# THE INTERNATIONAL YEAR BOOK AND STATESMEN'S WHO'S WHO

THE

# INTERNATIONAL YEAR BOOK

AND

# STATESMEN'S WHO'S WHO

# 1978

Compiled by: Robert M. Bradfield

Research: Jean-Pierre Keillor, BA (Biographies Section),
Mervyn O. Pragnell (Countries Section)

Published by Kelly's Directories Limited

(*Registered Office*)

Neville House Eden Street Kingston upon Thames Surrey KT1 1BY

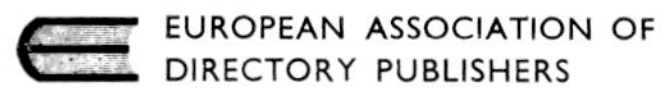


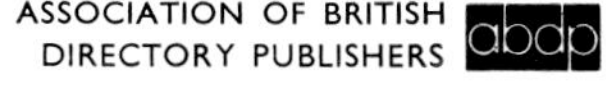

*First Published 1953*
*Twenty Sixth Edition Published 1978*



SBN 610 00513 8

ACKNOWLEDGEMENTS

The Publishers wish to thank the World Bank for allowing extracts from the World Bank Atlas to be reproduced in this publication.

The Publishers also wish to thank the Office of Population Censuses and Surveys (U.K.) for the demographic information reproduced in the United Kingdom section of this publication.

Printed in Great Britain by The Pitman Press, Bath

# CONTENTS

Every care has been taken to check the information supplied for the preparation of the articles in this volume but the publishers cannot accept responsibility for chance misstatements, omissions or inaccuracies. They will be glad to receive any authoritative corrections.

## PART ONE



## PART TWO



## PART THREE

# ABBREVIATIONS

| | |
|---|---|
| **A.A.** | Associate in Arts |
| **A.A.A.S.** | American Association for the Advancement of Sciences |
| **A.A.C.** | Army Air Corps |
| **A.A.F.** | Army Air Force |
| **A.A.S.A.** | Associate of the Australian Society of Accountants |
| **A.A.U.Q.** | Associate in Accountancy, University of Queensland |
| **A.B.** | Bachelor of Arts, Aktiebolaget |
| **A.C.** | Air Corps |
| | Companion of the Order of Australia |
| **A.C.A.** | Associate, Institute of Chartered Accountants |
| **A.C.G.I.** | Associate of City and Guilds of London Institute |
| **A.C.P.** | American College of Physicians |
| **A.C.S.** | American College of Surgeons |
| **A.C.T.** | Australian Capital Territory |
| **A.D.C.** | Aide-de-Camp |
| **Adj.-Gen.** | Adjutant-General |
| **Admin.** | Administration |
| **A.E.** | Agricultural Engineer |
| **A.E.C.** | Atomic Energy Commission |
| **A.E.F.** | American Expeditionary Forces |
| **A.F.C.** | Air Force Cross, Australian Flying Corps |
| **A.F.H.Q.** | Allied Force Headquarters |
| **A.F.Inst.Ae.S.** | Associate Eellow of Institute of Aeronautical Sciences |
| **A.F.R.Ae.S.** | Associate Fellow of the Royal Aeronautical Society |
| **A.G.** | Aktiengesellschaft (joint-stock company) |
| **a.i.** | ad interim. |
| **A.I.A.** | American Institute of Architects |
| **A.I.B.** | Associate of the Institute of Bankers |
| **A.I.C.A.** | Associate Member, Commonwealth Institute of Accountants |
| **A.I.C.E.** | Associate of Institute of Civil Engineers |
| **A.I.D.** | Agency for International Development |
| **A.I.F.** | Australian Imperial Forces |
| **A.I.L.** | Associate of the Institute of Linguistics |
| **A.I.M.E.** | American Institute ot Mining Engineers |
| | Associate of the Institute of Mining Engineers |
| **A.I.Mech.E.** | Associate of the Institution of Mechanical Engineers |
| **A.I.M.M.** | Associate of the Institution of Mining and Metallurgy |
| **A.Inst.C.E.** | Associate of Institution of Civil Engineers |
| **A.K.** | Knight of the Order of Australia |
| **A.L.A.** | American Library Association |
| **A.L.A.A.** | Associate, Library Association of Australia |
| **A.M.** | Master of Arts |
| | Member of the Order of Australia |
| **A.M.A.** | American Medical Association |
| **Amb. Ex. and Plen.** | Ambassador Extraordinary and Plenipotentiary |
| **A.M.I.C.E.** | Associate Member of the Institution of Civil Engineers |
| **A.M.I.E.E.** | Associate Member of the Institute of Electrical Engineers |
| **A.M.I.Mech.E.** | Associate Member of the Institution of Mechanical Engineers |
| **A.M.Inst.C.E.** | Associate Member of the Institution of Civil Engineers |
| **Am.Inst.E.E.** | American Institute of Electrical Engineers |
| **A.M.Inst.N.Z.E.** | Associate Member, Institute of New Zealand Engineers |
| **A.M.P.** | Advanced Management Program |
| **Am.Soc.C.E.** | American Society of Civil Engineers |
| **Am.Soc.M.E.** | American Society of Mechanical Engineers |
| **A.O.** | Officer of the Order of Australia |
| **A.O.C.** | Air Officer Commanding |
| **A.P.A.** | American Psychiatric Association |
| **A.R.A.** | Associate of the Royal Academy |
| **A.R.A.N.Z.** | Associate Registered Accountant of New Zealand |
| **A.R.C.** | American Red Cross |
| **A.R.C.V.S.** | Associate of the Royal College of Veterinary Surgeons |
| **A.R.I.B.A.** | Associate of the Royal Institute of British Architects |
| **A.R.I.C.** | Associate of the Royal Institute of Chemistry |
| **Ariz.** | Arizona |
| **Ark.** | Arkansas |
| **Arts. D.** | Doctor of Arts |
| **A/S** | Aktieselskap, Aktieselskab (Joint-stock company) |
| **A.S.C.E.A.** | American Society of Civil Engineers and Architects |
| **A.S.M.E.** | American Society of Mechanical Engineers |
| **Assn.** | Association |
| **Assoc.** | Associate |
| **A.S.S.R.** | Autonomous Soviet Socialist Republic |
| **Asst.** | Assistant |
| **A.U.S.** | Army of the United States |
| **B.** | born (née, nacido, geboren) |
| **B.A.** | Bachelor of Arts |
| **B.Agr.** | Bachelor of Agriculture |
| **B.Arch.** | Bachelor of Architecture |
| **B.A.Sc.** | Bachelor of Applied Science |
| **B.B.A.** | Bachelor of Business Administration |
| **B.B.C.** | British Broadcasting Corporation |
| **B.C.** | British Columbia |
| **B.C.E.** | Bachelor of Civil Engineering |
| **B.Ch.** | Bachelor of Surgery |
| **B.C.L.** | Bachelor of Civil Law |
| **B. Comm.** | Bachelor of Commerce |
| **B.D.** | Bachelor of Divinity |
| **Bd.** | Board |
| **B.D.Sc.** | Bachelor of Dental Science |
| **B.Ed.** | Bachelor of Education |
| **B.E.E.** | Bachelor of Electrical Engineering |
| **B.E.F.** | British Expeditionary Force |
| **BENELUX** | Belgian-Netherlands-Luxembourg Committee |
| **B. en H.** | Bachiller en Humanidades (Bachelor of Humanities) |
| **B.ès A.** | Bachelor of Arts |
| **B.ès L.** | Bachelor of Letters |
| **B.ès S.** | Bachelor of Science |
| **B.I.M.** | British Institute of Management |
| **B.I.S.** | Bank for International Settlements |
| **B.Jur. & Soc. Sc.** | Bachelor of Juridical and Social Science |
| **B.L.** | Bachelor of Law |
| **B.L.E.S.M.A.** | British Limbless Ex-Service Men's Assn. |
| **B. Litt.** | Bachelor of Letters |
| **B.M.A.** | British Medical Association |
| **Bn.** | Battalion |
| **Brig.** | Brigadier |
| **Brig.-Gen.** | Brigadier-General |
| **B.S.** | Bachelor of Science (U.S.A.) |
| | Bachelor of Surgery (G.B.) |
| **B.S.A.** | Bachelor of Science in Agriculture |
| **B.Sc.** | Bachelor of Science |
| **Bt.** | Baronet |
| **Bucks.** | Buckinghamshire |
| **B.V.Sc.** | Bachelor of Veterinary Science |
| **C.A.** | Central America |
| | Chartered Accountant |
| **Calif.** | California |
| **Cand. jur.** | Candidatus juris (Doctor of Law) |
| **C.A.R.I.F.T.A.** | Caribbean Free Trade Area |

| | |
|---|---|
| **C.B.** | Companion of the Order of the Bath |
| **C.B.E.** | Commander of Order of British Empire |
| **CBI** | Confederation of British Industry |
| **C.C.** | County Councillor |
| **C.D.** | Canadian Forces Decoration |
| **Cdr.** | Commander |
| **C.D.U.** | Christlich-Demokratische Union (Christian Democratic Union) |
| **C.E.** | Civil Engineer |
| **C.E.F.** | Canadian Expeditionary Force |
| **C.G.I.A.** | City and Guilds of London Insignia Award |
| **C.G.T.** | Confédération Générale du Travail (General Confederation of Labour) |
| **C.H.** | Companion of Honour |
| **Ch.B.** | Bachelor of Chemistry |
| **Ch.D.** | Doctor of Chemistry |
| **Ch.M.** | Master of Surgery |
| **Chmn.** | Chairman |
| **Cía.** | Compañía (Company) |
| **C.I.E.** | Companion of the Order of the Indian Empire |
| **Cie.** | Compagnie (Company) |
| **C.I.G.S.** | Chief of the Imperial General Staff |
| **C.-in-C.** | Commander-in-Chief |
| **C.I.O.** | Congress of Industrial Organizations |
| **C.M.** | Master in Surgery |
| **Cmdre.** | Commodore |
| **C.M.F.** | Commonwealth Military Forces |
| **C.M.G.** | Companion of the Order of St. Michael and St. George |
| **Cncl(r).** | Council, Councillor |
| **C.O.** | Commanding Office |
| **Co.** | Company |
| **Coll.** | College |
| **Colo.** | Colorado |
| **Comdr.** | Commander (Decorations) |
| **Comm.** | Commission |
| **Conf.** | Conference |
| **Conn.** | Connecticut |
| **Cons.** | Conservative |
| **Co-op.** | Co-operative |
| **Corp.** | Corporation |
| **C.P.M.** | Colonial Police Medal |
| **C.P.S.U. (B)** | Communist Party of the Soviet Union (Bolsheviks) |
| **C.R.A.** | Commander Royal Artillery |
| **C.S.I.** | Companion of the Order of the Star of India |
| **C.St.J.** | Commander of the Order of St. John of Jerusalem |
| **Cttee.** | Committee |
| **C.V.O.** | Commander of the Royal Victorian Order |
| **C'wealth** | Commonwealth |
| | |
| **D.** | died |
| **D.A.A. and Q.M.G.** | Deputy Assistant Adjutant and Quarter-master-general |
| **D.A.A.G.** | Deputy Assistant Adjutant-General |
| **Dau(s).** | daughter(s), (filles, hijas, Töchter) |
| **D.B.A.** | Doctor of Business Administration |
| **D.B.E.** | Dame Commander of the Order of the British Empire |
| **D.C.** | District of Columbia |
| **D.C.L.** | Doctor of Civil Law |
| **D.C.M.** | Distinguished Conduct Medal |
| **D.Com.** | Doctor of Commerce |
| **D.Com.L.** | Doctor of Commercial Law |
| **D.C.P.** | Diploma in Clinical Pathology |
| **D.C.S.** | Doctor of Commercial Sciences |
| **Dec.** | deceased |
| **D.Econ.** | Doctor of Economics |
| **Del.** | Delaware |
| **Deleg.** | Delegation |
| **D. en D.** | Docteur en Droit |
| **D.Eng.** | Doctor of Engineering |
| **D. en L.** | Doctor en Leyes (Doctor of Law) |
| **D.ê n M.** | Docteur en Médecine (Doctor of Medicine) |
| **Dept.** | Department |
| **D. ès L.** | Doctor of Letters |
| **D.F.C.** | Distinguished Flying Cross |
| **D.F.M.** | Distinguished Flying Medal |
| **D.H.L.** | Doctor of Humane Letters |
| **D.H.M.S.A.** | Diploma in the History of Medicine (Society of Apothecaries) |
| **D.I.C.** | Diploma of Imperial College |
| **D.in D.** | Dottore in Diretto (Doctor of Law) |
| **Dipl.Ing.** | Diplom Ingenieur (Diploma of Engineering) |
| **Dir.** | Director |
| **Dir.-Gen.** | Director-General |
| **Div.** | Division<br>Divorced |
| **D.K.** | Most Esteemed Family Order (Brunei) |
| **D.L.** | Deputy Lieutenant |
| **D.Litt.** | Doctor of Literature |
| **D.M.S.** | Decoration for Meritorious Service (South Africa) |
| **Dott.Ing.** | Dottore in Ingegneria (Doctor of Engineering) |
| **D.Ph.** | Doctor of Philosophy |
| **D.P.H.** | Diploma in Public Health (British) |
| **D.P.M.** | Diploma in Psychological Medicine |
| **D.Psych.** | Doctor of Psychology |
| **Dpty.** | Deputy |
| **Dr. Chem.** | Doctor of Chemistry |
| **Dr.h.c.Theol.** | Honorary Doctor of Theology |
| **Dr. Ing.** | Doktor Ingenieur (Doctor of Engineering) |
| **Dr. jur.** | Doctor juris (Doctor of Law) |
| **Dr.jur.sc.** | Doctor juridicae scientiae (Doctor of Juridical Science) |
| **Dr.jur.utr.** | Doctor juris utriusque |
| **Dr.rer.nat.** | Doctor rerum naturalium (Doctor of Natural Science) |
| **Dr.sc.oec.** | Doctor scientiae oeconomicae (Doctor of Economic Science) |
| **Dr.sc.pol.** | Doctor scientiae politicae (Doctor of Political Science) |
| **D.S.C.** | Distinguished Service Cross |
| **D.Sc.(Agric.)** | Doctor of Agricultural Science |
| **D.S.M.** | Distinguished Service Medal |
| **D.S.O.** | Distinguished Service Order |
| **D.T.M.** | Diploma in Tropical Medicine |
| **D.V.Sc.** | Doctor of Veterinary Science |
| **D.Zool.** | Doctor of Zoology |
| | |
| **ECA** | Economic Co-operation Administration |
| **ECAFE** | Economic Commission for Asia and the Far East |
| **ECE** | Economic Commission for Europe |
| **ECITO** | European Central Inland Transport Organization |
| **ECOSOC** | Economic and Social Council of the United Nations |
| **E.D.** | Australian Efficiency Decoration<br>Doctor of Engineering (U.S.A.) |
| **Educ.** | educated, (education, educación, Bildungsgang) |
| **EFTA** | European Free Trade Association |
| **E.K.D.** | Evangelische Kirche in Deutschland (Protestant Church in Germany) |
| **E.M.** | Earl Marshal |
| **En. Ex. and Min. Plen.** | Envoy Extraordinary and Minister Plenipotentiary |
| **E.O.P.H.** | Examined Officer of Public Health |
| **E.R.D.** | Emergency Reserve Decoration |
| **Est.** | Established |
| **e.t.** | en titre |
| **E.T.H.** | Eidgenässische Technische Hochschule |
| **ETOUSA** | European Theatre of Operations, United States Army |
| **EURATOM** | European Atomic Energy Community |
| **Exec.** | Executive |
| | |
| **F.A.A.** | Fellow of the Australian Academy of Science Fellow of the Australian College of Education |
| **F.A.C.E.** | |
| **F.A.C.P.** | Fellow of the American College of Physicians |
| **FAO** | Food and Agriculture Organization |
| **F.B.A.** | Fellow of the British Academy |
| **F.B.I.** | Federal Bureau of Investigation |
| **F.C.A.** | Fellow of the Institute of Chartered Accountants |
| **F.C.I.B.** | Fellow of the Corporation of Insurance Brokers |
| **F.C.I.C.** | Fellow of the Chemical Institute of Canada |
| **F.C.I.S.** | Fellow of the Chartered Institute of Secretaries |
| **F.C.O.** | Foreign and Commonwealth Office |
| **F.C.T.** | Federal Capital Territory |
| **F.C.W.A.** | Fellow of the Institute of Cost and Works Accountants |

| | |
|---|---|
| **Fed.** | Federation, Federal |
| **F.F.A.** | Fellow of the Faculty of Actuaries (Scotland) |
| **F.F.I.A.** | Fellow of the Federal Institute of Accountants |
| **F.I.A.** | Fellow of the Institute of Actuaries |
| **F.I.Ae.S.** | Fellow of the Institute of Aeronautical Sciences |
| **F.I.B.** | Fellow of the Institute of Bankers |
| **F.I.I.A.** | Fellow of the Institute of Industrial Administration |
| **F.I.I.M.** | Fellow of the Institute of Industrial Management |
| **F.I.M.** | Fellow of the Institute of Metallurgists |
| **F.Inst.F.F.** | Fellow of the Institute of Freight Forwarders |
| **F.Inst.P.** | Fellow of the Institute of Physics |
| **F.I.O.B.** | Fellow of the Institute of Building |
| **F.I.P.A.** | Fellow of the Institute of Public Administration |
| **F.I.R.E.** | Fellow of the Institution of Radio Engineers |
| **F.I.W.M.** | Fellow of the Institution of Works Managers |
| **F.I.W.S.P.** | Fellow of the Institute of Work Study Practitioners |
| **F.J.I.** | Fellow of the Institute of Journalists |
| **F.K.C.** | Fellow of King's College London |
| **Fla.** | Florida |
| **F.L.A.** | Fellow of the Library Association |
| **F.M.A.** | Fellow of the Museums Association |
| **F.N.Z.I.C.** | Fellow of New Zealand Institute of Chemistry |
| **F.O.** | Foreign Office |
| **F.P.S.** | Fellow of the Pharmaceutical Society |
| **F.R.A.C.I.** | Fellow of the Royal Australian Chemical Institute |
| **F.R.A.C.S.** | Fellow of the Royal Australian College of Surgeons |
| **F.R.Ae.S.** | Fellow of the Royal Aeronautical Society |
| **F.R.A.I.A.** | Fellow of the Royal Australian Institute of Architects |
| **F.R.A.S.** | Fellow of the Royal Asiatic Society<br>Fellow of the Royal Astronomical Society |
| **F.R.C.O.G.** | Fellow of the Royal College of Obstetricians |
| **F.R.C.S.** | Fellow of the Royal College of Surgeons |
| **F.R.Econ.S.** | Fellow of the Royal Economic Society |
| **F.R.E.I.** | Fellow of the Real Estate Institute (Australia) |
| **F.R.E.S.** | Fellow of the Royal Entomological Society |
| **F.R.G.S.** | Fellow of the Royal Geographical Society |
| **F.R.G.S.A.** | Fellow of the Royal Geographical Society of Australia |
| **F.R.Hist.S.** | Fellow of the Royal Historical Society |
| **F.R.I.B.A.** | Fellow of the Royal Institute of British Architects |
| **F.R.I.C.** | Fellow of the Royal Institute of Chemistry |
| **F.R.I.N.** | Fellow of the Royal Institute of Navigation |
| **F.R.S.A.** | Fellow of the Royal Society of Arts |
| **F.R.S.C.** | Fellow of the Royal Society of Canada |
| **F.R.S.E.** | Fellow of the Royal Society of Edinburgh |
| **F.R.T.S.** | Fellow of the Royal Television Society |
| **F.S.A.** | Fellow of the Society of Antiquaries |
| **F.S.A.Scot.** | Fellow of the Society of Antiquaries of Scotland |
| **F.S.A.S.M.** | Fellow of the South Australian School of Mines |
| **Ft.** | Fort |
| **F.T.I.** | Fellow of the Textile Institute |
| **F.Z.S.** | Fellow of the Zoological Society |
| **Ga.** | Georgia |
| **G.A.R.** | Grand Army of the Republic |
| **G.A.T.T.** | General Agreement on Tariffs and Trade |
| **G.B.E.** | Knight (or Dame) Grand Cross of the Order of the British Empire |
| **G.C.B.** | Knight Grand Cross of the Order of the Bath |
| **G.C.I.E.** | Knight Grand Commander of the Order of the Indian Empire |
| **G.C.M.G.** | Knight Grand Cross of the Order of St. Michael and St. George |
| **G.C.S.I.** | Knight Grand Commander of the Order of the Star of India |
| **G.C.V.O.** | Knight Grand Cross of the Royal Victorian Order |
| **Gebr.** | Gebrüder (Bros.. Brothers) |
| **Gen. Mgr.** | General Manager |
| **G.H.Q.** | General Headquarters |
| **G.L.C.** | Greater London Council |
| **G.M.** | George Medal |
| **G.m.b.H.** | Gesellschaft mit beschränkter Haftung (Company with limited liabilities) |
| **GNP** | Gross National Product |
| **G.O.C.** | General Officer Commanding |
| **G.O.C.-in-C.** | General Officer Commanding-in-Chief |
| **Govt.** | Government |
| **G.P.O.** | General Post Office |
| **H.B.M.** | Humming Bird Gold Medal (Trinidad) |
| **h.c.** | honoris causa |
| **H.E.** | His Eminence |
| **H.H.D.** | Doctor of Humanities (U.S.A.)<br>His Excellency |
| **H.M.** | His (Her) Majesty |
| **H.M.A.S.** | His (Her) Majesty's Australian Ship |
| **H.M.S.** | His (Her) Majesty's Ship |
| **Hon.** | Honourable, Honorary |
| **Hon. Consul** | Honorary Consul |
| **Hosp.** | Hospital |
| **H.Q.** | Headquarters |
| **H.R.H.** | His (Her) Royal Highness |
| **H.R.S.A.** | Hon. Member Royal Scottish Academy |
| **H.S.H.** | His (or Her) Serene Highness |
| **Ia.** | Iowa |
| **I.A.C.S.** | Indian Association for the Cultivation of Science |
| **I.A.E.A.** | International Atomic Energy Agency |
| **I.A.T.A.** | International Air Transport Association |
| **I.B.A.** | Institute of British Architects |
| **I.B.C.** | International Broadcasting Corporation |
| **I.B.C. Ltd.** | International Business Communications Ltd. |
| **I.B.E.** | Institute of British Engineers |
| **I.B.I.A.** | Institute of British Industrial Art |
| **I.B.R.D.** | International Bank for Reconstruction and Development |
| **ICAO** | International Civil Aviation Organization |
| **I.C.E.** | Institute of Civil Engineers |
| **I.C.S.** | Indian Civil Service |
| **Ida.** | Idaho |
| **I.D.E.P.** | Institute for Development and Economic Planning (Africa) |
| **ILEA** | Inner London Education Authority |
| **Ill.** | Illinois |
| **I.L.O.** | International Labour Office<br>International Labour Organization |
| **IMCO** | Inter-governmental Maritime Consultative Organization |
| **I.M.F.** | International Monetary Fund |
| **Inc.** | Incorporated |
| **Ind.** | Indiana |
| **Ind. Repub.** | Independent Republican |
| **Insce.** | Insurance |
| **Inst.** | Institute |
| **Instn.** | Institution |
| **Int.** | International |
| **IRO** | International Refugee Organization |
| **I.S.O.** | Companion of the Imperial Service Order |
| **I.T.U.** | International Telecommunication Union |
| **J.A.F.** | Judge-Advocate of the Fleet |
| **J.A.G.** | Judge-Advocate-General |
| **J.C.B.** | Bachelor of Common Law |
| **J.C.D.** | Doctor of Civil Law |
| **J.D.** | Doctor of Jurisprudence |
| **J.P.** | Justice of the Peace |
| **J.U.D.** | Doctor of both Canon and Civil Law |
| **Kan.** | Kansas |
| **K.B.E.** | Knight Commander of the Order of the British Empire |
| **K.C.** | King's Counsel |
| **K.C.B.** | Knight Commander of the Order of the Bath |
| **K.C.I.E.** | Knight Commander of the Order of the Indian Empire |
| **K.C.M.G.** | Knight Commander of the Order of St. Michael and St. George |
| **K.C.S.I.** | Knight Commander of the Order of the Star of India |
| **K.C.V.O.** | Knight Commander of the Royal Victorian Order |
| **K.G.** | Knight of the Order of the Garter |

## ABBREVIATIONS

| | |
|---|---|
| **K.-G.a.A.** | Kommandit-Gesellschaft auf Aktien (Private company partly organized as a joint-stock company) |
| **K.G.St.J.** | Knight of Grace of the Order of St. John of Jerusalem |
| **K.L.M.** | Koninklijke Luchtvaart Maatschappij N.V. (Royal Dutch Airlines) |
| **Km.** | Kilometre |
| **K.P.** | Knight of the Order of St. Patrick |
| **K.S.G.** | Knight of St. Gregory the Great |
| **K.St.J.** | Knight of the Order of St. John of Jerusalem |
| **K.T.** | Knight of the Order of the Thistle |
| **Kt.** | Knight |
| **Ky.** | Kentucky |
| **La.** | Louisiana |
| **Lab.** | Labour Party |
| **Lancs.** | Lancashire |
| **L.de Phil.** | Licencié de Philosophie (Licentiate in Philosophy) |
| **L.em C.** | Licenciado em Ciencia |
| **L.em D.** | Licenciado em Direito |
| **L.en C.E.** | Licenciado en Ciencias Económicas |
| **L.en L.** | Licenciado en Leyes |
| **L.en D.** | Licencié en Droit, Licenciado en Derecho |
| **L.ès L.** | Licencié ès Lettres |
| **L.ès Sc.** | Licencié ès Sciences |
| **L.H.B.** | Bachelor of Humane Letters |
| **L.H.D.** | Doctor of Humane Letters |
| **L.I.** | Long Island |
| **Lib.** | Liberal Party |
| **Lic. Econ.** | Licentiate in Economic Sciences |
| **Lic. Jur.** | Licentiate in Law |
| **Lic. L.** | Licentiate of Law |
| **Lic. Med.** | Licentiate in Medicine |
| **Lieut.** | Lieutenant |
| **Litt.D.** | Doctor of Letters |
| **LL.B.** | Bachelor of Laws |
| **LL.D.** | Doctor of Laws |
| **LL.L.** | Licentiate of Laws |
| **LL.M.** | Master of Civil and Canon Law, Master of Law |
| **L.M.** | Licentiate of Medicine |
| **L.N.** | League of Nations |
| **L.R.C.P.** | Licentiate of the Royal College of Physicians |
| **L.S.A.** | Licentiate of the Society of Apothecaries |
| **Ltd.** | Limited |
| **L.V.C.M.** | Licentiate Victoria College of Music |
| **M.** | married, marriage (marie, casado, verheiratet) |
| **M.A.** | Master of Arts |
| **M.Agr.** | Master of Agriculture (U.S.A.) |
| **Maj.** | Major |
| **Man. Dir.** | Managing Director |
| **Mapai** | Israel Labour Party |
| **Mapam** | Israel Marxist Party |
| **Mass.** | Massachusetts |
| **M.B.** | Bachelor of Medicine |
| **M.B.A.** | Master of Business Administration |
| **M.B.E.** | Member of the Order of the British Empire |
| **M.C.** | Military Cross |
| **M.Ch.** | Master of Surgery |
| **M.C.L.** | Master of Civil Law |
| **M.C.S.** | Master of Commercial Science |
| **M.D.** | Doctor of Medicine |
| **Md.** | Maryland |
| **M.E.** | Master of Engineering |
| **Me.** | Maine |
| **M.Ec.** | Master of Economics |
| **M.E.C.A.S.** | Middle East Centre for Arab Studies |
| **M.E.I.C.** | Member of the Engineering Institute of Canada |
| **Mem.** | Member |
| **M.Eng.** | Master of Engineering (Dublin) |
| **Mfg.** | Manufacturing |
| **M.F.H.** | Master of Foxhounds |
| **Mfr.** | Manufacturer |
| **Mgr.** | Monseigneur, Monseñor, Monsignor, Manager |
| **M.H.A.** | Member of the House of Assembly |
| **M.H.R.** | Member of the House of Representatives |
| **M.I.C.E.** | Member of the Institution of Civil Engineers |
| **M.I.Chem.E.** | Member of the Institution of Chemical Engineers |
| **Middx.** | Middlesex |
| **M.I.E. (Aust.)** | Member of the Institution of Engineers (Australia) |
| **M.I.E.E.** | Member of the Institution of Electrical Engineers |
| **Mij.** | Maatschappij |
| **M.I.Mech.E.** | Member of the Institution of Mechanical Engineers |
| **Min. Plen.** | Minister Plenipotentiary |
| **Minn.** | Minnesota |
| **Min.** | Ministry |
| **M.Inst.T.** | Member of the Institute of Transport |
| **M.I.Q.** | Member of the Institute of Quarrying |
| **M.I.R.E.** | Member of the Institution of Radio Engineers |
| **Miss.** | Mississippi |
| **M.I.D.** | Mentioned in Despatches |
| **M.I.T.** | Massachusetts Institute of Technology |
| **M.L.A.** | Member of the Legislative Assembly |
| **M.L.C.** | Member of the Legislative Council |
| **M.M.** | Military Medal |
| **Mo.** | Missouri |
| **M.O.H.** | Medical Officer of Health |
| **Mont.** | Montana |
| **M.P.** | Member of Parliament |
| **M.Ph.** | Master of Philosophy |
| **M.R.C.S.** | Member of the Royal College of Surgeons |
| **M.R.I.** | Member of the Royal Institution |
| **M.R.I.A.** | Member of Royal Irish Academy |
| **M.R.P.** | Mouvement Républicain Populaier |
| **M.S.** | Master of Sciences, Master of Surgery |
| **M.Sc.** | Master of Science |
| **M.S.M.** | Meritorious Service Medal |
| **Mt.** | Mount |
| **M.T.P.I.** | Member of the Town Planning Institute |
| **M.V.O.** | Member of the Royal Victorian Order |
| **My.** | Maatschappy |
| **N.A.A.F.I.** | Navy, Army and Air Force Institutes |
| **Nat.** | National |
| **Nat. Dem.** | National Democratic |
| **Nat. Lib.** | National Liberal |
| **NATO** | North Atlantic Treaty Organization |
| **N.B.** | New Brunswick |
| **N.C.** | North Carolina |
| **N.D.** | North Dakota |
| **N.E.** | North East |
| **Neb.** | Nebraska |
| **N.E.I.** | Netherlands East Indies |
| **N.Eng.** | New England |
| **N.E.R.A.** | Nat. Emergency Relief Admin. |
| **Nev.** | Nevada |
| **Nfd.** | Newfoundland |
| **N.G.I.V.** | Nishan Ghazee ge Izzaten Veriya (Maldives Decoration) |
| **N.H.** | New Hampshire |
| **N.I.R.A.** | National Industrial Recovery Administration (U.S.A.) |
| **N.R.A.** | National Recovery Administration |
| **N.R.T.** | Net Registered Tonnage |
| **N.S.A.I.V.** | Distinguished Order of Shaheed Ali (Maldives Decoration) |
| **N.S.W.** | New South Wales |
| **N.V.** | Naamloze Vennootschap (Limited Company) |
| **N.W.F.P.** | North West Frontier Province |
| **N.Y.** | New York |
| **N.Z.** | New Zealand |
| **O.** | Ohio |
| **OAS** | Organization of American States |
| **O.A.U.** | Organization of African Unity |
| **O.B.E.** | Officer of the Order of the British Empire |
| **O.C.** | Officer of the Order of Canada |
| **OCAS** | Organization of Central American States |
| **O.E.** | Order of Excellence (Guyana) |
| **OECD** | Organization for Economic Co-operation and Development |
| **O.F.S.** | Orange Free State |
| **O.J.** | Order of Jamaica |
| **Okla.** | Oklahoma |
| **O.M.** | Member of the Order of Merit |
| **O.P.E.C.** | Organization of Petroleum Exporting Countries |
| **O.R.C.** | Officers' Reserve Corps |
| **Ore.** | Oregon |
| **Ott.** | Ottawa |

| | |
|---|---|
| **O/Y or Oy.** | Osakeyhtio (Limited Company) |
| **Pa.** | Pennsylvania |
| **Parly.** | Parliamentary |
| **P.C.** | Privy Councillor |
| **P.C.B.** | Partido Colorado Batllista |
| **P.C.F.** | Parti Communiste Français (French Communist Party) |
| **P.D.R.Y.** | People's Democratic Republic of the Yemen |
| **P.E.I.** | Prince Edward Island |
| **P.E.N.** | Poets, Playwrights, Essayists, Editors and Novelists (Club) |
| **PEP** | Political and Economic Planning |
| **Ph.B.** | Bachelor of Philosophy |
| **Ph.D.** | Doctor of Philosophy |
| **Ph.L.** | Licentiate of Philosophy |
| **P.M.N.** | Panglima Mangka Negara (Malaysian Decoration) |
| **Pol.** | Political |
| **PPS** | Parliamentary Private Secretary |
| **P.Q.** | Province of Quebec |
| **Pres.** | President |
| **Privatdozent** | University teacher not belonging to professorial staff |
| **P.R.O.** | Public Relations Officer |
| **Prof.** | Professor |
| **psc.** | Graduate of Staff College |
| **P.S.M.** | Panglima Setia Mahkota |
| **P.S.T.** | Pacific Summer Time (U.S.A.) |
| **P.W.A.** | Portuguese West Africa |
| **PWC** | Pacific War Council (U.S.A.) |
| **P.W.U.** | Postal Workers Union |
| **Q.A.R.N.N.S.** | Queen Alexandra's Royal Naval Nursing Service |
| **Q.C.** | Queen's Counsel |
| **Q.M.** | Quartermaster |
| **Q.M.G.** | Quartermaster-General |
| **Q.P.M.** | Queen's Police Medal |
| **Q.R.V.** | Qualified Valuer, Real Estate Institute of New South Wales |
| **Q.S.M.** | Queen's Service Medal (N.Z. Awards) |
| **Que.** | Quebec |
| **R.A.** | Royal Academy, Royal Artillery |
| **R.A.A.F.** | Royal Australian Air Force |
| **R.A.C.** | Royal Armoured Corps |
| **R.A.F.** | Royal Air Force |
| **R.A.M.C.** | Royal Army Medical Corps |
| **R.A.N.** | Royal Australian Navy |
| **R.A.N.C.** | Royal Australian Naval College |
| **R.A.N.V.R.** | Royal Australian Naval Volunteer Reserve |
| **R.A.O.C.** | Royal Army Ordnance Corps |
| **R.A.S.C.** | Royal Army Service Corps |
| **R.B.K.** | Ranna Bandeiri Kilegefaan (Maldives Decoration) |
| **R.C.** | Roman Catholic |
| **R.C.A.F.** | Royal Canadian Air Force |
| **R.C.E.M.E.** | Royal Canadian Electrical and Mechanical Engineers |
| **R.C.N.C.** | Royal Corps of Naval Constructors |
| **R.D.I.** | Royal Designer for Industry (Royal Society of Arts) |
| **Regt.** | Regiment |
| **Ret.** | Retired |
| **Rev.** | Reverend |
| **R.F.A.** | Royal Field Artillery |
| **R.F.C.** | Royal Flying Corps |
| **R.I.I.A.** | Royal Institute of International Affairs |
| **R.M.A.** | Royal Marine Artillery<br>Royal Military Academy (Sandhurst) |
| **R.M.C.** | Royal Military College |
| **R.N.** | Royal Navy |
| **R.N.A.S.** | Royal Naval Air Service |
| **R.N.V.R.** | Royal Naval Volunteer Reserve |
| **R.N.Z.A.F.** | Royal New Zealand Air Force |
| **R. of O.** | Reserve of Officers |
| **R.P.F.** | Rassemblement du Peuple Français (Rally of the French People) |
| **R.S.F.S.R.** | Russian Soviet Federal Socialist Republics |
| **Rt. Hon.** | Right Honourable |
| **R.W.A.F.F.** | Royal West African Frontier Force |
| **S.** | son, sons, (fils, hijos, Söhne) |
| **S.A.** | Société Anonyme, Sociedad Anónima (Limited Company) |
| **S.A.E.** | Société Anonyme Egyptienne (Egyptian Limited Company) |
| **Sask.** | Saskatchewan |
| **S.B.** | Bachelor of Science |
| **S.C.** | South Carolina |
| **ScD** | Doctor of Science |
| **SEAC** | South East Asia Command |
| **Secy.** | Secretary |
| **SHAEF** | Supreme Headquarters, Allied Expeditionary Force |
| **SHAPE** | Supreme Headquarters, Allied Powers in Europe |
| **S.I.P.R.I.** | Stockholm International Peace Research Institute |
| **S.J.D.** | Doctor of Juristic Science |
| **S.N.C.F.** | Société Nationale des Chemins de Fer Français (National French Railway Company) |
| **Soc. Dem.** | Social Democrat |
| **Socy.** | Society |
| **S.P.A.** | Società per Azioni (Joint-stock company) |
| **S.Pk.** | Sitara-e-Pakistan |
| **S.S.** | Steam Ship |
| **S.S.M.** | Seri Setia Mahkota |
| **S.S.R.** | Soviet Socialist Republic |
| **Supt.** | Superintendent |
| **S.W.P.A.** | South West Pacific Area |
| **T.C.D.** | Trinity College, Dublin |
| **T.D.** | Territorial Decoration |
| **Tenn.** | Tennessee |
| **Tex.** | Texas |
| **Treas.** | Treasurer |
| **T.U.C.** | Trades Union Congress |
| **T.V.A.** | Tennessee Valley Authority |
| **T.W.U.** | Transport Workers' Union |
| **U.A.P.** | United Australian Party |
| **U.D.C.** | Urban District Council |
| **U.K.** | United Kingdom |
| **UNA** | United Nations Association |
| **UNDP** | United Nations Development Programme |
| **UNESCO** | United Nations Educational, Scientific, and Cultural Organization |
| **U.N.I.C.E.** | Union des Industries de la Compagnie Europe |
| **U.N.I.C.E.F.** | United Nations Children's Fund |
| **U.N.I.D.O.** | United Nations Industrial Development Organization |
| **U.N.I.P.E.D.E.** | Union Internationale des Producteurs et Distributeurs d'Energie Electrique |
| **U.N.I.T.A.R.** | United Nations Institute for Training and Research |
| **Univ.(s)** | University, Universities |
| **UNO** | United Nations Organization |
| **U.N.R.R.A.** | United Nations Relief and Rehabilitation Administration |
| **U.P.** | Uttar Pradesh, United Provinces |
| **U.P.U.** | Universal Postal Union |
| **U.S.A.** | United States of America |
| **U.S.J.O.C.** | Union of Sephardic Jews and Oriental Committees |
| **U.S.S.** | United States Ship |
| **U.S.S.R.** | Union of Soviet Socialist Republics |
| **U.S.W.S.A.** | U.S. War Shipping Administration |
| **Ut.** | Utah |
| **U.T.S.I.K.** | All Russian Central Executive Ctte. |
| **Va.** | Virginia |
| **V.C.** | Victoria Cross |
| **V.D.** | Victorian Decoration, Volunteer Officers Decoration |
| **Vic.** | Victoria |
| **V.R.D.** | Royal Naval Volunteer Reserve Officers' Decoration |
| **W.A.** | Western Australia |
| **W.A.A.C.** | Women's Army Auxiliary Corps |
| **W.A.A.E.** | World Assn. for Adult Education |
| **W.A.A.F.** | Women's Auxiliary Air Force |
| **Wash.** | Washington (state) |
| **W.E.A.** | Workers Educational Association |
| **W.E.U.** | Western European Union |
| **W.F.T.U.** | World Federation of Trade Unions |
| **WHO** | World Health Organization |
| **Wilts.** | Wiltshire |
| **Wis.** | Wisconsin |
| **W. Va.** | West Virginia |
| **Wyo.** | Wyoming |
| **Y.M.C.A.** | Young Men's Christian Association |
| **Yorks.** | Yorkshire |
| **Y.W.C.A.** | Young Women's Christian Association |

# WHAT'S ALL THIS ABOUT GENETIC ENGINEERING?

by

DAVID A. HOPWOOD

John Innes Professor of Genetics in the University of East Anglia, Norwich

During the last three or four years revolutionary developments have taken place in a new area of biology which is being called genetic engineering. Probably these same advances would not have been viewed as quite so dramatic, even by the biologists involved, if they had been documented only at meetings of scientists and in the specialist scientific press. But this did not occur. Instead, the media and many different sections of society have had a field day discussing, not so much the scientific developments themselves, but the moral, economic and historical issues which were variously felt to stem from the new techniques and their results. Something new and exciting was seen to be happening and the experiments rapidly began to be discussed in emotional and in some cases hysterical terms, with calls even for their complete prohibition.

What is this new field of scientific activity and why does it cause concern? What are the techniques? How might they be applied in the foreseeable future? And what is being done to ensure that they do not have undesirable consequences?

## WHAT IS GENETIC ENGINEERING?

Two essentially distinct concepts have come to be described by the same title. The original use of the term was to denote attempts which might be made in the future to change the genetic make-up of of human beings by artificial means: either to correct a congenital defect such as haemophilia or diabetes, or perhaps to change mental or physical characteristics to more "desirable" alternatives. It is easy to see why a fear of possible abuse, or indeed of any manipulation other than the correction of an obvious disease condition, would raise deep-felt antagonism to such manipulations, especially since public concern was already aroused several decades ago by books such as Aldous Huxley's *Brave New World* and by reports of experiments carried out in Nazi Germany.

The other use of the term genetic engineering is to describe experiments which have already become possible as a result of recent scientific discoveries and which, for reasons that will become clear later, are better referred to as "recombinant DNA experiments". These are at the centre of the recent furore. Their objective is to transfer artificially some of the genes from one form of life to another into which they would not naturally find their way. In other words we aim to create a hybrid between two organisms which are unable to mate with one another, by by-passing the normal biological barriers which separate them. So far the recipients of the "foreign" genes have been bacteria, and the experiments have had one of two main aims. In some experiments the bacterium has been used as a convenient living "test-tube" in which to propagate individual foreign genes so as to make enough of them to analyse chemically. In others the objective is to create new strains of bacteria capable of making useful pharmaceuticals under the direction of the foreign genes; for example human insulin might be made by introducing the appropriate human gene into bacteria which could be grown on an industrial scale.

Some of the techniques that have been used to create these artificial hybrids are extremely imaginative, the results already obtained are of great scientific interest, and some exciting practical applications may be not far off. So why could the experiments cause alarm? The reason is that the artificially created hybrid microbe *might* become dangerous in some way, either because of side effects of the new properties deliberately conferred on it, or because of the actions of genes inadvertently introduced into the bacterium along with those known to the experimenter. The microbe might itself cause disease; or it might transfer genetic material to human cells to make them cancerous; or it might simply colonize the environment in such a way as to upset the normal ecological balance. Because fundamentally new combinations of genes can be rapidly created by the new techniques, it is a reasonable concern that the normal processes of evolution which lead to the mutual adaptation of disease organisms and their hosts or of different forms of life in the same habitat would not have time to occur, so that a rogue organism *might* be created, capable of causing an uncontrollable epidemic or an ecological disaster. It was this concern that prompted several of the pioneers of the new techniques to publish a letter in the scientific press in July 1974[1] calling attention to the possible risks involved, and suggesting a temporary self-imposed moratorium on a limited group of experiments until a wider cross-section of the scientific community could assess any possible hazards. Little did they suspect what a Pandora's Box they had opened. Not only did the possible microbiological hazards of the work cause considerable alarm but ethical criticisms were also levelled at the experiments by those who saw them as logical steps towards making possible the eventual genetic manipulation of people: the earlier meaning of the term genetic engineering. I shall return, at the end of this article, to the ways in which the possible microbiological risks are being assessed, reduced and legislated about as a result of the publicity which followed the original letter.

## WHAT ARE THE RECOMBINANT DNA TECHNIQUES?

The inherited characteristics of organisms, be they bacteria or human beings, are determined by their genes. All genes are segments of very long molecules of the chemical called DNA (deoxyribonucleic acid) which makes up the chromosomes. Each gene is a particular sequence of the four chemical sub-units of DNA, the bases which we can call A, T, G and C. About a thousand bases constitute each gene. The information carried by the exact sequence of bases in all the genes of an organism is expressed as the diverse proteins that make the organism what it is. The DNA molecule is actually a double-stranded structure consisting of two chains of bases coiled around each other and the sequence of bases in one chain determines the sequence in its partner because the double molecule can be assembled only when each type of base is paired with is particular complementary type (A with T, T with A, G with C and C with G). Thus we speak of complementary base pairs in a double stranded DNA.

Sexual reproduction brings together the sets of genes of two organisms (or the complete set of one and a few genes of the other)) and sorts out a complete set of genes from the mixture. If the two parents are not identical, new combinations of genes, not seen in either parent, can arise: these produce *recombinant* individuals, e.g., a brown-eyed fair-haired person can be a recombinant from a marriage of brown-eyed black-haired and blue-eyed fair-haired people. Natural recombination between the genes of two organisms occurs only if the organisms are physically and physiologically similar enough to mate and if their sets of genes – their DNA molecules – are similar enough along most of their length to recognise each other and exchange segments. In practise these conditions are satisfied only when the prospective parents are rather closely related: they belong to the same species.

The recombinant DNA technique opens up a whole new range of possibilities because it overcomes completely the barriers which normally limit gene exchange to members of the same species. There are several steps in the procedure, which can be summarised as follows. We extract pure DNA chemically from two organisms without damaging the genetic information it carries, cut the DNA of each organism in particular places, rejoin the cut segments in new combinations, and introduce the hybrid (recombinant) DNA molecules into organisms of one or other of the parental types (or of a third type) in such a way that they can become part of the set of genes of the new organism, reproducing themselves along with the resident genes.

Most of the necessary techniques, such as methods for extracting and purifying DNA, have developed gradually over many years but the key discovery, made about five years ago, was the means of joining genetically unrelated DNA molecules. The most interesting way in which this can be done is through the action of enzymes – called restriction enzymes – which are found naturally in various bacteria and which recognise specific sequences of base pairs in double stranded DNA, cutting the chains across at these positions. The recognition sites, different for each restriction enzyme, typically consist of four or six base pairs and have the special property of being symmetrical, and therefore identical when viewed from opposite ends of the molecule for example:,

– – – A G C G C T – – →
← – – T C G C G A – – –

Moreover, in the case of many of the enzymes – the most useful for the construction of recombinant DNA – the two chains of the DNA are cut at staggered but symmetrical positions. As a result the cut molecules produced by the enzyme's action have single-stranded protrusions, and these are all identical and complementary to one another because of the symmetry of the recognition sequence. Usually the molecules fall apart at the sites of cutting, but the experimenter can choose alternative conditions in which the cut ends will find one another and hold together (by virtue of the exact match between the complementary bases of the single stranded protrusions) long enough for another type of enzyme, called ligase, to re-seal the cuts in the chains. Thus undamaged double stranded DNA is restored. Because of the marvellous specificity of each type of restriction enzyme and because the recognition sequence for that enzyme will occur – probably essentially by chance – at certain positions in the DNA of *all* organisms, groups of genes from any two

[1] Science, Vol. 185, p. 303, 1974

completely unrelated forms of life can be permanently joined together by cutting the DNA from both organisms with the same enzyme and mixing and sealing together the resulting fragments.

The construction of such recombinant DNA molecules is now rather straightforward, but their introduction into a living organism in such a way that they will become a permanent part of its genetic complement requires a special situation. It is not enough for the recombinant DNA molecules to enter the recipient cells. Genes do not have a general capacity for automatic self-reproduction, even inside cells. They must be joined to particular structures ("replicators") which have such a capacity and these then ensure the reproduction of all the genes linked to them. One or a few replicators are present in the chromosomes of bacteria and those of higher organisms but because the sheer size of the chromosomes renders them excessively delicate it is so far impossible to isolate whole intact chromosomes from cells and to re-introduce them into other cells. However, many bacteria possess much smaller extra chromosomes, called plasmids, which carry relatively few genes and which are small enough to be isolated, manipulated with enzymes, and taken up again by their bacterial hosts without damage. These plasmids can be used as the vehicles or *vectors* for the introduction and maintenance of foreign genes: they form one half of the recombinant DNA mixture, with the foreign or donor DNA as the other. Those plasmid vectors that have been harnessed so far are confined to bacteria. Plasmids may occur in some other microorganisms such as yeasts, and might be found in higher forms of life, although this seems unlikely. However, alternative vectors are provided by the DNA of viruses, which can be modified to accept foreign DNA and then colonise host cells without killing them.

Recombinant DNA technology is itself undergoing a rapid evolution. One development is the replacement of natural vectors by more suitable vehicles which have themselves been engineered from parts of plasmids and viruses. Another is the discovery of vectors for a much wider range of organisms. Ingenious solutions are also being found to the problem of recognising the desired recombinants, which may be very rare, particularly when we wish to transfer to a new host one particular gene from an organism whose complete set of genes runs to many thousands. All these problems are capable of ingenious solutions, but this will take time and effort.

Perhaps a more fundamental problem is the difficulty of persuading foreign genes to work satisfactorily – to *express* themselves – when they have been introduced into the new intracellular environment of a different organism. Although the chemical processes in all organisms, and this includes the expression of their genes, are remarkably similar, they are not identical. A particularly significant gulf seems to separate bacteria from all other forms of life. Moreover, higher organisms express particular groups of their genes only in certain tissues – insulin is made only in specialized pancreas cells, growth hormone only in the pituitary gland – and complex control sequences of bases in the DNA are involved. In order to achieve the expression of such genes in bacteria it will probably be necessary to eliminate, modify or replace such control sequences. These operations are now within reach, particularly since it is becoming possible to synthesise by chemical means quite long runs of double-stranded DNA and recombine these into vectors. Thus tailor-made control sequences are a possibility.

## APPLICATIONS OF RECOMBINANT DNA

A large area of recombinant DNA work does not aim to make a recombinant organism with useful or interesting properties. It is the donor DNA itself, inserted into a bacterium on a suitable vector, which is of interest. The technique is simply an incredibly powerful tool for making quantities of a particular gene or control region picked out from the total complement of DNA of a higher organism.

The complete set of DNA of each human cell contains about three billion ($3 \times 10^9$) base pairs. This total DNA could be cut into fragments with a restriction enzyme whose recognition site occurs on average every few thousand base pairs (every few genes) apart and the fragments could be inserted at random into a plasmid vector and introduced into a culture of bacteria. Different bacteria could then be grown into separate cultures, and the one which carries a certain donor DNA fragment could be recognised. A particular human gene or short run of genes could thus be propagated by growing the new bacterial strain on a suitably large scale – perhaps a few litres of culture. The recombinant DNA vector could be extracted from the cells and the inserted DNA sequence could be accurately cut out again from the vector with the same restriction enzyme that was used to insert it. It could then be analysed chemically, for example by determining its complete base sequence by techniques which, also, have been recently perfected. Thus the secrets of gene and chromosome organisation will be found out; for example the nature of DNA sequences that lie next to genes and control their expression or the structure of the sites at which cancer-inducing viruses insert themselves into chromosomes to upset the normal controls of cell division. In these ways, serious diseases may well be better understood and the improved knowledge may lead to better methods of treatment.

The other main part of the recombinant DNA field involves experiments in which the recombinant *organism* is to be used or studied. In this area, in contrast to the first, the main emphasis has already been on applications and a considerable commercial impetus has been felt even though actual commercialisation of any product stemming from recombinant DNA technology is probably still some years away. Many of the big pharmaceutical companies are investing in recombinant DNA programmes, at least of an exploratory kind. Examples have been proposed of expensive, rare or currently unavailable but medically important macromolecules which could be manufactured industrially by microorganisms in processes comparable with the "fermentations" used to make the much simpler antibiotics rather than being extracted from animal or human sources. Insulin has been talked about most but it may turn out not to be the best example because it is after all obtainable from slaughter-house material and any new process would have to compete with current methods. Perhaps more valuable new fermentation products that might be made by bacteria containing human genes would be human antibodies, blood clotting Factor VIII for the treatment of haemophilia, or even human interferon for the combat of virus diseases. Formidable problems remain to be solved before any of these possibilities are realised. Probably expression of a human gene in a bacterium will be achieved quite soon,[2] but much work will need to be done before a bacterial culture makes a sufficient concentration of the product to be a commercially viable proposition.

In the shorter term we can probably expect less spectacular applications of recombinant DNA techniques in areas closer to traditional fermentation processes: the ability to make a product will be transferred from one microorganism to another that is more easily grown on a large scale; the yield of a product will be increased by having the genes on a vector present in the host cell in many copies; or a new antibiotic will be manufactured by recombining genes controlling different but related steps in the synthesis of two existing antibiotics.

In the field of recombinant DNA research, very few scientists are concerned with genetic engineering in the "other" sense of manipulating the genes of people, and even fewer have any stomach for the moral issues involved. However, this may at least in part reflect the fact that techniques and knowledge have not reached the stage at which such manipulations would become possible, and important moral decisions may have to be made at a later date. No such ethical problems surround the manipulation of plants. Indeed, the prospect of using recombinant DNA techniques to help breed improved types of crop plants – in particular to introduce bacterial genes determining the ability to fix atmospheric nitrogen and so make the plants independent of nitrogenous fertilizers – was one of the main arguments for recommending that recombinant DNA work should go on, under suitable safety provisions, in the first British Government Report on the subject.[3] Such a prospect is still some way off but is sufficiently exciting to stimulate a search for suitable vectors on which to introduce foreign genes into plants.

## THE REGULATION OF RECOMBINANT DNA RESEARCH

A small proportion of biologists argue that any attempt to regulate this research is an intolerable infringement on their individual freedom. At the other extreme, some people harbour such a deep fear of the possible microbiological dangers of the experiments or of the misuse of their outcome in the manipulation of people that they call for a complete ban on the work. In between, the vast majority accept the need for some form of control, on the grounds of microbiological safety, even if only to allay public concern. However, they argue at length over the severity of possible controls and over the best way to administer them; not surprisingly since all the possible hazards are conjectural.[4] From all this argument, a pattern is beginning to emerge and several countries, led by Britain and the U.S.A., are evolving systems of guidelines which specify a series of levels of "physical containment". These range from conditions in a routine microbiological laboratory to those already used for handling the most dangerous known pathogens. Each class of experiment is assigned an appropriate containment level according to the degree of possible danger which might be posed if a recombinant microbe were to escape from the experiment into the environment. For example it is generally felt that the transfer of DNA from a higher organism, such as a mammal, into a bacterium might be more risky than engineering gene exchange between two kinds of bacteria because the latter is more likely to have happened occasionally in Nature and the resulting new combinations could therefore already have been subjected to natural selection. In parallel with physical containment is "biological containment" in which special fastidious strains of bacteria are being developed as hosts for recombinant DNA so that, even if they were to find their way out of the laboratory, the bacteria would be unable to survive. Use of such strains allows for a lower level

[2] Something close to this has just been reported (*Science*, Vol. 198, p. 1056, 1977): the expression of a gene for somatostatin. In this experiment the gene itself was synthesized chemically – a feasible undertaking since it is less than 50 base pairs long – rather than being fished out from the total DNA of a mammalian cell.
[3] Report of the Working Party on the Experimental Manipulation of the Genetic Composition of Micro-Organisms (Cmnd. 5880, HMSO, January 1975).
[4] S. N. Cohen, *Science*, Vol. 195, p. 654, 1977.

of physical containment, less expensive to build and less irksome to work in, for any particular experiment.

When it comes to administration of the guidelines, the situation is still very fluid and most countries have yet to take any official action. In the U.S.A., various specific recombinant DNA bills have been drafted, but the form of eventual legal controls is still far from clear. Britain has dealt with the problem by setting up a Genetic Manipulation Advisory Group (GMAG),[5] with lay and scientific membership, which has to be notified of the intention to carry out any experiment involving recombinant DNA, however trivial, and of the containment provisions to be used. Prior permission to proceed must be sought for experiments in the higher categories of possible risk. This system of control shows every sign of working satisfactorily

What began as a call for a short breathing space on the part of the scientists first exploring this field has escalated into a world-wide discussion which has already led to the expenditure of large sums of money on laboratory safety features. On the credit side, scientific knowledge is flowing from the experiments in an ever-increasing flood and the first practical applications may be just around the corner. However things turn out, the mid-1970's will surely be a fascinating period for scientific historians of the twenty-first century and later to look back upon.

[5] Report of the Working Party on the Practice of Genetic Manipulation (Cmnd. 6600, HMSO, August 1976.)

# INTERNATIONAL ORGANIZATIONS

# I. United Nations

## STRUCTURE

THE name 'United Nations' was devised by the late President Roosevelt, and was first used in the Declaration by United Nations of 1 January, 1942, when representatives of 26 nations pledged their governments to continue fighting together against the Axis powers.

The Charter of the United Nations was drawn up by the representatives of 50 countries at the Conference on International Organization, which met at San Francisco from 25 April to 26 June 1945, and was signed on the latter date. The representatives worked on the basis of principles which had been formulated by representatives of the United Kingdom, the U.S.A., the Soviet Union and China at Dumbarton Oaks from August to October 1944. The States invited to the San Francisco Conference were those which had declared war on the Axis powers and adhered to the Declaration by United Nations of 1 January 1942. In this declaration the 26 nations which were the original signatories and the 21 others which subsequently adhered to it formally subscribed to the purposes and principles of the Atlantic Charter and agreed not to make a separate peace. The invitation to Poland was held over owing to the fact that a Provisional Government of National Unity had not yet been formed. Four other countries were invited by the Conference itself, making a total of 51. These 51 states are the original members of the United Nations. The United Nations officially came into existence on 24 October 1945, when the United Kingdom, the U.S.A., France, the U.S.S.R. and China, and a majority of other signatories, ratified the Charter. All the signatories had ratified it by 31 December 1945, Poland having signed on 15 October. The aims and ideals of the United Nations are set forth in the Preamble to the Charter, which states that the Peoples of the United Nations are determined to prevent war, 'reaffirm faith in fundamental human rights, in the dignity and worth of the human person, in the equal rights of men and women and of nations large and small'; to maintain treaty obligations and the observance of international law; and to 'promote social progress and better standards of life in larger freedom'. Nothing in the Charter authorizes the United Nations to intervene in matters which come essentially within the national province of any state. However, the Charter states, this principle shall not prejudice the application of enforcement measures under Chapter VII concerning action with respect to threats to the peace, breaches of the peace and acts of aggression.

The official languages are Chinese, English, French, Russian and Spanish, and the working languages are English and French. Russian and Spanish are also working languages of the General Assembly. Membership is open to all peace-loving nations who are prepared to accept the obligations of the Charter, and is effected on the recommendation of the Security Council by the General Assembly. In December 1973 there was a total of 134 members (including the 51 Charter members).

The Headquarters of the United Nations is in New York City U.S.A.

The 148 Member States of the United Nations, and the date of admission to the Organization, are as follows:

| | |
|---|---|
| Afghanistan | 19 November 1946 |
| Albania | 14 December 1955 |
| Algeria | 8 October 1962 |
| Angola | 1 December 1976 |
| *Argentina | 24 October 1945 |
| *Australia | 1 November 1945 |
| Austria | 14 December 1955 |
| Bahamas | 18 September 1973 |
| Bahrain | 21 September 1971 |
| Bangladesh | 17 September 1974 |
| Barbados | 9 December 1966 |
| *Belgium | 27 December 1945 |
| Benin[1] | 20 September 1960 |
| Bhutan | 21 September 1971 |
| *Bolivia | 14 November 1945 |
| Botswana | 17 October 1966 |
| *Brazil | 24 October 1945 |
| Bulgaria | 14 December 1955 |
| Burma | 19 April 1948 |
| Burundi | 18 September 1962 |
| *Byelorussian SSR | 24 October 1945 |
| *Canada | 9 November 1945 |
| Cape Verde | 16 September 1975 |
| Central African Empire[2] | 20 September 1960 |
| Chad | 20 September 1960 |
| *Chile | 24 October 1945 |
| *China[3] | 24 October 1945 |
| *Colombia | 5 November 1945 |
| Comoros | 12 November 1975 |
| Congo | 20 September 1960 |
| *Costa Rica | 2 November 1945 |
| *Cuba | 24 October 1945 |
| Cyprus | 20 September 1960 |
| *Czechoslovakia | 24 October 1945 |
| Democratic Kampuchea[4] | 14 December 1955 |
| Democratic Yemen | 14 December 1967 |
| *Denmark | 24 October 1945 |
| Djibouti | 21 September 1977 |
| Dominican Republic | 24 October 1945 |
| *Ecuador | 21 December 1945 |
| *Egypt[5] | 24 October 1945 |
| *El Salvador | 24 October 1945 |
| Equatorial Guinea | 12 November 1968 |
| *Ethiopia | 13 November 1945 |
| Fiji | 13 October 1970 |
| Finland | 14 December 1955 |
| *France | 24 October 1945 |
| Gabon | 20 September 1960 |
| Gambia | 21 September 1965 |
| German Democratic Republic | 18 September 1973 |
| Germany, Federal Republic of | 18 September 1973 |
| Ghana | 8 March 1957 |
| *Greece | 25 October 1945 |
| Grenada | 17 September 1974 |
| *Guatemala | 21 November 1945 |
| Guinea | 12 December 1958 |
| Guinea Bissau | 17 September 1974 |
| Guyana | 20 September 1966 |
| *Haiti | 24 October 1945 |
| *Honduras | 17 December 1945 |
| Hungary | 14 December 1955 |
| Iceland | 19 November 1946 |
| *India | 30 October 1945 |
| Indonesia[6] | 28 September 1950 |
| *Iran | 24 October 1945 |
| *Iraq | 21 December 1945 |
| Ireland | 14 December 1955 |
| Israel | 11 May 1949 |
| Italy | 14 December 1955 |
| Ivory Coast | 20 September 1960 |
| Jamaica | 18 September 1962 |
| Japan | 18 December 1956 |
| Jordan | 14 December 1955 |
| Kenya | 16 December 1963 |
| Kuwait | 14 May 1963 |
| Lao People's Democratic Republic | 14 December 1955 |
| *Lebanon | 24 October 1945 |
| Lesotho | 17 October 1966 |
| *Liberia | 2 November 1945 |
| Libyan Arab Republic | 14 December 1955 |
| *Luxembourg | 24 October 1945 |
| Madagascar | 20 September 1960 |
| Malawi | 1 December 1964 |
| Malaysia[7] | 17 September 1957 |
| Maldives | 21 September 1965 |
| Mali | 28 September 1960 |

* Original Member.

| | |
|---|---|
| Malta | 1 December 1964 |
| Mauritania | 27 October 1961 |
| Mauritius | 24 April 1968 |
| *Mexico | 7 November 1945 |
| Mongolia | 27 October 1961 |
| Morocco | 12 November 1956 |
| Mozambique | 16 September 1975 |
| Nepal | 14 December 1955 |
| *Netherlands | 10 December 1945 |
| *New Zealand | 24 October 1945 |
| *Nicaragua | 24 October 1945 |
| Niger | 20 September 1960 |
| Nigeria | 7 October 1960 |
| *Norway | 27 November 1945 |
| Oman | 7 October 1971 |
| Pakistan | 30 September 1947 |
| *Panama | 13 November 1945 |
| Papua New Guinea | 16 September 1975 |
| *Paraguay | 24 October 1945 |
| *Peru | 31 October 1945 |
| *Philippines | 24 October 1945 |
| *Poland | 24 October 1945 |
| Portugal | 14 December 1955 |
| Qatar | 21 September 1971 |
| Romania | 14 December 1955 |
| Rwanda | 18 September 1962 |
| Samoa | 16 December 1976 |
| Sao Tome and Principe | 16 September 1975 |
| *Saudi Arabia | 24 October 1945 |
| Senegal | 28 September 1960 |
| Seychelles | 21 September 1976 |
| Sierra Leone | 27 September 1961 |
| Singapore | 21 September 1965 |
| Somalia | 20 September 1960 |
| *South Africa | 7 November 1945 |
| Spain | 14 December 1955 |
| Sri Lanka | 14 December 1955 |
| Sudan | 12 November1956 |
| Swaziland | 24 September 1968 |
| Sweden | 19 November 1946 |
| *Syria Arab Republic[3] | 24 October 1945 |
| Thailand | 16 December 1946 |
| Togo | 20 September 1960 |
| Trinidad and Tobago | 18 September 1962 |
| Tunisia | 12 November 1956 |
| *Turkey | 24 October 1945 |
| Uganda | 25 October 1962 |
| *Ukrainian SSR | 24 October 1945 |
| *USSR | 24 October 1945 |
| United Arab Emirates | 9 December 1971 |
| *United Kingdom of Great Britain and Northern Ireland | 24 October 1945 |
| United Republic of Cameroon | 20 September 1960 |
| United Republic of Tanzania[6] | 14 December 1961 |
| *United States of America | 24 October 1945 |
| Upper Volta | 20 September 1960 |
| *Uruguay | 18 December 1945 |
| *Venezuela | 15 November 1945 |
| Vietnam | 21 September 1977 |
| Yemen | 30 September 1947 |
| *Yugoslavia | 24 October 1945 |
| Zaire | 20 September 1960 |
| Zambia | 1 December 1964 |

*** Original Member**

[1] Formerly Dahomey

[2] Formerly Central African Republic

[3] By resolution 2758 (XXVI) of 25 October 1971, the General Assembly decided "to restore all its rights to the People's Republic of China and to recognize the representatives of its Government as the only legitimate representatives of China to the United Nations, and to expel forthwith the representatives of Chiang Kai-shek from the place which they unlawfully occupy at the United Nations and in all the organizations related to it".

[4] Formerly Cambodia

[5] Egypt and Syria were original Members of the United Nations from 24 October 1945. Following a plebiscite on 21 February 1958, the United Arab Republic was established by a union of Egypt and Syria and continued as a single Member. On 13 October 1961, Syria, having resumed its status as an independent State, resumed its separate membership in the United Nations. On 2 September 1971, the United Arab Republic changed its name to Arab Republic of Egypt.

[6] By letter of 20 January 1965, Indonesia announced its decision to withdraw from the United Nations "at this stage and under the present circumstances". By telegram of 19 September 1966, it announced its decision "to resume full co-operation with the United Nations and to resume participation in its activities". On 28 September 1966, the General Assembly took note of this decision and the President invited representatives of Indonesia to take seats in the Assembly.

[7] The Federation of Malaya joined the United Nations on 17 September 1957. On 16 September 1963, its name changed to Malaysia, following the admission to the new federation of Singapore, Sabah (North Borneo) and Sarawak. Singapore became an independent State on 9 August 1965 and a Member of the United Nations on 21 September 1965.

[8] Tanganyika was a Member of the United Nations from 14 December 1961 and Zanzibar was a Member from 16 December 1963. Following the ratification, on 26 April 1964, of Articles of Union between Tanganyika and Zanzibar, the United Republic of Tanganyika and Zanzibar continued as a single Member, later changing its name to United Republic of Tanzania on 1 November 1964.

The six main organs of the United Nations are:

The General Assembly
The Security Council
The Economic and Socia Council
The Trusteeship Council
The International Court of Justice
The Secretariat

# THE GENERAL ASSEMBLY

PRESIDENT

(Thirty-first Session, 1976)
Shirley H. Amerasinghe (Sri Lanka)

The General Assembly comprises all member states, each of which may have not more than five representatives and may decide the way in which to choose its representatives, but has only one vote. It meets regularly once a year, but special sessions can be convened at the request of the Security Council, of a majority of members or of one member supported by a majority of members.

Its functions are: To consider and make recommendations on the principles of general co-operation in the maintenance of international peace and security, including the principles governing disarmament and the regulation of armaments:

To discuss any problem affecting peace and security and, except where a dispute or situation is currently being discussed by the Security Council, to make recommendations on it. (The Assembly in 1950 decided that if the Security Council, because of lack of unanimity of the permanent members, fails to exercise its primary responsibility for the maintenance of international peace and security in any case where there appears to be a threat to the peace, breach of the peace, or act of aggression, the Assembly shall consider the matter immediately with a view to making recommendations to Members for collective measures, including in the case of a breach of the peace or act of aggression, the use of armed force when necessary):

To discuss and, with the same exception, to make recommendations on any question within the scope of the Charter affecting the powers and functions of any organ of the United Nations:

To initiate studies and make recommendations to promote international political co-operation, the development of international law and its codification, the realization of human rights and fundamental freedoms for all, and international collaboration in economic, social, cultural, education and health fields:

To receive and consider reports from the Security Council and other organs of the United Nations:

To make recommendations for the peaceful settlement of any situation, regardless of origin, which might impair friendly relations among nations:

To supervise, through the Trusteeship Council, the execution of the Trusteeship Agreements for areas not designated as strategic:

To elect the ten non-permanent members of the Security Council, the 27 members of the Economic and Social Council, those members of the Trusteeship Council which are elected; to take part (with the Security Council) in the election of the judges of the International Court of Justice; and, on the recommendation of the Security Council, to appoint the Secretary-General:

To consider and approve the budget of the United Nations, to apportion the contributions among members, and to examine the administrative budgets of specialized agencies.

The General Assembly deals with its work through seven main committees on each of which all members are entitled to be represented:

I Political and Security Committee (including the regulation of armaments).
Special Political Committee (to share the work of the first committee above).

II Economic and Financial Committee.

III Social, Humanitarian and Cultural Committee.

IV Trusteeship Committee (including non-self-governing territories).

V Administrative and Budgetary Committee.

VI Legal Committee.

The Chairmen of the above main committees in 1972 were Radha Krishna Ramphul (Mauritius); Hady Touré (Guinea); Bruce Rankin (Canada); Carlos Giambruno (Uruguay); Zdenek Cernik (Czechoslovakia); Motoo Ogiso (Japan); Erik Suy (Belgium).

In addition to these main committees, the Assembly may constitute other committees on which all members have the right to be represented. Preparatory Committees have been set up for the Second United Nations Development Decade, which started in 1970 and for the UN Conference on the Human Environment (Stockholm 1972).

There are also two procedural committees, the Credentials Committee of nine members appointed by the Assembly and the General (or Steering) Committee composed of 25 members (the President of the Assembly, 17 Vice-Presidents and the seven Main Committee Chairmen).

As a rule, the Assembly refers all questions on its agenda to one of the main Committees, to a joint committee, or to a specially appointed *ad hoc* committee. These committees then submit proposals for approval to a plenary meeting of the Assembly. Voting in committees and sub-committees is by simple majority. The Assembly may adopt resolutions without reference to any committee. The Assembly is further assisted by two standing committees: the Advisory Committee on Administrative and Budgetary Questions, comprising nine members, and the Committee on Contributions (ten members).

Budget appropriations for the United Nations financial year, 1973, amount to $225,920,420. By a General Assembly Resolution of 20 December 1961 and subsequent resolutions the Secretary-General was authorized to issue United Nations Bonds.

## THE SECURITY COUNCIL

*The Presidency of the Council is held monthly in turn by the Member States in English alphabetical order.*

THE Security Council comprises five permanent members and ten non-permanent members elected for a term of two years by the General Assembly.

Terms of office of temporary members of the Council end on 31 December of the year given in parentheses below:

| | | |
|---|---|---|
| Benin (1977) | India (1978) | Romania (1977) |
| Canada (1978) | Libya (1977) | U.S.S.R. |
| China | Mauritius (1978) | United Kingdom |
| France | Pakistan (1977) | United States |
| Germany (Federal Republic of) (1978) | Panama (1977) | Venezuela (1978) |

Its functions are: To maintain international peace and security in accordance with the Purposes and Principles of the United Nations:

To investigate any dispute or situation which might lead to international friction:

To recommend methods of adjusting such disputes or terms of settlement:

To formulate plans for the establishment of a system to regulate armaments:

To determine the existence of a threat to the peace or act of aggression and to recommend what action should be taken:

To call on Members to apply economic sanctions and other measures short of war in order to prevent or stop aggression:

To take military action against an aggressor:

To recommend the admission of new members and the terms on which states, non-members of the United Nations, may become parties to the Statute of the International Court of Justice:

To exercise the trusteeship functions of the United Nations in 'strategic areas':

To submit annual and special reports to the General Assembly.

The Security Council is primarily responsible for maintaining peace and security. Voting on all matters other than questions of procedure, when a decision is by an affirmative vote, of any nine members, requires the vote of nine members including the concurring votes of permanent members; but any member, whether permanent or not, may not vote when it is a party to a dispute.

The Council is so organized as to be able to function continuously and a representative of each of its members must always be present at the headquarters of the United Nations. It may meet at places other than at headquarters if considered advisable.

A country which is a member of the United Nations but not of the Council may take part in its discussions when the Council considers that country's interests are particularly affected. Both members and non-members are invited to take part in the Council's discussions when they are parties to disputes under the Council's consideration. In the case of a non-member the Security Council lays down the conditions under which it may participate.

The *Military Staff Committee*, which is composed of the Chiefs of Staff of the five permanent members or their representatives, according to the Charter, advises and assists the Security Council on such questions as the Council's military requirements for the maintenance of peace, the strategic direction of armed forces placed at its disposal, the regulation of armaments, and possible disarmament.

The *Disarmament Commission* was established by the General Assembly on 11 January 1952 to function under the Security Council, and by a decision of the 13th session of the General Assembly is now comprised of all members of the Organization. It replaces the Atomic Energy Commission, which was dissolved by the General Assembly, and the Commission for Conventional Armaments, which was dissolved by the Security Council.

The 1960s saw a number of encouraging achievements in the field of disarmament. On the eve of that decade in December 1959 the Antarctic Treaty was signed. In 1961, the Soviet Union and the United States succeeded in working out the Joint Statement of Agreed Principles for Disarmament Negotiations. The Agreed Principles were welcomed by the General Assembly and recommended by it as the basis for negotiations on general and complete disarmament. In 1963, the Treaty to Ban Nuclear Weapon Tests in the Atmosphere, in Outer Space and Under Water was signed. In late 1966 agreement was reached on the Outer Space Treaty banning nuclear and other weapons of mass destruction from that environment. In 1967 the Treaty for the Prohibition of Nuclear Weapons in Latin America was concluded. In 1968, the Treaty on the Non-Proliferation of Nuclear Weapons was completed and signed. All these treaties have entered into force.

The year 1970 marked the 25th Anniversary of the United Nations and it also marked the first year of the Disarmament Decade declared by the United Nations.

## THE ECONOMIC AND SOCIAL COUNCIL

THE Economic and Social Council is composed of 54 members States. Terms of office of members of the Council end on 31 December of the year given in parentheses listed below.

Afghanistan (1978)
Algeria (1978)
Argentina (1977)
Austria (1978)
Bangladesh (1978)
Bolivia (1978)
Brazil (1978)
Bulgaria (1977)
Canada (1977)
China (1977)
Columbia (1979)
Cuba (1978)
Czechoslovakia (1977)
Denmark (1977)
Ecuador (1977)
Ethiopia (1977)
France (1978)
Gabon (1977)
Germany (Fed. Rep. of) (1978)
Greece (1978)
Iran (1979)
Iraq (1979)
Italy (1979)
Jamaica (1979)
Japan (1977)
Kenya (1977)
Malaysia (1978)
Mauritania (1979)
Mexico (1979)
Netherlands (1979)
New Zealand (1979)
Nigeria (1978)
Norway (1977)
Pakistan (1977)
Peru (1977)
Phillipines (1979)
Poland (1979)
Portugal (1978)
Rwanda (1979)
Somalia (1979)
Sudan (1979)
Syria (1979)
Togo (1978)
Tunisia (1978)
Uganda (1978)
Ukraine (1979)
U.S.S.R. (1977)
United Kingdom (1977)
United States (1979)
Upper Volta (1979)
Venezuela (1978)
Yemen (1977)
Yugoslavia (1978)
Zaire (1977)

Retiring members are eligible for re-election.

Its functions are: To be responsible, under the authority of the General Assembly, for the economic and social activities of the United Nations:

To make or initiate studies, reports and recommendations on international economic, social, cultural, educational, health and related matters:

To promote respect for and observance of human rights and fundamental freedoms for all:

To call international conferences and prepare draft conventions for submission to the General Assembly on matters within its competence:

To negotiate agreements with the specialized agencies, defining the terms on which they shall be brought into relationship with the United Nations:

To co-ordinate the activities of the specialized agencies by means of consultation with them and recommendations to them, and by means of recommendations to the General Assembly and members of the United Nations:

To perform services, approved by the Assembly, for members of the United Nations and the specialized agencies upon request:

To consult with non-governmental agencies concerned with matters with which the Council deals.

The Council functions through commissions, sub-commissions and committees.

Four Regional Economic Commissions have also been established.

Members are elected by the Council and are nominated by countries in order to secure balanced representation in each Commission.

The United Nations Children's Fund (UNICEF) was established by the General Assembly on 11 December 1946 and functions under the supervision of the Economic and Social Council. It aids children and adolescents, particularly those in devastated countries. In 1950, greater emphasis began to be placed on the long-range needs of children and their continuing needs, particularly in under-developed countries. The Fund is administered by an Executive Director (appointed by the Secretary-General) under the guidance of an Executive Board of 30 nations, which determines allocations of sums, programmes, etc. The Executive Board is elected by the Economic and Social Council.

## THE TRUSTEESHIP COUNCIL

THE Trusteeship Council is composed of member states administering trust territories, permanent members who do not and a certain number of other members elected for three-year terms by the General Assembly to ensure that the Council is made up of an equal number of administering and non-administering members.

The members of the Council are China, France, U.S.S.R., U.K. and U.S.A. The Administering member is the U.S.A.

The Council's functions are: To formulate a questionnaire on the political, economic, social and educational advancement of the inhabitants of Trust Territories, on the basis of which administering authorities are to make annual reports: To examine and discuss reports from administering authorities: To examine petitions in consultation with the administering authorities: To make periodic inspection visits at times agreed upon with the administering authority.

Since 1947, the United Nations entered into a total of 11 Trusteeship Agreements. Nine of them provided for the transfer to U.N. trusteeship of certain territories formerly administered as mandates by the League of Nations, nine of the Agreements came to an end by February 1968.

The two remaining territories are: New Guinea, a former German territory, administered by Australia; and the Pacific Islands, composed of the former Japanese-mandated islands of the Marshalls, Marianas (with the exception of Guam) and Carolines (a strategic trust territory administered by the U.S.A. under an agreement approved by the Security Council in April 1947).

## THE INTERNATIONAL COURT OF JUSTICE

ESTABLISHED at The Hague in 1946, the Court functions under the authority of the United Nations, of which it is one of the judicial organs. Its judges (15) are chosen by majority votes in both the General Assembly and the Security Council. Their salaries are paid by the United Nations. They are nominated by the national groups in the Permanent Court of Arbitration, and by groups representing members of the United Nations who are not represented at that court. The selection from among the candidates rests with the General Assembly and the Security Council. Each of the judges must be of a different state, and not being representatives of their respective countries, or being responsible to any government; they enjoy complete judicial independence. A judge who may be a citizen of a state involved in a dispute is not debarred from taking part in the hearing, but he may not preside; and if the Court does not include such a judge the litigating state in question may nominate one of its own to sit for the occasion. No reference is made to the nationality of the judges, either during the hearing of cases, or when judgments or opinions are delivered. Their term of office is nine years, and they can be dismissed only by the unanimous vote of their colleagues. Nine judges form a quorum. The enforcement of their judgments rests with the Security Council. The official languages of the Court are English and French.

The Court's jurisdiction is limited. It can deal only with cases brought by sovereign states; it can adjudicate only with the consent of the parties; it can deal only with civil matters; it cannot handle criminal cases. It can consider cases for advisory opinions which are laid before it by the General Assembly, the Security Council or by certain specialized agencies.

The law which the Court administers is derived from (1) international treaties binding on the parties; (2) international customary law; (3) the general principles of law recognized by civilized nations, and (4) case law embodying decisions on points of international law, and the published works of expert jurists. The Court is not bound by precedent or by its own previous decisions.

The following was the composition of the court in 1977. The judges are listed in the official order of precedence. The nine-year term ends for each judge in the year indicated below:

Eduardo Jimenez de Arechaga (Uruguay) (1979) President
Nagendra Singh (India) (1982), Vice-President
Isaac Forster (Senegal) (1982)
Andre Gros (France) (1982)
Manfred Lachs (Poland) (1985)
Hardy C. Dillard (United States) (1979)
Louis Ignacio-Pinto (Dahomey) (1979)
Federico de Castro (Spain) (1979)
Platon D. Morozov (USSR) (1979)
Sir Humphrey Waldock (United Kingdom) (1982)
Jose Maria Ruda (Argentina) (1982)
Hermann Mosler (Federal Republic of Germany) (1985)
Taslim O. Elias (Nigeria) (1985)
Salah El Dine Tarazi (Syria) (1985)
Shigeru Oda (Japan) (1985)

The Court may adjudicate, and its findings may be correct; but it does not follow that it will be obeyed in all cases. For example, in the case of the United Kingdom against Albania arising out of the mining of the Corfu Channel, judgment was given against Albania, but the damages awarded by the Court, £843,947, have never been paid. On the other side, when the Court upheld Britain's ownership of the Minquiers and Ecrehous islets lying between Jersey and the French mainland, its decision was accepted by France.

The Court's jurisdiction has been challenged more than once, and the Court has found itself incompetent to judicate, as in the claim of the United Kingdom against Persia in the matter of the Anglo-Iranian Oil Company, in the Ambatielos case between Greece and the United Kingdom (when the latter challenged the Court's jurisdiction), and in the dispute between Italy, the United Kingdom, France and the United States as to the ownership of gold looted from the National Bank of Albania in Rome by the Germans in 1944. In this case Italy objected to the Court's competence, and the Court had to hold that it could not decide on the merits of the claim in the absence of Albania's consent.

On 18 July 1966, the Court delivered its Judgment in the second phase of the South West Africa cases (Ethiopia *v.* South Africa; Liberia *v.* South Africa). These cases, relating to the continued existence of the Mandate for South West Africa and the duties and performance of South Africa as Mandatory thereunder, were instituted by applications of the Governments of Ethiopia and Liberia filed in the Registry on 4 November 1960. By an Order of 20 May 1961 the Court joined the proceedings in the two cases. The Government of South Africa raised preliminary objections to the Court's proceedings to hear the merits of the case, but these were dismissed by the Court on 21 December 1962, the Court finding that it had jurisdiction to adjudicate upon the merits of the dispute. By its Judgment, the Court, by the President's casting vote—the votes being equally divided, seven-seven—found that the Applicant States could not be considered to have established any legal right or interest in the subject matter of their claims and accordingly decided to reject them.

## SECRETARIAT

THE Secretariat is composed of the Secretary-General, the chief administrative officer of the United Nations, who is appointed by the General Assembly on the recommendation of the Security Council, and such staff as the Organization may require.

The Secretary-General acts in that capacity at all meetings of the General Assembly, the Security Council, the Economic and Social Council and the Trusteeship Council, and performs such other functions as are entrusted to him by these organs. He is required to submit an annual report to the General Assembly on the work of the Organization. One of the special powers of the Secretary-General is the fact that he may bring to the attention of the Security Council any matter which in his opinion may threaten the maintenance of international peace and security.

The principal members are:

*Secretary-General:*
Dr. Kurt Waldheim (Austria)

*Under-Secretaries-General:*
C. V. Narasimhan (India), Inter-Agency Affairs and Co-ordination.
R. Guyer (Argentina), Special Political Affairs.
B. Urquhart (U.K.), Special Political Affairs.
Ming-chao Tang (Peoples' Republic of China), Political Affairs and De-colonization.
William Buffum (U.S.A.), Political and General Assembly Affairs.
A Shevchenko (U.S.S.R.), Political and Security Council Affairs.
E. Suy (Belgium), Legal Counsel.
Gabriel van Laethem (France), Department of Economic and Social Affairs.
George Davidson (Canada), Administration and Management.
Helmut F. Debatin (controller).
Bohdan Lewandowski (Poland), Conference Services.
V. Winspeare Guicciardi (Italy), Director-General of the UN Office at Geneva.
Abderrahman Khane (Algeria), Executive Director, UN Industrial Development Organization.
G. Corea (Sri Lanka), Secretary-General of UNCTAD.
H. R. Labouisse (U.S.A.), Executive Director of UNICEF.

*Administrator, United Nations Development Programme:*
Bradford Morse (U.S.A.).

*Executive Director United Nations Environment Programme*
Mostafa Talba (Egypt).

*Assistant Secretaries-General:*
M. H. Gherab (Tunisia), Director of Personnel.
I. T. Kittani (Iraq), Executive Assistant to the Secretary-General.
Genichi Akatani (Japan), Office of Public Information,
Robert Ryan (U.S.A.), Office of General Services.

*Regional Commissions:*
Adebayo Adedeji (Nigeria), Executive Secretary, Economic Commission for Africa. J. B. P. Maramis (Indonesia), Executive Secretary, Economic and Social Commission for Asia and the Pacific. J. Stanovik (Yugoslavia). Executive Secretary, Economic Commission for Europe. Davidson Nicol (Sierra Leone), Executive Director of United Nations Institute for Training and Research.

## UNITED NATIONS COMMISSIONS

THE United Nations and its related network of commissions and specialized agencies have set up multilateral technical assistance programmes for international sharing of the technical knowledge and skills essential to supplement the efforts of the less developed countries for economic and social progress. The General Assembly set up the United Nations Development Programme, an amalgamation of the Special Fund and the Expanded Programme for Technical Assistance, on 22 November 1965.

The United Nations has enabled the nations of four great regions—Europe, Asia and the Far East, Africa, and Latin America—to co-operate in solving common economic difficulties through its regional economic commissions in Geneva, Bangkok, Addis Ababa and Santiago (Chile).

The United Nations High Commissioner for Refugees (UNHCR) assists and protects 2·5 million refugees in many parts of the world (High Commissioner: Prince Sadruddin Aga Khan). The United Nations Relief and Works Agency (UNRWA) aids over 1·2 million refugees from Palestine in the Middle East (Commissioner: Thomas McElhiney).

## INTERNATIONAL ATOMIC ENERGY AGENCY

International Atomic Energy Agency: this agency, established to promote the peaceful uses of atomic energy and prevent their diversion to military uses, came into existence on 29 July 1957. The International Atomic Energy Agency is an autonomous member of the United Nations system. The I.A.E.A. fosters and encourages the peaceful uses of atomic energy throughout the world and provides assistance to developing countries for this purpose. It organizes technical meetings, publishes scientific literature, establishes safety standards for all types of nuclear activities, prepares feasibility and market studies for nuclear power and operates three laboratories. It applies safeguards to nuclear materials in more than sixty countries to ensure that they are used only for their intended peaceful purposes. The entry into force in March 1970 of the treaty on the non-proliferation of nuclear weapons required the 'Non-nuclear-Weapon' states party to that treaty to conclude agreements with the agency to apply safeguards to all nuclear materials in all their peaceful nuclear activities. Such states are at present party to the treaty.

In 1977 the number of I.A.E.A. member states amounted to 110.

The principal organs of the I.A.E.A. are the general converence and the board of governors. The secretariat is headed by a director general. The general conference consists of all member states of the agency. The board of governors consists of 34 members. The members of the board of governors during 1977–1978 are: Argentina, Australia, Austria, Belgium, Brazil, Bulgaria, Canada, Czechoslovakia, Ecuador Egypt, France, Federal Republic of Germany, Ghana, India, Iran, Italy, Japan, Kuwait, Malaysia, Mexico, Niger, Nigeria, Norway, Pakistan, Panama, Peru, Portugal, Republic of Korea, Romania, Senegal, Tunisia, Union of Soviet Socialist Republics, United Kingdom of Great Britain and Northern Ireland, United States of America,

Chairman of the Boards is H.E. Mr. Khor Eng Hee (Malaysia), Vice-Chairman: Mr Karel Barabas (Czechoslovakia), Mr. Reinhard Loosch (Federal Republic of Germany).

Members of the agency's scientific advisory committee are: Professor H. G. Carvalho, Brazil; Dr. Floyd Culler, United States of America; Professor I. Dostrovski, Israel; Dr. M. A. El-Guebeily, Egypt; Dr. B. Goldschmidt, France; Professor W. Haefele, Federal Republic of Germany; Dr. T. Ipponmatsu, Japan; Dr. W. B. Lewis, Canada; Dr. I. D. Morokhov, Union of Soviet Socialist Republics; Dr. W. C. Marshall, United Kingdom of Great Britain and Northern Ireland; Dr. H. N. Sethna, India; Professor B. F. Straub, Hungary.

*Director General:* Dr. Sigvard Eklund. *Deputy Directors General:* John A. Hall (Administration); Hidetake Kakihana (Research and Isotopes); Rudolf Rometsch (Safeguards); Helio F. S. Bittencourt (Technical Assistance and Publications); Ivan S. Zheludev; (Technical Operations). Assistant *Director General for External Relations:* David A. V. Fischer. *Address:* Kärtnern Ring 11, P.O.B. 590 A-1011 Vienna I.

# II. Specialized Agencies

## FOOD AND AGRICULTURE ORGANIZATION OF THE UNITED NATIONS (FAO)

FAO was founded at a conference in Quebec in 1945. Its objectives are to increase world agricultural, fisheries and forestry productivity and to improve conditions of life of people engaged in these fields.

FAO began with 44 member countries; by the end of 1975 there were 136 members.

FAO collects and disseminates statistics and technical information; it analyses trends and suggests policies to governments. It participates in international meetings for the exchange of information and the negotiation of agreements. It sends specialists to developing countries to help with technical problems and to plan development activities. Through cooperative arrangements with international banking groups it helps countries gain financing for development works.

The 18th session of the FAO Conference, meeting in November 1975, approved a budget of $167 million for the two years 1976–77.

*World Food and Agricultural Situation*

During the past year there has been a distinct improvement in the immediate world food and agricultural situation. Production in the developing countries and in North America and Oceania expanded in 1975 and prospects for the 1976 crops are generally good. Prices have consequently tended to ease and there has been some recovery both in the food consumption of developing countries and in world cereal stocks from the low levels of recent years.

Nevertheless, progress towards the longer-term goal of greater world food security has been disappointing. Measured against the need to improve nutritional levels, the trend in food production in developing countries remains inadequate. In spite of higher priority for agriculture in many of these countries, recent production increases must be mainly attributed to better weather.

World cereal stocks increased in 1975–76 for the first time in three years. This, however, has only brought them back to 13 per cent of annual consumption, or about the same proportion as in 1973–74, when the situation was considered precarious. They are still some 35 to 45 million tons below the level of 17 to 18 per cent of annual consumption which is regarded by FAO as a minimum safe level for world food security. However, the present favourable production prospects may further replenish stocks in 1976–77. Hence the urgent necessity that the many signatories of the International Undertaking on World Food Security substantiate their pledges concerning international coordination and nationally-held stocks.

Recent trends in world trade in agricultural products have been unfavourable for developing countries. Their earnings from agricultural exports fell substantially in 1975, and recent price changes have generally operated against them. Negotiations on trade and related matters continued through 1976 but virtually no progress can be recorded.

In 1975 there was encouraging expansion in the amount of international development assistance available for agriculture in the Third World. However, bilateral assistance to agriculture from the Development Assistance Committee countries of the OECD (Organization for Economic Co-operation and Development) dropped sharply in 1975, and in the fiscal year 1975–76 there was also a fall in commitments to agriculture by the World Bank, the major source of lending for the agricultural sector.

*The FAO Conference*

The 18th session of the FAO Conference was held in November 1975. Five newly-independent countries were admitted to the Organization, bringing its membership to 136 nations: Bahamas, Cape Verde, Grenada, Papua New Guinea and Surinam.

The opinion prevailed among Conference delegates that the key to long-term solution of the world food problem lies in greatly increased production in the developing countries. However, lasting improvement in the world food situation, while dependent on technical, commercial and financial action, also involved political and social change. Hopes were expressed that the International Fund for Agricultural Development, proposed by the World Food Conference, would soon be established. The Conference recognized that the fertilizer problem at present handicaps efforts to increase production in developing countries. Although the supply situation has eased and prices have declined, the poorer countries do not have the necessary foreign exchange for imports.

The session reviewed the status of the International Undertaking on World Food Security, an FAO initiative aimed at achieving a co-ordinated system of national food stock policies which would guarantee at least a safe minimum of basic food stocks. The 59 countries which have so far subscribed to the undertaking account for about 95 per cent of world cereal exports and more than half of such imports. To be fully effective; however, the cooperation of all countries is necessary and governments were invited to join the Undertaking or to support its broad objectives.

Remedial action to beat the shortage of pulp and paper predicted for the 1980's and the current dearth of fuel wood was proposed by the Conference. Although 55 per cent of the world's forests are in developing countries, these account for only 6·2 per cent of pulp and paper production capacity and they import virtually all their supplies of such products. Investment in developing their milling industry is encouraged. The Conference advocated consideration of an international research centre or programme to develop operational techniques for manufacturing pulp and paper from mixed tropical hardwoods, which constitute the most abundant natural forests in the Third World.

Industrialized countries were urged to assist developing countries in setting up their own forest industries for the local manufacture of wood products. Attention was drawn to the importance of silviculture and delegates were told that indiscriminate tree-felling is largely to blame for the droughts and floods which have occurred during the past few years. Finally, the tendency to sacrifice forest land for additional farming and grazing land was questioned. FAO urged the adoption of rational land use in lieu of haphazard agricultural practices which often result in stable forest land being turned into poor or degraded crop land.

*Funds for Field Work*

Approximately four-fifths of the funds received by FAO are spent on field activities. The largest source of finance is the UN Development Programme (UNDP) which in 1976 accounted for about $107 million disbursed by FAO on some 600 large-scale and small-scale projects. These will eventually involve an outlay of some $498 million.

A liquidity crisis which hit UNDP late in 1975 caused FAO to cut or suspend a number of projects with a consequent drop in expenditure from the 1975 total of $120 million.

Broadened activities of the Sahel Inter-State Committee for Drought Control and the establishment of "le Club des Amis du Sahel" in 1976 added coordinating responsibilities to the tasks which FAO's Sahel Unit is performing in the programme of seminars, information support and technical consultations on behalf of the drought-prone area.

A $45 million three-year programme was initiated in 1976 by the bilateral agencies of Denmark (DANIDA), Finland, Norway (NORAD), and Sweden (SIDA) in cooperation with FAO to assist newly-independent countries. The Mozambique Government has requested the Organization to implement some $15 million worth of projects under Trust Fund arrangement with the Nordic donors.

Plans for the establishment of the FAO/Near East Cooperative Programme went forward. The amount pledged to the Programme in 1976 totalled $29 million, and 64 projects were approved for submission to donor countries. Donor support was confirmed for five regional and eight national projects, and financial commitments amounted to $15 million.

There was a growing number of requests for FAO assistance through unilateral Trust Fund agreements under which countries finance FAO execution of part of their national development programmes. New Trust Fund projects became operational in Iran, Iraq and Libya. FAO will execute the technical assistance and training components of projects financed by two World Bank loans to the People's Democratic Republic of Yemen.

The FAO/Government Cooperative Programme was joined by new donors wishing to channel part of their development aid through the Organization. Belgium contributed $5.6 million to the financing of projects in Senegal. The first Trust Fund operation undertaken by the USA in this Programme involved assistance to rehabilitation projects in the Sahel. Switzerland helped some UNDP/FAO projects affected by the liquidity crisis. Germany and Holland committed large amounts for the Food Security Assistance Scheme. Canada and the Nordic donors increased their support.

In 1976, FAO set up its own Technical Cooperation Programme to deal with emergency situations and provide in areas not covered by existing field programmes. The sum of $18·5 million was ear-marked for the 1976–77 biennium, and the first projects under the Programme were approved towards the end of 1976.

*Investment*

Developing countries seeking capital for agricultural improvement turn increasingly to FAO for assistance in presenting the information required by multilateral, regional and national financing institutions. During 1976 efforts to improve the social and economic conditions of the poorest farmers accounted for a large proportion of the agricultural projects prepared by FAO and accepted by the World Bank. The Bank approved a loan of $60 million for a $143 million plan for irrigation, land reclamation, roads and bridges, water supply, electricity and fuelwood plantations which will affect 15,000 villages in Korea and some four million people, or about 30 per cent of the country's rural population.

More than 900,000 rural poor in Bangladesh will benefit from a $25 million project which is expected to increase jobs by 25 per cent and rice production by some 75,000 tons annually through better irrigation, credit facilities for farmers and strengthened institutions. Provision of agricultural inputs, modern infrastructure and social services under a $13 million project in Bolivia should give higher living standards to 10,000 rural families on the high plateaux—the Altiplano—and increase production of vegetables, cereals, milk and meat by local farmers.

Credits granted in 1976 by the International Development Association, the "soft loan" affiliate of the World Bank, will help to set up a quality seeds industry in Pakistan. The $56 million project will cover research, multiplication, processing certification, storage and marketing. In Yemen, some 5,000 farm families will be involved in a $7·7 million effort to increase production through the provision of farm equipment, feeder roads, extension services and safe water. Approximately 2,500 farm families in the arid northwest region of Somalia will be able to produce more food as new or repaired earthen embankments collect precious rainfall, small irrigated farms are developed and extension services invigorated under a $13 million project.

Improved export earnings from Afghanistan's meat and livestock products, better flocks and higher incomes for its partly nomadic sheep herders are the targets of a $18 million project which will help to set up sheep improvement centres, veterinary stations, a credit structure and technical training, in addition to providing new wells and access roads.

Regional Banks' increased emphasis on agricultural development broadened the scope of FAO cooperation in 1976. Planning in conjunction with the Inter-American Development Bank covered rural development in Panama, fisheries in Chile, Ecuador, Guatemala and Jamaica, irrigation in Haiti, forestry in Paraguay and Peru, and marketing and research in Jamaica.

Nearly all the agricultural projects financed by the African Development Bank and Fund were drawn up with FAO assistance. Projects for smallholder forestry in Cameroon, cacao development in Gabon, livestock production in Ethiopia, oil palm growing in the Central African Republic, irrigation in Upper Volta, tea in Rwanda and seeds in Mali were all approved for financing. Malawi was allocated $6 million for roads, produce stores, health centres, crop and stock protection, training, credit and extension services to help 7,000 farm families which depend on their output of maize, peanuts, tobacco and pulses.

Joint investment work with the Asian Development Bank has resulted in a $17 million project which will provide Afghanistan with quality wheat and cotton seed and fruit tree seedlings and should increase crop yields by ten to 20 per cent.

The FAO/Bankers Programme, which helps national development banks in the Third World to formulate investment projects, acquired new members in 1976. Work undertaken during the year included oil palm development in Thailand, fisheries in Indonesia and Morocco, mechanized rice production in Sierra Leone, forest settlement in Brazil, wood industries in Pakistan, sugar production in Colombia and Venezuela, and sugar storage in the Philippines.

Agreement was reached for cooperation with the Arab Fund for Economic and Social Development, and working arrangements were negotiated with the Kuwait Fund, the Islamic Development Bank and the Corporación Andina de Fomento.

*World Food Programme*

During 1976 the resources committed by the Programme since its inception in 1962 reached more than $3,000 million. WFP, which was established under the auspices of the UN and FAO, has made these resources available to some 800 social and economic development projects in 105 countries and to an estimated 230 emergency relief operations in more than 90 countries.

The target for the Programme's food aid pledges for the 1975–76 biennium was set at $440 million in 1974, but at the end of August 1976 pledges stood at $667 million, or more than 50 per cent above the target. Additional pledges enabled the Programme to enter into commitments for an amount of almost $600 million for 1976, compared with $368 for 1975 and $105 million for 1974.

A pledging target of $750 million for the two-year period 1977–78 was agreed to in October 1975 by WFP's 24-nation governing body, the Intergovernmental Committee, and by August the following year pledges had already reached $554 million. As a result of recommendations at the World Food Conference in November 1974, the Programme's governing body was reconstituted, and it has now become the Committee on Food Aid Policies and Programmes (CFA), a 30-nation body charged with the additional responsibilities of coordinating international food aid.

New projects approved by the CFA in 1976 represented an outlay of $554 million—the highest amount ever approved in one year. The largest of these was a three-year project with a total value of more than $60 million for Bangladesh, for reactivating many of its great waterways which had become silted up and unusable. Other major projects approved included resettlement of nomads and farmers in Somalia over three years at a cost of $21 million, $15 million for developing agriculture and resettling farmers in the Salikh and Euphrates basins of Syria, and two projects expansions and one new project in Pakistan at a total cost of more than $25 million.

Some $40 million of the Programme's resources was allocated for emergency aid during the year.

*Fisheries*

Estimated at some 70 million tons, the 1975 world catch matched the 1974 level. However, the supply of fish for direct human consumption, as opposed to fish meal for stock feeding, reached a record of some 50 million tons compared with a little more than 37 million tons in 1965, a rate of expansion greater than that of the world population.

Fishery projects operating during the year totalled 137, of which 40 were supported by national development agency contributions amounting to $11·7 million. Working closely with regional fishery commissions, FAO was involved in the operation of one global, 12 inter-regional and 17 regional projects to the value of $16·8 million Regional projects now cover the Indian Ocean, the South China Sea, the Gulf States, West African countries, the Western Central Atlantic and the Southern Ocean.

Short-term projects carried out in 1976 proved that modest inputs of technical assistance can produce speedy and often far-reaching results. Demonstrations of fishing methods in Yemen increased the catch rate of sardines to a level ensuring the viability of a profitable fish meal operation. Similar assistance to Bangladesh led to the identification of a quality control problem which was handicapping exports and demonstrations of remidial measures. FAO's Technical Cooperation Programme also partnered the rehabilitation of small-scale fisheries in the Philippines where operations had been affected by the recent earthquake.

The year 1976 was marked by more or less general recognition of the authority of coastal states over fisheries in the 200-mile zone. This development, combined with increasing pressure on fishery resources, implied new responsibilities for the countries concerned, which must now come to grips with problems of evaluation and resource management.

Augmented demand for FAO assistance has been acknowledged through support for expanded training facilities for the transfer of skill and technology from developed countries, the stimulation of international and private funding and the identification of opportunities for investment. Programmes were undertaken in Southwest Asia, the Far East and West Africa to improve the performance of small-scale fisheries on which the living conditions of millions of fishermen and ancillary workers depend.

In addition to the training element provided in many FAO field research projects, the Organization cooperated with the *Centre national pour l'Exploitation des océans* on stock assessment courses for French-speaking scientists, with the Norwegian International Development Agency (NORAD) on acoustic methods of resource survey, for Latin American scientists, and with the International Commission for the Conservation of Atlantic Tunas on tuna population dynamics. Technical papers on the construction of small fishing vessels, and manuals and guidelines on various types of fishing gear and on monitoring fish abundance were issued in new or revised form. Concurrently with advice on methods of quality control and fish inspection, audio-visual aids were devised for use in on-the-spot training.

A Regional Seminar on Fish Marketing was jointly planned with the Organization of American States in Lima, Peru. The Regional project for the establishment of a market information service for fish products in the Latin American Region completed its first phase. Workshops were organized on the business aspects of small-scale fishery enterprises and on development planning.

Regional collaboration emphasized pooling of data and co-ordination of national expertise. During 1976, working parties studied resources off West Africa and the shrimp stocks in the Malacca Strait and off coasts of Iran and the Arabian Peninsula. Inland fishery resources in Asia and the Caribbean were likewise investigated. The decline in whale stocks was discussed at a Consultation on Marine Mammals organized in Bergen, Norway, with support from the UN Environment Programme (UNER) and various governments. More than 400 participants representing 48 countries attended the World Conference on Aquaculture—or fish farming—held in Kyoto, Japan.

The protection of aquatic resources against pollution is a matter of increasing concern. The General Fisheries Council for the Mediterranean, one of FAO's eight Fishery bodies, is co-ordinating the execution of four pilot projects involving more than fifty research centres. Their participation is financially assisted by UNDP. The Aquatic Sciences and Fisheries Information System (ASFIS) was accepted as a UN Information System in 1976. In view of the increasing volume of information on marine and freshwater resources and their environment, FAO with the assistance of national input centres and the Inter-governmental Oceanographic Commission, is developing the services of ASFIS and disseminating its products in Member Countries. The FAO Council approved the statutes of a new Inland Fishery Commission for Latin America.

The first issue of a series of detailed regional bulletins of fishery statistics for the Mediterranean and the East Central Atlantic was published.

*Forestry*

More than 300 FAO experts—36 of them from developing countries—worked in the forests of 72 countries during 1976, helping their governments to operate 166 projects ranging from pulp and paper production to wildlife conservation and sawmilling.

The forests of Northern Thailand produce 70 per cent of the nation's timber output yet shifting cultivation, with consequent erosion and floods, has been destroying 40–50,000 ha. of forest annually. The demand for agricultural and forest products grows as living standards rise and in 1968 Thai became a net importer of wood for the first time in its history. Government efforts to change time-honoured but unrewarding methods, were supported by the Mae Sa Watershed and Forest Land Use project in Chiang Mai province, launched by UNDP/FAO. The result has been the adoption of intensive forestry practice combined with improved measures for settled agriculture such as horticulture, animal husbandry and small-scale crop production. New forms of land tenure, incentives and assistance with technical inputs have encouraged farmers' cooperation. The successful outcome of the project, which was scheduled for completion at the end of 1976, has induced the government to establish a Watershed Management Division to extend these activities to other areas.

FAO provided $600,000 worth of equipment under a UNDP/FAO project now helping India in its attempt to raise annual production of paper to two million tons by 1980. The current gap between national output and the mounting demand for paper, paperboard and newsprint has to be met by costly imports. The government is probing the country's forests in search of alternative raw materials, particularly the many species of hardwood and fast-growing trees. Any solution to the problem of processing these new varieties must hinge on technology and the project includes assistance to the Forest Research Institute, Dehra Dun and improved training facilities at the Institute of Paper Technology, Saharanpur. It is also enabling Indian research trainees to study in Australia, Czechoslovakia, Finland, Japan, the Netherlands, Norway, Sweden and the United Kingdom.

Institution-building assistance to Honduras led to the establishment of an organization for the promotion of forest protection and timber processing and marketing, which netted a profit of $3 million by the end of the year.

A training project for sawmilling in Nigeria, financed by a FAO/Finland Trust Fund, has set up an engineering extension service and a mobile saw-repairing unit. Both the unit and a training programme are run by local staff trained under the project and activities will be expanded on completion of the project sawmill.

The crocodile—properly managed—will be the opportunity for deprived groups living in economically marginal areas of

Papua New Guinea (PNG) to improve their living conditions and contribute to the national development process. The only saleable resource available in many parts of the country is the crocodile skin, for which there is steady world demand and declining supply. The country could increase its returns up to 1,000 per cent through the adoption of modern breeding and conservation methods and the limitation of local cropping to the crocodile population's annual surplus. The three-year project sponsored by UNDP/FAO which started operations in late 1976 will assist the government to establish legislative protected areas for wild crocodile and other wildlife management and evaluate the environmental effects of sustained-yield crocodile harvesting. Government extension personnel will be trained in crocodile husbandry and skin marketing. Backed by associated village farming units, annual production is expected approximate a current value of nearly $2 million, which will be reflected in higher incomes for the rural workers involved.

In 1976, FAO and the Swedish International Development Agency (SIDA) launched a five-year programme titled "Forestry for Community Development" aimed at promoting a "self-help" approach which will enable villages and rural settlements to draw the best returns from locally available resources in terms of production, consumption, inputs—including labour—and the marketing of any surplus. The combination of traditional craftsmanship, rational practices and team work is expected to raise levels of employment and income and link the community more closely with the rest of the nation. The Programme will emphasize "Blacksmith Technology"—local manufacture of simple equipment using low-cost machinery, mechanical components and material readily obtainable on the domestic market.

A consultation on the role of forestry in a rehabilitation programme for the Sahel, organized by FAO at the request of the Sahel Inter-State Committee for Drought Control was held in Dakar, Senegal, and attended by officials of the governments concerned and by representatives of multilateral and bilateral funding agencies. FAO helped the Secretariat of the UN Desertification Conference to prepare a feasibility study on the establishment of a Southern Sahara Green Belt. Three Forestry Conservation Guides went to press during the year.

With financial assistance from the UN Environment Programme (UNEP), FAO started a project for the conservation of forest genetic resources. Seeds and funds have been distributed for the establishment of conservation stands of tropical pines and eucalypts in developing countries.

A comprehensive survey of issues raised by the inroads on tropical moist forests and the problem of harvesting their wood without jeopardizing the environment was commissioned by FAO in 1974 and completed in 1976. The findings led to proposals for systematic and concerted action by FAO, forestry institutes, universities, development agencies and donors. Since tropical forest products are one of the largest commodity exports of developing countries, a new FAO service, launched in 1976, will provide monthly information on tropical hardwood trade.

The Pulp and Paper Industries Development Programme, in which UNDP and FAO cooperate with the World Bank, UNESCO and the UN Industrial Development Organization (UNIDO), carried out feasibility surveys during 1976 in the developing regions and data were assembled on which to base industrial planning directed towards a measure of self-sufficiency. A study has been made of the technical and economic problems connected with the establishment of small "quality paper" mills based on mechanical pulp technology. Mixed tropical forests constitute the only fibre resource for pulp and paper manufacture in many developing countries and FAO published an evaluation of the subject in 1976, together with a study on the pulp and paper-making properties of fast-growing plantation wood species.

The rapid expansion of wood-based panel industries during the past two decades has been matched by that of individual mill dimensions, which are now unsuitable for the requirements of many developing countries. FAO is building up a "Portfolio of small-scale wood-based panel mills" containing designs and case studies arranged for convenient consultation. Models from the Portfolio have already been the subject of investment negotiations with several developing countries.

An Association of Latin American Centres of Forestry Education was founded in the course of a FAO/SIDA Seminar on Forestry Development held in Quito, Ecuador, with the participation of directors, instructors and representatives of Latin American forestry schools and services. FAO/SIDA workshops on forestry development and planning were conducted in India and the Philippines, and an evaluation report was published on methods used in a multipronged pioneering project carried out in Malaysia with FAO assistance and involving the many aspects of forestry planning. A comparative study prepared in 1976 puts forward suggestions for the improvement of public forest administrations in six African countries.

*Land and Water*

The increasing demand for food has to compete with mounting pressure on the world's limited water resources for industrial, domestic and power requirements. FAO advocates an integrated approach to the need for irrigation, drainage, erosion control and water and has prepared proposals which will be made available to developing countries. The FAO Irrigation and Drainage Paper Series, of which sixteen papers were reprinted in 1976 to meet continuing demand, reached its 29th publication with a practical field manual on "Water Quality for Agriculture".

Field assistance was extended to Kenya for the development of irrigation schemes in arid pasture lands where recent droughts and the population pressure sparked Government action to avert famine. A water supply project operating in the Maktong river basin covering 32,000 sq. km. in Korea is dealing with the additional problem of periodical intrusions of sea water. Physical and mathematical models of the river estuary were constructed to simulate tidal and saline movements. The project includes investment options for the construction of additional storage, sewage treatment installations and estuary barrage.

A three-year course on the technology, economics and management of groundwater pollution, organized with FAO assistance and financed by the UN Development Programme (UNDP) provided academic and on-the-spot training in France, Spain, United Kingdom and USA. The outcome of this successful project has been analysed by the teachers and trainees in a 300-page publication which reviews the financial aspects and the benefits of pollution control in groundwater systems.

Twenty-seven field projects dealing with soil fertility and fertilizers were financed by UNDP in 1976. The regional programme for applied research in land and water use in the Near East will in its first phase cover eight countries. With financial assistance from the UN Environment Programme (UNEP), and the cooperation so far of eight countries in Africa and seven in Latin America, a project investigating biological nitrogen fixation as a cheap source of nitrogen started its first phase.

Under FAO's Cooperative Programme with the Swedish International Development Agency (SIDA), a regional workshop was held in Bangkok on the use of organic material as fertilizer in Asia. It was attended by research and operationally responsible personnel from many parts of the world and will be followed by similar meetings in Africa, the Near East and Latin America.

More than 30 countries were involved in the worldwide Trace Element Study undertaken by the FAO/Finland Cooperative Programme. National seminars on the use of mineral and organic fertilizer were held in Sierra Leone, Upper Volta and Zambia under the Norwegian Cooperative Programme. An Expert Consultation on Soil Conservation took place in Rome.

Action was initiated in Africa on the operational phase of a three-year project, financially supported by the UN Environment Programme (UNEP), for a World Assessment of Soil Degradation. The World Map of Desertification, prepared with the support of UNEP and in cooperation with UNESCO and the World Health Organization (WHO) to call governments' attention to vulnerable areas and to stimulate international action, will be ready for presentation at the UN Conference on Desertification scheduled for 1977.

Action was initiated on appraising land use by agroecological zones, aimed primarily at determining the potential of the developing world's land resources for agricultural development.

FAO's Fertilizer Programme helped to organize some 3,000 trials and more than 7,000 demonstrations on farmers' lands. Eighty training courses were attended by 3,000 local technicians. Nearly 10,000 farmers participated in pilot schemes for the improvement of fertilizer distribution, supply and credit facilities. FAO and the Netherland Government shared the cost of a course on fertilizer extension work organized by the International Agricultural Centre at Wageningen, Netherlands, for ten counterpart staff from developing countries.

*International Fertilizer Supply Scheme*

By October 1976, a total of $165 million had been pledged

to the FAO International Fertilizer Supply Scheme in fertilizer supplies, cash and services. During 1976, 60 fertilizer assistance operations were initiated or completed. They involved the shipment of about 270,000 tons of fertilizer —valued at $75 million—to 39 of the neediest developing countries in Africa, 18 in Asia and three in Latin America.

*Plant production and protection*

Higher yields from industrial, horticultural and field food crops, their protection against pests and diseases, seed and plant production, and crop forecasting methods were priority objectives of FAO during 1976.

With the assistance of the FAO-based secretariat of the International Board for Plant Genetic Resources, missions visited North and West Africa, several countries of South America, India and Pakistan to collect primitive cultivars threatened with extinction. Intensified cooperation with the World Meteorological Organization (WMO) centred around weather monitoring in relation to crop forecasting for the Organization's Global Information and Early Warning System, advance estimates of water available during the cropping season in the drought-prone Sahel Zone of Africa and participation in working groups of the Commission of Agricultural Meteorology.

FAO's Seed Industry Development Programme, in which 54 countries and three technical agencies participate, helped Member States to prepare programmes of seed production, processing, distribution and quality control. Reports on African and Asian countries were circulated in order to stimulate assistance from regional development banks, the World Bank, non-governmental organizations and private seed companies. Nearly $5 million have been committed by various sources or are under negotiation for the execution of field projects. Work continued on the establishment of regional seed production activities in the countries serviced by the Sahel Inter-State Drought Control Committee (CILSS)—Chad, Gambia, Mali, Mauritania, Niger, Senegal, Upper Volta and by the Cartagena Agreement Group comprising Bolivia, Chile, Columbia, Ecuador, Peru and Venezuela.

The Swedish International Development Agency (SIDA) financed a joint four-year research project on barley and spring wheat in Egypt, Ethiopia, India, Iran, Pakistan and Turkey, coupled with eight-month training courses in Sweden for nationals of those countries. Four more fellows completed their nine-month training course on durum wheat in Italy. A project financed by Saudi Arabia enabled nine persons from Near East and North African countries to start a one-year training course in systems of farming in Australia. Participants from African and Asian countries attended the sixth FAO/SIDA training course on Seed Technology in Kenya.

The International Institute of Tropical Agriculture in Ibadan, Nigeria, acting on behalf of FAO and the UN Development Programme (UNDP), organized field trials and extension staff training in modern rice technology. High yielding varieties introduced under a co-ordinated trials system launched by the 13 countries of the West African Rice Development Association (WARDA) are being tested locally in conjunction with a training programme.

Oil palm breeding, coconut improvement and large-scale government programmes for hybrid seednut production generated requests for FAO Assistance in Latin America Asia and the Far East. Field planting on 600 hectares of seed garden in Indonesia was completed in 1976 and is expected to provide sufficient seednut to replant some 30,000 ha. annually in a few years' time.

The impact of FAO's assistance to Thailand rubber production, involving agronomic research, processing and marketing studies and multi-level training over a number of years, culminated in action by the World Bank. The investment project agreed on will affect some 1,230,000 hectares, 95 per cent of which are small holdings that need replanting. The planned annual rehabilitation of 48,000 ha. should increase yields nearly six-fold and the income from a two-hectare farm is expected to rise from $350 to $1,750 annually when the plantation has reached full maturity. Increased production and better quality of vegetable seeds and planting material have been achieved by the newly-founded National Institute of Horticulture in Nigeria and the Horticultural Research Centre in Iran.

Smaller FAO projects have been successful in many countries and progress is reported from the Central African Republic, Ivory Coast, Rwanda and Senegal which have increased their production of tomatoes, onions, peppers and indigenous vegetables for local consumption and export markets. Kenya farmers trained with international assistance are now producing high value crops for export and collecting greatly increased incomes from comparatively small plots of land.

An experimental and demonstration centre for protected vegetable production was set up in Kuwait to help reduce the country's dependence on imported vegetables, promote investment opportunities and provide guidance for Gulf States and neighbouring areas with similar climatic characteristics.

A research network on olive production, originally organized with the cooperation of seven Mediterranean countries, has been extended to another eight countries in Europe, North Africa and the Near East. Data collected will be channelled through the International Information System for Agricultural Services and Technology (AGRIS) for distribution to olive oil producing countries. Members of the network will offer seminars and training courses for young researchers. A date palm research centre has been established in Iraq to help governments co-ordinate action to improve date production, processing and marketing.

The increased use of pesticides in developing countries motivated FAO action on various fronts. Training seminars were held in Chile, Peru and Pakistan. A programme for monitoring the environmental impact of pesticides was launched in cooperation with the UN Environment Programme (UNEP). Governments were assisted in modernizing methods of detecting and measuring pesticides residues in food and other material liable to contamination. The results of the FAO World Survey on the resistance of stored grain pests were published in 1976.

Eight Associate Experts were assigned to countries in Africa and South America for field work under the FAO International Programme on Horizontal Resistance (IPHR) which is designed to strengthen the pest and disease resistance of local varieties of major crops. Courses in Latin America on Crop Loss Assessment and Horizontal Resistance were attended by 56 trainees from Argentina, Brazil, Chile, Paraguay and Uruguay.

As a result of action undertaken with FAO guidance by some 60 countries and territories in Africa, the Middle East and South West Asia, the locust recession was maintained for the 14th year running and the risk of losses to an estimated $20 billion worth of agricultural crops, grasslands and forests was averted in areas prone to food shortages. Specific control operations were carried out in 15 countries ranging from India and Pakistan through Saudi Arabia to Sudan and Algeria.

Pilot evaluation undertaken in Pakistan's Vertebrate Pest Control Centre project showed that improved rodent control techniques in rice fields produced a crop increase equivalent to 50 times the cost of damage control. Similar improvements were obtained in the protection of stored grain against rodents.

*Policy Analysis*

By the end of 1976, FAO had 21 teams in the field helping governments to plan and analyse agricultural development, policy and budgetting. Agricultural economist and planning experts were provided for 25 FAO-operated projects, for nine projects managed by other members of the UN system, for missions organized by international and regional agencies and for individual consultancies to developing countries.

Long experience with assistance to regional integration scheme enabled FAO to make a substantial contribution to the "Group of 77" Conference on economic cooperation among developing countries which was held in Mexico. After helping with preparatory work, FAO participated in a seminar on agricultural planning conducted in Indonesia under the aegis of the Association of South-eastern Asian Nations. Similar support was extended to the seminars organized by the Maghreb Permanent Consultative Committee (CPCM). An analysis of Latin America's four integration schemes—Central American Common Market (CACM), Caribbean Common Market (CARICOM), Latin America Free Trade Association (LAFTA) and the Andean Pact—was prepared for inclusion in the State of Food and Agriculture for 1976.

The FAO regional study on the seven Sahelian countries (Chad, Gambia, Mali, Mauritania, Niger, Senegal, Upper Volta) was completed in 1976 and presented to the Inter-State Committee for Drought Control in the Sahel (Comité Inter-Etats de Lutte contre la Sécheresse au Sahel—CILSS) at the inaugural meeting of the "Club des Amis du Sahel" in Dakar, Sénégal. The study helped to muster support for the promotion of dryland farming, irrigated agriculture, livestock development and fisheries. Country studies undertaken for Ghana, Tanzania and Zambia provided the governments concerned with guidelines for development planning.

The emphasis in training programmes for agricultural planning is shifting from sector to project analysis. FAO organized a seminar in Dakar for French-speaking West African countries and participated in courses held in Tunis and Kuwait and in a course for Brazilian planners held in France. The major event in this field during 1976 was FAO's eighth agricultural planning course for Spanish-speaking member countries, which lasted four months and was attended by some 25 participants from 19 countries.

After completion of an agriculture sector analysis model for Tunisia, preparations were initiated for a similar project to be carried out in cooperation with the Government of Malaysia.

FAO continued to assess food and fertilizer import requirements and the outlook for agricultural export earnings in 45 developing countries most seriously affected by present economic crises and national calamities. The findings were used in evaluating requests for assistance received by the UN Special Fund and as background for deliberations of the Conference on International Economic Cooperation convened in Paris.

*Commodities and Trade*

By the end of 1976, 85 Member Governments of FAO, the European Economic Commission and the Central American Economic Integration Secretariat (SIECA) had agreed to join the Organization's Global Information and Early Warning System. During the year, the System kept a continuous watch on world food prospects and issued 12 Food Outlook reports, eleven monthly reports on Food Crops and Shortages, and a series of reports on the urgent cereal import requirements of the most severely affected developing countries. There were also 30 Special Crop Reports alerting major donors of food aid as to impending crop failures and the likelihood of food shortages in developing countries. The European Economic Commission, as well as the United Kingdom Disaster Unit and the U.S. Government, frequently called on the System to assess the situation in countries requesting emergency food aid.

In 1976, the Director-General formally established the Food Security Assistance Scheme (FSAS) to manage activities which had been operating experimentally for the past two years. The Scheme is designed to assist developing countries to formulate their national food security policy, identify supporting projects and mobilize the external resources required. The Federal Republic of Germany, the Netherlands, Norway and Switzerland have pledged several million dollars to the Scheme, while other countries are providing help in specific cases.

Four advisory missions were sent out in 1976 to Haiti, Indonesia, Tanzania and Tunisia, which have subscribed to the International Undertaking on World Food Security. Detailed projects were prepared for a number of countries in the Sahel region of West Africa, Cape Verde, Guinea Bissau, Tanzania and Bangladesh, and several of them have entered into operation. The Government of Nigeria set up a Trust Fund to finance FAO assistance in carrying out a strategic food reserve project. The project involves setting up storage and stock management systems, training of personnel and the adoption of national grain reserve policies. Notes on progress reported in planning and implementing cereal reserve stocks are distributed periodically to countries and organizations at their request.

The FAO Inter-governmental Group on Tea discussed the draft of a long-term agreement between exporting and importing countries, based on a system of "standby" export quotas. The Intergovernmental Group on Meat, after two years preparatory work, adopted a set of guidelines as a "code of conduct" for national and international trade policies in the livestock sector. The informal international stabilization arrangements on jute and on hard fibres were reactivated by the respective FAO Groups in 1976, after a lapse of several years.

*Director-General:* E. Saouma (Lebanon)

*Deputy Director-General:* Roy I. Jackson (United States of America).

*Independent Chairman of the Council:* Gonzalo Bula Hoyos (Colombia).

*Address:* Viale delle Terme di Caracalla, Rome.

# GENERAL AGREEMENT ON TARIFFS AND TRADE (GATT)

THE General Agreement on Tariffs and Trade entered into force on 1 January 1948. Originally intended as an interim arrangement, it was negotiated in 1947 by the member countries of a Preparatory Committee simultaneously engaged in drawing up the charter for an International Trade Organization that would have been a specialized agency of the United Nations. This Havana Charter was abandoned when it became clear that it would not be ratified. The General Agreement was thus left as the only multilateral treaty laying down agreed rules for the conduct of world trade. The 83 countries (September 1977) that are contracting parties to GATT carry on well over four fifths of world trade. A further 28 countries apply GATT rules in their trade.

*Functions*

GATT provides a framework for international trade relations and a forum in which countries can discuss and settle trade problems as they arise, and can negotiate to reduce trade barriers.

Chief among the multilateral rights and obligations laid down by the General Agreement is that of most-favoured-nation treatment: contracting parties must grant each other treatment as favourable as they give to any country in the application and administration of import and export duties and charges. Permitted exceptions to this rule of non-discrimination are customs unions and free-trade areas, preferences already existing when the Agreement was signed, and certain preferences (see below) for and among developing countries. A second basic principle is that protection should be given to domestic industry only through the customs tariff, and not through other commercial measures. The use of quantitative restrictions for protective purposes is thus forbidden, although they can be introduced, in specified circumstances, to re-establish a country's balance of payments, to protect domestic industries from products imported in such quantities that they cause or threaten serious injury to the domestic producers, or to meet the special problems of developing countries. Provision is made for the reduction of tariffs through multilateral negotiations, and a stable and predictable basis for trade is provided by the binding of the tariff levels negotiated.

These basic principles are applied flexibly. The Agreement itself specifies a number of exceptions, and individual countries may be permitted to digress from the common rules by the vote of a specific and carefully-defined waiver of obligations.

Consultation to avoid damage to the trading interests of contracting parties is another fundamental principle of GATT, and may concern disputes arising between individual countries or problems of world trade as a whole.

About two-thirds of all GATT members are developing countries. Their special trade problems and their need to open up markets for their exports are recognized in several provisions of the General Agreement, in particular in its Part IV, and in the work programme of GATT. Part IV provides, for example, that in trade negotiations developing countries are not expected to offer contributions inconsistent with their individual development, financial and trade needs. A Committee on Trade and Development supervises the implementation of Part IV and coordinates GATT activities on behalf of developing countries. GATT members in 1971 relaxed the usual rules against discrimination to permit introduction by developed countries of generalized preferences in favour of developing countries, and the exchange of preferences, on a multilateral basis, among a number of developing countries. Courses are provided to train government officials in trade policy. In 1964 GATT established an International Trade Centre (operated since 1968 in conjunction with UNCTAD) to help developing countries, through training, advice and market information, to improve the marketing of their exports.

'The substantial reduction of tariffs and other barriers to trade' is specified as a principal aim of the General Agreement. It has been the objective of a long series of GATT negotiations, including major negotiating conferences held in 1947 (in Geneva), in 1949 (Annecy, France), in 1951 (Torquay, England), in 1956 (Geneva), in 1961–61 (Geneva, the 'Dillon Round'), in 1964–67 (Geneva, the 'Kennedy Round').

In September 1973, at a meeting in Tokyo, Ministers of 102 countries agreed unanimously to launch new multilateral trade negotiations in GATT. The 'Tokyo Declaration', which specifies the aims of the negotiations, provides that they shall cover both tariffs and non- tariff barriers to trade in industrial and agricultural products, including tropical products, and lays particular stress on the need to find solutions to the trade problems of developing countries, which participate in the negotiations on special and more favourable terms. Substantive negotiations began early in 1975 in Geneva.

The "Tokyo Round" trade negotiations are the most comprehensive, and probably also most thoroughly prepared, ever undertaken. Detailed information on tariffs, non-tariff measures and trade flows has been recorded and analysed, and possible solutions to some important non-tariff distortions of trade have already been worked out. The negotiations are guided by a Trade Negotiations Committee, on which all the 97 participating governments are represented. Specialized groups are negotiating on tariffs, non-tariff measures, the special problems of agriculture, and tropical products (an area given special priority) and others are examining possibilities for co-ordinated reduction of trade barriers in selected sectors, the adequacy of the multilateral safeguard system, and possibilities for improving the international framework for the conduct of world trade.

*Finance*

Member governments contribute to the annual budget in accordance with a scale of contributions which is assessed on their share of the total trade of all GATT members.

*Publications*

Basic Instruments and Selected Documents, 4 volumes and 23 supplements, 1952–77. International Trade (Annually), GATT Activities (Annually).

*Director-General:* Olivier Long. *Address:* Centre William Rappard, 154 rue de Lausanne, 1211 Geneva 21.

# INTERNATIONAL BANK FOR RECONSTRUCTION AND DEVELOPMENT (WORLD BANK)

THE Articles of Agreement of the International Bank for Reconstruction and Development (known informally as the World Bank) were drawn up by the United Nations Monetary and Financial Conference at Bretton Woods in July 1944. The Bank came into existence on 27 December 1945 when the Articles had been signed by 28 governments, and it began operations on 25 June 1946. Since 1947 the Bank has been affiliated with the United Nations as a Specialised Agency.

All members of the Bank must first join the International Monetary Fund, although the two institutions are independent of one another. As of 1 July 1977, 129 countries were members of the Bank.

*Purposes*

The Bank's purposes are: To assist in the reconstruction and development of territories of members by facilitating the investment of capital for productive purposes; to promote private foreign investment and, when private capital is not readily available on reasonable terms, to supplement private investment by providing loans for productive purposes out of its own capital, funds raised by it, and its other resources; to promote the balanced growth of international trade and the maintenance of equilibrium in balances of payments by encouraging international investment for the development of the productive resources of its members.

*Operations*

During the financial year ended 30 June 1977 the Bank made 161 loans totalling $5,759 million in 55 countries. Bank disbursements during the year totalled $2,636 million. Loans totalling $876 million were made for development of transportation. Electric power development accounted for $785 million. Bank loans for finance companies and industry totalled $1,452 million; and for agricultural development $1,638 million. The remainder of $1,008 million lent in the developing countries included loans for education, telecommunications, water supply and sewerage systems, family planning, tourism, urbanization and general development. Up to 30 June 1977 the Bank had made 1,452 loans in 98 countries and territories totalling $38,610 million.

The following tables show cumulative lendings by purpose and areas up to 30 June 1977:

| *By Purposes* | *Amount (In millions of U.S. $)* |
|---|---|
| Agriculture and rural development | 6,780 |
| Industry and Development Finance Companies | 7,666 |
| Education | 1,224 |
| Electric Power | 8,455 |
| Non-Project | 1,854 |
| Population | 120 |
| Technical Assistance | 30 |
| Telecommunications | 934 |
| Tourism | 247 |
| Transportation | 9,588 |
| Urban Development | 368 |
| Water Supply and Sewerage | 1,344 |
| International Finance Corporation | 570 |
| Total | $39,180* |

*Includes cancellations and refundings amounting to the equivalent of $1,003 million.

| *By Areas* | *Amount (In millions of U.S. $)* |
|---|---|
| Eastern Africa | 2,477 |
| Western Africa | 2,016 |
| Europe, Middle East, North Africa | 11,392 |
| Latin America and Caribbean | 12,050 |
| East Asia and Pacific | 7,602 |
| South Asia | 3,073 |
| Total by Areas | $38,610 |
| International Finance Corporation | 570 |
| | $39,180* |

*Includes cancellations and refundings amounting to the equivalent of $1,003 million.

The unsatisfactory history of many pre-war foreign loans led the Bank's founders to prescribe strict standards for its lending. The Bank may lend to member governments, governmental agencies or private enterprises; if the borrower is not a government, the guarantee of the member government concerned is required. All loans must be for productive purposes. Before lending, the Bank studies the economic position of the country concerned and satisfies itself that the country can earn the foreign exchange needed for repayment. It also examines, on the spot, the economic and technical justification for the project and requires regular reports on the project's progress after the loan is made.

The rate of interest charged by the Bank on its loans is related primarily to the cost of funds it borrows in the capital markets through the sale to investors of its bond and note issues. Adjustments in the Bank's lending rate reflect the changing costs to the Bank of funds it raises in these markets. Changes in the lending rate, however, affect only loans made subsequent to such adjustments.

The Bank continued to foster close co-ordination of external assistance to developing nations through the 15 co-ordinating groups it has taken the lead in creating. These groups were created at the request of the developing countries whose development programmes have attracted sufficient support to justify them. Twelve meetings of Bank-sponsored aid groups were held in the last fiscal year. The Bank is also a participant in five co-ordinating groups organized under other auspices. As in previous years representatives of the International Monetary Fund, the OECD and the United Nations Development Programme and of the relevant regional development banks attended meetings of World Bank sponsored co-ordinating groups.

The Bank's technical assistance work continues to be an important part of its operations. During the fiscal year ended 30 June 1977, it agreed to act as Executing Agency for 10 new projects financed by the United Nations Development Programme (UNDP).

The Bank's technical assistance work continues to be an important part of its operations. Most of this assistance is provided in the course of Bank project, sector and economic work, but to an increasing extent Bank financing incorporates a separate technical assistance component. In the fiscal year ended 30 June 1977, 162 lending operations made specific provision for technical assistance aggregating $189 million.

In addition, the Bank continued to serve as Executing Agency for preinvestment projects financed by the United Nations Development Programme (UNDP). At the year's end the Bank was Executing Agency for 59 projects, of which 10 were new, and had completed 170 projects. The new projects include one in Malaysia designed to strengthen the country's capacity for project identification, preparation and implementation. This is the largest project the Bank has thus far executed for the UNDP. Other new projects include the design of a master plan for water resource development and use in Egypt; a major irrigation study in Nepal; technical assistance to the National Development Bank in Paraguay; a review of the Railway Development Plan in Argentina; technical assistance to the domestic contracting industry in Jamaica; and planning assistance in the Sudan.

The activities of the Bank in the fields of agriculture, education, water supply and wastes disposal, and industry, continued to be assisted by formal co-operative arrangements with the Food and Agriculture Organization of the United Nations (FAO), the United Nations Educational, Scientific and Cultural Organization (Unesco), the World Health Organization (WHO) and the United Nations Industrial Development Organization (UNIDO). The Bank and WHO have also been co-ordinating their activities in the field of population and during the year began consideration of modes and scope of collaboration in the health sector.

During the year, 290 senior officials from developing countries participated in 11 Washington courses on development problems conducted by the Economic Development Institute, the Bank's staff college which helps to train senior officials of the developing countries in development techniques. A further 621 officials received training in 24 courses held overseas, in which the Economic Development Institute participated or to which it lent its support in collaboration with national governments or with regional organizations.

A number of studies both theoretical and practical were undertaken in the year with a view to refining existing techniques or analysis and judgment on policy questions.

The Convention on the Settlement of Investment Disputes between States and Nationals of Other States came into force on 14 October 1966, 30 days after the deposit of the twentieth instrument of ratification. Under the Convention, which was prepared by the Executive Directors and staff of the Bank with the assistance of many legal experts over a period of several years, an International Centre for Settlement of Investment Disputes has been established providing facilities for the settlement, by voluntary recourse to conciliation or arbitration, of investment disputes between contracting States and foreign investors who are nationals of other contracting States.

The Convention had been signed by 72 countries and ratified by 67 of them.

*Capital Structure*

The Bank obtains its funds from three sources: the paid in capital provided by its member governments, its accumulated earnings, and its own borrowings in the capital markets of the world. The capital stock of the Bank is expressed in terms of United States dollars of the weight and fineness in effect on 1 July 1944. At 30 June 1977 the authorised capital of the Bank, in terms of 1944 dollars, was $34,000 million, of which $25,589 million had been subscribed. Only one-tenth of this total is actually paid in; the remainder is subject to call by the Bank if needed to meet its obligations and thus, in effect, provides the backing of many governments for the sale of Bank bonds and notes. The Bank has borrowed in Belgium, Canada, France, Germany, Italy, Japan, Kuwait, Lebanon, Libya, the Netherlands, Saudi Arabia, Sweden, Switzerland, United Arab Emirates, the United Kingdom, the United States and Venezuela in the respective currencies of those countries, and in Austria, Iran, Nigeria, Oman and Yugoslavia for United States dollars. It has also sold issues denominated in United States dollars to Central Banks and other Governmental Agencies in some 70 countries and to International Organizations. The outstanding funded debt of the Bank as of 30 June 1977 was $18,477 million. In addition the Bank replenishes its lending fund by selling part of its loans to investors. Sales of principal amounts of its own loans totalled $2,742 million, of which all but $69 million was sold without the Bank's guarantee. The Bank also uses for lending amounts arising from the repayment of loans.

*Organization*

All the powers of the Bank are vested in a Board of Governors composed of one Governor and an alternate appointed by each member country. This Board meets annually, two consecutive years in Washington, D.C., and the third year in the capital of another member country. Most of its powers have been delegated to the Executive Directors, of whom five are appointed by the five largest shareholders, and 15 are elected by the remaining members. The operations of the Bank are carried on by an international staff headed by the President, who is selected by the Executive Directors. The President is *ex officio* Chairman of the Executive Directors and chief of the Bank's operating staff; he is responsible, subject to the direction of the Executive Directors on policy questions, for the conduct of the Bank's business, and for the organization, appointment, and dismissal of its officers and staff.

*President:* Robert S. McNamara (U.S.A.). *Headquarters:* 1818 H Street, N.W., Washington, D.C., 20433, U.S.A. (New York Office: 120 Broadway, New York, N.Y. 10005, U.S.A. European Office: 66 Avenue d'Iena, 75116 Paris, France. London Office: New Zealand House, Haymarket, London, SW1 Y4TE). *Cable Address:* INTBAFRAD.

## INTERNATIONAL CIVIL AVIATION ORGANIZATION (ICAO)

THE Convention on Civil Aviation was adopted by the representatives of 52 states at the Chicago International Civil Aviation Conference on 7 December 1944. The ICAO was formally established on 4 April 1947, 30 days after the convention had been ratified. The member-countries number 140.

*Purposes*

The aims and objectives of ICAO, as stated in Article 44 of the Convention, are to develop the principles and techniques of international air navigation and to foster the planning and development of international air transport so as to (*a*) ensure the safe and orderly growth of international civil aviation throughout the world; (*b*) encourage the arts of aircraft design and operation for peaceful purposes; (*c*) encourage the development of airways, airports, and air navigation facilities for international civil aviation; (*d*) meet the needs of the peoples of the world for safe, regular, efficient and economical air transport; (*e*) prevent economic waste caused by unreasonable competition; (*f*) ensure that the rights of contracting states are fully respected and that every contracting state has a fair opportunity to operate international airlines; (*g*) avoid discrimination between contracting states; (*h*) promote safety of flight in international air navigation; (*i*) promote generally the development of all aspects of international civil aeronautics.

*Organization*

The Organization's machinery consists of an Assembly, a Council and a Secretariat.

The Assembly, composed of delegates from member nations, meets at least once in a three-year period.

The Council is composed of representatives of 30 nations elected by the Assembly for a three-year term. In the election, adequate representation is given to states of chief importance in air transport, states which make the largest contribution to the provision of facilities for civil air navigation and states whose inclusion will ensure that all regions of the world are represented.

The Council is the executive body of the Organization. It has many functions in the technical, economic and legal fields of aviation; one of its most important functions is the adoption and amendment of the ICAO International Standards and Recommended Practices (Annexes to the Convention on International Civil Aviation) which are designed to produce safety, regularity and efficiency in air navigation.

The principal subsidiary organs are the Air Navigation Commission, the Air Transport Committee, the Committee on Joint Support of Air Navigation Services, the Finance Committee, and the Legal Committee. ICAO's budget for 1976 was U.S. $14,074,000 (net). The grand total expenditure by ICAO technical assistance in 1976 was U.S. $25,443,149 as participant in the United Nations Development Programme and other U.N. assistance programmes.

*President of the Council:* Assad Kotaite. *Secretary General:* Yues Lambert. *Headquarters:* P.O. Box 400, 1000 Sherbrooke W., Montreal, Quebec H3A 2R, Cana2da.

## INTERNATIONAL DEVELOPMENT ASSOCIATION (IDA)

THE International Development Association, an affiliate of the International Bank for Reconstruction and Development (*q.v.*) originated in a resolution submitted by Senator A. S. Mike Monroney to the United States Senate at the end of 1957. His proposal received the support of the U.S. Administration, which sponsored it at the 1959 Annual Meeting of the Bank. In accordance with a resolution dated 1 October 1959 of the Governors of the Bank, Articles of Agreement for IDA were drawn up by the Bank's Executive Directors, and were submitted to member governments of the Bank in February 1960. IDA formally came into existence on 24 September 1960 when 15 countries had signed the Articles of Agreement. Membership of IDA is open to all members of the Bank. By 1 July 1977 membership included 117 countries.

### *Purposes*

The purposes of IDA, as set out in the Articles of Agreement, are: To promote economic development, increase productivity and thus raise standards of living in the less-developed areas of the world included within the Association's membership, in particular by providing finance to meet their important developmental requirements on terms which are more flexible and bear less heavily on the balance of payments than those of conventional loans, thereby furthering the developmental objectives of the International Bank for Reconstruction and Development and supplementing its activities.

### *Capital Structure*

The initial subscriptions of each member country of IDA are proportioned to that member's subscription to the capital stock of the Bank. For purposes of subscriptions, IDA members are divided into two groups: wealthier countries pay their subscriptions entirely in convertible form, and less developed countries pay only 10 per cent of their subscriptions in convertible form. The remaining 90 per cent is paid in each member's national currency and cannot be used by IDA for lending to other countries without the member's consent.

The bulk of usable resources available to IDA has been contributed by the first group, known as Part I countries, namely Australia, Austria, Belgium, Canada, Denmark, Finland, France, Germany, Iceland, Italy, Ireland, Japan, Kuwait, Luxembourg, the Netherlands, New Zealand, Norway, South Africa, Sweden, the United Kingdom and the United States. Like their original subscriptions to IDA, the contributions of Part I members to the four replenishments of IDA resources have been made on a fully convertible basis. By 30 June 1977, usable funds that have been made available to IDA amounted to $11,789 million. The cumulative total of IDA commitments at that date was $11,783 million; aggregate disbursements totalled $22,247,000.

### *Operations*

By 30 June 1977 IDA had extended 753 credits amounting to the equivalent of $11,397 million to help finance development projects in 68 member countries. Credits have been made for a term of 50 years, with no repayment for ten years, then 1 per cent per annum for the next ten years and 3 per cent per annum for 30 years.

Although its Articles of Agreement give IDA wide latitude in the terms on which it may offer financing, development credits have so far been extended on identical terms to all recipient countries. Each has been for 50 years, interest free, with a ten-year period of grace before repayment begins. A service charge of ¾ of 1 per cent per annum, payable on the amounts withdrawn and outstanding, is made to meet IDA's administrative costs. Repayment is due in foreign exchange.

### *Organization*

The structure of IDA is adapted to administration by the Bank. Each member country of IDA is represented by the same Governor and Executive Director as represents it for the Bank. The Governors have delegated to the Executive Directors the same broad powers as have been so delegated in the affairs of the Bank. The President of the Bank is *ex officio* President of IDA and Chairman of the IDA Executive Directors. The officers and staff serve IDA as well.

***President:*** Robert S. McNamara (U.S.A.). ***Headquarters:*** 1818 H Street, N.W., Washington, D.C. 20433, U.S.A. (New York Office: 120 Broadway, New York, N.Y. 10005, U.S.A. European Office: 66 Avenue d'Iena, 75116 Paris, France. London Office: New Zealand House, Haymarket, London, SW1 Y4TE).

## INTERNATIONAL FINANCE CORPORATION (IFC)

THE International Finance Corporation (IFC) was established by member governments in July 1956 as an affiliate of the World Bank. Its objective is to assist less developed member countries by helping to promote the growth of the private sector of their economies. Total membership was 106 countries at 30 June 1977. As of that date, IFC's subscribed share capital amounted to $108·3 million.

IFC provides risk capital for productive private enterprises in the less developed countries, assists the development of local capital markets and seeks to stimulate the international flow of private capital. IFC makes direct investments in projects that either establish new businesses, or expand, modernize or diversify existing businesses, usually by subscribing to shares in conjunction with a long-term loan. IFC often carries out standby and underwriting arrangements; provides technical and financial assistance to private development finance companies; and encourages the participation of private investors in its own commitments. IFC neither seeks nor accepts government guarantees in its operations.

Expansion and diversification have been the main features of IFC's recent operations. In the fiscal year ended 30 June 1977 the Corporation's commitments amounted to $206·7 million to 34 enterprises. Among the industries represented were steel, pulp and paper, development finance companies, capital markets institutions, textiles, chemicals, food processing, construction materials, mining, general manufacturing and tourism. The cumulative total of gross commitments made by the Corporation amounted to over $1,712 million at 30 June involving over 292 enterprises in some 62 countries in which others had concurrently invested approximately $7,262 million.

Net income for the fiscal year ended 30 June 1977 amounted to $8·9 million (1976: $7·7 million). The cumulative net earnings of IFC, amounting to $87·3 million at June 30, 1976, have been transferred to surplus and allocated to a General Reserve. The total paid-in capital and General Reserve amounted to $195·7 million. For additional resources IFC borrows from the World Bank and other sources and IFC seeks to sell participations in its loans and to revolve its equity portfolio (sales of $67·7 million in FY1977).

To provide for a future increase in capital resources, IFC's Board of Directors has recommended to its Board of Governors that the members should increase IFC's equity capital by $480 million over the period 1978–82.

***President:*** Robert S. McNamara. ***Executive Vice-President:*** Moeen A. Qureshi. *Headquarters:* 1818 H Street, N.W., Washington, D.C. 20433, U.S.A. (New York Office: 120 Broadway, New York, N.Y. 10005, U.S.A. *Paris Office:* 66 Ave. d'Iéna, 75116 Paris, France. *European Office:* New Zealand House, Haymarket, London, S.W.1. *Tokyo Office:* 5–1 Nibancho, Chiyoda-Ku, Tokyo 102, Japan. *Regional Mission in Eastern Africa:* Extelcoms House, Haile Selassie Avenue, Nairobi, Kenya; *Regional Mission in East Asia:* World Bank Group, Central Bank of the Philippines, Manila, Philippines. *Cable Address:* CORINTFIN.

## INTERNATIONAL LABOUR ORGANIZATION (ILO)

ESTABLISHED in 1919 (when its Constitution was adopted as Part XIII of the Treaty of Versailles), the I.L.O. was for many years associated with the League of Nations. In 1946, it became the first specialized agency associated with the United Nations. In 1969 it was awarded the Nobel Peace Prize. Members of the U.N. wishing to be admitted to the I.L.O. have only to accept the obligations of the I.L.O. Constitution. Other countries may be admitted to the Organization by a two-thirds vote of the International Labour Conference. The number of I.L.O. member countries stood at 135 on 31 July 1977.

*Purposes*

The I.L.O. was founded to advance the cause of social justice and, in so doing, to contribute to the establishment of universal and lasting peace. One of its primary functions has always been to raise standards by building up a code of international labour law and practice. This remains true despite the many new directions into which the Organization's activities have extended since the end of the Second World War. International labour standards are set by the International Labour Conference in the form of Conventions and Recommendations. Since the establishment of the I.L.O., a total of 149 Conventions and 157 Recommendations have been adopted. Taken together, these form the International Labour Code.

Each Convention is a legal instrument regulating some aspect of labour administration, social welfare or human rights; it is conceived as a model for national legislation. Recommendations, too, are designed to guide governments. Member countries are obliged to report periodically on the implementation of the Conventions they have ratified and also on their position with respect to Conventions they have not ratified and to the Recommendations.

Research and publishing have traditionally been, and still are, important aspects of the work of the I.L.O. The Organization periodically convenes regional labour conferences and contributes through its industrial committees, to the solution of social and labour questions of concern to particular industries. Other temporary and permanent commissions and committees have played an important part in the development of the I.L.O.'s programme. Meanwhile, the technical co-operation activities of the I.L.O. have expanded rapidly to the point where they now account for more than half of the work of the Organization.

The I.L.O., like other specialised agencies in the U.N. family, is a partner in the United Nations Development Programme. In 1976, some $40,000,000 was spent by the I.L.O. under this Programme to provide technical assistance to recipient countries. In addition, the I.L.O. provides technical assistance under its own budget. This is of the order of $5 million a year in 1978–79. Other sources off unding for such activities are trust fund arrangements with donor and recipient countries. These arrangements resulted in an expenditure of some $8,700,000 in 1975. Under these programmes of assistance, the I.L.O. had on assignment during the middle of 1977 some 630 experts serving in some 100 countries. The I.L.O.'s net expenditure budget for 1976–77 was set at $169,074,000.

The major fields of I.L.O. operational activity are: human resources development )including vocational training and management development); employment promotion and planning; social institutions development (including labour law, labour relations, labour administration, workers' education and co-operatives); and the promotion of fair working conditions (including such matters as remuneration, hours of work, occupational safety and health, and social security). A World Employment Conference held in Geneva in June 1976 worked out a programme of action aimed at important changes in world development strategy with emphasis on increased productive employment. The programme would seek satisfaction of the basic needs of the least privileged population groups within the next 25 years.

A parallel International Programme for the Improvement of Working Conditions and the Working Environment is also under way, with multidisciplinary teams of I.L.O. specialists advising member countries, on request, on how to improve the working environment.

The I.L.O.'s International Institute for Labour Studies at Geneva serves as an advanced staff college in social and labour policy, bringing together from all parts of the world persons with experience in labour questions, representing employers' organisations, management, workers' and government circles. The International Centre for Advanced Technical and Vocational Training, established by the I.L.O. at Turin, provides advanced training in management, technology and teaching methodology for persons primarily from developing countries who are considered suitable for more advanced training than any they could obtain in their own countries or regions.

*Organization*

The International Labour Conference is the supreme deliberative body of the I.L.O. It meets annually at Geneva. National delegations are composed of two Government delegates, one Employers' delegate and one Workers' delegate. Delegates can speak and vote independently.

The Governing Body, elected by the Conference, functions as the Organisation's executive council. It meets four times a year and is composed of 28 Government members, 14 Employers' members and 14 Workers' members.

*Chairman.* Mr. Joseph Morris; *Employers' Vice-Chairman:* G. Bergenström.

The International Labour Office is the Organisation's secretariat, operational headquarters, research centre and publishing house.

*Director-General:* Francis Blanchard (France).
*Address:* International Labour Organisation, CH-1211 Geneva 22, Switzerland.

## INTER-GOVERNMENTAL MARITIME CONSULTATIVE ORGANIZATION (IMCO)

IMCO, a specialized agency of the United Nations, deals with the technical aspects of shipping, with special emphasis on safety of life at sea, prevention of pollution of the sea from ships, and on certain maritime legal problems. Established by a U.N. Maritime Conference at Geneva in 1948, its headquarters are in London. Membership in July 1977 comprised 103 countries.

*The Assembly* of IMCO, consisting of representatives from all Member States, is the sovereign body of the Organization, and normally meets every two years.

*The Council* of eighteen Member States is elected by the Assembly for a term of two years; it meets twice a year and is IMCO's governing body between sessions of the Assembly. At present, the Chairman of the Council is Rear Admiral R. Y. Edwards (U.S.A.) and its members are Algeria, Argentina, Australia, Belgium, Brazil, Canada, China, the Federal Republic of Germany, France, Greece, India, Indonesia, Italy, Japan, Nigeria, Norway, Poland, U.S.S.R., the U.K. and the U.S.A.

*The Legal Committee* was established by the Council in June 1967 to deal initially with problems connected with the loss of the tanker *Torrey Canyon*, and subsequently with any legal problems laid before IMCO. Membership is open to all IMCO Member States.

*The Maritime Safety Committee*, of 16 Member States, is elected by the Assembly for a term of four years, and deals with the technical questions submitted to IMCO. At present the Chairman is Dr. L. Spinelli, (Italy), and its members are Argentina, Canada, Egypt, the Federal Republic of Germany, France, Greece, Italy, Japan, Liberia, Norway, Pakistan, Spain, U.S.S.R., the U.K., the U.S.A. and Yugoslavia. It has established the following specialized sub-committees.

*Sub-Committee on Cargoes and Containers.* Has drawn up regulations for carriage of grain in bulk and the Code of Safe Practice for Bulk Cargoes, which will be kept up to date. *Sub-Committee on the Carriage of Dangerous Goods.* Has drawn up International Maritime Dangerous Goods Code, which will be kept up to date. *Sub-Committee on Fire Protection.* Deals with fire protection measures for ships, including tankers. *Sub-Committee on Life-Saving Appliances.* Deals with questions pertaining to life-saving equipment. *Sub-Committee on Radio-communications.* Deals with questions pertaining to radio-communications from the viewpoint of safety at sea. Responsible for periodic revision of the International Code of Signals. *Sub-Committee on Safety of Navigation.* Deals with questions pertaining to safety of navigation, including those relevant to new types of craft. *Sub-Committee on Ship Design and Equipment.* Has produced codes for the construction and equipment of ships carrying dangerous chemical substances and for ships carrying liquefied gases in bulk; aims to recommend suitable design criteria, constructional standards and other safety measures. *Sub-Committee on Standards of Training and Watchkeeping:* aims to produce international standards in this field; *Sub-Committee on Sub-division of Stability.* Examines watertight sub-division of passenger ships, intact stability of passenger and cargo ships, sub-division and damage stability of cargo ships. *Sub-Committee on Safety of Fishing Vessels.* Deals with safety aspects of fishing vessels, including operation; is working on a Convention on Safety of Fishing Vessels.

*The Marine Environment Protection Committee,* a permanent subsidiary organ of the Assembly was established in November 1973. It executes and co-ordinates all activities of IMCO relating to the prevention and control of pollution from ships. Membership is open to all IMCO Member States. The present Chairman is Mr. P. Eriksson of Sweden.

*The Facilitation Committee* is a subsidiary body of the Council. Its task is to standardize and simplify documentation concerning ships' arrival and departure, cargo and passengers, implementation of the Convention of Facilitation and introduction of measures to that end. It also advises the Secretary-General in connexion with his duties as the depository of the Facilitation Convention. At present the Chairman is Mr. P. Vandensteen (Belgium). Membership is open to all Contracting Parties to the Convention of Facilities of International Maritime Traffic, 1965, and to all IMCO Member States.

*The Committee on Technical Co-operation* is a subsidiary body of the Council and performs advisory functions in respect of IMCO's programme of technical assistance to developing countries. Membership of the Committee is open to all Member States of IMCO. The present Chairman is Captain T. Soerahardja of Indonesia.

The budget for 1976 was £3,199,800.

*The Secretariat* is composed of international civil servants and works in London. *Secretary-General:* C. P. Srivastava. *Address:* IMCO, 101–104, Piccadilly, London, W.1.

## INTERNATIONAL MONETARY FUND (IMF)

THE International Monetary Fund was established on 27 December 1945, when representatives of 29 countries contributed 80 per cent of the original quotas agreed at the Bretton Woods Conference.

Its purposes are: To promote international monetary co-operation and the expansion of international trade; to promote exchange stability, maintain orderly exchange arrangements among members, and avoid competitive exchange depreciations; to assist in the establishment of a multilateral system of payments in respect of current transactions between members and in the elimination of foreign exchange restrictions which hamper world trade; to alleviate any serious dis-equilibrium in members' international balance of payments by making the resources of the Fund available to them under adequate safeguards, so that they would not resort to measures that might endanger national or international prosperity.

The 'Special Drawing Rights' (SDR) 29,700 million which the Fund holds in gold, special drawing rights and currencies provides a reserve on which members may draw, with its agreement, to meet foreign obligations during periods of temporary difficulty in their international balance of payments. The use of Fund resources is linked to a member's efforts to reduce exchange and trade restrictions, and to establish currency convertibility. The introduction of special drawing rights (SDRs) enabled the Fund to supplement the reserve assets of members that are participants in the Special Drawing Account. (Until 1 July 1974 one special drawing right was equal in value to 0·888671 gram of fine gold, or $1·20635 at the U.S. dollar parity established in October 1973; since that date, one SDR has been set equal to a weighted basket of the currencies of the 16 countries that had a share in world exports of goods and services in excess of 1 per cent on average over the 5-year period 1968–72.)

The Fund acts as a continuing forum for the consideration of foreign exchange and payments problems in which members are encouraged to avoid the use of restrictive practices and maintain an orderly pattern of exchange rates. A request for Fund assistance is considered in the light of the member's fiscal and monetary policies, and its co-operation with the Fund's principles.

Each member of the Fund undertakes to establish and maintain an agreed par value for its currency, and to consult the Fund on any changes in excess of 10 per cent of the initial parity. Countries retaining exchange controls are required to hold annual consultations with the Fund regarding these restrictions and the balance of payments justification for them. The Fund's financial assistance takes the form of a foreign exchange transaction in which the member pays to the Fund an amount of its own currency equivalent to the amount of foreign currency it wishes to purchase. The member is then expected to "repurchase" its own currency within three or five years with a payment of gold, SDRs, or convertible currency acceptable to the Fund.

A major step towards the establishment of a multilateral system of world payments was taken in February 1961, when ten countries (Belgium, France, Germany, Ireland, Italy, Luxembourg, the Netherlands, Peru, Sweden and the United Kingdom) accepted the convertibility obligations for their currencies under Article VIII of the Fund's Articles of Agreement. Members accepting the provisions of this Article must obtain the Fund's agreement before adopting restrictions on current international transactions or engaging in multiple exchange rates and discriminatory currency practices. Previously, Canada, the Dominican Republic, El Salvador, Guatemala, Haiti, Honduras, Mexico, Panama and the United States had already accepted these obligations. A total of 42 countries out of the Fund's 126 members has now accepted Article VIII status, the United Arab Emirates, and Oman are the most recent members to accept Article VIII status. Practically all currencies used to finance international trade and payments are now convertible under Article VIII.

Five general reviews of the adequacy of members' quotas were carried out by the Executive Director. Three of these have led to general and selective increases. Most quotas were increased by 50 per cent, and some by larger percentages, in September 1959 and succeeding months; by a further 25 per cent (more for 16 countries) in February 1966 and succeeding months; and by a further 30 per cent in December 1970. The total of members' quotas stood at SDR 29,189·4 million on 30 June, 1975.

The Fund is also authorized under its Articles of Agreement to supplement its resources by borrowing. In January 1962, a four-year agreement was concluded with ten industrial members which undertook to lend the Fund up to US $6,000 million in their own currencies, if this should be needed to forestall or cope with an impairment of the international monetary system. These arrangements, which have since been extended to 1980, were used to finance large drawings made in 1964, 1965, 1968, 1969 and 1970. All Fund borrowings under the arrangements have been repaid and, at the end of June 1975, the amount available was the equivalent of SDR 5,912·8 million.

In September 1967, following a study of the broader question of the adequacy of international liquidity, the Board of Governors at the Fund's Annual Meeting in Rio de Janeiro approved an outline plan for deliberate reserve creation in the form of special drawing rights in the Fund. The necessary Amendment to the Fund's Articles of Agreement was approved by the Governors in May 1968 and went into effect on July 28 1969 after being approved by the required three-fifths of the Fund's members having four-fifths of the total voting power. The Special Drawing Account, established in July 1969, is open to all Fund members undertaking its obligations. In September 1969, the Fund's Managing Director proposed to the Board of Governors that an allocation of SDRs to member countries totalling approximately SDR 9·5 billion over the first basic period of three years should be made. The first allocation of close to SDR 3·5 billion was made to 104 participants in the Special Drawing Account on 1 January 1970; the second of over SDR 2·9 billion was made to 109 participants on 1 January 1971; and the third of SDR 2·9 billion was made to 112 participants on 1 January 1972. The total allocation amounted to SDR 9,314·8 million over the first three year basic period. Since 1 January 1970, SDRs have been actively used in transactions between participants, and these transactions totalled the equivalent of SDR 2·4 billion at the end of June 1975. The Fund itself requires and uses SDRs in its General Account, whose holdings included SDR 524·7 million as of 30 June 1975.

Following serious monetary disturbances in 1971, the Board of Governors called for a complete study of all aspects of the international monetary system with a view to its improvement or reform. A Report on Reform of the International Monetary System was submitted to the Board at the 1972 Annual Meeting in Washington. During the Annual

Meeting the Committee of the Board of Governors on Reform of the International Monetary System and Related Issues—which subsequently became generally known as the Committee of 20—met at both the Ministerial and Deputies level to advise and report to the Board on all aspects of the international monetary system, including proposals for any amendments to the Fund's Articles of Agreement. The Committee of 20 met at both the Ministerial and Deputies level on numerous occasions prior to its last meeting on 12–13 June 1974. Following this final meeting the Executive Directors of the Fund submitted to the Fund's Board of Governors a resolution to create an Interim Committee of the Board of Governors to serve until a permanent Council of Governors can be established through an amendment of the Fund's Articles of Agreement. The Interim Committee met in January 1975 in Washington, in June 1975 in Paris and again in Washington on 31 August, immediately prior to the 1975 Annual Meetings of the Fund and the World Bank. The Committee reviewed the subject of Fund quotas, proposals for the amendment of the Fund's Articles of Agreement, including the role of gold and exchange arrangements, and the world economic situation.

Countries with the five largest quotas in the Fund as of 30 June 1975 were the United States (SDR 6,700 million), the United Kingdom (SDR 2,800 million), Germany (SDR 1,600 million), France (SDR 1,500 million), and Japan (SDR 1,200 million). On the same date, members' outstanding drawings had risen to the equivalent of SDR 6,891·8 million, and undrawn balances under stand-by arrangements with 11 members amounted to SDR 257·3 million. Drawings on the Fund since March 1947, when it began operations, totalled the equivalent of SDR 32,241·9 million, while repayments had risen to the equivalent of SDR 17,590·0 million.

The United States made its first drawing of US $125 million in various European currencies in February 1964, and subsequent transactions raised its total drawings on the Fund to SDR 3,552·0 million by 30 June 1975. All these drawings have been repaid.

Drawings on the Fund were made by the United Kingdom on sixteen separate occasions, totalling the equivalent of SDR 7,867·6 million. Outstanding drawings at the end of June 1975 were equivalent to SDR 463·0 million.

In addition to the United Kingdom, two other industrial countries (Denmark and Italy) had drawings on the Fund outstanding at the end of June 1975 equivalent to SDR 4·1 million and SDR 1,927·0 million respectively. Eight other developed countries had drawings outstanding on the same date, amounting to the equivalent of SDR 865·9 million. Also 53 less-developed countries had drawings outstanding amounting to the equivalent of SDR 3,211·7 million. Of these 13 Latin American countries accounted for the equivalent of SDR 769·4 million; five Middle Eastern countries for the equivalent of SDR 309·8 million; 11 Asian countries for the equivalent of SDR 1,528·4 million; and 24 African countries for the equivalent of SDR 604·2 million.

Up to 1961, drawings on the Fund were made chiefly in dollars, but since then drawings have been made in other currencies, including Argentine and Mexican pesos, Australian and Canadian dollars, Austrian schillings, Finnish Markkaa, Brazilian cruzeiros, Venezuelan bolivares, Belgian and French francs, Deutsche marks, Japanese yen, Netherlands guilders, pounds sterling, Iranian rials, Irish pounds, Spanish pesetas, Kuwaiti dinars, Malaysian dollars, Danish and Norwegian kroner, Saudi Arabian riyals, Swedish kroner, Italian lire, and South African rand.

The Fund's administrative budget for 1974–75 was SDR 46·0 million.

*Managing Director and Chairman of the Executive Board:* H. Johannes Witteveen. *Headquarters:* Washington, D.C. 20431, U.S.A.

## INTERNATIONAL TELECOMMUNICATION UNION (ITU)

Founded in Paris in 1865 as the International Telegraph Union, the International Telecommunication Union (ITU) took its present name in 1932 and became a Specialized Agency of the United Nations in 1947. The Union is governed by the International Telecommunication Convention which entered into force on 1 January 1975.

With a membership of 153 countries (as of 13 August 1977), the ITU acts to encourage world co-operation in the use of telecommunications of all kinds, to promote technical development and to harmonize national policies in the field. It also plans, co-ordinates and regulates all kinds of telecommunications, including satellite telecommunications.

### *Organization*

The supreme organ of the ITU is the Plenipotentiary Conference, which meets at intervals of normally five years and lays down general policy. The Plenipotentiary Conference reviews the International Telecommunication Convention, elects an Administrative Council composed of 36 Members of the Union, which meets once a year to examine and approve the annual budget, to supervise the administrative functions, and to co-ordinate the activities of the four permanent organs at the Union's Headquarters. These permanent organs are: the General Secretariat, the International Frequency Registration Board (IFRB), the International Telegraph and Telephone Consultative Committee (CCITT), and the International Radio Consultative Committee (CCIR).

The General Secretariat is responsible for the administration of the Union's Headquarters, the publication of ITU conference documents, regulations, manuals, etc., as well as for arranging conferences and meetings, and ensuring technical co-operation with Member countries. The IFRB's main task is to ensure that radio frequencies which countries assign to their radio stations (and which they have notified to the Board) will not cause harmful interference to other stations. The CCITT is concerned with the standardization of telephone and telegraph equipment as well as with questions dealing with tariffs concerning these services. The CCIR, on the other hand, deals with the standardization of radio equipment. Their Recommendations have an important influence on telecommunication scientists and technicians, operating administrations and companies, manufacturers and designers of equipment the world over.

World Administrative Conferences are held for revision of Administrative Regulations, and Regional Administrative Conferences are called to discuss specific telecommunication questions of a regional nature.

*Secretary-General:* Mohamed Mili (Tunisia). *Deputy Secretary-General:* Richard E. Butler (Australia). *Headquarters:* Place des Nations, 1211 Geneva 20, Switzerland.

## UNITED NATIONS EDUCATIONAL, SCIENTIFIC AND CULTURAL ORGANIZATION (UNESCO)

UNESCO was established on 4 November 1946, when the instruments of acceptance of 20 signatories of its Constitution were deposited with the Government of the United Kingdom. This followed a Conference of the representatives of 43 countries meeting in London, who laid down the basis of the Organization at the recommendation of the United Nations Conference of San Francisco.

### *Purposes*

The purpose of UNESCO, as stated in Article 1 of its Constitution, is 'to contribute to peace and security by promoting collaboration among the nations through education, science and culture in order to further universal respect for justice, for the rule of law and the human rights and fundamental freedoms which are affirmed for the peoples of the world without distinction of race, sex, language or religion by the Charter of the United Nations'.

UNESCO's programme has two main aspects: its traditional activities—such as exchange of information and preparation of international conventions—designed to further international co-operation; and operational involvement in development projects.

In the field of education, UNESCO works both to extend educational opportunities for children and to raise educational levels among adults. To further the basic concept of free, compulsory education, UNESCO is currently operating large-scale regional programmes in Africa, Asia and Latin America. These programmes concentrate on educational planning, teacher training, curriculum improvement, text-book production and better techniques for building schools. Two major works on education have been published as the result of an international commission set up under the chairmanship of Mr. Edgar Faure, former French Prime Minister and Minister of Ecucation. This commission undertook a comprehensive investigation of the whole range of education and educational strategies and its findings have been published in several languages under the title "Learning to Be" and its companion volume "Education on the Move".

In the field of science, UNESCO encourages scientific research and its application to development as well as for the improvement of living conditions. The organization's programme stresses surveys of natural resources and research in the marine sciences. UNESCO has carried out surveys of the world's major seismic zones with the aim of improving observatories as well as codes for earthquake-proof construction. It maintains Regional Centres for Science and Technology for the Arab States, South Asia, Southeast Asia, Africa, and Latin America. While continuing to encourage research on problems of the arid zones and desertification, UNESCO is now concentrating on the direct application of the benefits of science and technology for the developing countries. To help meet the 'environmental challenge' a new international research programme on *Man and the Biosphere* (MAB) was launched in 1970, and aims at close co-operation between ecologists and social scientists, underlining UNESCO's awareness of the importance of sociological factors in this field. The organization has also prepared natural resources maps, begun an International Geological Correlation Programme, studied the causes of natural disasters and undertaken the establishment of a science information system (UNISIST). In the social sciences, the UNESCO programme features two main themes: the teaching of social sciences and their application, and fundamental research, and the study of sociological problems connected with development and human rights.

UNESCO's programme also endeavours to strengthen international understanding by broadening public knowledge of various cultures. It also seeks to increase access to culture through promoting wide-scope cultural policies. The organization's cultural activities cover several different aspects: Research in the humanities, spreading knowledge of art and literature, safeguarding of cultural heritages, development of museums and libraries. An international campaign for safeguarding the monuments of Nubia resulted in the rescue of 22 temples threatened by flood waters of the Aswan High Dam, among them the temple of Abu Simbel, which was dismantled in its entirety and moved to a new site. A similar operation is now under way to save the temples on the island of Philae. International campaigns were also launched to save Borobudur, Indonesia, Moenjodaro, Pakistan, Venice and the Acropolis in Greece.

In the field of communication, UNESCO seeks to extend the use of press, films, radio and television in creating international understanding; to remove barriers to the international flow of information; and to expand communication facilities in under-developed countries, including services such as libraries and archives as well as mass media. UNESCO's Library and Documentation service began an International Information System on Research Documentation (ISORID) which computerizes a collection of research projects and reports that are then made available to interested institutions and specialists. The Organization has also carried out a feasibility study on the use of a regional satellite for educational purposes in eight Latin American countries.

Finally, an exchange of persons service provides information on opportunities for international exchanges of students, teachers and workers and administers fellowships.

*Organization*

UNESCO is operated by a General Conference composed of representatives of Member States which meets every two years and decides the policy, programme and budget of the Organization; an Executive Board consisting of 45 members elected by the General Conference as representatives of their respective governments, which supervises the execution of the programme; and an international secretariat headed by a Director-General.

In October 1977, 142 countries were members of UNESCO.

The regular budget for UNESCO for 1977–78 was $224,413,000, which was met by assessments on Member States.

*Director-General:* Amadou Mahtar M'Bow (Senegal). *Headquarters:* 7 Place de Fontenoy, Paris 75700.

# UNIVERSAL POSTAL UNION (UPU)

THE first attempt at drawing up a broad multilateral postal agreement was made by an International Postal Conference which met in Paris in 1863. Eleven years later the first International Postal Congress met in Berne and was attended by delegates from 22 countries. On 9 October 1874, the Congress signed an International Postal Treaty which became effective on 1 July 1875. The second Postal Congress, held in 1878, changed the name of the organization from General Postal Union to Universal Postal Union and the name of the basic act to Universal Postal Convention.

Since its foundation, the U.P.U. has held 17 Congresses. The last one took place in Lausanne in 1974, and the next one will take place in Brazil (Rio de Janeiro) in 1979. The Union is now governed by the Constitution of the U.P.U., adopted in 1964, and by the Acts resulting from the Lausanne Congress which came into force on 1 January 1976. The U.P.U. became a specialized agency of the United Nations in 1948.

U.P.U.'s budget for 1978 sets an expenditure ceiling of 16,160,000 Swiss francs (U.S. $6,542,500 at 31 August 1977). These expenses are borne jointly by all member countries, which for this purpose are divided into eight contribution classes; the contributions vary according to class, in the ratio of 1 for class 8 to 50 for class 1.

At 31 August 1977 the U.P.U. numbered 158 member countries.

The purposes of the Union are: To form a single postal territory for the reciprocal exchange of letter-post items; to ensure the organization and improvement of the various postal services; to promote in this sphere the development of international collaboration; to participate in technical assistance in the postal field. Such assistance is furnished from three sources: Multilateral aid accorded by the United Nations Development Programme (U.N.D.P.), the U.P.U. Special Fund (voluntary contributions from member countries) and direct bilateral technical assistance between postal administrations.

*Organization*

The Universal Postal Congress, the supreme legislative authority of the Union, consists of representatives of all member countries and is convened in principle every five years. Its main function is to study and revise the Acts of the Union, taking as a basis proposals put forward by member countries, the Executive Council or the Consultative Council for Postal Studies.

The Executive Council, composed of 40 members elected by Congress, meets each year at U.P.U. headquarters. It ensures the continuity of the Union's work between Congresses, supervises the activities of the International Bureau, undertakes studies, draws up proposals, and makes recommendations to Congress. It is reponsible for encouraging, supervising and co-ordinating international co-operation in the form of postal technical assistance and vocational training.

The Consultative Council for Postal Studies, composed of 35 members elected by Congress, meets annually, in principle at U.P.U. headquarters. It is responsible for organizing studies of major problems affecting postal administrations in all U.P.U. member countries, in the technical, operational and economic fields and in the sphere of technical co-operation. The C.C.P.S. also provides information and opinions on these matters, and examines teaching and training problems arising in the new and developing countries.

The International Bureau, a central office functioning at Berne, is responsible for the co-ordination, publication and dissemination of all manner of information about the international postal services. At the request of the parties concerned, it gives opinions on disputes. It considers requests for amendments to the Acts of the Union, gives notice of changes adopted and takes part in the preparation of the work of Congress; it provides secretarial services for U.P.U. bodies and promotes technical assistance.

*Director-General of International Bureau:* Mohamed Ibrahim Sobhi (Egypt). Headquarters: Weltpoststrasse 4, 3000 Berne 15, Switzerland. Tel: 031/432211.

# WORLD HEALTH ORGANIZATION (WHO)

The origin of the World Health Organization may be traced to a proposal made by the representatives of Brazil and China during the San Francisco Conference in April 1945 that an international health organization should be set up. Instructed by the Economic and Social Council, the Secretary-General of the United Nations convoked an International Health Conference in New York in June 1946. At its conclusion on 22 July 1946, the Constitution of the World Health Organization was accepted by 61 states and two of them, China and the United Kingdom of Great Britain and Northern Ireland, achieved the distinction of becoming the first full members of WHO by signing the document without reservation.

An Interim Commission carried on until, on 7 April 1948, the World Health Organization came into formal existence upon ratification of its Constitution by 26 Member States of the United Nations.

The Organization has 150 Member States and two Associate Members.

The objective of the World Health Organization is the attainment by all peoples of the highest possible level of health.

The WHO Constitution defines health as 'a state of complete physical, mental and social well-being and not merely the absence of disease or infirmity'.

In accordance with its constitutional responsibilities, the Organization (*a*) acts as the directing and co-ordinating authority on international health work; (*b*) furnishes technical assistance and emergency aid upon the request of governments; (*c*) stimulates and advances work to eradicate epidemic, endemic and other diseases; (*d*) promotes, in co-operation with other specialised agencies where necessary, the improvement of nutrition, housing, sanitation, recreation, economic or working conditions and other aspects of environmental hygiene; (*e*) promotes maternal and child health and welfare and fosters the ability to live harmoniously in a changing total environment; (*f*) fosters activities in the field of mental health; (*g*) promotes improved standards of teaching and training in the health, medical and related professions; (*h*) promotes and conducts research in the field of health; (*i*) promotes co-operation among scientific and professional groups; (*j*) maintains international services in epidemiology and statistics; (*k*) proposes international conventions and regulations in international health matters; (*l*) establishes international standards for biological and pharmaceutical products; (*m*) provides information, counsel and assistance in the field of health; and (*n*) assists in developing an informed public opinion on matters of health.

### *Organization*

The Organization's policy-making body is the World Health Assembly comprising delegates of Member States. An Executive Board is composed of 30 persons technically qualified in the field of health and designated by 30 Members elected by the Assembly. The Secretariat, appointed by the Director-General, consists of technical and administrative staff working at Headquarters in Geneva, the regional offices and on field projects.

Six Regional Organizations have been set up. Each consists of a regional committee, composed of representatives of Member States and Associate Members in the region, and a regional office functioning under a Regional Director who is appointed by the Executive Board in agreement with the Regional Committee. They are: Region for Africa—Brazzaville; Region of the Americas—Washington (Pan American Sanitary Bureau); Eastern Mediterranean Region—Alexandria; European Region—Copenhagen; South-East Asia Region—New Delhi; Western Pacific Region—Manila.

The Thirtieth World Health Assembly composed of delegates of 142 of *WHO*'s 150 Member States, met in Geneva in May 1977. The United Nations and many other international bodies were represented.

### *Activities in 1977*

The drive to eradicate smallpox made further progress during the year. Three countries in Asia (Bhutan, India and Nepal) and nine in Central Africa (Burundi, Cameroon, Central African Empire, Chad, Congo, Equatorial Guinea, Gabon, Rwanda and Zaire) were certified by WHO inquiry commissions to have eradicated the disease. In eastern Africa, however, the disease still maintained its foothold in Somalia. Special case search activities were carried out in Somalia and the two countries bordering it, Kenya and Ethiopia. By mid-September, a total of 3,132 cases of smallpox had been reported to WHO—3,127 of them from Somalia and five from northern Kenya.

The World Health Assembly met in May and adopted a budget of $165,000,000 for WHO's work in 1978. Other decisions taken by the Assembly included the following:

*Social target:* The Assembly decided that the main social target of WHO in the coming decades should be the attainment by all citizens of the world by the year 2000 of a level of health that will permit them to lead a socially and economically productive life.

*Economies in budget:* The Assembly approved proposals for the phased reduction of posts and of certain establishment and other costs, including the phasing out of projects that have outlived their utility, in order to make available substantial resources ($41 million) for new and expanded programmes during 1978–81.

*Nutrition problems:* The Assembly recognized that malnutrition was "one of the major health problems in the world" and that "dietary defiats in the developing countries and excesses and imbalances in developed countries" were affecting the health of populations in both groups of countries. Governments were urged to give high priority to food and nutrition problems within their health programmes.

*Primary health care teams:* More effective use should be made of nursing/midwifery personnel by involving them, together with other members of the health team, in the planning and management of primary health care and vaccination programmes an as teachers and supervisors of primary health care workers.

*Toxic effects of chemicals:* WHO should accelerate and make more effective the evaluation of health risks from exposure to chemicals and promote the use of experimental and epidemiological methods that will produce internationally comparable results.

*Tropical diseases:* The Assembly noted with satisfaction the progress made towards the establishment of WHO's Special Programme for Research and Training in Tropical Diseases, and the development of its initial activities in cooperation with the United Nations Development Programme, the World Bank and Member States.

*Cancer:* Bearing in mind the growing significance of the cancer problem for the developing as well as the developed countries, the Assembly requested the continuation of efforts on cancer control and research, training of qualified cancer specialists, and the establishment of favourable conditions for exchanges of experience on all aspects of the problem.

*Traditional medicine:* The Assembly approved WHO's efforts to initiate studies on the use of traditional systems of medicine in conjunction with modern medicine, and urged interested governments to give adequate importance to the utilization of their traditional systems of medicine with appropriate regulations as suited to their national health systems.

*Health legislation:* The Assembly requested the Director-General to strengthen WHO's programme in the field of health legislation with a view to assisting Member States, upon their request, in the development of appropriate health legislation adapted to their needs.

*Aid to strife-torn areas:* In separate resolutions, the Assembly requested the Director-General to continue and intensify WHO's assistance to Lebanon, Cyprus, Democratic Kampuchea, Lao People's Democratic Republic, and the Socialist Republic of Viet Nam, as well as to refugees and displaced persons in the Middle East.

### *World Health Day*

World Health Day, 7 April 1976, was devoted to the theme "Immunize and Protect your child". The day marked the twenty-ninth anniversary of the coming into force of WHO's constitution. "Down with High Blood Pressure" is the theme selected for World Health Day, 1978.

The budget for 1978 is U.S. $165,000,000.

*Director-General:* Dr. H. Mahler (Denmark), *Headquarters:* Avenue Appia, 1211 Geneva 27, Switzerland.

# WORLD METEOROLOGICAL ORGANIZATION (WMO)

THE World Meteorological Organization (WMO) is a Specialized Agency of the United Nations created to co-ordinate and improve the services rendered by meteorology throughout the world to various human activities. The earth's atmosphere is a whole which cannot be divided to conform to political frontiers. Moreover, weather and climate in one place are influenced by conditions in distant areas. For these reasons, the nations of the world recognized as early as the last century the necessity of international co-operation to study the vagaries of the weather and to apply the knowledge gained for the benefit of mankind. (Membership of the Organization has now reached 146, consisting of 139 States and seven Territories, each maintaining its own meteorological service.)

The basic programme of WMO is the World Weather Watch (WWW) a remarkable example of international co-operation, which consists of a worldwide meteorological system composed of the co-ordinated facilities and services provided by individual Members, supplemented by international organizations. Its primary purpose is to ensure that all Members obtain meteorological and other related environmental information they require for carrying out the most efficient and effective meteorological and other related environmental services, both as regards applications and research. The information required by Members includes both observational data and processed information. The information must be received by Members in a timely and co-ordinated fashion, and also be in a convenient format for manual or automatic processing.

WWW has now been in operation since 1968 and plans for further development were approved by the Seventh World Meteorological Congress (Geneva, April/May 1975). Its essential elements are a global observing system, including the most advanced remote sensing techniques from meteorological satellites, and automatic devices for *in situ* observations on land, at sea or in the air, a global data-processing system based on World, Regional and National Meteorological Centres equipped, as necessary, with powerful computers, and a global telecommunication system, linking meteorological centres and meteorological services. A scheme for the constant monitoring of the operation and performance of the WWW has been set up recently.

The WWW is a dynamic system, flexible enough to be adapted to incorporate scientific advances and new technology. New techniques of observations, telecommunications and data processing are being introduced as soon as they prove to be sufficiently reliable and economical.

WWW is being implemented through the application of the basic principle that each country will provide facilities and services which fall within its own territory but those developing countries which are unable to do this are being assisted, as far as possible, through the United Nations Development Programme (UNDP), Funds-in-Trust (FIT) arrangements, through bilateral agreements or through the Voluntary Assistance Programme (VAP) of WMO. VAP, which commenced operations at the beginning of 1968 is supported by donations from Members of cash, equipment or services. In the first nine years of the operation of the VAP (1968–1976) a total of 254 projects were completed and implementation of a further 210 projects had been undertaken with either full or partial support. An estimated $4·1 million were spent by WMO Members in 1976 on assistance under VAP

Under FIT arrangements WMO provides technical assistance through projects which are financed by a national government, either the government of the country where the project is being carried out or the government of another country which wishes to support the project. Four projects were under implementation in 1976 at a cost of approximately one-half million U.S. dollars.

Through its participation in the United Nations Development Programme, WMO assists many countries in the development of their meteorological and hydrological services and the training of personnel by supplying equipment for observing networks; international experts for advisory, training and operational missions; fellowships for training abroad, and support for training seminars. Advice is given on subjects ranging from the application of meteorology in special fields (e.g. utilization of data from meteorological satellites) to the establishment, organization and operation of national meteorological and hydrological services. Some large-scale economic development projects of the UNDP have been undertaken in a number of countries to enable them to provide information needed for the development of water resource potential (e.g. irrigation, hydroelectric power and flood control projects) and agriculture and to develop institutions for the training of personnel and the performance of research. In 1976, WMO provided technical assistance to 94 countries in the form of projects financially supported by the UNDP, VAP, FIT, UNEP and the regular budget of the Organization. The cost of assistance provided in 1976 for projects for which WMO was the executing agency of UNDP was U.S. $6·8 million.

One of the roles of WMO is to encourage and assist in co-ordinating meteorological research activities among Member countries, to organize joint multi-national research projects, to facilitate the exchange of scientific information and data and to sponsor and publish the proceedings of international conferences and symposia aimed at advancing knowledge in the atmospheric sciences. The WMO body with overall responsibility for the research programme is the Commission for Atmospheric Sciences (CAS).

The fields to which highest priority is at present being given within WMO are weather prediction, weather modification, climate changes and the interactions between atmospheric phenomena and other environmental parameters (e.g. sea waves, ice and snow cover, river and lake levels) with a view to forecasting environmental conditions as a whole rather than simply the state of the atmosphere.

One of the major undertakings at present is the Global Atmospheric Research Programme (GARP) which the Organization is carrying out jointly with the International Council of Scientific Unions (ICSU). The objective of GARP is to study the relevant atmospheric processes with a view to improving the accuracy of forecasts over periods of up to several weeks and acquiring a better understanding of the physical basis of climate. GARP is an international scientific effort in theoretical research and complex field experiments. The first such experiment, the GARP Atlantic Tropical Experiment (GATE) took place in 1974. An even more ambitious project, the First GARP Global Experiment, is planned for 1978/1979 which, as its name implies, will be on a world-wide scale.

WMO has recently stepped up its activities in the field of weather modification. In particular, the Organization is sponsoring the Precipitation Enhancement Project (PEP), an internationally planned, executed and evaluated experiment lasting several years, with the object of obtaining scientifically convincing evidence as to the feasibility of artificially increasing rainfall by significant amounts under specified conditions.

Considerable work is being done in connexion with studies of the physical aspects of climatic fluctuations. This entails assessing the possible natural causes of changes in climate (such as variations in solar activity, volcanic eruptions or changes in oceanic properties) as well as the consequences of man's activities (such as the release of heat, gases and particulate matter into the atmosphere and changes in the properties of the Earth's surface). The planning of a World Climate Programme is now in progress.

Research into the physical and chemical characteristics of the various components of the atmosphere, including pollutants, is a prerequisite for the overall studies aimed at safeguarding human life and health. For example, a close study is being made of stratospheric ozone in view of the vital role it plays in preventing dangerous amounts of ultraviolet radiation from reaching the lower levels of the atmosphere and the surface of the Earth.

Tropical meteorology is another important part of the WMO research programme. In many countries in the tropics, the national economy and even the lives of the inhabitants may depend upon the movement and evolution of tropical cyclones or the timely arrival of rainfall. Thus, the object is to achieve greater accuracy in forecasting such critical meteorological events.

The WMO Meteorological Applications and Environment Programme is aimed at the application of a knowledge of meteorology and climatology to human activities. The range of this programme is wide. In the field of transportation, services to aviation and marine interests cover those needed for safe and efficient operations as well as providing for special warning services in safeguarding human life and property. In addition, services to marine interests cover the needs of coastal developments such as harbour development, coastal defence measures and off-shore drilling. The agro-meteorological aspects cover the meteorological and climatological needs of all facets of agriculture, although there is particular emphasis on food production and the security of world food supplies through the methodology of crop/weather relationships. The study of the effects of climatic fluctuations, particularly in relation to food production and crop relations, form another part of this programme. WMO has agreed to provide the meteorological input to the FAO Early Warning System. Other important aspects of this work relate to the agricultural development of arid lands and problems of desertification, including studies on drought. Meteorological aspects of forest development and management as well as those of forest fires are also covered.

Studies of the social and economic benefits of the application of meteorology are being carried out both in developing and developed countries; important areas of study include the value of meteorological services to the construction industry, to the tourist industry and to human recreation. Studies on solar and wind energy and on meteorological aspects of human settlements are also under way.

Meteorological and climatological aspects of air and marine pollution are also an important facet of this programme. As regards air pollution, WMO has the prime responsibility of organizing a global network of background air pollution observing stations to provide the basic data against which long-term changes can be compared. As regards marine pollution, a pilot project is under way in collaboration with the Inter-governmental Oceanographic Commission using the facilities of the World Weather Watch, the Marine Meteorological Services Systems and the Integrated Global Ocean Station System (IGOSS).

The purpose of the WMO hydrology and water resources development programme is to promote world-wide co-operation in the evaluation of water resources and to assist in their development through the co-ordinated establishment of hydrological networks and services, including data collection and processing, hydrological forecasting and warnings and the supply of meteorological and hydrological data for design purposes. International projects are developed by relevant constituent bodies of the Organization or by joint action with other international organizations. The primary components of the programmes are: technical projects within the WMO Operational Hydrology Programme; institutionalized co-operation between hydrological services on regional and global levels; participation in the programmes of other organizations, such as the International Hydrological Programme of Unesco, in such fields as water balance, water quality and inland water pollution monitoring, environmental monitoring and integrated river basin development.

The WMO Operational Hydrology Programme (OHP) includes activities pertaining to: measurement of basic hydrological elements from networks of meteorological and hydrological stations; collection, transmission, processing, storage, retrieval and publication of basic hydrological data; hydrological forecasting; development and improvement of relevant methods, procedures and techniques.

These activities often result in the preparation of guidance material which is promulgated by WMO in an appropriate form.

The regular publications of WMO include Technical Notes, Manuals, Guides. Final Reports of Meetings, the quarterly WMO Bulletin, reports on marine science affairs, special environmental reports, operational hydrology reports GARP publications and an International Cloud Atlas in several volumes, one of which contains 121 black-and-white and 103 colour photographs of all types of cloud.

WMO's structure comprises the World Meteorological Congress which meets once every four years and includes representatives from all Member Governments of the Organization; the Executive Committee of 24 directors of National Meteorological Services; six Regional Associations which deal mainly with regional aspects of the WMO programmes, including the international exchange of meteorological observations and the network of reporting stations; and eight technical Commissions dealing respectively with atmospheric sciences, basic systems, instruments and methods of observation, agricultural meteorology, aeronautical meteorology, marine meteorology, special applications of meteorology and climatology, and hydrology.

The WMO Secretariat, headed by the Secretary-General, has a headquarters staff establishment of about 300. Towards the end of 1977 the number of experts in the field was about 100. The Secretariat acts as a link between the meteorological services of the world, undertakes technical studies and acts as the administrative, documentary and information centre of the Organization.

The Organization's regular budget for the four-year period 1976–79 amounts to US $40,542,000. This figure does not incorporate WMO's participation in technical assistance programmes mentioned above.

*Officers: President:* M. F. Taha (Egypt). *Vice-Presidents:* 1st—A. H. Parvis Navai (Iran); 2nd—Ju. A. Izrael (U.S.S.R.). 3rd—J. E. Echeveste (Argentina). *Secretary-General:* D. A. Davies (U.K.). *Deputy Secretary-General:* R. J. Schneider (Switzerland): *Address:* 41 Avenue Giuseppe-Motta, Geneva, Switzerland.

# III. Affiliated Agencies of the United Nations

## THE INTERNATIONAL UNION FOR CONSERVATION OF NATURE AND NATURAL RESOURCES (IUCN)

An independent nongovernmental body founded in 1948, at an international conference at Fontainebleau, France, sponsored by UNESCO and the French Government, to promote scientifically based action for the conservation of wild living resources.

*Aims:* To encourage and facilitate cooperation between governments, national and international organizations and persons concerned with the conservation of nature and natural resources; to promote in all parts of the world national and international action in respect of the conservation of nature and natural resources; to encourage scientific research related to the conservation of nature and natural resources and to disseminate information about such research; to promote education in and disseminate widely information on the conservation of nature and natural resources and in other ways to increase public awareness of the conservation of nature and natural resources; to prepare draft international agreements relating to the conservation of nature and natural resources and to encourage governments to adhere to agreements once concluded; to assist governments to improve their legislation relating to the conservation of nature and natural resources; and to take any other action which will promote the conservation of nature and natural resources.

*Functions:* To monitor the state of the planet's living resources—the plants, animals and ecosystems on which the survival and wellbeing of humanity depend; to determine scientific priorities for conservation action; to mobilize the scientific and professional resources to investigate the most serious conservation problems and recommend solutions to them; to develop, within a coherent global strategy, programmes of action to protect, sustain and use rationally the most important and threatened species and ecosystems; to assist governments and other bodies to devise, initiate and carry out projects for the conservation of wild living resources.

At present IUCN has 424 voting members in 102 countries, these members being States (48), government agencies (109) and nongovernmental organizations (267). The State members of IUCN are: Australia, Bangladesh, Belgium, Benin, Canada, Chad, Democratic Kampuchea, Denmark, Ecuador, Egypt, Ethiopia, Finland, France, Federal Republic of Germany, Greece, Iceland, India, Iran, Iraq, Israel, Italy, Ivory Coast, Kenya, Lao People's Democratic Republic, Libyan Arab Jamahiriya, Luxembourg, Madagascar, Malaysia, Mauritania, Mauritius, Mongolia, Morocco, Nepal, Netherlands, New Zealand, Norway, Oman, Pakistan, Samoa, Senegal, Socialist Republic of Viet Nam, Sudan, Switzerland, Thailand, United Kingdom, Venezuela, Zaire, Zambia.

IUCN also has several hundred individual Subscribers and Friends.

In addition, IUCN maintains a global network of more than 700 scientists and professionals organized into six commissions covering: threatened species; national parks and other protected areas; ecology; environmental planning; environmental policy, law and administration; and environmental education.

The members and commissions, and the many other scientists and professionals with whom they and the IUCN secretariat are in touch, provide the authoritative information and advice on which IUCN bases its programmes.

Essential information is published in key source documents, notably the *Red Data Book* (describing all threatened species of mammals, birds, amphibians and reptiles, and fish) and the *United Nations List of National Parks and Equivalent Reserves.*

IUCN is now preparing a World Conservation Strategy which is intended: to identify the principal ways in which species and ecosystems are depleted, degraded or destroyed; to define effective preventive or remedial action (by governments, intergovernmental bodies and nongovernmental bodies); and to propose priorities for action.

The Strategy will draw upon the accumulated expertise of IUCN's members and commissions as well as many other organizations and individuals. From it IUCN will derive its own three-year programme, and also develop programmes for World Wildlife Fund (WWF), for which IUCN acts as scientific adviser.

Two-thirds of IUCN's income come from the United Nations Environment Programme (UNEP) and World Wildlife Fund. Members supply about a fifth, and the balance comes from smaller grants and contracts. The IUCN budget for 1977 was Sfrs. 5,000,000.

IUCN has formal working relations with a wide range of intergovernmental and international nongovernmental organizations. Among UN bodies (ECOSOC, FAO, UNEP, UNESCO, UNIDO, WHO and WMO), IUCN works especially closely with UNEP, FAO and UNESCO—all members, with IUCN, of the Ecosystem Conservation Group, set up by UNEP to help coordinate the conservation work of the four organizations.

IUCN has special relationships with the Council of Europe, the Organization of African Unity, and the Organization of American States, and with the following nongovernmental organizations: International Association on Water Pollution Research, International Council for Bird Preservation, International Council of Scientific Unions, International Geographical Union, International Society for the Protection of Animals, International Youth Federation for Environmental Studies and Conservation, and World Wildlife Fund.

*Organization:* IUCN consists of: (a) the General Assembly; (b) the Council; (c) the Bureau; (d) the Commissions; and (e) the Director General.

*General Assembly:* The highest policy organ of IUCN, consisting of the delegates of the members of IUCN meeting in session. The Assembly meets in ordinary session every third year.

Since the inaugural meeting at Fontainebleau in 1948, the General Assembly has met at Brussels, Belgium (1950), Caracas, Venezuela (1952), Copenhagen, Denmark (1954), Edinburgh, Scotland (1956), Athens, Greece (1958), Warsaw, Poland (1960), Nairobi, Kenya (1963), Lucerne, Switzerland (1966), New Delhi, India (1969), Banff, Canada (1972), Kinshasa, Zaire (1975), Geneva, Switzerland—extraordinary session (1977). The 14th General Assembly is scheduled to take place in Ashkhabad, Turkmenian SSR in September/October 1978.

*Council:* Composed of: (i) the President of IUCN; (ii) 24 regional Councillors (three from each of the following regions: (a) Africa; (b) Central and South America; (c) North America and the Caribbean; (d) East Asia; (e) West Asia; (f) Australia and Oceania; (g) East Europe; (h) West Europe); (iii) five co-opted Councillors; (iv) six Chairmen of the Commissions.

The President, regional Councillors and Chairmen of Commissions are elected by the Assembly. The co-opted Councillors are appointed by the elected members of the Council.

The Council also appoints the Chairman and members of the Bureau, up to four Vice-Presidents, and the Treasurer of IUCN.

The Council meets at least once a year.

*Bureau:* Composed of: (a) Chairman of the Bureau and up to five members; (b) President, Vice-Presidents and Treasurer of IUCN. The Bureau meets at least twice each year.

*Commissions:* Commission on Ecology; Commission on Education; Commission on Environmental Planning; Commission on Environmental Policy, Law and Administration; Commission on National Parks and Protected Areas, Survival Service Commission.

*Council of IUCN*[1]

*President:* Professor D. J. Kuenen, Netherlands.

*Vice-Presidents:* Professor A. G. Bannikov, U.S.S.R.; Mr. Eskandar Firouz, Iran; Dr. D. F. McMichael, Australia; Dr. Lee M. Talbot, U.S.A.; Dr. David P. S. Wasawo, Kenya.

*Treasurer:*[2] Mr. Robert E. Boote, U.K.

*Chairman of the Bureau:*[3] Mr. Maurice F. Strong, Canada

*Councillors:* Professor Pierre Aguesse, France; Dr. E. O. A. Asibey, Ghana; Dr. José Candido de Melo Carvalho, Brazil; Mr. William G. Conway, U.S.A.; Dr. Marc J. Dourojeanni, Peru; Dr. Martin H. Edwards, Canada; Mr. Y. Fukushima, Japan; Dr. Pierre Goeldlin, Switzerland; Dr. A. Inozemtsev, U.S.S.R.; Professor M. Kassas, Egypt; Dr. Ashok Khosla, India; Ing. Edgardo Mondolfi, Venezuela; Dr. Muema Ngoy Toka, Zaire; Lic. Andrés Rozental, Mexico; Professor Otto Soemarwoto, Indonesia; Lic. G. Stutzin, Chile.

*Chairman, Commission on Ecology:* Professor J. D. Ovington, Australia.

*Chairman, Commission on Education:* Dr. L. K. Shaposhnikov, U.S.S.R.

*Chairman, Commission on Environmental Planning:* Professor D. Ogrin, Yugoslavia.

*Chairman, Commission on Environmental Policy, Law and Administration:* Mr. Wolfgang E. Burhenne, FRG.

*Chairman, Commission on National Parks and Protected Areas:* Dr. Kenton R. Miller, U.S.A.

*Chairman, Survival Service Commission:* Sir Peter Scott, U.K.

*Deputy Chairmen of Commissions*[4]

*Deputy Chairman, Commission on Ecology:* To be appointed.

*Deputy Chairman, Commission on Education:* Mr. Lars-Erik Esping, Sweden.

*Deputy Chairman, Commission on Environmental Planning:* Mr. V. C. Robertson, U.K.

*Deputy Chairman, Commission on Environmental Policy, Law and Administration:* To be appointed.

*Deputy Chairman, Commission on National Parks and Protected Areas:* Mr. Harold K. Eidsvik, Canada.

*Deputy Chairman, Survival Service Commission:* Mr. John Perry, U.S.A.

*Notes*

1 New organ, for which the functions under the revised IUCN Statutes, as adopted by the 13th (Extraordinary) General Assembly, April 1977, have been assumed by the former Executive Board until September 1978, when the 14th General Assembly will elect a new Council.

2 New office created under revised Statutes (April 1977).

3 New office created under revised Statutes (April 1977).

4 New offices, with appointment by Council. A Deputy Chairman acts in the place of his Commission's Chairman whenever the Chairman is unable to attend a meeting of Council. Deputy Chairmen of Commissions may also attend meetings of Council at which their respective Chairman is present; on such occasions the Deputy Chairmen are regarded as observers without voting rights.

*Bureau of IUCN*

*Chairman:* Mr. Maurice F. Strong, Canada.
*Members:* Professor A. G. Bannikov, U.S.S.R.; Mr. Robert E. Boote, U.K.; Mr. Wolfgang E. Burhenne, FRG.; Mr. William G. Conway, U.S.A.; Mr. Eskandar Firouz, Iran; Dr. Pierre Goeldlin, Switzerland; Professor M. Kassas, Egypt; Professor D. J. Kuenen, Netherlands; Dr. D. F. McMichael, Australia; Dr. Lee M. Talbot, U.S.A.; Dr. David P. S. Wasawo, Kenya.

*Director General and Secretariat*

*Director General:* Dr. David A. Munro.

*Headquarters:* 1110 Morges, Switzerland. Telephone (021) 71.44.01.

*Telegrams:* UNICORN Morges.
*IUCN Environmental Law Centre:* 214 Adenauerallee, 53 Bonn, Federal Republic of Germany. Approximately 40 staff.

*Publications:* Bulletin (monthly in English, French and Spanish); Annual Report; *Red Data Book*: *United Nations List of National Parks and Equivalent Reserves*: Books on conservation and development, land and freshwater animals' marine and coastal ecology and management, national parks and other protected areas, and regional conservation; Environmental Policy and Law Papers. A catalogue of IUCN publications is available on request.

*IUCN Executive Board* (1975–78)

*President:* Professor D. J. Kuenen, Netherlands.

*Vice-Presidents:* Professor A. G. Bannikov, U.S.S.R.; Mr Eskandar Firouz, Iran; Dr. D. F. McMichael, Australia; Dr. Lee M. Talbot, U.S.A.; Dr. David P. S. Wasawo, Kenya.

*Members:* Professor P. Aguesse, France; Dr. E. O. A. Asibey, Ghana; Mr. Robert E. Boote, U.K.; Mr. William G. Conway, U.S.A.; Dr. Martin H. Edwards, Canada; Mr. Y. Fukushima, Japan; Professor Pierre Goeldín, Switzerland; Dr. A. Inozemtsev, U.S.S.S.R.; Professor M. Kassas, Egypt; Dr. Ashok Khosla, India; Ing. E. Mondolfi, Venezuela; Dr. Muema Ngoy Toka, Zaire; Lic. Andrés Rozental, Mexico; Professor Otto Soemarwoto, Indonesia; Lic. G. Stutzin, Chile.

*IUCN Commissions*

*Commission on Ecology:*

Chairman: Professor J. D. Ovington, Australia.
Vice-Chairman: Dr. Arturo Gómez-Pompa, Mexico.

*Commission on Education:*

Chairman: Dr. L. K. Shaposhnikov, U.S.S.R.
Vice-Chairmen: Mr. Lars-Erik Esping, Sweden; Dr. M. Makagiansar, Indonesia.

*Commission on Environmental Planning:*

Chairman: Professor D. Ogrin, Yugoslavia.
Vice-Chairmen: Mr. R. J. Benthem, Netherlands; Mr. V. C. Robertson, U.K.

*Commission on Environmental Policy, Law and Administration*

Chairman: Professor Lynton K. Caldwell, U.S.A.
Vice-Chairmen: Mr. B. N. Bogdanov, U.S.S.R.; Mr. W. E. Burhenne, Federal Republic of Germany.

*Commission on National Parks and Protected Areas:*

Acting Chairman: Mr. Theodor R. Swem, U.S.A.
Vice-Chairmen: Dr. Marc U. Dourojeanni, Peru; Mr. P. H. C. Lucas, New Zealand; Dr. P. M. Olindo, Kenya.

*Survival Service Commission:*

Chairman: Sir Peter Scott, U.K.
Vice-Chairmen: Mr. John Perry, U.S.A.; Mr. M. K. Ranjitsinh, India.

## SPECIES IN DANGER OF EXTINCTION

CLASS: MAMMALIA

MONOTREMES
Long-beaked echidna
MARSUPIALS
Parma wallaby
Bridle nail-tailed wallaby
Crescent nail-tailed wallaby
Western hare-wallaby
Banded hare wallaby
Yellow-footed rock wallaby
Desert rat-kangaroo
Northern rat-kangaroo
Lesueur's rat-kangaroo
Leadbeater's possum
Scaly-tailed possum
Queensland hairy-nosed wombat
Red-tailed phascogale
Dibbler
Narrow-nosed planigale
Kimberley planigale
Long-tailed sminthopsis
Eastern jerboa marsupial
Thylacine
INSECTIVORA
Cuban solenodon
Haitian solenodon
Mindanao gymnure
Russian desman
Pyrenean desman
CHIROPTERA
Indiana bat
Hawaiian hoary bat
Ozark big-eared bat
Virginian big-eared bat
Spotted bat
PRIMATES
Black lemur
Red-fronted lemur
Sclater's lemur
Sanford's lemur
Mongoose lemur
Red-tailed sportive lemur
Nossi-bé sportive lemur
White-footed sportive lemur
Grey gentle lemur
Broad-nosed gentle lemur
Hairy-eared dwarf lemur
Fat-tailed dwarf lemur
Coquerel's mouse lemur
Fork-marked mouse lemur
Indri
Verreaux's sifaka
Perrier's sifaka
Western woolly avahi
Aye-aye
Buff-headed marmoset
Golden lion tamarin
Golden-headed tamarin
Golden-rumped tamarin
Goeldi's marmoset
White-nosed saki
Bald uakari
Red uakari
Black-headed uakari
Yellow-tailed woolly monkey
Woolly spider monkey
Tana River mangabey
Lion-tailed macaque
Zanzibar red colobus
Tana river red colobus
Uhehe red colobus
Olive colobus
Nilgiri langur
Golden langur
Pig-tailed langur
Snub-nosed langur
Douc langur
Kloss's gibbon
Pileated gibbon
Orang-utan
Chimpanzee
Pygmy chimpanzee
Gorilla
Mountain gorilla
EDENTATA
Giant anteater
Maned sloth
Giant armadillo
Brazilian three-banded armadillo
Lesser pichiciego
Greater pichiciego
LAGOMORPHA
Ryukyu rabbit
Volcano rabbit
Assam rabbit
Sumatra short-eared rabbit
RODENTIA
Delmarva Peninsula fox squirrel
Ebian's palm squirrel
Wilson's palm squirrel
Menzbier's marmot
Vancouver island marmot
Mexican prairie dog
Utah prairie dog
Big-eared kangaroo rat
Morro Bay kangaroo rat
Texas kangaroo rat
Salt-marsh harvest mouse
Block Island meadow vole
Beach meadow vole
Thin-spined porcupine
Chinchilla
Bushy-tailed hutia
Dwarf hutia
Jamaican hutia
Bahamian hutia
Cuvier's hutia
Dominican hutia
CETACEA
Indus dolphin
Fin whale
Blue whale
Humpback whale
Bowhead whale
Black right whale
CARNIVORA
Wolf
Northern rocky mountain wolf
Red wolf
Northern Simien fox
Northern kit fox
Small-eared dog
Maned wolf
Bush dog
Asiatic wild dog
African wild dog
Spectacled bear
Baluchistan bear
Glacier bear
Mexican grizzly bear
Barren-ground grizzly bear
Polar bear
Giant panda
Black-footed ferret
Marine otter
La Plata otter
Southern river otter
Giant otter
Cameroon clawless otter
Malabar large-spotted civet
Malagasy civet
Falanouc
Fossa
Brown hyena
Barbary hyena
Turkmenian caracal lynx
Spanish lynx
Ocelot
Texas ocelot
Eastern cougar
Clouded leopard
Formosan clouded leopard
Asiatic lion
Indian tiger
Caspian tiger
Siberian tiger
Javan tiger
Chinese tiger
Bali tiger
Sumatran tiger
Indochinese tiger
Leopard
Barbary leopard
South Arabian leopard

CARNIVORA (*cont.*)
Anatolian leopard
Amur leopard
Sinai leopard
Snow leopard
Jaguar
Cheetah
Asiatic cheetah
PINNIPEDIA
Galapagos fur seal
Juan Fernandez fur seal
Guadeloupe fur seal
Japanese sea lion
Laptev walrus
Kurile harbour seal
Saimaa seal
Mediterranean monk seal
Caribbean monk seal
Hawaiian monk seal
PROBOSCIDAE
Asian elephant
SIRENIA
Dugong
North American manatee
South American manatee
West African manatee
PERISSODACTYLA
Przewalski's horse
Asiatic wild ass
Indian wild ass
Syrian wild ass
African wild ass
Mountain zebra
Mountain tapir
Central American tapir
Malayan tapir
Great Indian rhinoceros
Javan rhinoceros
Sumatran rhinoceros
Northern square-lipped rhinoceros
Black rhinoceros
ARTIODACTYLA
Pygmy hog
Pygmy hippopotamus
Vicuna
Wild bactrian camel
Himalayan musk deer
Black muntjac
Fea's muntjac
Persian fallow deer
Kuhl's deer
Swamp deer
Manipur brow-antlered deer
Thailand brow-antlered deer
Formosa sika
Ryukyu sika
North China sika
Shansi sika
South China sika
Thorold's deer
Corsican red deer
Shou
Barbary deer
Kashmir stag
Yarkand deer
Bactrian deer
M'Neill's deer
Tule elk
Key deer
Columbia white-tailed deer
Cedros' Island deer
South Andean huemal
North Andean huemal
Marsh deer
Pampas deer
Lower Californian pronghorn
Sonoran pronghorn
Western giant eland
Asiatic buffalo
Tamaraw
Lowland anoa
Mountain anoa
Gaur
Banteng
Kouprey
Wild yak
European bison
Jentink's duiker
Lechwe
Arabian oryx
Scimitar-horned oryx
Addax
Bontebok
Hunter's hartebeest
Tora hartebeest
Swayne's hartebeest
Black wildebeest
Zanzibar suni
Beira antelope
Black-faced impala
Dibatag
Sand gazelle
Moroccan dorcas gazelle
Saudi Arabian gazelle
Pelzeln's gazelle
Arabian gazelle
Cuvier's gazelle
Slender-horned gazelle
Mhorr gazelle
Rio de Oro dama gazelle
Speke's gazelle
Sumatran serow
Szechwan takin
Golden takin
Arabian tahr
Nilgiri tahr
Walia ibex
Pyrenean ibex
Markhor
Kabul markhor
Straight-horned markhor
Chiltan markhor
Bighorn sheep

BIRDS
SPHENISCIFORMES
Galapagos Penguin
STRUTHIONIFORMES
Arabian ostrich
TINAMIFORMES
Black headed tinamou
Barred tinamou
PODICIPEDIFORMES
Atitlan or giant pied-billed grebe
Andean eared grebe
Junin grebe
Alaotra grebe
Titicaca grebe
PROCELLARIIFORMES
Short-tailed albatross
Dark-rumped petrel
Black-capped petrel
Black petrel
Westland black petrel
New Zealand Cook's petrel
Chatham Islands petrel
Reunion petrel
Cahow
Macgillivray's petrel
Pterodroma phaeopygia phaeopypia
PELECANIFORMES
Galapagos flightless cormorant
King shag
Chinese egret
Japanese white stork
Japanese crested ibis
Giant ibis
Waldrapp
ANSERIFORMES
White-winged wood duck
Cuban tree duck
Tule white-fronted goose
Aleutian Canada goose
Hawaiian goose or nene
Cape Barren goose
Auckland Island flightless teal
New Zealand brown teal
Campbell Island flightless teal
Madagascar teal
Mexican duck
Laysan duck
Hawaiian duck or koloa
FALCONIFORMES
Californian condor
ACCIPITRIDAE
African lammergeyer
Reunion harrier
Christmas Island Goshawk
Anjouan Island sparrow hawk
Cuba sharp-shinned hawk
Galapagos hawk
Hawaiian hawk
Monkey-eating eagle
Spanish imperial eagle
Southern bald eagle
Everglades kite
Grenada hook-billed kite
Cuba hook-billed kite
FALCONIDAE
Aldabra kestrel
Seychelles kestrel
Teita falcon
Kleinschmidt's falcon
Mauritius kestrel
Guadalupe kestrel
American peregrine falcon
GALLIFORMES
Marianas megapode
Palau megapode
Maleo
Red-billed curassow
Cozumel curassow
Horned guan
White-headed Curassow
Attwater'sprairiechicken
Greater prairie chicken
Masked bobwhite
Tadjoura francolin
Swierstra's francolin
Blyth's tragopan
Tibetan Blyth's tragopan
Cabot's tragopan
Western tragopan
Chinese Monal
Sclater's Monal
White-eared pheasant
East Tibetan white-eared pheasant
South Tibetan white-eared pheasant
Brown-eared pheasant
Edwards' pheasant
Imperial pheasant
Swinhoe's pheasant
Elliot's pheasant
Eastern Hume's pheasant
Hume's pheasant
Mikado pheasant
Cheer pheasant
Palawan peacock pheasant
Malaysian peacock pheasant
GRUIFORMES
Whooping crane
Cuban sandhill crane
Mississippi sandhill crane
Florida sandhill crane
Japanese crane
Siberian white crane
Hooded crane
Black-necked crane
Auckland Island rail
Yuma clapper rail
Lord Howe Wood rail
Zapata rail
Platen's Celebes rail
Eastern weka
Henderson Island rail
Jamaican Black rail
San Cristobal Mountain rail
Hawaiian gallinule
Takehe
Horned coot
Kagu
Great Indian bustard
CHARADRIIFORMES
New Zealand shore plover
Eskimo curlew
Auckland Island snipe
Snares Island snipe
Stewart Island snipe
Antipodes Island snipe
Chatham Island snipe
Hawaiian stilt
Audouin's gull
Japanese ancient murrelet
COLUMBIFORMES
Moheli green pigeon
Cloven-feathered dove
Giant imperial pigeon
Mindoro imperial pigeon
Chatham Island pigeon
Azores wood pigeon
Puerto Rico plain pigeon
Madeira long-toed pigeon
Tenerife long-toed pigeon
Ryukyu wood pigeon
Mauritius Pink pigeon
Seychelles Turtle dove
Grenada dove
Marquesas ground dove
Tooth-billed pigeon
PSITTACIFORMES
Kakapo or owl parrot
Tahiti blue lory
Ultramarine lory
Eastern thick-billed parrot
Western thick-billed parrot
St. Vincent parrot
Imperial parrot
Bahamas parrot
St. Lucia parrot
Puerto Rico parrot
Seychelles vasa parrot
Mauritius ring-necked parakeet
Masked parakeet
Golden-shouldered Paradise parakeet
Hooded paradise parakeet
Orange-bellied parakeet
Turquoise parakeet
Splendid parakeet
Horned parakeet
Loyalty Islands parakeet
Forbe's parakeet
Orange-fronted parakeet
Norfolk Island parakeet
Antipodes Island parakeet
S. W. Australian ground parrot
Tasmania ground parrot
S. E. Australian ground parrot
Australian night parrot
CUCULIFORMES
Prince Ruspoli's turaco
Cocos mangrove cuckoo
Red-faced malkoha
STRIGIFORMES
Soumagne's owl
Giant scops owl
Seychelles owl
Virgin Islands screech owl
Mrs. Morden's owlet
New Zealand laughing owl

STRIGIFORMES (*cont.*)
Puerto Rico short-eared owl
Anjouan scops owl
CAPRIMULGIFORMES
Hispaniolal Least pauraque
Puerto Rico whippoorwill
APODIFORMES
Scarce swift
Luanda swift
Pygmy swift
CORACIIFORMES
Long-tailed ground roller
Narcondam hornbill
PICIFORMES
Tristram's woodpecker
Grand Bahama red-bellied woodpecker
Abaco red-bellied woodpecker
Watling Island red-bellied woodpecker
Okinawa woodpecker
Cuban ivory-billed woodpecker
Ivory-billed woodpecker
Imperial woodpecker
PASSERIFORMES
Masafuera creeper
Sclater's spinetail
Red-rumped ant-thrush
Euler's flycatcher
Cocos Island flycatcher
Koch's pitta
South Island bush wren
North Island bush wren
Stead's bush wren
Small-billed false sunbird
Noisy scrub-bird
Rufous scrub-bird
Raza Island lark
Kupe mountain bush shrike
Norfolk Island starling
Ponape mountain starling
Rothschild's starling
South Island kokako
North Island kokako
South Island pipio
North Island pipio
South Island saddleback
North Island saddleback
Lord Howe currawang
Hawaiian crow
Grauer's cuckoo shrike
Reunion cuckoo shrike
Mauritius cuckoo shrike
Guadeloupe rock wren
Socorro Island wren
St. Lucia wren
Guadeloupe house wren
St Vincent wren
Pribilov wren
Fair Isle wren
St Kilda wren
Charles Island mockingbird
Socorro Island thrasher
Martinique trembler
Martinique white-breasted thrasher
St. Lucia white-breasted thrasher
Tanzania dappled bulbul
Dappled bulbul
Mauritius olivaceous bulbul
Rufous-headed robin
Cebu black shama
Seychelles magpie-robin
Isle of Pines solitaire
St. Vincent thrush
Ashy ground thrush
Tristan starchy
Inaccessible Island starchy
Nightingale Island starchy
Kauai thrush
Molokai thrush
Puaiohi
Teital olive thrush
Grey-headed blackbird
Grand Cayman thrush
St. Lucia forest thrush
Victoria Western whipbird
Western whipbird
York Peninsular Western whipbird
Lower Yangtze-kiang crow tit
White-necked rock-fowl
Grey-necked rock-fowl
Rodriguez warbler
Seychelles warbler
Nihoa millerbird
Nauru Nightingale warbler
Watut leaf warbler
Western bristlebird
Western rufous bristlebird
Codfish Island fernbird
Eyrean grass-wren
Guadeloupe kinglet
Rueck's blue flycatcher
Palau fantail
Chatham Island robin
Scarlet breasted robin
Tahiti flycatcher
Maupiti Island flycatcher
Coq de bois
Seychelles black flycatcher
Truk monarch
Tinian monarch
Kauai Oo
Stitchbird
Helmeted honeyeater
Truk great white-eye
Ponape great white-eye
Fernando poo speirops
Seychelles white-eye
Slender-billed vireo
Molokai creeper
Kauai alauwahio
Maui akepa
Oahu creeper
Maui creeper
Nukupuu
Maui nukupuu
Kauai akailoa
Hawaiian Nukupau
Maui parrotbill
Palila
O'u
Crested honeycreeper
Semper's warbler
Bachman's warbler
Kirtland's warbler
Cocos yellow warbler
Barbados yellow warbler
Seychelles fody
Mauritius fody
Pink-billed parrot finch
Gaudeloupe house finch
McGregor's house finch
Cocos Island finch
Baer's cardinal
Tumaco seedeater
Sao Miguel bullfinch
Warsangli linnet
Inaccessible Island bunting
Wilkin's bunting
Nightingale Island bunting
Charles Island ground finch
Colombian red-eyed cowbird
Nicaragua grackle
Slender-billed grackle
Grand cayman troupial
Rufous-sided towhee
Ipswich sparrow
Zapata sparrow
Oriente sparrow
Cape Sable sparrow
Dusky seaside sparrow
Guadeloupe junco
Baer's mountain finch
Garlepp's mountain finch

CLASS: AMPHIBIA
CAUDATA
Japanese giant salamander
Chinese giant salamander
Lake Patzcuaro salamander
Lake Lerma salamander
Santa Cruz long-toed salamander
Axolotl
California tiger salamander
Gold-striped salamander
Desert slender salamander
Kern Canyon slender salamander
Tehachapi slender salamander
Larch Mountain salamander
Jemez Mountain salamander
Texas blind salamander
Shasta salamander
Limestone salamander
Olm
SALIENTIA
Coromandel frog
Stephen's Islands frog
North Island frog
Cape platana
Israel painted frog
Italian spade-foot toad
Amargosa toad
Black toad
Houston toad
Sonoran green toad
Golden toad
Mt Nimba viviparous toad
Pine Barrens tree frog
Illinois chorus frog
Seychelle Islands frog
Goliath frog
Vegas Valley leopard frog

REPTILIA
TESTUDINES
River terrapin, (Tuntong)
Bog turtle
South American red-lined turtle
Aquatic box turtle
Western gopher tortoise
Berlandier's gopher tortoise
Pancake tortoise
Madagascar spider tortoise
South Abermarle tortoise
Abingdon saddlebacked tortoise
North Albermarle saddlebacked tortoise
Chatham Island tortoise
James Island tortoise
Duncan saddlebacked tortoise
South-West Albermarle tortoise
Hood saddlebacked tortoise
Tagus Cove tortoise
Indefatigable Island tortoise
Cowley Mountain tortoise
Geometric tortoise
Mediterranean spur-thighed tortoise
Radiated tortoise
Madagascar tortoise
Loggerhead turtle
Flatback green turtle
Green turtle
Eastern Pacific green turtle
Hawksbill turtle
Atlantic ridley turtle
Pacific ridley turtle
Leathery turtle
South American river turtle
Terecay turtle
Short-necked turtle
CROCODYLIA
American alligator
China alligator
Spectacled caiman
Rio Apaporis caiman
Magdalena caiman
Paraguay caiman
Broad-nosed caiman
Chaco broad-nosed caiman
Black caiman
Dwarf caiman
Smooth-fronted caiman
American crocodile
African slender-snouted crocodile
Orinoco crocodile
Australian freshwater crocodile
Morelet's crocodile
Nile crocodile
New Guinea crocodile
Mindoro crocodile
Mugger (marsh crocodile)
Ceylon swamp crocodile
Estuarine crocodile
Cuban crocodile
Siamese crocodile
Dwarf crocodile
West African dwarf crocodile
Congo dwarf crocodile
False gavial
GAVIALIDAE
Indian gavial, gharial
RHYNCHOCEPHALIA
Tuatara
SQUAMATA
Serpent Island gecko
Reticulated velvet gecko
Round Island day gecko
Rodriguez day gecko
Sail-fin lizard
Galapagos marine iguana
Narborough Island marine iguana
Albemarle marine iguana
Santa Cruz marine iguana
San Cristobal marine iguana
Genovese marine iguana
Pinta marine iguana
Hood Island iguana
Fiji banded iguana
Barrington land iguana
Galapagos land iguana
Blunt-nosed leopard lizard
Andros Island ground iguana
Turks and Caicos ground iguana
Mona Island rhinoceros iguana
Filfola lizard

SQUAMATA (*cont.*)
- St. Croix ground lizard
- Orange-throated race runner
- Macabé Forest skink
- Round Island skink
- Cape Verde giant skink
- California legless lizard
- Beaded lizard
- Mexican beaded lizard
- Chaipan beaded lizard
- Rio Fuerto beaded lizard
- Reticulated gila monster
- Gila monster
- Banded gila monster
- Central Asian grey monitor
- Komodo dragon

SERPENTES
- Round Island boa
- Southern rubber boa
- Cuban boa
- Puerto Rican boa
- Jamaica boa
- Indian Python
- Burmese python
- San Joaquin whipsnake
- Almeda striped racer
- Giant garter snake
- Two-striped garter snake
- San Francisco garter snake
- Central Asian cobra
- Ogmodon (Fiji snake)
- Schweizer's Lebetina viper
- Aruba Island rattlesnake
- Arizona ridge-nosed rattlesnake

PISCES
- Shortnosed sturgeon
- Lake sturgeon
- Atlantic sturgeon
- Amur sturgeon
- Kalugar
- Asian bonytongue
- Longjaw cisco
- Mexican golden trout
- Lahontan cutthroat trout
- Greenback cutthroat trout
- Bonneville cutthroat trout
- Pinte cutthroat trout
- Rio grande cutthroat trout
- Humboldt cutthroat trout
- Kern rainbow trout
- Gila trout
- Ala balik
- Sunapee trout
- Apache trout
- Blueback trout
- Beloribitsa
- Olympic mudminnow
- Cicek
- Desert dace
- Humpback chub
- Mohave chub
- White River spinedace
- Spikedace
- Moapa dace
- Woundfin
- Ikan temoleh, pla eesok
- Miyako tanago, Tokyo bitterling
- Modoc sucker
- Shortnose sucker
- Cui-ui
- Ayumodoki
- Mexican blindcat
- Widemouth blindcat
- Toothless blindcat
- Nekogigi
- Giant catfish
- Catfish
- Ozark cavefish
- Devils Hole pupfish
- Comanche Springs pupfish
- Tecopa pupfish
- Nevada pupfish
- Warm Spring pupfish
- Owens Valley pupfish
- Pahrump killifish
- Big Bend gambusia
- Clear Creek gambusia
- Pecos gambusia
- San Marcos gambusia
- Gila topminnow
- Monterrey platyfish
- Waccamaw silverside
- Unarmored threespine stickleback
- Rough sculpin
- Roanoke bass
- Suwannee bass
- Fountain darter
- Niangua darter
- Waccamaw darter
- Maryland darter
- Balkhash perch

PLANTS
- Vavaloa
- Mt. Athos fumitory
- Mt. Athos woad
- Canelillo
- Silene genistifolia
- Redbark camellia
- Grantham camellia
- Franklinia
- Panama mangrove
- Philip Island hibiscus
- Hibiscadelphus bombycinus
- Hibiscadelphus giffardianus
- Hibiscadelphus hualalaiensis
- Hibiscadelphus wilderianus
- Lebronnecia kokioides
- Keraudrenia macrantha
- St. Helena redwood
- St. Helena ebony
- Lowan phebalium
- Ford's tree of heaven
- Plectomirtha baylisiana
- Noble amherstia
- Flamboyant
- Gigasiphon macrosiphon
- Phillip Island glory pea
- Jade vine
- Collenette's korokio
- Pullea perryana
- Foetidia asymmetrica
- Natokely
- Hydrodea cryptantha
- Longwood samphire
- Mt. Athos woodruff
- Sibthorp's chamomile
- Henderson beggar tick
- Yellow Athos knapweed
- Pink Athos knapweed
- Mt. Athos hawksbeard
- Taygetos hawksbeard
- Virgin everlasting
- Georgia plume
- Vinous heath
- Golden bell heath
- Jasmine-flowered heath
- Juno heath
- Mt. Athos thrift
- Palinuri auricula
- Elingamita johnsonii
- Toxocarpus schimperianus
- Three kings trumpet flower
- Hawaiian plantain
- Tree amaranth
- Marsh rose
- Blushing bride
- Bollusiella maudae
- Lady's slipper orchid
- Cooktown orchid
- Dendrobium ostrinoglossum
- Dendrobium tofftii
- Diplocaulobium masonii
- Disa charpentierana
- Proud diuris
- Pterygodium flanaganii
- Philippine garland-flower
- Three kings cabbage tree
- Benguet lily
- Poor knights brush lily
- Coco de mer

## THE UNITED NATIONS DEVELOPMENT PROGRAMME PREINVESTMENT AND TECHNICAL ASSISTANCE TO DEVELOPING COUNTRIES

THE United Nations Development Programme (UNDP) works with over 140 governments and nearly 20 international agencies for worldwide economic growth, the increased output of goods and services, and improvements in the quality of life. The UNDP was established by the General Assembly in 1965, through a merger of the United Nations Expanded Programme of Technical Assistance and the United Nations Special Fund. Today it is the world's largest multilateral channel for technical co-operation in development.

The UNDP's activities are primarily directed toward helping developing nations make fuller, more effective use of available natural resources and human talents and energies. Toward this end, it supports some 8,000 projects in agriculture, industry, education, power production, transport, communications, health, public administration, housing, trade, and other related fields. These projects form part of three-to-five-year "country programmes" which are closely linked with overall national development plans. During the current country programming cycle (1977–1981), nearly half of all UNDP assistance will go to countries with per capita GNPs of under $150, and two-thirds to those where the figure is $300 or less.

Backed by UNDP funding of about $406 million in 1976, projects are largely carried out by the Agencies of the UN development system—with FAO, ILO, the World Bank, UNIDO, UNESCO, WHO, and the UN's Office of Technical Co-operation handling a major share of the work. Certain projects, however, are implemented directly by UNDP itself, and a small but growing number are being executed by developing country governments.

During 1976, projects make available to the developing countries each year the knowledge and experience of 8,600 experts . . . 5,200 fellowships for advanced study abroad . . . some $43 million worth of equipment, from computers to basic hand tools . . . and specialized technical services valued at about $33 million.

Project work covers five main fields:

—Surveying and assessing such development assets as farm lands and forests; rivers and sub-surface waters; mineral deposits; fuel reserves; and manufacturing, commercial and export potentials.

—Stimulating capital investments to help realize these possibilities.

—Training in a wide range of vocational and professional skills.

—Transferring appropriate technologies, and stimulating the growth of local technological capabilities.

—Economic and social planning . . . with particular emphasis on meeting the needs of the least developed countries and the poorest segments of the population, and on development co-operation among neighbouring countries.

The total cost of all currently operational projects (on their completion) will exceed $5,000 million. Approximately 45 per cent of this amount is financed by the UNDP . . . whose resources come from the yearly voluntary contributions of virtually every member of the UN or its affiliated Agencies. The remainder—of more than matching value—is furnished by the developing countries themselves through their provision of national personnel, project buildings and other facilities, and locally available supplies and services. In 1975 total expenditures from both these sources reached the $1,000 million dollar level for the first time.

Since 1959, more than $20,000 million dollars in development investments—from internal and external, public and private sources—have followed the findings of UNPD-supported surveys and feasibility studies. By way of example, investments reported for three recent typical years will provide developing countries with a $2·5 billion to increase agricultural productivity, $1·9 billion to expand industrial output, $3·7 billion to broaden and modernize transport and communications networks, and $1·6 billion for natural resources development.

Many millions of men and women have been equipped with new skills as teachers and industrial instructors; managers, supervisors, entrepreneurs, and product marketers; administrators and civil servants; farming and forestry specialists; factory workers and public utilities technicians; engineers, scientists and medical personnel.

The Administrator of the UNDP is appointed by the UN Secretary General with the approval of the General Assembly, and is responsible to a 48-nation Governing Council representing all major regions and both donor and recipient countries. The United Nations Fund for Population Activities, the Revolving Fund for Natural Resources Exploration, the United Nations Volunteers, the United Nations Capital Development Fund, and the United Nations Sahelian Office also report to UNDP's Governing Council. In addition to setting general policy guidelines, the Governing Council examines and approves the volume of assistance allocated to each country over successive five-year cycles, and must similarly approve all Country Programmes.

The UNDP maintains field offices in over 100 developing countries. They are headed by senior officials, known as Resident Representatives, to whom much of the responsibility for the Programme's operations has been delegated in a recent far-reaching process of decentralization.

Further information on UNDP may be obtained by writing to the Division of Information, United Nations Development Programme, United Nations, New York, New York 10017, U.S.A.

## UNITED NATIONS FUND FOR POPULATION ACTIVITIES (UNFPA)

Created in 1967 as a Trust Fund for population activities, in 1972 UNFPA was placed under the authority of the United Nations General Assembly, with the Governing Council of the United Nations Development Programme as its governing body.

*Aims and Purposes:*

The aims and purposes of the United Nations Fund for Population Activities are:

To build up, on an international basis, the knowledge and the capacity to respond to needs in the population and family planning fields and to promote co-ordination in planning and programming.

To promote awareness, of the implications of population problems; of the human rights aspects of family planning; and of strategies to deal with them, in accordance with the plans of each country.

To extend assistance to developing countries at their request in dealing with their population problems; such assistance to be afforded in forms and by means requested by the recipient countries.

To play a leading role in the United Nations system in promoting population programmes and to co-ordinate projects supported by UNFPA.

*Organization*

Following a decision of the 27th General Assembly late in 1972, naming the UNDP Governing Council the Fund's governing body, the Fund reports to the twice-yearly meetings of the Council. In addition advice is taken from the Inter-Agency Consultative Committee which brings together United Nations agencies and related organizations which execute projects financed by the Fund or which run parallel programmes. Another advisory body is composed of governmental and private agencies in countries which contribute to the Fund, as well as international organizations active in population.

Resident Representatives of the UNDP in developing countries assist governments to formulate requests for assistance and coordinate the work of members of the United Nations family of agencies engaged in population programmes. They help governments identify areas where population activities could make the best contribution to national development and advise the Fund so that resources supplement and do not compete with other efforts. Most requests come from governments, but requests from non-governmental organizations are also channelled through the Resident Representatives. In countries where Fund involvement is particularly heavy the Resident Representative's staff is strengthened by UNFPA Field Coordinators who monitor and advise on activities in their areas. By the end of 1976, 22 of these co-ordinators had taken up their posts.

*Resources*

The Fund's financial resources are provided by voluntary contributions mainly from governments; 89 governments had pledged a total of over $318 million up to 31 December 1976.

This level of activity makes the Fund the fastest-growing organization in the UN family. Contributions have grown from $20·4 million from 22 donors between 1967 and 1970, to $27·8 million from 39 donors in 1971, $30·6 million from 43 donors in 1972, and $42·5 million from 50 donors in 1973. The total for 1974 was $54·7 million, was the total for 1975 was $63·6 million. In 1976 the total was slightly over $79 million bringing cumulative contributions to the Fund to ove $318 million. In 1975, the total of the Fund's allocations and grants was $87·8 million.

*UNFPA Programming*

At the end of 1976 the Fund was supporting a total of more than 1,000 projects and programmes affecting 103 countries. This was in addition to research projects and other activities. New projects for 1977 were expected considerably to increase this figure. Most of these projects were executed by appropriate agencies of the United Nations family rather than by the UNFPA itself. Others were being carried out by the governments concerned or their agents.

The Fund has remained scrupulously neutral. To quote a Fund report to the Governing Council of the United Nations Development Programme: "The Fund does not prescribe any particular population policy, or any particular approach, but provides assistance as requested and with due regard for national and regional differences. Population programmes are supported as integral and complementary to and not as substitutes for the promotion of economic and social development."

The World Population Conference held in Bucharest in 1974 adopted a World Population Plan of Action which will assist countries in formulating their national population programmes and in contemplating future international involvement.

UNFPA has been asked to co-ordinate population activities brought out by the decisions of the Conference calling for a review of the whole question of integrating population assistance with the wider framework of economic and social development assistance.

*Executive Director:* Rafael M. Salas (Philippines) who shold the rank of an Under-Secretary General of the United Nations.

## UNITED NATIONS ENVIRONMENT PROGRAMME (UNEP)

Today, more than ever before, people everywhere are aware of the need to take action to protect the human environment. All indications are that if the present trends are allowed to continue, future life on earth will be endangered.

More than 20 years ago these potential perils to the human race began to be stressed at United Nations conferences. It was not until the late 1960s however that this cluster of technological and social questions were discussed in the United Nations as "problems of the human environment".

The United Nations Environment Programme has its origins in the first UN Conference on the Human Environment which was held in Stockholm in 1972. The Conference was convened to bring to the attention of governments and the people of the world evidence that man's activities were damaging the natural environment and were giving rise to serious risks for the survival and well-being of man himself.

The General Assembly of the United Nations in 1972 declared itself "Convinced of the need for prompt and effective implementation by Governments and the international community of measures designed to safeguard and enhance the environment for the benefit of present and future generations of man".

The Governing Council of the UNPE met for the first time in Geneva in 1973 and adopted the following General Policy Objectives:

1. To provide, through interdisciplinary study of natural and man-made ecological systems, improved knowledge for an integrated and rational management of the resources of the biosphere, and for safeguarding human well-being as well as ecosystems.

2. To encourage and support an integrated approach to the planning and management of development, including that of natural resources, so as to take account of environmental consequences, to achieve maximum social, economic and environmental benefits.

3. To assist all countries, especially developing countries, to deal with their environmental problems and to help mobilize additional financial resources for the purpose of providing the required technical assistance, education, training and free flow of information and exchange of experience, with a view to promoting the full participation of developing countries in the national and international efforts for the preservation and enhancement of the environment.

At its Second Session, held in Nairobi in 1974, the Council selected specific areas of concentration for the programme.

At each session of the UNEP Council the Executive Director presents a study compiled from many sources on 'The State of the Environment'. He also presents a review of the current activities in the areas identified by the Council for priority action. From these assessments of environmental conditions, it is expected that the policies and programmes of governments, international organizations, and UNEP itself will be influenced.

The Executive Director is Mostafa K. Tolba of Egypt. Mr. Tolba, a microbiologist, was Chairman of the Egyptian delegation at the United Nations Conference on the Human Environment, held in Stockholm in June 1972, and also served as Vice-President of the Conference.

In 1973 the General Assembly of the United Nations approved that a UN Conference on Human Settlements should be held in 1976 and accepted Canada's offer to act as host for the Conference which will be held in Vancouver, British Columbia, 11 June 1976.

The Conference, also known as HABITAT, adopted a Declaration of Principles and a series of recommendations to meet the urgent needs of housing shortages, contrasting crises of urban and rural communities, the proper use of land, access to essential services, and public involvement in remedial action.

It also adopted a resolution calling for action to set up a new United Nations machinery concerned exclusively with human settlements, including an intergovernmental body and a central secretariat.

The United Nations Conference on Desertification, due to take place from 29 August to 9 September 1977, probably in Nairobi, is the outcome of a resolution passed in the General Assembly of the United Nations in 1974 calling for international co-operation in trying to stop desertification. This is the process of arid lands spreading as a result of several causes including the action of Man. One-ninth of the Earth's surface, inhabited by 60 million people, is affected by this "march of the deserts" outward to engulf former arable land.

At the fifth session of the Governing Council Mr. Tolba said 'The ultimate goal of everything we do in the years ahead will remain the proper management of human activities which affect the environment. Management is relevant to every area with which we deal—to arid lands and tropical forests as much as to energy, water and respect for the outer limits of the biosphere. Whether we set up projects, organize environmental management training, publish guidebooks or offer assistance in catalytic ways, the end product is management. Governments are rightly looking to UNEP now to help them achieve effective environmental management and to offer them guidance in practical, usable form. . .

In connexion with our future work, there is one particular implication of environmental assessment that I would like to stress. It is clear that in the course of its job, UNEP will review actions, or inactions, which put the environment at serious risk. The issue may be a broad one, such as the use of the global commons, or a relatively narrow one, relating to a particular pollutant or development project. It is not likely to be identified initially in UNEP but by a national institution or service, or a non-governmental organization. But if it relates to a risky action of global significance, the issue will almost certainly involve UNEP in a form of confrontation at one level or another with whatever interests are supporting that action.'

*Address:* United Nations Environment Programme, P.O. Box 30552, Nairobi, Kenya. Cables: "UNITERRA" Nairobi. Telephone: 333930. Telex: 22068.

# UNITED NATIONS CHILDREN'S FUND (UNICEF)

*Legal basis*

The United Nations Children's Fund (UNICEF) was created by a resolution of the General Assembly at its first session (Resolution 57(I), 11 December 1946). Taking account of the effect of subsequent amendments, UNICEF is a continuing Fund to help advance the welfare and development of children in developing countries.

*Executive Board*

UNICEF is governed by an Executive Board of 30 countries, ten of which are elected each year by the Economic and Social Council for a term of three years, which is renewable. The Executive Board determines UNICEF's assistance programmes and commits its funds. The Board meets once a year. Its report is considered by the Economic and Social Council and, through it, by the General Assembly.

The membership of the Board for the period 1 August 1977 to 31 July 1978 is:

Afghanistan
Barbados
Benin
Bolivia
Brazil
Bulgaria
Canada
Chile
France
Federal Republic of Germany
Guinea
Indonesia
Italy
Japan
Jordan
Morocco
Netherlands
Norway
Pakistan
Philippines
Poland
Sweden
Switzerland
U.S.S.R.
United Kingdom
United Republic of Cameroon
United Republic of Tanzania
United States
Yugoslavia
Zambia

The officers of the Board for 1978–79 are: *Chairman (Executive Board):* Ferdinand Leopold Oyono (United Republic of Cameroon); *Chairman (Programme Committee):* Mrs. Sadako Ogato (Japan); *Chairman (Committee on Administration and Finance):* Pieter van Buren (Netherlands) *First Vice-Chairman:* Zaki Hasan (Pakistan); *Second Vice-Chairman:* Boguslaw Kozusznik (Poland); *Third Vice-Chairman:* Paal Bog (Norway); *Fourth Vice-Chairman:* Marcosde Candau (Brazil).

*Secretariat*

The Executive Director, Mr. Henry R. Labouisse, heads a secretariat, with headquarters at United Nations, New York, an office in Geneva and field offices in developing countries.

*Revenue*

The revenue of UNICEF comes from voluntary contributions by governments, private organizations and individuals.

*Assistance Policy*

UNICEF assistance supports services and projects benefiting children and mothers which are planned and undertaken by the national authorities concerned. The material support UNICEF can offer takes the form of supplies and equipment as well as stipends for training; UNICEF can also offer programming and planning advice. Patterns of co-operation are based on each country's own priorities of children's needs, and possibilities of action. Among the on going fields of co-operation are services for the improvement of maternal and child health, child nutrition, family and child welfare, basic education and special assistance programmes in the wake of disasters—natural or man-made.

*Technical Advice*

The advice of the specialized and technical agencies of the United Nations system is available to UNICEF and to the countries concerned for technical aspects of the assisted projects, and UNICEF does not duplicate their professional services.

*Control of Expenditure*

The Board approves 'commitments' to projects for assistance, usually extending over several years. The field office serving the country concerned 'calls-forward' annual requirements within the commitment, in accordance with the progress of the assisted project. Supplies are then procured and shipped to the country, where the field office helps and observes their delivery and use. UNICEF's internal audit checks the delivery of UNICEF assistance. UNICEF'S accounts are audited by the external auditors of the United Nations and the financial report goes to the General Assembly.

*National Committees*

National Committees may be set up in contributing countries in accordance with their laws and practices, in most cases, on the initiative of private citizens. They accept the obligations, defined by the Executive Board, of a 'UNICEF National Committee.' They spread information about the needs of children in developing countries, and the possibilities of action through UNICEF. Usually, they are also responsible for the distribution and sale of UNICEF greeting cards, and they may arrange other fund-raising campaigns. In their activities they usually benefit from widespread voluntary help.

*Non-Governmental Organizations*

Non-governmental organizations are often leaders in providing services to children in the developing countries. They offer UNICEF information and advice on the basis of their experience and some have become partners in projects of mutual interest. Many co-operate with UNICEF in information and fund-raising work. An NGO Committee for UNICEF comprises 106 member organizations having consultative status with the organizations.

# IV. Inter-Governmental Organizations

## AGENCY FOR INTERNATIONAL DEVELOPMENT (AID)

THE Agency for International Development (AID) is a semi-autonomous agency of the Department of State administering overseas economic assistance programmes of the United States. Its purpose is assisting recipient nations reach the point where increased human and capital resources, combined with ability to attract outside investment and credit, will sustain satisfactory economic growth.

AID programmes are devised to fit special country circumstances. Consideration includes country relationships with other aid donors. A large share of bilateral aid is in fact closely co-ordinated with these through groups organized by the IBRD, OECD, or other organizations. In Latin America aid is provided in the framework of the Alliance for Progress. From the AID appropriation, the United States made voluntary contributions of $184 million to international organizations and programmes during fiscal year 1972, an increase of more than $32 million over the previous year's total. The largest contribution during fiscal year 1972 was $85 million for the United Nations Development Programme.

In developing country programmes AID continues to emphasize assistance for agriculture, health and education in a context of long-range planning, self-help, and private investment in international development. With the establishment in 1967 of the Office of the War on Hunger, AID added new emphasis in family planning and population problems. Nutrition, including development of food from the sea, is also receiving increased attention.

The basic financial instruments of AID are Development Loans, Technical Assistance Grants, and Supporting Assistance. Development Loans totalling $696 million were committed in fiscal year 1971. They were divided into three major categories:

*Project loans* finance specific undertakings. They are used for capital investments necessary to build infrastructure such as roads, schools, power dams, railways, sewage systems or irrigation systems, and may also be used for technical assistance activities.

*Programme loans* finance the import of commodities needed to sustain overall economic development activity. Imports may include raw materials, industrial equipment and machinery, and spare parts and are usually associated with fiscal, monetary, or import reforms or with other self-help steps affecting the overall economy.

*Sector loans* closely integrate both capital and technical resources to spur the development of a particular sector in the country, such as agriculture or education. These loans contribute to the introduction of new policies or reforms by the borrowing country in the particular sector and may involve improved sector planning and increased allocation of host country resources to the sector.

Project, sector, and programme loan commitments in fiscal year 1972 totalled $610 million, some $86 million less than the previous fiscal year.

AID authorized 57 project loans amounting to $318 million in 20 countries including several regional projects. Of these, 13 loans amounting to more than $60 million were in transportation; nine more in agriculture totalled $58 million; 15 loans with an overall value of $99 million were for power and other industrial projects; and eight loans of $53 million were for private enterprise promotion. The remaining $48 million included loans for health, education, community and municipal development, and housing.

Sector loans to assist development in particular economic sectors totalled $106 million, with Colombia receiving the largest share—$89 million for its urban, agriculture and education sectors. Other sector loans were made to the agriculture sector in Ethiopia, $ 15 million; and $2 million for the agriculture sector (cereals) in Central and West Africa.

AID programme loan commitments in fiscal year 1972 totalled $184 million, a decrease of $132 million from the fiscal year 1971. Indonesia received the largest share of the programme funds committed—$75 million; with Pakistan accounting for another $60 million. Bolivia received $32 million; Tunisia $11 million and Nigeria $6 million.

In addition two loans were made from funds other than the development loan appropriation—one to Nigeria, $3·4 million, for a police staff college, and one to support the Indus Basin Development Fund, $13·8 million.

United States disaster relief assistance to other nations is coordinated by an office in AID. This programme, using contingency funds, provides help in disasters, and in fiscal year 1972 committed a total of $1·6 million for emergency relief.

AID shares with the Department of Agriculture operation of Food for Peace, under which food and fibre are sold overseas for local currency, or under long-term dollar credit, or are donated for humanitarian or emergency purposes and food-for-work activities. In the field many such programmes are carried on by voluntary agencies.

AID is headed by an Administrator, with the rank of Under-Secretary of State, and a Deputy Administrator. Field operations are directed by Assistant Administrators of regional bureaus for the Near East and South Asia, Africa, and Latin America, and are carried out by missions in the field. In addition to the geographic bureaus, the Bureau for Supporting Assistance specializes in economic aid to countries whose economic advancement would otherwise be impaired by their national security considerations.

In December 1972 AID had 11,277 employees in Washington and overseas, including 5,824 U.S. nationals. In South Vietnam AID employees number about 1,674, of which 364 are U.S. nationals.

The fiscal year 1972 commitments for economic assistance activities administered by AID was $2,072 million; for military assistance under the Foreign Assistance Act, $1,096 million.

The Agency for International Development was created by the Foreign Assistance Act of 1961, combining the functions of the International Co-operation Administration and the Development Loan Fund, plus local currency loan activities of the Export–Import Bank.

*Address:* Agency for International Development, Department of State, Washington, D.C. 20523, U.S.A.

## CARIBBEAN COMMUNITY (CARICOM)

*Establishment and functions.* The Treaty establishing the Caribbean Community, including the Caribbean Common Market, and the Agreement establishing the Common External Tariff for the Caribbean Common Market, were signed by the Prime Ministers of Barbados, Guyana, Jamaica, and Trinidad and Tobago at Chaguaramas, Trinidad on 4 July, 1973, and entered into force on 1 August 1973. Six Less Developed countries of Carifta signed the Treaty of Chaguaramas on 17 April 1974. They were Belize, Dominica, Grenada, St. Lucia, St. Vincent and Montserrat, and the Treaty came into effect for those countries on 1 May 1974. Antigua acceded to Membership on the 4 July 1974 and on the 26 July, the Associated State of St. Kitts–Nevis–Anguilla signed the Treaty of Chaguaramas in Kingston, Jamaica and became a Member of the Caribbean Community.

The Caribbean Community has three areas of activity: economic integration (that is, the Caribbean Common Market which replaced CARIFTA); co-operation in non-economic areas and the operation of certain common services; and co-ordination of foreign policies of Independent Member States.

The Caribbean Common Market provides for the establishment of a Common External Tariff (and common protective policy and the progressive co-ordination of external trade policies); the adoption of a Scheme for the Harmonization of Fiscal Incentives to Industry: double taxation arrangements among member countries; the co-ordination of economic policies and development planning; and a Special Regime for the Less Developed Countries of the Community.

*Composition of the 12 Member Countries:* Antigua, Barbados, Belize, Dominica, Grenada, Guyana, Jamaica, Montserrat, St. Kitts-Nevis-Anguilla, St. Lucia, St. Vincent and Trinidad and Tobago.

*Structure.* The *Heads of Government Conference* is the principal organ of the Community, and its primary responsibility is to determine the policy of the Community. It is the final authority of the Community and the Common Market, and for the conclusion of treaties and relationships between the Community and international organizations and States. It is responsible for financial arrangements for meeting the expenses of the Community.

The *Common Market Council* is the principal organ of the Common Market and shall consist of a Minister of Government designated by each Member State. Decisions in both the Conference and the Council are, in the main, taken on the basis of unanimity.

The *Secretariat,* successor to the Commonwealth Caribbean Regional Secretariat, is the principal administrative organ of the Community and of the Common Market. The Secretary-General shall be appointed by the Conference on the recommendation of the Council for a term not exceeding five years and may be reappointed. The Secretary-General shall act in that capacity in all meetings of the Conference, the Council, and of the institutions of the Community.

Institutions of the Community, established by the Heads of Government Conference, are: Conference of Ministers responsible for Health; Standing Committees of Ministers responsible for Education, Industry, Labour, Foreign Affairs, Finance, Agriculture, Transport, and Mines, respectively.

*General Publications:* CARIFTA and the New Caribbean; From CARIFTA to Caribbean Community; The Economics of Devaluation Under West Indian Conditions; The Caribbean Community—A Guide; The Caribbean Examinations Council Comes Into Being; A Guide for the Use of Exporters and Importers; The Brussels Tariff Nomenclature; Treaty Establishing the Caribbean Community, 4 July 1973; One Year of CARICOM; Common External Tariff; Manual of the Administration of the Scheme for the Harmonization for Fiscal Incentives to Industry in CARICOM Countries.

*Secretary-General:* Mr. Joseph A. Tyndall (Acting)
*Address:* Caribbean Community Secretariat, The Bank of Guyana Building, P.O. Box 607, Georgetown, Guyana. *Tel.:* 69280-9. *Cable Address:* CARIBSEC GUYANA. *Telex:* GY263.

# CENTRAL TREATY ORGANIZATION (CENTO)

A Pact of mutual defence which was signed by Turkey and Iraq on 24 February 1955, and was joined later by the United Kingdom, Pakistan and Iran (it was then known as the Baghdad Pact). The U.S.A. became a full member of its major committees; it is also represented at the council meetings by observers; and in 1958 entered into agreements designed to give effect to co-operation with the Pact countries. Bilateral defence agreements between the U.S.A. and Turkey, and Turkey, Iran and Pakistan, were signed at Ankara in March 1959. Iraq withdrew from the Pact in March 1959, and headquarters were transferred from Baghdad to Ankara in October 1958. On 21 August 1959 the Baghdad Pact became the Central Treaty Organization (CENTO).

Under the Pact the contracting parties agree to co-operate in security and defence measures, to refrain from interference in each other's internal affairs, settle disputes between themselves in accordance with the U.N. Charter, and not to enter into any international obligations inimical to the Pact, which remains in force for five years but is renewable for additional five-year periods.

To achieve greater co-ordination in defensive military planning a Permanent Military Deputies Group was established in January 1960. The Group is composed of senior officers of the equivalent rank of Lieutenant General from each of the five CENTO countries.

CENTO regional economic development projects in such fields as agriculture, minerals development, health, scientific co-operation and communications were approved in 1957. The communications projects include a railway which links Turkey and Iran across Lake Van. The United States has contributed approximately $2 in grant assistance to Iran and has made available over $24 million (Turkey $16·5 million, Iran $7·8 million) in long-term low-interest loans. The Turkish and Iranian Governments have almost doubled this sum in their local currency contributions to the project. The first completed 100 kilometre stretch of railway between Mus and Tatvan in Turkey was officially inaugurated by the Turkish Prime Minister in October 1964. The whole railway has now been completed, and was inaugurated by H.I.M. The Shahanshah of Iran, and H.E. Cevdet Sunay, The President of Turkey, in September 1971.

Progress is also being made on a year-round all-weather road to link Turkey and Iran. The new CENTO road starts at Cizne in south-east Turkey and joins with the main Iranian trunk road system at Zenjan, midway between Tehran and Tabriz. The United Kingdom has supplied a mechanical road building unit valued at £100,000 and has provided a further £100,000 of equipment to assist in building the Iranian section of the road.

Construction work to extend the Iranian railroad eastwards to join with that of Pakistan is due for completion in 1980. Construction has already been completed on a new road across central Iran to Quetta and Karachi in Pakistan, and a southern road from Lasbella westwards to Pishin (Nikshahr), Char Bahar (Iran), and the main Iranian trunk road system.

About £183,000 of equipment has been provided by the United Kingdom to develop the Turkish Black Sea port of Trabzon. The United Kingdom has also supplied equipment to help develop the Turkish Mediterranean port of Iskenderun.

The first phase of a high-frequency telecommunications link between London and CENTO regional capitals was inaugurated in June 1961. This linked London–Istanbul, London–Ankara and London–Tehran. The second phase to link London–Karachi, London–Rawalpindi is now completed. For both phases the United Kingdom is providing just over £650,000.

The CENTO microwave telecommunications project (for which the United States has contributed $18·37 million and Iran, Pakistan and Turkey have contributed about $8 million in local currency) links Ankara, Tehran and Karachi and many cities in between by means of radio-telephone. The system comprises 88 relay stations and has a capacity of 600 channels. However, this system is currently being up-dated to provide up to 1,800 channels.

The CENTO regional airway project provides for a fully controlled route between Ankara–Tehran–Karachi, including navigational aids, ground communication services between key traffic control points, air to ground communications and trained personnel to operate and maintain the system, all of which will conform with standards of the International Civil Aviation Organization (ICAO) of the U.N. The United States has contributed $6·3 million. Each of the CENTO countries is contributing the local currency costs of the project, as well as land, access roads, buildings and personnel for training, operating and administering the project. To assist in weather forecasting and night safety, the United Kingdom has provided some £200,000 worth of meteorological equipment.

The CENTO Multilateral Technical Co-operation Fund, to which all member governments contribute, provides training for region government nominees in various fields of economic development within the CENTO region. Specialists, students and industrial trainees receive instruction and exchange information among the three region member countries. In addition, the United Kingdom provides specialist training in England for candidates from the region countries under its technical assistance programme.

*Secretary-General:* Mr. Ümit Halûk Bayülken (Iran), who completed a three-year tour of duty in February 1975.
*Address:* Central Treaty Organization, Ankara, Turkey.

## THE COLOMBO PLAN

THE PLAN had its inception at a meeting of the Commonwealth Foreign Ministers in Colombo in January 1950. Political independence having been achieved, economic development had become an urgent problem in South and South-East Asia. Gradually, as confidence in the Plan developed, its membership grew, both of countries within the region and of countries outside the region, from the original seven Commonwealth countries in 1950 to 27 today, including 16 non-Commonwealth countries, in 1973.

The area has extended beyond South and South-East Asia; now it extends from Iran in the west to the Philippines in the east, from the Republic of Korea in the north to Indonesia in the south, embracing a population of over 1,050 million people.

What was once a Commonwealth idea has grown into an international co-operative effort. The present members of the Plan are: (within the region) Afghanistan, Bangladesh, Bhutan, Burma, Fiji, India, Indonesia, Iran, Khmer Republic, Republic of Korea, Laos, Malaysia, Republic of Maldives, Nepal, Pakistan, Papua New Guinea, Philippines, Singapore, Sri Lanka, Thailand and Republic of Vietnam, and (outside the region) Australia, Canada, Japan, New Zealand, the United Kingdom and the United States of America.

There is no overall Colombo Plan programming; it is a collective concept of the countries' own efforts, assisted by other members. There is no master plan for the area of South and South-East Asia, no compulsion from outside. Operationally speaking, the basic factor of the Colombo Plan is that all aid is bilaterally negotiated. The receiving country determines its needs and begins negotiations with a donor country on the best way to fulfil them. Nobody from outside intervenes or interferes; co-operation and equality among members is emphasized. Although the original plans were multilateral in approach, bi-lateral arrangements have become the accepted pattern.

The organization in which the Plan revolves is under four heads: the Consultative Committee (the top policy-making body consisting of Ministers of member governments), the Colombo Plan Council for Technical Co-operation (representatives of all the Colombo Plan countries resident in Colombo), the Colombo Plan Bureau (which serves as a participating body at Consultative Committee meetings, services the Council, records the technical assistance given in the area, and disseminates information of the Plan as a whole), and the Colombo Plan Staff College for Technician Education, which is located in Singapore (established in 1974 as the first 'Multilateral' Colombo Plan project). The College's main functions are to: (i) undertake programmes in Staff development and training of technician education staff; (ii) conduct study conferences and courses for senior administrators in technician education; (iii) promote and undertake research in the special problems of technician education and training within the region; and (iv) provide advisory and resources services in technician education and training to countries, both within and outside the region; and develop programmes of intra-regional training through the holding of seminars and Colloquia.

Assistance is given on a government-to-government basis; non-government organizations may also receive assistance, but such requests must be sponsored by the government of the country concerned. Assistance takes two principal forms: (1) capital aid in the form of grants for national development projects, and commodities including food-grains, fertilizers, consumer goods, specialized equipment including machinery, farm and laboratory equipment, and transport vehicles; and (2) technical co-operation represented by services of experts and technicians, facilities for study in advanced technology in various fields to trainees from South and South-East Asia; and the supply of special equipment for training and research and intra-regional training.

Broadly speaking, all fields of socio-economic development are covered by the Plan's assistance programmes, such as scientific development of agriculture; reclamation of waste land and land management; irrigation and power projects including nuclear energy; pest control and prevention and treatment of plant diseases; animal husbandry services; consumer, small-scale and village industries; development of railways, ports and harbours, national highways and roads; and training abroad of students from the area.

The Plan is a co-operative effort and every country tries to help. The capacity to assist is, however, dependent on the state of development, financial resources and other factors. Those countries which have rendered both capital aid and technical assistance are Australia, Canada, Japan, New Zealand, United Kingdom and United States of America. Countries of the area, Burma, India, Korea, Malaysia, Pakistan, Philippines, Singapore, Sri Lanka and Thailand have given technical assistance to one or more countries of the Plan region.

From 1950 to December 1975, 112,985 trainees and students had received technical training and 29,034 experts and 268 volunteers and equipment to the value of U.S. $698·1 million had been provided. During 1975, 6,804 trainees and students received training; 2,007 experts and 268 volunteers were sent out; value of equipment supplied was $23·0 million; total value of cooperation activities from the inception of the Plan to December 1975 was over $2,554·9 million, spent in the proportion of 18 per cent on trainees and students, 52 per cent on experts and volunteers and 30 per cent on technical equipment. Of the 6,804 training and student places offered in 1975, Britain was the major donor country, providing 2,080 places, i.e. 30 per cent of the total. Australia (1,484) was the second largest donor, closely followed by Japan (1,331) and the United States (1,308). Indonesia was the largest recipient of training and student awards during 1975 with 857 awards, followed by India (776), Thailand (746) and the Philippines (552). Of the 2,007 experts provided in 1975, Japan was the major donor country, providing 955 assignments, i.e. 48 per cent of the total. Australia (517) was the second largest donor followed by the United Kingdom (269) and the United States (216). A total of 268 Volunteers was provided by three major donors i.e. Britain (149), Japan (60) and Australia (59) during the period 1975. Papua New Guinea was the largest recipient of experts (89) during 1975 followed by Malaysia (41), Nepal (32) and the Philippines (25). Aid provided under the Colombo Plan by the main group of donor countries (Australia, Canada Japan, New Zealand, the United Kingdom and the U.S.A.) since the beginning of the Plan has been approximately U.S. $44·875 billion. According to latest figures *Australia* provided $1,138·95 million for capital aid projects and technical assistance up to 1974; *Britain's* expenditure since the beginning of the Colombo Plan up to the end of 1974 was $2,896·56 million; *Canada* had spent a total of $1,834·12 million; *Japan* up to the end of 1974 had spent $5,591·91 million; *New Zealand's* expenditure since the inception of the Plan amounted to approximately $88·36 million; *United States* assistance amounted to $33,325·50 million up to the end of 1974.

## THE COMMONWEALTH

THE Commonwealth is a voluntary association of sovereign nations representing about one quarter of the world population. It evolved from the British Empire and may be traced from the introduction of responsible government in Canada in the 1840s. Similar constitutional developments followed in Australia, New Zealand and South Africa. At the 1926 Imperial Conference, Britain and the four Dominions were described as 'autonomous communities within the British Empire, equal in status, in no way subordinate one to another in any aspect of their domestic or external affairs, though united by a common allegiance to the Crown and freely associated as members of the British Commonwealth of Nations'. Formal legal recognition of this change in status was given by the Statute of Westminster in 1931.

The Commonwealth began to assume its modern character when India and Pakistan became members in 1947 and Sri Lanka (then Ceylon) in 1948. In 1949 India decided to become a republic yet wished to remain in the Commonwealth. It was then agreed that allegiance to the same monarch need no longer be a condition of membership but the Queen remains the symbol of the free association of independent member nations and as such is the Head of the Commonwealth.

In 1965 the Commonwealth Secretariat was established, to be at the service of and financed by all members collectively; until then a British government department had co-ordinated Commonwealth relations.

There are now 36 member countries, whose combined population is about one billion. They are:

| | |
|---|---|
| Australia | Malaysia |
| The Bahamas | Malta |
| Bangladesh | Mauritius |
| Barbados | Nauru |
| Botswana | New Zealand |
| Britain | Nigeria |
| Canada | Papua New Guinea |
| Cyprus | Seychelles |
| Fiji | Sierra Leone |
| The Gambia | Singapore |
| Ghana | Sri Lanka |
| Grenada | Swaziland |
| Guyana | Tanzania |
| India | Tonga |
| Jamaica | Trinidad and Tobago |
| Kenya | Uganda |
| Lesotho | Western Samoa |
| Malawi | Zambia |

The relationship between these members is a relationship between equals. Nauru is a special member; it participates in functional meetings and activities and is eligible for Commonwealth technical assistance, but does not take part in meetings of Commonwealth Heads of Government.

The Commonwealth also includes the self-governing states associated with Commonwealth members and the remaining dependent territories. These are eligible for Commonwealth technical assistance and take part in a variety of Commonwealth activities. Their combined population is about five million. Several are approaching independence.

**The self-governing states associated with Britain**, which have a constitutional status amounting to slightly less than independence, are: Antigua, Dominica, St. Kitts-Nevis-Anguilla, St. Lucia and St. Vincent.

**Britain's remaining dependencies** include: Bermuda, Belize (formerly British Honduras, internally self-governing since 1964), British Solomon Islands Protectorate, British Virgin Islands, Cayman Islands, Falkland Islands, Gibraltar, The Gilbert Islands, Hong Kong, Montserrat, Pitcairn, St. Helena, Tuvalu, and Turks and Caicos Islands.

The Cook Islands are a self-governing territory in association with New Zealand. Niue and the Tokelau Islands are New Zealand island territories. Australia's external territories include Norfolk Island, Cocos (Keeling) Islands and Christmas Island. (There are also certain Antarctic and island territories of Australia, Britain and New Zealand without permanent populations.)

*Principles*

The Commonwealth has no constitution, but its members adhere to the principles which were unanimously approved by Commonwealth Heads of Government in Singapore in 1971.

These principles include support for the United Nations and its efforts to remove the causes of tension between nations, and belief in the liberty of the individual, in equal rights regardless of race, colour, creed or political views, and in the inalienable right to participate in free and democratic political processes. Racial prejudice is recognized as an unmitigated evil to be combated in each member nation, and opposition to all forms of colonial domination and racial oppression is expressed.

Believing that present disparities of wealth between different sections of mankind create world tensions, Commonwealth members seek to overcome poverty, ignorance and disease, raise standards of life and achieve a more equitable international society. To this end, the Declaration of Commonwealth Principles continues, they aim to bring about the free-est possible flow of international trade on terms fair to all, taking into account the special requirements of the developing countries, and to encourage the flow to the latter of adequate resources, both governmental and private, to assist sustained investment and growth.

The Declaration expresses the conviction that the Commonwealth is one of the most fruitful associations for removing causes of war, promoting tolerance, combating injustice and fostering development. Its constructive, multinational approach, based on consultation, discussion and co-operation, and its use of many channels for exchanges of knowledge and views, can increase understanding between peoples, contribute to the enrichment of life for all, and provide a powerful influence for peace among nations.

*The Secretariat*

The Commonwealth Secretary-General, who has access to Heads of Government and is responsible for the organization of their meetings, maintains close contacts with member countries and is the head of the Commonwealth Secretariat. Mr. Shridath S. Ramphal, who had been Minister of Foreign Affairs and Justice of Guyana, was appointed by Heads of Government as Secretary-General from July 1975. He succeeded Mr. Arnold Smith, of Canada, who became the first Secretary-General in 1965, when the Secretariat was established, and was re-appointed for a further five-year term in 1970. The Secretariat is responsible to Commonwealth governments collectively, is the main agency for multilateral communication between them and provides the central organization for joint consultation and co-operation in many fields. It is staffed by officers from member countries and is financed by contributions from member governments on an agreed scale. Its net budget for 1977–78 is £2,150,690.

The Secretariat organizes meetings and conferences and co-ordinates many Commonwealth activities. Besides promoting consultation, it disseminates information on a wide range of activities. The Secretariat's functions are shared among divisions responsible for: international affairs, economic affairs, education, export market development, law, food and rural development, applied studies in government, youth activities and information. Scientific and health matters are dealt with through a Scientific Adviser and a Medical Adviser.

The Secretariat also provides expert technical assistance for economic and social development through the multilateral Commonwealth Fund for Technical Co-operation which supplies experts for assignments in developing member countries, and supports education and training in developmental fields. The CFTC's budget for 1977–78 is £11 million.

The Secretariat maintains archives on international issues, and prepares papers which present a combination of Commonwealth knowledge and views. Because of its neutral position, the Secretariat has been able to make its good offices available in cases of dispute.

The Secretariat organizes and services meetings of Heads of Government, of Ministers, and of Commonwealth officials and experts on many subjects. Following discussions by Heads of Government at Kingston, Jamaica in May 1975 on the need for a new international economic order, the Secretary-General assembled a group of experts to make practical proposals for closing the gap between rich and poor countries. Reports produced by this group of experts have been influential both with member Governments and in discussions at the United Nations. A team of industrial specialists was asked by the Secretary-General in 1976 to propose practical measures for speeding the process of industrialization in Commonwealth developing countries.

The headquarters of the Secretariat are in London, at Marlborough House, which was made available as a Commonwealth centre by the Queen.

*Meetings of Heads of Government*

At the summit of the pyramid of inter-governmental Commonwealth meetings are those of Heads of Government, at which international developments, both political and economic, are reviewed and ways of developing co-operation among member countries are examined. There is no other forum in which Heads of Government of such a wide variety of countries can meet together periodically for an informal exchange of views. The proceedings are private, and the exchanges, while friendly, are frank and uninhibited.

No precise rules of procedure govern Heads of Government meetings, which operate not by voting but by consensus. The aim is to ensure that all Commonwealth governments have a common understanding of what may be at stake and appreciate the motives and purposes underlying the policies which each is separately pursuing. In fact, a wide measure of agreement is normally attained.

The situation in southern Africa, specially the Rhodesian problem, has for long been a major concern of the Commonwealth. Heads of Government have consistently affirmed their support for Rhodesian independence on the basis of majority rule. They have also been concerned with the need for faster progress towards a more equitable global social order. "Heads of Government reiterated that the independence of Zimbabwe must be achieved on the basis of majority rule, and agreed that it was necessary to exert maximum pressure on the illegal Smith regime. They noted that the armed struggle had become complementary to other efforts to secure independence for Zimbabwe, and that its maintenance was inevitable. While they welcomed the renewed attempts to reach a negotiated settlement, doubts were expressed about the prospects for their success...

Heads of Government condemned South Africa for the military and economic support which it continues to give to the illegal regime. In particular, they deplored and condemned the provision of military equipment and the supply of petroleum and petroleum products which buttress the illegal regime. They therefore called on South Africa to desist forthwith from complicity in repression and on all countries to take effective steps to ensure that South Africa no longer sustains the illegal regime in defiance of the resolutions of the Security Council. . . .

Heads of Government condemned South Africa's continued illegal occupation of and its military presence in Namibia. They recognized that the heroic people of Namibia have had to resort to several methods, including the armed struggle, to achieve their liberation. They reaffirmed the inalienable right of the people of Namibia to self-determination, independence and territorial integrity. They also reaffirmed the right of the people of Namibia to choose their own government in free elections under United Nations supervision and control. They rejected as totally unacceptable to the Commonwealth, and to the international community as a whole, any arrangements for independence based on the system of "bantustans" and apartheid and on the exclusion of SWAPO from participation in the electoral process. Accordingly they called on South Africa to act immediately to end its illegal occupation, to release all political prisoners and, in consultation with the appropriate organs of the United Nations, to transfer power within the framework of principles established by United Nations resolutions and in particular Security Council Resolution 385 of 30 January 1976. Heads of Government noted that two of their members were involved in the five-power initiative in relation to Namibia and expressed the hope that it would contribute to this purpose. In this connection they urged the international community to take urgent action to apply an immediate arms embargo against South Africa and to make such an embargo effective. . . .

The member countries of the Commonwealth, embracing peoples of diverse races, colours, languages and faiths, have long recognized racial prejudice and discrimination as a dangerous sickness and an unmitigated evil and are pledged to use all their efforts to foster human dignity everywhere. At their London Meeting, Heads of Government reaffirmed that apartheid in sports, as in other fields, is an abomination and runs directly counter to the Declaration of Commonwealth Principles which they made at Singapore on 22 January 1971. . . .

Mindful of these and other considerations, they accepted it as the urgent duty of each of their Governments vigorously to combat the evil of apartheid by withholding any form of support for, and by taking every practical step to discourage contact or competition by their nationals with sporting organizations, teams or sportsmen from South Africa or from any other country where sports are organized on the basis of race, colour or ethnic origin. . . .

Heads of Government recognized that the North-South dialogue had advanced since their Kingston Meeting and welcomed the steps which had been taken by developed and developing countries prior to and at the Conference on International Economic Co-operation to strengthen international co-operation and foster the recovery of the world economy. They noted that participants in CIEC considered that it had contributed to a broader understanding of the international economic situation, and that the intensive discussions had been useful to them. In the view of the developing members of the Commonwealth, however, the specific measures agreed upon were inadequate either by comparison with their needs or as a contribution towards the introduction of the New International Economic Order. Heads of Government called for renewed and more intensive efforts to pursue and advance the North-South dialogue in a constructive spirit in the responsible international institutions.

Heads of Government considered the Final Report of the Commonwealth Group of Experts which they set up at their Kingston Meeting. They congratulated the members of the Group on the expeditious and conscientious manner in which they discharged their mandate. While recognizing that some elements of the Report differ from the positions of some governments, they endorsed the Report as a constructive contribution towards developing a specific action programme. They agreed that many of the proposals contained in the Report should be implemented with urgency and be incorporated in comprehensive and mutually reinforcing national and international policies to provide greater opportunity for development to the developing countries. Such policies should reinforce the efforts of developing countries to achieve self reliance in satisfying their basic needs as soon as possible. They decided to refer the Report of the Group of Experts to Commonwealth Finance Ministers together with the decisions on economic issues taken at this Meeting as a basis for further action at the international level. They asked the Secretary-General to ensure that the Report was brought to the attention of the wider international community.

Heads of Government welcomed the agreement at CIEC that a Common Fund should be established as a new entity to play a key role in achieving the objectives of the Integrated Programme for Commodities as set out in Resolution 93 (IV) at Nairobi. They also noted the agreement that the specific purposes and objectives of a Common Fund as well as its other constituent elements will continue to be negotiated in UNCTAD. They agreed to work towards the early establishment of the Fund. To this end they asked the Secretary-General to establish a small technical working group drawn from Commonwealth countries to examine the issues which need to be addressed in further work in UNCTAD and their report should inform Commonwealth leaders on the range of objectives and purposes for which the Common Fund might be used, its methods of operation and the measures to be adopted to help developing countries which are net importers of the commodities concerned, with a view to facilitating greater progress at the UNCTAD Conference in November. . . .

Cognisant of the accumulated evidence of sustained disregard for the sanctity of life and of massive violation of basic human rights in Uganda, it was the overwhelming view of Commonwealth leaders that these excesses were so gross as to warrant the world's concern and to evoke condemnation by Heads of Government in strong and unequivocal terms. Mindful that the people of Uganda were within the fraternity of Commonwealth fellowship Heads of Government looked to the day when the people of Uganda would once more fully enjoy their basic human rights which now were being so cruelly denied. . . .

In reaffirming once again their position of solidarity with the Government and people of the Republic of Cyprus and their support for General Assembly Resolution 3212 (XXIX), Security Council Resolutions 365 (1974) and 367 (1975), further endorsed and supplemented by subsequent UN resolutions on Cyprus, Heads of Government expressed deep concern that these resolutions have remained unimplemented. They called for their urgent implementation in all their parts and for continued efforts through the intercommunal talks to reach freely a mutually acceptable political settlement. . . .

Heads of Government earnestly hope that negotiations towards a Middle East peace settlement will soon be resumed and will prove successful. . . .

They renewed their conviction that no real progress towards peace in the area is possible until the relevant resolutions of the United Nations are implemented and the right of the Palestinian people to their homeland is recognized. While urging all parties concerned vigorously to renew their efforts for the establishment of a durable peace in the area, Heads of Government called for the early convening of the Geneva Conference with the full participation of the authentic and lgitimate representatives of the Palestinian people. Most Heads of Government recognized that the Palestine Liberation Organization is the only legitimate representative of the Palestinian people.

Heads of Government reviewed the question of Belize and reaffirmed their full support for the aspirations of its people for early independence. They called upon all states to respect the right of the people of Belize to self-determination, independence and territorial integrity. They acknowledged that there could be no settlement of the question without the full consent of the Government and people of Belize, and pledged their co-operation in securing such a settlement. To this end they agreed to establish a ministerial committee of the Governments of Barbados, Canada, Guyana, India, Jamaica, Malaysia. Nigeria and Tanzania to meet with the Secretary-General to keep under review the situation relating to the efforts of the people of Belize in pursuit of their legitimate aspirations for self-determination and independence; to assist the parties concerned in finding early and effective arrangements for the independence of Belize on the basis of views expressed at Meetings of Commonwealth Heads of Government and in accordance with the Charter and relevant resolutions of the United Nations; to make recommendations; and to render all practicable assistance in achieving these objectives."

Recent decisions have concerned the Commonwealth Fund for Technical Co-operation, the Commonwealth Youth Programme, the Commonwealth Book Development Programme, the Commonwealth Information Programme, and a Programme for Applied Studies in Government.

Meetings of Heads of Government are held in various Commonwealth capitals approximately every two years, the latest being in London (1969), Singapore (1971), Ottawa (1973) and Kingston (1975) and London (1977). The next meeting is to be held in Lusaka in 1979.

*Economic affairs*

Commonwealth Finance Ministers meet annually to discuss international monetary and other economic issues. Their meetings. which are preceded by meetings of senior finance officials, take place shortly before the annual meetings of the International Monetary Fund (IMF) and the World Bank. The wide identity of views on major issues which generally emerges at these meetings makes for a greater impact internationally than would be the case were such views conveyed merely by individual, or even by regional groups of, Commonwealth states.

The discussions at recent Finance Ministers' meetings have centred on international monetary reform, the situation of developing countries most severely affected by rises in import prices. the terms of trade for primary producers, the need to control inflation while avoiding recession, the work of international agencies like the IMF and the World Bank, and on future trade relations between Commonwealth countries and the enlarged European Economic Community (EEC). Other subjects discussed have included the international negotiations under the General Agreement on Tariffs and Trade (GATT) and development assistance.

Ministers concerned with food production and rural development met in London in 1975 to follow up discussions among Commonwealth delegates to the World Food Conference in Rome. As a result of their recommendations, a new division was created in the Secretariat to promote Commonwealth co-operation to raise living standards in rural areas where the majority of Commonwealth people live.

*Development Assistance*

There has been a steady increase in bilateral aid between Commonwealth countries in recent years. Britain, Canada, Australia and New Zealand provide substantial amounts of aid, earmarking over 70 per cent of their bilateral aid to Commonwealth developing countries. Other donor countries include Nigeria, India, Malaysia and Singapore. Some of the bilateral aid is given under regional schemes, such as the Colombo Plan (which began as a Commonwealth scheme but which now includes many non-Commonwealth countries).

Complementary to bilateral aid is the assistance given through the Commonwealth Fund for Technical Co-operation (CFTC), which was established within the Secretariat in 1971. The multilateral Fund provides technical assistance for economic and social development in Commonwealth developing countries. All Commonwealth countries contribute to the Fund's resources, the more developed members, particularly Canada and Britain, being the major contributors, while Nigeria became the third largest contributor in 1974–75.

Through its General Technical Assistance Programme, the CFTC provides advisers and experts to developing countries, and commissions feasibility studies for development projects. The number of long-term (six months and over) experts rose to nearly 300 in mid-1977. Under its Education and Training Programme, nationals of developing countries are helped to study or be trained abroad, chiefly in other such countries. Over 500 projects, many involving several students, are supported annually. A team of headquarters specialists provide advice in key areas, particularly on the legal and financial aspects of mineral and oil exploitation. CFTC funds also support the work of divisions in the Secretariat concerned with export market development, food production and rural development, and raising skills in public administration.

Member governments have substantially increased their contributions to the CFTC each year, enabling it to maintain a steady expansion in activities. It plans to spend £11 million in 1977–78, against £8 million in 1976–77.

*Education*

Commonwealth Education Conferences are held approximately every three years. They are attended by ministers of education and their senior officials.

The 1977 conference, held in Ghana, focused on the economics of education and on the ways in which education could contribute to economic development. It prepared the ground for the formation of an association of polytechnics in Africa, and discussed measures to promote teaching about the Commonwealth. The Commonwealth Education Liaison Committee (CELC), established in 1959, provides a forum for the consideration of matters of principle arising out of conference recommendations. Its members act as the main link between Commonwealth governments and the Commonwealth Secretariat on education subjects. It keeps developments in education under review and provides advice on questions referred to it by the Secretariat.

The Commonwealth Secretariat plays a co-ordinating part in Commonwealth educational co-operation, organizing conferences, preparing and publishing reports and specialist papers and helping to assess future needs in order to provide a basis for educational planning. The Secretariat is able to disseminate information on a wide range of research and experimentation to assist governments to improve the quality of education and keep down costs.

Much of the educational co-operation between Commonwealth countries is bilateral. The Commonwealth Scholarship and Fellowship Plan, is basically a series of bilateral agreements under which member governments award scholarships and fellowships at their universities and other institutions of higher learning to men and women from other Commonwealth countries. The Association of Commonwealth Universities was founded in 1913, and now has a membership of 190 institutions, prepares annual reports on the Plan, which are published by the Commonwealth Secretariat.

There are many direct links between universities in different Commonwealth countries, which make possible collaboration in research projects as well as exchanges of teaching and research staff. Schoolteachers are linked by such organizations as the League for the Exchange of Commonwealth Teachers and the Association of Commonwealth Teachers, which arranges holiday tours.

*Youth*

A Commonwealth Youth Programme was approved at the first meeting of Commonwealth Ministers concerned with youth matters, in Lusaka early in 1973. The Programme's continuance beyond its initial phase of three years was approved by Heads of Government in 1975.

The Programme which is administered by the Commonwealth Secretariat, operate three regional centres (in Guyana, India and Zambia), which help to train administrators and key youth workers, and which ensure that the programme's activities are as widespread as possible. Other components of the Youth Programme's activities include: fellowships for applied research with particular reference to youth matters bursaries for training courses; study fellowships to enable youth personnel to visit Commonwealth countries other than their own to study new developments; and a Commonwealth youth information service.

Other Commonwealth youth activities are arranged by non-governmental organizations with which the Youth Programme maintains close liaison.

*Health*

The first Commonwealth Medical Conference was held in Edinburgh in 1965; subsequent conferences have been in Kampala (1968), Mauritius (1971), and Colombo (1974). The last conference was held in New Zealand in November 1977, on the theme of community health. Delegations are normally headed by Ministers of Health. Mutual assistance in medical education, the planning and development of health services, the training of ancillary staff, the supply of medical equipment and the provision of research facilities are prominent among the subjects discussed at these meetings.

The 1974 conference in Sri Lanka focused on the allocation of scarce resources for the improvement of health. Education, training and research were seen as the main fields for co-operation. The conference made recommendations on the migration of doctors, on training health administrators and para-medical staff, on the preparation of medical text-books, and on the bulk purchase of drugs. The conference also discussed family planning, rural health services and the use of medical statistics.

Regional co-ordination and co-operation in health activities among members of the Commonwealth is now well established. In the Caribbean, meetings of Health Ministers set guidelines for the work of the Caribbean Community in the health field. Similar co-operation has been developed in Africa, where there exist Health Secretariats, linked with the Commonwealth Secretariat, in Lagos, for West Africa, and in Arusha, for east, central and southern Africa.

To maintain continuity between conferences, discussions between Commonwealth representatives also take place before the annual meetings of the World Health Assembly in Geneva, and these are sometimes accompanied by separate discussions between representatives of various Commonwealth regional groups.

There are associations linking doctors, nurses and pharmacists in the Commonwealth.

*The Law*

The legal systems of Commonwealth countries have many features in common: shared legal traditions, similar courts and procedures, and a community of outlook among members of the legal profession, many of whom received their early training in the same Inns of Court and universities.

An important step towards preserving and strengthening the bond between Commonwealth lawyers was taken in 1955 with the holding of the first Commonwealth Law Conference in London. This was organized by bar associations and law societies and was attended by some 600 lawyers. Subsequent conferences have been held every five years, in Ottawa (1960), Sydney (1965) New Delhi (1971) and Edinburgh (1977).

It is now the practice for Law Ministers to have regular meetings: the last two meetings were in Lagos (1975) and Winnipeg (1977). These meetings are organized by the Commonwealth Secretariat whose legal division informs member governments of legal developments in other countries and organizes various forms of co-operation in legal matters. To help governments meet a shortage of legislative draftsmen which has hampered social and economic reforms in many countries, the Secretariat has organized regional schemes for training legal draftsmen.

At their Winnipeg meeting in 1977, Law Ministers reviewed Commonwealth legal co-operation, and considered such matters as the delays in the administration of justice, the relationship between the courts and the executive, sentencing and rehabilitation procedures, the training and use of legal and para-legal staff, compensation to victims of crime, and the work of law reform agencies.

There are three Commonwealth professional associations in the legal field: the Commonwealth Legal Bureau, the Commonwealth Magistrates Association, and the Commonwealth Legal Education Association.

*Parliamentarians*

Regular consultation and the exchange of information and visits between Commonwealth parliamentarians are promoted by the Commonwealth Parliamentary Association. Founded in 1911, this is an association of members of Commonwealth parliaments, who are united by community of interest, respect for the rule of law and the rights of the individual citizen, and in the pursuit of the ideals of parliamentary democracy. The Association now has more than 100 branches in Commonwealth legislatures.

Commonwealth Parliamentary Conferences are held annually by the Association; the 1977 Conference was in Canada. The General Council of the Association has its annual meetings during these conferences, and the executive committee of the Council meets twice a year in various Commonwealth centres. The Association's headquarters are in the Houses of Parliament at Westminster.

*Scientific Research*

Commonwealth Scientific Conferences were held in 1936, 1946 and 1952, but it was subsequently decided that intergovernmental discussion of scientific matters could be best conducted through meetings of the Commonwealth Science Council (formerly Committee). This Council, consisting of representatives of 26 participating governments, meets biennially and the 1976 meeting was held in Colombo, Sri Lanka. The Science Adviser to the Commonwealth Secretary-General is the Secretary of the Council, the headquarters of which are in London. An executive Committee meets several times a year and the Secretary makes visits to member countries.

In recent years the Commonwealth Science Council has been primarily concerned with helping scientific agencies in the developing countries of the Commonwealth to plan their research and development activities, and also to advise aid authorities in the developed countries on the assistance these agencies require.

Seminars and workshops bring together Commonwealth scientists on a regional basis are arranged to promote the exchange of views and experiences and to develop co-operation in particular fields of scientific activity. The Council's work has recently focused on such matters as the storage of food products, standards for industrial products, scientific communication, management of research and non-conventional energy for rural use.

Operating under the aegis of the Council are two specialist bodies. The Commonwealth Committee on Mineral Resources and Geology and its Commonwealth Geological Liaison Office link government organizations concerned with geology and mineral investigation. Besides supplying information the Committee also assists with recruitment. The Permanent Committee of the Commonwealth Collection of Micro-organisms fosters the maintenance and expansion of culture collections, makes available the cultures in them and publishes directories of collections and lists of species.

Ten Commonwealth Mining and Metallurgical Congresses have been held. the most recent being in Canada in 1974.

Another group of institutions concerned with ensuring that the results of research are made available to research workers throughout the Commonwealth are the Commonwealth Agricultural Bureaux, which now comprise four institutes and ten bureaux. The four institutes are: The Commonwealth Institute of Entomology; The Commonwealth Mycological Institute; The Commonwealth Institute of Helminthology; The Commonwealth Institute of Biological Control.

*The Professions*

Although there have long been links between professional people in the Commonwealth, there has been a tendency to follow political evolution and discontinue branch relationships with parent societies in Britain. At the same time, the need to establish soundly-based national and Commonwealth-wide professional organizations has grown, and in 1966 a unique international institution, the Commonwealth Foundation, was formed by Commonwealth Heads of Government to promote and strengthen links between individual members of the professions and between professional societies throughout the Commonwealth.

The objects of the Foundation are to encourage and support fuller representation at conferences of professional bodies within the Commonwealth; assist such bodies to hold more conferences between themselves; facilitate the exchange of visits among professional people; stimulate the flow of information between professional organizations; assist with the setting-up of national professional institutions and associations; promote the growth of Commonwealth-wide associations or regional Commonwealth associations; and in exceptional cases to help associations or individuals whose activities lie outside the strictly professional field but fall within the general ambit of the Foundation's operations.

Besides helping existing associations of doctors, architects and engineers, the Foundation has helped professional people in several other fields to form Commonwealth-wide associations. These include veterinarians, lawyers, surveyors, geographers, pharmacists, nurses, magistrates, librarians and museum curators. It has also helped in the establishment of national professional centres to serve several disciplines, ten centres are now functioning and five others are planned.

The Foundation, now supported by 35 governments, has an annual income of £675,000.

*Communications*

The first conference of Commonwealth Postal Administrations was held in London in 1971. Subsequent conferences have taken place in Trinidad and Tobago in 1973 and in Sri Lanka in 1976. The fourth conference is due to be held in Malaysia in 1978. These conferences allow senior postal officials to discuss matters of common interest such as rate fixing and the development of air mail, and to harmonize Commonwealth views on issues to be discussed at Universal Postal Congresses.

The Commonwealth Telecommunications Bureau is made up of two parts: the Commonwealth Telecommunications Council and the Commonwealth Telecommunications Conference. It promotes the efficient use and development of the Commonwealth telecommunications system, one of the world's largest commercial networks. Its last conference was in Sydney in 1977.

The Commonwealth Air Transport Council links civil aviation authorities in member countries, reviews the progress and development of civil aviation communications, and advises governments on matters which are referred to it.

*Information and the Media*

One of the oldest Commonwealth organisations concerned with the media is the Commonwealth Press Union, which was founded in 1909. Its present membership of over 600 includes most of the major newspapers, periodicals and news agencies in Commonwealth countries. The objects of the Union include the defence of the freedom of the press; the securing of cheaper and better telecommunications services; the education, training and exchange of journalists throughout the Commonwealth; and the improvement of reporting facilities for the Commonwealth Press as a whole.

The Diplomatic and Commonwealth Writers' Association, based in London, holds regular meetings and discussions, often with visiting speakers.

The Commonwealth Broadcasting Association, comprising

national public service broadcasting organizations in Commonwealth countries, was established in 1945 and has a small secretariat in London. The Association organizes biennial Boradcasting Conferences for Commonwealth countries, and organizes training courses for broadcasting staff, with assistance from the Commonwealth Secretariat through the Commonwealth Fund for Technical Co-operation.

Under the Commonwealth Information Programme, the Commonwealth Secretariat produces and distributes public information material on Commonwealth affairs and institutions, and the information services of member countries play their part in publicizing general Commonwealth activities as well as dealing with national affairs. The Secretariat maintains a general enquiry point and information room at Marlborough House.

A series of reference publications (including the quarterly 'Commonwealth Record' and 'Commonwealth Diary' and the 'Notes on the Commonwealth') are produced in the Secretariat and given a wide distribution. A full publications list is available.

The Secretariat works closely with the Commonwealth Institute, which is concerned with educating and informing public opinion, particularly in Britain, about the Commonwealth, and with many other Commonwealth non-governmental organizations.

*Commonwealth Studies*

There are two Institutes of Commonwealth Studies, both in Britain. The first, in the University of London, was established in 1949 to promote advanced studies of Commonwealth affairs. The other Institute, at Oxford, is a teaching centre for administrators and diplomatists from developing countries and in collaboration with senior members of the University undertakes research and bibliographical work. The Institute works closely with Queen Elizabeth House, another centre for studies concerning developing countries.

There are now some 260 universities in the Commonwealth. In most of them some aspect of Commonwealth affairs is the subject of study and research.

Journals of Commonwealth affairs, with multinational editorial boards, include 'Commonwealth', published by the Royal Commonwealth Society, 'The Round Table' and the 'Journal of Commonwealth Political Studies'. These are published in Britain, but most journals of international affairs throughout the Commonwealth devote much of their coverage to Commonwealth countries.

*Societies*

The largest of the many general Commonwealth bodies is the Royal Commonwealth Society, whose London headquarters offer club amenities, a library and a wide range of Commonwealth meetings, conferences. Club facilities are also provided by the Royal Over-Seas League in London, formed in 1910 to promote friendship and understanding between the people of the Commonwealth. Other societies include the English-Speaking Union of the Commonwealth, Victoria League for Commonwealth Friendship, and the Commonwealth Countries League. The general co-ordination of the activities of these and other Commonwealth societies is the function of the Joint Commonwealth Societies' Council which organizes joint meetings and ceremonies, and is responsible for arrangements for the celebration of Commonwealth Day in London and for the distribution of the Queen's Commonwealth Day message.

*The Arts and Sport*

Achievement in the arts throughout the Commonwealth has both richness and variety and this is made evident by the regular performances, given by dancers and musicians from all parts of the Commonwealth, (and by film shows) at the Commonwealth Institute's theatre in London. Exhibitions of the work of Commonwealth artists are mounted in the Institute's art gallery.

As in other fields, in fiction, poetry and drama the English language acts as a bridge between dissimilar cultures, and world literature owes much to the work of well-known Commonwealth writers.

Commonwealth Games have been held ten times. The venue for the 1974 Games was Christchurch, New Zealand, and the next will be in Edmonton, Canada in August 1978.

Apart from the Games it has become a tradition for certain Commonwealth countries to meet in top-class cricket, rugby and hockey matches.

## THE COUNCIL FOR MUTUAL ECONOMIC ASSISTANCE—CMEA (COMECON)

THE Council for Mutual Economic Assistance (CMEA) is an international organization for economic co-operation of a new type, which pools the efforts of sovereign and equal socialist states. The underlying working principles of CMEA are socialist internationalism, respect for state sovereignty, independence and national interests of the member-states, non-interference in the internal affairs of one another, full equality, the voluntary principle, mutual benefit and comradely assistance.

When it was founded in 1949, CMEA included Bulgaria, Czechoslovakia, Hungary, Poland, Romania, and the USSR, as well as Albania (which in practice ceased to participate in CMEA activities in 1961). In September 1950 the German Democratic Republic joined CMEA. The Mongolian People's Republic has been a CMEA member since 1962 and Cuba since 1972. Under the terms of an agreement signed in 1964 Yugoslavia has been taking part in the work of some CMEA organs concerned with matters of mutual interest. Representatives of the Democratic Republic of Vietnam, the Korean People's Democratic Republic, the People's Democratic Republic of Laos and the People's Republic of Angola attend meetings of a number of CMEA organs as observers. In May 1973 Finland signed an agreement on co-operation with CMEA. Agreements on co-operation with CMEA were also signed by Iraq in July 1975 and by Mexico in August 1975.

As stated in the CMEA Charter, adopted in 1960, the Council is called upon to promote the concerting and coordination of the member-countries' efforts, the planned development of their economies, the acceleration of economic and technological progress, a higher level of industrialization in industrially less developed countries, a continuous growth of labour productivity and a steady rise of the living standards in the CMEA countries.

The methods of CMEA work have been changing and improving at various stages of its activity. The meeting of the party and government leaders of the CMEA countries held in 1962 emphasized that the key element of the Council's activity was coordination of national economic plans on the basis of the "Fundamental Principles of International Socialist Division of Labour".

The highest organ of CMEA is its session which is convened on a rotational basis in the capitals of the member-countries at least once a year. The session considers fundamental problems, determines major policies of the Council and sets up such organs as are necessary for the discharge of the Council's functions.

The Executive Committee of the Council consists of representatives of all CMEA countries at the level of deputy head of government and holds its meetings once every two months. It directs the coordination of economic development plans and the work of the Council's Standing Commissions and Secretariat. The Council has more than 20 branch commissions, and other working organs. The Secretariat is in charge of organizational matters and also conducts economic surveys and studies and prepares material for the meetings of Council organs. The Secretary of the Council is N. V. Faddeyev (USSR).

An important part in the CMEA system is played by the International Bank of Economic Co-operation founded in 1963 in pursuance of an agreement on multilateral settling of accounts in transferable roubles. The Bank ensures the efficient and prompt settlement in regard of reciprocal trade between the member-countries, scientific and technological co-operation, non-commercial and other payments.

On 5 February 1971 an agreement came into force on the setting up of the International Investment Bank of which all the CMEA countries are members. The bank is designed to develop a system of medium-term and long-term crediting of measures to promote international socialist division of labour and specialization and co-operation of production, above all joint efforts to step up economic co-operation between the CMEA countries.

The 25th CMEA Session held in Bucharest 27–29 July 1971, at a heads-of-government level unanimously adopted the Comprehensive Programme for the Further Intensification and Improvement of Co-operation and the Development of Socialist Economic Integration. The programme is the result of a collective effort of the CMEA members to be implemented step by step within 15–20 years.

The Comprehensive Programme views integration as an objective historical process of development of world socialism.

which brings closer together the economies of the socialist countries and shapes an up-to-date and highly efficient structure of their economies, gradually evens out the levels of their economic development, promotes strong and durable links between the key branches of economy, science and technology, expands and consolidates on this basis the international market of these countries and improves their commodity-money relations. The basic method of international socialist division of labour will remain the co-ordination of long-term and five-year national economic plans, including joint planning of whole branches of economy. The programme prescribes the specific methods and time limits of implementing co-operation related to such important economic problems as the supply of fuel, raw materials and modern equipment for the national economy and meeting the demand of the population for industrial goods and foodstuffs.

Any country which is not a member of CMEA may participate, fully or in part, in implementing the measures planned by the Comprehensive Programme.

In order to expand and improve co-operation the 25th Session formed the CMEA Committee for Co-operation in Planning and transformed the Standing Commission for Coordination on Scientific and Technological Research into the CMEA Committee for Scientific and Technological Co-operation.

The CMEA member-states work in close co-operation with many foreign countries irrespective of their socio-political structures. In 1975 CMEA maintained various kinds of economic and scientific-technological relations with over 30 international organizations at governmental and non-governmental levels. In October 1974 CMEA received the status of official observer at the United Nations.

In almost 30 years of co-operation the CMEA countries have made considerable progress in all spheres of social, political and economic life. Since 1949 the industrial output of these countries has increased more than 14-fold, and national income 9·5 fold. Many new branches of industry have been established and hundreds of major economic projects have been completed.

The 31st CMEA session held in Warsaw in June 1977 reviewed the work of the Council and discussed key issues for future progress and the special report "The 60th Anniversary of the Great October Socialist Revolution and Fraternal Co-operation Among the CMEA Member-States."

The session considered the main ways of implementing the Comprehensive Programme. Special attention was given to the fuel and power programme for the economies of all the socialist countries, particularly questions such as the more rational and wiser use of power resources, atomic energy development and rationalization of the fuel and power balance.

Scientific and technological co-operation and ways to improve it were also thoroughly discussed. The session approved the programme for co-ordinating national economic development plans. *Address:* 56 Prospect Kalinina, Moscow 121205, U.S.S.R. Tel.: 290–91–11, 290–91–12.

# COUNCIL OF EUROPE

THE Statute bringing into existence the Council of Europe was signed at St. James's Palace, London, on 5 May 1949 (one year after The Hague Congress had called for its creation). The requisite seven ratifications were obtained shortly afterwards and in August 1949 the principal organs of the Council—the intergovernmental Committee of Ministers and the parliamentary Consultative Assembly—opened their first meetings in Strasbourg, where the Secretariat-General had already been installed.

## STATUTE OF THE COUNCIL OF EUROPE

The Statute is the Constitution of the Council of Europe. It defines its aims and governs the conditions of entry of new Members. It also provides for the organs of the Council and determines their competence.

### *Aims of the Council*

Article 1 of the Statute states that 'the aim of the Council of Europe is to achieve a greater unity between its Members for the purpose of safeguarding and realizing the ideals and principles which are their common heritage and facilitating their economic and social progress'. The Statute goes on to state that this aim shall be pursued through the organs of the Council by discussion of questions of common concern and by agreements and common action in economic, social, cultural, scientific, legal and administrative matters and in the maintenance and further realization of human rights and fundamental freedoms.

This reference to human rights is taken up again in Articles 3 and 4, in which acceptance of 'the principles of the rule of law' is made a condition of membership of the Council. The 'agreements and common action' referred to have mainly taken the form of European Conventions, of which there are now 89 (September 1976), covering such matters as human rights, social security, patents, the peaceful settlement of disputes, education, and a large number of social and legal questions.

The functions of the Council are thus general and extend to all fields of European co-operation, with the sole exception of questions of national defence excluded by Article 1 (*d*).

### *Member States*

The ten Governments which originally signed the Statute were Belgium, Denmark, France, Ireland, Italy, Luxembourg, the Netherlands, Norway, Sweden and the United Kingdom. During its first Session held in August 1949, the Committee of Ministers invited Greece, Turkey and Iceland to join the Council; Turkey and Greece in fact sent representatives to the first Session of the Consultative Assembly, while Iceland became a member in March 1950. Countries which have joined subsequently are the Federal Republic of Germany (Associate Member 1950, full Member 1951), Austria (1956), Cyprus (1961), Switzerland (1963), Malta (1965), and Portugal (1976). The Saar, admitted as an Associate Member in 1950, ceased to have separate representation in the Council at the end of 1956, following its political integration into the Federal Republic of Germany. Greece withdrew from the Council in December 1969, but was readmitted in November 1974.

'Any European State which is deemed to be able and willing to fulfil the provisions of Article 3 (regarding the respect of human rights and fundamental freedoms) may be invited to become a member of the Council of Europe by the Committee of Ministers.' By statutory resolution the Ministers have agreed that such invitations shall be launched only after consultation of the Assembly. The Ministers have also stated their willingness to admit non-member countries to certain activities of the Council: An example is the participation of Finland, the Holy See, and Spain which take part on an equal footing in the elaboration and execution of the Council's cultural and educational programme.

### *Budget*

Each member bears the expenses of its own representation in the Committee of Ministers and in the Consultative Assembly. The expenses of the Secretariat-General and all other common expenses are shared among Member States. As regards expenses arising out of the application of so-called Partial Agreements, i.e., agreements subscribed by certain Members only, only the subscribing countries contribute. Examples are the Resettlement Fund, in which 15 countries participate, together with the Holy See and Liechtenstein, and certain social activities taken over from Western European Union. In 1977 the Budget of the Council of Europe totalled about 135 million French francs in all.

### *Committee of Ministers*

The Committee of Ministers is the executive organ of the Council of Europe. It alone can accept the text of Conventions or Agreements and take the decision to open them to signature; it makes recommendations to Governments and may require them to inform it of what action they have taken in regard to such recommendations; it 'decides with binding effect all matters relating to the internal organization and arrangements of the Council of Europe'. It consists of the Foreign Ministers of Member States, who usually meet only twice a year; decisions are taken in their place and name by a body of high-ranking national officials known as the Ministers' Deputies. These meet for a week to ten days every month.

Article 17 of the Statute empowers the Committee of Ministers 'to set up advisory committees or commissions for such specific purposes as it may deem desirable'; considerable use has been made of this facility. It is the usual practice for the Ministers, when confronted with a Recommendation of the Assembly on a technical subject, to entrust its examination to such a committee of governmental experts. Such committees have been constituted in eight clearly defined sectors: human rights, social and economic problems, education and cultural co-operation, youth, public health, protection of the natural and man-made environment, local authorities and legal affairs.

*Parliamentary Assembly*

The Assembly consists of 154 representatives from the 19 member countries. The size of delegations varies from 18 (United Kingdom, Federal Republic of Germany, Italy and France) to three (Luxembourg, Cyprus, Malta and Iceland) according to the population of the member concerned. Representatives are elected by Parliament from among its members or are appointed from among the members of Parliament in such a manner as it shall decide, and, although they speak and vote in all freedom, according to their conscience and convictions as individuals, their party affiliations are taken into account so as to mirror the strength of the democratic parties in their particular national assemblies. Five international political groups, namely the Christian Democrat group, the Socialist group, the Liberal group, the Group of Independent Representatives and the Communist group have been formally recognized. Each of them has a chairman, who may initiate discussions or appoint spokesmen in Assembly debates. Representatives must be Members of Parliament. Each representative is entitled to a substitute who may speak and vote in his stead.

A proposal in its final form may be either a Recommendation or a Resolution. The former, which must receive a two-thirds majority of representatives present and voting is, after adoption, communicated by the President of the Assembly to the Committee of Ministers for their decision. A Resolution may be adopted by a simple majority only. It gives formal expression to the opinion of the Assembly on a particular point.

The first President of the Parliamentary Assembly was Mr. Paul-Henri Spaak (Belgium). Following his resignation in 1951, Mr. François de Menthon (France) was elected to the post, and was succeeded in 1954 by Mr. Guy Mollet (France). Mr. Fernand Dehousse (Belgium) was elected to replace Mr. Mollet in April 1956, and was re-elected in April 1957 and April 1958. The President from April 1959 until his death seven months later was the Rt. Hon. John Edwards (United Kingdom). In 1960 Mr. Per Federspiel (Denmark) was elected; he was succeeded in 1963 by M. Pierre Pflimlin (France). Sir Geoffrey de Freitas (U.K.), was elected President in May 1966. He was succeeded in May 1969 by Mr. Olivier Reverdin (Switzerland), whose office expired in May 1972. M. Giuseppe Vedovato (Italy) was elected President in May 1972, succeeded by Mr. Karl Czernetz (Austria) in April 1975.

*Joint Committee*

The task of co-ordinating the work of the two principal organs of the Council of Europe devolves mainly on the Joint Committee. This is a joint consultative committee, without power to take executive decisions. It is composed of members of the Assembly and of the Committee of Ministers.

*European Commission and Court of Human Rights*

The European Convention for the Protection of Human Rights and Fundamental Freedoms entered into force on 3 September 1953. It has been ratified by Austria, Belgium, Cyprus, Denmark, France, Federal Republic of Germany, Greece, Iceland, Ireland, Italy, Luxembourg, Malta, the Netherlands, Norway, Sweden, Switzerland, Turkey, and the United Kingdom.

As a result of the entry into force of the Convention, the Commission of Human Rights was established on 18 May 1954, when its members were elected by the Committee of Ministers in accordance with the procedure laid down in the Convention (Article 21).

The Commission adopted its Rules of Procedure on 2 April 1955. These Rules were revised in December 1974. The Commission is competent to hear, according to Article 24 of the Convention, complaints between Contracting Parties and also, subject to the conditions laid down in Article 25, complaints by individuals against Contracting Parties. The latter competence was achieved on 5 July 1955 after the sixth acceptance of the optional clause concerned but it is restricted to claims against the Contracting Parties who have accepted this competence, i.e., to date Austria, Belgium, Denmark, Federal Republic of Germany, Iceland, Ireland. Italy, Luxembourg, the Netherlands, Norway, Sweden, Switzerland, and the U.K., including nine non-metropolitan territories. The Commission has up to now received about 8,000 of these 'individual applications', of which about 160 so far have been ruled admissible. There have also been several inter-State applications. The President of the Commission is Mr. James Fawcett (United Kingdom).

The European Court of Human Rights was constituted in 1959 after eight States accepted its compulsory jurisdiction (Article 46). To date, fourteen States have accepted this jurisdiction, Austria, Belgium, Denmark, France, the Federal Republic of Germany, Iceland, Ireland, Italy, Luxembourg, the Netherlands, Norway, Sweden, Switzerland and the United Kingdom. The judges are elected by the Parliamentary Assembly from a list of persons nominated by the member States of the Council of Europe. Cases may be referred to the Court by the Commission and/or a State, on termination of proceedings before the Commission. Judgments of the Court are final and binding. The Court may in certain circumstances afford "just satisfaction" to the victim of a violation of the Convention. To date, the Court has given twenty-six judgments. The Court may give advisory opinions at the request of the Committee of Ministers. Mr. Giorgio Balladore Pallieri (Italian) is the acting President.

*Council for Cultural Co-operation (CCC)*

The CCC was created in 1962 to draw up proposals concerning the cultural policy of the Council of Europe, to co-ordinate and give effect to the overall educational and cultural programme and to allocate the resources of the Cultural Fund. In accordance with the European Cultural Convention, its membership includes not only the 19 member States of the Council of Europe but also Finland, the Holy See and Spain, which have acceded to this Convention.

The assets of the Cultural Fund are distinct from those at the disposal of the Council of Europe's general budget. They are used to finance the intergovernmental programme of the C.C.C. in the implementation of which non-governmental organizations play their part. The budget of the Fund for 1974 amounted to some £475,000.

Since 1970 the programme of the CCC has been geared to the two concepts of Permanent Education and Cultural Development, as guidelines for helping governments to adapt the educational and cultural systems of Europe to the needs of European society twenty years ahead and to achieve a greater harmonization between them. Particular attention is given in education to curriculum development, to the initial and continued training of educationalists, to the impact of the new educational technology and to assessment and guidance facilities. In the cultural field the programme deals in particular with the management of cultural affairs at national and local level and with the factors determining the cultural enrichment of the individual: facilities, animation methods, programmes, etc.

Important work is also being done in the field of educational documentation and research (EUDISED project).

Youth problems are under constant review. In 1972, the European Youth Centre which had operated on an experimental basis until 1971, moved into a residential building especially designed and built for it. A European Youth Foundation, the creation of which was decided by the Committee of Ministers in December 1971, began to operate in May 1973. A scheme 'Sport for All' has also been launched within the cultural development programme.

Finally, certain subjects directly affecting understanding between the European nations, such as modern language teaching, history and geography teaching and the revision of textbooks and atlases, and 'European studies' have been investigated in detail.

Numerous publications have been issued, particularly in the series 'Education in Europe'. Moreover, two periodicals: 'Information Bulletin of the Documentation Centre for Education in Europe' and the review 'Education and Culture' are available free of charge to educationalists.

*European Committee on Legal Co-operation (CDCJ)*

This body was set up in 1963 to implement the Council of Europe's legal programme. The committee is composed of delegations (governmental experts) from each of the member States and three representatives of the Parliamentary Assembly (i.e. of the legal committee).

Out of the many items on its agenda, the committee is at present working on several aspects of the reform of family law (legal representation and custody of minors, equality of spouses, etc.), on those concerning the protection of the individual in administrative law, the legal protection of consumers, the protection of the international data flow and the economic and other obstacles to civil proceedings, inter alia abroad.

*The European Committee on Crime Problems (CDPC)*

The CDPC was set up in 1957 to implement the Council of Europe's programme in the field of penal law, penology and criminology. It is composed of a delegation from each Member State; it operates through a number of select committees and working groups and is assisted by the Criminological Scientific Council.

Among its present activities are decriminalization, remand in custody, economic criminality, female criminality, crimes of violence, control of fire-arms, hardcore offenders in prisons and the theft of art objects.

The CDPC has over the years elaborated a series of Conventions, such as the Extradition Convention, the Convention for the Suppression of Terrorism and the Convention on Mutual Assistance in Criminal Matters.

*Secretariat-General*

The Secretariat-General (about 750 officials, drawn from the Member States) is governed partly by the Statute, partly by internal Administrative Regulations. The Statute provides that the Secretary-General, the Deputy Secretary-General and the Clerk to the Assembly shall be appointed by the Consultative Assembly on the recommendation of the Committee of Ministers.

### SURVEY OF ACHIEVEMENTS

On 6 May 1976, the Committee of Foreign Ministers of the Council of Europe adopted a five-year plan of intergovernmental co-operation to be undertaken by the 19-nation Organization in Strasbourg. The plan, which is to be reviewed every two years to take account of political developments and progress achieved, covers eight key areas: human rights, social and socio-economic questions, education and culture, youth, public health, environment and regional planning, local and regional government, legal co-operation. The implementation of this programme will result in the conclusion of new European agreements and charters as well as in the pooling of national experience and resources.

The Council's work has ranged very widely, from matters of major political and economic concern to such technical questions as the exchange of television programmes and co-operation in the punishment of road traffic offences. In general, it may be said that the guiding principles behind the Council's 'legislative' work, as exemplified in its series of more than 90 European Conventions and Agreements, are to standardize national laws as much as possible in particular fields, and to make the collective resources of Member countries available to all their citizens on a footing of equality. In the legal field, the adoption of the European Convention on the Suppression of Terrorism which was signed by 17 member* States in 1977. Of particular significance also in 1977 was the adoption of a European Convention on the Legal Status of Migrant Workers as well as the adoption of a Resolution on Women's employment.

In the political field the Assembly holds regular debates on general policy and formulates foreign policy recommendations for the guidance of the Ministers. It has also had much to say on the internal organization of Europe: The Council played an important role in securing the establishment of the European Coal and Steel Community, and various specialized bodies dealing with, *inter alia*, agriculture, civil aviation and posts and telecommunications. Particularly close relations are maintained with the OECD and with the European Communities (European Economic Community, European Coal and Steel Community, European Atomic Energy Community). An annual joint meeting is held between the Parliamentary Assembly and the European Parliament of the 'Nine'. The majority of European (and some world) inter-governmental organizations submit regular reports for debate by the Parliamentary Assembly, which has long been recognized as the 'Forum of Europe'.

The Committee of Ministers has discussed, on several occasions, the follow-up to the Final Act of the Helsinki Conference. In the course of these discussions there was a wide convergence of views, particularly in the preparation of the Belgrade meeting.

The Parliamentary Assembly also had many important debates on this subject.

Through the initiative of the Council of Europe a number of Ministerial Conferences (Education, Preservation and Rehabilitation of the Cultural Heritage of Sites and Monuments, Regional Planning, Environment, Family Affairs, and Labour and Social Affairs, Justice) have been set up which have special working relationships with the Council of Europe. The Council continues to provide assistance to the Conferences and makes use of their findings. The Conference of Local and Regional Authorities of Europe (CLRAE), which has its own Charter but functions within the framework of the Council, enables local authorities to play a more direct part in developing European unity. One of its chief activities is regional planning on the European scale. The Conference of Local and Regional Authorities of Europe meets every year.

The Council's work in the social field has centred on obtaining full reciprocity and equality of treatment in matters of social security, on an extensive public health programme which includes the grant of medical fellowships to enable doctors and para-medical staff to acquaint themselves with new techniques in other countries, and on the preparation of a European Pharmacopœia. The European Social Charter, which came into force in 1965, goes some way towards guaranteeing internationally certain economic and social rights.

The establishment of the Resettlement Fund was a very noteworthy achievement for the Council of Europe and in 1976 it celebrated 20 years of its existence.

With 15 member States, the main objective of the Fund is to give financial aid,* particularly in the spheres of housing, vocational training, and regional planning and regional development.

The value of loans granted by the Resettlement Fund since its inception total 330 million U.S. dollars.

*President of the Parliamentary Assembly:* Karl Czernetz.

*Secretary-General:* Georg Kahn-Ackermann. *Deputy Secretary-General:* Sforza Galeazzo Sforza; *Clerk to the Assembly:* John Priestman. *Address:* Council of Europe, 67006 Strasbourg-Cedex, France. Phone: (88) 614961. *Telex:* 870943.

* Excluding Ireland and Malta.

* Refugees, repatriated persons, migrants and population surpluses.

# THE EUROPEAN COMMUNITY

THE 'Common Market' which the United Kingdom joined at the tbeginning of 1973 formally consists of three Communities: he European Coal and Steel Community (ECSC); the European Economic Community (EEC); and the European Atomic Energy Community (Euratom). The ECSC was established by the Treaty of Paris, signed on 18 April 1951 and in force from 23 June 1952; the EEC and Euratom were established by the Treaties of Rome, signed on 25 March 1957 and in force from 1 January 1958.

These three Communities are composed of identical Member States: at present Belgium, Denmark, Germany, France, Ireland, Italy, Luxembourg, the Netherlands and the United Kingdom; and their institutional structures were amalgamated in July 1967 under the Merger Treaty of 8 April 1965. They are therefore usually known, together, as the 'European Community'.

*Origins of the Community*

The 'Schuman declaration' of 9 May 1950 is generally regarded as the genesis of the European Community. Acting upon a draft drawn up by the then head of the French national planning board, Jean Monnet, the French Foreign Secretary Robert Schuman proposed 'to place the whole of the production of coal and steel in France and Germany under a common high authority in an organization open to the participation of the other countries of Europe.' Six countries—Belgium, France, Germany, Italy, Luxembourg and the Netherlands—entered into negotiations, and within a year had signed the Treaty of Paris.

Under the Treaty a common market for coal, iron ore, steel and scrap was created (coal, iron-ore and scrap on 10 February 1953, steel on 10 May 1953 and special steels on 1 August 1954): customs duties, quantitative restrictions and other barriers to trade **were then largely abolished** between the six Member States.

Meanwhile, on 24 October 1950, the French Prime Minister René Pleven had suggested the creation of a European Defence Community, and an EDC Treaty was signed in Paris by the six Member States of the ECSC on 27 May 1952. On 30 August 1954, however, it was rejected in the French National Assembly on a procedural vote. The EDC proposals were shelved, as was the draft treaty for a European Political Community, covering foreign policy.

The success of the ECSC, however, encouraged the preparation of plans for further integration in the economic field. At the beginning of June 1955 the foreign ministers of the ECSC states met at Messina, and asked the Belgian representative, Paul Henri Spaak, to prepare a report on a complete merger of the six economies, and also on a common organization for the development of nuclear energy. A treaty-drafting conference was agreed upon a year later; and on 25 March 1957 the Rome Treaties were signed, establishing the EEC and Euratom.

*The Community and the United Kingdom*

The United Kingdom had declined to participate in the negotiations that led to the establishment of the ECSC; but an Agreement of Association with the Community was signed on 21 December 1954. This set up machinery for regular consultations in a Council of Association between the British Government, the National Coal Board and the Iron and Steel Board on the one hand, and the ECSC High Authority on the other. In 1957 an agreement was reached in the Council for mutual steel tariff reductions which was implemented in February of the following year.

Following the Messina conference in 1955, a representative of the British Government attended the early meeting of the Spaak Committee. The U.K., however, did not join in the formation of the EEC and Euratom. Instead, the British Government proposed the creation of a wider European Free Trade Area, and negotiations were started within the framework of the Organization for European Economic Co-operation (OEEC). The result was the formation in 1960 of a free trade area (the EFTA) comprising the seven non-EEC members of the OEEC: Austria, Denmark, Norway, Portugal, Sweden, Switzerland and the United Kingdom, (Finland became an associate member of EFTA in March 1961, and Iceland a full member in March 1970).

There followed a period in which attempts were made to 'build bridges' between the Six (the Community) and the Seven (the EFTA). In August 1961 these culminated in requests by Ireland, Denmark and the United Kingdom—followed by Norway in April 1962—for negotiations aimed at eventual membership of the Community. At the end of 1961 Austria, Sweden, and Switzerland also applied for association with the Community.

Negotiations between the U.K. and the Community opened in Brussels on 8 November 1961, and continued throughout 1962. On 13 January 1963, however, the French President de Gaulle declared at a press conference that Britain was not ready for Community membership; and on 29 January the negotiations were broken off. On 10 May 1967, Denmark, Ireland and the United Kingdom submitted a formal application for Community membership, followed by Norway on 21 July. The Community's Council of Ministers, however, were unable to agree on the opening of negotiations, and the applications were allowed to 'lie on the table'.

On 1 and 2 December 1969 a summit meeting of the Heads of State or Government of the six Community countries was held at the Hague; and this agreed in principle to the enlargement of the Community. Accordingly, on 20 June 1970, membership negotiations were opened in Luxembourg between the Community Member States and Denmark, Ireland, Norway and the United Kingdom.

On 22 January 1972, the Accession Treaties to the Community were signed. A referendum in Ireland approved membership on 10 May; and the same result was obtained in a Danish referendum on 2 October; but in Norway membership was rejected in a referendum on 26 September. In the U.K. the European Communities Act received the Royal Assent on 17 October 1972. On 1 January 1973 Denmark, Ireland and the United Kingdom thus became Member States of the European Community.

United Kingdom membership was confirmed by referendum on 5 June 1975.

*Community Institutions*

The European Community is administered by four main institutions: the Commission, the Council of Ministers, the European Parliament and the Court of Justice.

In July 1967 the High Authority of the ECSC and the Commissions of the EEC and Euratom were amalgamated to form the single Community Commission. Today it consists of 13 members—two each from France, Germany, Italy and the United Kingdom, one each from Belgium, Denmark, Ireland, Luxembourg and the Netherlands. Commissioners are appointed for a four-year renewable term by the national governments; but once appointed, they are pledged to act independently in the Community interest. The Commission President from the beginning of 1977 is the former British Cabinet Minister, Roy Jenkins. Decisions of the Commission are reached, where necessary, by simple majority vote.

The staff of the Commission, largely stationed in Brussels and Luxembourg, numbers some 7,300, including translators and interpreters. There are 19 Directorates-General[1] (each Commissioner is responsible for one or more of them); and ten specialized services.[2]

The *Council of Ministers* comprises one representative of ministerial rank from each of the nine Member States, the particular ministers at any one meeting depending on the subject under discussion. The Presidency of the Council is held for six-month terms by the Member States, in the alphabetic order of their names in their respective languages (e.g. for the first half of 1977 the United Kingdom; for the second half Belgique/Belgie; for the first half of 1978 Danmark; for the second half of 1978 Deutschland).

Council decisions are normally taken unanimously—since the 'Luxembourg agreement' of 28 January 1966 there has been an understanding that no Member State will be outvoted where a vital national interest is concerned. Under Article 148 of the EEC Treaty, however, provision is made for voting by simple majority, or by weighted, qualified majority. For weighted voting, France, Germany, Italy and the U.K. have ten votes each, Belgium and the Netherlands have five eache Denmark and Ireland have three each, and Luxembourg two, Out of the total vote of 58, 41 are needed for a qualified majority; in certain cases there must also be at least six Member States voting in favour.

Much of the detailed preparatory work for the Council—and in practice much of the decision-taking—is carried out by the Committee of Permanent Representatives (Coreper). These are the Member States' 'ambassadors' to the Community. Detailed preparatory work is also carried out within the context of the Council by working parties consisting of representatives from the appropriate national ministries and departments.

The Council has its own Secretariat, consisting of about 1,200 officials, including linguistic staff, mostly stationed in Brussels.

The *European Parliament* (called the 'Assembly' in the Treaties) currently consists of 198 Members, chosen by, and from among the Members of the nine national parliaments. France, Germany, Italy and the UK send 36 Members each; Belgium and the Netherlands 14 each; Denmark and Ireland 10 each; and Luxembourg six. The political balance of each national delegation usually reflects that of the home parliament: for example, the UK delegation in October 1976 consisted of 18 Labour Members (12 from the House of Commons, six from the House of Lords), 16 Conservatives (12 from the House of Commons, four from the House of Lords), one Liberal (from the House of Commons) and one Member of the Scottish National Party (from the House of Commons).

Full sittings of the Parliament take place, on average, for one week in the month, either in Strasbourg or in Luxembourg. The main working units of the Parliament, however, are the twelve specialized standing committees, which each meet for about four days in the month, usually in Brussels. The committees are: Political Affairs; Legal Affairs; Economic and Monetary Affairs; Budgets; Social Affairs, Employment and Education; Agriculture; Regional Policy, Regional Planning and Transport; Environment, Public Health

[1] I External relations; II Economic & Financial Affairs; III Industry & Technology; IV Competition; V Social Affairs; VI Agriculture; VII Transport; VIII Development & Co-operation; IX Personnel & Administration; X Information; XI Internal Market; XII Research, Science & Education; XIII Dissemination of Technical & Scientific Information; (XIV now no longer in existence); XV Financial Institutions and taxation; XVI Regional Policy; XVII Energy & Euratom Safeguards and Control; XIX CommunityBudgets; XX Financial Control.

[2] Secretariat-General; Legal Service; Spokesman's group; Statistical Office; Joint Research Establishments; Administration of the Customs Union; Environmental and Consumer Service; Euratom Supply Agency; Security Office; and Official Publications Office.

and Consumer Protection; Energy and Research; External Economic Relations; Development and Cooperation; and Rules of Procedure and Petitions. During 1976 a Control Sub-Committee of the Budgets Committee was established to supervise Community expenditure in conjunction with the new Court of Auditors (i.e. to act as a Public Accounts Committee).

The Members of the Parliament sit in six political groups (membership in January 1978 in parentheses): Communists and Allies (17); Socialists (65); Christian Democrats (53); European Progressive Democrats (19); European Conservatives (18); and Liberals and Democrats (23). There are also three independents.

The President of the Parliament is elected by its Members, for a one-year renewable term, in March. Parliamentary business is controlled by the 'enlarged bureau' consisting of the President, the 12 Vice-presidents (elected, by custom, on the basis of political and national balance) and the six leaders of the political groups.

The permanent secretariat of the Parliament, stationed mainly in Luxembourg, numbers some 1,500, including linguistic staff.

Article 138 of the EEC Treaty provides for the Parliament to be elected, eventually, by direct universal suffrage. A Community Act was signed in September 1976 providing for the first elections to be held, probably in 1978 or 1979. The Parliament is to be enlarged to 410 Members, distributed: France, Italy, the United Kingdom and Germany, 81 each; the Netherlands 25; Belgium 24; Denmark 16; Ireland 15; and Luxembourg six. For the first elections, each country will be able to decide separately on the system of voting, but work will begin on devising a common system for later elections. The elected Parliament will have a fixed term of five years.

Decisions on the distribution of the U.K.'s 81 seats between England, Scotland, Wales and Northern Ireland; the system of voting; the franchise; the method of drawing up constituency boundaries; election expenses, etc. are now being taken by Parliament at Westminster. The Government published a Bill on 24 June 1977, which was given a second reading on July 7. It was given another second reading on 24 November; and on 13 December the House of Commons decided in favour of the traditional "first-past-the-post" system of voting for Britain.

The *Court of Justice*, situated in Luxembourg, consists of nine judges, assisted by four advocates-general, appointed by the Member States for six-year renewable terms. Under Article 167 of the EEC Treaty, they are chosen from among persons, irrespective of nationality, 'whose independence is beyond doubt'. Decisions of the Court are taken by simple majority.

The Court has some 250 officials, including linguistic staff.

In addition to these four main institutions, there are over 70 consultative and specialized Community bodies.

The most important of these is the *Economic and Social Committee*, a 144-member body representing employers' organizations, trade unions and other—including consumer—interests in equal numbers. France, Germany, Italy and the U.K. have 24 seats each; Belgium and the Netherlands 12 each; Denmark and Ireland nine each; and Luxembourg six. There is a similar body, the 81-member *Consultative Committee*, which fulfils a similarr ole for matters covered by the ECSC Treaty.

Other bodies include: the Monetary Committee; the Economic Policy Committee; the Committee of Central Bank Governors; the Committee of the European Social Fund; the Standing Committee on Employment; the Administrative Commission for the Social Security of Migrant Workers; the Transport Committee; the Scientific and Technical Committee of Euratom; the Nuclear Research Consultative Committee; the Scientific and Technical Research Committee (CREST); the 'Article 113' Committee covering trade negotiations with third countries; the 17 agricultural management committees; and now the Committee for Regional Policy and the Regional Fund Committee. For the most part, these bodies consist of experts appointed by national governments to advise and co-ordinate policy with the Commission.

There is also the independent *European Investment Bank* established under Article 129 of the EEC Treaty. It operates on a non-profit-making basis; and is capitalized by subscriptions from the Member States—current capital 3,543·75 million EUA (£2,335 m.). Funds are borrowed on capital markets both within and outside the Community.

Borrowers from the Bank can be private firms, public enterprises or financial institutions, but projects must assist in the development of less advanced regions or be of some other Community interest. In addition, under the terms of different association or cooperation agreements with the Community, EIB activities have gradually been extended to more than 60 other countries outside the Community, most of them in the "third world".

In 1976 the Bank's total financing operations amounted to 1,273·3 million EUA (£839 m.), of which 1,086 m. EUA (£716·6 m.) were for investment in the Community. 187·3 million EUA (£123·4 m.) outside.

*Legislation.* Under the Treaties, proposals for legislation or action within the context of the Community emanate from the Commission. In practice, the Commission often prepares proposals in response to resolutions of the Council of Ministers, or of the 'European Council'—the name given to the now regular summit conference of heads of state or government. The European Parliament is also able to call for action by the Commission through the preparation of an 'own initiative' report by one of its specialized committees.

Commission proposals are, in any case, usually tabled formally only after discussion with interest groups, the Parliament's committees, etc. They are then sent to the Council of Ministers, which is in some cases obliged by the Treaties to, and in most cases does, forward them immediately to the Parliament for its opinion. Where appropriate, the Economic and Social Committee (or the Consultative Committee) is also consulted. In the Parliament the proposals are first discussed in one of the specialized committees, and a report prepared for debate in full session. The Commission is present throughout.

The proposals are also discussed in the Council of Ministers: probably by a working party first, then by the Coreper, and finally (if controversial) by the appropriate ministers. Again, the Commission is present throughout. The final decision is reached by the Council on the Commission's text. Under Article 149 of the EEC Treaty, the Commission may alter its original text at any time before the Council reaches its final decision 'in particular where the Assembly has been consulted on that proposal'.

Though the majority of Community decisions are reached in this way, the Commission has certain direct powers, notably in the field of agricultural management, and when acting as the High Authority of the ECSC.

The results of the Community legislative process can be *regulations*, directly applicable like national legislation; or *directives*, with implementation left to the national legislative process.

*Constitutional Functions.* Though the Commission is appointed by the Member States, it is thereafter directly responsible to the European Parliament. The Commission must make an annual report to the Parliament; and individual Commissioners must attend sittings of Parliament to answer oral questions, reply to debates, etc. The Commission must also reply to Members' questions for written answer.

Parliament also has the power to dismiss the Commission as a whole by a motion of censure. This must be passed by a two-thirds majority of those voting and with over 99 votes in favour (i.e., a majority of total Members).

As well as the initiator of Community legislation, the Commission is also the 'guardian' of the Treaties and of Community decisions. It is empowered to take legal proceedings against, for example, firms for breach of fair competition rules, and even against national governments.

The final arbiter on all legal questions under the Community Treaties is the Court of Justice. It deals with disputes between Member States; between the Member States and Community institutions; and between Community institutions, and firms, individuals, etc. Increasingly it also interprets Community law at the request of national courts.

The Council of Ministers acts collectively as a Community institution; its Members, however, are individually responsible to the nine national parliaments. A number of these parliaments have therefore established formal procedures for scrutinizing proposed Community legislation in advance of Council decisions. In the U.K., for example, the House of Lords has set up a Select Committee on the European Communities, and the House of Commons a Select Committee on European Secondary Legislation (usually called the scrutiny committees). These report to their respective Houses as to whether proposals raise important questions of policy, principle or legal effect.

To a very limited extent the Council of Ministers is also responsible to the European Parliament. By convention, Ministerial representatives of the Council Presidency attend Parliament sittings, answer questions from Members and occasionally reply to debates together with the Commission.

*Budgetary Power.* The Council of Ministers is the principal decision-taking body of the Community. In the budgetary field, however, it now shares power with the European Parliament. Under a revision of Article 203 of the EEC Treaty in April 1970, Parliament has from the beginning of 1975 had final powers of amendment over the 'non-obligatory' portion of the Community budget—about 25 per cent of the total in 1978. A further revision of the Treaty signed in July 1975 also gives the Parliament formal powers to reject the Budget as a whole.

In the event of disagreement between the Council and Parliament on budgetary matters, there is a formal 'conciliation' procedure, which can also be activated on all legislative proposals "with budgetary consquences".

The July 1975 Treaty also provided for the establishment of a completely independent Court of Auditors to supervise the management of Community funds.

*Community Policies: Internal*

The first economic purpose of the Community is the creation of a single market out of the separate economies of the nine Member States.

*The Common Market* for coal, iron-ore, steel and scrap was established by the original six Member States under the ECSC Treaty. Under the EEC Treaty, customs duties on all trade among the six was abolished by July 1968, eighteen months ahead of schedule. Those involving the three new Member States were eliminated by July 1977. All quantitative restrictions on trade between the six were abolished by the end of 1961, and have now also been eliminated by the new Member States.

The removal of non-tariff barriers to trade—in particular those arising from differences in law between different countries—is a continuing process. Under the ECSC Treaty, discrimination in freight-charges (e.g., extra charges at frontiers) were abolished, and international through-rates applied. Similar arrangements under the EEC Treaty were in effect by 1961.

In the field of fiscal frontiers, all the nine Member States had adopted some form of Value Added Tax by 1 April 1973, and steps have been taken to establish a common VAT base. Other indirect taxes (e.g., excise duties) are ultimately to be made more uniform.

In order to remove technical barriers to trade—divergent specification standards, health and safety rules, etc.—a programme of harmonization was adopted in 1969 and another in 1973. By February 1975 the Council of Ministers had agreed over 60 directives in this field.

Linked to the removal of institutional barriers to trade is the Community's *competition policy*. Under the ECSC and EEC Treaties, the Commission is empowered to take action against cartel agreements and practices—whether by privately or publicly-owned bodies—if they distort trade between Member States: e.g., price discrimination, price fixing, market-sharing, unjustifiable restrictions of output or discriminatory supply conditions. The Commission has widespread powers of investigation and can, if necessary, impose fines. Since 1972 many types of national discrimination in awarding public contracts have been barred: major public civil engineering and building contracts must be advertised in the Community's *Official Journal*. The Commission can also take steps to prevent the abuse of dominant or monopoly positions (again by privately or publicly-owned bodies). Under the ECSC Treaty, mergers need prior authorization, and it is intended that this should eventually apply generally.

*Free movement of persons*. This was established in the original six Community countries by 1939, and has applied to the new Member States since their accession at the beginning of 1973. Any national of a Community Member State can look for and take a job in another Member State without a work permit and with the right of residence for both self and family. Discrimination in recruitment, pay, terms of employment, etc., on grounds of nationality is prohibited (except in government service); and social security rights are preserved on movement between Community countries.

Some 40 Community directives have also begun to remove national restrictions on the *right of establishment:* i.e., the ability to set up a business in another country. The Community is also promoting the mutual recognition of professional qualifications, degrees, etc.

The *free movement of capital*, through the abolition of exchange controls is one of the EEC Treaty objectives. The original six Member States removed restrictions on certain capital movements within the Community by 1962, and the new Member States will have done the same by 1978. International monetary instability, however, has recently obliged several Member States to make use of the provision in the Treaties for 'protective measures in the field of capital movements', so that the establishment of a completely liberalized Community capital market is unlikely in the near future.

*Industrial Policy*. Under the ECSC Treaty the Community's coal industry was substantially restructured during the contraction of the late fifties and sixties and in 1977, under the Commission's 'Davignon' plan for steel, a system of minimum prices and reference prices was introduced to help EEC steelmakers meet the recession, as part of a similar restructuring of the steel industry. Proposals are also under discussion to give similar help to sectors in special difficulty, e.g. shipbuilding and textiles. EEC countries have also agreed in principle to collaborate in the production of civil aircraft and in 1976 a common programme of research and development was agreed in the data processing sector to supplement national programmes.

The European Atomic Energy Community ("Euratom") founded in 1958 made little progress until 1973 when its scope was extended to cover a wider field of scientific research. Euratom now concentrates on a number of agreed common scientific projects which are largely carried out under contract by national research institutes and by the Community's own Joint Research Centre facilities at Geel (Belgium), Karlsruhe (Germany), Ispra (Italy) and Petten (Netherlands).

The Community's industrial policy is associated with the harmonization of company law and of safety standards, consumer protection, environmental policy and state aids to industry. In the case of cars, by 1976 safety regulations relating to manufacture had been almost entirely placed on a Community footing.

*Social Policy*. The ECSC is pledged under its Treaty 'to promote the improvement of the living and working conditions of the labour force in each of the industries under its jurisdiction', and in the EEC Treaty there are similar objectives for the Community economy in general. One important application under the ECSC has been action through the Retraining and Settlement Fund to help workers in the Community's coal and steel industries meet the effects of increased competition, restructuring and technological change. The Fund provides resettlement grants, tiding-over allowances and wage-supplements in new jobs for up to two years, the other half being met by the Member State concerned. Up to the end of 1973 over half a million workers had been helped by the fund. The European Social Fund, established under the EEC Treaty, has provided similar help for workers in other industries. Up to the end of 1973 the Social Fund and Member States had aided more than two million workers in such industries as shipbuilding and textiles. Since 1972, retraining grants can be given in advance of actual redundancies.

Under the ECSC Treaty, the Community has also contributed towards the construction of over 140,000 houses for coal and steel workers. Under all three Treaties there has been both research and legislation to improve health and safety standards. At the end of 1973 the Community agreed on a three-year programme to help migrant workers, promote equal pay, etc.

In 1976 the Court of Justice held that the EEC Treaty on equal pay has direct effect in the member states.

*Regional Policy*. Under the ECSC Treaty, loans have been provided for general industrial development in order to provide new jobs for displaced coal and steel workers. In 1974 the Community agreed to set up a Regional Development Fund with resources of some £540 million over the three years 1975–77. A new fund is being set up under the 1978 Budget. Finance is available for projects which fit in with the national governments' regional development strategies. In addition, regional development projects can obtain low-interest loans from the European Investment Bank.

Regional development aid by a Member State is excluded from the general competition rules banning trade-distorting subsidies. The Commission, however, is empowered to keep system of aid 'under constant review'.

*Agriculture*. This is one of the industries for which the EEC Treaty lays down specific common policies. Each of the Member States, before membership, had its own system for maintaining farm incomes and stabilizing agricultural markets, and the objective of the Common Agricultural Policy (CAP) has been to replace these with a Community system.

The CAP covers most major agricultural products except mutton and lamb, and potatoes. Prices for each product agreed each year by the Council of Ministers are maintained by support buying of surpluses and by variable levies on imports (and refunds on exports) when world prices are lower, export levies when they are higher. The three new Member States are due to apply the CAP in full by 1978.

The CAP also provides finance for structural reforms in

agriculture: modernization, the creation of larger holdings, etc.

In recent years, the CAP has run into a number of difficulties. The first of these has been created by changes in the parities of Member States' currencies: it has been found necessary to introduce special exchange rates and 'compensatory amounts' (i.e., levies and subsidies) on products crossing borders between Member States. Secondly, there has been the problem of surpluses ('mountains'). Finally, there have been rising costs. A complete review of the CAP is now under way.

The EEC Treaty also specifically requires the establishment of a *common Transport policy*. So far, however, action has tended to be piecemeal, and major problems remain unsolved: for example, the liberalization of cross-frontier road haulage.

In 1973 the Council of Ministers adopted an *Action Programme for the Environment*. This includes not only research projects, but also proposes specific measures of control in areas like the lead content of petrol, waste disposal, pesticides, etc.

Also in 1973, the Commission made proposals for an initial programme of *Consumer Information and Protection*, including action on health and safety standards, unfair sales practices, labelling, etc. Earlier in the year a 25-member Consumers' Consultative Committee was set up, comprising representatives from national consumer associations and similar bodies.

One of the proposals examined by the Spaak committee after the Messina conference of 1955 was for the creation of a European University. The proposal was shelved until 1972, when the then six Member States signed an agreement establishing a postgraduate European University Institute in Florence. A Community Vocational Training Centre has also been opened in Berlin. Other elements of a Community *Training and Education* policy are under examination.

*Economic and Monetary.* The Member States of the Community are committed by the EEC Treaty to 'co-ordinate their economic policies'. A Short-Term Economic Policy Committee of national officials was established in 1960, and a similar Medium-Term Economic Policy Committee in 1964 (these are now combined in the Economic Policy Committee). The Commission itself publishes annual economic forecasts; and in 1967 the Council of Ministers adopted the first Community five-year economic programme. This, however, like its subsequent updated versions, was purely indicative.

Upheavals in the international monetary system during the late 1960s prompted the Community to plan jointacti on in this field. In February 1970 a Community reserves pool of over £1,000 million was established to provide 2–3 month aid to any Member State in difficulties. The Council of Ministers, in the same month, appointed a committee to investigate the creation of a common currency and common reserves. Its report (the Werner Report) was published just over a year later, and envisaged a three-stage plan leading to full economic and monetary union by 1980. The plan was launched in 1971, and in 1972 both the existing Community and the applicant States narrowed the margins of fluctuation of their currencies to create 'the snake in the tunnel'. Almost immediately, however, the Pound was floated, and both the U.K. and Ireland left the 'snake'. In the following year the Italian Lira floated and in 1974 the French Franc. The Franc returned in 1975 for a brief period, but is now floating again.

Despite these setbacks, a European Monetary Co-operation Fund was set up in 1973, and in 1974 agreement was reached to launch an initial 3,000 million dollar Community loan to help Member States in balance of payments difficulties. and to re-cycle petrodollars. Though the 1980 target date for economic and monetary union still stands officially, new methods of monetary co-operation are now under study.

### *External Relations*

In addition to the removal of internal barriers and the development of common internal policies, the creation of the Community has meant the development of common policies towards the rest of the world.

First, a *common trade policy* has involved the replacement of existing national tariffs by a single Community tariff. By the end of the ECSC transitional period, on 10 February 1958, a common tariff on steel imports from non-Community countries (based on the formula 'Benelux plus two') was established. The EEC common external tariff (CET), based on the average of the six national tariffs it superseded, was achieved in parallel with internal free trade by July 1968. There is a common list of products that can be imported freely, a common procedure for quotes, a joint anti-dumping policy and common rules on such matters as classification, bonding, etc. The new Member States adjusted to the CET by July 1977.

The Community is also developing a *common aid policy*. One important element is the generalized system of preferences (GSP), under which manufactured products from the less-developed countries are admitted into the Community duty-free, subject to a 'ceiling' for each product. The Community also operates joint programmes of financial aid: these, together with the programmes of Member States individually, make the Community the biggest source of official aid for the less developed world. Most recently, the Community has become a major source of food aid, in particular grain, butter-oil and skimmed milk powder.

One development of great importance has been the steadily growing number of countries with individual *association or trade agreements* with the Community—already over 75.

Greece was the first country to sign an association agreement under Article 238 of the EEC Treaty, on 9 July 1961. Turkey followed on 12 September 1963. In addition, the Yaoundé Convention of 1 July 1963 associated 18 independent states of Africa and Madagascar with the Community under Part IV of the EEC Treaty. A number of Commonwealth countries also reached association agreements with the Community during the 1960s: Nigeria in July 1966, and Kenya, Uganda and Tanzania, under the Arusha Convention of 26 July 1968. Agreements of varying duration were also signed with Morocco, Tunisia, Israel, Spain, Malta, Mauritius, Egypt, Lebanon, Yugoslavia, Cyprus, Uruguay, India, Brazil and the Argentine.

The enlargement of the Community from six to nine Member States made it necessary to negotiate agreements with the seven remaining EFTA countries. By 1977, therefore, an industrial free trade area will come into being covering the nine Community Member States and Austria, Finland, Norway, Sweden and Switzerland (Iceland and Portugal have a longer transition period).

Outside Europe, the Lomé Convention (replacing Yaoundé and Arusha) was signed in February 1974 with 46 African, Caribbean and Pacific (ACP) countries: former Yaoundé countries, 22 Commonwealth countries and a number of others. The Convention came into force in April 1976 and gives the ACP countries free access to Community markets for 96 per cent of their exports; financial assistance of some £1,600 million over the next five years; and commodity agreements for such products as coffee, cotton, copra and iron-ore. The first meeting of the ACP-EEC Council of Ministers was held in Brussels on 14–15 July 1976. Further accessions to the Convention have now brought the number of ACP states to 52.

Agreements of various kinds have been concluded or are under negotiation with several other countries, including India, Pakistan, Sri Lanka, Thailand, Indonesia, the Philippines and Bangladesh. There are now links with 14 Mediterranean countries—special co-operation agreements were signed with the Maghreb countries of Algeria, Morocco and Tunisia in April 1976, and with Egypt, Jordan and Syria on 18 January 1977. An agreement with Israel was signed on 8 February 1977. Australia, Canada and New Zealand benefit from arrangements made in the enlargement negotiations.

In *international negotiations* on matters covered by the treaties, the Community negotiates as a single unit from a common position: in the 1964–67 'Kennedy Round' and the current round of tariff-cutting within the GATT, for example. Where possible, the Community also tries to reach common positions in fields not strictly covered by the treaties. Such a common position was recently achieved in the Conference on Security and Co-operation in Europe (CSCF), and at recent sessions of the UN Law of the Sea Conference.

The Member States, indeed, are now increasingly seeking to co-ordinate their external policies. In 1970, the original six Member States set up the 'Davignon Committee' of the political directors from the Foreign Ministries. This committee (now of nine) meets at least four times a year. There are also regular twice yearly meetings of the Foreign Ministers or Secretaries. Both the Davignon Committee and the Council of Foreign Ministers report regularly to the European Parliament, which holds debates on foreign policy and defence matters as well as economic subjects.

### *Community Finance*

The operating expenditure of the Community in 1978 will be some £8¼ billion, about 70 per cent of it on running the Common Agricultural Policy. The High Authority of the ECSC obtained its income from direct levies on coal and steel capacity, and until 1971 the EEC and Euratom were financed by various national contributions. At the end of 1969, however, a marathon sitting of the Council of Ministers agreed that from the beginning of 1975 the Community would be self-financing. Its income would derive from: the levies on agricultural imports—these became the Community's 'own resources' from 1971; customs duties on other imports from outside the Community; and the product of (up to) a 1 per cent Value Added Tax.

Failure to arrive in time at a common VAT base, however, has meant that a proportion of Community expenditure has, until the end of 1977, been financed out of GNP-related national contributions. The 1978 Budget is the first to be financed entirely out of the Community's own resources. As a result of re-negotiations by the U.K. during 1974, a new correcting mechanism has also been established, providing refunds for any Member State whose share of the budget is significantly in excess of its share of Community GNP.

Community financial transactions have, up to 1978 been expressed in terms of the unit of account (u.a.). This is fixed at the value of one 'pre-Smithsonian' U.S. Dollar (i.e., its value before devaluation in 1971, or 0·88867088 gram of fine gold). In relation to payments into and out of the Community Budget, the Pound Sterling has been worth 2·4 u.a. For calculating agricultural prices, however, the Pound (the so-called 'Green Pound') has been worth around 1·75 u.a. The European Investment Bank has used a 'basket' of currencies, weighted to take account of trade, etc. This new European Unit of Account is now replacing the old gold unit in general Community use. It is currently worth about 65p.

*The Future*

The political purpose of the Community, declared in the preamble to the EEC Treaty, is to' lay the foundations of an ever closer unity among the peoples of Europe'. The summit conference at Paris of October 1972 (which included both the current and applicant Member States) proclaimed the objective of 'transforming, before the end of the present decade . . . the whole complex of the relations of Member States into a European Union'. A report on how this is to be effected was prepared by the Belgian Prime Minister, Leo Tindemans, for the summit at the end of 1975.

*Addresses:*

*Commission of the European Communities:* 200 rue de la Loi, 1049 Brussels, Belgium.

*Council of the European Communities:* 170 rue de la Loi, 1040 Brussels, Belgium.

*European Parliament:* Centre Européen, Plateau du Kirchberg, Luxembourg.

The Commission and the Parliament each have an information office in London at 20 Kensington Palace Gardens, W8 4QQ (Tel.: 01-727 8090 and 01-229 9366 respectively).

## EUROPEAN FREE TRADE ASSOCIATION (EFTA)

THE original member-countries of this Association are Austria, Denmark, Norway, Portugal, Sweden, Switzerland, and the United Kingdom (the 'Outer Seven'). It was established on 3 May 1960, following the ratification of the Treaty of Stockholm. An Association agreement with Finland was signed on 27 March 1961 and came into force on 26 June 1961. The Association was set up following the breakdown of negotiations with the six Common Market countries (Belgium, France, German Federal Republic, Italy, Luxembourg and the Netherlands) and the 11 other members of OEEC, for the formation of a European Free Trade Area. From 1 March 1970 Iceland has been a member of EFTA.

The objectives of EFTA are to promote, by abolishing customs tariffs and quantitative restrictions on industrial goods, economic expansion, full employment, increased productivity, the rational use of resources. financial stability, and a higher standard of living; to ensure that trade within EFTA takes place in conditions of fair competition; to avoid significant disparity in the supply of basic materials; and to contribute to the harmonious development of world trade. The principal long-term aim of the EFTA countries is the early establishment of a multilateral association for the removal of trade barriers and closer economic co-operation between the members of the former OEEC, including the members of the EEC.

During 1967 the U.K., Denmark and Norway applied for membership of the EEC and the other EFTA countries declared their intention to participate in an enlarged European market, in a way compatible with their neutral status (Austria, Finland, Sweden, Switzerland) or their special economic position (Portugal). In June 1970 negotiations were begun between the U.K., Denmark and Norway on the terms of their accession to the EEC.

Eighteen months later the negotiations were completed, and on 22 January 1972 the three countries signed the Treaty of Accession to the European Communities. By that time the six other EFTA countries—Austria, Finland, Iceland, Portugal, Sweden and Switzerland—had begun negotiations aimed essentially at establishing free trade in industrial goods between each of them and the enlarged EEC. These negotiations were successfully concluded in July 1972. On the assumption that all the nine agreements are ratified in time, the new arrangements come into force on 1 January 1973. Even before the negotiations were completed tentative discussions were begun between the six EFTA countries not acceding to the EEC about the future of EFTA. They agreed that the Stockholm Convention, appropriately modified, should continue to be the legal instrument for administering free trade between them, and that there would continue to be a need for an executive organ and for a permanent Secretariat.

*Tariffs.* As regards industrial goods, elimination of tariffs was achieved by 31 December 1966, the original timetable which foresaw their final abolition by 1 January 1970 having been accelerated by decision of the Ministerial Council Meeting in Lisbon in May 1963. The main exception to this rule concerns most manufactured imports into Portugal, which is following a slower time-table for tariff reduction and into Iceland which was given a transitional period of ten years for the progressive elimination of its tariffs. The removal of Customs duties applies to all duties of a protective character, only fiscal duties being unaffected. There are special arrangements on some agriculture, fish and marine products, designed to facilitate trade between member countries whose economies depend to a great extent on exports of these products. Bilateral agreements have been concluded to this effect.

Member-states do not have a common external tariff in relation to countries outside the area. 'Origin' rules have therefore been worked out to identify the products of member-countries to which the tariff reductions will apply. Member-countries are also free to take action which they consider necessary for the protection of their essential security interests and their balance of payments. In certain circumstances a member-state may also take action where the application of the Convention leads to serious difficulties in a particular section of industry. There are also provisions in respect of competition, subsidies, and restrictive business practices.

A major part of EFTA's work in recens years has been devoted to the removal of non-tariff barriers to trade such as differing national standards or technical requirements. EFTA's approach is to encourage the work done in more comprehensive international organizations, to harmonize national requirements; and at the same time to reduce the trade impact of the existing differences. To this end it has devised schemes relating to electrical products, pharmaceuticals, pressure vessels, ships' equipment, agricultural machinery and gas appliances.

*Secretary-General:* Bengt Rabaeus; *Deputy Secretary-General:* Alfred Wacker. *Headquarters:* 9–11, rue de Varembé, Geneva, Switzerland.

## INTERNATIONAL CRIMINAL POLICE ORGANISATION (INTERPOL)

FOUNDED Vienna 1923; reconstituted with headquarters in Paris 1946. *Purpose:* Mutual assistance between police authorities of all the different States in the suppression of ordinary law crimes. *Members:* Algeria, Argentina, Australia, Austria, Bahamas, Bahrain, Bangladesh, Belgium, Benin, Bolivia, Brazil, Burma, Burundi, Cameroon, Canda, Central Africa Empire, Chad, Chile, China (Republic of), Colombia, Congo, Costa Rica, Cuba, Cyprus, Denmark, Dominican Republic, Ecuador. Egyptian Arab Republic, El Salvador, Ethiopia, Fiji, Finland, France, Gabon, Federal Germany, Ghana, Greece, Guatemala, Guinea, Guyana, Haiti, Honduras, Iceland, India, Indonesia, Iran, Iraq, Irish Republic, Israel,

Italy, Ivory Coast, Jamaica, Japan, Jordan, Kenya, Khmer Republic, Korea (Republic of), Kuwait, Laos, Lebanon, Lesotho, Liberia, Libya, Liechtenstein, Luxembourg, Madagascar, Malawi, Malaysia, Mali, Malta, Mauritania, Mauritius, Mexico, Monaco, Morocco, Nauru, Nepal, Netherlands, Netherlands Antilles, New Oman, New Zealand, Niger, Nigeria, Norway, Pakistan, Panama, Papua New Guinea, Paraguay, Peru, Philippines, Portugal, Qatar, Romania, Rwanda, Saudi Arabia, Senegal, Seychelles, Sierra Leone, Singapore, Somalia, Spain, Sri Lanka, Sudan, Surinam, Swaziland, Sweden, Switzerland, Syria, Tanzania, Thailand, Togo, Trinidad and Tobago, Tunisia, Turkey, Uganda, United Arab Emirates, United Kingdom, U.S.A., Upper Volta, Uruguay, Venezuela, Yemen (Arab Republic of), Yugoslavia, Zaire, Zambia. *Structure:* General Assembly (which elects President, Vice-Presidents, Executive Committee and the Secretary-General). *Finance:* Contributions from governments. *Activities:* The General Secretariat in Paris co-ordinates the activities of police authorities of the member-states in international affairs and centralizes documentation relative to the movements of international criminals. Controls its own radio network of 53 stations. *Publications:* International Criminal Police Review (ten issues annually, in English, French and Spanish); semi-annual List of Selected Articles, selected from 220 reviews of 53 countries (in English and French); Reports submitted to the General Assembly; Reports submitted to the Commission on Narcotic Drugs and the International Narcotics Control Board. *President: Secretary-General:* J. Nepote. *Address:* International Criminal Police Organization—Interpol, 26 rue Armengaud, 92 Saint Cloud, France. Tel.: 602-5550.

## THE LEAGUE OF ARAB STATES

THE Pact establishing the League of Arab States was signed at Cairo on 22 March 1945. It was the culmination of a long struggle for unity among the many members of the Arab family.

Long before World War I there had been a movement for unity, but the peace settlement of 1919, placing the greater part of the Arab world—Syria, Lebanon, Palestine, Transjordan and Iraq—temporarily under British and French control, came as a check to these aspirations.

As a result, however, of World War II, these mandated territories, excluding Palestine, attained independence. While the war was still in progress, a Conference of Arab States met at Alexandria. Representatives of the Governments of Egypt, Syria, Lebanon, Transjordan, Iraq, Saudi Arabia and Yemen took part in the Conference. A delegation of the Palestinians also attended.

The Pact drafted the framework of the Arab League, the essence of which is that the Arab states, while uniting for joint action, maintain their own individual sovereignty.

The following year the Pact establishing the Arab League on this basis was signed by representatives of Egypt, Lebanon, Syria, Transjordan, Iraq, Saudi Arabia and Yemen.

The purpose of the League is to bring about a closer union, and political and economic collaboration between the different Arabian states. Arising from this an agreement for collective defence and economic co-operation was signed by the Arab states at Cairo in 1950.

The constitution of the Arab League lays down that other Arab countries may join on attaining independence. The League now comprises 21 members—Morocco, Mauritania, Algeria, Tunisia, Libya, Egypt, Sudan, Somalia, Lebanon, Syria, Palestine, Jordan, Iraq, Kuwait, Saudi Arabia, Democratic People's Republic of Yemen, Yemen Arab Republic, Qatar, Bahrain, Oman and the Arab Emirates Federation.

The organization consists of a General Council, Permanent Committees, a general secretariat and some affiliated organizations. The Arab League Council is the highest executive authority representing the member states. Its task is to adopt resolutions and see to it that they are implemented. Its main purpose is to act as mediator in any dispute which may threaten the peace between members or between them and another power. The Council meets in ordinary session twice a year in March and September and in extraordinary session whenever it is deemed necessary.

The permanent committees study the subjects of their specialization and refer them to the Council for approval. There are permanent committees for, political, cultural, social, health, economic, legal and communication affairs, as well as, information, petroleum, financial, administration, and liaison.

The general secretariat is the organ which is in charge of implementing the Council's resolutions. It is headed by the Secretary General who is elected for a five-year term of office, subject to renewal. He is helped by Assistant Secretaries General (elected by the Secretary General). The League Council elects the General.

The General Secretariat comprises departments for political, economic, social, legal, information and communication affairs, in addition to Palestine, financial, protocol and secretariat affairs departments.

The general secretariat's headquarters are in Cairo, and the Secretary General, Mahmoud Riad, has the status of Ambassador. The general secretariat has information offices abroad. The Arab League has a permanent delegation in both New York and Geneva, as well as offices in Washington, San Francisco, Chicago, Dallas, Bonn, London, Paris, Rome, Ottawa, Madrid, Buenos Aires, Brasilia, Santiago, New Delhi and Tokyo. In Nairobi, Dakar and Lagos, there are representatives of the League attached to some Arab Embassies.

Stemming from the Arab League is a defence council, a unified Arab military command, an economic council, an economic unity council, an Arab civil aviation council, an Arab exhibitions authority and an Arab cinematographic authority. There are also Unions of Arab Broadcasting Stations, Air Transport, International Tourism, News Agencies, Telecommunications, Automobile clubs and Tourism, as well as an Arab Agricultural Union, an Arab Scientific Union, an Arab Universities Union, a General Union of Arab Publishers. Arab organizations for standardization, Administrative sciences, social defence against crime, labour, agricultural development, petroleum exporting countries, as well as an Arab educational, cultural and scientific organization. Special Arab agencies, Arab center for the study of arid zones, Arab fund for economic and social development, Arab Academy for maritime transport, industrial development center for Arab states, Arab institute for forestral studies.

The Arab League is committed by its charter and functions to ensure Arab cooperation for the achievement of freedom, security, and progress.

## NORTH ATLANTIC TREATY ORGANIZATION (NATO)

THE North Atlantic Treaty was signed in Washington 4 April 1949, and after ratification by all the parties entered into force on 24 August 1949.

The Treaty has two aspects. In the preamble the parties express their determination to safeguard 'the freedom, common heritage and civilization of their peoples, founded on the principles of democracy, individual liberty and the rule of law'. They, therefore, agree that 'an armed attack against one or more of them in Europe or North America . . . shall be considered an attack against them all' and that if such an attack occurs each of them 'in exercise of the right of individual or collective self-defence recognized by Article 51 of the Charter of the United Nations' will take 'such action as it deems necessary, including the use of armed force . . .'. By Article 2, the parties agree to contribute toward 'the further development of peaceful and friendly international relations by strengthening their free institutions, by bringing about a better understanding of the principles upon which these institutions are founded, and by promoting conditions of stability and well-being'.

The Members are Belgium, Canada, Denmark, France, Federal Republic of Germany (acceded 9 May 1955), Greece (acceded 18 February 1952), Iceland, Italy, Luxembourg, Netherlands, Norway, Portugal, Turkey (acceded 18 February 1952), United Kingdom, and United States.

In March 1947, President Truman declared that the U.S.A. should 'support free peoples who are resisting attempted subjugation by armed minorities or by outside pressure . . .'. This statement, later known as the Truman doctrine, was made in the course of a request to the United

States Congress to appropriate $400 million worth of aid to Greece and Turkey as an emergency measure.

Four-Power negotiations in the Council of Foreign Ministers, where attempts had been made to draft peace treaties, finally broke down in December 1947. After this Mr. Ernest Bevin, the then British Foreign Secretary, had private and informal talks with his American colleague, General George Marshall. Mr. Bevin said he had been forced to reach the conclusion that for the foreseeable future there was no hope of the Kremlin dealing with the West on any normal terms. To safeguard Western civilization, Mr. Bevin said, it would be necessary to establish 'some form of union, formal or informal in character, in Western Europe, backed by the United States and the Dominions'. In January 1948, Mr. Bevin spoke in the House of Commons of the need to extend the 1947 Dunkirk Treaty of Co-operation between France and Britain to other European countries. His initiative was welcomed in Europe and led to the signature on 17 March 1948, by the Foreign Ministers of Belgium, France, Luxembourg, the Netherlands and the United Kingdom, of the Brussels Treaty (for complete details refer to *The International Year Book and Statesman's Who's Who* for 1955). It provided for joint defence against aggression in Europe, economic, social and cultural co-operation and the establishment of permanent consultative machinery. The Brussels Treaty was the direct precursor of the North Atlantic Treaty. Both treaties provided for collective self-defence in accordance with Article 51 of the United Nations Charter; they are not regional arrangements of the kind envisaged in Articles 52 and 53. In October 1954, in the Paris Agreements, the Brussels Treaty was revised and extended to include Italy and Western Germany, the new organization being called the Western European Union.

From the beginning, the United States and Canada declared their support for the Brussels Treaty.

On 11 June 1948, the United States Senate adopted a resolution presented by Senator Arthur Vandenburg, which affirmed the determination of the United States 'to exercise the right of individual or collective self-defence' and recommended the 'association of the United States with such regional and other collective arrangements as are based on continuous self-help and mutual aid, and as affect its national security'.

Negotiations between the Brussels Powers and Canada and the United States began in the summer of 1948. Other European Powers were invited to adhere to the proposed North Atlantic Treaty, which was signed on 4 April 1949.

NATO is not a supranational body. It is an international organization in which the members retain their full national sovereignty, while practising the principles of interdependence.

The *North Atlantic Council*, composed of representatives of the governments of the 15 member countries, is the highest authority in NATO on both civil and military matters. From April 1952 until October 1967 it was organized in permanent session in Paris. The Council then transferred its Headquarters to Brussels, where it now functions permanently. Two or three times a year the Council is attended by Ministers.

The *Secretary-General* is Chairman of the Council. He is responsible for organizing its work with the assistance of the International Staff-Secretariat, permanent Council Committees and temporary working groups. The first Secretary-General was Lord Ismay (U.K.), who was succeeded in May 1957 by M. Paul-Henri Spaak (Belgium), in April 1961 by Mr. Dirk Stikker (Netherlands), in August 1964 by Mr. Manlio Brosio (Italy), and in October 1971 by Mr. J. M. A. H. Luns (Netherlands).

The *Military Committee*, composed of one of the Chiefs-of-Staff or their representatives of each member country possessing armed forces (except France), is the chief military authority. The Chairman, who is elected by the Committee for a 2–3 year tour, is General Herman F. Zeiner Gundersen (Norway) (elected April 1977).

The *Command Structure* consists of the European Command (Supreme Allied Commander Europe, General Alexander M. Haig, U.S.A.), the Atlantic Ocean Command (Supreme Allied Commander Altantic, Admiral Isaac C. Kidd, U.S.A.), the Allied Channel Command, Allied Commander-in-Chief (Admiral Sir Henry Leach, U.K.) and the Canada-United States Regional Planning Group.

*Achievements* of NATO. Since 1949, the ability of members of the Atlantic Community to resist armed attack has greatly improved. NATO armed forces have increased in size and efficiency and their fire power and common strategy have been considerably developed. The provision of common military installations, known as 'infrastructure', on the basis of a cost-sharing formula. has included the construction of some 220 airfields for jet aircraft, more than 5,300 miles of fuel pipe-lines and storage tanks with a total capacity of 440 million gallons put under construction, an extensive early warning radar network, and 'forward scatter' telecommunications systems. The largest single project authorized by the Council—NADGE (Nato Air Defence Ground Environment) has now been completed and provides continuous warning and response to hostile aircraft and missiles throughout nine European countries from Norway to Turkey. The production capacity of member countries in such fields as aircraft, ammunition and electronics has greatly increased, and programmes of correlated production have been initiated. A certain number of standardization agreements have been reached by member countries. An equilibrium between the military requirements and the economic needs of the Alliance is maintained by a continuous defence planning procedure under which target force goals are projected ahead for five-year periods.

Since 1954, the NATO military forces have been further strengthened, and continuing reappraisals of defence planning, in view of the introduction of nuclear weapons, have been carried out.

The Treaty invited the signatory countries to consult together and to engage in self-help and mutual aid; it also provided for the establishment of the North Atlantic Council, which furnishes the member governments with the forum, system and structure to enable them to carry out these obligations. During the XXVth anniversary year (1974), the Heads of Government signed in Brussels a Declaration on Atlantic Relations reaffirming the aims and ideals of the 1949 Atlantic Pact.

In addition to the considerable development of political consultation, NATO keeps under review aspects of economic matters affecting the Alliance, promotes scientific and technological development to stimulate governmental action on ecological problems.

*Publications:* NATO Review (a bi-monthly magazine); NATO: Facts and Figures; The NATO Handbook; The Atlantic Alliance and the Warsaw Pact; Non-military Co-operation in NATO; Aspects of NATO (Specialized pamphlets); NATO Pocket Guide (statistics of member countries); Man's Environment and the Atlantic Alliance.

NATO Headquarters is in Brussels. *Address:* NATO, 1110 Brussels, Belgium.

## THE ORGANIZATION FOR ECONOMIC CO-OPERATION AND DEVELOPMENT (OECD)

OECD came into existence on 30 September 1961, after ratification of a convention signed on 14 December 1960. The new Organization succeeded the OEEC (Organisation for European Economic Co-operation) which was limited to European countries. The latter had been founded in April 1948, and was created both to administer American aid offered under the Marshall Plan and to undertake a joint effort for European economic recovery from the effects of the second World War.

As a result of the reconstitution of the Organization, Canada and the United States, formerly Associated countries, became full members, while the Organization's objectives were enlarged notably by including action in favour of the developing world. Japan, Finland, Australia and New Zealand joined in 1964, 1969, 1971, and 1973 respectively.

OECD consists at present of 24 Members: Australia, Austria, Belgium, Canada, Denmark, Finland, France, West Germany, Greece, Iceland, Ireland, Italy, Japan, Luxembourg, Netherlands, New Zealand, Norway, Portugal, Spain, Sweden, Switzerland, Turkey, United Kingdom, and the United States. Yugoslavia participates in the Organization's work with a special status. Briefly defined, the aims of the Organization are to promote economic and social welfare throughout the OECD area by assisting its Member Governments in the formulation of policies designed to this end and by co-ordinating these policies; and to stimulate and harmonize its Members' aid efforts in favour of developing countries.

The supreme body of OECD is the Council on which each Member country is represented by a Permanent Representative having the rank of an ambassador. It meets regularly (usually once a week) at Official level (the Permanent Representatives) under the chairmanship of the Secretary-General and from time to time (usually once a year) at Ministerial level, presided over by a Minister elected annually. The Council is responsible for all matters of general policy and may establish subsidiary bodies as required to achieve the objectives of the Organization. The Council's decisions, which are binding for all Member Governments, require unanimity.

The Council designates each year 14 of its Members to form the Executive Committee, whose general task is to prepare the work of the Council. Apart from its regular (weekly) meetings, the Executive Committee meets several times a year in 'Special Sessions' attended by senior government officials.

The major part of OECD's work is prepared and carried out in numerous specialized bodies, called either Committees or Working Parties (more than one hundred). All Members are normally represented on these bodies, but some are of a restricted nature, in which case only certain countries designated by the Council are allowed to take part in their activities. Some of the Committees meet occasionally at Ministerial level.

The Council, Committees and subsidiary bodies are serviced by an international Secretariat, independent of any national government and headed by the Secretary-General.

The following is a brief description of the tasks of OECD's main bodies:

*Economic Policy*

The main organ for the consideration and direction of economic policy among the Member countries is the *Economic Policy Committee*. This Committee, which comprises governments' chief economic advisers and central bankers, meets two or three times a year to review the economic and financial situation and policies of Member countries with a view to attaining the Organization's objectives. The EPC has three major working parties dealing with economic growth (WP2), the international payments equilibrium (WP3) and costs and prices (WP4).

The *Economic and Development Review Committee* is responsible for the annual examination of the economic situation of Member countries. Usually, a report is issued each year on each country, after an examination carried out by a panel of representatives of a number of other Member countries; this process of mutual examination, which consists in a confrontation exercise, had developed within the OEEC and has now been extended also to other branches of the Organization's work (agriculture, manpower and social affairs, scientific policy and development aid efforts).

*Energy*

The work of the Organization in the field of energy includes co-ordination of Members' energy policies; assessment of short-, medium- and long-term energy prospects; a long-term programme of energy conservation, development of alternative energy sources and energy research and development with the aim of reducing excessive dependence on oil; a system of information on the international oil and energy markets; and improvement of relations between oil-producing and oil consuming countries with a view to developing a stable international energy trade as well as the rational management and use of world energy resources in the interest of all countries.

This work is carried out in OECD's *International Energy Agency* (IEA), an autonomous body in which 19 Member countries of the OECD participate, as well as within the context of OECD as a whole under the *Committee for Energy Policy*. The IEA has developed specific programmes for co-operation in the above areas, as well as a system of demand restraint and oil supply allocation for use in case of emergency. The IEA's policies are determined by its Governing Board (with weighted majority voting in some cases), assisted by a Management Committee and four Standing Groups.

*Development Assistance*

The Development Assistance Committee consists of representatives of the main OECD capital-exporting countries: Australia, Austria, Belgium, Canada, Denmark, Finland, France, Germany, Italy, Japan, the Netherlands, New Zealand, Norway, Sweden, Switzerland, the United Kingdom and the United States together with those of the Commission of the European Community. The members of the Committee have agreed to secure an expansion of the aggregate volume of resources made available to developing countries and to improve their effectiveness. This Committee consults on methods for making national resources available for assisting countries and areas in the process of economic development anywhere in the world, and for expanding and improving the flow of development assistance and other long-term funds.

The principal tasks of the High-Level Group on Relations between Member Countries and Developing Countries are to identify new constructive approaches on selective substantive issues in this field and to give support and new impetus to negotiations in other bodies. A Technical Co-operation Committee has the task of drawing up and supervising the programmes of technical assistance arranged for the benefit of Member countries, or areas of *Member* countries, in the process of development.

*The OECD Development Centre* (a semi-autonomous body) has been set up for the collection and dissemination of information in this field and research into development problems.

*International Trade*

The activities of the *Trade Committee* are aimed at maintaining the degree of trade liberalization achieved, avoiding the emergence of new trade barriers, and improving further the liberalization of trade on a multilateral and non-discriminatory basis. These activities include examination of issues concerning trade relations among Member countries as well as relations with non-Member countries, in particular developing countries. The existing procedures allow, *inter alia*, any Member country to obtain prompt consideration and discussions by the Trade Committee of trade measures taken by another Member country which adversely affect its own interests.

The task of the High-Level Group on Commodities is to find a more active and broader approach to commodity problems, notably with a view to contributing to a greater stability in the markets.

*Financial and Fiscal Affairs*

The progressive abolition of obstacles to the international flow of services and capital is the responsibility of various OECD Committees. The *Invisibles Committee* watches over the implementation of the Codes of Liberalization of Invisible Transactions and of Capital Movements. The Committee for International Investment and Multinational Enterprises prepared a Code of Behaviour (called "Guidelines") for multilateral enterprises recommended to the latter by all Member governments; the Committee is to follow up the implementation of these guidelines in order to improve the effectiveness of co-operation among Member countries in the fields of international investment and multinational enterprises. Other specialized committees have been set up to deal with financial markets, fiscal matters, restrictive business practices, tourism, maritime transport and consumer policy etc.

*Agriculture and Fisheries*

The *Committee for Agriculture* reviews major developments in agricultural policies, deals with the adaptation of agriculture to changing economic conditions, elaborates forecasts of production and market prospects, holds consultations on import and export practices and assesses implications of world developments in food and agriculture for Member countries' policies.

A separate *Fisheries Committee* carries out similar tasks in its own sector.

*Environment*

The *Environment Committee* is responsible for the economic and policy aspects of OECD's work in this field. The Committee is assisted by various specialized Groups. Its work has led to agreements adopted by Member countries setting out guiding principles on the international trade aspects of environment policies (e.g. the "Polluter pays" principle), while other agreements were adopted concerning the use of environmentally dangerous chemical substances, noise, waste and coastal management. The Committee deals, moreover, with policies for air and water management, urban environment, noise abatement, trans-frontier pollution, and monitors the evolution of environmental quality.

*Science, Technology and Industry*

The Committee for Scientific and Technological Policy is responsible for encouraging co-operation among Member countries in the field of scientific and technological policies with a view to contributing to the achievement of their economic and social aims.

The Industry Committee has overall responsibility for all aspects of the Organization's work in the industry field which require co-operation and confrontation among Member governments. It examines the short and medium-term trends in industry and the longer-term structural changes that are taking place, as well as the applicability and effectiveness of the industrial and regional policy measures that can be deployed to deal with the current or emerging situation.

*Manpower, Social Affairs and Education*

The *Manpower and Social Affairs Committee* is concerned with the development of manpower and selective employment policies to ensure the utilization of manpower at the highest possible level and to improve the quality and flexibility of working life as well as with the integration of social policies. Its work includes such aspects as the role of women in the economy, industrial relations, intra-European migration movements and the development of social indicators.

The *Committee for Education* relates educational planning to educational policy and evaluates the implications of policy for the allocation and use of resources. The Committee reviews educational trends, develops statistics and indicators and analyses policies for greater equality of educational opportunity, new options for youth and learning opportunities for adults.

Together, the Manpower and Education Committees seek to provide for greater integration of manpower and educational policy.

The OECD's *Centre for Educational Research and Innovation* (CERI) promotes and supports the development of research activities in education together with experiments of an advanced nature designed to test innovations in educational systems and to stimulate research and development.

*Road Research*

The Steering Committee for Road Research is responsible for the promotion of international co-operation in road construction, safety, traffic and urban transport research; the aim of this activity is to define the scientific and technological basis needed to assist governments of Member countries in decision-making on road transport. An International Road Research Documentation Scheme ensures the systematic exchange of information and current programmes.

*Nuclear Energy*

The main function of the *OECD Nuclear Energy Agency* (NEA), a semi-autonomous body, is to promote international co-operation within the OECD area for the development and application of nuclear power for peaceful purposes. This it does through international research and development projects, and through the exchange of scientific and technical experience and information. The Agency has also for many years contributed to the development of uniform standards governing nuclear safety and health protection, and a uniform legislative regime for nuclear liability and insurance. NEA comprises a Steering Committee for Nuclear Energy and 12 technical Committees and Study Groups.

*Future Development of Advanced Industrial Societies*

A research project on the Future Development of Advanced Industrial Societies in Harmony with that of Developing Countries ("Interfutures") is to help governments of industrialized countries to prepare their long-term policy options in the context of international relations. Sixteen OECD countries participate in this project.

*Officers of the Organization* (as at end-September 1976)

*Secretary-General (and Chairman of the Council at Official Level):* Jonkheer Emile van Lennep (Netherlands); *Deputy Secretaries-General:* Charles G. Wootton (U.S.), Gérard Eldin (France); *Special Counsellor to the Secretary-General on Energy Problems and Executive Director of the International Energy Agency:* Ulf Lantzke (Germany); *Secretary-General's Economic Adviser:* Stephen Marris (U.K.); *Special Counsellor to the Secretary-General on Development Questions:* Enrico Macchia (Italy); *President of the Development Centre:* vacant; *Director General of the Nuclear Energy Agency:* Ian G. K. Williams (U.K.); *Director of the Centre for Educational Research and Innovation (CERI):* James Gass (U.K.); "Interfutures Project": Jacques Lesourne (France).

# ORGANIZATION OF AMERICAN STATES (OAS)

THE Organization of American States celebrated its 86th anniversary on Pan American Day, 14 April 1976. It is the oldest international organization in the world created by governments to preserve the peace, ensure freedom and security, and promote the welfare of the peoples of its member states. The O.A.S. has a membership of 25 nations representing over 500 million inhabitants from Alaska to Argentina.

The Organization maintains peace in these countries by preventing possible causes of difficulties and mediating any disputes that might arise in the member states. It provides for joint action in the event of aggression from forces within or outside the Western Hemisphere, and is concerned with solving political, legal, social and economic problems affecting the people of the Americas.

The basic Charter of the O.A.S., adopted in 1948 at Bogotá, Colombia, gave a permanent juridicial structure to the Organization and defined its principles, purposes and policies. Since the adoption of the original Charter, it has been deemed necessary to broaden the range of O.A.S. activities. At the Third Special Inter-American Conference in 1967 the Charter was modified. The amended Charter became effective on 27 February 1970.

The Charter of 1970 establishes a General Assembly as the supreme authority of the Organization. Under the General Assembly are three councils of equal rank: The Permanent Council; the Inter-American Economic and Social Council; and the Inter-American Council for Education, Science and Culture.

In addition there are six other major O.A.S. organs: The Meetings of Consultation of Ministers of Foreign Affairs; the Inter-American Juridicial Committee; the Inter-American Commission on Human Rights; the General Secretariat; the Specialized Conferences; and the Specialized Organizations.

In 1958, Juscelino Kubitschek, then President of Brazil, first urged a co-operative hemispheric development effort known as 'Operation Pan America'. This resulted in the creation of the 'Committee of Twenty-One', representing all 21 of the American Republics which, at an historic meeting in Bogotá, Colombia, in September 1960, produced a blueprint for hemispheric action spelled out in the Act of Bogotá.

The Act of Bogotá had as its objectives the promotion of a social development programme which included measures for the improvement of rural living and land use, the examination of the existing legal and institutional system with respect to land tenure, agricultural credit, and fiscal policies related to agriculture.

In March 1961 President John F. Kennedy called for an 'Alliance for Progress' under which the American peoples would translate words into concrete action to make a genuine development breakthrough.

Specific plans for accelerating the economic and social progress of the Latin American countries within the framework of Operation Pan America and the Alliance for Progress were crystallized at the Special Meeting of the O.A.S. Economic and Social Council at the Ministerial Level, held at Punta del Este, Uruguay, in August 1961.

The Charter of Punta del Este was signed on 17 August, with only Cuba abstaining. In the 'Declaration to the Peoples of America', which precedes the Charter, the 20 American republics pledged themselves to work in the coming years towards the following goals:

To improve and strengthen democratic institutions through the application of the principle of self-determination by the people; to bring about a substantial and steady increase in the average income in order to narrow the gap between the standard of living in the Latin American countries and that enjoyed in the industrial countries; to carry out urban and rural housing programmes; to encourage programmes of agrarian reform; to assure fair wages and working conditions, establish effective systems of labour-management relations, and procedures for co-operation among government authorities, employers' associations and trade unions; to wipe out illiteracy, extend primary education to all Latin Americans, and provide broader facilities for secondary and higher education; to promote programmes of health and sanitation; to reform tax laws and redistribute the national incomes to benefit those who are most in need; to maintain monetary and fiscal policies which would guarantee the greatest possible price stability; and to stimulate private enterprise; prevent excessive price fluctuations in basic Latin American exports, and accelerate the integration of Latin America as already begun through the General Treaty of Economic Integration of Central America and through the Latin American Free Trade Association.

The O.A.S. Programme of Technical Co-operation, (now known as Co-operation for Development) which was inaugurated in 1951, instituted the fellowship programme, which since 1961 has trained thousands of potential leaders in every conceivable field of endeavour that might contribute to the social, economic and cultural progress of the Latin American nations.

In October 1961 the Government of Peru formally asked the O.A.S. Council to call a Meeting of Consultation of Ministers of Foreign Affairs under the 1947 Inter-American Treaty of Reciprocal Assistance and requested that the Council, acting as a Provisional Organ of Consultation, investigate alleged violations of human rights in Cuba and activities aimed at overthrowing legitimately constituted governments. Upon consideration of all reports, the Eighth Meeting of Consultation resolved that the present Government of Cuba, which had officially identified itself with a Marxist-Leninist government, was incompatible with the principles and objectives of the Inter-American System, and that this incompatibility excluded the present Government of Cuba from participation in the Inter-American System. Only the current regime, however, has been banished from the councils and activities of the O.A.S. Cuba, as a nation, is still considered a member state. In 1975 the Sixteenth Meeting of Consultation in San José, Costa Rica, resolved to leave the States Parties to the Rio Treaty free to normalize relations with the Republic of Cuba.

In 1967 two members of the British Commonwealth, Trinidad and Tobago, and Barbados became the twenty-second and twenty-third members of the O.A.S. In 1969 Jamaica became the twenty-fourth member, Grenada the twenty-fifth in 1975 and Surinam became the twenty-sixth in 1977.

A Meeting of American Chiefs of State was held in Punta del Este in April 1967. At this time the leaders of the American nations reaffirmed their adherence to the goals of the Alliance for Progress; pledged their countries to even greater efforts to secure a better and richer life for all Americans; and embraced a programme of action to use the fruits of education, science and technology to benefit their peoples. O.A.S. regional development programmes in those fields now support more than 200 multinational centres for training and research throughout Latin America.

The so-called 'War of 100 Hours' between Honduras and El Salvador broke out in July 1969. A Thirteenth Meeting of Consultation formally convened 31 July. However, the O.A.S. Council, acting as a Provisional Organ of Consultation, had been actively and effectively engaged in damping down hostilities almost as soon as they began. Within four days a cease-fire had been arranged, and soon thereafter the belligerents agreed to withdraw all troops from each other's territory. The governments of El Salvador and Honduras were instructed by the Thirteenth Meeting of Consultation to re-establish diplomatic relations as soon as possible and to settle their boundary disputes. Since that time the O.A.S. has been working with the governments of both Honduras and El Salvador to find permanent solutions to several long-standing problems which combined to produce tensions and frictions between the two nations.

A signing of the 'Act of Managua' between the two Central American countries designed to put an end to a rash of border incidents between the two countries.

In 1973 the General Assembly created a Special Committee for the purpose of restructuring the inter-American system so that it may respond adequately to the new political, economic, social, and cultural situations in the member States and in hemisphere and world conditions. The 1974 meeting of the Assembly established that the Special Committee was to give priority to 'Inter-American co-operation for integral development' and 'collective economic security for development'. In 1975 the Special Committee prepared a Protocol of Amendment to the Rio Treaty that was signed at a meeting in San José, Coasta Rica in that year. The General Assembly of 1975, held in Washington, D.C., elected Alejandro Orfila of Argentina as Secretary-General of the O.A.S., and Jorge Luis Zelaya Coronado of Guatemala as Assistant Secretary-General.

In 1976 the General Assembly approved, among others, several resolutions on human rights, the Trade Act of 1974 of the United States, and transnational enterprises. The General Assembly proclaimed the 'Decade of Women 1976–1985: Equality, Development, and Peace.'

The 1977 General Assembly, held in Grenada, was the scene of an intense debate on the subject of human rights; the Permanent Council also was instructed to study co-operation for the prevention and punishment of acts of terrorism. The Assembly declared 1978 Inter-American Rural Youth Year.

*Secretary-General*, Alejandro Orfila (Argentina). *Assistant Secretary-General*, Jorge Luis Zelaya Coronado (Guatemala). *Executive Secretary for Education, Science and Culture*, Eduardo Gonzalez Reyes. *Executive Secretary for Economic and Social Affairs*, Annibal V. Villela. *Assistant Secretary for Management*, Ronald Scheman. *Assistant Secretary for Co-operation for Development*, Santiago Meyer. *Address:* Organization of American States, 17th Street and Constitution Avenue, N.W. Washington, D.C. 20006, U.S.A.

# THE SOCIALIST INTERNATIONAL

THE first International—the International Working Men's Association—was formed in London as early as 1864 and lasted until 1876. In Britain the first Trade Union Congress was not held until 1868, and the Labour Representation Committee, from which the Labour Party developed, did not come into being until 1900. In other countries, too, the labour movement was at an early stage of growth, and consequently the first International lacked solid foundations and collapsed 12 years after its formation.

The second attempt was made in 1889. Over the years the Second International grew in size and prestige. But it was shattered by the outbreak of war in 1914. Moreover, the Bolshevik Revolution in Russia (1917) split the international Socialist movement. In 1919 the Bolsheviks established the Communist International (Comintern, or Third International). The Socialist parties could not accept the Communists' denial of liberty and democracy, nor their subservience to the Russian party; and in 1923 they reconstituted the Second International under the name of Labour and Socialist International (L.S.I.).

At its fourth Congress (1931), L.S.I. represented a total membership of well over six millions, drawn from nearly every country in Europe, but with few connections outside that continent; but the growth of Fascism in Europe eliminated one party after another, and the fourth Congress was also the last. Its Executive and Bureau continued to meet up to and even after the outbreak of World War II; but after the fall of France the L.S.I. ceased to function. The British, Swedish and Swiss parties were then virtually the only survivors.

The first step towards reconstruction was taken in May 1946 when a Socialist Information and Liaison Office (S.I.L.O.) was set up in Transport House, London. The fourth conference (Antwerp, November 1947) improved the working of the International Socialist Conference by the replacement of the Consultative Committee by a Committee of the International Socialist Conference (Comisco), which was given greater powers than the old committee; but its functions remained largely administrative.

This conference adopted a resolution to obtain a common Socialist policy on the Marshall Plan. There was no agreement on this issue. Whereas the Western European parties welcomed the Marshall Plan, the reactions of the Eastern European parties were governed by their collaboration with the Communists who had had to reject the Marshall offer and join in establishing the Cominform.

There was no adequate common basis between those Socialist parties which were collaborating with the Communists and the others. The Cold War precipitated a complete break; and the Communist seizure of power in Czechoslovakia (February 1948), and the creation of satellite countries, brought the Socialist leaders to submission, to be liquidated or forced to flee into exile. The meeting of Comisco held in London in March 1948 declared that the former Social Democratic Parties of Rumania, Bulgaria and Hungary had excluded themselves by their leaders' acceptance of absorption by the Communists. It also rejected those leaders of the Czech Social Democratic Party who had betrayed the party to the Communists. A final appeal was made to the Polish and Italian parties not to follow the path leading to absorption.

By the middle of 1948, therefore, the movement was rid of collaborationist parties and stood united on its basic principles and supported by more than 20 member parties. In March 1951 Comisco decided to reinstate the Socialist International in its traditional form.

The founding Congress of the reinstituted Socialist International was held in Frankfort-on-Main in July 1951. It is now composed of 56 Socialist and Labour Parties from all over the world, with an aggregate membership of almost 15 millions and representing an aggregate vote of over 80 millions. Twenty-two of the parties govern their countries, either alone or in coalition. Thus, almost 200 million people in all continents are living under democratic Socialist rule.

Since its founding congress subsequent congresses defined the attitude of the international Socialist movement owards the problems of Colonialism, the United Nations, the Special U.N. Fund for Economic Development, Middle East, Algeria, Hungary, Suez, nuclear and general disarmament, security and peace, nuclear tests, co-operation between developed and developing countries, European co-operation, Africa, Berlin, the Common Market, South Africa, Spain, Chinese aggression in India, Aden, Jews in the U.S.S.R., Viet-Nam, Cuba, Greece, Rhodesia, apartheid, Soviet intervention in Czechoslovakia, Nigeria-Biafra, youth revolt in modern society, development co-operation and economic aid and the general international situation, European Security, Chile, Portugal, Spain, and Cyprus.

The *Chairman* is Bruno Pittermann (former Vice-Chancellor, of Austria). *Vice-Chairmen* of the International are Pietro Nenni, former President of the Italian Socialist Party and former Foreign Minister; Sir Harold Wilson former Prime Minister; Willy Brandt, former West German Chancellor Chairman of the German Social Democratic Party; Golda Meir, former Prime Minister of Israel; François Mitterrand, First Secretary of the French Socialist Party; Sicco Mansholt, former Dutch President of the EEC; Giuseppe Saragat, former President of Italy; Trygve Bratteli, a former Chairman of the Norwegian Labour Party, former Prime Minister. *General Secretary:* Hans Janitschek. *Address:* 88A St. John's Wood High Street, London, N.W.8.

# THE SOUTH PACIFIC COMMISSION (SPC)

THE South Pacific Commission is an advisory and consultative body established under an Agreement signed in Canberra in 1947 by the six Governments then administering territories in the Pacific region (Australia, France, Netherlands, New Zealand, the United States of America, and the United Kingdom). Since the signature of the Agreement, the Netherlands have withdrawn (in 1962 when they ceased to administer the former colony of Dutch New Guinea, now West Irian), and independent Pacific states have become members of the Commission. Western Samoa became a Participating Government in 1964, the Republic of Nauru in 1969, the Dominion of Fiji in 1971 and Papua New Guinea in 1975.

The Commission's purpose is to promote the economic and social welfare of the peoples of the Pacific region for whom it works: these number some four and a half million and are scattered over 12 million square miles, less than two per cent of which is land.

Until 1974, Commissioners from the Participating Governments met in annual Session, while the South Pacific Conference, attended by delegates from the 20 countries and territories for which the Commission works, became an annual event in 1967 and made recommendation for the Session's consideration.

In October 1974, a Memorandum of Understanding, signed by Representatives of all Participating Governments at Rarotonga, Cook Islands, provided for the Commission and the Conference to meet in a joint annual session known as the South Pacific Conference. Each Participating Government and Territorial Administration has the right to send to the Conference one Representative (and Alternates), and each Representative has the right to one vote. The Sixteenth South Pacific Conference was held in Noumea, New Caledonia in 1976.

The Conference is assisted in its work by a Planning and Evaluation Committee which meets annually, and by a Committee of Representatives of Participating Governments which deals with certain administrative matters and nominates the Commission's Principal Officers.

The Commission's budget is derived from contributions from the Participating Governments in the following agreed proportions: Australia 30 per cent; United States 20 per cent; United Kingdom 16 per cent; New Zealand 16 per cent; France 14 per cent; Fiji, Nauru, Western Samoa and Papua New Guinea 1 per cent each. In recent years generous voluntary contributions have also been made by some Governments for special projects of regional interest.

Following the recommendations of a Review Committee that met in May 1976, the Sixteenth South Pacific Conference directed that the Commission carry out the following specific activities: rural development; youth and community development; *ad hoc* expert consultancies; cultural exchanges (in arts, sports and education); training facilitation; assessment and development of marine resources and research; and that special consideration be given to projects and grants-in-aid which do not necessarily fall within these specific categories but which respond to pressing regional or sub-regional needs or to the expressed needs of the smaller Pacific countries. The Committee also recommended that the three main sectors (health, social development and economic development) into which the Commission's work programme was formerly divided be abolished, and an integrated approach adopted.

The Commission's work programme for 1977 falls into the following main fields: food and materials (agriculture, plant protection, animal production); marine resources (artisanal and oceanic fisheries); rural management and technology (conservation of nature, environmental health, rural employment, appropriate technology); community services (community education and training, out-of-school youth education, family health, public health); information services and data analysis (socio-economics statistics unit, health information unit, English teaching materials unit, information and publications unit).

The professional officers visit the countries and territories of the region on request to assist with particular problems; arrange conferences and training courses; and write technical documents for the information of their colleagues both within the region and beyond.

The Commission makes funds available each year to assist with the provision of short-term consultant services; study visits within the region; student travel; and applied research activities.

Publications include the quarterly *South Pacific Bulletin* (English and French editions); the *Report of the South Pacific Conference*; and *Annual Report*; and a number of series of technical publications covering a wide variety of fields.

The Commission has a staff of about 100, most of whom are based at Headquarters in Noumea, New Caledonia. Others are stationed at the Community Education Training Centre, the Regional Media Centre and the Regional English Teaching Centre in Suva, Fiji, and at the Publications Bureau in Sydney, Australia. Official languages of the Commission are English and French.

The Commission's senior officers are: *Secretary-General*, Dr. E. Macu Salato; *Director of Programmes*, Dr. Guy Motha; *Director of Administration*, Dr. Frank Mahony.

Addresses for official correspondence—The Secretary General, The South Pacific Commission, B.P. D5, Nouméa Cedex, New Caledonia; for inquiries relating to publications —SPC. Publications Bureau, P.O. Box 306, Haymarket, N.S.W., 2000, Australia.

## WARSAW TREATY

THE Warsaw Treaty was signed by eight socialist countries on 14 May 1955, their attempts to secure the establishment of an all-European system of collective security having failed. The signatories were Albania, Bulgaria, Czechoslovakia, Hungary, the German Democratic Republic, Poland, Romania and the Soviet Union. Albania took no further part in the Treaty organization after 1962, and denounced the Treaty in 1968.

The final act that led to the setting up of the Warsaw Treaty organization was the ratification of the Paris agreements by the Western powers. These agreements provided for the formation of the West European Union, the remilitarization of West Germany and her inclusion in NATO.

Immediately after this the countries listed above met in Warsaw and signed the Treaty of Friendship, Co-operation and Mutual Assistance that has since become known as the Warsaw Pact.

The Warsaw Treaty is strictly defensive in character and its preamble states that the signatories will strive for the establishment of "a system of collective security in Europe based on the participation of all European states".

Member states are committed to refrain from the use or the threat of force in their international relations, but in the event of armed attack on any one of them they undertake to give immediate help, using all means that appear necessary, including the use of force. They also have an obligation to act in a spirit of friendship and co-operation with the aim of further developing and strengthening economic and cultural relations among themselves.

The Treaty envisages mutual consultations in all important international questions affecting their common interests. For the purpose of holding these consultations and of reviewing questions arising in connection with the implementation of the Warsaw Treaty the Political Concultative Committee was set up. In practice this Committee sonsists of representatives of the member states at the highest level.

The Treaty was signed for an initial period of 20 years with automatic prolongation for ten years for all states that do not announce their intention to denounce the Treaty during the year before the expiry of the term of operation. It is open to all states, regardless of their social and state system.

To ensure effective defence against possible aggression the Treaty participants decided to set up a Joint Armed Forces Command, consisting of the Commander-in-Chief of the Joint Armed Forces and his deputies. The Commander-in-Chief is appointed by decision of the member-states, while his deputies are appointed by the respective governments. These deputies command the national contingents which each member-state allocates to the Joint Armed Forces under Article 5 of the Treaty.

The Joint Command has jurisdiction only over those contingents of national troops which have been placed at its disposal by decision of the member-states.

The Treaty organization also has a Committee of Defence Ministers and a Military Council consisting of the Commander-in-Chief of the Joint Armed Forces, his deputies and the Chief of Staff of the Joint forces.

The Warsaw Treaty Organization attaches great importance to the question of collective security in Europe and has pointed out that the best way to ensure peaceful conditions for the development of the countries of Europe would be to replace the existing military groupings in Europe with an all-European collective security system. From the outset the Warsaw Treaty countries have expressed their readiness to come to terms with the NATO states on the abolition of all military blocs in the interests of peace in Europe. Reaffirming this in November 1976, they called for the Helsinki Conference participants to sign a treaty on the non-use of nuclear weapons, for moves to be made towards a world conference on disarmament, and also towards a world treaty on the non-use of force in international relations.

## WESTERN EUROPEAN UNION (WEU)

THE Brussels Treaty, signed in 1948 by Belgium, France, Luxembourg, the Netherlands and the United Kingdom, provided for collective self-defence and for collaboration in economic, social and cultural matters between the Five Powers. In 1950 the military activities of the Brussels Treaty Organization were transferred to NATO; the economic objects of the Treaty had been assured by OEEC. In June 1960 the social and cultural activities of the Organization were transferred to the Council of Europe in the interest of a rationalization of European institutions.

When it became clear that the proposed European Defence Community could not become a reality, a Nine-Power Conference was called in London on 28 September–3 October 1954 to consider how to ensure the full association of the Federal Republic of Germany with the West and an alternative plan for the organization of European defence providing for a German contribution and the full participation of the United Kingdom. This Conference was attended by Belgium, Canada, France, the Federal Republic of Germany, Italy, Luxembourg, the Netherlands, the United Kingdom and the United States of America.

The Conference agreed to end the Occupation regime in Germany, to recommend that Germany should accede to NATO, and to invite Germany and Italy to accede to the Brussels Treaty, suitably modified to emphasize the objective of European unity and strengthened to make it a more effective focus of European integration.

At the same time, the United Kingdom Government undertook to maintain on the mainland of Europe four divisions and the Second Tactical Air Force and not to withdraw them against the wishes of the majority of the Brussels Treaty Powers, except in the case of acute overseas emergency. The Federal Republic of Germany, for its part, undertook not to manufacture in its territory atomic, chemical or biological weapons.

Other decisions concerned the size of defence contributions and the organization of the control of armaments.

The decisions of the Nine-Power Conference were embodied in a series of Agreements approved by the Conference of Ministers held in Paris on 20–23 October 1954. These agreements comprised the following texts:

1. *Documents relating to the termination of the Occupation regime in the Federal Republic of Germany, and a Convention on the presence of foreign forces in Germany.*

These agreements are between Britain, France, the United States and Germany, on a basis of equality, and replace the Bonn Conventions, which were between the three Occupying Powers on the one hand and the Federal Republic on the other. By them the Federal Republic has full authority over its internal and external affairs (except for Allied reserved rights on Berlin and Germany as a whole).

The three Allied Powers have abandoned their rights to declare an emergency in the Federal Republic (and use their forces accordingly); but they retain the right in international law of any local military commander to take action if his forces are immediately menaced independently of a state of emergency.

Foreign forces remain in Federal Germany with the consent of the Federal Government, but the Allied Powers retain their rights under the Potsdam agreement to send troops into all Germany, including Berlin.

German financial support towards the cost of Allied troops will be on a sliding scale, viz., for the first 12 months of Germany's entry into NATO it will decrease from an annual rate of £400 million to £200 million, and thereafter the amount will be a subject for negotiation with the Federal Government.

Decartelization and deconcentration of industry have been dropped, but the existing Allied deconcentration programmes are being completed.

Germany now has freedom to resume civil aviation; but arrangements for additional or new flights have to be approved by the three Powers.

2. *Documents relating to the North Atlantic Treaty Organization*

Under these, the Federal Republic of Germany acceded to the North Atlantic Treaty, and it was agreed that all the forces of Member countries of NATO on the Continent (except those for the defence of overseas territories and other forces which NATO recognizes as suitable to remain under national control) are under the command of the Supreme

Allied Commander, Europe (SACEUR), who has been given increased powers over the location and use of forces under his command. He is empowered to make field inspections, inspect reserve formations, and control training on the mainland of Europe.

Formations of army group size or over are integrated; they cannot be composed of the forces of only one nation. The exception to the rule is the U.S. 7th Army in Germany, which is composed of American units only and may stay so. It is for SACEUR to decide what corps or divisions can be integrated; but no unit in NATO Central Command greater than a corps composed of the forces of one country is permitted.

3. *Documents relating to the revision and extension of the Brussels Treaty*

The preamble to the new Treaty lays down that its object is to 'promote the unity and encourage the progressive integration of Europe'. A new Article provides for close co-operation with NATO; another provides for a Council (which usually sits in London) with powers of decision; and a third establishes a W.E.U. Assembly composed of representatives of the Seven Powers who attend the Council of Europe Parliamentary Assembly, to which the Council must make an Annual Report on its activities.

Protocol II to the revised Treaty sets upper limits on the size of land and air forces which the members of W.E.U. will maintain on the continent in peacetime and place under the command of the Supreme Allied Commander. As regards Belgium, France, the German Federal Republic, Italy and the Netherlands, these limits are to be the same as in the Annex to the E.D.C. Treaty; for Luxembourg the limit is one regimental combat team; for the United Kingdom it is four divisions and the Second Tactical Air Force. The level of naval forces will be determined in the course of the NATO Annual Review. Under Article 3 of the Protocol it is agreed that the limits set to the armed forces of the member countries shall not be increased except by *unanimous agreement.* Secondly, the level of internal defence and police forces shall be established by common agreement. In the third place, under Article 6 of the Protocol the United Kingdom agrees to maintain on the continent four divisions and the Second Tactical Air Force, or other equivalent forces, and, except in the event of an acute overseas emergency, not to withdraw these forces against the wishes of the majority of her partners.

Protocol III contains the German undertaking not to manufacture atomic, chemical or biological weapons, or certain other weapons on a list (including guided missiles, warships and strategic bombers) which can be amended by the Council of W.E.U. by a two-thirds majority. The Federal Republic agrees to supervision to ensure that these undertakings are observed. The other members agree that their stocks of various weapons shall be subject to control.

Protocol IV provides for the *Agency for the Control of Armaments*, which has the task of ensuring that the commitments contained in Protocol III are observed. The Agency was set up in Paris. It receives reports from NATO and from Member States on their stocks of armaments on the continent, carries out inspections and test checks, verifies whether stocks do not exceed the agreed levels and reports any discrepancies or the manufacture of prohibited weapons to the Council of W.E.U. The latter can then take the matter up with the member concerned or take such other action as it deems necessary, acting by simple majority.

Production and standardization of armaments are the responsibility of the *Standing Armaments Committee* set up by Resolution of the Council of W.E.U. on 7 May 1955. Its task is to seek the most practical means of using the resources available to Member States for the equipment and supply of their forces and of sharing tasks in the best interests of all. The Committee was created as a result of the deliberations of the Working Party appointed during the Paris Conference in the previous October to study the French proposals for the production and standardization of armaments.

4. *Franco-German Agreement on the Saar*

One of the conditions laid down by the French Parliament for approving German rearmament was a solution of the Saar problem. The Franco-German Agreement of 23 October 1954 was concluded at the same time as the Paris Agreements. It provided that the Saar should be given a European Statute within the framework of W.E.U., subject to approval by referendum. The Council of W.E.U. accepted certain responsibilities under this Agreement, and appointed a Commission to supervise the referendum. However, the population of the Saar rejected the proposed European Statute by a referendum held on 23 October 1955. The Treaty was modified and its Protocols entered into force between the seven Member States on 6 May 1955.

*Secretary-General:* Edouard Longerstaey. The Agency for the Control of Armaments, the Standing Armaments Committee and the Office of the Clerk of the Assembly are at 43 Avenue du Président Wilson, Paris XVI. Western European Union has its headquarters in London. *Address:* 9 Grosvenor Place, London, SW1X 7HL. Tel.: 01-235 5351.

# V. Other International and National Organizations

## ADMINISTRATION—MANAGEMENT—PLANNING

**Association of Certified Accountants.** Incorporated by Royal Charter. Founded 1904. Is the second largest of the four bodies of professional accountants which are recognized by statute in the United Kingdom. Membership of 17,500 and over 70,000 registered students. Examinations are held twice yearly in the principal cities of the United Kingdom and Ireland, and in many centres overseas. *Secretary:* R. A. Dudman. *Address:* 22 Bedford Square, London, WC1B 3HS. Tel.: 01-636 2103. Telex: 24381.

**British Standards Institution (BSI).** The BSI is the national standards organization of the United Kingdom. Under its six Divisional Councils, reporting to the Executive Board, are 80 Standards Committees responsible for 1,000 active technical committees whose members are drawn from all sectors of the economy.

BSI has evolved over 7,000 British Standards and British Standard Codes of Practice for materials, products and processes, and installations. It administers certification schemes to British Standards and provides a wide range of testing and inspection facilities. BSI also operates the Technical Help to Exporters (THE) information service. In the wider international field BSI is an active member of both the International Organization for Standardization (ISO) and the International Electrotechnical Commission (IEC). The object of these bodies is to achieve international standards agreements which can be implemented by each country in drawing up its own national standards. For example there are ISO and IEC standards on test methods for basic materials such as coal and steel, on terminology and symbols for electrical plant and refractories; and on dimensional standards for many items such as screw threads, freight containers, radio valves and joints for laboratory glassware. BSI is also active in European organizations for the co-ordination of standards. Subscribing members of BSI are kept regularly in touch with standards developments through the monthly BSI News, through the Institution's Annual Report and its Yearbook. Information services are available on standards and related requirements in overseas countries, and the library at BSI's headquarters holds the standards of the national standards bodies all over the world. *Address:* 2 Park Street, London, WIA 2BS. Tel: 01-629 9000.

**European Committee for Standardization and European Committee for Electrochemical Standardization.** The European Committee for Standardization (CEN) was founded in 1960 to promote the development of trade and the exchange of services in Western Europe by the elimination of technical barriers. CEN comprises the national standards bodies of EEC and EFTA countries and Spain, and prepares European Standards of an industrial and commercial nature which, if accepted by a significant majority of CEN members, are published without variation of text as the national standard in the countries approving them. The European Committee for Electrotechnical Standardization (CENELEC) is the electrochemical counterpart of CEN and was established in

1972 as a result of the union of the earlier European Standardizing bodies, CENEL and CENELCOM. It consists of the national electrochemical committee of the EEC and EFTA member countries. *Address:* 1 rue de Varembé, 1211 Geneva 20, Switzerland.

**The Institute of Chartered Secretaries and Administrators** (formerly The Chartered Institute of Secretaries). Founded in 1891, and granted a Royal Charter in 1902. It is an examining and qualifying body which provides a professional organization for company secretaries and other administrators in industry, commerce and the public Service. While company secretaries are an important element in its membership, the Institute has members in senior administrative positions over a wide field, such as in the nationalized industries, local government, hospital boards, trade associations, learned and professional bodies as well as in banking, insurance and the building society movement. The activities of the Institute include the holding of conferences and meetings, publication of technical papers, research into administration and business and the provision of a library and information service. The total membership is over 45,000. The Institute has members in many parts of the world, particularly Australia (8,600), Canada (1,200), New Zealand (2,300), and South Africa (3,900), where there are divisions which have a degree of autonomy. Where numbers are smaller, organizations called associations have been set up. These are found in Ceylon, Cyprus, Ghana, Guyana, Hong Kong, India, Jamaica, Kenya, Malawi, Malaysia, Malta, Nigeria, Singapore, Trinidad, Uganda, and Zambia. In the United Kingdom and the Republic of Ireland there are about 23,000 members most of whom belong to one of 33 local branches. These branches not only fulfil a social purpose, but their meetings are often devoted to lectures and discussions on a considerable range of subjects of business and professional interest, and consequently they play an important part in keeping the Chartered Secretary informed of developments. The Institute has almost 26,000 registered students world-wide and, whenever it is practicable, student societies have been formed. The Institute's current examination scheme, which came into effect in 1975, consists of four parts with four subjects in each part and there are three streams: one for those in the company secretarial field, another for general/financial administrators and a third for employees in the public sector. The Institute attaches great importance to relevant practical experience, which, together with success in the examination, is an essential condition for election to Membership of the Institute and entitlement to use the designatory letters ACIS. Before election as a Fellow of the Institute (FCIS), a Member must have held a substantial post for a number of years. Publications include the monthly journal 'Professional Administration' and 'The Chartered Secretaries Manual of Company Secretarial Practice'. *President:* (1978) R. M. Clarke MC, JP, FCIS. *Secretary:* B. Barker, MBE, MA, FCIS. *Address:* 16 Park Crescent, London W1N 4AH Tel.: 01–580 4741.

**The Institute of Directors.** Founded in 1903, the Institute provides a powerful, representative voice for the nation's directors, whatever the size of their company.

There are 24 branches in the U.K. and Channel Islands and 14 overseas in which members play an active part. Branch functions include visits, lectures and meetings addressed by guest speakers.

The main aims of the institute are to provide an effective voice to represent its Members and to use their experience for the common good; and to encourage and help them to improve their professional competence as business leaders.

Major issues generally affecting directors are researched and cases argued and publicized. Recent examples are industrial democracy, anti-inflation measures, the case for the market economy and the role of the non-executive director. The Director General of the IOD is one of the first authorities to be asked for comment by the media on issues affecting business.

The Institute is often instrumental in improving draft legislation.

While it does not have the sanction of a trade union it is capable of being just as vociferous and a lot more cogent. Some 150 MPs are Fellows of the Institute, which has an active parliamentary panel.

*Education:* Effective leadership depends not only on personal qualities, but also on knowledge, awareness and acquired skills, including the ability to keep abreast of the constantly changing business environment. To help improve directors' personal performance, the IOD's expanding educational programme has become an integral part of its nationwide activities.

The IOD's policy of providing short courses, conferences and training facilities concentrated on areas of key importance to directors has been enlarged and improved in scope. Subjects include Boardroom Responsibilities, Finance for Non-Financial Executives, Balance Sheet Analysis, Foreign Languages, Quick and Effective Reading and Public Speaking. One-day courses help directors improve television interview techniques. Other business educational activities are designed to emphasise the 'transferable' skills of the director. Through guidance about courses held both in the U.K. and abroad, members are given the latest information about modern business education techniques.

*Books:* The Institute has published a number of works to promote a professional approach to boardroom activities. "Guidelines for Directors" is issued to all new members. Other publications include "Financial and Accounting Responsibilities of Directors", "Sources of Finance for the Smaller Company", "Guide to Share-ownership Schemes", a regular flow of brochures and studies on current issues which affect directors such as its "Submission to the Industrial Democracy Committee."

*Convention:* In addition to smaller conferences the IOD Convention is held once a year in London. A central theme is chosen and the speakers are selected from the most eminent, interesting and knowledgeable in the world.

*Services:* In addition to pursuing its two main aims the IOD provides personal services to meet members' requirements.

The 'Director' magazine which is mailed free to members monthly, is a leading business journal containing original interviews, incisive analysis and entertaining features, plus a section of Institute news.

Non-executive Directors are regarded by the Institute as valuable, though often misunderstood, assets to the boardroom. The IOD promotes their effective use by acting as a contact between suitable candidates and boards with a requirement for their experience and abilities.

The Library maintains a wide range of reference books and the main newspapers and magazines. Books may be borrowed and there is an extensive information service.

British Executive Services Overseas sends senior British businessmen—usually retired—to advise companies in developing countries.

The Retirement Advisory Bureau has put thousands of retired members in touch with voluntary and other organizations needing senior administrative help.

Advice is available on many subjects affecting the director. There are committees and advisers on such matters as company law, industrial relations, accounting, tax, executive health and the arts.

The Club is available to all members of the Institute and, for those able to make use of it, is alone worth more than the subscription for its extremely high standards. It is financed from its operations so that there is no disadvantage to members who are unable to use its excellent facilities.

*Medical Centre:* Members of the Institute are entitled to reduced fees at BUPA's Medical Centre for one of the world's most sophisticated health checks. This was devised and introduced by the IOD.

BUPA rates for private treatment insurance are reduced for IOD members.

*Chairman of the Council:* Denys Randolph; *President:* Lord Erroll of Hale; *Director-General:* Jan Hildreth,; *Address:* 116 Pall Mall, London, SW1Y 5ED. Tel.: 01-839 1233.

**Institute of Public Relations.** Founded in 1948 by a group of public relations officers from various fields including commerce, industry and central and local government. Membership is 2,000. The institute defines Public Relations Practice as the 'deliberate, planned and sustained effort to establish and maintain mutual understanding between an organization and its public'. It implies a two-way flow of information from the organization to the public and the public to the organization, the public relations officer providing the necessary channels, and using the various media of public relations. There are five categories of membership: Fellows (elected by the Council for outstanding service to the profession); Members, Associates; Affiliates (who, although interested in Public Relations, are not necessarily engaged in it); Overseas Associates. The Institute's examinations are administered by the Communication Advertising and Marketing Education Foundation (CAM) and lead to the CAM Diploma in Public Relations. The Institute encourages and fosters high professional standards among its members from the standpoints of both education and ethics. The Institute publishes a monthly Newsletter 'Communicator'.

An advisory service is available to individual members. *Officers: President:* Peter R. Hunt (1978). *Director:* Jimmy Wild. *Address:* 1 Great James Street, London, WC1N 3DA. Tel.: 01-405 5505.

**The International Organization for Standardization.** The International Organization for Standardization (ISO) was established in 1947, (in succession to the United Nations Standards Co-ordinating Committee), in order to reach international agreement on industrial and commercial standards.

ISO is the international specialized agency for standardization. The statutory object of the organization is to promote the development of standards in the world with a view to facilitating international exchange of goods and services and to developing co-operation in the sphere of intellectual, scientific, technological and economic activity.

ISO work covers virtually every area of technology, with the exception of electrotechnical questions which are the responsibility of ISO's affiliated sister organization the International Electrotechnical Commission (IEC), located at the same address as ISO.

ISO brings together the interests of producers, users (including consumers), governments and the scientific community in the preparation of International Standards.

ISO is the largest international organization for industrial and technical co-operation.

The Member Bodies of ISO are the national standards institutes in sixty-four countries. Only one body in each country may be admitted to membership.

Organizations concerned with standardization, but in whose countries there is not yet a fully developed standards activity, may join ISO as Correspondent Members. Most ISO Correspondent Members are in developing countries; in almost all cases they are governmental agencies. In 1977 there were 20 Correspondent Members of ISO. The United Kingdom is a founder member, and together with the United States, France, and the U.S.S.R., has had a continuous membership of the Council, the executive organ, since the foundation of ISO. The technical work of ISO is carried out through 1,700 technical committees, sub-committees and working groups. Some 100,000 experts throughout the world participate in this work. Each working day of the year nine ISO meetings are taking place somewhere in the world.

By mid-1977, the work of ISO had resulted in more than 3,400 International Standards, representing nearly 40,000 pages of concise reference data.

At present 340 international organizations have liaison status with ISO technical committee and sub-committees. *Address:* 1, rue de Varembé, Case postale 56 1211 Genève 20, Switzerland. *Tel.:* (022) 34 12 40; *Telegrams:* Isorganiz; Telex: 23 88 7 ISO CH.

**PEP (Political and Economic Planning)** is an institute that is independent, non-party, not run for profit, and recognized as an educational charity.

The object of PEP is to contribute to better planning and policy-making, particularly in government and industry and in the relations between them. The method is to carry out studies of selected problems and publish the results.

The studies are made by qualified research staff with advisory groups consisting mainly of people concerned professionally with the problems being studied. In this way modern methods of research in the social sciences are married with the judgment of those with practical experience.

Many of the subject studies by PEP have international implications and PEP therefore benefits from its close relations with research institutes on the continent of Europe, in the United States and elsewhere.

Officers of PEP are: *President:* Lord Roll. *Vice:Presidents:* The Lord Annan, The Lord Boyle, The Viscount Hall, E. M. Nicholson, The Rt. Hon. Lord Robens, O. W. Roskill, The Hon. Sir Marcus Sieff, H. Saunders, Dr. M. Young. *Board of Patrons:* Sir Alexander Cairncross, Sir Edmund Hall-Patch, Sir Patrick Hamilton, Bt. J. H. Hansard, L. E. Neal, The Rt. Hon. Lord Salter, Sir George Schuster, Sir Robert Shone, K. M. Lindsay, Sir Lincoln Steel. *Executive Committee:* Sir Montague Finniston, FRS (*Chairman*), Dr. M. Abrams (*Vice-Chairman*), P. Parker (*Vice-Chairman and Hon. Treasurer*). Professor Sir Hermann Bondi, The Lord Briggs, J. C. Burgh, Mrs. Jean Floud, G. G. Hulme, P. Jay, Dr. F. E. Jones, H. Laing, J. Lyons, Sir Ronald McIntosh, Professor Sir Claus Moser, R. O'Brien, Sir Alastair Pilkington, W. J. L. Plowden, Professor M. C. Posner, G. Radice, MP., T. Raison M.P., W. G. Runciman, D. Sieff, C. H. Urwin. *Joint Directors:* R. Davies, J. Pinder, OBE. *Address:* 12, Upper Belgrave Street, London, SW1X 8BB. Tel.: 01-235 5271.

**Society for Advancement of Management. An international professional organization for managers in industry, commerce, government and education. Founded in 1912 by the 'father of scientific management', Frederick W. Taylor.** *Purposes:* **Through research, discussion, publication, and** other appropriate means to promote scientific study of the **principles governing organized effort in industrial and economic life, including both labour and management, and the elimination of unnecessary effort and unduly burdensome toil. It is the only international management organization with local chapters throughout the world whose membership represents all functions and levels of management; its undergraduate members total 10,000 in more than 200 university chapters and continue through to an *Advanced Management Course* for high-level executives. Its senior membership numbers 6,500** in the U.S., Canada, and around the world. Now affiliated with the American Management Association, it works closely with many management groups operating in specialized fields. It offers a diversified programme of 'learning by doing' designed to help develop the technical, human relations, and conceptual skills required by the manager as he progresses through the various levels of management. Membership is limited to individuals who consistently exercise independent judgment in the application of the principles, theories and techniques of scientific management. ***Executive Director:*** Donald G. Begosh. *Address:* Society for Advancement of Management, 135 W. 50th Street, New York, N.Y. 10020 U.S.A.

## AGRICULTURE

**Australian Farmers' Federation (founded 1969).** ***Objects:*** **To** encourage and promote education, particularly among rural industries in Australia; to encourage and promote science, particularly in agriculture and in the rural sector; to encourage and promote research in agriculture and agricultural products and materials used in agriculture; to promote the interests of farmers by any lawful means; to promote unity of all Australian farmers and so establish one voice for each commodity industry, and one voice on general matters at both State and Federal levels.

National organizations affiliated to the Federation are (with the prefix 'Australian'): Apple and Pear Growers' Association, Cane Growers' Council, Citrus Growers' Federation, Dairy Farmers' Federation, Mushroom Growers' Association, Wheat Growers' Federation, Wool and Meat Producers' Federation, Rice-growers' Association of Australia. State organizations are: Council of Agriculture (Qld.); Farmers' Union of W. A., Queensland Farmers' and Graziers' Association, Tasmanian Farmers' Federation, United Farmers and Graziers of S.A.; United Farmers' and Woolgrowers' Association of N.S.W.; Victorian Farmers' Union. *President:* D. P. Eckersley, OBE. *Secretary:* A. S. Norquay. *Address:* G.P.O. Box 10, Canberra, A. C. T. 2600, Australia.

**Commonwealth Agricultural Bureaux.** General purposes and functions; The Bureaux was established in 1929 to act as clearing houses for the interchange of information of value to research workers in agriculture, animal health and forestry. **The contributing Governments are United Kingdom,** Canada, Australia, New Zealand, India, Sri Lanka, Ghana, Malaysia, Nigeria, Cyprus, Sierra Leone, Tanzania, Jamaica, Trinidad and Tobago, Kenya, Malawi, Zambia, The Gambia, Guyana, Botswana, Mauritius, Fiji, Bangladesh, The Bahamas, and Dependent Territories. The structure consists of four Institutes and ten Bureaux, under the general supervision of the Executive Council. The organization is subject to examination at Commonwealth conferences which take place quinquennially. Finances are made up by contributions from Member Governments and from the sales of publications. Annual budget for 1974–75, £3,285,000. *Secretary:* E. A. Runacres. *Address:* Commonwealth Agricultural Bureaux, Farnham House, Farnham Royal, Slough, SL2 3BN, England. Tel.: Farnham Common 2281.

**International Commission for Agricultural and Food Industries** (*Commission Internationale des Industries Agricoles et alimentaires*). Founded March 1934, Paris, by an intergovernmental agreement concluded on the initiative of the French Government. Initially, 34 members began the work of the Commission in 1905. *Purposes:* to study scientific, technical and economic questions directly or indirectly affecting the food, agricultural industries in various countries; to co-ordinate investigations in progress, collect and distribute relevant documentation, and to draw up informative plans; to ensure regular contact with governments and international organizations; to organize yearly congresses on scientific and technical problems. The information centre is managed through CDIUPA (Centre de Documentation des Industries Utilisatrices de Produits Agricoles, au C. E. R. D.I.A., Le Noyer Lambert, 91305, Massy). *President:* Prof. R. Ammon (W. Germany). *General Secretary:* R. Forestier. *Address:* 24, rue de Téhéran, 75008, Paris.

**The Soil Association.** A world wide charity, founded in 1946, to promote a fuller understanding of the vital relationship between soil, plant, animal and man. The Association believes that these are parts of one whole, and that nutrition derived from a balanced living soil is the greatest single contribution to health (wholeness). For this reason it encourages an ecological approach and offers organic husbandry as a viable alternative to modern intensive methods.

*Current Activities of the Soil Association*

To promote organic husbandry as a viable alternative to modern intensive methods.

To assist farmers, horticulturists and gardeners who wish to adopt organic methods.

To conduct courses on the principles and practices of organic husbandry as part of its expanding educational programme.

To publish basic information on organic practice to support this programme.

To promote research and arrange field trials in organic methods.

To take part in conferences, exhibitions, agricultural and horticultural shows in order to demonstrate the advantages of organic methods.

To provide qualified speakers.

To publish a Quarterly Review free to members and to provide a comprehensive Bookshop service.

The Association is supported by active Groups throughout the United Kingdom.

The Association has published a code governing methods of organic production to the highest quality. The Association has its own registered Trade Mark which it issues on licence to growers who conform strictly to this code. This Trade Mark on any produce for sale is a sign of its high organic quality. The Association sponsored the setting up of an independent farmers co-operative, Organic Farmers and Growers Ltd, to market organic produce.

As a Registered Charity the Association depends for support upon its 4,800 members (800 are Overseas) donations and its own hard work.

The President of the Soil Association is Dr. F. E. Schumacher C.B.E. There is an elected council.

*The General-Secretary:* Brigadier A. W. Vickers and the H.Q. Staff are at Walnut Tree Manor, Haughley, Nr. Stowmarket, Suffolk. IP14 3RS. Tel.: Haughley 235.

## ARTS

**British Academy.** The British Academy owes its origin to a meeting of Academies at Wiesbaden in October 1899, where it was resolved to set up an International Association of Scientific and Literary Academies throughout the world. In this new Association, whilst the Royal Society (q.v.) represented the United Kingdom in the section 'Natural Science' no existing institution was at that time deemed competent to represent the United Kingdom in respect of the humanities.

Accordingly, on the initiative of the Royal Society, the British Academy was created in 1901 for the purpose of representing 'Historical, Philosophical and Philological Studies' under conditions which would satisfy the requirements of the International Association. In the following year it was granted a Royal Charter by King Edward VII on the eve of his Coronation. The membership of the Academy was originally restricted to 100 Fellows. Over the years the Bye-Laws have been changed to increase this maximum number and in 1974 the total permitted number was raised to 350. Fellows become Senior Fellows at the age of 72, and as such are not included in this total.

At first the Academy was organised in four Sections, but these have subsequently been enlarged to fourteen, covering the fields of Ancient History, Medieval and Modern History, Biblical, Theological and Religious Studies, Oriental and African Studies, Classical Literature and Philology, Medieval and Modern Literature and Philology, Philosophy, Jurisprudence, Economics and Economic History, Archaeology, the History of Art, and Social and Political Studies. In summary, the Academy undertakes the following main functions: the support and development of nine British Schools and Institutes overseas: the provision of grants for research whether undertaken by individuals and institutions outside the Academy or by the Academy itself and its Fellows; the organization and publication of lectures in the appropriate fields; the maintenance of contacts with scholars abroad through the Union Académique Internationale, foreign academies, and participation in international congresses.

At the Annual General Meeting on 30 June 1977, Sir Isaiah Berlin, OM, CBE, was re-elected President of the British Academy. The other officers are: *Treasurer:* Professor W. G. Beasley; *Foreign Secretary:* Professor A. G. Dickens, C. M. G.; *Publications Secretary:* Dr. Robert Shackleton (to 31 December 1977); Professor J. M. Wallace-Hadrill (from 1 January 1978). The Secretary-designate is Mr. J. P. Carswell. The other members of the Academy's Council are: Professor L. J. Austin; The Revd. Professor J. Barr; The Very Revd. Professor M. Black; Sir Anthony Blunt, K.C.V.O.; Professor, A. J. Brown, C.B.E.; Sir Kenneth Dover; Professor J. D. Evans; Professor M. I. Finley; Sir John Habakkuk; Professor H. L. A. Hart; Professor F. S. L. Lyons-Professor J. Lyons; Dr. G. Marshall; Professor J. H. Plumb; Professor B. A. O. Williams.

*Address:* Burlington House, Piccadilly, London W1V 0NS.

## BANKING—FINANCE

**American Bankers Association. Organized in 1875, it is the national organization of banking, representing in its membership** 94 per cent of commercial banks in the United States. Its total membership consists of more than 13,000 banks and 241 multi-bank holding companies, including 95 members in 32 foreign countries. It is fundamentally an organization to promote the usefulness of banks. The Association serves the banking industry through a voluntary banker committee structure in the areas of Banking Professions, Education, Government Relations, Communications, Research and Planning, and Membership Relations. The Association operates more than 15 educational projects, including The American Institute of Banking, the Stonier Graduate School of Banking, National Trust School, the National School of Real Estate Finance, The National Instalment Credit School, National Personnel School, the National Commercial Lending School, Bank Card School, and the School for International Banking, The Association publishes monthly the magazines *Banking*, which is its official journal and *Capital*, a weekly newsletter. In addition to issuing studies, reports and informative bulletins, various Association working groups hold meetings throughout the United States to promote the exchange of information and ideas among bankers. The Association's governing bodies are the General Convention consisting of the membership, the Governing Council which serves as an advisory body to the Board of Directors, and the Board of Directors which administers Association affairs between conventions. *Address:* American Bankers Association, 1120 Connecticutt Ave., N.W., Washington, D.C. 20036, U.S.A.

**Export Credits Guarantee Department.** Established in June 1919 by the retrospective action of the Overseas Trade (Credits and Insurance) Act 1920 for the purpose of re-establishing overseas trade. The present basis of ECGD activities are the Export Guarantees Act, 1975, as amended by the International Finance, Trade and Aid Act 1977 and the Overseas Investment and Export Guarantees Act, 1972. The Minister responsible for ECGD is the Secretary of State for Trade. ECGD is a separate Government Department, which provides insurance for U.K. exporters against the major risks of exporting. These include: the insolvency of the buyer; failure on the part of the buyer to pay within six months of the goods being accepted; a general moratorium on external debt by the government of the buyer's country, or a third country through which payment must be made; any other action of the government of the foreign country which wholly, or partly, prevents performance of the contract; political events, economic, legislative or administrative difficulties occuring outside the U.K. which prevent or delay transfer of payments; war, civil war etc. outside the U.K. preventing performance of the contract, where the cause of loss is not normally commercially insurable; cancellation or non-renewal of an export licence or restriction by law on exportation. The policies offered include: Comprehensive policies for goods normally sold on not more than six months' credit, although these policies can be supplemented to cover certain engineering goods sold on up to five years' credit provided that there is an established pattern of trade; Specific policies for the sale of capital goods on medium term credit. Comprehensive policies can also be endorsed to cover stockholding overseas, sales from stock and sales to and by overseas associated companies. There is also cover available for external merchanting trade, payments for services, and sales by overseas subsidiaries. Direct and unconditional guarantees are made available to banks that provide finance for export. Guarantees are also issued to U.K. investors for new overseas investments. In the financial year ending 31 March 1977, the amount of exports insured by ECGD was £11,728 million. The headquarters of ECGD is Aldermanbury House, Aldermanbury, London, E.C.2.; and there are offices in Belfast, Birmingham, Bristol, Cambridge, Central London, Croydon, Glasgow, Leeds, Manchester, and North London.

**The Institute of Bankers.** Founded in London in 1879. Is a professional banking organization with a world-wide membership of over 110,000. Its function is to provide the educational foundation on which members can build a banking career and also to keep them in touch with developments in banking and business generally. There are three grades of membership: *Ordinary Members* who, to be eligible for election, must be on the staff of a bank; *Associates* (A.I.B.) who are elected exclusively from those members who have passed the Associateship examinations of the Institute; and *Fellows* (F.I.B.), elected by the Council, for those who have achieved senior professional status. In addition to its qualifying examination work the Institute offers facilities for career-long professional education and other activities of particular interest to senior bankers. At national level it organizes management education seminars and lectures, and publishes standard reference books e.g. *Questions on Banking Practice, Leading Cases in the Law of Banking,* as well as textbooks occasional papers and an official Journal. The Institute also maintains a large reference and lending Library and a comprehensive information service for use by members. So widespread is the Institute's membership, however, that much of its post-graduate work is done through local centres, of which there are 98 in England and Wales and eight overseas (Accra, Cyprus, Hong Kong, Kampala, Lusaka, Malta, Nairobi and Singapore). At the international level, the Institute was the originator of the annual International Banking Summer School, first held in Oxford in 1948. This has now taken place in 18 other countries, under the auspices of the banking association of the host country, but returns periodically to the United Kingdom. In this and other ways the Institute provides an influential forum for the exchange of ideas and information throughout the banking world.

*President,* Mr. M. G. Wilcox, MBE, FIB (1977–). *Secretary: General,* Geoffrey Dix. *Address:* 10 Lombard Street, London, EC3V 9AS.

## CHAMBERS OF COMMERCE

**The Association of British Chambers of Commerce.** Patron, H.M. Queen Elizabeth II. Formed 1860 by 16 chambers, who gave to it the principal task of collecting and co-ordinating their opinions and stating how, on balance, the best interests of the nation could be served. In fulfilling its role the A.B.C.C. presents British Chamber of Commerce views to Parliament, Ministers, and all government departments. It represents the movement on government committees. It maintains close and continuous contact with British and other chambers in foreign countries. Its representatives play an active part in the affairs of the Federation of Commonwealth Chambers of Commerce and the International Chamber of Commerce, and the Permanent Conference of the Common Market Chambers of Commerce. *Membership:* 90 chambers with an aggregate membership of 47,000 companies.

The Association is governed by a National Council consisting of the President, Chairman of Council, Deputy Chairman of Council and Hon. Treasurer of the A.B.C.C. and three representatives from each of the Regions and major Chambers of Commerce. The Regions are coincident with H.M. Government's division of the country into regions for various administrative purposes. The Association's committees, working parties of experts and *ad hoc* panels make their recommendations on national and international policy problems to the National Council prior to submission to the appropriate Minister or Government Department.

The President of the Association is Mr. Tom Boardman, the Chairman of Council is Mr. K. A. Millichap and the Director-General is W. A. Newsome. *Address:* 6-14, Dean Farrar Street, London, SW1H 0DX. Tel.: 01-222 0201. Telex, Chamcom London 888941.

**Federation of Commonwealth Chambers of Commerce.** The Federation came into being as a result of a series of congresses organized by the London Chamber of Commerce. The first was held in July 1886, the second in 1892 and from then on a series of triennial congresses was organized until the need was felt for some more permanent link between the Chambers of Commerce in the Empire than could be provided by these congresses. Accordingly the Federation was inaugurated in 1911, its name being changed several times in the intervening years, until in 1963 it adopted its present title.

Apart from London, Congresses have been held in Montreal, Sydney, Toronto, Cape Town, Johannesburg, Wellington, Canberra, Port-of-Spain, and Hong Kong.

Between congresses the work of the Federation is carried on by the Council which in turn elects an executive committee. The present membership comprises more than 350 Associations and Chambers.

The objects of the Federation are to provide a permanent link between the Chambers of Commerce and other trade organizations in the Commonwealth, and to express the views of commerce and industry on current economic problems.

A series of regular discussions on a bilateral basis between Commonwealth countries has also been developed.

*Director:* V. R. B. Smallwood, TD. *Address:* 69 Cannon Street, London, EC4N 5AB. Tel.: 01-248 4444.

**Chamber of Commerce of the United States of America.** Founded in 1912, the National Chamber is a federation of more than 4,000 Organization Members (local, state and regional chambers of commerce, and American Chambers of Commerce in Europe, Asia and Latin America, and trade and professional associations) and more than 65,000 Business Members (firms, corporations and individuals). Member of U.S. Council of International Chamber of Commerce and Council of the Americas. *Publications:* Washington Report (weekly); Nation's Business (monthly); other publications. *Address:* 1615 H Street, N.W., Washington, D.C., 20062, U.S.A.

**International Chamber of Commerce.** Founded in 1919 at Atlantic City, N.J., U.S.A. Aims: to secure effective and consistent action for the improvement of business conditions between nations and for the solution of international economic problems; to promote world trade generally. Members: the leading elements in business life from over 80 countries. In over 50 of these members have formed a 'National Committee' of the I.C.C. Members are of two kinds, Organization Members (national and local associations, federations and other organizations representing commerce, industry, finance, transport, etc., and not conducted for profit or political purposes) and Associate Members (individuals, firms and corporations engaged in various business activities). Activities: I.C.C.'s work is carried out by some 40 international commissions and committees composed of experts and international traders; the work falls into two broad categories: the study of major issues of general economic and monetary policy and of problems of a technical and purely practical character affecting the organization and functioning of international trade. The I.C.C. has Category 'A' status with the U.N. Economic and Social Council. It also participates in the work of the specialized agencies and other inter-governmental and private and international organizations. The I.C.C. Court of Arbitration (which has been in existence for 50 years) aims at securing a rapid settlement of differences arising among businessmen from different countries. The International Council of Marketing Practice of the I.C.C. was set up to combat unfair practices in the field of international advertising. The International Bureau of Chambers of Commerce fosters the exchange of information and ideas on the functions and administration of chambers of commerce throughout the world. The Commission on Asian and Pacific Affairs, with its Bangkok-based secretariat, studies the special problems of that area. Triennial Congresses are held for all members. The next (twenty-sixth) Congress will be held in Florida in October 1978. Annual Conferences are also held. *Publications:* A range of publications is issued on general and technical problems of international trade, investments, transport, legal affairs, etc.: a regular bulletin, ICC information, is sent to all members. *President:* (1975–76) John G. Crean (Canada). *Vice-President:* Rolf Stödter (Federal Germany). *Secretary-General:* Mr. Carl-Henrik Winqwist. *Address:* 38 Cours Albert 1,75008 Paris. Tel.: 359-05-92. Telex 65770. Liaison offices (with U.N.): New York, N.Y. 10036 (1212 Avenue of the Americas); Geneva (57 Route de Chêne); Bangkok (150 Rajbopitr Road). The British National Committee's address is 6-14 Dean Farrar St., London SW1H 0DT. Tel.: 01-222 3755.

**London Chamber of Commerce and Industry.** With a membership of 10,000, this is the largest Chamber of its kind in the world and represents the Greater London area which, in addition to its outstanding position as a centre of world commerce, is pre-eminent in the field of insurance and banking, and is the industrial hinterland of the Port of London. The London Chamber was founded in 1881, considerably later than some others in Britain, but it gained influence quickly. In 1898 the Chamber was given by statute the right to appoint representatives on the Council of Foreign Bondholders.

The Chamber's Council consists of elected members and representatives of 55 trade sections, eight standing committees and 48 affiliated trade associations. The standing committees, made up of experts in such subjects as transport, postal and telecommunications matters, taxation, rating, town planning and commercial education, prepare reports and provide advice as basis for action by the Council.

The Chamber has developed greatly its overseas activities in recent years, and now has five Regional Groups covering between them all the markets of the world. Within these Groups the Market Sections continue their activities, and have exchanged visits with Chambers of Commerce in a number of countries. The Chamber has also been responsible for booklets and pamphlets on a number of subjects.

Among the sections covering trades the canned goods section, for example, has long been accepted as speaking for the British importer and distributor. The Diamond, Pearl and Precious Stone Trade section has its own internationally known laboratory for testing gems.

The departments of the Chamber provide direct service to members, answering business enquiries, giving advice, and providing a wide variety of information on tariffs and regulations, trade opportunities and statistics, names of suppliers, etc. Over 120,000 enquiries are dealt with, and 300,000 Certificates of Origin and other certificates are issued annually.

The London Court of Arbitration (housed and staffed by the London Chamber which manages it in collaboration with the Corporation of London) is consulted on national and international arbitration questions. The Commercial Education department has examined 1$\frac{3}{4}$ million candidates in commercial subjects since its inception in 1892. The Private Secretary's Diploma offers a qualification which has aroused much interest.

The Chamber's building is the centre for trade organizations in London. It houses 80 independent trade associations, including the Federation of Commonwealth Chambers of Commerce, and the British Export Houses Association.

*President:* Sir Patrick Reilly, GCMG, OBE. *Chairman:* C. M. Hughes. *Director:* W. F. Nicholas, OBE. *Address:* 69 Cannon Street, London, EC4N 5AB. Tel: 01-248 4444.

## CHEMISTRY

**The Chemical Industries Association** (CIA) **was formed in 1966** as a result of an amalgamation between the former Association of British Chemical Manufacturers and the Association of Chemical and Allied Employers. *Activities:* The Association deals with a broad range of activities on behalf of the chemical industry. It is strictly non-political, is not a trading organization and does not concern itself with price or quota conventions. The Association has two Boards, each of which is supported by a wide range of specialist committees. The Trade Affairs Board acts as a co-ordinating body in the industry dealing with Government or Government Departments on matters affecting chemical manufacturers and all questions likely to promote industrial efficiency in the widest sense. The Industrial Relations Board, as its name implies, deals with industrial relations, including initial negotiations with the trade unions. Services for the industry are maintained through the Boards in specialized subjects, including chemical engineering research; chemical plant instrumentation; exchange of non-confidential industrial information; packaging; productivity techniques; safety; trade effluents and water supplies; and training, including the Scheme of Training for Qualified Chemical Operators. The Chemical Industry Safety and Health Council (CISHEC) is an integral part of CIA. *Membership:* Membership is open to all chemical companies with manufacturing facilities in the U.K. *Publications:* The Association issues an annual statistical publication: 'U.K. Chemical Industry Statistics Handbook'. It also has an extensive range of publications on the subjects indicated above which are available for purchase, of which a list is obtainable on request. *President:* A. S. Woodhams (Fisons Ltd.); *Chairman, Industrial Relations Board:* Dr. H. M. Kimberley (Albright and Wilson Ltd.). *Chairman, Trade Affairs Board:* B. Rigby (Laporte Industries Ltd.); *Director-General:* M. E. Trowbridge; *Deputy Director-General and Director, European Affairs:* H. W. Vallender OBE; *Director, Company Operations:* R. J. Grainger; *Director, Industrial Relations:* J. T. Collins; *Director, Economic Affairs:* Dr. P. G. Caudle; *Director, External Relations:* W. McMillan; *General Secretary:* A. J. Chant, *Address:* Alembic House, 93 Albert Embankment, London SE1 7TU; Tel.: 01-735 3001; Telex: 916672 CHEMIN G; Telegrams and Cables: CHEMINDSOC LONDON SE1 7TU,

## COMPUTERS

**Association for Computing Machinery Special Interest Group on Computer Uses in Education.** The Association of Computing Machinery carries out much of its activities through a collection of many special interest groups within the larger parent organization. SIGCUE is one of these groups, particularly concerned with the educational use of computers. The membership includes users of computers in courses in many areas, and also includes developers of such materials.

Computers, as a tool in the educational environment, have generally been accepted for administrative functions. Their role as facilitators of instructional processes is gradually emerging as systems are developed which ease student-instructor use and research demonstrates their utility. Many developmental centers, both in the United States and Europe, are actively engaged in producing material for elementary through post-graudate educational programs.

SIGCUE attempts to focus, both nationally and internationally, on such activity. It provides a forum through meetings and publications. SIGCUE publishes the SIGCUE *Bulletin*, a quarterly journal, and *Topics*, a periodic publication focusing on a specific aspect of instructional computing. Its membership list also is a key means of identifying who is most active in computer-based education.

*Chairman:* David R. Kniefel, Director of Academic Services, New Jersey Educational Computer Network, Inc., P.O Box 390, New Brunswick, N.J. 08903. *Vice-Chairman:* Stuart Milner, Center for Educational Technology, School of Education, The Catholic University of America, Washington, D.C. 20017. *Secretary-Treasurer:* Joyce Statz, Department of Computer Science, Bowling Green State University, Bowling Green, Ohio 43403. *Address:* 1133 Avenue of the Americas, New York, N.Y. 10036, U.S.A. Tel.: (212) 265-6300.

**The British Computer Society.** The British Computer Society is the leading learned and professional society for computing practitioners in the United Kingdom and draws its membership from the commercial and academic fields; a number of companies and educational institutions are also members. The job distribution of the 22,000 individual members includes, among others, computing management, programming, teaching and research and systems analysis and design.

The Society is involved in national and international affairs.

Nationally, the Society which is much concerned with the social impact of computers has advised Government on a number of important issues including privacy. The Society is also active in the promotion of standards, both ethical and technical.

Internationally, the Society is a founder member of the European Co-operation in Informatics (ECI), a partnership of European computer societies formed to be of the widest assistance to the members of the partner bodies in their professional development.

The Society is also founder member of the International Federation for Information Processing (IFIP) and is represented on most IFIP Technical Committees and Working Groups.

Domestically, the Society organizes meetings and symposia on country-wide basis, and has 43 branches which organize talks and discussions and has 40 specialist groups each covering a specific area of computing with working parties in the forefront of technical development.

The Society publishes quarterly a scientific journal and a bulletin of informed opinion and comment on the role and consequences of computing—economic, sociological, and technical. Immediate communication with members is provided by the Society's page in the weekly 'Computing'.

Entrance to the Society is by examination or the attainment of an equivalent educational standard combined with proven acceptable practical experience. Membership of the Society gives recognition of the professional standing of the individual and requires adherence to the Society's standards as set out in The Code of Conduct and The Code of Good Practice. The following people are the officers of the Society for the year 1975–76.

*President:* Prof. P. A. Samet; *Deputy-President:* Professor F. H. Sumner; *Treasurer:* Mr. J. L. Bogod.

**The Association for Development of Computer-based Instructional Systems (ADCIS).** The Association for Development of Computer-based Instructional Systems (ADCIS) is an international, not for profit, organization with members throughout the U.S., Canada and Europe representing elementary and secondary school systems, colleges and universities, business and industry, as well as military and government agencies. (Formerly known as ADIS.)

The purposes of this organization are to: (1) advance the investigation and use of computer-based instruction (CAI) and/or management (CMI); (2) promote and facilitate the interchange of information, programs and materials in the best professional and scientific tradition; (3) reduce redundant effort among developers; and (4) to specify requirements and priorities for hardware and software development, and encourage and facilitate their realization.

An informative newsletter is published six times a year so that members may keep up-to-date with the activities of other ADCIS members and with other CAI installations throughout the world. In addition, the newsletter provides a bibliography of current literature relating to computer-assisted instruction. Its columns are open to both members and non-members for communications of interest to other readers in the field of CAI/CMI.

ADCIS is a unique organization. Like other professional organizations, it sponsors regular conferences for the presentation of papers dealing with the broad aspects of theory, research, and utilization of CAI/CMI, thus fostering the exchange of scientific information. The 'profession' of computer uses in education, however, is a heterogeneous mixture of many disciplines, many approaches, many kinds of hardware and software. A common denominator which drew the early workers of ADCIS together was the use of common CAI equipment; the IBM 1500 Instructional System. These users set a tone for the organization of willingness and opportunity to exchange materials, practical techniques, and programs. This organization has been in existence since 1967.

ADCIS membership has since grown to include not only 1500 system users but users of almost every major CAI system being utilized today. An increasing number of mini-computer users for (CAI) has been noted recently. A broad range of CAI languages is represented also.

ADCIS membership falls into three categories as described below:

*Institutional Membership* is available to all installations which use computer systems for interactive instruction. Dues are $50 per year. One individual at the installation is designated as Institutional Representative for mailing and voting purposes.

*Associate Membership* is available to other organizations having interests which are allied to the purposes of ADCIS Dues are $100 per year. One individual represents the organization and receives the Newsletter and voting privileges.

*Individual Membership* is available to anyone who supports the purposes of this organization. Dues for those persons affiliated with an Institutional or Associate Member will be $20 per year (U.S. and Canada). and $30 per year (foreign). Individual membership dues for those persons *not* affiliated with an Institutional or Associate Member shall be $30 per year (U.S. and Canada) and $20 per year (foreign).

In 1977–78, there are close to 900 ADCIS members, of whom approximately 25 per cent are Institutional or Associate members.

In order to provide members with opportunities to discuss issues of particular interest, formal interest groups are and can be created. Each such interest group will elect a chairman and will have time allocated at organization meetings. Presently constituted are these interest groups: Health Sciences, Health Network. Elementary/Secondary/2-yr. College, and Systems Implementation. Special Interest Group for the Education of the Deaf, MiniComputer Users, PLATO Users, the Music Consortium.

Organizational meetings are held at least once a year. In addition to the formal presentation of papers and demonstrations, exchanges of instructional programs and ideas are facilitated.

Individual registration fee for an Association meeting is $30 for members, $40 for non-members, and $5 for full-time students. (An additional $10 is charged for persons who do not preregister.).

*President:* Dr. Alan Smith, *President-Elect:* Dr. Karen Duncan, *Secretary-Treasurer:* Joan Lauer Hayes.

For further information and membership, contact: Joan Lauer Hayes, ADCIS, Computer Center, Western Washington University, Bellingham, WA 98225, U.S.A.

## CO-OPERATION—CO-PARTNERSHIP

**European League for Economic Co-operation, ELEC (Ligue Européenne de Coopération Économique—LECE).** The aim is the study of economic and social problems which are related to European integration. It is a private association with scientific objective. The League has sections in 17 European countries. It was founded in 1946 by the former Prime Minister of Belgium, M. Paul van Zeeland. The League has held 12 International Conferences. It is a founder member of the European Movement; it has consultative status (Category II) in ECOSOC and in the Council of Europe (Strasbourg). *Publications:* more than 50 papers relating to the economic integration of Europe. *International President:* Count Boël (Belgium); *Secretary-General:* Mrs. Yvonne de Wergifosse (Belgium). *Address:* Ligue Européenne de Coopération Économique, avenue de la Toison d'Or, 1, Bte 11, 1060 Brussels.

**International Co-operative Alliance.** Founded in London in 1895 to unite co-operative organizations in one world confederation. *Aims:* to propagate co-operative principles and methods throughout the world; to promote co-operation in all countries; to safeguard the interests of the co-operative movement in all its forms; to maintain good relations between its affiliated organizations; to work for the establishment of lasting peace and security. The Alliance comprises 663,510 societies in 66 different countries, and its total affiliated membership is over 330 millions. The proportion of consumers' co-operatives, now a little over one third, has declined, partly due to the amalgamation of small societies, and partly as the representation of agricultural, fishery, credit, housing, workers' productive and artisan co-operatives has gained in importance in recent years. The I.C.A. Regional Office and Educational Centre for S.E. Asia was opened in New Delhi in November 1960. An I.C.A. Office for East and Central Africa was opened in Moshi, Tanzania, in 1968. The Alliance enjoys Consultative Status 'I' in the work of the Economic and Social Council of the United Nations, and has similar consultative relations with ILO, UNICEF, FAO, UNESCO. UNIDO, and UNCTAD. In conjunction with the second United Nations Development Decade the International Co-operative Alliance launched the Co-operative Development Decade, 1971–1980 to strengthen co-operative development throughout the world. *President:* Roger Kerinec; *Director:* Dr. S. K. Saxena. *Publications:* Review of International Co-operation (illustrated) quarterly in English, French, and Spanish; The Co-operative News Service (monthly); Consumers' Affairs Bulletin (English and French editions, monthly); Agricultural Co-operative Bulletin (monthly); Studies and Reports Series (occasional). *Address:* 11 Upper Grosvenor Street, London, W1X 9PA. Tel.: 01-499 5991/3.

**Industrial Participation Association.** Founded 1884 as *The Labour Association for promoting co-operative production based on the co-partnership of the workers.* From 1927 to 1972 it functioned under the title *Industrial Co-partnership Association,* when the present name was adopted. The Association is an independent voluntary organization concerned specifically with the development of all forms of employee participation. It provides a forum for the exchange of ideas and experience and is a centre of research information and advice. Its members include some hundreds of companies in both the private and public sectors of British industry, many of whom are acknowledged as leaders in the industrial relations field; representatives of trade unions and professional people. The Association is registered as a charity.

Four main types of employee participation have been distinguished:

1. Participation in ownership through shareholding, either individually or corporately through a trust, or through some form of common co-operative ownership.
2. Participation in the government of the enterprise, commonly through representation on the controlling board.
3. Participation in determining terms and conditions of employment, the traditional province of collective bargaining.
4. Participation in management, or sharing in making and taking decisions, about the running of the enterprise, which is the key issue today in industrial democracy.

The central feature of participation is the opportunity to influence and share consciously in making decisions. This takes in a wide spectrum of practices including productivity bargaining; works councils; various methods of communication including company newspapers and suggestions schemes; profit-sharing and employee shareholding; participative styles of management (management by consent); job enrichment and work-structuring; various forms of common and co-operative ownership; worker directors and so on.

The Industrial Participation Association does not advocate any one form of participation rather than others. It believes participation to be no one thing in isolation, but a combination of many, that can offer the individual higher work satisfaction and generate a sense of corporate identity and a sense of common purpose among all who work together in an enterprise.

Its services to industry, commerce and public corporation include: *research*; It serves as a 'think tank' and examines and comments on a wide range of new developments and proposals; *consultation*, both with senior management and employee representatives; *Conferences* and informal meetings, for the presentation of case studies of what different companies are doing, and to discuss special issues of topical interest; *Publications*, including the journal 'Industrial Participation', commentaries in current trends, Study Papers to examine major issues in depth, and a series of definitive handbooks on different aspects of employee participation.

For many years, as the Industrial Co-partnership Association, the association was concerned primarily with methods of financial participation, through profit sharing and employee shareholding, and with joint consultation. It maintains these interests, and is the leading independent authority on financial participation for all employees in the United Kingdom. But in recent years the range of its concerns have expanded to include the range of topics outlined above.

*Officers: President*, Sir Donald Barron. *Chairman*, Nigel Vinson; *Deputy-Chairman*, John Boyd, CBE. *Joint Honorary Treasurers*, John Franklin and H. S. Mullaly. *Directors:* Ian Gordon-Brown and D. Wallace Bell. *Address:* 78 Buckingham Gate, London, SW1E 6PQ. Tel.: 01–222 0351.

**Regional Co-operation for Development (RCD).** Regional Co-operation for Development (RCD) is a tripartite agreement between Iran, Pakistan and Turkey for closer economic, technical and cultural co-operation. Its aims are directed towards the promotion of the economic advancement and welfare of some one hundred and fifty million people who live within the region. The decision to form this economic grouping was taken on 21 July 1964, at the Instanbul Summit meeting of the Heads of State and Governments of the three countries concerned.

Further Summit meetings were held in Ramsar (Iran) in July 1967; In Karachi, Pakistan in December 1968; and in May 1970 at Izmir in Turkey, and again at Izmir in April 1976.

The 1976 RCD Summit Conference made a number of important decisions aimed at restructuring and widening the activities of RCD in the light of the developments that had taken place since its inception. These decisions and the aims and objective of the organization were subsequently embodied in the Treaty of Izmir, a new charter drawn up for RCD as directed by the illustrious Heads of State in Izmir. The Treaty, signed by the Foreign Ministers of Iran, Pakistan and Turkey in March 1977, also envisages the creation of a number of educational, training and research institutions and confers upon the RCD Secretariat the status of an international organization.

The past thirteen years have shown that the economic potential of RCD is considerable and its member countries, while retaining their traditional economic outlets to other parts of the world have consistently forged closer links in many fields such as technical assistance, joint industrial ventures, trade, communications and social and cultural relations.

*Different fields of co-operation*

*Industry.* The member Governments have attained reasonable success in establishing joint-purpose enterprises on the basis of equity participation and off-take guarantees. Three major projects of the first category have already gone into production. These are Bank Note and Security Papers Limited and RCD Ball-bearings Limited, both located in Pakistan, and the Iranian Aluminium Company located in Arak, Iran. In production on an off-take guarantee basis are: Tungesten Carbide, Borax/Boric Acid, Centrifugal/Special Filters, High Tension Insulators and Tetracycline projects located in Turkey and Ultramarine Blue project located in Pakistan. With a view to streamlining industrial co-operation within RCD, a Regional Survey of four industries has been recently completed by the experts of the member countries and more industries will be evaluated for regional collaboration in the near future.

*Petroleum and Petrochemicals.* Co-operation in this field among the RCD countries is progressing. Among the projects located within the region, the Glycerine project of Pakistan is already functioning and Turkey continues to import products of this plant.

*Trade.* From the very inception of the organization, steps were taken to increase the volume of intra-regional trade. These include the setting up of the RCD Chamber of Commerce and Industry, the RCD Shipping Services, the RCD Reinsurance Pools, the signing of the RCD Agreement on Trade and the RCD Union for Multilateral Payments Arrangement. Regarding the all-important subject of the elimination of barriers impeding intra-regional trade, a draft trade protocol and a list of goods in respect of which the three countries would allow each other concessions were prepared by the region's experts and high-level Government officials. These were submitted to the meeting of the Commerce Ministers of Iran, Pakistan and Turkey which convened in Tehran in April 1976. The Ministers agreed on a schedule for finalizing the necessary arrangements and it is expected that an RCD Protocol on trade would be signed in late 1977.

A decision of far-reaching importance in this field was taken at the Summit Conference held in Izmir in April 1976 for the setting up of an RCD Free Trade Area within a period of not exceeding ten years.

In the field of Insurance, the five RCD Re-insurance Pools, i.e. Fire, Marine, Accident, Aviation and Engineering, were merged into a single Pool with effect from 1 January 1975, as a first step towards the establishment of the proposed RCD Re-insurance Company. The unified Pool, which groups together 41 major insurance companies of the region, registered a premium income of \$2·50 million in its first year of activity as compared to \$1·77 million in the previous year. The latest development in the field of insurance is the setting up of a committee by the RCD Re-insurance Pool to prepare a feasibility study for a speedy establishment of the planned RCD Re-insurance Company. The Tehran-based RCD International School of Insurance, founded in 1970, as a non-profit-making college of advanced studies in insurance, has done much to achieve its objective of training insurance managers and technicians and conducting research in appropriate fields.

Regarding tourism, the member Governments have signed an agreement to co-operate in this field and the Heads of the three National Tourist Organisations met in May 1975 to find ways of better effecting such collaboration. An expert assigned by the United Nations to study the potential for tourism in the RCD countries toured the region in early 1975 and will shortly submit his report.

The most recent development in this field has been a meeting of the three Tourism Ministers in 1976. This gathering agreed on a number of measures to expand the tourism industry in the region and the Ministers met again in 1977 to review the progress made in respect of their decisions.

*Transport and Communications.* Co-operative efforts in this field have proved very fruitful. Arrangements, for example, have been made by the three member countries to institute reduce rates for intra-regional postal exchanges. Representatives from the three postal authorities signed a convention in April 1976 to found the South and West Asia Postal Union, which could be joined by other regional countries. Besides, the three postal authorities are exploring the possibility of manufacturing postal equipment and machinery in the region.

The RCD Shipping Services, with its headquarters in Istanbul, started operation on intra-regional routes in May 1966 and on the United States route in August 1966.

*Roads.* The RCD Highway is scheduled to be completed by the end of 1978.

In Iran, the Highway starts from the Turkish border and reaches the Pakistan border at Mirjaveh. The total length of the road is 2,650 km. of which only a stretch of about 500 km. between Shoregaz and Zahedan remains to be completed.

In Pakistan, the total length of the RCD Highway is 1,319 km. The portions yet to be completed are between Taftan and Baratgzai and between Wad and Kunar.

In Turkey, the total mileage is 1,206 km., and the road is now complete, 1,063 km. have a bituminous surface. There is an alternative highway beginning from the intersection of Ankara-Yozgat, its total length is 650 km. All of this road has bituminous surface of a high standard.

*Railways.* The Pakistan railway system is already linked to the Iran border city of Zahedan, while the railroad between Tehran and Zahedan is also complete but for a missing portion between Zahedan and Kerman, the survey of which was undertaken during 1976–77 and its construction completed by 1980.

The Irano-Turkish railways system, in operation since 1971, is linked by ferry service at Lake Van. A third ferry was introduced at Lake Van in December 1975 to increase the total capacity of the ferry services from 530,285 tons to 720,000 tons annually and a fourth ferry was added in October 1976 to increase the capacity to 960,000 tons. Work on the improvement of the railway and harbour facilities have also been started.

*Technical Co-operation.* Since the inception of the RCD Technical Co-operation Programme, more than 1,600 trainees, about 1,100 students and 70 experts from Iran, Pakistan and Turkey have visited the regional countries. In addition, forty-three seminars have been arranged under the auspices of RCD and seven more are scheduled for the current year. There have also been joint courses on Public Administraton, of which seven have been held so far.

*Co-operation in the fields of Culture and Information.* Keeping in mind the basic common cultural heritage of the three RCD partners, an attempt has been made to give it a deeper and wider content through the establishment of a cultural institute in Tehran, with branches in Pakistan and Turkey. The Institute has hitherto published about fifty-five books which include original works as well as translations. Among other activities of the RCD Cultural Institute is the publication of a quarterly journal in English.

There is a comprehensive cultural exchange programme embracing regular sports contests, a common youth movement, co-operation among women's organizations, visits of eminent personalities, artists, journalists, and so on. There is also continuous contact between the regional press media and radio and television organizations.

The RCD Secretariat has to date published sixty-one books in regional and extra-regional languages. Besides, it brings out an anniversary booklet and a diary each year, a magazine and a newsletter. *Address:* RCD Secretariat, 5 Los Angeles Avenue, P.O. Box 3273, Tehran, Iran. Cable: ARCIDEVELOP.

## CULTURAL AND EDUCATIONAL RELATIONS

**The British Council** was established in 1934 and received a Royal Charter in 1940. Its objects are to promote a wider knowledge of Britain and the English language abroad, and to develop closer cultural relations with other countries. Most of its funds are provided by Parliament. The total estimated expenditure for 1977–78 is £77·9 million of which £3·5 million represents agency work carried out on behalf of Government Departments and international organizations. The Council is governed by a Board of up to 30 members, six of whom are nominated by Ministers. There are advisory committees for Scotland and Wales and also advisory committees or panels for the main branches of the Council's work, namely drama, English teaching, fine arts, law, libraries, medical, music, publishing and science (including agriculture, engineering and technology and veterinary science). Subject to the supervision of policy by the Board, the day-to-day management of the Council is the responsibility of the Director-General. At the end of 1977 the Council was represented in about 80 countries. The Council's work broadly divides into five parts: English language teaching and other educational work, the printed word, the development of two-way contacts, the presentation of the arts and sciences overseas and the administration of educational aid and technical assistance programmes.

The Council's involvement in English teaching and science education are of long standing. In both, the emphasis is on the training of teachers and teacher-trainers and in giving advice and assistance in syllabus and curriculum reform. The Council co-operates with overseas governments by maintaining specialist officers at its overseas centres and by seconding or recruiting staff for key posts. There is a similar support for science education, though the activity is considerably smaller. Of lecturers supplied for summer schools and short courses for teachers overseas, over half are science and mathematics specialists and the rest are mainly concerned with English. In some countries, the Council is engaged in direct English teaching, particularly to specialist professional groups, and administration for British examinations in English is provided. Several hundred teachers of English, science and other subjects are recruited annually for schools, colleges and universities on short-term contracts. On behalf of the British Volunteer Programme the Council provides the administrative framework overseas for about 700 volunteers who serve for two years in the developing countries. The Council also maintains scientifically qualified officers in an increasing number of countries to promote liaison with British academic and professional scientists and to provide information on British Science, medicine and technology. There is also a cadre of educational technology officers.

In recent years other educational work has become one of the Council's most important areas of activity. In Europe and the developed world this chiefly consists of establishing links between academics and institutions and of co-operating in conferences and seminars. In developing countries the Council's Representatives have been the official Education Advisers to HM Missions since an agreement signed with ODM in 1970 and have gradually taken over responsibility for administering the British educational aid and technical co-operation programmes. In oil-rich countries the Council is pioneering a new role in paid educational services, which includes the design and mangement of educational development projects in association with British Universities and Polytechnics, LEAs, and at times with construction companies and equipment suppliers. Inevitably in many of these activities the Council co-operates closely with the Ministry of Overseas Development, the Technical Education, and Training Organization for Overseas Countries, and the BBC, educational institutions and local education authorities. Headquarters support for English teaching includes specialist language consultants, the English-Teaching Information Centre in London which maintains a specialist library and provides bibliographical and other information, and the English Language Teaching Institute, where English is taught and experimental material is developed. Headquarters support for general educational work consists of a body of advisers in mathematics and science teaching, curriculum reform, examinations, technical and vocational education, higher education schools and teacher education, non-formal education and systems analysis. In addition, the Council offers its own studio. There is also a specialist information service providing bibliographical and other information in support of work in science and education.

The Council runs or is associated with over 170 reference and lending libraries in 75 countries. In 1976–77 these libraries issued 6–7 million books to some 400,000 members. The Council continues to assist the development of libraries in the developing world. In 1976–77 the Council organized over 230 book exhibitions in which some 100,000 books were shown, accompanied in many cases by specialized periodicals. The Council is responsible for the preparation and dissemination of bibliographical information about British books and periodicals in various forms and its publications include the monthly 'British Book News', the bi-monthly series 'Writers and their Work', 'British Medical Bulletin', 'British Medicine', 'Educational Broadcasting International', 'Governmental Organization of Science and Technology,' 'Agricultural Education in Europe', 'British Scientific Documentation Services', and 'How to Live in Britain', a handbook for overseas students, and biennially 'Higher Education in the UK'. It also acts as agent for the Ministry of Overseas Development's Low-Priced Textbooks Scheme. Under the joint imprints of Individual British publishers and ELBS (English Language Book Society), tertiary level textbooks are produced in special cheap editions for students in developing countries. Over 700 titles have been published already under this Scheme and the 20 millionth copy will be published during 1978.

The Council's development of personal contacts between Britain and other countries in the educational, scientific, professional and cultural spheres is a two-way traffic. In the outward direction, it arranges and assists advisory and consultative tours by British experts, usually between 600 and 800 a year. It also assists in the selection of British students for about 240 scholarships offered by foreign governments and universities. In the inward direction, the Council assisted some 27,000 visitors in 1976–77, many of whom came under certain schemes, such as British technical assistance, United Nations, OECD, Commonwealth Education Co-operation and Council of Europe. Many also came privately, and some as holders of the Council's own awards. The Council makes grants for exchanges of young people with Europe and other parts of the world, being advised by working groups representing official and Government bodies. It runs annually 11 Summer Schools for teachers of English and up to 25 courses for professional people in a wide variety of subjects. The Council also acts for H.M. Government on matters affecting the welfare of overseas students in Britain. It provides services for students and professional visitors and runs 25 offices in Britain where assistance can be given to overseas students and visitors, and it administers schemes of higher education interchange with Europe and the Commonwealth.

The Council sponsors tours by British theatrical, ballet and opera companies, and orchestras, ensembles and soloists; mounts exhibitions of British painting and sculpture, reproductions, prints and photographs; sends British films overseas and maintains substantial libraries of British short documentary films for lending to local institutions; sponsors the recording of works of British composers, dramatists and poets, and maintains lending libraries of discs and tapes *Director-General:* Sir John Llewellyn, KCMG, DSc, LLD FRS(NZ). *Address:* 10 Spring Gardens, SW1A 2BN. Tel.: 01-930 8466; telegrams: Britcoun London. Telex: 916522.

**The Commonwealth Institute** is a grant-aided organization representative of the whole Commonwealth. Its purpose is to foster among the peoples of the Commonwealth, a greater knowledge of one another and a better understanding of the importance and worth of the Commonwealth association by information, education and cultural activities designed to promote among all its peoples a wider knowledge of one another and greater understanding of the Commonwealth itself. By an Order-in-Council, the Institute is, *inter alia*, specifically charged to co-operate with other agencies within the Commonwealth formed for similar purposes, and to do anything conducive to carrying these purposes into effect. Apart from a small endowment, its income is derived from annual grants from the Governments of the United Kingdom and all the other Commonwealth countries. Parliamentary responsibility for the Institute in the United Kingdom rests with the Secretary of State for Foreign and Commonwealth Affairs.

The Institute was founded in 1887 (as the Imperial Institute) to commemorate the Golden Jubilee of Queen Victoria. The original building in South Kensington, opened by Queen Victoria in 1893, was occupied until 1962 when the Institute removed to a new building in Kensington High Street, opened by the Queen on 6 November. The name was changed by the Commonwealth Institute Act of 1958. The Institute is managed by an independent Board of Governors under the chairmanship of Sir David Hunt, KCMG, OBE. All the member countries of the Commonwealth are represented on the Board by their High Commissioners in London. In addition, the Board includes representatives of Commonwealth, educational, commercial and other relevant interests, appointed by the Secretary of State for Foreign and Commonwealth Affairs, and assessors appointed by government departments with which the Institute is functionally associated.

The chief feature of the Institute is the permanent exhibition which depicts, country by country, the life and environment of the Commonwealth peoples. Each exhibition is individually designed to capture something of the country's unique atmosphere, using the latest exhibition techniques which range from models and displays to multi-screen slide presentations, film sequences and other audio-visual attractions. The exhibition galleries are open free to the public on weekdays from 10 a.m.–5.30 p.m. and on Sunday from 2.30–6 p.m.

Temporary exhibitions are arranged to mark special Commonwealth occasions and travelling exhibitions on Commonwealth themes are circulated to civic centres, libraries, schools and other institutions.

The Trade Centre is available for Trade shows and the display of all kinds of Commonwealth produce.

Within the exhibition galleries is The Shop, a joint Institute and Oxfam enterprise which offers a comprehensive selection of Commonwealth goods as well as a variety of publications, teaching aids, records, stamps, and posters. Catalogues are available on request from the Manager.

Adjuncts to the galleries are a cinema-theatre with daily filmshows and an art gallery with changing exhibitions of the work of Commonwealth artists. The Institute also has a library and a restaurant.

The educational activities of the Institute are highly developed and concentrate to a large degree on promoting knowledge of the Commonwealth among students pupils and in colleges and schools. Every year about 3,000 school parties visit the Institute many of whom have the opportunity to attend lessons in the Activities Room, where the accent is on involvement rather than a passive classroom situation. Wherever possible these lessons are given by a national of the country or area being studied. A Talk to Schools service operates in all types of schools throughout the British Isles. A schools information service offers information and help to teachers and students. Conferences are organized in all types of secondary schools and in colleges of education. Courses for teachers and student teachers take place at the Institute, as well as special programmes for primary and secondary pupils. Another extra-mural activity is the Commonwealth Caravan which takes to suitable centres (e.g. teachers' centres and museums) displays, people and a wide range of learning materials including artefacts, all relating to a Commonwealth country or countries.

The Institute's Library and Resource Centre contains books, press cuttings, newspapers and periodicals, slides, film strips, gramophone records, educational charts and maps, describing the contemporary Commonwealth. There is a special collection of Commonwealth literature in English. Much of the material in the Library and Resource Centre is bought overseas. The library is open to the general public for reference and information, and its free loan service is available to all. Bibliographies and lists of other materials are available on request.

In the evenings the cinema–theatre and the exhibition galleries are frequently the venue of entertainments, receptions and other cultural and social events.

*Director:* J. K. Thompson, CMG. *Deputy-Director:* F. Lightfoot, MBE. *Address:* Kensington High Street, London, W8 6NQ. Tel.: 01-602 3252.

**The Commonwealth Institute in Scotland** is responsible for the work in that country. Although it operates in harmony with the broad policy determined by the Board of Governors of the Institute in London, the Institute in Scotland has its own independent committee under the Chairmanship of Professor G. A. Shepperson, who is a member of the Board in London.

The premises occupied by the Institute in Scotland provides, besides office accommodation, a show-room for educational aids, a reading-room for teachers and students and a gallery which is in constant use for small art exhibitions, conferences and meetings. *Scottish Director:* C. G. Carrol. *Address:* 8 Rutland Square, Edinburgh EH1 2AS. Tel.: 0131-299 6668.

**The English-Speaking Union.** The English-Speaking Union of the Commonwealth (incorporated under Royal Charter) and its sister society, The English-Speaking Union of the United States, although legally and financially distinct from one another, co-operate very closely in promoting throughout all the Commonwealth countries, U.S.A. and Europe interchange, understanding and friendship between all citizens of this group of countries. Membership is open to men, women or corporate bodies possessed of Commonwealth, U.S. or European nationality, who support the movement's purposes, irrespective of language, race, colour, party, religion or class, The E.-S.U. of the Commonwealth has 83 branches, and the U.-S.U. of the U.S.A. has 76 branches. The approximate worldwide membership is 70,000 (36,500 in U.S.A.; 16,500 in the U.K.; 17,000 Overseas Commonwealth). Founded in 1918 (but incorporating the Atlantic Union—founded in 1897—and two newer bodies, the American and British Commonwealth Association and Books Across the Sea, both founded in 1941), the E.-S.U. of the Commonwealth is under the patronage of H.M. Queen Elizabeth II. The President is H.R.H. Prince Philip, Duke of Edinburgh. Its other principal officers are: Deputy-President, Vacant; Vice-Presidents, the Rt. Hon. James Callaghan, MP; The Rt. Hon. Mrs. Margaret Thatcher, MP; David Steel, MP; Sir Stuart Mallinson, CBE, DSO, MC. Separately organized from 1921, the E.-S.U. of the U.S.A. has as its principal officer, The Hon. Barry Bingham, Sr. (Chairman of the Board). Its headquarters are at 16 East 69th Street, New York City. The chief means by which the two unions promote their common purpose are provision of advice, introductions, hospitality, exchanges, travel grants, fellowships, scholarships, etc., to enable men and women to visit each other's countries. Other provisions are objective information (both written and through the medium of speakers), lectures, discussions and social functions. Dartmouth House in London, the International Center and club provided welcome hospitality and advice to many Commonwealth and American visitors. *Chairman:* Sir Patrick Dean, GCMG. *Director-General:* David Alexander, CB. *Director and Secretary:* A. Grego-Bourne. *Address:* Dartmouth House, 37 Charles Street, Berkeley Square, London, W1X 8AB. Tel.: Officeand Club: 01-629 0104.

**P.E.N. Founded 1921 by C. A. Dawson Scott, under the presidency of John Galsworthy. A world association of writers. *Purpose*: to promote and maintain friendship and**

ntellectual co-operation between writers in every country, in the interests of freedom of artistic expression and international goodwill. Is open to every writer of standing, without distinction of creed or race, who subscribes to these fundamental principles. Takes no part in party politics, and its aims are summarized in these two quotations from speeches by former presidents of P.E.N.: 'We writers of the P.E.N. want to serve humanity at large in the ways (perhaps the only ways) in which the written word and the makers thereof can serve humanity, by linking up country by country the love of literature and by helping to restore to a bleak and starved world a friendly atmosphere' (John Galsworthy). 'We of the P.E.N. are united upon this fundamental thing, we stand for faith in the freely-thinking, freely-speaking, freely-writing mind. . . . Faced with the uproar and violence of contemporary affairs, the P.E.N. in its own fashion maintains the concept of an intellectual and aesthetic world republic; it asserts its faith in the ultimate triumph of the free brotherhood of mankind' (H. G. Wells). There are 76 autonomous centres. The English Centre meets monthly at discussions, and lectures, and has organized several large-scale congresses. Distinguished writers and others are entertained. P.E.N. has given much care to refugee writers from Austria, Germany, Czechoslovakia, Poland, Spain, Hungary and other countries, and has raised funds on their behalf. Annual congresses have been held in most European capitals, as well as in New York, Tokyo, Rio de Janeiro Buenos Aires, Abidjan and Seoul. The initials P.E.N. stand for Poets, Playwrights, Editors, Essayists, Novelists, but membership is open to all writers and translators of standing, International Presidents serve for three years. At the 28th International Congress (London 1956) Charles Morgan was succeded by André Chamson, Alberto Moravia was elected in July 1959, and Dr. Victor E. van Vriesland succeeded him in October 1962, Arthur Miller in July 1965, Pierre Emmanuel in 1969, Heinrich Böll in 1971, Sir Victor Pritchett in 1974, and at the London Congress in 1976 Mario Vargas Llosa was elected. English Centre; *President:* Lettice Cooper; Vice-Presidents, Sir Isaiah Berlin, CBE, Norman Collins, Lettice Cooper, Sir Robert Mayer, Wyn Griffith, OBE, Kathleen Nott, I. A. Richards, CH, Noel Streatfeild, Dame Rebecca West, DBE; General Secretary, Josephine Pullein-Thompson. *Publications:* Mightier Than the Sword, seven of The Hermon Ould Memorial Lectures (Macmillan); New Poems—A P.E.N. Anthology (annual by Hutchinson); P.E.N. Bulletin of Selected Books (quarterly in English and French); P.E.N. Broadsheet. *International Secretary:* Peter Elstob. *International Treasurer:* Thilo Koch. *Address:* Glebe House, 62 Glebe Place, Chelsea, London, SW3 SJB. Tel.: 01-352 9549 or 6303; Cables: Lonpenclub, London, S.W.3.

**Rotary International.** Founded in February 1905 to encourage and foster the ideal of service as a basis of worthy enterprise and, in particular, to foster the development of acquaintance as an opportunity for service, high ethical standards in business and the professions, and the advancement of international understanding, goodwill and peace. *Activities:* Throughout the world, include general community-betterment undertakings, promotion of high standards in business and in the professions, and work for the development of better understanding among the people of the world; The 1977 Convention of Rotary International (held in San Francisco, California, U.S.A.) was attended by 14,620 Rotarians and members of their families from 96 countries. Through The Rotary Foundation, more than 7,300 educational grants have been awarded to young men and women to enable them to study in a country other than their own. Individual grants average more than $8,100. In addition, more than 4,195 young business and professional men have participated in an international group study exchange programme. *Membership:* As of August, 1977 17,371; Rotary Clubs with a membership of 811,750 business and professional executives in 152 countries. *Publications:* Convention Proceedings; The Rotarian; Revista Rotaria (in Spanish); Adventnre in Service (a book of basic information about Rotary); Seven Paths to Peace (a practical guide for the individual in contributing to world peace); Service is my Business (a book on the importance of high business and professional standards). *Officers* (1977–78); *President:* W. Jack Davis, Bermuda, *Treasurer and Director:* Burton E. Grossman, Tampico. Tamaulipas, Mexico, *General Secretary:* Harry A. Stewart, Evanston, Illinois, U.S.A. *Address:* 1600 Ridge Avenue, Evanston, Illinois, 60201, U.S.A.

**British Volunteer Programme.** The British Volunteer Programme was set up in 1962 following discussions between volunteer sending organisations and the forerunner of what is now the Ministry of Overseas Development. It was then decided that the British contribution of qualified young people to serve on volunteer terms for development assistance in third world countries should be undertaken by voluntary organisations which already had experience in this field. The British Government offered to meet 50 per cent of the costs. This has subsequently been increased to 75 per cent and, from 1976 80 per cent. The voluntary organizations concerned raise the balance of the funds required from non-governmental sources.

The British Volunteer Programme is the co-ordinating body for this service, facilitating co-operation between the organisations concerned in such matters as overall planning, recruitment, selection standards, terms of service for volunteers, insurance, training and other matters of common concern. The organisations at present operating the scheme are Catholic Institute for International Relations, International Voluntary Service, United Nations Association and Voluntary Service Overseas. The Secretariat for BVP is provided by the National Council of Social Service.

During 1976 over 1,300 graduate and qualified volunteers were serving in about 90 countries in Africa, Asia and Latin America as well as in island territories in the Pacific and Caribbean. The major fields of assistance are in secondary education, health services, agriculture and technical services of various kinds. All volunteers serve for two years as a minimum. Travel and incidental expenses are met and in the field they receive a maintenance allowance only equivalent to board, lodging and pocket money.

*Address:* 26 Bedford Square, London, WC1B 3HU. *Tel.:* 01-636 4066.

### DISASTERS AND DEVELOPMENT AID

**Christian Aid.** This organization is a division of the British Council of Churches and the overseas aid agency of the Council's 28 member churches. It is also a registered charity of national reputation, and has been one of Britain's fastest growing voluntary agencies.

Christian Aid started in 1944 when the British Council of Churches set up an agency to help hundreds of thousands of Europeans who lost their homes, their families, and in many cases even their countries. The organisation was called 'Christian Reconstruction in Europe', renamed in 1949 'Inter-Church Aid' and in 1964 became simply 'Christian Aid'. As its work was expanded into other areas of need outside Europe, the department was gradually transformed into an agency for development in Third World countries, mainly in the Commonwealth where the links with churches were strongest. This bias is still apparent today, although Christian Aid now annually supports several hundred projects in more than 100 countries.

Unlike other agencies, Christian Aid has no projects of its own or representatives overseas; it works entirely through local structures—mainly churches or voluntary organizations—and relies on a regional screening of projects by specialists. It also co-operates closely with the world-wide network of Christian Churches and Councils centred on the World Council of Churches in Geneva.

The Rev. Alan Booth, Christian Aid's director from 1970 to 1975, pointed out: 'Not only are poor communities capable of advancing their own development, once given the financial resources, but it is in their own interests that they do so and that they do not become dependent upon borrowed skills, foreign methods and expatriate personnel. So it is Christian Aid's policy to send money rather than people.'

More than half Christian Aid's annual income is collected during Christian Aid Week, in which about 500,000 accredited collectors knock on the doors of 80 per cent of the homes in Britain. Christian Aid Week raised £2,590,895 in 1976 compared with £1,951,931 in the previous year. Christian Aid's total income for 1975–76 (October to September), including the revenue from emergency appeals, denominational and other special appeals and from individual gifts and legacies, totalled £4,757,910.

Christian Aid's present director is The Rev. Dr. Kenneth Slack, formerly Moderator of the United Reformed Church; its associate director is Mr. Martin Bax. It has a staff of about 80 including headquarters staff, Overseas Aid and Education Departments, and a field staff of 45 in Britain and Ireland.

*Publications:* Annual Report, Christian Aid News, information packs on development topics and overseas projects, topic sheets and work sheets for schools; The Aid Booklets, jointly with Oxfam; posters and filmstrips.

*Address:* P.O. Box No. 1. London SW9 8BH (callers: 240/250 Ferndale Road, SW9). Tel.: 01-733 5500.

**Disasters Emergency Commitee.** Formed in 1964 primarily to act as an agency for appeals for the five main British charities concerned with overseas relief. Current member charities: British Red Cross Society, Christian Aid, Catholic Fund for Overseas Development, Oxfam, The Save the Children Fund and War on Want. The Organization came into being when it became clear that the power of an appeal to the public for aid to disasters overseas by use of the television medium was successful out of all proportion to any other means of appealing. Such successes of television appeals by individual charities began to cause intense competition for the right to make such appeals as well as proving a source of embarrassment to the television authorities.

The idea of joint action by the major charities was first proposed by the late Lord Astor, at that time Chairman of the Standing Conference of British Organisations for Aid to Refugees. Lord Astor suggested that the five major charities should form an unofficial committee under the Red Cross chairmanship for the purposes of co-ordinating their efforts following a major disaster. Thus during 1964 the Committee was formed of the five charities plus official representatives of the Foreign and Commonwealth Office, the Standing Conference for Refugees and the U.N. High Commissioner for Refugees as observers as and when necessary.

The Committee is not itself a registered charity but it is recognized by the Charity Commissioners as the operative agency through which the charities jointly launch television appeals to the public over the national networks following any major disaster overseas.

The members of the Committee can be called together at short notice on receipt of news of a major disaster. The decision whether or not to appeal is then taken on reports available from the League of Red Cross Societies or the International Committee of the Red Cross, the United Nations Disaster Relief Office and the agents of the other member charities, official reports from the Foreign and Commonwealth Office representatives and the news media. If it is decided to appeal, the Red Cross, which provides the Secretariat, immediately seeks permission from the BBC and Independent Broadcasting Authority for times on their respective networks, which is given free, usually at a peak viewing time, of a duration of about four to five minutes. A draft script is prepared and suitable appellants are decided on and approached.

The Committee is concerned to distinguish its disaster appeals from normal charitable appeals and it considers that it is providing a necessary channel for the public to contribute directly to the help of disaster victims. This distinction has been accepted in principle by the television authorities.

Donations from the public are paid into a central account operated by one of the charities, in rotation. Each member is allocated one-sixth of the appeal proceeds, as these become available, and each charity is responsible for the expenditure of its own share. The member charities then meet frequently to decide among themselves how the money collected can best be spent, based on information received directly from the country concerned through the Government, Red Cross and other reliable channels.

After the first emergency steps, during which joint actions are often undertaken by some or all of the six charities, each charity tends to use the balance of its allocation for differing forms of relief, according to its particular aims and objectives.

Co-operation with the Government has always been close and in several recent disasters the Government have assisted greatly in arranging air freight (RAF or civilian charter) and allowing the Committee members to fill the space with relief material as part of a joint effort.

The Disasters Emergency Committee has, to date, launched sixteen appeals raising in excess of £8·75 million. *Chairman:* Rt. Hon. Lord Gore-Booth, GCMG, KCVO. *Deputy-Chairman:* H. L. Kirkley, CBE. *Secretary:* Mr. P. A. Adams. *Address:* 9 Grosvenor Crescent, London, SW1X 7EJ. *Telephone:* 01-235 7260.

**Oxfam.** Oxfam exists to relieve poverty, distress and suffering in any part of the world. A voluntary organization without political or religious affiliations, it has grown from a small group concerned for the starving of war-torn Greece in 1942 to an agency helping about 1,000 projects in over 80 countries at any one time.

Oxfam originated as The Oxford Committee for Famine Relief in response to a short-term need and it remains equipped to rush vital supplies to the victims of earthquake, flood, famine and war. However, the main emphasis of its work has changed over the years, with the official contraction of its name to Oxfam: more than two-thirds of its funds now go to long-term development schemes, helping the needy to help themselves. These overseas programmes are not directly run by Oxfam. They are carried out by the most appropriate group on the spot—which may be a village committee, a hospital, a church organization or another agency—with funds from Oxfam. The key to this way of working is a network of experienced Field Directors based at seven offices in Africa, three in Latin America and six in Asia, helped by Assistants and in some cases technical specialists. They respond to and encourage requests for help, provide advice, and report on the needs and progress of the projects.

Recommendations from the field are processed in Oxford by Field Committees made up of honorary members knowledgeable in a particular subject or geographical area. They in turn are responsible to the Council of Management, an honorary body of 50 members, who take important decisions and are Oxfam's legal trustees.

The priorities for Oxfam help are on constructive self-help and on prevention rather than cure, but Oxfam does help some purely welfare and relief schemes.

In 1976–77, 67 per cent of Oxfam's aid went to development work: 28 per cent on health projects; 21 per cent on agricultural; 29 per cent on social development. The remaining 22 per cent was spent on humanitarian and emergency work.

Voluntary help is a vital component of Oxfam's work at all levels. Tens of thousands of supporters throughout Britain and in other parts of the world help with fund-raising, bringing in an income of £6·4 million in 1976–77. About a third of this sum came from a network of nearly 600 shops run almost entirely by unpaid helpers.

Opinion-forming plays an increasing part in Oxfam's work and in 1974 the Council of Management agreed that up to five per cent of donated funds, other than those given for specific emergencies overseas, should be set aside for educational activities in the U.K.

Oxfam works with young people within the formal school system, through youth clubs, college and university groups, and with adults through seminars and conferences.

The organization has close links with a number of other bodies: in particular with its sister organization in various parts of the world. They help fund projects through Oxfam and also support other projects directly. A recent initiative is the linking of six British based agencies concerned with poverty both in Britain and the Third World (Child Poverty Action Group, Help the Aged, Shelter, the United Nations Association, War on Want and Oxfam) in a campaign to combat poverty everywhere. In major emergencies Oxfam meets with five other charities (Christian Aid, Save the Children Fund, the Red Cross, War on Want, and the Catholic Fund For Overseas Development) under the Disasters Emergency Committee to consider a joint appeal and discuss what co-operation may be appropriate.

The assistance Oxfam provides throughout the world can and does help many communities to transform their lives. At the same time it is clear that the limited funds available are minute compared with the global needs. For this reason Oxfam seeks constantly to improve evaluation methods, to learn from and disseminate success and failure and to use each grant as a catalyst which generates other local initiatives, which it is hoped will advance the cause of the poor and lead to greater human fulfillment for mankind.

*Director:* Brian Walker. *Address:* 274 Banbury Road, Oxford OX2 7DZ. *Telephone:* 0865 56777. *Telex:* 83610.

**The Save the Children Fund.** The Save the Children Fund is an independent, voluntary organization, now fifty seven years old, whose purpose is the rescue in disaster and the longer term welfare of needy children, irrespective of nationality, race or religion. The ultimate aims are to create conditions in which children can grow to a healthy maturity and, in overseas projects, to train local workers where necessary in the professional and technical skills required for child welfare.

The Organization is currently helping children in nearly fifty countries with teams of more than a thousand field workers, nurses, welfare workers and administrators. For example, in Bangladesh, the Yemen, Sudan and Honduras teams are bringing much-needed mother and child health care. And in countries such as Upper Volta, Ethiopia, India and Swaziland, tens of thousands of children rely on the Fund for a daily meal. In Morocco and Lesotho, blind and handicapped children receive long-term care, and in Indonesia, scores of teenagers pass through The Save the Children Fund's Vocational Training Centre. In addition, more than fifteen thousand chidren benefit from individual and family sponsorship.

In the United Kingdom, help i s given to meet pressing needs not yet fully provided by public authorities. In over-crowded cities, high rise estates and in Northern Ireland, Save the Children runs over one hundred community play-groups for the under-fives. Also, the needs of children in hospital are met through hospital playgroups. Thousands of children make use of the opportunity for hobbies and recreation through the Fund's peripatetic youth service, and for children in need of long-term care there are four residential homes.

The Fund was founded by Eglantyne Jebb in 1919 who was responsible for drawing up the 'Rights of the Child' which was later adopted by the United Nations.

*Patron:* Her Majesty The Queen; *President:* H.R.H. The Princess Anne, Mrs. Mark Phillips, GCVO. *Chairman:* Dr. N. H. Moynihan, C st J, MA(Cantab), MB, BChir, MR.CS, LRCP, MRCGP. *Director General:* John Cumber. CMG, MBE, TD. *Hon. Treasurer:* E. Pollitzer, OBE. *Address:* 157 Clapham Road, London SW9 0PT. *Telephone:* 01-582 1414.

**Volunteers in Technical Assistance.** VITA, Inc. is a private, non-profit association of 5,000 volunteer scientists, engineers, agriculturalists and crafts and business people who respond by mail to requests for technical assistance from individual and groups in the developing countries. Problems are generally in the areas of food production, shelter, alternative energy sources, small business development, and other human services, including health, sanitation and water supply systems.

A small staff in a Washington, D.C. suburb receives the 1,200 annual requests and co-ordinates the problem-solving process. Volunteers apply the principles of appropriate technology to development questions by designing solutions which can be implemented by the requestors, using local skills and materials, and which are culturally and environ-mentally considerate.

VITA regularly undertakes special projects which promise wider impact and require longer term commitment than usual requests, sometimes including short, on-site con-sulting trips. VITA currently has a staff member in Upper Volta and a representative in Papua New Guinea on long. term assignments.

VITA also disseminates technical information through its library of appropriate technology and via its Publications Program, which currently has 45 'how-to' manuals that have been written or compiled entirely by VITA Volunteers. Many of these have been translated into Spanish, French or Portuguese, as well as English. The most popular title is VITA's *Village Technology Handbook*, a collection of plans and designs applicable to establishing the support systems necessary for a small community's survival. VITA publi-cations are distributed throughout the world.

VITA is supported by government and private foundation grants and corporate and individual contributions.

The current Executive Director is Tom Fox.

*Address:* 3706 Rhode Island Avenue, Mt. Rainier, Mary-land 20822 U.S.A.

## EDUCATION

**The Association of Commonwealth Universities.** Almost all universities of good standing in the Commonwealth are members of this Association, which is a voluntary organiz-ation founded in 1913, incorporated by Royal Charter and financed by the subscriptions of its 209 member institutions. Its affairs are controlled by a Council of executive heads representing those institutions in the different Common-wealth countries, and its functions include the provision of an administrative link between member universities through-out the Commonwealth and the organization of periodical conferences. The eleventh quinquennial Congress of the Uni-versities of the Commonwealth was held in Edinburgh in 1973 (next in Canada in 1978). A conference of executive heads of member institutions is held twice in each five-year period (next in Canada in 1978) and, between congresses, smaller meetings are held in different Commonwealth countries (last in Malta in 1977). The Association acts as an agency in London for overseas member universities wishing to invite applications for vacant posts on their academic staffs. It also undertakes certain responsibilities in connec-tion with the Commonwealth Scholarship and Fellowship Plan, particularly by providing the secretariat for the Commonwealth Scholarship Commission in the United Kingdom. It administers the Third World Academic Ex-changes Programme (funded by the Commonwealth Fund for Technical Co-operation), the Third World Academic Exchange Fellowship (financed by the Times Higher Edu-cational Supplement) and the A.C.U./Commonwealth Foundation Administrative Travelling Fellowships. The Association provides the secretariat for the Marshall Aid Commemoration Commission and the Kennedy Memorial Trust. It acts as a publications and information centre, and maintains a 10,000-volume reference library. *Publications* include the annual 2,600-page Commonwealth Universities Yearbook, Register of Research Strengths of Universities in Developing Countries of the Commonwealth, A.C.U. Bulletin of Current Documentation, Awards for Commonwealth University Staff 1978–80, Scholarships Guide for Common-wealth Postgraduate Students, 1977–79, Financial Aid for First Degree Study at Commonwealth Universities, 1978–79, reports of proceedings of the quinquennial Commonwealth Universities Congresses, Map of Commonwealth Universities. Compendium of University Entrance Requirements for First Degree Courses in the United Kingdom, Schedule of Post-graduate Courses in U.K. Universities, List of Academic Visitors to the U.K., and (jointly with the British Council) Higher Education in the United Kingdom: A Handbook for Students from Overseas and their Advisers. *Chairman* (1977–78): Dr. H. E. Duckworth. *Vice-Chairman* (1977–78): Dr. J. Steven Watson. *Hon. Treasurer* (1977–78): Dr. T. H. B. Symons. *Hon Deputy Treasurer* (1977–78): Sir Douglas Logan. *Immediate Past Chairman* Dr. Professor E. J. Borg Costanzi. *Secretary General:* Sir Hugh W. Springer. *Address:* The Association of Commonwealth Universities, 36 Gordon Square, London, WC1H 0PF. Tel.: 01-387 8572.

**United States-United Kingdom Educational Commission.** Was set up under an agreement signed by the United States and the United Kingdom Governments in May 1965 to replace the former United States Educational Commission in the United Kingdom which had been in existence since Septem-ber 1948. The unchanged purpose of the Commission is to administer the programme of educational exchange between the two countries provided for by the 1961 Fulbright-Hays Act (Public Law 87–256). Under the agreement the British Government will contribute 33.3 per cent and the United States Government 66.6 per cent of the funds placed at the Commission's disposal each year; originally the Com-mission's funds had all been provided by the United States from its sterling deposits in the United Kingdom.

Under the Fulbright programme awards are made to American citizens for lecturing, advanced research, post-graduate research or courses, and other educational activities in the United Kingdom and its dependent territories overseas. Awards are made too to British citizens to carry out similar activities in the United States. For all American Scholars awards cover round-trip travel, maintenance and tuition, where applicable. For British lecturers and Senior Research Scholars Travel Grants only are available, but for British graduate students a maintenance allowance is paid in addition to round-trip travel. The Commission can also finance visits and interchanges of students, trainees, teachers and in-structors and professors between the U.S. and the U.K. and its dependent territories. Also with the approval of the two Governments it can finance other related educational and cultural programmes. The Commission itself consists of seven American members appointed by the U.S. Ambassador in London, and of seven British members appointed by the Secretary of State for Education and Science.

*Hon. Chairman:* American Ambassador to the Court of St. James's. *Chairman:* Mr. Irving Sablosky, Cultural Attaché to the American Embassy. *Secretariat:* John O. A. Herrington, Executive director. *Address:* 6 Porter Street, London, W1M 2HR. Tel.: 01-486-7697.

**University of London Institute of Commonwealth Studies.** Established in 1949 to promote advanced study of the Commonwealth. Its field of interest is mainly, but not exclusively, that of the social sciences and recent history in relation to the countries of the Commonwealth. It encourages collaboration at post-graduate level between workers who are employing different techniques of research in the study of Commonwealth problems. It provides a meeting place for both post-graduate students and members of the academic staffs of Universities and research institutions in the United Kingdom and overseas. Courses are held for the M.A. in Area Studies (the Commonwealth). The Library places particular emphasis upon primary material relating to history, politics, economic and social development and demography; and with this object it regularly acquires official publications, statistics, guides to archives, etc., of the United Kingdom and Commonwealth countries. Books and papers are for reference only and may not be borrowed from the Library. Particulars of admission and forms of appli-cation may be obtained from the Assistant Secretary. *Address:* 27 Russell Square, London, WC1B 5DS.

**Pan American Institute of Geography and History.** Founded, Havana, 1928, to promote co-operation between the Ameri-can nations in the conduct of their cartographic, geographic, historical and geophysic activities. It serves as a medium for stimulating these activities, and for the dissemination of information. The Institute works directly with the cartographic, geographic, historical and geophysics institutions and provides help and advice when needed. It will aid a country in setting up specialized technical agencies versed in modern methods. The four Commissions (Cartography, Geography, History, Geophysics) of the Institute, and their Committees, together with the General Secretariat constitute the main working forces. Some 300 individuals from the Republics and Canada are actively working on the Institute's plans and programmes. *Membership:* Governments of Argentina, Bolivia, Brazil, Canada, Chile, Colombia, Costa Rica, Cuba. Dominican Republic, Ecuador, El Salvador, Guatemala, Haiti, Honduras, Mexico, Nicaragua, Panama, Paraguay, Peru, United States, Uruguay, Venezuela. *Finance:* Quota payments, fundamentally based on *per capita* income and the Pan American Union system. Average revenue is $320,000 a year. *Publications:* Revista Cartográfica; Folklore Americano y Boletín Aéreo; Revista Geográfica; Revista de Historia de América; Boletin Bibliográfico de Antropologia Americana, Revista Geofisica; (all these are published at intervals); monographs and reports. The library contains over 50,000 volumes. *Secretary-General:* Engr. Jose A. Saenz G. (Panama). *Address:* Ex-Arzobispado 29, México, 18, D.F. México.

### ENGINEERING

**Institution of Electronic and Radio Engineers.** The purpose of the organization is to promote the advancement of radio, electronics and kindred subjects by the exchange of information in these branches of engineering.

The Institution is a constituent institution of the Council of Engineering Institutions.

*Current Activities:* The Institution publishes original papers on research work and on engineering development. Conferences on topical subjects are held regularly. Meetings are held in London and at more than 30 centres throughout Great Britain, throughout the winter months as well as at centres in Canada, Hong Kong, India, New Zealand, Israel, and Pakistan.

*Publication: The Radio and Electronic Engineer.*

*Library:* The Institution has a library for the use of members. *Educational Activities:* The Institution is associated with the C.E.I. Examination. Representatives serve on the Joint Committee for Higher National Certificates and Diplomas in Electrical and Electronic Engineering and on advisory committees of polytechnics, colleges of technology and technical colleges.

*President:* Prof. W. A. Gambling D.Sc., CEng., FIERE. *Secretary:* Air Vice-Marshal S. M. Davidson, CBE, CEng., FIERE. *Address:* 99 Gower Street, London WC1E 6AZ. *Telephone:* 01-388-3071.

**Institution of Mechanical Engineers.** The Institution was founded in 1847, the first general meeting being held on Wednesday, 27 January 1847, at the Queen's Hotel, Birmingham, with Mr. McConnell, of Wolverhampton, in the chair. The headquarters of the Institution continued to be in Birmingham until 1877, when they were transferred to London, and from that year until 1899, when the building in Birdcage Walk was opened, the London meetings were held by courtesy of the Institution of Civil Engineers, in the hall of that Institution. In 1856 arrangements were made for the Summer Meeting of the Intitution to be held in provincial centres, the first of these provincial meetings being held in Glasgow, in September of that year, under the Presidency of Joseph Whitworth. The prosperity of the Institution dates from this innovation, the membership having grown from an almost stationary figure of just over 200 in 1849 to 1855, to over 70,000 at the present day. The list of Past Presidents of the Institution includes the names of many famous engineers among them being George Stephenson, the first President; Robert Stephenson, Sir Joseph Whitworth, Lord Armstrong, Robert Napier, John Ramsbottom, Sir William Siemens, Sir Frederick Bramwell, Thomas Hawksley and others.

*Objects:* To promote the development of Mechanical Engineering and to facilitate the exchange of information and ideas thereon and for that purpose: (a) To encourage invention and research in matters connected with Mechanical Engineering and with this object to make grants of money or books or otherwise to assist such invention and research; (b) To hold meetings of the Institution for reading and discussing communications bearing upon Mechanical Engineering or the application thereof or upon subjects relating thereto: (c) To print, publish and distribute the proceedings or reports of the Institution or any papers, communications, works or treatises on Mechanical Engineering or its application or subjects connected therewith; (d) To co-operate with Universities, other Educational Institutions and public Educational Authorities for the furtherance of Education in Engineering Science or Practice; (e) To all other things incidental or conducive to the attainment of the above objects or any of them.

The membership of the Institution includes the following classes: Fellows (FIMechF); Members (MIMechE); Hon. Fellows (HonFIMechE), Companions, Associates, Graduates and Students.

*President:* Professor Sir Hugh Ford D.Sc, PhD, FRS, CEng, FIMechE, FICE. *Secretary:* Mr Alex McKay, CB, CEng. FIMechE, FIEE. *Address:* 1 Birdcage Walk, Westminster SW1H 9JJ. *Tel.:* 01-839 1211. *Telex:* 917944.

### ENVIRONMENTAL

**The Conservation Society Ltd.** The Conservation Society was founded in 1966 by Dr. D. M. C. MacEwan, with the aim of alerting the public and the government to the dangers arising from the continuous growth of population, both national and world-wide. Since then, its aims have been broadened to include consideration of the dangers to the environment from industrial expansion, and present Society policy is based on the need for human societies to move without delay towards a size of population and way of life that is *sustainable*, i.e., one that does not depend on material growth, does not cause accumulating pollution, and is not based on the progressive depletion of irreplaceable resources.

The Society pursues these aims by publication of articles, arranging public meetings, through contacts with local and national government, and through the communications media.

The governing body of the Society is a Council, largely elected at the Annual General Meeting, and there is a central office with a staff of four to manage day-to-day business. Much of the Society's work, however, is done on a voluntary basis, through membership of Working Parties on particular subjects (transport, land use, family planning, etc.) and through the 60 branches now established throughout the country.

Total membership is at present 6,500, and all members receive the Society's journal 'Conservation News', published four times a year.

*President:* Lord Avebury. *Chairman:* Dr. Leonard Taitz. *Director:* (to whom general correspondence should be addressed): Dr. John Davoll. *Address:* 12a Guildford Street, Chertsey, Surrey KT16 9BQ, England. Telephone: Chertsey 60975 (STD Code 093 28).

**Friends of the Earth.** *General Introduction*: FOE Ltd. (Friends of the Earth) is an independent company, limited by guarantee, non-profit-making and with no party allegiance. It is associated with a further company, Earth Resources Research Ltd., which is a recognized charity.

The objects of FOE (together with its research arm, Earth Resources Research) are to work for the protection of the environment and to promote the conservation of natural resources and their rational use. The methods which it employs towards these objectives can be seen on three levels: first, by position research and publications, second by pragmatically (rather than ideologically) based campaigns in the political arena and third by fostering public involvement and concern by way of citizen groups and activities.

The research studies are carried out by qualified individuals who are employed for the purpose. It is also the role of these researchers to translate their findings into realistic legislative reforms and to present them in an understandable manner to a wide sector of the public. The research team is assisted by a full-time staff, expert in various functional aspects of the company. FOE (U.K.) employs nine full-time staff and a part-time consultant. There are 170 local community groups.

FOE (U.K.) is part of a world-wide federation, Friends of the Earth International, working for the same objectives. Each national group is autonomous, but all interact via a monthly newspaper and international meetings.

*Finance*

FOE depends for its funds on private donations and subscriptions, and on grants from foundations and similar bodies. FOE is most grateful to the individuals, firms and other bodies concerned.

*Current Activities of FOE:*

*Energy and the Environment.* This campaign covers all aspects of energy policy. In our current work, we are closely involved in the environmental implications of various sources of energy (most particularly nuclear power) and in evaluating and working towards energy conservation measures to reduce demand.

*Land Use and Food Supply.* A standing survey of Britain's dependence on imported food and a series of critical studies on our agricultural policies in the context of the growing world demand for food produce and agricultural raw materials.

*Transport.* A pragmatic campaign towards an integrated transport policy for Britain. Our expertise centres on the energetics of transport, the social equity of various modes and the long-term implications of encouraging the use of the private car.

*Wild Life Protection.* Two major campaigns are currently being waged: first, on the international front, towards protection for the endangered species of whale (FOE Ltd. is an observer to the International Whaling Commission); second, towards a set of legal reforms in the U.K. for incorporating into our law the International Union for the Conservation of Nature's convention on the trade in endangered species.

*Reuse, Resource Reduction and Recycling.* A comprehensive campaign in which the resource content of household waste is being evaluated towards a more efficient use and reduction of such 'waste'.

*International Marine Issues.* FOE (U.K.) is at the centre of Friends of the Earth International's efforts for the protection of the marine environment. Hitherto, this has involved a study of the environmental aspects of the UN Law of the Sea Conference and a close watching brief on the UN Intergovernmental Maritime Consultative Organization (with which FOE International has consultative status).

In addition to these areas of special interest, the staff are well acquainted with general aspects of environmental control and pollution. Whenever needed, the team is able to answer general enquiries from the public and specific enquiries from those more closely involved. The two organizations have a series of publications on each aspect of their work. Details of these are available on request.

*Key Personnel*

The current Director of Friends of the Earth is Tom Burke. The Director of Earth Resources Research is Graham Searle.

*Address:* 9 Poland Street, London W1V 3DG.

**International Society for the Protection of Animals.** Founded 1959. This is a Registered Charity in the U.K. and the U.S.A. Aims: To promote effective means for the protection and conservation of animals and the relief of suffering throughout the world; to maintain effective liaison between, and seek co-operation with, localized organizations having similar objectives; to provide facilities for membership of approved animal welfare societies and individuals interested in animal welfare; to seek recognition and representation on suitable bodies; to study international and national legislation relating to animal welfare; and to promote international efforts for the protection of animals. ISPA has consultative arrangements with the United Nations, the Council or Europe, and the European Community, and maintains a fully trained Field Staff.

*Executive Director:* Trevor H. Scott. *Address:* 106 Jermyn Street, London, SW1Y 6EE. Offices in Boston, U.S.A. and Bonn, W. Germany.

**The National Centre for Alternative Technology.** The object of the Centre is to encourage greater national self-sufficiency by showing more sustainable (and therefore less wasteful) methods of living. The Centre demonstrates the production of energy supplies from renewable resources (e.g., sun, wind, organic waste), techniques for energy conservation and storage; intensive organic horticulture. An information service has also been established at the Centre.

The reasons for our objectives are: (1) The belief that mankind must live within the Earth's limited natural resources; (2) The realization that affluence and 'quality of life' are not necessarily synonymous; (3) The moral indefensibility of running risks by using inadequately proven technologies; (4) The likelihood of social breakdown should present highly centralized systems fail, either through natural causes or sabotage.

*The Project.* The Centre, sponsored by the Society for Environmental Improvement Ltd., provides a formal entity where the practice of alternative technology (AT) can be carried out. (The term 'Alternative Technology' describes the ways and means of doing things with minimal adverse consequences, both environmentally and socially.) The project is detailed in the Appendix. Work commenced on 1 February 1974.

Full facilities exist for demonstration of existing techniques and equipment; development of new ideas to prototype stage; seminars; courses; reference library, catalogues of equipment available, etc. A small permanent staff is supported by volunteer labour.

The project aims to co-ordinate and educate the numerous individuals and groups who are interested/involved in the development and practise of AT—an urgent requirement if duplication and misapplied effort are to be prevented. A close liaison with both industry and universities is now being developed so that research projects can be co-ordinated, demonstrations can be carried out on the site and commercial production of successful equipment can be encouraged. The supporting staff live as a largely self-sufficient community, serviced by the energy sources demonstrated.

Although the project described here relates specifically to the U.K., the demonstration of AT has a global relevance. In developing countries, the need for energy systems which are low in capital cost (even if relatively heavy in labour use) is a high priority. As far as is known, there is no comparable centre in the world. Nevertheless, throughout the world there is a great deal of information and expertise available for use in such a centre. Entrance tickets, consultancy fees, sale of publications, workshop fees, and conference fees and combined with low expenses, will form the basis for the eventual self-funding of the project.

The site, a 30-acre disused slate quarry, has been generously made available to the Society for a peppercorn rental. Planning consent has been obtained. The Centre is sited 3 miles north of Machynlleth, which has facilities for accommodation and a good rail link with London. The realization of the project is acting as a powerful stimulant to the employment of AT and will not only provide a positive reduction to the scale of the problems which we face today, but also indicate a direction in which our civilization may move in greater safety and sanity.

*Council:* Gerard Morgan-Grenville (Chairman); Diana Brass, Michael Bray, Diana Eccles, Roderick James.

*Address:* Llwyngwern Quarry, Pantperthog, Machynlleth, Powys, Wales.

### *APPENDIX*

#### *Schedule of Projects*

The development and demonstration of the following Alternative Technologies:

*Energy:* To construct, adapt and/or install equipment of the following types:

(i) Water-powered: small-scale turbines, high-efficiency water-wheels, hydraulic ram.
(ii) Solar: flat-plate collectors, focusing collectors, solar-electric conversion, solar-heat engine, biological fuels.
(iii) Wind Power: savonious rotor, turbine, small and large propellers.
(iv) Gas: methane, hydrogen.
(v) Energy storage: small-scale systems applicable to (i)–(iv) above.
(vi) Heat exchangers: heat pump, domestic heat collector.
(vii) Distillation: wood alcohol.

*Recycling.* To show:

(i) Small-scale equipment: for anaerobic digestion of sewage for fertilizer (and methane).
(ii) Systems: for group collection of raw materials.

*Building.* To exhibit materials, equipment, and complete buildings:

(i) Materials and equipment: for the utilization of on-site and/or environmentally suitable materials.
(ii) Buildings: demonstrating low-energy techniques, including methods of better insulation and techniques for autonomous provision of average domestic needs.

*Food.* To show methods and equipment—especially applicable to urban and suburban situations—in use for intensive organic horticulture:

(i) Plant symbiosis
(ii) Greenhouse cultivation
(iii) Pisciculture
(iv) Composting

*Transport.* To set up a transport facility *vis à vis* Rail, road and canal: to demonstrate low-energy personnel/freight transport systems, including the use of energy derived from renewable resources.

*Education.* To prepare educational packs for use in primary and secondary schools.

*An office has been equipped to give an indication of:*

(a) The performance, availability and price of the equipment demonstrated at the Centre;
(b) Similar details of other equipment unsuited to the particular site;
(c) Books and papers and filmstrips on all aspects of AT;
(d) An index of sites where AT is in practical use;
(e) An index of individuals/groups concerned with AT development;
(f) A register of new techniques/applications in need of development or trials.

The Centre also has a workshop for

(a) The realization of the projects mentioned at the beginning of the Appendix.
(b) The subsequent development of new systems, and
(c) A lecture room for visiting groups and short courses.

*Address:* Llwyngwern Quarry, Pantperthog, Machynlleth, Powys, Wales. *Telephone:* Machynlleth 2400.

**The World Wildlife Fund.** An international, non-governmental organisation which raises funds to support wildlife conservation projects all over the world. It was established in 1961 and now has National organizations in 26 countries. Together the International Union for Conservation of Nature and Natural Resources, WWF screens projects submitted for funding and provides money for those which are in line with current priorities for the conservation of the world's natural resources. The projects passed are then published in a yearly Conservation Programme. Since its inception the World Wildlife Fund has given over U.S. $25 million to over 1,700 projects in over 100 countries. It also achieves conservation objectives by direct representations to relevant authorities.

The International Secretariat of WWF and its National organizations also act as centres for information on the world's threatened species of plants and animals, as well as wild places. Its publications include the World Wildlife Fund Yearbook which is published every year by the International Secretariat and is a complete illustrated record of WWF's activities and achievements, and the quarterly World Wildlife News. *President:* John H. Loudon. *Executive Vice-President:* Dr. Luc Hoffman. *Chairman:* Sir Peter Scott. *Directors-General:* Charles de Haes, Dr. F. Vollmar. *Address:* 1110 Morges, Switzerland. *Telephone:* Lausanne (021) 71 96 11 *Telex:* 25999 PANDA CH.

**Nature Conservancy Council.** This official body was set up under the Nature Conservancy Council Act, 1973, to be responsible for nature conservation and to foster its understanding. The term "nature conservation" covers wild plants and animals and geological and physiographical features.

Council's functions are to establish, maintain and manage National Nature Reserves in Great Britain: to provide advice to Ministers on the development and implementation of policies for or affecting nature conservation in Great Britain; to provide advice and disseminate knowledge about nature conservation; and to commission or support relevant research. Council also has power to undertake certain research and to pay grants for nature conservation projects. While discharging its functions it takes account of actual or possible ecological changes.

Members of Council are appointed by the Secretary of State for the Environment, in consultation with the Secretaries of State for Scotland and Wales. Under the Act Council appoints separate Advisory Committees for England, Scotland and Wales; it also has set up an Advisory Committee on Science.

By the end of June 1977, Council was responsible for 155 National Nature Reserves (NNR)—79 in England, 45 in Scotland, and 31 in Wales—covering 299,303 acres (or 121,122 hectares). Moreover, it had notified over 3,600 Sites of Special Scientific Interest (SSSI) to local planning authorities. Council has no rights over these Sites but planning authorities must consult it before granting permission for development on them.

Additional duties include responsibility for granting or approving certain licences in connection with Acts protecting wild creatures, wild plants, birds, deer, seals and badgers.

Council advises the Government on the United Kingdom's interests in international nature conservation and takes the lead in certain scientific and professional projects such as the work of the International Union for Conservation of Nature and Natural Resources. It also provides the official United Kingdom agency for the Council of Europe's Information Centre for Nature Conservation.

*Publications* include Annual Reports (available from H.M.S.O.), Nature Conservation and Agriculture and numerous leaflets on National Nature Reserves and specific conservation topics.

*Chairman:* Professor F. G. T. Holliday CBE, FRSE. *Director:* R. E. Boote, CVO. *Deputy Director:* D. F. B. O'Connor. *Chief Scientist:* Dr. D. A. Ratcliffe. *Great Britain Headquarters:* 19–20 Belgrave Square, London SW1X 8PY. Tel.: 01–235 3241. *Director, England:* Dr M. Gane, Calthorpe House, Calthorpe Street, Banbury, Oxon OX16 8EX. Tel. 0295 57603. *Director, Scotland:* Dr J. Morton Boyd, 12 Hope Terrace, Edinburgh EH9 2AS. Tel.: 031–447 4784. *Director, Wales:* Dr T. O. Pritchard, Penrhos Road, Bangor, Gwynedd LL57 2LQ. Tel.: 0248 4001.

## FOUNDATIONS—TRUSTS—FELLOWSHIPS

**The Carnegie Trust for the Universities of Scotland.** Founded by Andrew Carnegie in 1901 and incorporated by Royal Charter. He placed Bonds of the United Steel Corporation of the aggregate value of $10 million under the charge of 22 Trustees. The active administration was entrusted to an Executive Committee of nine. During World War I the Steel Bonds were converted into Government securities. In 1958 the Trust secured a supplementary Royal Charter extending its powers of investment to ordinary shares, and in 1966 a further supplementary Royal Charter giving still wider powers of investment. The Trust Deed comprises three clauses. Clause A relates to assistance to the Scottish universities for development in science and medicine and certain subjects in the arts faculty and for the stimulation of research. Clause B is concerned with assistance to necessitous students with their fees at the Scottish universities. Clause C is a more general clause, the provisions of which become operative only when the objectives of the other two clauses have been satisfied. The underlying principle of the Trust is that one-half of the annual income shall be devoted to each of Clauses A and B, with the proviso that any surplus from B shall be at the disposal of A. For many years the assistance to students with their fees absorbed practically the one-half of the annual income, but with the State's more generous provision (including payment of fees) to students since 1961, Carnegie Trust assistance has been substantially diminished as far as fees are concerned. The Trust, however, gives vacation awards. The present position is that capital grants on a quinquennial basis are made to each of the eight Scottish Universities. The Universities utilize their capital grants on projects which cannot normally be state-financed and have been approved by the Trust. The remainder of the income is spent for the most part on research scholarships, fellowships and grants in aid of research made to members of Scottish University staffs. *Secretary and Treasurer:* Anthony E. Ritchie, MA, BSc, MD, FRSE. *Address:* The Merchants' Hall, 22 Hanover Street, Edinburgh EH2 2EN. Tel.: 031-225 5817.

**Dartington Hall Trust.** When in 1925 Mr. and Mrs. L. K. Elmhirst bought Dartington Hall it was with the idea of using the estate as a centre where some of the problems facing rural England might be examined. At that time the decline in agriculture, inadequate social services and restricted opportunities for work and recreation had caused the drift of population to the towns to reach alarming proportions. It was decided at the outset that, apart from developing the natural resources of the land, the policy would be to introduce industry on a suitable scale and include education and the arts as essential elements. Dartington Hall is a Trust established in perpetuity in 1931 by the Elmhirsts and is administered by eight Trustees. In order to carry out the purposes of the Trust in education and research a number of departments were set up and the commercial enterprises formed into private limited companies. *Trustees:* M. A. Ash (Chairman), A. O. Elmhirst, P. Sutcliffe, M. Young, Mrs. R. W. Ash, Sir Alec Clegg, M.D. (John) Lane, and C. B. Zealley. *Address:* Dartington Hall, Totnes, South Devon, TQ9 6JE.

**Federal Trust for Education & Research.** The Federal Trust for Education and Research was founded in 1945 to stimulate study and spread understanding of international problems, and has concentrated attention in recent years on European issues. Its activities include the promotion and execution of research, the organization of conferences and seminars, and educational work with colleges and universities, schools, trade unions, etc. Its work is carried out by a small staff and a much larger number of voluntary part-time helpers: politicians, officials, professional people, businessmen and academics, who join study groups and contribute papers and discussion. International contacts are fostered and many studies are carried out in collaboration with institutes and individuals in other countries, especially in East and West Europe and North America. The conclusions of study groups are published as books or reports, but much importance is attached to the direct educational effects of participants in the conferences and meetings.

*Recent publications* include: 'Economic and Monetary Union in Europe', The Security of Western Europe', 'The Economics of Europe' (books), 'CAP and the British Consumer', 'The Economics of Renegotiation', 'Europe's Wider Horizons', 'Electing the European Parliament', 'European Monetary Integration', 'The Price of Europe', 'Economic Union in the EEC' (reports).

*Study groups* are currently at work or commencing shortly on: East-West Security; Industrial Policy; Industrial Democracy; Enlargement of the European Community.

The Federal Trust is a non-profit-making company limited by guarantee and supported by foundations and private donations.

*Trustees:* B. D. Barton, FCA, J. M. Bowyer, Francois Duchene, Sir John Foster, KBE, QC, Richard Mayne, Norman Hart, David Howell, MP, Christopher Layton, Roderick MacFarquhar, MP, John MacGregor, OBE, MP, John Pinder, OBE, Dr. Roy Pryce, D. W. Sanders, Dennis Thompson, Tim Sherwen, William Wallace. *Officials: Director*, Geoffrey Denton. *Assistant Director*, Geoffrey Edwards. *Consultant:* Bernard Burrows. *Address:* 12a Maddox Street, London W1R 9PL. Tel.: 492 0727/9.

**Ford Foundation.** Established in 1936 by Henry and Edsel Ford as a private, non-profit corporation serving the public welfare. It seeks to identify and contribute to the solution of problems of national and international importance. The Foundation works mainly by giving funds for experimental, demonstration, and development efforts likely to produce significant advances in its field of interest. The Foundation is directed by a board of 15 trustees of which Alexander Heard is Chairman, McGeorge Bundy is President. Since its inception, the Foundation has made commitments totalling $4·9 billion (U.S. billion = 1,000 million) including grants to more than 7,000 organizations and institutions, principally in the United States, but also in 96 other countries.

At the close of the fiscal year ending on 30 September 1976, the Foundation's assets were $2·4 billion. New charitable commitments during the fiscal year totalled $137 million.

Under its *National Affairs Division*, the Foundation's 1976 grants and other actions included support for civil rights legal defense funds; grants to the Voter Education Project and the Joint Center for Political Studies to increase minority participation in the political systems; support for five organizations working for women's rights under law; continued assistance to organizations engaged in analysis of public policies, monitoring of programs, and public information concerning child care; continued assistance for "supported-work", a national experiment to help dependent persons enter the workplace; continued support for minority-operated community development corporations; grants concerning the quality of working life, occupational health and safety, the needs of white ethnic neighborhoods and public policy issues related to employment; grants to the National Committee Against Discrimination in Housing and other groups to promote equal housing opportunities; $600,000 to the Manpower Demonstration Research Corporation to supervise and evaluate National Tenant Management Programs; continued support for public interest law firms; efforts to improve the criminal justice system including grants to the Vera Institute of Justice in New York, the National Prison Project of the American Civil Liberties Union, and the American Bar Association Fund for Public Education's *Corrections Magazine*, a quarterly on corrections policies and programs; grants for mediation and conflict resolution between government and various interest groups; $1 million supplementary grant to the Urban Institute for research on issues of concern to urban policy makers; support to various organizations working on urban economic policy and financial problems; and $2·4 million continued support for the Drug Abuse Council.

In *Resources and the Environment*, the Foundation's principal focus was public policy issues in nuclear energy development including a study administered by the Mitre Corporation entitled *Nuclear Power Issues and Choices*: support also was given for research on resources versus economic growth by Resources for the Future; analysis of land-use problems by the Urban Institute's Land Use Center; explorations in the use of mediation to resolve environmental disputes; support for public-interest law firms practicing in the environmental field; and support for research and training programs to improve resource management in the less-developed world.

In *Education and Research*, the Foundation continued support for open-learning experiments, where students receive academic credit for learning acquired outside the classroom; commissioned an inquiry into adult literacy in the United States; supported two studies on minority enrollment in colleges and universities; granted $6 million to the Educational Testing Service and the Council of Southern Universities to award fellowships to minority doctoral candidates preparing for college teaching careers; continued support to strengthen the academic, financial and management capabilities of selected black colleges; supported higher education opportunities for American Indians through grants to Bacone College and the Western Interstate Commission for Higher Education's Office for Planning and Resources in Minority Education; granted $252,000 to the Center for Puerto Rican Studies at the City University of New York for language studies, training of students and community leaders, and research on Puerto Rican students and faculty at the City University; grants to increase professional skills of state legislators and education departments in planning and financing higher education; supported studies on the academic labour market on issues such as affirmative action policies, factors influencing mobility of college teachers, and the impact of part-time faculty on the academic job market; gave $200,000 to the American Council on Education to establish a commission to undertake a broad national study of intercollegiate athletics; supported two campus-based women's research centers, the Center for Research on Women at Stanford University, and the Data and Analytic Research Center for the Study of Women at Radcliff University; gave $150,000 to the Women's Equity Action League Educational and Legal Defense Fund to monitor discrimination against women in national fellowships, college sports, and academic programs; continued efforts to help with problems of desegregating schools including a grant to LQC Lamar Society to work with local leaders in Dallas, Dayton, Omaha, and other cities to prepare various segments of their communities for court-ordered school desegregation; continued efforts to combat sex discrimination in schools; supported efforts to protect the rights of children including $750,000 to the Children's Defense Fund in Washington, D.C. to continue research and litigation on children's rights issues; continued to assist groups working for more equitable systems of school finance; supported work at the Education Development Center in Massachusetts to design a series of tests to measure mathematical reasoning ability; supported research on declining student scores on standardized achievement tests; and continued support for research at the Center for Genetic Epistemology on how children learn.

In the *Arts*, the Foundation made grants to eleven performing arts companies in a program of cash reserve grants to enable such groups to eliminate accumulated operating losses and create a capital reserve fund; supported a study by the National Committee for Cultural Resources on the future of America's arts organizations; supported the Theater Development Fund in efforts to advise performing arts groups in various cities of means of increasing audiences, such as day-of-performance ticket discounts, vouchers, and block ticket sales; supported the TAG Foundation which sponsors performances by modern dance companies and provides facilities in which they can perform before large audiences; continued its program to strengthen American conservatories of music by granting $200,000 to the Mannes College of Music in New York; continued to support efforts to teach music to school children by the Kodaly training method; gave $439,636 to the Co-ordinating Council of Literary Magazines for the support of "little magazines"; continued to support the training of minorities for professional careers in the arts through grants to the Washington, D.C. Workshop for Careers in Arts, and the New Federal Theater in New York.

In *Communications*, the Foundation continued to maintain a modest program in public television as its twenty-five-year program of large scale support for public television neared its end; it supported the Station Program Co-operative, a mechanism through which local stations participate in the selection and financing of national programming; gave $2 million to the Educational Broadcasting Corporation; continued support for the New American Television Drama Project which is producing original plays by American writers for broadcast; in journalism the Foundation sponsored a series of conferences on media and the law; provided mid-career fellowships for journalists in the fields of education, law, and international security and arms control;

continued a scholarship program for minority journalists attending graduate schools of journalism; continued support for the Aspen Institute Program on Communications and Society, which analyses national communications issues, and for the Cable Television Information Center of the Urban Institute, established to advise communities on franchising, regulation, and pblic-service applications of cable television.

In *Public Policy and Social Organization*, the Foundation granted $1 million to graduate public-policy training centers; $150,000 to Duke University and the Rand Corporation to prepare new teaching materials in public policy; supported Tax Analysts and Advocates in Washington, D.C. in monitoring changes in federal tax policy; supported a study by the University of Notre Dame on the status of Vietnam veterans, deserters, and draft evaders; supported conferences and studies on retirement issues; gave a grant to Brookings Institution for a study of the role of women in the U.S. armed forces; supported the Institute of Society, Ethics, and the Life Sciences in exploring ethical and social implications arising from advances in biomedical sciences.

In the *International Division*, the Foundation continued to assist agricultural programs including efforts to improve multiple cropping systems in Thailand, and the production of rice in Bangladesh and India, sorghum and millet in Brazil and Mali, and corn, wheat, and rice in Egypt; renewed assistance to international agricultural research centers in Asia, Africa, Latin America and the Middle East; helped establish the International Food Policy Research Institute in Washington, D.C.; assisted graduate training in agricultural economics and other rural social sciences in Pakistan, Nigeria, Brazil, the West Indies, and Mexico; supported training of educational researchers in Thailand, Colombia, and Guatemala, funded a research and fellowship competition in Brazil to stimulate the application of social science methods to educational problems; supported a fellowship program to help raise the professional qualifications of black faculty members in South Africa's segregated universities; supported a new program in urban studies at the College of Mexico; assisted efforts to train economists for work in government ministries at the universities of Nairobi and Dar es Salaam; continued to support scholarly exchanges between China and the United States arranged by the Committee for Scholarly Communications; funded research on the status of women in Colombia, and the impact of technology on the work of rural African women; supported a worldwide competition for research on international security and arms control; launched a new program for the protection of human rights including grants to the Writers and Scholars Educational Trust to publish the *Index on Censorship* and the University of Minnesota for an internship program in association with such organizations as Amnesty International and the International Commission of Jurists; began a fellowship program to enable young social scientists from the Mediterranean region to study in the United States; completed a major review of the state of reproductive and contraceptive knowledge; continued support for research and training in reproductive sciences and programs to improve population communications and the management of family planning.

**The Harkness Fellowships.** Inaugurated in 1925 by the Commonwealth Fund of New York, a philanthropic foundation endowed by the late Mrs. Stephen Harkness and the late Mr. and Mrs. Edward S. Harkness.

The Fellowships are under the patronage of Her Majesty The Queen. Twenty Fellowships are offered annually to men and women between the ages of 21 and 30 years in any profession or field of study provided both their secondary and further education (or equivalent professional experience in lieu of further education) has been wholly or mainly in the United Kingdom. Candidates must, by 1 September of the year of award, have a degree, *or* an equivalent qualification conferred by a professional body, *or* an outstanding record of achievement in the creative arts, journalism, or other comparable careers. In addition, M.B.A. candidates must have had substantial full-time administrative experience. Candidacy is not open to persons who, between their nineteenth birthday and taking up the award, will have lived in the United States for more than six consecutive months. The Fellowships are tenable in the United States for between 12 and 21 months. Selection of candidates is made after interview by the British Committee of Award. A limited number of awards is also available generally *by nomination*, to citizens of Australia and New Zealand. Further information is available from the Harkness Fellowships (U.K.). *Address:* 38 Upper Brook Street, London, W1Y 1PE. Australia: Mr. L. T. Hinde, Reserve Bank of Australia, Box 3947 GPO, Sydney, N.S.W. 2001, New Zealand: Mr. I. L. Baumgart, 27 Onehuka Road, Lower Hutt, New Zealand.

**King George's Jubilee Trust** is a permanent fund set up for the benefit of the young people of the United Kingdom. It was inaugurated on 1 March 1935 as a national thank-offering on the occasion of the Jubilee of the late King George V. The Trust is administered by a Council and Secretary who, with the Trustees, are appointed by the **Patron** of the Trust, who was the late King George VI and is now **H.M. Queen Elizabeth II. King George VI**, as Duke of York, was the first Chairman of the Council. The present Chairman is H.R.H. The Prince of Wales. Approximately £1 million was subscribed in response to the original appeal. The total amount of the Trust Fund at 31 March 1977 (including investments at cost or as valued at date of gift) amounted to £2,671,981. In 1960 the Trust launched a National Silver Jubilee Appeal for additional funds which resulted in an addition of some £825,000. Since its foundation in 1935 the Trust has given more than 3·18 million pounds in grants to youth organizations. It was King George's own wish that the fund should be used for the good of the young and, when he broadcast to his peoples on 6 May 1935, he said: 'It is to the young that the future belongs. I trust that through this Fund many of them throughout the country may be helped in body, mind and character to become useful citizens.' In these words the King summed up the task laid upon the Council by the Trust Deed which requires them to advance the physical, mental and spiritual welfare of the younger generation, especially of young persons who are aged 14 and upwards. The Trust discharges its responsibilities partly by making substantial annual grants to the national headquarters of the principal voluntary youth organizations; but because it was set up to benefit *all* the young people of Britain, many of whom do not belong to any youth organization, the Trust also initiates and assists projects of enquiry and research such as may help to develop and expand work for the well-being of young people generally. In order to assist the Council in distributing the money available to the best advantage, the Secretary discusses annually with the national headquarters of the major voluntary youth organizations their requirements for the coming financial year. The Trust is thus enabled to concentrate its aid on those essential requirements of each organization which cannot be met wholly from their own resources. The grants are distributed as widely as possible so that no part of the United Kingdom can feel that its needs have been overlooked. The Trust takes a particular interest in those aspects of youth work which by combining, in a manner acceptable to young people, life in the open air with adventure and character training can help to arouse in them the desire to become and remain fit in body and mind. The Trust also sponsors enquiries into the needs of young people and the problems which attend their upbringing by studying methods of making the best use of the available resources in money, manpower and effort, by promoting and aiding experiments with new types of youth work, and by publishing up-to-date information on these matters. *Secretary:* Sir Gerard Mansfield (acting). *Address:* 8, Buckingham Street, London, WC2N 6BU. Tel.: 01-930 9811/12.

**The National Trust for Places of Historic Interest or Natural Beauty**, exists to preserve the best of the countryside and the finest buildings for the enjoyment of future generations. It is a charity, independent of the State, financed by gifts, legacies and members' subscriptions and the income from its property. The National Trust was founded in 1895 by Sir Robert Hunter, Canon Rawnsley and Miss Octavia Hill, and in 1907 it was incorporated by an Act of Parliament which provides that land owned by the Trust may be declared inalienable. The Trust cannot mortgage or sell its inalienable land, which cannot be compulsorily acquired without the special authority of Parliament.

Some 400,700 acres are now owned by the National Trust in England, Wales and Northern Ireland (there is a separate National Trust for Scotland) and the Trust holds covenants in its favour over another 70,888 acres. Most of the Trust's land and buildings have been declared inalienable. A further Act of Parliament in 1937 enabled the National Trust to accept country houses, and their contents, with an endowment, for permanent maintenance, and for the donor and his descendants to live in the house as tenants of the Trust while giving regular public access. The properties of the Trust include more than 1,000 buildings, 1,100 farms, 160 historic houses and their collections, 66 gardens, and 45 nature reserves, as well as inland waterways and examples of industrial architecture. Membership of the Trust is now 550,000,

The minimum subscription is £5 a year, life members £75. There are also industrial and junior corporate membership schemes. *President:* H.M. Queen Elizabeth the Queen Mother. GBE. *Chairman:* The Lord Gibson. *Chairman of Properties Committee:* I. O. Chance, CBE. *Chairman of Finance Committee:* Mark Norman, OBE. *Director-General:* J. D. Boles. *Registered office:* 42 Queen Anne's Gate, London, SW1H 9AS. Tel.: 01-930 0211 and 1841.

**Nobel Foundation.** Established under the terms of the will of Dr. Alfred Bernhard Nobel, drawn up on 27 November 1895, which in its relevant parts runs as follows: 'The whole of my remaining realizable estate shall be dealt with in the following way: The capital (well over 31 million Swedish crowns, equal to about £1,650,000, or $8,610,000 at the rate of exchange then prevailing) shall be invested in safe securities and shall constitute a fund, the interest on which shall be distributed annually in the form of prizes to those who, during the preceding year, shall have conferred the greatest benefit on mankind. The said interest shall be divided into five equal parts, which shall be apportioned as follows: one part to the person who shall have made the most important discovery or invention within the field of physics; one part to the person who shall have made the most important chemical discovery or improvement; one part to the person who shall have made the most important discovery within the domain of physiology or medicine; one part to the person who shall have produced in the field of literature the most outstanding work of an idealistic tendency; and one part to the person who shall have done the most or the best work for fraternity between nations for the abolition or reduction of standing armies and for the holding and promotion of peace congresses. The prizes for physics and chemistry shall be awarded by the Swedish Academy of Science; that for physiological or medical works by the Caroline Institute in Stockholm; that for literature by the Academy in Stockholm, and that for champions of peace by a committee of five persons to be elected by the Norwegian Storting (Parliament). It is my express wish that in awarding the prize no consideration whatever shall be given to the nationality of the candidates, but that the most worthy shall receive the prize, whether he be a Scandinavian or not.' Only *members* of bodies all over the world mentioned in the Statutes are qualified to propose prize candidates. As there is no competition nobody can propose himself for a Nobel Prize.

In 1901 the individual prize amounted to 150,800 Swedish crowns; in 1976 it was 681,000. The main fund (from the interest of which the prizes accrue) as at 31 December 1975 amounted to 48,000,000 Swedish crowns. There are other funds apart, i.e., for the activities of the Nobel Institutes and for use (otherwise than for the award of prizes) in the promotion of purposes intended by the testator. The aggregate of prizes paid out to eate amounts to 65,140,778 Swedish crowns.

The bodies governed by the statutes are: Four *Prize-Awarding Institutions*—The Royal Academy of Sciences, the Karolinska Institutet, the Swedish Academy and the Norwegian Nobel Committee; five *Nobel Committees* (including the above-mentioned Norwegian committee, which is in itself a prize-awarding institution)—one for each prize section; five *Nobel Institutes*—two for the Royal Academy of Sciences and one for each of the three other prize-awarding bodies; the *Nobel Foundation* with its Trustees and Board. The number of prizes distributed between 1901 and 1975 is Physics 70, Chemistry 68, Physiology or Medicine 67, Literature 69, Peace 56. The presentation of the prize money, the Nobel gold medals and the diplomas takes place at ceremonies held in Stockholm and in Oslo on 10 December, the anniversary of the death of Alfred Nobel. The prizewinners in 1976 were: *Physics:* The prize was awarded by equal shares to: Burton Richter, b. 1931; U.S.A., Stanford Linear Accelerator Center, Stanford, California and Samuel C. C. Ting, b. 1936, U.S.A., Massachusetts Institute of Technology, Cambridge (European Center for Nuclear Research, Geneva, Switzerland) "for their pioneering work in the discovery of a heavy elementary particle of a new kind". *Chemistry:* The prize was awarded to: William N. Lipscomb, b. 1919; U.S.A., Harvard University, Cambridge, Mass. "for his studies on the structure of boranes illuminating problems of chemical bonding". *Physiology or Medicine:* The prize was awarded jointly to: Baruch S. Blumberg, b. 1925; U.S.A., The Institute for Cancer Research, Philadelphia, Pennsylvania and D. Carleton Gajdusek, b. 1923; U.S.A., National Institutes of Health Bethesda, Maryland, "for their discoveries concerning new mechanisms for the origin and dissemination of infectious diseases". *Literature:* The prize was awarded to: Saul Bellow, b. 1915; U.S.A. "for the human understanding and subtle analysis of contemporary culture that are combined in his work". *Peace:* Prize reserved.

*The Bank of Sweden Prize in Economics in Memory of Alfred Nobel:* The prize was awarded to: Milton Friedman, b. 1912; U.S.A., University of Chicago, Chicago, Illinois "for his achievements in the fields of consumption analysis, monetary history and theory and for his demonstration of the complexity of stabilization policy".

**The Nuffield Foundation.** Established by Lord Nuffield in April 1943 to promote the advancement of health and the prevention and relief of sickness by medical research and teaching; the advancement of social well-being by scientific research; the care and comfort of the aged; and the advancement of education.

The resources of the Foundation consist of the Nuffield Fund, provided by Lord Nuffield, and the Auxiliary Fund, for which the trustees may accept gifts and bequests from other persons wishing to advance the objects of the Foundation.

The two main funds within the Auxiliary Fund are the Oliver Bird Fund for the promotion of research into the prevention and cure of rheumatism, and the Elizabeth Nuffield Educational Fund, the object of which is to help women and girls domiciled in the United Kingdom to complete courses of study or training.

The Foundation's original programme paid particular attention to research in nuclear physics and to medical research, with emphasis on normal health rather than on specific diseases (an exception being rheumatism, dealt with under the Oliver Bird Fund).

The Foundation's interest in medical research has continued, while in science the emphasis has moved from nuclear physics to biology. The Foundation also gives support for social research and experiment. In education the Foundation has organized large-scale programmes for the revision of school curricula and supported educational innovations in the teaching of all subjects at the undergraduate level. Grants for the welfare of old people and for research into their needs have continued throughout the life of the Foundation, since 1947 principally through the National Corporation for the Care of Old People. The policy of awarding fellowships has continued over the whole period, though the schemes have been varied from time to time to serve different purposes and opportunities. Support is also given for research in parts of the Commonwealth overseas.

Patron: H.M. Queen Elizabeth the Queen Mother. Ordinary Trustees: W. R. Gowers, CBE, MA, the Rt. Hon. Lord Todd, MA, FRS (President), and the Rt. Hon. Lord Trend, GCB, CVO. Managing Trustees: Rt. Hon. Lord Todd, MA, FRS (Chairman), J. B. Butterworth, MA, W. R. Gowers, MA, Prof. H. L. Kornberg, MA, FRS, R. C. O. Matthews, CBE, MA, FBA, and Rt. Hon. Lord Trend, GCB, CVO, *Director:* Mr. John Maddox. *Deputy Director:* J. W. McAnuff. *Assistant Director:* Miss M. P. Thomas. *Finance Officer:* W. D. Scott. *Fellowships Adviser:* D. D. Yonge. *Accountant:* R. C. Marshall. *Address:* Nuffield Lodge, Regent's Park, London, NW1 4RS. Tel.: 01-722 8871.

**The Pilgrim Trust.** Founded in 1930 by the late Edward Stephen Harkness of New York, who placed in the hands of British Trustees a sum of £2 million, as a gift to Britain, to be used for some of her more urgent needs, and to promote her future well-being. The annual income of the Trust is about £450,000. Grants are confined to the United Kingdom of Great Britain and Northern Ireland and to objects which are charitable within the legal definition. From the foundation of the Trust until the outbreak of World War II the Trustees expended some 50 per cent of their income on schemes of social welfare. chiefly for the unemployed. Since 1945, with the extension of social legislation, the Trustees have been mainly concerned with the repair and preservation of ancient buildings, historical records and works of art. Preservation of the countryside also falls within the scope of their policy. The promotion of learning and scholarship is claiming a substantial proportion of the Trustees' resources. In recent years they have helped a number of learned societies to continue their work, made possible the reorganization of several famous libraries, and contributed towards the acquisition for the nation of rare books, manuscripts and artistic treasures. *Chairman:* The Rt. Hon. Lord Harlech, KCMG. *Secretary:* Sir Patrick Hancock, GCMG, KCB, KCVO. *Address:* Fielden House, Little College Street, Westminster, London SW1P 3SH. Tel.: 01-839 4727.

**Rhodes Trust.** The body administering the estate of the late Cecil Rhodes, and in particular the Scholarships established under his will in 1902. The scholarships are available to citizens of the British Commonwealth, South Africa, Rhodesia, United States of America, and Western Germany. Each scholarship has a present value of approximately £3,750 a year; it is tenable at the University of Oxford, and it may be held for two or three years. Rhodes directed that in the election of a student regard should be paid not only to his literary and scholastic attainments, but also to his moral force of character, his instinct to lead and his fondness for, and success in, outdoor sports. The stipend of a Rhodes Scholarship consists of a direct payment to the Scholar's College of approved fees, plus a maintenance allowance of £2,000 a year which is paid to the scholar. The scholarships are allocated annually as follows: one usually for each Province of Canada (Quebec and Ontario two each); one for each state of the Australian Commonwealth, and two for New Zealand. Three are awarded annually to Rhodesia and Zambia; two to India; and one each to Jamaica, and Bermuda. To the United States of America, four scholarships are assigned annually to each of eight regions and are awarded among candidates sent forward from each State in the region. There are two scholarships annually from Western Germany.

Since 1959 Scholarships have been awarded, usually in every third year in Ghana, Malta, Malaysia, Nigeria, Pakistan, and the British Caribbean (excluding Jamaica, which awards its own annual Scholarship created in the Founder's will). Candidates must be bachelors between 19 and 25 years of age; they must be citizens of the country from which they come, and except in a few special cases, must have graduated before arriving in Oxford. Since 1976, women have been eligible for Rhodes Scholarships on the same terms as male candidates have enjoyed since 1903 when the first Rhodes Scholar arrived at Oxford.

The number of Rhodes Scholars on stipend at Oxford during the period 1976–77 was 180. The eight present Trustees are: *Chairman:* The Viscount Harcourt, KCMG, OBE, VL; Professor D. K. Price, Jr.; Professor W. D. M. Paton, CBE, JP, DM, FRS; The Lord Blake, JP, FBA; The Hon. John Baring; M. J. Hussey; W. G. Barr, DL; R. T. Armstrong, CB, CVO. The Secretary to the Rhodes Trust and the Warden of Rhodes House, Oxford is Sir Edgar Williams, CB, CBE, DSO, DL. *Address:* Rhodes House, Oxford.

**The Rockefeller Foundation.** Received its charter from the legislature of the State of New York in May 1913, 'to promote the well-being of mankind throughout the world'. It is one of several philanthropic funds founded by the late Mr. John D. Rockefeller, who in 1901 had created the Rockefeller Institute for Medical Research (now Rockefeller University) and in 1902 founded the General Education Board to promote education within the United States 'without distinction of race, sex or creed'. The Rockefeller Sanitary Commission, organized in 1909 to work for the cure and prevention of hookworm disease, became part of the Foundation. When Mrs. Rockefeller died in 1918, Mr. Rockefeller established in her memory The Laura Spelman Rockefeller Memorial (LSRM) concerned largely with the advancement of the social sciences, child growth and parent education. In 1923 the International Education Board, founded by Mr. John D. Rockefeller, Jr., began activities which aided education on an international scale until its funds were exhausted in 1938. Next came the Spelman Fund of New York, active from 1928–48, created by a grant from the Laura Spelman Rockefeller Memorial at the time of its consolidation with the Rockefeller Foundation. It was concerned with the improvement of practices in public administration. In 1965 the General Education Board issued its final report, having expended its entire principal and income, $324,632,958, in its 63-year career. The Rockefeller Foundation's programme has evolved to meet changing needs. With the 1929 consolidation its activities were dedicated to the advancement of knowledge. In 1963, and again in 1974, the programme was redefined to give greater emphasis to the application of knowledge for human welfare, especially in the less developed areas of the world. In terms of general goals, the Foundation's activities are now concentrated in eight program areas: Conquest of Hunger, Educational Publishing, Population and Health, toward the resolution of Conflict in International Relations, Education for Development (in several of the developing countries), and Quality of the Environment; and especially in the United States, Equal Opportunity for All and Arts, Humanities, and Contemporary Values. Organizationally, the Foundation works through eight categories—Agricultural Sciences, Arts, Health Sciences, Humanities, Information Services, International Relations, Natural and Environmental Sciences, and Social Sciences, each with a director and staff. The professional staff is spread throughout the world. Except to a limited extent in agriculture, the Foundation does not itself engage in research. Integrated with the general programme are fellowship appointments for advanced training, awarded mainly to persons from the United States and from some of the developing countries. Gifts from Mr. Rockefeller and his son to the boards mentioned amounted to $469,554,976. The Rockefeller Foundation is managed by an independent non-salaried board of 21 trustees. Capital funds received from the founder between 1913 and 1929 amounted to $245·8 million. Both income and principal of the Foundation's general fund are available for appropriation. *Publications:* Annual Report; RF ILLUSTRATED; and occasional special reports. *Officers: Chairman of the Board of Trustees:* Theodore M. Hesburgh. *President:* John H. Knowles. *Vice-Presidents:* Allan C. Barnes, Ellsworth T. Neumann, and Sterling Wortman. *Secretary:* Laurence D. Stifel. *Treasurer:* Theodore R. Frye. *Comptroller:* Herbert Heaton. *Programme Directors:* John A. Pino for Agricultural Sciences, Howard Klein for Arts, Kenneth S. Warren for Health Sciences, Joel Colton for Humanities, Henry Romney for Information Services, Mason Willrich for International Relations, Ralph W. Richardson, Jr. for Natural and Environmental Sciences, and Joseph E. Black for Social Sciences. Solicitors: Patterson, Belknap, Webb, Tyler. *Address:* The Rockefeller Foundation, 1133 Avenue of the Americas, New York, N.Y. 10036, U.S.A.

**The Wellcome Foundation Limited.** The Wellcome Foundation Limited was founded in 1880 by Silas M. Burroughs and Henry S. Wellcome as a Partnership with the name Burroughs Wellcome Co. It was registered under its present title by Wellcome in 1924. Sir H. Wellcome died in 1936, having by his Will bequeathed his sole ownership of the shares of the Company to his Trustees who are known as The Wellcome Trust. It is to this trust, therefore, that all distributed profits are paid.

*The Wellcome Trust* is a recognized public charity and has for its main objects the advancement, throughout the world, of research in human and veterinary medicine and allied sciences, and the establishment or endowment of research museums and libraries. Benefactions allocated between the time of Sir Henry Wellcome's death and December 1976 total nearly £35,000,000. The Wellcome Foundation Ltd., still trades in several parts of the world under the name Burroughs Wellcome and Co. The Headquarters of the organization are situated in London.

*Production:* The principal chemical and pharmaceutical manufacturing unit of the group is at Dartford. Large-scale production of biological products is carried out at the Wellcome Research Laboratories, Beckenham, Kent. Also produced at Beckenham is a range of laboratory diagnostic reagents. *Research:* The research units of the Company in Great Britain comprise the Wellcome Research Laboratories, incorporating with it the Wellcome Laboratories of Tropical Medicine, at Beckenham, and the Wellcome Research Laboratories (Berkhamstead) engage in veterinary research. Abroad there are research laboratories at Releigh (N. Carolina, U.S.A.). Research is carried out under two main divisions, these being chemical and pharmaceutical work in the search for new drugs both synthetic and of natural origin, and biological investigation in the field of immunology. *Marketing:* Business in Britain is divided between the Wellcome and Calmic Medical Divisions, selling a range of human medical products and vaccines. Wellcome veterinary and Cooper agricultural and dairy hygiene products are supplied by the Veterinary and Agricultural Division. The Consumer Division supplies a range of household products, and the Industrial Division provides hygienic services and bulk chemicals to commerce and industry. *Subsidiaries:* Wellcome Reagents Ltd., Beckenham, Kent manufacture a range of laboratory diagnostics and reagents and Macdonald & Taylor Ltd., Royton, Lancs, make textile products for the Consumer Division. The overseas organization of the Wellcome business comprise subsidiaries in most parts of the world. *Wellcome Museum of Medical Science:* The Wellcome Museum of Medical Science, situated in the Wellcome Building, is devoted to the teaching of contemporary medicine with special reference to diseases of warm climates and human parasitology. Its displays are synoptic and include descriptions of vectors and reservoirs of tropical infections. The Museum is primarily intended for the use of doctors, but undergraduates in medicine and the natural sciences, nurses and members of other para-medical professions and, under certain conditions, biology students from science sixth forms, are admitted. Arrangements can be made for teachers to borrow equipment and material for use in the Museum's tutorial room, providing that prior notice has been given. The Museum is open from 9 a.m. to 5 p.m. except on Saturdays, Sundays and Public Holidays.

*Wellcome Institute for the History of Medicine:* The Wellcome Institute is owned by the Wellcome Trustees and is also housed in the Wellcome Building. It comprises an academic unit for the promotion of research into the history of medicine, which is affiliated to University College, London, a library of medical books, manuscripts and documents, which is one of the most important and comprehensive collections of it kind in the world, and a museum collection relating to the history of medicine, surgery and allied sciences. The museum collection is to be placed on indefinite loan to the Science Museum in South Kensington; displays will remain open to the public at the Wellcome Building until the transfer has been completed.

*Address:* The Wellcome Foundation Ltd., The Wellcome Building, 183 Euston Road, London, NW1 2BP.

## INDUSTRY—TRADE—COMMERCE

**Commonwealth Development Corporation.** CDC's constitution and powers are laid down by Acts of Parliament which charge the Corporation with the task of investing its funds, in countries in which it is empowered to operate, in development projects which will not only help to increase the wealth of the countries but also yield a reasonable return on the money invested. Its area of operations covers Commonwealth countries which have achieved independence since 1948, the remaining territories dependent upon Britain and, with Ministerial approval, any developing country outside the Commonwealth.

CDC is required to pay its way and operates on commercial lines. It does not make grants, but offers investment in the development of resources. In general, it chooses projects with regard to their development value to the country concerned rather than for their profitability. Close relations with overseas government are maintained through CDC's Regional offices in order to ensure that the orporation's activities are directed in such a way as bestCto promote the economic development of the countries concerned. The Corporation has powers to borrow up to £500 million on a long or medium term basis and £10 million on short term. It may borrow up to £480 million outstanding at any one time from the United Kingdom Exchequer. At 30 June 1977, the corporation had committed £316 million to its projects in Africa, the Caribbean, East Asia and the Pacific Islands. Of the total commitment £248 million had already been disbursed.

In the recent years the trend towards a new pattern of CDC projects could be seen to be developing. Alongside the loans for public utility (infrastructure) purposes and the investments in large scale industrial and agricultural estate projects CDC investment is increasingly directed to projects which involve association with and support of the peoples collectively and individually in the countries in which it operates. Such projects are smallholder schemes in agriculture (probably attached to nucleus estates), local development companies for industry and mortgage companies for the prospective house purchaser.

During the five-years 1975–79 CDC will aim to place its new commitments preponderantly in the poorer countries and into renewable natural resource projects i.e. agriculture, ranching, forestry and fisheries including associated processing plants.

CDC's Chairman and Board members are appointed by the Minister for Overseas Development. The Chairman and Board are responsible for CDC policy. The General Manager is responsible for all CDC operations. He is assisted by an Executive Management Board in London, comprising Head Office Controllers, Regional Controllers, and other senior executives. In each of its six regions of operation CDC has a regional Controller permanently resident. These are Caribbean, East Africa, Central Africa, Southern Africa, West Africa, and East Asia and Pacific Islands. Additionally there are representatives in Jamaica, Malawi, Malaysia, Pacific Islands, Indonesia, and Thailand.

As a matter of CDC policy CDC undertakes the training of local men for important executive posts. Training is carried out at regional offices and at Head Office in London; there is also a considerable amount of on-the-job training. Scholarships and bursaries are also offered. CDC has set up an agricultural management training centre in Swaziland, where prospective managers of agricultural schemes are taught management techniques and financial control. Students are drawn from CDC's own projects and from government and commercial sources in Africa and elsewhere.

The principal officers of the Corporation are: *Chairman:* Sir Eric Griffith-Jones, KBE, CMG, QC. *Deputy Chairman:* Lord Grey of Naunton, GCMG, GCVO, OBE. *Members:* W. J. M. Borthwick, DSC, Lord Campbell of Eskan, J. M. Clay, J. K. Dick, CBE, FCA, Lord Greenwood of Rossendale, PC, A. R. Melville, CB, CMG, J. M. H. Millington-Drake, G. F. Smith, CBE, Lord Walston of Newton, CVO JP. *General Manager:* P. Meinertzhagen, CMG.

*Address:* Commonwealth Development Corporation, 33 Hill Street, London, W1A 3AR. Tel: 01-629 8484; Telex No. 21431; Telegrams: Velop London Telex.

**Commonwealth Industries Association.** Owes its origin largely to the fact that in 1923, the government of the day had appealed to the country on the issue of Protection and Imperial Preference and failed to secure the necessary support. The followers of the Joseph Chamberlain policy were not prepared to accept this decision, however, and under the leadership of Lord Milner, L. S. Amery, Neville Chamberlain and the then Sir Henry Page Croft, it was decided to form an association which would disseminate educational matter on this policy. Prior to World War I this work had been carried out by the Tariff Reform League, which ceased to function during that war. A new organization commenced to operate in 1926 under the chairmanship of Lord Croft and was called the Empire Industries Association. In 1931 the constitution was altered. Mr. Amery became President and Lord Croft remained Chairman of the committee. Both died during their term of office. The work was intensified and achieved a considerable amount of success with the passing of the Import Duties Act and the Ottawa Agreements Act in 1932. The British Empire League was founded in 1895, and while its principles were the same as those of the Association, its activities took a different direction and its work became unnecessary and impossible; nor was there scope for the same kind of activity in the immediate post-war years. The two organizations amalgamated in 1947 and the name Empire Industries Association and British Empire League was adopted. In December 1960 the title was changed to the Commonwealth Industries Association. The objects at which this Association aims are the protection and encouragement of trade within the Commonwealth by deliberate Governmental policy, to develop industry, support British shipping and air services, attract private and public investment to the Commonwealth. The Association issues a Journal 'Britain and Overseas' edited by Edward Holloway. *President:* Sir John Reiss, BEM. *Chairman:* Neil Marten, MP. *Chairman of the Parliamentary Committee:* Paul Deane, MP. *Hon. Treasurer:* E. G. C. Voullaire. *Director:* Edward Holloway. *Secretary:* Miss H. V. L. Packer. *Address:* 55, Park Lane, W1Y 3DH. Tel.: 01-499 3000.

**Confederation of British Industry.** Established in 1965, the Confederation is the national spokesman and representative of British industry and those elements of British business which are closely associated with it. It combines in a single democratic and voluntary association the roles previously played by the British Employers' Confederation, the Federation of British Industries and the National Association of British Manufacturers. Membership consists of some 11,000 companies, over 200 trade associations and employers' organizations and most nationalized industries. The CBI's regular computerized Industrial Trends Survey is widely recognized as giving the most up-to-date picture of prevailing business conditions in the U.K. The CBI is so constituted that it sees the whole industrial pattern from a national viewpoint. It develops broad policies and deals with general problems that are the concern of more than one branch of industry. It acts as a national point of reference for those who seek the views of industry and business, and is recognized internationally as the representative organization of British industrial management. The CBI advises the Government on all aspects of Government policy affecting the interests of industry generally, both at home and abroad. While preserving strict political neutrality in national affairs, the CBI speaks for its members and fosters their interests by representing their collective views when any aspects of general policy, economic, labour, commercial or technical matters are being debated or formulated. By providing numerous advisory services the CBI offers its members practical assistance and advice with their problems. The CBI maintains a staff of about 400 in London and in its 10 offices in the administrative regions of England and in Northern Ireland, Scotland and Wales. It has representatives and correspondents in nearly 100 overseas countries. CBI policy is formed by its members. The governing body is the Council, which meets in London once a month. It consists of over 400 members including nominees of employers' organizations and trade associations, commercial associations and public sector members, representatives of CBI regional Councils and individuals chosen regionally or centrally to represent member companies. The President, who normally serves two years, acts as Chairman of the Council. Some 30 standing committees, served voluntarily by experienced businessmen, aid the Council in its work and advise it on all the main aspects of business policy. Largely through the separate and specially-constituted Smaller Firms Council the CBI does much work on behalf of smaller firms which comprise over one-third of the individual companies in membership. As well as ensuring the formulation of representative views at the centre, the CBI's regional organization of Councils and offices enables its members to debate problems within a local context. Home services to members include advice on industrial relations, training and education, employment legislation, taxation, rating and valuation, insurance, contracts, transport, British and European Standards, metrication, research, automation, design, fire prevention, noise abatement, water tariffs and trade effluent disposal. Overseas services include advice on agency law, tariffs, credit insurance, export and import controls, overseas investment, market reports, trade enquiries and export opportunities. The CBI is a member of the Council of European Industrial Federations, and of UNICE, and is in close liaison with the International Labour Organization, the Business and Industry Advisory Committee to OECD, and the international Chambers of Commerce. The CBI has been much involved with questions following entry into the European Economic Community from the point of view of British business and industry, and has its own office in Brussels. An important part of the Confederation's task is to promote and publicize the viewpoints of industry and business as widely as possible at home and overseas. *Publications* include a regular Members Bulletin, a quarterly CBI Review and others on Education and Training and Overseas Trade, Also a wide range of booklets and reports on economic, commercial, technical and labour questions. *Officers: President:* Lord Watkinson, PC, CH. *Director-General:* John Methven. *Deputy Directors-General:* J. Whitehorn, CMG, E. F. James, CMG, OBE. *Chief Economic Adviser:* Sir Donald MacDougall, CBE. *Consultant Social Affairs*; T. A. Swinden, CBE. *Administration Director and Secretary:* E. M. Felgate. *Company Affairs Director:* P. S. Taylor, MC. *Economic Director:* D. R. Glynn. *Education, Training and Technology Director:* M. O. Bury, OBE. *Director, Social Affairs:* R. J. V. Dixon. *Director, Social Affairs (Administration and Advisory Services):* H. M. L. Morton. *Director of Information:* Mrs D. Drake. *Membership Director:* to be appointed. *Overseas Director:* C. L. S. Cope. *Regional Smaller Firms Director:* N. Tate, C. Meakin. *Address:* Confederation of British Industry, 21 Tothill Street, London, SW1H 9LP. Tel.: 01-930 6711; Telegrams: Cobustry London SW1. Telex: 21332 Cobustry.

**The Industrial Society.** The Industrial Society promotes the fullest involvement of people in their work, to increase the effectiveness and profitability or the organisation and the satisfaction of the individual.

The Society is one of Britain's leading advisory and training bodies in man-management and industrial relations. It is an independent, self-financing organization and specializes in leadership, management-union relations, communication and involvement, terms and conditions of employment and the development of young employees.

The Society's services include in-company advice and training, courses and conferences, information, publications, filmstrips and a monthly magazine.

Its member organisations include industrial and commercial companies, trade unions, nationalised industries, central and local government departments and employers' associations.

The Society's 14,500 corporate members include industrial and commercial companies, central and local government departments, nationalized industries, trade unions, and employers' associations.

The Society earns 90 per cent of its revenue for services and 10 per cent from subscriptions. The cost of membership depends on the number of employees in an organization. Its 70 training advisers have wide, practical experience in industry, commerce and the public services. Regional departments exist which maintain regular contact with members throughout the British Isles.

The Society was founded in 1918 by Sir Robert Hyde. Its governing body is a council of leading managers and trade unionists.

The Society specializes in: leadership: providing practical training to increase the efficiency with which managers and supervisors lead those responsible to them. Management–union relations: making management–union relations more productive by ensuring that the proper roles of each are recognized and accepted. Communication and involvement: establishing systematic, face to face communication by briefing groups and consultative committees; advising on means for involving people more effectively in their work. Conditions of employment: improving terms and conditions of employment so that they encourage flexibility and co-operation. Development of young employees: encouraging attitudes of responsibility in young employees; improving their induction and training.

In addition, the Society provides training and advice on the particular needs of young employees and has departments specializing in leadership training, industrial relations, physical working conditions, and employee food services. The Overseas Department provides training courses for managers and personnel specialists from developing countries. Details from The Industrial Society, 48 Bryanston Square, London, W1H 1BQ. Tel: 01-262 2401.

**Metrication Board.** The Metrication Board was established in 1969 to co-ordinate the adoption of the metric system in the United Kingdom and to provide information on the change. This followed a statement in the House of Commons in 1965 by the President of, what was then, the Board of Trade, Mr. Douglas Jay.

The use of the metric system in contracts was permitted by the Metric Act 1864. The Act was found to be unsatisfactory because the use of metric weights and measures in trade and commerce was still excluded. In 1897 the Weights and Measures (Metric System) Act made the use of the metric system in trade and commerce lawful.

The provisions of the 1897 Act were re-enacted in the Weights and Measures Act 1963 which at the outset and for the first time provides that:

> "the yard or the metre shall be the unit of measurement of length and the pound or the kilogramme shall be the unit of measurement of mass by reference to which any measurement involving a measurement of length or mass shall be made in the United Kingdom".

The Act goes on to define the imperial units in terms of the international metric units:

> "the yard shall be 0·9144 metre exactly:
> the pound shall be 0·453 592 37 kilogramme exactly".

The Weights and Measures Etc. Act 1976 provides powers for the ultimate phasing out of the use of imperial units in particular sectors of trade. The Minister of State for Prices and Consumer Protection in April 1977 issued a Report to Parliament containing his proposals for completing the metric change trade by trade by 1981.

A Directive of the European Economic Community (76/770/EEC), dated 27 July 1976, amending an earlier Directive (71/354/EEC), dated 18 October 1971, on Units of Measurement prescribes a schedule of metric units to be adopted for use over a wide area, including the economic field, public health and safety and administration. This schedule has already been authorized in the United Kingdom. The Directive also fixes dates for the phasing out of certain imperial units. Some were phased out by December 1977; others by December 1979; and the future position of the remainder, which include most of the more commonly used imperial units, has to be reviewed by December 1979. The use of certain special units fixed by international agreements for air and sea transport and rail traffic is not affected.

*Publications:* Publications include a Bulletin entitled 'Going Metric' and leaflets on various aspects of metrication. *Chairman:* Max Wood, OBE. *Director:* F. Lacey. *Address:* 22 Kingsway, London, WC2B 6LE. Tel.: 01-242 6828.

**Ministry of Overseas Development.** The Ministry of Overseas Development deals with British Development Assistance to overseas countries. This includes both capital aid on concessional terms and technical co-operation (mainly in the form of specialist staff abroad and training facilities in the U.K.), whether provided directly to developing countries or through the various multilateral aid organizations, including the United Nations and its specialized agencies. *Address:* Ministry of Overseas Development, Eland House, Stag Place, London, SW1E 5DH. Tel.: 01-834 2377.

## LABOUR

**Iron and Steel Trades Confederation.** A British industrial union founded in January 1917 by the amalgamation of a number of unions which had previously existed to organize either separate sections of the industry or groups of workpeople employed in the industry. It is the principal union of the British iron and steel industry, and with the exception of blast furnace men in England and Wales and various craftsmen, caters for all workpeople, including clerical, technical and management grades, engaged in the industry and kindred trades. Membership in 1976 was 120,325. The principal objects of the Confederation are to regulate the relations between workmen and employers; to assist its members to obtain fair wages and conditions of employment; to maintain joint conciliation machinery for the settlement of disputes; to provide monetary benefits, legal assistance and educational facilities for its members. The Confederation endeavours, not without success, to encourage and persuade its members to take a responsible part in the conduct of their industry. Its leaders have always believed that disputes can be settled peaceably, and the fact that there has been no serious official strike of production workers in the British iron and steel industry for a great number of years is evidence of the harmonious relations which exist between the employers and the Confederation. This is due mainly to a traditional acceptance on the part of both sides, of the principle of collective bargaining and joint agreement. The industry's conciliation machinery has been described by a well-known social investigator as the 'best method of negotiation and conciliation of any industry in the country'. *General Secretary:* Mr. William Sirs. *Address:* Swinton House, 324 Gray's Inn Road, London, WC1 X8DD.

**The Trades Union Congress.** Came into being in 1868 and since that date has had a continuous existence as a voluntary association of British trade unions for industrial purposes. At the 1977 Congress the T.U.C. had an affiliated membership of 11,515,920 in 115 unions. The annual affiliation fee is 17p. for each member. During its rise to a position of standing in the life of the nation and in the affairs of international labour it has established its right to speak for the organized workers of Britain. Not only are unions representing the vast majority of British trade unionists affiliated to it but at no time in its history has there been any rival national organization to claim the allegiance of even a substantial minority.

Each year affiliated unions send delegates to a Congress to discuss and to declare opinion on common problems and to elect a General Council of 41 to give centralized leadership on broad national trade union policy. Through this General Council, which meet at least every month, the trade union movement keeps up regular relations with the Government, with employers' organizations and with a very large number of advisory and consultative bodies concerned in particular with social and economic problems affecting the public interest.

The method of electing the General Council has been devised to ensure that the members bring to their deliberations opinion and experience representative of the whole range of British industrial activity. No member sits as representative of his union, but being elected by Congress is responsible to Congress as a whole. The Chairman of the Council is elected each year by the Council.

Neither Congress nor the General Council can override the autonomy of the affiliated unions. However the moral authority of the Council is strong and there is readiness among affiliated organizations to accept their decisions. The Council do, however, have certain disciplinary powers as well as machinery to deal with any disputes between unions. The Council may also intervene in serious industrial disputes where there is a likelihood that a dispute will create a situation which might hit the jobs, pay and conditions of other bodies of workpeople affiliated to Congress. On such occasions the General Council or its officers move in full consultation with the unions concerned.

On the international front the T.U.C. is affiliated to the International Confederation of Free Trade Unions and the European Trade Union Confederation, and supports the work of the International Labour Organization, to which each year it is asked by the Government to nominate the British workers' delegate.

The work of the T.U.C. is served by a headquarters office supervised by a general secretary who is elected by Congress and who is a member of the General Council. He is aided by an assistant general secretary and a staff of officials organized on a departmental basis. The 1977–78 members of the General Council are: *Chairman:* D. Basnett (National Union of General and Municipal Workers); *Vice-Chairman:* Mrs. C. M. Patterson (Transport and General Workers' Union). Lord Allen, CBE (Union of Shop Distributive and Allied Workers); F. A. Baker (National Union of General and Municipal Workers); R. Birch (Amalgamated Union of Engineering Workers (Engineering Section)); R. N. Bottini, CBE (National Union of Agricultural and Allied Workers); R. W. Buckton (Associated Society of Locomotive Engineers and Firemen); J. Chalmers (Amalgamated Society of Boilermakers); F. J. Chapple (Electrical Electronic Telecommunication and Plumbing Union); A. M. G. Christopher (Inland Revenue Staff Federation); L. Daly (National Union of Mineworkers); G. A. Drain (National and Local Government Officers' Association); F. Dyson (National Union of Dyers, Bleachers and Textile Workers); J. F. Eccles (National Union of General and Municipal Workers); L. F. Edmondson (Amalgamated Union of Engineering Workers (Engineering Section)); A. M. Evans (Transport and General Workers Union); A. W. Fisher (National Union of Public Employees); K. Gill (Amalgamated Union of Engineering Workers (Technical, Administrative and Supervisory Section)); J. Gormley OBE (National Union of Mineworkers); C. D. Grieve (The Tobacco Workers' Union); L. G. Guy (National Union of Sheet Metal Workers); T. Jackson (Union of Post Office Workers); F. F. Jarvis (National Union of Teachers); C. Jenkins (Association of Scientific, Technical and Managerial Staffs); J. L. Jones MBE (Transport and General Workers' Union); W. H. Keys (Society of Graphical and Allied Trades); A. L. Sapper (The Association of Cinematograph, Television and Allied Technicians); H. Scanlon (Amalgamated Union of Engineering Workers (Engineering Section)); W . Sirs (Iron and Steel Trades Confederation); J. H. Slater (National Union of Seamen); G. F. Smith CBE (Union of Construction Allied Trades and Technicians); E. A. G. Spanswick (Confederation of Health Service Employees); K. R. Thomas (Civil and Public Services Association); C. H. Urwin (Tansport and General Workers' Union); S. Weighell (National Union of Railwaymen). *General Secretary:* Lionel Murray, OBE. *Assistant General Secretary:* Mr. Norman Willis. *Press Officer:* B. Murphy. *Address:* Congress House, Great Russell Street, London, WC1B 3LS. Tel.: 01-636 4030.

## LAW—GOVERNMENT—PARLIAMENT

**Commonwealth Parliamentary Association.** Founded 1911 as the Empire Parliamentary Association which consisted of Members of the British Parliament and of the then Dominion Parliaments. Later its scope was extended to include other Commonwealth legislatures. A General Council as the governing body representative of all Branches was formed in 1949. *Purposes:* To promote understanding and co-operation between Commonwealth Parliamentarians and respect for parliamentary institutions. It pursues these objectives by organizing annual Commonwealth and Regional Conferences and the interchange of parliamentary delegations. It provides the sole machinery for regular consultation between Commonwealth MPs. Branches exist in the Parliaments of: Australia, the Bahamas, *Bangladesh, Barbados, Botswana, Canada, Fiji, The Gambia, *Ghana, Grenada, Guyana, India, Jamaica, Kenya. Lesotho, Malawi, Malaysia, Malta, Mauritius, Nauru, New Zealand, *Nigeria, Papua New Guinea, *Seychelles. Sierra Leone, Singapore, Sri Lanka, *Swaziland, Tanzania, Tonga, Trinidad & Tobago, *Uganda, United Kingdom, Western Samoa, Zambia; the State Parliaments of Australia, the Provincial Parliaments of Canada, 20 of the State Parliaments of India, and 12 of the State Parliaments of Malaysia; the Parliaments of the Isle of Man, Jersey and *Northern Ireland; the Legislatures of Antigua, Belize, Bermuda, British Virgin Islands, Cayman Islands, Cook Islands, Dominica, Falkland Islands, Gibraltar, Gilbert Islands, Guernsey, Hong Kong, Montserrat, Northern Territory, Northwest Territories, St. Christopher-Nevis-Anguila, St. Helena, St. Lucia, St. Vincent, Sark, Solomon Islands, The Turks & Caicos Islands, Tuvalu, Yukon Territory. There are also Kindred Groups in the Congress of the United States and in the Republic of Ireland. *Activities:* Annual Plenary Conferences and Council meetings in various places in the Commonwealth; biannual Executive Committee meetings; regional conferences; Parliamentary seminars and study-group meetings; exchange of Inter-Commonwealth hospitality and information. *Parliamentary Information and Reference Centre:* A parliamentary information and reference centre has been established in the office of the General Council Secretariat. Its purposes are to provide a complete and prompt information service for Members and Branches of the Association; to publish monographs, bibliographies and shorter book lists for those working or studying in the parliamentary field, and to assemble through direct acquisition and exchanges with Members, Clerks of Parliament and Parliamentary Librarians a comprehensive collection of material on Commonwealth Parliaments and other Legislatures. *Publications:* The Parliamentarian, formerly Journal of the Parliaments of the Commonwealth (quarterly);

* At present in abeyance.

Annual Reports; Reports of Conferences and General Meetings, and pamphlets on Parliamentary topics. *Secretary-General:* Sir Robin Vanderfelt, KBE; *Editor of Publications:* Ian Grey. *Address:* Houses of Parliament, 7 Old Palace Yard, London, SW1P 3JY. Tel.: 01-219 4666.

**The European Movement.** Has its origins in the United Europe Movement founded by Sir Winston Churchill in 1946. Together with other organizations formed at this time on the Continent, the European Movement became the parent body for voluntary organizations working towards the general objective of a United Europe. In May 1948 the Movement organized a Congress of Europe in The Hague which laid the foundation for the Council of Europe formed in May 1949, the European Payments Union and ultimately the European Communities. Its Presidents of Honour include Harold Macmillan, and Jean Monnet. The European Movement (British Council) is the parent body in Britain for voluntary organizations working for the common goal of European economic and political union based on an enlarged Common Market with effective and democratically controlled institutions. Patrons of the British Council of the European Movement are James Callaghan, MP; David Steel, MP; Margaret Thatcher, MP. *Chairman:* Lord Thomson of Monifieth. *Director:* Ernest Wistrich. *Address:* Europe House, 1A Whitehall Place, London SW1A 2HA. Tel.: 01-839 6622.

**Hansard Society for Parliamentary Government.** Founded in 1944, this Society is a non-political, educational organization, to promote knowledge of and interest in parliamentary government. Membership is open to individuals and corporate bodies in all parts of the world. The Society is governed by a council which is elected by the members. The founder was the late Lord King-Hall. Publishes a quarterly journal, 'Parliamentary Affairs'. The Society arranges meetings; maintains an information department; conducts research into problems of parliamentary government and engages in other activities in accordance with its rules. It has been granted consultative status by U.N. Economic and Social Council; is an associate member of the International Political Science Association, and works closely with national and international organizations working in similar fields. Income is derived from members' subscriptions and donations, special grants, and any surplus which may accrue from the publication of books or similar activities. The work is supported by Conservative, Labour and Liberal parties in Britain, by leaders in industry, and by educationalists. *President:* The Rt. Hon. Lord Selwyn Lloyd, CH, CBE, TD, QC. *Chairman:* Professor J. P. Mackintosh, MP. *Secretary:* Maxine Vlieland. *Address:* 12 Gower Street, London WC1E 6DP. Tel.: 01-323 1131.

**International Bar Association.** Founded February 1947, the I.B.A. embraces 81 member organizations from 53 countries. Additionally over 4,000 members of the profession from all over the world are affiliated as Individual members. *Purposes:* to advance the science of jurisprudence in all its phases and particularly in regard to international and comparative law; to promote uniformity in appropriate fields of law, and the administration of justice under law among the peoples of the world; to promote in their legal aspects the principles and aims of the United Nations; to establish and maintain friendly relations among the members of the legal profession throughout the world; to co-operate with, and promote co-ordination among, international juridical organizations having similar purposes. The IBA has consultative status with the U.N. and Council of Europe. *Principal achievements:* organization of annual international Conferences; organization of Seminars on international legal subjects; adoption in 1956 of an International Code of Ethics for the Lega Profession; compilation of Legal Aid Facilities Report (in member countries) and in 1960 the organization of the International Legal Aid Association under the auspices of the I.B.A. with headquarters in London; formation in 1970 of a Section on Business Law, membership of which is open to all individual members, which publishes its own Quarterly Journal, the International Business Lawyer, and a Directory of its members; Formation in 1973 of a Section on General Practice, membership of which is also open to all individual members; Support given to member organizations where their independence or professional status may be threatened; recommendations concerning revision of UN Charter; Publication on International Shipbuilding Contracts; Draft Conventions on International Shipbuilding Contracts and on Administration of Foreign Estates; adoption by General Meeting at Salzburg (1960) of Resolution on Sovereign Immunity; other reports (International Judicial Co-operation, Legal Aspects of Atomic Energy, Monopolies and Restrictive Trade Practices, Protection of Investments, Pollution, Consumer Protection, etc.). *Publications:* International Bar Journal, The Association, its members and their activities, Professional Ethics, The International Business Lawyer, and Membership Lists of all I.B.A. member organizations and individual members and of members of the Section on Business Law, World Energy Laws (1975). *Officers:* President, Dr. Werner Deuchler (Germany); Vice-President, Sir William Carter. Secretary General, John P. Bracken (U.S.A.); Director-General, Sir Thomas Lund (U.K.); Treasurer, Dr. Harold Foglar-Deinhardstein (Austria), Assistant Secretaries General, Rolf Christophersen (Norway), Heinz Brangsch (Germany), Phillipe Gastambide (France), Roberto Reyes (Spain), Bert Early (U.S.A.). *Address:* Byron House, 7/9 St. Jame's Street, London SW1A 15E.

**International Law Association.** Founded Brussels 1873 under title of Association for Reform and Codification of the Law of Nations. The present title was adopted in 1895. The objects of the association are the study, elucidation and advancement of international law (public and private), the study of comparative law, the making of proposals for the solution of conflicts of law, and for the unification of law and the furthering of international understanding and goodwill. *Activities:* The Association at its Conferences has considered a large number of topics of public and private international law; notable among these were the York Antwerp Rules of General Average (1877) which were revised in 1890, in 1924, and promulgated in their present form at Copenhagen in 1950. Other achievements include the following: The Hague Rules of Affreightment (1921); Proposals for an International Penal Court (Vienna, 1926); The Warsaw-Oxford Rules on C.I.F. Contracts (1932); a Draft Convention for the Regulation of the International Sale of Goods, a general Form of J.J.F. (C.A.F.) Contract, and Draft Principles to govern Jurisdiction in Divorce and Nullity of Marriage (Oxford, 1932); The Copenhagen Rules on International Commercial Arbitration (1950); A Draft Convention on the Payment of Foreign Money Liabilities (Dubrovnik, 1956); A Draft Convention on Conflicts of Law relating to Companies (New York, 1958); A Model Act for the Recognition and Enforcement of Foreign Money-Judgments (Tokyo, 1964). The Helsinki Conference (1966) approved the first general codification of the law of international rivers by adopting the 'Helsinki Rules', which deal with pollution, navigation, equitable utilization, timber floating and the settlement of disputes. The 53rd Conference (1968) adopted eight resolutions on the Succession of new States to the treaties of their predecessors. The 55th Conference (1972) adopted Draft Conventions on Diplomatic and Territorial Asylum; Draft Articles on Flood Control and on Marine Pollution of Continental Origin; and Articles setting forth Principles of International Law as guidelines to the resolution of problems concerning the assumption and exercise of jurisdiction by States in connection with Restrictive Trade Practices (Anti-Trust Regulation). The 57th Conference (1976) approved Draft Conventions on the Unification of Certain Rules Relating to Hovercraft and on Jurisdiction in Traffic Accidents. *President:* Dr. Antonio Rodríguez Sastre. *Chairman of Executive Council:* Rt. Hon. Lord Wilberforce, CMG, OBE; *Director of Studies:* Professor D. P. O'Connell QC; *Secretary-General:* John B. S. Edwards. *Secretary:* Vanessa Hall-Smith. *Address:* 3 Paper Buildings, The Temple, London, EC4Y 7EU. Tel.: 01-353 2904; Cables: Paxuna London, EC4Y 7EU.

**Inter-Parliamentary Union.** A world association of parliamentarians which was founded in 1889. Present membership consists of National Groups in 73 countries. The organs of the Union are the plenary Conference, Inter-Parliamentary Council (two members from each National Group), Executive Committee (11 members), five Standing Study Committees, and the Secretariat under a permanent Secretary General. The President of the Council is elected for a term of three years, he is also *ex-officio* President of the Executive Committee. The Union customarily holds two series of meetings each year. In the spring, the Study Committees meet to discuss topics for possible inclusion in the agenda of the forthcoming Conference. The final agenda is fixed by the Council. The plenary Conferences usually take place in late summer. It is the duty of National Groups to bring the resolutions adopted at that time to the attention of their Parliaments and Governments and to do everything in their power to implement these resolutions. *President of the Inter-Parliamentary Council:* Sir Thomas Williams, QC,

MP, United Kingdom. *Members of the Executive Committee:* M. A. Ziai (Iran); *substitute to the President*: M. O. Ba (Senegal); J. Baumel (France); C. Borja (Brazil); E. Cuvelier (Belgium); P. Dapcevic (Yugoslavia); R. G. L. Fairweather (Canada); J. Finat (Spain); M. Tarabonov (Bulgaria); H. Young (Australia). *Secretary-General:* Pio-Carlo Terenzio (Italy). *Address:* Place du Petit-Saconnex 1209 Geneva, Switzerland.

**World Association of World Federalists.** WAWF Mouvement universel pour une fédération mondiale (MUFM); Asociación de Federalistas (AUFM); Weltbund der Weltföderalisten (WdW). Founded at Luxembourg in 1946, when plans were also made which led to the setting up of a European Union of Federalists. Became World Movement for World Federal Government at its First Congress in 1947 (the present title was adopted in 1956, but the French name remained unchanged). Aims: a federation of national organizations working for world federation having a defined sphere of jurisdiction functioning through a legislature to make a world law, a judiciary to interpret it, and an executive with powers to enforce it upon individuals, associations and states; and to increase clarification and understanding of political and other issues that have a direct bearing on the development of a world community, with emphasis on reform or the revision of the UN to give UN limited powers to prevent war and to increase the well-being of peoples everywhere without interfering with the internal affairs of the member states. Membership: affiliated and associated organizations 45 in 31 countries. *Publication:* Transnational Perspectives (four issues per annum). *President:* Hermod Lannung (Denmark). *UN Representative:* Donald F. Keys, 777 UN Plaza, New York City 10017. *Address:* Leliegracht 21, Amsterdam, Netherlands.

## METALLURGY

**International Institute of Welding.** *Objects:* to promote the development of welding by all processes, and encourage the development of welding, both as regards equipment and raw materials, and provide for the exchange of scientific and technical information relating to research and education; to assist in the formation of international standards, in collaboration with the International Organization for Standardization. The Institute does not engage in trade or commercial activities, and in particular does not concern itself with prices, wage rates, markets, or agencies. Membership is open to non-profit making organizations which are wholly or mainly concerned with the scientific and technical aspects of welding and of allied processes; organizations whose activities are wholly or mainly of a commercial or trade character are ineligible for membership. The technical work of the Institute is carried out by 16 Commissions, each devoted to a different aspect of welding, and on each of which every member country may be represented. The results of the Commissions' work have appeared in a number of books and booklets and, in particular. in the Institute's bi-monthly bilingual (English/French) journal 'Welding in the World'. Fifty-seven societies from 37 countries belong to the Institute. *Secretary- General:* P. D. Boyd, MA (U.K.). *Address:* 54 Princes Gate, Exhibition Road, London, SW7 2PG.

**The International Tin Research Council.** Founded in 1932 with the object of developing the consumption of tin. Is financed by the major tin producers of the world. The Council's headquarters and laboratories are at the International Tin Research Institute, Greenford, Middlesex, England. The Council also controls organizations for technical development of tin in other countries, namely: Tin Research Institute, Inc., Columbus, Ohio, U.S.A., Palo Alto, Calif., U.S.A.; Centre d'Information de l'Etain, Brussels; Zinn-Informationsbüro, Düsseldorf; Technisch Informatie Centrum voor Tin, The Hague; Centro d'Informazioni dello Stagno, Milan; Centro de Informações sobre Estanho, Rio de Janeiro; Japan Tin Centre, Tokyo; Australian Tin Information Centre, Sydney, Australia. The International Tin Research Institute is engaged on scientific researches to develop new uses for tin and to improve existing tin products and the processes by which they are made. The whole group of organizations controlled by the Council is engaged in spreading knowledge of tin throughout the world. This is effected by a variety of means; by contributing articles to the technical and trade press; by issuing practical handbooks covering all the main industrial applications of tin; by giving lectures to learned societies, educational institutions and industrial bodies; by taking part in exhibitions and trade fairs; by practical demonstrations of new and established processes; and by visits to users' works. Loans of lecture, display and teaching material relating to tin are also arranged. *Members of the Council:* H. E. General Rogelio Miranda B. H. Zannier V. (Bolivia); Usodo Notodirdjo (Chairman), V. S. Siahaan (Indonesia); Abdul Fatah bin Zakaria, W. T. Dunne (Malaysia); C. O; Agidi (Vice-Chairman), E. K. Furze (Adviser) (Nigeria); Prayot Ransiyanon, Pisoot Sudasna (Thailand); Kabeya Milambu, R. Van Achter (Zaire). *Director:* Dr. D. A. Robins, B.Sc, PhD, FIM, FInstP. *Assistant Director:* Dt. B. T. K. Barry, BSc(Eng), PhD, ARSM, DIC, FIM, MIMM. *Secretary and Administration Officer:* C. J. Faulkner, MIM, ARAeS. *Address:* International Tin Research Institute, Fraser Road, Greenford, Middlesex, UB6 7AQ, England. Tel.: 01-997 4254.

**The Welding Institute.** Provides, through its Research Division, a wide range of advisory and technical services to industry, and undertakes an intensive programme of research into welding processes, welding metallurgy and engineering aspects of welding construction. The Communications and Training Division arranges a programme of intensive courses in welding technology and non-destructive testing, conferences, seminars, exhibitions, special publications and information services. It represents every aspect of research and professional activities in the field of welding technology and has 1,500 Research Member companies and 5,000 professional members. *Serial Publications:* Metal Construction; Research Bulletin (Rresearch Members only); Welding Research International: Surfacing Journal. *Director-General:* Dr. A. A. Wells, FRS. *Address:* Head office and research centre, Abington Hall, Abington, Cambridge CB1 6AL (telephone 0223 891162); London office, 54 Princes Gate, SW7 2PG.

## PRESS

**Commonwealth Press Union.** Founded in 1909, is an association whose member-newspapers, periodicals and news agencies are published in all parts of the Commonwealth. The principal objects are to promote the welfare of the newspaper Press of the Commonwealth and of those concerned with the dissemination of news and information in newspapers and other periodicals. and to give effect to the opinion of members on all matters which affect the freedom and efficiency of the newspaper and periodical Press throughout the Commonwealth; to promote conferences of members in various parts of the Commonwealth; to watch for and oppose proposals likely to be harmful to Press freedom and the maintenance of an effective Press; to work for improved telecommunications for the reporting and transmission of news; to promote measures for the training and education of journalists throughout the Commonwealth. The Council in London is composed of leading representatives of the Press of Commonwealth countries. There are autonomous Sections in Canada, Australia, New Zealand, India, Rhodesia, Malaysia, Singapore, the West Indies, Sri Lanka, and Ghana. The Union holds an annual Conference in London and a Quadrennial Conference in some other part of the Commonwealth. The thirteenth such conference was held in Hong Kong in 1974 and the next major conference will be held in Canada in 1978. *President:* The Lord Astor of Hever; *Chairman of the Council:* Sir Edward Pickering; *Secretary:* Col. T. Pierce-Goulding, MBE, CD. *Address:* Studio House, 184 Fleet Street, London, EC4A 2DU. Tel.: 01-242 1056.

## RAILWAYS—TRANSPORT

**European Goods Time-table Conference.** Soon after World War I certain European railway administrations considered a plan to co-ordinate international movement of railway goods traffic. The statutes came into force on 1 January 1930, and the Czechoslovak Railway Administration was appointed the managing authority (actually the Administration functioned from 1924, when the plan was unofficial but in operation, and a time-table had been issued by the German Riech Railways in 1928). The activities of the Conference were interrupted by World War II, but were renewed in Prague in 1946. The Czechoslovak Administration was re-elected as the managing authority and also entrusted with the task of editing the International Time-table for Goods Trains (LIM), which was issued in 1949. At the meeting at Copenhagen (1948) it was decided to extend the activities of the Conference so as to include an addendum to LIM, to schedule the connections for wagons transporting parcels over the international system. In 1951 the name of the organization was changed to its present title (abbreviation LIM Conference). According to the Statute which came into force 1 June 1969. Amended statutes came into effect on 1 January 1953 and international agreement made possible the easier and quicker transportation of parcels, and the acceleration of the movements of wagons at the frontier stations. Membership of the Conference is open to all railway administrations. As the result of collaboration, speedier movement of goods traffic from one country to another is an accomplished fact. Member-countries of the Conference are Austria, Belgium, Bulgaria, Czechoslovakia, Denmark, France, Germany (Federal and Reich Railways), Greece, Hungary, Italy, Luxembourg, Netherlands, Norway, Poland, Romania, Spain, Sweden, Switzerland, Turkey, United Kingdom, and Yugoslavia. There are also two independent railway administrations, viz. Györ-Sopron-Ebenfurt Railways and Bernina Alps Bern-Lötschberg-Simplon Railways and two international railway societies Interfrigo and Intercontainer. Communications should be addressed to the Czechoslovak Railways (ČSD), Príkopy, 33, Prague, 1, Czechoslovakia.

**International Road Federation (I.R.F.)** is a non-profit making organization established in 1948 to encourage the development and improvement of roads and road transport throughout the world. The I.R.F. has offices in Washington and Geneva, and it has affiliated national organizations in some 90 countries throughout the world. I.R.F. arranges for advanced training in highway engineering and traffic studies; it collects and publishes economic and statistical information illustrating the advantages to be derived from good roads, and organizes international conferences on highway problems. I.R.F. is a highway consultant to UNO, in category II, and to the Council of Europe and has co-operating status with the Organization of American States and OECD. *European Address:* I.R.F., 63 rue de Lausanne, CH 1202 Geneva, Switzerland. Tel: Geneva 31:71:50; Telex 27 590. *North American Address:* I.R.F., 1023 Washington Building, Washington, D.C. 20005.

**International Union of Railways (UIC).** International collaboration between European railways first began in 1872 when the European Timetable Conference was formed. But it was only fifty years later, in 1922, that the International Union of Railways came into existence, its object being the standardization and improvement of railway equipment and operating methods with special regard to international traffic.

The UIC functions through three bodies: the General Assembly, effecting a periodical control and composed of representatives of all UIC Member Railways, the Board of Management, comprising representatives of 18 Member Railways and which undertakes the administration or control of the various Committees, Working Parties, Centres, Offices or Bureaux, and finally the General Secretariat, in Paris, which ensures liaison and co-ordination with participating or affiliated organizations, as well as a certain number of governmental and non-governmental organizations. The General Assembly appoints a 'UIC Chairman', who changes every two years and is chosen from the General Managers of the Unions' Member Railways.

At present railways from all over the world (African, Asian, European, South and North American) are members of the UIC. The total length of railway line operated by these systems is in the region of 483,000 km. or 302,000 miles and their annual traffic is in the region of 18 thousand million passengers while over three thousand million tonnes of freight are carried. The number of member railways is 77.

Among the most important UIC achievements since the end of the Second World War, mention should be made of the creation of introduction of: ORE (Office for Research and Experiments); '*Europ*' wagon fleet, enabling 310,000 freight wagons to be used jointly by a number of Railways; the standard numbering of freight stock, preparing for the future automation of traffic; Eurofima (financing of rolling stock); Interfrigo and Intercontainer; Trans-Europ-Express (TEE) network, the fatest and most luxurious train service in Western Europe; Trans-Europe-Express-Merchandise (TEEM), for the rapid transport of perishable foodstuffs between principal centres; Europabus (road transport for tourist); special season tickets such as Eurailpass, Student-Railpass, InterRail.

*Chairman:* W. Winkler, Vice-Minister of Transport and Assistant General Manager of the German State Railway. *Secretary-General:* Bernard de Fontgalland. *Chief Executive Officer:* Paul Ballet. *General Secretariat:* 14–16 rue Jean Rey, 75–Paris. Tel.: 273-01-20. Telex: 27835 Unionfer Paris.

**Office for Research and Experiments (ORE) of the International Union of Railways (UIC).** *Objects:* (1) the pooling of the results of the research and experiments carried out by the different Railways and the distribution, between its Members, of the necessary technical documentation; (2) the pooling of means of research; (3) the carrying out, on joint account, of certain investigations; (4) the examination, with a view to reduction in costs, of the rationalization of means of construction and of the possibility of dividing the work between the industries of the various countries.

The activities of the Office may be extended to cover every field of railway technology: rolling stock, permanent way, signalling and other installations, electrification, handling, questions of technical organization, etc.

ORE is directed by a Control Committee composed of Administrations nominated by the Board of Management of UIC, each of which delegates two qualified highly-placed railway officials. The Chairmen of the UIC Rolling Stock and Motive Power Committee, the UIC Way and Works Committee and the UIC Planning Committee are also members of the Control Committee. The member Administrations are from Alaska, Austria, Belgium, Bulgaria, Czechoslovakia, Denmark, Finland, France (including Parisian Transports), Germany (Eastern), Germany (Fed.), Greece, Hungary, India, Iran, Iraq, Ireland, Israel, Italy, Japan, Lebanon, Liberia, Luxembourg, Netherlands, Norway, Poland, Portugal, Romania, South Africa, Spain, Sweden, Switzerland (including the Berne–Lotschberg–Simplon Railway), Turkey, United Kingdom (including London Transport Executive), Western Australia, Yugoslavia, Zaire, Inter-frigo, Deutsche Schlafwagen Gesellschaft, and Intercontainer, Present Managing Administration Netherlands Railways. Chairman (Control Committee): P. Détappe (France). *Address:* ORE, Oudenoord, 60, NL-3513 EV UTRECHT, Netherlands.

## REFUGEES—MIGRATION

**Intergovernmental Committee for European Migration (ICEM).** Established in Brussels in 1951 to help solve the European population and refugee problems through migration. *Membership:* 33 nations. In addition, eight non-member governments and a large number of international governmental and non-governmental organizations have observer status at meetings of the ICEM Council. The 1977 annual budget was $30 million. Upon request from Member Governments, ICEM provides essential services such as selection counselling, orientation, medical examination, vocational and language training and organizes adaptation courses. Furthermore, the Committee arranges prompt and modern transportation at a moderate cost, assists in financing the movements of those refugees and migrants who are unable to meet their own expenses and takes part in embarkation, reception and integration procedures in the new country. One of the most important programmes is that of family reunion, whereby dependents join their respective family heads, who have already settled in overseas countries. ICEM coordinates its refugee activities with the U.N. High Commissioner for Refugees and with governmental and non-governmental organizations. Since 1952 ICEM has often been called upon to intervene in emergency situations to organize speedy evacuation of large refugee groups. This was the case of the Hungarian refugees in 1956–57, of the Czechoslovak refugees in 1968–69 and of the Asians expelled from Uganda in 1972, and 5,000 refugees from Chile in 1973–74 and is now assisting in a similar operation in respect of refugees from Indochina. On 30 June 1977, 53,407 persons had been re-settled.

ICEM's programme for Latin America aims at making a contribution to the solution of its economic and social problems by providing human capital alongside technical and financial aid given to Latin America under many bilateral and multilateral agreements. By recruiting and selecting Europeans in high-level trades and professions to occupy positions in Latin America for which qualified persons are not available locally, ICEM provides its member countries in Latin America with part of the indispensable resources of skill, expertise and experience to modernize and increase industrial production, introduce new agricultural methods and build up educational establishments. In the last twelve years some 16,000 professional and highly skilled immigrants have been placed through ICEM. ICEM has special means at its disposal to facilitate the social and material adjustment during the period after arrival of the carefully selected persons coming to Latin America under its auspices. It maintains close contact with other agencies working in Latin America in order to ensure that incoming high-level manpower is channelled to priority economic sectors. In May 1977, ICEM organized a Third International Seminar on Adaptation and Integration of Permanent Immigrants in Geneva, to discuss problems related to migrant information, orientation and counselling, language training, vocational training and educational adaptation, and it is proposed to maintain, through further Seminars (the last

Seminar was held in November 1975), a permanent exchange of information between governmental and non-governmental organizations and European and overseas governments.

In recent years, the combined yearly movements of nationals and refugees under ICEM auspices have totalled between 70,000 and 80,000. From 1952 to 30 June 1977, ICEM had assisted 2,225,280 migrants and refugees to resettle. *Address:* 16 Avenue Jean Trembley, Case 100, 1211 Geneva 19, Switzerland.

## RELIGION

**The Anglican Communion.** The Anglican Communion comprises all the Anglican or Episcopalian Churches and dioceses throughout the world. All are in full communion with the see of Canterbury.

The Assemblies of the Anglican Communion are given below.

*The Anglican Consultative Council.* The whole Anglican Communion is represented on this Council. The Council meets every two or three years. The chief officiates are:

*President:* The Archbishop of Canterbury.
*Chairman:* Mrs. Harold C. Kelleran.
*Secretary-General:* The Rt. Rev. J. W. A. Howe, 32 Eccleston Street, London, SW1W 9PY.

*The Lambeth Conference. President:* The Archbishop of Canterbury.

This is an assembly of all the Anglican bishops. The Assembly meets approximately every ten years. It last met in 1968 and the next meeting will take place at the University of Kent, Canterbury, 22 July to 13 August, 1978.

*Churches and Dioceses of the Anglican Communion:* These are comprised of the following:

*The Church of England:* 43 dioceses.
*The Church of England in Australia:* 24 dioceses.
*Igreja Episcopal do Brasil:* 5 dioceses.
*The Church of the Province of Burma:* 4 dioceses.
*The Anglican Church of Canada:* 30 dioceses.
*The Church of the Province of Central Africa:* 8 dioceses.
*The Anglican Church in Ceylon:* 2 dioceses which are expected to form part of the united Church of Lanka when this is inaugurated.
*Chung Hua Sheng Kung Hui (The Holy Catholic Church in China):* This Church had 15 dioceses, but contact now is only with the Diocese of Hong Kong and Macao.
*Iglesia Episcopal de Cuba:* One diocese, under a Metropolitan Council.
*The Church of the Province of the Indian Ocean:* 5 dioceses.
*The Church of Ireland:* 12 dioceses.
*Nippon Sei Ko Kai (The Holy Catholic Church in Japan):* 11 dioceses.
*The Episcopal Church of Jerusalem and the Middle East:* 4 dioceses.
*The Church of the Province of Kenya:* 7 dioceses.
*The Church of the Province of Melanesia:* 4 dioceses.
*The Church of the Province of New Zealand:* 8 dioceses.
*The Church of the Province of Papua New Guinea:* 5 dioceses.
*The Scottish Episcopal Church:* 7 dioceses.
*The Church of the Province of South Africa:* 16 dioceses.
*The Anglican Church in the Sudan:* 4 dioceses.
*The Church of the Province of Tanzania:* 9 dioceses.
*The Church of the Province of Uganda, Rwanda, Burundi and Boga-Zaire:* 22 dioceses.
*The Episcopal Church in the United States of America:* 111 dioceses, of which 92 are in the United States and the remainder in other parts of the world.
*The Church in Wales:* 6 dioceses.
*The Church of the Province of West Africa:* 21 dioceses.
*The Church of the Province of the West Indies:* 9 dioceses.
*Extra-Provincial Dioceses under the jurisdiction of the Archbishop of Canterbury:* 9.
*Council of the Church of East Asia* ((*Chairman:* The Bishop of Taiwan).
*South Pacific Anglican Council* (*Chairman:* The Archbishop of Papua-New Guinea).
*Consejo Anglicano Sud Americano* (*President:* Bishop Colin F. Bazley, Chile).

**Roman Catholic Church.** The supreme government of the Church is vested in the Pope, with the advice and assistance of the College of Cardinals and the Synod of Bishops. The College numbered 135 members in August 1977, of which 103 were less than eighty years of age and could cast a vote, therefore, in a Papal election. The Cardinal Vicar is the Pope's representative in the ordinary ecclesiastical administration of the diocese of Rome. The administration of general Church affairs is carried out under the Pope by the Roman Curia, which is composed of Sacred Congregations, Tribunals, Offices and Secretariats, each under the direction of a Cardinal. The most important Office is the Papal Secretariat or Secretariat of State, which works in close collaboration with the Council for the Public Affairs of the Church, the Cardinal Secretary of State being also Prefect of the latter-named Council. To co-ordinate the work of the Curia, the Cardinal Secretary of State convokes meetings of the heads of the different departments to consider matters of common interest. In the general business of co-ordination, a vital role is that of the *Sostituto* (or Under-Secretary) of the Secretariat of State, though this is not technically an office of the first rank. The Sacred Congregations are as follows: For the Doctrine of the Faith, the Eastern Churches, the Evangelisation of the Peoples, Bishops, Religious, Sacraments and Divine Worship, Clergy, Canonization of Saints, and Catholic Education. The three Tribunals are: the Supreme Tribunal of the Apostolic Segnatura, the Holy Roman Rota and the Apostolic Penitentiary. The five Offices are: the Prefecture of Economic Affairs, the Apostolic Chamber, the Administration of the Patrimony of the Holy See, the Prefecture of the Papal Household and the Statistical Office. The other Secretariats are those for the Promotion of Christian Unity, for Non-Christians and for Non-Believers. There are Councils on the Laity and for co-ordinating international relief ("Cor Unum"), and also various Permanent Commissions, the most important of which are those for Emigration and Tourism, for Latin America, for the study of Justice and Peace and on the Mass Media of Communications. In 1974, two new Commissions were instituted, for relations respectively with Judaism and Islamism. The Roman Congregations are composed of Cardinals resident in Rome and certain residential Archbishops and Bishops. Consultors to the Congregations and other departments of the Curia include bishops, priests, religious and lay-persons from many parts of the world. Papal representatives abroad number 37 Nuncios, 41 Pronuncios, all with diplomatic status, and 22 Apostolic Delegates. The Holy See also has permanent representatives at various international organisations, both governmental and non-governmental, including permanent observers at UNO, UNESCO and FAO. The ecclesiastical organization of the Church is headed by patriarchs, archbishops and bishops in countries under the common law of the church, abbots, prelates *nullius diocesos*, vicars apostolic and prefects apostolic (the last in countries designated missionary and under the Sacred Congregation for the Evangelisation of the Peoples). There are 2,219 Residential Sees; 1,980 Titular Sees; 101 Prelacies; 22 Abbacies *Nullius*; 11 Apostolic Administrations; 26 Exarchates (of the Eastern rite); 79 Apostolic Vicariates; 66 Apostolic Prefectures; 4 Missions "sui juris"; 26 *Vicariate Castrensi*; 98 Episcopal Conferences. It is estimated that of the world's population 20 per cent are Catholic. *Publications:* Acta Apostolicae Sedis (monthly; records Encyclicals and other papal pronouncements, Acts of the Sacred Congregations, Offices, etc.); Annuario Pontificio (year-book, deals with administration); Attività della Santa Sede (yearly, chronicling events of previous year); Osservatore Romano (semi-official daily newspaper with weekly editions in French, German, Spanish, Portuguese and English); International Fides Service (mission news throughout the world). The Vatican has its own radio station, Radio-Vatican, which broadcasts daily in 28 languages to almost all parts of the world. The Apostolic Delegate to Great Britain is His Excellency Most Rev. Bruno Heim (Titular Archbishop of Xanthus), 54 Parkside, London, SW19 5NF.

**The Salvation Army.** Its founder and first General was William Booth, who was born at Nottingham (England) on 10 April 1829 and died on 20 August 1912. He lived to establish Salvation Army work in 58 countries and colonies. Among his many works, his 'In Darkest England and the Way Out' became the blueprint of all the Army's subsequent social schemes and it was reprinted in 1970. A new book, 'In darkest England—Now' was published in February 1974. The Salvation Army serves in 82 countries and preaches the Gospel of Jesus Christ in 109 languages. The Corps and Outposts number 16,236, Social Institutions and Agencies 3,310, Schools 676 (with 122,303 pupils). Officers and Cadets 26,146. The number of periodicals published is 114, with a circulation per issue of 1,644,282. The social services embody hostels, canteens, homes, workshops, wood yards, employment bureaux, aid for ex-prisoners, homes for inebriates and children, women's industrial homes, approved schools, training homes for girls and mothers with children, maternity homes, farms, migration and settlement, goodwill centres, slum posts, clinics, dispensaries, hospitals (including leprosaria, etc.), institutes for the blind, homes for the aged, and also operate missing persons' bureaux throughout the world. The International Headquarters are centred in London. The Head is General Arnold Brown. The General, through the administrative departments, directs every part of the Army and every phase of its operations throughout the world. Subsidiary organizations in the United Kingdom are Salvationist Publishing & Supplies Ltd., Reliance Bank Ltd., Salvation Army General Insurance Corporation Ltd. The directors of these companies receive no fees, and as all the shares are held by The Salvation Army, profits are paid over to The Salvation Army for the promotion of its evangelical work. The William Booth Memorial Training College, London, prepares young salvationists for S.A. officership, but there are 43 other training colleges in various parts of the world. *Address:* International Headquarters, 101 Queen Victoria Street, London, EC4P 4EP.

**Friends (Quakers) World Committee for Consultation.** The Religious Society of Friends (Quakers) numbers about 198,000 members in different parts of the world; they belong to over 50 organized yearly meetings and groups. The following approximate figures indicate some of the largest concentrations of Friends: The Americas, 135,000; British Isles 22,200, East Africa, 34,000. Most of the Yearly Meetings are represented on the Friends World Committee for Consultation which was set up in 1937. The Committee aims to encourage and strengthen the spiritual life within the Society of Friends through such measures as worship intervisitation, study, conferences and a wide sharing of experience on the deepest spiritual level; to help Friends to gain a better understanding of the world-wide character of the Religious Society of Friends and its vocation in the world today; to promote consultation amongst Friends of all cultures, countries and languages. The Committee seeks to bring the different groups of Friends into intimate touch with one another seeking their common Quaker heritage, sharing experiences and coming to some measure of agreement in regard to their attitude to world issues; to promote understanding between Friends everywhere and members of other branches of the Christian Church and also of other religious faiths, and to interpret the specific Quaker message to those who seek further religious experience; and to keep under review the Quaker contribution in world affairs and to the world Christian mission: to facilitate the examination and presentation of Quaker thinking and concern in these fields; and to encourage Friends to co-operate as far as possible in joint action with other groups having similar objectives.

Every three years the FWCC meets in full in different areas of the world. The eighth Triennial Meeting was held in Kenya in 1961, the ninth in Ireland in 1964, the tenth in the U.S.A. in 1967, the eleventh in Sweden in 1970 and the twelfth in Sydney, Australia, 1973 and the Thirteenth in Hamilton, Ontario, Canada, 1976. There have been so far four World Conferences of Friends, the last being held in 1967 in North Carolina, U.S.A.

FWCC publishes twice a year an illustrated Bulletin, Friends World News which provides information about what Friends in different areas do and think. A sixth edition of the Handbook of the Religious Society of Friends was published in 1972, it gives the brief history of the different Yearly Meetings as well as a list of Quaker schools, Centres, and periodicals. This is supplemented by an annual Calendar of Yearly Meetings. A booklet entitled 'International Work of the Religious Society of Friends' was issued in 1972, and a new edition was published in 1975. FWCC is recognized by the United Nations as a 'non-governmental organization with consultative status'. In New York and in Geneva Friends work on United Nations affairs and try to encourage the spirit of reconciliation and goodwill.

The Central Office of the Friends World Committee for Consultation is at Drayton House, 30 Gordon Street, London, WC1H 0AX. Tel: 01-388 0497.

**World Council of Churches.** Constituted 23 August 1948. The representatives (coming from 44 countries) of 147 Christian Churches assembled in Amsterdam and unanimously passed the resolution by which the Council was established in accordance with the Constitution drafted at Utrecht in 1938. The Assembly represented the majority of the Protestant churches, almost all Anglican churches and several Orthodox churches. Since 1961 almost all other Orthodox churches have joined the Council. The Roman Catholic Church is not a member but sends delegated observers to the Council's meetings; a Joint Working Group of 18 representatives of the Roman Catholic Church and of the WCC meets regularly. The Council is a fellowship of churches 'which confess the Lord Jesus Christ as God and Saviour according to the Scriptures and therefore seek to fulfil together their common calling to the glory of the one God, Father, Son, and Holy Spirit'. It has no authority over its members but is at their service to facilitate their common action through inter-church aid, to assist them in their task of mission and evangelism, to promote the witness and the service of the Church in the world of nations and in all areas of social life, and to further the cause of Christian unity.

The World Council of Churches is constituted for the following functions and purposes:

(i) to call the churches to the goal of visible unity in one faith and in one eucharistic fellowship expressed in worship and in common life in Christ, and to advance towards that unity in order that the world may believe;
(ii) to facilitate the common witness of the churches in each place and in all places;
(iii) to support the churches in their world-wide missionary and evangelistic task;
(iv) to express the common concern of the churches in the service of human need, the breaking down of barriers between people, and the promotion of one human family in justice and peace;
(v) to foster the renewal of the churches in unity, worship, mission, and service;
(vi) to establish and maintain relations with national councils and regional conferences of churches, world confessional bodies, and other ecumenical organizations;
(vii) to carry on the work of the world movements for Faith and Order and Life and Work and of the International Missionary Council and the World Council on Christian Education.

The principal authority of the Council is the Assembly, which meets every six or seven years. It is composed of official representatives of the different member churches, now numbering 289. The staff is headed by the General Secretary. Various sub-units and departments are grouped into three Programme Units with collegiate leadership and the General Secretariat. The Programme Unit on Faith and Witness comprises the Faith and Order Secretariat, the Department on Church and Society, Dialogue with people of living Faiths and Ideologies, and the Commission on World Mission and Evangelism, and Theological Education. The Programme Unit on Justice and Service comprises the Commission on Inter-Church Aid. Refugee and World Service, the Commission on the Churches' Participation in Development, the Programme to Combat Racism, and the Commission of the Churches on International Affairs. The third Programme Unit is on Education and Renewal, and includes a new sub-unit on 'Renewal and Congregational life' besides those on Education, Youth and Women. The Department of Finance and Administration and the Department of Communication are directly related to the General Secretary, as is the New York Office of the WCC, and the Ecumenical Institute at Bossey (near Geneva) and the WCC Library. The headquarters of the WCC are in Geneva. *Address:* 150 route de Ferney, 1211 Geneva 20, Switzerland. Telephone: 333400. Telex: 23423 01K. The address of the New York Office is: 475 Riverside Drive, New York, N.Y. 10027, U.S.A.

## SCIENCE

**Commonwealth Science Council.** The Commonwealth Science Council (CSC), formerly known as the Commonwealth Scientific Committee, has its origins in the British Commonwealth Scientific Official Conference held in 1946. It consists of nominees of member countries who are usually senior officials in national science organizations or their equivalents, and its main objectives are to ensure the fullest possible collaboration in increasing the capabilities of its members to use science and technology for their economic and social development. The Council achieve this by facilitating joint projects by participating member countries on problems of common concern.

The CSC meets biennially and its between-meeting operations are controlled by an Executive Committee. The Science Adviser to the Commonwealth Secretary-General is the Secretary of CSC and its Executive Committee.

The member countries are: Australia, Bahamas, Bangladesh, Barbados, Botswana, Britain, Canada, Cyprus, Ghana, Guyana, India, Jamaica, Kenya, Lesotho, Malawi, Malaysia, Malta, Mauritius, New Zealand, Nigeria, Sierra Leone, Singapore, Sri Lanka, Tanzania, Trinidad and Tobago, Uganda and Zambia. *Chairman:* Dr. P. A. Munroe. *Secretary:* Mr. C. de Laet. *Deputy Secretary:* Mr. D. G.

Thomas. *Assistant Secretary:* Dr. M. N. G. A. Khan. *Address:* Marlborough House, Pall Mall, London, SW1Y 5HX. Tel.: 01-839 4561.

**European Organization for Nuclear Research (CERN).** Sponsored originally by UNESCO, but now entirely independent of that organization, CERN is an intergovernmental organization for nuclear particle physics research which is undertaken at its Laboratories near Geneva, mainly by visiting teams of European scientists. The research is aimed at understanding the nature of the elementary particles of matter. The 12 countries which signed the Convention in Paris in July 1953 are Belgium, Denmark, France, German, Federal Republic, Greece, Italy, Netherlands, Norway, Sweden, Switzerland, United Kingdom and Yugoslavia. Austria joined the Organization officially on 1 July 1959 and Spain on 1 January 1961. Yugoslavia withdrew on 1 January 1962, and was granted Observer status, a status which it now shares with Poland and Turkey. Spain withdrew at the end of 1968 leaving 12 Member States. CERN came into existence in September 1954, when the requisite number of countries had ratified the Convention. The construction of the laboratories in Geneva was started early in 1954, and the first of the two particle accelerators, a synchro-cyclotron (600 million electron volts) came into operation in August 1957. The larger machine, the proton synchroton (28 thousand million electronvolts) was finished in 1959. In September 1965, an agreement was concluded for the expansion of the Laboratory across the Franco-Swiss frontier. On the new part of the site, Intersecting Storage Rings have been built which, working in conjunction with the proton synchrotron, now allow a programme of colliding beam physics to be pursued.

In 1971 it was decided to build a new accelerator on territory adjacent to the existing site of CERN. The area covers 412 ha in France and 68 ha in Switzerland but the machine, a 400 GeV proton synchrotron—the Super Proton Synchrotron (SPS)—is built deep underground in a ring tunnel of 2·2 km diameter so that only a few buildings are visible on the surface amid farming and forestry land. During the first five years of the eight-year construction programme the SPS site became Laboratory II of CERN under its own Director-General. As from 1 January 1976 the laboratories have been united to form the single laboratory of the Organization. All Member States except Greece participate in the SPS construction programme.

The injector for the SPS is the existing Proton Synchrotron which thus has to perform the triple role of SPS injector, feed for the ISR and source of particle beams for experiments at energies up to 28 GeV. The new machine first accelerated protons to 400 GeV in June 1976 and the first experimental area to be served by the SPS later that year was that in the West zone of the old CERN site. In 1978 part of the new North experimental area will come into use and the remainder of it will be in operation at the completion of the project in February 1979.

CERN has achieved impressive results in its research, notably: strong interaction phenomena—the identification of new particles and the measurement of their properties, the structure and scattering of high energy particles; electromagnetic interaction phenomena—testing the application of the theory at very small distances; weak interaction phenomena—discovery of 'neutral currents', work on symmetry problems. *Officers: President:* P. Levaux (Belgium); *Vice: Presidents:* B. Grégory (France), A. C. Pappas (Norway); *Chairman of the Finance Committee:* M. Lemne (Sweden); *Chairman of the Scientific Policy Committee:* W. Paul (Fed. Rep. of Germany); *Executive Director-General:* J. B. Adams (U.K.); *Research Director-General:* L. Van Hove (Belgium); *Directorate Members:* F. Bonaudi (Italy), P. Falk-Variant (Switzerland), S. Fubini (Italy), R. Levy-Mandel (France), E. Lohrmann (Fed. Repub. of Germany), H. O. Wüster (Fed. Repub. of Germany). *Publications:* Scientific Reports; Annual Report; 'Cern Courier' (monthly), Technical Notebooks, Information Booklets, etc. *Address:* CERN CH 1211 Geneva 232 *telex:* Switzerland 2 36 98.

**The International Council of Scientific Unions (ICSU)**, is an international n n-governmental scientific organization composed of 18 international Scientific Unions, 67 National Members, eight Scientific and one National Associates. Since its creation in 1931, ICSU has adopted a policy of non-discrimination, affirming the rights of all scientists throughout the world—without regard to race, religion, political philosophy, ethnic origin, citizenship, sex or language—to join in international scientific activities.

The Council provides advice and assistance to scientists who are not included in its membership. Its principal objective is to encourage international scientific activity for the benefit of mankind. It does this by initiating, designating and co-ordinating international scientific research projects; the International Geophysical Year and the International Biological Programme are probably the best-known examples. ICSU acts as a focus for the exchange of ideas, the communication of scientific information and the development of standards in methodology, nomenclature, units, etc. The various members of the ICSU family organize in many parts of the world conferences, congresses, symposia, summer schools and meetings of experts, as well as General Assemblies and other meetings to decide policies and programmes. In 1976 about 250 were organized. A wide range of publications is produced, including newsletters, handbooks, proceedings of meetings, congresses and symposia, professional scientific journals, data, standards etc.

Committees or Commissions of ICSU are created to organize programmes in multi- or trans-disciplinary fields which are not completely under the aegis of one of the Scientific Unions such as Antarctic, Oceanic, Space & Water Research, Solar Terrestrial Relations and Problems of the Environment. Activities in areas common to all the Unions such as Teaching of Science, Data, Science and Technology in Developing Countries are also co-ordinated by Committees.

ICSU is currently launching a Solar System Programme, which will be concerned with furthering our understanding of the solar system and by studying the planets to develop a fuller understanding of the earth.

ICSU set up in 1976 a Committee on Genetic Experimentation (COGENE) to serve as a non-governmental interdisciplinary source of advice concerning recombinant DNA activities.

ICSU maintains close relations and works in co-operation with a number of international governmental and non-governmental organizations and in particular UNESCO (with which ICSU has taken the initiative in launching a number of international programmes such as the International Indian Ocean Expedition, the World Science Information System, International Geological Correlation Project etc.), and with WMO (with which ICSU has taken the initiative in lauching the Global Atmospheric Research Programme).

The General Assembly at its biennial meetings elects the is composed of the representatives of the National Members, Scientific Unions, and Scientific and National Associates. The General Assembly at its biennial meetings elects the Officers, ratifies the nominations of the Scientific Unions to the General Committee, elects the representatives of the National Members, approves the creation or dissolution of the Committees and Commissions and determines the general policy of the Council. To review the administration of the Council and to facilitate the work, the Assembly elects *ad hoc* committees from the delegates. There are also Standing Committees for Finance, Admission, Free Circulation of Scientists, and Safeguard of the Pursuit of Science.

The General Committee meets annually to review the international scientific scene, to study scientific problems, to encourage and co-ordinate co-operative activity between the Unions and other component parts of the Council and determines priorities among the scientific activities of the Council. The Committee consists of the Officers, 18 representatives of the Scientific Unions, and 12 representatives of the National Members.

The Executive Board, consisting of the President, the Vice-President, the Secretary-General, the Treasurer and the Past President and four ordinary members, two from the Unions and two from the National Members, directs the day-to-day affairs of the Council between sessions of the General Assembly.

The Council has a Secretariat, located at 51 boulevard de Montmorency, Paris 75016. The Secretariat assists the Secretary-General in the administration of the Council and serves as a focus for exchanges between all the Members of the ICSU family and with international governmental and non-governmental organizations. Four Secretariats of the Members of the ICSU family are also housed in the same building in Paris, made available by the French Ministry of Education through the Académie des Sciences.

The sources of funds are diverse. The major contribution is made by the National Members, who pay annual dues to ICSU, the Unions and some of the Committees. UNESCO makes available a subvention, which is currently of $243,200 per year, which is distributed by ICSU to Members of the ICSU family for scientific purposes. This represents about 28 per cent of the income. In addition grants have beenmade for various projects by the Commonwealth, Ford, Nuffield, Rockefeller and several other Foundations.

In recent years, the Members of the ICSU family have been

making an increased effort to assist and to provide information and education to scientists in developing countries in Asia, Africa and Latin America. This has resulted in a need, which ICSU is currently trying to fulfil, for increased funds and in addition, assistance from scientists. This assistance is given freely by scientists throughout the world, in their spare time, as a contribution towards international co-operation for the benefit of mankind. *Officers: President:* Professor F. B. Straub; *Vice-President:* Professor C. de Jager; *Secretary-General:* Sir John Kendrew; *Treasurer:* Professor D. A. Bekoe; *Past President:* Professor H. Brown. *Address:* ICSU Secretariat, 51 blvd. de Montmorency, 75016 Paris. Tel. nos.: 527 77.02; 525 03.29. Telex no.: 630553 F.

**International Hydrographic Organization (IHO).** Established 1921 as the International Hydrographic Bureau following First International Hydrographic Conference (London 1919). *Purpose:* To establish a permanent association between hydrographic offices of member states; to co-ordinate their work with a view to rendering navigation easier and safer in all seas; to endeavour to obtain uniformity in hydrographic documents and to advance the science of hydrograpny; to promote measures aimed at establishing and/or strengtnening the hydrographic capabilities of developing countries, through co-operative programmes and other appropriate means. Member governments number 47. International conferences held in Monaco at five-year intervals (1972, 1977, etc.). *Publications:* Periodical: International Hydrographic Review (semi-annual) and Supplements; International Hydrographic Bulletin (monthly); IHO Yearbook; I. H. Conference Reports of Proceedings; Repertory of Technical Resolutions; Convention on the IHO; and special publications on technical subjects: General Bathymetric Chart of the Oceans (GEBCO); Systems of Maritime Buoyage and Beaconage; Radio Aids to Maritime Navigation and Hydrography; Harmonic Constants (tidal); Hydrographic Dictionary, etc. *Directing Committee: President:* Rear-Admiral G. S. Ritchie, CB. DSC, FRICS, (UK). *Directors:* Rear-Admiral D. C. Kapoor AVSM (India). Captain J. E. Ayres (U.S.A.). *Address:* Avenue President J. F. Kennedy, Monte Carlo, Monaco. Telex: 469870 MCS CARLO ATTN INHORG.

**International Map of the World on the Millionth Scale (IMW).** Between 1891 and 1913 several proposals were made to produce a map of the world on the scale of 1:1,000,000. At an international conference in 1913 the original specifications were agreed upon and the setting up of the Central Bureau was approved. The main function of the Bureau was to serve as a liaison between governments for the exchange of information and to assist them in co-ordinating publication of the maps in a standardized form. Since 1913 a considerable number of sheets have been produced, but because of two world wars and other causes, progress was slower than was foreseen, and, moreover, the original specifications did not keep pace with modern requirements. Eventually (September 1953) the functions of the Bureau were transferred to the U.N. Cartography Section. The specifications of the IMW, with the exception of the hypsometric tints, were revised in 1962 at the United Nations Technical Conference on the IMW which was held in Bonn, Fed. Repub. of Germany, in 1962. These specifications are now available. Later on, specifications for the hypsometric tints were revised at the U.N. Technical Conference held in Edinburgh in 1964. *Address:* Cartography Section, Centre for Natural Resources, Energy and Transport, Department of Economic and Social Affairs, United Nations, New York, N.Y., 10017, U.S.A.

**International Solar Energy Society.** An interdisciplinary organization, founded in Arizona in 1954, to foster the science and technology relating to applications of solar energy, and to compile and disseminate information relating to all aspects of solar energy. The Society's interests include thermal utilization of solar energy (house and water heating and solar-driven air-conditioning), photovoltaic processes, photochemical and photobiological methods of producing fuel, and energy storage and conservation.

The Society publishes a journal six times a year. *The Journal of Solar Energy Science and Technology,* which includes in its contents scholarly articles, reviews, technical notes and abstracts from other solar energy journals. (Non-members of the Society may subscribe directly to the Journal by application to: The Subscription Manager, Headington Hill Hall, Oxford OX3 0BW, England). The Society also organizes international conferences on various aspects of solar energy utilization.

The Society headquarters are in The National Science Centre of Australia. In countries where sufficient interest exists, National Sections, which are largely autonomous have been established.

*U.K. Section:* Dr. J. Barber, c/o The Royal Institution, 21 Albemarle St., London, W.1., U.K. *A.N.Z. Section:* Mr. W. R. W. Read, P.O. Box 52, Parkville, Victoria, Australia. *Belgium Section:* Dr. J. Nasielski, Faculte des Sciences, Universite Libre de Bruxelles, Ave. F. D. Roosevelt 50, B-1050 Brussels, Belgium. *German Section:* Dr. Ing. W. Lenz, VDI—Gesellschaft Energietechnik, Postfach 1139, 4 Dusseldorf 1, W. Germany. *Dutch Section:* Dr. C. C. H. T. Daey Ouwens, Experimental Physics Laboratory, University of Utrecht, Sorbonnelaan 4, Utrecht, Holland. *Indian Section:* Dr. R. L. Datta, C.S.M.C., Research Institute, Bhavnagar (Gujarat), India. *Irish Section:* Mr. J. O. Lewis, School of Architecture, University College, Earlfort Terrace, Dublin 2, Ireland. *Italian Section:* Dr. V. Storelli, Via Crispi 72, 80121 Naples, Italy. *S. African Section:* Mr. W. Cawood, c/o National Building Research Institute, P.O. Box 395, Pretoria 0001, South Africa. *Scandinavian Section:* Mr. U. Rengholt, VV5—Tekniska Foreningen, Hantverkargatan 8, S-112 21 Stockholm, Sweden, and *U.S.A. Section:* Dr. H. P. Harrenstein, c/o Florida Solar Energy Centre, 300 State Road 401, Cape Canaveral, Florida 32920, U.S.A.

**Medical Research Council.** The Medical Research Council was set up under its present title by Royal Charter in 1920. Although responsible to the Secretary of State for Education and Science, it is a government agency rather than a government department.

As the main government agency in the United Kingdom for the promotion of medical research, the Council's general aim is the advancement of knowledge towards the relief of human suffering, but its particular role is to assist the balanced development of medical and related biological research in the country as a whole by providing support complementary to the resources of the universities and hospitals. It employs its own research staff, most of whom work in the sixty-six units maintained by the Council, and awards grants for both short-term and long-term projects in universities and other institutions. In addition, it offers fellowships, scholarships, and other awards for training in research methods.

The Council's area of interest is wide—from psychology to cancer, and from nutrition to molecular biology. In 1977 it employed approximately 4,000 staff, over a quarter of whom were medically or scientifically qualified.

The major part of the Council's budget is in the form of a parliamentary grant-in-aid, over which it has direct control, but further sums are received from the Health Departments and the Department of Employment for commissioned research which the Council undertakes for those Departments on a 'customer-contractor' basis. In the financial year 1976–77, the Council was responsible for the expenditure of nearly £53 millions.

Council membership on 1 October 1977 was: *Chairman:* (to be appointed). *Secretary:* J. L. Gowans. *Members:* Professor A. J. Buller, Sir Arnold Burgen, FRS, Professor W. J. H. Butterfield, OBE Professor, R. H. Cawley, Professor A. R. Currie, B. Davies MP, K. P. Duncan, Professor A. P. M. Forrest, Professor I. M. Glynn, FRS, Professor R. F. Mahler, Professor D. C. Phillips, FRS, J. J. A. Reid, Cicely Saunders OBE, Professor J. N. Walton, Sir Henry Yellowlees, KCB. *Address:* 20, Park Crescent, London W1N 4AL. Tel.: 01-636 5422.

**Oceanographic Institute** (Institut Océanographique). Founded 1906 by Prince Albert I of Monaco to promote the study and teaching of oceanographic science. The governing body is the Council of Administration, consisting of six Frenchmen. The Technical and Scientific Committee consists of 30 members, of whom one-third must be French. The Institute's teaching and research establishment consists of amphitheatres, room for application works and three research laboratories, physical oceanography, biological oceanography and physiology of marine animals, each with aquarium rooms. It is located in Paris. The Museum (with exhibition halls, aquarium and laboratories) is in Monaco. *Publications:* Annales de l'Institut Océanographique (edited in Paris); Bulletin de l'Institut Océanographique et les Résultats des Campagnes scientifiques de S.A.S. le Prince Albert Ier de Monaco (edited at Monaco). *Address:* 195 rue Saint Jacques, Paris 5.

**The Royal Society.** The Royal Society, or, more fully, the Royal Society of London for Improving Natural Knowledge, founded in 1660, occupies a unique place in the country's scientific affairs and is equivalent to national academies of sciences in other countries. Election to it is regarded by scientists as a high honour. The Queen is Patron. There are today three main categories of Fellowship: Royal Fellows, including the Queen Mother and a Royal Duke; Foreign Members, of whom there are about 70; and the main body of Fellows numbering about 850. Election to the Fellowship, which is for life, was in 1976 increased to 40 persons a year, The society is governed by a council of 21 members.

Its activities include the holding of scientific meetings; publication of research work, mainly in the *Philosophical Transactions* and the *Proceedings*; the presentation of medals; the giving of endowed lectures; and the award of research appointments and grants.

The international relations of the Royal Society are extensive. It represents Britain in the international unions comprising the International Council of Scientific Unions and appoints national committees for each of them. It also plays a leading part in international scientific programmes and promotes exchange visits of scientists with many academies throughout the world. Its international fellowship scheme to foster relations with scientists of Western Europe and many other countries receives financial support from the Government and other sources. *President:* the Rt. Hon. the Lord Todd, Master of Christ's College, Cambridge. The other Officers are: *Treasurer* and *Vice-President:* Dr. B. J. Mason, Director-General of the Meteorological Office; *Biological Secretary* and *Vice-President:* Professor D. C. Phillips, Professor of Molecular Biophysics in the University of Oxford; *Physical Secretary* and *Vice-President:* Sir Harrie Massey, emeritus professor of physics in the University of London and honorary research fellow in the department of physics and astronomy at University College, London; and *Foreign Secretary* and *Vice-President:* Dr. M. G. P. Stoker, Director, Imperial Cancer Research Fund Laboratories.

The other members of the Council elected for 1977 (or re-elected, marked *) were:

*Dr. S. Brenner, a member of the scientific staff at the Medical Research Council Laboratory of Molecular Biology, Cambridge.
*Professor J. Chatt, professor of chemistry in the University of Sussex and director of the Unit of Nitrogen Fixation, Agricultural Research Council.
*Sir Alan Cottrell, *Vice-President*, master of Jesus College, Cambridge.
*Professor G. S. Dawes, *Vice-President*, professor in the University of Oxford and director of the Nuffield Institute for Medical Research, University of Oxford.
Dr G. D. H. Bell, *Vice-President*, Formerly Director, Plant Breeding Institute, Cambridge.
Sir Angus Paton, *Vice-President*, Senior Consultant, Sir Alexander Gibb and Partners, Consulting Engineers.
Professor C. G. Phillips, Dr Lee's Professor of Anatomy in the University of Oxford.
Sir Peter Swinnerton-Dyer, Master of St Catharine's College, Cambridge and Professor of Mathematics in the University of Cambridge.
Professor W. F. Vinen, Poynting Professor of Physics in the University of Birmingham.
Dr D. T. N. Williamson, Formerly Group Director—Engineering, Rank Xerox Limited.
*Professor H. L. Kornberg, Sir William Dunn professor of biochemistry in the University of Cambridge.
*Professor R. A. Raphael, professor of organic chemistry in the University of Cambridge.
*Professor J. Sutton, *Vice-President*, professor of geology at the Imperial College of Science and Technology in the University of London.
*Dr R. Weck, CBE, director-general of the Welding Institute, Cambridge.
*Dr J. H. Wilkinson, chief scientific officer, National Physical Laboratory.

*Address:* 6 Carlton House Terrace, London, SW1Y 5AG. *Telephone:* 01-839 5561. *Telex:* 917876.

**Science Research Council.** The Science Research Council was set up in 1965, taking over six national research establishments and the basic research functions of the former Department of Scientific and Industrial Research. The Council supports basic research in astronomy, the biological, engineering, mathematical and physical sciences. It devotes most if its resources to: (a) helping university and polytechnic staff to carry out timely and promising basic research at the forefront of their subjects, in their own institutions, in one of the Council's own research establishments, via an international organization or elsewhere; and (b) providing studentships to enable high quality graduates to receive further training in methods of research or in a specialized branch of science or engineering of national importance.

The membership of the Science Research Council from 1 October 1977 will be as follows:
*Chairman:* (full-time) Professor G. Allen, FRS, Professor of Chemical Technology, Imperial College. *Members:* Professor Sir Granville Beynon, CBE, FRS, Professor of Physics, University College of Wales, Aberystwyth. Dr J. Birks, CBE, Technical Director and Deputy Chairman of the Executive Committee of BP Trading Limited. Professor Sir Herman Bondi, KCB, FRS, Chief Scientist, Department of Energy. Professor R. L. F. Boyd, CBE, FRS, Professor of Physics, University College, London. Professor J. Brown, Professor of Light Electrical Engineering, Imperial College. Professor W. E. Burcham, FRS, Professor of Physics, University of Birmingham. Dr P. F. Chester, Director of the Central Electricity Research Laboratories. Dr D. S. Davies, Chief Scientist, Department of Industry. Professor W. E. Farvis, OBE, FRSE. Professor of Electrical Engineering, University of Edinburgh. Department of the Environment. Professor J. H. Horlock, Vice-Chancellor, University of Salford. Professor J. L. Jinks, FRS, Professor of Genetics, University of Birmingham. Dr A. J. Kennedy, Director of BNF Metals Technology Centre. Sir Norman Lindop, Director, Hatfield Polytechnic. Professor J. C. Polkinghorne, FRS, Professor of Mathematical Physics, University of Cambridge. Professor Sir George Porter, FRS, Director, The Royal Institution of Great Britain. Mr D. H. Roberts, Plessey Components Ltd., Managing Director, Microsystems Division. *Address:* State House, High Holborn, London WC1R 4TA. *Telephone:* 01-242 1262.

## SOCIOLOGY

**Institute of Nutrition of Central America and Panama (INCAP).** Is an international scientific institution established by the Governments of Costa Rica, El Salvador, Guatemala, Honduras, Nicaragua and Panama for the purpose of studying the problems of human nutrition and assisting the participating countries in their solution. It is administered by the Pan American Sanitary Bureau, Regional Office for the Americas, of the World Health Organization. INCAP is carrying out studies of the nutritional status and dietary habits of the people of the region, the chemical composition and the biological value of the available plant and animal foods and the value of various types of supplementary feeding programmes. Its sound academic programme comprises: a a School of Nutrition with a four-year curriculum at the graduate level and four postgraduate courses; in public health with emphasis in nutrition and maternal and child care; in food sciences and animal nutrition; in food science and technology, and in biochemistry and human nutrition. In addition, it trains both professional and auxiliary personnel in public health nutrition and associated laboratory techniques and provides the member countries with basic material for popular nutrition education programmes. Through agreement signed by PASB and the United Nations University, in 1976 INCAP became the first Associated Institution of the UNU. An academic tutorial program was thus established for the training of fellows from any part of the world who have completed their university advanced studies at the Doctoral or Master of Science level. INCAP also participates in co-operative research programmes with agricultural institutions and other organizations in fields related to human nutrition in the area and publishes scientific papers, informative bulletins, books, annual reports, various other documents, and periodic compilations of scientific publications. *Address:* Instituto de Nutrición de Centro América y Panamá, Carretera Roosevelt, Zone 11, Guatemala, C.A.

**The Institute of Race Relations.** Founded as an independent body in 1958. It had its origin in the knowledge that race relations had become a fundamental factor throughout much of human society and, as such, deserved searching study. The main aims of the Institute are to promote study of relations between groups and to advise on proposals for improvement. Methods used to achieve these aims include the distribution of information in a wide range of books, journals and pamphlets and through an information service; the promotion of thought and discussion at meetings; the collection of material in the library and the investigation of race issues. Recently the Institute has responded to a changing situation by extending its work and services to minority groups and by recognizing the need for increased studies of problem (racial) societies. The Institute publishes *Race & Class* (formerly *Race*). Members of the Institute have use of the library service, receive regular information and elect the Council. *Director:* A. Sivanandan. *Secretary:* J. S. Bourne. *Address:* 247/249 Pentonville Rd., London, N1 9NG. *Telephone:* 01-837 0041.

**Inter-American Conference on Social Security,** inspired by the principles of social security approved by the tripartite Labour Conference of the American countries which are members of the International Labour Organization, is intended to facilitate and develop the co-operation of the social security administrations and institutions. Its constituent agencies are: (*a*) the Inter-American Conference on Social Security which functions through the holding of sessions; (*b*) the Permanent Inter-American Committee on Social Security, the executive body of the Conference, which functions through the holding of sessions and (*c*) the Executive Committee or Executive Body of the Permanent Inter-American Committee on Social Security. The Permanent Inter-American Committee is established with the functions of (*a*) giving effect to the resolutions and recommendations adopted by the Conference; (*b*) preparing the sessions of the Conference and fixing the agenda of the sessions; (*c*) contributing by every other means to the attainment of the purposes of the Conference. The Permanent Committee appoints an Executive Committee to act for it during the intervals between its sessions. *President:* Lic. Carlos Gálvez Betancourt (Mexico); *Vice-President:* Carlos Jacinto Chavarría (El Salvador); *Secretary-General and Treasurer:* Dr. Gastón Novelo (Mexico). *Finance:* The necessary funds for its budget are provided by (*a*) The American Government member of the Conference, (*b*) The International Labour Office and (*c*) The National Institutions for Social Security in Latin America. *Address:* Apartado 20532, Unidad Independencia, San Jéronimo Lidice, Mexico 20, D.F., Mexico.

**The International Planned Parenthood Federation,** unites 90 national family planning associations throughout the world. Its work is based on the belief that knowledge of planned parenthood is a fundamental human right and that a balance between world population and natural resources is a necessary condition of future happiness, economic progress and peace. Therefore, the Federation aims to advance knowledge and practice of contraception everywhere. Encouragement is given for the integration of family planning in health and social welfare programmes in developing countries, where medical facilities are being expanded, as well as in countries where contraception has previously been left outside public health programmes. It became a federation under its present present name in 1952 and is now incorporated in the U.K. by special Act of Parliament. The Federation has steadily increased its world-wide membership, and as it has grown in size so too has it grown in influence. As an international, non-governmental organization, the IPPF has consultative status with the United Nations and its major specialized agencies. Growth of the Federation has been made possible by the addition of government grants to the voluntary contributions which were the basis of its early finances. Twenty four governments now support the Federation; funds for 1978 are estimated at $40,350,000. The policies and activities of the Federation are directed by public-spirited men and women from all parts of the world who are elected by the Federation's six constituent regional councils to its Central Council. This group lays down guidelines for the work carried out by the Secretary-General and her professional staff in London and regional offices in Tunis, Colombo, Kuala Lumpur, London, Nairobi, and New York. The Federation provides member associations and the general public with information on all aspects of world population developments; assists in the formation of new family planning associations in non-member countries; supports the training of medical and paramedical personnel in the practical implementation of contraceptive services; and promotes and organizes international and regional meetings and conferences concerned with the exchange of ideas on these subjects. The Federation also encourages appropriate scientific research in biology, demography and sociology; methods of contraception; studies of fertility and sub-fertility; and family life and sex education. A new area of concentration is in the planned parenthood and womans development programme which seeks to implement the U.N. World Plan of Action of World Population Year, and International Woman's Year. *Publications:* The chief regular publication is 'People', a quarterly magazine in English, French ('Peuples') and Spanish ('Pueblos'). This magazine contains features and news touching on all aspects of population and family planning in a development context. The annual subscription (1977) U.K. only is £5·00 post paid. All other countries U.S. $15·00 airmail post paid. *President:* Mrs. A. Hussein. *Secretary-General:* Mr. Carl Wahren. *Address:* 18–20 Lower Regent Street, London, SW1Y 4PW. Tel.: 01–839 2911. Cables: IPEPEE London, SW1. Telex: 919573.

**The Royal Society of Health.** The Society was founded in 1876 to promote the health of the people. The scope of the Society covers preventive and social medicine, hospitals, mental health, health education, hygiene, public health, veterinary hygiene, the environment, and other fields. Membership (from all parts of the world) is not restricted to any one profession; it embraces medical officers, environmental health officers, nurses, chemists, dentists, social workers, nutritionists, veterinary officers, engineers, surveyors, architects and all who are in any way connected with health. It has branches in Australia, New Zealand, Hong Kong, Malta and the U.S.A. Examinations in Great Britain include hygiene in food retailing and catering, inspection of meat and other foods, nursery nursing, nutrition in relation to catering, air pollution, parentcraft and hone management and dental health. Examinations held in 30 centres overseas also include health engineering, public health inspection for general and local overseas appointments, health visiting, school hygiene and tropical hygiene. Besides frequent meetings in London and the provinces, a Health Congress is held annually, attended by delegates from many countries. The Library of the Society includes many historical volumes. *Publication:* The Journal. The Society is under the patronage of H.M. the Queen. *Address:* 13 Grosvenor Place, London, SW1X 7EN. Tel.: 01-235 9961.

## STAPLE PRODUCTS

**International Coffee Organization.** Membership in the International Coffee Organization is confined to Governments. Sixty-six governments are members of the International Coffee Agreement. The terms of the Agreement will remain in force until 30 September 1982. Forty-two governments have joined the Agreement as Exporting Members, and 24 as Importing Members.

The objectives of the new Agreement are:

To further international co-operation between coffee exporting and coffee importing countries in order that, through fair prices to consumers and markets for coffee at remunerative prices to producers, the economic diversification and development of coffee producing countries may be fostered, political and economic relations between producers and consumers be improved, the consumption of coffee be increased, supply be brought into reasonable balance with demand and excessive fluctuations in prices for coffee be avoided."

*Officers: Executive Director:* Alexandre F. Beltrão. *Deputy Executive Director:* T. M. Loudon. *Address:* 22 Berners Street, London, W1P 4DD.

**International Cotton Advisory Committee.** Is the outgrowth of an international cotton meeting (Washington 1939) of the governments of 12 of the principal cotton exporting countries. At present 47 governments are represented on the Committee. Since 1945 membership has been open to both producing and consuming countries, and for the past several years a standing invitation to join the Committee has been extended to all members of U.N. and FAO. The Committee, which is an inter-governmental organization, observes and keeps in close touch with developments affecting the world cotton situation; it disseminates statistics, and it suggests to the governments represented measures considered suitable for the furtherance of international collaboration. The 36th Plenary Meeting was held in Seoul, Republic of Korea in October 1977. Between Plenary Meetings a Standing Committee meets monthly in Washington. *Publications:* Cotton—Monthly Review of the World Situation, with Quarterly Statistical Bulletin; Annual Proceedings; special reports. *Address:* South Agricultural Building, Washington, D.C., 20250, U.S.A.

**International Rice Commission.** The International Rice Commission (IRC), which works within the framework of FAO, was established on 4 January 1949 with the object of promoting national and international action in respect of production, conservation, distribution and consumption of rice. Matters relating to trade are outside the purview of the Commission.

Present membership (open to all FAO member nations and associate members who accept the constitution of the IRC) of the Commission is 46 and represents all the rice-growing regions of the world. In 1972, IRC member countries accounted for 63 per cent of the world's area and 55 per cent of the world's output of rice.

The Commission keeps under review the scientific, technical and economic problems relating to rice, encourages and co-ordinates research, organizes (where necessary) co-operative projects and reports to the member countries and the Director-General of FAO on appropriate actions to be taken in furtherance of its objectives.

The Commission has established four subsidiary bodies—the Working Party on Rice Production and Protection (1950), the Working Party on Rice soils, water and fertilizer practices (1950), the Working Party on the Agricultural Engineering Aspects of Rice Production, Storage and Processing (1958) and the Rice Committee for the Americas (1964), to study and recommend on specific technical problems. The Rice Committee of the Americas was abolished in 1974.

Three Divisions of the Agriculture Department of FAO are engaged in IRC activities which are implemented in co-operation with member countries and international agencies. Notable progress in rice production, witnessed over the past 25 years, is attributable, at least in part to the direct and indirect roles of the IRC in the application of technology, implementation of co-operative programmes and dissemination of information. To cite but a few—the initiation of a japonica indica hybridization programme (1950), cataloguing of genetic stocks (1951) and international blast nursery (1961); holding of seminars on water and fertilizer management, on industrial processing and mechanization; and conduct of training courses in breeding and technology had their share of contribution to global rice development. *Address:* Agriculture Department, Food and Agriculture Organization of the United Nations, Via delle Terme di Caracalla, Rome, Italy.

**International Sugar Organization.** The International Sugar Agreement 1968, which governed the operations of the International Sugar Organization, ceased to exist at the end of 1973. The United Nations Sugar Conference, convened by the Secretary-General of UNCTAD during the spring and autumn of 1973, failed to resolve all the major issues of policy with which it was faced with a result that an Agreement with economic provisions could not be negotiated in the circumstances then prevailing.

Instead, the Conference concluded a new Agreement which came into effect on 1 January 1974. It contains no economic clauses but keeps in being the International Sugar Organization. The Council of the Organization, apart from the continuing duty of collecting statistical and other information on sugar, has been authorized to arrange for studies to be made and discussions to be held between Members and with non-Members and other organizations with a view to determining the basis for an Agreement that will be in the general interest, and particularly in the interest of developing countries. As a result, the Council has invited the Secretary General of UNCTAD to convene a United Nations Sugar Conference in the spring of 1977 for the purpose of negotiating a new Agreement with full economic provisions. In the meantime, the 1973 Agreement was extended for another year to 31 December 1977.

*Executive Director:* E. Jones-Parry. *Address:* 28, Haymarket, London, SW1Y 4SP.

**International Tea Committee.** About 1930, surplus supplies of tea on the world's markets and consequent uncertainty then prevailing, resulted in a reduction of prices to an unremunerative level to producers. A voluntary scheme of crop restriction met with only limited success, and negotiations for the regulation of exports from the tea-producing countries resulted in the International Agreement, which came into operation in April 1933 for a period of five years and was renewed from time to time. The last Agreement entered into on 8 May 1950 between India, Pakistan, Ceylon and Indonesia was for five years ended 31 March 1955 after which date it was not formally renewed. The Committee has, however, been maintained in being to act as an information centre and to collect and publish world-wide statistics on tea in respect of area, production, exports, imports, stocks, etc. The Committee is comprised of representatives of the Governments and tea industries of Sri Lanka, India, Indonesia, Kenya, Malawi, Mozambique, Bangladesh, Tanzania, Uganda. *Secretary:* Mrs. E. E. E. Mooijen. *Statistician:* Peter Abel. *Address:* Sir John Lyon House, 5 High Timber Street, Upper Thames Street, London, EC4V 3NH.

**International Whaling Commission.** The International Whaling Commission (IWC) was set up under the International Convention for the Regulation of Whaling which was signed in Washington on 2 December 1946 and came into force on 10 November 1948. Membership at present consists of 16 nations — Argentina, Australia, Brazil, Canada, Denmark, France, Iceland, Japan, Mexico, Netherlands, New Zealand, Norway, Panama, South Africa, U.K., U.S.A. and U.S.S.R.

The Commission meets once a year. Its main duties are to keep under review and, if necessary, amend the Schedule to the Convention which governs actual whaling operations. Measures currently in force include complete protection for certain species, maximum catches of whales in one season, open and closed seasons and areas, size limits below which whales of certain species may not be killed, prohibition on the capture of suckling calves, lactating females and females accompanied by calves. Other functions of the IWC are the collection and analysis of statistical and biological records, the study and dissemination of information as to the methods of maintaining and increasing whale stocks, the conduct and encouragement of research on whales and whaling and the operation of a system of international observers on factory ships and at land stations.

At its 27th meeting in 1975 the Commission adopted a new management policy under which all whale stocks are classified on the latest Scientific advice into three categories;

(i) *Protection stocks,* are those species which are more than 10 per cent below the level of their maximum sustainable yield (MSY). For these stocks there is *complete and automatic protection* and the species may not be hunted. All blue whales, humpback whales, gray whales, right whales, bowhead whales and nearly all fin and some sei and sperm whales are protected stocks.

(ii) *Sustained management stocks,* are those species whose stock levels are between 10 per cent below the level of the MSY and 20 per cent above it, and for these whales *catches* are permitted in carefully *controlled* numbers according to the *quota systems* in operation for each of these stocks in the area in which they occur. Nearly half of the stocks of sperm whales fall into this category, as well as some individual stocks of fin, sei and minke whales.

(iii) *Initial management stocks,* are those species whose abundance is more than 20 per cent above the MSY level. Commercial whaling in permitted on these stocks, again is strict accorance with the quotas set by the Commission, which are designed to ensure that stocks do not fall below optimum levels. Most stocks of minke whales, Bryde's whales and the remainder of the sperm whale stocks fall into this category.

The new management procedure represents a major step forward in the protection and conservation of the world's whale stocks. Under these arrangements the number of species of great whales caught commercially has been reduced to five; fin, sei, Bryde, minke and sperm. The Commission sets separate annual quotas for each of these species in each whaling area based on scientific assessments of each of the stocks concerned. Annual quotas are set at levels designed to ensure in the longer term that whale populations are maintained at optimum levels.

At its 1976 meeting the Commission fixed, after considering the data provided by the Scientific Committee on the state of the stocks, the following catch limits in each of the main whaling areas for the 1977/78 Antarctic season and the 1978 season elsewhere;

| *Ocean Region* | *Species* | *Quota* | *(previous)* | *Number of Stocks* |
|---|---|---|---|---|
| Southern Hemisphere | Sperm | 5,908 | (4,791) | 2 sexes 9 divisions |
| | Minke | 5,690 | (8,900) | 6 |
| | Sei | 771 | (1,863) | 2 |
| North Pacific | Sperm | 763 | (7,200) | females only |
| | Bryde's | 524 | (1,000) | 1 |
| | Minke | 400 | (541) | 1 |
| North Atlantic | Sperm | 685 | (685) | 1 |
| | Minke | 2,555 | (2,483) | 4 |
| | Fin | 459 | (455) | 4 |
| | (1,524 in 6 years 1977–82 off Iceland) | | | |
| | Sei | 84 | (132) | 1 |

In the case of sperm whales in the North Pacific, quotas of zero males and 763 females were set, compared with 4,320 males and 2,880 females in the previous season. However, a special meeting of the IWC Scientific Committee will be held in November to reconsider information on North Pacific sperm whale stocks before the start of the 1978 season. Depending on the outcome of these discussions the Commission Chairman may call a special meeting of the IWC to consider amending these quotas.
All other whale species and stocks are protected or have zero quotas until they have been fully assessed.
These include:

| | |
|---|---|
| Blue whales | world-wide |
| Humpbacks | world-wide |
| Right whales | world-wide |
| Gray whales | North Pacific |
| Fin whales | Southern Hemisphere |
| | North Pacific |
| | North Atlantic (West Norway, Faroe Island, Nova Scotia) |
| Sei whales | North Pacific |
| | North Atlantic (Nova Scotia) |
| | Southern Hemisphere (four areas) |
| Briyde whales | Southern Hemisphere |
| Mnke whales | North Pacific (except Western stock) |
| Bottlenose whales | North Atlantic |

At the 1977 Meeting the Commission also took steps to bring all medium-sized whales under its control. These include bottlenose, beaked, pilot and killer whales.

*Exemptions*

Under a long standing arrangement specified exemptions are permitted for the taking of prohibited species and undersized whales for local consumption by certain native races where the meat is an important part of the staple diet.

Because bowhead whales in Arctic regions, which have been protected from commercial exploitation for forty years, are endangered, the Commission decided in addition to prohibit the catching by native peoples which was previously permitted as a special exemption.

Other important decisions agreed to at the meeting were:

A further intensification of scientific research, including the humane killing of whales; new procedures for prior international scientific review of national special permit applications to take whales for scientific studies; adoption of a resolution urging member countries to ban the import of whale products from non-member nations; adoption of a resolution urging member countries engaged in whaling not to transfer whaling vessels, equipment and technology to non-member nations; agreement to call a broadly based international meeting in Copenhagen early in 1978 as a prelude to a new International Cetacean Convention, the draft text of which has been developed over the past three years; active co-operation with the Convention on International Trade in Endangered Species of Wild Fauna and Flora, so far as it concerns whale stocks.

The catch by IWC member nations from the 1976/77 Antarctic whaling season and the 1976 season outside the Antarctic was reported to the Commission by the Bureau of International Whaling Statistics as follows: (Provisional figures).

Four expeditions (two Japanese and two U.S.S.R.) operated in the Antarctic in the 1976/77 season and took the following numbers of whales (previous year's catch shown in brackets).

| | | |
|---|---|---|
| Fin whales | 0 | (206) |
| Sei | 1,858 | (1,820 Sei and Bryde's combined) |
| Bryde's | 225† | |

† (taken under special permit for scientific research)

| | | |
|---|---|---|
| Minke | 7,900 | (6,034) |
| Sperm | 4,075* | (7,046) |

* of which 2,073 (4,127) were captured in the Southern Hemisphere on the way to and from the Antarctic.

In the 1976 season outside the Antarctic eight land stations and three factory ships (two Russian and one Japanese) operated taking:

| | | |
|---|---|---|
| Fin whales | 275 | (429) |
| Sei | 6 | (2,089 combined) |
| Bryde's | 1,340 | |
| Minke | 3,479 | (3,659) |
| Sperm | 8,328 | (10,804) |

*Officers: Chairman:* A. G. Bollen (Australia). *Vice-Chairman:* T. Asgeirsson (Iceland). *Secretary:* Dr. R. Gambell.
*Address:* The Red House, Station Road, Histon, Cambridge, CB4 4NP, England. Tel.: 022023 3971.

**International Wheat Council.** Established 1 July 1949 under the provisions of the International Wheat Agreement, 1949, and continued in being under the Agreements of 1953, 1956, 1959, and 1962, the International Grains Arrangement, 1967, and the International Wheat Agreement, 1971. The 1971 Agreement was concluded at the United Nations Wheat Conference held in Geneva in January and February, 1971, and entered into force on 1 July 1971. Like its predecessor, it consists of two separate legal instruments: a Wheat Trade Convention and a Food Aid Convention, each requiring separate ratification. The International Wheat Council administers the Wheat Trade Convention.

The objectives of the Wheat Trade Convention, 1971 are, in brief: to further international co-operation in connection with world wheat problems; to promote the expansion of international trade in wheat and wheat flour; to contribute to the fullest extent possible to the stability of the international wheat market; and to provide a framework for the negotiation of a new international wheat agreement. An important feature of the Convention is the work of the Advisory Sub-Committee on Market Conditions which keeps the world market situation under continuous review. The results of these reviews are released to the public in the form of monthly reports. The Convention has at present 50 members, including nine exporting members, 40 importing members and the European Economic Community (and its nine member States), which is both an exporting and an importing member.

The Food Aid Convention is administered by the Food Aid Committee, an autonomous and independent body. The International Wheat Council also provides administrative services for the Food Aid Committee. The parties to the Convention agree to contribute as food aid to developing countries, wheat, coarse grains or products derived therefrom, suitable for human consumption, or the cash equivalent thereof. The minimum annual contributions of the nine donor members for the current year (1977/78) total 4,226,000 tons.

Both the Wheat Trade Convention and the Food Aid Convention were originally due to expire on 30 June 1974, but have been extended by successive Protocols. The current

(1976) Protocol, which entered into force on 1 July 1976, extends the two Conventions to 30 June 1978.

In view of the general desire of members of the Council for increased co-operation in wheat matters the Council, at its Seventy-second (Special) Session in February 1975, appointed a Preparatory Group to examine the possible bases for a new international arrangement to replace the International Wheat Agreement, 1971. The discussions in the Preparatory Group have covered, in some depth, a wide range of possible options particular attention being given to the associated technical issues. At its Eightieth Session in June 1977 the Council affirmed its determination to take all necessary steps for the active preparation of a new international arrangement. To this end, it agreed a timetable aimed at intensifying the work of the Preparatory Group. The latter reported further to the Eighty-first Session of the Council in November 1977. At that time, the Council reviewed progress and took a decision on the convening of a negotiating conference early in 1978. *Publications (Annual):* World Wheat Statistics, Review of the World Wheat Situation, Annual Report; *Publications (Monthly):* Wheat Market Report. *Executive Secretary:* J. H. Parotte. *Address:* Haymarket House, 28 Haymarket, London SW1Y 4SS. *Tel.:* 01-930 4128; *Telex:* 916128.

**International Wool Study Group.** First meeting held in London, March–April 1947. The terms of reference were: The Group shall comprise representatives of countries substantially interested in the production or consumption of wool; the Group shall meet at mutually convenient times and places to discuss common problems; it shall be free to make such studies of the world wool position as it sees fit, having regard especially to the desirability of providing accurate information regarding supply, demand, and development; it shall take into account the desirability of measures designed to stimulate world consumption of wool; to consider those problems which are unlikely to be resolved by the ordinary development of world trade in wool; to formulate and transmit recommendations to participating governments; to collect and collate necessary statistics. Member Governments of the Group are: Afghanistan, Argentina, Australia, Austria, Belgium, Canada, Chile, Colombia, Czechoslovakia, Denmark, Finland, France, Germany, Greece, Iceland, India, Iran, Iraq, Irish Republic, Israel, Italy, Japan, Lebanon, Libya, Mexico, Netherlands, New Zealand, Norway, Pakistan, Paraguay, Peru, Portugal, South Africa, Spain, Sweden, Switzerland, Syrian Arab Republic, Turkey, United Arab Republic, United Kingdom, United States, Uruguay. Relations are maintained with the Commonwealth Secretariat, the U.N. Food and Agriculture Organization, the U.N. Conference on Trade and Development, the Commission of European Economic Community, the International Bank for Reconstruction and Development, the Organization for Economic Co-operation and Development, the International Wool Secretariat, the International Rayon and Synthetic Fibres Committee, and the International Wool Textile Organization. The 8th Session of the Group took place in London in December 1964 and the 9th Session took place in December 1966. The Economics and Statistics Committee meets and prepares a report on the World wool situation for use of member governments each quarter, and a Management Committee acts between Sessions of the Group. The United Kingdom provides the Secretariat from the Department of Industry, Millbank Tower, Millbank, Westminster, London SW1P 4QU. Tel.: 01-211 5921.

**International Wool Secretariat, and The Wool Bureau Inc. (U.S.A.).** The International Wool Secretariat (IWS)—of which The Wool Bureau is the U.S. branch—exists to promote demand for wool. It was set up in 1937 in London by the Wool Boards of Australia, New Zealand and South Africa, its funds being provided by a statutory levy on wool grown in these three countries, and later, also by Government contribution. In July 1970, Uruguay, fifth biggest wool exporter in the world, became a contributing member of the IWS, joining the three foundation members—respectively first, second and fourth biggest wool exporters. Representatives of these countries are appointed to the Board of the IWS, which meets twice annually and determines policy. There are branches or technical service offices in Austria, Belgium, Canada (where the branch is known as the Wool Bureau of Canada), Denmark, Eire, Finland, France, West Germany, Greece, Hong Kong, India, Iran, Italy, Japan, South Korea, Mexico, Netherlands, Norway, Portugal, Spain, Sweden, Switzerland, Taiwan, Turkey, U.K., U.S.A., and Yugoslavia. The IWS's activities include end-product promotion, technical, economic and market research, product development and technical and fashion services. The IWS, through the IWS Nominee Co. Ltd., owns the Woolmark and the Woolblendmark. The Woolmark, the international symbol for pure new wool products, is now licensed for use by manufacturers in 44 countries, The Woolblendmark, the symbol for products made from fibre blends in which new wool predominates, is licensed for use in 28 countries. Both marks are protected in more than 100 countries. The IWS has a Technical Centre at Ilkley, Yorkshire, England, employing scientists and textile technologists to provide product and process development support to its global promotion programmes. A considerable amount of scientific research work is financed in many countries. The Wool Bureau, Inc., a branch of the IWS, has offices in New York. *Managing Director:* Dr. G. Laxter, PhD. *Address:* Wool House, Carlton Gardens, London, SW1Y 5AE and 360 Lexington Avenue, New York, U.S.A.

**Organization of the Petroleum Exporting Countries.** The principal aims of the Organization are the coordination and unification of the petroleum policies of Member Countries and the determination of the best means for safeguarding their interests, individually and collectively.

The Organization devises ways and means of ensuring the stabilization of prices in international oil markets with a view to eliminating harmful and unnecessary fluctuations, due regard being given at all times to the interests of the producing nations and to the necessity of securing a steady income to the producing countries; an efficient, economic and regular supply of petroleum to consuming nations; and a fair return on their capital to those investing in the petroleum industry.

Founder Members of the Organization are those countries which were represented at the First Conference, held in Baghdad, and which signed the original agreement of the establishment of the Organization.

Full Members are the Founder Members plus those countries whose applications for membership have been accepted by the Conference.

Any other country with a substantial net export of crude petroleum, which has fundamentally similar interests to those of Member Countries, may become a full Member of the Organization, if accepted by a majority of three-fourths of Full Members, including the concurrent vote of all Founder Members.

*Address:* Dr. Karl Lueger-Ring 10, 1010 Vienna, Austria.

## STATISTICS

**The International Statistical Institute.** The International Statistical Institute (ISI) was founded in London in 1885. It is an autonomous society devoted to the development and improvement of statistical methods and their application throughout the world; and to the promotion of statistical education and the international integration of statistics.

Since 1972 ISI has been engaged in a major operation; the World Fertility Survey a programme for assisting developing countries in collecting the best possible statistical information about human fertility. The programme is funded by the U.K. Fund for Population Activities and the U.S. Agency for International Development. A professional centre has been established in London (35-37 Grosvenor Gardens). The Projector Director is Sir Maurice G. Kendall.

ISI is an association consisting of members distinguished for their contributions to the development of statistical methods or to the administration of statistical services. There are elected members (five honorary and 868 ordinary) and 113 *ex officio* members, and 23 corporate members. Ten international organizations and 20 national statistical societies are affiliated with ISI. *Sections:* Bernoulli Society for Mathematical Statistics and Probability, International Association for Regional and Urban Statistics, International Association of Survey Statisticians, International Survey for Statistical Computing. *Publications:* International Statistical Review (three issues per annum), Bulletin of the ISI (containing the proceedings of the biennial sessions), Statistical Theory and Method Abstracts (four issues per annum), and occasional publications. The composition of the Bureau until 15 December 1977 is as follows: *President:* M. Macura (Yugoslavia), *President-Elect:* C. R. Rao (India), *Vice-Presidents:* D. Blackwell (U.S.A.), L. Bosse (Austria) (for Finance), G. Goudswaard (Netherlands), (for liaison with the Permanent Office), P.A.P. Moran (Australia), (for programmes of sessions), A. E. Sarhan (Egypt). *Permanent Office: Director—Secretary/Treasurer:* E. Lunenberg (Netherlands). *Address:* 428 Prinses Beatrixlaan, Voorburg, near The Hague, Netherlands. Tel.: 070-694341. Cables: Statist.

## TARIFFS

**International Bureau for Publication of Customs Tariffs** (Bureau International pour la Publication des Tarifs Douaniers). Founded 1890 to translate and to publish in English, French, German, Italian and Spanish the customs tariffs of all countries, together with such modifications as may be introduced from time to time. *Publication:* Bulletin International des Douanes (in five languages). *Membership:* 79 States. *Officers:* The Belgian Ministry for Foreign Affairs appoints the staff. *President:* Eduard Grandry, Secretary-General of the Belgian Ministry of Foreign Affairs and Foreign Trade. *Director:* J. Loth. *Deputy Director:* B. Denne. *Address:* rue de l'Association 38, B-1000, Brussels, Belgium.

## TELECOMMUNICATIONS

**The Commonwealth Telecommunications Bureau.** The Bureau is the Secretariat of the Commonwealth Telecommunications Organization, which replaced the Commonwealth Telecommunications Board on 1 April 1969. This Organization comprises periodical Commonwealth Telecommunications Conferences, a Commonwealth Telecommunications Council meeting once a year and the Commonwealth Telecommunications Bureau. The Partner Governments represented on the Council are: Australia, Bangladesh, Barbados, Botswana, Britain, British Overseas Territories and Associated States, Canada, Cyprus, Fiji, Ghana, Guyana, India, Jamaica, Kenya, Malawi, Malaysia, New Zealand, Nigeria, Papua New Guinea, Sierra Leone, Singapore, Sri Lanka, Tanzania, The Gambia, Trinidad and Tobago, Uganda, Zambia. The functions of the Bureau, which was incorporated in Britain by the Commonwealth Telecommunications Act, 1968, are to collect, maintain and disseminate such information and data as the Council may determine; to process material for conferences and meetings of the Council; to perform the accounting and clearing house functions of the Partnership; to maintain and distribute regulations as determined by the Council; and to perform such other duties as the General Secretary may direct. *General Secretary:* S. N. Kalra; *Chief of Computing Systems:* K. Bristow; *Chief of Operations:* Dr. F. A. L. Subaran; *Chief of Finance:* J. B. Elliot. *Chief of Administration:* R. J. Christoffersen. *Address:* 28 Pall Mall, SW1Y 5LP. Tel.: 01-930 5511.

**European Broadcasting Union** (Union Européenne de Radiodiffusion). Founded at Torquay February 1950, in succession to the International Broadcasting Union, which had itself been formed in 1925. *Purposes:* A non-governmental international organization, the EBU exists to safeguard the interests of member broadcasting organizations, and to assist the study and exchange of information on broadcasting. *Activities:* The main fields are programming, legal and technical. One of the best-known EBU activities in the sphere of programme exchange is *Eurovision*, involving the regular daily linking of 33 television services in 26 countries of Europe, the Middle East and North Africa by a terrestrial network and satellite and via satellite to other continents when required. Other preoccupations include seminars and workshops for directors and producers, educational broadcasting, assistance to broadcasting organizations in developing countries and patronage of radio and television festivals and competitions. In the legal field, the EBU watches over the interests of its Members regarding international and domestic legislation on broadcasting, particularly copyright. Technical interests include standardization, operational questions, reception protection and the monitoring of transmissions. Membership: 38 Active and Supplementary Active Members, and 67 Associate in 75 countries. *Structure:* General Assembly; Administrative Council (appointed by General Assembly); President: Sir Charles Curran (BBC, United Kingdom); Vice-Presidents: Mr. J. Autin (TDF, France); Dr. O. Oberhammer (ORF, Austria); Committees: Legal (Chairman, Mr. A. Scharf, ARD, Germany); Television Programme (Mr. O. Nes, NRK, Norway); Radio Programme (Mr. R. Wangermée, RTB, Belgium); Technical (Mr. Mr. C. Terzani, RAI, Italy). Secretary, General: Dr. R. de Kalbermatten (Switzerland). Director, Department of Legal Affairs: Dr. M. Cazé (France); Director, Technical Centre: Mr. R. Gressman (Germany); Director, Television Programme Department: Mr. M. Vilcek (Jugoslavia); Director, Radio Programme Department: Mr. A. M Dean (U.K.); Revenue: Members' dues. *Publications:* EBU Review monthly, in English and French, there are two separate editions, one published in Geneva (Programmes, Administration, Law), the other published in Brussels (Technical); monographs on general, legal and technical aspects of broadcasting; reports and lists of stations. *Address:* Seat, 1 rue de Varembé, Case Postale No. 193 CH-1211 Geneva 20, Switzerland. Telegrams: Uniradio Geneva; Telex: 22 230 Geneva; Telephone: Geneva 33 24 00. Technival Centre, 32 avenue Albert Lancaster, B-1180 Brussels, Belgium. Telegrams: Uniradio Brussels; Telex: 21 230 Brussels; Telephone: Brussels 374 58 30.

**Comité International Radio Maritime (CIRM).** Constituted in September 1928 by a number of companies applying radio to the maritime service. Its objective is co-operative action in the advancement and improvement of maritime radio service for the benefit of those associated with the sea. During the period 1929–38, CIRM was represented at all the radio conferences of the International Telecommunications Union (ITU). The work of CIRM was interrupted by World War II, but in 1947 it was reconstructed and legally constituted under Belgian law. Its position was further strengthened in 1951, when it was recognized by ITU as a specialized international organization. United Nations, UNESCO, and IMCO have given it similar recognition. Since 1947 CIRM has contributed to and represented the views of its members at all international radio and telecommunications conferences. The membership comprises 50 leading companies, widely distributed throughout the world, specializing in marine telecommunications. The structure is the Annual General Meeting, the Board of Directors (including the President and Vice-Presidents appointed by the members), the Technical Committee (under the chairmanship of the Secretary-General), the General Secretariat (London) and the Administrative Secretariat (Brussels). *President:* H. T. Hylkema (Radio Holland); *Vice-Presidents:* R. Bryssinck (SAIT Electronics, Brussels), H. Smith (ITT Mackay Marine, U.S.A.). *Directors:* D. P. Furneaux (Marconi International Marine Company, Chelmsford, U.K.), E. Gjeruldsen (UME, Oslo). A. Asurmendi (H.R.M. Madrid), C. Buhl (Dannebrog Electronics, Copenhagen), R. E. Simonds (RCA Corp., U.S.A.), R. Bertini (SIRM, Rome), M. de Saint-Denis (C.R.M., Paris), and G. Schachtschneider (DEBEG, Hamburg), *Secretary-General:* Col. J. D. Parker, BSc, MBE. *Address:* Pier Head House, Narrow Street, London, E14 8DQ. Tel.: 01-790 6604. Telex 88254. *Administrative Secretary:* Miss J. Castanheta, 66 Chaussée de Ruisbroek, Brussels, B-1190.

## TEXTILES

**Int. Fed. of Cotton and Allied Textile Industries.** (IFCATI) Founded 1904. Previously known as the International Federation of Master Cotton Spinners' and Manufacturer's Associations. The objects are to promote the common interest of its Members, viz. national associations and ther duly constituted trade organizations of spinners and manufacturers of cotton and allied fibres. There are also Associate Members, i.e. associations representing cotton exchanges, finishing trades and related textile merchants and other Organizations allied to the industry. The Member countries are Africa and Madagascar, Australia, Austria, Belgium, Canada, Denmark, Finland, France, Germany, Greece, India, Israel, Italy, Japan, Mexico, Netherlands, Norway, Portugal, Republic of Korea, Spain, Sweden, Switzerland, Turkey, Arab Republic of Egypt, U.K. and U.S. The controlling body is the Committee of Management, with proportionate representation of Member Associations and Associate Members. The sub-committees are the Joint Cotton Committee, Raw Cotton Merchants' Committee, Committee for European Affairs, Committee for Market Research and Sales Promotion, Committee for Man-made Fibres Statistical Committee and *ad hoc* technical sub-committees. Finance is in the form of an annual levy according to production and consumption of yarns. *President:* Tom Normanton, TD, MP (England). *Senior Vice-President:* Roger Sauvegrain (France). *Junior Vice-President:* Ichiji Ohtani. *Hon. Treasurer:* M. K. H. Vos (Netherlands). *Director:* Dr. Herwig Strolz. *Economist:* Peter N. Scott. *Address:* 29 Am Schanzengraben, Postfach 289, 8039 Zürich, Switzerland.

**International Wool Textile Organization.** *Purpose:* To maintain a permanent connection between the organizations in the wool textile industry of the various countries, represent the production, commerce and industry of wool textiles in all branches of international economic activity, promote, support or oppose measures affecting the industry, promote study and solution of economic and commercial problems, ensure functioning of the International Arbitration Agreement, and generally to initiate, promote and support measures recommended by competent associations and organizations. Membership of the Organization is dependent upon adherence to the International Wool Textile Arbitration Agreement. *Secretary-General:* W. H. Lakin, MA. *Address:* 19–21, Rue du Luxembourg, 1040, Brussels, Belgium.

**The Textile Institute.** Founded 1910 Royal Charter 1925 and supplemental Charter 1955, amended 1975) the international body for those concerned with any aspect of textiles and related industries. The Institute is concerned with education, professional standards, and the interchange of information by means of its publications, conferences, meetings, and information services. *Membership:* Companions, Fellows, Associates, Licentiates, and Ordinary Members. World-wide membership 8,700. There are Sections in U.K., and most major textile producing countries. *Publications:* The Textile Institute & Industry, and Journal of the Textile Institute (monthly), Textile Progress (quarterly); text books on textile subjects. *General Secretary:* R. G. Denyer BSc. *Address:* 10 Blackfriars Street, Manchester, M3 5DR, England. Tel.: 061-834 8457.

## TRANSPORTATION—SHIPPING

**International Cargo-Handling Co-ordination Association (I.C.H.C.A.).** Inaugurated January 1952, with the aim to promote the efficiency and the economy of the movement of goods from origin to destination by all means of transport. *Membership* (Corporate and Private) in 80 countries with National Sections in Argentina, Australia, Belgium, Brazil, Canada, Denmark, Finland, France, Germany, India, Israel, Italy, Japan, Malta, Netherlands, New Zealand, Norway, Portugal, South African Republic, Spain, Sweden, U.K. and U.S.A. Regional Sections in the Caribbean, and S.E. Asia. *President:* Mr. A. S. Mayne (Australia). *Chairman of International Council and Executive Board:* Mr. R. P. Holubowicz (U.S.A.). *Hon. Treasurer:* J. A. Jackson (Australia). *Secretary-General:* Mr. W. P. R. Finlay. *Address:* Abford House, 15 Wilton Road, London, SW1V 1LX.

**International Chamber of Shipping.** Founded 1921 as the International Shipping Conference. Present title adopted in 1948. Represents the national associations of private shipowners in Australia, Belgium, Canada, Colombia, Denmark, Finland, France, Federal Republic of Germany, Greece, India, Ireland, Italy, Japan, Kuwait, Liberia, Mexico, Netherlands, New Zealand, Norway, Philippines, Portugal, Spain, Sweden, Switzerland, U.K., U.S.A., Venezuela, Yugoslavia. Promotes internationally the interests of its members on matters of general policy, including navigation, safety, legal and insurance questions, pollution control, and trade documentation. *Chairman:* H. T. Beazley. *Secretary-General:* Rear Admiral P. W. W. Graham, CB, DSC. *Address:* 30/32 St. Mary Axe, London, EC3A 8ET.

**International Commission of Cape Spartel Light at Tangier.** (Commission Internationale du Phare du Cap Spartel à Tangier). Established 1865 by the convention between the Sultan of Morocco and the governments of Austro-Hungary, Belgium, France, Italy, Netherlands, Norway, Portugal, Spain, U.K. and U.S.A. Germany and Russia later accepted the Convention, but Russia no longer participates in the Commission. The purpose is to manage, maintain, and ensure the permanent neutrality of the Cape Spartel Light. Revenue is derived from the participating governments. *Address:* La Commission Internationale du Phare du Cap Spartel, Tangier, Morocco.

**International Maritime Committee (Comité Maritime International).** Founded Brussels 1897. Its object is to contribute by all appropriate means and activities to the unification of maritime and commercial law, maritime customs, usages and practices. Members are National Associations of Maritime Law in Argentina, Australia, Belgium, Brazil, Bulgaria, Canada, Chile, Denmark, Federal Republic of Germany, German Democratic Republic, Ecuador, Eire, Finland, France, Greece, India, Israel, Italy, Japan, Mexico, Morocco, Netherlands, Norway, Poland, Portugal, Spain, Sweden, Switzerland, Turkey, U.K., U.S.A., Uruguay, U.S.S.R., Venezuala, and Yugoslavia. *Activities:* International conferences have prepared draft conventions which have been submitted to diplomatic conferences concerning: collisions at sea, salvage and assistance at sea, limitation of the liability of owners of sea-going vessels, maritime mortgages and liens on ships, immunity of state-owned ships, arrest of sea-going ships, stowaways, unification of certain rules of law relating to bills of lading, civil and penal jurisdiction in matters of collision, liability of owners of ships propelled by nuclear energy, carriage of nuclear substances, registration of rights in respect of vessels under construction, unification of certain rules relating to the carriage by sea of passengers and their luggage, civil liability for oil pollution damage, etc. Other subjects, such as shipbuilding contracts, arbitration, general average, combined transport, etc., have been, or are being, studied. The last C.M.I. International Conference was held in Hamburg in 1974. The following subjects were on the agenda: Hague/Visby Rules on bills of lading, York/Antwerp Rules on general average, limitation of the liability of owners of seagoing vessels, shipbuilding contracts, and international arbitration in maritime matters. The next C.M.I. International Conference was held in Rio de Janeiro from 25th to 30th September 1977. *Officers:* President, Francesco Berlingieri; Vice-Presidents: William Birch Reynardson, London; Arthur M. Boal, New York; Andrei K. Joudro, Moscow; Walter Müller, Basel; Nagendra Singh, New Delhi; Takeo Suzuki, Tokyo; Jean Warot, Paris; Secr. Gen. Executive: Kaj. Pineus, Göteborg; Chief Legal Officer: Jan Ramberg, Stockholm; Secr. Gen. Administrative and Treasurer: Henri Voet, Antwerp; Chief Administrative Officer: Henry Voet-Génicot, 17 Borzestraat, B2000 Antwerp, Belgium. The C.M.I. Headquarters are situated at this address.

## WAR GRAVES AND MEMORIALS

**The Commonwealth War Graves Commission.** Founded by Royal Charter in 1917, is responsible for the permanent marking and care of the graves of members of the forces of the Commonwealth who lost their lives in the 1914–18 and 1939–45 Wars, and the commemoration by name of those who have no known grave. The war dead of the Commonwealth amounted to 1,115,000 during the 1914–18 War and to 580,000 during the 1939–45 War.

It is the Commission's duty permanently to commemorate all these dead individually by name. The principle of equality of treatment, irrespective of rank, civilian status, race or religion, underlies the Commission's work. The most important of the Commission's monuments is the individual headstone on each grave. These headstones, erected over more than one million graves, are uniform in design and each bears the national service or regimental badge of the man whose grave it marks, his rank, name, age and date of death, the emblem of his religious faith and in many cases a personal inscription chosen by the next-of-kin. In the war cemeteries the central monuments are the Cross of Sacrifice and the Stone of Remembrance. The latter is a symbol which can be accepted by people of every faith and on it are inscribed the words *Their Name Liveth for Evermore.* Trees, flowers and lawns frame these monuments and headstones. Three-quarters of a million whose graves are unknown or who were cremated are commemorated by name on special memorials built by the Commission. These range from small tablets bearing only a few names to great structures bearing many thousands, such as the Menin Gate at Ypres (54,400 names) and the Commonwealth Air Forces Memorial near Runnymede (20,500 names).

Seven governments (those of the United Kingdom, Canada, Australia, New Zealand, South Africa, India and Pakistan) are represented on the Commission and share the cost of its work in the proportion of the number of their graves. The President of the Commission is H.R.H. The Duke of Kent, GCMG, GCVO, and the Chairman is, *ex officio*, the United Kingdom Secretary of State for Defence. Members of the Commission comprise the High Commissioners in London of the participating Commonwealth countries, the South African Ambassador, the Pakistan Ambassador, the United Kingdom Minister for Housing and Construction, and nine non-official Commissioners, of whom one is appointed Vice-Chairman.

In countries containing many cemeteries and memorials, the Commission's rights are protected by war graves agreements made between the governments represented on the Commission and the foreign governments concerned.

The commission's permanent maintenance organization comprises a Head Office, six independent Area Offices, and a number of agencies. The addresses of the Commission's offices and agencies throughout the world are given in the Annual Report which may be obtained from the Director-General, to whom any enquiry about the Commission's work should be addressed. *Address:* Commonwealth War Graves Commission, 2 Marlow Road, Maidenhead, Berkshire, SL6 7DX. Tel: Maidenhead 34221.

# STATES

# OF THE WORLD

# FOREIGN MINISTRIES OF THE FIVE GREAT POWERS

## LIST OF CHARTS



(*See following pages*)

## UNITED KINGDOM OF GREAT BRITAIN AND NORTHER

*SECRETARY OF STATE FOR FOREIG*

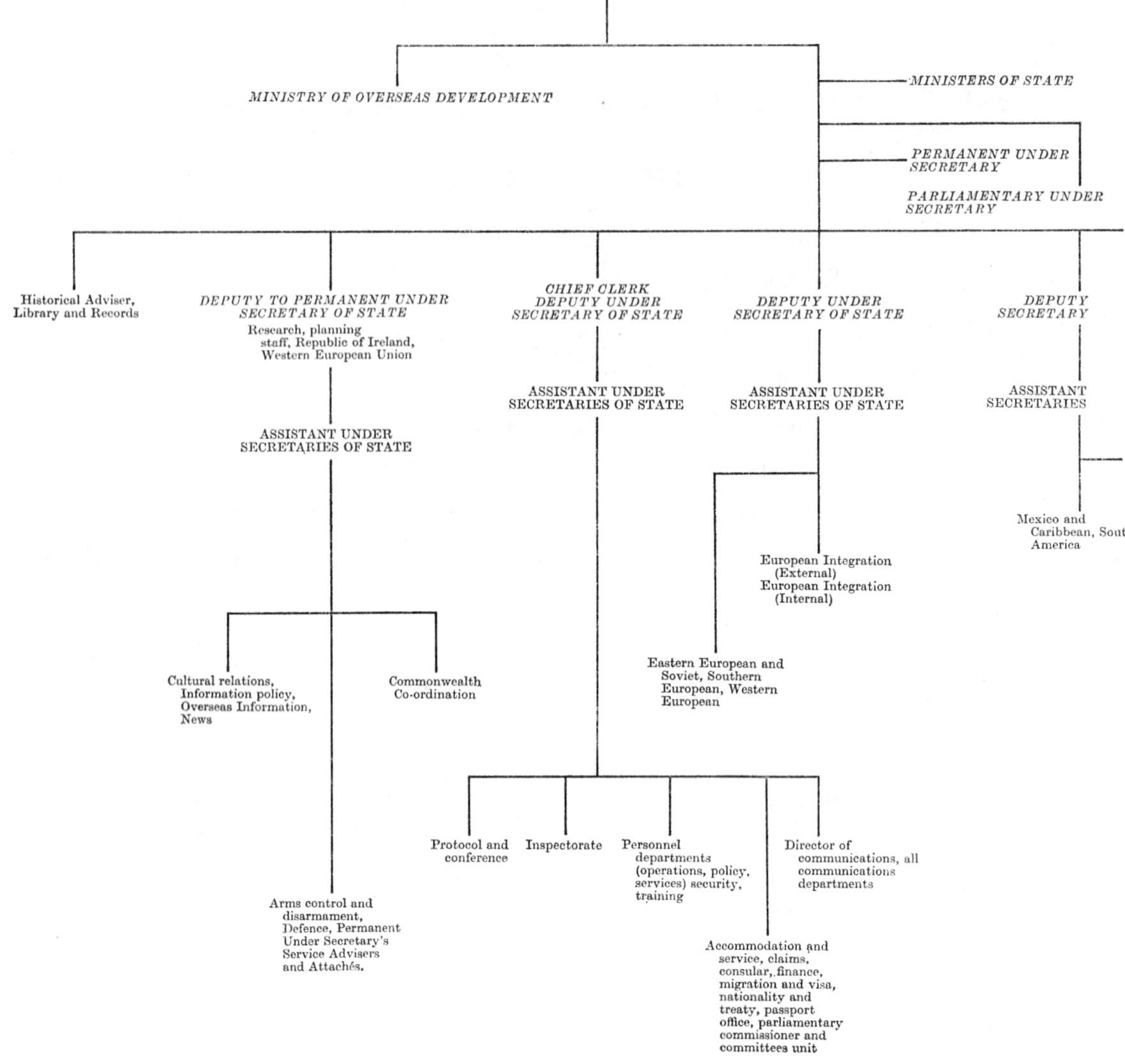
MINISTRY OF OVERSEAS DEVELOPMENT
MINISTERS OF STATE
PERMANENT UNDER SECRETARY
PARLIAMENTARY UNDER SECRETARY
Historical Adviser, Library and Records
DEPUTY TO PERMANENT UNDER SECRETARY OF STATE
Research, planning staff, Republic of Ireland, Western European Union
ASSISTANT UNDER SECRETARIES OF STATE
Cultural relations, Information policy, Overseas Information, News
Commonwealth Co-ordination
Arms control and disarmament, Defence, Permanent Under Secretary's Service Advisers and Attachés.
CHIEF CLERK DEPUTY UNDER SECRETARY OF STATE
ASSISTANT UNDER SECRETARIES OF STATE
Protocol and conference
Inspectorate
Personnel departments (operations, policy, services) security, training
Accommodation and service, claims, consular, finance, migration and visa, nationality and treaty, passport office, parliamentary commissioner and committees unit
Director of communications, all communications departments
DEPUTY UNDER SECRETARY OF STATE
ASSISTANT UNDER SECRETARIES OF STATE
European Integration (External) European Integration (Internal)
Eastern European and Soviet, Southern European, Western European
DEPUTY SECRETARY
ASSISTANT SECRETARIES
Mexico and Caribbean, South America

**IRELAND FOREIGN AND COMMONWEALTH OFFICE**
*AND COMMONWEALTH AFFAIRS*

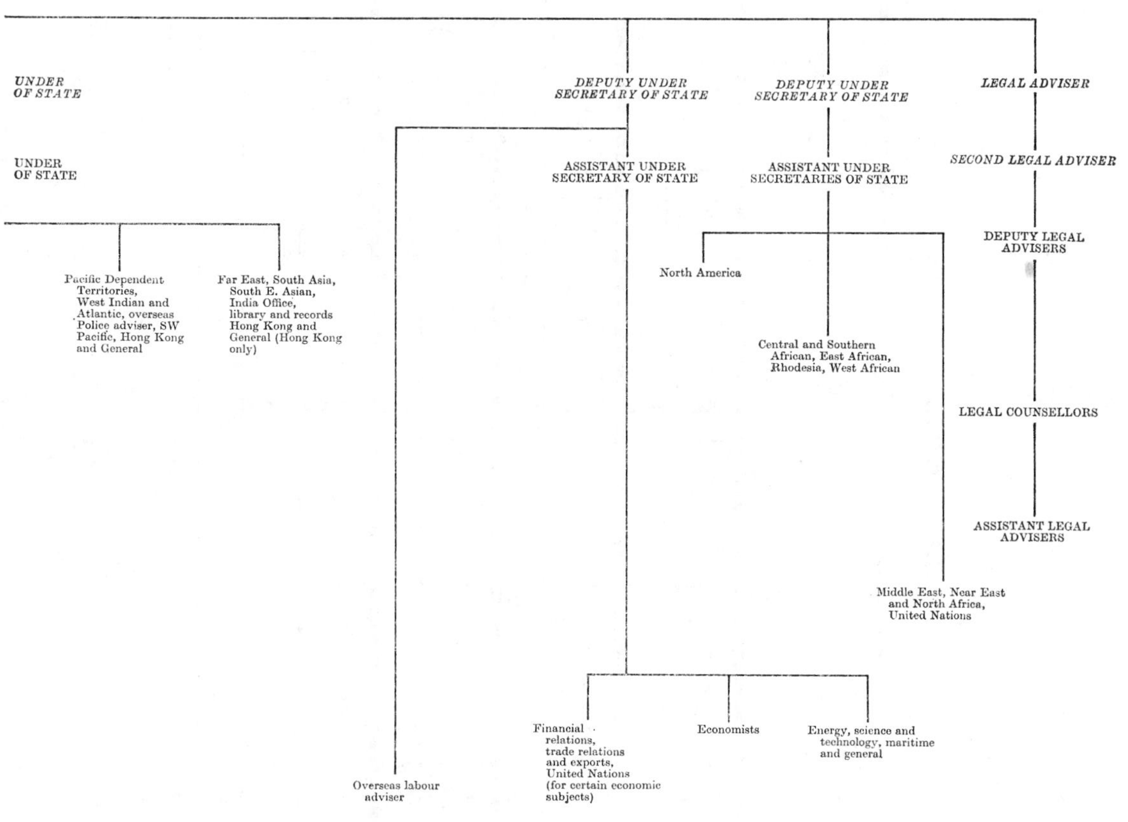

UNDER
OF STATE
DEPUTY UNDER
SECRETARY OF STATE
DEPUTY UNDER
SECRETARY OF STATE
LEGAL ADVISER
UNDER
OF STATE
ASSISTANT UNDER
SECRETARY OF STATE
ASSISTANT UNDER
SECRETARIES OF STATE
SECOND LEGAL ADVISER
DEPUTY LEGAL
ADVISERS
Pacific Dependent Territories, West Indian and Atlantic, overseas Police adviser, SW Pacific, Hong Kong and General
Far East, South Asia, South E. Asian, India Office, library and records Hong Kong and General (Hong Kong only)
North America
Central and Southern African, East African, Rhodesia, West African
LEGAL COUNSELLORS
ASSISTANT LEGAL
ADVISERS
Middle East, Near East and North Africa, United Nations
Financial relations, trade relations and exports, United Nations (for certain economic subjects)
Economists
Energy, science and technology, maritime and general
Overseas labour adviser

# UNITED STATES OF AMERICA
## DEPARTMENT OF STATE

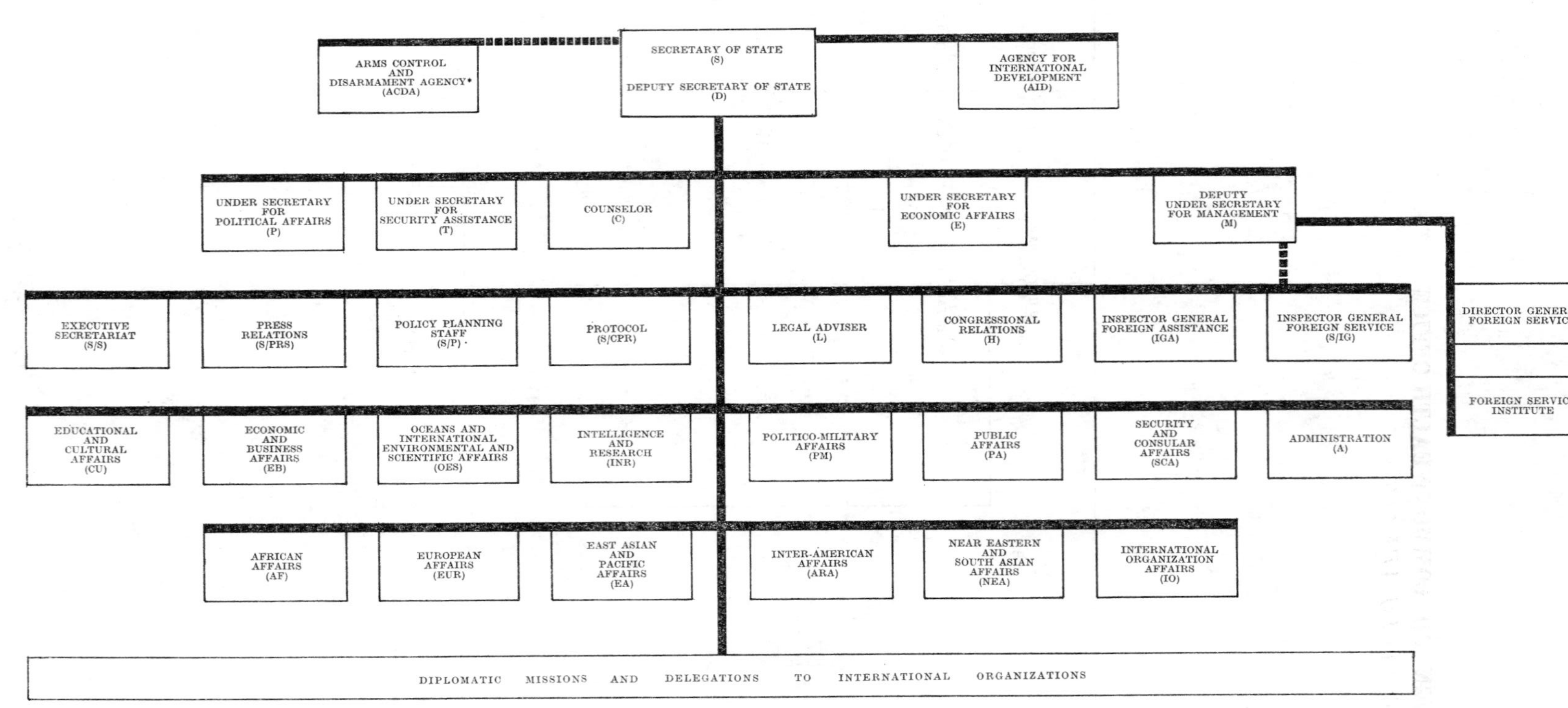


* A separate agency with the director reporting directly to the Secretary and serving as principal adviser to the Secretary and the President on Arms Control and Disarmament.

DECEMBER 1974

## FRANCE

# MINISTERE DES AFFAIRES ETRANGERES

Central Administration, 37 Quai d'Orsay, Paris 7

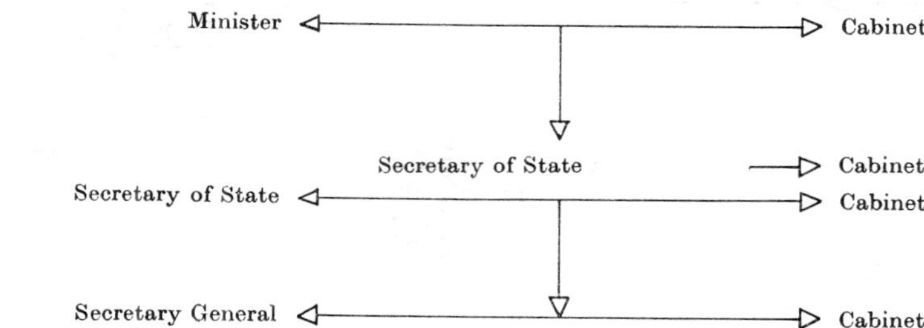


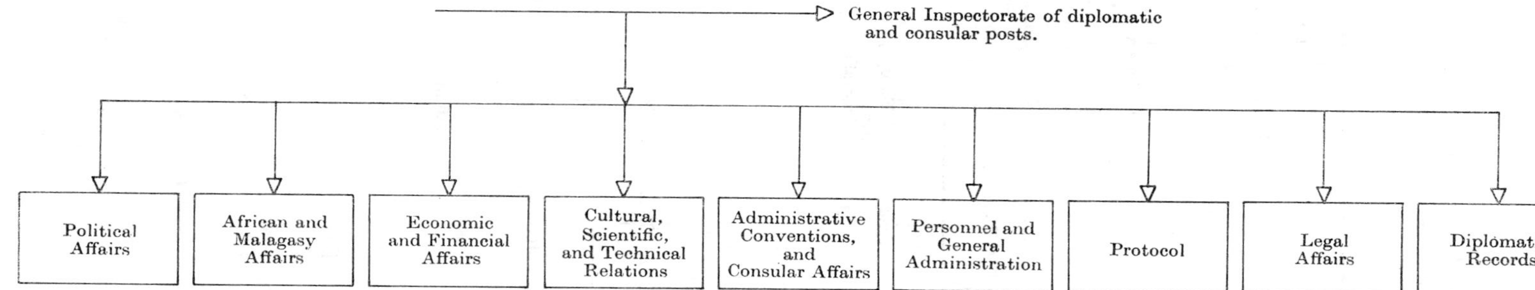

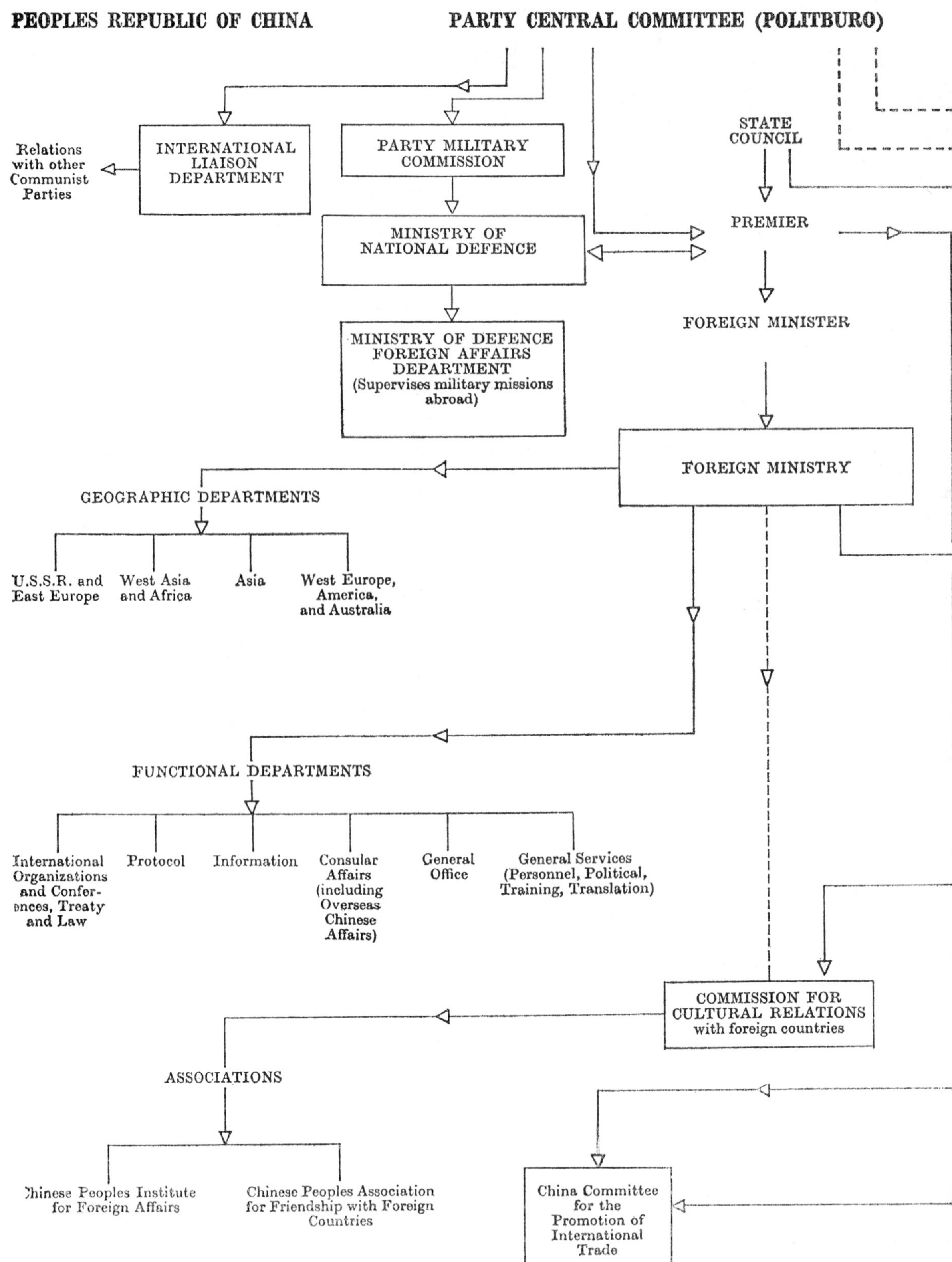
PEOPLES REPUBLIC OF CHINA
PARTY CENTRAL COMMITTEE (POLITBURO)
INTERNATIONAL LIAISON DEPARTMENT
Relations with other Communist Parties
PARTY MILITARY COMMISSION
MINISTRY OF NATIONAL DEFENCE
MINISTRY OF DEFENCE FOREIGN AFFAIRS DEPARTMENT (Supervises military missions abroad)
STATE COUNCIL
PREMIER
FOREIGN MINISTER
FOREIGN MINISTRY
GEOGRAPHIC DEPARTMENTS
U.S.S.R. and East Europe
West Asia and Africa
Asia
West Europe, America, and Australia
FUNCTIONAL DEPARTMENTS
International Organizations and Conferences, Treaty and Law
Protocol
Information
Consular Affairs (including Overseas Chinese Affairs)
General Office
General Services (Personnel, Political, Training, Translation)
COMMISSION FOR CULTURAL RELATIONS with foreign countries
ASSOCIATIONS
Chinese Peoples Institute for Foreign Affairs
Chinese Peoples Association for Friendship with Foreign Countries
China Committee for the Promotion of International Trade

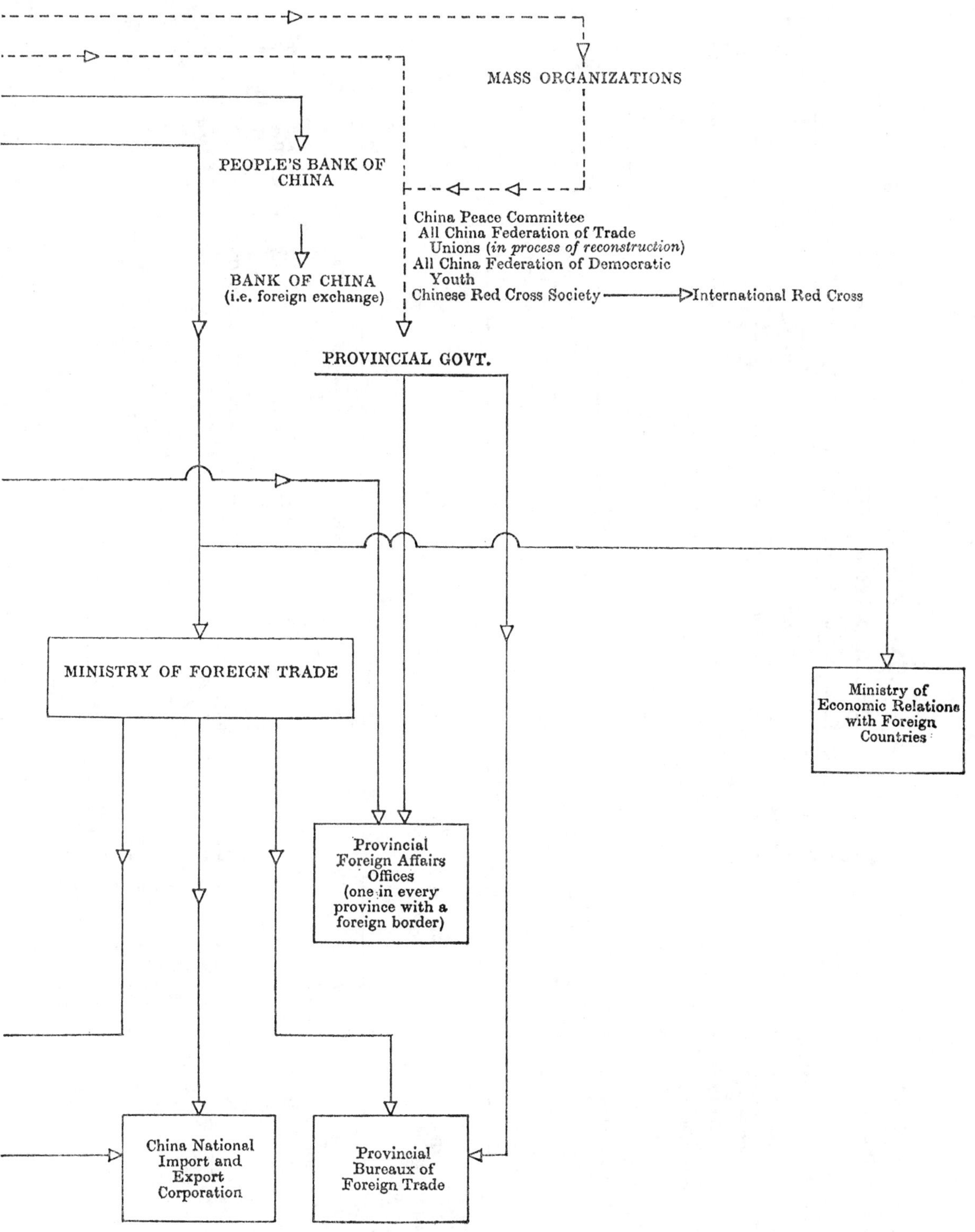

MASS ORGANIZATIONS
PEOPLE'S BANK OF CHINA
BANK OF CHINA
(i.e. foreign exchange)
China Peace Committee
All China Federation of Trade Unions (*in process of reconstruction*)
All China Federation of Democratic Youth
Chinese Red Cross Society
International Red Cross
PROVINCIAL GOVT.
MINISTRY OF FOREIGN TRADE
Ministry of Economic Relations with Foreign Countries
Provincial Foreign Affairs Offices (one in every province with a foreign border)
China National Import and Export Corporation
Provincial Bureaux of Foreign Trade

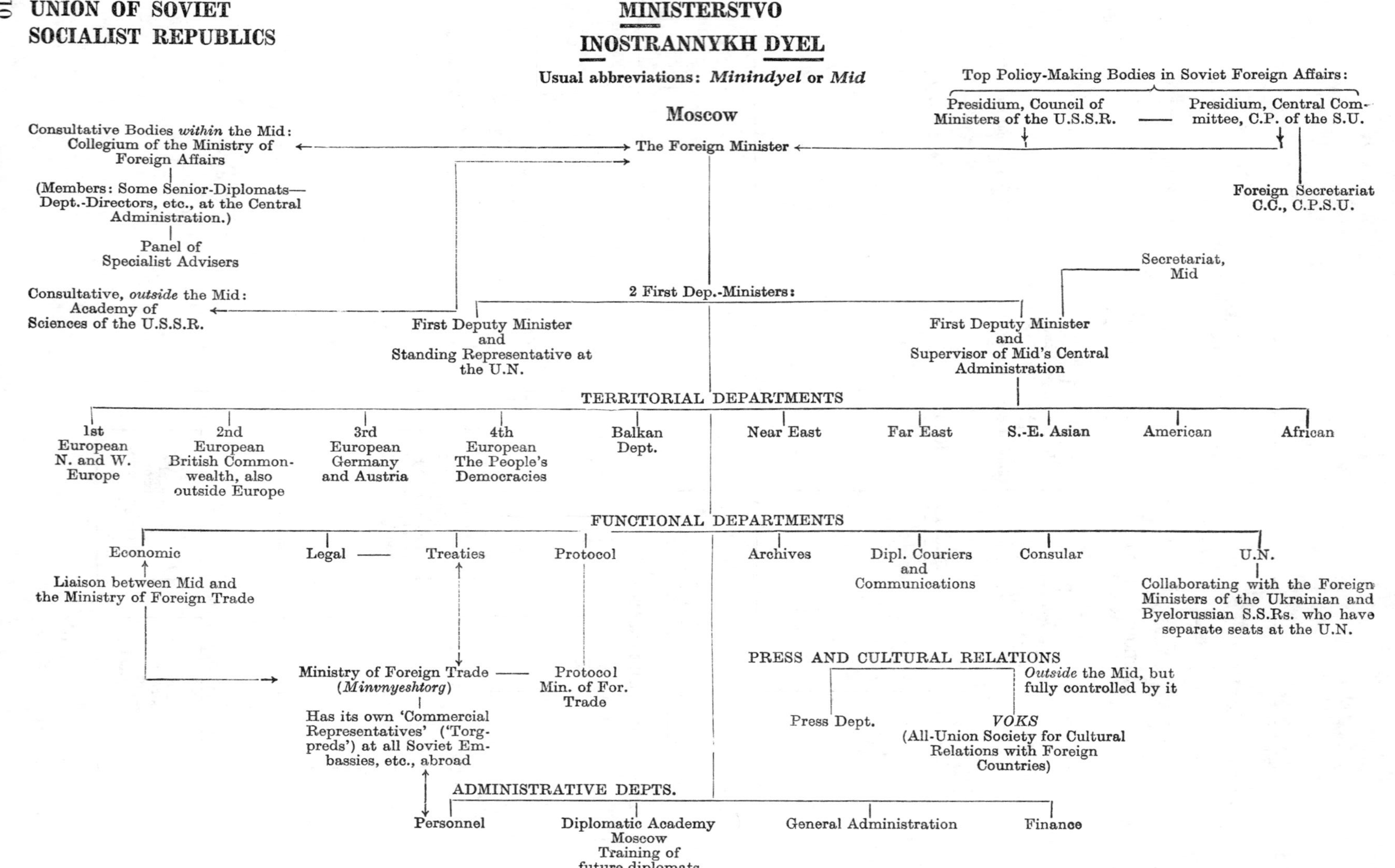
MINISTERSTVO
INOSTRANNYKH DYEL
Usual abbreviations: *Minindyel* or *Mid*
Moscow
Top Policy-Making Bodies in Soviet Foreign Affairs:
Presidium, Council of Ministers of the U.S.S.R.
Presidium, Central Committee, C.P. of the S.U.
Foreign Secretariat C.C., C.P.S.U.
The Foreign Minister
Consultative Bodies *within* the Mid: Collegium of the Ministry of Foreign Affairs
(Members: Some Senior-Diplomats—Dept.-Directors, etc., at the Central Administration.)
Panel of Specialist Advisers
Consultative, *outside* the Mid: Academy of Sciences of the U.S.S.R.
2 First Dep.-Ministers:
First Deputy Minister and Standing Representative at the U.N.
First Deputy Minister and Supervisor of Mid's Central Administration
Secretariat, Mid
TERRITORIAL DEPARTMENTS
1st European N. and W. Europe
2nd European British Commonwealth, also outside Europe
3rd European Germany and Austria
4th European The People's Democracies
Balkan Dept.
Near East
Far East
S.-E. Asian
American
African
FUNCTIONAL DEPARTMENTS
Economic
Liaison between Mid and the Ministry of Foreign Trade
Legal
Treaties
Protocol
Archives
Dipl. Couriers and Communications
Consular
U.N.
Collaborating with the Foreign Ministers of the Ukrainian and Byelorussian S.S.Rs. who have separate seats at the U.N.
Ministry of Foreign Trade (*Minvnyeshtorg*)
Protocol Min. of For. Trade
Has its own 'Commercial Representatives' ('Torgpreds') at all Soviet Embassies, etc., abroad
PRESS AND CULTURAL RELATIONS
*Outside* the Mid, but fully controlled by it
Press Dept.
*VOKS* (All-Union Society for Cultural Relations with Foreign Countries)
ADMINISTRATIVE DEPTS.
Personnel
Diplomatic Academy Moscow Training of future diplomats
General Administration
Finance

*A Note on Gross National Product (GNP)*

*The 1974 GNP in market prices and per capita GNP are calculated on the basis of the 1973–75 base period. With this method, GNP in domestic currency unit is first expressed in weighted average domestic prices of the base period 1973–75 and then converted into U.S. dollars by means of the weighted average exchange rate for the same base period. After adjusting it for the rate of U.S. inflation between the base period and the current year by means of the implicit U.S. GNP deflator for 1974, this estimate is divided by the midyear population to derive per capita GNP in current U.S. dollars. The per capita GNP estimates for 1973 and 1975 which are shown in the Annex together with the 1974 estimates are calculated on the basis of the same price and exchange rate after respective corrections for the rate of U.S. inflation between the base period and current years as these estimates are in current U.S. dollars. Thus, the year-to-year changes in the per capita GNP estimates reflect two factors: real per capita growth and the rate of U.S. inflation. The average annual rates of growth for population and per capita product for the periods 1960–74 and 1965–74 were computed by fitting a trend line to the logarithmic values of population and real GNP per capita over time. With this method all available observations in the relevant time periods are considered and the growth rates obtained reflect general trends rather than cyclical factors or irregular variations in any particular year.*

*The data shown provide only an approximate measure of economic conditions and trends. They are merely rough indicators of the absolute state of poverty in the developing world and reveal nothing about its distribution within countries.*

## METRIC ⟷ ENGLISH CONVERSION TABLES

### English to Metric

| **Length** | | |
|---|---|---|
| 1 mile | = 1.609 34 km | |
| 1 furlong (220 yd) | = 0.201 168 km | |
| 1 chain (22 yd) | = 20.1168 m | |
| 1 yd | = 0.9144 m | |
| 1 ft (foot) | = 0.3048 m | |
| 1 US Survey foot (12/39.370 m) | = 0.304 801 m | |
| 1 in (inch) | = 25.4 mm | = 2.54 cm |
| 1 milli-inch ('thou') | = 25.4 $\mu$m | |
| 1 rod, pole or perch (5.5 yd) | = 5.029 2 m | |
| 1 fathom (6 ft) | = 1.8288 m | |
| **Area** | | |
| 1 mile$^2$ | = 2.589 99 km$^2$ | = 258.999 ha |
| 1 acre (4840 yd$^2$) | = 4046.86 m$^2$ | = 0.404 686 ha |
| 1 yd$^2$ (square yard) | = 0.836 127 m$^2$ | |
| 1 ft$^2$ (square foot) | = 0.092 903 0 m$^2$ | = 929.030 cm$^2$ |
| 1 in$^2$ (square inch) | = 645.16 mm$^2$ | = 6.451 6 cm$^2$ |
| **Volume** | | |
| 1 yd$^3$ (cubic yard) | = 0.764 555 m$^3$ | |
| 1 ft$^3$ (cubic foot) | = 0.028 316 8 m$^3$ | = 28.316 8 dm$^3$ |
| 1 in$^3$ (cubic inch) | = 16.387 1 cm$^3$ | |
| 1 US barrel (petroleum) | = 0.158 987 m$^3$ | = 158.987 dm$^3$ |
| 1 gal (UK gallon) | = 4.546 09 dm$^3$ | |
| 1 US gal (231 in$^3$) | = 3.785 41 dm$^3$ | |
| 1 qt (quart) | = 1.136 52 dm$^3$ | |
| 1 pt (pint) | = 0.568 261 dm$^3$ | |
| 1 gill (1/4 pint) | = 0.142 065 dm$^3$ | |
| 1 fl oz (1/20 pint) | = 28.413 1 cm$^3$ | |

### Metric to English

| **Length** | | |
|---|---|---|
| 1 km | = 0.621 371 mile | |
| 1 m | = 1.093 61 yd | = 39.370 1 in |
| 1 cm | = 0.393 701 in | |
| 1 mm | = 0.039 370 1 in | |
| **Area** | | |
| 1 km$^2$ | = 247.105 acres | |
| 1 ha (hectare, 10 000 m$^2$) | = 2.471 05 acres | |
| 1 decare | = 0.247 105 acre | = 1 195.99 yd$^2$ |
| 1 a (are) | = 119.599 yd$^2$ | |
| 1 m$^2$ | = 1.195 99 yd$^2$ | |
| 1 mm$^2$ | = 0.001 550 00 in$^2$ | |
| **Volume** | | |
| 1 m$^3$ | = 1.307 95 yd$^3$ | |
| 1 dm$^3$ | = 0.035 314 7 ft$^3$ | |
| 1 cm$^3$ | = 0.061 023 7 in$^3$ | |
| 1 l (litre, 1 dm$^3$ exactly) | = 0.219 969 gal | = 0.264 172 US gal |

# Afghanistan

**Capital**—Kabul.

**Head of State** (President)—Mohammad Daoud.

**National Flag:** A tricolour pale-wise, black, red, green, bearing the state emblem which comprises two ears of wheat, a mehrab and monbar, an eagle and a rising sun; the ears of wheat are linked by a scroll inscribed 'Republic of Afghanistan', and above it '1352' (our year 1973).

## CONSTITUTION AND GOVERNMENT

AFGHANISTAN is an inland country of Asia bounded on the east and south by Pakistan, on the north and north-east by the U.S.S.R. and China, and on the west by Iran. Under the 1964 constitution, Afghanistan became a parliamentary democracy in which legislative authority rested with a National Assembly of two houses. The legislative, executive and judicial branches of government were separated. Certain powers, such as the appointment of the Prime Minister and judges of the Supreme Court, rested with the King, who was a constitutional monarch. This constitution replaced that which had been in force since 1933. The monarchy was overthrown in a military coup d'état in July 1973.

The country was ruled by Presidential Decree until February 1977 when a new Constitution was approved by a Loya Jirgah (Grand Assembly). Mohammad Daoud was elected President of the Republic for a term of six years. A one party system is in process of being set up.

## LOCAL GOVERNMENT

There are 26 provinces, each under a governor. They are Kabul, Parwan, Laghman, Nangahar, Logar, Katawaz and Urgun, Kalat, Kandahar, Uruzgan, Girishk, Chakhansur, Farah, Ghor, Herat, Badghis, Maimana, Shibergan, Mazar-i-Sharif, Bamiyan, Samangan, Baghlan and Pul-i-Khumri, Kunduz, Taleqan and Badakhshan, Wardak and Maidan, Ghazni, Paktya.

## LEGAL SYSTEM

Hitherto, Afghanistan has been ruled on the basis of Shariat or Islamic law. The 1964 constitution provided for the creation of a legal code, and for a new structure of courts. This consisted of a lower court in each 'wuluswal' (sub-province), and a court of appeal in each province, with a Supreme Court in Kabul. This system marked the complete separation of executive and judiciary for the first time. The independence of the Supreme Court was abolished by Presidential Decree in July 1973.

In late 1976 and early 1977 new Penal and Civil Codes were published.

## AREA AND POPULATION

The estimated area of Afghanistan is 250,000 square miles.

The population at mid-1974 is estimated at 16,311,000 and is of mixed origin. The projected population for 1985 will be approximately 25,000,000. The expectation of life at birth for both sexes, according to the United Nations Population Division, for the period 1965–70, was 37·5 years. The annual average population percentage growth rate for the period 1960–74 was 2·2, and for the period 1965–74 was also 2·2. There are approximately 8,200,000 Pathans; among these the Durranis predominate, especially in Kandahar. The languages spoken are Pushtu, Persian and Usbek.

The largest towns are Kabul, the capital (population about 500,000), Kandahar (115,000), Herat (62,000) and Mazar-i-Sharif (40,000), 1965.

## CURRENCY

The unit of currency is the 'afghani' weighing 10 grammes of silver ·900 fine, which is divided into 100 puls. Coinage consists of copper and cupro-nickel 25 and 50 puls, afghanis 1, 2 and 5. Currency notes of A/s 10, 20, 50, 100, 500, and 1,000 are in circulation. The open market rate fluctuates round 85 afghanis to the £1.

## FINANCE

The estimated domestic Revenue for 1974–75 was (in million afghanis) 10,250,100. Ordinary Expenditure was estimated at 6,538,000. Development Expenditure was 3,060,000. The GNP at market prices for 1974 was U.S. $ millions 1,880, and the GNP per capita at market prices for 1974 was U.S.$ 110. The annual average percentage growth rate of the GNP per capita for the period 1960–74 was 0·5 and for the period 1965–74 was 1·1. [*See the note at the beginning of this section concerning GNP.*]

## PRINCIPAL BANKS

**Da Afghanistan Bank.**

**Banke Millie.**

**Pashtani Tejaraty Bank.**

## PRODUCTION, INDUSTRY AND COMMERCE

**Agriculture.** The greater part of Afghanistan is more or less mountainous and too dry and rocky for successful cultivation. Satisfactory crops of fruit, cereals and vegetables are, however, grown in the fertile valleys. There are generally two crops a year, one of wheat, barley and lentils, and the other of rice, millet and maize. Schemes for irrigation are now in hand. A dam has been built on the Helmand River near Girishk in southern Afghanistan which has brought a considerable area of waste land under cultivation. Corn and cotton are already being grown in the area. Other land development schemes are in progress at Nangahar (77,000 acres), the Sarde dam area (43,655) and in the Parwan Valley. Fruit is extensively grown and forms the staple diet of large sections of the population. Sugar beet is also grown in Northern Afghanistan.

Sheep, especially the fat-tailed variety, are reared in large numbers and form the principal meat diet of the people. Wool and sheepskins are used for clothing and form important articles of export, particularly the Karakul variety. In 1955 Russian merino sheep were introduced, since they were thought to be better suited to the climate.

The following table shows the volume of Afghanistan's agricultural production during 1974–75 (in thousand metric tons):

| | |
|---|---|
| Wheat | 2,867 |
| Corn | 711 |
| Barley | 355 |
| Rice | 414 |
| | |
| Cotton (unginned) | 150 |
| Sugarbeet | 50 |
| Sugarcane | 65 |
| Oilseeds | 40 |
| Fruits | 840 |
| Vegetables | 700 |

**Mining.** There are three coal mines. A survey for oil is in progress. Beryllium, copper, lead, iron, coal, and petroleum await development. Lapis lazuli of the finest quality is produced.

Oil drilling in the north has produced disappointing results, but large natural gas resources have been discovered and an agreement for their exploitation was signed with the Soviet Union in 1963. The latter is now being piped to the Soviet Union and an agreement has now been signed to supply 2,800 million cubic metres in 1974.

**Industry.** There are a number of small textile factories at Kabul and Kandahar. For quality the native carpets and rugs are world famous. The chief centres of production are Daulatabad, Herat, Andkhoi and Mazar. Electric plants are in use at Kabul, Kandahar, Baghlan, Jalalabad, Mazar, Pul-i-Khumri Girishk, Bagram and Herat. Total (estimated) generating capacity was 486 million kWh in 1974–5, the major part of which is hydro.

## AFGHANISTAN

Afghanistan has two cement factories, one at Pul-i-Khumri and the other at Jabel-us-Seraj, with a total production of 500 tons a day.

There is a cotton spinning plant at Kunduz and cotton textile mills at Pul-i-Khumri, Bagramie, Gulbahar, Balkh and a number of smaller mills in the Kabul area. Four British-erected cotton-seed oil mills are in operation in the Kunduz area, and a fifth at Lashkargah, near Kandahar.

Woollen textiles are produced at Pul-e-Charki, near Kabul, and at Kandahar.

There are dried fruit processing and packing plants at Kabul and Kandahar.

The following table shows Afghanistan's estimated Major industrial output during 1974–75:

| *Product* | *Unit (thousand tons unless otherwise stated)* | 1974–75 |
|---|---|---|
| Cotton textiles | (m. metres) | 70 |
| Cotton (ginned) | — | 35 |
| Cement | — | 120 |
| Vegetable oil | — | 7·0 |
| Sugar | — | 8·0 |
| Soap | (million cakes) | 6·5 |
| Leather Shoes | (thousand pairs) | 300 |
| Coal | — | 145 |
| Natural Gas | (billion cubic feet) | 2·8 |

**Commerce.** Approximately half of Afghanistan's trade passes through Pakistan and half through Russia, the chief imports being wheat, cotton goods, sugar, hardware, petrol and oil. Exports include spices, fresh and dried fruits, karakul skins, carpets, cotton wool, and natural gas.

Apart from a ban on the import of certain goods there is no special import control. Importers, however, must hold trade permits issued annually by the Ministry of Commerce. There is a government monopoly of imports of petroleum products, sugar and tobacco products.

The following two tables show, respectively, the value in thousands of pounds sterling of imports into the United Kingdom from Afghanistan, and of exports from the United Kingdom to Afghanistan for the first six months of 1975.

| *Imports* | |
|---|---|
| Fruit and Vegetables | 511 |
| Hides, skins and furskins undressed | 181 |
| Textile fibres not manufactured, and their waste | 22 |
| Crude animal and vegetable materials | 18 |
| Textile yarn, fabrics, made-up articles, etc. | 766 |
| Non-metallic mineral manufactures | 2 |
| Machinery, other than electric | 4 |
| Electrical machinery, apparatus and appliances | 6 |
| Travel goods, etc. | 1 |
| Clothing | 25 |
| Footwear | 1 |
| Scientific instruments | 2 |
| Miscellaneous manufactured articles n.e.s. | 18 |
| Total | 1,557 |

*continued*

| *Exports* | |
|---|---|
| Dairy products and eggs | 66 |
| Cereals | 3 |
| Sugar, honey | 2 |
| Coffee, tea, cocoa, spices | 5 |
| Miscellaneous food preparations | 1 |
| Beverages | 30 |
| Tobacco | 31 |
| Hides, skins | 22 |
| Textile fibres, not manufactured | 7 |
| Petroleum and petroleum products | 246 |
| Chemical elements and their compounds | 4 |
| Dyeing, tanning, colouring materials | 5 |
| Medicinal and pharmaceutical products | 144 |
| Essential oils and perfume materials | 257 |
| Explosives | 16 |
| Plastic materials | 1 |
| Chemical materials | 3 |
| Rubber manufactures | 2 |
| Paper | 2 |
| Textile yarn | 135 |
| Non-metallic minerals | 13 |
| Iron and steel | 1 |
| Manufactures of metal n.e.s. | 326 |
| Machinery, other than electric | 159 |
| Electrical machinery | 111 |
| Transport equipment | 613 |
| Sanitary fixtures | 1 |
| Travel goods | 2 |
| Clothing | 19 |
| Footwear | 1 |
| Scientific instruments | 40 |
| Miscelleneous manufactured articles n.e.s. | 182 |
| Total | 2,471 |

The following table shows direction of trade for the period 1973–74 in U.S. $ millions.

| *Country* | *Exports* | *Imports** |
|---|---|---|
| Germany (West) | 6·9 | 4·5 |
| India | 27·2 | 21·6 |
| Pakistan | 23·0 | 5·3 |
| United Kingdom | 23·3 | 6·3 |
| U.S.A. | 2·1 | 6·0 |
| U.S.S.R. | 48·6 | 14·0 |
| Other countries | 28·0 | 26·6 |

* Excluding loan and grant imports.

### COMMUNICATIONS

**Several main roads are fit for motor traffic:**

(*a*) Internal: Kabul–Kandahar (310 miles); Kandahar–Herat (350 miles); Mazar-I-Sharif–Kabul (380 miles). Also Kabul–Khanabad–Faizabad (450 miles); Kabul–Gardez (80 miles); Herat–Maimana–Mazar–I-Sharif (500 miles) and Kabul–Bamiyan (140 miles are unsurfaced roads suitable only for vehicles with four wheel drive. They are usually impassable in winter.)

(*b*) Roads to the frontiers: Kabul–Khyber (175 miles); Kandahar–Chaman (70 miles) and roads from Herat to the Russian and Persian borders.

Minor roads fit for motor traffic in fine weather link the important districts and towns.

There are civilian airports at Kabul, Herat, Kandahar and Kunduz, and landing-grounds at Mazar-i-Sharif, Kunduz, Khost, Maimana, Bamian, Chakcharan, Lashkargah, Faizabad, Neemroz and Taluqan.

**Ariana Afghan Airlines Company Ltd.** (National carrier of Afghanistan) was established on 20 June 1955 and operates to Amritsar, New Delhi, Tashkent, Tehran, Damascus, Beirut, Istanbul, Rome, Frankfurt, Paris, London.

**Bakhtar Afghan Airlines.** Afghanistan's domestic carrier was established on 8 February 1968 and offers scheduled services to 15 points with Afghanistan.

Other airlines serving Afghanistan are: **Iran Air** twice weekly Tehran, Kabul; **Aeroflot** twice weekly Moscow, Tashkent, Kabul; **P.I.A.** twice weekly Peshawar–Kabul; **Indian Airlines** three times weekly to Delhi, once weekly to Amritsar.

NEWSPAPERS

The main newspapers at present published in Kabu are as follows:

**Anis.** Persian and Pushtu. Daily.

**Hewad.** Pushtu. Daily.

**Jamhouriat.** Persian and Pushtu. Daily

**Kabul Times.** English. Daily.

EDUCATION AND RELIGION

Education is free and nominally compulsory. There are elementary schools throughout the country, and high schools in Kabul and the provincial capitals. Kabul University was founded in 1932, and Jalalabad in 1963. There are also two training schools for teachers as well as technical, art, commercial and medical schools.

Islam is the predominant religion. Most of the inhabitants are of the Sunni sect but there is also a minority composed of Shiah Mohammedans. There are about 3,000 Jews.

# Albania

(REPUBLÍKA POPULLÓRE E SHQIPËRÍSË)

**Capital**—Tirana.

**Chairman of the Presidium of the People's Assembly** (President, Head of State)—Major-General Haxhi Lleshi.

**National Flag:** Red, bearing at the centre a double-headed eagle black, with wings displayed, under a star five-pointed red and bordered gold.

## CONSTITUTION AND GOVERNMENT

ALBANIA became an independent State on 28 November 1912, after 445 years of Turkish rule. The representatives of the Great Powers, at a conference held in London, agreed on the principles of Albanian autonomy, and decided on the frontiers of the country. Subsequently the German Prince William of Wied was chosen as the 'Mbret', or king, of Albania. He arrived at Durrës (Durazzo) in March 1914 but left the country in the following September after the outbreak of World War I.

Albania was occupied in turn by Austrian, French, Italian and Serbian troops, according to the changing fortunes of war. The secret Treaty of London in 1915 provided for the partition of most of Albania, assigning portions to Serbia, Montenegro and Greece. In 1917, however, Italy proclaimed the independence of Albania under Italian protection. A provisional government was established in 1918, but portions of the country were occupied by foreign troops until 1921.

In 1920 the Congress of Lushnja reasserted the national sovereignty and independence, elected a new government which moved into Tirana, the first post-war capital. The first free elections held immediately after resulted in an evenly divided parliament. After two uprisings in 1924 the country was proclaimed a republic, and a tribal chief named Ahmed Zogu was made president. On 1 September 1928 Albania was proclaimed a monarchy, and the President was enthroned as Zog I, King of the Albanians. He reigned until 1939, when on Good Friday, 7 April, Italian troops invaded the country, which was annexed to the Italian Crown.

In 1944 a provisional government was formed by the Democratic Front under Enver Hoxha. It was recognized by Allied governments on the understanding that free elections would be held. Elections held on 2 December 1945 on a single list sponsored by the Communist Party resulted in a victory for the Democratic Front, led by the Communist Party headed by Enver Hoxha. On 12 January 1946 the Constituent Assembly proclaimed Albania a republic

In 1946 the United Kingdom decided that no useful purpose could be served by opening diplomatic relations with Albania. The United States followed some months later. Albania was admitted a member of the U.N. in December 1955. A treaty was completed with Yugoslavia on 27 November 1946 providing for customs and currency union. When Yugoslavia left the Cominform in 1948 the Albanians remained in the Soviet bloc and the treaty was abrogated. Albania now has diplomatic relations with most foreign countries, with the notable exceptions of the United Kingdom, U.S.A., and U.S.S.R.

The Constitution was adopted in March 1946 and amended on 4 July 1950. Albania is a People's Republic. Its supreme legislative organ is the People's Assembly, elected for a term of four years, by all citizens of 18 years of age and over. One deputy is elected for every 8,000 inhabitants. The election of 10 July 1966 returned 240 deputies on a single list of the Democratic Front, in which the Party of Labour (as the Communist party is now called) plays the leading role.

The People's Assembly elects a Presidium, composed of a Chairman, three Deputy-Chairmen, one Secretary and ten Members. The Presidium convokes the People's Assembly twice a year; between the sessions, the Presidium exercises the functions of the Assembly. The People's Assembly appoints and removes from office the Government.

The leading political organization in Albania, and the guiding force in all spheres of social life at all levels, is the Communist 'Albanian Party of Labour' which is the basis and leader of the pro-regime mass organization called 'Albanian Democratic Front'. The Sixth Party Congress, held from 1 November to 7 November 1971, elected a Central Committee of 61 members and 36 alternate members. The Central Committee at its first meeting elected a Politburo of 13 members and 4 candidate members.

**The Politburo** (elected following 6th Party Congress in November 1971). Ramiz Alia, Beqir Balluku, Adil Çarçani, Kadri Hazbiu, Enver Hoxha, Hysni Kapo, Abdyl Këllezi, Spiro Koleka, Rita Marko, Manush Myftiu, Mehmet Shehu, Haki Toska, Koço Theodhosi.

Candidate members: Pirro Dodbiba, Petrit Dumo, Pilo Peristeri, Xhafer Spahiu.

Secretariat: Enver Hoxa (First Secretary). Haki Toska, Hysni Kapo, Ramiz Alia.

**The Presidium of the People's Assembly** (elected September 1966). *Chairman:* Haxhi Lleshi; *Vice Chairmen:* Rito Marko, Myslim Peza; *Secretary:* Bilbil Klosi; *Members:*Et-hem Barhani, Hito Çako, Myqerem Fuga, Enver Hoxha, Tonin Jakova, Vito Kapo, Spiro Moisiu, Pilo Peristeri, Xhafer Spahiu, Kahreman Ylli.

**Council of Ministers (1972)**

*Chairman of the Council of Ministers (Prime Minister):* Mehmet Shehu.
*Deputy Chairman of the Council of Ministers:* Beqir Balluku, Adil Çarçani, Spiro Koleka.
*Secretaries of the Central Committee:* Hysni Kapo, Ramiz Alia, Haki Toska, Manush Myftiu, Rita Marko.
*Minister of Foreign Affairs:* Nesti Nase.
*Minister of Finance:* Aleks Verli.
*Chairman of State Planning Commission:* Petra Dode.

## LOCAL GOVERNMENT

Albania, by the Law 'On the People's Councils' of 26 November 1953, with subsequent minor amendments, is divided into 26 regions (*rrathë*), and these are further divided into 51 towns (*qyteta*) and 125 rural districts (*lokaliteta*); the last-named include 2,833 villages (*fshatra*). Each of these administrative units is run by a People's Council, elected for a term of three years. The current tendency is towards decentralization, more power being given to the People's Councils.

## LEGAL SYSTEM

Justice is administered by a Supreme Court, elected by the People's Assembly for a term of four years, and by People's Courts and Military Tribunals. Judges of People's and Military Courts are elected by the people; they also may be recalled by the people.

The new Penal Code, introduced on 1 September 1952, is modelled on Soviet law. The Albanian Code, however, includes more severe penalties than the Soviet. Full penal responsibility starts at the age of 14; and for crimes against the State, for sabotage of State property, or economic sabotage—at 12.

*President of the Supreme Court:* Aranit Cela.

*Vice-Presidents:* Sami Baholli, Llazi Stratoberdha.

*Procurator-General:* Lefter Goga.

*Deputy Procurator-General:* Dhori Panariti.

## AREA AND POPULATION

The area of the country is approximately 10,629 sq. miles. In mid-1973 the estimated population was 2,295,000. The density of the population in 1969 was 72 persons per square kilometre.

The size and population of the regions is as follows:

| *Region* | *Area (sq. km.)* | *Population (1967)* |
|---|---|---|
| Berat | 1,066 | 104,390 |
| Dibra | 1,569 | 93,812 |
| Durrës | 861 | 155,780 |
| Elbasan | 1,505 | 130,430 |
| Fier | 1,191 | 139,175 |
| Gramsh | 699 | 24,095 |
| Gjirokastra | 1,137 | 49,170 |
| Kolonja | 804 | 18,685 |
| Korça | 2,181 | 159,115 |
| Kruja | 611 | 55,325 |
| Kukës | 1,564 | 58,880 |
| Lezha | 472 | 33,225 |
| Librazhd | 1,013 | 42,730 |
| Lushnja | 712 | 81,595 |
| Mat | 1,028 | 45,340 |
| Mirdita | 698 | 22,465 |
| Përmet | 938 | 30,340 |
| Pogradec | 725 | 42,775 |
| Puka | 969 | 27,568 |
| Saranda | 1,097 | 58,135 |
| Skrapar | 720 | 23,035 |
| Shkodra | 2,533 | 150,350 |
| Tepelena | 817 | 30,850 |
| Tirana | 1,186 | 241,900 |
| Tropoja | 1,043 | 25,570 |
| Vlora | 1,609 | 119,995 |
| Total | 28,748 | 1,964,730 |

Populations of principal towns in 1967 (estimates) were: Tirana, 169,300; Durrës (Durazzo), 53,160; Vlora (Valona), 50,351; Shkodra (Scutari), 49,830; Korça (Koritza), 45,858; Elbasan, 38,885; Berat, 23,895; Fier, 19,681; Kavaja, 18,800; Lushnja, 17,545; Gjirokastra, 15,590; Stalin City, 13,490.

The annual average percentage growth rate of the population for the period 1960–73 was 2·8, and for the period 1965–73 was 2·7.

## CURRENCY

In July 1947 the Albanian gold franc (franc ar) was replaced by the new monetary unit, the lek. 1 lek is divided into 100 qindar. In August 1965 a new lek was introduced. It is equal to 10 of the old leks.

## PRODUCTION, INDUSTRY AND COMMERCE

**Planning.** The economic help formerly given to Albania by the U.S.S.R. has been increasingly undertaken by China. The Albanian five-year plan launched at the beginning of 1960, which was to have been supported by a substantial long-term loan from the U.S.S.R., was replaced by a contract with the People's Republic of China said to amount to a long-term credit of roubles 112,500,000 (U.S. dollars 125,000,000). China agreed to supply equipment and technical help to assist the fulfilment of the third five-year plan. Besides this China supplied grain (purchased from Australia) to relieve a shortage due to three unsatisfactory harvests. Albania and China have signed a number of trade, cultural and military agreements in recent years.

Because of the withdrawal of Soviet assistance, the third five-year plan (1961–65) failed to be fulfilled by 3 per cent overall. The fourth five-year plan (1966–70) was fulfilled satisfactorily, and the fifth five-year plan (1971–75) has now been completed.

In several branches of industry and in regard to many important products the 1971–75 plans have been fulfilled and over-fulfilled. The tasks of the plan according to the respective branches were fulfilled as follows:

| | *Per cent* |
|---|---|
| Coal industry | 100 |
| Nickel | 104 |
| Copper | 102 |
| Engineering industry | 103 |
| Building material industry | 104 |
| Light industry | 103 |
| Food industry | 101 |

The genera /industrial production was fulfilled by 101 per cent achieving a four per cent rise as against 1974. In agriculture, during 1975, better advances were achieved than in any other year of the past 5-year plan. Thus, bread grains increased by about six per cent as against 1974 while the tasks of the wheat plan were overfulfilled by seven per cent. In other agricultural crops high indices were achieved: for example in cotton, sugarbeet, sunflowers, etc. Livestock production increased too. In 1975 as against 1974 more of the following were turned out: meat and milk five per cent, eggs eight per cent. The tasks of the plan were fulfilled in transport too which during 1975 fulfilled even better the demands of the economy for the transport of goods. The total volume of construction and assembly work foreseen by the plan increased by seven per cent as against 1974. The general volume of construction and assembly work envisaged in the plan registered a rise as against 1974 of seven per cent. The tasks of the 1975 plan for the construction of several major projects have entered their final phase, and during 1976 it is envisaged that those projects will go into operation. During 1975 education, culture, and the health service developed further in compliance with the needs of the economy and with the tasks set by the Party of Labour of Albania for the general educational and cultural elevation of the people and for the protection and insurance of their health.

Alongside the fulfilment in general of the tasks for the development of the people's economy and culture the tasks of the 1975 state budget with regard to national revenues were fulfilled by 99 per cent and expenditures by 96 per cent with a surplus of income over expenditure of 437 million leks.

In 1976 compared with 1975 total industrial output is expected to increase by 4·5 per cent. In 1976 it is also foreseen that the branches of the prediction of the means of production will increase their output by six per cent as against 1975. Very important tasks are set for the development of agriculture. Total agricultural production as against 1975 is foreseen to increase by 15 per cent. In 1976 as against 1975 the volume of construction and assembly work will increase by about six per cent.

The number of school pupils and students is expected to rise to 720,000. Important tasks are foreseen also for the increase in productivity through which about 30 per cent of the increase of industrial production will be achieved. In construction and assembly work productivity will increase by eight per cent. The state budget for 1976 has been worked out in compliance with the tasks of the plan for the economic and social development. It is foreseen that the budgetary revenue will increase by 2·4 per cent as against 1975 while expenditure will be six per cent greater. Expenditure for the sector of the people's economy represents 63·3 per cent of the total of expenditures of the state budget. Social and cultural expenditures 22·3 per cent: administrative apparatus 1·2 per cent: and for the country's defence 10·9 per cent.

## COMMUNICATIONS

The first standard-gauge railway was opened on 7 November 1947, and it covered a distance of 43 km. It connected the town and port of Durrës with Peqin via Kavaja. By 1970, Albania had a railway network with a total length of 205 km. including 10 km. of lines within industrial enterprises. A new line, some 50 km. long connecting Elbasan with Prenjas is at present under construction.

Between 1946 and 1969 about 2,300 km. of new first-class

roads were constructed, together with a further 2,400 km. of second- and third-class roads—increasing the 1945 total road network of 2,230 km. to approx. 7,000 km.

There is an oil pipe-line, connecting the Kuçova oilfields, near Berat, with the port of Vlora.

The general condition of roads is still unsatisfactory but plans are in hand to improve them to motor traffic standards.

The Italian airline, Alitalia, runs a regular weekly flight—Rome–Tirana. This is subsidized by the Italian government. There are also regular air services connecting Tirana with Belgrade, Berlin and Budapest.

In May 1973 a new tug-boat was launched at Durrës—30 km. long and with a speed of approximately 9 knots.

During the current Five Year Plan (1971–75) 25 steel ships will be built in the Durrës shipyards.

As a result of its expansion, the Albanian merchant navy could in 1973 carry seven times the volume of cargo possible in 1963.

On 8 December, 1973 it was announced that all Albanian villages were now linked to the telephone system—one year ahead of schedule.

Albania has the following ports: Shëngjin (San Giovanni di Medua). Durrës (Durazzo), Vlora (Valona), and Saranda (Porto Edda).

With the completion of the TV centre in Tirana, regular television transmissions began in 1971, initially for four hours daily.

### NEWSPAPERS

**Bashkimi.** Daily. Organ of the Democratic Front.

**Pioneri.** Weekly. Organ of the Union of Labour Youth.

**Hosteni.** Fortnightly. Satirical organ of the Union of Journalists.

**Zëri i Popullit.** Daily. Organ of the Party of Labour.

**Nëndori.** Monthly. Organ of the Union of Writers and Artists.

**Sporti Popullor.** Weekly. Organ of the Ministry of Education and Culture.

### HEALTH

In June 1973 a new spa was inaugurated at Leshovik, in south-eastern Albania. With 100 beds, this brings the number of Albanian spas to 6.

In May 1973 a new general hospital was opened in Rreshen, and in October 1973 a new pediatric hospital in Tirana and a maternity hospital in Vlora.

Among students who graduated from the State University of Tirana in 1973 were 413 doctors, dental surgeons and pharmacists.

In 1973 the Institute of Hygiene and Epidemiology produced a compound vaccine against diphtheria, tetanus and whooping cough, and a vaccine against cholera.

By the end of 1973 99·57 per cent of Albanian children had been vaccinated against measles.

By the end of 1973 every village in Albania had its own general clinic and child welfare clinic, and there was a cottage hospital and maternity hospital for every six villages. In addition every village had its own midwife.

In 1973 the Radiological Centre was opened, specialising in the use of radioactive isotopes in diagnosis and treatment.

By 1975 it is planned that there will be a doctor for every 850 inhabitants.

### EDUCATION

Ideological differences with the U.S.S.R. resulted in the return of Albanian students from Soviet schools and universities.

The first Albanian University was inaugurated in Tirana on 16 September 1957. Its official name is The State University of Tirana.

At the beginning of the school year in September 1973, 740,000 pupils and students enrolled in educational institutions—one in three of the population.

### ATOMIC ENERGY

On 23 August 1957, Albania became a member of the International Atomic Energy Agency. Albanian scientists are collaborating with the Chinese to produce Albania's first atomic weapon.

### RELIGION

There is no state religion in Albania. Islam claims 70 per cent of the population as Muslims, mainly of the Sunni and Bektashi sects; however, the conversion to Islam was imposed by the Turkish occupation authorities and was in large part a nominal one. The Catholic Church claims 10 per cent of the population as its adherents, mostly in the north, and the Greek Orthodox Church the remaining 20 per cent, mostly in the centre and south.

Since 1967 all religious buildings have either been demolished or transformed into cultural centres, except those considered to have historic or architectural importance, these being preserved as museums.

# Algeria

## (ALGERIAN DEMOCRATIC PEOPLE'S REPUBLIC)

**President**—Monsieur Houari Boumedienne.

**National Flag:** A crescent and star red on a field chequered white and green.

### CONSTITUTION AND GOVERNMENT

WITH the announcement of the result of the French Referendum held on 6–8 January 1961, the first stage of Algerian independence was concluded. The voting for the principle of Algerian self-determination was, in Metropolitan France, 15,200,073 in favour and 4,996,474 against; in Algeria itself the voting was for, 1,749,969; against, 767,546.

The military struggle for Algerian independence began seven years before (1954). A body known as the National Liberation Front, founded in 1954, organized active resistance to the French administration and army, and until the time of the cease fire there were open hostilities with the French. An attempt was made to delay independence by a secret organization of French officers and Civilians (OAS). This body was opposed to the policy of an independent Algeria.

The first free (extra-territorial) Algerian Government was formed in June 1958, in Cairo. This was appointed by a body known as The National Council of The Algerian Revolution. The provisional government Free Algerian President was Ferhat Abbas.

In the meantime negotiations of some kind had continued between the French and the Provisional Algerian Governments in spite of the highly disturbed state of the country. On 8 April 1962, a further referendum took place in France and Algeria concerning the Algerian settlement. The results were, for the settlement (independence of Algeria), 17,505,472 against, 1,794,553; abstentions, 6,580,772; spoiled votes, 1,102,477.

On 29 September 1962, the first territorial Algerian Government was formed. It was appointed by the Algerian Constituent National Assembly. Of its 179 members, 159 voted for the investiture of the Government.

On 19 June, 1965, Ben Bella was ousted from power and a new government formed under Colonel Houari Boumedienne.

At this moment a Council of the Revolution was formed. This council retains the sovereign authority.

#### Ministry

*President of the Council of the Revolution and of the Council of Ministers, Minister of Defence:* Houari Boumedienne.
*Minister of State:* Cherif Belkacem.

## ALGERIA

*Minister of Foreign Affairs:* Abdelaziz Bouteflika.
*Minister of Interior:* Colonel Abdelghani.
*Minister of Agriculture and Agrarian Reform:* Tayebi Larbi.
*Minister of State for Transport:* Rabah Ritat.
*Minister of Industry and Energy:* Belaid Abdessalem.
*Minister of Information and Culture:* Ahmed Taleb.
*Minister of Primary and Secondary Education:* Abdelkrim Ben Mahmoud.
*Minister of Higher Education and Scientific Research:* Mohamed Ben Yahia.
*Minister of Finance:* Smail Mahroug.
*Minister of Labour and Social Affairs:* Mohamed Mazouzi.
*Minister of Public Works:* Abdelkader Zaibek.
*Minister of Health:* Omar Boudjellab.
*Minister of Tourism:* Abdelaziz Maaoui.
*Minister of Justice:* Boualem Ben Hamouda.
*Minister of Commerce:* Layachi Yaker.
*Minister for Anciens Moudjahidines* (Veterans of War): Mahmoud Guennez.
*Minister of Youth and Sport:* Abdellah Fadel.
*Minister of Cultural and Original Education:* Mouloud Kassem.
*Minister of Posts and Telecommunications:* Said Ait Messaoudene.
*Under Secretary of State for Planning:* Kamed Abdullah Khodja.
*Under Secretary of State for Water:* Abdullah Arbaoui.

### AREA AND POPULATION

The area of Algeria is 2,381,000 sq. kilometres.

The population in mid-1974 was 15,215,000. The population of the *wilayas* (departments) was as follows:

Alger, 1,648,200; El Asnam, 789,600; Constantine, 1,513,000; Aurès, 765,000; Oran, 958,400; Saïda, 236,900; Tlemcen, 444,100; Saoura, 211,000; Annaba, 950,000; Sétif, 1,237,900; Mostaganem, 778,800; Tiaret Oasis, 362,000.

The annual average percentage population growth rate for the period 1960–74 was 3·2 and was 3·3 for the period 1965–74.

### CURRENCY AND FINANCE

The Algerian dinar, divided into 100 centimes replaced the franc in 1964

Budget figures for 1971 were (in million dinars): Revenue, 7,500; Expenditure, 4,900.

The GNP at market prices for 1974 was U.S. $ millions 11,100, and the GNP per capita at market prices for 1974 was U.S. $ 730. The annual average percentage growth rate of the GNP per capita for the period 1960–74 was 1·3 and for the period 1965–74 was 4·5. [*See the note at the beginning of this section concerning GNP.*]

### PRODUCTION, INDUSTRY AND COMMERCE

**Agriculture.** The coastal plains and valleys are very fertile and excellent crops are raised. Cereals are the most important.

The following table shows the allocation of agricultural lands at the completion of the first stage of the agrarian revolution at March 1973 in hectares:

| | |
|---|---|
| Total allocated area | 617,867 |
| Total number of beneficiaries | 43,784 |
| Groups for development: | |
| Number | 258 |
| Beneficiaries | 6,650 |
| Area | 59,291 |
| Individual parcels of land: | |
| Number | 1,120 |
| Area | 5,769 |
| Cooperatives for community exploitation: | |
| Number | 707 |
| Beneficiaries | 11,580 |
| Area | 97,583 |
| Cooperatives for production: | |
| Number | 1,349 |
| Beneficiaries | 24,434 |
| Area | 455,220 |

The following table shows the various uses to which agricultural land was put in the 1970–71 season in thousand has:

| | *Socialist sector* | *Private sector* | *Total* |
|---|---|---|---|
| Arable lands | 1,670 | 4,710 | 6,380 |
| Herbaceous cultivations | 999 | 2,300 | 3,299 |
| including cereals | 507 | 2,146 | 2,953 |
| Regenerating lands | 671 | 2,410 | 3,081 |
| Natural meadows | 13 | 20 | 33 |
| Vineyards | 252 | 40 | 292 |
| Orchards | 98 | 211 | 309 |
| Pastures and ranges | 264 | 35,119 | 35,383 |
| Unproductive lands | 71 | 299 | 370 |
| Total area: | 2,368 | 40,399 | 42,767 |

The following table shows the amount of agricultural produce for the year 1970–71 in thousands of quintals (for non-liquids) and in thousands of hectolitres for liquids, certain products figures are also given for the year 1971–72:

| | *Socialist sector* | *Private sector* | *Total* |
|---|---|---|---|
| Cereals | | | |
| Hard wheat | 2,709 | 5,231 | 7,940 |
| Soft wheat | 3,375 | 1,859 | 5,234 |
| Barley | 590 | 3,128 | 3,718 |
| Oats | 168 | 215 | 383 |
| Others (summer cereals) | 58 | 21 | 79 |
| Total: | 6,900 | 10,454 | 17,354 |
| Pulses | 242 | 245 | 487 |
| Potatoes | 1,271 | 1,466 | 2,737 |
| Tomatoes | 406 | 458 | 864 |
| Citrus (1971–72) | 4,695 | 636 | 5,331 |
| Olives (1971–72) | 508 | 1,241 | 1,749 |
| Dates (1971–72) | 114 | 1,487 | 1,601 |
| Figs | 36 | 475 | 511 |
| Tobaccos | 9 | 34 | 43 |
| Wines | 8,088 | 1,159 | 9,247 |
| Olive oil (1971–72) | 68 | 160 | 228 |

The following table shows in thousands of head, the livestock figures for 1971:

| | |
|---|---|
| Cattle | 922 |
| Sheep | 8,164 |
| Goats | 2,473 |
| Horses | 144 |
| Other equines | 431 |
| Camels | 184 |

**Mining.** The chief minerals are phosphates and zinc. The total mining output in 1963 was 1,950,000 tons. Total production capacity is estimated to be 3,500,000 tons.

**Oil.** The production of oil from the Sahara oilfields is continuing to increase. In 1967, 39,078,000 tons were produced as compared with 26,400,000 tons in 1964. The exports of oil are almost entirely to France and the other Common Market countries. Natural gas is an important item of export. 2,884,887 cubic metres were produced in 1966 and 1,593,672 cubic metres in the first six months of 1967.

**Livestock.** In 1967 in Northern Algeria there were 130,000 horses, 170,000 mules, 800,000 cattle, 2,321,700 goats, 7,130,000 sheep and lambs, and 300,000 asses.

**Fishing.** 4,000 people are engaged in fishing on 392 boats; in 1966 the total catch was 21,000 tons.

**Commerce.** The following table shows the value, in millions of Algerian dinar, of various groups of import and export commodities for the years 1971 and 1972.

| | 1971 | 1972 |
|---|---|---|
| Imports: | | |
| Food, drink, tobacco | 775 | 1,076 |
| Power, lubricants | 210 | 152 |
| Raw materials and semi-processed material | 428 | 450 |
| Semi-processed goods | 1,608 | 1,774 |
| Finished products: capital goods | 2,264 | 2,368 |
| consumer goods | 743 | 874 |
| Total | 6,028 | 6,694 |
| Exports: | | |
| Food, drink, tobacco | 514 | 536 |
| Power, lubricants | 3,149 | 4,816 |
| Raw materials and semi-processed material | 180 | 202 |
| Semi-processed goods | 123 | 123 |
| Finished products: capital goods | 198 | 132 |
| consumer goods | 43 | 45 |
| Total | 4,208 | 5,854 |

### COMMUNICATIONS

**Roads.** There are 18,200 kilometres of highways of which 8,900 kilometres are in the Saharan Departments.

**Railways.** Algeria has more than 4,000 kilometres of railway line open for passenger and goods traffic.

**Shipping.** In 1967 more than 16,000 merchant vessels entered Algeria's eight commercial ports carrying 3,650,000 tons of freight into the country and 18,690,000 tons out of it.

**Civil Aviation.** Services operated by CNAN = Compagnie Nationale Algerienne De Navigation. After independence an organization was set up to control the 65 airports and 135 private airports and to organize the safety control. In 1967 Air Algeria, the national airline, carried 367,016 passengers and 2,421,842 kilos of freight and mail. At present Air Algeria serves main centres within the country and in France, Further International links are being planned.

**Posts and Telephones.** There are 820 post offices in Algeria. Telephone subscribers number more than 60,000 and there are 1,188 exchanges.

### NEWSPAPERS

**El Moudjahid** Daily; Arabic. 2, Rue du Colonel Haouès, Algiers.

**Algerie-Actualite.** Daily; French. 20, Rue de la Liberté, Algiers.

**Revolution et Travail.** Weekly; Arabic and French. 48, Rue Khelifa Boukhalfa, Algiers.

**Revolution et Travail.** Daily; French. Maison du Peuple, Place du ler Mai, Algiers.

### EDUCATION AND RELIGION

Since Independence increased Arabization has been one of the aims of the education system. The teaching in primary schools is carried out almost entirely in Arabic. After the first three years of having been taught in Arabic, French is introduced as just another foreign language. In some secondary schools teaching is totally in Arabic, and in other secondary schools teaching is bilinguial with respect to Arabic and French. Big reforms are being effected in the Universities, with special regard to the economic and social needs of Algeria. The Universities offer courses in philosophy, psychology, sociology and literature, and law. In the teaching of law there are two distinct divisions, in one the teaching is entirely in French and in the other it is entirely in Arabic. Before Independence there was only one University and now there are three. Also most of the students are supported by Government grants. The technical college building programme is being constantly expanded.

The majority of the population is Moslem, with Europeans forming the main exception, in addition to a small Jewish community. There is a Roman Catholic archbishop and two bishops with about 400 clergy.

# Andorra

**Capital**—Andorra-la-Vella.

**National Flag:** A tricolour pale-wise, blue, yellow, red.

ANDORRA, officially known as Valls d'Andorra or Principat d'Andorra, comprises a group of valleys in the Central Pyrenees, enjoying a semi-independent and seignorial constitution of mediæval type. The seignorial rights are shared between the Spanish Bishop of Seu D'Urgell, Monsenyor Marti Alanis, and the President of the French Republic, representing the French State as successor to the rights of the Comte de Foix. The overlordship of this little country was for long in dispute between the Bishop of Seu D'Urgell and the Comte de Foix. It was made a Principality in 1278, and became a republic in 1806. The interest of the Comte de Foix passed to the kings of Navarre and through them to the French crown. The country is now administered by the General Council of the Valleys, consisting of 24 members, four of whom are elected from each of the six parishes. It is presided over by a Sindic, Sr. Julià Reig Ribó and a sub-Sindic who can be elected from the Council or from outside. The seigneurs are represented by two *Veguers* (vicars), who also act as a criminal court, along with the civil Judge of Appeal, two *Batlles* and two members of the council.

Civil disputes are dealt with by two *Batlles* appointed by the President of France and the Bishop. Appeals are dealt with by a judge appointed alternately by the seigneurs, and in the final instance by the Supreme Court of Andorra at Perpignan or by the Ecclesiastical Court of the Bishop of Seu D'Urgell.

Annual tributes are paid to the President of France (960 frs.) and to the Bishop of Seu D'Urgell (460 pesetas).

There is a good road connecting Andorra with the French and Spanish frontiers at Pas de la Casa and Farga de Moles respectively. There is a secondary road network which connects several villages of the country.

Andorra has an area of 465 square kilometres. Its length is 30 kilometres and its width 20 kilometres. The estimated population is 23,205 by the February 1973 Census, of whom about a third are native Andorrans.

Education, postal and telegraph services are provided by France and Spain. The country is linked with the rest of the world by automatic telephone service as well as telex.

The six cantons of Andorra are as follows: Canillo, Encamp, Ordino, Massana, Sant Julià de Lorià and Andorra-la-Vella.

Tourism is Andorra's main source of business; about two million visitors coming to the country each year. Cigarettes are made from locally grown tobacco. The Republic does a small import trade with Great Britain. Imports from the U.K. in 1971 amounted to at least £500,000, of which however a substantial proportion were imported through France. Direct exports from the U.K. to Andorra during the same period are not likely to have exceeded £150,000.

There are commercial broadcasting stations, 'Radio Andorra' and 'Sud-Radio', and a foreign owned hydro-electric generating station from which the owners export electricity.

Catalan is the official language but French and Spanish are also spoken.

The country has no official currency, but most transactions are carried out in Spanish Pesetas and French Francs, especially the former. The country's budget is expressed in Pesetas. There are no exchange restrictions and all currencies circulate freely.

# Angola

(REPUBLICA POPULAR DE ANGOLA)

**Capital**—Luanda (São Paulo de Luanda).

**President**—Dr. Agostinho Neto.

ANGOLA is on the west coast of Africa below the equator. It extends southward from the mouth of the Congo river for over 1,000 miles. It includes the territory of Cabinda, which runs for some eighty miles of coast north of the mouth of the Congo, but is separated from Angola itself by a strip of land along the north bank, where the Congo Republic pushes out to the Atlantic.

Angola became an independent country on 11 November 1975.

## AREA AND POPULATION

Angola covers an area of 1,246,700 sq. km. (over 481,000 sq. miles). The country is divided into 16 provinces: Kabinda, Zaire, Uige, Luanda, Kuanza Norte, Malange, Lunda, Benguela, Huambo, Bié, Moxico, Kuanza Sul, Moçamedes, Kuando Kubango, Huila and Kunene.

The population of Angola at mid-1974 was 6,050,000. The percentage population growth rate for the periods 1960–74 and 1965–74 was 1·4.

## CURRENCY AND FINANCE

The unit of currency is the Angola escudo at parity with the Portuguese unit.
The GNP at market prices for 1974 was U.S. $ millions 4,290 and the GNP per capita at market prices was U.S. $ 710. The annual average percentage growth rate of the GNP per capita for the period 1960–74 was 3·7 and for the period 1965–74 was 3·2. [*See the note at the beginning of this Section concerning GNP.*]

## PRODUCTION, INDUSTRY AND COMMERCE

Agriculture plays an important part in the life of the province, coffee, maize and sisal heading the list of exports. Angola is the fourth largest world coffee producer. Sugar, palm oil and cotton are also produced and exported in large quantities.

There are valuable diamond deposits, as well as copper, iron-tone and petroleum, manganese and mica.

There is as yet little industrial activity and the country has to import all machinery and nearly all textiles.

Imports and exports for 1973 are shown below (in thousand escudos) for the principal countries:

| *Country* | *Imports* | *Exports* |
|---|---|---|
| Portugal | 3,498,798 | 4,859,180 |
| Mozambique | 4,053 | 190,517 |
| Macao | 198,271 | 41 |
| West Germany | 1,726,327 | 968,288 |
| Belgo-Luxembourg | 452,992 | 211,948 |
| France | 893,075 | 283,199 |
| Netherlands | 330,755 | 482,119 |
| Italy | 503,245 | 215,886 |
| United Kingdom | 1,016,901 | 549,360 |
| Sweden | 219,418 | 18,000 |
| Switzerland | 194,290 | 56,475 |

*continued*

| *Country* | *Imports* | *Exports* |
|---|---|---|
| South Africa | 768,944 | 210,510 |
| Spain | 208,729 | 651,932 |
| Zaire | 9,641 | 363,000 |
| United States | 1,262,112 | 5,380,294 |

The following table shows the value of chief imports and exports for 1973 (in thousand escudos):

| *Commodity* | 1973 *Imports* | 1973 *Exports* |
|---|---|---|
| Live animals and animal products | 335,974 | 495,332 |
| Vegetable products | 620,456 | 5,975,078 |
| Fats and oils | 100,596 | 153,164 |
| Food, beverages, tobacco | 704,252 | 1,170,422 |
| Mineral products | 721,938 | 7,388,186 |
| Chemicals | 1,475,238 | 23,851 |
| Synthetic materials | 547,378 | 47,509 |
| Leather and leather products | 29,442 | 35,470 |
| Wood and wood products | 23,763 | 301,513 |
| Paper and paper products | 296,328 | 141,188 |
| Textiles | 1,391,338 | 1,143,743 |
| Misc. wearing apparel | 97,431 | 644 |
| Non-metallic mineral products | 16,814 | 1,999,553 |
| Machinery | 3,029,687 | 1,455 |
| Transport equipment | 1,801,076 | 8,370 |
| Precision instruments | 216,917 | 236,860 |
| Arms and ammunition | 14,703 | 90 |
| Misc. manufactures | 97,539 | 2,062 |
| Art works | 830 | 240 |

## COMMUNICATIONS

**Railways and Roads.** The internal railway system covers about 3,256 km. The country is linked up with Mozambique (East Africa) by a line starting at Benguela on the Atlantic coast, running through the southern tip of the Congo Republic across Zambia and Rhodesia and ending at Beira on the Indian Ocean. Angola is well provided with roads, totalling in length 35,500 km.

**Civil Aviation.** Airways cover over 14,000 km. There are services running from Luanda along the coast, southward to the end of the province at Port Alexandre and northward to Pointe Noire in the Congo Republic bloc. There are services north-east from Luanda to Brazzaville and to Kinshasu. There is also a line running inward from Benguela on the coast to the future capital Nova Lisboa and thence to Silva Porto and Vila Luso. It is intended to extend this service to the eastern frontier, where it will join a line to Elisabethville. From Luanda's international airport regular air connections are made to Maputo (Mozambique), S. Tomé e Príncipe, Lisbon, Algiers, Rome, Brazaville, Lagos, Libreville, Paris, and Moscow. TAAG (Angola Airways) is a national airline which also operates scheduled flights to most towns of the country.

**Shipping.** The main shipping ports are Luanda in the north and Lobito in the south.

# Argentina

(REPÚBLICA ARGENTINA)

**Capital.**—Buenos Aires.

**President**—Jorge Rafael Videla.

**National Flag:** A tricolour fesse-wise, light blue, white, light blue; the centre stripe charged with a sun in splendour gold with 32 rays, alternately straight and wavy.

## CONSTITUTION AND GOVERNMENT

THE independence of Argentina was declared in 1816 after a long war against Spanish rule. It was not, however, until 1853 that a Constitution was proclaimed and a stable government formed covering the whole country. Argentina declared war on Germany and Japan on 27 March 1945, and in April of that year General Farrell's revolutionary Government, which had deposed President Castillo, was recognized, after some delay, by the United States, Great Britain and other nations. Colonel Perón gained great influence in the Government, in which he was now Vice-President and Minister of War. He set himself to win the support of the working classes, but his attitude having antagonized sections of the army and the land-owning and business classes, in October 1945 he was forced to resign. Within a fortnight, however, Colonel Perón had assumed total power. He called for presidential elections in February 1946 and, having obtained a large majority of votes, was inaugurated as President on 4 June 1946. By 1952 he was in control of the country and had himself re-elected President for another period of six years, and promoted to the highest army rank—General of the Army.

After a period of nearly ten years, Perón was overthrown by a widespread military movement in September 1955 and fled the country.

After a short term as Provisional President of the Republic, nominated by a governing Junta created by the revolutionary forces, General Eduardo A. Lonardi resigned in favour of General Pedro Eugenio Aramburu who, with Rear-Admiral Isaac F. Rojas as Vice-President, made solemn promises that Argentina would return to its traditional democratic form of government. Nation-wide elections were held in 1958 and a Constitutional President, Dr. Arturo Frondizi, leader of the Intransigent Radical Party, was elected.

Following the Perónist victories in the elections of March 1962, the armed forces arrested Dr. Frondizi and the Chairman of the Senate, Dr. Guido, assumed the Presidency. The elections were later annulled and Congress declared to be in recess.

After 15 months of political uncertainty, new elections were finally held on 7 July 1963. These were won by the People's Radical Party, whose leader, Dr. Illía, assumed office as President on 12 October 1963.

Dr. Illía's government withstood pressures from right-wing military circles and Peronists, despite the ex-dictator's threatened return in 1964. The Peronists increased their representation in the lower house at the March 1965 elections.

Once again the military leaders were not prepared to tolerate such an increase of power for the Peronists and on 27 June 1966, the Army, supported by the Navy and Air Force, staged a coup d'état.

The temporary Junta of the three military commanders-in-chief dismissed President Illía and the Provincial Governors; the National and Provincial Legislatures were dissolved, as were also the political parties. A former Army Commander-in-Chief, Lt.-Gen. Juan Carlos Ongania, was appointed President, whereupon the Junta was dissolved. Brig.-Gen. Roberto Marcelo Levingston assumed office on 18 June 1970. The previous constitution, largely modelled on the Representative Federal System of the United States, was to remain in force insofar as it was consistent with the Statute and Objectives of the Revolution.

A general election was held on 11 March 1973. This was won by the 'Frente Justicialista de Liberation' (Coalition Party, whose head, Dr. Hector Campora, assumed the office of President on 25 May 1973. Dr. Campora resigned after being in office for six weeks. New Presidential elections were held on 23 September 1973. andGeneral Perón once again obtained a large majority of votes. Upon the death of General Perón in July 1974, Madam MariaP erón became President.

On 24 March 1976 the Armed Forces took over the government from the administration of Señora Perón.

### Ministry

*Minister of the Interior:* General de Brigada D. Albano E. Harguindeguy.
*Foreign Minister:* Vicealmirante D. Oscar A. Monte.
*Minister of Justice:* Brigadier Auditor, D. Julio Arnaldo Gómez.
*Minister of Defence:* Brigadier Mayor (RE), D. José María Klix.
*Minister of Economics:* Dr. José Alfredo Martínez de Hoz.
*Minister of Culture and Education:* Dr. Juan José Catalán.
*Minister of Labour:* General de Brigada, D. Horacio Tomás Liendo.
*Minister of Social Welfare:* Contraalmirante, D. Julio Juan Bardi.
*Minister of Planning:* General de División, Ramón G. Díaz Bessone.

## LEGAL SYSTEM

The legal system is administered by Federal and provincial courts, the former dealing only with cases of national or inter-provincial character. The Federal courts consist of a Supreme Court at Buenos Aires and Federal Appeal Courts in the major cities of the Interior—La Plata, Parana, Córdoba, Rosario, Bahia Blanca, Mendoza, Resistencia and Tucumán. In each Province there are a Supreme Court, courts of First Instance and minor courts.

### Supreme Court of Justice

Doctor Eduardo A. Ortiz Basualdo (President).

**Attorney General:** Doctor Enrique Carlos Petracchi.

## AREA AND POPULATION

| *Jurisdiction and region* | *Area (sq. kms.)* | *Population (thousands) (est.)* |
|---|---|---|
| **Whole Country** | 2,777,815 | 23,364 |
| Federal District (City of Buenos Aires) | 192 | |
| Province of Buenos Aires | 307,569 | 8,775 |
| ,, Chaco | 99,633 | 567 |
| ,, Corrientes | 89,355 | 564 |
| ,, Entre Rios | 76,216 | 812 |
| ,, Formosa | 72,066 | 234 |
| ,, Misiones | 29,801 | 443 |
| ,, Santa Fé | 133,007 | 2,136 |
| ,, Córdoba | 168,854 | 2,060 |
| ,, La Pampa | 143,440 | 172 |
| ,, San Luis | 76,748 | 183 |
| ,, Jujuy | 53,219 | 302 |
| ,, Salta | 154,775 | 510 |
| ,, Santiago del Estero | 135,254 | 495 |
| ,, Tucumán | 22,524 | 766 |
| ,, Catamarca | 99,818 | 172 |
| ,, La Rioja | 92,331 | 136 |
| ,, Mendoza | 150,839 | 973 |
| ,, Neuquén | 94,078 | 155 |
| ,, San Juan | 86,137 | 384 |
| ,, Chubut | 224,686 | 190 |
| ,, Rio Negro | 202,590 | 263 |
| ,, Santa Cruz | 243,943 | 84 |
| Territory of Tierra del Fuego | 20,710 | 8 |

**Chief Cities:** Buenos Aires, Rosario, Córdoba, La Plata, Tucumán, Mendoza, Santa Fé and Corrientes. Other important towns are Mar del Plata, Bahia Blanca and Paraná.

The population of the Federal Capital as at December 1962 was 2,994,565. That of Greater Buenos Aires is around 7 million.

### Vital Statistics

The total population figure for mid-1974 was 24,646,000. The annual average percentage population growth rate for the period 1960–74 was 1·5, and for the period 1965–74 was 1·5.

# ARGENTINA

## CURRENCY

From 1 January 1970 the new unit of currency, the 'Statute 18,188 Peso', came into force, being the equivalent of 100 of the old 'national currency pesos'. The 1 peso note and the coins of 50, 20 and 1 centavo of the new monetary unit are already in circulation. However, the notes and coins of the national currency peso are still legal tender, and are gradually being over-stamped with the value they now hold by virtue of the Statute 18,188, that is to say the hundredth part of the value printed on them. The actual exchange rate is 10·56 Statute 18,188 Pesos to the Pound Sterling (previously 840 national currency pesos). The rate of exchange in 1976 for the U.S. dollar was 1 U.S $ = ps250·00.

## FINANCE

The following table shows the national product and expenditure for 1975 in millions of pesos. The '$' in the sign for the pesos:

| | 1975 (*mill $*) |
|---|---|
| Gross domestic product | 381,654 |
| Gross domestic investment | 68,137 |
| Private consumption | 312,299 |
| Gross domestic product, per capita | 1,840 |

The GNP at market prices for 1974 was in millions U.S. $37,380, and per capita U.S. $1,520. The annual average percentage growth rate of the GNP per capita in U.S. $ for the period 1960–74 was 2·8 and for the period 1965–74, 2·9. [*Refer to note at beginning of this section concerning GNP.*]

## PRINCIPAL BANKS

**Banco Central de la República Argentina.** Est. 1935 Sole Bank of Issue for Argentina; all the share capital is owned by the state; Balance Sheet at 31 December 1960 showed assets ps 167,318,984,730; deposits accounts ps 27,208,523,230; banknotes in circulation ps 152,750,000,000; gold reserve (1962) ps 12,810,000,000. *Head Office:* Reconquista 258, Buenos Aires.

**Banco de la Nación Argentina.** Est. 1891; Balance Sheet at 31 December 1971 showed capital $220,365,000 and reserves $199,727,000. *Head Office:* Bartolomé Mitre 326, Buenos Aires; 217 Branches.

**Banco Nacional de Desarrollo.** Capital at 31 December 1974, $A400,000,000. Reserves $A378,704,681. *Head Office:* 25 de Mayo 145, Buenos Aires.

**Banco de la Provincia de Buenos Aires.** Balance Sheet at 31 December 1972 showed capital $246,000,000 and reserves $260,459,564·41. *Head Office:* San Martín 137, Buenos Aires. 226 Branches.

**Banco de Italia y Rió de la Plata, S.A.** (Chairman and Managing Director, Mr. M. Baratella), Est 1872; Balance Sheet at 30 November 1976 showed capital ps 2,205,886,086 and reserves ps 3,970,538,120. *Head Office:* Bartolomé Mitre 402/468, Buenos Aires. 68 Branches; Representative Office at Rome (Italy).

**Banco de Londres y America del Sud** (Bank of London and South America Ltd.). *Chief Office:* Reconquista 151, Buenos Aires.

**Banco Español del Rio de la Plata.** Est. 1935. Balance Sheet at 31 December 1962 showed capital $m/n. 250,000,000; reserves $m/n. 649,200,000. *Head Office:* Cangallo 402, Buenos Aires; 46 Branches and Agencies.

**The First National Bank of Boston.** Balance Sheet at 31 March 1971 showed capital $2,191,354; reserves $25,054,922. *Head Office:* Florida 99, Buenos Aires.

**The First National City Bank of New York.** Balance Sheet at 31 December 1964 showed capital $m/n. 30,000,000; reserves $m/n. 659,269,677. *Head Office:* Bartolomé Mitre 502, Buenos Aires.

**The Royal Bank of Canada.** Balance Sheet at 30 September 1965, showed capital $m/n. 12,000,000; reserves $m/n. 454,499,000. *Head Office:* San Martin 95, Buenos Aires.

## PRODUCTION, INDUSTRY AND COMMERCE

**Agriculture.** Argentina is one of the world's largest producers and exporters of agricultural and pastoral products. Of a total land area of approximately 700 million acres, farms occupy about 425 million. About 60 per cent of the farmland is in pastures, 10 per cent in annual crops, 5 per cent in permanent crops and the remaining 25 per cent in forest and wasteland. A large proportion of the land is still held in large estates devoted to cattle raising but the number of small farms is increasing. The principal crops are wheat, maize, oats, barley, rye, linseed, sunflower-seed, alfalfa, sugar and cotton. Argentina is preeminent in the production of beef, mutton and wool, being self-sufficient in basic foodstuffs and conducting a large export trade in many others. Pastoral and agricultural products provide more than 90 per cent of Argentina's exports and they originate mainly from the pampas or rich central plain which embraces the provinces of Buenos Aires, Santa Fé, Entre Ríos, Córdoba and La Pampa.

The following table gives some figures in connection with agricultural production in thousands of tons for the years 1959–60 and 1974–75:

| *Product* | 1959–60 *th. tons* | 1974–75 *th. tons* |
|---|---|---|
| Wheat | 5,837·0 | 5,970·0 |
| Maize | 4,108·0 | 7,700·0 |
| Linseed | 825·0 | 380·7 |
| Rice | 190·0 | 351·0 |
| Grain sorghum | 609·0 | 4,830·0 |
| Sunflower | 802·0 | 732·0 |
| Sugar cane | 10,089·0 | 16,000·0 |
| Grapes for wine-making | 1,996·4 | 3,100·0 |
| Cotton | 281·0 | 541·0 |
| Tobacco | 41·3 | 97·8 |
| Tea | 25·9 | 130·0 |
| Oranges | 484·0 | 783·0 |
| Apples | 431·0 | 608·0 |
| Pears | 112·8 | 97·2 |
| Wool | 192·0 | 155·0 |
| Fish | 100·0 | 277·6 |
| Beef meat | 1,892·8 | 2,448·0 |
| Cattle, as at 30 June, 1974 | | |
| Beef cattle (thous. head) | 43,509 | 56,300 |
| Sheep (thous. head) | 43,457 | 34,830 |

The area under wheat is now approximately 6½ million hectares and the area of maize at around 4·7 million hectares. Considerable progress has been made since 1945 in expanding the production of plantation crops such as rice, tea, sugar, tobacco, cotton, groundnuts and fruit and there are now exportable surpluses in some instances. The vine is cultivated in the provinces of Mendoza, San Juan and Río Negro and there is a large and growing wine industry centred on Mendoza. Olives, citrus and deciduous fruits are cultivated on a large scale.

The products of stock raising account for about 50 per cent of total exports; they include chilled, frozen and canned meat (of which the U.K. is the biggest single buyer), wool and hides.

Cattle raising is Argentina's oldest industry. Meat refrigeration is under state control exercised through the Argentine Meat Board, which extends its supervision to all stages of cattle raising, from breeding to distribution. The products of stock raising include wool (10 per cent of the world output), hides, horsehair and a wide range of by-products.

**Fishing.** The volume of fish caught in 1971 (including fresh water varieties and shellfish) amounted to 201,746 tons. The processing of fish was carried out by 196 establishments, which together produced, among other items, 15,489 tons of fish preserves and 19,198 tons of fishmeal.

**Mining.** Oil is found in many parts of the Republic and is obtained to a considerable extent at Comodoro Rivadavia (Chubut), Mendoza, Plaza Huincul (Neuquen), Tartagal (Salta), Tierra del Fuego and in other districts. A natural gas pipeline between Comodoro Rivadavia and Buenos Aires has been in operation since 1949. An oil pipeline from Campo Durán (Salta) to a refinery in San Lorenzo (Santa Fé) was put in service in March 1960 as was also a natural gas pipeline from the same source to the outskirts of Buenos Aires.

Coal, lead, zinc, tungsten, iron ore, sulphur, mica and salt are the chief minerals being exploited. There are small worked deposits of beryllium, manganese, bismuth, uranium, antimony, copper, kaolin, arsenate, gold, and silver. Coal production varies from 350,000 to 400,000 metric tons per year; this is produced at the Rio Turbio mine in the province of Santa Cruz.

**Industry.** Argentine industries received a powerful stimulus during World War II owing to the shortage of manufactured goods and the absence of foreign competition. The principal industries are meat refrigeration and packing, flour milling, sugar refining, wine making, oil extraction, textile, tobacco, chemical, rubber, glass and ceramics, vehicles and machinery and leather. Argentina has a new and expanding motor-car industry, mostly developed with foreign capital. There are 15 cement factories in operation.

**Commerce.** The following tables give estimated export and import values in million U.S$ for 1976:

| *Country* | 1976 |
|---|---|
| Brazil | 422 |
| Italy | 372 |
| Holland | 355 |
| United States | 270 |
| USSR | 219 |
| Japan | 209 |
| W. Germany | 205 |
| Cuba | 168 |
| Spain | 155 |
| United Kingdom | 121 |
| France | 103 |
| Mexico | 52 |

| *Country* | 1976 |
|---|---|
| United States | 537 |
| Brazil | 371 |
| W. Germany | 341 |
| Japan | 250 |
| Italy | 153 |
| United Kingdom | 129 |
| France | 106 |
| Bolivia | 98 |
| Switzerland | 69 |
| Canada | 49 |
| Holland | 44 |
| Belgium | 41 |

The following table shows production figures for various commodities for the years 1960 and 1975:

| *Commodity* | *Measure* | 1960 | 1975 |
|---|---|---|---|
| Petroleum | Thous. $m^3$ | 10,152·9 | 22,979·5 |
| Mineral coal (for sale) | Thous. tn. | 119·7 | 502·1 |
| Wine | Thous. hectol. | 15,826·0 | 21,400·0 |
| Sugar | Thous. tn. | 782·4 | 1,270·3 |
| Sulphuric Acid | Thous. tn. | 132.0 | 226·5 |
| Portland cement | Thous. tn. | 2,613·8 | 5,464·5 |
| Pig iron | Thous. tn. | 180·7 | 1,037·8 |
| Crude steel | Thous. tn. | 300·0 | 2,269·7 |
| Finished rolled iron | Thous. tn. | 773·1 | 2,899·3 |
| Quebracho extract | Thous. tn. | 126·3 | 67·6 |
| Iceboxes | Units | 225,875 | 239·7 |
| Automotive vehicles | Units | 89,338 | 240,049 |
| Tractors | Units | 20,229 | 19,120 |
| TV sets | Units | 125,000 | 282·0 |
| Cellulose pulp | Thous. tn. | 73·3 | 321·0 |
| Paper and cardboard | Thous. tn. | 290·8 | 750.0 |
| Motor petrol | Thous. $m^3$ | 2,635·3 | 5,186·1 |
| Gas oil | Thous. $m^3$ | 759·2 | 5,544·0 |
| Diesel oil | Thous. $m^3$ | 1,106·3 | 731·5 |
| Electric power from public power stations | Thous. kWh | 7,863 | 24,754·2 |

## COMMUNICATIONS

**Railways.** There are 42,000 km. of railways all of which are now state operated. In 1965, 23,460,000 tons of cargo and 481,779,000 passengers were carried. A direct weekly railway service was started in 1954 between Buenos Aires and Antofagasta, Chile, via Salta.

**Shipping.** The State-owned merchant fleet totals about 1,265,843 tons. In 1965, 12,000,000 tons of shipping cleared Argentine ports.

**Flota Mercante del Estado and Flota Argentina de Navegación de Ultramar**; have been amalgamated to form a state operated undertaking (E.L.M.A.); motor vessels 30, steam vessels 14; total tonnage 384,363 T.D.W. and Corrientes 389. *Services operated:* to Brazil, Chile, Caribbean, Gulf of Mexico, U.S. North Atlantic ports, Mediterranean, Northern Europe and the Near and Far East. *Head Office:* 25 de Mayo 459, Buenos Aires, Argentina.

**Civil Aviation.** There are numerous air-services between Argentina and South and Central American Republics, U.S.A. and the chief European countries. During 1970, Argentine Airways made 61,011 flights, carrying 2,607,400 passengers, and transported 292,787,000 tons/km. of goods.

**Aerolineas Argentinas (Empresa del Estado)**; President, Brigadier Jose Maria Klix; a state organization under the Secretary of State for Public Affairs and Transport. *Services operated:* Buenos Aires–Sao Paulo–Rio de Janeiro–Madrid–Rome–Frankfurt–London–Zurich. Buenos Aires–Sao Paulo–Rio de Janeiro–New York. Buenos Aires–La Paz–Lima–Miami. Buenos Aires–Santiago de Chile–Lima–Bogatá–Mexico–Los Angeles. Buenos Aires–Porto Alegre–Rio de Janeiro. Buenos Aires–Montevideo. Buenos Aires–Punta del Este. Buenos Aires–Asuncion de Paraguay. Buenos Aires–Santiago de Chile. Buenos Aires (Chile). *Head Office:* Paseo Colón 185, Buenos Aires, Argentina.

## NEWSPAPERS

**La Prensa.** 1869. Morning daily and Sundays. Avenida de Mayo 567, Buenos Aires. Owned by La Prensa Corporation. Publisher and Editor: Dr. Alberto Gainza Paz. Circulation 300,000.

**La Nación.** 1870. Morning daily and Sundays. San Martin 350, Buenos Aires. Editor: Dr. Bartolomé Mitre. Circulation 250,000.

**Clarin.** Morning daily and Sunday. Piedras 1743, Buenos Aires. Editor and owner: Dr. Roberto Noble. Circulation 420,000.

**La Razón.** 1905. Evening newspaper. Avenida de Mayo 729, Buenos Aires. Independent. Editor: Sr. Ricardo Peralta Ramos. Circulation 500,000.

**La Opinión.** Morning daily and Sunday. Reconquista 585, Beunos Aires. Director: Jacobo Timerman.

## ATOMIC ENERGY

Areas in Argentina are being exploited for atomic materials, and beryllium is being mined. A refinery at Ezéiza near Buenos Aires has already produced some refined uranium. The Argentine atomic Energy Commission carries out elementary atomic research in the Establishment at Buenos Aires. The latest published plans contemplate the building of two atomic power plants.

In 1958 progress had been made by the inauguration of Argentina's first reactor. It is a small research unit which came into operation on 20 January. The unit is producing a limited quantity of isotopes.

## EDUCATION

Primary education is compulsory and free in the State schools. In 1972 there was a Secondary School enrolment of 1,058,945 pupils and Elementary School enrolment of 3,699,007 pupils.

In 1972 there were twelve national universities, eight provincial universities and 24 private universities. In 1970 there were 297,529 university students.

Illiteracy, which stood as high as 35·1 per cent in 1914, has been reduced to 7·5 per cent.

## RELIGION

The Roman Catholic Church is recognized in the Constitution of the Republic, but all creeds are respected. About 93·6 per cent of the population belongs to the Roman Catholic faith.

# Australia

(MEMBER OF THE COMMONWEALTH)

**Capital**—Canberra.

**Sovereign**—H.M. Queen Elizabeth II.

**National Flag**: On the British Blue Ensign, a large star and Southern Cross white.

## CONSTITUTION AND GOVERNMENT

ON 1 January 1901 the colonies of New South Wales, Tasmania, Western Australia, South Australia, Victoria and Queensland were federated under the name of the 'Commonwealth of Australia'. The designation 'Colonies' was at the same time changed into that of 'States'.

On 7 December 1907 the Commonwealth and the State of South Australia entered into an agreement for the surrender to and acceptance by the Commonwealth of the Northern Territory. The Territory was formally transferred to the Commonwealth on 1 January 1911 and became the Northern Territory of Australia.

An area of 2,330 square kilometres of the State of New South Wales was transferred to the Commonwealth on 1 January 1911 as the seat of government of the Commonwealth, and became the Australian Capital Territory. It was increased on 4 September 1915 by an area of 70 square kilometres at Jervis Bay, New South Wales.

Under the provisions of the Commonwealth of Australia Constitution Act, 1900 government is based essentially on the British Parliamentary system. There are two Houses—a Senate and a House of Representatives. The Senate is composed of senators for each State, directly chosen by the people of the State voting as one electorate. Senators are chosen for a term of six years, but half retire at the end of every third year. An equal number of Senators is returned by each State. By an Act of 18 May 1948 their number was increased from 36 to 60. Two senators have since 1973 represented the Australian Capital Territory and the Northern Territory respectively.

The total number of the House of Representatives must be as near as possible double that of the Senate. The States are represented on a population basis, with a minimum of five members for each original State. The Northern Territory is represented by one member and the Australian Capital Territory by two members. Members are elected for the duration of Parliament, which is limited to three years. For the purpose of elections to the House of Representatives, each State is divided into single constituencies corresponding with the number of members. In both Houses members are elected by persons who have attained the age of 18 years. Voting is compulsory.

According to the Constitution any proposed law for the alteration of the Constitution must, in addition to being passed by an absolute majority of each House, be submitted to a referendum of the electors in each State, and must further be approved by a majority of the States and the electors who voted, before it can be presented for Royal Assent.

In theory, executive power is vested in the Governor-General, who is advised by an Executive Council over which he presides. In practice, policy is decided by the Ministers of State under the chairmanship of the Prime Minister. The Ministry is collectively responsible for the government of the country to the House of Representatives, and should resign if it ceases to command a majority there.

### Governor General

His Excellency Professor Sir Zelman Cowen Kt, CMG, QC.

### Cabinet (as at 20 December 1977)

*Prime Minister:* The Rt. Hon. John Malcolm Fraser, CH., MP.
*Deputy Prime Minister and Minister for Trade and Resources:* Douglas Anthony.
*Minister for Industry and Commerce:* Philip Lynch.
*Minister for Primary Industry:* Ian Sinclair.
*Minister for Administrative Services:* Senator Reginald Withers.
*Minister for Employment and Industrial Relations:* Anthony Street.
*Minister for Transport:* Peter Nixon.
*Treasurer:* John Howard.
*Minister for Education:* Senator John Carrick.
*Minister for Foreign Affairs:* Andrew Peacock.
*Minister for Defence:* James Killen.
*Minister for Social Security:* Senator Margaret Guilfoyle.
*Minister for Finance:* Eric Robinson.
*Minister for Aboriginal Affairs:* Ian Viner.
*Minister for Health:* Ralph Hunt.
*Minister for Immigration and Ethnic Affairs:* Michael MacKellar.
*Minister for Northern Territory:* Evan Adermann.
*Minister for Construction:* John McLeay.
*Minister for National Development:* Kevin Newman.
*Minister for Science:* Senator James Webster.
*Minister for Post and Telecommunications:* Anthony Staley.
*Attorney-General:* Senator Peter Durack.
*Minister for Productivity:* Ian MacPhee.
*Minister for Business and Consumer Affairs:* Walter Fife.
*Minister for Special Trade Representations:* Victor Garland.
*Minister for Environment, Housing and Community Development:* Raymond Groom.
*Minister for Home Affairs and Capital Territory:* Robert Ellicott.

### Non-Cabinet Ministers

*Attorney-General:* Senator Peter Drew Durack.
*Minister for Special Trade Negotiations with the European Economic Community:* The Hon. John Winston Howard, M.P.
*Minister for Health:* The Hon. Ralph James Dunnet Hunt, M.P.
*Minister for Immigration and Ethnic Affairs:* The Hon. Michael John Randall MacKellar, M.P.
*Minister for the Northern Territory:* The Hon. Albert Evan Adermann, M.P.
*Minister for Aboriginal Affairs and Minister assisting the Minister of Finance:* The Hon. Robert Ian Viner, M.P.
*Minister for Post and Telecommunications and Minister assisting the Treasurer:* The Hon. Eric Laidlaw Robinson, M.P.
*Minister for Construction:* The Hon. John Elden McLeay, M.P.
*Minister for Environment, Housing and Community Development:* The Hon. Kevin Eugene Newman, M.P.
*Minister for Science:* Senator The Hon. James Joseph Webster.
*Minister for the Capital Territory and Minister assisting the Prime Minister in The Arts:* The Hon. Anthony Allan Staley, M.P.
*Minister for Productivity, Minister assisting the Prime Minister in Women's Affairs, and Minister assisting the Minister for Employment and Industrial Relations:* The Hon. Ian Malcolm MacPhee, M.P.

## PARLIAMENT

### The Senate

*President:* Senator the Hon. Condor Louis Laucke

The State of the Parties at the end of July 1977 was as follows: Liberal Party, 28; National Country Party, 8; Australian Labor Party, 27; Independent, 1.

### House of Representatives

*Speaker:* Rt. Hon. B. M. Snedden, QC, MP.

The State of the Parties at the end of July 1977 was as follows:

Liberal Party, 68; National Country Party, 23; Australian Labor Party, 36.

## LOCAL GOVERNMENT

By the Commonwealth of Australia Act 1900 it was provided that each State of the Commonwealth shall, subject to the Constitution, continue as at the establishment of the Commonwealth, or, as at the admission or establishment of the State, as the case may be, until altered in accordance with the Constitution of the State. At the head of each State is a Governor representing the Sovereign; and a Cabinet represented by the Premier. The legislatures consist of upper and lower houses, except in the case of Queensland where the upper house was abolished in 1922. The functions discharged by the State Governors vary according to local conditions. General education, health, police, the operation of railways, transport undertakings and public utilities are generally administered by the State Governments.

## LEGAL SYSTEM

The judicial power in Australia is vested in the federal High Court of Australia, federal courts created by Parliament and State courts invested with federal jurisdiction.

The High Court has both original and appellate jurisdiction. It consists of a Chief Justice and six other Justices. Sittings are held in the capitals of the different States, the Court sitting in each State one or more times each year. The High Court functions as a general court of appeal from the Supreme Courts of the States and Territories.

Parliament has created four other federal courts: the Federal Court of Australia, the Federal Court of Bankruptcy, the Australian Industrial Court and the Family Court of Australia.

The judicial power of the States and Territories is vested in the Supreme Court and other courts of the respective States and Territories. Each State Supreme Court consists of a Chief Justice and a varying number of other Judges. The denominations and functions of intermediate and lower courts vary from State to State. All State courts of general State jurisdiction have also been vested with federal jurisdiction.

The judges of the federal courts are:

**High Court of Australia**

*Chief Justice:* Rt. Hon. Sir Garfield Edward John Barwick, GCMG.

**Federal Court of Australia**

*Chief Judge:* Hon. Sir Nigel H. Bowen.

**Australian Industrial Court**

*Chief Judge:*

**Federal Court of Bankruptcy**

Hon. Justice Charles A. Sweeney, CBE.
Hon. Justice Bernard B. Riley.

**Family Court of Australia**

*Chief Judge:* Vacant.

## AREA AND POPULATION

| State | Area (square kilometres) | Estimated 31 December 1976 Males (000's) | Females (000's) | Persons (000's) | Estimated 30 June 1976 (a) Males (000's) | Females (000's) | Persons (000's) |
|---|---|---|---|---|---|---|---|
| New South Wales | 801,600 | 2,464·2 | 2,468·7 | 4,932·9 | 2,455·8 | 2,458·4 | 4,914·3 |
| Victoria | 227,600 | 1,878·5 | 1,886·3 | 3,764·8 | 1,870·1 | 1,875·9 | 3,746·0 |
| Queensland | 1,727,200 | 1,067·6 | 1,053·9 | 2,121·5 | 1,063·2 | 1,048·5 | 2,111·7 |
| S. Australia | 984,000 | 633·4 | 635·3 | 1,268·7 | 629·9 | 631·7 | 1,261·6 |
| W. Australia | 2,525,500 | 603·2 | 580·5 | 1,183·7 | 596·8 | 573·0 | 1,169·8 |
| Tasmania | 67,800 | 205·1 | 204·2 | 409·3 | 204·1 | 203·3 | 407·4 |
| N. Territory | 1,346,200 | 57·4 | 46·5 | 103·9 | 56·2 | 45·2 | 101·4 |
| A.C.T. | 2,400 | 104·8 | 101·4 | 206·2 | 103·2 | 100·1 | 203·3 |
| Australia Total | 7,682,300 | 7,014·3 | 6,976·9 | 13,991·2 | 6,979·4 | 6,936·1 | 13,915·5 |

(a) Census results adjusted to allow for net under enumeration.

The estimated population in each State or Territory represents the population ascertained from the Census, plus recorded natural increase and recorded net gain from overseas migration for that State or Territory; gains and corresponding losses that result from movements between States and Territories are also taken into account insofar as they are recorded as transfers of State of residence under child endowment procedures or Commonwealth electoral procedures or are indicated by the results of any special count. Holiday, business or other similar short-term movements between States and Territories are not taken into account. As complete records of interstate migration are not available, the estimated State populations so derived are approximate, and are subject to revision when the actual population of each State is ascertained at the next census.

Capital city statistical divisions with their estimated populations at 30 June 1976: Sydney, 3,021,299, Melbourne, 2,603,578; Brisbane, 957,710; Adelaide, 900,379; Perth, 805,489; Hobart, 162,059; Canberra Statistical District, 214,678[(a)]; Greater Darwin, 43,344.

(a) Includes Queanbeyan in N.S.W. (18,920).

**Vital Statistics**

| | 1973 | 1974 | 1975 | 1976 |
|---|---|---|---|---|
| Marriages | 112,700 | 110,673 | 103,973 | [1]109,981 |
| Births | 247,670 | 245,177 | 223,012 | [1]227,645 |
| Deaths | 110,822 | 115,833 | 109,021 | [1]112,654 |

[1]preliminary

**Immigration and Emigration.** Permanent arrivals in 1976 amounted to 58,317 of whom 18,426 were citizens of U.K. and Ireland. Permanent departures totalled 26,733. In 1975 corresponding figures were 54,117 arrivals, including 18,286 citizens of U.K. and Ireland and 29,084 departures.

## CURRENCY

Decimal currency was introduced in February 1966. The unit is the dollar, which is divided into 100 cents. Notes are issued by the Reserve Bank in denominations of $1, $2, $5, $10, $20 and $50. The one-cent and two-cent coins are bronze, and the five-cent, ten-cent, twenty-cent and fifty-cent coins are cupro-nickel.

The total value of notes outstanding at 30 June 1977 was $3,290·8 million.

Since October 1968 the Royal Australian Mint in Canberra, opened in 1965, has been the only mint in Australia producing coins.

## FINANCE

Revenue and expenditure of the Commonwealth Consolidated Revenue Fund for 1976–77 and estimates for 1977–78 are given below (thousand $A):

| | 1976–77 | 1977–78 (est.) |
|---|---|---|
| Revenue | 21,436,302 | 24,404,326 |
| Expenditure | 21,436,302 | 24,404,326 |

Details of Expenditure (in thousand $A):

| | 1976–77 | 1977–78 (*est.*) |
|---|---|---|
| Debt charges | 696,051 | 916,611 |
| Departmental salaries and administration expenses | 3 123,145 | 3,371,211 |
| National Welfare Fund | 5,920,382 | 6,579,422 |
| Capital Works and Services | 978,673 | 736,374 |
| Payments to States | 6,696,135 | 7,289,697 |
| All other expenditure | 4,021,916 | 5,511,011 |
| Total Expenditure | 21,436,302 | 24,404,326 |

Details of Revenue (in thousand $S):

| | 1976–77 | 1977–78 (*est.*) |
|---|---|---|
| Customs | 1,273,521 | 1,408,000 |
| Excise | 2,485,792 | 2,792,500 |
| Sales tax | 1,650,318 | 1,865,000 |
| Income taxes | 13,974,480 | 15,985,000 |
| Pay roll tax | 21,298 | 23,500 |
| Estate duty | 76,044 | 80,000 |
| Gift duty | 11,486 | 13,000 |
| Other items | 1,943,363 | 2,237,326 |
| Total Revenue | 21,436,302 | 24,404,326 |

## PRINCIPAL BANKS[1]

**Australia and New Zealand Banking Group Limited.** (Chairman, Mr. A. Mackinnon, DSO, MC.) Consolidated balance sheet at 30 September 1975 showed assets $A7,501,998 million; deposits, current accounts, etc. $A5,585,564 million. Over 1100 branches in Australia, New Zealand, Fiji, Papua New Guinea, Solomon Islands and New Hebrides. Subsidiaries include Australia and New Zealand Savings Bank Limited; Deposits, etc. $A1,334·8 million and Esanda Limited: Borrowings $527·6 million. *Administrative Headquarters:* 351 Collins Street, Melbourne, 3000. *Registered Office:* 71 Cornhill, London EC3V 3PR.

**Australia and New Zealand Savings Bank Limited.** (Chairman, C. H. Rennie.) Balance sheet at 30 September 1974 showed total assets $1,155·7 million; depositors' balance $1,082·1 million. *Head Office:* 394–396 Collins Street, Melbourne 3000. 1,176 branches and agencies in Australia.

**Bank of Adelaide.** (Chairman, The Hon. Sir Arthur Rymill, MLC.) Est. 1865. Balance sheet at 30 September 1974 showed assets $294·5 million; deposits and current accounts $206·4 million. *Head Office:* 81 King William Street, Adelaide, 5001. 98 branches and 74 agencies.

**Bank of Adelaide Savings Bank Limited.** (Superintendent J. S. Hiller.) Est. 1962. Balance sheet at 30 September 1976 showed total assets $137·5 million; depositors' balances $129·3 million. *Head Office:* 81 King William Street, Adelaide, 5000. 101 branches and 163 agencies in Australia.

**Bank of New South Wales.** (President, Sir John Cadwallader.) Est. 1817. Balance sheet at 30 September 1974 showed assets $7,511 million; deposits and current accounts, $6,073 million. *Head Office:* 60 Martin Place, Sydney. 1,310 branches and agencies in Australia.

**Bank of New South Wales Savings Bank Limited.** (Chief Manager, J. W. Twycross.) Ext. 1956. Balance sheet at 30 September 1975 showed total assets $A2,023·8 million; depositors' balances $A1,922 million. *Head Office:* 60 Martin Place, Sydney 2000. 3,718 branches and agencies in Australia.

**C.B.C. Savings Bank Limited.** (General Manager, V. E. Martin.) Balance sheet at 30 June 1976 showed total assets $693·2 million; depositors' balances $653·6 million. *Head Office:* 343 George Street, Sydney 2000. 545 branches and 108 sub-branches and receiving offices in Australia.

**The Commercial Bank of Australia, Limited.** (Managing Director, D. W. Stride.) Balance sheet at 30 June 1974 aggregate assets $2,996·9 million; deposits and current accounts $1,866·4 million. 768 branches and agencies of which 107 are in New Zealand, two in the United Kingdom, one in the New Hebrides and a Representative Office in Japan, Singapore and New York. *Head Office:* 335–9 Collins Street, Melbourne; Chief Office in New Zealand: 328–30 Lambton Quay, Wellington.

**Commercial Banking Company of Sydney Limited.** (Chairman, Sir Gregory B. Kater.) Est. 1834. Consolidated balance sheet at 30 June 1974 showed assets $2,689 million; Trading Bank deposits and other accounts $1,192 million. *Head Office:* 343 George Street, Sydney, 2000. 633 branches and receiving offices in Australia.

**Commonwealth Banking Corporation.** (Chairman, Professor L. F. Crisp; Managing Director, R. S. Elliot.) Est. 1960. Controlling body for its three member banks, the Commonwealth Trading Bank of Australia, Commonwealth Savings Bank of Australia and Commonwealth Development Bank of Australia. *Head Office:* Martin Place, Sydney 2000.

**Commonwealth Development Bank of Australia.** (General Manager, Alwyn Richards.) Est. 1959. Member bank of Commonwealth Banking Corporation. Balance sheet at 30 June 1976 showed assets $381·4 million, capital $61·7 million. *Head Office:* First Floor, Prudential Building, 39 Martin Place, Sydney 2000. Branches in State Capital Cities and agents throughout Australia.

**Commonwealth Savings Bank of Australia.** (General Manager, I. R. Norman.) Est. 1912, Member bank of Commonwealth Banking Corporation since 1960. Balance sheet as at 30 June 1976 showed total assets $5,738·1 million; depositors' balances $5,430·9 million. *Head Office:* Martin Place, Sydney 2000. 7,461 branches and agencies.

**Commonwealth Trading Bank of Australia.** (General Manager, J. F. Lavan.) Est. 1953. Member bank of Commonwealth Banking Corporation since 1960. Balance sheet as at 30 June 1976 showed assets $4,741·1 million; deposits and current accounts $4,634·3 million. *Head Office:* Martin Place, Sydney 2000. 1,226 branches and agencies.

**Martin Corporation Group Ltd.** (Chairman, Sir James Vernon; Managing Director, D. S. Nicol.) Est. 1966. Assets as at 31 August 1976, were $A92,000,000; deposits and current accounts $A83,000,000. *Head Office:* 22nd Floor, Goldfields House, 1 Alfred St., Sydney, N.S.W. 2 branches.

**The National Bank of Australasia Limited** (and its wholly owned subsidiary The National Bank Savings Bank Ltd.). (Chairman, Sir James Forrest.) Est. 1858. Balance sheet at 30 September 1976 showed assets $5,610,386,000; depositors' balances $3,834,300,000. *Head Office:* 31 Queens Street, Melbourne 3000. 881 branches and agencies in Australia.

**National Bank Savings Bank Limited.** (Chairman, Sir James Forrest.) Balance sheet at 30 September 1973 showed total assets $623 million; depositors' balances $594·4 million. *Head Office:* 271–285 Collins Street, Melbourne 3000. 1,220 branches and agencies in Australia.

**Reserve Bank of Australia.** (Governor, Mr. H. M. Knight). Est. 1911 as Commonwealth Bank of Australia and reconstituted under Reserve Bank Act 1959. Sole bank of issue for Australia and Territories. Balance Sheet at 30 June 1976 showed assets $6,370·7 million; deposits and other accounts $2,967·4 million. Australian notes on issue $2,921·4 million. A gold reserve against issue is not required. *Head Office:* 65 Martin Place, Sydney 2000.

**State Bank of South Australia.** (General Manager, Mr. J. C. Taylor; Chairman, Mr. G. F. Seaman, CMG. B.Ec, AUA, FASA.) Est. 1896. Assets as at 30 June 1976, $374,280,795. *Head Office:* 51 Pirie Street, Adelaide, S.A. 5000, Australia. 52 branches.

**The Savings Bank of South Australia.** (General Manager, A. G. Shepherd, A.A.S.A.; Chairman, R. D. Bakewell, B.Sc. (Econ.), FRIPA, FAIM). Est. 1848, Total funds at 30 June 1977, $914,704,000; depositors balances $842,842,000. *Head Office:* 97–105 King William St., Adelaide, South Australia. 143 branches.

[1] All dollar figures refer to Australian dollars.

## PRODUCTION, INDUSTRY AND COMMERCE

**Agriculture.** The total area under cultivation in 1975–76 amounted to 14,640,000 hectares, of which 8,633,000 grew wheat. Principal crops with areas and production (1975–76) are shown as follows:

| *Crop* | *Area in millions of Hectares* | *Production millions of tonnes* | |
|---|---|---|---|
| Wheat (for grain) | 8·6 | 12·0 | tonnes |
| Oats | 1·0 | 1·1 | ,, |
| Maize | 0·05 | 0·1 | ,, |
| Hay | 0·2 | 0·7 | ,, |
| Sugar cane | 0·3 | 22·0 | ,, |
| Barley | 2·3 | 3·2 | ,, |
| Sorghum | 0·5 | 1·1 | ,, |

There were, in 1975–76, 63,061 bearing hectares of grapes, producing 268,848 tonnes of drying grapes (fresh weight); 22,069 tonnes of table grapes and 418,490 tonnes of wine grapes. Wine production was 231,792,000 litres.

Pastoral production and in particular sheep farming are of prime importance in Australia's economy. Wool alone contributes about one-tenth of the total value of Australian exports.

The following table gives agricultural production figures for 1975–76:

| *Commodity* | *Unit* | 1975–76 |
|---|---|---|
| Wool | '000 tonnes | 754 |
| Whole milk | 1,000 litres | 6,257,082 |
| Butter | 1,000 kg | 147,635 |
| Cheese | ,, | 112,617 |
| Condensed milk | ,, | 72,387 |
| Powdered milk | ,, | 199,838 |
| Beef and veal | tonnes | 1,840,415 |
| Mutton and lamb | ,, | 587,720 |
| Pork | ,, | 173,825 |
| Bacon and ham | | |
| Bone-in | ,, | 15,986 |
| Bone-out (Includes canned bacon and ham.) | ,, | 38,531 |
| Apricots | ,, | 26,202 |
| Apples | ,, | 274,831 |
| Bananas | ,, | 97,080 |
| Citrus fruits | ,, | 443,599 |
| Peaches | ,, | 79,066 |
| Pears | ,, | 140,143 |
| Plums and prunes | ,, | 26,504 |
| Pineapples | ,, | 102,935 |

At 31 March 1976 there were 33,434,000 cattle, 148,643,000 sheep and 2,173,000 pigs.

**Forestry.** Australia's forest areas are concentrated mainly around the wetter coastal belts and eastern highlands which receive rainfall sufficient for the growth of commercial timber. The trees are predominantly evergreen hardwoods of the genus Eucalyptus which includes forest giants such as Mountain Ash (*Eucalyptus regnans*) in the south-east of the continent and Karri (*Eucalyptus diversicolor*) in the west.

Forest reserves are adequate to provide for current needs for native hardwoods, but a quantity of hardwoods for special purposes is imported. The respective State and Australian Forest Authorities pursue an active policy of afforestation with exotic and indigenous softwoods in order to reduce Australia's present dependence on imported softwoods.

Estimated local value of forestry production for 1975–76 was $209·3 million. This figure includes the value of logs, hewn timber (including hewn sleepers), and other forest products such as charcoal, eucalyptus oil, sandalwood and substitutes, gums and tanning bark.

A new development in the forestry industry has been the establishment in recent years of four woodchip plants all of which are exporting chips to Japan.

During 1975–76 wood pulp production was 576,958 tonnes of chemical, mechanical and other pulp. Paper and paper board are manufactured throughout Australia, although the industry is centred chiefly in Victoria, Tasmania, and New South Wales. A wide range of products is manufactured including newsprint, wrapping, printing, writing and other papers and a variety of paper boards. Other manufactured timber products include plywood, veneers and manufactured boards.

Sawn timber output from all Australian mills for 1975–76 was 3,462,000 cubic metres.

**Fishing.** Fish stocks in Australian waters, although varied in species, are small by comparison with the stocks of the Northern Hemisphere. In 1975–76, 57,097 tonnes live weight of fish, 33,874 tonnes gross weight of crustaceans and 21,618 tonnes in-shell weight of molluscs were taken. The main types of fish taken were: Tuna, Shark, Mullet, Flathead, Australian Salmon, Mackerel, Whiting, Snapper, Ruff, and Morwong. Australian imports of edible fisheries products during 1975–76 totalled $68·7 million. The total value of Australian exports of edible fisheries products during 1975–76 was 83·1 million. Rock lobster exports amounted to approximately 46 per cent of this amount.

Pearl and trochus shell are taken in the tropical waters off northern Australia, with catches of 396·4 tonnes of pearl shell and manufacturing shell produced from pearl culture operations in the 1975 season.

Whaling was restricted to one shore-based station in W. Australia. In 1976, 995 whales were taken which produced 35,190 barrels of oil, to the value of $A2,240,000.

The local value of the recorded production of the fisheries industry, including whaling, was $A137,348,000 in 1975–76.

**Industry.** The following table shows the value added in manufacturing and gas and electricity establishments 1973–74 and 1974–75.

| *Industry Sub-division* | *$A million* 1973–74 | 1974–75 |
|---|---|---|
| Food, beverages and tobacco | 2,126 | 2,651 |
| Textiles, clothing and footwear | 1,157 | 1,106 |
| Wood, wood products and furniture | 753 | 845 |
| Paper and paper products, printing | 1,111 | 1,279 |
| Chemical, petroleum and coal products | 1,076 | 1,173 |
| Non-metallic mineral products | 664 | 768 |
| Basic metal products | 1,331 | 1,638 |
| Transport equipment | 1,337 | 1,611 |
| Fabricated metal products; other machinery and equipment | 2,861 | 3,378 |
| Miscellaneous manufacturing | 733 | 790 |
| Total manufacturing | 13,149 | 15,240 |
| Gas | n.a. | 1,235 |
| Electricity | n.a. | 151 |
| Total *Value Added*[1] | n.a. | 16,626 |

[1] Sales, transfers out, and other operating revenue, plus increase (or less decrease), in the value of stocks, less purchase, transfers in and selected expenses.

**Mining.** The full extent of Australia's mineral wealth is not known, since large areas have not yet been systematically prospected.

The following table shows the principal metallic content of minerals produced, and the production of coal, crude oil and natural gas for 1974–75 and 1975–76.

| *Mineral* | *Unit* | 1974–75 | 1975–76 |
|---|---|---|---|
| Copper | tonne | 235,590 | 218,296 |
| Lead | ,, | 416,500 | 396,664 |
| Zinc | ,, | 508,174 | 479,263 |
| Tin | ,, | 10,168 | 9,685 |
| Nickel | ,, | 49,106 | 80,953 |
| Bauxite[1] | thousand tonne | 22,205 | 19,755 |
| Iron | ,, | 60,860 | 58,263 |
| Tungsten ($WO_3$ content) | tonne | 1,576 | 2,124 |
| Gold | thousand grams | 15,061 | 16,901 |
| Silver | ,, | 729,913 | 721,544 |
| Titanium ($TiO_2$ content) | tonne | 839,720 | 889,460 |
| Zircon ($ZrO_2$ content) | ,, | 322,299 | 316,131 |
| Coal (black) | thousand tonne | 70,142 | 69,269 |
| Coal (brown) | ,, | 24,441 | 26,711 |
| Crude oil | thousand cu. m. | 23,096 | 23,839 |
| Natural gas | mil cu. m. | 4,633 | 5,172 |

[1] Quantity shown is gross output.

Total value added of the mining industry in 1974–75 was $A2,650·1 million and in 1975–76 $A3,076·0 million.

**Overseas Trade.** The value of Australia's exports was $A9,600,748,000 in 1975–76 compared with $A8,725,774,000 in 1974–75; the values of Australian imports for the same periods were $A8,240,187,000 and $A8,079,853,000 respectively, yielding trade surpluses of $A1,360,561,000 for 1975–76 and $A645,921,000 for 1974–75.

## AUSTRALIA

The following table shows the value of principal articles exported in 1973–74, 1974–75 and 1975–76 (in thousand $A):

| *Description* | 1973–74 | 1974–75 | 1975–76 |
|---|---|---|---|
| Butter | 41,880 | 33,833 | 63,659 |
| Cheese | 28,936 | 34,639 | 35,177 |
| Milk and cream | 73,539 | 87,511 | 86,798 |
| Barley | 68,463 | 186,682 | 200,827 |
| Wheat | 517,114 | 1,027,947 | 921,492 |
| Flour (plain white) | 20,196 | 48,993 | 38,458 |
| Meat and meat preparations | 795,212 | 443,767 | 667,907 |
| Fruit and vegetables | 111,884 | 99,208 | 103,964 |
| Sugar (cane) | 223,315 | 644,499 | 569,835 |
| Hides and skins | 150,574 | 104,196 | 146,339 |
| Wool | 1,156,564 | 753,492 | 961,900 |
| Coal | 348,397 | 721,466 | 1,023,455 |
| Iron ore concentrates | 498,664 | 706,404 | 770,998 |
| Lead ores and concentrates | 19,445 | 13,223 | 19,044 |
| Zinc ores and concentrates | 45,631 | 58,872 | 62,224 |
| Titanium and zirconium | 73,703 | 127,217 | 130,792 |
| Lead and lead alloys | 120,675 | 132,038 | 111,129 |
| Zinc and zinc alloys | 69,809 | 78,526 | 70,816 |

The following table shows the value of imports for 1974–75 and 1975–76 (in thousand $A):

| *Commodity* | 1974–75 | 1975–76 |
|---|---|---|
| Food and live animals | 302,492 | 274,812 |
| Beverages and tobacco | 74,566 | 90,164 |
| Crude materials, inedible, except fuels | 389,868 | 387,382 |
| Mineral fuels | 724,312 | 806,926 |
| Animal and vegetable oils and fats | 43,272 | 42,293 |
| Chemicals | 785,997 | 709,240 |
| Manufactured goods | 1,495,625 | 1,460,061 |
| Machinery and transport equipment | 3,059,258 | 3,177,195 |
| Miscellaneous manufactures | 960,641 | 1,049,952 |
| Unclassified commodities and transactions | 124,650 | 159,654 |
| Total merchandise trade | 7,960,683 | 8,157,681 |
| Non-merchandise trade | 119,170 | 82,506 |
| Total imports | 8,079,853 | 8,240,187 |

The following table shows imports into Australia from principal countries for 1974–75 and 1975–76 (in thousand $A f.o.b.):

| *Country of Origin* | 1974–75 | 1975–76 |
|---|---|---|
| Belgium–Luxembourg | 73,026 | 69,969 |
| Canada | 217,100 | 204,080 |
| China—excl. Taiwan Province | 81,150 | 68,942 |
| —Taiwan Province only | 113,103 | 134,223 |
| France | 139,838 | 138,766 |
| Germany, Federal Republic of | 580,039 | 543,618 |
| Hong Kong | 172,240 | 216,512 |
| India | 57,840 | 50,053 |
| Italy | 208,818 | 192,230 |
| Japan | 1,420,862 | 1,609,559 |
| Kuwait | 118,618 | 125,817 |
| Malaysia | 58,800 | 82,116 |
| Netherlands | 123,399 | 129,258 |
| New Zealand | 183,910 | 250,510 |
| Papua New Guinea | 34,179 | 36,399 |
| Saudi Arabia | 171,136 | 236,020 |
| Singapore | 126,905 | 160,319 |
| Sweden | 183,229 | 166,982 |
| Switzerland | 104,790 | 105,352 |
| United Kingdom | 1,214,426 | 1,108,680 |
| United States of America | 1,668,181 | 1,655,802 |

The following table shows exports to principal countries for 1973–74, 1974–75 and 1975–76 (in thousand $A f.o.b.):

| *Country* | 1973–74 | 1974–75 | 1975–76 |
|---|---|---|---|
| Belgium–Luxembourg | 59,379 | 73,543 | 125,262 |
| Canada | 173,465 | 288,906 | 243,617 |
| China—excl. Taiwan Province | 162,550 | 253,967 | 219,791 |
| —Taiwan Province only | 76,505 | 80,950 | 114,143 |
| Egypt, Arab Republic of | 76,401 | 134,573 | 162,754 |
| France | 199,060 | 175,069 | 206,545 |
| Germany, Federal Republic of | 181,287 | 308,503 | 294,518 |
| Hong Kong | 114,074 | 105,179 | 147,392 |
| Indonesia | 106,467 | 175,251 | 161,331 |
| Italy | 132,816 | 150,042 | 206,671 |
| Japan | 2,158,141 | 2,396,265 | 3,162,722 |
| Korea, Republic of | 54,772 | 123,215 | 120,224 |
| Malaysia | 117,637 | 194,370 | 172,735 |
| Netherlands | 89,430 | 145,898 | 173,196 |
| New Zealand | 449,085 | 529,270 | 455,297 |
| Papua and New Guinea | 133,042 | 193,806 | 174,719 |
| Philippines | 79,228 | 99,721 | 93,517 |
| Singapore | 147,677 | 206,480 | 185,334 |
| South Africa, Republic of | 90,280 | 97,861 | 90,958 |
| United Kingdom | 457,499 | 474,838 | 406,083 |
| United States of America | 749,797 | 831,496 | 968,322 |
| U.S.S.R. | 154,215 | 243,086 | 372,783 |

### COMMUNICATIONS

*Minister:* The Hon. P. J. Nixon, MP.
*Secretary:* C. C. Halton.

The Department is an Australian Government Department with responsibilities which include:

*Air Transport.* Investigate aircraft accidents, incidents and defects, and enforce safety regulations; Administration of Air Navigation Charges Scheme; the rationalization and licensing of air transport services; approval of fares, freight rates and timetables for airline operations and administration of financial arrangements in relation to airlines; issue of approvals for export of aircraft and permits for import of aircraft and administration of aircraft acquisition policies; negotiation and administration of international air transport agreements and the regulation of international flights and air services; assisting in the formulation of policy relating to airlines which are authorities of the Australian Government or in which the Australian Government is a share holder; provision, operation and maintenance of air navigation facilities; functional design, operations and maintenance of aerodromes and related facilities and arranging for their provision in collaboration with other departments; licensing and authorization of places for use as aerodromes; control of buildings and marking of obstructions likely to endanger air navigation in the vicinity of aerodromes; determining the rules of the air and general conditions of flight over Australian Territory; establish standards and certify airworthiness requirements for aircraft; approve and supervise aircraft design; licensing of flying school and training organizations and supervision of their activities; licensing of pilots, navigators, radio operators, flight engineers and aircraft maintenance engineers and technicians and supervision of licenced personnel; provision, operation and maintenance of aeronautical communications systems; specify and make arrangements for provision of meteorological services; establish and operate air traffic control, aeronautical information and search and rescue services; establish policy and implement procedures relating to noise abatement and security on and in the vicinity of aerodromes; development of business concessions and control of surface traffic at airports.

*Surface Transport.* Administration of the Commonwealth grants for roads; research into road safety especially in the development of vehicle safety and pollution standards and uniform traffic codes, and the implementation and administration of policy arising from the handling of explosives and transport of dangerous goods; development of Australian and State railway systems; standardization of railway gauges; programme specific grants to the States for urban transport improvement projects; investigation and development of suitable plans; formulation of policy in regard to overseas and coastal shipping; including the licensing of vessels to trade on the Australian coast; provision of adequate shipping services to meet the needs of the export trade; oversight manning of Australian ships and the examination of sea-going personnel; surveys of ships to ensure compliance with international safety and pollution regulations; investigations on behalf of Courts of Marine Inquiry; provision, installation and maintenance of maritime navigational aids; oversight the functioning of the National Plan (Oil Pollution); operate the Marine Search and Rescue Centre; develop maritime communications and traffic separation systems; objective appraisals and studies of the economics of surface transport.

*Australian Transport Advisory Council:* administration of this Council (comprising State Ministers for Transport, the Ministers for the Capital Territory and the Northern Territory, with the Australian Minister for Transport as Chairman) which advises the Australian and State Governments on transport problems and policies, seeks to promote coordination in transport development, and carries out research into matters affecting transport in Australia.

There are five Statutory Authorities responsible to the Minister for Transport.

Australian Shipping Commission: operating as Australian National Line. Responsible on behalf of the Australian Government for the management and operation of its own commercial ships.

Australian National Airlines Commission: operating as Trans-Australia Airlines. Responsible on behalf of the Australian Government for the management and operation of its own commercial aircraft.

Australian National Railways Commission: management and operation of the Railways owned by the Australian Government, and the Tasmanian Railways and non-metropolitan railways of South Australia which now come under the control and management of the Commonwealth government.

Commonwealth Bureau of Roads: investigation of matters related to roads and road transport for the purpose of assisting the Australian Government in considering financial assistance to States or for other Australian Government purposes.

Road Safety and Standards Authority: promotion of Road Safety promotion of means for control of vehicle emissions and consumer protection in relation to motor vehicles.

The principal ports are: Sydney, Botany Bay, Newcastle, Port Kembla (New South Wales); Melbourne, Geelong, Westernport, Portland (Victoria); Brisbane, Gladstone, Weipa, Townsville, Hay Point (Queensland); Port Adelaide, Whyalla, Port Stanvac, Port Lincoln, Port Pirie (South Australia); Fremantle, Dampier, Port Hedland, Kwinana, Yampi Sound, Geraldton, Albany, Bunbury, Cape Lambert (Western Australia); Hobart, Burnie, Launceston, Devonport, Port Latta (Tasmania); Darwin, Gove, Groote Eylandt (Northern Territory).

**Railways.** At 30 June 1976, there were 40,753 route kilometres open. During 1975–76, 317,213,000 passengers were carried and 104,355 tonnes of revenue goods and livestock, Gross earnings were $939,751,000 and working expenses (excluding debt charges) $1,306,115,000.

**Shipping.** The following are the principal shipping lines:

**Associated Steamships Pty. Ltd.**; (Chairman, Sir Ian Potter); share capital, nominal $10,000,000, paid up $6,800,000; subsidiary of Bulkships Limited; *services operated:* between Australian ports. *Head Office:* 90 William Street, Melbourne, Victoria 3000.

**Australian National Line**; (Australian Shipping Commission); Chairman, N. G. Jenner: the Australian government shipping line; capital and reserves $42,800,000. Vessels 34; total tonnage 702,915 deadweight; *services operated:* Melbourne–Tasmania Searoad Service, Melbourne–Sydney–Brisbane–North Queensland–Port Kembla–Adelaide–Geelong–Tasmania Searoad service, South ports–Darwin container service, Australia–Japan service, Australia–East Asia service, Australia–Europe/U.K. service, Australia–West Coast North America service, bulk cargoes between Australian ports. *Head Office:* 65 Riverside Avenue, South Melbourne, Victoria 3205.

**Broken Hill Pty. Co. Ltd.**; (Chairman, Sir Ian McLennan); share capital, nominal $600,000,000, paid up $392,074,484; steam 6, motor 11, gas turbine 2, total 644,609 deadweight; *services operated:* carrying raw materials in bulk to the steel works operated by this company and its subsidiaries at Newcastle, Port Kembla, Whyalla and Kwinana and also for export; the distribution of steel products. *Head Office:* 140 Williams Street, Melbourne, Victoria 3000.

**Bulkships Limited**; (Chairman, Sir Ian Potter); share capital nominal $30,000,000, paid up $18,751,000; major subsidiaries: Associated Steamships Pty. Ltd., Bulkships Container Pty. Ltd.: motor vessels 1, total tonnage 15,693 deadweight. Vessel operated by Associated Streamships Pty. Ltd. *Head Office:* Tower 1, TNT Plaza, Lawson Square, Redfern, Sydney, 2000.

**Bulkships Container Pty. Ltd.**; (Chairman, Sir Ian Potter); Nominal and paid-up capital $10,000; subsidiary of Bulkships Limited; motor vessels 4, turbine vessels 1, total tonnage 66,187 gross; on bareboat charter. *Head Office:* 90 William Street, Melbourne, Victoria 3000.

**Howard Smith Industries Pty. Ltd.**; (Chairman, W. Howard-Smith); share capital, nominal $9,074,999, paid up $3,775,003; motor vessels 6; total tonnage 121,072 tonnes deadweight, plus 7 wholly owned tugs and with other subsidiary companies of Howard Smith Limited are joint owners of 35 tugs; services operated: crude and refined petroleum products, bulk cargoes between Australian ports; towage. *Head Office:* Level 22, 1 York Street, Sydney, New South Wales, 2000. This company is a wholly owned subsidiary of Howard Smith Limited. Authorized Capital $50,000,000; Issued Capital $25,442,073.

**Western Australian Coastal Shipping Commission**; motor vessels 4; total tonnage 22,503 gross; *services operated:* cargo from Fremantle to North West Australian ports and Darwin. *Head Office:* 6 Short Street, Fremantle, Western Australia, 6160.

**Union Steam Ship Co. of New Zealand Ltd.**; employs 2 gas turbine-electric vessels of 8,348 tons gross carrying general cargo to and from Tasmania. *Managing Agents in Australia:* 90 William Street, Melbourne, Victoria 3000.

**Airlines.** The following are the principal airlines:

**Ansett Airlines of Australia**; (Chairman Sir Reginald Ansett, KBE; General Manager: F. Pascoe, CBE); *services operated:* throughout Australia, associated Ansett Airlines of New South Wales, Ansett Airlines of South Australia, Mac. Robertson Miller Airline Services. *Head Office:* 489 Swanston Street, Melbourne.

**Trans-Australia Airlines**; operated by Australian National Airlines Commission; established 1946 by the Commonwealth Government of Australia. (Chairman: Mr. K. H. Vial, CBE. General Manager: L. L. McKenzie); *services operated:* internal Australian. *Head Office:* 50 Franklin Street, Melbourne, Victoria.

**Qantas Airways Ltd.**; (Chairman: Sir Lenox Hewit OBE. General Manager: Mr. K. R. Hamilton); share capital: $75 million (authorized share capital), $64·4 million (issued share capital); *services operated:* Kangaroo Route–Sydney (Melbourne) to London via Singapore or Bombay; Sydney to Rome or Paris via Bangkok; Southern Cross Route–Sydney/Melbourne to San Francisco and Vancouver via Fiji and Honolulu; Orient Route–Sydney to Manila, Hong Kong and Tokyo; Papua New Guinea Route–Sydney and Brisbane to Port Moresby; Wallaby Route–Sydney to Johannesburg via Maritius; Trans Tasman Route–Brisbane, Sydney and Melbourne to Auckland, Wellington and Christchurch; Pacific Islands Route–Sydney to Norfolk Island, Sydney to Noumea. *Head Office:* Qantas House, 70 Hunter Street, Sydney. N.S.W., 2000.

**Connair Pty. Ltd.**; *Services operated:* services operated throughout the Northern Territory; most popular tourist routes being Alice Springs to Ayers Rock. *Head Office:* 51 Todd Street, Alice Springs, Northern Territory 5750. Telephone 52-1755; Telex AA81285.

**MacRobertson Miller Airline Services**; a division Transport Industries (operations) Pty. Ltd. (General C. N. Kleinig); *services operated:* Perth–Darwin–Gove, extensive inter-connecting services between these points. *Head Office:* 26 St. George's Terrace, Perth, Western Australia, 6000 (P.O. Box W.2092.)

**East-West Airlines Ltd.**; share capital, $858,342; *services operated:* internal. *Head Office:* Tamworth, New South Wales, 2340.

**Posts, Telegraphs and Telephones.** These operate under the control of the Postmaster-General, with a Director of Posts and Telegraphs in each State.

At 30 June 1975, there were 5,772 telephone exchanges, 5,266,845 telephone instruments and 3,539,020 telephone services in operation.

As from 1 July 1975 the Australian Post Office was divided into the Australian Postal Commission and the Australian Telecommunications Commission.

**Broadcasting and Television.** The Australian Broadcasting Commission operates national broadcasting stations in all state capitals, and also in regional areas. At 30 June 1976 there were 91 medium-wave, 6 short-wave domestic and 12 short-wave oversea stations; 120 medium-wave commercial stations operated under licence.

Television services in Australia operate under the general control of the Australian Broadcasting Control Board, and comprise the National Television Service and the Commercial Television Service. Operations commenced in September 1956, and have extended to all State capitals and most country centres. At 30 June 1976 when there were 84 National Stations and 48 Commercial Stations in operation.

**Satellite Communications.** The Overseas Telecommunications Commission (Australia) operates three ground stations which provide international services via the Intelsat communications satellites located over the Indian and Pacific oceans. The stations are sited at Moree, N.S.W., Ceduna, S.A., and Carnarvon, W.A. The Commission also operates a tracking, telemetry and control station, under contract to Intelsat, at Carnarvon.

The Department of Science maintains and operates a scientific satellite tracking station at Orroral Valley, near Canberra, on behalf of the U.S. National Aeronautics and Space Administration (NASA). The Department operates two other stations at Tidbinbilla and Honeysuckle Creek, also near Canberra, for tracking spacecraft engaged on planetary and interplanetary missions. By agreement, the facilities of these stations are available for use by local scientists, e.g. in radio astronomy, when they are not being used for NASA work.

Under an agreement between Australia and Japan, the Department of Science is funding the purchase, installation and operational costs of a Turn Around Ranging Station at Orroral Valley to help maintain the Japanese Geostationary Meteorological Satellite, launched on 14 July 1977, in its correct position. The Bureau of Meteorology is installing a receiving station at its head office in Melbourne to obtain weather data from the satellite when it begins regular transmission early in 1978. The Agreement provides for special observations to be transmitted to the Bureau when Australia is threatened by, or under the direct influence of, severe weather conditions such as tropical cyclones.

Consideration is being given to the establishment of reception, processing and analysis facilities to handle earth resources data transmitted from the U.S. LANDSAT series of satellites, Alice Springs, N.T., is favoured as the site for the receiving station.

None of the facilities are used for educational purposes.

## ATOMIC ENERGY

Australia has been a member of the International Atomic Energy Agency since its inception in 1957, and has a seat on the Board of Governors as the most advanced country in atomic energy in the South-East Asia and the Pacific Region. Australia has Government to Government agreements with Canada, Japan and the United States of America for the exchange of information on the peaceful uses of atomic energy. The Australian Atomic Energy Commission, an authority set up by the Federal Government in 1953 under the Atomic Energy Act, also has agreements for cooperation with the United Kingdom Atomic Energy Authority and the Commissariat à l'Energie Atomique in France. On 23 January 1973, Australia ratified the Treaty on the Non-Proliferation of Nuclear Weapons and the agreement giving effect in Australia to the Treaty safeguards provisions was signed on 10 July 1974. The Australian Atomic Energy Commission has representatives at the Australian High Commission in London and at the Australian Embassies in Tokyo, Vienna and Washington.

At 30 June 1977, Australia's reasonably assured uranium resources recoverable at a cost of up to US $80 per kilogram uranium (US $30 per pound $U_3O_8$) totalled 289,000 tonnes uranium. Estimated additional resources in the same cost range totalled 44,000 tonnes uranium. The total of 289,000 tonnes uranium represents 20 per cent of the Western World's reasonably assured resources recoverage at a cost of up to US $80 per kilogram uranium. These uranium resource estimates are expressed in terms of uranium recoverable after due allowance has been made for ore dilution, and for mining and milling losses. With continued exploration it would not be unreasonable to expect that substantial further additions to resources may be delineated in the future. By world standards most of the major Australian deposits contain relatively high-grade ore, much of which is recoverable by opencut mining. Despite their isolated location and the high cost of labour in Australia, production costs should compare favourably with those obtaining overseas. Uranium mining and processing resumed at Mary Kathleen, Queensland, in 1976. Proposals for mining and processing the Ranger uranium deposit in the Northern Territory were the subject of a public environmental inquiry which began in September 1975. Taking of evidence was completed in July 1976 and final submissions to the inquiry were made in August 1976.

The Australian Atomic Energy Commission is continuing research and development into uranium enrichment with high priority on techniques using gas centrifuge technology and lasers. The centrifuge project began in 1965 and is now the largest single development program within the Commission. Machines have been developed and single units and cascades have operated satisfactorily over extended periods.

Other key areas of Commission activity are in the assessment of nuclear power systems; fuel cycles; planning of standards, licensing and regulatory controls of a possible uranium industry and for future nuclear power reactors in this country; and developments in the use of radioisotopes and radiation. Research has been particularly active in the field of nuclear medicine and important developments have been made in the production of radio-pharmaceuticals based on technetium 99m. The Commission produces cobalt 60 teletherapy sources for cancer treatment, and exports high-activity sources to New Zealand and Asia. During the past twelve years, the Commission has undertaken research into the application of radioisotope techniques to chemical analysis in industry. The widest field of application is in the mineral industry for on-stream measurement of the concentration of valuable elements such as copper, lead, zinc, tin, and nickel in processing plant slurries. Systems based on these methods are being marketed world-wide under licence to the Commission. The Inquiry Commission produced a First Report in October 1976 and a Second Report (final report) in May 1977.

On 24 May 1977, the Commonwealth Government announced its policy on nuclear safeguards. On 25 August 1977, the Government announced its decision to allow development of the Ranger uranium deposit to go ahead, and to consider further development on the basis of stringent criteria concerning the environment and concerning aboriginal welfare. A series of Ministerial Statements, Background Papers, etc., was released by the Australian Government Publishing Service under the title "Uranium—Australia's Decision" following the announcement in Parliament.

The Australian Atomic Energy Commission's Research Establishment at Lucas Heights, near Sydney, is the major centre for nuclear research and information in Australia. It represents a capital investment of $37 million in buildings and specialized equipment, including a ten megawatt thermal, high flux nuclear research reactor, HIFAR, a 100 kilowatt thermal physics research reactor, "Moata", a split-table critical facility, and much other equipment unique in Australia. In addition to Commission use, these facilities are made available for work by universities and other organizations. This is arranged normally through the Australian Institute of Nuclear Science and Engineering, an organization jointly sponsored by the Commission and the Australian universities. The Commission, in association with the University of New South Wales, conducts an Australian School of Nuclear Technology at Lucas Heights. The School is open to students from overseas as well as from Australia.

**NEWSPAPERS**

**The Australian:** 2 Holt Street, Sydney, 2010.

**Daily Mirror:** 2 Holt Street, Sydney, 2010.

**Daily Telegraph:** 2 Holt Street, Sydney, 2010.

**Sunday Mirror:** 2 Holt Street, Sydney, 2010.

**Sunday Telegraph:** 2 Holt Street, Sydney, 2010.

**The News:** Circulation 175,000. 116 North Terrace, Adelaide, 5001.

**The Sunday Mail:** 116 North Terrace, Adelaide, 5001.

**Truth:** 402 LaTrobe Street, Melbourne, 3000.

**Sunday Sun:** Brunswick Street, Valley, Brisbane, 4006.

**The Sunday Times:** 34–42 Stirling Street, Perth.

**Northern Territory News:** Mitchell Street, Darwin.

**Sydney Morning Herald:** 235/243 Jones St., Broadway, N.S.W. 2007.

**The Sun:** 235/243 Jones Street, Broadway, Sydney 2007.

**The Age:** 250 Spencer Street, Melbourne, 3000.

**Sun News-Pictorial:** 44–74 Flinders Street, Melbourne, 3000.

**Herald:** 44–74 Flinders Street, Melbourne.

**Brisbane Telegraph:** Campbell Street, Bowen Hills, Brisbane, 4006.

**Courier-Mail:** Campbell Street, Bowen Hills, Brisbane, 4006.

**Advertiser Newspapers Ltd.:** G.P.O. Box 339, 121 King William Street, Adelaide, 5000.

**Daily News:** 125 St. George's Terrace, Perth, 6000.

**The West Australian:** Newspaper House, 125 St. George's Terrace, Perth, 6000.

**Mercury:** 93 Macquarie Street, Hobart, 7000.

**The Canberra Times:** Circulation 42,955. 18 Mort Street, Canberra, 2601.

**The Australian Financial Review.** Five times weekly. Printed by John Fairfax and Sons Ltd. at Jones Street, Broadway, Sydney, 2007.

**EDUCATION AND RELIGION**

School attendance is compulsory throughout Australia between the ages of six and, at least fifteen. In all States tuition at government primary and secondary schools is free. There were in 1976, 7,306 government primary and secondary schools and 2,138 non-government primary and secondary schools. Teachers numbered 129,668 in government schools and 29,717 in non-government schools; there was an enrolment of 2,335,431 in government schools and 624,819 in non-government schools.

In 1976 there were 18 operative universities, 6 in New South Wales, 3 in Victoria, 3 in Queensland, 2 in South Australia, 2 in Western Australia, one in Tasmania and one in the Australian Capital Territory. The total number of students at universities in 1976 was 153,960 with a full-time equivalent teaching staff of 11,502. In 1976 there were 83 operative colleges of advanced education, with an enrolment of 134,614 students.

Under the Constitution of the Commonwealth no religion may be established by the Commonwealth law, and no law may be passed prohibiting the free exercise of any religion. In addition, no religious test may be imposed as a condition of appointment to any office or public trust under the Commonwealth.

# Australian States

## NEW SOUTH WALES

**Capital:** Sydney.

**Governor:** Sir Roden Cutler, VC, KCMG, KCVO, CBE, K St J.

**Area:** 801,428 sq kilometres.

**Population** at 31 December 1975; 4,810,900. Chief cities with populations as estimated at 30 June 1975: Sydney (Statistical Division), 2,922,760; Newcastle (Statistical District), 363,010; Wollongong (Statistical District), 211,240; Wagga Wagga, 32,510; Albury, 32,250; Broken Hill, 28,160; Tamworth, 25,360; Orange, 24,830; Goulburn, 22,160; Lismore, 21,650; Armidale, 20,300; Queanbeyan, 20,070.

**Legislature.** The Parliament of New South Wales consists of two Chambers, the Legislative Assembly and the Legislative Council. The Assembly (the principal house) consists of 99 members, elected, on a system of universal adult suffrage, for a maximum period of three years. The Council is a House of 60 members. At elections held every third year, a group of 15 members is elected for 12 years. The electoral body comprises the members, for the time being, of the two Houses, who record their votes at simultaneous sittings of both Houses.

Representation of the parties (30 August 1976): Legislative Assembly: Liberal Party and Country Party 47; Australian Labor Party 50; Independent 1; vacancy 1; Legislative Council: Australian Labor Party 24; Liberal and Country Parties 34; Independent 1; vacancy 1.

**Ministry** (9 August 1976)

*Premier:* Hon. N. K. Wran, QC, MLA.
*Deputy Premier, Minister for Public Works, Minister for Ports, and Minister for Housing:* Hon. L. J. Ferguson, MLA.
*Treasurer:* Hon. J. B. Renshaw, MLA.
*Minister for Transport and Minister for Highways:* Hon. P. F. Cox, MLA.
*Attorney-General:* Hon. F. J. Walker, LLM, MLA.
*Minister for Mines, Minister for Energy, and Minister for Industrial Relations:* Hon. P. D. Hills, MLA.
*Minister for Planning and Environment and Vice-President of the Executive Council:* Hon. D. P. Lander, LLB, MLC.
*Minister for Decentralization and Development and Minister for Primary Industries:* Hon. D. Day, MLA.
*Minister for Education:* Hon. E. L. Bedford, BA, MLA.
*Minister for Local Government:* Hon. H. F. Jensen, MLA.
*Minister for Lands:* Hon. W. F. Crabtree, MLA.
*Minister for Health:* Hon. K. J. Stewart, MLA.
*Minister for Consumer Affairs and Minister for Co-operative Societies:* Hon. S. D. Einfield, MLA.
*Minister of Justice and Minister for Services:* Hon. R. J. Mulock, LLB, MLA.
*Minister for Sport and Recreation and Minister for Tourism:* Hon. K. G. Booth, MLA.
*Minister for Conservation and Minister for Water Resources:* Hon. A. R. L. Gordon, MLA.
*Minister for Youth and Community Services:* Hon. R. F. Jackson, MLA.
*Minister Assisting the Premier:* Hon. W. H. Haigh, MLA.

**Supreme Court**

*Chief Justice:* Hon. Laurence Whistler Street.

*President Court of Appeal:* Hon. Athol Randolph Moffitt.

*Chief Judge at Common Law:* Hon. Robert Lindsay Taylor.

*Chief Judge of the Family Law Division:* Hon. David Meyer Selby, ED.

**State Government Finance:** For the year 1974–75: Revenue and Expenditure figures were $A2,452,089,000 and $A2,492,634,000.

**Production;** Local value of primary commodities produced (excluding mining) in 1974–75 was $A1,525,383,000. The chief primary commodities were agriculture, $A697,853,000; livestock slaughterings, $A300,244,000; livestock products, $A451,191,000.

Imports and exports through N.S.W. ports in 1974–75 were $A3,494,781,000 and $A1,979,005 respectively. Principal imports were machinery, textiles, motor vehicles chemicals, petroleum, paper products, iron and steel, foodstuffs, and medical apparatus. Principal exports were wool, wheat, coal, meat, iron and steel, chemicals, raw sugar, and machinery.

## QUEENSLAND

**Capital:** Brisbane.

**Governor:** His Excellency Commodore Sir James Maxwell Ramsay, CBE, DSC.

**Area:** 1,728,000 sq kilometres.

**Population;** Cities and towns with population over 10,000 as at 30 June 1976 are: Brisbane Statistical Division, 985,920 (including cities of Brisbane, 717,170; Ipswich, 71,270; Redcliffe, 40,220); Gold Coast, 91,925; Townsville, 83,065; Toowoomba, 69,930, Rockhampton, 53,475; Cairns, 35,605; Bundaberg, 31,840; Mount Isa, 27,305; Maryborough, 22,185; Mackay, 21,670, Gladstone, 19,825; Gympie, 11,535.

**Legislature.** The Legislative Council was abolished in 1922. There is now only one Chamber, the Legislative Assembly, comprising 82 members, who are elected by all persons aged 18 years and over for a period of three years. The General Election on 7 December 1974 resulted in the following representation of parties: National Party, 39; Liberal Party, 30; Australian Labor Party, 11; North Queensland Party, 1; Independent, 1.

*Note.*—The National and Country Parties form a coalition Government.

**Ministry** (at 30 June 1977)

*Premier:* Hon. Johannes Bjelke-Petersen, MLA.
*Treasurer:* Hon. William Edward Knox, MLA.
*Minister for Mines and Energy:* Hon. Ronald Ernest Camm, MLA.
*Minister for Industrial Development, Labour Relations and Consumer Affairs:* Hon. Frederick Alexander Campbell, MLA.
*Minister for Community and Welfare Services and Sport:* Hon. John Desmond Herbert, MLA.
*Minister for Primary Industries:* Hon. Victor Bruce Sullivan, MLA.
*Minister for Tourism and Marine Services:* Hon. Allen Maxwell Hodges, MLA.
*Minister for Water Resources:* Hon. Neville Thomas Eric Hewitt, MM., AFM., MLA.
*Minister for Transport:* Hon. Keith William Hooper, MLA.
*Minister for Local Government and Main Roads:* Hon. Russell James Hinze, MLA.
*Minister for Police:* Hon. Thomas Guy Newbery, MLA.
*Minister for Lands, Forestry, National Parks and Wildlife Service:* Hon. Kenneth Burgoyne Tomkins, MLA.
*Minister for Health:* Hon. Llewellyn Roy Edwards, MLA.
*Minister for Education and Cultural Activities:* Hon. Valmond James Bird, MLA.
*Minister for Works and Housing:* Hon. Norman Edward Lee, MLA.
*Minister for Aboriginal and Islanders Advancement and Fisheries:* Hon. Claude Alfred Wharton, MLA.
*Minister for Justice and Attorney-General:* Hon. William Daniel Lickiss, MLA.
*Minister for Survey and Valuation:* Hon. John Ward Greenwood, MLA.

**Legal System**

*Chief Justice:* Hon. Sir Charles Gray Wanstall.

**District Courts**

*Chairman of the Judges:* William Murray Grant-Taylor.

**Finance.** Budget figures for 1975–76 were: Revenue, $1,349,513,000; Expenditure, $1,348,799,000. Estimates for 1976–77 were $1,596,457,000 and $1,597,022,000 respectively.

**Production.** The value (gross) of primary production (excluding mining) in 1975–76 was $1,322,566,000. It was made up as follows: crops, $851,854,000; livestock disposals, $243,151,000; livestock products, $180,968,000; forestry, $28,647,000; fishing, $17,137,000; and hunting, $810,000. Value of manufacturing (value added) in 1074–75 was $1,618,730,000.

Overseas imports for 1975–76 were valued at $634,893,000, exports at $2,322,021,000. The chief exports were minerals, $926,251,000; meat, $253,732,000; sugar, $561,335,000,

## SOUTH AUSTRALIA

**Capital:** Adelaide.

**Governor:** Keith D. Seaman, OBE.

**Area:** 984,375 square kilometres.

**Population** (Census June 1976, 1,261,600): Chief cities with populations are: Adelaide, 857,066; Whyalla, 33,825; Mount Gambier, 19,292; Port Pirie, 15,005.

**Legislature.** There is a Legislative Council, composed of 22 members, and a House of Assembly with 47 members, both Chambers being elective. A system of preferential voting is in operation.

Representation of the parties after the July 1975 election was (a) House of Assembly: Labor, 23; Liberal Party of Australia, 20; Liberal Movement 2; Country Party 1; Independent 1; (b) Legislative Council: Labor, 10; Liberal Party of Australia, 9; Liberal Movement 2.

**Ministry**

*Premier and Treasurer:* Hon. Donald Allan Dunstan, QC, MP.
*Deputy Premier, Minister of Works and Minister of Marine.* Hon. James Desmond Corcoran, MP.
*Minister of Mines and Energy, and Minister for Planning:* Hon. Hugh Richard Hudson, MP.
*Minister of Health and Chief Secretary:* Hon. Donald Hubert Louis Banfield, MLC.
*Minister of Transport and of Local Government:* Hon. Geoffrey Thomas Virgo, MP.
*Minister of Lands, Minister of Irrigation, Minister of Re-*

*patriation and Minister of Tourism, Recreation and Sport:* Hon. Thomas Mannix Casey, MLC.
*Minister of Education:* Hon. Donald Jack Hopgood, MP.
*Minister of Agriculture, Minister of Forests and Minister of Fisheries:* Hon. Brian Alfred Chatterton, MLC.
*Minister of Labour and Industry:* Hon. John David Wright, MP.
*Minister of Community Welfare:* Hon. Ronald George Payne, MP.
*Attorney-General and Minister of Prices and Consumer Affairs:* Hon. Peter Duncan, MP.
*Minister for the Environment:* Hon. Donald William Simmons, DFC, MP

**Law and Justice**

The judicial system includes a Supreme Court (and Circuit Courts) with a Chief Justice and nine puisne judges, District Criminal Courts, Local Courts, Courts of Summary Jurisdiction, Licensing Court, Court of Insolvency exercising Federal jurisdiction in bankruptcy, Industrial Tribunals which comprise an Industrial Commission and Conciliation Committees, Juvenile Courts and Adoption Courts.

**Finance.** For the year 1975–76 Revenue was $1,036,985,000, Expenditure $1,034,698,000 and for 1976–77 was Revenue $1,174,025,000, Expenditure $1,183,180,000.

**Production.** In 1975–76 the gross value of primary production (excluding mining), was $712,044,000 and in 1974–75 the value added by factory production was $1,335,276,000. In 1975–76 direct overseas exports were valued at $685,029,000, direct overseas imports $501,476,000.

## TASMANIA

**Capital: Hobart.**

**Governor:** Sir Charles Stanley Burbury, KBE.

**Area: 26,383 sq. miles.**

**Population** (Census count of 30 June 1976 adjusted for under-enumeration): 407,360. Chief urban centres are: Urban Hobart, 161,320; Urban Launceston, 63,629; Burnie-Somerset, 19,473; Devonport, 19,189.

**Legislature.** The Parliament has two houses: the Legislative Council and the House of Assembly. All adults 18 years and over vote to elect both houses. The Council consists of 19 members elected for six years. Three members retire each year, except in every sixth year when four retire.

There are five House of Assembly divisions, corresponding to the Federal electoral divisions, each returning seven members elected under a system of proportional representation. The term of the House of Assembly is four years. The last general election was held on 11 December 1976 and resulted in the re-election of the Labor Government led by the Hon. W. A. Neilson. The seven-seat majority enjoyed by the Government following the 1972 election was reduced to a single seat majority; the Labor Party holding 18 seats and the Liberal Party, led by the Hon. E. M. Bingham, 17 seats. The Labor Cabinet was made up of ten members from the Assembly and one from the Council.

Following elections for four seats held on 28 May 1977 (at which the sitting members were returned) the Legislative Council comprised two Labor members and 17 with no party affiliations.

**Ministry** (January 1977)

*Premier, Treasurer and Minister for Planning and Development,* Hon. W. A. Neilson, MHA.
*Deputy Premier and Minister for Industrial Relations and Health,* Hon. D. A. Lowe, MHA.
*Minister for Main Roads, Transport and Local Government,* Hon. D. J. Baldock, MHA.
*Minister for Primary Industry:* Hon. E. W. Barnard, MHA.
*Minister for Tourism and the Environment:* Hon. M. T. C. Barnard, MHA.
*Minister for Education, Recreation and the Arts,* Hon. N. L. C. Batt, MHA.
*Minister for Resources and Energy:* Hon. G. D. Chisholm, MHA.
*Minister for Housing and Construction and Minister Assisting the Deputy Premier:* Hon. H. N. Holgate, MHA.
*Minister for Social Welfare and Child Care and Minister Assisting the Premier:* Hon. M. R. Polley, MHA.
*Attorney-General and Minister for Police and Emergency Services:* Hon. B. K. Miller, MLC.

**Supreme Court of Tasmania**

*Chief Justice:* Hon. G. S. M. Green.

**Finance** (Consolidated Revenue Fund). For 1975–76 Revenue was $322,090,682; Expenditure $A317,946,696.

**Industry.** The value added by the various sectors of Tasmanian industry was: manufacturing, 1974–75, $402 million (1973–74, $340 million); mining, 1975–76, $81 million (1974–75, $73 million); wholesale, 1968–69, $61 million; retail, 1968–69, $79 million. The gross value of primary production (excluding mining) in 1975–76 was 198 million (1974–75, $197 million). Chipped, ground and flaked wood production in 1975–76 was 2·4 million tonnes, while exports of woodchips to Japan totalled 1·7 million tonnes.

In 1977, the output capacity of turbines in the State's hydro-electric integrated network was 1,452,400 kW. This total includes 240,000 kW contributed by the Bell Bay thermal, oil-fired power station. The Gordon River Power Development, Stage I, is expected to be completed by early 1978 and will have an initial generating capacity of 288,000 kW. A 140 metre high dam on the Gordon River plus two smaller dams on the Huon and Serpentine Rivers and a levee have been completed. The resultant Lake Pedder (filled) and Lake Gordon (to fill during 1978) will have a total surface area of just over 500 square kilometres. Construction of a power development in the catchment of the Pieman River on the west coast has commenced. This scheme is scheduled for completion during 1985 and is planned to have an installed generating capacity of 420,000 kW. Cheap bulk electricty for industrial use has attracted to Tasmania a number of major industries, principally associated with metal refining (e.g. zinc, aluminium, iron ore pelletizing, and ferro-alloy production) and paper and newsprint production.

**Commerce.** The total value of imports into Tasmania in 1974–75 was $530 m (1973–74, $452 m). The total value of exports from Tasmania in 1974–75 was $638 m (1973–74, $699 m). The value of exports overseas in 1975–76 was $251 m (1974–75, $226 m). Principal overseas exports are ores and concentrates, refined metals, woodchips, fresh fruit, greasy wool, meat, cheese and butter.

**Communications.** Physical isolation from other Australian States has been greatly reduced; jets fly Hobart–Melbourne in about an hour, and there are regular interstate and intrastate services to other main centres. Several roll-on roll-off type vessels provide regular shipping services for freight and passengers between Tasmania and the mainland states.

## VICTORIA

**Capital: Melbourne.**

**Governor:** Hon. Sir Henry Winneke, KCMG, OBE, K. StJ., QC.

**Area:** 227,600 sq. kilometres.

**Population** at the census of 30 June 1976 was 3,745,981. Populations of principal cities were: Melbourne Urban Area, 2,479,400; Geelong, 122,000; Ballarat, 60,700; Bendigo, 50,100.

**Legislature.** There are two legislative chambers, the Legislative Council and the Legislative Assembly. The Legislative

Council consists of 40 members, elected for a term of six years, one member from each of the 22 provinces retiring every third year.

The Legislative Assembly consists of 81 members, elected for the duration of Parliament, which is limited to three years.

Representation of the parties (election of March 1976): Labor Party, 30; Liberal Party 78; National Party of Australia (Victoria), 12; Independent Labor, 1.

**Ministry**

*Premier, Treasurer and Minister of the Arts:* Hon. R. J. Hamer, ED, MLA.
*Deputy Premier and Minister of Education:* Hon. L. H. S. Thompson, CMG, MLA.
*Minister of State Development and Decentralization, and Tourism:* Hon. D. G. Crozier, MLC.
*Minister of Housing, and Planning:* Hon. G. P. Hayes, MLA.
*Minister of Transport:* Hon. J. A. Rafferty, MLA.
*Minister of Fuel and Power and Mines:* Hon. J. C. M. Balfour, MLA.
*Chief Secretary:* Hon. V. O. Dickie, MLC.
*Attorney-General:* Hon. Haddon Storey, QC, MLC.
*Minister of Conservation, Lands, and Soldier Settlement:* Hon. W. A. Borthwick, MLA.
*Minister of Labour and Industry, Consumer Affairs:* Hon. R. R. C. Maclellan, MLA.
*Minister of Agriculture:* Hon. I. W. Smith, MLA.
*Minister of Public Works:* Hon. R. C. Dunstan, DSO, MLA.
*Minister of Local Government and Federal Affairs:* Hon. A. J. Hunt, MLC.
*Minister of Health:* Hon. W. V. Houghton, MLC.
*Minister of Social Welfare and Minister of Youth, Sport and Recreation:* Hon. B. J. Dixon, MLA.
*Minister of Water Supply and Forests:* Hon. F. J. Granter MLC.
*Minister of Special Education:* Hon. A. H. Scanlan, MLA.
*Immigration and Ethnic Affairs and Assistant Minister of Health:* Hon. Walter Jona, MLA.

**Supreme Court of Victoria**

*Chief Justice:* Hon. Sir John Young, KCMG.

**Finance** (Consolidated Fund). Budget figures for 1975–76 were: Receipts, $2,568,196,507; Payments, $2,568,196,507.

**Rural Production.** In 1975–76 there were 58,468 rural holdings with an area of 15,144,404 hectares of which 1,850,509 hectares were under crops during the year. Gross value of rural production was $1,258 million.

**Secondary Production.** At 30 June 1975 there were 11,758 manufacturing establishments in which 306,509 males and 132,069 females were employed. The principal industrial sub-divisions were: Transport equipment 61,902 persons. Basic metal products 13,054 persons; fabricated metal products 38,656 persons. Other machinery and equipment 69,727 persons. Clothing and footwear; 49,598 persons. Food beverages, and tobacco 61,210 persons. Most of the manufacturing activity is concentrated in the Melbourne Statistical Division. Important country manufacturing centres are Geelong, Ballarat, Bendigo and Latrobe Valley. Value added in the course of manufacture was $5,171 million.

Imports for 1975–76 totalled $2,875·342 million, exports 1,818·244 million (preliminary figures).

## WESTERN AUSTRALIA

**Capital:** Perth.

**Governor:** His Excellency Air Chief Marshal Sir Wallace Kyle, GCB, KCVO, CBE, DSO, DFC, K. StJ.

**Lieut.-Governor:** His Excellency The Hon. Sir Francis T. P. Burt, KCMG.

**Area:** 2,525,500 sq. kilometres.

**Population.** Census at 30 June 1976: 1,169,844. Chief centres of population are: Perth (including Fremantle), 805,700, Kalgoorlie (including Boulder), 19,900, Bunbury, 19,500, Geraldton, 17,600, and Albany, 12,600.

**Legislature.** In this State both Chambers are elective. There are 32 members of the Legislative Council, each of the provinces returning two members, one of whom retires triennially. At each triennial election the member elected holds office for a term of six years.

The Legislative Assembly is composed of 55 members, who are elected for a term of three years. A system of preferential voting is in operation.

Representation of the Parties: Assembly representation as at 30 June 1977 was: Liberal Party, 27; Australian Labor Party, 22; National Country Party, 6. Council representation was: Liberal Party, 18; Australian Labor Party, 10; National Country Party 4.

**Ministry** (30 June 1977)

*Premier, Treasurer and Minister Co-ordinating Economic and Regional Development:* The Hon. Sir Charles Walter Michael Court, OBE, MLA.
*Deputy Premier, Chief Secretary, Minister for Police and Traffic, and Minister for Regional Administration and the North-West:* The Hon. Desmond Henry O'Neil, MLA.
*Minister for Fisheries and Wildlife, Tourism, Conservation and the Environment, and Leader of the Government in the Legislative Council:* The Hon. Graham Charles MacKinnon, MLC.
*Minister for Agriculture:* The Hon. Richard Charles Old, MLA.
*Minister for Works, Water Supplies and Housing:* The Hon. Raymond James O'Connor, MLA.
*Minister for Labour and Industry, Consumer Affairs, and Immigration:* The Hon. William Leonard Grayden, MLA.
*Attorney General and Minister for Federal Affairs:* The Hon. Ian George Medcalf, ED., LLB., MLC.
*Minister for Education, Cultural Affairs, and Recreation:* The Hon. Peter Vernon Jones, MLA.
*Minister for Industrial Development, Mines, and Fuel and Energy:* The Hon. Andrew Mensaros, MLA.
*Minister for Local Government, and Urban Development and Town Planning:* The Hon. Edgar Cyril Rushton, MLA.
*Minister for Health and Community Welfare:* The Hon. Keith Alan Ridge, MLA.
*Minister for for Transport:* The Hon. David John Wordsworth, MLC.
*Minister for Lands and Forests:* The Hon. Margaret June Craig, MLA.

**Supreme Court of Western Australia**

*Chief Justice:* Hon. Sir Francis T. P. Burt, KCMG.

**Finance.** For the year 1975–76: Revenue was $950,861,398 and Expenditure was $950,267,621

**Production.** In 1975–76 the gross value of primary production excluding mining in thousand dollars was:

| | |
|---|---|
| Agriculture— | |
| Crops | 595,481 |
| Livestock Slaughterings and Other Disposals | 113,605 |
| Livestock Products | 286,788 |
| Forestry | 21,784 |
| Fishing and Whaling | 41,965 |
| Hunting | 1,744 |

Value added in mining for the year 1975–76 was $769·0 million; turnover was $1,167·7 million. Value added in manufacturing for the year 1975–76 was $911·0 million; turnover was $2,368·0 million.

# THE TERRITORIES OF AUSTRALIA

Territories under the control of the Commonwealth Government are administered in four groups, as follows:

(1) The Australian Capital Territory including Jervis Bay, by the Minister for the Capital Territory.

(2) The Northern Territory of Australia and the Territory of Ashmore and Cartier Islands by the Minister for the Northern Territory.

(3) The Territories of Cocos (Keeling) Islands, Christmas Island, Norfolk Island and the Coral Sea Islands by the Minister for Administrative Services.

(4) The Territory of Heard and McDonald Islands and the Australian Antarctic Territory by the Minister for Science.

The Australian Antarctic Territory, estimated area 6,199,846 square kilometres of a total of approximately 13,991,340 square kilometres for the Antarctic Continent, was established by an Order in Council, dated 7 February 1933, which placed under the control of the Commonwealth that part of the Territory in the Antarctic Seas which comprises all the islands and territories, other than Adelie Land, situated south of the 60th parallel of south latitude, and lying between the 160th and 45th meridians of east longitude.

## NORFOLK ISLAND

**Administrator**; D. V. O'Leary, VRD.

Norfolk Island, discovered by James Cook in 1774, lies in the Pacific Ocean about 1,676 kilometres north-east of Sydney.

The Island is about 8 kilometres long and 5 kilometres wide, with an area of 3,454 hectares. There is a permanent population of about 1,600 persons and tourism, the basis of the Island's economy, attracts some 20,000 visitors annually.

Inaccessible cliffs form most of the Island's 32 kilometre-long coastline. Jetties at Kingston in the south of the Island and Cascade Bay on the north-east coast provide landing places for lighters serving ships offshore. The Island relies mainly on regular air services for passenger transport.

The climate is mild and subtropical, with rainfall distributed evenly throughout the year.

In the early years of Australia's settlement Norfolk was a dreaded penal station. It has been administered as an Australian territory since 1914, retaining its historic interest and examples of early convict architecture.

An Administrator, responsible to the Minister for Administrative Services, represents the Government on the Island. A Norfolk Island Council, with eight members elected biennially, is empowered to consider and tender advice to the Administrator (who is also ex-officio voting chairman) on any matter affecting the peace, order and good government of the Island. The Council must be consulted on certain legislative and financial matters.

The Supreme Court for Norfolk Island sits as required. A Court of Petty Sessions exercises jurisdiction equivalent to similar mainland courts.

Education is free and compulsory for children between six and fifteen years of age. A number of scholarships and bursaries is available for secondary education on the mainland.

About half of the workforce is employed in the tourist industry. Agriculture and livestock are a source of income for a few Islanders but primary production is inadequate for local needs and foodstuffs are imported from the mainland and New Zealand.

The sale of postage stamps provides a major item of revenue for the Island. Philatelic items available at 1 July 1977 were the 1976–77 Butterflies and Moths Definitive Series, Queen Elizabeth II Coil Stamps and Commemoratives marking the 150th Anniversary of the Second Settlement and Silver Jubilee.

A Royal Commission into the affairs of Norfolk Island has recently been conducted and its report is under consideration.

## CHRISTMAS ISLAND

**Administrator**; W. Worth, OBE.

Christmas Island, a major source of phosphate fertilizer for Australia and New Zealand, is in the Indian Ocean, 2,623 kilometres north-west of Perth.

Rising steeply to a central plateau covered in tropical rain forest, the Island is about 135 square kilometres in area and has a mild climate, with seasonal rain between November and April.

Australia has administered the Territory since 1958. An Administrator, responsible to the Australian Minister for Administrative Services, represents the Government on the Island.

The Australian Government's involvement in phosphate mining began in 1948 while the Island was a dependency of the then British Colony of Singapore. Together with the New Zealand Government, it established by mutual agreement (reframed in 1958) the Christmas Island Phosphate Commission which employs the British Phosphate Commissioners (BPC) as managing agents, to carry out actual operations.

During the year ended 30 June 1977, 995,650 tonnes of phosphate rock, 123,260 tonnes of phosphate dust and 15,285 tonnes of citraphos dust were shipped from the Island.

Some 3,200 people are resident on the Island, comprising more than 1,800 Chinese, 900 Malays and 370 Europeans. There is no indigenous population.

Asian workers have been employed in the phosphate industry since mining began in 1899. Phosphate industry employees engaged after 1965 have worked on restricted-term contracts, with repatriation at the end of the term (usually three years).

The present population is made up largely of people who arrived during the past 30 years, or who were born in the Territory. Under provisions of the Christmas Island Act 1958, many are now Australian citizens. On 1 December 1976 a Government-sponsored resettlement scheme commenced to assist there long-term residents who wish to resettle outside the Island.

Education in the Territory is provided to secondary and tertiary technical levels and is based on an Australian-oriented curriculum.

Two unions are registered: the Union of Christmas Island Workers and the Police Association. An industrial Arbitrator for the Territory was appointed on 6 July 1976.

Transport to and from the Island is by regular air charter out of Perth via the Cocos (Keeling) Islands. The BPC operate an air charter between Singapore, Kuala Lumpur and the Island, and ships owned or chartered by the BPC run between the Island and ports in Australia, New Zealand, Singapore and Malaysia.

The Territory issues its own stamps. Philatelic items available at 1 July 1977 were the Ships and Famous Visitors Definitives and a Silver Jubilee Commemorative. The Territory issues its popular Christmas series stamps at Christmas time each year.

## COCOS (KEELING) ISLANDS

**Administrator**; R. J. Linford.

The 27 coral islands which form the two atolls of the Territory of Cocos (Keeling) Islands lie in the Indian Ocean, 2,768 kilometres north-west of Perth.

The northern atoll is a single uninhabited island, North Keeling. The southern atoll is a horseshoe-shaped chain, containing five major islands, two of them inhabited. Together, the atolls have an area of about 14 square kilometres.

West Island, about 10 kilometres long, is the largest island in the group. The Territory's administrative community of some 100 persons and the airport are located there.

Nearby Home Island is the headquarters of the Clunies Ross Estate. Since 1827, successive generations of the Clunies Ross family have developed substantial coconut plantations in the Islands, creating an economy based solely on the production and export of copra. The Estate exports several hundred tonnes of copra annually.

Some 320 Cocos Islanders are housed in the Estate settlement on Home Island. The Islanders are the descendants of the original labourers, mostly of Malay origin, who were brought to Cocos between 1827 and 1831.

At one time, the Islanders numbered over 2,000 but between 1948 and 1958 the majority were resettled, mainly in North Borneo (now part of Malaysia) and in Singapore and Christmas Island.

Australia has administered the Territory since 1955. An Administrator, responsible to the Australian Minister for Administrative Services, represents the Government in the Islands.

The Clunies Ross Estate meets the daily administration costs of the Home Island community, with the exception of education, medical and dental services subsidized by the Australian Government. The Cocos Islanders are dependent on the Estate for employment.

The Islands are not self-sufficient. Fish are caught locally but other foodstuffs, fuels and consumer items are imported from mainland Australia and Singapore.

The Territory is serviced by a regular air charter from Perth and a shipping charter from Singapore via Perth every six months.

The Administration maintains a radio teletype and radio telephone service on behalf of the Overseas Telecommunications Commission, linking West Island with Perth. It also operates a non-commercial broadcasting station for the Home and West Islands communities and a non-official Post Office on behalf of the Postal and Telecommunications Department. Philatelic items available at 1 July 1977 were the General Series Stamps 1976, Ships.

Education in the Territory is provided to primary level at the schools on Home and West Islands. Secondary education is available by correspondence or attendance at mainland schools.

In accordance with Article 73(e) of the United Nations Charter, the Australian Government reports regularly to the UN Secretary-General on economic and social progress in the Territory.

### CORAL SEA ISLANDS

The Coral Sea Islands Territory comprises scattered reefs and islands, often little more than sandbanks, spread over a sea area of 1,035,995 square kilometres with only a few square kilometres of land area. The sea area lies between the Great Barrier Reef and longitude 157°10′E.

In 1968, the British Government formally recognized the control which Australia had exercised over the islands for a number of years. The Australian Government then declared the islands an Australian territory by the Coral Sea Islands Act of 1969.

The islands, or cays, are formed largely of coral and sand. Some have a cover of grassy or scrub-type vegetation. The better known among them are Cato Island, Chilcott Islet in the Coringa Group, and those of the Willis Group. The islands are unpopulated due to their size and to the absence of permanent fresh water. However, they support large populations of sea birds.

A lighthouse has been erected on Bougainville Reef and beacons operate on the Frederick and Lihou Reefs. A three-man meteorological station has provided a service since 1921 and there is an unmanned weather station on Cato Island.

Most of the islands have been surveyed, and are visited regularly by Royal Australian Navy vessels. The Government has control over the activities of visitors to the Territory.

By ordinance, the laws of the Australian Capital Territory apply in the Coral Sea Islands Territory. The Minister for Administrative Services is responsible for matters affecting the Territory.

# Austria

(REPUBLIK ÖSTERREICH)

**Capital**—Vienna.

**President**—Dr. Rudolf Kirchschlaeger.

**National Flag:** Three stripes fesse-wise, red, white, red.

### CONSTITUTION AND GOVERNMENT

AUSTRIA was liberated by the Allied Powers in the spring of 1945. A provisional government took over in April 1945. Ten years later Austria became completely independent and the last forces of occupation left the country.

Austria's present Constitution goes back to the Constitution of 1929, which again came into force with effect from 19 December 1945.

The supreme head of the Republic is the Federal President, who appoints the Chancellor and, on his proposal, other members of the Federal Government. At present there is a cabinet formed by the Austrian Socialist Party (SPÖ). The Austrian People's Party (ÖVP) and the Liberal Party (FPÖ) represents the parliamentary opposition.

There are two Houses of Parliament, the Upper House or 'Bundesrat' having 58 members, and the Lower House or 'Nationalrat' having 183 members. Members are elected for a period of four years. Voting is by secret ballot and by a system of proportional representation. There are nine major constituencies. All men and women aged 19 years and over are entitled to vote.

#### Ministry

*Chancellor*, Dr. Bruno Kreisky.
*Vice-Chancellor and Minister of Social Affairs*, Ing. Rudolf Häuse.
*Minister of the Interior:* Otto Rösch.
*Minister of Justice:* Dr. Christian Broda.
*Minister of Transport:* Erwin Lanc.
*Minister of Foreign Affairs:* Dr. Willibald Pahr.
*Minister of Finance:* Dkfm. Hannes Androsch.
*Minister of Agriculture*, Dip. Ing. Dr. Oskar Weihs.
*Minister of Defence:* Brig. Karl Lütgendorf.
*Minister of Education:* Dr. Fred Sinowatz.
*Minister of Trade and Industry:* Dr. Josef Staribacher.
*Minister of Building:* Josef Moser.
*Minister of Science and Research:* Frau Dr. Hertha Firnberg.
*Minister of Health and Environment:* Frau Dr. Ingrid Leodolter.

### LOCAL GOVERNMENT

Austria is divided into nine counties (Länder), each one having its own Provincial Government with a Provincial Governor (Landeshauptmann) at its head, elected by the Provincial Diet (Landtag).

#### County Governors (Landeshauptmänner)

| | |
|---|---|
| Vienna (*Vienna*) | Bürgermeister Felix Slavik |
| Burgenland (*Eisenstadt*) | Theodor Kery |
| Carinthia (*Klagenfurt*) | Hans Sima |
| Upper Austria (*Linz*) | Dr. Erwin Wenzl |
| Lower Austria (*Vienna*) | Andreas Maurer |
| Salzburg (*Salzburg*) | Dr. Hans Lechner |
| Styria (*Graz*) | Dr. Friedrich Niederl |
| Tyrol (*Innsbruck*) | Ök. Rat Eduard Wallnöfer |
| Vorarlberg (*Bregenz*) | Dr. Herbert Kessler |

### LEGAL SYSTEM

The Austrian legal system is based on the principle of the division between administrative and judicial power. The Supreme Courts are the 'Verfassungsgerichtshof', 'Verwaltungsgerichtshof' and the 'Oberste Gerichtshof'. There are also four high provincial courts, 20 district courts and 230 local courts.

#### Supreme Constitutional Court

*President:* Prof. Dr. Walter Antoniolli.
*Vice-President:* Prof. Dr. Leopold Werner.

#### Supreme Administrative Court

*President:* Dr. Sergius Borotha.
*Vice-President:* Dkfm. Dr. Henus Porias.

#### Supreme High Court

*President:* Dr. Franz Pallin.
*Vice-President:* Dr. Franz Berger.

### AREA AND POPULATION

The total area of Austria is 83,849 sq. km.

The population at mid-1974 was 7,550,000. The annual average percentage population growth rate for the period 1960–74 was 0·5, and for the period 1965–74 was 0·5.

### CURRENCY

The basic unit of currency is the schilling, made up of 100 groschen. The rate of exchange in 1972 was 60·42 schillings to the pound sterling or 23·14 schillings to the U.S. dollar. There are metal coins of 2, 5, 10 and 50 groschen and of 1 schilling and 5 schillings, silver coins of 10, 25 and 50 schillings. Bank notes are issued of 20, 50, 100, 500 and 1,000 schillings.

**FINANCE**

Budget figures for 1972 (million schillings) are: Revenue 113·4; Expenditure 122,820. Budget figures for 1971 were: Revenue 100·9, Expenditure 110·7.

The chief items of revenue were Turnover Tax, Income Tax, Trade Tax. Austria's holdings of foreign exchange and gold amounted to 48,800 million schillings at 31 December 1971.

The GNP at market prices for 1974 was U.S.$ millions 33,310, and GNP per capita at market prices for 1974 was U.S.$ 4,410. The annual average percentage growth rate of the GNP per capita for the period 1960–74 was 4·4, and for the period 1965–74 was 5·0. [*See the note at the beginning of this section concerning GNP.*]

**PRINCIPAL BANKS**

**Bank für Arbeit und Wirtschaft Aktiengesellschaft.** Est. 1947. (General Manager, Walter Flöttl; Chairman of the Supervisory Board, Fritz Klenner) Assets as at 31 Dec. 1976, AS 30,707,566,607; deposits and current accounts AS 30,084,089,595. *Head Office:* 1010 Vienna, Seitzergasse 2–4. 27 branches.

**Creditanstalt-Bankverein.** (Chairman of the Managing Board, Dr. Heinrich Treichl.) Est. 1855. *Head Office:* Schottengasse 6, A–1010 Vienna. 88 branches.

**Girozentrale und Bank der österreichischen, Sparkassen Aktiengesellschaft.** (General Manager, Dr. Karl Pale.) *Head Office:* Schubertring 5, 1011 Vienna.

**Österreichische Länderbank A.G.** (Chairman of the Managing Board and Chief Executive Officer, Dr. W. Erndl.) Est. 1880. *Head Office:* Vienna. 82 branches.

**Oesterreichische Nationalbank.** (Austrian National Bank). (President, Hans Kloss RPD, LLD.) Est. 1923; Bank of Issue. *Head Office:* P.O. Box 61 A-1011 Vienna. 7 branches.

**PRODUCTION, INDUSTRY AND COMMERCE**

**Agriculture.** The total area under cultivation in 1970 was 1,543,666 hectares. The area and yield of the principal crops for 1971 were as follows:

| *Product* | *Area (thousand hectares)* | *Yield (thousand metric tons)* |
|---|---|---|
| Wheat | 273 | 974 |
| Barley | 294 | 1,015 |
| Oats | 98 | 283 |
| Rye | 145 | 488 |
| Potatoes | 105 | 2,716 |
| Sugar beets | 39 | 1,590 |

**Livestock.** In 1970 there were 2,488,000 head of cattle 3,091,000 pigs and 113,000 sheep.

Dairy produce in metric tons:

| | 1970 | 1971 |
|---|---|---|
| Milk yield | 3,298,601 | 3,282,000 |
| Butter | 40,697 | 40,584 |
| Cheese | 45,707 | 48,180 |

**Forestry.** The forests are one of Austria's great national assets. In 1971, 3,096,332 cubic metres of sawn wood were exported, together with 354,640 cu. m. of logs and 15,765 cu. m. of firewood.

The table below shows timber production:

| | 1970 (*cubic metres*) | 1971 |
|---|---|---|
| Timber for manufacture | 9,000,048 | 8,571,376 |
| Wood for fuel | 2,122,148 | 2,024,497 |

**Mining.** Production (in tons) is shown below:

| *Chief Products* | 1970 | 1971 |
|---|---|---|
| Brown coal (lignite) | 3,669,558 | 3,770,000 |
| Iron Ore | 3,996,700 | 4.171,000 |
| Lead-Zinc Ore | 219,407 | 382,000 |
| Copper Ore | 168,911 | 195,000 |
| Magnesite (crude) | 1,609,340 | 1,556,000 |

**Industry.** The largest oil refineries, coal extraction factories, mines and mineral refineries, iron and steel manufacturers, machinery and shipbuilding factories were nationalized in 1946, along with three banks and, in 1947, six electrical power companies.

| *Branch of Industry* | *Number of Establishments* Dec. 1971 | *Number of Workers December* 1971 |
|---|---|---|
| Iron and metal goods | 712 | 62,491 |
| Stone and pottery | 620 | 28,503 |
| Textiles | 721 | 65,557 |
| Other clothing | 658 | 38,770 |
| Machines | 624 | 71,180 |
| Chemicals | 699 | 61,310 |
| Paper | 82 | 17,371 |
| Paper processing and printing | 165 | 10,571 |
| Leather | 132 | 17,287 |
| Electro-industry | 309 | 63,641 |
| Timber industries | 512 | 27,711 |
| Iron and steel mines and works | 155 | 59,607 |
| Glass factories | 61 | 9,914 |

The following table shows indices of industrial production (1964 = 100):

| *Industrial Branch* | 1970 | 1971 |
|---|---|---|
| Mining | 84·9 | 87·7 |
| Oil | 128·9 | 135·6 |
| Iron and stee | 127·0 | 126·4 |
| Other metals | 129·0 | 134·3 |
| Foundry products | 127·1 | 126·3 |
| Iron and metalware | 146·1 | 160·0 |
| Machinery | 161·1 | 178·2 |
| Vehicles | 133·4 | 141·5 |
| Electrical engineering | 187·4 | 196·5 |
| Glass | 125·1 | 143·9 |
| Chemicals | 174·4 | 123·5 |
| Paper products | 145·5 | 150·3 |
| Paper processing | 163·8 | 182·7 |
| Wood processing | 154·0 | 179·6 |
| Leather | 98·6 | 99·3 |
| Textiles | 135·6 | 147·3 |
| Food | 131·1 | 135·1 |
| Tobacco | 122·0 | 124·8 |

**Commerce.** The following table shows imports and exports (in thousand schillings) for 1971:

| *Main Product Groups* | *Imports* | *Exports* |
|---|---|---|
| Food | 8,141,116 | 3,535,240 |
| Beverages and tobacco | 817,803 | 202,086 |
| Crude materials, inedible, except fuels | 7,992,440 | 7,373,414 |
| Mineral fuels, lubricants and related materials | 8,492,093 | 1,598,607 |
| Animal and vegetable oils and fats | 933,650 | 39,995 |
| Chemicals | 9,755,555 | 4,611,629 |
| Manufactured goods classified chiefly by material | 21,938,226 | 30,495,260 |
| Machinery and transport equipment | 35,748,579 | 19,708,307 |
| Miscellaneous manufactured articles | 10,638,457 | 11,407,513 |
| Miscellaneous transactions and commodities N.E.S. | 17,696 | 18,627 |
| Total | 10,445,791 | 78,990,678 |

## AUSTRIA

The following table shows imports and exports (in thousand schillings) from and to principal countries for 1971:

| *Country* | *Imports* | *Exports* |
|---|---|---|
| Germany (West) | 42,843,807 | 18,111,308 |
| Germany (East) | 646,210 | 842,421 |
| Italy | 6,973,265 | 7,328,862 |
| Yugoslavia | 1,186,313 | 3,332,306 |
| Poland | 1,360,709 | 1,248,601 |
| Switzerland | 7,740,245 | 8,819,597 |
| Czechoslovakia | 2,122,848 | 1,733,525 |
| Belgium–Luxembourg | 1,770,025 | 996,719 |
| Hungary | 1,548,383 | 2,221,947 |
| France | 3,835,709 | 1,837,363 |
| United Kingdom | 6,913,600 | 5,660,607 |
| Netherlands | 2,942,186 | 2,325,857 |
| Portugal | 416,813 | 653,050 |
| Norway | 474,229 | 1,069,929 |
| Denmark | 1,418,720 | 1,750,259 |
| Sweden | 2,947,879 | 3,092,228 |
| U.S.S.R. | 2,685,000 | 1,738,242 |
| U.S.A. | 3,869,177 | 3,185,085 |

### COMMUNICATIONS

In 1971 47·1 million tons of freight were imported, exported, or carried through Austria in transit. 24·1 million tons were transported by rail, 5·5 by ship, and 11·8 by road.

**Roads.** In 1971 there were 9,259 kilometres of toad and 6,634 bridges maintained by the Federal State, and 24,852 kilometres of road and 8,904 bridges by the Federal Provinces.

**Railways.** Austrian Railways are almost completely nationalized. The total length of the track in 1971 was 5,898 kilometres; 2,402 kilometres are already electrified. 176·4 million passengers travelled by rail in 1971.

**Shipping.** Austria has no sea frontier, but cargo is carried on the Danube. The following table shows the volume of goods traffic in 1970 and 1971.

| *Goods* | *Transported (in tons)* 1970 | 1971 |
|---|---|---|
| Coal and Coke | 1,478,924 | 1,150,763 |
| Iron Ore | 1,033,696 | 993,920 |
| Iron and Steel | 675,288 | 658,633 |
| Oil and Products | 2,635,000 | 1,818,871 |
| Cereals | 90,803 | 60,901 |
| Others | 4,101 | 1,468 |

Owing to the conclusion of trade agreements in recent years, Danube traffic is increasing steadily. The main Austrian shipping companies are the D.D.G.S. (Danube Steamship Company) and the C.O.M.O.S. (Continental Motor Shipping Company).

**Civil Aviation.** Austria's six airports handled 47,721 departures and landings in 1971.

**Telegraph and Telephones.** Telegraph and telephone are State operated. In 1971, 4,026,695 telegrams were sent, and 1,546,719 telephones were in operation.

**Broadcasting and Television.** There are three groups of broadcasting stations serving 2,159,574 radios. In 1971 1,586,114 television licences were issued.

### NEWSPAPERS

In 1970 there were 31 morning, 4 Monday and 141 weekly newspapers. The official organ is the Wiener Zeitung in Vienna.

**Unabhängige Kronen-Zeitung.** F. 1900. Independent. Muthgasse 2, Vienna 19.

**Kurier.** F. 1954. Independent. Lindengasse 52, Vienna 7.

**Arbeiter-Zeitung.** F. 1889. Socialist. Morning. Rechte Wienzeile 97, Vienna 5.

**Kleine Zeitung.** F. 1904. Independent. Schönaugasse 64, 8010, Graz.

**Die Presse.** F. 1848. Independent. Muthgasse 2, Vienna 19.

**Saltzburger Nachrichten.** F. 1946. Independent. Bergstrasse 12. 5021, Salzburg.

### EDUCATION

The whole educational system is supported by the state. Elementary education is free and compulsory. It normally begins in that school year which follows the day of the 6th birthday, and lasts nine years.

There were in the scholastic year 1971–72 5,818 elementary schools with an enrolment of 974,345 and 788 high schools with 232,292 pupils. There are four universities: Vienna (19,267), Graz (7,151), Innsbruck (6,860), and Salzburg (3,088).

On the third level of education there are also two technical universities, Vienna (6,748) and Graz (4,080), a mining college at Leoben (700), an agricultural college (1,151), a veterinary college (510), a commercial college (4,139), an academy of fine arts (477), an academy of applied arts (546), an academy of music and dramatic art (365), which are all at Vienna, and academies of music and dramatic art at Salzburg (465) and Graz (431), and a college of Social Sciences at Linz (1,865). There is also since 1969 a University of educational sciences in Klagenfurt.

### RELIGION

There is complete freedom of religion in Austria, although the population is predominantly Roman Catholic. There are two Roman Catholic Archbishoprics, Vienna, with bishoprics at St. Pölten, Linz and Eisenstadt in addition, and Salzburg with bishoprics also at Graz-Seckau, Gurk, Innsbruck and Feldkirch.

# Commonwealth of the Bahamas

(MEMBER OF THE COMMONWEALTH)

**Capital**—Nassau.

**Governor**—Sir Milo Boughton Butler, KCMG, GCVO, JP.

The country consists of an archipelago of 700 islands and more than 1,000 cays of which only 30 are inhabited, in the North Atlantic off the southeast coast of Florida. The principal islands are New Providence (containing the capital Nassau), Abaco, Harbour Island, Eleuthera, Inagua, Exuma, Cat Island, Long Island, Long Cay, the Biminis, San Salvador (or Watlings Island), Grand Bahama, Crooked Island, Acklins Island, Mayaguana, Andros Island, the Berry Islands, Ragged Island and Cat Cay.

Apart from a period in the early 1780s when Nassau was occupied by the Spaniards, the islands have been in British hands since 1647, when the 'Company of the Eleutherian Adventurers' was formed in London for the purpose of colonizing and developing the islands. An Act of Parliament was passed on 31 August 1649 which confirmed the Adventurers as proprietors of the islands.

## CONSTITUTION AND GOVERNMENT

In January 1964, a Constitution was introduced providing for internal self government with a Cabinet system, after having a representative form of Government since 1729.

Qualification for membership of the House of Assembly requires that a member shall be a British subject of 18 years or upwards, and shall have been resident in the country for a period of not less than five years before the date of his nomination.

Electoral system: The House of Assembly Elections Act provides for adult suffrage. Women are eligible for election to the House of Assembly.

On 20 December 1967, a seven-man committee was appointed to make recommendations for constitutional advance to full internal self-government. A majority report, recommended that the Premier should in future be consulted about the selection of a new Governor; that the Senate should consist of 15 members—ten appointed by the Governor on the advice of the Premier, and five on the advice of the Leader of the Opposition; that the functions of the Advisory Committee on the prerogative of mercy should be transferred to the Cabinet; that in the conduct of Bahamian external affairs and matters of defence, the Government of the Bahamas should be consulted in advance; and that there should be single-member constituencies.

In the General Election held on 10 April 1968, the Progressive Liberal Party won 29 seats in the House of Assembly, and the United Bahamian Party seven. One representative of the Labour Party, and one Independent (the Speaker of the House), were returned as before.

The formal proposals of the Bahamas Government, and the comments of the Opposition parties, were received in London during August 1968, and served as the basic working documents for a discussion at Marlborough House.

It was agreed that the territory should in future be known as 'The Commonwealth of the Bahama Islands', and that the Premier should be known as the 'Prime Minister'. The British Government retained the ultimate responsibility for appointing the Governor, but would consult the Government of the Bahamas informally to ensure that the needs of the territory were fully, fairly and satisfactorily met. The Conference also agreed that there should be a new post of Deputy Governor, the holder of which would, whenever necessary, act for the Governor and assist him in the exercise of special responsibilities.

It was agreed that the Senate should in future be composed of 16 members, of whom nine would be appointed by the Governor, on the advice of the Prime Minister, four on the advice of the Leader of the Opposition, and three after consultation with the Prime Minister and such other persons as the Governor, in his discretion, may decide to consult. The period for which the Senate might delay non-money bills and taxation bills would be reduced from 15 to nine months.

The Governor would retain ultimate responsibility for the Royal Bahamas Police Force and for internal security, but as soon as the new Constitution came into force, he would delegate immediate responsibility these for matters to a Minister designated on the advice of the Prime Minister. This Minister would keep the Governor and the Security Council informed on all important matters of policy within the field of entrusted responsibility.

A Security Council would be set up. This would consist of the Governor, the Prime Minister, another Minister, and such other persons as the Governor might appoint after consulting the Prime Minister. The Council would discuss matters of policy relating to external affairs, defence, the police and internal security, and advise the Governor on the discharge of his ultimate responsibility for the Police and internal security. In the discharge of this responsibility, he would not be obliged to accept the advice of the Council, and might, at his discretion, act on his own account, and give to the Commissioner of Police such instruction as he might think fit.

The Governor would retain his present special responsibility for defence and external affairs, but would be required to consult Bahamas Ministers through the Security Council on matters which involved the political, economic or financial interests of the territory. The British Government would delegate to the Government of the Bahamas the authority to negotiate and conclude trade agreements with other countries concerning the treatment of goods, or agreements with Commonwealth countries, or the United States, of a purely local concern, or relating to technical assistance or emigration.

When the decision was made that the Commonwealth of the Bahamas should move toward becoming an independent nation it was accepted by the governing Progressive Liberal Party, the opposition Free National Movement and the splinter Labour Party that "Independence" should be the theme of the next General Election. The Government effectively carried out a programme of educating the people of the Bahamas on Independence through seminars and conferences and panel discussions. The Opposition voiced its objection to Independence for the Bahamas "at this time".

The General Elections were held on 19 September 1972, and the Progressive Liberal Party was returned with an overwhelming majority, taking 29 of the 38 seats while the Opposition held on to 9. The sole Labour member and one Independent were defeated.

As this was a clear indication that the people favoured Independence, talks were arranged for 12–20 December 1972, in London. Independence was agreed to and the Bahamas became a nation on 10 July 1973. The first Governor-General of the Bahamas, Sir Milo Boughton Butler, GCMG, a Bahamian, was inaugurated on 1 August 1978, thus putting an end to a long line of Royal Governors.

### Cabinet

*Prime Minister and Minister of Economic Affairs:* The Hon. Lyden O. Pindling, PC, MP.

*Deputy Prime Minister and Minister of Finance:* The Hon. Arthur D. Hanna, MP.

*Minister of Tourism:* The Honourable C. T. Maynard, MP.

*Minister of Education and Culture:* The Honourable L. N. Coakley, MP.

*Minister of Labour and National Insurance:* The Honourable C. Darling, MP.

*Minister of Health and Works and Utilities:* The Honourable A. Loftus Roker, MP.

*Minister of Home Affairs:* The Honourable Darrell E. Rolle, MP.

*Minister of External Affairs and Attorney General:* The Honourable Paul L. Adderley.

*Minister of Agriculture and Fisheries and Local Government:* The Honourable R. F. Anthony Roberts, MP.

*Minister of Transport:* The Honourable George A. Smith, MP.

*Minister of Development:* The Honourable Alfred Maycock, MP.

## AREA AND POPULATION

The total area of the country is 5,380 sq. miles.

The population at mid-1974 was 199,000. The annual

average percentage growth rate for the period 1960–74 was 4·0 and for the period 1965–74 was 3·7. The majority of the inhabitants are of the Negro race. New Providence including Nassau had an estimated population of 112,500 at the end of 1973.

Births in 1973 numbered 4,419 and there were 1,180 deaths (excluding still births).

## FINANCE

The rate of inflation shown in the Bahama's Retail Price Index for 1976 was 4·2 per cent.

The main sources of revenue are customs duties, the receipts from fees, post office and public utilities.

The Bahamas have adopted a decimal currency. Notes are issued in denominations of B$100, B$50, B$20, B$10, B$5, B$3, B$1, and 50 cents; and coins in denominations of B$5, B$2, B$1, 50 cents, 25 cents, 15 cents, 10 cents, 5 cents and 1 cent.

The GNP at market prices for 1974 was U.S. $ millions 490, and the GNP per capita at market prices was U.S. $2,460. The annual average percentage growth rate of the GNP per capita for the period 1960–74 was 1·6, and for the period 1965–74 was −1·7. *[See the note at the beginning of this section concerning GNP.]*

## BANKS

**Bank of Montreal (Bahamas and Caribbean) Limited.** Est. 1970. (Managing Director, Harry G. Ackstein; Chairman, Kendal G. L. Isaacs, CBE, OC.) Assets as at 30 September, 1976; U.S. $188,360,618. *Head Office:* Harrison Building, P.O. Box N7118, Marlborough Street, Nassau, Bahamas. 3 branches.

**Bank of London and Montreal Limited.** Est. 1958. (Chairman, W. H. Sweeting, CMG, CBE.) Assets as at 30 September, 1976, $390,539,237; deposits and current accounts $355,836,660. *Head Office:* International Banking and Trusts Departments. King and George Streets, P.O. Box N-1262, Nassau, N.P., Bahamas. Number of branches and agencies, Guatemala 7, Honduras 6.

**Bahamas International Trust Company Limited.** Est. 1957. (Managing Director, Ralph S. Owers FCIS, FIB.; Chairman, Gordon W. P. Camble). Assets as at 30 November, 1976. B$16,866,446; deposits and current accounts B$13,518,056, *Head Office:* Bank Lane, P.O. Box N7768, Nassau, Bahamas.

## PRODUCTION AND COMMERCE

**Agriculture.** In 1975, 20·7 per cent of the $74,294,140 worth of foodstuffs consumed in the Bahamas was produced locally. In addition, cucumbers and tomatoes to the value of $312,694, were exported, mainly to the United States of America. There are strong indications that the Bahamian Export Trade in Agricultural Produce may be revived.

Some of significant development which will influence the future of agriculture in the Bahamas are:

The Bahamas Land Resource Survey which has indicated that about 200,000 acres of prime agricultural land occur on Abaco, Andros and Grand Bahama.

The Bahamas Agricultural Research Training and Development Project, a joint United States Agency for International Development/Bahamas Government undertaking. Under the provisions of the Project, Bahamians have been trained at different levels in various agricultural skills, Land Tenure Policies have been revived, an Agricultural Loan Guarantee Fund has been established in order to encourage commercial Banks to make loans for farming purposes and strong support has been given to the Co-operative movement.

The formation of Production Co-operatives, the expansion of the Farmer Services Division of the Ministry of Agriculture and Fisheries, the construction of Product Collecting and Grading Depots in five farming areas and the allocation of Crown Land for agricultural purposes.

It definitely seems that farming in the Bahamas, despite some disappointments such as the closing down of the Sugar Estate on Abaco, will become a more important Sector of the Economy.

**Industry.** Several light industries have been established on both Grand Bahama and New Providence in response to special encouragement Legislation, these include garment manufacturing, ice, furniture, purified water, plastic containers, perfumes, industrial gases, jewellery and others.

Larger industrial activities in the Bahamas, to a greater extent in Grand Bahama include: oil refining, oil transshipment, manufacture of alcoholic beverages, pharmaceuticals, aragonite mining, solar salt production and manufacture of steel piping.

Two industrial parks, one in New Providence and the other in Grand Bahama have been developed as part of the industrialization programme.

**Commerce.** The total imports for the year 1975 amounted to B$2,696,903,595, and exports to B$2,508,332,684. The main exports are salt, crawfish, pulpwood, cement, rum, aragonite, hormones, petroleum products.

## COMMUNICATIONS

**There are steamship services between the Bahamas and England (mainly cargo), Canada and the United States. In 1976, 632 freighters, 30 naval vessels and 559 cruise ships arrived at the port of Nassau with a total of 746,681 tons of cargo.**

**Most of the passenger traffic is now by air; Pan American World Airways, Eastern Airlines, Delta, Air Jamaica and International Bahama Airlines operate frequent daily services. There is direct communications with London and New York by the planes of B.O.A.C., Qantas and P.A.A., Trans Canada Airlines operate frequent services to Nassau from Toronto, Montreal and Tampa, and Eastern Airlines provide a daily service from Fort Lauderdale and Miami, Eastern Airlines and National also operate to a number of other points in the U.S.A.**

**Flamingo Airlines, and Delta provides Daily service between Boston, Newark, New York, Nassau and Freeport. Bahamas Air, the new flag carrier, and Island Flying Service provide commercial and charter services to the U.S.A. and within the Bahamas. Charter services are also operated between Nassau and Florida.**

## EDUCATION

The following table shows the number of schools by type, student enrolment and staff for 1975–76:

| | *Primary* | *Secondary* | *All-Ages* | *Primary* | *Secondary* | *All-Ages* | *Total* |
|---|---|---|---|---|---|---|---|
| Number | 57 | 23 | 104 | 17 | 10 | 15 | 226 |
| Students | 18,864 | 16,742 | 11,433 | 4,406 | 5,172 | 3,388 | 60,010 |
| Trained Staff | 542 | 506 | 311 | 146 | 155 | 102 | 1,762 |

NOTE: Teachers with academic degree only are not now considered as trained Teachers.

# Bahrain

**Capital**—Manama.

**Ruler**—H.H. Shaikh Isa bin Sulman Al Khalifa.

**National Flag:** Red; a white stripe pale-wise at the hoist, with a serration of eight teeth towards the fly.

THE Bahrain Islands are a small group lying some twenty miles off the east side of the Arabian mainland. Bahrain itself, the largest of the six islands comprising the group, is some thirty miles in length and about ten miles wide. The principal other island is Muharraq, connected to Manama, the capital of Bahrain, by a causeway a mile and a half long. Other islands are Sitra, joined to Bahrain by a bridge, which is the main anchorage and lies close to the refinery situated on Bahrain island. This anchorage affords twenty-four hour service to ships and tankers. Also Nebih Salih, famous for its fresh water springs, and Howar. The island of Bahrain is low-lying, the highest point being Jebel Dukhan in the centre of the island, a hill of some 450 feet. A new harbour has been built by the Bahrain Government to the East of the capital of Manama named Mina Salman. It was opened by His Highness, the Ruler, on 31 May 1962. It provides berths for six ships.

On 14 August 1971, full independence was proclaimed, the treaty arrangements with Britain being terminated, and a new treaty of friendship was signed with Britain the next day. On 17 August, Shaikh Isa took the title of Amir. In September Bahrain became a member of the Arab League and the UN.

Bahrain has always been the centre of the famous pearl fishing industry of the Arabian Gulf; in recent years, however, the industry has declined greatly, partly owing to the competition of the Japanese cultured pearl.

The islands' main source of revenue is oil. Bahrain's first oil well was "spudded in" in 1931. The Bahrain Petroleum Company (BAPCO)—a subsidiary of Socal—acquired the mining lease in 1934. In 1975 the Bahrain Government assumed a direct 60 per cent interest in the Bahrain oil field and natural gas production, together with related crude oil and gas facilities of Bapco. Bahrain's oil reserves are limited and production continues to show a steady decline. In 1975 the Refinery throughput was 215,500 barrels per day. Crude oil from the Dammam field in Saudi Arabia is carried via a 34-mile long pipeline to the Bahrain refinery. Some 61,000 barrels of crude oil are currently produced daily from the Bahrain zones. Natural gas reserves, however, are plentiful and 250 million cubic feet of natural gas are produced daily. Bapco employs nearly 4,000 people of whom 88·8 per cent are Bahraini and 5·9 per cent are British. The efinery is one of the largest in the Middle East.

Bahrain is perhaps one of the most developed of the Gulf shaikhdoms, having been, for many centuries before the discovery of oil, an important trading centre.

Social development has been matched by industrial and commercial progress. The first spectacular step forward was the establishment of Aluminium Bahrain—Alba. The smelter now produces over 120,000 tonnes of aluminium annually.

The Government is firmly committed to a policy of industrial diversification. Recent years have seen an increase in both small scale industrial development and in the establishment of service industries for the whole Gulf area.

### Cabinet Ministers

*Prime Minister:* His Excellency Shaikh Khalifa bin Sulman Al-Khalifa.
*Heir Apparent and Minister of Defence:* His Excellency Shaikh Hamad bin Isa Al-Khalifa.
*Minister of Foreign Affairs:* H. E. Shaikh Mohamed bin Mubarak Al-Khalifa.
*Minister of Finance and National Economy:* H. E. Mr. Ebrahim Abdul-Karim.
*Minister of Justice:* H. E. Shaikh Abdulla bin.
*Minister of Education:* H. E. Shaikh Abdul Aziz bin Mohamed Al-Khalifa.
*Minister of Health:* H. E. Dr. Ali Fakhro.
*Minister of Commerce, Agriculture and Economy:* H. E. Mr. Habib Kassem.
*Minister of Labour and Social Affairs:* H. E. Shaikh Isa bin Mohamed Al-Khalifa.
*Minister of Development and Engineering Services:* **H. E. Mr. Yousif Ahmed Al-Shirawi.**
*Minister of State for Legal Affairs:* Dr. Husain Mohammed Al-Baharna.
*Minister of State for Cabinet Affairs:* Mr. Jawad Salim Al Urayyed.
*Cabinet Secretary:* Mr. Saeed Zeera.
*Minister of Information:* H. E. Tariq Abdulrahman Almoayyed.
*Minister of Housing:* H. E. Shaikh Khalid bin Abdulla Al-Khalifa.
*Minister of Communications:* H. E. Ibrahim Humaidan.
*Minister of Works, Power and Water:* H. E. Majid Jawad Al-Jishi

### AREA AND POPULATION

The total area of the Islands is about 255 square miles The population at mid-1974 was 245,000. The annual average percentage growth rate of the population for the period 1960–74 was 3·4, and for the period 1965–74 was 3·1.

### CURRENCY

In October 1965, a new currency came into use. The unit is the Bahrain dinar, divided into 1,000 units called fils.

### FINANCE

The GNP at market prices for 1974 was US $ millions 580 and the GNP per capita for 1974 was US $2,350. The annual average percentage growth rate of the GNP per capita for the period 1960–74 was n.a., and for the period 1971–74 was 21·2. [*See the note at the beginning of this section concerning GNP.*]

Commercial banks in Bahrain include: National Bank of Bahrain, Bank of Bahrain and Kuwait, British Bank of the Middle East, Grindlays Bank, Citibank, Chase Manhattan Bank, Arab Bank, Rafidain Bank, Banque du Caire, Chartered Bank, Benk Melli Iran, Bank Saderat Iran, Habib Bank, United Bank, Algemene Bank, Continental Bank, Banque de Paris et des Pays Bas, National Bank of Abu Dhabi.

Thirty-two international banks are licensed for offshore banking operations from branches in Bahrain. A further number have representative offices in Bahrain.

Banking and exchange operations in Bahrain are controlled by the Bahrain Monetary Agency.

### PRODUCTION, INDUSTRY AND COMMERCE

Despite the small average annual rainfall of only four inches, one-twentieth of Bahrain consists of cultivated gardens and groves, the chief crops being dates, citrus and paw paw fruits, almonds, lucerne and vegetables. Bahrain is being developed as a major manufacturing state, the first important enterprise being the Aluminium Bahrain smelter.

Traditional industries, pearling, boat building, and weaving have tended to decline as the Government's policy of industrial diversification has developed.

Although oil reserves are limited natural gas is plentiful and among the new industries likely to be attracted to Bahrain are those which plan to make use of it.

Service industries of all kinds are of steadily increasing importance. Many local and foreign industries attracted by the lack of taxation and by the facilities provided at the industrial areas at Mina Sulman and Sitra are now fully established.

Bahrain is being developed as a regional centre for business and banking. An off-shore banking centre was established in 1975 and many prominent international banks have been granted licenses.

In 1975 work began on a major project to construct a 500,000 DWT Dry Dock for supertankers. The Arab Shipbuilding and Repair Yard (ASRY), a multinational venture organized by OAPEC, will be operational in 1977.

**Free Transit Area.** Bahrain became a Free Transit Area on 1 January 1958. Goods from any country except Israel may now pass through Bahrain without payment of any duty and may be stored in the Customs Area for the first 14 days without charges. Storage charges are taken by weight (for sacks) BD. 1,200 fils/cubic ton, and by measurement for cases and bundles, 50 fils/cubic foot per 14 days. Porterage, crane and pier fees are the same as for direct imports.

The following table shows the value of imports and exports for the year 1975 in Bahrain dinars. In this table 'n.e.s.' means 'not elsewhere specified'.

## BAHRAIN

| Commodity | Imports | Exports |
|---|---|---|
| Live animals | 1,026,234 | |
| Meat and meat preparations | 2,990,502 | 256,844 |
| Dairy products and eggs | 3,053,494 | 147,361 |
| Fish and fish preparations | 205,633 | 800,180 |
| Cereals and cereal preparations | 3,000,941 | 357,272 |
| Fruit and vegetables | 5,704,181 | 1,067,814 |
| Sugar, sugar preparations and honey | 2,356,822 | 299,651 |
| Coffee, tea, cocoa and spices | 3,279,099 | 1,836,146 |
| Animal feeding stuff | 317,138 | 31,880 |
| Miscellaneous food preparations | 1,044,054 | 80,959 |
| Beverages | 2,701,686 | 376,741 |
| Tobacco and tobacco manufactures | 3,263,457 | 1,594,921 |
| Hides and skins undressed | 788 | 20 |
| Oil-seed, nuts and kernels | 26,460 | 3,082 |
| Wood, lumber and cork | 1,916,560 | 38,821 |
| Textile fibres and waste | 71,491 | 732 |
| Crude fertilizers | 289,473 | 1,033 |
| Metal ores and scrap | 238,203 | 22,444 |
| Crude animal and vegetable materials n.e.s. | 432,543 | 226,171 |
| Coal, coke and briquettes | 1,702 | |
| Petroleum and products | 3,971,987 | 331,076 |
| Gas natural and manufactured | 248,546 | 37,275 |
| Animal oils and fats | 19,688 | 1,443 |
| Fixed vegetable oils and fats | 268,111 | 3,288 |
| Oils and fats, processed and waxes | 197,289 | 2,424 |
| Chemical elements and components | 7,710,358 | 152,191 |
| Tar and chemicals from oil and gas | 4,289 | 73 |
| Dyeing, tanning and colouring materials | 1,431,298 | 140,160 |
| Medical and pharmaceutical products | 1,684,532 | 56,055 |
| Essential oils etc. | 3,508,069 | 792,485 |
| Fertilizers manufactured | 21,624 | |
| Explosives | 28,086 | |
| Plastic materials | 514,938 | 25,750 |
| Miscellaneous chemical materials | 1,943,118 | 23,937 |
| Leather and leather manufactures n.e.s. | 49,441 | 825 |
| Rubber manufactures n.e.s. | 952,615 | 22,378 |
| Wood and cork manufactures | 3,066,064 | 71,640 |
| Paper, paperboard and manufactures thereof | 2,843,667 | 153,299 |
| Textile, yarn fabrics etc. | 12,718,530 | 5,427,341 |
| Iron and steel | 13,413,596 | 7,110,416 |
| Non-ferrous metal | 1,659,746 | 32,154,258 |
| Manufactures of metal n.e.s. | 12,779,622 | 1,566,057 |
| Machinery excluding electric | 45,158,796 | 5,626,899 |
| Electrical machinery | 24,042,952 | 3,446,433 |
| Transport equipment | 85,973,394 | 13,090,992 |
| Sanitary, plumbing, lighting equipment | 1,715,417 | 143,872 |
| Furniture | 3,125,728 | 309,835 |
| Travel goods, handbags, etc. | 1,484,825 | 956,880 |
| Clothing | 9,874,771 | 5,588,648 |
| Footwear | 4,390,429 | 3,343,360 |
| Scientific etc. instruments | 4,518,199 | 1,146,370 |
| Miscellaneous manufactured articles n.e.s. | 7,847,473 | 3,569,109 |
| Special transactions | 68,116 | 74,094 |
| Zoo animals, dogs, etc. | 700 | |
| War firearms ammunition | 20,825 | |
| Total (all imports and exports) | 229,509,141 | 83,952,193 |

### COMMUNICATIONS

Steamships make periodic calls. Owing to its geographic position Bahrain is a regular port of call for many of the airlines, including the British Airways service. In addition, Gulf Air runs a regular service with the Arabian mainland, with Qatar, the U.A.E., Muscat, Bombay, Karachi, and London.

Bahrain's Earth Station links Bahrain and most of the Gulf with the United Kingdom and many other countries, through a multitude of telephone, telegraph/telex and data circuits.

Regular lines of cargo vessels with passenger accommodation serve Bahrain and almost every ship plying the Arabian Gulf stops here. The main shipping agencies (all in Manama) are:

**Gray, Mackenzie & Co., Ltd.**

B.I.S.N.: India, Pakistan, Gulf and return: one vessel nine days each way.
Australia, Colombo, Pakistan, Gulf: one vessel per month.
Far East and Gulf: one vessel per month.
Strick line: England, Europe, Gulf and return: five vessels per month.
Hansa Line: Germany, Europe, Gulf, America: five vessels per month.

**Yusuf bin Ahmed Kanoo**

Nedlloyd Lines: U.S./Middle East Service: U.S.A. East Coast, Gulf: one vessel per month. Europe/Middle East Service: North Europe, London, Gulf: two vessels per month.

Nedlloyd and Hoegh Lines: U.S.A. West Coast, Far East, Ceylon, India, Pakistan, Gulf: one vessel per month.

Royal Interocean Lines, combined service with Mercury Shipping Co. Ltd.; S. and E. Africa, Gulf: one to two vessels per month.

Kuwait Shipping Company: Europe/Middle East Service: North Europe, London, Liverpool, Gulf: one or two vessels per month. Far East/Middle East Service: Japan, Hong Kong, Singapore, Gulf: one vessel per month. U.S.A./Middle East Service: U.S.A. East Coast, Gulf: one vessel per month. Australia/Middle East Service: Australia, Gulf: one vessel every two months. Iraqi Maritime Transport Company Ltd.: North Europe, London, Gulf: one vessel every two months.

Pan-Islamic Steamship Company Ltd.: Pakistan, Gulf: Passenger-cum-cargo service: two vessels per month.

**United Travel and Shipping Agency**

Johnson Line: Far East, Colombo, India, Pakistan, Gulf: two vessels per month.

Concordia Line: U.S.A. East Coast, Gulf: two vessels per month.

Nouvelle Compagnie Havraise Peninsulaire: North Europe, Genoa, Gulf: one vessel per month.

Compagnie Maritime Belge: North Europe, Gulf: one vessel per two months.

**International Agencies Co. Ltd.**

Shipping: Travel: Insurance: Manufacturers' representatives. P.O. Box 584, Bahrain.

**The Gulf Agency Co. (Bahrain), Ltd.**

**Al-Sherif Shipping Agency**
Hellenic Line: U.S. East Coast, Mediterranean, Red Sea, Arabian Gulf and return: one vessel per month.

Karachi Steam Navigation Co.: Ceylon, India, Pakistan, Arabian Gulf and return: one vessel per month.

**Civil Aviation.** As an airport, Bahrain is one of the main staging ports between England and the Far East for British Airways and Air Ceylon. It is the Arabian Gulf's main air communication centre, and is at present being expanded. From here, Gulf Air run services to the Arabian mainland, Qatar the Trucial Coast, Muscat, Bombay, Karachi; and London whilst Kuwait Airways, Iraqi Airways, M.E. Airlines, Air India, Iran Air, P.I.A., Qantas, T.M.A., Lebanese International Airlines and Saudi Arabian Airlines all call regularly and Aden Airways run a fortnightly plane. Lately, B.E.A. has linked up with Bahrain, and charter aircraft also land frequently. Bahrain was the first airport in the world to receive a scheduled Concorde aircraft flight. The airliner is in regular service to London.

# The People's Republic of Bangladesh

## (MEMBER OF THE COMMONWEALTH)

**Capital**—Dacca.

**President**—Major-General Ziaur Rahman.

### CONSTITUTION AND GOVERNMENT

The present government is headed by President and Chief Martial Law Administrator, Major-General Ziaur Rahman. The people have reposed their confidence in his leadership through a country-wide referendum held on 30 May, 1977.

The Constitution of Bangladesh provides a presidential system of Government where the President is the executive head. The constitution is based on four principles, namely, Absolute Trust and Faith in Almighty Allah, Nationalism, Democracy and Socialism meaning economic and social justice. The Constitution provides for a single chamber of Parliament consisting of 315 members, including 15 women members directly elected by the people. The term of the parliament is five years. The next general election is to be held in December, 1978.

#### The President's Council of Advisors

*Chief of Naval Staff and Deputy Chief Martial Law Administration-in-Charge of Ministry of Flood Control, Water Resources and Power, Shipping and Communication:* Rear-Admiral M. H. Khan.
*Chief of Air Staff and Deputy Chief Martial Law Administrator in-Charge of Civil Aviation and Tourism:* Air-Vice-Marshal A. G. Mahmood.
*Minister of Land Administration, Rural Development and Cooperatives:* Kazi Anwarul Huq.
*Minister of Planning:* Dr. M. N. Huda.
*Minister of Public Works and Urban Development:* Dr. Mohammad Abdur Rashid.
*Minister of Population Control and Family Planning:* Dr. Mohammad Ibrahim.
*Minister of Relief and Rehabilitation:* Mrs. Benita Roy.
*Minister of Ministry of Health Division, Labour and Social Welfare:* Col. (Rtd) M. M. Haque.
*Minister of Agriculture:* Mr. Azizul Huq.
*Minister of Information and Broadcasting:* Mr. Akbar Kabir.
*Minister of Commerce:* Mr. Mohammad Saifur Rahman.
*Minister of Foreign Affairs:* Professor Mohammad Shamsul Haq.
*Minister of Education, Cultural Affairs and Sport:* Professor Syed Ali Ahasan.
*Minister of Textiles:* Dr. Mozaffar Ahmed.
*Minister of Industries:* Mr. Jamal Uddin Ahmed.
*Minister of Petroleum and Minerals:* Mr. Ashfaque Hossain Khan.
*Minister of Food:* Mr. Abdul Momen Khan.
*Minister of Jute:* Mr. S. M. Safiul Azam.

### AREA AND POPULATION

The estimated population of Bangladesh in mid-1974 was 76,200,000. The population of the principal towns (1971 estimate) is Dacca, 915,000; Chittagong, 457,700; Khulna, 403,400; Naryanganj, 389,000.

The annual average population growth rate percentage for the period 1960–74 was 2·5, and for the period 1965–74 was 2·3.

### CURRENCY

The Bangladesh currency has the Paisas as the basic unit. There are 100 Paisas to one Taka.

### FINANCE

The Revenue Budget for the year 1974–75 shows a revenue receipt of Takas 470·23 Crores against which the expenditure balanced.

The GNP at market prices for 1974 was U.S. $ millions 7,910, the GNP per capita for 1974 was U.S. $100·0. The annual average percentage growth rate of the GNP per capita for the period 1960–74 was −0·5, and for 1965–74 was −1·9. [*See the note at the beginning of this section concerning GNP.*]

### PRODUCTION, INDUSTRY AND COMMERCE

The economy of Bangladesh is predominantly agricultural. More than 80 per cent of the population is employed in agricultural production, and about 64 per cent of the total land area is under cultivation. The production figures of the main agricultural crops in 1975–76 were rice 12·561 million tons; wheat 0·251 million tons; jute 5·00 million tons; sugarcane 5·886 million tons; tea 6,993 million lbs; fish 0·806 million metric tons.

The industry of the country is primarily agricultural. The main industrial products for 1975–76 were jute manufacture 0·441 million tons; printing paper 6,873 tons; newsprint 20,045 tons; sugar 87 thousand tons; yarn 89 thousand tons; cloth 70 thousand tons; mineral resources include proved reserves of methane gas amounting to 8·29 to 9.36 trillion cubic feet and 1,600 million tons of superior quality coal. The government has recently liberalized its industrial policy giving more facilities to private sector and foreign investment.

The items that earn the bulk of foreign exchange are jute, jute goods, tea, hide and skins, newsprint, fish and handicrafts.

# Barbados

(MEMBER OF THE COMMONWEALTH)

**Capital**—Bridgetown.

**Governor-General**—Sir Deighton Harcourt Lisle Ward, GCMG.

### CONSTITUTION AND GOVERNMENT

BARBADOS is an island in the West Indies to the East of the Windward Islands. It was occupied by the English in 1627. Unlike most of the neighbouring islands, it never passed out of British possession.

Barbados has one of the oldest constitutions in the Commonwealth and one in which conventions play an important part.

The Legislature consists of the Governor-General, a Senate and a House of Assembly. The Senate comprises 21 members appointed by the Governor-General. Of these, 12 are appointed on the advice of the Prime Minister, two on the advice of the Leader of the Opposition and the other seven by the Governor-General alone. The House of Assembly consists of 24 members elected every five years by adult suffrage. In 1963 by an Act of the Legislature the voting age was reduced to 18.

The Cabinet consists of the Prime Minister and not less than five other Ministers (at present eight) appointed by the Governor-General on the advice of the Prime Minister, and it is the principal instrument of policy.

The Governor-General appoints as Prime Minister the person who appears to him to be best able to command a majority in the House of Assembly. On the advice of the Prime Minister the Governor-General also appoints other Ministers and the Ministers without Portfolio who become members of the Cabinet.

Barbados became an independent sovereign state on 30 November 1966 following elections held on 3 November.

**Ministry** (8 September 1976)

*Prime Minister, Minister of Finance and Planning:* J. M. G. Adams.
*Minister of Caribbean Affairs, External Trade, Industry and Tourism:* Bernard St. John.
*Minister of Labour and Community Services:* Lionel Craig.
*Attorney General, Minister of External Affairs:* Henry Forde.
*Minister of Agriculture, Food and Consumer Affairs:* Charles Bolden.
*Minister of Health and National Insurance:* Miss Billie Miller.
*Minister of Housing and Land, Leader of the Senate:* Ronald Mapp.
*Minister of Communications and Works:* Lloyd Brathwaite.
*Minister of Education and Community Development:* Louis Tull.

### AREA AND POPULATION

Barbados is nearly 21 miles long and 14 miles wide and contains an area of about 166 square miles. The population at mid-1974 was 214,000. The inhabitants are chiefly of African descent. Persons of European descent represent only 5·1 per cent of the population, and those of mixed European-African descent 17·2 per cent. The annual average percentage population growth rate for the period 1960–74 was 0·2 and for the period 1965–74 was 0·3.

### FINANCE

The budget figures for 1975–76 were; Revenue $203 million Expenditure $207·6 million.

The Public Debt at was $·184 million. The estimates given below of GNP per capita and its growth rate are tentative.

The GNP at market prices for 1974 was U.S. $millions 290, and the GNP per capita at market prices was U.S. $1,200. The annual average percentage growth rate of the GNP per capita for the period 1960–74 was 5·2, and for the period 1965–74 was 5·2. [*See the note at the beginning of this section concerning GNP.*]

### PRODUCTION AND COMMERCE

The main crop grown in Barbados is sugar, which constitutes the chief wealth of the island.

The values of various exports in 1974 were; sugar, $52,184,510; rum, $4,974,871; molasses, $7,885,827. In 1974 the value of imports was $85,878,073; and the value of exports was $27,153,831.

### COMMUNICATIONS

There are no railways on the island. The Chief Technical Director is responsible for the maintenance of the main roads. The total length of road open for traffic is 1,020 miles, of which 740 miles have an asphalt surface.

Regular steamship services include those of the Booker Line, Hapaglloyd Line, Himmelman Supply Co., Lion Ferry A/B Line, Polish Ocean Line, Cunard Line, Holland/America Line, Swedish/American Line, Norwegian/Caribbean Line, Black Sea Shipping Co., Baltic Shipping Cruises, Italian Line, Great Lakes Trans-Caribbean Line, Tropical Shipping, Vinke and Co. Ltd., Harms Brothers Line, Sun Line, Delian Cruises, Pacific Far East Line, Navios Corporation, and Navigan Corporation, Booth-Lamport and Holt New York/West Indies Services, Compagnie Générale Transatlantique, West Indies Shipping Service, Harrison Line, Royal Netherlands Steamship Company, Saguenay Shipping Ltd., Westfall-Larsen, Boomerang, Geest Lines.

The new Deep Water Harbour which was opened on the 6 May 1961, is in full operation. It provides berths for eight ships between 500 and 600 feet in length including one specially built for bulk loading sugar. It has a minimum depth of 32 feet L.W.O.S.T. All berths for ships are provided with bunker fuel, fresh water and telephone.

### AIR TRANSPORT

Grantley Adams International Airport is owned and operated by the Government of Barbados. Services are provided by British Airways, B.W.I.A., Quebecair, Pan-American, Air Canada, L.I.A.T., S.A.S., A.L.M., Cubana Airlines, V.I.A.S.A., I.C.A., Eastern Transair, and Wardair. During 1974, 363,092 passengers arrived at Seawell International Airport and 369,295 departed.

### TELEPHONE SERVICE

The entire island is provided with a telephone service by the Barbados Telephone Co. Ltd., a aubsidiarq of Continental Telephone Corporation, U.S.A. At 31 July, 1976 there were 26,000 telephones. The system is entirely automatic and is served by seven exchanges.

A 24-hour-a-day overseas radio-telephone service is operated to all parts of the world. There is an internal telegraph system, but external systems are operated by Cable and Wireless (W.I.) Ltd., and the Western Union Telegraph Co.

The Congor Bay Earth Station was opened in 1972 by Cable and Wireless Ltd. It provides Barbados with direct access to the global space communication system and now allows for the handling of every form of telecommunication service, including inter-continental colour television.

### NEWSPAPERS

**The Advocate-News.** F. 1895. Daily. Bridgetown.

**The Beacon.** F. 1946. Weekly. Bridgetown.

**Sunday Advocate-News.** F. 1946. Weekly. Bridgetown.

**Barbados Observer.** F. 1934. Weekly. Bridgetown.

**The Truth.** F. 1955.Bi-weekly. Bridgetown.

**The Democrat.** F. 1970. Weekly. Bridgetown.

### EDUCATION

There are 120 primary schools, 10 newer and 10 older secondary schools which are maintained entirely from Government funds. At the close of the school year (1976–77) the number of pupils was 36,000 in primary schools, 12,000 in secondary (newer) schools and 5,674 in secondary grammar schools. There are 18 approved independent secondary schools with 6,393 pupils.

Since January 1962 education in all government schools

has been free. About 700 bursaries are provided each year for children who attend approved independent secondary schools. These schools are also aided by government each year. Pupils are prepared for G.C.E. examinations.

Erdiston Training College for teachers provides courses for teachers of this island and some of the Windward and Leeward Islands. There are 252 students in residence.

Further education is provided by the Barbados Evening Institute, the Samuel Jackman Prescod Polytechnic, and the Barbados Hotel Training School.

The Housecraft Centre in Bridgetown and 13 other centres in the island provide training for about 1,500 persons each year in Home Economics.

The Barbados Community College started classes in January 1969. There are at present seven Divisions in the Community College, viz.:— Liberal Arts, Fine Arts, Science, Commerce, Technology, Community Services and Health Sciences. An Agricultural Division is being planned.

The University of the West Indies College of Arts and Sciences in Barbados registered its first students in October 1963. First degrees were presented in February 1967 by the Chancellor of the University. It has 1,000 students for the academic year 1976–77 drawn from the English-speaking Caribbean countries.

Government expenditure on education for 1975–76 was $41 million.

### RELIGION

The population is almost wholly Christian and the Anglican Church, the membership of which comprises approximately 70 per cent of the population, is now dis-established.

# Belgium

**Capital**—Brussels.

**Sovereign**—H.M. King Baudouin.

**National Flag**: A tricolor, pale-wise, black, yellow, red.

### CONSTITUTION AND GOVERNMENT

BELGIUM was united to Holland by the Congress of Vienna (1815), but in 1830 a revolution broke out in Brussels and the Belgian Provinces seceded and formed themselves into an independent state. A constitution was adopted in 1831, which declared that Belgium was a constitutional hereditary monarchy. A National Congress elected Prince Léopold of Saxe-Coburg, King of the Belgians and he ascended the throne on 21 July 1831. When King Léopold III abdicated on 17 July 1951, he was succeeded by his eldest son, the present monarch, King Baudouin on 17 July 1951.

Belgium is a constitutional monarchy, with King Baudouin as the reigning Monarch.

The Government and administrative structure of Belgium is laid down by the Constitution promulgated in 1831.

The Constitutional structure of Belgium comprises the traditional allocation of public authority to three main powers: the Legislative, the Executive and the Judiciary.

The Executive authority (the power to issue decrees implementing laws, the conduct of foreign policy, the maintenance of law and order, military matters, etc.) is vested in the King, assisted by the Government headed by the Prime Minister. Ministers are politically responsible to Parliament.

Parliament is bi-cameral. Members of both Houses (Senate and House of Representatives) are elected by the citizens by proportional representation. The Executive, the House of Representatives and the Senate jointly possess the Legislative power.

As a result of the elections of 17 April 1977, Parliament is now composed as follows:

| *Parties* | *House* | *Senate* |
|---|---|---|
| Christian Social Party (PSC-CVP) | 80 | 70 |
| Socialist Party (PSB-BSP) | 62 | 52 |
| Party des Réformes et de la Liberté de Wallonie and Partij voor Vrijheid en Vooruitgang (PRLW-PVV) | 31 | 24 |
| Front des Francophones (FDF) and Rassemblement Wallon (RW) | 15 | 15 |
| Volksunie (VU) | 20 | 17 |
| Liberal Party (PL) | 2 | 2 |
| Communist Party (PC) and Union Démocratique et Progressiste (UDP) | 2 | 1 |
| number of seats | 212 | 181 |

It should be noted that:

1. The FDF (Democratic French-speaking Front) stood for election only in Brussels.

The Rassemblement Wallon (Walloon Assembly) stood in all parts of the French-speaking area of the country.

The FDF and Rassemblement Wallon had formed an alliance and appeared on the voting lists under the same number.

2. The Volksunie is a flemish Nationalist Party.

3. The CVP (Christian People's Party) is the Flemish wing of the social democracy, the PSC (Christian Social Party) being the Walloon wing of the same party.

4. The PSB-BSP is the Belgian Socialist Party.

5. The PL (Liberal Party) and the PRLW and PVV (Parti des Réformes et de la liberté de Wallonie—Partij voor Vrijheid en Vooruitgang) are parties representative of the Middle Classes.

The present coalition is composed of the PSC-CVP, PSB-BSP, FDF and VU.

**H.M. BAUDOUIN** Albert Charles Léopold Axel Marie Gustave, King of the Belgians; born at the Château de Stuyvenberg, 7 September 1930; succeeded his father on his abdication 17 July 1951; married on 15 December 1960 to Fabiola de Mora y Aragón, daughter of the Count de Mora and Marquess of Casa Riera.

Brothers and Sisters of the King: (a) Full brother and sister, issue of the 1st marriage of King Léopold III: 1. Princess JOSÉPHINE CHARLOTTE Ingeborg Élisabeth Marie José Marguerite Astrid; born at Brussels, 11 October 1927; married at Luxembourg, 9 April 1953, Jean, Hereditary Grand Duke of Luxembourg and has issue. 2. Prince ALBERT Felix Humbert Theodore Christian Eugene Marie, Prince of Liège; born 6 June 1934; married (civilly and religiously) 2 July 1959 Donna Paola Margherita Maria-Antonia Consiglia, born at Forte dei Marmi (Lucques, Italy) 11 September 1937; daughter of late Prince Fulco Ruffo di Calabria. (b) Half brother and sisters, issue of the 2nd marriage of King Léopold III: 3. Prince ALEXANDRE Emmanuel Henri Albert Marie Léopold; born at the Château de Laeken, 18 July 1942. 4. Princess MARIE CHRISTINE Daphné Astrid Élisabeth Léopoldine; born at the Château de Laeken, 6 February 1951. 5. Princess MARIAESMERALDA Adelaide Lilian Anne Léopoldine; born at the Château de Laeken, 30 September 1956.

Father of the King: H.M. LÉOPOLD III Philippe Charles Albert Meinrad Hubert Marie Miguel, formerly King of the Belgians; born at Brussels, 3 November 1901; succeeded his father King Albert 17 February 1934; abdicated the throne in favour of his eldest son, Brussels, 17 July 1951; married firstly at Stockholm (civilly), 4 November and at Brussels (religiously), 10 November 1926 Princess Astrid (born at Stockholm, 17 November 1905, killed in a motor accident at Küssnacht, Switzerland, 29 August 1935), youngest daughter of Prince Carl of Sweden, Duke of Västergötland; secondly at the Château de Laeken (religiously), 11 September and (civilly) 6 December 1941, Marie Lilian (born at Highbury, London, 28 November 1916) daughter of late Henri Baels.

Uncle and Aunt of the King: Children of King Albert (born 8 April 1875, died 17 February 1934): 1. Prince CHARLES Théodore Henri Antoine Meinrad, Count of Flanders, Regent of the Kingdom of Belgium form 20 September 1944 until the return of King Léopold III, 21

July 1950; born at Brussels, 10 October 1903. 2. Princess MARIE JOSÉ Charlotte Sophie Amélie Henriette Gabrielle; born at Ostende, 4 August 1906; married at Rome, 8 January 1930, Umberto II, formerly King of Italy and has issue.

**Ministry** (3 June 1977)

*Deputy Prime Minister and Minister for Public Service:* Léon Hurez.
*Deputy Prime Minister and Minister for National Defence:* Paul Vanden Boeynants.
*Minister of Justice:* Renaat Van Elslande.
*Minister of Foreign Affairs:* Henri Simonet.
*Minister of Economic Affairs:* Willy Claes.
*Minister of Social Security and Secretary of State for Social Walloon Affairs:* Alfred Califice.
*Minister of Communications:* Jozef Chabert.
*Minister of Education (Dutch):* Jef Ramaekers.
*Minister of Agriculture and Middle Classes:* Antoine Humblet.
*Minister of Dutch Culture and Flemish Affairs:* Mrs. Rika De Backer van Ocken.
*Minister of Education (French):* Joseph Michel.
*Minister of Public Health and Environment:* Luc Dhoore.
*Minister of Finance:* Gaston Geens.
*Minister of External Trade:* Hector De Bruyne.
*Minister of Overseas Development:* Lucien Outers.
*Minister of PTT and Brussels Affairs:* Léon Defosset.
*Minister of Pensions:* Jan Wijninckx.
*Minister of Employment and Labour:* Guy Spitaels.
*Minister of Interior:* Henri Boel.
*Minister of Scientific Policy:* Jan Vandekerckhove.
*Minister of French Culture:* Jean-Maurice Dehousse.
*Minister of Public Works and Walloon Affairs:* Guy Mathot.

## LOCAL GOVERNMENT

The country is divided into nine provinces and 2,539 communes which enjoy a large measure of local autonomy. Voting in communal elections is by proportional representation.

## LEGAL SYSTEM

There is a Supreme Court, three courts of appeal at Brussels, Ghent and Liège, assize courts for the trial of political and criminal cases and 26 courts of first instance. Minor crimes and misdemeanours are dealt with by local justices of the peace.

**Supreme Court**

*Premier President:* J. Bayot.
*President of the Court:* M. Van Beirs.
*Procurator General:* W. Ganshof van der Meersch.
*First Advocate General:* P. Mahaux.

## POPULATION

The following table shows the population of the provinces:

| *Province* | *Census of 31 December* 1973 |
|---|---|
| Antwerpen-Anvers | 1,550,494 |
| Brabant | 2,206,054 |
| Hainaut-Henegouwen | 1,321,258 |
| Liége-Luik | 1,016,333 |
| Limburg-Limbourg | 672,024 |
| Luxembourg-Luxemburg | 218,183 |
| Namur-Namen | 385,705 |
| Oost-Vlaanderen-East Flanders | 1,320,033 |
| West-Vlaanderen-West Flanders | 1,066,508 |
| Total | 9,756,590 |

The most important towns in 1973 including suburbs are Brussels, 1,063,274; Antwerp, 926,079; Ghent, 475,305; Liége, 620,309; Charleroi, 458,134.

| | 1972 | 1973 |
|---|---|---|
| Marriages | 74,584 | 73,464 |
| Births | 134,437 | 129,425 |
| Deaths | 116,743 | 118,313 |

The density of population is, perhaps, greater than in any other country in Europe. The average in 1972 was about 314 per square kilometre. The French-speaking provinces are Hainaut, Liège, Luxembourg and Namur, with the Nivelles district of Brabant. North of a line passing through Kortryk and Brussels, Flemish is the dominant language. Bruges and Antwerp are in the Flemish north, which includes the administrative divisions of Antwerp itself, West Flanders, East Flanders, Limburg and the Leuven and Halle-Vilvoorde districts of Brabant and contains rather more than half of the total population.

The annual average population growth rate percentage for the period 1960–74 was 0·5, and for the period 1965–74 was 0·3.

## CURRENCY

The franc is the basic unit of currency. There are metal coins of 25 and 50 centimes and 1, 5, 10, 20, 50 and 100 francs. The notes are of 20, 50, 100, 500 and 1,000 francs.

## FINANCE

Ordinary budget figures for 1972 (in million francs) were: Revenue, 366,033·5; Expenditure, 371,102·4.

National Debt at 31 December 1972 (million francs): Consolidated Internal, 558,752·7; External 8,166·1; Short and Middle Term Internal 141,375·9, External 22,321·8.

The GNP at market prices for 1974 was U.S.$ millions 55,430 and the GNP per capita at market prices was U.S.$ 5,670. The annual average percentage growth rate of GNP per capita for the period 1960–74 was 4·5 and for the period 1965–74 was 4·9. [*See note at the beginning of this section concerning GNP.*]

## PRINCIPAL BANKS

The central bank and bank of issue is the Banque Nationale de Belgique, Brussels. Under a law of 1948 the Government is able to control the composition of the Board and Management Committee of the Banque Nationale.

In the public interest the law prescribes a minimum capital for banks and forbids them to engage directly in industry, whilst the State exercises a certain supervision over banking business through the Commission Bancaire.

**Banque Nationale de Belgique.** (Governor, Cecil de Strycker. Established 1850; sole Bank of Issue for Belgium, half the share capital is owned by the State; Balance Sheet at 31 December 1976 showed assets F. 349,663,511,512; current and sundry accounts F. 4,547,195,606; gold reserve F. 71,821,213,379; banknotes in circulation F. 307,197,380,600. *Head Office:* Bd. de Berlaimont, 5, B-1000 Brussels; two Branches in Belgium, one in Luxembourg, 32 Agencies in Belgium.

**Société Générale de Banque S.A.** (Chairman of the Board, G. Dirckx, Chairman Executive Committee, R. Henrion.) Established 1965 through merger of Banque d'Anvers, Banque de la Société Générale de Belgique and Société Belge de Banque. Balance sheet on 31 December 1975 showed assets B. F. 510,041,808,600; deposit and current accounts B. F. 287,685,153,469. *Head Office:* 3 Montagne du Parc, Brussels; 1000 Branches and Offices.

**Amro Bank Voor België N.V.** (Chairman, H. N. Wakkie.) Established 1937; Balance Sheet at 31 December 1975 showed assets FB. 6,790,700,465, deposits and current accounts FB. 1,512,257,266. *Head Office:* Vestingstraat 74, 2000 Antwerp, Belgium.

**Banque de Bruxelles.** (Chairman, Louis Camu.) Established 30 January 1935, in conformity with Banking Law of 1934, to take over the banking business of the former Banque de Bruxelles (Established 1871); Balance Sheet at 31 March 1973 showed assets F. 245,979,153,326; deposits and current accounts F. 119,971,927,012. *Head Office:* 2 Rue de la Régence, Brussels; 985 Branches and Agencies throughout Belgium.

**Banque de Commerce, S.A.** (President, Jan de Spot.) Established 1893; Balance Sheet at 31 December 1973 showed assets BF. 20,000,624,996; current and deposit accounts BF. 7,052,121,586. *Head Office:* Antwerp, Lange Gasthuisstraat 9; 20 Branches and Agencies in Antwerp, Brussels, Liège and Ghent.

**Banque Diamantaire Anversoise, s.a.** (Chairman, Paul-Emmanuel Janssen.) Established 1934; Balance Sheet at

31 March 1977 showed assets F. 6,057,550,309; deposit and current accounts F. 2,048,849,721; Capital and Reserves F. 642,107,684. *Head Office:* Antwerp, Belgium.

**Crédit Lyonnais S.A.** (branch) see France.

**Kredietbank,** (President of the bank, Luc Wauters.) Established 1935; Balance Sheet at 31 March 1974 showed assets F. 181,247,157,307; deposits and current accounts F. 161,752,386,809. *Head Office:* 7 Arenbergstraat, B-1000 Brussels.

**Banque Belgo-Centrade S.A.** (President, Yves de Hennin de Boussu Walcourt; Managing-Director, Alberto Forte.) Established 1963; Assets as at 30 September 1976, BF. 2,418,579,738; deposits and current accounts BF. 323,220,160. *Head Office:* 107 Rue du Commerce, B-1040 Brussels; Number of branches 1.

**Benelux Bank Banque Du Benelux.** (President, Robert Plouvier; Chairman of the management committee, Jo Holvoet.) Established 1954. Assets as at 3 December 1976. BF. 14,287,961,035; deposits and current accounts BF. 13,703,707,343. *Head Office:* Grote Markt 9, 2000, Antwerp; Number of branches 4.

## PRODUCTION, INDUSTRY AND COMMERCE

**Agriculture.** Though highly industrialised, Belgium has a flourishing agricultural activity employing a large proportion of the population.

Belgium is almost self-supporting as regards meat production and has a surplus for export as well as some milk products, sugar and flax, and a choice of first-class horticultural and agricultural products such as wheat, grains and cheese. Nevertheless Belgium normally imports large quantities of Dutch produce, mostly butter, cheese and some horticultural goods.

Horticulture supplies most of the country's needs. Production of fruits, vegetables and flowers is large enough to allow quantities to be exported.

The following table shows the area of land under cultivation in thousands of acres for the years 1973–74:

| *Type of crop* | 1973 *th. acres* | 1974 *th. acres* |
|---|---|---|
| *Agriculture* | | |
| Cereals | 1,106 | 1,077 |
| Vegetables | 7 | 10 |
| Industrial crops | 283 | 289 |
| Potatoes | 105 | 99 |
| Fields and meadows | 1,883 | 1,860 |
| Fodder roots | 68 | 66 |
| Green fodder | 138 | 156 |
| Other crops | 4 | 4 |
| Total agriculture | 3,594 | 3,561 |
| *Horticulture* | | |
| Market gardening | 68 | 74 |
| Fruit crops | 43 | 41 |
| Flowers and tree nurseries | 9 | 9 |
| Horticultural crops consumed by the producer | 6 | 5 |
| Total horticulture | 126 | 129 |
| Osier-beds and fallow fields | 15 | 9 |
| Total area under cultivation | 3,735 | 3,699 |

The following table shows the total production of agricultural and horticultural crops in thousands of tons for the years 1973–74:

| *Type of crop* | 1973 *th. tons* | 1974 *th. tons* |
|---|---|---|
| Wheat | 969 | 997 |
| Rye | 62 | 49 |
| Barley | 707 | 690 |
| Oats | 246 | 222 |
| Sugar beet | 5,482 | 4,625 |
| Coffee chicory | 31 | 32 |
| Flax (straw) | 46 | 62 |
| Potatoes | 1,396 | 1,710 |
| Mangel-wurzels | 2,542 | 2,346 |
| Grass crops | 1,914 | 1,727 |
| Ordinary clover (hay) | 34 | 29 |
| Vegetables | 1,228 | n.a. |
| Fruit | 326 | n.a. |

The following table shows numbers of livestock for the years 1973–74:

| *Types of animal* | 1973 | 1974 |
|---|---|---|
| Horses | 56,150 | 52,964 |
| Cattle | 2,961,564 | 3,044,000 |
| Including: dairy cows | 1,057,884 | 1,078,388 |
| Pigs | 4,629,889 | 5,026,348 |
| Sheep | 101,343 | 111,015 |
| Goats | 4,610 | 5,242 |
| Rabbits | 138,181 | 133,865 |
| Apiculture: | | |
| Strawhives | 1,615 | 1,700 |
| Boxes with mobile frames | 24,885 | 25,396 |

**Fishing.** The total weight of fish landed and sold in 1974 amounted to 84,114,000 lbs.

**Forestry.** The Belgian forests cover about 267,627 hectares, approximately 88 per cent of the total territory in 1971.

**Mining and Metal Industries.** Belgium is an important producer of coal, pig iron, steel and such non-ferrous metals as zinc, copper, lead, tin, cobalt and radium; non-ferrous raw materials are imported in part from Zaire.

The following shows the production of unwrought metals for 1974 (thousand tons):

| | |
|---|---|
| Iron Ore | 121·0 |
| Cast Iron | 12,811·3 |
| Crude Steel | 15,970·8 |
| Rolled Steel | 11,962·3 |

The following table shows the volume of production (in thousands of tons) of various products for 1974:

| *Product* | 1974 *th. tons* |
|---|---|
| Coal | 7,981 |
| Coke | 7,981 |
| Pig iron | 12,811 |
| Crude steel | 15,971 |
| Rolled steel | 11,962 |
| Non-ferrous metals (1st and 2nd smelting) | 848 |
| Non-ferrous metals (semi-products) | 543 |
| Woollen yarns | 78 |
| Cotton yarns | 86 |
| Synthetic threads and fibres | 29 |
| Woollen fabrics | 31 |
| Cotton fabrics | 67 |
| Bricks, in millions of pieces | 1,328 |
| Cement | 7,348 |
| Glass | 1,294 |
| Paper and cardboard | 841 |
| Primary nitrogen | 573 |
| Compound fertilizers | 1,662 |
| Processing of crude petroleum | 29,699 |

## BELGIUM

**Commerce.** The following tables show trade by principal countries (in million francs):

| Country | Imports 1972 | Imports 1973 |
|---|---|---|
| West Germany | 166·4 | 212·3 |
| France | 133·0 | 160·5 |
| Netherlands | 109·0 | 135·5 |
| UK | 43·6 | 55·9 |
| U.S.A. | 38·4 | 48·1 |
| Italy | 28·4 | 32·1 |
| Zaire | 13·2 | 23·0 |
| Sweden | 13·8 | 16·1 |
| Saudi Arabia | 12·4 | 14·3 |
| Switzerland | 8·4 | 11·0 |
| Japan | 8·6 | 10·4 |
| Canada | 6·4 | 8·2 |
| Republic of South Africa | 5·8 | 7·6 |
| Iran | 5·2 | 7·1 |
| U.S.S.R. | 4·6 | 6·9 |
| Brazil | 3·8 | 6·2 |
| Spain | 4·7 | 6·1 |
| Libya | 1·4 | 5·5 |
| Kuwait | 5·8 | 5·0 |
| Argentine | 3·7 | 4·3 |
| Norway | 3·2 | 4·2 |
| Australia | 2·9 | 4·1 |
| Other places | 59·1 | 68·2 |
| Total | 681·8 | 852·6 |

| Country | Exports 1972 | Exports 1973 |
|---|---|---|
| West Germany | 176·5 | 205·8 |
| France | 144·3 | 180·8 |
| Netherlands | 132·1 | 155·2 |
| U.S.A. | 43·4 | 48·8 |
| Italy | 32·4 | 42·0 |
| U.K. | 31·5 | 40·3 |
| Switzerland | 14·8 | 18·1 |
| Sweden | 12·1 | 15·2 |
| Denmark | 6·8 | 10·2 |
| Spain | 7·3 | 8·6 |
| U.S.S.R. | 4·0 | 8·2 |
| Japan | 4·8 | 7·8 |
| Norway | 5·6 | 6·6 |
| Austria | 4·6 | 6·0 |
| Greece | 4·4 | 6·0 |
| Zaire, Rwanda and Burundi | 5·6 | 5·9 |
| Israel | 4·6 | 5·6 |
| Poland | 2·5 | 4·8 |
| Brazil | 3·2 | 4·4 |
| Algeria | 3·1 | 4·2 |
| Canada | 3·7 | 4·0 |
| Finland | 2·5 | 3·9 |
| South Africa | 2·4 | 3·5 |
| Portugal | 2·4 | 3·5 |
| Hong-Kong | 2·5 | 3·3 |
| Other places | 53·9 | 67·5 |
| Total | 711·0 | 870·2 |

The following tables show imports and exports of industrial goods for the years 1973–74. The figure shown against each entry refers to the percentage of the whole that commodity has.

| *Imported Goods* | 1973 | 1974 |
|---|---|---|
| Steel | 3·5 | 3·9 |
| Mechanical engineering | 29·4 | 24·8 |
| Non-ferrous metals | 5·2 | 5·1 |
| Textiles | 9·5 | 8·2 |
| Chemicals | 7·6 | 9·3 |
| Foodstuffs, beverages and tobacco | 12·1 | 10.0 |
| Diamond industry | 4·4 | 3·3 |
| Coal and coke | 2·1 | 2·5 |
| Oil industry | 6·0 | 10·8 |
| Miscellaneous industry | 7·8 | 8·1 |
| Other sectors | 12·4 | 14·0 |
| Total | 100·0 | 100·0 |

| *Exported Goods* | 1973 | 1974 |
|---|---|---|
| Steel | 15·6 | 17·7 |
| Mechanical engineering | 24·0 | 21·5 |
| Non-ferrous metals | 6·0 | 6·0 |
| Textiles | 11·4 | 10·2 |
| Chemicals | 10·3 | 13·0 |
| Foodstuffs, beverages and tobacco | 9·2 | 8·2 |
| Diamond industry | 3·7 | 3·0 |
| Coal and coke | 0·2 | 0·2 |
| Oil industry | 2·7 | 3·1 |
| Miscellaneous industries | 7·8 | 7·3 |
| Other sectors | 9·1 | 9·8 |
| Total | 100·0 | 100·0 |

### COMMUNICATIONS

**Railways.** A Public Board with privately held preference shares, the 'Société Nationale des Chemins de Fer Belges', (Director General, Fernand Delory) operates a network of 4,081 kilometres of track on the 1 January 1973.

**Shipping.** In 1973 the merchant fleet was composed of 89 ships of 1,091,984 gross tonnage. Antwerp, the chief port, is one of the largest on the continent and the main distributing centre for Western and Central Europe. In 1973, 18,708 vessels with a total tonnage of 51,024 (1,000 NRT tons) also entered the port of Antwerp. In 1972, 33,768 vessels entered Belgium maritime ports and unloaded 97,296,887 tons of merchandise.

**Armement Deppe.** (Chairman, A. André-Dumont.); *services operated:* Continent to Puerto Rico, Florida and U.S. Gulf Ports and vice-versa; Continent to Mexico and vice-versa, and Continent to Pacific Coast of South America and vice-versa. *Head Office:* 11 Meir, B-2000 Antwerp.

**Compagnie Maritime Belge (CMB)**, S.A. (Chairman P. E. Corbiau); motor vessels 33; total gross tonnage 637,000; *services operated:* from Europe to U.S.A., Canada, Florida, Puerto Rico, Mexico, East and West Coast of South America, Far East, West, East and South Africa, Persian Gulf; European coastal container service; U.S.A.—Canada to West Africa. *Head Office:* 61 St. Katelijnevest, 2000 Antwerp.

**Civil Aviation.** Civil aviation is administered by the Minister of Communications. Air transport and general policy matters are dealt with by the 'Administration de l'Aéronautique' (Director General Willy Vanderperren). *Head Office:* W.T.C.-Tower 1-8th Floor, Boulevard Emile Jacqmain, 162, Bte 60, 1000 Brussels.

The main airports are operated by a government agency, the 'Regie des Voies Aériennes' (Director General Léon Godart). *Head Office:* 41, Avenue des Arts, B-1040 Brussels. Main international airports are at Brussels National, Antwerp, Ostend, Charleroi (Gosselies), Liège (Bierset). Air services link Brussels with most of the capitals of Europe and the Middle East, Zaire and South Africa, East and West Africa, the U.S.A., Canada and Mexico, Far East.

**SABENA—Société anonyme belge d'Exploitation de la Navigation aerienne.** (Chairman of Board, Gaston Coppée);

share capital 1,373,679,000 Belgian francs; *services operated:* Brussels to New York, Montreal, Mexico, Casablanca, Tunis, Havana, Tangier, Algiers Dubai, Dakar, Conakry, Abidjan, Monrovia, Kano, Lagos, Douala, Libreville, Kinshasa, Entebbe, Nairobi, Bujumbura, Kigali, Dar-Es-Salaam, Abu Dhabi, Baghdad, Johannesburg, Beirut, Cairo, Istanbul, Teheran, Tel-Aviv, Dharan, Bombay, Bangkok, Kuala Lumpur, Singapore, Jakarta, Manila, Tokyo, and principal European cities. *Air Terminus:* rue Cardinal Mercier, 35, 1000 Brussels.

**SOBELAIR—Société Belge de Transport Par Air, S.A.** (Chairman, G. Kreveld; Managing Director, M. Dans); share capital 125,100,000 Belgian francs; *services operated:* all over the world on a charter basis. *Head Office:* 4, Rue de Hornes, 1050, Brussels.

**BIAS—International S.A.** (Managing director. Charles Van Antwerpen); share capital 20,000,000 Belgian francs; *services operated:* all over the world on a charter basis. *Head Office:* Antwerp Airport—Antwerp 1.

**Telephones and Telegraphs.** These are operated under the direction of the Minister of Communications. At 31 December 1972 there were 2,305,218 telephone instruments in use, representing approximately one instrument per 5 of the population of 9,726,850.

**Broadcasting.** The broadcasting service is operated by the Radiodiffusion-Télévision Belge (R.T.B.) (Director-General: for French transmissions R. Wangermee, for Flemish transmissions P. Vandenbussche). There are three transmissions in French and three in Flemish and there is one short-wave station. Radio licence holders numbered 3,559,958 on 31 December 1972. On 31 December 1972 the number of T.V. licence holders was 2,288,567.

### NEWSPAPERS

**La Libre Belgique.** 1884. Catholic Independent. Morning daily. Circulation 150,000. 83, boulevard E. Jacqmain, Brussels.

**De Standaard (Nieuusblad).** 1923. Catholic. Daily. Circulation 335,790. Em. Jacqmainiaan, 127, 1000-Brussels.

**La Dernière Heure.** 1906. Liberal. Daily evening. Circulation 169,984. 52 rue du Pont-Neuf, Brussels.

**Le Soir.** 1887. Independent. Daily. Circulation 234,371. 112 rue Royale, and 21 place de Louvain, Brussels.

**Het Laatste Nieuws.** 1888. Liberal. Daily. Circulation 287,609. Editor, U. van Maele. 105 Jacqmainlaan, 1000-Brussels.

**La Meuse, La Lanterne.** 1855. Independent. Daily. Circulation 180,000. 10 Boulevard de la Sauvenière, Liège.

**Gazet van Antwerpen.** 1891. Christian Democrat. Circulation 193,000. 46 Nationalestraat, Antwerp.

**Het Volk, De Nieuwe Gids, De Antwerpse Gids.** 1891. Catholic. Circulation 222,508. Forelstraat 22, Ghent.

**De Nieuwe Gazet.** Independent. Circulation 296,750. Antwerp.

### ATOMIC ENERGY

In 1950, a Commissioner for Atomic Energy was appointed with the task of promoting and supervising all initiatives aimed at the national development of nuclear energy. This post is at present held by Prof. Paul De Groote.

Fundamental research, theoretical and experimental, is conducted mainly in academic establishments and is co-ordinated by the Institut Interuniversitaire des Sciences Nucléaires (I.I.S.N.), founded in 1947. The chairman is Mr. Jean Willems.

Most of the applied nuclear research is carried out at the Centre d'Etude de l'Energie Mucléaire (C.E.N.), a body which came into existence in 1952. It is headed by a board of directors composed of representatives of Government departments, universities and industry. The chairman of the board is General-Major G. Letor.

The object of C.E.N. is to further peaceful applications of atomic energy, operate research facilities and train specialists at all levels. The establishment is located at Mol, some 50 miles north-east of Brussels, where there are three reactors and two critical assemblies in operation, with supporting laboratories for physics, health physics, chemistry, electronics, metallurgy, technology and radiobiology.

BR 1 is a graphite moderated, gas-cooled, research reactor which went critical in 1956.

The 50 MWe high flux materials testing BR2 reactor has been in use since 1961.

The 11·5 MWe pressurized water reactor, BR 3, was inaugurated in 1962 and for 2 years produced electricity for the grid. It has since been modified to accommodate a Vulcain core and, as BR 3 Vulcain, went into operation in December 1966.

The first large scale nuclear power station is the 266 ME(e) SENA plant: This is a PWR, built joint by the Belgian utility Centre et Sud and Electricité de France, on a site at Chooz near Givet, on the Franco-Belgian border. It was completed in April 1967, and is producing electricity for the French and Belgian grids. Two other power stations, of 600 MWe each, are planned, one on the Scheldt near Antwerp, the other on the Meuse near Nuy.

An important item on the Belgian national programme is the development of the Vulcain reactor, of Belgian design. This is based on the spectral shift principle and is particularly suitable for small and medium power reactors both for ship propulsion and land based plants. Since 1962, the U.K.A.E.A. and Belgian industry have been associated in this work, in which the Centre d'Etude de l'Energie Nucléaire also takes an active part.

The Belgo Nucléaire company, founded in 1957 by private companies in various industrial branches, specializes in the construction of reactors and critical assemblies, the manufacturing and reprocessing of fuel elements, including plutonium, the treatment and disposal of radioactive wastes and the uses of radioisotopes. Its chairman is Mr Marcel de Merre.

The firm 'Métallurgie et Mécanique Nucléaires' (M.M.N.) (chairman Mr. Marcel de Merre), established in 1958, specializes in the production of reactor materials, reactor fuels and auxiliary parts for reactors.

In addition to these, a number of firms, large and small, in various branches of the economy, have created sections specially devoted to nuclear activities.

Most companies concerned with nuclear energy have joined to form a professional association called 'Groupement Professionnel de l'Industrie Nucléaire'. Chairman: Mr. F. Seynaeve.

**International Cooperation.** Belgium is a member of the European Atomic Energy Community (EURATOM) which came into being with the Treaty of Rome in 1958. It is also a member country of the Organisation for Economic Cooperation and Development (O.E.C.D.) and of the International Atomic Energy Agency (I.A.E.A.). It also shares in the activities of the European Organisation for Nuclear Research (C.E.R.N.) and of the European Energy Society founded in London in 1954.

The first European plant for reprocessing irradiated fuel, EUROCHEMIC, which is a joint undertaking of thirteen O.E.C.D. countries, including Belgium, is located at Mol, in the immediate vicinity of the Belgian nuclear centre.

### RELIGION

There is no established religion but the majority of the inhabitants are Roman Catholic. There is full religious freedom and the State does not interfere in the internal affairs of the churches, paying part of the income of ministers of all denominations out of the national treasury.

### EDUCATION

Education is free and compulsory for both sexes, and excellent facilities are available for primary, secondary and higher education. There are universities at Brussels, Louvain, Ghent and Liège. Louvain is the largest and oldest, having been founded in 1426.

# Benin

**Capital**—Porto Novo.

**President**—Major Mathieu Kerekou.

**National Flag**: Green vertical stripe at the hoist, two horizontal stripes in yellow and red.

### CONSTITUTION AND GOVERNMENT

DAHOMEY, a former French territory, became independent on 1 August 1960. It is not a member of the French Community, but has co-operation agreements with France.

Major Kerecou established a government on 26 October 1972.

### AREA AND POPULATION

The area of the country is 122,600 sq. km. and the population over 2,500,000. Cotonou (120,000) is the chief port and business centre. The capital, Porto Novo, has a population of 85,000. Other important towns are Abomey, Ouidah and Parakou. The population at mid-1974 was 3,027,000. The annual average percentage population growth rate for the period 1960–74 was 2·7 and for the period 1965–74 was 2·7.

### CURRENCY AND FINANCE

The unit of currency is the Central African franc. The estimated budget for 1971 was: Expenditure, 11,800 million fr. CFA; Receipts, 10,400 million fr. CFA.

The GNP at market prices for 1974 was U.S. $ millions 370, and the GNP per capita at market prices was U.S. $120. The annual average percentage growth rate of the GNP per capita for the period 1960–74 was 0·7, and for the period 1965–74 was 0·8. [*See the note at the beginning of this section concerning GNP.*]

### PRODUCTION, INDUSTRY AND COMMERCE

Chief products are palm oil, maize, millet and sorghum. Potatoes, rice, beans and fruit are also grown. The livestock population is estimated at 300,000 cattle, 600,000 sheep and goats and 190,000 pigs. Fishing is important and about 3,000 tons are exported to Togo and Nigeria. There are four factories for palm-oil production at Avrankou and G'Bada, Bohicon and Ahazon. There is a brewery and other small industrial holdings.

### COMMUNICATIONS

There are about 6,000 km. of roads, of which roughly 10 per cent are paved. Railways connect Cotonou with Parakou, Pahou with Segboroue and Cotonou with Pobe. There is an airport at Cotonou. In 1966, 2,211 planes landed there, with 14,891 passengers and 367 tons of freight. There are over 70 post offices and about 2,200 telephones. Radio Dahomey broadcasts from Cotonou.

In 1966, 571 ships (tonnage 1,547,000) landed at Cotonou. 265,000 tons of freight were unloaded, and 4,117 passengers arrived. A modern harbour is now being built.

Radio Dahomey, the government station, broadcasts from Cotonou to about 30,000 people.

### EDUCATION

There are about 136,000 pupils in primary, secondary and technical schools.

# Bhutan

(DRUK-YUL)

**Capital**—Thimphu.

**Ruler**—The Druk Gyalpo, Jigme Singhye Wangchuck.

**National Flag**: Divided diagonally; fly to hoist yellow over orange; a dragon centred white, clasping jewels in the claws.

BHUTAN, a fully sovereign, independent kingdom is situated in the eastern Himalayas, bounded on the north and north-west by China, and to the south, west and east by India.

The form of Government, which formerly consisted of a dual rule—by the Deb Raja on the temporal side and the Dharma Raja (Shabdung Rimpoche) on the spiritual side—was changed in 1907 when the Tongsa Penlop, Ugyen Wangchuck was elected as the sole ruler on a hereditary basis. The recent changes made in the Constitution have converted absolute monarchy to a constitutional monarchy.

Under a treaty concluded with the East India Company in 1774, Bhutan had undertaken to pay an annual tribute of five horses and to prevent incursions into Indian territory. However, since such incursions did not stop, a number of punitive expeditions were arranged resulting in the occupation of various *duars* (passes) by the British. Under a fresh treaty signed in 1865 Bhutan ceded the *duars* to the Government of India and received in return an annual subsidy of Rs.50,000. In 1910 the treaty was amended increasing the amount of allowance to Rs.100,000 and placing Bhutan's external relations under the guidance of the Government of India.

The National Assembly (Tsogdu) was established in 1953. The Tsogdu has a three-year term and meets twice yearly in spring and autumn. Its present strength is 150 members, of whom 110 are indirectly elected by villages. Ten seats are reserved for ecclesiastical bodies and the remainder are occupied by officials; the Ministers, their deputies and members of the Royal Advisory Council. The Tsogdu enacts laws, advises on constitutional and political matters and debates all important issues. Both the Royal Advisory Council and the Council of Ministers are responsible to it.

In the matter of Foreign Affairs Bhutan follows a foreign policy of non-alignment and has been a member of the Non-aligned Movement since 1973. Bhutan was admitted to the United Nations by a unanimous vote in the General Assembly in 1971. She is also a member of the Universal Postal Union, the Colombo Plan for Co-operative Economic Development in South and South East Asia, the Economic and Social Commission for Asia and the Pacific and the United Nations Conference on Trade and Development. She has treaty relationships with the Government of India on the basis of cooperation and friendship.

The Government of Bhutan initiated a programme of planned development in 1961 and the first five-year plan was carried out during the period 1961–66. It was financed by grants from the Government of India totalling approximately Rs. 10·5 crores and the plan achieved its object in providing a sound economic and social foundation upon which more advanced plans could be based. The second five-year plan was launched in 1966 with India agreeing to contribute up to Rs. 20 crores towards the total proposed outlay of Rs. 22·15 crores. India also assisted by sending technical experts and administrators, by giving Bhutanese subjects technical training in India, by granting scholarships to Bhutanese students, by supplying food grain and other essential items in short supply, by providing foreign exchange for essential imports and by subsidizing the repair of flood damage caused in 1968. The second five-year plan ended in March 1971. The third five-year plan (1971–76) stressed the need to continue development of the infrastructure facilities such as construction of roads, bridges, power supply, and on development of agriculture, education and health. The total expenditure was Nu. 461 million. The fourth five-year plan began in 1976 with an outlay of Nu. 778 million.

### AREA AND POPULATION

The area of Bhutan is 18,000 square miles.

The population of Bhutan at mid-1974 was 1,150,000. The annual average percentage population growth rate for the period 1960–74 was 2·3, as it was also for the period 1965–74.

## PRODUCTION, INDUSTRY AND COMMERCE

The following figures concerning the GNP are tentative. The GNP at market prices for 1974 was U.S. $millions 80 and the GNP per capita was U.S. $70. The annual average percentage growth rate of the GNP per capita for the period 1960–74 was −0·3 and for the period 1965–74 was −0·2. [*See the note at the beginning of this section concerning GNP.*]

**Agriculture.** The Department of Agriculture has set up a large number of modern agricultural farms, seed-growing farms and research stations with the object of increasing food production. Emphasis is placed upon the following: Regional specialization of crops; the provision of better seeds, implements and fertilizers; the introduction of new and improved crops, the popularizing of fruit and vegetable growing and research.

Since 1961 eight livestock farms and one sheep and one yak development project have been set up, 14 District Veterinary Dispensary and six Veterinary Sub-centres have been established. There are also three pisiculture units, seven cattle artificial insemination centres, one liver fluke eradication and stagger disease eradication scheme.

**Forestry.** During the first Five Year Plan from 1961 to 1966 the forest department spent a sum of Nu. 30·7 lakhs. During the second Five Year Plan from 1966 to 1971 this expenditure went up to 71·8 lakhs—in the third Five Year Plan 1971 to 1976 the expenditure was further increased to 252·8 lakhs. The revenue of the forest department has steadily increased from a figure of 6·00 lakhs in 1959–60 to 37 lakhs in 1976–77. During this period 17 sawmills, one match factory, one veneer factory, one pencil slate factory, one resin distillation factory and one lemon grass distillation plant have been set up. Mechanization of logging operations has been started.

**Industry and mining.** Recent development projects include wood-work, bamboo work and weaving centres at different places; light industries in the field of timber, food preservation and liquor have been established. In addition, matches, soap, candle, carpets, textiles and similar products are being produced within the country. A cement plant with a production capacity of 1,000 tons a day is being installed at Pugli in southern Bhutan and it is expected to go into production during 1978. The mineral deposits including dolomite, graphite, gypsum, limestone, coal, lead, zinc, marble and slate deposits found in the country are being carefully exploited.

**Power.** Hydro-electric projects are located in Thimphu, Paro, Wangdiphodrang, Tashigang, Gidakhom and Mongar (completed during 1976–77). So far 16 towns and 49 villages have been electrified. Work on the construction of the 336 megawatt Chukha hydro-electric project which started in 1975 is likely to be completed by 1981.

## COMMUNICATIONS

**Roads.** More than 1,500 kilometres of roads (most of which are surfaced) now connect different parts of the kingdom. In addition, surfaced roads now link the important border towns of Phuntsholing, Gaylegphug, Sarbhang, and Samdrup Johkhar in southern Bhutan to towns in West Bengal and Assam in India. There are two airfields in the kingdom, Paro and Yangphulla, and numerous helicopter stations.

**Road Transport.** The State Transport Department operates a fleet of 74 buses. Lorries for carrying goods are all now in the private sector.

**Posts, Telegraphs and Telephones.** There are 61 post offices, four telegraph offices and 24 radio wireless stations in the kingdom. In addition, 15 telephone exchanges provide telephone services in the main towns. A teleprinter service now links Thimphu to the rest of the outside world.

## EDUCATION

At present, there are 110 schools (85 primary schools, 14 junior high schools, six central schools, one teacher's training institute, two technical schools, two schools for Buddhist studies and one junior college) and 19,000 student/trainees. There are no private schools in the country. About 500 students are receiving higher education and training in India, Australia, New Zealand, Japan, Singapore, United Kingdom, Switzerland, Austria and the United States of America.

## MEDICINE AND HEALTH

There are five hospitals, 50 dispensaries and three leprosy hospitals functioning in Bhutan.

# Bolivia

## (REPÚBLICA DE BOLIVIA)

**Capital**—Sucre.

**Seat of Government**—La Paz.

**President**—Colonel Hugo Banzer Suarez.

**National Flag:** A tricolour fesse-wise, red, yellow and green. The national coat of arms bears the mountain of Potosí, a tree, a wheatsheaf and a llama.

### CONSTITUTION AND GOVERNMENT

BOLIVIA is situated near the middle of South America, being bounded on the north and east by Brazil, on the south by Paraguay and Argentina, and on the west by Chile and Peru.

Bolivia became an independent republic in 1825. The first Constitution was framed in 1826. The executive power is in the hands of the President elected for a period of four years with a cabinet of 15 ministers.

Since President Banzer took over in August 1971, Bolivia has enjoyed seven years of uninterrupted political stability. President Banzer has stated that in 1980 he will relinquish his office. It is important to note that the Banzer regime, while military in nature, carries the support and backing of the private sector, and the public in general. In this regard, the Government has devised a system of "Civil Service" in which individuals from the private sector, i.e. leading bankers and industrialists, actually take part in governmental policy-making and planning. As a result of this close-knit coordination, the industrial, agricultural and banking activities of Bolivia have expanded at unprecedented rates.

### LOCAL GOVERNMENT

The nine departments into which Bolivia is divided are each governed by a prefect in whom is vested the supreme administrative and military authority. They are appointed by the President. The departments are sub-divided into 87 provinces administered by sub-prefects. The provinces are divided into cantons which are administered by *corregidores* appointed by the sub-prefects.

### LEGAL SYSTEM

There is a Supreme Court of nine judges sitting at Sucre. It is divided into two sections of four judges each to try civil and criminal cases, the Chief Justice presiding over both sections. There are in addition District Courts sitting in each department and local judges to try minor cases.

### AREA AND POPULATION

The area and population (estimated, 1971) of the departments are shown below. The capitals of each follow the names of the departments in brackets:

| *Department* | *Area (sq. km.)* | |
|---|---|---|
| La Paz (La Paz) | 133,985 | 1,484,100 |
| Cochabamba (Cochabamba) | 55,631 | 777,800 |
| Potosi (Potosi) | 118,218 | 657,700 |
| Santa Cruz (Santa Cruz) | 370,621 | 712,400 |
| Chuquisaca (Sucre) | 51,524 | 357,700 |
| Tarija (Tarija) | 37,623 | 226,800 |
| Oruro (Oruro) | 53,588 | 310,900 |
| Beni (Trinidad) | 213,564 | 164,800 |
| Pando (Cobija) | 63,827 | 34,300 |
| Total | 1,098,581 | 4,726,500 |

The Departmental capitals (with populations est., in 1976) are La Paz, 654,700; Oruro, 124,100; Cochabamba, 204,400; Potosí, 77,200; Santa Cruz, 255,500; Sucre, 63,200; Tarija, 39,000; Trinidad, 27,500; Cobija, 3,600. The annual average population growth rate percentage for the period 1960–74 was 2·5 and for the period 1965–74 was 2·2.

### CURRENCY AND FINANCE

The monetary unit has been the Peso Boliviano (Sb.) since July 1962. The exchange rate is approximately Sb. 34·50 = £1·00.

Since 1972 a decree was issued to encourage foreign investment in the field of mining, agriculture and industry.

Bolivia's external debt was (U.S.) $499,800,000 in December 1970.

The GNP at market prices for 1974 was U.S.$ millions 1,550 and the GNP per capita for 1974 was U.S. $280. The annual average percentage growth rate of GNP per capita for the period 1960–74 was 2·5 and for the period 1965–74 was 2·2. [*See the note at the beginning of this section concerning GNP.*]

### PRINCIPAL BANKS

**Banco Central de Bolivia.** (President: Lic. Manuel Mercado.) Established under Bolivian Law 1911 as Banco de la Nación Boliviana and reorganized in 1928. The bank was nationalized in 1939 and the Government became the sole stockholder. By a law of 1945 the Banco Central de Bolivia was divided into two departments (each completely independent of the other): the Banking Department, which was given a commercial function, and the Monetary Department, operating as a central bank. By a law of 1970 the Banking Department is now the Banco del Estado, and the Monetary Department continues to be the Banco Central. The latter has the sole power of note issue and must maintain a legal reserve equal to the amount of notes in circulation; fifty per cent of such reserve must be in gold and foreign exchange, and fifty per cent in securities. By the end of 1976 the Central Bank's net gold and foreign exchange reserves amounted to U.S. $103·5 million. The country has (up to January 1974) a Stand-by agreement of up to U.S. $27·3 million with the International Monetary Fund. Money in circulation at the end of 1972 totalled $b 2,153 million. The State obligations with the Central Bank rose to $b 2·666·8 million (excluding interests) by the end of 1972. The balance sheet of the Central Bank at 31 December 1972 showed assets of $b 5·066 million. *Head Office:* La Paz, Bolivia.

### PRODUCTION, INDUSTRY AND COMMERCE

**Agriculture.** Eastern Bolivia, approximately two-thirds of the country, is potentially rich for agriculture and almost any crop can be grown. In October 1952 the Government of the M.N.R. Party effected agrarian reforms. The main crops are sugar, rice and potatoes. The following table shows the value of some agricultural products in 1974 (metric tons):

| *Commodity* | *Metric Tons* |
|---|---|
| Rice | 75,380 |
| Sugar | 2,049,700 |
| Potatoes | 748,840 |
| Cotton | 26,700 |
| Corn | 276,660 |
| Bananas | 377,890 |
| Coffee | 13,870 |

**Mining.** The wealth of the country depends mostly on the mining industry, tin and other minerals representing 84 per cent of the total exports. As a tin producer, Bolivia ranks second to Malaya. Production in 1975 was 28,324 tons. The tin production for 1976 was 28,122 tons. Other minerals produced are gold, silver, copper, lead, zinc, antimony, tungsten and asbestos. In addition, Bolivia has enormous deposits of rich iron haematite in the Mutun area. On 1 November 1952 the Government of Dr Paz Estenssoro nationalized the three major mining concerns of Patino, Hochschild and Aramayo. About half of Bolivia's tin production is purchased by the United Kingdom.

Petroleum and especially natural gas have been located in large quantities. They are now being exploited by the state organization Y.P.F.B. The industry is an important factor in the national economy. Crude petroleum is exported at the rate of 45,000 barrels daily.

In 1976 the national production of petroleum was as follows (cu. meters):

| | 1976 |
|---|---|
| Crude petroleum | 6,361,40 |
| Gasoline | 539,50 |
| Kerosene | 171,30 |
| Diesel oil | 216,70 |
| Fuel oil | 215,40 |

**Forestry.** There are large areas of tropical forest, but their exploitation has been retarded by lack of transport facilities.

**Industry.** There are at present few industrial establishments, and the country relies on imports for the supply of most consumer goods. However, as a result of a new investment law passed in 1965, and 1972, industrial activity has increased. The ban in 1968 on the import of domestically produced articles is likely further to stimulate Bolivian industry.

The value of Electricity in millions of kw/h for the years 1974 and 1975 was respectively 993, and 1,057.

## COMMUNICATIONS

**Roads.** There are about 37,313 km. of roadways in service, and there will be approximately 50,366 km. in 1980.

**Railways.** The railways extend for 2,200 miles. There are two lines from La Paz to the Chilean coast—to the seaport of Arica, on the frontier between Chile and Peru; and to Antofagasta. La Paz is also linked up with Mollendo on the Peruvian coast, through the railway to Guaquí, on the Bolivian-Peruvian frontier, and thence by steamer across Lake Titicaca to Puno in Peru.

There is rail connection between La Paz and Buenos Aires by the line running south through Oruro to Villazón, on the frontier between Bolivia and Argentina and continuing to La Quiaca, where it joins up with the Argentinian railways.

There is a railway from Santa Cruz in the centre of the country, to the Brazilian frontier town of Corumbá and from Santa Cruz to Yacuiba on the Argentine frontier. These lines link up with the railways to São Paulo and Buenos Aires respectively. The railway from Cochabamba to Santa Cruz is under construction. When completed, it will unite the port of Santos in Brazil with the port of Arica in Chile, crossing all Bolivia from East to West.

**Civil Aviation.** Many parts of the country can be conveniently reached only by air. An internal service linking La Paz with the main cities is provided by the Lloyd Aereo Boliviano, which also connects La Paz with Lima, Arica in Chile and São Paulo in Brazil. Aerolineas Argentinas have a weekly service between La Paz and Buenos Aires. From Europe to the U.S.A. there are numerous airlines which connect with planes to Bolivia. All aeroplanes of these lines stop in Lima, Peru from whence the large planes of Braniff International, Iberia and Lufthansa, fly to El Alto airport, La Paz.

**LAB-Lloyd Aereo Boliviano S.A.** (General Manager, Gral. Federico Casanovas V.) Share capital, nominal $b. 200,000,000, paid-up $b. 64,711,246,70; domestic service and international service from Bolivia to Buenos Aires (Argentina), Salta (Argentina), San Pablo (Brazil), Arica and Santiago, Chile, Lima (Peru), Asunción (Paraguay), Panamá (Panamá), Miami, Florida (U.S.A.). *Head Office:* Casilla 132, Cochabamba (Bolivia).

**Posts, Telegraphs and Telephones.** There were 17,500 km. of telegraph lines in 1962; 201 post offices, 591 telegraph offices. There is a telephone service in the major towns. Remote parts of the country are connected to the capital by wireless.

**Broadcasting.** There is one official radio broadcasting station and two television stations. There are also about 45 private, commercial and trade union owned stations. Telex services are in operation in the main cities.

## NEWSPAPERS

**El Diario.** F. 1904. Circ. 45,000. Indep. Empresa Editora 'El Diario' S.A.

**Presencia.** F. 1952. Circ. 35,000. Indep. Empresa Editora 'Presencia'.

**Ultima Hora.** F. 1929. Circ. 9,800. Indep. Empressa Editora Boliviana 'Khana Cruz'.

**Los Tiempos.** F. 1967. Circ. 17,000. Editorial Canelas Cochabamba.

**Jornada.** F. 1964. Circ. 4,000. Empresa Jornada.

## EDUCATION AND RELIGION

Elementary education is free and compulsory for all children between the ages of seven and 14, but the illiteracy rate is very high. Schools are maintained by the municipalities and the State. In 1965, there were some 5,100 rural schools and 1,400 urban schools, with a total of 24,000 teachers and 650,000 pupils. 1,055,000 children between 5–14 are in school. 51·3 per cent of the population are literate.

There are universities at La Paz, Sucre, Cochabamba, Oruro, Potosí, Santa Cruz and Tarija. The University of St. Francis Xavier at Sucre, founded in 1624, is one of the oldest in America.

The established religion is the Roman Catholic, but other forms of worship are permitted. There are two Archbishoprics, La Paz and Sucre. Suffragans to the Archbishop of La Paz are the Bishops of Cochabamba, Oruro, Coroico and Corocoro. The Archbishop of Sucre has suffragan bishops at Potosí, Tarija and Santa Cruz de la Sierra. There are also five Vicars Apostolic at Beni, Chaco, Chiquitos, Pando and Reyes.

# Botswana

(MEMBER OF THE COMMONWEALTH)

**Capital**—Gaborone.

**President**—H.E. Sir Seretse Khama, KBE, LL.D., MP.

## CONSTITUTION AND GOVERNMENT

BOTSWANA is bounded on the south and east by the Republic of South Africa, on the northeast by Rhodesia, on the north by the Zambesi and Chobe Rivers, and on the west by the territory of Namibia. The chief tribes are the Bamangwato, Bangwaketse, Bakwena, Batawana, Bakgatla, Bamalete, Batlokwa and Barolong.

The Batswana appealed to Britain for help in 1895 after trouble with the Boers and the whole of Botswana (then Bechuanaland) was proclaimed a protectorate. In 1963 constitutional discussions took place and in 1964 proposals were accepted by Britain as a basis for revision of the Constitution. On 1 March 1965 a general election was held and self-government was inaugurated. In February 1966, at the Independence Constitutional Conference in London it was agreed that Bechuanaland would become a republic within the British Commonwealth on 30 September 1966 under the name of Botswana.

The Head of State is the President who is elected for the period of five years of the National Assembly. He is also the executive head of Government and is a member of, and presides over, a Cabinet consisting of the Vice-President and seven other Ministers drawn from the National Assembly and two Assistant Ministers.

The legislative power of the Republic is vested in the Parliament of Botswana, which consists of the President and the National Assembly. The National Assembly consists of 32 elected members, four specially elected members and the Attorney-General who can speak but not vote in the Assembly.

Under the Constitution there is also a House of Chiefs with advisory functions. It consists of the Chiefs of the eight principal tribes of Botswana as permanent *ex-officio* members, four other members elected by and from among the sub-chiefs in the Chobe, Francistown, Ghanzi and Kgalagadi Districts, and three specially elected members. The House of Chiefs is available to advise the Government in the exercise of its responsibilities. The National Assembly is prohibited from proceeding with any bill which particularly affects a defined range of subjects relating to matters of tribal concern, unless a draft of it has been referred to the House of Chiefs.

The country's first general election, based on universal adult suffrage, was held on 1 March 1965. A total of 140,789 people voted: 28 seats went to the Botswana Democratic Party (leader Sir Seretse Khama), and three to the Botswana People's Party (leader Mr. P. Matante).

Elections were held again in October 1969 when the Botswana Democratic Party again gained the majority of seats—24. The Botswana People's Party retained their three, three others went to the Botswana National Front (leader, B. Gaseitsiwe) and one to the Botswana Independence Party (leader, M. K. Mpho).

In the general elections held in October 1974 the Botswana Democratic Party was returned with an increased majority—27 seats. The Botswana People's Party had two, the Botswana National Front two and the Botswana Independence Party one seat.

### Cabinet

*The President:* Sir Seretse Khama, KBE, MP.

*The Vice-President and Minister of Finance and Development Planning:* The Hon. Dr. Q. K. J. Masire, JP, LL.D, MP.

*The Minister of Foreign Affairs:* The Hon. A. M. Mogwe, MBE., MP

*The Minister of Education:* The Hon. K. P. Morake, MP.

*The Minister of Mineral Resources and Water Affairs:* The Hon. M. K. Segokgo, MP.

*The Minister of Commerce and Industry:* The Hon. G. Chiepe, MBE., LLD., MP.

*The Minister of Local Government and Lands:* The Hon. L. Makgekgenene, MP.

*The Minister of Health:* The Hon. M. P. K. Nwako, MP.

*The Minister of Information and Broadcasting:* The Hon. D. K. Kwelagobe, MP.

*Attorney-General:* The Hon. M. D. Mokama.

*Assistant Minister of Finance and Development Planning:* The Hon. P. S. Mmusi, MP.

*Assistant Minister of Local Government and Lands:* The Hon. L. M. Seretse, MP.

## LOCAL GOVERNMENT

The new system of local government is based upon nine District Councils and three Town Councils (Gaborone, Lobatse and Francistown). Revenue comes mainly from a Local Government Tax on income, levied on people resident in a council area.

## LEGAL SYSTEM

The Botswana Court of Appeal succeeds the Court of Appeal for Basutoland, Bechuanaland and Swaziland, which was established in 1954. It has jurisdiction in respect of criminal and civil appeals emanating from the High Court of Botswana. Further appeal lies in certain circumstances to the Judicial Committee of the Privy Council.

The High Court for Botswana succeeds the High Court for Bechuanaland, which was established in 1938. It has jurisdiction in all causes and proceedings whatsoever, both criminal and civil, arising in the country. The Court consists of the Chief Justice and such number, if any, of Puisne Judges as may be prescribed from time to time.

There are Subordinate Courts and African Courts with limited jurisdiction in each of the twelve administrative districts of the country.

## AREA AND POPULATION

The country has not been surveyed as a whole, but its area is estimated at 570,000 sq. km.

The population at mid-1974 is estimated at 654,000, and an over-all population density of one person per sq. km. The annual average percentage population growth rate for the period 1960–74 was 1·9, and for the period 1965–74 was 1·9. The capital and seat of government, Gaborone, has a population of 18,436. The other towns are Francistown (19,903), Selebi-Pikwe (18,000), Lobatse (12,920), and Orapa (2,000). Botswana has some of the largest tribal villages in Africa. The biggest are Serowe (43,186), Kanye (39,220), Molepolole (31,986), Mochudi (21,382), Mahalapye (14,657), Maun (12,154), and Ramotswa (11,572).

## CURRENCY AND FINANCE

South African currency is used (R1·00 = £0·55p sterling). Budget estimates for 1975/76 are: Revenue, R73,274,560; Expenditure, R73,274,560, more than double the figures for 1973/74 which stood at R40,934,150 and R40,934,150 (actual) respectively. These figures exclude revenue and expenditure from the Commonwealth Development Corporation Fund and grants from the British Government.

Estimated development revenue and expenditure for 1975/76 was R51,831,313, which was below the figure for 1974/75 which stood at R60,484,750 and that for 1973/74 at R52,962,334. The decrease was largely due to the completion of major development projects, namely the Selebi-Pikwe copper mining complex and the Shashe power scheme, which had involved importation of large quantities of capital equipment. Development funds came from the World Bank, the African Development Bank, Canada, the United Kingdom, United States of America, Sweden, Denmark and others.

The GNP at market prices for 1974 was U.S. $ millions 190, and the GNP per capita for 1974 was U.S. $290. The annual average percentage growth rate of GNP per capita for the period 1960–74 was 4·8 and for the period 1965–74, 6·2. [*See the note at the beginning of this section concerning GNP.*]

The chief items of revenue were taxes and duties, customs and excise, posts and telegraphs, government property and licences. The chief items of expenditure were education, medical services, works and communications, agriculture, posts and telegraphs and development.

## PRODUCTION

Although the first steps have been taken to diversify the economy with the introduction of industrial and mining developments, the bulk of Botswana's population still depends largely on agriculture. The export of beef accounts for a large proportion of the country's foreign trade and is the major source of cash income. The cattle population grew to 2,300,000 head in 1975. Approximately half of this national herd is owned by about 10 per cent of the farmers, and over 25 per cent of the farmers have no cattle at all. Arable farming, therefore, is the only way by which the average farmer can provide for his family. The serious drought in the years of 1961–66 brought crop production to a virtual halt. Good rains the following year renewed agricultural activity but the yield was very small because of the low acreage that was cultivated. The reason for the low acreage planted was that either the draught oxen had died of starvation in the drought or were disposed of at the abattoir. In the last decade, therefore, Botswana has moved from a position of self-sufficiency in basic foods to being an importer of foodstuffs. Arable production can be increased by increasing the amount of arable land cultivated. It is estimated that in the years 1969/70 out of the available arable acreage of about 1·2 million acres, only 537,000 acres were planted.

In order to improve the quality of the indigenous cattle and small stock, a number of livestock improvement schemes have been introduced. Compulsory free vaccinations are carried out annually in order to control certain diseases.

**Commerce.** The following table shows estimated values (in millions of Rands), of principal imports for 1974:

| *Commodity* | *Value* |
|---|---|
| Food and live animals | 11·5 |
| Beverages and tobacco | 4·6 |
| Crude materials, inedible, except fuel | 1·4 |
| Mineral fuels, lubrications and related materials | 5·6 |
| Animal and vegetable oils and fats | 0·2 |
| Chemicals | 4·2 |
| Manufactured goods classified chiefly by material | 30·7 |
| Machinery and transport equipment | 48·9 |
| Miscellaneous manufactured articles | 12·3 |
| Commodities and transactions not classified according to kind | 2·6 |
| **Total** | 122·0 |

The following table shows values (in millions of Rands), of principal exports for 1974:

| *Commodity* | *Value* |
|---|---|
| Meat and meat products | 15·7 |
| Diamonds | 25·0 |
| Copper-nickel matte | 8·0 |
| Other commodities | 6·1 |
| **Total** | 54·8 |

**Mining.** One of the most important mineral discoveries made in Botswana recently was the discovery in 1966/67 of a new kimberlite province at Orapa, on the northern fringe of the Kgalagadi Desert, which has the world's second largest diamond bearing pipe, surpassed only by the Williamson pipe in Tanzania. A diamond mine was opened and full scale production began in July 1971. The mine is already Botswana's largest earner of foreign currency.

In July 1975 agreement was reached to establish Botswana's second diamond mine at Letlhakane, 40 km south-east of the existing mine at Orapa, following the successful conclusion of De Beers sampling programme on two kimberlite pipes in the area.

Copper and nickel were discovered in the Selebi-Pikwe area, 55 miles south-east of Francistown, in 1964 and a decision was taken to develop a mine. The copper-nickel mine came on stream in 1974 and cost R170 million to bring to production including infrastructure costs of R53 million. The mines at Selebi-Pikwe and Orapa are expected to provide the Government with a direct revenue of over R14,000,000 annually from 1975 onward.

A coal mine was opened at Morupule close to Palapye in 1973 and even larger coal resources were blocked out at Mmamabule and west of Morupule. Considerable reserves of copper have been outlined at Matsitama and nickel/copper at Selkirk/Phoenix while a gypsum mine will soon be developed in the Topisi area. On the Sau Pan of the Makgadikgadi Salt Pans vast reserves of salt, soda ash and salt cake have been proved and a mine is expected to be established there in the late 1970s.

## COMMUNICATIONS

There is a railway line running through Botswana 394 miles in length, which enters the country at Ramathlabama Spruit, 16 miles north of Mafeking. It is owned and operated by Rhodesia Railways.

The roads from railway stations and sidings to the principal villages serve for motor transport, but about 50 miles west of the railway the tracks are very sandy and generally unsuitable for motor traffic except on a few routes. There are about 83 km of tarred and approximately 8,000 km of gravelled or earth roads. All telegraph and telephone lines in the country were purchased by the Government in January 1957. At the end of 1972 there were 4,563 telephones and 11,743 licensed radio sets.

Air Botswana operates internal flights between Gaborone, Shashe, Selebi–Pikwe, Francistown and Maun in conjunction with Esquire Airways once a week, and a regular service between Johannesburg, Gaborone, and Francistown in conjunction with South African Airways. Zambia Airways operates directly from Lusaka, Zambia once a week.

## EDUCATION

In 1975 there were 327 primary schools, 15 secondary schools, two vocational schools, three teacher training schools, and fifteen other types of schools in Botswana. Enrolments were 115,052 in primary schools, 8,434 in secondary schools, 440 in vocational schools and 531 in teacher training schools.

All but three of the primary schools are run down by the District Councils and Township authorities, and are financed from local government revenues assisted by government grant-in-aid. Seven secondary schools are government controlled, five are private institutions and four are run by missions.

# Brazil

(REPÚBLICA FEDERATIVA DO BRASIL)

**Capital**—Brasília.

**President**—General Ernesto Geisel.

**National Flag:** Green, bearing at the centre a diamond yellow charged with a blue celestial globe; inscribed in green on white round the equator, 'Ordem e Progresso'.

## CONSTITUTION AND GOVERNMENT

BRAZIL was discovered on 22 April 1500 by the Portuguese admiral Pedro Alvares Cabral, and claimed for the mother country. There followed a policy of colonization, with the Portuguese starting, in the 17th century, sugar plantations worked by negro slaves brought from Africa. The discovery of gold and diamonds in the 18th century provided a further impetus to colonization and development.

Following the Napoleonic upheaval in Europe, the Portuguese Royal Family and court fled to Brazil and their presence set the stage for great developments. Brazil was raised to the status of a United Kingdom with Portugal and Algarves, and, on his return to Portugal in 1821, the King, yielding to popular demand, left his son to rule Brazil as Regent. In 1822, Prince Pedro proclaimed the country's full independence from Portugal and, until 1889, Brazil developed as an Empire ruled by a branch of the Braganza family, the unifying power of the monarchy making for an enviable cohesion unknown in other parts of South America.

A bloodless revolution, precipitated by the dissatisfaction of the landowning classes with the monarchy over the emancipation of the slaves, and having its roots in the republican sentiments of certain sections of the intelligentsia and the army, forced the abdication of Emperor Pedro II in 1889. Under the Constitution of 1891 Brazil became a Federal Republic, governed by a bi-cameral National Congress, with the executive power vested in a President elected for a term of four years.

Following close on the stress and strain of the 1929 depression, and after the disputed result of the 1930 election, Dr. Getulio Vargas, Governor of Rio Grande do Sul, seized power. A constituent assembly was called and in 1934 the new Constitution was produced, and Dr. Vargas elected as President. In 1937 Dr. Vargas cancelled the forthcoming presidential elections, dissolved Congress and all political parties and proceeded to govern by decree, but in spite of the authoritarian character of the régime, the rate of national development was accelerated and great progress was made towards industrialization. In 1942 Brazil broke off relations with the Axis Powers and in 1944 entered the war on the side of the Allies. During the war there was a boom in industrial activity owing to the shortage of foreign manufactured goods brought about by the war and the rise in prices of Brazilian export products.

In 1945, giving in to popular clamour for the return to constitutional government, Dr. Vargas called for presidential elections but was ousted before these were held. General Dutra, ex-War Minister, was elected and following elections for the National Congress, his Social Democratic Party won over half the total vote. Whilst General Dutra governed provisionally by decree the two Chambers sitting as a Constituent Assembly framed the new Constitution which came into force on 18 September 1946. A Presidential election was held on 3 October 1950, and Dr. Vargas was elected.

Getulio Vargas was President until August 1954 when he was forced to renounce his governorship.

The vice-president Café Filho succeeded him until 10 November 1955 when, in consequence of a political coup, Nereu Ramos, President of the Chamber of Deputies, became the head of the government to make sure that in January, 1956, Juscelino Kubitschek, the elected candidate, assumed the government.

The Constitution provides that legislative power is exercised by the National Congress, which is composed of the Chamber of Deputies and the Federal Senate.

The Chamber of Deputies is elected by proportional representation in the States, the Federal District and the Territories. The number of Deputies is fixed by the new Constitution put in force on 15 March 1967 in such a proportion as not to exceed one for each 300,000 inhabitants up to 25 Deputies, and beyond this limit, one for every million inhabitants. Each territory has one Deputy, and the minimum number for each state is seven.

The Federal Senate is elected by the majority principle on the basis of three Senators for each state. The Senatorial mandate is eight years, and the representation of each state is renewed every four years, alternately, by one-third and two-thirds. The Congress meets in the Capital of the Republic from 1 March to 30 June, and form 1 August to 30 November.

The Deputies and Senators receive an annual salary, as well as an allowance for expenses. The salaries are divided into two parts—one which is fixed and is paid during the course of the year, and the other variable, according to their attendance.

Executive power is exercised by the President of the Republic, who is elected for a term of four years. The Vice-President is elected at the same time, and he succeeds the President in the case of the post becoming vacant. The President is assisted by a Cabinet composed of a number of Ministers of State.

Political parties with programmes subversive to democratic principles and fundamental human rights can be banned. This was taken to apply to the Communist party, and on 7 May 1947 the Electoral High Court decided by three votes to two to declare it illegal. In the following January all the Communist Deputies and Senators, and the 18 members of the Municipal Council of Rio de Janeiro, where they constituted the largest single party, were unseated.

After the resignation of Jânio Quadros, João Goulart (the vice-president) was confirmed President of the Republic by Congress under the Parliamentary Regime with a Prime Minister and a Cabinet. However, on 6 January 1963, a popular plebiscite restored the Presidency in Brazil and João Goulart governed without a Prime Minister and with thirteen ministries.

On 31 March 1964, a revolution overthrew the government of João Goulart who fled to Uruguay.

The Brazilian Congress then elected General Humberto de Alencar Castello Branco President of Brazil, for the remaining period of 18 months, prior to the 1965 presidential elections which eventually were postponed for one year. On 3 October 1966 Congress elected Marshal Artur de Costa e Silva as President. He took office on 15 March 1967. In 1969 Congress elected General Emílio Garrastazu Médici as President. He took office on 15 October 1969. General Médici's Successor is Ernesto Geisel. Mr Geisel up to that time had been chairman of the state oil corporation Petrobrás. Mr Geisel took over formally in March 1974 for a five year term. An amendment to the Constitution now provides for the election of the President for a six year term by an Electoral College and delegates from the State Legislatures.

### Cabinet

*Minister of Agriculture:* Dr. Alysson Paulinelli.
*Minister of Air:* Tenente Brigadeiro do Ar Joelmir Campos de Araripe Macedo.
*Minister of Education and Culture:* Ney Amintas de Barros Braga.
*Minister of Finance:* Prof. Mario Henrique Simonsen.
*Minister of Foreign Affairs:* Ambassador Antonio Francisco Azeredo da Silveira.
*Minister of Health:* Prof. Paulo de Almeida Machado.
*Minister of Industry and Commerce:* Angelo Calmon de Sá.
*Minister of Justice:* Dr. Armando Ribeiro Falcão.
*Minister of Labour:* Dr. Arnaldo da Costa Prieto.
*Minister of Mines and Energy:* Dr. Shigeaki Ueki.
*Minister of the Navy:* Squadron-Admiral Geraldo Azevedo Henning.
*Minister of Transport:* General Dirceu de Araujo Nogueira.
*Minister of the Army:* Gen. Sylvio Couto Coelho da Frota.
*Minister for Communications:* Captain Euclydes Quandt de Oliveira.
*Minister of Internal Affairs:* Dr. Mauricio Rangel Reis.
*Minister of Social Welfare:* Dr. Luiz Gonzalga do Nascimento e Silva.

## LOCAL GOVERNMENT

The States of Brazil have separate legislatures, administrations and judiciaries. They have their own Constitutions and may make their own laws, provided that these accord with the constitutional principles of the Union. Inter-state taxation is forbidden, but export taxes are allowed up to 3 per cent ad valorem. Each State has its own legislature, the members of which are elected by popular vote, as are the state governors.

The administration of justice is by Federal Courts and State Courts. The Federal Courts comprise:

### LEGAL SYSTEM

1. The Federal Supreme Court, sitting at Brasília composed of 11 judges appointed by the President of the Republic, after their selection has been approved by the Federal Senate.

2. The Federal Court of Appeal, which has both primary and appellate jurisdiction. It is composed of 13 judges appointed by the President of the Republic (subject to the approval of the Federal Senate) and made up of eight judges from among magistrates and five from among lawyers and members of the Attorney-General's Office.

3. Military judges and Courts.

4. Electoral judges and Courts, consisting of (*a*) Electoral High Courts, (*b*) Regional Electoral Courts, (*c*) Electoral Boards and (*d*) Electoral Judges.

5. Labour Judges and Courts, comprising (*a*) Labour High Courts, (*b*) Regional Labour Courts, (*c*) Board of Judges of conciliation and judgment.

The functions of the Labour Judicature are to conciliate and judge individual and collective disputes between employers and employees as well as controversies arising out of labour relations controlled by special legislation.

The State courts administer justice according to the State law except in Brasília, where Federal Justice is administered.

**The Supreme Court**

*President:* Carlos Thompson Flores.
*Vice-President:* Olavo Bilac Pinto.
*Director-General:* Pedro José Xavier Mattoso.

### AREA AND POPULATION

| *Regions* | *Area (sq. km.)* | *Population Census 1970, September* |
|---|---|---|
| **Northern Region** | | |
| Rondônia | 243,044 | 116,620 |
| Acre | 152,589 | 218,006 |
| Amazonas | 1,564,445 | 960,934 |
| Roraima | 230,104 | 41,638 |
| Pará | 1,248,042 | 2,197,072 |
| Amapá | 140,276 | 116,480 |
| **Total Northern Region** | 3,554,180 | 3,650,750 |
| **North-east Region** | | |
| Maranhão | 328,663 | 3,037,135 |
| Piauí | 250,934 | 1,734,865 |
| Ceará | 148,016 | 4,491,590 |
| Rio Grande de Norte | 53,015 | 1,611,606 |
| Paraíba | 56,372 | 2,445,419 |
| Pernambuco | 98,281 | 5,252,590 |
| Fernando Noronha | 26 | 1,311 |
| Alagoas | 27,731 | 1,606,174 |
| **Total North-east Region** | 963,038 | 20,180,690 |
| **Eastern Region** | | |
| Sergipe | 21,994 | 911,251 |
| Bahia | 561,026 | 7,583,140 |
| Minas Gerais | 587,172 | 11,645,095 |
| Espírito Santo | 45,597 | 1,617,857 |
| Rio de Janeiro | 42,912 | 4,794,578 |
| Guanabara | 1,356 | 4,315,746 |
| **Total Eastern Region** | 1,260,057 | 30,867,667 |
| **Southern Region** | | |
| São Paulo | 247,898 | 17,958,693 |
| Paraná | 199,554 | 6,997,682 |
| Santa Catarina | 95,985 | 2,930,411 |
| Rio Grande do Sul | 282,184 | 6,755,458 |
| **Total Southern Region** | 825,621 | 34,641,244 |
| **West Central Region** | | |
| Mato Grosso | 1,231,549 | 1,623,618 |
| Goiás | 642,092 | 2,997,570 |
| Federal District | 5,814 | 546,015 |
| **Total W. Central Region** | 1,879,455 | 5,167,203 |
| **TOTAL BRAZIL** | 8,511,965 | 94,508,554 |

Principal cities with population above 300,000 (1970, Census) are: São Paulo, 5,978,977; Rio de Janeiro, 4,315,746; Belo Horizonte, 1,255,415; Recife, 1,084,459; Porto Alegre, 903,175; Salvador, 1,027,142; Fortaleza, 872,702; Curitiba, 624,362; Belém, 642,514; Brasília, 546,015; Goiânia, 389,784; Niterói, 330,396.

The population at mid-1974 was 103,981,000. The annual average percentage growth rate of the population for the period 1960–74 was 2·9 and for the period 1965–74 was also 2·9.

### CURRENCY AND FINANCE

The unit of currency is the 'Cruzeiro', made up of 100 centavos.

**Federal Budget** (All expressed in thousands of Cruzeiros)

| | 1975 *thousand Cruzeiros* |
|---|---|
| *Revenue* | |
| Taxation | 81,760,300 |
| Patrimonial | 410,500 |
| Industrial | 33,100 |
| Sundry | 3,177,461 |
| *Expenditure* | |
| Congress and Auxiliary bodies | 677,195 |
| Executive (*Total*) | 36,792,615 |
| Presidency | 904,603 |
| Ministries | |
| Air | 2,703,035 |
| Agriculture | 895,219 |
| Education and Culture | 3,893,359 |
| Finances | 978,327 |
| Army | 4,647,265 |
| Communications | 662,532 |
| Industry and Commerce | 107,350 |
| Justice | 473,864 |
| Interior | 1,339,205 |
| Navy | 2,575,019 |
| Mines and Energy | 450,461 |
| Foreign Affairs | 443,800 |
| Health | 829,384 |
| Social Welfare | 2,356,899 |
| Labour | 352,700 |
| Transport | 5,631,913 |
| Judiciary | 646,862 |

The GNP at market prices for 1974 was U.S. $ millions 95,920, and the GNP per capita for 1974 was U.S.$920. The annual average percentage growth rate of the GNP for the period 1960–74 was 4·0, and for the period 1965–74 was 6·3 [*See the note at the beginning of this section concerning GNP.*]

### PRINCIPAL BANKS

(All money figures in Cr. $.)

**Banco BoaVista S.A.** (President, Candido Guinle de Paula Machado.) Est. 1924; capital, Cr. $101,245,030·00; loans and discounted bills, Cr.$2,174,074,875·93; deposits, Cr. $1,449,746,337·58. *Head Office:* Praça Pio X 118-A-ZC-00A, Rio de Janeiro, Brazil; 45 branches.

**Banco Brasileiro de Descontos, S.A.** (President, Amador Aguiar.) Figures as of June, 1977: Capital, $1,800,000,000, reserves and funds, $3,020,855,410·52; deposits; $25,143,999,782·55. *Head Office:* Avenida Ipiranga 210, São Paulo, 811 branches. *Telex:* 11-23171.

**Banco Comercial do Parana S.A.** (President, Adolpho de Oliveira Franco.) Capital, Cr. $22,500,000·00; loans and discounted bills, Cr. $173,263,440·00; deposits, Cr. $274,102,679·00. *Head Office:* Rua 15 de Novembro, 310 Curitiba (Pr), Brazil. 156 branches.

**Banco Comércio Industria de Minas Gerais S.A.** (President, Dr. Ruy de Castro Magalhães.) Capital and reserves, Cr. $117,447,118 (U.S. $19,973,999); loans and discounts, Cr. $488,341,453 (U.S. $83,051,267); deposits, Cr. $516,374,456 (U.S. $87,818,785). *Head Office:* Rua Espírito Santo, 593 Belo Horizonte, M.G., Brazil. 219 branches, of which 10 operating Foreign Exchange.

**Banco da Bahia S.A.** (President, Clemente Mariani.) Capital, Cr. $35,000,000·00; reserves and funds, Cr. $56,339,383·02; loans and discounted bills, Cr. $639,566,174·18. *Head Office:* Rua Miguel Calmon 32, Salvador, Bahia; 217 branches.

**Banco de Credito Real de Minas Gerais S.A.** (President, Dr. M. A. G. de Souza.) Capital, Cr. $166 million; loans and discounted bills, Cr. $2,681,880,557·07. deposits, Cr. $1,823,727,794·53. *Head Office:* Rua Halfeld, 505, Juiz de Fora, Minas de Gerais; 116 branches.

**Banco do Brasil, S.A.** (President, Nestor Jost.) Est. 1808; the bank is controlled by the Government, which owns 57·8 per cent of the share capital; capital and reserves: Cr. $225,007,602·53; loans and discounted bills: Cr. $1,455,708,567·29; deposits: Cr. $1,816,837,780·53; Total resources Cr. $10,311,157,825·96. *Head Office:* Brasília; 797 branches in Brazil and 14 abroad.

**Banco do Estado de Minas Gerais, S.A.** (President, Dr. A. T. Caldeira.) Capital, Cr. $275,000·00; loans and discounted bills, Cr. $6,268,375,427·42; deposits, Cr. $4,523,201,675·03. *Address:* Pça. Sete de Setembro, Belo Horizonte, Minas Gerais; 28 branches and agencies.

**Banco do Estado de São Paulo, S.A.** (President, Dr. Joffre Alves de Carvalho) Est. 1926; 76,53 per cent of the capital is owned by the State of São Paulo Government; capital, Cr. $1,785,000,000·00; loans and discounted bills, Cr. $37,642,567,546·16; deposits, Cr. $15,201,988,504·21 as at 30 June 1977. *Head Office:* Praça Antonio Prado, 6, São Paulo, Brazil—Telex 1172121/4; 322 branches. New York: 270, Park Avenue, suit 1470, New York, N.Y. 10017—Telex-BESP UI 03005–422450; LONDON: Plantation House, 31–35 Fenchurch Street, London EC3M 3NA—Telex–0307–888839–BANESPA IDN; TOKYO: Fuji Building, 10th floor, Room 1020/21 Marunouchi, 3–23 Chiyoda-Ku—Telex–Tobesp J. 26825; *Representative Offices:* FRANKFURT: 6000 Frankfurt/Main—Bockenheimer Landstrasse 51–53/14° Etagee—Telex–BESP D 414356; BEIRUTH: Saint Charles City Center—Triangular Building, 4th floor Telex—Arabesp–Cable: Arabespa–P.O. Box 155082; ASSUNCION: Calle Azara esquina Yegros–Telex–305–349–PY–BANESPA, Casilla Del Correo 2211; GRAND CAYMAN (Caribe): P.O. Box 501 Grand Cayman–Cayman Islands–B.W.I. Contacts: New York.

**Banco do Commercio e Industria de São Paulo, S.A.** (President, Roberto F. Amaral.) Est. 1889; capital, Cr. $69,000,000·00; loans and discounted bills Cr. $592,450,000·00; deposits, Cr. $949,067,000·00. *Head Office:* 289 Rua 15 de Novembro, São Paulo; 231 branches.

**Banco do Estado do Rio Grande do Sul, S.A.** (Director and Vice-President, Assis A. De Souza.) Capital, Cr. $253,125,000; loans and discounted bills, Cr. $9,166,989,417·26; deposits, Cr. $4,630,682,165·10. *Head Office:* Rua Capitão Montanha 177, Porto Alegre; 203 branches.

**Banco do Estado do Rio de Janeiro, S.A.** (President, Olympio Pinto Reis Filho). Statement of condition as at 30 June 1977: Capital, Cr. $410 million; loans and discounted bills, Cr. $12,343,394,555·95; deposits, Cr. $10,437,319,002·58. *Head Office:* Av. Nilo Peçanha 175, Rio de Janeiro; 182 branches.

**Banco do Nordeste do Brazil S.A.** (President, Antonio Nílson Craveiro Holanda.) Capital, Cr. $700,000,000 (U.S. $64,814,814·81); loans and discounted bills, Cr. $11,015,367,237·55 (U.S. $1,019,941,410·88); deposits, Cr. $2,097,112,517·51 (U.S. $194,177,084·95). *Head Office:* Fortaleza, Ceará; 76 branches.

**Banco Francês E Italiano Para A America Do Sul S.A. Sudameris** Est. 1949. (President, Rogerio Giorgi; Managing Director, Giovanni Lenti.) *Head Office:* Rua Bela Vista, 739 São Paulo, 59 branches.

**Banco Industria e Comercio Sta. Catarina S.A.** (President, Genesio M. Lins.) Capital, 7,500; loans and discounted bills, 34,631; deposits, 53,301. *Head Office:* Caixa Postal No. 5, Itajai, Santa Catarina; 112 branches.

**Banco Nacional S.A.,** (President, Eduardo de Magalhães Pinto.) Balance Sheet at 31 December 1976 shows Capital, Cr. $443,330,642·00; capital and reserves, Cr. $954,200,098; loans, Cr. $9,413,933,539; deposits, Cr. $9,253,268,453. *Presidency:* Av. Rio Branco, 123-4° andar, Rio de Janeiro (GB); *International Department Headquarters:* Ave Rio Branco -123-2° andar, Rio de Janeiro (RJ) Genival de Almeida Santos (Executive Director).

**Banco Noreste do Estado do São Paulo S.A.** (President, Jorge W. Simonsen.) Balance Sheet at 31 Dec., 1976. Capital, Cr. $200,000,000; loans and discounted bills, Cr. $2,396,953,615; deposits, Cr. $2,734,825,871. *Head Office:* Rua Alvares Penteado 216, São Paulo, Brazil; 86 branches.

**Banco Real, S.A.** (Director President, Dr. Aloysio de Andrade Faria.) Capital and reserves, Cr. $1,451,598,051·34; loans and discounted bills, Cr. $9,003,039,258·64; deposits, Cr. $9,143,681,504·04; total resources (31 December 1976) Cr. $197,626,042,403·22. *Head Office:* Rua Boa Vista, 274, São Paulo, 549 branches throughout the country and the following branches abroad: New York, Los Angeles, Grand Cayman, Nassau, Curaçao, Panama, Bogata, Côte D'Ivoire, Chile and London.

**Banco Sul Brasileiro S.A.** Successor of Banco Nacional do Comercio S.A., Banco Industrial e Comercial do Sul S.A., Banco da Província do Rio Grande do Sul S.A., as from January 1, 1973; capital and reserves, 456,366,186·99; loans and discounted bills, 2,373,186,573·86; deposits, 1,791,122,309·02. *Head Office:* Rua 7 de Setembro 1028 Porto Alegre R.G.S., Brazil, 345 branches.

**Uniãco de Bancos Brasileiros S.A.** (Acting President, Walther Moreira Salles.) Capital, Cr. $294,000,000·00; deposits, Cr. $3,236,458,906·33. *Head Office:* Rua do Ouvidor, 91 Rio de Janeiro, Gb.

**Banco Mercantil de São Paulo S.A.** (President, Gastão Eduardo de Bueno Vidigal.) Capital and reserves, $232,578,610; loans, $930,752,673; deposits, 1,079,500·410. *Head Office:* Avenida Paulista, 1450, São Paulo; 218 branches.

## PRODUCTION, INDUSTRY AND COMMERCE

**Agriculture.** Despite the development rapidly proceeding in other spheres of production, Brazil is still largely an agricultural country. There is a wide range of soils and climates which enable a diversity of crops and plants to flourish. Brazil is the world's largest producer of coffee, manioc, cane sugar, oranges, beans and bananas. The country's coffee output is more than 40 per cent of the world total. The bulk of the coffee crop is grown in the states of Parana (most important), São Paulo, Matto Grosso, Minas Gerais, Rio de Janeiro and Espirito Santo. Large plantations of over 100,000 trees are the rule. The Government regulates the sales, the growers receive a variable subsidy on each bag. Brazil is the second largest producer of corn and citrus fruits, and stands third in sugar cane and cocoa.

Maize is the principal cereal crop, and production comes second only to that of the United States. Wheat is the main cereal deficiency, but the yield has been increased to 30 per cent of domestic requirements.

The cotton crop is gaining in importance, and accounts for about two-thirds of the South American output. The crop is grown in the states of São Paulo, Minas Gerais, Parana, Gojas, and in Northeast.

Other important crops are rice, beans and cassava, which are grown for domestic consumption. There is a large area under tobacco, but almost two-thirds of the crop is consumed at home. Soybean production has developed tremendously. In 1975 it became Brazil's largest source of export revenue and Brazil became the world's second largest producer in the world of soybean.

Conditions are excellent for fruit growing, as the wide range of climate enables fruit trees from all the intermediate zones between temperate and tropical to be planted successfully. The fruits cultivated on the largest scale are bananas, oranges and pineapples, which are exported in large quantities, but there are also good crops of apples, pears, grapes, plums and peaches in the southern states.

The southern part of Brazil is eminently suitable for the cultivation of the vine. Restriction of planting to the finest strain and the application of modern processes of wine-making have gone far to raise the quality of the product.

The estimated production figures for agricultural products for 1975 are:

| Crop | m Tons |
|---|---|
| Maize | 16,414,794 |
| Rice | 7,537,589 |
| Cotton, raw | 1,755,424 |
| Beans | 2,271,421 |
| Coffee | 1,392,000 |
| Sugar cane | 88,411,712 |
| Wheat | 2,090,990 |
| Soya | 9,717,353 |
| Cocoa | 230,000 |
| Potatoes | 1,668,874 |
| Oranges (th. fruit) | 31,671,818 |

**Forestry.** The forests of Brazil cover an area of about 1,350,000 sq. miles. The tropical forests are rich in oil-bearing plants, gums, resins, balsams, wax, essences, fibres and medicinal raw materials. In the south of the country there are vast areas of pine woods which constitute a valuable source of wealth, the standing timber being estimated at 200 million trees. The lumber is of fine quality, and is exported under the name of Parana Pine. The most valuable of the forest trees is the Carnauba, an imposing palm growing along the river banks on the north-east, which supplies a wax in high demand for such varied applications as floor polishes, gramophone records, carbon paper and explosives. A number of factories extract tannin from native bark and wood. The quebracho, or axe-breaker tree, also yields a valuable dyestuff. 95 per cent of cocoa production comes from Bahia. The cinchona or quina tree, from which quinine is derived, does well in the south. Other drugs such as strychnine, theobromine, atropine and curare are obtained from plants.

The Brazil nut tree is native to the Amazon valley, and large quantities of nuts are exported, chiefly to Great Britain and the United States.

In 1974, 9,275 tons of oiticica oil, and 155,793 tons of castor oil were exported.

**Mining.** There are important mines in Brazil of iron ore, manganese, bauxite, nickel, uranium, tin ore, diamonds, industrial diamonds, gems, nickel, zinc, and the rare minerals niobium, thorium, scheelite.

Brazil produces 90 per cent of the world supply of gems, such as aquamarines, topazes, amethysts and tourmalines and is becoming an important producer of emeralds.

Brazil has the world's largest reserves of iron ore of the richest content—60 per cent purity—estimated at 60,000 million tons. in 1973, 56 million tons were produced and 44 million tons exported. In 1974 production reached 75 million tons and 59·5 million tons were exported. Exports are made mainly through the ore loading terminal at Tubarão, in the State of Espirito Santo, and at the ports of Rio de Janeiro and Sepetiba, both in the State of Rio de Janeiro. The principal buyers are the United States, Germany and Japan. In the long term Brazil may become the world's leading exporter of iron ore, due to a recent find in the Carajas mountain range, with estimated reserves of more than 17,000 million tons. By 1980 exports from the Carajãs reserves alone will reach 20 million tons. These deposits will be explored jointly by *Companhia Vale do Rio Doce* (51 per cent of the shares) and the United States Steel Corporation, with British, Spanish and Japanese capital. The *Companhia Vale do Rio Doce* is the biggest producer and exporter of iron ore in Brazil and the fifth largest in the world. Its production of iron pellets alone reached eight million tons in 1974.

Brazil has proved deposits of manganese of 130 million tons, being one of the largest suppliers of this mineral.

Total reserves of bauxite are estimated at 443 million tons and rich deposits have been located in the lower Amazon region, on the Trombetas River, and in Paragominas in Pará with reserves estimated at 365 million tons of ore of 50 per cent purity. In 1973 bauxite production reached 849,218 tons. Over the next few years, government investments in this sector will reach U.S. $1,000 m. A joint venture with a Japanese company is providing an additional investment of U.S. $640 m.

Known reserves of nickel were estimated at 53 million tons but new deposits have recently been discovered, in São João do Piaui and Barro Alto in Goiás. It is possible that the new reserves reach more than 400 million tons. The largest single reserves are at Niquelândia, also in Goiás. All of Brazil's ferro-nickel comes from the State of Minas Gerais and is mainly produced by the *Companhia Morro do Niquel* (a subsidiary of the *Société de Nickel*) and by *Companhia Niquel do Brasil.*

The recent confirmation of important uranium reserves, in Araxá in the State of Minas Gerais should be of great value to Brazil's nuclear energy plans At 1·3 per cent purity the ore is of excellent quality.

**Commerce.** The following tables show the exports and imports by countries for 1973 and 1974:

| *Exports* | 1973 (*U.S. $m.*) | 1974 (*U.S. $m.*) |
|---|---|---|
| United States | 1,213 | 1,731 |
| West Germany | 601 | 788 |
| Argentine | 197 | 319 |
| Japan | 322 | 538 |
| United Kingdom | 202 | 243 |
| Italy | 185 | 202 |
| France | 167 | 210 |
| Sweden | 88 | 144 |
| Venezuela | 42 | 63 |
| Denmark | 30 | 30 |

| *Imports* | 1973 (*U.S. $m.*) | 1974 (*U.S. $m.*) |
|---|---|---|
| United States | 1,122 | 1,713 |
| West Germany | 554 | 570 |
| Argentine | 198 | 302 |
| Italy | 351 | 357 |
| Netherlands | 621 | 605 |
| Japan | 425 | 557 |
| United Kingdom | 312 | 375 |
| France | 209 | 269 |
| Belgium-Luxembourg | 156 | 145 |
| Sweden | 93 | 72 |

The following tables show the exports and imports by principal products for 1975:

| *Exports* | 1975 (*U.S. $m.*) |
|---|---|
| Coffee, raw | 855 |
| Cotton, raw | 97 |
| Iron ore | 908 |
| Sugar cane | 813 |
| Cocoa beans | 220 |
| Pinewood | 55 |
| Castor oil | 51 |
| Maize | 156 |
| Cocoa butter | 60 |
| Meat, frozen and tinned | 98 |
| Tobacco | 141 |
| Others | 5,207 |

| *Imports* | 1975 (*U.S. $m.* FOB) |
|---|---|
| Crude petroleum and bituminous mineral oils | 2,759 |
| Wheat | 471 |
| Wirebar copper | 328 |
| Jet-engined aircraft | 179 |
| Tractors | 166 |
| Telephone and telegraph apparatus and parts | 6 |
| Aluminium | 131 |
| Apples | 55 |
| Iron and steel plate | 369 |
| Codfish | 45 |
| Soluble naphtha | 4 |

## COMMUNICATIONS

**Railways.** In 1970 the total length of track of the Brazilian railways was 30,473 km., of which about 2,311 km. are electrified. The railways use tracks of five different gauges, but 90 per cent of the track is one metre gauge.

**Shipping.** The number of vessels on the Brazilian register in 1974 was 665, with a total tonnage of 4,109,843.

The number of vessels entering Brazilian ports in 1974 was 31,154, with a tonnage of 176,439,607.

Brazil has 975 natural ports, 231 of them sea-ports and 744 situated at the mouths of rivers. 25 of these ports are fully equipped with cranes and warehouses. The chief ports are Rio de Janeiro, Santos, Recife, Pôrto Alegre and Rio Grande. The government-owned shipping companies dominate coastal shipping. The Loide Brasileiro and the National Company of Coastal Navigation are responsible for half of all shipping operations, and between them operate a third of the 300 vessels engaged in the coastal trade. Another government firm FRONAPE is responsible for the transport of oil in tankers. The remainder of the merchant marine is in private ownership.

The following are the chief shipping lines:

**Loíde Brasileiro.** 50 vessels. Tonnage 335,266.

**Emprêsa de Bavegação da Amazônia S.A.** 26 vessels. Tonnage 16,226.

**Civil Aviation.** Owing to its great size and the impossibility of establishing an adequate system of roads through the forest areas, the development of civil aviation has been of great importance in maintaining communication between the different parts of the country. A network of more than 20 internal air routes has been established linking all the principal towns and carrying passengers, freight and mail. In addition the principal international airlines maintain regular air services between Rio de Janeiro and the chief European capitals. Pan American Airways have regular services to New York and there are numerous services between Brazil and the other South and Central American States, and Africa, provided in the main by the Brazilian airline Varig. Regular schedules by Concorde from Paris began in 1976.

In 1976 6·6 million passengers were carried and there were 431·8 million tons/km of freight flown.

Brazil has 1,453 airports of which 103 are used by regular commercial flights and 35 by jet aircraft. Apart from VASP, owned by the State of São Paulo, all the airlines, including VARIG, the international line, and Cruzeiro do Sul, the main line for South America, are privately owned.

The following are the principal airlines:

**SC—Serviços Aereos Cruzeiro do Sul, S.A.**; *services operated:* Domestic routes and to Argentina, Uruguay, Bolivia, Peru, French Guiana and Guyana, and Surinam. *Address:* Av. Rio Branco, 128-8th (P.O. Box 190-ZC-00). Rio de Janeiro, Brazil.

**VARIG, S.A.** (Viação Aérea Rio Grandense) Capital Cr. $310,800,000. Three per cent owned by State of Rio Grande do Sul (Brazil); 57 per cent by the Foundation Ruben Berta of VARIG Employees; Services operated: out of Rio de Janeiro between Buenos Aires, Montevideo, Santiago de Chile, Asuncion, Lima, Bogotá ,Caracas, Mexico, Los Angeles, Miami, New York, Lisbon, Madrid, Oporto, Rome, Geneve, Zurich, Paris, London, Frankfurt, Copenhagen, Johannesburg, Luanda, Tokyo and serving 64 cities in Brazil. *Head Office:* Av Almte Silvio Noronha, 365–Rio de Janeiro–Guanabara–Brazil. 20,000 ZC-39.

**Telegraphs and Telephones.** The Brazilian postal and telegraph services are controlled by the 'Empresa Brasileira de Correios e Telégrafos'.

The telephone systems are chiefly local. There exists a satellite tracking station and the subscriber trunk dialling services have been greatly expanded. Today, nearly 200 cities are provided with direct dialling services. Instruments in use numbered 2,626,090 in 1973.

**Broadcasting.** The number of broadcasting stations operating was 999 in 1973. There are 64 television stations.

## NEWSPAPERS

**O Estado de S. Paulo.** 1875. Daily. Liberal. Editor, Julio de Mesquita Neto. Rua Major Quedinho 28, São Paulo SP.

**Jornal do Brasil.** 1891. Publisher: M.F. do Nascimento Brito. Avenida Brasil 500, Rio de Janeiro.

**Diário de Notícias.** 1930. Editors, Ondina Portella Ribeiro Dantas and João Portella Ribeiro Dantas. Avenida Almirante Barroso 4A, Rio de Janeiro.

**Ultima Hora.** Daily. Rua Sotero dos Reis, 62, Rio de Janeiro GB.

**O Globo.** Editor in Chief: Roberto Marinho. Circulation: Sunday, 320,000; Monday, 237,000, Tuesday to Saturday, (one edition), 210,000 daily. Rua Irineu Marinho, 35, RJ GB Brasil.

## EDUCATION

The Brazilian Constitution makes elementary education compulsory, and free between the ages 7 to 14. In 1973 there were 176,906 primary schools (with 18,573,193 students) and 10,585 secondary schools (with 1,477,656 students). In 1974 there were 835 establishments of higher education, including 57 universities. The estimated enrolment of students in Brazilian universities in 1974 was 1,000,000.

## OIL

Until 1953, when Petrobrás (Brazil's state-owned oil company) was formed, crude oil production was only about 2,000 barrels a day, and the domestic refining capacity was only slightly over double this figure. Granted the exclusive rights for exploration and production, Petrobrás quickly set about creating a large-scale oil industry. In 1975 domestic production had reached 310,000,000 barrels, equivalent to 28 per cent of the country's consumption. Because Brazil is self-sufficient in refining imports are limited to crude petroleum, plus a few specialized products and limited quantities of certain fuels needed to balance the yield-breakdown of the domestic crude oil. Private oil companies still have a small share in the refining, but they play an important role in the distribution of refined products. Petrobrás has recently embarked as a policy of "risk contracts" with foreign companies willing to prospect for oil on Brazilian soil. In December 1974 Petrobrás confirmed the discovery of an oil-bearing calcareous structure off Campos in Rio de Janeiro state. The discovery, in the Garoupa area, 50 miles off the coast, means a new and important source of oil to be added to the other new finds in the North-east now coming into production. Petrobrás is also mounting a heavy exploration programme in the Amazon region and, by 1977, plans to process about 100,000 barrels of oil a day out of the shale deposits that stretch from São Paulo to Rio Grande do Sul. All this may mean oil self-sufficiency by 1980, when estimated consumption will reach 1·2 million barrels a day.

## ATOMIC ENERGY

A National Research Council was set up in April 1951 for the development of atomic energy. An indispensable device for atomic research, one synchro-cyclotron (21-inch), similar to the one existing in the University of Chicago, was partially constructed in Brazil and is now operating. A 170-inch synchro-cyclotron has been built in the Marine Arsenal, Rio de Janeiro. A 5-megawatt research reactor, partially built in Brazil, is working in the University of São Paulo. A smaller one is in Rio de Janeiro. Small reactors ('sub-critical') and nuclear research institutes are being set up in various universities, including those in Minas Gerais and Pernambuco.

Plans for the construction of a power reactor of 500 megawatts for the production of electrical energy in the Central-Southern Region (the most densely populated) have been completed. It will start operating in 1976–77.

Brazil was a supporter and signatory of the Latin America treaty banning the use of nuclear weapons, but has not signed the Geneva treaty on non-proliferation of nuclear weapons lest it might interfere with plans for using nuclear energy for economic development purposes.

The country's first commercial reactor is already under construction at Angra dos Reis, in the State of Rio de Janeiro. The reactor is of the conventional, enriched-uranium type, will have an initial capacity of 760,000 kilowatts and will begin operating in the near future. Administration and operation will be turned over to Centrais Elétricas de FURNAS. By 1985 three more powerful reactors will be in operation. By means of a recent treaty, West Germany is to supply Brazil with a complete package of nuclear fuel services and reactors for its nuclear energy industry.

## RELIGION

The population of Brazil is almost entirely Roman Catholic, although there is a minority of over 2,000,000 Protestants. Connection between Church and State was abolished in 1889, restored in 1934 and again abolished under the 1946 constitution. There is freedom of worship for all denominations.

# Brunei

(MEMBER OF THE COMMONWEALTH)

**Capital**—Bandar Seri Begawan.

**Sultan**—Duli Yang Maha Mulia Paduka Seri Baginda Sultan dan Yand Di-Pertuan Sir Muda Hassanal Bolkiah Mu'izzad-din Waddaulah DK, PSSUB, DPKG, DPKT, FSPNB, PSNB, PSLJ, SPMB, PANB, GCMG, DK (Kelantan), DK (Johore), Sultan dan Yang Di-Pertuan Negeri Brunei Darul-Salam.

**British High Commissioner**—J. A. Davidson, OBE.

Brunei is a State on the north-west of Borneo. It was at one time a powerful State, the authority of whose rulers extended over the northern part of the island of Borneo. Its importance gradually declined and the State fell into decay. The district of Sarawak was ceded to Sir James Brooke piecemeal between 1841 and 1890. In 1888 an agreement was concluded between the Sultan and the British Government under which the control of foreign relations was placed in the hands of Her Majesty's Government, whilst internal affairs were left to the Sultan. A further agreement was made in 1905, by which a British Resident was appointed to advise and assist in the administration of the State. The post of British Resident was abolished in 1959 when the Sultan of Brunei promulgated the first written Constitution and entered into a new agreement with Her Majesty the Queen. The British Government continued to be responsible for defence and external affairs, and a High Commissioner was appointed. On 23 November, 1971 an amendment to the 1959 agreement was signed. Under the amended agreement, Brunei ceased to be a British protected state and enjoys full internal self-government. Britain continues to be responsible for Brunei's external affairs. The Agreement provides for consultation between the two countries in the event of an external threat to Brunei.

The supreme executive authority of the State is vested in the Sultan. There are three councils, the Privy Council, the Council of Ministers and the Legislative Council. The Sultan presides over the Privy Council and the Council of Ministers. The speaker heads the Legislative Council. General internal administration is carried out by the Mentri Besar. The seat of Government is in Bandar Seri Begawan, which is situated near the Brunei River about nine miles from its mouth. There are four administrative districts under the charge of District Officers who are responsible to the Mentri Besar.

## POPULATION

The population at mid-1974 was 150,000. The average annual percentage growth rate of the population for the periods 1960–74 was 4·6 and for the period 1965–74 was 3·9.

## CURRENCY AND FINANCE

The unit of currency is the Brunei dollar. Public revenue in 1974 amounted to B$975,000,000 and expenditure to B$220,000,000. In addition B$60,000,000 was expended out of the Development Fund. Brunei depends primarily on its oil industry which employs about 11 per cent of the entire working population.

## COMMERCE

Production of crude petroleum in 1974 was 70,300,000 barrels, and of natural gasoline 151,700 million cubic feet. 80 per cent of Brunei's oil exports are shipped to Japan. Under the terms of a 20 year contract signed in 1972 Brunei also supplies Japan with about 5 million tons of natural gas per year. As a result of an agreement announced on 16 April 1975, the Brunei Government has acquired a substantial shareholding in Brunei Shell Petroleum, the company which conducts the extraction of oil from the Brunei fields. Liquefication of natural gas is conducted jointly by Shell, the Brunei Government and Japanese interests.

The value of principal exports in 1974 was B$2348·7 million.

Value of imports by section in 1974 in millions of Brunei dollars:

| | $ |
|---|---|
| Food | 62·3 |
| Beverages and tobacco | 9·9 |
| Crude materials, inedible, except fuels | 5·8 |
| Mineral fuels, lubricants, and related materials | 7·2 |
| Animal and vegetable oils and fats | 3·1 |
| Chemicals and products of chemical industries | 36·8 |
| Manufactured goods (classified chiefly by material) | 183·6 |
| Machinery and transport equipment | 113·2 |
| Miscellaneous manufactured articles | 22·8 |
| Total | 444·7 |

The GNP at market prices for 1974 was U.S.$ millions 990, and the GNP per capita at market prices was U.S. $6,630. The annual average percentage growth rate of the GNP per capita for the period 1960–74 was 2·4, and for the period 1965–74 was 5·7. [*See the note at the beginning of this Section concerning GNP*].

# Bulgaria

(NARODNA REPUBLIKA BULGARIA)

**Capital**—Sofia.

*Chairman of the State Council:* Todor Zhivkov.

**National Flag:** A tricolour fesse-wise, white, green, red, charged on the white with the emblem of state: a lion rampant white in a wreath of corn, over a red scroll inscribed in gold '681 1944', and under a star five-pointed red.

## CONSTITUTION AND GOVERNMENT

THE earliest inhabitants of the area now known as Bulgaria were the Thracians, who during the 6th and 7th centuries A.D. were absorbed by the Slavonic immigrants into the Balkans. In the second half of the 7th century the Proto-Bulgarians inhabited the region to the north of the Danubian delta. In a struggle against Byzantium together with the Slav tribes from North Bulgaria they formed the First Bulgarian State in 681. From 803 until 814 Krum reigned over the Bulgarians. The Byzantine Emperor Niceph orus undertook three expeditions against him in the last of which he was killed. Krum eventually conquered Serdica today called Sofia and many Slav regions.

Christianity was accepted in the reign of Boris in 864. The invention of the Slavonic Script created conditions for the development of original national culture. The Bulgarian literature had an influence on Serbian, Russian and Rumanian literature. The zenith of Bulgarian power was reached in the reign of Simeon 'Emperor and Autocrat of all the Bulgars and Greeks' (893–927). He defeated the Byzantines, twice capturing Adrianople.

In 1018 the Byzantine Emperor, Basil II (the 'Bulgar Slayer') overthrew the first Bulgarian Empire; but it was revived in 1187 by the brothers Peter and Assen, who led an insurrection and established the Second Bulgarian Kingdom. From 1218–41 the country once again enjoyed prosperity under Tsar Ivan Asen II, who conquered Albania, Epirus and South-East Thrace.

From the beginning of Ottoman rule in 1396 the Bulgarian people carried on a severe struggle for their liberation which was manifest in a number of uprisings. 'The Slav–Bulgarian History' written in 1762 by Father Paissi marked the beginning of the Bulgarian national revival, a period in which the Bulgarian nation was formed and a national and democratic revolution was prepared and took place in the country.

In the 19th century a revolutionary organization was set up in Bulgaria, headed by the prominent Bulgarian revolutionaries and democrats Georgi S. Rakovski, Vassil Levski, Lyuben Karavelov, Hristo-Botev, and many others. The April uprising, which occurred in 1876, marked the climax of the people's struggles. Its suppression led to the declaration of the Russo-Turkish War of Liberation (1877–1878) in which many Bulgarian voluntary detachments took part. After the signing of the San-Stefano Peace Treaty, the Third Bulgarian State was formed, including the country's present-day territories, the greater part of European Turkey and the whole of Macedonia. According to the decision of the Congress of Berlin (1878), Bulgaria was divided into a Principality of Bulgaria (North Bulgaria) and an autonomous region, called Eastern Rumelia (South Bulgaria). The rest of the Bulgarian lands remained under Ottoman domination.

In 1885 the principality of Bulgaria was united with Eastern Rumelia and in 1908 the independent Bulgarian Kingdom was proclaimed.

In 1912 Bulgaria formed an alliance with Greece, Serbia and Montenegro (the so-called Balkan Alliance) and took part in the Balkan War (1912–1913) for the liberation of the Bulgarian lands which were still under Ottoman domination. In 1915 Bulgaria became involved in the First World War on the German side. In September 1918 the Southern Front of the Bulgarian army was broken through by the Allied Forces. The retreating soldiers rose and proclaimed Bulgaria a republic. The uprising was suppressed with the help of the German army. According to the Neuilly Peace Treaty, Bulgaria lost part of its territory—the Western Regions, the Stroumitsa district, Western Thrace and South Dobroudja. After the war the revolutionary movement in the country gained strength. The prestige of the Party of Left-Wing Socialists (founded in 1891), which in 1919 was renamed the Bulgarian Communist Party, and the Bulgarian National Agrarian Union grew. In 1919 an Agrarian Government, headed by A. Stamboliiski, was formed, which carried out a number of progressive reforms. On 9 June 1923, that government was overthrown by a Fascist coup d'état and A. Stamboliiski was killed. In September 1923 the first anti-fascist uprising in the world broke out in Bulgaria, which was firmly suppressed. On 19 May 1934, another Fascist coup d'état took place, which established an authoritarian regime and gradually led to an overt Monarchal-Fascist dictatorship.

In 1941 German troops were permitted to enter the country and the Government declared war on Great Britain and the U.S.A., though not on the U.S.S.R. A mass anti-fascist partisan movement spread out all over the country.

On 26 August 1944 the Government stated that Bulgaria was neutral in so far as the war between the Soviet Union and Germany was concerned and attempts were made to approach Great Britain and the U.S.A. for peace terms. The U.S.S.R., however, refused to recognize Bulgaria's so-called neutrality and demanded that she should declare war on Germany. Having received no satisfactory reply, the Soviet Union declared war on Bulgaria on 5 September 1944. The advance of the Soviet Army onto Bulgarian territory coincided with the People's uprising which overthrew the monarcho-facist dictatorship. The government of the Fatherland took over and was composed of representatives of the Bulgarian Communist Party the Bulgarian Agrarian Union, the Social Democratic Party, the Zveno political circle, and independent intellectuals. On 10 September 1944, Bulgaria declared war on Germany and participated in the last stage of the war. The Armistice with the Allies was signed in Moscow on 28 October 1944.

In November 1945 Georgi Dimitrov, founder of the Fatherland Front, returned to Bulgaria after 22 years of exile. On 15 September 1946, after a referendum, Bulgaria became a People's Republic.

On 23 and 27 December 1947, industry, mines and banks were nationalized.

In April 1976 the XIth Congress of the Bulgarian Communist Party adopted the directives for the country's economic development in the 1976–1980 period.

The Constitution of the People's Republic of Bulgaria which is now in force was proclaimed on 18 May 1971 (the former dates from 4 December 1947). It provides for a single-chambered legislature: the National Assembly. In consists of 400 national representatives elected for five years in constituencies with an equal number of inhabitants. All Bulgarian citizens, both men and women, are eligible for election and may vote at the age of 18, with the exception of those who have been deprived by the courts of their civil and political rights. The National Assembly is the supreme organ of state power. It unites the legislative and executive activities of the State and exercises supreme control. A high and constantly functioning organ of state power is the State Council which deals with the fundamental problems of social management and the development of the country. It consists of a Chairman, deputy-chairmen, secretary and members. It is elected by the National Assembly, is responsible and accounts to it for all its activities. The Council of Ministers (the Government) is a high executive and administrative organ of state authority and is elected by the National Assembly.

**State Council of the People's Republic of Bulgaria** (elected on June 16, 1976)

*Chairman:* Todor Zhivkov.

*First Deputy Chairman:* Peter Tanchev.

*Deputy Chairman:* Peko Takov, Georgi Djagarov, Mitko Grigorov.

*Secretary:* Nikola Manolov.

*Members:* Alexander Lilov, Boris Velchev, Grisha Philipov, Pencho Kubadinski, Ivan Mikhailov, Tsola Dragoicheva, Todor Stoichev, Drazha Vulcheva, Misho Mishev, Angel Balevski, Angel Shishkov, Elena Lagadinova, Emil Khristov, Evgeni Mateev, Zhivko Zhivkov, Yaroslav Radev, Stoyan Tonchev, Lalyu Ganchev, Ivanka Dikova, Nayda Ferkhadova, Radi Kouzmanov.

**Council of Ministers of the People's Republic of Bulgaria** (elected on June 16, 1976).

*Chairman:* Stanko Todorov

*First Deputy-Chairman:* Tano Tsolov.

*Deputy-Chairman and Chairman of the Committee for state and People's Control:* Krastyu Trichkov.

*Deputy-Chairman and Chairman of the State Planning Committee:* Kiril Zarev.
*Deputy-Chairman:* Mako Dakov, Andrei Loukanov.
*Minister of Finances:* Belcho Belchev.
*Chairman of the Committee for Science, Technical Progress and Higher Education:* Nacho Papazov.
*Chairman of the Committee for Arts and Culture:* Lyudmila Zhivkova.
*Minister of the Interior:* Dimiter Stoyanov.
*Minister of Defence:* Gen. Dobri Djourov.
*Minister of Foreign Affairs:* Peter Mladenov.
*Minister of Education:* Prof. Nencho Stanev.
*Minister of the Mineral Resources:* Stamen Stamenov.
*Minister of Supplies and State Reserves:* Nikolai Zhishev.
*Minister of Energy:* Nikola Todoriev.
*Minister of Chemical Industry:* Georgy Pankov
*Minister of Machine-Building and Metallurgical Industry:* Nikola Kalchev.
*Minister of Electronic and Electrotechnical Industry:* Yordan Mladenov.
*Minister of Light Industry:* Stoyan Zhulev.
*Minister of Agriculture and Food Industry:* Gancho Krastev.
*Minister of Construction and Architecture:* Grigor Stoichkov.
*Minister of Transport:* Vassil Tsanov.
*Minister of Internal Trade:* Geogi Karamanev.
*Minister of Foreign Trade:* Ivan Nedev.
*Minister of Forests and Wood Industry:* Yanko Markov.
*Minister of Communications:* Pando Vanchev.
*Minister of Public Health:* Dr. Angel Todorov.
*Minister of Justice:* Svetla Daskalova.
*Minister without portfolio, Ambassador of the People's Republic of Bulgaria to the USSR:* Dimiter Zhulev.
*President of the Bulgarian National Bank:* Vesselin Nikiforov.
*Chairman of the Supreme Court:* Angel Velev.
*Prosecutor-General:* Ivan Vachkov.

**Political Parties**

The Bulgarian Communist Party was founded on 20 July 1891 at the Bouzloudja Congress, held on the initiative of Dimiter Blagoev as Bulgarian Social Democratic Party. In 1903 it purged its ranks and became the revolutionary Marxist vanguard of the Bulgarian proletariat, assuming the name of Bulgarian Workers' Social Democratic Party (left-wing socialists)—BWSDP. In 1919 it was renamed the Bulgarian Communist Party. After the defeat of the 1923 September anti-Fascist uprising, it became illegal. In 1927 it organized the Workers' Party as a legal revolutionary organization of the proletariat, and was merged with it in 1938–39 under the name of Bulgarian Workers' Party (BWP). It became the organizer and leader of the Bulgarian people's anti-Fascist struggle. After 9 September 1944, it became a guiding political force; at its Fifth Congress (1948) it was renamed the Bulgarian Communist Party (BCP). The BCP had 755,679 (1 April 1974) members. Its main organ is the newspaper *Rabotnichesko Delo,* and its theoretical one the magazine *Novo Vreme.*

Other political groups are the Bulgarian Agrarian Union (120,000 members), the Fatherland Front (3,783,565 members, 30 April 1974), and the Dimitrov Young Communist League (1,300,000 members, 1973).

**Politburo of the Bulgarian Communist Party** (elected at the XIth Congress of the Bulgarian Communist Party, April, 1976).
*Members:* Alexander Lilov, Boris Velchev, Grisha Philipov, Ivan Mikhailov, Pencho Kubadinski, Stanko Todorov, Tano Tsolov, Todor Zhivkov, Tsola Dragoicheva.
*Candidate Members:* Krastyu Trichkov, Peko Takov, Peter Mladenov, Dobri Djourov, Todor Stoychev, Drazha Vulcheva.
*Secretaries of the Central Committee of the Bulgarian Communist Party:* First Secretary, Todor Zhivkov; Secretaries, Boris Velchev, Alexander Lilov, Grisha Philipov, Ivan Prumov, Ognian Doynov.
*Members of the Secretariat of the Central Committee:* Dr. Vladimir Bonev, Georgi Yordanov, Sava Dalbokov, Misho Mishev.

## LOCAL GOVERNMENT

**Local Organs of State Power.** There are 28 districts and 1,260 municipalities (31 December 1972). The people's councils are collective organs of state authority and people's self-government. They are municipal, regional and district and are elected by the population in the area of the district and municipality for a term of two-and-a-half years, They are periodically called to sessions. The people's councils take decisions on questions of local significance within the limits of their competence in conformity with the laws and general directives of the superior organ of state power. They are in charge of education, culture and public health; they supervise the preservation of socialist property and public order; they manage the respective offices, enterprises and economic organizations; implement tasks of national importance; help and supervise the activity of the co-operative farms and help in strengthening the defence of the country. From among their members, the people's councils elect executive committees who are their executives and managing bodies. On the basis of the council decisions and the decrees of the superior organ of state power and government, the executive committees manage the council's daily work, direct and supervise the work of the executive committees and of the inferior people's councils in their area. In the execution of their tasks the district and municipal people's councils and executive committees rely on the initiative and broad participation of the people (through the permanent committees at the people's councils) and on the political, trade union, mass and other organizations. All decisions of the municipal people's councils which are contrary to the law, can be repealed by the district people's councils, and their decisions—by the State Council. The executive committees of the municipal people's councils are subordinate both to the people's council which has elected them and to the superior organs of the state administration (to the executive committees of the district people's councils and to the Council of Ministers). All state enterprises in the area of the districts are under the management of the executive committees of the district people's councils, except those which are under a direct central management and under the committees and central departments attached to the ministries.

## AREA AND POPULATION

The country's total area is 110,990 sq. km.

After several changes in the administrative division of the country, in January 1959 the existing 13 Provinces and 117 Districts were replaced by the following 30 new, smaller Provinces: Blagoevgrad, Bourgas, Varna, Veliko Turnovo, Vidin, Vratsa, Gabrovo, Kurdzhali, Kiustendil, Lovech, Mihailovgrad, Pazardzhik, Pernik, Pleven, Plovdiv, Razgrad, Roussé, Silistra, Sliven, Smolyan, Sofia, Stara Zagora, Tolbukhin, Turgovishte, Haskovo, Shoumen, Yambol and the towns of Sofia, Plovdiv and Varna which form administrative units of their own. In 1964, 28 re-grouped districts were established, and Plovdiv and Varna were included in the districts.

The population at mid-1974 was 8,676,000.

The population at 31 December 1971 for the principal towns was as follows: Sofia, 910,272; Plovdiv, 265,605; Varna, 239,879; Roussé, 158,270; Bourgas, 139,687; Stara Zagora, 115,538; Pleven, 103,277; Sliven, 86,297; Pernik, 81,227; Yambol, 77,302; Shoumen, 75,370; Tolbukhin, 70,633.

The annual average percentage population growth rate for the period 1960–74 was 0·7 and for 1965–74 was 0·6.

## CURRENCY AND FINANCE

The unit of currency is the *lev* of 100 *stotinki.* In May 1952 a currency reform linked the *lev* with the Soviet rouble. Bulgaria thus became the third country to base its currency on the rouble, Poland and Rumania having done so a few months previously. Under the reform old and new *leva* were exchanged in the ratio of 100 for 4.

In January 1962 a further exchange was made, 1 new *lev* being substituted for 10 old *leva.*

The gold content of the *lev* (1962) was 0·759,578. The rate of exchange is: 1 rouble = 1·30 *leva* for commercial payments and 1 rouble = 0·78 *leva* for non-commercial payments.

National income rose from 2,745 m. leva (1956) to 14,325 m. leva in 1975.

Revenue and expenditure for 1974 are shown below (in million leva):

| | |
|---|---|
| Revenue (including 5,853 leva from the national economy) | 8,059 |
| Expenditure (including 3,939 leva for financing the national economy, 2,609 leva for education, science, culture, the health service and national insurance) | 8,044 |

Since 1953 the 'unified' budget consists of both State and Local People's Council's budgets; it also includes the Social Security Fund and pensions.

# BULGARIA

Bulgaria has received several credits from the U.S.S.R. since 1944.

The GNP at market prices for 1974 was U.S. $millions 15,420, and the GNP per capita for 1974 was U.S. $1,780. The annual average percentage growth rate of the GNP per capita for the period 1960–74 was 4·5 and for the period 1965–74 was 3·5. [*See the note at the beginning of this section concerning GNP.*]

## BANKING

On 27 December 1947 a State monopoly of banking was instituted. All banking and financial institutions were nationalized and amalgamated into two large banks—the National Bank of Bulgaria (President: Kiril Zarev) and the Bulgarian Bank of Investments. In 1966, the Bulgarian Bank of Investments merged with the Bulgarian National Bank. The State Savings Bank (established in 1951) took on the crediting of the housing construction. The Bulgarian Foreign Trade Bank was established on 1 August 1964. It is a joint stock company, 70 per cent of whose capital belongs to the National Bank.

## PRODUCTION, INDUSTRY AND COMMERCE

**Planning.** State economic planning began in the spring of 1947, when the National Assembly voted the Two-Year Plan. All privately owned industrial enterprises were nationalized; their number was reduced and their size increased. Five five-year plans have been completed. The sixth runs from 1971 to 1975. Essentially the aim has been to provide Bulgaria with a heavy industry, exploit her natural resources, both mineral and hydro-electric potential, as well as to mechanize her agriculture. In 1972 industrial output was 43 times bigger than in 1939 (production of capital goods 117 times bigger). The following table shows the production of chief commodities in 1975:

| *Commodity* | *Unit* | **1975** |
|---|---|---|
| Coal | 1,000 metric tons | 28,290 |
| Steel | ,, ,, ,, | 2,265 |
| Pig Iron | ,, ,, ,, | 1,565 |
| Zinc | ,, ,, ,, | — |
| Lead | ,, ,, ,, | — |
| Nitrogen fertilizer | ,, ,, ,, | 379·9 |
| Phosphate fertilizer | ,, ,, ,, | 245·9 |
| Soda Ash | ,, ,, ,, | 1,009·21 |
| Sulphuric acid | ,, ,, ,, | 853 |
| Cement | ,, ,, ,, | 4,400 |
| Iron Ore (iron content) | ,, ,, ,, | 748[1] |
| Crude oil | ,, ,, ,, | 122 |
| Power | million kwh | 25,232 |

[1]Excluding production at mining of drifts.

Bulgaria is an industrial and agricultural country with a developed industry and large-scale socialist agriculture. In 1972, 64 per cent of the national product was created by industry, and over 51 per cent of the national income, agriculture contributed 16 per cent of the national product and 23 per cent of the national income.

**Agriculture.** Bulgaria possesses very fertile soil and a favourable climate. The total arable land amounts to 4·8 million hectares. At the end of 1974 there were 462 co-operative farms and 130 state farms. On the basis of the existing co-operative and state farms, 162 agro-industrial complexes had been set up by 1974, each with 245,302 hectares, 6,527 employees, and 652 tractors (15 h.p.) on an average. They include 85 per cent of the public categories of farms, 81 per cent of the arable land and 73 of the man-power in agriculture. Irrigation is being applied on a large scale. In 1972 22 per cent of the arable land was irrigated.

The following official statistics give quantities, in thousand metric tons, of basic crops produced in 1975:

| *Crops* | **1975** |
|---|---|
| Wheat | 2,742 |
| Barley | 1,707 |
| Maize | 3,025 |
| Sunflower seed | 419 |
| Cotton unginned | 32 |
| Oriental tobacco | 135 |
| Sugar beet | 2,010 |
| Tomatoes | 578 |
| Dessert grapes | 191 |
| Wine grapes | 551 |

**Livestock.** The following table shows the numbers of various farm animals, in thousands, for 1975:

| *Type* | *th.* |
|---|---|
| Cattle | 1,656 |
| Pigs | 3,889 |
| Sheep | 10,020 |
| Poultry | 38,057 |

The following table gives some figures for agricultural production for 1975:

| *Output of:* | | 1975 |
|---|---|---|
| Meat | (slaughterhouse weight) (1,000 metric tons) | 659 |
| Milk | (million l.) | 1,747 |
| Wool | (1,000 tons) | 34 |
| Eggs | (millions) | 1,845 |

**Forestry.** The principal timber woods are oak and beech and the past and present plans contain considerable provision for re-afforestation, and the improvement of road communications to exploit existing inaccessible resources.

Bulgaria's largest forests are in the Rila, Rhodopes, Pirin and Balkan Mountains. 74·8 per cent of the forests are deciduous and 25·2 per cent are coniferous. In 1971, 3·76 million cubic metres of round and hewn timber were produced.

**Commerce.** In 1972 Bulgaria's trade with the principal countries was as follows (million leva):

| *Country* | *Exports* | *Imports* |
|---|---|---|
| Great Britain | 28·6 | 41·1 |
| Austria | 25·8 | 34·4 |
| East Germany | 218·5 | 270·5 |
| West Germany | 73·0 | 91·1 |
| Italy | 81·4 | 71·0 |
| Poland | 115·1 | 119·6 |
| Rumania | 57·7 | 48·0 |
| Soviet Union | 1,596·7 | 1,447·8 |
| Hungary | 47·2 | 66·7 |
| France | 28·0 | 29·3 |
| Czechoslovakia | 135·2 | 174·6 |
| Switzerland | 43·3 | 29·5 |
| Yugoslavia | 51·8 | 37·0 |
| Cuba | 24·9 | 28·6 |
| India | 35·2 | 25·1 |

## COMMUNICATIONS

**Railways and Roads.** In 1972 there were 6,127 kms. of rail track. Passengers carried in 1972 totalled 100·8 million, freight, 73 million tons. The principal railways are: (1) Dragoman–Sofia–Plovdiv–Svilengrad–Bulgaria (Part of the international railway Munich–Istanbul), (2) Sofia–Plovdiv–Stara Zagora–Bourgas, (3) Sofia–Carlovo–Varna (Bourgas) (known as Sub-Balkan Line, opened 21 December 1952—shortest route between the capital and the Black Sea), (4) Sofia–Isker Gorge–Pleven–Gorna Oriachovitsa–Varna, (5) Sofia–Plevin–Oriachoritsa–Roussé, (6) Roussé–Gorna Oriachovitsa–Stara Zagora–Dimitrovgrad–Kurdzhali–Padkova (known as the Trans-Balkan Railway), (7) Shoumen–Karnobat, (8) Shumen–Karnoblat, (9) Sofia–Radomir–(Stanke Dimitrov)–Blagoevgrad V. Kulata (Sofia–Aegean Line), (10) Sofia–Isker Gorge–Mezdra–Vidin Vidin, (11) Roussé–Varna.

There were 30,784 kms. of roads in 1970.

**Shipping.** At the end of 1972 Bulgaria had 132 cargo ships with a loading capacity of 875,380 tons and 22 passenger ships with 3,292 passenger berths. During 1972, 19·8 million tons of cargo and 935,000 passengers were transported. In 1972 there were, in the inland waterway fleet, 11 passenger ships with 2,256 seats.

**Civil Aviation.** In 1970 Balkan Bulgarian Airlines had 237 planes. There are 28,145 km. of lines services, of which 3,245 km. are in the country.

There are foreign lines from Sofia to Athens, Istanbul, Damascus, Beirut, Baghdad, Cairo, Khartoum, Amsterdam, Benghari, Berlin, Brussels, Vienna, Copenhagen, London, Moscow, Paris, Rome, etc.

**Post, Telegraphs and Telephones.** These are state-owned. All towns are linked by a telegraph system, and almost all towns and villages by telephones. In 1975 there were 2,485 post offices and 777,127 telephones.

**Broadcasting.** All radio stations are owned and operated by the State. There are eight principal broadcasting stations, two in Sofia. Since 1959 Sofia has had a television broadcasting centre with regular transmissions. In 1975 there were 40 radio transmitters of a total capacity of 3,638 kW.; 1·92 million radio subscribers 548 radio programme hours a week. There were also 3 television stations; 9 television transmitters; 1,507,700 television subscribers.

## NEWSPAPERS

**Rabotnichesko Delo** (circulation 677,000). Central Committee of the Bulgarian Communist Party.

**Zemedelsko Znamé** (circulation 177,000). Agrarian National Union.

**Otechestven Front** (circulation 231,000). Fatherland Front.

**Narodna Mladezh.** Dimitrov Union of Peoples' Youth. (Circulation 237,000.)

**Trud.** Newspaper, daily. Pub. by the Central Council of the Bulgarian Trade Unions (circulation 166,000).

**Vecherni Novini** (evening paper; circulation 65,000). Sofia Town Peoples' Council, and Sofia Town Party Committee (BCP).

## EDUCATION

Education (beginning from the grade schools and up to the higher education institutions) is entirely free and is run by the State.

The school system is divided into three stages—elementary, secondary and higher. Elementary education is obtained in Children's Schools (3–7); in Basic Schools (4 years' course of lower elementary education), which is compulsory at the age of 7; and in Progymnasia (a 3-year course of higher elementary education—now being extended to 4 years—preparing the pupils for school certificate), which is also free and compulsory. Unified secondary schools have been organized after the Soviet Union model.

Higher education is provided at the Universities of Sofia, Plovdiv, and Veliko Turnovo, and at the other institutions of higher learning in Sofia, Plovdiv, Varna, Roussé, Bourgas, Gabrovo, Svishtov, and Haskovo.

In 1971 there were 110 students per 10,000 people. Education statistics for 1975–76 are as follows:

| *Institution* | *Number of establishments* | *Teaching Staff* | *Students* |
|---|---|---|---|
| General educational polytechnic schools | 3,747 | 56,082 | 1,098,889 |
| Schools for the mentally deficient and physically handicapped | 125 | 2,293 | 18,139 |
| Vocational technical schools | 8 | 180 | 9,708 |
| Secondary vocational technical | 307 | 9,245 | 136,566 |
| Secondary special and art schools | 246 | 9,983 | 140,721 |
| Semi-higher institutes | 28 | 982 | 19,779 |
| Higher educational institutions | 27 | 11,248 | 106,055 |
| Kindergartens | 7,553 | 27,137 | 393,000 |

## RELIGION

The majority of the believers in the country belong to the Eastern Orthodox Church. The National Congress of the Orthodox Church, assembled in May 1953 in Sofia, re-established the Bulgarian Patriarchate, which had been abolished for centuries. On 4 July 1971 Metropolitan Maxim of Lovech was elected Patriarch (lay name: Marin Minkov) to replace Patriarch Kiril (lay name: Konstantin Markov) who died on 7 March1971. Of the smaller religious bodies the largest is the Moslem community (headed by a Chief Mufti), to which belongs the Turkish minority. The Roman Catholics are about 50,000, the Protestants 20,000, and there is a small number of Israelites and Armenian Gregorians.

# Burma

**Capital**—Rangoon.

**President of the Socialist Republic of the Union of Burma and Chairman of the Council of State:** U Ne Win.

**National Flag:** Red; a canton blue charged with a star five-pointed white surrounded by five smaller, similar stars.

## CONSTITUTION AND GOVERNMENT

THE Union of Burma became an independent Sovereign State outside the British Commonwealth on 4 January 1948. Prior to 1937 it had formed part of British India, but in that year it became a separate territory with a large measure of self-government.

Burma was occupied by Japanese forces from early in 1942 that August 1945, and during that time the civil administration functioned in India. A new Executive Council was appointed in September 1946 comprising leading members of the main political parties; and a conference was held in London between the British Government and Representatives of this Council in January 1947, when an agreement was reached recognising the Council as an interim government.

Elections were held in April 1947 for a Constituent Assembly.

In March 1962, the administration of U Nu was removed and a Revolutionary Council formed, the Chairman being General U Ne Win.

The new State Constitution of the Socialist Republic of the Union of Burma was adopted by a consensus of all the people given by a national referendum held in December 1973, in which 90·19 per cent of the people who had the right to vote, voted for its adoption.

The adoption of the State Constitution of the Socialist Republic of the Union of Burma was proclaimed by the Proclamation No. 110 dated 3 January 1974.

The structure of the Constitution allows for a *Pyithu Hluttaw* (Assembly of People's Representatives), a Council of State, a Council of Ministers, a Council of Peoples' Justices, a Council of Peoples' Attorneys and Council of Peoples' Inspectors. *Pyithu Hluttaw* is the supreme assembly. The lists of members of the Council of State and the Council of Ministers are as follows:

### Council of State

*Chairman:* General U Ne Win (Rangoon Division).
*Secretary:* General San Yu (Rangoon Division).
U Kyaw Soe (Pegu Division).
U Kyaw Sein (Tenasserim Division).
U Khin Za Moong (Chin State).
U Khin Maung (Mon State).
U Soe Hlaing (Shan State).
U Sein Win (Tenasserim Division).
U Sao Ohn Hnya (Kayah State).
U Tin Thein (Mandalay Division).
U Saw Ohn (Shan State).
U Dingra Tang (Kachin State).
U Ba Nyein (Magwe Division).
U Min Thein (Irrawaddy Division).
Dr. Maung Maung (Mandalay Division)
Dr. Maung Lwin (Mandalay Division).
U Mahn San Myat Shwe (Karen State).
U Hla Tun Pru (Arakan State).
Dr. Hla Han (Irrawaddy Division).
U Lwin (Mon State).
U Lwin (Magwe Division).
U Tha Din (Pegu Division).
U Thaung Kyi (Sagaing Division).
U Thaung Tin (Rangoon Division).
U Thaung Dan (Sagaing Division).
U Than Sein (Magwe Division).
Dr. Thein Aung (Irrawaddy Division).
Thakin Aung Min (Chin State).
U Maung Maung Kha (Rangoon Division), Prime Minister.

### Council of Ministers

*Prime Minister:* U Maung Maung Kha.
*Minister for Planning and Finance:* U Than Sein.
*Minister for Home and Religious Affairs:* Col. Sein Iwin.
*Minister for Industry* (1): Col. Tint Swe.
*Minister for Industry* (2): Col. Maung Cho.
*Minister for Transport and Communications:* U Tun Lin.
*Minister for Mines and Labour:* U Kyaw Zaw.
*Minister for Construction:* U Htin Kyaw.
*Minister for Cooperatives:* U Tun Tin.
*Minister for Social Welfare:* U Van Kulh.
*Minister for Foreign Affairs:* U Hla Phone.
*Minister for Education:* Dr. Khin Maung Win.
*Minister for Defence:* General Kyaw Htin.
*Minister for Health and Information:* U Kyi Maung.
*Minister for Agriculture and Forests:* U Ye Gaung.
*Minister for Trade:* U Hla Aye.
*Minister for Culture:* U Aye Maung.

## LEGAL SYSTEM

There are four levels of courts under the Council of Peoples Justices, namely State Judges' Committees, Divisional Judges' Committees, Township Judges' Committees, Ward Judges' Committees and Village-tract Judges' Committees.

## AREA AND POPULATION

The total area of the Union is 261,789 sq. miles.

The total population in mid-1974 was about 29,521,000. The chief towns with populations are: Rangoon 3,180: Mandalay 417,000; Moulmein 202,000; Bassein 336,000; Akyab 143,000; Taunggyi 149,000.

The annual average percentage growth rate of the population for the period 1960–74 was 2·2, and for the period 1965–74 was 2·2.

## CURRENCY

The unit of currency is the kyat, with 100 py as being equal to one kyat. One pound sterling is worth K. 13·4, and one U.S. dollar is worth K 7·00 (at April 1976).

## FINANCE

Budget estimates for 1975–76 were: Revenue, 14,472·4 million kyats; Expenditure, 15,521·4.

The GNP at market prices for 1974 was U.S. $ millions 2,910. The annual average percentage growth rate of the GNP per capita for the period 1960–74 was 0·7 and for the period 1965–74 was 0·8. [*See the note at the beginning of this section concerning GNP.*]

## PRINCIPAL BANKS

**The Union Bank of Burma.** *Head Office:* 24–26 Sule Pagoda Road, Rangoon. All private banks including branches of foreign banks were nationalized in February 1963. All the banks and the insurance board were merged into a single Union Bank in 1969.

## PRODUCTION, INDUSTRY AND COMMERCE

**Agriculture.** Burma's economy is based primarily on agriculture, which employs about 80 per cent of the working population and accounts for 75 per cent of exports. Efforts are being made to improve the quality and to increase the output of selected crops. Among the selected crops paddy, cotton, sugar cane and jute are proving successful. Sown acreage continues to rise especially for paddy, sesamum, cotton and wheat.

Prior to World War II Burma stood fifth on the list of the world's rice producers, and the largest exporter of rice in the world.

Oxen and buffaloes are used for ploughing. There were in 1974–75 3,700,000 draught cattle, oxen, 574,000, draught buffaloes and 7,475 tractors.

The total agricultural production for 1974–75 is estimated at Ks. 6,15518 million (calculated at yearly current price).

The following table shows production of principal crops for 1972–73, and 1973–74:

| Crop | thousand tons | |
|---|---|---|
| | 1972–73 | 1974–75 |
| Paddy | 7,241 | 8,466 |
| Pulses | 162 | 174 |
| Groundnuts (in shell) | 377 | 405 |
| Sesamum | 69 | 152 |
| Cotton | 43 | 37 |
| Jute | 88 | 78 |
| Sugar cane | 2,000 | 1,661 |
| Burmese tobacco | 50 | 32 |
| Virginia tobacco | 16 | 10 |

**Forestry.** Burma's forests cover 261,228 square miles and possess about 76 per cent of the world's supply of teak and the most important kinds of hardwood. Since 1963 the State Timber Board has controlled teak production.

The following table shows production of timber for 1974–75 (estimated):

| Timber | thousand cubic tons 1974–75 (*estimates*) |
|---|---|
| Teak | 250 |
| Hardwood | 858 |

Burma also produces 660,000 tons of other hardwoods, and timber for the construction of railway sleepers, marine piles, gates, etc. Burma's hardwoods including teaks are found in the mixed deciduous forests of the plains and foothills everywhere except in the Delta and southern Tenasserim.

**Mining.** Although the output of petroleum is small by world standards, it is by far the most valuable of Burma's mineral assets. The output is now low as compared with before the 1939–45 war, when the production of crude oil was nearly 300,000,000 gallons from some 4,400 wells. The oil industry was then in the hands of the Burma Oil Company, but its oil installations and refineries were completely destroyed in 1942. A Joint Oil Venture Agreement was signed in Rangoon on 12 January 1954 between the Burma Government and three British oil companies led by the Burma Oil Company Ltd., whereby the Burmese Government acquired a 33 per cent interest in the producing and refining of oil in Burma with liberty to increase this percentage to any limit as and when it desired. In 1963 the Burma Oil Company was nationalized. There were 474 oil wells in the year 1974–75 and the total crude oil production was 7·63 million U.S. barrels.

The following table shows the quantity of minerals and ores produced in 1974–75:

| | 1974–75 *tons* |
|---|---|
| Zinc concentrates | 7,000 |
| Copper matte | 140 |
| Nickel speiss | 72 |
| Refined lead | 8,700 |
| Lead sulphide concentrates | 2,452 |
| Tin concentrates | 719 |
| Tungsten concentrates | 414 |
| Antimonial lead | 244 |
| Tin/Tungsten mixed concentrates | 100 |
| Tin/Tungsten scheelite mixed concentrates | 600 |
| Antimony | 1,050 |

**Industry.** The following table gives value of industrial production in a hundred thousand K.

| *Industry* | 1974–75 *100,000 Kyat* |
|---|---|
| Food and beverages | 33,881 |
| Clothing and wearing apparel | 5,094 |
| Construction materials | 3,677 |
| Personal goods | 1,336 |
| Household goods | 204 |
| Printing and publishing | 541 |
| Industrial raw materials | 2,455 |
| Minerals | 4,684 |
| Agricultural equipments | 385 |
| Industrial equipments | 87 |
| Transport vehicles | 1,057 |
| Electrical goods | 387 |
| Workshops | 2,168 |

**Commerce.** The following table shows the value of some exports in a hundred thousand K.):

| *Commodity* | 1974–75 |
|---|---|
| Agricultural products | 2,183 |
| Forest products | 1,466 |
| Minerals and gems | 578 |

The principal countries to which Burma exports her goods are Japan, India, U.S.A., W. Germany, Britain, Netherlands, Italy, U.S.S.R. and Pakistan. The principal countries from which she imports goods are Japan, India, Pakistan, South East Asia countries and West European countries.

## COMMUNICATIONS

**Railways.** In 1974–75, 2,687 miles of railway were in operation. In 1974–75, 59·5 million passengers and over 2·0 million tons of freight were carried.

**Roads.** Road transportation, in 1974–75, carried 196·5 million passengers and 1·2 million tons of freight.

**Shipping.** Owing to the mountainous nature of Burma's land boundaries, the country is dependent for external traffic on sea communication and airlines. Internally, Burma is well supplied with navigable waterways. The Irrawaddy is navigable up to Bhamo, 900 miles from the sea, while its main tributary, the Chindwin, is navigable for nearly 400 miles. The Irrawaddy delta with its numberous creeks provides a sea-board for all types of craft and has nearly 1,700 miles of navigable water. There are in addition 60 miles of navigable canals.

Inland waterways transportation carried, in 1974–75, 9·8 million passengers and 1·9 million tons of freight.

The inland water transport of Burma has been nationalized and the Inland Water Transport Board is now responsible for carrying passengers, goods, supplies, mails, etc. on the main Irrawaddy, the Chindwin and the Irrawaddy delta.

Coastal Shipping.—In 1974–75, the overseas and coastal transportation hauled about 435,000 tons of cargo and 2,000 passengers.

**Civil Aviation.** Burma Airways Corporation (formerly known as Union of Burma Airways). The Corporation was formed as Union of Burma Airways in October 1958 for the purpose of implementing the Nationalization of Transport Order of 1948. This was superseded by the Union of Burma Airways Order, 1950. With the passing of the Union of Burma Airways Board Act in 1952, a new statutory board was constituted, with a full time Chairman and six other members. However, the Board was reformed into Burma Airways Corporation in 1972. The number of passengers carried on Internal flights in 1975–76 was 398,946. The internal freightage figure for 1975–76 was 3,894 tons. The external figures for 1975–76 are 43,085 passengers and 557 tons of freight respectively. Services operated embrace 33 domestic stations, whilst external services cover Thailand (Bangkok), India (Calcutta), Nepal (Kathmandu) and Singapore. *Head Office:* 104, Strand Road, Rangoon. *Telex: BM* 2002 *RGN BAC. Cable: UNION AIR RANGOON. Sita:* (*AIRLINE COMMUNICATION*) *RGN D Z UB.*

**Posts, Telegraphs and Telephones.** In 1974–75 there were approximately 1,100 post offices in Burma. The internal system of communications is chiefly by radio. There is a telephone system in almost all the towns. There were approximately 30,259 telephones in 1974–5. Automatic operation was installed in 1959. The number of telegraph offices in the period 1974–75 was 283.

## NEWSPAPERS

**Loketha Pyuthu Nezin.** F. 1963. Burmese. 212 Theinbyu Street, Rangoon. Official newspaper. Circulation about 100,000.

**The Mirror** (Kye-mon). F. 1957. Burmese. 77, 52nd Street, Rangoon. Circulation 72,500.

**The Vanguard Daily** (Botataung). F. 1958. Burmese. 22–30 Strand Road, Rangoon. Circulation 68,000.

**The Working People's Daily.** F. 1964. English, 212 Theinbyu Street, Rangoon. Circulation Weekdays; 20,000, Sunday, 20,000.

**The Guardian.** F. 1956. English. 392–396 Merchant Street, Rangoon. Circulation 12,000.

**Hantha-Waddy Daily.** F. 1889. Burmese. 96 Bogyoke Aung San Road, Mandalay. Official newspaper. Circulation about 20,000.

**Myan-ma-alin.** F. 1914. Burmese. 58 Kominkochin Road, Rangoon. Official newspaper. Circulation 22,000.

## EDUCATION

A unified system of education has been introduced since 1948. There are now three grades of schools, Primary, Middle and High. Burmese has replaced English as the medium of instruction. English as a compulsory second language is introduced from the fifth grade. Education is free. Plans are going forward for compulsory education.

The following table gives some statistics in connection with the Burmese educational system for the year 1974–75:

| *Type of Institution* | *No. of schools* | *No. of teachers* | *No. of students* |
|---|---|---|---|
| Primary Schools | 19,399 | 73,653 | 3,449,552 |
| Middle Schools | 1,202 | 17,967 | 762,871 |
| High Schools | 571 | 8,794 | 182,848 |
| Academy for the Development of National Group Teachers' Training Institute | 1 | 57 | 680 |
| Teachers' Training Schools | 12 | 238 | 3,236 |
| Teachers' Training Colleges | 3 | 131 | 662 |
| Technical High Schools | 8 | 353 | 3,442 |
| Technical Institutes | 6 | 219 | 3,329 |
| Technical Teachers' Training Course | 1 | 4 | 30 |
| Agriculture High Schools | 13 | 79 | 1,980 |
| Agriculture Institutes | 2 | 50 | 600 |
| Other Vocational Schools | 15 | 166 | 1,335 |
| Agricultural Special School (Silk worms) | 2 | 10 | 400 |
| Engineering evening classes | 8 | 124 | 3,189 |
| Universities and Colleges: | | | |
| Arts and Science Universities | 2 | 1,117 | 22,446 |
| Intermediate Colleges | 7 | 642 | 16,352 |
| Institute of Medicine | 3 | 602 | 4,486 |
| Institute of Animal Husbandry and Veterinary Science | 1 | 43 | 933 |
| Institute of Economics | 1 | 212 | 4,938 |
| Rangoon Institute of Technology | 1 | 300 | 3,884 |
| Institute of Agriculture | 1 | 93 | 959 |
| Institute of Education | 1 | 163 | 3,535 |
| Institute of Dental Medicine | 1 | 52 | 308 |
| Post-Graduate Course for Medicine | 1 | 180 | 124 |
| Total | 21,262 | 105,249 | 4,472,119 |

There is a Social Welfare Directorate endeavouring to impart social education along with eradication of illiteracy. A training camp is now in operation to train organizers to carry out the work. There are also special schools for the deaf and dumb and blind.

## RELIGION

About 90 per cent of the Burmese people are Buddhists. All persons are, however, guaranteed freedom of religion and worship.

# Burundi

**Capital**—Bujumbura.

**President**—Lieutenant-Colonel Jean-Baptiste Bagaza.

**National Flag:** On a field quartered wedge-wise crimson and green, a saltire white; at the centre, a white disc charged with three stars red.

## CONSTITUTION AND GOVERNMENT

FORMERLY a part of the territory of Ruanda-Urundi, Burundi became independent in 1962. The country was ruled as a constitutional monarchy under Mwambi (King) Mwambutsa IV until 1966, when a series of political intrigues resulted in a *coup d'état* led by a 26-year-old army captain, Michel Micombero.

## AREA AND POPULATION

The area of Burundi is about 27,834 sq. km.

The population at mid-1974 was 3,655,000. The annual average percentage growth rate of the population for the periods 1960–74 and 1965–74 was 2·0. The Hutu, the Tutsi and the Twa are the three main ethnic groups. There are about 3,500 Europeans. Bujumbura, the capital, has about 70,000 inhabitants.

## CURRENCY AND FINANCE

The unit of currency is the Rwanda-Burundi franc. There has been a budget deficit since 1954. In 1963 it was about 250 million francs. In 1965 estimated revenue was 1,273 million francs and expenditure, 1,158 million francs. The 1971 budget was 2,121 million Burundi francs.

## PRODUCTION, INDUSTRY AND COMMERCE

The area is mostly agricultural. Main food crops are beans, cassava, maize, sweet potatoes, peas, groundnuts, and sorghum. Cotton and coffee are the main export crops. The coffee crop for 1969 was 14,500 tons. There are about half a million cattle, 358,000 goats and 141,000 sheep. The annual fishing catch from Lake Tanganyika is about 9,600 tons.

The GNP at market prices for 1974 was U.S. $ millions 330 and the GNP per capita for 1974 was U.S. $90. The annual average percentage growth rate of the GNP per capita for the period 1960–74 was 1·3 and for the period 1965–74, 1·3. [*See the note at the beginning of this section concerning GNP.*]

## COMMUNICATIONS

There are 25 miles of paved roads and lake services from the capital to Tanganyika. Bujumbura has an international airport and there are services to Europe and other African countries.

## EDUCATION

There are about 107,000 pupils in missionary schools and about 3,400 in state primary schools. There are nine secondary schools, three teachers' colleges and a university college at Usumbura.

# United Republic of Cameroon

(FRANC ZONE)

**Capital**—Yaounde.

**President**—Ahmadou Ahidjo.

**National Flag**: Three vertical stripes of green, red, and yellow of equal width, stamped with one gold star in a vertical red stripe.

## CONSTITUTION AND GOVERNMENT

The name Cameroon is derived from the Portuguese word Cameroes—meaning shrimps. In 1472 a Portuguese sailor named Fernando Po arrived at the river in Douala and discovered so many shrimps there that he decided to call it Rio dos Cameroes (Portuguese for River of Shrimps). It was from this word Cameroes, that the territory derived its name.

The territory was colonized by the Germans in 1884, and after the end of the 1914–18 war, Cameroon was mandated by the League of Nations to the French and British Governments. France took the greater sector then known as East Cameroon, while Britain took responsibility for West Cameroon, then known as 'Cameroon under British Administration'. In a common administration with Nigeria on 1 January 1960, the French sector became independent under the new name of Cameroon Republic. To attain independence for Southern Cameroon a plebiscite was held on 11 February 1961 under United Nations supervision the result of which was overwhelmingly in favour of independence with the Cameroon Republic but with a strip of the Northern Section to remain with Nigeria. Unification was achieved on 1 October 1961 with the Federal Republic of Cameroon as the new name.

On 20 May 1972, as the result of a national referendum, the creation of a unitary, bilingual and pluricultural state—'The United Republic of Cameroon' was overwhelmingly approved and the new Constitution came into force on 2 June 1972. French and English are the two official languages.

### Cabinet

By Presidential decree signed on 30 June 1975, the Government of the United Republic of Cameroon was announced. Its composition is as follows:

*Prime Minister:* Mr. Biya Paul.
*Minister of State in charge of the Armed Forces:* Sadou Daoudou.
*Minister of State in charge of Equipment and Housing:* Enoch Kwayeb.
*Minister of State in charge of Territorial Administration:* Ayissi Mvodo Victor.
*Minister of State in charge of Posts and Telecommunication:* Egbe Tabi Emmanuel.
*Minister in charge of Missions at the Presidency of the Republic:* Sengat Kuo Francois.
*Minister in charge of General State Inspection and Administrative Reform:* Onana Awana Charles.
*Minister in charge of Missions at the Presidency of the Republic:* Yadji Aboudlaye.
*Minister of Foreign Affairs:* Keutcha Jean.
*Minister of Economy and Planning:* Youssoufa Daouda.
*Minister of National Education:* Bidias A Ngon.
*Minister of Public Health:* Fokam Kamga Paul.
*Minister of Animal Breeding and Industries:* Dr. Maikano Abdoulaye.
*Minister of Agriculture:* Andze Gilbert.
*Minister of Finance:* Yondo Marcel.
*Minister of Justice, Keeper of the Seals:* Doumba Charles.
*Minister of Public Service:* Vroumsia Tchinaye.
*Minister of Mines and Power:* Elangwe Henry.
*Minister of Youths and Sports:* Tonye Mbog Felix.
*Minister Delegate at the Presidency in charge of Relations with the Assemblies:* Bongwa Christian.
*Minister of Social Welfare:* Delphine Tsanga.
*Minister of Labour and Social Insurance:* Dontsop Paul.
*Minister of Information and Culture:* Ze Nguele Rene
*Minister of Transport:* Dr. Monie Nkengong John.
*Vice-Minister of Agriculture:* Awounti Chongwain Joseph.
*Vice-Minister of Foreign Affairs:* Ndam Njoya.
*Vice-Minister of Finance:* Hamadou Moustapha.
*Vice-Minister of Economy and Plan:* Naah Robert.
*Vice-Minister of National Education:* Njeuma Dorothy.
*Vice-Minister of Territorial Administration:* Yang Philemon.

Mr. Philemon Beb à Don, previously Ambassador Extraordinary and Plenipotentiary of Cameroon in the Federal Republic of Germany, is the Director of the Civil Cabinet at the Presidency with Ministerial rank.

## AREA AND POPULATION

Shaped like a triangle, Cameroon is bordered on the north by the Republic of Chad, the west by Nigeria, the east by the Central African Republic and on the south by Congo Brazzaville, Gabon and Equatorial Guinea. It lies between the second and the thirteenth parallels, and its altitude varies between 0 and 13,354 feet (Mount Cameroon).

The population of Cameroon at mid-1974 was 7,120,000. The annual average percentage population growth rate for the period 1960–74 was 2·0 and for the period 1965–74 was 2·0.

Yaoundé the capital 180,000 inhabitants; Douala, commercial capital, 250,000; Nkongsamba, 71,000; Bafoussam, 56,000; Foumban, 38,000; Victoria, 32,000; Garoua, 28.000; Maroua, 24,000; Ngaoundéré, 20,000; and Buea, 13,000.

## CURRENCY AND FINANCE

The currency used in Cameroon is the franc.

The credits listed on the operational budget for 1975–76 were distributed as follows:

| | % | *millions CFA francs* |
|---|---|---|
| Armed forces | 13·6 | 10,957 |
| Education | 12·8 | 10,298 |
| Health and social services | 6·5 | 5,227 |
| Services affiliated with the Presidency | 6·3 | 5,106 |
| Equipment, housing, public lands | 5·8 | 4,672 |
| Finance | 4·8 | 3,860 |
| Territorial administration | 3·9 | 3,139 |
| Agriculture | 3·7 | 2,988 |
| Post and telecommunications | 2·9 | 2,369 |
| Youth and sports | 1·2 | 985 |
| Information and culture | 1 | 806 |
| Ranching and animal industries | 1 | 800 |
| Transportation | 0·9 | 694 |
| Industrial and commercial development | 0·7 | 550 |
| Mining and power | 0·5 | 429 |
| Miscellaneous | 8·8 | 7,064 |
| Common expenditures | 13·2 | 10,644 |
| State activities | 10·8 | 8,725 |
| Servicing the Foreign Debt | 1·6 | 1,287 |
| Total | 100 | 80,600 |

The GNP at market prices for 1973 was U.S. $ millions 1,760 and the GNP per capita at market prices for 1974 was U.S. $250. The annual average percentage growth rate of the GNP for the period 1960–74 was 3·9 and for the period 1965–74 was 4·0. [*See the note at the beginning of this section concerning GNP.*]

## BANKS

**Banque Camerounaise de Développement.** Yaoundé. 6 Branches.

**Société Camerounaise de Banque.** 9 Branches.

**Société Générale de Banques au Cameroun.** 3 Branches.

**Banque Internationale pour le Commerce et l'Industrie du Cameroun.** 10 Branches.

**Banque Internationale de l'Afrique Occidentale.** 6 Branches.

## COMMUNICATIONS

**Roads.** There are 1,500 km of tarred trunk and city roads, 5,200 km of secondary roads linking towns and villages, and 17,000 km of usable roads. About 50,000 vehicles or more circulate throughout the territory. Distances between main cities are as follows: Yaoundé–Sangmelima (170 km); Edea–Douala (96 km); Douala–Foumban via Nkongsamba, Bafang and Bafoussam (371 km); Douala–Tiko–Victoria (50 km); Buea–Kumba (80 km); Douala–Maroua (1,665 km). Yaoundé is connected to the Central African Republic by road via Yaoundé–Abong–Mbang–Bertoua–Batouri–Berberati (600 km). Douala–Gabon (Oyem) 660 km.

**Railways.** The oldest railway in the country links Yaoundé–Douala (308 km) and Douala–Nkongsamba (172 km). The newly constructed Mbanga–Kumba railroad is 29 km long, but the longest rail link is the trans-Cameroonian linking Yaoundé to Ngaoundéré (628 km) in the north. It will eventually be extended to Chad and the Central African Republic.

**Airlines.** Cameroon has 18 airports of various categories. The main ones are Douala, which is of international class, and Yaoundé and Garoua which can take planes as large as DC-6's. Those of Ngaoundére, Maroua, Koutaba, Yagoua, Kaele, Tiko, Bali, and Mamfe have sufficiently wide runways to accommodate DC-4s. 'Cameroon Airlines' the national carrier, operates all internal flights as well as international flights to Europe.

**Ports.** Among the four operating maritime ports in Cameroon, Douala is the busiest and most important. Tiko and Bota ports come next followed by the port of Kribi. During the months of July, August and September the Benoue river is used for shipping goods to and from northern Nigeria.

## PRODUCTION

Cameroon is basically an agricultural country, but it already possesses a relatively large number of industrial plants. Its geographic position enables it to offer a varied range of products, of which the principal ones are: cocoa, coffee, wood, banana, cotton, rubber, palm oil, palmetto oil, tea and ground-nuts. Stock-rearing is extremely important in the North and Central parts of the country.

The following table gives some agricultural statistics for the Central Rural Development Division for the 1974–75 season:

| | *Area planted (1,000 ha)* | *Yield (kg/ha)* | *Total production (1,000 t)* | *Quantities sold (1,000 t)* |
|---|---|---|---|---|
| Millet and sorghum | 501 | 700 | 350 | 110 |
| Corn | 492 | 1,200 | 590 | 250 |
| Rice | 22 | 900 | 19 | 10 |
| Sugar cane | 40 | 5,700 | 228 | 120 |
| Potatoes | 63 | 2,500 | 157 | 85 |
| Yams and sweet potatoes | 445 | 4,000 | 1,780 | 590 |
| Cassava | 479 | 3,900 | 1,868 | 625 |
| Macabo and taro | 532 | 3,000 | 1,596 | 530 |
| Plantain bananas | 647 | 4,200 | 2,717 | 910 |
| Leguminous vegetables | 150 | 550 | 82 | 42 |

**Commerce.** The following table shows imports and exports by principal countries for 1974 (value million C.F.A. francs):

| | *Exports* 1974 | *Imports* 1974 | *Balance* |
|---|---|---|---|
| E.E.C. Countries (Total) | 85,091,539 | 74,148,972 | +10,942,567 |
| France | 31,002,549 | 49,343,657 | −18,341,108 |
| Netherlands | 35,087,448 | 2,321,562 | +32,765,886 |
| West Germany | 8,148,678 | 9,687,376 | −1,538,698 |
| Italy | 6,186,816 | 5,914,817 | +271,999 |
| Benelux Countries | 3,057,545 | 2,194,522 | +863,023 |
| United Kingdom | 1,253,013 | 3,890,267 | −2,637,254 |
| Ireland | 8,342 | 148,891 | −140,549 |
| Denmark | 347,148 | 647,890 | −300,742 |
| Spain | 3,605 | 868 | +2,737 |
| U.S.A. | 4,615,390 | 6,528,388 | −1,912,998 |
| Economic Union for Central African States and Chad (Total) | 7,758,012 | 6,385,731 | +1,372,281 |
| Tchad | 876,666 | 93,801 | +782,865 |
| Central African Republic | 1,286,947 | 84,502 | +1,202,445 |
| Gabon | 3,802,067 | 5,331,803 | −1,519,736 |
| Congo | 1,792,332 | 875,625 | +916,707 |
| Japan | 3,399,276 | 2,395,890 | +1,003,386 |
| U.S.S.R. | 3,835,207 | 406,169 | +3,429,038 |
| People's Republic of China | 17,938 | 2,536,412 | −2,518,474 |
| Senegal | 78,226 | 413,985 | −335,759 |
| Ivory Coast | 1,147,450 | 371,018 | +776,432 |
| Canada | 811,859 | 474,956 | +336,903 |

## NEWSPAPER

**La Presse du Cameroun, F. 1927; daily. Bilingual, French-English. P. O. Box 584, Douala.**

## EDUCATION

In 1969–70 there were 1,822 public and 2,468 private primary schools with a total of 887,000 pupils. There were about the same number of public and private secondary schools with a total of 63,906 pupils. There is one university at Yaoundé with about 1,000 students.

# Canada

(MEMBER OF THE COMMONWEALTH)

**Capital**—Ottawa.

**Sovereign**—H.M. Queen Elizabeth II.

**Governor-General**—The Rt. Hon. Jules Léger.

**National Flag:** A single maple leaf with eleven points on a white square, flanked by vertical red bars one half the width of the square.

## CONSTITUTION AND GOVERNMENT

THE Government of Canada was established under the provisions of the British North America Act 1867. This statute of the Imperial Parliament as amended from time to time forms the written basis of the Constitution of Canada. For the first time in history, the Canadian Constitution combined the British Cabinet system of responsible government, with a Canadian adaptation of the United States principle of federation. The provinces united under this Act were Upper and Lower Canada (now Ontario and Quebec), Nova Scotia and New Brunswick. Provision was made for the later admission of British Columbia, Prince Edward Island, the Northwest Territories and Newfoundland. The province of Manitoba, formed out of the Northwest Territories, was admitted on 15 July 1870, British Columbia on 20 July 1871 and Prince Edward Island on 1 July 1873. The new provinces of Alberta and Saskatchewan were admitted on 1 September 1905. Newfoundland entered the Dominion on 31 March 1949 as the result of a plebiscite held in July 1948.

The several stages in the development of the states of the Dominion have been described in the reports of successive Imperial Conferences including that held in London in 1926, which defined the group of self-governing communities consisting of the United Kingdom and the Dominions as 'autonomous communities within the British Empire, equal in status, in no way subordinate one to another in any aspect of their domestic and foreign affairs, though united by a common allegiance to the Crown and freely associated as members of the British Commonwealth of Nations'. Simultaneously with this change in the constitutional relationship between the several parts of the British Commonwealth of Nations, there developed as a complementary aspect of nationhood the assumption by the Dominions of further rights and responsibilities of sovereign states in their relations with other nations, including the exercise of treaty-making powers and the establishment of separate diplomatic representation in other countries. Remaining limitations on the legislative autonomy of the Dominions were removed by the Statute of Westminster of 1931.

The Queen is represented in Canada by a Governor-General who holds in all respects the same position in relation to the administration of public affairs in Canada as Her Majesty holds in Great Britain.

The Canadian Parliament comprises the Queen (represented by the Governor-General), the Senate and the House of Commons. The Governor-General is appointed by the Queen, on the advice of the Prime Minister of Canada, usually for a term of five years.

Canada's system of government is based on that of the British by which a Cabinet (composed of members of the House of Commons or the Senate) is responsible to Parliament. The Cabinet is actually a committee of the Queen's Privy Council for Canada. The Cabinet is responsible to the House of Commons and, following established precedent, resigns office when it becomes evident that it no longer holds the confidence of the people's representatives. Members of the Cabinet are chosen by the Prime Minister; each generally assumes charge of one of the various Departments of Government. The Senate consists of 104 senators, of whom 24 are from Ontario, 24 from Quebec, ten from Nova Scotia, ten from New Brunswick, four from Prince Edward Island, six from Manitoba, six from British Columbia, six from Alberta, six from Saskatchewan, six from Newfoundland, one from the Yukon and one from Northwest Territories

Senators were originally appointed for life. However, in 1965 it was provided by an Act of the Parliament of Canada that members of the Senate summoned after 2 June 1965 shall hold office only until they reach the age of seventy-five. Senators are appointed by the Governor-General on the recommendation of the Prime Minister. Senators must be at least thirty years old at the time of their appointments and own property to the value of $4,000 within the province for which they are appointed.

The House of Commons is elected by popular vote for a period not exceeding five years. In 1952, through an amendment to the British North America Act, it was provided that the number of Members of the House would be 265 and that the representation of the provinces would forthwith and thereafter on the completion of each decennial census, be adjusted by such authority, in such manner and from such time, subject to certain rules, as the Parliament of Canada from time to time provided.

The Representation Commissioner Act, setting up the office and duties of the Representation Commissioner, was given Royal Assent on 21 December 1963. The Electoral Boundaries Readjustment Act, providing for the establishment of provincial Electoral Boundaries' Commissions to provide for, and report upon, the re-adjustment of the representation of the provinces in the House of Commons (in accordance with the findings of the Census of 1961), received Royal Assent on 20 November 1964. The Governor in Council declared (Proclamation, 16 June 1966) that the new representation would become effective as from the dissolution of the then-existing Parliament.

After the Election of 8 July 1974, representation in the House of Commons was as follows: Ontario, 88; Quebec, 74; Nova Scotia, 11; New Brunswick, 10; Manitoba, 13; B.C., 23; Prince Edward Island, 4; Saskatchewan, 13; Alberta, 19; Newfoundland, 7; Yukon Territory, 1; Northwest Territories, 1. The present total is 264.

The House of Commons is composed of natural-born or naturalised subjects of the Queen; no property qualification is necessary. The franchise is conferred upon all British subjects, men and women, who are 18 years old and who have been ordinarily resident in Canada for 12 months prior to polling day. For electoral purposes each province is divided into districts, returning a member on a plurality of votes taken by ballot.

**Federal Cabinet** (July 1977)

*Prime Minister:* The Right Honourable Pierre Elliott Trudeau.
*Deputy Prime Minister and President of the Queen's Privy Council for Canada:* Allan Joseph MacEachen.
*Minister of Industry, Trade and Commerce:* Jack Horner.
*Minister of Finance:* Jean Chrétian.
*Minister of Labour:* John Carr Munro.
*Revenue Minister:* Joseph Guay.
*Minister of Justice and Attorney General of Canada:* Stanley Ronald Basford.
*Secretary of State for External Affairs:* Donald Campbell Jamieson.
*President of the Treasury Board:* Robert Knight Andras.
*Minister of Transport:* Otto Emil Lang.
*Minister of Supply and Services:* Jean-Pierre Goyer.
*Minister of Energy, Mines and Resources:* Alastair William Gillespie.
*Minister of Agriculture:* Eugene Francis Whelan.
*Minister of Indian Affairs and Northern Development:* Huge Faulkner.
*Minister of State for Urban Affairs:* André Ouellet.
*Minister of Veterans Affairs:* Daniel Joseph MacDonald.
*Minister of National Health and Welfare:* Marc Lalonde.
*Minister of Communications:* Jeanne Sauvé.
*Leader of the Government in the Senate:* Raymond Joseph Perrault.
*Minister of National Defence:* Barnett Jerome Danson.
*Minister of Public Works:* Judd Buchanan.
*Minister of Fisheries and the Environment:* Roméo LeBlanc.
*Minister of Regional Economic Expansion:* Marc Lessard.
*Minister of Manpower and Immigration:* Jack Sydney George Cullen.
*Minister of State, Small Business:* Leonard Stephen Marchand.
*Secretary of State of Canada:* John Roberts.
*Minister of National Revenue:* Monique Bégin.
*Postmaster General:* Jean-Jacques Blais.
*Solicitor General of Canada:* Francis Fox.
*Minister of Consumer and Corporate Affairs:* Warren Allmand.
*Minister of State, Fitness and Amateur Sport:* Iona Campagnolo.
*Minister without Portfolio:* John Henry Horner.

**Parliament**

**House of Commons.** Party representation in the House of Commons as of 8 July 1974, with party leadership in brackets, was as follows: Liberals, 141 (Rt. Hon. Pierre Elliot Trudeau); Progressive Conservatives, 95 (C. Joe Clark); New Democratic Party, 16 (Ed. Broadbent); Social Credit, 11 (Réal Caouette); Independent, 1.

## LOCAL GOVERNMENT

All the legislatures of the Canadian Provinces are unicameral. The Queen is represented by a Lieutenant-Governor appointed by the Governor-General in Council, and governs with the advice and assistance of he Ministry or Executive Council, which is responsible to the Legislature and resigns when it ceases to enjoy the confidence of that body.

## LEGAL SYSTEM

The administration of justice in Canada follows the English system, by means of judges, police magistrates and justices of the peace.

Judges of Superior Courts, who are chosen from among leading members of the Bar, are appointed till aged 75 or 70, depending on the court, by the Governor-General. The highest court is the Supreme Court of Canada, sitting in Ottawa. It consists of a chief justice and eight puisne judges, and holds three sessions a year.

There is one other court—the Federal Court of Canada, which is also a Court of Admiralty, and has its own judges. It may sit anywhere. Included in the Provincial Courts are the Supreme or High Court, the Court of Queen's Bench, the Court of Appeal, Superior Courts, Country Courts, District Courts.

**Supreme Court of Canada**

*Chief Justice:* Rt. Hon. Bora Laskin.

**Federal Court of Canada**

*Chief Justice:* Hon. W. R. Jackett.

## AREA AND POPULATION

*Rural and Urban Population, Canada and Provinces,* 1971[1]

| *Province or Territory* | *Land Area Sq. miles* | *Total Population* | *Urban*[2] | *Rural* |
|---|---|---|---|---|
| Newfoundland | 143,045 | 557,725 | 298,800 | 223,305 |
| Prince Edward Island | 2,184 | 118,229 | 42,780 | 68,860 |
| Nova Scotia | 20,402 | 828,571 | 447,400 | 341,555 |
| New Brunswick | 27,835 | 677,250 | 361,145 | 273,410 |
| Quebec | 523,860 | 6,234,445 | 4,861,240 | 1,166,520 |
| Ontario | 344,092 | 8,264,465 | 6,343,630 | 1,359,480 |
| Manitoba | 211,775 | 1,021,506 | 686,445 | 301,805 |
| Saskatchewan | 220,182 | 921,323 | 490,630 | 435,610 |
| Alberta | 248,800 | 1,838,037 | 1,196,250 | 431,620 |
| British Columbia | 359,279 | 2,466,608 | 1,654,410 | 530,215 |
| Yukon Territory | 205,346 | 21,836 | 11,215 | 7,170 |
| Northwest Territories | 1,253,438 | 42,609 | 16,830 | 17,980 |
| Total | 3,560,238 | 22,992,604 | 16,410,780 | 5,157,525 |

[1] Figures may not add, owing to rounding.
[2] Includes persons living in centres of 1,000 or more.

Chief cities and towns with populations (1976 Census).

Population for Census Metropolitan Areas, 1971 and 1976

| | 1971[1] | 1976 |
|---|---|---|
| Calgary, Alta. | 403,300 | 469,900 |
| Chicoutimi-Jonquière, Qué. | 126,400 | 128,600 |
| Edmonton, Alta. | 496,000 | 554,200 |
| Halifax, N.S. | 250,500 | 267,900 |
| Hamilton, Ont. | 503,100 | 529,300 |
| Kitchener, Ont. | 238,500 | 272,100 |
| London, Ont. | 252,900 | 270,300 |
| Montréal, Qué. | 2,729,200 | 2,802,400 |
| Oshawa[2], Ont. | 120,300 | 135,100 |
| Ottawa-Hull, Ont., Qué. | 619,800 | 693,200 |
| Ontario (part) | 474,100 | 521,300 |
| Québec (part) | 145,600 | 171,900 |
| Québec, Qué. | 501,300 | 542,100 |
| Regina, Sask. | 140,700 | 151,100 |
| St. Catharines-Niagara, Ont. | 285,800 | 301,900 |
| St. John's, Nfld. | 131,800 | 143,300 |
| Saint John, N.B. | 106,700 | 112,900 |
| Saskatoon, Sask. | 126,400 | 133,700 |
| Sudbury, Ont. | 157,700 | 157,000 |
| Thunder Bay, Ont. | 114,700 | 119,200 |
| Toronto, Ont. | 2,602,000 | 2,803,100 |
| Vancouver, B.C. | 1,082,300 | 1,166,300 |
| Victoria, B.C. | 195,800 | 218,200 |
| Windsor, Ont. | 248,700 | 247,500 |
| Winnipeg, Man. | 549,800 | 578,200 |

[1] Based on 1976 Area.
[2] Not a Census Metropolitan Area in 1971.

# CANADA

**Vital Statistics**

| | Live births | | Deaths | | Natural increase[1] | | Infant mortality[2] | | Maternal mortality | | Marriages | |
|---|---|---|---|---|---|---|---|---|---|---|---|---|
| | No. | Rate[3] | No. | Rate[3] | No. | Rate[3] | No. | Rate[4] | No. | Rate[5] | No. | Rate[3] |
| 1966 | 387,710 | 19·4 | 149,863 | 7·5 | 237,847 | 11·9 | 8,960 | 23·1 | 135 | 3·5 | 155,596 | 7·8 |
| 1976 | 370,894 | 18·2 | 150,283 | 7·4 | 220,611 | 10·8 | 8,151 | 22·0 | 88 | 2·4 | 165,879 | 8·1 |
| 1968 | 364,310 | 17·6 | 153,196 | 7·4 | 211,114 | 10·2 | 7,583 | 20·8 | 99 | 2·7 | 171,766 | 8·3 |
| 1969 | 369,647 | 17·6 | 154,477 | 7·4 | 215,170 | 10·2 | 7,149 | 19·3 | 77 | 2·1 | 182,183 | 8·7 |
| 1970 | 371,988 | 17·5 | 155,961 | 7·3 | 216,027 | 10·2 | 7,001 | 18·8 | 75 | 2·0 | 188,428 | 8·8 |
| 1971 | 362,187 | 16·8 | 157,272 | 7·3 | 204,915 | 9·5 | 6,356 | 17·5 | 66 | 1·8 | 191,324 | 8·9 |
| 1972 | 347,319 | 15·9 | 162,413 | 7·4 | 184,906 | 8·5 | 5,938 | 17·1 | 54 | 1·6 | 200,470 | 9·2 |
| 1973 | 343,373 | 15·5 | 164,039 | 7·4 | 179,334 | 8·1 | 5,339 | 15·5 | 37 | 1·1 | 199,064 | 9·0 |
| 1974 | 345,645 | 15·4 | 166,794 | 7·4 | 178,851 | 8·0 | 5,192 | 15·0 | 35 | 1·0 | 198,824 | 8·9 |
| 1975 | | | | | | | | | | | 197,585 | 8·7 |

[1] Excess of births over deaths. [2] Deaths under one year of age. [3] Per 1,000 population.
[4] Per 1,000 live births. [5] Per 10,000 live births.

*Percentage Distribution of Population by Age Group and Sex as at 1 June, 1975*

| | Male | Female |
|---|---|---|
| 0–4 years | 7·9 | 7·5 |
| 5–14 years | 19·1 | 18·2 |
| 15–24 years | 19·7 | 19·1 |
| 25–34 years | 15·6 | 15·3 |
| 35–44 years | 11·5 | 11·1 |
| 45–64 years | 18·7 | 19·2 |
| 65–74 years | 4·9 | 5·7 |
| 75+ years | 2·5 | 3·9 |

*Age-Specific Fertility Rates per 1,000 Women, by Age Group for 1965–74 (exclusive of Newfoundland)*

| Year | 15–19 | 20–24 | 25–29 | 30–34 | 35–39 | 40–44 | 45–49 |
|---|---|---|---|---|---|---|---|
| | | | | *Total Women* | | | |
| 1965 | 49·3 | 188·6 | 181·9 | 119·4 | 65·9 | 22·0 | 2·0 |
| 1966 | 48·2 | 169·1 | 163·5 | 103·3 | 57·5 | 19·1 | 1·7 |
| 1967 | 45·2 | 161·4 | 152·6 | 91·8 | 50·9 | 15·9 | 1·5 |
| 1968 | 43·0 | 152·6 | 148·7 | 86·3 | 44·8 | 13·8 | 1·4 |
| 1969 | 42·2 | 147·7 | 149·8 | 85·0 | 42·6 | 12·5 | 1·1 |
| 1970 | 42·8 | 143·3 | 147·2 | 81·8 | 39·0 | 11·3 | 0·9 |
| 1971 | 40·1 | 134·4 | 142·0 | 77·3 | 33·6 | 9·4 | 0·6 |
| 1972 | 38·5 | 119·8 | 137·1 | 72·1 | 28·9 | 7·8 | 0·6 |
| 1973 | 37·2 | 117·7 | 131·6 | 67·1 | 25·7 | 6·4 | 0·4 |
| 1974 | 34·2 | 110·3 | 128·2 | 65·3 | 22·5 | 5·4 | 0·4 |
| | | | | *Married Women (legitimate live births only)* | | | |
| 1965 | 481·9 | 307·4 | 209·7 | 130·6 | 71·9 | 24·3 | 2·3 |
| 1966 | 465·8 | 280·2 | 187·3 | 112·5 | 62·5 | 21·0 | 2·0 |
| 1967 | 409·7 | 271·8 | 174·0 | 99·3 | 54·5 | 17·3 | 1·6 |
| 1968 | 372·8 | 259·2 | 169·9 | 93·0 | 47·4 | 14·9 | 1·5 |
| 1969 | 350·4 | 249·5 | 172·5 | 91·1 | 44·7 | 13·3 | 1·2 |
| 1970 | 338·8 | 244·6 | 169·8 | 87·4 | 40·7 | 11·9 | 1·0 |
| 1971 | 360·5 | 221·3 | 166·5 | 84·8 | 36·3 | 10·2 | 0·7 |
| 1972 | 233·7 | 200·0 | 170·4 | 80·0 | 31·2 | 8·4 | 0·6 |
| 1973[1] | — | — | — | — | — | — | — |
| 1974[1] | — | — | — | — | — | — | — |

[1] Intercensal estimates of population by marital status are not available as yet for 1973 and 1974 and therefore fertility rates for married women have not been calculated.

*Expectation of Life at Birth, 1931, 1941, 1951, 1956, 1961, 1966 and 1971*

| 1931 | | 1941 | | 1951 | | 1956 | | 1961 | | 1966 | | 1971 | |
|---|---|---|---|---|---|---|---|---|---|---|---|---|---|
| Male Years | Female Years | Male Years | Female Years | Male Years | Female Years | Male Years | Female Years | Male Years | Female Years | Male Years | Female Years | Male Years | Female Years |
| 60·00 | 62·10 | 62·96 | 66·30 | 66·33 | 70·83 | 67·61 | 72·92 | 68·35 | 74·17 | 68·75 | 75·18 | 69·34 | 76·36 |

## CURRENCY

The unit of currency is the dollar ($) of 100 cents. The Royal Canadian Mint has issued metal coins of 1, 5, 10, 25 and 50 cents and of $1. The Bank of Canada issues notes ranging from $1 to $1,000.

## FINANCE

The principal items of revenue for the years 1974–75 and 1975–76 are shown below:

| *Source* | 1974–75 $ | 1975–76 $ |
|---|---|---|
| *Tax Revenue:* | | |
| Income tax | 14,780,931,211 | 18,291,896,889 |
| Excise taxes | 3,313,511,721 | 4,227,932,835 |
| Customs import duties | 1,808,860,186 | 1,887,211,598 |
| Excise duties | 747,959,844 | 815,521,260 |
| Oil export taxes and charges | 1,669,369,708 | 1,062,929,509 |
| Miscellaneous | 7,378,292 | 11,336,681 |
| *Non-Tax Revenues* | 2,580,747,563 | 2,862,544,648 |
| Total Revenues | 24,908,758,525 | 29,159,373,420 |

The principal items of ordinary expenditure for the years 1974–75 and 1975–76 are shown below. Some of the departmental totals are not comparable from year to year due to the transfer between departments of various expenditure items.

| *Item* | 1974–75 $ | 1975–76 $ |
|---|---|---|
| Agriculture | 665,947,151 | 651,092,048 |
| Communications | 60,604,029 | 65,406,184 |
| Consumer and Corporate Affairs | 49,377,682 | 61,666,521 |
| Energy, Mines and Resources | 1,366,503,835 | 1,828,778,161 |
| (incl. Atomic Energy) | (97,818,195) | (104,922,440) |
| Environment | 384,984,343 | 452,575,696 |
| External Affairs | 549,644,602 | 678,483,922 |
| Finance (incl. Public Debt Charges) | 6,006,431,520 | 6,914,826,227 |
| Governor General and Lieutenant Governors | 1,911,136 | 2,333,391 |
| Indian Affairs and Northern Development | 673,692,919 | 843,071,146 |
| Industry, Trade and Commerce | 451,169,584 | 628,044,010 |
| (incl. Statistics Canada) | (94,050,535) | (103,374,481) |
| Justice | 61,892,225 | 82,315,145 |
| Labour | 35,261,536 | 39,745,789 |
| Manpower and Immigration | 1,685,259,229 | 1,836,251,042 |
| (incl. Unemployment Insurance) | (877,904,038) | (922,653,022) |
| National Defence | 2,513,079,988 | 2,973,680,285 |
| National Health and Welfare | 5,200,727,697 | 8,934,644,453 |
| National Revenue | 354,894,628 | 395,263,781 |
| Parliament | 51,232,347 | 66,967,138 |
| Post Office | 737,863,737 | 912,874,883 |
| Privy Council | 52,817,181 | 32,089,055 |
| Public Works | 524,896,570 | 622,907,752 |
| Regional Economic Expansion | 441,776,143 | 488,831,364 |
| Science and Technology | 166,671,759 | 194,894,951 |
| (incl. National Research Council) | (169,286,885) | (188,582,183 |
| Secretary of State | 1,156,266,285 | 1,323,116,111 |
| Solicitor General | 451,924,759 | 584,299,820 |
| (incl. Royal Canadian Mounted Police) | (282,597,987) | (362,672,288) |
| Supply and Services | 90,885,123 | 97,892,696 |
| Transport | 1,305,781,145 | 1,202,836,268 |
| Treasury Board | 113,811,984 | 142,091,157 |
| Urban Affairs | 278,879,990 | 439,867,516 |
| (incl. Central Mortgage and Housing Corporation) | (226,058,513) | (366,963,942) |
| Veterans Affairs | 620,681,826 | 684,409,366 |
| Total Expenditure | 26,054,870,953 | 33,181,255,878 |

The Gross National Expenditure and Gross National Product for 1976 were $184·5 thousand million, the Net National Income at factor cost was $142·5 thousand million, the Personal Income, and Personal Disposable Income were $151·6 thousand million and $122·0 thousand million respectively.

The tables below give the revenue and expenditure for the Federal Government for the year ended 31 March 1976.

| *Source* | *Revenue* $'000 | *Per-centage* |
|---|---|---|
| Taxes | | |
| Personal income taxes | 12,709,172 | 36·6 |
| Corporation income taxes | 5,748,176 | 16·6 |
| Tax on certain payments and credits to non-residents | 481,349 | 1·4 |
| Motive fuel taxes | 425,084 | 1·2 |
| General sales taxes | 3,514,806 | 10·1 |
| Alcoholic beverage taxes | 548,443 | 1·6 |
| Tobacco taxes | 647,088 | 1·9 |
| Taxes on other commodities and services | 84,575 | 0·2 |
| Customs duties | 1,887,212 | 5·4 |
| Estate taxes | 10,869 | — |
| Unemployment insurance contributions | 1,948,762 | 5·6 |
| Universal pension plan levies | 1,456,898 | 4·2 |
| Oil export tax | 1,062,930 | 3·1 |
| Other taxes | 468 | — |
| Total taxes | 30,525,832 | 88·0 |
| Natural resource revenue | 28,361 | 0·1 |
| Privileges, licences and permits | 49,544 | 0·1 |
| Sales of goods and services | 968,747 | 2·8 |
| Return on investments | 2,176,739 | 6·3 |
| Contributions to non-trusteed public service pension plans | 305,026 | 0·9 |
| Postal revenue | 560,823 | 1·6 |
| Bullion and coinage | 36,694 | 0·1 |
| Fines and penalties | 18,904 | — |
| Miscellaneous | 32,409 | 0·1 |
| Total Gross Revenue | 34,703,079 | 100·0 |

| *Function* | *Expenditure* $'000 | *Per-centage* |
|---|---|---|
| General government | 1,873,292 | 5·1 |
| Protection of persons and property | 3,396,519 | 9·2 |
| Transportation and communications | 2,478,979 | 6·7 |
| Health | 2,781,531 | 7·5 |
| Social welfare | 12,385,378 | 33·6 |
| Education | 1,177,886 | 3·2 |
| Natural resources | 1,981,203 | 5·4 |
| Agriculture, trade and industry, tourism | 1,917,737 | 5·2 |
| Environment | 290,431 | 0·8 |
| Recreation and culture | 345,676 | 0·9 |
| Labour, employment and immigration | 444,045 | 1·2 |
| Housing | 337,711 | 0·9 |
| Foreign affairs and international assistance | 747,866 | 2·0 |
| Supervision and development of regions and localities | 141,702 | 0·4 |
| Research establishments | 503,116 | 1·4 |
| General purpose transfers to other levels of government | 2,687,521 | 7·3 |
| Transfers to own enterprises | 521,338 | 1·4 |
| Debt charges | 2,831,846 | 7·7 |
| Other | 1,101 | — |
| Total Gross General Expenditure | 36,844,878 | 100·0 |

## PRINCIPAL BANKS

**Bank of Canada.** (Governor, G. K. Bouey.) Established 1935; sole Bank of Issue for Canada; all the share capital is owned by the Minister of Finance; Balance Sheet at 30 June 1976 showed paid-up capital $5,000,000; assets $10,946,481,610·49; deposits $3,047,917,885·72; banknotes in circulation $7,181,408,441·74. *Head Office:* 234 Wellington Street, Ottawa K1A OG9.

**Bank of Montreal.** (Chairman of the Board, G. Arnold Hart). Established 1817; Balance Sheet at 30 April 1975, showed paid-up capital $68,344,000; assets $18,566,490,000; personal savings $6,367,910,000; other deposit and current accounts $10,445,410,000. *Head Office:* 129 St. James Street West, Montreal, 1,201 Branches.

**Bank of Nova Scotia.** (Chairman of the Board, T. A. Boyles; Deputy Chairman of the Board, A. H. Crockett; President and Chief Executive Officer, C. E. Ritchie). Established 1832; Balance Sheet at 30 April 1974 showed paid-up capital $34,708,000; assets $11,784,694,126; personal savings $3,213,488,857, other deposit and current accounts $7,392,875,219. *Head Office:* Halifax, Nova Scotia. *General Office:* 44 King Street West, Toronto, Ontario. 966 branches throughout Canada and abroad.

**Toronto Dominion Bank.** (Chairman and Chief Executive Officer A. T. Lambert.) Established 1856; Balance Sheet at 30 April 1976 showed assets $5,639,580,000; total deposits $14,010,843,000. *Head Office:* Toronto Dominion Centre, Toronto. Over 885 Branches.

**Banque Canadienne Nationale.** (Chairman of the Board, Louis Hébert; President and Chief Executive Officer, Germain Perreault). Established 1874; Balance sheet at 31 October 1976 showed assets $5,674,756,636; personal savings deposits $2,117,189,263; and current accounts $2,526,723,497; one subsidiary in Paris (France)—Banque Canadienne Nationale (Europe); a representative office in London (England)—Banque Canadienne Nationale. An Agency in New York, N.Y. U.S.A. Banque Canadienne Nationale. *Head Office:* 500 Place d'Armes, Montréal, Québec, Canada, H2Y 2W3. 418 Branches.

**Canadian Imperial Bank of Commerce.** (Chairman and Chief Executive Officer; J. P. R. Wadsworth; President, Deputy Chairman, and Chief Operating Officer, R. E. Harrison.) Merger 1961; Balance Sheet at 30 April 1976 showed assets $24,534,028,000; personal savings deposits $8,940,211,000; other deposit accounts $13,470,981,000; paid-up capital $69,680,000. *Head Office:* Commerce Court, Toronto. 1,771 Branches.

**Mercantile Bank of Canada.** (Executive Vice-President, W. A. Prisco.) Established 1953; at 31 October 1976, Balance Sheet showed assets of $1,708,093,219; personal savings $11,463,818, other deposit accounts $54,050,773, paid up capital $40,000,000. *Head Office:* 625 Dorchester Boulevard West, Montreal. 12 Branches and one representative office. Affiliated with First National City Bank, New York.

**Provincial Bank of Canada.** (President, Léo Lavoie.) Established 1900; Balance Sheet at 30 April 1974 showed assets $2,308,918,628; paid-up capital $11,700,000; personal savings $822,192,940; and other deposit and current accounts $1,367,958,185. *Head Office:* 221 St. James Street, Montreal. 317 Branches and Agencies.

**Royal Bank of Canada.** (Chairman and President, W. Earle McLaughlin.) Established 1869; Balance Sheet at 31 October 1975 showed assets $25,211,131,473; personal savings $7,847,904,895; other deposit accounts $10,245,416,048. *Head Office:* 1 Place Ville Marie, Montreal 113, 1,605 Branches.

**Unity Bank of Canada.** (President, T. L. Avison, Chairman, Dr. G. S. Mann,) Established 1972. Assets as at 30 April 1976, $172,987,383; total deposits, $148,784,083. *Head Office:* 85 Richmond St. West, Toronto, Ontario, M5H 2C9. 20 Branches.

**Bank of British Columbia.** (Chairman, A. E. Hall; President, T. W. Pilley.) Established 1967. Assets as at 30 April 1976, $730,984,000; paid-up capital $7,658,000; personal savings $218,312,000; other deposit and current accounts $457,917,000. *Head Office:* 1725 Two Bentall Centre, Vancouver, B.C. V7X 1K1, 30 Branches.

## PRODUCTION, INDUSTRY AND COMMERCE

**Agriculture.** Agriculture, including stock raising and horticulture, is one of the most important industries, employing (1976) 5·0 per cent of the total gainfully occupied population.

Livestock on farms as at 1 July 1976 comprised 14,676,000. cattle and calves, 641,300 sheep and lambs, and 5,558,900 (April 1977) pigs.

Total production of poultry meat in 1976 was 1,009,337,000 pounds, and eggs 437,098,000 dozens.

The total milk production in 1976 was estimated at 16,941,879,000 pounds. Dairy factory production was: butter, 261,329,000 pounds; cheddar cheese, 171,979,000 pounds; concentrated milk products, 706,476,000 pounds; ice cream mix, 30,983,000 gallons.

Production figures for fruit for the year 1976 in tons were: apples, 438,556; peaches, 55,594; strawberries, 20,018; grapes, 93,741; cherries, 14,973; pears 31,567; raspberries, 5,989; plums and prunes, 7,801; blueberries, 11,027.

Maple syrup produced in 1976 amounted to 1,747,000 gall. and maple sugar production was 395,000 pounds. Production of honey in 1976 was 56,095,000 pounds, and for 1975, 46,419,000 pounds (estimated).

The table below shows the estimated area; yield and production of principal field crops for 1975–1976:

| | *Area* | | *Yield per acre* | | *Total production* | |
|---|---|---|---|---|---|---|
| | 1975 | 1976 | 1975 | 1976[1] | 1975 | 1976 |
| | acres | | | bu. | | |
| Canada: | | | | | | |
| Winter wheat | 455,000 | 520,000 | 49·2 | 47·4 | 22,405,000 | 24,648,000 |
| Spring wheat[2] | 19,317,800 | 23,759,200 | 26·5 | 31·1 | 511,910,000 | 739,678,000 |
| Durum wheat | 3,650,000 | 3,250,000 | 25·5 | 30·8 | 93,200,000 | 100,000,000 |
| All wheat | 23,422,800 | 27,529,200 | 26·8 | 31·4 | 627,515,000 | 864,326,000 |
| Oats for grain | 5,958,000 | 6,105,000 | 48·6 | 52·7 | 289,619,000 | 321,676,000 |
| Barley for grain | 11,041,200 | 10,721,200 | 39·6 | 44·1 | 437,251,000 | 473,245,000 |
| Fall rye | 748,500 | 762,000 | 26·3 | 27·9 | 19,695,000 | 21,239,000 |
| Spring rye | 42,000 | 37,000 | 21·2 | 23·0 | 890,000 | 850,000 |
| All rye | 790,500 | 799,000 | 26·0 | 27·6 | 20,585,000 | 22,089,000 |
| Flaxseed | 1,400,000 | 875,000 | 12·5 | 13·4 | 17,500,000 | 11,700,000 |
| Mixed grains | 1,835,400 | 1,737,000 | 48·9 | 47·9 | 89,807,000 | 83,158,000 |
| Corn for grain | 1,569,000 | 1,669,000 | 91·5 | 86·7 | 143,493,000 | 144,669,000 |
| Buckwheat | 47,200 | 54,000 | 19·1 | 14·4 | 901,000 | 776,000 |
| Peas, dry | 74,500 | 62,000 | 24·1 | 26·7 | 1,793,000 | 1,655,000 |
| Beans, dry | 162,000 | 159,000 | 20·5 | 21·3 | 3,322,000 | 3,387,000 |
| Soybeans | 390,000 | 370,000 | 34·6 | 25·0 | 13,478,000 | 9,250,000 |
| Rapeseed | 4,320,000 | 1,985,000 | 17·8 | 20·7 | 77,100,000 | 41,000,000 |
| | | | | cwt | | |
| Potatoes[3] | 260,300 | 283,600 | 185·9 | 205·3 | 48,390,000 | 58,229,000 |
| | | | | lb. | | |
| Mustard seed | 163,000 | 128,000 | 678 | 902 | 110,500,000 | 115,400,000 |
| Sunflower seed | 62,000 | 50,000 | 1,065 | 1,060 | 66,000,000 | 53,000,000 |
| | | | | ton | | |
| Tame hay | 13,014,000 | 13,013,000 | 1·99 | 1·95 | 25,933,000 | 25,322,000 |
| Fodder corn | 997,900 | 1,038,600 | 13·23 | 13·16 | 13,202,000 | 13,665,000 |
| Field roots | 5,000 | 4,300 | 12·46 | 13·09 | 62,300 | 56,300 |
| sugar beets | 79,485 | 79,120 | 13·07 | 16·14 | 1,039,037 | 1,276,867 |

[1] As indicated on basis of conditions on or about November 15.
[2] Includes relatively small estimates of winter wheat.
[3] Potatoes grown mainly for sale.

| Kind | Number | 1975–76 Value | Average Value |
|---|---|---|---|
| | | Dollars | |
| Wildlife— | | | |
| Badger | 5,124 | 156,441 | 30·53 |
| Bear | | | |
| Black or brown | 3,531 | 154,523 | 43·76 |
| Grizzly | 8 | 1,520 | 190·00 |
| White | 406 | 192,700 | 474·63 |
| Beaver | 334,924 | 6,723,401 | 10·07 |
| Cougar | 58 | 9,570 | 165·00 |
| Coyote or prairie wolf | 61,779 | 3,150,383 | 50·99 |
| Ermine (weasel) | 76,199 | 68,113 | 0·89 |
| Fisher or pekan | 8,698 | 702,997 | 80·82 |
| Fox | | | |
| Blue | 116 | 6,599 | 56·89 |
| Cross and red | 55,064 | 2,555,659 | 46·41 |
| Silver | 583 | 26,738 | 45.86 |
| White | 26,797 | 724,678 | 27·04 |
| Not specified | 10,125 | 559,508 | 55·26 |
| Lynx | 13,162 | 2,845,416 | 216·18 |
| Marten | 53,108 | 910,787 | 17·15 |
| Mink | 69,901 | 1,106,189 | 15·82 |
| Muskrat | 2,102,016 | 7,412,311 | 3·53 |
| Otter | 16,005 | 1,156,679 | 72·27 |
| Rabbit | 865 | 131 | 0·15 |
| Raccoon | 79,253 | 1,513,926 | 19·10 |
| Seals | | | |
| Fur seal—North Pacific[1] | 6,609 | 232,067 | 35·11[2] |
| Hair seal | 161,082 | 2,907,054 | 18·05 |
| Skunk | 747 | 1,102 | 1·48 |
| Squirrel | 445,507 | 320,128 | 0·72 |
| Wildcat | 3,103 | 295,069 | 95·09 |
| Wolf | 4,879 | 300,667 | 61·62 |
| Wolverine | 871 | 133,497 | 153·27 |
| Sub-total | 3,540,520 | 34,167,853 | — |
| Ranch-raised | | | |
| Fox | 1,923 | 349,505 | 181·75 |
| Mink | 958,088 | 19,425,356 | 20·28 |
| Sub-total | 960,011 | 19,774,861 | — |
| Total | 4,500,531 | 53,942,714 | — |

[1] Commonly known as Alaska fur seal. The value figures are the net returns to the Canadian Government for pelts sold.

[2] The gross average realized price per pelt sold in 1974–75 was $66·83 and $78·84 in 1975–76.

| Industrial groups | Estimated value of factory shipments 1976 |
|---|---|
| | thousand $ |
| Foods and beverages | 17,140,200 |
| Tobacco products | 743,400 |
| Rubber and plastics | 2,249,600 |
| Leather | 692,100 |
| Textiles | 2,789,100 |
| Knitting mills | 605,900 |
| Clothing | 2,430,200 |
| Wood | 4,795,800 |
| Furniture and fixtures | 1,457,000 |
| Paper and allied industries | 8,113,900 |
| Printing, publishing and allied industries | 3,159,300 |
| Primary metals | 7,149,000 |
| Metal fabricating (except machinery and transportation equipment) | 6,753,000 |
| Machinery (except electrical) | 3,969,400 |
| Transportation equipment | 13,401,100 |
| Electrical products | 4,857,000 |
| Non-metallic mineral products | 2,857,200 |
| Petroleum and coal products | 7,354,900 |
| Chemical and chemical products | 5,623,400 |
| Miscellaneous manufacturing industries | 2,024,700 |
| Total | 98,166,200 |

**Mines and Minerals.** The following table shows the quantities and values of principal minerals produced in 1976.

| | | 1976 Quantity ('000) | Value in thousand $ |
|---|---|---|---|
| *Metallics* | | | |
| Antimony | lb. | — | 7,270 |
| Bismuth | ,, | 337 | 2,491 |
| Cadmium | ,, | 2,843 | 7,462 |
| Calcium | ,, | 1,229 | 1,521 |
| Cobalt | ,, | 3,027 | 11,769 |
| Columbium ($Cb_2O_5$) | ,, | 3,650 | 6,935 |
| Copper | ,, | 1,647,141 | 1,126,156 |
| Gold | troy oz. | 1,686 | 207,796 |
| Indium | ,, | .. | .. |
| Iron ore | ton | 62,721 | 1,241,263 |
| Iron, remelt | ,, | .. | 65,086 |
| Lead | lb. | 571,175 | 129,388 |
| Magnesium | ,, | 12,914 | 12,248 |
| Mercury | ,, | — | — |
| Molybdenum | ,, | 31,780 | 91,873 |
| Nickel | ,, | 578,693 | 1,232,143 |
| Platinum group | troy oz. | 430 | 48,790 |
| Selenium | lb. | 568 | 9,134 |
| Silver | troy oz. | 40,887 | 175,128 |
| Tantalum ($Ta_2O_5$) | lb. | .. | .. |
| Tellurium | ,, | 53 | 529 |
| Thorium | ,, | .. | .. |
| Tin | ,, | 606 | 1,873 |
| Tungsten ($WO_3$) | ,, | .. | .. |
| Uranium ($U_3O_8$) | ,, | 13,356 | .. |
| Yttrium ($Y_2O_3$) | ,, | .. | .. |
| Zinc | ,, | 2,292,118 | 862,296 |
| Total metallics | | | 5,241,151 |
| *Non-metallics* | | | |
| Arsenious oxide | lb. | — | — |
| Asbestos | ton | 1,707 | 445,523 |
| Barite | ,, | .. | 1,860 |
| Diatomite | ,, | .. | .. |
| Feldspar | ,, | .. | .. |
| Flurospar | ,, | .. | 2,246 |
| Gemstones | lb. | .. | 414 |
| Grindstone | ton | .. | .. |
| Gypsum | ,, | 6,240 | 22,906 |
| Helium | Mcf. | .. | .. |
| Iron oxides | ton | — | — |
| Lithia | lb. | — | — |
| Magnesitic dolomite, brucite | ton | .. | 5,116 |
| Mica | lb. | .. | .. |
| Nepheline syenite | ,, | 596 | 10,828 |
| Nitrogen | Mcf. | .. | .. |
| Peat moss | ton | 387 | 22,500 |
| Potash ($K_2O$) | ,, | 5,650 | 361,442 |
| Pyrite, pyrrhotite | ,, | 34 | 240 |
| Quartz | ,, | 2,619 | 13,895 |
| Salt | ,, | 6,338 | 75,691 |
| Soapstone and talc | ,, | 71 | 1,774 |
| Sodium sulphate | ,, | 540 | 24,878 |
| Sulphur, in smelter gas | ,, | 859 | 15,454 |
| Sulphur, elemental | ,, | 4,166 | 63,339 |
| Titanium dioxide, etc. | ,, | .. | 74,410 |
| Total non-metallics | | | 1,142,516 |
| *Mineral fuels* | | | |
| Coal | ton | 27,900 | 604,000 |
| Natural gas | Mcf. | 3,067,367 | 2,466,621 |
| Natural gas by-products | bbl. | 104,053 | 794,325 |
| Petroleum, crude | ,, | 489,610 | 4,128,458 |
| Total fuels | | | 7,993,404 |

*continued*

| | | 1976 *Quantity* ('000) | *Value in thousand $* |
|---|---|---|---|
| *Structural materials* | | | |
| Clay products | | — | 92,110 |
| Cement | ton | 10,858 | 339,159 |
| Lime | ,, | 2,012 | 54,099 |
| Sand and gravel | ,, | 273,000 | 320,800 |
| Stone | ,, | 96,100 | 209,600 |
| Total structural materials | | | 1,015,768 |
| Grand total 1975 | | | 15,392,839 |

. . not available
— nil or zero

**Forestry.** The forested areas of Canada are about 1,259,192 sq. miles or 35 per cent of the total land area. The total stand of timber of merchantable size is estimated to be 673,160,000,000 cu. feet. There are more than 150 native tree species, of which 31 are conifers, producing the commercially more important softwoods. Spruce, of which there are five species, is the most important softwood. It is particularly valuable for pulp, owing to its light colour, freedom from resins and the characteristics of its fibres.

Balsam and Douglas fir come next in importance to spruce. The Douglas fir is Canada's largest tree. Other softwoods are pine, cedar, hemlock and larch. Western red cedar (Thuja Plicata) produces a particularly useful and durable timber, which is used extensively where durability and resistance to decay are important. Only 10 per cent of the nation's deciduous trees or "hardwoods", have commercial significance. Poplar is the most important hardwood. Birch and maple are used for veneers and plywood as well as for furniture and cabinet work, etc. The total value of lumber shipments in 1974 was $1,877,695,000.

**Fishing.** Canada's fishing grounds fall naturally into three main divisions, Atlantic, fresh water and Pacific. The total value of fishery products in 1975 was $713,338,000.

Landed values of the main species of sea fish in 1975 were: salmon, $106,809,000; herring, $100,500,000; cod, $74,646,000; lobster, $68,282,000; redfish, $47,122,000; flounders and soles, $48,861,000. Value of freshwater fish sales from May 1, 1975 to April 30, 1976 was $22,072,000.

Canada's oldest primary industry provides a livelihood to some 57,000 fishermen, with 325 fish processing establishments employing an additional 16,987 persons in 1975. Foreign trade in fish and fishery products totalled $581,849,000 in 1975. Canadian exports accounted for 77·0 per cent of this amount.

**Fur Trading.** Fur farming is carried on in all provinces of Canada.

The table on page 77 shows the number and value of pelts produced, by kind, for 1975–76.

**Industry.** The table on page 77 shows the estimated value of products by industrial groups for 1976.

**Commerce.** The tables below show imports and exports by principal countries for the years 1975 and 1976:

*Exports by Leading Countries* 1975–76

| *Country* | 1975[1] ($'000) | 1976[2] ($'000) |
|---|---|---|
| United States | 21,029,639 | 25,122,901 |
| Japan | 2,117,266 | 2,386,190 |
| United Kingdom | 1,766,455 | 1,826,797 |
| West Germany | 601,170 | 694,778 |
| Italy | 473,998 | 547,917 |
| U.S.S.R. | 418,454 | 535,224 |
| Belgium/Luxembourg | 376,597 | 472,154 |
| Netherlands | 473,781 | 442,327 |
| France | 341,686 | 393,464 |
| Australia | 245,990 | 359,067 |
| Venezuela | 319,931 | 355,317 |
| Brazil | 196,201 | 327,588 |
| Cuba | 225,489 | 258,387 |
| Mexico | 218,940 | 212,903 |
| People's Republic of China | 376,422 | 195,819 |
| India | 200,621 | 152,926 |
| Norway | 170,447 | 151,605 |
| Iran | 147,219 | 143,838 |
| Spain | 113,652 | 126,601 |
| Poland | 116,368 | 123,956 |
| Other countries | 2,394,717 | 2,383,094 |
| All Countries | 32,325,043 | 37,212,853 |

[1] Revised.
[2] Preliminary by order of rank.

*Imports by Leading Countries* 1975–76

| *Country* | 1975[1] ($'000) | 1976[2] ($000) |
|---|---|---|
| United States | 23,559,280 | 25,661,677 |
| Japan | 1,205,316 | 1,523,727 |
| Venezuela | 1,106,751 | 1,295,110 |
| United Kingdom | 1,221,969 | 1,153,318 |
| West Germany | 795,154 | 817,855 |
| Iran | 758,077 | 695,426 |
| Saudi Arabia | 745,961 | 481,614 |
| France | 487,414 | 437,721 |
| Italy | 379,557 | 365,369 |
| Australia | 344,756 | 340,836 |
| South Korea | 166,385 | 303,251 |
| Taiwan | 181,904 | 292,061 |
| Hong Kong | 170,930 | 285,181 |
| Sweden | 264,851 | 262,232 |
| Yemen | 196,655 | 201,715 |
| Netherlands | 158,589 | 181,179 |
| Switzerland | 179,255 | 162,923 |
| Brazil | 170,217 | 160,777 |
| South Africa | 193,822 | 159,136 |
| Nigeria | 78,371 | 155,860 |
| Other countries | 2,270,299 | 2,453,974 |
| All Countries | 34,635,513 | 37,390,942 |

[1] Revised.
[2] Preliminary by order of rank.

The value of exports for 1975 and 1976 by commodity is shown in the table below:

*Leading Commodity Exports* 1975–76

| *Commodity* | 1975[1] ($'000) | 1976[2] ($'000) |
|---|---|---|
| Passenger automobiles and chassis | 3,068,759 | 3,637,845 |
| Crude petroleum | 3,051,511 | 2,286,675 |
| Motor vehicle parts (except engines) | 1,618,409 | 2,189,175 |
| Pulp | 1,830,500 | 2,176,963 |
| Newsprint | 1,744,029 | 1,998,296 |
| Wheat | 2,001,152 | 1,707,822 |
| Natural gas | 1,092,168 | 1,616,490 |
| Lumber, softwood | 948,722 | 1,609,994 |
| Trucks, truck tractors and chassis | 1,080,275 | 1,403,551 |

*continued*

| *Commodity* | 1975[1] ($'000) | 1976[2] ($'000) |
|---|---|---|
| Iron ores and concentrates | 686,356 | 920,463 |
| Motor vehicle engines and parts | 519,209 | 776,627 |
| Coal and other crude bituminous substances | 493,579 | 560,878 |
| Petroleum and coal products | 638,474 | 558,788 |
| Fertilizers and fertilizer material | 456,357 | 547,209 |
| Barley | 442,192 | 542,362 |
| Nickel in ores, concentrates and scrap | 516,316 | 524,200 |
| Copper and alloys | 475,631 | 522,583 |
| Asbestos | 303,761 | 475,893 |
| Aluminum (including alloys) | 439,065 | 466,569 |
| Nickel and alloys | 416,575 | 443,592 |
| Other commodities | 10,502,003 | 12,246,878 |
| All commodities | 32,325,043 | 37,212,853 |

[1] Revised.
[2] Preliminary by order of rank.

The value of imports for 1975 and 1976 by commodity is shown in the table below:

*Leading Commodity Imports* 1975–76

| *Commodity* | 1975[1] ($'000) | 1976[2] ($'000) |
|---|---|---|
| Motor vehicle parts except engines | 3,700,025 | 4,387,804 |
| Crude petroleum | 3,301,924 | 3,273,927 |
| Sedans, new | 2,289,991 | 2,444,324 |
| Trucks, truck tractors and chassis | 809,877 | 839,681 |
| Other telecommunications and related equipment | 448,347 | 560,903 |
| Miscellaneous equipment and tools | 434,139 | 542,837 |
| Motor vehicle engines | 437,287 | 507,922 |
| Special transactions, trade | 324,711 | 504,708 |
| Motor vehicle engine parts | 390,701 | 460,868 |
| Wheel tractors, new | 372,872 | 438,948 |
| Other end products, inedible | 358,848 | 436,337 |
| Electronic computers | 343,350 | 428,355 |
| Organic chemicals | 365,287 | 413,397 |
| Other passenger automobiles and chassis | 259,422 | 359,198 |
| Televisions, radios and phonographs | 221,424 | 342,049 |
| Outerwear, excluding knitted | 201,937 | 341,848 |
| Other motor vehicles | 324,198 | 336,548 |
| Other chemical products | 307,405 | 334,628 |
| Paper and paperboard | 269,782 | 330,267 |
| Meat, fresh and frozen | 180,145 | 329,662 |
| Other commodities | 19,293,841 | 19,776,731 |
| All commodities | 34,635,513 | 37,390,942 |

[1] Revised.
[2] Preliminary by order of rank.

## COMMUNICATIONS

**Railways.** Canadian railway history began in the mid 1830's with the opening for traffic of a 16-mile line between St. John's and Lapráirie, Quebec on 21 July 1836, six years after the first railway in England. By 1867 there were 2,500 miles of railway line.

There were three great periods of railway construction in Canada: the 1850's, when the Grand Trunk and the Great Western Railways were built; the 1870's and 1880's, when the Intercolonial and the Canadian Pacific Railways were built; and the 1900 to 1917 period which saw construction of the Grand Trunk Pacific, the National Transcontinental and the Canadian Northern.

The Canadian Pacific Railway was completed in 1885. The Canadian National Railways, a name applied in 1918 to all government-owned and controlled lines, had its origin in Canada's first major railways. The system embraces numerous other railways and is successor to the original enterprises of 1850–1917.

Today, the Canadian National and Canadian Pacific Railways are the two main systems in Canada. Together they accounted for about 89 per cent of the country's 43,941 miles of first main track in 1975; about 88 per cent of the 1,820,882,670 passenger miles; and over 86 per cent of the 135,081,938,061 freight ton miles during 1975. The major roads and some smaller railways also provide related services such as steamship, trucking, airline, telecommunication, and hotel operations.

In all, some 24 companies provide over 99 per cent of the railway transportation in Canada. Several of these are subsidiaries of United States lines operating between the two countries. In 1975 railways in Canada loaded 228 million tons of freight and received another 21 million tons from U.S. connections, for a total tonnage carried of 249 millions.

**Shipping.** Legislation regarding all phases of shipping was consolidated under the Canada Shipping Act (Revised Statutes of Canada 1970, C. 5–9), which incorporates in the shipping law of Canada, features of international agreements and of British and previous Canadian legislation. Since all waterways, including inland canals and inland lakes and rivers, are open on equal terms (except for the coasting trade) to all countries, the commerce of Canada is not solely dependent upon Canadian shipping. Nevertheless, the greater part of the inland and coastwise traffic is carried in ships of Canadian registry.

Every ship that falls under the definition of 'British Ship', given in section six of the Canada Shipping Act, and is controlled as to management and use in Canada, must, unless registered elsewhere in the Commonwealth be registered in Canada. This does not apply to ships not exceeding 15 tons register and wholly engaged in coastal and inland navigation, nor to yachts not exceeding 20 tons register wherever employed.

As of 1 January 1977, there were 31,953 ships of Canadian Registry: 564 were over 1,000 gross tons.

During 1976 the volume of cargo handled at Canadian ports was 307·6 million tons, carried in 136,009 vessels arriving and departing in all waterborne trade. Canadian registered vessels carried 29·8 per cent of the 188·8 million tons handled in international shipping. In coastal shipping Canadian-registered vessels carried 94·8 per cent of the total cargo.

Chief ports from the viewpoint of foreign cargo handled are Sept Iles, Montreal, Vancouver, Hamilton, Halifax, Thunder Bay, Sault Ste. Marie, Saint John, Toronto, Port Cartier, Quebec, Port Alfred and Baie Comeau.

**Algoma Central Railway, Marine Division.** Sault Ste. Marie, Ontario. Four Dry Cargo; 99,675 deadweight tons (Great Lakes); five self-unloaders; 109,885 deadweight tons (Great Lakes).

**British Colombia Ferry Corporation.** 818 Broughton Street, Victoria B.C. V84 1E4.

**Canada Steamship Lines (1975) Limited,** P.O.B. 100, Montreal, P.Q. H3C 2R7. 31 Dry Cargo; 660,000 deadweight long tons (Great Lakes and Ocean Services).

**Canadian National Railways,** P.O. 8100, Montreal 101, P.Q. 19 Ferries and Passenger/cargo vessels; 81,433 gross tons (East Coast).

**Hall Corporation Shipping Ltd.,** 4333 St. Catherine Street West, Montreal H32 1P9, P.Q. (Great Lakes and St. Lawrence River and coastal transport). One Self-unloader; 11,000 deadweight tons (East Coast and Lakes); five Dry Cargo bulk carriers; 128,300 deadweight tons (Great Lakes); 11 Tankers; 87,600 deadweight tons (East Coast, Lakes and Deep Sea; total 17 ships; 226,900 deadweight tons.

**Hindman Transportation Co. Ltd.**, 1105 1st Avenue East, Owen Sound, Ontario. Four Dry Cargo; 44,350 deadweight tons (Great Lakes).

**N. M. Paterson & Sons Ltd.**, 276 St. James Street West, Montreal, P.Q. 15 Dry Cargo Vessels; 194,700 deadweight tons (Great Lakes and coastal).

**Quebec & Ontario Transportation Co. Ltd.**, 21 Allanburg Road, Thorold, Ontario, L2V 3Z5, Nine Dry Cargo: 82,375 deadweight tons (Great Lakes); and Two Dry Cargo: 15,941 deadweight (Ocean).

**Scott Misener Steamships Ltd.**, P.O. Box 100, 115 Dieppe Rd., St. Catharines, Ontario L2R 6S1. 10 Dry Cargo Vessels; 228,867 deadweight tons; including one Self-unloader; 24,496 deadweight tons (Great Lakes).

**Leitch Transport Ltd. and Upper Lakes Shipping Ltd.**, 49 Jackes Avenue, Toronto, Ontario M4T 1E2. 26 bulk carriers (six of which are self-unloaders); 717,863 summer deadweight tons (Great Lakes and Coastal).

**Civil Aviation.** Civil aviation comes under the jurisdiction of the Federal Government; it is administered under the authority of the Aeronautics Act and the National Transportation Act.

The Aeronautics Act has been divided into three parts. Part I deals with registration of aircraft, licensing of airmen, airports and facilities for air navigation, air traffic control, accident investigation and safe operation of aircraft. Part II is concerned with the economics of commercial air services and Part III deals with internal administration and the implementation of enactments.

On international routes schedules services are offered by the two national flag carriers (Air Canada and CP Air). A co-operative scheme of limited competition in the international market has enabled the Canadian airlines to strengthen their position to compete with foreign airlines. Charter flights for groups of people are also offered by these airlines but there are many charter flights operated by the Regional carriers and by other Canadian airlines as well.

The following are the chief Canadian airlines:

**Air Canada.** (President and Chief Executive Officer Claude I. Taylor.) Share Capital $5,000,000. *Services operated:* Europe – Shannon – London – Prestwick – Paris – Frankfurt – Zurich – Copenhagen; to United States – New York – Boston – Cleveland – Chicago – Los Angeles – San Francisco – Houston – Dallas – Tampa – Miami; to Bermuda and Caribbean – Antigua – Barbados – Trinidad – Nassau – Freeport – Kingston, Jamaica – Montego Bay – Guadeloupe – Martinique – Havana; International charter and scheduled domestic to all parts of Canada. *Head Office:* 1 Place Ville Marie, Montreal H3B 3P7, Quebec.

**Eastern Provincial Airways (1963) Limited.** *Services operated:* scheduled and non-scheduled internal mainly in Maritime provinces and Newfoundland. *Head Office:* P.O. Box 5001, Gander, Newfoundland A1V 1W9.

**Pacific Western Airlines Limited.** *Services operated:* scheduled services serving British Columbia, Alberta, Saskatchewan, Washington and the N.W. Territories. The Company also operates international passenger and cargo charters. *Head Office:* Vancouver, International Airport, B.C.

**Quebecair.** *Services operated:* scheduled services in the province of Quebec—Worldwide charter services—specialized services through four subsidiaries: Northern Wings Ltd., Northern Wings Helicopters Ltd., Air Fecteau, Air Gaspé.

**CP Air—Canadian Pacific Air Lines.** (President and Chiet Executive Officer Ian A. Gray.) *Services operated:* Vancouver – Calgary – Edmonton – Winnipeg – Amsterdam; Hong Kong – Tokyo – Vancouver – Lima – Santiago – Buenos Aires; Sydney – Nandi (Fiji) – Honolulu – Vancouver – Amsterdam; Montreal – Toronto – Mexico City; Toronto – Montreal – Lisbon – Madrid – Amsterdam – Milan – Rome – Athens – Tel Aviv; Los Angeles – San Francisco – Vancouver; international charter and scheduled domestic services serving Montreal, Ottawa, Toronto, Winnipeg, Edmonton, Calgary and Vancouver; and within British Columbia and Yukon. *Executive and Administrative Office:* One Grant McConachie Way, Vancouver International Airport, B.C. V7B IVI .

**Transair Ltd.** Scheduled services in central and western Canada and in the Northwest and Yukon Territories; charter services throughout Canada and from bases in Canada to the U.S.A., Mexico, the Caribbean and Europe; charter helicopter services throughout Canada; operates Boeing 707, Boeing 737, Fokker F 28 jet aircraft in addition to turbo prop transport aircraft, and a range of piston and turbine helicopters.

**Nordair Ltee – Nordair Ltd.** Regular scheduled services from Montreal to Chibougamau, Fort Chimo, Val d'Or, Fort George, Great Whale, and Deception Bay in the Province of Quebec; Frobisher Bay, Resolute Bay, Lake Harbour, Pangnirtung, Cape Dyer, Broughton Island, Clyde River, Cape Dorset, Coral Harbour, Hall Beach, Igloolik, and Pelly Bay, in the Northwest Territories; Ottawa, Hamilton, and Windsor in the Province of Ontario and Pittsburgh, Pennsylvania, U.S.A. Charter services throughout the world. *Head Office:* P.O. Box 4000, Dorval, Quebec H4Y 1B8.

**Telegraphs and Telephones.** There were nine telegraph and cable companies operating in Canada during 1975. Public telegraph service is provided by the railway companies through their telecommunications departments. Pole line mileage in 1975 was 32,152 while wire mileage totalled 767,609

In 1975 there were 13,165,000 telephones in use.

**Broadcasting.** Established in 1936, the Canadian Broadcasting Corporation provides Canada's publicly-owned national broadcasting service, presenting radio and television programmes to English- and French-speaking audiences from coast to coast.

The Canadian Broadcasting Corporation owned and operated 694 undertakings consisting of 50 AM and 77 FM radio undertakings, 284 low power relay transmitters, 280 television undertakings and 3 shortwave transmitters.

In April 1976, over 98 per cent of the households in Canada had radios and over 96 per cent. television sets.

The Canadian Radio-Television Commission (CRTC) was established in 1968 to administer and regulate broadcasting in Canada. The Commission consists of five full-time members and 10 part-time members chosen regionally and appointed by the Governor in Council.

As of 31 March, 1977, 1,826 broadcasting undertakings had been licensed in Canada. Of these there were 421 AM and 278 FM radio stations, 285 low-power relay transmitters, 8 shortwave transmitters and 834 television stations including 475 cable television systems.

Originating stations totalled 614 and were distributed as follows:

| *Province* | *AM* | *FM* | *TV* | *SW* |
|---|---|---|---|---|
| Newfoundland | 24 | 4 | 7 | |
| Prince Edward Island | 4 | | 1 | |
| Nova Scotia | 20 | 7 | 5 | 1 |
| New Brunswick | 17 | 4 | 4 | 1 |
| Quebec | 80 | 26 | 20 | |
| Ontario | 98 | 49 | 27 | |
| Manitoba | 19 | 7 | 6 | |
| Saskatchewan | 21 | 8 | 8 | |
| Alberta | 32 | 10 | 12 | |
| British Columbia | 54 | 12 | 10 | |
| Yukon Territory | 2 | | 1 | |
| Northwest Territories | 6 | 7 | | |

## NEWSPAPERS

**Calgary Herald.** F. 1885. Evening. Circulation 120,000.

**Edmonton Journal.** F. 1903. Evening Circulation 175,000.

**Halifax Chronicle-Herald and Mail Star.** F. 1844. Morning and Evening. Circulation 116,000.

**Le Journal de Montreal.** F. 1964. French. Morning. Circulation 152,000.

**London Free Press.** F. 1849. Morning and evening. Circulation 129,000.

**Montreal Gazette.** F. 1778. Morning. Circulation 131,000. 1,000 St. Antoine Street, Montreal 101.

**Montreal La Presse.** F. 1884. French. Evening. Circulation 195,000.

**Montreal-Matin.** F. 1930. French. Morning. Circulation 129,000.

**Montreal Star.** F. 1869. Evening. Circulation 188,000.

**Ottawa Citizen.** F. 1844. Evening. Circulation 93,215.

**Quebec Le Soleil.** Evening. French. Circulation 150,000.

**Regina Leader-Post.** F. 1883. Evening. Circulation 67,000.

**The Spectator (Hamilton).** F. 1846. Evening. Circulation (ABC figs. 31 March 1976) 140,000.

**Toronto Star.** F. 1892. Evening. Circulation 542,832.

**Toronto Globe and Mail.** F. 1844. Morning. Circulation 63,271.

**Toronto Sun.** F. 1971. Morning. Circulation 130,000; Sunday 250,000.

**Vancouver Sun and Province.** F. 1886. Morning and Evening. Ind. Circulation 393,000.

**Winnipeg Free Press.** F. 1874. Evening. Circulation 140,000.

**Winnipeg Tribune.** F. 1890. Evening. Circulation 75,000.

## EDUCATION

The British North America Act designated education as a provincial responsibility except for certain special areas reserved for the Federal Government, such as schools for the indigenous population, inmates of penitentiaries, and the armed services. The Federal Government also contributes to vocational education and higher education.

Education at the elementary and secondary levels is provincially administered, although the local school districts administer the schools under the School Law. Education is free and compulsory in all provinces for ages 7 to 14 or 15. The costs of public elementary and secondary education are met through local tax levies on real estate, and grants from the provincial governments.

Despite certain differences there is a basic pattern to the various provincial systems. Each province has established a Department of Education operating under the direction of a cabinet minister and has enacted a School Law or Laws governing the establishment of public schools, conditions of attendance, qualifications of teachers and other requirements. Quebec differs from the other provinces in that it operates a dual system—the Roman Catholic, which has developed in the French tradition; and the Protestant, which is similar to the systems in force in the other nine provinces. In Newfoundland the schools are denominational, but operate under uniform regulations regarding attendance, curricula, teacher qualifications, etc.

To meet the rapid increase in university enrolments, many new universities have been or are being built, while established ones are expanding. Institutions of higher education are relatively autonomous and determine their courses, standards, admission requirements and fees.

Schools of technology, open to high school graduates, provide advanced training of a practical nature designed to fit persons for skilled occupations just below the professional level.

The table below gives the number of schools, teachers and enrolment in Elementary and Secondary, and Post-Secondary schools, 1975–76.

*Statistics of Education* 1975–76

| | *Elementary and Secondary* | | | *Post Secondary* | | |
|---|---|---|---|---|---|---|
| *Province* | *No. of Schools* | *Full-time Teachers* | *Full-time Enrolment* | *No. of Schools* | *Full-time Teachers* | *Full-time Enrolment* |
| Newfoundland | 723 | 7,674 | 158,240 | 7 | 840 | 8,154 |
| Prince Edward Island | 72 | 1,483 | 27,911 | 3 | 185 | 2,175 |
| Nova Scotia | 640 | 11,006 | 205,072 | 24 | 1,790 | 20,782 |
| New Brunswick | 526 | 7,970 | 166,114 | 12 | 1,170 | 12,455 |
| Quebec | 2,909 | 77,120 | 1,486,288 | 84 | 15,310 | 193,974 |
| Ontario | 5,022 | 95,983 | 2,058,371 | 54 | 16,970 | 220,160 |
| Manitoba | 818 | 12,514 | 242,729 | 13 | 1,890 | 21,705 |
| Saskatchewan | 1,053 | 11,283 | 228,218 | 9 | 1,580 | 16,824 |
| Alberta | 1,343 | 24,219 | 448,801 | 24 | 4,010 | 47,223 |
| British Columbia | 1,792 | 27,765 | 566,236 | 24 | 4,310 | 48,815 |
| Yukon | 25 | 285 | 4,975 | — | — | — |
| Northwest Territories | 62 | 685 | 12,484 | — | — | — |
| DND Schools (Overseas) | 11 | 300 | 4,624 | — | — | — |
| Total | 14,996 | 278,287 | 5,610,063 | 254 | 48,055 | 592,267 |

## ATOMIC ENERGY

Canada's atomic energy programme had its beginning during the Second World War, when a joint Canadian–British laboratory was established in Montreal under the direction of the National Research Council of Canada. The laboratory was moved later to a new site at Chalk River, Ontario, where a small heavy water moderated reactor, ZEEP, in 1945 became the first nuclear reactor to be built and operated outside the United States.

When the war ended and the U.K.–Canada partnership was dissolved, it was decided by the Canadian government to press ahead with a programme of research and development aimed at utilizing nuclear energy for peaceful purposes. The year 1947 saw the commissioning at Chalk River of the heavy water moderated NRX reactor, which for some years was the most powerful research reactor in the world. In 1957, came NRU, with 10 times the initial power of NRX, and experimental facilities that helped keep Canada in the forefront of nuclear science and technology.

As a result of the expansion of the nuclear programme and its increasing commercial implications, a Government-owned Crown company, Atomic Energy of Canada Limited, was incorporated in 1952 to take over nuclear R & D in Canada from the National Research Council.

AECL has three main functions: research and development in the field of nuclear energy; the development of economic nuclear power; and the production and marketing of radioactive isotopes and equipment for the treatment of cancer. In addition, the company's responsibilities were extended in 1968 to include the export marketing of nuclear power stations and the production of heavy water for use in nuclear plants of Canadian design.

Most of AECL's effort has been directed toward the development of a nuclear power system that will best serve Canadian requirements, and at the same time will be commercially competitive on the international market. The system chosen and put into practical large-scale application, uses heavy water (deuterium oxide) as the reactor moderator and natural uranium as the fuel. Called CANDU, for Canada Deuterium Uranium, it has a number of attractive features, including very low fuel costs and a simple and efficient fuel cycle.

As of 1972, seven nuclear power stations of Canadian design were either in operation or being built. Five were in Canada, one was in India and one in Pakistan. Total design capacity was more than 6 million kilowatts. Additionally, work had started in India on another station which although designed in that country, was based on the CANDU system and was so identified.

The largest CANDU station to be committed, and the second largest nuclear plant to be ordered anywhere in the world up to that time, was the 3 million kilowatt Bruce nuclear generating station of Ontario Hydro, a public utility. Site work started in 1969, and the first of four 750,000 kilowatt reactors is expected to begin producing power in 1976. In 1973, Ontario Hydro's 2·2 million kilowatt Pickering nuclear power station, consisting of four 540,000 kilowatt units, came into full production.

Pickering is situated near the city of Toronto. The Bruce plant is being built on the shore of Lake Huron, near Canada's first commerical-size nuclear power station, Douglas Point. Completed in 1966, the 200,000-kilowatt Douglas Point plant produced its first power early in 1967. The station was built by AECL and is being operated by Ontario Hydro.

At the same site as the Bruce and Douglas Point stations, AECL began building (1969) a heavy water production plant with a capacity of 800 tons a year. It is scheduled to commence operation in 1975.

In the Province of Quebec, work was well advanced on a 250,000 kilowatt nuclear power station designed and built by AECL, with the co-operation of the Quebec Hydro-Electric Commission. Known as Gentilly, the station is a prototype. Like all CANDU stations, it is heavy water moderated and natural uranium fuelled, but it uses boiling light water for the coolant instead of heavy water. Gentilly is scheduled for completion in 1971.

In the radioisotope field, AECL is a major world-supplier of Cobalt-60, as well as a leader in the design, manufacture. and supply of teletherapy machines for the treatment of cancer and of large-scale industrial irradiators for the sterilization of medical supplies. More than 700 cobalt beam therapy units produced by AECL are in service in 52 countries. The company also supplies other radioisotopes and smaller irradiators for research and other uses.

AECL's principal research and development centres are the Chalk River Nuclear Laboratories (CRNL) at Chalk River, Ontario and Whiteshell Nuclear Research Establishment (WNRE) at Pinawa, Manitoba.

Chalk River employs some 2,336 persons, of whom 476 are professional scientists and engineers. Facilities include the two major research reactors, NRX and NRU, and three smaller reactors; laboratories for engineering, metallurgy, physics, chemistry, biology and medicine; a tandem Van de Graaff accelerator, a precision beta-ray spectrometer, mass spectrometers and numerous other instruments.

WNRE has 784 employees, of whom 180 are professionals. Although it has only been in operation since 1963, the establishment has already begun to acquire an international reputation for the quality of its work. The primary facility is a research reactor, WR-1, that is moderated with heavy water and cooled with a mixture of organic compounds. The first reactor of its kind in the world, WR-1 has given Canada a leading position in organic coolant technology, as well as proving itself to be particularly useful for the testing of materials for advanced nuclear power reactors.

Besides the work done in its own laboratories, AECL has additional research and development carried out, on a contract basis, by private industry and universities.

Another large AECL establishment is Power Projects, at Sheridan Park, Ontario. Employing 1,088 persons, Power Projects is responsible for nuclear power system design, nuclear engineering consulting services, the development and testing of major equipment for nuclear plants and the project management of certain nuclear power stations.

The Commercial Products group, at South March, Ontario, processes and sells radioisotopes produced in Canadian reactors and develops, designs, makes and markets associated equipment. Commercial Products is administered as a separate financial entity within the company, and follows normal commercial practices in its operations. It employs 613 persons.

Over-all direction and administration of AECL is provided from a relatively small Head Office, in Ottawa, in which are located the offices of the President and some other senior executives. Also at Head Office is the Nuclear Power Marketing group, which is concerned with the offshore marketing of the CANDU system.

From the inception of Canada's nuclear programme, international collaboration has played an important role. The early, close association with Britain and the U.S.A. has been maintained and senior officials of AECL meet annually with their counterparts of the UKAEA and the USAEC. Meetings are held each year also with representatives of the Commissariat à l'Energie Atomique of France.

When the International Atomic Energy Agency was formed in 1957, Canada was given a permanent seat on the Board of Governors, in recognition of its leading position in the development of peaceful uses of nuclear energy.

The incipient atomic energy programme in India is largely the result of the co-operation and technical assistance provided by Canada under an agreement between the two Commonwealth countries. The Indian programme has now matured to the point where the country is largely self-sufficient in nuclear power technology.

There are a number of other countries and agencies with whom there is active co-operation, and still more with whom there are agreements for exchange of information.

Two other federal government agencies are directly concerned with the atomic energy programme in Canada. One, the Atomic Energy Control Board, is the prime regulatory body for controlling the development, application and use of atomic energy. It also acts as technical consultant to the government on such international matters as nuclear safeguards. The other, Eldorado Nuclear Limited, operates a uranium mine and the only uranium refinery in Canada and carries out research into uranium extraction and refining processes. Currently under construction are plants for the production of zirconium and natural uranium hexafloride.

## RELIGION

Canada has complete freedom of worship and about 30 denominations are represented, almost all of which are Christian in form. The Roman Catholic Church is the largest single body, numbering 9,975,000, representing 46·2 per cent of the population, followed by United Church of Canada, 3,768,000 (17·5 per cent), Anglican Church of Canada, 2,544,000 (11·8 per cent), Presbyterian, 872,000 (4·0 per cent), Lutheran, 716,000 (3·3 per cent) and Baptist, 667,000 (3·1 per cent). These figures are for census year 1971.

# Canadian Provinces

## ALBERTA

**Capital**—Edmonton.

**Lieutenant-Governor**—His Honour Ralph G. Steinhauer.

**Area**—255,285 sq. miles (including 6,485 sq. miles water).

**Population**—1,817,000 (April 1976). Cities (June 1975): Edmonton, 451,600; Calgary, 453,800; Lethbridge, 44,500; Medicine Hat, 30,100; Red Deer, 30,100; Drumheller, 5,800; Camrose, 9,200; Wetaskiwin, 6,600; Grande Prairie, 16,600; Lloydminster, 5,200.

**Constituted as a province of the Dominion of Canada: 1** September 1905.

**Legislature:** (Term five years). Representation of the parties: Progressive Conservative, 69; Social Credit, 4; Independent 1; New Democratic Party, 1.

**Ministry**

*Premier, President of Executive Council:* Hon. Peter Lougheed.
*Deputy Premier and Minister of Transport:* Hon. Dr. Hugh M. Horner.
*Minister of Energy and Natural Resources:* Hon. Donald R. Getty.
*Minister of Federal and Intergovernmental Affairs, and Gov't House Leader:* Hon. Louis D. Hyndman.
*Provincial Treasurer:* Hon. C. Mervin Leitch.
*Attorney General:* Hon. James L. Foster.
*Minister of Labour:* Hon. Neil S. Crawford.
*Minister of Social Services and Community Health:* Hon. W. Helen Hunley (Miss).
*Minister of Hospitals and Medical Care:* Hon. Gordon T. W. Miniely.
*Minister of Housing and Public Works:* Hon. William J. Yurko.
*Minister of Environment:* Hon. David J. Russell.
*Minister of Agriculture:* Hon. Marvin E. Moore.
*Minister of Advanced Education and Manpower:* Hon. Dr. Albert E. Hohol.
*Minister of Education:* Hon. Julian G. J. Koziak.
*Solicitor General:* Hon. Roy A. Farran.
*Minister of Business Development and Tourism:* Hon. Robert W. Dowling.
*Minister of Utilities and Telephones:* Hon. Dr. Allan A. Warrack.
*Minister of Government Services, also responsible for Culture:* Hon. Horst A. Schmid.
*Minister of Recreation, Parks and Wildlife:* Hon. J. Allen Adair.
*Minister of Consumer and Corporate Affairs:* Hon. Graham L. Harle.
*Minister of Municipal Affairs:* Hon. Dick Johnston.
*Associate Minister, Energy and Natural Resources responsible for Public Lands:* Hon. D. W. Schmidt.
*Ministers Without Portfolio:* Hon. Stewart A. McCrae; Hon. Dallas W. Schmidt; Responsible for Native Affairs: Hon. Robert J. Bogle.

**Supreme Court** (Appellate Division):

*Hon. Chief Justice of Alberta:* William A. McGillivray.

**Supreme Court** (Trial Division):

*Hon. Chief Justice:* James Valentine Hogarth Milvain.

**Supreme Court** (District Court):

*Hon. Chief Justice:* JohnNicholas Decore.

**State Finance.** Budget figures estimated for the year ending, 31 March 1978 are; Revenue.[1] $3,577·0 million. Expenditure $3,329·1 million.

Personal income per capita was $6,775 in 1976.

[1]Excludes funds allocated to the Alberta Heritage Savings Trust Fund.

**Agriculture.** Of the surveyed area of the province (about 85 million acres), approximately 70 million acres may be classed as capable of agricultural development. Up to the present, however, only 40 per cent of this area has been brought under cultivation.

Alberta farmers' cash receipts in 1976 totalled $1,822,578,000, of which crops contributed $911 million, livestock and products $891 million and other sources $20 million.

**Mineral Production.** The estimated value of minerals produced in 1976 increased by $1,258 million above 1975 to $6,996 million. The major increases were in oil, natural gas, and natural gas by-products. Coal production was estimated at 11,780 thousand tons for 1976.

**Manufacture.** The value (in thousand $) of manufacturers shipments increased from $4,718,106,000 in 1975 to 5,273,383,000 in 1976.

The value of Manufacturers Shipments—Alberta 1975 and 1976 (in thousand $) is shown in the table below:

| *Industry* | 1975 | 1976[1] |
|---|---|---|
| | *(Preliminary figures)* | |
| Food and Beverage Products | 1,683,139 | 1,758,756 |
| Textile Products | 25,206 | 24,914 |
| Wood Products | 259,531 | 326,850 |
| Furniture and Fixtures | 50,075 | 51,608 |
| Paper and Allied Products | 175,570 | 177,258 |
| Printing, Publishing and Allied Products | 136,116 | 150,263 |
| Primary Metal Products | 324,370 | 295,664 |
| Metal Fabricating Products | 228,021 | 328,147 |
| Machinery | 127,447 | 153,227 |
| Transportation Equipment | 203,948 | 221,426 |
| Electrical Products | 81,910 | 85,224 |
| Non-Metallic Mineral Products | 231,156 | 318,013 |
| Petroleum and Coal Products | 700,467 | 940,252 |
| Chemical and Chemical Products | 280,700 | 283,758 |
| Miscellaneous Manufacturing | 32,415 | 35,248 |
| Total[2] | 4,718,106 | 5,273,383 |

[1] Revised.
[2] Totals include estimates for several industry groups which cannot be shown separately due to confidentiality provisions of the Statistics Act.

**Retail Trade.** The value of retail trade total for Alberta increased from $4,557 million in 1975 to an estimated $5,290 million in 1976.

**Universities.** University of Alberta, Edmonton (Established 1906). Total enrolment full-time; 1975–76, 19,736.

University of Calgary (gained autonomy in 1966). Total enrolment full-time; 1975–76 10,950.

University of Lethbridge (Established 1967). Total enrolment full-time; 1975–76, 1,340.

# BRITISH COLUMBIA

**Capital**—Victoria.

**Lieutenant-Governor**—Col. The Honourable Walter Stewart Owen, QC, LLD.

**Area**: 366,255 sq. miles.

**Population**: 2,491,000 (estimated 1976). Chief cities are (1974 estimate); Metropolitan Vancouver, 1,137,000; Metropolitan Victoria (revised), 208,000.

**Admitted to the Dominion**: 20 July 1871.

**Legislature**: (Term five years). Representation of the Parties (May 1976); New Democratic Party, 18; Social Credit, 35; Liberal, 1; Progressive Conservative, 1.

**Executive Council**:
*Premier and President of Council:* Hon. William Richards Bennett.
*Provincial Secretary, Deputy Premier, and Minister of Recreation and Travel Industry:* Hon. Grace Mary McCarthy
*Attorney-General:* Hon. Garde Basil Gardom, QC.
*Minister of Finance:* Hon. Evan Maurice Wolfe.
*Minister of Agriculture:* Hon. James J. Hewitt.
*Minister of Education:* Hon. Patrick Lucey McGeer.
*Minister of Municipal Affairs and Minister of Housing:* Hon. Hugh Austin Curtis.
*Minister of Mines and Petroleum Resources:* Hon. James R. Chabot.
*Minister of Labour:* Hon. Louis Allan Williams.
*Minister of Health:* Hon. Robert Howard McClelland.
*Minister of Highways and Public Works:* Hon. Alexander Vaughan Fraser.
*Minister of Energy, Transport and Communications:* Hon. Jack Davis.
*Minister of Human Resources:* Hon. William Nick Vander Zalm.
*Minister of Consumer and Corporate Affairs:* Hon. Kenneth Rafe Mair.
*Minister of Environment:* Hon. James Arthur Nielsen.

**Judiciary.** *The Court of Appeal* of British Columbia consists of a Chief Justice, the Hon. John L. Farris and nine Puisne Justices.

**The Supreme Court.** The Supreme Court of British Columbia is comprised of a Chief Justice, the Hon. Nathaniel Theodore Nemetz and 25 Puisne Justices. The Chief Justice is also responsible for general supervision of 31 County Court Judges in the Province. (Preceding courts appointed by Federal Government.)

**Provincial Court of British Columbia.** There are a Chief Judge, Lawrence C. Brahan and about 100 provincially appointed judges. The Provincial Court also has about 150 provincially appointed judges.

**Provincial Finance.** Total provincial revenues and expenditures for 1976–77 were estimated to be $3,587,200,000 and $3,615,200,000 respectively.

The Government operates a hospital insurance scheme giving universal coverage after a qualifying period of three months' residence in the province. In 1968 the Province came under a national medicare scheme which is financed partially by premiums, partially by Federal moneys and the remainder, including Premium Subsidies, by the Provincial Government.

**Production.** Almost 55 per cent of British Columbia's land area is forest and supports 285,423 million cubic feet of merchantable timber, more than half the total Canadian forest resource. The Provincial Government owns or administers 95 per cent of the forest area. Forest based industries accounted for an estimated 41 per cent of factory shipments in 1976. The total British Columbia timber cut in 1976 was 2,561 million cubic feet. Exports of the Province's forest products were valued at $3,190 million (Canadian) in 1976.

Copper, coal, crude oil, natural gas, zinc and molybdenum are the most important minerals produced. Total mineral production in 1976 was estimated to be $1,486·1 million. In British Columbia, production in 1976 of the leading metals was copper, 273 million kg. for a value of $397 million; zinc 113 million kg. worth $68 million; molybdenum 14 million kg. worth $89 million. The production of coal in 1976 —as 7·5 million metric tonnes, crude oil, 2·3 million cubic meters; and natural gas 8,800 million cubic meters. The total value of fossil fuels produced in 1976 was $687 million. The estimated net generation of electric power in British Columbia in 1976 amounted to 34,280 million kWh.

Almost three per cent of the total land area of the Province or 6·5 million acres is arable or potentially arable. Another 2·5 million acres is estimated as suitable for range land. The value of farm cash receipts was $436·8 million in 1976.

In 1976 fish landings totalled 383·9 million pounds. Salmon and herring were the leading species with 121·8 million pounds of salmon caught and 178·8 million pounds of herring taken by British Columbia fishermen. Exports of fish and marine products originating in the Province were estimated to be valued at $175·5 million in 1976.

The 1976 value of products shipped from British Columbia based factories is estimated at $8·7 billion. Processing primary resources (forests, mineral, agriculture and fisheries) dominates activity in British Columbia's manufacturing industry. However shipbuilding, truck manufacturing, and electrical equipment production are rapidly expanding sectors. Supplying equipment to the large integrated resource industries (logging equipment, sawmill and mining machinery, winches, etc.) is also important to the Provinces manufacturing industry.

Estimated value of British Columbia product exports through all Canadian customs ports in 1976 amounted to $5·3 billion.

**Communications**

*Railways.*—British Columbia is served by both national railways as well as the British Columbia Railway (formerly called the Pacific Great Eastern Railway) and several American lines. The Canadian National Railways, with 1,415 miles of first main track in the Province, connects Prince Rupert, Kitimat, and Prince George with Edmonton, Alberta, and points east. It also links Vancouver and the south central region of the Province with Edmonton. The Canadian Pacific Railway operates 1,814 miles of first main track and joins Vancouver and the southern region of the Province with Calgary and Lethbridge, Alberta, and points east. Both the CNR and CPR operate lines on Vancouver Island. The British Columbia Railway, with 1,260 miles of main track has its southern terminus at North Vancouver and serves central and northern British Columbia, with present terminals at Fort St. James, Fort Nelson, Dawson Creek, and Mackenzie. The British Columbia Railway in December of 1969 announced the 419 mile extension of its line from Fort St. James to Dease Lake. Subsequent to federal-provincial negotiations, construction was halted in the spring of 1977 with 113 miles completed. The Northern Alberta Railway connects with the British Columbia Railway at Dawson Creek.

Five American rail lines—the Milwaukee, the Union Pacific, the Spokane International, the Northern Pacific, and the Burlington Northern—serve British Columbia points directly or interchange with Canadian railways at, southern border points. Also, a number of industrial railways the British Columbia Harbours Board Railway, and the railway freight service of the British Columbia Hydro and Power Authority serve the Lower Mainland area.

*Shipping.*—The major ports are Vancouver, New Westminster, Victoria, Nanaimo and Prince Rupert. The volume of coastwise shipping in 1975 was 10·8 million tons loaded and 10·6 million tons unloaded. International deep-sea shipping handled in British Columbia ports during 1975 totalled 37·2 million tons.

The British Columbia Ferries connect Vancouver Island with the Mainland and provide passenger and freight service to many other coastal points. In the twelve months ended 31 March 1976 the 26 ships carried 9·8 million passengers and 3·8 million vehicles. Black Ball Transport Inc., Washington State Ferries and Canadian Pacific Steamships provide service between Vancouver Island and the United States. The Alaska State Ferries connect Prince Rupert with centres in Alaska.

*Air Lines.*—There are 77 air carriers based in British Columbia. Vancouver and Victoria are connected with the other parts of Canada by airways, two of which are transcontinental. In addition, there are a number of intra-provincial and interprovincial air routes and regular scheduled routes between Vancouver and many world centres.

**Universities.** The Universities in the Province had a full-time enrolment of 32,203 for 1975–76. The universities are University of British Columbia, Vancouver; University of Victoria, Victoria; Simon Fraser University, Burnaby; The Regional Colleges are Camosun, Victoria; Capilano, West Vancouver; Cariboo, Kamloops; Douglas, New Westminster; Fraser Valley, Abbotsford; Malaspina, Nanaimo; New Caledonia, Prince George; Okanagan, with branches at Kelowna, Salmon Arm and Vernon; Selkirk, Castlegar; Vancouver City (Langara Campus), Vancouver; British Columbia Institute of Technology, Burnaby.

# MANITOBA

**Capital**—Winnipeg.

**Lieutenant-Governor**—Hon. F. L. Jobin.

**Area**—251,000 sq. miles.

**Population:** 1,028,500 (estimate). Chief cities are: City of Winnipeg, 552,500; Brandon, 32,460; Flin Flon, 9,560; Portage la Prairie, 13,250; Thompson, 20,620.

**Admitted to Confederation: July 15, 1870.**

**Legislature:** (Term 5 years). Standing in the Legislature at 1 June, 1977 are New Democratic Party 31; Conservative 23; Liberal 3.

**Ministry**

*Premier, Minister of Dominion-Provincial Relations, Minister charged with the Administration of the Manitoba Hydro Act,* Hon. Edward Schreyer.
*Attorney General:* Hon. Howard Pawley.
*Minister of Mines, Resources and Environment Management:* Hon. Sidney Green.
*Minister of Agriculture:* Hon. Samuel Uskiw.
*Minister of Health and Social Development:* Hon. Laurent Desjardins.
*Minister of Industry and Commerce:* Hon. Leonard Evans.
*Minister of Highways:* Hon. Peter Burtniak.
*Minister of Tourism, Recreation and Cultural Affairs:* Hon. Ben Hanuschak.
*Minister of Public Works:* Hon. Russell Doern.
*Minister of Northern Affairs:* Hon. Ronald McBryde.
*Minister of Labour:* Hon. Russell Paulley.
*Minister of Education:* Hon. Ian Turnbull.
*Minister of Consumer Corporate, and Internal Services:* Hon. René Toupin.
*Minister of Municipal Affairs:* Hon. Billie Uruski.
*Minister of Finance and Urban Affairs:* Hon. Saul Miller.
*Minister of Renewable Resources and Transportation Services:* Hon. Harvey Bostrom.
*Minister responsible for Corrections and Rehabilitation:* Hon. J. R. Boyce.

**Manitoba Court of Appeal**

*Chief Justice of Manitoba:* Samuel Freedman.

**Manitoba Court of Queen's Bench**

*Chief Justice:* A. S. Dewer.

**State Finance:** Budget figures for 1977–78 are: Revenue, $1,158 million; Expenditure, $1,166 million.

**Production.** Gross provincial income for 1976 was $7·9 million,* an increase of about 14 per cent over 1975. In 1976 personal income amounted to $6·5 billion; labour income $4·2 billion; farm cash income $888 million; private and public investment $2·1 billion. Manitoba primary resource production gross output for 1976 is estimated at $1·5 billion.

* Canadian million.

**Universities.** University of Manitoba, in Winnipeg, founded 1877, 15,000 students (full-time). St. Boniface College (French language), 150 students. University of Winnipeg, founded 1967, 3,000 students. University of Brandon, founded 1967, 1,600 students.

# NEW BRUNSWICK

**Capital**—Fredericton.

**Lieutenant-Governor**—His Honour H. J. Robichaud.

**Area**—28,253 sq. miles.

**Population:** 681,000 (1975). Chief cities with populations are: Fredericton, 42,000 (Est.); Moncton, 47,890; Saint John, 106,745.

**One of the four original provinces** (entered Confederation 1867).

**Legislature:** (Term five years). Representation of the parties following the election of 18 November 1974; Conservative, 33; Liberal, 25.

**Ministry**

*Premier:* Hon. Richard B. Hatfield.
*Minister of Justice:* Hon. Rodman E. Logan, QC.
*Minister of Finance:* Hon. Lawrence Garvie.
*Minister of Natural Resources:* Hon. Roland C. Boudreau.
*Minister of Education:* Hon. Charles G. Gallagher.
*Minister of Supply and Services:* Hon. Harold N. Fanjoy.
*Minister of Agriculture and Rural Development:* Hon. Malcolm Macleod.
*Minister of Health:* Hon. Brenda M. Robertson.
*Minister of Labour and Manpower:* Hon. Paul S. Creaghan, Q.C.
*Minister of Municipal Affairs:* Hon. Horace B. Smith.
*Minister of Transportation:* Hon. Wilfred G. Bishop.
*Minister of Commerce and Development:* Hon. Gerald S. Merrithew.
*Minister of Fisheries:* Hon. Omer Leger.
*Minister of Tourism and Environment:* Hon. Fernand Dube QC.
*Minister of Youth, Recreation and Cultural Resources:* Hon. Jean-Pierre Ouellet.
*Minister of Social Services:* Hon. Leslie Hull.
*Provincial Secretary:* Hon. Paul S. Creaghan, QC.
*Minister of Treasury Board:* Hon. Jean-Maurice Simard.
*Minister of Historical Resources:* Hon. Charles, G. Gallagher.
*Chairman, N. B. Electric Power Commission:* Hon. G. W. N. Cockburn.

**New Brunswick Court of Appeal and Chancery Division**

*Chief Justice:* Hon. Charles J. A. Hughes.

**New Brunswick Court of Queen's Bench**

*Chief Justice:* Hon. A. J. Cormier.

**Finance.** Budget figures for the year ending 31 March 1977 were: Revenue, $991·6 million; Expenditure, $983·4 million.

**Education.** Public education is free and non-sectarian. There are four universities. The University of New Brunswick, at Fredericton, is supported by the province. It was founded in 1785 and had 5,204 full-time students in 1974–75, to it is affiliated St. Thomas University, formerly of Chatham, with 812 students; the Mount Allison University, founded 1858, at Sackville has 1,405 students. The University of Moncton, founded in 1963, amalgamated the several French language colleges; St. Joseph's, founded 1864, College de Bathurst, and College St. Louis at Edmundston. The University of Moncton had an enrolment of 3,081 students in 1974–75. In September 1976 there were 163,830 pupils in the province's school system.

It is predicted that 162,250 pupils will be in the provinces school system in September 1977.

**Manufactures.** Forest products; pulp, paper and timber form the major manufacture group, followed by foods, oil refining, shipbuilding and general manufacturing, including electronics, cooking and heating equipment, chemicals and fertilizers and diversified other products. Saint John is the principal manufacturing centre. Total value of manufactured products was $1,096,100,000 in 1973.

**Agriculture and Livestock.** The total land area is 17,685,120 acres of which about 85 per cent is forested. The Province is the largest potato-producing area of Canada, grown chiefly in the upper Saint John River Valley. Dairy farming is next in importance. Together, the potato industry and the dairy industry accounted for 58·3 per cent of total farm cash receipts in New Brunswick in 1976, or $63,150,000. This figure does not include dairy supplementary payments or Federal deficiency payments for potatoes which together account for another $2,113,000., or 2·0 per cent. These are by no means the only significant agricultural products of New Brunswick.

**Fishing.** The chief commercial fish are lobsters, sardines, herring, cod haddock and salmon etc., with an estimated market value of $25,000,000 in 1976.

**Minerals.** Extensive zinc, lead and copper deposits are now being mined in the north-eastern part of the Province with a smelter having recently come into operation. Further processing of New Brunswick metals include a lead smelter at Belledune. Total mineral production was valued at $255,057,000 in 1975, Coal continues to be mined on a decreasing scale with lesser amounts of non-metallic minerals.

## NEWFOUNDLAND AND LABRADOR

**Capital**—St. John's.

**Lieutenant-Governor**—The Honourable Gordon A. Winter.

**Area—156,185 sq. miles.**

**Population**: 557,725 (1 June 1976) Chief Towns with population (over 4,000) are: St. John's, 86,500; (Metropolitan Area, 143,300); Corner Brook, 25,100; Labrador City, 12,000; Stephenville, 10,200; Mount Pearl, 10,100; Conception Bay South, 9,700; Gander, 9,300; Grand Fall 8,700; Happy Valley-Goose Bay, 8,000; Windsor, 6,300; Channel-Port aux Basques 6,100; Marystown, 5,900; Carbonear, 5,000; Wabana, 4,800; Botwood, 4,500; Deer Lake, 4,500; Bishops Falls, 4,500; Bonavista, 4,200; Bay Roberts, 4,000.

**Admitted to the Dominion: 31 March 1949.**

**Legislature**: (Term five years). Election held 16 September 1975 (and one by-election): Progressive Conservative, 30; Liberal, 16; Liberal Reform Party, 4 Independent Liberal Party, 1.

**Ministry**

*Premier:* Hon. Frank D. Moores.
*President of the Council:* Hon. Dr. T. C. Farrell.
*Minister of Consumer Affairs and Environment:* Hon. A. J. Murphy.
*Minister of Education:* Hon. H. W. House.
*Minister of Finance and President of the Treasury Board:* Hon. C. W. Doody.
*Minister of Fisheries:* Hon. W. C. Carter.
*Minister of Forestry and Agriculture:* Hon. E. Maynard.
*Minister of Health and Minister of Rehabilitation and Recreation:* Hon. H. A. Collins.
*Minister of Industrial and Rural Development:* Hon. J. H. Lundrigan.
*Minister of Justice and Minister Responsible for Intergovernmental Affairs:* Hon. T. Alex Hickman.
*Minister of Mines and Energy:* Hon. B. A. Peckford.
*Minister of Municipal Affairs and Housing:* Hon. Jerome Dinn.
*Minister of Social Services:* Hon. R. C. Brett.
*Minister of Tourism:* Hon. T. V. Hickey.
*Minister of Transportation and Communications:* Hon. James Morgan.

**Supreme Court of Newfoundland and Labrador**

*Chief Justice:* Hon. R. S. Furlong, MBE.

**Finance.** Estimated budget figures for 1977–78 were: Current and Revenue; Estimated Expenditures (Budgetary), $1,168,278,200.

**University.** Memorial University of Newfoundland, founded 13 August 1949, in succession to the Memorial University College, founded 1925. Number of students, winter 1977, Full-time undergraduate, 5,393; Part-time undergraduate (on campus), 1,006; Part-time (off campus), 1,032; Total Post-graduate, 730; Total enrollment, 8,161. Regional College of Memorial University of Newfoundland in Corner Brook: Number of students, winter, 1977, Full-time undergraduate, 607; Part-time undergraduate (on campus), 26. For major faculties: Students on work terms under the cooperative program, 214; students working as interns or residents in hospitals, 133. A new campus was opened by Mr. Eleanor Roosevelt on 9 October 1961. The new campus at the Regional College was opened by Hon. Premier Frank D. Moores on 24 October 1975.

*Chancellor:* Dr. G. A. Frecker.

*President:* Dr. Moses Morgan.

## NOVA SCOTIA

**Capital—Halifax.**

**Lieutenant-Governor**—The Hon. Clarence L. Gosse, MD, CM, FRCS.

**Area—21,425 sq. miles.**

**Population**: (1976 Census): 828,571 an increase of 39,611 or five per cent over the five-year period from 1971. The population of cities and larger towns in the 1976 Census is: Halifax, 117,800; Dartmouth, 65,300; Sydney 30,600; Glace Bay, 21,800; Truro, 12,800; Amherst, 10,200; New Glasgow, 10,600.

**One of the four original provinces** (entered Confederation 1867).

**Legislature: (Term five years maximum). Representation of** the parties: Liberal, 31; Progressive Conservative, 12; New Democratic, 3.

**Ministry**

*Premier and President of Executive Council:* Hon. Gerald A. Regan, QC.
*Minister of Finance and Deputy Premier:* Hon. Peter Nicholson, QC.
*Attorney General and Minister in Charge of Administration of the Human Rights Act:* Hon. Leonard L. Pace, QC.
*Minister of Social Services and Minister Responsible for Status of Women:* Hon. W. M. MacEachern.
*Minister of Development, Minister in Charge of Administration of the Civil Service Act and Minister in Charge of Administration of the Research Foundation Corporation Act:* Hon. A. M. Sandy Cameron.

*Minister of Education:* Hon. George M. Mitchell, QC.
*Minister of Labour and Minister in Charge of the Housing Development Act:* Hon. Walter R. Fitzgerald.
*Minister of Recreation:* Hon. A. Garnet Brown.
*Minister of Fisheries:* Hon. Daniel S. Reid, MD.
*Minister of Public Works and Minister in Charge of Administration of the Liquor Control Act:* Hon. Benoit Comeau.
*Minister of Municipal Affairs:* Hon. Glen M. Bagnell.
*Minister of Tourism:* Hon. Maurice E. DeLory, MD.
*Minister of Mines and Minister in Charge of the Nova Scotia Energy Council:* Hon. J. William Gillis.
*Minister of Highways:* Hon. J. Fraser Mooney.
*Minister of Agriculture and Marketing and Chairman of the Treasury Board:* Hon. John Hawkins.
*Minister of Health, Minister in Charge of Administration of the Drug Dependency Act and Registrar General:* Hon. Maynard C. MacAskill, MD.
*Minister of Lands and Forests, Minister of the Environment, Minister in Charge of Administration of the Emergency Measures Organization (NS) Act and Regulations:* Hon. Vincent J. MacLean.
*Minister of Consumer Affairs, Minister in Charge of the Residential Tenancies Act:* Hon. Guy A. C. Brown.
*Provincial Secretary, Minister in Charge of Administration of the Communications and Information Act:* Hon. Harold M. Huskilson.

**Supreme Court of Nova Scotia**

*Chief Justice:* Ian Mackeigan, Q.C.

**Provincial Finance** for the year ending 31 March 1976, Revenue was $764,117,432; Expenditure $755,554,187.

**Production.** Approximately 7·6 per cent of the total land area of Nova Scotia or 989,037 acres was classified as farm land in the 1976 census. This census showed 3,441 farms (with sales of over $1,200 in 1975) in the province. In 1976, farm cash income was $124,029 million.

Fisheries accounted for 6·7 per cent of the net value of commodity production in 1975. In 1976 land value amounted to $101·9 million. Fish products is one of the leading manufacturing industries with the marketed value in 1975 in the region of $208·6 million.

There are about 10·8 million acres of forested lands in Nova Scotia or about 78 per cent of the total land area. Roughly 26 per cent is held by the Crown (24 per cent provincial and 2 per cent federal); 21 per cent in private ownerships of 1,000 acres and over and 52 per cent in private ownerships under 1,000 acres in size. Primary forest products include sawlogs, pulpwood, pit props, poles and piling, veneer logs and Christmas trees. Secondary activity includee sawmilling, pulp and paper manufacturing, other wood-using industries (planing mills, box and barrel factories, etc.), and boatbuilding yards. The total value of primary and secondary products was approximately 294·9 million in 1974.

Principal minerals mined in Nova Scotia are gypsum, salt and coal. Total value of mining in Nova Scotia in 1976 was $117·2 million, a 15·6 per cent increase from 1975.

In 1976 the value of manufacturing shipments was $1,978·8 million. Oil refining, fish processing, primary steel operations, pulp and paper manufacturing, tyre manufacturing, sawmilling and a variety of food processing operations are the provinces main primary industries.

Construction occupies a position second only to manufacturing in the total net value of production. In 1976 total value of construction was estimated to be $852 million. In 1977 it is expected to be $949 million. Employment in this industry stood at approximately 24,000 in 1976.

**Communications.** Nova Scotia has a network of 15,659 miles of roads. Of this total over 5,850 miles are paved.

There are approximately 1,214 miles of railway track, owned mainly by the Canadian National Railways. During 1976, over 9·5 million tons of freight were loaded on the railways.

In 1976, more than 23,000,000 tons of cargo were loaded and unloaded in Nova Scotian ports—approximately 50 per cent and 30 per cent of the cargo were handled at the Port of Halifax and Port Hawkesbury respectively.

**Education.** Almost all elementary and high school education is handled by compulsory free public schools, over 632 in number. There are, in addition, a number of private schools and business colleges. General administration of the public schools is controlled by the provincial Department of Education, but local boards are directly responsible for their operation. There are 12 institutions of higher learning.

# ONTARIO

**Capital**—Toronto.

**Lieutenant-Governor**—Hon. Pauline M. McGibbon, OC, BA, LLD, DU, DHumL, BAA (Theatre), Hon. FRCPS (C.)

**Area**—412,582 sq. miles.

**Population:** 8,264,465 (Census 1976). Chief cities with population, census June 1976: Toronto Metropolitan Area, 2,803,100; Ottawa (including Hull), 693,200; Hamilton, 529,300; London 270,300; Windsor, 247,500; Kitchener, 272,100; St. Catharines, 123,300; Thunder Bay, 119,200; Oshawa, 135,100; Sudbury, 157,000; Sault Ste. Marie, 81,000; Niagara Falls, 69,400; Brantford, 66,900; Guelph, 67,500; Kingston, 56,000; Peterborough, 59,600; Sarnia, 55,500; Cornwall, 46,100.

**One of the four original provinces** (entered Confederation in 1867).

**Legislature:** (Term five years). Representation of the parties, June 1977 election: Progressive Conservative, 58; Liberal, 34; New Democratic Party, 33.

**Executive Council**

*Premier and President of the Council:* Hon. William G. Davis, QC.
*Provincial Secretary for Justice and Solicitor-General:* John Macbeth.
*Provincial Secretary for Social Development:* Margaret Birch.
*Provincial Secretary for Resources Development:* René Branelle.
*Treasurer and Minister of Economics and Intergovernmental Affairs:* W. Darcy McKeough.
*Chairman, Management Board of Cabinet:* James Auld.

**Ministers**

*Minister of Agriculture and Food:* William Newman.
*Attorney-General:* Roy McMurtry.
*Minister of Colleges and Universities:* Dr. Harry Parrott.
*Minister of Community and Social Services:* Keith Norton.
*Minister of Consumer and Commercial Relations:* Sidney Handleman.
*Acting Minister of Correctional Services:* John MacBeth.
*Minister of Culture and Recreation and Government House Leader:* Robert Welch.
*Minister of Education:* Thomas Wells.
*Minister of Energy:* James Taylor.
*Minister of the Environment:* George Kerr.
*Minister of Government Services:* James Auld.
*Minister of Health:* Dennis Timbrell.
*Minister of Housing:* John Rhodes.
*Minister of Industry and Tourism:* Claude Bennett.
*Minister of Labour:* Dr. Bette Stephenson.
*Minister of Natural Resources:* Frank Miller.
*Minister of Revenue:* Margaret Scrivener.
*Minister of Transportation and Communications:* James Snow.
*Chairman of Cabinet and Minister without Portfolio:* Lorne Henderson.

**Supreme Court of Ontario** (Court of Appeal)

*Chief Justice:* Hon. Willard Z. Estey.

*Chief Justice of the High Court:* Hon. G. T. Evans.

**Provincial Finance**

| | 1976–77* | 1977–78† |
|---|---|---|
| | *(in thousands of dollars)* | |
| Gross Revenue[1] | 10,514,328 | 11,983,000 |
| Gross Expenditure[1] | 11,743,046 | 12,975,000 |

† Estimate.
[1] Excludes Ontario Hydro debenture transactions by province.

**Production.** Ontario's gross provincial product increased from \$65·3 billion* to an estimated \$75 billion* in 1977. Real output rose 4·9 per cent and prices rose 9·4 per cent in 1976 The value of retail trade in 1976 was \$21·1 billion.

**Education.** Enrolment of full-term degree undergraduates in provincially assisted universities in 1976–77 was as follows: Brock University, 2,483; Carleton University, 7,760; University of Guelph 8,944; Lakehead University, 2,188; Laurentian University, 2,969; McMaster University, 8,796; University of Ottawa, 9,153; Queen's University, 9,145; University of Toronto, 26,187; Trent University, 2,438; University of Waterloo, 13,229; University of Western Ontario, 15,614; Wilfrid Laurier University, 2,925; University of Windsor, 6,601; York University, 11,709. Ryerson Polytechnic, 3,745; Total, 133,936.

* Canadian Dollars.

## PRINCE EDWARD ISLAND

**Capital**—Charlottetown.

**Lieutenant-Governor**—Gordon L. Bennett.

**Area**—2,184 sq. miles.

**Population:** 119,000. Chief towns with populations are: Charlottetown, 19,100; Souris, 1,600; Summerside, 9,400.

**Admitted to the Dominion:** 1 July 1873.

**Legislature:** (Term five years). Representation of the parties, 1976: Liberal, 24; Progressive Conservatives, 8; Vacant, 0.

**Executive Council**

*Premier, and Attorney General:* Hon. Alexander B. Campbell.
*Minister of Education:* Hon. W. Bennett Campbell.
*Acting Minister of Finance:* Hon. W. Bennett Campbell.
*Minister of Agriculture and Forestry:* Hon. A. E. (Bud) Ings.
*Minister of Municipal Affairs; Minister of the Environment and Minister of Tourism, Parks, and Conservation:* Hon. Gilbert R. Clements.
*Provincial Secretary:* Hon. Arthur MacDonald.
*Minister of Public Works and Highways:* Hon. Bruce L. Stewart.
*Minister of Health, Minister of Social Services:* Hon. Catherine S. Callbeck.
*Minister of Fisheries and Minister of Labour:* Hon. George R. Henderson.
*Minister of Industry and Commerce, and Minister of Development:* Hon. John H. Maloney, M.D.
*Minister Responsible for the P.E.I. Housing Corporation:* Hon. George A. Proud.

**Supreme Court of Prince Edward Island**

*Chief Justice:* J. P. Nicholson.

**State Finance.** Budget figures for the year ended 31 March 1977 were: Revenue, \$189,453,000; Expenditure, \$189,016,900.

**Education.** There is one university in Prince Edward Island (established 1969). The forecasted enrolment for 1977–78 is 1,500 full-time students.

Holland College, a college of Applied Arts and Technology (established 1969) is the home of the Atlantic Police Academy. The forecasted enrolment for 1977–78 is 750.

## QUEBEC

**Capital**—Quebec.

**Lieutenant-Governor**—Hon. Hugues Lapointe.

**Area**—596,336 sq. miles.

**Population:** 6,234,400 (June 1, 1976). Chief towns with populations: Laval, 228,000; Quebec, 187,800; Montreal, 1,060,000; Verdun, 67,400, Trois Rivieres, 51,700; Sherbrooke, 75,100.

**One of the four original provinces** (entered Confederation 1867).

**Legislature** The provincial government is administered by a lieutenant-governor, and a National Assembly. The Assembly is elected for five years. Since 1966, citizens 18 years of age and over are entitled to vote. Women have the vote and can be elected to the Legislature. The National Assembly consists of 110 members. Each of the 110 electoral districts forms an electoral division and sends one member to represent it.

Representation of the parties in the National Assembly (1976): Liberal, 21; Social Credit 1; Parti Québécois, 7; P.N.P. 1; Union Nationale, 11.

**Ministry** (26 November 1976)

*Prime Minister and President of the Executive Council:* Rene Levesque.
*Deputy Minister and Minister of Education:* Jacques-Yvan Morin.
*House Leader and Minister of State Responsible for Parliamentary Reform:* Robert Burns.
*Minister of Intergovernmental Affairs:* Claude Morin.
*Minister of Finance and Minister of Revenue:* Jacques Parizeau.
*Minister of State Responsible for Cultural Development:* Camille Laurin.
*Minister of State Responsible for Social Development:* Pierre Marois.
*Minister of State Responsible for Economic Expansion:* Bernard Landry.
*Minister of State Responsible for Planning:* Jacques Leonard.
*Minister of Justice:* Marc-Andre Bedard.
*Minister of Transport, Public Works and Supply and Services:* Lucien Lessard.
*Minister Responsible for the Environment:* Marcel Leger.
*Minister Responsible for Youth, Recreation and Sports:* Claude Charron.
*Minister Responsible for Energy:* Guy Joron.
*Minister of Consumers Affairs, Cooperatives and Financial Institutions:* Mme. Lise Payette.
*Minister of Agriculture:* Jean Garon.
*Minister of Social Affairs:* Denis Lazure.
*Minister of Municipal Affairs:* Guy Tardif.
*Minister of Labour and Manpower and Minister of Immigration:* Jacques Couture.
*Minister of Cultural Affairs and Minister of Communications:* Louis O'Neill.
*Minister of Natural Resources and Minister of Lands and Forests:* Yves Berube.
*Minister of Industry and Commerce:* Rodrigue Tremblay.

*Minister of Tourism, Fish and Game:* Yves Duhaime.
*Minister of Civil Service and Vice-President of the Treasury Board:* Denis de Belleval.

**Quebec Court of Appeal**

*Chief Justice:* Lucien Tremblay.

**Quebec Superior Court**

*Chief Justice:* Jules Deschenes.

**State Finance** for the year 1975–76 was: Revenue, $7,917,715,907; Expenditure, $8,791,121,754; and Net debt, $4,023,754,725.

**Production.** In 1976 farm cash receipts were: crops, 122·7 thousands; livestock and products $1,099·2 million; other, 162·4 million. Estimated gross value of mining production on 1976 was $1,533,006,000. Chief minerals are iron ore, copper, asbestos, zinc and gold. In 1976 estimated value of shipments in all manufacturing industries was $25,706,100,000 External trade; Exports, 1976: $6,364,770,129; principal commodities; printing paper; aluminium; iron, copper and other ores and concentrates; highway vehicles; asbestos; aircraft and parts; machinery and equipment; pulp; lumber, etc. Imports, 1976: 8,773,648,917. Total wages and salaries, 1976: $23,914,500,000. Retail trade, 1976: $14,262,884,000.

**Universities.** The Province has seven universities: three Catholic universities, Laval (Quebec) founded in 1852, Montreal University, opened in 1876 as a branch of Laval and erected independently in 1919, and Sherbrooke University granted a charter in 1954; and three Protestant universities, McGill (Montreal) founded in 1821, Bishop's (Lennoxville) founded in 1845, and Sir George Williams University (Montreal) granted a charter in 1948. Since 9 December 1968, there is the University of Quebec, a state-run university. In 1976–77 there were 75,035 full time students registered in the universities of Quebec and 66,037 part time students.

## SASKATCHEWAN

**Capital**—Regina.

**Lieutenant-Governor**—Hon. George Porteous, MBE, CM.

**Area**—251,700 sq. miles.

**Population:** 945,000 (estimate). Cities and population figures are as follows: Regina, 154,100; Saskatoon, 135,200; Moose Jaw, 34,100, Prince Albert, 30,800; Swift Current, 14,800; Yorkton, 15,000; North Battleford, 13,500; Estevan, 9,100; Weyburn, 9,400; Lloydminster, 4,800; Melville, 5,400.

**Admitted to the Dominion:** 1 September 1905.

**Legislature: (July 1977). Representation of the Parties:** NDP (New Democratic Party) 39; Liberal n.a.; Progressive Conservative n.a.

**Ministry** (as at 2 August 1977).

*Premier and President of the Executive Council:* Hon. A. E. Blakeney.
*Department of the Attorney General:* Hon. R. J. Romanow.
*Department of Mineral Resources:* Hon. J. R. Messer.
*Department of Finance:* Hon. W. E. Smishek.
*Department of Labour:* Hon. G. T. Snyder.
*Department of Northern Saskatchewan:* Hon. G. R. Bowerman.
*Department of the Environment:* Hon. N. E. Byers.
*Department of Telephones:* Hon. N. E. Byers.
*Department of Municipal Affairs:* Hon. G. MacMurchy.
*Department of Highways and Transportation:* Hon. E. Kramer.
*Provincial Secretary:* Hon. E. Cowley.
*Department of Health:* Hon. E. Tchorzewski.
*Minister of Revenue:* Hon. W. A. Robbins.
*Department of Co-operation and Co-operative Development:* Hon. W. A. Robbins.
*Department of Consumer Affairs:* Hon. E. C. Whelan.
*Department of Agriculture:* Hon. E. E. Kaeding.
*Department of Tourism and Renewable Resources:* Hon. A. Matsalla.
*Department of Social Services:* Hon. H. H. Rolfes.
*Department of Culture and Youth:* Hon. E. B. Shillington.
*Department of Government Services:* Hon. E. B. Shillington.
*Department of Education:* Hon. D. L. Faris.
*Department of Continuing Education:* Hon. D. L. Faris.
*Department of Industry and Commerce:* Hon. N. Vickar.
*Speaker of the Legislative Assembly:* Hon. J. E. Brockelbank.

**Saskatchewan Court of Appeal**

*Chief Justice:* Edward M. Culliton.

**Saskatchewan Court of Queen's Bench**

*Chief Justice:* F. W. Johnson.

**Provincial Finance**

| For fiscal year 1976–77 | |
|---|---|
| Budgetary Cash Inflow | $1,330,236,000 |
| Budgetary Cash Outflow | $1,328,235,000 |

**Production.** The estimated total net value of commodity production for 1976 was $4,080 million.
The average estimated wheat crop harvested in 1976 amounted to 36·5 bushels per acre. The following table gives the agricultural production figures for 1976.

| | *Production (tons)* | *Acreage* |
|---|---|---|
| Wheat | 548,000,000 | 17,400,000 |
| Oats | 103,000,000 | 1,850,000 |
| Barley | 135,000,000 | 3,500,000 |
| Rye | 9,300,000 | 350,000 |
| Rape Seed | 19,400,000 | 850,000 |
| Flax | 3,800,000 | 225,000 |

The livestock figures as at July 1976 were as follows: Cattle, 2,910,000; Swine, 523,000; Sheep, 99,000. Poultry (Placements) estimated, Chickens, 8 m; Turkeys, 950,000.
The value of mineral production in 1976 was Petroleum, $443·7 million; Natural gas, $10·6 million; Coal, $15·2 million; Gold, $2·1 million; Silver, $1·4 million; Copper, $14·5 million; Zinc, $6·4 million; Potash, $358·5 million; Salt, $3·5 million; Uranium, $44·8 million.

**University.** University of Saskatchewan at Saskatoon (founded 1907). Number of students for the year 1976–77, approximately 11,600 University of Regina, 1976–77, approximately, 6,600.

# YUKON TERRITORY

**Seat of Government**—Whitehorse.

**Area**—207,076 sq. miles, including 1,730 sq. miles of fresh water.

**Population**—21,392 (Preliminary, 1 June, 1976).

**Government.** The Yukon was made a distinct territory in 1898 and its constitution is now defined in the Yukon Act. The Yukon Act provides for a Chief Executive, styled Commissioner, who is appointed by the Federal Government, and an Elected Territorial Council of members having a four-year tenure of office. The legislative powers of the Yukon Territorial Council are generally the same as those of a provincial legislature with certain exceptions. A six-member Executive Committee is responsible for the co-ordination of government activities and advises the Commissioner in carrying out his duties as defined in the Yukon Act. The executive Committee includes the Commissioner, an Assistant Commissioner (Executive) appointed by the federal government, an Assistant Commissioner (Administrative) appointed by the Commissioner, and three members of the Territorial Council who are appointed by the Territorial Council. These elected members of the Executive Committee are Dan Lang (responsible for Education and Yukon housing), Flo Whyard (responsible for Health, Welfare and Rehabilitation) and Ken McKinnon (responsible for Local Government). The Territory is represented in the Federal House of Commons by one member (E. Nielsen, Progressive Conservative).

**Commissioner:** Arthur M. Pearson.

**Finance.** Total expenditure for the year ending 31 March 1976 was $71,718,216.

**Production.** Mining is the chief industry. Value of mineral production for 1975 was $220,928,000. Production figures for 1975 were:

| *Metals* | *Quantity* | *Dollar Value* |
|---|---|---|
| Copper | 24,021,000 lbs | 14,413,000 |
| Gold | 21,100 ozs | 2,849,000 |
| Lead | 197,475,000 lbs | 39,495,000 |
| Silver | 6,172,000 ozs | 28,445,000 |
| Zinc | 268,012,000 lbs | 93,804,000 |
| *Non-metals* | | |
| Asbestos | 118,500 tons | 41,475,000 |
| Coal | 23,400 tons | 421,000 |

It is estimated that 340,108 tourists visited Yukon in 1975, a 4·5 per cent increase over the previous year. The tourists spent approximately $27,338,000.

**Communications.** There are 58·1 miles of railway line in the Yukon. The Yukon River, 1,979 miles long, is navigable for small boats for 1,777 miles. An all-weather gravelled highway (the Alaska Highway) is 1,221 miles from Dawson Creek, B.C. to Yukon–Alaska border—593 miles of this road are in the Yukon.

**Education.** For the 1975–76 school year, there were 23 schools in Yukon and a total of 5,315 kindergarten—Grade 12 students. In addition to the courses given in the Yukon Vocational and Technical Centre, Yukon offers a limited number of post-secondary courses through the University of Alberta. The government provides assistance to students requiring further education elsewhere.

# NORTHWEST TERRITORIES

**Capital**—Yellowknife.

**Area**—The Northwest Territories comprise (1) all that part of Canada North of the 60th parallel of north latitu, deexcept the portions thereof within the Yukon Territory and the Provinces of Quebec and Newfoundland; and (2) the islands in Hudson Bay, James Bay and Ungava Bay, except those islands within the Provinces of Manitoba, Ontario and Quebec.

**Population**—37,800 (including, 7,180 Indians and 13,354 nuit). (The term 'Inuit' is a generic word for 'Eskimo'.)

**Government.** The Northwest Territories Act provides for the appointment of a Commissioner to administer the government of the Territories under instructions from time to time by the Governor in Council or the Minister of Indian and Northern Affairs.

The Act, as amended in 1974, also provides for a Council of 15 members, elected to represent such electoral districts in the Territories as are named and described by the Commissioner in Council.

With the movement of the territorial government to Yellowknife in September 1967, the Territorial Administration assumed responsibility for most provincial type services, including Education and Public Works. The Northern National Resources and Environment Branch will continue to be responsible for natural resources.

**Mineral Products.**

The following table shows the preliminary figures for value and quantity of minerals for 1975:

*continued*

| | *Quantity* | *Value Canadian $s* |
|---|---|---|
| Gold | 186,000 oz. | 30,752,000 |
| Silver | 2,174,000 oz. | 9,821,000 |
| Copper | 551,000 lbs. | 351,000 |
| Lead | 151,555,000 lbs. | 30,841,000 |
| Zinc | 293,392,000 lbs. | 110,022,000 |
| Total value | | 181,787,000 |

**Forest Products.**

The following table shows the quantity and value of Forest Products for 1975–76:

| | *Quantity* | *Value Canadian $s* |
|---|---|---|
| Lumber (board feet) | 7,195,000 | 1,295,100 |
| Cordwood (cords) | 2,000 | 55,000 |
| Round Timber (linear feet) | 197,346 | 35,522 |
| Total value | | 1,385,622 |

**Territorial Council**

***Commissioner:*** Stuart M. Hodgson.

***Deputy Commissioner:*** John H. Parker.

***Members of the Council:***

David H. Searle Q.C. (Yellowknife South), Speaker of the Council; Donald M. Stewart (Hay River), Deputy Speaker; Arnold McCallum (Slave River); Peter Fraser (MacKenzie Great Bear); Ipeelee Kilabuk (Central Baffin); William A. Lafferty (MacKenzie Liard); William Lyall (Central Arctic); Thomas H. Butters (Inuvik); Peter Ernerk (Keewatin); Dave Nickerson (Yellowknife North); Bryan R. Pearson (South Baffin); Ludy Pudluk (High Arctic); John Steen (Western Arctic); Richard Whitford (Great Slave Lake).

# Cape Verde Islands

(ILHAS DE CABO VERDE)

**Capital**—Praia.

The Cape Verde Islands became independent on 5 July 1975.

## AREA AND POPULATION

THE Islands of Cape Verde lie about 400 miles off the west coast of Africa opposite Cape Verde, near Dakar (Senegal Republic). They consist of 10 main islands and some islets. The islands are divided into two groups, those lying to the north are called Barlavento (windward) and those to the south are called Sotavento (leeward).

There are six islands in the first group: Santo Antão, São Vicente, Santa Luzia, São Nicolau, Boa Vista and Sal. The four in the southern group are São Tiago (Santiago), Fogo, Brava and Maio.

The capital Praia, is situated at the south end of São Tiago. The islands cover an area of 4,033 sq. km. and had a population of 201,549 at census of December 1960.

There are 12 *concelhos* (councils or boroughs) with two courts of justice and ten municipal courts, under the judicial district of Lisbon.

The population at mid-1974 was 290,000. The annual average percentage growth rate of the population for the period 1960–74 was 2·9, and for the period 1965–74 was 3·1.

## CURRENCY AND FINANCE

The currency is Portuguese.

The GNP at market prices for 1974 was U.S. $ millions 14 and the GNP per capita at market prices was U.S. $470. The annual average percentage growth rate of the GNP per capita for the period, 1960–74 was 4·7 and for the period 1965–74 was also 4·7.

## PRODUCTION, INDUSTRY AND COMMERCE

The chief products are salt, coffee, hides, tunny, bananas, physic-nuts and pozzolana.

In 1970 there were 2,236 asses; 3,512 pigs; 4,207 cattle; 8,072 goats.

The main commodity of both import and export, forming about three-quarters of the total, is oil, as the Island of São Vicente is the fuelling station for vessels going to South America.

The following list shows the principal exports for 1970 (in thousand escudos):

| *Commodity* | 1970 |
|---|---|
| Live animals; animal products | 10,254 |
| Vegetable products | 11,774 |
| Food, beverages, tobacco | 15,250 |
| Mineral products | 3,491 |
| Transport equipment | 1,348 |
| Miscellaneous | 78 |

The following list shows the principal imports for 1970:

| *Commodity* | 1970 |
|---|---|
| Live animals and animal products | 10,005 |
| Vegetables | 92,292 |
| Oils and fats | 16,147 |
| Food, beverages, tobacco | 60,534 |
| Mineral products | 34,500 |
| Chemicals | 23,338 |
| Synthetics | 5,454 |
| Leather | 1,509 |
| Wood and wood products | 8,254 |
| Paper products | 6,016 |
| Textiles | 40,661 |
| Misc. wearing apparel | 8,214 |
| Non-metallic mineral products | 11,027 |
| Metal and metal products | 20,400 |
| Machinery | 66,204 |
| Transport equipment | 23,483 |
| Miscellaneous | 6,161 |

Imports and exports for 1970 by principal country are shown below (in thousand escudos):

| *Country* | 1970 *Imports* | 1970 *Exports* |
|---|---|---|
| Portugal, metropolitan | 269,889 | 33,049 |
| Overseas provinces | | |
| Port Guinea | 2,350 | 1,727 |
| Angola | 77,441 | 467 |
| Mozambique | 5,105 | N.A. |
| West Germany | 4,685 | 15 |
| Netherlands | 12,908 | 1 |
| Italy | 1,627 | 1 |
| United Kingdom | 14,921 | 526 |
| Congo (Leopoldville) | N.A. | 841 |
| United States | 15,425 | 6,093 |
| Canada | 3,470 | N.A. |

## COMMUNICATIONS

There are three airports on the island of Sal, S. Vicente and Santiago.

The telegraph system extends 524 km. There are 29 telegraph stations and two wireless stations. Telephone lines are 379 km. in length.

# Central African Empire

(MEMBER OF THE FRENCH COMMUNITY)

**Capital**—Bangui.

**Emperor**—General Jean Bedel Bokassa.

**National Flag:** On a field divided by a crimson upright, and parti of four fesse-wise, blue, white, green, yellow. star five-pointed yellow at the upper hoist.

### CONSTITUTION AND GOVERNMENT

ON 13 August 1960 the independence of the Central African Republic (as it was then called), was proclaimed by the Prime Minister, M. David Dacko. The attachment of the Republic to the French Community was stressed. On 20 September the Empire was admitted to the U.N.

An army coup overthrew the government of President Dacko and Colonel Bedel Bokassa assumed power as chief of state.

### AREA AND POPULATION

The Republic has an area of 617,000 sq. km.

The population of the Central African Empire in mid-1974 was 1,748,000. The annual average percentage growth rate of the population for the period 1960–74 was 2·2, and for the period 1965–74 was 2·2. Bangui, the capital, has 82,000 inhabitants.

### FINANCE

The 1971 budget was balanced at 12,538 million frances CFA. The GNP at market prices for 1974 was U.S.$ millions 370 and the GNP per capita at market prices for 1974 was U.S. $210. The annual average percentage growth rate of the GNP per capita for the period 1960–74 was 0·4 and for the period 1965–74 was 0·8. [*See the note at the beginning of this section concerning GNP.*]

### PRODUCTION AND COMMERCE

The resources of the Empire are mainly agricultural. Mist important crops are cotton, millet and sorghum, maize, groundnuts and coffee. Diamonds represent the chief mineral wealth. The deposits are of an alluvial type.

The production figures (in metric tons) for 1971 for some agricultural products are: Cotton, 54,000; Maize, 48,000; Coffee, 12,359.

# Chad (Tchad)

**Capital**—Ndjaména.

**President**—Félix Malloun.

**National Flag:** A tricolour pale-wise, blue, yellow, red.

### CONSTITUTION AND GOVERNMENT

ON 10 August 1960 Chad proclaimed its independence within the French Community in accordance with agreements signed with France in July. The following day M. François Tombalaye was elected President by the National Assembly. President Tombalaye was killed in the military uprising of April 1975. In 1975 President Malloun took office. The Republic was admitted to the U.N. on 20 September 1960.

### AREA AND POPULATION

Chad has an area of 1,284,000 sq. km. and is situated in what was previously known as French Equatorial Africa with a population at mid-1974 of 3,952,000. The annual average percentage growth rate of the population for the period 1960–74 was 1·4 and for the period 1965–74 was 2·0 Ndjaména, the capital, has 300,000 inhabitants.

### FINANCE

The budget for 1973 showed expenditure: 17,018,051,000 francs CFA; Receipts: 17,018,051,000 francs CFA.

The GNP at market prices for 1974 was U.S.$ millions 410 and the GNP per capita at market prices for 1974 was U.S. $100. The annual average percentage growth rate of the GNP per capita for the period 1960–74 was −1·2 and for the period 1965–74 was −1·5. [*See the note at the beginning of this section concerning GNP.*]

### PRODUCTION AND COMMERCE

The economy is based mainly on agriculture, including the breeding of cattle. Livestock is the first truly national resouce. Chad has 4,500,000 cattle, and 4,000,000 sheep and goats. Cotton is the main export crop. The record production figure is that of 1969, with 47,000 tonnes of fibre cotton. In 1971 the total value of imports was 17,220 million francs CFA, exports were 7,787 million francs CFA.

# Chile

## (REPÚBLICA DE CHILE)

**Capital**—Santiago.

**President**—General Augusto Pinochet.

**National Flag: Divided fesse-wise white and red; a canton blue charged with a star five-pointed white.**

**Government Junta**

General Augusto Pinochet.
Admiral José Toribio Merino.
Air Marshal Gustavo Leigh.
General (Carabineros) César Mendoza.

**Cabinet**

*Minister of Finance:* Señor Sergio De Castro.
*Minister of Economy:* Señor Pablo Barahona.
*Minister of Justice:* Srta. Mónica Madariaga.
*Minister of Labour:* Señor Sergio Fernández.
*Minister of Health:* Air Brigade General Fernando Matthei Aubel.
*Minister of Defence:* General Herman Brady.
*Minister of Land:* General of Carabineers Lautaro Recabarren.
*Minister of Transport:* General Raúl Vargas M.
*Minister of Mines and Energy:* Señor Enrique Valenzuela B.

### AREA AND POPULATION

The areas and population of the various provinces in 1970 are given below:

| *Province* | *Area (sq. kilometres)* | *Population* |
|---|---|---|
| Tarapacá | 58,073 | 161,906 |
| Antofagasta | 125,306 | 288,604 |
| Atacama | 78,266 | 155,854 |
| Coquimbo | 38,847 | 414,297 |
| Aconcagua | 9,874 | 188,308 |
| Valparaíso | 5,118 | 828,270 |
| Santiago | 17,686 | 3,266,149 |
| O'Higgins | 7,106 | 348,037 |
| Colchagua | 8,327 | 212,448 |
| Curicó | 5,266 | 141,824 |
| Talca | 10,141 | 276,382 |
| Maule | 5,697 | 106,882 |
| Linares | 9,414 | 229,545 |
| Nuble | 13,951 | 382,878 |
| Concepción | 5,681 | 722,863 |
| Arauco | 5,240 | 119,931 |
| Bio Bio | 11,135 | 226,242 |
| Malleco | 14,095 | 233,435 |
| Cautín | 18,377 | 520,012 |
| Valdivia | 18,472 | 348,129 |
| Osorno | 9,263 | 193,078 |
| Llanquigüe | 18,205 | 224,438 |
| Chiloé | 27,014 | 132,935 |
| Aisén | 103,584 | 50,656 |
| Magallanes | 116,759 | 98,391 |

The principal towns with their populations, according to official estimates for 1970, are: Santiago 2,555,887; Valparaíso (including Viña del Mar) 493,565; Concepción 198,425; Valdivia 82,188; Temuco 100,677; Talca 91,318, Osorno 74,090; Chillán 87,250; Antofagasta 117,733; Los Angeles 47,585; Punta Arenas 66,335.

**Vital Statistics** (per 1,000 of population):

| | 1971 |
|---|---|
| Marriages | 8·6 |
| Births | 27·6 |
| Deaths | 8·4 |

The population at mid- 1974 was 10,408,000. The annual average percentage growth rate of the population for the period 1960–74 was 2·2 and for the period 1965–74 was 1·9.

The great majority of the population is of mixed Spanish and 'Indian' origin. The remaining element of the Araucanian race (one of the original 'Indian' tribes), known as 'Mapuches', now number only about 65,000 and are mostly centred round the southern town of Temuco. The British community in Chile numbers about 10,000.

### CURRENCY

From 29 September, 1975 the currency unit is the Peso, which replaced the Escudo (1 Peso = 1·000 Escudos). The parity of the Peso with foreign countries is fixed by the Banco Central and is altered periodically in order to maintain a realistic relationship between the escudo and foreign currencies. In October 1975, the rate of exchange was 6·7 pesos per dollar.

### FINANCE

Current revenue in 1974 was Eq 2,660,406 million; of this total, Eq 1,699,361 million came from taxation, 257,309 from other current sources and 703,737 were capital revenues. Current expenditure in 1974 (January–November) totalled Eq 1,357,019 million and capital expenditure 663,359 million.

The GNP at market prices for 1974 was U.S.$ millions, 8,680, and the GNP per capita at market prices was U.S.$830. The annual average percentage growth rate of the GNP per capita for the period 1960–74 was 1·7, and for the period 1965–74 was 1·3. [*See the note at the beginning of this section concerning GNP.*]

### PRINCIPAL BANKS

**Banco Central de Chile.** Est. 1925; sole Bank of Issue for Chile; Balance Sheet at 30 June 1971 showed assets E°.19,527·3 million; deposits on current accounts E°.13,207·3 million; gold reserves E°.572·4 million; banknotes and coins in circulation E°.7,705·4 million. *Head Office:* Augustinas 1180, Santiago. 14 Branches.

**Banco de Chile.** Est. 1894; Balance Sheet at 31 December 1976 showed capital and other reserves over $1,971,582,454. *Head Office:* Santiago. 52 Branches and Agencies.

**Banco del Estado de Chile.** Est. 1953. Balance Sheet at 30 June 1973 showed capital and other reserves of E°. 2,292,131,001·60. *Head Office:* Alameda B. O'Higgins 1111, Santiago. 171 Branches.

**Banco Osorno y la Union.** Balance Sheet at 31 December 1963 showed assets E°.498,010,932·6; capital and reserves E°.30,341,872·76. *Head Office:* Osorno. 7 Branches.

**Banco Español—Chile.** Chief Executive Officer, Miguel Otero Lathrop. Capital and reserves, 30 June 1976, U.S.$19,071,773. *Head Office:* Santiago.

**Banco Sudamericano.** Est. 1944; capital and reserves, 30 June 1967, E°.33·9 million. *Head Office:* Santiago.

**Banco de Credito e Inversiones.** Condensed Balance Sheet as of 31 December, 1975:

| *Assets* | | |
|---|---|---|
| Cash and Due from Banks | US $ | 22,732,763 |
| Loans | | 7,310,681 |
| Customer' Acceptances | | 24,255,746 |
| Investments | | 5,500,261 |
| Bank Premises | | 19,244,176 |
| Other Fixed Assets | | 2,311,736 |
| Other Assets | | 26,666,717 |
| Total | US $ | 108,022,084 |

| *Liabilities* | | |
|---|---|---|
| Demand Deposits | US $ | 26,438,742 |
| Time Deposits | | 4,496,180 |
| Guarantees and Acceptances | | 22,246,910 |
| Liabilities with Correspondents | | 7,220,081 |
| Other Liabilities | | 21,395,766 |
| Capital and Reserves | | 26,224,405 |
| Total | US $ | 108,022,084 |

*Head Office:* Huerfanos 1134, Santiago de Chile. *Cable Address:* "Bancredito", Santiago de Chile. *Postal Address:* Casilla 136 D, Santiago de Chile. *Telex:* 40477 CREBC CL or BANCRED SGO 373 or 3520012 BANCRED. *Telephone:* 713132, Santiago de Chile.

## PRODUCTION, INDUSTRY AND COMMERCE

**Agriculture.** Agricultural activity is carried on mainly in the centre of the country. Here both the soil and the climate are more favourable. The extreme north is mostly desert and in the far south it is extremely wet and cold. Magallanes, however, lends itself to sheep-breeding and Yugoslavian and British subjects have played an important part in this activity.

The most important crops are: wheat, maize, potatoes, oats, barley, beans, beet, rape and rice. In the richer areas of the centre, vines and fruit are of great importance; peaches, apples and pears are produced as well as cantaloupe and water melons, plums, nuts, apricots and dessert grapes. Chile exports wines and fruit.

The climate and land of the Magallanes region are particularly suited to the raising of sheep. Wool and frozen lamb provide substantial sources of foreign exchange. Many of the sheep farmers are British subjects. Throughout the country there are nearly 6·7 million sheep, and cattle number some 2·8 million. Chile is not self-supporting for beef and Argentina has to supply a proportion of Chile's needs.

Fruit growing has been largely developed in the region north and south of Valparaiso and near Valdivia in the south. Grapes, peaches, plums, melons, apples and pears are exported to the United States and other countries. The land is particularly suited to the growing of grapes, and the wine produced is reputed to be the best in South America. The wine industry employs 300,000 workers and produces approximately 100 million gallons per year. Dried fruits of excellent quality are prepared and about a half of the produce is exported.

The value of fruit exports for the year 1976 was approximately U.S. $38·0 million.

**Forestry.** Chile has about 5 million hectares of workable forests, located predominantly in the southern area. Apart from the timber, cellulose and paper industries have been developed, both of which export part of their production. In 1975 the value of these exports amounted to 84 million dollars. In the same period of the previous year, the figure was eight million dollars.

Chile also exports timber. The figures for the period mentioned in the years 1973 and 1974 in respect of products exported are 1·4 and 2·1 million dollars respectively.

**Fishing.** The edible varieties of sea fish off the whole length of the Chilean coast are many and excellent. There are three whaling stations which process annually some 3,000 carcases, and also numerous fish and shellfish preserving industries. Chile exports seafood, the value thereof for the first four months of 1973 being 0·8 million dollars. For the same months of 1974, the figure was 1·2 million.

**Mining.** Chile is the principal mineworking country of South America and one of the world's largest copper producers. The most important copper mines belong to the State. Chile also produces iron, coal, nitrate of soda, lead, sulphur, molybdenum, salt and oil.

The following table shows the amount of minerals mined for *two* periods in 1973 and 1974.

| *Mineral Products Mined* | *January–May* 1973 | *January–May* 1974 |
|---|---|---|
| Copper (tons) | 226,760 | 305,838 |
| Iron (long tons) | 3,796·3 | 4,114·4 |
| Coal (tons) | 527,105 | 592,096 |
| Nitrate of soda (tons) | 284,980 | 299,394 |

**Industry.** Chilean industry represents approximately 25 per cent of the Gross National Product, its annual growth rate being of the order of seven per cent. Between January and April 1974 industrial exports were 58·9 million dollars. Chile possesses iron and steel, oil and petrochemical fertilizers and every kind of article for the home.

## COMMUNICATIONS

**Railways.** The total length of railway line in Chile amounts to 8,415 km., of which 1,921 are privately owned. The Chilean State Railway system runs from Iquique in the north to Puerto Montt in the south. The sections from Valparaiso to Santiago and from Santiago to Chillán and Concepción have been electrified. This is the first stage of a gradual electrification programme for the whole southern main line to Puerto Montt. The Transandine Railway connects Santiago with Buenos Aires and there are lines from Arica—La Paz (Bolivia), Antofagasta-La Paz, Antofagasta-Salta (Argentina). The Chilean section of the last-named line is operated by the British-owned Antofagasta (Chile) and Bolivia Railway.

**Shipping.** A number of shipping companies run regular services from Chile to European and United States ports via the Panama Canal and Magallanes Straits. Chilean and Argentine lines connect Valparaiso with Rio de Janeiro and Buenos Aires via Magallanes Straits.

**Compañía Sud Americana de Vapores.** Services operated: west coast of South America, U.S.A., North European ports. *Head Office:* Valparaiso Blanco 895 P.B.O. 49-V; (Chile) and Agustinas 1235 P.B.O. 3207, Santiago de Chile.

**Compañía Chilena de Navegación Interoceanica.** *Services operated* (a) Monthly sailing from Chile to River Plate and Brazil via Magellan Straits and return; (b) Monthly sailing from Chile and Peru to Japan, S. Korea, Taiwan, the Philippines and North Pacific.

**Civil Aviation.** Chile is covered by a number of commercial airlines, domestic and foreign. The principal Chilean line is LAN—**Linea Aérea Nacional.** *Head Office:* Los Cerrillos Airport, Santiago. Agencies throughout Chile and in Argentina, Uruguay, Peru, Panama and the U.S.A. In 1974 the passenger-kilometre figure was 1·159 million, and the ton-kilometre figure was 51·2 million.

There is a fleet consisting 4 Boeing 707-320's, 5 Boeing 727-100's, 2 CVL 6-R and 9 Hawker Siddeley 748s.

## NEWSPAPERS

**El Mercurio.** Morning. Right Independent. Circulation 110,000–125,000, Sunday 210,000.

**La Nación.** Morning. Santiago. Government owned. Circulation 70,000.

**La Tercera de la Hora.** Santiago. Morning tabloid. Independent Radical. Circulation 75,000.

**El Mercurio.** Valparaiso. Morning. F. 1827. Independent. Circulation 55,000.

**La Unión.** Morning. Valparaiso. Conservative. Circulation 35,000.

**Clarin.** Santiago. Independent.

**Las Ultimas Noticias.** Midday. Independent. Santiago. Circulation 85,000.

There are 20 other newspapers of importance and a number of smaller papers.

## ATOMIC ENERGY

An Atomic Energy Committee (as a first step towards a Commission) has been set up. The University of Chile has a nuclear physics laboratory. Chile has signed with the United States an Atoms for Peace Agreement (August 1955) and a Co-operative Uranium Exploration Agreement (April 1956).

The University of Chile provides courses in radiochemistry in various faculties. An experimental nuclear reactor has been installed at the Nuclear Investigation Centre.

## EDUCATION AND RELIGION

The education given by the State is free. Basic education is compulsory (eight years). An 1973 the total number on the register was 2,314,283. Of this figure, 471,673 registrations were in respest of private educational establishments and the remainder for State schools.

There is no state religion, but the greater part of the inhabitants are Roman Catholic.

# China

## People's Republic of China

### (ZHONGHUA RENMIN GONGHEGUO)

**Capital**—Peking.

**Head of State**: In 1975 the post of head of state was abolished. Until his death in 1976, some of the duties normally undertaken by a head of state were performed by Chu Teh, Chairman of the National People's Congress.

**National Flag**: Red, charged at the upper hoist with a star of five-points gold, representing the Chinese Communist Party; round it in the fly side in an arc are four smaller similar stars representing the four class alliance of the 'New Democratic Period'.

#### CONSTITUTION AND GOVERNMENT

THE formal announcement of the creation of the Chinese People's Republic occurred on 1 October 1949 (National Day). A Chinese People's Political Consultative Conference (CPPCC) acted as a constituent assembly and adopted the Common Programme of the CPPCC, the organic law of the CPPCC and the organic law of the Central People's Government of the Chinese People's Republic.

In this, a 'New Democratic Period', the state organs were to serve a four class bloc (workers, peasants, petty bourgeoisie and 'national capitalists') in which the workers were to play the leading role. Emphasis was placed upon friendship with the Soviet Union, land reform, the abolition of 'imperialist privileges', the suppression of counter revolutionaries, industrialization upon Soviet lines and support for the North Korean war effort.

The most important governmental organ was the Central Peoples Government Council which was simultaneously a legislative, executive and judicial organ. The most important subordinate organ was the Government Administration Council controlling all economic and other ministries and headed by a Premier and five deputy premiers. All ministries were responsible to four committees of the GAC; those of political and legal affairs, finance and economics, culture and education and people's control. All heads of committees and ministers were appointed by the CPGC. Mao Tse-tung was Chairman of the CPPCC and its standing committee as well as the CPGC. Chou En-lai was appointed Premier of the GAC. The country was divided into six large administrative regions with a considerable degree of local autonomy.

In 1954 a National People's Congress was elected by universal suffrage and The Common Programme replaced by a constitution based on the Soviet Constitution of 1936. This held that the country was in a transitional stage in its progress towards a socialist society. The six administrative regions were abolished and the CPPCC became a purely advisory organ.

According to the 1954 constitution, the National People's Congress elected Mao Tse-tung as Chairman of the People's Republic. In this post, Mao was constitutionally commander of the armed forces and Chairman of the National Defence Council. He might, when necessary, convene supreme state conferences that included the People's Republic Vice-Chairmen, the Chairman of the Standing Committee of the National People's Congress and the Premier of the State Council.

The National People's Congress was elected for a term of four years and met normally once a year prior to the Cultural Revolution. A Second NPC took office in 1959 which replaced Mao Tse-tung as Chairman by Liu Shao-ch'i and a third took office in 1965, which reconfirmed Liu's position. The standing committee of the National People's Congress, headed first by Liu Shao-ch'i and later by Chu Teh, appears to have enjoyed limited power in initiating policy.

The State Council was formed, according to the constitution of 1954, to replace the GAC and was headed until 1976 by Premier Chou En-lai. It is the leading executive body in the government and, in addition to the Premier, consists of a number of vice-premiers and the heads of all ministries and commissions. Provision was made for a secretariat (inner cabinet) to carry out the day to day work of the government.

In 1957 local Party Committees achieved a degree of decision-making power far greater than they had during the early 1950s. Radicalization in this period led to a general move away from the Soviet type structure and placed stress on small self-sufficient organic communities at local level (people's communes) which were to be organs of government, education, defence (militia) and production. The huge centralized ministerial hierarchies were simplified and formal control structures abolished.

The three years of natural calamities (1959–61), together with internal opposition, brought the 'Great Leap Forward' (1958–59) to an end and there was a partial recentralization of administration. Large administrative regions were brought back in a limited form as Party structures. A change in the nature of Party organs which allowed them to become associated with bureaucratic rather than political goals led to a crisis within the Communist party. This was one of the major reasons why Mao Tse-tung launched the Cultural Revolution of 1966–69, which sought to completely reorganize the structure of both Party and government.

Red Guards and Red Rebels were urged to seize power from 'people in authority walking the capitalist road.' The aim in 1967–68 was to form revolutionary committees at all levels of administration consisting of representatives of the old leadership, new rebel organizations and the People's Liberation Army. Some of these were formed quite smoothly, others required military intervention. Revolutionary committees modelled on this pattern exist now at almost all levels below that of province, though both the "rebel" and military components have declined in power.

In 1968, Liu Shao-ch'i, the Chairman of the People's Republic, was stripped of all posts and, in the period which followed, it is claimed that Lin Piao, Minister of Defence and Vice-Chairman of the Party sought to replace him. Following an attempted coup in 1971, Lin Piao died en route for the Soviet Union and the restructuring of Party and state administration, begun in 1969, was carried through to completion. During recent years, organizations dismantled during the Cultural Revolution such as the Communist Youth League and the labour unions, have been revived. Many senior officials who disappeared from their posts in the Cultural Revolution, have returned to their old or similar posts.

The completion of the post Cultural Revolution reforms was signalled by the convocation of a Fourth National Peoples Congress in 1975. The Congress approved a new constitution replacing that of 1954. It abolished the post of Chairman of the People's Republic and, for the first time, explicitly specified the role of the Communist Party in the state structure. The new NPC Standing Committee consisted of a Chairman (Chu Teh, until his death in 1976) and 22 Vice-Chairmen and the new State Council consisted of a Premier (Chou En-lai and later Hua Kuo-feng), 12 Vice-Premiers and 29 ministries or commissions (as opposed to 48 prior to the Cultural Revolution).

It would appear, however, that the general regularization of administration in the early 1970s was resisted by a number of senior members of the leadership. After initiating a number of political campaigns (1973–76), senior members were removed from office, following the death of Mao in September 1976 and subjected to severe criticism.

**The Chinese Communist Party.** The Chinese Communist Party (CCP) was founded in July 1921 in Shanghai. After a period of collaboration with the Kuomintang (Nationalist Party) 1923–27, a split occurred which developed into civil war. The Chinese Soviet Republic was proclaimed in 1931 and defeated in 1934. Following this the Red Army embarked on the Long March to Yenan. In January 1935 at the Tsunyi Conference Mao Tse-tung became Chairman of the Party, and this post he held until his death in 1976. During the Sino-Japanese War the CCP maintained an independent regime in Yenan which was the centre of a network of loosely federated 'liberated areas'. An uneasy truce with the Kuomintang was in effect 1936–41. In 1946 civil war was resumed, ending with the ultimate victory of the CCP. Since 1921, the Party has held ten national congresses, the last being in 1973 when membership was stated to be 28 million. The leadership of the party is as follows:

*Chairman:* Hua Kuo-feng.

*Vice-Chairmen:* Yeh Chien-ying, Teng Hsiao-p'ing.

*Politburo:* Wei Kuo-ch'ing, Yeh Chien-ying, Liu Po-ch'eng, Hsü Shih-yu, Hua kuo-feng, Chi Teng-k'uei, Wu Te, Wang

Tung-hsing, Ch'en Yung-kuei, Ch'en Hsi-lien, Li Hsien-nien, Li Te-Sheng, Teng Hsiao-p'ing.

*Alternate Members of the Politburo:* Wu Kuei-hsien, Su Chen-hua Ni Chih-fu, Saifudin.

*Full Members of the Central Committee* (1973): 195 members.

*Alternate Members of the Central Committee* (1973): 124 members.

## LEGAL SYSTEM

The Supreme Peoples Court is the highest judicial body in the country. Below the Supreme Court is a network of courts extending down to urban ward (*qu*) level.

According to the 1954 constitution, a Supreme People's Procuratorate was set up to ensure the strict observance of the law by all government institutions, officials, and citizens in the country, to investigate, prosecute and sustain the prosecution of criminal cases, to ensure that the activities of control departments conformed to the law and that the execution of judgements in criminal cases and the activities of departments in charge of reform through labour also conformed to the law. The old procuratorial organs exercised independent power, without the interference of local organs of state and were responsible only to higher levels of the Procuratorate. Under the 1975 constitution, the "functions and powers of procuratorial organs are exercised by the organs of public security at various levels". This change reflects the ever increasing stress on informal control through the Party.

There has been a steady decline in the importance of formal legal machinery and minor disputes are usually settled outside the courts usually by local Party committees. There is no clear-cut distinction between the Party and the Judiciary.

## THE PEOPLES LIBERATION ARMY

Estimates of current strength of the PLA vary between 2,800,000 and 3,500,000. It consists of: Main forces: 121 infantry divisions, ten armoured divisions, three cavalry divisions, four airborne divisions, 40 artillery (including AA) divisions, 41 railway and construction engineer divisions. Local forces: 65 infantry divisions and 110 independent regiments. The air force comprises some 4,250 combat aircraft of which the majority are fighters—modified MIG 17s, 19s and 21s (as well as a new Chinese designed Mach fighter, the F-9.) Recently great attention has been focussed on building up a missile capability. MRBMs with a range of 600–700 miles are in operation but may be replaced by IRBMs, also operational, with a range of 1,500–1,750 miles. A multi-stage ICBM with a range of 3,000–3,500 miles has been developed and some may have been deployed but full scale testing has not yet been carried out. So far China has conducted 18 nuclear tests. The navy is divided into three fleets, the North Sea Fleet, the East Sea Fleet and the South Sea Fleet and consists of eight destroyers, ten destroyer escorts, 15 patrol escorts, one submarine (G class with ballistic missile tubes), 55 other submarines, 30 submarine chasers, 100 missile patrol boats, 30 minesweepers, 220 MTBs and hydrofoils, 320 motor gunboats, 482 other craft. The greater part of the PLA is deployed along the frontier as a deterrent against possible attack. China is currently faced by 45 Soviet regular divisions along the Soviet frontier.

The PLA has always performed an important subsidiary role in production, administration, education and propaganda. A modern technical army on Soviet lines was built up during and following the Korean War (1951–59), but following the dismissal of Defence Minister P'eng Teh-huai in 1959, Lin Piao was entrusted with the task of reforming military structure and training more along the lines advocated by Mao during the Civil War than along the modern Soviet lines. This ensured the loyalty of the Army to Mao during the Cultural Revolution (with very few exceptions). The PLA became for a time a substitute Party following dismantling of Party structures in 1967. In recent years the Army has played an important role in economic as well as political work. At the time of the Ninth Party Congress 46 per cent of the members of the new Central Committee held army posts, though with the Tenth Congress this figure declined to 31 per cent and with the death of Lin Piao the army has receded from civilian administration.

Defence expenditure is probably about $17 billion.

Recently considerable attention has been focused on building up a People's Militia and there have been new calls for technical modernization.

## AREA AND POPULATION (1976)

| *Province or provincial level administrative unit* | *Population in millions* | *Provincial capital* | *Area (in square kms.)* |
|---|---|---|---|
| Peking municipality | 8 | — | 17,100 |
| Shanghai municipality | 10 | — | 5,800 |
| Hopei | 40 | Shihchiachuang | 191,600 |
| Tertsin municipality | 7 | — | 11,100 |
| Shansi | 23 | Taiyuan | 157,100 |
| Shantung | 68 | Tsinan | 153,300 |
| Honan | 60 | Chengchow | 167,000 |
| Liaoning | 33 | Shenyang (Mukden) | 151,000 (1970) |
| Kirin | 23 | Ch'angch'un | 187,000 (1970) |
| Heilungkiang | 32 | Harbin | 463,600 (1970) |
| Inner Mongolia Autonomous Region | 8 | Huehot | 600,000 (1970) |
| Shensi | 26 | Sian | 195,800 |
| Kansu | 18 | Lanchow | 366,500 |
| Ninghsia Hui Autonomous Region | 3 | Yinch'uan | 66,400 |
| Tsinghai | 3 | Hsining | 721,000 |
| Sinkiang, Uighur Autonomous Region | 10 | Urumchi | 1,646,800 |
| Kiangsu | 55 | Nanking | 102,200 |
| Chekiang | 35 | Hangchow | 101,800 |
| Anhui | 45 | Hofei | 139,900 |
| Hupei | 40 | Wuhan | 187,500 |
| Hunan | 40 | Changsha | 210,500 |
| Kiangsi | 28 | Nanchang | 164,800 |
| Fukien | 20 | Foochow | 123,100 |
| Kwangtung | 54 | Kwangchow | 231,400 |
| Kwangsi Chuang Autonomous Region | 31 | Nanning | 220,400 |
| Kweichow | 24 | Kweiyang | 174,000 |
| Szechwan | 80 | Chengtu | 569,000 |
| Yunnan | 28 | Kunming | 436,200 |
| Tibetan Autonomous Region | 2 | Lhasa | 1,221,600 |
| Total | 847 | | 9,597,000 |

The population of China at mid-1974 was 809,251,000. The percentage population growth rate for the period 1960–74 was 2·9 and for the period 1965–74 was 2·7.

**The Chinese People's Republic is bounded by the Yellow Sea, East China Sea and the following countries:**

| | |
|---|---|
| North | **USSR border in dispute—talks intermittently in progress.** |
| North East | **Korea (no border agreement).**<br>**USSR (border disputed).** |
| South | Democratic Republic of Vietnam (no border agreement but no dispute).<br>**Burma (border agreement 1960).**<br>**India (border disputed).**<br>**Pakistan (border agreement 1963).**<br>**Bhutan (no agreement).**<br>**Nepal (border agreement 1961).**<br>**Laos (no agreement).**<br>**Sikkim (no agreement).** |

**Party authority is divided into large regions as follows:**

1. **North East.**
2. **North China.**
3. **East China.**
4. **Central South China.**
5. **South West.**
6. **North West.**

Provinces, autonomous regions and directly administered cities are subdivided into:

| | |
|---|---|
| Special districts | 174 |
| Autonomous zhou (Minority nationality areas) | 29 |
| Leagues (Only in Inner Mongolia) | 7 |
| Administrative areas | 1 (Hainan Island) |

Apart from Peking, Shanghai, and Tientsin, that rank at provincial level, there are 178 municipalities of which the largest are:

Shenyang (Mukden)
Kwangchow (Canton)
Chungking
Nanking
Tsingtao
Harbin
Sian
Talien (Dairen)

Below special district level are:

| | |
|---|---|
| Counties (*xian*) | 2,012 |
| Autonomous counties (Minority nationality areas) | 66 |
| Banners (Inner Mongolia only) | 53 |
| Autonomous banners (Inner Mongolia only) | 3 |
| *zhen* (In Yunnan province) | 1 |

(1974 figures)

**Nationalities.** There are 52 officially recognized national minorities. According to 1957 data, these comprised 38 million people scattered over 50–60 per cent of the area of China. Most minority people, however, live in West China. The following are the largest:

| | *million* |
|---|---|
| Chuang (Zhuang) | 7·78 |
| Hui (Moslem) | 3·93 |
| Uighur | 3·90 |
| Yi (Lolo) | 3·26 |
| Tibetan | 2·77 |
| Miao | 2·68 |
| Manchu | 2·43 |
| Mongol | 1·64 |
| Pu Yi | 1·31 |
| Korean | 1·25 |

Where there is sufficient concentration these minority nationalities are organized into:

autonomous regions (provincial level)
autonomous *zhou* (special district level)
(alliances)
autonomous counties
(banners)

The smallest recognized nationality is the Hoche which comprises 600 people only.

## CURRENCY AND FINANCE

China's currency is the 'People's Currency' (Renminbi, or RMB). The basic monetary unit is the yuan and the currency system is decimal. Thus, one yuan equals ten chiao (pronounced mao); and one chiao equals ten fen. Yüan notes are issued in denominations of 1, 2, 5 and 10 yüan.

Since the introduction, after 1949, of the RMB on a nationwide basis, and especially since currency unification in 1952, currency values have remained remarkably stable—in dramatic contrast to the grossly inflated currency of the pre-1949 Nationalist government. Currency stability is one of the reasons given for the large increase in bank deposits.

In 1969, Peking sought wider recognition for the RMB as an international trading currency.

Budgetary information is scarce and only the genera outlines of Chinese policy are discernible. An overall, unchanging aim has been that the budget should always show a surplus, and deficit financing and the adoption of inflationary policies are therefore not practised. Avoidance of external debt has been an object of Chinese foreign trade policy, but more surprisingly, efforts have also been made to remove all internal debts. By the end of 1968, China claimed to have neither external nor internal debts—even to the extent of having redeemed all national bonds.

The apparent trade deficits of 1973–5 does not necessarily indicate a change in policy and in 1976 a trade surplus was once again recorded.

The GNP at market prices for 1974 was U.S.$ millions 244,640 and the GNP per capita at market prices was U.S.$ 300. The annual average percentage growth rate of the GNP per capita for the period 1960–74 was 5·2 and for the period 1965–74 was 4·6. [*See the note at the beginning of this section concerning GNP.*]

## PRODUCTION, INDUSTRY AND COMMERCE

**The Development of the Domestic Economy since 1949.** The First Five-Year Plan was inaugurated in 1953. Over 60 per cent of the total investment was allocated to industry (of which 90 per cent was for heavy industry), while the agricultural sector received well under 10 per cent.

The Second Plan (1958–62) was based on the intensive utilization of under-employed labour combined with the promotion of technological dualism ('walking on two legs'), designed to maximize agricultural growth without affecting the programme of industrialization. At the same time, the rural population was organized into communes. This policy was the basis of the Great Leap Forward of 1958.

Targets became increasingly unrealistic and output figures were grossly exaggerated. From 1959–61 extreme natural calamities caused a severe economic crisis which compelled the government to introduce wheat imports. After 1962, however, the economy recovered rapidly.

The Third Five-Year Plan began in 1966. China's planners were probably hoping for an annual growth rate of four to five per cent though this aim was frustrated somewhat by the Cultural Revolution in 1967. Figures quoted by the Premier, Chou En-lai, in early 1971 however are consistent with this figure for industrial production and show a growth rate of three to three and a half per cent for agricultural and industrial production combined. A Fourth Five Year Plan began in 1971 and a Fifth in 1976. Estimates of China's GDP very widely. A reasonable American estimate for 1974 was 266 billion Yüan. It would be misleading to convert this figure into U.S.$ at the official exchange rate and an adjusted rate to allow for price differences gives an approximate figure of $190 billion, showing a per capita GDP of about $200.

**Agriculture.** Mechanization in agriculture has so far only been carried out on a limited scale and in the last two years long term plans have been put forward for accelerated mechanization.

Natural conditions in 1967 were exceptionally favourable for agriculture and a 'bumper harvest' was achieved. Even the most pessimistic estimate suggests an output of 214 million tonnes and the true figure may have been nearer 220 million. In the following year (1968), the combination of only average conditions plus the adverse effects of the Cultural Revolution caused a decline in total grain production.

Until 1971 there was a steady increase in grain output and official figures claim an output of 246 million tonnes for that year. In 1972 however, China suffered the worst drought in nine years (in North China) and grain production fell to some 240 million tonnes. It is significant to note that a similar catastrophe in the early 1960s caused considerable hardship whereas today the decline in production seems to have been successfully absorbed given good reserves and continuing imports. The 1975 grain output was probably some 275 million tonnes rising to 285 in 1976.

The chief food crop is rice (representing over 40 per cent of total grain production) followed by wheat, kaoliang (sorghum) and other cereal grains. Soya production is also at a high level though output fell slightly in 1972. In many parts of south China, two or more crops are grown a year.

Throughout the 1960s China continued to import wheat. It is likely that the continued imports represent a deliberate choice by the Chinese—allowing them to extend the arable area of economic crops, such as cotton, or high value food crops, such as rice.

China is the third-largest producer of cotton in the world and cotton occupies second priority in agricultural production. 1974 production has been estimated at 2·5 million tonnes.

**Livestock.** Most of the work of ploughing and harrowing is still done by animals (mainly oxen and water-buffaloes, but also horses, donkeys and mules). In 1967, the population of 'large animals' (i.e. oxen, water-buffaloes, horses, etc.) was put at 97·0 million. In 1967, the numbers of sheep and goats were estimated to be 127·0 million. The pig population in 1973 was about 200 million. Chickens, ducks and geese are also raised in large numbers and are an important source of peasant income in some areas.

**Industry.** Rapid industrial growth during the First Five-Year Plan period was perhaps the most outstanding short-term economic achievement of the new government. In the initial period of the Great Leap Forward, the high rate of industrial growth continued and reached a peak in 1959, but thereafter it suffered a sharp decline. Recovery started in 1962 and was completed by 1966. Industrial policy during these recovery years emphasized the development of a small number of key industries rather than the overall expansion of the industrial base. This policy was also followed in the late 1960s. By the mid 1960s considerable stress was placed on the development of rural light industry which was a continuation of the policy of 1958.

At the end of 1966, work in factories was affected by the Cultural Revolution and 1967 industrial production showed a decline over the 1966 level. In 1968, the worst excesses of the previous years were dispelled and the downward trend reversed. The upward trend continued in 1969 with a further rise of about 10 per cent. Future growth in industry can be expected to be relatively slow. Nevertheless, in the context of Asia, China now stands as an industrial power of some consequence.

A suggested index of industrial production for 1967–72 is shown below:

| | |
|---|---|
| 1967 | 92 |
| 1968 | 101 |
| 1969 | 112 |
| 1970 | 125 |
| 1971 | 135 |
| 1972 | 145 |
| 1973 | 153 |
| 1974 | 160 |
| 1975 | 180 |
| 1976 | 189 |

Some individual industries are examined in the following sections:

(1) Coal. Estimate for 1976: 450 million tons.

(2) Electric power. Estimated production of electric power in 1971 was 270 billion KWh.

(3) Petroleum. Since 1965, China has been self-sufficient in crude oils. In addition, China now claims to be able to produce a complete range of petroleum products. Production figures for crude oil are indicated below:

| | *million tonnes* |
|---|---|
| 1970 | 20 |
| 1971 | 26 |
| 1972 | 30 |
| 1973 | 50 |
| 1974 | 60 |
| 1975 | 72 |
| 1976 | 84 |

(4) Iron and Steel. Estimates of steel production are given below:

| | *million tonnes* |
|---|---|
| 1969 | 12–13 |
| 1970 | 18 |
| 1971 | 21* |
| 1972 | 23 |
| 1973 | 24 |
| 1974 | 25 |
| 1975 | 25 |
| 1976 | 21 |

* Official figure.

One of the main deficiencies of China's iron and steel industry has been, and remains, its inability to produce certain high-quality steel products and some alloy steels. As a result, imports of such goods—from Japan and Western countries—were found necessary throughout the 1960s.

(5) Cement. Cement production in 1965 was below the previous peak level of 1960, but this was probably regained in 1966. The general decline in industrial activity in 1967 was a factor in the decline in cement output of that year (to about 10 million tons), but recovery in 1968 brought production back to the 1965 level. Spectacular growth in the 1970s was due to the establishment of large numbers of small plants which now produce some 60 per cent of the total output of 42 million tons (1976).

(6) Chemical fertilizers. Since priority was given to agriculture in the early 1960s, the chemical fertilizer industry has been developed rapidly. After a temporary setback in 1961–62, production has increased steadily. Western estimates in 1968 put China's output at above five million tonnes though in 1971 Chou En-lai claimed an output of 14 million tonnes which he anticipated would rise to 30–35 million tonnes by 1975. A current estimate is 30 million tonnes of which 60 per cent is produced in small rural plants.

(7) Synthetic fibres. The 1960s saw increasing emphasis on the development of synthetic fibres as a means of making China's textile industry less dependent on agricultural raw materials. This development has entailed the import of synthetic fibres and synthetic fibre plants.

(8) Machine building industry. Production in the machine-building industry grew rapidly after 1957 to reach a peak in 1960; there followed a sharp fall and a rapid recovery to a new peak level in 1966. Since then progress has been maintained.

**Foreign Trade.** Until the Sino-Soviet split of 1960, China's trade was orientated towards the Soviet Union and, to a lesser extent, Eastern Europe; after 1961, trade with Asian Socialist countries became much more important. Economic relations with Western European countries (especially Italy, West Germany, and the U.K.) have grown steadily since the easing of trade restrictions with China in the mid-1950s. China has also engaged in trade with a number of other countries: most important is Japan, who, in recent years, has become China's principal trading partner ($3,790 million in 1975). The recent easing of restrictions on U.S.–China trade resulted for a time in the U.S. becoming China's number two trading partner ($876 million in 1973) though by 1975, the U.S. had slipped to sixth place. Hong Kong and Malaysia are important as sources of foreign exchange. Canada and Australia have supplied a large percentage of China's wheat imports. In the last two years China has imported a large number of complete industrial plants from overseas though there is known to be internal opposition to this policy.

China's main exports consist mainly of petroleum, rice and other food products.

The following table shows China's trade balances, 1974–76 (in U.S.$ millions):

| | *Exports* | *Imports* | *Total Trade* | *Balance* |
|---|---|---|---|---|
| 1974 | 5,140 | 6,375 | 11,515 | −1,230 |
| 1975 | 5,565 | 6,400 | 11,965 | −835 |
| 1976 | 5,660 | 4,964 | 10,624 | +696 |

The following table shows China's foreign trade by area in U.S. million $.

| | *Total Two-Way Trade* | | | *Rank* | | |
|---|---|---|---|---|---|---|
| *Country* | *1975* | *1974* | *1973* | *1975* | *1974* | *1973* |
| Japan | 3,790 | 3,330 | 2,021 | 1 | 1 | 1 |
| Hong Kong | 1,035 | 895 | 796 | 2 | 3 | 3 |
| West Germany | 750 | 650 | 487 | 3 | 4 | 4 |
| France | 550 | 345 | 231 | 4 | 8 | 11 |
| Malaysia/ Singapore | 530 | 550 | 460 | 5 | 6 | 5 |
| United States | 460 | 1,070 | 876 | 6 | 2 | 2 |
| Romania | 440 | 300 | 265 | 7 | 10 | 9 |
| Canada | 430 | 575 | 409 | 8 | 5 | 6 |
| Australia | 410 | 465 | 247 | 9 | 7 | 10 |
| United Kingdom | 310 | 330 | 340 | 10 | 9 | 7 |
| Soviet Union | 280 | 280 | 272 | 11 | 11 | 8 |
| Italy | 275 | 220 | 196 | 12 | 12 | 12 |

### COMMUNICATIONS

**Roads.** In 1949, there were 80,768 km. of roads in China, but by 1957 this had risen to 254,624 km. In 1959 and 1960, China claimed to have further increased this to 400,000 and 480,000 km. respectively, though these figures may be exaggerated. In 1957 freight turnover by motor vehicles was only 3,940 million ton-km., or 2·93 per cent of the total. Road development has been particularly rapid in Inner Mongolia and other National Minority Areas.

**Railways.** The total railway network now stands at 120,000 km. Rapid expansion of China's railways was given high priority in the Fourth Five Year Plan.

**Shipping.** The Yangtze River is navigable for ships up to 10,000 tons as far as Wuhan, 600 miles upstream, and for smaller ships, a thousand miles further. The river serves the important industrial cities of Shanghai and Wuhan, as well as Nanking and Chungking. The length of waterways navigable by steamboats was about 40,000 km. in 1958. There is some evidence that, with the expansion of railways, the volume of freight carried on the inland waterways has declined since 1958.

In 1976, the Chinese merchant fleet was estimated at 5 million tonnes deadweight.

Chinese ships, however, only meet part of China's needs, the remainder being moved in chartered vessels. Since 1958 the shipbuilding industry has expanded rapidly especially in Shanghai and Talien. Both of these centres have the capacity to produce 24,000 ton ships. Despite this growth, China still buys large numbers of ships (mainly second hand) from overseas. Recently much attention has been devoted to containerization.

**Air Traffiç.** Civil air traffic has developed rapidly since the 1960s. China's General Administration of Civil Aviation (CAAC) aircraft operate nine overseas routes and 119 domestic routes. There are 23 air services linking China with other countries and China has signed air transport agreements with over 30 countries. China currently operates seven international airports and intends to expand rapidly the CAAC network. She has recently purchased a large number of aircraft from overseas (including the Concorde). The total number of flights per week stands at 328.

**Telecommunications.** Provisional estimates suggested that in 1964, there were 8 million radio receivers. In 1965 there were about 100,000 television receivers. Reports for 1969 stated that the radio network was being expanded in many provinces. It has been estimated that the total number of wired radio loudspeakers in the country exceeds 50 million. In the past few years considerable attention has been paid to improving China's communication links with the outside world. Agreements with foreign countries have been concluded establishing satellite communications systems.

### NEWSPAPERS

**People's Daily (Renmin Ribao).** Organ of the Central Committee of the Chinese Communist Party.

**Guangming Ribao.** Originally represented the views of minority parties but recently has reflected editorial line of Peoples Daily.

**Jiefangjunbao.** The organ of the Chinese Peoples Liberation Army.

**Xinhua News Release.** Published in Chinese, English and a number of other languages.

In addition, each province and major municipality publishes a daily newspaper.

### ATOMIC ENERGY

Nuclear research dates from the early 1950s when China received a certain amount of Soviet help including the supply of an experimental nuclear reactor (1957). The open split with the Soviet Union led her to redouble her own efforts to develop a nuclear capacity. By 1963, a 7,000 kilowatt atomic reactor had been completed and a cyclotron producing alpha particles constructed. Since then China has carried out eighteen major nuclear tests.

### DIPLOMATIC RELATIONS

During the past six years, China has been making strenuous efforts to 'normalize' diplomatic relations with the West. China currently maintains diplomatic relations with over 100 countries. The visits of President Nixon and Prime Minister Tanaka to Peking signalled a new era in China's foreign relations. Mutual liaison offices have been established in Peking and Washington. A resolution passed by the 26th General Assembly of the United Nations in 1971 recognized the lawful right of the Peoples Republic of China to the seat reserved for China in the United Nations and since that time China has played an active part not only in the General Assembly and Security Council but also in many of the U.N. agencies and conferences called by the U.N.

### EDUCATION

Recently a wide-ranging "revolution in education" has been under way and the whole field is in a state of flux. A new principle of "open-door education" has been adopted which aims at a much closer identification of educational institutions with the rest of society. Many schools run their own productive units and students at all levels are required to spend some time in factory and agricultural work. It is now extremely difficult to graduate directly from secondary to tertiary level without having spent two years in the factories and communes. The following are the major types of schools:

*Primary* (5 years): 1,090,000 schools with 150 million students.

*Secondary* (4–5 years): 123,000 schools with 44·6 million students (these are sometimes divided into upper and lower secondary schools though increasingly these two types are combined).

*Technical secondary:* 3,000 schools with 900,000 students.

*Ordinary tertiary* (3 years): 400 colleges with 500,000 students.

There are also a number of special types of tertiary institutions. Recently great attention has been devoted to the establishment of "July 21st colleges" (now approximately 6,000) to provide technical training for factory workers and peasants and "May 7th Colleges" concerned with the political training of administrative, technical and educational codres. Schools at all levels might be organized on a part-work part-study basis. At local levels there are a number of "people-run" schools, the funding for which is provided by the local community. It is now claimed that 95 per cent of children of primary school age attend school.

### RELIGION

There are some 50 million moslems in China, mainly in North China (Hui nationality) and in Sinkiang (Uighurs, Kazakhs, etc.). Islam appears still to be thriving in Islamic minority areas. There are a few Jews of Chinese race in Kaifeng though the synagogue is no longer used as such.

Despite Red Guard attacks on Christian churches, no official line has been adopted concerning the suppression of religion. Indications are that the less radical policies adopted since the Ninth Party congress will mean a continuation of the policy of official discouragement but legal tolerance. Since the Cultural Revolution a number of Christian churches have been reopened.

## TIBET

**Capital**—Lhasa.

*Chairman of the Revolutionary Committee of the Tibet Autonomous Region:* Jen Jung.

European relations with Tibet began in 1626, when António de Andrada, a Portuguese Jesuit father, became the first European known to have entered the country. Two other Jesuits, Johann Grueber, an Austrian, and Albert d'Orville, a Belgian, were the first Europeans to enter Lhasa. Under Warren Hastings there were attempts to extend British influence, but these failed despite the visits of George Bogle, in 1774, of Lt. Samuel Turner, in 1783, and one Manning who reached Lhasa in 1811. During the 19th century Europeans were excluded from Tibet. Nevertheless, a few missionaries and explorers, as, for example, E. R. Huc and J Sabet (both

French), or the brothers Henry and Richard Strachey, succeeded in travelling through portions of the country. In 1902 there were reports of a Russo-Chinese agreement regarding spheres of influence in Tibet. In consequence the then Viceroy of India, the Marquess Curzon, proposed to send a mission with an armed escort to Lhasa. Lieut.-Col. (later Sir Francis) Younghusband commanded the expedition which in 1904 fought its way to Lhasa. The Dalai Lama fled to Mongolia and in his absence a treaty was concluded with the Tibetan delegates. In 1906 there was a Convention between Britain and China which recognized China's sole right to concessions in Tibet, and in 1907 an agreement between Great Britain and Russia over Tibet. In 1910, however, the Dalai Lama found it expedient to take refuge in India, where he remained until 1912. The Tibetans rose in revolt against the Chinese, whose troops in Lhasa were compelled to surrender. In 1913 a treaty was concluded between Mongolia and Tibet. By resolutions of a conference between the British and Chinese at Simla in October 1913, Tibet was to be given internal autonomy, though Britain recognized Chinese suzerainty over Tibet.

## CONSTITUTION AND GOVERNMENT

On 23 May 1951 an 'Agreement of the Central Peoples Government and the Local Government of Tibet on Measures for the Peaceful Liberation of Tibet' was signed in Peking by the Chinese Central Peoples Government, the Panchen Lama (Panchen Erdeni) and Ngapo Ngawang Jigme. In February 1952 the Tibet PLA Military Area was set up with General Chang Kuo-hua as commander and Ngapo Ngawang Jigme as 1st Deputy Commander. In April 1952 an anti-Chinese 'Peoples Council' was set up which demanded the removal of the Chinese troops and agitated for revolt. Its leaders were removed from their posts and the Dalai Lama officially disbanded the body whereupon the 'Peoples Council' went underground until the rebellion of 1959. During 1951–59 the PLA undertook various construction projects in Tibet.

In April 1956 a Preparatory Committee was formally inaugurated for the Tibet autonomous region with the Dalai Lama as Chairman and Panchen Erdeni as 1st Vice Chairman, Chang Kuo-hua as 2nd Vice Chairman and Ngapo Ngawang Jigme as Secretary General. During this period the religious structure of the country was not radically altered and in 1957 the Chinese Communist Tibet Work Committee said that it would not carry out 'democratic reform' during the period of China's Second Five-Year Plan. During 1958 a number of disturbances took place in Tibet. On 10 March 1959 the Tibet Local Government led an open rebellion against the PLA presence which the PLA put down. The Dalai Lama fled to India and the Panchen Erdeni then became acting Chairman of the Preparatory Committee for the Tibet Autonomous Region. The Tibet Local Government was dissolved. After the rebellion, 'democratic reform' was commenced and numbers of refugees made their way to India. In December 1964 the Dalai Lama was officially removed from his post as Chairman of the Preparatory Committee by the 151st Plenum of the State Council.

In 1965 the Tibet Autonomous Region that was to be administered in the same way as the other autonomous regions in China was formally inaugurated and Ngapo Ngawang Jigme was elected Chairman. The Panchen Erderi was removed from his post. During the Cultural Revolution, Red Guard units and revolutionary rebel units were formed in Tibet, and on 5 September 1968 a Revolutionary Committee was set up under the Chairmanship of Tseng Yung-ya (Deputy Political Commissar of the Military Region). During recent years there have been several unconfirmed reports of sporadic fighting still continuing in Tibet.

## AREA AND POPULATION

The area of the Tibetan Autonomous Region is 1,221,600 sq. km. In 1957, the population was 1,270,000.

## PRODUCTION. INDUSTRY AND COMMERCE

**Agriculture.** Tibet remains largely an agrarian area. Due to the limitations imposed by natural and geographical conditions, Tibetan grain production has always been insufficient to meet demand, and reports of loans of seeds and grain in the 1950s from Peking suggested that this shortage had not been overcome. After the 1959 uprising, full-scale land reform took place, which was said to have resulted in higher yields. New crop varieties were also introduced including high-value vegetable crops, such as tomatoes, peppers and cucumbers.

Livestock rearing has traditionally been important in Tibet, and further development has been fostered. In 1963 Tibet was acknowledged to be one of China's most important livestock breeding areas. Total livestock population in that year was put at 13·2 million.

**Industry.** During the early 1960s 67 factories were set up for the production of electricity, coal, cement and certain light industrial goods. Further progress in industry was reported during the Cultural Revolution.

**Commerce.** Wool is the main export but Yak products and medicinal herbs are also exported.

## COMMUNICATIONS

By 1965, three main roads linked Tibet with the rest of China: the 2,413 km. Szechwan-Tibet Highway from Ch'eng-tu to Lhasa; the Tsinghai-Tibet Highway from Sining to Lhasa; and the Sinkiang-Tibet Highway which was opened as early as 1957.

# Colombia

## (REPÚBLICA DE COLOMBIA)

**Capital**—Bogotá D.E.

**President**—Alfonso Lopez Michelsen.

**National Flag:** A tricolour fesse-wise, yellow, blue, red, the yellow to half the depth of the flag.

### CONSTITUTION AND GOVERNMENT

UP to the beginning of the eighteenth century what is today the Republic of Colombia was known as the Vice-Royalty of New Granada, governed by the King of Spain. The Colombians rose against Spanish rule in 1810 and, after a bitter struggle, gained their independence in 1819. The State of Greater Colombia was then constituted, composed of what is today Venezuela, Ecuador, Panama and Colombia. In 1830 Venezuela and Ecuador seceded and the remaining part became the United States of New Granada. In 1858 a Centralist form of government was adopted, the eight Sovereign States which made up the Union relinquished their autonomous powers to the central government, becoming Departments ruled by a Governor appointed by the President. In 1903 the Department of Panama broke away to become a separate republic.

The Constitution of 1886, with several amendments, is the Basic Law of the Nation. The Legislative Branch is composed of a Senate and a House of Representatives. Its members are chosen by direct vote of the electorate, for a four-year term. Congress meets in Bogotá every year for a session of at least 150 days. The President, also elected by direct vote, serves for four years and cannot be re-elected for the immediately following presidential term. The Constitution guarantees freedom of speech, press, and assembly as well as all other basic rights.

Since 1958 the country has been ruled by a coalition of the two principal parties—the Liberals and the Conservatives. Under the terms of the 1958 Constitutional Amendment, the Presidency is alternated between the popularly elected candidate of each party. Thus, in 1958, Dr. Alberto Lleras Camargo, a Liberal, was elected President. He was replaced at the end of his term by Dr. Guillermo Leon Valencia, a Conservative who served between 1962 and 1966. Dr. Carlos Lleras Restrepo became the next President, for the period 1966–70. Dr. Misael Pastrana Borrero, the fourth and last President of the National Front coalition, was elected in 1970 and will serve until 1974.

In 1971, a third party, the Alianza Nacional Popular, made up of splinter groups of the two traditional parties, was formed. Since 1971 yet another party has been formed, the Unión Nacional de Oposición. The composition of the Congress elected in 1974 is as follows:

| | *Senate* | *House of Representatives* |
|---|---|---|
| Liberals | 66 | 113 |
| Conservatives | 37 | 66 |
| Alianza Nacional Popular | 7 | 15 |
| Unión Nacional de Oposición | 2 | 5 |

**Cabinet***

*Minister of Finance:* Abdon Espinosa Valderrama.
*Minister of Defence:* Abraham Varon Valencia.

* On 29 September 1977 eleven Ministers resigned from a coalition government, leaving only the two above named individuals.

### LOCAL GOVERNMENT

The nation is divided into 23 departments (states), four Intendencies and four Commissaries (national territories). The departments are subdivided into municipalities (counties). The State Governors are appointed by the President and the State and Municipal Assemblies are elected by direct suffrage. The Intendencies and Commissaries are administered by the Central Government.

### LEGAL SYSTEM

The Judiciary functions independently of the other two branches of government. The Supreme Court of Justice is composed of 16 Justices, chosen by its own members and serves a period of five years. It acts as a Court of Appeals for civil, criminal and constitutional cases. There are a number of lower courts, such as the district courts which function in each department and try civil and criminal cases. There is no capital punishment in Colombia.

### AREA AND POPULATION

The area of population of the Departments, Intendencies and Commissaries are shown below:

| *Department* | *Capital* | *Area (sq. kilometres)* | *population 1975 (estimated)* |
|---|---|---|---|
| Antioquia | Medellín | 63,000 | 3,096,230 |
| Atlántico | Barranquilla | 3,452 | 1,020,360 |
| Bolívar | Cartagena | 26,392 | 827,970 |
| Boyacá | Tunja | 60,133 | 978,120 |
| Caldas | Manizales | 7,231 | 698,400 |
| Cauce | | | 603,180 |
| César | Valledupar | 24,431 | 359,770 |
| Córdoba | Monteria | 25,175 | 659,140 |
| Cundinamarca (Excluding Bogotá) | Bogotá | 23,444 | 1,103,290 |
| Chocó | Quibdo | 47,468 | 206,520 |
| Guajira | **Neiva** | 19,828 | **188,655** |
| Huila | Riohacha | 21,000 | 482,250 |
| Magdalena | Santa Marta | 22,264 | 629,130 |
| Meta | Villavicencio | 85,220 | 266,845 |
| Nariño | Pasto | 32,373 | 830,839 |
| Norte de Santander | Cúcuta | 20,192 | 733,290 |
| Quindío | Armenia | 1,825 | 325,217 |
| Risaralda | Pereira | 4,014 | 456,020 |
| Santander | Bucaramanga | 30,318 | 1,161,080 |
| Sucre | | | 364,140 |
| Tolima | Ibague | 32,393 | 917,490 |
| Valle del Cauca | Cali | 20,430 | 2,322,160 |
| Bogotá | Special District | | 3,193,805 |

The population of the principal cities, as follows: Bogotá, 2·5 million; Medellin 1·5 million; Cali, 1 million; and Barranquilla, 900,000. The population at mid-1974 was 23,125,000.

The annual average percentage growth rate of the population for the period 1960–74 was 2·9 and for the period 1965–74 was 2·8.

### CURRENCY AND FINANCE

The monetary unit of Colombia is the peso (Col. $). There are coins of 1, 2 and 5 cents (centavos), made of steel-copper alloy and 10, 20 and 50 cent coins minted from a steel-nickel alloy. Notes are issued in the following denominations: 1, 2, 5, 10, 20, 50, 100, 200 and 500 pesos. At the end of 1974 the currency circulation amounted to Col. $16,533 million.

Since the suspension of the gold standard in 1931, the peso has fluctuated. During the last few years the rate of exchange has been as follows: U.S. $1·00 = Col. $17·90 at the end of 1968, Col. $18·91 in 1969, Col. $19·31 in 1970 Col. $20·82 at the end of 1971, and Col. $32·94 at the end of 1975.

The purchase of foreign exchange in the open market was suspended in 1966 and replaced by a 'Capital Market' and an 'Exchange Certificate' through which private foreign loans are repaid, foreign owned companies remit their profits abroad and imports are financed and paid for.

The GNP at market prices for 1974 was U.S.$ millions 11,640, and the GNP per capita at market prices was U.S.$500. The annual average percentage growth rate of the GNP per capita for the period 1960–74 was 2·6, and for the period 1965–74 was 2·8. [*See the note at the beginning of this section concerning GNP.*]

### PRINCIPAL BANKS

**Banco de la Republica.** (General Manager, Dr. Miguel Garcia Herreros.) Est. 1923. Sole Bank of Issue for Colombia

Balance Sheet at 31 December 1963 showed assets p. 8,458,645,687; sight deposits p. 2,067,160,934; Banknotes in circulation p. 2,661,020,490. *Head Office:* Carrera 7 Avenida Timenez, Bogotá. 24 Branches and Agencies.

**Banco Central Hipotecario.** (Manager, Javier Ramirez Soto.) Est. 1932; Balance Sheet at 31 December 1976 showed assets Col. p. $21,432,864; deposits Col. p. $9,577,055. *Head Office:* Carrera 6a, No. 15–32/48, Bogotá. 47 Branches.

**Banco Comercial Antioqueño.** (President, Vicente Uribe Rendon.) Est. 1912; Balance Sheet at 31 May 1971 showed assets Col.$2,775,834,000; sight deposits Col.$1,664,065,000. *Head Office:* Medellin. 69 Branches and Agencies.

**Banco de Bogota.** (President, Jorge Mejia Salazar.) Est. 1870; Balance Sheet at 31 December 1974 showed assets Col. p. 14,160,421,123; sight deposits Col. p. 1,102,733,440. *Head Office:* Bogotá, Colombia. 225 Branches.

**Banco de Columbia.** (President, Jaime Michelson Uribe.) Est. 1874; Balance Sheet at 31 December 1971 showed assets Col. p. 4,882,174,558·15; deposits Col. p. 3,644,887,532. *Head Office:* Bogotá. 200 Offices in Colombia and seven offices in Panama.

**Banco de los Andes.** (Acting Manager, Augusto Restrepo.) Capital p. 9,760,000 paid up; Balance Sheet at 31 December 1963 showed assets p. 246,066,476; deposits p. 123,896,868.

**Banco del Comercio.** (General Manager, Camilo Herrera Prado.) Balance Sheet at 31 December 1976: assets p. $13,247,427,717·69 Deposits p. $5,519,113,735·36. *Head Office*: Bogotá. 120 Branches.

**Banco Franco Colombiano.** Bogotá, Barranquilla, Buenaventura, Medellin.

**Banco Industrial Columbiano.** (General Manager, Ivan Correa Arungo.) Balance Sheet at 30 June 1962: assets p. 397,087,000; deposits p. 289,408,000.

**Banco Popular.** (President, Dr. Eduardo-Nieto Calderón.) Grant loans to middle and lower classes specially to small and medium-size industry. Its functions are directed to the democratization of credit and to help development business. Has special public auction services, international division and all banking services through 170 Branches in Colombia. Paid-up capital (including Reserves) P.$775,405,000. Assets P.$7,653,713. *Head Office:* Calle 17 743, Bogota, Colombia, S.A.

**Banco Cafetero.** (General Manager, Rodrigo Munera M.) Grants special credits to coffee growers, promotes agricultural development. It started with working capital of Col. $50,000,000. First to experiment in specialized credit in South America. Balance Sheet at 30 June 1971 showed assets Col. $4,104,828,964; deposits Col. $2,962,611,678. Paid-up capital Col. $325,000,000.

**Banco Ganadero.** (General Manager, Arturo Bonnet Trujillo.) Established 1956 and founded to serve the interests of the cattle industry. Authorized capital p. 100,000,000; paid-up p. 59,500,000. Balance Sheet at 31 December 1964, showed total assets p. 436,735,312; deposits p. 125,263,546. *Head Office:* Bogotá. 18 Branches.

**Caja de Crédito Agrario.** (General Manager, José Elías de Hierro.) Capital 464,434,580. Legal reserve 340,666,590. Assets at 31 December 1963, 2,717,045,703.

**Branches of Foreign Banks**

**Bank of London & Montreal Limited.** Bogotá, Barranquilla Bucaramanga, Cali, Manizales, Medellín, Pasto and Pereira

**The First National City Bank of New York**—Bogotá.

**The Royal Bank of Canada**—Our Telex 044609 Bogotá.

**Banco Francés e Italiano para la América del Sud**—Bogotá.
**Banque Nationale de Paris**—Bogotá, Barranquilla, Buenaventura, Medellin.

## PRODUCTION, INDUSTRY AND COMMERCE

**Agriculture.** Agriculture is the most important sector of the Colombian economy. With a wide variety of soils and climates, the country produces a wide range of crops, both for the home market and for export. The annual growth in agriculture has increased from approximately 3 per cent over many years to an average of 5·2 per cent for the past four years. This is sufficient to keep pace with population growth—3·2 per cent—allowing for export and import substitution. Expansion has been particularly rapid in grain sorghum, soyabeans, cotton, sugar and rice.

Coffee is the most important agricultural product. It accounts for one-tenth of the gross domestic products, one-tenth of the central government revenues and almost two-thirds of the foreign exchange earnings of the country. Approximately two million Colombians make their living from coffee farming. Colombian coffee is of mild, high quality variety and has the highest selling price of all coffees in the international market. Other important export crops are bananas, cotton and sugar cane.

**Forestry.** There are over 150 million acres of forest but these have not been exploited to any extent. The trees are mostly hardwoods, unsuitable for building purposes, but a certain amount of lumber is produced for cabinet making. Various drugs and dye woods as well as rubber are collected from the forests.

**Industry.** This sector is the most dynamic of the Colombian economy. Since 1953 it has shown an average annual increase of 6·7 per cent. Of particular importance has been the growth of the domestic engineering industries.

**Mining.** Colombia is rich in mineral wealth, specially in precious metals. There are also substantial deposits of iron, coal and petroleum in the country.

**Oil.** Colombia has had a substantial production of petroleum. However, due to the increase in the internal demand for this product, the country will become a net importer of petroleum products, unless new reserves are found. The internal market is supplied by Ecopetrol (Colombian National Petroleum Company) but a number of foreign companies, such as British Petroleum, and Shell, operate in the country.

**Commerce.** Colombia's foreign trade reached the sum of U.S. $3,300 million in 1974 of which exports amounted to U.S. $1,509 million and imports to U.S. $1·78 million. The principal articles imported were: wheat and flour, U.S. $80 millions; soybean U.S. $10 millions; barley, U.S. $9 million; cocoa U.S. $11 million; chassis, U.S. $56 million; tractors, U.S. $45 million.

The main exports were: Coffee U.S. $625 million; beef U.S. $37 million; flowers U.S. $15 million; beans U.S. $14 million; bananas U.S. $27 million; sugar U.S. $96 million; tobacco U.S. $22 million; chemical products U.S. $65 million. fur and leather U.S. $16 million; timber U.S. $18 million; books U.S. $14 million, cotton U.S. $86 million, and textiles U.S. $184 million.

Colombia's principal trading partners, and the value of trade (in million U.S. $) are shown in the following table:

| *Country* | *Exports (million U.S.$)* | *Imports (million U.S.$)* |
|---|---|---|
| United States | 456 | 756·8 |
| West Germany | 169 | 160·5 |
| France | 29 | 72·3 |
| United Kingdom | 49 | 54·7 |
| Netherlands | 60 | 45·4 |
| Japan | 23 | 139·4 |
| Spain | 46 | 48·1 |
| Ecuador | 46 | — |
| Sweden | 34 | — |
| Switzerland | — | 58·7 |
| Venezuela | 71 | — |
| Chile | — | 40·5 |
| Canada | — | 4·0 |
| Panama | 69 | — |
| Peru | 42 | — |
| Argentina | 27 | — |

The following table shows the volume of production for the years 1973–74 taking as a base 1970 = 100:

| *Sector* | 1973 | 1974 |
|---|---|---|
| Farming and stock-farming | 113·6 | 120·1 |
| Agriculture | 115·4 | 120·4 |
| Livestock | 111·6 | 119·5 |
| Other production | 112·2 | 120·4 |
| Game-shooting and fishing | 170·1 | 101·5 |
| Forestry, felling and pruning | 125·0 | 134·4 |
| Minerals | 99·4 | 92·7 |
| Oil | 83·8 | 76·7 |
| Metalliferous ores | 104·1 | 115·6 |
| Non-metalliferous ores | 140·7 | 145·6 |
| Manufacturing industry | 129·1 | 136·3 |
| Other manufactures | 131·8 | 139·5 |
| Small and artisan industry | | |
| Handicrafts | 113·1 | 117·4 |
| Building (Total) | 121·1 | 126·7 |
| Private | 127·6 | 140·4 |
| Public | 117·0 | 118·1 |
| Commerce | 123·2 | 130·7 |
| Transport | 122·0 | 133·3 |
| Communications | 141·2 | 168·8 |
| Electricity, gas and water | 135·6 | 145·3 |
| Finance and property | 139·1 | 160·6 |
| Net housing rents | 118·9 | 127·3 |
| Personal services | 123·0 | 130·6 |
| Government services | 127·1 | 130·1 |

## COMMUNICATIONS

**Railways.** The Colombian National Railways (a state owned enterprise) operates a unified network of lines totalling 3,436 km. This system has access to the Pacific at Buenaventura and to the Atlantic at Santa Marta and links all of the major regions of the country. Traffic achieved a record 1·159 million-ton-km in 1969. However, competition from some major highway projects is expected to result in substantial diversion of traffic from some routes. Passenger travel has been declining at 6 per cent per annum and, in 1969, the railway carried only one million passengers, or 28 per cent less than in 1968.

**Highways.** Colombia has some 45,000 km of roads, of which about 5,000 are paved. The total number of road vehicles, 260,000 in 1968, has been increasing at about 4 per cent annually.

**Civil Aviation.** Colombia's very difficult terrain encouraged the early development of air service for internal as well as for international transport. There are about 700 aircraft landing facilities in the country. International air service is provided by a number of carriers with several daily flights from the American continent and Europe. These are: B.O.A.C., Avianca, Lufthansa, Air France, Varig, K.L.M., Viasa, Iberia, Lan Chile, Braniff, Aerolineas Argentinas, etc.

The principal Colombian airlines are:

**AVIANCA.**—Aerovías Nacionales de Colombia S.A. (President, Dr Ernesto Mendoza.) Est. 1919. *Services operated:* Colombia, Venezuela, Puerto Rico, Spain, France, Germany, Chile, Switzerland, Ecuador, Peru, Argentina, Brazil, Panama, Mexico and the United States. *Head Office:* Bogotá. It is the oldest airline in America, both north and south, founded under the name of SCADTA it has been in continuous operation since 1919.

**SAM.** *Head Office:* Calle 52 52–11 P.O. Box 1085, Medellin Colombia. *Services operated:* Colombia and Central America, Miami (cargo service).

**AEROCONDOR.**—Aerovías Condor de Colombia. *Head Office:* Cra. 10 No. 24–55, Bogotá. *Services operated:* Colombia, United States, Aruba, Curaçao, Haiti, Guatemala, Dominican Republic.

**Shipping.** The principal Colombian line is the Flota Mercante Gran Colombiana which is jointly owned by Colombia and Ecuador. It has expanded and modernized its fleet from 19 owned and 15 chartered vessels with a capacity of 84,000 tons to 22 owned and 35 chartered ships with a capacity of 151,664 tons. *Services operated:* Japan, Atlantic and Gulf ports of the U.S., Canada, Atlantic and Mediterranean ports of Europe, Caribbean, Ecuador and Venezuela.

Other important lines are Agromar, with services to Venezuela, Brazil, Uruguay and Argentina and **NAVENAL.**

**Telegraph and Telephones, Broadcasting.** There are nearly 200 commercial radio stations in the country and two nation-wide television networks of which one is educational. There is also a local T.V. channel in Bogotá and soon local channels will be added in Medellín, Cali, and Barranquilla.

The number of automatic telephone lines in Colombia has about doubled—from 270,000 in 1960 to 560,000 in 1969. All but 17,200 lines are automatic. The telephone density of the country has increased from 1·75 in 1960 to about 2·75 telephones per hundred of the population in 1969. About 109 cities and towns have automatic telephone service with an additional 360 which have manual lines. Overseas calls are placed through the satellite service. There is also a nation-wide and international telegraph and telex service.

## NEWSPAPERS

**El Tiempo.** Morning. F. 1911. Liberal. Bogotá. Circulation 204,300; (Sunday) 390,000.

**La Republica.** Morning. Conservative. Bogotá. Circulation 95,137.

**El Espectador.** Morning. F. 1887. Liberal. Bogotá. Circulation (weekdays) 200,000; (Sunday) 300,000.

**El Siglo.** Morning. Conservative. Bogotá. Circulation 55,800.

**El Colombiano.** Morning. Conservative. Medellín. Circulation 80,000.

**El Pais.** Morning. Conservative. Cali. Circulation 62,000.

**Occidente.** Morning. Conservative. Cali.

**El Vespertino.** Afternoon. F. 1965. Liberal. Bogotá. Circulation 60,000 (no Sundays).

**El Espacio.** Afternoon. Liberal. Bogotá.

## ATOMIC ENERGY

In June 1958, a United Nations Atomic Energy Mission visited Colombia. The Mission was composed of a considerable number of experts of various nationalities and its main purpose was to study the possible requirements of atomic energy for peaceful purposes in Latin American countries. As far as Colombia is concerned, though there is an Institute of Nuclear Affairs in Bogotá, the economic situation of the country does not permit more than a token interest in atomic matters. In certain quarters there are great hopes of earning more foreign exchange by selling Colombian uranium, but no proper survey has yet been made on the country's uranium resources nor have communications in the areas where there are known to be deposits been brought up to the necessary standard.

## EDUCATION AND RELIGION

Primary education is free and even though there are not sufficient schools to provide education for all, some regions of the country have reached the national goal and provide facilities for every child of school age. The Government also carries out a campaign to eradicate illiteracy.

Columbia is predominantly a Catholic country but every other major religion is practised in the nation, with absolute freedom.

# The Comoros State

**Capital**—Moroni.

**Head of State**—Ali Soilih.

The Comoros consists of the Islands of Mayotte[1], Anjouan, Grande Comoro and Moheli, and is situated about 310 miles from Madagascar. The archipelago was previously an administrative region of Madagascar but from 1 January 1947 it was given the status of an Overseas Territory with administrative and financial autonomy.

On the 6 July 1975 there was a unilateral declaration of independence. The inhabitants of the island of Mayotte, which, together with the islands mentioned above, formed a French Overseas Territory, declined to be associated with the declaration of independence. On 11 November 1975. The Comoros State was accepted into the United Nations.

The French Parliament adopted a law on 31 December 1975 which recognised the independence of the islands of Grande Comoro, Anjouan and Moheli. In a referendum on the island's future on 8 February 1976 the inhabitants of Mayotte cast 99·4 per cent of their votes in favour of the island remaining a part of the French Republic. In a further referendum on 11 April 1976 Mayotte voted to abandon its status as a French Overseas Territory. A bill was adopted by the French National Assembly on 14 December 1976 granting to Mayotte the status of territorial entity ("collectivité territoràle") with the French Community.

**Council of State**

Ali Soilih
Mohamed Hasan Aly
Tadjidine B. S. Massonde
Abdellah Mohamed
Mouzawoir Abdallah

### AREA AND POPULATION

The total area of the islands forming the archipelago is about 849 sq. km.

The population at mid-1974 was 265,000. The annual average percentage growth rate for the period 1960–74 was 2·2 and for the period 1965–74 was 2·1.

### FINANCE

The GNP at market prices for 1974 was U.S. $ millions 60, and the GNP per capita at market prices for 1974 was U.S. $230. The annual average percentage growth rate of the GNP per capita for the period 1960–74 was 3·1 and for the period 1965–74 was 1·6. [*See the note at the beginning of this Section concerning GNP.*]

### AGRICULTURE

The principal food crops are rice, cassava, corn, sweet potatoes and such European vegetables as egg plant and tomatoes. Tropical fruits, bananas, oranges, tangerines, lemons, mangos, etc., grow in abundance. The chief industrial crop is vanilla, other crops are perfume plants, e.g. jasmine, basil, and spices as well as coffee and sisal. There are numerous coconut palms which furnish copra, one of the chief export products.

### COMMUNICATIONS

The Comoro Islands have a total of 435 miles of roads, 370 miles of which are passable during all the seasons of the year. In 1960 the various ports of the Comoros handled 600 ships and 23,000 metric tons of goods.

### EDUCATION

In 1960 nearly 4,500 pupils were receiving elementary education in 48 French schools. Two secondary schools prepared nearly 200 students for the 'Baccalaureat'.

[1] The following text is a quotation from the *Note D'Actualite* dated 31 October 1975, published by the French government:

'A bill dealing with the consequences of *Comoran* self-determination was adopted.

From the date of promulgation of this legislation, Grand Comoro, Anjouan and Mohli will cease to be part of the French Republic. Within the two months following promulgation, the population of Mayotte will be called upon to decide on its inclusion in the new Comoran State. In the event of a refusal, it would be called upon within two months to choose the status it would wish to see applied to Mayotte within the French Republic.

The Government spokesman pointed out that if Mayotte refused to become part of the New Comoran State, it would be able to opt for the status of Overseas Department or Overseas Territory of the French Republic.'

# Republic of Congo

**Capital**—Brazzaville.

**Head of State**: Col. Joachim Yhombi-Opango.

**National Flag**: Green and crimson, divided by a bend sinister, yellow.

### CONSTITUTION AND GOVERNMENT

The independence of the Republic of Congo within the French Community was proclaimed on 15 August 1960. On 20 September the Republic was admitted to the U.N.

### AREA AND POPULATION

The area of the Republic is 342,000 sq. km.

The population in mid-1974 was 1,300,000. The annual average percentage growth rate of the population for the period 1960–74 was 2·3 and for the period 1965–74 was 2·3.

### FINANCE

The GNP at market prices for 1974 was U.S. $millions 610, and the GNP per capita at market prices was U.S. $470. The annual average percentage growth rate of the GNP per capita for the period 1960–74 was 2·8, and for the period 1965–74 was 4·0. [*See the note at the beginning of this section concerning GNP.*]

In 1972 the budget was balanced at 21,800 million francs CFA.

### PRODUCTION AND COMMERCE

Resources include timber, groundnuts, sugar cane, palm cabbages and manioc (the base of tapioca). There are mineral deposits chiefly of copper and tin. The sources of hydraulic energy are still to be exploited. A first step in this direction was the creation of the company 'L'Energie Electrique de l'Afrique Equatoriale Française' whose first project was the construction of a dam on the D'Juwe (a tributary of the Congo) to supply Brazzaville. The dam will have a capacity of 10,000 kWh.

In 1972 trade with the United Kingdom was: imports, £1,698,000; exports, £1,074,000.

# Costa Rica

(REPÚBLICA DE COSTA RICA)

**Capital**—San José

**President**—Lic. Daniel Oduber Q.

**National Flag**: Parti of five fesse-wise, dark blue, white, red, white, dark blue, the red stripe being twice the width of the others.

### CONSTITUTION AND GOVERNMENT

THE Republic of Costa Rica, the most southerly State of Central America, lies between Nicaragua and Panama, and between the Caribbean Sea and the Pacific Ocean. Costa Rica formed part of the Spanish Empire until 1821 when the country became independent. From 1824 to 1839 it belonged to the Confederation of Central America, but since that time has been an independent state.

The Constitution dates from 1871, but has been modified on several occasions since that time and lastly in 1949. Under the Constitution, legislative power is vested in a single Chamber of Representatives or Constitutional Congress made up of 57 Deputies who are elected for four years. All male and female citizens who are 20 years of age and over are entitled to vote. Constitutional power is in the hands of a President who is elected for a term of four years. President Lic. Daniel Oduber Q. was elected in February 1974. At the Congress elections, the state of the parties became: National Unification Party, 16; Liberation Party, 27; Socialist Action Party, 2; National Democrat Party 1; National Independent, 6; Renovación Democratica, 3; Unión Cartaginesa, 1; Republicano Nacional, 1.

#### Ministry

*Finance:* Lic. Federico Vargar Peralta.
*Foreign Affairs:* Lic. Gonzalio Facio.
*Interior, Police and Justice:* Sr. Milton Arias Calro.
*Agriculture:* Lic. Eneigua Azofeifa.
*Public Transport:* Ing. Alvaro Jenkins.
*Culture, Youth and Sports:* Lic. Fernando Volio.
*Public Health:* Dr. Hernan Weinstok.
*Labour and Social Welfare:* Lic. Rafael Angel Rojas, J.
*Economics Industry and Commerce:* Lic. Rodolfo Quinós Gonzalez.
*Public Security:* Mario Charpantier.
*Minister of the Presidency:* Lic. Guido Séanz.
*Education:* Lic. Fernando Volio.

### LEGAL SYSTEM

In addition to the Supreme Court, there are four Appeal Courts and a Court of Cassation. Minor crimes and misdemeanours are dealt with by provincial courts and local justices.

The President of the Supreme Court is Lic. Cato Albán, and the 16 other members of the Courts of Cassation and Appeal form the Supreme Court.

### AREA AND POPULATION

The area of Costa Rica is about 19,883 sq. miles.

The population at 1 July 1976 was 2,017,986 divided among the seven provinces as follows: San José 747,059; Alajuela, 349,528; Cartago, 220,312; Heredia, 143,262; Guanacaste, 193,619; Puntarenas, 238,252; Limón, 125,954. The annual average percentage growth rate of the population for the period 1960–74 was 3·1 and for the period 1965–74 was 2·9.

The chief towns are San José, 230,935; Alajuela, 35,287; Cartago, 13,351; Heredia, 24,545; Liberia, 11,179; Puntarenas, 27,349, Limón, 30,664.

### CURRENCY

The unit of currency is the colón of 100 centimos. There are cupro-nickel and brass coins of 5, 10, 25 and 50 centimos and 1 colón and 2 colónes. Banknotes of various denominations are in circulation (5, 10, 20, 50, 100, 500 and 1,000 colónes).

### FINANCE

Revenue in 1974 totalled 1,669,644,987 colónes, with 1,619,916,192 expenditure. The Central Government Debt at 31 December 1972 was 2,628,176,000·00 colónes.

The following are details of the budget for the fiscal year 1973 (in millions of colónes):

| | |
|---|---|
| *Expenditures* | |
| Public Debt Service | 287·9 |
| Social Services: | |
| Education | 495·3 |
| Public Health | 90·7 |
| Public Works | 236·7 |
| Public Security | 32·7 |
| Other expenditure | 725·9 |

The GNP at market prices for 1974 was U.S. $millions 1,610, and the GNP per capita at market prices was U.S. $840. The annual average percentage growth rate of the GNP per capita for the period 1960–74 was 2·9, and for the period 1965–74 was 3·7. [*See the note at the beginning of this section concerning GNP.*]

# COSTA RICA

## PRINCIPAL BANKS

**Banco Central de Costa Rica:** (President, Bernal Jiménez M; Manager, Rigoberto Navarro M., Est. 1950; now acts as sole bank of issue, and custodian of the nation's reserves; total assets at 31 December 1975 ₡3,551,241,655·90; note circulation ₡974,316,960·00. *Head Office:* San José

**Banco Nacional de Costa Rica.** (Manager, Elías Quirós.) Est. 1914 for development and commerce; total assets at 31 December 1970 ₡744,977,167; deposits ₡528,922,950; capital and reserves ₡80,248,876. 75 branches and 59 Rural Credit Board. *Head Office:* San José.

**Banco de Costa Rica.** (Manager, Boris Méndez.) Est. 1877; Commercial Bank; total assets at 31 December 1971 ₡844,377,827 19 branches. *Head Office:* San José.

**Banco Anglo Costarricense.** (Manager, Guido Goicoechea Q.) Est. 1863; Commercial Bank; total assets at 30 June 1975 ₡1,054,689,947·00; deposits ₡640,748,242·00; capital and reserves ₡49,937,789·00. *Head Office:* San José; 12 branches.

**Banco Crédito Agricola de Cartago.** (Manager, Hernán Levia). Total assets at 30 June 1973 ₡214,100,000; deposits ₡110,100,000·00; capital and reserves ₡37,731,500·00. *Head Office:* Cartago; 4 branches.

## PRODUCTION, INDUSTRY AND COMMERCE

**Agriculture.** *Coffee.* In 1969–70 the coffee crop reached a total of 1,838,010 quintals.

*Cocoa.* A draft law to establish a Cocoa Defence Board was submitted to the Ministry of Economy and Finance for consideration by the municipal and provincial authorities of Limón, the main cocoa growing province in the country. The proposed legislation is aimed at regulating in an equitable manner the relations between cocoa growers and exporters for their mutual benefit, whilst promoting national production. In 1970, 90,745 quintals were produced.

Values of the exports of the main crops in 1975 and 1976 (in thousand $ U.S.):

| | 1975 | 1976 |
|---|---|---|
| Bananas | 112,898 | 74,188 |
| Coffee | 96,907 | 97,269 |
| Cocoa | 5,318 | 3,415 |
| Sugar | 42,005 | 16,904 |
| Livestock | 5,921 | 695 |

*Tobacco.* The Legislative Assembly approved legislation establishing a Tobacco Defence Board. The Board will consist of five members, representing the Government, the tobacco manufacturing companies and the growers. The Board will recommend to the National Production Council the prices to be paid to growers according to quality and type of leaf, as well as the production quotas to be granted to individual growers. Production in 1968–69 was 34,092 quintals.

*Honey.* The U.S. is a substantial consumer of Costa Rican honey. According to figures released by the Ministry the production of honey in Costa Rica was 853,285 lb. In 1963 production was about 476 tons of which about 388 tons were exported. The export value was $115,614.

**Forestry.** Costa Rica's extensive forests have remained only partially exploited. In 1962 about 50 million board feet of timber were produced by the saw mills. Exports, consisting mainly of a soft wood used in the plywood industry, were valued at about 300,000 U.S. dollars.

**Commerce.** Main imports and exports by countries for 1976 (in thousand U.S. dollars):

| *Country* | *Exports* 1976 | *Imports* 1976 |
|---|---|---|
| United States | 199,893 | 238,731 |
| Canada | 1,196 | 15,618 |
| Netherlands Antilles | 222 | 5,831 |
| Netherlands | 16,290 | 8,663 |
| United Kingdom | 723 | 23,337 |
| Colombia | 456 | 7,015 |
| Belgium–Luxembourg | 9,515 | 6,809 |
| Germany | 55,822 | 39,429 |
| Italy | 10,476 | 9,381 |
| Japan | 8,199 | 61,241 |
| Other countries | 190,513 | 277,914 |

**Industry.** *Petroleum.* A company, *La Petrolera de Costa Rica*, affiliated to the Union Oil Co. of California, has begun operations in the country. New borings have been made, and yields of oil have resulted from two of them, but not in economic quantities. In accordance with their contract, the Company's working is restricted to an area of 150,000 hectares in the Province of Limón.

There are no commitments elsewhere in the country, so that the Government is free to offer concessions on the basis of a 50/50 sharing agreement as between the Government and the private concessionaire. The suggested regulation is that there should be a payment of 12·5 per cent of the value of the crude product as payment on account of the 50 per cent payable to the Government on the refined product.

A Petroleum Law is now in the process of being drafted, but it has not yet reached the Legislative Council.

*Electricity.* Investment made by the Costa Rica Electrical Institute (ICE), an autonomous Government institution, in 1968 was $3,674,628. On 16 October 1968, 93 per cent of the shares of the National Energy and Light Co. (C.N.F.L.) were acquired by I.C.E. In 1968 C.N.F.L. made total investments of $602,205.

In 1963, I.C.E. began work on the Cachi hydro-electric scheme, which was completed in 1967, at a total cost of $23,645,285. Operations began in 1967, and its installed capacity was 64,000 kW.

The total electrical energy produced by Costa Rica's power plants in 1968 was 761,854,628 kWh. These plants have a total installed capacity of 206,630 kW.

## COMMUNICATIONS

**Roads.** There are almost 23,091 km. of roads, mostly unsurfaced. The Costa Rican portion of the Pan-American Highway is about 660 km. long.

**Railways.** Costa Rica has 1,064 kilometres of railways, all of 42 inch gauge, of which 297 are owned by the United Fruit Company. The Northern Railway, 604 kilometres, connecting San José with Limón, is British-owned.

The Ferrocarri Eléctrico al Pacífico, 151 kilometres, connecting San José with Puntarenas, is an autonomous government institution.

### Civil Aviation

**LACSA—Lineas Aereas Costarricenses, S.A.** Chairman, Dr. Antonio Peña Chavarria; Executive President, Capt. Otto Escalante. W. 33⅓ per cent share capital is owned by the State; *services operated:* San José–Tocumen (Panama), San José–Miami, San José–Mexico, San José–Grand Cayman, San José–San Salvador, San José–Barranquila, Colombia, San José–Maracaibo and Caracas, Venezuela. *Head Office:* Apartado 1531, San José, Costa Rica.

**Telegraphs and Telephones.** Wireless communication with all parts of the world is maintained by the Compañía Radiografica Internacional de Costa Rica. Inland services are Government owned and controlled. The Government has 28 wireless telegraph offices in the local network.

In keeping with Law 3226, since 28 October 1963 the Costa Rican telephone system has been operated by I.C.E. In December 1968, there were 13 telephone exchanges handling 33,316 telephones; there were 29,286 subscribers, of which 17,381 were residential, 7,982 commercial, 1,531 duplex, 313 public, and 2,079 PBX. There are 26,589 kilometres of trunk lines, and 148,552 kilometres of pairs in urban circuits, of which 97,361 comprise the primary network, and 51,191 the secondary network; both figures include overhead, underground and screened cables.

**Broadcasting.** There are 43 medium wave and seven short wave transmitting stations.

### NEWSPAPERS

**La Nacion.** Independent. Morning. Editor, Guido Fernández. San José. Circulation 80,557.

**La Republica.** Independent. Morning. Editor, Rodrigo Madrigal Nieto. San José. Circulation 27,000.

**La Prensa Libre.** Independent. Afternoon. Editor, Andrés Borrasé. San José, Costa Rica. Circulation 48,200.

### ATOMIC ENERGY

A National Atomic Energy Commission was formed in September 1957 under the auspices of the University of Costa Rica.

In April 1958 the Interamerican Institute of Agricultural Science (Instituto Interamericano de Ciencias Agricolas), who maintain an agricultural research station at Turrialba, approximately 60 kilometres from San José, inaugurated an experimental gamma ray irradiation field with equipment supplied by the United States Atomic Energy Commission. It is used for experiments on tropical and sub-tropical plants such as coffee, cocoa and bananas. An isotope laboratory was opened at the same time.

In view of the considerable hydro-electric resources suitable for further development it seems unlikely that the construction of nuclear power stations will be considered for the next few years.

### EDUCATION

Primary education is compulsory and free. In 1976 there were 2,934 primary schools with 375,108 pupils. There are secondary schools with 143,390 pupils and 8,830 professors.

Higher education is provided at the University of Costa Rica, situated at San José. In 1974 there were 19,544 pupils and 766 professors.

### RELIGION

Roman Catholicism is the state religion but there is complete freedom of worship for others.

# Cuba

## (REPÚBLICA DE CUBA)

**Capital**—Havana.

**President**—Fidel Castro Ruz.

**National Flag:** Parti of five fess-wise, alternately blue and white; at the hoist, pointing towards the fly, a triangle red charged with a star five-pointed white.

### CONSTITUTION AND GOVERNMENT

Cuba belonged to Spain until 10 December 1898 when sovereignty was handed over in accordance with the terms of the Paris Treaty which put an end to the intervention of the U.S. Armed Forces in Cuba's fight against Spanish domination.

Cuba was then under U.S. military rule until 1902. In 1901 the States' Government imposed on the Constituent Assembly the Platt Amendment, which became an annex to the Constitution, establishing the right of the United States to intervene in Cuba's internal affairs.

The mediatized Republic inaugurated in 1903 lasted until 1959 when, after a battle, the forces led by Comandante Fidel Castro Ruz, overthrew Batista's dictatorship.

With the advent of the Revolution on 1 January 1959, a Fundamental Law had to be promulgated adapted to the conditions of that occasion; thus it was that the Fundamental Law of the Republic came into force on 7 February 1959, adapating the 1940 Constitution to the new situation and its consequent development.

Various laws aimed at achieving the objectives of the Revolutionary Government has been promulgated since then, each subject to further revision. In fact these laws have been different interpretations of the best methods of organizing the State and its resources for the benefit of the people, in the light of experience.

On 16 April 1961, Comandante Fidel Castro proclaimed the Revolution to be Socialist on the eve of the attack in Bahia de Cochinos made by mercenary troops sent in by the U.S government; it was defeated in less than 72 hours.

The Cuban Communist Party is the leading party of the government and of the state.

The party is led by a Central Committee with an eight-member Political Bureau, a six-member secretariat and an Organizing Secretary.

### POLITICAL BUREAU

Comandante Fidel Castro Ruz.
Comandante Raúl Castro Ruz.
Dr. Osvaldo Dorticós Torrado.
Comandante Juan Almeida Bosque.
Comandante Ramiro Valdés Menéndez.
Dr. Armando Hart Dávalos.
Comandante Guillermo García Fría.
Comandante Sergio del Valle Jiménez.

#### Secretariat

Comandante Fidel Castro Ruz.
Comandante Raúl Castro Ruz.
Dr. Osvaldo Dorticós Torrado.
Companero Blas Roca Calderió.
Comandante Faure Chomón Mediavilla.
Dr. Carlos Rafael Rodríguez.

#### Organizing Secretary

Dr. Armando Hart Dávalos.

#### Executive Committee

The Executive Committee of the Council of Ministers consists of the Prime Minister who presides, and a number of Vice prime ministers.

#### Council of Ministers

The Council of Ministers consists of the Prime Minister, the Vice prime ministers and the heads of all central state agencies with the rank of ministries.

The following is the list of the Council of Ministers:

*Prime Minister:* Dr. Fidel Castro Ruz.
*First Deputy Prime Minister and Minister for Armed Forces:* Cdte de Div. Raúl Castro Ruz.
*Deputy Prime Ministers,* Cdte. de la Revolucion Ramiro Valdes Menendez; Cdte. de la Revolucion Guillermo Garcia Fria; Sr. Flavio Bravo Pardo; Sr. Belarmino Castilla Más; Sr. Diocleo Torralba González; Dr. Carlos Rafael Rodriguez; Sr. Joel Domenech Benitez.
*Minister for Foreign Affairs:* Dr. Raúl Roa García.
*Minister of Justice:* Dr. Armando Torres Santrayill.
*Minister of Interior:* Sr. Sergio del Valle.
*Minister of Communications:* Sr. Pedro Guelmes González.
*Minister of Foreign Trade,* Sr. Marcelo Fernandez Font.
*Minister of Internal Trade:* Sr. Serafín Fernández Rodriguez.
*Minister of Chemical Industry:* Sr. Antonio Esquivel Yedra.
*Minister of Mining and Geology:* Sr. Manuel Cespedes Herrandez.
*Minister of Sidero-Mechanic Industry:* Sr. Lester Rodriguez Pérez.
*Minister of Electricity Industry:* Sr. José Luis Beltran Fernandez.
*Minister of Light Industry:* Sra. Nora Frometa Silva.
*Minister of Public Health:* Dr. José A. Gutiérrez Muñiz.
*Minister of Education:* Sr. José Fernandez Alvarez.
*Minister of Labour:* Sr. Oscar Fernandez Padilla.
*Minister of Merchant Marine and Ports:* Sr. Angel Joel Chaveco Morales.
*Minister of Transport:* Sr. Enrique Lussón Battle.
*Minister of the Sugar Industry:* Ing. Marcos Lage Cuello.
*Minister of the Food Industry:* Sr. José A. Naranjo Morales.
*President, National Bank:* Sr. Raúl León Torras.
*Minister of Industrial Development:* Ing. Angel Gomez Trueba.

*Minister of Industrial Construction:* Sr. Raciel Alvarez.
*Ministsr of Social and Agriculture Buildings Development:* Sr. Levi Farah Balmaseda.

## LEGAL SYSTEM

There is a Supreme Court consisting of civil, criminal and administrative departments in Havana and Courts of Appeal in each of the provinces. The provinces are divided into judicial districts, with courts for civil actions and municipal courts for minor offences.

*President of the Supreme Court:*
Enrique Hart.

## AREA AND POPULATION

Cuba has a total area of 42,892 sq. miles. The population at mid-1974 was 9,090,000. The annual average percentage growth rate of the population for the period 1960–74 was 2·0 and for the period 1965–74 was 1·8.

The areas and population of the six provinces are shown below:

| *Province* | *Area* (*sq. km.*) | *Population* 1965 |
|---|---|---|
| Havana | 8,221 | 2,023,600 |
| Pinar del Rio | 13,500 | 555,800 |
| Matanzas | 8,444 | 447,000 |
| Las Villas | 21,411 | 1,178,800 |
| Camaguey | 26,346 | 785,400 |
| Oriente | 36,602 | 2,443,600 |

The chief towns and the numbers of their inhabitants according to the 1970 Census are: Havana, 1,755,360; Holguín, 422,329; Camaguey, 196,854; Santiago de Cuba, 372,007; Santa Clara, 331,655; Cienfuegos, 225,615; Matanzas, 160,097.

## CURRENCY

The monetary unit is the peso consisting of 100 centavos. The current rate of exchange is 2·40 pesos to one pound sterling. The U.S. dollar ceased to be legal tender in Cuba on 30 June 1961. Notes in circulation are issued by the National Bank of Cuba in denominations of 100, 50, 20, 10, 5 and 1 pesos.

## FINANCE

The GNP at market prices for 1974 was U.S. $ millions 6,480. The annual average percentage growth rate of the GNP per capita for the period 1960–74 was −0·9 and for the period 1965–74 was −0·6. [*See the note at the beginning of this Section concerning GNP.*]

## BANKS

All banks were nationalized in 1960.

**National Bank of Cuba.** *Head Office:* Cuba No. 402, Havana. Branches: 6 Provincial Offices, 52 Regional Offices and 204 Agencies. *Cable:* Bancuba—Telex Nos. 124 and 146. President: Lcdo. Raúl León Torras. Vice-President: Mr. Julio A. Imperatori. London Representative Office: Market Buildings, 29 Mincing Lane, London, E.C.3. *Cable:* Bancubarep. *Telex:* 883693. Tl. 6232707.

## PRODUCTION, INDUSTRY AND COMMERCE

**Agriculture.** Until the Revolution, the economy was essentially an agricultural one, with a predominance of extensive single-crop production, and the consequent existence of large estates. With these conditions it was therefore essential to introduce a system of Agrarian Reform, which made owners of more than 100,000 small producers by expropriating estates of over 165 acres, and substantially modifying the land in Cuba by investing a large amount of resources and effort.

Cuba's soil is fertile and up to two annual crops can therefore be obtained. Sugar production is the main source of foreign exchange earnings. In 1970 production was 8,537,600 tons which is the highest ever, and what is more the highest cane sugar production achieved by any country. In order to mechanize agriculture, 56,166 tractors and 7,205 cane sugar lifters were imported in the period 1959 to 1970.

There are many natural resources that can be exploited to promote agricultural development at an industrial level, in particular underground waters which provide highly aquiferous zones over some 16·4 thousand square miles.

The water capacity in the dams prior to 1959 was 982 million cubic feet which by 1970 had been increased to 27,955 million cubic feet.

In 1969, 1,347,000 acres were under irrigation. Cuba's hydraulic potential is 741 thousand million cubic feet.

**Livestock.** In 1962 there were 6,100,000 cattle, 194,000 sheep, 412,000 horses, 31,000 mules, 3,000 asses, 1,900,000 pigs and 162,000 goats.

**Forestry.** Cuba's economic policy in the forestry sector is aimed at developing the resources and exploiting the country's forests at national level. They used to cover an area equivalent to 50 per cent of the territory but in 1959 after many decades of indiscriminate felling only 10 per cent of the area of the country remained afforested. The forests contain many valuable cabinet woods such as mahogany and cedar, the latter being used locally for the manufacture of cigar boxes.

**Fishing.** Cuba's fishing platform is very important—about 500 different species and varieties of edible fish live around the island.

Ever since the Revolution, Cuba's catch has steadily increased; one of the contributing factors to this success has been the acquisition of modern boats built with the latest technological skills, which have enabled the radius of operation to be extended beyond the insular platform, and new techniques are being used which have led to considerable production increases.

Only 21·9 thousand tons of fish were landed in 1958 as against 90·5 thousand tons in 1970.

Cuba's fishing exploitation and development policy is the responsibility of the National Fisheries Institute which has a Fisher Research Centre and a River Re-population Centre.

**Commerce.** Cuba's chief exports are sugar, tobacco and minerals. Sugar accounts for almost 85 per cent of the total value of exports, minerals for about 6 per cent and tobacco for 5 per cent. Total estimated value of exports in 1964 was 713·7 million dollars; and of imports 1,104·7 million.

**In 1963 the value of sugar and tobacco exports** (thousand pesos) was as follows: raw sugar cane, 378,738; refined sugar cane, 39,271; syrup, 13,586; tobacco leaf (untreated), 16,142; tobacco leaf (processed), 1,782; tobacco (twisted), 6,272; cigarettes, 911.

The following tables show percentage value of imports and exports by selected countries 1969 and 1970:

| *Imports* | 1969 (*million U.S.* $) | 1970 |
|---|---|---|
| **Total** | 1,167,667·9 | 1,300,459·0 |
| **Bulgaria** | 25,270·3 | 23,312·2 |
| **Canada** | 13,954·9 | 27·968·3 |
| **Czechoslovakia** | 28,833·9 | 3,248·7 |
| German Democratic Republic | 43,166·8 | 49,986·7 |
| Japan | 9,623·6 | 31,496·4 |
| U.S.S.R. | 659,886·5 | 686,852·6 |
| United Kingdom | 40,140·8 | 58,548·4 |
| Algeria | 2,348·5 | 4,262·5 |

| *Exports* | 1969 (*million U.S.* $) | 1970 |
|---|---|---|
| **Total** | 663,543·1 | 1,043,434·9 |
| **Bulgaria** | 26,997·3 | 28,825·5 |
| **Canada** | 6,849·5 | 8,835·5 |
| **Czechoslovakia** | 43,071·4 | 49,230·8 |
| German Democratic Republic | 37,741·5 | 48,791·8 |
| Japan | 65,266·3 | 105,983·4 |
| U.S.S.R. | 233,050·2 | 529,110·7 |
| United Kingdom | 14,243·9 | 19,439·4 |

**Mining.** In spite of her relatively limited area, Cuba has an abundance of minerals of various kinds, although some of the extremely important ones are absent e.g. coal and phosphorites and a little oil is extracted.

The greatest importance is attached to deposits containing nickel, cobalt and iron whose known reserves are in the region of several hundred million tons. Cuba's laterite deposits are of world importance. Moa, Nicaro and Pinares de Mayarí. all in the province of Oriente, are the main ones. There are also large reserves of chromite, magnetite, manganese and copper. To a lesser extent, lead, zinc, gold, silver and tungsten.

There are large reserves of limestone, rock salt, gypsum and dolomite, and there are also large kaolin and marble deposits on the Island of Pines. In 1964, production was: nickel and cobalt oxide, 18,861 tons; nickel and cobalt ore, 2,009,000 tons; nickel and cobalt sulphate, 14,005 tons; nickel and cobalt sinter, 17,701 tons; manganese sinter, 70,347 tons.

**Industry.** There are a number of factories manufacturing consumer goods for local consumption, including cotton and rayon textiles, rayon yarn, staple fibre and tyre yarn (the latter is also exported), leather and rubber footwear, tyres and tubes, cement, paints, soap, beer and mineral waters, matches, leather goods, pharmaceuticals, aluminium ware and cardboard boxes. The manufacture of cigars and cigarettes is the best-known export industry. 90 per cent of all industry is controlled by the Government.

## COMMUNICATIONS

**Roads and Railways.** The highway network consists of approximately 18,932 km. of which approximately 8,000 km. are surfaced. The most important roads are the 1,444-kilometre central highway and the White Road, which is 110 km. long and connects Havana and Matanzas. 800 km. of roads are being built in Oriente Province. Up to 1970 over 3,240 km. of highways and roads have been built. There has been a large increase in the number of buses; in 1970 urban buses carried a total of 1,124,140·1 thousand passengers.

Cuba's national rail network has 14,797 km. of track in operation, of which only 3,179 km. are narrow gauge.

**Shipping.** Cuba's merchant navy has grown rapidly since 1959; her 14 vessels with 58·0 thousand tons dead weight had increased by 1970 to 51 vessels and a dead weight of 437·8 thousand tons.

**Civil Aviation.** Cuba has a civil airline covering national and international routes; internally there are flights from Havana to Santiago de Cuba, Baracoa, Guantánamo, Camaguey, Cienfuegos, Island of Pines and other places; there are international air services to Prague, Madrid, Chile, and Mexico.

**CCA—Compania Cubana de Aviacion.** The Company is an all-Cuban enterprise. Resources more than $17,000,000; *services operated:* Havana–Gander–Madrid, Havana–Mexico, Havana–Santiago de Cuba, and internal, Havana–Baracoa. *Head Office:* 105 Calle 23, Vedado, Cuba.

**ECCA—Empresa Consolidada Cubana De Aviacion.** Resources 100 per cent Cuban enterprise. *Services operated:* Havana–Madrid, Havana–Praga, Havana–Mexico. Routes covering all national territory. *Head Office:* 23/64 La Rampa, Vedado, Havana, Cuba.

**Telegraphs and Telephones.** There are national telex, telegraph and telephone networks. In 1970 there were 2,693,000 telephones installed and 5,569 exchanges and public telephones. The public telephone service is free of charge.

**Broadcasting and Television.** Cuba has its own radio and television network. There are two television stations in Havana and a provincial one in Oriente.

## NEWSPAPERS

**Granma Weekly Review.** Sunday, editions in English, French and Spanish. P.O. Box 6260, Havana 6, Cuba.

**Hoy.** Morning, except Monday. Prado y Teniente Rey, Havana. Circulation 232,000.

**La Tarde.** Evening. Gral. Suarez, Plaza de la Revolucion, Havana. Circulation 85,000.

**Revolución.** Morning. Havana. Circulation 180,000.

## EDUCATION AND RELIGION

From 1959 and after the 1961 campaign against illiteracy, Cuba has seen a new stage in the development of education based on training through qualified scientific and technical instruction and a marxist culture.

There are three universities in Cuba; the 1958–59 academic year registration figures of 25,514 students rose to 330,050 in the 1970–71 academic year. These universities have Faculties of Technology, Agricultural Sciences, Medical Sciences, Humanities and Institutes of Economics and Education.

The primary schools had 700,000 pupils in the 1958–59 school year and 1,600,000 in 1967–70.

Another aspect developed in Cuba in the field of education has been adult education, involving millions of Cubans.

There is no established church, though most of the population is Roman Catholic.

# Cyprus

(REPUBLIC OF CYPRUS)

(MEMBER OF THE COMMONWEALTH)

**Capital**—Nicosia.

**President**—Spyros Kyprianou.

**National Flag:** White; at the centre the Island in gold above two olive branches crossed.

## CONSTITUTION AND GOVERNMENT

THE island was declared an independent sovereign state on 16 August 1960. Under the Constitution of the Republic of Cyprus the island is administered by a Council of Ministers (seven Greek and three Turkish) with a Greek President and a Turkish Vice-President, elected for a five-year term of office by the Greek and Turkish communities respectively. The Council of Ministers is appointed by the President and the Vice-President.

Legislative power rests with the House of Representatives, which is elected for five years.

In 1963 difficulties arose in connection with the implementation of certain provisions of the Constitution and in December 1963 armed clashes took place between the Turkish Cypriots and Government Forces. A United Nations Peace Keeping Force is now stationed in Cyprus following a resolution of the Security Council. A mediator was also appointed to find a solution to the Cyprus problem. His report containing his recommendations was, however, rejected by the Turkish Cypriots and by Turkey which was one of the guarantors of the Zurich Agreement which led to the Independence of Cyprus.

Since January 1964 the Turkish members of the Executive have ceased taking part in the work of the Council of Ministers and the Turkish members of the House of Representatives have also ceased attending the House. Equally the Turkish Civil Servants have abandoned their posts.

Following an acute crisis in November 1967 Special Envoys were sent to the area by President Johnson and U.N. Secretary-General U Thant in an effort to avert the conflagration which seemed imminent.

The U.N. Security Council dealt with the situation and extended the stationing of the Peace Force in Cyprus and the Secretary-General offered his good offices to the parties to help find a solution to the outstanding issues, and these were accepted.

Following these developments respresentatives of the Greek and Turkish Cypriots started direct talks in June 1968 with a view to finding a formula reconciling the different views.

Among the questions to be solved is that of local government. In May 1969, the government submitted to the Turkish side, proposals to achieve a successful outcome of the talks.

On 15 July 1974 mainland Greek officers of the Greek Cypriot National Guard launched a coup d'état against President Makarios. The leaders of the coup subsequently claimed that President Makarios was dead although this was not the case and the President was in due course rescued by RAF helicopter from Paphos in Western Cyprus and then flown from the British Sovereign Base area, to the United Kingdom.

The coup was followed on 20 July 1974 by Turkish military intervention. On the same day the United Nations Security Council called for a cease-fire which, following agreement by Greece and Turkey, was on 22 July. The British Government then obtained the agreement of Greece and Turkey to hold talks between the guarantor States in Geneva. The first stage of the Geneva conference took place between 25 and 30 July. The talks reconvened in Geneva on 8 August and on 12 August the Turkish delegation demanded a constructive reply to their proposal for a clearly defined Turkish Cypriot zone covering a third of the island. The talks broke down on 13 August when the Turkish Government refused to extend its deadline for a decision on its proposals and Turkish forces subsequently moved to extend their control over Northern Cyprus. A further cease-fire was effected on 16 August.

The United Nations Secretary-General visited Cyprus in late August 1974 and arranged that the Intercommunal talks between Mr Clerides, the then acting-President of Cyprus, and Mr Denktash, the Turkish Cypriot leader, should be resumed under the auspices of the United Nations in Nicosia. This phase of negotiations lasted until February 1975 when Mr Denktash declared his so-called "Turkish Federated State of Cyprus". However, discussion in the Security Council led to a further resumption of the talks in April 1975 since when there have been six rounds of talks.

On 3 August 1977 President Makarios died.

## LEGAL SYSTEM

Legal institutions are the Supreme Court of the Republic, the Assize Courts and the District Courts, and the Communal Courts.

The Supreme Court is composed of more than five, but not exceeding seven Judges, one of whom is the President of the Court. The Supreme Court adjudicates exclusively and finally: on all constitutional and administrative law matters, including any resources that any law or decision of the House of Representatives, or the Budget, is discriminatory against either of the two communities; on any conflict of competence between state organs in the Republic, decision questions of the unconstitutionality of any law, or on any question of interpretation of the Constitution in case of ambiguity, as well as recourses for annulment of administrative acts, decisions or omissions.

All judicial power in civil and criminal matters is also exercised by the Supreme Court and its subordinate courts. The Supreme Court is the highest appellate Court in the Republic and has jurisdiction to hear and determine all appeals from any Court; it has exclusive jurisdiction to issue orders in the nature of habeas corpus, mandamus, prohibition, quo warranto and certiorari, and it has original jurisdiction in admiralty and matrimonial matters.

There are six Assize Courts and six District Courts, one for each district. The Assize Courts have unlimited criminal jurisdiction and power to order compensation up to £800. These Courts are normally composed of a President of a District Court who presides, and two District Judges nominated by the Supreme Court.

The six District Courts consist of one or more Presidents and such District Judges as the Supreme Court may direct.

The District Courts exercise original civil and criminal jurisdiction, the extent of which varies with the composition of the Bench. In civil matters (other than those within the jurisdiction of Supreme Court) a District Court composed of not less than two and not more than three Judges has unlimited jurisdiction. A President or a District Judge sitting alone has jurisdiction up to £500, and is also empowered to deal with any action for the recovery of possession of any immovable property, and certain other specified matters.

In criminal matters the jurisdiction of a District Court is exercised by its members sitting singly and is of a summary character. A President or a District Judge sitting alone has power to try any offence punishable with imprisonment up to three years, or with a fine up to £500, or with both, and may order compensation up to £500.

Civil disputes relating to personal status of members of the Turkish community are dealt with by two Communal Courts; there is also a communal appellate court to which appeals may be made from the decisions of the courts of first instance.

There is a Greek Orthodox Church tribunal having exclusive jurisdiction in matrimonial causes between members of the Greek Orthodox Church. The decisions of this tribunal are appealable to the appellate tribunal of that Church.

## AREA AND POPULATION

The area of the island is 3,572 square miles.

The *de jure* population in mid-1973 amounted to 639,000. It consists of 82 per cent Greek Cypriots and 18 per cent Turkish Cypriots (small minorities of Armenians, Maronites and Latins are included in the Greek Cypriot percentage). The chief towns are Nicosia, the capital, with a population of 117,000, Limassol 80,600, Famagusta 39,400, and Larnaca 19,800.

The Greek Cypriot populations of Famagusta and Kyrenia have abandoned these towns, which are under Turkish occupation.

## FINANCE

Revenue and Expenditure for two Calendar Years (in £ sterling):

| *Ordinary* | 1974 | 1975 |
|---|---|---|
| Revenue | £55,207,730 | £56,025,900 |
| Expenditure | £60,840,032 | £67,745,048 |
| Development | £10,612,956 | £11,894,869 |

The figures for development expenditure do not include loans advanced by Government to local authorities and Semi-Government Institutions for carrying out development projects.

## BANKING

Bank's deposits at 31 December 1975 were C£247·9 m. as against C£229·9 m. in 1974. Bank's advances and loans were C£218·5 m. The country's foreign exchange reserves as the end of December 1975 were C£89·0 m.

**Central Bank of Cyprus.** (Governor, C. C. Stephani.) Est. 1963. Responsible for the issue of currency, the regulation of money supply and credit, administration of the Exchange Control Law and the foreign exchange reserves of the Republic. The bank acts as a banker to the Government and the commercial banks operating in Cyprus.

## PRODUCTION, INDUSTRY AND COMMERCE

Agriculture is the industry which provides the greatest employment in the island. The following table gives some figures appertaining to agricultural economics:

| | 1974 | 1975 |
|---|---|---|
| (*a*) Employment: % of economically active population | 33·1% | 23·2% |
| (*b*) % of Gross Agricultural Product to G.D.P. | 17·82% | 16·82% |
| (*c*) Gross Agricultural Product in Value terms | £50·2 m. | £40·3 m. |

Principal agricultural products are: citrus, potatoes, vine products, cereals, carobs, olives, carrots, almonds, tobacco and onions.

The figures for principal agricultural products for 1975 are as follows in thousands of tons:

| | |
|---|---|
| Wheat | 32·0 |
| Barley | 50·0 |
| Potatoes | 110·0 |
| Carrots | 3·2 |
| Wine | 10,820·0 (gallons) |
| Carobs | 20·0 |
| Olives | 13·0 |
| Oranges | 32·0 |
| Grapefruits | 35·0 |
| Lemons | 11·0 |
| Grapes | 170·0 |

Mining is carried on in various parts of the island and the following minerals are extracted: cupreous concentrates, cement-copper, cupreous pyrites, iron pyrites, asbestos, chromium ore and concentrates, gypsum and earth colours.

The total value of minerals exported in 1973 was £10,691,373. Cupreous concentrates, iron and cupreous pyrites, cement, copper and asbestos are the principal mineral exports.

Manufacturing output is estimated at about £111·5 m. in 1974. The contribution in value of gross output of each branch of the manufacturing sector for 1974 (thousand £s) was as follows:

| | 1974 |
|---|---|
| Food industries | 23,789 |
| Beverages | 15,156 |
| Tobacco | 2,751 |
| Textiles | 3,388 |
| Clothing and footwear | 12,144 |
| Wood and cork | 1,641 |
| Furniture | 3,978 |
| Paper | 2,022 |
| Printing | 3,677 |
| Leather | 1,261 |
| Rubber articles | 659 |
| Chemical | 3,707 |
| Petroleum products | 14,571 |

*continued*

| | 1974 |
|---|---|
| Non-metallics | 7,153 |
| Metal goods | 5,980 |
| Machinery | 2,001 |
| Electrical equipment | 951 |
| Transport | 3,579 |
| Miscellaneous | 3,066 |

The following table shows imports and exports by commodities for the year 1975 (in C£):

| | *Imports* | *Exports* |
|---|---|---|
| Food | 24,345,747 | 19,090,320 |
| Beverages and Tobacco | 2,338,987 | 5,845,995 |
| Crude materials | 1,284,477 | 8,872,663 |
| Mineral fuels | 18,067,228 | 236,818 |
| Natural oils | 2,746,308 | 96,417 |
| Chemicals | 10,246,184 | 442,027 |
| Manufactured goods | 28,726,113 | 9,477,350 |
| Machinery and transport | 17,498,564 | 4,596,190 |
| Miscellaneous manufactured goods | 7,296,490 | 6,538,387 |
| Miscellaneous | 1,159,053 | 816,231 |
| Total | 113,709,151 | 56,012,398 |

## COMMUNICATIONS

Limassol is the main sea port. In 1974, 2,031 steamships (tonnage 3,310,096) and 48 sailing vessels (tonnage 5,575) engaged in foreign trade entered Cyprus Ports. In 1975 the comparable figures were: 2,519 steamships (tonnage 3,230,428) and 12 sailing vessels (tonnage 1,388).

There were (December 1975) 139,300 road motor vehicles, including 85,160 private and 13,210 motor cycles.

In 1975 there were 31 main post offices and 553 agencies.

A new airport has been constructed at Larnaca from which flights operate on a scheduled basis to Europe, the Middle East and the Arabian Gulf. International operations at Larnaca commenced on the 8 February 1975.

During the period 8 February 1975 to 31 December 1975, two airlines, Cyprus Airways and Olympic Airways operated scheduled services to Athens, Beirut, Cairo, London, Salonica and Tel-Aviv. Air passenger traffic in, out and through Larnaca Airport in 1975 amounted to 179,171.

The Nicosia Flight Information Centre controls and safeguards movements of aircraft through the Eastern Mediterranean which in 1975 reached the figure of 73,756, an increase of 11·2 per cent over 1974.

In 1975 there were 21,750 car radio licences, 91,020 household radio licences and 58,490 television licences.

## NEWSPAPERS

There are 1 English, 10 Greek and 2 Turkish daily newspapers, and 6 Greek and 1 Turkish weekly in addition to Government publications.

## EDUCATION

In March 1965 a Ministry of Education was established to which all functions concerning Greek education, as well as education of all minorities except the Turkish, have been transferred. Turkish education remains under the control of the Turkish Community.

Elementary education is mainly public, while in the case of secondary education, 11·5 per cent is provided by the private sector. Third level education in Cyprus is mostly pursued abroad, mainly in Greece, the U.K., France, the U.S.A., and the Soviet Union. Expenditure of Public sector on education has been 3·8 per cent of the GNP, while that of Public and Private sectors amounted to 6·5 per cent of the GNP in 1974–75.

## RELIGION

Population according to religion has not greatly changed since the 1960 census. During that period 77 per cent Greek Orthodox belonged to the Cypriot Church and 18·3 per cent were Moslem Turkish. The remainder comprised members of various religions. The Cypriot Church is a branch of and in communion with the Orthodox Eastern Church. It is, however, independent, in that the Archbishop of Cyprus is not subordinate to any Patriarch.

# Czechoslovakia

(ČESKOSLOVENSKÁ SOCIALISTICKÁ REPUBLIKA)

**Capital**—Prague.

**President**—Dr. Gustáv Husák.

**National Flag:** Divided fesse-wise white and red; at the hoist, point to the fly, a triangle blue full depth.

## CONSTITUTION AND GOVERNMENT

THE Czechoslovak Socialist Republic is a federal State of two nations of equal rights, the Czechs and Slovaks. Geographically it consists of Bohemia, Moravia and parts of Silesia, which constitute the Czech Socialist Republic, and of Slovakia, which constitutes the Slovak Socialist Republic. Besides the two fraternal nations proper, the Czech and the Slovak, the country was also inhabited up to the end of the Second World War by a fairly numerous minority of Germans and Magyars. In accordance with the Potsdam Agreement of the three Great Powers, the German minority was transferred to Germany after the end of the war. On the basis of a bi-lateral agreement between Czechoslovakia and Hungary, a part of the Magyars who had been living in Slovakia were exchanged for Slovaks still living in Hungary. According to the 1976 figures, there are 595,000 Hungarians, 78,000 Germans, 67,000 Poles and 60,000 Ukrainians in Czechoslovakia.

The Czechoslovak State came into existence on the 28 October 1918 after the defeat and disintegration of the Austro-Hungarian monarchy. The official proclamation of the Republic by the first Czechoslovak National Assembly took place on the 14 November 1918 and Professor T. G. Masaryk was elected as its first President.

In September 1938 Adolf Hitler demanded from Czechoslovakia the cession of the so-called Sudeten area and by the Munich Agreement on 29 September 1938 between Great Britain, Germany, France and Italy, these districts were annexed by the German Reich on the understanding that no further demands were to be made. The second President of the Republic, Dr. Eduard Beneš, resigned from office and went abroad. On 15 March 1939 Germany invaded and occupied the Czech Provinces of Bohemia, Moravia and Silesia, whilst Hlinka's separatist party proclaimed, with the approval and assistance of Germany, the formation of a so-called independent Slovak State. This state of affairs was never recognized by the Soviet Union, the United States, Great Britain and France. The Munich Agreement was never recognized by the Soviet Union on the grounds that it would have no standing in international law and was thus invalid. This view was confirmed by Italy on 26 September 1944, and by the French National Committee on 29 September 1942 who each declared the Agreement invalid. The position of the British Government was explained on 5 August 1942, when they declared that as Germany had deliberately destroyed arrangements concerning Czechoslovakia in which U.K. participated, the British Government regard themselves as free to form any engagements in this respect.

In July 1940 the first provisional Czechoslovak Government was established in London.

On his return to Czechoslovakia in April 1945 President Beneš formed a new government, with Zdeněk Fierlinger (Social Democrat) as Prime Minister.

The Constituent National Assembly was elected in May 1946. The elections confirmed the fact that the Communist Party, which won the largest number of votes, was the leading force in the National Front. Besides the position of Prime Minister, the Communists had various important ministries, such as the Ministry of the Interior. The fact that the Communists strengthened their leading positions in other ways as well during 1947, led some representatives of the other parties to work against the National Front programme which they themselves accepted in 1945. As a result of this 12 ministers handed in their resignation on 20 February 1948. The crisis was resolved constitutionally by President Beneš accepting the resignations of the ministers, and, on the proposal of the Prime Minister, appointing new ministers. The National Front was re-established with the help of representatives of the Czechoslovak people, from all the political parties, mass organizations and religious bodies. On 25 February 1948, Klement Gottwald formed a new Government of the re-established National Front.

On 14 June 1948 Klement Gottwald was unanimously elected President of the Czechoslovak Republic, following the resignation of Dr. Beneš, who was seriously ill and who died in September of the same year. On 15 June a new Cabinet under Antonín Zápotocký was formed. Of its 22 members, 12 were Communist and three Social Democrats, but on 27 June the Social Democratic Party merged with the Communist Party. Since 1948, cultural and economic co-operation with the Soviet Union and other socialist countries has been greatly increased.

In March 1953 President Gottwald died, Prime Minister Zápotocký was elected the new President. Czechoslovakia, the German Democratic Republic, Yugoslavia and Rumania are the only Socialist countries which have retained the office of the Presidency of the State.

President A. Zápotocký died in November 1957. Antonín Novotný, the First Secretary of the Communist Party of Czechoslovakia, was elected as the new President. On 22 March 1968 Mr. Antonín Novotný resigned as President of Czechoslovakia. General Ludvík Svoboda was unanimously elected as President on 30 March 1968, and re-elected on 22 March 1973. Dr. Gustáv Husák was elected President of the Republic on 29 May, 1975.

### The National Front

The political embodiment of the alliance of the working people is the National Front, associating all political parties and social organizations (Trade Unions, the Socialist Union of Youth, etc.) headed by the Communist Party of Czechoslovakia. The other political parties are the Czechoslovak Socialist Party, the Czechoslovak People's Party (these two in the Czech lands only), the Slovak Freedom Party and the Slovak Revival Party (in Slovakia only). The Communist Party of Slovakia is the territorial party organization of the Communist Party of Czechoslovakia.

In 1968 it was decided to transform the hitherto unitary Czechoslovak Socialist Republic into a federation consisting of two national republics, the Czech Socialist Republic and the Slovak Socialist Republic to ensure full equality of both nations. The pertinent constitutional law on the federation of Czechoslovakia was passed by the National Assembly on 28 October 1968, and the federation came into force on 1 January 1969. The new law replaces some chapters of the existing Constitution.

The federal structure of the Czechoslovak Socialist Republic is based on two main principles—that of the parity of the two nations, and the ban of outvoting the representatives of one nation by those of the other nation in affairs concerning essential national interests.

The supreme organ of state power in the Czechoslovak Socialist Republic is the Federal Assembly (parliament), which elects the President of the Republic for a five-year term of office. The Federal Assembly consists of two chambers of equal rights—the House of the People and the House of Nations. The composition of the House of the People corresponds to the composition of the population of the Republic—of its two hundred deputies, 137 are elected in the Czech Socialist Republic, 63 in the Slovak Socialist Republic. The House of Nations has 150 deputies on parity basis: 75 are elected in the Czech Socialist Republic, 75 in the Slovak Socialist Republic. The House of Nations represents the equality of the constitutional status of both national republics. Concurrent membership in both houses of the Federal Assembly is not possible.

The head of the Czechoslovak Socialist Republic is the President, elected by the Federal Assembly. The President appoints the Federal Government of the Republic which is accountable to the Federal Assembly and the Government Programme is subject to its approval.

The Federal Government is the supreme executive organ of state power in Czechoslovakia; it consists of a premier, deputy premiers and ministers. It has 16 federal ministries, of which three—the Ministry of Foreign Affairs, the Ministry of National Defence and the Ministry of Foreign Trade—have exclusive authority in the whole Federation, i.e. there are no corresponding portfolios in the governments of the national republics. The other federal ministries, the State Planning Commission and the Committee of People's Control of ČSSR, share authority with bodies of the two republics, i.e. there are corresponding portfolios in the national governments. The federal ministries, the Committee of People's Control and the State Planning Commission are headed by ministers.

Both nations in the federation have their own governments and parliaments, the Czech National Council (200 deputies) and the Slovak National Council (150 deputies), which are the supreme organ of state power in each republic, the supreme representative body and the sole legislative body. They are elected for five-year terms of office. The Chairman of the Czech National Council is Evžen Erban; the Chairman of the Slovak National Council Ondrej Klokoč. The governments of the national republics are appointed by the respective National Council.

It is the duty of each National Council to deal with the activities and suggestions advanced by the National Committees, to pass constitutional and other laws of its republic, to deal with principal questions of internal policy, to discuss programme statements of the government of the republic, etc.

**Presidium of the Central Committee of the Communist Party of Czechoslovakia**

**Members**

Vasil Biľak
Peter Colotka.
Karel Hoffmann
Václav Hůla
Gustáv Husák
(General Secretary)
Alois Indra
Antonín Kapek
Josef Kempný
Josef Korčák
Jozef Lenárt
Lubomír Štrougal

**Alternate members**

Miloslav Hruškovič
Jan Baryl

**Government**

*Prime Minister:* Dr. Lubomír Štrougal.
*Deputy Prime Ministers:* Prof. Dr. Peter Colotka; Ing. Václav Hůla (simultaneously Chairman of the State Planning Commission); Josef Korčák; Prof. Dr. Karol Laco; Ing. Jindřich Zahradník; Ing. Rudolf Rohlíček, Josef Šimon.

*Minister of Foreign Affairs:* Ing. Bohuslav Chňoupek.
*Minister of National Defence:* General of the Army Ing. Martin Dzúr.
*Minister of the Interior:* Dr. Jaromír Obzina.
*Minister of Finance:* Ing. Leopold Lér.
*Minister of Labour and Social Affairs:* Michal Štancel'.
*Minister of Foreign Trade:* Ing. Andrej Barčák.
*Minister in charge of the Federal Price Office:* Michal Sabolčík.
*Minister of Telecommunications:* Ing. Vlastimil Chalupa.
*Minister, Chairman of the Committee of People's Control of ČSSR:* Dr. František Ondřich.
*Deputy Prime Minister, Chairman of the State Planning Commission:* Ing. Václav Hůla.
*Minister of Fuels and Power:* Vlastimil Ehrenberger.
*Minister of Metallurgy and Engineering:* Zdeněk Půček.
*Minister for Technological and Investment Development:* Ing. Ladislav Šupka.
*Minister of Transport:* Vladimír Blažek.
*Minister of Agriculture and Food:* Ing. Josef Nágr.
*Minister of general Engineering:* Ing. Pavol Bahyl.

## LEGAL SYSTEM

Proceedings before the courts in the Czechoslovak Socialist Republic concerning matters of civil law are regulated by the Rules of Civil Procedure. All judges are elected. The principle of two instances is in force, according to which matters in the first instance are decided by district courts, in the second instance by regional courts.

All trials and legal actions are to be held in public. The Supreme Court acts only as a court of appeal in cases in which the regional court has passed a decision and in cases when the prosecutor general has lodged a complaint against violation of the law.

Criminal proceedings have three main stages; preliminary proceedings carried out by the prosecuting organs under the supervision of the Procurator as a result of which the Procurator either presents the indictment or discontinues the prosecution; proofs accumulated in the course of preliminary proceedings are examined and assessed by judges at one hearing at which a verdict and sentence is given; an appeal may be filed against the decision of any court, the decision of the appeal court being final. Criminal proceedings before military courts are regulated by the same provisions pertaining to civil criminal courts.

The extension of the jurisdiction and responsibility of the National Committees administrative processes has been newly regulated by Government Ordinance No. 91/1960 which came into force on 1 July 1960.

*Procurator-General:* Dr. Ján Feješ.

*President, Supreme Court:* Dr. Josef Ondřej.

## AREA AND POPULATION

Czechoslovakia has a total area of 49,374 sq. miles.

The old historic provinces of the Czech lands—Bohemia and Moravia-Silesis—and Slovakia, were abolished as administrative units in December 1948, and were succeeded by 19 regions in the whole of Czechoslovakia; the number was reduced to 10 in 1960.

On 31 December 1976 the population was 14,973,792, of which 10,158,434 were in the Czech regions and 4,815,358 in Slovakia.

Recent figures of the area and population of the new counties and the population of the cities are as follows:

| *Region* | *Area (km.²)* | *Population 1 January* 1975 |
|---|---|---|
| Prague (Capital City) | 491 | 1,173,031 |
| Central Bohemia | 11,208 | 1,137,755 |
| South Bohemia | 11,348 | 672,943 |
| West Bohemia | 10,871 | 878,943 |
| North Bohemia | 7,810 | 1,144,884 |
| East Bohemia | 11,240 | 1,230,833 |
| South Moravia | 15,028 | 1,999,413 |
| North Moravia | 11,067 | 1,891,702 |
| Bratislava, (Capital of Slovak Socialist Republic) | 368 | 345,515 |
| West Slovakia | 14,859 | 1,641,704 |
| Central Slovakia | 17,976 | 1,469,704 |
| East Slovakia | 16,179 | 1,332,685 |

| *Cities* | *Population* 31 *December* 1976 |
|---|---|
| Prague | 1,175,522 |
| Brno | 363,179 |
| Bratislava | 320,025 |
| Ostrava | 316,919 |
| Plzeň | 162,902 |
| Košice | 180,792 |
| Havířov | 93,039 |
| Olomouc | 97,504 |
| České Budějovice | 84,639 |
| Karviná | 81,711 |
| Liberec | 83,156 |
| Ústí nad Labem | 76,945 |
| Pardubice | 88,478 |
| Hradec Králové | 89,192 |
| Gottwaldov | 79,609 |
| Kladno | 62,950 |
| Most | 60,935 |
| Teplice | 52,869 |
| Nitra | 68,099 |
| Presov | 63,779 |
| Karlovy Vary | 61,002 |
| Most | 60,935 |

## CURRENCY

The parity of the Czechoslovak crown is fixed at 0·123426 grams of fine gold, as from 1 June 1953. The rate of exchange of the rouble was fixed at Kčs. 8·00 = 1 rouble and Kčs. 5·77 for 1 U.S. Dollar (1976).

In 1964 a new tourist exchange rate, advantageous to foreign visitors, was introduced.

## FINANCE

Budget estimates for 1976 (in thousand million new crowns) were: Revenue, 292,165; Expenditure, 290,071; Corresponding figures for 1975 were 278,113 and 273,774 respectively.

Receipts from the socialized sector of the national economy in 1976 were 245,7 m. crowns, while individual taxation amounted to 32,8 m. crowns.

# CZECHOSLOVAKIA

The expenditure of the 1976 budget provided 141·8 m. crowns for the development of the national economy, 121·9 m. crowns for cultural and social services, 20·4 m. crowns for national defence.

The GNP at market prices for 1974 was U.S. $ millions 48,860, and the GNP per capita at market prices was U.S. $3,330. The annual average percentage growth rate of the GNP per capita for the period 1960–74 was 2·4, and for the period 1965–74 was 2·5. [*See the note at the beginning of this section concerning GNP.*]

## BANKING

The banking and credit system is now entirely run by the State through the following banks: the State Bank of Czechoslovakia, the Investment Bank, the Živnostenská Bank, which has a branch in London, the Czechoslovak Commercial Bank and the State Savings Banks. The State Bank is the only bank issuing short-term credits and for current and deposit accounts both in Czechoslovakia and abroad. It has 134 branches in all. The State Savings Banks receive savings from the population and grant loans. The Živnostenská Banka, National Corporation, caters more particularly for the private accounts of foreigners.

## PRODUCTION, INDUSTRY AND COMMERCE

**Planning.** The targets of the 1949–53 Five-Year Plan were considerably increased in 1951. This revised plan is claimed to have been fulfilled, but there were serious shortfalls in production of black coal and iron ore, while output of electricity and farm products was far too small for domestic needs.

The second plan (1956–60) called for a 50 per cent increase in industrial production. The figure was raised to 54·4 per cent in 1957. The third plan (1961–65) was suspended in 1962 because of underfulfilment and annual plans formulated for 1963, 1964 and 1965. In the course of the fourth Five-Year Plan (1966–70) industrial production rose by over 38·8 per cent. Industrial production rose by 38 per cent in the fifth Five-Year Plan (1971–75). The sixth Five-Year Plan (1976–80) envisages a 32–34 per cent increase in industrial production.

In 1976 there were 2·7 million persons employed in the whole of industry.

**Agriculture.** In 1976 there were 4,907,000 hectares of arable land, 1,753,000 hectares of permanent grass and pasture land and 4,511,000 hectares of forest. Although farming is cooperative, the land is personal property of the member. who owns it. In all Co-operatives the members are paid soley on the basis of work done.

There are 2,097 Co-operatives working on 4,420,882 hectares of land (average 2,183 hectares per Co-operative) and 213 State Farms working on 1,394,000 hectares of land (average 6,544 hectares per Farm). Altogether 777,205 private farmers hold 346,941 hectares of land (average 0·5 hectare per holding).

In 1976 there were 1,003,000 people working in agriculture. In 1976 there were 141,123 tractors, 50,088 tractor ploughs, 20,018 harvesters and 27,484 planting machines.

The following tables shows the harvest for 1975 and 1976 in thousands metric tons:

| *Product* | 1975 | 1976 |
|---|---|---|
| Wheat | 4,202 | 4,807 |
| Rye | 530 | 561 |
| Maize | 843 | 514 |
| Oats | 591 | 379 |
| Barley | 3,114 | 2,901 |
| Potatoes | 3,565 | 4,214 |
| Sugar beet | 7,734 | 5,248 |

In 1976 the livestock population was as follows: Cattle 4,654,000, pigs 6,820,000, chickens and other poultry 44,142,000, sheep 797,000, horses 57,000.

Timber is an important industry. Production in 1976 was 17,144,979 cu. metres.

**Mining.** Minerals and metals produced comprise coal (hard and soft), iron, graphite, silver, copper, lead and uranium. The chief coalfields are at Chomutov, Ostrava, Most, Sokolov and Teplice. The uranium mines are at Jáchymov, Karlovy Vary, Mariánské Lázně, Příbram-Dobříš and Ústi.

Rock salt comes from Eastern Slovakia.

**Industry.** Principal industrial products are fertilizers, glassware, kaolin, paper, yarns, footwear, and engineering in all branches.

The following table shows the industrial production for 1975 and 1976 (million metric tons):

| *Commodity* | 1975 | 1976 |
|---|---|---|
| Hard coal | 28·1 | 29·1 |
| Lignite and Brown coal | 83·5 | 86·8 |
| Crude oil | 0·14 | 0·13 |
| Iron ore | 1·8 | 1·9 |
| Coke | 10·9 | 10·9 |
| Pig iron | 9·3 | 9·5 |
| Crude steel | 14·3 | 14·7 |
| Rolled products | 10·0 | 10·4 |
| Sulphuric acid | 1·2 | 1·2 |
| Fertilizers (N content) | 0·5 | 0·6 |
| Fertilizers (P content) | 0·4 | 0·4 |
| Cement | 9·3 | 9·6 |
| Cotton (m. metres) | 555·2 | 530·3 |
| Shoes (and other) (m. pairs) | 125·4 | 127·8 |
| Paper | 0·8 | 0·8 |
| Electricity (m. kWh.) | 59,277·0 | 62,746·0 |

**Commerce.** The following table shows the pattern of export/import trade with European countries for 1976 (million crowns):

| *Country* | *Imports* | *Exports* |
|---|---|---|
| Austria | 1,756 | 1,230 |
| West Germany | 3,198 | 2,748 |
| United Kingdom | 1,143 | 788 |
| Sweden | 376 | 394 |
| Finland | 212 | 172 |
| Italy | 714 | 681 |
| Netherlands | 791 | 575 |
| France | 954 | 563 |
| Belgium | 679 | 314 |

The pattern of export/import trade with Eastern European Countries for 1976 (million crowns):

| | *Imports* | *Exports* |
|---|---|---|
| U.S.S.R. | 18,230 | 17,696 |
| East Germany | 6,568 | 6,550 |
| Poland | 5,032 | 4,902 |
| Hungary | 3,336 | 3,328 |
| Bulgaria | 1,536 | 1,473 |
| Yugoslavia | 1,644 | 1,903 |
| Rumania | 1,680 | 1,759 |

The total value of exports in 1976 was 52,137 m. Kčs.; that of imports was 55,996 m. Kčs.

## COMMUNICATIONS

In 1976 there were 13,186 kilometres of railway track, nearly 73,677 kilometres of roadway and 2,807 kilometres of electrified railway track. In 1976, the railway effected 461,696 passenger journeys.

In 1976 there were 2,743,387 telephones, 3,265,348 radio licences and 3,793,488 television licences.

The main airports are at Prague, Brno, Bratislava, Olomouc and Košice.

**ČSA—Československe Aerolinie;** ***services operated:*** Prague to principal European capitals, Near Middle and Far East, Canada and U.S.A. (from May 1970), West and North Africa and internal. *Head Office:* Revoluční 1, Prague, Czechoslovakia.

## ATOMIC ENERGY

In Czechoslovakia work on nuclear physics was started in 1945. There was, however, no significant expansion in research into nuclear physics and radio-chemistry until 1955 when the Soviet Government offered Czechoslovakia scientific and technical assistance in research and the use of atomic energy. Agreements between the two countries were made in the same year.

The Soviet Union has sent Czechoslovakia an experimental reactor with an output of 2,000 kW and a cyclotron for the speeding of alpha particles to produce energy up to 25 million kW. These two installations, which are essential for basic research in nuclear physics, have been set up in the newly built Institute of Nuclear Physics administered by the Czechoslovak Academy of Sciences.

A further Soviet-Czechoslovak agreement provides for Soviet assistance in planning and erecting the first Czechoslovak nuclear power station with an output of 150 MW. Another Soviet-Czechoslovak agreement, concluded in April 1970, provides for Soviet assistance in planning and erecting the second and third Czechoslovak nuclear power stations, each of an output of 880 MW. The main equipment will be delivered by the Soviet Union.

A faculty of technical and nuclear physics has been established at the Charles University in Prague, and an industrial school of nuclear technique founded for the training of specialized personnel. A number of Czechoslovak scientific workers are taken on at research institutes under the Soviet Academy of Sciences for short-term or long-term study.

In March 1956 Czechoslovakia became a member of the Joint Institute for Nuclear Research which has been established on Soviet initiative and has its headquarters in the Soviet Union.

## EDUCATION

The Prague Charles IV University founded in 1348 was the first in Europe north of the Alps and east of France.

There are 36 institutions of higher learning. Apart from the older universities in Prague, Brno, Bratislava and Olomouc, four new universities have been founded since 1961.

In 1976 there were 106 university faculties with 168,310 students.

Primary education comprises the basic nine-year schools. Secondary education is divided between those schools which provide further general education and those which provide specialized vocational or technical education.

In 1976, 1,882,371 pupils attended 8,550 basic nine-year schools, 137,062 attended 339 secondary schools of a general nature, and 307,303 attended the specialized and technical schools which numbered 588.

## RELIGION

There has been no post-war census of the religious denominations of the population but the dominant religion is Roman Catholicism. In 1949 the government took over the administration of churches.

# Denmark

(KONGERIGET DANMARK)

**Capital**—Copenhagen.

**Sovereign**—Queen Margrethe.

**National Flag:** Red, with a white cross, the upright slightly towards the hoist.

## CONSTITUTION AND GOVERNMENT

DENMARK'S first free and democratic Constitution dates from 1849. It has been revised several times. The latest Constitution dates from 5 June 1953.

The form of government is a limited (constitutional) monarchy. The legislative authority rests jointly with the Crown and Parliament (Folketing). Executive power is vested in the Crown, and the administration of justice is exercised by the courts. The Sovereign can constitutionally 'do no wrong'. She exercises her authority through the Ministers appointed by her. The Ministers are responsible for the government of the country. The Constitution establishes the principle of Parliamentarianism under which individual ministers or the whole Cabinet must retire when defeated in Parliament by a 'vote of no confidence'. The Prime Minister can ask the Queen to dissolve Parliament and issue writs for an election.

The Sovereign acts on behalf of the State in international affairs. Except with the consent of the Parliament, she cannot, however, take any action which increases or reduces the area of the Realm or undertake any obligation, the fulfilment of which requires the co-operation of the Parliament or which is of major importance. Nor can the Sovereign, without the consent of the Parliament, terminate any international agreement which has been concluded with the consent of the Parliament.

Apart from defence against armed attack on the Realm or on Danish forces, the Sovereign cannot, without the consent of the Parliament, employ military force against any foreign power.

Through the Constitution of 5 June 1953, the bi-cameral legislature was replaced by one chamber, the Folketing, consisting of not more than 179 members, two of whom are elected on the Faroe Islands and two in Greenland. Danish nationals with permanent residence in Denmark have the franchise and are eligible. The age-limit is 20 years. The members of the Folketing are elected for four years. Election is by a system of proportional representation, with a direct and secret ballot on parties or candidates in large constituencies. A bill adopted by the Folketing may be submitted to referendum, when such referendum is claimed by not less than one-third of the members of the Folketing and not later than three days after the adoption. The bill is void if rejected by a majority of the votes cast, representing not less than 30 per cent of all electors.

**Reigning Royal Family.** Evangelical-Lutheran.—The reigning house of Glücksburg is a branch of the ancient house of Oldenburg. Prince Christian of Schleswig-Holstein-Sonderburg-Glücksburg, son of Duke Wilhelm of Schleswig-Holstein-Sonderburg-Glücksburg, was designated as successor to King Frederik VII (of the elder line) by the treaty of London of 8 May 1852 and by the Danish succession act of 31 July 1853 and ascended the throne as Christian IX, King of Denmark, 15 November 1863, on the death of King Frederik VII. According to a new succession act of 27 March 1953, the throne is hereditary for descendants of King Christian X (grandson of King Christian IX), male or female, sons taking precedence of daughters in order of age. A childless king would be succeeded by his brother or sister, the same rules being applied. The children of a sovereign and of the heir to the throne have the title prince or princess of Denmark, Royal Highness; other members of the family are prince or princess of Denmark, Highness.

**H.M. QUEEN MARGRETHE II OF DENMARK** (Alexandrine Thorhildur Ingrid). Born at Amalienborg Castle, Copenhagen, 16 April 1940; eldest daughter of King Frederik IX (born 11 March 1899, died 14 January 1972) and Queen INGRID, born Princess of Sweden, on 28 March 1910; succeeded to the throne on the death of her father; married at Copenhagen, 10 June 1967, Count Henri Laborde de Monpezat (from then named Prince Henrik of Denmark).

Children: 1. Frederik born 26 May 1968. 2. Joachim born 7 June 1969.

Sisters of the Queen:—1. Princess BENEDIKTE Astrid Ingeborg Ingrid; born at Amalienborg Castle, Copenhagen, 29 April 1944; married at Fredensborg, 3 February 1968, Prince Richard of Sayn-Wittgenstein-Berleburg and has issue. 2. Princess ANNE-MARIE Dagmar Ingrid; born at Amalienborg Castle, Copenhagen, 30 August 1946; married at Athens, 18 September 1964, Constantine, Ex-King of the Hellenes and has issue.

Uncle of the Queen: Prince KNUD Christian Frederik Michael; born at Sorgenfri Castle, 27 July 1900, died 14 June 1976; married at Fredensborg Castle, 8 September 1933, his first cousin Princess Caroline-Mathilde (born at Jaegersborghus, 27 April 1912), daughter of Prince Harald of Denmark.

Children:—1. Princess ELISABETH Caroline-Mathilde Alexandrine Helena Olga Thyra Feodora Estrid Margarethe Desirée; born at Copenhagen, 8 May 1935. 2. H. E. INGOLF Christian Frederik Knud Harald Gorm Gustav Viggo Valdemar Aage, Count of Rosenborg; born at Sorgenfri Castle, 17 February 1940; renounced his title and rights of succession to the throne of Denmark on his marriage 13 January 1968. 3. H. E. CHRISTIAN Frederik Franz Knud Harald Carl Oluf Gustav Georg Erik, Count of Rosenborg; born at Sorgenfri Castle, 22 October 1942; renounced his title and rights of succession to the throne of Denmark on his marriage 27 February 1971.

First Cousins of the late King Frederik IX: Children of his uncle, Prince Harald (born 8 October 1876, died 30 March 1949); married 28 April 1909, Princess Helena (born 1 June 1888, died 30 June 1962), daughter of Friedrich Ferdinand, Duke of Schleswig-Holstein-Sonderburg-Glücksburg:

1. Princess CAROLINE-MATHILDE Louise Dagmar Christiane Maud Augusta Ingeborg Thyra Adelheid; born at Jaegersborghus, 27 April 1912; married at Fredensborg Castle, 8 September 1933, her first cousin, Knud, Prince of Denmark, and has issue. 2. Prince GORM Christian Frederik Hans Harald; born at Jaegersborghus, 24 February 1919. 3. H.E. OLUF Christian Carl Axel, Count of Rosenborg; born at Copenhagen, 10 March 1923, renounced his title and rights of succession to the throne of Denmark on his marriage 4 February 1948.

First Cousins of the Late King Christian X: Children of his uncle, Prince Valdemar (born 27 October 1858, died 14 January 1939):

1. Prince AXEL Christian Georg; born at Copenhagen, 12 August 1888; died 14 July 1964; married at Stockholm, 22 May 1919, Princess Margaretha (born at Stockholm, 25 June 1899), eldest daughter of Prince Carl of Sweden, Duke of Västergötland.

Sons:—1. Prince GEORG Valdemar Carl Axel; born at Bernstorffshöj, nr. Gentofte, 16 April 1920; married at Glamis Castle, Angus, 16 September 1950, Anne Ferelith (born at Washington, 4 December 1917), formerly wife of Viscount Anson (elder son of 4th Earl of Lichfield) and daughter of late Hon. John Bowes-Lyon, son of 14th Earl of Strathmore and Kinghorne. 2. H.E. FLEMMING Valdemar Carl Axel, Count of Rosenborg; born at Stockholm, 9 March 1922; renounced his title and rights of succession to the throne of Denmark on his marriage 24 May 1949.

2. Princess MARGRETHE Françoise Louise Marie Helene; born at Bernstorffshöj, 17 September 1895 (Catholic); married at Copenhagen, 9 June 1921, René, Prince of Bourbon-Parma, died 30 July 1962, and has issue.

### Cabinet

*Prime Minister:* Anker Jørgensen.
*Minister for Foreign Affairs:* K. B. Andersen.
*Minister for Finance:* Knud Heinesen.
*Minister for Economic Affairs:* Per Haekkerup.
*Minister for Commerce:* Ivar Nørgaard.
*Minister for the Interior:* Egon Jensen.
*Minister for the Environment and for Cultural Affairs:* Niels Matthiasen.
*Minister for Social Affairs:* Eva Gredal.

*Minister for Labour:* Erling Jensen.
*Minister for Justice and for Defence:* Orla Møller.
*Minister for Education:* Ritt Bjerregaard.
*Minister for Fisheries:* Svend Jakobsen.
*Minister for Inland Revenue:* Jens Kampmann.
*Minister for Ecclesiastical Affairs and for Greenland:* Jørgen Peder Hansen.
*Ministsr for Agriculture:* Poul Dalsager.
*Minister for Public Works and Communication:* Kjeld Olesen.
*Minister without portfolio with a view particularly to matters of foreign policy:* Lise Østergaard.
*Minister for Housing:* Ove Hove.

## LOCAL GOVERNMENT

The Danish local government system was, from its inception at the beginning of the 19th century, a two-tier system outside the system of 87 boroughs, which were all county boroughs. The upper tier, the 25 counties and the 87 boroughs, was made responsible for the hospital services and the construction and maintenance of major roads.

A reorganization of the structure of local government was implemented and since 1 April 1970 Danish local government has been a two-tier system with 14 counties at the higher level, and 273 local authorities at the lower level. The Capital Copenhagen and Frederiksberg do not come within the administrative boundaries of any counties.

This reorganization brought changes to the older system in two respects: (1) The status of borough was abolished, all lower tier local authorities were given a similar status with responsibility exclusively for local affairs. The counties are still responsible for the hospital service and major roads. In addition some powers within the sphere of physical planning were conferred on the counties. (2) The number of counties was brought down from 25 to 14 which meant a total reduction in the number of upper tier authorities from 112 to 14. The reason for this change has been that development—mainly specialization—within the hospital service required a minimum population in each county which could only be reached by a reduction in the number of the counties and to some extent a redrawing of boundaries between the existing counties.

The county authority is The Council elected for 4 years and consisting of 13 to 31 members depending on the population of the county. The Council elects its own chairman who is a fulltime leader of the administration. His title is burgomaster.

Municipalities each have a council of 5 to 31 elected members, depending on their population, each council electing its chairman (burgomaster) from its members. The burgomaster is the chief executive officer, but there will also be a chief officer with status as public servant.

In addition to the local government reform of 1970 a reform was implemented 1 April 1974 establishing a third-tier council with a constitution similar to the counties. The Metropolitan Council is responsible for the overall development within Metropolitan Copenhagen.

The City of Copenhagen has an unique constitution. The 55-member council (Borger-repraesentationen) elects an executive committee (Magistraten) consisting of a Chief Burgomaster (Overborgmesteren), and 10 members (5 Burgomasters, 5 Aldermen); the members of the Magistracy cannot be members of the Council. Each Burgomaster heads an administrative department.

Local authorities exercise their powers under central government control in so far as some decisions are due for approval. The most important means of control is the restriction on raising a loan without approval and nullifying illegal decisions.

The supreme supervisory authority is the Minister of the Interior. Direct control is exercised by the Ministry over the county authorities and the Copenhagen and Frederiksberg authorities. Supervision, to ensure that local government in Copenhagen is being lawfully carried out, is performed on behalf of the Ministry of the Interior by the Prefect (Overpraesidenten). The supervision of local authorities is in the hands of local supervising authorities known as Supervisory Committees, of which there is one in each county. The Supervisory Committee is a corporate body, its chairman being the county prefect (amtmand). He is the senior civil servant of the county and has an university degree in law. Apart from the amtmand the Supervisory Committee consists of four members elected by the county council from its members.

## LEGAL SYSTEM

The administration of justice is based upon an Act which came into force in 1919. The Supreme Court is the highest tribunal of the country and consists of a President and 14 judges. Next come the two *Landsretter*, one of which acts for the islands and one for Jutland (including North Slesvig). These courts hold assizes in various places in their respective districts. In Copenhagen there is a lower court called the Town Court (*Byretten*). The remainder of the country is divided into 84 Lower Court Jurisdictions.

As a general rule each case is dealt with in two courts only. Civil cases of slight importance and criminal cases in which juries are not compulsory are heard in the lower courts and appeals go to the *Landsret*. Cases of greater importance are heard in the *Landsret* and may be carried up to the Supreme Court.

Juries are compulsory for the more serious criminal cases, which are always tried before the *Landsret*.

There are a few special courts of which the most important is the Maritime and Commercial Court in Copenhagen, which tries cases involving legal questions arising out of shipping and commerce. The court is formed by a professional judge and two to four non-legal experts. There is also a Permanent Arbitration Court for the settlement of disputes regarding labour agreements. Military courts have been abolished.

## AREA AND POPULATION

The total area of the Kingdom of Denmark is about 44,474 sq. kilometres, including the Faroe Islands in the Atlantic Ocean, which have an area of about 1,400 sq. kilometres.

The total population at mid-1974 was 5,050,000. Approximately 69 per cent live in towns. Copenhagen is the only large city. The largest towns are Aarhus, Odense, Aalborg, Esbjerg, and Randers.

The annual average percentage growth rate of the population for the periods 1960–74 and 1965–74 was 0·7.

## CURRENCY

The unit of currency is the *krone* of 100 øre. There are base metal coins in denominations of 5, 10 and 25 øre, 1 and 5 kroner. Banknotes have been issued in values of 10, 50, 100, 500 and 1,000 kroner.

The old par value fixed by the Coinage Act of 23 May 1873 is 0·403.226 gramme, the present par value, notified by the International Monetary Fund is 0·118,489 gramme of fine gold.

## FINANCE

The Finance Bill is presented to the *Folketing* shortly after Parliament assembles in October. After being passed and having received the royal assent, the Act comes into force for the following financial year, which begins on 1 April and ends on 31 March.

In 1976–77 the total revenue stated in the finance bill was Kr. 66,996 million and the total expenditure stated in the finance bill was Kr. 79,270 million.

The GNP at market prices for 1974 was U.S. $ millions 32,470, and the GNP per capita at market prices was U.S. $6,430. The annual average percentage growth rate of the GNP per capita for the period 1960–74 was 3·8, and for the period 1965–74 was 3·4. [*See note at the beginning of this section concerning GNP.*]

## PRINCIPAL BANKS

**Danmarks Nationalbank.** (Governor, Erik Hoffmeyer). Est. 1818 as "Nationalbanken i Kjöbenhavn". Since 1936 a national autonomous institution with a general capital fund subscribed by the government; Sole Bank of Issue for Denmark; Balance Sheet at 31 December 1975 showed assets Kr. 24,873,006,855; deposits and current accounts Kr. 3,677,918,955; gold reserve Kr. 480,965,461; banknotes in circulation Kr. 8,205,808,050; coins in circulation Kr. 698,414,324. *Head Office:* 5 Havnegade, DK 1093 Copenhagen K; 2 branches.

**Kjøbenhavns Handelsbank.** (Managing Directors, Bendt Hansen, A. Bagge-Petersen, H. C. Bang, H. Gade, H. E. Johansen, H. C. Østergaard). Est. 1873; Balance Sheet at 31 December 1975 showed assets Kr. 25,004,698,000; deposits Kr. 17,215,767,000; share capital Kr. 700,000,000; reserves Kr. 1,245,081,000. *Head Office:* 2 Holmens Kanal, DK 1091 Copenhagen K. Branches and sub-branches all over the country.

**Den Danske Bank af 1871 Aktieselskab.** (Managing Directors, S. O. Sørensen, H. Maegaard Nielsen, Tage Andersen, E. Bagger). Est. 1871; Balance Sheet at 31 December 1975 showed risk-bearing loan capital and share capital Kr. 644,625,000; reserves Kr. 1,040,173,106; assets

Kr. 22,216,908,001; deposits Kr. 15,280,808,100. *Head Office:* 12 Holmens Kanal, DK 1092 Copenhagen K; 268 branches.

**Privatbanken, Aktieselskab.** (Managing Directors: A. Schmiegelow, M. Staal, Hans Paaschburg) Est. 1857; Balance Sheet at 31 December 1975 showed assets Kr. 15,486,855,000; deposits, current and other accounts Kr. 11,911,442,000; share capital Kr. 388,500,000, *Head Office:* 4 Børsgade, DK 1249 Copenhagen K; 209 branches.

**Andelsbanken A/S,** Danebank (Chief General Manager: P. Nyboe Andersen; General Managers: S. A. Andersen and Kjeld Knudsen). Est. 1925; Balance Sheet at 31 December 1975 showed assets Kr. 8,087,074,448; capital and reserves Kr. 629,784,331. *Head Office:* 4A Vesterbrogade, DK 1620 Copenhagen V. 288 branches.

**Den Danske Provinsbank.** (General Managers, Erik Rahbek, Niels Schack-Eyber, Erik Nærø, Eigil Hastrup). Est. 1957 being a merger of Aarhuus Privatbank, Fyens Disconto Kasse, and Aalborg Diskontobank. Balance Sheet at 31 December 1975 showed assets Kr. 7,403,776,214; deposits and current accounts Kr. 5,488,236,716; share capital Kr. 265,500,000; reserves Kr. 390,762,011. *Head Office:* 4-6 Kannikegade, DK 8100 Aarhus C, 1 Flakhaven DK 5100 Odense, 10 Gammel Torv, DK 9000 Aalborg, 1 Nygade, DK 1003 Copenhagen K. 143 branches.

**Arbejdernes Landsbank.** (Managing Directors, G. Schmidt Laursen and S. Nibelius). Est. 1919; Balance Sheet at 31 December 1975 showed assets Kr. 2,448,521,274; deposits Kr. 1,836,580,358; share capital Kr. 84,010,000; reserves Kr. 142,057,333. *Head Office:* 5 Vesterbrogade, DK 1502 Copenhagen K; 32 branches.

**Fællesbanken for Danmarks Sparekasser A/S.** (Managing Directors, H. Hermansen and Poul Tage Madsen. Est. 1924 as D. B. Adler and Co. Bank A.S. In 1950 name changed as above. Fællesbanken is a commercial bank, jointly owned by the Danish savings banks; Balance Sheet at 31 December 1975 showed assets Kr. 2,267,850,879 deposits Kr. 967,541,817; share capital Kr. 75,000,000; reserves Kr. 88,493,557. *Head Office:* 24 Borgergade, DK 1347 Copenhagen K. 11 branches.

**Jyske Bank.** (Managing Directors, E. Christensen, E. Danielsen, T. Graversen, P. Norup, S. A. Schmidt). Est. 1917; Balance Sheet at 31 December 1975 showed assets Kr. 2,134,050,755; deposits Kr. 1,156,036,470: share capital Kr. 72,000,000; reserves Kr. 128,719,508. *Head Office:* 8–10 Vestergade, DK 8600 Silkeborg; 61 branches.

**Sjællandske Bank.** (Managing Directors, J. Tarp, E. Johansen, H. Navntoft Pedersen, N. Westergaard-Olsen). Est. 1890; Balance Sheet at 31 December 1975 showed assets Kr. 2,027,116,039; deposits Kr. 1,151,142,477; share capital Kr. 75,000,000; reserves Kr. 107,359,666. *Head Office:* 100 Nørregade, DK 4100 Ringsted; 56 branches.

## PRODUCTION, INDUSTRY AND COMMERCE

**Agriculture.** The agricultural area is about 2,900,000 hectares or 67 per cent of the total area. 61 per cent of the agricultural area is devoted to cereals, 25 per cent to grass and green fodder, 10 per cent to root crops and four per cent to other crops. Denmark's farm produce comes from holdings and farms. In 1976 there were 36,900 smallholdings of less than ten hectares, 76,800 medium-sized farms of 10–50 hectares and 10,500 large holdings of over 50 hectares.

Production from livestock for 1975–76 is given below (thousand tons):

| | |
|---|---|
| Milk | 5,080 |
| Butter | 147 |
| Cheese | 150 |
| Beef and veal | 258 |
| Pork | 766 |
| Poultry | 91 |
| Eggs | 73 |

In 1976 there were 3,095,000 cattle, 7,701,000 pigs and 8,088,000 poultry. The figure for poultry is merely that of chickens for slaughter. The total chicken population was 14,773,000, there were also 259,000 turkeys, 658,000 ducks and 69,000 geese. About 10,300,000 pigs are killed annually.

In 1975/76 an area of roughly 24,000 hectares was devoted to horticulture and fruit growing. The area is less than one per cent of the agricultural area.

**Fishing.** In 1975 sea fishing was carried on by about 7,444, motor driven vessels and 3,112 non-powered vessels. The total yield in the year 1975 was about 1,730,000 metric tons valued at Kr. 1,439,000 million. The fish caught are chiefly cod, mackerel, haddock, flatfish, herrings, eels, lobsters and shrimps.

**Industry.** Danish industry, including handicrafts, employs about 638,000 persons. Main industries include the food industry and iron and metal industry. The main organization of Danish industry is the Federation of Danish Industries (Industriraadet) whose address is H. C. Andersen's Boulevard 18, DK-1553 Copenhagen V. *Managing Director:* Ove Munch. *Chairman:* H. Brüniche-Olsen. The Federation is concerned with all aspects of industrial activity in Denmark with the exception of collective agreements.

**Commerce.**

Apart from the normal import and export trade there is a fairly extensive transit trade, with Denmark as an intermediate station. Almost the whole of this transit trade goes via Copenhagen, and much of it through the Free Port. The most important groups in this trade are soft goods, mineral oils and machinery.

Denmark was a member of the European Free Trade Association which included U.K., Norway, Sweden, Switzerland, Austria and Portugal. The Association is commonly called 'The Seven'. On 1 January 1973 Denmark entered the European Common Market.

## COMMUNICATIONS

**Railways.** There are about 2,600 kilometres of railway (including ferry crossings) in Denmark, on which 80 per cent belong to the State, and 20 per cent (mostly branch lines of small importance) are owned by private companies. Nearly all the shares of the private companies belong to the state and local governments. Trains cross the Great Belt between Funen and Zealand on the Danish State Ferries. There are also rail and car ferry services connecting Denmark with Sweden via Copenhagen–Malmö and Elsinore–Helsingborg and with the Continent via Rödby Faerge-Puttgarden.

**Shipping.** In view of Denmark's geographical situation and formation shipping plays a large part in her system of communications.

Apart from regular services between Denmark and the main foreign ports, Denmark's merchant shipping has taken an important part in the international carrying trade.

The port of Copenhagen is an independent institution on the board of which are representatives of the government, parliament, the city corporation and the large trade organizations. Chairman of directors is E. Andersen. The Free Port of Copenhagen is owned by the Copenhagen Port Authority, but is worked by a joint stock company which has provided warehouses, cranes, etc.

Other important ports are Aalborg, Aarhus, Odense, Esbjerg and Nyborg. In 1974 there were 45,317 ships, net registered tonnage 28,452,000, at the principal Danish ports. They discharged 38,878,000 tons of cargo and loaded 15,060,000 tons.

The following are the chief shipping companies:

**A. P. Møller** (Chairman, Maersk McKinney Møller); vessels 97; tonnage 2,928,153 gross; *services operated:* A. P. Møller—under the name of Maersk Line—maintains regularly scheduled cargo liner service linking the Far East with USA, Europe, Africa and the Middle East, and USA with the Middle East. Furthermore, A. P. Møller operates a large fleet of tankers, bulk vessels, reefers and supply vessels. *Head Office:* Kongens Nytorv, Copenhagen, Denmark.

**The East Asiatic Co. Ltd.** (Chairman, Mogens Pagh); share capital Kr. 500,000,000; motor vessels 28 total tonnage 499,731 gross, 643,044 DW.; *services operated:* Europe–Far East (as partners in ScanDutch), Europe–Australia (as partners in ScanAustral), Europe – Pacific Coast U.S.A. – Canada (as partners in Johnson ScanStar), Europe – West Africa, Europe – India-Pakistan – Sri Lanka – Bangladesh, Europe – Indonesia, Europe – New Zealand, British Columbia – U.S. East Coast, Far East – Europe (Bulk service in cooperation with Ben Line. Transpacific service Far-East-Canadian and U.S. West Coasts. *Head Office:* 2 Holbergsgade DK 1099 Copenhagen K, Denmark. *Telegrams:* Orient.

**J. Lauritzen A/S**; vessels 20; total tonnage 283,645 tons d.w.; *services operated:* Tankers, drillships, refrigerated and dry cargo transport. Year round refrigerated services: Ecuador/Japan/Medt./Persian Gulf, New Zealand/Japan.—*Seasonal* *refrigerated services:* South America/U.K., Continent, Scandinavia. New Zealand/U.K., Continent, Scandinavia. South Africa/U.K., Continent, Scandinavia. Arctic and Antarctic trade. *Head Office:* Hammerensgade 1, DK-1260 Copenhagen, Denmark.

**DFDS A/S—The United S.S. Co. Ltd.**; (General Managers, Erik Heirung, B. P. C. Walker, L. Juul Jørgensen); share capital d.Kr. 150,000,000; vessels 20; total tonnage 71,016 DW., 111,225 gross; *services operated:* throughout European waters, the Mediterranean, Middle East, U.S. Gulf, and South America. *Head Office:* Sankt Annae Plads 30, DK-1295 Copenhagen, Denmark.

**Civil Aviation.** There are regular air services between Copenhagen Airport, and most of the larger cities of Western Europe and other continents except Australia.

**DDL—Det Danske Luftfartselskab A/S** (Danish Air Lines) (Chairman, Haldor Topsøe; General Manager, H. Bech-Bruun); share capital Kr. 90,800,000 divided into A: Kr. 50,800,000 (50 per cent owned by the state). B: Kr. 5,000,000 (100 per cent owned by the state). C: Kr. 35,000,000 (50 per cent owned by the state). DDL is a partner in the Scandinavian Airlines System (SAS) which operates all services. *Head Office:* Nørre Farimagsgade 5, DK-1364 Copenhagen K.

**SAS—Scandinavian Airlines System;** (President: Knut Hagrup, Exec. Vice-Presidents: K. A. Kristiansen, Björn Törnblom, Carl-Erik Lindh, Gunnar Sandberg); a consortium partnered by Danish, Norwegian and Swedish Airlines (DDL, DNL, ABA) in proportion 2 : 2 : 3 for the operation of joint traffic from Scandinavia to rest of Europe, North, Central and South America, Africa, Near and Far East. *Head Office:* Bromma Airport, S-161 87 Bromma, Sweden. *Regional Offices:* At Kastrup Airport, Copenhagen, Denmark, Fornebu Airport, Oslo, Norway and Bromma Airport, Stockholm, Sweden.

There are also major Danish charter operators such as Sterling Airways and Maersk Air as well as a number of private companies providing internal services.

Regular domestic services are operated by SAS and DANAIR (owned by SAS, Maersk Air and Cimber Air).

**Telegraphs and Telephones.** The telegraph services are solely under state management. There were in 1977, 721 telegraph stations. A total of 1,361,000 telegrams was dealt with.

The inter-provincial telephone services are run by the state, but most of the local services are carried on by three companies with government concessions. There was a total of 1,835,000 subscribers and about 6·6 million kilometres of lines. In 1976 there were 2,514,000 telephones in use. By August 1977, there were 1,845,768 radio and T.V. licence holders.

**Broadcasting.** The broadcasting services are owned and operated by the state. Radio Denmark is a public institution, which has a monopoly of all sound and television broadcasting.

## NEWSPAPERS

**Aalborg Stiftstidende.** F.1767. Circulation 73,137 weekdays; 101,775 Sundays.

**Aarhuus Stiftstidende.** F.1794. Circulation 67,692.

**Aktuelt.** F. 1872. Morning. Social Democrat. Editors: Bent Hansen, Harry Rasmussen. Circulation: 71,600 weekdays, Sunday 136,100. Milnersvej 43.3400 Hillerød.

**Berlingske Tidende.** F. 1749. Morning. Independent. Conservative. Circulation 140,000 (Sundays 255,000). Editors, Aage Deleuran and Niels Nørlund. Pilestraede, DK-1147 Copenhagen.

**B.T.** F. 1916. Afternoon. Independent. Circulation 240,000. Editor, Morten Pedersen. Kr. Bernikowsgade 6, DK-1147 Copenhagen.

**Fyens Stiftstidende.** F.1772. Circulation 54,844.

**Politiken.** F. 1884. Morning. Independent. Circulation 118,007 (Sundays 187,240). Editors, Herbert Pundik, Bent Thorndahl, Managing Director, Ernst Klaebel.

## ATOMIC ENERGY

Following a reorganization within Danish energy administration the Danish Atomic Energy Commission—established in 1955—was abolished by an Act of 28 April 1976.

The Commission's Research Establishment Risø—located on and next to a small peninsula, Risø, in Roskilde Fjord, 27 miles west of Copenhagen—continues as a national laboratory under the Minister for Trade and Industry (who is also the Minister responsible for Energy). Chairman of the Board: Erik Ib Schmidt; Managing Director: Niels W. Holm.

The research facilities include a heavy-water-moderated, 10 MW reactor, a 14 MeV electron linear accelerator, cobalt radiation sources, and a hot cell facility. The establishment carries out research and development, and acts as consultant with regard to the peaceful application and control of atomic energy. The main research fields include reactor technology, uranium prospecting and extraction, basic and applied physics and chemistry, as well as agricultural research.

Since 1 February 1976 the Inspectorate of Nuclear Installations—established in 1973 under the Danish Atomic Energy Commission—is placed under the Ministry for the Environment.

Some of the tasks previously the responsibility of the Danish Atomic Energy Commission, such as collaboration with international and foreign organizations within the nuclear field, is now handled by the Danish Energy Agency established by the above Act of 28 April 1976 under the Minister for Trade and Industry.

## EDUCATION

In Denmark education is compulsory for a period of nine years. Compulsory education may be fulfilled either through attending the "Folkeskole" or private schools or through home-instruction, the only requirement being that the instruction given should be comparable to that offered in the "Folkeskole".

Primary education takes place in nine-year comprehensive elementary schools which are in practise not streamed, and no examinations are held during this period. The children pass through the nine forms according to age. A certain differentation may, however, take place in the 8th and 9th forms in foreign languages, mathematics, and physics/chemistry. At the termination of the 9th form the leaving examination of the municipal primary and lower secondary school may be passed in the following subjects: Danish, mathematics, English, German and physics/chemistry. Besides this there is a possibility at the end of the teaching period (in the 8th, 9th or 10th forms) of passing the above mentioned leaving examination in the following subjects: needlework, woodwork, domestic science, French, Latin and typing.

In the 10th form—lower secondary education—a certain differentation may take place. Optional subjects may be studied. The pupils may choose German, French, mathematics, physics/chemistry, and a number of practical and creative subjects. Instruction in this form must not, however, be vocationally biased.

At the termination of the 10th form the pupils may pass either the leaving examination of the municipal, primary and lower secondary school in the subjects Danish, mathematics, English, German, and physics/chemistry, or they may pass the extended leaving examination of the municipal, primary and lower secondary school in the same subjects. Having completed the compulsory education the pupils may continue their education either in a three-year Gymnasium (Grammar School) ending with the "studentereksamen" (Certificate of Education) or in courses leading to the "HF-eksamen" (2 year) (Higher Preparatory Examination).

Admission to the Gymnasium is possible after the 9th form. Normally the pupil shall have followed education in German as an optional subject in the 7th to 9th form, and he shall have passed the leaving examination of the Folkeskole in some specified subjects: Danish and arithmetic/mathematics for both branches of the Gymnasium, English, German and Latin for the linguistic branch, physics/chemistry for the mathematics/science branch. It is also required that his former school states that he is qualified for the education in the Gymnasium. For pupils applying for admission after the 10th form the advanced leaving examination of the Folkeskole can replace the leaving examination after the 9th form.

The formal requirements for entrance are the equivalent of 10 years schooling including instruction in mathematics, English and German.

In 1974–75 there were 2,279 primary and lower secondary

schools with 807,879 pupils and a teaching staff of 51,350. In 1974–75 there were 112 Gymnasia with 40,939 pupils and 92 HF Courses to Higher Preparatory Examination with 12,203 pupils. The number of teachers in the Gymnasia and the Courses to Higher Preparatory Examination were 5,133.

The local authorities are responsible for the provision of primary schools, and there are both State and Municipal Secondary as well as private schools. Instruction is free in State and Municipal schools, whereas fees are charged in private schools.

There are five universities in Denmark: Copenhagen, Arhus, Odense, Roskilde and Alborg.

### RELIGION

The Evangelical Lutheran Church is the established church to which the Sovereign must belong. There is, however, complete religious toleration, and no civil liabilities attach to dissenters.

### FAROE ISLANDS

The Faroes constitute a group of islands in the Atlantic Ocean north-west of Scotland and form a separate Danish territory enjoying a wide range of home rule. The total area of the islands is 540 sq. miles with a population of 41,575 (1977). There are 18 inhabited islands. The *Rigsombudsmand* is the highest representative of the Danish state in the islands. Local legislation and administration are carried out by an elected assembly called the *Lagting*, which comprises 26 members. The seats in the *Lagting* are distributed as follows: People's Party 5, Independence Party 6, Unionist Party 5, Social Democrats Party 7, Self-Government Party 2, and Progress Party 1.

The economic life of the islands depends principally on fishing; 26 per cent of the economically active persons living directly on the proceeds of this industry. In 1976 the total catch of fish was approximately 340,000 tons.

### GREENLAND

Greenland, Denmark's former colony, was incorporated as an integral part of the Danish Realm by the Constitution of 5 June 1953, which also gave Greenland two representatives in the Folketing. Greenland is the largest island in the world, with a total area of about 840,000 sq. miles. Of these, 114,600 sq. miles are made up of coastal tracts. The islands along the coast aggregate 17,300 sq. miles, while the inland ice covers 708,100 sq. miles. In 1977 approximately 50,000 persons were living in Greenland. The population has more than doubled in the past half century.

The majority of the nationals live by hunting, fishing, etc. Within the area of mineral resources there is an export of the hard minerals zinc, and lead, and in 1975 the first off-shore oil and gas concessions were granted to 21 of the internationally known oil companies. Other articles for export are frozen fish, frozen and canned shrimps and other fishery products, hides and furs. In 1976 the total catch of fish and shrimps was around 49,000 tons.

Communities of hunters of arctic animals have during the last 40 years become fishing villages where the inhabitants now fish for cod, salmon and shrimps. Greenland's fishing catch is sold on the world markets. Canneries and freezing plants for shrimps and fish have been established. While fishing is the main industry, there is some sheep farming.

Central administration is carried out by the Landshøvding (Governor) assisted by a staff of administrative and technical experts. The population elects a National Council (Landsråd) and a number of District Councils.

# Djibouti

**Capital**—Djibouti

**Chief Administrator**: Christian Dublanc.

Djibouti is the former Territory of Afars and Issas (forming French Somaliland) and is situated on the north-east coast of Africa opposite Aden and between Eritrea and the Somali Republic.

A referendum was held on 19 March 1967 to decide for or against continued association with France. The result was 22,555 votes for staying in the French Community and 14,606 votes against. Consequently, a revised status for the territory was brought into effect, providing for a certain measure of autonomy; only finance, defence, external affairs and internal security being reserved for the French Government.

On 12 May 1967 the Parliament of French Somaliland unanimously voted to change the name of the country to the French Territory of Afars and Issas.

On 26 June 1977 the new Republic of Djibouti came into existence, it having been decided by France in 1976 that self-determination should be achieved.

The Prime Minister is Mr. Hassan Ghouled.

### LEGAL SYSTEM

Justice is administered by a Court of Appeal and a Court of First Instance seated at Djibouti.

### AREA AND POPULATION

The territory has an area of 23,000 sq. km.

The total population at mid-1974 was 103,000. The annual average percentage growth rate of the population for the period 1960–74 was 1·9 and for the period 1965–74 was 2·2.

### CURRENCY

The currency is the Djibouti franc which is related to gold and, for exchange purposes, to the U.S. dollar at a fixed rate.

### FINANCE

The GNP at market prices for 1974 was U.S.$ millions 180, and the GNP per capita at market prices was U.S.$ 1,720. The annual average percentage growth rate of the GNP per capita for the period 1960–74 was 9·9 and for the period 1965–74 was 11·3. [*See note at the beginning of this Section concerning GNP.*]

### COMMUNICATIONS

There is a railway running inland from Djibouti to Addis Ababa which is one of the principal means of communication between Ethiopia and the outside world. There are two important kinds of trade, (*a*) trans-shipment, victualling and bunkering at Djibouti; (*b*) transit trade via the Djibouti–Addis Ababa railway.

# Dominican Republic

## (REPÚBLICA DOMINICANA)

**Capital**—Santo Domingo

**President**—Dr. Joaquín Balaguer

**National Flag:** Quarterly, 1st and 4th blue, 2nd and 3rd red; over all a white cross charged at the centre with the national coat of arms.

### CONSTITUTION AND GOVERNMENT

THE island of Santo Domingo was discovered by Christopher Columbus on 5 December 1492. He took possession in the name of the King and Queen of Spain, and christened the island 'La Española', now called Hispaniola. The city of Santo Domingo was founded by his brother Bartolome Columbus on 4 August 1496. This is the oldest city of the American Continent and was for fifty years the royal capital of the Spanish Empire in the Americas.

The discovery of the enormous wealth of Mexico and Peru caused a decline in its importance and for the next two hundred years there followed a period of lawlessness and neglect. The western end of Santo Domingo was invaded by the French in 1691, and by the Treaty of Ryswick in 1697, Spain ceded the part of the island which is now the Republic of Haiti to France. In 1795 the whole of the island passed under French rule. The Spanish colonists rebelled against the French in 1808, and in 1821 declared their independence. Before the Dominicans could firmly establish their freedom the country was again invaded by the negro inhabitants of Haiti, and the colony was occupied by the Haitians for 22 years.

On 27 February 1844 the Spanish inhabitants, having expelled the invaders, set up the Dominican Republic. Sixteen years later the republic was annexed to Spain by its own President but after two years the Dominicans again rebelled, and after a bitter struggle succeeded in regaining their independence.

The Dominicans again lost their sovereignty in 1916, when the country was occupied by United States Marines, who set up a military government that remained in power until 1924, when the Dominicans regained their independent status and adopted a new Constitution.

A revised Constitution was passed by President Bosch's Government in 1963 but this lapsed during the Constitutionalist Revolution of 1965, and the Constitution now in force was passed by President Balaguer's Government in November 1966. Executive power is vested in the President who is elected by direct vote of the people. His term of office is four years, and he is eligible for re-election. The President appoints the members of his Cabinet without reference to Congress. With effect from August 1957, the post of Vice-President has also been created.

Congress is composed of Upper and Lower Chambers. The Senate has 27 Senators, one for each province and one for the district of Santo Domingo. The Chamber of Deputies is composed of 74 Deputies, one for each 50,000 inhabitants or fraction of more than 25,000 in each province, with the provision that no province shall be represented by less than two members. The members of both chambers are elected by popular vote for a term of four years, and an alternative for each member in the event of a vacancy is elected at the same time as the member. All Dominicans over the age of 18 and married women under 18, (except members of the Armed Forces), are eligible to vote.

Following the assassination of General Trujillo, who had ruled the country as dictator for over 30 years, elections were held in December 1962, resulting in an overwhelming victory for Prof. Juan Bosch and his party, the Partido Revolucionario Dominicano. The inauguration of Prof. Bosch as President took place on 27 February 1963. On 25 September, less than seven months later, President Bosch was deposed by a military junta in a bloodless coup d'état. Executive powers were later vested in a civilian junta which ruled for 19 months. On 24 April 1965, an Army revolt broke out espousing the return of ex-President Bosch and constitutional government. Civil war between the rump of the army and the rebels followed. On 30 April 1965, a force of 23,000 U.S. Marines and Army were landed. The capital remained divided between the rival factions and the U.S. forces. On 3 September 1965, Dr. Héctor Garcéa-Godoy was installed as Provisional President under the Institutional Act. His task was to prepare the country for the elections which took place on 1 June 1966. These were won by the Partido Reformista of Dr Joaquín Balaguer, who was formally inaugurated as President on 1 July 1966. Both houses of the National Congress resumed sitting in July 1966.

The Partido Reformista and Dr. Balaguer were returned to power in the elections held in May 1970 and May 1974.

### POLITICAL PARTIES

Following the revolution of 1930, a single union party was formed known as the Partido Dominicano. After the assassination of General Trujillo six opposition parties were formed. Ten parties took part in the 1966 elections but only the Partido Reformista of Dr. Balaguer and the Partido Revolucionario Dominicana of Professor Bosch secured seats in Congress.

In the 1970 elections five parties took part. The Partido Revolucionario Dominicana abstained. The Partido Reformista secured 84 seats in the congress and two of the opposition parties, the Movimiento de Integración Democrática Antireelectionista of former Vice-President Lora and the Partido Quisqueyano Demócrata of ex-General Wessin y Wessin, secured 15 seats.

In the 1974 elections the Partido Reformista was virtually unapposed. All opposition parties except one withdrew their candidates due to a disagreement with the government on voting procedures. The only opposition party to contest the election was the tiny Partido Demócrata Popular, which gained two congressional and four city council seats.

### LOCAL GOVERNMENT

The Dominican Republic is divided for administrative purposes into 26 provinces (excluding the National District) whose administration is the responsibility of a Civil Governor appointed by the President. Each province consists of two or more *comúnes* and in the principal of these is situated the Capital of the Province. The *común* is governed by a locally elected county council or *Ayuntamiento de Regidores* and consists of a city or town and its surrounding rural district which is divided into *secciones*. The chief administrative officer of the city or town is the *Alcalde* who is elected by the people of the *común*; and the *secciones* are governed by an *Alcalde Pedáneo* who is appointed by the *Ayuntamiento*.

Elected local government officials serve a term of two years.

### LEGAL SYSTEM

The judicial branch of the government is made up of the Supreme Court, of a president and judges chosen by the Senate, District Courts of Appeal, Courts of First Instance and local Justices or *Alcaldes*.

**Supreme Court of Justice—1975**

| | |
|---|---|
| *President:* | Lic. Nestor Contín Aybar. |
| *Judge (First Substitute President):* | Lic Fernando Ravelo de la Fuente. |
| *Judge (Second Substitute President):* | Lic. Dr. Manuel A. Amiama. |

*Secretary:* Dr. Ernesto Curiel, junior.

### AREA AND POPULATION

The total area is estimated at 48,442 sq. km. The population of the Republic at mid-1974 was 4,562,000. The annual average percentage growth rate of the population for the period 1960–74 was 2·9, and for the period 1965–74 was 2·9.

The chief cities and towns with populations (1970) are: National District (including Santo Domingo), 817,467; Santiago de los Caballeros, 244,794; San Cristóbal, 105,904; La Vega, 155,537; La Romana and Higuey, 117,213; Azua, 54,404; Puerto Plata, 74,480.

### CURRENCY

In 1947 the *peso oro* (RD$) of 100 *centavos* was adopted as the unit of currency. There are metal coins of 1 to 50 centavos and banknotes of 1 to 1,000 pesos. The Peso is at par with the U.S. dollar.

### FINANCE

Government Revenue and Expenditure for the years 1974–75 were as follows:

| | 1974 *RD $ million* | 1975 *RD $ million* |
|---|---|---|
| Revenue | 521·6 | 486·3 |
| Expenditure | 512·6 | 486·3 |

## DOMINICAN REPUBLIC

The GNP at market prices for 1974 was U.S. $ millions 2,960, and the GNP per capita at market prices was U.S. $650. The annual average percentage growth rate of the GNP per capita for the period 1960–74 was 3·1, and for the period 1965–74 was 5·.5 [*See the note at the beginning of this section concerning GNP.*]

The external debt outstanding at 31 December 1974 was U.S. $383·5 million.

The balance of payments habitually shows a slight deficit (1973 was an exception) and a larger deficit was realized in 1975.

### BANKS

**Banco Central de la República Dominicana.** Est. 1947. Bank of Issue. *Head Office:* Santo Domingo.

**Banco de Reservas de la República Dominicana.** *Head Office:* Santo Domingo.

**Banco Agricola de la Republica Dominicana.** *Head Office:* Ave. George Washington, Santo Domingo.

**Banco de Credito y Ahorros.** *Head Office:* Santo Domingo.

**Banco Popular Dominicano.** *Head Office:* Santo Domingo.

**Royal Bank of Canada.** *Head Office:* Santo Domingo.

**Bank of Nova Scotia.** *Head Office:* Santo Domingo.

**Chase Manhattan Bank.** *Head Office:* Santo Domingo.

**First National City Bank.** *Head Office:* Santo Domingo.

**Bank of America.** *Head Office:* Santo Domingo.

### PRODUCTION, INDUSTRY AND COMMERCE

**Agriculture.** About 55 per cent of the working population are engaged in agriculture, which is by far the largest source of wealth.

The following table shows production value of principal sectors for the years 1971–72, the latest available figures:

| *Commodity* | *Thousands of pesos* 1971 | 1972 |
|---|---|---|
| Agriculture | 248,514·1 | 275,116·8 |
| Cattle | 112,583·7 | 112,502·6 |
| Mining | 23,565·6 | 51,426·9 |
| Industry | 306,177·7 | 347,325·4 |
| Construction | 100,644·3 | 128,001·3 |
| Commerce | 272,930·0 | 332,145·0 |
| Transport | 112,214·8 | 130,762·6 |

**Forestry.** There is no reliable information available on Dominican hardwoods, but the tropical forests are believed to contain various species, including satinwood, cigar box cedar, lignum vitae, and mahogany.

**Industry.** Important industrial products are ferro-nickel, gold, silver, textiles, cement, bottles, soap, paint, paper, cigarettes, milk products, vegetable oil, biscuits and matches. Production of cement is about 640,000 metric tons a year, a million tons of bauxite is exported annually.

Electricity production capacity has been steadily growing and in 1973 had reached 1,196,750 Mwh.

**Commerce.** With the achievement of self-sufficiency in rice production in the 1930's, the Dominican Republic became a food surplus area and exporter. Sugar, coffee, cocoa and tobacco are the traditional exports, but government policy is to diversify food production, shifting the emphasis from sugar to other foods, which will complement the sugar economies of the neighbouring islands. In the long term the Government envisages the role of the 'Granary of the Caribbean' for the Republic. Sugar and its products are the principal exports. The Dominican Republic had a regular favourable trade balance until 1964, when imports overtook exports. There was a favourable balance again in 1965 when all trade was depressed, but since 1966 the balance has continued to be adverse.

The table below shows values of exports in 1973 and 1974 according to principal countries of destination (in thousand RD $):

| *Exports* | 1973 | 1974 |
|---|---|---|
| U.S.A. | 267,448 | 414,447 |
| Netherlands | 38,661 | 47,950 |
| Puerto Rico | 32,541 | 42,896 |
| Morocco | 12,820 | 21,260 |
| Spain | 13,361 | 20,412 |
| France | 10,657 | 15,204 |
| United Kingdom | 7,822 | 13,969 |
| Algeria | 4,811 | 13,579 |
| Japan | 8,528 | 11,495 |
| Belgium/Luxembourg | 11,289 | 8,293 |
| Canada | 2,263 | 7,702 |
| Total | 450,897 | 650,847 |

Values of the principal exports for 1973 and 1974 are shown below (in thousand RD $):

| *Commodity* | 1973 | 1974 |
|---|---|---|
| Sugar | 186,615 | 323,309 |
| Ferro-nicke | 85,949 | 93,097 |
| Cocoa | 19,593 | 44,098 |
| Coffee | 39,751 | 38,582 |
| Tobacco | 29,507 | 37,913 |
| Bauxite | 14,835 | 17,756 |
| Molasses | 9,513 | 13,555 |
| Meats | 10,099 | 9,273 |
| Furfural | 7,844 | 7,959 |
| Total | 450,897 | 650,847 |

### COMMUNICATIONS

**Roads.** The modern four-lane concrete highways are being extended. The remainder of the country is well served by first- and second-class roads.

**Railways.** There are about 1,444 kilometres of railway lines, on the sugar estates, but there are no passenger services, except for a short stretch that runs between Sánchez and La Vega.

**Civil Aviation.** Airlines passing through Santo Domingo include Pan American, Iberian Airways, Aerocondor (Colombia), Dominican Airlines, Venezuelan National Airlines (VIASA), A.L.M. and Eastern Airlines. The international airport at Punta Caucedo is used by jet and other aircraft. Another airport is being constructed near Puerto Plato on the north coast.

**Telegraphs and Telephones.** Telegraphic communication is operated by the Government.

There are about 14 telephone exchanges including Government exchanges connected with other 44,000 instruments.

**Broadcasting.** There is one Government television and radio station, and three private television stations, in Santo Domingo, and there are more than 90 private radio stations throughout the country. Radio receivers number about two million; there are at least 150,000 television sets.

### NEWSPAPERS

**Listin Diario.** Morning. Santo Domingo. Circulation 38,000.

**El Caribe.** Morning. Santo Domingo. Circulation 36,000.

**El Nacional.** Santo Domingo. 30,000.

**Ultima Hora.** Santo Domingo. 18,000.

### EDUCATION

Primary education is free and compulsory. In June 1975 there were 5,249 primary schools (with a total registration of 963,600 pupils), 997 secondary schools (175,400) and 4 universities (30,867). In addition there were a number of trade schools, with a total registration of 32,518 pupils of whom 27,436 were enrolled in office employee and salesman courses.

### RELIGION

The established religion is Roman Catholic, other forms of religion are permitted. A Concordat with the Holy See was signed in 1954.

# Ecuador

## (REPÚBLICA DEL ECUADOR)

**Capital—Quito**

**Members of the Supreme Council of Government**

Vice-Admiral Alfiedo Poveda Burbano.
Divisional General Guillermo Durán Arcentales.
Brigadier General Louis Leoro Franco.

**National Flag:** A tricolour fesse-wise, yellow, blue, red, the yellow half the depth of the flag, which bears at its centre the national coat of arms; a condor, Mount Chimborazo and four signs of the zodiac.

### CONSTITUTION AND GOVERNMENT

THE Republic of Ecuador is bounded on the north by Colombia, on the east and south by Peru, and on the west by the Pacific Ocean.

After the discontinuance of Spanish rule, it became part of the original republic of Gran Colombia, founded by Simón Bolívar in 1819. The Republic split up in 1830, and the Presidency of Quito became the new Republic of Ecuador. Since that time there have been many constitutions, the latest having been promulgated in 1967.

Executive power is vested in the President of the Republic, who is elected by popular vote for a term of four years. He cannot be re-elected until four years after his retirement. Legislative power is in the hands of the National Congress.

**Ministry**

*Minister of Government:* Col. Bolivar Jarrin Cahueñas.
*Minister of Foreign Affairs:* Lcdo. José Ayala Lasso.
*Minister of Education:* Gen. Fernando Dobronsky Ojeda.
*Minister of Labour and Social Services:* Col. (r) Jorge Salvador Chiriboga.
*Minister of Finance:* Econ. Santiago Sevilla Larrea.
*Minister of Natural Resources and Energy:* Gen. Eduardo Semblantes Polanco.
*Minister of Public Health:* Dr. Asdrúbal De la Torre.
*Minister of Agriculture:* Gen. Oliverio Vázcones Salvador.
*Minister of Public Works:* Gen. Angel Polivio Vega Mora.
*Minister of Defence:* Gen. (r) Andrés Arrata Macias.
*Minister of Industry and Commerce:* Ing. Galo Montaño Pérez.
*Secretary-General of the Administration:* Commandant Victor Hugo Garcés Pozo.

### LOCAL GOVERNMENT

The country is divided into 20 Provinces, each of which is administered by a Governor appointed by the Minister of the Interior. Their subdivisions, or cantons, are administered by Political Chiefs and elected Cantonal Councillors and the parishes by Political Lieutenants.

### LEGAL SYSTEM

**Supreme Court**

*President:* Dr. Luis Jaramillo Perez.

*Ministro Fiscal:* Dr. Gonzalo Gallo Subía.

### AREA AND POPULATION

The area of the country has never been measured, but the latest estimate gives the total of approximately 261,492 sq. km.

The total population at mid-1974 was 6,952,000.

The chief towns with estimated populations are Quito, 782,600; Guayaquil, 907,000; Cuenca, 104,400; Ambato, 182,400.

The annual average percentage growth rate of the population for the period 1960–74 was 3·4 and for the period 1965–74 was also 3·4.

### CURRENCY

The unit of currency is the sucre, of 100 centavos. Banknotes have been issued by the Banco Central del Ecuador in denominations of 5, 10, 20, 50, 100, 500 and 1,000 sucres. The coins are 5, 10, 20, 50 centavos and 1 sucre.

### FINANCE

Budget figures for 1976 (in million sucres) were: Revenue, 7,384; Expenditure, 7,384.

Currency in circulation at 31 December 1976 was 21,463 million sucres. The external Debt was 731 million dollars in 1976.

The GNP at market prices for 1974 was U.S. $ millions 3,310, and the GNP per capita at market prices was U.S. $480. The annual average percentage growth rate of the GNP per capita for the period 1960–74 was 2·4, and for the period 1965–74 was 2·9. [*See the note at the beginning of this section concerning GNP.*]

### PRINCIPAL BANKS

**Banco Central del Ecuador.** Est. 1927; Sole Bank of Issue; part of the share capital is owned by the state; Balance Sheet at 31 December 1973 showed assets sucres 15,120,851,553; deposits and current accounts sucres 4,969,526,283; banknotes in circulation sucres 3,883,155,762; gold reserve 656,299,000. *Head Office:* Av. 10 De Agosto, Plaza Bolívar, Quito; 12 Branches.

**La Previsora Banco Nacional de Credito.** (President, Ernesto Amador Ycaza.) Est. 1920; Balance Sheet at 30 June 1976 showed assets sucres 5,692,759,466·15; deposits and current accounts sucres 2,438,228,753·03. *Head Office:* 9 de Octubre No. 110, P.O. Box 44, 161 and 1324, Guayaquil, Ecuador; 11 Branches.

### PRODUCTION, INDUSTRY AND COMMERCE

**Agriculture.** The principal agricultural products (volume in thousand metric tons, value in million $U.S.) of Ecuador, in the order of their importance as exports in 1975–76 are shown in the following table:

| Product | 1975 Volume | 1975 Value | 1976 Volume | 1976 Value |
|---|---|---|---|---|
| Bananas | 1,352·6 | 142·4 | 1,229·6 | 136·7 |
| Cocoa | 37·8 | 42·3 | 91·1 | 205·4 |
| Coffee | 62·6 | 64·3 | 22·2 | 32·5 |
| Percentage | 19·1 | 27·7 | 16·6 | 33·2 |

Agricultural production is shown below:

| Product | 1975 metric tons | 1976 metric tons |
|---|---|---|
| Potatoes | 499,371 | 532,774 |
| Cacao | 73,715 | 65,192 |
| Rice | 162,306 | 198,663 |
| Maize | 293,639 | 293,607 |
| Wheat | 64,647 | 65,000 |
| Barley | 62,801 | 62,872 |
| Sugar cane | 7,723,420 | 3,765,588 |
| Coffee | 76,437 | 87,101 |
| Cotton | 30,210 | 27,000 |
| Bananas | 2,569,452 | 2,570,952 |

**Livestock.** 1976 estimated figures were: cattle, 2,792,690; sheep, 2,792,640; pigs, 2,733,630.

**Mining.** Gold, silver, copper, lead and zinc are all found and there are some exports of copper and lead as well as the precious metals. Vast reserves of petroleum have recently been discovered in the Amazon Basin. In 1973 petroleum production was 76·2 million barrels, and that of refinery products, 406·8 million gallons. Sulphur has also been discovered in the north part of the Andes.

**Industry.** Industrial development has increased notably in the last ten years with the help of the Industrial Development Law, which gives protection and benefits such as exemptions from import and sales tax. There are a number of mills producing cotton and cotton goods, also woollen and knitted goods, as well as factories for shoes, leather goods and rayon productions. There are also flour and sugar mills and plants for the refining of edible oils and salt. Building materials produced include nails, cement blocks and cement.

Industrialization in Ecuador is being helped by the increased exploitation of hydro-electric resources. Estimated output of electricity for industry in 1972 was 375,180,396 kWh—33·58 per cent of total production. Large sums of money have been invested in the textile industry since 1949. Ecuador produces a hand-loomed tweed-type woollen cloth of interest to tourists, and attempts are being made to introduce more modern methods and dyes into this home industry.

There are flour mills in various parts of the country, and imports of flour have been replaced by wheat imports. Cement production has been augmented by the erection of two new factories. Two new ceramics factories have begun production. Panama hats are made mostly in the neighbourhood of Cuenca and Jipijapa.

The following table shows production of principal commodities for 1975 and 1976:

| *Item* | *Measure* | 1975 | 1976 |
|---|---|---|---|
| Gold | Oz. troy | 8,157 | 11,014 |
| Cement | Metric tons | 603,722* | 607,948* |
| Petroleum | Thousand barrels | 58,753 | 68,362 |
| Paraffin | Thousand galls. | 5,680 | 6,079 |
| Diesel oil | Thousand barrels | 3,162 | 2,885 |
| Sugar | Metric tons | 273,886* | 309,491* |
| Beer | Thousand litres | 101,039* | 116,094* |
| Cigarettes | ,, packets | 197,027* | 318,002 |

* Provisional Figures.

**Commerce.** Exports by main countries in 1975 and 1976 (in thousand U.S. dollars):

| *Country* | 1975 | 1976 |
|---|---|---|
| United States | 419,885 | 391,580 |
| United Kingdom | 1,909 | 1,775 |
| Columbia | 24,672 | 71,829 |
| Belgium and Luxembourg | 13,260 | 20,765 |
| Japan | 8,487 | 14,019 |
| Italy | 17,486 | 19,342 |
| Chile | 70,662 | 77,130 |
| Germany | 31,122 | 43,910 |
| Canada | 4,885 | 19,434 |

The following table shows values of main commodities exported in 1975 and 1976:

| *Commodity* | 1975 (*thousand sucres*) | 1976 (*thousand sucres*) |
|---|---|---|
| Balsa | 214,700 | 216,125 |
| Bananas | 3,560,825 | 3,417,225 |
| Cocoa | 1,057,100 | 813,025 |
| Coffee | 1,608,500 | 5,134,225 |
| Pharmaceutical products | 81,350 | 102,975 |
| Panama hats | 163,150 | 156,175 |
| Crude petroleum | 12,896,675 | 14,129,400 |
| Figs | 58,300 | 77,525 |
| Sea products | 920,850 | 848,275 |
| Sugar | 376,725 | 122,250 |
| Others | 1,448,200 | 24,225 |

The following table shows values of main commodities imported during 1975 and 1976:

| *Item* | 1975 (*thousand sucres*) | 1976 (*thousand sucres*) |
|---|---|---|
| Non-durable consumer goods (food, drink, tobacco, clothing) | 1,540,025 | 1,474,850 |
| Consumer durables (domestic appliances and equipment, furniture, vehicles, weapons and military equipment) | 1,522,600 | 1,004,600 |
| Petrol, lubricants and associated products | 342,975 | 185,475 |
| Raw materials and intermediate products for agriculture | 744,500 | 573,725 |
| Raw materials and intermediate products for industry | 7,028,200 | 8,884,350 |
| Construction materials | 1,457,675 | 1,687,050 |
| Capital goods for agriculture | 915,125 | 637,550 |
| Capital goods for industry | 6,401,325 | 6,347,950 |
| Transport equipment | 3,540,350 | 3,971,850 |
| Others | 88,325 | 60,675 |

## COMMUNICATIONS

**Railways.** The railways are under state management and cover a total length of 1,064·9 kms. The Quito-San Lorenzo line is 373·1 kms long, and meets the transport needs of the northern and western provinces of Imbabura and Esmeraldas.

Quito, the capital, is connected with the main port, Guayaquil, by a narrow-gauge railway system covering a distance of 452 kilometres. Some 3,654,175 passengers and about 139,578 tons of freight are carried annually.

**Shipping.** A total of 2,114 foreign ships called at Ecuadorean ports in 1976, unloading a net cargo tonnage of 2,763,866 tons. Of these vessels, 146 were American, 264 German, 172 British, 259 Colombian, and 107 Swedish.

**Aviation.** All the important towns are connected by Ecuadorian air services. There are also foreign air services such as K.L.M., Air France, Apsa, Avianca, Braniff, Lan Chile, Lufthansa, Iberia and Air Panama.

The national air services are operated by: Aerotur, Agro Aéreo, Atesa, Americana, Andes, Labores Aéreas, Lansa, San, Saeta, Savac, Tao, TAME, Viansa y Compañia Ecuatoriana de Aviación, VAO.

### Telecommunications

*Telegraphy:* National system, the system consists of point to point radio relay teletype circuits connecting the capital of the provinces to the principal cities Quito and Guayaquil. The rural telegraph system consist mainly of Morse circuits (14,000 KM appr.) on open wire lines.

The international system consists partly of H.F. circuits and partly of radio relay and satellite circuits (via Colombia).

There are telex-exchanges in Quito and Guayaquil (200 subs. approximately) connected by different carriers to the U.S.A., Europe and neighbouring states.

*Telephony:* National system, the local telephone service is automatic in Quito, Guayaquil the capitals of the provinces and in several smaller towns.

Number of subscribers: 106,000, of which 82,000 in Quito and Guayaquil.

The trunk service is fully automatic between Quito and Guayaquil, and for the rest mainly semi-automatic.

The International system, International circuits are partly M.F., partly radio relay and partly by satellite.

Direct communications exist with New York, Madrid and the capitals of neighbouring states.

The service is semi-automatic with Colombia, and for the rest, manual.

A satellite communications system is being set up at the Valle de los Chillos station (Pichincha province).

**Broadcasting.** There are 244 commercial radio stations, with over 3,500,000 listeners; and 16 television stations with 450,000 viewers (1970).

## NEWSPAPERS

**El Comercio.** F. 1906. Morning. Independent. Quito. Circulation 85,000 (Sundays 120,000).

**El Telegrafo.** F. 1884. Morning. Independent. Guayaquil. Circulation 20,000, Sunday 35,000.

**El Universo.** F. 1921. Morning. Independent. Guayaquil. Circulation 85,000 (Sundays and Mondays 105,000).

**La Prensa.** Evening. Guayaquil. Circulation 10,000.

**Ultimas Noticias.** F. 1938. Evening. Independent. Quito. Circulation 32,000 (Saturdays 45,000).

**El Tiempo.** F. 1965. Morning. Independent. Quito.

**El Mercurio.** F. 1920. Morning. Independent. Cuenca. Circulation 12,000.

### EDUCATION

Education is free and compulsory, and there are secondary schools and colleges throughout the country as well as 17 advanced educational institutions, including music schools, 14 universities and three technical institutes. During the 1972–73 school year there were 15,983 children at kindergarten schools, 1,101,586 pupils at primary schools, 268,888 students at secondary schools.

There were 57,677 students at the country's main University of Quito.

### RELIGION

There is no state religion, and all creeds have freedom of worship. The Catholic Church is represented by a cardinal archbishop.

### GALAPAGOS ISLANDS

The Province of Galapagos (formerly Island Territory) (capital Puerto Baquerizo Moreno) was created by Supreme Decree No. 164 of 18 February 1973, published in the official register No. 256 of 28 February 1973.

The province covers an area of 7,876·7 square kilometres and its population was estimated in 1974 as 4,058 inhabitants.

Owing to the position of the islands and the influence of ocean currents the climate of the Galapagos is hot and dry in the low-lying areas and moist and temperate in the higher ones, manifesting itself rather as a variety of microclimates.

The Galapagos islands lie in the dry zone of the Equatorial Pacific, 1,000 kilometres from the coast of Ecuador. The main islands are Santa Isabel, San Cristóbal and Santa Cruz.

The islands, of volcanic origin, were formed by uplifting of the sea bed, and their structure therefore differs from that of the mainland.

In view of the islands' special features the Government has declared them a National Park, and UNESCO regards them as a natural laboratory for the study of the rarest biological species, to which scientists, naturalists and others anxious to learn about them may have access. The Charles Darwin Foundation is currently working on the conservation of and research into the islands.

The islands are of little commercial importance, although on the direct route from Panama to Australia and New Zealand, but produce a certain amount of salt, hides and fish. Tourism is their main attraction.

# Egypt

(ARAB REPUBLIC OF EGYPT)

**Capital**—Cairo.

**President**—Mohamed Anwar El-Sadat.

**National Flag:** Horizontal tricolour, red, white and black; the white stripe is charged with two green stars of five points.

### CONSTITUTION AND GOVERNMENT

ON 18 June 1953, the Egyptian Revolution proclaimed the termination of the monarchy and its replacement by a republican regime. Since that time there have appeared a number of national documents defining the framework of the social, economic and political system of the State as well as the system of government. The two main documents are: (1) The Charter of National Action proclaimed on 21 May 1962, which is considered the basic document expressing the philosophy of national action in all home and foreign affairs; (2) The Provisional Constitution, issued on 25 March 1964, which defines the form of government, the rights of citizens and the competence of the State organs. The President of the Republic is in charge of the executive authority. He nominates the Prime Minister and members of the government. On 15 March 1965, President Gamal Abdel Nasser was elected for six years. On 19 June 1967, he took the office of Prime Minister besides his post as President of the Republic, and formed a Cabinet comprising four Vice-Presidents and 23 Ministers. On 20 March 1968, a new Cabinet was formed with President Nasser as Prime Minister. On 28 September 1970, President Nasser died and Anwar El-Sadat became President.

The 1973 Arab-Israeli war commenced on 6 October. The full effects of the subsequent cease-fire and peace negotiations have yet to be evaluated.

**Cabinet** (26 April 1974)

*First Deputy Prime Minister:* Dr. Abdul Aziz Hegazy.
*Deputy Prime Minister and Minister of the Interior:* Mamduh Salem.
*Deputy Prime Minister and Minister of Wakfs:* Dr. Abdu Aziz Kamel.
*Deputy Prime Minister and Minister of War:* Field Marshall Ahmed Ismail.

The other portfolios are given as follows:—

*Minister of Transport Communications and Marine Transport:* Eng. Abdel Fattah Abdullah.
*Minister of Foreign Affairs:* Muhammad Ibrahim Kamal.
*Minister of Higher Education and Scientific Research:* Dr. Ismail Ghanem.
*Minister of Tourism and Civil Aviation:* Ibrahim Naguib Ibrahim.
*Minister of Power:* Ahmed Sultan.
*Minister of Social Affairs:* Dr. Aisha Rateb.
*Minister of Planning:* Dr. Ismail Sabry Abdullah.
*Minister of State for Sudanese Affairs:* Dr. Osman Badran.
*Minister of Health:* Dr. Mahmud Mahfuz.
*Minister of Manpower:* Salah Eddin Gharib.
*Minister of Information:* Dr. Ahmed Kamal Abul Magd.
*Minister of War Production:* Lt. Gen. Ahmed Kamal el Badry.
*Minister of Culture:* Yusselflel Sabal.
*Minister of Agriculture and Land Reclamation:* Dr. Mohamed Moheb Zaky.
*Minister of State for Local Government and People's Organization:* Dr. Fuad Mohieddin.
*Minister of Petroleum:* Ahmed Ezz Eddin Hilal.
*Minister of Industry and Mining:* Ibrahim Salem Mohmadein.
*Minister of Insurances:* Dr. Hassan Ahmed el Sherif.
*Minister of State for Presidential Affairs:* Abdul Fattah Abdallah.
*Minister of Al Azhar Affairs:* Sheikh Abdul Aziz Mohamed Issa.
*Minister of Maritime Transport:* Abdul Moty Ahmed Ismail El. Araby.
*Minister of Foreign Trade:* Fathy Ahmed el Matbuly.
*Minister of State for Cabinet Affairs:* Dr. Yehia Abdul Aziz el Famal.
*Minister of State for People's Assembly Affairs:* Albert Barsum.
*Minister of Housing and Reconstruction:* Osman Ahmed Osman.
*Minister of Irrigation:* Ahmed Aly Kamal.
*Minister of Finance:* Mohamed Abdul Fattah Ibrahim.
*Minister of Supply and Home Trade:* Mohamed El Hady el Maghraby.
*Minister of Justice:* Dr. Mustafa Abu Zeid.
*Deputy Minister of Youth:* Dr. Abdul Hamid Hassan.

**Political Organization**

The Arab Socialist Union (A.S.U.) is the political party organization in the U.A.R. Its membership is open to all citizens and its main objectives are the realization of sound democracy and the socialist revolution, and the safeguarding of the guarantees embodied in the National Charter.

## LEGAL SYSTEM

The National Courts are as follow:

1. Court of Cassation, a bench of five judges, which constitutes the highest court of appeal in both criminal and civil cases.
2. Courts of Appeal, of three judges each, situated at Cairo, Alexandria, Asyut, Mansura and Tantar. Appeals are heard from the decisions of the Central Tribunals.
3. Assize Courts, of three judges, which deal with all cases of serious crime.
4. Central Tribunals, of three judges, which deal with ordinary civil and commercial cases.
5. Summary Tribunals, presided over by a single judge, which hear civil disputes in matters of up to £E.250, and criminal offences punishable by a fine or by imprisonment of up to three years.

## LOCAL ADMINISTRATION SYSTEM

This was introduced in 1960 with a view to giving the people an active share in administering and organizing their own affairs in a concerted effort with the Central Government. Accordingly, local councils were set up on governorate, city and village levels. Each of these Councils has a legal entity, and is financially autonomous.

## AREA AND POPULATION

The area of the country is estimated at 386,198 sq. miles of which some 13,500 sq. miles are inhabited.

The population in mid-1974 was 36,350,000. The annual average percentage growth rate of the population for the period 1960–74 was 2·5 and for the period 1965–74 was 2·4. Population in different governorates distributed as follows according to July, 1970 population estimate census:

| | | | |
|---|---|---|---|
| Cairo | 4,961,000 | Menufiya | 1,529,000 |
| Alexandria | 2,032,000 | Kaliubiya | 1,379,000 |
| Port Said | 313,000 | Giza | 1,934,000 |
| Suez | 315,000 | Fayum | 1,008,000 |
| Ishmalia | 2,215,000 | Beni Suef | 977,000 |
| Beheira | 395,000 | Minya | 1,813,000 |
| Damietta | 472,000 | Assiut | 1,487,000 |
| Kafr El Sheikh | 1,234,000 | Sohag | 1,764,000 |
| Gharkiya | 2,080,000 | Qena | 1,559,000 |
| Dakahliya | 2,492,000 | Aswan | 651,000 |
| Sharkiya | 2,344,000 | | |

## CURRENCY

The monetary unit is the Egyptian pound of 100 piastres. Silver coin is legal tender only up to £E.1, and nickel or bronze coins up to 10 piastres. Banknotes are issued by the National Bank in various denominations of 5, 10, 25 and 50 piastres and £E.1, 5 and 10.

## FINANCE

Total public expenditure in the 1970–71 budget was set at £E.1,911 million. The net national income for 1971–72 was £E.2,783 as compared with 2,670 in 1969.

Appropriations for the Government administrative machinery, public bodies, economic organizations and special financing funds totalled £E.1,882·2 million as against last year's budget figure of £E.1,658·3 million.

The GNP at market prices for 1974 was U.S. $ millions 10,210, and the GNP per capita at market prices was U.S. $280. The annual average percentage growth rate of the GNP per capita for the period 1960–74 was 1·5, and for the period 1965–74 was 1·0. [*See the note at the beginning of this section concerning GNP.*]

## PRINCIPAL BANKS

**National Bank of Egypt.** (Chairman, Mr. M. A. M. Roushdy.) Established 1898; Balance Sheet at 31 December 1976 showed capital and reserves, £E.28,778,550; investments, Securities and other investments, £E.78,252,590; discounts, advances and sundry debit balances £E.607,652,637; deposits, £E.525,853,275. *Head Office:* 24 Sherif Street, Cairo. 93 Branches.

**Banque de Port-Said.** Established 1929 as Banque Belge et Internationale en Egypte—nationalized on 1 December 1960. (*Managing Director:* Mohamed Fahmi Rizk). Balance-sheet at 31 March 1969 showed capital, reserves and provisions, £E.7,512,000; loans and investments, £E.82,864,000; deposits, £E.100,737,000. *Head Office:* 155 Mohamed Farid Street, Cairo.

**Banque Misr.** (Chairman, Ahmed Fouad.) Established 1920. Balance Sheet at 30 June 1970 showed capital, 2,000,000; reserves and provisions, £E.25,536,994; loans and investments, £E.122,957,942; deposits, £E.187,588,406. *Head Office:* 151 Mohamed Farid Street, Cairo.

**Central Bank of Egypt.** Established 1961. (Governor and Chairman of the Board, Mr Mohamed Abdel Fattah Ibrahim.) Balance sheet at 30 June 1977 showed total assets, banking dept., £E.1,860,288,000; deposits and other credit accounts, £E.1,719,459,000. *Head Office:* 31 Kasr El Nil Street, Cairo.

## PRODUCTION, INDUSTRY AND COMMERCE

**Agriculture.** The cultivatable area of Egypt is comparatively small in proportion to the whole, being confined to the Nile valley and delta and the oases. The development of agriculture depends almost entirely on irrigation from the flood waters of the Nile. Barrages have been erected at several places to conserve flood water and to ensure adequate supplies during the growing season. The benefits accruing from the Aswan High Dam project, now completed are an expansion of the cultivatable area by 1·3 million feddans; the conversion of 700,000 feddans from the basis irrigation system to perennial irrigation; an adequate supply of water for the irrigation of the present and newly cultivated areas, as well as the land under reclamation; an increase in the productivity of the cultivated land; a major expansion in the cultivation of the rice crop for export; and the generation of an electric power of about 10 million kW annually, to be used for industrial and agricultural development.

According to the new Agrarian Reform Law a limit of 100 feddans is imposed on individual holdings. The remainder has been taken over by the Government against payment of compensation in the form of bonds issued by the State. The Government has already started redistributing the requisitioned land among the small farmers at a very low price to be paid over a period of thirty years, about one million feddans of feudal lands were expropriated of which 838,000 have been redistributed to 418,000 families. Smallholders join Agricultural Co-operatives, which act as a banker to them and also supply their requirements of seed, fertilizer, cattle and equipment.

A three-crop rotation system is used in most areas, one-third of the area for cotton and the remainder divided among such crops as wheat and clover.

£E.37,700,000 were allocated to the agricultural sector from the 1969–70 budget, of which £E.26,300,000 is for irrigation purposes. This will be spent on completing the conversion of basin into perennial irrigation in an area of 26,000 feddans; starting the conversion of another 60,000 feddans from basin to perennial irrigation; improving irrigation in 33,000 feddans and improving drainage facilities in an area of about 170,000 feddans.

The following table shows the acreage and production of main agricultural crops for 1973:

| *Crop* | *Unit* | *Area in Feddans* | 1973 *Average crop yield per Feddans* | *Total yield* |
|---|---|---|---|---|
| **Cotton** | Kentar[1] | N.A. | N.A. | N.A. |
| **Wheat** | Ardeb[2] | 1,247,578 | 9·82 | 12,246,426 |
| **Barley** | ,, | 84,009 | 9·50 | 798,126 |
| Fenugreek | ,, | 25,951 | 4·92 | 127,644 |
| Maize-Indian Corn | ,, | 1,303,079 | 11·75 | 15,313,587 |
| Egyptian millet | ,, | 462,780 | 12·70 | 5,877,887 |
| Rice | Dariba[3] | 997,072 | 2·41 | 2,406,678 |
| Beans[4] | Ardeb | 270,016 | 6·51 | 1,759,029 |
| Lentils | ,, | 74,412 | 5·18 | 385,341 |
| Egyptian lupines | ,, | 9,324 | 4·27 | 39,744 |
| Chick-peas | ,, | 8,402 | 4·84 | 40,624 |
| Peanuts (ground nuts) | ,, | 29,402 | 11·72 | 344,554 |
| Sesame seeds | ,, | 36,218 | 4·93 | 178,570 |
| Winter onions | Kentar | 98,250 | 47·00 | 4,566,467 |
| Flax (Straw) | ,, | 39,571 | 55·00 | 2,194,224 |
| Linseed | Ardeb | 39,571 | 4·20 | 166,198 |

[1] 1 Kentar = 44·9 kilograms.
[2] 1 Ardeb = 198 litres.
[3] 1 Dariba = 120 kilograms.
[4] Excluding areas where yield is consumed fresh.

The following table shows the value (in thousands £E.) of imports and exports for 1973:

| | *Imports* | *Exports* |
|---|---|---|
| *Country group* | | |
| Arab countries | 24,971 | 30,874 |
| East European countries | 109,925 | 243,864 |
| Western European countries | 122,803 | 95,843 |
| Asian countries | 30,700 | 51,542 |
| African countries | 4,210 | 5,948 |
| North American countries | 45,458 | 6,999 |
| Central American | 15 | 1,577 |
| South American | 1,074 | 7,329 |
| Oceanic countries | 18,366 | 92 |
| Ships and free zones | 3,595 | 129 |
| Total | 361,117 | 444,197 |

## COMMUNICATIONS

**Roads.** Total length of roads is 21,637 km., of which 16,182 km. are paved.

**Railways.** The State railway system covers 4,446 kilometres, besides 2,554 km. which represent the length of storage, extra tracks and service tracks; there are 750 railway stations. In 1966–67 over 6,529 million passenger km., and about 43 million ton km., were run.

**Shipping.** The three chief ports are Alexandria, Port Said and Suez. In 1965–66 20,635 ships (259,322,000 tons) passed through the Suez Canal. In 1970 2,920 ships cleared the port of Alexandria and a new vessel, the S.S. *Goumhouriai Misri* (12,000 tons) of the Khedivial Mail Line made its maiden voyage to the United States. It was bought from Canada along with another vessel, now renamed the *Makka* which is being used mainly for the pilgrim traffic to Saudi Arabia.

**Principal Shipping Lines—Egyptian Navigation Company.** (Chairman, Mr. Hussein Yakout Zaher.) Vessels, 38; total tonnage 218,000; *services operated:* Liner service all over the world. *Head Office:* 2 El Nasr Street, Alexandria. *Cable Address:* Arabnavi-Alexandria.

**United Arab Maritime Co.** (Chairman, M. Hehia Ramadan.) Vessels 37; total tonnage 169,460 tons gross. *Head Office:* 2 Rue de l'Ancienne Bourse, Alexandria. *Cable Address:* ARABHAVI.

**Civil Aviation. EgyptAir.**
*Internal Flights:* Luxor, Aswan, Abm Simpel. *External Flights:* Benghazi, Tripoli, Algiers, Khartoum, Entebbe, Nairobi, Dar-es-Salaam, Kano, Lagos, Accra, Abidjan, Beirut, Damascus, Baghdad, Amman, Kuwait, Doha, Jeddah, Aden, Bombay, Manilla, Tokyo, Athens, Rome, Zurich, Paris, London, Frankfurt, Munich, Copenhagen, Nicosia, Karachi, Aleppo, Dhahran, Bahrain, Abu Dhabi, Dubai Sharjah, Sanaa, Vienna.
*Address:* Head Office: Egyptair, Cairo International Airport, Cairo, A.R.E.

**Posts, Telegraphs and Telephones.** Both these services are owned and operated by the Egyptian State Telegraphs and Telephones Department. The number of automatic telephone lines in 1967 was estimated at 262,500, including public call offices.

In 1969–70. there were 1,447 government post offices and 1,390 postal agencies, plus 1,767 mobile offices and 2,492 private stations. 45,328,000 letters went out of the country and 54,841,000 letters were sent within the country.

**Broadcasting.** This is a State service. Daily broadcasting transmission hours in 1970 were 159 hours and 12 minutes, while TV average daily transmission was 19 hours and 56 minutes. Only owners of television sets pay an annual licence fee.

## NEWSPAPERS

**Al-Akhbar.** F. 1944. Arabic. Morning. Independent. Al-Sahafa Street, Cairo.

**Al-Gomhouria.** F. 1954. Arabic, Morning. Independent. 24 Galal Street, Cairo.

**Journal du Commerce et de la Marine.** F. 1909. French and English. Evening. P.O. Box 813, Alexandria.

**Al-Ahram.** F. 1875. Arabic. Morning. Independent. Sharia El-Galaa, Cairo.

**Egyptian Gazette.** F. 1880. English. Morning. 24 Sharia Zakaria Ahmed (ex Gala), Cairo.

**Le Journal d'Egypte.** F. 1936. French. Morning. Cairo.

## ATOMIC ENERGY

Construction of a plant for producing atomic fuel from uranium has been completed. This is the second factory of its kind. The first, which uses monazite as raw material, was opened in 1963.

Research is being carried out to extract pure uranium from raw uranium found in the eastern desert region of the A.R.E.

## EDUCATION

In February 1953 Law No. 210, was issued, for the reorganization of primary schools. According to this law elementary and primary schools form one stage known as primary which lasts for six years from six to 12 years of age. This stage is compulsory. Now the term primary comprises both primary and old elementary. The following figures give a comparison between the 1952–53 figures for education, and those of 1971–72.

| | 1952–3 | 1971–2 |
|---|---|---|
| Primary stage | 1,392,741 | 3,878,017 |
| Elementary stage | 351,834 | 925,227 |
| General secondary schools | 92,063 | 312,462 |
| Secondary technical schools | 18,838 | 289,812 |
| Teachers training schools | 23,636 | 27,237 |

Compulsory education is free, including meals.

There are five state universities already functioning, Cairo University (previously Fouad University, founded 1908, taken over by Government 1925), Alexandria University (previously Farouk University, founded 1942) and Ain Shams University (formerly Ibrahim), Asyut and Al-Azhar. The number of University students in 1969–70 was 161,517; the number of students in higher institutes was 38,892.

## THE SUEZ CANAL

The Suez Canal is the shortest and most economical route between East and West.

The Canal is 101 miles long excluding the approach channels. It permits the passage of vessels with 38 ft. draught, and its minimum width at 33 ft. is 300 ft. In 1965 the number of vessels passing through the Canal reached 20,289, an increase of 139 per cent compared with 1955, while tonnage reached 246,817, an increase of 213 per cent over the same period.

The Nasser Project aims at widening the Canal to allow two-way traffic and deepening it to accommodate ships with 45 ft. draught and 70,000 tonnage.

The Canal remained unused due to the exigencies of the Middle East situation from June 1967 to June 1975.

# El Salvador

(REPÚBLICA DE EL SALVADOR)

**Capital**—San Salvador.

**President**—General Carlos Romero.

**National Flag:** A tricolour fesse-wise, blue, white, blue, the centre stripe charged with the national coat of arms: a triangle bearing five mountains under a cap of liberty.

## CONSTITUTION AND GOVERNMENT

El Salvador, the most densely populated state in the continent of America, became an Independent Republic in 1841 when the Central American Federation, which had comprised the States of Guatemala, El Salvador, Honduras, Nicaragua and Costa Rica, was dissolved. From December 1948 to September 1950 the country was governed by a Junta named the Council of Revolutionary Government, which came into power as the result of a revolution on 14 December 1948. The Constitution of 1886, which had previously been amended several times was repealed and presidential elections were held in March 1950 with for the first time in the country's history, universal male and female suffrage. A Constituent Assembly was elected at the same time and a new Constitution was promulgated. This Constitution was revised in January 1962. The President is elected for a term of five years beginning on 1 July. He may not succeed himself nor extend his term of office. The Legislature consists of a Legislative Assembly of 52 members elected for a two-year term.

President Lemus, who had been elected in 1956 for a six-year term, was overthrown in October 1960. The six-man Junta de Gobierno which took his place was itself overthrown in January 1961; and a five-man Directorio Civico-Militar took its place. The Directory enacted a sweeping programme of social reforms and held elections for a Constituent and Legislative Assembly in December 1961. This Assembly amended the 1950 Constitution and elected a provisional President; and then became the Legislative Assembly. Presidential elections were held in April 1962, at which the only candidate was Lieutenant-Colonel Julio A. Rivera, a former member of the Directory who had resigned in September 1961 to lead the new Partido Conciliación Nacional. This Party won all the seats in the Legislative elections in December 1961. From 1 July 1967 to 1 July 1972 Colonel Fidel Sánchez Hernández was in power.

Proportional representation was introduced in August 1963 and new legislative elections were held under this system in March of 1964, 1966, 1968 and 1970. In the latter elections the Government party won 39 seats in the Assembly and the three Opposition parties, 13 seats between them. Presidential elections were held on 25 February 1972, and Colonel Arturo Armando Molina, the Government party candidate and former Private Secretary to the Presidency, secured a narrow majority. The Government controlled National Assembly ratified the result. Colonel Molina took office on 1 July 1972.

### Cabinet

*Minister of Foreign Affairs:*
*Minister of Interior:* Col. Agustín Martinez Varela.
*Minister of Education:* Dr. Rogelio Chavez.
*Minister of Public Health and Social Assistance:* Dr. Julio Astacio.
*Minister of Defence:* Col. Carlos Humbarto Romero.
*Minister of Finance:* Dr. Vicente Amado Gavidia H.
*Minister of Economy:* Dr. Guillermo Hidalgo Qüelh.
*Minister of Public Works:* Ing. Antonio Jorge Seaman.
*Minister of Agriculture:* Mr. Roberto Eladio Castillo.
*Minister of Justice:* Dr. José Enrique Silva.
*Minister of Labour and Social Insurance:* Dr. Rogelio Chávez.
*Secretary of Economic Planning:* Lic. Atilio Vieytez.
*Under Secretary for Economic Integration:* Lic. Carlos Valencia Valladares.
*Secretary General to Presidency:* Dr. Enrique Mayorga R.
*Secretary Principal to the Presidency:* Major and Dr. Mauricio Vides Casanova.
*Private Secretary to the Presidency:* Col. Anibal Figueroa Velarde.

**Legislative Assembly** (Elections of March 1970): Partido Conciliación Nacional, 39; Partido Demócrata Cristiana, 8; Partido Popular Salvadoreño, 4; Frente Unido Democratico Independiente, 1.

## LEGAL SYSTEM

There is a Supreme Court of Justice, several courts of first and second instance, a court of third instance and some minor courts. The Supreme Court appoints judges of the first instance, whilst judges of second and third instance are elected by the National Assembly. All judges serve for a term of three years.

*President of the Supreme Court:* Dr. Francisco Armando Arias.

## AREA AND POPULATION

The population at mid-1974 was 3,887,000.
The Departments (with population) in June 1971 were:

| | |
|---|---|
| Department of Ahuachapán | 177,958 |
| Department of Santa Ana | 336,287 |
| Department of Sonsonate | 228,338 |
| Department of Chalatenango | 172,408 |
| Department of La Libertad | 283,727 |
| Department of San Salvador | 730,894 |
| Department of Cuscatlán | 155,635 |
| Department of La Paz | 181,578 |
| Department of Cabañas | 129,145 |
| Department of San Vicente | 156,710 |
| Department of Usulután | 292,494 |
| Department of San Miguel | 316,280 |
| Department of Morazán | 155,508 |
| Department of La Unión | 224,048 |

The annual average percentage growth rate of the population for the period 1960–74 was 3·4 and for the period 1965–74 was 3·4.

## CURRENCY

The unit of currency is the *colón* of 100 *centavos* which is issued in denominations of 1, 2, 5, 10, 15 and 100 colónes; 25 and 50 centavos; 1, 5 and 10 centavos.

## FINANCE

The approved 1972 Budget is Ȼ367,717,590. Of this figure Ȼ301,393,260 is budgeted for operating expenses, and Ȼ66,324,330 for capital expenditure. Tax revenues are expected to account for Ȼ291,900,000, with the balance made up of non-tax revenues of Ȼ21,100,000, and loans from international organizations amounting to Ȼ44,931,000. The 1972 figures represent an increase of Ȼ89,447,590 over the 1970 budget with Ȼ30,874,320 of this increased amount being allocated to the Ministry of Education.

The GNP at market prices for 1974 was U.S. $ millions 1,590 and the GNP per capita at market prices for 1974 was U.S. $410. The annual average percentage growth rate of the GNP per capita for the period 1960–74 was 1·8 and for 1965–74 was 1·0.

## BANKS

**Banco Central de Reserva de El Salvador.** (President, Ing. Edgardo Suarez Contreras.) Established 1934, nationalized 1961; Sole Bank of Issue for El Salvador; Balance Sheet showed assets Ȼ767,806,926, including Ȼ250,835,218 gold and foreign exchange; deposits at sight Ȼ265,092,240 cash in circulation Ȼ166,354,662. *Head Office:* San Salvador. *Branches:* Santa Ana, Sonsonate, and San Miguel. Correspondents in the interior 14, Correspondents abroad, 15.

## PRODUCTION, INDUSTRY AND COMMERCE

**Industry.** Local industry has considerably improved in recent years and products manufactured now include first-class cotton and artificial fibre textiles, iron and steel rods, bars and angles, air conditioning equipment, refrigerators, locks, electric irons, petrol and other petroleum derivatives, cement, fertilizers, instant coffee, beer, cigarettes, insecticides, clothing, etc. A new plant to produce pharmaceuticals with over 50 per cent British investment will start to operate at the end of this year. The Salvadorean Institute for Industrial Development (INSAF) continue to provide financial and technical assistance to new and already established industrial firms. A silver mine located in the eastern section of the country was re-opened this year under their auspices. Laws are now in force to encourage and protect foreign investments. Special grants are given to industries which export their output to the Central American common market.

### COMMUNICATIONS

**Railways and Roads.** There are two rail systems, the Salvador Railway and the American-owned international Railways of Central America. The first-named railway connects the capital with Acajutla and Santa Ana while the second system has a line from the port of La Unión via San Salvador to Zacpa (Guatemala) and Puerto Barrios.

There are 8,641 kms. of roads in El Salvador of which 959·6 are asphalt including the Salvadorean Section A of the Pan-American highway.

**Shipping.** The principal ports are Acajutla, La Libertad and La Unión. 498 ships with a gross total tonnage of 5,652,372 tons called at El Salvador ports in 1968.

**Civil Aviation.** TACA, Pan American Airways, T.A.N., LA NICA and LACSA airlines connect El Salvador with the U.S.A., Mexico, Central and South America. There were 4,370 commercial air landings in 1968. The enlarged Ilopango airport was opened to jet aircraft in May 1964.

**Posts and Telegraphs.** There are 317 post office and telegraph offices throughout the country. The automatic telephone system is being greatly enlarged and now covers most of the towns of the interior with a population of over 1,500 people.

**Broadcasting.** There are 26 broadcasting stations operating on 34 wavelengths, and five television stations. Three of these television stations are commercial stations, and the remaining two are devoted to education.

### NEWSPAPERS

**La Prensa Grafica's.** 3a Calle Pte. No. 130, Apartado Postal (06) 202, San Salvador, El Salvador, Central America. Morning circulation = 61,090, Sunday Circulation = 104,124. Certified by the Audit Bureau of Circulations (ABC). The above figures cover a six month period ending on 31 March 1975. (Newspaper Publisher's Statement.) Circulation 56,400.

**El Diario de Hoy's.** 8a Calle Poniente 215, San Salvador. Morning Circulation = 95,327, Sunday Circulation = 99,695. Certified by the Audit bureau of Circulations (ABC). The above figures cover a three month period ending on 31 March 1977. (Newspaper Publisher's Statement.)

**Diario Latino.** Afternoon. 23 Avenida Sur, Ap. 96, San Salvador. Circulation 38,000.

**El Mundo.** Evening. 2A Avenida Norte 711, San Salvador. Circulation 24,000.

### EDUCATION AND RELIGION

Primary education is free and obligatory. In 1972 562,354 pupils were registered for primary education and 86,853 pupils for secondary education. There is also a national university which had 22.342 students in 1972. The José Simeón Canãs University has 9,430 students, The Government of President Sanchez Hernandez completed its election pledge of building a school a day throughout its tenure of office.

Roman Catholicism is the dominant religion though all creeds are tolerated.

# Equatorial Guinea

**Capital**—Malabo (formerly Santa Isabel).

**President**—Francisco Macías Nguema Byogo.

**National Flag:** Three horizontal stripes, green, white and red, with a triangle of blue on the staff side and the national coat of arms in the centre.

### CONSTITUTION AND GOVERNMENT

Equatorial Guinea consists of several islands in, or close to, the Gulf of Guinea, and territory on the West coast of the mainland of Africa bordering the Gulf of Guinea.

This area previously formed part of Spain's overseas territories. In July 1959 the colony was made an integral part of Spain as the Equatorial Region, divided into two provinces and Africans became technically full Spanish citizens. This policy of assimilation was pursued till 1964 when a measure of autonomy was granted to the Region to answer nationalist clamours for independence. After protracted negociations with Spain, independence was granted on 12 October 1968 with Francisco Macías Nguema Byogo elected as first President of the new Republic, whose first constitution recognized a fair amount of autonomy to the insular province of what was then Fernando Poo. Relations with Spain became strained in early 1969 and, after an abortive coup against the President, a mass exodus of the Spanish population took place in 1969 provoking a near collapse of the economy. Since then, the Republic is under the authoritarian rule of the President who has parried many attempted coups, merged all parties into his own Partido Unico Nacional De Los Trabajadores (1970), assumed complete powers and was appointed Life President on 14 July 1972. Whatever economic life survived in the early 1970's was further weakened by chaotic management, lack of funds and expertise, loss of about one quarter of the national population to neighbouring countries and Spain, and the departure of most of the Nigerian field-workers on cocoa estates on the main island. The new constitution of July 1973 abolished whatever autonomy had been granted to Fernando Poo and the Republic is now administered as a single unit by the President, while a nominal Assembly has been retained.

For administrative purposes it is still divided into two provinces, one insular, the other continental. The first, formerly named Fernando Poo, now Macías Nguema Byogo (from the President's name) includes (a) the island of that name with the capital Malabo (formerly Santa Isabel) of the Republic; (b) the island of Pigalu (formerly Annobón) several hundred miles to the south, in the southern hemisphere. The province of Rio Muni consists of the mainland territory of that name, the off-shore islands of Elobey Chico, Elobey Grande and Corisco and other smaller islands nearby.

### AREA AND POPULATION

The estimated population of Equatorial Guinea at mid-1974 was 318,000. The annual average percentage growth rate of the population for the period 1960–74 was estimated at 1·8 and for the period 1965–74 at 1·3.

Macías Nguema Byogo (Fernando Po) including Pigalu (17 sq. km) is 2,034 sq. km in area. The climate is tropical and this area is subject to violent windstorms. A highly fertile volcanic soil coupled with abundant rain make it particularly suitable to cocoa growing.

The population of Fernando Po was 60,000 in 1960. Since then, no census seem to have taken place and while it was reported that its population reached 90,000 in recent years, it is safe to assume that with the departure of Nigerians and Equato-Guinean citizens into exile, this figure is no longer valid. The Bubis are the native tribe.

The area of Rio Muni is 26,017·5 sq km. including Corisco (15 sq. km) and the Elobeys islands (2·5 sq. km). The population of Rio Muni was 184,000 in 1960. The figure is unknown for recent years. The main city on the mainland is Bata which the President has endowed with a new harbour. Most of the inhabitants are of the Fang tribe.

The main cities are Malabo (Santa Isabel) the capital of the Republic and Bata (the capital of Rio Muni Province), other towns are Luba (San Carlos) on the main island and various Rio Munian harbours such as Rio Benito and Puerto Iradier or inland administrative centres: Micomeseng, Niefang, etc. As the entrance of foreigners into the country is screened by the President's office, no first-hand impartial report on Equatorial Guinea has appeared for years and no statistical figures have been released by the authorities either. Those which exist are educated guesses or extrapolation at best.

The official language is Spanish.

### CURRENCY AND FINANCE

The unit of currency is the ekuele. 1 ekuele = 1 Spanish peseta.

## EQUATORIAL GUINEA

The GNP at market prices for 1974 was given at U.S. $millions 90, and the GNP per capita at market prices was U.S. $290. The annual average percentage growth rate of the GNP per capita for the period 1960–74 was −0·5, and for the period 1965–74 was −3·7. [*See the note at the beginning of this section concerning GNP.*]

**PRODUCTION, INDUSTRY AND COMMERCE**

The principal products are cocoa, timber and coffee. Other products are bananas and palm oil. It is estimated that production of cocoa has declined to one third (about 12,000 metric tons in 1974) of its pre-independence level. Coffee (7,200 tons in 1974) and timber (920,000 cubic meters in 1974) have better weathered the vagaries of the post-independence situation. Spain still continues to buy a certain quota of cocoa at above world market prices, as a policy of subsidizing her former colony economy.

Exports are mainly to Spain, West Germany, the United Kingdom and the U.S.A.

Imports largely consist of consumer goods and machinery. Guinea has little industry and as yet no exploitation of mineral resources, although there is evidence that minerals exists.

# Ethiopia

**Capital**—Addis Ababa.

**National Flag:** A tricolour fesse-wise, green, yellow, red.

**CONSTITUTION AND GOVERNMENT**

ETHIOPIA can claim considerable antiquity as an independent African state but the present territorial form dates from the late 19th century. The country is at present in a transitional state.

In 1955, a new Constitution was promgated, lureplacing that of 1931. Under this there were two Chambers, a Senate whose members continued to be appointed by the Emperor and a Chamber of Deputies with members who were elected throughout Ethiopia and Eritrea on a system of universal suffrage for men and women over 21 years old. The first General Election was held in 1957, followed by others in 1961, 1965, 1969, and 1973. The Chamber of Deputies had a limited but not insignificant authority, and a certain measure of fiscal control. The Prime Minister had power to select his own ministers for approval by the Emperor. Following military intervention in 1974 and the deposition of Emperor Haile Sellassie on 12 September of that year, the constitution was abolished. Ethiopia is now governed by a Provisional Military Administrative Council (the Dergue) which rules by decree.

From 1952–1962 Eritrea was federated with Ethiopia, retaining its own Assembly and having control over certain spheres of Government. In 1962, Eritrea was incorporated in Ethiopia as a province.

The present chairman of the Dergue is Lt. Colonel Mengistu Haile Mariam. He succeeds Brig. General Teferi Banti who was killed in February 1977 following a conflict within the military council. Brig. General Teferi was himself appointed to replace the original chairman of the PMAC Maj. General Aman Andom who was shot dead in November 1974.

The PMAC has pursued a socialist and increasingly Marxist policy. They have introduced rural and urban land reform and have nationalized most sectors of industry and commerce. The senior members of the Dergue are:—

*Chairman:* Lt. Col. Mengistu Haile Mariam.
*Vice-Chairman:* Lt. Col. Atnafu Abate.

**LOCAL GOVERNMENT**

For purposes of local government the country is divided into 14 administrative regions as follows, shoa, Gojjam, Wollega, Gondar, Tigre, Eritrea, Wollo, Hararghe, Arssi, Sidamo, Katta, I'llubabor, Bale and Gamu Gofa.

Each region is divided into provinces, which in turn are divided into districts and localities. The latter number over 1,000.

**LEGAL SYSTEM**

The legal system of Ethiopia has been reorganized on modern lines. An additional penal code was introduced in November 1974. The death penalty has been retained for serious offences.

**AREA AND POPULATION**

Ethiopia is situated on the east side of Africa above the equator, lying between the White Nile and the Red Sea. It is bounded on the north and west by the Sudan, east by the Red Sea and French Territory of the Afars and Issas, south-east by the Somali Republic, and south by Kenya. It was formerly cut off from the sea on all sides, but the federation with Eritrea which came into effect in September 1952 gave free access to the coast. The country is mountainous, with high plateaux and deep ravines. The total area is approximately 395,000 sq. miles.

The inhabitants are mainly Hamitic, with some Semitic admixture; numerically, the largest element is the Gallas approx. 45 per cent) but the Amharas and Tigrais who together make up about 33 per cent of the population have always supplied the Imperial House. Other smaller racial groups are the Somalis, Gurages, Afar, Shankallas and Falashas.

The estimated population in mid-1974 was 27,240,000. The annual average percentage growth rate of the population for the period 1960–74 was 2·2 and for the period 1965–74 was 2·5.

The principal towns are Addis Ababa, the capital, with over 912,000 inhabitants; Asmara, with 250,000; Dessie, 50,000; Jimma 47,000; Dire Dawa, 67,000; Harar, 48,000; Gondar, 39,000 and Massawa, 21,000, Nazret 45,000.

**CURRENCY AND FINANCE**

In October 1976 a new currency was introduced. The Ethiopian dollar was replaced by the Girr which has the same exchange rate on the international market. As before each Girr is divided into 100 cents and the denominations of notes and coins has not changed

Ethiopia is a charter member of the International Monetary Fund, the International Bank for Reconstruction and Development and the African Development Bank.

The GNP at market prices for 1974 was U.S. $ millions 2,660, and the GNP per capita at market prices was U.S.$10. The annual average percentage growth rate of the GNP per capita for the period 1960–74 was 2·2, and for the period 1965–74 was 1·5. [*See the note at the beginning of this section concerning GNP.*]

Estimated Government revenue and expenditure for 1975–76:

| | |
|---|---|
| Revenue Eth. $ | 1,174,899,200 |
| Expenditure Eth. $ | 1,330,966,574 |

**PRINCIPAL BANKS**

**National Bank of Ethiopia.** (Governor: Ato Legesse Tikehere.) Balance Sheet at 6 June 1976 showed assets Eth. $1,372,120,525, notes in circulation Eth. $781,912,967. Other sight liabilities Eth. $1,072,473,802. Address: P.O. Box 5550, Addis Ababa.

**Commercial Bank of Ethiopia.** (A/General Manager: Dr. A. Birara). Address: P.O. Box 255, Addis Ababa. Balance Sheet at 31 December 1976 showed deposits of Girr 908,885,236 and assets of Girr 1,075,296,593. The Commercial Bank of Ethiopia which is a state controlled bank, replaced the former State Bank of Ethiopia at the end of 1963.

**The Addis Ababa Bank S.C.** (Managing Director: Ato Debebe H. Yohannes). Balance Sheet at 31 December 1972 showed deposits of E$68,588,861 and assets of E$77,883,759. National and Grindlays Bank Ltd., London, has a 40 per cent shareholding in this bank. *Address:* P.O. Box 751, Addis Ababa.

**The Agricultural and Industrial Development Bank S.C.** (A/Managing Director: Ato Addis Anteneh.) Formed in November 1970 from an amalgamation of the Development Bank of Ethiopia and the Ethiopian Investment Corp. S.C. to encourage and promote agricultural and industrial development. The issue capital is E$100,000,000. *Address:* P. O. Box 1900, Addis Ababa.

## PRODUCTION, INDUSTRY AND COMMERCE

**Agriculture.** The main wealth of Ethiopia is pastoral and agricultural. The full agricultural potential, is however, not likely to be realized until modern methods of stock breeding, agriculture, land tenure reform and much improved and an entirely new transport infrastructure are effectively introduced and soil erosion and de-afforestation checked.

There is a good, but seasonal, rainfall and crops are numerous. Barley, wheat, peas and beans grow at altitudes of 5,000 to 9,000 feet, maize and millet at lower altitudes. Teff, a grass-like grain peculiar to the country, is highly esteemed, and the flour baked in flat cakes is used as bread; wheat, millet and other cereals are similarly used. Oil seeds, sugar cane and coffee are also grown, coffee forming the chief export crop. Large scale growing of cotton is well established and expanding.

Fruit is grown on the lower slopes, principally bananas, citrus fruits and grapes do well at somewhat higher altitudes. Soft fruit is grown in the neighbourhood of Addis Ababa.

Cattle herding is carried on jointly with agriculture on the plateaux, and it is estimated that there are 24 million head of cattle in the whole country. These are mostly cattle belonging to the zebu type, which is humped, and they are used both for work and for milk. Sheep and goats are also kept (24 million), but the wool is of poor quality. The horses are small and sturdy, and are found all over the uplands, as are mules, which are used mainly for transport in broken country. Poultry is also plentiful and development of poultry farming is planned.

In the damp, sub-tropical regions of the south-west the forest areas are a potential source of wealth. Valuable cedar is found and other hardwoods. Eucalyptus is planted round most of the big towns and forms an important source of fuel. There is big game. Game laws, exist, however, and licences are required for hunting.

**Mining.** The traditional small scale exploitations of salt, gold and platinium will soon be supplemented. Exploitation by Japanese interests of considerable deposits of copper in Eritrea has been held up by the conflict between Eritrean separatists and the Ethiopian Government. Oil exploration in the Ogaden has discovered encouraging traces of oil and natural gas. There are large reserves of potash in the Dandkil Depression but lack of demand has inhibited exploitation so far. Other mineral deposits of various kinds are known to exist and surveys are in progress.

**Industry.** Industrial development has taken place in Addis Ababa, Asmara and Dire Dawa. There were about 500 industrial establishments of various kinds, but they are mostly small. The general policy is of import substitution. The largest areas of capital investment are the railways, sugar factories, cement, cotton, flour, oil crushing mills, meat canning, pharmaceuticals, pulp and paper, tyres and textile mills (cotton and wool). A small steel rolling mill is operating. More cement factories are projected. A pulp and paper mill went into production in April 1970. and a rubber tyre plant in October 1972. The hydro-electric plant at Koka Dam, capable of producing 110 million kW in an average year, began to operate in May 1960. A second dam on the Awash began operation in 1967 and a third production late in 1969. A new hydro-electric dam on the Finchaa River in the Blue Nile basin to produce 100 MW was also inaugurated in November 1973. Smaller thermal stations as well as diesel plants are in operation elsewhere.

**Commerce.** Ethiopia benefitted considerably in 1972 and 1973 from the world boom in certain basic commodities (e.g. hides and skins). From 1973–75 exports declined in value due to lower prices and the effects of drought and crop disease. In 1974–75 exports were Eth. $478·2 m. and imports Eth. $683·8 m. Coffee remains the principal export crop. Other exports include hides and skins, pulses, oilseeds, fruit and vegetables. Chief among imports are motor vehicles and spares, petroleum and products, specialized machinery, tyres and clothing.

The following table shows the value of major commodities of exports by country of destination for 1972 in thousands of Ethiopian dollars:

| | |
|---|---|
| *Coffee* | |
| United States | 127,438 |
| West Germany | 13,818 |
| Italy | 3,650 |
| Saudi Arabia | 6,529 |
| Japan | 5,615 |
| France | 3,724 |
| Norway | 1,285 |
| Sweden | 587 |
| China (mainland) | 3,629 |
| Others | 16,279 |
| **Total** | **182,554** |
| *Hides and Skins* | |
| United Kingdom | 6,462 |
| Italy | 16,810 |
| United States | 3,304 |
| France | 4,408 |
| West Germany | 1,798 |
| U.S.S.R. | 3 |
| Greece | 1,708 |
| Lebanon | 1,160 |
| Iran | 106 |
| Others | 11,835 |
| **Total** | **47,594** |
| *Oil Seeds* | |
| United States | 707 |
| Italy | 3,138 |
| Japan | 13,866 |
| Greece | 3,120 |
| Southern Yemen | 1,342 |
| United Kingdom | 1,155 |
| *Oil Seeds* | |
| Lebanon | 723 |
| Saudi Arabia | 2,972 |
| West Germany | 834 |
| Israel | 2,438 |
| U.S.S.R. | 6,310 |
| Others | 12,163 |
| **Total** | **48,768** |
| *Vegetables, Fresh and Frozen* | |
| West Germany | 5,701 |
| Territory of Afars and Issas | 1,651 |
| Italy | 5 |
| Ceylon | 6,877 |
| Saudi Arabia | 7,923 |
| United Kingdom | 1,848 |
| France | 1,900 |
| Japan | 743 |
| Southern Yemen | 107 |
| Sudan | 150 |
| Israel | 494 |
| Lebanon | 260 |
| Jordan | 456 |
| Others | 6,855 |
| **Total** | 34,975 |

The following table shows the value of major commodities, in thousands of Ethiopian dollars, of imports by country of origin for 1972:

| | |
|---|---|
| *Clothing* | |
| China (mainland) | 448 |
| Japan | 1,358 |
| Hong Kong | 877 |
| West Germany | 344 |
| India | 599 |
| Italy | 1,057 |
| Poland | 146 |
| Czechoslovakia | 213 |
| United Kingdom | 452 |
| Israel | 153 |
| Hungary | 510 |
| United States | 131 |
| Korea South | 326 |
| Others | 819 |
| **Total** | 7,433 |

*continued*

| *Road Motor Vehicles and Parts* | |
|---|---|
| Italy | 23,826 |
| West Germany | 9,553 |
| United Kingdom | 4,818 |
| France | 3,476 |
| United States | 8,186 |
| U.S.S.R. | 663 |
| Japan | 4,376 |
| Others | 7,977 |
| Total | **62,875** |

| *Petroleum and Products* | |
|---|---|
| Iran | 25,560 |
| United States | 2,484 |
| Saudi Arabia | 243 |
| Italy | 2,093 |
| Southern Yemen | 1,953 |
| United Kingdom | 1,213 |
| Others | 2,188 |
| Total | 35,734 |

| *Machines for Special Industries* (Major supplier Countries) | |
|---|---|
| France | 126 |
| Italy | 1,786 |
| West Germany | 2,515 |
| United States | 4,910 |
| United Kingdom | 1,280 |
| Netherlands | 2,753 |
| Japan | 144 |
| India | 12 |

| *Rubber articles not elsewhere specified* (Major supplier countries) | |
|---|---|
| Japan | 12,040 |
| United Kingdom | 1,236 |
| Italy | 760 |
| West Germany | 279 |
| Israel | 553 |
| United States | 491 |
| France | 646 |
| China (mainland) | 426 |

## COMMUNICATIONS

**Railways.** Addis Ababa is linked by rail to the port of Djibouti in the Republic of Djibouti. This railway line was cut in May 1977 after guerrillas of the Western Somali Liberation Front had dynamited several bridges. Repairs were expected to take some months. The distance is 487 miles and can be covered in 24 hours. There is also a railway from the Eritrean port of Massawa to Asmara (the capital). Normally more than half Ethiopia's foreign trade is moved by rail but guerrilla action in 1977 caused disruption to this traffic.

**Roads.** Much improvement and extension of all-weather trunk highways has been and is being undertaken. The Imperial Highway Authority had spent a sum of E $592·6 million in constructing 9,370 kilometres of all-weather roads following its establishment in 1951.

The Fourth Highway Programme to construct 770 km. of primary all-weather roads, 700 km. of feeder roads, and 300 km. of secondary roads at a cost of E $280 million, began in 1968 and was completed in April 1974. The 5th programme worth approximately U.S.$30 million is currently underway.

In 1972 there were about 55,000 motor vehicles registered in Addis Ababa of which about 80 per cent are private cars.

**Posts and Telegraphs.** Mail is carried mainly by air. Urban delivery is to Post Office Boxes only. A telecommunications system operates throughout the country. International services are available from Addis Ababa and Asmara.

**Civil Aviation.** Ethiopian Airlines (P.O. Box 1755, Addis Ababa) operates scheduled internal air services to all important provincial centres by piston engined aircraft International scheduled services by jet aircraft are operated from Addis Ababa, Asmara and Dire Dawa to Abu Dhabi, Accra, Aden, Athens, Bahrain, Bombay, Cairo, Dar-es-Salaam, Djibouti, Douala, Entebbe, Frankfurt, Jeddah, Khartoum, Kigali, Kinshasa, Lagos, London, Paris, Nairobi, Rome, Peking and Sanaa.

**Broadcasting.** The Ethiopian Broadcasting Service operates both sound and television services (the latter at present for the capital and surrounding areas only, maximum radius 170 km.; but plans exist to expand the service throughout the country). Sound broadcasts are made in Amharic, Tigriniya, Tigre, English, Arabic, Galigyao, French, Somali and Atar and television in Amharic, English and French. Commercial publicity is accepted.

Radio voice of the Gospel was taken over by the government in March 1977 and renamed Radio Voice of Revolutionary Ethiopia.

There are estimated to be 500,000 sound and 12,000 television receivers in Ethiopia.

## NEWSPAPERS

The Ministry of Information and National Guidance publishes daily newspapers and other periodicals in the vernacular and other languages. The principal dailies are *Addis Zemen* (Amharic), *Ethiopian Herald* (English), *Hebret* (Tigriniya) and *Addis Soir* (French).

## EDUCATION AND RELIGION

In 1971 there were 1,321 Government, 394 Mission, 619 private and 120 Church schools. In 1971 there were 790,812 pupils studying in primary, secondary and special schools served by 18,891 teachers; approximately 5,300 were following higher education courses. In 1962 the Haile Selassie I University was formed from the existing organs of higher education. It is now intended that the provincial colleges be developed into Universities in their own right. In 1971 2,400 students were studying abroad.

An educational television service has been in operation in the Addis Ababa area since 1965. It caters for about 54,000 students in 66 schools.

The Ethiopian Orthodox Church, a Christian Church of monophysite belief, is the constitutionally Established Church of the State. Formerly subject to the spiritual authority of the Orthodox Church of Alexandria, the Ethiopian Orthodox Church is now entirely independent. The present Patriarch, Aba Melaku Wolde-Mikael, was consecrated in July 1976 in Addis Ababa by Archbishops of the Ethiopian Church. Non-christians (Moslems and pagans) form a majority within the Empire and their freedom of worship is guaranteed by the Constitution.

# Fiji

(MEMBER OF THE COMMONWEALTH)

**Capital**—Suva.

**Governor-General**—Ratu (Chief) Sir George Cakobau, GCMG, OBE.

**National Flag:** Azure blue, with the Union Jack in the top left hand corner and the shield of the Fiji coat-of-arms in the fly.

## CONSTITUTION AND GOVERNMENT

Fiji is an independent state within the Commonwealth. The advisory service commissions, the Public Service, Judicial and Legal Services and Police Service Commissions, became executive under the new constitution. There is a bicameral Parliament, consisting of a nominated Senate and elected House of Representatives, and a Cabinet, presided over by a Prime Minister. The constitution contains a statement of Fundamental Rights and Freedoms.

The Cabinet is directly responsible to Parliament and consists of the Prime Minister, the Attorney-General and any other Ministers the Governor-General may appoint on the recommendation of the Prime Minister. There are at present 14 members.

The constitution provides for an ombudsman to investigate complaints concerning the actions of governmental authorities. Fiji's first Ombudsman, Mr. Justice Tikaram, took office on 1 March 1972.

## LOCAL GOVERNMENT

Development of urban local government institutions has gone ahead rapidly during the past few years, with a progressive transfer of authority in the smaller urban areas from officials to local boards and committees. There are now nine proclaimed urban local authorities in Fiji responsible for promoting health, welfare and good government of towns. A Local Government Act was approved in February 1972 which did away with the distinction between towns and townships; created a new concept of urban districts and provided for a common roll system of elections in municipalities in Fiji. Municipal elections on this system were held in November 1972 in Suva and Lautoka, which had previously used communal voting rolls. The common roll system was already in use in other towns in Fiji.

## FIJIAN ADMINISTRATION

The Fijian Administration constitutes a form of rural local government system established in 1876 but revised in 1945 and 1968 and having jurisdiction over all Fijians. At the apex of the Fijian Administration is the Great Council of Chiefs, presided over by the Minister for Fijian Affairs and Rural Development and comprising 30 members elected from the 14 Provincial Councils; the 22 Fijian elected members of the Legislature; up to seven members appointed by the Governor-General; and up to eight members appointed by the Minister for Fijian Affairs and Rural Development. The Council considers legislation affecting the rights and welfare of Fijians, which is referred to it by the Government and makes recommendations. It also advises the Government on general matters for the welfare and good government of Fijians. There is a Fijian Affairs Board presided over by the Minister for Fijian Affairs and Rural Development which has power to make regulations binding on all Fijians and exercises a degree of financial and other control over the Provincial Councils. Members of the Provincial Councils are elected on a full adult franchise among Fijians. The Councils can make by-laws, levy rates and draw up their own budgets. There are standing committees on health, agriculture, finance and staffing and education.

## LEGAL SYSTEM

Justice is administered by the Fiji Court of Appeal, the Supreme Court and the Magistrates' Courts. The judiciary consists of the Chief Justice, who is appointed by the Governor-General after consultation with the Prime Minister and the Leader of the Opposition, and four Puisne Judges, two stationed in Suva and the others at Lautoka. The Court of Appeal, presided over by the Chief Justice, has jurisdiction to hear and determine appeals from the Supreme Court, which is itself an appellate court from the decisions of the Magistrates' Courts. Appeals lie from the Court of Appeal to the Judicial Committee of the Queen's Privy Council. The Supreme Court is a superior court of record with unlimited original jurisdiction to hear and determine any civil or criminal proceedings including those involving interpretation of the constitution.

## AREA AND POPULATION

Fiji has a total land area of 7,055 square miles consisting of 844 islands, including atolls and reefs. About 100 are permanently inhabited and many more used for planting food crops or as temporary habitations during the turtle fishing season.

The population at mid-1974 was 564,000. The percentage average annual growth rate for the period 1960–74 was 2·6 and for the period 1965–74 was 2·2.

The 1976 census taken in September was 588,068. The 1976 total was made up of the following breakdown (1966 census figures in brackets): 259,932 Fijians (202,176); 292,896 Indians (240,960); 10,276 Part-Europeans (9,687); 4,929 Europeans (6,590); 6,822 Rotumans (5,797); 4,652 Chinese (5,149); 7,291 other Pacific Islanders (6,095); and 1,270 others (273).

## CURRENCY AND FINANCE

Fiji issues its own currency, the Fiji Dollar which was allowed to float with sterling when Britain let the £ float on foreign exchange markets in June 1972. On 10 September, 1973, the Fiji dollar was again revalued to £Stg.100·00 = F$1·602 while continuing to float. In August 1976, a central rate of US$1·1151 = F$1·00 was declared to the International Monetary Fund. No par value has yet been established. With effect from 7 April, 1975 the rate of exchange between the Fiji dollar and the US dollar has been determined daily on a basis of a trade weighted basket. The decimal currency system was introduced in 1969. A number of trading banks are established in Fiji: they include branches and agencies of the Bank of New South Wales, the Bank of New Zealand, the Australia and New Zealand Banking Group Limited, the First National City Bank of New York, the Bank of Baroda and Barclays Bank International Ltd. There are branches of the Savings Bank of Fiji throughout the country. The Fiji Development Bank provides loan assistance to firms and industrial and agricultural enterprises. A Central Monetary Authority, set up under Act No. 1 of 1973, commenced operations on the 1st July, 1973.

Public Accounts. For budget purposes revenue and expenditure are divided into two parts: operating and capital. Operating (recurrent) revenue comes mainly from taxation, customs and excise duty, licences and fees. The total estimated operating revenue for 1977 is about $134·28 million. According to the 1977 estimates, the two highest percentages of this total will account for revenue derived from customs and excise duty and licences and income tax collections.

Total Operating revenue and expenditure figures for the years 1973–76:

*$F million*

| | 1973 | 1974 | 1975 | 1976 |
|---|---|---|---|---|
| Total Revenue | 72·5 | 80·9 | 113·3 | 128·8 |
| Total Operating expenditure | 70·4 | 79·0 | 108·4 | 129·7 |

The biggest single items of operating expenditure in 1976 were for education, works and public debt (i.e. the repayment of loans raised for financing the capital budget).

In the 1977 estimates, the Ministry of Education, Youth and Sport, the Ministry of Health and expenditure on public repayments are expected to account for the largest percentage increases of total ordinary expenditure over the 1976 figures. The percentages are 23·25, 8·74 and 21·97 respectively. Capital budget estimates, although presented at the same time as the operating budget, form part of the five-year development programme. Expenditure from the Capital Fund in 1977 is estimated at $54·92 million. The largest portions of this total will be spent under the Infrastructure sector (46·02 per cent) and Economic Services (22·97 per cent).

The GNP at market prices for 1974 was U.S.$ millions 470, and the GNP per capita at market prices was U.S.$840. The annual average percentage growth rate for the period 1960–74 was 3·2 and for the period 1965–74 was 5·4.

## PRODUCTION, INDUSTRY AND COMMERCE

**Agriculture, Fisheries and Forestry.** Some 600,000 acres (243,000 hectares) of land in Fiji are in agricultural use. The cultivable land is confined to major river valleys, deltas and coastal flats. Sugar cane is the principal cash crop, accounting for more than two-thirds of Fiji's export earnings; about one-quarter of the population depend on it directly for their livelihood. Total production in 1976 amounted to 291,179 tonnes. Sugar cane is grown by nearly 16,000 independent farmers on holdings averaging about 10 acres (4 hectares).

In April 1973, Government purchased 98 per cent of the shares held by Colonial Sugar Refining Company in the South Pacific Sugar Mills Limited and set up the Fiji Sugar Corporation to carry on milling operations. The Corporation has the monopoly right to manufacture raw sugar. Coconuts, Fiji's second major cash crop provides coconut oil and other products for export and employs nearly as many workers as the sugar industry. Coconut oil is also used in the domestic manufacture of food products, soaps and detergents. The 1976 crop of 26,570 tonnes shows a lack of growth of copra production over the past years. However, extensive replanting has been carried out recently and should soon show results. Ginger is the third major export crop, replacing bananas which has declined through disease and hurricanes. Other agricultural products include cocoa, maize, tobacco and a variety of fruits and vegetables. Efforts are being made to develop the production of rice, so that the country can become self-sufficient in one of its staple foods. Three production areas, Rewa, Navua and Dreketi are being developed for double-cropped irrigated rice. There are nine agricultural research stations located in the different ecological zones.

There is a small but developing livestock industry. Development plans are underway to achieve self-sufficiency in beef by 1980 and to modernize the factory producing butter and sterilized milk. Pork and poultry production have been increasing rapidly and should meet local demand within three years. Efforts are being made to improve goat production to meet demand and to substitute mutton imports.

Although there is no large-scale fishing industry, plans are in hand to exploit the substantial skip-jack tuna resources for the local market and for canning. More up-to-date methods of fishing are being introduced and training and marketing assistance is given to fishermen. Other development programmes include aquaculture, mariculture and intensified marketing assistance with suitably located cold-storage and ice-making facilities.

Forestry has an important place in the economy in that it supplies the bulk of local needs for timber and timber products. The main objectives of the government's forestry policy are to ensure the best possible use of indigenous species of timber and to plant other species to meet future domestic needs, as well as supplying a surplus for export. A timber inventory has been made of the major islands. A sizeable pine afforestation programme has been implemented with the aim of planting 186,000 acres by 1988. As at the end of March 1976 some 50,558 acres have been planted with 13,800 acres going in each year. The first local veneer plant began operations in 1970. The government gives assistance by way of subsidized seedlings.

Government provides extension and research services, agricultural subsidies, training and marketing services.

**Mining.** Fiji has a variety of mineral resources, and exploration activity on the two large islands of Viti Levu and Vanua Levu is quite intense. Large areas of land are under licence to many companies and the outlook is reasonable that at least one more major mine may eventuate in the next decade. The most interesting exploration is being carried out in the Namosi area of Viti Levu where over 70 diamond drill holes have been completed so far to delineate a low grade porphyry copper deposit. The Emperor Gold Mining Company continues to be the only mine in production. With the recent high price of gold the company is now paying back the loan it received from the Government during leaner times. The company has stated that its gold reserves should keep the mine operating for another twenty years. A bauxite mine which was being developed by the Japanese in southern Vanua Levu was aborted in early 1973 because of the world financial situation. Two offshore areas are being actively explored for oil in the northern and eastern shores of Viti Levu under establishment agreements between the Government and two oil companies. Extensive seismic and aero-magnetic surveys have so far been carried out and it is hoped that a decision will be made in the near future on drilling.

**Manufacturing.** Fiji produces a range of industrial products. Manufacturing now accounts for 22·8 per cent of the gross domestic product of the country.

Apart from traditional items like raw sugar and copra oil, it has other processing facilities like, rice and flour milling, steel rolling, saw milling, building materials like portland cement and concrete blocks and pipes, paints, roofing materials, various steel wires, PVC pipes and gutters, aluminium doors and windows, screens, wall panels or marble lustre and electrical products like electrical conduits, switchboards, fluorescent lights, etc.

It has built up facilities for production of coaches, boats, steel tanks, copra dryers and other steel fabrications, including solar heaters and tanks.

It produces various food items like meat, poultry, milk, butter, bread and biscuits, ice cream, fruit juices and pulps, soft drinks and beer and various confectionery as well as cigarettes and tobacco.

Besides a variety of other consumer goods like footwear, garments, suitcases, umbrellas, various plastic and aluminium household goods, cultured pearls and jewellery, soaps and detergents, various stypes of handicrafts such as masi, mats, baskets, shell products, etc., are also produced.

A wide variety of packaging materials and metal and plastic containers are produced.

To aid expansion of the manufacturing sector, the government offers various types of incentives to investors.

## COMMUNICATIONS

**Satellite Communications.** In 1971 the United States National Aeronautics and Space Administration (NASA) made the radio relay (voice) portion of the ATS-1 (Applications Technology Satellite number one) Satellite available for educational experiments, the University of Hawaii was granted use of the Satellite for a project called PEACESAT (Pan Pacific Educational and Communication Experiments by Satellite). This network extends to nine territories, and in which Fiji is also included.

In 1973, the University of the South Pacific was granted use of the Satellite for its own experimental programme and it has set up nine ground stations within its regional centres. Eight are currently operating and the remaining one will be fully activated in future. The stations are located at as follows:

(1) University of the South Pacific, Suva, Fiji.
(2) USP Regional Centre, Nuku'alofa, Tonga.
(3) Scientific Research Division, Premier's Department, Rarotonga, Cook Islands.
(4) USP Regional Centre, Honiara, Solomon Islands.
(5) Education Department, Niue.
(6) USP Regional Centre, Tarawa, Gilbert Islands.
(7) Kaweni Teachers' College, Port Villa, New Hebrides.
(8) Education Department, Apia, Western Samoa.
(9) Education Department, Tuvalu to be installed by the end of this year (1976).

The USP network has 10 hours per week on the satellite.

There are six areas of experimentation which are as follows—

(1) *The USP External Classroom*—Students in USP's correspondence courses take part in tutorial sessions with their tutors and course supervisors on the Suva campus.
(2) *Regional Curriculum Development*—The United Nations Development Programme team based at USP, Suva, utilize the network to assist in the co-ordination of their activities in the area of regional Curriculum development.
(3) *Continuing Education*—Individuals and groups use the network for a wide range of discussions, seminars, guest lectures, and meetings. The participants are researchers and workers in fields such as medicine, agriculture, planning, rural development, natural resources etc.
(4) *Information Exchange*—This is designed to determine the effectiveness of direct two-way or multi-way communication channel as a means of facilitating the exchange of selective information such as library needs, USP regional reports, administration meetings, etc.

(5) *PEACESAT Network*—The aims and objectives of the PEACESAT network are similar to those of the USP network. The control of the PEACESAT network is with the University of Hawaii.

(6) *Multi Link Experiments*—The USP joins other satellite users for special programmes such as National Eduation Association Pan-Pacific Satellite sessions. These experiments join the Alaska Network, PEACESAT, and USP network. Additionally USP has regular sessions with Alaska.

**System Operation.** There is a single channel of communication which can be used for voice, facsimile, teletype or slow-scan television transmissions. The single channel means that only one station can talk at a time. If more than two terminals are participating it is necessary to say 'over to Tonga' or 'over to Wellington' to avoid confusion.

All the locations have facilities such as loudspeakers or headphones for listening, and a microphone for transmitting, to allow group participation.

**Scheduling procedures.** Certain times are set for enquiries and requests. The terminal managers are present on these occasions to discuss network operations. Requests for time on the satellite are made to the terminal managers in the location and the scope for exchange topics is limitless. The terminal managers give assistance in making the programmes as beneficial as possible by suggesting formats and styles which have been found, through the limited experience, to be most effective.

**Funding and Costs.** NASA's ATS-1 is available at no cost to users. But the cost of setting up the ground terminals is met by the users. The USP network funding has been provided from two sources, the Carnegie Corporation of New York and the United Nations Development Programme team in Suva. The funds are used to pay salary of Project Manager, to cover equipment and installation costs for stations and to finance the terminals within the network.

The costs of running and maintenance are met from the USP funds.

**Air Services.** An increasing number of international and regional air services are operated through Nadi International Airport, situated on the west coast of Viti Levu, connecting Fiji with Australia, New Zealand, North and South America and other parts of the world. The other main airport, Nausori, has been developed to cope with increased local services. Labasa airport has recently been upgraded and there is provision for improvements to Savusavu and Matei airports. There is an airstrip at Bureta, Ovalau, and in 1972 the first airstrip for the outer islands, the forerunner of others, was opened at Lakeba in Lau. There is provision for airstrips at Gau and Koro islands, and it is government's intention to build one outer island airstrip per year during Development Plan VII (1976–1980).

Early 1975, the Fiji Government acquired a 62 per cent shareholding in the regional airline, Air Pacific, in which Qantas, Air New Zealand, British Airways and other Pacific Territories hold minority shares.

Air Pacific operates services within Fiji and regional services in the South-West Pacific. It has recently begun operating services to Auckland and Brisbane.

Fiji has concluded bilateral air traffic rights agreements with the governments of Chile, New Zealand, Australia, United Kingdom, India and Singapore.

Agreements with the United States and France have yet to be concluded.

Fiji Air Services Limited, the country's domestic airline, operates scheduled and charter flights to some of the smaller airstrips.

**Ports and Shipping.** Suva, Fiji's main seaport, has an excellent natural harbour and its facilities have been brought up to a high standard by a modernization scheme. The other major ports are Lautoka and Levuka. There are roadstead anchorages for overseas vessels at Malau, near Labasa, and at Savusavu. Management of the principal ports is being transferred from Government to a Ports Authority. Local commercial shipping companies operate small ships to outer islands of the group. International cargo and passenger ships call in large numbers and there has been an increase in cruise liners visiting Fiji. A Hydrographic Survey Unit was formed in 1970. The Government Shipyard at Suva completed its first commercial vessel at the end of 1970 and subsequently has built two more sister vessels for the same owner. During Development Plan VI 14 vessels were built for Government and private owners and plans are in hand for a further 34 vessels to be built in the next five years.

**Roads.** There are 1,849 miles of public roads maintained by the Fiji Government of which 173 miles are bitumen surfaced. Work is now under way on the reconstruction of approximately two-thirds of the main road between Suva and Nadi which will add a further 67 miles to the total of bitumen sealed roads. The construction of a new gravel surfaced highway on Vanua Levu to link the towns of Savusavu and Labasa has reached the half way stage and work is now commencing on the section through rugged terrain in the centre of the island. In addition to the expansion and upgrading of the main road network considerable effort is being applied to the construction of rural roads which are opening up large areas for agricultural and forestry developments. Urban roads are also being improved to meet the needs of the rapidly increasing traffic.

**Telecommunications.** Internal telephone services are being continually extended throughout Fiji to help promote trade and commerce in all areas and to assist Government administration. New public radio telephone stations are being installed each year and postal agencies built, in outlying areas. There are automatic exchange in most towns with full subscriber trunk dialling facilities. Fiji is a telecommunication centre for the South Pacific Region, and is linked by the Commonwealth Pacific Telephone Cable (COMPAC) with Australia, New Zealand and the international telecommunications network. The telex system with international subscriber dialling to most world-wide destinations is growing fast and used extensively by airlines, travel agents, hotels, banks and business concerns. Fiji participates in a Regional Telecommunication Training Centre which has been established in Suva by the International Telecommunication Union, under the auspices of the United Nations Development Programme and with support from the Australian and New Zealand Governments.

**Education.** School attendance is not compulsory in Fiji. In 1976 about 96 per cent of children aged 6—13 were attending school. The long-term intention of the Government is to provide 10 years of free education for every child. The gradual abolition of tuition fees began with Class I in1973 (by 1974 about 36,700 children in classes 1 and 2 have benefited) and will extend to cover all classes in due course.

In 1976, the total national primary roll was 133,400 whilst the total national secondary roll was 30,700. The total roll for technical and vocational schools was about 2,000. There were 760 schools (primary and secondary) scattered over 55 islands, staffed by about 6,000 teachers. About 29 per cent of Fiji's total population were enrolled full-time at schools and colleges in 1976 compared with 16·1 per cent in 1946.

The Government is giving special attention to increasing the provision of vocational and technical training at all levels and to encouraging secondary and higher education. New courses are being designed to prepare students for life in modern Fiji so that they can take a more active part in the country's development. Full-time vocational education is provided by the Derrick Technical Institute, the School of Maritime Studies, the School of Hotel and Catering Services and at the Ratu Kadavulevu School. Courses are also available in Agricultural Engineering, carpentry and joinery. A three-year post-secondary course for Diploma in Tropical Agriculture is provided at the Fiji College of Agriculture and after completing the course students will qualify for services in General Agriculture, Fisheries or Animal Science.

A pilot scheme for post-Form V Multi-Craft course was introduced in Rotuma Junior Secondary School in 1974. Similar courses will gradually be introduced into other secondary schools located in rural areas before consideration can be given to schools located in urban areas.

A number of secondary schools also offer courses in Field Husbandry and Animal Husbandry. Navuso Agricultural School provides a two-year general residential course in Tropical Agriculture and runs a three-year Student–Farmer Scheme for boys who have completed its residential course or others whose interest lie in Agriculture. The Agricultural College at the Marist Training Centre on Taveuni also provides for adults a course in general agriculture. There is a forestry training school at Lololo, Lautoka.

Of the three teacher training colleges, the largest, at Nasinu, near Suva, is run by the Government. Two smaller teacher-training colleges, the Corpus Christi Training College and the Fulton Missionary College, are run by missions. The University of the South Pacific provides two pre-service courses for secondary teachers, a correspondence course for untrained teachers and an in-service training and re-training courses.

The University of the South Pacific opened in February 1968 at Laucala Bay, Suva, to meet the needs for higher education of the communities of the South Pacific. In 1974 there were 981 full-time students at the University, 135 students studying by correspondence for the Diploma in Education and 154 part-time students. Some 780 of the full-time students in 1974 were from Fiji. The University in 1974 had three schools—Social and Economic Development Natural Resources and Education.

Medical training is provided at the Fiji School of Medicine, founded in 1878. It has been reorganized and extended a number of times and now serves as a regional centre for medical training in the Pacific area, providing a five-year diploma course in medicine, a three-and-a-half year diploma course in dentistry and ancillary courses in such subjects as public health inspection, physiotherapy, dietetics and laboratory technology. There is also provision for post-graduate training at universities overseas. Basic nursing training is given at the Central Nursing School in Suva, which also accepts some students from other Pacific Islands. The School has a branch at Lautoka.

The main libraries are at Suva and Lautoka and there are also public libraries at Nadi, Ba, Sigatoka and Labasa. A book box scheme operates in a number of other centres. There is a "National Archives" library, confined mainly to Fijiana and Oceania. Attached to the "National Archives" is the Sir Alport Barker Memorial Library, equipped with reading room. In the Western Pacific Archives are kept records of official publications of British administration in the Pacific and of two Pacific Island Territories.

The Fiji Museum in Suva contains a fine historical and ethnological collection relating to Fiji and Western Pacific Territories. There is a growing emphasis on Fijian natural history.

### RELIGION

The principal religions in Fiji are Christianity and Hinduism though a proportion of the population is Moslem.

# Finland

(SUOMEN TASAVALTA—REPUBLIKEN FINLAND)

**Capital**—Helsinki

**President**—Urho Kaleva Kekkonen

**National Flag:** Rectangular with an ultramarine cross on a white field. The cross divides the flag into four rectangular areas of equal height. The Finnish Standard, used only by the President of the Republic and State Institutions, bears the Finnish coat of arms in the middle of the blue cross.

### CONSTITUTION AND GOVERNMENT

FROM 1154 to 1809 Finland formed a part of the kingdom of Sweden. It then became an autonomous Grand Duchy connected with Russia until 6 December 1917, the date of Finland's declaration of independence. A republican constitution was laid down by the Form of Government Act promulgated at Helsinki 17 July 1919, and other constitutional laws. Sovereign power belongs to the people represented by the delegates assembled in Parliament, who hold legislative power in conjunction with the President. Supreme executive power is vested in the President of the Republic, who is assisted for the general government of the State by a Council of State (Cabinet) consisting of a Prime Minister and the necessary number of ministers.

The President is elected by an Electoral College of 300 members chosen by general election. His term of office is six years. The President's powers are extensive. He controls foreign policy and he can dissolve Parliament.

Parliament consists of a single chamber of 200 members elected for four years. Voting at a general election is by secret ballot and is based on a system of proportional representation. All persons of 20 years and over are entitled to vote. Parliament elects its own Speaker and two Deputy Speakers who, together with the Chairmen of the various Committees, form the Speaker's Council. As a kind of substitute for an upper chamber there is a Grand Committee of 45 members, chosen by Parliament. It considers and expresses an opinion on Bills or matters relating to taxation or loans coming up before Parliament in full session.

Legislation may be initiated either by the Government or by members of Parliament. Bills involving legislation, taxation or government loans are required to be read three times at different meetings of Parliament in full session. After the first reading the bill goes to the Grand Committee which reports on it and appends any eventual recommendations. The Bill then comes up for a second reading. If the report of the Grand Committee is accepted unaltered, the second reading is declared closed, failing which the Bill goes back to the Grand Committee which now reports on the amendments passed by Parliament, which then makes its final decision in full session at a third reading.

During the Second World War Finland became involved in three wars. The first, the so-called Winter War against the U.S.S.R., came to an end by a peace concluded on 13 March 1940. The outbreak of the second war was the result of the German invasion of U.S.S.R. in June 1941. In 1944 Finland broke off relations with Germany and her satellites. On 19 September she concluded an armistice with the Governments of the U.S.S.R. and the United Kingdom. Not only did Finland withdraw from the war, but she declared war on the German Reich and drove the German troops from Finnish Lapland. A treaty of peace was signed in Paris on 10 February 1947 between Finland and the U.S.S.R., the United Kingdom and the other members of the United Nations with whom she had been at war.

Under the terms of the Moscow treaty of 1940 Finland ceded to the Soviet Union about 10 per cent of her territory including the whole of the Karelian Isthmus, the city of Viipuri and Viipuri Bay with the islands thereof, the western and northern coastal area of Lake Laatokka with the towns of Käkisalmi, and Sortavala, a number of islands in the Gulf of Finland.

The Treaty of Paris drew the frontiers as they existed after the Peace of Moscow with one exception. The province of Petsamo on the Arctic Ocean was ceded to the Soviet Union. The total area ceded as the result of these two treaties amounted to about 46,000 sq. km. The entirepopulation of the ceded area, 417,000 persons, was resettled in the remaining parts of the country.

The Porkkala area near Helsinki, which in 1944 was leased to the Soviet Union for 50 years, was returned to Finland in January 1956. In 1962, the Soviet Union agreed to lease back to Finland the southern sector of the important Saimaa Canal, which had been ceded by Finland under the Peace Treaty. The rebuilt Canal was re-opened for traffic in 1968.

Finland is a member of the United Nations, the O.E.C.D. and the Nordic Council, and joined EFTA as an associated member in 1961.

#### Cabinet

*Prime Minister:* Kalevi Sorsa (SDP).
*Deputy Prime Minister and Minister of Agriculture and Forestry:* Johannes Virolainen (CP).
*Foreign Minister:* Matti Väyrynen (CP).
*Minister of Justice and the Interior:* Tuure Salo (LPP).
*Minister of the Interior:* Eino Uusitalo (CP).
*Minister of Defence:* Taisto Tähkämaa (CP).
*Minister of Finance:* Paul Paavela (SDP).
*Minister of Economics and Finance:* Esko Rekola (no party).
*Minister of Education and the Interior:* Lars Gestrin (SPP).
*Minister of Education (Deputy):* Kalevi Kivistö (FPDL).
*Minister of Communications and Agriculture and Forestry:* Veikko Saarto (FPDL).
*Minister of Trade and Industry:* Eero Rantala (SDP).
*Minister of Social Affairs and Health:* Pirkko Työläjärvi (SDP).
*Minister of Social Affairs and Health (Deputy):* Veikko Martikainen, (CP).
*Minister of Labour:* Arvo Aalto (FPDL).

(CP = Centre Party, SDP = Social Democratic Party, FPDL = Finnish People's Democratic League, SPP = Swedish People's Party, LPP = Liberal People's Party).

#### Parliament

### LOCAL GOVERNMENT

For purposes of State Government the country (formerly divided into ten counties) now consists of 12 provinces subdivided into communities with extensive autonomous municipal self-government elected by the local population. The head of each province is a Provincial Governor. Local government is concentrated in 84 urban and 380 rural communes.

There is a sharp dividing line between state and local affairs. In practice communes are allowed to manage all local matters concerning public order, economic activity and social welfare not expressly reserved by legislation for the Government.

Many matters within the sphere of local government are, however, controlled by the central government. This is the case with elementary schools, sanitation, municipal town planning, building inspection, etc. Loans for a period exceeding five years cannot be raised without prior government approval. Local taxation is based on an income tax of the same percentage for all size of income. In most cases the appointment of local government staffs rests wholly with local government bodies, but there are certain exceptions. Presidents of the municipal courts are appointed by the Supreme Court from among nominees put forward by the municipalities. The basis of local government is provided by the communal elections held every fourth year in October at which the communal councils are elected. The towns have a special city executive at the head of which is a mayor elected for life by the municipal council. In addition the executive comprises members elected for a term of years, usually from the municipal council. At the head of the communal administration is the chairman of the communal council. In rural communes the body corresponding to the town executive is the Communal Board.

The Åland Islands, with a predominantly Swedish-speaking population of about 22,300 have a peculiar position in so far as they enjoy a certain amount of autonomy including legislative powers within limits specified in the Åland Self-government Act. The population of Åland elects its own Parliament (*Landsting*) with 40 members. The Parliament appoints the members of the Province Government (*Landskapsstyrelse*) which is the central administrative body of the province. The legislative power of the Ålandic Parliament extends to the cultural, social and economic fields, whereas civil and penal laws as well as laws relating to legal procedure are within the exclusive competence of the State Parliament. The President of the Republic has an absolute veto with regard to laws passed by the Ålandic Parliament.

The administration on the fields covered by the Ålandic legislation is executed by Ålandic authorities subcordinated to the Province Government. The expenses incurred are refunded to the Province on the basis of a calculation made by the Åland Delegation, which is headed by the Åland Governor and to which the Finnish Government and the Åland Parliament appoint each two members. This Delegation also gives its opinions about the laws passed by the Åland Parliament and the decrees passed by the Province Government.

The Self-Government Act also contains provisions aiming to preserve the Swedish language as the only official language of Åland and to prevent the purchasing of real estate by persons who have not acquired domiciliary rights. These rights, which usually can be acquired by an immigrant only five years after he has settled in Åland, are also a prerequisite for participating in the local and provincial elections.

## LEGAL SYSTEM

The lowest courts are the District Circuit Courts and the corresponding Town Courts. The former consist of a judge with legal training and not less than five and not more than seven local jurors. These are not jurymen in the English sense but paid laymen permanently appointed to assist the judge, who may form his own judgment unless it is unanimously opposed by the jurors. The District Court judges are appointed by the Supreme Court. The country is divided into 73 districts each with its own judge.

A Town Court is a tribunal consisting of no less than three judges, the Chairman of which is a Burgomaster appointed by the Supreme Court. The other members of the Town Court, who are not necessarily lawyers, are elected by the Municipal Council and appointed by the provincial government concerned. In the larger cities, the Town Courts consist of several sections. The first section is generally headed by the Burgomaster, and the others by the eldest member of the section. The Chairmen are necessarily lawyers and at least in the larger cities the rule is for the other members also to be trained lawyers.

There are four Courts of Appeal to which appeal against decisions by District or Town Courts may be taken. In matters of minor importance the decision of the Court of Appeal is final; in others further appeal may be brought to the Supreme Court. Trials for treason and high treason are always commenced in a Court of Appeal, which is also the court of first instance for offences committed in an official capacity by the judges of inferior courts and higher officials.

The public prosecutor in the District Courts is the local Sheriff, in the Town Courts, the City Attorney, in the Courts of Appeal, the Attorney attached to the court, and in the Supreme Court, the Chancellor of Justice or a person appointed by him.

For matters relating to the partition of land, there are special Land Partition Courts from whose decisions appeal can be brought to the Supreme Court. There is also a special Insurance Court which deals with appeals against decisions by private insurance companies or the State Insurance office relating to compensation for labour accidents while at work.

**The Supreme Court.** The Supreme Court of Justice situated in Helsinki, consists of a Chief Justice and at least 21 Justices, controls the administration of justice in the lower courts, appoints judges, and nominates members of the Supreme Court of Justice, who are appointed by the President of the Republic.

**The Supreme Administrative Court.** This is the highest tribunal for appeals in administrative cases.

A general control is exercised over the administration by the oikeuskansleri (justitiekansler) (Chancellor of Justice) and the Eduskunnan oikeusasiamies (Riksdagens justitieombudsman) (Parliamentary Ombudsman). The Chancellor of Justice is the chief public prosecutor, and acts as counsel for the government. The Parliamentary Ombudsman, appointed by Parliament, exercises supervision over the general administration of justice.

## AREA AND POPULATION

The area is 337,032 square kilometres, of which inland waters form 9·4 per cent, forests 56·5 per cent, cultivated land 7·9 per cent. The total land area is distributed among different classes of owners approximately as follows: private 61 per cent, State 29 per cent, joint stock companies, etc. 8 per cent, municipalities and parishes, 2 per cent.

Total population is 4·17 million. Density of population in South Finland is 46·2, in North Finland 4·0 and in the country as a whole an average of 15·5 inhabitants to the sq. km. 41 per cent of the population inhabit the rural areas, 59 per cent the towns and urban districts.

There are two main linguistic groups, the Finnish-speaking and the Swedish-speaking which formed in 1970 respectively 93·2 per cent and 6·6 per cent of the population. The Swedish-speaking population is concentrated in the central part of the West coast, on the South coast and on the Åland Islands. The population of Helsinki was 85·3 per cent Finnish-speaking in 1970. There is a third small group, the Lapps in Northern Finland, which numbered 2,240 in 1970.

**Vital Statistics** (per 1,000 of population):

| | 1975 | 1976 |
|---|---|---|
| Marriages | 7·1 | 6·9 |
| Births | 14·1 | 14·0 |
| Deaths | 9·4 | 7·4 |
| Infant deaths (per 1,000 births) | 10·0 | 10·5 |

The population at the end of 1976 was 4,733,000. The annual average percentage growth rate the population for the period 1960–73 was 0·3 and for the period 1970–75 was 0·4.

At 31 December 1976 the estimated populations of the principal towns were: Helsinki 493,300, Tampere 166,100, Turku 164,500, Lahti 94,900, Espoo 123,900, Oulu 92,600, Pori 80,300, Kuopio 72,300, Jyväskylä 62,100, Lappeenranta-Villmanstrand 53,300, Vantaa, 122,300, Vaasa 53,900.

## CURRENCY

The unit of currency is the markka' which is divided into 100 penni. 6·99 marks are equivalent to £1.

## FINANCE

Revenue and expenditure for 1975–76 are shown below (in million new marks):

| | 1975 | 1976 |
|---|---|---|
| Taxes and similar revenue | 21,617 | 27,888 |
| Other revenue | 2,825 | 2,298 |
| Redemptions of state loans | 337 | 397 |
| Long-term borrowing | 988 | 1,587 |
| Total | 25,767 | 32,170 |

| | 1975 | 1976 |
|---|---|---|
| Consumption expenditure | 7,097 | 8,311 |
| Transfer expenditure | 12,805 | 14,876 |
| Real investments | 3,144 | 3,759 |
| Financial investments | 2,958 | 3,526 |
| Other expenditure | — | — |
| Redemptions of long-term loans | 496 | 484 |
| Total | 27,546 | 31,288 |

In 1976 the external debt was 2,248 million marks and the internal debt 1,820 million marks.

The GNP at market prices for 1974 was U.S.$ millions 22,030, and the GNP per capita at market prices was U.S.$4,700. The annual average percentage growth rate of the GNP per capita for the period 1960–74 was 4·6, and for the period 1965–74 was 5·2. [*See the note at the beginning of this section concerning GNP.*]

## PRINCIPAL BANKS

**Suomen Pankki Finlands Bank.** (Governor: Mauno Koivisto.) Est. 1811; Sole Bank of Issue for Finland; under the guarantee and supervision of the Parliament there being no shareholders; Balance Sheet at 30 June 1977: assets mks. 9,609,158,155; gold reserves mks. 127,010,577; notes and coins in circulation mks. 3,154,359,144. *Head Office:* Snellmaninaukio, P.O. Box 160, SF-00101, Helsinki 10; 12 Branches.

**Bank of Helsinki Ltd.—Helsingin Osakepankki—Helsingfors Aktiebank.** (Chief General Manager: Filip Pettersson.) Est. 1913; Balance Sheet at 31 December 1976 showed assets 2,462,895,735,48 mk; deposits and current accounts 2,098,982,013,29 mk. *Head Office:* Aleksanterinkatu 1700100 Helsinki 10, 121 Branches.

**Kansallis-Osake-Pankki.** (Chief General Manager: Veikko Makkonen). Est. 1889; Balance Sheet at 30 June 1975 showed assets 11,223,159,215 Fmk; deposit and current accounts 9,031,371,818 Fmk. *Head Office:* Aleksanterinkatu 42, Helsinki 10; 424 Branches.

**Osuuspankkien Keskuspankki Oy-Andelsbankernas Centralbank Ab-Central Bank of the Co-operative Banks of Finland Ltd.** (President: Seppo Konttinen.) Est. 1902. Commercial bank which is the Central Bank of 384 local Co-operative Banks. Balance Sheet at 31 December 1975 showed 3,174 million mks.; public deposits and current accounts 144 million mks.; Banks deposits and current accounts 145 million mks. *Head Office:* Arkadiankatu 23, Helsinki 10. Cables: oko Helsinki. Telex: 12-714a-bokohe sf. Telephone: 4041.

**Skopbank** (formerly **Säästöpankkien Keskus-Osake-Pankki) Central-Aktie-Bank.** (Chief General Manager: Matti Ranki.) Est. 1908. Commercial Bank which is the Central Bank of the Finnish Savings Banks; Balance Sheet at 31 July 1977 showed assets 3,147,556,782 Fmks; public deposits and current accounts 264,460,321 Fmks. Bank's, deposit and current accounts 1,997,822,403 Fmks. *Head Office:* Aleksanterinkatu 46, SF-00100 Helsinki 10; 1,277 Savings Bank offices.

**Postipankki-Postbanken.** (Chief General Manager: Heikki Tuominen.) Est. 1886. Balance Sheet at 31 December 1975 showed assets 7,423·1 million mks.; deposit and current accounts 5,509·8 million mks. *Head Office:* Unioninkatu 20, Helsinki 7; 3,132 offices.

**Säästopankkien Keskus-Osake-Pankki** (see also **Skopbank**).

**Union Bank of Finland** formerly: Pohjoismaiden Yhdyspankki Oy.—Nordiska Föreningsbanken Ab. (Chairman and President: Mika Iiivola.) Est. 1862; Balance Sheet at 30 June 1976 showed assets mks. 12,189,164,915; deposits and current accounts mks. 9,874,790,299. *Head Office:* Alek santerink 30, Helsinki; 354 Branches and Sub-branches.

## PRODUCTION, INDUSTRY AND COMMERCE

**Agriculture.** In 1976 approximately 10·9 per cent of the labour force was employed in agriculture, which, however, accounted for only 5·7 per cent of the net domestic product.

Low productivity is mainly due to the climate. The cereal crops, especially in the northern part of the country, are not entirely safe owing to frosts in late summer, but as agricultural production is mostly based on fodder crops, the climate does not form an obstacle to rational production.

The opportunities for horticulture are limited owing to the cold climate. Apples are the only fruit grown on a large scale. Pears, plums and cherries can only be grown in the very southern-most parts of the country. There are about 260,000 farms, most of them having less than ten hectares arable area. Due to the losses of about 10 per cent of agricultural areas in consequence of the wars 1939–45, a wide land reform has been necessary. In 1976 the livestock population included 33,300 horses, 1,815,300 cattle, 111,400 sheep and 1,096,700 pigs, and 9,098,200 poultry.

The following table shows the area under cultivation and the total produce for the principal field crops for the year 1976:

| *Crop* | *Area (in thousand hectares)* | *Yield (in thousand tons)* |
|---|---|---|
| Wheat | 219·7 | 654·1 |
| Rye | 65·2 | 178·2 |
| Barley | 506·7 | 1,553·4 |
| Oats | 551·1 | 1,572·9 |
| Field Hay | 592·4 | 2·426·5 |
| Potatoes | 52·7 | 947·9 |

**Forestry.** The forests of Finland cover an area of 18·7 million hectares. Pine and spruce are the most important trees, covering 43·9 per cent and 37·2 per cent of the total forest area respectively. The birch is a valuable species too. Approximately 23·6 per cent of the forest area is exploited by the state, 65·3 per cent by private ownership and the remaining 11·1 per cent worked by wood-working enterprises, communes and parishes.

In 1976 3,860,944 cu. m. of sawn timber, and 673,373 cu. m. of veneers and plywood were exported.

Forest management in Finland is carried out on the basis of a sustained yield. There is a special law concerning private forestry which prohibits destructive cuttings and a law of forest improvement which provides state subsidies for improvement of the production of wood. The state forest service takes care of the government owned forests. The maintenance of private forestry is carried out mainly by voluntary organizations of forest owners. The University of Helsinki has a faculty of forestry and there are 25 forestry schools in the country. The Forest Research Institute does extensive research work including a general survey of forest resources and of the use of wood. There are many other organizations dealing with different aspects of forestry.

**Fishing.** The type of fish caught around the coast of Finland is conditioned by the unusual freshness of the Baltic which in the Gulf of Bothnia and the Gulf of Finland is of insignificant salinity. The most important fish from the economic point of view is the little Baltic herring of which approx. 69·5 mill. kg. were caught in 1976. Another important salt water fish is the sprat, used mainly for the canning industry.

**Mining.** The number of useful minerals found in Finland is not small. The main metallic deposits are copper, nickel, zinc, chromium and iron ore.

There are 13 ore mines operating. Output in 1971 was 7·3 million tons. The metal production of Finland in 1976 was (in 1,000 tons):

| | | | |
|---|---|---|---|
| Raw iron | 1,329 | Cathode nickel | 7·6 |
| Sulphur | 86 | Vanadium pentoxide | 2·7 |
| Zinc | 111 | Cobalt | 0·9 |
| Ferro-chromium | 40 | Cadmium | 0·4 |
| Cathode copper | 38 | | |

Small quantities of selenium (9,931 kg), mercury (13,186 kg), silver (24,051 kg) and gold (817) are mined annually.

**Industry.** The following table shows the index of industrial production for the year 1976.

| Volume (1970 = 100) | 1976 |
|---|---|
| Total industry | 125 |
| Woodworking | 82 |
| Paper | 99 |
| Metal-working | 129 |
| Foodstuffs | 110 |
| Textile | 126 |
| Printing | 137 |
| Chemicals | 170 |
| Ceramics, glass, etc. | 145 |
| Mining and quarrying | 100 |

Although the forest industry still leads in exports, the metal and shipbuilding industries have become more important. In 1976, production figures for pulp and paper industry were as follows (in thousand metric tons): Chemical wood pulp, 3,447; mechanical wood pulp (for sale), 23; newsprint, 991·5; printing and writing papers, 1,258; kraft paper, 431; cardboard, 1,327; fibre board, 141.

26 per cent of the total labour force are engaged in industry.

In 1976 the total consumption of electric energy in Finland was about 31,770 million kWh, 30 per cent of the demand for electric power was covered from water power resources. The total demand of energy is estimated to increase until the year 1980 up to 50,000 and until the year 1985 up to 70,000 million kWh.

The total amount of water power that can be economically harnessed is estimated as giving an average annual output of 17,537 million kWh. Of this amount 11,600 million kWh were in operation and 150 million kWh under construction in 1976.

**Commerce.** The following table shows imports by countries of purchase, exports by countries of sale for 1976 (million marks):

| *Country* | *Imports* | *Exports* |
|---|---|---|
| Total | 28,555 | 24,505 |
| United Kingdom | 2,277 | 3,493 |
| Austria | 420 | 170 |
| Belgium-Luxembourg | 508 | 418 |
| Denmark | 861 | 938 |
| France | 785 | 867 |
| West Germany | 4,571 | 2,408 |
| Italy | 527 | 386 |
| Netherlands | 863 | 741 |
| Norway | 867 | 832 |
| Portugal | 86 | 71 |
| Sweden | 5,201 | 4,350 |
| Switzerland | 956 | 405 |
| United States | 2,154 | 659 |
| Czechoslovakia | 136 | 134 |
| East Germany | 137 | 205 |
| Poland | 478 | 269 |
| Soviet Union | 5,132 | 4,903 |
| Brazil | 177 | 121 |
| Japan | 445 | 165 |
| Canada | 117 | 144 |
| Spain | 364 | 242 |
| Hungary | 123 | 132 |

The following table shows imports and exports in money value and percentage terms for various economic organizations.

| | *Imports (1,000 Fmk)* | *Exports (1,000 Fmk)* |
|---|---|---|
| EFTA | 7,559,042 | 5,860,090 |
| EEC | 10,422,566 | 9,378,332 |
| COMICON | 6,065,830 | 5,683,788 |
| | *(per cent)* | *(per cent)* |
| EFTA | 23·2 | 23·1 |
| EEC | 34·7 | 38·1 |
| COMICON | 21·8 | 23·7 |

The following tables show exports and imports of the various categories of goods for 1975 and 1976 (million marks):

| *Imports* | 1975 | 1976 |
|---|---|---|
| Raw materials and producer goods | 17,057 | 17,828 |
| Fuels and lubricants | 1,670 | 1,581 |
| Investment goods | 5,223 | 4,972 |
| Consumer goods | 3,989 | 4,102 |

| *Exports* | 1975 | 1976 |
|---|---|---|
| Agricultural products | 385 | 721 |
| Wood industry products | 2,177 | 2,892 |
| Paper industry products | 7,225 | 7,860 |
| Metal engineering industry products | 5,357 | 6,892 |
| Textile industry products | 1,847 | 1,936 |

## COMMUNICATIONS

**Roads.** The length of public highways in Finland in 1975 was 73,341 (of which 30,132 were paved). The number of registered motor vehicles in 1976, was 1,032,884 cars.

**Railways.** Length of State railways, 5,957 km, of which 395 km have been electrified. In 1976 the railways carried 23·4 million tons of commercial goods and 37·0 million passengers.

**Shipping.** Finland's merchant fleet numbered, in 1976, 442 vessels with a gross tonnage of 2,090,000 In the same year 16,378 vessels with aggregate tonnage of 32,930,000 entered Finnish ports and 16,590 vessels totalling 33,334,000 tons departed.

Owing to the improvement of road net, and transport equipment the significance of inland waterways transport on the chain of lakes and rivers is at present of little importance, being limited mainly to timber floating only. To facilitate transport from eastern Finland the Saimaa Canal the southern part of which has been leased from the U.S.S.R., was enlarged and opened in 1968.

The following are the principal shipping lines:

**Finland Steamship Co. Ltd., EFFOA.** (Managing Director, R. G. Ehrnrooth); share capital 48,000,000·00 marks; motor vessels 37; total tonnage 189,779 d.w.t.; new buildings 6; total tonnage of new buildings 96,200 d.w.t.; *services operated:* Sweden, Levant ports, East Coast of South America, Tramp Trade; lines operated by Oy Finncarriers Ab: United Kingdom–Ireland, Holland–Belgium, France, Germany, Poland, Denmark, Sweden, western Mediterranean ports and Morocco. *Head Office:* Eteläranta 8, 00130 Helsinki 13, Finland.

**Oy Finnlines Ltd.;** (Managing Director, H. Holma); 34 vessels, 237,577 brt, 258,922 dwr; *services operated:* U.S. East Coast–Continent–Finland–U.S. Gulf–Continent–U.K.–Scandinavia (Atlantic Gulf Service)–Finland–U.K.–Western Mediterranean–Biscay–Finland, Finland–Germany via Sweden, Finland U.K., Ocean Cruises (Passenger Service); Finland –Germany–Denmark (Ferry Service), Finland–U.K. (Finanglia Line). *Head Office:* Korkeavuorenkatu 32, 00131 Helsinki 13.

**Civil Aviation. Finnair Oy;** (Managing Director, Gunnar Korhonen); share capital 60,000,000 new marks 75·2 per cent owned by the state); aircraft: 2 DC-8-62CFs-8 Super Caravelles, 5 Convair Metropolitan 8 DC-9-10s-2 DC-10-30, 1 DC-8-62, 6 DC-9-51, 9 DC-9-14/15; *services operated:* Rome, Montreal, Bangkok, Gothenburg; from Turkey to Stockholm and Copenhagen, from Vaasa to Umeå and Sundsvall. Domestic services to 20 destinations. *Head Office:* Mannerkeimintie 102, P.O. Box 6, 00250 Helsinki 25, Finland.

**Telecommunications.** Finnish telegraph, telex and long distance telephone services are operated by the Posts and Telegraphs (PTT). Local telephone services are operated by the PTT in an area covering 76 per cent of the total area of the country while in the remaining area local telephone services are operated by privately-owned telephone enterprises under the control of and concession given by the PTT. As most densely populated areas are served by the latter systems 22·6 per cent of all telephones are connected to their networks. The total number of telephones in the country was 1,833,993 at the end of 1975.

**Broadcasting.** Oy Yleisradio Ab. (The Finnish Broadcasting Co. Ltd.). *Chairman of the Governors:* Atte Pakkanen. *Director-General:* Erkki Raatikainen. *Head Office:* Helsinki.

The state owns 98 per cent of the company share capital and the remainder is divided among groups and associations representing various interests. There are three radio programmes covering the whole country and two television channels. On 30 June 1974 there were 1,983,087 receivers' licences, 1,249,748 television licences, and 93,730 colour television licences.

## NEWSPAPERS

In 1971 there were 91 daily newspapers (of which 12 were printed in Swedish) and 119 local papers in Finland. The circulation of all daily newspapers totalled over 2,340,000.

**Aamulehti.** Circulation 120,000. Editor, Raino Vehmas.

**Helsingin Sanomat.** F. 1889. Morning. Independent. Circulation (weekdays) 355,900; (Sundays) 407,312. Chairman Aatos Erkko. Managing Director Väinö J. Nurmimaa. Editors, Teo Mertanen, Heikki Tikkanen, Keijo Kylävaara, Simopekka Nortamo, Helsinki.

**Hufvudstadbladet.** F. 1864. Morning. Independent. Swedish. Circulation 66,000. Editor, Jan-Magnus Jansson, Helsingfors.

**Ilta-Sanomat.** Circulation 126,000. Editor-in-chief, Martti Huhtamäki, Managing editors, Mikko Saukkonen, Leevi Korkkula.

**Turun Sanomat.** 127,694. (Sundays 130,528). Editor, Keijo K. Kulha.

**Uusi Suomi.** F. 1847. Morning. Independent. Circulation approx. 11,000. Editor, Johannes Koroma.

## ATOMIC ENERGY

Because the increased exploitation of hydro-electric power resources is impossible, and consumption increase must be covered by thermal capacity, the use of nuclear energy is of particular interest to the Finnish power economy.

A special Law on Atomic Energy was issued in October 1957 and a Law on Protection Against Radiation has been in force since 1 July 1957. The Law on Atomic Energy is very liberal and its main purpose is to ensure safety, protect the public interest, and enforce the international safeguard regulations. A licence is required for all cartage, and possession of fissionable material, utilization of a reactor, or facilities designed to produce materials of this kind. Prospecting and mining are excluded from the provisions of this law. The licensing authority is the Ministry of Trade and Industry assisted by the Institution of Radiation Physics as a control authority. Finland has also entered into agreement with the International Atomic Energy Agency on the application of safeguards in accordance with the Treaty on Non-Proliferation of Nuclear Weapons and put all her peaceful nuclear activities under the control of the Agency.

The Atomic Energy Commission was established in October 1958. It acts as an advisory body to the Ministry of Trade and Industry, follows development in the field of atomic energy, makes appropriate proposals to the Ministry of Trade and Industry and maintains contact with foreign organizations.

There are several enterprises working in the field of nuclear energy. The state-owned Imatran Voima Osakeyhtiö (Imatra Power Company) is constructing a nuclear power plant of 2 × 420 MW at Loviisa and has plans for additional units to be started later. Similar plans are under consideration within the privately owned industries which produce about one-half of the total electricity. Sixteen private utilities and companies have formed a joint company, Teollisuuden Voima Oy, to take care of nuclear power production. They have not yet, however, placed any orders. For equipment and machinery production eight big metal industry enterprises have formed a joint company, Oy Finnatom Ab. The Technical Research Centre of Finland has one Truga Mk. II research reactor and the Helsinki Technical University has in addition a subcritical assembly for training purposes.

Finland is a member of the International Atomic Energy Agency and participates in the OECD Halden Reactor Project. As one of the Scandinavian countries Finland participates in several joint Scandinavian undertakings like information services, research, safety and other co-operative arrangements. Nuclear engineering is taught at the Helsinki University of Technology, and nuclear physics, chemistry, etc., at the Helsinki University.

Prospecting for uranium, thorium and other ores which are used in reactors is done by the state and private enterprise. Some fairly good deposits have been found.

## EDUCATION

Primary education is compulsory and free. There are about 4,700 primary schools in Finland with a total of over 460,000 pupils. The primary school proper is on a 6–7 year basis and the second stage of primary education, the civic school, extends over 2–3 years. The pupils who go on to secondary schools leave the primary schools after the fourth grade. Completion of the primary school course (the primary school proper and the civic school) is a basic qualification for admission to vocational schools. There are about 590 vocational schools and colleges with a total enrolment of more than 100,000 students. Those who have completed the five-year junior secondary school course may apply for admission either to the senior secondary school or to vocational colleges. After having completed the three-year senior secondary school course and passed the matriculation examination, students may be admitted to universities or institutes of higher education. There are more than 670 secondary schools in Finland with a total of about 337,000 students.

From the existing parallel forms of education, the primary school and the civic school and the junior secondary school, a nine-year Basic School of the comprehensive type will be formed to replace the existing forms of education. Completion of the Basic School will fulfil the requirements of compulsory education. The school reform will be implemented gradually during 1972–77.

Over half the 600 secondary schools are privately owned, but receive state subsidies for 85–90 per cent of their expenditure. The other secondary schools are state or municipal schools. The vocational training schools and institutes are owned by the state, the municipalities and organizations, and may also be privately owned. They are also state subsidized.

In 1971, Finland had 17 universities and institutes of higher education. The largest of these is the University of Helsinki with more than 24,000 students. The other universities and institutes of higher education are the Swedish-language university Åbo Academy, the universities of Jyväskylä, Oulu, Turku, Tampere, Kuopio and Joensuu, the Technical University of Helsinki, Tampere and Lappeenranta, the Helsinki, Turku and Vaasa Schools of Economics, the Swedish School of Economics in Helsinki, the School of Economics of Åbo Academy, and the Veterinary College.

Nearly 50 per cent of the 60,000 students (approx.) in the above-mentioned institutes of higher education are women.

The State finances about 75–100 per cent of the total expenditure of the universities and institutes of higher education.

By the 1977–78 school year the whole country will have transferred from the old school system to the new comprehensive education system. Compulsory education consists of the full course of the nine-year comprehensive school, in which instruction is principally the same for all students. Tuition is free for everybody. The comprehensive school is divided into a six-year lower level and a three-year upper level. The lower level is provided by about 4,100 schools and the upper level by some 600 schools. In 1977, the number of students in the comprehensive school system was about 650,000.

After the comprehensive school the student may transfer either to an upper secondary school or a vocational education institution. The upper secondary school provides a three year course of general education. At the end of the upper secondary school the students take the so called matriculation examination. After having passed this examination they are qualified to seek admission to the institutions of higher education, or vocational education institutions with similar entrance requirements. In 1976, the number of upper secondary schools was about 460, the total enrolment being about 95,000. In the same year, about 35,000 new students registered in the upper secondary schools, a number equivalent to about 45 per cent of the age group of 16-year-olds.

The vocational education institutions are either vocational schools (for skilled manual work) or institutes (for managerial tasks and planning). They are based on the course of the comprehensive school or the upper secondary school. They offer about 650 different courses, lasting one to four years. In 1976, the number of vocational education institutions was about 600, with an enrolment of about 130,000 students. About 72,000 new students, 17,000 of them upper secondary school leavers, registered in the same year.

The comprehensive and the upper secondary schools are, with some exceptions, run by the municipalities. The vocational institutions are either municipal (48 per cent), State-run (22 per cent), or private (30 per cent). The State covers the greater part of the recurrent costs of the comprehensive schools (70 per cent), the upper secondary schools (85 per cent), and the vocational education institutions (75 per cent).

In 1977, Finland had 17 universities and other institutions of higher education. The largest of them is the University of Helsinki with slightly more than 20,000 students (in 1976). The other universities and institutions of higher education are the Swedish-language university Åbo Academy, the Universities of Jyväskylä, Oulu, Turku, Tampere, Kuopio and Joensuu, the Helsinki, Tampere and Lappeenranta Universities of Technology, the Helsinki, Turku and Vaasa Schools of Economics, the Swedish School of Economics in Helsinki, the School of Economics at Åbo Academy, and the Veterinary College.

About 50 per cent of the 73,000 (in 1976) students in the above-mentioned institutions of higher education are women.

The State finances about 90 per cent of the total expenditure of the universities and other institutions of higher education.

### RELIGION

The National Churches are the Evangelical-Lutheran Church of Finland, to which about 93 per cent of the people belong, and the Greek Orthodox Church. The Greek Orthodox Church is, in spite of its comparatively few adherents (about 60,000), is also a National Church with the same rights as the Evangelical-Lutheran Church. Its bishops are thus also appointed by the President of the Republic from among three candidates put forward by the church authorities. Entire freedom is allowed to other religions and denominations The minority groups are small. The various Free Churches (Free Church of Finland, Methodist, Baptist, Adventist) number only about 16,500.

# France

## (RÉPUBLIQUE FRANÇAISE)

**Capital**—Paris.

**President**—Valéry Giscard d'Estaing.

**National Flag**: A tricolour pale-wise, blue, white, red.

### CONSTITUTION AND GOVERNMENT

THE first Constituent Assembly of the Fourth Republic passed a new Constitution on 19 April 1946. The Draft of this Constitution was submitted by referendum to the French electorate, and was rejected.

The Second Constituent Assembly, elected on 2 June 1946, passed a revised Constitution on 29 September 1946. This Constitution was passed by referendum, and came into force on 24 December 1946.

On 2 June 1958, the de Gaulle Government received from The National Assembly by a vote of 350 to 161, and from The Council of The Republic (on 3 June) by a vote of 256 to 30 a mandate to prepare a draft of a new constitution.

On 28 September the Constitution was submitted to a Referendum with the following results: Total of the electorate 26,603,464; Number of votes cast, 22,293,301; Ayes, 17,668,790; Noes, 4,624,511.

The Executive is composed of the President and a government headed by the Prime Minister. The President is elected by direct universal suffrage, for a seven-year term. He appoints the Prime Minister, and on his recommendation, the other government members. He accredits ambassadors and envoys. He negotiates and ratifies treaties. In domestic matters, he presides over the Council of Ministers, signs ordinances, promulgates law and can ask Parliament for a new reading of any Bill. He can institute constitutional reform and call for a referendum on important Bills. He is empowered to dissolve Parliament. According to the famous article 16, the President takes on exceptional powers in an emergency situation. After consultation with the Prime Minister and the government, he may 'take the measures required by these circumstances'.

The Prime Minister directs the Government's actions. He ensures the execution of laws, makes civil and military appointments (subject to the President's authority). He is responsible for national defence. The cabinet is responsible to the National Assembly. It can be forced to resign only if a motion of censure, signed by at least ten per cent of the N.A. members, is passed by an absolute majority of that assembly. Motions of censure can be brought forward only on the government's programme, on a statement of general policy or on a text which it wants passed.

The legislative branch consists of a National Assembly and a Senate. The Assembly is elected by direct universal suffrage for a five-year term. It is composed of 490 members, of whom 473 represent Metropolitan France, ten the Overseas Departments and seven the Overseas Territories.

Senators are elected by indirect suffrage for nine years, by an electoral college composed of National Assembly members, the General Departmental Councils, and the delegates of the Municipal Councils. One-third of the Senate is renewed every three years. There are 283 Senators—264 from Metropolitan France, 13 from the Overseas Departments and five from the Overseas Territories. The remaining six represent French communities in foreign countries.

A member of parliament may not hold ministerial office, membership of the Constitutional Council or any non-elected public appointment.

Parliament passes laws on all matters involving individual rights and the organization of the State. The Prime Minister, as well as members of parliament, has the right to initiate legislation. If the normal procedures for settling disagreement between the two houses fail, the National Assembly makes the final decision. Parliament may delegate some or all of its powers to the Government. Parliament controls Government action by oral and written questions, by interpellation (calling the Government to explain its general policy) and by censure motions. Conversely, the Government may place on the agenda of either house motions it wants discussed, it may oppose amendments, and may appeal to the country by means of referendum.

The Constitutional Council, the Economic and Social Council and the Council of State help the executive and legislative branches.

The Constitutional Council has nine members. It ensures that the Constitution is respected. The President, the Prime Minister and the Presidents of the two houses of Parliament have the authority to refer a matter to the Council. It also examines the procedural regulations of Parliament, settles contested elections and supervises referendums.

The Economic and Social Council is an advisory body of 205 members appointed for five-year terms. The members come from labour unions and professional organizations and represent the country's economic and social interests.

The Council of State has two functions. It advises the Government on drafting Bills, decrees and ordinances; and it is the highest administrative court of law.

The death of President Georges Pompidou occurred on 2 April 1974. On 19 May M. d'Estaing was elected President.

**Government** (30 March 1977)

*Prime Minister, Minister of Economy and Finance:* Raymond Barre.

*Keeper of the Seals, Minister of Justice:* M. Alain Peyrefitte.

*Minister of Foreign Affairs:* M. Louis de Guiringaud.
*Minister of the Interior:* M. Christian Bonnet.
*Minister of Defence:* M. Yvon Bourges.
*Minister of Cooperation:* M. Robert Galley.
*Minister for Culture and the Environment:* M. Michel d'Ornano.
*Minister Delegate for the Economy and Finance:* M. Robert Boulin.
*Minister of Equipment and Area Planning:* M. Jean-Pierre Fourcade.
*Minister of Education:* M. René Haby.
*Minister of Agriculture:* M. Pierre Méhaignerie.
*Minister of Industry, Trade and Artisan Industries:* M. René Monory.
*Minister of Labour:* M. Christian Beullac.
*Minister of Health and Social Security:* Mme Simone Veil.
*Minister of Foreign Trade:* M. André Rossi.

## LOCAL GOVERNMENT

In France, the commune is the basic geographical unit of French local government. It has at all times been acknowledged. Roman law recognized it, it was confirmed in medieval times, as far as towns were concerned, by the procedure of enfranchisement, and the Monarchy recognized it for the rural communities. The area covered by a commune can vary widely. Towns and villages, urban and rural communes, where one category ends and the other begins is difficult to determine. Statistical services habitually apply the term 'rural' to any commune with an aggregate population of less than 2,500. The French communal patchwork features a multiplicity of small communes.

In view of the population growth and industrialization of the last two decades, however, the communal structures no longer reflect the demographic and economic realities of present day France. It is therefore essential that administrative boundaries be brought more into line with the natural communities by this evolution, especially in urban areas.

In rural areas, a very large number of communes lack the minimum demographic substance indispensible to administrative life. By grouping together, they can considerably improve the management and output of local public services, distribute costs more fairly over their populations, and rationalize policies of local public utilities and services. What is sought is to facilitate mergers or other forms of association.

The system in force prior to an Act of 16 July 1971 was not effective enough in encouraging groupings. In ten years, only 746 communes merged into 350 municipalities. On the other hand, 1,108 multipurpose inter-communal syndicates were created affecting a population of 12,951,000, as well 90 districts grouping 686 communes, and seven urban communities grouping 237 communes.

*The Act of 16 July 1971.* The three fundamental principles underlying this act are:

1. Highly diversified solutions should be applied to a communal context, itself widely varying according to regions. These solutions are, depending on circumstances:

(*a*) The merger. Two or more communes disappear into one bigger unit.

(*b*) The multi-purpose inter-communal syndicate. The object of this syndicate is to run services which the member communes cannot, or no longer wish to provide individually.

(*c*) The district. A district is a public establishment which has the same object as an inter-communal syndicate, but asserts a closer solidarity between the communes involved. The district has certain powers of decision of its own over its organization and financing. Also, unlike the syndicate, a number of competences are transferred to it compulsorily.

(*d*) The urban community. This solution is applicable to large urban concentrations made up of several aggregated communes totalling not less than 50,000 inhabitants. Its purpose is to pool a field of competences wide enough to allow for a modernization of administrative structures and a rational financing, it is therefore a closer and more far-reaching form of association than the district.

2. Because it offers a lasting solution to the problems facing communes, the merger formula will be attempted whenever it seems to be the most rational solution.

3. Mergers and other forms of association are to be brought about only by liberal and democratic procedures, with inducements.

## LEGAL SYSTEM

Petty civil and police court cases are dealt with in courts presided over by Justices of the Peace. The Correctional Courts deal with more serious criminal cases. In these courts there is no trial by jury, the cases being dealt with by Courts of First Instance. There are 27 Courts of Appeal which deal with appeals from the Courts of First Instance, and the Correctional Courts. Very serious crimes, such as murder, are dealt with by Courts of Assize, which sit in every Department. In these cases there is a jury of seven persons.

The final Court of Appeal is the Court of Cassation. Appeals to this court may, however, be made only on points of law. If the Court of Cassation decides that the law has been wrongly interpreted, the case is remitted to another Court of Appeal.

According to the law of 22 July 1947 the High Court of Appeal (Cassation) is composed of a First Président, four Présidents of the Court, 60 puisne judges, one Procedure. Général, ten Advocats Général, a Registrar in Chief and five others.

The Chief Officers of the Court of Cassation are as follows:

*First Président:* M. Maurice Aydolot.

*Procurator-General:* M. Touffait.

*Chief Registrar:* M. Depeyrot.

**The Supreme Court of Justice.** The Supreme Council of Justice (Conseil Supérieur de la Magistrature) is composed of 14 members: The President of the Republic Chairman; The Keeper of the Seals, Minister of Justice, Vice-Chairman; Six persons elected for six years by the National Assembly, by a two-thirds majority, outside its members, six deputy-members being elected in the same conditions; Six persons designated as follows: Four members of the magistrature elected for six years, representing each category of the magistrature, in the conditions laid down by law, four deputies being elected in the same conditions; Two members appointed for six years by the President of the Republic outside Parliament and the magistrature, but within the judicial profession, two deputies being appointed in the same conditions.

The decisions of the Supreme Council of Justice are made by a majority vote. When votes are equally divided, that of the President prevails.

The President of the Republic appoints the magistrates, with the exception of the public prosecutor upon presentation by the Supreme Council of Justice.

The Supreme Council of Justice ensures, in accordance with the law, the discipline of these magistrates, their independence and the administration of the tribunals.

The magistrates are irremovable.

At mid-1973 the population of France was 52,160,800.

## AREA AND POPULATION

The area of France is 54,907,800 hectares. In 1974, 49,908,100 hectares of French territory was devoted to agriculture, i.e. 90·9 per cent of its total area.

If the non-agricultural areas of France were to be grouped together in the centre, they would extend over the departments of Allier, Cantal, Puy-de-Dôme, Haute-Loire, Creuse, Corrèze and Haute-Vienne as well as four fifths of the department of the Loire, while the whole of the remainder would represent France's agricultural land.

The following table shows the average annual population growth during the three periods 1954–1962, 1962–1968, 1968–1975, that is, between the most recent censuses.

The figures give the average percentage increase during the periods under consideration. The table distinguishes between the natural increase (excess of births over deaths) and the migratory increase (excess of immigrants over emigrants) broken down into two categories, namely foreigners and French repatriates.

Average Annual Population Increase in France

| | *Annual percentage rate of change* | | |
|---|---|---|---|
| *Breakdown of increase* | *1954–1962* | *1962–1968* | *1968–1975* |
| Net natural increase | +0·7 | +0·7 | +0·6 |
| Net migratory increase | +0·4 | +0·5 | +0·2 |
| of which: repatriates | +0·1 | +0·3 | — |
| others | +0·3 | +0·2 | +0·2 |
| Total increase | +1·1 | +1·2 | +0·8 |
| Total increase (including repatriates) | +1·0 | +0·9 | +0·8 |

The table shows a clear slow-down in population growth in the last intercensal period compared with the two preceding ones. This slow-down is caused by a fall in both the natural rate of increase (the birth rate dropped from 18·1 per cent in 1964 to 15·2 per cent in 1974) and in the net migratory increase (except in the case of "other migrations", made up mostly of foreign nationals).

A major cause of the slow-down is the fall in the net migratory increase of repatriates (+0·1 per cent from 1954 to 1962: repatriates from Indo-China and North Africa; +0·3 per cent from 1962 to 1968, when the bulk of repatriations from Algeria took place; no repatriations occurred during the most recent period). But even if no account is taken of repatriates, the reduction in the rate of increase is substantial.

To sum up: between 1968 and 1975, the annual average rate of increase in population was 0·8 per cent of which three-quarters is accounted for by the excess of births over deaths and one-quarter by that of immigrants over emigrants.

The following table shows the population of the Regions of France to the nearest 100 in 1975.

| *Regions* | *Population* 1975 |
|---|---|
| Region Parisienne | 9,863,400 |
| Champagne-Ardenne | 1,342,100 |
| Picardie | 1,677,200 |
| Haute-Normandie | 1,597,400 |
| Centre | 2,147,300 |
| Basse-Normandie | 1,304,400 |

*continued*

| *Regions* | *Population* 1975 |
|---|---|
| Bourgogne | 1,568,000 |
| Nord | 3,918,200 |
| Lorraine | 2,331,300 |
| Alsace | 1,515,200 |
| Franche-Comte | 1,059,000 |
| Pays de la Loire | 2,765,400 |
| Bretagne | 2,598,000 |
| Poitou-Charentes | 1,527,300 |
| Aquitaine | 2,546,000 |
| Midi-Pyrenees | 2,260,000 |
| Limousin | 738,500 |
| Rhone-Alpes | 4,781,200 |
| Auvergne | 1,330,500 |
| Languedoc-Roussillon | 1,789,100 |
| Provence-Cote-D'Azur | 3,664,900 |
| Corse | 220,000 |
| France (Total) | 52,674,000 |

## CURRENCY

**The unit of currency was changed in 1959 to the New Franc and in 1963 to the Franc. There are nickel alloy coins in circulation of ½, 1, 5 and 10 francs and 5, 10 and 20 centimes There are also banknotes with a value of 10, 50, 100 and 500 francs.**

## FINANCE

The following table shows the breakdown of expenditure, in millions of Francs, between Ministries according to the 1977 budget:

| *Ministries and Services* | *Running exp.* | *in %* | *Capital exp.* | *in %* | *Total* | *in %* |
|---|---|---|---|---|---|---|
| Foreign Affairs | 3,398 | 1·10 | 73 | 0·13 | 3,471 | 0·95 |
| Agriculture | 14,045 | 4·55 | 2,008 | 3·63 | 16,053 | 4·41 |
| Ex. Servicemen | 10,945 | 3·55 | — | — | 10,945 | 3·01 |
| Trade and Artisan industries | 51 | 0·01 | 43 | 0·07 | 94 | 0·02 |
| Cooperation | 1,958 | 0·63 | 613 | 1·10 | 2,571 | 0·71 |
| Cultural Affairs | 1,475 | 0·47 | 392 | 0·71 | 1,867 | 0·51 |
| Overseas Departments | 355 | 0·11 | 222 | 0·40 | 577 | 0·16 |
| Economy and Finance: I. Common expenditure | 90,156 | 29·20 | 3,402 | 6·15 | 93,558 | 25·70 |
| II. Financial services | 10,719 | 3·47 | 139 | 0·25 | 10,858 | 2·98 |
| Education and Universities: Education | 54,963 | 17·80 | 3,205 | 5·79 | 58,168 | 15·98 |
| Universities | 8,920 | 2·89 | 1,569 | 2·83 | 10,489 | 2·88 |
| Equipment | 6,096 | 1·97 | 8,409 | 15·19 | 14,505 | 3·98 |
| Industry and Research | 5,232 | 1·69 | 3,411 | 6·16 | 8,643 | 2·37 |
| Home Affairs | 11,770 | 3·81 | 1,811 | 3·27 | 13,581 | 3·73 |
| Home Affairs (Repatriates) | 80 | 0·02 | — | — | 80 | 0·02 |
| Justice | 2,982 | 0·96 | 152 | 0·27 | 3,134 | 0·86 |
| Quality of Life: I. Environment | 103 | 0·03 | 116 | 0·21 | 219 | 0·06 |
| II. Youth and Sport | 1,914 | 0·62 | 466 | 0·84 | 2,380 | 0·65 |
| III. Tourism | 55 | 0·01 | 54 | 0·09 | 109 | 0·03 |
| Prime Minister's services: | | | | | | |
| I. General services | 2,914 | 0·94 | 531 | 0·96 | 3,445 | 0·95 |
| II. Official Journals | 128 | 0·04 | 2 | 0·00 | 130 | 0·03 |
| III. Secretariat-General of National Defence | 13 | 0·00 | 19 | 0·03 | 32 | 0·00 |
| IV. Economic and Social Council | 49 | 0·01 | — | — | 49 | 0·01 |
| V. General Planning Commission | 33 | 0·01 | 11 | 0·02 | 44 | 0·01 |
| Overseas Territories | 350 | 0·11 | 106 | 0·19 | 456 | 0·12 |
| Transport: I. Common section | 58 | 0·02 | 23 | 0·04 | 81 | 0·02 |
| II. Overland transport | 11,585 | 3·75 | 546 | 0·99 | 12,131 | 3·33 |
| III. Civil Aviation and meteorology | 1,179 | 0·38 | 1,488 | 2·69 | 2,667 | 0·73 |
| IV. Merchant Navy | 1,349 | 0·44 | 1,201 | 2·17 | 2,550 | 0·70 |
| Labour and Health: I. Common section | 1,167 | 0·38 | 27 | 0·04 | 1,194 | 0·33 |
| II. Labour | 8,309 | 2·69 | 189 | 0·34 | 8,498 | 2·33 |
| III. Health | 11,853 | 3·84 | 1,151 | 2·08 | 13,004 | 3·57 |
| Defence | 44,443 | 14·39 | 23,933 | 43·25 | 68,376 | 18·78 |
| Total | 308,647 | | 55,312 | | 363,959 | |

The GNP at market prices for 1974 was U.S. $ millions 285,780, and the GNP per capita at market prices was U.S. $5,440. The percentage growth rate of the GNP per capita for the period 1960–74 was 4·4, and for the period 1965–74 was 4·8. [*See the note at the beginning of this section concerning GNP.*]

## BANKS

**Banque de France.** (Governor, Bernard Clappier.) Est. 1800; sole Bank of Issue for France; all the share capital is owned by the State; Balance Sheet at 31 December 1974 showed assets F.191,272,595,729. *Head Office:* 39 rue Croix-de-Petits-Champs, Paris. 236 Offices and Branches.

# FRANCE

**Banca Commerciale Italiana** (France) S.A. (President. Frédéric Berbigier.) Est. 1918; Balance Sheet at 31 December 1972 showed assets F.508,901,845; deposit accounts F.442,425,165. *Head Office:* 14 Rue Halévy, Paris 9e. 15 Branches.

**Banque des Antilles Françaises,** (President, René Arnaud). Head Office in Paris; see Guadeloupe and Martinique.

**Banque Internationale pour l'Afrique Occidentale, S.A.** (President, J. Dromer.) Est. 1965; Balance Sheet at 31 December 1975 showed assets fr.3,177,341,509·47; deposits fr. 1,731,000,000. *Head Office:* 9 Avenue de Messine, Paris 8e. 77 Branches, subsidiaries and affiliates in West and Central Africa, Greece and Germany in West and Central Africa.

**Banque de l'Indochine, S.A.** (President, François de Flers.) Balance Sheet at 31 December 1968 showed assets fr. 2,875,463,798; current accounts fr.423,929,213. *Head Office:* 96 Boulevard Haussmann, Paris. 19 Branches.

**Banque de Madagascar et des Comores.** (President, Maurice Gonon.) Est. 1925; Bank of Issue for the Comores only (since 1 April 1962); Balance Sheet at 31 December 1973 showed assets and liabilities F.482,577,144; capital; F.14,430,000. *Head Office:* 23 Avenue Matignon, Paris (8ème). 1 Branch: Comores. Agencies: Marseille, Toulon.

**Banque Nationale de Paris "Intercontinentale"** (since 27 April 1972) formerly Banque Nationale pour le Commerce et l'Industrie (Afrique); Est. 1940; Chairman Pierre Ledoux; General manager André Beronie; Balance sheet at 31 December 1974 showed assets FF. 1,511,198,242·53; deposits and current accounts FF. 1,383,096,802·88; *Head Office:* 1 Boulevard Haussmann 75009 Paris; 3 Branches.

**Banque de Paris et des Pays-Bas, S.A.** (Chairman, Jacques de Fouchier.) Est. 1872; Balance Sheet at 31 December 1973 showed assets F.13,564,576,783; current accounts F.3,709,000,000. *Head Office:* 3 Rue d'Antin, Paris. 32 Branches.

**Banque Nationale de Paris.** (Hon. Chairman, P. Ledoux.) Balance Sheet at 31 December 1972 showed assets F.101,134,034,488·10. *Head Office:* 16 Boulevard des Italiens, Paris. Over 2,000 Branches and affiliates.

**Banque Nationale pour le Commerce et l'Industrie (Ocean Indien) formerly Credit Foncier de Madagascar, S.A.** (President Director General, André Beronie.) Est. 1919; Balance Sheet at 31 December 1974 showed assets FF. 946,617,889·46 deposits and current accounts FF. 1,140,333,845·93. *Head Office:* 7 Place Vendôme, Paris. 15 Branches.

**Crédit Commercial de France, S.A.** (Chairman, Jacques Merlin.) Est. 1894; Balance Sheet at 31 December 1974 showed assets F.20,710,000,000; total deposits F. 19,042,000,000. *Head Office:* 103 Avenue des Champs-Elysées, 75008 Paris; 263 Branches.

**Crédit du Nord, S.A.** (President, Antoine Dupont Fauville.) Est. 1848; Balance Sheet at 31 December 1976 showed assets F.23,814,057,420; call and term deposits F. 20,611,697,183, Paris.

**Credit Foncier de France.** (Governor, Roger Goetze.) **Est.** 1852; Balance Sheet at 31 December 1976 showed assets F.61,225,865,856. *Head Office:* 19 Rue des Capucines, Paris.

**Crédit Industriel et Commercial.** (Chairman, Ch. de Lavaréne.) Est. 1859; Balance Sheet at 31 December 1976 showed fr.16 assets fr.16,401,855,524·16; and liabilities total,401,855,524·16. *Head Office:* 66 Rue de la Victoire, Paris 9e, France. *London Office:* 74 London Wall, E.C.2. *New York Office:* 280 Park Avenue, N.Y. 10017.

**Crédit Lyonnais.** (Chairman, C. Pierre Brossolette.) Est. 1863, nationalised 1 January 1946. According to the Law of Jan. 1 1973 stipulating acquisitions of shareholdings by staff of nationalised banks, the shares to personnel involved 326,307 units, that is 6·798 per cent of the equity. Balance Sheet at 31 December 1976 showed assets FF.181,022,702,109·40; total deposits 147,898 (in million FF.) *Head Office:* 18 Rue de la République. Lyons. *Central Office:* 19 Boulevard des Italiens, Paris. 2400 Branches in France and abroad. Affiliated Branches in U.S.A., Canada, South America, Africa, Middle East and Asia-Oceania.

**Fidelity Bank (France).** (Chairman, Jacques de Dumast, General Manager, John H. Newton,) Assets at 31 December 1976 F.445,932,710; deposits and current accounts, F424,802,805. *Head Office:* 104, Avenue des Champs-Elysées, 75008 Paris.

**Hongkong and Shanghai Banking Corporation, The.** Branch in Paris. See Hong Kong.

**Ottoman Bank** (branch in Paris) see Turkey.

**Société Centrale de Banque, S.A.** (Président, Gonzague de Lavernette.) Est. 1880; Balance Sheet at 31 December 1962 showed assets F.1,532,611,638·04; deposits and current accounts F.1,170,226,347·28. *Head Office:* 43 rue Cambon, Paris; *Registered Office:* 5 Bd. de la Madeleine, Paris. 24 Branches.

**Messieurs Hottinguer & Cie.** Established 1786. (Partners, Baron Hottinguer; Jean C. Hottinguer; Comte de Boissieu; Pierre Hottinguer; Henri Hottinguer; Jean Philippe Hottinguer; Paul Hottinguer–Sogefi; Manager, Charles de Pourtalès; Armand de Baudry d'Asson; Bernard Chatenet; Jean Luc Barthelemy; Françoir de Beco-Louis Benedetti. Assets as at 31 December 1974 FF.358,010,751; deposits and current accounts FF.224,752,000. *Head Office:* 38 rue de Provence, 75009 Paris. Tele: 285.05.61—Telex: 65664.

**Société Lyonnaise de Dépôts et de Crédit Industriel, S.A.** Established 1865. (President, Henri Arminjon.) Assets as at 31 December 1974, Fr.8,891,203,592; deposits and Current accounts Fr.6,018,596,268. *Head Office:* 8 rue de la République Lyon 1; Number of branches 260.

**The Royal Bank of Canada (France)** S.A. Established 1919. (President, A. de Takacsy.) Assets as at 31 December 1974, F.1,436,396,078·21. *Head Office:* 3 Rue Scribe, 75009-Paris. Tel. 742-02-40, Telex: 22671; Number of Branches 3.

**Société Générale pour favoriser le Développement du Commerce et de l'Industrie en France, S.A.** (Chairman, Maurice Laure; Vice-Chairman, Jean Richard; Deputy General Managers, Jean-Paul Delacour, Marc Vienot, Pierre Muron, Jean Starck). Est. 1864; 95 per cent of share capital are owned by the State; Balance Sheet at 31 December 1973 showed assets F.101,034,966,584·86; deposits F.97,658,751,447·21. *Head Office:* 29 Boulevard Haussmann, 75009, Paris. Offices and agencies in London, Manchester; 2200 branches in France; branches and subsidiaries in Belgium, Luxembourg, the Netherlands, Spain, Austria, Germany, Switzerland, Africa, Morocco, Tunisia, the Comoro Islands, New-Caledonia, Tahiti, Brazil, Argentina, Lebanon, Japan and United States. Representative offices in U.S.S.R., Mexico, Italia, Iran, Australia, Indonesia, South Africa, Canada. Hong-Kong, Pakistan, Malaysia, Singapore.

**Société Générale Alsacienne de Banque.** *Head Office:* Strasbourg, 4, rue Joseph-Massol (Bas-Rhin).

**Société Lyonnaise de Dépôts & de Crédit Industriel, S.A.** (President, G. Brac de La Perriere.) Est. 1865; Balance Sheet at 31 December 1966 showed assets F.12,817,373,961; total deposits F.12,272,192.524. *Head Office:* 8 Rue de la République, Lyons. 346 Branches.

**Société Marseilles de Crédit.** (President and General Manager, Edouard de Cazalet.) Est. 1865; Balance Sheet at 31 December 1966 showed assets fr.1,722,894,990; deposits, current and other accounts fr.1,523,221,250. *Head Office:* 75 Rue Paradis, Marseilles. 92 Branches.

**Société Nancéienne et Varin-Bernier.** (President, Jean Roquerbe.) Est. 1881; Balance Sheet at 31 December 1973 showed assets F.4,746,811,559·70. *Head Office:* 4 Place André Maginot, Nancy. 166 Branches.

### AGRICULTURE

French farming land (49,908,100 hectares) consists mainly of arable land and grazing land (natural meadows and grassland), the reason for the importance of French crop growing and livestock farming.

Arable land accounts for an area of 16,914,300 hectares, while natural meadows and grasslands account for an area of 13,596,600 hectares.

The following table shows the land usage in France:

| *Type* | *(1000 hectares)* |
|---|---|
| Arable land | 16,914·3 |
| Permanent grassland | 13,596·6 |
| Woods, forests, poplar plantations, osier beds | 14,576·9 |
| Orchards, olive groves, walnut plantations, chestnut plantations | 303·4 |
| Vineyards | 1,310·2 |
| Market and vegetable gardens, flower nurseries | 329·6 |
| Tree nurseries | 18·5 |
| Associated ponds and pools | 118·8 |
| Uncultivated agricultural land | 2,739·8 |
| Total Agricultural Land | 49,908·1 |
| Non-Agricultural Land | 4,999·7 |
| Total area | 54,907·8 |

The following table gives production figures for some agricultural commodities in 100 tonne measures for 1975:

| *Commodity* | *100 tonnes* |
|---|---|
| Soft Wheat | 142,293 |
| Durum Wheat | 7,841 |
| Barley | 93,357 |
| Sweetcorn | 81,636 |
| Rice | 457 |
| New Potatoes | 4,628 |
| Old Potatoes | 57,793 |
| Cauliflowers | 4,599 |
| Artichokes | 1,143 |
| Carrots | 5,181 |
| Melons | 1,540 |
| Salad vegetables | 4,214 |
| Tomatoes | 6,388 |
| Peaches | 1,049 |
| Pears | 3,810 |
| Apples | 19,346 |
| Plums | 258 |
| Cherries | 825 |
| Wine: "appellation d'origine contrôlée" (1,000 hectolitres) | 10,169 |
| Wine: "vin délimité de qualité supérieure" | 2,820 |
| Other Wines | 43,044 |
| Wines suitable for production of brandies | 9,942 |

The following table shows the livestock slaughtered in 1975 in thousands:

| | | | |
|---|---|---|---|
| Beef Cattle | | 4,599·0 | |
| | bulls | | 609·7 |
| | bullocks | | 1,019·7 |
| | cows | | 2,969·6 |
| Veal Cattle | | 3,233·7 | |
| | calves | | 2,054·4 |
| | heifers | | 1,179·3 |
| Pigs | | 15,648·5 | |
| | porkers | | 15,184·4 |
| Sheep | | 7,139·5 | |
| | lambs | | 6,003·5 |
| Goats | | 200·2 | |
| Horses | | 158·4 | |

Livestock producer groups are one of the basic methods of promoting economic organization of this sector of farming, improving production and marketing. In 1974, there were 484 groups in the "livestock rearing and meat production' sector (227 in 1969), and 151 in the poultry sector (123 in 1969).

In addition, rearing contracts for butcher's and breeding animals provide producers with the credit facilities they need and price guarantees.

The following table shows poultry meat production for 1974–75 in 1,000 tonnes:

| | 1974 | 1975 |
|---|---|---|
| | *1,000 tonnes* | |
| Main types of poultry | 631·2 | 628·0 |
| including chickens | 523·1 | 516·2 |
| Other types of bird | 201·9 | 190·9 |
| including ducks | 39·1 | 38·2 |
| turkeys | 117·0 | 105·1 |
| guinea fowl | 33·8 | 35·1 |
| geese | 12·0 | 12·5 |
| Total | 833·1 | 819·9 |

There have been radical technical and economic changes in the production of poultry over the past few years. It is the sector which has adapted most readily to industrialization.

There has been a steady increase in production, with productivity reaching almost its maximum level. In 1975, the output of chicken meat alone exceeded 500,000 tons, while the output of other poultry was 320,000 tons.

France has many breeds of sheep:
Mainly wool-producing: merino wool, i.e. Rambouillet, early Arles lambs and merino wool sheep in the East;
Mainly meat-producing: Ile-de-France, Berrichon du Cher, Southdown and Charmoise; "black head" breeds of English origin such as Suffolk and Hampshire; and grassland breeds such as Texel, Bleu du Maine, Cotentin and Avranchin;
Mainly milk-producing: Lacaune, Bearnaise, Manech and the Corsican breed.

Finally, there are many other local breeds which are particularly well suited to difficult environmental conditions, especially in the Massif Central, Pyrenees and Southern Alps.

For many years now, two foreign breeds have been imported to improve the prolificacy of French breeds: Romanov sheep from Russia, and Finnish sheep.

The number of milk ewes has fallen from 6,012,000 head in 1968 to 5,432,200 in 1975.

**Mining.** The mineral resources of France include iron, potassium, sulphur, and bauxite, which is by far the most important. France's main deficiency is in coal and she is forced to rely on imports to the extent of one-third of her needs. Lorraine is rich in deposits of iron ore, and France is, after the U.S.A. and the Soviet Union, the largest producer of iron in the world.

Production of *Charbonnages de France*, the French coal agency, totalled 31·2 million tons in 1972, a decrease of 3·4 million tons (−9·8 per cent) compared with 1971. The number of miners decreased from 58,819 at the end of 1971 to 51,543 at the end of 1972, a decrease of 12·4 per cent; and the number of surface workers went from 30,680 to 29,196, a decrease of 4·9 per cent. The average yield of miners in 1972 was 2,792 kilograms compared with 2,705 kilograms in 1971, an increase of 3·2 per cent. Total sales of coal by coal mines were estimated at 22·7 million tons, a decrease of 12·4 per cent compared with 1971. Coal covers 25 per cent of French energy needs (excluding petroleum) and coal mined in France accounts for 16 per cent of French needs.

**Industry.** France's industrial production has doubled in the past ten years. France is one of the world's most important industrial countries, with highly developed mechanical engineering, automobile and textile industries.

The following table gives production figures of a few commodities for 1974 in thousands of tonnes:

| *Commodity* | | 1974 |
|---|---|---|
| Iron ore | | 54,264 |
| Pig iron | | 22,512 |
| Crude steel | | 27,012 |
| Sulphuric acid | | 4,688 |
| Paper and cardboard | | 1,986 |
| Private cars | (no. of) | 2,544,491 |

French foreign trade showed a surplus in 1972. Exports totalled 133,482,000 francs and imports 127,906,000 francs. Export figures exceeded import figures by 5,576,000 francs compared with 1971 when the surplus was 1,290,000 francs.

Compared with 1969, the 1970 increase was 18·2 per cent for imports and 27·6 per cent for exports. These figures compared with respective increases of 11·6 per cent and 14·7 per cent in 1971 and 15·2 per cent in 1972. However, the covering rate continued to increase as follows:

1969 93·6%
1970 101·3%
1971 103·8%
1972 104·4%

The following table shows values of imports and exports by countries for 1972 (in millions of francs).

| *Country* | *Imports (c.i.f.)* | *Exports (f.o.b.)* |
|---|---|---|
| Belgium and Luxembourg | 15,442 | 15,014 |
| Germany (Fed. Rep.) | 30,219 | 27,816 |
| Italy | 13,838 | 15,106 |
| Netherlands | 8,391 | 7,166 |
| United Kingdom | 7,061 | 7,180 |
| Denmark | 640 | 1,076 |
| Ireland | 348 | 305 |
| Algeria | 1,702 | 2,382 |
| Australia | 1,202 | 409 |
| Brazil | 1,083 | 951 |
| Canada | 1,135 | 1,338 |
| China | 529 | 301 |
| Czechoslovakia | 316 | 323 |
| Finland | 671 | 566 |
| Germany (Dem. Rep.) | 416 | 703 |
| Greece | 421 | 1,195 |
| India | 363 | 340 |
| Iraq | 1,634 | 373 |
| Iran | 952 | 621 |
| Ivory Coast | 1,084 | 1,147 |
| Japan | 1,855 | 1,157 |
| Kuwait | 1,966 | 193 |
| Lebanon | 90 | 595 |
| Libya | 1,272 | 665 |
| Mexico | 114 | 381 |
| Morocco | 1,254 | 1,237 |
| New Zealand | 407 | 60 |
| Norway | 617 | 802 |
| Poland | 595 | 766 |
| Portugal | 356 | 794 |
| Romania | 447 | 682 |
| Saudi Arabia | 2,711 | 259 |
| Senegal | 676 | 671 |
| South Africa | 646 | 927 |
| Spain | 2,656 | 3,269 |
| Sweden | 2,616 | 1,814 |
| Switzerland | 3,236 | 6,645 |
| Tunisia | 342 | 895 |
| Turkey | 336 | 510 |
| U.S.A. | 11,022 | 6,993 |
| U.S.S.R. | 1,487 | 1,718 |
| Yugoslavia | 473 | 869 |
| **Total** | **135,741** | **131,483** |

**Forestry.** One-fifth of the total area of France is covered with forest, but the country's need for timber still exceeds production. Under a government re-afforestation plan, however, it is hoped that the State will not only be able to supply all home needs in future, but will have a surplus for export. Ownership of forest lands is divided as follows:

| | *Hectares* |
|---|---|
| State | 1,668,900 |
| Departments, Communes and public organizations | 2,523,500 |
| Private individuals and companies | 8,567,600 |

## COMMUNICATIONS

**Railways.** The Société Nationale des Chemins de Fer (S.N.C.F.) has control over the railways and in January 1969 employed a staff of 319,000. Annual traffic on the railways is some 67,700 million ton-kilometres of goods.

The S.N.C.F. was set up in 1938. It is not a State service but a limited company in which the state is the biggest share-holder.

Since the end of the war an intensive modernization programme has been in effect—the replacement of steam by electric and diesel locomotives. By the end of 1969, 9,500 km. of track (i.e. 25 per cent of the system carrying 75 per cent of the traffic) had been electrified.

The express services are reputed to be the fastest in the world. Running time from Paris to Marseilles in 1965 was 7 hours, 10 minutes.

France is at present experimenting with a new means of transport—the 'aerotrain' invented by the French engineer Bertin. This vehicle which glides on an air cushion along a single track of concrete is expected to reach speeds of up to 250 mp.h. Experiments with an 80 passenger model have been carried out on a special 12 mile track out of Orleans towards Paris.

The French railways had a record year in 1972. Passenger traffic, totalling 43·2 thousand million passenger-kilometres (635 million passengers), increased by 5 per cent compared with 1971. The increase was especially high in traffic on high-speed and express trains (6 per cent) and on trains servicing the Paris suburbs (6·9 per cent). However, traffic on slow trains continued to decrease (−4·7 per cent compared with 1971).

Freight traffic totalling 68·4 thousand million ton-kilometres, increased by only 2 per cent compared with 1971. The drop in coal transport was quite high (−18 per cent). The leading industrial products which increased were: motor vehicles (+18 per cent); building materials (+5·7 per cent); ores (+3·4 per cent); chemical products (+4·5 per cent). The increase for agricultural products was quite high: cereals (+ 9 per cent), fruit and vegetables (+7 per cent).

**Shipping.** The French Commercial fleet consisted of 510 ships at the end of 1972 as follows: 24 passenger liners; 35 freighters; 128 tankers.

The principal passenger ports are Calais, Dieppe, Marseilles, Boulogne, Dunkirk, Le Havre and Cherbourg; the principal freight ports are Le Havre, Marseilles, Rouen, Bordeaux and Nantes-St. Nazaire. The total of goods loaded and unloaded in 1968 amounted to 33,316,000 tons and 136,350,000 tons respectively.

The following are the principal shipping lines:

**Compagnie Fabre-Société Générale de Transports Maritimes**; (President, Pierre C. Fabre); share capital fr. 60,892,200; motor vessels 8, and many chartered ships; total tonnage 58,536 T.D.W.; *services operated:* from Marseilles and West Mediterranean ports to Morocco ports, West Africa Coast (SNCDV) lines). French West Indies and Guyana, South Africa and Far East (CMCR lines). *Head Office:* 70–72 rue de la République,Marseil les (2e), France. Phone (91) 91 90 30. Telex 44 0905.

**Compagnie de Navigation Mixte**; (Chairman, Gérard de Cazalet); share capital fr. 15,000,000; motor vessels 4, steam vessels 4; total tonnage 38,111; *services operated:* passenger and merchant between France and North Africa and Balearic Islands. *Head Office:* 1 La Canebière, Marseilles, France.

**Compagnie des Messageries Maritimes**; (President, Roger Carour); share capital fr. 40,000,000 (the majority owned by the state); motor vessels 34, total tonnage 385,900; *services operated:* From Europe to French Somaliland — Ceylon — India — Pakistan — Bangla Desh — Malaysia — Singapore — Thailand — Indonesia — Viet Nam — Cambodia — Philippines — Hong Kong — Taiwan — Korea — Japan — Tahiti — New Caledonia — Australia — New Hebrides — New Zealand — East Africa — Madagascar — Reunion — Mauritius — South Africa — Brazil — Uruguay — Argentina. *Head Office:* 12 Boulevard de la Madeleine, Paris 9, France.

**Compagnie Maritime des Chargeurs Réunis**; (Chairman, Francis C. Fabre); share capital fr. 133,231,950; vessels 39; total tonnage 330,070 dead weight; *services operated:* South Africa, Far East — U.S.A. — West Africa — Far East — West Africa. *Head Office:* 3 Boulevard Males-herbes, Paris 8e, France.

**Maritime Compagnie Générale**; (Chairman, Jacques Friedmann); share capital NF. 130,616,265; steam and motor vessels 77; total tonnage 1,770,000 gross r.t.; *services operated: Container services:* to the U.S. East Coast and Canada (within Atlantic Container Line ACL), to the West Coast of North America (within Europacific), to the South

East Asia and the Far East (within ScanDutch), to the Australia and New Zealand (within the Australia New Zealand Europe Container Service ANZECS), to the Middle East, North Africa and Corsica within its affiliated Sudcargos, to the Caribbean (within Caribbean overseas Line CAROL), to the South Africa (within South Africa Europe Container Service SAECS), *Conventional deep sea services:* to the Caribbean, Central America, Southern America, East Africa, the Indian Continent and Pacific Islands. *And a number of short sea services:* in the Mediterranean, North Sea and Baltic by roll-on/roll-off. *Head Office:* Tour Winterthur, 102 Quartier Boieldieu, Cedex 18, 92085, PARIS LA DEFENSE.

**Société Navale Delmas-Vieljeux**; (Chairman, Tristan Vieljeux; Assistant Managing Director, Patrice Vieljeux); share capital fr. 35,000,000; motor vessels 15, steam vessels 9; total tonnage 170,950 T.D.W.; *services operated:* Hamburg—Rotterdam — Antwerp — Dunkirk — La Havre — Bordeaux and West African ports; Hamburg, Copenhagen, Rotterdam, Antwerp and Red Sea ports and East Africa. *Head Office:* 29 Rue Galilée, Paris 16e, France. *Branch Offices* and *Agencies:* **Dunkirk:** Société Navale Delmas Vieleux, 8 place de l'Yser; **Le Havre:** Société Navale Delmas Vieljeux, P.O. Box 98; **Rouen:** Société Navale Delmas Vieljeuc, 4 rue du Bac; **La Rochelle-Pallice:** Société Navale Delmas Vieljeux, P.O. Box 45; **Bordeaux:** Société Navale Delmas Vieljeux, 15 quai Louis XVIII; **Dakar:** Union Senegalaise d'Industries Maritimes, P.O. Box 164; **Kaolack:** Union Senegalaise d'Industries Maritimes, P.O. Box 144; **Ziguinchor:** Union Senegalaise d'Industries Maritimes; **Sassandra:** Société Navale Delmas Vieljeux; **Abidjan:** Société Navale Delmas Vieljeux, P.O. Box 1281; **Cotonou:** Société Navale Delmas Vieljeux, P.O. Box 213; **Douala:** Société Navale Delmas Vieljeux, P.O. Box 263; **Kribi:** S.A. de Transports et d'Acconage de Kribi, P.O. Box 18; **Libreville:** Société Navale Delmas Vieljeux, P.O. Box 77; **Port-Gentil:** Société Navale Delmas Vieljeux, P.O. 522; **Pointe-Noire:** Société Navale Delmas Vieljeux, P.O. Box 679.

### Civil Aviation

**Air France**; (President, Pierre Giraudet); share capita fr. 1,761,200,000; *services operated:* Paris to chief capitals of Europe, U.S.A., Canada, West Indies, South America, Far East and French Africa. *Head Office:* 1 Square Max Hymans, Paris 15, France.

**Compagnie Air Transport**; (President, L. J. Ottensooser); share capital fr. 3,500,000; *services operated:* Le Touquet—Lydd (Ferryfield), Calais—Southend, Cherbourg—Hurn. These routes are operated jointly with British United Air Ferries (formerly 'Silver City Airways Ltd.' and 'Channel Air Bridge'). *Head Office:* 5 Avenue Hoche, Paris 8e, France.

**U.T.A.—Union de Transports Aériens.** (President, Francis C. Fabre.) A French private company incorporated in France. Capital fr. 68,934,950; *services operated:* Paris to West, Central, Equatorial and Southern Africa, Far East, Australia, the Pacific area and the West Coast of the U.S.A.

U.T.A. carried 625,991 passengers and 51,426 tons of freight during 1974. Its network has a total length of 258,000 km and it serves 40 countries. The jet fleet comprises 10 DC.8s and 4 DC.10s series 30.

**Posts, Telegraphs and Telephones.** Telephone subscribers in 1966 numbered 3,150,853. In 1966 there were about 56,114 km. of long-distance cables and over 13,000 post offices. There were 4,774 million letters and 250·9 million packages carried in 1966.

## NEWSPAPERS

**L'Aurore.** F. 1944. Anti-communist. Circulation 500,000. Director: Madame Francine Lazurick. Editors-in-chief: Gilbert Guilleminault, Dominique Pado, José Van den Esch, Roland Faure. *Address:* 100 rue de Richelieu, Paris 2.

**France-Soir.** F. 1941 as Defence de la France. Circulation 633,000. *Address:* 100 rue Réaumur, Paris 2.

**Paris-Jour.** F. 1959. Morning. Independent. Circulation 302,400. *Address:* 37 Rue de Louvre, Paris.

**Le Figaro.** F. 1826. Morning. Independent. Circulation 500,000. *Address:* 14 Rond-Point des Champs-Elysées, Paris 8.

**L'Humanité.** F. 1904. Morning. Communist. Director Etienne Fajon. *Address:* 6 Boulevard Poissonière, Paris 9. Code Postal 75440, Paris Cedex 09.

**Paris-Presse L'Intransigeant.** F. 1944. Evening. Circulation 300,000. *Address:* 37 rue du Louvre.

**Le Parisien.** F. 1944. Morning. Circulation 900,000. *Address:* 124 rue Réaumur, 75 080 Paris, Cedex 02.

**Le Monde.** F. 1944. Evening. Circulation 431,536. *Address* 5 rue des Italiens 75427 Paris Cedex 09.

## EDUCATION

Education is compulsory from the age of six to 16 years, and is provided either by the free and non-sectarian schools controlled by the State (approximately four-fifths of the total school population), or by private schools either completely independent or helped in some measures by the State. The school leaving age was raised to 16 in 1967. There are, roughly, 9,500 infant schools for children under six years and 63,000 elementary schools for children from 6 to 11 years. To provide a teaching stafi in primary schools the state trains some 43,000 teachers of both sexes in training colleges in the various departments. It is compulsory for each department to provide at least two training colleges for this purpose, one for men and one for women.

Secondary education is also free and compulsory from 11 to 16 years of age, without any entrance examination. Children can choose between three different sections with a common programme but different teaching methods. At 15 they opt either for long studies: three years leading to baccalauréat and access to higher education; or short studies: (a) either one year intensive practical training, (b) or two years in technical colleges leading to industrial, commercial or administrative formation, (c) or three years' apprenticeship with 300 hours yearly at school. For the lower secondary cycle (11–15 years of age) the *lycées* and *collèges d'enseignement général* are rapidly being replaced by *collèges d'enseignement secondaire* which will, in 1975, be the sole establishments for children of this age. Lycées will continue only for the long High Secondary cycle leading to the baccalauréat.

Teachers in secondary schools must possess:

1. In the first cycle a diploma obtained after 2 year's university studies plus a teaching certificate: the CAPCEG.
2. In the 2nd cycle a masters' degree plus a teaching certificate: the CAPES.
3. In technical colleges, various technical qualifications plus a teaching certificate: the CAPET.

The following table gives the number of pupils in State Schools, 1973–74:

| | |
|---|---|
| Pre-schools | 1,891,000 |
| Elementary | 4,022,000 |
| Lower Secondary cycle | 2,564,000 |
| Higher Secondary cycle (long) | 741,000 |
| Higher Secondary cycle (short) | 552,000 |
| Specialized education | 73,000 |
| Apprenticeship | 77,000 |
| Total | 9,920,000 |

To this number must be added over 2,000,000 children in private education.

Higher Education in France is practically free (apart from examination and library fees), and open to all students, French and foreign, who can justify the baccalauréat or a foreign title admitted as equivalent. The total of students in universities, *Grandes Ecoles et Ecoles Normales* is over 750,000.

Lecturers in universities must have obtained an 'agrégation' and Heads of Department a Doctorat d'Etat.

The universities of France are of ancient foundation. The University de Paris à la Sorbonne, for example, was founded in 1253; the University de Montpellier, with its famous Faculty of Medicine, in 1289; the University de Toulouse, noted for its studies in Spanish Literature and history, in 1229. Altogether there are now 90 universities and university centres in France. On the same level but with a highly competitive entrance examination are the Grandes Ecoles such as the Polytechnique, the Ecole Normale Supérieure and Ecole Centrale, which receives the elite of the French students.

## ATOMIC ENERGY

The French Atomic Energy Commission (C.E.A.) is responsible for research development and the production of fissile materials. Its costs, which have trebled since 1959, amount to about 4·5 per cent of the national budget.

French uranium production in 1957 was 400 tons, and had risen to almost 1,925 by 1970. Three principal deposits which are workable have been discovered in La Vendée, Limousin and Le Forez, and the plant has been installed.

Reserves of uranium in France at 1 July 1970 were estimated at 51,600 tons compared with 54,200 tons six months earlier. The C.E.A. is participating in uranium mining in Gabon and Madagascar, and is prospecting on the Niger and in the Central African Republic.

A centre for processing natural uranium into plutonium and then into uranium 235 has been completed at Marcoule. Now constructed are an isotope separation plant at Pierrelatte, this plant produces very highly enriched uranium 235); and a plutonium extraction plant at La Hague.

There are numerous nuclear electricity-producing power plants planned. Some are designed to study the application of foreign and new techniques. The Franco-Belgian power station at Chooz, built with Euratom assistance, will use the American enriched uranium process; the plant at Brennilis is heavy water moderated, thus permitting a saving of uranium. Others will use the natural uranium-graphite-carbon dioxide gas system. These comprise three stations at Chinon. The three Chinon reactors are of these ratings for nett power output: Chinon I, 68,000 kW, Chinon II, 170,000 kW, Chinon III, 375,000 kW. Another (480,000 kW) is at Saint-Laurent-des-Eaux and the last (500,000 kW) is at Saint-Vulbas.

In 1967, nuclear power stations produced 2,560 million kWh. By 1972 the production of nuclear electricity should have reached 5 per cent of the total production.

In February 1971 it was decided to build three new 850,000 kW nuclear power stations, and the work was to be put in hand over the next two years. A decision in principle was also taken to build about another six nuclear power stations, so that the total power production envisaged will be almost 8 million kW.

### RELIGION

France is mainly Roman Catholic, with not more than about a million Protestants. Neither Catholics nor Protestants, however, are in any way associated with the State, which by a law of 1905, separated itself entirely from the Church.

# Overseas Departments

## FRENCH GUIANA

## (*La Guyane*)

**Prefect**: Jean Le Direach.

The territory of French Guiana is situated on the North-East coast of South America. Previously a colony, its status was changed to that of an overseas Department on 19 March 1946. It is administered by a Prefect and an elected Council of 12 members. It is represented in the National Assembly, the Council of the Republic and the Assembly of the French Union by one Deputy in each.

It has an area of about 34,000 sq. miles; The population is approximately 60,000. The chief town is Cayenne (population 25,000).

Guiana is an agricultural country but it is short of farmers. Guiana has 32,000 sq. miles of forest, 1,000 sq. miles suitable for grazing and the same for agriculture. The forests are therefore the largest potential source of wealth, and various timber industries are to be developed: wood peeling, veneering, panelling, cellulose, paper pulp. In 1969 58,040 logs were felled and stripped for export.

Cayenne is a port of call for airliners of Pan American Airways on the service from Buenos Aires to New York. There is also a service of Air France connecting with Trinidad and Martinique.

The few exports (gold, timber and rum) do not cover more than 7 per cent of imports, the latter extending to all the necessities of life and exceeding 80 million francs.

Attempts to diversify crops are impeded by the narrow limits of the home market. However, forest activities are being developed, as well as plantations of rice, sugar-cane, pineapples and cocoa, livestock breeding and especially fisheries, mainly shrimps.

Since 1965, one company has been operating 40 trawlers and has its own dockyard, its cold store, and its units for treating shrimps 15 km. from Cayenne. 98 per cent of the fisheries' output is exported to the United States.

The building of a space centre at Kourou was no doubt the most important event in the history of Guiana. This centre is particularly suitable for putting synchronous or stationary satellites in orbit, an advantage in space telecommunications, and the *Centre National d'Etudes Spatiales* (CNES—National Centre of Space Studies) allows the space organizations of the countries wishing to do so to make use of its exceptional advantages. Kourou was the equatorial launching site for the European rockets designed by Eldo. 250,000 acres of savanna have been developed (approaches, ancillary installations, firing sites, and technical and administrative installations for a staff of 3,000).

The actual firing zone consists of four areas. The east end, six miles from Kourou, is reserved for probe-rocket launchings and was opened in April 1968 with the launching of the scientific rocket *Véronique*. Next comes the *Diamant* area, opened in March 1970 with the launching of the German satellite *Dial* on a *Diamant B* rocket. Further west is the area for heavy boosters. The centre is now working on the *Ariane* (European launcher) project.

A second company, established at the mouth of the Maroni, fishes and processes prawns in the same conditions. Investment prospects are expected in this sector in the coming years.

Guiana has a variety of mineral resources, including gold, (mined since the nineteenth century), tantalite, bauxite, etc. Industrial activities are on a small scale, owing chiefly to the shortage of manpower, but efforts to develop local processing industries (forest products, pineapples, rum) are meeting with some success and a start has been made on light engineering manufactures for export.

A space centre at Kourou was completed. It is the only rocket range in the world where both polar and equatorial orbits can be obtained.

### EDUCATION

98 per cent of school-age children attend classes. There are 43 primary schools, 4 secondary schools including 1 lycée, 2 technical schools of secondary level, and 8 private schools. In higher education, only law courses are being offered so far, which prepare students for the first year of the 'licence' degree.

## GUADELOUPE AND ITS ISLANDS

**Prefect**: M. J. Le Cornel.

The Department of Guadeloupe, situated in the West Indies, consists of two large islands, Guadeloupe (chief town La Basse Terre) and Grand Terre (chief town Pointe-à-Pitre), and five smaller islands—Marie Galante, Les Saintes, Désirade, St. Barthélemy and St. Martin. Its status was changed from that of a colony to an overseas Department on 19 March 1946. The administration is in the hands of a Prefect and an elected Council of 36 members. Guadeloupe sends three Deputies to the National Assembly, two Senators and one Councillor to the Economic Council.

Justice is administered by a Court of Appeal, an Assize Court and a Court of First Instance at Basse Terre and a Court of First Instance at Pointe-à-Pitre.

The Department has an area of 656 square miles, the population is approximately 334,000. The chief towns, with populations, are Pointe-à-Pitre 29,522, Basse-Terre 15,690, Moule 16,111. The chief crops are sugar and bananas. Exports are almost entirely to the French Union.

There are direct steamship lines between Guadeloupe and France and the United States. Air services are provided by Air France to Paris via New York and by P.A.A. to New York.

**BANKS**

**Banque des Antilles Françaises** (Formerly Banque de la Guadeloupe). (Manager, D. Labbe.) Head Office in Paris. Branch in Pointe-à-Pitre; Agencies Bass Terre and Saint Martin.

**Credit Guadeloupeen S.A.** (Président, G. Beuzelin.) Est.1926; Balance Sheet at 31 December 1973 showed assets fr. 169,057,445·29; deposits and current accounts fr. 126,593,775·27. *Head Office:* 28 Rue Achille René-Boisneuf, Pointe-à-Pitre. 1 Branch.

**Banque Antillaise.** (President, Cherdieu D'Alexis.)

**Banque des Antilles Françaises.** (Chairman, Claude Rispal.) *Head Office:* See Guadelope and Martinique (General Manager, Clause Garcin).

**Banque Nationale de Paris.** (Director, M. Dubois.) *Head Office:* Pointe-à-Pitre, 22 rue A. René-Boisneuf.

**Banque Royale du Canada.** (Manager, J. C. Paradis.) *Head Office:* 30 rue Frébault, Point-a-Pitre, Guadeloupe.

**Banque des Antilles Françaises.** (President, Cherdieu V. Alexis.) 21 rue Gambetta. *Head Office:* Pointe-à-Pitre.

**Credit Agricole Mutuel.** (Director, S. Laboisiere.) *Head Office:* Pointe-à-Pitre, Rue Gouverneur Général Felix Eboué (prolongée).

## MARTINIQUE

Prefect: Paul Noirot-Cosson.

The status of Martinique, a large island in the West Indies, was changed from that of a colony to a Department of France on 19 March 1946. It is administered by a Prefect and an elected Council. Martinique sends three Deputies to the National Assembly, two Councillors to the Council of the Republic and one delegate to the Assembly of the French Union.

Justice is administered by a Court of Appeal, a Court of Assize, a Commercial Court and a Court of First Instance. These are situated at Fort-de-France. There are five justices of the peace in the principal communities of the island.

The total area is 386 square miles; population (1967) was 320,000; the chief town and port is Fort-de-France with a population of 110,000. The chief crops are sugar and bananas, and a substantial area is devoted to the production of food for local consumption.

Fort-de-France is a regular port of call for French and American steamers. There is a direct air service to Paris by Air France.

**BANKS**

**Banque des Antilles Françaises.** (Banque de la Guadeloupe, de la Martinique et l'Union-Bank réunies.) (President: Andre Gaverioux.) Branches in Guadeloupe, Pointe-à-Pitre, Basse, Terre, also in Martinique (Fort de France) and in Saint Martin (Marigot).

**Credit Martiniquais, S.A.** (Managing-Chairman, André Garcin.) Est. 1922; Balance Sheet at 31 December 1966 showed assets fr. 144,307,730; deposits and current accounts fr. 133,548,182. *Head Office:* Fort-de-France, Martinique, French West Indies. 3 Branches.

## REUNION ISLAND

*(Île de la Réunion)*

Prefect: Bernard Landouzy.

La Réunion, or Bourbon, is an island in the Indian Ocean, 420 miles east of Madagascar. It has belonged to France since 1645 and its status was changed from that of a colony to an overseas Department on 19 March 1946. It is administered by a Prefect and an elected Council. It is represented in the National Assembly by three Deputies, in the Senate by two Councillors, and in the Conseil Economique by two delegates.

The area of La Réunion is approximately 251,000 hectares; population 570,000. The chief town is St. Denis with a population of 85,444. Other towns are St. Paul (43,128) and St. Pierre (40,355).

**BANK**

**Banque de la Réunion.** (President, R. de la Fortelle.) **Est.** 1849; Capital fr. C.F.A. 200,000,000. *Head Office:* 15 Rue Jean Chate St. Denis, La Réunion. *Branch:* St. Pierre, La Réunion.

## SAINT-PIERRE AND MIQUELON

Prefect: Pierre Eydoux.

The archipelago of Saint-Pierre and Miquelon, situated off the south coast of Newfoundland, comprises three main islands: Saint-Pierre, Langlade, and Miquelon. The last two have in fact been united during the last 75 years by a low sandy isthmus. There are also about a dozen small islets.

The Department is represented in the French Parliament by one Deputy and one Senator, both elected.

The General Council, composed of 14 elected members, is responsible for local finances and certain statutory matters concerning the management of territorial affairs.

On the local level, the Department is divided into two communes: the commune of Saint Pierre, which includes Ile aux Marins; and the commune of Miquelon-Langlade. Elected municipal councils administer both communes.

The economy is based on fishing and, to a lesser extent, on the raising of fur-bearing animals and tourism. Agriculture, which is limited to vegetables, does not meet domestic needs. The total area is 42 sq. kilometres with a population of 5,840 (1965).

The greater part of Saint-Pierre Miquelon imports come from Canada.

**BANK**

**Banque des Îles Saint-Pierre et Miquelon S.A.** (Manager. G. Roulet.) Est. 1889; Balance Sheet at 31 December 1974 showed assets fr. 18,165,105, deposits fr. 15,270,136. *Head Office:* Saint-Pierre, La Réunion.

# Overseas Territories

The status of the Overseas Territories is regulated by Articles 72–76 of the New Constitution of 1958. In each territory there is a repre sentative of the French Goverement, the Governor or High Commissioner, who is the trustee of the powers of the Republic. He is the head of the administration of the territory, and is responsible for his actions to the Government. There is an elected assembly in each territory.

The French Overseas Territories now consist of the following: Territory of Afars and Issas, Comoro Islands, St. Pierre and Miquelon, New Caledonia, Polynesia, and the Pacific Islands of Wallis and Futuna. At the end of 1959, the islands as the result of a referendum became an integral part of the French Republic with the status of an Overseas Territory.

The French Southern and Antarctic regions are in a special category. They consist of the Islands of Saint Paul and New Amsterdam, the Kerguelen and Crozet Archipelagos and the Adelie Lands. The resources of the territories have not yet been much exploited. The Kerguelen archipelago has agricultural possibilities. From a very small number of wild sheep, native to the islands, 500 head have been raised since 1954. The scientific stations of the territories made important contributions to the work of the geophysical year.

## POLYNESIA

**Capital**—Papeete (Tahiti).

**Governor**: Charles Schmitt.

French Polynesia (French Settlements in Oceania) comprises a large number of islands scattered over the Eastern Pacific, grouped together for administrative purposes as follows:

1. Society Islands, comprising two groups, the Windward Islands (Îles du Vent) and Leeward Islands (Îles-sous-le-Vent). The chief of the Windward Islands is Tahiti (1,042 sq. km.); other islands are Moorea (132 sq. km.), Tetiaroa, Maiao-Iti and Mehetia. The Leeward Islands comprise Huahine, Raïatea, Tahaa, Borabora, Motu-Iti, Maupiti, Mopélia, Bellingshausen and Scilly and have a population of about 12,000.
2. Tuamotu Islands comprising 56 islands, with a total area of 800 sq. km., lying to the east of Tahiti and with a population of 5,127.
3. Gambier Islands lying to the south-east of Tuamotu comprising four islands and a score of islets of no importance. They have an area of 185 sq. km. and a population of 1,569. The chief town is Rikitea on the island of Mangoreva.
4. Marquesas Islands, discovered by the Spanish navigator Mendana de Nyra in 1595. He named the islands Marquesas in honour of the Marquesa de Mendoza, wife of the Viceroy of Peru. There are eleven islands of which the chief is Nuku-Hiva. The total population is about 2,000.
5. Tubuaï or Austral Islands lying to the south-east of Tahiti. They comprise Rurutu (1,174), Tubuaï (1,006), Rimatara (695), Raïvavaé and Rapu-Iti (298).
6. Clipperton Islands, the most easterly of the French possessions in the Pacific, is an atoll comprising two islands, L'Île de l'Est and L'Île de l'Ouest. The total area is only 750 nectares.

In 1965 the population was 85,000.
The chief town, Papeete, had a population of 12,428.

The territory is administered by a governor who resides at Papeete, seat of the local assembly of 20 members. The islands of the archipelago as a whole are divided into Districts which have elected native chiefs at their head. French Overseas administrators are responsible for the general administration of the area.

In Polynesia, copra, coffee and vanilla are exported. While the working of the phosphate mines is on the point of ending, the production of mother-of-pearl is holding its ground.

The unit of currency is the fr. C.F.P. (franc de la Communauté Française du Pacifique), which is worth 5·5 metropolitan francs.

## NEW CALEDONIA AND DEPENDENCIES

### (*Nouvelle Calédonie et Dépendances*)

**Capital**—Noumea.

**High Commissioner**: M. Jean Gabriel Eriau.

New Caledonia is an island some 240 miles long by almost 40 miles wide, situated in the South Pacific 700 miles east of Queensland. The territory also includes a number of groups of small islands, the chief of which are the Loyalty Islands. It is administered by a High Commisioner resident at Noumea. He is assisted by a Territorial Assembly, which is elected by universal franchise and which appoints a council of government. The territory is represented in the French Parliament by one Senator and one Deputy.

French justice is administered. There are a Court of Appeal at Noumea, an Assize Court and a Court of First Instance as well as Justices of the Peace.

The whole territory has an area of approximately 19,000 sq. kilometres and a population (April 1976) of 133,233 made up of 55,598 Melanesians, 50,757 Europeans, 15,907 Wallisians and Tahitians and 10,910 Vietnamese, Indonesians and Chinese. 50 per cent of the population live in Noumea and its environs.

Exports were valued at 25,500 million CFP in 1975 and 26,200 million CFP in 1976. New Caledonia's only natural wealth is mineral. The economy is entirely based on the export of nickel mattes, ferro-nickel and nickel ore. Exports of mineral products accounted for over 96 per cent of exports in 1974. Exports of iron-ore ceased during 1969. New Caledonia had been undergoing an economic boom until 1971 but exports of nickel ore were then reduced because of the world over-supply of nickel. There have been continuing delays in proposed new nickel projects. The only nickel metal producer, Société Le Nickel, had to obtain State aid in 1974. Agriculturally the Territory is poor. Small quantities of subsidized coffee and copra are exported but the beef cattle population of just over 85,000 no longer meets the Territory's needs. The number of tourist entries in 1976 was 34,983.

The following table shows values (in millions of francs CFP) of principal exports for 1975 and 1976:

| *Commodity* | 1975 | 1976 |
|---|---|---|
| Nickel-ore | 4,819 | 6,495 |
| Refined nickel metals | 17,261 | 18,330 |
| Coffee and Trocas | 1,204 | 1,308 |

The cost of living index rose slowly during 1976, the index for December 1976 being only 6·4 per cent higher than at the beginning of the year.

Imports were valued at 27,049 million CFP in 1975 and 24,200 million in CFP 1976. The value of imports from France dropped from 11,396 million CFP in 1975 to 9,370 million CFP in 1976. Australia's exports to New Caledonia over the same period were valued at 2,597 million CFP in 1975 increasing to 3,164 million CFP in 1976.

The following table shows values (in millions of francs CFP) of principal imports for 1975 and 1976:

| *Commodity* | 1975 | 1976 |
|---|---|---|
| Foodstuffs | 5,139 | 5,172 |
| Mineral Products | 6,106 | 6,231 |
| Textiles | 1,400 | 1,116 |
| Metals and Metal Products | 1,951 | 1,466 |
| Machinery and Electrical | 3,422 | 2,704 |
| Transport Equipment | 2,928 | 2,260 |

The principal suppliers of the territory were:

| *Country* | 1976 |
|---|---|
| France | 38·8% |
| Australia | 13·1% |
| E.E.C. | 11·0% |
| United States | 4·4% |

A new satellite earth receiving/transmitting station became operational at Nouville (Novméa) at the end of July 1976. The facility has substantially improved international communications between New Caledonia, Europe, Australia, and New Zealand.

# WALLIS AND FUTUNA

## (*Pacific*)

**Chief Administrator:** Henri Beaux.

On 27 December 1959 the Pacific islands of Wallis and Futuna elected by referendum to become an integral part of the French Republic with the status of an Overseas Territory of the Republic. The final results of the referendum were as follows: *Wallis*, votes cast 2,261, in favour 2,261. *Futuna*, 1,148, in favour 888. The nationals of Wallis and Futuna living in New Caledonia and New Hebrides also voted, the electors in New Caledonia casting 929 votes with 925 in favour; those living in New Hebrides casting 238 votes with 233 in favour.

Wallis numbers 5,380 inhabitants and Futuna about 3,000 of Melanesian origin.

**Commerce and Industry.** The principal cash crop of the Islands is copra, but an attempt is being made to add pepper, coffee and stockfarming. The chief food crops of the islands are taro, yams, cassava, bananas and arrowroot. The most common domestic animals are pigs though poultry is raised in abundance. Fishing is practised throughout the Islands; trochus is one of the principal resources, about 10 metric tons are exported each year.

**Communications.** Sea communications are provided by coastal vessels and cargo steamers. The territory has several seaplane bases and two airports. There is a principal road that goes all around Wallis Island and several interior roads are suitable for automobile traffic.

**Education.** Education is provided by the missionaries. Educational facilities include a school in Mata-Utu. The French government pays a subsidy to the missionaries for education, in particular for the development of technical training.

# ANTARCTIC AND SUBANTARCTIC LANDS

## (*Territoire des Terres Australes et Antarctiques Françaises*)

**Chief Administrator:** Yves Gibeat.

At the southern extremity of the Indian Ocean, France possesses a number of islands that are grouped, together with the French portion of the Antarctic continent, into one administrative framework. These territories have been given the overall name of *Territoire des Terres Australes et Antarctiques Françaises*.

These lands, which are more than 15,000 kilometres away from France, have in common their antarctic and subantarctic fauna, the fact that they were uninhabited until very recent times, and their extremely limited economic activity. But since the end of the second world war, they have served as a base for scientific activities. France exercises full sovereignty over the Southern Islands, while, as concerns the lands forming part of a the Antarctic continent itself, she has accepted the terms of the Washington Treaty of the Antarctic. The islands and territory involved are:

### SAINT-PAUL AND AMSTERDAM

Saint-Paul, situated at 38°S. lat. and 77°E. long. is a small island of about seven sq. kilometres. Amsterdam lies at 37°S. lat. and 70°E. long. It, like Saint-Paul, is a volcanic island. The central peak of its volcanic cone is Mont Dives (881 m.).

### THE CROZET ARCHIPELAGO

This archipelago is formed by two groups of islands, some 100 km. apart, between 50 and 53°E. long. and at 46° lat.

### KERGUELEN

Kerguelen consists of one large island, called Grande Tene, closely surrounded by 85 smaller islands, and countless islets and rocks. Grand Terre has an area of 6,675 sq. kilometres. The groups total area is 7,215 sq. kilometres. Kerguelen is situated at a mean latitude of 49° 15′, its mean longitude is 69° 30′.

### TERRE ADÉLIE

The French Antarctic territory is a narrow section of a circle covering some 432,000 sq. kilometres of that continent. In the absence of natural frontiers, it can only be determined by reference to the order of 1 April 1938, whereby 'The islands and territories situated south of the 60th Parallel of latitude and between the 136th and 142nd meridians east of Greenwich are under French Sovereignty'.

# Gabon

(MEMBER OF FRENCH MONETARY ZONE)

**Capital**—Libreville.

**President**—Omar Bongo.

**National flag:** Three horizontal stripes, green, yellow and blue.

### CONSTITUTION AND GOVERNMENT

GABON, a former part of the French territory of Equatorial Africa became independent on 17 August 1960.

Executive power rests with the President, elected by universal suffrage for a seven-year term. He names cabinet ministers and takes special powers in times of 'grave danger or menace to the country'. There is an elected National Assembly of 47 members. Their term is seven years.

### AREA AND POPULATION

The area of the country is 267,000 square kilometres. The population of Gabon at mid-1974 was 528,000. The annual average percentage growth rate of the population for the period 1960–74 was 1·2 and for the period 1965–74 was 1·5. Principal towns are Libreville and Port-Gentil.

### FINANCE

The GNP at market prices for 1974 was U.S. $millions 1,030, and the GNP per capita at market prices was U.S. $1,960. The annual average percentage growth rate of the GNP per capita for the period 1960–74 was 4·7, and for the period 1965–74 was 6·4. [*See the note at the beginning of this section oncerning GNP.*]

### PRODUCTION, INDUSTRY AND COMMERCE

Food production, mainly manioc and bananas, is insufficient for local needs. Forests cover half of the country and Gabon is an important producer of bark. Minerals are the country's most important resource. In 1971 the following commodities (among others) were produced: Manganese, 1,900,000 tons; Petrol, 5,784,766 tons; Uranium, 1,400 tons. Industrial plant consists of sawmills, a petroleum refinery, a brewery, a cement factory and a textile complex, a flour mill and a refinery for uranium.

In 1971 a five-year plan, designed to take important steps towards the achievement of Gabon's full economic potential, was introduced. Completion is scheduled for 1975.

Principal imports are: machinery, consumer goods, and food.

Principal exports are: wood, crude petroleum, uranium, manganese and gold.

### COMMUNICATIONS

There are about 4,500 km. of roads, of which a fourth are national routes. The number of motor vehicles in use is estimated to exceed 8,000. Libreville and Port Gentil are the main ports. River traffic is very important for the transport of raw materials. At the main airports landings and take-offs amount to approximately 60,000 annually.

### EDUCATION AND RELIGION

In 1968 there were 647 primary schools, 10 secondary schools and 22 technical schools. There were 85,000 pupils at primary schools and 5,200 at lycées and colleges.

45 per cent of the population is Roman Catholic, 10 per cent are Protestant and 0·5 per cent are Muslims.

# The Republic of The Gambia

(MEMBER OF THE COMMONWEALTH)

**Capital**—Bathurst.

**President**—H.E. Sir Dawda Kairaba Jawara, KtB.

### CONSTITUTION AND GOVERNMENT

THE Gambia is one of the great rivers of West Africa which flows into the Atlantic Ocean through a large estuary, measuring at its entry into the sea nearly eight miles across. The Gambia extends for 300 miles on both banks of the river from its mouth.

The Gambia became a Republic on 24 April 1970, with Sir Dawda Jawara as its first President, Head of State and Commander-in-Chief of the Armed Forces.

The executive power of the Republic is vested in the President subject to the provisions of the Constitution.

The result of a general election held in March 1972 was as follows: People's Progressive Party, 28; United Party, 3; Independents, 1.

#### Ministry

*President:* H.E. Sir Dawda Kairaba Jawara, KtB.
*Vice-President and Minister of External Affairs:* Andrew David Camara.
*Minister for Local Government, Lands and Mines:* Alhaji Yaya Ceesay.
*Minister of Agriculture and Natural Resources:* Alhaji Alieu Badara N'Jie.
*Minister of Health and Labour:* Alhaji Kalilou Singhateh.
*Attorney-General:* Mohamadu Lamin Saho.
*Minister of Works and Communications:* Alhaji Sir Alieu Sulayman Jack.
*Minister of State, Information, Broadcasting and Tourism:* B. L. K. Sanyang.
*Minister of State for Education, Youth and Social Welfare:* Alhaji Momadu C. Cham.

The House of Parliament consists of a Speaker, elected by the House; the Attorney-General, who is a nominated member; 32 elected members; four elected Head chiefs, elected by the Head chiefs; and three nominated members appointed by the President. The three nominated members have no voting rights. A deputy Speaker is elected by the House from among its own members. The President may attend and address the House at any time.

The capital is Bathurst (31,000), which is also the main commercial centre. It is administered by a City's Council consisting of 15 elected members and five nominated members. Other centres, none of which exceeds 5,000 inhabitants are the five Divisional Headquarters—Brikama, Mansa Konko, Kerewan, Georgetown, Basse, and the river ports of Kaur and Kuntaur.

In the rural areas the 35 traditional Districts presided over each by a Chief, have been grouped into six Area Councils containing a majority of elected members. Each Council has its treasury and is responsible for local government services, the Chiefs retaining powers of customary law.

### LEGAL SYSTEM

The Chief Justice, appointed by Letters Patent under the Public Seal, constitutes the Supreme Court. Appeals from the Supreme Court lie to the Gambia Court of Appeal: appeals from subordinate Courts and Moslem Courts lie to the Supreme Court. The legal system is founded on English common law.

### AREA AND POPULATION

The total area is slightly over 4,000 square miles.

The population at mid-1974 was 506,000. The annual average percentage growth rate of the population for the period 1960–74 was 2·2, and for the period 1965–74 was 2·2.

Apart from some hundreds of Europeans, Lebanese and Mauretanians residing in or near Bathurst, the population is African, mainly of the following tribes—Mandinkas Fulas, Woloffs, Sarahulis and Jolas.

### CURRENCY

The unit of currency is the *dalasi*, and 100 *bututs* equal one *dalasi*.

### FINANCE

The GNP at market prices for 1974 was U.S. $millions 90, and the GNP per capita at market prices was U.S. $170. The annual average percentage growth rate of the GNP per capita for the period 1960–74 was 3·8, and for the period 1965–74 was 3·2. [*See the note at the beginning of this section concerning GNP.*]

Revenue and expenditure for 1971–72 were (in thousand dalasi), 20,052 and 20,728 respectively; for 1972–73, 19,652 and 19,986 respectively.

### COMMERCE

Total value of imports from July, 1970 to June 1971 was D42,627,565. Chief items for that period 1970–71 in D'000 were: rice, 1,502; wheat 773; sugar 2,205; beverages 847; cigarettes aud tobacco 2,210; petroleum products 1,321; cotton fabrics 8,200; other fabrics 561; bags and sacks 405; cement 857; corrugated iron sheets 727; machinery (except electrical) 1,739; batteries and accumulators 288; radio receiving sets 940; motor cars and lorries 1,739; apparel 920.

Total value of exports from July 1970 to June 1971 was D29,894,620. Chief items for that period 1970–71 (D'000) were: groundnuts 30,578 tons, value D14,965; groundnut oil 14,032 tons, value D10,495; palm kernels 2,307 tons value D737; groundnut cake and meal 12,800 tons value D3,348; smoked fish and molluscs 792 tons value D211.

### COMMUNICATIONS

There are 794 miles of roads in The Gambia; 185 miles are bitumen surfaced and 315 are of Public Works Department gravel road. These are all-season roads. The remainder are Commissioner's roads.

The Gambia Airways Limited, act as sales agents for all air services from Bathurst, i.e. Caledonian/British United Airways, Ghana Airways, Nigeria Airways and Air Senegal.

There are no internal services as such operating in the country.

### NEWSPAPERS

**Gambia News Bulletin.** F. 1943. Thrice weekly. Information Officer, Banjul.

**Gambia Echo.** F. 1933. Weekly. Editor: J. R. Forster. Gambia Echo Syndicate, Bathurst, P.O. Box 84.

**The Progressive.** Twice weekly. Editor: Mr. MBacke N'Jie, 15 Louvel Square, Bathurst.

**The Gambia Onward.** Thrice weekly. Editor: R. Allen, 46 Grant Street, Banjul.

**The Nation.** Fortnightly. Editor: W. Dixon Colley, 3 Box Bar Road, Bathurst.

**The Gambia Outlook.** Twice weekly. Editor: M. B. Jones, 76 Perseverance Street, Bathurst.

### EDUCATION

There are 94 Primary Schools and 24 Secondary Schools, with a total enrolment of 22,569 pupils, including 6,642 girls.

There are 251 students, including 32 females, at the Yundum Teacher Training College. A Vocational Training Centre operates in Bathurst, with courses in Carpentry and Joinery, Mechanical Engineering, Craft Practice, Masonry, Clerical Studies, Motor Mechanics, Welding and Fitting.

Government Expenditure on education in 1971–72 was D2,534,150.

# Germany

## Federal Republic of Germany

(BUNDESREPUBLIK DEUTSCHLAND)

**Capital**—Bonn.

**President**—Walter Scheel.

**National Flag:** A tricolour fesse-wise, black, red, gold.

### CONSTITUTION AND GOVERNMENT

THE Basic Law for the Federal Republic of Germany was promulgated in the Federal Gazette on 23 May 1949, and came into force the next day. Previously on 23 May the Parliamentary Council had stated in a public meeting held in Bonn that the Basic Law enacted by them on 8 May 1949 had been approved by the parliaments of more than two-thirds of the German Länder concerned.

The Basic Law is based on the principle of representative democracy, and its constitutional character is laid down in Article 20, which runs as follows:

1. The Federal Republic of Germany is a democratic and social federal state.
2. All state authority emanates from the people. It shall be exercised by the people by means of elections and prebiscites and by separate legislative, executive and judicial organs;
3. Legislation shall be limited, subject to the constitutional order, to the executive and the administration of justice, legislation and the law;
4. Germans shall have the right to resist any person or persons seeking to abolish that constitutional order should no other remedy be possible.

The deputies of the *Bundestag* (Federal Diet) are elected by the people for a term of four years by direct vote. Details concerning the procedure of voting and the number of seats are determined by a special federal law. Deputies elected in the first general elections numbered 402; in the general elections of 1965 deputies elected numbered 518 including the members from Berlin.

The principal functions of the *Bundestag* include legislation, election of the Federal Chancellor, election of the President of the Federal Republic (within the Federal Assembly), parliamentary control of the Federal Government.

Agreements signed in Paris on 23 October 1954 ended the Allied occupation of Western Germany and restored to the Federal Government full sovereignty over all internal and external affairs.

On 8 May 1955, the Federal Government became the fifteenth member of NATO, and has undertaken the full duties and enjoys the rights of this partnership. Government representatives have since been actively co-operating with the General Secretariat at NATO, with SHAPE and with other NATO organizations. The newly organized German Bundeswehr has been placed at the disposal of NATO as the allied German fighting force. But the Federal Republic undertakes not to make use of her armed forces for the purposes of the re-unification of Germany, or otherwise for the expansion of her territories. According to the Treaties of Paris for protection of the Free World, the following NATO member nations maintain military forces in the Federal Republic: U.S.A., Great Britain, France, Canada, the Netherlands, and Belgium. Since 1956 the Federal Republic voluntarily contributed a substantial amount towards the costs of maintenance of the allied military establishments in her territory.

The Federal Republic was also invited to become a member of the Western European Union, a body which has grown out of the Brussels Treaty of 1948 then directed against Germany. Western Germany is now allied in the W.E.U. with Britain, France, Italy, Holland, Belgium and Luxembourg.

## GERMANY

**Cabinet**

*Federal Chancellor:* Helmut Schmidt (SPD).
*Head of the Chancellor's Office:* Manfred Schüler (SPD).
*Minister of State:* Hans-Jürgen Wischnewski (SPD).
*Vice Chancellor and Minister of Foreign Affairs:* Hans-Dietrich Genscher (FDP).
*Ministers of State:* Dr. Klaus von Dohnanyi (FDP), Dr. Hildegard Hamm-Brücher (SPD).
*Secretaries of State:* Günther van Well, Dr. Peter Hermes.
*Federal Minister of the Interior:* Werner Maihofer (FDP).
*Parliamentary Secretaries of State:* Gerhart Baum (FDP), Andreas von Schöler (SPD).
*Secretaries of State:* Günter Hartkopf, Siegfried Fröhlich.
*Federal Minister of Finance:* Hans Apel (SPD).
*Parliamentary Secretaries of State:* Karl Haeser (SPD), Rainer Offergeld (SPD).
*Secretaries of State:* Karl Otto Pöhl, Joachim Hiehle.
*Federal Minister of Economics:* Otto Graf Lambsdorff (FDP).
*Parliamentary Secretary of State:* Martin Grüner (FDP).
*Secretaries of State:* Detlef-Carsten Rohwedder, Otto Schlecht.
*Federal Minister of Defence:* Georg Leber (SPD).
*Parliamentary Secretary of State:* Andreas von Bülow (SPD).
*Secretaries of State:* Helmut Fingerhut, Karl Schnell.
*Federal Minister of Justice:* Hans-Jochen Vogel (SPD).
*Parliamentary Secretary of State:* Hans de With.
*Secretary of State:* Günther Erkel.
*Federal Minister of Youth, Family and Health:* Antje Huber (SPD).
*Parliamentary Secretary of State:* Karl Fred Zander (SPD).
*Secretary of State:* Hans-Georg Wolters.
*Federal Minister of Regional Planning, Housing and City Planning:* Karl Ravens (SPD).
*Parliamentary Secretary of State:* Dieter Haack (SPD).
*Secretary of State:* Hubert Abress.
*Federal Minister of Education and Science:* Helmut Rohde (SPD).
*Parliamentary Secretary of State:* Björn Engkolm (SPD).
*Secretary of State:* Reimut Jochimsen.
*Federal Minister of Food, Agriculture and Forestry:* Josef Ertl (FDP).
*Parliamentary Secretary of State:* Georg Gallus (FDP).
*Secretary of State:* Hans-Jürgen Rohr.
*Federal Minister of Labour and Social Affairs:* Herbert Ehrenberg (SPD).
*Parliamentary Secretary of State:* Hermann Buschfort (SPD).
*Secretaries of State:* Reinhard Strehlke, Anke Fuchs.
*Minister for Research and Technology:* Hans Matthöfer (SPD).
*Parliamentary Secretary of State:* Volker Hauff (SPD).
*Secretary of State:* Hans-Hilger Haunschild.
*Federal Minister of Transport, Posts and Telecommunications:* Kurt Gscheidle (SPD).
*Parliamentary Secretaries of State:* Ernst Haar (SPD), Lothar Wrede (FDP).
*Secretaries of State:* Heinz Ruhnau, Dietrich Elias.
*Federal Minister for Economic Cooperation:* Marie Schlei (SPD).
*Parliamentary Secretary of State:* Alwin Brück (SPD).
*Secretary of State:* Udo Kollatz.
*Federal Minister for Inner-German Relations:* Egon Franke (SPD).
*Parliamentary Secretary of State:* Egan Höhmann (SPD).
*Secretary of State:* Dietrich Spangenberg.
*Head of the Federal Press Office:* Secretary of State Klaus Bölling.

**Parliament**

**Bundestag** (Federal Diet).
*President:* Kar C'arstens (CDU).
Representation of the Parties in 1976 was: Christian Democratic Union-Christian Social Union (C.D.U./C.S.U.) 243; Social Democrats (S.P.D.) 214; Free Democrats (F.D.P.) 39.

There are also 22 deputies from West Berlin without voting power with the following numerical distribution amongst three parties: C.D.U. 11; F.D.P. 1; S.P.D. 10.

**Bundesrat** (Federal Council)

The Bundesrat is an assembly of representatives of the Federal States (Länder) carrying out Acts of Government to participate in the legislation and administration of the Federation. The rights of the Bundesrat are, among others, as follow:

The Bundesrat can introduce bills as well as give its opinion on bills introduced by the Federal Government. It may declare or deny its consent to certain bills, particularly those touching the Federal character of the Republic. With regard to all other bills the Bundesrat may, within three weeks of the receipt of a bill adopted by the Bundestag, demand that a Committee for joint consideration of bills, composed of members of the Bundestag and Bundesrat, be convened. If this Committee does not reach an agreement within a week the Bundesrat can enter a veto, which, however, may be rejected by the Bundestag. The Bundesrat approves the delegation of federal commissioners to Land authorities. Concurrently with the Bundestag, it can swear in and impeach the Federal President and it has ultimate control of the Länder police forces. The Bundesrat also has electoral rights in respect of judges of the Constitutional Courts.

*President:* Dr. Bernhard Vogel (C.D.U.)

| *Land* | *Representation* |
|---|---|
| Bavaria | 5 |
| Berlin (Consultative) | 4 |
| Bremen | 3 |
| Hamburg | 3 |
| Hesse | 4 |
| Lower Saxony | 5 |
| North Rhine-Westphalia | 5 |
| Rhineland-Palatinate | 4 |
| Schleswig-Holstein | 4 |
| Baden-Württemberg | 5 |
| Saarland | 3 |
| Total | 45 |

**LEGAL SYSTEM**

(1) Judicature is exercised by the courts. In addition to constitutional jurisdiction, there are the following branches of jurisdiction: ordinary jurisdiction, labour jurisdiction, administrative jurisdiction, fiscal jurisdiction and social jurisdiction.

(2) The constitutional courts adjudicate upon constitutional disputes to the extent explicitly assigned to them by the Basic Law or any other law.

(*a*) The Federal Constitutional Court is competent mainly to adjudicate upon:

(1) the interpretation of the Basic Law in disputes concerning the extent of the rights and obligations of any one of the highest Federal organs;
(2) the constitutionality of laws;
(3) the compatibility of Land legislation with Federal legislation;
(4) disputes between the Federation and Länder;
(5) the constitutionality of political parties;
(6) constitutional complaints.

The Federal Constitutional Court, which sits at Karlsruhe, consists of two Chambers.

(*b*) Most of the Länder have Land Constitutional Courts, which are competent to deal with constitutional disputes within individual Länder.

(3) (*a*) The ordinary courts adjudicate upon all civil disputes and in criminal cases. They are also competent in voluntary jurisdiction (guardianship, probate, land register, and register matters).

(*b*) Ordinary courts are—the municipal courts, the district courts, the regional courts, the Federal Court of Justice.

(*c*) In civil and criminal cases, the municipal courts and district courts are courts of the first instance; the district courts are also appellate and complaint instances against decisions of municipal courts. The regional courts are competent in civil cases to deal with appeals and complaints against decisions taken by district courts in the first instance, and in criminal cases for the review on points of law of appeal judgments passed by district courts. In matters of voluntary jurisdiction, the regional courts are generally a further complaint instance.

(*d*) The Federal Court of Justice (seat: Karlsruhe) is competent:

in civil cases for reviews of judgments passed by regional courts,
in criminal cases for high treason, treason, and a few other cases in the first and last instance; for reviews of judgments of large criminal divisions and courts of assizes as an appellate instance, except where the competence of the regional court is substantiated.

(4) The labour courts adjudicate upon disputes in labour matters. They are courts of the first instance. The district labour courts are competent to adjudicate upon appeals and complaints against judgments passed by the labour courts. The Federal Labour Court, which sits at Kassel, is a reviewing instance.

(5) The administrative courts adjudicate upon disputes under public law of a non-constitutional nature, except where such are explicitly assigned to another court. The system of judicature and the procedure of the administrative courts are laid down in the Administrative Judicature Act. Normally, those concerned have the right of appeal or complaint to the regional administrative court against judgments passed by administrative courts of the first instance. In certain cases provided for by law, judgments passed by regional administrative courts are subject to review, which lies with the Federal Administrative Court in Berlin.

(6) The fiscal courts adjudicate upon all disputes under public law concerning taxes. They are courts of the first instance, whilst the Federal Fiscal Court is a court of the second instance. It sits at Munich.

(7) The social courts adjudicate upon disputes under public law concerning matters of social insurance, unemployment insurance, and any other matters incumbent upon the Federal Board of Labour Exchanges and Unemployment Insurance, as well as matters of war victims benefits. They are courts of the first instance. The Land Social Courts are competent to adjudicate upon appeals and complaints against decisions taken by the Social courts. The Federal Social Court, which sits at Kassel, is a reviewing instance.

**Federal Constitutional Court** (Bundesverfassungsgericht)

*President:* Dr. Ernst Benda.
*Vice-President:* Dr. Wolfgang Zeidler.

**Supreme Federal Court**

*President:* Dr. Robert Fischer.

**Federal Administrative Court** (Bundesverwaltungsgericht)

*President:* Dr. Walther Fürst.

## AREA AND POPULATION

All statistical data relates to the Federal Republic of Germany including Berlin (West). Any deviations have been indicated.

Owing to the war and the partition of the former *Deutsches Reich* there has been a great movement of population from East to West. In 1939 the population of the area now included in the Federal Republic was 43,008,300. At 31 Dec. 1975 it was 61,640,000.

Area and population of the Federal Republic are shown below:

| *District* | *Area (sq. km.)* | *Population* |
|---|---|---|
| Schleswig-Holstein | 15,678 | 2,579,600 |
| Hamburg | 753 | 1,751,600 |
| Lower Saxony | 47,417 | 7,259,200 |
| Bremen | 404 | 728,800 |
| North Rhine-Westphalia | 34,057 | 17,245,500 |
| Hesse | 21,112 | 5,583,800 |
| Rhineland-Palatinate | 19,835 | 3,700,800 |
| Baden-Wüttemberg | 35,751 | 9,239,400 |
| Bavaria | 70,547 | 10,852,800 |
| Saarland | 2,568 | 1,111,900 |
| Berlin (West) | 480 | 2,047,900 |
| Federal Republic | 248,602 | 61,640,000 |

Vital statistics for the year 1975 are as follows:

| | |
|---|---|
| Marriages | 386,681 |
| Births | 600,512 |
| Deaths | 749,260 |

Chief cities and towns with populations over 100,000 are 31 December 1972):

| | | | |
|---|---|---|---|
| Berlin (West) | 1,984,800 | Mülheim a.d.Ruhr | 191,800 |
| Hamburg | 1,717,400 | Mainz | 181,100 |
| München | 1,312,900 | Solingen | 176,700 |
| Köln | 985,600 | Ludwigshafen am Rhein | 174,300 |
| Essen | 679,100 | Freiburg im Breisgau | 171,400 |
| Frankfurt am Main | 642,300 | Osnabrück | 163,900 |
| Dortmund | 625,100 | Mönchengladbach | 151,100 |
| Düsseldorf | 663,500 | Bremerhaven | 144,500 |
| Stuttgart | 594,300 | Darmstadt | 140,800 |
| Bremen | 572,900 | Remscheid | 135,500 |
| Nürnberg | 497,000 | Regensburg | 133,500 |
| Hannover | 560,800 | Oldenburg | 133,300 |
| Duisburg | 597,700 | Wolfsburg | 130,100 |
| Wuppertal | 408,600 | Saarbrücken | 125,900 |
| Gelsenkirchen | 339,800 | Recklinghausen | 124,900 |
| Bochum | 339,100 | Heidelberg | 122,600 |
| Mannheim | 328,400 | Offenbach am Main | 119,900 |
| Bielefeld | 320,900 | Koblenz | 119,700 |
| Bonn | 281,000 | Göttingen | 119,100 |
| Kiel | 268,800 | Neuss | 117,800 |
| Karlsruhe | 263,400 | Salzgitter | 117,600 |
| Augsburg | 257,000 | Würzburg | 114,100 |
| Wiesbaden | 252,200 | Leverkusen | 109,000 |
| Oberhausen | 242,600 | Heilbronn | 105,400 |
| Aachen | 239,600 | Bottrop | 104,400 |
| Lübeck | 237,600 | Wilhelmshaven | 104,300 |
| Krefeld | 221,500 | Fürth | 103,900 |
| Braunschweig | 220,200 | Herne | 103,700 |
| Kassel | 212,900 | Trier | 102,700 |
| Münster (Westf.) | 200,500 | Rheydt | 101,800 |
| Hagen | 197,800 | Kaiserslautern | 101,600 |

## CURRENCY

The *Deutsche Mark* of 100 *Pfennige* is the basic unit of currency, the rate of exchange of the pound sterling has been floating since 23 June 1972. Banknotes and coins were issed by the Bank Deutscher Länder from 1 August 1957 Deutsche Bundesbank. On 8 July 1950 the right of coinage was assumed and exercised again by the Federal Republic. There are notes of DM. 5, 10, 20, 50, 100, 500 and 1,000 and metal coins of 1, 2, 5, 10 and 50 Pfennige and DM. 1, 2, 5, and 10.

## FINANCE

The following table gives some figures concerning money and capital for the years 1974 and 1975:

| | *Billions of DM.*[1] 1974 | 1975 | *Per cent changes* |
|---|---|---|---|
| *Deposits from nonbanks with credit institutions*[2] | | | |
| Demand | 109·5 | 130·0 | +18·7 |
| Time | 210·3 | 205·0 | −2·5 |
| Savings (deposits and certificates) | 334·3 | 408·6 | +22·2 |
| Total deposits | 654·1 | 743·6 | +13·7 |
| *Loans to domestic enterprises and private individuals*[2] | | | |
| Short-term | 178·6 | 170·2 | −4·7 |
| Medium-term | 79·5 | 77·6 | −2·4 |
| Long-term | 398·4 | 441·4 | +10·8 |
| Total | 656·5 | 689·2 | +5·0 |
| *Securities*[2] | | | |
| Securities in circulation (in billions[1] of DM) | | | |
| Bonds and notes | 267·9 | 316·9 | +18·3 |
| Stocks (face value) | 70·2 | 75·6 | +7·7 |
| Stock-price index[3] (29.12.1972 = 100) | 81·5 | 93·7 | +15·0 |
| Average dividends of stocks quoted (per cent)[2] | 13·73 | 13·67 | |
| Yield of stocks quoted (per cent)[2] | 4·36 | 3·52 | |
| Yield of bonds and notes (per cent)[3] | 10·2 | 8·6 | — |

[1] 1 billion = 1,000,000,000.
[2] At end of year.
[3] Annual average.

# GERMANY

## PRINCIPAL BANKS

**After the war the German big bank branches—Commerz bank, Deutsche Bank and Dresdner Bank—were de centralized on *Land* level. The establishment of three over-regional banking districts in the Federal Territory by the 'Ordinance on the Districts of Business for Credit Institutes' (Gesetz über den Niederlassungsbereich von Kreditinstituten) of 29 March 1952 rendered it possible to re-combine these institutes to three successor institutes each, which were legally independent.**

**Under the 'Gesetz zur Aufhebung der Beschränkung des Niederlassungsbereichs von Kreditinstituten' of 24 December 1956 the successor institutions of the large banks were enabled to re-amalgamate.**

**After the authorization given by the competent general meetings the following banks have availed themselves of this right since 1 January 1957: The group 'Deutsche Bank' now 'Deutsche Bank Aktiengesellschaft' in Frankfurt/Main, and the group 'Dresdner Bank', now 'Dresdner Bank Aktiengesellschaft' in Frankfurt/Main and since 1 July 1958: the group 'Commerzbank' now 'Commerzbank Aktiengesellschaft' in Düsseldorf.**

**Bank für Gemeinwirtschaft Aktiengesellschaft.** ***Address:*** **Mainzer Landstrasse 16–24, Frankfurt am Main.**

**Bank fur Handel und Industrie Aktiengesellschaft,** Est. 1949. (General Managers: Dr. Hans Born, Eberhard Linnenkamp, Dr. Joachim Meyer-Blücher. Chairman, Jürgen Ponto.) Assets at 31 December 1976: DM.5,280,103,728; deposits and current accounts DM.4,844,837,059. *Head Office:* 1 Berlin 12, Uhlandstrasse 9–11. 72 Branches.

**Bankhaus B. Metzler seel. Sohn & Co.,** Est. 1674. (Personal Liable Partners: Albert von Metzler, Dr. Gustav von Metzler, Karl-Oskar Koenigs, Christoph von Metzler, Friedrich von Metzler, Brian D. Townsend.) Assets at 31 December 1976, DM.572,816,231·82; deposit and current accounts DM.460 Mio. *Head Office:* 6000 Frankfurt (Main) 1/Germany, Neue Mainzer Strasse 40–42.

**Bankhaus Burgardt + Bröckelschen A.G.** Est. 1929. (Managing Board: Dr. Peter Brauns (Düsseldorf), Franz Josef Hentrei (Dortmund), M. Aldo Nicolai (Düsseldorf).) Assets at 30 June 1975, DM.399 million; deposits and current accounts DM.342 million. *Head Office:* 4600 Dortmund, P.O. Box 255, Westenhellweg 22–24. *International Dept.:* 4000 Düsseldorf, P.O. Box 1613, Jacobistrasse 3. Offices in Düsseldorf and Dortmund.

**Bayerische Hypotheken-und Wechsel-Bank.** Est. 1835. Balance Sheet at 31 December 1976 shows total assets, DM.33,869,907,480·56; deposits DM.19,013,902,281·59. *Head Office:* Munich.

**Berliner Bank Aktiengesellschaft,** Est. 1950. (Chairman, Klaus Schütz.) Assets at 31 December 1974, DM.4,127,316,041·30; deposits and current accounts, DM.3,874,985,666·73. *Head Office:* 1 Berlin 12, Hardenbergstr, 32. 77 Branches.

**Berliner Handels- und Frankfurter Bank,** Est. 1856. (Managing Partners: Dr. Gottheiner, H. H. Jacobi, Dr. H. Ch. Schroeder-Hohenwarth, K. Subjetzki, R. v. Tresckow. Chairman, Dr. E. v. Schwartzkoppen.) Assets at 31 December 1976 (consolidated), DM.14,803 million; deposits and current accounts DM.8,412 million. *Head Office:* D-6000 Frankfurt am Main 1, P.O. Box 2301. 35 Branches.

**Chartered Bank, The,** branches at Hamburg, Frankfurt am Main, and Dusseldorf; see Great Britain.

**Commerzbank Aktiengesellschaft,** Est. 1870. Chairman of the Supervisory Board: Paul Lichtenberg. Consolidated Balance Sheet at 31 December 1976: capital and reserves DM.1,901,767,098; total assets DM.63,274,737,229. Total deposits DM.48,624,018,266. *Central Offices:* Dusseldorf, Breite Strasse 25; Frankfurt 1 Main, Neue Mainzer Strasse 32–36, Hamburg, Ness 7–9. All international divisions in Frankfurt/Main. 850 branches in Germany and West Berlin, foreign branches in Brussels, Chicago, London, New York, Paris, and Tokyo. Co-operating internationally in Europartners group with Banco di Roma, Banco Hispano Americano and Crédit Lyonnais.

**DG Bank Deutsche Genossenschaftsbank. Est. 1949 (until 31 Dec. 1975, Deutsche Genossenschaftskasse). (Chairman, Managing Board: Dr. Felix Viehoff.) Assets at 31 December 1974 (consolidated), DM.33,340,901,977; deposits and current** accounts DM.20,841,703,330. *Head Office:* Taunustor 3, Postfach 2628, D-6000 Frankfurt (Main).

**DGL-BANK Deutsche Gewerbe- und Landkreditbank AG,** Est. 1923. (Executive board (management): Wolfgang Hempel, Bertold Meier, K. H. Netsch, Dr. Erich Wecks. Chairman of the board of directors, Dr. Karl-Herbert Schneider-Gädicke.) Assets at 31 December 1976, Cash and Banks DM.640,267,082·71; Investments DM.177,881,105·07; Loans and discounts DM.1,177,774,790·88; other assets DM.17,581,156·25; total DM.2,013,504,134·91; deposits and current accounts, DM.1,886,521,337·47; other liabilities DM.51,619,527·74; capital DM.55,000,000; surplus profits and reserves DM.20,362,657·18. *Head Office:* 6000 Frankfurt/Main 1. Mainzer landstrasse 47, P.O. Box 2607. 4 Branches.

**Deutsche Bank Aktiengesellschaft,** Est. 1870. *Central Office:* Frankfurt am Main, Junghofstrasse 5–11; Grosse Gallusstrasse 10–14; Düsseldorf Königsallee 47, Statement—31 December 1976: Assets DM.67,361,370,614; liabilities DM.67,361,370,614. Over 1,100 branches in the Federal Republic of Germany. Speakers of the Board of Managing Directors: Dr. F. Wilhelm Christians, Dr. W. Guth. Chairman of the Supervisory Board: F. H. Ulrich.

**Deutsche Bundesbank.** President, Dr. Otmar Emminger. On 1 August 1957, the Land Central Banks and the Berlin Central Bank were merged with the Bank deutscher Länder and became the Deutsche Bundesbank. Sole Bank of Issue. Balance Sheet at 31 December 1976 showed assets DM. 128,500,267,772·74 deposits. DM.57,979,470,225·0; banknotes in circulation DM.59,038,317,260·0. *Address:* Wilhelm-Epstein-Strasse 14, Frankfurt am Main 50.

**Deutsche Länderbank A.G.,** Est. 1909. (Chairman, Jürgen Ponto.) Assets at 31 December 1976, DM.3,224,745,691; deposits DM.2,798,872,176. *Head Office:* 6000 Frankfurt am Main 17, Bockenheimer Landstrasse 23.

**Dresdner Bank Aktiengesellschaft.** Est. 1872. (Chairman of the Supervisory Board, Dr. Hermann Richter.) Balance Sheet at 30 June 1977: capital and reserves DM. 2,388,138,400; showed assets DM.55,717,621,000; deposits and current accounts DM.49,691,040,000. *Head Office:* Gallusanlage 7, Frankfurt am Main. 844 Branches.

**Handelsbank Heilbronn A. G.,** Est. 1901. (General Managers: Dr. H. Braun; Dr. O. K. Deutelmoser; H. Diem. Dr. H. Mattes. Assets at 31 December 1975, DM.978,113,880; deposits and current accounts DM.896,868,961. *Head Office:* P.O.B. 2140, Allee 11 D 7100 Heilbronn. 35 Branches.

**The Hongkong and Shanghai Banking Corporation,** branch at Hamburg and Frankfurt; see Hong Kong.

**Kreissparkasse Saarbrücken,** Est. 1858. (President, Werner Klumpp; Chairman, Ferdinand Paffrath. Assets at 31 December 1974, DM.1,374,267,482·72; deposits and current accounts DM.1,306,081,660·21. *Head Office:* D-6600 Saarbrücken, Postfach 184. 71 Branches.

**Sparkasse in Bremen,** Est. 1825. (Members of the Board of Managing Directors Rolf Speckmann, Friedrich Rebers, Dr. iur. Heinrich Frick; Chairman of the Board of Governors, Hans Koschnick, Mayor). Total assets at 31 December 1975, DM.4,377·5 million, deposits and current accounts DM. 3,627·8 million. *Head Office:* Am Brill, 2800 Bremen. 88 Branches.

**Volksbank Remscheid eG.,** Est. 1927. (Chairman, Heinrich Hübeler; Members of Board, Friedhelm Pflanz, Otto Pixberg. Assets at31 December 1975 DM.302,144,821·19; deposits and current accounts DM.259,946,667·57. *Head Office:* Volksbank Remscheid eG. D-563 Remscheid-Lennep, Kölner Str. 64. 11 Branches.

**Württembergische Bank,** Est. 1871. (Managers: Dr. Hanns Goeser, Dr. Manfred Prechtl. Deputy Managers: Erwin Funk, Dieter Maier. Foreign Manager: Siegfried Huck. Chairman: Robert Gleichauf, Minister of Finance of Land Baden-Württemberg.) Assets at 31 December 1976, DM. 2,248,672,267; deposits and current accounts DM. 2,039,443,677. *Head Office:* D7000—Stuttgart 1, Postfach 142, Kleiner Schlossplatz (FRG). 16 Branches.

Agriculture, Forestry, and Fisheries

| Crop | Area (in thousand hectares) | | | Total yield (in thousand tons) | | |
|---|---|---|---|---|---|---|
| | 1971 | 1972 | 1973 | 1971 | 1972 | 1973 |
| Rye | 865 | 843 | 739 | 3,032 | 2,917 | 2,576 |
| Wheat | 1,544 | 1,626 | 1,603 | 7,142 | 6,608 | 7,134 |
| Winter grains | 41 | 36 | 30 | 156 | 127 | 116 |
| *Total bread grain* | 2,450 | 2,505 | 2,372 | 10,330 | 9,653 | 9,827 |
| Barley | 1,505 | 1,549 | 1,671 | 5,774 | 5,997 | 6,622 |
| Oats | 836 | 808 | 821 | 3,037 | 2,887 | 3,045 |
| Summer grains | 342 | 324 | 315 | 1,210 | 1,143 | 1,109 |
| *Total cattle grain* | 2,683 | 2,680 | 2,808 | 10,021 | 10,027 | 10,777 |
| *Total grain* | 5,133 | 5,185 | 5,180 | 20,351 | 19,680 | 20,604 |
| Potatoes | 554 | 503 | 481 | 15,175 | 15,038 | 13,676 |
| Sugar beet | 315 | 331 | 352 | 14,409 | 14,656 | 15,858 |
| Colza and rape | 95 | 106 | 108 | 228 | 249 | 222 |
| Tobacco | 4 | 4 | 4 | 9 | — | 12* |
| Hops | 15 | 18 | 20 | 24 | 30 | 37* |

* Preliminary results.

**Livestock.** The following table shows livestock in thousand head for the years 1971–73:

| Livestock | 1971 | 1972 | 1973 |
|---|---|---|---|
| Horses | 265·3 | 283·3 | 319·7 |
| Cattle | 13,637·7 | 13,891·9 | 14,363·9 |
| Pigs | 19,984·5 | 20,028·2 | 20,451·6 |
| Sheep | 850·2 | 907·5 | 1,015·5 |
| Goats | 43·2 | 39·9 | 38·0 |
| Chickens* | 100,297·5 | 100,401·1 | 97,544·2 |
| Geese | 414·0 | 408·4 | 336·9 |
| Ducks | 1,469·5 | 1,364·3 | 1,262·2 |
| Bee colonies | 989·2 | 945·4 | 837·5 |

* Excluding guinea-fowl and bantam-fowl.

**Forestry.** Germany has extensive forests which constitute an important part of the country's economy. At the 1971 census the total forest area of the Federal Republic was 7,000,900 hectares, of which about 31 per cent hectares were state-owned, about 25 per cent hectares corporation-owned, and about 44 per cent privately-owned.

**Fishing.** The following table shows yield (tons) and value thousand DM.) of fisheries (nominal catch) for 1971–73:

| Category | 1971 | 1972 | 1973 |
|---|---|---|---|
| Total yield | 492,641 | 407,974 | 458,072 |
| Total value | 356,039 | 333,884 | 429,215 |
| Yield, deep-sea steamer | 345,438 | 270,530 | 316,040 |
| Value, deep-sea steamer | 268,853 | 237,118 | 319,379 |
| Yield, lugger herring | 7,612 | 6,900 | 7,606 |
| Value, lugger herring | 4,380 | 4,242 | 5,630 |
| Yield, coastal and deep-sea cutter | 139,591 | 130,544 | 134.426 |
| Value, coastal and deep-sea cutter | 82,807 | 92,524 | 104,206 |

**Industry.** The Federal Republic is predominantly industrial. Its principal industries are coal mining, iron and steel production, machine construction, the electrical industry, the steel, plate and metal industry, chemicals, textiles and food

The following table gives various statistics for Agriculture, Forestry, and Fisheries for the years 1960, 1970, and 1974:

| | Unit | 1960 | 1970 | 1974 |
|---|---|---|---|---|
| *Acreage* | 1,000 ha | 24,734 | 24,777 | 24,731 |
| Agriculturally used area | 1,000 ha | 14,266 | 13,578 | 13,344 |
| Wood area | 1,000 ha | 7,106 | 7,170 | 7,145 |
| Building and farmsteads | 1,000 ha | 819 | 1,048 | 1,147 |
| Other areas | 1,000 ha | 2,542 | 2,981 | 3,095 |
| *Agricultural holdings* | 1,000 | 1,618 | 1,244 | 1.067 |
| incl. with agriculturally used area of . . . ha | | | | |
| 1 to under 2 | 1,000 | 230 | 155 | 127 |
| 2 to under 5 | 1,000 | 387 | 251 | 197 |
| 5 to under 20 | 1,000 | 629 | 500 | 405 |
| 20 to under 100 | 1,000 | 136 | 174 | 197 |
| 100 and over | 1,000 | 3 | 3 | 4 |
| *Agricultural labour*[1] | 1,000 | 3,850 | 2,766 | 2,553[3] |
| incl. family labour | 1,000 | 3,306 | 2,574 | 2,292[3] |
| *Harvested quantities* | | | | |
| Grain | 1,000 t | 15,531 | 17,297 | 22,653 |
| Potatoes | 1,000 t | 24,545 | 16,250 | 14,548 |
| Fruit | 1,000 t | 4,225 | 3,282 | 2,282 |
| Vegetables | 1,000 t | 1,299 | 1,368 | 1,182 |
| Wine must | 1,000 hl | 7,433 | 9,889 | 6,805 |

| | Unit | 1960 | 1970 | 1974 |
|---|---|---|---|---|
| *Livestock population* | | | | |
| Cattle | 1,000 | 12,872 | 14,026 | 14,420 |
| Pigs | 1,000 | 15,787 | 20,969 | 20,213 |
| Horses | 1,000 | 712 | 253 | 325 |
| Milk production | 1,000 t | 19,264 | 21,856 | 21,508 |
| Quantities slaughtered[2] | 1,000 t | 2,791 | 3,894 | 4,114 |
| Timber-cutting | 1,000 fm | 25,148 | 28,196 | 30,680[4] |
| Landings of sea fisheries | 1,000 t | 593 | 591 | 493 |

1 On holdings with 2 ha and over. Excl. Hamburg, Bremen and Berlin.
2 Home reared animals.
3 1972/73.
4 1973.

The following tables show industry turnover, and the index of net industrial production (base year for index of 100, 1970 for net industrial production) for various years:

| *Industry* | Unit | 1960 | 1970 | 1974 |
|---|---|---|---|---|
| Local units | Number | 56,156 | 56,219 | 54,543 |
| Persons engaged | 1,000 | 8,081 | 8,603 | 8,144 |
| Manhours worked | mn | 13,393 | 12,246 | 10,445 |
| Total wages and salaries | 1,000 mn DM | 51 | 126 | 182 |
| Turnover | 1,000 mn DM | 266 | 529[5] | 750[5] |
| incl. foreign turnover | 1,000 mn DM | 41 | 102 | 181 |
| Consumption of coal | mn t[3] | 78 | 55 | 50 |
| Consumption of fuel oil | mn t | 9 | 32 | 30 |
| Consumption of electricity | 1,000 mn kwh | 78 | 133 | 158 |
| *Index of orders received* | | | | |
| Manufacturing[2] | 1970=100 | 52[4] | 100 | 139 |
| Primary and producers' goods industries | 1970=100 | 56[4] | 100 | 154 |
| Investment-goods industries | 1970=100 | 47[4] | 100 | 134 |
| Consumer-goods industries | 1970=100 | 54[4] | 100 | 128 |
| *Production index* | | **1962** | 1970 | **1974** |
| Total industry | **1970=100** | **66** | **100** | **112** |
| Mining | 1970=100 | 107 | 100 | 91 |
| Manufacturing | 1970=100 | 65 | 100 | 111 |
| Primary and producers' goods industries | 1970=100 | 59 | 100 | 116 |
| Investment-goods industries | 1970=100 | 64 | 100 | 107 |
| Consumer-goods industries | 1970=100 | 73 | 100 | 108 |
| Food, beverages and tobacco industries | 1970=100 | 72 | 100 | 114 |
| Public power supply industry | 1970=100 | 51 | 100 | 151 |
| Construction industry | 1970=100 | 75 | 100 | 105 |
| *Index of labour productivity* | | | | |
| per person engaged | 1970=100 | 69 | 100 | 116 |
| per wage earner | 1970=100 | 65 | 100 | 121 |
| *Output of selected products* | | 1960 | 1970 | 1974 |
| Hard coal (output) | mn t | 142 | 111 | 95 |
| Electricity production | 1,000 mn kwh | 116[8] | 243 | 312 |
| Gas production | 1,000 mn $m^3$ | 28[8] | 41 | 48 |
| Cement (excl. cem. clinker) | 1,000 t | 24,905[8] | 38,325 | 35,977 |
| Pig iron and ferro alloys | 1,000 t | 25,739[8] | 33,627 | 40,221 |
| Raw steel | 1,000 t | 33,428[8] | 44,315 | 52,602 |
| Rolled steel | 1,000 t | 22,531 | 32,291 | 39,612 |
| Virgin aluminium | 1,000 t | 169 | 309 | 689 |
| Sulph. acid (as $SO_3$) | 1,000 t | 2,588 | 3,620 | 4,188 |
| Petrol, special and testing benzines | 1,000 t | 5,906 | 14,103 | 16,638 |
| Fuel oils | 1,000 t | 13,712 | 62,170 | 62,802 |
| Plastics | 1,000 t | 1,019 | 4,360 | 6,314 |
| Chemical fibres | 1,000 t | 282[8] | 724 | 940 |
| Sawn wood | 1,000 $m^3$ | 7,739[8] | 9,383 | 9,905 |

*continued*

| *Industry* | Unit | 1960 | 1970 | 1974 |
|---|---|---|---|---|
| Paper and paperboard | 1,000 t | 3,439 | 5,692 | 6,919 |
| Passenger cars[6] | 1,000 | 1,818[8] | 3,528 | 2,840 |
| Radio sets | 1,000 | 4,313[8] | 6,729 | 5,340 |
| Television sets | 1,000 | 2,164 | 2,927 | 4,293 |
| Beer | 1,000 hl | 47,324[8] | 81,624 | 87,688 |
| Cigarettes | 1,000 mn | 72 | 130 | 143 |
| *Handicrafts*[7] | | | | |
| Persons engaged | 1,000 | 3,478[9] | 3,911 | 3,801 |
| Turnover | 1,000 mn | 84[9] | 173[10] | 231[10] |

In general local units employing 10 and more persons; excl. electricity and gas construction.
[2] Excl. food, beverages and tobacco industries.
[3] In terms of hard coal.
[4] Excl. the Saar and Berlin.
[5] Excl. turnover (value added) tax.
[6] Incl. estate cars.
[7] Excl. subsidiary establishments.
[8] Excl. Berlin.
[9] 1961; excl. the Saar and Berlin.
[10] Incl. turnover (value added) tax.

The following tables show the value in millions of DM of various types of goods imported and exported to and from the Federal Republic, and also by Country of destination. and origination for the years 1974 and 1975:

| *Exports and Imports* | 1974 (*in millions of DM*) | 1975 | *Per cent changes* |
|---|---|---|---|
| *Foreign trade by commodity groups* | | | |
| Total Exports | 230,578 | 221,600 | −3·9 |
| of which | | | |
| Machinery | 45,701 | 46,594 | +2·0 |
| Motor vehicles | 27,545 | 29,785 | +8·1 |
| Chemicals | 33,649 | 27,620 | −17·9 |
| Electrical engineering | 21,445 | 21,458 | +0·1 |
| Iron and steel | 19,798 | 16,694 | −15·7 |
| Food, beverages & tobacco | 8,406 | 8,553 | +1·8 |
| Textiles | 8,691 | 7,805 | −10·2 |
| Metal goods | 6,982 | 6,410 | −8·2 |
| Total Imports | 179,733 | 184,448 | +2·6 |
| of which: | | | |
| Petroleum, natural gas & bituminous minerals | 24,328 | 22,146 | −9·0 |
| Agricultural & forestry products | 19,638 | 19,973 | +1·7 |
| Chemicals | 15,092 | 14,344 | −5·0 |
| Food, beverages & tobacco | 13,335 | 14,106 | +5·8 |
| Machinery | 10,092 | 11,581 | +14·8 |
| Textiles | 9,947 | 10,548 | +6·0 |
| Electrical products | 9,517 | 10,507 | +10·4 |
| Motor vehicles | 5,769 | 8,592 | +48·9 |
| *Foreign trade by area* | | | |
| Total Exports | 230,578 | 221,600 | −3·9 |
| to EEC countries | 103,516 | 96,553 | −6·7 |
| of which: | | | |
| France | 27,345 | 25,968 | −5·0 |
| The Netherlands | 23,470 | 22,192 | −5·4 |
| Belgium-Luxemburg | 17,584 | 16,868 | −4·1 |
| Italy | 18,731 | 16,191 | −13·6 |
| to EFTA countries | 49,892 | 47,974 | −3·8 |
| of which: | | | |
| Austria | 10,152 | 9,824 | −3·2 |
| Switzerland | 11,536 | 9,568 | −17·1 |
| Sweden | 7,873 | 8,090 | +2·9 |
| Norway | 2,980 | 3,488 | +17·1 |
| to U.S.A. & Canada | 19,236 | 15,063 | −21·7 |
| to Eastern Europe | 15,878 | 17,410 | +9·6 |
| to other industrial countries | 9,943 | 8,146 | −18·1 |
| to developing countries | 32,113 | 36,454 | +13·5 |
| Total Imports | 179,733 | 184,448 | +2·6 |
| from EEC countries | 86,147 | 91,343 | +6·0 |
| of which: | | | |

*continued*

| | 1974 (*in millions of DM*) | 1975 | *Per cent changes* |
|---|---|---|---|
| The Netherlands | 25,219 | 25,733 | +2·0 |
| France | 20,898 | 22,148 | +6·0 |
| Italy | 14,976 | 17,229 | +15·0 |
| Belgium-Luxemburg | 15,917 | 15,831 | −0·5 |
| from EFTA countries | 22,229 | 23,477 | +5·6 |
| of which: | | | |
| Switzerland | 4,879 | 5,472 | +12·2 |
| Sweden | 4,280 | 4,252 | −0·7 |
| Austria | 3,516 | 3,789 | +7·8 |
| Norway | 1,816 | 1,870 | +3·0 |
| from U.S.A. & Canada | 15,970 | 15,983 | +0·1 |
| from Eastern Europe | 8,403 | 8,657 | +3·0 |
| from other industrial countries | 6,791 | 8,116 | +19·5 |
| from developing countries | 40,193 | 36,872 | −8·3 |

## COMMUNICATIONS

**Railways.** German railways (*Deutsche Bundesbahn*) are nationalized. In 1976 there were 28,576 km of railway track. There were 8,605 locomotives in operation.

**Shipping.** On 31 December 1976 the merchant fleet comprised 2,197 with a total tonnage of 7,485,497 (vessels primarily engaged in carrying seaborne commercial traffic of 50 m³ = 17·65 gross registered tons or over and moved by mechanical power). The total net tonnage of vessels cleared and entered with cargo in international traffic amounted to 193,139,000 in 1973. The chief ports are Hamburg, Bremen, Bremerhaven, Brake, Nordenham, Emden, Wilhelmshaven, Lübeck, Kiel and Flensburg.

**Argo Nah-Ost Linie GmbH**; Managing Owner: Max Adler. *Services operated:* Hamburg, Bremen, Rotterdam, Antwerp, to U.A.R., Algeria, Bulgaria, Cyprus, Malta, Greece, Lebanon Libya, Syria, Rumania, Tunisia and Turkey. *Head Office:* Tiefer 12 (28) Bremen.

**Argo Reederei Richard Adler & Söhne**; (Managing Partners: Richard Adler and Max Adler); motor vessels 18; *Services operated:* Hamburg to London, Bremen to London, Bremen, Hamburg to Hull and other ports on the East Coast U.K. and Scotland, Rhine ports to Hull; Bremen to Finland, Rotterdam to Finland, Amsterdsm to Finland; Bremen to East Norway; Hamburg, Bremen, Rotterdam to French Channel and Atlantic ports; The Mediterranean Service is run under Argo Nah-Ost Linie GmbH. *Head Office:* Tiefer 12, 28 Bremen. *Branch Office:* Mattenwiete 6, Hamburg 11, Adler & Söhne.

**Cosima—Poseidon—Schiffahrt GmbH**; (Managing Directors: Dr. Dietrich Heitmüller, Dr. Jens Karsten, Ing. grad. Ernst Willner). Managing owners for 11 motor vessels; 1 motor tanker; services operated: world wide. Under construction: 4 motor vessels. *Head Office:* Ballindamm 17, Hamburg 1.

**DAL Deutsche Afrika-Linien GmbH. & Co.** (Chairman, Frau Liselotte v. Rantzau, ne. Essberger; Managing Directors, A. Schwencke, Dr. Rolf Stödter, Dieter Seidel, Ludwig Bielenberg, R. Brennecke; Norbert Bellstedt, C.-T. Hubrich, O. W. Sieb, Willi Wassmann (deputies)); motor vessels 20. *Services operated:* Canary Islands and West Africa under Woermann-Linie, to South and East Africa under Deutsche Ost-Afrika-Line. *Head Office:* Hamburg-Altona, Palmaille 45.

**Deutsche Dampfschifffahrts-Gesellschaft 'Hansa'**; (Managing Directors: H. C. Helms. W. Döhle, F. Schäfer, B. Teuber, K.-J.P. v. Quistorp); 78 vessels totalling 366,902 GRT, carrying capacity 519,482 metric tons. 7 vessels are being built with a total metric tonnage of 62,491 and carrying capacity of 65,516 metric tons. The total charter tonnage is 96,388 tdw disposed amongst 14 vessels; *services operated:* Hamburg, Bremen, Rotterdam, Antwerp, Marseilles and Genoa to Egypt, Jordan, Saudi-Arabia, Sudan, French-Somaliland, Aden, Eritrea, Oman, Bahrein, Kuwait, Iraq, Iran, Pakistan, India, Ceylon, Burma, Madagascar, further from East Coast U.S.A. to Red Sea ports, Arabia, Oman and Kuwait also to Iran and Iraq. Full container service. *Head Office:* Schlachte 6, 28 Bremen.

**Gehrckens H. M**; (Managing Directors: Heinrich M. Gehrckens, Dr. I. Greis); motor vessels 7; *services operated:* from Hamburg to Finland and Sweden, also from Continental ports to West Africa. *Head Office:* Beim neuen Krahn, 2, 2 Hamburg 11.

**Hamburg-Suedamerikanische Dampfschifffahrts-Gesellschaft Eggert & Amsinck**; (Managing Directors: de la Trobe, Herbert Amsinck, Dietrich Foepfel); motor vessels 24; total tonnage 128,344 G.R.T.; *services operated:* passenger and freight service between Hamburg, Bremen, Rotterdam, Antwerp to Brazil and South American ports, Canada and U.S.A. *Head Office:* Ost-Weststrasse 59, Hamburg 11.

**Hapang-Lloyd Aktiengesellschaft**; *Executive Board:* H. J. Kruse (Speaker); K.-H. Sager (Deputy Speaker), Dr. K.-H. Necker, Dr. H. J. Stöcker, Dr. H. Willner; (Chairman of the Supervisory Board) Dr. A. Kleffel; cargo vessels 52; passenger ship 1; total tonnage 837,858 G.R.T., 815,323 tdw. *Services operated:* U.S.A., East Coast; North Pacific; U.S. Gulf/South Atlantic; West Indies; Mexico; Venezuela/Columbia/Costa Rica; Central America/West Coast; Northern Brazil; South America/West Coast; U.S.A. and Canada/West Coast; Far East, Indonesia, Australia, New Zealand; The Canary Islands.

**Horn-Linie**; (Director: E. Schmidt); motor vessels 2; *services operated:* from Hamburg, Bremen, Rotterdam, Antwerp to Atlantic Colombia, Costa Rica; to Puerto Rico, Dominican Republic, Haiti and Jamaica; to Trinidad, Venezuela, Curacao, Aruba. *Head Office:* Baumwall 3, Hamburg 11.

**Oldenburg-Portugiesische Dampfschiffs-Rhederei; Kusen, Heitmann & Cie., K.G.**; (Director, Peter Hansen); motor vessels 7; *services operated:* Continental ports to Morocco, Canary Islands, South Spain, North and East Spain, Portugal. Algeria. *Head Office:* Kajen 10, Hamburg 11.

**Poseidon Schiffahrt GmbH**; (Managing Directors: Dr. Dietrich Heitmueller, Dr. Jens Karsten; Deputy Directors: Klaus Brigmann, Klaus Schmidt-Rieche). Managing Owners for 2 turbine tankers; services operated: world wide. *Head Office:* Ballindamm 17, Hamburg 1.

**Rickmers-Linie K.G.**; (Managing Director: Claus Rickmers); motor vessels 5; *services operated:* from Hamburg, Bremen, Rotterdam, Antwerp and French ports to Malaya, Thailand, Hong Kong and China. *Head Office:* Beim Neuen Krahn, Hamburg 11.

**Rudolf A. Oetker**; (Proprietor, Rudolf A. Oetker); motor vessels 18; steam ships 1; total tonnage 30,143 G.R.T.; *services operated:* from Continental ports to Greece, Turkey, Syria, Cyprus, Lebanon, Egypt, Israel and Bulgaria, Algeria, Tunisia, Libya, Rumania. *Head Office:* Ost-Weststrasse 59 Hamburg 11.

**Schuldt H**; (Managing Director: Kurt Sieh, E. Sieh, B. Todsen); motor vessels 16; total tonnage 90,000 G.R.T.; *services operated:* from Continental ports to N. Africa, E. Mediterranean, Black Sea, Gulf of Agnaba, Bermudas, Mexico Atlantic, U.S. Gulf and South Atlantic, also world wide fully refrigerated vessels' services. *Head Office:* Ballindamm 8, 2 Hamburg 1.

**Sloman Neptun** Schiffahrts-Aktiengesellschaft; (Managing Directors: J. Willhöft, W. Holtz, W. Krieger), motor vessels 15; total tonnage 40 108, 2. *Services operated:* Regular Liner Service: Norway, Sweden, Spain, Portugal, South-coast U.K., Belgium, Holland, West Africa, North Pacific, North Africa. International Chartering, Container Facilities, Through Cargoes, Seismic Sea Explorations, LPG Tankers, Chemical Tankers O.N.E. Shipping Ltd., Refrig. Cargo Vessels. *Head Office:* Langenstr. 52+54, Bremen. *Branch Offices:* Bremen, Rotterdam, Madrid, Hamilton (Bermuda).

**Sloman, Rob. M. jr.**; (Managing partners: Henry S. Edye, Claus Edye, Michael Reincke. Managing Director: Werner Krieger); motor vessels 3; *services operated:* Continental ports to East Coast Spain, Algeria and Tunisia; West Africa; also tramp and reefer services. *Head Office:* Baumwall 3, Hamburg 11.

**Verband Deutscher Reeder e.V.**; *Head Office:* 2 Hamburg 36. Esplanade 6.

**Civil Aviation.** The "Deutsche Luft Hansa Aktien-Gesellschaft", Berlin was established on 6 January 1926 to succeed "Deutscher Aero Lloyd" and "Junkers Luftverkehr AG". It started air transport operations on 6 April 1926 and operated, amongst others, the first Berlin–Koenigsberg night flight, the first transoceanic postal service between Europe and South America in 1934 and in 1937/39, regular test flights over the North Atlantic. The company was reorganized on 6 January 1953 in Cologne as "Aktiengesellschaft fuer Luftverkehrsbedarf (Luftag)", which became "Deutsche Lufthansa AG" on 6 August 1954. It again undertook regular flights on 1 April 1955.

82·2 per cent of the shares are held by the Federal Republic of Germany and other public corporations. Main subsidiaries: Condor Flugdienst GmbH; Delvag Luftfahrtversicherungs-AG; Lufthansa Service GmbH; Lufthansa Commercial Holding GmbH. The fourth largest international airline, Lufthansa operates 93 jet aircraft (Summer 1977), has 5 more jets on order for delivery 1977/78, and options on 8 other aircraft. The route network exceeds 260,790 miles, covering 114 airports. In 1976 Lufthansa aircraft flew 147,763 flights of over 119 million miles and carried 11,223,404 passengers and 304,927 metric tons of freight. About 50 per cent of revenue arises outside Germany. Employees at 31 December 1975 numbered 25,340.

*Directors:* (Chairman, Board of Executives) Dr. H. Culmann, R. Abraham, G. Fruehe, Professor H. Suessenguth, Flight Captain W. Utter.

Capital: Total: authorized and issued DM600,000,000. Ordinary shares (DM.50): authorized and issued 10,420,000 shares. Preference shares: authorized and issued 1,580,000 shares. Debentures and loan stock: Total value issued DM.95,649,000. *Head Office:* 5000 Koln 21, Von-Gablenz-Strasse 2–6 Germany. Telephone: Cologne (02 21) 82 61, Telex: 8 87 35 31.

**Posts, Telegraphs and Telephones.** Postal, telegraph and telephone services are operated by the *Deutsche Bundespost.* The number of telephones in use at 31 December 1976 was 21,200,000, representing one instrument per 3·5 of the population.

**Broadcasting.** Broadcasting is operated by 12 companies having corporation status. The principal stations are Westdeutscher Rundfunk/Köln, Norddeutscher Rundfunk/Hamburg, Bayerischer Rundfunk/München and Zweites Deutsches Fernsehen/Mainz. On 30 June 1977 radio licence-holders numbered 20,457,741, television licence-holders numbered 18,718,623 (only holders subject to charges).

## NEWSPAPERS

**Frankfurter Allgemeine Zeitung.** Frankfurt am Main, Hellerhofstrasse 2–4. Editors: Bruno Dechamps, Jürgen Eick, Fritz Ullrich Fack, Joachim Fest, Johann Georg Reissmüller, Erich Welter. Verlag Frankfurter Allgemeine Zeitung GmbH.

**Die Welt.** Kölner Str. 99,5300 Bonn, Bad Godesberg.

**Süddeutsche Zeitung**. 8000 München 2, Sendlingerstr. 80 Süddeutscher Verlag GmbH.

**Der Tagesspiegel**. Berlin 30, Potsdamer Str. 87 Herausgeber: F. K. Maier. Verlag der Tagesspiegel GmbH.

**Berliner Morgenpost**. Berlin 61, Kochstraße 50, Ullstein GmbH (Axel Springer Verlag A.G.).

**Stuttgarter Zeitung**. Stuttgart, Eberhardstr. 61 (Turmhaus). Editor: J. Eberle; Stuttgarter Zeitung Verlagsgesellschaft, Eberle & Co.

**Bild Zeitung**. Hamburg 36, Kaiser-Wilhelm-Strasse 6, Axel Springer Verlag A.G.

**Frankfurter Rundschau**. Frankfurt am Main, Grosse Eschenheimer Strasse 16–18. Verlag: Druck-und Verlagshaus Frankfurt am Main GmbH.

**Hamburger Abendblatt**. Hamburg 36, Kaiser-Wilhelm Strasse 6, Axel Springer Verlag A.G.

**B.Z.** Berlin 61, Kochstraße 50. Ullstein GmbH. (Axe Springer Verlag A.G.)

## ATOMIC ENERGY

Subsequent to the removal in 1955 of the restrictions previously placed on nuclear research, a period of energetic planning and rapid promotion began in close co-operation between government, industry and the universities in the field of the peaceful research into the utilization of nuclear energy.

A new Federal Ministry for Atomic Affairs was established with the task of defining the objectives of governmental promotion in this field, and of taking the lead in elaborating related problems at Federal level. In the meantime, this Ministry has been renamed 'Federal Ministry for Research and Technology', on account of the major expansion of its competences. At present the Ministry comprises, in addition to a Division for Energy Research, Commodities and Biology/ Medicine, Divisions for Space Research, Data Processing, International Relations and Research Policy, and is currently headed by Hans Matthoefer.

The work of the Ministry is concentrated on nuclear research and development, particularly on the promotion of new reactor lines with great development potential (high-temperature reactors with steam turbines, fast breeder reactors, and controlled thermonuclear fusion), and activities concerning the fuel cycle (the supply of natural uranium, uranium enrichment, reprocessing and waste disposal). Furthermore, promotion is given to intensive research work on the safety of reactors and other nuclear facilities, and activities directed at reducing the environmental pollution load.

In addition, basic nuclear research is supported on a broad basis, ranging from high-energy physics, solid state and heavy ion research to radiation biology and radiation medicine. All the work done in this field has been summarized in four Nuclear Programmes. At present, an Energy Programme is being drawn up for the years 1977–81 comprising also non-nuclear Research and Development.

Up to the end of 1971, the Ministry was advised on the formulation and execution of these tasks by the German Atomic Energy Advisory Commission, which was composed of leading representatives from science, industry and government. This body was disbanded at the end of 1971, and—owing to changed requirements—replaced by a system of advisory bodies, either directly task-oriented, or set up to follow programmes on a shortlived or long-term basis.

In the Federal Republic of Germany, particularly in the field of light water reactors (LWR), the break-through was made with regard to the commercial utilization of nuclear energy. As a result of the successful operation of the LWR demonstration power stations (each with a capacity of approx. 250 MWe) at Gundremmingen, Lingen and Obrigheim, proof could be given that this type of nuclear power station is economic, reliable and—in particular—safe. The two first fully commercial nuclear power stations at Würgassen and Stade, each with a capacity of 670 MWe, went into operation at the beginning of 1972. They were followed by the 1200 MWe LWR Station Biblis A in early 1975. A further 12 stations of about 12,000 MWe are under construction and eight stations of about 10,200 MWe are on order. The 'Otto Hahn', the first nuclear-propelled merchant vessel in Western Europe has been operating successfully since 1968.

Four small experimental power stations (with capacities ranging between 20 and 60 MWe) serve for training purposes or to try out new reactor lines, e.g. the AVR at Jülich for the high-temperature reactor, and the KNK at Karlsruhe for the sodium-cooled Fast Breeder.

The construction of two prototype nuclear power stations, each with a capacity of 300 MWe, one with a high-temperature reactor and steam turbines in Schmehausen (THTR 300) and the other with a sodium-cooled fast breeder reactor (in co-operation with Belgium and the Netherlands) at Kalkar (SNR 300) is well underway. A pilot enrichment plant using the gas ultra centrifuge technique (in co-operation with Great Britain and the Netherlands) is in operation at Almelo in the Netherlands.

At the eight nuclear research centres, which are financed chiefly by the Federal Government (accommodating approximately 11,000 members of staff), both problems of basic research are tackled, particularly with the use of large-scale equipment (e.g. accelerators and research reactors), and technological development work. The tasks of these centres are now also taking in non-nuclear activities to an increasing degree.

## EDUCATION

*Schools providing general education:* Primary and post-primary schools (Grund- und Hauptschulen), special schools (Sonderschulen), intermediate schools (Realschulen), high schools (Gymnasien) Primary schools: Attendance is compulsory for all children having completed their sixth year of age. Compulsory education extends to nine years. The first four (or six) years at primary school are attended by all children. Thereafter the children may attend postprimary schools (Hauptschulen), intermediate schools, high schools and other schools of general secondary education. Special schools: For retarded, physically or mentally handicapped and socially maladjusted children. The intermediate school comprises six, the high school nine years of schooling after four years of primary school. The successful completion of the final class of the intermediate school permits entry in qualified occupations not requiring academic education. The final high school certificate entitles the holder to enter any institution of higher education.

*Schools providing vocational education:* Part-time, full-time and advanced full-time vocational schools (Berufs-, Berufsaufbau-, Berufsfach-, Fachober und Fachschulen[1]). Running parallel to the occupation, part-time vocational school offer six to 12 hours per week of additional compulsory schooling. After having completed compulsory schooling, all young people who are apprentices in some other employment or even unemployed have to attend them in general up to the age of 18 years or until the completion of the practical vocational training. Full-time vocational schools comprise courses of at least one year. They are attended instead of the part-time vocational schools and serve in particular to prepare for commercial, and domestic occupations as well as specialized occupations in the field of handicrafts. "Fachoberschulen" provide an advanced vocational-cum-general education following intermediate school that leads to entry into Fachhochschule; for pupils with completed apprenticeship, reduction to one year. Advanced full-time vocational schools provide additional schooling in the occupation practised so far. They are attended by pupils having completed their 18th year of age. Courses from half a year to three or even more years are offered.

In November 1975, there were 1,835 part-time vocational schools with 1,635,960 pupils (657,471 girls); 465 full-time and part-time vocational schools with 27,786 pupils (6,515 girls); 2,609 full-time vocational schools with 300,422 pupils (199,736 girls); 893 Fachoberschulen with 118,675 pupils (34,948 girls). 3,068 advanced vocational schools with 205,661 pupils (119,280 girls). In all schools of initial vocational education together there were 52,251 teachers (17,467 female): in the schools of further education and re-training there were 7,204 teachers (3,332 female).

*Institutions of higher education:* Universities and equivalent institutions (Wissenschaftliche Hochschulen); teacher training colleges and equivalent institutions (Pädagogische Hochschulen und entsprechende Einrichtungsen) higher technical colleges (Fachhochschulen, the former Ingenieurschule" and "Höhere Fachschuleu"), colleges of music (Hochschulen für Musik), fine arts (Hochschulen für bildende Künste), television and film (Hochschule für Fernsehen und Film) and the college for physical education (Sporthochschule) in Köln.

[1] Fachschulen für Technik and Schulen des Gesundn beitswesens included.

*Universities and equivalent institutions of higher education:* During the winter term 1975/76 there were 104 academic institutions of higher education (universities, Gesamthochschulen, technical universities, theological colleges, teacher training colleges) with 675,903 students; 26 Kunsthochschulen with 15,343 students; 134 higher technical colleges (Fachhochschulen) with 145,833 students. In some cases various types of the above institutions have been integrated into Gesamthochschulen (comprehensive institutions of higher education).

**RELIGION**

There is no state religion. Protestants and Roman Catholics are the largest religious bodies in the Federal Republic, the former comprising 49·0 per cent of the total population and the latter 44·6 per cent according to Census 1970.

# Länder

The jurisdiction of the *Länder* and the Federation and their mutual relations are set forth in the Basic Law for the Federal Republic, promulgated on 23 May 1949. Each *Land* has its own parliament and government. The *Länder* exercise their right to participate in forming the will of the Federation through the *Bundesrat* (see page 223). Each *Land* has its own representation at the seat of the Federal Government. The Federal character of the Basic Law is safeguarded by the provision that any law amending the Basic Law requires the approval of two-thirds of the members of the *Bundestag* and two-thirds of the votes of the *Bundesrat*. In view of the Federal character of the Basic Law an amendment to it by which the organization of the Federation into *Länder* and the basic co-operation of the *Länder* in legislation are affected is inadmissible.

The numbers of votes each *Land* has in the *Bundesrat* is proportionate to the size of its population. *Länder* with up to two million inhabitants have three votes, *Länder* with more than two million inhabitants four votes, and those with more than six million inhabitants five votes. The decisions of the *Bundesrat* are prepared by Committees.

## BADEN-WÜRTTEMBERG

**Capital**—Stuttgart.

Baden-Württemberg has been created by uniting the former countries Württemberg-Baden, Baden and Württemberg-Hohenzollern. It consists of four administrative areas as follows: Stuttgart, Karlsruhe, Freiburg und Tübingen.

**Area:** 35,751 sq. km.

**Population** (1 January 1976): 9,152,700, of which 4,395,000 are males and 4,757,700 females.

The population figures for some of the main towns are (31 December 1975):
Stuttgart 600,000; Mannheim 314,000; Karlsruhe 280,000; Freiburg im Breisgau 175,000; Heidelberg 129,000; Heilbronn 113,000.

**Legislature:** (Election of 23 April 1972).
*President:* Camill Wurz
Representation of the **Parties:**

| | |
|---|---|
| Christian Democratic Party (CDU) | 65 |
| Social Democratic Party (SPD) | 45 |
| Free Democratic Party (FDP/DVP) | 10 |
| | 120 |

**Finance.** Budget figures for 1976 (in DM. million) were 20,901.0.

**Principal Industries.** In 1975 1,439,000 people were employed in 10,802 industrial concerns with a total turnover of 123,025,000,000 D. Marks, of which 29,485,000,000 D. Marks were in foreign business. The following are the chief industrial concerns with the number of establishments in brackets (local units with more than ten employees); Mechanical engineering (1,406); Textile industry (1,021); Electrical engineering (836); Iron. steel, sheet and metal goods industry (652); Manufact. of motor vehicles (162).

**Agriculture.** The total arable land is 1,735,000 hectares. Forested area covers 1,301,400 hectares. Areas and yield of the chief crops in 1975 were:

| *Crop* | *Area (in thousand hectares)* | *Yield (in thousand tons)* |
|---|---|---|
| Wheat | 241·0 | 1,011·4 |
| Barley | 177·4 | 577·8 |
| Oats | 100·0 | 314·7 |
| Corn | 26·2 | 154·6 |
| Potatoes | 46·9 | 1,748·8 |
| Sugar Beet | 25·1 | 978·0 |
| Tobacco | 1·8 | 4·8 |
| Vineyards | 24·7 | 1,848·0 |
| Hops | 1·2 | 2·0 |
| Rye | 15·7 | 56·7 |

**Livestock**

Livestock population was as follows (in thousands):

| | 1975 |
|---|---|
| Horses | 40·3 |
| Cattle | 1,827·4 |
| Pigs | 2,056·4 |
| Sheep | 161·7 |
| Poultry | 7,560·4 |

## BAVARIA

**Capital**—Munich.

**Area:** 70,547 sq. km.

**Population** (31 December 1975): 10,810,392 of which 5,152,006 are males and 5,658,383 females.

The population figures for some of the main towns are (31 December 1975):
Munich 1,314,800; Nuremberg 499,000; Augsburg 249,900; Regensburg 131,800; Würzburg 112,500; Fürth 101,600.

**Legislature:** Representation of the parties following the election of 27 October 1976 was as follows: Christian Social Union (CSU) 132, Social Democratic Party (SPD) 64, Free Democratic Party 8.

**Livestock.** Livestock population for 1975–76 was as follows (in thousands):

| | 1975 | 1976 |
|---|---|---|
| Horses | 48·0 | 50·2 |
| Cattle | 4,605·6 | 4,575·2 |
| Pigs | 3,892·1 | 3,970·8 |
| Sheep | 261·4 | 271·0 |
| Goats | 10·5 | 10·5 |
| Poultry | 15,116·5 | 15,136·3 |
| Bee colonies | 336·3 | 336·3 |

**Agriculture.** The total arable land in Bavaria is 2,118,400 hectares.

Forested areas cover 2,310,200 hectares. Areas and yield of the crops in 1976 were:

| *Crop* | *Area (in thousand hectares)* | *Yield (in thousand tons)* |
|---|---|---|
| Rye | 79·0 | 219·0 |
| Wheat | 499·7 | 1,982·0 |
| Barley | 439·4 | 1,499·3 |
| Oats | 169·6 | 474·8 |
| Potatoes | 159·2 | 4,053·3 |
| Sugar beet | 91·9 | 4,077·0 |
| Hops | 18·4 | 26·7 |
| Clover | 122·8 | 805·6 |
| Lucerne | 27·7 | 186·3 |

**Principal Industries.** Electrical engineering, machine construction, clothing, textile industry, car building, chemical industry, stones and earths, wood processing, graphic industry, ceramics industry, fine mechanics and optics, and breweries, oil and plastics working.

**Finance.** The budget figure for 1976 (in DM. million was): Total: 24,132·2.

# BERLIN

Greater Berlin remains under a Four Power status. The Allied Kommandantura (the Quadripartite Allied Government) governed in fact all four sectors of the city until July 1948, when the Soviet element withdrew unilaterally and set up a separate municipal government in Berlin (East). Within the Allied Kommandantura, the Three Powers continue to exercise supreme authority in Berlin (West).

According to the constitution of the Federal Republic and to the constitution of Berlin, Berlin is simultaneously a Land of the Federal Republic, being represented in the Bundestag and Bundesrat although without the right of voting, and a City. It is governed by a House of Representatives of at least 200 members, the executive power being vested in the Senat, which consists of the Governing Lord Mayor (Regierender Bürgermeister), the Deputy Mayor and not more than 16 Senators. The following figures refer to Berlin (West).

**Area:** The area of Western Berlin is 480 sq. km. (the area of greater Berlin being about 883 sq. km.). The British sector of 164 sq. km. comprises the administrative districts of Tiergarten, Charlottenburg, Wilmersdorf, Spandau. The American sector covers 211 sq. km. and consists of the districts of Kreuzberg, Neukölln, Tempelhof, Schöneberg, Zehlendorf and Steglitz. 105 sq. km. is the area of the French sector comprising the districts of Wedding and Reinickendorf.

**Population** (31 December 1973): 2,047,948 of which 903,945 are males and 1,144,003 females.

**Legislature:** (Election of 2 March 1975):

*President of House of Representatives:* Peter Lorentz (CDU).

Representation of the parties: Social Democratic Party (SPD) 67; Christian Democratic Union (CDU) 68; Free Democratic Party (FDP) 11.

Unallotted seats remain reserved for the Soviet Sector.

**Agriculture.** The total arable land is 1,701 hectares. Forested areas cover 7,721 hectares.

**Finance.** Budget figures for 1974 (in DM. million) were: Revenue, 12,065·1; Expenditure, 12,123·7.

**Principal Industries.** Electrical, textiles and clothing, food and beverages, machinery, printing and publishing, chemicals, mechanical industry. Total turnover: 24,345 DM. million.

# BREMEN

## (*Land Freie Hansestadt Bremen*)

The Land Freie Hansestadt Bremen is formed by the two cities Bremen and Bremerhaven.

**Area:** 404 sq. km.

**Population** (1 January 1974): 728,843 of which 343,389 are males and 385,454 females.

Towns populated by more than 50,000 are (1 January 1974): Bremen, 584,265 and Bremerhaven, 144,578.

**Legislature:** (Election of 10 October 1971). Representation of the Parties: Social Democratic Party (SPD) 59; Christian Democratic Party (CDU) 34; Free Democratic Party (FDP) 7.

**Finance.** Budget figures for 1976 (in DM. million) were: Revenue, 3,662·5; Expenditure, 3,619·7.

**Livestock.** Livestock population of principal sorts was as follows:

| | 1974 | 1975 | 1976 |
|---|---|---|---|
| Horses | 1,346 | 1,429 | 1,600 |
| Cattle | 18,250 | 17,838 | 17,055 |
| Pigs | 6,990 | 6,567 | 9,074 |

**Principal Industries.** Steel production, shipbuilding, manufacture of motor vehicles and aircraft, machinery, electrical, textiles, fish curing, fish canning, brewing, coffee roasting, processing of mineral oil, smoking-tobacco and cigarettes.

# HAMBURG

## (*Freie und Hansestadt Hamburg*)

**Area:** 753 sq. km.

**Population** (31 December 1976): 1,698,615 of which 788,035 are males and 910,580 females.

**Legislature:** (Election of 3 March 1974). Representation of the Parties: Social Democratic Party (SPD) 56; Christian Demosratic Party (CDU) 51; Free Democratic Party (F.D.P.) 13.

*President of Parliament:* Herbert Dau.

**Finance.** Budget figures for 1977 were (in DM. million): Revenue, 8,685·6; Expenditure, 8,811·89.

**Livestock** (in thousands):

| | 1971 | 1972 | 1973 | 1975 |
|---|---|---|---|---|
| Horses | 2·2 | 2·5 | 3·1 | 3·2 |
| Cattle | 15·2 | 15·9 | 15·9 | 14·5 |
| Pigs | 15·8 | 14·8 | 13·0 | 10·8 |

**Principal Industries.** Shipbuilding, machinery, motor vehicles, electrical engineering, precision instruments and optics, mineral oil, dyes and varnishes, rubber, chemicals, vegetable oil, margarine, and cigarettes.

The following table shows the trade figures for 1971–1976 in million DM.:

| | 1974 | 1975 | 1976 |
|---|---|---|---|
| Foreign Trade (Importers and Exporters): | | | |
| Imports | 39,975 | 36,137 | 41,855 |
| Exports | 15,867 | 13,776 | 16,003 |
| Turnover of Wholesale Trade | — | — | — |
| Turnover of Retail Trade | 11,971 | 12,858 | 13,892 |
| Turnover of Industry | 26,939 | 26,371 | 27,460 |

# HESSE

## (*Hessen*)

**Capital**—Wiesbaden.

The State of Hesse comprises the areas of the former Prussian provinces 'Kurhessen' and 'Nassau' (excluding the exclaves formerly belonging to Hesse and the rural counties of Westerwaldkreis and Rhine-Lahn), and of the former 'Volksstaat Hessen' the provinces Starkenburg (including parts of Rheinhessen east of the Rhine river) and Oberhessen.

**Area:** 21,112 sq. km.

**Population** (31 December 1976): 5,538,432 of which 2,657,126 are males and 2,881,306 females.

The population figures for some of the main towns are (31 December 1976):
Frankfurt am Main 641,000; Wiesbaden 269,700; Kassel 201,700; Lahn 155,200; Darmstadt 139,300; Offenbach am Main 113,100.

**Legislature** (Landtag): (Election of 27 October 1974). Representation of the Parties: Social Democratic Party (SPD) 49; Christian Democratic Party (CDU 53; Free Democratic Party (FDP) 8.

*President:* Hans Wagner (CDU).

**Finance.** Budget figures for 1975–6 (in DM. million) were:

Revenue: 1975 = 10,344·2 1976 = 11,374·7
Expenditure: 1975 = 12,374·8 1976 = 13,661·4

**Agriculture.** The total arable land is 561,300 hectares. Forested areas cover 831,800 hectares.

Areas and yield of the chief crops in 1976 were:

| *Crop* | *Area (in thousand hectares)* | *Yield (in thousand tons)* |
|---|---|---|
| Rye | 46·5 | 156·3 |
| Wheat | 144·1 | 561·9 |
| Barley | 125·0 | 448·9 |
| Oats | 87·5 | 240·1 |
| Potatoes | 33·7 | 673·2 |
| Sugar beet | 24·8 | 976·9 |
| Clover | 11·2 | 48·8 |
| Lucerne | 4·4 | 27·9 |

**Livestock** (in thousands):

| | 1974 | 1975 | 1976 |
|---|---|---|---|
| Horses | 29·3 | 30·1 | 30·8 |
| Cattle | 901·6 | 888·0 | 862·2 |
| Pigs | 1,469·3 | 1,389·0 | 1,384·5 |
| Sheep | 133·6 | 133·8 | 125·0 |
| Poultry* | 5,848·6 | 5,382·5 | 5,113·5 |

* Excluding guinea-fowl and bantam-fowl.

**Principal Industries.** The following chief industrial concerns are arranged in order of importance: Chemicals; machinery; electricals; foodstuffs and stimulants; motor-cars; tin and metal ware; plastics products industry; stones and earths; caoutchouc and asbestos; steel and light metal construction; printing and allied industries; wood working; foundry; clothing.

# LOWER SAXONY

## (*Niedersachsen*)

**Capital**—Hanover.

**Area:** 47,430 sq. km.

**Population** (1975): 7,238,000 of which 3,464,000 are males and 3,774,000 females.

The population figures for some of the main towns are (1 March 1974):
Hannover 573,000; Braunschweig 271,400; Osnabrueck 164,100; Oldenburg 133,700; Wolfsburg 132,000; Salzgitter 120,100; Goettingen 119,100; Hildesheim 107,300; Wilhelmshaven 104,200.

**Legislature** (Landtag): (Election of 9 June 1974):
*President:* Heinz Müller.
Representation of the parties: Social Democratic Party

(SPD) 67; Christian Democratic Party (CDU) 77; Democratic Party (FDP) 11.

**Finance.** Budget figures for 1972 (in DM. million) were: Revenue, 10,489·2; Expenditure, 10,523·6.

**Principal Industries.** Crude oil and coal mines, iron and metal ore mining potash, stones and earths, iron, steel and metals, chemicals, plastics, wood, rubber, machines, motor cars, shipbuilding, electrotechnics, textiles, clothing, food-stuffs.

**Agriculture.** The total arable land is 1,588,372 hectares. Forested area cover 943,666 hectares.
The following are the areas and yield of the chief crops for the year 1973:

| *Crop* | *Area (in thousand hectares)* | *Yield (in thousand tons)* |
|---|---|---|
| Rye | 306·2 | 1,030·6 |
| Oats | 197·0 | 762·9 |
| Wheat | 241·7 | 1,092·9 |

*continued*

| *Crop* | *Area (in thousand hectares)* | *Yield (in thousand tons)* |
|---|---|---|
| Barley | 380·8 | 1,455·9 |
| Potatoes | 96·0 | 2,791·6 |
| Sugar beet | 121·0 | 4,902·9 |

**Livestock** (in thousands):

| | 1971 | 1972 | 1973 |
|---|---|---|---|
| Horses | 63·8 | 66·5 | 75·1 |
| Cattle | 2,707·6 | 2,783·6 | 2,921·2 |
| Pigs | 5,905·5 | 5,789·0 | 5,869·0 |
| Sheep | 125·7 | 127·7 | 130·2 |
| Goats | 3·3 | 3·0 | 2·4 |
| Poultry | 35,112·8 | 37,099·5 | 34,773·3 |
| Bee colonies | 70·8 | 78·0 | 54·4 |

# NORTH RHINE-WESTPHALIA

## (*Nordrhein-Westfalen*)

**Capital**—Düsseldorf.

On 23 August 1946, the Land North Rhine-Westphalia of today was constituted from three of five administrative districts of the former Prussian province Rhineland, viz. the administrative district Düsseldorf, Cologne and Aachen, added to which was the former Prussian province Westphalia, consisting of the administrative districts Münster, Minden and Arnsberg. With effect from 21 January 1947, the former Land Lippe was incorporated into the Land North Rhine-Westphalia and combined with the administrative district Minden. With effect from 9 June 1947, the administrative district Minden altered its name to administrative district Detmold. In the course of the communal reorganization of the land North Rhine-Westphalia, the administrative district of Aachen was dissolved on 4 August 1972 and merged with the administrative district of Köln.

**Area**: 34,057 sq. km.

**Population**: 31 December 1975: 17,129,615.
The population figures of some of the main towns are (31 December 1975):
Köln 1,013,000; Essen 677,500; Düsseldorf 664,300; Dortmund 630,000; Duisburg 591,600; Bochum 414,800; Wuppertal 405,300; Gelsenkirchen 322,500; Bielefeld 316,000; Bonn 283,000; Münster 264,500; Mönchengladbach 261,300; Aachen 242,400; Oberhausen 237,100; Hagen 229,200; Krefeld 228,400; Bottrop 197,800; Herne 190,500; Mülheim a.d. Ruhr 189,200; Leverkusen 165,900; Neuss 148,100; Remscheid 133,100; Recklinghausen 122,400.

**Legislature**: (Election of 4 May 1975).
*President:* Dr. Wilhelm Lenz.
Representation of the parties: Christian Democratic Party (CDU) 95; Social Democratic Party (SPD) 91; Free Democratic Party (FDP).

**Finance.** The budget figure for 1975 (in million DM.) was: Expenditure, 34,605·7.

**Agriculture.** The total arable land is 1,107,857 hectares. Forested areas cover 803,630 hectares.
Areas and yield of the chief crops in 1975 were:

| *Crop* | *Area (in thousand hectares)* | *Yield (in thousand tons)* |
|---|---|---|
| Wheat | 212·3 | 1,005·2 |
| Rye | 113·4 | 436·1 |
| Barley | 314·1 | 1,425·2 |
| Oats | 151·1 | 593·6 |
| Potatoes | 38·3 | 1,095·4 |
| Sugar beet | 88·2 | 3,471·3 |

**Livestock.** In 1975 livestock was numbered as follows (in thousands): horses, 83·7; cattle, 1,909·8; pigs, 4,328·9; sheep, 173·9; poultry, 16,958·7.

**Principal Industries.** Coal mining, iron and steel foundries, machinery, textiles, chemicals, iron, steel, metalware.

| *Production* | *Unit* | 1975 |
|---|---|---|
| Hard coal | 1,000 tons | 83,419 |
| Coke | ,, | 29,173 |
| Lignite | ,, | 107,426 |
| Briquettes of lignite | ,, | 4,984 |
| Pig iron | ,, | 19,393 |
| Raw steel ingots | ,, | 25,547 |
| Rolled steel | ,, | 17,210 |
| Drawn wire | ,, | 1,160 |
| Castings (iron, steel and malleable) | ,, | 1,784 |
| Cement | ,, | 13,317 |
| Burnt lime | ,, | 5,589 |
| Bricks | 1,000 m$^3$ | 1,986 |
| Fireproof products | 1,000 tons | 1,247 |
| Sulphuric acid (incl. production of cokeries) | ,, | 1,847 |
| Nitrogenous fertilizer (incl. production of cokeries) | ,, | 683 |
| Paints and varnishes | ,, | 669 |
| Machines for mining industry | ,, | 235 |

*continued*

| *Production* | *Unit* | 1975 |
|---|---|---|
| Cranes and hoisting machinery | ,, | 69 |
| Installation and implements | ,, | 49 |
| Cables and electric lines | ,, | 278 |
| Springs of all kinds | ,, | 168 |
| Locks and fittings | ,, | 208 |

*continued*

| *Production* | *Unit* | 1975 |
|---|---|---|
| Needles | tons | 2,588 |
| Tools of all kinds | mil. DM. | 1,038 |
| Spun yarns | 1,000 tons | 175 |
| Electric power | mill. kWh. | 146,113 |

## RHINELAND-PALATINATE
## (*Rheinland-Pfalz*)

**Capital**—Mainz.

**Area**: 19,838 sq. km.

**Population** (31 December 1976): 3,649,001, of which 1,740,467 are males and 1,908,534 females.

The population figures for some of the main towns are (31 December 1976):
Mainz 183,900; Ludwigshafen am Rhein 166,000; Koblenz 116,900; Kaiserslautern 100,300; Trier 99,100.

**Legislature**: (Election of 9 March 1975).

*President:* Albrecht Martin.

Representation of the parties: Christian Democratic Party (CDU) 55; Social Democratic Party (SPD) 40; Free Democratic Party (FDP) 5.

**Finance.** Budget figures for 1975 (in DM. million) were: Revenue, 7,218·7; Expenditure, 8,360·4.

**Agriculture.** The total arable land is 505,776 hectares. Forested areas cover 751,680 hectares. Areas and yield of the chief crops in 1976 were:

| *Crop* | *Area (in thousand hectares)* | *Yield (in thousand tons)* |
|---|---|---|
| Rye | 37·1 | 104 |
| Wheat | 122·1 | 385 |
| Barley | 130·0 | 341 |
| Oats | 63·0 | 101 |

*continued*

| *Crop* | *Area (in thousand hectares)* | *Yield (in thousand tons)* |
|---|---|---|
| Potatoes | 32·6 | 603 |
| Sugar beet | 27·3 | 1,189 |
| Vineyards | 64·6 | 6,028 |

**Livestock** (in thousands):

| | 1974 | 1975 | 1976 |
|---|---|---|---|
| Horses | 19·3 | 20·2 | 21·0 |
| Cattle | 684·0 | 675·8 | 654·0 |
| Pigs | 710·7 | 677·0 | 683·1 |
| Sheep | 75·1 | 77·6 | 83·0 |
| Poultry* (chicken) | 4,506·7 | 4,295·8 | 4,312·5 |

* Excluding guinea-fowl and bantam-fowl.

**Principal Industries.** Chemicals and chemical products: machinery; stone quarrying, clay and sand pits; footwear; motor vehicles; metal products; beverage industries.

## SCHLESWIG-HOLSTEIN

**Capital**—Kiel.

The Land Schleswig-Holstein was constituted from the province Schleswig-Holstein of the former Land Prussia. In November 1945 a territorial interchange of minor importance was made between Kreis duchy Lauenburg and Mecklenburg.

**Area**: 15,678 sq. km.

**Population** (31 December 1975): 2,582,412, of which 1,238,750 are males and 1,343,662 females.

The towns populated by more than 50,000 are (31 December 1975): Kiel 262,100; Lübeck 232,200; Flensburg 93,200; Neumünster 84,700; Norderstedt 61,500.

**Legislature** (Election of 13 April 1975):
President of the Landtag: Dr. Helmut Lemke.

Representation of the parties: Christian Democratic Party (CDU) 37; Social Democratic Party (SPD) 30; Free Democratic Party (FDP) 5; South Schleswig Association (Danes) (SSW) 1.

**Finance.** Budget figures for 1975 (in DM. million) were: Revenue and Expenditure 5,984·2383.

**Agriculture** (1975). The total arable land is 634,620 hectares. Forested area covers 137,300 hectares.

| *Crop* | *Area (in thousand hectares)* | *Yield (in thousand tons)* |
|---|---|---|
| Rye | 75·9 | 236·9 |
| Wheat | 113·8 | 636·8 |
| Barley | 126·5 | 558·0 |
| Oats | 110·6 | 402·3 |
| Mixed grain | 8·1 | 18·7 |
| Potatoes | 7·6 | 159·1 |
| Sugar beet | 20·7 | 734·9 |
| Oleaginous fruits | 44·2 | 102·5 |

**Livestock** (in thousands):

| | 1974 | 1975 |
|---|---|---|
| Horses | 28·6 | 30·6 |
| Cattle | 1,507·0 | 1,525·4 |
| Pigs | 1,567·3 | 1,619·6 |
| Sheep | 113·2 | 121·1 |
| Goats | — | — |
| Poultry* | 4,468·5 | 4,380·1 |
| Bee colonies | 35·5 | 34·4 |

* Excluding guinea-fowl and bantam-fowl.

**Principal Industries.** The following chief industrial concerns are arranged in order of importance in 1975: machinery, shipbuilding; meat manufacturing; milk products; fishing and fish products; electrical engineering; prints; chemicals; mineral oil manufacture; stones and earth; foreign visitors

# SAARLAND

**Capital**—Saarbrücken.

**Area:** 2,568 sq. km.

**Population** (30 June 1976): 1,092,900, of which 518,800 are males and 574,000 are females. Saarbrücken, the principal town, has 204,300 inhabitants (30 June 1976).

By the Treaty of Versailles the Saar Territory was placed for 15 years under the control of the League of Nations and at the end of this period the territory reverted to Germany, following a plebiscite.

In March 1945 the Saar was occupied by U.S. Forces and was part of the French Zone of Occupation from 1945 until 1947.

The Saar, separated *de facto* from the rest of Western Germany in 1947, has been in economic union with France since that time.

An agreement on the future political status of the Saar (so-called European Statute) was signed between Germany and France on 23 October 1954, but rejected by the Saar population in a referendum on 23 October 1955. Of the valid ballots 67·7 per cent were cast against, and 32·3 per cent in favour of the Statute.

As a result of the success at the polls of the Christian Democratic Party by a narrow majority in December 1955, and with the support of the two other pro-German parties, the Government became committed to the policy of unification with Western Germany. On account of the German-French agreement on the Saar of 27 October 1956, signed in Luxembourg on 31 December 1956, the Saar Territory was incorporated in the German Federal Republic on 1 January 1957. Its reintegration with the Federal Republic of Germany was completed by 5 July 1959.

**Legislature** (Landtag): (Election of 4 May 1975).

*President:* Dr. Hans Maurer (CDU).

Representation of the parties:

| | |
|---|---|
| Christian Democratic Party (CDU) | 25 |
| Social Democratic Party (SPD) | 22 |
| Free Democratic Party (FDP) | 3 |
| | 50 |

**Finance.** Budget figures for 1976 (in DM. million) were: Revenue, 2,598·5; Expenditure, 2,612·9

**Agriculture.** The total arable land is 65,600 hectares. Forested area covers 81,000 hectares. Areas and yield of the chief crops in 1976 were:

| *Crop* | *Area (in thousand hectares)* | *Yield (in thousand tons)* |
|---|---|---|
| Wheat | 12·0 | 36·9 |
| Rye | 7·5 | 20·9 |
| Barley | 12·6 | 33·1 |
| Oats | 9·0 | 16·8 |
| Potatoes | 6·7 | 89·9 |

**Livestock** (in thousands):

| | 1974 | 1975 | 1976 |
|---|---|---|---|
| Horses | 3·8 | 4·0 | 4·1 |
| Cattle | 74·5 | 72·7 | 69·3 |
| Pigs | 66·3 | 52·5 | 50·4 |
| Sheep | 10·2 | 10·3 | 9·6 |
| Goats | 0·4 | 0·3 | 0·3 |
| Poultry* | 629·4 | 631·4 | 591·7 |

* Excluding guinea-fowl and bantam-fowl.

**Mining.** Coal mines and iron and steel works are the basis of the Saar economy, and almost one-third of the working population is employed in these industries. In 1973 the Saar coal mines produced 9·2 million tons of coal; the average shift output amounted to 4,074 kg. The five iron foundries had 17 blast furnaces working and produced 5·0 million tons of pig-iron and 5·7 million tons of crude steel.

The following table shows production of coal, iron and steel for five representative years (in thousand tons):

| *Year* | *Hard coal* | *Crude steel* | *Pig iron* |
|---|---|---|---|
| 1972 | 10,429 | 4,998 | 4,468 |
| 1973 | 9,175 | 5,713 | 4,975 |
| 1974 | 8,929 | 6,368 | 5,533 |
| 1975 | 8,974 | 4,650 | 4,081 |
| 1976 | 9,295 | 4,965 | 4,408 |

Apart from the foundries of Völklingen-Burbach, Dillingen, Neunkirchen, Brebach, Bous and the iron works of Homburg, St. Ingbert, Dillingen and Hostenbach, the Saar economy has 208 enterprises of all sizes of the iron-manufacturing industry. In 1976 the iron-producing industry employed about 36,520 persons out of a total employed population of 411,500.

# German Democratic Republic

## (DEUTSCHE DEMOKRATISCHE REPUBLIK)

**Chairman of the Council of State**—Erich Honecker.

**Prime Minister**—Willi Stoph.

**National Flag:** A tricolour fesse-wise, black, red, gold; centred, the coat of arms: a hammer and compass within a wreath of grain.

**Chairman of the Council of Ministers:** Willi Stoph.

### CONSTITUTION AND GOVERNMENT

After the unconditional surrender of Germany on the 8 May 1945 the declaration on the subjection of Germany was signed on the 5 June by the government representatives of France, Great Britain, the U.S.S.R., and the U.S.A. An Allied Control Council was set up with its seat in Berlin and the supreme power in matters affecting Germany as a whole was transferred to it. The decree defining the occupation zones was signed. The general administration of Berlin was taken over by the Inter-Allied Military Command. The Potsdam agreement of the 2 August 1945 laid down the principles for a peaceful and democratic Germany: the complete extermination of German nazism and militarism and their roots, so that "Germany can never again threaten her neighbours or the maintenance of peace throughout the world"; the destruction of the national socialist party "with its associated organizations and sub-organizations", guarantees being provided so that they "cannot reappear in any other form"; the elimination of the excessive concentration of economic power in the form of monopoly agreements; the treatment of Germany as an economic unit; the establishment of the Oder and Neisse (Lausitzer) rivers as Germany's eastern frontier.

In June 1945 parties and organizations were permitted in the Soviet occupation zone and their proposals for the provision of administrations for Saxony, Saxony-Anhalt, Thuringia, Brandenburg and Mecklenburg-Vorpommern were confirmed. The first elections in the provinces of the Soviet occupation zone took place in the autumn of 1946. In this zone the directions in the Potsdam agreement were carried out in full. On the 18 March 1948 the second German People's Congress elected a German People's Council of 400 members to represent the whole of Germany.

The German Democratic Republic was founded in Berlin on the 7 October 1949. At its ninth session the German People's Council resolved to transform itself into the Provisional People's Chamber of the GDR. On the 11 October 1949 at a general assembly of the Provisional People's Chamber and the Provisional Provincial Chambers, Wilhelm Pieck, the SED chairman, was elected President of the GDR. At the third session of the Provisional People's Chamber on the 12 October 1949 Otto Grotewohl was confirmed as Minister President (Premier).

#### The People's Chamber

*President:* Horst Sindermann (SED).
*Deputy:* Friedrich Ebert (SED).

The supreme organ of power in the GDR is the People's Chamber, whose 500 representatives are elected at free, universal, and secret elections. The People's Chamber is the legislative and executive body. It determines the aims of the development of the GDR. The members of the People's Chamber conduct regular consultations and debates and account for their activities to the electors.

Laws are voted by the People's Chamber, as the sole organ for making the constitution and the laws. The constitution may be changed by law by the People's Chamber only with the consent of at least two thirds of the members.

Every citizen over the age of 18 is entitled to vote and may be elected. Of the 500 elected members of the People's Chamber in 1976, 57 per cent are by social origin workmen. 168 members are women, 40 members under 25 years. Party members:

| | | | |
|---|---|---|---|
| SED | 127 | CDU | 52 |
| FDGB | 68 | LDPD | 52 |
| DBD | 52 | FDJ | 40 |
| NDPD | 52 | DFD | 35 |
| Kultursbund der DDR (GDR Culture Fedn.) | | | 22 |

#### Council of State

On the 12 September 1960 the fourteenth session of the People's Chamber passed the law for the formation of the GDR National Council which, between the meetings of the People's Chamber, whose elected organ it is and to which it is responsible, carries out the duties arising from the laws and resolutions of the People's Chamber. After the expiry of the period for which the People's Chamber has been elected, the National Council continues its activity until the new National Council has been elected by the People's Chamber. The chairman of the National Council publishes the laws passed by the People's Chamber in the law gazette.

### COUNCIL OF STATE OF THE GERMAN DEMOCRATIC REPUBLIC

*Chairmen:*
Erich Honecker (SED)
Willi Stoph (SED)

*Deputy Chairmen:*
Horst Sindermann (SED)
Friedrich Ebert (SED)
Gerald Götting (CDU)
Dr. Manfred Gerlach (LDPD)
Prof. Dr. Heinrich Homann (NDPD)
Ernst Goldenbaum (DBD)

*Members:*
Kurt Anclam (LDPD)
Erich Correns (ptl.)
Willi Grandetzka (DBD)
Prof. Kurt Hager (SED)
Brunhilde Hanke (SED)
Prof. Dr. Lieselott Herforth (SED
Friedrich Kind (CDU)
Margarete Müller (SED)
Bernard Quandt (SED)
Prof. Albert Norden (SED)
Dr. Klaus Sorgenicht (SED)
Paul Strauss (SED)
Ilse Thiele (SED)
Harry Tisch (SED)
Paul Verner (SED)
Rosel Walther (NDPD)

*Secretary:*
Heinz Eichler (SED)

#### Council of Ministers

The Council of Ministers conducts all government business. As the organ of the People's Chamber, it is responsible and accountable to that body for its activities. The largest group in the People's Chamber provides the chairman of the Council of Ministers. The formation of the Council is entrusted to the chairman and the Council constitute the presidium from among themselves.

*Council of Ministers of the German Democratic Republic*[1]

*Chairman of the Council of Ministers:* Willi Stoph (SED)
*First Deputies of Chairman:* Werner Krolikowski (SED), Alfred Neumann (SED).
*Deputy Chairman and Chairman of the National Contracts Court:* Manfred Flegel, (NDPD).
*Deputy Chairman and Minister of Justice:* Hans-Joachim Heusinger, (LDPD).
*Deputy Chairman and Minister for Construction of General and Agricultural Machinery and Vehicles:* Günther Kleiber, (SED).
*Deputy Chairman and Minister for Materials:* Wolfgang Rauchfuss, (SED).
*Deputy Chairman and Minister for Protection of the Environment and Water Management:* Dr. Hans Reichelt, (DBD).

[1] The Chairman, the First Deputy Chairmen, the Deputy Chairmen and the Ministers, Siegfried Böhm, Walter Halbritter, Heinz Kuhrig, constitute the Presidium of the Council of Ministers of the GDR.

*Deputy Chairman and Chairman of the National Planning Commission:* Gerhard Schürer, (SED).
*Deputy Chairman and Minister for Posts and Long Distance Communication:* Rudolph Schulze, (CDU).
*Deputy Chairman:* Dr. Gerhard Weiss, (SED).
*Deputy Chairman and Minister for Learning and Technology:* Dr. Herbert Weiz, (SED).
*Minister for Traffic Communications:* Otto Arndt, (SED).
*Minister for Light Industry:* Dr. Karl Bettin, (SED).
*Minister for Geology:* Dr. Manfred Bochmann, (SED).
*Minister of Finance:* Siegfried Böhm, (SED).
*Minister for Secondary and Vocational Education:* Prof. Hans-Joachim Böhme, (SED).
*Minister for Trade and Supply:* Gerhard Briksa, (SED).
*Minister of the Interior:* Friedrich Dickel (Colonel-General), (SED).
*Minister of Foreign Affairs:* Oskar Fischer, (SED).
*Minister for Production of Machine Tools and processing Machinery:* Dr. Rudi Georgi, (SED).
*Minister for the Glass and Ceramic Industries:* Werner Greiner-Petter, (SED).
*Minister and Head of the Prices Bureau attached to the Council of Ministers:* Walter Halbritter, (SED).
*Minister for Culture:* Hans-Joachim Hoffmann, (SED).
*Minister for National Defence:* Heinz Hoffmann (General in the Army), (SED).
*Minister for People's Education:* Margot Honecker, (SED).
*Minister for Construction:* Wolfgang Junker, (SED).
*Minister for Land, Forestry and Food Production:* Heinz Kuhrig, (SED).
*Minister, Chairman of the Workers and Peasants Inspection Committee:* Heinz Matthes, (SED).
*Minister of Health:* Prof. Dr. sc. med. Ludwig Mecklinger (OMR), (SED).
*Minister of National Security:* Erich Mielke (Colonel-General), (SED).
*Minister for Coal and Energy:* Klaus Siebold, (SED).
*Minister for Mines, Metallurgy and Potash:* Dr. Kurt Singhuber, (SED).
*Minister for Overseas Trade:* Horst Sölle, (SED).
*Minister for Electro-technology and Electronics:* Otfried Steger, (SED).
*Minister for Industry at Regional Level and for the Foodstuffs Industry:* Dr. Udo-Dieter Wange, (SED).
*Minister for the Chemical Industry:* Gunther Wyschofsky, (SED).
*Minister for Construction of Heavy Machinery and Plant:* Gerhard Zimmermann, (SED).
*Deputy Chairman of the National Planning Commission:* Dr. Kurt Fichtner, (SED).
*President of the State Bank of GDR:* Horst Kaminsky, (SED).
*Secretary to the National Planning Commission:* Heinz Klopfer, (SED).
*Mayor of Berlin, the GDR State capital:* Erhard Krack, (SED).

*Local Representative Bodies of the People*

The above bodies are the elected national organs of power in the regions, districts, towns and municipalities. On their own responsibility and on the basis of the law they decide on all matters affecting their territory and its citizens.

*Political Parties and Mass Organizations*
*Parties*

1. German Socialist Party of Unity
   The SED was formed in April 1946 from the merging of the KPD and SPD.
   First secretary of the SED: Erich Honecker
2. German Democratic Peasants Party (DBD)
3. German Christian-Democratic Union (CDU)
4. German Liberal-Democratic Party (LDPD)
5. German National-Democratic Party (NDPD)

*Mass Organizations*

1. Free German Trade Union Federation (FDGB)
2. Society for German-Soviet Friendship (DSF)
3. German Democratic Women's Federation (DFD)
4. Free German Youth (FDJ)
   The FDJ leads the "Ernst Thälmann" Pioneer Organization
5. GDR Culture Federation
6. German Gymnastic and Sports Federation (DTSB)

*Other Social Organizations:*

People's Solidarity
Union of the GDR Consumer Associations
Urania—Society for the Propagation of Scientific Knowledge
Chamber of Technology
Peasants Mutual Assistance Union (VdgB)
Society for Sport and Practice (GST)
German Red Cross in the GDR (DRK)
Anti-fascist Resistance Fighters Committee
GDR Peace Council, and others.

## LEGAL SYSTEM

In the GDR the law is administered by the supreme court, the regional courts, the district courts and by the social courts (conflict and commissions and arbitration commissions). All judges' and lay assessors are elected through the People's Representative Organization. All members of the social courts are directly elected by the citizens. The supreme court is the highest organ for the administration of the law. The president and the judges of the Supreme Court and also the public prosecutor are elected by the People's Chamber, to which they are responsible; between the sittings of the Chamber, they are responsible to the National Council.

Penal responsibility is determined by the law of the GDR and the basic legal standard is the 1968 GDR penal code.

In the publicly owned concerns and institutions of the GDR, conflict commissions operate; they consider workmen's differences, petty penal offences, disputes about civil rights and others of a straightforward kind. The arbitration commissions fulfil similar functions in residential areas. The co-operation of the citizens in the administration of justice is ensured by law.

**Supreme Court of the GDR**

*President:* Dr. Heinrich Toeplitz.
*Vice-Presidents:* General Major Dr. Günter Sarge, Dr. Werner Strasberg.

*Supreme National Association of the Bar of the GDR*
*Attorney General:* Dr. Josef Streit.

**Supreme Court**

*President:* Dr. Heinrich Toeplitz (CDU).

*Vice-Presidents:* Peter-Paul Siegert, Walter Ziegler.

## AREA AND POPULATION

The total area of the German Democratic Republic is 108,179 sq. km. The population at 31 December 1976 was 16,767,030 i.e. 155 people per sq. km. 75·5 per cent of the population are urban dwellers.

Chief cities and towns with population are (1976): Berlin, Hauptstadt, 1,106,200; Leipzig, 564,500; Dresden, 510,400; Karl-Marx-Stadt, 307,500; Magdeburg, 279,400; Halle, 234,200; Rostock, 217,000; Erfurt, 205,400; Zwickau, 122,100; Potsdam, 121,900; Gera 117,300; Schwerin, 110,000; Cottbus, 101,200; Jena, 100,800; Dessau, 100,700.

The 15 *Bezirke* (areas) are called after their respective chief towns. The following table shows the population (units) and area of the *Bezirke* ($km^2$) in 1976:

| | *Population* | *Area, km²* |
|---|---|---|
| Hauptstadt Berlin | 1,106,200 | 403 |
| Cottbus | 874,000 | 8,262 |
| Dresden | 1,825,800 | 6,738 |
| Erfurt | 1,238,200 | 7,349 |
| Frankfurt | 690,200 | 7,186 |
| Gera | 737,200 | 4,004 |
| Halle | 1,863,500 | 8,771 |
| Karl-Marx-Stadt | 1,962,200 | 6,009 |
| Leipzig | 1,435,400 | 4,966 |
| Magdeburg | 1,283,300 | 11,525 |
| Neubrandenburg | 625,000 | 10,792 |
| Potsdam | 1,117,100 | 12,572 |
| Rostock | 871,200 | 7,074 |
| Schwerin | 589,100 | 8,672 |
| Suhl | 548,200 | 2,856 |
| DDR | 16,767,030 | 108,179 |

At 30 September 1976 the working population of the German Democratic Republic was 8,018,300 of which 49·9 per cent was women.

## CURRENCY

The unit of currency is the Mark der Deutschen Demokratischen Republik of 100 pfennige. 1 M is equal to 0·3999902 grammes of gold. The Mark is now worth 0·405 roubles. The U.S. $ equals 2·22 M.

### FINANCE AND BANKING

The following table shows the items of revenue and expenditure for the years 1975 and 1976 (in millions of marks):

| | 1975 | 1976 |
|---|---|---|
| Revenue | 114,662 | 117,588 |
| Expenditure | 114,160 | 117,128 |
| Expenditure on: | | |
| Public education | 8,276 | 8,907 |
| Art and culture | 1,953 | 2,044 |
| Public health and social services | 29,246 | 30,492 |

Among the banking institutions the most important are the Staatsbank der Deutschen Demokratischen Republik, Berlin, which is the Bank of Issue, the Industrie und Handelsbank der Deutschen Demokratischen Republik, Berlin, and the Deutsche Aussenhandelsbank AG, Berlin. President of the Staatsbank der Deutschen Demokratischen Republik: Horst Kaminsky.

### PRODUCTION, INDUSTRY AND COMMERCE

**Industry.** Breakdown of National Income (in the Marxist economics sense, the total production of material goods minus the amount corresponding to depreciation of the production apparatus. Not, therefore, corresponding to the GNP) according to forms of ownership:

| *Form of Ownership* | *Total* | | *Of which industry and prod. trades (excl. building trade)* | |
|---|---|---|---|---|
| | 1970 | 1976 | 1970 | 1976 |
| | *Percentages* | | | |
| Socialist Enterprises | 85·6 | 95·8 | 82·8 | 96·8 |
| People's Enterprises (nationalized) | 68·9 | — | 79·7 | 95·6 |
| Co-operative Enterprises | 16·8 | — | 3·2 | 1·2 |
| Enterprises with State participation and commission contract | 8·8 | 0·8 | 11·6 | 0·0 |
| Private Enterprises | 5·6 | 3·4 | 5·6 | 3·2 |

3·1 million hectares of land have been sequestered and given to farmers.

The first half-year plan started in 1948. It was followed by a two-year plan (1949–50) and a five-year plan (1951–55). The last five-year plan was concluded in 1975.

The following table shows the manufacture of selected products for 1975–76:

| *Product* | *Unit* | 1975 | 1976 |
|---|---|---|---|
| Electric energy | million kwh | 84,505 | 89,150 |
| Crude lignite | 1,000 tons | 246,706 | 246,897 |
| Brown coal briquettes | 1,000 tons | 48,938 | 48,679 |
| Sulphuric acid | 1,000 tons $H_2SO_4$ | 1,002 | 957 |
| Diesel fuel | 1,000 tons | 4,853 | 5,108 |
| Potassium fertilizer | 1,000 tons $K_2O$ | 3,019 | 3,161 |
| Nitrogen fertilizer | tons N | 538,336 | 776,121 |
| Phosphate fertilizer | tons $P_2O_5$ | 427,350 | 423,276 |
| Synthetic rubber | tons | 143,916 | 145,473 |
| Synthetic fibres | 1,000 tons | 112 | 118 |
| Pig iron | 1,000 tons | 2,456 | 2,528 |
| Ingot steel | 1,000 tons | 6,472 | 6,732 |
| Rolled steel | 1,000 tons | 4,281 | 4,593 |
| Products from second stage processing | 1,000 tons | 2,793 | 3,008 |
| Private cars | units | 159,147 | 163,970 |
| Tractors | units | 4,027 | 4,018 |
| Agricultural machinery | million marks* | 2,744 | 2,945 |
| Printing and duplicating machines | million marks* | 466 | 481 |
| Metal cutting machine tools | million marks* | 1,255 | 1,412 |
| Electronic equipment | million marks* | 1,493 | 1,709 |
| Semi conductor equipment | million marks* | 719 | 866 |
| Data processing and office equipment | million marks* | 2,033 | 2,173 |
| Electrical household goods | million marks* | 1,027 | 1,076 |
| Electric washing machines | 1,000 | 374 | 390 |
| Household refrigerators | 1,000 | 527 | 554 |
| Vacuum cleaners | 1,000 | 773 | 840 |
| Television sets | 1,000 | 509 | 561 |
| Radios | 1,000 | 1,070 | 1,122 |
| Typewriters | 1,000 | 408 | 407 |
| Straw cellulose | 1,000 tons | 435 | 424 |
| Paper | 1,000 tons | 796 | 799 |
| Shoes | 1,000 pairs | 79,014 | 80,067 |
| Leather shoes | 1,000 pairs | 39,122 | 42,813 |
| Textiles | 1,000 $m^2$ | 862,338 | 890,358 |
| Cotton and cotton-type textiles | 1,000 $m^2$ | 429,364 | 426,060 |
| Knitted underwear | 1,000 | 161,538 | 163,005 |

* At 1975 prices.

The following table is a summary of the production index (1970 = 100):

| | 1975 | 1976 |
|---|---|---|
| Chemical industry | 149 | 158 |
| Metallurgy | 139 | 147 |
| Building materials industry | 140 | 147 |
| Machine and vehicle construction | 132 | 141 |
| Electrical engineering, Electronics, equipment construction | 155 | 170 |
| Light industry (excluding textile industry) | 133 | 141 |
| Textile industry | 129 | 136 |
| Industry as a whole | 136 | 144 |

3·1 million persons are employed in industry.

In 1976, the gross industrial production amounted to 220 (at 1975 prices) thousand million marks. The most important spheres of industry are: machine and vehicle construction (49,693 million marks); the chemical industry (31,529 million marks); and electrical engineering (electronics) equipment construction (21,643 million marks). In 1976, total investments within the national economy amounted to 45·5 thousand million marks, of which 22·7 million thousand million marks were industrial investments.

Investment means is mainly spent on modern machines and equipment, on mechanizing and automating the production processes as well as for modernization of old equipment. In brown coal mining the DDR takes first place in the world.

**Agriculture.** The total arable land was 6,292,872 hectares in 1976. Meadows and pastures covered 1,295,091 hectares, forests and woodland 2,950,994 hectares. Of this 5,938,586 hectares is under the control of socialist agriculture.

The following table shows the yield per hectare (five year averages) of principal crops:

| *Annual average* | *Cereal crops* | *Of this Wheat* | *Rye* | *Pota-toes* | *Sugar beet* |
|---|---|---|---|---|---|
| | | 100 *kilograms per hectare* | | | |
| 1956–60 | 24·8 | 31·2 | 21·1 | 171·3 | 262·5 |
| 1961–65 | 25·8 | 31·5 | 21·2 | 165·7 | 243·7 |
| 1966–70 | 29·8 | 36·5 | 23·7 | 184·8 | 313·4 |
| 1971–75 | 36·2 | 40·7 | 27·8 | 170·8 | 279·0 |
| 1972–76 | 35·9 | 39·9 | 27·5 | 165·6 | 265·9 |

**Commerce.** Although the chief trade of the German Democratic Republic is with the Soviet Union and other Socialist countries, the trade with Western Europe is substantial and has considerably increased in the last few years.

The following table shows the value of total turnover by the principal countries (million valuta-marks)

| *Country* | 1975 | 1976 |
|---|---|---|
| U.S.S.R. | 26,539·4 | 27,785·1 |
| Czechoslovakia | 6,913·2 | 7,519·7 |
| Federal Republic of Germany | 4,989·5 | 5,441·5 |
| Poland | 6,619·5 | 7,476·8 |
| Hungary | 4,029·7 | 5,104·2 |
| Bulgaria | 2,385·5 | 2,767·8 |
| Romania | 2,015·8 | 3,043·3 |
| France | 1,143·9 | 1,669·4 |
| Great Britain | 1,055·2 | 2,612·2 |
| West Berlin | 1,485·1 | 1,918·5 |
| Netherlands | 1,186·6 | 1,158·0 |
| Sweden | 993·3 | 1,152·2 |
| U.S.A. | 1,086·8 | 2,241·6 |

The following table gives some important exports for 1976:

| *Commodity* | *Unit* | 1976 |
|---|---|---|
| Diesel fuel | 1,000 tons | 1,423·7 |
| Petrol | 1,000 tons | 416·1 |
| Machine-tools for metal cutting-machining | million marks | 1,177·8 |
| Agricultural machines | million marks | 966·4 |
| Cars | units | 81,025·0 |
| Motor-cycles above 50 $cm^2$ | units | 45,477·0 |
| Furniture | million marks | 654·7 |
| Cameras | 1,000 | 515·5 |
| Typewriters | 1,000 | 344·1 |
| Cotton and cotton-type fabrics | 1,000 $m^2$ | 31,950·0 |

The following table gives some important imports for 1976:

| *Commodity* | *Unit/Value* | 1976 |
|---|---|---|
| Crude oil | 1,000 tons | 18,036 |
| Coal | 1,000 tons | 6,096 |
| Iron-ore | 1,000 tons Fe | 2,053 |
| Bauxite | 1,000 tons | 261 |
| Machine-tools for metal cutting-machining | million marks | 516 |
| Paper | 1,000 tons | 229 |
| Machines for textile and leather industry | million marks | 474 |
| Cotton fabrics | 1,000 $m^2$ | 114,630 |
| Leather shoes | 1,000 pairs | 4,590 |
| Wine and champagne | 1,000 hectolitres | 1,466 |
| Cigarettes | million | 7,676 |
| Wheat | 1,000 tons | 1,691 |

The Total value of imports in 1976 was 45,921·0 million valuta-marks (39,289·0 in 1975). Total value of exports in 1976 was 39,535·5 million valuta-marks (35,104·6 in 1975).

## COMMUNICATIONS

In 1976, there were 14,306 km. of railway lines, 47,530 km. of classified roads and 2,538 km. of navigable waterways.

Interflug flies on 48 routes and has agency-contracts with 151 foreign airlines.

In 1976 passenger road traffic was 21,870 million passenger-km. and freight road traffic 18,655 million ton-km.

Comparative 1976 figures for the railroads were 21,955 million passenger-km. and 51,792 million ton-km.

Rostock is the country's largest port and is being enlarged (11·5 million tons in 1976).

## EDUCATION

*Education and Training:* The educational and training institutions in the GDR have a uniform socialist cultural character. They comprise the people's education and culture, professional training, universities and the vocational system and also the instruction and further education of the working population. In detail, the whole system is divided into the pre-school institutions, the ten-grade polytechnic secondary schools for general education, the advanced polytechnic secondary schools (university entrance), special schools for physically and mentally handicapped children, establishments for professional training including professional training with university entrance, the vocational schools, universities and institutes of university status, and establishments for the instruction and further education of the working population. The determining factor in the uniform socialist educational system, the construction of which goes back to a resolution of the GDR People's Chamber in 1965, is the socialist general education.

*Education for the People:* (a) Pre-school education. The pre-school training organizations take children in day nurseries from the age of one year. After the age of 3, children are prepared in kindergartens for the transfer to schools for general education. In 1976 there were 11,714 of these establishments in the GDR, caring for a total of 671,281 children.

(b) Ten-grade polytechnic secondary schools for general education. These guarantee the constitutional right of all children to secondary education. A uniform syllabus provides continuous education and instruction in mathematics, natural science, sociology, German and foreign languages, music and aesthetic subjects, and sport. The feature of secondary education schools in the GDR is the polytechnic instruction and training, which overcomes the separation of school from ordinary life. In 1976, 2,649,158 pupils attended these polytechnic secondary schools for general education.

(c) Continuation polytechnic secondary schools. In conjunction with the tenth grade, these schools prepare a proportion of the young people in two school years for admission to university. At the conclusion of the twelth grade, students gain their university entrance. In 1976 there were 284 of these establishments with 47,562 students.

*Advanced education:* This covers the whole of the higher education establishments in the GDR. At present these number 54 (of which 7 are universities). In 1976 there were 130,201 registered students.

## RELIGION

In the GDR freedom of conscience and belief is guaranteed by the constitution. Every citizen has the right to profess a religious belief and carry out religious practices. There is no state church. State and church, school and church are separated.

There are eight evangelical regional churches in the GDR with some 7,500 church communities. The catholic church, except in three small areas, is scattered; there are 27 other religious communions.

# Ghana

(MEMBER OF THE COMMONWEALTH)

**Capital**—Accra.

**Head of State**—Col. I. K. Acheampong.

**National Flag:** On a tricolour fesse-wise, red, gold, green, a star five-pointed centred black.

## CONSTITUTION AND GOVERNMENT

GHANA (or the Gold Coast, as it used to be called) lies on the West coast of Africa between 1° 12′ east and 3° 15′ west longitude and 11° 11′ north latitude. It is bounded on the south by the Gulf of Guinea, on the east by the Republic of Togo, on the north by Haute Volta and on the west by the Ivory Coast.

The first contact of the Gold Coast with Europe was probably made by Portuguese navigators who visited the country in the second half the 15th century in search of gold, ivory and spices. So much gold was obtained in the district between rivers Ankobra and Volta that the Portuguese named the country Mina, meaning 'Mine', and the French, Côte de l'or or the Gold Coast, a name later adopted by the English and applied to the whole country.

In 1782, the Portuguese built Elmina Castle as a permanent trading post. So profitable did the traffic in slaves and gold become that other European traders also entered the field.

When in 1872 the Danish and the Dutch Governments withdrew from the country, the Colonial Office in Britain decided not to leave the Gold Coast but rather to turn it into a crown colony. As a result, the southern section of the country became a British Crown Colony. From this base, the British administration became involved in a series of wars resulting in the final defeat and annexation of Ashanti in 1901. A protectorate was declared over the North (then the Northern Territories) in 1898, and in 1919, after World War I, part of the German protectorate of Togoland became a British mandated territory. Later, after World War II, the protectorate was administered by Britain as part of the Gold Coast, and following a plebiscite held in 1956, became part of the country on the attainment of independence.

On 6 March 1957, the Gold Coast became an independent State, and was renamed Ghana after one of the ancient Sudanese empires which flourished between the fourth and tenth centuries. On 1 July 1960 Ghana became a Republic within the Commonwealth.

On 24 February 1966, the Ghana Armed Forces and the Police, in a popular coup d'état, overthrew the dictatorial regime of the late Dr. Kwame Nkrumah which had ruled the country since the attainment of independence. A National Liberation Council, formed after the coup, administered the country. After the General Election of 29 August, 1969 the Council handed over power to a civilian government led by Dr. K. A. Busia.

However, the Ghana Armed Forces had to take over the reins of government again on 13th January 1972.

### National Redemption Council

*Chairman of NRC and Head of State:* Col. I. K. Acheampong.
Brig. N. Y. R. Ashley-Lassen (*Chief of Defence Staff*).
Col. J. C. Adjeitey.
Maj. Kwame Baah.
Maj. A. H. Selormey.
Maj. K. B. Agbo.
Maj. R. J. Felli.
Mr. J. H. Cobbina (*Inspector-General of Police*).
Mr. E. N. Moore (*Attorney-General*).

### Commissioners in charge of Ministries

*Commissioner in charge of Defence, Finance and Sports:* Col. I. K. Acheampong.
*Chief of Defence Staff and Commissioner in charge of Special Duties:* Brig. N. Y. R. Ashley-Lassen.
*Commissioner in charge of Agriculture:* Col. F. G. Bernasko.
*Commissioner in charge of Economic Planning:* Major R. J. A. Felli.
*Commissioner in charge of Education, Youth and Culture* Col. E. O. Nyante.
*Commissioner in charge of Foreign Affairs:* Major Kwame Baah.
*Commissioner in charge of Health:* Major A. H. Selormey.
*Commissioner in charge of Industries:* Lt.-Col. P. K. Nkegbe.
*Commissioner in charge of Information:* Col. C. R. Tachie-Menson.
*Inspector-General of Police and Commissioner in charge of Internal Affairs:* Mr. J. H. Cobbina.
*Attorney-General and Commissioner in charge of Justice:* Mr. E. N. Moore.
*Commissioner in charge of Labour, Social Welfare and Co-operatives:* Major K. B. Agbo.
*Commissioner in charge of Lands and Mineral Resources:* Major-General D. C. K. Amenu.
*Commissioner in charge of Local Government:* Major-General N. A. Aferi.
*Commissioner in charge of Trade and Tourism:* Alhaji Lt.-Col. D. A. Iddisah.
*Commissioner in charge of Transport and Communications:* Major Kwame Asante.
*Commissioner in charge of Works and Housing:* Col. R. E. A. Kotei.
*Commissioner in charge of NRC Affairs:* E. K. Buckman.

## LEGAL SYSTEM

Under a declaration issued by the N.L.C. on 12 September 1966, the Courts of Ghana have been re-constituted as follows:

1. A supreme court of judicature, consisting of the Court of Appeal and the High Court, which shall be Superior Courts of Ghana.
2. Circuit Courts.
3. District Courts of two grades designated District Courts (Grade 1) and District Courts (Grade 2) known as Inferior Courts and
4. Such other inferior courts as may be provided by law.

## AREA AND POPULATION

The area of the country is 92,100 square miles.

The population at mid-1974 was 9,610,000. Breakdown of the population into the country's regions shown below:

| *Region* | *Population* (1970) | *Area* (*sq. miles*) |
|---|---|---|
| Western | 768,312 | 9,236 |
| Central | 892,593 | 3,815 |
| Eastern | 1,262,882 | 7,698 |
| Volta | 947,012 | 7,943 |
| Ashanti | 1,477,397 | 9,417 |
| Brong-Ahafo | 762,673 | 15,273 |
| Northern | 728,572 | 27,175 |
| Upper | 857,295 | 10,458 |
| Greater Accra | 848,925 | 995 |

The annual average percentage growth rate of the population for the periods 1960–74 and 1965–74 was 2·6.

The chief cities and towns with populations: Accra (capital), 633,880; Sekondi-Takoradi, 161,071; Cape Coast, 71,594; Koforidua, 69,804; Ho, 46,348; Kumasi, 342,986; Sunyani, 61,772; Tamale, 98,818; Bolgananga, 93,182.

## FINANCE

The following table shows the balance of payments position for some recent years:

| *Balance of Payments* | 1970 | 1971 |
|---|---|---|
| | $ million | |
| Trade balance f.o.b. | +87·7 | −13·9 |
| Freight and insurance | −45·4 | −46·7 |
| Investment income | −40·3 | −41·7 |
| Other | −17·1 | −18·0 |
| Transfers | −11·3 | −7·7 |
| Current account balance | −26·4 | −128·0 |
| Long term capital | | |
| Private | +18·8 | +77·0 |
| Official | +45·4 | +29·3 |
| Basic Balance | +37·8 | −21·7 |

The GNP at market prices for 1974 was U.S. $millions 4,130 and the GNP per capita at market prices was U.S. $430. The annual average percentage growth rate of the GNP per capita for the period 1965–74 was −0·2, and for the period 1960–74 was 0·3. [*See the note at the beginning of this section concerning GNP.*]

The Ghanaian currency has now been decimalised. The cedi equals 100 pesewas.

## BANKS

**Bank of Ghana.** Central bank and the sole bank of issue. It started operations on 1 August 1957 with an authorized and paid-up capital of ₵2,000,000. Since March 1965, the authorized capital has been raised to ₵20,000,000 while the paid-up capital has risen to ₵10,000,000. The Bank issued the Ghana Pound Currency for the first time on 14 July 1958 to replace the currency of the West African Currency Board, which was in circulation at the time. On 19 July 1965, decimal currency was introduced to replace the Ghana Pound. The Governor of the Bank is Dr. Amon Nikoi.

**Ghana Commercial Bank.** Established February 1953. State owned. Paid up capital ₵14 million; deposits and other accounts ₵759·2 million (June 1976). *Chairman & Managing Director*, T. E. Anin. More than 108 branches, and 21 sub-branches. *Head Office:* P.O. Box 134, Accra. *London Office:* 69 Cheapside, London, E.C.2.

**Standard Bank Ghana Limited.** *Head Office:* P.O. Box 768. Accra, 28 Branches.

**Barclays Bank of Ghana Limited.** *Head Office:* P.O. Box 2949, Accra. 48 Branches.

## PRODUCTION AND COMMERCE

The great majority of the people of Ghana are engaged in the cultivation of crops for their own consumption. The most important export crop is cocoa.

A very special achievement in the country's economic performance during 1972 was the reversal of the large balance of trade deficit of 1971 into a surplus of ₵174 million. This favourable development was carried into the first half of 1973. Below are the relevant figures:

| | *Imports ₵ million* | *Exports ₵ million* | *Balance of trade* |
|---|---|---|---|
| January–December 1971 | 445·3 | 380·2 | − 65·1 |
| January–December 1972 | 396·2 | 570·1 | +173·9 |
| January–May 1973 | 205·1 | 318·4 | +113·3 |

The following table gives some information on exports by product for the first eleven months of 1971 at annual rate:

| *Product* | *₵ million* | *per cent* | *per cent change 1970–71* |
|---|---|---|---|
| Cocoa | 212·0 | 55 | −30 |
| Logs and sawn timber | 32·9 | 8 | −13 |
| Gold | 27·4 | 7 | + 7 |
| Diamonds | 9·5 | 3 | −28 |
| Manganese | 6·7 | 2 | − 8 |
| Bauxite | 2·2 | 1 | +69 |
| Re-exports | 8·3 | 2 | +20 |
| Other | 88·9 | 23 | − 1 |
| Total | 387·9 | 100 | −18 |

The following table gives some information concerning exports by country of destination for the first eleven months of 1971 at annual rate:

| *Country* | *₵ million* | *per cent* | *per cent change 1970–71* |
|---|---|---|---|
| USA | 88·1 | 23 | + 5 |
| UK | 85·3 | 22 | −15 |
| West Germany | 40·4 | 10 | −11 |
| Other EEC | 56·4 | 15 | −15 |
| Japan | 31·3 | 9 | + 3 |
| Other (including re-exports) | 86·4 | 22 | −49 |
| Total | 387·9 | 100 | −18 |

The following table gives some information on imports by product for the first eleven months of 1971 at annual rate:

| *Product* | *₵ million* | *per cent* | *per cent change 1970–71* |
|---|---|---|---|
| Machinery and transport equipment | 135·1 | 30 | +25 |
| Manufactures | 120·3 | 27 | + 3 |
| Chemicals | 74·0 | 16 | +13 |
| Food and drink | 67·5 | 15 | −18 |
| Fuel | 27·0 | 6 | +13 |
| Raw materials | 12·5 | 3 | +38 |
| Other | 14·2 | 3 | +58 |
| Total | 450·6 | 100 | + 8 |

The following table gives some information on imports by country of origin for the first eleven months of 1971 at annual rate:

| *Country* | *₵ million* | *per cent* | *per cent change 1970–71* |
|---|---|---|---|
| UK | 112·1 | 25 | +13 |
| USA | 70·0 | 16 | − 9 |
| West Germany | 56·9 | 13 | +30 |
| Other EEC | 51·2 | 11 | +12 |
| Japan | 42·2 | 9 | +66 |
| Other | 118·2 | 26 | − 4 |
| Tota | 450·6 | 100 | + 8 |

**Agriculture.** The food crop trade is more extensive and possessed of a much higher degree of organization than is generally appreciated. Following the pattern in previous years, the main source of the country's food supply is derived from peasant farming. The remainder was provided by large-scale farms which also produced crops such as sugar cane, oil palm, rubber and kenaf as raw material for local industries. The distribution of food to the growing urban communities continues to present a problem and the Government has set up a task force, under the Ministry of Agriculture, to deal with it. Imported foods include substantial quantities of wheat (meal and flour), sugar, rice, meat and fish. The following table gives some selected output data for agricultural production for the years 1970 and 1971:

| *Product* | 1970 *th. tons* | 1971 *th. tons* |
|---|---|---|
| Cocoa (year to 30 Sept.) | 409 | 386 |
| Maize | N.A. | 378 |
| Cassava | N.A. | 2,400 |
| Yams | N.A. | 1,900 |
| Logs and sawn timber, million cu. ft. | N.A. | N.A. |

# GHANA

## COMMUNICATIONS

**Civil Aviation.** The new terminal of the Kotoka International Airport at Accra was formally opened in February, 1969. The 9,600 ft. runway is capable of taking the largest and fastest aircraft and facilities at the airport have been designed to meet international standards. There are internal airports at Kumasi, Takoradi and Tamale (now being extended and developed), together with a landing strip at Sunyani which is being developed into an airport. Wa, Navrongo, Yendi and Wenchi afford landing strips only.

About 17 companies operate aircraft into and out of the country. Ghana Airways, a wholly Government-owned corporation, operates one VC 10, one H.S.748 aircraft, one DC3, one F.28 and one Viscount. In addition to its internal flights, the Corporation operates international flights with a number of West African States, Europe and the Middle East. In 1969, the number of passengers carried by Ghana Airways totalled 121,225, compared with 104,998 in 1968, an increase of 16,227. Total freight carried by the Corporation's planes was 1,049,801 Kg. in 1969, compared with 1,383,300 Kg in 1968.

Work on recabling the lighting system at Kotoka International Airport has been completed at a cost of N₵200,000. There are plans for the airport to have its own standby generator capable of catering for all electrical requirements during power failures.

British Overseas Airways Corporation, one of the companies operating aircraft into and out of the country, ended its operations in Ghana on 2 April 1971; British Caledonian Airways has taken over the service.

**Railways.** The railway system forms a letter 'A' with Kumasi at the apex and Accra and Takoradi at the feet. The cross piece consists of the line from Huni Valley near Tarkwa to Kotoku, some 20 miles north of Accra. There are in addition a number of branch lines radiating from the main lines, with an important extension to Tema and thence to Shai Hills. Total route mileage is 805 miles of 3 ft 6 in. gauge track.

The Railways and Ports Authority is to modernize the rail terminals at Kumasi and Accra; a project estimated to cost N₵3 million. In addition the Authority is to recondition some of its rolling stock and to take delivery of 150 wagons to improve the transport of cocoa and timber. Some recent statistics are:

| *Item* | | 1967–68 | 1968–69 |
|---|---|---|---|
| Passenger miles | '000 | 253,219 | 269,809 |
| Freight | '000 tons | 1,678 | 1,523 |

**Roads.** There are over 19,000 miles of roads of which 5,680 miles were maintained by the Public Works Department as at December 1969. In addition approximately 3,100 miles of non-surfaced road are maintained by the regional organizations. The construction and maintenance of secondary and feeder roads is undertaken by district and local councils with the aid of Government funds.

The Accra/Tema motorway was completed in 1965. Plans for extending the motorway north of Accra were shelved in 1966 although there has subsequently been some extension of the motorway to the east and north of Accra.

**Air.** The new terminal of the Kotoka International Airport at Accra was formally opened in February 1969. The 9,600 ft. runway is capable of taking the largest and fastest aircraft and facilities at the airport have been designed to meet international standards.

**Shipping.** About 29 shipping companies operate services into and out of the country giving direct connections with all continents. The Government-owned Black Star Line now has 16 vessels with a gross tonnage of 117,197·41, compared with a fleet strength of 14 with a gross tonnage of 103,187 at the end of 1968. The company at present operates fast cargo-passenger services between West Africa and the United Kingdom/Continent as far as the Baltic Sea; between West Africa and Canada and the United States including the Gulf of Mexico; and between West Africa aud ports of the Mediterranean and Adriatic. The tonnage of cargo carried by the Black Star Line during 1969 was 695,458 tons deadweight, compared with 597,739 tons in 1968.

The Black Volta rises in the hills near Soukouraba and the White Volta rises near Quahigouga, both in the Upper Volta. These two rivers converge some 280 miles from the sea on the Ashanti-Northern Region border and become the River Volta which flows into the sea at Ada. This river is navigable for light draught launches as far as Akuse, and with the exception of the Krachi rapids, can be used for canoe traffic during certain seasons of the year as far as Yeji. The Akosombo Dam, completed in 1965, has greatly increased its river transport potential. The Ankobra River is navigable for many months of the year by surf boats and light draughts launches for a distance of 50 miles. The Tano, connected with Half Assini by the main lagoon, is navigable for light draught launches and canoes as far as Tanoso, a distance of about 60 miles.

## NEWSPAPERS

**The Mirror:** Weekly. P.O. Box 742, Brewery Road, Accra. Circulation 103,000.

**The Daily Graphic:** Daily. P.O. Box 742, Brewery Road, Accra. Circulation 190,000.

**The Ghanaian Times:** Daily. P.O. Box 2638, Accra.

**The Pioneer.** Daily. Independent. P.O. Box 235, Kumasi.

**Spokesman:** Twice weekly. P.O. Box 7687, Accra.

**Weekly Spectator:** Weekly. P.O. Box 2638, Accra.

**The Echo:** Weekly. P.O. Box 3640, Accra.

**Business Weekly:** Weekly. P.O. Box 2351, Accra.

**Legon Observer:** Fortnightly. P.O. Box 11, Legon, Accra.

**Drum:** Monthly. P.O. Box 1197, Accra.

**Flamingo:** Monthly. P.O. Box 3075, Accra.

**Ghana Trade Journal:** P.O. Box 2351, Accra.

## EDUCATION

The System of Education in Ghana begins with Primary education. Education at this level is free and compulsory for all children aged six and above. In 1969–70 there were 10,660 primary and middle schools with a total enrolment of 1,400,000 pupils; at the end of the academic year there were 112 Secondary schools with a total enrolment of 49,182 pupils.

There are three universities—the University of Ghana, the University of Science and Technology and the University College of Cape Coast. In 1972–73 the student population at the University of Ghana stood at 2,556, the University of Science and Technology, 1,765, and the University of Cape Coast, 1,100.

# Greece

(ELLINIKI DIMOCRATIA)

**Capital**—Athens.

**President**—Constantine Tsatsos.

**National Flag**: A white cross on a canton blue with nine stripes fesse-wise, five blue and four white.

## CONSTITUTION AND GOVERNMENT

GREEK independence was proclaimed on 25 March 1821, when a successful revolt against the Ottoman Empire began. It brought to an end four centuries of Turkish domination. The new kingdom of Greece was guaranteed by the three major powers, Great Britain, Russia and France at the London Convention in 1830. The Crown was offered to Prince Otto of Bavaria, who ascended the throne in 1833 as Otto I. He was expelled from Greece in 1862, and Prince William, son of the Danish King, was chosen King George I of the Hellenes in his place. He reigned until his assassination in 1913. King Constantine, his son, then came to the throne and reigned until 1922, although his reign was interrupted by a period of abdication in favour of his son Alexander. He than resigned in favour of his son King George II. Between the years 1924 and 1935, Greece became a Republic, but in October 1935 it was again declared a kingdom and the 1911 constitution was reinstated, replacing that of the Republican interlude. A plebiscite of 3 November 1935 resulted in an overwhelming vote in favour of the return to the throne of King George II.

On 28 October 1940 Italy invaded Greece following an unacceptable ultimatum which was rejected by the Prime Minister, Metaxas. In the ensuing counter-attacks, the Greek armies threw the enemy back and pursued him into his Albanian base. On 6 April 1941, Germany came to the aid of the hard-pressed Italians, striking through Bulgaria and forcing the capitulation of the Greek Army in Albania on 20 April. On 27 April the Germans entered Athens in force. For three years Greece was under foreign occupation during which time the Greek Resistance movement never ceased its struggle against the invader. The German-Italian-Bulgarian occupation lasted until October 1944. In September 1946 a plebiscite recalled King George II. He died on 1 April 1947 and was succeeded by his brother Paul. King Paul died 6 March 1964 and was succeeded by his son, Constantine.

The constitution was amended on 1 January 1952. There is a Council of State, of not more than 21 members, which exercises a specified jurisdiction over the administration. Its members are appointed for life, on the proposal of the Cabinet.

In April 1967 a *coup d'état* took place as a result of which the Army took over power. A new National Government was formed, headed by Constantine Kollias, the Supreme Court Public Prosecutor.

A new Constitution was approved by referendum on 29 September 1968 and came into force from 15 November 1968.

On 1 June 1973 Greece was declared a republic. On 29 June 1973 a referendum was held to approve the republic and the installation of Georges Papadopoulos as president for 7 years. However, in November 1973 Georges Papadopoulos was removed from the Presidency and replaced by General Phaidon Ghisikis.

On 24 July 1974, after the abortive coup against the late President Markarios of Cyprus and the Turkish invasion of the island the Greek military government, faced also by serious domestic problems, was forced to hand power back to the politicians. Mr. Constantine Karamanlis, prime minister in the period 1955–63, formed a provisional government of National Unity with politicians from the main pre-1967 parties and elections were held on 17 November 1974. Karamanlis won the elections decisively and formed the government listed below. On 9 December 1974 a referendum was held to decide the monarchy issue. This resulted in a pro-republican vote of 69·5 per cent. The new republican Constitution was enacted by Parliament in June 1975 and Mr. Constantine Tsatsos was elected President of the Republic (between December 1974 and June 1975 the presidential duties were provisionally discharged by Mr. M. Stassinopoulos, ex-Chairman of the Council of State). There follows a list of the present cabinet ministers:

### Cabinet

*Prime Minister:* Mr. Constantine Karamanlis.
*Deputy Premier:* Constantine Papaconstantinou.
*Minister of Coordination and Planning:* George Rallis.
*Minister of Defence:* Evanghelos Averoff.
*Minister of Foreign Affairs:* Panayotis Papaligouras.
*Minister of Interior:* Christophoros Stratos.
*Minister of Public Order:* Anastasios Balkos.
*Minister of Finance:* Yiannis Bouttos.
*Minister of Trade:* George Panayotopoulos.
*Minister of Industry:* Miltiadis Evert.
*Minister of Public Works:* Nikos Zardinidis.
*Minister of Shipping:* Emmanuel Kefaloyiannis.
*Minister of Agriculture:* Athanasios Taliadouros.
*Minister of Labour:* Constantine Laskaris.
*Minister of Justice:* George Stamatis.
*Minister of Education and Religion:* Ioannis Varvitsiotis.
*Minister of Culture and Science:* George Plytas.
*Minister of Communication:* Alexandros Papadongonas.
*Minister of Social Services:* Spyros Doxiadis.
*In Charge of Prime Minister's Office:* Constantine Stefanopoulos.
*Minister of Northern Greece:* Nikolaos Martis.
*Minister Without Portfolio;* (EEC Affairs): George Kondoylorgis.

## LEGAL SYSTEM

Justice is administered by the Supreme Court, Courts of Appeal and Courts of First Instance. Judges are appointed for life, retiring at the age of 65. There are also minor courts for the trial of petty offences, and a Court of Accounts, whose members are appointed for life, but who are obliged to retire from the service upon reaching the age limit.

*President of the Supreme Court:* Constantinos Zacharis.
*First Vice-President of Supreme Court:* Constantinos Marmaras.
*Second Vice-President of Supreme Court:* Spiros Gaggas.

## AREA AND POPULATION

Greece has an area of 50,942 sq. miles. The population of the country at mid-1974 was 9,020,000.

| | 1971 |
|---|---|
| Central Greece (including Athens, Piraeus, and Euboea) | 3,532,318 |
| Peloponnese | 986,912 |
| Ionian Islands | 184,443 |
| Thessaly | 659,913 |
| Macedonia | 1,890,684 |
| Epirus | 310,344 |
| Crete | 456,642 |
| Aegean Islands (including Cyclades and Dodecanese) | 417,813 |
| Thrace | 329,582 |

The annual average percentage growth of the population for the period 1960–74 was 0·6, and for the period 1965–74 was 0·5.

Population density was 66·5 per square kilometre in 1971. The rural and semi-urban population (living in communes of less than 10,000 people) amounted to 4,101,152 (census 1971) which represented 46·8 per cent of the total population.

The principal towns with populations are Greater Athens (including Athens, the port of Piraeus aud their suburbs) 2,540,241; Athens (municipal), 67,023; Piraeus, 187,458, Salonica, 345,799.

## CURRENCY AND FINANCE

The unit of currency is the drachma. In December 1970 there were 38,878·1 million drachmas in circulation.

In 1970 the gross national income was provisionally 65,130·30 million drachmas at current prices (1971) and the gross expenditure of the economy was 65,126·0 million drachmas at current prices (1971).

## GREECE

The GNP at market prices for 1974 was U.S. $ millions 18,830, and the GNP per capita at market prices was U.S. $2,090. The annual average percentage growth rate of the GNP per capita for the period 1960–74 was 6·8, and for the period 1965–74 was 6·5. [*See the note at the beginning of this section concerning GNP.*]

### PRINCIPAL BANKS

**Bank of Greece.** (Governor, Xenophon E. Zolotas). Established 1927; Sole Bank of Issue for Greece; Balance Sheet at 31 December 1975 showed assets and liabilities Drs. 267,998,368,588; deposits Drs. 94,274,718,546. *Head Office:* E. Venizelos Avenue, Athens.

**Commercial Bank of Greece.** Established 1907; Balance Sheet at 31 December 1976 showed assets Drs.106,231,762,845; deposits Drs. 57,549,718,027. *Head Office:* 11 Sophocleous Street, Athens; 196 branches, and 11 foreign exchange offices.

**Ionian and Popular Bank of Greece.** Established 1958 through the merger of the Greek branches of 'Ionian Bank Ltd.', established 1839, and the 'Banque Populaire', established 1905. Balance Sheet at 31 December 1976 showed assets Drs. 45,721,603,672; deposits Drs. 22,597,055,461. *Head Office:* 45 Eleftheriou Venizelou Avenue, Athens 132; 107 branches, and five foreign exchange offices.

**National Bank of Greece.** (Governor Professor Angelos Angelopolous.) Established 1841. Balance sheet at 31 December 1976 showed assets Drs. 297,956,441,188; deposits Drs. 200,719,135,086. *Head Office:* 86 Eolou Street (Cotzia Sq.) Athens; 333 Greek, 19 foreign branches.

**National Mortgage Bank of Greece.** (Governor, Elias D. Krimpas.) Established 1927. Balance Sheet at 31 December 1971) showed assets Drs. 15,860,876,973; deposits Drs. 3,877,974,306. *Head Office:* 40 Venizelou Avenue, Athens.

### PRODUCTION, INDUSTRY AND COMMERCE

**Agriculture.** Greece is mainly an agricultural country, 40·0 per cent of the working population being employed on the land. Only 39 per cent of the total area, however, is suitable for cultivation. Of the total area of 35,565,700 acres, 6,631,400 are forests, 15,086,000 meadowland, while 4,483,000 acres are devoted to cereals (3,707,000 in winter and 776,000 in spring). 490,000 acres are used for grapes, 1,165,000 acres for fruit, olives, tobacco, cotton and other industrial crops.

In respect to exports tobacco is one of the most important and accounts by value for nearly one-sixth of Greece's total exports. Other exported commercial crops are: raisins (currants and sultanas), olives and olive oil, citrous, dry figs, wine, cotton, etc. Livestock was considerably reduced during the German occupation. Sheep and goat rearing is vital to the economy, yielding milk, butter, cheese and wool.

The following table shows the main crops with outputs (in thousand metric tons) for 1970 and 1971:

| *Crop* | 1970 | 1971 |
|---|---|---|
| Wheat | 1,930·2 | 1,905 |
| Barley | 718·3 | 780 |
| Oats | 106 | 113 |
| Rice | 81·4 | 68 |
| Potatoes | 731·2 | 628 |
| Cotton | 326·3 | 359 |
| Tobacco | 90·2 | 88 |
| Mustard | N.A. | N.A. |
| Sultanas | 73·8 | 79 |
| Currants | 93·8 | 88 |
| Grapes | 192·7 | 184 |
| Citrus | 684·2 | 520 |
| Olive Oil | 190 | N.A. |
| Olives | 50·1 | 107·9 |

**Mining.** Though Greece's mineral resources are limited, they are varied. The main deficiency is coal, of which both reserves and production are small. There are deposits of iron ore of high content, iron pyrites, copper, zinc, lead, manganese, sulphur, aluminium, antimony, nickel. Marble is also quarried. Output (in thousand metric tons) of main mineral ores for 1973 was as follows: lignites 13,211; bauxites 2,748; iron 1·5; magnesite 1,068; manganese 42; barytes 124.

**Industry.** The rapidly developing Greek industry, aided by foreign enterprise, contributes to the rising technological level of the Greek economy, and promotes quantitative and qualitative diversifications in the pattern of the national income. This has resulted in an improvement in the living conditions of the Greek people and the expansion of the local market and has brought about a decisive rebuilding of the country's foreign trade. Between 1967 and 1969 industrial production increased by 45 per cent, at an annual rate of about 10 per cent. The industries which had grown up between the wars were almost totally destroyed in World War II and in the subsequent civil war, which lasted till 1949 and thus delayed reconstruction.

In terms of OECD industrial production rates, Greece ranks today among the first countries, with an annual growth rate of 11 per cent (1970). The increase was most pronounced in the base metals industry (31 per cent in 1969). Such expansion, together with the setting up of new industries, guarantee the development and diversification of Greek industrial production.

Many large industrial units have come into operation (e.g. blast furnaces, nitrogen plants, Pirelli, Thessaliki Paper and Pulp, Aluminium of Greece, Esso-Pappos, etc.). The following table shows gross domestic product of manufacturing for 1972.

| *Product* | *In drachmas at 1971 prices* |
|---|---|
| | 1972 |
| Food, beverages and tobacco | 22,732,556 |
| Textiles | 11,970,086 |
| Clothing | 2,927,592 |
| Wood and furniture and cork | 2,331,710 |
| Paper and printing | 3,402,880 |
| Chemicals | 5,285,841 |
| Non-metallic minerals | 3,391,430 |
| Basic metal industries | 5,900,671 |
| Metal products, engineering and electrical goods | 2,312,950 |
| Transport equipment | 327,561 |

**Commerce.** The following table shows the value of principal imports in 1974 (thousand drachmas):

| *Commodity* | 1974 |
|---|---|
| Foodstuffs and live animals | 14,395,798 |
| Raw materials | 12,445,496 |
| Fuel-Lubricants | 29,231,160 |
| Machinery, transport equipment | 37,007,382 |

The following table shows the value of principal exports in 1974 (thousand drachmas):

| *Commodity* | 1974 |
|---|---|
| Fruits (dried) | 2,999,992 |
| Fresh fruits (inc. nuts) | 3,220,451 |
| Tobacco (unmanufactured) | 5,109,331 |
| Cotton | 1,581,228 |
| Skins and hides | 1,110,718 |
| Aluminium | 2,886,633 |
| Miscellaneous | 4,652,995 |

The following table shows the balance of payments situation and the value of exports and imports for the year 1974 in million drachmas.

| *Country* | *Imports* | *Exports* | *Trade balance* |
|---|---|---|---|
| Total | 132,181 | 60,890 | 70,291 |
| U.S.A. | 12,102 | 3,687 | 8,415 |
| Canada | 1,532 | 585 | 947 |
| Argentina | 799 | 33 | 766 |
| Brazil | 590 | 45 | 545 |
| Uruguay | 125 | — | 125 |
| West Germany | 21,418 | 12,861 | 18,557 |
| France | 9,354 | 3,633 | 5,721 |
| Belgium–Luxembourg | 3,706 | 2,113 | 1,593 |
| Holland | 4,628 | 2,879 | 1,749 |
| Austria | 2,402 | 704 | 1,698 |
| Denmark | 574 | 268 | 306 |
| Switzerland | 2,142 | 460 | 1,682 |
| Norway | 635 | 183 | 452 |
| Sweden | 2,407 | 1,109 | 1,298 |
| Portugal | 195 | 98 | 97 |
| Turkey | 746 | 421 | 325 |
| Spain | 1,132 | 1,876 | 744 |
| U.S.S.R. | 1,798 | 2,429 | 631 |
| Bulgaria | 418 | 575 | 157 |
| East Germany | 777 | 763 | 14 |
| Hungary | 298 | 541 | 243 |
| Poland | 954 | 1,007 | 53 |
| Romania | 944 | 989 | 45 |
| Czechoslovakia | 840 | 885 | 45 |
| Yugoslavia | 1,187 | 2,584 | 1,397 |
| Finland | 878 | 90 | 788 |
| Egypt | 297 | 948 | 651 |
| Israel | 775 | 201 | 574 |
| Japan | 7,268 | 930 | 6,338 |
| Unspecified | 45 | 65 | 20 |

In 1971, the value of exports in U.S. dollars was 2,135,546,000, and the value of imports was in U.S. dollars 1,990,023,000.

## COMMUNICATIONS

**Roads.** A tremendous improvement of the road network was brought about in recent years. The total length of the network is 35,445·17 km., of which 8,004·2 km. are national roads.

All the cities, towns and most of the tourist sites on the mainland are connected by privately owned and operated motor coaches and buses. Villages are connected by buses with the main towns in their vicinity.

Total motor vehicles in the country at the end of 1974 were 648,154. These included 380,388 passenger cars (of which 355,779 were of private use and 24,609 public use taxis), 12,953 buses (of which the majority are for public transport and the rest belong to private enterprises, schools, etc.), 170,789 trucks and 84,024 motorcycles. Of the buses, 2,967 are used for urban transportation. It is estimated that buses throughout the country transport about 175 million passengers a year.

Athens and Piraeus are also served by electric trolley buses, while an electric railway runs, partly underground, from Piraeus through Athens to Kifissia.

**Railways.** There is one main railway network operating in Greece, the Greek Railways Organization (OSE). It is the outcome of a merger of the Greek State Railways, connecting Athens with Thessaloniki and the main towns in central and northern Greece and the Piraeus–Athens–Peloponnese Railways (S.P.A.P.), connecting the capital with the main towns in the Peloponnese.

The length of the OSE network is 2,571 km.

The country's total railway network is 2,543 kms. (or 1,580 miles) long. In 1974, about 12 million passengers and 3·2 million tons of freight were transported by rail.

**Shipping.** In June 1974, the Greek Merchant Fleet comprised 3,145 ships with a total tonnage of 24,080 thousand GRT, which means an increase of 70 per cent over the past four years. If the other Greek owned ships under foreign flags are included, it is the largest merchant fleet in the world with 3,364 ships of more than 30 million GRT. Shipping has become a factor of decisive importance to the country's economy. In 1970 the remittances of shipowners and of 100,000 Greek seamen came to a total of $280 million (i.e. about half the value of exports). Shipbuilding activities increase day by day with the establishment of new shipyards in various parts of the country.

**Airlines.** Athens is linked by air with about thirty towns or islands in the country and with all continents abroad.

In 1974, there were 27,712 internal flights for 1,581,570 passengers. All in all (for both domestic and international flights), there were 59,158 aircraft departures, 59,120 aircraft arrivals, 3,325,000 passenger departures and 3,264,307 passenger arrivals, in addition to 1,035,667 passengers on transit.

*The following are the principal shipping lines:*

**Hellenic Lines Ltd.**, controlling 38 vessels with a total tonnage 414,718 T.D.W.; *services operated:* England - Continent - Mediterranean - Black Sea ports; North America - Mediterranean ports - North America - Red Sea - Persian Gulf ports; North America - India - Pakistan ports; North America - South and East Africa ports; Mexico Gulf ports - Mediterranean ports - Black Sea ports; Mexico Gulf ports - Red Sea - Persian Gulf ports; Mexico Gulf ports - India - Pakistan ports; Mexico Gulf ports - South and East Africa ports; Mediterranean ports - South and East Africa ports. *Head Office:* Filonos 61/65 Piraeus.

**Hellenic Mediterranean Lines Co. Ltd.**, controlling 5 passenger vessels with a total tonnage 28,000; *services operated regularly* Patras - Igoumenitsa - Corfu - Brindisi. Venice - Piraeus - Rhodes - Limassol - Famagusta - Haifa - Naples - Marseilles - Heraklion (Crete). Also 7-day cruises to Greek islands and Turkey per m.s. Aquarius now under construction. *Head Office:* Electric Railway Building, Piraeus.

**National Hellenic American Line.** One (1) linear, with a total tonnage 21,329 registered tons (Queen Frederica); *services operated:* Mediterranean ports - Canada - New York. *Head Office:* 10 Venizelou St., Athens.

**Petros Nomikos Ltd.** 4 passenger vessels with a total tonnage of 7,626 G.R.T.; *services operated:* Piraeus - Brindisi/Ancona, Aegean cruises and inter-island services. *Head Office:* Tanpy Building, Piraeus.

**Ch. M. Sarlis & Co.** 9 cargo vessels with a total tonnage of 10,168 registered tons; *services operated:* between Adriatic-Greek, Turkish and Black Sea ports and between Adriatic, Libyan and Tunisian ports, and between Adriatic, Cyprus, Syrian and Lebanese ports. *Head Office:* Electric Railway Building, Piraeus.

**Civil Aviation.** Greece is well served by airlines. In addition there is one national airline maintaining domestic as well as international services. The principal airport is at Elliniko, near Athens.

**Olympic Airways.** Greece's national airline, maintains international services to 24 cities on the five continents of the world, and also flies to 34 cities and islands within Greece; *Services operated:* Athens - New York, v.v.; Athens - Paris - New York, v.v.; Athens - Paris - New York, v.v.; Athens - Montreal - Chicago, v.v.; Athens - Montreal, v.v.; Athens - Bangkok - Singapore - Sydney, v.v.; Athens - Nairobi - Johannesburg, v.v.; Athens - London, v.v.; Athens - Thessaloniki - London, v.v; Athens - Corfu - London, v.v.; Rhodes - Athens - London, v.v.; Heraklion - Athens - London, v.v.; Athens - Paris, v.v.; Athens - Frankfurt - Paris, v.v.; Athens - Zurich - Amsterdam, v.v.; Athens - Geneva - Brussels, v.v.; Athens - Zurich - Dusseldorf, v.v.; Athens - Rome, v.v.; Athens - Milan - Dusseldorf, v.v.; Athens - Thessaloniki - Frankfurt, v.v.; Athens - Thessaloniki - Dusseldorf, v.v.; Athens - Thessaloniki - Stuttgart, v.v.; Athens - Vienna - Frankfurt, v.v.; Athens - Nicosia, v.v. Nicosia - Athens - London, v.v.; Athens - Istanbul, v.v.; Athens - Cairo, v.v.; Athens - Tel Aviv, v.v; Kos - Frankfurt - Kos, v.v.; Athens - Frankfurt - Dusseldorf - Frankfurt - Athens. *Head Office:* 96–100 Syngrou Ave., Athens 404. *London Office:* 141 New Bond Street, W1Y 0BB.

**Broadcasting.** Radio and Television services come under EIPT (Ethnicon Idryma Radiophonias-Tileoraseos), the Hellenic National Radio-Television, which is an organization sponsored by the state. Besides the stations operated by EIPT, there are Radio and Television Transmitters operated by the Armed Forces.

Radio Athens has three medium-wave transmitters (150 kW, 50 kW and 15 kW) and two short-wave transmitters (100 kW each), for external broadcasting.

There are also 37 FM transmitters of 3 or 10 kW (ERP) throughout Greece. Regional AM stations are at Thessaloniki, Corfu, Zakynthos (50 kW each), Rhodes, Chania (Crete), Komotini (5 kW each), Volos, Amalias (1 kW each) and Patrai (0·25 kW). For Television programmes, originated from Athens, there are 17 transmitters of 30/6 or 10/2 kW (ERP). There is a licence fee, for radio receivers only, of 160 drachmas per annum.

### NEWSPAPERS

There are four morning papers published in Athens: **Akropolis, Vima, Eleftheros Kosmos**; five evening papers: **Hestia, Vradyni, Apogevmatini, Ta Simerina, Nea**; three papers dealing with economics: **Imerisia, Naftemboriki, Express**; and three foreign language papers: **d'Athenes**, Athens News, **Athens Daily Post and Messager.**

### ATOMIC ENERGY

The Greek Atomic Energy Commission was organized in 1954 under Law 2750/54, and thereafter the law was reviewed and revised twice (Nos. 3277/55 and 3891/58). In October 1960 the Law was revised once again bringing the G.A.E.C. directly under the Prime Minister of Greece (No. 4115/60).

The Greek Atomic Energy Commission is an independent Governmental Agency responsible for all matters relating to planning, research, development and applications in the field of Nuclear Energy in Greece.

The Governing body of the Greek Atomic Energy Commission (Administrative Committee) consists of a chairman, vice-chairman and six members with a scientific director.

In common with similar organizations in other countries the policy of the Commission is to encourage, promote and support research work, to plan, erect and equip the necessary laboratories where research will be carried out and to sponsor the extension of research in all branches of nuclear science. The Commission is also responsible for the import and export of isotopes and for the supervision of their application, the development of studies relating to the radioactivity of the country's subsoil as well as for national surveys for the purpose of locating nuclear raw materials.

With these aims in view, the Commission has established relations with such International Organizations as the International Atomic Energy Agency, in Vienna and CERN in Geneva. Also, the Commission has established relations with national atomic energy commissions in other countries.

The Commission also is concerned with the training of personnel in nuclear safety, the detection of radioactive contamination, and the measures to be taken in contaminated areas. It will also deal with public education in matters connected with atomic energy, and particularly in connection with safety measures.

It is recognized that the prospecting for, and exploitation of, radioactive and related minerals will call for new legislation, and in fact a law has already been enacted to regulate such matters. Prospecting has, of course, already begun.

Greece entered into a bi-lateral co-operation agreement with the United States for the acquisition of a nuclear research reactor which was to be completed in July 1961. The reactor is of the swimming-pool type 1 MW.

The reactor is located at the 'Democritus' nuclear research centre at Aghia Paraskevi, near Athens. The centre consists of reactor, physics, electronics, chemistry, biochemistry, experimental medicine, biology and health physics laboratories.

### EDUCATION

Public education is provided free of all charges in Greece from nursery to university level. This includes both tuition and textbooks. The state budget for education in 1975 provides expenditures of Drs. 14,164 million, in addition to Drs. 3,430 earmarked for infrastructure state investments (principally for the erection of school buildings).

Nursery schools for children of six years and under in 1974–75 numbered 3,275 with a staff of 3,648 for 105,084 children.

Primary education, which runs for six grades, is compulsory. In 1974–75, there were 9,705 primary schools with a teaching staff of 29,804 for 926,628 boys and girls.

Secondary education, which also continues for six years, was provided for by 1,105 schools with 19,279 teachers and 521,141 pupils.

Technical and professional training is provided for by 460 public schools for 40,319 pupils, and 706 private schools for a further 76,687 pupils.

An estimated 84,600 young men and women are receiving university education at the hands of 5,038 professors and assistants. Institutions of higher learning include the Universities of Athens, Thessaloniki, Patras and Ioannina, the planned Universities of Rethymnon (Crete) and Komotini (Thrace), the National Metsovion Polytechnic, the School of Economic and Commercial Sciences, The Pantios School of Political Sciences, the Industrial Schools of Piraeus and Thessaloniki, the Athens Agricultural School, the School of Fine Arts, the Physical Education Academies of Athens and Thessaloniki and a number of education academies, in addition to the military, naval and air academies.

The 1971 census indicated that there were 210,520 higher education graduates in Greece (152,420 men and 58,100 women), 81,440 holders of technical or vocational training diplomas (58,600 men and 22,840 women), 790,200 secondary school graduates (419,700 men and 370,500 women) and 3,613,720 primary school graduates (1,956,860 men and 1,656,860 women).

Greece has a long tradition in athletics. The Olympic Games were the most famous athletic event of ancient times, held every four years at Olympia, in South-Western Greece. The first modern Olympic Games were held in Athens stadium in 1896.

The Government's General Secretariat for Athletics exercises supervision over 2,000 athletic clubs. About 90 per cent of club members are men. Of the total membership, 67 per cent are engaged in group sports (principally football, but also basketball and volleyball), 10 per cent in swimming and other water sports, 12·5 per cent in track and field and the rest in other sports. There are 191 national stadia, 23 national swimming pools and more than 500 training grounds scattered throughout the country.

### RELIGION

The established religion of Greece is that of the Greek Orthodox Church and it is estimated that over 96 per cent of the people adhere to this church. Other religions are tolerated and freedom of worship is guaranteed by the constitution, proselytising and any other intervention against the established religion being prohibited. In spiritual matters. the Greek Church is subject to the authority of the Œcumenical Patriarch at Constantinople, but its Government is vested in a permanent council, the Holy Synod, under the presidency of the Archbishop of Athens and All Greece.

# Guatemala

(REPÚBLICA DE GUATEMALA)

**Capital**—Guatemala City.

**President**—Gen. Kjell Laugerud García.

**National Flag:** A tricolour pale-wise, blue, white, blue, charged with a badge centred and inscribed 'Libertad 15 de Septiembre 1821'.

## CONSTITUTION AND GOVERNMENT

GUATEMALA is situated in Central America, bounded on the north and west by Mexico, on the south by the Pacific and El Salvador, on the east by Honduras, the Gulf of Honduras and Belize (formerly British Honduras).

The country was conquered by the Spaniards about 1523 and was a Spanish colony till 1821. It then joined the Confederation of Central America, but became an independent republic on 17 April 1839.

Since President Ubico was deposed in 1944, there have been radical changes in Guatemala. His successor, President Arevalo, launched a modest programme of social reform, and when he retired in 1950, President Arbenz—who secured 65 per cent of the votes—continued on reformist lines. But his Agrarian Reform Law, aimed at dividing the large estates amongst the landless peasants, aroused fierce opposition amongst his political enemies. Their leader, Colonel Castillo Armas, was arrested in 1950 after leading an abortive revolt. He escaped from prison in 1951 and organized armed opposition forces outside Guatemala.

In June 1954 Colonel Castillo Armas overthrew the Arbenz regime. On 8 July a Military Junta was created, and on 1 September Colonel Castillo Armas became President. Colonel Castillo Armas was confirmed by popular vote as President until 15 March 1960. At the same time a National Constituent Assembly was elected and drafted a new Constitution (March 1956).

President Castillo Armas was assassinated on 26 July 1957. Deputy President Lic. González Lopez assumed the Presidency.

After the result of elections held on 20 October 1957 was disputed by supporters of General Miguel Ydígoras Fuentes, the chief complainant, and following popular demonstrations, a Military Junta took over the government on 24 October, annulling the elections. New elections were held on 19 January 1958, and were won by Ydígoras Fuentes, though without a legal majority. Congress proclaimed him President and he took office on 2 March 1958. He was deposed on 31 March 1963 by the Army, which handed executive and legislative powers to its senior officer, Col. Enrique Peralta Azurdia, the Minister of Defence. After three years of military rule, a new constitution was promulgated on 15 September 1965. Elections took place in March 1966, and Dr. Méndez Montenegro was inaugurated as President on 1 July. In March 1970 Col. Carlos Arana Osorio was elected President. As a result of elections held on 3 March 1974, General Kjell Laugerud García became President on 1 July. The Christian Democrats protested strongly that their candidate had polled the most votes, and opposition members of Congress boycotted the session in which Kjell Laugerud was confirmed the winner. Presidential elections are to be held early in 1978.

### Ministers

*Minister of the Interior:* Lic. Donaldo Alvarez Ruíz.
*Minister of Foreign Affairs:* Lic. Adolfo Molina Orantes.
*Minister of Finance:* Lic. Jorge Lamport Rodil.
*Minister of the Economy:* Lic. Ramiro Ponce Monroy.
*Minister of Communications and Public Works:* Ing. Ricardo Arguedes Martínez.
*Minister of Agriculture:* Gen. Fausto David Rubio Coronado.
*Minister of Education:* Lic. Guillermo Putzeys Álvarez.
*Minister of Public Health:* Dr. Julio Benjamín Sultán Berkowitz.
*Minister of Labour:* Lic. David Corzo de la Roca.
*Minister of Defence:* Gen. Fernando Romeo Lucas García.

## LOCAL GOVERNMENT

The country is divided for administrative purposes into 22 departments: Guatemala, San Marcos, Huehuetenango, Alta Verapaz, Baja Verapaz, Quezaltenango, Quiché, Jutiapa, Escuintla, Suchitepéquez, Chimaltenango, Chiquimula, Santa Rosa, Totonicapán, Sololá, Jalapa, Zacapa, Retalhuleu, Sacatepequez, Izabal, Progreso and Petén. Each has a governor appointed by the President.

## LEGAL SYSTEM

The judiciary comprises a Supreme Tribunal, courts of appeal and courts of first instance. The judges of the Supreme Tribunal and the appeal courts are appointed by the Congress. The judges of courts of first instance are appointed by the chief justice.

## AREA AND POPULATION

The estimated population in mid-1974 was 5,284,000. The annual average percentage growth rate of the population for the period 1960–74 was 2·3 and for the period 1965–74 was 2·1. Prior to the earthquakes of February 1976 the largest cities had populations (to the nearest hundred) as follows: Guatemala City 700,000, Quezaltenango 100,000 and Escuintla 90,000.

## CURRENCY

The unit of currency is the *quetzal* of 100 *centavos*, equivalent to the U.S. dollar. There are silver coins of 5, 10, 25 and 50 *centavos* and copper coins of 1 and 2 *centavos*. There are paper notes of 50 centavos 1, 5, 10, 20, 100 *quetzales*.

The money supply at the end of December 1976 was Q583·6 million.

## FINANCE

The GNP at market prices for 1974 was U.S. $millions 3,060 and the GNP per capita at market prices was U.S. $580. The annual average percentage growth rate of the GNP per capita for the period 1960–74 was 3·3 and for the period 1965–74 was 3·8. [*See the note at the beginning of the section concerning GNP.*]

Following the February earthquakes the 1976 budget was revised by Q.100 million to Q.673·6 million as against a final 1975 budget of Q.422·6 million. The total public debt at the end of 1975 was Q.456·6 million of which Q.169·5 million was externally financed.

## PRINCIPAL BANKS

**Banco de Guatemala.** Established 1946. (President, M. M. Escobar.) Sole bank of issue for Guatemala. Balance Sheet at 31 March 1976 showed assets Q.836,281,793·66; notes and coins in circulation Q.253,814,332·59. *Head Office:* Guatemala City.

**Bank of London and Montreal.** (Manager: S. Jeffreys.) Established Guatemala 1920. Balance sheet at 30 June 1977 showed assets Q.100,436,369·53. Deposit and current account Q.85,028,539·56. Branch and 3 Agencies in Guatemala City; 3 out-of-town Agencies.

**Banco Agricola Mercantil.** Established 1926; Balance Sheet at 30 June 1974 showed assets Q.72·9 million. *Head Office:* Guatemala City. 13 Branches.

**Bank of America NT & SA.** Established 1957. (Manager, W. H. Snodgrass.) Balance sheet at 30 June 1974 showed assets Q56,410,423·68. Branch and two agencies in Guatemala City.

## PRODUCTION, INDUSTRY AND COMMERCE

**Agriculture and Fishing.** Guatemala is mainly an agricultural country. Much of the soil is fertile, and climatic conditions allow a variety of crops to be grown. Maize, wheat, beans and rice are widely grown for domestic consumption.

The four most important export crops are coffee (1977 forecast exports U.S. $millions 350–400), cotton (U.S. $millions 100), sugar (U.S. $millions 110) and bananas. Coffee production in 1976–77 was expected to reach 2·5 million bags. The cotton crop in 1976 produced an estimated 532,500 bales. Sugar production in 1976 was 600,000 tonnes and is forecast at 635,000 tonnes for 1977. Banana production in 1976 amounted to 571,000 tons compared with 520,000 tons in 1975 when 230,000 tons were exported. The fishing industry continues to develop, in 1975 exports were valued at Q4·1 m, an increase of nearly 30 per cent over the 1974 figure. Livestock production has also greatly expanded and meat exports are now among the top five export categories. Performance in the export sector has been satisfactory but not in the domestic sector where since 1973 there has been a deficit in basic grain production. In response the Government has introduced measures including the mandatory growing of grains in certain farm size categories, price support, and financial and technical assistance to farmers, increasing these measures following the earthquakes early in 1976.

**Forestry.** There are large areas of forest, much of which, including the rich Petén region, remains to be exploited, but at the same time some areas of the country are now suffering from deforestation. Annual timber production averages 184,000 cubic metres; exports were prohibited following the February 1976 earthquakes.

Next to Mexico, Guatemala is the chief source of *chicle* gum for the manufacture of chewing-gum. Exports of *chicle* in 1975 decreased in value to Q.0·8 m. (1·6 m in 1974).

**Mining.** The outlook for the mining industry has improved with the commencement of exploratory activities by the nickel mining company Exploraciones y Explotaciones Mineras de Izabal (Exmibal). Exmibal has built a processing complex at Chulac-El Estor which began operations in July 1977 and will produce 14,000 tons of dry nickel daily; this is to make the commodity the second most important export after coffee.

Exmibal has also been granted 40-year concessions to develop deposits of nickel iron ore, chrome and cobalt at El Amate (Alta Verapaz) and Xaan (Izabal).

In 1971–72 2·6 million kg. of marble were produced, valued at Q.0·4 million.

Export production of zinc and lead and other concentrates in 1975 amounted to about 21,893,600 kgs. with a value of Q.8·2 m.

Oil has been discovered at Rubelsanto. Exploration continues onshore and in Guatemalas offshore areas along the Atlantic coast. The reserves of the Rubelsanto field have been estimated at some 27·3 m barrels and the daily capacity was expected to reach 5,000–6,000 barrels in 1978, ensuring self sufficiency. A 200 km pipeline is to be built to carry petroleum from Rubelsanto to Livingston, on the Gulf of Honduras, at a cost of Q.30 m.

**Tourism.** Tourism has become a major source of foreign exchange and brought in some U.S. $millions 85 in 1975, and is forecast to reach nearly U.S. $100 m in 1977.

**Commerce.** The following table shows the volume and value of main categories of exports in 1974 (in million kilos and million quetzales).

| *Commodity* | *Volume* | *Value (f.o.b.)* |
|---|---|---|
| Food products | 751·9 | 243·9 |
| Beverages and tobacco | 4·1 | 3·6 |
| Non-edible raw materials, except fuels | 184·4 | 69·0 |
| Fuels and lubricants, minerals and similar | 4·8 | 0·1 |
| Animal and vegetable fats and oils | 6·2 | 2·3 |
| Chemical products | 25·4 | 31·5 |
| Manufactured goods classified by material | 107·8 | 58·9 |
| Other manufactured goods including transport equipment and materials | 11·4 | 26·9 |

The following table shows the Volume and Value of main categories of imports in 1974 (in million kilos and million quetzales):

| *Commoditty* | *Volume* | *Value (c.i.f.)* |
|---|---|---|
| Food products | 154·6 | 30·6 |
| Beverages and tobacco | 2·1 | 1·4 |
| Non-edible raw materials, except fuels | 64·9 | 10·8 |
| Fuels and lubricants, minerals and similar | 1,031·6 | 35·2 |
| Animal and vegetable fats and oils | 10·0 | 3·7 |
| Chemical products | 305·1 | 94·2 |
| Manufactured goods classified by material | 238·8 | 109·4 |
| Transport machinery and materials | 48·2 | 109·8 |
| Other manufactured goods | 12·0 | 35·7 |

In 1975 exports f.o.b. were valued at Q.623·5 m (Q.572·1 m in 1974), the main items were coffee (Q.164·2 m), sugar (Q.115·6 m), cotton (Q.76·0 m), bananas (Q.17·1 m) and fresh meat (Q.17·0 m).

In 1975 imports c.i.f. were valued at Q.732·7 m compared with Q.700·5 m in 1974, their volumed ecreased to 1,839 m kilos (1,935 m in 1974).

In 1976 exports f.o.b. and imports c.i.f. were valued at Q.740 m and Q.840 m respectively.

## COMMUNICATIONS

**Railways and Roads.** There are nearly 1,000 miles of railway track most of which is operated by the Government-owned Ferrocarril de Guatemala (FEGUA). The main line runs from Puerto Barrios on the Atlantic coast via Guatemala City to San José on the Pacific coast, branches from this line connect with the Mexican and El Salvador borders.

The railway, and road, system suffered some damage as a result of the February 1976 earthquakes with some 60 km of railway track requiring reconstruction and 400 km of road.

The roads have been improved in recent years and at the end of 1973 totalled 14,000 km of which 2,619 km were asphalted. The axes of the road system are formed by the Pan American Highway linking Mexico with El Salvador, the Pacific Highway which follows the coastline and the Atlantic Highway which links Puerto Barrios and San Jośe via Guatemala City. Bus and truck lines connect Guatemala City with the most important interior cities and neighbouring countries.

**Shipping.** The chief ports are Puerto Barrios, Santo Tomás de Castilla (formerly Matías de Gálvez) and Livingston on the Atlantic and San José and Chamoerico on the Pacific; the latter was being redeveloped with capacity to simultaneously berth four 15,000 ton vessels in 1977 at a cost of Q.45 m; while Santo Toma's de Castilla was expanded at a cost of Q.3·5 m. The pier at Puerto Barrios was severely damaged by the 1976 earthquakes.

External shipping services are maintained chiefly by the United Fruit Co. with sailings to Puerto Barrios from New York, New Orleans and the Gulf ports, other lines also provide service on these routes. Grace Lines serve the U.S. West Coast and the Pacific ports of Guatemala whilst various companies provided services between Guatemala and Europe. Guatemala also has interests in a number of small shipping lines providing regional services.

**Civil Aviation.** There is an international airport at Guatemala City and 46 other designated commercial landing fields. There are air connections with the other republics of Central America and the United States by Pan American Airways, Transportes Aeros Centroamericanos (TACA), Servicios Aéreos Hondurenos SA (SAHSA), Iberia, Braniff. Sabena, Air Panama, Lufthansa, KLM and Mexicana de Aviación.

A new international airport is to be built at Santa Elena Petén at a cost of Q.21 m.

The principal national airline is:

Empresa Guatemalteca de Aviación (Aviateca); a mixed-capital company; services operated: internal and to Miami and New Orleans. *Head Office:* Aeropuerto 'La Aurora,' Guatemala City. Aviateca operates in almost all Departments of the Republic.

**Posts, Telegraphs and Telephones.** These services are under the general control of the Ministry of Communications and Public Works. The Government agency, Empresa Guatemalteca de Telecomunicaciones (GUATEL), established in 1967, now operates the national telephone system and is responsible for radiotelegraphic and radiotelephonic services within the Republic and to Mexico and elsewhere abroad. A total of 57,000 telephone lines is to be installed by June 1978 at a cost of U.S. $11·5 m by an American firm. Telegraph services link important points in the Republic and connect with services in other parts of Central America and Mexico. Telex services link the main centres.

There are over 84 broadcasting stations in Guatemala of which over 20 are in the City. There are 2 television stations.

NEWSPAPERS

**Prensa Libre**: 13 Calle 9–31, Zona 1, Daily morning (ex. Sun.) circulation 60,000. Guatemala City.

**Impacto**: 9a Calle 'A' 1–56, Zona 1, Guatemala City. Daily.

**Diario de Centro América**: 9a Avenida 11–34, Zona 1, Guatemala City. Evening.

**El Imparcial**: 7a Calle 10–54, Zona 1, Guatemala City. Evening.

**La Hora**: la Avenida 9–18, Zona 1, Guatemala City. Evening.

**El Guatemalteco** (Government Gazette): 7a Avenida and Calle 18 de Septiembre, Zona 1, Guatemala City. Evening.

**El Grafico**: 14 Ave. 4–33 Zona 1 Guatemala City. Morning and evening.

**Diario 'La Tarde'**: 14 Ave. 4–33 Zona 1 Guatemala City Evening Paper.

**La Nación**, 2 Calle 6-51, Guatemala City Zona 2. Daily.

EDUCATION AND RELIGION

It is estimated that in 1975 47·3 per cent of the population was literate. There are four universities and 3 schools of social welfare, rural welfare, and nursing.

Roman Catholicism is the religion most widely practised. Other religions have complete freedom of worship.

There is one Archbishopric, that of Guatemala City, with bishoprics at Quezaltenango and Verapaz.

# Guinea

(THE REPUBLIC OF GUINEA)

**Capital**—Conakry.

**President**—Ahmed Sékou Touré.

**National Flag**: A tricolour pale-wise, red, gold, green.

## CONSTITUTION AND GOVERNMENT

THE former French Guinea is in north-west Africa, north-west of Sierra Leone and south-east of Senegal. As the result of a referendum on 28 September 1958, Guinea's independence of the French Community was proclaimed.

Guinea retained French as the official language. Official cultural and diplomatic relations with France were broken in 1965. Private commercial links between the two countries have persisted.

The Republic's relations with Ghana were broken following Nkrumah's overthrow. and in 1960 agreement for a union of Guinea with Mali and Ghana materialized. However, the union envisaged in the 1960 agreement did not materialize.

On 22 November 1970 a seaboroe attack was made on Conakry. A Security Council investigation commission established that the attack was launched from neighbouring Portuguese Guinea and that Portugal had supported Guinean exiles. The successful defence of the capital was followed in January 1971 by the establishment of a Revolutionary Tribunal to judge those captured at the time of the attack and those judged to be internal accomplices. Many Guineans and a few foreigners were sentenced to death or life imprisonment.

## AREA AND POPULATION

The area of the Republic is about 95,000 square miles.

The population of Guinea at mid-1974 was 5,390,000. The annual average percentage growth rate of the population for the period 1960–74 was 2·8, and for the period 1965–74 was 2·8. Essentially, the Republic is populated by three tribes, the Fulani (over one million), the Malinké (850,000) and the Soussou (300,000). The largest population centre is Conakry, the capital and port city, with a population in excess of 150,000.

## FINANCE

The GNP at market prices for 1974 was U.S. $millions 630, and the GNP per capita at market prices was U.S. $120. The annual average percentage growth rate of the GNP per capita for the period 1960–74 was 0·0, and for the period 1965–74 was 0·1. [*See the note at the beginning of this section concerning GNP.*]

## COMMUNICATIONS

In 1968 there were 4,725 miles of road, of which 3,075 were improved. Of particular importance is the highway across Liberia which provides an outlet to the South and the port of Monrovia in Liberia for products of the forest area of Guinea. There are 511 miles of railways, the main Conakry—Niger line runs about 415 miles from Conakry to Kankan, but is in poor condition. Two smaller lines run from Conakry to the FRIA aluminium project and the iron ore development in Boké to Port Kakande on the Atlantic Ocean.

Conakry is the chief port and has recently been greatly improved with the creation of additional deep-water docking facilities and construction of important ore-loading and fruit-loading facilities.

The main international airport is at Conakry and a new airport has been opened at Faranah. There are also airports at Kankan, N'zerekore, Labe and Boke.

There are cable connexions with France, Pernambuco, Freetown and Moravia, and there is a wireless station at Conakry with communications throughout West Africa. In 1966, there were about 6,000 telephones.

## EDUCATION

In 1965–6 there were over 150,000 pupils in primary schools, 16,698 pupils in the secondary general schools, 5,018 vocational students and 822 teacher-training students. About 18 per cent of the primary school age children are at school.

Literacy in Guinea is estimated at five to ten per cent.

## PRODUCTION AND COMMERCE

The budget balancing figure for 1971–72 was 27,800,000 Guinea francs.

The chief products of Guinea are agricultural. The main staple food crops are rice, manioc, millet, corn and sweet potatoes. The main cash crops are bananas, palm nuts and kernels, coffee, peanuts and pineapples, all of which are major agricultural exports. There is a substantial mineral production. Large deposits of bauxite and iron ore contribute greatly to the nation's income. Preliminary bauxite exploration agreements have been signed with Alusuisse and the Yugoslavs. These are for deposits at Tongue and Dabola respectively. Work is also underway for the Soviet bauxite project at Kindia which is scheduled to begin exporting ore by early 1974. An eventual output of 3 million tons is anticipated. Diamonds and gold are also found. The country has a valuable livestock population and hides and skins and breeding animals are exported to neighbouring countries.

The principal countries from which imports are received are France, United States, Federal Republic of Germany, United Kingdom, and countries in the Communist bloc.

The principal countries to which commodities are exported are Norway, United States, Cameroon, and countries in the Communist bloc.

# Guinea—Bissau

## (GUINÉ)

**Capital**—Bissau.

**President of the Council of State**—Luiz de Almeida Cabral.

### AREA AND POPULATION

Guinea is situated on the west coast of Africa, to the south of Gambia. It borders on Senegal and Guinea Republics. The province includes the island of Bolama, and the archipelago of Bissangos (Bijagos). The capital, Bissau, occupies a central position on the coast and is the principal port. The province covers an area of 36,125 sq. km.

The population at mid-1974 was 520,000. The annual average percentage growth rate of the population for the period 1960–74 was −0·4, and for the period 1965–74 was −0·7.

It is divided into 12 *concelhos* (councils or boroughs) Bolama, Bissau, Bissora, Cacheu, S. Domingos, Farim, Mansoa, Bafatá, Gabu, Catió, Fulacunda and Bijagós. There is one tribunal of justice, under the judicial district of Lisbon.

### FINANCE

The GNP at market prices for 1974 was U.S. $millions 210, and the GNP per capita at market prices was U.S. $390. The annual average percentage growth rate of the GNP per capita for the period 1960–74 was 3·5 and for the period 1965–74 was 5·2. [*See note at the beginning of this section concerning GNP.*]

### PRODUCTION, INDUSTRY AND COMMERCE

Imports and exports by principal countries are shown below for 1970 (in thousand escudos):

| *Country* | 1970 *Imports* | 1970 *Exports* |
|---|---|---|
| Portugal, metropolitan | 434,884 | 78,913 |
| Cape Verde Islands | 3,497 | 1,438 |
| Angola | 15,439 | 1,570 |
| Mozambique | 6,517 | N.A. |
| Macao | 20,388 | N.A. |
| West Germany | 36,657 | 3,710 |
| Belgo-Luxembourg | 6,079 | 40 |
| France | 23,191 | 195 |

*continued*

| *Country* | 1970 *Imports* | 1970 *Exports* |
|---|---|---|
| Netherlands | 22,333 | 1,790 |
| Italy | 10,387 | N.A. |
| United Kingdom | 46,320 | 30 |
| Sweden | 1,928 | N.A. |
| Switzerland | 4,977 | N.A. |
| Madagascar | N.A. | N.A. |
| Rhodesia, Zambia and Malawi | 10,348 | N.A. |
| United States | 9,087 | N.A. |
| Canada | 5,891 | N.A. |
| Curaçao | 2,715 | N.A. |
| Japan | 218,700 | N.A. |

The following table shows exports for 1970 (in thousand escudos):

| *Commodity* | 1970 |
|---|---|
| Vegetable products | 80,333 |
| Oils and fats | 7,645 |
| Food, beverages, tobacco | 2,110 |
| Leather goods | 767 |
| Wood products | 2,841 |

The province's wealth lies in its agriculture. The main agricultural products are groundnuts, coconuts, palm oil and rice. About 46,000 tons of groundnuts are produced annually and about 14,000 tons of coconuts. Palm oil production is about 2,700 tons a year and rice 128,349 tons. Timber, wax and hides are also produced.

### COMMUNICATIONS

The chief port is Bissau. The length of the roads is approximately 3,102 km. and there were in 1961 1,230 km. of telegraph lines. There are 2 radio stations.

# Guyana

## (MEMBER OF THE COMMONWEALTH)

**Capital**—Georgetown.

**President**—Arthur Chung.

**Flag:** Red triangle with black border pointing from hoist to fly, on a yellow triangle with white border all on a green field.

GUYANA, the former colonial territory of British Guiana, lies on the mainland of the South American continent. Its northern coastline, about 270 miles long, borders the Atlantic Ocean from the eastern mouth of the Orinoco river on the west, to the Corentyne river on the east. Guyana is bounded on the south and south-west by Brazil, on the east by Surinam (Netherlands Guiana), and on the northwest by Venezuela. It had been in British hands since 1814, when it was ceded to Great Britain by the Dutch. Guyana became independent and the twenty-third member of the Commonwealth on 26 May 1966 and the 119th Member of the United Nations on 20 September 1966. The country became a Co-operative Republic on 23 February 1970.

### CONSTITUTION AND GOVERNMENT

The Independence Constitution was agreed to at the London Constitutional Conference in November 1965. It provides for a Republic State of Guyana, with a President elected by a simple majority vote of elected members of the National Assembly. The Constitution provides for citizenship and the safeguard of fundamental freedoms of the individual. It also retains the electoral system of Proportional Representation or "single list" system, each voter casting his vote for a party list of candidates. The President must exercise all his powers in accordance with Ministerial advice. The Prime Minister is the member of the Assembly, who, in the judgement of the President, is best able to command the confidence of a majority of members of that chamber. The Prime Minister and Cabinet are responsible collectively to the National Assembly which consists of 66 members, 53 of whom were elected by secret ballot. The voting age has been reduced to 18. Amendments to important sections of the Constitution require the support of a majority of voters in referendum, or in certain circumstances, a two-thirds majority of all members of the National Assembly. The Constitution recognizes the role of the Leader of the Opposition and provides for consultation with him, by the Prime Minister, in a number of important matters. An important and characteristically modern feature of the Constitution is its provision for the appointment of an Ombudsman. The life of Parliament is five years, and is presided over by a Speaker who may or may not be a member of Parliament.

#### Cabinet

*Prime Minister:* L. F. S. Burnham, OE, SC.
*Deputy Prime Minister, and Minister of National Development:* Dr. P. A. Reid.
*Minister of Economic Development and Co-operatives:* H. D. Hoyte, SC.
**Minister of Health, Housing and Labour:* H. Green.
**Minister of Energy and Natural Resources:* H. O. Jack.
**Minister of Finance:* F. E. Hope.
*Minister of Works and Transport:* S. S. Naraine, AA.
**Minister of Trade and Consumer Protection:* G. A. King.
**Minister of Agriculture:* G. B. Kennard, CCH.
**Minister of Foreign Affairs and Justice:* F. R. Wills, SC.
*Minister of Information:* S. M. Field-Ridley.
*Minister of Parliamentary Affairs and Leader of the House:* B. Ramsaroop.
*Minister of Home Affairs:* C. V. Mingo.
**Minister of Education, Social Development and Culture:* V. R. Teekah.

* Non-elected Ministers.

### AREA AND POPULATION

The area of Guyana is approximately 83,000 square miles.

The population at mid-1974 was 791,000. The annual average percentage growth rate of the population for the periods 1960–74 and 1965–74 was 2·4. The population of Georgetown at the end of 1976 was 59,600.

The population (Registrar General's Estimate December 1976) was made up as follows: East Indians, 362,700; Negro, 218,400; White, 2,100; Chinese, 3,400; Mixed etc., 73,300; Portuguese, 5,600; Amerindians, 34,300; other races 800.

### LEGAL SYSTEM

The Roman-Dutch law was in force in the Colony until 1 January 1917, at which date the Civil Law of British Guiana Ordinance, Chapter 7, came into force. This enactment, along with two others, was the outcome of a Common Law Commission and Statute Law Committee and purports to substitute for Roman-Dutch law the English Common Law.

The Criminal Law is similar to that obtaining in England and is codified. The administration of the law is similar to that of the United Kingdom and responsibility is exercised on behalf of the Government by the Director of Public Prosecutions. The Chancellor is head of the Judiciarh and the Chief Justice, Justices of Appeal and a number of Puisne Judges and Magistrates are answerable to him.

### FINANCE

Budget figures for 1977 were: Revenue, G\$497·6 million; Expenditure, G\$795·1 million.

In addition to the recurrent expenditure of G\$411·1, G\$134·8 million is estimated for development projects in 1977.

The GNP at market prices for 1974 was U.S. \$millions 390 and the GNP per capita at market prices was U.S. \$500. The annual average percentage growth rate of the GNP per capita for the period 1960–74 was 1·5 and for the period 1965–74 was 1·1 [*See the note at the beginning of this section concerning GNP.*]

### PRODUCTION INDUSTRY AND COMMERCE

The main products of Guyana are sugar, rum and molasses, rice, bauxite, timber, diamonds, gold and balata. Sugar and its by-products furnished 30·5 per cent in value of the total exports.

The forests represent one of Guyana's most important natural resources. They extend over approximately 70,000 square miles, representing 87 per cent of the total land area. The principal timber production is from greenheart, mora, and crabwood. Exploitation of the forest is entirely by private agency, mainly operating under licence on State lands. Gold, diamonds, and bauxite are also important.

Bauxite is obtained from open-cast mines and is processed by crushing, washing and drying. A G\$60 million plant for the processing of alumina is also in operation. This Industry which was nationalized on 15 July 1971, and which is now known as the Guyana Bauxite Company Limited, was formerly owned and operated by the Demerara Bauxite Company Limited, of Canada, a subsidiary of Alcan Limited.

The pattern of trade has followed that of most developing countries in that exports which were almost entirely agricultural or forest products and untreated minerals are steadily including more products of secondary industries using these materials; and imports, which were almost entirely consumer goods, are including more capital goods in order to reduce the dependence on consumer imports by encouraging the increase in local production of food, as well as in manufacturing industries. As part of this policy a ban on the importation of certain items of food, for which there are local substitutes, was recently introduced.

The following table shows the quantity and value of principal exports for the year 1976.

| *Articles* | *Unit* | *Quantity* | *Value* (\$G) |
|---|---|---|---|
| Sugar (unrefined) | tons | 296,773 | 233,743,308 |
| Rice | tons | 70,681 | 73,593,324 |
| Molasses (inedible) | cwt. | 1,229,225 | 6,019,769 |
| Shrimps | lbs. | 1,455,740 | 12,908,293 |
| Alumina | tons | 246,926 | 61,156,670 |
| Alumina hydrate | tons | 17,777 | 3,262,683 |
| Bauxite, calcined | tons | 730,706 | 190,671,444 |

*continued*

| *Articles* | *Unit* | *Quantity* | *Value* ($G) |
|---|---|---|---|
| Bauxite, dried refactory | tons | — | — |
| Bauxite, other | tons | 810,920 | 33,103,584 |
| Diamonds | carat | 11,789 | 801,720 |
| Timber | ct. ft. | — | 9,700,185 |
| Rum | p. gal | 2,223,725 | 10,360,740 |

The following table shows the production figures for the year 1976.

| *Articles* | *Unit* | *Quantity* |
|---|---|---|
| Sugar (unrefined) | tons | 332,457 |
| Rice | tons | 110,000 |
| Molasses | lbs. | 23,800,009 |
| Shrimp | lbs. | — |
| Alumina | tons | 246,524 |
| Alumina hydrate | tons | 18,822 |
| Bauxite, calcined | tons | 729,160 |
| Bauxite, dried refactory | tons | — |
| Bauxite, other | tons | 968,575 |
| Diamonds | carat | 13,533 |
| Timber | ct. ft. | 8,913,150 |
| Rum | p. gal. | 4,604,694 |

The following table shows the value (in G$) of foreign trade with the United Kingdom.

| *Imports* | 1974 | 1975 | 1976 |
|---|---|---|---|
| Imports | 116,170,372 | 173,920,894 | 213,487,854 |
| Domestic exports | 123,477,065 | 240,993,166 | 180,146,907 |
| Re-exports | 793,814 | 1,474,082 | 3,162,636 |

The following table shows the value of foreign trade.

| | 1974 | 1975 | 1976 |
|---|---|---|---|
| Imports | 563,511,275 | 806,435,131 | 927,299,407 |
| Domestic exports | 589,662,040 | 832,016,872 | 660,865,251 |
| Re-exports | 6,538,363 | 17,461,229 | 16,121,391 |

## COMMUNICATIONS

There are 1,810·29 miles of roads and vehicular trails. Of the three main rivers, the Demerara, the Essequibo and the Berbice, the Demerara is navigable by ocean-going vessels of moderate draft i.e. 20 feet, for 60 miles from Georgetown, while the Essequibo and the Berbice are navigable for 35 and 100 miles respectively from Georgetown, by ships with drafts of 17 feet. Beyond these distances ocean-going vessels cannot travel due to the narrowness of the rivers, but there are long stretches of water in the upper rivers navigable by launches.

Guyana Airways Corporation operates an internal air transport service and charter services to neighbouring territories. The International Airport at Timehri serves Pan American Airways, British Airways, K.L.M., British West Indian Airways, Air France, Cubana Airlines and Cruzerio Do Sul (Brazil), and there are services to Trinidad, Barbados, other of the West Indian Islands and neighbouring countries.

There is a Central Telephone Exchange and many small automatic exchanges in the rural areas are also in operation.

A Tropospheric Scatter System, is operated by Cable and Wireless (W.I.) Ltd. It provides for a maximum of 64 channels linking Guyana with the rest of the world via Trinidad, the nearest point for connection in the Company's broad band system.

## EDUCATION

The government took the forward step in September 1976 for the total responsibility of education from nursery school to university, thus bringing to an end any form of private ownership of schools. In September 1976, the total number of schools was as follows: Nursery, 400; Primary, 445; Secondary, 57; University, 1. This take-over of private and denominational schools by Government makes it possible for a child to receive free education from nursery to University.

In order to make education serve the needs of the society, agricultural, technical education, home economics and commercial education have formed an integral part of the educational system. There are now five technical and vocational schools and two schools for the teaching of home economics and domestic crafts. Training in Co-operatives is provided by the Kuru-Kuru Co-operative College and agriculture by the Guyana School of Agriculture and the Burnham Agricultural Institute. The training of primary and secondary school teachers is under-taken by three institutions. Higher education is also provided by the University of Guyana which was established in 1963 with faculties of Natural Science, Social Science, Art, Technology and Education as well as first year students in Law.

## NEWSPAPERS

**Sunday Chronicle:** F. 1881. Industrial Estate, Ruimveldt. Circulation 610,089.

**Daily Chronicle:** F. 1881. Industrial Estate, Ruimveldt. Circulation 21,026.

**Guyana Graphic:** F. 1944. Daily, Bel Air Park. Circulation 30,000.

**Sunday Graphic:** F. 1944. Weekly, Bel Air Park. Circulation 50,000.

**Mirror:** F. 1962. Lot 8, Ruimveldt, Industrial Estate, Georgetown. Circulation 15,796 (daily); 22,616 (Sunday).

**New Nation:** Weekly. 131 Crown and Albert Streets, Georgetown. Circulation 18,000.

## RELIGION

The following shows membership of the various religious denominations at the census of 1960:

Anglican, 117,060; Roman Catholic, 94,497; Presbyterian, 52,104; Methodist, 26,387; Pentecostal, 4,435; Moravian, 3,703; Baptist, 2,804; Hindu, 261,094; Others, 132,483.

# Haiti

(RÉPUBLIQUE D'HAÏTI)

**President**—M. Jean-Claude Duvalier.

**Capital**—Port-au-Prince.

**National Flag:** Two vertical bands, black (next to staff) and red; arms in centre on a white background.

## CONSTITUTION AND GOVERNMENT

THE Island of Hispaniola, of which the Republic of Haiti forms about one-third, was discovered by Columbus in 1492. At the time of its discovery, the Island had a large native population, but in the course of a few years the natives were almost completely exterminated. In order to provide labour for the plantations, the Spaniards introduced Negro slaves from the west coast of Africa, and the present population is chiefly of negro origin. In 1697, Spain ceded Haiti, which was then known as Saint Domingue, to France. The French Revolution had its effects on Saint Domingue, and an insurrection of the slaves was suppressed by General Leclerc. But resistance continued, and in 1804, the former French colony was declared an independent republic named *Haiti* or *The Land of the Mountains*. The United Kingdom recognized the republic in 1825.

General Magloire's six years of office as President of the Republic came to an end in December 1956. When he tried to prolong his term beyond the constitutional limit, he was forced by a general strike to resign and to go into exile. A series of short-lived provisional Governments followed, until in June 1957 a military junta assumed power and under its control elections were held on 22 September, following which Dr. François Duvalier was declared elected as President of the Republic for a 6-year term.

In May 1961 he took the oath of office for his second term. On 30 April 1961, a single Legislative Chamber was elected for a 6-year term. On 14 June 1964, after a national referendum, Dr. Duvalier was elected President for Life. Dr. Duvalier died on 21 April 1971. He was succeeded as President for Life on the same day by his son, Jean-Claude Duvalier, whom he had nominated as his successor under Article 102 of the constitution of 1964 as amended on 14 January 1971. Since that time the political situation has been stable, the economic situation has improved considerably, and the aid-donor countries and the international development agencies are showing much greater readiness to contribute to the economic development of Haiti.

## LOCAL GOVERNMENT

The country is divided into Departments—North, North-East, North-West, Artibonite, Centre West, South-West, South and Grand Anse. In turn these Departments are divided into arrondissements, which are again divided into communes. In each commune there is a Mayor who takes care of communal interests. Mayor of Port-au-Prince: Député M. Antoine Herard.

## LEGAL SYSTEM

Justice is administered by one Supreme Court, or Court of Cassation and by lower courts including Courts of Appeal, Civil Courts and Magistrate Courts.

*The President of the Court of Cassation:* Maître Fournier Fortuné.

## AREA AND POPULATION

The area of the Republic including offshore islands is estimated at 10,700 sq. miles.

The population at mid-1974 was 4,514,000. The annual average percentage growth rate of the population for the period 1960–74 was 1·6 and for the period 1965–74 was also 1·6. The population is predominantly negro although there are numbers of mulattos. The official language is French, but the majority speak only Creole.

Chief towns with populations are Port-au-Prince, 250,000 (1960 census), estimated 500,000 (1971 census); Cap Haitien, 30,000 (1960 estimate); Les Cayes, 14,000 (1960 estimate).

## CURRENCY

U.S. currency, along with the gourde of 100 centimes, is legal tender in Haiti. Banque National de la République d'Haiti notes in denominations of 500, 250, 100, 50, 20, 10, 5, 2 and 1 gourdes (1 U.S. $ = 5 gourdes) and coins of 5, 10, 20 and 50 centimes.

## FINANCE

Revenue and expenditure budgeted for the year 1974–75 are balanced at U.S.$ 38·9 millions for the year 1973–74 they were balanced at U.S.$ 32·2 million. There is also considerable non-fiscalized (and unpublished) revenue—i.e. from the Tobacco Monopoly.

By the end of 1973 Haiti had built up a modest exchange reserve of some $20 million but this has been eroded by the oil price increases since then, and by the rising cost of other essential imports; Haiti's balance of payments position is thus once more a little tight. But it is confidently expected she will be able to pay her way with the help of International Monetary Fund drawing rights.

The GNP at market prices for 1974 was U.S. $ millions 750, and the GNP per capita at market prices was U.S. $170. The percentage growth rate of the GNP per capita for the period 1960–74 was —0·1, and for the period 1965–74 was 0·7. [*See the note at the beginning of this section concerning GNP.*]

## PRINCIPAL BANK

**Banque Nationale de la République d'Haiti.** (Pretident, M. Antonio Andre.) Established 1881; Sole Bank of Issue for Haiti; all the share capital is owned by the State; Balance Sheet at 30 September 1973 showed assets Gourdes 685,386,872·33; banknotes in circulation (not including dollar notes) Gourdes 128,607,466·00. *Head Office:* Angle des Rues Férou et Américaine, Port-au-Prince; 8 Branches and 3 Agencies.

There are seven banks operating in Haiti: Banque Nationale de la République d'Haiti, Royal Bank of Canada, First National City Bank of New York, Bank of Nova Scotia, Populaire Colombo-Haitienne, Bank of Boston, Banque de l'Union Haitienne, and Banque Nationale de Paris.

## PRODUCTION, INDUSTRYAND COMMERCE

**Agriculture.** Haiti is almost entirely an agricultural country. Coffee accounts for about one-third of the total exports and is still a mainstay of the country's economy. Other important crops are sisal, sugar, cocoa, cotton and various kinds of oil seed.

**Industry and Commerce.** Exports of bauxite began in 1957. Production of copper in the Terre Neuve area started in 1960 but was suspended as uneconomic at the end of 1971. Deposits of copper recently discovered are now being investigated by test drilling, and may turn out to be important. Industry is still on a small scale but the last few years or so have seen a steady and considerable expansion of light industry taking advantage of cheap labour to assemble or manufacture labour intensive goods for the U.S. market (baseballs, underwear, electronic equipment, etc.). Exports of manufactures now rank second after coffee at about 20 per cent of total exports.

The following figures show the estimated value of exports (in million U.S.$) for 1972–73 (the Haitian fiscal year 1 October to 30 September).

| *Commodity* | 1972–3 |
|---|---|
| Coffee | 20·6 |
| Sisal | 1·2 |
| Sugar | 2·5 |
| Bauxite | 6·5 |
| Copper | — |
| Essential oils | 3·7 |
| Industry | 10·7 |

The value of merchandise imports (f.o.b.) and exports (f.o.b.) for the years 1972–73 in U.S. $million was 76·7 and 51·3 respectively.

The adverse balance of visibles is normally covered by invisibles (tourism and remittances from Haitians overseas).

### COMMUNICATIONS

There are about 100 miles of railway track used exclusively for the transport of sugar cane.

Haiti is well served by air from New York and Miami, Kingston, Puerto Rico, the French Antilles, etc., with daily services to the North and the South. The airlines touching Port-au-Prince International Airport include Pan American, Air France, American Air Lines, Eastern Airlines, ALM. Internal air services are operated by Turks and Caicos Airways.

Freight sailings to North and South America, Europe and the West Indies (except Cuba) are frequent.

Existing roads have for years been in a poor state of repair but are being rapidly improved. Roads in the south of the country are sometimes impassable for light vehicles during the rainy season, but the Inter American Development Bank is financing the construction, which has recently started of an all-weather road to Cayes (capital of the South), and the World Bank has financed a similar road to Cap Haitien (Capital of the North) now under construction.

The French government has financed a new road from Port-au-Prince to Jacuel, and is under construction.

There are four religious broadcasting stations, 21 commercial stations and one television station.

There are four French daily newspapers. Total circulation is very small.

The National Bank of Haiti now owns a controlling interest in the Telephone Company, (51 per cent), the balance remaining in Canadian hands. The expansion and improvement of service continue. External telephone, telegraph and postal services are reasonably good, though airmail is apt to be slow and erratic.

### EDUCATION

Primary education is free and theoretically compulsory, but the rate of illiteracy is very high at about 70 per cent. Higher education is provided by the University of Haiti with its Faculties of Medicine, Pharmacy and Dentistry; Law, Economics and International Studies; Agronomy and Veterinary Science; the Polytechnic School (architecture and engineering); the Institute of Ethnology and the School of International Studies. There are also two Teachers' Training Colleges and a Military Academy.

### RELIGION

Officially, Haiti is a Roman Catholic country with an Archbishop and a full hierarchy; many Protestant denominations have their adherents—Episcopal, Baptist, Methodist, etc. The folk religion is Voodoo.

# Honduras

## (REPÚBLICA DE HONDURAS)

**Capital**—Tegucigalpa.

**Head of State**—General de Brigada, Juan Alberto Melgar Castro.

**National Flag:** A tricolour fesse-wise, blue, white, blue with 5 stars blue five-pointed centred.

### CONSTITUTION AND GOVERNMENT

HONDURAS has been an independent Republic since 15 September 1821. A new Constitution was enacted by a Constitutional Assembly on 6 June 1965 which provides for executive power to be vested in the President, who is elected for a term of 6 years by popular vote. He is assisted by a Cabinet of 11 Ministers. The Constitution provides for a single-chambered Legislature, the Congress of Deputies, consisting of 64 members (one for every 30,000 inhabitants) elected by popular vote for a term of 6 years. The Congress meets on 21 November each year for a session of not less than 100 days nor more than 150 days under the new Constitution of 6 June 1965. A commission of five members is in permanent session during the recess.

#### Ministry

*Minister of Internal Affairs and Justice:* Col. Alfonso Flores Guerra.
*Minister of Foreign Affairs:* Dr. Roberto Palma Gálvez.
*Minister of Defence and Public Security:* Col. Omar Zelaya.
*Minister of Economy:* Lic. J. Vicente Diaz.
*Minister of Treasury:* P. M. Porfiuo Zavala.
*Minister of Education:* Prof. Lidia Williams de Arias.
*Minister of Communications:* Ing. Mario Flores Theresin.
*Minister of Health:* Dr. Enrique Aguilar Paz.
*Minister of Labour:* Adalberto Discua.
*Minister of Natural Resources:* Lic. Rafael Leonardo Callejas.
*Minister of Culture, Tourism and Information:* Col. y Lic. Efrain Lisandro Gonzales Muñoz.
*Executive Secretary of the Superior Executive Council of Economic Planning:* Lic. Arturo Corleto.
*Executive Director of the National Institute of Agriculture:* Lic. Flavio Salgado.

The Liberal Party won the elections of 10 October 1954, but did not obtain the required absolute majority over the Nationalists to secure the Presidency and Vice-Presidency. The new Congress should then have met on 5 December to decide the Presidential succession, but as it appeared unlikely that any party would have the required majority, Don Julio Lozano Diaz, as Acting President, declared a state of emergency on 6 December and assumed full powers as Supreme Chief of State. He was overthrown on 21 October 1956 by a Military coup, and the Military Junta of Government assumed power. On 21 July 1957 an Electoral Law was decreed and following free and secret elections in September 1957, when the Liberal Party gained a sweeping victory, Dr. Ramon Villeda Morales was inaugurated as constitutional President for a term of six years on 21 December 1957.

On 3 October 1963, Dr. Villeda Morales, whose term was due to expire in December 1963, was overthrown by the armed forces, and an administrative cabinet was appointed by the former C.-in-C. of the Armed Forces.

On 16 February 1965 elections for a Constituent Assembly took place resulting in a win for the Nationalist Party who elected the President. In March 1971 another election took place and Dr. Ramon Ernesto Cruz was elected President.

Another military coup took place on 4 December 1972 and from 1975 General de Brigada Juan Alberto Melgar Castro became head of state.

### LEGAL SYSTEM

There is a Supreme Court of 9 Judges and an Attorney-General who are elected for 6 years. There are also Appeal Courts and Departmental and local Justices who are appointed by the Supreme Court.

#### Supreme Court

*President:* Alberto Maleano.

### AREA AND POPULATION

The total area of Honduras is approximately 43,227 sq. miles, and lies between latitude 13° and 16°30′N and longitude 83° and 89°41′W.

The population at mid-1974 was 2,806,000. The annual average percentage population growth rate for the period 1960–74 was 2·7, and for the period 1965–74 was 2·7.

The inhabitants speak various languages, but Spanish is the official language of the country. The Republic is divided into 18 Departments, of which the newest, Gracias a Dios, formed on 21 February 1957, replaces the territory known as Mosquitia together with parts of the Departments of Colón and Olancho. Chief towns with populations are: Tegucigalpa 253,200, San Pedro 136,900, La Ceiba 45,900, Tela 38,100 and Puerto Cortés 37,800.

### CURRENCY AND FINANCE

The unit of currency is the *Lempira* of 100 *centavos*. Its value is fixed at 50 cents, United States currency. There are nickel copper coins of 20, 50 and 100 centavos, nickel coins of

5 and 10 centavos and 1 and 2 centavos copper pieces. Banknotes are issued in denominations of 1, 5, 10, 20, 50 and 100 lempiras.

The GNP at market prices for 1974 was U.S.$ millions 950, and the GNP per capita at market prices was U.S. $340. The annual average percentage growth rate of the GNP per capita for the period 1960–74 was 1·6, and for the period 1965–73 was 1·2. [*See the note at the beginning of this section concerning GNP.*]

## PRINCIPAL BANKS

**Banco Central de Honduras.** This is a Central Bank; all shares are held by the Government. (President, Alberto Galeano M.) Established 1950; Bank of issue; Balance Sheet at 31 May 1972 showed assets Lempiras 269,003,322,28; deposits Lempiras 61,843,782,42; banknotes in circulation Lempiras 81,855,853; coins in circulation Lempiras 8,895,637,40. *Address:* P.O. Box C-58, Tegucigalpa, D.C. Honduras, C.A.

**Banco Atlantida.** (President, Dr. José T. Mendoza.) Established 1913; Balance Sheet at 31 December 1971; assets Lempiras 129,269,283; deposits Lempiras 113,168,146. *Head Office* in Tegucigalpa, 46 Branches and Agencies throughout the country.

**Banco Nacional de Fomento.** (President, Lic. G. Medina Santos.) Established 1960. Balance Sheet at 31 December 1964 showed assets Lempiras 40,737,079; deposits Lempiras 5,538,454. *Head Office:* Tegucigalpa, Honduras. 17 Branches.

**Banco del Ahorro Hondureño.** *Head Office:* Tegucigalpa, Branch in San Pedro Sula.

**Bank of London and Montreal Ltd.** Branches in Tegucigalpa, San Pedro Sula, La Ceiba and Puerto Cortéz.

**Bank of America.** Tegucigalpa. Branch in San Pedro Sula.

**Banco de Los Trabajadores.** Branch at Edificio América 6-C, San Pedro Sula, Cortés.

## PRODUCTION, INDUSTRY AND COMMERCE

**Agriculture.** Production, in metric tons, of the principal agricultural products for the year 1975 is shown in the table below:

| | 1975 (*metric tons*) |
|---|---|
| Bananas | 266,585,400 |
| Plantain | 1,382,500 |
| Tobacco | 2,272,900 |
| Beans | 3,264,100 |
| Coffee | 47,331,700 |
| Cotton fabrics | 396,200 |
| Sugar | 5,717,500 |

**Forestry.** The State Corporation for Forestry Development (COHDEFOR) was created by Decree No. 103 of 10 January 1974 with the objective of enforcing policies for the attainment of optimum profitability in the exploitation of National Forest resources and also protect, operate and improve the resources. Its aim is to implement joint ventures in wood processing and resin extraction; to centralize wood exports; to provide counselling and technical assistance to the private sector of the wood industry; and to organize new businesses and cooperatives in the Honduran rural areas.

**Mining.** Honduran mineral resources have not been fully exploited. The value of the exports for 1969 are shown below:

| *Commodity* | 1969 |
|---|---|
| Iron and steel scrap | 52,662 |
| Zinc ore and its concentrates | 3,332,459 |
| Silver ores and ore concentrates | 7,758,492 |
| Silver and its alloys | 1,762,014 |
| Gold filings | 188,514 |
| Gold bars | 201,192 |

**Commerce.** Value of imports for 1971 are shown in the table below (in millions of Lempiras):

| *Product* | 1971 |
|---|---|
| Food products | 31·2 |
| Drinks and tobacco | 1·7 |
| Non-edible raw materials | 3·6 |
| Mineral fuels and lubricants | 34·9 |
| Animal and vegetable oils and fats | 4·2 |
| Chemical products | 60·4 |
| Manufactured articles | 110·5 |
| Machinery and transport equipment | 112·6 |

The value of exports for 1971 are shown in the table below (in millions of Lempiras):

| *Product* | 1971 |
|---|---|
| Bananas | 191·4 |
| Coffee | 46·0 |
| Timber | 38·4 |
| Silver, lead and zinc | 6·8 |
| Refrigerated meats | 28·2 |
| Beans | 48·0 |
| Tobacco | 4·2 |

## COMMUNICATIONS

There are about 1,000 miles of railways in operation in the Northern Region used for the transportation of bananas. There is increasing road transport for passengers and freight. There is an asphalted road from Tegucigalpa to San Pedro Sula. There is a road under construction from Tegucigalpa to Danli. There is also a good asphalted road connecting Danli, Nicaragua, and Danli. Asphalted roads also connect San Pedro Sula and Santo Rosa, also San Pedro Sula, Tela, and La Ceiba. In 1969 there were 1,958 banana wagons and 75 passenger coaches. Inland communications are maintained by improved air serviecs. There are altogether nearly 100 airports or airstrips in the larger and smaller towns of which only 35 are fullys erviceable and 25 can take twin-engined passenger aircraft. The Tegucigalpa road is asphalted and good.

In April 1971 there were 91 radio stations. There were also four television stations three in Tegucigalpa and one in San Pedro Sula, with booster stations in La Ceiba, Copan, Siguatepeque, Omoa and Choluteca.

**Aero-Servicios HD243.** President, W. Kivett, Jr.; Vice-President: G. J. Kivett; Adviser: H. S. Kivett, *Services operated:* Scheduled freight within Honduras, and Charter flights to over 100 locations throughout Central America. I.A.T.A. Associate Airline. Cessna and Piper Aircraft.

**Servicio Aéreo de Honduras, S.A.** (President, General Oswaldo López A.); share capital $200,000 (20 per cent owned by the State); *services operated:* Guatemala, twice daily; Nicaragua, once daily; Costa Rica, ten times a week; San Andrés y Panama, four times a week; Belize H.B., once a week; New Orleans, four times a week. *Head Office:* Avenida Colón y Cuarta Calle, Tegucigalpa D.C. Honduras, C.A.

**Transportes Aereos Nacionales (TAN).** (General Manager, Ing. Roberto Galvez B.). Passenger and cargo service, international and inland.

Six large commercial radio stations and 60 others serve about 180,000 receivers. There are four television stations transmitting to over 6,500 sets.

## NEWSPAPERS

**El Dia**: Afternoon. Independent. Tegucigalpa.

**La Prensa.** Morning. San Pedro Sula.

**El Tiempo.** Morning. Independent. San Pedro Sula.

**El Cronista** Independent. Evening. Tegucigalpa.

**El Pueblo.** Liberal. Evening. Tegucigalpa.

There are also small newspapers published in Tela, La Ceiba and El Progreso.

### EDUCATION AND RELIGION

Primary education is free and nominally compulsory for children between the ages of 7 and 15. At Tegucigalpa there is a University with Faculties of Law, Economics, Pedagogy, Medicine, Pharmacy and Engineering. The Rector is Lic. Jorge Arturo Reina Idiaques. At San Pedro Sula there is a Centre of Pre-University Studies for the faculty of Economics. At La Ceoba there is a School of Agricultural Science.

The Constitution guarantees freedom to all religious sects. The bulk of the inhabitants are, however, Roman Catholic.

# Hungary

## (MAGYAR NÉPKÖZTÁRSASÁG)

**Capital**—Budapest.

**Chairman of the Presidium of the People's Republic**—Pál Losonczi.

**National Flag:** A tricolour fesse-wise, red, white, green.

### CONSTITUTION AND GOVERNMENT

IN June 1941 Hungary entered the war against the U.S.S.R. and by December she was also at war with the U.S.A. and the United Kingdom. In March 1944 German troops occupied Hungary and installed a Government which was entirely pro-German. On 15 October 1944 the Regent Horthy issued a proclamation declaring Hungary's withdrawal from the war. The Hitlerite forces removed Horthy and in his stead placed the Szálasi Arrow Cross government in power. Soviet forces had by then entered the country. Budapest fell in February 1945 after a 7-weeks siege in which the Germans destroyed all the Danube bridges, and the city suffered severe damage. The country was wholly cleared of German troops by 4 April. In the meantime a new government had been set up under Soviet auspices in December 1944. In February 1946 Hungary was proclaimed a republic and Dr. Zoltán Tildy became President. A Treaty of Peace between Hungary and the Allied and Associated Powers was signed in Paris on 10 February 1947. This treaty restored the frontiers of 1 January 1938.

The People's Republic of Hungary is governed according to the Constitution adopted in August 1949 and amended by Parliament in April 1972. Parliament (one House of Representatives now consisting of 352 members) wields theoretically the supreme power; it elects a Presidential Council of 21 members, the Presidium of the People's Republic. This Presidium carries out the duties of Head of State and exercises legislative powers between the sessions of Parliament. Election both to Parliament and to local councils is for five years, by universal adult (over age of 18) suffrage. The last elections to Parliament took place on 15 June 1975 when 7,527,169 people out of a total electorate of 7,760,464 cast their votes. Under amendments to the electoral law adopted by Parliament in October 1970, the sole right to adopt candidates for both parliamentary and local council seats is now vested in the nomination meetings which are held in each constituency before an election and which are open to all on the electoral register. These meetings have a right to nominate two or more candidates for the seat in question, but for the nomination to be valid the candidate must receive the backing of 30 per cent of those at the meeting.

In 1975 elections two candidates stood in 34 parliamentary constituencies (out of a total of 352) and in three instances where no candidate received more than half the votes cast, by-elections had to be held. Local council elections were held in April 1973 when 7,319,436 people voted out of a total electorate of 7,459,030. More than one candidate was nominated for 1,707 seats (out of a total of 67,114).

The Constitution proclaims that the bulk of the means of production is publicly owned; a new feature under the 1972 amendments is that state owned and co-operatively owned property are given equal status. Protection for persona private property is guaranteed while the state recognizes the usefulness of the activities of small producers, in so far as private property and private initiative does not harm public interest.

New provisions introduced into the Constitution in 1972 include the right of every citizen to claim financial care in the case of old age, sickness or disability, and a guarantee of freedom for creative work in the arts and sciences.

More weight is now placed on local government, with an increase in both the autonomy and sphere of activities of local councils.

There is one political party—the Hungarian Socialist Workers' Party, which was formed on 1 November 1956 as a successor to the dissolved Hungarian Working People's Party. The latter party was formed in 1948 from a merger of the Communist and Social-Democratic Parties, and was dissolved during the uprising in October 1956. The Hungarian Socialist Workers' Party held its 11th Congress in March 1975, when a Central Committee of 125 members was elected. Membership of the party was 754,353–91,956 more than at the 10th Congress in 1971. The following Political committee of 13 members was elected by the new Central Committee.

Since the Congress there has been an exchange of party cards, involving a discussion with all members. As a result there has been a small turnover of membership with 2·7 per cent resigning, but others joining. Membership on December 31, 1976 was 765,566.

**Political Committee**

*First Secretary:* János Kádár.

György Aczél.
Antal Apró.
Valéria Benke.
Béla Biszku.
Jenő Fock.
Sándor Gáspár.
Dezső Nemes.
Károly Németh.
György Lázár
László Maróthy
Miklós Óvári
István Sarlós

Two additional members were co-opted in July 1975:

Pál Losonczi
István Huszár

**Secretariat**

*First Secretary:* János Kádár.

Béla Biszku.
Miklós Ovári.
Sándor Borbély (appointed Oct. 1976).
Imre Györi.
Károly Németh.
András Gyenes

**Control Committee**

*President:* János Brutyó.
*Secretary:* János Venéczi.

Oszkár Barinkai.
Mrs. József Csikesz.
Emil Kimmel.
Mátyás Klaukó.
Mrs. József Nagy.
Mrs. László Németh.
József K. Papp.
Sándor Sebes.
József Suhajda.
Sándor Szerényi.
János Tausz.
Gyula Uszta.
Tibor Vágvölgyi.
Mrs. Lajos Farkas.
Ferenc Kárpati
Árpád Kovács.
Zoltán Lantos.
Frigyes Molnár.
Ferenc Petrák.
Imre Somogyi.
István Tóth.
Mihály Vaskó.

**Presidium of the People's Republic**

*President:* Pál Losonczi.
*Vice-Presidents:* Dr. Rezsö Trautmann. Sándor Gáspár.
*Secretary:* Lajos Cserterki.

**Council of Ministers**

*Chairman of the Council of Ministers:* György Lázár.
*Deputy Prime Ministers:* György Aczél, Ferenc Havasi, János Borbándi, István Huszar, Gyula Szekér.
*Minister for Foreign Affairs:* Frigyes Puja.
*Minister of Interior:* András Benkei.

*Minister of Defence:* Lajos Czinege.
*Minister of Finance:* Dr. Lajos Faluvégi.
*Minister of Justice:* Dr. Mihály Korom.
*Minister of Metallurgy and Machine Industry:* Tivadar Nemeslaki.
*Minister of Heavy Industry:* Dr. Pál Simon.
*Minister of Light Industry:* Mrs. János Keserü.
*Minister of Foreign Trade:* Dr. József Biró.
*Minister of Construction and City Planning:* Dr Kálmán Ábrahám.
*Minister of Transport and Communications:* Árpád Pullai.
*Minister of Agriculture and Food:* Dr. Pál Romány.
*Minister for Culture:* Imre Pozgai.
*Minister for Education:* Dr. Károly Polinszky.
*Minister for Health:* Dr. Emil Schultheisz.
*Minister of Labour:* Dr. Fereuc Trethon.
*Minister of Home Trade:* Dr. Vilmos Sághy.
*President of the State Planning Commission and President of the Nat. Planning Office:* István Huszár.
*President of Nat. Technical Development Committee:* Dr. Miklós Ajtai.
*President of National Assembly (Speaker):* Antal Apró.

## LOCAL GOVERNMENT

Prior to 1950 Hungary was divided into 25 counties which varied greatly in area and population. At the beginning of 1950 new administrative divisions were made in an endeavour to achieve more equality. There are now 19 counties (megye), of which 11 have populations of from 200–400,000 people, the other eight have larger populations.

The present divisions of the country are as follows:

| *County* | *Capital* |
|---|---|
| Pest | Budapest |
| Komárom | Tatabánya |
| Fejér | Székesfehérvár |
| Nógrád | Salgótarján |
| Győr-Sopron | Győr |
| Veszprém | Veszprém |
| Zala | Zalaegerszeg |
| Somogy | Kaposvár |
| Baranya | Pécs |
| Tolna | Szekszárd |
| Bács-Kiskun | Kecskemét |
| Szeded | Szeged |
| Békés | Békéscsaba |
| Szolnok | Szolnok |
| Hajdú-Bihar | Debrecen |
| Szabolcs-Szatmár | Nyiregyháza |
| Heves | Eger |
| Borsód-Abaúj-Zemplén | Miskolc |
| Vas | Szombathely |

## LEGAL SYSTEM

The organization of law courts is regulated by a law passed n January 1954, which was amended by Parliament in June 1972. There is a Supreme Court in Budapest, district courts which try first degree cases. The Supreme Court is also a Court of Appeal. Special courts exist for trying military offences. Cases in all courts are tried by an official judge and Supreme Court judges are elected by Parliament. Lay judges, all of whom are elected, are subject to recall.

The President, judges and lay judges of the Supreme Court are elected by Parliament. Similar officials for district courts are elected by district councils, and for county courts by county councils. Under the new 1972 legislation all judges are elected for an indefinite period instead of periods of five and three years as earlier.

A new Hungarian Criminal Code was introduced in 1962. A new Civil Code came into force on 1 May 1960. Extensive penal reform measures, introduced on 1 March 1967, included provisions for employment of all detained persons in useful work, paid for at trade union rates, and educational facilities for all prisoners.

Other new provisions under the 1972 Act include the introduction of a single system of professional judges to decide in certain defined cases; provisions for economic and labour arbitration courts to be transformed into courts of law; and the setting up of economic and labour boards at the Supreme Court.

Further new legislation, this time to simplify criminal procedure, was adopted by Parliament in March 1973. New provisions include the presumption of innocence until a defendant is proved guilty, the obligation of the prosecution to provide material evidence of guilt, whether the defendant pleads innocent or guilty, and greater differentiation in dealing with minor offences and more serious crimes.

In July 1953, Hungary established the Office of the Procurator-General, based on the Soviet model of that institution, The Office is independent of both the State Executive and the Judicial Authorities. It watches over the lawfulness of decisions taken by Ministers and local authorities. The Office must take note of complaints from the public and act quickly. New legislation defining the work of this office was introduced in June 1972, mainly aimed at simplifying procedures and promoting consistent interpretations of legal provisions. More attention was also focused on protecting consumer interests.

*President of the Supreme Court:* Dr. Ödön Szakács.
*Procurator-General:* Dr. Károly Szijártó.

## AREA AND POPULATION

Hungary has an area of 35,893 square miles (93,011 sq. km.) and a population of 10,625,000 (January 1977).

The principal cities and towns with population (1977) are: Budapest, 2,083,000 (19·6 per cent of the total population); Miskolc, 203,000; Debrecen, 190,000; Szeged, 171,000; Pécs, 164,000; Győr, 120,000.

## CURRENCY

On 1 August 1946 a new unit of currency was introduced to replace the paper pengő, which was by that time completely valueless. The new unit, the forint, which is divided into 100 Fillér, should correspond to 0·0757 gr. of fine gold. The National Bank is required to keep reserves of 25 per cent in gold or foreign exchange in order to cover the banknotes in circulation and other liabilities on sight.

## FINANCE

Estimated budget figures for 1977 were: Revenue, 359,000 million forints; Expenditure, 362,000 million forints. Actual figures for the 1976 budget were: Revenue, 320,400 million forints; Expenditure, 322,900 million forints.

The annual budget has been running at a deficit since the introduction of economic reforms in 1968 under which more income remains with the individual enterprises and less is paid into the national exchequer—although this still provides the bulk of revenue. This situation was aggravated by the increase in prices on the world market in 1973–75, which affected the country's balance of trade adversely after 1973. Nevertheless the deficit for 1975—2,960 million forints—was about 2,000 millions less than estimated and was 500 million forints down on that for 1974. In 1976 this downward trend continued and the deficit was 2,500 million forints, about 500 million less than planned. Long term plans aim at restoring the balance of the economy by 1980.

## PRINCIPAL BANKS

**National Bank of Hungary** (Magyar Nemzeti Bank). *President:* Dr. Mátyás Timár. First Deputy-President: Miklós Pulai. Deputy-President: János Fekete, Chief of Board of Exchange. Central Bank of Issue. From January 1972 has provided finance for factories, enterprises and co-operatives. It is a member of the International Bank of Co-operation, Moscow, and a shareholder in the Basle Bank for International Settlements. *Head Office:* 8–9, Szabadság-tér. H-1850 Budapest V., Hungary. Subsidiaries: Hungarian International Bank Ltd., 95, Gresham Street, London E.C.2, and Central Weschel-und Creditbank AG, 1010 Wien I, Karntner Str. 43.

**State Development Bank.** Established 24 September 1948. (As from January 1972 legal successor of former Hungarian Investment Bank). Financing state investments and their control, Deák Ferenc u.5, Budapest V.

**Hungarian Foreign Trade Bank Ltd.** (Chairman: Jenö Baczoni, General Director: Dr. István Salusinszky, Deputy General Director: Gáspár Gáspár). Handles all monetary transactions with foreign countries and grants letters of credit for imports and exports. Budapest V, Szent István tér II.

**National Savings Bank.** (Managing director, Jenö Szirmai.) This bank is now handling accounts for local government authorities and local council development funds. Other financial business transacted includes: the acquisition of bank deposits for building, various consumer credits, funds for building and construction of communal housing and open spaces, the operation of sports-accountancy, TOTO and the LOTTO lotteries. Under a relatively new service this bank also handles accounts for foreign nationals, including interest-bearing foreign exchange accounts, which carry interest in the currency of the deposit. In the case of withdrawals, these can be converted into forints or withdrawn in foreign currency. The Foreign Exchange Department has contacts with a number of banks abroad, including the Midland Bank in London for £ sterling accounts. *Head Office:* Budapest V, Münnich Ferenc u. 16. Branch offices throughout the country. Inspection is by the Savings Bank General Directory of The Ministry of Finance.

## PRODUCTION, INDUSTRY AND COMMERCE

**Planning.** Hungary embarked on a planned socialist economy in 1947. Natural resources, banking and transport are all state-owned; the state sector today contributes 93 per cent of all industrial output, a further 6 per cent comes from firms in co-operative ownership and 1 per cent from the private sector. State and co-operatively owned companies handle 97 per cent of transport and home trade, while 94 per cent of the agricultural land is state-owned or co-operative.

Economic development has been geared to a succession of three and five year plans. After the immediate task of post-war reconstruction, these were first aimed at promoting extensive industrial growth, but since the mid 1960s the emphasis has been on restructuring and modernizing industry, with a swing away from material-consuming to labour-consuming branches of industry. Today the dominant sector of the economy, industry contributed nearly 45 per cent of the national income in 1974, compared with 26 per cent in 1950.

Methods of planning have changed; in the initial period direct central guidance was applied to almost every detail, with factories receiving instructions for the quantity, pattern and rate of expansion of production. In the 1960s however when possibilities for extensive development were coming to an end and intensive development was felt to be increasingly important, changes in planning were introduced. After a number of years of preparation, a sweeping reform of economic management was introduced in 1968.

The main characteristics were: greater independence for factories and other enterprises to promote efficiency, and a greater role for market forces. A two-level system of planning was introduced in which central state bodies provided economic incentives to direct the economy, rather than issuing detailed directives. This has led to an acceleration in the growth of the national income from an annual average of 4·1 per cent (1961–65) to 6·3 per cent (1971–75).

Main targets of the fourth five year plan (1971–75) were overfulfilled; national income rose by 35 per cent, industrial production by 38 per cent and agricultural output by 18 per cent. Real wages went up by 16 per cent and real incomes by 26 per cent. Trade turnover increased at a rate in excess of the growth of national income with the value of exports and imports increasing by 60 per cent against the 45–50 per cent planned. Over the five years, trade closed with a small active balance with the rouble accounting area but a strong deficit with the dollar accounting area, because of price trends on the world market.

On a national economic level, investments in all branches were higher than planned. In the incomes field wages for industria and building workers went up at a faster than average rate, while in the social services sector, the most important measures were aimed at raising the living standards of the elderly and of large families. In 1975 the nominal monthly average earnings were 35 per cent higher than in 1970; retail prices were 15·8 per cent higher and the consumer price index, which also covers services, was 14·6 per cent up in the five years.

The new fifth year plan (1976–80) was adopted by Parliament in December 1975. The major targets include: a 30–32 per cent increase in national income; 33–35 per cent increase in industrial output and 16–18 per cent increase in agricultural output. Foreign trade turnover is expected to go up by 40 per cent. Real wages are scheduled to go up by 14–16 per cent and real incomes by 18–20 per cent. It is aimed to restore the balance of the economy during this period—first of all by increased productivity and effectiveness. The growth in domestic use (consumption + accumulation) is scheduled to rise by 23–25 per cent, slower than the national income. A larger proportion of the net social income will be withdrawn by the central budget under new economic regulators which came into force on 1 January, 1976. There will also be a slight decline in the growth rate of investments. Labour productivity is scheduled to go up by 32–34 per cent—about six per cent per annum.

Plans for industry include further modernization of the structure of production and an average overall increase of six per cent per annum is aimed at for industrial production. There will be selective development and a greater concentration of investments. The production of electrical energy should go up by seven per cent per year and electrical energy requirements are expected to climb from 25,000 million kwh in 1975 to 35,000 million kwh in 1980. Imports of electrical energy will also go up. Most rapid development will be in the chemical industry where plans call for an annual increase in production of over nine per cent. Within light industry, the re-equipment of the textile and ready made clothing industries is to continue.

Plans for agriculture call for a 3·2–3·4 per cent annual increase in output on the average, in line with the increase in recent years. Development will be centred on mechanization; large scale farming is expected to increase share in the total output from 64 per cent to 70 per cent.

A new State Planning Commission, to improve economic planning and co-ordinate the work of various economic bodies, was set up by the government in June 1973. Operating directly under government jurisdiction, it replaces the earlier government economic commission.

The new Commission was first headed by Mr. György Lázár until his appointment as Prime Minister in May 1975. He was succeeded by Deputy Prime Minister István Huszár. Members include the Ministers of Finance, Foreign Trade and Labour. Work will include the co-ordination of the planning activities of the various ministries and national bodies, the submission of proposals concerning the national economic plant to the government, and supervision of how proposals adopted are carried out. The Commission is expected to contribute to better investment efficiency and to help harmonize planning at home with economic activities abroad.

**Agriculture.** In March 1945 a Land Reform law divided up all estates of more than 240 acres—47·9 per cent of the agricultural land. 642,342 persons received 4,510,000 acres of land.

Since 1948 State farms and co-operative farms have been developed. In March 1956 membership of co-operative farms totalled 269,575 families; there were 4,982 farms covering 3,321,500 acres. Together with State farms they covered more than one-third of the total cultivated land at the beginning of 1956. Under the impact of the insurrection in October 1956, 3,037 co-operative farms were dissolved. But recovery was rapid, particularly in 1959, and by Spring 1961 there were 1,200,000 members of co-operatives, farming 2,600,000 acres. During the 1960s the trend has been towards farming on a larger scale with smaller farms merging. In 1976 there were 147 state farms, compared with 333 in 1960, and 1,470 co-operative farms, compared with 4,507 in 1960. Active earners in the co-operative farms (members and employees) numbered 623,700 in 1976; 147,500 were employed on state farms. The total number of persons employed in agriculture fell from 1,866,000 in 1960 to 1,015,500 in 1976 (active earners). Together with state farms, 94 per cent of arable land is now being farmed socially.

The following table shows the production of principal crops (in thousand metric tons) for 1974, 1975 and 1976:

| *Crop* | 1974 | 1975 | 1976 |
|---|---|---|---|
| Wheat | 4,968 | 4,005 | 5,138 |
| Rye | 175 | 147 | 156 |
| Barley | 894 | 699 | 746 |
| Oats | 78 | 87 | 86 |
| Maize | 6,194 | 7,088 | 5,189 |
| Potatoes | 1,364 | 1,268 | 1,060 |
| Sugar beet | 3,707 | 4,089 | 3,923 |
| Rice | 56 | 69 | 55 |

In 1976 53·2 per cent of the land was arable, 1·7 per cent gardens, and 1·8 per cent orchards, 2·1 per cent vineyards, 4·0 per cent meadow, 9·8 per cent pasture, 16·7 per cent forest, 0·4 per cent reeds and 0·3 per cent fish ponds.

Livestock figures are as follows:

| *Animals* | 1976 (*June*) | 1976 (*Dec.*) |
|---|---|---|
| Pigs | 7,629,000 | 7,854,000 |
| Cattle | 1,951,000 | 1,887,000 |
| Horses | — | 147,000 |
| Sheep | — | 2,347,000 |

**Mining.** Coal production, which reached a peak total of 31,548,000 tons in 1964 (more than treble the pre-war level), has been cut back in the last few years as greater use is made of oil and natural gas. Output in 1976 was 25,257,000 tons; it is planned to keep annual output at around the 25 million ton mark over the next few years but new mines are being opened up—in particular lignite is to be used extensively to feed new, on-the-spot thermal power stations. Output is expected to rise to between 35 and 40 million tons a year by 1990.

Steel and iron production has been helped considerably by the erection of the large Danube Iron and Steel Works on the Danube (at Dunaújváros) 40 miles from Budapest, which went into production early in 1954. At the end of 1960 the hot-rolling mill at Dunaújváros went into production. This makes Hungary independent of thin-sheet imports.

Hungary's most important ore is bauxite, used in the production of aluminium. Reserves are estimated to be between 18 and 20 per cent of the world's total. Mining is carried on mainly in the Bakony and Vertes mountain regions.

Under the agreement concluded with the Soviet Union in November 1962 Hungary exports increasing quantities of alumina for processing in the Soviet Union. The entire amount is returned in the form of aluminium ingots. By 1980, Hungary expects to export an annual 330,000 tons of alumina and to receive 165,000 tons of aluminium ingots in return three times as much as she now produces.

Hungary's aluminium industry is becoming increasingly important and the new agreement will speed its development. Sizeable deposits of copper have also been located at Recsk in northern Hungary, combined with deposits of lead and zinc. As the copper field is concentrated, it is thought that this ore may come to rival bauxite in importance in the years to come. An annual output of between 7–8 million tons of copper has been predicted, enough to cover all domestic needs.

Oil and natural gas fields discovered near Szeged in Southern Hungary in the early 1960s have turned out to be the richest in the country. Output from the Szeged basin oil field neared one million tons in 1971, and surpassed this in 1972. The other principal oil fields are in the Lispe and Lovaszi region (county Zala).

Extensive natural gas fields have also been located at Hajdúszoboszló in Eastern Hungary.

**Industry.** The table below gives the chief production figures for 1976:

| *Product* | 1976 *metric tons* |
|---|---|
| Aluminium | 70,499 |
| Alumina | 736,000 |
| Bauxite | 2,918,000 |
| Coal | 25,257,000 |
| Pig Iron | 2,221,000 |
| Steel | 3,652,000 |
| Rolled Steel | 2,859,000 |
| Crude oil | 2,142,000 |
| Electricity (mil. kWh.) | 22,040 |
| Cement (tons) | 4,298,000 |
| Sugar | 363,345 |
| Woollens (sq. m.) | 41,272,000 |
| Cotton fabrics | 352,453,000 |
| Shoes (prs.) | 44,567,000 |
| Fertiliser (nitrogen) | 2,398,000 |
| Sulphuric acid | 617,000 |
| Natural gas (mil. cu. m.) | 6,083 |

According to official estimates industrial output today is ten times the pre-war level. The growth of industrial production averaged an annual 10 per cent between 1950 and 1967 compared with a growth rate of just under 1 per cent on the average between 1918 and 1938.

In 1976 1,794,000 were employed in industry, 422,200 in the building industry, 1,015,500 in agriculture, 50,500 in forestry, 402,900 in transport, 467,400 in trade, 70,500 in water conservancy and 870,200 in other occupations.

**Commerce.** Foreign trade is governed by a new act which was adopted by Parliament in October 1974 and came into force at the beginning of 1975. This lays down that foreign trade is a state monopoly; the activities covered by the act are international trade in goods and services, international co-operation and specialization in production and trade, economic ventures abroad and the commercial activity of aliens in Hungary.

Foreign trade is carried out in part through state trading companies, but since 1968 many manufacturing and other economic enterprises have been authorized to carry out foreign trade activities. The 1974 act lays down that these rights are granted by the Minister of Foreign Trade to a company when it is felt that to do so is in accord with the interests of the national economy and that the company concerned has the economic, organizational and other conditions necessary to ensure the successful conduct of such trade. Authorization can be withdrawn if these conditions cease to exist or if the company contravenes the act.

Production co-operation agreements with Western firms have been a new feature of Hungary's foreign trade in the last few years and a new company specializing in such deals, Interco-operation Co. Ltd., was set up in 1971. In addition since 1972 it has also been possible to set up economic associations within Hungary, with foreign participation. The first mixed enterprise of this type involving a Western firm was set up in June 1974 between Volvo of Sweden and the Mogürt Foreign Trade Company for the production of cross-country vehicles, with Hungary contributing 52 per cent of the invested capital and Sweden 48 per cent.

Legal provisions for foreign companies trading with Hungary to set up their own offices within the country was a new feature of the 1974 Foreign Trade Act, with the proviso that these activities should be in harmony with the interests of the Hungarian national economy and foreign trade policy. At the same time Hungarian economic bodies were authorized to set up companies abroad, or to participate in existing foreign companies.

Because Hungary has to import much of her raw materials and energy, the price increase on the world market between 1973 and 1975 had a deleterious effect on the economy and the country's foreign trade. Balance of trade surpluses in 1972 and 1973 were followed by deficits in 1974, 1975 and 1976 and one of the objectives of the new five year plan (1976–80) is to correct this and restore the balance.

Imports from dollar accounting countries totalled 13,787 million exchange forints in value in 1973, 21,868 million forints in 1974 and 21,117 million forints in 1975.

In 1976 foreign trade figures were calculated in commercial rate forints instead of the exchange rate forints used in earlier years. Imports from dollar accounting countries totalled 108,800 million forints.

Trade with the United Kingdom accounts for about two per cent of Hungary's imports and 1 per cent of exports (3 per cent of exports to non-Comecon countries). In 1975 imports from the U.K. totalled £44·5 million and exports £26·1 million.

In 1976 imports from the U.K. totalled £49·5 million and exports £30·7 million.

The following table shows the value of imports from nine Western countries in 1976 expressed in million commercial rate forints:

| *Country* | 1976 |
|---|---|
| Austria | 11,028·7 |
| Western Germany | 22,042·0 |
| Italy | 9,191·0 |
| Switzerland and Lichtenstein | 5,761·4 |
| Belgium-Luxemburg | 2,631·5 |
| France | 5,384·1 |
| Holland | 3,624·1 |
| Sweden | 3,321·3 |
| United Kingdom | 4,589·3 |

Total exports to dollar accounting countries in 1976 were 101,300 million commercial rate forints.

The following table shows the value of exports to nine Western countries in 1975 expressed in million commercial rate forints:

| *Country* | 1976 |
|---|---|
| Austria | 7,475·1 |
| Western Germany | 16,293·1 |
| Italy | 8,216·5 |
| Switzerland/Licht. | 4,695·9 |
| Belgium/Luxembourg | 827·3 |
| France | 3,805·5 |
| Netherlands | 2,147·9 |
| Sweden | 2,128·3 |
| United Kingdom | 2,703·8 |

The following table shows some of the most important commodities imported in 1976.

| Commodity | 1976 |
|---|---|
| | tons |
| Coal | 1,297,000 |
| Crude oil | 8,785,000 |
| Iron ore | 4,234,000 |
| Foundry coke | 1,271,000 |
| Raw oxhide | 23,600 |
| Fuel oil | — |
| Timber (cubic metres) | 840,000 |
| Rolled steel | 623,000 |
| Passenger cars (units) | 83,300 |
| Lorries (units) | 15,678 |
| Chemical fibres | 52,900 |
| Cotton | 87,000 |

In 1976 the value of imports from rouble accounting countries was 121,200 million commercial rate forints and exports totalled 103,500 million forints. Trade with the U.S.S.R. accounts for about one-third of the total.

The following table shows some of the most important commodities exported in 1976:

| Commodity | 1976 |
|---|---|
| | tons |
| Wheat | 707,000 |
| Petrol | 97,000 |
| Diesel oil | 213,000 |
| Bauxite | 633,000 |
| Alumina | 628,000 |
| Flour | — |
| Salami | 6,200 |
| Slaughtered poultry | 102,900 |
| Rolled steel | 1,084,000 |
| Buses (units) | 9,414 |
| Leather footwear (pairs) | 20,500,000 |
| Wine (hectol.) | 1,794,000 |
| Cattle, slaughtered | 161,000 |
| Fruit | 429,000 |
| Maize | 966,000 |
| Eggs (million) | 388 |
| Sunflower oil | 31,600 |
| Aluminium | 53,900 |
| Cotton piece goods (mill. m.) | 102,800 |
| Knitted goods | 6,500 |
| Ready made clothing (pieces) | 16,295,000 |
| Raw meat | 66,200 |

## COMMUNICATIONS

Although Hungary has no sea-board, her shipping company MAHART operates both river transport on the Danube and sea-going ships which transport goods to ports throughout the world. Her international air line operates in Europe, the Middle East and Scandinavia. The international airport is Ferihegy (Budapest). In 1976 the Hungarian State Railways had 13,669 kilometres length of railway track in operational use, including 1,303 kilometres of electrified line. The length of navigable rivers is 1,688 km. and there are 29,915 km. of roads, including 28,510 km. of dust-free roads.

The following is the airline:

**Malév** (Magyar Légiközlekedési Vállalat-Hungarian Air Lines).

*Services operated:* Budapest–London, Budapest–Rome, Budapest–Milan, Budapest–Prague, Budapest–Munich, Budapest–Frankfurt, Budapest–Paris, Budapest–Zurich, Budapest–Frankfurt, Budapest–Paris, Budapest–Zurich, Budapest–Athens–Cairo Budapest–Warsaw, Budapest–Bucharest –Istanbul, Budapest–Damascus, Budapest–Berlin, Budapest –Erfut, Budapest–Leipzig, Budapest–Sofia, Budapest–Warsaw–Leningrad, Budapest–Bucharest, Budapest–Moscow Budapest–Belgrade–Tirana, Budapest–Vienna, Budapest–Vienna–Brussels, Budapest Zurich–Madrid, Budapest–Dresden, Budapest–Prague–Amsterdam, Budapest–Munich–Amsterdam, Budapest–Copenhagen, Budapest–Helsinki, *Address:* 5 Vörösmarty tér, Budapest V 1367. *London Office:* 10 Vigo Street, London, W.1.

There are also services to Burgas, Constanta, Dubrovnik, Kiev, Rijeka, Split and Varna.

## NEWSPAPERS

**Népszabadság:** Central paper of the Hungarian Socialist Workers' Party. Daily. Budapest VIII, Blaha Lujza tér 3.

**Magyar Nemzet:** Patriotic People's Front. Budapest VII, Leninkrt 9–11.

**Népszava:** Hungarian Trade Unions. Budapest VII, Rákoczi u. 54.

**Esti Hirlap:** Political evening paper. Budapest VIII, Blaha Lujza tér 3.

**Magyar Hirlap:** Political Daily. Budapest VII Lenin Krt 9–11.

## ATOMIC ENERGY

It was not until the setting up of the Central Physics Research Institute in 1950 that high-standard, large-scale experiments could be conducted.

An experimental atomic reactor of 2 MW capacity, built with the help of the Soviet Union in the Buda Hills above Budapest, began working on 25 March 1959. The installation is fully automatic.

The reactor is primarily for research work and particularly for the training of nuclear technicians; but it also supplies isotopes, previously obtained abroad, to Hungarian industrial, medical and scientific establishments.

The six departments of the Institute are concerned with the most important problems of atomic and nuclear physics: spectroscopy, cosmic rays, electromagnetic waves, atomic physics, radiology and ferromagnetic waves.

Two achievements of the atom physics department are worth mention: the construction of a 4,500,000 volt Van de Graaf accelerator, of which there are only a few in Europe of similar performance, and the working out of the fissioning cross-section of uranium and thorium. The great powers leading in nuclear physics research made public the fissioning cross-section of uranium for the first time at the Geneva atomic conference in 1969. The information published shows that the fissioning cross-section calculated by Hungarian scientists was sound.

The radiology department of the Institute has constructed an apparatus which measures a millionth of a microgram. In the electromagnetic wave laboratory measurements are being carried on which have proved to be among the most precise in the world.

The leading research workers of the Institute regularly publish their work in *Acta Physica*, the foreign language periodical of the Hungarian Academy of Sciences, and are in contact with their colleagues abroad.

Under an agreement signed on 22 December 1959, Hungary and the Soviet Union are co-operating on the design of experimental and power atomic reactors. The two countries are carrying out joint work on the use of isotopes, exchanging designs and documentation and assisting each other in the manufacture and design of various instruments.

Work on the site of Hungary's first atomic power station started at Paks on the Danube in 1969, but the opening of the plant, originally scheduled for 1975, has been postponed. The first 440 MW unit is now due to go into operation in 1980; three further units of this size will raise capacity to 1,760 MW by 1984. Eventual capacity will be 6,000 MW and it is planned to reach this in the first half of the 1990s. Work on the first power plant buildings started in 1975 and installation work is scheduled to begin in 1977. Under an agreement between the Soviet and Hungarian governments, the Soviet Union is supplying the plans and technology and some of the major operation units including the reactor itself. The power station will be of the VVER (Voronezh pressurized water) type. Among those now working at Paks are 40 Hungarian engineers and 300 workers who have gained practical experience of nuclear power plant construction at Lubmin in the German Democratic Republic where they have worked for 3½ years.

A small experimental training reactor which will be used in part to help train personnel for the Paks power station, has been completed at the Budapest Technical University.

## EDUCATION

The Hungarian Academy of Sciences has 93 members and 115 corresponding members.

*President of the Hungarian Academy of Sciences:* Janos Szeutágothai.
*Vice-Chairmen:* Géza Bognár, András Somos, Imre Szabó.
*General Secretary:* Ferenc Márta.
*Deputy General Secretaries:* Béla Kőpeczi, István Láng.

There are 56 universities and university colleges in the country, the oldest and most important being in Budapest, Pécs, Szeged and Debrecen. Since 1950 the Technical University in Budapest has undergone considerable expansion and new technical universities have been established at Miskolc, Veszprém and Szolnok. Other new establishments include the University of Agrarian Sciences at Gödöllő, the Budapest University of Economics, the Foreign Language Academy and the School of Journalism, both in Budapest, and a number of new colleges and institutes throughout the country.

After a rapid expansion of higher educational facilities in the years immediately after the war and during the First Five-Year Plan, attention is now being focused on raising academic standards.

In 1976–77 there were 1,072,423 pupils at primary schools (6–14 years), 373,372 at secondary schools (14–18), 158,000 in apprentice training, and 110,528 at universities and colleges.

# Iceland

## (LÝDVELDID ÍSLAND)

**Capital**—Reykjavík.

**President**—Dr. Kristján Eldjarn.

**National Flag:** Blue, bearing a red cross bordered white.

### CONSTITUTION AND GOVERNMENT

ICELAND was settled and colonized between the years A.D. 874–930 by Norwegians. A Republic was established in 930, when a Central Parliament for all Iceland, the *Althing*, was established at Thingvellir. The Republic came to an end in 1262–64, when the Icelanders made a Treaty of Union with the Crown of Norway in which they accepted its supremacy. In 1380 Iceland came under the Danish Crown as a result of the Chalmar Union. The Icelandic people maintained that they had accepted the supremacy of the King but not that of the Danish Government. But in spite of this they had no more than provincial autonomy far into the 19th century.

In 1874 Iceland was granted a constitution by which the people were allowed to voice in the management of some of their own affairs, but this did not satisfy national aspirations and there was a long struggle for constitutional freedom which at last came to an end in 1918. In that year an Act of Union was passed, the Parliament of both countries acknowledging Iceland to be a sovereign state having the King in common with Denmark. It also provided that after 1940 either party could request negotiations regarding its future and, if no agreement be concluded within three years, either Parliament might, by a two-thirds majority, resolve that the Act be cancelled, subject to confirmation by plebiscite. Denmark being under German occupation in 1940, no negotiations were possible and Iceland adopted a temporary regency. A plebiscite for the purpose of determining a form of government was held in 1944 and as a result the Republic of Iceland was declared on 17 June 1944.

Under the Constitution executive power is exercised by the President and other governmental authorities specified by the Constitution whilst judicial power is exercised by the Judiciary. The President acts through his ministers. He is not answerable for his official actions, whereas the Cabinet, headed by the Prime Minister, is responsible for all acts of government. The President has power to appoint and dismiss ministers, to make appointments to all the more important official posts, to make treaties with other nations and to summon Parliament. He can dissolve Parliament if he thinks fit. He may refuse to ratify a law passed by Parliament but it does not become void thereby. Ratification lies with a plebiscite to whose judgment the law must be submitted as soon as circumstances permit.

The ministers forming the Government are appointed by the President but they must have the confidence of Parliament, and if they are unable to command a parliamentary majority the Government must resign. Ministers need not necessarily be elected members of Parliament but they have seats in the house according to their office and have freedom of speech there and the right of introducing bills. They have, however, no right to vote unless they are also members of the Parliament.

Parliament is divided into two Houses, an Upper House and a Lower House. There are no separate elections for the two houses. After a General Election has taken place a joint Parliament chooses one-third of the members to sit with the Upper House and each party has to nominate representatives to it in proportion to its total number of members. There are 60 members of Parliament who are elected for a normal term of four years in one of two ways: (1) Proportional Election, (2) Compensatory or Equalizing Election. By the first method districts or towns elect eight members. There are 11 compensatory seats to make up the balance between parties, so that each party has seats as near as possible in proportion to the total number of votes obtained in the General Election as a whole.

**Ministry** (Coalition Cabinet formed on 28 August 1974)

*Prime Minister:* Geir Hallgrímsson (Ind.).
*Foreign Minister:* Einar Agústsson (Prog.).
*Minister of Justice and of Commerce:* Ólafur Jóhannesson (Prog.).
*Minister of Industries and Social Affairs:* Gunnar Thoroddsen (Ind.).
*Minister of Finance:* Matthias A. Mathíesen (Ind.).
*Minister of Fisheries and Health and Social Security:* Matthías Bjarnason (Ind.).
*Minister of Agriculture and of Communications:* Halldór E. Sigurðsson (Prog.).
*Minister of Education:* Vilhjálmur Hjálmarsson (Prog.).

**Parliament**

THE ALTHING

*President of the United Althing:* Asgeir Brarnason.
*Speaker of the Upper Chamber:* Th. G. Kristjánson
*Speaker of the Lower Chamber:* Mrs. R. Helgadóttir.

Party representation is as follows: Independence Party 25; Progressives 17; People's Union 11; Social Democrats 5; Liberal Lefts 2.

### LEGAL SYSTEM

The highest court in Iceland is called *Haestiréttur*, which is a Supreme Court of Appeal of five judges. Nearly all cases on which lower courts have given judgment may be referred here for appeal. There are 26 judges of lower courts who are called *sýslumenn* and *baejarfógetar*. In addition to their judicial duties they act as tax collectors for the Treasury, control police and direct local government. There is also a number of special courts, such as the Maritime and Commercial Courts, Boundaries Court and the Court of Labour Disputes, etc. All judges are appointed by the Minister of Justice and cannot be removed except under the age limit or because of misconduct in the performance of their duties.

**Supreme Court**

Einar Arnalds
Benedikt Sigurjonsson
Logi Einarsson
Armann Snævarr
Magnús Torfason

### AREA AND POPULATION

Iceland has an area of 39,000 sq. miles with a coastline of 3,700 miles. The population in 1976 was 220,000.

The annual average percentage growth rate of the population for the period 1960–74 was 1·4 and for the period 1965–74 was 1·2.

The chief towns with populations are Reykjavik, the capital, 84,500; Akureyri, 12,300; Hafnarfjördur, 11,100; Kopavogur, 12,090; Vestmannaeyjar, 4,906.

The following table shows the vital statistics for the year 1974:

| | 1974 |
|---|---|
| Marriages | 1,897 |
| Births | 1,233 |
| Deaths | 1,497 |

### CURRENCY

The unit of currency is the króna (plural krónur). The rate of exchange is approximately 330 (approximately) kronur to the pound sterling.

### FINANCE

Budget figures for 1970 (in 1,000,000 Kr) were: Revenue, Kr.8,396; Expenditure, Kr.8,187.

The Public Debt at the end of 1970 (in 1,000,000 Kr.) amounted to 3,547 of which the public debt (in 1,000,000 Kr.) was 532.

The GNP at market prices for 1974 was U.S. $ millions 1,200, and the GNP per capita at market prices was U.S. $5,430. The annual average percentage growth rate of the GNP per capita for the period 1960–74 was 3·1, and for the period 1965–74 was 2·4. [*See the note at the beginning of this section concerning GNP.*]

### PRINCIPAL BANKS

**Central Bank of Iceland. Est. 7 April 1961, in succession to Landsbanki Islands, the Central Bank. Sole Bank of Issue**

for Iceland. An independent State-owned institution under separate management. Balance sheet at 31 December 1972 showed assets kr. 17,058,688,993. Bank notes and coins in circulation kr. 2,286,592,975. Foreign liabilities 3,701,333,038. Capital and reserves kr. 818,469,220. *Head Office:* Reykjavik, Iceland.

**Landsbanki Islands, The National Bank of Iceland.** (General Managers: Björgvin Vilmundarson, Jóns H. Haralz and Helgi Bergs.) Balance Sheet at 31 December 1976 showed assets kr. 51,388,301,761; deposits kr. 24,473,731,340 reserves kr. 2,243,265,338 *Head Office:* Reykjavik. 21 Branches.

**Bunadarbanki Islands** (Agricultural Bank). Reykjavík.

**Utvegsbanki Islands,** successors from 1930 to Islandsbanki. A State-owned bank since 3 June 1957. Balance Sheet at 31 December 1973 showed assets kr. 5,990,998,175; deposits on current accounts kr. 1,190,076,368. *Head Office:* Reykjavík.

**Iceland Bank of Commerce Ltd.** (Verzlunarbanki Islands h.f.). Reykjavík.

**Industrial Bank of Iceland** (Idnadarbanki Islands h.f.). Reykjavík.

**Co-operative Bank of Iceland** (Samvinnubanki Islands). Reykjavík.

## PRODUCTION, INDUSTRY AND COMMERCE

**Commerce.** The following table gives the supply and use of resources in Kr. million at current prices for 1974 and 1975. The figures for 1975 are provisional.

| | 1974 | 1975 |
|---|---|---|
| Private consumption | 90,630 | 121,540 |
| Public consumption | 14,430 | 19,300 |
| Gross fixed asset formation | 45,150 | 63,560 |
| *Expenditure on final domestic use* | 150,210 | 204,400 |
| Change in stocks of export products and livestock | 2,578 | 3,680 |
| *National expenditure* | 152,788 | 208,080 |
| Exports of goods and services | 48,080 | 72,190 |
| Imports of goods and services | 63,610 | 93,570 |
| *Gross national product (market prices)* | 137,258 | 186,700 |
| Depreciation | 17,175 | 28,366 |
| *Net national product (market prices)* | 120,083 | 158,334 |
| Indirect taxes | 36,360 | 51,460 |
| Subsidies | 7,800 | 11,100 |
| *Net national income* | 91,523 | 117,974 |
| Net income to abroad | 1,915 | 4,863 |
| *Net domestic income* | 93,438 | 122,837 |

**Agriculture.** Only a small portion of Iceland is suitable for cultivation. The main crops are hay, potatoes, turnips, carrots, cabbage and vegetables grown in similar districts to that of Iceland. The agricultural population is engaged in the rearing of livestock, especially sheep.

**Fishing.** Iceland has always been 90 per cent dependent on its fishing catch, and lacks raw materials for the production of other goods for export. Nevertheless, Iceland today is industrializing as far as her limited capital resources permit. The following tables give details for 1975 of catches of fish and size of fishing fleet:

| | 1975 *thousand tons* |
|---|---|
| *Catches* | |
| White fish | 407,973 |
| Herring | 30,059 |
| Capelin | 452,893 |
| Shrimp, lobster and shellfish | 13,412 |
| Other | 2,533 |

| | |
|---|---|
| *Fishing fleet (end of year)* | |
| Number of fishing vessels | 907 |
| Total size; GRT | 98,975 |

Protective clothing for trawler men, insulating material for building and processed building stone are all being manufactured now. A factory for making electric motors has been established as well as a fertilizer plant. A cement factory is in operation. A new project is the manufacture of salt—at present imported—using the hot springs at Krisuvik to evaporate sea-water.

## COMMUNICATIONS

The Mercantile Marine of Iceland at the end of 1975 comprised 87 vessels totalling 75,841 gross tons. The chief shipping companies are the Iceland Steamship Company Ltd., Eimskipafélag Islands H.F., the Shipping Department of the Federation of Iceland Co-operative Societies, and Jöklar Ltd., which maintain regular sailings between Icelandic ports and the United Kingdom, the United States and the European continent.

There are no railways in Iceland. Internal travel is exclusively by road or air services. There are regular external air services between Iceland and Great Britain and the Scandinavian countries. Reykjavík, Keflavík and Reykjavik are ports of call for airliners on the trans-Atlantic air routes.

Civil aviation in Iceland is controlled by the Aeronautic Board. There are Customs Airports at Reykjavík and Keflavík.

The following are the Icelandic airlines:

**Flugfélag Íslands h.f., Icelandair.** *Services operated:* Reykjavík and Glasgow, London, Frankfurt, Oslo, Copenhagen and internal. *Head Office:* Reykjavík Airport, Reykjavík, Iceland. 330,000 passengers carried during 1974.

**Loftleidir** Icelandic scheduled services from New York and Chicago to London, Glasgow, Copenhagen, Stockholm, Oslo and Luxembourg, via Keflavík. *Address:* Loftleidir Icelandic, Reykjavík Airport, Reykjavík, Iceland.

## NEWSPAPERS

**Morgunbladid.** F. 1913. Daily. Independence Party Reykjavík.

**Dagbladid.** F.1975. Sidumuli 12, Reykjavik. Circulation 24,500.

**Timinn.** F. 1917. Daily. Progressive Party. Circulations 18,000. Reykjavík.

**Thjodviljinn.** F. 1935. The Socialist Unity Party. Reykjavík.

**Visir.** F. 1910. Daily. Independent. Sídumúla 14, Reykjavik. Circulation 24,000. Editor-in-Chief: Thorsteinn Pálsson.

**Althýdubladid.** F. 1916. Daily. Labour. Reykjavík.

## EDUCATION

Education is compulsory for all from 7–15 years of age. There are primary schools, secondary, agricultural and technical schools. There are grammar schools at Reykjavík and Akureyri and Laugarvatn and a university at Reykjavík founded in 1911.

## RELIGION

The Evangelical Lutheran Church is the Established Church of Iceland. Complete religious freedom is allowed to every denomination.

# India

## (MEMBER OF THE COMMONWEALTH)

**Capital**—New Delhi.

**President**—N. Sanjuva Reddy.

**National Flag:** A tricolour fesse-wise, saffron, white, green, the white charged with the Chakra of Asoka, the Buddhist ruler, in dark blue centred.

### CONSTITUTION AND GOVERNMENT

INDIA became an independent State as the result of the Indian Independence Act, 1947, which provided for the setting up of two independent Dominions, to be known as India and Pakistan. The Act declared that, from the 15 August 1947, His Majesty's Government of the United Kingdom should have no responsibility as respects the governing of any of the territories which immediately before that date were included in British India. As a consequence of this Act the old Indian legislature ceased to function, and its powers were taken over by the Indian Constituent Assembly. The most important function of the Constituent Assembly was the drafting of a new Constitution, which was finally adopted on 26 November 1949. By this Constitution India became a sovereign independent republic on 26 January 1950. The conference of Commonwealth Prime Ministers had previously reached a unanimous agreement regarding Indian relations with the Commonwealth. It was agreed that India should be accepted as a full member of the Commonwealth. India, although a republic, accepted the Sovereign as 'the symbol of the free association of its independent member nations, and as such the head of the Commonwealth'.

The chief features of the new Constitution are the disappearance of Princely India, and the creation of a President and a Cabinet system of government, sovereignty of the people, adult suffrage, joint electorates, the abolition of Privy Council jurisdiction and the substitution of that of the Supreme Court, the abolition of titles and untouchability, and civil equality irrespective of religion. India is a Union of 22 States and nine Union Territories. The executive of each State consists of a Governor appointed by the President and a Council of Ministers. The Union Territories are administered by the President acting through an administrator.

The President is the head of the executive, and the supreme commander of the defence forces of the Union. He is elected by an electoral college consisting of the elected members of both Houses of Parliament and the Legislative Assemblies of the States. He holds office for five years and is eligible for re-election. The President is constitutionally the head of the Union, and is not expected to govern. His functions are similar to those of the Governor-General in the former régime. He summons, prorogues and dissolves the Lok Sabha, he appoints all the higher officials, consents to bills, proclaims emergencies and promulgates ordinances.

There is also a Vice-President who is *ex-officio* Chairman of the Council of States. He is elected by members of both Houses of Parliament and holds office for five years.

Actual executive power is in the hands of a Council of Ministers with the Prime Minister at the head. His position is similar to that of the Prime Minister in Great Britain; in fact the constitution follows closely the model of the British parliamentary system.

The Indian Parliament consists of the President and two Houses: Lok Sabha (House of the People) and Rajya Sabha (Council of States). The Council of States has not more than 250 representatives of the States. At present it has 244 members including 12 nominated members. The nominated members represent literature, science and social services. The Council of States is not subject to dissolution, but one-third of the members retire every second year. The House of the People consists of 525 members elected from the States and Union Territories on the basis of adult franchise, the constituencies being so demarcated that there is not less than one member for every 75,000 of the population, and not more than one member for every 50,000. Two Anglo-Indian members are nominated by the President.

The official language of the Indian Union is Hindi, in Devanagari script, and all forms of numerals are in international form. English, however, will continue to be used for official purposes for the transaction of business in Parliament. The language of the Supreme Court and the High Court and all Acts, regulations, rules, orders, etc., is English; with translations into Hindi.

The first Indian General Election was held on varying dates between October 1951 and February 1952, the spread-over being necessary owing to the huge area of the country, the size of the electorate, the varied climatic conditions and the desire to avoid interference with agricultural operations.

One of the most interesting features of the elections was the allotment of familiar symbols, such as a cow or plough, to different political parties and their candidates. This procedure was devised to enable the overwhelming number of illiterate voters to exercise their franchise with comparative ease. To prevent impersonation at the polling booth the election official, who supplied the ballot paper, checked the voter's name and marked his left forefinger with indelible ink.

**Cabinet Ministers** (6 March 1977).

*Prime Minister:* Shri Morarji R. Desai.
*Minister of Home Affairs:* Chaudhuri Charan Singh.
*Minister of Defence:* Shri Jagjivan Ram.
*Minister of Information and Broadcasting:* Shri L. K. Advani.
*Minister of Agriculture and Irrigation:* Shri Surjit Singh Barnala.
*Minister of Petroleum, Chemicals and Fertilizers:* Shri H. N. Bahuguna.
*Minister of Works and Housing and Supply and Rehabilitation:* Shri Sikander Bakht.
*Minister of Law, Justice and Company Affairs:* Shri Shanti Bhushan.
*Minister of Education, Social Welfare and Culture:* Shri Pratap Chandra Chunder.
*Minister of Railways:* Prof. Madhu Dandavate.
*Minister of Commerce and Civil Supplies and Cooperation:* Shri Mohan Dharia.
*Minister of Industry:* Shri George Fernandes.
*Minister of Tourism and Civil Aviation:* Shri Purushottam Kaushik.
*Minister of Health and Family Planning:* Shri Raj Narain.
*Minister of Finance and Revenue and Banking:* Shri H. M. Patel.
*Minister of Steel and Mines:* Shri Biju Patnaik.
*Minister of Energy:* Shri P. Ramachandran.
*Minister of External Affairs:* Shri Atal Bihari Vajpayee.
*Minister of Parliamentary Affairs and Labour:* Shri Ravindra Varma.
*Minister of Communications:* Shri Brij Lal Verma.

**Parliament**

**House of the People**

The number of seats allotted to each of the States and Union Territories is as follows:

| **States** | *Number of seats* |
|---|---|
| Andhra Pradesh | 41 |
| Assam | 14 |
| Bihar | 53 |
| Gujarat | 24 |
| Haryana | 9 |
| Karnataka | 27 |
| Kerala | 19 |
| Madhya Pradesh | 37 |
| Tamil Nadu | 39 |
| Maharashtra | 45 |
| Nagaland | 1 |
| Orissa | 20 |

*continued*

| States | *Number of seats* |
|---|---|
| Punjab | 13 |
| West Bengal | 40 |
| Rajasthan | 23 |
| Uttar Pradesh | 85 |
| Jammu and Kashmir | 6 |
| Himachal Pradesh | 4 |
| Mainpur | 2 |
| Meghalaya | 2 |
| Tripura | 2 |
| Sikkim | 1 |
| **Union Territories** | |
| Delhi | 7 |
| Pondicherry | 1 |
| Andoman and Nicobar Islands | 1 |
| Mizoram | 1 |
| Arumachal Pradesh | 1 |
| Chandigarh | 1 |
| Dadra and Nagar Haveli | 1 |
| Goa, Daman and Diu | 2 |
| Lakshadweep | 1 |
| Sub-Total | 523 |
| Anglo-Indian Presidential Nominees | |
| Total | 525 |

## LEGAL SYSTEM

Article 372 of the Constitution provides, *inter alia*, that, subject to the other provisions of the Constitution, all the laws in force in the territory of India immediately before the commencement of the Constitution shall continue in force therein, until altered, repealed or amended by a competent legislative or other competent authority.

Article 124 provides for the establishment of a Supreme Court of India consisting of a Chief Justice of India and of not more than 13 judges. Every judge shall be appointed by the President, and shall hold office until he attains the age of 65 years. The Supreme Court has exclusive final jurisdiction in any dispute between (*a*) the Government of India or one or more of the States, (*b*) the Government of India and one or more of the States on one side or one or more of the States on the other and (*c*) between two or more States.

The Appellate jurisdiction of the Supreme Court extends over all appeals from judgment, decree or final order of the High Court in civil, criminal or other proceedings if the High Court certifies that the case involves a substantial question of law as to the interpretation of the Constitution. Appeals also lie in other specified civil and criminal cases.

Provision is made in Articles 214–237 of the Constitution for the establishment of High Courts and subordinate courts in the States. Judges of the High Courts are appointee by the President and hold office until they attain the age of 60 years. The High Courts have powers of superintendence over all subordinate courts within their respective jurisdictions.

Civil courts are competent to try all accused persons duly committed, and to inflict any punishment authorized by law, but sentences of death are subject to confirmation by the highest court of criminal appeal in the State. There are magistrates courts for the trial of petty offences, and courts of small causes for the trial of money cases up to Rs.500.

### Supreme Court

*Chief Justice:* Hon. M. H. Beg.

## AREA AND POPULATION

*Note on statistical matter relating to India:* Indian numerical data often contain references to the quantities 'lakh' and 'crore', one lakh = 100,000, one crore = 10,000,000.

The population of India at mid-1974 was 595,586,000. The annual average percentage growth rate of the population for the periods 1960–74, 1965–74 was 2·3.

After China, India is the most thickly populated country in the world, and the population is rapidly increasing.

The following table shows the area of the States and Territories and the population at the 1971 census.

| *State/Union Territory* | *Area in sq. kilometres*[1] | *Population 1971 (Provisional)* (*in thousands*) | *Density of Population per sq. km* |
|---|---|---|---|
| India | 3,287,782 | 548,159,652 | 178[3] |
| *States* | | | |
| Andhra Pradesh | 276,814 | 43,502 | 157 |
| Assam[4] | 78,523 | 14,625 | 186 |
| Bihar | 173,876 | 56,353 | 324 |
| Gujarat | 195,984 | 26,697 | 136 |
| Haryana | 44,222 | 10,036 | 227 |
| Himachal Pradesh | 55,673 | 3,460 | 62 |
| Jammu & Kashmir | 222,236[5] | 4,616 | N.A. |
| Karnataka | 191,773 | 29,299 | 153 |
| Kerala | 38,864 | 21,347 | 549 |
| Madhya Pradesh | 442,841 | 41,654 | 94 |
| Maharashtra | 307,762 | 50,412 | 164 |
| Manipur | 22,356 | 1,072 | 48 |
| Meghalaya | 22,489 | 1,011 | 45 |
| Nagaland | 16,527 | 516 | 31 |
| Orissa | 155,782 | 21,944 | 141 |
| Punjab | 50,362 | 13,551 | 269 |
| Rajasthan | 342,214 | 25,765 | 75 |
| Sikkim | 7,299 | 209 | 29 |
| Tamil Nadu | 130,069 | 41,199 | 317 |
| Tripura | 10,477 | 1,556 | 149 |
| Uttar Pradesh | 294,413 | 88,341 | 300 |
| West Bengal | 87,853 | 44,312 | 504 |
| *Union Territories* | | | |
| Andaman & Nicobar Islands | 8,293[2] | 115 | 14 |
| Arunachal Pradesh | 83,578 | 467 | 6 |
| Chandigarh | 114 | 257 | 2,257 |
| Dadra & Nagar Haveli | 491 | 74 | 151 |
| Delhi | 1,485 | 4,065 | 2,738 |
| Goa, Daman & Diu | 3,813 | 857 | 225 |
| Lakshadweep | 32 | 31 | 994 |
| Mizoram | 21,087 | 332 | 16 |
| Pondicherry | 480 | 471 | 983 |

[1] Provisional, as on 1 July 1971.
[2] As on 1 January 1966.
[3] Density worked out after excluding population and area figure of Jammu and Kashmir.
[4] As reorganized on 21 January 1972 according to North-Eastern Areas (Reorganization) Act, 1971.
[5] Includes area under occupation of Pakistan and China.

N.A.—Not Available.

Population of principal towns of 100,000 and over at the census of 1971 (in thousands) (please note that the Indian States named below are those nameable before the creation of certain new states in 1971. The precise disposition of the various towns in the new states has not yet been ascertained. Ed.)

| ANDHRA PRADESH | |
|---|---|
| 1. Hyderabad | 1,798 |
| 2. Visakhapatnam | 362 |
| 3. Vijayawada | 343 |
| 4. Guntur | 269 |
| 5. Warangal | 207 |
| 6. Rajahmundry | 188 |
| 7. Kakinada | 164 |
| 8. Kurnool | 136 |
| 9. Nellore | 133 |
| 10. Eluru | 127 |
| 11. Nizamabad | 114 |
| 12. Machilipatnam (Bandar) | 112 |
| 13. Tenali | 102 |
| ASSAM | |
| 1. Gauhati | 122 |

BIHAR

| | | |
|---|---|---|
| 1. | Patna | 490 |
| 2. | Jamshedpur | 465 |
| 3. | Dhanbad | 433 |
| 4. | Ranchi | 256 |
| 5. | Gaya | 179 |
| 6. | Bhagalpur | 172 |
| 7. | Darbhanga | 132 |
| 8. | Muzaffarpur | 127 |
| 9. | Bokaro Steel City | 108 |
| 10. | Monghyr | 102 |
| 11. | Bihar | 100 |

GUJARAT

| | | |
|---|---|---|
| 1. | Ahmedabab | 1,588 |
| 2. | Surat | 471 |
| 3. | Baroda | 467 |
| 4. | Rajkot | 300 |
| 5. | Bhavnagar | 226 |
| 6. | Jamnagar | 214 |
| 7. | Nadiad | 108 |

HARYANA

| | | |
|---|---|---|
| 1. | Rohtak | 124 |
| 2. | Ambala Cantt. | 102 |

JAMMU AND KASHMIR

| | | |
|---|---|---|
| 1. | Srinagar | 403 |
| 2. | Jammu | 155 |

KERALA

| | | |
|---|---|---|
| 1. | Cochin | 438 |
| 2. | Trivandrum | 409 |
| 3. | Calicut | 333 |
| 4. | Alleppey | 160 |
| 5. | Quillon | 124 |

MADHYA PRADESH

| | | |
|---|---|---|
| 1. | Indore | 572 |
| 2. | Jabalpur | 533 |
| 3. | Gwalior | 406 |
| 4. | Bhopal | 392 |
| 5. | Durg-Bhilainagar | 245 |
| 6. | Ujjain | 209 |
| 7. | Raipur | 205 |
| 8. | Sagar | 154 |
| 9. | Bilaspur | 130 |
| 10. | Ratlam | 118 |
| 11. | Burhanpur | 105 |

MAHARASHTRA

| | | |
|---|---|---|
| 1. | Greater Bombay | 5,968 |
| 2. | Nagpur | 866 |
| 3. | Poona | 853 |
| 4. | Sholapur | 398 |
| 5. | Kolhapur | 259 |
| 6. | Amravati | 193 |
| 7. | Malegaon | 191 |
| 8. | Nasik | 176 |
| 9. | Thana | 170 |
| 10. | Akola | 168 |
| 11. | Ulhasnagar | 168 |
| 12. | Aurangbad | 150 |
| 13. | Dhulia | 137 |
| 14. | Nanded | 126 |
| 15. | Ahmednagar | 117 |
| 16. | Sangli | 115 |
| 17. | Jalgaon | 106 |

MYSORE

| | | |
|---|---|---|
| 1. | Bangalore | 1,648 |
| 2. | Hubli-Dharwar | 379 |
| 3. | Mysore | 355 |
| 4. | Manglore | 214 |
| 5. | Belgaum | 213 |
| 6. | Gulbarga | 145 |
| 7. | Bellary | 125 |
| 8. | Devanagere | 121 |
| 9. | Bijapur | 103 |
| 10. | Shimoga | 102 |
| 11. | Bhadravati | 101 |

ORISSA

| | | |
|---|---|---|
| 1. | Cuttack | 194 |
| 2. | Rourkela | 172 |
| 3. | Behrampur | 117 |
| 4. | Bhubaneswar | 105 |

PUNJAB

| | | |
|---|---|---|
| 1. | Amritsar | 432 |
| 2. | Ludhiana | 401 |
| 3. | Jullundur | 296 |
| 4. | Patiala | 151 |

RAJASTHAN

| | | |
|---|---|---|
| 1. | Jaipur | 613 |
| 2. | Jodhpur | 318 |
| 3. | Ajmer | 262 |
| 4. | Kota | 213 |
| 5. | Bikaner | 188 |
| 6. | Udaipur | 162 |
| 7. | Alwar | 100 |

TAMIL NADU

| | | |
|---|---|---|
| 1. | Madras City | 2,470 |
| 2. | Madurai | 548 |
| 3. | Coimbatore | 353 |
| 4. | Salem | 308 |
| 5. | Tiruchirapalli | 306 |
| 6. | Tuticorin | 154 |
| 7. | Nagercoil | 141 |
| 8. | Thanjavur | 140 |
| 9. | Vellore | 138 |
| 10. | Dindigul | 127 |
| 11. | Singanallur | 113 |
| 12. | Tiruppur | 113 |
| 13. | Kumbakonam | 112 |
| 14. | Kanchipuram | 110 |
| 15. | Tirunelveli | 108 |
| 16. | Erode | 103 |
| 17. | Cuddalore | 101 |

UTTAR PRADESH

| | | |
|---|---|---|
| 1. | Kanpur | 1,273 |
| 2. | Lucknow | 826 |
| 3. | Agra | 637 |
| 4. | Varanasi | 582 |
| 5. | Allahabad | 513 |
| 6. | Meerut | 367 |
| 7. | Bareilly | 326 |
| 8. | Moradabad | 272 |
| 9. | Aligarh | 254 |
| 10. | Gorakhpur | 230 |
| 11. | Saharanpur | 225 |
| 12. | Dehra Dun | 199 |
| 13. | Jhansi | 198 |
| 14. | Rampur | 161 |
| 15. | Shahjahanpur | 144 |
| 16. | Mathura | 140 |
| 17. | Firozabad | 133 |
| 18. | Ghaziabad | 128 |
| 19. | Muzaffar Nagar | 114 |
| 20. | Farrukhabad-cum-Fatehgarh | 111 |
| 21. | Faizabad | 109 |
| 22. | Mirzapur-cum-Vindhyachal | 105 |

WEST BENGAL

| | | |
|---|---|---|
| 1. | Calcutta | 7,005 |
| 2. | Durgapur | 207 |
| 3. | Kharagpur | 161 |
| 4. | Asansol | 157 |
| 5. | Burdwan | 144 |

CHANDIGARH

| | | |
|---|---|---|
| 1. | Chandigarh | 257 |

DELHI

| | | |
|---|---|---|
| 1. | Delhi | 4,065 |

MANIPUR

| | | |
|---|---|---|
| 1. | Imphal | 100 |

## VITAL STATISTICS

**Birth and Death Rates.** There is a difference in the birth and and death figures based on the registration data (R) and those estimated (E) by the census data. This is explained by the fact that many births and deaths go unregistered in the country. The table below gives the birth and death rates per thousand during the five decennia up to 1970:

| *Decade* | 1921–30 | | 1931–40 | | 1941–50 | | 1951–60 | | 1961–70[1] | |
|---|---|---|---|---|---|---|---|---|---|---|
| | R | E | R | E | R | E | R | E | R | E |
| Birth Rate | 33 | 46·4 | 34 | 45·2[2] | 28 | 39·9 | 22 | 41·7 | N.A. | 39·9 |
| Death Rate | 26 | 36·3 | 23 | 31·2[2] | 20 | 27·4 | 11 | 22·8 | N.A. | 18·1 |

[1] Provisional, based on Expert Committee Population Projections.
[2] Unofficial estimates.
N.A.—Not available.

**Life Expectancy.** Estimates of life expectancy for males and females at decennial censuses since 1901 are given in the Table below. There has been a steady though slow increase in life expectancy during the successive decades, and accelerated increase during 1951–60. The sharp drop in life expectancy during 1911–20 was largely attributable to the influenza epidemic. The table below gives life expectancy from 1901 to 1970:

| Expectation of life at birth | 1901–1910 | 1911–1920 | 1921–1930 | 1931–1940 | 1941–1950 | 1951–1960 | 1961–1970[1] |
|---|---|---|---|---|---|---|---|
| Males | 22·59 | 19·42[2] | 26·91 | 32·09[2] | 32·45 | 41·90 | 47·0 |
| Females | 23·31 | 20·91[2] | 26·56 | 31·37[2] | 31·66 | 40·60 | 45·6 |

[1] Provisional, based on Expert Committee Population Projections.
[2] Unofficial estimates.

**Age Structure.** The following Table shows the percentage of different age groups to the total population according to the 1971 census.

| Age Group | 0 to 14 | 15 to 19 | 20 to 24 | 25 to 29 | 30 to 39 | 40 to 49 | 50 to 59 | 60+ | Age not stated |
|---|---|---|---|---|---|---|---|---|---|
| Percentage of total population | 42·0 | 8·7 | 7·9 | 7·4 | 12·6 | 9·3 | 6·1 | 6·0 | N |

N—Negligible.

**Sex Ratio.** The sex ratio of the population has been generally adverse to females, i.e., the number of males has exceeded that of the females. In certain States, however, the tendency has been otherwise.

The States that show a sex ratio exceeding 1,000 in favour of females are Kerala (1,016) and Dadra and Nagar Haveli (1,007). In Manipur, Orissa, Goa, Daman and Diu, Mizoram and Pondicherry, the sex ratio which was in favour of females till 1961 has now changed in favour of males.

**Family Planning.** Family Planning as an official programme was adopted in 1952. The First Five Year Plan recognized that a rapidly growing population would be more a source of embarrassment than of help in raising the standard of living of the people. The aim was to reduce the birth rate to a level the national economy could sustain. The Second Five Year Plan emphasized that a higher rate of population growth was bound to affect adversely the rate of economic advance and the living standards per capita. During these two Plans (1951–1961), the family planning programme was taken up in a modest way with a clinical approach. The stress was mainly on research in the field of motivation, communication, demography, physiologyof reproduction and on the extension of Central and State organizations in providing clinical services. The programme was reorganized in the Third Plan after the publication of the 1961 census results which showed a higher growth rate than anticipated. The clinical approach was supplemented by an extended approach under which information concerning contraceptives, services and supplies of contraceptives were taken to the people. A full-fledged Department of Family Planning was created in 1966 in the Ministry of Health, Family Planning and Urban Development. During the three Annual Plans (1966–69) the family planning programme, which was described as the 'king pin' of the Plan, was given vastly increased funds. In the Fourth Plan, the programme was given the 'highest priority'.

The programme aims at reducing the annual birth rate from about 39 per thousand in 1969 to 25 by 1980–81. The operational goals are adoption of family planning by the people as a way of life through group acceptance of a small family norm, personal knowledge of family planning methods and ready availability of supplies and services. For its success, the programme should cover about 10 crore couples in the reproductive age-group to motivate them to adopt family planning. So far, 1·6 crore couples have been protected.

The programme is implemented through the State Governments as a Centrally-sponsored scheme.

The Central Family Planning Council advises on family planning at the national level. A number of central committees, like the Research Co-ordination Committee, have been set up to study the progress of research programmes.

Voluntary organizations and private medical practitioners are also used in the family planning campaign. Nearly 300 voluntary organizations are participating in the family planning programme. At present 2,032 urban centres and 5,234 rural centres are functioning in the country along with 35,234 sub-centres.

IUCD and sterilization services are offered through both mobile and static units. During 1975–76, 5·9 lakh insertions were carried out and 26·27 lakh persons were sterilized, the highest in any year since the inception of the family planning programme. In the period 1952–75 a total of 162·5 lakh sterilizations and 54·37 lakh IUCD insertions were completed giving a rate of 27·3 and 9·1 per 1,000 population respectively.

Nirodh (condoms) are presently distributed over the country by three methods, namely, a Free Supply Scheme, a Depot Holder Scheme and a Commercial Distribution Scheme.

Nirodh and other conventional contraceptives are distributed free to interested couples under the Free Supply Scheme through family planning centres and sub-centres numbering about 40,000. In addition, family planning field workers also distribute conventional contraceptives free during their field visits. Under the Depot Holder Scheme, Nirodh is sold through selected rural post offices at 5 paise for 3. Under the Commercial Distribution Scheme, six of the country's largest and most experienced consumer goods marketing companies are selling Nirodh through their regular network of salesmen, distributors, wholesalers and retailers. The sales of Nirodh under this scheme have increased from 1·57 crore male contraceptives during 1968–69 to 6·4 crore male contraceptives in 1974–75.

The oral pill was introduced as a pilot project in the family planning programme in 1967. 319 Oral Contraception Projects have been commissioned so far.

To propagate the message of family planning among women attending hospitals for delivery and abortion, a Post-partum Programme was started in 1969 in 59 selected hospitals. Since then 255 more hospitals have been covered under the programme.

## HEALTH

Planned development of over two and a half decades has resulted in vastly improved health facilities. The number of doctors and hospital beds has increased by more than two and a half times, and that of nurses by more than five times. The number of medical colleges has increased from 30 before the first plan to 106 as at present. In rural areas, there are 5,320 primary health centres and 33,291 sub-centres (15,299 in the health and 17,992 in Family Planning side in December 1975 whereas none existed before 1971.) Malaria, Tuberculosis and Cholera which used to take a heavy toll of life have been controlled to a varying degree. No case of plague has been reported in the country since 1967. Small-pox which was a dreaded disease has been non-existent since July 1975. The general death rate has come down from 27·4 per thousand in 1949–50 to 14·4 per thousand in 1974 and life expectancy at birth has increased from 32 years to 50 years in the same period.

**Nutrition.** Surveys conducted in different parts of the country have revealed that under-nutrition and malnutrition are prevalent in large sections of the population. The most affected segment is the vulnerable population consisting of young children and expectant and nursing mothers. To protect their health, various nutrition programmes have been launched by the Ministries of Health and Family Planning, Agriculture and Education and Social Welfare. Important among them are the School Meal Programme for primary school children and the Crash Feeding Programme (supply of toned milk and fortified bread) to pre-school children in city slums and tribal areas in different States. The number of beneficiaries covered by the two schemes up to 15 February 1973 was about 1·6 crores. In addition, a Supplementary Feeding Programme for children in the age group 3–6 through Balwadis is being implemented in rural areas. Production and consumption of nutritious foods by the rural community is also encouraged. Other measures include supplies of concentrated doses of Vitamin A to children to control blindness, and a supply of tablets containing ferrous sulphate and folic acid to expectant mothers and pre-school children.

The Nutrition Advisory Committee of the Indian Council of Medical Research sponsors schemes for nutrition research, besides advising the Government of India on nutrition matters.

**Water Supply and Sanitation.** The National Water Supply and Sanitation Programme was launched in 1954 as part of the Health Plan to assist the states in their urban and rural water supply and sanitation schemes so as to provide adequate water supply and sanitation facilities in the entire country. A Central Public Health and Environmental Engineering Organization (C.P.H.E.E.O.) was also set up in 1954 to provide technical advice and guidance to state governments in the preparation and execution of their schemes. The programme and the organization were transferred to the Union Ministry of Works and Housing in February 1973. By March 1976, 1,770 towns had been provided with water supply benefiting a population of ten crores (about 90 per cent of the total urban population). Also 200 towns with a population of four crores (36 per cent of the total urban population) had been provided with a partial sewerage system. Of the 5·76 lakh villages, about 64·00 with a total population of about five crores had been provided with piped water supply and hand pump tube wells up to March 1976. Of the remaining villages, about 4·22 lakhs have some kind of water supply, like conserved wells and springs, but in about 90,000 villages water is not available within a depth of 15 metres or a distance of 1·6 km. The Fifth Plan makes an allocation of Rs. 564·23 crores for this purpose under the Minimum Needs Programme. This is an addition to Rs. 440 crores allotted for urban water supply and sewerage. Apart from the programmes in the state sector, C.P.H.E.E.O. administers six central programmes which have a total provision of Rs. 16·60 crores in the Fifth Plan.

## FINANCE

The GNP at market prices for 1974 was U.S. $ millions 80,410, and the GNP per capita at market prices was U.S. $140. The annual average percentage growth rate of the GNP per capita for the period 1960–74 was 1·1, and for the period 1965–74 was 1·3. [*See the note at the beginning of this section concerning GNP.*]

The following table shows the budgetary position of the government of India for the periods 1974–75, and 1975–76:

| *Major Head* | 1974–75 (*Revised*) | 1975–76 *Budget* (*in crores of rupees*) |
|---|---|---|
| I. **Revenue account** | | |
| A. Revenue | 6,484.7 | 6,875·1 (7,092·4) |
| B. Expenditure | 5,860·0 | 6,490·9 |
| C. Surplus (+) or deficit (−) | +624·7 | +384·2 (+601·5) |
| II. *Capital account* | | |
| A. Receipts | 3,492·4 | 3,951·2 |
| B. Disbursements | 4,742·2 | 4,799·6 |
| C. Surplus (+) or deficit (−) | −1,249·8 | −848·4 |
| III. *Overall surplus* (+) *or deficit* (−) (IC+IIC) | −625·1 | −464·2 (−246·9) |
| *Financed by:* | | |
| A. Treasury bills increase (+) or decrease (−) | −425·1 | −238·8 |
| B. Cash balances decrease (−) or increase (+) | −200·0 | −8·1 |
| (i) opening balance | +258·2 | +58·2 |
| (ii) closing balance | + 58·2 | +50·1 |

*National and per capita incomes.* National income in India is defined as the sum of incomes accruing to factors of production supplied by normal residents of the country before deduction of direct taxes. It is identically equal to net national product at factor cost. The table below gives the estimates of national and per capita incomes for selected years since 1960–61, at current and 1960–61 prices, as compiled by the Central Statistical Organization:

| Item | 1960–61 | 1970–71[1] | 1972–73[1] | 1973–74[1] | 1974–75[2] |
|---|---|---|---|---|---|
| Net national product (Rs crores) | | | | | |
| at current prices | 13,263 | 34,476 | 39,573 | 49,148 | 60,120 |
| at 1960–61 prices | 13,263 | 19,033 | 19,077 | 20,034 | 20,075 |
| Per capita net national product (Rs) at current prices | 305·6 | 637·3 | 700·4 | 851·8 | 1022·4 |
| at 1960–61 prices | 305·6 | 351·8 | 337·6 | 347·2 | 341·4 |
| Index number of net national product with 1960–61 as base | | | | | |
| at current prices | 100·0 | 259·9 | 298·4 | 370·6 | 456·0 |
| at 1960–61 prices | 100·0 | 143·5 | 143·8 | 151·1 | 151·4 |
| Index number per capita net national product with 1960-61 as base | | | | | |
| at current prices | 100·0 | 208·5 | 229·2 | 278·7 | 334·6 |
| at 1960-61 prices | 100·0 | 115·1 | 110·5 | 113·6 | 111·7 |
| Gross national product (Rs crores) | | | | | |
| at current prices | 13,999 | 36,558 | 42,077 | 51,902 | 63,375 |
| at 1960–61 prices | 13,999 | 20,334 | 20,460 | 21,403 | 21,478 |
| Index number of gross national product | | | | | |
| at current prices | 100·0 | 261·1 | 300·6 | 370·8 | 452·7 |
| at 1960–61 prices | 100·0 | 145·3 | 146·2 | 152·9 | 153·4 |

[1] Provisional. [2] Quick Estimates.

*Note:* The present estimates of National product for 1970–71 and 1971–72 are not strictly comparable with the estimates of 1960–61 to 1969–70. This is mainly because of methodological changes in the estimates of 'Construction' and use of revised data for 'Other Services'. Marginal changes have also been made in the industrial classification to conform to the National Industrial Classification (1970).

The table below gives the share of public and private sectors in domestic product at current prices in Rs crores:

| Item | 1960–61 | 1971–72[1] | 1972–73[1] | 1973–74[1] |
|---|---|---|---|---|
| **Gross domestic product (total)** | **14,071** | **39,105** | **42,388** | **52,234** |
| | **(100.0)** | **(100.0)** | **(100.0)** | **(100.0)** |
| Gross product of public sector | 1,538 | 6,146 | 6,803 | 7,739 |
| | (10.9) | (15.7) | (16.0) | (14.8) |
| Administrative departments | 735 | 2,697 | 2,926 | 3,299 |
| | (5.2) | (6.9) | (6.9) | (6.3) |
| Department enterprises | 586 | 1,596 | 1,700 | 1,741 |
| | (4.2) | (4.1) | (4.0) | (3.3) |
| Non-departmental enterprises | 217 | 1,853 | 2,177 | 2,699 |
| | (1.5) | (4.7) | (5.1) | (5.2) |
| Gross product of private sector | 12,533 | 32,959 | 35,585 | 44,495 |
| | (89.1) | (84·3) | (84.0) | (85·2) |
| **Net domestic product (total)** | **13,335** | **36,826** | **39,884** | **49,480** |
| | **(100.0)** | **(100.0)** | **(100.0)** | **(100.0)** |
| Net product of public sector | 1,422 | 5,687 | 6,267 | 7,095 |
| | (10.7) | (15.4) | (15.7) | (14.3) |
| Administrative departments | 735 | 2,697 | 2,926 | 3,299 |
| | (5.5) | (7.3) | (7.3) | (6.7) |
| Departmental enterprises | 522 | 1,493 | 1,575 | 1,602 |
| | (3.9) | (4.0) | (4.0) | (3.2) |
| Non-departmental enterprises | 165 | 1,497 | 1,766 | 2,194 |
| | (1.3) | (4.1) | (4.4) | (4.4) |
| Net product of private sector | 11,913 | 31,139 | 33,617 | 42,385 |
| | (89.3) | (84.6) | (84.3) | (85.7) |

[1] Provisional.
Note: Figures in brackets indicate percentage share.

## CURRENCY

On 1 April 1957, a decimal system based on the *paisa* (0·01 rupee) was introduced in India. On that date, new coins and postage stamps were issued.

To replace the original division of three *pies* to a *pice* (*paisa*), four *pice* to an *anna* and 16 *annas* to the *rupee*, the coinage is now divided into *rupees* and *paise*, 100 *paise* being the equivalent of a *rupee*. The new series has the units two paise, five paise and ten paise.

## BANKS

**Reserve Bank of India.** (Governor, Shri S. Jagannathan.) Est. 1935; Sole Bank of Issue for India; the Bank was nationalized 1 January 1949; Balance Sheet at 30 June 1974 showed assets (issue department) Rs.6509,89,63,352·50; (banking department) Rs.2591,20,30,398·44; total gold reserves Rs.182,53,04,731·42; notes in circulation Rs. 6472,72,04,191·50. *Head Office:* Central Office, Shaheed Bhagat Singh Road, Fort, Bombay–400 001.

**Allahabad Bank.** (Chairman and Mg. Director, S. D. Varma.) Est. 1865; Balance Sheet at 31 December 1974 showed assets Rs. 289,92,51,823·31; deposits and current accounts Rs. 239,24,49,177·69. *Head Office:* 14 India Exchange Place, Calcutta –700001: 388 Branches.

**Bank of Baroda.** (Chairman, Mr. R. C. Shah.) Est. 1908. Assets as at 31 Dec. 1976: RS. 1669,44,96,027·33 deposits and current accounts Rs. 1257,60,70,561·89. *Head Office:* Bank of Baroda, Head Office, Post Bag No. 506, Mandvi, Baroda 390006, India. 1,118 branches, 1,076 in India and 42 abroad.

**Bank of India.** (Chairman and Managing Director, C. P. Shah.) Est. 1906; Balance Sheet at December 1976 showed assets Rs. 1830,74,68,376; deposits and other accounts Rs. 1412,20,39,321. *Head Office:* 'Express Towers'. Nariman Point, Bombay 400 021. 960 Branches including 17 overseas branches and one affiliated office.

**Central Bank of India.** (Chairman and Managing Director D. P. F. Gutta.) Est. 1911; Nationalised on 19 July 1969. Wholly owned by the Government of India. Balance Sheet at 31 December 1976 showed assets Rs. 166,16,287,939. *Head Office:* Chander Mukhi, Nariman Point, Bombay 400 021. Number of Branches: 1,419.

**Chartered Bank, The.** (24 Branches.) See United Kingdom.

**State Bank of India** (formerly the Imperial Bank). (Chairman, R. K. Talwar.) Est. 1955. Authorized Capital: Rs. 20,00,00,000. Issued, subscribed and paid up capital Rs.5,62,50,000. Reserve Fund and other reserves Rs. 219,075,052. *Central Office:* P.O. Box No. 12, Bombay 1. Over 3,000 offices as at 31 December 1973.

**Indian Bank Limited.** Est. 1907; Balance Sheet at 31 December 1965 showed assets Rs.65,23,50,075 deposit and current accounts Rs.58,35,29,824. *Head Office:* Indian Chamber Buildings, Madras. 175 Branches.

**Indian Overseas Bank Limited.** (Chairman, R. N. Chettur.) Est. 1937; Balance Sheet at 31 December 1971 showed assets Rs. 174,69,29,553; deposits and other accounts Rs. 131,60,07,391. *Head Office:* Mount Road, Madras. 300 Branches.

**Mercantile Bank Limited.** Branches at Bombay and Calcutta. See Hong Kong.

**Grindlays Bank Limited.** See United Kingdom.

**Punjab National Bank.** (Chairman and Managing Director, Shri P. L. Tandon.) Est. 1895, nationalized on 9 July 1969; Balance Sheet at 31 December 1969 showed assets of over 758 crores rupees, deposits and other accounts over 620 crores rupees. *Head Office:* 5, Parliament St., New Delhi. Over 900 Branches throughout India.

**United Commercial Bank.** (Chairman and Managing Director, V. R. Desai.) Est. 1943; Balance Sheet at 31 December 1976 showed Paid-up Capital Rs. 50 million; Reserves Rs. 60 million; Deposits Rs. 7,883 million. *Head Office:* 10 Brabourne Rd. Calcutta-70000. Branches: 912 in India and nine overseas.

## PRODUCTION, INDUSTRY AND COMMERCE

**Planning.** The Draft Fourth Five-Year Plan aims at increasing development in conditions of stability and reduced uncertainties particularly in respect of agricultural production and great dependence on foreign aid. The Draft Fourth Plan envisages a total outlay of Rs.24,398 crores, with Rs. 14,398 in the public sector and Rs.10,000 crores investment in the private sector. One of the major aims of the plan is to provide more employment in the rural and urban sectors on an increasing scale.

**Agriculture.** Nearly 70 per cent of the people in India are dependent for their living on agriculture and allied activities which account for about 44 per cent of the national income. Agriculture not only supplies raw materials for some of the major industries such as cotton and jute textiles and sugar, but also provides a large proportion of the country's exports.

**Agricultural Census.** An agricultural census, taken up for the first time in India in 1970–71, has been completed in most of the States. The data being compiled relate to the structure of agricultural holdings, area under crops and land utilization, irrigation, details of tenancy, use of fertilizers, agricultural machinery, implements and livestock.

Land utilization statistics are available for 30·60 crore hectares or 93·3 per cent of the total area of 32·8 crore hectares. The following table gives details of land utilization in India for 1970–73:

*(crore hectares)*

| | 1970–71[1] | 1971–72[1] | 1972–73[1] |
|---|---|---|---|
| Total geographical area | 32·88 | 32·88 | 32·88 |
| Total reporting area for land utilization | 30·55 | 30·62 | 30·62 |
| 1. Forests | 6·58 | 6·57 | 6·74 |
| 2. Not available for cultivation: | | | |
| (i) Area put to non-agricultural uses | 1·64 | 1·66 | 1·63 |
| (ii) Barren and uncultivable lands | 2·83 | 2·98 | 2·75 |
| *Total* | 4·47 | 4·64 | 4·38 |
| 3. Other uncultivated land, excluding fallow lands: | | | |
| (i) Permanent pastures and grazing lands | 1·32 | 1·31 | 1·29 |
| (ii) Land under tree crops and groves | 0·44 | 0·44 | 0·46 |
| (iii) Cultivable waste | 1·75 | 1·58 | 1·58 |
| *Total* | 3·51 | 3·33 | 3·33 |
| 4. Fallow lands: | | | |
| (i) Current fallows | 1·06 | 1·24 | 1·58 |
| (ii) Others | 0·86 | 0·82 | 0·91 |
| *Total* | 1·92 | 2·06 | 2·49 |
| 5. Net area sown: | 14·10 | 14·02 | 13·68 |
| Area sown more than once | 2·49 | 2·49 | 2·47 |
| Total cropped area | 16·59 | 16·51 | 16·15 |

[1]Provisional.

Of the net area under cultivation, 22·2 per cent is irrigated. Between 1950–51 and 1972–73, the net irrigated area increased by 1·10 crore hectares as shown in the table below:

*(crore hectares)*

| *Source of irrigation* | 1972–73[1] | *Increase* (+) *or decrease* (−) |
|---|---|---|
| Canals | 1·31 | +0·48 |
| Tanks | 0·36 | — |
| Wells | 1·30 | +0·70 |
| Other sources | 0·22 | −0·08 |
| *Total* | 3·19 | +1·10 |

[1]Provisional

The two outstanding features of agricultural production are the wide variety of crops and the preponderance of food over non-food crops. The table below shows the area under major crops in 1950–51, 1971–75.

(thousand hectares)

| Crops | 1950–51 | 1971–72[1] | 1972–73[1] | 1973–74 | 1974–75[2] |
|---|---|---|---|---|---|
| Rice | 30,810 | 37,758 | 36,688 | 38,286 | 37,922 |
| Jowar | 15,571 | 16,777 | 15,513 | 16,716 | 15,856 |
| Bajra | 9,023 | 11,773 | 11,817 | 13,934 | 11,261 |
| Maize | 3,159 | 5,668 | 5,838 | 6,015 | 5,921 |
| Ragi | 2,203 | 2,425 | 2,329 | 2,360 | 2,529 |
| Small millets | 4,605 | 4,477 | 4,265 | 4,567 | 4,510 |
| Wheat | 9,746 | 19,139 | 19,463 | 18,583 | 18,108 |
| Barley | 3,113 | 21,455 | 2,449 | 2,650 | 2,931 |
| *Total Cereals* | 78,230 | 100,472 | 98,362 | 103,111 | 99,038 |
| Gram | 7,570 | 7,912 | 6,967 | 7,761 | 7,150 |
| Tur | 2,181 | 2,346 | 2,424 | 2,646 | 2,540 |
| Other pulses | 9,340 | 11,893 | 11,524 | 13,020 | 12,888 |
| *Total Foodgrains* | 97,321 | 122,623 | 119,277 | 126,538 | 121,616 |
| Potatoes | 240 | 492 | 505 | 543 | 594 |
| Sugarcane (gur) | 1,707 | 2,390 | 2,452 | 2,752 | 2,771 |
| Black pepper | 80 | 119 | 120 | 122 | 122 |
| Chillies | 592 | 753 | 682 | 739 | 710 |
| Ginger | 17 | 25 | 23 | 25 | 25 |
| Tobacco | 357 | 458 | 445 | 462 | 409 |
| Groundnut | 4,494 | 7,510 | 6,990 | 7,024 | 7,167 |
| Castoseeds | 555 | 453 | 426 | 546 | 582 |
| Sesamum | 2,204 | 2,392 | 2,288 | 2,386 | 2,246 |
| Rapeseed and mustard | 2,071 | 3,614 | 3,319 | 3,457 | 3,607 |
| Linseed | 1,403 | 2,064 | 1,726 | 2,038 | 1,984 |
| Cotton | 5,882 | 7,800 | 7,679 | 7,574 | 7,621 |
| Jute | 571 | 815 | 700 | 793 | 665 |
| Mesta | n.a. | 296 | 293 | 370 | 316 |
| Tea | 314 | 357 | 359 | 360[3] | 362[3] |
| Coffee | 91 | 138 | 146 | 155 | n.a. |
| Rubber | 58 | 209 | 213 | 218 | 221 |
| Coconut | 622 | 1,088 | 1,099 | 1,102 | 1,116 |

[1] Revised estimates. [2] Final estimates
[3] Provisional. n.a.—Not available.

There are three main crop seasons, *kharif*, *rabi* and summer. The major *kharif* crops are rice, jowar, bajra, maize, cotton, sugarcane, sesamum and groundnut. The major *rabi* crops are wheat, barley, gram, linseed, rapeseed and mustard. Rice, maize and groundnut are grown in summer season also.

The following table gives the quantity of principal crops:

(thousand tonnes)

| Crops | 1950–51[1] | 1972–73[2] | 1973–74[2] | 1974–75[2] |
|---|---|---|---|---|
| Rice (cleaned) | 22,058 | 39,245 | 44,051 | 40,253 |
| Jowar | 6,250 | 6,968 | 9,097 | 10,221 |
| Bajra | 2,680 | 3,929 | 7,519 | 3,231 |
| Maize | 2,357 | 6,388 | 5,803 | 5,723 |
| Ragi | 1,353 | 1,923 | 2,072 | 2,031 |
| Small millets | 1,776 | 1,552 | 1,966 | 1,823 |
| Wheat | 6,822 | 24,735 | 21,778 | 24,235 |
| Barley | 2,518 | 2,379 | 2,371 | 3,150 |
| *Total Cereals* | 45,814 | 87,119 | 94,657 | 90,667 |
| Gram | 3,823 | 4,537 | 4,099 | 4,056 |
| Tur | 1,813 | 1,928 | 1,409 | 1,818 |
| Other Pulses | 3,561 | 3,442 | 4,500 | 4,523 |
| *Total Foodgrains* | 55,011 | 97,026 | 104,665 | 101,064 |

*continued*

(thousand hectares)

| Crops | 1950–51[1] | 1972–73[2] | 1973–74[2] | 1974–5[2] |
|---|---|---|---|---|
| Potatoes | 1,832 | 4,451 | 4,861 | 6,171 |
| Sugarcane (cane) | 70,490 | 124,867 | 146,805 | 140,196 |
| Black Pepper | 20 | 26 | 29 | 28 |
| Chillies (dry) | 358 | 412 | 497 | 450 |
| Ginger (dry) | 14 | 34 | 38 | 39 |
| Tobacco | 257 | 372 | 462 | 395 |
| Groundnut (nuts in shell) | 3,319 | 4,092 | 5,932 | 4,991 |
| Castorseed | 107 | 145 | 229 | 216 |
| Sesamum | 422 | 385 | 485 | 408 |
| Rapeseed and mustard | 768 | 1,808 | 1,704 | 2,211 |
| Linseed | 364 | 428 | 504 | 538 |
| Cotton (lint) ('000 bales)[7] | 3,039[7] | 5,735 | 6,309 | 7,080 |
| Jute (dry fibre) ('000 bales)[4] | 3,497 | 4,978 | 6,220 | 4,488 |
| Mesta (dry fibre) ('000 bales)[4] | 659 | 1,112 | 1,456 | 1,327 |
| Tea | 275[5] | 456 | 472 | 490[6] |
| Coffee | 25[5] | 91[6] | 86[6] | 92[6] |
| Rubber | 14[5] | 112 | 125 | 130 |
| Coconut (crore nuts) | 358[5] | 600 | 585 | 596 |

[1] Adjusted. [2] Revised estimates. [3] Final estimates
[4] 180 kg each. [5] Unadjusted figures. [6] Provisional.
[7] 170 kg each.

The food situation in the country which had been extremely difficult during 1972–74 showed a continuous improvement from October 1974 onwards. The main features of the food situation during 1975–76 were plentiful market supply, comfortable stock position with the Government, easiness in market prices and reduced prices on public distribution. The production of foodgrains which had remained practically stagnant between 1971–72 and 1974–75 mainly on account of adverse weather conditions had surpassed all previous records during 1975–76. According to latest indications, the target fixed for the Kharif foodgrain had exceeded 11·8 crore tonnes as against the target of 11·4 crore tonnes.

**Irrigation.** The vulnerability of India's agriculture owing to the vagaries of the monsoon has made it imperative to accord irrigation a high place in the national development plans. About 725 major and medium projects were taken up after Independence, of which 440 have been completed and many others have started yielding partial benefits. The irrigation potential of major and medium projects has been doubled and there has been an appreciable increase in the irrigated area. The total irrigated area in the country, which was about 2·26 crores hectares in 1950–51, rose to about 4·54 crore hectares in 1975–76. The total cropped area in 1974–75 was about 16·90 crore hectares.

A broad assessment of the water resources of the country by different agencies places the total average annual surface run-off as varying from 167,300 crore cubic metres to 188,100 crore cubic metres and the approximate annual groundwater recharge as 42,400 crore cubic metres. The utilizable surface and groundwater resources were assessed by the Irrigation Commission in 1972 as 87,000 crore cubic metres. Against this, the utilization, which was about 17,250 crore cubic metres in 1950–51, had risen to about 34,300 crore cubic metres by March 1975.

With the possibilities of diverting the normal flow of rivers into irrigation canals having been almost exhausted, effort is now directed at impounding by dams the surplus river flows during the monsoon for use in dry weather and the development of groundwater in minor irrigation programmes.

In 1951, the irrigated area from major and medium projects was 97 lakh hectares. By 31 March 1975, 421 out of a total of 690 major and medium projects taken up since 1951 had been completed and an additional potential of 1·2 crore hectares was estimated to have been created. The table below shows the growth of irrigation potential and the corresponding utilization from major and medium projects since the advent of planning:

(*lakh hectares*)

| | *Additional potential at the end of* | | | | |
|---|---|---|---|---|---|
| | 1st Plan | 2nd Plan | 3rd Plan | 4th Plan | 5th Plan |
| Potential | 25 | 46 | 69 | 115 | 174 |
| Utilization | 15 | 34 | 55 | 98 | 173 |

The total investment on major and medium irrigation projects between 1951–52 and 1975–76 was 3,915 crores and on flood control and drainage works Rs 434 crores. The outlay for 1976–77 is Rs. 615 crores and Rs. 59 crores respectively.

**Plantation Crops.** Tea, coffee and rubber plantations together cover only about 0·4 per cent of the cropped area; yet tea is the second largest foreign exchange earner for the country. These industries, concentrated largely in the north-east and along the south-west coast, employ over 12 lakh workers.

*Tea:* The production of tea in 1974 was the highest ever recorded. It was 49 crore kg. The 1973 production was 47·19 crore kg. The production during 1975–76 was 48·7 crores kg. Export earnings from tea in 1975–76 totalled Rs. 236·81 crores as compared to Rs. 228·06 crores during 1974–75.

During the past few years there has been an increase in the production and export of instant tea. In the five-year period, 1966–70, production increased ten-fold, from 30,354 kg in 1966 to 3·16 lakh kg in 1970. Foreign exchange earnings went up twenty times during the same period, from Rs 5.35 lakhs to Rs 105 lakhs. In terms of quantity, exports went up from 13,608 kg to nearly 3·20 lakh kg. However, during 1973, production declined to 2·14 lakh kg. and exports to 2·43 lakh kg valued at Rs 76 lakhs. The exports of instant tea were of the order of Rs 2·55 lakh kgs. in 1974–75 and 4·78 lakh kg in 1975–76 valued at Rs 85·63 lakhs and Rs 191·62 lakhs respectively.

The Tea Board, which is the principal agency for the development of the tea industry, is implementing a number of schemes to increase production. These include long-term loans to tea estates, provision of facilities for acquiring machinery on hire-purchase basis and grant of subsidy to the industry for replanting over-aged tea bushes. A Tea Trading Corporation at Calcutta has also been set up which markets Indian tea in consumer packs in certain selected countries.

*Coffee:* Production of coffee during 1974–75 was 92,000 tonnes. It comprised 62,000 tonnes of Arabica and 30,000 tonnes of Robusta. Total exports of coffee were of the order of 66·65 crores in 1975–76 as against Rs. 51·36 crores in 1974–75.

The Coffee Board, which is responsible for the development of coffee industry, has undertaken a coffee development plan to improve the yield and quantity of coffee. For this purpose, it advances loans to coffee growers. In 1973–74, Rs one crore were made available to planters.

*Cardamom:* India is the largest exporter of cardamom and accounts for 70 per cent of the world trade. Production in 1975–76 was about 3,000 tonnes. Export earnings during 1975–76 were valued at Rs. 18·6 crores as against Rs 13·3 crores in 1974–75.

*Rubber:* The output in 1975–76 was 137,750 tonnes as against 130,143 tonnes during 1974–75. Owing to increased indigenous availability of rubber, the Government of India banned the import of natural rubber during 1973–74.

The Rubber Board assists the industry in its problems and decides on major issues pertaining to it. It introduced a replanting subsidy scheme in 1957, under which Rs 7·95 crores were granted as subsidy up to 31 May, 1976.

**Land Reform.** Immediately after independence, land reform measures were initiated in the country. The objectives of the land reform policy were set out by the planners as the removal of such institutional and motivational impediments to the modernization of agriculture as were innate in the agrarian structure inherited from the past and the reduction of gross inequalities in the agrarian economy and rura society which stemmed from unequal rights in land.

The objectives were translated into the following programmes of action: (a) the abolition of the prevalent intermediary system between the State and the tiller of the soil; (b) conferment of ownership rights on the cultivating tenant in the land held under their occupation; (c) imposition of a ceiling on agricultural land holdings as a measure contributing to the modernization of agriculture and to eliminate absentee landlordism; (d) rationalization of the record of rights in land so as to make it reflect the rights of tenants, share croppers and other categories of insecure land holders and (e) consolidation of holdings with a view to making easier the application of modern techniques of agriculture, provision of dependable irrigation facilities, etc.

More than a dozen states have enacted laws conferring ownership rights on the cultivating tenants. Notable among them are Maharashtra, Gujarat, Kerala, Karnataka, Assam, Himachal Pradesh, Jammu and Kashmir, Rajasthan, Madhya Pradesh and Orissa.

By land ceiling measures, ten lakh hectares of land have been declared surplus. About 5·1 lakh hectares have been actually taken over by the State; a little over 3·5 lakh hectares have so far been distributed among 6·1 lakh allottees.

| *State* | *Level of ceiling* (*hectares*) |
|---|---|
| Andhra Pradesh | 4·05–21·85 |
| Assam | 6·74[1] |
| Bihar | 6·07–18·21 |
| Gujarat | 4·05–21·85 |
| Haryana | 7·25–21·85 |
| Himachal Pradesh | 4·05–12·14[2] |
| Jammu & Kashmir | 3·68– 7·77[3] |
| Karnataka | 4·86–21·85 |
| Kerala | 4·86– 6·07 |
| Madhya Pradesh | 4·05–21·85 |
| Maharashtra | 7·25–21·85 |
| Manipur | 10·12[4] |
| Orissa | 4·05–18·21 |
| Punjab | 7·00–21·80 |
| Rajasthan | 7·25–21·85[5] |
| Tamil Nadu | 4·86–24·28 |
| Tripura | 2·00– 7·20[6] |
| Uttar Pradesh | 7·25–18·21 |
| West Bengal | 5·00– 7·00 |

[1] Actual area of the orchard, subject to a maximum of 2·02 hectares in excess of the ceiling, can be retained.
[2] In certain specified areas up to 28·33 hectares.
[3] Orchards in excess of the ceiling can be retained subject to an annual tax.
[4] To be revised.
[5] In certain specified areas up to 70·82 hectares.
[6] Standard hectares.

**Fisheries.** The production of fish in the country is estimated to have gone up from 17·69 lakh tonnes in 1968–69 to 22·55 lakh tonnes in 1974–75 (14·71 lakh tonnes of marine and 7·84 lakh tonnes of inland).

The exports of marine products in 1975–76 reached a level of 54,463 tonnes earning Rs 124·53 crores in foreign exchange.

The export of marine products, which stood at 38,900 tonnes valued at Rs 59·72 crores in 1972–73, rose to 52,300 tonnes valued at Rs 89·51 crores in 1973–74, showing an increase cf 34 per cent in quantity and 50 per cent rise in terms of value.

Under the balance trade and payments to arrangement with Bangladesh, fish worth Rs 1·08 crores was imported in 1975–76 against a target of Rs 3·50 crores.

The Fifth Plan envisages introduction of 4,750 additional mechanized boats. Currently about 12,300 boats are in operation compared to 10,500 boats at the end of the fourth plan.

To stimulate deep-sea fishing, infra-structural facilities are being provided at various major and minor ports. Work is in progress on the construction of fishing harbours at the major ports of Madras, Cochin and Vishakhapatnam. A fishing harbour is to be built at Calcutta, Honnarar (Karnataka), Dhmra (Orissa), Malipatnam and Kodyakkarai (Taiml Nudu). In addition, fishing harbours capable of handling large-sized fishing vessels are nearing completion at Karwar, Port Blair, Tuticorin and Vizhinjam. Plans have also been formulated for the construction of self-contained fishing harbours at 13 other sites. Apart from these projects, landing and berthing facilities on a limited scale have been provided at 70 sites. The UNDP project for the pre-investment survey of fishing harbours is being continued with assistance from the Swedish International Development Agency.

**Livestock.** The government is working on programmes to develop the milk-yielding capacity of well-defined breeds by selective breeding. It is also working to upgrade nondescript cattle.

The programmes for the development of animal husbandry and dairying aim at augmenting the supply of nutritive foods like milk, eggs and meat and helping the small and marginal farmers to diversify their economic activities.

*Cattle:* Cross-breeding of indigenous cows with bulls of exotic dairy breeds is encouraged for augmenting milk production. Programmes for selective breeding in recognized breeding tracts and for upgrading of nondescript animals with recognized dairy breeds are being continued. To support the cross-breeding programme, about 500 exotic dairy cattle of Jersey and Friesian breeds were imported during 1973–74. Five central cattle breeding farms have been established for raising high quality bulls of Sindhi, Tharparkar and Jersey breeds and Murrah and Surti breeds of buffalo.

To locate superior germplasm of important national breeds and their utilization for improvement, a Central Herd Registration Scheme is in operation at state livestock farms and breeding tracts of milch breeds. A Central Frozen Semen Bank has been established at Hessarghatta (Bangalore) for the production of frozen semen from high quality bulls of exotic and indigenous breeds. In addition, establishment of frozen semen stations, as a centrally-sponsored programme, has also been taken up at 5 Intensive Cattle Development Project areas.

Under the Intensive Cattle Development programme being implemented since 1964–65, 70 projects have been set up in different parts of the country. Another important cattle development scheme is the key village scheme. At present, there are 640 key village blocks. The central government has established seven regional stations in different agro-climatic conditions in the country for fodder production and demonstration. These fodder stations provide in-service training as well as training to farmers. They also hold 'field days' during different crop seasons for popularizing the production of nutritive green fodders to meet the needs of exotic cross-bred and indigenous milch animals.

*Sheep:* A central sheep breeding farm has been set up at Hissar with Australian assistance for Corriedale breed of sheep. The farm has a flock strength of 3,500 Corriedale sheep. Corriedale rams are supplied to various states, to Haryana Agricultural University and to Indian Veterinary Research Institute, Izatnagar, for breeding trials. Short-term training courses for state sheep husbandry officers and a sheep shearing training course are being organized since 1972–73.

Under a centrally-sponsored scheme, establishment of five large sheep breeding farms one each in Andhra Pradesh, Jammu and Kashmir, Karnataka, Rajasthan and Uttar Pradesh was started under the Fourth Plan. These farms will be fully established during the Fifth Plan. Sites for two more farms have been selected, one in Bihar and the other in Madhya Pradesh.

In order to produce exotic germplasm for sheep improvement work in the states, 1,222 Merino sheep from USSR were imported during 1973–1974.

*Poultry:* Poultry development programmes are continuing both in the public and private sectors. The estimated production of eggs in 1973–74 totalled 770 crores as against the Fourth Plan target of 800 crores. The poultry industry has also made a major breakthrough in the direction of attaining self-sufficiency in respect of genetically superior chicks. Intensification of the scientific poultry breeding programme at government farms has enabled the production of strain crosses which have given performance comparable to, and in many cases, better than the exotic hybrids available in the country.

The three central poultry breeding farms distributed 3·1 lakh chicks for breeding purposes to the States and private poultry farms during 1975–76.

*Pigs:* All the eight modern bacon factories and pork processing plants established during the Third and Fourth Plan periods have gone into production. During 1973–74, about 1,000 tonnes of pork and pork products were produced at these factories. Some of these factories have diversified their products and are handling different types of meat in addition to pork and pork products.

So far, 52 pig farms and 174 piggery development blocks have been established. The regional pig breeding stations produce selected breeds of pigs for multiplication and distribution in the piggery development blocks. About 10,000 exotic pigs are now available in these farms for upgrading local stock.

**Forestry.** Forests in India occupy an area of about 750 lakh hestares and account for 22·8 per cent of the total geographical area. The percentage of forest area in the country is rather low as compared to most of the countries of the world. The National Forest Policy, revised in 1952, lays down that the area under forests be steadily raised to 33·3 per cent of the total geographical area, the proportion being 60 per cent in the Himalayas, Deccan and other mountainous tracts and 20 per cent in the plains. With the growth in population, urbanization and demands for agricultural land, there has been a shrinkage of forest area. Any increase in area under forests is more than offset by the utilization of forest areas for river valley projects, rehabilitation of displaced persons, extension of area under plantations of commercial and food crops and establishment of industries and townships. Considerable improvement has, however, been brought about by scientific management over large areas.

The table on page 207 top, LHS shows the classification of area under forests in 1972–73[1] and 1973–74[1]:

**Mining.** The following table shows the quantity and value of some minerals and ores produced in 1974 and 1975:

| *Mineral* | *Unit* | 1974 *Quantity* | *Total Production* *Value* (*Rs.* '000) | 1975 *Quantity* | *Value* (*Rs.* '000) |
|---|---|---|---|---|---|
| *Total value of all minerals* | | | 8,617,601 | | 10,588,735[1] |
| **Fuels** (*total value*) | | | 6,153,657 | | 7,903,719 |
| Coal | '000 tonnes | 84,102 | 4,260,365 | 95,931 | 5,456,519 |
| Lignite | ,, | 3,044 | 136,414 | 2,822 | 126,465 |
| Natural gas[2] | crores cubic metres | 101·0 | 36,450 | 125·1 | 45,970 |
| Petroleum (crude) | '000 tonnes | 7,490 | 1,720,428 | 8,277 | 2,274,765 |
| **Metallic minerals** (*total value*) | | | 1,121,191 | | 1,336,884 |
| Bauxite | '000 tonnes | 1,114 | 30,810 | 1,270 | 29,726 |
| Chromite | tonnes | 396,535 | 48,973 | 499,248 | 68,158 |
| Copper Ore | '000 tonnes | 1,429 | 155,821 | 1,831 | 200,418 |
| Diaspore | tonnes | 3,122 | 516 | 2,510 | 612 |
| Gold[3] | kilograms | 3,145 | 125,369 | 2,824 | 117,796 |
| Iron ore (total) | '000 tonnes | 35,485 | 597,620 | 41,297 | 740,359 |
| Lead concentrates | tonnes | 10,969 | 15,677 | 13,830 | 19,208[4] |
| Manganese ore | '000 tonnes | 1,502 | 98,004 | 1,531 | 102,484 |
| Silver[3] | kilograms | 4,581 | 4,665 | 2,582 | 2,555 |

*continued*

| Mineral | Unit | 1974 Quantity | Total Production Value (Rs. '000) | 1975 Quantity | Value (Rs. '000) |
|---|---|---|---|---|---|
| Tungsten concentrates | kilograms | 23,365 | 1,316 | 37,538 | 2,319 |
| Zinc concentrates | tonnes | 29,060 | 42,420 | 38,339 | 53,249[4] |
| **Non-Metallic minerals** (*total value*) | | | 1,342,753 | | 1,348,132 |
| Agate | tonnes | 988 | 183 | 1,583 | 312 |
| Apatite | tonnes | 12,034 | 1,398 | 24,762 | 2,188 |
| Phosphorite | ,, | 433,438 | 167,430 | 429,109 | 197,629 |
| Asbestos | ,, | 23,272 | 5,915 | 20,551 | 6,095 |
| Ball-clay | ,, | 22,396 | 444 | 25,263 | 496 |
| Barytes | ,, | 143,541 | 3,069 | 170,693 | 3,692 |
| Calcite | ,, | 25,336 | 556 | 12,760 | 249 |
| Chalk | ,, | 54,336 | 1626, | 44,866 | 1,316 |
| Clay (others) | '000 tonnes | 229 | 612 | 158 | 507 |
| Corundum | tonnes | 337 | 175 | 307 | 168 |
| Diamond | carats | 20,975 | 12,366 | 19,827 | 9,452 |
| Dolomite | '000 tonnes | 1,195 | 32,442 | 1,453 | 35,388 |
| Emerald (crude) | carats | 2,990 | N.D. | 38,180 | N.D. |
| Emerald (dressed) | ,, | — | — | N.A. | N.A. |
| Felspar | tonnes | 54,496 | 1,313 | 38,216 | 917 |
| Fireclay[5] | '000 tonnes | 802 | 10,236 | 628 | 7,570 |
| Fluorite (concentrates)[6] | tonnes | 10,709 | 11,840 | 10,217 | 12,443[4] |
| Garnet (abrasive) | ,, | 3,702 | 258 | 4,351 | 290 |
| Garnet (gem variety) | kilogram | 632 | 11 | 153 | 1 |
| Graphite | tonnes | 26,456 | 2,374 | 18,891 | 1,743 |
| Gypsum | '000 tonnes | 1,073 | 15,536 | 810 | 12,001 |
| Jaspar | tonnes | 1,550 | 78 | 1,505 | 75 |
| Kaolin[7] (total) | '000 tonnes | 426 | 19,196 | 336 | 16,556 |
| Natural[8] | ,, | 315 | 4,500 | 241 | 3,170 |
| Processed[9] | ,, | 111 | 14,696 | 96 | 13,386 |
| Kyanite | tonnes | 45,337 | 10,400 | 50,301 | 13,153 |
| *Limestone and other calcareous materials* | | | | | |
| Limestone | '000 tonnes | 25,816 | 406,102 | 25,759 | 381,117 |
| Lime kanker | ,, | 295 | 2,688 | 281 | 2,691 |
| Lime shell | '000 tonnes | 89 | 3,692 | 98 | 3,047 |
| Calcareous sand | | 729 | 1,516 | 902 | 1,991 |
| Magnesite | tonnes | 265,532 | 21,553 | 313,415 | 27,132 |
| Mica (crude) | ,, | 13,804 | 24,263 | 11,244 | 22,230 |
| Mica (waste) | ,, | 4,951 | N.A. | 4,024 | N.A. |
| Ochre | ,, | 80,500 | 1,661 | 89,739 | 1,759 |
| Pyrites | ,, | 35,660 | 8,202 | 50,633 | 12,169 |
| Pyrophyllite | ,, | 15,562 | 409 | 11,474 | 219 |
| *Quartz and Silica* | | | | | |
| Quartz | '000 tonnes | 161 | 2,168 | 158 | 2,178 |
| Quartzite | ,, | 162 | 3,413 | 122 | 3,389 |
| Silica sand | ,, | 401 | 6,534 | 369 | 6,283 |
| Moulding sand | ,, | 69 | 384 | 67 | 388 |
| Sand (others) | | 969 | 2,801 | 982 | 3,623 |
| Salt (rock) | ,, | 5,273 | 897 | 3,331 | 566 |
| Sillimanite | tonnes | 2,950 | 1,013 | 8,116 | 2,438 |
| Slate | ,, | 4,905 | 348 | 3,323 | 199 |
| Staurolite | tonnes | 21 | 11 | 11 | 6 |
| Steatite | '000 tonnes | 293 | 11,603 | 189 | 6,553 |
| Sulphur | tonnes | 3,400 | 2,555 | 6,200 | 5,081 |
| Vermiculite | ,, | 2,895 | 218 | 2,195 | 112 |
| Wollastonite | ,, | 954 | 29 | 1,102 | 31 |
| Minor minerals (value) | | | 539,468 | | 539,468[4] |

[1] Includes estimates for 'minor minerals'.
[2] Relates to gas utilised.
[3] Relates to metal.
[4] Estimated.
[5] Includes partly the output of fireclay incidentally recovered from the collieries.
[6] Source: Gujarat Mineral Development Corporation Ltd.
[7] Also known as chinaclay.
[8] Kaolin natural refers to the mineral produced and consumed as such.
[9] Kaolin processed refers to the kaolin obtained after processing the run of nine materials.
N.A. Not available.
N.D. Not determined.

| Description | 1972–73[1] | 1973–74[1] |
|---|---|---|
| | (lakh hectares) | |
| 1. *From point of view of exploitation* | | |
| (a) Exploitable (forests in use) | 437 | 427 |
| (b) Potentially exploitable | 161 | 178 |
| (c) Others | 153 | 144 |
| Total | 751 | 749 |
| 2. *By Ownership* | | |
| (a) State | 714 | 713 |
| (b) Corporate bodies | 22 | 24 |
| (c) Private individuals | 15 | 13 |
| Total | 751 | 750 |
| 3. *By Legal status* | | |
| (a) Reserved | 381 | 381 |
| (b) Protected | 243 | 242 |
| (c) Unclassed | 127 | 127 |
| Total | 751 | 750 |
| 4. *By Composition* | | |
| (a) Coniferous | 42 | 42 |
| (b) Non-coniferous (including bamboo) | 709 | 708 |
| Total | 751 | 750 |

[1]Provisional.

Gold is produced in Mysore State from the Mysore, the Nundydroog, Ooregum and Champion Reef mines, as well as the Hutti mines in Hyderabad.

India is the largest producer of muscovite block mica and mica splittings, about 80 per cent of the world's supply of dressed mica blocks, condensers and splittings being supplied by her. She has extensive reserves of this mineral, and the world markets have generally been controlled by the supply of Indian mica, which comes chiefly from Hazaribagh district of Bihar, the Nellore district of Madras and in several areas of Rajasthan. The phlogopite variety of mica is obtained from Travancore.

Until the beginning of the Second Plan, the country's only producing oilfield was in Assam. The Oil and Natural Gas Commission has since carried out a survey, as a result of which drilling is in progress in Gujarat, Assam, Punjab, Uttar Pradesh, Bihar, Madras and West Bengal. Oil has been discovered in commercial quantities in Gujarat and is being produced at the rate of 6,000 metric tons per day.

**Industry.** The following table shows the industrial production for the years 1974–76:

| | 1974–75 | 1975–76[1] |
|---|---|---|
| *I. Mining* | | |
| 1. Coal (including lignite) (lakh tonnes) | 916 | 1,027 |
| 2. Iron ore (lakh tonnes)[2] | 370 | 415 |
| *II. Metallurgical Industries* | | |
| 3. Pig iron (lakh tonnes) | 76·4 | 84·7 |
| 4. Steel (lakh tonnes) | 64·6 | 74·5 |
| 5. Finished steel (lakh tonnes) | 51·6 | 54·9 |
| 6. Steel castings ('000 tonnes) | 64 | 60 |
| 7. Aluminium (virgin metal) ('000 tonnes) | 126·6 | 187·0 |
| 8. Copper (virgin metal) ('000 tonnes) | 12·8 | 17·1 |
| *III. Mechanical Engineering Industries* | | |
| 9. Machine tools (Rs crores) | 90·4 | 112·7 |
| 10. Railway wagons ('000 no.)[3] | 11·0 | 12·2 |
| 11. Automobiles ('000 no.)[4] | 81·3 | 72·7 |
| (i) Commercial vehicles ('000 no.)[5] | 40·2 | 43·8 |
| (ii) Passenger cars etc. ('000 no.) | 41·1 | 28·9 |
| 12. Motor cycles and scooters ('000 no.) | 149·6 | 182·7 |
| 13. Power-driven pumps ('000 no.) | 282 | 277 |
| 14. Diesel engines (stationary ('000 no.) | 110·5 | 134·3 |
| 15. Bicycles ('000 no.) | 2,384 | 2,364 |
| 16. Sewing machines ('000 no.) | 327 | 264 |
| *IV. Electrical Engineering Industries* | | |
| 17. Power transformers (lakh kva) | 125·3 | 139·3 |
| 18. Electric motors ('000 hp) | 3,644 | 3,581 |
| 19. Electric fans (lakh no.) | 22·5 | 22·1 |
| 20. Electric lamps (lakh no.) | 1,498 | 1,553 |
| 21. Radio receivers ('000 no.) | 1,949 | 1,543 |
| 22. Electric cables and wires | | |
| (i) Aluminium conductors ('000 tonnes) | 28 | 59·1 |
| (ii) Bare copper conductors ('000 tonnes) | 1·2 | 1·3 |
| *V. Chemical and Allied Industries* | | |
| 23. Nitrogenous fertilizers ('000 tonnes of N) | 1,185 | 1,535 |
| 24. Phosphatic fertilizers ('000 tonnes of $P_2O_5$) | 327 | 320 |
| 25. Sulphuric acid ('000 tonnes) | 1,417 | 1,416 |
| 26. Soda ash ('000 tonnes) | 516 | 555 |
| 27. Caustic doda ('000 tonnes) | 426 | 470 |
| 28. Paper and paper board ('000 tonnes) | 826 | 831 |
| 29. Rubber tyres | | |
| (i) Automobile tyres (lakh nos.) | 48·3 | 47·4 |
| (ii) Bicycle tyres (lakh nos.) | 250·5 | 242·5 |
| 30. Cement (lakh tonnes) | 147·3 | 172·3 |
| 31. Refractories ('000 tonnes) | 753 | 729 |
| 32. Petroleum products refined | 196 | 210 |
| *VI. Textiles Industries* | | |
| 33. Jute textiles ('000 tonnes) | 1,049 | 1,302 |
| 34. Cotton yarn (crore kg) | 102·5 | 100·5 |
| 35. Cotton cloth (crore metres) | 826·7 | 812·6 |
| (i) Mill sector (crore metres) | 445·0 | 402·6 |
| (ii) Decentralized sector (crore metres) | | |
| 36. Rayon yarn ('000 tonnes)[6] | 115·9 | 104·3 |
| 37. Art silk fabrics (crore metres) | 86·3 | 87·5 |
| 38. Woollen manufactures | | |
| (i) Woollen and worsted yarn (lakh kg) | — | — |
| (ii) Woollen and worsted fabrics (lakh metres) | — | — |
| *VII. Food Industries* | | |
| 39. Sugar (Oct.-Sept.) (lakh tonnes)[7] | 47·9 | 42·2 |
| 40. Tea (crore kg) | 49·4 | 48·2 |
| 41. Coffee ('000 tonnes) | 90·0 | 83·0 |
| 42. Vanaspati ('000 tonnes) | 353 | 489 |
| *VIII. Electricity generated* (crore kwh)[8] | 7,058 | 7,984 |

[1] Provisional.
[2] Excludes output in Goa up to 1969–70.
[3] Excludes output in railway workshops.
[4] Includes landrovers, jeeps, utilities, station wagons and vans.
[5] Includes buses, trucks, tempos and three and four wheelers.
[6] Includes viscose yarn, staple fibre and acetate yarn.
[7] Relates to December 1975-May 1976.
[8] Relates to public utilities only.

It is estimated that India has reserves of water power equivalent to 30 to 40 million kilowatts. Installed capacity by March 1966 in the public utilities was 9027019 lakh kWh. From 58583 lakh kWh in 1951 capacity had increased to 329901 lakh kWh in 1966.

The cotton industry is the largest. It has over 1,500 factories and mills—for weaving, spinning and pressing—and is the largest possessed by any single country. Rice mills number nearly 2,000 and there are over 1,000 general engineering workshops. There are also more than 1,000 tea factories and over 800 printing and bookbinding establishments. There are nearly 500 sugar factories in the country and about 450 oil mills. Iron and steel output for 1965 was over 11 million tons. Two hundred new engineering and metal factories have come into existence.

**Commerce.** The following tables show a summary of the imports and exports for some years in Rs. lakhs:

| *Imports* | 1973–74 | 1974–75 |
|---|---|---|
| Iron and steel | 24,946 | 41,728 |
| Machinery other than electric | 42,664 | 39,675 |
| Petroleum products | 14,319 | 20,205 |
| Transport equipment | 9,497 | 12,290 |
| Electric machinery and appliances | 12,998 | 15,013 |
| Raw cotton | 5,205 | 2,667 |
| Wheat, unmilled | 34,610 | 69,818 |
| Petroleum, crude and partly refined | 41,709 | 95,490 |
| Chemical elements and compounds | 10,966 | 17,882 |
| Manufactures of metals | 2,189 | 2,726 |
| Textile yarn and thread | 348 | 999 |
| Copper | 7,083 | 7,299 |
| Zinc | 2,772 | 5,536 |
| Rice | 645 | 1,217 |
| Medicinal and pharmaceutical products | 2,643 | 3,406 |
| Fresh fruits and nuts | 3,640 | 4,717 |
| Raw wool and hair | 2,095 | 2,748 |
| Paper and paper-board | 2,892 | 5,843 |
| Oilseeds, nuts and kernels | 737 | 1,007 |
| Coal-tar, dyestuffs and natural indigo | 377 | 318 |
| Aluminium | 287 | 299 |
| Milk and cream, dried or condensed | 1,499 | 1,825 |
| Raw jute and waste | 1,222 | 375 |
| Vegetable oils | 5,694 | 1,230 |
| Total (including other items) | 295,537 | 451,993 |

N.A.—Not available.

| *Exports* | 1973–74 | 1974–75 | 1975–76 |
|---|---|---|---|
| Jute manufactures (excluding twist and yarn) | 22,573 | 29,403 | 24,528 |
| Tea | 14,603 | 22,806 | 23,681 |
| Cotton manufactures (excluding twist and yarn) | 23,989 | 21,511 | 21,301 |
| Textile fabrics (other than cotton and jute) | 3,684 | 2,683 | 2,398 |
| Textile articles (other than cotton and jute mfrs, woollen carpets, carpeting floor rugs and mattings) | 1,071 | 1,460 | 1,755 |
| Textile yarn and thread | 3,049 | 3,763 | 2,267 |
| Ores of non-ferrous base metals and concentrates | 1,999 | 3,044 | 4,381 |
| Lather | 16,657 | 13,388 | 19,129 |
| Raw cotton (excluding linters and waste) | 3,242 | 1,522 | 3,924 |
| Fresh fruits and nuts (excluding oilnuts) | 7,898 | 12,113 | 10,219 |
| Crude vegetables materials, inedible | 5,844 | 8,953 | 7,140 |
| Raw wool | 704 | 657 | 358 |
| Sugar (including molasses) | 4,259 | 33,933 | 47,382 |
| Iron ore and concentrates | 13,287 | 16,039 | 21,379 |
| Tobacco, unmanufactured | 6,841 | 8,036 | 9,310 |
| Vegetable oils (non-essential) | 3,165 | 3,366 | 3,329 |
| Crude minerals (excluding coal, petroleum, fertilizer materials and precious stones) | 2,153 | 3,335 | 3,144 |
| Woollen carpets, carpeting floor rugs and mattings | 2,406 | 3,364 | 964 |
| Iron and steel | 2,618 | 2,106 | 6,818 |
| Coffee | 4,601 | 5,136 | 6,665 |
| Hides and skins, undressed | 138 | 29 | 15 |
| Petroleum products | 1,225 | 1,363 | 1,888 |
| Coal, coke and briquettes | 309 | 680 | 1,669 |
| Total (including other items) | 252,340 | 332,883 | 394,162 |

The following tables show imports and exports (in Rs. lakhs) by principal countries for 1973–75 and 1973–76:

| *Imports* | 1973–74 | 1974–75 |
|---|---|---|
| U.S.A. | 49,843 | 72,909 |
| U.K. | 25,217 | 21,340 |
| Germany (West) | 20,579 | 30,687 |
| Iran | 26,758 | 47,266 |
| Japan | 25,953 | 45,347 |
| Italy | 4,940 | 7,838 |
| France | 7,029 | 8,116 |
| U.S.S.R. | 25,473 | 40,249 |
| Belgium | 6,571 | 10,190 |
| Switzerland | 1,692 | 3,652 |
| Australia | 4,381 | 11,848 |
| Malaysia | 3,209 | 1,120 |
| Saudi Arabia | 13,135 | 29,765 |
| Canada | 11,586 | 13,042 |
| Czechoslovakia | 2,671 | 3,331 |
| Bangladesh | 1,704 | 918 |
| Burma | 7 | 1 |
| Netherlands | 5,656 | 4,759 |
| Singapore | 972 | 722 |
| Sweden | 2,393 | 2,599 |
| Egypt | 2,590 | 2,283 |
| Kenya | 1,743 | 983 |
| Sudan | 2,193 | 503 |
| Total (including other countries) | 295,537 | 451,993 |

| *Exports* | 1973–74 | 1974–75 | 1975–76 |
|---|---|---|---|
| U.K. | 26,314 | 31,226 | 40,356 |
| U.S.A. | 34,592 | 37,493 | 50,774 |
| U.S.S.R. | 28,603 | 42,135 | 41,278 |
| Japan | 35,875 | 29,665 | 42,688 |
| Australia | 5,078 | 6,141 | 4,767 |
| Sri Lanka | 984 | 2,685 | 2,301 |
| Germany (West) | 8,679 | 10,617 | 11,782 |
| Canada | 3,109 | 4,418 | 4,243 |
| Burma | 154 | 465 | 891 |
| Egypt | 1,488 | 5,255 | 10,029 |
| France | 4,970 | 8,632 | 8,401 |
| Argentina | 642 | 1,063 | 398 |
| Sudan | 1,859 | 6,646 | 3,651 |
| Malaysia | 2,463 | 2,926 | 3,235 |
| Singapore | 4,354 | 3,679 | 4,223 |
| Netherlands | 7,334 | 7,175 | 7,518 |
| Czechoslovakia | 4,379 | 6,038 | 3,439 |
| Kenya | 1,028 | 1,540 | 1,556 |
| Italy | 6,935 | 5,243 | 7,872 |
| Nigeria | 1,149 | 2,161 | 3,714 |
| Cuba | — | — | — |
| New Zealand | 1,355 | 2,074 | 1,287 |
| Bangladesh | 5,878 | 4,220 | 6,213 |
| Indonesia | 2,678 | 5,096 | 5,292 |
| Total (including other countries) | 252,340 | 332,883 | 394,162 |

## COMMUNICATIONS

**Roads.** The Indian road network is one of the largest in the world. In 1974–75, the road length was 11·89 lakh km as against 4 lakh km in 1950–51. The road development programme in the Fifth Plan will lay emphasis on (i) completion of works spilling over from the Fourth Plan; (ii) widening to four-lanes of certain sections of the national highways; (iii) construction of byepasses around congested cities, replacing railway level crossings with over or under bridges, strengthening of pavements and widening to two-lanes of certain remaining single lane sections; (iv) removal of missing links; and (v) development of rural roads under the Minimum Needs Programme.

**Railways.** The Indian Government railway system with a route length in 1974–75 of 60,301 km is the largest in Asia and the fourth largest in the world. The railways ran daily 10,800 trains, covering a distance of about 12·5 lakh km. operated 7,085 stations, carried over 73 lakh passengers and about 5·5 lakh tonnes of freight. The operational fleet consisted of 11,113 locomotives, 36,566 coaching vehicles and 384,283 wagons. They employed 14·3 lakh persons. The total investment was Rs 5,050 crores and the revenue Rs 1,408 crores.

As a result of planned development spread over two decades (1951–1973), the number of passenger and goods traffic has more than doubled. The number of locomotives has increased by 74 per cent, coaching vehicles by more than 95 per cent and wagons by about 87 per cent.

There has also been a progressive increase in expenditure on the development of railways under the five year plans. It was Rs 423·23 crores, Rs 1,043·69 crores, Rs 1,685·8 In the Fourth Plan, the expenditure was Rs 1,419·76 crores and in the first year of Fifth Plan it was Rs 346·68 crores. The proposed outlay under the Fifth Plan is Rs 2,350 crores, besides Rs 200 crores allocated for transport projects in the metropolitan cities of Bombay, Calcutta, Delhi and Madras.

The table below gives some statistics for the period 1950–75.

| *Year* | *Route length (kilometres)* | | | *Running Track* | *Passengers* | *Goods* |
|---|---|---|---|---|---|---|
| | *Electrified* | *Non-electrified* | *Total* | *(km)* | *(lakhs)* | *(lakh tonnes)* |
| 1950–51 | 388 | 53,208 | 53,596 | 59,315 | 12,840 | 930 |
| 1955–56 | 388 | 54,623 | 55,011 | 60,845 | 12,750 | 1,159 |
| 1960–61 | 748 | 55,499 | 56,247 | 63,602 | 15,940 | 1,562 |
| 1965–66 | 2,423 | 55,976 | 58,399 | 68,375 | 20,820 | 2,030 |
| 1969–70 | 3,553 | 56,131 | 59,684 | 71,251 | 23,380 | 2,079 |
| 1970–71 | 3,730 | 56,060 | 59,790 | 71,669 | 24,311 | 1,965 |
| 1971–72 | 3,952 | 56,115 | 60,067 | 73,225 | 25,356 | 1,978 |
| 1972–73 | 4,055 | 56,094 | 60,149 | 73,664 | 26,530 | 2,013 |
| 1973–74 | 4,191 | 56,043 | 60,234 | 74,104 | 26,537 | 1,849 |
| 1974–75 | 4,397 | 55,904 | 60,301 | 74,197 | 24,290 | 1,966 |

**Shipping.** India is the second largest ship-owning country in Asia and though it ranks seventeenth in the world, Indian ships operate on most of the sea routes of the world.

The shipping tonnage on 1 April 1975 was 38·29 lakh GRT (with another 18·00 lakh GRT on order) as against 3·72 lakh GRT on 1 April 1951. Of this, the central government undertakings owned 15·02 lakh GRT, *i.e.*, 48·8 per cent. The number of ships was 274 as against 94 on 1 April 1951. The Filth Plan envisages a target of 96 lakh GRT including 10 lakh GRT on order.

The following are the principal shipping lines:

**Bharat Line Ltd.**: vessels 1, total tonnage, 4,933 grt; *services operated:* coastal trade of India. *Head Office:* Kundan Kunj, Bhavnagar. *Principal Office in India:* 104 Apollo St., Bombay 1.

**India Steamship Co. Ltd.**: (Chairman, K. K. Birla; Chief Executive, Capt. J. C. Anand; share capital, paid up Rs. 520,000,000; vessels 22; total tonnage 206,759 grt, 291,472 dwt; *services operated:* India–U.K. and Continent, India–U.S.S.R.–Poland and A.R.E., India–Bulgaria and Rumania, India–Adriatic Ports of Italy–Yugoslavia and Scandinavia. India–Bangladesh, West Asian (Gulf) Ports, Aden, East African Ports, Red Sea Ports and coastal trade of India. *Head Office:* India Steamship House, 21 Old Court House Street, P.O. Box 2090, Calcutta.

**Mogul Line Ltd.**: (Chairman, Shri C. P. Srivastava; Managing Director, Shri J. G. Saggi); Share Capital, authorized Rs. 2,00,00,000, paid-up Rs. 1,01,19,000; steam vessels 3; motor vessels 2; tanker 1; Gross Registered tonnage 50,648; Pilgrim/Passenger/Cargo. *Services operated:* Indian Coast, Bombay/Cochin/Colombo–Red Sea ports, India–Bangla Desh, Bombay–West Asia Gulf ports, Repatriate service from Burma to Madras; cruises from Bombay/Cochin to Ceylon–Malaysia–Singapore; *Registered Office:* 16 Bank Street, Fort, Bombay 1.

**Scindia Steam Navigation Co. Ltd.**; (Chairman, Krishnaraj M. D. Thackersey); share capital Rs 25,000,000; motor and steam vessels, 46; total tonnage 574,026 gross; *services operated:* India–Bangladesh–Pakistan–U.K.-Continent; India–Bangladesh–Poland; U.K.–Continent–Red Sea; India–Bangladesh–Straits–Mediterranean–Adriatic; Mediterranean–Adriatic–West Asia (Gulf); India–Bangladesh–A.R.E.–Red Sea; India–Bangladesh–West Asia (Gulf); India–Bangladesh–Black Sea Ports; India–Bangladesh–East and West Africa–Mediterranean–Adriatic; India–Bangladesh–Sri Lanka to U.S. Atlantic Gulf Ports–Mexico–Kingston and other Caribbean Ports and from U.S. East Coast–Gulf–Mexico to Far East–India–Sri Lanka–Bangladesh; India–Bangladesh–Strait Ports–Far East–Japan to U.S. Canada Pacific Coast and from U.S. Canada Pacific Coast to Far East–India–Sri Lanka–Bangladesh; India–Bangladesh–Sri Lanka to East Canada; Great Lakes to India–Sri Lanka–Bangladesh; India–Bangladesh–Pakistan–Burma–Sri Lanka. *Head Office:* Scinidia House, Narottam Mararjee Marg, Ballard Estate, Bombay 400038.

**Shipping Corporation of India**; (Chairman, C. P. Srivastava); cargo vessels, 61; passenger-cum-cargo, 6; tankers, 8; bulk carriers, 11; ore-oil-grain carriers, 6; coastal coal carriers, 3; timber carrier, 1; total number of vessels, 96; total tonnage, 1,205,132 G.R.T.; 1,882,483 D.W.T. *Services operated:* Australia, New Zealand, Japan, West Asia (Red Sea and Gulf), East Africa, U.S.S.R. and Black Sea ports, U.K.–Continent, Poland, G.D.R. U.S.A., Canada (Atlantic and Pacific Coast), Arab Republic of Egypt, Adriatic and Mauritius. *Head Office:* Steelcrete House, 4th Floor, Dinshaw Wacha Road, Bombay 20 BR.

**Civil Aviation.** Civil aviation in India has made rapid progress since Independence. During 1974. India aircraft flew both on scheduled and non-scheduled services, about 5·39 crore km as against 2·16 crore km in 1947. They carried about 28·4 lakh passengers and 52,232 tonnes of cargo and mail in 1972 as compared to 3·1 lakh passengers and 45·6 lakh kg of cargo and mail in 1947.

**Posts, Telegraphs and Telephones.** Postal services in India are controlled by the government. The number of post offices was 116,991 in March 1976; the number of kilometres of surface mail routes in 1969–70 was 665,443. The number of articles handled totalled 617·62 and the number of money orders issued was 9·48 crores.

The telegraph and telephone systems are controlled by the Director-General of Posts and Telegraphs, whose office is attached to the Ministry of Communications of the Government in India.

**Broadcasting.** All-India Radio is attached to the Department of Information and Broadcasting of the Government of India. It is the largest broadcasting organization in Asia and the fourth largest in the world. It has a network of 66 broadcasting centres, broadcasting in 14 Indian languages and in English. In addition, external transmissions are broadcast in a number of foreign languages, making 32 languages in all. They cover the Middle East, East and South Africa and East and South Asia. These transmissions are radiated from Delhi. Broadcasting stations have individual transmissions and are situated at Lucknow, Patna, Calcutta, Cuttack, Madras, Tiruchirapalli, Bombay, Shillong-Gauhati, Nagpur, Vijawoda, Baroda, Allahabad, Jullundur, Ahmedabad, Dharwar, Mysore, Calicut, Trivandrum, Hyderabad and Aurangabad among others. The number of domestic broadcast receiver licences is now 1·48 crores. Television transmissions began in 1959 in New Delhi. There are more than 275,000 television sets in operation.

## NEWSPAPERS

**Amrita Bazar Patrika.** English. Circulation 90,484. Calcutta.

**Ananda Bazar Patrika.** Bengali. Circulation 305,752 Calcutta.

**Free Press Journal.** Circulation 83,391. Bombay.

**Hindustan.** Hindi. Circulation 81,333. Delhi.

**Hindustan Times.** English. Circulation 198,979 Delhi.

**Indian Express.** English. Circulation 72,347. Delhi.

**Jugantar.** Bengali. Circulation 196,676. Calcutta 3.

**Lok Satla.** Marathi. Circulation 118,598. Bombay.

**Statesman.** English. Circulation 210,000. Calcutta and Delhi.

**The Hindu.** English. Circulation 236,643. Mount Road Madras 600002.

**Times of India.** English. Bombay, Delhi and Ahmedabad.

## ATOMIC ENERGY

India has a considerable programme of research and development of atomic energy for peaceful purposes. It is initially directed to the production of electric power and of isotopes for industry, agriculture and medicine.

The Atomic Energy Commission, founded in 1948, is co-operating with the Tata Institute of Fundamental Research (founded 1945) in connection with the training of scientists in nuclear physics. To ensure a steady supply of trained personnel a programme has been worked out to complete the training of 200 annually.

There is a thorium/uranium plant at Trombay. A uranium mill is to be set up at Jagunda, location of a major source of uranium ore. Travancore Minerals Ltd. produces ilmenite and monazite, and Indian Rare Earths Ltd. produces rare earth compounds.

Considerable work has been done in setting up the first atomic power plant at Tarapur. It should have a capacity of 380 megawatts and is likely to begin working during the Fourth Plan. A second nuclear power station of 200 mw. capacity is to be set up at Rana Pratapsagar, in Rajasthan, and a third of 400 mw. capacity at Kalpakkam, in Madras.

## EDUCATION

The literacy rate in India has gone up from 16·6 per cent in 1951 to 29·45 per cent in 1971. Four out of five children in the age group 6–11 are today at school as compared to one out of three two and a half decades ago. Primary education is now free in all the states and compulsory in most of the states. There were about 8·58 crore students in schools in 1973 as against 2·58 crores in 1950–51. At the university stage, the number of students increased by more than eight times and that of colleges more than five times.

Education in India is primarily the responsibility of state governments but the union government has also been entrusted with certain responsibilities specified in the Constitution. These include co-ordination of educational facilities, determination of standards of higher education, scientific and technical education, research, and promotion of Hindi and all other Indian languages. Most of the educational development plans are formulated and implemented with some assistance from the central government, which is also responsible for the running of five central universities of Aligarh, Banaras, Delhi, Jawaharlal Nehru and Visva Bharati and other similar institutions. It also runs 219 Kendriya Vidyalayas (central schools) in different parts of the country. A special responsibility of the union government is the promotion of the education of the weaker sections.

An Education Commission was appointed in 1964 with Dr. D. C. Kothari as chairman to advise the union government on a national pattern and development of education. Based largely on its recommendations, the government formulated a National Policy on Education which was issued in the form of a government resolution in 1968. The key points were: (i) free and compulsory education up to the age of 14; (ii) improved status, emoluments and education of teachers; (iii) three-language formula and development of regional languages; (iv) equalisation of education of science and research; (v) development of education for agriculture and industry; (vi) improvement in quality and production of inexpensive text-books; and (vii) investment of 6 per cent of national income in education.

Emphasis was also laid on the spread of literacy and adult education and promotion of games and sports.

The Education Commission has suggested a uniform pattern of 15 years' duration leading to the first degree (10 years of high school education, two years of higher secondary education and three years for the first degree course).

The new pattern has been adopted in Andhra Pradesh, Assam, Bihar, Giujarat, Jammu, Kashmir, Karnatakn; Kipalm. Kaharashtra, Sikkism, Tripura, Uttar Pradesh, and West Bengal among States and Andaman and Nicobar islands, Arunachal Pradesh, Charndigarh, Dodran and Nolor Haveli, Delhi, Goa, Daman and Dirs and Lakhadee among union territories. The States of Horyana, Himachal Pradesh, Manitur, Nagaland, Orissor, Royasthan and Tamil Nadu propose to adopt the new pattern from 1977–78/ 1978–79.

In the two decades of planned development since 1951, the number of educational institutions[1] has more than doubled. The number of teachers has gone up by about three times and that of students by about 3½ times. The achievements during the last two decades and targets of the Fifth Plan are given in Table 5.1. Expenditure on education also went up from Rs 153 crores in the First Plan to Rs 781 crores in the Fourth Plan. The proposed outlay for the Fifth Plan is Rs 1,726 crores. The table below gives details of the expenditure.

| *Major heads* | *First three Plans* | *Fourth Plan* | | *Fifth Plan* | |
|---|---|---|---|---|---|
| | | *Estimated expenditure (Rs crores)* | *Percentage* | *Proposed outlay (Rs crores)* | *Percentage* |
| Elementary education } Secondary education } | 556·0 | 241·3 | 30 | 743·0 | 43 |
| | | 140·4 | 18 | 241·0 | 14 |
| University education | 149·0 | 198·9 | 25 | 337·0 | 20 |
| Social education | 11·0 | 4·1 | 1 | 35·0 | 2 |
| Cultural programmes | 10·0 | 11·1 | 2 | 35·0 | 2 |
| Other educational programmes | 96·0 | 82·4 | 11 | 171·0 | 10 |
| *Total:* General education | 822·0 | 678·2 | 87 | 1,562·0 | 91 |
| Technical education | 194·0 | 102·4 | 13 | 164·0 | 9 |
| *Grand Total* | 1,016·0 | 780·6 | 100 | 1,726·0 | 100 |

[1] Estimated.

Broadly speaking, the Fourth Plan aimed at making progress towards implementing the Constitutional Directive of free and compulsory education for the age group 6–14. At secondary and higher stages of education more emphasis has laid on consolidation and diversification so as to meet the diverse needs of trained manpower of requisite standard. However, as the table below shows, targets laid down for elementary education were not realised in full, more so in case of girls. The anticipated enrolment in secondary education also showed a shortfall, but that in higher education was exceeded.

(*in lakhs*)

| *Age group/classes* | | 1969–70 | | 1974–75 (*target*) | | 1974–75 (*likely position*) | | 1975–76 (*target*) | |
|---|---|---|---|---|---|---|---|---|---|
| 6–11/I-V | | | | | | | | | |
| | Boys | 347·70 | (95) | 405·59 | (102) | 404·60 | (102) | 416·08 | (100) |
| | Girls | 207·16 | (50) | 259·06 | (69) | 258·78 | (70) | 269·85 | (72) |
| | *Total* | 554·85 | (73) | 664·65 | (86) | 663·38 | (86) | 685·92 | (88) |
| 11–14/VI-VIII | | | | | | | | | |
| | Boys | 92·75 | (47) | 111·76 | (51) | 111·96 | (50·5) | 117·73 | (53) |
| | Girls | 37·04 | (20) | 50·29 | (25) | 51·09 | (24) | 55·54 | (26) |
| | *Total* | 129·79 | (34) | 162·05 | (36) | 163·05 | (38) | 173·27 | (39) |
| 14–17/IX-XI-XII | | | | | | | | | |
| | Boys | 47·24 | (10) | 65·74 | (32) | 61·60 | (31) | N.A. | |
| | Girls | 16·06 | (27) | 24·73 | (13) | 23·40 | (12) | N.A. | |
| | *Total* | 63·30 | (18) | 90·47 | (23) | 85·50 | (22) | N.A. | |
| 17–23/University stage | *Total* | 22·37 | | 26·60 | (3·9) | 30·00 | (4·4) | N.A. | |

*Note:* Figures in brackets indicate enrolment as percentage of the population of relevant age group.

The Fifth Plan lays emphasis on (i) ensuring equality of educational opportunities as part of the overall plan of ensuring social justice; (ii) establishing closer links between the pattern of education, on the one hand, and the needs of development and the employment market, on the other; (iii) improvement of the quality of education imparted; and (iv) involvement of the academic community, including students, in the tasks of social and economic development.

*Elementary Education:* Under a Directive Principle of State Policy, free and compulsory education is to be provided for all children up to the age of 14. In pursuance of this directive, all states have introduced free education for children in the age group 6–11. It is also free for children in the age aroup 11–14 in all states except Orissa, Uttar Pradesh and West Bengal. Even in these states, girl students and students from backward communities get free education.

All states have compulsory Primary Education Acts except Meghalarya, Sikkim, Manipur, Nagaland and Tripura. Of the union territories, Andaman and Nicobar Islands, Chandigarh and Delhi have such legislation. However, even where such legislation exists, penal clauses are seldom enforced because of socio-economic reasons. Instead, incentives such as mid-day meals, free books and uniforms are provided to attract children to school.

*Secondary Education:* Education is free up to the secondary stage in Andhra Pradesh, Gujarat, Karnataka, Kerala, Tamil Nadu, Andaman and Nicobar Islands, Arunachal Pradesh and Lakshadweep and in government institutions in Jammu and Kashmir, Nagaland, Dadra and Nagar Haveli and Pondicherry. It is free for girls in Madhya Pradesh, Children belonging to the scheduled castes and tribes get free education in all the states.

*Higher and University Education:* Higher education is imparted through arts and science and professional colleges, research institutions and universities.

There are at present 102 universities besides 10 institutions of national importance and nine institutions deemed to be universities. These institutions are also deemed to be universities for the purposes of the University Grants Commission Act, 1956. Many of the research laboratories and institutions are recognised by the Association of Indian Universities as centres of higher research.

## RELIGION

The following Table shows the population of major religious communities along with their percentage to total population and the percentage increase during the decennium 1961–71.

| *Religious community* | 1961[1] *Population* | *Percentage to total population* | 1971 *Population* | *Percentage to total population* | *Percentage increase 1961–71*[3] |
|---|---|---|---|---|---|
| Hindus | 366,501,267 | 83·50 | 453,436,630 | 82·72 | 23·69 |
| Muslims | 46,939,791 | 10·70 | 61,418,269 | 11·20 | 30·84 |
| Christians | 10,726,373 | 2·44 | 14,225,045 | 2·60 | 32·58 |
| Sikhs | 7,845,170 | 1·79 | 10,378,891 | 1·89 | 32·28 |
| Buddhists | 3,250,227 | 0·74 | 3,876,947 | 0·71 | 17·33 |
| Jains | 2,027,267 | 0·46 | 2,604,837 | 0·48 | 28·49 |
| Others[2] | 1,608,118 | 0·37 | 2,221,038 | 0·40 | 19·62 |
| Total | 439,234,771 | 100·00 | 548,159,652 | 100·00 | 24·80 |

[1] 1961 figures exclude the figures for Arunachal Pradesh as the all-India census schedule was not canvassed throughout that Pradesh then.
[2] Includes figures for 'religion not stated.'
[3] Percentage increase (1961–71) of each religion has been calculated on comparative area figures of 1961–71.

# Indian States and Territories

## ANDHRA PRADESH

**Capital**—Hyderabad.

**Acting Governor**—Mrs. Sharda Mukherje.

**Area**: 276,814 sq. km.

**Territory.** The State of Andhra was founded on 1 October 1953. Under the reorganization, out of the composite Madras State, it received territory from Hyderabad.

**Population**: 43,502,708. The language of the people of the State is Telugu. Hyderabad, the capital, has a population of 2,787,693.

The principal languages are Telegu and Urdu.

**Legislature**: *Number of seats in Leglislative Council:* 90; *Number of seats in Legislative Assembly:* 287.

## ASSAM

**Capital**—Shillong.

**Governor**—L. P. Singh.

**Area**: 205,677 sq. km. (includes Meghalaya and NEFA).

**Territory.** The State of Assam comprises the former Province of Assam, the North-East Frontier Agency, the Khasi States and a number of other small Princely States. Its borders were unaffected by the States Reorganization Act, 1956.

**Population**: 14,625,159 (1971). Chief cities and towns with estimated populations (census of 1961): Shillong, 102,398; Gauhati, 100,707; Dibrugarh, 37,991; Silchar, 34,059; Nowgong, 28,257; Dhubri, 22,787; Barpeta, 21,137.

Principal languages are Assamese and Bengali.

**Legislature.** There is no Legislative Council in Assam. *Number of seats in Legislative Assembly:* 114.

**Education.** The University of Gauhati was established in 1948. In 1963, enrolment was 30,351. There are also 38 arts and science colleges, 12 professional colleges and one special education college.

There are about 20,000 schools, with 1·5 million pupils. The literacy rate is 27·4 per cent.

**North East Frontier Agency.** This territory is administered by the Governor of Assam. It has an area of 31,436 sq. miles and a population of 336,558.

## BIHAR

**Capital—Patna.**

**Governor**—Jagan Nath Kaushal.

**Area**: 173,876.

**Territory.** Under the Transfer of Territories Act (1956) West Bengal receives territory from Bihar, namely, part of Kishangunj, part of Gopalpur, a sub-division of the Manbhum District and the Patamda station of Police.

**Population**: 56,353,369. Chief cities and towns with provisional populations (census of 1961): Patna, 364,595; Jamshedpur, 328,044; Gaya, 151,105; Bhagalpur, 143,850; Ranchi, 140,253.

The principal language is Hindi.

**Legislature.** *Number of seats in Legislative Council:* 96; *Number of seats in Legislative Assembly:* 318.

**Education.** The University of Patna was established in 1917. The five other universities are Bihar University, Muzaffarpur; Bhalzapur University; Ranchi University; Darbhanga Sanskrit University; and Magadha University, Gaya.

There are about 37,000 primary schools, 4,500 middle schools and 1,500 high schools. There are also 230 schools for professional training.

The literacy rate is about 18 per cent.

## GUJARAT

**Capital**—Gandhinagar.

**Governor**—K. K. Viswanathan.

**Area**: 195,984 sq. km.

Established on 1 May 1960, following the division of the bilingual Bombay State, Gujarat comprises the former States of Saurashtra and Kutch and the Gujarati-speaking area in the north of the former Bombay State.

**Population**: 26,697,475 (1971). Chief cities with populations (1961 census): Ahmedabad, 1,206,001; Baroda, 298,398; Surat, 288,026; Rajkot, 194,145; Bhaunajar, 176,473; and Yamnagar, 148,572.

The principal language is Gujarati.

**Legislature.** There is no Legislative Council in Gujarat. *Number of seats in Legislative Assembly:* 182.

**Education.** There are three universities, Gujarat, Maharaja Sayajirao University and Sardar Vallabhbhai Vidyapeeth. There are about 55,000 university students. 18,500 primary schools, 1,100 secondary schools and 8,000 special schools have a total of about 2,800,000 pupils.

## HARYANA

**Capital**—Chandigarh.

Governor—H. S. Barar

**Territory.** Under the Punjab Reorganization Act 1966, the State of Haryana was formed on 1 November 1966 out of the Hindi-speaking areas of Punjab. It consists of the districts of Hissar, Mohindergarh, Gurgaon, Rohtak, Karmal, Ambala and Jind.

**Area**: 44,222 sq. km.

**Population**: 10,036,808.

**Legislature.** *Number of seats in Legislative Council:* —; *Number of seats in Legislative Assembly:* 81.

## HIMACHAL PRADESH

**Capital**—Simla.

**Governor**—Amin-ud-din.

**Territory.** Himchal Pradesh became a Union Territory in 1949. It originally consisted of the districts of Mahasu, Sirmur, Mandi, Chamba, Bilaspur and Kinnaur. Under the Punjab Reorganization Act, 1966 the Hill areas of Punjab were transferred to Himachal Pradesh, doubling its size and population.

**Area:** 55,673 sq. km.

**Population:** 3,460,434 (1971).

**Legislature.** *Number of seats in Legislative Council:* —; *Number of seats in Legislative Assembly:* 68.

**Education.** In 1964 there were six arts and science colleges, one professional college and two special education colleges.

## JAMMU AND KASHMIR

**Capital**—Srinagar, (Summer); Jammu, (Winter).

**Governor**—L. K. Jha

**Area and Population.** The total area of the state is 222,236 sq. km. and the population is 4,616,632, 80 per cent of whom are Moslem. The country is mainly agricultural and the Government has introduced a number of land reforms whereby land in excess of 22·75 acres has been transferred from the owner to the actual farmer. Forestry accounts for another large source of revenue, some 10,000 sq. miles of the territory being given over to it. Chief cities with populations: Srinagar, 295,084; Jammu, 02,738. The principal languages are Kashmiri, Dogri and Urdu.

**Legislature.** *Number of seats in Legislative Council:* 36; *Number of seats in Legislative Assembly:* 75.

**Education.** Since 1953, education has been free throughout the State from the Primary to the University stage. This has resulted in an increase by about 70 per cent in the amount budgeted for education. Over 150,000 students have benefited by this reform.

The University of Jammu and Kashmir, with 23 affiliated colleges, has about 10,500 students.

## KARNATAKA

**Capital**—Bangalore.

**Governor**—Giovind Narain.

**Area:** 191,773 sq. km.

**Territory.** The State of Mysore comprises the former Princely State of Mysore, more than doubled in size in 1956 by the addition of the Kannada-speaking area of Bombay, Hyderabad, Madras and Coorg.

**Population:** 29,299,014 (1972). Chief cities and towns with populations: Bangalore, 1,206,961; Mysore, 253,865; Hubli-Dharwai, 248,489; Kolar Mangalore, 170,253; Gold Field City, 146,811; Belgaum, 146,790. The principal language is Kannada.

**Legislature.** *Number of seats in Legislative Council:* 63; *Number of seats in Legislative Assembly:* 216.

**Justice.** There are, besides the High Court, 74 Criminal and 45 Civil Courts.

**Education.** The University of Mysore, with four university colleges and 66 affiliated colleges had 36,469 students in 1964. Other institutions of higher learning are Karnalak University at Dharwar, Bangalore University and the Indian Institute of Science, also at Bangalore. The literacy rate is about 25 per cent.

## KERALA

**Capital**—Trivandrum.

**Governor**—N. N. Wanchoo.

**Area:** 38,864 sq. km.

**Territory.** The State of Kerala was formed in 1956 out of most of the former Malayalam-speaking State of Travancore-Cochin, together with the Malabar District of Madras.

**Population:** 21,347,375 (1961). Chief cities and towns with populations: Cochin-Ernakulan-Alwaye, 313,030; Trivandrum, 302,314; Calicut, 248,548; Alleppey, 138,834. The chief language is Malayalam.

**Legislature.** There is no Legislative Council in Kerala. *Number of seats in Legislative Assembly:* 133.

**Education.** With 47 per cent literacy, Travancore-Cochin stands foremost among the Indian States in educational advancement. There are 45 Colleges (mostly affiliated to the Travancore University), including those for medical, engineering and other technical education, 613 High Schools, 855 Middle Schools, 4,219 Primary Schools, and about 175 special schools for various subjects in arts and crafts. More than 1,800,000 of the population of the State are school-going children. Another 28,000 youths undergo university education. Out of the children in the age-group of five to ten in the State, 95 per cent are actually attending schools.

## MADHYA PRADESH

**Capital**—Bhopal.

**Governor**—S. N. Sinha.

**Territory.** The State of Madhya Pradesh originally comprised the former central Provinces and Berar and 15 Princely States. In 1956 its borders were substantially redrawn. It lost territory in the south-west (Berar) to Bombay and acquired the former States of Bhopal, Madhya Bharat and Vindhya Pradesh, all originally Princely States or Unions of such States.

**Area:** 442,841 sq. km.

**Population:** 41,653,119. Chief cities and towns with populations: Indore, 394,941; Jabalpur, 367,014; Gwalior, 300,587; Bhopal, 222,948; Ujjain, 144,161; Raipur, 139,792.

The principal language is Hindi.

**Legislature.** Although the Constitution (Seventh Amendment) Act, 1956, provides for the creation of a Legislative Council in Madhya Pradesh, it has not yet been constituted in the State. *Number of seats in Legislative Assembly:* 296.

**Education.** There are eight universities—the University of Sangar (founded 1946), Jabalpur University (1957), Vikram University (1957), Indira Kala Sangeet Vishwavidyalaya (1958), Indore University (1963), Gawlior University (1963), Jabalpur Agricultural University (1963) and Ravishankar University (1964).

There are over 33,000 schools, with about 2·5 million pupils. The literacy rate is almost 17 per cent.

## MAHARASHTRA

**Capital**—Bombay.

**Governor**—Sardiq Abi.

**Territory.** Established on 1 May 1960 following the division of the bi-lingual Bombay State, Maharashtra comprises the area of the former Bombay State south and east of the Surat District (including Vidarbha).

**Area**: 307,762 sq. km.

**Population:** 50,412,235 1971). The principal language is Marathi.

**Legislature.** *Number of seats in Legislative Council:* 78; *Number of seats in Legislative Assembly:* 270.

**Education.** There are six universities. Bombay University, founded in 1857, is the oldest and largest.

There are almost 3,000 secondary schools and 25,000 primary schools, with a total enrolment of almost 5·5 million. The literacy rate is about 30 per cent.

## MANIPUR

**Capital**—Imphal.

**Governor**—L. P. Singh.

**Area:** 22,346 sq. km.

**Population:** (1963) 780,037. Chief cities and towns with populations (census of 1951): Imphal is the only town and has a population of 110,847.

**Legislature** Assembly 60.

**Education.** There are two Arts Colleges teaching up to the Degree Course. There are also 22 special education colleges and one professional college.

## MEGHALAYA

**Capital**—Shillong.

**Governor**—L. P. Singh.

**Area:** 22,489 sq. km.

**Population:** 1,011,699.

**Legislature**: Assembly 60.

## NAGALAND

**Capital**—Kohima.

**Governor**—L. P. Singh.

**Territory.** Under the Constitution (Thirteenth Amendment) Act 1962, the areas comprised in the Naga Hills–Tuensang Area, known by the name of Nagaland, became a separate State of the Union.

**Area:** 16,527 sq. km.

**Legislature**: Assembly 60.

**Population**: 516,449 (1971).

**Legislature.** There is no Legislative Council in Nagaland. *Number of seats in Legislative Assembly:* 52.

## ORISSA

**Capital**—Bhubaneswar.

**Governor**—Bhagwat Dayal Sharma.

**Area:** 155,842 sq. km.

**Population**: 21,944,615 (1971). Chief cities and towns: Cuttack (146,308 inhabitants); Puri, Bhubaneswar.

The principal language is Oriya.

**Legislature.** There is no Legislative Council in Orissa. *Number of seats in Legislative Assembly:* 147.

**Education.** In 1964 there were 33 arts and science colleges, 23 professional colleges and six special education colleges.

## PUNJAB

**Capital**—Chandigarh.

**Governor**—Mahendra Mohan Chaudhury.

**Territory.** By the Punjab Reorganization Act, 1966, the Punjab became a unilingual state. The predominantly Hindi-speaking areas were formed into the new state of Harjana, while the Hill areas merged with the contiguous state of Himachal Pradesh.

**Area**: 50,362 sq. km.

**Population**: 13,551,060 (1971). Chief cities with populations: Amritsar, 398,047; Jullundur, 265,030; Ludhiana, 244,032; Ambala, 181,747; Patiala, 125,234.

Principal language is Punjabi.

**Legislature.** The Legislative Council in Punjab was abolished, with effect from 7 January 1970. *Number of seats in Legislative Assembly:* 104.

**Education.** Punjab University at Chandigarh has 107 affiliated colleges. The other two universities are Kurukshetra University (established 1956) and Punjabi University at Patiala (1962). In 1963 there were about 900,000 pupils in secondary schools and 1·5 million in primary schools.

## RAJASTHAN

**Capital**—Jaipur.

**Governor**—Raghukul Tilak.

**Area**: 342,214 sq. km.

**Population**: 25,724,142 (1971). Chief cities and towns with populations (census of 1961): Jaipur, 403,444; Ajmer, 231,240; Jodhpur, 224,760; Bikaner, 150,634; Kotah, 120,345; Udaipur, 111,139.

Principal languages are Rajasthani and Hindi.

**Legislature.** There is no Legislative Council in Rajasthan. *Number of seats in Legislative Assembly:* 184.

**Education.** Rajasthan University, with four university colleges and 65 affiliated colleges, had 28,000 students in 1964. Other universities are Jodhpur University and Rajasthan Agricultural University.

## SIKKIM

**Capital**—Gangtok.

**Governor**—B. B. Lal.

The Himalayan State of Sikkim has an area of 2,745 sq. miles and a population of 209,843.

**Legislature**: Assembly 32.

**Finance.** Revenue is Rs. 10 million per year.

## TAMIL NADU

**Capital**—Madras.

**Governor**—Probhu Das Patwari.

**Territory.** The State of Tamil Nadu comprises the large Tamil-speaking remnant of the former Province of Madras. In 1953 it lost its northern areas to Andhra and in 1956 some of its western districts to Mydore and Kerala. It acquired, however, in 1956 a small Tamil-speaking portion of Travancore-Cochin.

**Area**: 130,069 sq. km.

**Population**: 41,199,168 (1971). Chief cities and towns with estimated populations (census of 1961): Madras, 1,729,141; Madurai, 424,810; Coimbatore, 286,305; Tiruchirrappalli, 249,862; Salem, 249,145; Palavamcottai, 190,048; Tuticorin, 127,356; Vellore, 122,761; Kurichi, 119,310; Thanjavur, 111,099; Nagercoil, 106,207.

The principal language is Tamil.

**Legislature.** *Number of seats in Legislative Council:* 63; *Number of seats in Legislative Assembly:* 234.

**Education.** The University of Madras was established in 1857 and had (in 1966) an enrolment of about 75,000 students. Annamalai University, established 1929, has over 3,000 students.

There are over 1,000 high schools, 23,500 primary schools and 3,600 basic schools, with a total enrolment of approximately 3,700,000 pupils.

The literacy rate is a little over 31 per cent.

## TRIPURA

**Capital**—Agartala.

**Governor**—L. P. Singh.

**Area**: 10,477 sq. km.

**Population**: 1,556,342. There are no large towns.

**Legislature.** *Number of seats in Legislative Council:* —. *Number of seats in Legislative Assembly:* 60.

**Education.** In 1964 there were two arts and science colleges, five professional colleges and one special education college.

## UTTAR PRADESH

**Capital**—Lucknow.

**Governor**—M. Channa Reddy.

**Territory.** The State of Uttar Pradesh comprises the former United Provinces and the Princely States of Benares, Tehri-Garhmal and Rampur.

**Area**: 294,413 sq. km.

**Population**: 88,341,144. Chief cities and towns with populations: Kanpur, 971,062; Lucknow, 655,673; Agra, 508,680; Varanasi, 489,864; Allahabad, 430,730; Meerut, 283,997; Bareilly, 272,828; Moradabadad, 191,828; Saharanpur, 185,213; Aligarh, 185,020; Gerakhpur, 180,255.

The principal language is Hindi.

**Legislature.** *Number of seats in Legislative Council:* 108; *Number of seats in Legislative Assembly:* 425.

**Universities.** The University of Agra, established in 1927, has an enrolment of 52,636 students. Enrolment in other universities in 1964 comprised Benares Hindu University, established 1916, 7,634; Lucknow University, established 1920, 14,711; Aligarh Muslim University, established 1916, 5,073; Roorkee University, established 1948, 1,838; Allahabad University, established 1887, 8,317.

## WEST BENGAL

**Capital**—Calcutta.

**Governor**—A. L. Dias.

**Area:** 87,853 sq. km.

**Population:** 44,312,011 (1971). Chief cities with populations: Calcutta, 2,927,289; Howrath, 512,598; South Suburbs, 341,712; Asansol, 168,689; Bhatpara, 147,630; Kharagpur, 147,253; Bally, 130,896; Kamarhatti, 125,457; South Dum Dum, 111,284.

The principal language is Bengali.

**Legislature.** The Legislative Council was abolished with effect from 1 August 1969. *Number of seats in Legislative Assembly:* 280.

**Education.** The University of Calcutta, established in 1857, had an enrolment of 119,542 during 1963–64. This figure includes the number of students of the University only and excludes the number of students of other colleges.

Other universities are Visva Bharati, the University of Jadarput, Burdwan University and Kalyani University.

# Union Territories

## ANDAMAN AND NICOBAR ISLANDS

**Chief Town**—Port Blair.

**Chief Commissioner**—S. M. Krishnatry.

This chain of islands, with an area of 8,293 sq. km., lies in the eastern part of the Bay of Bengal about 800 miles to the east and south-east of Madras. The total population is about 115,133 of whom two-thirds are to be found in the Andamans, where the majority live within a radius of 15 miles of Port Blair, the capital.

**Legislature**

There is no elected or nominated legislature; government is administered by the President of the Union of India acting through a Chief Commissioner and an Advisory Council of five members.

**Education.** There is a Government High School in Port Blair teaching students up to the Matriculation Standard. There are a number of Primary Schools in the villages. There is also a government-aided private institution called the Modern Preparatory School for children in Port Blair. For higher education, students have to go to the mainland of India.

## ARUNCHAL PRADESH

**Capital**—Itanacar.

**Lt.-Governor**—K. A. A. Raja.

**Area:** 83,578 Sq. km.

**Population:** 1,167,511.

## CHANDIGARH

**Headquarters**—Chandigarh.

**Chief Commissioner**—T. N. Chatuvredi

As a result of the Punjab Reorganization Act, 1966, the City of Chandigarh became a Union Territory. The city is also joint capital of the States of Punjab and Haryana.

Population of the Territory is 89,000.

**Area Approx.:** 115 sq. km.

**Population:** 257,251.

## DADRA AND NAGAR HAVELI

**Headquarters**—Silvassa.

**Administrator**—S. K. Banerji.

This territory was integrated with the Union of India on 11 August 1961. Principal languages are Gujorati and Portuguese.

**Area:** 491 sq. km.

**Population:** 74,170 (1971).

## DELHI

**Capital**—Delhi.

**Lieutenant Governor**—Kohli.

**Territory.** The Territory of Delhi comprises the cities of Old and New Delhi and the areas immediately surrounding them. Its area is 1,483 sq. km. and its population is 4,065,698.

Delhi became a Union Territory on 1 November 1956. It is administered by the Union Minister of Home Affairs with the aid of an Advisory Council.

**Finance.** Budget estimates for 1967–68 (in lakh Rs.) were: Revenue, 3630·8; Expenditure, 3778·93.

**Education.** About 51 per cent of the population are literate.

The University of Delhi, with 34 constituent colleges has about 23,000 students.

## GOA, DAMAN AND DIU

**Capital**—**Panaji.**

**Lt.-Governor**—S. K. Banerji.

The former Portuguese territory was united with India on 20 December 1961.

**Area:** 3,813 sq. miles.

**Population:** 857,771.

**Legislature.** *Number of seats in Legislative Council:* —. *Number of seats in Legislative Assembly:* 32.

## LAKSHADWEEP

**Chief Town**—Kavarathi.

**Administrator**—M. C. Verma.

This group of small islands lies between 100 and 200 miles off the south-west coast of India. The islands were, prior to 1956, administered by the State of Madras. Total area is 32 sq. km. and population is about 31,810. The Administrative Headquarters is at Kozhikode (formerly known as Calicut) in Kerala.

The principal language is Malayalam, but Mahl is spoken in Minicoy.

## MIZORAM

**Capital**—Aizawl.

**Lt. Governor**—S. P. Mukherjee.

**Area:** 21,087 sq. km.

## PONDICHERRY

**Capital**—Pondicherry.

**Lt.-Governor**—Kulkarni

The Government of India, in agreement with the Government of France, took over the administration of the French Establishments in India (Pondicherry, Karaikal, Yamam and Mahe) in 1954. A Treaty, ceding these territories to India, was signed in 1956 and ratified by the French Assembly in 1962. The total area is 480 sq. km. and the population 471,707. Principal languages are Tamil and French.

**Legislature.** *Number of seats in Legislative Council:* —. *Number of seats in Legislative Assembly:* 30.

# Indonesia

(REPUBLIK INDONESIA)

**President**—Gen. Soeharto.

**Capital**—Jakarta.

**National Flag:** Divided fesse-wise, red and white, in the proportion two to three.

## CONSTITUTION AND GOVERNMENT

THE Republic of Indonesia consists of the islands of Java, Sumatra, Kalimantan (except Sarawak, Brunei and Kucing) Sulawesi, and New Guinea except the Eastern part together with many thousands of smaller islands. Until 1945 these islands comprised the Netherlands East-Indies, which were governed by the mother country.

A Round Table Conference held at The Hague, 1949, ended the state of 4½ years of intermittent fightings and negotiations between the Netherlands and Indonesia. It resulted in the recognition by the Netherlands Government of the irrevocable and complete sovereignty of Indonesia, on 29 December 1949.

The status of West-Irian, now called Irian-Jaya (the Indonesian name for West New-Guinea), which was part of the former Netherlands East-Indies, was to be determined by further negotiations between the two sovereign states within 12 months after the recognition of Indonesian sovereignty. Negotiations on this problem failed, resulting in a unilateral abrogation of the Round Table Agreements by Indonesia, early in 1956. Indonesia twice attempted through the United Nations General Assembly sessions, in 1956 and 1957, to get the negotiations reopened. During 1962 negotiations reached, in August, a settlement by which the administration of West-Irian would be carried on for interim period by a United Temporary Executive Authority (U.N.T.E.A.) and in May 1963 would pass to Indonesia. After an act of Free Choice was held in that territory, under the auspices of the U.N., the U.N. General Assembly in its 24th session, held on 6 November 1969, took note of the official return of that territory of West-Irian to the Republic of Indonesia.

A Netherlands-Indonesian Union having no organ of power was set up (at the same time as the recognition of sovereignty), and it was agreed that a Union Conference should take place twice each year to solve any mutual problems.

According to the (Dutch) 1949 Constitution, Indonesia was a Federation of States; this became unitary on 15 August 1950 which constituted a return to the original Republican Constitution of 1945.

Indonesia at present is divided into 27 Provinces, with regional autonomy granted according to the natural division of the country. The following is the division of the territory into 22 first level autonomous regions: East-, Central- and West-Java; Aceh; North- and West-Sumatra; Riau; Djambi; South-Sumatra; Central-, West-, South- and East-Kalimantan; North, Central, South, South-West and South-East Sulawesi; Bali; West-Nusa Tenggara; East-Nusa Tenggara; Maluku; Irian-Jaya; the special Territory of Jakarta Raya; and the special Territory of Yogyakarta.

The Senate, which consisted of delegates from the former constituent States of the Federation, was abolished with the formation of the Unitary State. Since unification, legislative power has been vested in the single chamber of the House of Representatives.

Indonesia's first General Elections took place on 29 September 1955, when 82 per cent of all registered voters came to the polls, while voters of 34 out of 208 electoral regencies were allowed to vote at a later date. Elections to form a Constituent Assembly to draft a Constitution took place on 16 December 1955, three months after the first General Elections.

The Western type of parliamentary democracy followed so far was not suitable for Indonesia.

In trying to find a way out, a new concept of democracy was introduced based on the traditional principle of 'musjawarah and mufakat' which is 'consultation and agreement'. Neither the term 'guided democracy' nor the political ideas it connotes are new, but were enunciated by the pre-war Nationalist Movements.

When the Constituent Assembly failed to reach a two-thirds majority of voters on the recommendation of the Government to return to the Constitution of 1945, President Sukarno by special decree on 5 July 1959, ordered the re-application of the 1945 Constitution and at the same time the dissolving of the Constituent Assembly.

In January 1960, President Sukarno took control of the political parties. He also set up a supreme State body called the People's Consultative Assembly, as stipulated in the 1945 Constitution, consisting of the members of the current House of Representatives, plus representatives of the regions and the functional groups, and entrusted with the task of mapping out the broad lines of State policy. In March 1960, Parliament was prorogued, to be organized on the basis of the 1945 constitution.

An attempt by the communists to overthrow the government in September 1965 was suppressed by the army, and on 18 October the Communist Party was banned.

Dr. Sukarno was declared President for life by the Consultative Assembly in May 1963. This title was abolished, however, on 5 July 1966 by a decision of the fourth session of the Provisional People's Consultative Assembly. On 25 July General Soeharto became Commander-in-Chief for the Restoration of Order and Security, and in February 1967 Dr. Sukarno handed over all his powers to Gen. Soeharto. In March 1968 General Soeharto was elected President of the Republic by the provisional People's Consultative Assembly.

The Cabinet is headed by President General Soeharto, assisted by Sri Sultan Hamengkubuwono as Vice-President. In addition, there are 18 full Ministers, each heading a department, and four Ministers of State.

The results announced on the 13 May 1977 for the General Election held on 2 May 1977 were as follows: Persatuan Partai Pembangunan, 18,350,141; Golkar, 39,078,426; Pari Demokrasi Indonesia, 5,445,413.

### Composition of the Indonesian Development Cabinet

*Minister of Home Affairs:* Lt. Gen. Amir Machmud.
*Minister of Foreign Affairs:* H. Adam Malik.
*Minister of Defence and Security concurrently Commander in Chief of the Armed Forces:* General Maraden Panggabean.
*Minister of Justice:* Dr. Mochtar Kusumaatmadja.
*Minister of Information:* Mashuri, LLD.
*Minister of Finance:* Prof. Dr. Ali Wardhana.
*Minister of Trade:* Drs. Radius Prawiro.
*Minister of Agriculture:* Prof. Dr. Ir. Thojib Hadiwidjaja.
*Minister of Industry:* Lt. Gen. Mohammad Jusuf.
*Minister of Mining Affairs:* Prof. Dr. Ir. Mohammad Sadli.
*Minister of Public Works and Electric Power:* Ir. Sutami.
*Minister of Communications:* Prof. Dr. Emil Salim.
*Minister of Education and Culture:* Dr. Sjarif Thayeb.
*Minister of Health:* Prof. Dr. G. A. Siwabessy.
*Minister of Religious Affairs:* Prof. Dr. H. A. Mukti Ali.
*Minister of Social Affairs:* H. M. S. Mintaredja, LLD.
*Minister of Manpower, Transmigration and Co-operatives:* Prof. Dr. Soebroto.
*Minister of State for Economic, Financial and Industrial Affairs, concurrently Chairman of the National Development Planning Body (BAPPENAS):* Prof. Dr. Widjojo Nitisastro.
*Minister of State for Public Welfare:* Prof. Dr. Sunawar Sukowati.
*Minister of State for Administrative Reforms and concurrently Vice-Chairman of BAPPENAS:* Dr. J. B. Sumarlin.
*Minister of State for the coordination of Research:* Prof. Dr. Soemitro Djojohadikoesoemo.
*Minister of State for Administrative and Financial Affairs of Non-Departmental Government Agencies and concurrently State Secretary:* Sudharmono, LLD.

## AREA AND POPULATION

The twin islands of Java and Madura have a population of approximately 76,102,406 people to-day. The average density per square km. is about 565 on the two islands, while on some parts of the islands the figure increases to about 1,000 per square mile. On the other hand, the average density for Sumatra is only 38 per sq. km., and for Kalimantan only 7·6 per sq. km.

The population at mid-1974 was 128,400,000. The annual average percentage growth rate of the population for the period 1960–74 was 2·1, and for the period 1965–74 was 2·3.

The following table shows the areas of various parts of Indonesia with their approximate populations:

| *Territory* | *Area (sq. kilometres)* | *Population* |
|---|---|---|
| West-Java | 49,118 | 21,600,000 |
| Central-Java | 34,503 | 21,800,000 |
| East-Java | 47,366 | 25,500,000 |
| Java alone has a population of | 130,987 | 69,000,000 |
| Sumatra | 541,174 | 20,800,000 |
| Kalimantan (Borneo) | 550,848 | 5,100,000 |
| Sulawesi (Celebes) | 277,654 | 8,000,000 |
| Maluku (Moluccas) | 83,675 | 1,000,000 |
| Irian-Jaya (W. Irian) | 412,781 | 900,000 |
| Bali | 5,623 | 2,100,000 |
| West Nusa Tenggara | 21,740 | 2,200,000 |
| East Nusa Tenggara | 48,889 | 2,200,000 |
| Total | 2,027,087 | 119,200,000 |

## CURRENCY

The monetary unit is the rupiah which is divided into 100 sen. An export premium of Rp. 9·25 is given on every U.S. dollar or hard currency equivalent paid to the Government for export proceeds. There are special exchange rates for foreign tourists.

## FINANCE

As from 1 April 1969, Indonesia entered into its first year of implementation of its first Five Year Development Plan and on 1 April 1973 entered its last year of implementation of its first Five Year Development Plan. The Second Five Year Development Plan commenced on 1 April 1974. In this context, the financial policies are designed to further encourage and accelerate the expansion of production to create more employment opportunities, more equal distribution of development gains, and the financing of social services while remaining committed to maintaining stability.

The total state revenue for 1972–73 was Rp. 573,600,000,000 and the total State expenditure was Rp. 437,500,000,000.

The GNP at market prices for 1974 U.S.$millions 21,780, and the GNP per capita at market prices was U.S. $170. The annual average percentage growth rate of the GNP per capita for the period 1960–74 was 2·1, and for the period 1965–73 was 4·1. [*See the note at the beginning of this section concerning GNP.*]

## BANKS

**Bank Bumi Daya.** (President, R. A. B. Massie S.H.; Managing Directors, Martojo Koento, R. Prasodjo, R. S. Natalegwa.) Established 1959 as Bank Umum Negara; on 17 August 1965 name changed to Bank Negara Indonesia Unit IV; on 31 December 1968 name changed as above. A State-owned commercial bank. Balance Sheet at 31 March 1973 showed total assets Rp. 274,342,671,000; capital paid up Rp. 300,000,000; reserves Rp. 6,252,847,000; deposits Rp. 130,336,808,000. *Head Office:* Djl Kebonsirih 66–70, P.O. Box 106, Djakarta. Cable address: Bunegpusat; Bunegluar for Head Office International Dept. Telex No. 0114277 (Head Office). Overseas representative offices: 50–53 Caxton House, 1 Duddell Street, Hong Kong; Max Havelaarlaan 121, 2nd floor Amstelveen, and Frederiksplein 1, Netherlands; 66–68 Cecil Street, Singapore. 50 branches in Indonesia.

**Bank Nusantara.** Capital Rp. 2,000,000. *Head Office:* 18 Purwodinatan Tengah, Semarang.

**The HongKong and Shanghai Banking Corporation.** Branch and sub-office in Jakarta. See Hong Kong.

**Indonesian Mercantile Bank Ltd.** *Head Office:* 33 Kebon Sirih, Djakarta.

**N.V. Bank Djakarta.** Capital Rp. 5,000,000. *Head Office:* 22–23 Asemka, Djakarta, Indonesia.

**The Indonesian National Commercial Bank Ltd.** *Head Office:* Djl. Sutomo 314, Medan, Sumatra.

**Bank Pembangunan Indonesia** (State Bank for development, incorporating former Bank Industri Negara). *Head Office:* 2–4 Gondangdia Lama. President: Mr. Kuntoadji, Managing Director: Mr Priasmoro Prawiroardjo.

**Bank Pembangunan Swasta** (Finances private development in the productive sector).

**American Express Bank.**

**Citibank, N.A.** (Vice-President, J. J. Collins). Branches in Indonesia, established in 1968. *Head Office:* P.O. Box 2463, Djakarta.

## PRODUCTION, INDUSTRY AND COMMERCE

**Forestry.** During the last five years an inventory was made of forest area in Indonesia. The following table shows the result of this survey:

| *Survey Type* | *Hectares* | *Percentage of the total acreage of forest land* |
|---|---|---|
| 1. Air survey | 15,531,000 | 11% |
| 2. Field survey | 31,500,000 | 25% |
| 3. Air photo estimates | 14,732,000 | 8% |

In the last four years (1969–72) 76,000 hectares of forest land have been replanted, while afforestation has been carried out on 470,000 hectares. The replanting and rehabilitation of forest land are meant to increase timber production. Efforts have been made to minimize the dangers of both floods and droughts.

**Livestock.** The development of animal husbandry is important for increasing food supplies, such as meat, eggs and milk. Animal husbandry also contributes to Indonesia's foreign exchange earnings. Livestock is mostly produced by small holders.

The following table shows the meat production figures for 1970–73 in 1000 kg units, and the percentage growth for the years 1968–73:

| *Kind of Meat* | 1970 | 1971 | 1972[1] | 1973[2] | *Average growth* 1968–1973 (%) |
|---|---|---|---|---|---|
| Cow | 167,285 | 177,176 | 196,080 | 213,882 | 5·5 |
| Buffalo | 49,176 | 52,083 | 57,127 | 62,954 | 5·3 |
| Goat | 12,200 | 12,921 | 13,915 | 15,435 | 6·0 |
| Sheep | 10,304 | 10,986 | 12,206 | 12,206 | 5·6 |
| Hog | 34,655 | 36,764 | 38,620 | 41,355 | 4·8 |
| Horse | 7,784 | 830 | 732 | 807 | 2·8 |
| Fowl | 39,736 | 42,086 | 48,140 | 66,848 | 7·7 |
| Total | 313,621 | 332,164 | 365,600 | 403,487 | 5·7 |

[1] Corrected Figures.
[2] Provisional Figures.

The following table shows the agricultural production figures for a few commodities for three years:

| *Year* | *Meat* | *Milk* | *Eggs* |
|---|---|---|---|
| | *tons* | *litres* | |
| 1970 | 313,621 | 29,304,000 | 1,054,920,000 |
| 1971 | 314,017 | 67,125,000 | 1,323,540,000 |
| 1972 | 354,251 | 37,694,000 | 1,711,900,000 |

# INDONESIA

**Agriculture.** Rice is the most important staple food of Indonesia. Priority is given to the production of rice. The production of rice between the years 1968–1971 showed an increase. However in 1972 a severe drought led to a decrease especially in the regions of Central-Java, South Sulawesi, South Sumatra, East Nusa Tenggara, and other regions. The rice area in 1972 that suffered from drought and floods was 160,000 hectares.

The following table shows the average paddy yields in quintals per hectare for the years 1970–73:

| | 1970 | 1971 | 1972 | 1973[1] |
|---|---|---|---|---|
| Java | 35·17 | 36·65 | 35·78 | 37·36 |
| Outside Java | 26·45 | 26·12 | 27·52 | 29·39 |
| Indonesia | 31·06 | 31·70 | 32·00 | 33·73 |

[1] Provisional figures.

The following table gives some output figures for legumes for the years 1970–73:

| *Year* | *Harvested area 1,000 ha* | | *Average yields Quintal/ha* | | *Production 1,000 tons* | |
|---|---|---|---|---|---|---|
| | *Peanuts* | *Soybeans* | *Peanuts* | *Soybeans* | *Peanuts* | *Soybeans* |
| 1970 | 380 | 695 | 7.40 | 7·17 | 281 | 498 |
| 1971 | 376 | 680 | 7·55 | 7·59 | 284[1] | 516 |
| 1972[1] | 354 | 697 | 7·97[1] | 7·43 | 282 | 518 |
| 1973[2] | 407 | 751 | 7·45 | 5·94 | 303 | 446 |

[1] Corrected figures.
[2] Provisional figures.

**Fisheries.** The catch of sea fish for the years 1970–71 was 802,000 tons and 824,000 tons respectively, that for fresh water fish was 447,000 tons and 402,000 tons respectively.

**Mining.** The following table shows the relative and absolute production figures for 1970–71, and 1971–72:

| | *Unit* | 1970–71 | 1971–72 | % *Increase* |
|---|---|---|---|---|
| Crude oil | million barrels | 324·2 | 341·5 | 5·3 |
| Tin | thousand tons | 19·1 | 20·5 | 7·3 |
| Coal | ,, | 175·4 | 196·8 | 12·2 |
| Bauxite | ,, | 1,207·7 | 1,288·1 | 6·6 |
| Nickel | ,, | 689 | 850 | 23·4 |
| Gold | kilograms | 225·4 | 343·4 | 34·4 |
| Silver | tons | 9·2 | 8·1 | 12·0 |
| Iron sand | thousand tons | — | 298·5 | — |

**Industry.** The following table shows industrial production for the year 1973–74:

| *Item* | *Thousands of indicated unit* | 1973–74 |
|---|---|---|
| Batteries | pc | 140 |
| Radios | set | 900 |
| Television sets | set | 70 |
| Electric bulbs | pc | 16,000 |
| Sewing machines | | 500 |
| Motorcars | | 36 |
| Motor cycles | | 132,000 |
| Dry Batteries | | 132,000 |
| Galv. iron sheets | ton | 70 |
| Steel wire | ton | 30 |
| Steel pipe | ton | 80 |
| Concrete, iron | ton | 120 |

## COMMUNICATIONS

The total length of railways open to public traffic in 1963 was 6,640 km. The number of passengers carried was about 125,000,000, and the freight about 5,000,000 tons.

The upgrading targets on roads for 1969 covered 2,156·7 km of roads and 236 bridges. Satisfactory progress has been made. Various highways, particularly those in West Java have been completed or nearing completion, such as the highways between Djakarta–Tijirebon, Djakarta–Bandung and many others in Central and East Java.

The Government has created a State inter-island shipping line, PELNI, which took over the service operated by the Dutch Royal Steam Packet Company.

The rivers of East Sumatra and Kalimantan (Borneo) form an important means of communication. Because their upper reaches have not been fully explored in many cases, exact figures are not readily available. The River Rokan is over 120 miles long and is navigable for 70 miles; the Kampar is navigable for 18 miles by very large vessels; the Djambi has a maximum navigability of 500 miles and the Musi is navigable for 54 miles by large vessels and has a maximum navigability of 330 miles. In Borneo the Kapuas is navigable by small steamers up to approx. 400 miles. The other great rivers of Borneo, the Barito (with its associated rivers) and the Kurei are navigable for a great part of their length but no exact figures are available.

During 1954 the Indonesian Government virtually nationalized the Garuda Indonesian Airways which was formerly a mixed enterprise with the K.L.M. Royal Dutch Air Lines holding 50 per cent of the shares. In March 1954 a revised agreement was signed enabling the Indonesian Government to purchase the K.L.M. shares for 15 million guilders.

Besides internal services there are flights to Manila, Bangkok, Hong Kong, Tokyo, Karachi, Cairo, Rome and Amsterdam.

## NEWSPAPERS

**Kompas.** F. 1965. Morning daily. Circulation: 249,253. Printed in Indonesia. P.O. Box 615, 7AK.

**Angkatan Bersendjata.** Djakarta.

**Meredeka.** Djakarta.

**Pikiran Rakjat.** Daily. Circulation: 50,000. Jalan Asia-Afrika 77 Bandung.

**Suara Merdeka.** General Newspaper. Published daily except Sundays. Circulation: 60,000. Jalan Merak II a Semarang.

**Berita Yuda.** Djalan Lapangan Banteng. Barat 22, Djakarta.

**Sinar Harapan.** Daily. Djl. Pintu Besar Selatan No. 93, Djakarta-Kota.

**Warta Minggu.** Djakarta, (Sunday) 35,000.

**Warta Harian.** Daily. Circulation 45,000. Chief-editor: Marcus Rebong. 29 Sukardjowirjopranoto, Djakarta.

## ATOMIC ENERGY

Development work on an atomic energy programme is at present being carried out at Bandung, Bogor, Djakarta and Jogjakarta. Consideration is being given to the construction of training and research reactors at Bandung and Jogjakarta, which would serve as the centres for a nuclear research and training programme. Considerable efforts are being made by Indonesian officials, scientists and members of the university faculties, but outside assistance will be required to carry out the development programme for the utilization of atomic energy in agriculture, medicine and industry. A nuclear reactor is being built at Bandung under the 'Atoms for Peace' programme of the U.S.A. (began March 1964).

Considerable agricultural research is being carried out both at Bogor and at Gadjah Mada University.

Possible future developments in the field of medicine are the establishment of a radioisotope therapy laboratory at the projected Cancer Institute at Djakarta, and of a second laboratory and measurement clinic for diagnostic studies in the Djakarta Centra Hospital.

In 1958 the Government established a Council for Atomic Energy to advise them about developments in this field. An Institute of Atomic Energy has also been formed to regulate and supervise all nuclear energy matters in Indonesia. The Institute is under the direct supervision of the President.

In July 1965 the Institute for Atomic Energy was upgraded to Ministry level and renamed the National Atomic Energy Agency.

## EDUCATION AND RELIGION

In all the State Universities the use of Bahasa Indonesian as the language of instruction is obligatory but foreign lecturers are allowed to use English besides Bahasa-Indonesian.

The following table gives some educational statistics for the years 1970–73:

| | 1970 | 1971 | 1972 | 1973 |
|---|---|---|---|---|
| Dept. of Ed. and Culture: | 190,905 | 205,400 | 218,640 | 231,420 |
| Public | 116,805 | 124,400 | 128,650 | 131,350 |
| Private | 74,180 | 81,000 | 89,990 | 100,070 |
| Non Dept. of Ed. and Culture: | 89,980 | 91,865 | 94,700 | 97,880 |
| Public | 53,660 | 55,465 | 57,480 | 59,045 |
| Private | 36,320 | 36,400 | 37,220 | 38,835 |
| Total Public | 170,465 | 179,865 | 186,130 | 190,395 |
| Total Private | 110,500 | 117,400 | 127,210 | 138,905 |
| Total | 280,965 | 297,265 | 313,340 | 329,300 |

Most Indonesians are Muslims, but there are also Hindus and Bhuddists, and there are important Christian groups all over the archipelago. In line with the Pantca Sila, all religions are respected and protected.

# Iran

## (PERSIA)

Capital—Tehran.

Sovereign—Mohammad Reza Pahlavi Ariyamehr, Shahanshah of Iran.

**National Flag**: Length to width 3:1, a tricolour fesse-wise, green, white, red.

## CONSTITUTION AND GOVERNMENT

PRIOR to 1906 the Shah of Persia ruled with despotic power. Owing to discontent with a deficient and corrupt administration, a revolutionary movement became active and the Shah eventually acceded to the popular demand and granted a constitution. This provided for the establishment of a legislature consisting of two Houses, the Senate and a National Assembly (*Majlis*).

After World War I the country was in a state of disorder, but a strong man arose in the person of Reza Khan, who became Prime Minister and re-established order. The reigning Shah, who had been absent from the country for some years, was finally deposed by the *Majlis* in 1925 and Reza Khan Pahlavi was elected Shah. After the Nazi attack on the U.S.S.R. in 1941 the Allies intervened and British and Soviet forces entered the country. The Shah abdicated on 16 September 1941 and left the country. He was succeeded by his son Mohammad Reza Pahlavi, who agreed to rule as a constitutional monarch. His coronation took place on 26 October 1967.

The *Majlis* consists of 268 members, who are elected by direct and secret ballot. The Shah appoints the Prime Minister who forms the Council of Ministers which must have the approval of the *Majlis*. The Senate has 60 members, half of whom are appointed by the Shah and the other half elected.

**Reigning Royal Family.** Moslem (Shiites). Reza Shah Pahlavi; born 18 March 1878; died 26 July 1944. Entered the service of the Persian Cossack Brigade in 1900 and became Sardar-Sepah (commander-in-chief of the army) and Minister of War in 1921 and President of the Council in 1923. After the deposition of Shah Ahmed of the former dynasty of the Kadjars, he became regent of the Persian Empire and head of the provisional government, 31 October 1925. He was elected hereditary sovereign by the national constituent assembly, 12 December 1925, ascended the throne 14 December 1925, and was crowned 25 April 1926.

**H.I.M. MOHAMMAD REZA PAHLAVI ARYAMEHR,** Shahinshah of Persia; born at Tehran, 26 October 1919, son of Reza Shah Pahlavi (born 18 March 1878, died 26 July 1944); succeeded to the throne on his father's abdication 16 September 1941; married firstly at Tehran, 16 March 1939 (marriage dissolved by divorce at Cairo, 19 November 1948), Princess Fawzieh (born at Alexandria, 5 November 1921), daughter of Ahmed Fouad I, King of Egypt; secondly at Tehran, 12 February 1951; (marriage dissolved by divorce at Tehran, 6 April 1958), Soraya, daughter of Khalil Esfandiari Bakhtiari; thirdly at Tehran, 21 December 1959, Farah Diba, daughter of late Captain Suhrab Diba.

Daughter by first marriage: Princess SHAHNAZ Pahlavi; born at Tehran, 27 October 1940; married at Tehran, 12 October 1957, Ardeshir Zahedi, and has issue. Son by third marriage: Prince REZA Pahlavi; born at Tehran, 31 October 1960, proclaimed Crown Prince, 6 November 1960; Princess Farah Naz; born at Tehran, 12 March 1963; Prince Ali Reza; born at Tehran, 1966; Princess Leila; born at Tehran, 1970.

The Imperial Family: 1. Princess SHAMS Pahlavi; born at Tehran, 18 October 1917; married. 2. Princess ASHRAF Pahlavi; born at Tehran, 26 October 1919 (twin with the Shah); married. 3. The late Prince ALI REZA Pahlavi; born at Tehran, 1 April 1922; killed in a plane crash, 26 October 1954. 4. Prince GHOLAM REZA Pahlavi; born at Tehran, 14 May 1923; married. 5. Prince ABDOL REZA Pahlavi; born 1924; married. 6. Prince AHMAD REZA Pahlavi; born 1925; married. 7. Prince MAHMUD REZA Pahlavi; born 1926; married. 8. Princess FATIMEH Pahlavi; born 1930; married. 9. Prince HAMID REZA Pahlavi; born 1932; married.

### Cabinet

*Prime Minister:* Amir Abbas Hoveyda.
*Foreign Minister:* Abbas Ali Khalatbari.
*War Minister:* Gen. Reza Azimi.
*Minister of the Interior and Employment:* Amir Ghassen Moini.
*Minister of Economic and Financial Affairs:* H. Ansari.
*Minister of Information and Tourism:* Karimpasha Bahadori.
*Minister of Education:* Manouchehr Ganji.
*Minister of Science and Higher Education:* Abdol Hosain Samii.

*Minister of Mines and Industries:* Farrokh Najmabadi.
*Minister of Co-operatives and Rural Affairs:* Reza Sadaghiani.
*Minister of Posts, Telephones and Telegraphs:* Karim Motamedi.
*Minister of Trade:* Manoochehr Taslimi.
*Minister of Housing and City Planning:* Homayoun J. Ansari.
*Minister of Social Affairs:* Amir Ghassem Moieni.
*Minister of Agriculture and National Resources:* Mansur Rouhani.
*Minister of Energy:* Iraj Vahidi
*Minister of State and Head of Plan and Budget Organization:* Abdul Majid Majidi.
*Minister of Roads:* Ibrahim Farahbakshan.
*Minister of Health:* Shojaeddin Sheikh Al Eslamzadeh.
*Minister of Arts and Culture:* Mehrdad Pahlbod.
*Minister of Justice:* Gholamrez Kianpour.
*Minister of Labour:* Manouchehr Azeman.
*Minister Without Portfolio:* Ezatollah Yazdanpanah.
*Minister Without Portfolio:* Manuchehr Kalali.
*Minister of State and Executive Assistant to Prime Minister:* Hadi Hedayati.
*Minister of State:* Safi Asfia.

## LOCAL GOVERNMENT

For purposes of local government Iran is at present divided into 14 numbered Provinces, each under a Governor-General, and 9 counties, each under a Governor. Each Province (*Ustan*) is divided into Sub-Provinces (*Shahrestan*) and Districts (*Bakhsh*).

## LEGAL SYSTEM

The judicial system is modelled on that of France. There is a Court of Cassation, which sits at Teheran, and several district courts of appeal. Minor cases and civil cases are dealt with by justices of the peace and magistrates.

In the field of judicial administration Equity Courts and Arbitration councils have been set up whose members are directly elected by the people. Both institutions serve as civil courts, handling over 80 per cent of petty cases.

*President of the Supreme Court:* Emad-ud-Din Mir Mutahhari.

## AREA AND POPULATION

The total area of Iran is 628,000 sq. miles.

The population in mid-1974 was 33,100,000.

The annual average percentage growth rate of the population for the period 1960–74 was 3·3, and for the period 1965–74 was 3·2.

The latest estimates of population for the larger towns are: Tehran, 3,923,000; Tabriz, 477,000; Isfahan, 546,000; Mashad, 533,000; Abadan, 300,000; Shiraz, 340,000.

## CURRENCY

The unit of currency is the *Rial*. There are metal coins of 1, 2, 5, 10 and 20 rials and banknotes in denominations from 50 to 10,000 rials issued by the Central Bank.

## FINANCE

Budget estimates for 1971–72, 1970–71 (in million rials) were 548·5 and 454·3 respectively.

The fiscal year extends from 21 March to 20 March.

The GNP at market prices for 1974 was U.S. $ millions 41,440, and the GNP oer capita at market prices was U.S. $1,250. The annual average percentage growth rate of the GNP per capita for the period 1960–74 was 6·7 and for 1965–74 was 7·7. [*See the note at the beginning of this section concerning GNP.*]

## PRINCIPAL BANKS

A Central Bank was created by a law (the Monetary and Banking Law), approved on 28 May 1960. Mr. Mohammed Yeganeh is the Governor. Balance Sheet of Central Bank at 20 March 1974 showed: assets (billions Rs.) 599·5; deposits (Government) Rs. 128, Municipalities and other Government Agencies, Rs. 25, Banks, Rs. 83·1, capital, Rs. 5 notes issued, Rs. 103.

**Bank Bimeh Iran.** Established 1958. (President, Dr. Mohammad Reza Tehrani.) Assets as at 21 May 1975, Rls. 15,694,823,975; deposits and current accounts, sight deposits: Rls. 4,932,963,483, time deposits: Rls. 3,610,014,255. *Head Office:* 420 N. Saadi Ave., Tehran 11, Iran. 44 Branches.

**The Bank of Iran & The Middle East.** Established 1959. (Chief Executive & General Manager, Mr. M. H. Vakili; Chairman, Dr. G. H. Khoshbin.) Assets as at 20 March 1975, Rls. 11,007,383,031; deposits and current accounts 8,322,928,080. *Head Office:* Avenue Ferdowsi, Kucheh Berlin, P.O. Box 1680 Tehran. Branches 12; Provincial Branches 7.

**The Irano British Bank.** Established 1958. (Chairman & Managing Director, H. E. Abbas Gholi Neysari.) Assets as at 20 March 1977, Rls. 8,594,416,928; deposits and current accounts Rls. 11,332,141,639. *Head Office:* 638 Avenue Saadi, P.O. Box 1584, Tehran. 22 Branches.

**Bank Melli Iran.** Established 1928. (President, Youssof Khoshkish.) Assets as at 21 May 1975 (including contra accounts totalling Rls 102,660,383,592) Rls 431,812,288,725; deposits and current accounts Rls 281,938,782,965. *Head Office:* Ferdowsi Ave, Tehran. 1,500 Branches.

## PRODUCTION, INDUSTRY AND COMMERCE

**Agriculture.** Iran is still mainly an agricultural country though industrialization is taking place at a considerable rate. Most years there is enough food produced for home consumption, and in good years there is a considerable quantity for export. Crop land area is estimated at 18 million hectares. Much more land than this is cultivated at different times, but labour and water are limited and it is not all bearing at the same time. About a third of the area cultivated is dependent on irrigation. Irrigation methods used to consist only of ditches cut on gentle slopes to bring water from higher ground, animal lifts from wells and, where the slopes are steep, tunnels carrying water from the heights. The town of Kerman is supplied with its entire water supply by one such tunnel. Today a great deal of dam building, both for irrigation and electricity generation, has taken place and is being continued on a wide scale.

The main cereals are wheat, barley and rice. Cotton, sugarbeet and tobacco are the main commercial crops, cotton being the most important.

Production of the main crops in 1970–71 (thousand metric tons) was: wheat, 3,800; rice, 1,060; cotton, 450; sugar beet, 4,000; tea (dried), 13.

Livestock in the country is estimated at: cattle, 5,230,000; sheep, 31,130,000; asses and horses, 474,000; camels, 198,000; goats, 13,380,000.

Fruit grown includes apricots, mulberries, plums and grapes; vegetables include cucumbers, tomatoes, melons, pumpkins and gourds.

**Fishing.** The National Fisheries Company and the Southern Fisheries Company, both Government agencies, are responsible for the fishing industry in the Caspian and the Persian Gulf respectively. Exports of caviar were worth about 420 million rials in 1969–70. The production of caviar from the Caspian Sea was about 200 tons in 1973.

**Mining.** Iran is rich in minerals and the present modest exploitation is likely to be considerably expanded in the coming years. Principal exports are lead, zinc and chromite, with silver occurring as a by-product of the lead and zinc smelting. There are extensive reserves of copper, also of iron ore and coal which will be used for Iran's nascent iron and steel industry. Mercury, molybdenum and gold occur and the geology also favours tin. Limestone, marble, travertine and phosphate deposits occur widely.

**Oil.** Until the passing of the oil nationalisation law on 1 May 1951, Iranian oil was the property of the Anglo-Iranian Oil Company under a concession from the Iranian Government. Following the passing of the law, however, British members of the staff were gradually withdrawn until the last one had left by 4 October in the same year.

In 1971, 263·4 million long tons of crude oil were produced.

The arrangement between the Consortium and the National Iranian Oil Company continues. It is that the Consortium pays the Company for all oil required for export. The payment is made in kind in crude oil up to a certain percentage of the total export. Oil and oil products for internal consumption in Iran are to be sold to the Company substantially at cost. The Company undertakes to produce a certain proportion of oil for domestic needs, and to organise the distribution of oil and oil products internally. In 1971 Iran's income from the export of oil, including oil delivered to the N.I.O.C., was about 160,000 million Rls of which 80 per cent was allocated to the Plan Organization and the balance between the N.I.O.C. and the Ministry of Finance. Total oil production in 1969 was 168 million metric tons.

As from 21 March 1973 Iran took over all downstream operations.

**Industrial Development.** Industrial development in Iran dates from 1934. Previously, industry was confined to small workshops producing foodstuffs and clothing. The most important industry was carpet weaving. There is now larger scale production of textiles, food, chemicals, cement and light metal and many other important basic and secondary industries have been and are being established.

The Fourth (Five Year) Plan began in early 1968. It provides for the expenditure of 568,000 million Rials allocated as follows: agriculture 8·5 per cent; mining and manufacturing, 19·8 per cent; petroleum and natural gas, 11·8 per cent; water and power, 15 per cent; others 44·9 per cent.

**Commerce.** The following table shows the value of imports (incl. oil) by principal countries for the period 1970–71 in Rials million.

| | *Imports* |
|---|---|
| W. Germany | 26,613 |
| U.S.A. | 16,630 |
| U.K. | 12,448 |
| Japan | 15,394 |
| France | 5,925 |
| Italy | 5,198 |
| Netherlands | 3,605 |
| U.S.S.R. | 9,980 |
| India | 3,292 |
| Belgium | 4,016 |
| Switzerland | 2,361 |
| Yugoslavia | 1,820 |
| Sweden | 2,220 |
| Austria | 1,241 |
| Australia | 1,504 |
| Rumania | 2,387 |
| Czechoslovakia | 1,589 |

The following table shows the value of exports (excl. oil) by principal countries for the period 1970–71 in Rials million.

| | *Exports* |
|---|---|
| Japan | 1,262 |
| U.K. | 743 |
| India | 192 |
| South Africa | 391 |
| U.S.A. | 1,845 |
| Netherlands | 349 |
| Singapore | 37 |
| Pakistan | 3 |
| U.S.S.R. | 4,809 |
| W. Germany | 2,999 |
| France | 1,168 |
| Aden | 1,041 |
| South Korea | 550 |
| Italy | 4,888 |
| Canada | 37 |
| Australia | 17 |
| Hong Kong | 99 |

## COMMUNICATIONS

**Railways.** There were no railways in Iran before 1927. The Trans-Iranian railway was built on the orders of Reza Shah Pahlavi, who abdicated in 1941. It extends from Bandar Shahpur on the Persian Gulf to Bandar Shah and Gorgan on the Caspian, via Ahwaz, Arak, Qum, Tehran and Savi, a distance of 1,427 kilometres. It has 93 stations and rises 2,176 metres above sea level in the mountains. At present, the Iranian State Railways have a total of 4,509 kilometres of main lines over which trains are regularly circulating pulled by diesel electric locomotives of the most modern kind.

**Shipping.** The chief ports are on the Persian Gulf. They are Abadan, from which refined petroleum products are exported; Kharg, the crude oil export terminal; Bandar Mah-Shah (shortly to replace Abadan for export of refined products); Khorramshahsr; Bandar-Shahpur; Bandar Abbass Lavan and Bushehr. These ports deal with most of the Persian overseas trade. In 1967 Iran formed its own shipping line, called Arya National Shipping Line, based on the Persian Gulf. In the Caspian Sea, traffic between the U.S.S.R. and Iran is carried on entirely by Soviet vessels.

**Civil Aviation.** There is direct communication between Tehran and the chief European capitals by the Iran National Airlines Corporation, B.O.A.C. and most European airlines. Internal services are operated by Iranair. Iranair started service to Europe in July 1965. *Head Office:* Mahrabad Airport, Iran Air Head Office Building, Tehran. Iran.

**Iran National Airlines Corporation.** (Chairman and Managing Director, Ali Mohammed Khademi). *Head Office:* Mehrabad Airport, Iran Air Head office Building, Tehran.

**Posts, Telegraphs and Telephones.** There are some 400,000 telephones in Iran, 230,000 of these in Tehran and 170,000 in the provinces.
A Telecommunications Research Centre started operations in 1972.

## NEWSPAPERS

**Ettela'at.** Tehran. F. 1925.

**Kayhan.** Kh. Ferdowsi, Tehran.

**Kayhan International.** Daily. Circulation 15,000.

**Ayandegan.** Tehran. Circulation 20,000.

**Tehran Journal.** Tehran. Circulation 12,000.

**Zan-e-Ruz.** Weekly. Circulation 150,000.

## EDUCATION

When compulsory primary education was established by Reza Shah the Great over 40 years ago, there were no more than 36,000 children attending school. In 1972–73 over five million children were attending many thousands of primary and secondary schools all over the country. The figure represents a sevenfold increase during the past 18 years. This does not include Literacy Corps schools and literacy classes.

Primary education for five years, is compulsory for all children, while textbooks and stationery are also supplied free of charge during the first four years of schooling.

An increasing number of children are now proceeding to secondary schools after obtaining their primary education certificate.

During the past few years the Government has taken steps to encourage private investment in education and as a result thousands of primary schools and hundreds of privately-owned secondary schools have come into being in Tehran and in the major provincial centres.

Following the motto "The Affairs of the People Should Be Handed Over to the People," the Government is now helping to create city and provincial education organizations which will take over, under overall Government control, the entire secondary schooling machinery of their region.

Iran has eight universities, three in Tehran and one in Shiraz, Tabriz, Ahwaz, Mashad and Esfahan respectively. There are also 12 institutes of higher education, four teachers training colleges, an important college of advanced technology in Abadan, and colleges of agriculture in Karaj, Rezaiyeh and Kerman.

Vocational training schools also exist in Tehran, Shiraz, Tabriz, Rasht and a number of other cities.

Over 97,000 students are at present attending undergraduate and postgraduate courses at these universities and colleges, while a further 30,000 are studying abroad, chiefly in Europe and North America.

In recent years much emphasis has been put on improving the higher education facilities as well as expanding research. A Ministry of Science and Higher Education was established in 1967 and charged with the task of streamlining and coordinating the affairs of universities, colleges and research institutes.

In 1968 the principles of education reform were formulated at a meeting presided over by the Shahanshah. Since then these reforms have been carried out, with the result that the quality of higher education has improved considerably.

During the fourth Development Plan existing universities have been expanded and new colleges of advanced technology have been created.

In recent years the Government has been working on several plans to expand vocational training schools and reorienting universities towards the training of skilled personnel and technicians required by Iran's rapidly expanding industries.

According to a new Royal Decree issued on 23 February 1974 all elementary and secondary education will be free as from the 1975 academic year.

**RELIGION**

The official religion is the Shi'a Muslim creed, but there are tribes, notably the Kurds and Baluchis, who are mainly Sunni Muslims. There are also Jewish, Christian and Zorastrian elements.

# Iraq

(IRAQI REPUBLIC)

**Capital**—Baghdad.

**President**—Ahmed Hassan Al-Bakr.

**National Flag:** A tricolour pale-wise, red, white, black; on the white three stars five pointed centred green.

## CONSTITUTION AND GOVERNMENT

IRAQ was freed from Turkish rule during the later stages of World War I. Its independent status was recognised by the Allied powers, and the League of Nations appointed Great Britain as the mandatory power. A provisional Arab Government was set up in 1920 to administer the country. Faisal, the third son of King Hussain of the Hedjaz, was chosen as the King of Iraq in 1920.

A constituent Assembly was convened on 21 March 1924, and drafted a constitution which came into effect on 21 March 1925. It provided that Iraq should be a constitutional hereditary monarchy, with a Parliamentary form of government.

On 30 June 1930 a treaty was concluded between Great Britain and Iraq which provided that Great Britain should renounce the mandate and recommend Iraq for admission to the League of Nations. This came about on 4 October 1932.

On 14 July 1958 a revolution led by the army took place in Iraq, the first results of which were the ending of the monarchy and the proclamation of a republic.

A government was formed in which the nationalist movement were represented. This government was headed by Brigadier Abdul Karim Qasim with a Council of Sovereignty consisting of General Najib Rubai, Mohammed Mahdi Kubba and Khalid Nakshabandi.

The first country to recognise the Iraqi Republic was the United Arab Republic. It was followed by the Soviet Union. Recognition by other states came in rapid succession in July, and Great Britain and the United States gave recognition at the beginning of August.

Following negotiations between the Government of Iraq and the Oil companies, the Government had to announce in December 1961 its control over 99 per cent of the Iraq Petroleum Company's concession area. In September of the some year, a Kurdish rebellion erupted in the north of Iraq. That revolt, the failure of the claim made by Qassem's Government upon Kuwait, the deterioration of the political and economic situation and Iraq's isolation from the Arab countries, all led to the creation of difficulties for the government.

On 8 February 1963 the Arab Ba'ath Socialist Party led an armed popular revolution, whose vanguard was the army. Abdul Karim Qassem was executed on the following day. The post of president was assumed by Abdul Salam Aref who later reneged against the Ba'ath Party on 18 November 1963 by leading a military *coup d'etat*. On 13 April 1966 Abdul Salem Aref was killed in a helicopter crash near Basra. Three days later his brother, Abdul Rahman Aref, was chosen as President.

On 17 July 1968 the Arab Ba'ath Socialist Party carried out a revolution which put an end to the unpopular rule of Abdul Rahman Aref. President al-Bakr become President of the Republic and Prime Minister.

### Cabinet

*President of the Republic, Chairman of the Revolutionary, Command Council, Secretary of the Regional Leadership of the Arab Ba'ath Socialist Party in Iraq:* Mr. Ahmed Hassan al-Bakr.
*Deputy Chairman of the Revolutionary Command Council, Deputy Secretary of the Regional Leadership of the Arab Ba'ath Socialist Party:* Mr. Saddam Hussain.
*Vice-President (Kurdish citizen):* Mr. Taha Muhiddin Ma'rauf.
*Minister of Communications:* Mr. Sa'doun Ghaidan.
*Minister of Interior:* Mr. Izzat al-Douri.
*Minister of Industry and Minerals:* Mr Flayeh Hassan al-Jassim.
*Minister of Health:* Dr. Riyadh Ibrahim Hussain.
*Minister of Youth:* Mr. Na'im Haddad.
*Minister of Oil:* Mr. Tayeh Abdulkarim.
*Minister of Education:* Mr. Mahammed Mahjoub
*Minister of Higher Education and Scientific Research:* Mr. Ghanem Abdul Jalil.
*Minister of Information:* Mr. Tareq Aziz.
*Minister of External and Internal Trade:* Mr. Hikmat al-Azzawi.
*Minister of Foreign Affairs:* Dr. Sa'doun Hammadi.
*Minister of Labour and Social Affairs:* Dr. Izzat Mustafa.
*Minister of State for coordination between Autonomy organs and the Central Authority:* Mr. Hamed al Juburi.
*Minister of Finance:* Dr. Sa'di Ibrahim.
*Minister of Justice:* Dr. Mundhir al-Shawi.
*Minister of State for Unity Affairs:* Dr. Abdulla al-Khudhair.
*Minister of Agriculture and Agarian Reform:* Dr. Hassan Fahmi Juma'.
*Minister of Public Works and Housing:* Mr. Taha al-Jazrawi.
*Minister of Transport:* Mr Abdul Sattar Sherif.
*Minister of Irrigation:* Dr. Mukarram al-Talabeni.
*Minister of Municipalities:* Mr. Anwar Abdul Qadir.
*Minister of State for Foreign Affairs:* Mr. Hisham al-Shawi.
*Minister of State:* Mr. Aziz Rashid Aqrawi.
*Minister of State:* Mr. Ubaidulla Mustafa al-Barzani.
*Minister of State:* Mr. Aziz Sharif.
*Minister of State:* Mr. Amer Abdulla.
*Minister of Awqaf:* Mr. Abdul Sattar Jawari.

### Political Parties

In September 1954 all political parties were abolished by a new Government law which abrogated the 1922 decree permitting the formation of new parties. Five organizations were affected: the Independence Party, the Umma Socialist Party, the United Popular Front, the Constitutional Union Party and the National Democratic Party. Political parties were permitted to be formed on 6 January 1960. The following parties were licensed thereafter: National Democratic Party, National Progressive Party, Iraqi Islamic Party, Kurdish Democratic Party and Iraqi Communist Party. Licences were refused to a group representing the majority of the former Iraqi Communist Party, the Republican Party and the Liberation Party. Following the coup of February 1963 all political parties except the Ba'ath were suspended, and after the November coup this too was suspended. On 14 July 1964 the formation of an Arab Socialist Union on single party lines was announced.

In July 1967 the Arab Baath Socialist Party assumed power and became the leading party in Iraq, and on 17 July, 1973 the ABSP announced the formation of a National Progressive Front with the Iraqi Communist Party and some independent national elements.

## LOCAL GOVERNMENT

Iraq is administratively divided into 16 Mahafdha (provinces). Each Liwa is administered by a Muhafdh. The Liwa is subdivided into smaller administrative units *Qadhas*, which in turn are subdivided into smaller units called *Nahiyas*.

## LEGAL SYSTEM

The Iraqi Judicial System consists of courts of first instance, courts of appeal, and a high court for ultimate appeal. Peace Courts consider minor civil cases. The Court of First Instance is of two types, the Court of First Instance with Limited Jurisdiction which deals mainly with civil and commercial cases the value of which does not exceed 500

Dinars, and the Court of First Instance with Unlimited Jurisdiction, which considers civil and commercial cases irrespective of their value.

Courts of Appeal consider objections against the decisions of the Courts of First Instance.

On the penal side, the Penal Courts form the lowest courts in grade. A penal court is established in the district of each civil Court of First Instance.

In every District of Appeal there is a Court of Sessions which consists of three judges under the Presidency of the President of the Court of Appeal or one of his Vice-Presidents.

On the personal status side, there are the Shari'a Courts. The Court of Cassation is the highest judicial tribunal in the land. It sits in Baghdad, and consists of a President and a number of Vice-Presidents and not less than fifteen permanent judges, delegated judges and reporters as necessity requres. A technical Bureau has been established in the Court of Cassation to carry out the work of abstracting and classifying the legal principles which are contained in its judgments. In addition to the Courts mentioned above, there is the Revolutionary Court which deals with cases affecting the security of the State in political, financial, economic and other spheres.

There are also the Courts for the Execution of Judgments, which are set up in every Civil Court of First Instance and presided over by the judge of the said Court.

## AREA AND POPULATION

The following table shows live births, deaths, and infant deaths registered at health institutions (by governates) for 1973.

| Governorate | *Live Births* | | | *Deaths* | | | *Infant Deaths* | | |
|---|---|---|---|---|---|---|---|---|---|
| | *Male* | *Female* | *Total* | *Male* | *Female* | *Total* | *Male* | *Female* | *Total* |
| Nineveh | 8,294 | 6,983 | 15,277 | 1,816 | 1,068 | 2,884 | 166 | 110 | 276 |
| Kirkuk | 3,114 | 2,481 | 5,595 | 786 | 440 | 1,226 | 26 | 19 | 45 |
| Diala | 2,442 | 2,053 | 4,495 | 504 | 392 | 896 | 11 | 8 | 19 |
| al-Anbar | 2,279 | 1,761 | 4,040 | 445 | 211 | 656 | 80 | 39 | 119 |
| Baghdad | 42,272 | 36,910 | 79,182 | 8,188 | 6,305 | 14,493 | 1,595 | 1,177 | 2,772 |
| Wasit | 2,223 | 1,786 | 4,009 | 839 | 725 | 1,564 | 13 | 3 | 16 |
| Babylon | 4,556 | 3,818 | 8,374 | 1,479 | 1,155 | 2,634 | 151 | 95 | 246 |
| Kerbela | 2,405 | 2,221 | 4,626 | 1,368 | 1,161 | 2,529 | 118 | 95 | 213 |
| al-Qadisiya | 1,802 | 1,522 | 3,324 | 1,028 | 776 | 1,804 | 113 | 62 | 175 |
| al-Muthanna | 525 | 446 | 971 | 365 | 396 | 761 | 3 | 1 | 4 |
| Maysan | 1,709 | 1,360 | 3,069 | 971 | 857 | 1,828 | 8 | 7 | 15 |
| Thi-Qar | 2,421 | 1,914 | 4,335 | 1,508 | 1,529 | 3,037 | 9 | 10 | 19 |
| Basrah | 10,508 | 9,400 | 19,908 | 2,336 | 2,051 | 4,387 | 289 | 174 | 463 |
| Autonomous Region: | | | | | | | | | |
| D'hok | 727 | 559 | 1,286 | 228 | 157 | 385 | 25 | 28 | 53 |
| Arbil | 2,125 | 1,952 | 4,077 | 562 | 263 | 825 | 31 | 22 | 53 |
| al-Sulaimaniya | 1,895 | 1,924 | 3,819 | 564 | 277 | 841 | 43 | 28 | 71 |
| Total | 89,297 | 77,090 | 166,387 | 22,987 | 17,763 | 40,750 | 2,681 | 1,878 | 4,559 |

**Vital Statistics:**

The population at mid-1974 was 10,770,000. The annual average percentage growth rate of the population for the period 1960–74 was 3·2 and for the period 1965–74 was 3·3.

## CURRENCY

The unit of currency is the Iraqi *Dinar*, one *Dinar* is equal to £1·78 sterling.

There are bronze coins of 1 fils and cupro-nickel coins of 5, 10, 25, 50 and 100 fils. Notes are issued in denominations of $\frac{1}{4}$, $\frac{1}{2}$, 1, 5 and 10 dinars.

## FINANCE

The GNP at market prices for 1974 was U.S. $ millions 12,000, and the GNP per capita at market prices was U.S. $1,110. The annual average percentage growth rate of the GNP per capita for the period 1960–74 was 4·0 and for the period 1965–74 was 4·8. [*See the note at the beginning of this section concerning GNP.*]

## PRINCIPAL BANKS

**Central (formerly National) Bank of Iraq.** Bank of Issue; Balance Sheet at 30 April 1976 showed assets D.1,326,233,292,669; current accounts D.179,640,314,513. *Head Office:* Rashid Street, Baghdad.

Except for the state-owned Rafidain Bank the other banks (including foreign owned banks) were nationalised on 14 July 1964, and were later amalgamated into new groups:

**Commercial Bank of Iraq** (comprising the Credit Bank of Iraq, The Commercial Bank of Iraq, and the Bank of Baghdad.) *Head Office:* Baghdad.

**Al-Rashid Bank,** comprising Al-Rashid Bank, the Eastern Bank and the United Bank of Iraq.

## PRODUCTION, INDUSTRY AND COMMERCE

**Agriculture.** The main crops of Iraq are classed under two groups:

A. Winter crops: including wheat, barley, flax, vetch, broad beans, berseam (Egyptian clover), onions, turnips and lentils.

B. Summer crops: including dates, cotton, rice, tobacco, maize, sesame, millet, alfalfa, green gram, potatoes and ground nuts.

As regards the main horticultural crops, Iraq produces citrus fruits, truck crops. dates, fruit crops and nuts.

**Mining.** Geological exploration and prospecting work have proved the presence of big deposits of copper and sulphur in the northern parts of Iraq. Production of sulphur has already commenced.

**Oil.** Oil was first discovered in Iraq in 1927, in the Kirkuk area. The production of crude oil is estimated to be in the region of 45 million tons annually. On 1 June 1972 the revolutionary government in Iraq nationalized the Iraq Petroleum Company which came to be known as the Iraq Company for Oil Operations. On 1 March 1973 the Mosul Petroleum Company was merged with the Iraq company for Oil Operations.

On 7 October 1973 the shares belonging to the American companies, Standard became the property of the Iraq National Oil Company. These shares constitute 23·75 per cent of the total shares of the Basrah Petroleum Company.

On 21 October 1973 the share of the Dutch Oil Company in the Basrah Petroleum company, amounting to 14·25 per cent of the total shares of the company, was nationalized and became the property of the Iraq Petroleum Company. In 1973, gross crude oil production in Iraq amounted to 736,588,000 barrels.

There are seven oil refineries in Iraq, five of which are under Government supervision. The State is now undertaking the distribution and marketing of refined oil products, which were done in the past by the Khanaqin Oil Company.

The following table shows the quantities of crude oil produced in Iraq for the period 1970–75 in thousands of barrels:

| *Year* | *Daily Average* | *Annual Total* | *Accumulated* |
|---|---|---|---|
| 1965 | 1,312·6 | 479,099 | 4,849,235 |
| 1966 | 1,392·2 | 508,141 | 5,357,376 |
| 1967 | 1,228·1 | 448,239 | 5,805,615 |
| 1968 | 1,503·3 | 550,208 | 6,355,823 |
| 1969 | 1,521·2 | 555,241 | 6,911,064 |
| 1970 | 1,546·0 | 564,308 | 7,475,372 |
| 1971 | 1,694·2 | 618,375 | 8,093,747 |
| 1972 | 1,469·8 | 536,502 | 8,630,249 |
| 1973 | 2,018·0 | 736,588 | 9,366,837 |
| 1974 | 1,976·0 | 719,275 | 10,086,112 |
| 1975 | 2,162·0 | 825,533 | — |

**Industry.** The years since 1968 have witnessed major developments in the field of industry. The allocation of Government money for the industrial sector in the national development plan over the years 1970–1974 was 207·25 million dinars. This sum was later increased to 391 million dinars.

According to the 1971 statistics; there were 1,330 major industrial undertakings in Iraq, embracing the public, private and mixed sectors, covering numerous and diverse industries. The Government of Iraq allocated money for the development of heavy industries in Iraq. Work has already started on the iron and steel complex in the south, the petrochemical complex, and other major projects.

Under an agreement with the Soviet Union in 1959 industrial plants, including a canning, a pharmaceutical factory, textile mills and a small steel mill are to be built. There are independent plans to build a paper mill, rayon and petro-chemical industries.

## COMMUNICATIONS

**Railways.** According to the 1972–73 statistics, the number of passengers was 3,330,000, and the total quantity of railway freight was 3,327,000 tons. The Iraqi State Railways owns a total of 7,101 locomotives, passenger wagons and freight trucks. The total length of railways is 2,203 kms. (standard gauge 1,130 kms., metric gauge 1,073 kms.).

**Civil Aviation.** By virtue of its geographical position Iraq is served by most of the important airlines of the world. There are four civil airports in Iraq. The International Baghdad Airport (which is the only international airport), the Basrah airport, the Mosul airport and the Bamerni airport. The Iraqi Airways was established in 1947 and was attached administratively and financially to the Iraqi State Railways. In 1961 a law was passed under which the Iraqi Airways became managed by an independent board of management. Iraqi Airways has eight modern aircraft of the Trident, Boeing 707 and Boeing 73 types. It will operate Boeing 747 aircraft on the new routes due to be opened very shortly. Iraqi Airways has witnessed a rapid expansion in recent years. The Iraqi Airways intends to open new offices abroad and new services covering various parts of the world.

**Posts, Telegraphs and Telephones.** Posts, telegraphs and telephones are owned by the Government. The estimated number of telephones in 1971 was 119,600. The number of foreign telegrams sent was 219,797 and the number received was 291,083.

**Broadcasting.** Broadcasting and television are operated by the Iraqi Government. The principal stations are at Baghdad, but there is a nation-wide network.

## NEWSPAPERS

**Al Jumhuriyyah. F.** 1963. Baghdad. Circulation 20,000.

**Al-Fajr Al-Jadid. F.** 1959. Baghdad.

**Baghdad Observer.** F. 1967. Circulation 7,000. Editor-in Chief, Abdul Jabbar El-Shatab. P.O. Box 257, Baghdad.

## EDUCATION AND RELIGION

Allocations to Education in the 1976 Budget, amounted to: 168,400,000 million Iraqi Dinars. All foreign and private schools are nationalized. Therefore, they have become completely free, as the rest of Iraqi schools. All Universities and colleges including that of Medicine and Law are free. Since 1974, the state started to bear the expenses of books and all other equipment needed by students, in addition to tuition which was free to begin with.

It is important to note that there is no discrimination on the basis of sex, religion, or race, as far as admission to schools and universities is concerned. The only factor is the student's academic standard.

According to the 1973–74 statistics, there were 6,731 primary schools with 1,408,929 pupils, and 1,093 high schools with 33,349 students.

In 1973, the number of students admitted to Iraqi universities and higher institutes was 58,351 (males: 42,455, females: 15,896). The Women's College (formerly al-Tahrir for Girls) was closed several years ago. The women students were transferred to the College of Arts.

# Ireland

**Capital**—Dublin.

**President**—Dr. Patrick Hillery.

**National Flag**: A tricolour pale-wise, green, white, orange.

## CONSTITUTION AND GOVERNMENT

IRELAND is a sovereign, independent, democratic State. An armed insurrection against British rule in Ireland took place in Dublin in April 1916. A republic was proclaimed but the revolt was repressed and a number of leaders were shot. In spite of this, republicanism made great headway and at the General Election of December 1918 the Sinn Fein (Republican Party) won 73 seats out of a total of 105. They refused to take their seats at Westminster but instead they constituted themselves as an Irish Legislature (*Dáil Éireann*). On 21 January 1919 the establishment of a Republic was ratified, and a revolutionary government with Eamon de Valera as President was elected. The armed struggle against Great Britain was renewed and continued until 1921; hostilities ceased and a treaty between the two countries was signed on 6 December 1921, by which Dominion Status was accepted for the time being under the name of *Saorstát Éireann* (Irish Free State); the border between *Saorstát Éireann* (26 counties) and *Northern Ireland* (six counties) was fixed in December 1925.

The Constitution of *Saorstát Éireann* came into operation on 6 December 1922. Certain provisions which were regarded as contrary to national sentiments were gradually removed by successive amendments in the period to December 1936 and, on 1 July 1937, a new Constitution was enacted by plebiscite. This Constitution, which came into operation on 29 December 1937, restores the former name of Ireland (Éire) and declares the national territory to consist of the whole island of Ireland, its islands and the territorial seas. It provides, however, that, pending the re-integration of the national territory, the laws enacted by the Parliament established by the Constitution shall have the like area and extent of application as those of *Saorstát Éireann*, which did not include six countries of the province of Ulster (Antrim, Armagh, Derry, Down, Fermanagh and Tyrone) known as 'Northern Ireland'.

The Constitution was amended by referendum on the 10 May 1972, to allow Ireland to become a member of the European Economic Community.

The President of Ireland is elected by direct vote of the whole electorate and holds office for a term of 7 years.

The Parliament (*Oireachtas*) consists of the President and two Houses, a House of Representatives (*Dáil Éireann*) and a Senate (*Seanad Éireann*). The *Dáil* consists of 148 members elected by adult suffrage on a system of proportional representation for a term not exceeding 5 years. Of the 60 members of the Senate, 11 are nominated by the *Taoiseach* (Prime Minister), 6 are elected by the Universities and the remaining 43 are elected from 5 panels of candidates, established on a vocational basis, representing the following public services and interests: (1) national language and culture, literature, art, education and such professional interests as may be defined by law for the purpose of this panel; (2) agriculture and allied interests, and fisheries; (3) labour, whether organized or unorganized; (4) industry and commerce, including banking, finance, accountancy, engineering and architecture; (5) public administration and social services, including voluntary social activities.

### Ministry

*Taoiseach* (*or Prime Minister*): Jack Lynch.
*Tanaiste* (*or Deputy Prime Minister*), *Minister for Finance and Minister for the Public Service:* George Colley.
*Minister for Health and Minister for Social Welfare:* Charles J. Haughey.
*Minister for Fisheries:* Brian Lenihan.
*Minister for Transport and Power and Minister for Posts and Telegraphs:* Pádraig Faulkner.
*Minister for Agriculture:* James Gibbons.
*Minister for Industry and Commerce:* Desmond O'Malley.
*Minister for Defence:* Robert Molloy.
*Minister for Justice:* Gerard Collins.
*Minister for Foreign Affairs:* Michael O'Kennedy.
*Minister for the Environment:* Sylvester Barrett.
*Minister for Labour:* Gene Fitzgerald.
*Minister for the Gaeltacht:* Denis Gallagher.
*Minister for Education:* John P. Wilson.
*Minister for Economic Planning and Development:* Martin O'Donoghue.

### Parliament

In Dáil Éireann, (House of Representatives), the state of the parties on 5 July 1977 was as follows: Fianna Fáil 84, Fine Gael 43; Labour 17; Independents 4.

*Chairman:* Joseph Brennan.

*Chairman:* Sean Treacy.

Seanad Éireann (Senate) is made up as follows: Members nominated by Taoiseach 11; University members 6; Cultural and Educational Panel 5; Agricultural Panel 11; Labour Panel 11; Industrial and Commercial Panel 9; Administrative Panel 7.

## LOCAL GOVERNMENT

At present the elected local authorities comprise 27 county councils, 4 county borough corporations, 7 borough corporations, 49 urban district councils and 28 town commissions. All the members of these authorities are elected under a system of proportional representation, normally every five years. All residents of an area who have reached the age of 18 are entitled to vote in the local election for their area. Women are eligible for election as members of local authorities in the same manner and on the same conditions as men. The minimum age for membership is 18 years.

The local authorities are concerned mainly with physical planning and development, the provision of infrastructure, environmental and amenity services and, to a lesser extent, with protective and regulatory services. Their principal functions may be classified under the headings Planning and Development, Housing, Roads and Sanitary and Environmental Services. Because of the small size of their administrative areas the functions which are actually carried out by town commissioners and some urban district councils have tended to become increasingly limited.

The local authorities have a system of government which combines an elected council and a whole-time manager. The elected members have specific functions reserved to them which include the making of rates (local tax), the borrowing of money, the adoption of development plans, the making, amending or revoking of by-laws and the nomination of persons to other bodies. The managers, who are paid officers of the local authorities, exercise all the executive functions of the local authorities, and have control over all the officers and employees of their authorities. The manager for a county council is manager also for every borough corporation, urban district council, and board of town commissioners whose functional area is wholly within the county.

The revenue expenditure of local authorities is financed by a local tax on the occupation of property (called rates), grants and subsidies from the central government and payments for certain services which they provide. Capital expenditure is financed mainly by means of borrowing from the Local Loans Fund, which is operated by the central government, and from banking and insurance institutions.

## LEGAL SYSTEM

The Constitution provides that Justice shall be administered in public in Courts established by law by Judges appointed by the President on the advice of the Government. These Courts consist of Courts of First Instance and a Court of Final Appeal, called the Supreme Court. The Courts of First Instance are the High Court with full original jurisdiction and the Circuit and District Courts with local and limited jurisdiction. The Judges of all Courts are, under the Constitution, completely independent in the exercise of their judicial functions and their remuneration may not be reduced during their terms of office. A Judge may not be removed from office except for stated misbehaviour or incapacity and then only on resolutions passed by both Houses of the Oireachtas (Parliament). Judges of the Supreme, High and Circuit Courts are appointed from among practising barristers. Judges of the District Court (styled District Justices) may be appointed from among practising barristers or practising solicitors. The jurisdiction and organization of the Courts are dealt with in the Courts (Establishment and Constitution) Act, 1961, and the Courts (Supplemental Provisions) Acts, 1961 to 1973.

The Supreme Court, which consists of the Chief Justice (who is *ex officio* an additional judge of the High Court) and five ordinary judges, has appellate jurisdiction from all decisions of the High Court. The President may, after consultation with the Council of State, refer a Bill, which has been passed by both Houses of the Oireachtas, to the Supreme Court for a decision on the question as to whether such Bill or any provision or provisions thereof is or are repugnant to the Constitution. The High Court, which consists of the President of the High Court (who is *ex officio* an additional judge of the Supreme Court) and seven ordinary judges, has full original jurisdiction in and power to determine all matters and questions, whether of law or fact, civil or criminal. In all cases in which questions arise touching the validity of any law having regard to the provisions of the Constitution, the High Court alone exercises original jurisdiction. The High Court on Circuit acts as an appeal court from the Circuit Court.

The Court of Criminal Appeal consists of the Chief Justice or an ordinary Judge of the Supreme Court together with the President of the High Court and an ordinary judge of the High Court or two ordinary judges of the same. It deals with appeals by persons convicted on indictment where the appellant obtains a certificate from the trial Judge that the case is a fit one for appeal, or, in case such certificate is refused, where the Court itself, on appeal from such refusal, grants leave to appeal. The Central Criminal Court consists of a Judge or Judges of the High Court, to whom is assigned, for the time being, the duty of acting as and constituting the Court. The Court sits at such times and in such places as the President of the High Court may direct and tries criminal cases which are outside the jurisdiction of the Circuit Court or which may be sent forward for trial from the Circuit Court on the application of the Director of Public Prosecutions or the accused person.

The country is divided into a number of circuits for the purposes of the Circuit Court. The President of the Circuit Court is *ex officio* an additional judge of the High Court. The civil jurisdiction of the Circuit Court is limited to £2,000 in contract and tort, hire-purchase and credit-sale agreement proceedings, and £5,000 in equity (including probate and administration); where the parties consent the jurisdiction is unlimited. In criminal matters the Court has jurisdiction in all cases except murder, treason, piracy and allied offences. The Circuit Court acts as an appeal court from the District Court.

The District Court has a summary jurisdiction in a large number of criminal cases where the offence is not of a serious nature. In civil matters the Court has jurisdiction in contract and tort (except slander, libel, criminal conversation, seduction, slander of title, malicious prosecution and false imprisonment) and in hire-purchase and credit-sale agreement proceedings where the claim does not exceed £250.

All criminal cases except those dealt with summarily by a Justice in the District Court are tried by a Judge and Jury of twelve. Juries are also used in very many civil cases in the High Court. In a criminal case the jury must be unanimous in reaching a verdict but in a civil case the agreement of nine members is sufficient.

**Supreme Court**

*Chief Justice:* Thomas F. O'Higgins.

*Judges:* Brian C. Walsh, Frank Griffin, Weldon R. C. Parke, Seamas Henchy, John Kenny

**High Court**

*President of the High Court:* Thomas A. Finlay.

*Judges:* George D. Murnaghan.
Sean De Buitleir.
John Gannon.
Liam Hamilton.
Thomas A. Doyle.
James McMahon.
Herbert R. McWilliam.
Declan Costello.
James A. D'Arcy.

*President of the Circuit Court:* Thomas J. Neylon.

## AREA AND POPULATION

The whole of Ireland is 32,051 sq. miles in area, of which the Irish Republic covers 26,600 sq. miles. The 1971 population of all Ireland was 4,514,313 comprising 2,978,248 in the 26 counties and 1,536,065 in the six North-Eastern Counties.

Population of each Province, County and County Borough in 1966 and 1971, Area and Number of persons per square mile.

| *Province, County or County Borough* | *Population* 1966 | 1971 | | | *Area* | | *Persons per Sq. Mile* |
|---|---|---|---|---|---|---|---|
| | *Persons* | *Persons* | *Males* | *Females* | *Acres* | *Sq. Miles* | |
| **Total** | **2,884,002** | **2,978,248** | **1,495,760** | **1,482,488** | **17,023,661** | **26,599** | **112** |
| **Leinster** | **1,414,415** | **1,498,140** | **737,460** | **760,680** | **4,851,369** | **7,580** | **198** |
| Carlow | 33,593 | 34,237 | 17,502 | 16,735 | 221,485 | 346 | 99 |
| Dublin Co. Borough | 567,802 | 567,866 | 267,801 | 300,065 | 28,519 | 45 | 12,744 |
| Dun Laoghaire Borough | 51,811 | 53,171 | 24,063 | 29,108 | 4,179 | 7 | 8,143 |
| Dublin* | 175,434 | 231,182 | 114,144 | 117,038 | 195,052 | 305 | 758 |
| Kildare | 66,404 | 71,977 | 37,279 | 34,698 | 418,644 | 654 | 110 |
| Kilkenny | 60,463 | 61,473 | 31,828 | 29,645 | 509,431 | 796 | 77 |
| Laoighis | 44,595 | 45,259 | 23,805 | 21,454 | 424,892 | 664 | 68 |
| Longford | 28,989 | 28,250 | 14,891 | 13,359 | 257,936 | 403 | 70 |
| Louth | 69,519 | 74,951 | 37,511 | 37,440 | 202,806 | 317 | 237 |
| Meath | 67,323 | 71,729 | 36,977 | 34,752 | 577,823 | 903 | 79 |
| Offaly | 51,717 | 51,829 | 27,029 | 24,800 | 493,636 | 771 | 67 |
| Westmeath | 52,900 | 53,570 | 27,544 | 26,026 | 435,606 | 681 | 79 |
| Wexford | 83,437 | 86,351 | 43,768 | 42,583 | 581,031 | 908 | 95 |
| Wicklow | 60,428 | 66,295 | 33,318 | 32,977 | 500,328 | 782 | 85 |
| **Munster** | **859,334** | **882,002** | **447,271** | **434,731** | **5,961,804** | **9,315** | **95** |
| Clare | 73,597 | 75,008 | 39,002 | 36,006 | 787,704 | 1,231 | 61 |
| Cork Co. Borough | 122,146 | 128,645 | 61,731 | 66,914 | 9,229 | 14 | 8,921 |
| Cork | 217,557 | 224,238 | 115,055 | 109,183 | 1,834,092 | 2,866 | 78 |
| Kerry | 112,785 | 112,772 | 58,404 | 54,368 | 1,161,706 | 1,815 | 62 |
| Limerick Co. Borough | 55,912 | 57,161 | 27,626 | 29,535 | 4,705 | 7 | 7,775 |
| Limerick | 81,445 | 83,298 | 43,160 | 40,138 | 658,948 | 1,030 | 81 |

*continued*

| *Province, County or County Borough* | *Population* | | | | *Area* | | *Persons per Sq. Mile* |
|---|---|---|---|---|---|---|---|
| | 1966 | 1971 | | | | | |
| | *Persons* | *Persons* | *Males* | *Females* | *Acres* | *Sq. Miles* | |
| Tipperary, N.R. | 53,843 | 54,337 | 28,190 | 26,147 | 493,258 | 771 | 71 |
| Tipperary, S.R. | 68,969 | 69,228 | 35,333 | 33,895 | 558,034 | 872 | 79 |
| Waterford Co. Borough | 29,842 | 31,968 | 15,421 | 16,547 | 2,423 | 4 | 8,444 |
| Waterford | 43,238 | 45,347 | 23,349 | 21,998 | 451,705 | 706 | 64 |
| Connacht | 401,950 | 390,902 | 203,694 | 187,208 | 4,230,720 | 6,611 | 59 |
| Galway | 148,340 | 149,223 | 77,842 | 71,381 | 1,467,670 | 2,293 | 65 |
| Leitrim | 30,572 | 28,360 | 15,269 | 13,091 | 376,764 | 589 | 48 |
| Mayo | 115,547 | 109,525 | 56,402 | 53,123 | 1,333,940 | 2,084 | 53 |
| Roscommon | 56,228 | 53,519 | 28,294 | 25,225 | 608,540 | 951 | 56 |
| Sligo | 51,263 | 50,275 | 25,887 | 24,388 | 443,806 | 693 | 73 |
| Ulster (part of) | 208,303 | 207,204 | 107,335 | 99,869 | 1,979,768 | 3,093 | 67 |
| Cavan | 54,022 | 52,618 | 27,819 | 24,799 | 467,162 | 730 | 72 |
| Donegal | 108,549 | 108,344 | 55,424 | 52,920 | 1,193,621 | 1,865 | 58 |
| Monaghan | 45,732 | 46,242 | 24,092 | 22,150 | 318,985 | 498 | 93 |

* Excluding Dun Laoghaire Borough.

Chief cities with populations (Census 1971) are: Dublin County Borough 567,866, Cork County Borough 128,645, Limerick County Borough 57,161, Waterford County Borough 31,968, Dun Laoghaire Borough 53,171.

| | 1972 | 1973 | 1974 | 1975 | 1976* |
|---|---|---|---|---|---|
| Marriages | 22,302 | 22,816 | 22,833 | 21,280 | 20,431 |
| Births | 68,527 | 68,713 | 68,907 | 67,178 | 68,167 |
| Deaths | 34,381 | 34,192 | 34,921 | 33,173 | 33,284 |

* Provisional.

## CURRENCY AND FINANCE

The unit of currency is the Irish pound. The foreign exchange value of the Irish pound is held at par with the £ sterling. The principal estimated items of revenue for 1977 are:

| | *£m* |
|---|---|
| Customs duties | 30·0 |
| Excise duties | 460·0 |
| Income tax | 544.0 |
| Corporation Tax, etc. | 82·0 |
| Value Added Tax | 334·0 |
| Stamp duties | 20·8 |
| Estate, etc. duties | 4·5 |
| Capital Taxes | 9·5 |
| Motor-vehicle duties | 42·5 |
| Post Office services | 125·5 |
| Total (incl. other items) | 1,811·3 |

The principal estimated items of current expenditure for 1977 are:

| | *£m.* |
|---|---|
| Debt service | 448·1 |
| Agriculture | 133·1 |
| Education | 253·1 |
| Transport | 66·7 |
| Post Office | 84·7 |
| Defence | 86·4 |
| Justice (including Gardaí) | 66·9 |
| Social Welfare | 288·4 |
| Health | 299·7 |
| Superannuation | 52·7 |
| Industry | 65·0 |
| Total (incl. other items) | 2,029·0 |

Revenue and Expenditure (actual) for Jan–December 1976 were £1,470·20 million and £1,671·64 million respectively.

The last fifteen years have witnessed a significant diversification of the Irish Economy with a major expansion of the industrial sector, which now accounts for about 36 per cent of National Income. In common with many other developed countries, Ireland was affected by the International recession of 1974–75; after growing at an average annual rate of 4·5 per cent in the period 1968–73, real GNP grew by only 1·7 per cent in 1974 and declined by 0·7 per cent in 1975.

The recovery commenced towards the middle of 1975 and in the following year GNP grew by three per cent in real terms. The balance of payments deficit which had fallen from £280 million in 1974 to only £18 million in 1975, widened again to £150 million in 1976 as a result of an increase in the trade gap associated with the higher level of economic activity. The official external reserves rose for the third year running; in 1976 they increased by £280 million implying a net capital inflow of £430 million.

## BANKS

**Central Bank of Ireland** (Governor: C. H. Murray; Established 1943; Bank of Issue. All the capital is owned by the State. Balance Sheet at 31 December 1976 showed assets £1,271, 566, 400; Gold reserve £7,603,429; Bank notes in circulation £345,259,189. *Address:* P.O. Box 61, Dublin 2.

**Bank of Ireland** (Governor: William D. Finlay). Established 1783; Bank of Issue; Consolidated Balance Sheet of the Bank of Ireland and its subsidiaries at 31 March 1977 showed assets £1,754,474,000; Deposit, current and other accounts £1,589,999,000. *Head Office:* Lower Baggot Street, Dublin 2. 372 Brances.

**Allied Irish Banks Ltd.** (Chairman: Niall Crowley.) Consolidated Balance Sheet of the Bank and Subsidiary Companies at 31 March 1977 showed assets £1,784,733,000; Deposit, Current and other accounts £1,642,729,000. On 1 April 1972, by virtue of Agreements and existing legislation, the banking businesses of the Munster & Leinster Bank Ltd., Provincial Bank of Ireland Ltd. (other than its Royal Avenue Office, Belfast) and the Royal Bank of Ireland Ltd., were transferred to Allied Irish Banks Ltd., of which those Banks are wholly owned subsidiaries. *Head Office:* Lansdowne House, Ballsbridge, Dublin 4. 323 Branches.

**Chase and Bank of Ireland (International) Ltd.** (President, Edward R. McCutcheon) Associated with the Chase Manhattan Group and the Bank of Ireland Group. *Address:* Stephen Court, St. Stephen's Green, Dublin 2. Branches: Belfast and Shannon.

**Northern Bank Ltd.** (Chairman: W. L. Stephens, DSO, VRD, DL). Established 1824; Balance Sheet at 31 December 1975 showed assets £512,885,000; Deposit, current and other accounts £454,930,000. *Head Office:* 16 Victoria Street, Belfast. *Dublin Office:* 112–113 Grafton Street, Dublin. 167 Branches, 98 Sub-Branches.

**Ulster Bank Ltd.** (Chairman, Sir Robin Kinahan, ERD, JP, LLD, DL). Established 1836; Balance Sheet at 31 December 1975 showed assets £522,666,000. Deposit, current and other accounts £452,481,000. *Dublin Office:* College Green. *Head Office:* Donegall Place, Belfast. 142 Branches.

## PRODUCTION, INDUSTRY AND COMMERCE

**Agriculture.** Ireland is principally an agricultural country. The greater part of the land is devoted to the production and feeding of livestock and a considerable portion is also under corn and root crops.

The following table shows the acreage of the principal crops as at 1 June 1975*:

| *Crops* | *Area (acres)* |
|---|---|
| Wheat | 117,700 |
| Oats | 124,200 |
| Barley | 586,500 |
| Rye | 1,000 |
| Beans and Peas | 7,000 |
| Potatoes | 97,600 |
| Turnips | 57,300 |
| Mangels | 10,800 |
| Sugar Beet | 82,200 |
| Fodder Beet | 6,800 |
| Other root and green crops | 32,300 |
| Fruit (including Horticultural Flowers and Bushes) | 8,800 |
| Hay (incl. grass for silage) | 2,570,500 |
| Pasture | 8,275,200 |

Livestock on farms on 1 June 1975* comprised 6,927,300 cattle; 3,796,000 sheep; 843,000 pigs; 431,300 turkeys; 102,100 geese; 168,500 ducks; 9,710,500 fowl; total milk production, 909·5 million gallons; butter production 1,675,100 cwt.; shorn wool production, 14,990,000 lbs., eggs, 6,032,400 gt. hundreds.

* Preliminary estimate.

**Industry.** The principal industries are food processing, tobacco manufacturing, metal trades, vehicle assembly, electrical machinery, clothing and footwear, printing and paper, chemicals and drugs.

The following table shows the value of the gross output for the principal industries for the year 1973.

| *Commodity* | *Gross output thousand £* |
|---|---|
| Tobacco | 85,867 |
| Creamery, butter, cheese, condensed milk, chocolate crumb, ice cream and other edible milk products | 232,822 |
| Grain milling and animal feeding stuffs | 93,150 |
| Bacon factories | 84,605 |
| Assembly construction and repair of mechanically propelled road and land vehicles | 77,200 |
| Manufacture and refining of sugar and manufacture of cocoa, chocolate, and sugar confectionery | 51,761 |
| Bread, biscuit and flour confectionery | 48,845 |
| Slaughtering preparation and preserving of meat other than by bacon factories | 149,066 |
| Brewing | 51,390 |
| Metal trades (excluding machinery) | 99,707 |
| Printing, publishing and allied trades | 50,288 |
| Manufacturing of paper and paper products | 45,081 |
| Chemicals and drugs | 56,488 |
| Manufacture of electrical machinery | 81,513 |
| Clothing and footwear (wholesale factories) | 78,259 |
| Cement, concrete and structural clay products, asbestos goods, etc. | 61,504 |
| Building, construction | 107,756 |
| Gas, water, electricity | 104,212 |
| Mining, quarrying and turf production | 62,018 |

**Mines and Minerals.** The average number of persons engaged in mines and quarries in 1973 was 5,980 of whom 305 are employed in the coal mines. The output for 1973 was 72,800 tons of coal.

**Commerce.** The following table shows the value of principal exports by commodities for 1975 and 1976 (in million £1):

| *Commodity* | 1975 | 1976 |
|---|---|---|
| Live animals | 123·6 | 108·3 |
| Meat and meat preparations | 239·8 | 211·6 |
| Dairy products and eggs | 152·7 | 201·2 |
| Fish and fish preparations | 13·6 | 19·7 |
| Cereals and cereal preparations | 15·1 | 16·5 |
| Fruit and vegetables | 16·0 | 19·7 |
| Sugar, sugar preparations and honey | 18·0 | 28·6 |
| Coffee, tea, cocoa and spices | 23·2 | 28·9 |
| Feeding stuffs for animals (excl. unmilled cereals) | 13·1 | 18·3 |
| Misc. food preparations | 27·5 | 52·4 |
| Beverages and tobacco | 31·3 | 38·0 |
| Hides, skins, furskins | 9·9 | 13·8 |
| Textile fibres and waste | 11·4 | 19·2 |
| Metal ores and scrap | 29·9 | 25·3 |
| Other raw materials | 15·9 | 19·7 |
| Fuel | 5·4 | 5·7 |
| Petroleum and products thereto | 13·7 | 6·6 |
| Animal and veg. oils and fats | 6·3 | 8·1 |
| Chemicals | 108·2 | 167·2 |
| Leather, leather mnfrs. and dressed furskins | 13·3 | 17·5 |
| Rubber manufactures | 16·3 | 26·4 |
| Wood and cork manufactures | 4·9 | 8·7 |
| Paper, paper board and manufactures | 17·1 | 17·2 |
| Textile yarn, fabrics etc. | 79·1 | 118·4 |
| Non metallic mineral manufactures | 27·6 | 32·2 |
| Iron and steel non ferrous metals | 12·2 | 15·1 |
| Manufactures of metal nes. | 30·2 | 44·1 |
| Machinery (non-electric) | 86·4 | 140·1 |
| Electrical machinery, goods, etc. | 48·8 | 76·6 |
| Transport equipment | 26·0 | 37·1 |
| Clothing and footwear | 57·5 | 68·5 |
| Professional scientific, etc. goods, watches and clocks | 35·4 | 53·7 |
| Other manufactured articles | 47·9 | 67·3 |
| Parcel post and special transactions | 70·1 | 96·3 |
| Total | 1,447·4 | 1,857·9 |

The following tables show import and export value in £ millions by principal countries for 1975 and 1976:

| | *Imports* | |
|---|---|---|
| *Country* | 1975 | 1976 |
| | *£m.* | *£m.* |
| Great Britain | 768·3 | 1067·3 |
| Northern Ireland | 64·4 | 84·6 |
| Germany (Federal Republic) | 119·6 | 159·8 |
| United States of America | 122·4 | 199·0 |
| Netherlands | 54·8 | 74·3 |
| Czechoslovakia | 5·2 | 6·2 |
| France | 85·9 | 109·8 |
| Canada | 17·6 | 29·8 |
| Belgium and Luxembourg | 30·7 | 45·0 |
| Finland | 18·9 | 21·7 |
| Sweden | 36·2 | 41·9 |
| India | 9·1 | 8·7 |
| Japan | 29·9 | 51·7 |
| Italy | 42·7 | 59·8 |
| Argentina | 3·0 | 7·2 |
| U.S.S.R. | 18·1 | 22·1 |
| Denmark | 13·3 | 20·3 |
| Poland | 13·7 | 15·4 |
| Switzerland | 12·2 | 17·7 |
| Saudi Arabia | 26·7 | 22·3 |
| Spain | 11·0 | 16·1 |
| Morocco | 4·3 | 4·2 |

*continued*

| Country | Imports | |
|---|---|---|
| | 1975 | 1976 |
| Iran | 28·1 | 38·7 |
| Norway | 8·4 | 11·6 |
| South Africa | 6·1 | 8·5 |
| Brazil | 4·1 | 9·6 |
| New Zealand | 4·1 | 7·6 |
| Ghana | 5·9 | 8·5 |
| Israel | 3·8 | 5·8 |
| Kuwait | 32·5 | 19·5 |
| Portugal | 6·0 | 7·0 |
| Austria | 5·2 | 6·5 |
| Iraq | 5·1 | 5·7 |
| Hong Kong | 4·5 | 8·4 |

| Country | Exports | |
|---|---|---|
| | 1975 | 1976 |
| Great Britain | 628·5 | 743·1 |
| Northern Ireland | 153·5 | 161·9 |
| Germany (Federal Republic) | 114·5 | 160·8 |
| United States of America | 87·9 | 128·5 |
| Netherlands | 85·6 | 109·7 |
| France | 63·5 | 95·1 |
| Canada | 16·8 | 20·7 |
| Belgium and Luxembourg | 53·0 | 83·5 |
| Sweden | 15·3 | 21·9 |
| Japan | 9·1 | 23·6 |
| Australia | 9·9 | 17·9 |
| Italy | 39·5 | 43·0 |
| Portugal | 1·1 | 7·1 |
| Denmark | 5·3 | 11·6 |
| Poland | 3·2 | 5·8 |
| Switzerland | 7·0 | 11·7 |
| Spain | 11·2 | 12·7 |
| Nigeria | 11·5 | 17·0 |
| Mexico | 1·2 | 6·0 |
| Venezuela | 2·8 | 3·2 |
| Norway | 3·7 | 10·2 |
| South Africa | 7·3 | 5·6 |
| Finland | 4·6 | 5·1 |
| Greece | 1·7 | 4·0 |
| Austria | 3·4 | 6·2 |
| Israel | 5·2 | 3·4 |
| U.S.S.R. | 10·1 | 1·9 |
| Iran | 5·6 | 9·6 |
| Libya | 4·4 | 11·6 |
| Gambia | 4·4 | 4·1 |
| Algeria | 2·6 | 3·2 |
| Iraq | 1·0 | 6·8 |
| Saudi Arabia | 1·3 | 4·5 |

**Fishing.** Ireland's fisheries fall into two divisions, sea and inland. Landings of sea fish in 1976 amounted to 73,868 metric tonnes valued at £12,435·713. Landings of the main freshwater species, salmon, amounted to 1,492 metric tonnes valued at £5,301,737. Total employment in the industry (excluding distribution) is approximately 9,350, of whom 2,495 are full time and 4,898 part time sea fishermen. Exports of fish and fishery products in 1976 totalled 39,265 metric tonnes valued at £20·6 million.

## COMMUNICATIONS

**Railways.** The principal transport system is that of Córas Iompair Éireann which operates co-ordinated rail, road passenger and freight services covering most of the country.

For the year ended 31 December 1975 the total length of track was 1,247 miles, the total number of passengers carried by rail was 13,891,000, freight (rail) carried amounted to 3,244,000 tons and passenger receipts amounted to £9,727,000 and freight receipts to £8,447,000.

**Shipping.** In 1976 the number of ships with cargo and in ballast, in the foreign trade, which arrived at Irish ports was 11,780 (18,960,765 net registered tons); of these, 1,358 (2,299,072 net registered tons) were of Irish nationality.

**Civil Aviation.** The principal airports are Shannon Airport (Co. Clare), Dublin Airport and Cork Airport, all of which are owned by the State, and managed on behalf of the Minister by the State-sponsored company Aer Rianta Teoranta.

Shannon airport is a Customs-free Airport. The development and promotion of industrial and tourist activity at and in the region of the Airport are the responsibility of the Shannon Free Airport Development Company Limited.

The national airlines are Aer Lingus Teoranta and Aerlinte Éireann Teoranta. The capital position of each of these companies at present is:

**Aer Lingus:** Authorized Capital 6,500,000 Ordinary Shares of £1 each; 15,000,000 Preferred Ordinary Shares of £1 each. Issued Capital; 6,393,003, Ordinary Shares fully paid; 15,000,000 Preferred Ordinary Shares fully paid. Shareholders: Minister for Finance and Government nominees, Aerlinte Éireann Teoranta.

Aer Lingus operates domestic services from Dublin to Shannon and Cork Airports. The company operates international services from Dublin to Amsterdam, Barcelona, Belfast, Birmingham, Bristol, Brussels, Cardiff, Copenhagen, Dusseldorf, Edinburgh, Frankfurt, Geneva, Glasgow, Jersey, Leeds, Bradford, Liverpool, London, Lourdes, Madrid, Manchester, Milan, Munich, Paris, Rome and Zurich, and also from Shannon to Belfast, Dusseldorf, London and Paris. Aer Lingus also operates services from Cork to Birmingham, London, Manchester and Paris.

**Aerlinte:** Authorized Capital: 10,000,000 "A" Shares of £1 each; 10,000,000 "B" Shares of £1 each. Issued Capital: 7,217,042 "A" Shares fully paid; 10,000,000 "B" Shares fully paid. Shareholders': Minister for Finance and Government nominees.

Aerlínte operates transatlantic services between Shannon and Boston, Chicago, Montreal and New York. The services begin and end at Shannon but under an interchange arrangement with Aer Lingus, connecting services are provided between Shannon and Dublin Airport, between Shannon and Belfast and between Shannon and London.

The Head Offices of Aer Rianta, Aer Lingus, and Aerlinte are at Dublin Airport.

**Telegraphs and Telephones.** The telegraph and telephone systems are under the control of the Department of Posts and Telegraphs. The number of telephones at 31 December 1976 was 440,000.

**Broadcasting and Television.** The national television and radio services are operated by Radio Telefís Éireann, an autonomous statutory corporation created by the Broadcasting Authority Act, 1960. The Radio Telefís Éireann Authority comprises nine members appointed by the Government. RTE's television service was inaugurated on 31 December 1961 and provides national coverage—reception is available to 98 per cent of the population though five main transmitters at Maghera, Co. Clare, Mullaghanish, Co. Cork, Truskmore, Co. Sligo, Kippure, Co. Dublin and Mount Leinster, Co. Carlow and twenty-one low-power satellite transposers. Television transmission (excluding schools broadcasting) average 55 hours weekly during the year. Programmes are broadcast in both Irish and English.

The national line-standard is 625 lines. At 30 April 1977 the total number of television licences was 573,574 (including 19,350 outstanding licences). RTE is financed as to current expenditure by nett licence revenue and the proceeds of the sale of advertising time on both radio and television. The annual licence fee for television is £18·50 for monochrome and £31 for colour as from 1 April 1977. The radio licence was abolished as from 1 September 1972.

The national radio service commenced on 1 January 1926, and until the passing of the 1960 Act was administered by the Department of Posts and Telegraphs. RTE operates three medium-frequency transmitters, Tullamore, 530 m. (500 kW, day-time; 150 kW, night-time), Dublin 240 m. (5 kW) and Cork, 240 m. (10 kW). In addition, RTE programmes are radiated by a VHF/FM network co-sited with the five main television transmitters.

Total broadcasting time for the year ended 30 September 1976: television 3,196 hours; radio 6,120 hours. Local programming from the Cork radio transmitter totalled 287 hours. Approximately 46 per cent of the total hours broadcast on television was home-produced.

**Radio na Gaeltachta a new radio network to serve the scattered Irish-speaking communities in the western half of Ireland, was inaugurated on 2 April 1972. This Irish-language service is radiated locally from the following medium frequency transmitters: Conamara 556 m. (2 kW),**

Tír Chonaill 240 m. (10 kW) and Corca Dhuibhne 312 m. (1 kW). It is also broadcast on a national basis from five VHF transmitters co-sited with the television transmitters. The main studio control for Radio na Gaeltachta is at Casla, Co. Galway, with subsidiary studios at Na Doirí Beaga, Co. Donegal and Baile nan Gall, Co. Kerry.

## NEWSPAPERS

**Irish Times:** F. 1859. Daily. Independent, morning. 11-13, D'Olier St. Dublin 2. Circulation 66,829.

**Irish Independent:** F. 1905. Non-party. Daily morning. Independent House, Middle Abbey Street, Dublin. Circulation 174,539.

**Irish Press:** F. 1931. Daily. Morning, Independent, Irish Press House, Lr. O'Connell Street, Dublin. Circulation 89,161.

**The Cork Examiner:** F. 1841. Independent. Daily/Morning. 95 Patrick Street, Cork. Circulation 64,274.

**Evening Herald:** F. 1891. Non-party. Daily/Evening. Independent House, Middle Abbey Street, Dublin 1. Circulation 117,320.

**Evening Echo:** F. 1892. Daily/Evening. 95 Patrick Street, Cork. Circulation 35,981.

**Sunday Independent:** F. 1905. Non-party Weekly. Independent House, Middle Street, Dublin 1. Circulation 285,286.

**Evening Press:** F. 1954. Daily (evening). Irish Press House, Lr. O'Connell Street, Dublin 1. Circulation 151,078.

**The Sunday Press:** F. 1949. Independent, weekly. Irish Press House, Lr. O'Connell Street, Dublin 1. Circulation 396,313.

**Sunday World:** F. 1973. Weekly. 18, Rathfarnham Road, Terenure Dublin 6. Circulation 288,516.

## EDUCATION

**Elementary.** Elementary education is free and is given in some 3,396 National Schools. The average daily enrolment of pupils in 1976 was 527,000 pupils. The percentage average daily attendance is still about 90·2 per cent. There are now about 17,600 teachers. There are six Colleges of Education for the training of primary school teachers all of which are co-educational. The estimated State expenditure on elementary education for 1977 (1 January–31 December) is £110,353,000, excluding the cost of administration.

Satisfactory progress is being maintained in relation to provision of up-to-date facilities and accommodation for primary school pupils, and special measures are taken in the interest of disadvantaged children.

**Special Education.** Within the general framework of the system of national education special provision is made for handicapped and deprived children in special schools which are recognised on the same basis as primary schools, in special classes attached to ordinary schools and in certain voluntary centres where educational services appropriate to the needs of the children are provided. Categories of handicapped children catered for include visually handicapped, hearing impaired, physically handicapped, mentally handicapped, emotionally disturbed, itinerants and other socially disadvantaged children. Provision is also being made on an increasing scale for children with dual or multiple handicaps. In each case a programme suited to the needs of the particular kind of handicap is provided and new school buildings have been provided or are planned to cater for the special educational requirements of the handicapped child. The number of children in each class in such schools is very much smaller than in ordinary classes in a primary school and because of the size of the catchment areas involved an extensive system of school transport has been developed. Many handicapped children who have spent some years in a special school or class are integrated into normal schools for part of their school career, if necessary with special additional facilities such as nursing services, special equipment, etc. For others who cannot progress with the ordinary school system the special schools or classes provide both the primary and secondary level of education. In addition to the services being provided on a full-time basis many children are being catered for by the provision of part-time teaching facilities in hospitals, child guidance clinics, rehabilitation workshops, special "Saturday-morning" centres and home teaching schemes.

**Secondary Education.** Voluntary Secondary Schools are under private control and are conducted in most cases by religious orders; all schools are in receipt of grants from the State and are open to inspection by Inspectors of the Department of Education. The number of recognized secondary schools during the school year 1976/77 was 537 and the number of pupils in attendance 189,445. Total estimated State expenditure for 1977 (Janary/December) is £68,649,000.

Grants for the provision of a wide range of audio-visual teaching aids are available to secondary schools. The schools television service "Telefis Scoile" provides programmes in Irish, English, History, Geography, Mathematics and Science subjects for senior and junior pupils. The vast majority of secondary schools now have at least one television receiving set, purchased with the aid of a State grant.

Vocational Education Committee schools provide courses of general and technical education, apprentice training, courses of technician training and courses leading to professional qualifications (i.e. architecture, engineering, accountancy). These schools are controlled by local Vocational Education Committees and are maintained partly from the rates and partly by State grants. The estimated State expenditure for 1977 (January/December) is £47,666,000 excluding the cost of administration, and the estimated expenditure from the local rates, for the same period is £1,912,936.

**Comprehensive Education.** Comprehensive Schools which have been established in recent years and are financed by the State combine academic and technical subjects in one broad curriculum so that each pupil may have a range of educational options structured to his particular needs, abilities and interests available to him. Pupils are prepared for State examinations and for entrance to Universities and Institutes of further education. To date, 13 comprehensive schools have been built.

**Community Education.** Community Schools continue to be established through the amalgamation of existing voluntary secondary and Vocational Education Committee Schools, where this is found feasible and desirable, and in new areas where a single larger school is considered preferable to two smaller schools under separate managements. These 24 schools cater for all aspects of second-level education and provide adult education facilities in the areas in which they are situated. They also make facilities available to voluntary organizations and to the adult community generally. The estimated State expenditure on running costs for Comprehensive and Community Schools for 1976 (January/December) is £6,869,000.

**Regional Technical Colleges.** Regional Technical Colleges have been set up in eight provincial centres: Athlone, Carlow, Cork, Dundalk, Galway, Letterkenny, Sligo and Waterford. The colleges provide apprentice, technician, professional as well as general and adult education courses. The estimated State expenditure on the colleges for 1977 (January/December) including capital costs and student aid is £9,403,000.

**Third Level Education.** University Education is provided by the National University of Ireland, founded in Dublin in 1908, and by the University of Dublin (Trinity College) founded in 1592. The National University comprises 3 constituent colleges—University College, Dublin; University College, Cork; and University College, Galway.

St. Patrick's College, Maynooth, Co. Kildare, is a national seminary for Catholic priests and a pontifical university with the power to confer degrees up to a doctoral level in philosophy, theology and canon law. It now admits lay students (men and women) to the courses in arts, celtic studies, science and education which it provides as a "recognized" college of the National University. Besides the University medical schools, the Royal College of Surgeons in Ireland, which is a long established independent medical school, provides medical qualifications which are internationally recognized. Third-level courses with a technological bias, leading to degree, diploma and certificate qualifications are also provided by the National Institute for Higher Education, Limerick.

Full time instruction in agriculture is provided for all sections of the farming community. There are four State agricultural colleges administered by the Department of Agriculture and Fisheries, and seven similar private State-aided agricultural colleges, at each of which a standard one-year course in agriculture is given. Second-year courses in general agriculture and more specialized courses in farm machinery, dairying, pig husbandry and in beef cattle and sheep production are provided at a number of these colleges, all of which are residential. Scholarships on a liberal scale tenable at these institutions are awarded by County Committees of Agriculture. For persons interested in farming who are unable to avail themselves of these facilities or who require preparatory instruction before entering one of the agricultural colleges the Committees of Agriculture conduct winter classes in agriculture and horticulture at convenient local centres. The Advisory Service employed by the County Committees of Agriculture provide a continuing educational programme for the agricultural population. This programme is implemented through a wide range of activities from farm walks through lectures and part-time courses to short residential courses at the Agricultural Colleges, and caters for the needs of young people entering farming, practising farmers, farm workers and farmers' wives. A special scheme of vocational training for persons engaged in agriculture aged 18 years or over is operated by the Committees under the terms of Directive 72/161/EEC. The Scheme forms part of the EEC common measures for the structural improvement of agriculture and is aimed at enabling farmers, farm workers and family helpers to acquire the knowledge and skills necessary to meet the needs of modern farming. The Scheme provides for day release and residential courses at basic and advanced levels covering the main farm enterprises (including horitculture and farm home management). Participants receive a minimum of 100 hours' training under the Scheme. A scheme of farm apprenticeships providing for up to four years practical training on approved farms and a three year trainee farmer scheme (involving only one year away from home) are administered by the Farm Apprentice Board.

There are six State-aided residential colleges of rural home economics at each of which a one-year course is provided, mainly in dairying, poultry-keeping and domestic economy subjects. Co. Committees of Agriculture also provide scholarships to these colleges. A 3 year diploma course in Farm Home Management is provided at the Munster Institute, Cork, a residential school administered by the Department of Agriculture. It also provides courses in poultry-husbandry and management.

Courses in horticulture are provided at the National Botanic Gardens, Dublin and at Kildalton Agricultural and Horticultural College, County Kilkenny, both administered by the Department of Agriculture and Fisheries. Courses are also provided for boys at one of the State-aided agricultural colleges and for girls by the Irish Countrywoman's Association.

The Department of Agriculture and Fisheries award a number of University scholarships each year leading to the Degrees of B.Agr.Sc. and B.Sc. (Dairying) and a number of bursaries to the course for Diploma in Dairy Science. Post-graduate scholarships in agricultural advisory work are also awarded annually.

### RELIGION

At the census of 1971 there were 2,795,666 Catholics, 97,739 Church of Ireland and 30,579 other denominations.

# Israel

(MEDINAT YISRAEL)

**Capital**—Jerusalem.

**President**—Ephraim Katzir.

**National Flag:** White, charged with a star six-pointed centred blue, composed of two interlaced equilateral triangles, between two blue fesse-wise stripes.

### CONSTITUTION AND GOVERNMENT

THE State of Israel is a Republic headed by a President elected by the Knesset (Parliament). The independence of the State of Israel was proclaimed on 14 May 1948 with the termination of the British Mandate over Palestine. It followed a resolution of the United Nations General Assembly of 29 November 1947 which recommended the partition of Mandatory Palestine into independent Jewish and Arab States.

The two temporary governing bodies of the new State until the elections were held in 1949 were the Provisional State Council (37 members) presided over by Dr. Chaim Weizmann and acting as the supreme legislative authority, and a Provisional Government under the Premiership of David Ben-Gurion.

The United Nations Partition resolution was immediately followed by Arab attacks on the Jewish population. On 15 May 1948 the armies of five Arab States invaded the nascent State of Israel.

After almost a month of heavy fighting a first truce of four weeks' duration was arranged on 11 June 1948. Hostilities recommenced on 8 July after the Arab governments had declined an extension of the truce. A second truce was arranged on 18 July 1948. Armistice agreements were concluded with Egypt, Lebanon, Jordan and Syria in 1949.

On 5 June 1967, war broke out between Israel and Egypt, Jordan and Syria following the blockage of the Tiran Straits by Egypt and attacks by Jordan and Syria on Israel. Israeli forces overran the Sinai peninsula, the West Bank of the Jordan, the Syrian Heights and captured the Old City of Jerusalem. The whole of Jerusalem was reunified under Israel sovereignty on 29 June. A cease fire was agreed on 10 June.

Israel has been a member of the United Nations since 11 May 1949.

Israel has no Constitution in the ordinary meaning of that term. Some years ago, a proposal to enact a written Constitution was, after exhaustive debates, rejected by a majority vote of the Knesset. Instead it was decided to enact from time to time fundamental laws which eventually, taken together, would form a Constitution. To date, four such laws have been enacted: the Law of the Knesset, 1958, the Israeli Lands Law, 1960, the Law of the President, 1964, and the Law of the Government in 1968. The Law of Human Rights is in preparation. They can be altered only by a vote representing the absolute majority of Knesset members. There are, however, in existence a number of ordinary laws dealing with constitutional matters, such as the Law and Administration Ordinance, 1948, the Knesset Elections Law, 1955, the State President (Tenure) Law, 1951, the Judges Law, 1953, and the State Comptroller Law, 1949.

The Law of Return, 1950, providing that 'Every Jew shall be entitled to come to Israel as an immigrant,' the Nationality Law, 1952, and the Women's Equal Rights Law, 1951, also belong to this type of constitutional legislation.

Fundamental human and civil rights and freedoms such as freedom of worship, freedom of speech, of association, assembly and of the press, and the free exercise of any profession, trade or business, although not laid down in any enactment, exist and form part of the law of Israel, much on the same lines as in England. As in England they are safeguarded by writs of habeas corpus, mandamus, etc. The right to hold property, subject to law and to the power of the State to require land for public purposes on payment of compensation assessed by the District Court, is also recognized.

There is an extensive labour legislation, a law providing for free elementary education and a National Insurance Law, 1953, providing, *inter alia*, for accident insurance and old age pensions.

The Government consists of the Prime Minister and a number of Ministers who may or may not be Members of the Knesset. There may also be Deputy Ministers appointed from among the Members of the Knesset. The President entrusts a Member of the Knesset with the formation of a Government, which then must obtain a vote of confidence from the Knesset. It may be ousted from office by a parliamentary vote of censure and may also resign by its own decision as a result of the resignation of the Prime Minister.

The Knesset is a one chamber parliament consisting of 120 members. It is elected for a four-year term. The system of election is proportional representation, secret ballot and universal direct suffrage. The first Knesset was elected on 25 January 1949 with 86 per cent of the electorate going to the polls. As no party has so far commanded an absolute majority, all cabinets have been based on coalitions. During the term of the Fifth Knesset the Labour Alignment was formed by the Mapai and Achdut Ha'avoda parties; The Herut-Liberal Bloc was formed by Herut and a part of the Liberal Party; the Independent Liberal Party and the Israel Labour List (Rafi) were formed: and the Communist Party split into two sections. At the beginning of 1967 part of the Herut section of the Herut-Liberal Bloc broke away and was recognized as a separate faction in the Knesset.

In January 1968, the parties Mapai, Ahdut Ha'avoda and Rafi, the Israel Labour List, merged to become the Israel Labour Party. On 5 June 1967, the Cabinet was enlarged by the co-option of representatives of Rafi (as it then was) and the Herut-Liberal bloc (Gahal). The latter resigned from the Cabinet in August 1970 over the Government's acceptance of the United States peace initiative.

On 6 October 1973 Syria and Egypt simultaneously attacked Israel on two fronts. Fighting continued in the Yom Kippur War until the 24 October. On 22 October the Security Council formally adopted Resolution 338 calling for a cease fire and implementation of Resolution 242 of 22 November 1967. Fighting continued for another 36 hours and when the cease fire went into effect United Nations military observers and a United Nations Emergency Force were sent into the area. On the 11 November, Israel and Egypt signed a six point agreement designed to stabilize the cease fire. A Middle East peace conference was convened in Geneva on the 21 December 1973. Israel, Egypt and Jordan participated, Syria stayed away. As a result, an agreement was concluded between Israel and Egypt on the separation of forces, the implementation of which was completed on 4 March 1974. An agreement on the separation of forces between Israel and Syria was signed in Geneva on 31 May 1974, a further agreement was initiated by both parties on 1 September 1975 when there were further territorial adjustments towards a final settlement.

**Cabinet**

*Prime Minister:* Menachem Begin.
*Minister of Finance:* Simha Erlich.
*Minister of Commerce, Industry and Tourism:* Yigal Horowitz.
*Minister of Defence:* Ezer Weizman.
*Speaker of Knesset:* Yitzhak Shamir.
*Minister of Housing:* Gideon Patt.
*Minister of Health:* Eliezer Shostak.
*Minister of Absorption:* David Levi.
*Minister of Infrastructure and Energy:* Yitzhak Moda'i.
*Minister of Agriculture:* Ariel Sharon.
*Minister of Foreign Affairs:* Moshe Dayan.
*Minister of Interior:* Yosef Burg.
*Minister of Education:* Zevulun Hammer.
*Minister of Religious Affairs:* Aharon Abu Hatsira.

## LOCAL GOVERNMENT

Local government is by means of municipal corporations, local councils and regional councils, the latter dealing with agricultural problems, security, health, social welfare of groups of settlements situated in the same area. There are 31 municipalities (2 Arab), 115 local councils (46 Arab and Druze), and 48 regional councils (one Arab) comprising representatives of 700 villages.

## LEGAL SYSTEM

The Knesset is the only institution in the State whose authority to legislate is primary and unlimited. A number of other authorities, such as the Government, Ministers, Municipal Councils and others have the power to make regulations with legislative effect within the limits laid down by the Knesset. Much of the English law, which was introduced during the British Mandate, as well as certain parts of the original Turkish law, is still in force. Certain provisions of the Mandatory law which was in force at the time of the Proclamation of Independence were specifically repealed.

One of the first laws to be repealed was the British White Paper of 1939 restricting immigration and the transfer of land. Matters of personal status are within the jurisdiction of religious courts of the several religious communities. The parents' right to ensure religious education for their children is established by the State Education Law of 1953.

There is, besides, judicial autonomy for the three main religious communities in all matters affecting personal status (marriage, divorce, etc.), which cases are heard by the relevant religious authority, Jewish, Christian or Moslem.

Municipal Courts exist in certain of the municipal areas, Magistrate's Courts in the districts and sub-districts and District Courts at Jerusalem, Tel Aviv, Haifa and Beersheba. There are also tribunals for special cases.

The Supreme Court sits as a Court of Civil Appeal, Criminal Appeal, a High Court and a Special Tribunal. It is composed of a President (Mr Y. Sussman), a Deputy President and eight justices (A. Witkon, H. Cohn, Itshak Kister, M. Etzioni, M. Landau, Z. Berinson, E. M. Manny and I. Kahan). All judges are appointed by the President on the advice of an Appointments Committee.

## AREA AND POPULATION

The total population of Israel in mid-1972 was 4,249,000. The annual average percentage population growth rate for the period 1960–74 was 2·2 and for the period 1965–74 was 1·9. The non-Jewish population is as follows: 392,500 Moslems, 84,500 Christians and 41,600 Druze and others. The population of the major cities (May 1973) was as follows: Tel-Aviv-Jaffa, 367,600, Jerusalem 326,400, Haifa 225,800 and Ramat Gan 121,000. The Druze Community is recognized as an autonomous body with full rights.

Hebrew and Arabic are the official languages of the State. Arabic is used officially for the benefit of the Arab citizens. Government publications appear in Arabic and Hebrew. Stamps, banknotes and coins have Arabic inscriptions and provision is made in the Knesset for the simultaneous translation of Hebrew speeches into Arabic and vice-versa.

**Vital Statistics:** Marriages, births and deaths for 1974 were: (per 1,000) Births, 27·7; Marriages, 9·5, Deaths, 7·1; Infant Deaths, 23·5.

## CURRENCY AND FINANCE

The unit of currency is the Israel pound (I£), which is divided into 100 *agorot* (singular *agora*). There are coins of 1, 5, 10, 25, 50 and 100 *agorot* and banknotes for I£1, 5, 10, 50 and 100.

**Budgets of the State of Israel**

| | *Ordinary* |
|---|---|
| Revenue for 1973–74 | IL16,102,900,000 |
| Revenue for 1974–75* | IL31,915,500,000 |
| Revenue for 1975–76* | IL44,520,000,000 |

* Estimates.

The GNP at market prices for 1974 was U.S. $ millions 6,850, and the GNP per capita at market prices was U.S. $3,460. The annual average percentage growth rate of the GNP per capita for the period 1960–74 was 5·3, and for the period 1965–74 was 5·8. [*See the note at the beginning of this section concerning GNP.*]

## PRINCIPAL BANKS

**Bank Kupat-Am Le-Israel Ltd.** (Chairman, Mr. B. Yekutieli.) Established 1918. Assets as at 31 December 1974, IL351,547,272; deposits and current accounts, IL336,631,906. *Head Office:* 13, Ahad Ha'am Street, Tel-Aviv, Israel. 17 Branches.

**Bank of Israel.** (Governor, Mr. M. Sanbar). Established 1 December 1954 in pursuance of the Bank of Israel Law passed on 24 August 1954. The Bank of Israel is the sole Bank and Fiscal Agent in Israel of the Government and sole Bank of issue. Authorised capital I£10m.; Balance Sheet at December 1974 showed total assets I£20,265,887; notes and coins in circulation I£3,319,126. *Head Office:* Mizpah Bldg., Jaffa Road, Jerusalem. There are two branches in Israel. Agencies: Ashdod, Beer Sheba, Eilat, Hadera, Natanya, Petah Tiqvah, Rehovoth Safad, and Tiberias for the supply of currency.

**Bank Lemelacha Ltd.** (Acting Chairman, Brian D. Wine; Managing Director, Y. Gal'on.) Established 1954. Assets as at 31 December 1975, IL306,869,526; deposits and current accounts, IL232,402,249. *Head Office:* 18, Shoken Street, Tel-Aviv, Israel. 16 Branches.

**Bank Leumi le-Israel B.M.** (formerly Anglo-Palestine Bank Ltd., originally incorporated in 1902 under the name of Anglo-Palestine Company Ltd.) (Chairman of the Board and Chief Executive: F. I. Japhet); Consolidated Statement of

Condition of the Bank and its Subsidiaries as at 30th June 1977 showed Assets IL. 91,014,383,000 (US$9,689,803,000*), Deposits IL. 65,381,115,000 (US$6,960,769,000). *Head Office:* Tel Aviv. 316 branches and offices of the Group in Israel and abroad. *U.K. Subsidiary:* Bank Leumi (U.K.) Ltd., Head Office and West End Branch, 4–7 Woodstock Street, London W1A 2AF; City branch—Bow Bells House, 11 Bread Street, London EC4P 4BT. *U.S. Subsidiaries:* Bank Leumi Trust Company of New York, 579 Fifth Avenue, N.Y., N.Y. 10017; branches—11 Leumi Securities Corporation, 18 East 48th Street, N.Y. 10017; New York Agency: 579 Fifth Ave., N.Y. 10017; Branches—Chicago: 100 North La Salle St., Chicago, Ill. 60602; Beverly Hills—Los Angeles; 9731 Wilshire Blvd. Beverly Hills, Calif. 90212; Cayman Island Branch; Georgetown, Grand Cayman Island. Swiss Subsidiary: Bank Leumi Le-Israel (Switzerland); Zurich Head Office: Claridenstrasse 34, Zurich 8022; Geneva Branch: Rue du Rhone 80, Geneva 3. French Subsidiary: Bank Leumi Le-Israel (France) S.A., 30 Boulevard des Italiens, 75009 Paris; Benelux Subsidiary: Luxinvest S.A., 3 Rue Belliard, Bruxelles 1040, Belgium. Representative Offices: Florida; Toronto; Argentina; Brazil; Venezuela; Zurich; Frankfurt a/Main; Milan; Johannesburg; Hong Kong; Leumi International Investments N.V., Curacao.

* Rate of Exchange as at 30th June 1977: U.S. $ 1 = IL. 9·3928.

**Israel Discount Bank Ltd.** 27–29 Yehuda Halevy St., Tel-Aviv f. 1935 as Palestine Discount Bank Ltd., name changed 1957; cap. funds IL. 727·8 m. (consolidated: IL. 913·5 m., including capital notes and minority interest) Consolidated total Assets IL. 36,809 m. (31 December, 1976). *Chairman:* Daniel Recanati. 159 branches in Israel, 2 in New York, 1 in Nassau, 1 in Luxembourg and 1 in Grand Caymen Luxembourg 1, and Grand Cayman, 1.

**Bank Hapoalim B.M.** (Chairman of Board of Management, J. Levinson). Established 1921. Balance Sheet at 31 December 1976 showed assets I£62,821,273,000; current and deposit accounts I£55,912,065,000. *Head Office:* 50 Rothschild Blvd., Tel Aviv. Over 280 branches of the Bank's group in Israel.

*Branches abroad:*

London (City Branch), 22/23 Lawrence Lane, London EC2V 8DA; London West End branch, 8-12 Brook Street, London W1Y 1AA; New York Branch, 10 Rockefeller Plaza, New York, N.Y. 10020. Representative offices in Zurich, Johannesburg, Buenos Aires and Sao Paulo.

## PRODUCTION, INDUSTRY AND COMMERCE

**Agriculture.** Jewish agricultural settlement in Palestine in modern times began with the establishment of the first Jewish agricultural school Mikve-Israel in 1870. The first agricultural settlement, Petach Tikva, was founded in 1878 and was followed by the establishment of a number of other Jewish villages.

The Zionist movement fostered the idea not only of a return to the homeland but also of a return to the soil and the creation of a land settlement and a farming society in Palestine.

The idea of a communal agricultural settlement was first evolved in the early years of the 20th century and the first such 'kibbutzim'—Degania—was established in 1909.

Today there are many forms of agricultural settlement ranging from the collective farm to the private village and privately-operated plantation. Much of the land suitable for cultivation or afforestation is owned by the Jewish National Fund. This land cannot be sold and is allotted to prospective settlers on the basis of a 49-year hereditary lease. By the end of 1974 there were 697 Jewish and 88 non-Jewish rural settlements.

The following table shows the agricultural production of selected items for 1976 (in tons, except where otherwise designated):

| *Product* | *Tons* |
|---|---|
| Citrus Fruit | 1,505 |
| Grapes | 92 |
| Bananas | 57 |
| Other fruit | 144 |
| Wheat | 203 |
| Groundnuts | 24 |
| Cotton lint | 54 |
| Cotton seed | 87 |
| Sugar beet | 324 |
| Vegetables, Potatoes and Onions | 759 |
| Poultry meat | 190 |
| Cattle meat | 40 |
| Fish | 24 |
| Milk (million litres) | 670 |
| Eggs (millions) | 1,710 |

Israel's agricultural development is largely dependent upon expansion of the irrigation system.

The northern area of the Negev has been brought under cultivation during recent years. The Yarkon-Negev water pipeline which carries approximately 100 million cu.m. per year was inaugurated in 1955 and has enabled the irrigation of further 200,000 dunams (50,000 acres). The Negev, south of Beersheba, is largely desert, but it is being rehabilitated. In the course of 1964 the Israel Water Project came into operation, and water from Lake Kinneret (Sea of Galilee) now flows through the 108 in. Pipeline to the South; this is designed to alleviate, at least partially, the needs of certain areas where present resources are now being overexploited.

A countrywide development plan for the utilization of all water resources was carried out during the last few years. This plan is on the basis of regional projects which are interrelated and forms a national grid for an overall water supply network.

Water consumption in agriculture in 1974–75 was 1,230 million cubic m. Total cultivated area in 1974–75—4,350,000 dunams of which 1,825,000 dunams were under irrigation.

The plans for agricultural development stress the improvement of agricultural methods, achievement of larger production figures per unit and introduction of new crops. Among the new successfully grown crops are: cotton, groundnuts, sugar beet, sisal and various kinds of tropical fruit.

Other industrial crops include tobacco and oil crops. The Hula swamps in north of the country have been successfully drained and brought under cultivation, adding 15,000 acres to Israel's agricultural area. Special attention is paid to regrassing and development of pasture land; cattle and sheep breeding have been expanded in recent years. Poultry is the main source of meat, supplying two-thirds of the total meat consumption.

The most important feature of Israel's agriculture was the growth of agricultural exports. The value of fresh agricultural products exported increased from U.S. $157 million in 1971 to U.S. $375 million in 1976–77, beside the traditional export of citrus at the value of US $185 million. The following exports in 1976–77 were:

| *Exports* | *Value U.S. $ million* |
|---|---|
| Vegetable | 45 |
| Fruits (other than citrus) | 26 |
| Flowers | 28 |
| Field crops (cotton & groundnuts) | 56 |
| Seeds | 5 |
| Livestock & Poultry products | 30 |

**Forestry.** The total afforested area in Israel (1973–74) amounted to 584,000 dunams of which 108,000 is Government owned, 462,000 by the Jewish National Fund (JNF) and by others, 14,000.

**Mining.** Prior to the establishment of the State of Israel, the only mineral resources exploited were the Dead Sea chemicals.

After 1948 a serious geological survey was undertaken and large deposits of phosphates, copper, bitumen, manganese, iron, granite, marble, clay, feldspar, silicate sand, etc. have been discovered; oil was first struck in 1955 in the South and a second oilfield was opened up in 1957. In 1960 the output of oil reached 15 per cent of Israel's annual consumption. In 1970–71, 83,000 tons of oil were pumped and the gas wells at Rosh Zohar produced the equivalent of 123,000 tons of oil.

## ISRAEL

In 1973 crude oil production in Israel was 45 million litres and natural gas production was 66 million cubic metres.

A basic industry utilizing these local natural resources came into being. The mineral deposits, however, are in many cases not very rich and do not lend themselves to easy exploitation. Intensive scientific and technological aid is necessary to ensure the best possible exploitation of this mineral wealth.

The overall responsibility for the utilization of these resources and the establishment of basic industries rests with the Ministry of Development. The actual mining and processing are carried out by a number of development companies controlled by the Ministry of Development and of which the Government is a shareholder. In 1957 a Technological Advisory Board which includes some of the world's technological authorities, as well as Israeli experts, was established to direct and develop the exploitation of the country's resources.

A copper processing plant has been established on the site of King Solomon's historical mines. The running-in of the plant took place in spring 1958 and regular production started March 1959. The output was 5,300 tons in 1959–60 and 6,000 tons in 1960–61. The final target is 14,000 tons. In 1974–75 Timna Copper Mines Ltd. produced 9,500 tons of copper.

**Industry.** An indication of the development of Israel's industries is shown by the rise in electricity consumption. This was 246,000,000 kWh in 1949 and 7,915,100,000 kWh in 1974–75.

Industries have greatly expanded to include textiles, diamond polishing, building materials, foodstuffs, woodworking and others. Major industries include heavy chemicals, motor vehicle assembly, large diameter concrete irrigation pipes, electrical refrigerators, air conditioning units, electric motors and tyres, electronic equipment, plastics, pharmaceuticals and ceramic ware.

Modern sugar plants, cotton gins, a paper mill, a steel rolling mill, up-to-date airplane assembly and repair shops, shipyard, and other marine repair installations, and a further wide range of manufacturing enterprises have been established.

Most of Israel's mineral resources are in the Negev, and have been discovered through extensive geological surveys since the achievement of independence. Previously, only the Dead Sea potash was exploited on a fairly large scale.

Israel is one of the few countries in the world possessing deposits of the principal raw materials—phosphates and potash—for the three main types of fertilizers in common use.

The Government gives every facility for the investment of foreign or local capital.

On 30 September 1970, the total value of the assets of development undertakings, most of them financed by the State, was IL 2,035 million, including IL 1,076 million in electricity installations. Their exports earned $23 million f.o.b. in the first half of 1970/71.

Large quantities of Negev minerals are exported to Asia and East Africa through the Red Sea port of Eilat, and there are good prospects of further expansion.

The Dead Sea is known to contain billions of tons of magnesium chloride, common salt, potassium chloride, magnesium bromide, and calcium chloride. The output of potash was 950,000 tons in 1975. Bromine and a variety of its derivatives are manufactured.

Chemicals and Phosphates Ltd. operates plants in Haifa. Its production in 1971–72 amounted to 390,000 tons of various products, and its exports earned U.S. $900,000. Phosphates Ltd. operates a plant at Oron in Negev and this produced 790,000 tons of phosphates in 1971.

About a million tons a year of phosphate rock are mined at Oron in the Negev. A large chemical complex has now been completed at Arad; it earns $18 million a year from exports and export premiums.

The chemical industry has an annual output of the value $400 million, 30 per cent of this output is exported.

At an investment of $15 million, a plant for the production of 46,000 tons of magnesium and 80,000 tons of hydrochloric acid a year is also being erected in the Arad area.

**Commerce.** Israel's foreign trade, though still showing an adverse balance, reflects a steady improvement in the position of exports. In 1973, exports amounted to more than 46 per cent of imports.

The following tables show the value of imports and exports in 1975:

**Imports by Economic Destination** in 1975 (in million $)

| *Commodity* | 1973 |
|---|---|
| Consumer goods | 319·6 |
| Raw materials | 3,175·8 |
| Investment goods | 647·8 |

**Main Exports** in 1975 (in million $)

| *Commodity* | 1975 |
|---|---|
| Citrus fruits | 176·7 |
| Other agricultural exports | 101·1 |
| Industrial exports | 1,022·2 |
| Diamonds | 641·0 |

The following table shows the imports and exports by main countries of purchase and destination for 1975 (in thousand $):

| | *Imports* 1975 | *Exports* 1975 |
|---|---|---|
| *Europe* | 2,205,916 | 984,868 |
| United Kingdom | 682,917 | 171,591 |
| West Germany | 591,291 | 160,826 |
| Netherlands | 165,105 | 129,347 |
| Belgium and Luxembourg | 143,983 | 80,877 |
| France | 129,893 | 112,694 |
| Switzerland | 101,711 | 80,916 |
| Italy | 167,103 | 56,576 |
| Sweden | 53,179 | 27,874 |
| Rumania | 28,199 | 17,941 |
| Finland | 28,405 | 12,131 |
| Yugoslavia | 11,770 | 14,966 |
| *Asia* | 124,961 | 417,463 |
| Japan | 85,367 | 107,184 |
| Hong Kong | 3,686 | 113,224 |
| Iran | 4,163 | 119,864 |
| *America* | 1,038,015 | 388,556 |
| USA | 939,986 | 308,026 |
| Canada | 28,057 | 29,781 |
| South America | 89,025 | 36,219 |
| *Australia and New Zealand* | 3,774 | 18,946 |

### COMMUNICATIONS

**Roads.** There are more than 6,200 miles of roads, 2,700 miles being maintained by the Government, alone or with local authorities, 3,250 miles by local authorities themselves, and the rest by private bodies.

Large sums have been invested in road making, widening and alignment to keep pace with economic expansion and the rapid growth in the number of private and commercial vehicles. In 1974/75. IL 309·3 million was spent on road development.

The highways connecting Eilat to Haifa provide for the first time in history a satisfactory link between the Red Sea and the Mediterranean; a start has been made in using it for a land-sea service carrying goods between Europe and East Africa, a kind of 'dry-land Suez Canal'.

Buses operated by cooperatives are the principal means of passenger transport, with the railways second and *sherut* taxis (plying along fixed routes for fixed fares) a good third. There were 5,615 buses in 1974 and five *sherut* taxi services running between the major towns.

Fares, routes and frequency of services are supervised by the Ministry of Transport.

There were 267,425 private cars in 1974. In 1960 there was one car for every 50 inhabitants, by 1973 the ratio was nearly 1:15.

**Railways.** The railways are State-owned. There are 484 miles of main lines and 291 miles of branch lines in operation.

The extension to the Negev is very important for the development and population of that area. The line, which was lengthened from Beersheba to Dimona in 1965, reached the phosphate works at Oron in 1970, with a Spur to Tzefa, near Arad.

**Shipping.** Israel's major deep water port on the Mediterranean is Haifa, with a subsidiary harbour at the mouth of the Kishon river nearby. A modern port in the South of Israel's Mediterranean has been built at Ashdod, replacing the port of Tel-Aviv which has been closed.

The following table shows freight handling figures for various ports for 1974:

| | *Freight Traffic (tons)* |
|---|---|
| Haifa port | 4,139,000 |
| Ashdod port | 1,774,000 |
| Eilat port | 337,000 |
| Unloading—total | 6,250,000 |
| Haifa port | 1,082,000 |
| Ashdod port | 2,188,000 |
| Eilat port | 450,000 |
| Loading—total | 3,720,000 |

The Port of Eilat on the Red Sea is of supreme importance for trade with Asia and Africa. A 16-inch oil pipeline links Eilat with Haifa.

At the beginning of 1974 there were 106 ships in the merchant fleet with a gross weight of 2,304,253 tons.

**Civil Aviation.** The chief airport is at Lod. In 1974, 9,182 planes landed, 870,600 passengers arrived; 876,000 passengers departed, 28,191 tons of freight were loaded; and 20,860 tons unloaded.

Below is shown the principal airline:

**EL-AL, Israel Airlines, Ltd.** (Managing Director, Mr. M. Hod); Issued Capital I£55,500,000. The company serves the following cities: Tel Aviv, Amsterdam, Athens, Brussels, Bucharest, Constanza, Copenhagen, Frankfurt, Geneva, Istanbul, Johannesburg, Lisbon, London, Mexico, Montreal, Munich, Nairobi, New York, Nice, Nicosia, Paris, Rome, Teheran, Vienna, Zurich, and has a fleet of 14 Boeings, including 4 Boeing 747s. In 1976–77 El-Al carried 901,880 passengers.

*Head Office:* Ben Gurion International Airport, Lod.

**Posts, Telegraphs and Telephones.** In 1974–75 there were 591 post offices and postal agencies. A further 43 mobile post offices serve 636 rural settlements. Over 72,000 accounts were handled by the Post Office Bank. The total sum of transactions handled by the Post Office exceeded IL 16,000 million. There are 91 telephone exchanges in the country. In 1974 the number of operating telephone sets was 698,800. In 1973, 56,300 telephones were installed. Communications by radio telegraph and radio telephone are maintained with most countries in the world. A telex service was inaugurated recently. In December 1959 Israel was linked to the International Telex network. A satellite communication station has been operating since 1972 for telephone telegraph and telex communication as well as for television and radio broadcasts and computer and metereological data.

## CULTURE

**Theatre.** Israel has three main professional companies—Habimah, the Israel National Theatre; Kameri Theatre and Haifa Municipal Theatre. Apart from these three theatres there are revue companies and amateur groups scattered throughout the country. Several companies, most of them satirical revues, perform in languages other than Hebrew, especially for new immigrants. The Israel National Opera was re-opened in 1958.

There is an annual Festival of Music and Drama. It is held at the Roman Amphitheatre in Caesarea and in other towns throughout the country, during July and August.

**Music.** The leading orchestra in Israel is the Israel Philharmonic Orchestra which gives a series of concerts for 32,000 subscribers (135 each season)—a world record. The orchestra now has a permanent home of its own; the 3,000-seat Fredric R. Mann Auditorium in Tel Aviv. A number of other orchestras and numerous musical ensembles in settlements also give concerts regularly. Every three years a world-wide meeting of Jewish Choirs takes place in Israel. There have been International Harp Contests in Israel.

**Literature.** Israel publishes almost 4,000 books every year. A novel by an established writer would reach a circulation of fifteen to forty-five thousand copies (in a population of 3 million). Most European and other classics have been translated into Hebrew, as well as contemporary world literature. The country has 4 literary monthlies and 5 literary supplements to daily newspapers. The 1966 Nobel Prize winner was the Israeli writer, S. J. Agnon

## NEWSPAPERS

There are 11 daily newspapers (two of them afternoon) published in Hebrew, four in Arabic and nine in other languages. There are over 550 other periodicals, including some 70 Government publications. About 65 are weeklies and 150 fortnightlies or monthlies. Over 300 periodicals appear in Hebrew, 50 in English and others are published in Arabic, Bulgarian, French, German, Hungarian, Ladino, Persian, Romanian, Russian, Spanish and Yiddish.

**Ha'aretz.** 21, Salman Schocken St., P.O. Box 233 Tel-Aviv. F. 1918. Hebrew morning. Independent.

**Davar.** 45 Sheinkin St., Tel-Aviv. Hebrew, morning, Histadrut. F. 1925.

**The Jerusalem Post.** P.O. Box 81, Jerusalem, F. 1932. English, morning, daily excpt Saturdays.

**The Jerusalem Post International Edition.** P.O. Box 81, Jerusalem, Israel (or 110 East 59th Street, New York, N.Y., 10022). F. 1959. English.

**Ma'ariv.** 2 Carlebach St., Tel-Aviv. F. 1948. Hebrew, evening. Independent. Circulation 210,000.

**Uj Kelet.** 52 Harakevet St., Tel-Aviv. F. 1918. Hungarian. Morning. Circulation 20,000.

**Yediot Ahronot.** 5 Yehuda Mozes St., Tel-Aviv. F. 1939. Hebrew, evening. Independent. Circulation daily 130,000; weekend 18,000.

## ATOMIC ENERGY

In view of the scarcity of local fuel resources, and the important role which atomic energy is bound to play in Israel very soon, work in the field of atomic energy was started immediately after the establishment of the State.

This work which is directed and supervised by the Atomic Energy Commission appointed by the Prime Minister in 1952. The Commission, composed of leading personalities in science, industry, economics and administration, advises the Government on nuclear research and development, and supervises the execution of policy.

Israel has to research centres: the Sorek Nuclear Research Centre and the Negev Nuclear Research Centre.

The main areas of research and study are: nuclear physics and chemistry, reactor engineering, radiation research, application of isotopes, metallurgy, electronics, radiobiology, nuclear medicine, nuclear power and desalination.

Some of the research projects are carried out in co-operation with the institutes of higher education in Israel, the International Atomic Energy Agency in Vienna, Euratom and other institutions abroad.

The research centres provide the following national services: health physics, including film-badge service; isotope production and molecule labelling; activation analysis; irradiation; advice to industry and institutions; training of personnel; technical courses; documentation.

Israel has arrangements for co-operation in the peaceful uses of atomic energy with a number of countries.

Israel awards fellowships to other countries, both through the International Atomic Energy Agency and directly and from time to time acts as host-country to international panels and courses. Her own scientists are active participants in courses, symposia and panels arranged by the IAEA and other organizations.

## EDUCATION

Israel has universal, free and compulsory primary education for all children between the ages of 5 and 15. Young people below the age of 18 who have not completed elementary schooling must attend special classes. The language is Hebrew in all Jewish schools and Arabic in all Israel Government Arab schools.

In 1969 the Knesset approved re-organization of the school system into 6 years' primary; 3 years' junior secondary and 3 years' senior secondary.

In 1974–75 there were 6,620 educational institutions, 59,195 teaching posts and the total of pupils attending numbered 1,014,414, of which 53,000 were in academic institutions and 89,350 were in other institutions.

The following table gives some educational statistics for 1974–75:

98 per cent of all children belonging to the age groups covered by the State Compulsory Education Law attend kindergartens and elementary schools. This percentage is among the highest in the world. The last year of kindergarten is compulsory.

**Higher Education**

*The Hebrew University*
In 1974–75 had 15,500 students (compared with 1,000 in 1948). About 200 of the students are Arabs and Druzes; 4,000 come from abroad. Teaching staff numbers 1,857.

*The Technion, Israel Institute of Technology*
In 1974–75 undergraduates numbered 8,550. In addition, there are: 3,000 post-graduate students, 1,709 in the Junior Technical College, 2,788 in the school for Senior Technicians and over 11,000 on extension courses. The teaching staff number 1,317.

*Tel Aviv University*
Founded in 1956. In 1974–75 there were 12,900 students and an academic staff of 2,403.

*Bar Ilan University*
A campus of 22 buildings at Ramat Gan near Tel Aviv. There are 7,000 students at Bar Ilan University, students and a teaching staff of 886. Here there is compulsory study of Jewish Subjects.

*Haifa University*
Founded 1963. Faculties of Humanities and Social Sciences. This University had in 1974–75 4,850 students and an academic staff of 778. Some 380 students are Arabs and Druzes; some 750 students have come from abroad.

*Ben Gurion University of the Negev*
Founded in 1965 at Beersheba. 1974–75 enrolment: 3,750 undergraduate students. Teaching staff of 862.

*The Weizmann Institute of Science*
The Institute in Rehovot is devoted to fundamental research in the natural sciences. Its 400 projects include such fields as cancer research, immunology, genetics, organic and physical chemistry (including isotope research), experimental and theoretical nuclear and elementary particle physics, solid-state and chemical physics, seismology, applied mathematics, design and construction of computers, biophysics, biochemistry and polymers and plastics.

There are also areas more specifically related to Israel's own problems, such as desalination and hydrology.

In 1972–73 the Institute's staff numbers about 2,100 including 176 Senior Academic staff and 550 students.

**RELIGION**

There is a Ministry for the supervision of religious affairs, with departments for all creeds—Jewish, Christian, Moslem and Druze.* The religious affairs of each community are otherwise under the full control of the religious order concerned. The Jewish Sabbath and Holy Days are observed as holidays by the State, but provision is also made for the observance of similar days according to other faiths.

* The Druze community is one holding distinctive religious beliefs of a Gnostic character.

# Italy

(REPUBBLICA ITALIANA)

**Capital**—Rome.

**President**—Giovanni Leone.

**National Flag:** A tricolour pale-wise, green, white, red.

**CONSTITUTION AND GOVERNMENT**

THE seizure of Rome by Italian forces in 1870 and the consequent withdrawal of the Pope into the Vatican, followed by King Victor Emanuel II's entry into the city, which was then declared the capital of the Kingdom of Italy, marked the end of the long struggle for Italian unity and independence, in which Mazzini's idealism, Garibaldi's militant nationalism and Cavour's diplomacy paved the way for the emergence of the Italian nation under the House of Savoy.

In the summer of 1943 the Allies invaded Italy. Mussolini resigned from the premiership of the Fascist régime which he had held since 1922, and power was transferred to Marshal Pietro Badoglio under King Victor Emanuel III. The King retired on 5 June 1944 and Crown Prince Umberto became Lieutenant-General of the Kingdom. Following the King's abdication on 9 May 1946, Umberto succeeded him as King Umberto II.

On 2 June 1946 a referendum was held which revealed that out of a total electorate of 28,005,449, the number of Italians in favour of a republican form of government was 12,717,923, as opposed to 10,719,284, who cast their vote for the Monarchy. Broadly speaking, the North was Republican in temper, the South Monarchist in its loyalties.

On the announcement of the result of the referendum on 10 June, Italy became a Republic, and in accordance with this result, King Umberto left the country on 13 June, bringing to an end the reign of the House of Savoy. The first elections held concurrently with the Referendum brought the Catholic Christian Democrats to power with the Communists and the Socialists. The first government was a coalition of the three parties under the premiership of Christian Democrat Alcide de Gasperi. In July 1947, de Gasperi dissolved the government and reformed it, leaving out the parties of the Left.

The first republican constitution was adopted by the Constituent Assembly on 22 December 1947, and came into force on 1 January 1948. The Constitution describes Italy as 'a democratic republic founded on work, with sovereignty vested in the people, to be exercised in the forms and within the framework of the Constitution'. Parliament is bicameral and consists of a Chamber of Deputies and a Senate. The lower chamber is elected by direct and universal adult suffrage for five years, the number of deputies is 630. The Senate is elected regionally, the number of Senators is 315. Each region returns at least 7 senators except Valle D'Aosta, which returns only 1. In addition the President of the Republic can nominate 5 senators for life from among men eminent in the public, scientific and cultural life of the country.

The President of the Republic is elected by the two chambers sitting in joint session to which are added 3 delegates from each Regional Council. The successful candidate must poll a two-thirds majority, but after three inconclusive ballots, an absolute majority is decisive. The President can dissolve Parliament, except in the course of the last six months of his seven years tenure of office.

Article 94 of the Constitution asserts the principle of cabinet responsibility, and the newly constituted cabinet must obtain a vote of confidence within ten days of its coming to office. An adverse vote in parliament does not suffice to unseat a government. It can only be forced to resign by a deliberate vote of censure. Ministers are responsible collectively for the policy of the Government and individually for the actions of their departments.

Legislative power is vested in the Government, both chambers and such other bodies on whom it has been conferred by the Constitution. The President promulgates laws, but his acts are only valid if counter-signed by the minister concerned.

The Constitution is notable for certain features designed to bar the way to unconstitutional developments and the abuse of power. Thus it provides for a Constitutional Court not unlike the U.S.A. Supreme Court, whose duty it is to pronounce on the constitutionality oi laws and decrees. Allowance is made for a eferendum to the people on controversial issues and for considerable local autonomy, aimed at avoiding excessive centralization.

**Trieste**

IN October 1954 the Governments of United Kingdom, United States, Italy and Yugoslavia signed a 'practical' agreement in London concerning the Free Territory of Trieste which ended the nine-year territorial conflict between Italy and Yugoslavia. Italy was given the northern part of the Territory—formerly known as Zone A—an area of about 223 square kilometres which contains the city of Trieste and the port of Trieste. A narrow coastal strip connecting Trieste with Italy was also part of the adjustment. Yugoslavia was given the former Zone B in the southern part of the territory and certain port facilities in Trieste which Italy undertook to maintain as a free port. Careful provision was made to protect the rights of the Yugoslav minority—estimated at 30,000—in the area under Italian administration. Following the signing of the agreement the Allied Military Government handed over Zone A to full Italian civilian administration and the Allied troops were withdrawn from the former Free Territory.

The population of the Trieste area was, at 24 October 1971 census, 300,304, the majority (271,879) being in the city of Trieste.

**Ministry**

*Prime Minister:* Giulio Andreotti.
*Minister of Foreign Affairs:* Arnaldo Forlani.
*Minister of Interior:* Francesco Cossiga.
*Minister of Justice:* F. Paolo Bonifacio.
*Minister of the Budget:* Tommaso Morlino.
*Minister of Finance:* F. Maria Pandolfi.
*Minister of Defence:* Vito Lattanzio.
*Minister of the Treasury:* Gaetano Stammati.
*Minister of Education:* F. Maria Malfatti.
*Minister of Public Works:* Antonio Gullotti.
*Minister of Agriculture:* Giovanni Marcora.
*Minister of Transport and Civil Aviation:* Attilio Ruffini.
*Minister of Posts and Telegraphs:* Vittorino Colombo.
*Minister of Industry and Commerce:* Carlo Donat-Cattin.
*Minister of Labour and Social Security:* Tina Anselmi.
*Minister of Foreign Trade:* Rinaldo Ossola.
*Minister of Mercantile Marine:* Francesco Fabbri.
*Minister of State-subsidized Industries:* Antonio Bisaglia.
*Minister of Public Health:* Luciano Dal Falco.
*Minister of Tourism and Entertainment:* Dario Antoniozzi.
*Ministers without Portfolio:* Tommaso Morlino, Ciriaco de Mita.
*Minister of Art, Environment and Research:* Mario Pedini.

**Legislature**

Official figures for the vote for the Senate and Chamber of Deputies at the election of 20 June 1976 are:

| *Parties* | *Senate* | *Chambers of Deputies* |
|---|---|---|
| Christian Democrats | 12,215,036 | 14,211,005 |
| Socialists | 3,208,382 | 3,541,383 |
| Social-Democrats | 965,478 | 1,237,483 |
| Republicans | 845,629 | 1,134,648 |
| Communists | 10,631,871 | 12,620,509 |
| Liberals | 436,506 | 478,157 |
| M.S.I.-Destra Nazionale | 2,088,318 | 2,243,849 |
| Others | 1,029,731 | 1,248,543 |

## LOCAL GOVERNMENT

The Republic is divided into regions, provinces and communes, and the constitution specifically promotes local automony and the decentralisation of national services. The functions of the 20 autonomous 'regions' are defined by the Constitution, and the regions enjoy certain legislative and administrative rights in local matters as well as a degree of financial autonomy.

A government commissioner maintains national control, co-ordinating regional administration with the policy of the Republic.

## LEGAL SYSTEM

The legal system is constituted by a Court of Cassation, in Rome, 23 Appeal Court Districts (plus three Appeal Court Sections) and 159 Tribunals. There are also 899 *Mandamenti*, each having its own magistracy (*Pretura*). In Italy are in existence 85 Assize Courts and also *Uffici Conciliatori*, which deal with petty plaints connected with civil business.

## AREA AND POPULATION

The following table shows the area and resident populations of the regions at 31 December 1976.

| *Regions* | *Area (sq. km.)* | *Population 1976 (thousands)* |
|---|---|---|
| Piedmont | 25,399·25 | 4,542,000 |
| Valle d'Aosta | 3,262·26 | 114,000 |
| Lombardy | 23,850·30 | 8,865,000 |
| Trentino Alto-Adige | 13,613·09 | 869,000 |
| Veneto | 18,365·26 | 4,360,000 |
| Friuli Venezia Giulia | 7,844·73 | 1,244,000 |
| Liguria | 5,413·65 | 1,864,000 |
| Emilia and Romagna | 22,122·76 | 3,946,000 |
| Tuscany | 22,991·70 | 3,578,000 |
| Umbria | 8,456·04 | 799,000 |
| Marche | 9,693·52 | 1,396,000 |
| Lazio | 17,202·60 | 4,958,000 |
| Abruzzi | 10,794·09 | 1,220,000 |
| Molise | 4,437·62 | 330,000 |
| Campania | 13,595·33 | 5,334,000 |
| Puglia | 19,346·97 | 3,818,000 |
| Basilicata | 9,992·27 | 617,000 |
| Calabria | 15,080·26 | 2,048,000 |
| Sicily | 25,708·45 | 4,902,000 |
| Sardinia | 24,089·66 | 1,568,000 |
| Total | 301,259·81 | 56,322,000 |

The chief towns with populations are: Rome, 2,883,000; Milan, 1,705,000; Naples, 1,993,000; Turin, 1,790,000; Genoa, 800,000; Palermo, 673,000; Bologna, 485,000; Florence, 464,000.

**Vital Statistics**

| | 1974 | 1975 | 1976 |
|---|---|---|---|
| Marriages | 404,082 | 374,364 | 355,273 |
| Births | 882,459 | 836,688 | 789,678 |
| Deaths | 528,461 | 550,552 | 546,912 |

## CURRENCY AND FINANCE

The lira is the basic unit of currency.

Budget figures for 1974 were: Revenue, 22,080,400 million lire and Expenditure, 26,744,100 million lire.

During 1974 the internal National Debt increased by 9,222,000 million lire and at 31 December 1974 it stood at 27,703,400 million lire.

The total currency circulation (banknotes, coins and treasury notes) was 10,273,100 million lire for 31 December 1973.

The GNP at market prices for 1974 was U.S.$ millions 156,510 and the GNP per capita at market prices was U.S.$2.820. The annual average percentage growth rate of the GNP per capita for the period 1960–74 was 4·2, and for the period 1965–74 was 4·4. [*See the note at the beginning of this section concerning GNP.*]

## PRINCIPAL BANKS

**Banca D'Italia.** (Governor, Dr. Paolo Baffi.) Established 1893; Sole Bank of Issue for Italy; capital is owned by credit, provident and insurance institutions; Balance Sheet at 31 December 1975 showed assets. L.36,986,320,576,304; banknotes in circulation L.12,921,254,566,000; gold reserve L.1,804,287,663,615. *Head Office:* 91, via Nazionale, Rome; 97 branches.

**Banca Cattolica del Veneto, S.p.A.** (President, Gr. Uff. Dr. Massimo Spada.) Established 1892; Balance Sheet at 31 December 1972 showed assets L.775,976,235,989; current accounts L. 762,478,209,557. *Head Office:* 25, via S. Corona, Vicenza; 173 branches and offices.

**Banca Cesare Ponti Spa.** (President, G. L. Ponti; Chairman, R. Tarquini.) Established 1906; Assets as at 31 December 1974, L.60,681,406,130; deposits and current accounts L.58,499,367,620. *Head Office:* Piazza Duomo, 19 Milan. 11 branches.

**Banca Commerciale Italiana, S.p.A.** (Chairman, Prof. Dott. Innocenzo Monti.) Established 1894; Part of the share capital is owned by the Istituto per la Ricostruzio ne Industriale (I.R.I.) which is a State-owned company; Balance Sheet at 31 December 1976 showed assets (excluding 'contra accounts') Lit. 15,242,236,231,978; deposits and current accounts Lit. 13,491,225,574,972. *Head Office:* 6, Piazza della Scala, 20121 Milan; 321 branches in Italy and 25 branches and representative offices abroad.

**Banca d'America e d'Italia, S.p.A.** (Chairman Cav. Lav. Rag. Vincenzo Polli Dott. Managing Director Antonio Tonello; General Manager Sig. Manilo Sesenna.) Established 1917; Balance Sheet at 31 December 1975 showed assets L.1,594,789,291,166; deposits and current accounts L.1,418,876,047,600. *Head Office:* 5, via Manzoni, 20121 Milan: 85 branches and offices.

**Banco Di Desio E Della Brianza S.p.A.** (President, Dott. Ing. Pietro Gavazzi; Chairman, Dott. Mario Veneziani.) Established 1909. *Head Office:* Via XXIV Maggio 1 20033 Desio (Milan). 25 branches.

**Banca Mutua Popolare Di Verona.** (President, Marani Giorgio.) Established 1867. Assets as at 31 December 1974, L.638,827,887,743; deposits and current accounts, L.413,995,572,667. *Head Office:* Piazza Nogara 2, Verona. Branches: n. 15 Agenzie in Verona; n. 55 Filiali nella Provincia di Verona e Brescia.

**Banca Nazionale dell'Agricoltura, S.p.A.** (President, Dott. Gaetano Ennio Barilla.) Established 1921; Balance Sheet at 31 December 1972 showed assets L.2,523,167,162,230; deposits and current accounts L.1,852,940,881,964. *Head Office:* via Lovanio 16, Rome; 148 branches and offices.

**Banca Nazionale del Lavoro**—Incorporated by Decree. (President, Antigono Donati.) Established 1913; Balance Sheet at 31 December 1976 showed assets L.20,971,472,671,680; deposits and current accounts L.18,252,810,814,278 (including the special Credits Section). *Head Office:* 119, via Vittorio Veneto, Rome.

**Banca Popolare di Milano**—Soc. Coop a R. L. (Prof. Avv. Schlesinger Piero.) Established 1865 Balance Sheet at 31 December 1976 showed assets L.4,637,965,005,536; deposits and current accounts L.2,541,087,923,467. *Head Office:* 4 piazza Meda, Milan; 290 branches throughout Italy; Branches abroad in London, New York, Madrid, Barcelona; Representative Offices: Brussels, Buenos Aires, Caracas, Chicago, Frankfurt/Main, Houston, Kuala Lumpur, Los Angeles, Mexico City, Montreal, Paris, Rio de Janeiro, São Paulo, Singapore, Sydney, Tehran, Tokyo.

**Banca Popolare di Novara**—Soc. Coop. (President, Avv. Roberto Di Tieri.) Established 1871; Balance Sheet at 31 December 1976 showed assets L.4,539,723,779,612; deposits and current accounts L.3,682,123,466,249. *Head Office:* 12, via Negroni, Novara. 332 branches and offices.

**Banca Provinciale Lombarda, S.p.A.** (President, Gr. Uff. Rag. Luigi Colombo.) Established 1932; Balance Sheet at 31 December 1972 showed assets L.886,617,735,643; deposits and current accounts L.815,888,788,314. *Head Office:* 4, via G. Sora, Bergamo; 110 branches and offices.

**Banca Toscana, S.p.A.** (President, Enzo Balocchi.) Established 1904; Balance Sheet at 31 December 1976 showed assets L.2,514,471,623,931; deposits and current accounts L.2,185,864,075,719. *Head Office:* 4, Via del Corso, Florence; 175 branches and offices.

**Banco Ambrosiano, S.p.A.** (President, Roberto Calui.) Established 1896; Balance Sheet at 31 December 1976 showed assets L.2,600,779,430,477 (Contra accts. excluded); deposits and current accounts L.2,279,127,141,259. *Head Office:* 2, via Clerici, Milan; 61 branches and offices.

**Banco di Napoli**—Incorporated under public law. (President, Prof. Paolo Pagliazzi.) Established 1539; Balance Sheet at 31 December 1974 showed assets L.5,246,627,743,385, deposits and current accounts L.4,278,743,773,269. *Head Office:* 177–178, via Toledo, Naples; 511 branches and offices.

**Banco di Roma, S.p.A.** (President, Cav. di Gr. Cr. Avv. Vittorino Veronese.) Established 1880; Part of the share capital is owned by Istituto per la Ricostruzione Industriale (I.R.I.); Balance Sheet at 31 December 1972 showed assets L.8,645,772,957,341; deposits and current accounts L.5,760,149,298,010. *Head Office:* 307, via del Corso, Rome; 250 branches and offices in Italy and abroad.

**Banco di Santo Spirito, S.p.A.** (President, Vincenzo Firmi). Established 1605; Balance Sheet at 31 December 1976 showed assets L.3,376,474,518,723; deposits and current accounts L.2,901,026,528,207. *Head Office:* 18, Piazza del Parlamento, Rome; 205 branches and offices.

**Banco di Sicilia—Public Credit Institution.** (Chairman, dott. Ciro de Martino); Capital funds L.166,931,626,287. *Head Office:* Via Mariano Stabile, 182, Palermo; Chief Foreign Department: Via del Corso, 271, Roma; 284 branches and agencies in Italy, one branch in New York. Representative offices in Abu Dhabi, Brussels, Budapest, Copenhagen, London, Paris, Frankfurt/Main and Zurich.

**Credito Commerciale, S.p.A.** (President, Dr. Ing Carlo Pesenti.) Established 1907; Balance Sheet at 31 December 1976 showed assets L.1,556,557,527,490; deposits and current accounts L.1,194,940,176,891 *Hcad: Office* 4, via Armorari, Milan; 61 branches and offices.

**Credito Italiano, S.p.A.** (Chairman, Prof. Dott. Silvio Golzio.) Established 1870; Part of the share capital is owned by the Istituto per la Ricostruzione Industriale (I.R.I.) which is a State-owned company; Balance Sheet at 31 December 1976 showed assets L.12,441,513,885,732 deposits and current accounts L.11,320,890,806,370. *Head Office:* Piazza Cordusio, Milan; 366 branches and offices.

**Istituto Bancario San Paolo di Torino**—Incorporated by Decree. (President, Prof. Dr. Luciano Jona; General Manager, Dr. Luigi Arcuti.) Established 1563: Balance Sheet at 31 December 1975 showed assets L.7,561,149,649,324; deposits L.7,561,149,649,324. *Head Office:* 156 Piazza San Carlo, Turin; 258 branches and offices.

**Monte dei Paschi di Siena**—Public Law Credit Institution (President, Avv. Danilo Verzili.) (Chairman, Mr. D. Verzili; General Manager, Mr. G. Cresti.) Bank established 1472; Balance sheet as at 31 December 1974 showed Reserve Funds: L.158,073,967,787, Deposits: L.3,316,320,000,000, Assets: L.5,159,504,434,120. *Head Office:* 3 Piazza Salimbeni, Siena; 363 branches and offices. Rep. Offices in London and Frankfurt/M.

## PRODUCTION, INDUSTRY AND COMMERCE

**Agriculture.** The area under cultivation and including forest was on 30 June 1975, 270,434 sq. km. out of a total area of 301,260 sq. km. The balance of 30,826 sq. km. is unproductive land. According to the census of 1961, there are 5,657,446 people engaged in agriculture, nearly one-quarter of the working population. About 650,000 hectares have been appropriated and reallotted to some 115,000 families under the 1950 land reform laws.

Italy produces a wide variety of fruit and vegetables, and a large surplus of these, particularly her citrus crop, are exported. She is also an exporter of certain types of wine.

1976 figures for livestock were as follow: cattle, 8,812,600; pigs, 9,097,300; sheep and goats, 9,393,400; horses, mules and donkeys, 540,600. There are now 819,334 tractors in use in Italy.

The following table shows the production of principal crops for the years 1974, 1975 and 1976:

| *Crop (in thousand metric tons)* | 1974 | 1975 | 1976 *(provisional)* |
|---|---|---|---|
| Wheat | 9,695 | 9,610 | 9,528 |
| Rye | 37 | 37 | 35 |
| Barley | 559 | 648 | 760 |
| Oats | 462 | 506 | 440 |
| Maize | 5,043 | 5,326 | 5,337 |
| Rice (paddy) | 997 | 1,009 | 907 |
| Sugar beet | 7,711 | 12,536 | 15,442 |
| Kidney beans (fresh) | 264 | 278 | 283 |
| Kidney beans (dry) | 112 | 106 | 110 |
| Peas (fresh) | 268 | 264 | 253 |
| Peas (dry) | 5 | 5 | 5 |

*continued*

| *Crop (in thousand metric tons)* | 1974 | 1975 | 1976 (*provisional*) |
|---|---|---|---|
| Broad beans (fresh) | 115 | 118 | 121 |
| Broad beans (dry) | 268 | 252 | 239 |
| Chick peas | 19 | 18 | 17 |
| Lentils | 3 | 3 | 2 |
| Total grapes | 11,809 | 10,917 | 10,547 |
| Olives | 2,323 | 3,371 | 1,820 |
| Tobacco | 93 | 113 | 106 |
| Citrus fruit | 2,934 | 2,812 | 3,100 |
| Fodder | 38,271 | 38,546 | — |
| Apples | 1,886 | 2,127 | 2,143 |
| Tomatoes | 3,637 | 3,512 | 2,985 |

**Industry.** The industrialization of Italy did not begin until the 20th century. Today Italy possesses large mechanical, metallurgical, textile and chemical industries. Owing to the lack of natural resources, Italy's industrial development has been in the direction of the manufacturing industries, entailing a precarious dependence on imports of basic raw materials from abroad. The total power generated in 1973 was 142,266 million kWh, of which 39,129 million were generated by hydroelectric plants.

The following table shows the production figures for certain commodities for 1976 (provisional):

| | |
|---|---|
| Steel (tons) | 23,446,624 |
| Sulcis coal (Sardinia) (tons) | — |
| Crude oil (Sicily) (tons) | 820,745 |
| Electricity (kWh million) | 155,833 |

In 1961, substantial plans were formulated for the industrial development of Southern Italy. The regions scheduled for assistance are: Southern Continental Italy, Sardinia, Sicily, The Lazio Districts, the Islands of Elba, Giglio and Capraia.

The assistance planned includes the extension and development of existing undertakings and the creation of new ones.

To encourage this development, there is to be substantial tax reduction, or, in some cases, tax exemption. Capital grants are to be available to small and medium sized industries. A joint-stock enterprise (Istituto lo Sviluppo delle Attivita Produttive) with an initial capital of 2 billion lire will finance and promote the development of industry in Southern Italy.

Production of motor vehicles for 1975 and 1976 is shown in the following table:

| *Commodity* | 1975 | 1976 |
|---|---|---|
| Cars | 1,348,544 | 1,471,308 |
| Trucks up to 1·5 tons | 43,666 | 54,974 |
| Trucks up to 2·5 tons | 21,506 | 24,440 |
| Trucks up to 3·5 tons | 9,243 | 4,731 |
| Trucks up to 5 tons | 3,869 | 4,418 |
| Trucks up to 7 tons | 2,416 | 2,734 |
| Trucks over 7 tons | 22,973 | 23,001 |
| Light motor buses | 2,000 | 1,046 |
| Average buses | 848 | 1,111 |
| Heavy buses | 3,564 | 2,914 |
| Total | 1,458,629 | 1,590,677 |

Production of some industrial products in 1975 and 1976 (in thousand metric tons):

| | 1975 | 1976 |
|---|---|---|
| Iron ores | 631·5 | 514·2 |
| Mercury ores | 231·8 | 140·0 |
| Lead ores | 42·3 | 37·3 |
| Zinc | 234·1 | 247·7 |
| Sardianian coal | — | — |
| Lignite | 2,050·3 | 2,028·0 |
| Pig iron | 11,350·3 | 11,630·6 |
| Crude steel | 21,832·3 | 23,446·6 |
| Mercury | 1·1 | 0·8 |
| Aluminium | 194·0 | 213·0 |
| Lead | 37·6 | 45·2 |
| Zinc | 176·6 | 201·7 |

Imports and exports by principal countries for the years 1975 and 1976 (in million lire) are shown below:

| *Country* | *Imports from* | | *Exports to* | |
|---|---|---|---|---|
| | 1975 | 1976 | 1975 | 1976 |
| Argentina | 216,262 | 342,312 | 115,066 | 113,249 |
| Austria | 392,993 | 639,906 | 482,512 | 726,997 |
| Australia | 172,931 | 326,171 | 136,121 | 216,041 |
| Zaire | 102,369 | 99,712 | 39,999 | 29,255 |
| Belgium–Luxembourg | 793,761 | 1,334,688 | 766,203 | 1,194,324 |
| Brazil | 231,685 | 367,365 | 352,962 | 361,623 |
| Canada | 365,239 | 472,690 | 229,124 | 294,086 |
| China Mainland | 34,631 | 129,511 | 95,723 | 104,246 |
| Denmark | 271,345 | 322,937 | 168,388 | 260,512 |
| Egypt (UAR) | 108,393 | 317,112 | 248,684 | 243,692 |
| France | 3,354,770 | 4,928,258 | 3,025,299 | 4,650,521 |
| Germany | 4,316,247 | 6,167,224 | 4,293,155 | 5,854,854 |
| Greece | 159,354 | 241,394 | 341,799 | 480,313 |
| India | 55,811 | 122,401 | 57,568 | 54,780 |
| Indonesia | 35,679 | 99,435 | 56,031 | 46,175 |
| Iran | 741,932 | 1,056,729 | 370,263 | 642,996 |
| Iraq | 1,093,660 | 1,130,748 | 169,707 | 206,297 |
| Kuwait | 233,910 | 176,156 | 76,436 | 153,889 |
| Lebanon | 1,262 | 3,738 | 119,060 | 27,332 |
| Libya | 216,864 | 1,375,817 | 674,961 | 835,281 |
| Malaya | 74,090 | 130,666 | 15,484 | 22,458 |
| Morocco | 94,366 | 84,276 | 70,548 | 117,380 |
| Mexico | 54,041 | 33,060 | 87,087 | 92,609 |
| Netherlands | 1,189,153 | 1,711,324 | 971,014 | 1,264,753 |
| Norway | 100,402 | 103,694 | 79,265 | 123,053 |
| Pakistan | 23,478 | 41,286 | 42,983 | 49,728 |
| Panama | 28,195 | 33,255 | 22,435 | 29,360 |
| Poland | 200,765 | 281,557 | 204,451 | 275,615 |

| Country | Imports from | | Exports to | |
|---|---|---|---|---|
| | 1975 | 1976 | 1975 | 1976 |
| Portugal | 41,182 | 61,811 | 113,198 | 175,445 |
| Saudi Arabia | 1,531,528 | 2,101,494 | 209,664 | 555,635 |
| Spain | 184,865 | 303,168 | 469,124 | 609,291 |
| Sweden | 336,270 | 400,494 | 260,598 | 380,567 |
| Switzerland | 583,440 | 867,283 | 862,035 | 1,147,910 |
| Syria (UAR) | 210,803 | 255,364 | 104,916 | 189,950 |
| Turkey | 65,223 | 183,767 | 318,035 | 455,049 |
| Union of South Africa | 358,651 | 573,138 | 222,594 | 224,881 |
| United Kingdom | 839,545 | 1,263,628 | 1,046,512 | 1,484,208 |
| United States | 2,193,760 | 2,854,319 | 1,489,646 | 1,998,367 |
| USSR | 587,357 | 1,140,373 | 667,031 | 821,015 |
| Venezuela | 104,503 | 180,421 | 210,499 | 305,169 |
| Yugoslavia | 223,698 | 380,755 | 505,780 | 450,963 |

The quantities of main exports and imports (in tons) for 1975 and 1976 are:

| *Exports* | 1975 | 1976 |
|---|---|---|
| Marble and alabaster | 413,400 | 484,222 |
| Petrol | 4,023,251 | 4,782,854 |
| Petroleum | 2,039,283 | 2,131,797 |
| Gas-oil | 5,940,684 | 4,596,640 |
| Chemical fertilizer | 968,432 | 1,362,564 |
| Rice | 450,353 | 398,535 |
| Fruits, fresh and dried | 1,413,736 | 2,058,558 |
| Wine (hectolitres) | 22,942,272 | 13,009,030 |
| Chemicals | 5,945,837 | 4,495,654 |
| Building materials | 1,580,442 | 2,292,189 |
| Lime, cement and chalk | 850,828 | 926,394 |
| Vermouth (hectolitres) | 1,205,244 | 1,129,295 |
| Total (all exports) | 50,569,773 | 54,310,964 |

| *Imports* | 1975 | 1976 |
|---|---|---|
| Wheat | 1,612,171 | 2,450,660 |
| Coffee | 201,393 | 211,066 |
| Dried, salted fish | 33,074 | 37,039 |
| Olive oil | 85,119 | 79,150 |
| Edible oil and fats | 247,726 | 325,212 |
| Industrial oil and fats | 108,573 | 114,476 |
| Coal | 12,421,900 | 11,811,782 |
| Iron ore | 15,649,164 | 17,052,892 |
| Other metallic ores | 2,695,746 | 2,887,297 |
| Iron and steel ingots | 292,609 | 574,367 |
| Rolled iron and steel | 3,044,197 | 4,551,022 |
| Raw cotton in bulk | 197,553 | 216,333 |
| Crude mineral oil | 94,443,439 | 98,997,505 |
| Common wood, sawn | 2,181,237 | 2,790,260 |
| Paper and cardboard | 359,502 | 476,306 |
| Total (all imports) | 191,128,010 | 203,135,555 |

**Mining.** Italy possesses meagre raw materials and inadequate fuel and mineral resources, and is consequently a heavy importer of coal, oil and petroleum products, iron ore, pyrites and iron and steel scrap. To make up for her lack of fuel, Italy has gone a long way towards developing her water power resources and possesses one of the largest hydro-electric industries in Western Europe.

**Commerce.** Italy's imports normally exceed her exports. To make up the adverse balance of trade she has relied on invisible exports such as receipts from tourists, shipping and the substantial remittances from Italian emigrants.

Her chief imports are raw materials for her industries and basic food-stuffs. Italy's principal exports are textiles, machinery and motor cars, fruit and vegetables.

## COMMUNICATIONS

**Railways.** There is in Italy a total of 20,176 km. of track, of which 16,077 are State-owned. In 1975 the railways carried 490,653,000 passengers and 45,707,000 metric tons off reight.

**Shipping.** On 1 January 1977 the Italian merchant fleet consisted of 3,253 vessels aggregating 11,241,185 gross tons. There were 1,796 motor vessels of 100 gross tons and over: 1,457 motor vessels of less than 100 gross tons.

**Achille Lauro,** vessels 42; total tonnage 600,000 G.R.T. (approx.) gross; *services operated:* Italy—West Indies, Australia, South Pacific, Mexico, also tramps and tankers. *Head Office:* Lauro Building, Via Nuova Marittima, Naples, Italy.

**'Adriatica' di Navigazione S.p.A.** (Chairman, Giuseppe Salomone); share capital L.3,000,000,000; passenger vessels 6, cargo vessels (ro/ro) 7, full container ships 2, hydrofoils 2; total tonnage 61,789 gross; *services operated:* Italy – Eastern Mediterranean – North Europe. *Head Office:* Zattere 1411, Venice, Italy.

**Giacomo Costa fu Andrea,** vessels 12, total tonnage 109,911 gross; *services operated:* Mediterranean and North and South America. Mediterranean and Caribbean cruises. *Head Office:* Via G. D'Annunzio 2, P.20, Genoa, Italy.

**ITALIA di Navigazione-Società pèr Azioni,** (Chairman, Adm. G. R. Lorenzini); share capital L.4,000,000,000; motor vessels 18; total tonnage 328,211; *services operated:* Italy to North, Central and South America, Atlantic and Pacific; Trieste to North and Central America, North Pacific; cruises in Caribbean Sea. *Head Office:* Piazza De Ferrari 1, Genoa, Italy.

**'Italnavi' Soc. di Navigazione Per Azioni,** vessels 9; total tonnage 287,198 gross; *services operated:* tankers, ore/oil carriers, O.B.O. *Head Office:* Via Roma 1, Genoa, Italy.

**Lloyd Triestino,** (Chairman, Alfredo Berzanti); share capital L.6,000,000,000; motor vessels 27; total tonnage 207,166; *freight services operated:* to Australia, New Zealand, India, Pakistan, Far East and South, East and West Africa. *Head Office:* Piazza Unità d'Italia 1, Trieste.

**Societá Italiana di Armamento 'Sidarma',** (President, Clemente Gandini); share capital L.60,000,000; motor vessels 10, total tonnage 74,432 gross; *services operated:* West Africa, Portugal, Central and South America. *Head Office:* Zattere 1404, Venice, Italy.

**'Tirrenia' S.p.A.N.,** (Chairman, Admiral Stegano Pugliese); share capital L.3,000,000,000; motor vessels 25, steam vessels 4; total tonnage 93,517; *services operated:* Northern Europe and the Mediterranean. *Head Office:* Rione Sirignano 2, Naples, Italy.

**Civil Aviation. Alitalia—Linee Aeree Italiane S.P.A.,** (president, Giorgio Tupini); share capital L.50,000,000,000, *services operated:* Rome to Abidjan, Addis Ababa, Accra, Algiers, Amsterdam, Asmara, Athens, Bangkok, Barcelona, Belgrade, Bengazi, Beirut, Bombay, Bucharest, Buenos Aires, Boston, Brussels, Cairo Caracas, Casablanca, Chicago,

Cologne, Copenhagen, Dakar, Dar-es-Salaam, Detroit, Douale, Dubrovnik, Dusseldorf, Entebbe, Frankfurt, Jeddah, Johannesburg, Geneva, Hong Kong, Karachi, Khartoum, Kinshasa, Istanbul, Lisbon, Lagos, Lima, London, Lusaka, Madrid, Malta, Mauritius, Melbourne, Mogadishu, Monaco, Montevideo, Montreal, Moscow, Nairobi, New Delhi, New York, Nice, Nicosia, Paris, Philadelphia, Rio, Sao Paolo, Sydney, Singapore, Santiago, Stockholm, Stuttgart, Tananarive, Tehran, Tel-Aviv, Tripoli, Tunis, Tokyo, Toronto, Vienna, Warsaw, Washington, Zurich, Manchester and Kanoo (only cargo) and internal. *Head Office:* Palazzo Alitalia Piazzale guilio Pastore, 0144 Rome, EUR, Italy.

**ITAVIA S.P.A.**, (President, Avv. Aldo Davanzali). Share capital L.1,800,000,000. *Head Office:* 43 via Sicilia, Rome.

## NEWSPAPERS

**Il Popolo.** F. 1944. Christian Democratic. Daily. Rome.

**La Voce Repubblicana.** Republican. Daily. Rome.

**Corriere della Sera.** F. 1876. Democratic. Milan.

**L'Umanità.** F. 1970. Social Democrat. Daily. Rome.

**Avanti!.** Socialist. Via Guardiola 22, Rome.

**Il Messaggero.** Centre. Via d. Tritone 152, Rome.

**Il Tempo.** F. 1944. Piazzo Colonna, 366-Rome.

**L'Unità.** F. 1924. Communist. Via dei Taurini, 19, Rome.

**Avvenire.** F. 1968. Catholic. Piazza Duca d'Aosta 8/B, Milan.

## ATOMIC ENERGY

At the present time the chief Italian organizations interested in these problems are: The National Committee for Nuclear Energy (CNEN) and The National Institute of Nuclear Physics (INFN). On the industrial side: the Società Ricerche Impianti Nucleari (SORIN) owned by Fiat and Montecatini; the AGIP Nucleare owned by ENI and the Centro Informazioni Studi Esperienze (CISE) owned by ENEI together with other industries.

Two nuclear power plants are now completed in Italy: the Latina 200 MWe gas-graphite plant and the Garigliano 150 MWe boiling-water plant. A third plant, of 250 MWe pressurized water type, is now under construction at Trino Vercellese, near Vercelli.

The National Committee for Nuclear Energy (CNEN) was established by Law N. 933 of 11 August 1960, which also provided for a four-year appropriation.

The present structure of CNEN derives from the transformation of the National Committee for Nuclear Research (CNRN), established by a Decree of the Prime Minister dated 26 June 1925, for the purpose of creating a technical research coordination and Government advisory body in the field of nuclear energy.

Today, the National Committee for Nuclear Energy is a public entity operating under the supervision of the Ministry of Industry and Trade and following the policies laid down by a Committee of Ministers composed of the Prime Minister and of the Ministers of Foreign Affairs, Interior, Treasury, Industry and Trade and Public Education.

The organs of CNEN are: the President (a position held ex officio by the Minister of Industry and Trade); the Steering Commission and the Secretary General, who is the Committee's executive officer.

The Committee's organization comprises nine Divisions, three major Research Centres (Casaccia Nuclear Studies Centre, Frascati National Laboratories and Bologna Computer Centre), each comprising an adequate number of Laboratories and Groups specializing in various operating and study techniques and two main pilot plants now under construction (Brasimone Organic Moderated 30 MWt Reactor and Rontondella Spent Fuel Reprocessing Plant). In addition, CNEN avails itself of the services of several other Study Centres attached to the major Italian universities.

The Committee has a technical staff of experts and specialists in the field of nuclear energy totalling about 1,500 persons; including administrative personnel the Committee's total staff is over 2,000 strong.

Based on these structures, the activities of CNEN develop along the following lines:

(1) Conducting and promoting nuclear research and experimentation;
(2) Exercising high-level scientific and technical supervision of the activities connected with the use of raw materials and special fissionable materials and with the production of nuclear power;
(3) Promoting and encouraging the technical training of experts on nuclear power and its uses; disseminating knowledge of nuclear problems;
(4) Maintaining and fostering technical-scientific co-operation with international and foreign agencies operating in the nuclear field.

CNEN may also finance, support financially and grant contributions to university institutions or other public institutions for studies, research and experimentation in the field of nuclear energy and for the implementation of previously approved specific and particular programmes.

For the performance of the functions of CNEN in the 1960–64 five-year period, the sum of 80 billion Lire has been appropriated.

For the second five-year programme a financement of 140 billion Lire is foreseen.

## EDUCATION

In 1975 (1975–76 academic year), there were 33,534 primary schools attended by 4,835,449 children; 9,800 schools providing education at lower secondary level with 2,761,959. At the upper secondary level, there were 4,228 technical, vocational and art schools attended by 1,321,209 pupils; 836 schools and institutes for pupils intending to take up a career in teaching, with an enrolment of 196,496; and 1,728 classics and science lycées with 560,055 pupils. There were 60 universities and institutes of advanced learning with a student body of 935,795.

## RELIGION

Article 7 of the Constitution states that both State and Church are independent and sovereign in their respective spheres. Their relations are still governed by the Lateran Pact of 1929, according to which the Roman Catholic religion is recognized as the state religion, though the Constitution affirms the freedom of worship and equality before the law of all creeds. The great majority of the Italian population are Catholics (99·6 per cent).

# Ivory Coast

## (REPUBLIQUE DE CÔTE D'IVOIRE)

**Capital**—Abidjan.

**President**—Félix Houphouet-Boigny.

**National Flag:** Vertical tricolour, orange, white and green.

### CONSTITUTION AND GOVERNMENT

FROM 1904 until 1960, when the country became independent, the Ivory Coast was a French territory. The country has signed agreements of cooperation with France, but is not a member of the French Community. The executive consists of a government of eighteen ministers, the executive of a legislative assembly of 85 members. All of them belong to the Rassemblement Démocratique Africain.

**Cabinet**

*President of the Republic:* Félix Houphouet-Boigny.
*Minister of State:* Auguste Denise.
*Minister of State in charge of the Interior:* Mathieu Ekra.
*Minister of State with responsibility for Public Health and Population:* Mr. Jean-Baptiste Mockey.
*Minister of State:* Mr. Loua Diomande
*Minister of State:* Mr. Nanlo Bamba.
*Keeper of the Seals, Minister of Justice:* Mr. Camille Alliali.
*Minister of Foreign Affairs:* Mr. Arsène Assouan Usher.
*Minister of Defence and the Civil Service:* Mr. Kouadio M'Bahia Blé.
*Minister for the Economy and Finance:* Mr. Henri Konan Bédié.
*Minister for Building and Town Planning:* Mr. Alexis Thierry Lebbé.
*Minister for the Plan:* Mr. Mohammed Diawara.
*Minister of Agriculture:* Mr. Abdoulaye Sawadogo.
*Minister for Scientific Research:* Mr. Jean Guédé Lourougnon.
*Minister for Technical Education and Vocational Training:* Mr. Ange Barry-Baptesti.
*Minister of National Education:* Mr. Paul Yao Akoto.
*Minister of Trade:* Mr. Maurice Seba Gnoleba.
*Minister of Public Works and Transportation:* Mr. Désiré Boni.
*Minister for Livestock Production:* Mr. Dicoh Garba.
*Minister of Labour:* Mr. Albert Vanie Bi Tra.
*Minister for Youth, Popular Education and Sport:* Mr. Etienne Ahin.
*Minister of Information:* Mr. Laurent Dona Fologo.
*Minister of the Budget:* Mr. Abdoulaye Kone.
*Minister of Mining:* Mr. Paul Gui Dibo.
*Minister for Water and Forestry:* Mr. Koffi Attobra.
*Minister for Primary Education and Educational Television:* Mr. Pascal Dikebié N'Guessan.
*Minister for Cultural Affairs:* Mr. Jules Hié Nea.
*Minister for Internal Security:* Mr. Gaston Ouassenan Kone.
*Minister for Cooperation:* Mr. Clément Paul Meledje.
*Minister of Postal and Telecommunications:* Mr. Bangali Kone.
*Minister for the Navy:* Mr. Lamine Fadiga.
*Minister for Public Services:* Mr. Kei Boguinard.
*Minister for Women's Status:* Mrs. Jeanne Gervais.
*Minister of Tourism:* Mr. Ibrahima Kone.
*Minister of Social Affairs:* Mr. Alphonse Yao Kouman.
*Minister for the Protection of Nature:* Mr. Tabley Dacoury.
*Minister with responsibility for Relations with the National Assembly:* Mr. Emile Brou.

### LEGAL SYSTEM

There is a court of original jurisdiction. There are also two courts of second instance and the Supreme Court, with appellate jurisdiction.

*President of the Supreme Court:* Alphonse Boni.

### AREA AND POPULATION

The total area of the country is 322,460 sq. km.

The population at mid-1974 was 6,387,000. The average annual percentage growth rate of the population for the period 1960–74 was 3·6, and for the period 1965–74 was 4·0.

### CURRENCY AND FINANCE

The unit of currency is the Central African franc. The details of budgets allowed for are: 1969, 46 milliards 500 millions de F.C.F.A.; 1970, 57 milliards 500 millions de F.C.F.A.; 1971, 62 milliards 700 millions de F.C.F.A; 1972, 68 milliards 200 million de F.C.F.A.

The GNP at market prices for 1974 was U.S. $ millions 2,930, and the GNP per capita at market prices was U.S. $460. The average annual percentage growth rate of the GNP per capita for the period 1960–74 was 3·5, and for the period 1965–74 was 2·7. [*See the note at the beginning of this section concerning GNP.*]

### PRODUCTION, INDUSTRY AND COMMERCE

The Ivory Coast is the most prosperous of the West African regions. It produces coffee, cocoa beans and timber. There are about 280,000 cattle, 350,000 sheep, 410,000 goats and 50,000 pigs. There are factories for production of palm-oil, canned fruit and fruit juice.

Coffee is the most important of the agricultural crops of the Ivory Coast; plantings cover 650,000 hectares, provide a living for about 2,000,000 people (almost half the total population) and the crop harvested in 1970 was 310,000 tons.

Cocoa, once the second most valuable crop, has been supplanted by wood. Export (particularly of hard redwoods) has developed at such speed and on such a scale that, although plans for re-planting are being implemented, there is some risk of temporary over-felling.

Other products of importance are cotton, rubber, palm oil and copra.

The following table shows the gross output by the major economic sectors of the economy for the years 1971–74:

*Gross Output by Sector (CFA billions)*

| | 1971 | 1972 | 1973 | 1974 | % Contribution 1974 |
|---|---|---|---|---|---|
| Agriculture, Livestock, Forestry, Fishing | 117·6 | 125·1 | 159·2 | 194·0 | 28·8 |
| Industry | 68·0 | 79·1 | 87·0 | 119·6 | 17·8 |
| of which: | | | | | |
| Manufacturing Industries | 62·0 | 71·9 | 78·9 | 108·7 | 90·1 |
| Extractive Industries | 1·2 | 1·5 | 1·8 | 1·8 | 1·5 |
| Electricity, Water | 4·8 | 5·7 | 6·3 | 9·1 | 7·6 |
| Building, Public works | 33·4 | 32·5 | 34·5 | 38·5 | 5·7 |
| Transportation | 37·6 | 42·2 | 53·1 | 65·0 | 9·7 |
| Services and Commerce | 108·8 | 114·2 | 136·6 | 204·5 | 30·4 |
| Import Duties and Taxes | 29·4 | 32·1 | 39·5 | 51·4 | 7·6 |
| Total | 394·8 | 425·2 | 509·9 | 673·0 | 100.0 |

The following table shows chief imports for 1976:

| | (Quantity) Tons | (Value) Million CFA FR |
|---|---|---|
| Fish, shell-fish, molluscs | 86,045 | 6,489 |
| Milk products | 31,443 | 7,001 |
| Edible fruits and vegetables | 17,193 | 2,058 |
| Cereals: | 119,508 | 5,353 |
| Rice | 2,315 | 371 |
| Wheat | 113,766 | 4,853 |
| Sugar and Confectionery | 19,749 | 2,491 |
| Processed Food: | | |
| Meat and Fish | 3,273 | 1,013 |
| Fruits and Vegetables | 8,393 | 1,286 |
| Drinks | 68,726 | 5,195 |
| Tobacco | 3,542 | 2,099 |

*continued*

| | Quantity Tons | (Value) Million CFA RF |
|---|---|---|
| Building materials | 863,434 | 6,697 |
| Clinker | 715,069 | 4,294 |
| Oil products | 1,635,838 | 39,965 |
| Crude Oil | 1,529,626 | 35,692 |
| Chemical products | 37,675 | 5,251 |
| Pharmaceutical products | 2,700 | 5,449 |
| Fertilizers | 69,514 | 2,034 |
| Plastics | 27,071 | 7,065 |
| Rubber | 10,124 | 5,439 |
| Paper, board, stationery | 51,308 | 9,859 |
| Threads and Textiles | 23,130 | 14,216 |
| Cotton material | 8,785 | 7,823 |
| Clothes and hosiery | 1,846 | 2,554 |
| Stone, ceramic, glassware | 6,863 | 1,034 |
| Iron work | 169,240 | 24,103 |
| Metal products | 7,754 | 6,471 |
| Machinery and Appliances: | | |
| Mechanical | 29,465 | 37,731 |
| Electrical | 12,559 | 17,320 |
| Road transport material | 44,657 | 40,260 |
| Precision material | 894 | 3,503 |
| Other goods | 134,435 | 48,671 |
| | 3,486,384 | 311,607 |

The following table shows the amounts and values of various commodities exported from the Ivory Coast in 1976:

| Commodity | Quantity in tons | Value in F.C.F.A. (millions) |
|---|---|---|
| Cocoa beans | 194,949 | 71,396·8 |
| Cocoa butter | 12,113 | 10,593·8 |
| Cocoa (in bulk) | 20,056 | 9,291·3 |
| Green coffee | 322,826 | 132,757·2 |
| Coffee extract | 2,424 | 2,421·2 |
| Fresh bananas | 98,647 | 3,149·2 |

*continued*

| Commodity | (Quantity) in tons | Value in F.C.F.A. (millions) |
|---|---|---|
| Fresh pineapple | 61,315 | 2,771·6 |
| Canned pineapple | 59,600 | 7,486·3 |
| Pineapple juice | 12,041 | 646·2 |
| Palm kernels | 28,508 | 1,177·2 |
| Palm oil | 91,861 | 7,783·3 |
| Palm cakes | 1,231 | 30·4 |
| Cola nut | 36,996 | 900·4 |
| Processed fish and shell-fish | 9,473 | 3,095·0 |
| Raw rubber | 17,476 | 3,952·2 |
| Timber | 2,787,128 | 78,318·5 |
| Raw timber | 2,492,778 | 62,356·9 |
| Sawn timber | 239,451 | 10,934·6 |
| Veneer and plywood | 9,338 | 1,187·1 |
| Diamonds | | 282·2 |
| Oil products | 488,309 | 15,166·1 |
| Cotton | 18,976 | 5,565·3 |
| Other products | 294,286 | 36,716·8 |
| Total | 4,558,215 | 392,501·0 |

**France is the Ivory Coast's most important foreign trade partner.**

## COMMUNICATIONS

**There is a railway line from Abidjan to La Leraba and on to Upper Volta. In 1969 the railway carried 2·4 million passengers and 774,000 tons of freight. Total receipts were 3,120 million fr. C.F.A. There are about 28,000 miles of roads, of which less than 1,000 are paved. In 1966, 5,167 planes arrived at Abidjan airport, carrying 65,473 passengers. The main ports are Abidjan, Sassandra and Tabou. In 1966. 2,448 ships (of a total tonnage of 7,076,000) entered Abidjan, 11,170 passengers landed and 19,009 left by sea.**

## EDUCATION AND RELIGION

**In 1970–71 there were about 385,047 Primary school pupils with approximately 8,450 teachers and about 46,000 Secondary school pupils with approximately 1,846 teachers.**

**About one-tenth of the population is Christian and about 20 per cent is Moslem.**

# Jamaica

(MEMBER OF THE COMMONWEALTH)

**Capital**—Kingston.

**Governor-General**—H.E. The Most Honourable Florizel Augustus Glasspole, ON., CD.

**Flag:** On a field quartered wedge-wise green and black, a gold saltire.

## CONSTITUTION AND GOVERNMENT

JAMAICA is situated in the Caribbean Sea, 100 miles west of Haiti and 90 miles south of Cuba. It was discovered by Christopher Columbus on 4 May 1494. It remained a Spanish possession until 1655, when it was attacked by a force under Admiral Penn and General Venables, sent out by Cromwell against Hispaniola and capitulated on 11 May 1655. Regular civil government was established in 1661 by Charles II, who appointed General Edward Doyley Governor-in-Chief with an elected council.

In August 1962, Jamaica became independent after over 300 years as a British colony.

This development came with the after-effects of the decision taken by the people of Jamaica through a referendum in September 1961 to secede from the Federation to the West Indies.

The House of Representatives is elected at least once every five years by universal adult suffrage and consists of 60 members. The member of the House who, in the opinion of the Governor-General, can best command the confidence of a majority of the members of that Chamber is appointed Prime Minister by the Governor-General.

The Senate consists of 21 persons, thirteen of whom are appointed by the Governor-General on the advice of the Prime Minister and the remaining eight on the advice of the Leader of the Opposition.

Any Bill except a Money Bill may be introduced in either House, but a Money Bill may be introduced only in the House of Representatives. For a Bill to become Law, it must first be passed by both Houses, either without amendment or with only such amendments as are agreed to by both Houses. The Bill must then be assented to by the Governor-General. The Senate has no power to delay a Money Bill for longer than one month, or any other kind of Bill for longer than seven months against the wishes of the House. A Bill on its rejection by the Senate, unless the House of Representatives otherwise resolves, may be presented to the Governor-General for assent.

General control and direction of Government policy rests in the hands of the Cabinet, which is collectively responsible to Parliament. The Cabinet must consist of the Prime Minister and not less than eleven other Ministers appointed from both Houses by the Governor-General on the advice of the Prime Minister. Not less than two nor more than four Ministers may be appointed from the Senate.

The Governor-General, acting on the advice of the Prime Minister, may also appoint Parliamentary Secretaries and Ministers of State from both Houses; but there may not at any time be more than four Parliamentary Secretaries appointed from the Senate. It is the duty of the Parliamentary Secretaries and Ministers of State to assist Ministers in the performance of their functions. At present the Cabinet consists of the Prime Minister and 19 other Ministers, not more than four of whom may sit in the Senate. There are also 19 Parliamentary Secretaries.

The Ministers who sit in the House are charged by the Governor-General on the recommendation of the Prime Minister with responsibility for the general direction of the work of their Ministries and the Civil Service Departments specified in their portfolios.

The People's National Party with 47 seats, holds a majority in the House, the Opposition being the Jamaica Labour Party with 13 seats.

The constitution also provides for the Chief Justice and the President of the Court of Appeal to be appointed by the Governor-General acting on the recommendation of the Judicial Service Commission.

*Prime Minister:* Hon. Michael Manley.

## LOCAL GOVERNMENT

The Island is divided into 14 parishes, two of which, namely, Kingston and St. Andrew, are amalgamated for local government purposes. Their affairs are conducted by the Kingston and St. Andrew Corporation. The local authorities in other parishes are called Parish Councils, and there is one in each parish.

The local authorities are responsible for the administration of all local government matters, the most important of which is the maintenance of water supplies, municipal and parochial rates, markets and the administration (under the guidance of the Board of Supervision) of poor relief, maintenance of parochial roads, street lighting and sanitation. In the Kingston–St. Andrew area the maintenance of water supplies is under the control of a separate body—the Water Commission.

Local government revenue, which is derived from local rates and taxes, is supplemented by assistance grants from the Central Government.

The Chairmen of the Parish Councils are also Mayors of the principal towns:

*Trelawny:* Beriah Henlon.
*St. Ann:* Sam Campbell.
*St. Mary:* Noel Walker.
*Portland:* Conrad Francis.
*St. Thomas:* Byron Gayle.
*Kingston and St. Andrew:* George Mason.
*St. Catherine:* Cecil Bramwell Clare.
*Clarendon:* Irvine Francis.
*Manchester:* Cecil Charlton.
*St. Elizabeth:* J. A. G. Myers.
*Westmoreland:* John Mailer.
*Hanover:* Lloyd Spence.
*St. James:* Cecil Donaldson.

## LEGAL SYSTEM

Justice is administered in the island by the Supreme Court, the Resident Magistrates' Courts, the Traffic Court and the Courts of Petty Sessions, the Gun Court and the Family Court. Judges of the Supreme Court are the Chief Justice, a Senior Puisne Judge and seven Puisne Judges. There is a Court of Appeal consisting of the President appointed by the Governor-General on the recommendation of the Prime Minister after consultation with the Leader of the Opposition, the Chief Justice, three other Judges, and any others as may be prescribed by Parliament. The Traffic Court is presided over by a Resident Magistrate. Petty Sessions are presided over by Justices of the Peace or by the Resident Magistrates of the parish.

The Family Court, the first of which was officially opened in November 1975, has jurisdiction over all matters related to family life, with the exception of divorce.

*Chief Justice, Supreme Court of Jamaica:* Hon. Kenneth G. Smith, OJ.

## AREA AND POPULATION

Jamaica is 146 miles long and its greatest width is 51 miles. Its total area is 4,411 sq. miles.

The population of Jamaica at mid-1974 was 2,008,000. The annual average percentage growth rate of the population for the periods 1960–74 and 1965–74 was 1·7.

## CURRENCY AND FINANCE

Jamaica changed to a decimal currency system in September 1969.

Revised budget estimates for 1976–77 were: Revenue, J$612 million. Expenditure J$1,289·5 million.

These figures include recurrent revenues, capital revenues, loan receipts, recurrent estimates and capital estimates of expenditure.

The Public Debt at March 1977 was J$1,430·3 million, an increase of 40·1 per cent over the 1976 figure.

The GNP at market prices for 1974 was U.S. $ millions

2,390, and the GNP per capita at market prices was U.S. $1,190. The annual average percentage growth rate of the GNP per capita for the period 1960–74 was 3·6 and for the period 1965–74 was 4·5. [*See the note at the beginning of this section concerning GNP.*]

## BANKS

**Bank of Jamaica:** Sole bank of issue. It administers currency and external reserves, acts as bankers to the government, and is responsible for management of the National Debt and administration of foreign exchange control. P.O. Box 621, King Street, Kingston, Jamaica. Cables Reserve, Kingston. Telex: 2165.

The following commercial banks operate in Kingston, and branches throughout the island:

**Bank of Montreal (Ja.) Ltd., Bank of Nova Scotia (Ja.) Ltd., Barclays Bank International Ltd., Canadian Imperial Bank of Commerce, First National City Bank, First National Bank of Chicago (Ja.) Ltd., Jamaica Citizens Bank Ltd., Royal Bank Jamaica Ltd.**

## PRODUCTION, INDUSTRY AND COMMERCE

Jamaica's economy is basically agricultural, with agriculture employing over 35 per cent of the island's labour force. The two principal export crops are bananas and sugar, but a variety of minor crops, including coffee, cocoa, pimento, ginger and citrus are also exported. Through the Agricultural Development Corporation and the Agricultural Marketing Corporation, the government provides instruction in agricultural techniques, as well as providing the farmer with finance and with guaranteed marbets.

Since 1959, manufacturing has grown from the processing of a few agricultural products into the production of a range of commodities dependent on both local and foreign raw materials.

Export earnings from bauxite and alumina totalled J$393·1 million in 1976.

The number of visitors (excluding Armed Forces) to Jamaica was 469,200 in 1976 spending approximately J$96·1 million. 75·2 per cent of these visitors came from the U.S.A., 18·5 per cent from Canada, Europe and U.K., and 6·3 per cent from the Commonwealth Caribbean, Latin America and others.

The total value of imports and exports for the years 1975–76 are shown below (million J$):

| | 1975 | 1976 |
|---|---|---|
| Imports | 1,021·4 | 846·2 |
| Exports | 721·7 | 581·8 |

The value of principal exports during 1976 was as follows: sugar, J$156·0 m.; aluminium, J$274·1; bauxite, J$119 m; bananas, J$12·8 m.; others J$119·9 m.

Imports from the United Kingdom in 1976 totalled J$90,331 m. and exports totalled J$99,073 m.

## COMMUNICATIONS

The Jamaica Railways Corporation, a statutory body, operates the railway system, having a total track mileage of 229. The main line is from Kingston to Montego Bay, in the parish of St. James, a distance of 113 miles.

The Island has 2,720 miles of main roads. There are also 7,600 miles of parochial or subsidiary roads, of which more than half are suitable for light motor traffic.

Air Jamaica (1968) Ltd. is the national airline, flying to Miami, Nassau, Chicago, Detroit, Toronto, Philadelphia, Montreal, New York and London. The operating fleet at 31 December 1976 consisted of two DC-8-61s, one DC-8-62, three DC-8-51s, and three DC-9-30, four Boeing 727-200. The scheduled revenue passengers carried in 1975 totalled 696,843, compared to 686,112 in 1974.

There are two international airports, Norman Manley Airport, at Palisadoes near Kingston, and Sangster's Airport at Montego Bay. Twelve scheduled airlines provide freight and passenger services to North, South and Central America, the Caribbean area and Europe. Scheduled internal routes are operated by Trans-Jamaica Airlines Ltd.

The Post and Telegraphs Department of the Ministry of Public Utilities, Communications and Transport operates the country's internal and external postal service and the internal telegraph service. External telegraph services are provided by Jamaica International Telecommunications Ltd. (JAMINTEL) established in 1971 jointly by the Government and Cable and Wireless (West Indies) Ltd. to take over responsibility for all international communications. There are 314 post offices and 472 postal agencies.

There were 108,000 telephones in operation at the end of December 1976. Jamaica is linked to the U.S.A., by submarine telephone cable operated by JAMINTEL and American Telephone & Telegraph, operated by the Jamaica Telephone Company.

So far as broadcasting is concerned there is Radio Jamaica, Ltd., a commercial organization and also the Jamaica Broadcasting Corporation (J.B.C.), a publicly owned corporation. The J.B.C. also operates a television service for approximately 56·5 hours a week. Educational programmes are transmitted for 18·75 hours each week during the school term.

The Government is served by the Agency for Public Information (A.P.I) formerly Jamaica Information Service (J.I.S.) which operates through publications, radio, television, recordings and film.

## NEWSPAPERS

**Daily Gleaner.** F. 1834. Daily, Morning. North Street, Kingston.

**Public Opinion.** F. 1937. Friday. 2 Torrington Road, Kingston.

**The Voice.** F. 1952. Friday. 98 Duke Street.

**The Daily News.** F. 1973. 58 Half Way Tree Road, Kingston 10 Ja. Ed. Canute James. Circulation 30,000 daily.

## EDUCATION

In 1975 there were 804 primary and special schools (enrolment 440,525); 103 schools offering Secondary Education (enrolment 113,922), and four Comprehensive High Schools (enrolment 3,176). There are two Vocational Schools, six Technical High Schools, seven Teacher Training Colleges, the College of Arts, Science and Technology (C.A.S.T.), and the Mona Campus of the University of the West Indies.

## RELIGION

Today the great majority of Jamaicans are Christians and almost every Christian denomination and sect is represented here. There are also very small Jewish, Hindu, Moslem and Baha'i communities. Religious freedom is safeguarded in the country's constitution.

# Japan

## (NIPPON KOKU—"LAND OF THE RISING SUN")

**Capital**—Tokyo.

**Sovereign**—Emperor Hirohito.

**National Flag:** White, with a red sun.

### CONSTITUTION AND GOVERNMENT

The ancestors of the Japanese people are generally believed to be an ethnic group, now known as the Yamato Race, which gradually asserted its supremacy over other warring tribes and clans during the first three or four centuries A.D. The Yamato leaders are generally accepted as the ancestors of the Japanese Imperial Family. The succession to the throne was settled on the male heirs of the Imperial House by the Constitution of 11 February 1889. In the absence of a direct descendant, the succession falls on the nearest prince and his descendants.

The whole of the executive power, according to the Constitution of 1889, was invested in the Emperor, who exercised that power with the advice of ministers whom he himself had appointed.

After the Second World War a new Japanese Constitution was established, proclaiming that the sovereign power resides in the people. This new Constitution, which was passed in the Japanese Congress in October 1946, was promulgated by the Emperor the following month and came into force on 3 May 1947.

The new Constitution deprived the Emperor of all executive power. It abolished the peerage, renounced war, granted votes to women and established many other democratic rights.

The legislative power rests with a bicameral Congress, consisting of a House of Representatives and a House of Councillors. There are 491 members in the House of Representatives, who are elected for a period of four years. In the House of Councillors there are 252 members, one half of whom are elected every three years.

The executive power is in the hands of the Prime Minister and his cabinet. The Prime Minister is elected from among the members of Congress by the members themselves.

**Recent Political History.** 15 August 1945: The unconditional surrender to the United Nations; 8 September 1951 Japanese Peace Treaty was signed, the Japan-U.S. Treaty was signed; 28 February 1952: The Japan-U.S. Administrative Agreement was signed; 8 March 1954: The Japan-U.S. Mutual Security Act was signed; 1 June 1954: The Self-defence Force Law was signed; 12 December 1956: Japan became a member of the United Nations 25 February 1957: Kishi Cabinet was formed 1 October 1957: Japan was elected as one of non-permanent members of the Security Council, United Nations; 25 December 1959: Democratic Socialist Party was formed; 19 January 1960: The Japan-U.S. New Security Treaty was signed; 2 March 1960: The Japan-U.S.S.R. Trade Agreement was signed; 15 July 1960: Kishi Cabinet resigned; 19 July 1960: Ikeda Cabinet started; 9 November 1964: Ikeda Cabinet resigned; and Sato Cabinet started; January 1967: The Liberal Democratic Party under Prime Minister Sato was returned for a second term, and for a third term in December 1969; June 1970: The Japan-U.S. Mutual Security Pact was renewed for another ten years; June 1971: The Okinawa Reversion Agreement (yet to be ratified) was signed by Japan's Foreign Minister Kiichi Aichi and Secretary of State for the U.S.A. Mr. William Rogers.

**Reigning Royal Family.** Shintoist.—As a result of a law of the Imperial House 11 February 1889 (revised 15 January 1947), succession to the throne is in the male line.

**H.M. HIROHITO**, Emperor of Japan; born at Tokyo, 29 April 1901; eldest son of Emperor Taisho (Yoshihito) (born 31 August 1879, died 25 December 1926), by his wife Sadako (born 25 June 1884, married 10 May 1900, died 17 May 1951); daughter of Prince Michitaka Kujo; succeeded his father, having been Regent from 25 November 1921; married at Tokyo, 26 January 1924, Princess Nagako (born at Tokyo, 6 March 1903); daughter of late Prince Kunihiko Kuni.

Children: 1. The late Princess SHIGEKO (Terunomiya) born at Tokyo, 6 December 1925; married at Tokyo, 13 October 1943 (Prince) Morihiro Higashikuni, and had issue (died at Tokyo, 23 July 1961). 2. Princess SACHIKO (Hisanomiya); born at Tokyo, 10 September 1927, died at Tokyo, 8 March 1928. 3. Princess KAZUKO (Takanomiya); born at Tokyo, 30 September 1929; married at Tokyo, 20 May 1950, Toshimichi Takatsukasa. 4. Princess ATSUKO (Yorinomiya); born at Tokyo, 7 March 1931; married at Tokyo, 10 October 1952, Takamasa Ikeda. 5. Crown Prince AKIHITO (Tsugunomiya); born at Tokyo, 23 December 1933; married at Tokyo, 10 April 1959, Michiko Shoda. 6. Prince MASAHITO (Hitachinomiya); born at Tokyo, 28 November 1935, married at Tokyo, 30 September 1964, Hanako Tsugaru. 7. Princess TAKAKO (Suganomiya); born at Tokyo, 2 March 1939; married at Tokyo, 10 March 1960. Hisanaga Shimazy.

Brothers of the Emperor: 1. The late Prince YASUHITO (Chichibu); born at Tokyo, 25 June 1902, died at Kugenuma, 4 January 1953; married at Tokyo, 28 September 1928, Setsuko (born in London, 9 September 1909), daughter of late Tsuneo Matsudaira, Japanese Ambassador in London 1929–35. 2. Prince NOBUHITO (Takamatsu); born at Tokyo, 3 January 1905; married at Tokyo, 4 February 1930, Kikuko (born at Tokyo, 26 December 1911), daughter of late Prince Yoshihisa Tokugawa. 3. Prince TAKAHITO (Mikasa); born at Tokyo, 2 December 1915; married at Tokyo, 22 October 1941, Yuriko (born at Tokyo, 4 June 1923), 2nd daughter of late Viscount Masanari Takagi and has issue·

**Cabinet** (28 November 1977)

*Prime Minister:* Takeo Fukuda.
*Minister of Justice:* Mitsuo Setoyama.
*Foreign Minister:* Sunao Sonoda.
*Minister of Finance:* Tatsuo Murayama.
*Minister of Education:* Shigetami Sunada.
*Minister of Health and Welfare:* Tatsuo Ozawa.
*Minister of Agriculture-Forestry:* Ichiro Nakagawa.
*Minister of International Trade and Industry:* Toshio Komoto.
*Minister of Transport:* Kenji Fukunaga.
*Minister of Post and Telecommunications:* Yasushi Hattori.
*Minister of Labour:* Katsushi Fujii.
*Minister of Construction:* Yoshio Sakurauchi.
*Minister of Home Affairs:* Takenori Kato.

### LOCAL GOVERNMENT

The country is divided for administrative purposes into 47 prefectures, and these are divided into municipalities, towns and villages. Each of these has an elected representative assembly.

Each of the prefectures has a governor who is elected by the people in the area comprised in the prefecture, and each town and village has a mayor and an assembly elected in the same way.

The prefectural assembly is responsible for health, educational and other matters in the whole area.

### LEGAL SYSTEM

A Supreme Court was established by the Constitution which came into force in May 1947. The Emperor appoints the Chief Justice. The Cabinet appoints the judges, but these must be reviewed by the electorate at the first general elections of the House of Representatives following their appointment. The Supreme Court, which consists of 15 judges, can decide on the Constitutional validity of any act of the Legislature or of the Executive. There are also district and local courts.

*President of the Supreme Court:* Tomokazu Murakami.

### AREA AND POPULATION

Japan consists of 4 large and many small islands of a total area of 369,778·13 square kilometres and a population 118,012,000 (1980 estimate). Japan proper consists of Honshu (or mainland), 230,531·9 sq. k.; Shikoku, 18,765·80 sq. k.; Kyushu, 41,969 sq. k.; Hokkaido, or Yezo, 78,511 sq. k.; Okinawa, 2,389 sq. k. The various parts of China which had been throughout the years of Japanese expansion and aggression leased or annexed, e.g. Formosa and the Kwantung Province, reverted to Chinese sovereignty after the War of 1939–45.

The population of Tokyo in March 1976 was 8,613,618 in the Ku area and 11,161,201 in the metropolitan area. The other chief cities had the following populations: Osaka, 2,769,271; Kyoto, 1,458,955; Nagoya, 2,079,062; Yokohama, 2,633,148; Kobe, 1,362,356; Fukuoka, 1,002,214; Kawasaki, 1,017,243; Sapporo, 1,225,888.

The following table gives the list of the prefectures with their areas and populations (in thousands) 1974.

| *Prefecture* | *Population* (1000) | *Area*[1] ($km^2$) | *Population density* |
|---|---|---|---|
| Japan | 113,086 | 377,582 | 304 |
| Hokkaido | 5,394 | 83,514 | 69 |
| Hokkaido | 5,394 | 83,514 | 69 |
| Honshu | 90,022 | 230,929 | 390 |
| Tohoku region | 9,306 | 66,961 | 139 |
| Aomori-*ken* | 1,483 | 9,615 | 154 |
| Iwate-*ken* | 1,394 | 15,277 | 91 |
| Miyagi-*ken* | 1,982 | 7,291 | 272 |
| Akita-*ken* | 1,238 | 11,610 | 107 |
| Yamagata-*ken* | 1,226 | 9,326 | 131 |
| Fukushima-*ken* | 1,982 | 13,782 | 144 |
| Kanto region | 33,261 | 32,315 | 1,029 |
| Ibaraki-*ken* | 2,378 | 6,090 | 390 |
| Tochigi-*ken* | 1,715 | 6,414 | 267 |
| Gumma-*ken* | 1,776 | 6,356 | 279 |
| Saitama-*ken* | 4,962 | 3,799 | 1,306 |
| Chiba-*ken* | 4,264 | 5,119 | 833 |
| Tokyo-*to* | 11,661 | 2,145 | 5,435 |
| Kanagawa-*ken* | 6,504 | 2,391 | 2,720 |
| Chubu region | 19,382 | 66,749 | 290 |
| Niigata-*ken* | 2,405 | 12,577 | 191 |
| Toyama-*ken* | 1,079 | 4,252 | 254 |
| Ishikawa-*ken* | 1,082 | 4,196 | 258 |
| Fukui-*ken* | 779 | 4,189 | 186 |
| Yamanashi-*ken* | 786 | 4,463 | 176 |
| Nagano-*ken* | 2,032 | 13,585 | 150 |
| Gifu-*ken* | 1,889 | 10,596 | 178 |
| Shizuoka-*ken* | 3,340 | 7,772 | 430 |
| Aichi-*ken* | 5,989 | 5,118 | 1,170 |
| Kinki region | 20,649 | 33,046 | 625 |
| Mie-*ken* | 1,638 | 5,774 | 284 |
| Shiga-*ken* | 1,006 | 4,016 | 251 |
| Kyoto-*fu* | 2,452 | 4,613 | 532 |
| Osaka-*fu* | 8,341 | 1,860 | 4,484 |
| Hyogo-*ken* | 5,034 | 8,369 | 601 |
| Nara-*ken* | 1,100 | 3,692 | 298 |
| Wakayama-*ken* | 1,078 | 4,723 | 228 |
| Chugoku region | 7,424 | 31,858 | 233 |
| Tottori-*ken* | 586 | 3,492 | 168 |
| Shimane-*ken* | 771 | 6,627 | 116 |
| Okayama-*ken* | 1,829 | 7,084 | 258 |
| Hiroshima-*ken* | 2,671 | 8,459 | 316 |
| Yamaguchi-*ken* | 1,566 | 6,099 | 257 |
| Shikoku | 4,070 | 18,797 | 217 |
| Tokushima-*ken* | 809 | 4,145 | 195 |
| Kagawa-*ken* | 971 | 1,880 | 516 |
| Ehime-*ken* | 1,476 | 5,665 | 261 |
| Kochi-*ken* | 814 | 7,107 | 115 |
| Kyushu | 12,541 | 42,094 | 298 |
| Fukuoka-*ken* | 4,359 | 4,950 | 881 |
| Saga-*ken* | 842 | 2,419 | 348 |
| Nagasaki-*ken* | 1,577 | 4,104 | 384 |
| Kumamoto-*ken* | 1,731 | 7,400 | 234 |
| Oita-*ken* | 1,200 | 6,331 | 189 |
| Miyazaki-*ken* | 1,100 | 7,734 | 142 |
| Kagoshima-*ken* | 1,734 | 9,157 | 189 |
| Okinawa | 1,059 | 2,249 | 471 |
| Okinawa-*ken* | 1,059 | 2,249 | 471 |

[1] Figures for prefectures do not add up to the total because of the exclusion of the areas in dispute concerning boundaries.

The total population at mid-1974 was 109,670,000. The annual average percentage growth rate for the period 1960–74 was 1·1 and for the period 1965–74 was 1·2.

## CURRENCY

The unit of currency is the yen. The value of the yen before World War II was 28·81 U.S. cents. Since April 1949 it has been 0·2778 cents ($1 = 300 yen). The exchange rate to £1 is about 525 yen.

Coins in circulation are of aluminium (1 yen), copper (5 and 10 yen), nickel (50 yen) and silver (100 yen), and noter of 10,000 yen have been issued since December 1958. At ths end of 1974 notes in circulation amounted to ¥.116,678 million.

## FINANCE

The following table shows the Revenue in General Accounts in 100 million yen for several fiscal years:

| *Fiscal year* | *Total* | *Taxes* | | | | |
|---|---|---|---|---|---|---|
| | | *Total* | *Income tax* | *Corporation tax* | *Liquor tax* | *Customs duties* |
| 1965 | 37,731 | 29,668 | 9,704 | 9,271 | 3,529 | 2,220 |
| 1970 | 84,592 | 70,771 | 24,282 | 25,672 | 6,136 | 3,815 |
| 1975 | 214,734 | 132,730 | 54,823 | 41,279 | 9,140 | 3,733 |
| 1976[1] | 246,502 | 149,890 | 64,010 | 46,080 | 10,710 | 4,330 |
| 1977[2] | 285,143 | 175,260 | 73,480 | 58,130 | 10,580 | 5,270 |

| *Fiscal year* | *Stamp duties* | *Monopoly profits* | *Government enterprise profits and receipts*[3] | *Miscellaneous* | *Public bonds* | *Surplus during previous fiscal year* |
|---|---|---|---|---|---|---|
| 1965 | 827 | 1,804 | 402 | 1,699 | 1,972 | 1,358 |
| 1970 | 2,187 | 2,744 | 313 | 3,199 | 3,472 | 1,906 |
| 1975 | 4,798 | 3,405 | 346 | 7,857 | 52,805 | 12,793 |
| 1976[1] | 5,300 | 6,238 | 342 | 8,149 | 73,750 | 2,833 |
| 1977[2] | 7,140 | 5,490 | 1,397 | 10,357 | 84,800 | 699 |

[1] Revised budget. [2] Original budget.
[3] Including receipt from liquidation of Government property.

The following table shows the Expenditure in General Accounts in 100 million yen for several fiscal years:

| *Fiscal year* | *Total* | *Social securities* | *Education and culture* | *National debt* | *Pensions* | *Transfers to local governments* |
|---|---|---|---|---|---|---|
| 1965 | 37,230 | 5,457 | 4,957 | — | 1,681 | 7,162 |
| 1970 | 81,877 | 11,515 | 9,652 | 2,870 | 2,979 | 17,716 |
| 1975 | 208,609 | 41,356 | 27,075 | 11,024 | 7,590 | 33,511 |
| 1976[1] | 246,502 | 48,293 | 30,581 | 18,430 | 9,877 | 39,422 |
| 1977[2] | 285,143 | 56,919 | 34,301 | 23,487 | 11,620 | 49,326 |

| Fiscal year | National defence | Public works | Economic cooperation | Small business measures | Foodstuff control | Other |
|---|---|---|---|---|---|---|
| 1965 | 3,056 | 7,261 | 124 | 178 | 1,298 | 6,055 |
| 1970 | 5,906 | 14,406 | 920 | 500 | 4,884 | 10,529 |
| 1975 | 13,861 | 34,870 | 1,675 | 1,246 | 9,146 | 27,255 |
| 1976[1] | 15,228 | 37,923 | 1,822 | 1,481 | 9,016 | 34,428 |
| 1977[2] | 16,906 | 42,810 | 2,109 | 1,729 | 8,288 | 37,647 |

[1] Revised budget. [2] Original budget.

The GNP at market prices for 1974 was U.S. $ millions 446,026 and the GNP per capita at market prices was U.S. $4,070. The annual average percentage growth rate of the GNP per capita for the period 1960–74 was 8·8 and for the period 1965–74 was 8·5. [*See the note at the beginning of this section concerning GNP.*]

## PRINCIPAL BANKS

**Bank of Fukuoka, Ltd.** Established 1945. (President, Toshiaki Yamashita; Chairman, Gojiro Arikawa.) Assets as at 31 March 1976 ¥1,251,090,228,000; deposits and current accounts ¥1,071,365,610,000. *Head Office:* 13–1 Tenjin 2-chome, Fukuoka-city, Japan. 151 Branches.

**Bank of Japan.** (Governor, Teiichira Morinaga; Deputy Governor, Haruo, Mayekawa.) Established 1882; Central Bank and Sole Bank of Issue for Japan; Balance Sheet at 31 March 1976 showed assets ¥15,876,868 million; gold bullion ¥30,890 million, total banknotes in circulation. ¥11,276,000 million. *Head Office:* 2-2-1 Hongoku-cho, Nihonbashi, Chuo-ku, Tokyo. 33 Branches.

**Bank of Tokyo Limited.** (President, Soichi Yokoyama.) Established 1946; Balance Sheet at 31 March 1976 showed assets ¥8,073,141,256; deposits and debentures ¥4,480,342,955. *Head Office:* Nihembashi, Chuo-ku, Tokyo. Branches and agencies: Japan 31; overseas 39. Affiliates and subsidiaries 19; associated institutions 11.

**Chartered Bank.** (Three branches); see United Kingdom.

**Chuo Trust & Banking Co., Ltd.** Established 1962. (President, Hisao Fukuda; Chairman, Keitaro Nagato.) Assets as at 31 March 1977, ¥1,526,847,740,000; deposits and current accounts ¥1,420,391,488,000. *Head Office* No. 3, Kyobashi 1-chome, Chuo-ku, Tokyo 104, Japan. Number of Branches: Domestic 42; Overseas 2 (New York, London Rep. Office).

**Dai-Ichi Kangyo Bank Limited** was formed 1 October 1971 by the merger of The Dai-Ichi Bank Limited with The Nippon Kangyo Bank Limited, (Chairman, Shojiro Nishikawa; President, Shuzo Muramoto) Balance Sheet at 31 March 1977 showed assets 12,782,387 million yen; deposits 8,608,763 million yen. *Head Office:* 6-2, Marunouchi 1-chome, Chiyoda-ku, Tokyo. 100 Branches and agencies: Japan 313 in all principal cities; Overseas 7: Representative Offices 10; Subsidiaries 3; Affiliated and associated companies 15; Other investments in overseas financial institutions 4.

**Fuji Bank Limited.** (President, Takuji Matsuzawa.) Established 1880; Balance Sheet at 31 March 1977 showed assets of ¥10,897,742 million; deposits ¥7,434,911 million. *Head Office:* 1-chome, Otemachi Chiyoda-ku, Tokyo. Agency in New York and branches in London, Düsseldorf, Seoul, Los Angeles, Singapore, Chicago. Nine overseas representative offices in Djakarta, Hong Kong, Sao Paulo, Beirut, Toronto, Chicago, Tehran, Paris and Sydney.

**Hokuriku Bank, Ltd.** Established 1943. (President, Seisuke Mase.) Assets as at 31 March 1977. Total Assets 1,831,569 (In millions of yen); deposits and current accounts, Total deposits 1,449,098 (In millions of yen). *Head Office:* 2-26, Tsutsumicho-dori, 1-chome, Toyama city, Japan. 144 Branches.

**Hongkong and Shanghai Banking Corporation.** Branches in Kobe, Osaka and Tokyo. See Hong Kong.

**Industrial Bank of Japan, Limited.** Established 1902. (President, Kisaburo Ikeura; Chairman, Isao Masamune). Assets as at 31 March 197 (in thousands), U.S. $32,379,039 (¥8,978,707,487); debentures and deposits U.S. $26,121,491 *Head Office:* 3-3, Marunouchi 1-chome, Chiyoda-ku, Tokyo. Number of Branches: 16 in Japan; 1 Agency, 2 overseas, 8 overseas representatives.

**Mercantile Bank Limited.** Branch in Nagoya. See Hong Kong.

**Mitsubishi Bank Limited.** (Chairman of the Board and President, Toshio Nakamura.) Establis hed 1919; Balance Sheet at 31 March 1977 showed total assets: ¥10,477,929,910,000; deposits: ¥7,195,184,394,000. *Head Office:* 7-3, Marunouchi 2-chome Chiyoda-ku, Tokyo. 194 branches throughout Japan. Agency: Los Angeles; Branches: New York, Chicago, London, Düsseldorf, Seoul, Singapore. Representative offices: Toronto, Sao Paulo, Paris, Beirut, Hong Kong, Jakarta, Sydney.

**Mitsui Bank Limited.** (President Joji Itakura.) Established 1876; Balance Sheet at 31 March 1977 showed assets ¥7,889,484 million; deposits ¥5,174,897 million. *Head Office:* 1-2, Yurakucho 1-Chome, Chiyoda-ku, Tokyo. 166 offices, with overseas offices in New York, Los Angeles, London, Brussels, Bangkok, Bombay, Singapore, and Düsseldorf.

**Nippon Trust and Banking Co., Ltd.** Established 1927. (President, Shigeyasu Fukawa; Chairman, Shoji Shimomura.) Assets as at March, 1977, Yen. 1,110,654,975,000, U.S. $4,005,022,000 (¥1 = 0·003606); deposits and current accounts Yen. 822,811,844,000; U.S. $ 2,967,060. *Head Office:* 1-8 Nihombashi 3-chome, Chuo-ku, Tokyo. 34 Branches.

**Sanwa Bank Limited.** (President, Toshio Akashi; Chairman, Daigo Miyadoh.) Established 1933. Paid-up capital ¥89,100 million. Balance Sheet at 31 March 1977 showed assets ¥10,272,664 million; deposits ¥7,041,320 million. *Head Office:* 10, Fushimimachi 4-chome Higashi-ku, Osaka. 226 Branches.

**Sumitomo Bank Limited.** Established 1895. Capital ¥80,000 million. Paid-up capital ¥66,000 million. Balance Sheet at 31 March 1973 showed assets ¥9,133,576 million; deposits ¥5,982,617 million. *Head Office:* 22, Kitahama 5-Chome Higashi-ku, Osaka. 202 Offices.

**Sumitomo Trust & Banking Co., Ltd.** Established 1952 (President, Koji Makino; Chairman, Sen-ichi Okudaira.) Assets as at 31 March 1977, ¥4,957,858 million; deposits and current accounts ¥4,459,613 million. *Head Office:* 15, Kitahama 5-chome, Higashi-ku, Osaka. Number of Branches: 43 (Domestic), 2 (London, New York), 1 Representative Office (Frankfurt).

**Tokai Bank, Ltd.** Established 1941. (President, Shinichi Tani; Chairman, Shigemitsu Miyake). Assets as at 31 March 1976, U.S. $24,211,319; deposits and current accounts U.S.$ 15,980,781. *Head Office:* 21–24 Nishiki 3-chome, Naka-ku, Nagoya, Japan. Domestic Branches 213; Overseas Branches and Agencies 4; Representative Offices 6.

**Toyo Trust and Banking Co., Ltd.** Established 1959, (President, Mr. Chigazo Morita; Chairman, Mr. Masao Ohtsuka.) Assets as at 31 March 1977, ¥2,765,208 (in millions of yen); deposits and current accounts ¥2,590,154 (in millions of yen). *Head Office:* 9-1, 1 Chome Nihonbashi, Chuo-ku, Tokyo. 42 Branches in Japan; London Rep. Office: 6th Floor, Gillett House, 55 Basinghall St., London EC2V 5EE; New York Rep. Office: 140 Broadway, New York NY 10005, U.S.A. Hong Kong Rep. Office: 26th Floor, Alexandra House, 16-20 Chater Road, Central, Hong Kong.

**Yasuda Trust and Banking Company, Limited.** Established 1925. (President, Shoji Kamai.) Assets as at 31 March 1977, Yen 3,383,486 million; deposits and current accounts Yen 3,174,772 million. *Head Office:* 2-1, Yaesu 1-chome, Chuo-ku, Tokyo, Japan. 42 Branches in Japan; London and New York Branches.

## PRODUCTION, INDUSTRY, AND COMMERCE

**Agriculture and Forestry.** Rice, which is Japan's main crop, accounted for 39 per cent of the total value of agricultural production in 1975, or 13·2 million tons. Due to the mechanization of rice production and the refinement of rice cultivation skills, the production of rice per hectare increased to 4·8 tons in 1975 compared with 3·8 tons in 1955.

The total production of wheat and barley was 0·4 million tons in 1975. The ratio of wheat and barley production in value to the total agricultural output dropped to 0·6 per cent in 1975 from 3·0 per cent in 1965. Demand for wheat has increased every year despite the decreasing domestic production. As a result, imports rose year after year until they amounted to 5·7 million tons in 1975, accounting for 102 per cent of domestic consumption.

Vegetable production stood at 15·2 million tons in 1975. The share of vegetables in the total agricultural production was 16 per cent second only to rice. Due to the introduction of sophisticated methods of vegetable cultivation in recent years, seasonal variations in shipment volume have diminished markedly.

Pulse production was 0·4 million tons in 1975, of which soy beans constituted 0·1 million tons. Soy beans imports totalled 3·3 million tons in 1975, supplying 95 per cent of the domestic demand.

The following tables give some agricultural production figures for selected years:

| *Year* | *Area planted (1,000 hectares)* | *Production (1,000 tons)* | *Yield per hectare (tons)* | *Imports (1,000 tons)* | *Domestic consumption (1,000 tons)* |
|---|---|---|---|---|---|
| | | Rice | | | |
| 1960 | 3,308 | 12,858 | 3·89 | 219 | 12,618 |
| 1965 | 3,255 | 12,409 | 3·81 | 1,052 | 12,993 |
| 1970 | 2,923 | 12,689 | 4.34 | 15 | 12,200 |
| 1974 | 2,724 | 12,292 | 4·51 | 63 | 12,033 |
| 1975 | 2,764 | 13,165 | 4·76 | 29 | 11,964 |
| | | Wheat | | | |
| 1960 | 602 | 1,531 | 2·54 | 2,660 | 3,965 |
| 1965 | 476 | 1,287 | 2·70 | 3,532 | 4,631 |
| 1970 | 229 | 474 | 2·07 | 4,621 | 5,207 |
| 1974 | 83 | 232 | 2·80 | 5,483 | 5,517 |
| 1975 | 90 | 241 | 2·69 | 5,715 | 5,578 |
| | | Barley | | | |
| 1960 | 402 | 1,206 | 3·00 | 30 | 1,165 |
| 1965 | 245 | 721 | 2·94 | 512 | 1,271 |
| 1970 | 146 | 418 | 2·87 | 1,072 | 1,474 |
| 1974 | 60 | 182 | 3·03 | 2,038 | 2,086 |
| 1975 | 61 | 174 | 2·86 | 2,117 | 2,150 |

All the figures in the table immediately below are to be interpreted in terms of 1,000 tons:

| *Item* | 1960 | 1965 | 1970 | 1974 | 1975 |
|---|---|---|---|---|---|
| Potatoes | 3,594 | 4,056 | 3,611 | 2,942 | 3,261 |
| Soybeans, dried | 418 | 230 | 126 | 133 | 126 |
| Cucumbers | 462 | 773 | 965 | 963 | 1,023 |
| Tomatoes | 242 | 532 | 790 | 822 | 1,024 |
| Eggplants | 449 | 623 | 722 | 663 | 668 |
| Cabbages | 686 | 1,157 | 1,437 | 1,433 | 1,423 |
| Chinese cabbages | 998 | 1,541 | 1,739 | 1,712 | 1,587 |
| Spinach | 231 | 322 | 363 | 335 | 346 |

*continued*

| *Item* | 1960 | 1965 | 1970 | 1974 | 1975 |
|---|---|---|---|---|---|
| Welsh onions | 410 | 568 | 614 | 555 | 555 |
| Onions | 601 | 860 | 973 | 1,031 | 1,032 |
| Lettuce | — | 48 | 164 | 246 | 258 |
| Japanese radishes | 2,859 | 3,085 | 2,748 | 2,724 | 2,545 |
| Taros | 496 | 478 | 542 | 430 | 370 |
| Mandarin oranges | 894 | 1,331 | 2,552 | 3,383 | 3,665 |
| Apples | 876 | 1,132 | 1,021 | 850 | 898 |
| Grapes | 155 | 225 | 234 | 295 | 284 |
| Japanese pears | 240 | 346 | 445 | 508 | 460 |
| Peaches | 170 | 229 | 279 | 263 | 271 |
| Persimmons | 337 | 346 | 343 | 284 | 275 |
| Tobacco | 121 | 192 | 150 | 151 | 166 |
| Crude tea | 78 | 77 | 91 | 95 | 105 |
| Sugar beet | 1,074 | 1,813 | 2,332 | 1,878 | 1,759 |

Owing to the mountainous nature of the country not more than one-sixth of its area is available for cultivation. There were in 1973 over 24,483,000 hectares of forest, of which 11 million hectares were national forests and 1·4 million hectares were private forests. The soil is only moderately fertile, but intensive cultivation secures good crops. The tobacco-plant, tea-shrub, potato, rice, wheat and other cereals are all cultivated; rice is still the staple food of the people (about 12,000,000 metric tons produced in 1973) although consumption of wheat-based foodstuffs has dramatically increased of late. The floral kingdom is rich, beautiful, and varied, though scented flowers are comparatively few. Fruit is abundant, including the orange, persimmon and loquat; European fruits, such as apples, strawberries, pears, grapes, figs and peaches are produced, and the American navel orange is extensively grown. Mulberry trees are now cultivated on only 161,600 hectares (about one third of the pre-war area) and silk is playing a reduced part in Japanese exports.

**Livestock.** In 1974 there were about 1,752,000 milk cows, 1,898,000 beef cattle, 66,230 horses, 8,018,000 swine and 15,730 sheep.

**Mining.** At the end of 1971, 180,000 workers engaged in mining included some 29,195 metal miners, 26,916 non-metal miners, 41,338 coal miners and 1,462 petroleum mine workers.

The following table shows the production figures for minerals and petroleum in 1973:

| *Mineral* | *Unit* | 1973 |
|---|---|---|
| Crude petroleum | thousand k. litres | 817 |
| Coal | thousand m. tons | 22,414 |
| Iron Ore | thousand m. tons | 729 |
| Manganese ore | thousand m. tons | 189 |
| Copper ore | thousand m. tons | 91 |
| Zinc ore | thousand m. tons | 264 |
| Gold ore | kg. | 5·9 |
| Pyrites | thousand m. tons | 1·3 |
| Sulphur (Refined) | thousand m. tons (1971) | 65 |
| Limestone | thousand m. tons | 164,374 |

Japan has large deposits of coal, with reserves amounting to 20,246 million metric tons. The post-war record production was 54,484 tons in 1961. Today, the Coal Association (18 large firms) own 79 mines. 37 per cent of the national output is accounted for by about 545 coal mines which belong to the Coal Mining Industry Federation. They are known as 'medium and small mines'.

**Fishing.** Japan is the foremost fishing country in the world. In pre-war years Japanese catch averaged about 4,300,000 tons, more than double the output of the U.S., the second most important fish-producing nation.

# JAPAN

The following table gives fishing catch figures (in tons) for some recent years:

| *Species* | 1970 | 1971 | 1972 | 1973 | 1974 |
|---|---|---|---|---|---|
| Saltwater (marine fisheries and culture in marine water) | | | | | |
| Herring | 97,374 | 100,483 | 62,198 | 82,658 | 76,274 |
| Sardines | 441,589 | 495,904 | 527,157 | 730,962 | 724,672 |
| Horse mackerel | 269,300 | 315,494 | 193,969 | 183,069 | 216,352 |
| Mackerel | 1,301,819 | 1,253,892 | 1,189,910 | 1,134,502 | 1,330,625 |
| Scurry | 93,129 | 190,288 | 196,615 | 406,445 | 135,462 |
| Yellowtail | 98,175 | 109,845 | 126,651 | 133,185 | 133,662 |
| Skipjack | 231,865 | 191,656 | 253,936 | 318,292 | 373,573 |
| Tuna | 291,017 | 307,965 | 318,090 | 330,282 | 748,950 |
| Swordfish | 66,733 | 52,506 | 48,357 | 44,937 | 348,712 |
| Salmon and Trout | 117,896 | 139,320 | 119,685 | 136,124 | 132,531 |
| Halibut, Flounder, etc. | 295,410 | 347,697 | 356,845 | 388,544 | 356,749 |
| Cod | 2,463,829 | 2,802,763 | 3,122,889 | 3,129,383 | 2,964,295 |
| Shark | 50,564 | 43,689 | 42,669 | 42,215 | 39,909 |
| Sea Bream | 38,796 | 30,378 | 34,188 | 32,949 | 29,497 |
| King Mackerel | 19,870 | 17,444 | 20,857 | 13,955 | 21,149 |
| Flying Fish | 10,139 | 14,076 | 11,021 | 9,898 | 10,003 |
| Mullet | 8,707 | 8,905 | 7,973 | 6,057 | 6,019 |
| Freshwater (inland sea fisheries and culture) | | | | | |
| Salmon and Trout | 13,803 | 16,734 | 17,069 | 21,315 | 22,246 |
| Common Carp | 19,908 | 22,453 | 27,533 | 31,650 | 32,021 |
| Eel | 19,456 | 16,857 | 15,773 | 16,969 | 19,160 |

**Industry.** The following tables show production figures of yarns (in tons), and fabrics (in square meters), for 1972 and 1973:

| *Yarns* | 1972 | 1973 |
|---|---|---|
| Rayon filament yarn | 82,670 | 91,158 |
| Spun Rayon yarn | 203,368 | 181,901 |
| Cotton yarn | 555,140 | 554,898 |
| Spun Silk yarn | 2,917 | 2,878 |
| Wool yarn | 196,409 | 198,390 |

| *Fabrics* ($m^2$) | 1972 | 1973 |
|---|---|---|
| Rayon filament fabric | 264,405 | 272,643 |
| Spun Rayon fabric | 718,248 | 737,855 |
| Cotton fabric | 2,264,148 | 2,380,434 |
| Silk fabric | 189,745 | 188,453 |
| Wool fabric | 543,728 | 469,770 |
| Synthetic fabric | 2,717,931 | 2,922,134 |

The following table shows production of some important industrial products in 1972 and 1973:

| *Production* | 1972 | 1973 |
|---|---|---|
| Electricity (mill. kWh) | 414,291 | 470,150 |
| Gas (m. kcal) | 586,861 | 653,447 |
| Ferro-alloys (thousand tons) | 1,743 | 2,035 |
| Pig Iron (thousand tons) | 74,055 | 90,007 |
| Steel rolled product (thousand tons) | 74,924 | 91,128 |
| Crude steel (thousand tons) | 96,900 | 119,322 |
| Sulphuric acid (tons) | 6,691,976 | 7,116,296 |
| Steel vessels | 12,768 | 14,734 |
| Passenger cars | 4,022,289 | 4,471,000 |
| Motor-cycles | 3,565,000 | 3,763,000 |
| T.V. Receivers | 14,300,000 | 14,414,000 |
| Radio Receivers | 76,833,000 | 24,484,000 |
| Paper (thousand tons) | 7,471,242 | 8,222,182 |

**Commerce.** The following tables gives some export and import figures in millions of dollars:

| *Year* | *Total valve* | | *Asia (total)* | | *China* | |
|---|---|---|---|---|---|---|
| | *Exports* | *Imports* | *Exports* | *Imports* | *Exports* | *Imports* |
| 1965 | 8,452 | 8,169 | 2,747 | 2,731 | 245 | 225 |
| 1970 | 19,318 | 18,881 | 6,033 | 5,553 | 569 | 254 |
| 1974 | 55,536 | 62,110 | 18,188 | 29,273 | 1,984 | 1,305 |
| 1975 | 55,753 | 37,863 | 20,488 | 28,345 | 2,259 | 1,531 |
| Year | (Taiwan) | | Hong Kong | | India | |
| 1965 | 218 | 157 | 288 | 35 | 204 | 184 |
| 1970 | 700 | 251 | 170 | 92 | 103 | 390 |
| 1974 | 2,009 | 955 | 1,360 | 274 | 595 | 658 |
| 1975 | 1,822 | 812 | 1,378 | 245 | 471 | 658 |
| Year | Indonesia | | Iran | | Korea, Rep. of | |
| 1965 | 205 | 149 | 58 | 247 | 180 | 41 |
| 1970 | 316 | 637 | 179 | 995 | 818 | 229 |
| 1974 | 1,450 | 4,572 | 1,014 | 4,766 | 2,656 | 1,568 |
| 1975 | 1,850 | 1,850 | 3,430 | 1,854 | 2,248 | 1,308 |
| Year | Kuwait | | Malaysia | | Pakistan | |
| 1965 | 41 | 306 | 75 | 263 | 104 | 27 |
| 1970 | 94 | 308 | 166 | 419 | 138 | 42 |
| 1974 | 279 | 2,132 | 708 | 979 | 226 | 75 |
| 1975 | 367 | 2,012 | 566 | 691 | 290 | 89 |
| Year | Philippines | | Saudi Arabia | | Singapore | |
| 1965 | 240 | 254 | 48 | 231 | 124 | 33 |
| 1970 | 454 | 533 | 84 | 435 | 423 | 87 |
| 1974 | 911 | 1,105 | 677 | 5,238 | 1,388 | 619 |
| 1975 | 1,026 | 1,121 | 1,351 | 6,135 | 1,524 | 399 |

*continued*

| Year | *Total value* | | *Asia (total)* | | *China* | |
|---|---|---|---|---|---|---|
| | *Exports* | *Imports* | *Exports* | *Imports* | *Exports* | *Imports* |
| Year | Thailand | | Europe (total) | | Belgium | |
| 1965 | 219 | 131 | 1,297 | 1,002 | 49 | 25 |
| 1970 | 449 | 190 | 3,363 | 2,555 | 154 | 74 |
| 1974 | 951 | 686 | 10,276 | 6,930 | 483 | 230 |
| 1975 | 959 | 724 | 10,346 | 5,778 | 410 | 161 |
| Year | France | | Germany, Fed. Rep. of | | Italy | |
| 1965 | 49 | 62 | 215 | 223 | 52 | 38 |
| 1970 | 127 | 186 | 550 | 617 | 192 | 134 |
| 1974 | 736 | 592 | 1,498 | 1,454 | 416 | 462 |
| 1975 | 699 | 501 | 1,661 | 1,139 | 334 | 365 |
| | Netherlands | | Norway | | Spain | |
| 1965 | 119 | 43 | 79 | 9 | 22 | 20 |
| 1970 | 277 | 104 | 184 | 34 | 104 | 28 |
| 1974 | 1,055 | 222 | 471 | 89 | 209 | 127 |
| 1975 | 726 | 214 | 523 | 76 | 302 | 115 |
| Year | Sweden | | Switzerland | | United Kingdom | |
| 1965 | 61 | 34 | 62 | 70 | 205 | 163 |
| 1970 | 99 | 89 | 168 | 177 | 480 | 395 |
| 1974 | 336 | 250 | 373 | 453 | 1,530 | 878 |
| 1975 | 384 | 199 | 348 | 417 | 1,473 | 810 |
| Year | North and Central America (total) | | Canada | | Cuba | |
| 1965 | 2,933 | 2,040 | 214 | 357 | 3 | 29 |
| 1970 | 7,095 | 6,886 | 563 | 929 | 39 | 111 |
| 1974 | 16,578 | 16,312 | 1,587 | 2,676 | 203 | 444 |
| 1975 | 14,697 | 14,929 | 1,151 | 2,499 | 439 | 343 |
| Year | Mexico | | United States | | South America (total) | |
| 1965 | 41 | 145 | 2,479 | 2,366 | 248 | 391 |
| 1970 | 94 | 151 | 5,940 | 5,560 | 596 | 976 |
| 1974 | 305 | 308 | 12,682 | 12,682 | 2,875 | 1,759 |
| 1975 | 348 | 212 | 11,149 | 11,608 | 1,368 | 1,701 |
| Year | Argentina | | Brazil | | Africa (total) | |
| 1965 | 44 | 48 | 27 | 50 | 818 | 353 |
| 1970 | 96 | 154 | 167 | 218 | 1,423 | 1,099 |
| 1974 | 440 | 229 | 1,389 | 657 | 4,930 | 2,935 |
| 1975 | 363 | 213 | 927 | 883 | 5,557 | 2,320 |
| Year | Liberia | | South Africa | | Oceanic (total) | |
| 1965 | 371 | 17 | 137 | 120 | 404 | 652 |
| 1970 | 588 | 32 | 329 | 314 | 802 | 1,812 |
| 1974 | 2,345 | 36 | 959 | 763 | 2,689 | 4,888 |
| 1975 | 2,585 | 16 | 872 | 868 | 2,295 | 4,788 |
| Year | Australia | | New Zealand | | USSR | |
| 1965 | 313 | 552 | 61 | 61 | 168 | 240 |
| 1970 | 589 | 1,508 | 114 | 158 | 341 | 481 |
| 1974 | 1,998 | 4,025 | 485 | 402 | 1,096 | 1,418 |
| 1975 | 1,739 | 4,156 | 393 | 367 | 1,626 | 1,170 |

## COMMUNICATIONS

**Railways and Roads.** The total length of railway track in 1973 was 45,518 km. of which 40,402 km. was owned by Japan National Railways and 5,116 km. by private companies. At the end of 1972 the rolling stock of the National Railways included 459 steam locomotives, 1,997 electric locomotives and 1,946 diesel locomotives.

Receipts from passenger fares on the National Railways totalled ¥965,645 million and receipts from freight charges were ¥229,689 million.

The total length of roads at the end of 1972 was 1,049,497 km. of which national highways comprised 32,877 km. In 1973 there were over eleven million passenger cars and over six million trucks.

**Shipping.** The Japanese merchant fleet in 1971 numbered 8,635 vessels of 30,431,000 gross tons. There were 5,648 cargo vessels of 18,211 tons, 2,370 tankers of 11,722,000 tons, 617 passenger ships of 498,000 tons. Fishing vessels in 1973 numbered 399,023 craft of 2,712,030 tons.

**Civil Aviation.** In December 1973 there were 1,325 aircraft registered in Japan and Japanese air services carried over 22 million passengers and 174,266 tons of goods in the same year.

In 1967 Japan Air Lines started round the world air transport services, carrying 2,498,746 passengers on international scheduled services in 1973.

**Telegraphs and Telephones.** In 1973 there were almost 35 million telephones and over 24 million subscribers.

**Broadcasting.** In 1972 there were 914 radio stations of which 706 were owned by the Japan Broadcasting Corporation and 158 were privately owned. In the same year the Japan Broadcasting Corporation owned 3,333 television stations and private concerns owned 1,411.

In March 1973 television subscribers numbered over 24 million; 87 per cent of the households have television.

## EDUCATION

Education is compulsory and free from the age of six for nine years. Primary education is given up to the age of 12, after which the children go to junior secondary schools for another three years. They may then continue in a senior secondary or highers chool.

In 1972 there were 24,325 primary schools with 9·7 million pupils and 10,868 junior secondary schools with 4·7 million pupils. Senior secondary schools numbered 4,798 with 4·7 million pupils.

Senior secondary schools (3-year course) are mainly established and maintained by prefectures, and are co-educational. They have several courses in general, agricultural, commercial, technical, mercantile marine, radio-communication and home-economics education, etc. There are 2- or 3-year junior colleges and 4-year universities. Many 4-year universities have graduate schools.

Japanese is said to be one of the Altaic group of languages and remained a spoken tongue until the fifth–seventh centuries A.D., when the Chinese characters came into use. Most Japanese who have received school education can read and write the Chinese characters in current use (about 1,800 characters) and also the syllabary characters called Kana. English is the best known foreign language. It is compulsory in almost all colleges and universities and optional in almost all middle and high schools.

The six principal Universities are at Tokyo, Kyoto Sendai (Tohoku University), Fukuoka (Kyushu University), Sapporo (Hokkaido University) and Osaka. In addition there are 500 colleges and institutions of university rank.

## ATOMIC ENERGY

The visit to Japan of Sir C. Hinton, the British atomic energy expert, in 1956 served to heighten public and official interest in atomic energy development and to focus attention on the possible contribution which the United Kingdom might make in this field. The Atomic Energy Research Institute now has four research reactors in operation. The Japan Atomic Power Company started to operate its first nuclear power station (166,000 kW) in 1967.

## NEWSPAPERS

At the end of October 1974 total circulation was 59,100,000 copies.

**Asahi Shimbun. F. 1879.** Morning and Evening. Independent. Tokyo, Osaka, Nagoya, Kita-Kyushu and Sapporo. 2–6–7 Yuraku-cho, Chiyoda-ku, Tokyo 100.

## JAPAN

**Mainichi Shimbun.** F. 1872. Morning and Evening. Tokyo, Osaka, Chubu, Kyushu, Hokkaido. 1-1-1, Hitotsubashi Chiyoda-ku, Tokyo.

**Nihon Keizai Shimbun.** F. 1876. Circulation, Morning 1,635,122, Evening 1,092,319. Tokyo.

**Sankei Shimbun.** F. 1933. Morning and Evening. Tokyo, Osaka.

**Yomiuri Shimbun.** F. 1874. Morning and Evening. Tokyo, Osaka, Kitakynshu, Takaoka and Sapporo.

**Hokkoku Shimbun.** F. 1942. Morning and Evening. Hokuriku.

**Kahoku Shimpo.** F. 1897. Tohoku.

### RELIGION

The principal religions practised by the Japanese are Mahayana Buddhism and Shintoism, but there are many different sects. All other religions are permitted. In 1970 there were 2,896 churches and chapels belonging to the Roman Catholic, the Greek Orthodox and Protestant Churches. The Roman Catholic Archbishop of Tokyo has suffragan bishops at Fukuoka, Nagasaki, Osaka, Sendai and Yokohama. The Nippon Seikokai (Holy Catholic Church of Japan), which is an autonomous branch of the Anglican communion, has eight Japanese bishops. There is also a United Protestant Church.

# Jordan

(EL MAMLAKA EL URDUNIYA EL HASHIMIYA)

**Capital**—Amman.

**Sovereign**—King Hussein I.

**National Flag:** A tricolour fesse-wise, black, white, green; at the hoist a full-depth triangle red, point to the hoist, charged with star seven-pointed white.

### CONSTITUTION, GOVERNMENT, AND RECENT HISTORY

THE Hashemite Kingdom of Jordan lies between Israel and Iraq, with Syria to the north and Saudi Arabia to the south.

It comprises the former Emirate of Transjordan and that part of Palestine which remained in Arab hands after the Arab-Israel war of 1948–49, with the exception of the Gaza Strip. During the war of June 1967 Israel occupied both East Jerusalem and West Jordan as far as the Jordan River.

On 25 November, 1971, the Arab National Union was established. The Union is a social and political organization whose aim is to channel the efforts of all Jordanians towards the political, economic and social development of the country. The constitution of this organization is the National Charter.

In an attempt to consolidate national unity, King Hussein, on 15 March, 1972, presented 'The United Arab Kingdom' plan to be implemented after the liberation of the West Bank. The plan provides for the creation of a federal state composed of two regions: Palestine (the West Bank and any other liberated territories) with Jerusalem as its capital, and Jordan (the East Bank) with Amman as its capital. The King would be Head of State, but each region would have control of its internal affairs through an elected legislative council. Executive power in each region would reside in a governor and an executive council. The proposed federal government would have jurisdiction in matters of defence, foreign policy and national economy. The inhabitants of the two regions would elect a federal parliament and there would be a federal council of ministers.

*The Ramadan War (6 October, 1973)*

Notwithstanding Security Council Resolution 242, efforts towards a peaceful settlement in the Middle East failed and a war commenced on 6 October 1973 on both the Syrian and Egyptian fronts. It was a confrontation which involved land, sea and air forces. The Egyptian forces crossed the Suez Canal and after two days of fighting were able to achieve control of the East Bank of the Canal, breaking through the Israeli 'Barlev Line'. On the Syrian front, the Syrian forces were able to break through the Israeli lines.

From the first day of the war, Jordan's forces were alerted and its reserves were called to arms; the Supreme Defence Council mobilized all the Kingdom's potential for the war effort. During the first days of the war, the role of the Jordanian Army was confined to protecting the left flank of the Syrian forces by holding Israeli forces on the Jordanian front and preventing them from taking the offensive on the Syrian front. Jordan, at a later stage, sent two armoured brigades and a divisional command to fight on the Syrian front. Jordanian troops engaged the enemy in two major battles. Jordan's participation had the full accord of Syria and Egypt. Jordanian forces were engaged in fighting until the cease-fire of 24 October, which was called for by resolution 338 adopted two days earlier by the UN Security Council. These forces withdrew from the Syrian front in late December to confront new Israeli military concentrations on the Jordanian front.

The consequences of the October war affecting Jordan include the resumption of the Kuwaiti financial aid and the resumption of diplomatic relations with Tunisia and Algeria. The war resulted in the emergence of oil as a weapon in the battle, whereby the oil-producing Arab countries decided to reduce production and apply an oil embargo on countries supporting Israel.

An Arab Summit Conference was held in Algeria from 26 to 28 November to coordinate the Arab views regarding the peace talks which might emerge as a result of the October war. A communique was issued confirming the readiness of the Arabs to establish peace in the Middle East on the basis of two principles:

1. The withdrawal of Israel from all occupied territories, including Jerusalem.
2. The restoration to Palestinians of their legitimate national rights. The Jordanian views regarding this issue called for:

1. The withdrawal of Israel from all Arab territories occupied in 1967.
2. Rejection of any partial settlement; and
3. Recognition of the rights of Palestinians to self-determination and giving the Palestinians the right to determine their future after liberation.

*The Geneva Conference*

The Geneva Peace Conference was called to assemble by the Governments of the United States and the Soviet Union. The invitation was sent to the Governments of Syria, Jordan, Egypt and Israel to attend the conference under the auspices of the United Nations and the co-chairmanship of the USA and USSR. The Conference held its first meeting on 21 December, 1973. All parties concerned sent delegations, except Syria. The Conference lasted for two days and it was agreed to postpone further sessions to a later stage. In the meantime military working committees were formed to discuss the disengagement of forces on the Suez Canal front. The Head of the Jordanian delegation, Prime Minister Zaid Rifa'i, proposed that disengagement of forces be applied on the Jordanian front too since Jordan had fought three wars with Israel i.e., in 1948, 1967 and 1973.

In his speech at the Geneva Conference, Prime Minister Zeid Rifa'i outlined the views of the Jordanian government regarding the achievement of a peaceful settlement. These were:

1. Israel's complete withdrawal from all Arab territories which it occupied since June 5th, 1967. A programme of implementation and a time-table for this withdrawal should be drawn up and agreed upon.
2. International boundaries of the States of the area must be recognized and respected, as well as the territorial integrity, sovereignty and independence of these states.
3. Wherever there are no international boundaries between an Arab State and Israel, such boundaries are to be established by agreement and on the basis of the inadmissibility of the acquisition of territory by force.
4. The right of every state in the area to live in peace within secure and recognized boundaries free from threats or acts of force must be pledged and guaranteed.
5. The legitimate rights of the Arab people of Palestine must be fulfilled in accordance with the resolutions of the United Nations; and the Palestinian refugees must exercise their rights of repatriation and/or compensation in accordance with law and justice.
6. Arab Jerusalem is an inseparable part of the occupied Arab territories; therefore, Israel is to relinquish its authority over it. Arab sovereignty must be restored in the Arab

sector of the City. The Holy Places of all Three Divine religions must be preserved, protected and respected, and free access for the followers of these three religions must be secured and maintained.

In January 1974, Dr. Henry Kissinger, U.S. Secretary of State, visited the Middle East and his efforts resulted in an agreement signed on 18 January, 1974, between Israel and Egypt on the disengagement of their forces. The agreement stipulates the withdrawal of Israeli forces to a line along the western base of the mountains in Sinai east of the Suez Canal.

Jordan is a constitutional monarchy. The Executive consists of a Council of Ministers and the Legislature of a Senate (30 persons nominated by the King) and a House of Representatives consisting of 60 elected members.

**Reigning Royal Family.** Moslem (Sunnite).—Members of this branch of the Hashemite dynasties were hereditary Emirs of Mecca from 1201. Hussein Ibn Ali, Grand Sherif of Mecca, proclaimed the independence of the former Turkish province of Hedjaz, 5 June 1916, and took the title King of the Hedjaz in November 1916, the title King of Arabia, 21 June 1917, and of Caliph, 7 March 1924. His son Abdullah Ibn Hussein was Emir of Transjordan. Emir Abdullah assumed the title King, 25 May 1946. When the treaty of recognition of sovereignty was ratified, 17 June 1946, the name of the territory was changed to the Hashemite Kingdom of the Jordan.

**H.M. HUSSEIN I ibn Talal,** King of the Hashemite Kingdom of the Jordan; born 14 November 1935; succeeded to the throne on the deposition of his father King Talal I, 11 August 1952; under a Council of Regency of three during his minority; ascended the throne 2 May 1953; married at Amman, 19 April 1955, Princess Dina Abdel Hamid, daughter of Siadet El Sharif Abdel Hamid, whom he subsequently divorced. Married at Amman on 25 May 1961 to Muna al Hussein, daughter of Col. Walter Gardiner. Known as Her Royal Highness Princess Muna al Hussein. He was subsequently divorced. Married at Amman on 24 December 1972 to Alia Touqan who had the title of Queen Alia. She died on 9 February 1977 in an air crash.

Daughter:—Princess ALYIA; born at Amman, 3 February 1956. Son (by second marriage) Prince Abdullah, born at Amman, 29 January 1962. Prince Faisal, born at Amman, 11 October 1963. Twin daughters, Princess Aisha and Princess Zeine, born 23 April 1968, daughter of Princess Haya, born 3 May 1974. A prince, Price Ali was born on 23 December 1975.

Brothers and Sister of the King: 1. Crown Prince MOHAMMED; born 1940. 2. Crown Prince HASSAN heir apparent; born 1948. 3. Princess BASMAH; born 1951.

Parents of the King: TALAL I ibn Abdullah, formerly King of the Hashemite Kingdom of the Jordan; born at Mecca, 26 February 1909, died 8 July 1972 at Istanbul son of King Abdullah I ibn Hussein (born 1882, assassinated at Jerusalem, 20 July 1951), succeeded his father under the Regency of his brother Emir Naif until 5 September 1951, and was deposed in favour of his eldest son 11 August 1952; married at Amman, 27 November 1934, Sherifa Zeine, daughter of Sherif Jamil.

Uncle and Aunts of the King: 1. Princess HAYA; born at Constantinople, 1907/08. 2. Prince NAIF; born 1914/15; married at Cairo, 7 October 1940, Princess Mihr Sultane (born at Istanbul, 14 April 1920), daughter of Prince Abdur Rahime Effendi, and grand-daughter of Sultan Abdul Hamid II of Turkey. 3. Princess MUNIRA; born at Mecca, 1915/16. 4. Princess MAKBOULA; born at Mecca, 1917/18.

Grandmother of the King: Queen MUSBAH, daughter of Emir Nazir ibn Ali; born at Mecca, 1884/85; married to King Abdullah I at Constantinople, 1904/05; died on 15 March 1961.

**Ministry**

*Prime Minister and Minister for Defence and Foreign Affairs:* Mudar Badran.
*Minister of Education and Minister of State for Prime Ministry Affairs:* Dr. Abdul Salam Al-Majali.
*Minister for Information:* Adnan Abu Odeh.
*Minister of Tourism and Antiqities:* Ghaleb Barakat.
*Minister of Justice:* Ahmad Abdul Kareem Al-Tarawneh.
*Minister of Agriculture:* Salah Jum'a.
*Minister of State for Foreign Affairs and Minister of Development and Construction:* Hasan Ibrahim.
*Minister of Labour:* Isam Ajlouni.
*Minister of Islamic Property Affairs and the Holy Places:* Kamil Al-Shareef.
*Minister of Supply:* Marwan Al-Kassem.
*Minister of Interior:* Suleiman Arar.
*Minister of Communications:* Abdul Ra'oof Al-Rawabdeh.
*Minister of Rural and Municipal Affairs:* Ibrahim Ayoob.
*Minister of Youth and Culture:* Shareef Fawaz Sharaf.
*Minister of Trade and Industry:* Dr. Najm Eldeen Al-Dajani.
*Minister of Finance:* Mohammad Al-Dabbas.
*Minister of Public Works:* Sa'id Beeno.
*Minister of Transport:* Ali Soheimat.

**AREA AND POPULATION**

The total area of the country is 34,607 sq. miles.

The population at mid-1973 was 2,620,000. The annual average percentage growth rate of the population for the period 1960–74 was 3·3 and for the period 1965–74 was 3·4. At the end of 1971, the population of Amman, the capital and district was estimated at 691,120.

**CURRENCY**

Jordan has its own currency, the unit being the Jordan Dinar (JD), which is divided into 1,000 fils, Jordan is a member of the Sterling Area. In December 1976, £ = JD. 0·568. Currency in circulation as at December 1976 was JD. 164,930,000. Jordan coins are issued in values of 1–250 fils, and notes in values of J.D. ½–10.

**FINANCE**

The following table gives the balance of payments situation for the years 1974,1975, and 1976 in J.D. millions:

| | 1974 | 1975 | 1976 |
|---|---|---|---|
| Visible Trade Balance | −105·93 | −184·06 | −270·03 |
| Invisible Balance | +22·13 | +65·73 | +170·82 |
| Net goods and Services | −83·80 | −118·33 | −99·21 |
| Net Transfer payments | +86·74 | +139·80 | +126·55 |
| Balance on current Account | +2·94 | +21·47 | +27·34 |
| Balance on capital Account | +10·88 | +44·11 | −31·19 |
| Errors and Omissions | −7·08 | −14·84 | +1·51 |
| Balance of monetary movements | −6·74 | −50·74 | +2·34 |

(1) An increase in assets is shown by minus sign and a decrease by a plus sign.

An increase in liabilities is shown by a plus sign and a decrease by a minus

The estimated figures for revenue and expenditure for 1971 are J.D. 78·6 m. and JD. 90·5 m.

The GNP at market prices for 1974 was U.S. $ millions 1,120, and the GNP per capita at market prices was U.S. $430. The annual average percentage growth rate of the G.N.P. per capita for the period 1960–74 was 0·9, and for the period 1965–74 was −2·5. [*See the note at the beginning of this section concerning GNP.*]

**BANKS**

**Arab Bank Limited.** (Chairman, Abdul Majeed Shoman.) Est. 1930; Balance Sheet at 31 December 1976 showed assets JD. 1,372 million; Deposits and other accounts JD. 682 million (JD = $3·00). *Head Office:* Amman, Jordan, 55 Branches.

**Grindlays Bank Ltd.** (12 branches and one sub-branch).

**British Bank of the Middle East,** Amman. 4 Branches.

**Central Bank of Jordan,** Amman.

**Bank Almashrek S.A.L.,** Amman.

**Cairo-Amman Bank,** Amman. 12 Branches.

**Jordan National Bank S.A.** *Head Office:* Amman, Jordan. Beirut Branc., Lebanon.

**Rafidain Bank,** Amman. 2 Branches.

**Arab Land Bank.** Statement of 31 December 1972 showed Paid Up Capital, L.E. 600,000; Reserves and Provisions, L.E. 751,908. *Head Office:* 33, Abdul Khalik Sarwat Street Cairo, U.A.R. *Jordan Regional Office:* Amir Muhammed Street, Amman.

## JORDAN

**Bank of Jordan.** Amman. (Chairman of the Board, and General Manager, H. S. Kurdi); Statement of Condition 31 December 1975 showed liabilities and assets of JD. 22,590,108. 17 Branches.

### PRODUCTION, INDUSTRY AND COMMERCE

**Agriculture.** Jordan is essentially an agricultural country and its prosperity in normal times depends entirely on the success of its cereal crops. Approximately 85 per cent of the working population are engaged in agriculture.

Wheat is the main crop, and some 2·2 million dunums (1 acre = 4·046 dunums) were sown in 1972; in addition 600,000 dunums of barley were sown.

Agricultural production for 1974 for the East Bank only is shown in the following table.

| *Product* | *Tons* |
|---|---|
| Wheat | 244,500 |
| Barley | 40,200 |
| Tobacco | 1,548 |
| Tomatoes | 133,500 |
| Olives | 40,500 |
| Grapes | 17,000 |
| Citrus fruits | 33,600 |
| Water melons | 46,600 |

**Industry.** Apart from agriculture, Jordan's main industry is phosphate mining. In addition to a petroleum refinery and a cement plant, there are numerous small manufacturing industries, mainly in the Amman district.

Production of the principal industries in 1976 is given in the following table.

| *Product* | *Quantity* |
|---|---|
| Phosphate | 1,767,933 tons |
| Cement | 533,000 tons |
| Petroleum products | 1,041 tons |
| Detergents | 7,548 tonf |
| Cigarettes | 2,408 tons |
| Spirits and alcoholic drinks | 6,614,800 litres |
| Electricity | 501,000 KWh |
| Textiles | 916,000 yards |
| Fodder | 50,000 tons |

**Commerce.** Main imports are foodstuffs, chemicals, rubber, textiles, iron and steel, machinery and electrical equipment.

Main exports are agricultural products and phosphates (1,767,000 tons in 1976).

Total 1976 trade: Imports JD. 349,500; exports J.D. 49,500.

1,064 vessels called at Aqaba port in 1976 and total tonnage handled was 3,000,503 tons.

Below are imports and exports (million JD) by countries during 1976.

*Imports*

| *Country of Origin* | 1976 |
|---|---|
| Arab Common Market Countries | 18·8 |
| Other Arab Countries | 42·1 |
| EEC Countries | 120·8 |
| United States | 31·0 |
| Japan | 21·5 |
| Socialist Countries | 25·1 |
| Other Countries | 90·2 |
| Total | 349·5 |

*Exports*

| *Country of Destination* | 1976 |
|---|---|
| Arab Common Market Countries | 13·4 |
| Other Arab Countries | 10·5 |
| EEC Countries | 2·5 |
| Japan | 1·9 |
| Socialist Countries | 7·3 |
| Other Countries | 13.9 |
| Total | 49·5 |

[1] **Arab Common Market Countries:** Arab Republic of Egypt, Iraq, Syria and Sudan.

[2] **EEC:** UK, France, W. Germany, Italy, Denmark, Holland, Belgium and Ireland.

[3] **Socialist countries:** China, USSR, E. Germany, Romania, Hungary, Bulgaria, Poland, Czechoslovakia.

### COMMUNICATIONS

There are 450 kilometres of railway in the country, excluding the new track being laid south of Ma'an as part of the Hedjaz Railway reconstruction now suspended.

Over 2,000 kilometres of asphalted roads connect Jordan's main towns including a good highway from Amman to Aqaba, Jordan's only outlet to the sea. In addition there are some 2,500 kilometres of other roads.

In 1970 the number of vehicles (for the East Bank only) was 24,279.

**Posts, Telegraphs and Telephones.** The Trunk Telephone System extends to the principal towns, and calls can be made to Iraq, Syria and Lebanon, Egypt and London. There are 25,000 telephones. Mail, air mail and telegraph services are regular. A Telex system was started in 1969, and in 1971 there were 100 subscribers.

**Aviation.** Alia, the Royal Jordanian Airline was established in 1963 to succeed Jordan Airways Co. Alia at present covers Frankfurt, London, Rome, Paris, Copenhagen, Athens, Istanbul, Madrid, Aquaba, Beirut, Cairo, Nicosia, Benghazi, Jedda, Kuwait, Dhahran, Dubai, Doha, Abu Dhabi, Tehran, and Karachi.

### NEWSPAPERS

There are three daily newspapers, al-Dustour, al-Urdon and al-Rai; five weekly, Amman al-Masaa, al-Hawadith, al-Liwa, al-Suhufi, al-Sabah; and one monthly, al-Sharia (Islamic magazine).

### EDUCATION AND RELIGION

Education is mainly in the hands of the Government. The following table shows the numbers and percentage of students in comparison with the respective age-population in the country, during the scholastic year 1975–76:

| *Type of School* | *Age* | *Age-population* | *No. of students* | *Percentage* |
|---|---|---|---|---|
| Kindergarten | 3–5 | 214,994 | 15,107 | 7·5 |
| Elementary | 6–11 | 349,002 | 371,631 | 106·9 |
| Preparatory | 12–14 | 139,390 | 100,678 | 72·5 |
| Secondary | 15–17 | 122,284 | 42,648 | 34·9 |
| Higher Studies | 18–23 | 188,980 | 9,302 | 4·9 |

In 1975–1976 Jordan University had a teaching staff of 345 and 5,307 students (1,283 in the Faculty of Arts, 1,092 in the Faculty of Economics and Commerce, 1,119 in the Faculty of Sciences and 414 in the Faculty of Islamic Law).

The official religion is Moslem (Sunni) but there is a relatively large Christian minority.

# Democratic State of Kampuchea

**Capital**—Phnom-Penh.

**Head of State**—Khieu Samphan.

**National Emblem:** A factory, amid rice fields, encircled by sheaves of rice.

## CONSTITUTION AND GOVERNMENT

CAMBODIA, one of the former Protectorates of French Indo-China, is bounded on the south and on the east by South Vietnam, on the north by Laos and Siam, on the west by Siam and on the southwest by the Gulf of Siam. A French Protectorate was established over the country in 1863. On 9 March 1945 the Japanese Army took control of the country from the French civil and military authorities. Since the Protecting Power could no longer carry out its obligations, King Norodom Sihanouk proclaimed the independence of Cambodia on 12 March 1945. After the defeat of Japan the French authorities regained control; a *modus vivendi* was signed on 7 January 1946 and a preliminary agreement fixed the relationship between the Kingdom of Cambodia and France. A new political structure of democratic tendencies was created, an electoral law was passed and elections for a National Consultative Assembly took place on 1 September 1946. On 9 September 1946 the territories annexed by force by Siam in July 1941 were reincorporated in Cambodia.

The first Cambodian Constitution was promulgated on 6 May 1947. Elections to the National Legislative Assembly took place on 21 December 1947. By a treaty of 8 November 1949, Cambodia was established as an autonomous state functioning within the French Union as an Associated State.

In 1954, there was fighting between Vietminh regular troops who engaged Royal Cambodian forces. In July 1954, an agreement was arrived at at the Geneva Conference which resulted in the withdrawal of Vietminh troops from Cambodia.

In January 1955, the financial and economic union with France came to an end and in March King Sihanouk abdicated in favour of his father, King Norodom Suramarit. Elections took place in September with Sihanouk's party, the Sangkum (Popular Socialist Community) winning all the seats. Sihanouk became Prime Minister and on 25 September Cambodia became an independent sovereign state. In 1960, on the death of the king, Prince Sihanouk resigned the premiership and became head of state.

Prince Sihanouk consistently affirmed Cambodia's neutrality, believing that only in this way could its future independence be assured. As time passed, however, Cambodia's neutrality increasingly favoured the communist powers—the Thais and southern Vietnamese, Cambodia's neighbours and traditional enemies were both allied with the United States. As fighting intensified in Vietnam, Sihanouk attempted to prevent it from spreading to Cambodia. He was unable to stop North Vietnamese and NLF units from using the Cambodian border area as a staging post and sanctuary or to prevent air raids on their camps.

In March 1970, while Sihanouk was abroad, his cabinet led by Prime Minister Lon Nol announced radical changes in foreign and domestic policy, presenting Vietnamese communist forces with an ultimatum ordering them to withdraw from Cambodia. On 18 March Sihanouk was deposed and Cheng Heng, President of the National Assemby became Head of State. In October Cambodia was declared a republic.

By this date, Cambodia was deeply involved in the Vietnam war. South Vietnamese troop entered the country soon after Sihanouk's fall to back up the small, ill-equipped Cambodian army against the Vietnamese communists and an embryo Cambodian resistance movement, the National United Front of Cambodia (NUFC) founded in March 1970. Between May and July 1970, American troops also entered the Cambodian border area in strength, possibly intending to drive the North Vietnamese and NLF from their sanctuaries.

In May 1970, Prince Sihanouk announced from Peking the formation of the Royal Government of National Union (RGNUC) with himself as head of state. In Cambodia, the resistance movement which was based on an alliance between the Cambodian communist party (driven underground in 1962) and Sihanouk's supporters, grew in strength. Backed by the Vietnamese communists it gained control of much of the countryside. In 1973, most of the RGNUC ministerial posts held by Sihanouk's followers in exile were transferred to guerrilla leaders in Cambodia.

In January 1975, a major offensive by NUFC forces gave the guerrillas control of the Mekong river, a vital government supply route and cut off Phnom Penh, the capital, which was bombarded. In early April, Lon Nol who had succeeded Cheng Heng as President of the republic, left the country. On 17 April 1975, government forces surrendered and NUFC troops entered Phnom Penh. On 9 September 1975, Sihanouk returned to Cambodia as Head of State.

In January 1976, at a national congress, the NUFC was reported to have drawn up a new constitution and in March the election of a People's National Assembly composed of 250 farmers', workers' and soldiers' representatives was announced. In April, this assembly was reported to have chosen a new government and State Praesidium. In the same month, Sihanouk resigned as Head of State and was replaced by Khieu Samphan, the former Minister of Defence.

None of Sihanouk's supporters were included in the new government which also apparently severed all links with non-communist nationalists. In September 1977 the existence of the ruling Cambodian Communist party was officially confirmed. Its Secretary is the Prime Minister, Mr Pol Pot.

### Cabinet

*Prime Minister:* Pol Pot.
*Deputy Prime Minister, Minister for Foreign Affairs:* Ieng Sary.
*Deputy Prime Minister, Minister for National Defence:* Son Sen.
*Deputy Prime Minister, Minister of Economy:* Von Vet.
*Minister of Information and Propaganda:* Hou Nim.
*Minister of Social Action:* Mrs. Ieng Thirith.
*Minister of Public Works:* Toch Phoeun.
*Minister of Health:* Thiunn Thioeun.
*Minister of Culture and Education:* Mrs. Yun Yat.
*President of Judiciary Committee:* Kang Chap.
*Chairman of Committee for Industry:* Cheng An.

*State Praesidium*
*Chairman:* Khieu Samphan.
*First Vice-Chairman:* So Phim.
*Second Vice-Chairman:* Nhim Ros.
*High Counsellor:* Penn Nouth.
*Chairman of People's Assembly:* Nuon Chea.

## AREA AND POPULATION

The total area of Cambodia is 70,000 square miles and the estimated population in 1977 was around 5 million. In 1975, the country was divided into 22 provinces and four municipalities. The principal towns are Phnom Penh, the capital, Kompong Cham, Battambang, Pursat, Kompong Thom and Kompong Som, Cambodia's main seaport. In 1974, Phnom Penh's population, swollen by refugees from the war, was estimated at two million. When the new government took control in April 1975, it ordered the evacuation of Phnom Penh and other towns which were left virtually empty while the inhabitants departed to the countryside to work on the land. In 1977, the population of Phnom Penh was estimated at 20,000.

## CURRENCY AND FINANCE

The unit of currency is the riel. It was valued in October 1977 at 211·236 to the pound sterling.

During the war, in spite of substantial foreign aid, Cambodia had a large budget deficit—a record 17,600 million riels in 1972. Between January 1972 and January 1974, prices rose by 472 per cent. In 1975 it was reported that money was no longer being used in Cambodia and that there were no markets.

## PRODUCTION, INDUSTRY AND COMMERCE

**Agriculture.** Rice is Cambodia's chief crop and before war broke out in 1970, 2·5 hectares of rice land yielded some

3·8 million tons. By the 1972–73 season, output had fallen to 1 million tons and instead of providing some 40 per cent of Cambodia's export earnings, rice was being imported. When the war ended, the new government's most pressing problem was to increase rice supplies to feed a population forced into the towns by the fighting and which had come to rely on foreign, particularly American, assistance. Town dwellers were sent to the countryside to work in the fields, the army was also reported to be taking part in production and the government emphasized that no cultivable land should be left untilled.

The rice crops in 1975 and 1976 were said to be good ones, although in 1976 it was reported that the planted area had fallen substantially. In 1977, although the rice growing area had fallen still further, the government had concentrated manpower on new irrigation projects and paddy output was said to have risen from two to four tons per hectare with two to more than three crops annually in some places. The state has made it clear that it intends to establish a self-sufficient, agriculturally based society. There is now no privately held land and labourers are reported to receive no wages. A rice ration and other necessities are distributed by local committees.

Other Cambodian crops include maize, pulses, pepper, kapok, fruits of many kinds, soya beans, sugar, groundnuts, castor oil, cotton, jute, coffee and tobacco. Rubber is Cambodia's most important industrial crop, with output averaging 50,000 tons a year before 1970. The plantations were badly damaged by the fighting and production came virtually to a standstill in 1971. In 1972, 15,000 tons were produced and production continued at a reduced level until the end of the war in 1975. The RGNUC has nationalised the plantations, which were mostly French owned, and has begun to clear, replant and (eventually) enlarge them.

The livestock population before 1970 consisted of 1,850,000 cattle, 730,000 buffalo, 1,100,000 pigs, 50,000 horses and 1,000 domestic elephants. Fishery production averaged 200,000 metric tons.

There is a great variety of hardwoods in the forests. Forestry production before the war was estimated as follows: timber, 101,000 cubic metres; lumber, 321,000 cubic metres; charcoal, 11,000 metric tons. Wood oil, resin and gamboge are also produced.

**Industry.** Between 1955 and 1967, Cambodia invested more than 6 million riels in industrial development. With the help of foreign aid, by 1969, factories making cement, paper, plywood, textiles, alcohol, cigarettes, jute bags, tyres, fertilisers and soap were in operation. In 1968, a new hydro-electric dam at Kirirom was completed. In 1969, 130,000 kwh of electricity was generated throughout the country. An oil refinery at Kompong Som, finished in 1968, was able to meet all Cambodia's needs in 1969.

Industrial plant throughout the country was heavily damaged during the war. When the new government took over in 1975 all private industry was nationalized and reconstruction began with priority being given to power plants, water works and factories producing necessities such as textiles, cement and pharmaceuticals. By September 1977, it was reported that 200 factories and power stations had resumed production including the rubber processing plant, textile mills, tyre, battery and shoemaking factories in Phnom Penh and textile mills and sack factories in Battambang. All production, however, was on a very limited scale. Cement and machine plants were also said to be back in operation. Output at the rubber processing plant in Phnom Penh was put at 40 to 50 tons of cured rubber a day. Some new enterprises had been set up in Phnom Penh—a ship building yard, a vehicle repair plant, acid works and a machine tool plant.

All industry in Cambodia is hampered by an acute shortage of machinery and spare parts. The government has said that tools are being made from war scrap and has called for the development of traditional handicrafts and cottage industry to provide essentials such as wooden and metal tools, bricks, tiles, pumps, rice mills, cloth and utensils.

**Commerce.** Cambodia's chief exports before the war were rice, rubber, cattle, timber, pepper and maize. It imported metals, machinery, vehicles, mineral products including petroleum, manufactured goods, chemicals and textiles.

After the fall of Lon Nol's government in 1975, trade came virtually to a standstill, although some border dealing with Thailand continued, the Thais providing oil and salt in exchange for Cambodian fish and lumber. In 1976, however, Cambodia began to export its surplus rice to finance essential imports. Phnom Penh said that 150,000 tons of rice were exported in 1976 and it was also reported that Cambodia had sold 13,000 tons of rubber to China and North Korea. Small quantities of teak, fruit, jewels and hides were also exported. By 1977, Cambodia had set up a small trade mission in Hong Kong.

In 1976 and 1977, Cambodia imported only such necessities as spare parts for vehicles and machinery, electric generating and transmission equipment, DDT and medicines, water pumps, chemicals and machinery for latex processing. In March 1977 it was announced that Japan would export 10,000 tons of steel products to Cambodia.

## COMMUNICATIONS

Before 1970, Cambodia had some 3,000 miles of motorable road. A railway, 370 miles in length ran from the port of Kompong Som via Phnom Penh to Battambang and the Thai border. During the war, roads, railway and bridges were heavily damaged and overland communications virtually paralysed.

When the fighting ended in 1975, repair work began promptly and by 1977 all major roads were reported to have been repaired and the railways to have resumed normal service.

There are airports at Phnom Penh and Siem Reap which before 1975 could handle international traffic and at major provincial towns such as Battambang, Kompong Cham and Kratie. Phnom Penh airport, heavily damaged in the last stages of the war, is back in operation. In October 1976, a fortnightly airlink to Hanoi and Ho Chi Minh City was established and there are monthly flights to Pakse and Vientiane in Laos.

Cambodia has a sea port at Kompong Som and river ports at Phnom Penh and Kompong Chhang. All these are reported to have been repaired after war damage. Cambodia's rivers are an important means of communication and work is underway to clear the Mekong below Phnom Penh of sunken vessels. Some shipping and ferries had resumed operations by August 1975.

## EDUCATION AND RELIGION

The population is almost entirely Buddhist. Before 1975 there was freedom in matters of belief.

In 1970–71 there were 1,490 primary schools with 337,729 pupils. There were 95 secondary schools with 81,611 pupils; 9 universities with 48 Faculties, 12 'grandes écoles' with 14,560 students and 99 technical schools. All these were apparently closed by the new government in 1975. It has established a new basic system emphasizing practical rather than academic education.

# Kenya

(MEMBER OF THE COMMONWEALTH)

**Capital**—Nairobi.

**President**—Hon. Mzee Jomo Kenyatta, MP.

## CONSTITUTION AND GOVERNMENT

THE Republic of Kenya lies across the Equator on the eastern seaboard of Africa. It is bounded on the north by the Sudan and Ethiopia, on the east by the Indian Ocean and Somalia, on the south by Tanzania and on the west by Uganda and Lake Victoria.

From the narrow, tropical, coastal belt the land rises towards the great plateau of East Africa. The Highlands, which include some of the best agricultural land in Africa, rise from the plateau at about 5,000 feet. The country is divided by the Rift Valley which runs from Lake Turkama in the north southwards to where it splits the Highlands. Kenya's arid northern region stretches from near the coast to the foothills of Mount Kenya and to Lake Turkana. This region, which covers more than half the country, is sparsely populated and hot, with a low rainfall.

In 1887 the Imperial British East African Company obtained, from the Sultan of Zanzibar, a concession of the Sultan's mainland dominions consisting of a strip of land, extending ten miles inland along the coast from the Tanganyika border to Kipini together with the islands of the Lamu Archipelago.

In 1895 the British Government declared an East African Protectorate over the whole of the territory now known as Kenya, including the coastal strip. In 1906 the Protectorate was placed under a Governor and Executive and Legislative Councils were constituted.

By the 'Kenya Annexation Order in Council 1920' that part of the territory outside the mainland dominions of the Sultan of Zanzibar was recognized as a Colony; the coastal strip remaining a Protectorate, in respect of which an annual rent of £10,000 was paid to the Sultan.

By an Order in Council of 1954 a Council of Ministers was set up, to be the principal instrument of government, with six Official Members, two Nominated Members, and six Unofficial Members appointed by the Governor. The latter were appointed from the Elected and Representative Members of the Legislative Council.

By 1958 the number of Ministers in the Council of Ministers had been increased to 16 and the number of African elected Members rose from eight to 14. Twelve new seats were created for 'Specially Elected Members'.

At the Kenya Constitutional Conference held in London in January/February 1960, the Secretary of State circulated some constitutional suggestions relating to changes in the structure of the Legislative Council. These changes culminated in the General Election of May 1963, and the introduction of the New Constitution for internal self-government.

On 12 December 1963, Kenya became an Independent State and a member of the Commonwealth. One year later, on 12 December 1964, Kenya assumed Republican status.

The Cabinet consists of the President and 22 Ministers who are collectively responsible to the National Assembly.

The National Assembly is composed of 158 members representing each of the existing districts, elected by universal adult suffrage and based on single-member constituencies. A further 12 Members representing special interests are nominated by the President.

Powers of local administration are held by Provincial Authorities in seven provinces and the Nairobi Area.

## LEGAL SYSTEM

Justice is administered by the Supreme Court, which consists of the Chief Justice and eleven puisne judges. The court sits in Nairobi, Mombasa and other centres, and appeals lie to the Court of Appeal for Eastern Africa. There are many subordinate courts presided over by resident magistrates or by administrative officers holding first, second or third class magisterial powers. A limited number of courts have special jurisdiction in respect of Muslims.

## AREA AND POPULATION

The total area of Kenya is approximately 224,960 square miles including 5,171 square miles inland water.

Most of the population is concentrated into a relatively small portion of the country in the south-west where the rainfall is inadequate. The population at mid-1974 was 12,910,000. The annual average percentage growth rate of the population for the period 1960–74 was 3·2, and for the period 1965–74 was 3·4. The largest African tribes are the Kikuyu (1,642,000) the Luo (1,148,000) the Lukyu (1,086,000) and the Kamba (933,000). Of the 139,000 Asians in Kenya, about two-thirds are Hindus, Sikhs and Muslims. The majority of the 40,500 Europeans are of British origin.

## CURRENCY

A new currency came into circulation on 14 September 1966. As formerly, when the currency was controlled by the East African Currency Board, the official units are cents and shillings. Kenya shillings 14·32 = K. £1 sterling. There are 100 cents in a shilling.

## FINANCE

The GNP at market prices for 1974 was U.S. $millions 2,610 and the GNP per capita at market prices was U.S. $200. The annual average percentage growth rate of the GNP per capita for the period 1960–74 was 3·2, and for the period 1965–74 was 3·5. [*See the note at the beginning of this section concerning GNP.*]

Approved estimates of expenditure for the financial year 1972–73 were: £122,594,600 on Recurrent Account, £28,645,800 on Development Account. The corresponding figures of actual expenditure and revenue in 1971–72 were: Recurrent expenditure, £120,506,100; Development expenditure, £16,445,427.

## BANKS

**Central Bank of Kenya.**

**National Bank of Kenya, Ltd.** Executive Chairman: S. M. Githunguri. Directors: L. O. Kibinge, P. J. Mwangola, E. Matu Wamae, R. K. Cheshire, R. Kemoli, J. Oyugi. General Manager & Secretary: J. T. Carr. Balance sheet at 30 June 1976 showed paid-up capital Shs. 45,000,000; deposits: Shs. 1,036,856,420; Advances: Shs. 665,382,280; Cash on hand and with Central Bank of Kenya Shs. 108,614,320. *Head office:* National Bank House, Harambee Avenue, P.O. Box 41862, Nairobi. Cables: Natbank, Nairobi Telex: 22619 Nairobi. Branches: Nairobi (3), Mombasa, Nakuru and Kisumu.

**Kenya Commercial Bank, Ltd.** *Head Office:* Nairobi.

**Barclays Bank International.**

**Standard Bank of S. Africa.**

**Ottoman Bank.**

**Lombard Bank.**

**Bank of Baroda.**

## PRODUCTION, INDUSTRY AND COMMERCE

**Agriculture.** Agriculture is the mainstay of Kenya's economy. More than 80 per cent of the population is engaged on the land, while agriculture and livestock provide over 85 per cent of the country's export earnings.

The progress of African farming is largely a result of the development of cash crops on consolidated and enclosed farms, a process started by the Swynnerton Plan, whose purpose was to develop a modern system of farming by Africans.

Promising results have been achieved from irrigation schemes, in particular the Mwea Tebere scheme in Embu district where rice is the chief cash crop. On the Lower Tana River a three-year pre-investment survey of the irrigation potentialities of the area is being undertaken.

In 1961, the Government introduced settlement schemes for African farmers in the formerly exclusive European farming areas of the Highlands. It is planned to settle between 50,000 and 75,000 families on one million acres of land, at a cost of £27·5 million.

Owing to the variation of altitude from sea level to over 9,000 feet, Kenya lends itself to the production of a wide range of crops. In the areas of 5,000 feet and above, coffee, tea, pyrethrum, maize, wattle bark and wheat, barley and oats are the principal crops. At the lower altitudes sisal, cotton and oilseeds are most important. Other crops grown in various parts of the country include beans, potatoes, sorghums, millets, pulses, coconuts, cashew nuts, sugar cane, vegetables, fruit and essential oil plants.

Kenya has an expanding livestock industry. Much of the country is suited to ranching and there is an important dairy industry in the areas of higher rainfall. Dairy products such as butter, cheese, milk, ghee and eggs are exported. Rearing of wool sheep and of pigs is being expanded to provide all local requirements as well as for export.

**Forestry.** The forests produce a large number of valuable woods varying with their situation. On the coast, mangrove poles and bark and muhugu timber (*Brackylaena*) are the main products. In the highland forests are found large quantities of pencil cedar and such other timbers as *Podocarpus*, East African olive, cypress and camphor, also large areas of bamboos.

There are 6,719 square miles of gazetted forests in Kenya. This represents just over 3 per cent of the total land area. In 1963, 43,032 tons (50 cu. ft. true measure per ton) of indigenous softwoods (*Juniperus procera* and *Podo carpus* spp.), 41,820 tons of exotic softwoods (*Cupressus lusitanica*, *Pinus radiata* and *P. patula*) and 11,710 tons of hardwoods were sold from forest reserve.

In the last quarter of a century there has been a vigorous programme of afforestation and re-afforestation with quick growing exotic softwoods, which now total over 160,000 acres. It is planned that by 1980 over 300,000 acres will have been established. The stage has been reached where the development of major forest industries based on these resources is a very real possibility.

**Fishing.** There is a substantial fishing industry on Lakes Victoria, Baringo and Naivasha. The coastal fisheries and those of Lake Turkana are being developed.

**Minerals.** The mineral resources of Kenya have not yet been fully developed, but traces of most of the important minerals have been found and the work of the Geological Survey is making steady progress. Soda ash is at present the most important mining product.

The following table shows some raw material production (value in thousand £k):

| *Raw Material* | 1973 | 1974 |
|---|---|---|
| Barytes | 21,085 | — |
| Carbon dioxide | 162,500 | — |
| Copper | — | — |
| Diatomite | 27,302 | 39,768 |
| Felspar | 10,250 | — |
| Fluorspar Ore (Fluorite) | 306,742 | — |
| Garnets | 41,208 | 70,605 |
| Gold | 4,091 | 11,000 |
| Guano | 14,428 | 10,984 |
| Limestone products | 227,441 | — |
| Magnesite | 12,136 | — |
| Magnetite | 123,450 | 98,900 |
| Salt (Crude) | 27,631 | — |
| Salt (Refined) | 270,433 | 195,962 |
| Sand | 20,238 | — |
| Sapphire | 50,399 | — |
| Soda Ash | 2,087,194 | 2,243,932 |
| Soda crushed raw | 39,159 | 12,469 |

**Industry.** Manufacturing accounts for nearly 11 per cent of the gross domestic product. More than half of the manufacturing industry is based on processing of primary agricultural products. The manufacture of cement for export and local consumption is important, in addition to shirt and garment, plastics, textiles and blanket manufacturing and food product industries.

Nairobi remains the chief industrial centre and it is still the headquarters of many commercial organizations operating throughout East Africa. Among the more important industries established in Nairobi are: brewing, soft drinks, flour milling, pharmaceuticals, small textile and knitwear factories, cigarette manufacture, clothing and footwear, foodstuffs manufacture, light engineering and soap-making.

Mombasa also has a big industrial complex and the port itself has ship-repairing facilities. The first oil refinery in East Africa is at Mombasa. There are good prospects for industries in Western Kenya where there is a high density of population. Several small industries exist at Nakuru, Kisumu, Eldoret and Thika.

The Coast area is supplied by a modern steam generating station at Mombasa with an installed capacity of about 40 Megawatts. The areas from Nairobi westward to the Uganda boundary (a distance of about 300 miles) are principally supplied from a comprehensive transmission system fed from a capacity of over 100 Megawatts. Kenya is at present developing a hydrogeneration complex at Seven Forks, about 70 miles from Nairobi.

**Commerce.** Kenya, Tanzania and Uganda are subject to a common customs tariff and trade statistics are shown separately for each territory. Freedom of interterritorial trade is secured by tripartite agreements which provide for the transfer of goods under a system of consignor's declarations.

Kenya's total domestic exports in 1971 were £73,185,000 and imports £184,105,000. Britain has traditionally been her best customer and still takes more of her exports than any other country, with West Germany in second place, the U.S.A. in third place. Kenya's imports also come mainly from Britain, with Japan in second place and the U.S.A. in third place.

The following table shows values of principal imports for 1973 and 1974 (th £k):

| | 1973 | 1974 |
|---|---|---|
| Crude petroleum | 17,557 | 67,027 |
| Motor vehicles and chassis | 11,464 | 22,226 |
| Agricultural machinery and tractors | 3,284 | 3,284 |
| Industrial machinery (including electrical) | 38,861 | 40,479 |
| Iron and steel | 14,410 | 26,958 |
| Cotton fabric | 618 | 1,272 |
| Synthetic fibre fabric | 6,749 | 8,253 |
| Paper and paper products | 10,171 | 17,497 |
| Pharmaceutical products | 3,944 | 6,546 |
| Fertilizers | 4,331 | 15,271 |

During 1973 and 1974 values of principal items exported were as follows (th £k):

| | 1973 | 1974 |
|---|---|---|
| Coffee, unroasted | 35,776·7 | 38,387·4 |
| Tea | 16,963·8 | 19,386·8 |
| Petroleum products | 9,488·4 | 26,184·9 |
| Meat and products | 3,761·3 | 4,512·5 |
| Pyrethrum extract | 2,920·3 | 4,536·3 |
| Sisal | 4,776·8 | 16,956·6 |
| Hides and skins, undressed | 5,186·1 | 4,441·5 |
| Wattle extract | 1,214·6 | 1,434·1 |
| Soda ash | 2,815·6 | 2,703·6 |
| Cement | 2,565·8 | 3,986·5 |
| Beans, peas, etc. | 1,173.2 | 1,544·6 |
| Cashew nuts, raw | 608·9 | 1,612·9 |
| Wool | 806·5 | 692·0 |
| Animal feed | 962·7 | 296·8 |
| Cotton, raw | 1,373·1 | 1,135·7 |
| Pineapples, tinned | 1,481·2 | 1,411·6 |
| Butter and ghee | 691·8 | 458·5 |
| Wood carvings | 755·1 | 620·6 |
| Metal scrap | 530·8 | 768·6 |
| Wattle bark | 135·3 | 70·3 |
| All other items | 28,648·1 | 31,804·3 |

## COMMUNICATIONS

**Roads.** Kenya has about 44,932 kilometres of public roads, of which about 3,103 kilometres are bitumen-surfaced (1971). The main roads—11,662 kilometres of them—where not bitumenized, are gravel-surfaced and usually 'all-weather' roads, except during excessive rains. Kenya's Development Plan, 1966–70, provides for an expenditure of about £21·5 million for reconstruction and improvement of roads.

**Railways.** There are about 1,270 route miles of railway operated by the East African Railways and Harbours. The main railway line runs from Mombasa, through Kenya to Uganda. In 1969 the Railways worked goods traffic amounting to 2,615 million ton-kilometres.

**Shipping.** Mombasa is the largest port in East Africa, serving not only Kenya but also Uganda and parts of Tanzania. There are 15 deep water berths together with an oil berth and a new oil jetty for the modern larger tankers. In 1971, 1,859 ships called, and a total of 5,570,000 metric tons of dry cargo was handled (excluding oil in bulk).

**Civil Aviation.** East Africa's own airline, East African Airways Corporation, operates a network of domestic routes linking Kenya with Tanzania and Uganda. It also operates international routes from Nairobi to London and other European Centres, Bombay, Karachi, Bangkok, Hong Kong and Central Africa. In 1965 its aircraft flew over 8·8 million revenue-earning miles. Aircraft movements in and out of Nairobi averaged over 1,200 per month with 46,000 passengers and 750,000 kilogrammes of freight.

**Broadcasting.** The Voice of Kenya operates a National Sound Service in Swahili and a general service in English, which are transmitted from Nairobi in the medium wave and short wave bands.

Additional vernacular languages are also transmitted from the new medium wave transmitter station sited at Ngong, near Nairobi. Programmes are directly relayed using either Post Office circuits, VHF/FM links or VF multi-channel circuits. Sound broadcasts totalling 467 hours per week are transmitted in several languages, covering all parts of Kenya.

The television service operates over a total of 68 hours per week, of which 33 hours are provided for the radio trade for engineering and demonstration purposes. The transmitter is some 14 miles from Nairobi, and gives a primary service to about 50 miles and a secondary service to 100 or more miles in radius. During the early part of 1964 an experimental relay service covering the Western Kenya area was replaced with a permanent relay service offering excellent coverage for a distance of about 40 miles to the West of Timboroa and a secondary service up to 60–70 miles. The main transmitter operates in band 1, channel 4 and the Timboroa relay in band 1, channel 2, both using CCIR 625 lines.

All radio and television services accept commercial advertisements and sponsored programmes.

## NEWSPAPERS

**East African Standard.** F. 1902. English morning, daily. Circulation 32,000. P.O. Box 30080, Nairobi.

**Daily Nation and Friday Nation.** F. 1960. English, morning. Circulation 79,226. Box 49010, Nairobi.

**Taifa Leo.** F. 1960. Daily, morning. Swahili. Circulation 27,000. P.O. Box 9010, Nairobi.

**Sunday Post.** F. 1936. English, weekly. Circulation 22,000. P.O. Box 30127, Nairobi.

**Baraza.** Swahili weekly. Circulation 45,000. P.O. Box 30080, Nairobi.

**Sunday Nation.** F. 1960. English weekly. Circulation 70,100. P.O. Box 49010, Nairobi.

## EDUCATION

The main event of 1976 was the meeting of the National Committee for Educational Objectives and Policies. Primary education was the area chosen to receive improvement in the 1974–1978 Development Plan. The Kenya Government retaining responsibility for secondary schools, teacher training colleges, certain national institutions, and higher education as a whole. All schools are integrated. In the past few years many 'Harambee' secondary schools have been established, built and run on a 'self-help' basis by local communities.

**Primary Education.** Primary education is a seven year course leading to the Certificate of Primary Education. There are three private schools, similar to preparatory schools in the United Kingdom, which prepare pupils for the U.K. common entrance examination. In 1974 there were 6,123 primary schools with 2,734,398 pupils.

**Secondary Education.** There are about 590 secondary schools in Kenya which prepare students for the East African School Certificate Ninety-four of these schools provide Advanced Certificate of Education courses.

The full secondary course covers a period of six years. After four years candidates sit for the East African School Certificate. Selected students are then given an additional two years to prepare for the Advanced Certificate Examination.

In 1974 there were 140,000 secondary school pupils.

**Teacher Training.** There are at present 17 teacher training colleges. The number of student teachers in training in 1974 was 8,200. A new Technical Teachers College will open shortly at Nairobi. Eight technical and trade schools prepare students for artisan employment in industry, and in crafts in which they can be self-employed. In 1974, 2,400 trainees were attending courses at technical and trade schools. The Kenya Polytechnic, which was established in 1961, provides technician level. In 1974 there were over 3,800 full and part time students at the Polytechnic. The Mombasa Polytechnic is also running similar courses.

**Higher Education.** The University of Nairobi provides degree courses in Agriculture, the Arts and Architecture, Education, Medicine and the Sciences, Engineering, Economics, Surveying, Commerce, Law, Journalism, Pharmacy and Dentistry.

In 1974, 3,976 Kenya students were studying at the University of Nairobi. In addition over 5,500 students were taking courses of higher education overseas in 1974.

# Korea

KOREA is a peninsula on the east coast of Asia, jutting southwards towards Japan. Its total area is 85,228 sq. miles. Its northern frontier lies along the borders of Manchuria, with a small portion touching Siberia. Its sea boundaries are formed by the Yellow Sea on the west, the Sea of Japan on the east, and the East China Sea on the south. Japan is separated from it by the Korea Strait, or Straits of Shimonoseki.

Its early history is shrouded in antiquity, but the semi-mythical figure known variously as Tangoon, Tankun or Dan Goon is supposed to be the founder of the State about 2400 B.C. The name Chosun, meaning 'Land of Morning Calm', was given to it by him, and afterwards adopted by the Japanese. Tai-Han is the Korean name.

The people are quite distinct from either the Chinese or Japanese, although greatly influenced by both in the course of their history. Wars and invasions have been frequent. The Koreans proper are believed to be a mixture of Mongolian and Caucasian stock.

They have a reputation for ingenuity, and claim a number of inventions, including the spinning wheel, movable type, astronomical and surveying instruments, the mariner's compass and the observation balloon, all dating from between A.D. 1300 and 1600. A simplified phonetic alphabet was also introduced, although some writing is still based on Chinese pictographs. In the same period, the Admiral Yi Soon-Sin is credited with the invention of the world's first armour-plated battleship, a turtle-decked boat which he used to defeat the Japanese navy.

Korea's recent history begins in 1905, when it became a protectorate of Japan. This was the result of the Russo-Japanese War, and five years later Japan annexed Korea as part of her empire. The situation remained unchanged until 1945, when the collapse of Japan led to the occupation of the country by U.S.S.R. and American forces.

For military convenience the peninsula was divided into two sections along the 38th parallel, the U.S.S.R. occupying the northern zone and the Americans the southern zone and it was agreed that Korea should be placed under a four-power trusteeship for 'a period of up to five years', the final object being to give the country full and unified independence.

For this purpose the General Assembly of the United Nations created a Temporary Commission on Korea in 1947 to help in the establishment of a Korean national government through general elections. The U.S.S.R. boycotted the Commission, however, and refused permission for it to enter the north. As a result, the Interim Committee of the General Assembly authorized the Commission to observe elections in South Korea only, and these took place on 10 May 1948. In September of the same year elections were held independently of the U.N. Temporary Commission in the north, and the government so elected proclaimed itself the government of all Korea.

Thus Korea, which had been a single and unified State for over four thousand years, became divided into North and South, with separate governments each claiming the whole of the country. On 25 June 1950 armed forces from the North invaded the Republic of Korea. The United Nations Security Council came to the assistance of the Republic. U.N. and Republic of Korea forces advanced as far as the Yalu River, but were forced to retreat to Seoul by the intervention of the Chinese Army on the side of the North Koreans, on 26 November 1950.

On 23 June 1951, Mr. Y. A. Malik, President of the Security Council, asked for a cease-fire. Truce talks were held which resulted in the conclusion of an armistice agreement on 27 July 1953.

The war in Korea lasted three years and one month. It was estimated to have cost more than 2 million casualties (including civilians) and to have left something like 10 million persons homeless. Korea remains divided into two parts, North Korea and South Korea with a continuous state of tension making peace always precarious.

# Korean Democratic People's Republic

(NORTH KOREA)

**Capital**—Pyongyang.

## CONSTITUTION AND GOVERNMENT

THE first session of the fifth Supreme People's Assembly ratified the new constitutional law—the Socialist Constitution of the Democratic People's Republic of Korea 27 December 1972, replacing the old constitution of 1948.

According to the new constitution, 'the DPRK is an independent socialist state which represents the interests of all Korean people'.

The highest power is *the Supreme People's Assembly* (SPA), composed of deputies elected on the principle of universal, equal and direct suffrage by secret ballot. Its term of office is four years.

Regular sessions are convened once or twice a year by a Standing Committee of the SPA and extraordinary sessions when it deems necessary, or on the request of a minimum of one third of the deputies.

The present fifth SPA is composed of 541 deputies elected in December 1972. The permanent body of the SPA is a Standing Committee.

*Chairman of the Standing Committee:* Hwang Jang Yop.

In accordance with a new constitution, the state structure has been greatly changed. An entirely new institution is the office of President.

The President of the DPRK is the head of state and represents the state power. He is elected by the SPA for the term of four years. The President directly guides the Central People's Committee; when necessary, convenes and presides over meetings of the Administration Council (Cabinet); is the Supreme Commander of entire Armed Forces of the DPRK and the Chairman of the National Defence Commission; ratifies or abrogates treaties concluded with foreign countries; receives foreign envoys' letters of credence, etc. He is responsible to the SPA for his activities.

*The President of the DPRK:* Kim Il Sung.
*The First Vice-President:* Kim Il.
*Vice-Presidents:* Choi Yong Kun, Kang Ryang Wook, Kim Tong Gyoo.

Another new institution according to the 1972 Constitution is the Central People's Committee (CPC) which is 'the highest leadership organ of state power in the DPRK'. It exercises such functions as shaping the internal and external policies; directing the work of the Administration Council and the local People's Assemblies; directing the work of judicial and procuratorial organs; supervising the execution of the constitution and laws; declaring a state of war, etc. The CPC is headed by the President of the DPRK and is responsible to the SPA for its activities.

The administrative and executive body of the highest organ of power is the Administration Council (AC). It works under the guidance of the President of the DPRK and the CPC. The AC is composed of the Premier (elected by the SPA on the recommendation of the President of the DPRK), Vice-Premiers, ministers and other members that are deemed heeded.

**Administration Counçil** (Cabinet, June 1976)

*Premier:* Pak Sung Chul.
*Vice-Premiers:* Hu Dam, Li Keun Mo, Jung Joon Ki, Hong Sung Nam, Kim Yung Joo.
*Chairman of the State Planning Committee:* Hong Sung Nam.
*Minister of the People's Armed Forces:* O Jin Woo.
*Minister of Foreign Affairs:* Hu Dam.
*Minister of Public Security:* Li Jin Soo.
*Chairman of the Heavy Industry Committee:* Yoon Myung Geun.
*Chairman of Machine-Building Industry:* Kim Hyun Myung.
*Minister of Ship-Machine-Building Industry:* Han Sung Ryong.

*Minister of Chemical Industry:* Koong San Man.
*Chairman of the Agricultural Committee:* Suh Kwan Hi.
*Chairman of the Transport and Communications Committee:* Kang Song San.
*Minister of Fisheries:* Kim Yoon Sang.
*Minister of Building Materials Industry:* Moon Pyung Il.
*Chairman of the Committee of Service for the People:* Li Yung Soon.
*Chairman of Education Committee:* Kim Suk Ki.
*Minister of Culture and Art:* Li Chang Sun.
*Minister of Higher Education:* Song Son P'il.
*Minister of Finance:* Kim Kyung Ryun.
*Minister of Foreign Trade:* Kye Eung Tai.
*Minister of External Economic Affairs:* Chun Song Nam.
*Minister of Construction:* Pak Im Taie.
*Minister of Labour Administration:* Chung Too Hwan.
*Minister of Public Health:* Pak Myung Bin.
*Minister of Elementary and Middle Education:* Kim Soo Gook.
*Minister of Sea Transport:* Li Chul Bon.

## LOCAL GOVERNMENT

The local organs of power are the People's Assemblies (PA) of the province (or municipality directly under central authority), city (or district) and county. The People's Committees are the local organs of power when the PAs at the corresponding levels are not in session. The administrative and executive bodies of the local power organs are the Administrative Commissions. The term of office of the PA of province is four years and that of the PA of the city (district) or county two years.

## LEGAL SYSTEM

Justice is administered by the Central Court, provincial courts, the people's courts of cities and counties and special courts in accordance with Chapter Ten of the Constitution.

The officials of the Courts are elected to their office. The President of the Central Court is elected by the SPA. The Central Court's judges and people's assessors by the Standing Committee of the SPA, and the courts of the province and the people's courts are elected by the people's assemblies of the corresponding levels. The term of their office is the same as that of the PA, i.e. four, or two years.

Justice is administered by the court composed of one judge and two people's assessors. The Central Court supervises the judicial work of all courts.

*President of the Central Court:* Pang Hak Se.

The Central Court is responsible for its work to the SPA, the President of the DPRK and the CPC.

Procuration affairs are conducted by the Central Procurator's Office, procurator's offices of the province, city (district), county and the special office. They supervise to see that the state laws are properly observed by the state institutions, enterprises, social co-operative organizations and by citizens; and supervise to see that the decisions and directives of state organs conform to the constitution, the laws and ordinances of the SPA or the President, and decrees of the CPC, etc.

The President of the Central Procurator's Office is appointed or removed by the SPA. The Central Procurator's Office is responsible for its work to the SPA, the President of the Republic, and the CPC.

*President of the Central Procurator's Office:* Chung Dong Chul.

### Political Structure

There are three political parties of which the *Worker's Party of Korea* (WPK)—a type of marxist–leninist party—has a leading role in the whole society. The party was originally formed by Kim Il Sung as the North Korean Organizing Committee of the Communist Party of Korea in October 1945. After merging with the New Democratic Party in August 1946, it developed into the North Korean Worker's Party. After merging with the South Korean Worker's Party in June 1949, it changed its name to the Worker's Party of Korea. In 1975 it had 2,000,000 members.

The Central Committee of the Worker's Party of Korea was last elected in November 1970.

*General Secretary:* Kim Il Sung.

The other two political parties are the *North Korean Democratic Party*, founded in November 1945 (Chairman: Kang Ryang Wook) and the *Religious Chungwoo Party*, founded in October 1945 (Chairman: Kang Jang Su).

**Overseas Policy.** According to Article 16 of the new Constitution, the DPRK establishes diplomatic as well as political, economic and cultural relations with all countries which are friendly towards her, on the principles of complete equality, independence, mutual respect, non-interference in each other's internal affairs and mutual benefits.

'The State, in accordance with the principles of Marxism–Leninism and proletarian internationalism, unites with the socialist countries, unites with all the peoples of the world opposed to imperialism and actively supports and encourages their struggles for national liberation and their revolutionary struggles.'

One of the aims of the DPRK's foreign policy is to obtain world support for her plan for the unification of Korea.

In 1974, the permanent mission of the DPRK to the U.N. at Geneva and the permanent observer office in the U.N. in New York were established.

In June 1976 the DPRK maintained regular diplomatic relations at ambassadorial level with nearly 95 states in four continents. In September 1975, she was a member of 140 international organizations.

The Foreign Ministers Conference of Non-Aligned States (Lima, August 25, 1975) unanimously decided to admit the DPRK as a full member of the Non-Aligned Movement.

In April 1975, President Kiru Il Sung visited the People's Republic of China and in May–June 1975 Romania, Algeria, Mauretania, Bulgaria and Yugoslavia.

### North–South Korean Relations

The 28th session of the General Assembly of the U.N. decided unanimously, without voting, to dissolve at once the U.N. Commission for the Unification and Rehabilitation of Korea and expressed the hope that both sides of the Korean dispute would continue their talks in the spirit of the North–South Joint Statement of 4 July 1972.

The 30th session of the U.N. General Assembly in 1975 discussed the Korean situation with the participation of the D.P.R.K., as well as the Republic of Korea's representatives. Two conflicting resolutions on Korea were passed at the 30th U.N. session.

The draft resolution co-sponsored by 43 countries, including Algeria, the U.S.S.R., the P.R.C. etc. and supported by the D.P.R.K., cf. Government Statement of 11 August 1975, stated that "it is necessary to dissolve the United Nations Command and withdraw all the foreign troops stationed in South Korea under the flag of the U.N."; it also called upon "the real parties to the Armistice Agreement to replace the Korean Military Agreement with a peace agreement as a measure to ease tension and maintain and consolidate peace in Korea"; also it urged the North and the South "to observe the principles of the North-South joint statement and . . . remove the military confrontation and maintain a durable peace in Korea, conducive to accelerating the independent and peaceful reunification of the country".

For the first time, a resolution supported by the D.P.R.K. was passed in the First Committee, 51 to 38 with 50 abstentions, and ratified by General Assembly, 54 to 43 with 42 abstentions, on 18 November 1975.

In fact, the dialogue between the North and South became deadlocked in 1975–76, and the preliminary meetings and contacts, including those of the Red Cross, ended without positive results.

On 4 March 1976, the Standing committee of the D.P.R.K. Supreme People's Assembly sent a letter to the Parliaments and governments of all countries of the world in connection with the tension created, of late, in Korea. Many countries expressed active support for this letter.

The Central Committee of the Democratic Front for the Reunification of the Fatherland and the Pyongyang side of the North–South Co-ordination Commission issued a joint statement on 3 July 1976, on the occasion of the fourth anniversary of the publication of the North–South Joint Statement. It stressed again that the most reasonable way of discussing and solving the question of the country's reunification was to convene a Great National Congress. The statement recalled the North–South Joint Statement of 4 July 1972, whose keynotes are the three principles of independence, peaceful reunification and national unity and accused the South authorities that they have used the dialogue for perpetuating the national split.

## AREA AND POPULATION

North Korea covers an area of 121,193 sq. km. The population at the end of 1963 was 11,568,000, the population at mid-1974 was 15,443,000. The annual average percentage growth rate of the population for the period 1960–74 was 2·8, and for the period 1965–74 was 2·8.

## CURRENCY AND FINANCE

The basic unit of currency is the won. 1 won comprises 100 jon. Budget figures (in million won):

| | 1975 | 1976 (*estimated*) |
|---|---|---|
| Revenue | 11,586 | 12,513 |
| Expenditure | 11,367 | 12,513 |

The 1975 state budgetary revenue surpassed the 1974 figures by 15·7 per cent. Expenditure was 98·7 per cent of the planned figure and 17·7 per cent over the previous year. The state revenue was in excess of 218 million won.

The Government allotted 16·4 per cent of the total budget to defence in 1975.

The national income in 1974 was 1·7 times the 1970 figure.

In 1974, taxation was abolished, the prices of manufactured goods were cut by 30 per cent on average.

## PRINCIPAL BANK

**Central Bank of the Democratic People's Republic of Korea.** Established 1946. (President, Mr. Byon Seung Woo. *Head Office:* Nammoon Dong, Central District, Pyongyang. Number of Branches etc. 221.

## PRODUCTION, INDUSTRY AND COMMERCE

**Mining.** Korea is known for its rich underground resources. So far over 300 kinds of ores have been discovered, some 200 of which are of economic value.

Korea ranks within the first ten in the world in deposits of gold, tungsten, molybdenum, graphite, magnesite, limestone, mica, barytes, fluorspar, etc. And she has rich deposits of iron ore, coal, lead, zinc, copper, aluminium, fire-resisting material, rare minerals, manganese, nickel and other valuable ores.

**Industry.** According to the report of the Central statistical board of 22 September 1975, the Six Year Plan, 1971–76, was fulfilled one year and four months earlier than schedule.

At the end of August 1975, the annual gross industrial output was 2·2 greater than that in 1970, the means of production was increased 2·3 times and that of consumer goods 2·1 times.

In the period from 1971–August 1975 the average annual rate of growth of industrial production reached 18·4 per cent.

In the period from 1971–August 1975, 1,055 modern factories and a large number of workshops were built and put into operation. The second-stage project of the Pukchang thermal power plant, the first-stage project of the Sodusu power station and the project of the Unggi thermal power plant were completed. The large furnace, the continuous sintering furnace, and the No. 3 and 4 coking batteries were installed in the Kim Chaek Iron Works. The construction of April 13 iron works, the reduced pellet shop of Hwanghae iron and steel Works, the No. 3 steel shop of the Songjin steel works and No. 2 steel shop of the Kangson steel works were likewise completed. The Puraesan cement factory, the expansion project of the production capacity of vinalon and vinyl chloride of the February 8 Vinalon Complex in Hungnam, the projects of the Sungni Chemical plant, phosphatic fertilizer factories with a total capacity of one million tons, the Kumsong Tractor Plant, the October 30 bearing factory, the Sariwon textile mill, the knitwear mill of Pyongyang, Siniju, Wonsan and Hamhung, the Pyongynag leather shoe-making factory etc. were also completed.

In the same period, the engineering industry increased by 2·4 times. The breakdown of this increase is as follows: heavy machine industry 2.2 times, machine tool industry 2·6 times and farm machine production 3·6 times.

The engineering industry produced modern plant equipment including metallurgical and chemical plants and various kinds of machinery. It successfully manufactured 300 h.p. bulldozers, 10-cubic meter excavators, 2,500-h.p. medium-speed engines, 3,000-h.p. high-speed engines, 50,000 kW generators, 200,000 kVa transformers, 2,500-h.p. diesel locomotives, 100-ton trucks, 18-metre turning lathes, 20,000-ton cargo ships etc.

The following are the latest available official figures for industrial output of some important commodities:

| *Commodity* | *Unit* | 1970[1] | 1976[2] | *Rate of*[3] *fulfilment of* 1976 *goals, per cent* | *Growth compared with* 1970 *times* |
|---|---|---|---|---|---|
| Electricity | milliard kWh | 16·5 | 28–30 | 102 | 1·7 |
| Coal | million tons | 27 | 50–53 | 101 | 1·8 |
| Pig and granulated iron | million tons | | 3·5–3·8 | 92 | 1·7 |
| Steel | million tons | 2·2 | 3·8–4 | 86 | 1·5 |
| Machine tools | unit | | 27,000 | 111 | 2·4 |
| Tractors | unit | | 21,000 | 101 | 8·7 |
| Chemical fertilizers | million tons | 1·5 | 2·8–3 | 109 | 2 |
| Cement | million tons | 4 | 7·5–8 | 91 | 1·7 |
| Fabrics | million meters | 400 | 500–600 | 116 | 1·8 |
| Shoes | million pairs | | 70 | 115 | 2·2 |
| Marine products | million tons | | 1·3–1·6 | 104 | 1·5 |

[1] The last year of the Seven Year Plan.
[2] Targets of the Six Year Plan announced at the 5th Congress of the WPK.
[3] by August 1975.

**Agriculture.** The collectivization and nationalization of the rural economy were fully completed by 1958. Since 1966 all co-operative farms have been exempt from the agricultural tax-in-kind. The technical reconstruction of the rural economy has been realized successfully with the support of heavy industry. An advance was made in the comprehensive mechanization of agriculture. The number of tractors per one hundred hectares of arable land rose to 2·25, and to 3·4 in the plain area in 1974 in comparison to 1·8 in 1972 (in terms of 15 h.p. units).

In 1974–75, the mechanization level of major categories of farm work reached in sillage of paddy and non-paddy fields, thrashing, fodder crushing and transport 100 per cent in rice—transplanting 92, harvesting 66 and reseeding 55 per cent. In 1975, rice transplanters were for the first time successfully used on a large scale.

The completion of irrigation has been successfully carried out. During the plan period 45 reservoirs and 3,872 water pumping and drainage stations were constructed and the acreage of irrigated non-paddy fields was increased 1·9 times, the acreage under water-sprinkling systems increased 3·4 times in comparison to 1970.

The total length of the network of water channels was over 40,000 kilometres in 1975. In 1974–75 the quantity of chemical fertilizers applied showed a two-fold increase compared with 1970 to exceed one ton per chongbo, (0·99 hectare).

Grain harvest increased to more than 7 million tons in 1974 and to 7·7 million tons in 1975. The country's 1974 average per chongbo grain yield was 5·9 tons of rice and five tons of maize.

In 1974, the output increased 1·4 times in meat, 1·8 times in eggs, 2·2 times in cocoons, 1·5 times in fruits and 1·4 times in vegetables as compared with the 1970 figures.

In the four and a half years from 1971 to June 1975, the acreage of the reclaimed tideland has doubled, 203,000 chongbo of land has been claimed, and the fruit farms have been enlarged still further to 300,000 chongbo.

In the last ten years the state has built a great number of production units for co-operative farms. More than 560,000 modern rural dwelling houses and a large number of nurseries, kindergartens, clubhouses, hospitals and various other cultural and public service establishments were built at state expense in the same time.

### COMMUNICATIONS

During 1971–75 160 km. railway sections were newly electrified. The electrification of the major trunk lines has been completed (especially the line Pyongyang–Sinijoo Pyongyang–Hamheung–Chungjin–Hoeryong–Najin – Chungjin, and Pyongyang–Sariwon). The important East–West line Kanggye–Hyesan–Musar in the northern mountain area, the railway construction Kujang–Parwon, Pukchang–Toksong, and the electrification of the line Susong–Musan, have been progressing throughout 1975.

The second line of the subway Metro was open for service in 1975 in Pyongyang.

During 1971–August 1975 420 km. new railway lines had been laid. The railway freight traffic rose 1·7 times, auto freight traffic 1·8 times and shipping freight traffic 1·7 times. The introduction of bus services to the rural villages has been completed.

### EDUCATION

Primary education became compulsory in 1956 and compulsory middle school education was enforced in 1958. In 1967 universal nine-year compulsory technical education began.

Tuition fees were abolished on 1 April 1959 at schools of all levels up to higher educational institutions.

In 1973, the SPA of the DPRK adopted a law of compulsory ten-year senior middle school education (4–6 system) and a compulsory one-year pre-school education for the Six-Year Plan. This system had been fully introduced by 1 September 1975. By April, 1975 more than 5·6 million students or one third of the population have received a compulsory eleven-year education.

Nearly one million students study at higher schools and universities and colleges. These have trained one million technicians and specialists up to the present.

The DPRK had 60,000 nurseries and kindergartens, 4,700 primary schools, 4,100 senior middle schools, more than 600 higher specialized schools and 150 universities and colleges in 1975.

According to The Law on the Nursing and Upbringing of Children, which came into force on 1 June 1976, the DPRK educates all the children in nuseries and kindergartens at state expense. 3,500,000 children were in kindergarten and nursery schools in 1976.

# Republic of Korea

(SOUTH KOREA)

**Capital**—Seoul.

**President**—Park Chung Hee.

**National Flag:** A white field bearing a disk (the *Taeguk*) divided fesse-wise by an S-shaped line, red over blue; on the white field corner, parallel black bars broken and whole, to symbolize natural opposites.

### CONSTITUTION AND GOVERNMENT

THE first representative government of Korea was formed in August 1948. It is based on a presidential system similar to that of the United States. After the April Revolution (1960), the Constitution was amended giving greater power to the legislature. In May 1961, with the emergence of the military government, the National Assembly was dissolved.

The constitutional amendments submitted by the military government to a national referendum were adopted on 5 December 1962. The new constitution came into force on 17 December 1963, the day of the first convocation of the National Assembly which is constituted pursuant to this constitution. By adoption of newly amended constitution, short-lived parliamentary system was abolished, and the Presidential system re-established.

On 17 October 1972 an Emergency Presidential Decree was promulgated. After a national referendum a new constitution was adopted on 21 November 1972. Under the new Constitution on 15 December 1972, 2,359 deputies to the National Conference for Unification were elected. These deputies in turn re-elected on 23 December 1972 Park Chung Hee for a six year Presidential term. There are 219 seats in the National Assembly. This National Assembly came into existence because of an electoral decision. The relevant election having been held on 27 February 1973. 73 seats of this National Assembly were elected by the National Conference for Unification. After a quarter of a century of hostilities talks began between the Northern and Southern parts of the country.

The first conference between North and South was held on 29 August 1972 in Pyongyang. The participants were the respective Red Cross Societies of the two parts of Korea.

The first political meeting on 12 October 1972 was held at Panmunjom between the South and North Co-ordinating Committees.

**Cabinet**

*President:* Park Chung-Hee.
*Premier:* Choe Gyu-ha.
*Deputy Premier and Economic Planning Minister:* Nam Deok-u.
*Foreign Minister:* Park Tong-Jin.
*Minister of Finance:* Yong-Hwan Kim.
*Home Minister:* Kim Chi-yeo.
*Minister of Justice:* San-Duk Hwang.
*Minister of Defence:* Jyong-Chul Suh.
*Minister of Education:* Kee-Chun Yoo.
*Minister of Agriculture and Forestry:* Choe Gak-kyu.
*Minister of Commerce and Industry:* Ye-Joon Chang.
*Minister of Construction:* Kim Jae-gyu.
*Minister of Health and Social Affairs:* Shin Hyeon-hwak.
*Minister of Transport:* Kyung-Nok Choi.
*Minister of Communications:* Soung-Toe Chang.
*Minister of Culture and Information:* Won-Kyong Lee.
*Minister of Science and Technology:* Hyung-Sup Choi.
*Minister of Government Administration:* Heung-Sun Shim.
*Minister of National Unification:* Sang-Guine You.
*Ministers without Portfolio:* Byung Hee Lee, Tae-Hoe Koo.

### LOCAL GOVERNMENT

At present The Republic of Korea is divided into nine provinces, and two special cities. Seoul and Pusan, ranking as Provinces headed by appointed governors and mayors who are responsible to the Executive Branch of the National Government through the Ministry of Home Affairs.

Since the establishment of the Republic of Korea, both local self-government system and direct government control system were tried alternately. At present, governors of provinces and other officials are directly appointed by the Government. The newly amended constitution stipulates that provinces and lower territorial sub-divisions shall have elected councils with limited legislative powers.

### LEGAL SYSTEM

Judicial Power is vested in courts composed of Judges. There are three types of courts: The Supreme Court which is the highest court of the State, Courts of Appeal, and District Courts. The Supreme Court has the power to change laws, when they are judged not to be constitutional; it also has the power to decide the manner in which the law is to be interpreted in particular cases, or when in fact the law as constituted is applicable. It is also authorized to dissolve political parties. It consists of up to 16 judges, who are appointed by the President upon the recommendation of the Chief Justice, after they have been selected by the Judge Recommendation Council.

### AREA AND POPULATION

The area of South Korea, below the Southern Demilitarized Zone, is 98,477·48 sq. kilometres.

The population at mid-1973 was 32,905,000. The annual average percentage growth rate of the population for the period 1960–73 was 2·2 and for the period 1965–73 was 1·9. The following table shows populations of the nine provinces and of the cities of Seoul and Pusan, which have provincial status (1975).

| *Province or town* | *Population* |
|---|---|
| Seoul City | 6,884,000 |
| Pusan City | 2,451,000 |
| Kyonggi Province | 4,036,000 |
| Chungchong North Province | 1,522,000 |
| Chungchong South Province | 2,947,000 |
| Cholla North Province | 2,455,000 |
| Cholla South Province | 3,984,000 |
| Kyongsang North Province | 4,856,000 |
| Kyongsang South Province | 3,279,000 |
| Kangwon Province | 1,862,000 |
| Cheju Province | 412,000 |

## CURRENCY AND FINANCE

On 9 June 1962, the monetary unit became the won. Bank note denominations are, 5, 10, 50, 100, 500, 1,000, 5,000 and 10,000 won. The number of types of coins in circulation has been increased to five, i.e. 1, 5, 10, 50, and 100 won.

The total national budget for 1974 was W. 1,034,832,000,000.

The GNP at market prices for 1973 was U.S.$ millions 13,250, and the GNP per capita at market prices was U.S. $400. The annual average percentage growth rate of the GNP per capita for the period 1960–73 was 7·1, and for the period 1965–73 was 8·7. [*See the note at the beginning of this section concerning GNP.*]

## BANKS

**Bank of Korea.** (Governor, Sung Whan Kim.) Est. 1950; Bank of Issue; note issue 229·7 billion won at the end of 1972. *Head Office:* Seoul, Korea.

*Commercial Banks:* Commercial banks in Korea are characterized by a branch banking system with a nationwide network of branch offices. The six commercial banks are The Choheung Bank, The Commercial Bank of Korea, The First Bank of Korea, The Han-il Bank, The Bank of Seoul, The Korea Trust Bank.

*Special Banks.* The Korea Development Bank, The Korea Exchange Bank, The Medium Industry Bank, The Citizens National Bank, The Korea Housing Bank, The National Agricultural Co-operative Federation and The Central Federation of Fisheries Co-operatives.

*Local Banks:* Pusan Bank, Taegu Bank and eight others.

## PRODUCTION, INDUSTRY AND COMMERCE

**Agriculture.** Grain production, living environment, dietary and other agricultural patterns are being changed in line with the rapid industrialization of the country. Farmland owned per household increased from an average of 0·8 hectares in 1960 to 0·94 hectares in 1974. The total Cultivated Land is 2,238,432 hectares (of which 1,268,949·8 hectares are rice paddies). 1975 figures: Rice: 4,669,000 metric tons.

Korea's major agricultural products are rice, barley, soyabeans, and potatoes, rice being the staple grain. The country, because of antiquated farming methods and increasing population (now brought down to 1·65 per cent growth) has to import large amounts of grain, but self-sufficiency in grain supply is planned by 1976. To secure maximum agricultural acreage, the Government has classified 'absolute farmland' (which cannot be converted for any non-farming purpose) and 'convertible farmland'. Development of the basins of four major rivers for agricultural purposes is well under way.

**Fishing** is a growth industry. Deep-sea fishing fleets increased from 3 ships (431 tons gt) in 1960 to 833 ships (585,000 mt) in 1975. In 1975, the 833 Korean deep-sea fishing vessels were engaged in 21 fishing grounds around the world—173 in the Atlantic, 112 in the Indian Ocean and 261 in the Pacific.

The Government plans a U.S. $360,877,500 inshore fishing development programme 1974–81 to increase the annual incomes of fishing households by 304 per cent by 1981, the target year of the fourth Five-Year Economic Development Plan.

**Mining and Manufacturing Industry.** Industrial growth has been very rapid in the late 60s and early 70s. There are now some 30 industrial complexes throughout the country, and the Government has ambitious programmes to develop further industrial facilities under its five-year economic development plans which started in 1962. In March 1974 was announced construction of six more industrial bases for shipbuilding, non-ferrous, machine and combined chemical industries. In the ten years ended December 1973 the national economy grew at an average of 10 per cent yearly (highest growth: 1969 with 15·9 per cent). In 1975 per capita GNP rose to U.S. $531 with a predicted figure for 1981 of U.S. $1,284. This economic growth was spearheaded by brisk production activities in the mining and manufacturing industry which increased by 18·2 per cent (1970), 16·9 per cent (1971), 15·4 per cent (1972) and 29·3 per cent (1973). The growth rate in the mining and manufacturing industrial sector for 1974 was set at 15 per cent. Taking into account the unfavourable economic situations caused by the oil crisis, the Government set the economic growth rate for 1974 rather conservatively at 8 per cent. In manufacturing industry, the nation achieved a real growth of 9·4 per cent in 1974. The light industrial sector grew by 21·7 per cent while the heavy industrial sector grew by 6·9 per cent. Growth rates for other sectors are: textiles: 16·7 per cent; footwear: 39·1 per cent; paper manufacturing: 16·5 per cent. For the exploitation of various mineral resources to meet any prolonged energy crisis, the Government plans an investment of U.S. $438,250,000 by 1976. So long as the mining and manufacturing industry grows at a steady pace, Korea should have little trouble in achieving the major economic targets set under its long-range economic development programme—U.S. $13,000 million in exports and U.S. $1,300 in per capita GNP annually around 1980. Korea lacks major raw materials. Therefore the Government has been taking various counter-measures, including launching reinforced 'resources diplomacy' toward nations abundant in raw materials.

## COMMUNICATIONS

**Motorways.** Motorways connect virtually all corners of the country from the capital city of Seoul, and two more motorways are scheduled for completion by 1977. Total length of roads: 46,035 km (including 1,142 km motorways).

**Railways.** Railways are the major method of long-distance transportation, and the railway network comprises 5,600 km railroads, 600 locomotives (diesel and steam), 18,000 passenger and freight cars, and related facilities. In 1974, total train passengers numbered 160,236,000; ship passengers 6,668,962; and total freight handled 132,571,000 tons.

**Aviation.** Civil commercial aviation has developed fast. The flag-carrier Korean Air Lines (KAL), although only formed in 1969, by mid-1974 had a fleet of nearly 90 planes, including 27 passenger aircraft (two of them being Boeing 747 jumbo jets). KAL flies as far as Los Angeles across the Pacific, to Paris across the North Pole, and to South-east Asian countries. The company plans to initiate routes to New York and to other European countries in the near future. Kimpo International Airport, the gateway to Korea, is being expanded (1974) at a total cost of U.S. $1,774,850 to handle more effectively the increasing traffic volume. There are two more international airports: Pusan (second largest city) and Cheju.

**Shipping.** In marine transportation, total tonnage of vessels in 1974 was 1,877,239 gt (cargo ships: 707,350 gt; oil tankers: 674,546 gt; fishing vessels: 458,806 gt; passenger liners: 19,263 gt; others: 33,695 gt).

**Posts, Telegraphs and Telephones.** Post Offices at the end of 1974 totalled 1,921, with 18,396 post boxes, 19,623 PO boxes, 166 motor vehicles, 5,686 bicycles and 8,591 mainmen employed by the Ministry of Communications. In 1974 a total of 640 million mail items were received and 743 million delivered, including 38 million air and surface mail items from overseas.

Telephone subscribers totalled 727,400 at October 1973, with 49 international telecommunication lines, 155 international telephone lines and other international communications facilities. Direct dialling began between Seuol and Pusan in 1972 and will be extended throughout the country by 1976. In major cities, wireless facilities are used for coastal communications and also emergency communication networks. By 1976, micro-wave facilities with about 4,380 circuits are expected to be in operation.

Korea maintains a scatter system with Japan and semi-auto telephone exchanges with Japan and the U.S.A. A satellite receiving earth station was dedicated in Kumsan in 1970 and facilities for 39 circuits have been installed throughout Korea, with preparations for installing a further 120 circuits completed.

### EDUCATION AND RELIGION

In April 1972 there were over 8 million students and 179,015 teachers, with scholarships and grants available. Primary school attendance is compulsory, 98 per cent of the primary school-age population attending. Almost 90 per cent of the population is literate, and there are adult education programmes in all areas.

Korea has adopted a school system, dividing education into six-year elementary schools, three-year middle schools, three-year high schools and four-year colleges or universities. Educational Statistics for the year 1972 are:

| | *Schools* | *Pupils* | *Teachers* |
|---|---|---|---|
| Primary | 6,269 | 5,692,285 | 107,259 |
| Middle | 1,916 | 1,832,092 | 43,155 |
| High | 1,015 | 839,318 | 27,834 |
| Colleges and Universities | 69 | 178,650 | 9,253 |

There are 74 graduate schools (which grant master's degrees in two years and doctor's degrees in four years) with 8,681 students and 141 professors. At the primary level the number of pupils per classroom does not exceed 60 in urban areas, 65 in rural areas. Textbooks will be distributed free by 1976.

Shamanism had been the sole and indigenous religion of Korean ancestors until Buddhism was introduced from China in 372 A.D. to rule the religious life until the end of the Koryo Dynasty. In the early days of the Yi Dynasty, Confucianism came to dominate the religion and thought of the Korean people.

In 1758 and in 1884, Catholicism and Protestantism were introduced respectively and began to spread during the latter half of the 19th century.

The following figures are based on the 1973 religious census:

| *Belief* | *Followers* | *Churches, etc.* | *Clergy, etc.* |
|---|---|---|---|
| Buddhist | 7,986,000 | 1,912 | 18,629 |
| Confucian | 4,423,000 | 231 | |
| Chondogyo | 718,000 | 140 | |
| Other Asian | 2,233,000 | | |
| Catholic | 790,000 | 438 | 3,487 |
| Protestant (50 denominations) | 3,463,000 | 13,417 | 17,562 |

All the major religions administer institutions of higher education, most of them also sponsor secondary or primary schools and many have associated hospitals or social welfare organizations.

# Kuwait

**Capital**—Kuwait City

**Head of State**—His Highness Shaikh Jabir al-Ahmed al-Jabir al-Sabah.

**National Flag:** On a tricolour fesse-wise, green, white, red, a wedge at the hoist black.

### CONSTITUTION AND GOVERNMENT

KUWAIT is an independent Arab State situated at the north-west of the Persian Gulf.

Constitutional government was introduced in January 1963 when a 50 member National Assembly was elected, the electorate consisting of all adult Kuwaiti males. Under the Constitution, which was introduced at the same time, the Assembly must pass all laws, and approve the heir apparent nominated by the Amir. The Amir appoints the Prime Minister, who can appoint his Ministers from the members of the Assembly or from outside. The Assembly has the right to pass a vote of no confidence in any Minister except the Prime Minister.

### POPULATION

The mid-1974 population was 930,000. The annual average percentage population growth rate for the period 1960–74 was 9·1, and for the period 1965–74 was 7·8.

### CURRENCY AND FINANCE

The unit of currency is the Kuwait dinar. It was introduced in 1961.

The GNP at market prices for 1973 was U.S. $ millions 10,610, and the GNP per capita at market prices was U.S. $12,050. The annual average percentage growth rate of the GNP per capita for the period 1960–74 was −2·7, and for the period 1965–74 was −2·3. [*See the note at the beginning of this section concerning GNP.*]

**Banks.** The National Bank of Kuwait Ltd., a Kuwaiti bank, was established in 1952. The Commercial Bank of Kuwait (S.A.K.) (a Kuwaiti bank) was established on 15 April 1961 and a further Kuwaiti bank, the Gulf Bank, K.S.C., opened in October 1961. The Al Ahli Bank was formed in May 1967. The Bank of Kuwait and the Middle East K.S.C. opened in December 1971, taking over the branches of the British Bank of the Middle East, whose 1942 concession then expired. The Central Bank, opened in May 1969, controls all banking transactions.

### PRODUCTION, INDUSTRY AND COMMERCE

The main source of state revenue is royalties and income tax on oil production. The Kuwait Oil Company Limited was awarded the concession to explore for and produce oil in the state of Kuwait in 1934. In May 1962, the Company relinquished about 50 per cent of its original concession area. Production, which in 1946 was 17 million tons, reached 143,724,505 tons in 1973. The main oilfields are situated at Magwa and Burgan in the south of Kuwait and at Raudhatain in the north. The latter is connected by a 30-inch pipeline to Mina al-Ahmadi. The centre of the Company's administrative activity is at Ahmadi. The refinery at Mina al-Ahmadi can process 250,000 barrels of crude oil per day. It supplies middle distillates, marine diesel fuel oils and residual fuel oil, and various products including petrol for the local market. Natural gas extracted from crude oil is used to provide power for the State and the Kuwait Oil Company, and liquid petroleum gas is also produced.

In October 1960 the Kuwait National Petroleum Company was established. The Kuwait Government owns 60 per cent of the shares in this Company, which in June 1961 took over the distribution of petroleum products in Kuwait from the K.O.C. Ltd. This company has built a refinery at Shuaiba to process about 100,000 barrels a day and has negotiated a concession for the areas relinquished by K.O.C. in conjunction with the Spanish company, Hispanoil.

The off-shore area of Kuwait was conceded to the Shell Company in November 1960, and the agreement was signed in January 1961. Exploratory drilling began in 1962, but was suspended in the autumn of 1963.

Kuwait and Saudi Arabia enjoy equal rights in the Partitioned Zone to the south of Kuwait. The concession to exploit the Kuwaiti share of the on-shore oil resources was awarded to the American Independent Oil Company (Aminoil) in 1947, the Saudi concession going to the Getty Oil Company. Aminoil's production totalled 3,650,000 tons in 1973.

In 1958 both Kuwait and Saudi Arabia awarded concessions for their respective half interests in the Neutral Zone off-shore area to a Japanese undertaking, the Arabian Oil Company (Japan) Ltd., whose centre of activity is at Ras al-Khafji in the south of the Neutral Zone. The first shipment of crude oil was made in March 1961 and production in 1973 was about 10,000,000 tons, of which half pertains to Kuwait.

The face of Kuwait town has been greatly changed by this sudden influx of wealth; schools, roads and hospitals have been built, the latter being equipped with the most up-to-date equipment. The Kuwait University was opened in November 1966. Fresh water, which has always been a problem, is now being provided from distillation plants at a rate of approximately 10,030,000,000 gallons per annum. In 1961 a natural source of fresh water was discovered at Raudhatain in the north of the State. This has been developed to produce 5 million gallons per day for at least 20 years, and a pipeline has been built to carry the water to Kuwait town. In February 1964 Kuwait signed an agreement with Iraq which would allow her to draw up to 120,000,000 gallons a day from the Shatt-al-Arab, but the scheme has not yet been implemented.

**Commerce.** The port of Kuwait is traditionally an entrepôt for goods for the interior and for the export of skins and wool. With the development of the oil industry the importance of entrepôt trade has diminished. There has been a considerable increase in traffic through the port in recent years. The oil production figure for 1974 was 929·4 barrels.

The value of the 1974 exports was 3,213 million Kuwait Dinars, and the value of imports was 449 million dinars.

## COMMUNICATIONS

Shuwaikh, the port of Kuwait City, can handle up to 1,400,000 tons of cargo annually. Ships of British, Dutch, Norwegian, Kuwaiti and other lines make regular calls at Kuwait. B.O.A.C., Kuwait Airways, and many other airlines operate regular services. Wireless communication, telephones and postal services are managed by the Ministry of Posts, Telegraphs and Telephones of the Government of Kuwait, using a communications satellite ground station and other sophisticated equipment.

# People's Democratic Republic of Laos

**Capital**—Vientiane.

**President**—Prince Souphanouvong.

**National Flag:** Horizontal stripes red blue red with a white circle in the centre.

## CONSTITUTION AND GOVERNMENT

LAOS, originally a Protectorate of French Indo-China, is bounded on the west by Siam and Burma, on the north by China, on the east by Viet-Nam and on the south by Cambodia. The country became a French Protectorate in 1893. On 9 March 1945 the Japanese took control of the country and abolished the French Protectorate. The independence of Laos was proclaimed on 15 April 1945 and a Laotian Government under Japanese protection was installed. After the Japanese capitulation on 15 August the French authorities regained control. After 15 September, however, Chinese troops who had been allotted the task of disarming the Japanese to the north of the 16th parallel gradually occupied the greater part of the country. A rebel Laotian government—the Lao Issara (Free Laos)—was formed acting in collaboration with the Viet Minh. Early in 1946 the French progressively reoccupied Laos and the greater part of the country was under their control by the middle of the year, while the Lao Issara formed a government in exile in Bangkok. A *modus vivendi* was signed on 27 August between France and the King of Laos. It confirmed the unity and partial independence of Laos and foreshadowed a new democratic political structure. Deputies were elected to a National Constituent Assembly in January 1947 and on 11 May 1947 the new constitution was proclaimed by the king. Laos was declared a parliamentary, constitutional monarchy, the king ruling through ministers responsible to a National Assembly elected for five years.

In 1949, the Lao Issara split. One group led by Prince Souvanna Phouma returned to Laos and accepted limited independence under the French. By a treaty signed in Paris in July and ratified on 2 February 1950, Laos became, like Cambodia, an Associated State within the French Union. Meanwhile the other faction of the Lao Issara organized a resistance movement called the Pathet Lao (Land of the Lao) in northern Laos. By 1953, Pathet Lao and Viet Minh forces had control of the north eastern provinces in which a Pathet Lao administration was established.

Full independence from French rule was established in 1953 and in 1954, when the Geneva Agreements ended the first Indochina war, Laos was recognized as a neutral state. After lengthy negotiations an agreement was signed in 1957 between the two Lao sides. This provided for elections and for the political and military integration of both factions in a coalition government. Elections were held in 1958, but the coalition rapidly disintegrated and the Pathet Lao leaders returned to their base areas. After a military coup d'etat in 1960, a new Vientiane government led by Prince Souvanna Phouma re-opened talks with the Pathet Lao. This government was itself ousted later in the year by right wing leaders and fighting broke out between Souvanna Phouma's supporters (the neutralists) and the Pathet Lao on one side and the right wing on the other. The latter was supported by the United States of America, while the Pathet Lao and neutralists were backed by the communist powers.

In 1962 a new Geneva Agreement was signed. Laos was again recognised as a neutral state and a new tripartite (right-left-neutral) coalition government with Souvanna Phouma as Premier was set up. As before, it was not able to bring the Pathet Lao and the right wing together. In 1963, Pathet Lao ministers again returned to their base areas and by 1964 fighting was in progress between right and left wings, with the neutralists split between the two sides. Nine years of war followed, with the Vientiane government receiving substantial military support from the United States and the Pathet Lao from North Vietnam. In 1973 a third ceasefire agreement was signed and a third coalition government formed—the Provisional Government of National Union, headed once more by Souvanna Phouma. A National Political Consultative Council to make policy recommendations was also established, headed by the Pathet Lao leader Prince Souphanouvong (Souvanna Phouma's half brother).

From the beginning, political initiative lay with the well organized Pathet Lao. By June 1974, a decision had been taken to dissolve the largely right wing National Assembly. This was carried out in April 1975 and in May after skirmishing between the two sides, a series of anti-right wing demonstrations demanding reform preceeded the take over of American property and the resignation and exile of rightist ministers and senior army officers. By August 1975, Pathet Lao forces had moved into former right wing strongholds. Local elections were held in October and November and in early December, at a national congress of 270 People's Representatives, the monarchy was abolished and the coalition government dismantled. King Srisavang Vatthana abdicated, a new government including all the most senior Pathet Lao leaders was named and a 45 member People's Supreme Council, headed by the new President, Prince Souphanouvong was set up to revise the constitution.

In 1977, strained relations with Thailand and the activities of right-wing rebels operating along the border led to the ex-king being placed under house arrest and a tightening of internal security.

### Members of the Government

*Prime Minister:* Kaysone Phomivane.
*Vice-Premier and Minister of Finance:* Nouhak Phoumsavanh
*Vice-Premier and Minister of Education, Sport and Religion:* Phoumi Vongvichit.
*Vice-Premier and Minister of Foreign Affairs:* Phoune Sipraseuth.
*Vice-Premier and Minister of Defence:* Khamtay Siphandone.
*Ministers of the President's Council:* Saly Vongkhamsao, Chanmy Douangphoukeo, Maychantane Sengmany, Sisavat Keobounthanh.
*Minister in Charge of Premier's Office:* Sali Vongkhamsao.
*Chief of National Planning Committee:* Ma Khai Khamphithoun.
*Minister of Interior: Veterans and Social Welfare:* Somsune Khamphithoune.
*Minister of Information, Propaganda, Culture and Tourism:* Sisana Sisane.
*Minister of Justice:* Kou Souvannemethi.
*Minister of Communications, Public Works and Transport:* Sanan Southichak.
*Minister of Health:* Souk Vongsak.
*Minister of Agricultural Production, Forestry and Irrigation:* Khamsouk Saygnaseng.
*Minister of Industry and Commerce:* Maysouk Saysompheng.
*Minister of Posts and Telecommunications:* Khampheng Boupha.
*Supreme Counsellor of the President:* ex-King Srisavang Vatthana.
*Counsellor of the Government:* Prince Souvanna Phouma.

There are also 19 Vice-Ministers.
*Supreme People's Council.*
*President:* Prince Souphanouvong.
*Vice-Presidents:* Sisounthone Lovonsay, Faydang Lobliayao, Khamsouk Keola.
*Secretary General:* Khamsouk Keola.
*Vice-Secretaries General:* Xay Phetrasy, Souvannarath.

## AREA AND POPULATION

The area of the country is approximately 91,000 square miles. It is landlocked and mountainous. The population is estimated at roughly three million persons. Less than half of the inhabitants of Laos are ethnic Lao; the rest are tribal groups living mainly in the mountain areas. Among the more important of these are the Black and White Thai, the Meo and the Yao. In the towns there are sizeable Vietnamese and Chinese communities. Per capita income is estimated at US $75 per annum.

The country is divided into 16 provinces, each headed by a provincial governor. The principal towns are Vientiane, the administrative capital, population about 180,000, Luang Prabang, the royal capital, pop. 35,000, Savannakhet, pop 80,000 and Pakse, pop. 80,000.

## CURRENCY AND FINANCE

The unit of currency is the kip. The kip valued in October 1977 at approximately 352 to the pound sterling.

From 1964–1975, the stability of the kip was underwritten by the Foreign Exchange Operations Fund (FEOF) supported by Britain, France, Japan, Australia and the United States which matched the contributions of the others. The fund, amounting to some US $ 22 million a year, provided balance of payments aid and helped to cover Laos's large budgetary deficit. However, in 1975, the United States suspended aid to Laos and withdrew from future contributions to the FEOF. At the same time the demand for foreign currency increased as Laotians opposed to the new government went into exile. As a result the kip plummeted, falling from a stable 500 to the US dollar in the 1960s to its lowest level of 14,000 to the US dollar in June 1975. At that point the government introduced a new kip exchanging at the rate of one to twenty old kip. In 1976, FEOF opertions ended completely. In spite of strict controls on the export of foreign currency the government has been unable to stabilise the kip. Border disputes with Thailand and distribution problems within Laos have led to shortages, forcing up the price of food and other necessities. The government has been forced to increase the money supply to pay officials and provide compensation for nationalised businesses. Not only foreign currency but food supplies have continued to cross the Thai border in exchange for consumer goods formerly financed by the FEOF and in abundant supply. In 1977, the official exchange rate was 200 kip to the US dollar while the blackmarket rate soared to 2,000 to the US dollar.

In November 1976, a new agricultural tax was imposed to provide the government's main source of revenue. In 1977, it was announced that 54·71 per cent of that year's budget would be allocated to developing economic and cultural affairs, the balance going to defence, public order, administration and propaganda.

## PRODUCTION, INDUSTRY AND COMMERCE

Eighty per cent of the population of Laos works on the land and rice is the principle crop. The country, however, is not self-sufficient. The war devastated large areas of land and in 1976, out of four million hectares of cultivable land, only 500,000 hectares were actually being farmed. Barely three per cent of the rice area is irrigated, agricultural machinery is scarce and distribution poses a constant problem—because of bad communications, rice surpluses in the richer southern provinces have been regularly smuggled across the border to Thailand while the government has been forced to import rice to feed less productive areas. Before 1975, rice imports were running at 100,000 tonnes a year.

Aiming for self-sufficiency within two or three years, in 1976 the government announced plans to expand the cultivated land area, introduce double cropping and give priority to irrigation works and hydroelectric projects. It also intends to move gradually towards collective farming with agricultural co-operatives being set up immediately in re-settled areas devastated by the war. By the end of 1976, 40,000 hectares of land had been reclaimed. Some state farms had also been set up and governments had established and staffed their own farms outside Vientiane.

The 1975 rice crop was a good one, but in 1976 and 1977 production was severely affected by drought and pests. In September 1976, Laos appealed to the United Nations Food and Agriculture Organisation for aid to save the rice crop in the northern provinces. In spite of a surplus in the south, Laos was forced to import an estimated 120,000 tons or rice. In 1977, some southern provinces were themselves suffering from drought and the government called on people to conserve rice, prevent hoarding and to plant as many kinds of additional starch crops as possible. An additional complication was a new tax on agricultural production imposed in November 1976, which allied to the shortage of consumer goods, discouraged farmers from attempting to produce more.

In January 1977, Laos had 400,000 cattle, eight million pigs and 500,000 poultry. 16 centres had been established to step up the production of draught and meat animals. The government is also planning to develop forestry and agricultural crops for export. Tobacco, cotton and coffee are grown in Laos and there is a great variety of hardwood in the forests, including teak and rosewood. The forests have, however, been considerably damaged by the war and by "slash and burn" methods of agriculture.

In November 1975, the government legalized the production of opium under state control for sale to the pharmaceutical industry. Opium has been traditionally grown by the mountain tribes and exported in unknown quantities. Production is estimated at about 50 tons a year.

Laos has deposits of tin, coal, iron and potash. Apart from the tin, these are largely unexploited. Tin production stood at 1,262 tons in 1969 from two mines near Thakhek in central Laos. Electricity production in 1969 was 20·7 million khW. In August 1972 construction of the Nam Ngum dam, 45 miles north of Vientiane was completed. Initial output was 35,000 kW. Until 1974 much of this energy went to Thailand as payment for debts incurred through the use of Thai electric power.

There is little industry, though small factories exist producing alcohol, soft drinks, textiles, soap, matches and rubber sandals. In 1977, 21 war damaged factories had been repaired and two new ones—producing farm tools and asbestos tiles—set up. There are plans to build factories for processing forestry and agricultural products, but in 1977 most enterprises were running down through a lack of raw materials.

Tension between Laos and Thailand was largely responsible for these shortages. Since Laos is landlocked, 70–80 per cent of its imports and nearly all exports are transported across Thailand. A Thai embargo, officially confined to strategic goods and imposed only during September in practice severely restricted all imports throughout 1977 and cut down the flow of foreign aid so that industrial essentials such as oil, steel, cement and spare parts only trickled into the country. Exports also were brought to a virtual standstill. Thailand's embargo was lifted in October 1977.

In the past, Laos's exports have been negligible, earning between US$ 2·1 million and US$ 4 million between 1968 and 1974 and consisting principally of tin, timber, raw cotton and unroasted coffee. In 1975, the government said that imports in future would be restricted to essentials while efforts would be made to step up exports. In 1976, Laos exported timber valued at US$ 5 million, tin valued at US$ 2 million while electric power from the Nam Ngum hydroelectric project was sold to Thailand for around US$ 1 million. In 1977, Thailand refused transit to timber, and tin shipments came to a halt as the result of a dispute between the government and the tin mines' former French operators.

Laos has signed aid agreements with the U.S.S.R., China, Vietnam, Japan, West Germany, Sweden and Holland. In 1975 an agreement with North Vietnam provided for the shipment of goods across North Vietnam and the use of North Vietnamese ports for some Laotian trade. Another agreement with united Vietnam allowing Laos to import and export goods through the port of Da Nang was signed in July 1977. Cambodia has also allowed Laos to move goods across its territory to the port of Kompong Som.

## COMMUNICATIONS

There are no railways in Laos. In 1974 the Laotian government decided to revive a plan first proposed before World War II to build a railway from Thakhek in central Laos to Tap An in North Vietnam where it could be linked with the North Vietnamese railway system. In 1977 work had not yet commenced.

In 1977, Laos had 9,700 miles of road, with 800 miles sealed—the rest, surfaced with dirt and gravel, become unusable during the rainy season. Vietnam is helping to improve existing highways and build new ones, including one linking the Plain of Jars in central Laos with Vinh in central Vietnam and another from Savannakhet in the south to the Vietnamese port of Da Nang. Other roads are being built with Chinese assistance in Laos's northern provinces including an all-weather road from Yunnan to the former royal capital of Luang Prabang. Route 13 from southern Laos to Vientiane is being enlarged. Vehicles and petrol are in short supply.

The River Mekong is an important means of communication. It is navigable, depending on the season, for ships of 200 gross tons from Luang Prabang to Vientiane and thence to Savannakhet and Pakse.

Laos has 115 airfields. The largest are at Vientiane, which handles international flights, Luang Prabang, Savannakhet and Pakse. The national airline flies to Hanoi, Ho Chi Minh City, Bangkok, Phnom Penh and Hong Kong as well as operating domestic services.

## EDUCATION AND RELIGION

In 1972, there were at least 240,354 primary school children, 7,917 in secondary schools, and 5,708 students in higher education. In 1976, there were 2,000 students at Vientiane University. Students are also studying in the U.S.S.R. and China.

The religion is Buddhism and there are no Christians except among Europeans and Vietnamese.

# Lebanon

(LUBNAN)

**Capital**—Beirut.

**President**—Elias Sarkis (elected 23 September 1976).

**National Flag:** Stripes fesse wise, red, white, red, each red stripe half the width of the white, which bears a cedar tree in the centre.

## CONSTITUTION AND GOVERNMENT

LEBANON consists of a narrow coastal strip at the eastern end of the Mediterranean. It extends northward from Israel to a point 15 miles above Tripoli, a distance of 120 miles. In no part is it more than 35 miles in width. It was formerly part of the Ottoman Empire, but was captured from the Turks by Allied Forces in 1918. Both Lebanon and Syria were then administered by the French under mandate until 1941 when the two countries were proclaimed separate and independent.

The Republic of Lebanon came into being on 1 January 1944. On that date, under an agreement reached the previous November between representatives of Lebanon and the French National Committee of Liberation, all powers hitherto exercised by the French were formally handed over to the new Lebanese Government and the evacuation of foreign troops was completed in 1946.

The Constitution is democratic in principle. All citizens are equal in law, and personal freedom and freedom of the press is guaranteed and protected. By convention, however, the President is always a Maronite Christian, the Premier a Sunni Muslim and the Speaker of the Chamber a Shia Muslim. Men and women over the age of 21 have the right to vote and to be elected to Parliament.

The President is Head of the State, and is elected for a term of six years. Executive power under the President is exercised by the Cabinet. Legislative power is in the hands of Parliament, which is elected for four years, and consists of a single Chamber of 99 members. The last elections were held in April, 1972. The President has the power to dissolve Parliament.

The Speaker of the House is Kamal el Asa'ad.

Fighting existed in the Lebanon from April, 1975 to November, 1976. During this period various short cease fire agreements were effected but with the deployment of an Arab League peace keeping force fighting was brought to a halt.

Cabinet (9 December 1976)

*Prime Minister, Minister of Economy and Commerce, Industry, Oil and Information:* Dr. Selim al-Hoss.
*Minister of Foreign Affairs and Defence and Deputy Prime Minister:* Mr. Fuad Butros.
*Minister of the Interior and Housing:* Dr. Salah Salman.
*Minister of Finance:* Mr. Farid Raphael.

## LOCAL GOVERNMENT

Lebanon is divided for administrative purposes into the five areas of Beirut, South Lebanon, North Lebanon, Bekaa and Mount Lebanon, and there is an administrative government in each of these districts.

## LEGAL SYSTEM

The legal code is a local application of the French Code Napoléon and the Ottoman Civil Code. There is a Court of Cassation in Beirut, a Court of Appeal and Courts of First Instance. There are also Islamic Courts for dealing with the personal status of Muslims and the registration of their births, marriages and deaths.

## AREA AND POPULATION

The area of Lebanon is 3,600 square miles.

The population at mid-1974 was 3,065,000. The average annual percentage growth rate of the population for the period 1960–74 was 2·7 and for the period 1965–74 was 2·8. The capital is Beirut, with a population of about 800,000. Tripoli has a population of 210,000. The only other towns of importance are Zahle and Sidon which, however, have populations of probably less than 150,000.

**Vital Statistics:**

| | 1971 |
|---|---|
| Marriages | 16,516 |
| Births | 76,099 |
| Deaths | 12,799 |
| Divorces | 1,382 |

## CURRENCY

Currency is issued by the Banque du Liban, the Lebanese central bank which commenced operations on 1 April 1964. The unit is the Lebanese pound (£L) which contains 100 piastres. There are coins of 5, 10, 25 and 50 piastres and notes of £L.1, £L.5, £L.10, £L.25, £L.50 and £L.100. Lebanon has a free market and the pound fluctuates. The current exchange-rate (1971) is 7·85 Lebanese £s to £1 sterling.

## FINANCE AND BANKS

There are just over 70 banks operating in Beirut which is one of the world's important centres for money exchange; these include two British banks, namely The British Bank of the Middle East and The Eastern Bank Ltd. A central bank, the Banque du Liban, began operating on 1 April 1964.

Revenue is collected by direct and indirect taxes, although 41 per cent of the annual revenue comes from indirect taxes. The main source is customs duties which accounts for over 26 per cent of the total revenue.

Estimated expenditure in the ordinary and annexed budgets for 1970 and 1971 was £Leb.816·9 million and £Leb.871·3 million respectively.

The GNP at market prices for 1974 was U.S. $millions 3,290, and the GNP per capita at market prices was U.S. $1,070. The annual average percentage growth rate of the GNP per capita for the period 1960–74 was 3·1, and for the period 1965–74 was 3·7. [*See the note at the beginning of this section concerning GNP.*]

The total expenditure allowed for in the 1972 budget was £Leb.964,800,000.

**Bank of Beirut and the Arab Countries S.A.L.** (Chairman, T. S. Assaf.) Est. 1957; Capital L£5m.; deposits L£108·3m. (in 1970).

**Banque al-Ahli (Banque Nationale) Foncière, Commerciale et Industrielle S.A.L.** *Address:* Rue Foch, Beirut, P.O.B. 2868.

**Banque Audi S.A.L.** Balance sheet at 31 December 1972 showed assets £185,929,448·12. *Address:* rue Al Arz, Imm. Beydoun, P.O. Box 2560.

**Banque de Crédit Agricole, Industriel et Foncier.** *Address:* P.O. Box 3696, Beirut. *Cables:* BCAIF. *Telex:* Dibank 20887.

**Banque de Crédit National S.A.L.** *Address:* rue Allenby, Beirut, P.O. Box 204.

**Banque de l'Industrie et du Travail, S.A.L.** *Address:* B.I.T. Building, rue Riad Solh, P.O. Box 3948, Beirut.

**Banque du Liban et d'Outre-Mer** (S.A.L.). *Address:* P.O.B. 11-1912, Beirut. *Telex:* 21380 LE.

**Banque Libanaise pour le Commerce S.A.L.** *Address:* P.O.B. 1126, Beirut, Lebanon.

**Banque Libano-Bresilienne S.A.L.** *Address:* P.O.B. 3310, Maarad St., Beirut.

**Banque de la Mediterranee S.A.L.** President and General Manager, Joseph A. El-Khoury; Capital £L5 million; Deposits 167 million (1974). *Address:* Allenby Street, P.O.B. 348, Beirut.

**Banque Misr-Liban (S.A.L.).** *Address:* rue Riad El Solh, Beirut.

**Banque Nasr Libano-Africaine S.A.L.** *Address:* B.P. 798 Tayara Bldg., Foch St., Beirut.

**Banque Sabbag S.A.L.** *Address:* P.O.B. 144, Hamra Street, Sabbag Centre, Beirut.

**Banque Saradar S.A.L.** *Address:* Kassatly Bldg., Fakhry Bey St., Beirut, P.O.B. 1121.

**Banque S. Shoucair S.A.L.** *Address:* B.P. 224, Allenby St., Beirut.

**Banque G. Trad (Crédit Lyonnais) S.A.L.** *Address:* Weygand St., Beirut.

**Beirut-Riyad Bank S.A.L.** *Address:* Beirut-Riyad Bank Bldg., Riad Solh St., P.O.B. 4668, Beirut. *Telex:* Baberi 20610 LE.

**Continental Development Bank, S.A.L.** *Address:* Beydoun Bldg., Arz St., Beirut, P.O.B. 11-3270.

**Federal Bank of Lebanon S.A.L.** Member, of the Association of Banks in the Lebanon, President, and Chairman of the Board, M. Saab; Managing Director, Ayoub-Farid Saab; Manager, G. A. Khoury; Manager, Foreign Department, A. Atamain. *Address:* Parliament Square, P.O.B. 2209, Beirut. *Cable Address:* FEDERALIBAN. Telex No.: FEDRAL 20267 LE.

**Intra Bank.** *Address:* Abdel Aziz St., Beirut.

**MEBCO BANK—Middle East Banking Co. S.A.L.** *Address:* B.P. 3540, Beydoun Bldg., Beirut.

**Rifbank S.A.L.** *Address:* Head Office: B.P. 5727, rue Trablos, Beirut.

**Société Bancaire du Liban S.A.L.** *Address:* P.O. Box 110.435, rue Allenby, Beirut; P.O.B. 435.

**Société Générale Libano-Européenne de Banque S.A.L.** *Address:* P.O.B. 2955, Beirut.

**Société Nouvelle de la Banque de Syrie et du Liban S.A.L.** *Address:* P.O.B. 957, Beirut.

**Trans Orient Bank S.A.L.** *Address:* P.O. Box 6260, Beirut. *Telex:* 20925 LE.

*Principal Foreign Banks*

**Algemene Bank Nederland N.V.** (*General Bank of the Netherlands*). *Address:* Amsterdam; P.O.B. 3012, Beirut.

**Arab Bank Ltd.** *Address:* Amman; Beirut.

**Arab African Bank.** *Address:* P.O.B. 11–6066, Riad el Solh St., Beirut.

**Arab Libyan Tunisian Bank,** *Address:* Riad Solh Shaker Oueyni Build. Beirut. Telegraphic address: Lituban; *Telex:* Latban 20712/21582 LE.

**Banco Atlantico.** *Address:* Barcelona 8, Spain; Arab Bank Bldg., Riad Solh St., Beirut.

**Banco di Roma.** *Address:* Rome, Italy; Beirut.

**Bank of America (National Trust and Savings Assen.).** *Address:* San Francisco; P.O.B. 3965, Beirut.

**Bank of Nova Scotia.** *Address:* Toronto, Ont.; Riad el Solh St., P.O.B. 4446, Beirut.

**Bank of Tokyo.** *Address:* Tokyo; Arab Bank Bldg., P.O.B. 1187, Beirut.

**Bank Saderat Iran.** *Address:* Teheran, Iran; Beirut.

**Bankers Trust Co.** *Address:* New York, U.S.A.; Shaker Oueini Bldg., Place Riad Solh, P.O.B. 6239, Beirut. **Banque Francaise Pour le Moyen-Orient S.A.L.** Beirut.

**Banque Libano-Francaise-Beyrouth.** *Address:* 1 Rue Riad El Solh; Beirut.

**Banque Nationale de Paris "Intercontinentale".** *Address:* B.P. 1608, Beirut.

**Banque pour le Developpement Commercial:** *Address:* Geneva, Switzerland; Beirut.

**Bayerische Vereinsbank.** *Address:* Munich; K.L.M. Bldg., rue de l'Armee, B.P. 3247, Beirut.

**Berliner Bank.** *Address:* Berlin; P.O.B. 3247, Beirut.

**British Bank of the Middle East.** *Address:* London; Beirut; brs. at Ras Beirut, St. Georges' Bay, Mazra'a and Tripoli.

**Chase Manhattan Bank, N.A.** *Address:* New York; P.O.B. 11.3684, Beirut.

**Chemical Bank.** *Address:* 20 Pine St., New York 10015; P.O.B. 7286, Riad el Solh St., Beirut.

**Commercial Bank of Czechoslovakia.** *Address:* Prague, Czechoslovakia; Representative Office for Lebanon and Syria: B.P. 5928, Beirut.

**Commerzbank A.G.** *Address:* Düsseldorf, Frankfurt, Hamburg, Berlin, German Federal Republic; P.O. Box 3246, Beirut.

**Dresdner Bank A.G.** *Address:* Frankfurt/Main, Federal Republic of Germany; Imm. Starco, B.P. 4831, Beirut.

**The Eastern Bank Ltd.** *Address:* London; P.O.B. 3996, Riad el Solh St., Beirut.

**First National City Bank.** *Address:* New York, N.Y. 10022; P.O.B. 3648, Beirut.

**Frankfurter Bank.** *Address:* Frankfurt, German Federal Republic; P.O.B. 3247, Beirut.

**Habib Bank (Overseas) Ltd.** *Address:* Karachi, Pakistan; Beirut.

**Handels- U. Gewerbebank Heilbronn A.G.** *Address:* Heilbronn (Neckar), German Federal Republic; P.O.B. 3247, Beirut.

**Jordan National Bank, S.A.** *Address:* Amman, Jordan; Beirut. Branch Lebanon.

**Manufacturers Hanover Trust Co.** New York *Address:* P.O. Box 11-5133 B.I.T. Bldg., Riad el-Solh St., Beirut.

**Morgan Guaranty Trust Co.** *Address:* New York, U.S.A.; P.O.B. 5752, Beirut-Riyad Bank Bldg., rue Riyad Solh, Beirut.

**Moscow Narodny Bank Ltd.** *Address:* Head Office: London E.C.4; Beirut Branch: P.O.B. 5481, Beirut.

**Norddeutsche Kreditbank.** *Address:* Bremen, German Federal Republic: P.O.B. 3247, Beirut.

**Rafidain Bank.** *Address:* Head Office: Baghdad, Iraq; Beirut Branch: Bazirkan St., Beirut, P.O.B. 1891, Beirut.

**Royal Bank of Canada (Middle East) S.A.L.** *Address:* Toronto, P.O.B. 2520, SFAH Bldg., Kantari, Beirut.

**Saudi National Commercial Bank.** *Address:* Jeddah, Saudi Arabia; P.O.B. 2355, Beirut.

**Société Centrale de Banque.** *Address:* Paris, France; rue Omar Daouk, Beirut.

**Vereinsbank in Hamburg.** *Address:* Hamburg, German Federal Republic; P.O.B. 3247, Beirut.

**Westfalenbank.** *Address:* Bochum, German Federal Republic; P.O.B. 3247, Beirut.

---

**Association of Banks in Lebanon.** (President: Dr. Assaad Sawaya; General Secretary: Dr. P. Nasrallah.). Member Banks: 73; Members representative offices: 39. *Address:* P.O.B. 976, Beirut.

## PRODUCTION, INDUSTRY AND COMMERCE

**Agriculture.** About 12 per cent (1967) of the Lebanese national income derives from agriculture, and some 55 per cent to 60 per cent of the population obtain all or part of their living on the land. One of the major problems is irrigation although some progress is being made in extending the cultivated area. The major part of agricultural investment at the moment is being put into increasing the fruit output.

According to the latest figures from the Lebanese Ministry of Agriculture, the land is apportioned as follows (in hectares):

| *Irrigated* | *Dry* | *Fallow* | *Other* | *Total* |
|---|---|---|---|---|
| 63,979 | 152,199 | 174,745 | 632,100 | 1,023,023 |

The Cedars of Lebanon are unfortunately much reduced in numbers, but efforts are being made towards reafforestation. The chief crops grown are apples and other summer fruits, citrus fruits. vines, olives, potatoes and other vegetables, and Turkish tobacco. The following table gives some statistics for the principal crops:

| | *Area (1,000 hectares)* | | *Production (1,000 tons)* | | *Yield (tons per hectare)* | |
|---|---|---|---|---|---|---|
| | 1972 | 1973 | 1972 | 1973 | 1972 | 1973 |
| Wheat | 50·5 | 50·1 | 63·7 | 55·2 | 1·3 | 1·1 |
| Barley | 7·8 | 7·3 | 7·6 | 6·5 | 1·0 | 0·9 |
| Sugar beet | 3·8 | 2·5 | 190·0 | 139·4 | 50·0 | 55·4 |
| Potatoes | 9·2 | 8·9 | 116·5 | 116·2 | 12·7 | 13·1 |
| Onions | 1·6 | 1·5 | 29·5 | 31·2 | 18·0 | 20·7 |
| Tobacco | 7·8 | 7·5 | 9·5 | 9·9 | 1·2 | 1·3 |
| Citrus fruit | 11·9 | 11·9 | 296·2 | 306·7 | 27·4 | 26·4 |
| Apples | 12·8 | 12·3 | 220·4 | 166·2 | 19·1 | 15·1 |
| Grapes | 17·8 | 18·2 | 109·4 | 107·5 | 6·3 | 6·1 |
| Olives | 28·1 | 30·2 | 39·6 | 32·3 | 1·5 | 1·2 |
| Tomatoes | 4·6 | 4·5 | 72·6 | 59·1 | 15·9 | 13·6 |

The following tables gives some livestock figures for 1972 and 1973:

| | 1972 | 1973 |
|---|---|---|
| | *thousands* | *thousands* |
| Goats | 355 | 330 |
| Sheep | 239 | 226 |
| Cattle | 90 | 84 |
| Donkeys | 28 | 27 |
| Poultry | 20,164 | 19,359 |

**Industry.** According to the latest figures there were at the end of 1968, 6,981 factories employing 68,460 workers and representing an investment of £L.1,068 million. The more important manufactures are: textiles, cement, wooden and metal furniture, plastics, footwear, sugar refining, vegetable oils and fats, beer, cotton yarn, plywood and tanned leather.

Two pipelines reach the sea through Lebanon, one belonging to the Iraq Petroleum Company ending at Tripoli, where there is a small refinery, the other belonging to Trans-Arabian Pipeline Company ending at Zahrani near Sidon where a refinery was opened in 1955.

Lebanon runs a flourishing tourist industry, and considerable investment has been put into hotel development and the construction of a large casino. Many of the visitors come from Arab countries; Western visitors in general stay a relatively short time in Lebanon, although their *per capita* expenditure is believed to be higher than that of the remaining visitors.

The following table shows the value of imports and exports for 1970 and 1971 by area (in £Leb. thousands):

| *Imports* | 1970 | 1971 |
|---|---|---|
| Precious Metals, Stones, Jewellery and Coins | 432,947 | 304,584 |
| Vegetable Products | 234,795 | 237,959 |
| Machinery and Electrical Apparatus | 239,336 | 282,274 |
| Textiles and Products | 222,125 | 284,802 |
| Non-precious Metals and Products | 184,301 | 202,642 |
| Transport Vehicles | 129,115 | 170,396 |
| Animals and Animal Products | 126,264 | 122,916 |
| Industrial Chemical Products | 152,820 | 182,041 |
| Mineral Products | 129,112 | 139,487 |
| Beverages and Tobacco | 97,435 | 142,273 |

| *Exports** | 1970 | 1971 |
|---|---|---|
| Vegetable Products | 99,459 | 121,598 |
| Precious Metals, Stones, Jewellery and Coins | 62,256 | 51,413 |
| Animals and Animal Products | 37,286 | 55,050 |
| Machinery and Electrical Apparatus | 65,701 | 98,702 |
| Non-precious Metals and Products | 53,288 | 80,230 |
| Textiles and Products | 57,247 | 79,527 |
| Beverages and Tobacco | 54,758 | 49,445 |
| Transport Vehicles | 48,290 | 57,997 |

* Including re-exports.

## COMMUNICATIONS

**Railways.** The total length of railway line in Lebanon is estimated at 254 miles, of which 203 are standard gauge and 51 narrow gauge. A narrow-gauge line, operated by the Damas, Hama et Prolongement Chemin de Fer under a concession granted in 1891 (now nationalized), runs from Beirut to Rayak (in the Bekaa) and thence to Damascus. A standard-gauge line runs from Beirut to Tripoli and thence to Aleppo. A line exists from Beirut southwards to the Israeli frontier, but this line is in use only as far as Sidon.

**Shipping.** The chief ports are Beirut and Tripoli, the latter being used mainly by tankers for Iraqi oil. The following table shows the activity of Beirut Port for 1971 and 1972:

| | *Ships Entered* | | *Merchandiser (Metric tons)* | |
|---|---|---|---|---|
| | *Number* | *Tonnage* | *Entered* | *Cleared* |
| 1971 | 3,320 | 4,837,003 | 2,456,517 | 626,384 |
| 1972 | 3,586 | 6,197,000 | 2,665,000 | 678,000 |

**Civil Aviation.** Lebanon possesses one international airport and two military airfields: one in the Bekaa Valley and one in the north of the country, near Tripoli. The modern and well equipped international airport (Beirut International Airport) lies about seven kilometres from Beirut and serves many of the world's international airlines, as well as the local airlines. Traffic handled at the International Airport in 1971 and 1972 was as follows:

| | *Aircraft using airport* | *Passengers using airport* | *Freight through airport (metric tons)* |
|---|---|---|---|
| 1971 | 39,643 | 1,832,514 | 69,742 |
| 1972 | 38,735 | 2,090,634 | 87,991 |

2,476 tons of mail were handled at the airport in 1970 compared with 2,274 tons in 1969.

A customs-free shopping area for the benefit of transit passengers only is available.

**MEA. Middle East Airlines Airliban.** Founded in 1945, regular services throughout Europe, the Middle East, and Africa. The fleet consists of 3 Boeing 707/320Cs, 16 Boeing 707/720Bs, and 3 Boeing 747s. *Chairman and President:* Sheikh Najib Alamuddin. *General Manager:* Asad Nasr. *Head Office:* Airport Blud., P.O. Box 206, Beirut.

**TMA—Trans-Mediterranean Airways.** (President and Chairman: Munir Abu Haidar.) *All-cargo services operated:* regular flights from Beirut to Tokyo via South Asia and from there across the Pacific to New York via Anchorage and across the Atlantic to Europe and back to Beirut, and vice-versa. Also there are regular flights to Khartoum, Benghazi, and Tripoli (Libya). TMA is operating in addition to the round the world route, all its European and Far East Services with Boeing 707/320C jet equipment. *Head Office:* Beirut International Airport, P.O. Box 3018, Beirut.

**Telephones, Broadcasting and Television.** The telephone service in Lebanon is state-owned and controlled by governmental departments. In Beirut a new and entirely automatic service was opened on 1 May 1954.

Broadcasting is the responsibility of the Minister of Information. There are two commercial television companies: the Lebanese Television Company (C.L.T.) opened in 1959, and the Television Company of Lebanon and the Near East (Tele-Orient) opened in 1962.

### NEWSPAPERS

Over 30 daily papers, in four languages, are published in Beirut. The leading ones are:

**al-Anwar.** F.1959. Independent. Daily Arabic (includes weekly supplement). Prop.: Said Freiha; Editor: Issam Freiha. Circulation 69,150. Published by Dar Assayad S.A.L.

**Daily Star.** English. Circulation 19,220. P.O. Box 11987, Beirut, Lebanon. *Telex:* Hayat 22137 LE.

**An-Nahar.** Arabic. F. 1933. Circulation 55,997. Rue Banque du Liban-Hamra, Press Co-operative Bldg., P.O. Box 11-226. Beirut, Lebanon.

**Hayat.** Arabic. F. 1945. Circulation 34,100. Rue Ghalghoul. P.O. Box 987.

**Lissan-Ul-Hal.** Arabic. F. 1877. Circulation 32,500. Rue Châteaubriand, P.O. Box 4619.

**Assayad.** F. 1943. Circulation 67,650. Dar Assayad S.A.L., P.O. Box 1038, Beirut.

**Achabaka.** F. 1955. Circulation 121,575. Dar Assayad S.A.L., P.O. Box 1038, Beirut

**L'Orient-Le Jour.** French. F. 1924. Circulation 21,000. Rue Hamra, St., Beirut.

**Le Jour.** French. F. 1964. Circulation 10,500. Rue Hamra, P.O .Box 2,488.

### EDUCATION

The Lebanon is the centre of education for the Middle East. Most schools of the secondary class are privately owned. There are many Government-owned schools, mostly of the primary type. There are four universities in Beirut, namely the American University of Beirut, the Jesuit University College, the Lebanese University run by the Ministry of National Education and the Arab University of Beirut. The American University at Beirut is the largest one outside the U.S.A. There are many Moslem secondary schools for young men and women. There are two mission schools. There is a school of fine arts which gives courses in architecture, music and painting. This is privately owned. Students from Egypt, Iraq, Syria and other countries go to Beirut to study law, medicine, dentistry and political science at the Universities. Literacy is as high as 70 per cent.

### RELIGION

The chief religions of Lebanon are Christianity and Islam. About half the population are Christian: they are mainly of the Maronite sect but there are also Greek, Syrian, Armenian and Roman Catholics, Greek and Armenian Orthodox, and Chaldeans and Protestants. Lebanon is reputed to have the oldest Christian communities in the world. The Muslims belong mainly to the Sunni and Shia sects. There is also a large Druze community. The numbers of adherents of the main churches are approximately as follows: Maronites, 424,000; Sunni Muslims, 286,000; Shia Muslims, 250,000; Greek Orthodox, 150,000; Armenian Orthodox, 69,000; Druze, 88,000; Greek Catholics, 91,000; Protestants, 14,000; Armenian Catholics, 14,500; and Jews, 6,600.

# Lesotho

## (MEMBER OF THE COMMONWEALTH)

**Capital**—Maseru.

**Head of State**—His Majesty King Moshoeshoe II.

### CONSTITUTION AND GOVERNMENT

THE Territory of Lesotho (formerly Basutoland) is bounded on the west and north by the Orange Free State, on the east by Natal and on the south by the Cape Province. Basutoland first became a British Protectorate in January 1868, after an appeal by the Basotho, who were at war with the Boers. The country remained in an unsettled condition until it was annexed to the Cape Colony in 1871. In 1884 the Territory was separated from the Cape Colony, and Government was carried on under the direct control of the Imperial Government.

Until 1959 the Territory was governed by a Resident Commissioner under the direction of the High Commissioner for Basutoland, the Bechuanaland Protectorate and Swaziland. For fiscal and other purposes the country is divided into nine districts. There was until 1959 an annual session of the Basutoland Council which consisted of 99 members, all Africans, 36 being elected (four each from nine District Councils) six represented various associations, five were nominated by the Government, and the rest represented the Chieftainship.

In 1959 Basutoland was granted a Constitution under an Order-in-Council made by Her Majesty the Queen. The Legislative Council, known as the Basutoland National Council consisted of 80 members divided equally between elected and non-elected members. The Council received wide legislative powers, and acted as a consultative body on such legislative matters as were reserved under the constitution to the High Commissioner.

In May 1965, a pre-independence constitution was introduced, under which the powers of the Paramount Chief were those of a constitutional monarch, exercised on behalf of the Queen and in her name.

In June 1966 the Basutoland Independence Conference was held in London. It was agreed that Basutoland should become independent under the name of Lesotho on 4 October 1966. The independence constitution follows in most respects the constitution of 1965. The principal changes arise from the establishment of the Paramount Chief as King, and the transfer of the remaining powers and responsibilities exercised by the British Government Representative to the Lesotho Government.

The Parliament of Lesotho consists of the King, the Senate, comprising the 22 principal chiefs and 11 other persons nominated by the King, and an elected National Assembly of 60 members.

**KING MOSHOESHOE II**, King of Lesotho since the establishment of the new Constitution 1966. Born 2 May 1938. Educated at Roma College, Lesotho, Amplefarth College and Corpus Christi College, Oxford University. Married 23 August 1962 to Princess Tabitha 'Masentle, daughter of Chief Lerotholi Mojela. Reigned as Paramount Chief of Basutoland 1960–66.

Children of the King: 1. Prince Letsie David, Principal Chief-designate of Matsieng Ward and heir apparent to the Throne; born 17 July 1963. 2. Prince Seeiso Simeone; born 16 April 1966. 3. Princess Constance Christina Sebueng; born 24 December 1969.

Parents of the king: Seeiso Griffith, late Paramount Chief of Basutoland and 'Ma-Bereng.

#### Cabinet

*Prime Minister and Head of Government:* Dr. Leabua Jonathan.

*Deputy Prime Minister and Minister of Works:* Chief N. S. 'Maseribane.

*Minister of Foreign Affairs:* Mr. C. D. Molapo.

*Minister of Finance, Planning and Statistics:* Mr. E. R. Sekhonyana.

*Minister of the Interior:* Mr. J. Rampeta.
*Minister to the Prime Minister:* Mr. P. Lehloenya.
*Minister of Agriculture and Co-operatives:* Mr. J. R. L. Kotsokoane.
*Minister of Education:* Mr. A. S. Mohale.
*Minister of Health:* Chief P. 'Mota.
*Minister of Sports, Culture and Community Development:* Mr. A. S. Ralebitso.
*Minister of Information and Broadcasting:* Mr. M. Lerotholi.
*Minister of Transport and Communications:* Mr. P. M. Peete

**Ministers of State.**

*Minister of State for Health:* Mr J. Mothepu.
*Ministers of State in the Prime Minister's Offices:* Mr. T. Leretholi, Mr. P. T. Khasoane.

## AREA AND POPULATION

The area of the territory is 11,716 square miles. A belt between 20 and 40 miles in width, lying along the western and southern boundaries and comprising about one-third of the total, is classed as 'Lowland', i.e. between 5,000 and 6,000 feet above sea level. The remaining two-thirds are classed as 'Foothills' and 'Highlands', mostly at altitudes of 7,000 to 9,000 feet but rising in the east to the high peaks (10,500 to 11,425 feet) of the Drakensburg range, which forms the boundary with Natal.

The mid-1974 population was 1,191,000. The annual average percentage population growth rate for the period 1960–74 and the period 1965–74 was 2·2. In the lowlands the population density varies between 100 and 300 persons per square mile. The principal town is Maseru, with an estimated population of 16,000.

The term Basotho as applied to the inhabitants of Lesotho has primarily a political rather than an ethnical significance. It applies specifically to those groups of various tribal origin which now acknowledge the authority of the King of Lesotho.

## LEGAL SYSTEM

The head of the Judiciary is the Chief Justice, appointed by the King, on the advice of the Prime Minister. The courts of law are: the Court of Appeal, the High Court, the Subordinate Courts and the Basotho Courts.

## FINANCE

The unit of currency is the South African rand (100 cents = 1 Rand).

The territory is grant-aided and receives an annual development grant from the United Kingdom Government. The principal sources of revenue are customs and excise duties, direct personal tax and income tax, mohair and wool export duty. The principal exports are wool, mohair and hides. Some diamonds have been found in the Territory recently.

The GNP at market prices for 1974 was U.S.$ millions 170, and the GNP per capita at market prices was U.S. $140. The annual average percentage growth rate of the GNP per capita for the period 1960–74 was 4·2, and for the period 1965–74 was 3·7. However the estimates of the GNP per capita and its growth rate are tentative. [*See the note at the beginning of this section concerning GNP.*]

## PRODUCTION INDUSTRY AND COMMERCE

**Agriculture.** Agriculture and animal husbandry constitute Lesotho's sole major industry. Production on arable land consists of crops of maize, sorghum and beans in summer, and wheat, peas, barley and oats in winter. The fertility of the soil in the lowland arable region is very low and yields are poor. In the mixed farming areas of the foothills soil fertility is much greater. Under conditions of normal seasonal rainfall, while much of the yield is used for subsistence, there are exportable surpluses of most crops, although large quantities of maize are imported annually. In periods of short rainfall and drought substantial imports of foodstuffs are necessary.

Soil erosion is Lesotho's principal problem. The soil conservation programme of the Agricultural Department includes the protection of arable land by mechanically dug, graded contour furrows (terracing), the planting of grass buffer strips, grass runways and trees and the construction of small dams. The government plan to build a large poultry plant at the Maseru station to hold 80,000 pullets has now been completed.

The chief source of wealth lies in the keeping of livestock. Sheep, angora goats and to a lesser extent, cattle, are of major economic importance, wool and mohair being Lesotho's principal exports. The desire amongst farmers to maintain flocks of superior sheep is increasing and in March 1969, 153 high quality Merino rams were imported. The number of livestock in 1967 was 375,709 head of cattle, 96,894 horses, 58,945 donkeys, 2,654 mules, 1,526,442 sheep and 890,628 goats.

During 1968–69 it was estimated that between 80,000 and 90,000 bags of wheat were exported.

**Industry.** Geological surveys of Lesotho have been discouraging about the mineral resources of the country except for diamonds. Diamond claims are worked by Basotho concession holders at Letseng-la-Draai and a prospecting area at Kao has been leased to the De Beers/Anglo-American Corporation group. Diamond exports during 1971 were 6,814·6 at a value of 212,043·75 rands.

Industrial development is steadily growing, a new candle factory is now in production, two well-established printing enterprises, a tyre company and a factory making building materials are situated at Maseru. There are plans to set up a maize milling plant at Maseru and work on the new project is currently being carried out. The average number of people employed in industry in 1966 was 1,880.

During the past year three new factories came into operation. Two of these are in our new industrial area at Ficksburg Bridge. They are a clothing factory and a factory for the design and production of electric lamps and a variety of light fittings. A diamond cutting and polishing factory was opened in Maseru.

Five new factories will commence operations in the new year. These will include another pottery, a workshop to make jewellery, a tractor assembly plant and a maize mill which will also include the manufacture of balanced cattle feed. We also started negotiations for factories to make umbrellas and electric generators.

**Commerce.** Since there are no manufacturing industries, Lesotho must import consumer goods and capital items as well as a certain amount of agricultural produce and livestock.

The following table shows export values for selected goods for the year 1971 in thousand rands:

| | 1971 |
|---|---|
| Cattle | 606 |
| Sheep | 87 |
| Other live animals | 7 |
| Wheat | 140 |
| Peas and Beans | 187 |
| Other Foodstuffs | 11 |
| Total live animals and foodstuffs | 1,038 |
| Wool | 322 |
| Mohair | 325 |
| Hides and Skins | 22 |
| Diamonds | 241 |
| Other crude materials | 3 |
| Total crude materials | 913 |
| Other exports | 245 |
| Total | 2,196 |

The following table shows the import values for selected goods for the year 1971 in thousand rands:

| | 1971 |
|---|---|
| Foodstuffs and livestock | 5,640 |
| Beverages and tobacco | 1,256 |
| Crude materials | 579 |
| Mineral fuels and lubricants | 1,723 |
| Animal and vegetable oils | 277 |
| Chemicals | 1,845 |
| Manufactured goods classified by material | 5,912 |
| Machinery and transport equipment | 4,114 |
| Miscellaneous manufactured goods | 5,989 |
| Commodities n.e.s. | 662 |
| Total | 27,997 |

### COMMUNICATIONS

There are no railways in Lesotho with the exception of two miles of the South African Railways, which enters Lesotho at Maseru from the Orange Free State. A good main road runs from Butha Buthe in Northern Lesotho to Mohale's Hoek in the south. It connects all the Government Stations with the exception of Qacha's Nek and Mokhotlong. Qacha's Nek is accessible by road from Matatiele in East Griqualand and a jeep service up the Sani Pass to Mokhotlong has recently come into operation.

There are air-strips in the Territory of Maseru, Mokhotlong, Sehonghong and Semongkong and a number of other strips mainly used by traders for transporting merchandise to and from their stores, and for the disposal of mail.

In 1964 there were 12 post offices, 52 postal agencies and 16 telephone exchanges (of which one, at Maseru, is automatic). There are telephone and telegraph links with other countries through South Africa.

### EDUCATION

Though school attendance is not compulsory, about three-quarters of Basotho children attend school for some period between the ages of 5+ and 20+. Attendance of boys is adversely affected by the Basotho father's insistence on their performing herding duties between the ages of 8+ and 14+. Education is mainly in the hands of the Church of Lesotho, Roman Catholic and English Church Missions, each of which receives a grant-in-aid from the Government to meet the cost of teachers' salaries in aided schools. There were 1,029 aided primary schools in 1967 and 48 unaided. Secondary institutions numbered 44 of which 26 were aided secondary schools, seven Teacher Training schools and 11 Technical and Vocational schools. Primary enrolment in 1967 was 167,803 and secondary enrolment was 3,201, Teacher Training and Technical and Vocational schools enrolment was 625 and 389 respectively. The number of teachers in 1967 in primary schools was 3,065, in secondary schools 170, in Teacher Training schools 56 and in Technical and Vocational schools 38. There is one university (formerly known as Pius XII College now known as the University of Botswana, Lesotho and Swaziland as it serves these three areas) situated at Roma, 22 miles from Maseru.

# Liberia

**Capital**—Monrovia.

**President**—William R. Tolbert, Jr.

National Flag: Eleven stripes fesse-wise, alternately red and white; a canton blue charged with a star five-pointed white.

### CONSTITUTION AND GOVERNMENT

LIBERIA is an independent Negro Republic situated on the coast of West Africa between Sierra Leone and the Ivory Coast and touching the Republic of Guinea in the north. It stretches inland for a distance of about 200 miles, the boundary being determined by the Anglo-Liberian Agreement of 1885 and the Franco-Liberian Agreements of 1892 and 1907–10. The Republic of Liberia was founded by The American Colonization Society as a home for freed American Negro slaves. A settlement was first made in 1822 and on 26 July 1847 the Independent Republic was proclaimed. The new State was recognised by Great Britain in 1848 and subsequently by the other great powers.

The Government of Liberia is patterned after that of the United States, having its authority divided into three separate and distinct branches—the Legislative, the Executive and the Judicial.

The Legislative branch consists of two separate Houses—the House of Representatives and the Senate. The Senate is composed of eighteen members elected from each of the nine Counties. They hold office for a period of six years. The House of Representatives is composed of 65 members elected from the nine Counties and each member holds office for four years.

The supreme executive power is vested in the President who is elected by popular majority vote and holds office for a period of eight years in the first place. He can be re-elected for four-year periods. He is assisted by a Cabinet.

Both men and women are entitled to vote.

The President, R. Tolbert, Jr., was upon President Tubman's death on the 23 July, 1971, immediately sworn into office to complete the latter's unexpired term. and on January, 1972 was inaugurated into office for a four year term.

**Cabinet** (September, 1973)

*President:* Dr. William R. Tolbert Jr.
*Minister of Foreign Affairs:* Cecil C. Dennis.
*Minister of Finance:* Mr. Edwin Williams.
*Attorney General:* Clarence L. Simpson Jnr.
*Postmaster General:* McKinley A. DeShield.
*Minister of National Defence:* Allen H. Williams.
*Minister of Local Government, Rural Development and Urban Reconstruction:* Everett J. Goodridge.
*Minister of Education:* Jackson Doe.
*Minister of Public Works:* Gabriel J. Tucker.
*Minister of Agriculture:* James T. Phillips Jnr.
*Minister of Health and Welfare:* Oliver Bright.
*Minister of Commerce, Industry and Transportation:* William E. Dennis Jnr.
*Minister of Information, Cultural Affairs and Tourism:* Dr Edward B. Kesselly.
*Minister of Planning and Economic Affairs:* D. Franklin Neal.
*Chairman, Public Utilities Authority:* Taylor E. Major.
*Minister of State for Presidential Affairs:* Hon. E. Reginald Townsend.
*Ministry of Action for Development and Progress:* Mr. Julius Cooper.
*Minister of Lands and Mines:* Nyema Jones.
*Minister of Youth and Labour:* J. Jenkins Peal.

### LEGAL SYSTEM

The Republic of Liberia is divided into ten Judicial Circuits. The Circuit Courts have civil, criminal, equity, admiralty and probate jurisdictions. Cases of magnitude originate in these Courts and are conducted under the principles of code-pleading adopted since 1856. Previous to that time the system was governed by Common LawProcedure. The General practice of the Liberian Courts is similar to that of the Federal practice of the United States of America. American and British standard works are accepted as legal authorities where there are no statutes governing the issue involved. Petty cases travel juridically from Magistrates Court or a Court of Petty Session to the Circuit Courts and from the latter an appeal may be taken to the Supreme Court for final adjudication.

Laws have been collected in the Liberian Code of Laws, 1956, to which additional volumes are to be added from time to time.

### AREA AND POPULATION

The total area is about 43,000 sq. miles.

The population at mid-1974 was 1,500,000. The annual average percentage growth rate of the population for the periods 1960–74 and 1965–74 was 3·3. The capital—Monrovia—has an estimated population of 110,000.

Other towns with populations varying from 4,000 to 8,000 are: Robertsport, Buchanan, Greenville, Harper City, Sanquellie, Gbarnga, Ganta, Tchien, Tappita, Zorzor, Voinjama and Kolahun.

### CURRENCY

The unit of currency is the Liberian dollar, which is at parity with the United States dollar. The greater part of the money in circulation consists of American notes and coinage. There are Liberian coins of copper and silver in denominations of 1, 2, 5, 10, 25, 50 cents and $1.00.

### FINANCE

The GNP at market prices for 1974 was U.S. $millions 580, and the GNP per capita at market prices was U.S. $390. The annual average percentage growth rate of the GNP per capita for the period 1960–74 was 2·2, and for the period 1965–74 was 4·1. [*See the note at the beginning of this section concerning GNP.*]

## BANKS

**Bank of Liberia Inc.** Established 28 July 1955. President: Lawrence A. Morgan; Chairman of the Board: Ernest E. Dennis; Executive Vice-President: Cosimo Boscaino. *Head Office:* Monrovia.

**First National City Bank (Liberia).** Formerly the Bank of Monrovia, wholly owned subsidiary of Citibank, N.A., New York. *Head Office:* P.O. Box 280, Monrovia, Liberia. Number of Branches etc. 1.

**Tradevco. The Liberian Trading and Development Bank Ltd. Monrovia.**

**The International Trust Co. of Liberia Inc.** Monrovia.

**Commercial Bank of Liberia.** Monrovia.

**The Chase Manhattan Bank.** N.A. P.O. Box 181, Monrovia.

**The Chase Manhattan Bank,** N.A. P.O. Box 47, Harbel.

**Union National Bank (Liberia) Inc.** Established 1962. Associated with the Union National Bank (S.A.L.) of Beirut, Lebanon. *Head Office:* Monrovia.

## PRODUCTION, INDUSTRY AND COMMERCE

Agricultural land is rich, inexpensive and plentiful in Liberia. A wide variety of crops are grown profitably and more could be grown on plantations for export or for sale to local plants which could be established for processing to supply the local market or for export. Commodities which offer promise of successful cultivation on plantations include oil palms, coconut palms, citrus fruits, rubber, pineapples, tomatoes, okra, beans, soya beans, corn, rice, banana, cassava, coffee, cocoa, suar cane, eddoes, cucumber, ginger, etc.

### Exports.

*Iron ore.* Liberia's export earnings are still heavily dependent on two primary commodities—iron ore and rubber. Iron ore continues to be far the most important. During the first three quarters of 1974 iron ore accounted for 60 per cent of the total value of all exports. The value of iron ore exports for the period January to September was $159·4 million, 7 per cent more than for the same period in 1973. Total earnings were about $212·5 million, a $30·4 million increase over the 1973 figure.
*Rubber.* The value of rubber exports in 1974 was about $68·4 million compared to $42·9 million in 1973. This constitutes an increase of about 59·4 per cent more than the 1973 figure.
*Diamonds.* Diamond exports covering the period January to September 1974 amounted to $25·5 million compared to $44·7 million for the same period in 1973. Estimates for the fourth quarter of 1974 were about $8·0 million. Export earnings from diamonds for 1974 total about $33·5 million compared to $49·3 million in 1973. This represents a decrease of over 47·1 per cent compared to the 1973 export earnings.
*Timber.* Export earnings for logs and timber totalled about $14·8 million in 1974 compared to $16·6 million in 1973. This indicates a decrease in export earnings from logs and timber of about 12 per cent.
*Agriculture.* The value of exported agricultural commodities such as coffee, cocoa and palm kernel extracts as well as piassava totalled about $14·8 million in 1974 compared to $9·2 million in 1973, a 60 per cent increase over the 1973 figure.
*Total exports.* Total export earnings for 1974 were about $350·0 million compared to $324·0 million for 1973. This indicates a value increase of $26·0 million, an increase of 8 per cent for the 1974 reporting period.

### Imports.

*Equipment and machinery.* Machinery and transportation equipment imported into Liberia during the first three quarters of 1974 were valued at $58·1 million compared to $46·2 million during the same period in 1973. The 1974 total was about $77·4 million compared to $68·8 million in 1973, representing an increase of 12·5 per cent over the 1973 import figure for machinery and transportation equipment.
*Food, animals.* About $36·9 million was spent in 1974 on food and live animal imports, a 20 per cent increase over the $30·2 million expended in 1973.
*Fuel.* The value of mineral fuel imports significantly increased to $42·4 million during the first three quarters of 1974 as compared to $9·9 million for the same period in 1973, and totalled about $56·5 million by the end of the year compared to $13·2 million during 1973. This represented an increase of $43·3 million over and above the 1973 figure.
*Rice.* Rice imports reduced considerably during the first three quarters of 1974. The increase in 1974 was 47·6 million lbs. as compared to 79·6 million lbs. for the same period in 1973. However, the value for rice imported during the first three quarters of 1974 amounted to $9·7 million as compared to $9·0 million during the same period in 1973. Though there was a 40·1 per cent reduction in the volume of rice imported into Liberia, the increased value of rice imported during the first three quarters of 1974 showed a value increase of $0·7 million dollars. By the end of 1974 about $13 million was spent for the rice imports.
*Manufactured goods.* Manufactured goods imports amounted to $40 million during the first three quartes of 1974. In 1973 the figure was $39 million.
*Total imports.* Total imports for last year amounted to $286 million. compared to $193·5 million for 1973—a percentage increase of 48·1 per cent.

The favourable balance of trade for 1974 was $64 million. Total value of exports during the 1974 reporting period amounted to $350 million as compared to $324 million for 1973. The value of imports for 1974 was $286 million compare to $193·5 million in 1973. This means that the trade surplus of the country declined from $130 million in 1973 to $64 million in 1974. This is being blamed on the escalating costs of imported commodities.

The regional pattern of Liberia's imports shows that Europe continues to be Liberia's largest trading partner in terms of imports. This pattern commenced in 1969 and can be accounted for by the increase in trade with the Countries in the European Economic Community. Europe is followed by America, Asia and Africa and other regions in descending order. Although small in magnitude, imports from African countries have increased both absolutely and relatively over the reporting period.

## HEALTH AND SANITATION

Health and Sanitation are the responsibility of the National Public Health Service which is assisted by USAID (successor to the U.S. International Co-operation Administration) and the World Health Organization. There are a number of government hospitals and clinics, as well as those run by missionaries and by the large concessionary companies.

The Liberian Institute of the American Foundation for Tropical Medicine provides a research centre for the investigation of the attack on some of the complex diseases in the tropical and subtropical regions throughout the world.

## COMMUNICATIONS

**Railways.** A railway has been constructed for hauling iron ore from the Mano River and Bomi Hills mines to the Free Port of Monrovia for shipment. Another railway links the iron-ore mines at Nimba with the port of Buchanan 175 miles away. Another carries iron-ore from the Bong Hills to the port of Monrovia. The extensive rainfall in the country makes the building and maintenance of roads a difficult problem. Nevertheless, this project is being carried on throughout the country by the Government with satisfactory rapidity under the circumstances. The road system connects with that of Guinea and Sierra Leone. There are over 1,000 miles of State roads suitable for motor traffic as well as roads on private plantations.

**Shipping.** There is a good harbour constructed by the United States Government at Monrovia, which is a Free Port; and another at Buchanan, to handle iron ore from the Nimba Mountains.

During 1966 a total of 440 main line vessels entered the port and 4,737,332 tons of cargo were handled.

**Civil Aviation.** Air Liberia, which came into operation in April 1974, continues to progress steadily, but modestly, reports the Bureau of Transportation. The management of Air Liberia reports that a total of 7,771 passengers, 10,028 kilos excess baggage, 64,498 kilos of freight and 30,275 kilos of mail were transported during the first nine months of this year on the domestic routes: Monrovia–Sinoe–Cape Palmas–Sinoe–Monrovia; and Monrovia–Sinoe–Tchien–Cape Palmas–Sinoe–Monrovia.

On the international routes: Monrovia–Freetown, Freetown–Monrovia, Monrovia–Abidjan, Abidjan–Monrovia, 9,601 passengers, 10,129 kilos of excess baggage, 64,764 kilos of freight and 30,309 kilos of mail were transported.

Total revenue for the first nine months of 1974 was $478,748·00, while total revenue for the same period last year was $205,733·00, reflecting an increase of $273,015·00 or 133 per cent.

There are international airfields at Roberts Airport and James Spriggs Payne Airfield. Roberts Airport is a regular port of call for aircraft of U.T.A., Pan American Airways, Ghana Airways, Nigerian Airways, Air Liban, KLM, SAS, SWISS-AIR and Liberian National Airways. There are many other airstrips in the country, mainly suitable for lighter aircraft.

**Radio and Telephones.** There are internal radio links and a growing dial telephone system. The internal circuits are: Cape Palmas, Sinoe, Grand Bassa, Cape Mount, Tchien, Kolahun, Harbel—Firestone Plantations and Robertsfield. The international circuits are French Cable and Liberian Government Radio station.

### EDUCATION

Education is under the supervision of the Department of Education.

By the beginning of 1967 there was an estimated total of 150,000 pupils in attendance at all elementary and secondary schools: 77,289 in Government schools; 21,969 in missionary schools; 11,407 in schools operated by industrial enterprises. In 1966 there were some 3,658 teachers.

The University of Liberia is a new Institution, established in 1950, which absorbed the old Liberia College. According to the Act of the National Legislature, the University is composed of the following Colleges and Schools: The Louis Arthur Grimes School of Law and Government; The William V. S. Tubman School of Teacher Training; The Mary Ann Cheeseman School of Home Economics and Applied Science; The Thomas J. R. Faulkner School of Engineering and Applied Science; The Benjamin J. K. Anderson School of Commerce and Business Administration; The People's College of Mass Education; The School of Liberal and Fine Arts and The College of Forestry.

Other degree-granting institutions are: Cuttington College and Divinity school and Our Lady of Fatima College.

There are many government scholarship students studying at the University of Liberia. A new science building was opened in 1957. The University is assisted by UNESCO and FAO teaching staff as well as those supported by the British, West German and U.S. Governments. There is considerable help to education generally from USAID.

Enrolment figures for 1970 were as follows:

| | |
|---|---|
| University of Liberia | 1,500 students |
| Cuttington College | 515 students |
| Fatima College | 112 students |

### RELIGION

The natives in the interior are Christians, Mohammedans and Pagans. The Christian population comprises a large number of denominations, including Baptist, Methodist, Episcopalian, Roman Catholic, The Seventh Day Adventist, Assembly of God and several other smaller denominations throughout the country with headquarters in Canada, the United States of America, Eire, Sweden and Switzerland.

# Libyan Arab People's Republic

## (AL JUMHOURIYYA AL ARABIYYA AL LIBIYYA)

**Capital**—Tripoli.

**National Flag:** Three equal horizontal bands of red, white and black with golden eagle device in centre band.

### CONSTITUTION AND GOVERNMENT

THE LIBYAN ARAB PEOPLE'S REPUBLIC is situated on the north coast of Africa between Egypt in the east and Tunisia in the west. After the expulsion of the Italians and Germans in 1943, Libya was placed under military administration. According to the Peace Treaty signed in February 1947, Italy renounced all claims to its former possessions in Africa. The fate of the territories was to be settled by the Governments of the United States, Great Britain, France and the U.S.S.R., but the four Great Powers were unable to reach agreement and the case was submitted to the General Assembly of the United Nations.

In the meantime, in June 1949, the British Government recognized Emir Mohammed Idris el-Senussi as Emir of Cyrenaica, and he proclaimed the independence of the country and established a *de facto* government. After a great deal of controversy, the General Assembly, on 21 November 1949, resolved that Libya should become an independent sovereign state by the beginning of 1952.

The National Constituent Assembly of Libya, consisting of 60 delegates representing the three Libyan territories, held its inaugural session at Tripoli on 25 November 1950 in preparation for the unification and independence of the country by 1 January 1952. It adopted the resolution of 3 December 1950 by which it formally proclaimed Mohammed Idris el-Senussi, the Emir of Cyrenaica, as King of Libya. The Constituent Assembly prepared a constitution, which came into force with the formal declaration of independence on 24 December 1951.

On 1 September 1969, Libya became the Libyan Arab Republic, with sovereignty and supreme legislative and political authority vested in a Revolutionary Command Council composed of military officers. This Council appoints the Prime Minister and other ministers, and the Chairman is virtually Head-of-State, although on 2 April 1974 Colonel Qadafi withdrew from day-to-day administrative and political duties. The Libyan Royal Family is in exile in Egypt.

**Revolutionary Command Council** (January 1970)

*Chairman and Commander-in-Chief of the Armed Forces:* Mu'ammer al Qadafi.
*Members:* Major Abdul Salam Jalud, Major Mukhtar al Qarawi, Major Bashir al Hawadi, Major Abdul Munim al Huni, Lt. Col. Mustafa al Kharubi, Major Khweldi al Hameidi, Major Mohammed Najm, Major Awad Ali Hamza, Lt. Col. Abu Bakr Yunis, Major Omar al Muhaishi.

**Cabinet** (14 November 1974)

*Prime Minister:* Major Abdul Salam Jalud.
*Minister of Interior:* Major Khweldi al Humaidi.
*Minister of Foreign Affairs:* Major Abdul Munim al Huni.
*Minister of Planning and Scientific Research:* Major Omar al Muhaisli.
*Minister of Education:* Dr. Mohammed Ahmed Sharif.
*Minister of Communications:* Taha Sherif Ben Amer.
*Minister of Housing:* Mohammed Ahmed Mangoush.
*Minister of Justice:* Mohammed Ali Jiddi.
*Minister of Health:* Dr. Muftah al Usta Omar.
*Minister of Labour and the Civil Service:* Abdul 'Ati al Obeidi.
*Minister of Oil:* Izzedin al Mabruk.
*Minister of Agriculture and Agrarian Reform:* Mohammed Ali Tibbu.
*Minister of the Treasury:* Mohammed Zaruk Rajab.
*Minister of Economy:* Abu Bakr Ali Sharif.
*Minister of Industry and Minerals:* Jadallah Azuz Talhi.
*Minister of Social Affairs and Social Security:* Muhammed Abdussalam al Faituri.
*Minister of State for Agricultural Development:* Abdul Majid Qa'ud.
*Minister of State:* Muhammad Azzuwai.
*Minister of Municipalities:* Muftah Ali Ka'eba.
*Minister of Marine Transport:* Mansur Badr.
*Minister of Electricity:* Jum'a Al Arbash.
*Minister of State for Nutrition and Marine Wealth:* 'Amr Al Mugsi.

### LEGAL SYSTEM

It was decided to adopt Egyptian law as a basis for future legislation.

## AREA AND POPULATION

With a coastline of about 1,000 miles in extent on the Mediterranean, Libya is bounded by Tunisia, Algeria, Niger, Chad, the Sudan and Egypt. The area of the country has been estimated at approximately 680,000 sq. miles.

The population at mid-1973 was 2,352,000. The annual average percentage growth rate of the population for the period 1960–74 was 3·9 and for the period 1965–74 was 4.2.

Arabic is the official language. As the second language, English has largely replaced Italian.

## CURRENCY, FINANCE AND BANKING

The unit is the Libyan dinar but is divided into 1,000 dirhams. Banknotes are issued in LD.10, LD.5, LD.1, LD.½, LD.¼ denominations. Coinage for the new currency, which was introduced in 1971, have not yet been issued, and those for the old currency in 1, 5, 10, 20, 50, and 100 milliemes are still in use.

Details of Federal Budget 1974–75:

| | £L. millions 1974 | 1975 |
|---|---|---|
| *Expenditure* | | |
| General Budget | 310 | 437 |
| Development budget | 740 | 1,110 |
| Total | 1,050 | 1,547 |

The Central Bank of Libya was established in 1956 under the National Bank Law of 26 April 1955. The bank's authorized capital is £L. 1 mill. An Agricultural Bank has been established and its Head Office in Tripoli was opened in 1957. Branches have been opened in Benghazi, Sebha and other towns.

**Masraf Al Gumhouria.** Established 1969. (Chairman & General Manager, Shtewi K. Ettir Assets as at 31 December 1974, LD 194,314,180; deposits and current accounts Libyan Dinar 84,960,068. *Head Office:* Sh. Emhamed El Megarief, P.O. Box 3224, Tripoli Libyan Arab Republic. Number of Branches etc. 25.

**National Commercial Bank.** Established 1970. (Chairman, Bashir M. Sharif.) Assets as at 31 December 1974, LD 497,340,181; deposits and current accounts LD 175,594,806, 122,574,409. *Head Office:* P.O. Box 4647, Tripoli, Libya. Number of Branches etc. 18.

Libya left the sterling area in 1971. The currency in circulation in March 1975 was £L.306m.

The GNP at market prices for 1974 was U.S. $10,430 millions, and the GNP per capita at market prices was U.S. $4,440. The annual average percentage growth rate of the GNP per capita for the period 1960–74 was 12·5, and for the period 1962–74 was 6·5. [*See the note at the beginning of this section concerning GNP.*]

## PRODUCTION, INDUSTRY AND COMMERCE

**Industry.** Most of Libya's vast land area is desert and completely unproductive and only about 6 per cent of the country's area is under cultivation. By far the most important sector of the economy is the petroleum industry. Libya's first commercial oilfield was discovered in 1956 and this was put into production in 1961. Since then the growth of the oil industry has been remarkably rapid reaching a peak in 1970 of 132 million tons. In 1974 production reached about 100 million tons. In 1973 the Government nationalized 51 per cent of all foreign oil companies, and some companies have been nationalized 100 per cent. This sudden expansion of the oil industry has brought about great changes in the Libyan economy, and as a result the industries and services which are ancillary to the production of oil have kept in step with the expansion.

**Commerce.** The following table shows imports of selected commodities (LD thousands):

| *Commodity items* | 1971 | 1972 | 1973 (*six months only*) |
|---|---|---|---|
| Live cattle | 1,684 | 1,879 | 597 |
| Live poultry | 247 | 323 | 233 |
| Animal feed-stuffs | 4,191 | 4,318 | 3,692 |
| Pharmaceuticals | 5,798 | 6,521 | 4,744 |
| Fertilizers | 1,081 | 610 | 1,701 |
| Iron and steel reinforcing rods | 3,474 | 6,009 | 4,387 |
| Iron and steel pipes and tubes | 8,535 | 9,409 | 5,480 |
| Gas turbines (for electric power generation) | 1,861 | 24 | 779 |
| Agricultural machinery | 2,162 | 5,449 | 3,215 |
| Construction equipment | 3,630 | 12,368 | 9,018 |
| Pumps | 3,104 | 4,695 | 3,389 |
| Electrical engineering equipment and materials | 7,137 | 13,135 | 13,138 |
| Domestic electrical appliances including T.V. and radio sets | 5,325 | 7,419 | 5,229 |
| Telephone, telegraph and telecommunications equipment | 1,475 | 891 | 1,35 2 |
| Passenger motor cars | 11,575 | 13,075 | 9,20 2 |
| Buses | 1,196 | 292 | 108 |
| Lorries and trucks | 4,233 | 14,154 | 7,534 |
| Special purpose trucks, lorries and vans | 571 | 1,487 | 1,138 |
| Vehicle spare parts | 7,256 | 9,352 | 6,560 |
| Medical equipment and Furniture | 1,768 | 1,623 | 438 |

The following table shows the value in U.S. $ (millions) of imports from selected countries for 1973–74:

| *Imports* | 1973 | 1974 |
|---|---|---|
| U.K. | 37·1 | 145·0 |
| U.S.A. | 28·6 | 120·0 |
| Italy | 139·0 | 819·6 |
| West Germany | 56·0 | 393·4 |
| France | 44·1 | 379·8 |
| Total | 305·0 | 1,858·8 |

| *Petroleum Exports in barrels* | 1973 | 1974 |
|---|---|---|
| United Kingdom | 90,934,706 | 66,769,869 |
| West Germany | 181,451,836 | 120,424,059 |
| Italy | 206,578,743 | 183,535,281 |
| France | 44,252,071 | 32,415,681 |
| U.S.A. | 74,909,770 | 478,942 |
| Netherlands | 31,427,318 | 4,907,873 |
| Belgium | 19,896,461 | 10,824,471 |
| Spain | 11,996,376 | 20,017,161 |

## COMMUNICATIONS

Most goods and persons move by road. A good metalled road stretches from the Tunis frontier along the coast to the Egyptian frontier. Other good roads radiate from the main centres of population on the coast but do not penetrate far inland. A road links Sebha in the Fezzan with the main coast road.

Principal civil airports are at Tripoli International Airport, 17 miles south of Tripoli, and at Benina, inland from Benghazi. International airlines connect these airports with centres in Africa, the Middle East and Western Europe, and there is an internal service. There are minor civil airports at Sebha and a number of other towns.

The main harbours are at Tripoli and Benghazi, the latter being under reconstruction. Work on extending Tripoli port started in 1973. Installations for the export of oil have been built in the Gulf of Sirte at Mersa Brega, at Ras al-Sidr, Marsa el Nariga (Tobruk), and at Ras Lanuf.

### NEWSPAPERS

**Al Fajr al Jadid.** Government-owned. Daily except Fridays. Arabic. Tripoli.

**Al Balagh.** Independent. Three times weekly. 8,000. Arabic. Tripoli.

**Al Kifah.** Daily. Arabic. Benghazi.

### EDUCATION

During the academic year 1960–61 there were 649 primary, preparatory and secondary schools in Libya, with a total of 254,963 pupils. In 1968–69 there were 324,757 pupils at these levels and at all Libyan educational institutions a total of 333,324 students representing 20 per cent of the population. There are private schools run by foreign communities which accommodate pupils of mixed Christian and Moslem background. The Libyan University has eight Faculties: Arts, Commerce, Medicine and Law, at Benghazi, and Science, Agriculture, Engineering and Teacher Training, at Tripoli. A Faculty of Medicine opened towards the end of 1970. In 1961 the University had 700 students.

The latest figures are as follows:

| | *Schools* 1969–70 | *Pupils* 1970–71 (*est.*) |
|---|---|---|
| Primary | 1,224 | 348,708 |
| Preparatory | 123 | 41,016 |
| Secondary | 30 | 8,564 |
| T.T.C.'s | 16 | 4,651 |
| Vocational and Technical | 8 | 1,730 |
| University | | 4,600 |

### RELIGION

The religion of Libya is Islam, but there is freedom for the practice for all others.

# Liechtenstein

## (FÜRSTENTUM LIECHTENSTEIN)

**Capital**—Vaduz.

**Sovereign**—Prince Franz Josef II.

**National Flag:** Divided fesse-wise, royal blue and red, the blue charged with a princely crown, its top facing and near the hoist.

LIECHTENSTEIN is an independent principality on the eastern bank of the Rhine, situated between the Swiss cantons of St. Gallen and Graubünden and the Austrian province of Vorarlberg.

Its history dates back to the 14th century, when Graf Hartman von Montfort became the owner of the Castle of Vaduz, took residence there, calling himself Count of Vaduz, and reigned over the land. In 1396 his son obtained the confirmation of the Holy Roman Emperor that his estates were a Fief of the Empire. They thus became independent of the Dukes of Swabia, under whose authority they had theoretically still been. By this act the foundations of present-day Liechtenstein were laid.

The Montfort family ruled for 200 years. They eventually lost their fortunes through becoming involved in German civil wars and through quarrels amongst themselves and their neighbours. The last descendants pledged the County of Vaduz to the Brandis family, who took possession in 1416. In 1419 this family purchased the County of Schellenberg, and by 1434 the territory reached its present boundaries.

The country was raised to the status of a principality on 23 January 1719 by the Emperor Charles VI, under whose immediate authority it was placed, granting it the name of Liechtenstein after the name of the then ruling family.

As a result of the Napoleonic wars and the state of upheaval in Europe, the Holy Roman Empire was dissolved and the Emperor Francis I resigned, henceforth calling himself Emperor of Austria. The German princes who had been immediately under the Emperor now became independent; in this way Liechtenstein also became a sovereign state.

Twelve of these states were persuaded by Napoleon to form themselves into a league under his influence, called the *Rheinbund*. Liechtenstein was one of them, although she never took any active part. After the collapse of the *Rheinbund* and Napoleon had been banished to Elba, Liechtenstein joined in 1815 the German Confederation, of which she remained a member until its dissolution in 1866.

In 1852 the principality formed a customs union with Austria and in 1858 adopted the use of Austrian currency. This union endured until the dismemberment of the Austro-Hungarian Empire in 1918. Since 1921 Swiss currency has been in use in Liechtenstein, and in January 1924 a customs union was formed between the two countries. Switzerland also administers posts, telegraphs and telephones and also manages diplomatic and consular representation.

Liechtenstein today is a constitutional monarchy hereditary through the male line of the dynasty. But before ascending the throne the Prince must pledge himself in writing to respect the Constitution. The Constitution of 5 October 1921 provides for a *Landtag* of 15 members elected for four years by direct vote. In the 1970 General Election, the Patriotic Union Party won eight seats and the Progressive Citizens, seven. Every male over the age of 20 is entitled to vote.

In February 1974 the Progressive Citizens' Party won eight seats and the Patriotic Union Party seven.

**Reigning Royal Family.** Roman Catholic.—This ancient landed family of Lower Austria descends from Huc von Liechtenstein (1133–1156), who took his name from the fortress castle of Liechtenstein at Moedling, near Vienna. The dignity of Prince of the Holy Roman Empire and Hereditary Prince of Liechtenstein was conferred 20 December 1608, and the various estates were combined into the present-day principality of Liechtenstein 23 January 1719. There are other cadet lines besides the one shown below. Succession is in the male line and the members of the family have the title prince or princess of (von und zu) Liechtenstein, Serene Highness.

*Head of Government:* Dr. Walter Kieber.
*Vice-Chief of Government:* Hans Brunhart.
*Secretary-general:* Dr. Emil Schaedler.
*President of the Diet:* Dr. Gerard Batliner.

### LEGAL SYSTEM

The administration of justice is carried out in the name of the Prince by responsible judges. In matters of civil law, jurisdiction is exercised in first instance by the Lower Court (one judge), in second instance by the High Court, and in third instance by the Supreme Court of Justice. The High Court and the Supreme Court of Justice are corporate judicial bodies, each consisting of five judges. These bodies contain lay as well as professional judges.

In criminal cases jurisdiction is exercised in first instance by the Lower Court (petty offences), the Assize Court (misdemeanours), the Criminal Court (felonies), and the Juvenile Court. The Assize Court consists of five judges, the Juvenile Court consists of three judges, the Criminal Court of five. In criminal cases, too, the High Court and the Supreme Court of Justice function as second and third instances.

Appeal can be made against Government decisions and orders before the Administrative Tribunal (five judges), and, in certain cases as laid down by law, before the State Tribunal (five judges) as an administrative. The members both of the Administrative Tribunal and the State Tribunal enjoy judicial independence. The State Tribunal also functions as a Constitutional Court, and as such is competent, to decide about complaints as to the violation of citizens' rights as guaranteed in the Constitution.

### AREA AND POPULATION

The country comprises the former counties of Vaduz and Schellenberg. Liechtenstein consists of *Gemeinden* (communities) of Vaduz, Balzers, Planken, Schaan, Triesen and Triesenberg, Eschen, Gamprin, Mauren, Ruggell and Schellenberg.

The plain in the Rhine Valley occupies about one-third of the country. This is the real agricultural land of the Principality, as the rest of the country is mountainous in character. The mountain ranges that transverse the land in a south–north direction are foot-hills of the Rhätikon massif. In an isolated position in the valley stands the Eschnerberg (730 metres high), while the mountainous part of the east of the country is composed of three high-level valleys.

The total area is 160 sq. km. The population in December 1976 was 24,251. The inhabitants of the communities are as follows: Vaduz, 4,632, Triesen, 2,926, Balzers 3,059, Triesenberg 2,006, Schaan, 4,363, Planken 235, Eschen, 2,388, Mauren 2,361, Gamprin 711, Ruggell 1,007, Schellenberg 563.

## FINANCE

The income-tax rates range generally from 2·1 per cent to 25 per cent for individuals and from 7·5 per cent up to 20 per cent for businesses. The communes in general may impose taxes at about 2·5 times the rate levied by the government.

The revenue and expenditure (in Swiss Francs) for the year 1976 is shown below:

| | *Expenditure* | *Revenue* |
|---|---|---|
| Administration | 9,323,952·79 | 1,281,153·47 |
| Schools | 18,937,894·97 | 2,120,316·00 |
| Buildings | 4,669,335·80 | 614,662·40 |
| Agriculture and Forestry | 3,077,572·90 | 204,983·00 |
| Post, telegraphs and telephones | 15,509,901·55 | 33,367,650·07 |
| Justices and prisons | 4,177,823·40 | 6,925,515·50 |
| Health | 4,637,202·05 | 118,986·66 |
| Social Welfare | 13,775,803·98 | 288,010·60 |
| Interests | 30,966,759·41 | 118,806,251·65 |
| Deposit of funds, withdrawal of funds, depreciations | 74,840,262·82 | 16,292,968·40 |
| | 179,916,509·67 | 180,020,497·75 |
| Balance | 103,988·08 | |
| Total | 180,020,497·75 | 180,020,497·75 |

## PRINCIPAL BANKS

**Liechtensteinische Landesbank.** (President, Dr. Peter Ritter; Director, lic. oec. Werner Strub.) Est. 1861; Capital S.F. 44,500,000; reserves S.F. 23,500,000. Balance Sheet at 31 December 1976 showed assets S.F. 1,324,589,682·06; deposits S.F. 507,346,006·27. *Head Office:* Vaduz, Städtle 44. *Agency:* Eschen Schaan & Balzers. *Telephone:* 075/61166. *Telegrams:* Landesbank Vaduz. All engagements guaranteed by the State.

**Bank of Liechtenstein. Ltd.** (President, Adolf Ratjen.) Est. 1920; Capital S.F. 30,000,000; reserves 35,000,000. Balance Sheet at 31 December 1975 showed assets S.F. 885,207,000; deposits 105,858,000. *Office:* Vaduz. *Telex:* Vaduz 77865; *Telegrams:* Bank, Vaduz.

**Verwaltungs- und Privatbank Aktiengesellschaft.** Est. 1956. Capital S.F. 15,000,000. Open reserves 12,600,000; total assets S.F. 305,000,000.

## PRODUCTION, INDUSTRY AND COMMERCE

**Agriculture.** Between 1940 and 1964 Liechtenstein was transformed from an agricultural to an industrial state. The proportion of the agricultural population has sunk from 33 per cent in 1940 to 3·0 per cent in 1976.

Stockbreeding and dairy farming are the principal farming occupations.

Alpine farming is still of great importance. There are 3,500 hectares of alpine grazing-lands to which 1,900 head of cattle are taken for three months in the summer. This enables the farmers to keep their reserve stocks of fodder free for the winter.

About 25 per cent (4,000 hectares) of the land is useful area, whereof 25 per cent is open arable land. Only some 3,000 hectares are suitable for intensive cultivation. The chief crops are vegetables, maize and garden produce; bread-cereals and potatoes, however, have now lost their once dominant role. There are about 15 hectares devoted to wine-growing, with an average yield of 70,000 litres of wine annually.

**Forestry.** Forests cover an area of 5,454 hectares, of which about 2,237 hectares are of economic importance. 2,331 hectares of standard forests and 886 hectares of tree and bush plantations in steep areas are not exploited and serve purely protective purposes.

4,980 hectares (91 per cent) of the forest land are public property, and belong mostly to the 11 communes of the Principality. The timber yield from all public and private woodlands comes to 10–12,000 cubic metres annually. About 80 per cent of this is used productively (i.e. for building purposes and in industry), 15 to 20 per cent is used as firewood.

**Industry.** The boom in industry which set in after the Second World War was part of the all-European wave of economic growth. The number of people employed in industry in 1976 was 5,096. Wages and salaries paid out amounted to 152 million francs as opposed to 6 million.

There are about 45 modern factories. The main industries engaged in are metal manufacturing, textiles, ceramics, pharmaceuticals and the food industry.

Home industries have an important place in the economy. They consist largely of small and middle sized family businesses, geared almost exclusively to the home market.

The tourist industry is an important source of additional income. In 1976 there were 77,462 visitors to the country, as compared with 17,339 in 1954.

Industrial exports in 1976 totalled 597 million francs.

**Commerce.** Liechtenstein is closely connected with Switzerland by reason of the customs union, and most of the country's foreign trade is in consequence with Switzerland. Exports are potatoes, textiles, and the manufactured goods mentioned above; the chief imports are cotton, finished goods, machinery and foodstuffs.

In 1976 exports totalled 597 million Swiss francs, compared to 168 million in 1965. The main markets for industrial products (apart from Switzerland) are Germany, Great Britain, Austria, the U.S.A. and Italy. By commodities, the chief exports are screws, needles, machinery, chemicals, sausage skins and textiles.

## NEWSPAPERS

**Liechtensteiner Vaterland.** F. 1913. Circulation 5,000. Organ of the Patriotic Union Party—Conservative. Vaduz.

**Liechtensteiner Volksblatt.** F. 1866. Circulation 6,300. Organ of Progressive Citizens Party—Liberal. Schaan.

**Der Liechtensteiner Wochenspiegel.** F. 1964. Circulation 1,700. Neutral. Schaan.

## EDUCATION AND RELIGION

The Principality has 14 elementary schools, two "upper schools" (the upper school is obligatory for pupils that do not go on to secondary schools), 5 secondary schools and the Liechtenstein Gymnasium (higher secondary school) with a total of about 3,690 pupils and 200 teachers (in May, 1976). There is also an evening technical school and a school of music. There are also two schools for backward children, and two schools for mentally handicapped children.

Liechtenstein is a Roman Catholic country, and has been so from the earliest days of its existence. There are two Protestant Churches in the Principality. Protestants form 8·0 per cent of the population; 90·0 per cent is Catholic; 1·0 per cent are of other denominations. Liechtenstein forms part of the bishopric of Church.

# Luxembourg

## (GRAND DUCHÉ DE LUXEMBOURG)

**Capital**—Luxembourg.

**Sovereign**—H.R.H. The Grand Duke Jean.

**National Flag:** A tricolour fesse-wise, red, white, azure.

### CONSTITUTION AND GOVERNMENT

THE Grand Duchy of Luxembourg is a constitutional monarchy.

From 1815–66 Luxembourg formed part of the German Federation; but after the war between Austria and Prussia it broke away, refusing to join the new North German Confederation.

By the Treaty of London in 1867 the Grand Duchy was declared neutral, and its independence guaranteed by Great Britain, France, Italy, Austria, Prussia and Russia. It remained under the sovereignty of the House of Orange-Nassau until 1890, when William III died without male issue. According to the Nassau Family Pact of 1783 no female could succeed to the throne of the Grand Duchy. The sovereignty therefore passed to the Walramian branch of the family, Duke Adolphus of Nassau succeeding. But his son, William IV having no male issue, later adjusted the law of succession, in order to preserve Luxembourg's independence in favour of his daughter, Grand Duchess Marie Adelaide, who succeeded him on his death in 1912. The Grand Duchess, Charlotte, succeeded her sister, Marie Adelaide, after her abdication in 1919.

By Grand-Ducal Act of 28 April 1961 and in application of Art. 42 of the Constitution, H.R.H. Prince Jean, Hereditary Grand-Duke of Luxembourg, was appointed 'Lieutenant-Représentant de la Grande-Duchesse'. This appointment enabled him to exercise in the name of the Grand-Duchess, all the political and judicial prerogatives granted to the Sovereign. The Grand Duchess abdicated in November 1964, in favour of her son who became Grand Duke Jean.

Luxembourg's present Constitution was promulgated on 17 October 1868. Some important revisions were made in 1919, when the Constituent Assembly decided that the Sovereign Power resided in the Nation (Art. 32). All secret treaties were to be abolished (Art. 37). Deputies were to be elected on the basis of universal suffrage, pure and simple, by scrutiny of lists according to the rules of proportional representation (Art. 51).

The Head of the State takes part in the legislative power and exercises the executive power. The Constitution leaves to the Sovereign the right to organize the Government, which consists of a Minister of State, who is President of the Government, and at least three ministers.

Parliament consists of the Chamber of Deputies (59 members) and the Council of State (21 members chosen for life by the Sovereign, who each year chooses a President from among them). The Council of State deliberates on proposed laws and bills, and on amendments which might be proposed; it also gives administrative decisions and expresses its opinion on any other question referred to it by the Grand Duke or the Government.

Members of the Chamber of Deputies are elected for five years. There are four electoral districts: the North, Centre, South and East. All men and women aged 18 and over are entitled to vote, and all those over 21 are eligible for election.

**Government** (June 1974)

*President of the Government, Minister of State, Minister of Foreign Affairs, Overseas Trade and Sports:* Gaston Thorn.
*Minister of Labour and Social Security, Minister for the Family, Youth, Social Welfare:* Benny Berg.
*Minister of National Economy, Minister of the Middle Classes, Transport, Energy and Tourism:* Marcel Mart.
*Minister of Public Health and Environment, Minister of the Civil Service and Public Forces:* Emile Krieps.
*Minister of the Interior:* Joseph Wohlfart.
*Minister of Justice, Minister of National Education and Cultural Affairs:* Robert Krieps.
*Minister of Agriculture and Viticulture, Minister of Public Works:* Jean Hamilius.
*Minister of Finance and Planification of the Territory:* Jacques Poos.
*Secretary of State for Agriculture and Viticulture:* Pierre Berchem.
*Secretary of State for National Education:* Guy Linster.
*Secretary of State for Labour and Social Security:* Maurice Thoss.

**Conseil d'Etat**

*President:* A. Goldman.

*Vice-President:* F. Wirtgen.

*Councillors:*

| | |
|---|---|
| A. Origer | R. Schaak. |
| J. Kauffmann. | F. Zurn. |
| L. Schaus. | J. Foog. |
| R. Maul. | E. Reuter. |
| F. Worré. | A. Goedert. |
| A. Bonn. | E. Arendt. |
| F. Georges. | P. Beghin. |
| N. Droessaert. | J. Lahure. |
| F. Goerens. | Mme. A. Schwall-Lacroix. |

*Secretary:* G. Glodt.

**Chamber of Deputies.** Elections of 26 May 1974. Representation of the parties is as follows: Christian Social Party, 18; Socialist Party, 17; Democratic Group, 14; Communist Party, 5; Social Democratic Party, 5.

### LOCAL GOVERNMENT

For administrative purposes the Grand Duchy is divided into three districts; the districts are divided into 12 'cantons' and the 'cantons' into 'communes' which number 126 in all. Most of the 'communes' are further divided into electoral sections and accountancy sections. At the head of the districts are the 'Commissaires', who are directly responsible to the Ministry of the Interior corresponding to the British Home Office. The district does not correspond to local government; the 'Commissaire', who is a civil servant, has the right of supervision, especially with regard to financial control, which is exercised by a special service directly under the Ministry of the Interior. Luxembourg's local government is the 'conseil communal', which represents the 'commune'. The division of the 'commune' into sections is only a technical one.

### LEGAL SYSTEM

Justice is administered by the following courts:

1. High Court of Justice.

*President:* C. Biever.
*Attorney General:* H. Delvaux.

2. Courts of Appeal.

3. **District Tribunal.**

Luxembourg: *President:* H. Jacoby.
Diekirch: *President:* R. Everling.

### AREA AND POPULATION

The total area of Luxembourg is 2,586 sq. km.

The estimated total population at 31 December 1975 was 358,500.

The population of various towns and districts is as follows: Luxembourg, 78,300; Esch-Alzette, 27,700; Differdange, 18,300; Dudelange, 14,700; Pe'tange, 12,000.

The following table shows the vital statistics for 1974:

| | |
|---|---|
| Marriages | 2,202 |
| Births | 3,925 |
| Deaths | 4,315 |

### CURRENCY

The basic unit of currency is the franc, made up of 100 centimes. In accordance with a decree of 14 October 1944 the Luxembourg franc was fixed at par value with the Belgian franc and Belgian banknotes were made legal tender in the Grand Duchy. There are banknotes of 10, 20, 50 and 100 francs, and metal coins of 25 centimes, 1 franc and 5 francs.

**FINANCE**

The following table shows revenue and expenditure in million francs for two years:

| | 1974 (*estd.*) | 1975 (*estd.*) |
|---|---|---|
| Revenue | 20,209 | 25,664 |
| Expenditure | 20,334 | 25,301 |

**PRINCIPAL BANKS**

**Banque Internationale à Luxembourg, S.A.** (Chairman of the Board of Directors, Joseph Leydenbach.) Est. 1856; Sole Bank of Issue for Luxembourg. *Head Office:* 2 Boulevard Royal; 48 Agencies.

**Banque Générale du Luxembourg, S.A.** (President, Georges Schwall; Managing Director, Georges Arendt.) Est. 1919. *Head Office:* 14 Rue Aldringen. 44 Branches.

**Credit Lyonnais, S.A.**, see France.

**Kredietbank, S.A.**, 43 boulevard Royal, Luxembourg.

**PRODUCTION, INDUSTRY AND COMMERCE**

**Agriculture.** Out of a working population (full time occupied) of 146,800, 10,200 are employed in agriculture, and in 1973, 132,680 hectares were under cultivation. The principal crops for the year 1974 were as follows:

| *Product* | *Metric Quintal* |
|---|---|
| Wheat | 337,184 |
| Rye | 32,730 |
| Barley | 511,116 |
| Oats | 363,240 |
| Potatoes | 581,750 |

Wine production in 1974 was 138,000 hectolitres.

**Industry.** The mining and metallurgical industries are by far the most important in the country. The number of blast furnaces in operation in 1972 was 20. In 1971 the number of workers in the mining and metallurgical industries was 23,300.

Production for the year 1974 (in metric tons) is shown below:

| *Products* | 1974 |
|---|---|
| Iron ore | 2,686,000 |
| Pig iron | 15,469,000 |
| Steel | 6,448,000 |

Electric power output in 1974 was 2,078 million kWh.

**Commerce.** After World War I Luxembourg's customs union with Germany came to an end. Negotiations with Belgium were opened and agreement was reached in 1921, and a bill was passed for a 50 year economic union with Belgium. This union was dissolved in 1940 by the Germans, but was re-established after the liberation in May 1945.

77 per cent of exports went to EEC countries and 92 per cent of imports came from them in 1969.

**COMMUNICATIONS**

**Roads.** In 1975 there were 2,849 km. of national and 2,118 km. of local roads. On 1 January 1974, there were 119,659 passenger cars, 10,009 trucks, 680 buses, 4,185 road tractors and special vehicles and 9,785 agricultural tractors.

**Railways.** Luxembourg's railways are State-owned. In 1973 there were 271 km. of track.

**Civil Aviation.** There is one Luxembourg airline: Luxair. The chief airport is Luxembourg-Sandweiler (Findel).

**Posts, Telegraph and Telephones.** The length of telephone and telegraph lines is 2,072 km. The number of telephones in operation on 1.1.72 was 119,000. All postal, telegraph and telephone services are operated by the State.

**EDUCATION**

Education is compulsory for all children between the ages of six and 15. In 1972–73 primary schools had 35,525 pupils and 1,667 teachers. There are five secondary boys' schools, four state and seven private secondary girls' schools and 16 technical and vocational schools. Secondary schools had 8,425 pupils and 731 teachers.

**ATOMIC ENERGY**

In 1956 the National Council of Nuclear Energy (Conseil National de l'Energie Nucléaire) was set up in order to study the economic, legal, financial and technical aspects of the pacific use of nuclear energy, and to take part in the study and work of similar organizations abroad either national or supranational. Projects for a nuclear power plant are being studied.

**NEWSPAPERS**

**Luxemburger Wort.** F. 1848. Catholic. Morning. Circulation 74,391 (C.I.M.), Luxembourg.
**Journal d'Esch.** F. 1912. Labour. Circulation 32,000. Esch.
**Letzeburger Journal.** F. 1880. Liberal. Circulation 31,500. Luxembourg, Case Postale, 2101.

**RELIGION**

The majority of the population is Roman Catholic. At the last census there were 296,508 Roman Catholics, 2,946 Protestants, 643 Jews, 1,054 of other religions, 705 having no religious affiliation, and 12,938 without indication.

# Madagascar

## Democratic Republic of Madagascar

(MALAGASY REPUBLIC)

*(Part of the French Franc Area)*

**Capital**—Antananarivo.

**President**—Lt.-Com. M. Didier Ratsiraka.

**Flag:** Divided fesse-wise crimson and green; a white stripe pale-wise at the hoist.

### CONSTITUTION AND GOVERNMENT

MADAGASCAR is situated 240 miles off the east coast of Africa and is the fifth largest island in the world. It became a French colony in 1896.

Madagascar has elected to become a member state of the French Community in accordance with Article 76 of the Malagasy Republic proclaimed on 14 October 1958, and on 26 June 1960 the independence of the Republic was proclaimed. The territory is divided into six provinces: Tananarive, Diégo, Fianarantsoa, Majunga, Tamatave and Tulear.

*Chief of Government:* Gabriel Ramanantsoa.

**Cabinet**

*Prime Minister:* M. Justin Rakotoniaina.
*Minister of Defence:* Capt. Sibon Guy.
*Minister of Public Service and Works:* M. Marius Randranto.
*Minister of Posts and Telecommunications:* M. Rakotovao Andriantina.
*Counsellor to the President:* M. Lucien X. M. Andrianarahirjaka.
*Minister of Economy and Commerce:* M. Justin Rarivoson.
*Minister of Finance:* M. R. Razakaboana.
*Minister of Public Works:* M. Célestin Radio.
*Minister of Education:* M. Francois de P. Rabotoson.
*Minister of Rural Development:* M. Pierre Rajyaonah.
*Minister of Scientific Research:* M. R. Tiandrazana.
*Minister of Health:* M. Jean J. Séraphin.
*Minister of Justice:* M. G. T. Indrianjapy.
*Minister of the Interior:* M. Ampy Poetos.
*Minister of Foreign Affairs:* M. Bruno Rakotomavo.
*Minister of Youth:* M. Richard C. Remi.
*Minister of Population:* M. Said Aly.

### AREA AND POPULATION

The area of the main island is 592,000 sq. km.

The population at mid-1974 was 8,560,000. The annual average percentage growth rate of the population for the period 1960–74 was 2·7 and for the period 1965–74 was 2·8. The chief towns are Tananarive (300,000), Tamatave (55,000), Majunga (46,000) and Fianarantsoa (42,000). The inhabitants are of many different tribes and races.

### FINANCE

In 1968 total ordinary revenue amounted to 32,160·0 million francs FMG and total ordinary expenditure to 28,003·6 million francs FMG. The GNP at market prices for 1974 was U.S. $millions 1,570, and the GNP per capita at market prices was U.S. $180. The annual average percentage growth rate of the GNP per capita for the period 1960–74 was 0·1, and for the period 1965–74 was 0·3. [*See the note at the beginning of this section concerning GNP.*]

### PRODUCTION, INDUSTRY AND COMMERCE

The economy of Madagascar is predominantly agricultural. 88 per cent of the working population is engaged in agricultural pursuits. The most important crops produced are rice, coffee, sugar cane, corn, butter beans, sisal, cloves, tobacco and vanilla.

The livestock population is estimated at seven million cattle, 650,000 pigs, 350,000 sheep, and one million goats.

There are important mineral resources in Madagascar and in particular mica, graphite, uranium and chromite.

The following table shows the value in millions of U.S. dollars of imports and exports for 1975:

| *Country* | *Imports* |
|---|---|
| France | 132 |
| Qatar | 44 |
| People's Republic of China | 39 |
| Fed. Rep. of Germany | 32 |
| U.S.A. | 26 |
| Total | 358·8 |

| *Country* | *Exports* |
|---|---|
| France | 109 |
| U.S.A. | 67 |
| Australia, Caribbean, Pacific Group | 35 |
| Japan | 19 |
| Fed. Rep. of Germany | 15 |
| Total | 323·3 |

### COMMUNICATIONS

There are four railways in Madagascar with a total length of about 535 miles. In 1968, 3·62 million passengers and 1,482,000 metric tons were carried. Receipts were 2,352,000 francs.

In October 1964 national roads covered 18,800 miles of which 12,460 are permanent motorway.

There are three international airports, Arivoniamamo, Ivato and Majunga. Air France, Air Madagascar and Alitalia maintain regular air services between Paris, Rome and Tananarive as well as a number of internal services which link Tananarive with the principal towns of the island. In 1968, 198,365 passengers, 8,179 tons of freight and 916 tons of post were carried.

### EDUCATION

In addition to a large number of elementary and secondary schools, there are in Madagascar one vocational school, seven training centres, 101 district workshops, and one school of medicine and pharmacy. Total number of pupils in 1968 was 639,854 in primary schools, 38,794 in secondary schools and 8,238 in technical schools. The university of Tananarive has about 3,000 students.

# Malawi

(MEMBER OF THE COMMONWEALTH)

**Capital**—Lilongwe.

**President**—His Excellency Ngwazi Dr. Kamuzu Banda.

**National Flag:** Three equal horizontal stripes of black, red and green with a red rising sun superimposed in the centre of the black stripe.

### CONSTITUTION AND GOVERNMENT

A FORMAL British Protectorate was declared over the area now called Malawi in May 1891. It was then known as the British Central African Protectorate. For 16 years the territory was ruled by a Commissioner and Consul-General. In 1907 the territory was renamed Nyasaland, the title of Commissioner and Consul-General was changed to that of Governor, and the first Legislative Council was inaugurated.

The Council consisted of the Governor as President, and six other Members all nominated by the Governor, a pattern which was followed closely for the next 50 years. The first two African Members were appointed in 1948, and a third in 1953.

In July 1961 the Lancaster House Conference was held in London. This led to the introduction, in 1961, of an entirely new Constitution, providing for the direct election of Africans to the Legislative Council for the first time.

The Constitution introduced higher and lower qualitative franchise. With the Malawi Congress Party's overwhelming victory in the General Election of August 1961, elected Africans were, for the first time, in a majority. At the same time a Ministerial system was introduced, and Dr. Banda and four of his leading followers became Ministers, together with three *ex officio* and two nominated Ministers.

In February 1963 self-government became a fact when two of the *ex officio* ministers were replaced, leaving the Financial Secretary as the only non-elected Minister. At the same time Dr. Banda became Prime Minister and the Legislative Council was retitled Legislative Assembly.

On 6 July 1966 Malawi became a republic, two years after the attainment of Independence and the number of nominated members (nominated by the President to represent interests of the minority) was increased to five.

During the 1973 Annual Convention of the Malawi Congress Party, it was resolved that there should no longer be minority representation in Parliament, and pursuant to this resolution minority representation terminated in October 1973.

In the last General Election, April 1971, the size of the Assembly, now called the National Assembly, was increased to 75 (made up of 60 elected members and 15 nominated members) and all Malawi Congress Party candidates were returned unopposed.

In the 1976 General Election the number of constituencies returning elected Members of Parliament was increased to eighty-seven plus up to fifteen nominated members.

Following a unanimous resolution by the Malawi Congress Party Convention (Malawi's only political party), His Excellency Ngwazi Dr. Kamuza Banda was sworn-in on 6 July 1971 as Life President of the Republic of Malawi. Supreme executive authority is vested in the Life President and the Constitution of Malawi provides him with the power to select his Cabinet from within or outside Parliament.

**Cabinet** (August, 1976)

*Ministry of Justice, External Affairs, Agriculture and Natural Resources, Works and Supplies:* H.E. the Life President, Dr. H. Kamuzu Banda.
*Minister without Portfolio:* The Hon. A. A. Muwalo Nqumayo M.P.
*Minister of Youth and Culture:* The Hon. Gwanda Chakuamba Phiri M.P.
*Minister of Finance:* The Hon. D. T. Matenje M.P.
*Minister of Education and Minister of Health:* The Hon. R. T. C. Munyenyembe M.P.
*Minister of Trade, Industry and Tourism:* The Hon. E. C. I. Bwanali M.P.
*Minister of Organization of African Unity Affairs and Minister of Labour:* The Hon. W. B. Deleza M.P.
*Minister of Local Government, Community Development and Social Welfare:* The Hon. D. Kainja Nthara M.P.
*Minister of Transport and Communications:* The Hon. Robson Chirwa M.P.
*Minister for Northern Region:* The Hon. M. M. Lungu M.P.
*Minister for Southern Region:* The Hon. P. Makhumula Nkhoma M.P.
*Minister for Central Region:* The Hon. A. E. Gadama M.P.

### LEGAL SYSTEM

The Chief Justice is appointed by the President, but Puisne Judges are appointed on the advice of the Judicial Service Commission. There is a High Court and a Supreme Court of Appeal, from which one may appeal in certain cases to the Judicial Committee of the Privy Council.

### AREA AND POPULATION

Malawi is bounded on the south-east and south-west by Mozambique, on the north-east by Tanzania and on the north-west by Zambia. It is a strip of land some 520 miles long, varying in width from 50 to 100 miles. Total area is 45,748 sq. miles.

The population at mid-1974 was 4,958,000. The annual average percentage growth rate of the population for the period 1960–74 was 2·6, and for the period 1965–74 was 2·6. The main towns are Blantyre-Limbe (193,000), Lilongwe (102,000), and Mzuzu (14,675), and Zomba.

### CURRENCY AND FINANCE

The units of currency are the Tambala and the Kwacha. 100 Tambala(s) = 1 Kwacha (K1.00). 1 Kwacha = £0·50. The GNP at market prices for 1974 was U.S. $millions 660, and the GNP per capita at market prices was U.S. $130. The annual average percentage growth rate of the GNP per capita for the period 1960–74 was 3·9, and for the period 1965–74 was 4·7. [*See the note at the beginning of this section concerning GNP.*]

Budget figures for 1974–75 are (*a*) Revenue Account: Revenue, K78·8 million; Expenditure, K73·8 million; (*b*) Development Account: Revenue, K39·8 million; Expenditure, K40·8 million.

### BANK

**Commercial Bank of Malawi Ltd.** (affiliated with the Bank of America N.T. and S.A.). Chairman, L. W. Masiku; General Manager, John D. Hurd. Deposits and current accounts as at 30 June 1976, K29,045,586. *Head Office:* P.O. Box 1111, Blantyre. 10 Branches, 12 Agencies and 80 mobile agency stopping places.

### PRODUCTION, INDUSTRY AND COMMERCE

**Agriculture.** Five crops, tea, tobacco, groundnuts, sugar, and cotton, account for 77 per cent of agricultural exports. There is a need to produce high value crops to meet the heavy cost of transport to world markets. Maize, cassava and millet are the main food crops.

The main livestock products are beef, hides and skins. Dairy farms are maintained on estates near towns and ghee is produced in the Central and Northern Regions.

**Forestry.** Forests cover 8,890 square miles of the land area of Malawi. Of this, 3,743 are state-controlled forest reserves. However there is very little natural forest with timber suitable for general construction or joinery work. The only suitable indigenous tree is the Mlanje cedar which grows on Mlanje mountain above an altitude of 4,500 feet.

The country's planting programme did not start in earnest until the early 1950's and it is only now that supplies of local softwoods are beginning to come forward in reasonable quantities.

A major planting programme of 15,000 acres of timber per annum, adding to the 70,000 acres already established by 1975, is being carried out on the Vipya and its foothills to supply a bleached kraft pulp mill at Chintheche.

**Fishing.** Provisional figures of landings of fresh water fish in 1975 was 48,000 tons. With the country's shortage of animal protein, fish are a vital part of the population's diet and considerable attention is being given to the development of the fisheries on Lake Malawi, Lake Malcombe and Lake Chilwa, and Shire River.

**Industry.** The principal manufacturing industries are naturally associated with the existing agricultural economy. Wherever possible indigenous raw materials are used, but, since the home market is relatively undeveloped as yet, imported raw materials are also frequently required.

Products already manufactured in Malawi include soaps, polishes, edible oils and fats, cattle foodstuffs, flour, clothing and blankets, cigarettes and pipe tobaccos, cement, biscuits and confectionery, fishing nets, mineral waters, tea, rope, twines and yarns, toilet preparations, agricultural implements footwear and a wide range of metal products. Other industries are: brewing and distilling; spinning, weaving and dyeing of cotton textiles, using locally grown cotton; production and milling of sugar, and radio assembly and printing.

Industries now planned or in course of construction include production of extruded and injection-moulded plastic articles; and the manufacture of bicycle frames, etc.

In 1975, total exports were valued at K119·7 million, imports at £216·6 million.

### COMMUNICATIONS

There are 273 miles of railway line, while another railway line is under construction from Salima through Lilongwe, the Capital, to Mchinji on the border with Zambia; and a shipping service on Lake Malawi. The two main airports are at Chileka near Blantyre and at Lilongwe. Total road mileage is 6,808, of which over 900 miles are bitumenised There are 26,699 registered motor vehicles.

**Broadcasting.** Radio Malawi was established in 1963, when the Protectorate Government assumed responsibility for broadcasting. The service, now known as the Malawi Broadcasting Corporation, provides programmes in English and Chichewa.

### NEWSPAPERS

**The Daily Times.** Daily. English. Blantyre, Malawi.

**The Malawi News.** The official organ of the Malawi Congress Party. Weekly. English and Chichewa. Private Bag, 39, Blantyre.

### EDUCATION

In 1972 there were 397,632 primary pupils and 15,040 secondary pupils. The primary course is eight years, the secondary four. There are 13 teacher training colleges offering a two-year course. The University of Malawi has 1,100 students.

### RELIGION

The latest census figures show that there are about 1,073,000 Roman Catholics, 79,000 Anglican, Presbyterian Church of Central Africa 846,000, Moslem (approx.) 100,000.

# Malaysia

(MEMBER OF THE COMMONWEALTH)

**Capital**—Kuala Lumpur.

**Supreme Head of State**—His Majesty the Yang Di-Pertuan Agong (Tuanku Yahya Petra ibni Al-marhum Sultan Ibrahim, Sultan of Kelantan).

**National Flag.** On a field of fourteen stripes fesse-wise and counterchanged red and white, a canton blue charged with a crescent yellow and a star of the same with fourteen points.

### CONSTITUTION AND GOVERNMENT

ON 31 August 1957, Malaya became an independent sovereign nation within the Commonwealth of Nations. On 16 September 1963 a larger federation came into being whereby the Federation of Malaya, the State of Singapore (internally self governing since 1959) and the former territories of British North Borneo (Sabah) and Sarawak were federated under the title of Malaysia.

The federation then consisted of 14 states. To the nine Malay States (Sultanates) and the two former settlements—now States—Malacca and Penang, were added the State of Singapore, and the former territories of Sabah and Sarawak.

The general scheme of government is founded upon that of the former Federation of Malaya which adopted a constitution recommended by the Reid Commission in 1957. This provides for a Senate (Dewan Negara) and a House of Representatives (Dewan Ra'ayat). The Senate comprises two Senators nominated from each of the 13 States and 32 nominated by His Majesty the Yang Di-Pertuan Agong, making 58 in all. The Senate is presided over by a President. The House of Representatives is elected in single-member constituencies by citizens of 21 years and above. The House consists of 154 elected members, presided over by a Speaker.

Whilst the constituent states form a strong central government, the constitutional rights of the respective states are preserved.

Governmentally, the autonomy of the States within the federation is represented by the provision of constitutions for all the component States. Each State has a sovereign Ruler or Governor; each has transferred absolutely certain of its functions to the federal authority.

In August 1965, Singapore left Malaysia and has since been an independent republic within the Commonwealth. The territory of the former Federation of Malaya is known as Peninsular Malaysia and the States of Sabah and Sarawak.

Malaysia's third general election since independence took place on 10 May 1969. This was followed by violent communal rioting in Kuala Lumpur. The government then proclaimed a state of emergency and a National Operationt Council, to combat terrorism and maintain order was formed, headed by Tun Abdul Razak, the then Deputy Premier and Minister of Defence.

On 20 February 1971, Parliament re-convened after a lapse of 21 months. The Government felt that it has a duty to concentrate on nation building. To achieve this it has introduced the *Rukunegara* (national ideology) containing the five principles: Belief in God; Loyalty to King and Country; Upholding the Constitution; Rule of Law; and Good Behaviour and Morality.

On 24 August 1974, Malaysia held her fourth General Election. This was the first national election held under Prime Minister Tun Haji Abdul Razak bin Hussein. The National Front, is a confederation of eight political parties, namely, United Malays National Organization, (UMNO), Malaysian Chinese Association (MCA), Malaysian Indian Congress (MIC), Pan-Malayan Islamic Party (PAS), Gerakan Rakyat Malaysia (GERAKAN), People's Progressive Party (PPP), Sarawak United People's Party (SUPP) and Parti Pesaka Bumiputra Bersatu (PP BP); and was led by Tun Haji Abdul Razak bin Hussein. The National Front emerged victor, capturing 135 parliamentary seats out of 154.

On 21 June 1976 the United Sabah National Organization (USNO), BERJAYA (a newly formed party in Sabah) and the Sarawak National Party (SNAP) have been accepted into the National Front Coalition. The National Front now hold 143 of the 154 parliamentary seats and controls all state governments.

#### Cabinet

*Prime Minister and Minister of Defence:* Datuk Hussein b. Onn, SPMJ.

*Deputy Prime Minister and Minister of Education:* Dr. Mahathir b. Mohamad.

*Minister of Labour and Manpower:* Datuk Lee San Choon, SPMJ, KMN.

*Minister of Communications:* Tan Sri V. Manickavasagam, PMN, SPMS.

*Minister of Land and Regional Development:* Vacant.

*Minister of Trade and Industry:* Datuk Haji Hamzah b. Datuk Abu Samah, SMK, SIMP, SPDK.

*Minister of Science, Technology and Environment:* Tan Sri Ong Kee Hui, PMN, PNBS, PGDK.

*Minister of Home Affairs:* Tan Sri Hj. Muhammad Ghazali bin Shafie, PMN, SIMP, SPDK.

*Minister of Works and Utilities:* Datuk Hj. Abdul Ghani Gilong, SPDK, JP.

*Minister of Health:* Tan Sri Lee Siok Yew, PMN, PJK.

*Minister of Law:* Tan Sri Datuk Hj. Abdul Kadir b. Yusof, PMN, SPDK, SPMJ.

*Minister of Welfare Services:* Datuk Hajjah Aishah bte. Haji Abdul Ghani, DPMS.
*Minister of Information:* Datuk Amar Hj. Abdul Taib b. Mahmud, PDK, PGDK.
*Minister of Culture, Youth and Sports:* Datuk Abdul Samad b. Idris, JMN, PSK.
*Minister of Foreign Affairs:* Tengku Datuk Ahmad Rithauddeen Al-haj b. Tengku Ismail, PMK.
*Minister of Public Enterprises:* Datuk Hj. Mohamed b. Yaacob, PGDK, PMK, SMT.
*Minister of Housing and Village Development:* Datuk Michael Chen Wing Sum, DPMS.
*Minister of Primary Industries:* Datuk Musa Hitam, SPMJ.
*Minister of Finance:* Tengku Tan Sri Razaleigh Hamzah, PSM, SPMK.
*Minister of Agriculture:* Datuk Ali b. Hj. Ahmad, SPMJ.
*Minister of Local Government and Federal Territory:* Tuan Hj. Hassan Adli b. Hj. Arshad, JSM.
*Minister without Portfolio (In Prime Minister's Department):* Tan Sri Chong Hon Nyan, PSM, JMN.

## AREA AND POPULATION

Malaysia occupies two distinct regions—the Malay peninsula extending south-south-east from the Thai border, and the north-western coastal area of the island of Borneo, consisting of Sabah (North Borneo) and Sarawak. It has land frontiers with the Repubeic of Indonesia (about 900 miles) in the island of Borneo.

Malaysia has an area of 130,000 square miles.

The population at mid-1974 was 11,702,000. Of the total population approximately 9 million people are domiciled in the Malaysian peninsular and one million in Sabah and Sarawak. The annual average percentage growth rate of the population for the period 1960–74 was 2·6, and for the period 1965–74 was 2·6.

The population is made up of Malays and other indigenous people—the sea Dayaks (Ibans), Land Dayaks (Bidayuhs), Kadazans, Kenyahs, Melanaus and Muruts—as well as Chinese, Indians, Eurasians and many others. By ethnic origin:

| | |
|---|---|
| Malays and other indigenous people | 56 per cent |
| Chinese | 34 per cent |
| Indians | 9 per cent |
| Others | 1 per cent |

## CURRENCY AND FINANCE

The GNP at market prices for 1974 was U.S.$ millions 7,910, and the GNP per capita at market prices was U.S.$680. The annual average percentage growth rate of the GNP period 1960–74 was 3·9, and for the period 1965–74 was 3·8. [*See the note at the beginning of this section concerning GNP.*]
The unit of currency is the Malaysian dollar, divided into 100 cents.

The following table shows the federal government budgets for three years:

| | 1974 | 1975 | 1976 |
|---|---|---|---|
| | *Actual* | *Latest estimate* | *Budget estimates* |
| Current revenue | 4,788 | 4,815 | 5,100 |
| (i) Current Expenditure | 4,315 | 4,950 | 5,290 |
| (ii) Direct Development Expenditure | 1,107 | 1,073 | |
| (iii) Net Lending | 745 | 802 | |
| Total (i) + (ii) + (iii) | 6,167 | 6,825 | |
| Overall deficit | −1,379 | −2,010 | −2,173 |
| Sources of Finance: | | | |
| Domestic borrowing (net) | 826 | 1,300 | 1,350 |
| Foreign borrowing (net) | 223 | 860 | 785 |
| Special receipts | 31 | 32 | 40 |
| Change in assets | +299 | −182 | −2 |
| Total | 1,379 | 2,010 | 2,173 |

Source: *Economic Report 1975–76,* The Treasury Malaysia, Kuala Lumpur.

*The Achievement of the Second Malaysia Plan (1971–75).* In the main, the Malaysian economy achieved a creditable rate of growth during 1971–75. It is estimated that the Gross Domestic Product (GDP) at factor cost, in real terms, grew by 7·4 per cent per annum during the period as compared with the original SMP target of 6·8 per cent and the revised target in the Mid-Term Review (MTR) of 7·8 per cent. The shortfall with respect to the MTR target is largely attributable to the impact of world wide recession on the Malaysian economy. The average annual rate of growth of GDP was 8·4 per cent during 1971–74 as compared with 3·5 per cent in 1975.

The fastest growing sectors were transport, manufacturing, public administration and other services with average annual rates of growth of 12·6 per cent, 10·9 per cent, 8·6 per cent and 7·2 per cent respectively during the SMP period. However, in terms of its relative contribution to total growth, agricultural production, mainly arising from the oil palm sector, continued to predominate with over a quarter of the growth in real GDP. Manufacturing and trade accounted for 19·3 per cent and 14·4 per cent of the growth, whilst transport, administration and other services accounted for about 10 per cent each of the increase.

In the five-year period of the SMP, the economy achieved a rate of 3·3 per cent per annum in employment growth compared with 3·2 per cent per annum in the growth of labour force. This resulted in a net increase of some 588,000 new jobs.

Economic development during the SMP was largely stimulated by public sector expenditures for investment and consumption. Public investment was the most buoyant source of final demand in the course of the SMP. Although it constituted only 9·0 per cent of the cumulative GDP for the period, its rate of growth was an unprecedented 17·6 per cent per annum in real terms compared to 1·9 per cent under the First Malaysia Plan (FMP). The share of public investment to gross capital formation grew from 28·1 per cent in 1970 to 49·1 per cent in 1975.

Private investment experienced sharp cyclical fluctuations during the SMP Negative rates of growth were registered in 1972 and 1975 in contrast with an increase of 22·3 per cent between 1973 and 1974. Over the five year period, private fixed capital formation grew by 17·9 per cent per annum in current prices compared with 7·2 per cent per annum in real terms, reflecting the higher cost of imported capital goods.

*Third Malaysia Plan.* The Third Malaysian Plan (1976–1980) has been launched and carries a triple thrust: a major assault on poverty, a vigorous and continuous effort to restructure society and the strengthening of national security. The plan also lays greater emphasis on regional development that has been the case in the past. It also gives a very strong commitment to the promotion of a favourable climate for investment. Total investment under the TMP is estimated at more than $44 billion of which the Government's contribution will be $18·6 billion. The private sector is expected to invest $26·8 billion. Per capita income is expected to increase by $324 compared with $96 between 1970 and 1975.

The target for development expenditure by the public sector over the period of the TMP is estimated at $18·6 billion, of this amount, some 25·5 per cent will be invested in agriculture; 9·5 per cent in mining, manufacturing and commerce; about 16·6 per cent for social development including education, health and housing, with education itself accounting for 9 per cent of total development expenditure; 36·5 per cent for infrastructure development, the management of the environment and general administration; with 11·9 per cent for defence and security.

In comparison with the estimated growth in the labour force, employment is targetted to grow by 3·3 per cent per annum during the OPP (outline perspective Plan) period. In consequence, unemployment as a percentage of the labour force will be reduced from 7·4 per cent in 1970 and 7·0 per cent in 1975 to 6·1 per cent in 1980 and 3·6 per cent in 1990. By 1990, therefore, full employment of the labour force should be secured taking into account the fact that some 3 to 4 per cent of the labour force would conventionally comprise those in voluntary and fractional unemployment.

### JOHORE

*Head of State:* His Royal Highness Sultan Ismail ibni Al-Marhum Sultan Ibrahim.

Johore is the southernmost of the states which lie between the Straits of Malacca and the South China Sea. To the south of it are the Strait of Johore and the Causeway linking the state with the independent republic of Singapore. Johore covers an area of 7,330 square miles and has a population of 1,276,969. The capital is Johore Bahru. The state came under British protection by a treaty signed in 1885.

### KEDAH

*Head of State:* His Highness Tuanku Abdul Halim Mu'adzam Shah ibni Al-marhum Sultan Badlishah.

Extending along the north-western coast of the Malay Peninsula, Kedah has an area of 3,660 square miles and a population of 954,749. The state includes the sparsely populated Langkawi Islands. Its capital is Alor Star. In 1511 Kedah came under the suzerainty of its neighbour, Siam, and remained thus until 1909, when the signing of an Anglo-Siamese treaty transferred suzerainty to Britain.

### KELANTAN

*Regent:* His Highness Tengku Ismail Petra ibni Tuanku Yahya Petra.

One of the northern states of Malaysia, Kelantan has as its neighbours Perak, Pahang and Trengganu. It has a relatively short seaboard and only one port, Tumpat. Malaysia-Singapore Airlines serve the towns of Kota Bharu, Kuala Trengganu and Kuantan. Its area comprises 5,750 square miles. Much of the southern part of the state is still jungle and it also contains Gunong Tahan (7,186 ft.). Kelantan has a population of 686,266 and its capital is Kota Bharu. The state was under Siamese protection until 1909, when a treaty was concluded with Great Britain.

### MALACCA

*Head of State:* His Excellency the Governor of Malacca, Tan Tun Syed Zahiruddin bin Syed Hassan.

This historic state lies on the western side of the peninsula bordering the Straits and with Negri Sembilan to the north and Johore to the south of it. Covering an area of 640 square miles, the land is largely devoted to the production of padi and rubber. The population in 1970 was 481,491. Its capital is the ancient port of Malacca, to which, from the fifteenth century onwards, came traders from many nations. Malacca's history was eventful; first the Portuguese then the Dutch seized the port, then came the British, during the Napoleonic wars. In 1818, however, it was returned to the Dutch but by treaty of 1824 returned once again to the British.

### NEGRI SEMBILAN

*Head of State:* His Royal Highness the Yang Di-Pertuan Besar of Negri Sembilan Tuanku Ja'afar Al-Haj ibni Al-Marhum Tuanku Abdul Rahman Al-Haj.

The state is bordered by Selangor, Pahang, Malacca and Johore, and has a seaboard of about 30 miles, on the Malacca Strait. Its area is 2,580 square miles, population (1970) 481,491, and the capital is Seremban. Negri Sembilan means Nine States, the name deriving from nine districts, parts of which have since been incorporated in adjacent states. Although so named, the present state of Negri Sembilan now consists of six political units and was formed in 1895. Although from 1844 onwards Britain's influence had been exercised in the state, in an advisory capacity to the chiefs, active intervention came only in the latter part of the century, and was due to the growing importance of tin, one of Malaysia's foremost products, in the world economy.

### PAHANG

*Regent:* His Royal Highness Sultan Haji Ahmad Shah ibni Al-Marhum Sultan Aba Bakar Ri'ayatuddin Al-Mu'adzam Shah.

The largest state in Peninsular Malaysia, Pahang covers an area of 13,820 square miles, much of which is still unexplored jungle. Its coastline of 130 miles borders the South China Sea. It has a population of 775,440. Kuantan is the capital. In 1887 Pahang concluded its first treaty with Britain; a second one in the following year placed the state under British protection.

### PENANG

*Head of State:* His Excellency the Governor of Penang, Tun Haji Sardon bin Haji Jubir.

This state consists of the Island of Penang, a number of smaller islands and the mainland of Province Wellesley. Its total area is 390 square miles. Penang Island, which lies at the northern extremity of the Straits of Malacca, is about 15 miles long and nine miles broad. The mainland, facing it, is about eight miles wide and 45 miles long. The population is 775,440 and the capital is George Town. In the late eighteenth century the Island of Penang was ceded to the East India Company. The mainland strip was ceded to Britain in 1880.

### PERAK

*Head of State:* His Royal Highness Sultan Idris Al-Mutawakil Allahi Shah ibni Al-Marhum Sultan Iskandar Shah Kadasallah Shah.

This state which extends northwards to the border of Thailand and on its western side skirts the Straits of Malacca, contains some of the country's most productive tin mines within its 7,980 square miles. On the eastern side of the state, adjoining Kelantan and Pahang, lies the main mountain range. Perak has a population of 1,569,161, the second largest in Malaysia. Ipoh is the state capital. Early in the seventeenth century the Dutch built up powerful trading connections with Perak and their influence predominated until 1818, in which year Britain secured a treaty that gave her subjects the right to free trade in the state. In 1874 the Perak chiefs accepted a British Resident.

### PERLIS

*Head of State:* His Royal Highness Tuanku Syed Putra ibni Al-Marhum Syed Hassan Jamalullil.

The smallest of the Malay States, Perlis lies between two provinces of Thailand and the Malay state of Kedah, and was in fact a part of the latter until the Siamese occupation in 1721. Perlis came under British suzerainty as the result of an Anglo-Siamese Treaty, and the state concluded a treaty with Britain in 1930. The capital is Kangar. The state covers an area of 310 square miles and its population is 120,991.

### SABAH

*Head of State:* His Excellency Datuk Hj Ahmad Koroh.

Sabah covers an area of 29,388 square miles with a coastline of about 900 miles washed by the South China Sea on the west and north, and the Sulu and Celebes Seas on the east.

Sabah is a mountainous country of dense tropical forests, with mountain ranges rising to 6,000 ft. However, rising to a height of 13,455 ft., Mount Kinabalu is the highest mountain in Malaysia and South East Asia.

On 31 August 1963, the country gained self-government and on 16 September 1963, Sabah joined the Federation of Malaysia as an independent state. The capital is Kota Kinabalu.

The population in 1970 was 654,949.

Only five to six per cent of Sabah is cultivated as agriculture is restricted by poor communications and a relatively small population.

Sabah has a good timber industry which plays an important part in the economy of the State.

## SARAWAK

*Head of State:* His Excellency the Governor of Sarawak, Datuk Pattingi Abang Mohamad Salahhuddin.

Sarawak in Borneo covers an area of approximately 48,250 sq. miles on the northwest coast of the island. The country is low-lying along the coast but inland there is a tangled mass of hills, its dominant feature being the multitude of rivers.

The population in 1970 was 977,438.

Sarawak's economy depends on agriculture, rubber being its chief product. There are about 6,000 sq. miles of swamp forest and they produce most of Sarawak's commercial timber. Sarawak's chief exports are petroleum, bauxite, rubber, pepper, timber and sago.

## SELANGOR

*Head of State:* His Royal Highness Sultan Salahuddin Abdul Aziz Shah ibni Al-Marhum Sultan Hishamuddin Alam Shah Al-Haj.

Selangor lies to the south of Perak and has an extensive seaboard on the Straits of Malacca. On that part of the northern border joining Pahang the country is mountainous. Selangor's population of 1,629,386 is the highest in Malaysia. The capital is Klang. In 1818 Britain concluded a commercial treaty with Selangor and subsequently an agreement of peace and friendship with Sultan Ibrahim Shah. This ruler's successor had difficulty in controlling his chiefs and anarchy prevailed until the state came under British protection in 1874.

## TRENGGANU

*Head of State:* His Royal Highness Tuanku Ismail Nasiruddin Shah ibni Al-Marhum Sultan Zainal Abidin.

Trengganu is one of the eastern states of the peninsula, its long coastline bordering the South China Sea. Its neighbouring states are Kelantan and Pahang. A good deal of the interior is mountainous, thickly forested and uninhabited. The state covers an area of 5,050 square miles and its population in 1970 was 405,539. The capital is Kuala Trengganu. British political influence began in 1909, with a treaty concluded with Siam, to which the state paid tribute. A second treaty in the following year brought Trengganu under British protection.

## PRINCIPAL BANKS

**Bank Negara Malaysia.** (Central Bank of Malaysia.) Established January 1959. Governor: Tan Sri Ismail bin Mohamed Ali. The bank has full currency issuing powers and is financial adviser and acts as a banker to the Malaysian Government.

**Algemene Bank Netherland, N.V., Kuala Lumpur.** 1 branch.

**Bangkok Bank Ltd.**

**Bank Bumiputra Malaysia Burhad.** Net Profit for year ending December 1975 M$5,453,921. 40 Branches.

**Bank Negara Indonesia 1946, 3 Malacca Street, Singapore 1.**

**Bank of America N.T. & S.A.**

**Ban Hin Lee Bank Bhd., Penang.**

**Bank of Canton Ltd., Kuala Lumpur.**

**Bank Kerjasama Rakyat Malaysia Bhd.** 11 branches.

**Bank of Tokyo Ltd.**

**Banque de l'Indochine.** 1 branch.

**The Chartered Bank.** 35 branches.

**The Chase Manhattan Bank N.A.**

**The Chung Kiaw Bank Ltd.** 34 branches.

**Co-operative Bank Malaysia Ltd.** 6 branches.

**Co-operative Central Bank Ltd.**

**Deutsch-Asiatische Bank.**

**Development and Commercial Bank (Ltd.) Bhd.**

**The Development Bank of Singapore Ltd.** DBS Building Shenton Way, Singapore 1.

**Citibank N.A.**

**Habib Bank.**

**Hock Hua Bank Bhd.**

**The Hongkong and Shanghai Banking Corporation.** branches. See Hong Kong.

**The Indian Bank Ltd.**

**The United Asian Bank Ltd.** 20 branches.

**Kwong Yik Bank Ltd.**

**Lee Wah Bank Ltd.** (Incorporated in Singapore in 1920). branches in Singapore and 9 branches in Malaysia.

**Malayan Banking Berhad.** 126 branches.

**Malayan Banking Ltd.** 126 branches.

**Mercantile Bank Ltd.** 12 branches. See Hong Kong.

**Oriental Bank Berhad.** (Chairman: T. S. H. bin Haji Mohd. Sidek.) *Head Office:* No 16, Jalan Silang, Kuala Lumpur 01-19.4 branches.

**versea Chinese Banking Corp. Ltd.** 42 branches.

**Overseas Union Bank Ltd.** 9 branches.

**Pacific Bank Bhd.** 1 branch.

**Public Bank Ltd.** 7 branches.

**Southern Banking Berhad.** 7 branches.

**The United Commercial Bank Ltd.** 2 branches.

**United Malayan Banking Corpn.** Bhd. 48 branches.

## PRODUCTION, INDUSTRY AND COMMERCE

The mainstay of the Malaysian economy is still agriculture. The Malaysian economy has traditionally been dependent on the production and export of primary commodities like rubber, tin, timber, iron-ore, pepper and coconut oil. The object of the government's agricultural diversification plan is to increase the cultivation of other promising crops like palm oil, rather than to replace the traditional ones.

The following table gives some figures for agricultural production for the year 1976:

| | 1976<br>*thousand tonnes* |
|---|---|
| Rubber | 1,480 |
| Rice | 1,407 |
| Timber: | |
| sawn logs | 16,270 |
| sawn timber (cu. metres) | 3,685 |
| Coconut oil | 66 |

The principle of diversification was applied not only to agriculture but also to export oriented industry. The economy was strengthened by a rapid growth of the manufacturing industries. This growth was oriented towards the home market and substantial import substitution especially in foodstuffs, beverages, tobacco products, petroleum products, cement, rubber and plastic goods, fertilizers, textiles and steel bars.

This industrial growth is based essentially on private enterprise assisted and encouraged by various Government Acts of legislation.

The Capital Investment Committee (CIC) directs the implementation of the nation's industrial development policy through the agency of the Federal Industrial Development Authority (FIDA).

Approvals in principle were given to 179 projects for pioneer status in 1973, compared with 158 in 1972. These projects were estimated to require a total investment of $375·3 million. These projects were estimated to employ 49,240 persons.

The following table shows the production index for the years 1972–74 for various products, taking 1968 = 100 for the Malaysian peninsular:

| *Industry* | 1972 | 1973 | 1974 |
|---|---|---|---|
| Processing of Estate type Agricultural Products in Factories off Estate | 164·8 | 182·2 | 210·4 |
| Food | 115·4 | 130·3 | 128·5 |
| Beverage | 135·9 | 169·7 | 195·1 |
| Tobacco Products | 130·6 | 154·5 | 967·5 |
| Textiles | 156·1 | 196·8 | 141·0 |
| Wood, Rattan, Mengkuang, Attap and Cork Products | 183·7 | 203·3 | 185·9 |
| Paper and Paper Products | 175·0 | 218·4 | 214·2 |
| Rubber Products | 139·8 | 166·5 | 161·7 |
| Chemicals and Chemical Products | 144·2 | 165·6 | 175·1 |
| Products of Petroleum and Coal | 96·6 | 99·1 | 101·5 |
| Non-Metallic Mineral Products | 129·2 | 147·0 | 154·6 |
| Basic Metal Industries | 192·2 | 225·5 | 237·5 |
| Metal Products | 171·7 | 242·8 | 267·5 |
| Electrical Machinery Apparatus, Appliances and Supplies | 192·4 | 200·6 | 247·0 |
| Transport Equipment | 268·3 | 393·0 | 531·4 |
| Other Pioneers | 313·6 | 474·5 | 906·0 |

The following tables show the value in M$ millions, and percentage change of various imports and exports for the year 1974:

| *Category* | *M$ million* | *Imports per cent* | *per cent change* 1973/74 |
|---|---|---|---|
| Machinery and transport equipment | 3,173·9 | 32·2 | + 78 |
| Manufactured Goods | 1,871·1 | 19·0 | + 50 |
| Food | 1,563·5 | 15·9 | + 45 |
| Mineral Fuels | 1,004·3 | 10·2 | +181 |
| Chemicals | 879·1 | 8·9 | + 67 |
| Inedible Crude Minerals | 538·8 | 5·5 | + 45 |
| Beverages and Tobacco | 114·9 | 1·2 | + 17 |
| Animals and Vegetable oils and Fats | 44·1 | 0·4 | + 64 |
| Other manufactured articles | 557·9 | 5·7 | + 68 |
| Other imports | 96·3 | 1·0 | + 39 |
| Total | 9,843·9 | 100 | + 66 |

| *Category* | *M$ million* | *Percentage* | *Change in per cent 1973/74* | |
|---|---|---|---|---|
| | | | *Vol.* | *Value* |
| Rubber | 2,886·7 | 28·3 | − 4 | + 15 |
| Tin | 1,514·9 | 14·9 | + 5 | + 69 |
| Saw logs | 1,032·4 | 10·1 | − 6 | + 5 |
| Sawn timber | 437·2 | 4·3 | −18 | − 22 |
| Palm oil | 1,086·0 | 10·7 | +13 | +133 |
| Palm kernel oil | 164·8 | 1·6 | +39 | +195 |
| Petroleum | 673·9 | 6·6 | −18 | +150 |
| Other exports | 2,393·5 | 23·5 | — | + 47 |
| Total | 10,189·4 | 100 | — | + 38 |

## COMMUNICATIONS

**Railways.** The main line, 488 miles long, follows the west coast and extends from Singapore in the south to Butterworth, opposite Penang Island, in the north. The railway, which has been extended from Prai to Butterworth, crosses the Prai River by a swing bridge which opened on 14 September 1967. The new Butterworth station is adjacent to the Penang Port Commission's pier where the ferry services to Penang operate. The new extension will also serve the new deep-water wharves for ocean-going ships in Butterworth.

From Bukit Mertajam the line branches off to the Thai border at Padang Besar, where connection is made with the State Railway of Thailand. Three through international passenger train services operate between Butterworth and Bangkok every week. The Bangkok to Sungei Golok express service has been extended to Tumpat on the east coast. There is also a through rail car service between Butterworth and Haadyai in Thailand.

On the West Coast of Sabah, there is a 100-mile rail network, running from Kota Kinabalu to the main towns of Papar, Beaufort and Tenom, and stopping at many smaller towns en route.

The East Coast line of Peninsular Malaysia, 327 miles long, runs from Gemas to Tumpat, near Kota Bahru. A 13-mile branch line from Pasir Mas, 16 miles south of Tumpat, makes connection with the State Railway of Thailand at Sungei Golok.

Branch lines serve railway operated ports of Port Dickson, Telok Anson and Port Weld as well as Port Swettenham and Jurong in Singapore.

There are several diesel rail car services in operation.

Air conditioned sleepers and buffet cars are operated on the main services.

**Shipping.** The chief ports are Penang, Port Kelang, Kota Kinabalu, Sandakan and Kuching.

The Port of Penang is administered by the Penang Port Commission and Port Swettenham by the Port Kelang Authority. All the five new wharves in Penang can accommodate containers discharged by ships and are geared to lorries or flat-bed trailers. Two of the five berths are designed to accommodate larger container cranes on the wharf should the demand develop.

The $37 million North Klang Strains project for the construction of four deep-water berths in Port Swettenham was completed in 1964. Work on an additional 2,800 feet of berths started in mid-1969 and is scheduled for completion in 1972.

In 1968, a Sabah Ports Authority was formed. The first port to be administered by the Authority is Kota Kinabalu but eventually it will extend its area of operation to all ports in Sabah. Negotiations have been concluded with the World Bank for a loan to expand the ports in Sandakan and Kota Kinabalu.

A new port will be constructed in Kuching at Pending Point in Sarawak to replace the existing port at Tanah Puteh. The new port when completed, will be able to take in ships of over 18,000 tons.

The Malaysian International Shipping Corporation (MISC) which has been designated as the national shipping line, was formed in 1968 with 30 per cent government equity participation. The MISC has already in service three vessels on the Far East–Europe run.

The Marine Department, with headquarters in Penang, administers the Merchant Shipping Ordinance, and a Light Dues Board maintains lights and navigational aids.

**Road Transport.** Malaysia's road system is extensive and good. In 1974, the road network spanning the country comprised 20,800 kilometres of roads of which over 80 per cent have a metalled surface. The number of motor vehicles amounted to 1,090,279 and this represents a ratio of one motor vehicle to every 14 persons in Malaysia.

Roads play a dominant role in the transport system in Peninsular Malaysia. Under the second Malaysian five-year development plan (1971–75) road traffic is expected to increase at an average rate of 9–12 per cent per year. To meet this growth in traffic, the present network will be improved and upgraded an new additions to the network will be made where no transport facilities are now available.

In Sabah, Australian financial and technical assistance are given to the East–West Highway, a new road project linking Sandakan with Kota Kinabalu. As part of Malaysia's contribution to the Asian Highway System, Kelantan will be linked to Penang while in South East Pahang, there will be the Kuantan–Segamat Highway.

The principal towns of Malaysia have their own regular scheduled bus services and all towns on the main highway are linked by long distance bus service.

**Civil Aviation.** Malaysia is well served with air transport. There are 19 aerodromes in Malaysia, including the international airports at Kuala Lumpur, Penang, and Kota Kinabalu. Kuala Lumpur's airport at Subang has a runway of 11,400 feet, the longest in Southeast Asia. Penang and Kota Kinabalu can accept Comet 4s, Caravelle jets and Boeing 737s with construction underway to cater for Boeing 707s.

Malaysia's new airline and flag-carrier was established in April 1971 as Malaysian Airline Ltd. (MAL). This was subsequently changed to Malaysia Airline System (MAS). 'MAS' which means gold in Bahasa Malaysian started operations on 1 October 1972, after Malaysia–Singapore Airlines ceased operations. In 1974 with a fleet of 24 aircraft, it provided flight services throughout the country. MAS has established offices in Sydney, Melbourne, and Perth in Australia; Los Angeles, San Francisco, and Chicago in the U.S.A.; London and Frankfurt in Europe; Tokyo, Bangkok, Hong Kong, Singapore, and Jakarta; and Kuwait in West Asia.

Malaysia Air Charter, a private charter company which operates light to medium aircraft, provides services to the smaller airstrips, in addition to carrying out photographic surveys and aerial crop spraying.

Malaysia practises the 'open-sky' policy whereby any carrier can be given landing rights without reciprocity.

International airlines operating through Kuala Lumpur are: Aeroflot, Air Ceylon, Air India, Air Vietnam, Alitalia, British Airways, Cathay Pacific Airways, China Airlines, Garuda Indonesian Airways, Japan Airlines, KLM-Royal Dutch Airlines, Qantas, Scandinavian Airlines System, Thai International Airways and UTA—Union de Transports Aeriens.

The administration of civil aviation is carried out by the Civil Aviation Department in Kuala Lumpur.

**Satellite Communication.** Malaysia has three transmitting/receiving stations capable of receiving and transmitting signals to an INTELSAT satellite. One of these stations is of the large or 'Standard A' type, the others are small or 'Standard B' type. One big and one small station are situated at Kuantan, the other small one being at Kota Kinabalu, Sabah. One of the functions of these three stations is to transmit television programmes of an educational kind to schools throughout Malaysia, both the peninsular and East Malaysia.

## NEWSPAPERS

**Malay Mail.** English. Afternoon. Circulation 44,000. Kuala Lumpur.

**New Straits Times.** English. Circulation 144,000. Kuala Lumpur.

**Tamil Nesan.** Tamil. Morning. Circulation 24,300. Kuala Lumpur.

**Sunday Echo.** Weekly. Circulation 34,000 P.O. Box 334, 216 Penang Road, Penang.

**Straits Echo.** English. Morning Circulation 28,000. 216, Penang Road, Penang.

**Kwong Wah Yit Poh.** Chinese. Morning. Circulation 45,196, *Head Office:* 2–4 Chulia Street Ghaut, Penang, Malaysia.

**Sing Pin Jih Pao.** Chinese. Morning. Circulation 45,319. Penang.

**Utusan Melayu.** Jawi (Bahasa Malaysia in Arabic script). Morning. Circulation 51,500. Kuala Lumpur.

**China Press.** Chinese. Daily. Morning. Circulation 38,816, London Representatives: Colin Turner (London) Ltd., 122 Shaftesbury Avenue, London, W1V 8HA.

**Berita Harian.** Bahasa Malaysia-Romanized. Morning. Circulation 48,000. Kuala Lumpur and Singapore.

**Utusan Malaysia.** Bahasa Malaysia-Romanized. Morning. Circulation 115,000. Kuala Lumpur.

**Utusan Zaman, Jawi.** (Bahasa Malaysia and Arabic script). Sunday. Circulation 53,000. Kuala Lumpur.

**Mingguan Malaysia.** Latin script (Bahasa Malaysia). Sunday. Circulation 218,000. Kuala Lumpur.

**Daily Express.** English/Bahasa Malaysia. Morning. Circulation 23,890. Kota Kinabalu, Sabah.

**Kinabalu Sabah Times.** English/Bahasa Malaysia/Kadazan and Chinese. Morning. Circulation 12,000. Kota Kinabalu.

**Malayan Thung Pau.** Chinese. Morning. Circulation 74,450 Kuala Lumpur.

**Nanyang Siang Pau.** Chinese. Morning. Circulation 178,350. Kuala Lumpur and Singapore.

**Overseas Chinese Daily News.** Chinese. Morning. Circulation 26,205. Kota Kinabalu.

**See Hua Daily News.** Chinese. Morning. Circulation 22,500. Kuching, and Sibu.

**Shin Min Daily News.** Chinese. Morning. Circulation 82,211. Kuala Lumpur.

**Sin Chew Jit Poh.** Chinese. Morning. Circulation 160,000. Singapore and Malaysia.

**Tamil Malar.** Tamil. Morning. Circulation 11,000. Petaling Jaya, Selangor.

## EDUCATION

The Education Ordinance, 1957 and the Education Act 1961, have the basic aim of providing six years of free primary education to every child. In addition national schools are given financial assistance (i.e. those using Bahasa Malaysia as a medium of instruction and those using English, Chinese and Tamil as media of instruction). In fact, the national education system is designed to promote national integration and unity. It therefore provides for an educational system in which Bahasa Malaysia will ultimately become the main medium of instruction and English a second language in all schools.

Malaysia now provides six years free primary education and since 1964 an additional three years of lower secondary education. In 1970, Bahasa Malaysia was introduced as the medium of instruction for English-medium primary schools. Consequently, by 1983, all courses other than languages, for new admission to universities will be conducted in Bahasa Malaysia. From 1974, all subjects in Form I have been taught in Bahasa Malaysia.

Promotion into upper secondary levels depends on the pupils' performance in the Lower Certificate of Education examination. They are then streamed into arts, science, technical or vocational courses. After two years the pupils will sit for either the Malaysian Certificate of Education or the Vocational Certificate of Education. If they do well, they can have another two years before sitting for their Higher School Certificate. This qualification entitles the pupil to go to a university.

There are now the following post secondary institutions of learning: Technical College, College of Agriculture, MARA Institute of Technology, and Tunku Abdul Rahman College in Kuala Lumpur and the Ungku Omar Polytechnic in Ipoh. The Technical College has been converted into the University of Technology with university status. The College of Agriculture has been merged with the University of Malaya Agriculture Faculty to form the Agriculture University.

The other three universities are the University of Malaya (1959) in Kuala Lumpur, the second is the University of Penang (1969) which has been renamed Universiti Sains Malaysia (Science University of Malaysia). Finally there is the Universiti Kebangsaan or the National University, established in 1970 which is at the moment in Kuala Lumpur. The National University plans to move to a 2,300-acre site in Bangi, 18 miles from Kuala Lumpur.

# The Republic of Maldives

**Capital**—Malé.

**President**—H.E. Amir Ibrahim Nasir, RBK, NGIV.

**National Flag:** Green, red-bordered and charged with a white crescent.

### CONSTITUTION AND GOVERNMENT

Maldives came under British protection in 1887 by an agreement between the Sultan and the Governor of Ceylon. On the Independence of Ceylon in 1948 a new agreement dated 24 April 1948 was signed between the Sultan and the British Government. Under this agreement, which was reaffirmed in 1953, Maldives remained under British protection but it was agreed that internal affairs would be the responsibility of the Sultan. A revised agreement in 1960 introduced certain changes with regard to the conduct of external relations by the Maldivian Government in economic and cultural fields and providing for the use of certain defence facilities on Gan Island by the British Government.

Maldives has been a member of the Colombo Plan since 1963 and of the United Nations since 1965.

#### Cabinet

*Minister of Justice:* Hon. Moosa Fathhi.
*Minister of Home Affairs:* Hon. Ibrahim Rasheed.
*Minister of Provincial Affairs:* Hon. Hassan Zareer.
*Minister of Fisheries:* Amir Ahmed Hilmy Faashana Kilegefaanu.
*Minister of Public Safety:* Amir Abdul Hannan Doshimena Kilegefaanu.
*Minister of Education:* Amir Abdul Sattar Faamuladeiri Kilegefaanu.
*Minister of Agriculture:* Hon. Ibrahim Shihab.
*Minister of Health:* Hon. Mrs. Moomina A. Ismail.
*Minister of Shipping:* Hon. Ali Umar Maniku.
*Minister of Transport:* Hon. Maumoon Abdul Gayoon.
*Attorney General:* Hon. Adnan Hussein.
*Speaker of the Majlis:* Sheikh Ahmed Shathir.

### LEGAL SYSTEM

The legislative body since April 1975 comprises 48 members of whom eight members are nominated by the President, two members elected by the people of Malé, and two members elected from each of the 19 atolls. Executive Power is vested in the President elected by popular vote for five years.

### AREA AND POPULATION

Maldives lies about 420 miles south-west of Sri Lanka and comprises just over 1,196 islands, of which 203 are inhabited. The population at mid-1974 was 116,000. The annual average percentage growth rate of the population for the period 1960–74 was 1·8, and for the period 1965–74 was 1·9.

### COMMERCE

The economy of the Republic is almost entirely dependent on the fishing industry. The principal export is dried fish ('Maldive fish') prepared from the bonito. Coconuts grow fairly well on the islands.

The GNP at market prices for 1974 was U.S. $ millions 10, and the GNP per capita at market prices was U.S. $100. The annual average percentage growth rate of the GNP per capita for the period 1960–74 was 0·8, and for the period 1965–74 was 0·4. [*See the note at the beginning of this section concerning GNP.*]

In 1975 the total value of exports was Rs. 10,029,321·71 and imports in the same year were Rs. 26,532,909·38.

The islands have no direct taxation or commercial banking system.

Besides Britain, the World Health Organization and the Colombo Plan are also assisting Maldives in her development.

# Mali Republic

**Capital**—Bamako.

**President**—Colonel Moussa Traore.

**Flag:** A tricolour pale-wise, green, yellow, red, charged with an idiogram of Man on the yellow centred black.

### CONSTITUTION AND GOVERNMENT

THE Republic of Mali, formerly the territory of French Sudan, became independent on 22 September 1960.

As a result of discussion between the Presidents of Ghana, Guinea and Mali at the end of 1960, a Union under the name of the Union of African States formally came into being on 21 July 1961.

The Charter of the Union is designed to strengthen friendship and co-operation between the member States and to guarantee, collectively, territorial integrity and co-operation in defence.

### LEGAL SYSTEM

In 1946, the traditional courts were abolished. Certain purely local judicial organization remains, however, whereby disputes between individuals can be heard.

There is a Court of the First Instance at Bamako with a circuit. There are Sectional Courts at Kayes, Segou and Skiasso with circuits.

### AREA AND POPULATION

The area of the Mali Republic is 1,204,021 sq. km.
The population at mid-1974 was 5,560,000. The annual average percentage growth rate of the population for the period 1960–74 was 2·2 and for 1965–74 was 2·1.

### CURRENCY AND FINANCE

The monetary unit is the franc malien.

The 1971–72 national budget balanced at 45,300 million fr.

The GNP at market prices for 1974 was U.S. $millions 450, and the GNP per capita at market prices was U.S. $80. The annual average percentage growth rate of the GNP per capita for the period 1960–74 was 0·9, and for the period 1965–74 was 0·4. [*See the note at the beginning of this section concerning GNP.*]

### PRODUCTION INDUSTRY AND COMMERCE

The Republic has a substantial agriculture foundation producing millet, rice, groundnuts, cotton, maize gum and kapok. In 1965 production of cotton was estimated at 22,000 tons. Animal husbandry is well developed. There are estimated to be 4·0 million cattle, 7·2 million sheep and goats, 0·32 million donkeys, 124,000 horses, 100,000 camels 11,000 pigs and 15 million poultry.

**Mining.** There are small deposits of gold, not generally regarded as economic to develop. 500 to 2,000 kg. of gold per annum is the estimated potential. The most interesting mineral deposits is one of pure salt at Agorgot, 700 km. from the capital. This is mined and transported in blocks weighing 30–40 kilos. Surveys indicate that there may be economic deposits of bauxite, zinc and lead.

**Forestry.** There are estimated to be 800,000 sq. km. of forest. 1,195,440 hectares of this area is reserved for hunting, mainly of elephants.

**Commerce.** Value (million fr. C.F.A.) of principal exports in 1965 was as follows: groundnuts, 555; cotton, 644. For imports, 1965 figures were: food and tobacco, 2,280; fuels, 637; raw material and semi-manufactures, 1,791; machinery, 2,121; consumer goods, 6,045. Total value of exports was 3,877 million fr. C.F.A. and of imports, 10,579 million fr. C.F.A.

### COMMUNICATIONS

There are at present about 13,000 km. of road, of which about 2,640 are federal road, 6,160 of secondary roads and about 5,000 km. of track. The roads in general are not satisfactory. 9,000 km. are covered only by roads and tracks which are unusable during the rains. 560 km. of road are tarred.

There are 641 km. of railroad which connects the Republic with the coast.

Air services from Bamako connected Mali with Paris, Abidjan and Dakar.

### EDUCATION

In 1965, there were 111,000 primary school children. In the secondary schools there was a total of 5,500 pupils, and there was a total of 900 pupils undergoing technical education.

# Malta

(MEMBER OF THE COMMONWEALTH)

**Capital**—Valletta.

**President of the Republic**—Dr. Anton Buttigieg, BA, LLD.

**National Flag:** On a field pale-wise, parti white and red; a canton bearing the George Cross.

## CONSTITUTION AND GOVERNMENT

THE Maltese Islands are situated in the Mediterranean Sea about 58 miles south of Sicily. Malta itself is about 17 miles in length and nine miles in breadth. Other islands in the group are Gozo and Comino.

Malta was in turn held by the Phoenicians, Greeks, Carthaginians and Romans, and was conquered by the Arabs in AD 870. In about the year 1127 it was joined to Sicily until 1530, when it was handed over to the Knights of St. John who ruled until dispersed by Napoleon in 1796. The Maltese rose in rebellion against the French and the Island was subsequently blockaded by the British Fleet. Malta passed under the British Crown by the free will of its people which was confirmed by the Treaty of Paris of 1814. The Island is one of the most important ports of call in the world.

On 15 April 1942, in recognition of the steadfastness and fortitude of the people of Malta during the Second World War, King George VI awarded the George Cross to the Island.

Malta became a republic on 13 December 1974. Several changes in the Constitution included the creation of the office of President to replace that of Governor-General. The Constitution also provides that the national language and the language of the Courts in Maltese but both Maltese and English are official languages.

The first Maltese-born Governor-General appointed by the present Labour Government in July, 1971 was nominated President of Malta on 13 December 1974.

Under the Constitution the office of President becomes vacant after five years from the date of appointment made by Resolution on the House of Representatives. He appoints the Prime Minister, choosing the Member of the House of Representatives whom he judges to be ablest to command the confidence of a majority of the Members, and on the advice of the Prime Minister he appoints the other Ministers, the Chief Justice, the Judges and the Attorney General.

### The Cabinet

The Cabinet consists of the Prime Minister and such number of other Ministers as recommended by the Prime Minister.

### Parliament

The House of Representatives consists of such number of members, being an odd number and divisable by the number of divisions as Parliament by law determines from time to time.

Each division returns such number of members, being not less than five and not more than seven, as Parliament by law determines from time to time. The electoral divisions are an odd number, being not less than nine and not more than fifteen, as Parliament determines from time to time.

At the moment the number of members is 55. From the forthcoming general elections the House of Representatives shall consist of sixty-five Members. By Act XII of 1975 Malta was divided into thirteen electoral divisions, each division returning five members.

The life of the House of Representatives, unless sooner dissolved, is five years, after which a general election is held.

Election is by universal adult suffrage on the principle of proportional representation. The age of majority is eighteen years.

### The Cabinet

*Prime Minister and Minister of Commonwealth and Foreign Affairs and Minister of the Interior:* Hon. Dom. Mintoff, BSc, BE and A, MA (Oxon) A and CE, MP.
*Minister of Justice, Lands, Housing and Parliamentary Affairs:* Hon. Joseph Cassar, BA, LLD, MP.
*Minister of Labour, Welfare and Culture:* Hon. Agatha Barbara, MP.
*Minister of Finance, Custom and People's Financial Investments:* Hon Joseph Abela, LLD, MP.
*Minister of Tourism:* Hon. Daniel Piscopo, BSc, MD, MP.
*Minister of Works and Sport:* Hon. Lorry Sant, MP.
*Minister of Development, Energy, Port and Telecommunications:* Hon. Wistin Abela, MP.
*Minister of Parastatal and People's Industries:* Hon. Freddie Micallef, MP.
*Minister of Trade:* Hon. Patrick Holland, LLD, MP.
*Minister of Health and Environment:* Hon. Vincent Moran, B. Pharm, MD, MP.
*Minister of Industry, Fisheries and Agriculture:* Hon. Danny Cremona, MP.
*Minister of Education:* Hon. Philip Muscat, BSc, MD, MP.
*Secretary to the Cabinet:* Mr. Albert Agius Ferrante, LP.

## AREA AND POPULATION

The Maltese Archipelago consists of three main islands with a total area of 121·8 square miles. Malta, the largest island, covers an area of 94·9 square miles. Gozo and Comino, the other two islands, have an area of 25·9 and 1·1 square miles respectively.

The Maltese population which, according to an estimate drawn by the Central Office of Statistics stood at 300,786 on the 31 December, 1974. The birth rate, in 1975 stood at 19·0 per thousand of the population. The death rate stood at 9·6 per thousand in 1975.

## PRODUCTION, INDUSTRY AND COMMERCE

The island is highly cultivated. Potatoes are the principal agricultural export, valued at £M1,532,000 and these take up approximately 20 per cent of the land under cultivation. Flowers, seed and plants, onions and tomatoes are also exported. The largest fruit crop is grapes, the bulk of which is taken up by local vintners for production of table wines.

Total output of manufacturing rose by £M33·1 million or 33 per cent to £M131·8 million, with most manufacturing activities increasing their output particularly the textile and clothing, food preparation and leather sectors.

Tourist inflow continued its upward trend with a total of 334,519 visitors in 1975.

**Commerce:** Principal imports in 1976 were as follows:

| | 1976 (*thousand £M*) |
|---|---|
| Food | 36,207 |
| Beverages and tobacco | 5,774 |
| Crude materials | 3,497 |
| Mineral fuels | 15,758 |
| Animal and vegetable oils and fats | 1,154 |
| Chemicals | 11,257 |
| Manufactures | 70,688 |
| Machinery and transport equipment | 34,316 |
| Miscellaneous transactions | 1,271 |
| Total | 179,923 |

The principal domestic exports in 1976 were as follows:

| *Commodity* | 1976 (*thousand £M*) |
|---|---|
| Potatoes | 1,532 |
| Onions | 173 |
| Cut flowers, etc. | 329 |
| Scrap metal | 568 |
| Motor cars | 235 |
| Textiles and yarns | 4,808 |
| Gloves | 424 |
| Rubber goods | 2,174 |
| Sanitary fixtures | 2,267 |
| Clothing | 38,223 |
| Plastic goods | 1,657 |

| Commodity | 1975 (thousand £M) |
|---|---|
| Cigarettes | 2,373 |
| Detergents | 357 |
| Food processed | 3,394 |
| Toys and games | 2,269 |
| Other | 19,329 |
| Total | 80,112 |

## FINANCE

The Budget for 1977–78 provides for a total expenditure of about £M 103 million which will be financed from current revenue of around £95 million and the balance in the Consolidated Fund carried forward from 1976/77. The major sources of revenue are Customs and Excise Duty, Income Tax, Central Bank profits, and Rent for Defence facilities, which among them are expected to contribute 69 per cent of total revenue. As regards expenditure nearly £32·5 million will be allocated to the Capital Programme.

## COMMUNICATIONS

**Roads.** There are about 770 miles of asphalted and macadamized roads. An efficient bus service operates to all parts of Malta from two termini at Valletta.

## BANK

**Bank of Valletta Ltd.** (Constituted as limited liability company by agreement between Government and Malta Development Corporation to assume business of National Bank of Malta Ltd.) Chairman, Dr. J. Agius, MD. Assets as at 31 December 1976, £M48,187,000; deposits and current accounts, £M44,059,000. *Head Office:* 45 Republic Street, Valletta, Malta. Branches, 30.

**Shipping. Malta, whose chief port and trade centre is Valletta,** is a port of call for most of the shipping lines serving the Mediterranean.

The principal port, Grand Harbour in Valletta, is a natural harbour and the approaches present no navigational difficulty. It has adequate shore facilities for handling import and export cargoes. Large ship repair facilities are available. With the opening of the Suez Canal an increase in both cargo traffic and repair facilities is envisaged.

Sea Malta Company Limited, the National Shipping Line is today running a Liner service between Antwerp, Felixstowe, Rotterdam, Malta and *vice versa.* It has also provided a regular Roll On/Roll Off service between the ports of Malta, Reggio Calabria, Livorno, Tripoli and Tunis.

**National Shipping Line. Sea Malta Company Limited.** (Chairman, A. Mizzi; Managing Director, P. Guez; Commercial Director, D. A. H. Howell; Operations Manager, D. L. Jones; Secretary/Financial Controller, J. T. Apps). *Head Office:* Europa Centre, P.O. Box 555, Floriana, Malta.

**Airline. Air Malta Company Limited.** (Chairman: Albert Mizzi, General Manager: M. M. Salim; Deputy General Manager: Vincent Falzon). *Head Office:* Europa Centre, Floriana, Malta. Telephone: 23271, 623246, Telex: MW389.

National carrier operating daily passenger and cargo scheduled services to Amsterdam, Brussels, Cairo, Frankfurt, London, Manchester, Paris, Rome, Tripoli, Tunis, Vienna and Zurich. Charter Services also operating to Europe and North Africa.

**Telecommunications and Broadcasting.** Telecommunications and Broadcasting are operated by the Telemalta Corporation (Chairman Mr. Godfrey Craig), 1 Pender Place, St. Andrew's Road, St. Julian's.

Malta and Gozo are covered by a telephone network providing over 38,000 exchange lines. These are serviced through a number of exchanges in Malta and Gozo and the system is being developed to provide for the next seven years. The Corporation is responsible for telegraph and telex services and provides these via a cable link and a microwave link with Sicily and radio links with the United Kingdom and France.

The Corporation has taken over sound and television broadcasting, formerly operated by Rediffusion (Malta) Ltd., and is also responsible for Radio Malta.

**Broadcasting.** The Broadcasting Authority is an independent statutory body set up in 1961 to control broadcasting services in Malta. Programmes are provided by the Telemalta Corporation.

## NEWSPAPERS

**Times of Malta**: F. 1935. Daily. 341 St. Paul's St., Valletta, P.O. Box 328. Cables: Progress Malta. Telex: Malta 341. Editor, Charles Grech Orr.

**The Sunday Times of Malta**: F. 1924. St. Paul Street, Valletta, P.O. Box 328. Cables: Progress Malta. Telex: Malta 341. Editor, Anthony Montanaro.

**The Bulletin**: Daily (English). Lux Press, Hamrun.

**L-Orizzont**: F. 1962. Daily in Maltese. Circulation 20,000. Editor, Carmel Micallef, Union Press, Workers' Memorial Building, Valletta.

**Malta News**: cir. 15,000. Daily in English. Union Press, Workers' Memorial Building, Valletta.

**Il-Hajja**: (Maltese), Daily, Blata-l-Bajda, P.O. Box 49, Valletta.

**Lehen-Is-Sewwa**: F. 1928. Weekly. Catholic Institute, Floriana.

**Il Mument**: (Maltese). Weekly. National Press, Our Lady of Sorrows St., Pieta.

**In-Nazzjon Taghna**: (Maltese). Daily. National Press, Our Lady of Sorrows St., Pieta.

**Is-Sebh**: (Maltese). Weekly. Freedom Press, Trunk Rd., Marsa.

**It-Torca**: (Maltese). Weekly. Worker's Memorial Bldg. South St., Valletta.

## EDUCATION

Education in Malta is in the hands of a Minister of Education and Culture. Included in the Ministry of Education and Culture are the following: the Education Department, Public Libraries, the National Museums, the National Theatre and The Sports Board.

There is an Advisory Council of Education, with members nominated by the Government and representing interested sectors, whose duties are to study educational matters referred to it by the Minister as well as other matters brought up by members.

The Director of Education who is in charge of the Education Department is aided by three Assistant Directors.

In Malta, there are government schools and private schools. Private Schools cater for about 17 per cent of the total school population at pre-primary, primary and secondary levels. The Government subsidizes private secondary schools, and some private primary schools on a per capita basis.

The government system provides education free of tuition fees at all levels. Books, milk and medical care are also provided free of charge at the Primary, Secondary, Trade and Technical levels.

Education is compulsory for all children between the ages of six and sixteen. Kindergarten education begins at four years. The primary school course lasts six years and begins at age five. At age eleven, or after the completion of full primary school course, students transfer automatically to 'area secondary schools'. In private secondary schools, entry is selective. The normal secondary school course lasts five years. Students can sit for their General Certificate of Education examinations (Oxford or London) at 'Ordinary' level at the end of the five-year course. Students who obtain the necessary 'O' level qualifications can continue their studies in Upper Secondary Schools.

Students who have completed at least three years of general secondary education can apply for admission to trade schools or technical institutes and continue their studies at Craft level. Entry into these schools is by ability and aptitude. Technician courses require higher entry qualifications, and are carried out in technical institutes, The Malta College of Arts, Science and Technology (Polytechnic) caters for higher technical, business and technological courses as well as further and adult education programmes.

The Government also provides evening courses in academic commercial and technical subjects in a number of centres.

## RELIGION

**The Roman Catholic religion is established by law as the religion of the country, but full liberty of conscience and freedom of worship are guaranteed.**

# Islamic Republic of Mauritania

**Capital**—Nouakchott.

**President**—Maître Mokhtar Ould Daddah.

**National Flag**: Gold five-pointed star and crescent in the centre of a green background.

## CONSTITUTION AND GOVERNMENT

MAURITANIA used to be a French colony. It had a government of its own for the first time in 1958 (internal autonomy). Independence was proclaimed on 28 November 1960 (full and complete sovereignty).

It has an elected National Assembly of 50 members and a Government composed of 15 ministers

## AREA AND POPULATION

The total area of the country is 1,030,000 square kilometres. The population in 1974 was 1,290,000. The annual average percentage growth rate of the population for the period 1960–74 was 2·1, and for the period 1965–74 was 2·5. The principal towns are: Nouakchott, Nouadhibou (once Port Etienne), Kaedi, Atar, F'Derik-Zouerate (once Fort H'Ouraud) and Akjoujt.

## CURRENCY AND FINANCE

The monetary unit is the ougiya which is divided into five khoums.

The budget for 1972 balanced at 10,004 million francs CFA.

The GNP at market prices for 1974 was U.S. $millions 380, and the GNP per capita at market prices was U.S. $290. The annual average percentage growth rate of the GNP per capita for the period 1960–74 was 3·8, and for the period 1965–74 was 1·3. [*See the note at the beginning of this section concerning GNP.*]

## PRODUCTION, INDUSTRY AND COMMERCE

Since 1963 when MIFERMA first exported iron ore, the gross national product has doubled and eoports have quntupled. The most important crops are millet, rice, maize. cowpea, dates, etc. Work is in progress for the cultivation of rice, millet and dates as well as experiments with sugar-cane and cotton.

Animal husbandry represents 72 per cent of rural production. There are about two million oxen, eight to ten million sheep and goats, one million camels and 200,000 donkeys and horses.

The rivers and lakes can yield as much as 15,000 tons of fish. In 1970 sea-fishing enabled 20,500 tons of fish to be exported in various forms.

The Akjoujt copper mine and the works for processing copper started operating at the end of 1970. On 1 June 1971 exports of copper concentrates were already equal to 2,000 tons.

In 1969, the total value of exports was 19,563 million CFA francs and imports 11,000 million CFA francs. In 1969 the main imports from France, expressed in French francs, were: sugar (5,600,000); cast iron and steel (7,900,000); pneumatic tyres (5,100,000); cars and lorries (4,400,000); railway plant and equipment, etc. (26,600,000). In 1970 9,200,000 tons of iron ore were sold. The principal buyers of iron are France, Great Britain, Italy and Germany; Japan is rapidly becoming an important buyer. Gum-arabic is essentially bought by France as well as the products from the fishing industries. In the year 1969–70, 7,500 tons of gum-arabic were exported.

## COMMUNICATIONS

There is a tarred road of about 500 km. rom Akjoujt to Ross. There are also about 1,200 km. of improved tracks and 5,000 km. of other tracks. In 1970 there were 8,500 vehicles.

A 675 km. rail line from F'Derik to Nouahbidou was opened in 1963 for the export of iron ore and for the commercial traffic of various products.

There are airports in the principal Mauritanian towns; those at Nouadhibou and Nouakchott can take four-engined jet planes.

Cansado (Nouadhibou) is a port for the ore-ships and Nouadhibou is a trade and fishing port. At Nouakchott the wharf has recently been doubled and a project for a deep-water port is in hand.

## EDUCATION

In 1970, about 28,000 pupils were receiving primary education, 3,500 secondary education and about 250 students were studying in various universities.

# Mexico

## (ESTADOS UNIDOS MEXICANOS)

**Capital**—Mexico City.

**President**—José Lopez Portillo.

**National Flag:** A tricolour pale-wise, green, white, red, the white charged with the national badge: on a prickly pear supported by a wreath of oak and laurel, an eagle holding in its beak a serpent.

### CONSTITUTION AND GOVERNMENT

Mexico is a Federal Republic, whose current Constitution dates from 5 February 1917; but it has been frequently, amended since that date. The Government is headed by the President, who is elected by direct popular vote for a period of six years.

The Congress of the Union, i.e. the legislative branch, consists of the Senate, with 60 members (two for each State, including the Federal District), elected for a period of six years, and the Chamber of Deputies, with 178 members. Deputies are elected on a basis of universal suffrage for a period of three years. There is one member for every 250,000 inhabitants or fraction exceeding 125,000. Members of both houses of Congress cannot be re-elected until a further six-year period has elapsed.

The President appoints the Governor of the Federal District and the Ministers who form part of the President's Cabinet.

There now follows a description of the parts of the Federation and the National Territory including a description of the political structure.

*Article 42* The national territory comprises:
I. That of the component parts of the Federation; II. That of the islands, including the reefs and keys in the adjacent seas; III. That of the Guadalupe and Revillagigedo islands in the Pacific Ocean; IV. The continental shelf and the submarine base of islands, keys and reefs; V. Territorial waters, subject to the extent and terms fixed by international law, and internal waters; and VI. The space above national territory, subject to the extent and conditions laid down by International Law.

N.B. Article 43 of the Political Constitution of the United States of Mexico was amended by Presidential Decree of 7 October 1974 to read as follows:

*Article 43* The component parts of the Federation are the States of: Aguascalientes, Baja California, Baja California Sur, Campeche, Coahuila, Colima, Chiapas, Chihuahua, Durango, Gunanajuato, Guerrero, Hidalgo, Jalisco, México, Michoacán, Morelos, Nayarit, Nuevo León, Oaxaca, Puebla, Querétaro, Quintana Roo, San Luis Potosì, Sinaloa, Sonora, Tabasco, Tamaulipas, Tlaxcala, Veracruz, Yucatán, Zacatecas and the Federal District. N.B. This means that the territories of Quintana Roo and Baja California Sur (Southern Lower California) were raised as from 7 October 1974 to the rank of States.

Source: Official Gazette published on 8 October 1974.

*CHAPTER X* National sovereignty and form of government.

*Article 39* National sovereignty essentially and originally resides in the people. All public power derives from and is instituted for the benefit of the people. The people have at all times the inalienable right to change or modify the form of their Government.

*Article 40* It is the will of the Mexican people to form themselves into a representative, democratic, federal Republic composed of States which are free and sovereign in all matters relating to their internal affairs, but united in a Federation established in accordance with the principles of this fundamental law.

*Article 41* The people exercise their sovereignty through the powers of the Union in those cases within the competence of the latter, and through those of the States in matters regarding their internal affairs, as respectively laid down by this Federal Constitution and the individual Constitutions of the States, which may in no circumstances contravene the provisions of the Pacto Federal (Federal Agreement).

*CHAPTER I* Division of Powers.

*Article 49* The Supreme Power of the Federation is divided into Legislative, Executive and Judicial for purposes of its exercise.

Two or more of such Powers may not be combined in a single person or corporation, nor may the legislative power be vested in an individual except in the case of special powers to the Executive of the Union as laid down in Article 29. In no other case, except as provided for in Article 131 (2), will special legislative powers be granted.

*CHAPTER II* The Legislative Power.

*Article 50* The Legislative Power of the United States of Mexico is vested in a General Congress, to be divided into two Chambers, the Chamber of Deputies and the Senate:

*Section I* Election and installation of Congress.

*Article 51* The Chamber of Deputies shall consist of representatives of the Nation, elected in their totality every three years by Mexican citizens.

*Article 52* One titular deputy shall be elected for every two hundred and fifty thousand inhabitants or fraction exceeding one hundred and twenty-five thousand, taking into account the General Census of the Federal District and that of each State; but in no case shall a State be represented by less than two Deputies.

*Article 54* Deputies shall be elected directly, subject to the provisions of Article 52, and shall be supplemented by party deputies, in both cases in compliance with the provisions of the Electoral Law, and in the second in accordance with the following regulations:

I. Any national political party obtaining one and a half per cent of the total votes in the country in the relevant election of deputies shall be entitled to have five of its candidates accredited as deputies, plus one extra, up to a maximum of twenty-five, for every additional half per cent of votes obtained.

II. If it achieves a majority in twenty-five or more electoral districts, it will not be entitled to have party deputies accredited, but if it is successful in a lesser number, provided it fulfils the requirements set out under (I) above, it will be entitled to have up to twenty-five deputies recognized, totalling those elected by majority vote and on a percentage basis.

III. The party deptuties will be accredited in strict descending order of votes received in comparison with other candidates of the same party throughout the country.

IV. Only national political parties which have secured registration under the Federal Electoral Law at least one year before the date of the election may accredit deputies under the terms of this Article, and

V. Majority and party deputies shall, as representatives of the Nation as laid down in Article 51, have the same standing and equal rights and obligations.

*Article 55* To be a deputy the following conditions must be met:

I. To be a Mexican citizen by birth, in exercise of his rights; II. To be at least twenty-one years of age on the date of the election; III. To be a native of the State in which the election takes place, or have been actually resident therein for more than six months prior to the date of the election. Residence rights are not lost through absence in discharge of public duties by popular election. IV. Not to be on active service in the Federal Army, nor hold office in the police or rural gendarmerie in the district in which the election takes place for at least ninety days beforehand; V. Not to be a Minister or Deputy Minister nor a Magistrate of the Supreme Court of Justice of the Nation unless he resigns such office ninety days before the election. State Governors may not be elected in the entities in their jurisdiction during their term of office even if they resign from their positions. Ministers of State Governments, and Federal or State judges and magistrates may not be elected in the entities in their respective jurisdictions unless they resign from their positions ninety days before the election. VI. Not to be a minister of any religious denomination, and VII. Not to be covered by any of the instances of incapacity specified in Article 59.

*Article 56* The Senate shall consist of two members for each State and two for the Federal District, all of whom shall be elected directly every six years.

The legislature of each State shall declare elected that person who has obtained a majority of the votes cast.

*Article 57* For each titular senator an alternate shall be elected.

*Article 58* To be a senator requires the same conditions as to be a deputy, with the exception of the age qualification, which shall be at least 30 years on the date of the election.

*Article 59* Senators and Deputies to the Congress of the Union shall not be eligible for re-election in the period immediately following. Alternate senators and deputies may be elected for the period immediately following on a titular basis, provided they have not served; but titular senators and deputies may not be elected for the period immediately following as alternates.

*Article 60* Each Chamber shall assess the elections of its members and resolve any doubts relating thereto. Its decision shall be final and unassailable.

*Article 61* Deputies and Senators enjoy immunity as regards any opinions expressed in the exercise of their functions and may in no circumstances be taken to task in this respect.

**Ministry**

*Office of the President of the Republic:* Lic. José Lopez Portillo.
*Ministry of the Interior:* José Reyes Heroles.
*Ministry of Foreign Affairs:* Santiago Roel Garcia.
*Ministry of National Defence:* Gen. Felix Galvan Lopez.
*Ministry of Naval Affairs:* Admiral Ricardo Chazaro Lara.
*Ministry of Finance and Public Credit:* Julio Rodolfo Moctezuma Cid.
*Ministry of Planning and Budgetary Affairs:* Carlos Tello Macias.
*Ministry of the National Heritage and Industrial Development:* José Andres Eteyza Fernandez.
*Ministry of Commerce:* Fernando Solana Morales.
*Ministry of Agriculture and Hydraulic Resources:* Mr. Francisco Merino Rabago.
*Ministry of Communications and Transport:* Emilio Mojica Montoya.
*Ministry of Development and Public Works:* Pedro Ramirez Vazquez.
*Ministry of Education:* Porfirio Muñoz Ledo.
*Ministry of Health and Welfare:* Emilio Martinez Manautou.
*Ministry of Labour and Social Security:* Pedro Ojeda Paullada.
*Ministry of Agrarian Reform:* Jorge Rojo Lugo.
*Ministry of Tourism:* Guillermo Rosell de la Lama.
*Department of Fisheries:* Fernando Rafful Miguel.
*Department of the Federal District, Governor:* Prof. Carlos Hank Gonzalez.

**Congress**

**Upper Chamber (Cámara de Senadores)**
**Under Constitution Amendment of 30 December 1942 the entire Senate is renewed every six years.**

***Speaker:*** **Changes each month except in period of recess.**
***Number of Members:*** **60.**

**Lower Chamber (Cámara de Diputados)**
**Under Constitution Amendment of 30 December 1942, the entire Chamber is completely renewed every six years.**

***Speaker:*** **Changes each month except in period of recess.**
***Number of Members:*** **178.**

## LOCAL GOVERNMENT

**Mexico is divided into 29 states, one federal district (Mexico City and environs) and two territories. Each has the right to manage its own affairs and, besides the federal legislation, has its own constitution, government and laws. The states levy their own taxes, but inter-state customs duties do not exist. Each state has its own governor, legislature, and judicature, elected by popular vote. The President appoints the governors of the territories and of the federal district. In the Federal District the office of Governor is discharged by a Chief of the Central Department which forms part of the Presidential Cabinet.**

| State | Governor: |
|---|---|
| Aguascalientes | Prof. J. Refugio Esparza Reyes |
| Baja California | Lic. Milton Castellanos Everardo |
| Baja California Sur | Lic. Angel César Mendoza Arámburo. |

*continued*

| State | Governor: |
|---|---|
| Campeche | Lic. Rafael Rodríguez Barrera |
| Coahuila | Prof. Oscar Flores Tapia |
| Colima | Lic. Arturo Noriega Pizano |
| Chiapas | Lic. Jorge de la Vega Domínguez |
| Chihuahua | Manuel Bernardo Aguirre |
| Durango | Dr. Héctor Mayagoitia Domínguez |
| Guanajuato | Lic. Luis H. Ducoing |
| Guerrero | Ing. Rubén Figueroa Figueroa |
| Hidalgo | Lic. José Luis Suárez Molina |
| Jalisco | Lic. Flavio Romero de Velasco |
| México | Dr. Jorge Jiménez Cantú |
| Michoacán | Lic. Carlos Torres Manzo |
| Morelos | Dr. Armando L. Bejarano |
| Nayarit | Col. Rogelio Flores Curiel |
| Nuevo León | Dr. Pedro G. Zorrilla Martínez |
| Oaxaca | Gen. Eliseo Jiménez Ruiz |
| Puebla | Dr. Alfredo Toxqui Fernández de Lara |
| Querétaro | Arq. Antonio Calzada Urquiza |
| Quintana Roo | Lic. Jesús Martínez Ross |
| San Luis Potosi | Lic. Guillermo Fonseca Alvarez |
| Sinaloa | Alfonso G. Calderón Velarde |
| Sonora | Sen. Alejandro Carrillo Marcor |
| Tabasco | Ing. Leandro Rovirosa Wade |
| Tamaulipas | Enrique Cárdenas González |
| Tlaxcala | Lic. Emilio Sánchez Piedras |
| Veracruz | Lic. Rafael Hernández Ochoa |
| Yucatán | Dr. Francisco Luna Kan |
| Zacatecas | Maj. Gen. Fernando Pámanes Escobedo |
| Federal District | Prof. Carlos Hank González (Appointed by the Government) |

## LEGAL SYSTEM

**There is a Supreme Court with 21 judges, circuit courts, and district courts.**

Chief Justice and Judges of the Supreme Court of Justice of the Nation.

*Chief Justice:* Lic. Agustín Téllez Cruces.

*Division One,*
*Presiding Judge:* Lic. Antonio Rocha Cordero
Lic. Ernesto Aguilar Alvarez
Lic. Mario S. Rebolledo F.
Lic. Manuel Rivera Silva
Lic. Fernando Castellanos Tena

*Division Two,*
*Presiding Judge:* Lic. José Alfonso Abitia Arzapalo
Lic. Jorge Iñarritu
Lic. Carlos del Río Rodríguez
Lic. Arturo Serrano Robles
Lic. Eduardo Langle Martínez

*Division Three*
*Presiding Judge:* Lic. Salvador Mondragón Guerra
Lic. David Franco Rodríguez
Lic. Raul Lozano Ramírez
Lic. Raul Cuevas Mantecón
Lic. J. Ramón Palacios V.

*Division Four*
*Presiding Judge:* Lic. Julio Sánchez Vargas
Lic. Ramón Cañedo Aldrete
Lic. Juan Moisés Calleja
Lic. María Cristina Salmorán de Tamayo
Lic. Alonso López Aparicio

*Auxiliary Division*
*Presiding Judge:* Lic. Jorge Olivera Toro
Lic. Luis Felipe Canudas Orezza
Lic. Gloria León Orantes
Lic. Anastacio González Martínez
Lic. Francisco Pavón Vazconcelos

# MEXICO

## AREA AND POPULATION

The following table gives the population figures for the parts of the Federation and the population of the State Capitals. These figures are an estimate as at 30 June 1977.

| *Unit* | *Area km²* | *Population* | *State Capital* | *Population* |
|---|---|---|---|---|
| Distrito Federal | 1,499 | 9,233,000 | Distrito Federal | 9,233,000 |
| Aguascalientes | 5,589 | 447,000 | Aguascalientes | 238,000 |
| Baja California Norte | 70,113 | 1,320,000 | Mexicali | 360,000 |
| Baja California Sur | 73,677 | 187,000 | La Paz | 75,000 |
| Campeche | 51,833 | 349,000 | Campeche | 98,000 |
| Chiapas | 73,887 | 1,984,000 | Tuxtla Gutiérrez | 96,000 |
| Chihuahua | 247,087 | 2,062,000 | Chihuahua | 386,000 |
| Coahuila | 151,571 | 1,363,000 | Saltillo | 233,000 |
| Colima | 5,455 | 332,000 | Colima | 73,000 |
| Durango | 119,648 | 1,149,000 | Victoria de Durango | 209,000 |
| Guanajuato | 30,589 | 2,895,000 | Guanajuato | 45,000 |
| Guerrero | 63,794 | 2,074,000 | Chilpancingo de los Bravo | 61,000 |
| Hildalgo | 20,987 | 1,435,000 | Pachuca de Soto | 102,000 |
| Jalisco | 80,137 | 4,294,000 | Guadalajara | 1,725,000 |
| México | 21,461 | 6,684,000 | Toluca de Lerdo | 153,000 |
| Michoacán | 59,864 | 2,872,000 | Morelia | 230,000 |
| Morelos | 4,941 | 905,000 | Cuernavaca | 357,000 |
| Nayarit | 27,621 | 725,000 | Tepic | 126,000 |
| Nuevo León | 64,555 | 3,456,000 | Monterrey | 1,132,000 |
| Oaxaca | 95,364 | 2,377,000 | Oaxaca de Juárez | 126,000 |
| Puebla | 33,919 | 3,133,000 | H. Puebla de Zaragoza | 516,000 |
| Querétaro | 11,769 | 638,000 | Querétaro | 167,000 |
| Quintana Roo | 50,350 | 138,000 | Chetumal | 37,000 |
| San Luis Potosí | 62,848 | 1,560,000 | San Luis Potosí | 303,000 |
| Sinaloa | 58,092 | 1,786,000 | Culiacán Rosales | 281,000 |
| Sonora | 184,934 | 1,468,000 | Hermosillo | 281,000 |
| Tabasco | 24,661 | 1,101,000 | Villahermosa | 162,000 |
| Tamaulipas | 79,829 | 1,968,000 | Ciudad Victoria | 123,000 |
| Tlaxcala | 3,914 | 512,000 | Tlaxcala de Xicothéncatl | 12,000 |
| Veracruz | 72,815 | 5,091,000 | Jalapa de Enríquez | 195,000 |
| Yucatán | 39,340 | 926,000 | Mérida | 250,000 |
| Zacatecas | 75,040 | 1,114,000 | Zacatecas | 71,000 |

The population at mid-1974 was 57,899,000. The annual average percentage growth rate of the population for the period 1960–74 was 3·4 and for the period 1965–74 was 3·5.

## CURRENCY

The unit of currency is the Peso of 100 Centavos. There are silver coins of 5 pesos, 1 peso, 50 cents and 25 cents; copper coins of the value of $0·5, 0·2, 0·1, 0·05, 0·01; and nickel coins of $0·1 and 0·05. There are banknotes for the following amounts: 10,000, 1,000, 500, 100, 50, 20, 10, 5 and 1 pesos. The currency was devalued in April 1954 (from 8·65 pesos to the U.S. $ to 12·50 pesos). The currency circulating on the 31 December 1971 was: notes held by the public (all figures refer to millions of pesos) 19,795·2; Coins held by the public 2,029·2; Current accounts (National Currency) 31,236·0; Total 53,060·4.

## FINANCE

The GNP at market prices for 1974 was U.S. $millions 63,050, and the GNP per capita at market prices was U.S. $1,090. The annual average percentage growth rate of the GNP per capita for the period 1960–74 was 3·3, and for the period 1965–74 was 2·8 [*See the note at the beginning of this section concerning GNP.*]

## PRINCIPAL BANKS

**Banco de México, S.A.** Est. 1925; Sole Bank of Issue or Mexico; 51 per cent of the share capital is owned by the State: Balance Sheet at 31 December 1975 showed assets 151,871·5 millions of pesos; deposits and current accounts 94,329·9 millions of pesos; banknotes in circulation 53,131·4 millions of pesos. *Head Office:* Avenida 5 de Mayo 2, Mexico 1, D.F. 8 Branches and 3 Agencies.

**Banco Nacional de Mexico, S.A.** (Director-General, Augustín F. Legorreta.) Est. 1884; Balance Sheet at 31 December 1974 showed assets 26,826,878,000 pesos; deposits and current accounts 24,544,452,000 pesos. *Head Office:* 44 Avenida Isabel la Católica, Mexico City. 316 Branches in Mexico and Offices in Frankfurt, New York, Los Angeles, Paris, Madrid, Tokyo.

**Banco de Comercio, S.A.** (Director General, Manuel Espinosa Yglesias.) Est. 1932. Total assets at 31 December 1975 U.S. $6,146,400,000. *Head Office:* Bolivar y Venustiano Carranza 44, Mexico City 1, DF. 556 Branch Offices, with offices in Los Angeles, New York, London, Madrid, Tokyo, also affiliated with Lilra Bank Ltd. London.

**Banco de Londres y Mexico, S.A.** (Director-General, Josr Antonio César.) Est. 1864; Balance Sheet at 31 Decembeé 1969 showed assets $3,812,585,823; deposits and current accounts $3,153,411,883. 133 Sub-offices and Branches. *Head Office:* Bolivar y 16 de Septiembre, Mexico City.

**Banco Internacional, S.A.** (Director, Jose V. Altamirano.) Est. 1941; Assets at 30 December 1969, $1,341,193,533; deposit and current accounts, $1,120,144,322. *Head Office:* Paseo de la Reforma No. 156, Mexico, D.F. 37 Branches and a special deposit Agency.

**Banco de Industria y Comercio, S.A.** (Director-General, Aarón Sáenz.) Est. 1932; Balance Sheet at 31 December 1969 showed assets $564,848,535; deposits and current accounts $457,157,250. *Head Office:* Balderas 26, Mexico I, D.F. 15 Branches.

**Banco Comercial Mexicano, S.A.** (Director-General, Felipe Sandoval Hoyer.) Est. 1934; Balance Sheet at 31 December 1969 showed assets $2,974,523,030; deposits and current accounts $2,480,169,783. *Head Office:* Victoria 14, Chihuahua, Chih. 120 Branches.

## PRODUCTION, INDUSTRY AND COMMERCE

**Forestry.** There are 18,639,402 hectares of forest with a great variety of timber of commercial importance, including pine, spruce, cedar, mahogany and rosewood. Chicle gum is harvested and exported for the manufacture of chewing gum.

The following table shows wood production for 1974 and 1975:

*Forestry Production*

| *Product* | *unit* | 1974 | 1975 |
|---|---|---|---|
| Sawn timber (including board for boxes) | $m^3$ | 3,626,850 | 3,438,524 |
| Coniferous | ,, | 3,353,526 | 3,163,452 |
| Non-coniferous | ,, | 273.324 | 275,072 |
| Sleepers (cross-ties) | ,, | 482,288 | 531,012 |
| Plywood and board | $m^2$ | 36,990,424 | 36,506,574 |
| Compressed board | $m^3$ | 93,800 | 23,298 |
| Fibreboard | ,, | 19,660 | 14,937 |
| Charcoal | ,, | 365,749 | 386,751 |
| Wood pulp (mechanical) | tonnes | 58,498 | 50,760 |
| Wood pulp (chemical) | ,, | 303,638 | 313,516 |
| Pulp of other fibres | ,, | 202,736 | 183,881 |
| Pulp of soluble types | ,, | 1,891 | 2,065 |
| Paper and cardboard | ,, | 1,253 688 | 1,136,733 |
| Non-timber | ,, | 109,803 | 111,441 |
| Spirits of turpentine | ,, | 4,489 | 3,297 |
| Almonds | ,, | 494 | 449 |
| Pitch or resin | ,, | 18,470 | 11,989 |
| Vegetable waxes | ,, | 1,427 | 1,905 |
| Chewing gum (chicle) | ,, | 1,401 | 984 |
| Tanning barks | ,, | 250 | 363 |
| Tree tops (cogollos) | ,, | 215 | 504 |
| Ixtle (agave) fibre | ,, | 7,360 | 8,425 |
| Fruit | ,, | 4,818 | 4,105 |
| Gums | ,, | 178 | 124 |
| Herbs | | 150 | 500 |
| Palm leaves (for hats) | ,, | 40 | 23 |
| Palm leaf ribs | ,, | 309 | 829 |
| Roots | ,, | 24 | 20 |
| Leaves | ,, | 3,863 | 3,525 |
| Rhizomes | ,, | 11,420 | 16,450 |
| Turpentine (resin) | ,, | 54,895 | 57,949 |
| Christmas trees | thousands of trees | 2 | 2 |

**Agriculture.** Agriculture is the primary Mexican industry. Mexico is self-sufficient in agricultural products. About 54 per cent of the population work on the land. About 19,109·06 million hectares are under cultivation. Sisal is largely grown in the southern state of Yucatán and is a chief source of wealth in the region.

The following table gives production figures for principal crops in 1975.

| *Crop* | *Cropped area Ha.* | *Production metric tons* |
|---|---|---|
| Coffee | 372,646 | 214,271 |
| Garlic | 6,600 | 32,076 |
| Sesame | 245,000 | 164,150 |
| Green alfalfa | 187,000 | 12,342,000 |
| Cotton (algodón pluma) | 260,000 | 230,000 |
| Bales of 230 kg. each | — | 1,000,000 |
| Cottonseed | — | 367,000 |
| Alpist | 7,600 | 11,400 |
| Unhusked rice | 196,000 | 509,600 |
| Clean rice | — | 336,336 |
| Pea (arvejón) | 4,500 | 2,835 |
| Oats (grain) | 130,000 | 91,000 |
| Oats (fodder) | 32,000 | 352,000 |
| Aubergine | 990 | 19,305 |
| Beet | 220 | 4,097 |
| Groundnut | 47,000 | 65,800 |
| Sweet potato | 11,000 | 121,000 |
| Sugar cane | 476,000 | 36,368,000 |
| Sugar | — | 2,816,016 |
| Safflower | 290,000 | 450,000 |
| Barley (grain) | 250,000 | 362,500 |
| Barley (fodder) | 3,200 | 65,600 |
| Onion | 26,000 | 301,600 |
| Pea (chícharo) | 15,500 | 49,600 |
| Dried chilli | 26,000 | 32,760 |
| Fresh chilli | 60,000 | 429,000 |
| String bean | 10,000 | 29,400 |
| Strawberry | 7,300 | 117,530 |
| Haricot bean | 1,800,000 | 918,000 |
| Edible chickpea | 60,000 | 88,800 |
| Fodder chickpea | 195,000 | 173,550 |
| Sunflower | 8,000 | 5,600 |
| Broad bean | 56,000 | 34,720 |
| Castor oil plant | 10,000 | 3,000 |
| Jícama (various tubercular plants) | 4,500 | 45,000 |
| Lentils | 7,800 | 6,630 |
| Linseed | 8,500 | 12,750 |
| Maize | 7,500,000 | 9,375,000 |
| Melon | 18,500 | 223,850 |
| Potato | 56,000 | 660,000 |
| Cucumber | 10,500 | 135,450 |
| Pineapple | 7,000 | 261,800 |
| Fodder beet | 3,800 | 99,180 |
| Watermelon | 30,000 | 351,000 |
| Brown millet | 15,500 | 37,975 |
| Sorghum (fodder) | 20,800 | 1,248,000 |
| Sorghum (grain) | 1,100,000 | 2,805,000 |
| Soya | 320,000 | 604,800 |
| Leaf tobacco | 44,000 | 70,400 |
| Tomato (red) | 70,000 | 1,127,000 |
| Tomato (green) | 11,000 | 80,850 |
| Wheat | 750,000 | 2,700,000 |
| Processed vanilla | 1,300 | 47 |
| Total | 14,399,610 | — |

Mexico is a large grower of vegetable fibres for rope making, cords, string, etc., and produces about half the world's supply of fibres for harvester twine.

**Oil and Natural Gas**

In 1974 production of natural gas amounted to 21,089 million cubic metres, and in 1975 to 22,273 million cubic metres.

Production of crude (oil and condensate) for 1974 was 238,271 thousand barrels, and for 1975 294,254 thousand barrels, including condensed crude and liquid absorption oil. In 1974 the number of development wells totalled 30,965 being unproductive and 244 productive. The total for 1975 was 26,654 being unproductive and 212 productive.

**Mining.** The following table shows mineral and metallurgical production for 1975:

*Precious metals*

Gold 4,501 kg.
Silver 1,182,822 kg.

| *Non-ferrous industrial metals* | *metric tons* |
|---|---|
| Antimony | 3,137 |
| Arsenic | 4,636 |
| Bismuth | 445 |
| Cadmium | 1,581 |
| Copper | 78,196 |
| Tin | 378 |
| Mercury | 490 |
| Lead | 178,615 |
| Tungsten | 277 |
| Zinc | 228,851 |
| *Metals and minerals for the steel industry* | |
| Coal | 176,839 |
| Coke | 2,088,004 |
| Iron | 3,369,258 |
| Manganese | 154,245 |

**Industry**

The following table shows values of principal industrial products for 1975:

| *Activity* | *Value of production Thousands of pesos* |
|---|---|
| Milling of wheat | 5,024,748 |
| Manufacture of oils, margarines and vegetable fats | 8,787,383 |
| Manufacture of animal feeds | 5,657,889 |
| Manufacture of beer | 10,232,323 |
| Manufacture of cigarettes | 5,154,827 |
| Manufacture of cellulose and paper pulps | 8,039,442 |
| Manufacture of tyres and tubes | 4,606,950 |
| Manufacture of cellulose fibres and other artificial fibres | 7,221,580 |
| Manufacture of fertilizers | 4,126,650 |
| Manufacture of soaps, detergents and other washing and cleaning products | 5,905,230 |
| Manufacture of hydraulic cement | 4,835,174 |
| Casting and primary rolling of iron and steel | 11,386,004 |
| Secondary rolling of iron and steel | 16,275,661 |
| Smelting, refining, rolling, extrusion and drawing of copper and alloys | 4,053,440 |
| Manufacture and assembly of motor vehicles, including automotive tractors for trailers | 24,203,274 |

**Commerce.** The following table shows the total imports and exports to and from principal countries for the year 1976 (in thousand pesos):

| | *(Preliminary figures) Thousands of pesos* |
|---|---|
| *Imports* | |
| West Germany (Federal Republic) | 6,426,078 |
| Dutch West Indies | 1,769,914 |
| Brazil | 1,813,467 |
| Canada | 2,057,000 |
| United States | 56,774,187 |
| France | 2,754,381 |
| Italy | 1,426,767 |
| U.K. | 2,741,488 |
| Sweden | 1,264,208 |
| Switzerland | 1,313,767 |
| Japan | 4,783,457 |
| *Exports* | |
| West Germany (Federal Republic) | 1,279,421 |
| Brazil | 2,640,827 |
| United States | 28,782,059 |
| Israel | 1,124,362 |
| Japan | 1,580,138 |
| Venezuela | 935,719 |
| Belgium–Luxembourg | 737,172 |
| Dutch West Indies | 619,614 |
| Italy | 605,023 |

The following table gives the value of exports or classified dutiable goods for 1976:

| *Commodity* | *Thousands of pesos* |
|---|---|
| Live cattle | 506,700 |
| Fresh or chilled tomato | 738,428 |
| Fresh fruit | 562,522 |
| Fresh, chilled or frozen shrimp | 1,622,402 |
| Raw coffee (beans) | 5,208,244 |
| Uncarded, uncombed cotton | 1,575,286 |
| Crude petroleum oils (or crude petroleum) | 8,396,514 |
| Sulphur | 750,156 |
| Fluorspar or fluorite | 587,737 |
| Vegetable or fruit preparations | 453,157 |
| Cinematographic or photographic film or plate, sensitized, but not printed | 451,285 |

*continued*

| *Commodity* | *Thousands of pesos* |
|---|---|
| Wood, cork, wicker, liana, and manufactured products | 493,147 |
| Cotton yarn | 425,991 |
| Cotton fabric | 703,178 |
| Henequen (sisal) products | 566,269 |
| Glass and glass products | 572,633 |
| Iron or steel pipe | 503,146 |
| Springs and iron or steel leaves | 403,341 |
| Refined zinc | 1,247,404 |
| Other metals and their products | 841,016 |
| Mechanically, electrically or electronically operated machinery and apparatus, and parts | 3,116,319 |
| Structures and parts for transport vehicles | 535,649 |
| Other manufactured products | 1,301,746 |

**The following table gives the value of principal imports for 1976.**

| *Commodity* | *Thousands of pesos* |
|---|---|
| Powdered, evaporated and condensed milk | 527,302 |
| Maize | 1,504,849 |
| Products of the book trade and graphic arts | 770,804 |
| Clothing, accessories and other textile products | 654,567 |
| Musical instruments and equipment for recording and reproducing sound or on television | 481,542 |
| Oil seeds and fruits | 2,123,683 |
| Oils and fats (animal and vegetable) | 549,400 |
| Asbestos, phosphates, clays and similar | 951,479 |
| Oil and its derivatives | 4,901,687 |
| Gasoline, except aviation gasoline | 1,011,003 |
| Gas oil or diesel oil | 1,073,606 |
| Fuel oil | 688,361 |
| Petroleum gas and other gaseous hydrocarbons | 1,569,506 |
| Inorganic chemicals | 1,536,618 |
| Organic chemicals | 5,584,109 |
| Fertilizers | 924,505 |
| Photographic or cinematographic products | 562,332 |
| Industrial preparations and mixtures (chemical industry) | 861,823 |
| Plastics and artificial resins | 2,142,143 |
| Natural, synthetic and artificial latex | 757,616 |
| Paper pulp | 868,792 |
| Paper and cardboard, mechanically made, in roll or sheet form | 1,741,544 |
| Aluminium and its products | 816,559 |
| Scrap and waste from iron and steel casting | 634,840 |
| Products of iron and steel casting | 5,258,470 |
| Assembly plant for cars produced in Mexico | 7,406,187 |
| Automobile spares | 1,579,538 |
| Tools, of ordinary metals | 580,649 |
| Machinery, apparatus and appliances (mechanical) | 22,727,082 |
| Machinery, electrical appliances and items for electrical engineering purposes | 7,749,947 |
| Items for railways (including rolling stock and spare parts) | 2,016,329 |
| Wheel or caterpillar tractors and combined units | 1,300,168 |
| Measurement and precision instruments and apparatus | 2,220,600 |

## COMMUNICATIONS

**Roads.** The road network in 1971 covered 77,572 km., 24,103 km. were surfaced and 44,660 km. paved.

**Railways.** 90 per cent of the Mexican railways are now the property of the nation and operated by the Government. There were in 1971 24,129 kilometres of track, with 1,059 locomotives and 28,002 wagons of all kinds. Tramways have about 297 km. of track. Metric tonnage of freight carried by Mexican National Railways in 1971 was 48,399,000 and 33,500,000 passengers were carried.

The following table provides some statistics concerning road transport for 1975:

| | *kilometres* |
|---|---|
| Total length of roads | 324,350 |
| Unsurfaced | 153,677 |
| Surfaced | 111,715 |
| Paved | 58,958 |
| Total vehicles registered | 3,831,707 |
| Cars | 2,669,213 |
| Buses | 49,264 |
| Trucks | 874,758 |
| Motorcycles | 238,472 |

The following table provides some figures for the railways for 1975:

| | |
|---|---|
| Length of railways (1975) | 24,985 km. |
| Passengers carried | 4,749 thousand |
| Passenger–kilometres | 4,198,419 thousand |
| Income from passengers | 311·15 million pesos |
| Freight carried | 61,569 thousand tons |
| Income from freight | 4,569,616 thousand pesos |

The following table gives the value of principal imports for 1976:

**Shipping.** The following table gives some figures for maritime freight loaded and unloaded per type of traffic for 1975:

| | | |
|---|---|---|
| Loaded | 33,932 | thousand tons |
| Deep sea | 13,981 | ,, |
| Coastal | 19,951 | ,, |
| Unloaded | 29,250 | ,, |
| Deep sea | 9,299 | ,, |
| Coastal | 19,951 | ,, |

**Civil Aviation.** The following table gives some statistics for air transport for 1975:

| | | |
|---|---|---|
| Mexican carriers. Flights | 204 | thousand |
| Passengers | 7,305 | ,, |
| Mail carried, including air postal parcels | 3,628 | tons |
| Foreign carriers. Flights | 32 | thousand |
| Passengers | 2,330 | ,, |
| Mail | 2,588 | tons |

**AEROMEXICO, Aeronaves de Mexico, S.A.** (Director General, Ing. Raymundo Cane Pereira); share capital M.$225,600,000; *services operated:* internal Mexico and to Philadelphia, Houston, Los Angeles, Miami, New York, Phoenix Tucson, Toronto, Canada, Panamá, Caracas, Madrid, Paris. *Head Office:* Boulevard Aeropuerto Central 161, Mexico 9, D.F.

**Posts, Telegraphs and Telephones.** The following table gives some figures concerning the telephone system for 1975:

| | |
|---|---|
| Telephone companies (number of) | 111 |
| Public | 16 |
| Private | 95 |
| Instruments in service | 2,796,366 |
| In public concerns | 2,782,260 |
| In private ,, | 14,106 |

**Broadcasting.** In 1975 there was a total of 711 radio stations of which 29 were government owned.

## NEWSPAPERS

**Ovaciones.** F. 1947. Morning circulation 178,300. Evening circulation 159,600. Lago Zirahuén 279, D.F.

**Esto.** F. 1941. Morning. Circulation 246,800. Guillermo Prieto 7, D.F.

**El Universal.** F. 1916. Morning. Independent. Circulation 139,242. Bucareli 8, D.F.

**Excelsior.** F. 1917. Morning. Independent. Circulation 149,572. Reforma 18, D.F.

**El Sol de Mexico.** F. 1965. Mid-day except Sundays, circulation 145,000. Morning circulation 157,000. 7 Guillermo Prieto, D.F.

**Novedades.** F. 1936. Morning. Circulation 140,773. Balderas y Morelos, D.F.

**La Prensa.** F. 1928. Morning. Circulation 185,361. 40 Basilio Badillo 40, D.F.

**El Heraldo de Mexico.** F. 1965. Morning. Circulation 161,768. Dr. Carmona y Valle 150, D.F.

## ATOMIC ENERGY

On 19 December 1955 the President of the Republic, Adolfo Ruiz Cortínes, issued the Law setting up the National Nuclear Energy Commission, as an organ of the Federal Government, in accordance with the Decree issued by the Congress of the United States of Mexico.

For the purposes of this law the following are atomic materials included in the National Mineral Reserves: uranium, thorium and in general any element from which energy can be obtained, by means of nuclear reactions, in large quantities, in the Commission's judgment.

The objectives of the Commission are: 1. The control, monitoring, co-ordination, development and undertaking of: exploration for and exploitation of deposits of atomic materials and others of specific use for the construction of atomic materials and others of specific use for the construction of atomic reactors; the possession of atomic materials; the export and import of such materials, with the specific authorization of the President of the Republic; the import and export of plant to harness nuclear energy; internal transport and trade in such items; the production and use of nuclear energy, primarily to meet national needs; scientific research in the field of nuclear physics and related scientific disciplines and techniques. 2. To advise the Government on legislation and on all matters related to this subject on which it may be consulted.

## EDUCATION

The following table gives some educational statistics for the year 1975–76:

| | Number of: | | |
|---|---|---|---|
| | *Schools* | *Teachers* | *Pupils* |
| Education prior to first grade | 4,156 | 14,073 | 537,090 |
| First grade | 55,618 | 255,939 | 11,461,415 |
| Second grade | 7,943 | 141,930 | 2,506,014 |
| General secondary | 6,798 | 110,921 | 1,898,053 |
| Bachillerato (school-leaving examination) | 1,145 | 30,809 | 60,791 |
| Other second-grade schooling | 2,329 | 19,655 | 321,456 |
| Second grade Normal schooling | 296 | 8,396 | 111,502 |
| Third grade | 503 | 45,025 | 501,250 |
| Higher Normal schooling | 26 | 2,394 | 41,139 |
| Specialised Normal schooling | 2 | 110 | 723 |

Primary education is free and compulsory. All official schools, private and co-educational, come under the control of the Secretary of Public Education.

## RELIGION

The predominant religion is the Roman Catholic (96 per cent of the population), but there is no state religion and there is freedom of worship for all denominations.

In 1970 the numbers of the various religions were as follows: Catholics 46,380,401; Protestants 876,879; Jews 49,181; Others 150,329; None 768,448.

# Monaco

## (PRINCIPAUTÉ DE MONACO)

**Capital**—Monaco-Ville.

**Sovereign**—Prince Rainier III.

**National Flag**: Divided fesse-wise, red and white.

### CONSTITUTION AND GOVERNMENT

MONACO is a small Principality situated on the shores of the Mediterranean and extending inland to the slopes of the Alpes-Maritimes. The total area is 168 hectares, or 415 acres. The population (Census 1971) was 23,285.

Its excellent position, sunny and sheltered from the winds, has attracted a settled population from ancient times. Used successively by the Phoenicians, the Phocaeans and the Romans, the port of Monaco was ceded in 1191 by the Emperor Henry VI to the Republic of Genoa, which established a fortress in 1215 on the headland commanding the entrance to the bay.

Towards the end of the 13th century the Grimaldi family (one of the most ancient families of Genoa, who governed as representatives of the Guelph party) were driven out of the town by a Ghibelline rising. On 8 January 1297 François Grimaldi, at the head of a troop of partisans, made himself master of the fortress and founded a dynasty, that of the family now reigning.

The principality of Monaco presents the peculiarity of being a territory hardly the size of a large town, which yet possesses all the institutions and machinery of a state. Its independence, recognized for many centuries, is assured today by a series of pacts with the principal Powers, and confirmed by the exchange of diplomatic and consular representatives. Among these pacts is the Convention signed on 10 April 1912 with France, establishing a customs union between the two states, and the treaty of goodwill of 17 July 1918, which settled the political relations of the two countries and which was amended by The Treaty of 18 May 1963.

The government of the Principality is carried on under the supreme authority of the Prince by a Minister of State, assisted by three State Counsellors. A Consultative Assembly, the Council of State, prepares laws and ordinances. Legislative power is exercised by the Prince and the National Council of 18 members, elected for four years by direct universal suffrage. Laws are promulgated by the Prince.

The State is divided into four sections: Monte Carlo, the Condamine, Monaco-Ville (the seat of the Government) and Fontvieille, the new industrial area.

The tourist trade, which is growing each year, particularly in summer, contributes largely to the economy of the Principality. A fairly intensive building programme has been undertaken since the war, and the residential population is increasing, attracted by the privileged financial position of the Principality, there being, except for French subjects, no Income Tax nor any Death Duties in direct line. There has also been a notable increase in the last few years in the number of foreign enterprises erecting factories in the Principality.

The Monte-Carlo Winter Season enjoys a world-wide reputation for the operas, plays, ballets and concerts which are given in the Monte-Carlo Opera House, built by Garnier on the model of the Paris Opera.

The Principality is being chosen more and more by a number of professions from overseas as the seat of their annual conferences.

The Port of Monaco, about 1,600 square metres in size, is principally a yachting harbour, but warships and submarines of various nationalities use it as a port of call.

The International Hydrographic Bureau, an independent organization formed by members of 33 States, co-ordinates the researches and activities of hydrographic services throughout the world.

### CURRENCY AND FINANCE

The Principality is served by a number of world-wide known banking institutions: Banca Commerciale Italiana (France); Banco di Roma (France); Barclays Bank S.A.; Credit Foncier de Monaco; Credit Lyonnais; Lloyds Bank Europe Ltd.; Société Marseillaise de Credit; Banque de Financement Industriel, Société Financière Monégasque, Société Financière Monégasque, Banque de l'Union Parisienne, Société de Banque et d'Investissements, Société Generale, Bank Nationale de Paris, American Express International Banking Corporation, Banque de Paris et des Pays-Bas.

The Princes of Monaco possess the right to coin money; coins of 1, 2, 5, 10, 20, 50 and 100 francs have recently been issued by the Princely Treasury. By an order of 2 January 1925 it is decreed that the currency of the French State and the notes of the Banque de France, together with the national currency, are the only legal tender in the Principality.

Budget figures for 1975 were: Revenue, 426,604,080 francs; Expenditure, 385,893,557.

# Mongolian People's Republic

(BÜGD NAIRAMDAH MONGOL ARD ULS)

**Capital**—Ulaanbaatar.

**Head of State**—Yu. Tsedenbal.

**National Flag**: A tricolour pale-wise, red, blue, red, with the red nearest the hoist charged with a mystical symbol (*soyombo*) under a star five-pointed all gold.

## CONSTITUTION AND GOVERNMENT

MONGOLIA first emerged as a state in the form of the Mongol empire founded by Genghis (Chingis) Khan (died 1227). After the fall of the Yüan or Mongol dynasty in China in 1368, Mongolia became the scene of civil wars for some 200 years. By 1636 the princes of Inner Mongolia had surrendered to the rising Manchu power, and in 1691 the nobility of Outer Mongolia also submitted.

The collapse of the Manchus in 1911 enabled the Mongol nobility to declare Mongolia a monarchy independent of China. They failed, however, to gain control of Inner Mongolia. In the confused years after the Russian revolution of 1917 Mongolia was re-occupied first by the Chinese and then by White Russian forces. A provisional revolutionary government was established in March 1921. The monarchy was restored, but in 1924 Mongolia was constituted a People's Republic.

Mongolia was neutral in the war against Germany, and declared war on Japan only on 10 August 1945. China recognized Mongolia's independence on 5 January 1946. In October 1948 Mongolia, till then in diplomatic relations only with the USSR, established relations with N. Korea, and subsequently with all the socialist countries, and with many others. Mongolia was admitted to the United Nations in October 1961. Diplomatic recognition was exchanged with the United Kingdom in January 1963, and embassies were established in Ulaanbaatar in 1965 and in London in 1969.

According to the Constitution of 1960 the supreme organ of state power is the People's Great Assembly (*Ardyn Ih Hural*). When this is not in session its functions pass to its Presidium. The Assembly is elected by universal direct suffrage every four years. It is the sole legislative body. It may add to or change the provisions of the constitution, and confirms other laws. It confirms annual plans for the national economy, and approves the budget and its implementation. It elects its presidium from its own members and has the power of appointing the members of the Council of Ministers and members of the Supreme Court and of appointing the State Procurator.

Among the powers of the Presidium are: all powers connected with the organization and work of the Assembly, including the convening of regular and irregular meetings and the calling of elections; all powers concerned with national defence and foreign relations, including the declaration of war when the Assembly is not in session.

The Council of Ministers is the supreme executive authority, responsible to the Assembly or to the Presidium. It consists of a Chairman, Vice-Chairmen, Ministers, and certain other senior officials.

**The Great People's Assembly:**

*Chairman:* N. Luvsanchültem.
*Vice-chairmen:* B. Shirendev, J. Lhagvasüren, N. Tsedenpil, M. Ahan.

**Presidium of the Assembly:**

*Chairman:* Yu. Tsedenbal.
*Vice-chairmen:* S. Jalan-Aajav, N. Luvsanravdan.
*Secretary:* Ts. Gotov.
*Members:* S. Bataa, G. Ochirbat, L. Tüdev, S. Udval, B. Lamjav.

**Parliamentary Group of the Assembly:**

*Chairman of the Executive Committee:* D. Tsevegmid.
*Vice-chairmen.* J. Avhia, Ts. Namsrai.
*Secretary:* D. Tsolmon.

**Council of Ministers:**

*Chairman:* J. Batmönh.

*First Vice-chairman and Chairman of the State Committee for Science and Technology:* D. Maidar.
*First Vice-chairman:* T. Ragchaa.
*Vice-chairman and Chairman of Building and Architecture Commission:* S. Luvsangombo.
*Vice-chairman and Chairman of the State Committee for Higher, Special Secondary, Technical and Vocational Education:* D. Tsevegmid.
*Vice-chairman and Chairman of the State Planning Commission:* D. Sodnom.
*Vice-Chairman:* Ch. Süren.
*Vice-Chairman and Chairman of the Commission for the Affairs of the Council for Mutual Economic Assistance (Comecon):* M. Peljee.
*Minister of Agriculture:* L. Rinchin.
*Minister of Fuel and Power:* P. Ochirbat.
*Minister of Geology and Mining:* Ch. Hurts.
*Minister of Light and Food Industries:* P. Damdin.
*Minister of Building and Building Materials:* O. Tleihan.
*Minister of Forests and Wood Industry:* D. Tseden.
*Minister of Transport:* B. Enebish.
*Minister of Water Economy:* B. Bars.
*Minister of Communications:* D. Gotov.
*Minister of Trade and Procurement:* D. Dorjgotov.
*Minister of Foreign Trade:* Yo. Ochir.
*Minister of Finance:* Ts. Molom.
*Minister of Foreign Affairs:* M. Dügersüren.
*Minister of Defence:* Army General B. Dorj.
*Minister of Public Security:* Lt. Gen. B. Dejid.
*Minister of Popular Education:* D. Ishtseren.
*Minister of Health:* D. Nyam-osor.
*Minister of Public Economy and Services:* O. Nyamaa.
*Minister of Justice:* D. Pürev.
*Minister of Culture:* S. Sosorbaram.
*Chairman of the People's Control Committee of the MPR:* L. Damdinjav.
*Chairman of the Central Statistical Directorate:* D. Dzagasbaldan.
*Chairman of the Board of the State Bank:* D. Danzan.
*President of the Academy of Sciences of the MPR:* B. Shirendev.
*Chairman of the State Committee for Labour and Wages:* M. Lhamsüren.
*Chairman of the State Committee for Information, Radio and Television:* S. Pürevjav.
*Chairman of the State Committee for Prices and Standards:* D. Byambasüren.
*Chairman of the Administration Office of the Council of Ministers:* B. Badarch.
*First Vice-chairman of the State Planning Commission with Ministerial Rank and Chairman of the State Material and Machinery Supply Committee:* B. Rinchinpeljee.
*First Vice-chairman of the State Planning Commission with Ministerial Rank and chairman of the State Committee for Foreign Economic Relations:* D. Saldan.

Other concurrent appointments held by ministers are:
*Chairman of the Supreme Council of the Union of Agricultural Co-operatives:* L. Rinchin.
*Chairmen of the Mongol sections of Intergovernmental Commissions for Economic, Scientific and Technical Cooperation:*
*Mongol-Soviet Commission:* D. Maidar.
*Mongol-Bulgarian Commission:* S. Luvsangombo.
*Mongol-GDR Commission:* D. Gombojav.
*Mongol-Hungarian and Mongol Polish Commissions:* T. Ragchaa.

### Central and Local Representation

The most recent elections for the Great People's Assembly were held in June 1977. 354 deputies (1973–336) were elected, of whom 84 represented Ulaanbaatar constituencies. 694,855 persons were entitled to vote for candidates on an official list of party and non-party candidates. 694,828 persons or 99·99 per cent of those who cast their votes did so for the official candidates.

Below national level deputies are elected by the same voters to local Assemblies of People's Deputies. The most recent elections were held in June 1975, when 14,415 deputies were elected to the following series of assemblies:

18 provincial (*aimag*) and 2 city (Ulaanbaatar and Darhan) assemblies: 1,981 deputies.

Raion (Ulaanbaatar city districts) assemblies: 422.
Provincial districts (*sum*): 9,646.

**Provincial towns: 1,513.**
**Town districts (*horoo*): 853.**

Local assemblies of people's deputies elect permanent commissions which are responsible for the implementation of national policies in specified sectors, for example social services, transport, finance, culture. An executive authority chosen by each local assembly from its members is responsible to the assembly for the implementation of its policies.

Local Assemblies are elected every three years.

**The Mongol People's Revolutionary Party**

The MPR is a single party state, whose policies are determined by the MPRP (founded as the Mongol People's Party. June 1920. First Party Congress March 1921. Renamed 1925.) At the time of the 17th Party Congress (June 1976), there were 66,933 full and candidate members.

The Central Committee of the Party consists of 91 full and 61 candidate members, elected by the plenary meeting of the Party. The Central Committee in turn elects its Political Bureau:

*Member of the Political Bureau and First Secretary of the Central Committee:* Yu. Tsedenbal.
*Members of the Political Bureau and Secretaries of the Central Committee:* N. Jagvaral, S. Jalan-aajav, D. Molomjamts.
*Members of the Political Bureau:* J. Batmönh, N. Luvsanravdan, D. Maidar, T. Ragchaa.
*Candidate Member of the Political Bureau and Secretary of the Central Committee:* D. Gombojav.
*Candidate Member of the Political Bureau:* B. Altangerel.
*Secretary of the Central Committee:* S. Sosorbaram.

The work of the Party is supervised by the Party Control Committee (*Chairman:* N. Luvsanravdan) and the Central Inspection Commission (*Chairman:* O. Nyamaa).

Below national level there are provincial (*aimag*) and town party committees and below this level, in provincial districts (*sum*), rural collectives, state farms, factories, offices, schools, etc., party committees, or party cells where the size of membership does not justify a committee. Where the number of party members does not justify the establishment of a cell, a section (*heseg*) may be established provided there are not less than three members.

Party discipline is laid down in the Party Rules revised most recently by the 16th Party Congress of 1971. Normally, a plenary congress of the Party should meet once every five years. More frequent meetings are prescribed for subordinate organs.

The Mongolian League of Revolutionary Youth has 140,000 members (August 1975) aged between 15 and 28.
*First Secretary of the Central Committee:* L. Tüdev.

**The Mongol People's Army:**

*Chief of the General Staff and First Vice-Minister of Defence:* Major General Ch. Pürevdorj.
*Head of the Political Directorate:* Lt. General D. Yondondüichir.
*First Deputy Head of the Political Directorate:* Major General S. Gombosüren.
*Head of the General Directorate of Construction Troops:* Major General D. Bavuu.
*First Vice-minister of Defence and Head of Civil Defence Directorate:* Major-General Ch. Tümendemberel.

Other appointments held by military officers:

*First Vice-minister of Defence and Chairman of the Society of Veterans of the Revolutionary Struggle:* Colonel General B. Tsog.
*Chairman of the Society for the Defence of the State:* Lieutenant-General J. Jamyan.
*Head of the General Directorate of Civil Air Transport:* Major General S. Shanjmyatav.
*Vice-minister of Public Security, Head of Directorate of Border and Internal Troops:* Major General Sh. Arvay.
*Head of Political Directorate of Border and Internal Troops:* Major General Sh. Dorj.

## LEGAL SYSTEM

Justice is administered by the Supreme Court, the Ulaanbaatar City Court, 18 provincial courts and local (*sum*) courts.
*Chairman of the Supreme Court:* R. Günsen.
*State Procurator:* J. Avhia.
*Minister of Justice:* D. Pürev.
*Minister of Public Security:* Lieutenant General B. Dejid.
*First Vice-minister of Public Security, Head of State Security Directorate:* P. Dechin.
*First Vice-minister of Public Security, Head of Militia Directorate:* Major General S. Büdragchaa.

## AREA AND POPULATION

Mongolia has an area of 1,564,660 sq. km. The population on 1 January 1977 was 1,511,900. One quarter of the population is estimated to live in Ulaanbaatar. There is a clear movement of population from rural areas to the towns, which now contain about 47·5 per cent of the total population. Some 250,000 people, or 22 per cent of the total population, also live in permanent quarters in the rural areas. In 1975 the birth rate was 39·4 per 1,000 and the death rate 10·0 per 1,000. Projections of population trends show a steady rise to a figure of between 4 and 4·8 million in 2,025. In 1969 Mongols formed approximately 87 per cent of the population, with 901,200 Halh Mongols forming 75·3 per cent of the total. Kazakhs, with 5·2 per cent, are the largest minority group. Russians and Chinese form very small groups.

## FINANCE

The national unit of currency is the *tögrög* which is divided into 100 *möngö*. The State Bank was founded in 1924.

The State Budget is as follows (million *tögrög*):

| | 1977 (*est.*) |
|---|---|
| Revenue | 3,312·0 |
| Expenditure | 3,300·0 |

## PLANNING, PRODUCTION AND COMMERCE

**Planning.** The fifth five-year plan expired at the end of 1975 and the sixth plan, published in April 1976, was approved by the Central Committee of the MPRP in June. The fifth plan is said to have achieved its overall objectives, though individual ministries, *aimags*, towns and enterprises were criticised for shortcomings. The sixth five-year plan covers a period, 1976–1980, which is described as critical for building the material and technical base for socialism and for further refining socialist social relations. The basic aims are to increase the social product, to raise profitability, to improve the quality of production, and to enhance the standard of living and the level of culture of the population.

In the rural economy a modest rise of about 7 to 9 per cent in the total number of livestock is proposed, and attention will be paid to promoting the raising of pigs, poultry and bees. Food production is expected to rise: meat by 20 to 24 percent, milk by 26 to 30 per cent, eggs 2·5 to 3 fold. Some 12 million hectares of land are to be provided with water and turned into pastureland, bringing the total area to 65 million hectares. Five state farms specializing in animal husbandry are to be established. Annual fodder production is to reach 850,000 to 870,000 tons, and further steps are to be taken to improve the emergency supply system. However, the main developmental effort will apparently be concentrated on a new virgin lands programme, under which 230,000 hectares of land will be brought under cultivation. (At present some 724,000 hectares have been brought under cultivation, of which 538,000 were sown in 1976). Eleven new state farms will be built, five of them entirely with Soviet money and labour and six with Mongol labour and Soviet assistance. All will be provided with Soviet equipment. The intention is to raise production to the following figures:

| | | |
|---|---|---|
| Grain: | 500,000 to 530,000 tons | (1975 average, 410,000 tons) |
| (Wheat: | 380,000 to 400,000 tons) | |
| Potatoes: | 60,000 to 65,000 tons. | |
| Vegetables: | 40,000 to 45,000 tons. | |
| Silage crops: | 140,000 to 146,000 tons. | |

Industrial production is expected to rise by up to 65 per cent. Labour productivity will rise by up to 38 per cent. These rises are to be achieved partly by further mechanization, by reducing time lost and by tightening up labour discipline. The fuel and power industry is to grow at a greater rate than other sectors. The third Ulaanbaatar power station and the Choibalsan city power station are to be enlarged, and a new big thermal power station is to be built in the central economic region. The country's central power network is to be connected with the USSR. Power generation is to rise to 1,440 million kwt/hrs by 1980. Coal production is to rise from 2·9 million tons in 1975 to 4·5 to

4·9 million tons by 1980. Existing mines at Nalaih, Sharyn gol, Aduunchuluun and Bayanteeg will be enlarged, and by 1979 a new coalfield at Baga nuur in the central economic region, capable of yielding 2 million tons a year, will come into production. Great attention will be devoted to mining of all sorts of minerals. Geological prospecting will be doubled, with the participation of experts from COMECON countries and mining production will increase six fold by 1980. The copper and molybdenum deposits now being developed jointly with the USSR at Erdenet ovoo, and described as among the ten largest such enterprises in the world, will start production in 1979 and will play a large part in the planned rise in Mongolia's exports. Communications will be further developed. In particular the Salhit-Erdenet line, already in operation, will be completed, together with a new line linking Baga nuur with the main system at Maan't.

Radio and television will be developed, with the number of television sets doubling. Regular use of the Soviet "Orbita" satellite system will enable the population to view programmes of social, political and cultural interest from many parts.

Continued attention will be paid to nature conservancy. (In this connection the setting up in late 1975 of the Natural Environment Protection Society should be noted. A thirteen-man praesidium was elected, the composition of which reflects the importance attached to the Society:

*Chairman:* D. Maidar.
*Vice-chairmen:* S. Luvsangombo, B. Shirendev.
*Secretary:* M. Dash.

Foreign trade turnover is expected to increase by 40 to 45 per cent compared with the period 1971–1975.

**Rural Economy.** Rural production is carried out in 259 co-operatives (*negdel*) and in 47 state farms (*sangiin aj ahui*). The latter include 11 fodder farms (*tejeeliin aj ahui*). There are also a number of research stations. Co-operatives concentrate on herding, while state farms are concerned primarily with crop cultivation, but this division is not absolute. Crop farming on some scale or other is in fact now practised in 80 per cent of agricultural enterprises.

The typical *negdel* consists of a number of brigades (*brigad*), each of which in turn usually consists of a number of camps (*suur'*) or sections (*heseg*). A camp is generally made up of a small number of households, the head of one of them acting as leader (*ahlagch*). *Negdel* and *sum* (county) are generally coextensive. Both *sum*-centre and brigade-centre consist of a core of permanent buildings used for offices, shops, school, clubs, Party-centre, hotel, etc., with the population living mostly in felt tents (*ger*). However, considerable efforts are being devoted to the erection of more fixed buildings in the countryside. One of a *negdel's* brigades may be concerned with craft production. Thus in 1973, out of a total of 870 brigades, 236 were concerned with crop-growing or auxiliary crafts. Members of co-operatives may retain animals up to a fixed maximum for their private support, all others being common property. Wages are paid in cash on a labour-day unit system. On average (1975) each *negdel* has 452,000 hectares of pastureland, 68,900 head of livestock, 27 tractors (in terms of units of 15 h.p.) and 13 vehicles. The average state farm has 9,500 hectares of arable land, 31,800 head of livestock, 220 tractors (units of 15 h.p.), 45 combines and 33 vehicles.

Livestock shelters and wells are of great importance in the rural economy, and during the period of the fifth five-year plan 16,600 shelters and 7,000 water points were put into operation. However, misuse and failure to carry out repairs mean that at any one time a considerable number of shelters and wells is unusable. Thus in late 1974 it was estimated that 12·9 per cent of all wells were not in operation.

The following table shows the number of livestock holdings in 1972 and 1975:

| *Livestock holdings* | 1972 | 1975 |
|---|---|---|
| Camels | 625,100 | 617,100 |
| Horses | 2,239,300 | 2,254,600 |
| Cattle | 2,189,400 | 2,427,000 |
| Sheep | 13,716,900 | 14,458,100 |
| Goats | 4,338,400 | 4,594,700 |
| Total | 23,109,100 | 24,351,500 |

Considerable losses in 1976 and 1977 are believed to have reduced the total to 21,000,000.

| *Livestock shelters* | 1965 | 1970 | 1975 |
|---|---|---|---|
| | 37,700 | 47,100 | 54,100 |

1,940 shelters were built in 1976.

| *Wells* | 1965 | 1970 | 1975 |
|---|---|---|---|
| Shaft wells | 14,000 | 20,000 | 25,200 |
| Bore wells | 700 | 1,400 | 2,900 |
| Total | 14,700 | 21,400 | 28,100 |

1,461 wells were put into use in 1976.

| *Sown area* | 1975 | 1976 | 1977 |
|---|---|---|---|
| | hectares 509,900 | hectares 538,100 | hectares 588,600 |

| *Crop production* | 1970 | 1975 |
|---|---|---|
| *Crop* | *Quantity (thousand tons)* | |
| Grain | 284·8 | 482·4 |
| Wheat | 250·2 | 365·7 |
| Barley | 9·0 | 64·1 |
| Oats | 23·9 | 49·4 |
| Other | 1·7 | 3·2 |
| Potatoes | 20·8 | 40·7 |
| Vegetables | 12·7 | 21·2 |
| Fodder | 34·7 | 164·5 |
| incl. Silage | 6·6 | n.a |

The grain harvest in 1976 amounted to 406,600 tons.

| *Hay* | 1970 | 1972 | 1973 | 1975 | 1976 |
|---|---|---|---|---|---|
| | | *(thousand tons)* | | | |
| | 522·2 | 645·7 | 808·9 | 958·0 | 941·2 |

The following table shows the hunting figures for the years 1965 and 1975:

| *Hunting* *Type of skin* | *Quantity* 1965 | 1975 |
|---|---|---|
| Marmot | 1,208,800 | 939,200 |
| Squirrel | 112,800 | 48,600 |
| Fox | 49,500 | (protected) |
| Corsac (Tartar Fox) | 36,200 | (protected) |
| Wolf | 3,600 | 4,500 |

**Industry.** The following are the figures for industrial production for 1975:

| *Commodity* | *Quantity* | |
|---|---|---|
| Electricity | (mill. kWh.) | 817·8 |
| Coal | (1,000 t.) | 2,719·6 |
| Fluorspar | (1,000 t.) | 290·6 |
| Bricks | (million) | 82·5 |
| Lime | (1,000 t.) | 35·8 |
| Timber | (1,000 cu. m.) | 975·7 |
| Sawn timber | (1,000 cu. m.) | 479·3 |
| Washed wool | (1,000 t.) | 11·6 |
| Felt | (1,000 m.) | 600·0 |
| Felt boots | (1,000 prs.) | 446·4 |
| Hides | (1,000 t.) | 1·1 |

*continued*

| *Commodity* | | *Quantity* |
|---|---|---|
| Skins | (1,000 pieces) | 3,193·3 |
| incl. kid | (1,000 pieces) | 833·3 |
| Leather boots | (1,000 prs.) | 1,780·1 |
| Leather coats | (1,000 pieces) | 58·3 |
| Matches | (million boxes) | 12·7 |
| Woollen textiles | (1,000 m.) | 910·8 |
| Industrial soap | (1,000 t.) | 3·0 |
| Toilet soap | (million bars) | 5·0 |
| Flour | (1,000 t.) | 105·7 |
| Bakery | (1,000 t.) | 38·4 |
| Confectionery | (1,000 t.) | 16·3 |
| Meat | (1,000 t.) | 53·7 |
| Sausages | (tons) | 1,391·7 |
| Fish | (tons) | 204·1 |
| Butter | (1,000 t.) | 3·2 |
| Alcohol | (1,000 litres) | 2,012·2 |
| Vodka | (1,000 litres) | 3,915·8 |
| Beer | (1,000 litres) | 7,206·5 |
| Tent frames | (1,000 sets) | 5·8 |
| Stationery | (mill. printers' sheets) | 274.1 |

The most significant new enterprise in the current five-year plan is the joint Mongol-Soviet copper and molybdenum mining and processing plant being built with massive Soviet hel at Erdenet-ovoo in Bulgan *aimag*, and the associated new town. Erdenet-ovoo already has some 10,000 inhabitants. A high-tension line has been built from Darhan, and a water-supply from the Selenge river, over 60 km. distant, is being laid down. Production and processing-capacity of 16 m. tons of ore a year are being provided for initially.

**Commerce.** In 1975 approximately 99 per cent of trade was with socialist countries, and almost all of this with COMECON.

Foreign trade increased by 13·4 per cent in 1976 compared with 1975.

### COMMUNICATIONS

The following tables show freight carriage and turnover for two years:

| *Freight carriage* | 1970 | 1975 |
|---|---|---|
| | *(in million tons)* | |
| Railway | 4·7 | 6.9 |
| Motor | 9·7 | 13·9 |
| Water | 0·03 | 0·05 |
| Total | 14·4 | 20·9 |

| *Freight turnover* | *(in million ton-km)* | |
|---|---|---|
| Railway | 1,527·6 | 2,150·2 |
| Motor | 623·8 | 952·6 |
| Water | 3·6 | 4·9 |
| Air | 1·5 | 3·0 |

Total freight turnover in the first half of 1977 was 1,756·2 ton-km.

Almost all passenger transport is by motor. In 1975, out of 88,100,000 passengers, 86,700,000 were carried by motor transport.

Ulaanbaatar is connected by rail with the TransSiberian system via Sühbaatar, Naushki and Ulan-Ude. and with the Chinese railways via Zamyn-Üüd. Choybalsan is connected with the TransSiberian system via Ereentsav and Borzya. The Sharyn Gol coalfield is connected by a branch line to the main railway system, and a branch has been built to Erdenet-ovoo.

External air services operate to Moscow and Irkutsk and to Peking. Internal services link Ulaanbaatar with all *aimag* centres, and there are also internal *aimag* services.

**Posts, Telegraphs and Telephones.** In 1975 there were 391 post offices, 211 telephone exchanges and 31,000 telephones.

**Broadcasting.** Radio programmes are carried by broadcast and by relay. Broadcasting began in 1934. Radio sets numbered 124,600 in 1976. A television service for Ulaanbaatar opened in November 1967. In 1976 there were 33,800 television sets.

T.V. ground stations at Ulaanbaatar, Choibalsan and Sainshand receive Soviet programmes from "Molniya" satellites. The station at Ulaanbaatar can transmit Mongolian T.V. to Moscow.

### NEWSPAPERS

There were in 1974, 38 newspapers and 31 magazines. Circulation figures for 1975 were 84,415,900 and 3,872,000 respectively. The main newspaper is *Unen* (Truth), the organ of the Central Committee of the Party and of the Government.

### HEALTH

The following table gives some statistics for the Mongolian Health Service:

| | 1970 | 1972 | 1975 |
|---|---|---|---|
| No. of fully trained doctors | 2,415 | 2,578 | 2,920 |
| (No. of doctors per 10,000 persons | 17·9 | 19·2 | 19·9 |
| No. of hospitals | 112 | 114 | 120 |
| No. of beds | 9,003 | 9,851 | 10,865 |

### EDUCATION

In 1975, 366,700 pupils were attending educational establishments of some sort. The following figures are available:

| | |
|---|---|
| General education day schools: | 320,300 |
| Technical schools: | 15,400 |
| Special technical middle schools: | 15,000 |
| Higher schools: | 16,000 |

In addition, 37,000 children attended 542 kindergartens in 1975.

### RELIGION

Freedom of religious belief and freedom of anti-religious propaganda are guaranteed by the constitution. However, organized religion functions only on a small scale.

# Morocco

## (MAGHREB EL AKSA)

**Capital**—Rabat.

**Sovereign**—H.M. Hassan II.

**National Flag**: Red, charged with a voided star five-pointed green, composed of interlaced triangles.

### CONSTITUTION AND GOVERNMENT

MOROCCO is an independent Arab Kingdom. From 1912 to 1956 it was administered as a French Protectorate in its southern half and as a Spanish Protectorate in the north. Tangier enjoyed a special international status. Morocco regained its independence in March 1956 under its late ruler, Mohammed V, who, on his death in February 1961, was succeeded by his son, the Crown Prince Moulay Hassan, who took the style of King Hassan II. Tangier lost its status as a free money market and free trade zone in 1960.

The late King, Mohammed V, gave an undertaking in 1960 that a Constitution would be enacted by the end of 1962. A Constitutional Council of 78 members was appointed towards the end of 1960, but due to internal differences did not begin work on the Constitution. A 'Basic Law', intended to serve as a temporary Constitution until the promulgation of the permanent one, was enacted in June 1961.

Under the Constitution promulgated on 14 December 1962, Morocco is a constitutional and democratic monarchy in which sovereignty belongs to the nation. The official language is Arabic. The King appoints ministers and promulgates legislation. Parliament consists of a Chamber of Representatives elected for four years by universal suffrage and a Chamber of Counsellors. Two-thirds of the members of the latter chamber are elected by electoral colleges composed of members of local assemblies and councils and the remaining one-third by local Chambers of Agriculture, Commerce and Industry and Handicrafts and representatives of trade unions. Members are elected to the Chamber of Counsellors for six years, half the seats falling vacant every three years.

On 8 June 1965, the king proclaimed a state of emergency and appointed a new cabinet headed by himself. Since then there have been a number of changes. In July 1970, the king proposed a new Constitution to the referendum of the Moroccan people who accepted it by a 98·7 per cent vote. This Constitution brings about several modifications to the 1962 Constitution, notably the creation of a single chamber composed of 240 deputies. Of these deputies 150 are elected by indirect vote through an electoral college representing the town councils, the regional assemblies, the chambers of commerce, industry and agriculture and the trade unions. Their elections were held on the 21 August 1970. On the 28 August 1970 there was a general election when 90 other deputies were chosen. On the 1 March 1971 the King proposed a new constitution to a referendum of the Moroccan people who accepted by a 96 per cent vote. The latest Constitution brings about several modifications to the 1970 Constitution.

#### Cabinet

*Prime Minister:* Ahmed Osman.
*Minister of Foreign Affairs and Cooperation:* Muhammad Boucetta (Istiqlal).
*Minister of Posts and Telecommunications:* Mahjoubi Ahardane (Mouvement Populaire).
*Minister of Cultural Affairs:* Muhammad Bahnini.
*Minister of Interior:* Muhammad Benhima.
*Minister of Justice:* Maati Bouabid.
*Minister of Equipment:* Muhammad Douiri (Istiqlal).
*Minister of Finance:* Abdellatif Ghissassi.
*Minister of Agriculture:* Mustapha Faris.
*Minister of Information:* Larbi Khattabi.
*Minister of Labour:* Muhammad Bouamoud.
*Minister of Administrative Affairs:* Muhammad Benyakhlef.
*Minister for Relations with Parliament:* Haddou Chiguer.
*Minister of Education:* Azzedine Iraki (Istiqlal).
*Minister of Youth and Sport:* Abdelhafid Kadiri (Istiqlal).
*Minister of Urban Affairs and Housing:* Abbes Fassi (Istiqlal).
*Minister of Transport:* Muhammad Nasser (MP).
*Ministsr of Trade and Industry:* Kamel Reghaye.
*Minister of Public Health:* Rahal Rahali (MP).
*Minister of Mines and Energy:* Moussa Saadi.
*Minister of Tourism:* Mansouri (MP).
*Minister of Handicrafts and Social Affairs:* Abdallah Gharnit.

#### Reigning Royal Family

Moslem.—The history of Morocco practically begins in the 8th century, with the introduction of Islam and the establishment of a branch of Mohammed's family, the Idrisis, contemporary with Haroun-al-Raschid. Nine native dynasties have succeeded one another, the present Alaouite having arisen in the 17th century.

### AREA AND POPULATION

The area of Morocco is about 180,000 sq. miles.

The population in mid-1974 was 16,291,000. The annual average percentage growth rate of the population for the period 1960–74 was 2·4 and for the period 1965–74 was 2·4. There are also 145,675 foreigners. This figure includes about 190,000 aliens, of whom 97,000 are French and 50,000 Spaniards.

### CURRENCY AND FINANCE

The Moroccan unit of currency is the Dirham, created on 1 July 1959 and composed of 100 Moroccan centimes. The present rate of exchange is 11·48 DH = £1, and 4·85 DH = U.S. $1. The fiscal year runs from January to December. 1965 revenue was 2,155 million dirhams and expenditure was 2,098 million dirhams.

The GNP at market prices for 1974 was U.S.$ millions 7,070, and the GNP per capita at market prices was U.S.$430. The annual average percentage growth rate of the GNP per capita for the period 1960–74 was 1·8, and for the period 1965–74 was 2·8. [*See the note at the beginning of this section concerning GNP.*]

### BANKS

**Banque Commerciale du Maroc.** (President, Raymond Belin.) Balance Sheet at 31 December 1970 showed assets Dh337,528,310; deposits Dh415,972,346. *Head Office:* 1 rue Idriss Lahrizi, Casablanca.

**Banque du Maroc.** Established 1 July 1959; Bank of Issue. *Head Office:* Rabat, Morocco. 15 Branches.

**Banque Marocaine du Commerce Exterieur,** affiliated to La Banque National de Paris.

**Worms et Cie** (branches at Casablanca and Rabat).

**Banque de Paris et des Pays Bas.**

**Société Marseillaise de Crédit.**

**Banque Commercial du Maroc.**

**Société Générale.**

**Banque Nationale pour le Commerce et l'Industrie.**

**The British Bank of the Middle East (Morocco).** (Casablanca and Tangier.)

**First National City Bank.** (Casablanca.)

### PRODUCTION, INDUSTRY AND COMMERCE

**Mining.** Phosphates are by far the most important of the minerals produced in Morocco. Production in 1967 was 10,058,400 tons, in 1968, 10,411,759 tons, and in the first five months of 1970, 12,546,897 tons.

The following table show the production of minerals in thousand tons, for two years:

| | 1972 | 1973 |
|---|---|---|
| Iron ore | 234 | 375 |
| Lead | 146 | 159 |
| Zinc | 36 | 33 |
| Cobalt | 11 | 10 |
| Crude petroleum | 28 | 42 |
| Chemical Manganese | 96 | 146 |

## MOROCCO

**Agriculture.** Morocco is essentially an agricultural country in spite of insufficient rain. The produce is very varied owing to a varied climate, almost European in the north, very dry in the interior and verging on tropical in the south. Most of the small holdings are worked in a very primitive manner, but there are more and more large mechanized farms coming into being for the main purpose of export. Legislation for expropriation of *lots de colonisation* (tribal land taken over by former Protectorate authorities) was enacted in 1963. About half of this land—250,000 hectares—has been taken over.

Wheat, barley, oats, maize, peas, lentils, potatoes and other vegetables are all grown, as well as cotton, flax and hemp. Morocco also produces essential oils, medicinal plants and forage for animals.

The following table shows the area in hectares of irrigated crops for the year 1972:

| | 1972 |
|---|---|
| Cereals | 51,600 |
| Rice | 2,300 |
| Legumes | 11,150 |
| Cotton | 16,200 |
| Sugar Beets | 34,150 |
| Citrus | 22,000 |
| Sugar Cane | 500 |
| Fodder crops | 25,850 |
| Olives | 8,700 |
| **Total** | **204,300** |

All citrus fruits (oranges, mandarins, lemons) are cultivated in Morocco and nearly all European fruits and nuts, but principally apricots, peaches and prunes in the north and dates in the south. Figs and olive trees grow everywhere. Acacia and eucalyptus trees are cultivated for tanning purposes, as well as cork trees, cedars, pines and cyprus.

After agriculture, stockraising forms the principal riches of Morocco, though herds are frequently depleted in dry weather.

In 1972–73 there were in the country (in thousand heads): 2,751 cattle; 13,241 sheep; 5,527 goats; 115 camels; 10 pigs.

**Fishing.** There is a great deal of fishing for tunny fish, mackerel, sardines and anchovies, much of which is tinned for export.

The Moroccan fishing fleet is composed of 500 vessels of varying tonnage of which 300 are vessels used for catching sardine. The chief fishing ports are Safi and Casablanca, both of which have storage and refrigerating facilities. The annual average catch of the various species is 220,000 tons of sardines, 10,000 tons of mackerel, 10,000 tons of tunny fish, and 2,000 tons of anchovies.

**Industry.** Manufacturing is still a relatively small sector of the Moroccan economy. The most important branch is the food products industry. Also there are textile and paper industries, assembly plants for cars, lorries and tractors and a number of light consumer goods industries. In 1968 the U.S.A. overtook Morocco as the world's largest exporter of phosphates. In 1965 a large chemical complex began operating at Safi, producing triple superphosphate and diammonium phosphates; in 1968 about 300,000 tons of superphosphates were produced. The tourist industry is of growing importance. It is estimated that some 588,000 tourists visited Morocco in 1968, and 914,292 in 1971.

**Commerce.** Morocco's main imports include food and beverages (especially sugar), industrial machinery and equipment, non-electrical metal products, fuel oil, and a wide range of consumer goods and finished products. Phosphates account for about 25 per cent of Morocco's exports. Next in importance are citrus fruits (about 14 per cent of exports) and other agricultural and mineral products (tomatoes, canned fish, lead ore, etc.).

The following table shows the Rank percentage value of exports to principal countries for 1972 and 1973:

| *Country* | *Percentage of total value* 1972 | 1973 |
|---|---|---|
| France | 32 | 34 |
| W. Germany | 9 | 10 |
| Italy | 9 | 7 |
| Spain | 5 | 5 |
| Netherlands | 4 | 4 |
| U.K. | 4 | 5 |
| U.S.S.R. | 4 | 3 |

The following table shows the weight and the value of principal imports by commodity for the years 1972 and 1973 in millions of dirhams:

| *Commodity* | *Weight (tons)* | *Value (th. dirhams)* | *Weight (tons)* | *Value (th. dirhams)* |
|---|---|---|---|---|
| | 1972 | | 1973 | |
| Dairy products | 22,768 | 69,658 | 25,754 | 72,588 |
| Coffee | 12,956 | 35,077 | 12,238 | 47,028 |
| Tea | 12,367 | 86,107 | 10,366 | 66,948 |
| Crude petroleum | 1,753,072 | 171,766 | 2,261,687 | 226,428 |
| Pharmaceuticals | 1,518 | 59,551 | 1,393 | 61,064 |
| Textiles | 2,235 | 29,776 | 2,180 | 31,751 |
| Cars | 3,223 | 26,454 | 5,240 | 41,761 |
| Sugar | 222,016 | 169,296 | 277,919 | 245,074 |

The following table shows the weight and the value of principal exports by commodity for the years 1972 and 1973

| *Commodity* | *Weight (tons)* | *Value (th. dirhams)* | *Weight (tons)* | *Value (th. dirhams)* |
|---|---|---|---|---|
| | 1972 | | 1973 | |
| Various fresh vegetables | 26,008 | 47,409 | 27,879 | 46,097 |
| Fresh tomatoes | 119,546 | 179,146 | 173,211 | 229,484 |
| Citrus Fruit | 585,641 | 428,519 | 699,637 | 494,080 |
| Potatoes | 82,910 | 46,802 | 90,150 | 55,666 |
| Fish Conserves | 45,977 | 134,394 | 65,760 | 189,546 |
| Wine in barrels | 63,056 | 30,944 | 133,039 | 88,699 |
| Phosphates | 13,580,791 | 673,209 | 16,101,895 | 788,055 |
| Manganese | 117,693 | 26,731 | 151,108 | 33,595 |
| Lead | 138,194 | 90,345 | 136,144 | 102,106 |

### COMMUNICATIONS

**Railways.** Morocco has 1,800 kilometres of normal track with lines from Casablanca to Algeria via Meknes and Oujda, Casablanca–Marrakesh, Casablanca–Tangier–Oujda–Colomb Bechar and Casablanca–Oued–Zem, also branch lines to the phosphate and coal mines. About 760 kilometres has been electrified.

The following table shows the main rail statistics for 1970 and 1971.

| | *passenger km.* | *tons km.* |
|---|---|---|
| 1970 | 522·2 m | 2,647·8 m |
| 1971 | 548·8 m | 2,695·7 m |

**Shipping.** At 1 January 1960 Moroccan vessels registered under the flag totalled 54,000 tons, as shown in the following table:

| *Type* | *Number of vessels* | *Tonnage* |
|---|---|---|
| Merchant marine | 29 | 20,730 |
| Ancillary craft | 468 | 17,330 |
| Fishing vessels | 2,708 | 15,820 |

In 1971 36 million tons of freight were handled in Moroccan ports and Casablanca dealt with 20·5 million tons.

Casablanca is by far the most important port of the Atlantic coast and in 1968 handled 2,313,221 tons of import freight and 9,104,846 tons of exports.

**Highways.** The following table indicates the lengths in kilometres of various types of highway and the stages of their development including projected schemes, as of the year 1971:

| | |
|---|---|
| *Main Highways* | *Kilometres* |
| Length projected | 7,620 |
| Length laid | 7,150 |
| Length paved | 7,120 |
| *Secondary Highways* | |
| Length projected | 7,285 |
| Length laid | 6,325 |
| Length paved | 5,840 |
| *Local Roads* | |
| Length projected | 36,630 |
| Length laid | 11,610 |
| Length paved | 8,620 |

**Civil Aviation.** Morocco is served by a number of foreign airlines as well as Royal Air Maroc. In 1973 there were 1,353,447 air passengers, and 11,235 metric tons of freight.

In 1971 there were 363,508 air passengers and 9,653 metric tons of freight.

**Royal Air Maroc (R.A.M.)** Casa/Anfa–Casablanca Télex: 21800. *Management:* President and Chairman of the Board Royal Air Maroc: Ahmed Lasky. Managing Director: Yaala Saïd Ben Ali. Commercial Director: Mohamed Kermoudi. Administrative Director: Abderrafih Tahiri. Technical Director: Hamayed el Mili Rafik. Operations Director: Colonel Mohamed Kabbaj. *Capital:* 75.600.000 DH. *State holding %:* 81.73%. *Personnel employed:* 2,700. *Fleet in operation* (April, 1976): 3 Boeing 737/200, 4 Boeing 727/200, 2 Boeing 707/320, 3 Caravelles. *Fleet on order:* December 1976: 1 Boeing 727/200, February 1977: 1 Boeing 727/200, May 1977: 1 Boeing 727/200. *Principal routes: Europe:* France – Switzerland – Belgium – Holland – West Germany – Italy – Austria – Portugal – Greece – Great Britain – Spain. *Africa:* Algeria–Tunisia–Libya–Egypt–Mauritania–Senegal–Ivory Coast–Canary Islands. *North America:* United States–Canada. *South America:* Brazil. *Middle East:* Saudi Arabia–Kuwait. *Domestic:* Casablanca–Rabat–Fes–Tangiers–Al Hoceima–Oujda–Marrakesh–Agadir–El Ayoun. Passenger-Km (RPKM) in 1975: 1.540.578.297 par/km. Freight and tonne-Km in 1975: 14.691.903 tonne/Km. Total tonne-Km (all services) in 1975: 163.889.328 tonne/Km.

**Posts, Telegraphs and Telephones.** All main towns have ample telegraph, telephone and postal facilities.

### EDUCATION AND RELIGION

The majority of schools are now the responsibility of the Ministry of Education, the number of private and foreign schools having been reduced during the last few years. The Koranic schools attached to mosques and Quaraouiyin University at Fez continue to function. So does a smaller, more recent foundation at Marrakesh. The University Mohammed V at Rabat has faculties of Letters, Science, Law and Medicine; and schools of Administration, Social Studies, Engineering and Education. Courses are offered not only for its own degrees but for the degrees of Bordeaux University.

In 1971 there were 2,476,072 children in primary schools, 911,227 in secondary schools, and 31,058 in higher education.

The majority of the population are Sunni Moslems, but there is a substantive Jewish population. Christian communities are made up entirely of non-Moroccans.

# Mozambique

(MOÇAMBIQUE)

**Capital**—Maputo.

**President**—Samora Moises Machel.

**Members of the Standing Political Committee of FRELIMO:**

| | |
|---|---|
| Samora Machel | Armando Guebuza |
| Marcelino dos Santos | Jorge Rebelo |
| Joaquim Chissano | Mariano Matsinha |
| Alberto Chipande | Sebastiao Mabote |
| Jacinto Veloso | Mario Machungo |

**Council of Ministers (Cabinet):**

*Minister for Development and Economic Planning:* Marcelino dos Santos.
*Ministsr for Foreign Affairs:* Joaquim Chissano.
*Minister for Defence:* Alberto Chipande (Vice-Ministers: Sebastiao Mabote and Armando Guebuza).
*Minister for Information:* Jorge Rebelo.
*Minister for Labour:* Mariano Matsinha.
*Minister for Industry and Commerce:* Mario Machungo.
*Minister of State in the President's Office:* Oscar Monteiro.
*Minister for Education and Culture:* Graca Machel.
*Minister for Agriculture:* Joaquim de Carvalho.
*Minister for Transport and Communications:* Jose Cabaco.
*Minister for Housing and Public Works:* Julio Carrilho.
*Minister for Justice:* Rui Baltazar dos Santos Alves.
*Minister for Finance:* Salomao Munguambe.
*Minister for Health:* Helder Martins.
*Vice-Minister for the Interior:* Daniel Mbanze.

### AREA AND POPULATION

Mozambique stretches along 2,570 km. of coast between the Rovuma River in the north and the Maputo River in the south. The landward border is 2,470 km. long. To the north is Tanzania and to the south, South Africa. On the west, Mozambique has borders with Malawi, Zambia, Southern Rhodesia, Swaziland and South Africa.

Mozambique covers an area of 783,030 sq. km.

Mozambique is divided into nine districts. Lourenço Marques, Gaza, Inhambane, Manica e Sofala, Tete, Zambézia, Moçambique, Cabo Delgado and Niassa. There are ten tribunals of justice and one municipal court, under the judicial district of Lourenço Marques.

The population at mid-1974 was 9,030,000. The annual average percentage growth rate of the population for the period 1960–74 was 2·0, and for the period 1965–74 was 2·2.

### CONSTITUTION AND GOVERNMENT

The People's Republic of Mozambique was created on 25 June 1975, following a ten-year armed struggle for independence from Portugal. The independence war was waged by the Front for the Liberation of Mozambique (FRELIMO), founded in Dar es Salaam in 1962. FRELIMO led a Transitional Government which included some Portuguese ministers from September 1974, when the war ended, until independence and the foundation of the People's Republic.

The constitution defines the country as a state based on people's democracy, guided by the political line laid down by FRELIMO, the leading force of the State and society. The supreme organ of the state is the People's Assembly, which shall have no more than 210 members. The constitution, approved by the Central Committee of FRELIMO on 20 June 1975, specifies that the first general elections for the People's Assembly should take place within a year of the holding of FRELIMO's Third Congress. This Congress took place in February 1977. In accordance with the decisions of that Congress, a Provisional National People's Assembly nominated by the Central Committee met, and on 1 September 1977 approved Mozambique's Electoral Law. This came into immediate effect, and from 25 September onwards, elections took place throughout the country for Local and City People's Assemblies. When elected, these bodies select members of higher organs: the District People's Assemblies. These in turn elect the ten Provincial People's Assemblies which elect the supreme state body, the National People's Assembly. (The whole process ended on 4 December 1977.)

The Constitution stipulates that the President of FRELIMO is also the President of the Republic and Commander-in-Chief of the Mozambican People's Liberation Forces. The President of FRELIMO is elected by the FRELIMO Central Committee.

The Third Congress ended the existence of FRELIMO as a front, membership of which had been open to any Mozambican who supported the struggle for national independence. A new party was created which, while retaining the name FRELIMO, is defined as a Marxist-Leninist vanguard party, membership of which is restricted to Mozambicans "entirely dedicated to the cause of the Party, the country, the people, and socialism, and who live exclusively from the fruits of their work".

The Congress elected as Party President Samora Moises Machel who, as President of the Front, had led the country to independence. Also elected at the Congress was a 67-member Central Committee, a ten-member Standing Political Committee, a Control Committee and a Secretariat.

The supreme body of FRELIMO is the Congress, to be held ordinarily every five years. Between Congresses the highest organ is the Central Committee, which elects from among its members the President of the Party, the Standing Political Committee and the Secretary and Deputy Secretary of the Control Committee. The Standing Political Committee leads the Party between the biennial ordinary sessions of the Central Committee and appoints the members of the Secretariat of the Central Committee.

## FINANCE

The budget for 1977 projects expenditures at 350 million dollars and revenues at 227 million dollars, thus forecasting a deficit of some 123 million dollars. But stringent control of expenditure has been made necessary by the shortage of resources, and it is hoped to reduce this deficit to 63 million dollars.

The last official balance of payments figures available for 1975 are shown:

| | |
|---|---|
| Trade balance | −4,092,698 contos |
| Invisibles | +5,197,069 contos |
| Capital balance | −1,992,369 contos |
| Total balance | −887,998 contos |

(One conto is 1,000 escudos. These are approximately 33 escudos to one U.S. dollar.)

The GNP at market prices for 1974 was U.S. $millions 3,030 and the GNP per capita at market prices was U.S. $340. The annual average percentage growth rate of the GNP per capita for the period 1960–74 was 2·8 and for the period 1965–74 was 3·5. [*See the note at the beginning of this section concerning GNP.*]

A 3,000 kW. thermal power plant is being installed at Nicala at a cost of some 25 m. escudos.

## PRODUCTION, INDUSTRY AND COMMERCE

Mozambique is chiefly an agricultural country. Among the principal export crops are *cashew nuts* (estimated exports for 1977: 20,000 tons); *sugar* (estimated production 1977–78 season; 290,000 tons); *tea* (annual production around 15,000 tons). About 6,000 tons of *cotton* are expected to be exported this year.

Total manufacturing production in 1975, was valued at 11,810,661 contos. Before independence, Mozambique's main trading partners were Portugal, South Africa and the United States, but the Country is now in the process of diversifying its trade—especially to include African and socialist countries.

## COMMUNICATIONS

The principal ports are Lourenço Marques in the south, Beira in the centre and Mozambique and Nacala in the north.

The province has roads extending 38,250 km. and a railway system covering 3,485 km. There is a good internal air service and there is a regular service to Rhodesia (Salisbury), Durban and to South Africa (Johannesburg).

Telegraph lines cover 14,242 km., with 223 stations and 25 wireless stations. Telephone lines extend over 47,312 km

# Republic of Nauru

(MEMBER OF THE COMMONWEALTH)

**Capital**—Owing to its small size and absence of urban development, Nauru has no Capital.

**President**—Bernard Dowiyogo.

**National Flag:** A Royal Blue background, representing the Pacific Ocean, with gold horizontal band, representing the Equator and white twelve pointed star, representing the Island's geographical position, with the points symbolising the original twelve tribes of Nauru.

### CONSTITUTION AND GOVERNMENT

The first European to visit Nauru was Captain John Fearn in 1798. He called it 'Pleasant Island', and noted that it was 'extremely populous' with 'houses in great numbers'. During the 19th Century, various Europeans settled on the Island, without it coming under the formal control of any European power. By the Anglo-German Convention of 1881, the Island was allocated to the German sphere of interest, and reverted to its native name of 'Nauru'. German occupation began on 1 October 1888. In 1899 when the missionaries arrived, education and Christianity were introduced to the Island.

Nauru was surrendered by the Germans to an Australian Expeditionary Force on 6 November 1914, when it passed under British Administration. In 1920, it became a British mandated territory under the League of Nations, under the joint trusteeship of Britain, Australia and New Zealand, with Australia being directly responsible for administration.

In August 1942, Nauru was occupied by the Japanese. It was re-occupied by Australia in September 1945. In November 1947, Nauru came under the trusteeship of the United Nations, although the three partner Governments retained their former responsibilities for its administration, with Australia in immediate control until 31 January 1968 when the Nauruans, under the leadership of Head Chief Hammer DeRoburt, achieved full independence for Nauru.

The President of Nauru is elected by Parliament, which consists of eighteen members, elected by Nauruan citizens who have attained the age of 20 years. It is mandatory for a General Election to be held not less than once every three years. On election, the President shall appoint four or five Members of Parliament to be Ministers of the Cabinet, in which the executive authority of Nauru is vested and over which the President presides. To qualify to be elected President, a person must be a Member of Parliament.

#### Cabinet

*Minister of External Affairs, Minister of Justice:* H. F. Bernard Dowiyogo, OBE, MP.

*Minister for Health and Education:* Hon. Laurence Stephen, MP.

*Minister for Internal Affairs, for Island Development and Industry, and for Civil Aviation:* Hon. Kenas Aroi, MP.

*Minister for Finance, Minister Assisting the President:* Hon. Kinza Clodumar, MP.

*Minister for Works and Community Services:* Hon. Ruben Kun, MP.

*Speaker:* Hon. David Peter Gadaraoa, MP.

*Deputy Speaker:* Hon. Derog Gioura, MP.

### AREA AND POPULATION

Nauru consists of a single island, approximately 8·2 sq. miles in area, situated in the Western Pacific Ocean to the North East of the Solomons and 26 miles South of the Equator. The mainland of Nauru merges directly with a fringing reef and, in consequence, the Island has no natural harbours. It is oval in shape and 12 miles in circumference, with a fertile coastal belt between 100 and 300 yards wide, rising inland to a plateau, the highest point of which is 213 feet above sea level.

The population is situated around the coastal belt. The most recent population figures give a total of 4,400 Nauruans, 1,900 other Pacific Islanders, 650 Chinese, 550 Caucasians. Total, 7,500.

The climate is tropical, tempered by sea breezes, with average shade temperatures varying between 76 and 93 degrees Fahrenheit. The average annual rainfall has been 81 in. over the past 20 years, but is subject to marked deviations. Cultivation is restricted, and local vegetation is chiefly confined to coconut palms and pandanus trees and some indigenous hardwoods.

### FINANCE

Australian currency is used, and a branch of the Bank of New South Wales is established on the Island. Although Nauru is not a member of the Australian monetary area, an agreement has been reached with the Commonwealth Government of Australia which secures for the Government of the Republic, and residents in Nauru, advantages similar to membership.

### PRODUCTION, INDUSTRY AND COMMERCE

The discovery and exploitation of phosphate forms an integral part of the history of Nauru. After the occupation by Germany in 1888, the Island fell within the trading sphere of the Jaluit Gesellshaft, a German Company whose interests were in buying copra and selling merchandise. As the result of an agreement reached between the Nauruans and the partner Governments in 1969, control of the phosphate industry which since 1907 had formed the Islands' chief and only significant source of income, passed to the Nauruans who set up the Nauru Phosphate Corporation. It is calculated that 35,000,000 tons of phosphate remain to be mined on Naura which, at the calculated extraction rate of about 2,000,000 tons per annum, limits the life of the industry to about 30 years. The current extraction rate, however, is 1,000,000 tons per annum. Phosphate is at present chiefly exported to Australia and New Zealand, although from 1969 some has also been exported to Japan. The claim is sometimes made that the per capita income of the Nauruans is the highest of any nation in the world, a calculation based on a total gross return of about $35,000,000 (Australian) per annum, from the sale of 1,000,000 tons of phosphate at $35 per ton, divided amongst a population of approximately 3,500 Nauruans.

Practically everything required on Nauru has to be imported. Apart from some chickens, pigs, cats and dogs, there are no animals and the erratic rainfall severely limits the local cultivation of food. Almost all food, therefore, consumed on the Island is imported, and much of the water as well.

### COMMUNICATIONS

Ships call regularly at Nauru to load phosphate but are occasionally compelled by strong Westerly winds to drift off-shore for many weeks at a time.

In addition to shipping the Island is at present served by two Air services: Air Nauru operates twice weekly services linking Nauru with Melbourne, Hong Kong, Japan (Kagoshima), Tarawa, Majuro, Noumea, Okinawa, Guam, Ponape, and Honiara. It operates a once weekly service between Nauru and Western Samoa, Fiji, Taipei, and the New Hebrides (Vila). The Air Nauru Fleet now consists of two Fokker Fellowship F.28's, one Boeing 737, and one Boeing 727. On the Island itself, there is a circular tar-sealed road, and some unsealed subsidiary roads, mostly used for transporting phosphate rock by lorry. There is a local bus service and private cars are prevalent.

# Nepal

**Capital**—Kathmandu.

**Sovereign**—H. M. King, Birendra Bir Bikram Shah Dev.

**National Flag:** Two right-angled triangles base to base at the hoist, crimson bordered blue, the upper bearing a moon crescent and the lower a sun in splendour.

## CONSTITUTION AND GOVERNMENT

NEPAL is an independent kingdom situated between India and the Tibet Autonomous Region of China. From 1846 until 1951 the country was ruled by a succession of hereditary Prime Ministers from the Rana family, the reigning family playing little part in the conduct of the State. The Rana Prime Ministers had a unique succession system in which all the eligible brothers and then the sons of the brothers took their turn in the Prime Ministership. In 1951, King Tribhuban re-assumed the powers of a constitutional monarch assisted by a Cabinet drawn partly from nominated politicians and partly from members of the Rana family. This was succeeded by a number of other Governments nominated from leading politicians, but it was not found possible to hold a general election until 1959. In this election the Nepali Congress Party won a large majority and a Government under Mr. B. P. Koirala as Prime Minister was appointed. In December 1960, King Mahendra, who had succeeded his father in 1955, again assumed full powers of government in order to be able himself to give closer direction to affairs. Between then and 1963 a four-tier system of indirect elections—the Panchayat system—was evolved. King Mahendra died in January 1972 and was succeeded by King Birendra. The first National Panchayat met on 14 April 1963 and has certain powers over legislation and ministers, though the latter are primarily responsible to the King.

In December 1975 several measures of constitutional reform were promulgated by King Birendra. These included increased representation in the National Panchayat, the reduction to a three-tier system of indirect elections, the opening of proceedings and of Panchayats to the general public and the constitutional status given to the National Campaign Central Committee whose duties are to explain and publicise the partyless panchayat system and to evaluate the performance of Panchayat members at every level.

**Reigning Royal Family.** Hindu.—This is the hereditary dynasty of the house of Shah ruling in Nepal since 1767.

Shri Panch Maharajadhiraja **BIRENDRA BIR BIKRAM SHAH DEV,** King of Nepal; born at Kathmandu, 28 December 1945; succeeded his father, King Mahendra Bir Bikram Shah Dev, (born 11 June 1920; died 31 January 1972). Sons: one. Daughters: one. In English the King is normally referred to as 'His Majesty King Birendra'.

## LOCAL GOVERNMENT AND LEGAL SYSTEM

The country is divided for administrative purposes into 14 Zones, each under an Anchaladish ,below which there are 75 Districts, and for speedy development the country is divided into four development regions, namely the Eastern, Central, Western and Far Western Development Regions. There are elected Panchayats at the village, District and National level. Justice is administered by District Courts of which there are 75. The next instance is the 14 Zonal Courts (not coterminous with the administrative Zones). The Supreme Court sits in Kathmandu, and four regional courts were opened in 1974.

## AREA AND POPULATION

The area of Nepal is 54,362 square miles.

The population in mid-1974 was estimated to be 12,320,000. The annual average percentage growth rate of the population in the period 1960–74 was 2·0 and for the period 1965–74 was 2·2. The capital, Kathmandu, has a population of 160,147. Other important towns are Patan, 62,874 and Bhadgaon, 42,710. The figures for these three towns include some outlying villages and rural areas.

## CURRENCY AND FINANCE

The unit of currency is the *rupee*, of 100 *pice*. The Nepalese rupee is 171 grains in weight, whereas the Indian rupee is 180.

Coins in circulation are of 1, 2, 5, 10, 25, 50 pice denominations. Notes, which were introduced in 1945, are of 1, 5, 10 and 100 rupees and in 1970 500 and 1,000 rupee notes were introduced. In 1976 a 50 rupee note was introduced.

In the year 1977–78 the regular budget expenditure is estimated at 938·5 m Nepalese rupees. Development expenditure is estimated at 2148·8 m. Ordinary revenue from taxation, internal loans etc. is expected to total 1,966·8 m; foreign aid grants 505·8 m, and foreign loans 614·6 m. (Exchange rate: on 19 August 1977: £1 = Rs21·53 buying and Rs21·75 selling).

The GNP at market prices for 1974 was U.S.$ millions 1,250, and the GNP per capita at market prices was U.S. $100. The annual average percentage growth rate of the GNP per capita for the period 1960–74 was 0·4, and for the period 1965–74 was 0·0. [*See the note at the beginning of this section concerning GNP.*]

## PRODUCTION, INDUSTRY AND COMMERCE

Agriculture tourism and forestry are the main sources of the country's wealth. About eight million acres are under cultivation. Rice, wheat and other grains are grown and large quantities are exported. Other products are jute, oilseeds and ghee, which is butter purified by boiling.

There are large forests, chiefly in the southern part of the country.

There is little industrial production, but there are jute, match and sugar factories at Biratnagar, Nepalgunj and Birgunj. A modern cigarette factory has been erected at Janakpur, a new sugar factory at Bhairawa, a leather and shoe factory and a Brick and Tile Factory at Kathmandu.

Three hydro-electric plants are in operation in the valley of Kathmandu. The Trisuli Valley hydro-electric project is now capable of supplying 18,000 kW.

Exploration for exploitable mineral resources has hitherto been disappointing, although there is a good deal of mica in the country.

The principal exports are rice, wheat, timber, cattle, hides, ghee, wool, herbs and some jute. The chief imports are cotton fabrics, sugar, cigarettes, metal goods, petrol and pharmaceuticals.

With effect from mid-July 1974 small industries having capital investment up to Rs 1 million in fixed assets may only be registered by Nepalese. Opportunities to establish medium-scale industries having investment up to Rs 5 million in fixed assets are granted to both Nepalese and non-Nepalese but preference is given to those having higher Nepalese participation. Nepalese and non-Nepalese are equally treated in the establishment of large-scale industries having investment more than Rs 5 million in fixed assets.

## COMMUNICATIONS

The first railway was opened in 1927 which ran from Amlekhganj, south of the capital, to Raxaul, in India. At present a small gauge line connects Janakpur, a town in eastern Nepal, with Jaynagar in India, and has been extended North-west of Janakpur for a further 15 miles.

The 72-mile motor road known as the Tribhuban Rajpath from Thankot to Bhainse, which completes the link between Kathmandu and Birganj was completed in 1958. A 114 km. road from Kathmandu to Kodari on the Tibetan frontier (Arniko Highway) has been built with Chinese Aid, and a 73 miles road from Adhabar to Dhalkebar (Simra/Janakpur) sector of the East/West Highway has been constructed with Russian aid. A similar road along the Rapti Valley connecting the Narayani River with the Tribhuban Rajpath at Hitaura has already been built by the Americans. India has completed the construction of the 279 km. Jhapa–Janakpur sector of the East/West Highway, and is constructing the Butwal–Nepalgunj sector of the East/West highway. The 128-mile Sunauli–Pokhara Road has been completed with Indian aid. A 176 km. road from Kathmandu to Pokhara, being constructed under Chinese aid, was completed in 1973. The Chinese have built a 27 km. ring road in the Kathmandu Valley. The 76-mile Naranghat-Butwal sector of the East–West Highway was constructed with British aid and was completed in 1975. The British have now started a 65 km. road from Dharan–Dhankuta. Kathmandu is connected to Trisuli by a 67 km. long road constructed with Indian aid. The roads inside Kathmandu Valley extend to 372 kms. 181 kms. of which are black-topped.

There are daily flights to New Delhi, sometimes direct and sometimes via Benares. There is a once-weekly direct flight to Dacca by Bangla Airlines. Thai International connects Bangkok to Kathmandu via Calcutta thrice a week. Royal Nepal Airlines fly to Bangkok thrice a week, and Union of Burma Airlines fly from Rangoon to Kathmandu twice a week via Calcutta. RNAC also fly once a week to Colomba.

Kathmandu is linked by telephone and wireless telegraphy to India.

**EDUCATION AND RELIGION**

According to 1976–77 statistics there were 8,768 primary schools with an enrolment of 643,835; 2,289 lower secondary schools with 188,688; and 526 secondary schools with 74,060 students. Besides Tribhuvan University at Kathmandu there are 65 campuses under 12 institutes. Total enrolment in campuses in 1976–77 is 20,527.

The religion of the majority of the people is Hinduism, though Buddhism, is also practised.

# The Netherlands

(KONINKRIJK DER NEDERLANDEN)

**Capital**—Amsterdam.

**Seat of Government**—The Hague.

**Sovereign**—H.M. Queen Juliana.

**National Flag**: A tricolour, fesse-wise, red, white, blue.

**CONSTITUTION AND GOVERNMENT**

THE foundation of the Dutch Republic was laid in 1579, when the northern provinces of the Netherlands united to form one front against Spain. Provision was made for a purely democratic form of government with a Statdtholder as the head. The first Statdtholder was William the Silent. Since then the leadership of the Netherlands has been entrusted to the House of Orange. The Royal succession is in the direct male line in the order of primogeniture. In default of male heirs succession falls to the female line. The Republic became a kingdom in 1815 after the defeat of Napoleon, and the first constitution was approved in that year.

The Constitution of the Netherlands guarantees fundamental democratic rights, including freedom of the press, religion and speech, and the right of association, assembly and petition. It declares the reigning monarch to be above the law and that the ministers shall be responsible to Parliament. The Head of the State is outside the above party politics. Criticisms of government policy on the part of the people's representatives are directed against the ministers. The Cabinet must resign when Parliament has lost confidence in, and denounces, it. If the Crown refuses to accept the resignation, Parliament is dissolved and a General Election follows.

Parliament, which is called the States-General, consists of two chambers, the second chamber being the more important of the two. There are 150 members elected by universal suffrage, on the system of proportional representation. All men and women who have reached the age of 18 are entitled to vote. Members are elected for a term of four years. The first chamber consists of 75 members who are elected for a term of six years (one half retiring every three years) by the Provincial States, that is, to say, provincial representative councils. The functions of the first chamber are restricted to approving or rejecting bills passed by the second chamber, without the power of inserting amendments. A Minister or Under-Secretary cannot be a member of the States-General, except during a transition period of three months. A member of the Cabinet may attend all meetings of the States-General without being entitled to vote.

The Council of State—consisting of the Queen as President, a Vice-President, 24 members and six extraordinary members—is a body which submits recommendations to the Crown (Sovereign and ministers) in matters of legislation and administration. The Council is divided into sections, one of which is the Administrative Disputes Section, which deals with administrative disputes. Moreover since the first of July 1976 the Council has a section charged with the Administrative jurisdiction.

**Reigning Royal Family.** Reformed.—This is the younger branch of the house of Nassau (see also LUXEMBOURG) descended from Otto, Count of Nassau-Siegen, who died circa 1290. The title of Prince of Orange dates from 1530. The title of King of the Netherlands was taken after the Napoleonic Wars, 16 March 1815. Succession is in the male and female lines since 29 March 1814. The daughters of the Queen are princesses of the Netherlands, princesses of Orange-Nassau, princesses of Lippe-Biesterfeld, Royal Highness.

**H.M. JULIANA** Louise Emma Marie Wilhelmina, Queen of the Netherlands, Princess of Orange-Nassau, Duchess of Mecklenburg, etc.; born at The Hague, 30 April 1909; succeeded her mother following her abdication 4 September 1948; married at The Hague, 7 January 1937, BERNHARD Leopold Frederik Everhard Julius Coert Karel Godfried Pieter, Prince of Lippe-Biesterfeld (born at Jena, 29 June 1911) (created H.R.H. The Prince of the Netherlands by Royal Decree 7 January 1937), elder son of Prince Bernhard of Lippe.

Daughters: 1. Crown Princess BEATRIX Wilhelmina Armgard; born at Soestdijk, 31 January 1938; married at Amsterdam, 10 March 1966, Claus George Willem Otto Frederik Geert von Amsberg (born at Dötzingen, 6 September 1926) (created H.R.H. Prince of the Netherlands, Jonkheer van Amsberg by Royal Decree 16 February 1966), son of Claus von Amsberg. They have three sons: Prince Willem-Alexander, Prince Johan Friso, Prince Constantijn. 2. Princess IRENE Emma Elisabeth; born at Soestdijk, 5 August 1939; married at Rome, 29 April 1964, Prince Carel Hugo de Bourbon Parma. They have two sons and two daughters: Prince Carlos, Princess Marguarita, Prince Jaime, Princess Maria Carolina. 3. Princess MARGRIET Francisca; born at Ottawa, Canada, 19 January 1943; married at The Hague, 10 January 1967, Pieter van Vollenhoven (born at Schiedam, 30 April 1939). They have four sons: Prince Maurits, Prince Bernhard, Prince Pieter-Christiaan, Prince Floris. 4. Princess MARIA CHRISTINA; born at Soestdijk, 18 February 1947; married at Utrecht, 28 June 1975, Jorge Guillermo. They have one Son: Bernardo Federico Tomas.

Mother of the Queen: WILHELMINA Helena Pauline Maria, formerly Queen of the Netherlands; born at The Hague, 31 August 1880, died 28 November 1962, daughter of Willem III, King of the Netherlands (born 19 February 1817, died 23 November 1890), by his 2nd wife Emma (born 2 August 1858, married 7 January 1879, died 20 March 1934), daughter of George Viktor, Prince of Waldeck and Pyrmont; succeeded her father under the Regency of her mother until her coming-of-age 31 August 1898; abdicated the throne in favour of her daughter and took the title 'Princess of the Netherlands' 4 September 1948; married at The Hague, 7 Feburary 1901, Duke HENDRIK (Heinrich) (born at Schwerin, 19 April 1876, died at The Hague, 3 July 1934) (created H.R.H. The Prince of the Netherlands by Royal Decree 6 February 1901), son of Friedrich Franz II, Grand Duke of Mecklenburg-Schwerin.

**THE NETHERLANDS**

**Ministry**

*Prime Minister:* Andreas van Agt.
*Minister of Interior and Deputy Prime Minister:* Hans Wiegel.
*Foreign Secretary:* Christoph van de Klaauw.
*Minister of Defence:* Roelof Kruisinga.
*Minister of Social Affairs:* Willem Albeda.
*Minister of Finance:* Frans Andriessen.
*Minister of Economic Affairs:* Gijsbert van Ardenne.
*Minister of Transport and Waterways:* Daniel Tuljnman.
*Minister of Education:* Arie Pais.
*Minister of Public Health and Environment:* Leendert Ginjaar.

*Minister of Development Cooperation:* Jan de Koning.
*Minister of Culture, Recreation and Social Welfare:* Mrs Mathilda Gardeniers.
*Minister of Agriculture and Fisheries:* Alphons vahr der Stee.
*Minister of Housing:* Pieter Beelaerts van Blokland.
*Minister of Justice:* Job de Ruiter.
*Minister of Science Policy:* Rinus Peijnenburg.

**The Council of State**

*President:* H.M. Queen Juliana.
*Other members of the Royal Family who have a seat in the Council are:* HRH The Prince of the Netherlands; HRH Princess Beatrix and HRH Prince Claus of the Netherlands.

*Vice-President:* M. Ruppert.

Members:

| | |
|---|---|
| J. M. Kan | Th. J. A. M. van Lier |
| A. A. M. Struycken | J. van der Hoeven |
| L. Brouwer | K. T. M. van Rijckevorsel |
| S. J. Baron van Tuyll van Serooskerken | R. van den Bergh |
| W. H. van den Berge | A. J. Hagen |
| Mrs. J. Zeelenberg | M. Troostwiyk |
| J. V. Rijpperda Wierdsma | W. Scholten |
| J. H. Beekhuis | P. J. Bovkema. |
| P. J. M. Aalberse | Th. E. E. van Schaik. |
| J. A. W. Burger | P. J. G. Kapteyn |
| G. H. Veringa | M. C. Verburg |
| J. M. Aarden | J. M. Polak |

**Parliament**

FIRST CHAMBER

*President:* Th. L. M. Thurlings

Representation of the Parties is as follows: Labour Party, 25 seats; Christian Democratic Appeal, 24 seats; People's Party of Freedom and Democracy, 15 seats; Party of Political Radicals, 5 seats; Communist Party, 2 seats; Political Reformed Party, 1 seat; Reformed Political Union, 1 seat; Pacifist Socialist Party, 1 seat; Farmers Party, 1 seat.

SECOND CHAMBER

*President:* A. Vondeling.

Representation of the Parties is as follows: Labour Party, 53 seats; Christian Democratic Appeal, 49 seats; People's Party of Freedom and Democracy, 28 seats; Democrats '66, 8 seats; Party of Political Radicals, 3 seats; Political Reformed Party, 3 seats; Communist Party, 2 seats; Democratic Socialists '70, 1 seat; Farmers Party, 1 seat; Reformed Political Union, 1 seat; Pacifist-Socialist Party, 1 seat.

**Chief Permanent Government Officials**

*Office of the Prime Minister, and Minister for General Affairs, Secretary-General:* D. M. Ringnalda.
*Ministry of Foreign Affairs, Secretary-General:* E. L. C. Schiff.
*Ministry of Justice, Secretary-General:* A. Mulder.
*Ministry of Home Affairs, Secretary-General:* P. van Dijke.
*Ministry of Education and Science, Secretary-General:* M. D- van Wolferen.
*Ministry of Finance, Secretary-General:* J. C. W. M. Huijs. mans.
*Ministry of Defence, Secretary-General:* G. H. J. M. Peijnenburg.
*Ministry of Housing and Physical Planning, Secretary-General:* Th. Quené.
*Ministry of Transport, and Public Works, Secretary-General:* P. C. de Man.
*Ministry of Economic Affairs, Secretary-General:* F. W. Rutten.
*Ministry of Agriculture and Fisheries, Secretary-General:* G. van Setten.
*Ministry of Social Affairs, Secretary-General:* W. A. van den Berg.
*Ministry of Cultural Affairs, Recreation and Social Work, Secretary-General:* J. van Viegen.
*Ministry of Public Health and Environmental Hygiene, Secretary-General:* P. Siderius.

## LOCAL GOVERNMENT

The Netherlands is divided for administrative purposes into 11 provinces. Each province has its representative council called the Provincial States (Provinciale Staten). The number of members varies with the size of the population in the province they represent. They are elected for four years by universal suffrage. In each province there is a committee of six members of the Provincial States with a Queen's Commissioner as chairman. These committees are called Deputy States (Gedeputeerde Staten). They are charged with executive power. One of their tasks is supervision of the financial side of municipal administration.

The municipalities (833 on 1 January 1978) are governed by Municipal Councils elected by universal suffrage. The number of members varies with the size of the population. The Municipal Councils are presided over by a Burgomaster, who is appointed by the Crown for six years. Each municipality has a committee of two to six members (Aldermen) charged with executive powers.

**Commissioners of the Queen**

| *Province* | *Name* |
|---|---|
| Drenthe | Mrs. A. P. Schilthuis. |
| Friesland | H. Rijpstra. |
| Gelderland | W. J. Geertsema. |
| Groningen | E. H. Toxopeus. |
| Limburg | J. Kremers |
| North Brabant | J. D. van der Harten. |
| North Holland | R. J. de Wit |
| Overijssel | J. L. M. Niers. |
| South Holland | M. Vrolijk. |
| Utrecht | P. J. Verdam. |
| Zeeland | C. Boertien. |

## LEGAL SYSTEM

The judiciary in the Netherlands is completely independent. All judges are appointed for life by the Sovereign, and in the case of the High Court, from a list prepared by the Second Chamber. The principal task of the High Court lies in guarding against erroneous application of the law and misuse of judicial powers by the lower courts. There are five Courts of Appeal, 19 Districts Courts and 62 Cantonal Courts. There is no trial by jury in the Netherlands.

**High Court**

*President:* C. W. Dubbink

**Courts of Appeal**

*President:* J. K. Schellenbach ('s-Hertogenbosch)
J. van Andel (Arnhem)
H. K. A. Stoffels (The Hague)
F. B. Dozy (Amsterdam)
J. J. Woltman (Leeuwarden)

## AREA AND POPULATION

At 1 January 1977 the estimated population was 13,814,495, The following table shows the population by provinces at 31 December 1976:

| *Province* | *Area (land) sq. km.* | *Population* |
|---|---|---|
| Groningen | 2,329·83 | 544,200 |
| Friesland | 3,340·13 | 566,000 |
| Drenthe | 2,645·09 | 409,800 |
| Overijssel | 3,804·08 | 992,900 |
| Gelderland | 5,010·29 | 1,653,500 |
| Utrecht | 1,328·32 | 873,700 |
| North Holland | 2,655·63 | 2,299,400 |
| South Holland | 2,869·06 | 3,049,500 |
| Zeeland | 1,789·95 | 335,600 |
| North Brabant | 4,911·13 | 1,991,100 |
| Limburg | 2,166·79 | 1,055,600 |
| Dronten | 296·82 | 17,200 |
| Southern Yssellake Polders | 666·41 | 23,400 |
| Central Population Register | | 2,000 |
| Total | 33,811·23 | 13,814,400 |

The Central Register of Population includes persons with residential qualifications but who have no fixed residence in any particular municipality.

**Vital Statistics.** The following table shows the vital statistics for two years 1975–76:

| | 1975 | 1976 |
|---|---|---|
| Marriages | 100,081 | 97,056 |
| Births | 177,876 | 177,090 |
| Deaths | 113,737 | 114,454 |

**CURRENCY**

The unit of currency is the guilder, or florin of 100 cents, four kwartjes (quarters), or ten dubbeltjes (ten-cent pieces); there are banknotes in denominations of from five to 1,000 guilders.

**FINANCE**

Revenue and expenditure of the Central Government for two years (in million guilders) are shown below:

| | 1975 | 1976 |
|---|---|---|
| Revenue | 58,540 | 65,362 |
| Expenditure | 68,364 | 80,472 |

The National Debt (in million guilders) was as follows:

| | 31 *Dec.* 1975 | 31 *Dec.* 1976 |
|---|---|---|
| Long-term debt | 34,777 | 40,983 |
| Treasury bills | 6,400 | 8,372 |
| Other floating debts balance | 5,600 | 6,651 |
| Gross total debt | 46,777 | 55,006 |
| Credit Netherlands Bank | 5,228 | 4,908 |
| Other credits | 1,849 | 2,219 |
| Net total debt | 39,700 | 47,879 |

The gross National Debt at March 1977 amounted to 57,899,000,000 guilders at home and nil guilders abroad. The net National Debt amounted to 51,418,000,000 guilders.

For 1973 about 30 per cent and for 1974 and 1975 about 31 per cent of the National Income, at market prices, was claimed for taxes. 1976: 31 per cent.

The GNP at market prices for 1974 was U.S. $71,120 million and the GNP per capita at market prices was U.S. $5,250. The average annual percentage growth rate of the GNP per capita for the period 1962–74 was 4·0, and for the period 1962–74 was 4·1. [*See the note at the beginning of this section concerning GNP.*]

**PRINCIPAL BANKS**

**Algemene Bank Nederland N.V.** (Dr. A. Batenburg, Chairman of the Managing Board.) Result of a merger between De Twentsche Bank N.V. and Nederlandsche Handel-Maatschappij N.V.; merged with Hollandsche Bank-Unie N.V. (see below) at the beginning of 1968. Consolidated balance sheet at 31 December 1976 showed assets Dfl. 55,905,487,000; deposits and current accounts Dfl. 50,092,961,000. *Head Office:* 32 Vijzelstraat, Amsterdam, P.O. Box 669. 646. domestic offices and 178 foreign branches.

**Amsterdam-Rotterdam Bank, N.V.** Consolidated Balance Sheet at 31 December 1972 showed assets fl. 21,220,116,000. Deposits, fl. 19,600,306,000. *Head Offices:* 595, Herengracht, Amsterdam-C. and 119 Coolsingel, Rotterdam, more than 750 Branches.

**Bank Mees & Hope N.V.** Established 1969 through a merger of Nederlandse Overzee Bank N.V. and Mees & Hope. Mees & Hope was established in 1966 through a merger of R. Mees & Zoonen (established 1720) and Hope & Co. (established 1762). Nederlandse Overzee Bank was formed in 1954 by a merger of Amsterdamsche Goederen-Bank N.V. with Nederlandsche Bank voor Zuid-Afrika N.V. (both established 1888). All shares of Bank Mees & Hope N.V. are owned by the holding company. Mees & Hope Group N.V., Balance Sheets at December 1974 showed Bank Mees & Hope N.V. assets Dfl. 5,510,192,217 and current accounts Dfl. 4,950,526,372. *Head Offices:* 548 Herengracht, Amsterdam; 93 Coolsingel, Rotterdam. 29 Branches.

**Bank Morgan Labouchere N.V.** Established 1917. (Chairman, J. H. I. van Eck.) Assets as at 31 December 1976, F.620,920,000; deposits F. 549,512,000. *Head Office:* 12, Tesselschadestraat, Amsterdam, P.O. Box 154.

**Banque de Paris et des Pays-Bas N.V.** Established 1872. (President, Willem Werner; Chairman, Gustave Bambaud.*:* Assets as at 31 December 1974, Dfls. 1,199,724,385, deposits and current accounts Dfls. 1,134,119,094. *Head Office*) NL-1001 Amsterdam, Herengracht 539–543. 16 Branches.

**Central Bank van Suriname.** Established 1957. (President V. M. de Miranda; Chairman, Mr. H. E. R. Rijsdijk.) Assets as at 31 December 1976; Sf. 235,029,821; deposits and current accounts Sf. 61,874,525. *Head Office:* Waterkant 2, Paramaribo P.O. Box 1801.

**Centrale Rabobank** (Coöperatieve Centrale Raiffeisen-Boerenleenbank G.A.) P.O. Box 8098, St Jacobsstraat 23, Utrecht, Netherlands. Established 1970. (Board of Managers: Dr. P. J. Lardinois, Chairmen, Dr. F. P. J. Bakx, Vice-Chairman, Dr. J. A. van Ogtrop, Dr. T. J. Jansen Schoonhoven, Dr. G. J. M. Vlak; General Manager International Division, G. N. Brands) International Division: *Main Office:* Utrecht, St. Jacobsstraat 23, P.O. Box 8098. Tel. (030) 369111, Telex 40200. Branches: Amsterdam, For. Exch. Dept., Keizersgracht 452, P.O. Box 3452. Tel. (020) 241552. Telex 15051. Rotterdam, Blaak 33, P.O. Box 1433. Tel. (010) 130992. Telex 23142. Subsidiaries: Hakrinbank N. V., Paramaribo; London and Continental Bankers Ltd., London; Rabomerica International Bank N.V., Amsterdam.

**De Nederlandsche Bank N.V.** (President, Dr. J. Zijlstra.) Established 1814; Sole Bank of Issue for the Netherlands; all the share capital is owned by the State; Balance Sheet at 31 December 1976 showed assets fl. 23,411·5; million guilders; domestic deposits 3,617·9 million guilders. *Head Office:* Westeinde 1, NL-1017ZN Amsterdam; *Postal Address:* P.O. Box 98, NL-1000 AB Amsterdam. 15 Branches.

**Hollandsche Bank-Unie, N.V.** (Dr. A. Batenburg.) Established 1914 as Hollandsche Bank voor Zuid-Amerika N.V. Merged with Algemene Bank Nederland N.V. at the beginning of 1968 (see above).

**Kas-Associatie, N.V.** (Managing Directors, Dr. F. Winkler, J. Giskes, C. P. Pluilaart.) Established 1806. Balance sheet at 31 December 1973 showed assets fl. 929,817,263; deposits and current accounts fl. 890,767,263 fl 37·3 million. *Head Office:* 172 Spuistraat, Amsterdam.

**Nederlandsche Middenstandsbank, N.V.** (President, W. E. S. Rom.) Established 1927; 23 per cent of the share capital is owned by the State; Balance Sheet at 31 December 1976 showed assets Dfl. 22,266,250,000 deposits and current accounts Dfl. 21,032,375,000. *Head Office:* 2, Eduard van Beinumstraat, Amsterdam, 447 Branches.

**Nederlandse Credietbank N.V.** (Managing Directors, J. A. H. Delsing, H. C. van Straateen, A. A. Gieben, J. Ch. Estourgie, C. Müller.) Established 1918; affiliated with The Chase Manhattan Bank, N.A. Balance sheet at 31 December 1974 showed assets Dfl. 4,816,920,781, deposits and current accounts Dfl. 4,605,915,135. *Head Office:* 458 Herengracht, Amsterdam. 118 Branches.

**Nederlandse Overzee Bank N.V.** See Bank Mees & Hope NV.

**N.V. Slavenburg's Bank,** (Chief General Manager, P. Slavenburg, General Managers, R. Slavenburg, J. van der Meer, J. W. Coert, S.P. van Eeghen, C. van Eeghen.) Established 1925; Balance sheet at 30 June 1975 showed assets Dfl. 15,596,629,000, deposits and current accounts Dfl. 14,730,878,000. *Head Office:* 2, Eduaard van Beinumstraat 2, Amsterdam, (P.O. Box 1800), 434 Branches.

**Van der Hoop, Offers & Zoon N.V.** Established 1807. (Genera Managers, C. Zwaan, Dr. W. H. Berghuis; Chairman

Jhr Mr. C. C. van Valkenburg.) Assets as at 1 January 1976, D.fl. 163,133,000; deposits and current accounts D.fl. 153,127,000. *Head Office:* 88, Westersingel, Rotterdam 2 Branches.

Combined Balance Sheet:

| Liabilities, 31 December | 1974 Fl. |
|---|---|
| Capital accounts | 1,774,000,000 |
| Savings & deposits | 35,581,000,000 |
| Total | 37,355,000,000 |

| Assets, 31 December | 1974 Fl. |
|---|---|
| Cash & Banks | 761,000,000 |
| Investments | 10,154,000,000 |
| Loans & Discounts | 25,178,000,000 |
| Premises | 1,262,000,000 |
| Total | 37,355,000,000 |

## PRODUCTION, INDUSTRY AND COMMERCE

**Agriculture.** Of the total land area of the Netherlands, 41 per cent is pasture, 23 per cent arable land, 9 per cent woodland and 4 per cent horticultural land.

As from 1970 some smaller holdings have been excluded from the surveys.

The areas of the principal field crops for 1975 and 1976 (in hectares) were as follows:

| *Product* | 1975 | 1976 |
|---|---|---|
| Autumn wheat | 64,864 | 109,045 |
| Spring wheat | 42,068 | 21,149 |
| Rye | 18,196 | 21,226 |
| Autumn barley | 6,065 | 9,526 |
| Spring barley | 77,069 | 51,833 |
| Oats | 34,346 | 25,360 |
| Peas | 6,026 | 4,499 |
| Colza (incl. rape seed) | 14,110 | 12,339 |
| Flax | 5,126 | 5,306 |
| Agricultural seed | 20,756 | 15,253 |
| Potatoes, edible* | 78,145 | 89,037 |
| Potatoes, industrial | 73,024 | 71,536 |
| Sugarbeets | 136,515 | 139,089 |
| Fodderbeets | 3,482 | 3,079 |

* Including early potatoes and seed potatoes.

The yield of the chief agricultural products for 1975 and 1976 (in metric tons) is shown below:

| *Crop* | 1975 | 1976 |
|---|---|---|
| Wheat | 527,793 | 709,585 |
| Rye | 62,815 | 65,321 |
| Barley | 335,924 | 263,397 |
| Oats | 158,127 | 103,390 |
| Field beans | N.A. | N.A. |
| Peas | 21,917 | 15,903 |
| Colza (incl. rape seed) | 36,600 | 34,207 |
| Potatoes, edible | 2,574,283 | 2,776,314 |
| Potatoes, industrial | 2,428,847 | 2,006,561 |
| Sugarbeets | 5,926,777 | 5,484,355 |

**Livestock**

| | 1975 | 1976 |
|---|---|---|
| Cattle | 4,956,303 | 4,964,101 |
| Pigs | 7,279,071 | 7,507,124 |
| Horses* | 22,569 | 18,743 |
| Sheep | 760,102 | 780,017 |
| Hens and Ducks | 68,707,000 | 69,202,000 |
| Turkeys | 1,539,650 | 1,350,015 |

* Three years old and over.

**Fisheries.** Fishing has always held an important place in Dutch trade.

The following table shows the volume (tons) and value (in guilders) of the total and herring catches for 1972–76:

| | *Total Catch* | | *Total Herring* | |
|---|---|---|---|---|
| | *tons* | *guilders* | *tons* | *guilders* |
| 1972 | 333,768 | 350,487,000 | 46,335 | 48,898,000 |
| 1973 | 322,991 | 419,528,000 | 61,838 | 70,817,000 |
| 1974 | 293,925 | 421,427,000 | 49,166 | 68,008,000 |
| 1975 | 309,908 | 468,559,000 | 59,394 | 85,370,000 |
| 1976 | 255,820 | 461,253,000 | 48,108 | 76,252,000 |

**Mining.** Coal mining in the South of Limburg is drawing to an end. Production in 1972 was 2,812,000 metric tons, in 1973 1,722,000 metric tons only in 1974: 758,000 metric tons. 1974 was the last year in which coal was extracted. There are salt deposits at Hengelo and Delfzijl, exploited by N. V. Koninklijke Nederlandsche Zoutindustrie. Production in 1973 was 3,044,000 metric tons, in 1974: 3,387,000 metric tons and in 1975: 2,690,000 metric tons. 1976: 3,026,000 metric tons. The mineral oil fields are being exploited by N. V. Nederlandsche Aardolie Maatschappij. Production of crude oil amounted to 1,597,000 metric tons in 1972, 1,492,000 metric tons in 1973; in 1974, 1,461,000 metric tons, and in 1975: 1,419,000 metric tons; in 1976: 1,371,000 metric tons. The largest gasfield in the world has been found near Groningen with reserves of 1,850·5 billion cubic metres at 1 January, 1976 and 1,770·9 billion cubic metres at 1 January, 1977. Other gasfields on shore have reserves of 286·7 (1976) and 258·6 (1977) billion cubic metres and the reserves in the continental shelf are 340·1 (1976) an 367·4 (1977) billion cubic metres. From the total reserves of 2,477·3 (1976) and 2,396·9 (1977) billion cubic metres, 629·1 billion cubic metres (1976) and 637·8 (1977) are as yet not proven. Production of natural gas increased from 58,420 million $m^3$ in 1972 to 70,834 million $m^3$ in 1973, 83,725 million $m^3$ in 1974, 90,853 million $m^3$ in 1975 and 97,302 million $m^3$ in 1976.

**Industry.** The following table gives figures about production and consumption of energy (in thousand T-cal):

| | *Total* | *Coal* | *Oil* | *Natural gas* |
|---|---|---|---|---|
| Production | | | | |
| 1972 | 527·9 | 19·7 | 16·4 | 491·5 |
| 1973 | 626·1 | 12·1 | 15·6 | 597·6 |
| 1974 | 732·4 | 5·3 | 15·7 | 708·5 |
| 1975 | 789·3 | — | 15·7 | 763·0 |
| Consumption (including bunkers) | | | | |
| 1972 | 703·8 | 30·8 | 386·1 | 286·6 |
| 1973 | 747·0 | 30·8 | 396·7 | 318·6 |
| 1974 | 705·0 | 28·9 | 334·0 | 339·2 |
| 1975 | 701·7 | 23·9 | 315·8 | 351·5 |

Not mentioned are small quantities for brown-coal and imported electricity and gas.

**Commerce.**

The following tables show imports and exports by principal commodities for the years 1975 and 1976 (in million florins):

| *Imports* | 1975* | 1976* |
|---|---|---|
| Food, beverages and tobacco | 10,836 | 12,333 |
| Chemical products | 5,660 | 7,243 |
| Mineral fuels | 15,027 | 19,692 |
| Wood and woodware, paper and paperware | 2,739 | 3,677 |
| Non-ferrous metals | 1,550 | 1,981 |
| Raw materials and rags for the textile industry | 1,074 | 1,296 |
| Fabrics, wearing apparel | 4,471 | 5,572 |
| Iron and steel scrap | 3,345 | 2,879 |
| Machinery, other than electric | 6,902 | 7,493 |
| Electro-technical material | 3,279 | 5,842 |
| Transport equipment | 5,124 | 5,483 |

* Exclusive of Belgium and Luxembourg.

| *Exports* | 1975* | 1976* |
|---|---|---|
| Meat, fish and products thereof | 4,374 | 4,684 |
| Milk, dairy produce and eggs | 3,312 | 3,936 |
| Fruit and vegetables | 2,772 | 3,622 |
| Mineral fuels | 13,092 | 15,790 |
| Chemical products | 11,301 | 13,783 |
| Raw materials and rags for textile industry | 1,271 | 1,442 |
| Fabrics, wearing apparel | 2,789 | 2,976 |
| Iron and steel scrap | 2,867 | 3,124 |
| Machinery other than electric | 5,203 | 6,112 |
| Electro-technical material | 5,345 | 6,516 |
| Transport equipment | 4,215 | 5,290 |

* Exclusive of Belgium and Luxembourg.

The total imports for 1976 were in volume 161,269,745 metric tons and in value fl. 91,084,698,817 (exclusive of Belgium and Luxembourg).

The total exports for 1976 were in volume 82,404,471 metric tons and in volume fl. 90,361,263,612 (exclusive of Belgium and Luxembourg).

| | 1975 | | 1976 | |
|---|---|---|---|---|
| | *Imports* | *Exports* | *Imports* | *Exports* |
| | (in thousand guilders) | | | |
| West Germany | 22,354,051 | 26,940,538 | 25,177,762 | 32,764,219 |
| U.S.A. | 8,777,327 | 2,439,888 | 9,585,322 | 3,011,700 |
| France | 6,773,918 | 9,127,244 | 7,336,289 | 11,273,951 |
| United Kingdom | 5,096,679 | 3,120,932 | 6,472,037 | 8,805,708 |
| Italy | 3,093,340 | 4,481,672 | 3,517,328 | 5,475,517 |
| Sweden | 1,716,288 | 1,895,534 | 1,993,151 | 2,196,577 |
| Switzerland | 1,130,759 | 1,155,184 | 1,317,212 | 1,317,850 |
| Japan | 1,285,590 | 382,954 | 1,667,335 | 506,272 |
| Denmark | 605,939 | 1,489,718 | 781,690 | 1,799,350 |
| Spain | 792,007 | 950,013 | 920,662 | 1,073,927 |
| Kuwait | 1,226,748 | 113,543 | 1,632,688 | 1,459,948 |
| Austria | 543,949 | 770,804 | 667,497 | 990,530 |
| Indonesia | 314,323 | 400,570 | 364,008 | 566,051 |
| Norway | 609,073 | 1,074,834 | 648,584 | 1,683,002 |
| Finland | 379,096 | 456,244 | 538,647 | 492,779 |

## COMMUNICATIONS

**Railways.** The Netherlands Railways N.V. own and operate the whole of the country's railway system. The total length of track in 1976 was 2,825 km. of which 1,719 km. is electrified. The number of passengers carried in 1976 was 171,500,000, Total goods traffic carried in the same year amounted to 18,800,000 tons.

**Shipping.** There was on 1 January 1977 a total of 690 ships under the Dutch flag, with a total G.R.T. of 5,077,000 of which 2·3 million is steam and 2·8 million motor. A total of 46,032 vessels entered Dutch ports during 1976. The chief ports are Rotterdam, Amsterdam, Vlaardingen, Hoek van Holland, Dordrecht, Delfzijl, Terneuzen and Flushing Rotterdam, the largest port in the world, has a berthing space at wharfs, buoys and sidequays of 48·4 miles for sea-going ships and berthing space for river barges of 27 miles. It is connected to the North Sea by open water called the *Nieuwe Waterweg*, 17·4 miles long, which is navigable by the largest ships. In Rotterdam in 1976 the total goods handled by sea was 283·1 million metric tons of which 147·1 million was crude oil.

The Dutch inland fleet of 1 January 1976 comprised 19,235 barges of which 11,729 were self-propelled with a total carrying capacity of 7,110,288 metric tons. Dutch barges in 1976 carried 178,968,000 tons of which 87,852,000 tons was international trade.

The following are the principal shipping lines:

**Holland America Line,** Holding N.V paid up share capital fl. 66,000,000; five cruise vessels, four specialized transport vessels, total tonnage 125,000 G.R.T.; *services operated:* world wide cruising services and specialized transport (integrated heavy loads). *Head Office:* Wilhelminakade, Rotterdam.

**Koninklijke Hollandsche Lloyd,** paid up share capital fl.7,500,000; vessels 7; total tonnage 54,127 B.R.T.; *services operated:* Bremen, Hamburg and Amsterdam–Brazil–Uruguay–Argentine. *Head Office:* Oostelijke Handelskade 12 Postbox 132, Amsterdam.

**Koninklijke Nedlloyd Groep N.V. (Nedlloyd Group),** controlling holding company of various transportation interests: Liner shipping (Nedlloyd Lines), tramping and tankers (Nedlloyd Bulk), Drillships operation (Neddrill), forwarding, road haulage, airfreight forwarding, storage and distribution (Damco International Transport), stevedoring, shipping agencies, storage, specialist road haulage, Rhine and inland shipping (Nedlloyd Ports and Specialised Transport Division), trading, services to industry, real estate management, hotel operation (Nedlloyd Industrial Services Division).

The Group also has interests in companies specialising in Ocean and port towage, salvage, supplying offshore drilling rigs, aviation, telecommunications, container handling, North Sea ferry services, travel agency, tour operation and exploration on the Dutch continental shelf.

Share capital plus reserves at 31 December 1976: Dfl. 1,649,815,000. *Head Office:* Houtlaan 21, Rotterdam. *Telegraphic address:* Nedlloydgroep. Telex: 27087.

**Nedlloyd** (Koninklijke Nedlloyd B.V.), a member of the Nederlandsche Scheepvaart Unie group of companies, also a partner in Scan Dutch Container Service to and from the Far East. 64 vessels 67,859,925 dwt; liner services between Europe and West Africa, South and East Africa, Malaysia, Singapore, Sabah, Indonesia, South Pacific Islands, New Zealand, Australia, the Arabian Peninsula, Iran, India, Sri Lanka, Bangladesh and Burma. Also between the North American Continent and South Africa, East Africa, the Arabian Peninsula, Iran, India, Pakistan, Ceylon and countries in South East Asia. *Head Office:* Van Vollenhovenstraat 3, Rotterdam, Telegraphic address: Nedlloyd.

**Nedlloyd Lines.** A member of the Nedlloyd group. *services operated:* Far East-Africa-S. America; Far East–W.C.L. America; S. Africa–Far East; Hong Kong–Straits–S. Africa; Far East–W. Africa; China–W. Africa; Far East–E. Africa; India–Australia; Australia–Singapore–Thailand; N.Zealand–E. Asia; Africa–N. Zealand; N. Zealand-Unit Express;

Asia–Australia Express; S. Africa–Australia. *Head office:* Nedlloyd Lijnen B.V. Houtlaan 21 3016 Da Rotterdam, The Netherlands, Telegraphic address: NEDSHIP.

**Holland Bulk Transport N.V.**, a member of the Nederlandsche Scheepvaart Unie group of companies; vessels: 12 bulk carriers and trampers 384,000 dwt. 6 tankers 861,000 dwt. *Head Office:* 3 van Vollenhovenstraat, Rotterdam. Telegraphic address: Hollandships Telex: 26005 HBT NL.

**Ruys Transport Groep B.V.** Deputy Managing Director: R. B. Lenterman; Director Transport Development: B. W. J. Steensma; Assistant Managing Director: B. H. Klaasman; Manager Marketing and Sales: G. C. Franken. The Ruys Transport Groep is one of the divisions of the Nederlandsche Scheepvaart Unie and comprises an internation group of transport companies. Their activities include stevedoring, domestic and international trucking of general cargo, liquids and gas; transportation of automobiles by truck; Rhineshipping; short-sea shipping; shipping agencies and chartering; local and international forwarding warehousing and distribution; offshore-activities; marine-supplies; airfreight forwarding and freight consulting. *Head Office:* 1 Parklaan, P.O. Box 720 Rotterdam. *Telephone:* 363522. Telegraphic address: Ruystransgroup.

**Scheepvaartunie Reis and Tourism Group N.V.**, a member of the Nederlandsche Scheepvaart Unie group of companies; travel agencies, tour operating, hotels, hotel management and Rhine travel. *Head Office:* Korte Vijverberg 5, The Hague.

**Van Nievelt, Goudriaan & Co. B.V.**, subsidiary of SHV Nederland N.V., Utrecht; motor vessels 17, (owned and/or in management), total tonnage 403,566 brt. *Services operated:* shipowners, owners' agents, liners agents, fleet management, chartering, charterers' agents, husbandry *Head Office:* 2, Veehaven, Rotterdam.

**Koninklijke Nederlandsche Stoomboot-Maatschappij B.V.** (K.N.S.M.), operating company of KNSM Group N.V. of which paid-up share capital is fl. 67,492,000,—. Data operating company K.N.S.M.: vessels 21; total gross tonnage 141,693; *Services operated:* Dutch and German ports to Baltic and Mediterranean ports, Guyanas, Antilles, Bahamas, Venezuela, Colombia, West Coast South America and Central America; Mediterranean ports to Caribbean, Colombia, Venezuela and Central America; East Coast U.S.A. and Gulf of Mexico to Antilles, Guyanas and Venezuela and Pto Limon. *Head Office:* Het Scheepvaarthuis, Prins Hendrikkade 108–114 Amsterdam-1001 or P.O. Box 209, Amsterdam-1000.

**Civil Aviation. KLM—Koninklijke Luchtvaart Maatschappij (Royal Dutch Airlines)**, was founded in 1919 by Dr. Albert Plesman. Issued share capital fl.710,572,500; *services operated:* Amsterdam to Canada, U.S.A., Mexico, Near East, Carribbean, Middle East, South Africa, Far East, Australia, South America and the principal cities of Europe. *Head Office:* Amsterdamscheweg 55, Amstelveen. Postal address P.O. Box 7700, Amsterdam International Airport Schiphol, The Netherlands. *Telephone:* Amsterdam 499123. *Telegraphic Address:* Transaera Amsterdam.

**Posts, Telegraphs and Telephones.** At 1 January 1977 there were 3,612,000 (26 per 100 inhabitants) telephone connections: the number of apparatuses was 5,412,000.

**Broadcasting.** There are seven national broadcasting organizations with a certain religious or political colour: N.C.R.V., K.R.O., A.V.R.O., V.A.R.A., T.R.O.S., V.P.R.O., and E.O.

There is also the 'Netherlands World Broadcasting Organization' (Stichting 'Radio Nederland Wereldomroep') at Hilversum, which broadcasts in seven foreign languages, particularly to the English-speaking world, the Middle East, Indonesia and South America.

Finally the 'Nederlanse Omroep Stichting N.O.S.' ('Netherlands Broadcasting Organization') is responsible for nationwide broacasts not coming under the responsibility of any of the denominational stations.

All these organizations are independent, but there is a Government Commissioner responsible to the Government for the fulfilment of ministerial decisions with regard to broadcasting.

On 1 January 1977, 3,754,000 television sets (27 per 100 inhabitants) were registered. Radio sets are not registered separately.

## NEWSPAPERS

**De Tijd.** F. 1845. Roman Catholic. Daily. N.Z. Voorburgwal 65, Amsterdam.

**De Volkskrant.** F. 1920. Independent Progressive. Daily (morning). Circulation 250,000. Wibautstraat 148–50, Amsterdam.

**Trouw.** F. 1943. Protestant. Box 85g Wibautstraat 131 Amsterdam.

**Het Vrije Volk.** F. 1900. Witte de Withstr. 25, Rotterdam.

**De Waarheid.** F. 1940. Communist. Keizersgracht 324 Amsterdam.

**NRC-Handelsblad**, combination of Nieuwe Rotterdamse Courant, founded 1844, and Algemeen Handelsblad (Amsterdam), founded 1824. Liberal. Westblaak 180, Rotterdam-3002.

**De Telegraaf-De Courant Nieuws van de Dag.** F. 1893. Independent. Basisweg 30, Amsterdam.

**Algemeen Dagblad.** F. 1879. Independent. Westblaak 180, Rotterdam.

**Het Parool.** F. 1940. Independent. Wibautstraat 131, Amsterdam.

## ATOMIC ENERGY

There are three undertakings concerned with atomic development. The Foundation Energy Centre (E.C.N.), The Institution for Fundamental Research in Connection with Atomic Materials and The Research Laboratory for Electrical Undertakings (K.E.M.A.). In addition to the E.C.N. there are now two other organizations concerned with research and development, The Reactor Committee of the Foundation for Fundamental Material Research (F.O.M.) and The Joint Establishment for Nuclear Energy Research (J.E.N.E.R.) with which the Norwegian Institute for Atomic Energy co-operates.

The Dutch Government is among those of the 27 countries who have signed a bilateral agreement with the U.S.A. in connection with atomic development.

At the end of 1975 there were two nuclear power stations for the production of electric energy; their total capacity amounted to 530 M.W.

## EDUCATION

Since 1 August 1975 there is compulsory education for children extending over a period of 10 years (from six or seven years of age through 15 or 16 years of age). Compulsory education is free.

In the school year 1975/76 there were 8,568 primary schools attended by 1,453,467 pupils, 885 special schools for mentally and physically handicapped children attended by 83,364 pupils.

Secondary general education is received by 766,391 pupils in 1,441 schools. Secondary vocational education is given in 1,438 junior vocational schools attended by 402,907 pupils, in 562 senior vocational schools attended by 114,287 pupils and 384 vocational colleges attended by 111,249 students.

Moreover 244,839 pupils are registered in part-time education (i.e. apprenticeship schemes, other part-time vocational and general education).

There are 14 universities attended by 127,644 students in 1976/77 (provisional data).

## RELIGION

Approximately 34 per cent of the population is Protestant and 40 per cent Roman Catholic. The majority of the Protestants belong to the Dutch Reformed Church; other Protestants belong to the Calvinist faith. Two per cent of the population belong to the smaller churches and 24 per cent of the population does not belong to any church. (Source: 14th Census of 28 February 1971.)

# Overseas Netherlands

The former Netherlands Colonies acquired a new status set out in a Decree proclaimed on 29 December 1954. The Charter of the Kingdom provides that the Overseas Territories of the Netherlands Antilles shall have what is essentially a commonwealth standing with independent governments and ministries but with a constitution within the framework of that of the Netherlands. They owe allegiance to the Netherlands Crown, and the Government and ministry are invested with the same responsibilities as those of the Netherlands itself. In both States the Crown is represented by a Governor. Each member of the Kingdom is independently administered but matters of mutual concern in the field of foreign policy and of defence, etc., are acted upon after consultation between the partners.

The Overseas Territory of Surinam became an independent Country on 25 November 1975.

## NETHERLANDS ANTILLES

### (*Nederlandse Antillen*)

The total area is 1,004 sq. km. and the population at 31 December 1972 was: 230,825 (Curacao: 150,008; Aruba: 61,294; Bonaire: 8,181; St. Maarten: 8,970; St. Eustatius: 1,401; Saba: 971).

**Government and Ministry**

*Minister-President and Minister for General Affairs, and Acting Minister of Finance:* R. J. Isa.
*1st Vice-Minister-President and Minister of Justice:* H. R. Dennert.
*2nd Vice-Minister-President and Minister of Economic Development:* F. J. Pijpers.
*Education and Cultural Affairs:* R. Elhage.
*Economic Affairs:* D. G. Croes.
*Traffic and Transport:* L. A. I. Chance.
*Public Health and Welfare:* Mrs. L. E. da Costa Gomez-Matheeuws.
*Labour and Social Affairs:* Dr. R. F. McWilliam.
*Minister Plenipotentiary at The Hague:* S. G. M. Rozendal.

#### FINANCE AND BANKING

Expenditure and Revenue in 1972 (million Antillian guilders, exchange rate 1 U.S. $ = 1,79 Antillian guilder):

| | *Expenditure* | *Revenue* |
|---|---|---|
| Central budget | 121·3 | 121·7 |
| Curacao separate budget | 102·7 | 102·9 |
| Aruba separate budget | 67·1 | 62·8 |

The central bank is the Bank van de Nederlandse Antillen, established in 1828, of which all shares are owned by the Government.

#### PRODUCTION, INDUSTRY AND COMMERCE

The chief industry is the refining of oil, imported from Venezuela. In the last few years however, the Government has succeeded in its efforts to attract foreign industries, e.g. Texas Instruments, the Continental Milling, the Dry-dock Company, etc., and to promote tourism. In 1971, 282,928 stay-over tourists visted the Netherlands Antilles.

Total exports and imports for 1971 were f.o.b.; Exports NAfl. 1,239 million and imports NAfl. 1,508 million c.i.f.

**Seat of Government**—Willemstad at Curaçao.

**Governor**—Dr. B. M. Leito.

#### GOVERNMENT

The Government of the Netherlands Antilles, an autonomous part of the Netherlands' Kingdom, is headed by a Governor. He has constitutional power. The Ministers are appointed by him in accordance with the parliamentary system and they are responsible for the executive to the legislature (The Staten). The 'Staten' consists of 22 members elected by general suffrage. The Netherlands Antilles are independent and have control of their own affairs. As to the affairs of the Kingdom of the Netherlands, which consist of the countries the Netherlands, Surinam and the Netherlands Antilles, the decisions therein are taken on a tripartite basis. This system was laid down in the Charter of the Kingdom which came into force on 29 December 1954. In conducting Kingdom affairs the Kingdom avails itself of the Netherlands constitutional institutions wherein the Netherlands Antilles represent their own interests with full voting power by means of their Minister Plenipotentiary (Mr. S. G. M. Rozendal, since March, 1971), who has the right of voice and vote in the Council of Ministers of the Kingdom, while there is also a provision enabling this Minister to exhibit the point of view of his country in the Council of Ministers and in the Parliament of the Kingdom. The Acting Governor is Mr. J. R. L. Beaujon (appointed 16 June 1970) and the Minister-President in office is Mr. R. J. Isa (appointed 15 November 1972).

#### LOCAL GOVERNMENT

In 1952 the Netherlands Antilles Island Regulation provided for island autonomy of each of the four insular communities, Aruba, Bonaire, Curaçao and the Windward Islands. The autonomous powers of the insular communities are divided systematically over the local institutions, i.e. the Island Council (Eilandsraad, consisting of members elected by general suffrage), the Executive Council (Bestuurscollege) which conducts most of the island executive, and the Lieutenant-Governor (the Gezaghebber), who is responsible for the maintaining of public peace and order.

The Netherlands Antilles consist of six islands in two groups, Curaçao, Aruba, Bonaire and 550 miles apart the Windward Islands, St. Maarten, St. Eustatius and Saba. Curaçao and Aruba are the main islands, but the other islands especially St. Maarten are also important regarding tourism.

# New Zealand

(MEMBER OF THE COMMONWEALTH)

**Capital**—Wellington.

**Sovereign**—H.M. Queen Elizabeth II.

**National Flag**: The Blue Ensign, charged in the fly with four stars five-pointed red and bordered white, to represent the Southern Cross.

## CONSTITUTION AND GOVERNMENT

THE first European to discover New Zealand was Abel Tasman who sighted the coast on 13 December 1642, but he did not land. Captain Cook, who visited the country in 1769, circumnavigated the islands and made friends with the native Maori tribes. In the early nineteenth century the country was frequented by whalers and casual traders. Some of these settled there and a small European and chiefly British population was gradually built up. The settlers contained a ruffianly element which made trouble with the Maoris. This led to the annexation of the country by the British Government, which felt itself responsible for the maintenance of order. In 1840 the Treaty of Waitangi, signed by Captain William Hobson, R.N., representing the British Government, and many Maori chiefs, transferred sovereignty over the country to Queen Victoria while guaranteeing native rights of ownership of land.

An Act granting representative institutions to the Colony was passed by the Imperial Parliament in 1852. Provision was made for the constitution of a General Assembly and for the division of the country into provinces. (These were abolished in 1875.) The present form of government dates from 1856, and the structure of local government from 1875. The designation of the Colony of New Zealand was changed to the Dominion of New Zealand on 26 September 1907.

In 1947 the New Zealand Government formally adopted the Statute of Westminster passed by the United Kingdom Government in 1931.

Under this, New Zealand attained complete autonomy. Legislative power is vested in the General Assembly, which now consists of the Governor-General and the House of Representatives, the former 'Upper House'—the Legislative Council—having been abolished since the end of 1950.

The House of Representatives consists of 87 members, 83 representing General electorates and four representing Maori electorates. After each five-yearly population census the boundaries of the European electorates are adjusted to allow for shifts in population. Elections are normally held every three years. The franchise extends to every British subject or Irish citizen, male or female, of 18 years of age, who has resided a minimum of one year in New Zealand and for three months in the electorate for which he claims to vote.

Legislative procedure is based on the British system. Bills are given three readings and discussed in committee. The first reading is voted on without comment; the second reading sees the proposals discussed as a whole; in committee (of the whole House) the clauses are thrashed out in detail; the third reading may, if the bill is very contentious, involve another debate, but it is generally formal only. When a bill has gone through this procedure it goes to the Governor-General for his assent.

New Zealand constitutional procedure is based on that of Great Britain. After a Parliamentary election the leader of the majority party becomes Prime Minister and selects the members of his Ministry. In the Cabinet, which may or may not comprise all the Ministers, is vested the supreme control of national policy within the limits of Parliamentary approval. There is a close relationship between the Cabinet and the Executive Council. All the Ministers, together with the Governor-General, comprise the Executive Council, which, among other things, advises the Governor-General and acts as one of the instruments for giving legal form to policy determined by Cabinet.

**Governor-General**—Sir Denis Blundell, KBE.

### Executive Council

His Excellency the Governor-General.

*Prime Minister, Minister of Finance, Minister in Charge of Legislative Department, Minister in charge of the New Zealand Security Intelligence Service, Minister in Charge of the Audit Department:* Rt. Hon. R. D. Muldoon.

*Deputy Prime Minister, Minister of Foreign Affairs and Overseas Trade*, Rt. Hon. B. E. Talboys.

*Minister of Labour and State Services:* Hon. J. B. Gordon.

*Minister of Agriculture and Maori Affairs, Minister in Charge of the Rural Banking and Finance Corporation:* Hon. D. MacIntyre.

*Minister of Trade and Industry:* Hon. L. R. Adams-Schneider.

*Minister of Justice:* Hon. D. S. Thomson.

*Minister of Energy Resources, Minister of Electrictiy, Minister of National Development, Minister of Regional Development:* Hon. G. F. Gair.

*Minister of Education and Science and Technology:* Hon. L. W. Gandar.

*Minister of Health and Immigration:* Hon. Air Commodore T. F. Gill.

*Minister of Transport, Civil Aviation and Meteorological Services and Railways:* Hon. C. C. A. McLachlan.

*Minister of Works and Development:* Hon. W. L. Young.

*Minister of Housing, Minister in charge of Public Trust Office:* Hon. E. S. F. Holland.

*Minister of Defence and Police, Minister in Charge of War Pensions, Minister in Charge of Rehabilitation:* Hon. A. McCready.

*Minister of Social Welfare, Minister in Charge of the Government Life Insurance Office, Minister in Charge of the State Insurance Office, Minister in Charge of the Earthquake and War Damages Commission:* Hon. H. J. Walker.

*Minister of Internal Affairs, Local Government, Recreation and Sport, and Civil Defence, Minister for the Arts:* Hon. D. A. Highet.

*Attorney-General: Minister of Customs, Postmaster-General:* Hon. P. I. Wilkinson.

*Minister of Lands, Forests, Minister for the Environment, Minister in Charge of the Valuation Department:* Hon. V. S. Young.

*Minister of Tourism, Minister in Charge of Publicity, Minister in Charge of the Government Printing Office:* Hon. H. R. Lapwood.

*Minister of Broadcasting, Minister of Statistics, Associate Minister of Finance, Minister in charge of the Inland Revenue Department, Minister in charge of Friendly Societies:* Hon. H. C. Templeton.

*Minister of Fisheries, Associate Minister of Agriculture:* Hon. J. B. Bolger.

The residence qualification for the House of Representatives has to be validated for election purposes by three months' residence in one electoral district. No elector can be registered on more than one electoral roll. The Maori (a branch of the Polynesian race which emigrated from the Pacific more than 700 years ago) have equal rights with Europeans in respect of election to the House. Like Europeans, they must have been resident at least three months in a Maori electoral district before they can be nominated or elected.

Those of mixed descent can register either for a European or a Maori electoral district.

Although the Maori representation is small, the use and maintenance of the language is ensured by the Standing Orders of the House. Important legislation relating to Maori affairs is officially translated.

New Zealand was the first country in the world to introduce women's suffrage. It came into effect in 1893, and women first became eligible to sit in the House of Representatives in 1919. In 1977, there were four women members.

In 1974, the voting age was reduced from 20 to 18 years.

### House of Representatives

*Speaker:* Hon. Sir Roy Jack.
Representation of the Parties following the Election of November 1975 was: Labour Party, 32; National Party, 55.

## LOCAL GOVERNMENT

In 1876, following the abolition of the provinces, local government assumed the form it still basically retains. Geographically, New Zealand is divided into 103 counties. Administratively, cities, boroughs and independent town districts are regarded as separate entities. There are 135 cities and boroughs, and seven independent town districts. When the population reaches 20,000 a borough may be proclaimed a city. In addition to their usual functions of regulations and governance, some city councils carry on trading enterprises, including bus services, gas and electric power supply. In addition there are a large number of boards administering various services such as land drainage, water supply, electric power, hospitals, harbours and pest control.

### LEGAL SYSTEM

The legal system is based upon the British pattern. The highest Court of first instance is the Supreme Court, consisting of a Chief Justice and 19 other Judges, all appointed by the Governor-General in the name of the Queen. Judges are removable only following an address to the Queen by Parliament. They retire at the age of 72 years. The Supreme Court is a single Court administering both law and equity and possesses by statute all jurisdiction necessary to administer the law of New Zealand. The Supreme Court also hears appeals from decisions of Magistrates' Courts and exercises a general supervisory jurisdiction over those Courts and other inferior courts and tribunals.

The Court of Appeal is the final and highest Court in New Zealand, although in certain cases there is an appeal from the Court of Appeal to the Privy Council. It consists of the Chief Justice (who is *ex officio* a member), a President and two members. The President and members of the Court of Appeal are also appointed Judges of the Supreme Court and may if necessary act as such. Conversely the Court of Appeal may in special cases be augmented by one or more Supreme Court Judges.

Magistrates' Courts are presided over by salaried Magistrates with professional qualifications, although occasionally lay Justices of the Peace sit in minor criminal cases.

There are also special Courts such as the Maori Land Court.

**Supreme Court**

*Chief Justice:* Rt. Hon. Sir Richard Wild, KCMG.

*Court of Appeal:* Rt. Hon. Sir Clifford Richmond, KB. (President).
Rt. Hon. Sir Owen Woodhouse, KB.

### AREA AND POPULATION

New Zealand is about 1,000 miles long, and nowhere wider than 280 miles. It comprises the North Island (area, 44,281 sq. miles) and the South Island (area, 58,093 sq. miles) and several smaller islands (some uninhabited) including Stewart Island and the Chatham Islands, which lie about 450 miles eastwards. The total area is 103,740 sq. miles.

At the census taken on 23 March 1976 the provisional population was 3,129,383

The following table shows the areas and populations of the statistical areas at the Census of 23 March 1976 at which 257,770 persons specified themselves as half or more N.Z. Maori.

| *Statistical Area* | *Area sq. miles* | *Population* |
|---|---|---|
| Northland | 4,883 | 106,960 |
| Central Auckland | 2,155 | 798,291 |
| South Auckland—Bay of Plenty | 14,187 | 471,665 |
| East Coast | 4,195 | 48,301 |
| Hawke's Bay | 4,260 | 144,963 |
| Taranaki | 3,750 | 107,081 |
| Wellington | 10,870 | 591,974 |
| Marlborough | 4,220 | 35,002 |
| Nelson | 6,910 | 75,544 |
| Westland | 6,010 | 24,050 |
| Canterbury | 16,779 | 428,445 |
| Otago | 14,070 | 188,812 |
| Southland | 11,460 | 108,995 |

For the 1971 census seven Statistical Divisions were created, each one comprising a central urban area together with the surrounding heavily populated areas with which it has close economic, social and geographical connections encompassing a total population of 75,000 or more. In addition there are ten Urban Areas with populations of over 20,000 but less than 75,000.

Census populations of the seven statistical Divisions and ten Urban Areas at 23 March 1976 were as follows:

| | |
|---|---|
| *Statistical Divisions* | |
| Auckland | 797,406 |
| Hamilton | 154,406 |
| Napier-Hastings | 109,010 |
| Palmerston North | 88,724 |
| Wellington | 349,628 |
| Christchurch | 325,710 |
| Dunedin | 120,426 |
| *Urban Areas* | |
| Whangarei | 39,069 |
| Tauranga | 48,153 |
| Rotorua | 46,650 |
| Gisborne | 31,790 |
| New Plymouth | 43,914 |
| Wanganui | 39,679 |
| Masterton | 21,001 |
| Nelson | 42,433 |
| Timaru | 29,958 |
| Invercargill | 53,762 |

The following table shows the vital statistics (European and Maori) for two recent years:

| | 1975 | 1976 |
|---|---|---|
| Marriages | 24,535 | 24,127* |
| Births | 56,639 | 55,120* |
| Deaths | 25,114 | 25,452 |

* Provisional

Over 75 per cent of the population live in the seven Statistical Divisions and ten Urban Areas combined while nearly 62 per cent live in the seven Statistical Divisions.

The following table shows the external migration for two years ended 31 March (Immigrants intending permanent residence, and New Zealand residents departing permanently).

| | 1976 | 1977 |
|---|---|---|
| Arrivals | 48,460 | 37,020 |
| Departures | 43,160 | 56,092 |

### METRICATION

New Zealand has converted to the metric system of weights and measures. The system used is a modern version of the metric system known as the International System or SI ('Systeme International d'Unites') which was adopted at the 1960 General Conference of the International Bureau of Weights and Measures in Paris.

### CURRENCY

New Zealand adopted a decimal currency on 10 July 1967 and the main unit of currency is now the New Zealand dollar. This is divided into 100 cents with 1, 2, 5, 10, 20 and 50 cent coins .The Reserve Bank of New Zealand, which is a State-owned institution, has the sole right of note issue. On 11 July 1974 exchange rates were; buying £0·6079 = NZ$1, selling £0·6042 = NZ$1.

Until 7 July 1973 the New Zealand dollar was linked with the U.S. dollar. On that date the New Zealand dollar was revalued by 3 per cent and the Minister of Finance announced that in future the value of the N.Z. dollar would be set in a "constant average relationship" with the currencies of New Zealand's main trading partners. On 9 September 1973 the New Zealand dollar was revalued by a further 10 per cent, devalued on 25 September 1974 by 9 per cent on 10 August 1975 by 15 per cent. On 30 November 1976 by seven per cent relative to all currencies except the Australian dollar and revalued by two per cent on 20 December 1976.

# NEW ZEALAND

## FINANCE

| | 1975–76 | 1976–77 |
|---|---|---|
| **Consolidated Revenue Account** | *thousand $* | *thousand $* |
| Income tax | 2,295,800 | 2,828,500 |
| Estate, racing and stamp duties | 107,600 | 119,000 |
| Sales tax | 311,400 | 353,300 |
| Beer duty | 48,400 | 46,500 |
| Customs duties | 217,000 | 352,900 |
| Motor spirits duty; mileage tax | 76,300 | 100,400 |
| Land tax | 3,600 | 6,900 |
| Motor vehicles fees and charges | 23,900 | 20,600 |
| Energy resources levy | — | 4,000 |
| Foreign travel tax | — | 4,900 |
| Foreign fishing vessel entry tax | — | 500 |
| **National Roads Fund** | | |
| Highways revenue | 101,300 | 107,400 |
| **Total Taxation** | 3,185,300 | 3,844,900 |

| | 1976–77 | |
|---|---|---|
| **Interest on Capital Liabilities** | *thousand $* | *thouand $* |
| Post Office | 19,876 | 28,702 |
| Electricity supply | 59,521 | 75,290 |
| Housing Corporation | 27,559 | 52,634 |
| Other accounts | 52,338 | 93,017 |
| Interest on other public money | 25,618 | 28,319 |
| Profits on trading undertakings | 11,803 | 11,839 |
| Departmental receipts | 57,192 | 137,631 |
| **Total Receipts, Consolidated Revenue Account and National Road Fund (incl. items not listed)** | 3,684,091 | 4,227,784 |

Expenditure from the Consolidated Revenue Account for the year 1976–77 amounted to $4,225,117,000. The gross Public Debt at 31 March 1977 amounted to $6,289,245,000, an increase of $731,308,000 as compared with a year earlier. Of this, overseas debt amounted to $1,826,607,000, an increase of $363,404,000 as compared with the position a year earlier.

By the middle of 1977 some progress had been made towards restoration of balance in the economy. The deficit in the current account of overseas exchange transactions in the year ended March 1977 was $861m an improvement of $156m on the previous March year. The terms of trade which at 31 March 1977 stood at 80 (1957 = 100) showed nevertheless only a marginal recovery from the lowest level experienced since the depression of the 1930's. Since 1973 they have deteriorated by between 35 and 40 per cent.

The Monetary and Economic Council reported that New Zealand is faced with a large deterioration in terms of trade causing a severe erosion of the country's purchasing power. It is estimated that real Gross Domestic Product will have grown only one per cent in the period 1974–76, but the deterioration in the terms of trade will have caused a loss of nine per cent in effective income.

Borrowing from overseas has continued. Amongst loans raised were two Swiss franc loans at $96·9m and two Euro-dollar loans at $160·8m a Deutschemark loan at $42·2m and a Dutch guilder loan at $31·5m. Among member-nations of the O.E.C.D., New Zealand's inflation rate, at 16·9 per cent, was one of the highest recorded in 1976.

Leading amongst the items which lead to an increase of 33 per cent in the value of exports in the year ending 30 June 1977 were wool rising from $456m to $644m meat from $593m to $754m and hide and skins from $77m to $127m.

The present tightening of economic control by the Government is likely to continue as the present demanding situation slowly improves. However, it seems possible that the suddenness of the effects of the Government's new policies may promote a delaying and damaging degree of social and industrial unrest.

## PRINCIPAL BANKS

**Reserve Bank of New Zealand.** (Governor, A. R. Low.) **Established 1934; Sole Bank of Issue for New Zealand; Balance Sheet at 31 March 1976 showed assets:**

| *Assets* | *N.Z. thousand $* | *Liabilities* | *N.Z. thousand $* |
|---|---|---|---|
| Gold and coin | 11,623 | Reserves | 35,712 |
| Overseas assets | 294,595 | Circulation | 401,013 |
| Investments | 807,956 | Deposits | 839,090 |
| Loan and discounts | 479,053 | Other liabilities | 412,496 |
| Other assets | 95,084 | | |
| Total | 1,688,311 | Total | 1,688,311 |

*Head Office:* P.O. Box 2498, Wellington.

**Australia and New Zealand Banking Group Ltd.** (Chairman: Mr. Angus MacKinnon) Consolidated balance sheet at 30 September 1974 showed assets $4,649,157,000; Deposits $A4,649,157,000. *Registered Office:* 71 Cornhill, London, EC3V 3PR; *Head Office for New Zealand:* 196 Featherston Street, Wellington. 200 offices throughout New Zealand. Wholly owned subsidiaries, A.N.Z. Savings Bank (New Zealand) Limited. Deposits $NZ114,383,000.

**BANK OF NEW ZEALAND.** (Chairman, L. N. Ross, CMG). Established 1861; share capital owned by State; Consolidated Balance Sheet 31 March 1977 showed assets $NZ1,956,117,000; Deposits $NZ1, 764,807,000. *Head Office:* Corner Lambton Quay and Customhouse Quay, Wellington. *London:* 1 Queen Victoria Street, EC4P 4HE and 28-30 Royal Opera Arcade SW1Y 4UY. Representative offices in Tokyo and Singapore; Bank Branches: 233 and 4 subbranches.

**National Bank of New Zealand Ltd.** (Chairman, Lord Lloyd.) Established 1872; wholly owned subsidiary of Lloyds Bank-Ltd., London. National Bank of New Zealand owns subsidiary company, National Bank of New Zealand Savings Bank Ltd. Consolidated Balance Sheet at 31 October 1976 showed assets £ sterling £496,892,439; deposits and current accounts £477,652,855. *Head Office:* 8 Moorgate, London, EC2R 6DB; 210 Branches and agencies throughout New Zealand, one branch in Rarotonga, representative offices in Tokyo, Singapore, Manila and New York.

**Bank of New South Wales.** (See Australia.) 159 Branches and agencies in New Zealand. Balance sheet at 30 September 1975 showed assets $A8,850,000,000, Deposit and current accounts $A7,302,392,000. *Chief Office in New Zealand:* 318·324 Lambton Quay, Wellington.

**The Commercial Savings Bank of Australia Ltd.** (General Manager, D. W. Stride.) Balance Sheet at 30 June 1974 aggregate assets $408·3 million; depositors' balances $386·8 million. 656 branches and agencies. *Head Office:* 335–9 Collins Street, Melbourne 3000.

**The Commercial Bank Savings Bank (N.Z.) Ltd.** (General Manager, D. W. Stride). Balance Sheet at 30 June, 1975, aggregate assets N.Z.$35·2 million; depositors' balances N.Z.$35·2 million. 110 branches and Agencies in New Zealand. *Head Office:* 335–9 Collins Street, Melbourne, 3000, *Chief Office* in New Zealand: 328-30 Lambton Quay, Wellington.

## PRODUCTION, INDUSTRY AND COMMERCE

**Agriculture.** Production from farms is the source of just under 90 per cent of New Zealand's export income. Livestock statistics as at 31 January 1977 show dairy stock as totalling 2,966,000, including 2,074,000 cows in milk during season; beef stock totalled 6,505,000 including 2,167,000 cows and heifers used for breeding during season; pigs totalled 536,000; and lambs totalled 39,699,000. The number of sheep totalled 56,400,000 at 30 June 1976.

Herd and flock sizes are steadily being increased to keep farming economic.

Liquid milk production during the year ended May 1976 amounted to 1,398·0 million gallons, of which only 122·3 million gallons was consumed as whole milk or cream. The remainder (bar wastage) was made into butter, cheese, milk powder, or casein.

New Zealand is now the world's leading meat exporting country. There are 42 freezing works from which the frozen meat is taken in specially insulated vans to the wharves and shipped abroad in vessels with specially fitted refrigeration chambers or containers.

The greater part of the arable land is under fodder crops; swedes, turnips, rape and kale are grown extensively. Over much of the country grass is the most valuable crop and provides all-the-year-round grazing for livestock. There is a considerable acreage under grass and clover harvested for seed.

Agricultural production during 1975–76 was valued at $1,796·7 1 million, an increase on the previous year's total of $1,371·8 million.

Over the last thirty years the volume of New Zealand's agricultural production has more than doubled.

New Zealand grows sufficient of most cereals to satisfy her own wants.

Estimated area and yield of principal crops for threshing for the year 1975–76 are as follows:

| *Crop* | *Area (hectares)* | *Yield (tonnes)* |
|---|---|---|
| Wheat | 100,000 | 375,000 |
| Oats | 12,000 | 40,000 |
| Barley | 83,000 | 283,000 |
| Maize | 26,000 | 180,000 |

**Forestry.** Figures issued by the New Zealand Forest Service for the year ended 31 March 1976 show that the output of roughsawn timber was 2,003,000 cubic metres. The output of the major species was as follows (in thousands of cubic metres): for the year ended 31 March 1976, rimu and miro, 266; matai, 20; kahikatea, 32; Douglas fir, 153; beech, 26; tawa, 21; and exotic pines, 1,427.

**Mining.** Coal is the most important mineral, the amount mined in 1976 being 2,486,904 tonnes. Important supplies of natural gas have been discovered and are now being developed. Development of an iron and steel industry, utilizing New Zealand's large resources of black iron-bearing sands, is proceeding and iron-sand concentrate is being exported to Japan. Other metals produced on a small scale include gold, silver, zinc, lead, cadmium, copper.

**Industry.** Other than census figures, the only regular survey of persons engaged in industry is made by the Department of Labour bi-annually as at mid-April and mid-October. The latest available estimate is for October 1976 and the total labour force (including armed services) was estimated to be 1,206,800 distributed as follows:

| | |
|---|---|
| Primary industry | 148,500 |
| Manufacturing industry | 289,500 |
| Building and construction | 90,600 |
| Wholesale and retail trade | 190,100 |
| Transport, storage and communication | 110,700 |
| Community and personal services | 269,100 |
| Finance; electricity, gas and water; armed forces; unemployed, etc. | 108,600 |

Among the 289,200 persons employed in manufacturing, 56,900 were engaged in manufacturing or processing foodstuffs, beverages and tobacco; 49,300 in textiles, clothing and leather; 29,900 in paper and paper products, printing and publishing; 22,300 in chemicals, petroleum, rubber and plastics; 24,400 in wood and wood products; 11,700 in non-metallic mineral products; and 94,700 in base metals, metal products, machinery and equipment, and other manufacturing industries.

The actual value of production in manufacturing is shown in the table below. These figures exclude Motor Vehicle Repairs. The figures cover an annual survey of 85 per cent of the labour force recorded under manufacturing above:

| | 1973–74 |
|---|---|
| Number of establishments | 7,690 |
| Number of persons engaged | 244,522 |
| Value of output (thousand $) | 5,250,878 |
| Net output (net value added) (thousand $) | 1,502,387 |

**Commerce.** Exports of principal commodities are shown below for 1975–76:

| *Commodity* | 1975–76* | |
|---|---|---|
| | *Quantity* (000 tonnes) | *Value* ($ *million*) |
| Beef | 217·8 | 228·7 |
| Veal | 16·4 | 12·6 |
| Lamb | 317·8 | 261·3 |
| Mutton | 86·2 | 33·7 |
| Cheese | 80·8 | 78·2 |
| Milk† | 145·9 | 82·8 |
| Butter | 24·3 | 27·0 |
| Casein | 215·3 | 60·4 |
| Newsprint and Machine Papers | 272·5 | 456·3 |
| Wool | 158·2 | 156·7 |
| Hides and Skins (number) | 29,996,000 | 77·0 |
| Total (incl. other) | — | 2,246 |

* Provisional.
† Dried and condensed.

The total value of imports during the year ended 30 June 1976 were $2,693 million C.D.V. (provisional figures). This compares with $2,492 million during 1974–75.

The values of some principal imports in the year 1975–76 (in N.Z. $ million) were: food and live animals, 133·6; beverages and tobacco, 25·1; crude materials (except fuel), 100·3; mineral fuels, lubricants and related materials, 395·3; chemicals, 307·4; manufactured goods, 558·3; machinery and transport equipment, 964·5; and miscellaneous manufactured articles, 178·0.

Imports and exports by principal countries for 1975–76 are shown below (in N.Z. thousand $):

| *Imports* | 1975–76* |
|---|---|
| **Commonwealth** | |
| United Kingdom | 457,345 |
| India | 22,447 |
| Australia | 514,464 |
| Canada | 53,454 |
| Sri Lanka | 3,849 |
| Malaysia | 19,121 |
| Hong Kong | 40,766 |
| **Others** | |
| U.S.A. | 394,779 |
| Belgium and Luxembourg | 16,797 |
| France and Monaco | 24,468 |
| Western Germany | 96,148 |
| Netherlands | 32,919 |
| Sweden | 49,764 |
| Switzerland | 20,572 |
| Japan | 401,987 |
| Italy | 33,372 |
| Saudi Arabia | 33,771 |
| Iran | 99,404 |

* Provisional

| *Exports* | 1975–76* |
|---|---|
| **Commonwealth** | |
| United Kingdom | 449,415 |
| India | 927 |
| Australia | 288,360 |
| Canada | 60,040 |
| Fiji | 30,846 |
| British West Indies | 30,398 |
| Malaysia | 26,130 |

*continued*

| *Exports* | 1975–76* |
|---|---|
| **Others** | |
| U.S.A. | 277,029 |
| Belgium and Luxembourg | 28,371 |
| France and Monaco | 65,376 |
| Western Germany | 61,578 |
| Italy | 38,028 |
| Netherlands | 35,101 |
| U.S.S.R. | 62,130 |
| Japan | 323,377 |
| Poland | 23,461 |
| China excluding Taiwan | 25,399 |
| Philippines | 34,749 |
| Peru | 16,514 |

* Provisional.

## COMMUNICATIONS

**Roads and Railways.** Except for about fifty kilometres of private railways, mainly serving collieries or sawmills, the whole system is State owned. There are 4,797 kilometres of State railway open for traffic. In 1975–76 gross revenue was $170,207,000 and expenditure $233,160,000. Passengers journeys numbered 20,035,000 (rail) and 13,193,000 tonnes of freight were carried.

The Railways Department also operates road services over more than 5,000 miles of highways.

Road-rail ferries cross Cook Strait to link the North and South Islands.

Formed roads totalled 95,026 kilometres at 31 March 1975. At 30 June 1976 motor vehicles licensed totalled 1,989,453 which includes 1,205,433 cars and 108,026 motor and power cycles.

**Shipping.** The total cargo handled at New Zealand ports in 1976 was 34,863,000 tonnes of which 16,308,000 tonnes was coastal cargo. In recent years the advent of containerisation and roll-on roll-off ships has revolutionised both overseas and coastal shipping. New Zealand's seaborne trade with both Europe and North America is now handled mainly by container ships, while much of the trans-Tasman and coastal trade is handled by roll-on roll-off ships. Lines operating regular sailings include A.C.T., PACE Line, Columbus Line, Farrell Lines, and the Union Steam Ship Company.

A subsidiary of the Government-owned N.Z. Shipping Corporation—the N.Z. Shipping Line—operates in conjunction with Shaw-Savill and Albion Co. Ltd., 2 container ships of 12,227 tons in the U.K.-N.Z. trade. The Corporation itself operates in the Coastal and Pacific islands trade a roll-on roll-off vessel, a bulk aluminium ore carrier and 2 other cargo vessels and will in 1978 introduce a 42,000 ton container vessel to the U.K. and continental service. *Head office:* 1 Brandon St., Wellington, N.Z.

**Civil Aviation.** During the year ended December 1975 a total of 2,312,000 passengers were carried on domestic scheduled services. Freight carried amounted to 61,200 tons. International services flying to and from New Zealand carried 1,179,000 passengers, 30,877 tonnes of freight, and 2,270 tonnes of mail.

The following are the chief New Zealand airlines:

**New Zealand National Airways Corporation.** (Chairman, C. W. Mace, CBE; Chief Executive and General Manager, D. A. Patterson); assets $73 million; *services operated:* Extensive internal air network throughout the North and South Islands. Booking agents for overseas airlines. *Head Office:* The Terrace, P.O. Box 96, Wellington.

**Air New Zealand Ltd.** (Chairman, Mr. C. J. Keppel; share capital $40 million, paid up capital $40 million (owned entirely by New Zealand Government). *Services operated:* Auckland–Sydney; Auckland–Melbourne; Auckland–Brisbane; Wellington–Sydney; Wellington–Melbourne; Wellington–Brisbane; Christchurch–Sydney; Christchurch–Melbourne; Christchurch–Brisbane; Auckland–Nadi; Auckland–Pago Pago; Auckland–Los Angeles (via Nadi/Honolulu); Nadi–Rarotonga; Auckland–Norfolk Island; Auckland–Noumea; Auckland–Los Angeles (via Honolulu); Auckland–Los, Angeles (via Tahiti); Auckland–Hong Kong (via Sydney; Auckland–Singapore. *Head Office:* Air New Zealand House, 1 Queen Street, Private Bag, Auckland.

**Telegraphs and Telephones.** These are operated by the State through the Post Office. There were 980,307 telephone subscribers in 1975.

**Broadcasting and Television.** From February 1977 the Broadcasting Corporation a publicly-owned corporation responsible to a Minister has united under one central Board TV1, TV2 and Radio New Zealand which, nevertheless, retain the maximum practical independence.

Radio New Zealand provides programmes for 52 medium-wave broadcasting stations (and 2 short-wave transmitters); 33 of them broadcasting advertising material. Some non-commercial stations provide a 24-hour service, commercial stations' hours vary, most being from 6.00 a.m. to late evening.

The television networks covers most of the populated areas of the country. At December 1976 there were operating five 300 kW transmitters, one 50 kW, 12 kW of from one to ten kW, and 197 installations of less than one kW. These transmitters provide coverage for 99 per cent of the population.

Colour transmissions using the 625 lines PAL system started from October 1973. Approximately ten per cent of households are equipped to receive transmissions or colour TV sets.

Broadcasting services are financed by advertising and a television licence fee is $NZ 27·50 p.a. A colour television licence is $NZ 45. For the year ended December 1976 there were 821,473 licensed television sets, of these 278,525 were for colour.

**Satellite Communications.** In 1971, an earth station was opened at Warkworth for international telecommunications traffic. The station is also used for live television relays from overseas, using a satellite over the Pacific Ocean.

The satellite system is not used for any educational purposes. The New Zealand government participates in the Earth Resources satellite programme.

## NEWSPAPERS

New Zealand has 40 daily newspapers with a total circulation of 1,070,000. A summary of the eight main daily newspapers is given below. These are published in the four main centres and have a total circulation of approximately 763,600.

**Auckland Star.** F. 1870. Evening. Circulation 133,000. Auckland.

**Christchurch Press.** F. 1861. Morning. Circulation 74 Christchurch.

**Christchurch Star.** F. 1868. Evening. Circulation 69,000. Christchurch.

**Dominion.** F. 1907. Morning. Circulation 77,000. Wellington.

**Evening Post.** F. 1865. Evening. Circulation 100,355. Wellington.

**Evening Star.** F. 1863. Evening. Circulation 25,000. Dunedin.

**New Zealand Herald.** F. 1863. Morning. Circulation 233,250. Auckland.

**Otago Daily Times.** F. 1861. Morning. Circulation 45,000. Dunedin.

## EDUCATION

Education is available on a free and secular basis in State primary and secondary schools. It is compulsory between the ages of 6 and 15 years. Bursaries are liberally available for University education. There are 2,215 public (State) primary and intermediate schools with 474,092 pupils and one Correspondence School with 1,021 pupils. Secondary education is provided in 299 State schools, comprising 257 secondary schools with 193,894 pupils, 42 district high schools with 2,856 pupils, and in addition one Correspondence School with 762 pupils. All of these secondary schools provide general courses of instruction up to the standard required for entrance to university or polytechnic. In 1975 there were 19,500 State primary school teachers and 10,660 State secondary school teachers.

All schools are for European and Maori children alike. In 1975, out of 98,251 Maori pupils attending primary and secondary schools, 95 per cent were attending State schools. Scholarships are available to Maori children living in rural areas where no secondary school is established to enable them to attend selected secondary schools as boarders.

Apart from the State system of education, there are a

number of private schools run by religious bodies or private individuals, but subject to State inspection. The majority are run by the Roman Catholic Church. In 1976 there were 325 primary with 49,899 pupils and 112 private secondary schools with 32,379 pupils.

There are six universities, those of Auckland, Waikato, Massey, Wellington, Canterbury, and Otago, and also one university college of agriculture, Lincoln (near Christchurch). The universities grant degrees in Arts, Science, Commerce, Law, Dentistry, Agriculture, Medicine, Engineering, Forestry, Home Science and Music.

University students comprise over one per cent of the population, there being 38,505 internal students in 1976 and an additional 6,314 extra-mural students.

There are technical institutes at Auckland, Hamilton, Wellington, Christchurch and Dunedin; they were attended by 4,513 full-time students and 97,689 part-time students in 1976. There were also 21,712 students on the roll of the Technical Correspondence Institute.

### ANTARCTIC ACTIVITIES

The Government is continuing its policy of maintaining Scott Base and scientific work in Antarctica has been continued. Further research investigations of national and international value have been initiated at the base. New Zealand scientists are co-operating with those of other countries through membership of the Scientific Committee of Antarctic Research of the International Council of Scientific Unions. At Scott Base the scientific programme in the fields of ionospherics, aurora, geomagnetism, seismology and meterorology have been continued, along with gravimetric and ice-breakout observations in the Ross Island–McMurdo Sound Region. At the joint United States–New Zealand station at Hallett a scientific programme in aurora, ionosphere, geomagnetism, and seismology has been carried out, with the addition of a study in earth currents. Geological and survey mapping of the Ross Dependency has resulted in a survey of Victoria land between Barne Inlet and Shackleton Inlet, approximately 5,000 square miles.

Non-Government projects have included biological investigation on Adelie penguins and Weddell seals in the McMurdo Sound area, investigation of temperature gradients in lakes and study of volcanic moraine fossiliferous deposits.

### RELIGION

There is no State church in New Zealand, nor State aid to any form of religion; nor do the majority adhere to one church. About 32 per cent of the population belong to the Church of England, 20 per cent are Presbyterians, 16 per cent Roman Catholic, and six per cent Methodists. There is a large number of small sects which have most of their adherents in the 14 major cities.

## OVERSEAS TERRITORIES

The island territories of New Zealand can be divided into three groups; the islands which form part of the Dominion proper: outlying islands which were in 1847 proclaimed to be within the geographical boundaries of New Zealand; and islands later annexed. The Cook Islands and Niue are another category. They enjoy self-government, with New Zealand taking responsibility for foreign affairs and defence.

### COOK ISLANDS

The Cook Islands can be divided into two geographical groups. The Southern mainly volcanic group, consisting of the islands of Rarotonga, Aitutaki, Mangaia, Atiu, Mauke, Mitiaro, Manuae, Takutea. It has the greater population and is by far the most fertile. The Northern group is for the most part coral atolls and consists of Palmerston atoll, Suwarrow, Pukapuka, Nassau. Manihiki, Rakahanga and Penrhyn. The total land area is 93 sq. miles.

The High Commissioner represents both the Queen and the government of New Zealand. On 4 August 1965 the Islands attained internal self-government. Executive power is vested in the Cabinet, consisting of the Premier and five other ministers. The new Constitution Act was passed by the New Zealand Parliament in November 1964, but it did not come into force until it had been endorsed by the 22-member Legislative Assembly of the Cook Islands, elected in April 1965.

New Zealand is responsible for the Islands' external affairs and defence, but the New Zealand Prime Minister consults the Premier. Cook Islanders remain citizens of New Zealand, and migrate freely to that country. New Zealand gives considerable financial aid in the form of grants and other forms of assistance.

The population of the Cook Islands on 1 December 1976 was 18,112.

Imports in 1973 amounted to $4,932,000. Exports in 1974 amounted to $1,892,000. Principal agricultural exports in 1974 were bananas (1,110 tons), copra (839 tons), fruit juices (565,547 gals.), canned fruit (94,952 gals.), fruit pulp and mandarins (583 tons). Clothing is also exported (in1970 it was the second largest export earner, after fruit juices) as are smaller quantities of tomatoes, pineapples, and taro.

Justice is administered by the High Court, the Native Land Court and the Native Appellate Court.

There are 24 Government primary schools in the Group, and, in addition, six Roman Catholic Mission primary schools, and one Seventh Day Adventist Mission primary school. Post-primary education is provided by four Government secondary schools and two mission schools on Rarotonga.

An international airport on Rarotonga was opened at the end of 1973.

### NIUE ISLAND

This is a dependency to the West of the Cook Islands group. It has an area of 100 square miles and population was estimated at 3,954 at 31 December 1976. There are on the island eight regional schools and one secondary school at Alofi. The main crop is coconuts, which occupy about 5,000 acres. The other crops of importance are taro. (350 acres), limes (42 acres), passion-fruit (35 acres), yams (25 acres), cassava (25 acres), and Kumaras (35 acres)s Bananas and pawpaws are also grown for local consumption. There are approximately 530 cattle in Niue and 50 sheep. The main livestock owned by Niueans are pigs and poultry.

Imports in 1973 amounted to $721,000 and exports to $137,000. Chief exports were passion fruit ($31,198), plaited ware ($14,277), honey ($10,404), and copra ($20,012). Trade is predominantly with New Zealand; other important trading partners are Fiji, Singapore, Australia and Japan.

Since 19 October 1974 Niue has been self-governing in free association with New Zealand. The constitutional arrangements are similar to those enjoyed by the Cook Islands, i.e. self-government, with New Zealand taking responsibility for foreign affairs and defence.

### KERMADEC ISLANDS

This is a group of five islands about 600 miles north-east of Auckland. They are Raoul (Sunday), Herald, Macaulay, Curtis and L'Esperance Islands. They are volcanic with a mild equable climate and rainfall plentiful but not excessive. Their total area is 8,208 acres. There are 10 inhabitants. All are government employees at the Meteorological Station.

### TOKELAU or UNION GROUP

This, the most northern territory, became a British Protectorate in 1877. It consists of the atolls of Atafu, Nukunono and Fakaofo. Each atoll consists of a number of islets varying in size and circling a lagoon. The islands have a total area of four sq. miles and population of 1,558 (30 June 1976). The Secretary for Maori and Island Affairs acts as Administrator through a District Officer of the Tokelau Islands Administration based in Apia, Western Samoa. Apart from coconuts (used in the manufacture of copra), agricultural products are of a basic subsistence nature, due partly to the poor soil. Fish and shellfish form a staple constituent of the diet of the inhabitants. The principal export is copra valued at $22,658 in the 1975–76 financial year.

### ROSS DEPENDENCY

By Imperial Order of Council of 30 July 1923, the coasts of the Ross Sea with the adjacent islands and territory between 160°E. and 150°W. longitude were proclaimed a British Settlement and placed under the jurisdiction of New Zealand. The settlement was formerly uninhabited, but in 1956–57 it became a base for New Zealand Antarctic expeditions and occupation has been continuous since then. A Ross Dependency Research Committee supervises New Zealands' scientific and industrial programme in the Dependency.

# Nicaragua

## (REPÚBLICA DE NICARAGUA)

**Capital**—Managua.

**President**—General Anastasio Somoza Debayle.

**National Flag:** A tricolour fesse-wise, blue, white, blue, the white charged with the national badge: five mountains and a cap of liberty on a triangle encircled in gold with 'Republica de Nicaragua—America Central'.

### CONSTITUTION AND GOVERNMENT

NICARAGUA is the largest of the republics of Central America. It is bounded on the north by Honduras, on the south by Costa Rica, on the east by the Atlantic and on the west by the Pacific.

The country became a colony of Spain in the early part of the 16th century. It declared its independence in 1821. For some time it formed part of the Republic of Central America but broke away in 1838 to become an independent state.

The present constitution was proclaimed on 11 November 1974. It was drawn up by a Constituent National Assembly. It provides for a Congress of two houses, consisting of 70 deputies and 30 senators with their respective substitutes, elected for a period of six years—42 deputies belong to the majority party and 28 to the minority, 18 senators for the majority party and 12 for the minority. Former presidents of the Republic are appointed senators for life. Executive power is vested in the President, who is elected for six years.

On 21 September 1956 the President, General Anastasio Somoza García, was shot and seriously wounded at a ball. As a result of his wounds, he died on 29 September. His son Colonel Luis Somoza Debayle, was elected President by Congress and took his seat on 1 October. He served until the end of the term in May 1957, and was re-elected for the next presidential term of six years.

On 3 February 1963, Dr. René Schick Gutierrez was elected President. President Schick died of a heart attack on 3 September 1966, and the Vice-President, Dr. Lorenzo Guerrero, took his seat for the remainder of the Presidential term.

General Anastasio Somoza Debayle started his six-year Presidential period on 1 May 1967. On May 1 1972 The National Constituent Assembly vested power in a provisional Junta comprised of members of the two traditional parties: Liberal and Conservative. The Governing National Council, a Triumvirate consisting of General Roberto Martinez Lacayo, Doctor Alfonso Lovo Cordero of the Liberal Party, and Doctor Edmundo Paguaga Irias, of the Conservative Party, were in Office until December 1974 when Popular elections took place.

On the 23 December 1972 an earthquake of force 6·25 on the Richter scale destroyed a large part of the capital city of Manaqua. An estimated ten to twelve thousand people were killed. Plans are now being put in hand for a complete rebuilding of the city.

#### Ministry

*Minister of Defence:* Colonel Herbert Sanchez.
*Minister of Foreign Affairs:* Alejandro Montiel Arguello.
*Minister of Interior:* J. Antonio Mora R.
*Minister of Economic Affairs:* Lic. Juan José Martinez.
*Minister of Finance:* General Gustavo Montiel.
*Minister of Education:* Helia Robles.
*Minister of Public Works:* Ing. Armel Gonzalez.
*Minister of Agriculture:* Ing. Klaus Sengleman.
*Minister of Labour:* Dr. Julio Cardoze.
*Minister of Health:* Adan Cajina.
*Minister of the National District Board:* Dr. Luis Valle Olivares (Major).

### LOCAL GOVERNMENT AND LEGAL SYSTEM

The country is divided into 16 departments, each of which is under a civil governor. There are 125 municipalities.

Judicial power is vested in the Supreme Court of Justice in Managua, with seven judges. There are Chambers of Second Instance at León, Masaya, Granada, Matagalpa and Bluefields and 153 judges of lower tribunals.

### AREA AND POPULATION

Nicaragua covers an area of 49,173 sq. miles. It has a coastline of about 327·5 miles on the Atlantic and 256 miles on the Pacific.

The population at mid-1974 was 2,041,000. The annual average percentage growth rate of the population for the period 1960–74 was 2·7 and for the period 1965–74 was 2·7.

About 998,000 of these live in the western part of the country. They are mostly of mixed Indian and Spanish descent. In the eastern part of the country are the banana plantations and here there are many negroes from the West Indies and natives of mixed Indian and negro blood.

The chief towns, with their populations, are Managua 410,067; León, 71,777; Matagalpa, 66,414; Granada, 44,281; Masaya, 39,545.

### CURRENCY

The unit of currency is the *córdoba* of 100 *centavos*. There are cupro-nickel coins of 5, 10, 25 and 50 *centavos* and banknotes of 1 to 1,000 córdobas.

National banknotes in circulation are in denominations of 1 to 1,000 *córdobas*.

### FINANCE

The GNP at market prices for 1974 was U.S. $ millions 1,360 and the GNP per capita at market prices was U.S. $670 The annual average percentage growth rate of the GNP per capita for the period 1960–74 was 3·0, and for the period 1965–74 was 1·5. [*See the note at the beginning of this section concerning GNP.*]

### PRINCIPAL BANKS

**Banco Central de Nicaragua.** (President Dr. Roberto I. Barquero.) Established 1961. Balance Sheet at 31 December 1976 showed assets of C.$2,071,875,682·49; capital and reserves C.$50,321,265,73; notes in circulation C.$768,946,023·05. *Head Office:* Managua, P.O. Box 2252,2253. *Cables:* Bancedenic. *Telex:* No. 1056.

**Banco Nacional de Nicaragua.** (President, Dr. José M. Castillo.) Established 1912; Government owned, all the share capital is owned by the State; Balance Sheet at 31 December 1970 showed assets C.$988·4 millions; deposits C.$211·4 millions; capital and reserves C.$175·9 millions. *Head Office:* Central Avenue, Managua. 20 Branches and 33 Agencies.

### PRODUCTION, INDUSTRY AND COMMERCE

**Agriculture.** Most of the national production is based on agriculture. The chief products are cotton fibre, coffee, sesame seed, cotton seed, bananas, corn, rice, sugar and meat.

Cotton is the most valuable crop and it accounts for one-third of the total value of exports.

Bananas, originally a very important source of revenue, contracted a disease which attacked the plantations some years ago, and greatly reduced production. By now the production is growing up in the Pacific coast.

Nicaragua is one of the leading cattle countries of Central America and for the past few years has exported boneless beef to the value of 12 million dollars annually.

There has been no census of the livestock population since 1963 when the figures were: horses 174,768; mules, 43,627; asses, 6,726; cattle 1,251,763; pigs, 422,598; poultry 2,253,090.

**Forestry.** The huge forests, much of it green hardwood, are found in the eastern part of the country, and mahogany, pine and red cedar are valuable woods used for export. Only the timber close to the chief rivers is cut, so that the logs may be floated down to the Atlantic.

### COMMUNICATIONS

**Railways and Roads.** The chief railway, the State-owned Pacific Railway, has a total length of 317 km. It links the capital with Granada, on Lake Nicaragua, where it connects with a steamer service to other towns. North-west from the capital the line runs to León, Chinandega and Corinto. At León it connects with a line to Río Grande.

In 1972 there were 12,902·2 km. of roads: 1,185 which are paved; 4,134 all season roads and 5,495 penetration roads.

The Inter-American highway runs for 385 km. from Honduras through Managua to Costa Rica.

**Shipping.** The chief seaports are Corinto, Puerto Somoza and San Juan del Sur, on the Pacific and Puerto Cabezas, Puerto Isabel and El Bluff, on the Atlantic. Corinto handles about 47 per cent of the seaborne trade of the country. The Marina Mercante Nicaraguense S.A. (Mamenic Line) is making good progress and operates regular services between Nicaragua, Central America, Hispaniola, United States and Europe.

**Civil Aviation**

PAWA (Pan-American World Airways) has a regular service from Managua to Central and South American countries and to the United States. Another American line, TACA (Transportes Aeros Centro-Americano) also connects Managua with other capitals of Central America, Mexico, New Orleans and Miami COPA (Compânia Panaméria de Aviacion) connects Managua with other capitals of Central America.

**La Nica—Lineas Aereas de Nicaragua.** (President General Anastasio Somoza D.) Share capital C.$12,000,000 (5 per cent owned by the State, 10 per cent by Pan American World Airways, Inc.); *services operated:* El Salvador, Mexico and Miami (U.S.A.) and internal. *Head Office:* Managua.

**Posts, Telegraphs and Telephones.** The State owns the telegraph and telephone services. In 1969, there were 6,904 km. of telegraph wire and 14,089 km. of telephone wire. There were 13,000 automatic telephones and 3,618 non-automatic telephones (latest available figures).

The All-American Cables and Radio Company has stations at Managua and San Juan del Sur. The Tropical Radio Telegraph Company also has a station at Managua and another at Bluefields, on the Atlantic coast.

The State-owned *Radio Nacional* has 50 broadcasting stations.

**NEWSPAPERS**

**Novedades.** Daily. Managua.

**La Prensa.** Daily. Managua.

**El Centroamericano.** Established 1917. Daily. León.

**El Mundo.** Daily. Granada.

**El Universal.** Daily. León.

**Extra.** Weekly. Managua.

**EDUCATION AND RELIGION**

There were 2,336 elementary schools with 360,000 pupils and 229 secondary and other schools with 32,953 pupils in 1972. There is now one university at Leon, where the former universities of Managua and Granada have been centralized. A Catholic university was founded at Managua in 1961.

Roman Catholicism is the predominant religion but there is complete religious freedom. There is an archbishopric at Managua and bishoprics at Matagalpa, León, Granada, Esteli, Juigalpa and Bluefields.

# Niger

## (RÉPUBLIQUE DU NIGER)

**Capital**—Niamey.

**President**—Lt. Col. Seyni Kountché.

**National Flag:** Three horizontal stripes, orange, white and green; the white charged with an orange disc.

**CONSTITUTION AND GOVERNMENT**

NIGER became independent in 1960. It had been a French colony since 1904. With independence, it left the French Community, of which it had been a member since 1958; but it has signed agreements of cooperation with France. The country was governed, until April 1974, by the President and a council of thirteen ministers and by the sixty member national assembly. In April 1974, Lt. Col. Kountche came to power, suspended the constitution. dissolved the National Assembly, and suppressed all political organizations. He then set up a Provisional Military Council with himself as President and eleven other officers.

**AREA AND POPULATION**

Total area of the country is 1,189,000 sq. km.

The population in mid-1973 was 4,480,000, of which about 4,000 are European. The population of the capital is about 90,000. The annual average percentage growth rate of the population for the period 1960–74 was 2·7, and for the period 1965–74 was 2·7.

**CURRENCY AND FINANCE**

The unit of currency is the Central African Franc. The GNP at market prices for 1974 was U.S. $ millions 540, and the GNP per capita at market prices was U.S. $120. The annual average percentage growth rate of the GNP per capita for the period 1960–74 was −1·8, and for the period 1965–74 was −3·8. [*See the note at the beginning of this section concerning GNP.*]

The 1975 budget was 15·3 million fr. CFA.

**PRODUCTION, INDUSTRY AND COMMERCE**

The mainstays of the economy are agriculture and livestock, which together employ about 90 per cent of the population. The principal crops for 1972–73 were: millet (800,000 metric tons); sorgum (200,000 metric tons); groundnuts (160,000 metric tons); paddy rice (31,000 metric tons); onions (20,302 metric tons); cotton seeds (6,000 metric tons). According to official estimates there are 2 million cattle, 7 million sheep and goats, 345,000 camels, 200,000 horses and 370,000 asses; poultry (est. 1975) 7,100,000. Industry is of minor economic importance, accounting for less than 10 per cent of the G.N.P. Industries already established include two groundnut oil extraction plants, a cement plant, a refrigerated abattoir, a tile factory, a soap and perfume factory, a plastics factory producing domestic articles and footwear, and a number of small metal-working units producing furniture and agricultural implements. Electricity consumption totalled about 59·8 million kW in 1973. A company has been formed to exploit reserves of uranium at Arlit, in the Air Mountains; production began in 1972 when 750 tonnes were produced. A second stage is proposed to increase output to 1,500 tonnes.

Imports were valued at 19 million francs CFA, and exports at 13,712 million francs CFA in 1973.

**COMMUNICATIONS**

The road network of Niger is 7,141 km long of which 793 km are tarred. 70,087 passengers used Niamey airport in 1973, and 7,097 metric tons of freight were moved. There are about 2,000 telephones and 40 post offices.

**EDUCATION**

There are 700 primary schools with 88,000 pupils, 23 secondary schools with 7,000 pupils and one technical school with 190 pupils.

# Republic of Nigeria

## (MEMBER OF THE COMMONWEALTH)

**Capital**—Lagos.

**Head of Government**—Lt. General Olusegun Obasanjo.

**National Flag**: A tricolour pale-wise, green, white, green.

### CONSTITUTION AND GOVERNMENT

THE Federal Republic of Nigeria is the largest single geographic unit along the west coast of Africa and occupies a position where the western and equatorial parts of the Continent of Africa meet. Its greatest length from east to west is over 1,120 miles and from north to south about 1,040 miles. Nigeria is bounded on the west by the Republic of Benin, on the north by the Niger Republic, on the east by the Republic of Cameroon and on the south by the Atlantic Ocean. The Atlantic coast line, variously referred to as Bight of Benin and Bight of Biafra, is about 500 miles long. The Republic of Nigeria is divided into 19 States, as follows: Anambra State, Bauchi State, Bendel State, Benue State, Borno State, Cross River State, Imo State, Kaduna State, Gongola State, Kano State, Kwara State, Lagos State, Niger State, Ogun State, Ondo State, Oyo State, Plateau State, Rivers State and Sokoto State.

At midnight, 30 September 1960 Nigeria became an independent state and a full member of the British Commonwealth.

Meeting on 7 October The Security Council unanimously approved Nigeria's application for admission to the U.N. This was sponsored jointly by Great Britain, Ceylon and Tunisia.

On 1 October 1963 Nigeria became a republic. The Constitution of the Federation was defined in 'The Nigeria (Constitution) Order in Council, 1960' which came into force on 1 October 1960.

The first general elections into the Federal Parliament after the country became a Republic were held on 30 December 1964. As in the 1959 elections, no single political party obtained an absolute majority and the President asked the outgoing Prime Minister and Deputy Leader of the Northern People's Congress, which won the largest number of seats, to form a government. A coalition government was formed consisting of the Northern People's Congress, the National Council of Nigerian Citizens and the Nigerian National Democratic Party. In spite of the coalition government, there was increasing loss of faith between the political parties and among the political leaders. This led to disturbances in parts of the country. The situation deteriorated to the extent that certain army officers attempted to sieze power on 15 January 1966. The Federal Council of Ministers decided to hand over voluntarily the administration of the country to the Nigerian Armed Forces on 16 January 1966.

The Federal Military Government suspended by a Decree the provisions of the Constitution of the Republic relating to the office of the President, the establishment of the Parliament, and the office of the Prime Minister, and the provisions of the Constitutions of the Regions relating to the establishment of the offices of the Regional Legislatures, Regional Governors, their Premiers and the Regional Executive Councils.

The Republic is at present administered by the Head of the Federal Military Government and Commander-in-Chief of the Armed Forces. In the States, military governments have been formed under Military Governors who are directly responsible to the Chief of Staff Supreme Headquarters.

It is the intention of the Federal Military Government to maintain law and order in the Republic until such time as a new Constitution, prepared in accordance with the wishes of the people, is brought into being. All political activities in the country have been banned and all political parties suspended. The Federal Military Government has fixed 1979 as the target date for a return to civilian rule.

A decree establishing the Constituent Assembly has therefore been promulgated. Nominations for elections into the Constituent Assembly ended on 30 June, 1977. The elections took place on 31 August. Altogether 203 members were elected by the Local Government Councils to represent their areas of jurisdiction in the assembly which will meet in Lagos to consider and ratify the draft constitution prepared by the Constitution Drafting Committee, launched in October 1976.

The assembly consists of 230 members. The selected members have been joined by the Chairman of the Constitution Drafting Committee (CDC); chairmen of the seven sub-committees of the CDC and about 20 other members to be nominated by the Supreme Military Council.

### LEGAL SYSTEM

The chief court is the Federal Supreme Court.

Magistrates' courts are established throughout the Federation and a well-organized system of native and customary law courts extends throughout the country.

### AREA AND POPULATION

The area of Nigeria is 923,000 square kilometres.

The population of Nigeria at mid-1974 was 73,044,000. The annual average percentage population growth rate for the period 1960–74 was 2·5, as it was also for the period 1965–74. It is distributed as follows: Lagos State, 1·9 million; Oyo State, 6·4 million; Ondo State, 3·3 million; Ogun State, 1·9 million; Bendel State, 3·1 million; Rivers State, 1·9 million; Cross River State, 4·4 million; Anambra State, 3·8 million; Imo State, 5·1 million; Bornu State, 3·6 million; Bauchi State, 3·0 million; Gongola State, 3·2 million; Kano State, 7·1 million; Sokoto State, 5·6 million; Kaduna State, 5·0 million; Niger State, 1·4 million; Benue State, 3·0 million, and Plateau, 2·5 million.

The population of the largest towns is: Ibadan, 627,379; Lagos, over 665,246; Kano, 295,432; Ogbomosho, 343,279; Port Harcourt, 179,563; Onitsha, 163,032; Ilorin, 208,546; Benin, 100,684; Ife, 130,050; Abeokuta, 187,292; Oyo, 72,000. There are several towns with a population of 20,000 or more.

### CURRENCY

The Central Bank of Nigeria has issued new currency notes as from 3 January 1968 in denominations of ₦20, ₦10, ₦5, ₦1, and 50k. The new notes are of the same sizes as the existing notes and they retain the main features of the existing notes.

The existing notes issued in 1959 and 1965 ceased to be legal tender as from 22 January 1968, on which day also the liability of the Central Bank to redeem the notes ceased.

The Nigerian £ is equivalent to 2·48828 grams fine gold. Foreign rates of exchange are quoted by the Central Bank and by Commercial banks in Nigeria.

On 1 January 1973 Nigeria adopted a decimal currency system. The unit of currency is the *naira* which is divided into 100 *kobo*. 1·56 *naira* is equivalent to one pound sterling.

### FINANCE

The GNP at market prices for 1974 was U.S. $ millions 20,810, and the GNP per capita at market prices was U.S. $280. The annual average percentage growth rate of the GNP per capita for the period 1960–74 was 2·9, and for the period 1965–74 was 6·0. [*See the note at the beginning of this section concerning GNP.*]

**National Development Plan.** The Third National Development Plan 1975–80 was officially launched on 24 March, 1975. During the Plan period, the aggregate investment to be undertaken by the Federal and State Governments in the various sectors of the economy will be in the order of ₦20 billion while the aggregate private sector investment programme is estimated at ₦10 billion giving a total investment of ₦30 billion. The Plan is the biggest and the most ambitious plan ever prepared for Nigeria, for the two last National Development Plans involved capital expenditure of ₦2·2 billion and ₦3 billion respectively. While the two last plans postulated growth rate of four per cent and 6 per cent respectively the present plan postulates a growth rate of over nine per cent. The size of the plan is designed to ensure a radical transformation of the national economy during the plan period.

The plan places emphasis on those sectors of the economy which directly affect the welfare of the ordinary citizen such as housing, water supplies, health facilities, education, general electrification and community development.

The Third National Development Plan represents a major milestone in the evolution of economic planning in Nigeria. Its size and magnitude reflect not only the considerably increased resources now available to Nigeria but also the Federal Military Government's determination to translate the country's vast potential into a permanent improvement in the living standard of all Nigerians.

## BANKS

**Arab Bank (Nigeria) Limited.** Established 1969. (Chairman, Mr. A. M. Shoman; Alternate, Mr. Khalid Shoman: Director, Mr. Mahmoud Beydoun; Alternate, Mr. Munib R. Masri; Managing Director, Mr. T. A. Sharaf.) Assets as at 31 December, 1974, N27,761,252,05, (US $45,050,959,82); deposits and current accounts N13,397,262,18 (US $21,741,077,07). *Head Office:* 36, Boalgun Square, P.O. Box 1114, Lagos, Nigeria. 3 branches.

## PRODUCTION, INDUSTRY AND COMMERCE

The Nigerian National Oil Corporation (NNOC) and nine oil producing companies in Nigeria signed agreements under which the N.N.O.C. acquired either 35 per cent or 51 per cent participating shares in each of the companies. The Federal Government raised its equity interest in the oil exploration industry to a minimum of 55 per cent with effect from April 1, 1974 through a participation agreement with the oil companies.

A decree establishing the Nigerian National Petroleum Corporation (N.N.P.C.) recently promulgated merged the Federal Ministry of Petroleum Resources and the Nigerian National Oil Corporation (N.N.O.C.) under the new organisation. The Corporation was set up to carry on, on behalf of the Government, exploration and prospecting, refining and processing of petroleum products, petroleum marketing, construction and operation of pipelines tankers and other methods of conveyance of crude oil, natural gas and their products.

The chief cash crops grown for export are cocoa, palm kernels, palm oil, groundnuts, benniseed and cotton. Other important agricultural and animal products are rubber, timber and hides and skins. Nigeria also exports tin ore and is the world's largest producer of columbite. The most important part of Nigerian agriculture still remains the production of foodstuffs for local consumption. The main food crops are yams, cassava, maize, rice, fruit, millet, beans and groundnuts.

A N20-million oil refinery, capable of supplying nearly all Nigeria's petroleum requirements, went into production in 1965. The refinery was shut down temporarily because of the civil war in the country, but has since resumed production.

A second refinery under construction at Warri will be 'on-stream' by April 1978, and the contract for the Kaduna refinery has already been awarded and should be ready by 1980.

Secondary industries now in production include cement manufacture, pottery, oil processing, breweries and mineral waters, canning, plastics, prestressed concrete, spinning, weaving, assembly plants, boat building, shoe making, etc.

## COMMUNICATIONS

Two major areas of investment in Nigeria's second National Development Plan are Transport and Communication. The size of the revised National Transport Programme is conservatively put at N885,563,377 as against the original Plan target of N486,838,000. The increase in the allocated amount is caused by changes in the scope of existing projects and the introduction of new ones. The Communication sector is part of a long-term programme began a few years back. The original planned expenditure for the sector was revised from N85·2 million to N112·9 million. The revision was mainly aimed at removing the problems arising from inadequate demand projections on which the programme and projects were based and correcting gross under-estimation of the size and costs of projects therefrom.

The Plan gives high priority to the improvement and expansion of external telecommunications services to link Nigeria with the outside world. This sub-sector has an allocation of about N12·1 million.

The Nigerian Railway Corporation took over control of the railway on 1 October 1955. The system comprises two main lines and several branches. It has a total length of about 2,992 kms. By June 1961, the number of passengers carried was 850,000 per month, about 100,000 more than the previous June.

The Sokoto and Niger States main lines run from Lagos to Maiduguri, a distance of 1,766·4 kms. The Eastern main line runs form Port Harcourt deep-water quay on the Bonny River north wards to Kaduna, a distanceof 910·4 kms; investment in the railway during the current development plan period will amount to N80,756,654 million. This allocation will be spent on track re-laying, re-grading and re-alignment, locomotive, rolling stock, building and equipment.

The rivers Niger and Benue are great navigable waterways and provide a means of communication over a large area of the country. Surveys to improve the navigability of both rivers and of the Niger Delta have been carried out by a Netherlands firm. A dam has been built across the Niger at Kainji.

Begun in 1964, the Kainji Dam took nearly five years to construct. More than half the ₦174 million it cost was provided through the International Bank for Reconstruction and Development, Italy, the United Kingdom, the Netherlands, the U.S.A., and Canada. In addition to providing flood control for the lower reaches of the Niger River to its confluence with the Kaduna River, and water for extensive agricultural irrigation schemes, the lake rising behind the Kainji Dam will furnish 10,000 tons of fish and an initial hydro-electric capacity of 320,000 kW, which is capable of increase to nearly one million kW. The lake will become 85 miles in length and cover an area of 480 sq. miles.

There are regular steamship services between Nigeria and Europe, America, South Africa, Australia, Far East and the West African territories. The two principal ports are Lagos and Port Harcourt. The two principal inland river ports are Burutu on the Niger and Warri on the Warri River. All ports are under the administration of the Nigerian Ports Authority. The Warri and Calabar ports are being further developed for ocean-going vessels and berthing facilities in the ports will be expanded at a cost of £N18 million by the construction of four new berths in Lagos, two in Calabar and two at Warri. The ports of Bonny (an oil terminal) and Koko will also be rebuilt. The Shell-BP has recently completed an oil terminal at Forcados at a cost of N50 million.

Nigeria has a large number of airfields which can be used at all seasons. Regular services are operated by Nigeria Airways, B.E.A., K.L.M., Sabena, Air France and Swissair, which connect with the capitals of Western Europe, and by Pan American Airlines to the U.S.A.

On 1 October 1958 the Nigeria Airways (W.A.A.C.) (Nigeria) Ltd. took over control of the internal and Lagos–London services previously operated by the West African Airways Corporation. The new Company is also operating the West African services previously maintained by W.A.A.C. except the Ghana internal services which have now been taken over by Ghana Airlines. Nigeria Airways is also to acquire a long-haul aircraft for its intercontinental routes, two medium-haul jet aircraft for internal and West African routes and four small passenger cargo aircraft. Several more airlines also operate from Lagos.

The international airports in Lagos and Kano are to be further developed to provide better service to airlines. The runway and aprons will be extended and new communications equipment installed.

There are 72,000 kilometres of roads. Most of the roads have gravelled or earth surfaces, but over 8,000 kilometres are now bitumen surfaced. The Onitsha Bridge, and the major road link between Ijebu-Ode and Benin, which reduces the journey from Lagos to Benin by 224 kilometres, opened in 1964. They will provide an entirely new service not only to the Eastern States but also to the Delta Area of the Bendel State. New roads and bridges, constructed to a very high standard, and the reconstruction of existing roads are the major projects in the current Development Plan. Four major roads will be constructed to link the rest of the country with the four sea ports and new road bridges will be built on the Niger and Benue rivers. A new Lagos–Ibadan expressway is being constructed at a cost of ₦8·8 million while the Eko bridge construction and the Apapa road and Western Avenue projects were completed at a cost of over £N18 million. The total expenditure on roads during the Plan period was £N166·3 million.

Telegraphs and telephone systems are owned and operated by the Government. A system of inland telegraphs connects the majority of the principal towns throughout the country. A major programme of expansion including a network of V.H.F. stations, installation of automatic telephone systems in the main towns and a countrywide system of postal offices and agencies is being developed. External telegraph services are owned and operated by Nigerian External Telecommunications Ltd. through stations at Lagos from which telegraphic communication is maintained with all parts of the world. Radio telephones and telex services connect Lagos with the United Kingdom, the United States and other countries.

A satellite telecommunications earth station is being built in Nigeria for the transmission and reception of messages and television signals through satellites. The earth station will go into service this year.

**NEWSPAPERS**

**Daily Express.** 5/11 Apongbon Street, Lagos.

**Nigerian Daily Sketch.** Ijebu By-pass, Ibadan.

**Nigerian Tribune.** Daily. 98 Shittu St., Adeoyo, Ibadan.

**Nigerian Tide.** 4 Ikwerre Road, Port Harcourt.

**Nigerian Herald.** Gen. Manager, Chief Abiodun Aloba. Telex: 33108 Herald Nigeria. (Kwara State Printing and Publishing Corp.), Offa Road, P.M.B. 1369, Ilorin, Kwara State, Nigeria.

**Nigerian Standard.** Daily. No. 5 Zaria By-Pass, Jos.

**Sunday Standard.** Weekly. No. 5 Zaria By-Pass, Jos.

**New Nigerian.** F. 1966. Daily. English. Circulation 69,267 Editor, Turi Muhammadu. P.O. Box 254, Ahmadu Bello Way, Kaduna, Nigeria.

**Daily Times.** Morning. 3, 5, and 7 Kakawa St., Lagos.

**Morning Post.** Malu Rd., Apapa.

**Nigerian Observer.** 18, Airport Road, Benin.

**West African Pilot.** 34, Commercial Avenue, Yaba.

**Rennaissance.** Star Printing and Publishing Co. Ltd., 9, Works Road, P.M.B. 1139, Enugu.

**Chronicle.** P.M.B. 1074, Calabar.

**EDUCATION**

There are at the moment ten Universities in the country. They are named in the table below:

| *Institution* | *Established* |
|---|---|
| The University of Ibadan at Ibadan | 1948 |
| University of Nigeria at Nsuka | 1960 |
| Ahmadu Bello University at Zaria | 1962 |
| University of Lagos at Lagos | 1962 |
| University of Ife at Ile-Ife | 1962 |
| University of Benin at Benin | 1970 |

Four other new Universities have been recently established, the Universities of Jos, Calabar, Maiduguri and Sokoto.

There are also three colleges in Port Harcourt, Ilorin and Kano affiliated to the Universities of Lagos, Ibadan and Ahmadu Bello respectively.

In addition, the government hopes to reform the contents of general education and make it more responsive to the socio-economic needs of the country and also eradicate illiteracy from society.

It is to this end that the Federal Military government took the bold decision to introduce free Universal Primary Education throughout the country.

The programme was introduced on a voluntary basis in September 1976 but by September 1979, it will be compulsory for all children of school age.

The Federal Government has earmarked N300 million for the implementation of the Universal free Primary Education during the Third National Development Plan.

In the 1977/78 academic session it is expected that over 2·3 million children would enrol for the programme.

**RELIGION**

There are over 19 million Christians in Nigeria, 26 million Moslems and 10 million with other religions. The distribution of populations according to Religion in the 1963 Census are as follows:

| | *Christians* | *Moslems* | *Others* |
|---|---|---|---|
| Northern States | 3,881,437 | 21,386,450 | 5,540,733 |
| Western States | 4,995,691 | 4,458,531 | 811,625 |
| Eastern States | 9,573,622 | 29,964 | 2,790,876 |
| Lagos State | 363,384 | 294,694 | 7,168 |
| Bendel | 1,393,009 | 106,857 | 1,035,973 |

# Norway

(NORGE)

**Capital**—Oslo.

**Sovereign**—King Olav V.

**National Flag:** Red, charged with a white cross bearing a cross of blue, the uprights slightly towards the hoist.

**CONSTITUTION AND GOVERNMENT**

THE present Norwegian Constitution was drafted by a National Assembly at Eidsvoll and proclaimed on 17 May 1814. Several modifications have been passed at various times. It lays down that the Kingdom of Norway is a free, independent, indivisible and inalienable Kingdom. Its form of government is a limited and hereditary monarchy. Executive power is vested in the King and legislation in the Parliament, the *Storting*. Three important general provisions in the Constitution are, first, that no person can be imprisoned without a trial, secondly, that there should be freedom of speech, printing and assembly, and thirdly, that no law may be given retrospective effect.

The *Storting* is composed of 155 members from 19 multi-member constituencies. All Norwegian subjects have the right to vote, provided that they are at least 20 years of age, and have not had their right to vote suspended. A ballot is written and sealed and takes place on the same day in September for all electoral districts. The number of representatives to be elected from each district is permanent in the Constitution. All men and women who are entitled to vote and have resided in Norway for ten years are eligible for election to the *Storting*. The electoral period is four years and the *Storting* cannot be dissolved during an electoral period.

At the first meeting of the *Storting*, it elects from among its members 39 to constitute the *Lagting*, while the rest form the *Odelsting* This division is of importance only with regard to proposals of laws which must be discussed separately in the *Odelsting* and the *Lagting*. All other decisions are made by the united *Storting*. The *Storting* may require modifications to be made in treaties with foreign powers and it is its prerogative when and where necessary to elect the heir to the throne, the King and the Regency.

The King exercises his executive authority through the cabinet, called the *Statsråd*, composed of the Prime Minister and at least seven ministers. The Ministers are entitled to be present during sittings of the *Storting* and to take part in discussions but not to vote.

**Reigning Royal Family.** Lutheran.—Prince Carl of Denmark (see DENMARK) was elected King of Norway 18 November 1905, on that country's separation from Sweden; crowned at Trondheim Cathedral, 22 June 1906. Succession is in the male line and the cadet members of the family are prince or princess of Norway, Royal Highness.

**H.M. OLAV V** (Alexander Edward Christian Frederik), King of Norway; born at Appleton House, Sandringham, 2 July 1903; son of King Haakon VII (born 3 August 1872, died 21 September 1957) by his wife Maud (born 26 November 1869, died 20 November 1938), youngest daughter of Edward VII, King of Great Britain and Ireland; succeeded to the throne on the death of his father; married at Oslo 21 March 1929, Princess Märtha (born at Stockholm, 28 March 1901, died at Oslo, 5 April 1954), 2nd daughter of Prince Carl of Sweden, Duke of Västergötland.

Children: 1. Princess RAGNHILD Alexandra; born at Oslo, 9 June 1930; married at Skaugum, Asker, 15 May 1953, Erling Sven Lorentzen, and has issue. 2. Princess ASTRID Maud Ingeborg; born at Oslo, 12 February 1932; married at Skaugum, Asker, 12 January 1961, Johan Martin Ferner, and has issue. 3. Crown Prince HARALD; born at Skaugum, Asker, 21 February 1937; married at Oslo, 28 August 1968, Miss Sonja Haraldsen, who then became Crown Princess of Norway. Children: Princess Märtha Louise, born at Oslo, 22 September 1971. Prince Haakon Magnus, born at Oslo, 20 July 1973.

**Ministry**

*Prime Minister:* Odvar Nordli.
*Minister of Foreign Affairs:* Knut Frydenlund.
*Minister of Municipal and Labour Affairs:* Leif Aune.
*Minister of Finances and Customs:* Per Kleppe.
*Minister of Defence:* Rolf Hansen.
*Minister of Ecclesiastical Affairs and Education:* Kjølv Egeland.
*Minister of Industry and Handicraft:* Bjarbfmar Gjerde.
*Minister of Trade and Shipping:* Hallvard Bakke.
*Minister of Communications:* Ragnar Christiansen.
*Minister of Fisheries:* Eivind Bolle.
*Minister of Environment:* Gro Harlem Brundtland.
*Minister of Social Affairs:* Ruth Ryste.
*Minister of Consumer Affairs and Government Administration* Annemarie Lorentzen.
*Minister of Justice:* Inger Louise Valle.
*Minister of Agriculture:* Oskar Øksnes.
*Minister without portfolio (law of the sea):* Jens Evensen.

**Parliament** (*Storting*). (Since 1973.)

*President:* Guttorm Hansen.
*Vice-President:* Svenn Stray.
*President of the Lagting:* Torild Skard.
*Vice-President:* Egil Aarvik.
*President of the Odelsting:* Per Borten.
*Vice-President:* Aase Lionæs.

The parties are represented as follows: Labour: 62, Conservative: 29, Centre: 21, Christian Democrats: 20, Socialist Electoral League: 16, Progress Party: 3, Liberals: 2, New Liberals: 1, Independent: 1.

## LOCAL GOVERNMENT

On 1 January 1977 Norway was divided into 47 urban and 407 rural municipalities. These have extensive local self-government. The Municipalities have taxation rights to enable them to undertake certain administrative services, including education and public health, public relief and building and maintenance of roads. The municipal councils are elected by proportional representation for a term of four years.

## LEGAL SYSTEM

The courts of general jurisdiction are the county and city courts, of which there are 106 throughout the country. Most civil cases are decided by a single professional judge; most criminal cases are decided by a professional judge assisted by two lay judges; minor severe criminal cases can be decided by a single professional judge, but only if the defendant admits his offence. Before a civil case reaches the court it has, as a rule, to be subjected to mediation by a conciliation council, consisting of laymen, who try to help the parties to come to an agreement. The conciliation councils have jurisdiction to decide cases of minor importance.

In the courts of appeal (of which there are five) a civil case is decided by three professional judges; lay judges may participate at the request of either party. Criminal cases originating in the lower courts may be retried by the courts of appeal when the question of guilt is at issue; otherwise they are appealed directly to the Supreme Court. The courts of appeal have original jurisdiction in criminal cases of a more severe character. In criminal cases the courts of appeal are composed of three professional judges; the question of guilt is decided by a jury of ten laymen.

The Supreme Court consists of 18 permanent judges (including the president). During a regular session of the court a case is decided by five judges. A committee of three judges of the Supreme Court deals with special cases and eliminates cases which do not require court session. In very important cases the court may sit in plenum.

## AREA AND POPULATION

Norway has a coastline of 2,650 km., taking no account of the numerous fjords and inlets. The total area is 323,886·2 sq. km. The total population at 1 January 1977 was 4,035,202.

The annual average percentage growth rate of the population for the period 1965–1974 was 0·8. For 1971–1975 it was 0·7.

Populations of principal towns are as follows:

Oslo, 462,497; Bergen, 212,755; Trondheim, 135,558; Stavanger, 87,360; Kristiansand, 60,037; Drammen, 50,821.

**Vital Statistics:**

| | 1972 | 1973 | 1974 | 1975 | 1976 |
|---|---|---|---|---|---|
| Marriages | 28,596 | 28,141 | 27,344 | 25,898 | 25,389 |
| Births | 64,260 | 61,208 | 59,603 | 56,345 | 53,474 |
| Deaths | 39,375 | 39,958 | 39,464 | 40,061 | |

* Preliminary figure

## CURRENCY

The unit of currency is the kroner of 100 øre. There are copper coins of 5 øre and nickel coins of 10, 25 and 50 øre and one and five kroner. Banknotes have been issued in denominations of 10, 50, 100, 500 and 1,000 kroner. The rate of exchange at the end of 1976 was 8,769 kroner to the pound sterling.

## FINANCE

**Budget Estimates 1977**

Central Government current net expenditures in millions of kroner:

| | |
|---|---|
| Administration | 3,327·6 |
| Defence | 5,738·7 |
| Justice and police | 1,260·8 |
| Education | 7,267·0 |
| Health services | 893·3 |
| Other social purposes | 6,939·8 |
| Price regulation | 3,471·1 |
| Industrial purposes | 14,759·3 |
| Interest on external debt | 850·0 |
| Interest on internal debt | 2,579·0 |
| Repayment of debt | 1,854·3 |
| Other expenditures | 8,064·1 |
| Total net expenditure (1976) | 46,560·9 |
| Total net expenditure (1977) | 57,005·0 |
| Total tax revenue (1976) | 35,570·4 |
| Total tax revenue (1977) | 40,116·0 |

The principal items of revenue are taxes on consumption and taxes on income and property. Direct taxes on income and property are paid to the municipalities as well as to the State. The National debt at 31 December 1976 amounted to 50,290 million kroner of which 9,560 million kroner were foreign loans.

The GNP at market prices for 1976 was U.S.$ millions 31,227 and the GNP per capita at market prices was U.S.$ 7,756. The annual average percentage growth rate of the GNP per capita for the period 1960–76 was 4·0 and for period 1965–76 was 3·8. [*See the note at the beginning of this section concerning GNP.*]

## PRINCIPAL BANKS

**Norges Bank.** (Governor, Knut Getz Wold.) Est. 1816; Sole Bank of Issue for Norway; the whole of the share capital is owned by the State; Balance Sheet at 30 June 1977 showed assets Kr.28,895,090,000; deposits and current accounts Kr.9,831,470,000; total banknotes in circulation Kr. 14,612,598,000 gold reserve Kr.247,740,000. *Head Office:* Bankplassen, Oslo; 20 Branches.

**Andresens Bank A/S.** (Managing Director, H. P. Schnitler.) Balance Sheet at 31 December 1976 showed total assets Kr. 4,026,832,096. *Head Office:* Torvgaten 2, Oslo 1.35 Branches.

**Bergen Bank** (Bergens Privatbank–Bergens Kreditbank AS merger 27 October 1975). Chairman, J. E. Greve; Deputy Chmn., J. Stove-Lorentzen; Managing Director, Finn B. Henriksen; Deputy Man. Dir., Finn Holck Pisani. Balance sheet total of new bank is (approx.) ten thousand million Kroners. About 100 offices and branches. There will be two main offices, in Bergen and Oslo. *Head Office:* 2 Torvalmenning, Bergen, Norway.

**Bergens Skillingsbank A/S.** Est. 1857; (Manager, Gunnar Lorentzen; Chairman, Nils Moe Nilssen.) Assets as at 31 December 1976, Kr.335,465,459; deposits and current accounts, Kr.318,202,156. *Head Office:* Raadstuplass 4, 5000 Bergen. Number of branches 3.

**Bøndernes Bank A/S.** (Chief General Manager, Vilhelm Kierulf.) Est. 1918; Balance Sheet at 31 December 1976 showed total assets Kr.1,406,554,615. *Head Office:* 23 Ovre Slottsgate., Oslo. 4 Offices and 11 Branches.

**Christiania Bank og Kreditkasse.** (Managing Director, Sven Viig and Tor Moursund). Est. 1848; Balance Sheet at 31 December 1976 showed total assets Kr. 8,145,525,853. *Head Office:* 7 Stortorvet, Oslo: The bank has 84 branches and offices in Norway, a wholly owned subsidiary in Luxembourg, Christiania Bank og Kreditkasse International S.A., and a Representative Office in New York.

**Den Norske Creditbank.** (Chairman, Sverre Grötter; Managing Director, Johan Melander.) Est. 1857; Balance Sheet at 30 June 1976 showed assets Lux.Fr.11,474,418,947. *Head Office:* 21 Kirkegaten, Oslo; 91 Branches.

**Fellesbanken A.S.** (Chairman, E. Torjusen; Managing Director, Victor Pedersen.) Est. 1919; Balance Sheet at 31 December 1972, showed assets Kr.2,124,502,664. *Head Office:* Kirkegaten 14, 16 & 18, Oslo; 9 offices and branches.

**Kristiansands og Oplands Privatbank A/S.** Est. 1926. President, Mr. Jørgen Øslebø; Chairman, Mr. Einar Rasmussen. Assets as at 31 December 1975, Nkr.413,888,902; deposits and current accounts, Nkr.302,087,633. *Head Office:* P.O. Box 202, N-4601 Kristiansand S. Number of Branches 5.

**Opplandsbanken A/S.** Est. 1929. President, Mr. Ansgar Wiken; Chairman, Mr. Sverre Askvig. Assets as at 31 December 1975, Nkr. 390,850,889; deposits and current accounts, 329,980,412. *Head Office:* Hunnsvn. 5, 2800, Gjoevik. Number of Branches 8.

**Oslo og Akershus Sparebank.** (Chairman, Erling H. Mathiesen; Managing Director, Arne Jensen.) Est. 1822; Balance Sheet at 31 December 1976 showed assets Kr.4,406,505,360, deposits and current accounts Kr.4,102,268,677. *Head Office:* Avre Slottsgate 3, Oslo 1. *Administrative Offices:* Tordenskioldsgate 8–10, Oslo 1; 84 offices.

## PRODUCTION, INDUSTRY AND COMMERCE

**Agriculture.** About 8·0 per cent of the population of Norway is occupied in agriculture and forestry. The total farm area amounts to 2·2 million acres, of which about three-fifths is temporary or permanent meadow land. Most of the farms are small and are worked personally by the owners and their families. The total grain crop in 1976 was estimated at 846,200 tons.

The area (in hectares) of the principal crops for the year 1976 was as follows:

| | | | |
|---|---|---|---|
| Wheat | 20,138 | Mixed grain } Peas } | 496 |
| Rye | 2,149 | | |
| Barley | 172,830 | Potatoes | 27,908 |
| Oats | 102,454 | Hay | 364,666 |

The livestock population in 1976 was as follows:

| | | | |
|---|---|---|---|
| Horses | 21,750 | Goats | 67,758 |
| Cattle | 921,231 | Pigs | 697,822 |
| Sheep | 1,667,488 | Hens | 3,798,369 |

Animal products in 1976 were as follows (in thousand metric tons): beef, 60; veal, 3; pork, 76; mutton, 16. Production of milk was 1,894,000 metric tons.

**Forestry.** The forests of Norway are estimated at about 65,000 sq. km. of productive woodland, and this woodland accounts for about 20 per cent of the total land area. Approximately 80 per cent of the forest land consists of coniferous trees. On the average, 8·5 million cubic metres are cut annually for industrial use, and 0·7 million cubic metres for fuel and domestic use. Of the cut, about 3·8 million cubic metres are used in the lumber industry, 4·5 million cubic metres for pulping and 0·2 million cubic metres for special timber. Paper and paper pulp cover eight per cent of Norway's total exports.

**Fisheries.** Fishing has always been one of the most important sources of income for Norway. The total number of persons engaged in fishing in 1975 was 35,261. A great deal of the fishing is seasonal and many of the fishermen have other occupations during the remainder of the year. The total yield of the fisheries in 1976 was 3,155,000 metric tons, with a value of 2·653 million kroner.

**Mining.** Production and value of the chief mineral products for the year 1975 are shown below:

| *Production* | *Quantity (metric tons)* | *Value (thousand kroner)* |
|---|---|---|
| Iron ore and ilmenite (60 per cent Fe) | 4,635,955 | N.A. |
| Copper ore and concentrates (21 per cent Cu) | 105,965 | 124,341 |
| Pyrites (41 per cent S) | 475,112 | 32,717 |
| Zinc ore and concentrates (50 per cent Zn) | 47,301 } | 56,449 |
| Lead ore and concentrates (63 per cent Pb) | 5,345 } | |
| Molybdenum ore (100 per cent $MoS_2$ | — | — |
| Quartz (97 per cent $SiO_2$) | 824,081 | 17,811 |
| Limestone (90 per cent $CaCO_3$) | 5,119,949 | 67,994 |

The structure of the manufacturing industry is to a large extent determined by the raw materials produced within the country and the abundant power resources of the Norwegian waterfalls. The annual production of electric power in 1974 was 73,036 million kWh and in 1975 76,700 million kWh. The following table gives details of the chief industries for the year 1975:

| *Group* | *Persons Employed* | *Gross value of Production (1,000 kr.)* |
|---|---|---|
| Coal mining | 702 | 100,953 |
| Crude petroleum and natural gas products | 1,015 | 4,295,778 |
| Metal ore mining | 4,961 | 1,066,822 |
| Other mining | 3,780 | 732,775 |
| Food manufacturing | 49,209 | 17,212,074 |
| Beverages | 4,736 | 1,555,601 |
| Tobacco products | 1,233 | 770,957 |
| Textiles | 12,560 | 1,876,795 |
| Wearing apparel, except footwear | 10,164 | 1,053,402 |
| Leather and leather products, except wearing apparel | 1,389 | 200,210 |
| Footwear | 1,818 | 197,138 |
| Wood and wood products, except furniture | 24,735 | 5,802,556 |
| Furniture and fixtures | 10,406 | 1,710,999 |
| Paper and paper products | 20,484 | 7,092,392 |
| Printing, publishing and industries | 33,254 | 4,319,920 |
| Industrial chemicals | 8,546 | 3,289,848 |
| Other chemical products | 7,851 | 2,219,012 |
| Petroleum refining | 685 | 4,166,630 |
| Petroleum and coal | 1,573 | 722,640 |
| Repair of rubber products | 2,878 | 423,115 |
| Plastic products | 7,520 | 1,351,023 |
| Ceramics | 1,654 | 181,697 |
| Glass and glass products | 2,194 | 350,369 |
| Mineral products not elsewhere classified | 8,989 | 2,417,044 |
| Iron, steel and ferroalloys | 16,550 | 5,264,951 |
| Non-ferrous metals | 12,186 | 5,385,946 |
| Metal products, except machinery and equipment | 28,469 | 4,941,675 |
| Machinery | 30,380 | 9,898,047 |
| Electrical apparatus and supplies | 23,544 | 4,774,540 |
| Transport equipment | 52,631 | 11,926,752 |
| Professional and scientific instruments, photographic and optical goods | 1,110 | 162,790 |
| Other manufacturing industries | 4,052 | 558,636 |

**Commerce.** The following table shows the value (in thousand kr.) of imports and exports by principal countries for the year 1976:

| Country | Imports | Exports |
|---|---|---|
| Denmark | 3,341,356 | 3,057,156 |
| Sweden | 11,110,582 | 6,137,209 |
| United Kingdom | 5,925,611 | 12,890,910 |
| Western Germany | 9,381,313 | 4,122,121 |
| U.S.A. | 3,956,225 | 2,031,250 |

The following table shows the value of imports (thousand kr.) by commodities for the years 1975 and 1976.

| Commodity | 1975 | 1976 |
|---|---|---|
| Grain and flour | 598,449 | 763,326 |
| Sugar | 547,903 | 477,655 |
| Coffee, tea, cocoa, etc. | 532,206 | 781,132 |
| Wine and spirits | 133,588 | 145,458 |
| Tobacco | 166,429 | 179,584 |
| Fodder stuffs | 88,582 | 109,902 |
| Oils and fats | 84,013 | 109,183 |
| Oilseeds, oilnuts etc. | 505,186 | 354,659 |
| Chemicals and dyestuffs | 3,853,806 | 3,451,903 |
| Fertilizers | 495,954 | 413,935 |
| Rubber and rubber articles | 502,271 | 561,232 |
| Hides and leather | 150,906 | 233,677 |
| Textile articles | 1,591,309 | 1,819,769 |
| Clothing | 1,662,979 | 2,049,322 |
| Fuel and lubricating oils | 4,968,915 | 6,781,527 |
| Iron and steel | 3,228,694 | 2,765,328 |
| Machinery and requisites | 9,788,145 | 11,398,411 |
| Ships | 6,585,208 | 8,103,241 |
| Other transport vehicles | 3,317,494 | 5,718,625 |
| Others | 11,743,799 | 14,315,046 |

The following table shows the value (in thousand kr.) of exports by commodities for the years 1975 and 1976:

| Commodity | 1975 | 1976 |
|---|---|---|
| Fish and herrings | 1,706,656 | 2,089,709 |
| Canned fish, etc. | 366,824 | 460,666 |
| Oils and fats | 703,816 | 500,986 |
| Chemical fertilizers | 973,908 | 759,551 |
| Paper pulp | 1,052,477 | 1,129,945 |
| Paper | 1,930,777 | 2,087,902 |
| Metals and ores | 7,040,989 | 8,438,136 |
| Machinery and parts | 4,016,366 | 4,131,060 |
| Other articles | 20,430,525 | 23,732,322 |

## COMMUNICATIONS

**Roads and Railways.** Practically all the railways in Norway are owned by the State. At the end of 1976 the State railway network included 4,241 km. of lines, of which 2,440 were electrically operated. The total receipts of the State railways for the year amounted to 1.308 million kroner and expenses to 1,880 million kroner. The State railways carried (as from 1976 altered way of calculating) 32·7 million passengers and 29·2 million metric tons of goods including 17·9 million metric tons of iron ore transported by the 'Ofot' railway).

At 31 December 1976 the total length of the roads was 78,116 km., including streets in towns.

**Shipping.** The Norwegian Merchant Fleet at 31 December 1976 consisted of 2,042 merchant vessels with an aggregate tonnage of 27,048,000 gross tons. These figures refer only to vessels of 100 gross tons and over, and exclude fishing and catching boats, floating whaling factories, tugs, salvage vessels and ice-breakers.

The merchant fleet was composed as follows: tanker fleet (including gas carriers) 15·4 million gross tons; Bulk carrier fleet (including combined carriers) 9·3 million gross tons; Passenger ships 0·5 million gross tons and other dry cargo fleet 1·9 million gross tons.

The whaling and fishing (of 100 gross tons and over, not included in the merchant fleet) consisted of 680 vessels of 229,000 gross tons.

At the same time 3·7 million GRT new ships were on order for Norwegian account.

Norwegian shipping is a private industry, wholly owned and operated by private individuals and companies. About 92 per cent of the fleet is transporting goods exclusively between foreign ports. Half the tonnage is engaged on timecharter and consecutive voyages of long duration.

The fleet serving international trade is managed by about 300 shipping companies. The following companies had more than 0·8 million GRT at their disposal as of 1 July 1975.

**Sig. Bergesen d.y. & Co.** (Partners: Sigval Bergesen d.y., Jacob Erland Jacobsen); total tonnage, 2,247,700 GRT. *Trades:* Tanker trade, combined trade. *Head Offices:* Drammensvn. 106, Oslo and N. Strandgt. 27, 4000 Stavanger.

**Fearnley & Eger A/S** (Chairman: Nils J. Astrup.) Total tonnage 941,467 GRT, consisting of liner vessels, bulk carriers, car/bulk carriers, tankers, LPG/Ammonia tankers and semi-submersible oil rigs.

**Leif Hoegh & Co. A/S** (Board of directors: Ove Høegh, Chairman; Christian A. Olsen, Vice-Chairman and President; Westye Høegh, Per. A. Flaate); total tonnage, 1,431,878 GRT. *Trades:* bulk liner, gas, car and combined. *Services operated:* Høegh Lines Round the World Service—US & Canada (all coasts) to Indonesia, Singapore, Colombo, Karachi and Persian Gulf and return via Indonesia, Singapore and west coast India/Ceylon to Canada & US (all coasts). Høegh Lines West Africa Service—Scandinavia, the Continent, UK, France and West Africa (Mauritania/Angola and return. *Head Office:* Parkveien 55, Oslo 2.

**Anders Jahre** (Partners: Anders Jahre, Jörgen Jahre and Björn Bettum); total tonnage, 1,711,665 GRT. *Trades:* tanker trade, tramp trade and passenger operations. *Services operated:* Oslo–Kiel–Oslo (passenger service). *Head Office:* P.O. Box 250, 3201 Sandefjord.

**Hilmar Reksten** (Partners: Hilmar Reksten, Audun Reksten, Johan Reksten); total tonnage, 1,183,723 GRT. *Trades:* Tanker trade, tramp trade. *Head Office:* Fjøsanger pr. Bergen.

**Wilh. Wilhelmsen** (Partners: Tom Wilhelmsen, Niels Werring Jr., Wihelm Wihelmsen; Managing Director, L.T. Løddesøl, Director, F. Scheie). Total tonnage, 2,285,316 DWT. *Trades:* Tanker, trade, bulk trade, offshore services, liner operations. *Services operated:* Between Europe and South Africa, New Zealand, Persian Gulf, India, Pakistan, Bangladesh Far East (as a partner in ScanDutch), Australia (as a partner in ScanAustral). Between Far East and Persian Gulf and between U.S. and Far East and U.S. and West Africa (the two last mentioned as a partner in Barber Lines). *Head Office:* Roald Ammundsensgt. 5, Oslo 1.

### Civil Aviation

**Braathen's South American and Far East Air transport A. S. (S.A.F.E.)** (President, Ludv. G. Braathen; Executive Vice-President, Bjørn G. Braathen). Share capital Kr.21,470,000; *services operated:* Charter flights to all parts of the world. Domestic routes: Oslo–Stavanger v.v.; Oslo–Kristiansand–Stavanger v.v.; Oslo–Trondheim v.v.; Oslo–Ålesund v.v.; Oslo–Kristiansund v.v.; Oslo–Lista v.v.; Oslo–Molde v.v.; Stavanger–Bergen–Ålesund–Trondheim–Bodø–Tromsø. *Head Office:* Ruseløkkvn. 26, Oslo 2.

**DNL—Det Norske Luftfartselskap A.S. (Norwegian Air Lines)** (Chairman, Jens Chr. Hauge; General Manager, Johan Nerdrum); share capital Kr. 129,976,000 (50 per cent owned by the State); DNL is the Norwegian partner in the Scandinavian Airlines System (SAS) which operates an extensive intercontinental and European route network including the following domestic services in Norway: Oslo–Bergen v.v., Oslo-Haugesund v.v.–Oslo–Trondheim–Bodø–Bardufoss–Tromsø v.v., Tromsø–Alta–Lakselv–Kirkenes v.v., and Oslo–Stavanger v.v., Oslo–Kristiansand S. v.v. and Bergen–Stavanger v.v. operated as domestic parts of international routes. *Head Office:* Oslo Airport, Fornebu.

**SAS—Scandinavian Airlines System** (President, Knût Hagrup; Executive Vice-Presidents, K. A. Kristiansen, Björn Törnblom and C. E. Lindh; Senior Vice-President, Gunnar Sandberg). A consortium partnered by Danish, Norwegian and Swedish Airlines (DDL, DNL and ABA) in proportion 2 : 2 : 3 for the operation of joint traffic from Scandinavia to rest of Europe, North, Central and South America, Africa, Near and Far East. SAS carried 7·2 million passengers in 1976–74. *Head Office:* Stockholm 161 87 Bromma 10. *Regional Offices:* Oslo, Copenhagen and Stockholm.

**Telegraphs and Telephones.** The telegraphs and principal telephone services are owned and operated by the State. During the year 1976, 1,554,000 telegrams were dispatched. Telez calls totalling 38,749,000 minutes were made. On 31 December 1976 the State Telegraph Administration and linked networks all had 1,476,091 telephones installed.

**Broadcasting.** At the end of the year 1976 the State Broadcasting Company "Norsk rikskringkasting" operated five stations on the long-wave band, 22 medium-wave, one short-wave stations and 391 V.H.F. transmitters in the three metre band. There were 1,302,192 registered licences. The annual cost of a licence is 60 kroner.

Regular television was started in the autumn of 1960. At the end of the year 1976 the State Broadcasting Company operated 817 television stations and transmitters. There were 1,078,965 registered licences, including 311,941 colour television licences. The annual cost of an ordinary licence is 320 kroner and the cost of a colour licence is 420 kroner (including the radio fee).

### NEWSPAPERS

**Aftenposten.** F. 1860. Conservative. Circulation for 1976. Mon.–Sat. morning 212,165; Special Sat. morning 236,766.

**Arbeiderbladet.** F. 1884. Labour. Circulation 69,115. Oslo.

**Dagbladet.** F. 1869. Liberal. Circulation 116,880. Oslo.

**Adresseavisen.** F. 1767. Conservative. Circulation 74,681. Trondheim.

**Bergens Tidende.** F. 1868. Liberal. Circulation 81,050. 5000 Bergen.

**Verdens Gang.** F. 1945. Independent. Circulation 130,716. Oslo.

Altogether 72 daily newspapers are issued in Norway, the daily net circulation in 1976 being 1,619,000. The total number of newspapers other than dailies is 82, of which 79 are issued two, three, four or five days per week and 3 are issued weekly. The net circulation is 409,000.

### ATOMIC ENERGY

Institutt for Atomenergi (IFA) is the national atomic energy research establishment. IFA's head office, laboratories and facilities for general nuclear research are situated at Kjeller near Oslo, where three research reactors have been built. The first reactor JEEP came into operation in 1951 and has been in almost continuous operation until 1967 when it was finally shut down. The second reactor at Kjeller the zero power reactor NORA was in operation from 1961 until 1968. A third reactor, JEEP II, was completed in course of 1966 and became critical in December 1966. JEEP II is used for production of radio-isotopes and as a neutron source for research on solid-state physics. At Kjeller are also laboratories for manufacturing radio-isotopes, metallurgical hot-cells and other facilities for applied nuclear research.

In Halden, 80 miles south of Oslo, a prototype boiling heavy water reactor of 25 MW heat capacity has been in operation since 1959 .The research at the Halden reactor is carried out as one of the joint projects of the OECD Nuclear Energy Agency (–NEA).

Apart from research and technical progress work being done at the Institute of Atomic Energy, the universities in Oslo and Bergen and the Norwegian Institute of Technology in Trondheim are engaged in research work in nuclear physics.

On 1 July 1973 the act concerning nuclear energy activities came in to force. In February 1973 the Nuclear Energy Safety Authority was established. It is directed by an executive board of seven members.

Norway has no uranium or thorium mines and only small deposits of fissionable materials have hitherto been discovered within her territory. Another material of great importance to nuclear energy production, heavy water, is however being produced in Norway in quantities of about 10–15 tons a year.

### EDUCATION

Since 1860 elementary education has been free of charge and compulsory for all Norwegian children between seven and 14 years of age. Work, which is now completed, has been done all over the country in extending the compulsory schools to include pupils of 15 and 16 years of age. With the exception of the few private schools, Norway's primary schools are maintained by public funds, the expense being divided between the central, provincial and local authorities. Dental and medical care and transport are provided.

After finishing their compulsory education the pupils might continue their education in one of the upper secondary schools, i.e. folk high schools, secondary general schools or vocational schools. The final examination of the upper stage of the secondary general school was earlier a condition for enrolling at the universities and equivalent institutions. It is now possible to enroll at the universities without this examination. The total number of pupils at October 1975 in the upper secondary schools was 152,000. The number of pupils in the upper stage of the secondary general school was 65,000. In the programmes of business, trade, craft, transport and communications, health, agriculture etc. in the vocational schools the number of pupils was 79,000.

At 1 October 1975 the number of pupils of 17, 18 and 19 years old as a percentage of the registered population was 62, 48 and 31 respectively.

In Norway, education at the third level is provided in universities or colleges. Institutions offering education at the third level, second stage are classified as universities. By this definition there were 13 universities in Norway at 1 October 1975: The Agricultural University of Norway, the University of Oslo, the Free Faculty of Theology, the State Veterinary College, the Oslo School of Architecture, the Norwegian College of Physical Education and Sports, the State Academy of Music, the National Academy of Liberal Arts, the University of Bergen, the Norwegian School of Economics and Business Administration, the University of Trondheim (College of Arts and Science and Norwegian Institute of Technology) and the University of Tromsø.

There are eight different types of colleges in Norway: District Colleges, colleges for teachers, colleges for engineers, schools of social sciences, schools for advanced nursing education, military colleges and other schools of higher learning. At 1 October 1975 there were 105 colleges in Norway.

The total number of students at universities and colleges was 66,628 at 1 October 1975, of these 40,774 were students at universities, 11,070 at colleges for teachers and 6,652 at colleges for engineers. The University of Oslo is the greatest educational institution in Norway, with 20,224 students.

### RELIGION

The Evangelical-Lutheran Church is the National Church of Norway, as laid down in section two of the Constitution. There is, however, complete freedom of religion. The Church is administered by the Ministry of Ecclesiastical Affairs and Education and all servants are thus subordinate to the King and Parliament. Approximately 94 per cent of the population belong to the State Church.

## SVALBARD

The archipelago of Svalbard includes all the islands situated between 10°–35° E. and 74°–81° N., that is Spitsbergen (formerly Vestspitsbergen), Nordaustlandet, Edgeøya, Barentsøya, Prins Karls Forland, Bjørnøya, Hopen, Kong Karls Land, Kvitøya, and many smaller islands. The total area is about 62,000 sq. km. (24,000 sq. miles); the largest island, Spitsbergen, covers 39,400 sq. km. (15,000 sq. miles).

Svalbard is believed to have been discovered in the late 12th century by Norwegians, but was re-discovered in 1596 by the Dutch navigator, Willem Barents.

During the 17th and 18th centuries whale hunting took place by British, Dutch, Danish-Norwegian, German and other whalers, and the three nations first mentioned tried to gain sovereignty. When the whaling died out, the interest in sovereignty also faded away. Russian fur hunters regularly wintered in the islands from about 1715 to about 1820, and from the end of the 18th century Norwegian trappers and sealers wintered in Svalbard.

Coal has been known in Spitsbergen for a long time, but it was not until about 1900 that the coalfields aroused economic interest, and the first mining started a few years afterwards. Coalmining is now the principal industry. in Svalbard. At present coal is mined in one Norwegian community (Longyearbyen) and in two Soviet communities (Barentsburg, Pyramiden). A second Norwegian mining community, Sveagrua, is being prepared for re-opening. In 1975 375,406 tons of coal were exported from the Norwegian mines and 456,179 from the Soviet mines.

By the treaty of 9 February, 1920, sovereignty was given to Norway and in 1925 Svalbard was officially taken over by this country as part of the Kingdom of Norway.

The total population as at 31 December 1976 was 3,495, of which 1,171 lived in Norwegian communities while 2,324 were residents of Soviet communities.

Five Norwegian Arctic meteorological stations are in operation; Bjørnøya (since 1920), Hopen (since 1945), Longyearbyen (since 1957), and Ny-Ålesund (since 1961). A Norwegian research station at Ny-Ålesund, administered by Norsk Polarinstitutt, was built in 1968, and since then geophysical observations and research have been carried out there.

## JAN MAYEN

A mountainous island about 380 sq. km. (145 sq. miles) in area, situated about 71° 00′ N. and 8° 30′ W. (between Iceland and Svalbard) entirely of volcanic origin. Beerenberg, its highest peak, reaches 2,277 m. (7,470 ft.), on the north-eastern side of which a major volcanic eruption started on 18 September 1970. The discovery of the island was claimed by several skippers at the beginning of the whaling period, but it is generally assumed that Henry Hudson was the discoverer. Its present name derives from the Dutch whaling captain Jan Jacobsz May, who indisputably landed there in 1614. The island came under Norwegian sovereignty in 1929. By a law of 27 February 1930, Jan Mayen was made part of the Kingdom of Norway. It is uninhabited, save for a meteorological station (established 1921), a LORAN station (1959) and a CONSOL station (1968). There is a landing strip for aircraft on the island.

## BOUVETØYA

**Bouvetøya** (Bouvet Island) is situated in the Southern Atlantic at 54° 26′ S. and 3° 24′ E., with an area of about 48 sq. km. (19 sq. miles). The island was discovered by the French naval officer Jean Baptiste Lozier Bouvet in 1739. In 1825 it was claimed for Great Britain by the British sealing skipper George Norris, who landed and hoisted the British flag. He had, however, no authorization, and the British Government did nothing to maintain the occupation.

On 1 December 1927 Captain Horntvedt, on the 'Norvegia'. Expedition sent out by Lars Christensen, claimed it for Norway, and by Order in Council of 23 January 1928, it was placed under the sovereignty of Norway. A diplomatic dispute concerning the claim arose between the United Kingdom and Norway, resulting in the renouncement of the British claim in November 1928. By law of 27 February 1930, the island became a Norwegian dependency.

## PETER I ØY (Peter I Island)

An almost completely ice-covered uninhabited Antarctic island of volcanic origin at 68° 48′ S. and 90° 35′ W., area about 180 sq. km. (69 sq. miles). Discovered in 1821 by the Russian Admiral von Bellingshausen. On 2 February 1929, Dr. Ola Olstad, leader of the II. 'Norvegia' Expedition, claimed it for Norway. On 1 May 1931, the island was placed under the sovereignty of Norway, and by Act of 24 March 1933, added to Norway as a dependency.

## DRONNING MAUD LAND (Queen Maud Land)

Part of Antarctica between 20° W. and 45° E. The land is highly ice-covered, and the coast mostly surrounded by extensive ice-shelves forming a high barrier towards the sea. The territory was first explored by Norwegian, German and U.S.A. expeditions. The first wintering took place at Maudheim (about 71° 03′ S. and 10° 56′ W.) by the Norwegian-British-Swedish Antarctic Expedition, 1949–52.

The Norwegian Antarctic Expedition, 1956–60, had its base at Norway Station (about 70½° S., 2½° W.). This station was taken over by South Africa, which closed it in 1962 and erected in the neighbourhood a new station, SANAE, which is still working. A second (small) South African station, of varying name and position, has been in operation from 1969. A Japanese station (Syowa) (69°00′ S. and 39° 35′ E.) was erected in February 1957 and is still working. A Soviet station (Lazarev) was erected near the shore about 12° E. in the season of 1959–60. A new Soviet station, Novolazarevskaja, which is still working, was erected about 90 km. inland. On 14 January 1939, Dronning Maud Land was pronounced Norwegian territory by the Norwegian Government. From 1957 the land has had the status of Norwegian dependency. Save for the above-mentioned stations the land is uninhabited.

# Oman

**Capital**—Muscat.

**Sultan**—Qaboos bin Said.

**National Flag:** Red, Green, and White. The dexter quarter of the field gules (by the hoist), the remaining three quarters per fess argent and vert over all, a bar gules charged with trophy of two crossed daggers.

## CONSTITUTION AND GOVERNMENT

THE independent Sultanate of Oman is situated at the easterly corner of Arabia. It was called the Sultanate of Muscat and Oman until 1970. Gwadur, situated on the Persian coast, formerly belonged to the Sultanate, but was transferred to Pakistan on 8 September 1958. The present Sultan who was born in 1940 succeeded his father Said bin Taimur on 23 July 1970, following a bloodless coup.

His Council of Ministers, as of 10 April 1976, comprises:

*Governor of the Capital and Personal Adviser to His Majesty:* Sayyid Thuwaini bin Shihab.
*Minister of Diwan Affairs:* Sayyid Hamad bin Hamud.
*Minister of Justice:* Sayyid Fahr hin Hamad al-Sammar.
*Minister of State for Foreign Affairs:** Mr. Qais Abdul Mun'im al Zawawi.
*Minister of Information and Culture:* Sayyid Fahd bin Mahmoud al Said.
*Minister of Communications:* Eng. Abdul Hafidh Salim Rajab.
*Minister of Education:* Ahmed Abdullah Ghazzali.
*Minister of Lands and Municipalities:* Dr. Asim Jamali.
*Minister of Social Affairs and Labour:* Mr. Khalfan bin Nasr al Wahaibi.
*Minister of Waqf and Islamic Affairs:* Sheikh Walid bin Zahir al Hin'ai.
*Minister of Omani Heritage:* Sayyid Faisal bin Ali al-Said.
*Minister of Public Works:* Mr. Karim Ahmed al Haremi.
*Minister of the Interior:* Sayyid Muhammad bin Ahmad.
*Minister of Commerce & Industry:* Mr. Mohammed Zubair.
*Minister of Agriculture, Fisheries Petroleum & Minerals:* Mr. Said Ahmed al Shanfari.
*Minister of Health:* Dr. Mubarak el Khadduri.
*Governor of Dhofar and Minister without Portfolio:* Sheikh Braik bin Hamud al Ghafari.
*Minister of Youth and Deputy Minister of Defence:* Sayyid Fahr bin Taimur al-Said.

* The Sultan acts as his own Minister of Foreign Affairs and of Defence.

Except for an area between Dibba and Kalba, belonging to Sharjah and Fujairah of the Union of Arab Emirates, on the east coast of the Musandam peninsula, the coast line of the Sultanate extends from just south of Tibat on the west coast of the peninsula to Ras Darbat Ali, a cape on the southern coast of Arabia about half-way to Aden and including the Sultan's southern province of Dhofar. Inland, the Sultanate border meets the desert sands of the Rub-al-Khali.

The Sultan is directly descended from the Arab Al Bu Said dynasty which rose to power in the middle of the 18th century. Another branch of the same family ruled in the island of Zanzibar until 1964. The Sultan has treaties of friendship and commerce with Britain, the United States, France, Holland and India.

The Sultanate consists of three divisions: a coastal plain, a range of hills and a plateau. The coastal plain varies in width from ten miles near Suwaiq to practically nothing in the vicinity of Matrah and Muscat where the hills descend abruptly into the sea. The mountain range runs generally from west to south-east. The hills are for the most part barren, but in the high area round Jabal Akhdar there is considerable cultivation. The plateau has an average height of 1,000 feet. In the valleys agricultural development has increased of recent years. North-west of Muscat the coastal plain is known as the Batinah, which is fertile and relatively prosperous. The coastline between Muscat and the fertile province of Dhofar is barren. Along the littoral rainfall is low and Muscat itself is judged to be one of the of the hottest harbours in the world. Special permission is required from the Ministry of the Interior for travel outside the Capita Area. The rocky coast-line and lack of shelter makes cruising in the waters difficult and dangerous.

The rebellion in Dhofar started in 1964 perhaps as a reaction to the harsh rule of Sultan Said bin Taimur. It developed into a guerrilla campaign organised by the Popular Front for the Liberation of Oman. This organisation received and still receives support and shelter from the Peoples Democratic Republic of Yemen. After the accession of Sultan Qabus steady progress was made in containing the rebellion. Military assistance was received from the United Kingdom (in the supply of seconded officers) and from Iran. The fighting was effectively ended in the last months of 1975 and the Sultan is now trying to consolidate the peace in Dhofar with a development programme.

## AREA AND POPULATION

The estimated area of the Sultanate is 120,000 sq. miles and the population. UN estimate in mid-1975, was 766,000, chiefly Arabs, except in the coastal towns of Muscat and Matrah where the population includes Baluchis, Indians Pakistanis and Zanzibaris. The total population of the towns of Muscat and Matrah was 28,000 in 1973. The annual average percentage population growth rate for the period 1960–74 was 3·1, and for the period 1965–74 was 3·1.

## CURRENCY AND FINANCE

On the 1 November 1972 a new currency called the Rial Omani was brought into circulation. The main unit is the Rial which is divided into 1000 new Baiza. There are notes of Rials 10, 5, 1, ¼, ½ and 100 Baiza and coins of Baiza 100, 50, 25, 10, 5 and 2.

The GNP at market prices for 1973 was U.S. $millions 610, and the GNP per capita at market prices was U.S. $840. The annual average percentage growth rate of the GNP per capita for the period 1960–73 was 13·5, and for the period 1965–73 was 19·4. [*See the note at the beginning of this section concerning GNP.*]

The following banks are established in Oman: British Bank of the Middle East; Chartered Bank; National and Grindlays Bank; National Bank of Oman; Arab Bank; Habib Bank; Bank of Oman and the Gulf; Arab African Bank; Arab European International Bank; Chase Manhattan; Banque de Paris et des Pays Bas; Bank Melli Iran; Bank of Oman, Bahrain and Kuwait; Arab International Bank for Foreign Commerce and Development; Bank of Credit and Commerce Int. SA.

Oman's imports were RO 231 million in 1975. Imports from the UK totalled £102 million in 1976 and Exports to the UK totalled £73 million in 1976.

## PRODUCTION, INDUSTRY AND COMMERCE

**Agriculture.** There is extensive date cultivation along the Batinah coast and in the valleys of the Interior and dates and dried limes are the principal export crops. Cereals are cultivated for local consumption. Other activities include coastal fishing and the raising of sheep, goats and camels by the inland tribes. Cattle are raised in the hills of Dhafar which receive the summer monsoon. Plans have been proposed to develop agriculture and fishing on a large scale.

**Industry.** The Oman Government took a 60 per cent share in Petroleum Development (Oman) Ltd. in July 1974. Shell now own 34 per cent. Production totalled 105·8 million barrels in 1974. A new oil concession inland south-west of Fahud was awarded to a joint French/Japanese company, Elf-Aquitane Sumitomo in May 1975.

**Development.** For many years the Sultanate was a poor country with a total annual income of less than £1,000,000. Since the advent of oil revenues in 1967 and the change of régime in 1970, prospects have improved and a wide-ranging development programme has been initiated with special emphasis on health, education and communications. The rapid increases in the price of crude oil late in 1973 have effectively quadrupled the income of the Sultanate (from RO 53 million in 1972 to RO 470 million in 1976. The total revenue is RO 495 million for 1976).

Total planned expenditure for 1977 is RO 621 million. In

Dhofar the new civil airport at Salalah is only planned, not under construction. Government centres are now being established in central as well as eastern areas of the province.

As part of the programme to improve health conditions new hospitals have been completed at the main provincial centres and there are a large number of health centres and dispensaries in lesser towns. There are now 13 hospitals and 150 doctors.

## COMMUNICATIONS

There are now 789 km of asphalt roads and 5,500 km of ungraded roads linking the coast with the interior and beyond to the towns of the United Arab Emirates.

The towns of Muscat and Matrah are linked by a tarmac road to Sohar in the north. This road provides access to the new International Airport at Seeb. The road from Nizwa to Seeb is complete. Roads from Ibri to al-Qabil (Buraimi) and from Sohar to Buraimi are under construction.

The port of call for steamers is Matrah, where eight deep-water berths have been completed in the new Port Qaboos. Other ports are Sohar, Sur and Khaburah, suitable only for local craft.

The post office in Muscat which was previously run by the G.P.O. London, was taken over by the Oman government on 30 April 1966, who now issue their own stamps. Cable and Wireless Limited maintain the telegraph and telephone service.

## EDUCATION

Education has seen enormous progress in the 4 years since the change of régime. Primary schools have increased from 3 to 180 and a number of secondary and specialized schools are being opened. But only 30 per cent of children of primary school age attend school at present. There are now in 1976 237 schools and 70,000 pupils.

# Pakistan

**Capital**—Islamabad.

**President**—Fazal Elahi Chaudry.

**National Flag:** Green, charged at the centre with a crescent and star five-pointed white; a white stripe pale-wise at the hoist to one-quarter width of the flag.

## CONSTITUTION AND GOVERNMENT

PAKISTAN became an Independent Sovereign State as a result of the Partition of India on 14 August 1947, and became a Republic within the Commonwealth on 23 March 1956, comprising the two provinces of East Pakistan and West Pakistan. On 7 October 1958, Major-General Iskander Mirza, the then President of Pakistan, issued a Proclamation abrogating the Constitution of 23 March 1956. General Muhammad Ayub Khan, Commander-in-Chief of the Pakistan Army, was appointed Chief Martial Law Administrator. On 27 October 1958, President Iskander Mirza decided, in the interest of the country, to step aside and handed over all the powers to General Muhammad Ayub Khan, who became the President of Pakistan with Presidential Cabinet to assist him. He was re-elected in January 1965.

Under the new Constitution announced by President Ayub on 1 March 1962, in the National Assembly elections on 23 March 1965, the Pakistan Muslim League won an absolute majority.

On 21 February, President Ayub announced his intention not to contest the Presidential Election due to be held on 23 March 1970. On 25 March 1969 he resigned in favour of General A. M. Yahya Khan, who immediately declared Martial Law throughout the country and became (as well as President of Pakistan) Chief Martial Law Administrator—a step made necessary by the seriously unsettled state of some parts of the country.

A general election was held on 7 December 1970, when 53 million people went to the polls to elect a Constituent Assembly. The balloting was secret, and based on the principles of 'one man, one vote' and universal adult suffrage.

Ten different political parties and 16 Independents won seats in the Constituent Assembly. The Awami League, headed by Sheikh Mujibur Rahman, obtained 167 seats; the Peoples' Party, led by Mr. Z. A. Bhutto, had 90 seats. Neither of these two political parties had a candidate elected from the other wing of Pakistan.

The National Assembly, under the Legal Framework Order 1970, was required to frame the Constitution within 120 days. The Assembly was scheduled by the President to meet on 3 March 1971.

In the interim period (Dec. 1970–Feb. 1971), political parleys were held and negotiations conducted among the various political party leaders, in particular Sheikh Mujib and Mr. Bhutto, with a view to arriving at a general agreement on the broad aspects of constitution-making. But there was complete stalemate.

The inaugural session of the Constituent Assembly, scheduled for 3 March 1971 was, therefore, postponed by the President until 25 March to allow more time for political leaders to reach agreement.

The postponement of the Constitutional Assembly was greeted in East Pakistan by rallies and demonstrations and by the launching of a 'Civil disobedience, non-co-operation' movement.

On the night of 25–26 March the Pakistan Army took action in an endeavour to ensure that no plans for a more serious uprising to establish an independent Republic of Bangladesh could be implemented.

In view of the grave situation, President Yahya Khan banned the Awami League as a political party, but general elections were not annulled. Subsequent events led to war between India and Pakistan and the occupation of East Pakistan by the Indian Army in December 1971. The Cease-fire was agreed upon by both countries on 17 December 1971. Subsequently the independent state of Bangladesh was created, comprising all that was East Pakistan.

President A. M. Yahya Khan resigned on 20 December 1971. Mr. Zulfikar Ali Bhutto was sworn-in as President and Chief Martial Law Administrator of Pakistan from the same date. Martial law was lifted on 21 April 1972 and President Bhutto was sworn in under the Interim Constitution as the first civilian president on the same date.

President Bhutto immediately made several important appointments at Central and Provincial levels and later named his cabinet. Provision was made for the eventual enlargement of his cabinet.

After assuming office President Bhutto took several steps that affected National policy, foreign policy and social reform. He also indicated that the permanent Constitution would be ready by 23 March 1973.

On 30 January 1972 Pakistan left the Commonwealth. Significantly President Bhutto annulled the results of the by-elections of East Pakistan, removed the ban on the National Awami Party and announced the unconditioned release of Sheikh Mujibar Rahman from house arrest.

On 14 August 1973 a new Constitution, already passed by the National Assembly on 10 April 1973, was adopted. Under this Constitution President Bhutto stepped down to become Prime Minister. Mr. Fazal Elahi Chaudry was elected as President of Pakistan in his place. Parliament consists of two houses: the Senate, which is the Upper House, and the National Assembly.

In July 1977 there was a military takeover headed by General Mohammad Zia-ul-Haq.

The Senate consists of sixty-three members. Each Provincial Assembly elects fourteen members (there are four provinces). Five are elected by the members from the Federally Administered Tribal Areas in the National Assembly and finally, two are chosen from the Federal Capital. The term of office of its members is four years, half of them retiring every two years, except in the case of the members elected by the Members from the Federally Administered Tribal Areas, of whom three shall retire after the expiration of the first two years and two shall retire after the expiration of the next two years.

The National Assembly consists of two hundred members elected by adult franchise. Ten additional seats have been reserved for women, these seats are held for ten years or until the next General Election, whichever is the later. Women are also eligible to contest elections against all the non-reserved seats.

Seats in the National Assembly have been allocated to Provinces, Federally Administered Tribal Areas, and the Federal Capital on the basis of population. The term of the National Assembly is five years.

## LEGAL SYSTEM

The Supreme Court of Pakistan is the highest Court of appeal in the country. The Court also exercises advisory and original jurisdiction in certain special cases. Besides the Chief Justice, there are six puisne Judges in the Court. There are three High Courts in Pakistan. The Constitution provides for a High Court in each Province, but this does not preclude two Provinces from having a common High Court, with the consent of the President. Under the High Courts, there are the Courts of District and Sessions Judges, Subordinate Judges and Magistrates.

The Constitution of Islamic Republic Pakistan provides for an independent Judiciary, which constitutes the greatest safeguard of the rights of citizens. Under the Constitution, each High Court has power to issue in appropriate cases directions, declarations, or writs of *Habeas Corpus*, *Mandamus*, *Certiorai* and *Quo-Warranto*.

The Constitution provides for a Supreme Judicial Council for the purpose of inquiring into the conduct of Judges. This Council consists of the Chief Justice of the Pakistan Court, the two next most senior judges of the Supreme Court, and two most senior Chief Justices of the High Court.

There is an Attorney-General, who is appointed by the President. He has the right of audience in all the courts of Pakistan.

### Supreme Court of Pakistan

*Chief Justice:* Muhammed Yaqub Ali.
*Attorney-General:* Mr. Yahya Bakhtiar.

## AREA AND POPULATION

The total area of Pakistan excluding Jammu and Kashmir, Gilgit, Baltistan, Junagarh and Manavadar, is 10,403 sq. miles.

The population of Pakistan at mid-1974 was 67,213,000. The annual average percentage growth rate of the population for the period 1960–74 was 2·9 and for the period 1965–74 was 2·9.

The following table shows the population of the chief cities according to the census of 1972:

| *City* | *Population (in thousands)* |
|---|---|
| Islamabad | 77 |
| Peshawar | 273 |
| Mardan | 109 |
| Rawalpindi | 615 |
| Gujrat | 100 |
| Sargodha | 203 |
| Lyalpur | 820 |
| Lahore | 2,148 |
| Multan | 544 |
| Bawawalpur | 134 |
| Sukkur | 159 |
| Hyderabad | 624 |
| Karachi | 3,469 |
| Quetta | 156 |
| Jhang | 136 |
| Kasur | 103 |

## CURRENCY

The unit of currency is the *Pakrupee* with a U.S. dollar equivalent of $0·09 for one rupee. The coins in circulation are minted at the Pakistan Government mint at Lahore. Notes are issued by the State bank of Pakistan in denominations of Rs. 5, 10, 50, and 100 in the name of the Government of Pakistan. One Rupee notes are issued by the Government and the State Bank incurs no liability on them.

A decimal system of currency was introduced on 1 January 1961. The rupee remains the unit, but it is now divided into 100 paisa instead of the original 64 small units. Smaller coins are 0·5, 0·25, 0·1, 0·05 and 0·01 rupee.

Currency in circulation at the end of June 1976 amounted to 11,032 million rupees.

## FINANCE

The GNP at market prices for 1974 was U.S. $millions 8,760. and the GNP per capita at market prices was U.S. $130. The annual average percentage growth rate of the GNP per capita for the period 1960–74 was 3·4, and for the period 1965–74 was 2·5. [*See the note at the beginning of this section concerning GNP.*]

The following table shows the Pakistan budget for the year 1976–77 in Rs million:

| | *Budget* 1975–76 | *Budget* 1976–77 |
|---|---|---|
| Total gross revenue receipts | 17,476·8 | 18,918·7 |
| Less revenue assignments to provinces | 2,505·8 | 2,775·4 |
| Net federal revenue expenditure | 14,971·0 | 16,143·3 |
| Non-development revenue expenditure | 14,895·0 | 16,147·1 |
| Surplus available for ADP | 76·0 | 03·8 |
| | 1975–76 *Revised* | 1976–77 *Budget* |
| *Capital* | | |
| Internal resources | 957·1 | 1,490·2 |
| External resources | 12,126·3 | 12,713·7 |
| Total resources | 13,083·4 | 14,203·9 |
| Development outlay | 14,595·4 | 17,000·0 |
| Gap. | 1,512·0 | 2,796·1 |

## PRINCIPAL BANKS

**State Bank of Pakistan.** (Governor and Chairman: Mr. Ghulam Ishaq Khan.) Established 1948. Central Bank and Sole Bank of Issue for Pakistan. Balance Sheet at 3 August 1973 showed total assets Pakistan Rs. 10,404,454,000; reserve fund Pakistan Rs. 147,500,000; deposits 5,290,515,000. *Head Office:* I.I. Chundrigar Road, Karachi. Cable address: Bankrate.

**Habib Bank Limited.** Established 1941. Balance Sheet at 31 December 1972 showed assets Pak. Rs. 8,603 million deposits and current accounts Pak. Rs. Rs. 6,163 million. *Head Office:* Habib-Bank Plaze, Karachi-21.

**National Bank of Pakistan.** Established 1949. *Head Office:* I.I. Chundrigar Road, Karachi; over 1,300 branches in Pakistan, and 17 foreign branches, and three Representative offices.

**Chartered Bank.** Six offices in Pakistan. See United Kingdom.

## PRODUCTION, INDUSTRY AND COMMERCE

**Agriculture.** The index of agriculture production which stood at 89 in 1948–49 rose to 186 in 1974–75. The index of food crops increased from 100 to 180; while that of other non-food crops rose from 100 to 178 and fibres from 100 to 218 during the period between 1959–60 and 1974–75.

The agriculture sector registered an annual growth rate of 1·5 per cent during 1950's, 3·4 per cent during the Second Plan period and 4·1 per cent during the Third Plan period. However, there has been a serious set-back to agriculture since the early seventies. Earlier shortfall in investment in the economy vitally affected agriculture. This, combined with a series of bad weather years slowed down the agricultural growth rate, during 1970–75 to less than one per cent. The year 1974–75 was a specially bad year for agriculture as the value added in the agriculture sector fell by about two per cent. The agriculture sector had similar experience during 1960–61, 1963–64 and 1965–66 in which agricultural production either recorded a fall or remained stagnant breaking the pattern of steady growth. The decline in agricultural production in 1974–75 is explained mainly by shortage of irrigation water, poor rains, and pest attack on sugarcane and cotton crops. The canal water flow at the farm gate fell to as low as 60 per cent during some critical months for important crops. Similarly, there were not sufficient rains when critically required although during the later period there were some rains which had a favourable impact on the crops. The delay in the commissioning of the Tarbela Dam further aggravated the situation.

One of the most important measures taken by the Government was land reforms introduced in March, 1972 which aimed at breaking the hold of the feudal lords over the rural masses. This was done by reducing the ceiling on individual holdings by two-thirds from 36,000 to 12,000 produce index units (P.I.Us). All concessions previously allowed, such as retention of 150 acres as orchards, gifts of land up to 18,000 P.I.Us to family dependents, exemptions allowed in case of hunting grounds, trusts, stud farms etc. were done away with. All land in excess of the ceiling was acquired by the State, without compensation, for free distribution among the landless or small tenants. The only concession allowed was for retention of areas up to 2,000 P.I.Us if the owner had adopted modern techniques of agricultural production by purchasing tractors and installing tubewells on his land on or before 20 December 1971. For effecting consolidation of land, persons affected were permitted to inter-change land with members of their families.

Up to June, 1975 the number of owners who filed declarations of land holdings was 10,267 for a total area of 10·80 lakh acres. The area which was allowed to be retained by the owners was 10·30 lakh acres, and 9·50 lakh acres were acquired by the Government. Out of the total of acquired land, 4·39 lakh acres were distributed among 54,550 small farmers/tenants, each getting an area equal to a subsistence holding.

The aerial spray covered an area of 30·83 lakh spray acres in 1973–71 which is estimated to increase to 39·55 lakh spray acres in 1974–75. Similarly the area covered by ground operations is esimated to have increased from 38·14 lakh spray acres in 1973–74 to 36·19 lakh spray acres in 1974–75. Plant spray operations were also undertaken in the private sector and about 17·82 lakh acres were covered during July–December 1974 compared with 5·08 lakh acres during the corresponding period last year.

The Federal Government is providing the serial plant protection services free of charge, in spite of considerable increase in pesticide prices in the international market. About 1,350 tons of pesticides costing Rs. 102·1 crore were to be imported during the current year. The provincial governments are also providing such services at subsidized rates.

*Rural Development:* A number of institutional changes were introduced to exploit the movement in growth in the rural areas, with particular emphasis on the winning of the farmer's participation in the activity. These changes aim at improving the relative position of agriculture in price relationships with the rest of the economy, along with an expansion of production, and mobilization and utilization of local resources. The measures taken by the Government to develop rural areas can thus be divided into three categories: (a) improving the price relationship of rural community, (b) mobilizing and utilizing the rural resources through institutional changes, and (c) improving rural infrastructure through various nation-building departments.

*Integrated Rural Development Programme:* The IRD programme was launched in July, 1972 with the purpose of improving the quality of life and socio-economic status of the people living in the rural areas. The term "Integrated Rural Development" has been defined as "a joint action by the farmers, nation-building departments and the private sector to improve the economic position of the rural population so that they can participate with dignity in the social, political and economic life of the nation".

It may also be noted that many facilities have been provided, to between 80,000 to 100,000 residents of each Markaz, by coordinating activities of various nation building departments. These activities include construction of road links, water supply, poultry farming, vegetable farming, bee farming, training and publicity, small and cottage industry, transport and farm development.

The principal crops and their yields for 1974–75 are shown below:

| *Crop* | 1974–75 |
|---|---|
| | *(in million tons)* |
| Rice (cleaned) | 2,544 |
| Wheat | 8,200 |
| Maize | 790 |
| Sugarcane | 25,146 |
| Cotton (lint) (th. Bales) | 2,890 |

**Mining.** A number of minerals have been found in Pakistan by geological survey but not yet worked, mining being confined to coal, gypsum, Fuller's earth, salt, steatite, chrome ore and petroleum. As far as coal is concerned, it has been estimated that the readily workable reserves in Pakistan amount to 165 million tons, but the seams are of poor quality and the coal is unsuitable for general purposes.

Chrome ore and gypsum come mainly from Baluchistan.

Oil production comes mainly from the Potowar Plain, from fields at Khaur, Dhulian, Joya Mair, Lakhran, Chakwal, Pathana and Meyal.

In Baluchistan Province, natural gas discovered in Sui continues to implement power supply of both domestic and industrial users, there being estimated reserves of considerable quantity.

Production figures of some minerals for the year 1975–76 were: Chromite, 23,000 tons; Gypsum, 590,000 tons; Limestone, 2,748,000 tons; Rock salt, 354,000 tons; coal (estimated) 1,328,000 tons; crude oil 2·2 million barrels; natural gas 179,500 million cu. ft.

**Industry** (the public sector):

During the 1974–75, the performance of State Enterprises under the Board of Industrial Management improved considerably. Their aggregate production showed an increase of over 21·8 per cent compared to 1973–74. All sectors except Chemical, recorded substantial increases in production levels. The Chemical sector, however, suffered a decline of 11·9 per cent due to marketing problems. Sales increased from Rs. 2,935·8 million to Rs. 4,838 million in 1974–75, making an increase of over 65 per cent. Net profits before tax were estimated at Rs. 254·5 million as compared to Rs. 174·8 million in the previous year, showing an increase of 46 per cent. New job opportunities were created for 4,857 persons during the year, and benefits available to workers in the State Enterprises included, *inter alia* group insurance, gratuity, conveyance or conveyance allowance, house or house rent allowance, medical care, regular attendance bonus, production bonus, dust allowance, fair price shop and subsidized canteen facilities, sports and recreational facilities and children education allowance. The expansion programme of the State Enterprises is being vigorously implemented and over a few years the Board of Industrial Management will invest over Rs. 2,880 million in steel, fertilizers, cement, light and heavy engineering, petro-chemicals and automobiles.

**Commerce.** The Government of Pakistan continues to pursue the free trade policies which were initiated after the devaluation of the Pak Rupee in May 1972.

There has been a sharp increase in Pakistan's exports during 1971–76. Exports have increased from $1,990 million in 1971 to $11,212 million in 1976. This trend has been stopped by the international recession which has seriously affected the volume and unit prices of Pakistan's major exports, especially cotton textiles. The Government of Pakistan has consequently abolished export duties on almost all items. Rice is now the major export item and accounts for more than a quarter of total export earnings. Other major exports are cotton, textiles, leather products, carpets, prawns, cement, and sports goods.

The import policy has been liberalized further despite severe pressure on the balance of payments, and due to higher unit prices of major imports especially oil, fertilizer and wheat, and a mounting imports bill.

There has been a sharp deterioration in Pakistan's terms of trade which has increased its trade deficit. It is estimated during 1974–75, terms of trade have deteriorated to the extent of costing Pakistan $700 million. Pakistan along with other most severely affected countries has financed its trade deficit by borrowing from IMF and friendly countries.

## COMMUNICATIONS

**Telephones.** The telephone and telegraphs system is owned and controlled by the Government and is being developed to serve the whole country. 78 Radio telegraph and telex links exist with a number of countries. 25,000 new telephones and 60 telephone exchanges were installed during 1974–75 bringing the total number of telephones to 226,000. It is proposed that 23,000 more telephone lines be installed during 1975–76.

**Railways.** The Pakistan Western Railway has 5,334 miles of track, it comprises three gauges and by far the greatest length is the broad, or 5 ft. 6 in. There are comparatively short lengths of metre gauge and narrow gauge lines.

Pakistan Western Railway has undertaken a number of new construction projects. The Hyderabad–Mirpurkhas Section has been converted into broad gauge. Likewise, a 77 miles long railway line between Jacobabad and Kashmore has been converted into broad gauge.

However, the biggest construction project undertaken by the Railway after independence is the Kot Abdu–Dera Ghazi Khan–Kashmore rail link, a length of 190 miles, at a cost of Rs. 14 crore 47.

**Shipping.** At present there is a sea port at Karachi. The second sea port at Phitti Creek about 26 miles east of Karachi known as Port Muhammad Bin Qasim is under construction. Pakistan's merchant fleet now consists of 43 dry cargo vessels, 4 passenger vessels, 4 passenger-cum-cargo vessels and one oil tanker having a total carrying capacity of 618,843 tons and 7,311 passengers. The national flag carriers now operate between Pakistan and U.K.–North Continent, U.S.A.–Canada, Adriatic–Turkey–Black Sea, Pakistan Gulf–Red Sea–Sri Lanka–China–Far East and Indonesia–Australia. There is a shipyard at Karachi, located on the major east and west Arabian sea route. This is laid out on modern lines, with up-to-date machinery and experienced and skilled personnel. Its principal activities include construction of all types of ships and floating crafts up to 30,000 DWT size; under-water ship repairs up to 25,000 DWT and floating ship repairs for all types and size of ships; manufactures of general engineering products and production of ferrous and non-ferrous castings.

**Civil Aviation.** The Pakistan International Airlines Corporation now owns besides other aircraft three Lockheed 1049-C Super-Constellations and Boeing 707 jets. They are used on the non-stop services namely Karachi–London, Karachi–Frankfurt, Karachi–Moscow, Karachi–Tehran–Ankara, Karachi–Jeddah, Karachi–Kabul, Karachi–Dar-es-Salam.

The Karachi Airport has good communications. It serves nearly all international trunk-routes. The following are the chief airlines operating through Karachi: B.O.A.C., Pan-American Air-Ways, Indian Airways Corporation, K.L.M. Royal Dutch Airlines, Air India International, Qantas Empire Airways, Air France, Scandinavian Airlines System, Transport Aerians Intercontinentaus, Iranian Airways Ltd., Air Ceylon, Ethiopian Airways, Swissair, Union of Burma Airways, Aryana Afghan Airlines, Transportes Aerios da India Portuguese and Lufthansa.

There are four flying clubs, The Karachi Aero Club, The Lahore Flying Club. The Peshawar Flying Club and the Multan Flying Club. All are open to the public for instruction in flying. The clubs are Government subsidised for the encouragement of flying.

**Posts, Telegraphs and Telephones.** The telephone system is owned and controlled by the Government and is being developed to serve the whole country. Radio telegraph links exist with the United Kingdom, Egypt, Switzerland, the U.S.A. and Persia.

## NEWSPAPERS

*Leading English Dailies*

**Dawn.** Karachi.

**Pakistan Times.** Lahore and Rawalpindi.

**Morning News.** Karachi.

**Indus Times.** Hyderabad.

**Eastern Examiner.** Chittagong.

**Khyber Mail.** Peshawar.

*Leading Urdu Dailies*

**Hurriat.** Karachi.

**Imroze.** Daily Circulation 75,000. Lahore and Multan. Editor, Zaheer Baber.

**Mashriq.** Karachi, Lahore, Peshawar, and Quetta.

**Nawa-i-Waquat.** Lahore, Rawalpindi and Multan.

**Jang:** Karachi, Peshawar, Rawalpindi, Quetta and London.

**Kohistan.** Lahore, Rawalpindi and Multan.

**Tameer.** Rawalpindi.

## SCIENCE AND ATOMIC ENERGY

For applied research, there are two important organizations in Pakistan. They are the Council of Scientific and Industrial Research and the Atomic Energy Commission. The former promotes scientific research with a view to industrial development and maximum utilization of resources; the latter deals with harnessing of atomic energy by conversion into electronic power and the application and uses of radio-isotopes and radiation sources in the solution of problems in the field of agriculture, industry and medicine.

Pakistan's first atomic reactor has since been set up at Islamabad. In addition, a nuclear power project with a generating capacity of 137 MW is also being set up in Karachi.

## EDUCATION AND RELIGION

Population by Religion—1961 census.

| | |
|---|---|
| Muslims | 41,666,153 |
| Caste Hindus | 203,794 |
| Scheduled Castes | 418,011 |
| Buddhists | 2,445 |
| Christians | 583,884 |
| Parsis | 5,219 |
| Others | 872 |
| Total Population | 42,880,378 |

The last population census in Pakistan was conducted in 1972. The census questionnaire sought, *inter alia*, data on the literacy of the people. The results of this census are still being evaluated. At the earlier census of 1961, 16·3 per cent of population aged 5 years and over was found to be literate. At that time the absolute number of the literate population was about 5·4 million.

In order to banish illiteracy the Government formulated an Education Policy in 1972 which aimed at providing universal primary education for boys by 1979 and for girls by 1984. Due to certain limitations these targets have now been revised and it is hoped that universal primary education for boys will be achieved by 1983, and for girls by 1987. Massive programmes for adult literacy and adult education are also envisaged in the Education Policy and a start has already been made. Adult literacy programmes have also been launched on radio and Television.

Expansion at primary level of education has been achieved during the two year period from 1974 to 1976. There were 1,988 more schools in 1975–76 as compared with 1973–74, as compared with 10 per cent additional enrolment during the two years period.

The number of secondary schools (middle and high) increased from 7,328 in 1973–74 to 7,976 in 1975–76. An increase of over 200 thousand pupils at secondary stage made the enrolment grow from about 1·5 million in 1973–74 to 1·7 million in 1975–76.

There were 184 institutions of technical and vocational education at the secondary level of education in 1973–74 as compared with 356 in 1975–76. The enrolment of polytechnic institutes and of the industrial and vocational schools increased by 9·3 per cent and 3·6 per cent respectively.

The improvement of existing colleges and opening of new ones resulted in an increase of nearly 16·8 thousand students raising their number from 194,800 in 1973–74 to 211,600 in 1975–76 which means an increase of 8·6 per cent over the period in question. Enrolment in the universities increased by 18·3 per cent in 1975–76 over 1973–74. Enrolment in the agriculture and engineering universities increased by about six per cent.

## THE MUSLIM CALENDAR

The Islamic era dates from prophet Muhammad's migration from Mecca to Medina, which is known as the Hejra. The current Muslim year 1392–93 corresponds to the current Christian year 1972–73. The following are the names of the muslim months, which are entirely lunar:

| | |
|---|---|
| 1. Muharram | 7. Rajab |
| 2. Safar | 8. Shaban |
| 3. Rabi Al-Awwal | 9. Ramadan |
| 4. Rabi Al-Thani | 10. Shawwal |
| 5. Jamadi Al-Awwal | 11. Dhu Al Qaadah |
| 6. Jamadi Al-Thani | 12. Dhu Al-Hijjah |

## PROVINCES

Pakistan consists of four provinces: The Punjab, North Western Frontier, Sind and Baluchistan. Before July 1970, these provinces constituted one single administrative unit.

Pakistan has been divided into the following divisions: Bahawalpur, Dera Ismail Khan, Hyderabad, Karachi, Kalat, Khairpur, Lahore, Malakand, Multan, Peshawar, Rawalpindi, Sargodha and Quetta, and 51 districts and agencies.

The Malakand Division has resulted from the merger of Swat, Dir, Chitral and the Malakand Agency with the headquarters at Saidu Sharif. It covers an area of 12,344 square miles.

Since the setting up of a democratic government in Pakistan under President Bhutto, each of the four provinces is governed by a Chief Minister who is assisted by his cabinet and a provincial Secretariat, headed by a Secretary. The Provincial Governors are, however, appointed by the President and holds office during his pleasure.

The Divisions are administered by respective Commissioners appointed by the President. The districts are under the executive control of Deputy Commissioners (or Collectors) who are responsible to the Provincial Governments.

## STATES

At the time of independence, the following States acceded to Pakistan and now form part of the country. They are Amb (174 sq. miles); Bahawalpur (17,708 sq. miles); Chitral (4,000 sq. miles); Dir (3,000 sq. miles); Kalat (72,944 sq. miles); Khairpur (20,293 sq. miles); Kharan (18,508 sq. miles); Las Bela (7,343 sq. miles); Makran (23,197 sq. miles); Swat (4,000 sq. miles).

The State of Jammu and Kashmir has an area of about 84,000 sq. miles with a population of five million, out of which 80 per cent are Muslims. It is still a disputed territory as under the United Nations resolution in 1949 its fate has to be decided by the people of the State by means of a free plebiscite to be held under the United Nations auspices.

The liberated territory of Jammu and Kashmir, called Azad Kashmir, comprises the districts of Muzaffarabad, Poonch and Mirpur and is administered by the Azad Jammu and Kashmir Government, headed by an elected President and Council of Ministers appointed by the Azad Kashmir President.

The Northern areas of Gilgit and Baltistan since their liberation from the Dogra Rule in August 1947, are the direct responsibility of the Government of Pakistan as regards administration and security pending the settlement of the future of the State of Jammu and Kashmir.

# Panama

## (REPÚBLICA DE PANAMÂ)

**Capital**—Panama City.

**President of the Republic**—Engineer Demetrio B. Lakas.

**Vice-President of the Republic**: Lic. Gerardo González V.

**National Flag**: Quarterly, 1st and 4th white, 2nd, red, 3rd, blue, the first quarter charged with a star five-pointed blue and the fourth with a like star red.

### CONSTITUTION AND GOVERNMENT

A Constituent Assembly of 505 Representatives elected by popular vote for a period of six years, on 6 August, 1972, approved a new Constitution on 11 October 1972. The same Assembly elected Engineer Demetrio B. Lakas as President of the Republic and Licentiate Arturo Sucre P. as Vice-President, for a period of six years, and granted General Omar Torrijos H. as leader of the Panamanian Revolution, extraordinary powers.

The Executive Power is in the hands of the President and Vice-President of the Republic assisted by the Cabinet of Ministers. The President may not be re-elected so as to have two successive periods in office. There is universal suffrage for all people over the age of 18.

Legislative Power is created by the National Assembly of Representatives of Burrow and the National Legislative Council.

**Ministry**

*Minister for Housing:* Lic. Tomás A. Duque.
*Minister for Foreign Affairs:* Licenciado Nicolás González Revilla.
*Minister for Public Works:* Ing. Néstor T. Guerra.
*Minister of Finance:* Licenciado Luis Adames.
*Minister for Government and Justice:* Lic. Jorge Castro.
*Minister of Education:* Dr. Aristedes Royo.
*Minister of Labour and Social Welfare:* Lic. Adolfo Ahumada.
*Minister of Health:* Doctor Abraham Saied.
*Minister for Agricultural Development:* Teniente Coronel Rubén D. Paredes.
*Minister for Trade and Industry:* Lic. Julio E. Sosa.
*Minister of Planning and Economic Policy:* Doctor Nicolás Ardito Barletta.

### LEGAL SYSTEM

*Chief Justice of the Supreme Court:* Lic. Juan Materno Vásquez.

### AREA AND POPULATION

Panama, which is composed of nine provinces and subdivided into 65 districts and an autochthonous region, has an area of 75,650 sq. km. not including the 1,432 sq. km. under the jurisdiction of the Panama Canal Zone.

In 1970 the population of the Republic was 1,428,082. No provision was made for sub-dividing the population into races, but the figures given in the 1940 census were 12·2 per cent white, 14·6 per cent negro, 71·8 per cent mixed blood and 1·4 per cent other races. The estimated total for the year 1976 was 1,718,700.

The census taken in the Canal Zone in 1970 gave the figures for that area as 44,198.

### CURRENCY

The unit of currency is the *balboa*, equal to one U.S. dollar. No Panamanian paper currency is issued, and U.S. dollar bills of all values are in circulation throughout the Republic; U.S. silver coinage is also tender. Panamanian metal coins of 1, 2½, 5, 10, 25 and 59 cents, 1 balboa, and 5 balboas are in circulation.

### FINANCE

Revenue for 1976 was (balboas) 514,992,936 and Expenditure for 1976 was (balboas) 548,128,422.

### PRINCIPAL BANK

**Banco Nacional de Panama.** (General Manager, Lic. Ricardo de la Espriella, Jr.) Established 1904; owned by the Panamanian Government; Balance Sheet at 31 December 1973 showed assets B.219,833,634; deposits B.158,879,403. *Head Office:* Casa Matriz, Panama City. 36 Branches.

| | |
|---|---|
| 1974 | 36 Branches |
| 1975 | 37 Branches |
| 1976 | 39 Branches |

### PRODUCTION, INDUSTRY AND COMMERCE

Only a small proportion of the total land area is cultivated, although there are large fertile areas suitable for agriculture. The chief crop is bananas, which are exported to the United States and count for about one-half of the total exports.

The following provisional table shows the value of the principal exports for 1975 and 1976 (in balboas):

| *Product* | *Value FOB in balboas* | |
|---|---|---|
| | 1975 | 1976 (*p*) |
| Bananas | 59,513,030 | 61,497,704 |
| Cocoa beans | 847,969 | 1,338,604 |
| Fresh, chilled or frozen prawns | 19,009,934 | 33,516,621 |
| Timber in the form of trunks and logs for sawing and veneers, or in rough planks | 31,901 | 4,479 |

(p) Cifrar preliminary.

* Boundaries of the City according to the Municipal Article 1, 23 June 1960.

Fuel, minerals, machinery and manufactured goods are Panama's main imports.

The U.S.A. in 1975 took 56·0 per cent of Panama's exports.

Sugar, coffee and rice are grown for local consumption.

Cattle raising is carried on successfully in the Savannah Country. Animals are slaughtered for consumption within the country and the hides exported.

There are large areas of forest land containing many valuable hard woods, especially mahogany, but their potentialities have not yet been fully exploited. Other forest products include sarsaparilla and ipecacuanha.

The Panama Canal has been a stable source of revenue for Panama. Under the original treaty of 18 November 1903 providing for the construction of the canal, the United States agreed to pay a lump sum of $10 million and an annual payment of $250,000 as from November 1912. This annuity was increased to $430,000 by a new treaty ratified by the United States in 1939.

Legislation incorporating certain changes in the operation of the canal was approved in September 1950, becoming effective on 1 July 1951. By this legislation the present Panama Canal Company came into being and was made responsible for the payment of Panama's annuity of $430,000 out of the tolls collected on vessels using the canal.

On 25 January 1955, in Panama City representatives of the United States and the Republic of Panama signed a Treaty of Mutual Understanding and Co-operation and a Memorandum of Understandings Reached.

The annuity payable by United States to Panama under the 1903 convention, as amended, is increased from $430,000 to $1,930,000. Actually this annuity is $2,328,000 because of the effect of the dollar devaluation.

In 1976 a total of 12,157 ships (ocean-going, over 300 tons) passed through the Canal, representing 117,212,266 long tons of cargo. Tolls levied amounted to $134,204,402. By 30 June 1976, 429,687 toll-paying, ocean-going commercial vessels had passed through the Canal since its opening on 15 August 1914.

### PANAMANIAN SHIPPING

The following tables show the number and total tonnage of seagoing vessels registered with the Merchant Navy on the 31 December 1974.

| | 1974 | |
|---|---|---|
| | *Number* | *Tonnage* |
| Less than 1,000 tons | 6,574 | 1,024,459 |
| Total | 8,843 | 17,319,007 |

### NEWSPAPERS

**Critica.** F. 1958. Circulation 27,000. Via Fernández de Córdoba, Apdo 665 Panama 9A.

**El Matutino.** F. 1969. Circulation 25,000. Via Fernández de Córdoba, Apdo. B-4, Panamá 9A.

**El Panama America.** F. 1929. Circulation 25,000. Via Fernández de Córdoba, Apdo B-4, Panama 9A.

**La Estrella de Panama.** Circulation 22,000. Calle D. H., Brid 8, Apdo 159, Panama City.

**La Hora.** Circulation 10,000. Apdo 1764, Panama City.

**La Republica.** F. 1977. Circulation 25,000. Via Fernández de Córdoba, Apdo. B-4. Panamá 9A.

**The Panama-American.** F. 1925. Circulation 12,000. Via Fernández de Córdoba, Apdo B-4, Panama 9A.

**The Star and Herald.** Circulation 13,000. Calle D. H., Brid 8, Apdo 159, Panama City.

### COMMUNICATIONS

In 1976 there were 7,671 kilometres of roads.

The principal railway runs between Panama City and Colón, for the greater part of its length through the Canal Zone territory. It is the property of the United States Government. There is also a Government-owned narrow-gauge railway with a terminus at Puerto Armuelles on the Pacific Coast, connecting Concepción, Pedregal and David.

The United Fruit Company now operates about 55 miles of line among the banana plantations of Bocas del Toro Province.

International Airlines connect Panama with the United States, Cuba and other Republics of South and Central America. The Compañia Panameña de Aviación provides an internal service.

### EDUCATION AND RELIGION

State education is free at all pre-university levels. First level, (general basic level), is compulsory.

The following (Provisional) table shows pupil registration in primary and secondary schools and at the Universities of the Republic for the academic year 1974–75:

| | 1974 | 1975 *Preliminary Figures* |
|---|---|---|
| Primary Schools | 328,460 | 342,600 |
| Secondary Schools | 123,310 | 125,746 |
| Universities | 24,204 | 26,289 |

There is complete freedom of worship. Over 93 per cent of the population is Roman Catholic.

# Papua New Guinea

**Administrative Centre**—Port Moresby.

**Head of State**—Her Majesty Queen Elizabeth II.

**Governor-General**—Sir Tore Lokoloko, GCMG.

**Prime Minister**—The Hon. Michael Thomas Somare, MP.

### CONSTITUTION

The Papua New Guinea Act 1949–74, approved the placing of the territory of New Guinea under the Trusteeship system of the United Nations with Australia as the sole administering authority, provided for the administrative union of that Territory with Papua as Papua New Guinea, and set up the basic legislative, executive and judicial organs of government of Papua New Guinea.

A Legislative Council which had been established under the Act was replaced in 1964 by a partly elected House of Assembly. In 1968 the House was increased in size from 64 to 94 elective seats, and in 1972 it was further increased to 100 seats representing 82 open electorates and 18 regional electorates. There were four official members appointed by the Governor-General of Australia; these withdrew from the House on the attainment of self-government on 1 December 1973.

After the elections in March 1972 a National Coalition Government was formed under the leadership of Mr. Michael Somare, as Chief Minister. There are nineteen ministers of the National Coalition Government. Since 1972 all functions of government have been progressively transferred to the Papua New Guinea Government from the Australian Government. Authority over defence and foreign relations was transferred on 6 March 1975.

On 18 June 1975, the House of Assembly resolved to nominate 16 September 1975 as the date of independence for Papua New Guinea.

A Constitutional Planning Committee was appointed in 1972 to prepare recommendations for the constitution of an independent Papua New Guinea. It delivered its report in 1974. A draft constitution was prepared and was considered during 1975 by the House of Assembly, meeting as the National Constituent Assembly. Final passage of the constitution is expected during August 1975, prior to to independence on 16 September.

Under the constitution, the House of Assembly will elect a Speaker from among its members. The Prime Minister will be appointed by the Head of State, acting in accordance with a decision of the Parliament. Other ministers will be appointed by the Head of State acting in accordance with the advice of the Prime Minister.

The Ministers will form the National Executive Council which has final executive and policy making authority over a wide range of government functions.

For the purpose of administration Papua New Guinea is divided into 20 districts, with a District Commissioner as representative of the central government in each.

The Supreme Court of Papua New Guinea is the highest judicial tribunal. It is a superior Court of Record, and consists of the Chief Justice and six judges. The courts of inferior jurisdiction are the District Courts, the Local Courts and Children's Courts, presided over by magistrates, and the newly formed Village Courts.

### PAPUA BACKGROUND

Papua was placed under the authority of the Australian Commonwealth in 1906, following the Papua Act of 1905. It lies wholly within the tropics, and has an area of about 16,100 square miles. Papua includes the islands of the Trobiands, Woodlark, D'Entrecasteaux and Louisiade groups together with Tagula and Rossel Islands. Papua is divided into six districts for administrative purposes, as follows: Western, Gulf, Central, Milne Bay, Northern, and Southern Highlands.

### NEW GUINEA BACKGROUND

New Guinea is a former German colony which passed after World War I to the control of the Commonwealth Government under mandate (1920). New Guinea came under the Trusteeship System established by the United Nations Charter in 1946. It comprises the mainland of North-East New Guinea (approx. 69,000 square miles) and New Britain, Bougainville, New Irland, New Hanover, Admiralty Islands and Buka (approx. 22,760 square miles).

### POPULATION

The population of Papua New Guinea at mid-1974 was 2,650,000. The annual average percentage growth rate for the period 1960–74 was 2·4, and for the period 1965–74 was 2·4.

### ECONOMICS

In 1974–75 the Papua New Guinea budget included planned expenditure of $321·2 million and estimated receipts of $311·2 million, indicating a deficit of $10 million. Estimated income in the budget included $83·2 million aid from Australia (including $4·5 million defence aid). Other aid from Australia in 1974–75 was an estimated $100 million for salaries and retirement benefits for Australian public servants supplied to the Papua New Guinea Government. With another $8·8 million (covering training, airport projects and some miscellaneous items), Australian aid to Papua New Guinea was estimated to total $192·0 million in 1974–75.

# PAPUA NEW GUINEA

The GNP market prices for 1974 was U.S.$ millions 1,250, and the GNP per capita at market prices was U.S.$ 470. The annual average percentage growth rate of the GNP per capita for the period 1960–74 was 4·2, and for the period 1965–74 was 4·1. [*See note at the beginning of this section concerning GNP.*] The copper deposit situated on Bougainville Island is estimated to contain 900 million tons of copper ore containing an average of 0·48 per cent copper, 0·36 dwt gold and some silver. Capital investment in the establishment of an open pit copper mine and facilities has amounted to $400 million and production of copper concentrates for export commenced in April 1972.

The value of the country's exports rose to $229·6 million in the 1972–73 financial year from $127·2 million in 1971–72. The large increase was mainly caused by high international prices for Papua New Guinea's new major export, copper ore, from the Bougainville copper project, and for a number of Papua New Guinea's traditional commodity exports (coffee, coconut products, and cocoa). The high prices persisted into 1974 but have since declined.

Visible imports in 1972–73 were $228·8 million, compared with $256 million in 1971–72. The 1971–72 figure was unusually high because of imports required for the Bougainville Copper project.

The search for new minerals has intensified. A further reserve of copper ore has been explored at Ok Tedi, in the Star Mountains, in the Western District. The Kennecott Company withdrew from negotiations with the Papua New Guinea Government about this resource, but the Government announced that it would continue exploration on its own behalf, and would enter negotiations with other international companies. Exploration continues for nickel near Bundi (Madang District), for copper near Frieda River (Western Highlands) and in other areas. The tuna and prawn fisheries are contributing to a substantial export income from marine produce, and there is a proposal to establish a fish cannery at Madang. The cattle industry numbers about 130,000 head. Secondary industry, although still small, is growing. Among the total of $229,614,000 for exports in 1972–73, principal exports were (in thousand $A):

| *Product* | $A *thousands* |
|---|---|
| Copper ore | 125,625 |
| Copra, coconut oil, nuts and kernels | 14,015 |
| Rubber | 1,998 |
| Timber, including plywood and veneers | 10,702 |
| Fish | 4,379 |
| Desiccated coconut | 1,192 |
| Palm oil | 1,148 |
| Re-exports | 29,072 |
| Cocoa | 11,175 |
| Coffee | 23,395 |

## DEVELOPMENT

In December 1972 the Government of Papua New Guinea presented its aims for economic and social development. The major objective is the improvement of the lives of the people and the central themes of the aims are, decentralisation, rural development, equitable distribution of incomes and self-reliance. A single year "Interim Improvement Program" was presented with the Papua New Guinea budget in August 1973 followed by a five-year "Improvement Program". A Central Planning Office was created in 1973 to co-ordinate Papua New Guinea's economic planning.

## INVESTMENT

The Government has a positive policy for the encouragement in Papua New Guinea of foreign investment which is in harmony with the objectives of the development plan and will, as far as practicable, meet such criteria as the provision of employment and training for local workers, the processing of local products, and the use of common user facilities such as roads, ports and other basic services.

There is no restriction on the repatriation by foreign investors of capital or profit and specific tax incentives and other attractions are offered as an encouragement to sound investment.

In October 1974, the Papua New Guinea House of Assembly passed the National Investment Development Authority (NIDA) Act. The first National Investment Priorities Schedule indicating the investment activities which would be particularly welcomed by the Papua New Guinea Government, was published in April 1975.

The provision of foreign enterprises for local equity participation is on a voluntary basis. However the Government has set up the Papua New Guinea Investment Corporation for the purpose of taking up equity in major investment projects financed by overseas capital, and holding such equity for future sale to the people of Papua New Guinea.

# Paraguay

(REPÚBLICA DEL PARAGUAY)

**Capital**—Asunción.

**President**—General de Ejército Alfredo Stroessner.

**National Flag:** Horizontal tricolour, red, white and blue with a centrepiece on one side formed by the national emblem of a yellow star surrounded by a wreath of palm and olive leaves. The centrepiece on the reverse side is the Treasury seal formed by a lion with the words 'Paz y Justicia' above it.

## CONSTITUTION AND GOVERNMENT

PARAGUAY is situated almost in the centre of South America, bounded on the east by Brazil, on the south by Argentina and on the west by Bolivia.

The country, which had been a colony of Spain since 1535, gained its independence in 1811. For over 50 years it was governed by dictators—Dr. José Gaspar Rodríguez de Francia, Carlos Antonio López and his son, Francisco Solano López. It was while the latter ruled that Paraguay was plunged into a devastating war against Brazil, Argentina and Uruguay. This went on for five years, ending in 1870 with the defeat of the Paraguayans and the death of their ruler. It is believed that some 500,000 Paraguayans were killed.

A new constitution replacing that of 1940 was drawn up by a Constituent Convention in which all legally recognized political parties were represented; it was signed into law on 25 August 1967. It is based on the principle of the separation of powers and provides for a President, a two-chamber Congress and independent Judiciary. The President and the two chambers (Senate and Deputies) are elected simultaneously every five years by universal suffrage (voting is compulsory for all citizens over 18). The next election is due in 1978. The Judiciary is appointed by the Executive. The President of the Republic is eligible for two terms of five years, either in succession or separated by an interval. Under Article 79 of the Constitution he can declare a state of Siege and decrees applying the state of Siege to the principal inhabited areas have been regularly enacted every ninety days.

The President appoints a cabinet of Ministers, who are not members of the Legislature. There are 30 Senators and 60 Deputies. Two-thirds of the seats in each chamber are allocated to the majority party: the remaining third are shared among the minority parties in proportion to the votes cast. When the congress is in recess the President may govern by decree through a Council of State consisting of the Ministers, and representatives of various bodies, including the armed forces.

The first elections under the new Constitution were held on 11 February 1968, and President Stroessner, who had been in office since 1954, was formally inaugurated on 15 August 1968, and re-elected for another period of five years in 1973.

The Membership of the two Chambers is as follows:

*President of the Senate:* Dr. Juan R. Chavez.

*Senate:*

| | | | |
|---|---|---|---|
| Colorados | 20 | Liberales | 1 |
| Radicales | 9 | Febreristas | 0 |

*President of the Chamber of Deputies:* Dr. J. Augusto Saldívar.

*Deputies:*

| | | | |
|---|---|---|---|
| Colorados | 40 | Liberales | 3 |
| Radicales | 16 | Febreristas | 1 |

### Ministry

*Minister of Foreign Affairs:* Dr. Alberto Nogués.
*Minister of the Interior:* Dr. Sabino Augusto Montanaro.
*Minister of Finance:* General (Retd.) César Barrientos.
*Minister of Industry and Commerce:* Dr. Delfin Ugarte Centurión.
*Minister of Defence:* General (Retd.) Marcial Samaniego.
*Minister of Justice and Labour:* Dr. Saúl González.
*Minister of Education and Worship:* Dr. Raúl Peña.
*Minister of Public Health and Social Welfare:* Dr. Adan Godoy Jiménez.
*Minister of Public Works and Communications:* General de División Juan A. Cáceres.
*Minister of Agriculture and Livestock:* Ing. Agr. Hernando Bertoni.
*Minister without Portfolio:* Arq. Tomás Romero Pereira.

### Judiciary

*President of the Supreme Court:* Dr. Juan Felix Morales.

## LOCAL GOVERNMENT

The country is divided into the capital district of Asunción and 19 departments—14 for Eastern Paraguay and four for Western Paraguay, the large tract of sparsely populated land known as the Chaco.

## LEGAL SYSTEM

There is a Supreme Court of Justice, which sits at the capital, Asunción. Under the new constitution it is composed of five judges. There are six departmental tribunals of first instance and two courts of appeal, one for civil and one for criminal offences. There are lower tribunals for minor offences.

## AREA AND POPULATION

The country is geographically divided into two parts, Eastern and Western Paraguay, by the river Paraguay, which flows from north to south. Western Paraguay, or the Chaco, is bounded on the south by the river Pilcomayo, which flows for some 400 miles along the frontier between Paraguay and Argentina till it joins the river Paraguay near Asunción. To the north and west of the Chaco lies Bolivia. The actual line of demarcation between the Paraguayan Chaco and Bolivia was the cause of war between the two countries (1932–35) and was finally settled at the Peace Treaty of 1939.

The total area of the country is 406,752 sq. km., Eastern Paraguay being 159,827 sq. km. and Western, 246,925 sq. km.

The population at mid-1974 was 2,484,000. The annual average percentage growth rate for the period 1960–74 was 2·6 and for the period 1965–74 was 2·6. The population of the capital according to the provisional census of 1972 was 387·676.

About 95 per cent of the population are in Eastern Paraguay.

| | | | |
|---|---|---|---|
| Concepción | 108,625 | Paraguarí | 205,284 |
| San Pedro | 137,295 | Alto Paraná | 86,761 |
| Cordillera | 193,144 | Central | 308,783 |
| Guirá | 33,502 | Neẽmbucú | 74,468 |
| Caaguazú | 56,341 | Amambay | 65,505 |
| Caazapá | 102,822 | Boquerón | 26,503 |
| Itapúa | 203,196 | Olimpo | 5,355 |
| Misiones | 70,096 | Pte. Hayes | 38,101 |

Except for the capital, there are no towns with a population substantially in excess of 30,000.

## PRINCIPAL BANKS

**Banco Central del Paraguay** (President, Dr. César Romeo Acosta); Established 1952; sole bank of issue for Paraguay; Balance Sheet at 30 December 1976 showed (in million guaraníes) the following: Gold and exchange reserves, 17,256, contribution to I.M.F., 1,823; loans and other investments, 12,266; other assets, 3,463.

**National Development Bank.** Handles internal loans. At April 1971, its assets totalled 8,916·9 million guaraníes. Independencia Nacional y 25 de Mayo, Asunción.

**Banco Paraguayo de Comércio S.A.** Ind. Nacional y Cerro Corá, Asunción.

**Banco Exterior S.A.**, (Director and President, M. Arburua); Established 1961; Capital, Gs. 300,000,000 Reserves, Gs. 137,645,541; Sinking Fund Gs. 139,819,868; Deposits, Gs. 3,182,132,870; Loans, 1,814,916,380. 25 de Mayo y Yegros, Asunció.

**Banco de Asuncion S.A.** 14 de Mayo y Palma.

The following foreign banks have branches in Asunción and in some of the principal towns: Bank of London & South America Ltd.; Banco de la Nación Argentina; Banco del Brasil; First National City Bank of New York; Banco Holandés Unido; Bank of America.

**Banco Alemán Transatlántico,** 14 de Mayo c/Estrella.

## PARAGUAY

### CURRENCY

The unit of currency is the guaraní, so called after the Guaraní Indians, the original inhabitants. It was introduced in 1943, replacing the old paper peso at the rate of 1 guaraní to 100 pesos. Notes are issued in denominations of 10,000, 5,000, 1,000, 500, 100, 50, 10, 5 and 1. While centimos are still legal tender they are rarely used in day to day business.

Notes in circulation in April 1975 were Gs. 7,640 million. Official exchange rate is Gs. 126 = U.S. $1.

### FINANCE

Revenue and expenditure for 1976 were (in million guaranies): Revenue (estimated) 61,655,603; Expenditure (estimated) 59,175,246.

Details of Budget (estimated) (million guaraníes):

| *Allocations by Departments* | 1976 |
|---|---|
| Presidency | 123 |
| Interior | 1,762 |
| External | 265 |
| Finance | 811 |
| Education and Worship | 2,709 |
| Agriculture and Livestock | 731 |
| Public Works and Communications | 3,376 |
| National Defence | 3,516 |
| Public Health and Social Welfare | 607 |
| Justice and Labour | 241 |
| Industry and Commerce | 107 |
| Ministry without Portfolio | 3 |
| Judiciary | |
| Chamber of Deputies and Senators | 124 |

The GNP at market prices for 1974 was U.S. $millions 1,270, and the GNP per capita at market prices was U.S. $510. The annual average percentage growth rate of the GNP per capita for the period 1960–74 was 2·0, and for the period 1965–74 was 2·5. [*See the note at the beginning of this section concerning GNP.*]

### PRODUCTION, INDUSTRY AND COMMERCE

**Agriculture.** The country has great agricultural possibilities. Cotton, tobacco, soyabeans and meat are the principal products. Other products are sugar cane, rice, essential oils, maize, oil-nuts such as ground-nuts, tung-nuts, etc. Production of soyabeans reached 250,000 tons in 1976.

**Forestry.** There are vast tropical forests with a great variety of trees, shrubs and plants. 118,304 tons of timber were exported in 1975. The Paraguayan tea, *yerba maté*, is collected in these forests but its value as a source of wealth has diminished considerably. Exports of *yerba maté* in 1975 were 679 tons. Extract of *quebracho*, from which tannin is extracted, is an export of declining importance. Exports of *quebracho* in 1975 amounted to 12,665 tons. Essential oils are extracted from several plants, of which, *petit grain* (leaf of bitter orange) used in perfume is the most important. The export of *petit grain* amounted to 278 tons in 1975.

There are deposits of iron, manganese and copper, but commercial exploitation is on a low scale.

**Industry.** The following table shows the production by principal commodities (in thousand tons, unless otherwise stated) for 1975:

| *Product* | 1975 |
|---|---|
| Hides | 12·4 |
| Preserved meat | 8·8 |
| Animal fat | 1·8 |
| Bone meal | 3·2 |
| Frozen meat | 3·2 |
| Cotton | 16·0 |
| Timber | n.a. |
| Tannin | 17·7 |
| Petit grain | 3·50 |
| Cement | 137·7 |
| Cigarettes (million pkts) | 41·6 |
| Matches (thousand boxes) | 23·9 |
| Electricity (thousand kWh) | 592 |
| Sugar | 51·8 |

**Commerce.** The following table shows 1975 imports and exports by country (in thousand U.S. $):

| *Country* | *Imports* | *Exports* |
|---|---|---|
| Argentine | 33,277 | 49,676 |
| United States | 21,776 | 15,521 |
| United Kingdom | 16,778 | 18,348 |
| Spain | 1,288 | 4,609 |
| France | 2,570 | 7,915 |
| Uruguay | 3,508 | 2,281 |
| Netherlands | 998·7 | 15,103 |
| Germany (W.) | 14,534 | 22,050 |
| Italy | 2,114 | 836 |
| Sweden | 3,141 | 26 |
| Belgium | 1,005 | 13,480 |
| Japan | 8,812 | 3,678 |
| Switzerland | 1,005 | 13,480 |
| Brazil | 37,150 | 5,661 |
| Total | 212,748 | 176,200BCP |

The following table shows the export figures by commodities for 1975 (in thousand U.S. $):

| *Commodity* | 1975 |
|---|---|
| Sawn wood | 22,184 |
| Manufactured wood products | 5,688 |
| Meat, processed beef | 32,221 |
| Hides | 1,978 |
| Frozen horse meat | 265 |
| Tobacco | 12,077 |
| Maize | [illegible]572 |
| Yerba maté | 269 |
| Fruit | 5,744 |
| Coffee | 8,718 |
| Cotton | 20,107 |
| Sugar | 6,657 |
| Oils | 10,614 |
| Tannin | 2,543 |
| Palm shoots | 3,121 |
| Soyabeans | 19,092 |
| Seeds for industrial use | 9,755 |
| Essential oils | |

The following table shows the import figures by commodities for 1975 (in thousand U.S. $):

| *Commodity* | 1975 |
|---|---|
| Foodstuffs | 8,808 |
| Drink and tobacco | 18,172 |
| Paper and board | 5,274 |
| Chemicals | 9,538 |
| Transports and accessories | 22,613 |
| Textiles | 3,741 |
| Agricultural equipment | 4,822 |
| Manufactured metal and hardware | 14,090 |
| Fuel and Lubricants | 38,443 |
| Machinery and engines | 36,626 |

Meat packing plants slaughtered 200,000 head of cattle for processing in 1972.

### COMMUNICATIONS

**Roads.** There are 810 kilometres of asphalted road in the country. One running from Asunción to Puerto Presidente Stroessner, and thence to Sao Paulo and Rio de Janeiro, another asphalted road connects Asunción to Ita Enriamada and from there across the river Paraguay by ferry to Pilcomayo and the road to Buenos Aires. Asphalting of the road Paraguari to Encarnación was completed in 1970, a start on the paving of the Trans-Chaco road, which links Asunción with Bolivia, has been made. The remaining roads (601 kilometres gravelled and 4,898 earth) are closed in wet weather.

**Rivers.** River transport plays a great part in the economy of Paraguay which, landlocked as it is, is fortunate in having the Paraguay–Paraná river system as a means of communication with the Atlantic. The capital, Asunción, on the southern part of the Paraguay, is the chief river port. From Asunción the river flows southward for about 150 miles, till, just above the Argentinian city of Corrientes, it joins the Paraná.which continues for another 800 miles through Argentina to the River Plate and Buenos Aires.

The Paraná, which is over 2,000 miles in length, flows down from Brazil, forming over 100 miles of the Paraguayan–Brazilian frontier and about 400 miles of the frontier between Paraguay and Argentina. It turns west at Encarnación to continue its journey to Corrientes. Both rivers are, however, extremely shallow so that shipping services are adversely affected whenever the water level falls.

The rivers are commercial highways for both internal and external traffic. The two principal foreign companies using the rivers are Flota Argentina de Navegación Fluvial and the Lloyd Brasileiro.

The Rotterdam–South American Line operates a service approximately once a month from N.W. European ports, and the Lamport and Holt Line also operates a direct monthly service between Great Britain and Paraguay. The service of both these lines is affected when the Paraguay–Paraná river depths drop below a certain level and goods have to be transshipped downstream.

**Railways.** The principal railway, Ferrocarril Carlos Antonio Lopez, links the capital with Encarnación in the South East of the country. From Posadas on the opposite side of the River Paraná there is a connection with the Argentine railway system.

**Airlines.** Nine airlines operate international services from Asunción as follows: Braniff International Airways; from Buenos Aires; and from New York, Miami, San Francisco, Los Angeles, Lima and La P az(four times weekly). Pluna (Primeras Láneas Uruguayas de Navegacion Aérea) to and from Montevideo (twice weekly). Aerolineas Argentinas on routes Asuncion via Corrientes or Resistencia to Buenos Aires (seven times weekly in each direction). Lineas Aéreas Paraguayas (LAP) to and from Lima twice weekly, to and from Buenos Aires direct six times weekly (and via Montevideo once weekly), and to and from Santa Cruz, Bolivia, once weekly. Varig on the route Asuncion, Foz de Yguazu, Sao Paulo, Rio de Janeiro (daily in each direction). Iberia on the route Madrid, Rio, Sao Paul once weekly. Lloyd Aéreo Boliviano Lima, La Paz, Cochamaba, Santa Cruz, Asuncion, once weekly.

**Broadcasting.** There are 30 commercial radio stations and one commercial television station in Paraguay.

### NEWSPAPERS

**La Tribuna.** Morning. Asunción.

**ABC Color.** Morning. Asunción. Est. 1967.

**Patria** (Official Journal of the Government Party). Morning. Asunción.

**El Radical.** Weekly political publication. Est. 1967.

**El Enano.** Weekly political publication.

**El Colorado.** Weekly political publication.

**Ultima Mora.** Daily. Afternoon.

### EDUCATION AND RELIGION

Primary education is free and compulsory. In 1973 there were 2,709 government primary schools with 459,393 pupils and 15,871 teachers; 600 Secondary schools with 75,000 students. There are approximately 13,000 students at the two universities, the national and the Catholic.

Catholicism is the established State religion, but there is complete freedom of worship.

# Peru

## (REPÚBLICA PERUANA)

**Capital**—Lima.

**President**—General Francisco Morales Bermúdez.

**National Flag**: A tricolour, pale-wise, red, white, red, the white charged with the national coat of arms: a guanaco pink on blue, a tree green on white, and a horn-of-plenty yellow on red.

### CONSTITUTION AND GOVERNMENT

PERU, originally the largest and most important of the Spanish Vice-royalties in South America, became an independent state 28 July 1821. The present constitution, dating from 9 April 1933, provides for a Senate and a Chamber of Deputies, both elected for six years. The President is also elected for six years by direct vote, and may not serve two terms in succession.

The Constitution was amended in 1936 to provide for the election of two vice-presidents, and further amendments in 1945 gave more power to congress at the expense of the executive. Voting is compulsory for all literate, married Peruvian men and women between the ages of 18 and 60, for all single literates between the ages of 21 and 60, also those between 18 and 21 who are legally released from parental tutelage; beyond 60 it is optional.

### LOCAL GOVERNMENT

The Republic is divided into 23 departments, 150 provinces and 1,425 districts. Each department is administered by a prefect appointed from Lima, each province by a sub-prefect and each district by a governing Council. The first municipal elections for 40 years were held on December 1963 to choose mayors and municipal councils.

### LEGAL SYSTEM

The Supreme Court at Lima consists of 15 judges chosen by the National Council of Justice, and five fiscals. The country is divided into 19 districts with 19 Superior Courts composed of 144 judges and 38 fiscals. In addition there are 240 courts of First Instance, 157 are civil courts and 83 criminal courts with a total of 157 fiscals. Superior and minor court judges are chosen by the Supreme Court and the National Council of Justice.

*President of the Supreme Court:* Dr. Francisco Velasco Gallo.
*President of the National Council of Justice:* Dr. Pedro Patron Faura.

### AREA AND POPULATION

The area of Peru is stated to be 1,285,215·6 sq. km. This figure includes part of Lake Titicaca whose total area is 8,400 sq. km. as well as islands off the coast 32 sq. km.

The mid-1974 population was 14,953,000. The annual average percentage growth rate of the population for the period 1960–74 and the period 1965–74 was 2·9.

The following table shows the area and population of the departments taken on 4 June 1972:

| *Department* | *Capital* | *Area (in sq. km.)* | *Population* |
|---|---|---|---|
| Amazonas | Chachapoyas | 41,297·12 | 196,469 |
| Ancash | Huaráz | 36,308·31 | 726,665 |
| Apurímac | Abancay | 20,656·56 | 307,805 |
| Arequipa | Arequipa | 63,527·62 | 530,528 |
| Ayacucho | Ayacucho | 45,503·04 | 459,747 |
| Cajamarca | Cajamarca | 35,417·81 | 916,331 |
| Callao | Callao | 73·82 | 315,605 |
| Cuzco | Cuzco | 84,140·98 | 708,719 |
| Huncavelica | Huncavelica | 22,870·96 | 331,155 |
| Huánuco | Huánuco | 35,314·57 | 420,764 |
| Ica | Ica | 21,251·39 | 357,973 |

*continued*

| *Department* | *Capital* | *Area (in sq. km.)* | *Populaion* |
|---|---|---|---|
| Junín | Huancayo | 32,354·42 | 691,216 |
| La Libertad | Trujillo | 23,241·32 | 806,368 |
| Lambayeque | Chiclayo | 16,585·90 | 515,363 |
| Lima | Lima | 33,894·97 | 3,485,411 |
| Loreto | Iquitos | 478,336·15 | 494,935 |
| Madre de Dios | Maldonado | 78,402·71 | 21,968 |
| Moquegua | Moquegua | 16,174·65 | 74,573 |
| Pasco | Cerro de Pasco | 21,854·07 | 176,750 |
| Piura | Piura | 33,067·12 | 854,668 |
| Puno | Puno | 67,386·15 | 779,594 |
| San Martín | Moyobamba | 53,063·60 | 224,310 |
| Tacna | Tacna | 14,766·63 | 95,623 |
| Tumbes | Tumbes | 4,731·62 | 75,399 |
| Total | | 1,280,219·32 | 13,567,939 |

Principal towns with populations (1971 estimate):

| | | | |
|---|---|---|---|
| Lima (Census 1972) | 3,593,787 | Cuzco | 106,000 |
| | | Trujillo | 145,000 |
| Callao | 322,000 | Iquitos | 83,000 |
| Arequipa | 181,000 | Juancayo | 82,300 |
| Chiclayo | 141,000 | Piura | 102,000 |

## CURRENCY

The unit of currency is the *sol*, divided into 100 *centavos*. There are alloy coins (70 per cent copper, 30 per cent zinc) for 1 sol, and also for 5, 10, 20, and 50 centavos; there are also alloy coins for 1 and 2 centavos (5 per cent copper, 95 per cent zinc). Banknotes are issued in 5, 10, 50, 100, 500 and 1,000 soles.

## FINANCE

The biennial Budget for 1972–73, in operation at the present time, includes a total authorised expenditure of 140,039 million soles. This budget has been the starting point for a total transformation in the system of studies, calculations and operation of the Peravian national budgets.

The GNP at market prices for 1974 was U.S. $millions 11,110, and the GNP per capita at market prices was U.S. $620. The annual average percentage growth rate of the GNP per capita for the period 1960–74 was 2·0, and for the period 1965–74 was 1·8. [*See the note at the beginning of this section concerning GNP*].

## BANKS

**Banco Central de Reserva del Peru.** (President, Dr. Emilio Barreto.) Est. 1922; Sole Bank of Issue for Peru; Balance Sheet at 31 December 1973 showed banknotes in circulation S.31,246,930·73 m.; reserves U.S. $430,183,091. *Head Office:* Esq. Lampe y Ucayali, Lima.

**Banco de Credito del Peru.** (President, Lizardo Alzamora Porras.) Est. 1889; Balance Sheet at 30 June 1975 showed capital and reserves S.1,319,789,819. *Head Office:* 499 Lampa, Lima. More than 205 Branches and Sub-Branches.

**Banco de Fomento Agropecuario del Perú.** (President, Ing. Edgardo Seoane.) Balance Sheet at 30 December 1971 showed capital and reserves S.1,786 m. *Head Office:* 543 Carabaya, Lima.

**Banco de la Nacion.** (President, Brig. Gen. Jorge Viale Solari.) Est. 1966. Financial Agent of the Government, Insurance Agent or State Assets. 492 Branches and Agencies. *Head Office:* Cuadra 5a, Av. Abancay, Lima.

**Banco Internacional del Perú.** (Chairman, David Landeo.) Est. 1897; Balance Sheet at 31 December 1972 showed capital and reserves S.665,289,846·00. *Head Office:* Plaza de la Merced, Lima. 103 Branches.

**Banco Popular del Perú.** (President, Luis Barúa Castañeda.) Est. 1899; Balance Sheet at 31 December 1971 showed reserves of S.600,000,000. *Head Office:* 380, Huallaga, Lima. 109 Branches and Agencies.

**Banco de Lima.** (President. Dr. Manuel Pablo Olaechea Dubois). Balance Sheet at 31 December 1974 showed capital and reserves of $212,541,235·45. *Head Office:* 698, Carabya, Lima. Correspondent of the Credit Lyonnais; Paris. 26 Branches.

**Banco Minero del Perú.** (President, Carlos Dongo Soria.) Balance Sheet at 31 December 1972 showed capital and reserves. S.741,806,000. *Head Office:* Av. Inca 6. de la Vega 1464, Lima.

**Banco Industrial del Peru.** (President, Ing. Luis Guiulfo Zender). Balance Sheet at 31 December 1974 showed capital S.1,917,090,606·83. Surplus, Profits and Reserves S.380,574,526·78. *Head Office:* Plaza G. Gastañeta 681, Lima 1.

**Banco Central Hipotecario del Perú.** (President, Dr. Arturo Seminario García.) Balance Sheet at 31 December 1973 showed capital and reserves S.221,642,370·03. *Head Office:* Carabaya 421, Lima. 17 main Branches and 16 Agencies.

**Banco Wiese Ltd.** (President, Dr. Guillermo Wiese de Osma.) Balance Sheet at 30 June 1973 showed capital and reserves S.398,035,210·12. *Head Office:* Lima. 1 Branch, 43 Agencies.

**Banco Continental.** (Chairman, Dr. Salvador Velarde.) Balance Sheet at 31 December 1973 showed capital and reserves S.665,686,000, total resources S.13,976,558,000. *Head Office:* 545, Lampa, Lima. 69 City offices in Lima and Callao. Branches in Arequipa, Iquitos, and Pucallpa.

**Banco Comercial del Peru.** (President, Francisco Mendoza W.) Balance Sheet at 31 December 1976 showed capital and reserves S,310,576,913·24. *Head Office:* Lima, 70 Branches.

## PRODUCTION, INDUSTRY AND COMMERCE

**Agriculture.** Agriculture plays an important part in the economy of the country, with 13·8 per cent of the land under cultivation. The Agrarian Reform Law, promulgated on 24 June 1969, has completely changed the structure of Peruvian agriculture. Through this Law, the land has been given to those who directly work it.

There is also a large area under orchard, mainly in the warmer valleys between the coast and the cordilleras, although exports are small and mainly to the surrounding South American countries. Pears, apples, oranges, pineapples, peaches, quinces, grapes and even dates, olives, and figs are all grown. There is also production of white and red wine for internal consumption.

Yields of the main crops at the end of 1971 are shown in the following table:

| *Crop* | *Yield in thousands of Metric tons* |
|---|---|
| Sugar cane | 8,562·0 |
| Fruit | 2,138·5 |
| Potatoes | 1,813·0 |
| Maize | 669·0 |
| Rice | 595·0 |
| Yucca | 503·0 |
| Vegetables | 475·5 |
| Cotton | 225·0 |
| Barley | 176·0 |
| Sweet Potatoes | 159·0 |
| Wheat | 126·0 |
| Coffee | 61·0 |

Smaller crops, but still yielding an exportable surplus, are quinine and other medicinal plants. Tea and tobacco are also grown but not exported.

**Livestock.** The wool clip for 1964 was approximately 15,195 metric tons. The wool clip comes partly from llamas, alpaca and huarizo, and partly from sheep.

Cattle are also bred at high altitudes, sometimes more than 14,000 ft. above sea level, and even sheep are reared at 10,000 ft. The export of hides and skins includes cattle hides, sheepskins, goatskins, peccary and alligator hides. The following table shows livestock figures for the year 1971:

| | 1,000 *Metric Tons* |
|---|---|
| Bovine | 3,784,377 |
| Ovine | 12,513,574 |
| Pigs | 1,688,234 |
| Fowl | 19,895,121 |

The World Bank made a loan of 5,000,000 U.S. $ in 1954 and another for the same amount in 1957 and 1960 to the Banco de Fomento Agropecuario to finance imports of machinery, livestock and materials needed to stimulate agricultural output.

**Forestry.** There is plenty of timber in the eastern regions of Peru but it is difficult to transport owing to the nature of the country. The main outlet for such traffic is the Amazon and its tributaries. There are very hard woods like *palo acero* (ironwood) and very soft woods like the famous balsa. Mahogany, cedar and oak all grow in abundance, and there are some exports of mahogany and cedar. In addition to the quinine plant there are cube, a powerful insecticide, and tara, about 2,500 tons of which are produced annually for tanning. Total wood exports in 1964 were valued at 6,422,000 soles.

**Fishing.** Since 1964, Peru has maintained its place as the first country in the world in the list of fishmeal producers.

The Peruvian fishmeal, of high protein content, is obtained from the anchovy. During 1971, 10·3 million metric tons of anchovies were caught yielding a production of close on 1,528,170 metric tons of fishmeal. The main buyers of Peruvian fishmeal are the Federal Republic of Germany and the United States. The commercialization of fishmeal is in the hands of the State under the organization called EPCHAP (Empresa Pública de Comercialización de Harina y Aceite de Pescado).

On the 25 March 1971 the General Law on Fishing was passed establishing the legal standard for this economic activity and setting-up the "Fishing Community" for the participation of fishermen in these companies.

**Mining.** Peru is rich in minerals. Lead, copper, silver, iron ore, zinc, tungsten, gold, bismuth, antimony, manganese and cadmium are all exported. Peru is the world's fourth largest producer of silver. There are also large deposits of coal in Peru, both anthracite and bituminous. The former is exported and the latter used for smelting purposes.

On the 8 June 1971 the General Mining Law was passed which has reformed the structure of this sector. Through this legislation there has been established a "Mining Community" which allows the workers some say in the running of the mines.

The State has nationalized, through "Minero-Perú", the production of minerals.

Recent discoveries of petroleum, both in the jungle and on the continental shelf, will probably mean a notable increase in the production of petroleum in Peru.

Petroleum production in 1972 was 25·6 million barrels (of 42 h.s. gallons).

The table below shows the quantity of minerals produced in 1971:

| *Mineral* | *Quantity* (000's) |
|---|---|
| *Metallic* | |
| Copper | 214·0 metric tons |
| Silver | 1,242·0 kilos |
| Lead | 172·0 metric tons |
| Zinc | 376·0 metric tons |
| Iron (concentrate) | 8,849·0 metric tons (gross) |
| Gold | 3,131·0 grammes |
| *Non-metallic* | |
| Coal | 92·0 metric tons |
| Petroleum | 22,588·0 barrels |

**Industry.** Although primarily an agricultural country, Peru has a number of manufacturing industries that are able to satisfy local demand. The textile industry, however, is the most important, being in a position to produce a large part of the cotton yarn, knitted goods and other wearing apparel required for home use, in addition to a large percentage of cotton piece goods. Shoes are also manufactured in sufficient quantity to satisfy local demand and are exported.

Other manufactures include cement, bricks, tiles, paint, aluminium ware, paper, furniture, glassware, chemicals, tyres, and rubber goods, canned fish and preserves.

During 1970, industrial production increased 11 per cent, after having remained relatively small in 1968 and 1969 when increases of 2·4 per cent and 0·3 per cent were registered, respectively. This increase was due to a greater use of installed capacity and to the increase in internal demand.

On the 27 July 1970 the General Law of Industries was passed which outlines the new strategy for the development of Peruvian industry.

The Law on Industrial Communities was passed on the 1 December 1970 through which workers can participate in the management and profits of companies.

**Commerce.** The trade balance for 1972 showed exports to the value of $944 millions, imports to the value of $796 millions, giving a trade surplus of $148 millions.

The following table shows the values of imports and exports by principal countries in 1972 (in thousands of Soles):

| *Country* | *Exports* | *Imports* |
|---|---|---|
| U.S.A. | 12,047 | 9,193 |
| Japan | 5,075 | 2,374 |
| Germany | 4,101 | 3,661 |
| Belgium | 1,273 | 669 |
| Netherlands | 2,500 | 713 |
| U.K. | 966 | 1,314 |
| Italy | 907 | 956 |
| Argentine | 574 | 750 |
| Chile | 498 | 326 |
| Canada | 280 | 1,231 |
| Ecuador | 167 | 301 |
| Switzerland | 108 | 879 |

The following table shows the value of exports during 1972 by principal commodities (in million dollars):

| *Commodity* | 1972 |
|---|---|
| Marine products | 280·1 |
| Cotton | 46·6 |
| Sugar | 77·1 |
| Coffee | 46·8 |
| Wool and fibres | 6·1 |
| Leather (untanned) | 1,386·0 |
| Fishmeal | 322·0 |
| Copper | 188·5 |
| Iron | 64·9 |
| Silver | 61·6 |
| Lead | 33·2 |
| Zinc | 69·0 |
| Non-traditional export products | 33·1 |

The following table shows the value of imports during 1971 by commodities (in million dollars):

| *Commodity* | 1971 |
|---|---|
| Capital goods for Industry | 164,308 |
| Capital goods for Agriculture | 14,299 |
| Capital goods for Transport | 29,985 |
| Chemical and Pharmaceutical products (semi-refined and refined) | 133,250 |
| Fuel and lubricants | 24,772 |
| Sunflower oil | 23 |
| Soya bean oil (gross) | 2,321 |
| Newspaper | 9,628 |
| Wheat | 52,263 |
| Bovine and ovine meat | 8,996 |
| Cattle on foot for consumption | 16,262 |

## COMMUNICATIONS

**Railways.** There are 19 lines in the Republic, nine of which are State owned. In 1962 there were 5,308,866 km. of main lines, and 559,796 km. of branch lines. Most lines are of standard gauge, and one, the Central Railway, is the highest standard-gauge railway in the world, reaching an altitude of 15,801 ft. In 1962 the total number of passengers carried was 4,142,232 and the weight of the goods amounted to 3,752,693 metric tons.

**Airlines.** There are air-mail and passenger services between Lima and all other South American republics, Europe and the U.S.A., including a twice weekly B.O.A.C. service between London and Lima, as well as an internal air network.

**Posts, Telegraphs and Telephones.** Post and telegraph services are controlled by the State. The public services of telecommunication passed to the State when Peru purchased the shares which ITT owned in the Peruvian Telephone Company, and, at the same time, taking charge of services operated by other companies.

On the 14 June 1969, Peru entered the Space Age in communications when the Lurín Satellite Station came into operation. International telephone, telex, telegraphic, radiographic, television and data processing are processed by this Station.

Entel-Peru (Empresa Nacional de Telecomunicaciones del Perú—the National Telecommunications Board) was created by Law on the 7 November 1969 for the operation, on behalf of the State, of telecommunication services in Peru.

### NEWSPAPERS

**El Peruano.** F. 1825. Official Gazette.

**El Comercio.** F. 1839. Morning. Independent. Lima.

**La Nueva Crónica.** F. 1912. Morning and afternoon. Independent. Lima.

**Expreso.** F. 1961. Morning. Independent. Lima.

**Ultima Hora.** F. 1950. Afternoon. Independent. Lima.

**Correo.** F. 1963. Morning. Independent. Lima.

**El Grafico.** F. 1963. Afternoon. Independent. Lima.

**Extra.** F. 1964. Afternoon. Independent. Lima.

**Ojo.** F. 1967. Morning. Independent. Lima.

### ATOMIC ENERGY

There are thought to be possibilities of sources of uranium in Peru and prospecting is going on. This, and all other matters relating to atomic energy, is under the supervision of the Board of Control of Atomic Energy. Also under the Board is an institute for instruction in nuclear matters. 'Atoms for Peace' agreements have been signed with the United States, making possible the supply of uranium from that country for both research and power reactors and financial assistance in the acquisition of a research reactor.

The Peruvian Atomic Energy Board has announced its decision to develop uranium deposits in the department of Cuzco which it claims are of very rich content. According to analyses, reported to have been confirmed by the U.S. Atomic Energy Commission, the minerals contain from 5·8 per cent to 9·2 per cent of radio active uranium.

Peru has acquired from the United States what is stated to be the largest cobalt bomb in Latin America, for use in the fight against cancer.

### EDUCATION AND RELIGION

The General Law on Education, passed on 21 March 1972 has created a new education system in Peru on three levels for the transformation of Peruvian society. The three levels are: Initial Education for children of less than six years of age; Basic Education which comprises nine grades and divided into three cycles to establish general information; and Higher Education, divided into three cycles, the first of which gives Master and the third of Doctor.
an option of the title of Bachelor, the second of Licenciate or

The new Law institutes and guarantees freedom of education as a right for everyone to be educated and to choose the form of their education. It also establishes the principle of bilingual education and due attention to local folklore.

There is now a total of 33 universities with 92,700 students in all.

Peru has freedom of religion, but the Roman Catholic religion is protected by the State.

# Republic of the Philippines

## (REPÚBLICA DE FILIPINAS)

**Capital**—Manila.

**President**—Ferdinand E. Marcos.

**National Flag:** Divided fesse-wise, blue and red; at the hoist a triangle white, point to the fly, bearing a yellow sun with eight three-pointed rays between three stars five-pointed yellow.

### CONSTITUTION AND GOVERNMENT

THE Republic of the Philippines, politically a constitutional Republic and geographically an archipelago, consists of some seven thousand islands in South east Asia.

The Philippines were first visited by Spaniards led by the Portuguese explorer Ferdinand Magellan in 1521. In a renewed expedition to the Philippines in 1565, the Spaniards took possession of the Island of Cebu in the central Philippines and from there gradually extended control over the rest of the country.

Spanish rule lasted in the Philippines until 1898. During the 300 odd years that Spain governed the country, there were numerous local revolts but the Spaniards consolidated their hold by introducing and encouraging the spread of Christianity, stimulating trade and commerce, establishing schools and hospitals and, not until the second half of the 19th century, did they see the need for political reforms. By then, Filipino agitation for reforms, led notably by such writers like Jose Rizal, Marcelo H. del Pilar, and Graciano Lopez Jaena was already at fever pitch. But the reform movement proved ineffective in evoking the necessary response from the lethargic Spanish authorities, and soon separatist activities began to sprout in the country. The most noted among these was the *Katipunan*, a secret society whose avowed purpose was the overthrow of Spanish rule.

On 30 December 1896, the Spanish government in the Philippines executed Rizal, the foremost of Filipino patriots. This act wrote *finis* to any further thought of reform and served to fortify the resolve of the Filipino people to be rid of Spanish rule. On 24 May 1898, a ranking leader of the Revolution, General Emilio Aguinaldo, announced the formation of a Filipino Dictatorial Government in order to buttress the struggle against Spain. On 12 June 1898 he proclaimed Philippine Independence, and shortly after, inaugurated a Revolutionary Government which took over the task of partly administering and partly restructuring the government. But the most memorable achievement of the Revolutionary Government was its promulgation of a democratic constitution which is regarded as the most noteworthy of its kind in East Asia during this period.

Unknown to the Revolutionary Government, a combination of circumstances began to conspire against the declaration of Filipino autonomy. Following U.S. Commodore Dewey's victory over the Spanish fleet in Manila Bay on 1 May 1898, the Americans steadily brought in reinforcements to Manila. Tensions between the Americans and the Filipinos built up until hostilities erupted. Superior American arms finally won. American authority was established over the entire country and pacification took less time than would have been normally necessary because of the promise of eventual autonomy. The Americans helped in rebuilding the shattered economy, established a nationwide educational system, brought in English as the official language and language of instruction, reorganized the governmental system and acquainted the people with the juridical and political institutions of Anglo-Saxon democracy. Passing through phases of increasing autonomy which was interrupted by three years of Japanese military occupation during the Pacific War of 1941–1945, the Philippines eventually regained its independence on 4 July 1946.

Between 1946 and 17 January 1973, the Republic of the Philippines operated according to the 1935 Constituion which provided for a tripartite system: the Executive, represented by a President who was elected by direct vote of the people for a four-year term, with a right to re-election, a bicameral Congress made up of Congressmen with a four-year term and Senators with a six-year term and a Judiciary, with the power of judicial review. The Constitution was nationalistic, contained a Bill of Rights, and some nationalistic provisions, and explicitly provided for a strong Chief Executive.

On 21 September 1972, in the face of anarchic conditions, the incumbent President, Ferdinand E. Marcos, declared a nationwide martial law, pursuant to powers expressly vested in him by the 1935 Constitution. In explaining his action, the President noted the existence of actual subversion and the continuing threat it posed to the democratic institutions of the Republic. Governing through constitutionally authoritarian means, i.e. upon means logically following from his constitutional power to declare martial law, the President issued a series of decrees designed to meet the danger of subversion, purge the government of grafters and time-servers, reorganize the government along lines of economy and efficiency, intensify the collection of taxes and determine a set of priorities requiring urgent government attention.

Martial law abolished the powerful and corrupt Congress and saw the adoption of a new Constitution which provides for the eventual adoption of a parliamentary government in the Philippines.

On 17 January 1973, President Marcos proclaimed the effectivity of a new Constitution following its approval by the Citizens Assemblies organized throughout the land. The Constitution was drafted by a duly-elected Constitutional Convention which approved the final version thereof on 30 November 1972.

The overwhelming ratification of the new Constitution by the Filipino people underscored and confirmed the need of immediate and massive social, political and economic reforms along constitutional lines.

The new Charter contains an expanded declaration of principles and state policies. Noteworthy among these are those concerned with the positive role of the State in regulating the use and enjoyment of private property, equitably diffusing property ownership and profits, affording protection to labour and providing social services. In the field of individual rights, a Bill of Rights, largely consisting of derivations from the concept of due process, is reaffirmed. A novel feature is the article on the duties and obligations, like the duty to vote and the duty to exercise one's rights responsibly.

The structure of Government consists of a President, a National Assembly composed of as many members as the law may apportion among the political divisions of the country, the Prime Minister and the Cabinet, and the Judiciary. The members of the National Assembly serve for six years unless they fail in a re-election bid in the event of the National Assembly being dissolved. The President functions as symbolic head of State. He proclaims the election of a Prime Minister, dissolves the National Assembly upon advise of the Prime Minister, and accepts the resignation of the Cabinet. The Constitution lodges the exercise of executive power in the Prime Minister with the assistance of the Cabinet. The Prime Minister is constitutionally the Head of the Government; he is elected by a majority of all the members of the National Assembly from among themselves. He continues in office as long as the National Assembly does not withdraw its confidence from him.

The seat of legislative power is the National Assembly. It regularly convenes once every year on the fourth Monday of July and continues in session until thirty days before its next regular session. Generally it exercise the following functions: to declare war, conduct inquiries in aid of legislation, to interpellate the Prime Minister and the Cabinet, to authorize the Prime Minister to carry out a declared national policy, to act on appropriations proposals of the Prime Minister, and to pass upon bills recommended by the Cabinet.

The Judicial power is vested in a Supreme Court and such inferior courts as the law may establish. The Supreme Court, composed of a Chief Justice and fourteen Associate Justices, may sit *en banc* or in two divisions in its deliverations. It has jurisdiction to hear and decide cases involving the constitutionality of a treaty, executive agreement or law, cases affecting ambassadors, other public ministers and consuls, petitions for special types of cases, review, revise, reverse, modify or affirm final judgments and decrees of inferior courts. In order to expidite the resolution of cases, the Constitution has broken fresh ground by requiring that the maximum period within which a case or matter shall be heard is eighteen months for the Supreme Court, twelve months for all inferior collegiate courts and three months for all inferior courts. The members of the Supreme Court and judges of the inferior courts shall be appointed by the Prime Minister.

The National Assembly, however, has not been convened since the people, through the Barangays (Citizens Assemblies) in the January 1973 referendum, voted to defer the holding of an interim National Assembly.

On 28–28 July 1973, a nationwide referendum participated in by more than twenty million members of the 54,470 Barangays of fifteen years of age and over, including illiterates, voted overwhelmingly in the affirmative on the sole question: "Under the present Philippine Constitution the President, if he so desires, can continue in office beyond 1973. Do you want President Marcos to continue beyond 1973 and finish the reforms he initiated under Martial Law?" A closer rapport between Government and people has become therefore a reality, as the Barangays had been established precisely to broaden the base of citizen participation in the democratic process and to afford ample opportunities for the citizenry to express their views on important national issues.

On 27–28 February, 1974 the Filipino people overwhelmingly voted for the continuation of martial law and gave the President a free hand in appointing local officials.

### The President's Cabinet

*Secretary of Foreign Affairs:* Carlos P. Romulo.
*Secretary of Finance:* Cesar E. A. Virata.
*Secretary of Justice:* Vicente Abad Santos.
*Secretary of Agriculture:* Arturo A. Tanco.
*Secretary of Public Works, Transportation and Communication:* Alfredo L. Juinio.
*Secretary of Education and Culture:* Juan L. Manuel.
*Secretary of Labor:* Blas F. Ople.
*Secretary of National Defense:* Juan Ponce Enrile.
*Secretary of Health:* Clemente S. Gatmaitan.
*Secretary of Trade:* Troadio T. Quiazon, Jr.
*Secretary of Social Services and Development:* Estefania Aldaba-Lim.
*Director-General of the National Economic Development Authority:* Gerardo Sicat.
*Secretary of Agrarian Reform:* Conrado F. Estrella.
*Secretary of Public Information:* Francisco S. Tatad.
*Secretary of Local Governments and Community Development:* Jose A. Roño.
*Secretary of Tourism:* Jose D. Aspiras.
*Secretary of Industry:* Vicente T. Paterno.
*Secretary of Public Highways:* Baltazar Aquino.
*Secretary of Natural Resources:* Jose J. Leido, Jr.
*Secretary of Youth and Sports Development:* Gilberto Duavit.

### Congress

#### Senate

*President:* Gil Puyat.
*President Pro Tempore:* José J. Roy.
*Majority Floor Leader:* Arturo Tolentino.
*Minority Floor Leader:* Gerardo Roxas.

#### House of Representatives

*Speaker:* Cornelio T. Villareal.
*Speaker Pro Tempore:* Jose Aldeguer.
*Majority Floor Leader:* Marcelino Veloso.
*Minority Floor Leader:* Justiniano Montano.

## LOCAL GOVERNMENT

Each province is governed by a Sangguniang Panlalawigan (Provincial Advisory Council). The Sangguniang Panlalawigan assumes all the old powers and responsibilities of the, now, defunct provincial board. The duties of the Sangguniang Panlalawigan include administrative functions like providing for the offices of provincial and court officials, courthouses, jailhouse and equipment. It is also responsible for appropriating money for the general welfare of the population of the province. The Sangguniang Panlalawigan is composed of the following members: (1) a former governor who acts as the presiding officer; (2) a former vice-governor; (3) former provincial board members; (4) the president of the provincial barangay federation; (5) the president of the provincial kabataang barangay federation; and (6) a representative from each sangguniang pambayan in the province.

## LEGAL SYSTEM

The judiciary comprises the Supreme Court, the Court of Appeals, the Courts of First Instance, the Municipal Courts, and City Courts of the chartered cities, and courts of special jurisdiction, such as Criminal Circuit Courts, Juvenile and Domestic Relations Courts and the Court of Agrarian Relations, the members of which are appointed by the Prime Minister. The Supreme Court consisting of a Chief Justice and fourteen associate justices shall have administrative supervision over all Courts and the personnel thereof.

## AREA AND POPULATION

The approximate area of the Philippines is 299,404 sq. km., of which 297,409 sq. km. comprises the land area.

The population at mid-1974 was 41,433,000. The percentage growth rate of the population for the periods 1960–74 and 1965–74 was 3·0. Chief cities and towns with their populations are: Manilla, 1,473,557; Quezon, 994,679; Cebu, 418,517; Davao, 515,520; Caloocan, 515,520.

The population is composed of 43 ethnographic groups, having 87 languages and dialects. Filipino, the national language, is based on Tagalog, one of the native languages.

# PHILIPPINES

## CURRENCY

The unit of currency is the peso of 100 centavos. The peso has been allowed to float. As of July 1976 the prevailing exchange rate is P.7·28 to U.S. $100. The new "Ang Bagong Lipunan" (The New Society) coinage series are in the following denominations: "1,000-piso", "100 piso", "50-piso", "5-piso" and the lesser "1-piso", 50, 25, 10, 5 and 1 "sentimo" coins. Bank notes are issued in denominations of 2, 5, 10, 20, 50 and 100 pesos.

## FINANCE

The GNP at market prices for 1974 was U.S. $ millions 13,650, and the GNP per capita at market prices was U.S. $330. The annual average percentage growth rate of the GNP per capita for the period 1960–74 was 2·4, and for the period 1965–74 was 2·7. [*See the note at the beginning of this section concerning GNP.*]

National government revenue, including non-tax revenues were estimated to have increased to P18,829 million in 1976 from the 1975 level of P16,780 million, representing a growth rate of 12·2 per cent. The total expenditure loomed larger than the receipts during 1976 principally because of the accelerated implementation of infrastructure and other development projects. Total expenditures were estimated to have increased from the 1975 level of P19,048 million to P21,814 million in 1976, a 14·5 per cent increase, while receipts were estimated to have grown by 12·2 per cent. Thus, a financial gap results amounting to P2,985 million and representing 2·3 per cent of GNP. The deficit was financed from net borrowings of P2,800 million and drawdown in cash balances amounting to P124 million.

Expenditure included P2,121·5 million on general public service; P2,752·0 million on national defenses; P2,140·7 million on education; P713·8 million on social security and welfare; P1,682·4 million on housing; P10,000·3 million on economic services; and P2, 169·7 million on debt services.

Total outstanding internal public debt as of 1976 stood at P26,855·9 million registering an increase of P6,520·8 million or 32 per cent over that of 1975. External debts as of December 31, 1976 amounted to P5,554 million, 48 per cent higher than the level outstanding as of end-1975. Of this amount, 47 per cent were obligations of the private sector; 40 per cent, the government sector; and 13 per cen, the Central Bank. The annual debt service burden stood below the statutory 20 per cent ceiling of the average past three-year foreign exchange receipts.

## PRINCIPAL BANKS

**Bank of the Philippine Islands.** Est. 1851. (President, Alberto F. de Villa-Abrille; Chairman, Enrique Zobel.) Assets as at 30 June 1975 stand at P. 1,852,121,295·00; demand deposits P. 477,825,292; time deposits, 746,396,352; deposits of banks, 5,672,628. *Head Office:* 6795 Ayala Avenue, Makati, Rizal. Number of branches 48.

**Central Bank of the Philippines.** Est. 1949. (Governor, Gregorio S. Licaros; Chairman of the Monetary Board, Gregorio S. Licaros.) Assets as at 30 June 1977, P. 27,556,797,885·57; deposit and current accounts P. 109,941,048·27. *Head Office:* Manila, Philippines. Number of Branches, 3 Regional Offices and 9 Regional Clearing Units.

**Far East Bank and Trust Company.** Est. 1960. (President, Augusto M. Barcelon; Chairman, Jose B. Fernandez, Jr.) Assets as at 21 June 1977 P. 2,095,919,199·90; deposits and current accounts P. 1,106,152,279·10. *Head Office:* Muralla, Intramuros, Manila, Philippines. Number of branches 26.

**Philippine National Bank.** (President, P. O. Domingo.) Est. 1916; 99 per cent of share capital is owned by the State. As of 30 June 1974, balance sheet showed total assets P. 8,964,238,765; total deposits, P. 5,586,091,845. *Head Office:* Manila. 9 Overseas offices, 161 domestic branches and agencies.

**Citibank.** As of 20 June 1977, balance sheet showed total assets P. 4,171,395,005·07; total deposits, P. 1,008,949,873·99. *Head Office:* Makati, Metro Manila.

**China Banking Corporation.** Total assets, P. 986·7 million; total deposits, P. 462·3 million. *Head Office:* Manila.

**Equitable Banking Corporation.** Total assets as of 31 December 1972, P. 736·5 million; total deposits, P. 507·7 million. *Head Office:* Manila.

**Philippine Commercial & Industrial Bank.** Total assets at 28 September 1974, P. 523·1 million; total deposits, P. 551·1 million. *Head Office:* Manila.

**Bank of the Philippine Islands.** Total assets as of 31 December 1972, P. 668·5 million; total deposits, P. 473·5 million. *Head Office:* Manila.

**Consolidated Bank & Trust Corporation.** Total assets as of 31 December 1976, P. 1,774,899,442·01; Total deposits; 1,154,601,296·74. *Head Office:* Manila.

**Rizal Commercial Banking Corporation.** Total assets as of 31 December 1972, P. 740·0 million; total deposits, P. 511·4 million. *Head Office:* Corner of Dasmariñas and Juan Luna Sts. Manila, R.O.P.

**Hongkong & Shanghai Banking Corporation.** Total assets as of 31 December 1972, P. 321·7 million; total deposits, P. 73·8 million. *Head Office:* Makati, Rizal. Branch in Iloilo.

**Chartered Bank.** Total assets as of 31 December 1972, P. 164·7 million; total deposits, P. 72·6 million. *Head Office:* Manila.

## PRODUCTION, INDUSTRY AND COMMERCE

The country's significant economic growth for CY 1976 was attributed largely to the performance of the productive sector, This sector, which accounted for more than 26 per cent of the gross domestic product (GDP), contributed almost one-fourth of the increase in GDP. This gain was due principally to the strength of the 22·2 per cent growth of sugar cane, notwithstanding falling export prices, and the 10·7 per cent growth of forestry.

**Agriculture.** The Philippines is predominantly an agricultural country. Considered the backbone of the country's economy, agriculture accounts for one-third of the gross domestic product, more than half the total employment in the country, and 70 per cent of commodity export earnings.

Rice, corn and coconut are the dominant crops, accounting for 82 per cent of the total effective crops, area. Sugar, fruit crops, vegetables and other crops account for the rest.

The table below shows the production of selected agricultural crops for 1975 and 1976:

VOLUME OF OUTPUT
(*in metric tons*)

| *Crop* | *1975* | *1976* | *Per cent Increase or (Decrease)* |
|---|---|---|---|
| Rice (unhusked) | 6,112,039 | 6,187,042 | 1·2 |
| Corn | 2,731,966 | 2,760,036 | 1·0 |
| Centrifugal sugar | 2,489,520 | 3,261,170 | 31·0 |
| Copra | 2,089,402 | 2,421,461 | 15·9 |
| Banana | 1,858,333 | 1,816,706 | (2·2) |

As of January 1976, government statistics show that there was a farm animal population of 46 million chickens, 4·1 million ducks, 6.4 million head of swine, 1·7 million head of cattle, and 2·7 million head of carabao. While the Philippines is about self-sufficient in poultry, eggs, and pork, it is still short of the country's requirement by 52 per cent. To meet the requirements, the government continues its present efforts to increase production under the Beef and Carabeef Program launched in November 1975.

Similarly, a 25-year plan for the National Dairy Development Program aimed at increasing the sufficiency level of domestic milk production has been initiated and is nearing completion.

The livestock and poultry sector registered a 2·1 per cent and 5·8 per cent growth rate respectively for 1976.

**Forestry.** Philippine rain forests are considered among the finest in the world. From its resources are obtained several forest products of economic importance and other immeasurable benefits. The Philippines was thought to have an exhaustible supply of forest products and at the same time was able to safeguard its watersheds and maintain ecological balance until the great floods of 1972 and 1974.

In this regard, the government embarked on a holistic ecosystem approach to forest resources management in the country through the Program for Forest Ecosystem Management (PROFEM) with the aim of preventing human destruction of forest resources, minimize the effects of floods, droughts, soil erosion and other destructive factors on the ecosystem and to increase public participation in agro-forestry activities.

**Fisheries.** Geographical location and physical attributes make the Philippines a natural fishing ground. Its vast territorial and insular water abound with rich fishery and aquatic resources. Undoubtedly, if such vast resources are efficiently developed and properly managed, the country could become a major fishing country.

In this direction, the government is undertaking an Integrated Fisheries Development Plan covering 1977 to 1981. The projects hope to accelerate fish production by 5·5 per cent annually and to meet the increasing consumption requirement and export demand for fish and fishery products. For CY 1976, the industry registered a 3·0 per cent growth rate.

**Mining.** The mining sector continued to be adversely affected by unfavorable price movements in the international market, although its real volume of production expanded. Government assistance helped the industry to overcome some of its difficulties.

However, by first quarter-1977, the Bureau of Mines reported that the industry is well on its way to a sustained recovery as the sector continues to enjoy high prices and strong world market demand for major mineral commodities particularly chromite and nickel during the first half of 1977. World prices have generally moved higher in most markets except for some major fluctuations evident in copper and gold as of mid-year.

Preliminary estimates for the first semester placed a total value of mineral production at P2·45 billion up by 18·38 per cent from the P2·07 billion during the same period in 1976.

Production values for almost all metallic minerals went up except lead which suffered from relatively low output due to depressed market conditions. Cooper's continuous recovery resulted in an increase of 10·63 per cent in volume and 15·85 per cent in value during the first six months. This was principally due to the improvement in copper prices which averaged 64 cents per pound during the semester despite fluctuations in June.

**Commerce.** General export trend was favorable with the exception of some principal exports like sugar, logs and copra. Notable gains were registered by the manufactured exports which increased by 45 per cent in 1976. Meanwhile, import restraint was pursued during the year. Priority was accorded to crude oil importation which increased by almost 16 per cent in 1976.

The following tables show imports and exports of principal commodities (in million dollars) for 1975 and 1976:

| *Exports* | *1975* | *1976* |
|---|---|---|
| 1. Centrifugal sugar | 581·0 | 435·2 |
| 2. Coconut oil | 231·0 | 284·4 |
| 3. Copper concentrates | 212·0 | 255·8 |
| 4. Copra | 172·0 | 145·4 |
| 5. Logs | 167·0 | 133·0 |
| 6. Bananas | 73·0 | 66·7 |
| 7. Gold from copper ores and concentrates | 53·3 | 57·1 |
| 8. Pineapples in syrup | 35·0 | 43·3 |
| 9. Molasses, inedible | 34·0 | 17·1 |
| 10. Copra cake or meal | 33·0 | 48·8 |

| *Imports* | *1975* | *1976* |
|---|---|---|
| 1. Mineral fuels, lubricants and other related materials | 653·4 | 867·3 |
| 2. Machinery other than electric | 424·0 | 591·8 |
| 3. Returned goods and special transactions | 183·6 | 297·6 |
| 4. Base metals | 295·7 | 262·8 |
| 5. Transport equipment | 265·3 | 244·1 |
| 6. Electric machinery, apparatus and appliances | 105·3 | 195·9 |
| 7. Cereals and cereal preparations | 154·9 | 169·2 |
| 8. Chemical elements and compounds | 216·1 | 153·1 |
| 9. Explosives and misc. chemical materials and products | 113·8 | 118·4 |
| 10. Manufacture of metals | 60·1 | 83·6 |

The country's leading trading partners for 1976 were the United States, Japan and Saudi Arabia, whose shares to total trade were 27·2 per cent, 26 per cent, and 4·9 per cent, respectively. The other leading trade partners which registered surpluses in the country's trade account were the Netherlands, the Union of Soviet Socialist Republic, the Federal Republic of Germany, Kuwait, United Kingdom and Australia.

## COMMUNICATIONS

The slow growth of water and air transport dampened the performance of the service sector composed of transport, communications and storage sector. Gross value added amounted to P3,491 million in 1976 as against P3,263 million in 1975. This represents an increase of 7·0 per cent in 1976 compared to 11·3 per cent in 1975. Storage registered the highest growth rate of 16·1 per cent, followed by communication with 11·0 per cent.

The Philippine National Railways operations declined by about 22·84 per cent (71,773 tons) from 315,135 tons of the preceding period of 243,162 tons of the current FY 1975–76. Likewise, revenue income dropped by about 13·77 per cent (P1,221,227)—from P8,871,023 to P7,649,796.

It could be gleaned from the figures that the decrease in volume of loading was much higher than the corresponding decrease in revenue. The disparity in the percentage may be attributed to increased freight rates instituted by the management starting the last fiscal period.

Passenger movement slightly slowed down by about 1·36 per cent (117,222) from 8,584,589 last year to 8,467,367 passengers this year (1976). In contrast, the corresponding revenue slightly improved by about 0·92 per cent (P471,108) from P51,101,987 to P51,573,095. Increased rates in passenger fares instituted recently by the company was responsible for such situation where revenue increased despite a decline in passenger movement during the period of one year.

Commodities transported thru the PNR from Jan.-June 1976 was 156,279 tons worth P6,448,695 of which 126,412 tons (P3,355,402) were transported through the facilities of the company's ordinary cars and 29,867 tons (P3,093,293) through its express cars. The total volume carried by the former was more than 4 times as much, while the corresponding value was only about equal to that carried by the latter. This shows that loadings through the express cars were mostly manufactures or commodities with higher prices.

As in previous surveys, agricultural products registered the highest movement, chalking a combined total of 83,380 tons valued at P1,383,485. Manufactures came in poor second for a combined total of 47,972 tons valued at P3,604,917.

During the first-half of the year ending June 1976, a total of 36,649 coastwise vessels with gross tonnage of 18,807,317 tons were registered as having entered 26 ports of entry. These figures show 2·85 per cent (1,074) and 7·19 per cent (1,258,472) increase over the number and tonnage of the same period in the preceding year. The rate of increase in the number of entered vessels was much less than the corresponding increase in total gross tonnage indicating acceptability for bigger vessels to cope with the growing demand for increased domestic trade and commerce.

By individual ports of entry. Cebu again registered the premiere position, both in number and gross tonnage of entered domestic vessels for the period while Manila (4,743 and 3,094,272).

38,394 coastwise vessels with a total gross tonnage of 18,648,804 were cleared in 26 ports of entry. The total number of cleared vessels was 2·18 per cent more than what was registered during FY 1974–75. Cebu registered the highest number of cleared vessels followed by Manila with 4,672 cleared vessels.

### Civil Aviation

**PAL—Philippine Air Lines Inc.** (President, Benigno P. Toda, Jr.); share capital pesos 25,000,000; *services operated:* Manila–Hong Kong; Manila–Honolulu–San Francisco; Manila–Taipei; Manila–Singapore; Manila–Kuala Lumpur; Manila–Jakarta; Manila–Port Moresby; Manila–Sydney–Melbourne; Manila–Tokyo; Manila–Bangkok–Karachi–Rome –Frankfurt–Amsterdam; and domestic services. *Head Office:* PAL Building, Ayala Avenue, Makati, Rizal, Philippines.

## NEWSPAPERS

**The Manila Chronicle.** F. 1945. English. Independent.

**The Manila Times.** F. 1945. English. Independent.

**The Daily Mirror.** F. 1948. English. Afternoon daily.

**The Evening News.** F. 1945. English. Afternoon daily. Audited circulation 1967, 39,630.

**Taliba.** Filipino daily.

**Manila Daily Bulletin.** F. 1900. English. Independent. Manila.

**Philippines Herald.** F. 1920. Morning. English. Manila.

**Fookien Times.** Afternoon. Chinese. Publishes also The Sunday Morning Journal and the Financial Journal. Combined circulation 25,000. Manila.

### EDUCATION

At the beginning of the American occupation in 1898 a system of public primary education was established. The English language is now spoken and understood by a large section of the population. All officials and employees in the Government, as well as a great number of business people, speak English, or at least understand the language. Sustained efforts in the area of education have raised the literacy rate of the country up to 83·4 per cent.

The public school system includes a university with various collegiate courses, normal, high, elementary and vocational schools. As of school year 1976–77, the actual number of public schools in the country stood at 32,659. The number of state colleges and universities (including the branches) stood at 77. Overall enrollment (public and private) for school year 1974–75 is 10·7 million.

### RELIGION

There are three principal religions—Roman Catholicism, which embraces about 84·9 per cent of the population, Protestantism which accounts for 3·1 per cent and Mohammedanism (4·3 per cent). In 1901 the Philippine Independent Church was established by Mons. Gregorio Agilpay, a Filipino priest who seceded from the Roman Catholic Church. The new religion retains most of the beliefs and rituals of the Catholic Church. His followers are estimated to be more than 1,500,000 scattered throughout the country. Protestantism came with the American occupation, and its adherents are spread throughout the islands. The Moors, numbering some 500,000 and professing Mohammedanism, inhabit the Sulu Islands and parts of the coastal regions in Mindanao, the second largest island in the Philippines.

# Poland

## (POLISH PEOPLE'S REPUBLIC)

**Capital**—Warsaw.

**President**—Henryk Jabłoński.

**National Flag:** Divided fesse-wise, white and red.

### CONSTITUTION AND GOVERNMENT

*DATES in Polish Political History.*—The Polish state arose in the second half of the 10th century, *circa* A.D. 960. Prince Mieszko I first ruler of Poland (Piast dynasty). A.D. 966—Christening of Mieszko I, the beginning of Christianization of Poland. King Bolesław Chrobry (992–1025) strengthened the power of the new state. 9th–12th century—Resistance to the German drive. 1138—Division of Polish territory between the sons of Duke Bolesław III. Growth of provincial divisions. 1320—Unification of the country by Władysław Łokietek. 1370—End of the Piast dynasty. 1386—State union with the Grand Duchy of Lithuania. 1386–1572—Rule of the Jagiellon dynasty. Poland's period as a great power. Victory of Polish and Lithuanian forces over Teutonic Knights at Grunwald (1410). Continued struggle against the Teutonic Order concluded by the victorious Treaty of Toruń (1466). 1569—Close union between Poland and Lithuania, the so-called Lublin union. 1572–1795—Period of elective monarchy and wars with Russia, Sweden and Turkey (Vienna liberated by King Jan Sobieski 1683). 1772—First partition of Poland, by Russia, Prussia and Austria. 1791—New constitution to effect the consolidation of the state. 1792—The war against Russia in defence of the constitution. 1793—Second partition. 1794—First great national uprising under the leadership of T. Kościuszko. 1795—Third (final) partition of Poland. 1807—Creation of the Duchy of Warsaw. 1815—Under the terms of the Congress of Vienna, Poland again partitioned and so-called autonomous Kingdom of Poland under Russian domination formed, in which in 1830–31 a national uprising called 'The November Uprising' took place and the Kingdom's autonomy was *de facto* liquidated. In 1846 radical national insurrection in Cracow suppressed by Austria (who made use of the peasants' rebellious attitude to the nobility). 1848—Insurrection movement grows in the area occupied by Prussia; revolutionary uprising in Austria. 1863–64—'January' national uprising in Russian Poland broke out. 1918 (November)—Independent Polish Republic formed as a result of the defeat of Germany and Austria-Hungary in World War I, of the October Socialist revolution in Russia and as a result of battles fought by the Polish soldiers. New frontiers fixed by the Treaty of Versailles (1919), the Treaty of Riga (1921) and of three Silesian uprisings against the Germans and the Plebiscite of Silesia (1921). 1926—Coup d'état by Józef Pilsudski. 1932—Non-aggression pact with U.S.S.R. 1934—Non-aggression pact with Germany. 1939—Denunciation of non-aggression pact by Hitler and signing by Poland of Pact of Mutual Assistance with Great Britain. 1939 (September) German invasion of Poland. Formation of Polish Government in exile. 1940—Underground resistance developed. The fight against fascism both within the country and, together with the Allies, on all fronts was carried on by the Polish people. 1943—Formation of Polish Patriotic Union in the U.S.S.R., and the Polish National Council 22 July 1944—Organization and manifesto of Polish Committee of National Liberation. (1 August–2 October)—Uprising against Germans in Warsaw. (December)—Formation of Polish Provisional Government in liberated territory. 1945 (January–May)—Liberation of Poland by the Soviet Army and Polish forces. (April)—Treaty of Friendship and Mutual Assistance between Poland and the U.S.S.R. (July–August)—The Potsdam Conference fixed the Polish-German frontier at the Oder-Neisse line. 1947 (January and February)—First Seym elected and formulation of so-called 'Little-Constitution'. 1948 (December)—Unification of workers' parties into the Polish United Workers' Party (PZPR). 1952 (22 July)—Constitution of the Polish People's Republic. 1956 (October)—8th Plenary Session of the Polish United Workers' Party. W. Gomulka elected 1st Secretary of the Central Committee of the Polish United Workers' Party (PUWP). 1957 (January)—Parliamentary elections which endorsed the programme of the 8th Plenary Sessions. 1957 (October)—Rapacki's plan concerning the creation of a nuclear-free zone in Central Europe. The last Seym elections took place in March 1976. 1964—Poland suggests Gomulka's plan for freezing nuclear and thermonuclear weapons in Central Europe. Poland proposed to the UN that a European security conference be called. On 7 December 1970 a Plenary Session of the Central Committee of the Polish United Workers' Party was held. E. Gierek was elected First Secretary of the Central Committee of the Polish United Workers' Party. In December 1976 the Seventh Congress of the Polish United Workers Party was held.

During World War II, of the 1939 population 6,028,000 people were wiped out and war devastation caused reduction of national industrial capital by some 38 per cent.

*Constitution and Government.*—The supreme organ of the State power is the Seym, which is elected by universal, equal, direct and secret suffrage for a period of four years. The Seym enacts laws, supervises the activities of other organs of State power and administration, approves national economic plans and votes annual budgets. It appoints and recalls the Government, namely the Council of Ministers, and its individual members, and elects the President of the Supreme Chamber of Control. Also, it elects from among its own members the Council of State (which is a collective Head of State and its chairman). The Council of State issues decrees having legal force between the Seym sessions, it ratifies and terminates international agreements, appoints and recalls representatives of the Polish People's Republic abroad and exercises the prerogative of mercy, appoints civil and military officers, appoints judges, and the Procurator-General.

The National* Councils, which the Council of State also supervises, are the State power organs in the rural communes, town-districts, towns and voivodships. To their sphere of competence belong: the laying down of guidelines and the designation of tasks in the economic, social and cultural domains within their respective areas; and they co-ordinate the work and needs of the local population with national tasks and requirements. The National* Councils are elected for periods of four years.

Legislative initiative is vested in the Seym, the Council of State and the Government.

The function of the Supreme Chamber is to control the economic, financial and administrative organization under the supervision of the Seym.

**Presidium of the Seym**

*Marshal of the Seym:* Stanisław Gucwa (United Peasant Party).

*Vice-Marshals of the Seym:* Piotr Stefański (Democratic Party).
Halina Skibniewska (Non-Party Member).
Andrzej Werblan (Polish United Workers Party).

**The Council of State**

*President:* Henryk Jabłoński.

*Vice-Presidents:*
Edward Babiuch.
Tadeusz W. Młyńczak.
Władysław Kruczek.
Zdzisław Tomal.

*Secretary:* Ludomir Stasiak.

**Members**

Edward Duda.
Edward Gierek.
Michał Grendys.
Eugenia Kempara.
Halina Koźniewska.
Konstanty Łubieński.
Józef Ozga-Michalski.
Bolesław Piasecki.
Henryk Szafrański.
Stanisław Wroński.
Jerzy Ziętek.

**Supreme Chamber of Control**

*President:* Mieczysław Moczar.

**The Council of Ministers**

**Presidium of Government**

*Chairman:* Piotr Jaroszewicz.

*Deputy Chairman:* Longin Cegielski, Mieczysław Jagielski, Franciszek Kaim, Józef Kepa, Kazimierz Olszewski, Jadeusz gyka, Jan Szydlak, Kazimierz Secomski, Jozef Tejchma, Tadeusz Wrzaszczyk.
*Member of Presidium of Government:* Kazimierz Barcikowski.
*Office of the Council of Ministers: Chief:* Tanusz Wieczorek.
*Spokesman to the Government:* Wtodzimierz Janiurek.
*Chairman, Planning Commission at the Council of Ministers:* Tadeusz Wrzaszczyk.
*Minister of Building and Building Materials Industry:* Adam Glazur.
*Minister of Finance:* Henryk Kisiel.
*Minister of Administration Local Economy and Preservation of the Environment:* Maria Milczarek.
*Ministry of Mining:* Wtodzimierz Lejczak.
*Minister of Foreign Affairs:* Emil Wojtaszek.
*Minister of Internal Trade and Services:* Adam Kowalik
*Minister of Foreign Trade and Shipping:* Jerzy Olszewski.
*Minister of Transport:* Tadeusz Bejm.
*Minister of Forestry and Timber Industry:* Tadeusz Skwirzyński.
*Minister of Communications:* Edward Kowalczyk.
*Minister of Science, Higher Education and Technology:* Sylwester Kaliski.
*Minister of National Defence:* General Wojciech Jaruzelski.
*Minister of Education:* Jerzy Kuberski.
*Minister of Labour, Wages, and Social Affairs:* Tadeusz Rudolf.
*Minister of Heavy and Agricultural Machine Industry:* Franciszek Adamkiewicz.
*Minister of Light Industry:* Tadeusz Kunicki.
*Minister of Engineering Industry:* Aleksander Kopeć.

* Although commonly called 'People's Councils' 'National Councils' (Rady Narodowe) is the correct term.

*Minister of Food Industry and Purchases:* Emil Kołodziej.
*Minister of Agriculture:* Kazimierz Barcikowski.
*Minister of Internal Affairs:* Stanisław Kowalczyk.
*Minister of Power Industry and Nuclear Energy:* Andrzej Szozda.
*Minister of Chemical Industry:* Henryk Konopacki.
*Minister of Material Economy:* Eugeniusz Szyr.
*Minister of Metallurgy:* Franciszek Kaim.
*Minister, Head of the Office for Denominational Affairs:* Kazimierz Kąkol.
*Minister without Portfolio, Chairman of the Main Office of the Central Union of Agricultural Cooperatives* ("Samopomoc Chłopska"): Jan Kamiński.
*Minister of Justice:* Ferzy Bafia.
*Minister of Health and Social Welfare:* Marian Sliwiński.
*Minister for War Veterans Affairs:* General Mieczysław Grudzień.

**Political Parties in Poland**

*Polska Zjednoczona Partia Robotnicza (PZPR)*—the Polish United Workers' Party.

Political Bureau of the P.U.W.P. Central Committee:

Edward Gierek.
Edward Babiuch.
Zdzisław Grudzień.
Henryk Jabłoński.
Mieczysław Jagielski.
Piotr Jaroszewicz.
Wojciech Jaruzelski.
Stanisław Kania.
Józef Kępa.
Stanisław Kowalczyk.
Władysław Kruczek.
Stefan Olszowski.
Jan Szydlak.
Józef Tejchma.

*Deputy Members:*
Kazimierz Barcikowski.
Jerzy Łukaszewicz.
Tadeusz Wrzaszczyk.

*Secretariat, PUWP Central Committee:*
Edward Gierek, First Secretary.

*Secretaries:*
Edward Babiuch.
Ryszard Frelek.
Stanislaw Kania.
Alojzy Karkoszka.
Jerzy Łukaszewicz.
Stefan Olszowski.
Józef Pińkowski.
Andrzej Werblan.
Zdzisław Żandarowski.

*Members:*
Zdzistaw Kurowski, Zbigniew Zielinski.

*Zjednoczone Stronnictwo Ludowe (ZSL)*—The United Peasants Party (UPP).

*Presidium of UPP Chief Committee:*

*President:* Stanisław Gucwa.

*Vice-Presidents:*
Józef Ozga-Michalski.
Zdzisław Tomal.

*Members of Presidium of UPP Chief Committee:*
Longin Cegielski.
Edward Duda.
Stefan Ignar.
Emil Kołodziej.
Józef Krotiuk.
Bernard Kus.
Witold Lipski.
Jerzy Maciak.
Roman Malinowski.
Bronisław Owsianik
Bolesław Strużek.
Aleksander Schmidt.
Tadeusz Skwirzyński.
Janina Szczepańska.
Jerzy Szymanek.

*Secretariat, UPP Chief Committee:*

*President:* Stanisław Gucwa.

*Secretaries:*
Edward Duda.
Roman Malinowski.
Bronisław Owsianik.
Jerzy Szymanek.

*Stronnictwo Demokratyczne (SD)*—Democratic Party (DP).

*Presidium of DP Central Committee:*

*Chairman:* Tadeusz Witold Młyńakak.

*Vice-Chairman:*
Tadeusz Kałasa.
giotr Stefański.

*Secretariat of DP Central Committee:*

*Chairman:* Tadeusz Witold Młyńczak.

*Secretaries:*
Krystyna Marszałek.
Zbigniew Rudnicki.
Zdzisław Siedlewski.

**Youth Organizations**

*Federacja Socjalistycznych Związków Młodzieży Polskiej*—The Federation of Socialist Unions of Polish Youth. The Chairman of the Main Council—Zdzisław Kurowski

*Związek Socjalistycznej Młodzieży Polskiej (ZSMP)*—Union of Polish Socialist Youth. Chairman of the Central Board—Krzysztof Trębaczkiewicz (on 28th April 1976 The Socialist Youth Union, Union of Socialist Rural Youth and Socialist Union of Young Soldiers merged to form Union of Polish Socialist Youth).

*Socjalistyczny Związek Studentów Polskich*—Socialist Union of Polish Students. Chairman—Eugeniusz Mielcarek.

*Związek Harcerstwa Polskiego (ZHP)*—The Polish Pathfinders Organization. Commandant of ZHP, Jerzy Wojciechowski.

*Front of National Unity:*
Chairman, Prof. dr. Henryk Jabłoński.

## LEGAL SYSTEM

In accordance with the Constitution of 22 July 1952, the administration of justice in Poland is carried out by the following: The Supreme Court, Voivodship Courts, District Courts and Special Courts. The main principles applied in the administration of justice are:

(1) A uniform administration of justice for all citizens;
(2) Judges are independent and subject only to the law;
(3) Judges are appointed by the Council of State;
(4) Court with corporate structure and including lay assessors;
(5) Public Court proceedings with right to legal representative.

The Constitution also envisages the appointment of a Chief Public Prosecutor, who 'safeguards the people's rule of law, watches over the protection of public property and ensures that the rights of citizens are respected'.

The Supreme Court is elected by the Council of State for a period of five years. The Chief Public Prosecutor reports to the Council on his activities.

*The President of the Supreme Court:* Włodzimierz Berutowicz.
*Procurator-General:* Lucjan Czubiński.

## AREA AND POPULATION

The area of Poland is 312,677 square kilometres, and the total length of her frontiers is 3,538 kilometres, the sea coast accounting for 694 km., including bays, and the land frontiers for 3,014 km.; the sea frontier is 524 km. long. As a result of territorial changes after World War II the whole territory of the state was shifted some 200 kilometres to the west. The areas east of the Bug were incorporated in the Union of Soviet Socialist Republics, and the territories on the Odra and Nysa Łużycka Rivers and the greater part of former East Prussia became part of Poland. Poland's frontier with the U.S.S.R. (1,244 km.) was generally agreed upon at Yalta (11 February 1945) and laid down in detail in Moscow (16 August 1945), it underwent minor changes in 1951. The 1,310 km. frontier with Czechoslovakia adjoins the Carpathians and the Sudeten lands. The frontier with the German Democratic Republic (460 km.) was fixed in a general way at Potsdam (2 August 1945) and worked out in detail with the government of the German Democratic Republic at Zgorzelec (Goerlitz) on 6 July 1950.

The whole area of the State is divided into 46 voivodships and three urban voivodships. The voivodships are sub-divided into 2,327 boroughs.

There are 29 towns with a population of more than 100,000, Warsaw, Łódź, Cracow, Wrocław, Poznań, Gdańsk, Szczecin, Katowice, Bydgoszcz, Lublin, Gdynia, Zabrze, Częstochowa, Bytom, Biatysłok, Gliwice, Radom, Chorzów, Sosnowiec, Ruda Śląska, Toruń, Kielce, Tychy, Wałbrzych, Bielsko Biała, Olsztyn, Opole, Rybnik, Wodzisław Śląski.

The total population on 31 December 1975 was 34,186,000 of which 19,031,000 belong to urban areas and 15,155,000 belong to rural areas. The area and population of the voivodships are as follows:

| *Voivodships* | *Area in thousand sq. km.* | *Population in thousands* |
|---|---|---|
| Poland | 312·7 | 34,186·0 |
| Biała Podlaska | 5·4 | 280·0 |
| Białystok | 10·0 | 618·0 |
| Bielsko Biała | 3·7 | 779·0 |
| Bydgoszcz | 10·3 | 995·0 |
| Chełm | 3·9 | 221·0 |
| Ciechanów | 6·4 | 399·0 |
| Częstochowa | 6·2 | 727·0 |
| Elbląg | 6·1 | 423·0 |
| Gdańsk | 7·4 | 1,249·0 |
| Gorzów Wielkpoplski | 8·5 | 434·0 |
| Jelenia Góra | 4·4 | 487·0 |
| Kalisz | 6·5 | 644·0 |
| Katowice | 6·6 | 3,488·0 |
| Kielce | 9·2 | 1,037·0 |
| Konin | 5·1 | 426·0 |
| Koszalin | 8·5 | 435·0 |
| Kraków—City | 3·2 | 1,120·0 |
| Krosno | 5·7 | 422·0 |
| Legnica | 4·0 | 414·0 |
| Leszno | 4·2 | 343·0 |
| Lublin | 6·8 | 885·0 |
| Łomża | 6·7 | 320·0 |
| Łodź—City | 1·5 | 1,079·0 |
| Nowy Sącz | 5·6 | 599·0 |
| Olsztyn | 12·3 | 663·0 |
| Opole | 8·5 | 971·0 |
| Ostrołęka | 6·5 | 362·0 |
| Piła | 8·2 | 417·0 |
| Piotrków Trybunalski | 6·3 | 583·0 |
| Płock | 5·1 | 481·0 |
| Poznań | 8·2 | 1,171·0 |
| Przemyśl | 4·4 | 374·0 |
| Radom | 7·3 | 678·0 |
| Rzeszów | 4·4 | 610·0 |
| Siedlce | 8·5 | 601·0 |
| Sieradz | 4·9 | 387·0 |
| Skierniewice | 4·0 | 389·0 |
| Słupsk | 7·5 | 356·0 |
| Suwałki | 10·5 | 415·0 |
| Szczecin | 10·0 | 854·0 |
| Tarnobrzeg | 6·2 | 535·0 |
| Tarnów | 4·2 | 578·0 |
| Toruń | 5·3 | 587·0 |
| Wałbrzych | 4·2 | 714·0 |
| Warsaw—City | 3·8 | 1,891·0 |
| Włocławek | 4·4 | 403·0 |
| Wrocław | 6·3 | 1,026·0 |
| Zamość | 7·0 | 472·0 |
| Zielona Góra | 8·8 | 580·0 |

## FINANCE

**State Budget** (in thousand million zlotys):

| *Budget* | 1973 | 1974 | 1975 |
|---|---|---|---|
| *Revenue* | | | |
| Total | 483·8 | 604·1 | 720·1 |
| of which: | | | |
| Turnover tax and tax on non-commodity operations of socialized enterprises | 181·4 | 233·3 | 274·2 |
| Payments arising from profits of socialized enterprises | 148·2 | 143·5 | 154·9 |
| Taxes and duties from the private sector | 10·9 | 11·6 | 12·8 |
| Taxes and duties from the population | 29·2 | 18·8 | 14·5 |
| Social security contributions | 28·8 | 33·3 | 39·3 |
| *Expenditure* | | | |
| Total | 482·2 | 602·3 | 714·7 |
| Current in which: | 380·6 | 490·5 | 594·4 |
| Socialized enterprises and other economic units | 169·2 | 257·9 | 317·6 |
| Social and cultural services | 88·5 | 98·8 | 111·2 |
| National defence | 40·4 | 43·7 | 47·6 |
| Administration | 26·0 | 29·3 | 32·0 |

## BANKS

**Narodowy Bank Polski** ( The National Bank of Poland). Est. 1945. (President, Prof. Dr Witold Bień.) *Head Office:* Świętokrzyska 11/21, 00–950 Warsaw, P.O. Box 1011.

## PRODUCTION, INDUSTRY AND COMMERCE

The share of foreign capital in 1937 amounted, according to official data, to 1,294 million zlotys, or 43·3 per cent of the capital of all active companies. It was much higher in certain industries: 87·5 per cent in the oil industry, 66·1 per cent in the electrotechnical industry, 59·9 per cent in the chemical industry, 81·3 per cent in power stations and waterworks, and 59·1 per cent in the insurance business. Moreover, there were 44 foreign companies (with executive boards residing abroad) with a total capital of 150 million zlotys. Poland was restricted to the role of supplier of food and raw materials. Raw materials, and foodstuffs at dumped prices were the main items in Poland's exports.

War devastation during World War II caused the reduction of the national industrial capital by some 38 per cent.

After the war Poland embarked upon a Socialist economy. On 3 January 1946, the National Home Council passed an act on the taking over by the State of the fundamental branches of the national economy. Mineral resources, forests, mines, roads, water resources, rail, road, water and air transport, banks, industrial establishments, trade enterprises, and public services were declared national property.

The nationalization of the means of production, exchange, transport and credit served as a basis for the development of the country's economic life within the framework of national economic plans: the Three-Year Economic Reconstruction Plan (1947–49), the Six-Year Plan for Economic Development (1950–55) and the Five-Year Plan (1956–60) whose central aim was to raise the living standards of the population and the Five-Year Plan (1961–65), the Five-Year Plan (1966–70), the Five-Year Plan (1971–75), and the Five-Year Plan 1976–80.

**Agriculture.** There are 19·3 million hectares of cultivatable land of which 14·8 million hectares are arable land. In 1944 agrarian reforms were carried out and some six million hectares of land were allocated between smallholders and landless peasants. The most common form of property is the private farm. In June 1975 there were about 3·4 million with a total of 15,179,000 hectares of cultivatable land. Co-operative farms are organized on a basis of voluntary association. In June 1975 there were 1,120 profit-sharing co-operatives with a total of 346,200 hectares of land. Apart from private and co-operative farms there were, in June 1975, 6,703 State farms (PGR) with a total of 3,981 thousand hectares of land. Of that number there were 3,660 state farms under the Ministry of Agriculture. The total area of cultivatable land was divided as follows: Private farms: 79·7 per cent, co-operative farms: 2·3 per cent, State farms: 16·6 per cent.

The following table shows harvests of principal field crops (in million tons) for 1974–1975:

| *Crop* | 1974 | 1975 |
|---|---|---|
| Four cereals | 21·4 | 18·0 |
| Wheat | 6·4 | 5·2 |
| Rye | 7·9 | 6·3 |
| Barley | 3·9 | 3·6 |
| Oats | 3·2 | 2·9 |
| Sugar beet | 13·0 | 15·7 |
| Potatoes | 48·5 | 46·4 |

The following table shows production of main animal products in 1974 and 1975:

| *Product* | 1974 | 1975 |
|---|---|---|
| Meat and offal (thousand tonnes) | 3,066·8 | 3,067·0 |
| Milk (million litres) | 16,165·6 | 15,882·7 |
| Eggs (millions) | 7,871·0 | 8,013·0 |
| Wool (tons) | 8,999·0 | 9,450·0 |

**Livestock.** In June 1975, the livestock population was as follows: cattle, 13,254,300; pigs, 21,310,800; sheep, 3,174,500; horses, 2,237,200.

**Forestry.** 8,550,800 hectares of the area of Poland are forests After the Second World War, the majority of forests became the property of the State. 103,600 hectares of land were afforested in 1975. The annual average production is about 22,300,000 cubic metres (in 1974 it was 24,198,700. Apart from the State-owned forests (93·3 per cent of total forest area), there are also forests classified as privately owned (6·7 per cent). They belong either to individual or collective owners.

**Industry.** The share of industrial production in the total value of the national product (at current prices) was 48 per cent in 1937, 61 per cent in 1955, 67 per cent in 1960, 70 per cent in 1963, and 73 per cent in 1972. The production of the most important items in 1974 and 1975 are given below:

| | *Unit* | 1974 | 1975 |
|---|---|---|---|
| *Iron and Steel:* | | | |
| *Metallurgy:* | | | |
| Iron ores | thousand tons | 1,296 | 1,192 |
| Steel (crude) | ,, | 14,566 | 15,004 |
| Rolled goods | ,, | 10,558 | 11,085 |
| *Non-ferrous Metals:* | | | |
| Crude zinc and lead ore | ,, | 4,154 | 4,598 |
| Crude copper ore | ,, | 13,815 | 16,963 |
| Zinc | ,, | 233 | 243 |
| High-tension cables | thousand km. | 123 | 143 |
| *Fuel-Industry:* | | | |
| Coal: hard | million tons | 162 | 172 |
| brown | ,, | 39·8 | 39·9 |
| Coke | thousand tons | 18·1 | 18·3 |
| Crude petroleum | ,, | 550 | 553 |
| Petrol (incl. synthetic) | ,, | 2,068 | 2,387 |
| Oil fuel | ,, | 3,216 | 3,986 |
| Natural gas | million $mt^3$ | 5,739 | 5,963 |
| *Power Industry:* | | | |
| Energy | milliard kWh | 91·6 | 97·2 |
| *Engineering Industry:* | | | |
| Transformers over 20 kWh | thousand units | 20·5 | 20·5 |
| Machines and equipment for chemical industry | thousand tons | 87·6 | 87·7 |
| Machines and equipment for food ind. | ,, | 64·8 | 75·9 |
| Textile machinery | ,, | 26·0 | 27·0 |
| Tractors (2 axle) | thousand units | 55·0 | 57·6 |
| Railway wagons: (standard gauge): passenger carriages | units | 588 | 543 |
| goods wagons | thousand units | 17·8 | 18·7 |
| Ships launched | thousand DWT | 678 | 1,023 |
| *Chemical Industry:* | | | |
| Sulphuric acid (in terms of 100 per cent) | thousand tons | 3,333 | 3,413 |
| *Fertilizers:* | | | |
| Nitrous (N) | ,, | 1,457 | 1,533 |
| Phosphoric ($P_2O_3$) | ,, | 823 | 929 |
| *Pharmaceutical Products (including medicinal herbs):* | million zl | 10,700 | 12,105 |
| *Textile Industry:* | | | |
| Cotton yarn | thousand tons | 215 | 212 |
| Wool yarn | ,, | 97·3 | 103 |
| Cotton fabrics | million m. | 885 | 928 |
| Woollen fabrics | ,, | 117 | 124 |
| Silk fabrics | ,, | 187 | 180 |
| *Salt Industry:* | | | |
| Salt | thousand tons | 3,295 | 3,524 |
| *Sea fishing:* | | | |
| Fish | ,, | 587 | 648 |

# POLAND

**Mining.** Poland's natura wealth consists of: coal (Upper Silesia and Watbrzych Basin and Lublin voiv.), brown coal (Konin voiv., Piotrkow voiv, Jelenia Gora voiv., and Lower Silesia), crude oil and natural gas (Krosno voiv.), iron ore (Silesia, Częstochowa voiv. and Łęczyca region), zinc ore (Silesia), copper ore (Lower Silesia), salt (Cracow voiv.), sulphur (Tarnobrzeg voiv.).

Coal mining is Poland's most important industry. Deposits of hard coal are estimated at 100 milliard tons (deepness 1,000 m.). There are substantial deposits of rock salt, limestone, gypsum and sulphur. Sulphuric acid and nitrogen compounds are the most important products of the mining industry.

**Commerce.** Main exports are coal, coke, rolled metal goods, zinc and sheet zinc, caustic soda, carbon electrodes, goods wagons, machine tools, metal working machines, ships, construction projects, cement, meat, eggs, sugar, salt, raw hides, deal boards and furniture. Main imports are iron ore, petroleum, fertilizers, cotton, wool, rolled products and metal working machines. The following tables show value of imports and exports by principal countries (in million zlotys):

| *Imports* *Selected Countries* | 1974 *in mill. zl* | 1975 *in mill. zl* |
|---|---|---|
| Total | 34,822·9 | 41,650·7 |
| *Europe:* | | |
| Albania | 45·6 | 59·8 |
| Austria | 1,079·9 | 1,528·2 |
| Belgium | 1,120·7 | 1,006·3 |
| Bulgaria | 608·6 | 616·5 |
| Czechoslovakia | 2,067·4 | 2,248·8 |
| Denmark | 389·2 | 488·2 |
| Finland | 149·1 | 210·9 |
| France | 1,178·7 | 1,986·9 |
| Greece | 114·1 | 122·8 |
| Spain | 157·6 | 220·2 |
| Netherlands | 872·8 | 1,084·9 |
| Ireland | 16·4 | n.a. |
| Iceland | 39·9 | 10·6 |
| Yugoslavia | 539·6 | 605·0 |
| German Dem. Rep. | 2,557·7 | 3,130·5 |
| German Fed. Rep. | 4,154·5 | 3,359·5 |
| Norway | 203·7 | 241·3 |
| Portugal | 35·8 | 22·7 |
| Rumania | 684·1 | 671·6 |
| Switzerland | 1,199·0 | 1,636·9 |
| Sweden | 1,087·5 | 1,430·8 |
| Hungary | 866·4 | 880·6 |
| United Kingdom | 1,675·2 | 2,226·7 |
| Italy | 1,141·3 | 1,388·7 |
| U.S.S.R. | 7,816·5 | 10,556·8 |
| *Asia:* | | |
| Afghanistan | 31·4 | 21·6 |
| Sri Lanka | 12·1 | n.a. |
| Chinese People's Rep. | 161·6 | 152·3 |
| Cyprus | — | n.a. |
| Viet-Nam Dem. Rep. | 8·9 | 11·6 |
| India | 266·5 | 344·7 |
| Indonesia | 32·1 | 19·4 |
| Iran | 37·0 | 45·4 |
| Japan | 770·6 | 966·5 |
| Korean People's Dem. Rep. | 41·2 | 60·2 |
| Lebanon | 8·7 | 20·0 |
| Malaysia | 55·5 | 47·7 |
| Mongolia | 16·8 | 17·2 |
| Pakistan | 26·3 | 55·3 |
| Thailand | 10·3 | 8·4 |
| Syria | 32·9 | 4·8 |
| Turkey | 31·5 | 42·3 |
| Bangla Desh | 16·0 | 29·3 |
| *Africa* | | |
| Algeria | 99·3 | 129·8 |
| Ghana | 9·2 | 39·3 |
| Guinea | — | — |
| Morocco | 277·1 | 353·3 |
| Nigeria | — | — |
| Sudan | 19·1 | 14·2 |
| Tunisia | 30·1 | 51·4 |
| Uganda | 11·1 | — |
| Ivory Coast | 8·5 | — |

*continued*

| *Imports* *Selected Countries* | 1974 *in mill. zl.* | 1975 *in mill. zl.* |
|---|---|---|
| U.A.R. (Egypt) | 113·6 | 184·8 |
| United Republic of Tanzania | 1·0 | — |
| *America:* | | |
| Argentina | 50·0 | 65·7 |
| Brazil | 144·3 | 212·7 |
| Chile | 57·3 | — |
| Equador | 7·4 | — |
| Canada | 197·3 | 185·5 |
| Columbia | 57·5 | 44·7 |
| Cuba | 54·4 | 75·9 |
| Mexico | 26·0 | 7·7 |
| Peru | 89·1 | 64·7 |
| U.S.A. | 1,573·4 | 1,958·6 |
| Uruguay | 10·7 | 14·8 |
| *Australia and Oceania:* | | |
| Australia | 222·6 | 174·0 |
| New Zealand | 56·2 | 57·4 |

| *Exports* *Selected Countries* | 1974 *in mill. zl* | 1975 *in mill. zl* |
|---|---|---|
| Total | 27,624·8 | 34,160·7 |
| *Europe:* | | |
| Albania | 31·6 | 34·4 |
| Austria | 457·6 | 519·0 |
| Belgium | 357·1 | 360·0 |
| Bulgaria | 756·7 | 893·6 |
| Czechoslovakia | 2,056·4 | 2,741·6 |
| Denmark | 442·8 | 556·7 |
| Finland | 443·2 | 489·0 |
| France | 911·3 | 1,087·6 |
| Greece | 122·1 | 188·0 |
| Spain | 247·5 | 376·6 |
| Netherlands | 324·7 | 468·3 |
| Ireland | 83·0 | 74·2 |
| Iceland | 43·8 | 12·1 |
| Yugoslavia | 532·8 | 724·2 |
| German Dem. Rep. | 2,479·9 | 3,151·3 |
| German Fed. Rep. | 1,742·5 | 1,777·7 |
| Norway | 158·4 | 243·0 |
| Portugal | 8·7 | 31·6 |
| Rumania | 593·4 | 752·8 |
| Switzerland | 327·7 | 428·1 |
| Sweden | 521·9 | 739·3 |
| Hungary | 789·5 | 1,021·0 |
| United Kingdom | 1,233·6 | 968·1 |
| Italy | 1,018·5 | 994·9 |
| U.S.S.R. | 7,875·3 | 10,766·3 |
| *Asia:* | | |
| Afghanistan | — | — |
| Saudi Arabia | 9·7 | 18·3 |
| Burma | — | — |
| Ceylon | 8·7 | — |
| Chinese People's Rep. | 148·7 | 212·6 |
| Cyprus | 8·5 | 5·7 |
| Viet-Nam Dem. Rep. | 41·3 | 44·1 |
| India | 311·8 | 358·2 |
| Indonesia | 110·8 | 119·6 |
| Iraq | 136·8 | 192·4 |
| Iran | 160·1 | 201·5 |
| Japan | 206·7 | 232·2 |
| Jordan | 5·4 | — |
| Korean People's Dem. Rep. | 35·7 | 38·0 |
| Kuwait | 19·7 | 25·5 |
| Lebanon | 54·4 | 73·4 |
| Mongolia | 14·6 | 16·0 |
| Pakistan (without Bangla Desh) | 36·1 | 64·3 |
| Thailand | 31·7 | 34·5 |
| Syria | 48·0 | 47·3 |
| Turkey | 86·2 | 114·8 |
| Bangla Desh | 25·8 | 8·4 |

*continued*

| *Exports Selected Countries* | 1974 *in mill. zl.* | 1975 *in mill. zl.* |
|---|---|---|
| *Africa:* | | |
| Algeria | 110·9 | 117·7 |
| Ethopia | — | — |
| Ghana | 24·2 | 6·0 |
| Guinea | — | — |
| Kenya | 6·4 | 3·0 |
| Liberia | 20·6 | 13·4 |
| Libya | 147·1 | 303·2 |
| Morocco | 83·6 | 111·9 |
| Nigeria | 27·8 | 63·8 |
| Sudan | 20·1 | 13·5 |
| Tunisia | 14·6 | 33·2 |
| U.A.R. (Egypt) | 142·5 | 109·7 |
| United Rep. of Tanzania | — | — |
| *America:* | | |
| Argenina | 56·2 | 108·6 |
| Brazil | 108·3 | 270·7 |
| Chile | — | — |
| Canada | 152·0 | 134·2 |
| Colombia | 29·5 | 9·9 |
| Cuba | 40·4 | 66·3 |
| U.S.A. | 861·3 | 777·9 |
| Uruguay | — | — |
| Venezuela | 5·4 | 10·0 |
| *Australia and Oceania:* | | |
| Australia | 46·0 | 24·3 |
| New Zealand | — | — |

Export of coal and coke accounted for 18·1 per cent of total exports in 1975 (11·2 per cent, 1970), 12·4 per cent in 1972 and 11·2 per cent in 1973. Export of iron and metallurgical products: steel, pig iron, ferro-alloys, etc., accounted for 9·3 per cent in 1970, 8·1 per cent of total export in 1971, 7·2 per cent in 1972, 7·3 per cent in 1973 and 6·8 per cent in 1975 (10·3 per cent, 1960). Export of machinery, industrial installations and transport equipment accounted for 41·7 per cent in 1970, 42·3 per cent of total export in 1971, 41·9 per cent in 1972, 41·5 per cent in 1973, and 41·4 per cent in 1975 (30 per cent, 1960).

## COMMUNICATIONS

In 1975 there were 8,127,000 radio subscribers, and 6,472,000 television subscribers.

Tonnage of merchant ships sailing under the Polish flag: 4,036,000 DWT. Railway track: 26,709 km. Roads (hard surfaced): 140,397 km. Navigable inland waterways: 6,895 km. Air routes: 59,638 km., in Poland: 5,707 km.

## NEWSPAPERS

In 1975 there were 87 periodicals of general information with an aggregate single circulation of 10,434 thousand copies. In that total there are 52 dailies and besides 2,650 magazines of 32,086 thousand copies.

Among the newspapers are:

**Trybuna Ludu** (The People's Tribune). Organ of the Central Committee of the Polish United Workers' Party. Circulation ca. 1,000,000 (Saturday-Sunday edition-ca. 1,400,000). Editor-in-Chief: Józef Barecki. Established 1948. Warsaw, Plac Starynkiewicza 7.

**Trybuna Robotnicza** (The Workers' Tribune). Organ of the District Committee of the Polish United Workers' Party in Katowice. Circulation 683,000. Editor-in-Chief: Jerzy Kułtuniak. Established 1945. Katowice, ul. Młyńska 1.

**Zielony Sztandar** (Green Banner). Main organ of the United Peasant Party. Circulation Mon.-Fri. 144,050. Sat. 164,400. Editor-in-Chief: Tzydor Adamski. Established 1931. Warszawa, ul. Grzybowska 4.

**Kurier Polski** (The Polish Courier). Circulation 161,700. Editor-in-Chief: Cezary Leżeński. Published by the Democratic Party. Established 1957. Warsaw, u. Hibnera 11.

**Gtos Pracy** (The Voice of Labour). Circulation 160,000. Editor-in-Chief: Wiesław Rogowski. Organ of the Central Council of Trade Unions. Established 1945. Warsaw, ul. Smolna 12.

**Sztandar Mlodych** (The Banner of Youth). Circulation 225,000. Organ of the Chief Council of the Federation of Socialist Unions of Polish Youth. Established 1950. Editor-in-Chief: Ryszard Łukasiewicz. Warsaw, ul. Wspólna 61.

**Express Wieczorny** (The Evening Express). Independent organ. Circulation 560,000. Editor-in-Chief: Michał Wojewódzki. Established 1946. Warsaw, Al. Jerozolimskie 125–127.

**Życie Warszawy** (Warsaw Life). Independent organ. Daily. Circulation ca. 360,000. Editor-in-Chief: Bohdan Rolinski. Established 1944. Warsaw, ul. Marszalkowska 3/5.

**Gromada—Rolnik Polski** (Rural Community—Polish Farmer). Circulation 397,059. Established 1947. Editor-in-Chief: Włodzimierz Chećko. Warsawa, ul. Smolna 12.

**Stowo Powszechne** (The Universal Word). Daily. Circulation 85,780. Editor-in-Chief: Janusz Stefanowicz. Organ of the Catholic Association 'Pax'. Established 1947. Warsaw, ul. Mokotowska, 43.

## HEALTH SERVICE

In 1975, there were 58,226 doctors (1949, 8,735); 15,949 dentists (1949, 1,756); 14,061 midwives (1949, 6,896); 14,496 chemists (1949, 3 455); 129,690 nurses (1949, 11,238). The Social Health Service provides free medical treatment for the whole of the working population. All chemists' shops and all in-patient establishments (sanatoria, hospitals, etc.) have also been nationalized.

## SCIENCE

The Polish Academy of Sciences was established in 1952. It is the supreme scientific institution in Poland. The Polish Academy of Science has 363 members in 1975. Professor Włodzimierz Trzebiatowski is president of the P.A. of S. and Professor Jan Kaczmarek is Scientific Secretary.

The Polish Academy of Sciences consists of the six following departments: (1) social sciences, (2) biological sciences, (3) mathematical, physical, chemical, geological and geographic sciences, (4) technical sciences, (5) agricultural and forestry sciences, (6) medical sciences.

The Polish Academy of Sciences co-operates in planning and co-ordination of scientific research in Poland. The Academy also conducts research in its own scientific institutes and independent scientific institutes and laboratories, which numbered 72 on 31 December 1975.

## ATOMIC ENERGY

The first radiological centre in Poland was organized in Warsaw in 1912. The general supervision of its work was in the hands of Maria Skłodowska-Curie.

At present scientific and technical activities in the field of nuclear energy are co-ordinated by the Minister of Power Industry and Nuclear Energy—Andrzej Szozda.

The Government Commissioner has direct supervision over the activities of the Institute of Nuclear Research in Warsaw and the Institute of Nuclear Physics in Cracow.

The Institute of Nuclear Research in Warsaw is the largest scientific institute in Poland and its 30 departments cover research in nuclear physics, chemistry, biology and various branches of the technical sciences.

The Central Laboratory for Radiological Protection in Warsaw is an organization responsible for radiological protection in Poland.

## EDUCATION

There are crèches for children up to three years, furnished, maintained by the Ministry of Health and Social Welfare and nursery schools for children from three to seven years maintained by the Ministry of Education. There are eight-year primary schools, four-year secondary general-educational, technical-educational schools and various vocational schools.

Higher education has been greatly expanded. There are 89 schools of higher education in Poland and ten universities, namely: The Warsaw University, the Jagiellonian University in Cracow, the A. Mickiewicz University in Poznań, the Łódz University, the B. Bierut University in Wrocław, the M. Skłodowska-Curie and the Catholic Universities in Lublin, the M. Kopernik University in Toruń, Silesia University in Katowice, and Gdańsk University, also ten Medical Academies seven Agricultural Colleges, six Schools of Economics, twelve of Education, one School of Social Studies, two Theological

Academies, six Fine Art Schools, seven Music Schools, three High Schools of Acting, an Academy of Mining and Metallurgy, nine Academies of Engineering and Technology (called Polytechnics) in Warszawa, Czestochowa, Gdańsk, Gliwice, Kraków, Łódź, Poznań, Szczecin and Wrocław, and eight Evening Colleges of Technology. There are also two Higher Naval Schools and six Physical Culture Academies.

The table shown on page 354 shows the present state of education.

### RELIGION

The majority of the Polish people are Roman Catholics. Cardinal Stefan Wyszyński is the Primate of Poland.

| | 1974–75* | | 1975—76* | |
|---|---|---|---|---|
| *Type of School* | *Number of Schools* | *Number of Pupils (in thousands)* | *Number of Schools* | *Number of Pupils (in thousands)* |
| Elementary schools | 16,106 | 4,453·4 | 14,738 | 4,309·8 |
| Towns | 3,884 | 2,281·0 | 3,855 | 2,378·4 |
| Villages | 12,222 | 2,172·4 | 10,883 | 2,071·4 |
| General secondary schools | 895 | 483·2 | 895 | 472·0 |
| Special schools | 670 | 89·2 | 682 | 84·1 |
| Elementary schools for adult education | 2,194 | 152·4 | 2,111 | 137·7 |
| Secondary schools for adult education | 360 | 165·3 | 373 | 150·0 |
| Higher schools | 89 | 426·7 | 89 | 464·9 |

There are also numerous secondary technical schools: in 1971–72: 9,023 schools—1,753·1 pupils, in 1972–73: 9,344 schools—1,829·7 pupils, in 1973–74: 9,480 schools—1,921·7 pupils, in 1974–75: 10,038 schools—2,013·3 pupils, in 1975–76: 10,095 schools—1,581·4 pupils (in thousands).

* Data for end of academic year.

# Portugal

## (REPÚBLICA PORTUGUESA)

**Capital**—Lisbon.

**President**—General Antonio Dos Santos Ramalho Eanes.

**National Flag**: Divided pale-wise green and red about 2 : 3 at the juncture a yellow armillary sphere charged with the arms of the former monarchy; a white shield bearing five blue shields, each with five disks white, the whole bordered red with seven yellow castles.

### CONSTITUTION AND GOVERNMENT

PORTUGAL first became an independent kingdom in 1139, when she seceded from Spain and Alfonso Henriques assumed the title of king. In 1580, on the death of King Henry of Portugal, the Portuguese crown devolved on Philip II of Spain. The Portuguese finally threw off the Spanish yoke in 1640, proclaiming the Duke of Bragança King John IV.

The Bragança dynasty remained on the throne of Portugal until 1910. In that year an armed rising in Lisbon drove the King and Royal family into exile and soon afterwards the Republic of Portugal was proclaimed.

In April 1974 a revolution took place and a provisional government was formed under General Spinola. The political process that started with the swearing in of the Provisional Government (May 1974) underwent various crises that culminated in sharp advances or set backs for the Revolution.

The Political Constitution, promulgated on 2 April 1976, declares that Portugal is a Republic. The State is democratic and is based on popular sovereignty, the respect and guarantee of fundamental rights and freedoms, pluralism of expression and democratic political organisation and which has the objective of assuring the transition to socialism.

Sovereignty, which is one and indivisible, lies in the people, who exercise it according to the forms foreseen in the Constitution.

Since the very outset, the MFA (the Armed Forces Movement) has been the guarantor of the democratic achievements and the revolutionary process. On 26 February 1976, the Armed Forces Movement and the political parties signed a Platform of Constitutional Agreement which is an integral part of the Political Constitution and will be in force for a transitional period of four years.

**Ministry** (January 1978)

*Prime Minister:* Mario Soares.
*Minister of Defence:* Colonel Mario Firmino Miguel.
*Assistant Prime Minister:* Antonio de Almeida Santos.
*Minister of Finance and Planning:* Victor Constancio.
*Minister of Internal Affairs:* Alberto Oliveira e Silva.
*Minister of Justice:* José Santos Pais.
*Minister of Foreign Affairs:* Victor de sa Machado.
*Minister of Administrative Reform:* Rui Pena.
*Minister of Agriculture:* Luis Salas.
*Minister of Industry:* Carlos Melancia.
*Minister of Commerce:* Basolio Horta.
*Minister of Labour:* Antonio Maldonado Gonelha.
*Minister of Education:* Mario Sottomayor Gardia.
*Minister of Social Affairs:* Antonio Arnaut.
*Minister of Transport:* Manuel Ferreira Lima
*Minister of Housing:* Antonio Sousa Gomes.

### LOCAL GOVERNMENT

For administrative purposes the country is divided into *concelhos* (boroughs) composed of *freguesias* (parishes) and grouped into districts. Within the *concelho* there exists a Municipal Assembly composed of representatives of the *freguesias* and corporative organizations in the *Concelho*. This Assembly is responsible for municipal administration, discusses and votes on annual schemes for development and improvement and elects members to the *Câmara Municipal* (Municipal Chamber). The *Câmara Municipal* carries out the effective administration of the Municipal Assembly's business. It is composed of *vereadores* (members) or councillors (two, four or six, according to the importance of the *concelho*) elected by the Municipal Assembly and of a President nominated by the Government.

There is no Municipal Assembly in the cities of Lisbon and Oporto, its duties being performed by the President of the Municipal Chamber assisted by the Directors of Services. The *Câmara Municipal* meets only once a month and consists of 12 members.

The *frequesia* is a section of the *concelho*, the administrative part of which is a *junta* (committee). A *regedor* (chairman) representing the municipal authority is responsible for the police. The District is an area in which the Civil Governor exercises his duties as representative of the Government.

The *concelhos* can constitute themselves into federations. The cities of Lisbon and Oporto, with their neighbouring municipalities, also constitute federations.

## LEGAL SYSTEM

For judicial purposes the whole of the Portuguese territory is subject to the jurisdiction of the Supreme Court of Justice, seated in Lisbon.

Portugal itself is divided into 169 *comarcas* (districts), each with its lower court. There are 33 lower courts in Lisbon and 17 in Oporto. There are also over 34 municipal courts.

There are three Courts of Appeal—in Lisbon, Oporto and Coimbra.

According to the Constitution, the constitutional illegality of ordinances promulgated by the President of the Republic may be called into question only by the National Assembly, either on its own initiative or on that of the Government and the National Assembly shall determine the effects of such illegality.

## AREA AND POPULATION

Portugal lies on the western side of the Iberian Peninsula, extending for about 561 miles down the coast and varying in width from 112 to 218 miles. Its area covers 88,860 sq. km., including the estuaries of Tejo, Sado and the Ria de Aveiro. The area of the Azores is 2,305 sq. km. and that of Madeira 797 sq. km.

At mid-1974 census the resident population of continental Portugal was 9,014,000. The population of the islands of Madeira and the Azores, which are politically an integral part of the country, was 600,000.

The average annual percentage growth rate of the population for the period 1960–74 was 0·0 and for the period 1965–74 was −0·1.

The General State Budget for 1976 forecasts a deficit of 35 thousand million escudos, i.e., about eight per cent of the national product.

The Budget which the VIth Government drew up, demonstrated the Governments' intention to appropriate larger sums to economic development expenditure (over 87 per cent more than in the previous year). The analysis of this expenditure is shown in the following table:

Public Investment Programme

| | % |
|---|---|
| Housing | 28·5 |
| Transport and communication | 14·8 |
| Education | 12·4 |
| Agriculture, forestry and livestock | 9·5 |
| Health | 4·3 |
| *Other expenditures* | |
| Aid to companies for capital increases | 10·8 |
| Subsidies to local governments for public works and equipment | 7·9 |

## CURRENCY

The unit of currency is the *escudo* of 100 *centavos*. There are silver coins of 20, 10, 5 and 2½ escudos; copper-nickel coins of 5 and 2½ escudos; alpaca coins of 1 escudo and ½ excudo; and bronze coins of 20 and 10 centavos.

Notes are issued in denominations of 20, 50, 100, 500 and 1,000 escudos. A *conto* is 1,000 escudos.

## FINANCE

At the end of 1967, the reserves held by the Bank of Portugal amounted to 22,739 million esc. which, with undertakings in foreign currency of 191 million esc. gave a total of 22,548 million esc. (about £331,500,000). The balance of payments of the escudo area has consistently shown surpluses since1962.

The GNP at market prices for 1974 was U.S. $millions 14,650, and the GNP per capita at market prices was U.S. $1,630. The annual average percentage growth rate of the GNP per capita for the period 1960–74 was 7·4, and for the period 1965–74 was 7·6. [*See the note at the beginning of this section concerning GNP.*]

## BANKS

**Banco de Portugal.** (Governor, José da Silva Lopes.) Established 1846; Sole Bank of Issue for Continental Portugal and adjacent islands (Madeira, Azores); Balance Sheet at 31 December 1975 showed assets E.193,254,448,099. *Head Office:* Rua do Comercio, 148, Lisbon, Portugal. 33 Branches.

**Banco de Angola.** Established 1926; Bank of Issue for Angola Province, commercial Bank for Portugal. Part of the share capital is owned by the State: Balance Sheet at 31 December 1973 showed assets E.46,190,341,493; deposits E.7,421,132,233; notes in circulation E.4,433,955,295. *Head Office:* Rua da Prata, 10 Lisbon, Portugal. 47 Branches.

**Banco Espirito Santo e Comercial de Lisboa.** (President, Dr. Amilcar Neto Contente.) Established in 1920 as Banco Espirito Santo, in 1937 became Banco Espirito Santo e Comercial de Lisboa; Balance Sheet at 31 December 1975 showed assets E.108,202,487,000; deposits E.32,474,978,000. *Head Office:* Rua do Comércio, Lisbon, Portugal. 100 Branches.

**Banco Nacional Ultramarino.** (President of the Executive Board, Dr. A. A. de Oliveira Pinto FIBA.) Established 1864; Bank of Issue for Macao; Balance Sheet at 31 December 1976 showed assets E.101,473,082,431$58, deposits 28,616,874,253$19. *Head Office:* Rua do Comércio, 84, Lisbon, Portugal. 130 Offices in Continental Portugal, 2 in Madeira, 2 in Azores, 1 in Macau. *London Representative Office:* 1/3 Abchurch Yard, London EC4N 7BH.

**Banco da Agricultura, S.A.R.L.** Established 1928. Assets as at 1974, Esc.19,791,570,000, (U.S. $494,789,250); deposits and current accounts 1974, Esc.8,566,626,000 (U.S. $214,165,650). *Head Office:* Rua da Assunção, 74 Lisboa 2. Number of Branches, 32.

**Banco Pinto & Sotto Mayor.** Established 1914. Government Owned. Assets as at 31 December 1974, Esc.56,980,724,426, excl. contigent items; deposits and current accounts, Esc.39,511,814,307. *Head Office:* Rua Do Ouro, Lisbon 2. 74 Branches in Portugal. Main branches and offices in France. Representative offices in San Francisco, Newark (U.S.A.), Toronto (Canada), Dusseldorf (Germany), Lausanne (Switzerland), Luxembourg and Cape Town (S. Africa).

**Banco Fonsecas & Burnay.** Established in 1861 as Fonsecas, Santos & Vianna, in 1937 became a limited company under the title Banco Fonsecas, Santos & Vianna, in 1967 merged with Banco Burnay (established 1875) and absorbed Banco Regional de Aveiro. On May 1, 1976 absorbed Casa Bancária Pancada, Morais and Cia; Nationalized in 1975. Balance Sheet at 31 December 1976 showed total assets E.62,252,084,484; deposits E.14,937,057,366. *Head Office:* Rua de Comércio, 132, Lisbon, Portugal.

## PRODUCTION, INDUSTRY AND COMMERCE

**Agriculture.** Portugal is still mainly an agricultural country. The following table shows yield of principal crops for the years 1975 and 1976:

| *Crop* | 1975 *th. metric. tons (Provisional figures)* | 1976 *th. metric tons (Provisional figures)* |
|---|---|---|
| Wheat | 686 | 671 |
| Rye | 144 | 123 |
| Rice | 121 | 89 |
| Potatoes | 923 | 853 |
| Maize | 462 | 360 |
| Oats | 122 | 104 |
| Barley | 94 | 81 |
| French Beans | 36 | 29 |

The wine industry is very important and about one-seventh of the production is exported. Production in 1975 was 11,086,000 hectolitres.

The following tables show export values of wine and Port wine to various areas of the world for the years 1974 and 1975 in thousands of escudos:

| Country | All Wines th. escudos 1974 | th. escudos 1975 |
|---|---|---|
| U.K. | 515,257 | 444,514 |
| Belgium and Luxembourg | 163,988 | 120,032 |
| France | 620,103 | 495,382 |
| Sweden | 52,566 | 51,624 |
| Switzerland | 99,950 | 66,770 |
| West Germany | 185,402 | 188,068 |
| U.S.A. | 672,236 | 166,770 |
| Italy | 150,570 | 89,095 |
| Denmark | 41,818 | 95,784 |

| Country | Port Wines th. escudos 1974 | th. escudos 1975 |
|---|---|---|
| U.K. | 444,960 | 378,237 |
| Belgium/Luxembourg | 156,577 | 111,803 |
| France | 617,875 | 494,187 |
| Sweden | 37,210 | 34,314 |
| Switzerland | 17,658 | 12,071 |
| West Germany | 160,932 | 162,689 |
| U.S.A. | 16,732 | 11,753 |
| Italy | 130,438 | 62,160 |
| Denmark | 81,369 | 78,900 |

**Fishing.** Portugal has a very important fishing industry. The chief fishing ports are Figueira da Foz, Leixões and Aveiro in the north; Lisbon, Peniche and Setúbal in the centre; Olhão, Portimão and Vila Real de Santo António in the south.

**Mining.**
The following table shows the production (in metric tons) of the principal minerals for the years 1973–74:

| *Mineral* | 1973 | 1974 |
|---|---|---|
| Coal | 220,807 | 230,210 |
| Copper (precipitated) | 532,401 | 510,571 |
| Wolframite | 2,428 | 2,544 |
| Tin ores | 2,413 | 2,267 |
| Kaolin | 761 | 618 |
| Iron | 34,950 | 27,400 |

Hydro-electric power has risen sharply since the opening of the new power-station at Castelo de Bode, Venda Nova, Belver, in January 1951, Salamonde in 1953, Cabril in 1954, Bouça, 1955, Paradela in 1956, Picote in 1958 and Miranda in 1960 and Alto Rabagâo and Bemposta in 1964.

**Commerce.** The following tables show imports and exports respectively by principal commodities (in thousand escudos) for the year 1975:

| *Imports* | 1975 |
|---|---|
| Petroleum and products | 11,703,164 |
| Iron and steel | 2,642,708 |
| Raw cotton | 3,104,633 |
| Motor vehicles | 3,848,466 |
| Wheat | 1,784,331 |
| Maize | 4,726,229 |
| Oil seeds | 866,196 |

| *Exports* | 1975 |
|---|---|
| Clothing | 6,783,694 |
| Wine | 2,754,428 |
| Cork | 2,719,884 |
| Pulpwood | 2,390,330 |
| Cotton yarn | 1,252,369 |
| Textiles | 3,328,336 |
| Resin | 730,176 |
| Sardines | 833,663 |

## COMMUNICATIONS

**Roads.** The total length of roads in Continental Portugal in 1970 was 30,165 miles. In 1970 there were 756,608 motor vehicles.

**Railways.** The total length of the railway system is 3,563 km. About half is owned by the State. In 1970 the number of passengers carried on the railways amounted to 144,757,000 and the merchandise totalled 3,927,000 tons.

**Shipping.** In 1965 Portugal had 24,638 registered vessels, including 18,363 fishing boats with a total of 842,163 tons. The merchant marine in 1965 comprised 1,166 vessels of 602,089 tons.

The number of ships entering Portuguese ports during 1965 totalled 16,124 of which 8,740 were Portuguese and 7,384 foreign vessels. The main ports of entry were Lisbon (5,899 ships), Setubal (964), Oporto and Douro (899) and Leixões (2,479). In 1965 the total tonnage of vessels entering was 45,159,101 tons. Of these 15,141,502 tons were Portuguese and 30,017,599 tons were foreign.

The following are the principal shipping lines:

**Companhia Portuguese de Transportes Maritimos.** (Chairman, Dr. Antonio Matias Fernandes). Share capital E.770,000,000: motor vessels thirty four; turbine vessels one; total tonnage 242,982 DWT; *services operated:* Madeira and Açores Islands, East Coast U.S.A., Portugal–France–N. Europe–U.K., North Europe–South Africa–Moçambique, Mediterranean–South Africa–Moçambique, North Europe–Angola, Mediterranean–Angola, Portugal–Angola. *Head Office:* Rua de S. Julião 63, Lisboa-2, Portugal, P.O. Box 2747, telephone 369621, telexes 12440 A/B/C CTMLX P.

**Companhia Nacional de Navegaçã.** (Chairman, Eng. Jose Rodu.) Share capital E.250,000,000; motor vessels 15, steam vessels three: total tonnage 122,128; *services operated:* to Portuguese and West Africa, Macao, Portuguese Timor. *Head Office:* Rua do Comércio, 85, Lisbon.

**Civil Aviation.**

The following are the principal airlines:

**T.A.P.—Transportes Aéreos Portugueses. S.A.R.I.** Total Company Employees (July 1977), 8,935. Pilots employed, 329. *Address:* Edifició 25, Instalações TAP, Aeroporto da Portel, Lisbon, Portugal. Telephone: 899121. *Cable Address:* AEROTAP. Official Airline Code: (TP).

**Sociedade Açoriana de Transportes Aéreos SARL.** Share capital ESP50,000,000; *services operated:* S. Miguel–Santa Maria–Terceira–Faial and Flores (Azores). *Head Office:* Avenida do Infante D. Henrique, Ponta Delgada, S. Miguel, Azores.

**Posts, Telegraphs and Telephones.** In 1965 the total length of all circuits was 89,750,000 km. Telegrams sent and received totalled 4,590,656.

There were 1,684,998 km. of telephone line operating, of which 781,473 km. were owned by the State and 903,525 km. by the Anglo-Portuguese Telephone Company. There were 550,490 telephones in service, of which 172,287 belonged to the State. Calls in 1965 numbered 803,718,000, nearly all of which passed through lines owned by the Anglo Portuguese Telephone Company.

**Broadcasting.** There are 15 State-owned broadcasting stations: two in Lisbon, two in Oporto, two in Portalegre, two in Coimbra, two in Faro and one each in Guarda, Castelo Branco, Setubal, Viseu and Ponta Delgada.

There are 23 privately-owned stations, six of which are in Lisbon, two in Santarém, five in Oporto, two in Viseu, one in Guarda and one in Vila a Real, four Azores and two in Funchal (Madeira).

In 1964 there were 1,126,990 receiving sets.

EDUCATION

In the school year 1964–65 there were 17,590 state schools (with 1,086,689 pupils) and 1,641 private schools (with 160,241 pupils). There were 17,120 State primary schools and 401 State secondary schools. Total of students was 1,246,930 and of teachers, 45,812. There were 31,575 students in higher schools—6,529 at the University of Coimbra, 9,761 at Lisbon, 4,717 at Oporto and 3,708 pupils at the other 51 schools of the same level.

NEWSPAPERS

**Novidades.** F. 1885. Daily. Morning. Lisbon.

**O Século.** F. 1881. Daily. Morning. Lisbon.

**A Voz.** F. 1927. Daily. Morning. Lisbon.

**Diário da Manhâ.** F. 1931. Daily. Morning. Lisbon.

**Diário de Lisboa.** F. 1921. Daily. Evening. Circulation 80,000.

**Diário Popular.** F. 1942. Daily. Evening. Lisbon, Circulation 80,000.

**Jornal do Comércio.** F. 1853. Daily. Morning. Rua Dr. Luís de Almeida e Albiquerque, 5, Lisbon.

**Republica.** F. 1911. Daily. Evening. Lisbon.

**O Primeiro de Janeiro.** F. 1868. Daily. Morning. Oporto.

**O Comércio do Porto.** F. 1854. Daily. Morning. Oporto.

**Jornal de Noticias.** F. 1888. Daily. Morning. Oporto.

**Diário do Norte.** F. 1949. Daily. Evening. Oporto.

**Diário do Alentejo.** F. 1931. Beja.

**Correio do Minho.** F. 1926 Braga.

**Diário de Coimbra.** F. 1930. Coimbr

**emocracia do Sul.** F. 1902. E'vora.

**Noticias de E'vora.** F. 1900. E'vora.

RELIGION

According to the Portuguese Constitution there is complete freedom of creed and worship, excepting in matters incompatible with the life and liberty of the individual and with good morals. While the Constitution maintains the régime of separation regarding the Catholic Church (or any other religion), the country is predominantly (96 per cent) Roman Catholic (22 per cent in the Portuguese African provinces).

# TIMOR

**Capital**—Dilly (Dili).

**Governor**—Brig. José Noguiera Valente Pirez.

TIMOR is a large island in the Malay Archipelago, off the north-west coast of Australia, about 700 km. from Port Darwin. Portuguese Timor is the eastern half of the island, the other half now belonging to Indonesia, to whom it was ceded by the Dutch in 1949.

The province includes the territory of Ocussi-Ambens, which extends for about 60 km. to a depth of 25 km. along the middle of the northern coast of Indonesian Timor.

The total area of the province is 14,925 sq. km. and the population is 517,079.

In Timor, the process of decolonization was crippled by the civil war that broke out among three political movements. Indonesia intervened and occupied the territory. Portugal asked the United Nations to intervene, and the Security Council demanded the withdrawal of the Indonesian forces. On 31 May 1976 the Popular Assembly of Timor, called into emergency session, with 28 delegates representing 13 regions, decided to ask Indonesia to annex Timor. Portugal has not recognized this deliberation because the problem falls within the scope of action of the United Nations.

FINANCE

Budget figures for 1969 were: Revenue, 136,008 contos; Expenditure, 170,358 contos.

PRODUCTION, INDUSTRY AND COMMERCE

The main products are coffee, copra, palm oil, rice, wax and hides.

In 1970 there were in the province 127,148 buffalo, 114,152 horses, 43,033 sheep, 217,011 goats and 224,268 pigs.

The following table shows imports for 1970 (in thousand escudos):

| *Commodity* | 1970 |
|---|---|
| Live animals; animal products | 5,676 |
| Vegetable products | 6,267 |
| Food, beverages, tobacco | 33,961 |
| Mineral products | 13,931 |
| Chemicals | 14,376 |
| Paper products | 4,273 |
| Textiles | 46,100 |
| Misc. wearing apparel | 5,221 |
| Non-metallic mineral products | 3,421 |
| Metal products | 23,387 |
| Machinery | 21,045 |
| Transport equipment | 16,542 |
| Miscellaneous | 3,050 |

The following table gives imports and exports by principal countries in 1970 (in thousand escudos):

| | 1970 *Imports* | 1970 *Exports* |
|---|---|---|
| Portugal, metropolitan | 52,592 | 13,147 |
| Mozambique | 23,178 | 467 |
| Macao | 37,298 | N.A. |
| West Germany | 2,787 | 1,650 |
| Netherlands | 5,912 | 34,453 |
| Denmark | 393 | 18,468 |
| United Kingdom | 8,042 | 476 |
| United States | 1,264 | 6,409 |
| Japan | 15,632 | N.A. |
| Singapore | 36,980 | 7,845 |
| Hong Kong | 5,221 | 2,139 |
| Australia | 15,203 | 91 |

The following table shows exports for 1970 (in thousand escudos):

| *Commodity* | 1970 |
|---|---|
| Live animals; animal products | 112 |
| Vegetable products | 93,683 |
| Oils and fats | 717 |
| Synthetics | 51 |
| Miscellaneous | N.A. |

EDUCATION

There are 105 primary schools with 6,269 pupils and a technical school with over 100 pupils.

COMMUNICATIONS

In 1961 the number of vessels entering the ports was 37. Total gross tonnage was 53,542.

There are seven airports and landing strips. Planes entering in 1960 numbered 252, all of which were Portuguese. Roads are 2,042 km. in length and the telegraph and telephone lines 3,953 km.

# MACAO[1]

## (*Macau*)

**Capital**—Macau.

**Governor**—Dr. José Manuel Nobre de Carvalho.

MACOS is situated at the entrance to the Canton River. The province includes the two small islands of Taipa and Coloane. It has an area of 16 sq. km. and the total population was 169,299 at the 1960 census. Nearly all of these (165,880) belong to the Mongolian races.

There is one tribunal of justice, under the judicial district of Lourenço Marques.

### CURRENCY AND FINANCE

The unit of currency is the *pataca*, which is equivalent to about 5·5 escudos.

Budget figures for 1969 were: Revenue, 297,735 contos; Expenditure, 287,873 contos.

### COMMERCE

Macao is an important centre of commerce and finance. Its wealth largely depends on transit and entrepôt trade.

Imports for 1970 are shown in the following table (in thousand patacas):

| *Commodity* | 1970 |
|---|---|
| Live animals; animal products | 213,450 |
| Vegetable products | 194,825 |
| Fats and oils | 20,558 |
| Food, beverages, tobacco | 187,139 |
| Mineral products | 112,562 |
| Chemicals | 66,350 |
| Synthetics | 67,169 |
| Wood and wood products | 49,518 |
| Paper products | 62,329 |
| Textiles | 584,038 |
| Misc. wearing apparel | 25,544 |
| Non-metallic mineral products | 59,326 |
| Metal products | 58,871 |
| Machinery | 94,655 |
| Transport equipment | 34,766 |
| Miscellaneous | 27,808 |

Exports for 1970 are shown in the following table (in thousand patacas):

| *Commodity* | 1970 |
|---|---|
| Live animals; animal products | 91,647 |
| Vegetable products | 4,884 |
| Food, beverages, tobacco | 45,911 |
| Chemicals | 104,377 |
| Synthetics | 5,921 |
| Leather products | 40,758 |
| Wood and wood products | 12,756 |
| Paper products | 7,315 |
| Textiles | 707,771 |
| Misc. wearing apparel | 75,416 |
| Non-metallic mineral products | 27,149 |
| Metal products | 15,047 |
| Transport equipment | N.A. |
| Miscellaneous | 38,603 |

The following table shows values of imports and exports (in thousand patacas) by country for 1970:

| *Country* | 1970 *Imports* | 1970 *Exports* |
|---|---|---|
| Portugal, metropolitan | 17,405 | 130,983 |
| Angola | N.A. | 98,402 |
| Mozambique | 25 | 73,519 |
| Timor | N.A. | 29,298 |
| West Germany | 7,348 | 185,970 |
| France | 7,869 | 167,838 |
| Italy | 6,636 | 34,893 |
| Norway | 347 | 8 |
| United Kingdom | 20,804 | 804 |
| United States | 27,323 | 105,806 |
| Canada | 1,877 | 3,816 |
| China (Communist) | 506,766 | 181 |
| Borneo | N.A. | N.A. |
| Hong Kong | 1,214,571 | 217,203 |
| Indonesia | 6 | 735 |

### COMMUNICATIONS

The number of steamships entering the port in 1963 was 4,322, totalling 2,753,706 gross tons.

[1]Macao is not a colony of Portugal, but is merely administered by the Portuguese.

# Qatar

**Capital—Doha.**

**Ruler—H.H. Sheikh Khalifa bin Hamad al-Thani.**

**National Flag: Maroon; a white stripe pale-wise at the hoist, with a serrated edge of nine and a half points.**

QATAR is a fully independent sovereign Arab state on the western shore of the Arabian Gulf. Its territory occupies a peninsula of approximately 4,000 square miles that projects true north into the Gulf for about 100 miles and has an approximate maximum width of 55 miles.

The capital, Doha, is situated on the eastern coast. Qatar's landward frontiers at the neck of the peninsula lie with the Kingdom of Saudi Arabia to the west and Abu Dhabi to the east.

The State's nearest seaward neighbour is Bahrain. The eastern, Iranian, shore of the Gulf is 120 miles off Qatar's rounded northern extremity Basra, the Iraqi port at the northern head of the Gulf, is 350 miles away and the southern Strait of Hormuz 310 miles. Qatar thus occupies an important pivotal position on the Gulf.

The mid-1973 population was 180,000. The annual average percentage growth rate of the population for the period 1960–73 was 8·5 and for the period 1965–73 was 8·9. The majority are concentrated in the capital town of Dona on the East coast.

The peninsula's terrain is flat except for the Dukhan anticline in the west. Blown sand covers much of the south and sand dunes predominate in the south-east.

Excavations carried out in the peninsula between 1956 and 1964 revealed it as one of the most prolific Stone Age areas on the Gulf. Other finds dating from about 300 BC indicated that the inhabitants clearly had long distance trading contacts.

In its modern history, there is clear evidence of Qatar's reluctance to accept foreign authority, first under the Turks and later under the British. From 1916 up to the present decade, Britain's relationship with Qatar developed until its role was limited to the exercise of purely technical and administrative functions in Anglo-Qatari affairs.

On 3 September 1971, Qatar's independence was proclaimed two days earlier the special treaty arrangements with Britain had been abrogated.

The Emir of Qatar and Head of State is His Highness Sheikh Khalifa bin Hamad al-Thani, who on 22 February 1972 assumed the emirship in a peaceful transfer of power based on a decision of the ruling al-Thani family.

Legislative procedures are controlled by a provisional Constitution promulgated in April 1970. A 14-man Council of Ministers assists the Emir in the discharge of duties. The membership of an Advisory Council was in 1975 enlarged by 10 to 30 and power to question ministers on budgetary and administrative matters added to its consitutional rights.

Islam is the official and dominant religion of the population, indigenous and migratory alike.

The official language of the State is Arabic but most senior Qatari departmental officials are fluent in English as well.

Western highlights of intensive Qatari international diplomacy throughout 1975 have been talks in Paris, between the Emir H.H. Sheikh Khalifa bin Hamad al-Thani, and the President of France, H.E. M. Valery Giscard d'Estaing, on economic, financial and political matters of mutual concern and the initialling, in London, of an Anglo-Qatari agreement designed to strengthen economic and commercial ties between the two countries.

Sheikh Khalifa also paid visits to Iran, Iraq, Tunis, Morocco, the United Arab Emirates and Oman. A number of Qatari—Western,—Arab and—African agreements were signed in 1975.

Qatar is a member of the United Nations and the Arab League, which it joined in the same month as its independence, September 1971.

**Cabinet**

*Minister of Foreign Affairs:* Shaikh Suhaim bin Hamad al-Thani.
*Minister of Economy and Commerce:* Shaikh Nasser bin Khaled al-Thani.
*Minister of Water and Electricity:* Shaikh Jassem bin Muhammad al-Thani.
*Minister of the Interior:* Shaikh Khaled bin Ahmad al-Thani.
*Minister of Industry and Agriculture:* Shaikh Faisal bin Thani al-Thani.
*Minister of Municipal Affairs:* Shaikh Muhammad bin Jaber al-Thani.
*Minister of Finance and Petroleum:* Shaikh Abdel-Aziz bin Khalifah al-Thani.
*Minister of Public Works:* Khaled bin Abdullah al-Atiya.
*Minister of Labour and Social Affairs:* Ali bin Ahmad al-Ansari.
*Minister of Transport and Communications:* Abdullah bin Nasser al-Suweidi.
*Minister of Public Health:* Khaled bin Muhammad al-Monal.
*Minister of Information:* Isa Ghanern al-Kawari.

**Finance.** The State's budget for the Moslem year 1396 (which began on 3 Jan. 1976) provides the following allocations for vital projects in the major sectors: heavy industry, QR 1,1495m (as opposed to QR 305m in 1975); housing, electricity, water, QR 858m (QR 602m in 1975); transport, communications, agriculture, QR 1,062m (QR 477m in 1975); education, health, information, QR 354m (QR275m in 1975); and security and justice QR 173m (QR 144m in 1975) The GNP at market prices for 1974 was U.S.$millions 1,380, and the GNP per capita at market prices was U.S. $7,240. The annual average percentage growth rate of the GNP per capita for the period 1960–74 was 5·5, and for the period 1965–74 was 8·1. [*See the note at the beginning of this section concerning GNP.*]

**Communications.** In 1975 HH The Amir inaugurated a powerful addition to the State's sound broadcasting services —a 750 kw mf transmitter intended to improve local daytime coverage and provide after-dusk services to most parts of the Middle East by means of a six-mast directional system. Colour accounts for over 50 per cent of the output of two television transmitters providing a total power of 200 kw.

**Telecommunications.** A QR 20 million earth satellite station was inaugurated in March 1976. Initially it is carrying 30 international telephone circuits, TV and radio traffic.

**Public Health.** The State's traditional policy of providing free health services to all residents of the peninsula, Qatari and non-Qatari alike, remains a source of local pride. The 1976 budget allocates QR 93m for health projects, the most important of which are a new 660-bed hospital in Doha and quarantine hospitals in Doha and Umm Said.

**Social Services.** The 1975 budget allocated QR 130m for the State's "popular" housing and home ownership schemes. Over 650 popular units have already been offered free of charge and 640 out of 890 now being built are similarly ear-marked. The 1976 budget allocates QR 50m for popular housing and QR 140m for land ownership.

**Public Utilities.** The Government is taking vigorous action to ensure the long term efficiency and quality of its water and electricity supply services. The 1976 budget allocates QR 399m for electricity projects and QR 185m for water projects.

**Infrastructure.** Road construction is a continual process throughout the peninsula and the 1976 budget allocates QR 140m to this end.

**Petroleum.** The Government in December 1974 decided to acquire the remaining 40 per cent share held in on-shore and off-shore crude oil recovery by the two foreign interim operators the Qatar Petroleum Company (QPC) and Shell Company of Qatar (Shell Qatar) respectively, and negotiations on details are proceeding.

H.H. The Emir recently stated that Qatar had decided to reduce its oil production in accordance with its own needs. It has also been officially stated that the State's direct income from oil will by 1980 represent only 15 per cent of its total revenue: the remainder will come from earnings from new petrochemical heavy and light industries. Total oil production in 1975 amounted to 159,483,709 barrels and exports to 156,606,664 barrels.

Thus, the Government continues with its well-known policy of promoting industrial diversification with the aim of reducing national dependence on oil revenues. Expansion of the productive fertilizer and cement factories is going on, as is work on a steel complex. A new NGL plant was inaugurated in May 1975 and a huge petrochemicals plant is under construction. A number of lighter industries are under study.

**Agriculture.** A five year plan designed to ensure total Qatari self-sufficiency in basic food supply—based on the results of a hydro-agricultural resources survey—is now in the final stages of preparation.

Meanwhile production of certain vegetables continues at a sufficiently high rate to justify the export of small surpluses and yields of fruit continue to increase.

A poultry farm at Umm Qarn was completed in October 1975 with a target of 1 million chickens and 10 million eggs. Work continues on a sheep farm.

**Fishing.** The Qatar National Fishing Co., incorporated in Doha in 1966 to fish for shrimp in territorial waters and process catches in a purpose-built and refrigerated factory, in 1974 exported 290,000 kilogrammes of head-off fish worth QR 1,232m, the bulk to Japan.

Doha is now the headquarters of the UNDP Regional Fisheries Survey.

**Education.** Since 1955, the school population has increased from 1,000 to over 26,000. In the same 20-year period the total of girls registered has risen from 50 (4·7 per cent compared with boys) to 13,000 (parity) and the total of girls schools from one (with a single teacher) to 45 (800 teachers).

Existing male and female teacher training colleges, established in 1933, will form the nucleus of Qatar's university, to be completed within three years at a cost of QR 500m.

## BANK

**Qatar National Bank S.A.Q.** Established 1965. (Chairman, H. E. Shaikh Abdul Aziz Ben Khalifa Al-Thani). Assets as at 31 December 1974, QR.1,414,468,290; deposits and current accounts, QR.526,118,503. *Head Office:* Central Office, P.O. Box 1000. 6 Branches.

# The Socialist Republic of Romania

**Capital**—Bucharest (Bucureşti).

**President of the Socialist Republic of Romania**—Nicolae Ceauşescu.

**National Flag**: A tricolour pale-wise, blue, yellow, red, the yellow bearing the emblem of the Republic.

## CONSTITUTION AND GOVERNMENT

THE Romanian national state was formed in 1859 through the union of the two principalities of Moldavia and Wallachia, under the rule of Prince Alexandru Ioan Cuza. Under his rule (1859–66) he promulgated a number of progressive laws concerning the land reform, the legislative and education system, the civil code. He was forced to abdicate in 1866; Prince Carol of Hohenzollern-Sigmaringen was then brought to the throne. In May 1877, Romania proclaimed her independence and entered the war against Turkey, on Russia's side. Through the Berlin Treaty (1878) Romania's independence was recognized. Three years later, she was recognized as a kingdom, Prince Carol being crowned king. In 1913, after participating in the second Balkan war, the Southern part of the Dobrogea became part of Romania.

During World War I. Romania fought alongside the Allied Powers (1916–18) and was partially and temporarily invaded by German troops. On April 9, 1918, Bessarabia united with Romania. After the dismemberment of the Austro-Hungarian Empire, Transylvania (on 1 December 1918) and Bukovina (on 28 November 1918) which up to then had been ruled by the Hapsburgs, united with Romania; and thus the bounds of the modern state were formed. In June 1940, Bessarabia and Northern Bukovina became part of the Soviet Union.

Through the Vienna Arbitration—30 August 1940—imposed on Romania by Germany and Italy, Northern Transylvania, mostly inhabited by a Romanian population, was ceded to Horthyist Hungary. According to the Craiova Treaty (7 September 1940), Southern Dobrogea came under Bulgarian rule. Antonescu's régime was set up in September 1940. In 1941 Romanian armies fought alongside the troops of Germany in the war against the Soviet Union. On 23 August 1944 the democratic forces grouped around the Romanian Communist Party organized the armed national anti-facist and anti-imperialist insurrection which overthrew Antonescu's régime and Romania joined the powers fighting against Germany.

Through the Paris Peace Treaty, signed on 10 February 1947, the frontiers were reorganized according to those existent on 1 January 1941 and the Vienna Dictate was cancelled. Romania pledged herself to pay the Soviet Union damages. The Allied Powers received compensations for their holdings in Romania in September 1939.

The Romanian People's Republic was proclaimed after the abdication of King Michael, on 30 December 1947. In 1948, the Romanian Communist Party united with the Social Democratic Party to form the Romanian Workers' Party (since 1965, the Romanian Communist Party). The elections to the Grand National Assembly were held the same year (1948). In view of these elections the political parties and organizations, (namely: the Romanian Worker's Party; the Ploughmen's Front; the National Popular Party and Madosz (Magyar Working People's Union of Romania)) formed a coalition under the name of the Popular Democracy Front with a single register of votes. On 28 March 1948—eight million voters, men and women (92·3 per cent of the number of voters), went to the polls. The Popular Democracy Front received 90·8 per cent of the total number of votes.

The Grand National Assembly consisted of:

| | *members* |
|---|---|
| Popular Democracy | 405 |
| National Liberal Party (Bejan) | 7 |
| Peasant Democratic Party (N. Lupu) | 2 |
| | 414 |

At the last election on 9 March 1975 of deputies for the Grand National Assembly almost 14·9 million voters went to the polls (99·96 per cent of the total number of electors); 98·81 per cent of them voted for the Front of the Socialist Unity candidates.

According to article 44 of the Constitution, the number of deputies in the Grand National Assembly is 349.

Romania's first democratic Constitution was adopted by the Grand National Assembly on 13 April 1948. It was replaced by the Constitution promulgated on 24 September 1952. A new constitution was adopted on 21 August 1965 by which Romania was proclaimed a Socialist Republic.

A new political organization, the Front of the Socialist Unity, was formed in November 1968 to make possible a more general participation in the drafting and implementation of R.C.P. policy by bringing the R.C.P. into more direct contact with other mass, trade and professional organizations. The President of the F.S.U. is Nicolae Ceauşescu.

The supreme body of state power, the only legislative body in the Socialist Republic of Romania, is the Grand National Assembly.

The deputies of the Grand National Assembly, 349 in number, are elected for a five-year period by the secret vote of all citizens over 18, in electoral districts, each district having an equal number of inhabitants. Deputies are proposed by citizens' organizations. The Grand National Assembly holds ordinary working sessions twice a year. The Grand National Assembly can be summoned to extra-ordinary session whenever necessary on the initiative of either the State Council, the Bureau of the Grand National Assembly, or at least on third of the total number of deputies. The Grand National Assembly must give its agreement when one of the deputies is arrested or brought to trial.

The Grand National Assembly elects the President of Socialist Republic of Romania and the State Council.

On 28 March, 1974, Nicolae Ceauşescu, General Secretary of the Romanian Communist Party, President of the State Council, was elected by the Grand National Assembly, the first President of the Socialist Republic of Romania. In the system of supreme organs of state power, the President of the Republic (elected for the duration of a legislature) fulfils the function of head of state and represents the state power in the internal and international relations of Romania, is supreme commander of the armed forces, president of the Defence Council, and fulfils the function of President of the State Council of the S.R.R.

The State Council of the Socialist Republic of Romania is the highest power in permanent session. However, the State Council is subordinate to the Grand National Assembly. The State Council consists of a President, Vice-Presidents, and members.

*Vice-Presidents of the State Council:* Emil Bobu, Stefan Peterfi, Ştefan Voitec.

The Council of Ministers, elected by the Grand National Assembly, is the supreme organ of the state administration. It is responsible to the Grand National Assembly for the activity carried out and—between the sessions of the Grand National Assembly—to the State Council. The latter can rescind the decisions taken by the government (by the Council of Ministers) if they are not conformable to the Constitution or any other law of the country.

The Constitution registers the role of the Romanian Communist Party as the leading political force in the Socialist Republic of Romania.

The supreme organ of the Romanian Communist Party is the Congress of the Romanian Communist Party which elects the Central Committee and the General Secretary of the Party. The Central Committee elects the Executive Political Committee, and the Secretariat.

**Executive Political Committee of the Central Committee of the Romanian Communist Party**

| | |
|---|---|
| Nicolae Ceauşescu | Lina Ciobanu |
| Manea Mănescu | Ion Dincá |
| Emil Bobu | Emil Drăgănescu |
| Cornel Burtică | Janos Fazekas |
| Elena Ceauşescu | Ion Ioniţă |
| Gheorghe Cioară | Petre Lupu |
| | Paul Niculescu |

| | |
|---|---|
| Gheorghe Oprea | Virgil Trofin |
| Gheorghe Pană | Iosif Uglar |
| Ion Păţan | Ilie Verdeţ |
| Dumitru Popescu | Vasile Vîlcu |
| Gheorghe Rădulescu | Ştefan Voitec |
| Leonte Răutu | |

**Deputy Members of the Executive Political Committee**

| | |
|---|---|
| Ştefan Andrei | Nicolae Giosan |
| Iosif Banc | Ion Iliescu |
| Ion Coman | Ştefan Mocuţa |
| Teodor Coman | Vasile Patilineţ |
| Mihai Dalea | Mihai Telescu |
| Miu Dobrescu | Ioan Ursu |
| Ludovic Fazekas | Richard Winter |
| Mihai Gere | |

**The Secretariat of the Central Committee of the Romanian Communist Party**

Nicolae Ceauşescu, *General Secretary*

| | |
|---|---|
| Ştefan Andrei | Aurel Duma |
| Iosif Banc | Dumitru Popescu |
| Emil Bobu | Ion Stănescu |
| Cornel Burtică | Iosif Uglar |
| Constantin Dăscălescu | Ilie Verdeţ |

**Council of Ministers of the Socialist Republic of Romania**

*Prime-Minister of Government:* Manea Mănescu.
*Vice Prime-Minister of the Government:* Gheorge Cioară.
*Vice Prime-Minister of the Government:* Emil Drăgănescu.
*Vice Prime-Minister of the Government and Minister of Home Trade:* Janos Fazekaş.
*Vice Prime-Minister of the Government:* Ion Ioniţă.
*Vice Prime-Minister of the Government and President of the State Planning Committee:* Mihai Marinescu.
*Vice Prime-Minister of the Government and Minister of Agriculture, and Food Industry:* Angelo Miculescu.
*Vice Prime-Minister of the Government:* Ion Stanescu.
*Vice Prime-Minister of the Government:* Cornel Burtică.
*Vice Prime-Minister of the Government:* Paul Niculescu.
*Minister of Education and Instruction:* Suzana Gâdea.
*Vice Prime-Minister:* Gheorghe Oprea.
*Vice Prime-Minister and Minister of Foreign Trade and International Economic Co-operation:* Ion Păţan.
*Vice Prime-Minister:* Gheorghe Rădulescu.
*Minister of External Affairs:* George Macovescu.
*Minister of National Defence:* General Ion Coman.
*Minister of Internal Affairs:* Teodor Coman.
*Minister of Finance:* Florea Dumitrescu.
*Minister of Metallurgy:* Nicolae Agachi.
*Minister of the Machine-Building Industry:* Ioan Avram.
*Minister of Mines, Oil and Geology:* Constantin Băbălău.
*Minister of Chemical Industries:* Mihail Florescu.
*Minister of Electric Power:* Trandafir Cocîrlă.
*Minister of Forest Economy and Building Materials:* Vasile Patilineţ.
*Minister of Light Industry:* Lina Ciobanu.
*Minister of Transports and Telecommunications:* Traian Dudaş.
*Minister of Labour:* Gheorghe Pană.
*Minister of Industrial Constructions:* Vasile Bumbăcea.
*Minister of Technical and Material Supply and for Fixed Assets Management Control:* Maxim Berghianu.
*Minister of Health:* Nicolae Nicolaescu.
*Minister of Justice:* Constantin Stătescu
*Minister of Tourism:* Ion Cosma.
*Chairman of the National Council for Science and Technology:* Ioan Ursu.
*Chairman of the Council of Socialist Culture and Education:* Miu Dobrescu.
*Chairman of the State Committee for Prices:* Gheorghe Gaston Marin.
*Chairman of Committee for Problems of People's Councils:* Josif Uglar.

Other members of the Council of Ministers are: Emilian Dobrescu—Minister-Secretary of State, Prime-Vice-President of the State Planning Committee; Dumitru Bejan—Minister-Secretary of State of the Ministry for Foreign Trade and International Economic Co-operation; Florin Iorgulescu—President of the National Council of Waters; Petre Blajovici—Minister-Secretary of State, Head of the Department for Food Industry; Marin Capisizu—Head of the Department for State Agriculture.

According to the provisions of the Constitution, the Council of Ministers also comprises, as members:
President of the Central Council of the General Union of Trade-Unions: Gheorghe Pană.
President of the National Union of Co-operative Production Farms: Constantin Dăscălescu.
President of the National Council of Women: Lina Ciobanu.
First Secretary of the Central Committee of the Union of Communist Youth: Ion Traian Stefănescu.

**The State Council of the Socialist Republic of Romania**

President of the Socialist Republic of Romania, President of the State Council: Nicolae Ceausescu.
Vice-President of the State Council: Emil Bobu.
Vice-President of the State Council: Ştefan Peterfi.
Vice-President of the State Council: Ştefan Voitec.

**Members of the State Council**

| | |
|---|---|
| Dan Anghel | Eduard Eisenburger |
| Ioan Anton | Ludovic Fazekas |
| Ioan Ceterchi | Ion Hortopan |
| Ion Dincă | Ioan Manciuc |
| Tamara Dobrin | Gheorghe Petrescu |
| Miu Dobrescu | Ion Popescu-Puţuri |

**Bureau of the Grand National Assembly**

*President of the Grand National Assembly:*
Nicolae Giosan
*Vice-Presidents of the Grand National Assembly:*

| | |
|---|---|
| Stefan Mocuţa | Gheorghe Puşcaş |
| Aneta Spornic | Virgil Teodorescu |

## LOCAL GOVERNMENT

Articles 86–100 of the Constitution establish as local organs of the State power, the People's Councils. The People's Council's are responsible for such matters as the defence of socialist property, the protection of citizen's rights, socialist legality, the maintenance of public order, and various cultural, economic and planning activities.

A People's Council also has the power to budget for local affairs; in addition it can elect and dismiss judges and people's assessors. The term of office of all district People's Councils, as well as that of the Bucharest municipality is five years. The term of office of municipal, town and communal People's Councils is two and a half years.

## LEGAL SYSTEM

In Romania, justice is administered according to the law by the Supreme Court, district courts and military courts.

The State controls sentencing bodies and the administration of punishment, in addition the state defends the socialist system, and the rights and interests of organizations and individual citizens. All prosecutions are under the aegis of the General Prosecutor. The prosecution organizations are classified as follows, general, district, local, and military. On 1 April 1950, the activity of lawyers was also recognized and they now form a College of Barristers.

*Chairman of the Supreme Court:* Justin Grioóras.
*General Prosecutor:* Nicolae Bobocea.

## AREA AND POPULATION

The area of the Socialist Republic of Romania is 91,700 sq. miles (237,500 sq. km.).

On 1 July 1976, the total population was 21,445,698.

In the period from 1948 to July 1975, urban population increased from 23·4 per cent of the total population to 43·8 per cent.

The census of 5 January 1977 recorded a total population of 21,559,416 inhabitants, of which 47·5 per cent urban population.

The territory is organized in districts, towns and communes. The more important towns are organized as municipalities. The capital is organized as a municipality with eight sectors (not subordinate to any district). On 1 January 1977, there existed 39 districts, 236 towns (out of which 47 are organized as municipalities) and 2,706 communes (147 of them being suburban communes, and 13,149 of them being villages).

| Districts | Area—(sq. km.) | Population on 5 January 1977 (in thousands) |
|---|---|---|
| Alba | 6,231 | 409·6 |
| Arad | 7,654 | 512·3 |
| Argeş | 6,801 | 631·9 |
| Bacău | 6,603 | 667·7 |
| Bihor | 7,535 | 633·1 |
| Bistriţa-Năsăud | 5,305 | 286·7 |
| Botoşani | 4,965 | 451·2 |
| Braşov | 5,351 | 582·9 |
| Brăila | 4,724 | 377·9 |
| Buzău | 6,072 | 508·4 |
| Caras-Severin | 8,514 | 385·6 |
| Cluj | 6,650 | 715·4 |
| Constanţa | 7,055 | 608·8 |
| Covasna | 3,705 | 199·1 |
| Dîmbovita | 3,738 | 493·5 |
| Dolj | 7,413 | 750·4 |
| Galaţi | 4,425 | 581·6 |
| Gorj | 5,641 | 348·5 |
| Harghita | 6,610 | 326·3 |
| Hunedoara | 7,016 | 514·5 |
| Ialomiţa | 6,211 | 372·7 |
| Iaşi | 5,469 | 729·2 |
| Ilfov | 8,225 | 780·4 |
| Maramureş | 6,215 | 492·8 |
| Mehedinţi | 4,900 | 322·4 |
| Mureş | 6,696 | 605·4 |
| Neamţ | 5,890 | 532·1 |
| Olt | 5,507 | 518·8 |
| Prahova | 4,694 | 817·1 |
| Satu Mare | 4,405 | 393·9 |
| Sălaj | 3,850 | 264·4 |
| Sibiu | 5,422 | 481·6 |
| Suceava | 8,555 | 634·0 |
| Teleorman | 5,872 | 523·0 |
| Timiş | 8,678 | 696·7 |
| Tulcea | 8,430 | 254·4 |
| Vaslui | 5,300 | 436·9 |
| Vîlcea | 5,705 | 414·4 |
| Vrancea | 4,863 | 369·7 |
| Municipiul Bucureşti | 605 | 1,934·0* |

* The suburban communes included.

| Municipalities (Towns) county residents | Population* 5 January 1977 (in thousands) |
|---|---|
| Alba Iulia | 41·5 |
| Arad | 171·1 |
| Piteşti | 123·9 |
| Bacău | 126·7 |
| Oradea | 171·3 |
| Bistriţa | 44·5 |
| Botoşani | 63·2 |
| Braşov | 257·2 |
| Brăila | 194·6 |
| Buzău | 97·8 |
| Reşita | 85·0 |
| Cluj-Napoca | 262·4 |
| Constanţa | 256·9 |
| Sfîntu Gheorghe | 40·7 |
| Tîrgoviste | 61·7 |
| Craiova | 222·4 |
| Galaţi | 239·3 |
| Tîrgu Jiu | 63·7 |
| Miercurea Ciuc | 31·1 |
| Deva | 60·5 |
| Slobozia | 30·1 |
| Iaşi | 264·9 |

* Towns belonging to municipalities and suburban communes exclusively.

| Population (Towns) | Population 5 January 1977 (in thousands) |
|---|---|
| Bucharest (Bucureşti) | 1,807·0 |
| Baia Mare | 101·0 |
| Drobeta-Turnu Severin | 77·0 |
| Tîrgu Mureş | 130·1 |
| Piatra Neamţ | 78·1 |
| Slatina | 45·0 |
| Ploieşti | 199·3 |
| Satu Mare | 103·6 |
| Zalău | 32·1 |
| Sibiu | 151·1 |
| Suceava | 62·9 |
| Alexandria | 37·4 |
| Timişoara | 268·8 |
| Tulcea | 61·8 |
| Vaslui | 39·4 |
| Rîmnicu Vîlcea | 66·1 |
| Focşani | 56·5 |

## CURRENCY, FINANCE AND BANKING

The Romanian monetary unit is the Leu (plural Lei). 1 Leu = 100 Bani.

In Romania, the following notes and coins are in circulation:

Banknotes issued by the National Bank of the Socialist Republic of Romania in notes of Lei 100, 50, 25, 10, 5, 3 and 1; and coins of 3 and 1 Lei and 5, 10, 15 and 25 Bani.

The monetary reform which took place on 15 August 1947, fixed a new gold standard for the Leu, the parity of 5·94 mg. gold having a title of 0·900. In 1952, by a new reform, the monetary signs were replaced, the parity being fixed at 1 Leu = 79·346 mg. fine gold. On 1 February 1954, the gold standard of the Leu was raised once more: 1 Leu = 0·148112 gr. of fine gold.

As a consequence of the raising of the gold standard of the Leu, new exchange rates in Lei were established, at the respective dates, for the foreign currencies, starting from their gold standard.

In Romania, the banks are State institutions. The former National Bank of Rumania, set up in 1880, was nationalized in December 1946. On 11 June 1948, the private banks were nationalised.

The financial-banking system of the Socialist Republic of Romania comprises the following banks: the **National Bank of the Socialist Republic of Romania** which, in the framework of the State plan for the country's development and according to its statutes directs the monetary circulation and is the only issuing bank.

**The Investments Bank** specializes in financing of the capital investments made by State enterprise, economic organizations and institutions, in granting long-term credits.

**The Bank for Agriculture and Food Industry** specializes in financing the production, the investments for agriculture and the food industry.

**The Romanian Bank of Foreign Trade** specializes in payment operations resulting from foreign relations.

**The Savings and Bank Deposits** (C.E.C.) mobilize the temporarily available financial resources of the population.

The State Budget (in thousand million Lei) for 1975 and 1976 is given below:

| | 1975 | 1976 |
|---|---|---|
| *Income* | 238·6 | 254·5 |
| Of which | | |
| Taxes on goods circulation | 42·1 | 44·9 |
| Quotas from profits on the enterprises of state economic organizations | 45·5 | 54·9 |
| Taxes and duties from the population | 20·2 | 23·8 |
| Income of State social insurances | 17·2 | 21·6 |
| *Expenditure* | 236·2 | |
| Of which | | |
| Financing of national economy | 155·8 | 165·7 |
| Financing of social and cultural activities | 50·9 | 55·3 |
| State defence | 9·7 | 10·6 |
| State power and administration, legal and prosecutors office | 2·7 | 3·0 |

# ROMANIA

## AGRICULTURE, INDUSTRY AND COMMERCE

Before the war Romania was an agrarian-industrial state. After World War II a vast programme of economic development was applied. As a result, in a relatively short period Romania has become a powerful industrial-agrarian state, with industry being fully developed and modernized, and agriculture progressing steadily.

The powerful development of the national economy was possible as a consequence of the great and ever increasing volume of investments. Between 1966–70 the national economy received 330,797 million Lei investments, 1·7 times more than in the preceding five-year period. The greatest part of the volume of investments was allotted to the sphere of material production. In 1971–75, 548,980 million Lei were invested in the national economy. In 1976, more than 149,000 million Lei were invested in the national economy.

As a result of the increased volume of investments and the increase of production in all branches, the national income became bigger every year so that in 1976 it was 11 times bigger than the national income in 1938—a summit year in the pre-war development of the Romanian economy.

**Agriculture.** At the end of 1976 Romania had a total agricultural area of 14,954·8 thousand hectares. Of this, 9,760·2 thousand hectares are arable land, 3,032·3 thousand are pastures, 1,404·3 thousand are hayfields, 326·9 thousand are vineyards and viticultural nurseries and 431·1 thousand are orchards and fruit-growing nurseries.

Until 1944 Romanian agriculture was very backward. In 1945 a law was promulgated by which 1,468,000 hectares were expropriated from the landowners. Most of this land was distributed to the peasants, over 900,000 families receiving more than 1·1 million hectares. The remainder of the land was nationalized.

In 1949, the organization of small peasant holdings into large co-operative units was begun. In spring 1962, co-operativization was completed.

The State assigned big budgetary funds for the technical and economic improvement of agriculture. Between 1966 and 1970, the capital State investments allotted to agriculture amounted to almost 51·6 thousand million Lei; in 1971–75, almost 77,000 million Lei were allotted to agriculture from state funds. At the end of 1976, there were in agriculture 128,024 tractors, 44,117 seed drills, 53,000 combine harvesters and numerous other agricultural machines. The chief field jobs are now mainly carried out by mechanized means. Increasing numbers of agricultural specialists are being trained. Each co-operative farm has at its disposal at least one expert with higher training.

At the end of 1976 there were 392 State agricultural enterprises, which possessed an agricultural area of 2,060·3 thousand hectares; 743 enterprises for the mechanization of agriculture and 4,649 agricultural co-operatives, possessing 9,055·2 thousand hectares of agricultural land. State units own 30·1 per cent of the agricultural area of the country and production agricultural co-operatives 60·5 per cent.

Between 1961 and 1965, the average annual yield for cereals was 10·9 million tons, between 1966–70 it was 12·7 million tons, and between 1971–1975 it was 14·8 million tons. In 1976, the total grain production was 19·8 million tons (wheat: 6·8 million tons; maize: 11·6 million tons); sunflower: 799·3 thousand tons; sugar beet: 5,910·6 thousand tons; potatoes: 4,788·4 thousand tons; vegetables: 3,592·9 thousand tons; grapes: 1,535·7 thousand tons; fruit: 1,349·9 thousand tons.

At the beginning of 1977 there were 6,351 thousand heads of horned cattle, 10,193 thousand pigs, 14,331 thousand sheep and 91·5 million fowls. The following table shows animal production for 1975 and 1976.

| | | 1975 | 1976 |
|---|---|---|---|
| Meat | thousand tons (live weight) | 2,012 | 2,157 |
| Milk | thousand hl. | 44,721 | 48,302 |
| Wool | thousand tons | 31·5 | 32·0 |
| Eggs | thousand million | 5·4 | 6·2 |
| Honey | thousand tons | 7·6 | 13·0 |

**Forestry.** In 1975, growing stock accounted for 6,315,800 hectares (26·6 per cent of the total land area). There are more than 80 species of trees, the most widespread being beech, coniferous trees and oak. 1976 production figures for the wood industry are as follows: timber, 4,311 thousand cu. m.; fibre boards, 578 thousand tons; plywood, 275 thousand cu. m. veneers, 71,885 thousand sq. m. The value of wood furniture production in 1975 was 10,886 million Lei.

**Industry.** This is the leading branch of the economy. In 1975 industrial production formed 64·7 per cent of the social output and 55·9 per cent of the national income. Until recently Romania was poorly developed industrially. After World War II a great process of industrialization developed. In 1948 the chief industrial, mining, banking, insurance and transport enterprises were nationalized.

Beginning with the year 1949, the State planned to raise, in as short a time as possible, Romania to the level of the developed countries. The long-term State economic plans are for a five or ten-year period. At the 10th Congress of the R.C.P., held in August 1969, the directives of the five-year plan for 1971–75 were issued.

The Romanian Communist Party Congress of November 1974 debated and adopted: The Romanian Communist Party Programme for the Creation of the Many-sidedly Developed Socialist Society and Romania's Advance Towards Communism; Directives Concerning the 1976–1980 Five-Year Plan and the Guide Lines of Romania's Economico-Social Development in the Period 1981–1990

For the 1976–80 five year plan it is hoped that approximately 1,000 million lei will be available for investment, in addition approximately 2,700 important industrial and agricultural units will be put into service.

The volume of funds invested for the social economic development of the country is growing every year. Between 1951–75, the volume of investments in the economy amounted to 549 thousand million Lei (277·2 thousand million Lei in industry). Over 314 thousand million Lei were invested in the socialist sector during the five-year plan 1966–70, of which 165 thousand million Lei went into industry.

In the development of industry, heavy industry takes first place, especially its main branches—mechanical engineering, energetics, metallurgy and chemicals. In 1975, the output of means of production was 72·5 per cent of the total industrial output. In 1976, there were 1,752 industrial enterprises, having 2,793,360 employees.

The average rate of growth of the total industrial output was of 12·9 per cent between 1951 and 1976. In that period the growth rate of the electrical and thermic industry was 15·3 per cent; of ferrous metallurgy 12·7 per cent; of machine manufacturing and metal processing 17·7 per cent; of the chemical industry 20·6 per cent; and of the output of consumer goods, 10·6 per cent.

The mining industries have developed greatly. New oil areas and reserves of ores and non-ferrous metals have been exploited.

The following table shows production of certain raw materials and fuels for 1975–76:

| *Product* | *Unit* | 1975 | 1976 |
|---|---|---|---|
| Iron ores | thousand tons | 3,065 | 2,835 |
| Crude coal extracted | thousand tons | 29,385 | 28,115 |
| Crude oil extracted | thousand tons | 14,590 | 14,700 |
| Methane gas extracted | million cu. m. | 27,001 | 29,834 |
| Oil-well gas | million cu. m. | 6,305 | 6,496 |
| Metallurgical coke | thousand tons | 2,277 | 2,472 |
| Salt | thousand tons | 3,833 | 4,210 |

The following table shows output of processed metals, (in thousand tons) for 1975–76:

| | 1975 | 1976 |
|---|---|---|
| Pig iron | 6,602 | 7,415 |
| Steel | 9,549 | 10,733 |
| Full finished roller goods | 6,810 | 7,305 |
| Steel pipes | 1,151 | 1,213 |

In 1966 a large iron-and-steel centre was put into operation in the town of Galați. In its final stage (1980) this centre will produce 7,280 thousand tons of steel per year, of which 6,700 thousand tons of converted steel.

In 1975 production in the mechanical engineering and metal-working industries was more than 123 times that of 1938. Some of the machines and equipment produced in 1976 were: power motors of over 0·25 kW with a total power of 6,265,000 kW; power generators totalling 2,234,000 kVA; 29,889 metal splintering machine tools; 87,857 tons of chemical processing equipment; 53,911 tractors and 121,138 motor vehicles.

The following table shows production of chemicals and related products for 1975 and 1976 (in thousand tons):

| | 1975 | 1976 |
|---|---|---|
| Caustic dosa (100% NaOH) | 566·0 | 673·0 |
| Calcinate soda (100% $CO_3Na_2$) | 693·0 | 814·0 |
| Sulphuric acid (100%) | 1,448·0 | 1,555·0 |
| Chemical fertilizers (100% active subst.) | 1,729·0 | 1,869·0 |
| Organic dyes | 11·8 | 179·0 |
| Chemical yarns and fibres | 159·0 | 465·0 |
| Plastic and synthetic resins | 575·0 | 610·0 |
| Cellulose and semicellulose (100% dry) | 98·9 | 95·2 |
| Synthetic rubber | 16·6 | 17·7 |
| Detergents | 4,526·0 | 5,083·0 |
| Tyres (thousand pieces) | 347·0 | |

Electrical power production came to 58,266 million kWh in 1976 which was 51·5 times the production figure of 1938.

In 1976 12,548 thousand tons of cement, 1,686 million pieces of masonry and ceramic blocks, 4,658,000 cu. m. prefabs of reinforced concrete slabs, 171 million tiles, 71,000,000 sq. m. of window panes (equivalent 2 mm. thickness), 4,311,000 cu. m. timber, a.o. were produced.

Production of consumer goods has increased 17 times since 1938. Output of consumer goods is shown in the following table:

| *Product* | *Unit* | 1975 | 1976 |
|---|---|---|---|
| Cotton fabrics and cotton type | mil. sq. m. | 591 | 677 |
| Woollen fabrics and woollen type | ,, | 96 | 105 |
| Silk fabrics and silk type | ,, | 89 | 106 |
| Knitted goods | mil. pieces | 203 | 246 |
| Footwear | mil. pairs | 161 | 96 |
| Radio sets | thousand items | 712 | 791 |
| T.V. sets | ,, | 512 | 548 |
| Electric washing machines for domestic use | ,, | 178 | 199 |
| Sewing machines for domestic use | ,, | 74 | 376 |
| Refrigerators | ,, | 332 | 815 |
| Meat | thousand tons | 713 | 815 |
| Meat products | ,, | 182 | 212 |
| Canned meat | ,, | 47 | 55 |
| Canned vegetables | ,, | 294 | 345 |
| Edible oils and fats | ,, | 321 | 322 |
| Sugar | ,, | 516 | 561 |

**Foreign Trade.** The consequent promotion of the technical progress, the diversification of production and the permanent raising of the quality of products have determined the increase of the volume of foreign trade, which in 1976 attained 60,798 million standard Lei (30,504 million Lei exports and 30,294 million Lei imports). The total volume of the foreign trade in 1976 shows an increase of 22 times as against 1950 and of 4·7 times as against 1965. The changes in the structure of production, especially in industry, had as a result modifications in the structure of Romania's foreign trade (see table at foot of page).

Chief exports are oil-processing equipment, equipment for cement plants, transport equipment, power equipment, machine tools, building equipment and materials, wood products, products and equipment for chemical industry, and food products etc.

An important place in Romania's foreign trade is that held by socialist countries and, in the first place by the Soviet Union. These relations are organized both in the framework of bilateral treaties, agreements or conventions, as well as through the Council of Mutual Economic Aid (C.A.E.R.).

Romania maintains economic relations of trade and co-operation with over 130 countries on all the continents. The following table shows the volume of foreign trade in 1975 and 1976 (in million standard Lei) with the principal countries:

| | 1975 | 1976 |
|---|---|---|
| **Total** | 53,095·4 | 60,798·4 |
| Arab Republic of Syria | 402·5 | 814·1 |
| Austria | 1,492·8 | 1,625·8 |
| Belgium | 541·4 | 739·9 |
| Brazil | 267·5 | 637·8 |
| Sri Lanka | 42·8 | 58·9 |
| People's Republic of China | 2,164·4 | 2,240·4 |
| Federal Republic of Germany | 5,039·1 | 4,644·4 |
| Yugoslavia | 1,209·8 | 1,402·7 |
| Finland | 53·4 | 67·3 |
| France | 1,689·2 | 2,156·9 |
| Great Britain | 1,503·4 | 1,568·6 |
| Denmark | 158·3 | 177·3 |
| German Democratic Republic | 2,909·0 | 4,253·6 |
| Greece | 630·3 | 907·9 |
| Hungary | 1,603·5 | 1,976·4 |
| India | 510·8 | |
| Italy | 2,273·4 | 1,956·4 |
| Japan | 1,089·1 | 905·4 |
| Democratic People's Republic of Korea | 185·1 | 163·2 |
| Libya | 933·3 | 1,273·4 |
| Lebanon | 462·6 | 383·3 |
| Netherlands | 1,019·1 | 1,266·8 |
| Albania | 81·2 | 104·9 |
| Bulgaria | 1,023·1 | 1,089·4 |
| Poland | 2,072·6 | 2,730·6 |
| Czechoslovakia | 2,446·7 | 2,685·0 |
| Spain | 535·8 | 298·3 |
| Sweden | 589·6 | 615·3 |
| Singapore | 157·1 | 166·9 |
| Switzerland | 2,068·5 | 1,339·5 |
| Turkey | 262·5 | 661·5 |
| Arab Republic of Egypt | 726·6 | 487·0 |
| U.S.S.R. | 9,857·5 | 10,863·7 |
| U.S.A. | 1,174·1 | 2,319·5 |
| Sudan | 66·5 | 88·8 |
| Democratic Republic of Viet-Nam | 57·8 | 48·1 |
| Israel | 298·3 | 215·9 |
| Iran | 1,702·1 | 2,434·2 |
| Mongolian People's Republic | 33·8 | 40·7 |
| Cuba | 127·3 | 160·6 |

| | *Exports (percentages)* | | | *Imports (percentages)* | | |
|---|---|---|---|---|---|---|
| | 1950 | 1975 | 1976 | 1950 | 1975 | 1976 |
| Machinery, and transport equipment for production | 4·2 | 25·3 | 25·7 | 38·3 | 34·7 | 31·8 |
| Fuel, mineral raw materials and metals | 33·8 | 22·3 | 8·3 | 23·5 | 38·2 | 41·0 |
| Chemical products, fertilizers and rubber | 1·7 | 10·8 | 3·0 | 4·5 | 6·5 | 6·8 |
| Building materials and appliances | 4·4 | 2·9 | 6·5 | 1·1 | 1·1 | 1·2 |
| Non-edible raw materials and processed products | 28·9 | 6·3 | 6·3 | 21·4 | 8·4 | 7·3 |
| Raw materials for the production of food wares | 11·6 | 5·7 | 9·7 | 0·7 | 5·0 | 6·4 |
| Food wares | 14·1 | 10·6 | 16·4 | 0·3 | 2·2 | 2·0 |
| Industrial goods of large consumption | 1·3 | 16·1 | | 10·2 | 3·8 | 3·4 |

## COMMUNICATIONS

**Roads.** Total length of the public roads at the end of 1976 was 77,768 km. of which 13,470 km. are modernized. The most important road junction is Bucharest. Main roads run to all industrial centres and to all important frontiers. In 1976 the passenger turnover by motor transport amounted to 850 millions and that of goods to 442 million tons.

**Railways.** The building of Romanian railways started with railway lines connecting the Danubian ports with the interior of the country. The first railway line put into operation was the Oravița-Baziaș line (1854). There followed later Giurgiu lines (1869). The total length of the railway network is at present of approximately 11,080 kilometres. The central point of the railway network is Bucharest.

Other important railway junctions are: Ploiești, Mărășești, Iași, in the east and south of the country; Roșiorii de Vede, Piatra Olt, Craiova in the south; Timișoara, Arad, Oradea in the west; Brașov, Simeria, Beiuș in the centre.

In 1976, the total freight turnover amounted to 711·7 million tons and the passenger turnover to more than 1,227 million passengers.

**Shipping.** The Black Sea and the river Danube make it possible to make great use of water-borne transport. 1,075 kms of the river Danube flow through Romania.

The economic importance of Danubian transports consists of the fact that, on the Romanian portion, ships with higher register tonnage (2,000 tons) can sail. Ships of 4,500 tons enter from the Black Sea on the Danube up to Galați. A great part of the commercial traffic between Central and Eastern Europe is carried on the Danube. The goods can be shipped directly from the merchant marine ships to the river ships and transported in the countries situated along the Danube as far as the Federal Republic of Germany.

The chief port is Constanța (11·7 million tons in 1974) which has been provided with modern loading and unloading facilities. Main river-and-sea ports are Brăila and Galați.

The most important waterways served by Romanian ships are:

Constanța–Varna–Istanbul–Salonika.
Constanța–Istanbul–Piraeus–Alexandria.
Constanța–Istanbul–Piraeus–Haifa–Beirut.
Constanța–Hamburg–Anvers–Rotterdam.
Constanța–Beirut–Latakia–Famagusta.
Constanța–Alexandria.
Constanța–Aschenod (Israel).

In 1976, the number of passengers carried by river boats amounted to 2,253,000 and the volume of goods to 6·7 million tons.

**Airlines.** The most important centre of air transport is Bucharest. It is from here that all airlines leave, both internal and international. Bucharest is served by two airports: The Băneasa Airport and the Otopeni International Airport, put into operation in 1970, serving an estimated 1·5 million passengers and with possibilities of extending to about 4 million. Flights on international and internal lines are provided by the Romanian state company TAROM (Romanian Air Transport) and LAR (the Romanian Air Lines); which makes use of the following types of planes: Boeing 707, I162, I118, BAC 1-11, and An 24.

Regular airlines connect daily or even several times, according to schedule, the capital with the following towns: Arad–Timișoara–Sibiu–Deva–Cluj–Satu Mare–Baia Mare–Tîrgu Mureș–Oradea–Bacău–Iași–Tulcea–Constanța–Craiova–Suceava.

Romania has regular air communications with: Budapest, Prague, Berlin, Amsterdam, Athens, Vienna, Cairo, Frankfurt, Warsaw, Kiev, Moscow, Odessa, Sophia, Belgrade, Brussels, Copenhagen, Rome, Zurich, London, New-York, Istanbul, Beirut, Tel Aviv, Amman, Teheran, Karachi, Peking.

Bucharest is also linked in the circuit of lines served by Air France, Interflug, JAT, KLM, Lufthansa, Lot, El Al, TABSO, Malev, CSA, AUA, Sabena, Swissair, Aeroflot, Alitalia, British Airways, SAS, Panam.

In 1976, the total number of air passengers was 1,351 thousand.

**Telephones and Broadcasting.** In 1938 Romania had two broadcasting stations, at Băneasa and Bod; in 1976, 64 stations were in operation. In 1938 there were 252,000 radio subscribers; in 1976, 3,104,000; 2,963,000 T.V. subscribers, and 984,000 telephone subscribers.

## NEWSPAPERS

In 1976 there were 59 newspapers of general information. The most important papers in Romania are:

**Scînteia.** Organ of the Central Committee of the RCP. Circulation nearly 1,500,000 copies. Bucharest.

**România Liberă.** Edited by the National Council of the Front of the Socialist Unity. Bucharest.

**Scînteia Tineretului.** Central organ of the Union of Communist Youth. Bucharest.

**Elöre.** Hungarian. Political daily paper.

**Neuer Weg.** German. Political daily paper. Bucharest.

32 daily newspapers have a combined day circulation of 3·5 million.

## EDUCATION

Illiteracy has been completely eliminated. In 1938 there were almost 4,000,000 illiterates and semi-illiterates. The educational reform which took plase in August 1948 altered the structure of education.

There were in 1976–77: 13,600 pre-school establishments, attended by 825,028 children; 15,005 general education schools and lycées of general culture attended by 3,496,785 pupils; 440 vocational schools attended by 119,311 pupils; 640 specialized lycées with 639,011 pupils; 137 technical schools of post-lycée specialization with 22,450 pupils; 156 master schools with 13,819 pupils and 67 art schools with 28,516 pupils.

There are also special schools (for children with various physical or psychic deficiencies) as well as various evening and extra-mural schools for adults who cannot leave their work but want to complete their education.

The general compulsory education lasts for ten years. As far back as 1948, the necessary conditions were ensured in order to enable all children to attend the first four grades. In the school year 1964–65, 8-year compulsory education was generalized. Through a law of 1968, ten-year education has become compulsory and the school starting age was reduced to six years. Education taxes have been discontinued.

In 1976–77 higher education consisted of universities and institutes with 139 faculties with a general enrolment of 174,888 students. Over 75,000 students live in students' hostels and nearly 63,000 students take their meals in students' canteens.

### The Academy of the Socialist Republic of Romania

The Academy is the highest authority in the field of science and culture in the country; it includes honorary members, full members and corresponding members elected from the scientists and artists who distinguish themselves by original works of theoretical and practical value. The Academy is organized in departments as follows: mathematics, physics, chemistry, technical sciences, biological, agricultural and forest sciences; geology, geophysics and geography; medical sciences; economic sciences and sociological sciences; philosophical, judicial, psychological sciences; historical sciences; philological sciences; a department of literature and art.

The Academy has two branches (in Iași and Cluj-Napoca), two scientific research bases (in Timișoara and Tg. Mureș).

The directing body of the Academy is the General Assembly of the members. Between the assemblies, the directing body is the Presidium of the Academy (composed of the Chairman of the Academy, Vice-Presidents, General Secretary, chairmen of the branches and of the departments and a delegate of the National Council for Science and Technology). The Chairman of the Academy: vacant.

The Academy publishes, through its own publishing house, '*Editura Academiei Republicii Socialiste România*', 55 reviews, 30 of which are translated into the main international languages.

In December 1965 the National Council for Science and Technology was created. It directs the scientific research activity carried out in the framework of the Academy, of the higher educational institutes, as well as in the framework of the ministries and of the other central bodies. The Chairman of the Council is Ioan Ursu.

The Academy of Medical Sciences was founded in 1969 to co-ordinate the medical and pharmaceutical research undertaken in Romania. It consists of 14 honorary members, 45 full members, and 28 corresponding members. The Chairman is Aurel Moga.

In 1969 The Academy of Agricultural and Forest Sciences was founded, which co-ordinates the agricultural and forest researches in Romania. Itis formed of 45 full members and 55 corresponding members. President of the Academy is Nicolae Giosan.

In 1970 the Academy of Social and Political Sciences of the Socialist Republic of Romania was created, with 118 full members and 92 corresponding members. Hon. President: Nicolae Ceauşescu. President: Mihnea Gheorghiu.

### HEALTH SERVICE

In 1975, the number of medical assistance beds was 196,236. That same year, there was one physician for every 624 inhabitants. Mortality decreased from 19·1 per 1,000 inhabitants in 1938 to 9·3 per 1,000 in 1975 and infant mortality in the same period from 179·0 per thousand born alive to 34·7 per thousand born alive.

### RELIGION

The State guarantees the free exercise of any religion. The religious groups have their own statutes. There are about 17,000 churches and chapels and numerous monasteries with over 18,000 clergymen and 2,000 monks and nuns.

The greater part of the population (some 13 million of them) belong to the Greek Orthodox creed. In 1948, the former Greek Catholics reverted to the Greek Orthodox Church. The rest of the believers belong to the following denominations: Roman Catholic, Protestant, Evangelical of Augsburg Confession, Mosaic, Baptist, Unitarian, Penticostal, Servian-Orthodox, Ancient Rite Christian, Seventh Day Adventists, Moslem, Evangelican Synodo-Presbyterian, Gospel Christian and Armeno Gregorian.

The Romanian Orthodox Church was organized as early as 1925 as a patriarchy. It has 13 dioceses with 106 archpriests districts, 11,000 churches, chapels and monasteries and hermitages, and a corresponding number of priests, deacons, cantors, monks and nuns necessary to the cult. The thirteen dioceses are grouped in the framework of the five metropolitan churches of Ugro-Vlahia, Moldavia and Suceava, Transylvania, Oltenia and Banat. For the training of its clergy, the church possesses two theological institutes of university standard (4-year education), six theological seminaries (5-year education), and one special theological seminary of 3-years.

The Roman Catholic Church is organized in two dioceses, the Bucharest archbishopric and the Alba Iulia bishopric. Both dioceses have over 900 churches and a corresponding number of clergymen. For the education of its clergy, there is a higher theological institute and a cantors school with tuition given in Hungarian at Alba Iulia and Romanian at Iasi.

The Protestant (Calvin) Church has two dioceses at Cluj-Napoca and at Oradea, with 24 deaneries and two archpriests. The Evangelical Augustan Church has one bishopric at Sibiu, ten deaneries and over 200 parishes. The Evangelical Synodo-Presbyterian Church has one superintendence at Cluj-Hapoca, three special districts with 38 parishes as well as the corresponding number of clergymen. The Unitarian Church has a bishopric at Cluj-Napoca and six deaneries. The training of the clergy of these churches is carried out in the Theological Institute of university standard in Cluj-Napoca.

The religious groups have their own printing establishments, publish books and reviews for the cult, manage workshops for cult handicrafts and own retirement and rest houses.

The clergy, churches and chapels, theological schools and general religious expenditure are maintained with funds resulting from free contributions, the incomes of their own properties and the wages and subsidies granted by the State through the Department of Cults.

The religious groups maintain relations with similar cults from abroad and with international religious organizations (the Oecumenical Council of Churches, the Christian Conference for Peace etc.).

# Rwanda

**Capital**—Kigali.

**President**—Juvenal Habyarimana.

**Flag**: On a tricolour pale-wise, green, yellow, crimson, an R centred black.

### CONSTITUTION AND GOVERNMENT

FORMERLY part of the United Nations Trust territory of Ruanda-Burundi which lies east of the Congo, Rwanda became a sovereign state on 1 July 1962. It became a member of the U.N. in September of the same year. Attempts to federate the northern territory of Rwanda with its southern neighbour Burundi failed and all common organizations came to an end in 1964.

Following a military coup on 5 July 1973, all political activity in Rwanda was suspended. The former Commander of the Rwandan Army became President of the Republic of Rwanda and President of the Committee for Peace and National Unity. He is supported by a cabinet of twelve Ministers.

### AREA AND POPULATION

The area is about 10,100 square miles. It is boarded to the south by Burundi, to the west by Zaire, to the north by Uganda and to the east by Tanzania. The seat of Government is Kigali.

The population in mid-1974 was 4,058,000. The annual average percentage population growth rate for 1960–74 was 3·3 and for 1965–74 was 2·9. The three ethnic groups are the Hutu (85 per cent), the Tutsi (14 per cent) and the Twa (1 per cent). There are about 2,000 Europeans of whom 60 per cent are Belgians.

### CURRENCY AND FINANCE

The unit of currency is the Rwanda franc. In the period 1963–65 the financial operations of the Central Government gave rise to large deficits which were financed mainly by short-term bank borrowing. In April 1966, a programme of stabilization measures was adopted which included the adoption of a unitary official rate of exchange of Rw. f. 100 per U.S. dollar. These measures have proved to be realistic and the country's economic situation has now begun to improve.

The following table gives some economic statistics for the year 1970:

| *Category* | *£ (millions)* |
|---|---|
| Gross Domestic Product | 88·2 |
| Total exports | 10·2 |
| Total imports | 12·1 |
| Aid | 7·9 |
| Imports from the U.K. | ·625 |
| Exports to the U.K. | ·362 |

The GNP at market prices for 1974 was U.S. $ millions 310 and the GNP per capita at market prices was U.S. $80. The annual average percentage growth rate of the GNP per capita for the period 1960–74 was −0·2, and for the period 1965–74 was 1·4. [*See the note at the beginning of this section concerning GNP.*]

### PRODUCTION, INDUSTRY AND COMMERCE

The territory is predominantly an agricultural country, with the larger proportion of agricultural production deriving from subsistence-type farming. The principal cash crops are coffee, pyrethrum and tea, with coffee accounting for more than half of the total exports. The possibilities of expanding exports of other crops such as fresh vegetables, tobacco and castor oil are being examined. Bananas, sweet potatoes, manioc, sorghum and beans are the main crops for domestic consumption.

A number of different minerals are produced in Rwanda, of which cassiterite is the most important in terms of both production and foreign exchange earnings. 1968 production was 1,747 metric tons. Other minerals mined include wolfram (1968—623 metric tons), colombo-tantalite (a side product of cassiterite) (1968—28 metric tons), and beryl (1968—148 metric tons). Industrial development is inhibited by the size of the domestic market. In addition to the primary processing of coffee and tea, rice and sugar are also produced on a factory scale. A pyrethin extraction plant will be in operation shortly. Light industry includes the manufacture of footwear, radios, paint and shirts.

Electricity is the most important source of power, mainly because of the requirements of the mines. There are four power-houses of which one is hydro-electric, two are thermal, while the fourth is hydro-electric and thermal combined. A pilot natural methane gas plant at Lake Kivu produces gas for use in a brewery at Gisenyi.

In 1967, visible exports were worth 1,480 million Rwanda francs (FOB), and imports totalled about 1,500 million francs (FOB). Foreign aid made up the trade deficit.

### COMMUNICATIONS

There is a road network of 1,666 miles of main roads (50 miles of macadamized road) and over 2,000 miles of secondary roads. Further road development is planned. There are two commercial airports located at Kigali and Gyangugu. A regular jet service operates between Kigali and Brussels. There are in addition landing strips in all the main provincial towns, and a regular non-jet service between Kigali and Kampala.

### EDUCATION

In 1968 there were 2,017 primary schools with 345,654 pupils and 104 secondary schools with 7,721 pupils. There is a university at Butare.

# San Marino

## (REPUBBLICA DI SAN MARINO)

**Capital**—San Marino.

**National Flag**: Divided fess-wise, white and blue, charged with the national arms within a wreath of oak and laurel.

### CONSTITUTION AND GOVERNMENT

SAN MARINO claims to be the oldestrep ublic in Europe. The date of its foundation is given as A.D. 301. The story is that it was founded by a Christian stone-cutter named Marino. The constitutional laws, however, as laid down in the *Statuta Illustrissimae Reipublicae Sancti Marini* are much later in origin, dating from the 12th century. The present constitution is based on the Statutes of 1600.

The Arengo, according to the old Statutes, was the Meeting of the Heads of Families, one from each household, and exercised the supreme powers of the State. In the 12th century it delegated its powers to the Sovereign Grand Council, and today the Arengo is virtually synonymous with the electoral body, being composed of all citizens who have reached the age of 21 and are in possession of civil and political rights. The Sovereign Grand Council (*Consiglio Grande e Generale*) of 60 members, is elected every five years by direct vote of all citizens over the age of twenty-one. Women voted for the first time in the 1964 elections. Every six months (in the middle of March and September) two members of the Council are nominated to act as Captains Regent (*Capitani Reggenti*). The Captains Regent hold executive power and represent the Republic in its relations with other countries. Their inauguration takes place on 1 April and 1 October each year with picturesque ceremony. They cannot be re-elected until three years have expired after their last term of office. The Captains Regent are personally responsible for the mandate assumed, and at the termination of their office are subject to a Syndicate to which any citizen may present his claims.

The Sovereign Grand Council also elects a committee of 12 members to act as a Supreme Court, known as the Council of XII, which has civil, penal and administrative functions and is the ultimate court of appeal.

There is a Congress of State, composed of ten members chosen by the Sovereign Grand Council, which in the past had exclusively consultative functions. Now, however, this organ is invested with directive and executive powers of government and is divided into ten departments.

### LEGAL SYSTEM

The legal system is composed of the following bodies:

1. Conciliatory Judge, who has power to judge civil cases up to a maximum of 10,000 lire.
2. Judge of First Hearing, called Commissary of the Law, who has power to judge all civil and penal cases where the maximum penalty does not exceed six months.
3. Penal Judge for penal cases which are beyond the competence of the Judge of First Hearing.
4. Judge for civil and penal appeals.
5. The Council of XII, whose members constitute the tribunal for third hearing.

### AREA AND POPULATION

The territory of the Republic covers an area of 61·19 sq. kilometres and lies between the Italian cities of Pesaro and Forli, 24 kilometres distant from the seaside resort of Rimini. The population in January 1974 was 19,100. The capital, San Marino, has a population of about 3,000. Other centres are Borgo Maggiore, Serravalle, Faetano, Chiesanuova, Montegiardino, Fiorentino, Domagnano and Acquaviva. The language is Italian.

### CURRENCY AND FINANCE

Italian currency is legal tender in San Marino, under terms of an agreement between the Republic and the Italian government. Such agreement was amended on 10 September 1971, and now the Government of San Marino also issues its own coins (500 lire, silver; 100 and 50 lire, steel and chrome; 20 lire, copper and aluminium; 10, five, and two lire, aluminium, magnesium, and manganese). In June 1974 the making of gold coinage was authorized. The coins are of the values one Scudi, and two Scudi. The Republic also issues its own postage stamps.

The San Marino budget for 1974 is of the order of L.12·2 billion. The revenue derives mainly from taxes, the sale of government monopoly goods, the postal services and an annual sum paid by the Italian government in return for various economic concessions.

There are no customs barriers whatever between San Marino and Italy.

### PRODUCTION, INDUSTRY AND COMMERCE

Tourism is the primary industry of the small Republic-which attracted three million visitors in 1974.

San Marino's economic resources are mainly agricultural. Wheat is the largest crop, and averages 36,000 quintals a year. Wine production is considerable and averages about 20,000 hectolitres a year. The quality of the wines, and particularly the Moscato, is widely recognized.

There is a small industrial production including textiles and cement. Small quantities of paper, leather, soap, paint and synthetic rubber are produced in the Republic.

San Marino's ceramic work dates from the 16th century, and is a considerable industry. It employs more than 400 skilled workers in ten workshops.

### COMMUNICATIONS

There is no rail service between San Marino and Italy, but the capital is linked with Rimini and the Italian 'autostrade' network by a modern highway. There is now a new funicular service from the city of San Marino to Borgo Maggiore (1 mile away). From there, there is a helicopter service to the international airport at Rimini. The network of roads in the Republic has a total length of 100 kilometres.

There is a telegraphic station in the capital and telephones throughout the whole country.

### EDUCATION AND RELIGION

In 1974 there were 19 elementary schools and 15 infant schools at various centres and a secondary school and a high school in the capital. The religion is predominantly Roman Catholic.

# São Tomé and Príncipe Islands

(SÃO TOMÉ E PRÍNCIPE)

**Capital**—São Tomé.

**President**—Manuel Pinto da Costa.

THE Islands of São Tomé and Príncipe are situated off the west coast of Africa in the Gulf of Guinea. The province includes the fort of São João Baptista de Ajuda on the Slave Coast.

## AREA AND POPULATION

The islands have an area of 964 sq. km.

The population at mid-1974 was 79,000. The annual average percentage growth rate for the period 1960–74 was 1·9 and for the period 1965–74 was 3·2.

The São Tomé and Príncipe Islands became independent on 12 July 1975.

## FINANCE

Budget figures for 1964 were: Revenue, 111·3 million escudos; Expenditure, 103·5 million escudos.

## PRODUCTION, INDUSTRY AND COMMERCE

The main products of the province are cocoa, coconuts, copra and palm oil.

The GNP at 1974 at market prices was U.S. $40 millions and the GNP per capita at market prices was U.S. $570. The annual average percentage growth rate of the GNP per capita for the period 1960–74 was 0·6, and for the period 1965–74 was −1·0. [*See the note at the beginning of this section concerning GNP.*]

## COMMUNICATIONS

In 1963 the number of vessels entering the ports was 993 totalling 1,284,560 gross tons. Nearly all these vessels (934) were Portuguese, totalling 1,040,642 gross tons. The number of planes entering 1963 was 588, all Portuguese. In 1963 roads extended for 323 km. There were, in 1963, two wireless stations. Telephone lines were 210 km. in length.

## EDUCATION

In 1962–63 there were 30 primary schools with 4,952 pupils, a secondary school with some 583 pupils and a small technical school.

# Saudi Arabia

(AL MAMLAKA AL ARABIYA AL-SAUDIYA)

**Capitals**—Mecca and Riyadh.

**Sovereign**—King Khalid Ibn Abdul Aziz Al Sa'ud.

**National Flag**: Green, bearing in white the Arabic inscription 'La ilaha illa Allah Muhammad rasul Allah' (There is no god but God, and Mohammed is his Prophet) over a white sword.

## CONSTITUTION AND GOVERNMENT

SAUDI ARABIA consists of the central plateau of Nejd, Al Ahassa and the coastal strips of Asir and the Hejaz on the Red Sea. It covers the greater part of the Arabian peninsula and its western coastline extends some 1,000 miles down the Red Sea to the boundaries of the Yemen. It was conquered by Ibn Saud, father of the present ruler, in the years between 1913 and 1926. Great Britain recognized the independence of the kingdom in 1927.

The name 'Saudi Arabia' was given to it by Ibn Saud in 1932, when he proposed to form a constitution covering the whole area. The only constitution as yet in force, however, is that issued for the Hejaz in 1926. In its present form it provides for a Central Council of Ministers, a consultative Legislative Assembly for Mecca, municipal councils for Mecca, Jeddah and Medina, and tribal councils elsewhere.

Ministers and council members are appointed by the King, who is also the religious leader of the people.

Mecca is the religious capital of Saudi Arabia and the Islamic religion, and Riyadh is the seat of government. There are no political parties in the country.

**Reigning Royal Families.** Moslem. This dynasty is descended from Muhammed Ibn Saud (died 1766), Emir of Daraiyya, who was proclaimed Imam and Protector of Islam. After many vicissitudes, the Emir Abdul Aziz re-established the authority of Al-Saud in Nejd and its dependencies, eventually as a separate kingdom; he proclaimed himself Sultan of Nejd 1917, King of the Hedjaz 8 January 1926, King of Nejd 4 January 1927 and King of Saudi Arabia 18–22 September 1932.

**H.M. KHALID ibn Abdul Aziz AL SAUD**, King of Saudi Arabia, Imam and Protector of the Faith; born at Riyadh, 1913; son of King Abdul Aziz ibn Abdul Rahman Al Feisal Al Saud (born October 1880, died 9 November 1953).

Brothers of the King: 1. Emir MUHAMMED ibn Abdul Aziz ibn Saud; born at Er-Riyadh, 1908; has issue. 2. Emir Fahad ibn Abdul Aziz ibn Saud; born at Er-Riyadh, 1922 has issue.

**Cabinet**

*Prime Minister:* H.M. King Khalid Bin Abdulaziz.
*Deputy Prime Minister:* H.R.H. Prince Fahd Ibn Abdulaziz.
*Second Deputy Premier and Commander of the National Guard:* H.R.H. Prince Abdullah Ibn Abdulaziz.
*Minister of Defence and Aviation:* H.R.H. Prince Sultan Ibn Abdulaziz.
*Minister of Public Works and Housing:* H.R.H. Prince Mutaib Ibn Abdulaziz.
*Minister of Interior:* H.R.H. Prince Naif Ibn Abdulaziz.
*Minister of Municipal and Rural Affairs:* H.R.H. Prince Majed Ibn Abdulaziz.
*Foreign Minister:* H.R.H. Prince Saud Al-Faisal.
*Minister of Higher Education:* Sheikh Hassan Ibn Abdullah Al-Sheikh.
*Minister of Finance and National Economy:* Sheikh Mohamed Abal Khail.
*Minister of Petroleum and Mineral Resources:* Sheikh Ahmed Zaki Yamani.
*Minister of Justice:* Sheikh Ibrahim Al-Sheikh.
*Minister of Transport:* Sheikh Hussein Mansouri.
*Minister of Education:* Dr. Abdulaziz Al-Khuwaiter.
*Minister of Labour and Social Welfare:* Sheikh Ibrahim Al-Ankari.
*Minister of Planning:* Sheikh Hisham Nazer.
*Minister of Haj and Endowment:* Sheikh Abdul Wahab Ahmed Abdul Wasei.
*Minister of Agriculture and Waters:* Dr. Abdulrahman Ibn Abdulaziz Ibn Hassan Al-Sheikh.
*Minister of Information:* Dr. Mohammad Abdu Yamani.
*Minister of Health:* Dr. Hussein Abdul Razak Al-Jazaeri.
*Minister of Trade:* Dr. Suleiman Al-Abdulaziz Al-Saleem.
*Minister of Posts, Telephones and Telecommunications:* Dr. Alawai Darweesh Kayal.
*Minister of Industry and Electricity:* Dr. Ghazi Abdulrahman Al-Qusaibi.
*Minister of State and Cabinet Member:* Sheikh Mohamed Ibrahim Masoud.
*Minister of State and Cabinet Member:* Dr. Abdullah Mohammad Al-Omran.
*Minister of State and Cabinet Member:* Dr. Mohammad Aldulatif Al-Milhem.

## LEGAL SYSTEM

The law of the country is based on the religious law of Islam, and sentences are based on the Koran and the Sunnat of the Prophet Mohammed. There is a Chief Judge who is responsible for the Department of Sharia Affairs. There are three grades of court and a supervisory committee, as follows:

1. Mahkamat Al-Omour Al-Mostaajalah, for dealing with minor misdemeanours and matters concerning the Bedouin tribes.
2. Al-Mahkamat Al-Shaariah Al-Koubra, situated in Mecca, Jeddah and Medina, for the trying of all cases not within the competence of the minor courts.
3. Courts of Appeal, or of Cassation, for the hearing of appeals from courts at 2 above.
4. Judicial Supervisory Committee, consisting of three members and a president appointed by the King. It is situated at Mecca, and supervises the work of the three types of court. A person found guilty of murder or a like offence by a Court of Appeal may appeal to the Committee, which will return the case to the lower court with recommendations, which do not have to be accepted.

*Chief Justice* (Mecca): Sheikh Abdulla Ibn Hassan.

*Chief Justice* (Medina): Abdul Aziz bin Salin.

## AREA AND POPULATION

The total area of the country is said to be 925,000 square miles.

The total population at mid-1974 was 8,008,000. The annual average percentage population growth rate for the periods 1960–74 and 1965–74 was 1·8.

The principal towns with estimated populations are: Mecca, 400,000; Jeddah, 650,000; Medina, 70,000; Riyadh, 700,000; Buraida, 60,000; and Hofuf, 50,000. Most of the population is nomadic, though there is a tendency by some to seek a more settled way of life.

## CURRENCY

The legal monetary unit is the rial, a silver coin containing 0·34 oz. fine. Exchange rate remains fairly steady at about 6·05 rials to the £ sterling, with minor seasonal fluctuations. There are silver coins for ¼, ½ and 1 rial, and a nickel guerch, 20 of which equal 1 rial (or 11 for certain official payments including Customs duties).

There is Official paper currency. The Saudi Arabian Government declares that they are fully backed by a reserve held by the Saudi Arabian Monetary Agency.

There are no exchange control regulations. Foreign banknotes can normally be freely exchanged into Saudi currency. For higher denominations the Saudi gold guinea (the same weight and fineness as the British sovereign) is the official currency although now seldom seen. Most have been withdrawn because of skilful replicas circulating on the market. The genuine Saudi sovereign has a fixed rate of 40 rials (about £7). Export of gold and silver coins without licence is prohibited as well as the import of these coins.

## FINANCE

Budget estimates for 1974 were: Revenue, 211,000,000,000 rials.

The GNP at market prices for 1974 was U.S. $ millions 22,670 and the GNP per capita at market prices for 1974 was U.S. $2,836. The annual average percentage growth rate of the GNP per capita for the period 1960–74 was 8·4 and for the period 1965–74 was 9·2. [*See the note at the beginning of this section concerning GNP.*]

## PRINCIPAL BANKS

**Saudi Arabian Monetary Agency.** Est. 1952. The Statement of Affairs as 31 December 1974 shows gold of the value Rls. 546·5 million, Foreign Exchange holdings Rls. 53,977·7 million, and Investments Rls. 24,431·7 million.

**National Commercial Bank.** Balance Sheet at February 1971 showed capital and reserves, SR. 66,000,000; total assets, SR. 1,660,760,000. *Head Office:* Jeddah.

The following banks have branches in Saudi Arabia: Arab Bank Limited (see Jordan); Banque de l'Indochine S.A. (see France); British Bank of the Middle East (see United Kingdom); First National Bank of Pakistan (see Pakistan); Bank of Cairo; First National City Bank of New York (see U.S.A.); Algemene Bank Nederland, N.V. (see Netherlands); Banque Misr; Banque de Liban et d'Outre Mer.

## PRODUCTION, INDUSTRY AND COMMERCE

**Agriculture.** Owing to the desert nature of the country there is not a great deal of agriculture, although wheat and barley are grown in the Nejd, and there is some export of dates. The main occupation of the people is the raising and export of camels, horses and sheep, with the export of hides and wool. Honey, clarified butter and fruit are also produced. At Al-Kharj, near Riyadh, some 2,000 acres of former desert have been reclaimed by means of irrigation. The total agricultural area is 92,970,000 hectares, of which 210,000 hectares is arable land and the rest pasture.

**Oil.** The oil-wells are situated on the Persian Gulf, and are worked mainly by the Arabian-American Oil Company. In December 1948 the previous ownership of this company was changed to 30 per cent each for Standard Oil of California, Standard Oil of New Jersey and the Texas Company and 10 per cent for Socony Vacuum Oil Company. In 1950, following negotiations, it was agreed that the Saudi Arabian Government and the Arabian-American Oil Company should share profits equally after deduction of operating expenses; but since 1952, before deduction of foreign, including U.S., income tax, a royalty is also paid.

The Ghawar field, which is the world's largest oilfield, is believed to hold at least as much as all the known U.S. reserves, about 28,000 million barrels. Another fifth of the total comes from the Safaniya field, the world's largest offshore field. Oil from these and other fields is piped through either the Trans-Arabian Pipeline Company's pipeline to the Mediterranean, where it is refined, or through a shorter pipeline to Bahrain, from where it is shipped either as crude or refined petroleum.

Other oil companies operating in Saudi Arabia include the Getty Oil Company, and the Arabian Oil Company, a joint Saudi-Japanese company.

Proven oil reserves in the whole country amount to about 30 per cent (approximately 100,000,000 barrels) of the world's total, which places Saudi Arabia second only to Kuwait in this respect.

Exploitation of natural gas resources has not progressed much. Apart from being used in large quantities for the repressurization of the oilfields, the difficulties and high cost of transportation make its further use at the moment impracticable.

**Commerce.** The chief imports are piece goods, motor vehicles machinery and electrical goods, and building materials especially cement and mild steel bars, and cereals, tea, sugar and rice. Oil makes up over 99 per cent of Saudi Arabia's exports.

## COMMUNICATIONS

**Roads and Railways.** The metalled roads in the country are the 45-mile stretch connecting Mecca with Jeddah and the recently completed roads between Jeddah and Medina, 450 km.; Mecca and Taïf, 75 km. There are numerous unmetalled roads and tracks which can be used by motor vehicles, such as the 829 miles of road between Mecca and Dhahran. Although there are a large number of buses and taxicabs the caravan is still a means of transport.

There is a main line railway running from Dammam, a port on the Persian Gulf, via Dhahran, Abqaiq, Hofuf, Haradh, El Kharj, to Riyadh, the capital. It is a journey of 357 miles and takes six hours.

**Shipping.** Jeddah is the main port of the Hejaz, both for commercial purposes and for the transport of pilgrims to Mecca, and services to India are operated by the Turner and Morris Steamship Co. There are also frequent services to Egypt by the Khedivial Steamship Co. Other ports are Yenbo Rabigh and El Wejh Jizan on the west and Dammam and Al-Khobar on the east coast.

The Arabian-American Oil Company has its main Persian Gulf port at Ras Tanura. The Company uses its own fleet of tankers to carry about 40 per cent of the oil exports.

**Civil Aviation.** In addition to the facilities offered by the Saudi Arabian Airlines services are operated by the following international airline companies: Aden Airways Arab Airways, Misrair, Air Liban, Ethiopian Airlines and Air France, K.L.M., B.O.A.C. and Middle East Airways also operate services to Dhahran airport.

**Saudi Arabian Airlines;** *services operated:* Algiers – Amman – Asmara –Baghdad – Bahrain – Beirut –Bombay –Cairo – Casablanca – Damascus – Doha – Dubai – Frankfurt – Geneva – Hodaida – Istanbul – Karachi – Khartoum – Kuwait – London – Oman – Paris – Port Sudan – Rome – Sanaa – Shiaz – Tripoli – Tunis – Jeddah. *Head Office:*

## SAUDI ARABIA

Saudia Building, P.O. Box 620, Jeddah. London office: 171 Regent Street, W.1.

**Broadcasting.** The Saudi Arabian Broadcasting System Mecca, operates several medium- and short-wave stations and broadcasts programmes in Arabic, English, French, Urdu, Indonesian, and Swahili languages. Wireless licences are not issued, but it is estimated that there are some 100,000 receiving sets in the country.

There are six television stations, located at Jeddah, Riyadh, Medina, Kassim, Dammam, and Abha.

### NEWSPAPERS

**Al Bilad.** Djeddah. Daily.

**Al Nadwa.** Mecca. Daily.

**Okaz.** Arabic Independent. F. 1960. Editor: Ali Hussein Shabakshy. Circulation 207,000. *Address:* Al Mina Street, Jeddah, Saudi Arabia.

**Al Medina.** Jeddah. Daily.

**Al Riyad.** Riyal. Daily.

### EDUCATION AND RELIGION

In 1954, the Ministry of Education initiated a school building programme, and the number of elementary schools has now been substantially increased. In 1959 a five year education plan was brought into operation. Since the formation of the Ministry of Education in 1954, expenditure on education has risen from just under SR 13 million to SR 196,500,000 in 1963. In 1963 there were 138,000 pupils in primary schools, about three times as many as in 1954. There were 13,000 pupils in intermediate schools, and 800 graduates from secondary schools. The education of girls is receiving more attention than previously, and in 1963 there were 30,000 girls in primary and secondary schools. Education at all levels is free. Approximately 1,000 students were engaged in further education abroad, about half of these in the United Arab Republic. There were 300 students at the Riyadh University, which has faculties of arts, science, commerce and pharmacy. There is also a college of engineering in Riyadh and a recently founded institute of public administration. In the future increasing emphasis will be given to technical and commercial schools, and the project for a new university at Jeddah is being actively pursued. There are several colleges at Mecca for the study of Islamic law and religion, and there is an Islamic University at Medina.

The religion practised is Islamic.

# Senegal

(MEMBER OF FRENCH COMMUNITY)

**Capital**—Dakar.

**President**—M. Léopold Sédar Senghor.

**Flag:** On a tricolour pale-wise, green, yellow, red, a star of the first five-pointed on the yellow centred.

### CONSTITUTION AND GOVERNMENT

THE former French West Africa now consists of a group of eight republics as follows: Mali (formerly Senegal and Sudan), The Ivory Coast, Upper Volta, Niger, Dahomey, Togoland and The Islamic Republic of Mauritania. Of these, Senegal and Sudan were first federated as the Mali Federation; but following a state of emergency proclaimed at the end of August 1960, the Legislative Assembly of Senegal met and decided to withdraw from the Federation. The leaders were invited to Paris to discuss the situation. Sudan is now The Republic of Mali.

The national sovereignty rests with the People who exercise their will through their representatives or by referendum. No section of the people nor any individual person may take on the sovereignty. All Senegalese nationals, of both sexes, who are of age and in possession of their civil and political rights may vote under the conditions laid down by the law.

**Ministry as at 26 March 1975.**

*Prime Minister:* Abdou Diouf.
*Minister of State in charge of relations with the Assembly:* Magatte Lô.
*Minister of State in charge of Home Affairs:* Jean Collin.
*Minister of State in charge of Finance and Economic Affairs:* Babacar Ba.
*Minister of State in charge of National Education:* Doudou N'Gom.
*Minister of Foreign Affairs:* Assane Seck.
*Keeper of the Seals, Minister of Justice:* A. Badara M'Bengue.
*Minister for the Armed Forces:* Amadou Clédor Sall.
*Minister of Rural Development and Hydraulics:* Adrien Senghor.
*Minister of Higher Education:* Ousmane Camara.
*Minister of Industrial Development and the Environment:* Louis Alexandrenne.
*Minister of the Plan and Cooperation:* Ousmane Seck.
*Minister for Public Works, Urbanism, and Transport:* Mamadou Diop.
*Minister of Culture:* Alioune Sène.
*Minister of Information and Telecommunications:* Daouda Sow.
*Minister of Public Health and Social Affairs:* Matar N'Diaye.
*Minister of Public Offices, Labour and Employment:* Amadou Ly.
*Minister of Youth and Sports:* Joseph Mathiam.
*Secretary to the Prime Minister in charge o the 'Promotion Humaine':* Ben Mady Cissé.

**Officers of the National Assembly**

*President:* Amadou Cissé Dia.
*Vice-Presidents:* Samba Gueye, Etienne Carvalho, Kabirou M'Bodj, Mme. Caroline Diop, Lamine Lô, Amadou Bouta Gueye.
*Secretaries:* Moussa M'Bengue, Moustapha Diouf.
*Questors:* Abdoul N'Diaye, Alioune Palla M'Baye.
*Doyen:* Pierre Senghor.

**The Economic and Social Council**

*President:* Amadou Karim Gaye.
*Vice-Presidents:* Paul Bonifay, Bassirou Gueye.
*Secretaries:* Idrissa Seydi, Mouhamadou Doudou N'daw.

### LEGAL SYSTEM

The Supreme Court decides constitutional questions and international obligations as well as disputes between the Executive and the Legislative bodies. It deals with abuse of power by the Executive. The Supreme Court is also a Probate Court and a Court of Appeal.

The Presidents of the various sections of the Supreme Court are given in the list below:

*1st President:* Mr. Kéba M'Baye.
*1st Section:*
*President:* Laïty Niang.
*Public Prosecutor:* Mme Kane.
*2nd Section*
*President:* Chéramy Bruno.
*3rd Section:*
*President:* Mendoumbé Sarr.
*Public Prosecutors:* Amadou Moctar Samb, Mamadou Sall.
*Clerk of the Court:* Mr. Salmone Fall.
*Public Prosecutors Office:*
*Attorney General:* Ousmane Goundiam.

### AREA AND POPULATION

The total area of the Republic is 197,161 sq. km.

The mid-1974 population of Senegal was 4,869,000, of whom there are about 50,000 non-Africans residing chiefly in Dakar. The average density of the population for the country as a whole is 19·5 inhabitants to the square kilometre.

The urban population represents about 30 per cent of the whole population. The annual average percentage population growth rate for the period 1960–74 was 2·6, and for the period 1965–74 was 2·7.

The principal towns are: Dakar, the capital, with about 600,000 inhabitants (its population is increasing at the rate of 7 per cent per annum because of a large migratory population); Kaolack with 96,000 inhabitants; Thiès with 91,000 inhabitants; Saint-Louis with 81,000 inhabitants; Ziguinchor with 46,000 inhabitants; Diourbel with 39,000 inhabitants and Tambacounda with 22,000 inhabitants.

The largest ethnic groups are the Wolof, Peul, Tukulor, Serer, Diola, etc.

## CURRENCY

Senegal belongs to the West African Monetary Union. The Central Bank of the West African States is the issuing Bank for this monetary union.

The currency of the West African Monetary Union is the C.F.A. Franc. 'C.F.A.' is an abbreviation for African Financial Community. Money and bills between the West African Monetary Union and France are freely transferable and for unlimited amounts.

The GNP at market prices for 1974 was U.S. $ millions 1,590, and the GNP per capita at market prices was U.S. $330. The annual average percentage growth rate of the GNP per capita for the period 1960–74 was −1·1, and for the period 1965–74 was −0·9. [*See the note at the beginning of this section concerning GNP.*]

## PRODUCTION, INDUSTRY AND COMMERCE

There are substantial resources in livestock, groundnuts, millet, maize and rice. Titanium concentrates and cement are produced.

The following table gives some information on agricultural production for the years 1970–71 and 1971–72:

| *Product* | *Metric Tons* 1970–71 | 1971–72[2] |
|---|---|---|
| Groundnuts[1] | 583,000 | 917,500 |
| Millet and Sorgho | 400,876 | 601,735 |
| Niebes | 17,777 | 21,875 |
| Rice | 90,545 | 101,700 |
| Maize | 38,746 | — |
| Manioc | 133,100 | — |
| Potato | 9,718 | — |
| Cotton | 11,610 | 18,318 |

[1] Edible groundnuts excluded.
[2] Provisional figures.

The following tables show the value of imports and exports for 1970 and 1971:

| | 1970 *Thousand tons* | 1970 *billion C.F.A. francs* | 1971 *Thousand tons* | 1971 *billion C.F.A. francs* |
|---|---|---|---|---|
| *Imports* | 1,177 | 53·6 | 1,358 | 60·56 |
| *Exports* | 1,888 | 42·2 | 2,003 | 34·7 |
| *Trading deficit* | | 11·4 | | 25·86 |

| | 1970 | 1971 |
|---|---|---|
| *Value of exports compared with imports* | 79% | 57% |

The following table gives figures for livestock for the year 1974:

| *Description* | 1974 |
|---|---|
| Cattle | 2,670,000 |
| Sheep | 1,930,000 |
| Goats | 875,000 |
| Pigs | 175,000 |
| Horses | 205,000 |
| Donkeys | 190,000 |
| Camels | 7,000 |
| Poultry | 5,300,000 |

The following shows the provisional production figures in metric tons of certain agricultural products for the years 1972–73 and 1973–74:

| *Product* | 1972–73 | 1973–74 |
|---|---|---|
| Groundnuts | 550,000 | 900,000 |
| Millet and Sorghum | 322,000 | 700,000 |
| Niebes | — | 26,000 |
| Rice | 49,000 | 110,000 |
| Maize | 39,000 | 60,000 |
| Cotton | 23,500 | 35,000 |

## COMMUNICATIONS

### Roads

Senegal has the best road network in West Africa. There are 2,243 km of paved bituminous roads, 643 km of laterite roads ready for covering with bitumen, and 5,200 km of unpaved roads accessible in all seasons and numerous tracks. This situation was the result of the application of a programme included in the first Four-Year Plan. In 1960, there were only 765 km of paved bituminous roads over nearly 10,000 km of tracks of all types which were mostly unusable in the rainy season. The Second Plan provided for the construction of 855 km of bituminous roads for an investment of nearly 6 billion C.F.A. Francs. The second plan proceeded with the objectives of the first plan. In 1969 the roads network comprised: 2,043 km of paved bituminous roads, 643 km of laterite roads ready for covering with bitumen, and 5,200 km of tracks accessible under all weather conditions. These investments total 3·5 billion C.F.A. Francs. The Third Plan, now in progress, aims at bringing the road network of Senegal to: 2,646 km of paved bituminous roads, 866 km of laterite roads, and 4,800 km of accessible tracks. The cost of these investments amounts to 7 billion 800 million C.F.A. Francs. At 1 January 1972 200 km of paved bituminous roads had been constructed under this plan which brings the total of roads covered with bitumen to 2,243 km.

### Railways

The railway network of the Senegal Railway has, at 1 January 1972, 1,186 km of railroad, consisting of: 1,034 km of main-lines, and 152 km of branch-lines (sidings, etc.). The main-lines comprise: 70 km two way line between Dakar and Thiès, and 964 km single track lines. The equipment includes: 32 main line locomotives, 13 rail-cars, 94 passenger-cars, and 1,100 goods wagons and sundries of which 144 are special wagons for transporting phosphates. The railways network extends towards Mali up to Bamako and crosses the frontier at Kidira. The annual budget of the railways is 3 billion C.F.A. francs.

### Civil Aviation

Senegal is linked by air to all the countries in the world. Dakar–Yoff international airport is regularly served by the large airline companies.

Senegal forms part of the international company AIR AFRIQUE which was founded by the Treaty of Yaoundé in 1961 with twelve African states and France.

This airline company's development means that Senegal and the other African states have direct traffic with Europe and America by means of a modern fleet of aircraft.

Senegal also operates internal services regularly between Dakar and twelve airports serving the principal towns and tourist centres of Senegal, the services are operated by SONATRA (Société Nationale des Transports Aériens).

The technical installations, regularity and safety of flights in each of the territories are, according to an agreement signed at Saint-Louis in 1959 by Senegal and other member countries, under the management and control of ASECNA (Agency for the Safety of Aerial Navigation in Africa and Malagasy) whose offices are situated in Dakar.

The major work planned in the Third Plan and now in course of execution represents 1 billion 318 million C.F.A. Francs.

The airport of Dakar–Yoff was one of the first to receive the supersonic airliner 'Concorde' in 1971, the landing and take-off were possible because of the high quality of the airport's technical installations.

The following table shows arrivals and departures of goods and passengers for the years 1970 and 1971 at the Dakar-Yoff airport.

| | 1970 | 1971 |
|---|---|---|
| Movement of commercial aircraft | 12,962 | 4,508 |
| Number of passengers: | | |
| Arrivals | 92,624 | 23,899 |
| Departures | 94,851 | 24,882 |
| Transit (A + D) | 134,315 | 29,568 |
| Total freight (in tons) | 5,877·2 | 1,683·5 |
| Arrivals | 2,320·4 | 679 |
| Departures | 3,556·8 | 1,104·5 |
| Post and other items | 782·5 | 219·3 |

The technical installations and substructure of the airport of Dakar–Yoff are currently being improved with a view to adapting them to the needs of modern aviation.

## EDUCATION

For the year 1971–1972 the Ministry of Education's budget stands at 6,675,000,000 CFA Francs.

The ever increasing number of children of school age is a problem in providing sufficient premises and teaching personnel. The quality of the teaching personnel in primary schools has, however, been improved owing to the qualifications now required (school certificate, teaching diploma, etc.)

### Primary School Education

In 1970–1971 there were 266,383 children attending school, as against 257,708 in the preceding year, of whom 101,451 were girls.

More than 86 per cent of the education budget is spent on public education.

In the year 1970–1971, there were 5,722 teachers, of whom 902 were ordinary teachers, 3,416 assistant teachers and 1,404 supervisors.

In 1972, the number of teachers rose to 6,500. The rate of school attendance remains at about 40 per cent for the whole country, though in the Cape Verde region it is more than 75 per cent.

In 1971, out of 35,961 pupils who sat for the examinations, 21,030 passed the Primary School Certificate. 7,778 pupils (25·6 per cent girls), were admitted to secondary schools, out of 44,315 candidates (in the previous year 7,463 pupils were admitted).

### Secondary Education

In 1970, there were 48,905 pupils (13,376 girls) in secondary schools. There were 621 students (of whom 197 girls) at teacher's training colleges.

In 1971, in the Higher School Certificate, out of 9,191 students 5,766 passed (of whom 2,743 automatically passed without having to take the oral) as against 9,734 candidates and 6,696 passes in 1970.

In the matriculation examinations, out of 2,391 candidates 1,289 passed as against 2,086 candidates and 1,085 passes in 1970.

### Further Education

In 1970–71, 4,092 students including 742 girls registered as students at Dakar University as against 3,054, including 598 girls, in the preceding year. For 1971–1972 there are 4,690 (including 886 girls) students registered.

## RELIGION

The main religions are Islam and Christianity.

# Republic of Seychelles

(MEMBER OF THE COMMONWEALTH)

**Capital**—Victoria.

**President**—Mr. France Albert René.

**Constitution and Government.** Seychelles became an independent republic on 29 June, 1976, and subsequently joined OCAM, the Lomé Convention and the Commonwealth. On 5 June, 1977, there was a *coup d'état*, after which Mr. France Albert René assumed presidential powers and suspended the constitution. At the same time, he announced that the laws of the country would remain unchanged except when altered by presidential decree; and that all international agreements and conventions to which the Republic had become party would be honoured. The National Assembly was suspended *sine die* and the Cabinet dissolved. In its place, the President appointed a smaller number of Ministers to administer specific portfolios. The Seychelles (Constitution) Proclamation, published on 28 June, 1977, requires the President as soon as possible to set up a Constitutional Council, headed by an international expert on constitutional law and comprising members drawn from the various sections of the Seychelles community, to ascertain the wishes of the people about what sort of a constitution they want and thereafter to make proposals for a constitution that will as far as possible include and take into account the wishes of the people, and give effect to their aspirations.

**Ministers**

*The President:* Mr. France Albert René.
*Minister of Foreign Affairs, Tourism and Civil Aviation:* Mr. Guy Sinon.
*Minister of Labour, Health and Welfare:* Mr. Matthew Servina.
*Minister of Works and Port:* Mr. Philibert Loizeau.
*Minister of Agriculture:* Dr. Maxime Ferrari, OBE.
*Minister of Education and Culture:* Mr. Jacques Hodoul.
*Minister of State in the President's Office for Internal Affairs:* Mr. Ogilvy Berlouis.
*Minister of State in the President's Office for Administration and Information:* Mr. James Michel.

(N.B. The functions of the Minister of Finance are performed by the President.)

## LEGAL SYSTEM

There is a Supreme Court and a Court of Appeal for Seychelles for both criminal and civil matters, with no right of appeal to the Judicial Committee of the Privy Council. The President appoints the Chief Justice and the President of the Court of Appeal and appoints the other judges in consultation with the Chief Justice. Judges may be removed for misbehaviour or incompetence on the advice of a special tribunal (the members of which shall hold, or shall have held, high judicial office); and for mental or physical incapacity on the advice of a panel of three medical doctors.

## AREA AND POPULATION

The total area of the Seychelles is 171·4 square miles. This figure includes the former British Indian Ocean Territories that were returned to the Seychelles on 29 June 1976.

The total population of the Seychelles at mid-1974 was 56,000. The annual average percentage growth rate of the population for the period 1960–74 was 2·1 and for the period 1965–74 was 2·0.

## FINANCE

The GNP at market prices for 1974 was U.S. $30,000,000 and the GNP per capita at market prices for 1974 was U.S. $520. The annual average percentage growth rate of the GNP per capita for the period 1960–74 was 2·6 and for the period 1965–74 was 3·7. [*See note at the beginning of this section concerning GNP.*]

## PRODUCTION, INDUSTRY AND COMMERCE

The following tables give some information on imports and exports:

*Exports*

| | *FOB Value (Rs. '000)* | | | *Percentages* | | |
|---|---|---|---|---|---|---|
| *Country* | 1974 | 1975 | 1976 | 1974 | 1975 | 1976 |
| Greece | — | — | 1,250 | — | — | 7 |
| Holland | 954 | 457 | 790 | 5 | 4 | 4 |
| Mauritius | 589 | 1,115 | 1,798 | 3 | 9 | 10 |
| Pakistan | 4,993 | 7,251 | 8,473 | 27 | 55 | 48 |
| Reunion | 266 | 480 | 2,121 | 1 | 4 | 12 |
| U.K. | 648 | 645 | 607 | 3 | 5 | 3 |
| U.S.A. | 4,032 | 1,575 | 1,567 | 22 | 12 | 9 |
| Others | 7,239 | 1,380 | 1,334 | 39 | 11 | 7 |
| Total | 18,721 | 12,903 | 17,940 | 100 | 100 | 100 |

*Imports*

| | *CIF Value (Rs. '000)* | | | *Percentages* | | |
|---|---|---|---|---|---|---|
| *Country* | 1974 | 1975 | 1976 | 1974 | 1975 | 1976 |
| Australia | 7,252 | 15,121 | 15,107 | 5 | 8 | 5 |
| Japan | 6,348 | 10,254 | 15,545 | 4 | 6 | 6 |
| Kenya | 32,395 | 37,267 | 46,408 | 20 | 19 | 16 |
| Singapore | 8,444 | 8,318 | 15,363 | 5 | 5 | 5 |
| South Africa | 15,851 | 14,642 | 20,916 | 10 | 8 | 7 |
| U.K. | 46,608 | 52,574 | 86,436 | 28 | 27 | 30 |
| U.S.A. | 5,718 | 6,400 | 11,666 | 4 | 3 | 4 |
| Yemen | — | 4,289 | 20,000 | — | 2 | 7 |
| Others | 37,878 | 42,489 | 59,181 | 24 | 22 | 20 |
| Total | 160,494 | 191,354 | 290,622 | 100 | 100 | 100 |

### COMMUNICATIONS

**Roads.** There is a total of 132·9 miles of roads, of which 89·9 miles are surfaced, and 43 miles are unsurfaced.

**Civil Aviation.** The following table gives some air Traffic figures for 1973–76:

| *Air Traffic* | 1973 | 1974 | 1975 | 1976 |
|---|---|---|---|---|
| *International* | | | | |
| Aircraft movements | 1,198 | 1,324 | 1,594 | 2,119 |
| Passengers off '000 | 25 | 30 | 40 | 54 |
| Passengers on '000 | 25 | 29 | 39 | 53 |
| Passengers in transit '000 | 32 | 34 | 33 | 41 |
| Freight off (mt) | 394 | 365 | 476 | 656 |
| Freight on (mt) | 69 | 100 | 120 | 177 |
| *Domestic* | | | | |
| Total passengers | 14,653 | 19,491 | 24,876 | 39,660 |
| of which visitors | 10,586 | 15,195 | 19,030 | 30,747 |

**Shipping.** The following table shows the number and type of ships calling at the main port, Port Victoria, for the years 1970–75:

| *Ships Calling* | 1970 | 1971 | 1972 | 1973 | 1974 | 1975 |
|---|---|---|---|---|---|---|
| General cargo | 123 | 121 | 120 | 103 | 76 | 96 |
| Bulk cargo | 35 | 30 | 33 | 33 | 26 | 30 |
| Naval vessels | 17 | 31 | 31 | 32 | 24 | 29 |
| R.F.A.(1) | 26 | 27 | 10 | 14 | 4 | 11 |
| Fishing | 112 | 72 | 73 | 47 | 43 | 56 |
| Research | 3 | 4 | 4 | 3 | — | 6 |
| Cruise ships | 18 | 20 | 8 | 10 | 6 | 9 |
| Yachts | 15 | 20 | 31 | 32 | 33 | 50 |
| Other | 9 | 15 | 14 | 19 | 11 | 15 |
| Total | 358 | 340 | 324 | 293 | 223 | 302 |

### EDUCATION

*Primary Education:* Primary Schooling is of six years' duration from the age of six. The main entry is in January at the beginning of the school year. English is the medium of secular (as distinguished from religious) instruction in all schools. The teaching of French begins in the fourth year in all Government and aided schools.

*Secondary Education:* Of the 1,655 children who completed primary schooling in 1975, 195 or 11·8 per cent proceeded to the two grammar schools, and 1,313 or 79·3 per cent entered a two-year course in the 13 junior secondary schools.

*Higher Education:* University entrance and higher professional training are available through the United Kingdom's Technical Assistance Programme, Commonwealth Scholarships and French Government Scholarships.

# Republic of Sierra Leone

(MEMBER OF THE COMMONWEALTH)

**Capital**—Freetown.

**President**—Dr. Siaka Stevens.

**Vice-President and Minister of State Enterprises**—Hon. S. I. Koroma.

**National Flag:** Parti of three fesse-wise green, white and blue.

### CONSTITUTION AND GOVERNMENT

THE colony originated in 1780 by the sale and cession of a portion of land by 'King' Naimbana and his subordinate chiefs to Captain John Taylor of His Britannic Majesty's brig 'Miro' for the purpose of securing a home on the African continent for a number of natives who, from circumstances, had been separated from their countries of origin and were destitute in and about London. The territory was added to from time to time by various concessions from native chiefs. On 21 August 1896 a proclamation was issued declaring a protectorate over the hinterland of Sierra Leone and ordinances were passed providing for the administration of this Protectorate.

The Colony and Protectorate was governed, under the provisions of the 1956 Constitution, by an Executive Council, over which the Governor presided. Under the Constitution of 14 August 1958, there was a House of Representatives consisting of 15 elected and two nominated members. 14 elected members were from the Colony, 24 from the Protectorate and one from the Bo region.

Under the interim Constitution of 1960 the Executive Council became the Cabinet over which the Prime Minister presided. On 27 April 1961 Sierra Leone became an independent sovereign state taking her place as a member of the British Commonwealth of Nations. Under the 1961 Constitution Her Majesty the Queen's representative was the Governor-General.

On 21 March 1967 the army assumed control of the government. On 23 March, a counter-coup by senior army officers and the police led to the formation of the National Reformation Council which suspended the Parliament and the offices of Governor-General and of Prime Minister.

Full Civilian Rule was restored in April 1968. In April 1971 the country attained Republican status, and Dr. Siaka Stevens who was then Prime Minister was appointed Executive President. At the end of his first five years in office in April 1976, he was re-elected for a second term.

The Sierra Leone Parliament presently consists of 12 paramount Chiefs representing the 12 Districts in the Provinces, 85 elected members and three members appointed by the President, who has powers to appoint up to seven.

*Vice-President and Minister of State Enterprises.* Hon. S. I. Koroma.
*Prime Minister and Minister of Housing and Country Planning:* Hon. C. A. Kamara-Taylor.
*Minister of Finance:* Hon. A. B. Kamara.
*Attorney-General:* Hon. F. M. Minah.
*Minister of Foreign Affairs:* Hon. Dr. Abdul Conteh.
*Minister of Development and Economy Planning:* Hon. S. A. J. Pratt.
*Minister of Agriculture and Natural Resources:* Hon. Bangali Mansaray.
*Minister of Trade Industry:* Hon. Dr. I. M. Fofanah.
*Minister of Transport and Communications:* Hon. A. B. M. Kamara.
*Minister of Education:* Hon. Abdul Karim Koroma.
*Minister of Interior:* Hon. K. C. Gbmanja.
*Minister of Health:* Hon. Desmond Luke.
*Minister of Works:* Hon. E. J. Kargbo.
*Minister of Information and Broadcasting:* Hon. Thaimu Bangura.
*Minister of Lands and Mines:* Hon. F. S. Conteh.
*Minister of Tourism and Cultural Affairs:* Hon. A. G. Sembu Forna.
*Minister of Social Welfare and Rural Development:* Hon. S. H. O. Gborie.
*Minister of Labour:* Hon. Formeh Kamara.
*Minister of Energy and Power:* Hon. S. B. Marah.
*Minister of State and Leader of the House:* Hon. Tom Smith.
*Resident Minister, Eastern Province:* Hon. A. G. Lappia.
*Resident Minister, Southern Province:* Hon. A. J. Sandy.
*Resident Minister, Northern Province:* Hon. J. A. Conteh.
*Minister of State:* Hon. Paramount Chief Dr. Jaia Kai Kai.
*Minister of State:* Hon. Paramount Chief Bai Kurr Kanasaky III.
*Minister of State:* Hon. Paramount Chief S. S. Mbriwa.
*Force Commander and Minister of State:* Hon. J. S. Momoh.
*Commissioner of Police and Minister of State:* Hon. P. C. Kaetu-Smith.

### AREA AND POPULATION

Sierra Leone covers an area of some 27,925 square miles. The population at mid-1974 was 2,911,000. The annual average percentage growth rate of the population for the period 1960–74 was 2·2 and for the period 1965–74 was 2·3.

For administrative purposes the country is divided into two units: (a) the Western Area, and (b) the Provinces. There are three provinces administered by Provincial Secretaries. The three provinces cover 12 districts which are administered by District Officers.

## CURRENCY AND FINANCE

In August 1964, a new decimal currency system was introduced. The Sierra Leone currency will be freely convertible into other currencies in the same way as the present West African currency. It is exchanged against sterling on demand. Paper currency 50 cents, 1, 2 and 5 Leone notes have been introduced. 1 Leone is worth 50p. As to coinage there are 1 c., 5 c., 10 c., 20 c. and 50 c. coins. As for conversion, 20 cents are the same as the present 10p, 10 cents will be 5p.

The estimated revenue for the year 1977–78 amounts to Le. 143·69 million, and total current expenditure is budgeted at Le. 105·5 million which include public debts charges of Le. 34·1 million.

The GNP at market prices for 1974 was U.S. $ millions 540, and the GNP per capita at market prices was U.S. $190. The annual average percentage growth rate of the GNP per capita for the period 1960–74 was 1·6, and for the period 1964–74 was 1·4. [*See the note at the beginning of this section concerning GNP.*]

## PRODUCTION, INDUSTRY AND COMMERCE

In the Western Area farming is largely confined to the production of cassava and garden crops, such as maize and vegetables for local consumption. In the Provincial Area the principal agricultural products include rice, which is the staple food of the country, and export crops such as palm kernels, cocoa beans, coffee and kola nuts.

The U.K. is Sierra Leone's most important trade partner. Imports from the U.K. in 1969 were valued at Le. 27,148,000 and were valued at Le. 12,770,000 in the first half of 1970. Exports to the United Kingdom were worth Le. 72,330,000 in 1969 and in the first half of 1970 were valued at Le. 42,020,000.

The total Import and Export duty figures for the period April to June 1972 were respectively Le. 92,137,952 and Le. 6,146,626.

Most important exports are cocoa, coffee, diamonds, kola nuts, palm kernels and piassava.

The following table gives the value in Le of imports by Principal Countries for the period April to June 1972:

| | *Imports* | *Domestic Exports* |
|---|---|---|
| **Sterling Area:** | | |
| United Kingdom | 5,947,329 | 8,842,203 |
| Hong Kong | 6,666,352 | 300 |
| India | 274,500 | — |
| Malawi | 210,880 | — |
| Trinidad | 182 | — |
| Other Countries | 28,705 | 24,677 |
| Total Sterling Area | 13,127,948 | 8,867,180 |
| **Non-Sterling Area:** | | |
| Belgium | 266,434 | 24,677 |
| Canada | 32,986 | 398,157 |
| China | 32,574 | 300 |
| Czechoslovakia | 505,731 | — |
| Denmark | 544,001 | 170,108 |
| Eire | 9,103 | — |
| France | 1,329,240 | 3,300 |
| German Federal Republic | 1,300,829 | 834,931 |
| Germany, East | 291,723 | — |
| Italy | 496,657 | — |
| Japan | 1,972,072 | 1,378,246 |
| Netherlands | 788,879 | 1,365,706 |
| Netherlands, West Indies | 502,445 | — |
| Sweden | 84,848 | — |
| Switzerland | 1,197,259 | 1,012,142 |
| U.S.A. | 1,345,234 | 1,923,468 |
| Venezuela | — | — |
| Other Countries | 35,238 | 329,019 |
| Total Non-Sterling Area | 9,735,253 | 7,440,054 |
| Ship's Stores | 329,019 | 17,212 |
| Total Domestic Exports | — | 16,324,446 |
| Re-Exports | — | — |
| **Total Imports/Exports** | 23,192,220 | 16,324,446 |

## COMMUNICATIONS

The phasing out of the railway has accentuated the demand for highway transport. The network of modern roads has considerably expanded in the last four years during which several highway projects were completed. These include the Bauya-Yonibana Road (37 miles costing Le. 0·93 million as it was gravel surfaced (Laterite) and not paved), Makeni-Matotoka Road (22 miles, costing Le. 5·22 million), Bo-Tajama Road (32 miles, costing Le. 7·08 million), Congo Cross Bridge and approaches (costing Le. 1·15 million).

Of particular benefit to land transport operators is the substantial completion and opening to traffic at the end of 1976–77 of the 16·5 miles rural section of the Freetown-Waterloo Road. The completion of this major highway project with financial assistance from West Germany represents 7·5 per cent of the target of 216 miles of improvement of primary and secondary roads as foreseen in the National Development Plan.

The 42-miles long Bo-Kenema Road has been completed and opened to traffic.

By the end of 1976–77, therefore, 29 per cent of the plan's target for primary roads would have been achieved.

Two major bridges, Mange bridge along the main highway to the neighbouring country of Guinea and Mano River across the river to Liberia were completed in 1975–76 while a third major bridge (Kambia) is under construction. These three bridges represent 75 per cent of the plan's target for major bridges and have replaced the ferries previously used by vehicles at river crossings.

In feeder road construction, the Co-operative for American Relief Everywhere (CARE) completed 100 miles in 1975–76 and 124 miles in 1976–77. These feeder roads of higher standards, if added to the 297 miles of lower standard penetration roads constructed or improved by CARE in 1974–75, give a total accomplishment of 80 per cent of the plan's target of 650 miles of feeder roads.

Since 1974 maintenance of all roads in Sierra Leone became the responsibility of the Ministry of Works.

The total length of roads up to date is 4,406 miles. About 665 miles are surfaced with bitumen (Paved) and the remainder are earth or gravel surfaced (laterite).

Total investment in the Transport and Communications Sector was Le. 15·4 million in 1976–77 representing a fall of 14·9 per cent, compared to Le. 19·5 million in 1975–76. In 1977–78, total investment is expected to reach Le. 15.5 million. Important projects in this sector include the rural sector of the Freetown-Waterloo road and the Makeni-Kabala road.

The Port of Freetown, which is one of the world's finest natural harbours, has a berth solid wall quay served by portal and mobile cranes and other mechanical handling equipment. Master porterage is in operation through three transit sheds. Water and oil bunkering is also available. Since the completion of the extension of the Queen Elizabeth The Second Quay at the end of 1969, four additional ships can now be accommodated at the same time in addition to existing facilities which accommodate two ships at a time.

The quay extension is 2,325 ft. long; depth of water at low tide at the quay side is 33 ft. Nine miles of tubular piles and 69 miles of sheet piles were sunk. Dredging amounted to 802,000 cubic yards sand-fill to 2,493,000. There are two additional sheds of 53,200 sq. ft. Regular mail vessel services to and from the United Kingdom are available and an increasing number of cargo vessels of several lines give a service between Freetown, the United Kingdom, the continent, North America, South Africa India and the Far East.

**Civil Aviation.** The following international airlines operate scheduled services through Freetown International Airport, Lungi.

Air Mali, British Caledonian Airways, C.S.A. Czechoslovakian Airlines, Cubana, Ghana Airways, K.L.M. Royal Dutch Airlines, Nigeria Airways, Sierra Leone Airways and U.T.A. French Airlines.

British Caledonian Airways operate two direct services a week to Europe. One in association with Sierra Leone Airways and two services serving Las Palmas and Casablanca en route to London, Gatwick. Ghana Airways and Nigeria Airways offer regular services to West African coastal destinations ranging from Dakar to Lagos.

Other European Airlines e.g. C.S.A. Czechoslovakian Airlines serve Prague; K.L.M. Royal Dutch Airlines has a weekly service to Amsterdam via Casablanca; and U.T.A. French Airlines serve Paris twice a week, one service being operated by a DC 10 aircraft.

Sierra Leone Airways domestic schedule serve, on a regular basis, Bo, Kenema, Yengema, Kabala, Gbangbatoke,

Bonthe and Lungi International Airport from their base at Hastings.

The Post and Telecommunications Department maintain a trunk network of 2,800 miles of telephone and telegraph route connecting Freetown with the Provinces. Freetown is served by a modern automatic telephone exchange and trunk telephone facilities which exist between Freetown, Bo, Kenema, Makeni and to her principal towns by landline and radio telephone.

There are 127 Post Offices and Postal Agencies. 58 are provided with telegraph facilities by means of landline and wireless. There are four new automatic telephone exchange systems in Freetown, Bo, Kenema, and Makeni.

The wired Broadcasting system in Freetown was replaced in 1963 by a Transistor Radio Service. In 1970 there were approximately 150,000 transistor radios in service.

The government continues to pursue vigorously its policy of development and expansion of the National Broadcasting Service. The first phase of this programme has been completed with the inauguration of the new and powerful 250 kilowatt shortwave transmitter station at Waterloo.

Work on the improvement of the Television Service is progressing satisfactorily and it is expected that the new 10 kilowatt, Bank III Television Transmitter Station at Leicester Peak will shortly be ready for commissioning. This will make it possible for two-thirds of Sierra Leone to receive television coverage for the first time in the nation's history. It is government's committed intention to make television accessible to all parts of Sierra Leone, and plans have already been worked out to achieve this goal during the current Parliament. It is also hoped that this development will be further greatly enhanced when the new Broadcasting House now under construction at New England Ville is completed.

## EDUCATION

In 1975–76, Primary Education was provided in 1,974 schools with an enrolment of 205,910. Primary Education is neither fee free nor compulsory, but the rate of fee is moderate and some equipment is provided free of charge. The percentage of children attending schools varies considerably in different parts of the country.

In 1975–76, the enrolment in the country's 132 Secondary Schools was 48,609. The main pattern of general secondary education has been the Grammar School type of instruction. The policy of diversification whereby Commercial, Agricultural, Technical and Vocational subjects can be introduced in all secondary schools has been proclaimed in the 1970 'White Paper' on Education policy.

The IDA Education Project seeks to improve commercial, agricultural and technical education to provide employable skills to secondary school leavers. As a short-term policy of the diversification of the curriculum, a pilot programme between 1970–73 was to cover 11 secondary schools and eventually all secondary schools.

Technical education is provided in two Technical Institutes situated in Freetown and Kenema and two Trade Centres situated in Freetown and Magburaka. There are also technical training programmes in some mining and industrial companies.

Teacher training at non-university level is provided at six teacher colleges which include five primary teacher-colleges and one secondary teacher-college—Milton Margai Teachers College. The primary teacher-training colleges offer a 3-year teacher certificate course for students with four years secondary education and those who pass the entrance examination. The Milton Margai Teachers Certificate (H.T.C.). Course is for students with 4 G.C.E. 'O' Level subjects.

Holders of the Higher Teachers Certificate are qualified to teach in the lower classes of secondary schools. The Department of Education at Fourah Day College and Njala University College provide teacher education at graduate level.

A year's Post Graduate Teacher Programme leading to Diploma in Education is pursued at Fourah Bay College. The Degree Programme at Njala University College leads to Bachelor of Arts and Bachelor of Science in Education.

In 1975–76 Bunumbu Teachers College was granted permission to conduct the HTC (Primary Programme). This course has strong rural community bias. Moreover, in teacher education, the Bunumbu Project has a purpose of educating and training primary school teachers for rural areas.

Fourah Bay College and Njala University College are the constituent Colleges of the University of Sierra Leone. Enrolment at Fourah Bay College and Njala University College in 1975–76 was 1,016 and 596 respectively. The Institute of Education exists as part of the University of Sierra Leone.

Early in 1970, a commission set up with the approval of Government completed its report on Higher Education in Sierra Leone and submitted it to the government. The report formed the basis of a National Education policy for Sierra Leone.

The University of Sierra Leone in collaboration with the Ministry of Education carried out the Sierra Leone Education Review which is in substance completed. The Ministry of Education coordinates Adult Education Programmes through the National Literacy Committee on which all the principal participating organisations in Adult Education are represented.

## RELIGION

Sierra Leone is Muslim and Christian.

# Singapore

(MEMBER OF THE COMMONWEALTH)

**President**—Dr. Benjamin Henry Sheares.

**National Flag:** Red over white, halved horizontally in ratio 2 : 3, at the top of the hoist a crescent moon sided by five stars in a circle, all in white.

## CONSTITUTION AND GOVERNMENT

Singapore was founded by Sir Stamford Raffles in 1819. In 1826, Singapore together with Malacca and Penang formed the Straits Settlements, with the Governor of Penang in overall responsibility of the administration. In 1832, Singapore became the administrative centre of the Straits Settlements which remanied under the control of the British East Indian Company until 1867, when Singapore became a British colony. After the Japanese occupation from 1942–45, Singapore moved gradually to self-government, which it achieved in 1959. In 1963, it became a state within the Federation of Malaysia. On 9 August 1965, Singapore ceased to be a part of Malaysia and became an independent nation; and a member of the Commonwealth on 15 October, 1965.

Head of State is the President, elected by parliament for a term of five years. The Cabinet is responsible to a parliament of 65 members.

### Cabinet

**Prime Minister:* Lee Kuan Yew.
*Deputy Prime Minister and Minister of Defence:* Dr. Goh Keng Swee.
*Minister for Health:* Dr. Toh Chin Chye.
*Minister for Foreign Affairs:* S. Rajaratnam.
*Minister for Labour:* Ong Pang Boon.
*Minister without portfolio:* Yong Nyuk Lin.
*Minister for National Development and Communications:* Lim Kim San.
*Minister for Culture:* Jek Yeun Thong.
*Minister for Social Affairs:* Othman bin Wok.
*Minister for Law and Environment:* E. W. Barker.
*Minister for Home Affairs:* Chua Sian Chin.
*Minister for Finance:* Hon Sui Sen.

* The Prime Minister also has responsibility for the Ministry of Education.

## AREA AND POPULATION

The total land area of the main island of Singapore together with the numerous outlying small islands is 596·8 square kilometres. The highest hill (Bukit Timah) is 177 metres above sea level and the longest river (Sungei Seletar) is about 14·5 kilometres long. The population is large for a country of its size with a density of 3,770 persons per square kilometre in 1975, but is not expanding too rapidly. The population growth rate is among the lowest in the region.

The average annual rate of growth of the population was 4·4 per cent for the period 1947–1957, 2·8 per cent for the period 1957–1970 and 1·6 per cent for the period 1970–1975.

The population was estimated at 2,249,900 as at 30 June 1975, comprising 1,148,200 males and 1,101,700 females; an increase of 30,800 persons as compared with 2,219,100 persons as at 30 June 1974. There were 1,712,800 Chinese, 338,800 Malays, 155,200 Indians and 43,100 persons of other ethnic groups in 1975. 76·1 per cent of the population were Chinese, 15·1 per cent Malays, 6·9 per cent Indians and 1·9 per cent persons of other ethnic groups.

The sex ratio in 1975 was 1,042 males per thousand females. Of the main ethnic groups, the Chinese and the Malays had fairly even sex distribution of 1,014 and 1,034 males per thousand females respectively. The Indians however, still have an uneven sex distribution of 1,433 males per thousand females.

About 46 per cent of the total population are below 20 years of age with a sex ratio of 1,058 males per thousand females in 1975.

Singapore remains as one of the healthiest countries. The crude death rate which was 20·8 per thousand population in 1941 declined to 13·3 per thousand in 1947 and to 5·1 per thousand in 1975. Infant mortality rate in 1975 was 13·9 per thousand live-births, a marked decline as compared with 87·3 per thousand in 1947. The expectation of life at birth in 1970 was 65·1 years for males and 70·0 years for females.

## FINANCE

The monetary unit is the Singapore dollar.

The GNP at market prices for 1974 was U.S. $ million 4,970, and the GNP per capita at market prices was U.S. $2,240. The annual average percentage growth rate of the GNP per capita for the period 1960–74 was 7·6 and for the period 1965–74 was 10·0. [*See the note at the beginning of this section concerning GNP.*]

The Budget Division of the Ministry of Finance is responsible for the control and administration of Government finances.

The Budget Division of the Ministry of Finance is responsible for the control and administration of Government finances.

Total government revenue collected in 1975 was $3,055 million, an increase of $602 million or 24·5 per cent over the figure for 1974. Of the total revenue, tax receipts amounted to $2,178 million—$1,483 million from direct taxes and $695 million from indirect taxes. While the main sources of direct tax revenue was income tax ($1,127 million) and property tax ($283 million), the indirect tax revenue came mainly from import duties ($228 million) and excise duties ($176 million).

*Annual Current Revenue*

| *Year* | *Revenue $ million* |
|---|---|
| 1960 | 311 |
| 1966 | 585 |
| 1967 | 663 |
| 1968 | 803 |
| 1969 | 934 |
| 1970 | 1,182 |
| 1971 | 1,420 |
| 1972 | 1,669 |
| 1973 | 2,073 |
| 1974 | 2,453 |
| 1975 | 3,055 |

For the current budget year 1976/1977 beginning on 1 April, 1976, social and community services have been allocated $802·7 million and economic services $172·8 million. Defence and security take about $859·1 million of the current budget. Development expenditure is estimated to reach $2,610·3 million. Of this, $902·1 million is for expenditure on Government projects while the remaining $1,708·2 million is set aside as loans to statutory authorities and Government-owned companies.

## BANKS

**Algemene Bank Nederland N.V.,** 2 Cecil Street, 1.

**American Express International, Inc.,** 6th Floor A.I.A. Building, Robinson Road, Singapore 1.

**American Express International Banking Corporation,** Shing Kwan House, Shenton Way, No. 4, 1.

**Asia Commercial Banking Corporation Ltd.** (Chairman, Ang Keong Lan BBM; Vice-Chairmen, K. C. Heng, D. T. K, Chua, C. C. Chung, C. P. Teck; Managing Director, D. B. H. Chew (Operations and Admin.); Managing Director, C. P. Tiong.) 104–106 Robinson Road, 1. Incorporated on 29 January 1959, with an authorised capital of $2 million. This amount was increased to $10 million on 28 July 1961, and to $30 million on 14 September 1971.

Authorised capital was increased to $100 million on 15 July 1974, with $32·5 million fully paid-up. Paid-up capital was increased to $40 million on 29 November 1975, and it was further increased to $50 million on 30 August 1976, to cope with expansion programmes.

**Asien-Pazifik-Bank A.G.,** 50 Collyer Quay, O.U.B. Shopping Centre, 1.

**Ban Hin Lee Bank, Berhad,** 52A Circular Road, S. 1.

**Banca Commerciale Italiana,** Shing Kwan House, 4 Shenton Way, 1.

**Bangkok Bank, Ltd.,** 55 New Bridge Road, S. 1.

## SINGAPORE

**Bank of America NT and SA** (incorporated in U.S.A. with limited liability), 24 Raffles Place, 1. Tel: 913322.

**Bank of China,** Battery Road, 1.

**Bank of Canton, Ltd.,** Denmark House, Raffles Quay, 1.

**Bank of East Asia, Ltd.,** 137 Market Street, 1.

**Bank of India,** 132/136 Robinson Road, 1.

**Bank Negara Indonesia,** 3 Malacca Street.

**Bank of Singapore, Ltd.,** 34 Market Street, 1.

**Bank of Tokyo, Ltd.,** 6/10 Phillip Street, 1.

**Banque de l'Indochine et de Suez,** Shenton House, Shenton Way, Singapore 1. Tel.: 2207111 (15 lines). Telex: (Forex) Indocab RS 24394. Telex: (General) Indocab RS 24435.

**Banque Nationale De Paris,** Overseas Union Shopping Centre, Mezzanine Floor, Raffles Quay, 1.

**Chartered Bank,** 28/30 Battrey Road, Post Box 1901, 1.

**Chase Manhattan Bank, N.A.,** 4, Shenton Way, 1.

**Chung Khiaw Bank, Ltd.,** 59/61 Robinson Road, 1.

**Development Bank of Singapore Ltd.,** DBS Building, Shenton Way, 1. Tel.: 2201111. Cables: DEVBANK; Telex: RS 24455.

**Dresdner Bank A.G.,** 6 Shenton Way, DBS Building, Singapore 1.

**Eastern Bank, Ltd.,** 18 Cecil Street, 1.

**Far Eastern Bank Ltd.,** 156 Cecil Street, 1.

**First National Bank of Chicago,** 49, Robinson Road, 1. Telephone: 912233.

**First National City Bank,** UIC Building, Shenton Way, 1.

**Habib Bank Ltd.,** Grand Building, Phillip Street, 1.

**Hongkong and Shanghai Banking Corporation, The.** 7 Branches. See Hong Kong.

**Indian Bank, Ltd.,** 4 D'Almeida Street, 1.

**Indian Overseas Bank,** 1 Collyer Quay, 1.

**Industrial and Commercial Bank Ltd., The.** ICB Building, 2 Shenton Way, Singapore 1. Cable Address: INDCOM BANK *Telex:* RS21112.

**Kwantung Provincial Bank,** 19/25 Cecil Street, 1.

**Kwong Lee Bank Bhd.,** 72 South Bridge Road, 1.

**Lee Wah Bank, Ltd.,** *Head Office:* 63 Robinson Road, Singapore, 1.

**Malayan Banking Bhd.,** Fullerton Sq., 1.

**Mercantile Bank, Ltd.,** 1 Branch. See Hong Kong.

**Mitsui Bank Ltd.,** 6 Robinson Road, 1.

**Moscow Narodny Bank Ltd.,** MNB Building, 50 Robinson Road, Singapore 1.

**United Malayan Banking Corporation Bhd.,** 66–68 South Bridge Road, 1.

**General Bank of the Netherlands,** 2 Cecil Street, 1.

**Oversea Chinese Banking Corporation, Ltd.,** OCBC Centre, Chulia Street, Singapore 1.

**Overseas Union Bank, Ltd.,** Raffles Place, Singapore 1.

**Four Seas Communications Bank Ltd.** (Chairman and Managing Director, Tan Siak Kew P. J. G.; Deputy Chairman and General Manager, L. H. Siang.) Est. 1906. At 31 December 1972 authorized capital totalled S$50,000,000; paid-up capital S$20,000,000; Capital Reserves S$12,059,704; deposits S$163,380,079; total resources S$254,935,122. (Formerly known as Sze Hai Tong Bank Ltd.), 57 Chulia Street, 1.

**United Overseas Bank Ltd.,** 1 Bonham Street, Raffles Place Singapore, 1.

**United Commercial Bank,** 1 D'Almeida St., S. 1.

**United Malayan Banking,** 66–68 South Bridge Road, 1.

With the exception of Asia Commercial Banking Corporation and Kwong Lee Bank, all the other banks are Authorised Dealers under the Exchange Control Ordinance.

### PRODUCTION, INDUSTRY AND COMMERCE

**Commerce.** Singapore is a commercial and trading centre of South-East Asia. In 1975, total external trade amounted to $32,028 million registering a decline of seven per cent as compared to an increase of 61 per cent in 1974. The decline which was in line with world-wide trends was caused by adverse world economic conditions.

Total external trade comprised of $12,758 millions exports and $19,270 million imports. Both were smaller than the previous year figures by ten per cent and six per sent respectively. The fall in imports was mainly in mineral fuels, vegetable oils and fats, chemicals, manufactured goods and machinery and transport equipment while that of exports was associated with crude materials, mineral fuels, animal and vegetable oils and fats and chemicals. Domestic exports, which accounted for about 60 per cent of total exports in 1975, registered a drop of ten per cent to $7,540 million while re-exports recorded a decline of nine per cent.

In contrast to sharp increases in prices in 1973 and 1974, prices of commodities traded remained fairly stable throughout 1975.

In 1975, USA accounted for 15 per cent of the total trade and replaced Japan as Singapore's leading partner. Malaysia was second while Japan third.

Since 1966 the balance of payments has been registering surplus every year. From 1967 to 1974 the overall surpluses averaged $684 million a year. In 1975, preliminary estimates indicated a surplus of $972 million.

In 1975, the recorded trade deficit amounted to $5,898 million, larger than the deficit of $5,541 million for 1974. Singapore has run a persistent trade deficit which has been largely offset by earnings from 'invisible' items and large capital inflows.

Net earnings from services increased to $4,221 million in 1975 from $2,906 million in 1974. The increase was mainly contributed by travel and other transportation and services, n.i.e. The net receipt from these two categories rose from $3,942 million in 1974 to reach $5,136 million in 1975.

Capital movements registered an inflow of $1,387 million in 1975. This was due to an inflow of $1,545 million of the non-monetary sector which was offset by an outflow of $158 million of the monetary sector (commercial banks).

The manufacturing sector comprised a wide range of industries including the processing of rubber, rattan and coconut oil, petroleum refining, shipbuilding and oil rig construction, sawmilling, steel rolling, printing and the manufacture of rubber footwear, soap, dry cell batteries, beer, soft drinks, tin containers, glass, textiles, garments, bricks, tiles, calculators, machinery and oil field equipment. The traditional concentration on the processing of primary products (rubber, rattan), the provision of docking facilities, light engineering works and motor assembly plant have been shifted in recent years to industries which require higher skills and technology such as ship-building, oil rig construction, metal working, manufacture of electrical appliances, semi-conductors, machinery and precision equipment and optical goods.

Total output of manufacturing industries engaging ten persons and over increased from $8,687 million in 1973 to $14,215 million in 1974. Value added was $3,579 million in 1974 as compared with $2,591 million in 1973. Employment rose from 201,813 in 1973 to 209,214 in 1974. The manufacturing sector contributed 24 per cent of the total Gross Domestic Product in 1974.

| | *Imports* ($ millions) | | *Exports* ($ millions) | | *Total Trade* ($ millions) | | % *of Singapore's Total Trade* | |
|---|---|---|---|---|---|---|---|---|
| *Country* | 1974 | 1975 | 1974 | 1975 | 1974 | 1975 | 1974 | 1975 |
| Australia | 571·0 | 661·5 | 687·7 | 637·2 | 1,258·7 | 1,298·7 | 3·6 | 4·1 |
| China | 643·9 | 682·0 | 125·8 | 98·5 | 769·7 | 780·5 | 2·2 | 2·4 |
| France | 234·2 | 266·8 | 262·9 | 224·7 | 497·1 | 491·5 | 1·4 | 1·5 |
| Germany, Fed. Rep. | 712·3 | 636·2 | 428·2 | 481·5 | 1,140·5 | 1,117·7 | 3·3 | 3·5 |
| Hong Kong | 470·9 | 427·8 | 901·4 | 937·0 | 1,372·3 | 1,364·8 | 4·0 | 4·3 |
| India | 167·0 | 137·0 | 70·5 | 99·5 | 237·5 | 236·5 | 0·7 | 0·7 |
| Iran | 1,066·0 | 1,000·8 | 53·2 | 63·8 | 1,119·2 | 1,065·6 | 3·2 | 3·3 |
| Italy | 237·1 | 211·7 | 177·8 | 123·4 | 414·9 | 335·1 | 1·2 | 1·0 |
| Japan | 3,653·9 | 3,254·3 | 1,610·5 | 1,112·9 | 5,264·4 | 4,367·2 | 15·2 | 13·6 |
| Kuwait | 1,216·5 | 601·3 | 24·6 | 36·4 | 1,241·1 | 637·7 | 3·6 | 2·0 |
| Malaysia, East | | | | | | | | |
| Sabah | 6·50 | 91·9 | 348·1 | 287·6 | 413·1 | 379·5 | 1·2 | 1·2 |
| Sarawak | 560·7 | 391·0 | 238·1 | 213·5 | 798·8 | 604·5 | 2·3 | 1·9 |
| Malaysia, Peninsular | 2,060·5 | 1,755·6 | 1,761·1 | 1,687·1 | 3,821·6 | 3,442·7 | 11·1 | 10·8 |
| Netherlands | 274·6 | 280·5 | 231·7 | 242·9 | 506·3 | 523·4 | 1·5 | 1·6 |
| Taiwan | 348·6 | 383·6 | 171·1 | 131·1 | 519·7 | 514·7 | 1·5 | 1·6 |
| Thailand | 542·6 | 406·3 | 343·2 | 445·4 | 885·8 | 851·7 | 2·6 | 2·7 |
| U.S.S.R. | 25·7 | 18·2 | 236·4 | 126·0 | 262·1 | 144·2 | 0·8 | 0·5 |
| United Kingdom | 996·3 | 956·0 | 574·5 | 539·8 | 1,570·8 | 1,495·8 | 4·5 | 4·7 |
| U.S.A. | 2,858·1 | 3,024·0 | 2,100·7 | 1,775·4 | 4,958·8 | 4,799·4 | 14·3 | 15·0 |
| Vietnam, Rep. | 29·3 | 17·7 | 511·8 | 182·4 | 541·1 | 200·1 | 1·6 | 0·6 |
| Others | 3,670·7 | 4,065·2 | 3,295·3 | 3,311·8 | 6,966·0 | 7,377·0 | 20·2 | 23·0 |
| *Total* | 20,404·9 | 19,270·4 | 14,154·6 | 12,757·9 | 34,559·5 | 32,028·3 | 100·0 | 100·0 |

## COMMUNICATIONS

**Roads.** Singapore has 2,167 kilometres of public roads, 1,716 kilometres of which have a permanent bituminous surface —usually bituminous—and the remaining 451 kilometres are unimproved roads.

**Rail.** The Malayan Railway System is owned by the Government of the Federation of Malaysia and serves Singapore and the Federation of Malaysia. The track is of metre gauge and the total route mileage is 1,654 kilometres. The railway enters the State of Singapore at the Johore Causeway and continues for a distance of 25·7 kilometres to the terminal station near Keppel Harbour. Branch lines link the railway with the Port of Singapore Authority area, and with the Jurong Industrial Estate.

**Air.** Singapore Airport is 12 kilometres from the city centre, and is connected to it by a fine fast double-carriage highway. It is an International Airport and one of the finest in South-East Asia. The runway has a length of 3,353 metres and a further extension of 670 metres is underway. Besides the national carrier, Singapore Airlines, 27 other international airlines operate scheduled services through Singapore to most parts of the world.

In 1975, the 29 scheduled airlines operated a total of 577 scheduled services a week. 59,916 aircraft movements were registered at the Singapore International Airport in 1975. During the same period approximately 3·9 million passengers used the Airport and the freight throughout was about 64,180 tonnes.

Singapore's general aviation airport, Seletar Airport recorded 98,264 aircraft movements.

During the same period 46,900 passengers passed through Seletar Airport and 1,741 tonnes of freight were handled.

**Shipping.** Singapore is the fourth busiest port in the world and the busiest in the Commonwealth. It is used by 250 major shipping lines covering services to all parts of the world. It is not only a great bunkering port, but is also one of the largest storing, blending and distributing oil centres in existence.

The fully-equipped East Lagoon Container Terminal of PSA inaugurated in June 1972 represents one of the largest investments undertaken by the Authority. To date, $140 million has been spent on this project. The terminal occupies an area of 27 hectares comprising three main berths of 914 metres (13·4 m depth at zero tide), a feeder berth of 213 metres (depth 13·8 metres at zero tide) and a cross berth of 213 metres. The main berth can accommodate three third-generation container vessels at one time.

There is a stacking yard of approximately 11 hectares, which can accommodate 8,000 containers. There are also three large container freight stations prividing 20,902 sq. m. of covered area for consolidation of cargoes and unstuffing of containers. The yard also has 64 outlet points to provide electrical power to refrigerated containers.

Operations at the Container Terminal are serviced by four quay cranes, two tango cranes, 15 van carriers and a fleet of forklifts, tractors and trailers. Container operations are kept track by the Authority's IBM 370 Model 145 computer system. The Container Handling Information System, operating in real-time mode and aided by visual display units and a tele-typewriter terminal installed within the Container Terminal Building. It monitors the movements of containers and subsequently uses the information stored for operational and billing purposes.

The Container Terminal continued to make good progress despite general downturn in world trade and cargo handling activities. In 1975, some 564 vessels berthed at the Container Terminal working 2·6 million tonnes of cargo in nearly 192,000 containers (TEU's). This represented an increase of 272 vessels and 665,000 tonnes (35 per cent) over 1974.

As at 31 December 1975, PSA employs 10,903 workers of which 8·2 per cent are senior officers, 51·2 per cent junior officers and 40·3 per cent daily-rated employees.

## NEWSPAPERS

There are four Chinese daily newspapers—Nanyang Siang Pau, Sin Chew Jit Poh, Shin Min Daily News and Min Pao Daily; two English daily newspapers—The Straits Times and New Nation (an afternoon paper); a Malay daily newspaper—Berita Harian; two Tamil daily newspapers—Tamil Murasu and Tamil Malar; one Malayalan newspaper—Malaysia Malayali; and a Punjabi weekly—Navjiwan.

Singapore is a major distribution centre for world news and seven major news agencies, Reuters, United Press International, Associated Press, Agence France-Presse, Kyodo News Service, and Tass News Agency—are based in Singapore.

## EDUCATION

There were 541 schools, comprising 263 Government schools, 218 Government-aided schools, and 60 private schools in Singapore in 1975.

There were 509,508 children and young people in full-time attendance at schools, 4,883 of whom were in registered kindergartens, 328,401 in primary schools, and 176,224 in secondary schools.

Four main languages (Malay, Chinese, Tamil and English)

are used, and all schools use identical syllabuses to foster national consciousness and unity.

In order to promote bilingualism, the study of a second language has been made compulsory. English is the compulsory language for pupils in the Malay, Chinese and Tamil streams, whilst pupils in the English stream offer Malay, Chinese or Tamil as their second language.

With rapid industrialization needing skilled technical manpower there is an emphasis on the teaching and acquisition of technical knowledge. With this aim in mind, all the boys and 54 per cent of the girls in secondary I and II classes follow a comprehensive curriculum covering both academic and technical subjects. Further technical education is available in 20 Secondary Technical and Bilateral Schools and 9 Vocational Institutes.

With increasing sophistication, the Educational Television Services transmit through the existing national television return during normal school hours educational programmes in different subjects specially geared for Primary and Secondary pupils.

# Somali Democratic Republic

**Capital**—Mogadishu.

**President of the Supreme Revolutionary Council**—Major General Mohamed Siad Barre.

**Flag:** Blue; a star five-pointed centred white.

## CONSTITUTION AND GOVERNMENT

THE Union of the British Protectorate of Somaliland and the Italian Trust Territory of Somalia was effected in the summer of 1960, and the independence of the new Republic was officially declared on 1 July. On 21 October 1969 the Armed Forces made a successful bloodless revolution against the Civilian Government. After the revolution, the country was renamed the 'Somali Democratic Republic', the constitution repealed, and the Parliament dissolved.

The country is now ruled by 21 members of the Supreme Revolutionary Council together with 18 Secretaries of State headed by Major-General Mohamed Siad Barre as the President of the Council and the Cabinet.

## AREA AND POPULATION

Somalia has an area of about 63·8 million hectares. About one-eighth of this area is suitable for cultivation. Only 5 per cent of these eight million hectares of arable land is estimated to be under the plough.

The population at mid-1974 was 3,100,000. The annual average percentage growth rate of the population for the period 1960–74, was 2·4 and for 1965–74 was 2·4. The chief towns are Mogadishu (350,000), Hargeisa (40,254), and Kismayo (17,872).

## CURRENCY AND FINANCE

The official unit of currency is the Somali shilling, divided into 100 cents. 6·23 So. Sh. = 1 U.S. Dollar.

The GNP at market prices for 1974 was U.S. $ millions 290, and the GNP per capita at market prices was U.S. $90. The annual average percentage growth rate of the GNP per capita for the period 1960–74 was −0·3, and for the period 1965–74 was 1·1. [*See the note at the beginning of this section concerning GNP.*]

Revenue and expenditure for 1971 and 1972 were (in million Somali shillings): Revenue 306 and 358; and Expenditure 306 and 358.

## PRODUCTION, INDUSTRY AND COMMERCE

**Agriculture and Forestry.** Somalia's territory can be divided as follows:

| | *Million Hectares* | *Percentage* |
|---|---|---|
| Area suitable for cultivation | 8·0 | 12·5 |
| Area suitable for livestock raising | 35·0 | 54·9 |
| Forest | 8·8 | 13·8 |
| Others | 12·0 | 18·8 |
| | 63·8 | 100·0 |

Forests cover an estimated 14 per cent of the total area. They consist mainly of bush, shrubs and thorn trees. Actual forests with acacias, euphorbias and other trees are situated along the two main rivers. Incense, myrrh and arabic gum are collected from free-growing trees in the North-Eastern part of the country.

**Mining.** No mineral deposits are at present being exploited for industrial use. But an official report affirms that Somalia possesses the largest deposits of gypsum in the world. Marble and apatite deposits have also been discovered. Moreover, iron ore and recently ore deposits of uranium, thorium and rare earth bearing minerals have been proven to exist in commercial quantities.

**Livestock.** Livestock is Somalia's most important renewable resource. A percentage of the population entirely depend on it for their livelihood and another percentage supplement their income from it.

**Fishing.** Somalia has a longer coastline than any African country, extending over 3,000 km. along the Gulf of Aden and the Indian Ocean. At present there are four fish processing plants along the Northern Coast (Alula, Candala, Habo and Laskore) and a lobster canning factory at Kismaio.

**Commerce.** The following tables show the value of exports and imports for 1970 and 1971 (in million Somali shillings):

| *Export by Selected Commodities* | 1970 | 1971 |
|---|---|---|
| Total | 224 | 246 |
| Food and live animals | 190 | 211 |
| live animals | 119 | 123 |
| cattle | 15 | 18 |
| goats | 41 | 41 |
| sheep | 42 | 46 |
| camels | 18 | 16 |
| Fish and fish prod. | 1 | 2 |
| Bananas | 62 | 63 |
| Hides, skins and fur skins | 14 | 18 |

| *Import by Selected Commodities* | 1970 | 1971 |
|---|---|---|
| Total | 322 | 447 |
| Cereals and cereal preparations | 55 | 104 |
| Sugar and sugar preparation | 0·9 | 111 |
| Tobacco and Tobacco manufactured | 6 | 10 |
| Petroleum and petroleum products | 20 | 18 |
| Textile yarn, fabrics, made up and related articles | 25 | 36 |
| Machinery and transport equipment | 53 | 55 |
| Medical and Pharmaceutical products | 8 | 14 |

Most of Somalia's exports go to Italy and the Arab States while its imports mainly come from Italy, Japan, U.K. and the U.S.S.R.

## COMMUNICATIONS

There are no railways and land transport is by motor services. In addition to its local airline (Somali Airlines), Somalia is served by modern international airlines, such as Alitalia, United Arab Airlines, Aeroflot and the East African Airlines.

Mogadishu is the main import harbour and Berbera (Livestock), Merca (Banana) and Kismaio (Banana) are the main export harbours.

## EDUCATION AND RELIGION

There were 69,524 students enrolled in both Government an private schools in the year 1971/72.

In 1971–72 there were 273 Public Schools and 75 Private Schools, in the same period there were 1,944 teachers in Public Schools and 548 teachers in Private Schools.

Most of the population are Sunni Moslems.

# Republic of South Africa

(REPUBLIEK VAN SUID-AFRIKA)

**Seat of Administration**—Pretoria.

**Seat of Legislature**—Cape Town.

**State President**—Dr. N. J. Diederichs.

**National Flag:** A tricolour fesse-wise, orange, white, blue; centred in the white the old Orange Free State flag conjoined towards the hoist with the Union Jack, and towards the fly with the old Transvaal Vierkleur.

## CONSTITUTION AND GOVERNMENT

THE constitutional basis of the Republic of South Africa is contained in the Republic of South Africa Constitution Act, 1961, which established, with effect from 31 May 1961, the Republic consisting of the four provinces: viz. the Cape of Good Hope, Natal, the Transvaal and the Orange Free State, which comprised the Union of South Africa immediately prior to the commencement of the aforementioned Act.

The head of the Republic is the State President who is elected by an electoral college consisting of the members of the Senate and the House of Assembly at a meeting specially convened for the purpose, and presided over by the Chief Justice or a judge of appeal designated by him.

The executive government of the Republic in regard to any aspect of its domestic and foreign affairs is vested in the State President, acting on the advice of the Executive Council which consists of the Ministers, not exceeding 18 in number, appointed by the State President to administer such Departments of State as the State President may establish. They must be members of either of the Houses of Parliament.

The legislative power of the Republic is vested in the Parliament, consisting of the State President, a Senate and a House of Assembly. A session of Parliament must be held once at least in every year.

The Senate consists of 54 members, ten being nominated by the State President (two for each of the four Provinces of the Republic of South Africa, two for South-West Africa) and 44 being elected (15 in Transvaal, 11 in the Cape Province, eight in Natal, eight in the Orange Free State and two in South-West Africa). The Separate Representation of Voters Act of 1951 in terms of which Coloured voters in the Cape Province were represented in the Senate was repealed in 1968. The position now is that in terms of section twenty-nine (2) (b) of the Republic of South Africa Constitution Act, 1961, the Coloured population of the Republic of South Africa is now represented (as from 1 July 1969) by the Coloured Persons Representative Council. At least one of the two senators nominated by the State President from each province should be thoroughly acquainted, by reason of official experience or otherwise, with the needs of the Coloured population in the province concerned for which he is nominated, and he should be capable, *inter alia*, of serving as the channel through which the interests of the Coloured population in the province concerned may be promoted. Similarly, in terms of the South-West Africa Affairs Amendment Act, 1949, one of the senators nominated from South-West Africa should be selected mainly on the ground of his thorough acquaintance with the reasonable wants and wishes of the Coloured races of the territory.

In each of the four provinces the senators are elected jointly by the sitting members of the House of Assembly and the provincial councillors for that province, and in South-West Africa by the members of the Legislative Assembly for the territory, together with the members of the House of Assembly for the territory.

Vacancies are filled in the same manner.

Senators normally hold their seats for five years, but the State President may at any time by proclamation in the Government Gazette, dissolve the Senate simultaneously with the House of Assembly. He may also dissolve the Senate at any time within 120 days of any dissolution of the House of Assembly or the expiry of the term of office of a Provincial Council. Nominated senators are required to vacate their seats if the Prime Minister vacates his office and another person becomes Prime Minister and the State President publishes a notice in the Government Gazette that a change of Government has occurred.

The House of Assembly consists of 166 members, 160 being directly chosen by the voters in the Republic of South Africa in electoral divisions as laid down in the Constitution, six being directly chosen by the voters in South-West Africa. Separate representation of Coloured voters in the Cape Province was abolished in 1968 and the Coloured population of the whole Republic is now represented (as from 1 July 1969) by the Coloured Persons Representative Council.

Parliament is the sovereign legislative authority in and over the Republic and has full power to make laws for the peace, order and good government of the Republic. Bills appropriating revenue or moneys or imposing taxation must originate in the House of Assembly.

Under the Republic of South Africa Constitution Act, 1961, the seat of Government is at Pretoria while the seat of the Legislature is at Cape Town.

In September 1966 the Prime Minister, Dr. H. F. Verwoerd, was assassinated. His place was taken by the former Minister of Justice, Mr. B. J. Vorster, who was duly elected leader of the National Party and became Premier on 13 September 1966.

### Ministry

*Prime Minister:* Mr. B. J. Vorster.
*Finance:* Senator O. P. F. Horwood.
*Defence:* Mr. P. W. Botha.
*Foreign Affairs:* Mr. R. F. Botha.
*Social Welfare, Pensions, Posts and Telecommunications:* Senator J. P. van der Spuy.
*Bantu Administration and Development and Information:* Mr. C. P. Mulder.
*Transport:* Mr. S. L. Muller.
*Water Affairs, Forestry:* A. J. Raubenheimer.
*National Education, Sport, Recreation:* Dr. P. G. J. Koornhof.
*Health Planning, the Environment and Statistics:* Dr. S. W v. d. Merwe.
*Public Works, Interior and Immigration:* Mr. A. L. Schlebusch.
*Labour and Mines:* S. P. Botha.
*Agriculture:* Mr H. Schoeman.
*Coloured, Rehoboth and Nama Affairs:* Mr. H. H. Smit.
*Economic Affairs:* Mr. J. C. Heunis.
*Tourism, Indian Affairs and Community Development:* Mr. S. J. M. Steyn.
*Justice, Police and Prisons:* Mr. J. T. Kruger.
*Education and Training:* Mr. W. A. Cruywagen.

### Deputy Ministers

*Bantu Development:* Dr. F. Hartzenburg.
*Bantu Administration and Education:* Dr. P. P. Treurnicht.
*Agriculture:* Mr. J. J. Malan.
*Social Welfare, Pensions, Planning, Environment, Statistics:* Mr. T. N. H. Janson.
*Information and the Interior:* L. Le Grange.

### Parliament

**Upper Chamber** (Senate):

*President:* Senator M. Viljoen.

The Parties are represented as follows: National Party, 43; United Party, 10; Progressive Reform Party, 2.

**Lower Chamber** (House of Assembly):

National Party, 123; United Party, 30; Progressive Reform Party, 12; South African Party, 6.

## PROVINCIAL SYSTEMS

The Republic of South Africa Constitution Act, 1961, provides that in each of the four provinces there shall be a Chief Executive Officer appointed by the State President in council and styled the Administrator of the province. All executive acts relating to provincial affairs are performed in the name of this officer. Preference is given, as far as possible, when appointing an Administrator, to a person resident in the province.

Each Provincial Council elects from among its members, or otherwise, four persons to form with the Administrator an Executive Committee for the province, the Administrator acting as Chairman.

The Provincial Council consists of the same number of elected members as there are electoral divisions of the House of Assembly, unless that number is under 25, as is the case in Natal and the Orange Free State, where the number of members of the Provincial Council is fixed at 25. There must be a session of the Council once in every year. The legislative powers of Provincial Councils are limited in general to matters of purely local concern. These include the control of primary and secondary education and the establishment, maintenance and management of hospitals, maternity homes, dispensaries, dental clinics, etc. The preservation of game and fish is under the control of the provincial administrations.

There are six Bantu homelands in number. They are: Ciskei, Lebowa, Venda, Gazankulu, Basotho Qwaqwa and Kwazulu. In South West Africa there are at present legislative councils in Kavango, Owambo and in the eastern Caprivi Zipfel which all enjoy considerable measures of self-government. The Transkei became Independent on 26 October 1976. Bophuthatswana became independent on 6 December 1977.

## LEGAL SYSTEM

South African Common Law is based on Roman-Dutch Law which was introduced to the Cape by the Dutch settlers in 1652. After the second British occupation of the Cape in 1806, South African law was influenced by English law, but when the Union of South Africa was established this influence diminished.

Roman-Dutch Law has been adapted over the years to suit the complex structure of the country. South African law consists of Common Law. Statute Law and Case Law, the latter being based on decisions of the Supreme Court.

Judicial authority is vested in the Supreme Court of South Africa (which consists of several Divisions), certain special courts (composed of judges of the Supreme Court of South Africa), several Lower Courts and courts of Bantu Chiefs and Headmen and of Bantu Affairs Commissioners.

The Appellate Division of the Supreme Court is the highest court in the Republic and South West Africa, and sits in Bloemfontein. This court consists of the Chief Justice and as many Judges of Appeal as the State President may stipulate. Its jurisdiction is confined to appeals.

Other Divisions are: The Provincial Division of the Cape of Good Hope, the Eastern Cape Division, the Northern Cape Division, the Natal Division, the Orange Free State Division. the Transvaal Division, the South West Africa Division, the Witwatersrand Local Division and the Durban and Coast Local Division. The Provincial Divisions consist of a Judge-President and as many judges as the State President may stipulate. Judges of the relative Provincial Divisions sit on the Durban and Coast Local Division and on the Witwatersrand Local Division.

Judges from the Supreme Court may not be removed from their posts except by the State President, following an address, submitted on grounds of misbehaviour or incapacity, from both Houses of Parliament during the same session.

Special Courts are the Special Criminal Court (this Court may be established to try offences such as high treason, public violence and revolt), the Water Court (settle disputes over riparian rights) and the Special Income Tax Court (to hear Income Tax Appeals against rulings made by the Secretary for Inland Revenue.)

Lower Courts are the Magistrates' Courts (there are 253 magisterial districts in South Africa), Children's Courts (adjudicating cases of neglect and ill-treated children) and Maintenance Courts (empowered to hear cases in regard to maintenance liability.)

Generally speaking, Bantu, in both civil and criminal matters, are subject to the ordinary laws and ordinary courts of the land. Certain special tribunals have, however, been established for the hearing of purely Bantu issues. Insofar as civil matters are concerned, the following special Bantu courts have been established:

1 Courts of Bantu Chiefs and Headmen in which civil suits arising out of Bantu law and custom between Bantu are heard by a Bantu chief, headman or chief's deputy on whom jurisdiction has been conferred by the Minister of Bantu Administration and Development. There is a right of appeal to the Bantu Affairs Commissioner.
2 Courts of Bantu Affairs Commissioners are established by the Minister of Bantu Administration and Development to try crimes committed by Bantu and to adjudicate disputes between Bantu. The jurisdiction of these courts is limited. The court of a Bantu Affairs Commissioner can apply Bantu law in cases between Bantu, insofar as it is not contrary to accepted legal practice and natural justice.
3 The Bantu Appeal Court deals with appeals against the verdicts of Bantu Affairs Commissioners.
4 Bantu Divorce Courts try cases concerning the dissolution of marriages and other matrimonial disputes.

**Supreme Court**
*Chief Justice:* Hon. F. L. H. Rumpff.

## AREA AND POPULATION

The total area of the Republic of South Africa is 1,182,486 sq. km., and the population at 6 May 1970 was 21,448,169. This was made up of 3,751,328 Whites; 15,057,952 Bantu; 2,018,453 Coloureds and Malays; 620,436 Asians.

The following table shows the area and population of the provinces according to the 1970 census, (excluding the population of the Bantu Homelands).

| *Province* | *Area in sq. miles* | *Population 1970 census)* |
|---|---|---|
| Cape of Good Hope | 278,465 | 4,235,523 |
| Natal | 33,578 | 2,140,166 |
| Transvaal | 110,450 | 6,388,870 |
| Orange Free State | 49,866 | 1,649,306 |

The 1976 midyear *estimate* of population (excluding the estimated population of Transkei) is Total: 24,033 thousand, whites 4,310 thousand, coloureds, 2,426 thousand, Asians 746 thousand, Blacks, 16,551 thousand.

The following table shows vital statistics for the years 1972–75 (latest year available):

| | | *Number* | | |
|---|---|---|---|---|
| *Series* | *Year* | *Whites* | *Coloureds* | *Asians* |
| Births | 1972 | 90,458 | 74,863 | 22,462 |
| | 1973 | 90,501 | 74,992 | 22,158 |
| | 1974 | 83,727 | 70,021 | 20,946 |
| | 1975 | 80,026 | 67,537 | 20,298 |
| Deaths | 1972 | 33,686 | 27,743 | 4,638 |
| | 1973 | 33,757 | 28,443 | 4,727 |
| | 1974 | 34,974 | 29,479 | 4,795 |
| | 1975 | 35,035 | 27,615 | 4,834 |
| Marriages | 1972 | 41,294 | 15,385 | 7,166 |
| | 1973 | 40,602 | 16,626 | 7,250 |
| | 1974 | 41,066 | 16,054 | 7,495 |
| | 1975 | 41,333 | 16,694 | 7,938 |
| Divorces | 1972 | 8,432 | 900 | 193 |
| | 1973 | 8,890 | 1,212 | 135 |
| | 1974 | 9,907 | 1,307 | — |
| | 1975 | 10,730 | 1,260 | — |

Compulsory registration of births and deaths of Bantu applied only to the urban areas up to 30 June 1952 from which date compulsory registration was extended to the rural areas. However, it will probably be some years before registration can be looked upon as reasonably complete.

Principal towns and populations:

| | 1970 (*census*) |
|---|---|
| Johannesburg | 1,432,643 |
| Cape Town | 1,096,595 |
| Durban | 843,327 |
| Pretoria | 561,703 |
| Port Elizabeth | 468,577 |
| Bloemfontein | 180,179 |
| East London | 123,294 |
| Kimberley | 103,789 |

The official languages of the Republic are English and Afrikaans.

## FINANCE

The currency unit in use in South Africa is the Rand, indicated by the symbol R. The Rand equals 100 cents. Coins in use are: in silver, R.1; in nickel, 50c., 20c., 10c., 5c.; in copper, 2c., 1c., ½c. Banknotes in use are: R.50, R.20, R.10, R.5, and R.2.

Revenue Account plus Bantu Education Account (million R.):

| | 1974–75 | 1979–76 provisional |
|---|---|---|
| Net ordinary revenue | 4,474·7 | 5,046·0 |
| Total expenditure i.r.o. Revenue Services plus Bantu Education Account | 4,293·7 | 5,183·7 |

**PRINCIPAL BANKS**

**South African Reserve Bank.** (Governor, Theunis Willem de Jongh.) Est. 1921; Sole Bank of Issue for South Africa and South Western Africa; Balance Sheet at 31 April 1977 showed assets R.3,057 million; deposits and current accounts R.491 million; banknotes in circulation R.1,176 million; gold reserve R.287 million. *Head Office:* Church Square, Pretoria. 9 Branches.

**Nedbank Limited** (Prior to 1 October 1971 Netherlands Bank of South Africa Limited.) Est. 1888. At 30 September 1975 assets totalled R.1,635,670,000 and in 1976 R.2,269,069,000; total public liabilities in 1975 R.1,506,928,000 and in 1976 R. 2,123,497,000. *Head Office:* 81 Main Street, Johannesburg; 146 offices in S.A., S.W.A.; affiliations in Rhodesia; *London Offices:* 37 Lombard Street, E.C.3., and 71 Haymarket, S.W.1. Representative offices in New York and Zurich.

**Volkskas Limited.** (Chairman, Dr. J. A. Hurter; Managing Director, Mr. D. P. S. Van Hyussteen.) Est. 1935; Balance Sheet at 31 March 1977 showed assets R.2,641,409,000; total public liabilities R.2,513,303,000. *Head Office:* Cor. Pretorius and Van der Walt Street, Pretoria. (P.O. Box 578). 573 Offices.

**The South African Bank of Athens Ltd.** *Head Office:* 103 Fox St., Johannesburg.

**French Bank of Southern Africa, Ltd.,** 50 Marshall Street, Johannesburg.

**The Stellenbosch District Bank Limited.** *Head Office:* Stellenbosch.

**Barclays National Bank Ltd.** The bank has 883 offices throughout South and South West Africa. *Head Office:* P.O. Box 1153, Johannesburg.

**Chase Manhattan Overseas Corporation.** *Representative:* S. Pryke, 6th Floor Homes Trust Bldng, 108 Fox Street, P.O. Box 9606, Johannesburg.

**First National City Bank (South Africa) Ltd.** *Head Office:* 60 Market Street, Johannesburg.

**Trust Bank of Africa Ltd.** P.O. Box 2116, Cape Town.

**PRODUCTION, INDUSTRY AND COMMERCE**

**Agriculture.** South Africa's development began in 1652 as an agricultural settlement. Until about 1870 agriculture remained the principal source of revenue. With the discovery of gold and diamonds the country entered a new phase in which mining was the chief source of income. Then, during and after the two world wars, manufacturing industry became increasingly more important. Although agriculture today only contributes about 8% of gross domestic production (7·6% in 1975), sufficient food is produced to meet the country's requirements. Agricultural produce accounts for about 40 per cent of the total value of South African exports excluding gold.

South Africa's land surface is utilized as follows:

| *Agriculture and Forestry* | *(million hectares)* |
|---|---|
| Cultivated | 11·62 |
| Timber plantations | 1·09 |
| Natural forest | 0·14 |
| Natural pastures | 90·74 |
| | 103·59 |
| Other uses cities, towns, roads etc. | 18·74 |
| | 122·33 |

The gross values of agricultural production of the main products in 1974–75 were as follows:

| | *(million Rands)* |
|---|---|
| *Field Crops* | |
| Maize | 580·8 |
| Wheat | 156·0 |
| Grain sorghum | 32·5 |
| Hay | 56·6 |
| Dry beans | 17·0 |
| Sugar cane | 148·7 |
| Tobacco | 32·0 |
| Cotton | 35·1 |
| Groundnuts | 53·4 |
| Sunflower seed | 29·2 |
| *Horticulture* | |
| Viticulture | 46·7 |
| Citrus | 55·5 |
| Sub-tropical fruit | 23·3 |
| Deciduous fruit and other | 85·7 |
| Vegetables | 89·4 |
| Potatoes | 54·2 |
| *Livestock* | |
| Wool | 106·3 |
| Karakul | 15·0 |
| Poultry slaughtered | 73·6 |
| Eggs | 61·9 |
| Cattle and calves slaughtered | 303·8 |
| Sheep and goats slaughtered | 130·2 |
| Pigs slaughtered | 52·6 |
| Fresh milk | 146·9 |
| Dairy products | 73·5 |
| *All Agriculture: Gross Value* | 2,524·0 |

Production of the main products were as follows:

| ('000 *tonnes*) | 1973–74 | 1974–75 |
|---|---|---|
| Maize | 11,105 | 9,806 |
| Sorghum | 682 | 552 |
| Wheat | 1,871 | 1,596 |
| Sugar cane | 15,454 | 16,896 |
| Apples | 260 | 307 |
| Pears | 92 | 106 |
| Total grapes | 978 | 1,130 |
| Total deciduous fruit | 1,526 | 1,715 |
| Oranges | 596 | 612 |
| Total citrus fruit | 751 | 777 |
| Total Sub-tropical fruit | 355 | 339 |
| Potatoes | 685 | 719 |
| Total vegetables | 1,855 | 1,903 |
| Beef and veal | 505 | 502 |
| Mutton and goats meat | 141 | 148 |
| Poultry | 193 | 224 |
| Eggs (million dozen) | 195 | 210 |
| Wool | 106 | 108 |

The South African Livestock inventory during 1973–74 was as depicted below:

| | *(thousands)* |
|---|---|
| Cattle | 12,986 |
| Woolled sheep | 22,708 |
| Non-woolled sheep | 7,788 |
| Goats | 5,501 |
| Horses | 338 |
| Donkeys and mules | 198 |
| Pigs | 1,209 |
| Poultry | 29,339 |

**Forestry. The total forest area is about 3,500,000 acres, or about 1 per cent of the total land area. Softwoods are imported from the U.S.A. and Canada; hardwoods, from South America and Japan. South Africa is the world's chief producer of wattle extract and in 1971, 58,261 metric tons were produced for export.**

## SOUTH AFRICA

**Mining. Since the discovery of gold in 1884, more than R.13,000 million worth of gold has been mined in South Africa, attracting more than R.1,500 million of new capital,** half of which came from overseas. The total value of South Africa's mineral sales amounted to R.3,540 million in foreign exchange in 1975, making it the fourth largest producer in the world of minerals. Output has been doubled every ten years. South Africa is the world's largest producer of gem diamonds, and one of the two largest producers of manganese, chrome, vanadium, vermiculite and industrial diamonds. It is also the third largest producer of asbestos. South Africa, the world's largest producer of platinum since 1953, also is one of the most important of the producers of uranium. Although constituting only 0·8 per cent of the world's surface South Africa produces about three-quarters of the world's gold (excluding production of the U.S.S.R.).

The following table shows quantities (thousand tons) of principal minerals sold by the Republic in 1975:

Mineral Production and Sales in 1975:

| *Product* | 1975 *Quantity tons* |
|---|---|
| Gold | 713,447 kg |
| Silver | 95,923 kg |
| Diamonds ct. | 8,012,631 |
| Uranium oxides (includes stockpile) | — |
| Metalic minerals: | |
| Antimony (ore concentrates) | 24,243 |
| Beryl (concentrates) | 16 |
| Bismuth (ore concentrates) | — |
| Chrome (ore concentrates) | 1,460,072 |
| Chrome (sand) | 531,423 |
| Copper (metal and concentrates) | — |
| Iron ores: | |
| Haematite | — |
| Magnetite | — |
| Lead (galena concentrates) | 5,557 |
| Lithium (ore concentrates) | — |
| Manganese (ores) | — |
| Nickel | — |
| Tantalite (concentrates), kg | — |
| Tin: | |
| Metal | 728 |
| Cassiterite (concentrates) | 2,416* |
| Titanium (ore concentrates) | — |
| Tungsten (ore concentrates) | — |
| ‡Vandadium | |
| Zinc (ore concentrates) | 108,992 |
| Zicronium (Baddeleyite) | 6,671 |
| Non-metallic minerals: | |
| Andalusite | 76,933 |
| Asbestos | — |
| Barytes | 795 |
| Coal: | |
| Bituminous | 67,297,891 |
| Anthracite | 1,823,033 |
| Corundum | 241 |
| Felspar | 42,935 |
| Fluorspar | 155,704 |
| Graphite | 742 |
| Gypsum | 477,378 |
| Iron Pyrites | 278,175¶‡ |
| Kieselguhr | 649 |
| Limestone and dolomite | 15,064,549 |
| Manganesite | 66,459 |
| Mica | 4,050 |
| Mineral Pigments | 4,352 |
| Phosphates (concentrates) | 1,646,475 |
| Salt | 248,012 |
| Silcrete | 8,080 |
| Silica | 1,135,559 |
| Silimanite (corundum) | 16,972 |
| Talc | 8,598 |
| Vermiculite | 192,691 |
| Wonderstone | 5,061 |
| Ornamental, building stone and sundry: | |
| Clay: | |
| Bentonite | 31,962 |
| China (kaolin) | 59,624 |
| Fire (raw and calcined) | 297,754 |
| Flint (raw and calcined) | 211,906 |
| Fuller's Earth | 263 |
| Granite or Norite | — |
| Marble | 4,693 |
| Shale (for cement manufacture) | 383,362 |
| Quartzite | — |
| Slate | — |
| Semi-precious stones | — |
| Other | — |

† Metal in concentrates.
* Pure.
‡ Sulphur content
¶ Includes Slag, Poly- and Metavandate and fused Pentoxide in $V_2O_2$ content.

**Industry.** The following table shows the gross value of industrial production for 1973 (in million R):

| *Industry* | 1973 |
|---|---|
| Processed foodstuffs | 1,977 |
| Beverages and tobacco | 593 |
| Textiles | 604 |
| Knitting mills | 81 |
| Clothing | 542 |
| Footwear | 115 |
| Wood and wood products | 172 |
| Furniture | 179 |
| Paper and paper products | 370 |
| Printing, publishing and allied industries | 278 |
| Leather and leather products | 37 |
| Rubber products | 195 |
| Basic industrial chemicals | 886 |
| Miscellaneous chemicals | 124 |
| Pharmaceutical preparations | 227 |
| Mineral products (non-metallic) | 509 |
| Basic iron and steel | 746 |
| Basic non-ferrous metals | 225 |
| Metal products | 1,036 |
| Machinery (excluding electrical) | 454 |
| Electrical machinery and equipment | 446 |
| Transport equipment | 190 |
| Motor vehicles | 708 |
| Miscellaneous | 427 |
| Total | 11,121 |

Source: Office of the Economic Adviser to the Prime Minister, Economic Development Programme for the RSA, 1974–1979.

**Commerce.** The following table shows imports by principal countries for the years 1975 and 1976 (in million R):

| *Countries* | 1975 | 1976 |
|---|---|---|
| Africa | 253·6 | 309·8 |
| Sweden | 102·6 | 89·5 |
| U.K. | 1,094·2 | 1,030·7 |
| Belgium | 104·7 | 85·8 |
| Netherlands | 141·4 | 148·2 |
| West Germany | 1,033·8 | 1,058·7 |
| France | 244·9 | 256·2 |
| Switzerland | 140·3 | 123·8 |
| Italy | 203·3 | 211·9 |
| Canada | 79·9 | 86·0 |
| U.S.A. | 984·1 | 1,266·8 |
| Japan | 611·5 | 600·4 |
| Australia | 86·2 | 89·0 |
| New Zealand | 8·7 | 5·5 |

Exports by principal countries 1975 and 1976 (in million R): *continued*

| *Countries* | 1975 | 1976 | *Country* | 1975 | 1976 |
|---|---|---|---|---|---|
| Africa | 423·8 | 453·1 | Italy | 92·2 | 143·5 |
| Sweden | 19·0 | 26·4 | Canada | 132·8 | 123·3 |
| U.K. | 928·1 | 997·0 | U.S.A. | 434·9 | 456·5 |
| Belgium | 120·1 | 190·1 | Japan | 491·7 | 514·8 |
| Netherlands | 88·9 | 124·8 | Australia | 29·3 | 40·9 |
| West Germany | 445·0 | 472·8 | New Zealand | 3·6 | 3·9 |
| France | 115·0 | 148·3 | | | |
| Switzerland | 171·9 | 165·5 | | | |

The following table shows the composition of South Africa's imports for three recent years:

| *Commodity* | 1973 | 1974[1] | 1975[1] |
|---|---|---|---|
| | | *R.million* | |
| Live animals; animal products | 38·5 | 60·5 | 54·2 |
| Vegetable products | 75·2 | 101·0 | 108·4 |
| Animal and vegetable fats and oils and their cleavage products; prepared edible fats; animal and vegetable waxes | 25·6 | 40·6 | 30·3 |
| Prepared foodstuffs; beverages, splints and vinegar; tobacco | 57·7 | 84·4 | 116·8 |
| Mineral products; | 38·6 | 95·7 | 77·5 |
| Products of the chemical and allied industries | 257·3 | 448·3 | 456·4 |
| Artificial resins and plastic materials, cellulose esters and ethers, and articles thereof; rubber, synthetic rubber, factice, and articles thereof | 139·1 | 278·0 | 200·1 |
| Raw hides and skins, leather, fur skins and articles thereof; saddlery and harness; travel goods, handbags and the like; articles of gut (other than silk-worm gut) | 19·6 | 23·6 | 22·2 |
| Wood and articles of wood; wood charcoal; cork and articles of cork; manufactures of straw, of esparto and of other plaiting materials; basketware and wickerwork | 52·3 | 63·8 | 55·1 |
| Paper-making material; paper and paperboard and articles thereof | 117·8 | 203·7 | 159·4 |
| Textiles and textile articles | 326·7 | 464·9 | 352·1 |
| Footwear, headgear, umbrellas, sunshades, whips, riding-crops and parts thereof; prepared feathers and articles made therewith; artificial flowers; articles of human hair, fans | 18·5 | 23·9 | 29·1 |
| Articles of stone, plaster, cement, asbestos, mica and similar materials; ceramic products; glass and glassware | 45·3 | 61·0 | 68·9 |
| Pearls, precious and semi-precious stones, precious metals, rolled precious metals, and articles thereof; imitation jewellery; coinage | 32·1 | 42·9 | 67·9 |
| Base metals and articles of base metal | 244·3 | 507·9 | 573·5 |
| Machinery and mechanical appliances; electrical equipment and parts thereof | 977·6 | 1,320·6 | 1,832·2 |
| Vehicles, aircraft, and parts thereof; vessels and certain associated transport equipment | 601·5 | 789·4 | 1,084·3 |
| Optical, photographic, cinematographic, measuring, checking, precision, medical and surgical instruments and apparatus; clocks and watches; musical instruments; sound recorders and reproducers and parts thereof | 129·3 | 179·4 | 206·6 |
| Miscellaneous manufactured articles | 31·4 | 42·1 | 45·8 |
| Total | 3,282·2 | 4,898·0 | 5,599·7 |

[1] Preliminary figures
Works of art, collector's pieces and antiques as well as other unclassified goods excluded.

The following table shows the composition of South Africa's exports for three recent years:

| *Commodity* | 1973 | 1974[1] | 1975[1] |
|---|---|---|---|
| | | *R.million* | |
| Live animals; animal products | 80·2 | 54·1 | 68·1 |
| Vegetable products | 232·5 | 403·1 | 491·8 |
| Animal and vegetable fats and oils and their cleavage products; prepared edible fats; animal and vegetable waxes | 12·6 | 40·6 | 30·8 |
| Prepared foodstuffs; beverages, spirits and vinegar; tobacco | 275·8 | 446·6 | 512·7 |
| Mineral products | 212·5 | 286·2 | 379·5 |
| Products of the chemical and allied industries | 86·9 | 116·0 | 135·1 |

*continued*

| Commodity | 1973 | 1974[1] | 1975[1] |
|---|---|---|---|
| | *R.million* | | |
| Artificial resins and plastic materials, cellulose esters and ethers, and articles thereof; rubber, synthetic rubber, factice, and articles thereof | 15·6 | 21·5 | 19·6 |
| Raw hides and skins, leather, fur skins and articles thereof; saddlery and harness; travel goods, handbags and the like; articles of gut (other than silk-worm gut) | 73·4 | 55·3 | 49·2 |
| Wood and articles of wood; wood charcoal; cork and articles of cork; manufactures of straw, of esparto and of other plaiting materials; basketware and wickerwork | 4·3 | 5·8 | 4·8 |
| Paper-making material; paper and paperboard and articles thereof | 66·6 | 96·1 | 77·7 |
| Textiles and textile articles | 206·1 | 152·3 | 164·5 |
| Footwear, headgear, umbrellas, sunshades, whips, riding-crops and parts thereof; prepared feathers and articles made therewith: artificial flowers; articles of human hair; fans | 1·3 | 1·6 | 1·6 |
| Articles of stone, plaster, cement, asbestos, mica and similar materials; ceramic products; glass and glassware | 10·8 | 14·2 | 18·8 |
| Pearls, precious and semi-precious stones, precious metals, rolled precious metals, and articles thereof; imitation jewellery; coinage | 478·7 | 710·5 | 988·8 |
| Base metals and articles of base metal | 362·4 | 488·8 | 495·6 |
| Machinery and mechanical appliances; electrical equipment and parts thereof | 106·4 | 129·3 | 149·6 |
| Vehicles, aircraft, and parts thereof; vessels and certain associated transport equipment | 32·8 | 45·3 | 52·9 |
| Optical, photographic, cinematographic, measuring, checking, precision, medical and surgical instruments and apparatus; clocks and watches; musical instruments; sound recorders and reproducers and parts thereof | 9·6 | 11·1 | 14·0 |
| Total | 2,417·7 | 3,339·5 | 3,922·7 |

[1] Preliminary figures.
Excluding miscellaneous manufactured articles, works of art, etc. and other unclassified goods.

## COMMUNICATIONS

**Roads.** There are about 39,800 km of surfaced and 146,000 km of unsurfaced roads—total 185,800 km (1974 figure). Licensed motor vehicles numbered 2,994,114 in 1975. This figure is growing 8 per cent a year.

**Railways.** South African Railways are entirely owned by the State and are operated by the Department of Railways and Harbours. All the chief ports of the Republic of South Africa are connected by rail with Johannesburg, Pretoria, Kimberley, Bloemfontein and other large towns in the interior, and the system extends to Windhoek, capital of South West Africa, and the two main South West African ports.

The track is narrow gauge of 1,065 mm. The total kilometre distance of open lines on 31 March 1976 was 20,092. In South-West Africa the railway kilometre distance was 2,340. On 31 March 1976 there were 2,018 steam locomotives, 1,528 electric locomotives and 973 diesel locomotives.

During 1975–76 the railway system transported 643 million passengers and 130 million tons of freight.

**Shipping.** The five main ports of the Republic of South Africa are Richards Bay, Cape Town, Durban, Port Elizabeth, and East London. During 1975–76, merchandise of 58 million metric tons was handled in all South African harbours.

**Civil Aviation.** Civil Aviation in South Africa is controlled by the Department of Transport.

The following State-owned airports are wholly administered by the Department of Transport:

Jan Smuts Airport, Johannesburg.
D. F. Malan Airport, Cape Town.
Louis Botha Airport, Durban.
J. B. M. Hertzog Airport, Bloemfontein.
Ben Schoeman Airport, East London.
J. G. Strijdom Airport, Windhoek.
H. F. Verwoerd Airport, Port Elizabeth.

At 13 other airports the Department provides air navigation services.

The air navigation services comprise *inter alia* modern aerodrome lighting, radio and radar aids for navigation, approach and landing, a network of inter-station and ground/air communications and personnel to provide Air Traffic Control and Flight Information Services.

South African Airways, as the national air carrier, operates scheduled international air services within Africa and to Europe, Australia, South America and the U.S.A.

Trek Airways of Johannesburg carry non-scheduled flights to Europe.

South African Airways, Commercial Air Services (Pty.) Ltd., Suidwes Lugdiens (Edms.) Bpk. and Namakwaland-lugdiens (Edms.) Bpk. operate scheduled air services within South Africa. There are, furthermore, many air carriers licensed in accordance with the Air Services Act (Act No. 51 of 1949), to operate non-scheduled air services.

Other carriers which maintain services to and from South Africa include Air Madagascar, Lesotho Airways, Botswana Airways, Air Malawi, and Swazi Air.

**Posts, Telegraphs and Telephones.** Postal, telegraph and telephone services are owned and operated by the Government. After 1924 morse code was gradually replaced by the teleprinter as a means of transmitting telegrams. On 23 February 1971 morse was used for the last time on an ordinary telegraph circuit. It is now used only by coastal radio stations for communication with ships at sea. Today the Post Office telegraph system handles 43,000 telegrams daily. There are 736 teleprinter-equipped telegraph offices which can dial one another direct. By the end of March 1975 the number of automatic exchanges had increased to 292 and the number of telephones in use to 1,979,598 of which 82·36 per cent were connected to automatic exchanges. There is a radio telephone service to all the principal countries of the world and direct services exist between the Republic and the United Kingdom, New York, Australia, the Argentine and Nairobi, also to Angola, France, Italy, Japan, Madagascar, Congo, Switzerland and West Germany.

In 1974–75 there were 2,937 post offices and 1,514,899,000 pieces of mail were handled.

Telegraph Traffic

| | 1939–40 | 1960–70 | 1973–74 | 1974–75 |
|---|---|---|---|---|
| Inland telegrams accepted | 6,863,187 | 12,848,624 | 11,966,917 | 12,471,321 |
| International telegrams accepted | 406,258 | 1,227,203 | 1,134,083 | 1,073,627 |

**The new Cape Town to Lisbon undersea cable connects to a global submarine cable network comprising 80,000 nautical route miles, providing 14,000 telephone channels. In the '70s this system will be supplemented by a global network of some six satellites, 40 ground stations and 6,000 telephone circuits.**

**Broadcasting.** There are eighteen separate programme services viz. English, Afrikaans, Springbok, Radio South Africa, Radio Highveld, Radio Good Hope and Radio Port Natal, Radio R.S.A. (External service) and the following in Bantu languages: Southern Sotho, Northern Sotho, Zulu, Xhosa, Tswana, Venda, Tsonga, Ovambo, Herero and Damara/Nama. With the exception of the English and Afrikaans services and Radio R.S.A. all the services carry advertising.

There are 86 F.M. transmitting stations in operation and 98·9 per cent of the total population can tune in to F.M. transmissions: 99 per cent of the Whites, 93·2 per cent of the Coloureds, 100 per cent of the Asians and 99·4 per cent of the Blacks.

The S.A.B.C. broadcasts 2,122½ hours a week in its 20 radio programme services and 37 hours a week in its television service.

At the end of 1975 there were approximately 2·5-million radio listeners' licence holders and at the end of June 1976, approximately 500,000 TV licence holders. There were 161,767 radio licence holders in 1936 and 2,400,000 in 1974. The cost of a radio listener's licence is R.6·60 a year, while a TV licence costs R.36 a year.

### NEWSPAPERS

**The Argus.** F. 1857. Afternoon. English. P.O. Box 56, Cape Town.

**The Cape Times.** F. 1876. Morning. English. P.O. Box 11, Cape Town.

**Die Burger.** F. 1915. Morning. Afrikaans. P.O. Box 692, Cape Town.

**Rand Daily Mail.** F. 1902. Morning. English. P.O. Box 1138, Johannesburg. Tel. No. 28–1500. Telex: 43–0014.

**Post.** Weekly. P.O. Box 1491, Durban, 4000.

**Die Transvaler.** F. 1937. Morning. Afrikaans. P.O. Box 5474, Johanneburg

**The Star.** F. 1887. Afternoon. English. P.O. Box 1014, Johannesburg.

**Die Vaderland.** Afternoon. Afrikaans. P.O. Box 845, Johannesburg.

**Hoofstad.** Afternoon. Afrikaans. P.O. Box 422, Pretoria.

**The World.** Daily. English. P.O. Box 6663, Johannesburg.

**Sunday Express.** Sunday. English. P.O. Box 1067, Johannesburg.

**Sunday Times.** Sunday. English. P.O. Box 1090, Johannesburg, 2000.

**Rapport.** Sunday. Afrikaans. P.O. Box 8422, Johannesburg.

**South African Financial Gazette.** Friday. English. P.O. Box 8161, Johannesburg.

**Post.** Sunday. English. P.O. Box 3413, Johannesburg. Non-White circulation (National).

**Diamond Fields Advertiser.** Morning. English. P.O. Box 610, Kimberley, 8300.

**Natal Witness.** Morning. English. P.O. Box 362, Pietermaritzburg.

**Natal Mercury.** Morning. English. P.O. Box 950, Durban.

**Daily News.** Afternoon. English. P.O. Box 1491, Durban.

**Sunday Tribune.** Sunday. English. P.O. Box 1491, Durban.

**Die Oosterlig.** Afternoon. Afrikaans. P.O. Box 525, Port Elizabeth.

**Weekend World.** Weekly. English. P.O. Box 6663, Johannesburg.

**Eastern Province Herald.** Morning. English. P.O. Box 1117, Port Elizabeth.

**The Evening Post.** Afternoon. English. P.O. Box 1121, Port Elizabeth.

**Pretoria News.** Afternoon. English. P.O. Box 439, Pretoria.

**Daily Dispatch.** F. 1872. Morning. English/Afrikaans. P.O. Box 131, East London, Cape Province.

### ATOMIC ENERGY

All matters relating to atomic energy in South Africa are under the statutory control of the Atomic Energy Board. It has responsibility for regulating the production and sales of uranium and the distribution of radioisotopes and for implementing a carefully drafted Research and Development Programme.

Much of the emphasis of the Programme is on the exploitation of the country's natural resources of materials having significance in nuclear technology. Where appropriate the Geological Survey and the Government Metallurgical Laboratory are undertaking portions of the Programme and a pilot uranium refining plant is now in operation at the latter establishment.

Investigations more specific to reactor technology and radioactivity will be undertaken at the National Nuclear Research Centre at Pelindaba some 18 miles west of Pretoria. The country's first research reactor, SAFARI I, with a 20 MW capacity, went critical in March 1965. A 3 MeV Van de Graaff particle accelerator is also operating.

South Africa is the third largest producer of $U_3O_8$ in the Western World. Economically exploitable deposits were estimated in 1961 to amount to 234,000 tons.

Scientists of the Atomic Energy Board have succeeded (July 1970) in developing a new process for uranium enrichment and they are at present engaged on the building of a plant for the enrichment of uranium based on this process.

The Uranium Enrichment Bill has been introduced into Parliament. It provides for the establishment of a body to be known as the Uranium Enrichment Corporation of South Africa Ltd.

### EDUCATION

The responsibility for education in South Africa has been delegated to a number of departments.

Primary and secondary education for Whites, as well as the training of teachers to a large extent, is administered by the four provincial education departments.

All types of Bantu education are controlled by the Republican Government through the Department of Bantu Education. The Departments for Coloured Affairs and Indian Affairs administer primary and secondary education and university, technical, vocational and special education for Coloureds and Indians.

Although education varies slightly at different stages in the different provinces the whole field covered in the period of 12 years primary and secondary education is essentially the same. In general education is compulsory for all White children up to the age of 16 years.

Institutions under the control of the Department of National Education include the technical colleges, housecraft and technical high schools, schools of industries and reform schools, state-aided vocational schools and state-aided special schools for the physically handicapped, including the blind, the deaf and dumb, the cerebral palsied and the epileptic in various sentres in the Republic. State expenditure by the Department of Education, Arts and Science including administration and expenditure connected with the above-mentioned institutions, Archives, Archaeological Survey, the Republic Observatory and subsidies to universities, libraries and other cultural institutions for the financial year was R.442,362,000 in 1976/77. The University of South Africa with 23,339 students in 1972, has its headquarters at Pretoria and conducts correspondence courses through its Division of External Studies. It also acts as an examining body. In 1974 there were 10 universities primarily for Whites (excluding the University of South Africa) and 95,879 White and 8,933 Non-White students enrolled

There are 5 universities for non-whites and in 1975 a total of 6,979 students enrolled.

The University of South Africa enrolled 40,207 students in 1975.

**RELIGION**

There is no State Church in South Africa. All denominations are, however, represented, and the three Dutch Reformed Churches (Nederduits, Gereformeerde, Nederduits Hervormde and Gereformeerde Kerk) have the greatest number of adherents.

The following table gives the number of adherents of the principal religions:

*Membership of Religious Denominations* 1970

| *Religion* | *Total* | *Whites* | *Coloureds* | *Asians* | *Blacks* |
|---|---|---|---|---|---|
| Total | 21,402,470 | 3,726,540 | 2,021,430 | 618,140 | 15,036,360 |
| Nederduitse Gereformeerd | | 1,487,080 | 573,400 | | |
| Gereformeerd | 3,329,710 | 113,620 | 3,940 | 830 | 924,820 |
| Nederduitsch Hervormd | | 224,400 | 1,620 | | |
| Church of the Province of South Africa | | | | | |
| Church of England in South Africa | 1,676,800 | 399,950 | 333,200 | 5,930 | 937,720 |
| Church of England—so stated | | | | | |
| Anglican—so stated | | | | | |
| Presbyterian | 454,460 | 117,250 | 7,560 | 320 | 329,320 |
| Congregational | 349,790 | 19,640 | 144,760 | 70 | 185,320 |
| Methodist | 2,151,840 | 357,410 | 115,810 | 2,540 | 1,676,080 |
| Lutheran | 884,120 | 40,620 | 83,510 | 250 | 759,740 |
| Roman Catholic | 1,844,270 | 304,840 | 195,630 | 13,820 | 1,329,930 |
| Bantu Separatist Churches | 2,761,120 | — | — | — | 2,761,120 |
| Other Christian | 2,344,450 | 431,990 | 379,620 | 26,840 | 1,506,000 |
| Jewish, Hebrew | 118,120 | 117,990 | 110 | 20 | * |
| Islam | 255,210 | 430 | 130,050 | 124,730 | * |
| Hindu | 423,300 | 120 | 620 | 422,560 | * |
| Other and unspecified | 4,809,280 | 111,200 | 51,590 | 20,230 | 4,626,260 |

* Not available

# Provinces of the Republic of South Africa

## CAPE OF GOOD HOPE

**Capital**—Cape Town.

**Administrator**—Dr. L. A. P. A. Munnik.

**Area:** 682,441 sq. km.
(Area of Transkei subtracted).

In April 1978 the 3,800 km of East Grigualard will be transferred to Natal.

**Population:** (census 1970) 4,235,523: white, 1,102,367; Bantu, 1,360,172; Coloured, 1,751,367; Asian, 21,617. Principal towns and population (census 1970) are as follows: Cape Town, 1,096,597 (White, 378,505; Coloured, 598,952; Asian, 11,263; Bantu, 107,877); Port Elizabeth, 468,499 (White, 149,569; Coloured, 112,154; Asian, 5,280; Bantu, 201,574); East London, 123,294 (White, 56,809; Coloured, 13,249; Asian, 1,994; Bantu, 51,244); Kimberley, 103,789 (White, 29,397; Coloured, 24,657; Asian, 938; Bantu, 48,797).

**Legislature:** Provincial council elections are held every five years. Representation at the last elections (March 1974) was as follows: United Party 15; National Party 37; Progressive Party 1.

The Executive Committee was formed by members of the National Party.

**Finance:** Loans are now granted to the provinces, so there is no provision for revenue and expenditure. In 1977/78 the subsidy and loan was R.540,572,000 (1976/77—R.504,087,000).

**Education:** The universities of the Province are those of Cape Town; Rhodes University, Grahamstown; University of Stellenbosch; University of Port Elizabeth and the University of Fort Hare, now under control of Bantu Education Department, and the University of the Western Cape for coloured persons. In 1974 there were 246,667 white pupils in Cape schools (including public, private, public aided schools). In 1976 there were 952 Indians in State and State aided schools in Cape Province and in 1973 (latest figures available) there were 515,105 pupils in State and State aided schools. In 1973, 3,919 coloured and Indian students enrolled at training colleges for C. and I. teachers. In 1976 there were 210,210 black pupils at schools in white areas.

## NATAL

**Capital**—Pietermaritzburg.

**Administrator**—Hon. W. W. B. Havemann.

**Area:** 33,578 sq. miles.

**Population:** (census 1970) 2,140,166; white, 442,499; coloured, 66,836; Asian, 514,810; Bantu, 1,116,499. Principal towns and populations are: Durban, 721,265 (white, 257,777; coloured, 43,396; Asian, 234,772; Bantu, 224,209); Pietermaritzburg, 158,921 (white, 45,503; coloured, 8,756; Asian, 36,400; Bantu, 68,762); Ladysmith, 28,554 (white, 8,177; coloured, 522; Asian, 6,031; Bantu, 13,884).

**Education:** University of Natal, founded 1909; formerly a constituent College of the University of South Africa; assumed university status 1949. University of Zululand (Bantu) founded in 1960. The University College, Durban for Asians (Indians) has been granted academic autonomy and as from 1971 will be known as the University of Durban-Westville.

In 1974 there were 101,949 white pupils in schools in Natal (including public, private and State aided schools). In 1976 there were 164,020 Indians in State and State aided schools and in 1973 (latest figures available) 22,432 coloureds in State and State aided schools. In 1973, 621 coloured and Indian students registered at teachers training colleges. In 1976 559 Black students enrolled at teacher training colleges in the white areas. In 1976 there were 202,522 black pupils in schools in white areas.

**Legislature:** Representation at the provincial elections of 1974 (elections are held every five years) was as follows:

| *Party* | *Seats* |
|---|---|
| United Party | 16 |
| Nationalist Party | 4 |
| | 20 |

**Finance:** Loans are now granted to the provinces so there is no provision made for expenditure and revenue. In 1977–78 the subsidy and loan was R.229,606,000 (1976–77—R.220,053,000).

## ORANGE FREE STATE

**Capital**—Bloemfontein.

**Administrator**—Hon. A. C. van Wyk.

**Area:** 49,866 sq. miles.

**Population:** (census 1970) 1,649,306: white, 295,903; coloured, 36,090; Asian, 5; Bantu, 1,317,308. Principal towns and populations are: Bloemfontein, 180,179 (white, 74,516 coloured, 10,152; Asian, 1; Bantu, 95,510); Kroonstad, 50,898 (white, 15,475; coloured, 1,316; Bantu, 34,107); Bethlehem, 29,460 (white, 9,332; coloured, 553; Bantu, 19,575.

**Legislature:** Representation of the parties in the 1974 provincial council elections (elections take place every five years) was as follows: National Party, 28; United Party nil.

**Finance:** Loans are now granted to the provinces. In 1977–78 the subsidy and loan granted was R.1,596,007,000 (1976–77—R.1,482,933,000).

**Education:** University of the Orange Free State, Bloemfontein, originally part of Grey College, founded 1855; constituted a University 18 March 1950. In 1974 there were 70,585 white pupils in schools in O.F.S. (including public, private and public aided schools.)

In 1973 there were 9,040 coloured pupils in State and State aided schools. In 1976, 324 black students enrolled at teachers training colleges in the white areas. In 1976 there were 291,021 black pupils in schools in white areas.

## TRANSVAAL

**Capital**—Pretoria.

**Administrator**—Hon. S. G. J. van Niekerk.

**Area:** 110,450 sq. miles.

**Population:** (census 1970) 6,388,870: white, 1,890,182; coloured, 150,853; Asian, 80,563; Bantu, 4,267,272. Principal towns and populations are: Johannesburg, 1,432,643 (white, 501,061; coloured, 82,639; Asian, 39,348; Bantu, 809,595); Pretoria, 561,703 (white, 304,618; coloured, 11,343; Asian, 11,047; Bantu, 234,695); Germiston, 139,472 (white, 101,211; coloured, 4,471; Asian, 2,158; Bantu, 31,632); Springs, 104,090 (white, 44,627; coloured, 2,234; Asian, 1,337; Bantu, 55,892); Benoni, 152,794 (white, 51,210; coloured, 538, Asian, 7,276; Bantu, 103,770); Krugersdorp, 91,202 (white, 34,844; coloured, 3,047; Asian, 711; Bantu, 52,600; Roodeport, 139,810 (white, 70,830; coloured, 2,351; Asian, 1,067; Bantu, 65,562).

**Legislature:** Provincial elections normally take place every five years. The last was in March 1965. The various political parties are represented as follows: Nationalist Party, 62; United Party, 14. Progressive, 3.

**Finance:** Loans are now made to the provinces. In 1977–78 the subsidy and loan was R.663,112,000 (1976–77—R.614,333,000).

**Education:** University of Pretoria founded in 1908, secured higher status on 10 October 1930. University of Witwatersrand, Johannesburg, founded 1904, constituted as a university on 1 March 1922. University of Potchefstroom founded 1905 with higher status on 17 March 1951. University of the North (Bantu) founded 1960. Rand Afrikaans University established 1966. In 1974 there were 471,494 white pupils in Tvl. schools (public, private and govt. aided schools). In 1976 there were 23,036 Indians in State and State aided schools and in 1973 there were 39,675 coloured pupils in State and State aided schools. In 1973, 542 coloured and Indian students registered at teachers training colleges. In 1976 there were 1,326 black students enrolled at black teacher training colleges in the white area of Transvaal (i.e. not including the Homelands). In 1976 there were 729,357 black pupils at schools in white areas.

# South-West Africa

(SUIDWES-AFRIKA)

**Capital**—Windhoek.

**Administrator**—Hon. B. J. van der Walt.

The territory of South-west Africa is bounded on the north by Angola and Zambia, on the east by Botswana and on the south by Cape Province of the Republic of South Africa. It was annexed by Germany in 1884 and was captured by South African forces in 1915. It is now administered by the Republic of South Africa in the spirit of the mandate from the former League of Nations, dated 17 September 1920.

Under the Union Act, No. 49 of 1919, the exercise of the mandate was vested in a Governor-General who delegated his powers to the administrator appointed by the Union Government. A limited measure of self-government was conferred upon the inhabitants by the Union Act No. 42, 1925. Fundamental and far-reaching changes in the constitutional position of the Territory were introduced by the passing of the South-West Africa Affairs Amendment Act, 1949 (No. 23 of 1949). The advisory Council was abolished as well as the nominated members of the Legislative Assembly. All 18 members of the Assembly are now elected by the registered voters of the Territory.

The Territory is represented in the Republic House of Assembly by six members duly elected by the registered voters of the Territory and in the Senate by four Senators, of which number, two are elected and two nominated by the State President. One of the nominated Senators is selected mainly on the ground of his thorough acquaintance, by reason of his official experience or otherwise, with the reasonable wants and wishes of the coloured races of the Territory.

As from 1 November 1951 the powers of the Governor-General under the Treaty of Peace and South-West Africa Mandate Act, 1919, and the delegated powers of the Administrator to legislate by Proclamation were abolished, so that only the Parliament of the Republic has power to legislate on those matters in respect of which the Legislative Assembly is not competent to legislate.

On 1 September 1975 a Constitutional Conference, consisting of elected and traditional representatives of the Territory's 11 population groups, formally commenced in Windhoek. The aim of the Conference was to decide the political future of the Territory.

The Conference already held four plenary sessions, while it also appointed committees to make conclusive studies of various aspects concerning for example, economic elevation, social development, educational facilities and constitutional possibilities. The Conference's constitutional committee is presently engaged in discussing constitutional proposals.

## LEGAL SYSTEM

By the Administration of Justice Proclamation, 1919, Roman-Dutch law as existing and applied in the Province of the Cape of Good Hope on 1 January 1920 was introduced as the common law of the Territory, and all existing laws in conflict therewith were to the extent of such conflict, repealed. Much of the statute law of the Union has been specifically extended to the Territory by Act of the Parliament of the Republic, by proclamation or ordinance, subject to amendments required by local circumstances.

There is a superior court, the Supreme Court of South Africa, S.W. Africa Division, consisting of two judges of which one is the Judge President. It has its seat at Windhoek, but may be held at other places appointed by the Judge President. In civil cases the judge sits alone, but in criminal cases the court is composed of the judge, who is the President, and two other assessor members, who must either be advocates or magistrates. There is no jury.

By proclamation No. 38 of 1920, circuit courts were established with a similar constitution to that of the High Court. The Territory is divided into two or more circuit districts, in each of which a circuit court is held at least twice a year. An appeal from the Supreme Court and from a circuit court lies to the Appellate Division of the Supreme Court of South Africa.

The Territory exclusive of Okavango, Owambo, Caprivi Zipfel and the Kaokoveld, is divided into 17 magisterial districts, wherein the various magistrates exercise certain administrative as well as judicial functions. Okavango, Owambo and Kaokoveld are also magisterial districts, but are under the control of the Bantu Affairs Commissioners of the Department of Bantu Administration and Development. In these four areas a system of indirect rule is in force and all civil disputes between natives, and all crimes committed by natives therein, except capital offences, are tried by Native Chiefs or Tribunal Councils consisting of Headmen, according to tribal law and custom. The Development of self-Government for the Native Nations in South-West Africa Act was passed by the South African Parliament in 1968, and in terms of this Act a Legislative Council and Executive Council have been established for Owambo, Kavango, and the Eastern Caprivi, which is the homeland of more than half the native population of the territory.

## AREA AND POPULATION

The total area of the territory is 824,269 km$^2$, including the area of Walvis Bay (1,124 km$^2$) which is part of the Republic of South Africa as a result of the area's proclamation as a British Crown Territory in 1878, and its subsequent annexation to the Cape of Good Hope in 1884. Certain islands along the coast of South West Africa are also part of the Republic of South Africa. The estimated population figures for 1974 are as follows: Total, 852,000 comprising 396,000 Ovambos, 99,000 Whites, 95,000 Damaras, 56,000 Hereros, 37,000 Namas, 56,000 Kavangos, 29,000 East Caprivians, 32,000 Coloureds, 19,000 Rehobothers, 26,000 Bushmen, 5,000 Tswanas and others and 7,000 Kaokovelders.

The capital is Windhoek, while principal towns are Walvis Bay, Keetmanshoop, Otjiwarongo, Tsumeb and Swakopmund.

**Finance:** In 1973 the Territory's Gross National Product totalled R.615·6 million. The total administrative costs of running the Territory were nearly R.384 million in 1974. The estimated South African expenditure in South West Africa amounts to about R.150 million for the book year 1974/75.

## PRODUCTION, INDUSTRY AND COMMERCE

The generally low rainfall prevailing in the Territory hampers agriculture. Practically the whole of the Territory is farmed under pastoral conditions. The Territory exports annually considerable numbers of cattle to the Republic, mainly for slaughter. In the south, farming is confined principally to sheep, especially karakul, and goats. In 1970 agriculture provided a total product worth R.64 million.

At Walvis Bay there is an important and growing fishing industry, with several factories engaged in canning, and in manufacturing fish meal and fish oil. At Luderitz there are similar industries, including a sealing undertaking and a producer of agar-agar. During the crawfish season from 70 to 100 cutters operate from Luderitz. The fishing industry's total sales in 1972 amounted to R.58·8 million.

The most important economic sector is, however, mining. It contributes about one-quarter of the Gross Domestic Product and provides employment for roughly 16,000 people. Diamonds, sales of which reached R.147 million in 1973, made the most valuable contribution. Other minerals include base minerals, blister copper, refined lead and low-grade uranium.

Other economic sectors are *inter alia* forestry and tourism, while the production and construction industries, commerce and banking and financial services also make significant contributions. Economic development is further being stimulated by Government-subsidized development corporations, such as the Bantu Development Corporation. The latter in 1973 had a budget of almost R.14 million, while it created employment opportunities for about 1,450 black South West Africans.

**Planning.** A five-year plan for the Territory evolved in 1963 by the Odendaal Commission, provided for accelerated progress for the inhabitants of the Territory in all spheres.

A huge hydro-electric power and transmission project based on the Kunene River is now in the process of being built at a cost of about R.225 million. This project is to entail the following: a power line from the hydro-electric station at Matala in Angola to the Owambo border and thence to Tsumeb; a regulating dam; hydro-electric generating plant at the Ruacana Falls; a power line from Ruacana linked to the Matala–Tsumeb line; power lines from Tsumeb to centres further south; a pumping plant and accessories at Calueque in Angola and a canal linking up with the existing Owambo canals.

## COMMUNICATIONS

Tarred roads in 1973 amounted to 2,772 km. Road bridges in the same year amounted to 350, while 23 additional bridges were under construction.

Aircraft of South African Airways make 20 direct return flights every week between centres in the Territory and the Republic. In addition, SAA's Boeing aircraft land at Windhoek twice a week *en route* from Johannesburg to overseas centres.

The railways in South West Africa were incorporated in the South African system from 1 April 1922, with headquarters at Windhoek. The length of railways in kilometers per 10,000 inhabitants in the Territory is 30·7, which is the highest comparative figure in Africa. Vehicle distances covered by road transport services were 7·93 million km in 1972/73, while trailer distances were 8·20 million km. In the same year the total tonnage of goods amounted to 353,356 tons.

The chief ports are Walvis Bay and Luderitz. In the financial year 1970–71, Walvis Bay handled 1,419,390 tons of cargo.

Telegraphs and telephone systems are operated by the Department of Posts and Telegraphs. In 1973 there were 38,746 telephones. A F.M. Radio service was introduced for Windhoek and surrounding areas and for Owambo. The value of telephone, telegraph and radio installations in the Territory amounted to R.35·81 million on 31 March 1973.

## EDUCATION

Education is free both for primary and secondary instruction. The number of schools for Blacks and Coloureds rose from 313 in 1960 to 598 in 1973; teachers from 1,310 in 1960 to 3,453 in 1973; and students from 43,000 in 1960 to 140,000 in 1973.

## HEALTH

Expenditure on health services in the Territory amounted to R.12·73 million in 1973/74. Hospitals and clinics totalled 183 in 1974, while there were 143 general medical practitioners, 19 specialists and 2,330 nursing staff in 1973.

# Spain

## (ESTADO ESPAÑOL)

**Capital**—Madrid.

**Sovereign**—King Juan Carlos I.

**National Flag:** A tricolour fesse-wise, red, yellow, red, the yellow in width equal to the two red stripes combined, the flag charged with the national arms, which bear an eagle black and are flanked by the Pillars of Hercules.

### CONSTITUTION AND GOVERNMENT

ON 14 April 1931 King Alfonso XIII, as a result of the Republican victory in the municipal elections, decided to leave the country. The Spanish Republic was then proclaimed and a provisional government formed. Later the Constituent Cortes assembled and the Republican Constitution was drawn up. Alcalá Zamora was elected President of the Republic.

At the general election in 1936 the Popular Front, a coalition of left-wing parties, gained a parliamentary majority over the right-wing coalition. The President, Alcalá Zamora, resigned and was succeeded by one of the chief leaders of the Popular Front, Manuel Azaña.

In July of the same year the country was embroiled in civil war, which raged for nearly three years. It is estimated that there were over one million dead.

The Civil War ended in March 1939 with the defeat of the Republican forces, and General Franco, the leader of the opposing forces, became the head of the Spanish State.

Three months later the National Council of all the parties—the traditionalists or monarchists, the *Falangistas* and the right-wing Acción Popular—united under the *Caudillo*, or leader, General Franco, met in Burgos to legislate for the country.

Three years later, on 17 July 1942, the present Spanish Cortes was established by law. In July 1945 the Cortes passed the *Fuero de los Españoles*, the Spanish Charter of Rights and in October of the same year a law was passed creating the institution of popular referendum for the final ratification of laws of outstanding importance.

This referendum was put to the test two years later on 18 July 1947, when the Law of Succession to the Headship of State, passed by the Cortes on 8 June 1947, was ratified.

On 14 December 1966, a national referendum gave a 'yes' vote to the Ley Organica de Eslado (Organic Law of the State), which changed the previous constitution considerably.

The Head of State, supreme representative of the nation, has among other duties, that of calling together the Cortes (Parliament) appointing and dismissing the Presidents of the Government and of the Cortes and of presiding over the meetings of the Consejo del Reino (Council of the Kingdom) and of the Consejo Nacional (National Council).

The President of the Government is appointed by the Head of State from among three candidates proposed by the Consejo del Reino (Council of the Kingdom): his term of office is for five years and he exercises in the name of the Head of State the national leadership of the Movement (Jefatura Nacional del Movimiento).

The Cortes in accordance with the new constitution is formed by the following groups of Procuradores (attorneys): (a) Members of the Government; (b) National Counsellors; (c) The Presidents of the Supreme Court of Justice, State Council, the Supreme Court of Military Justice, the Court of the Accounts of the Kingdom and the National Economy Council; (d) One hundred and fifty representatives of the Trade Unions; (e) A representative from the Municipalities of each Province, chosen by their Town Councils from among the Councillors and another from each Municipality of more than three hundred thousand inhabitants and from those of Ceuta and Melilla chosen by their Councillors; a representative from each Provincial Council and the Commonwealth of the Canary Islands chosen by their respective corporations from among their members, and the representatives of the Local Authorities of those territories not established as Provinces, chosen in the same way; (f) Two representatives of the Family for each Province elected by those who appear in the electoral rolls as heads of families and married women, as established by law; (g) University Rectors; (h) The President of the Institute of Spain and two representatives chosen from among the members of the Royal Academies which form part of it; the President of the Supreme Council for Scientific Research and two representatives of the same elected by its members; (i) The President of the Institute of Civil Engineers and a representative of the Associations of Engineers which form part of it; two representatives of the Colleges of Lawyers, two representatives of the Medical Colleges. One representative from each of the following Associations: Stock Exchange Agents, Architects, Economists, Chemists, Graduates and Doctors in Science and Arts, Graduates and Doctors in Chemistry and Physics, Notaries, Court Attorneys, Property Registrars, Veterinary Surgeons and other professional associations of University Graduates or equivalent which in future are recognized for this effect, who will be chosen by their respective official associations. Three representatives from the official Chambers of Commerce, one from the Chamber of Urban Proprietors and one representing the Tenants' Association, chosen by their Board of Directors or official organizations; (j) Those persons, up to the number of twenty five, who for their ecclesiastical, military or administrative rank, or for their services to the country, are appointed by the Head of State, after consulation with the Council of the Kingdom.

The establishment of the right of appeal as contrafuero (infringement 'ultra vires') constitutes an important innovation. Every legislative act or general rule of the Government which infringes the principles of the national Movement or the other fundamental laws of the Kingdom is contrafuero. As a guarantee of the principles and norms affected by contrafuero, the right of appeal to the Head of State is established.

With respect to the succession to the office of Head of State the following rules are established: Upon the office of Head of State becoming vacant, his powers will be assumed by a Regency Council, consisting of the President of the Cortes, the Prelate of highest rank and longest service as Counsellor of the Kingdom, and the Captain General, or in his default, the Lieutanant General on active service and with most years of service in the Army, Navy or Air Force.

If the Head of State dies or is declared incapable of carrying out his duties without having appointed his successor, the Regency Council will assume the powers, except that of revoking the appointment of any of the members of the Council itself, who will in any case, retain their appointments.

He will within three days summon the members of the Government and of the Council of the Kingdom to decide, in continuous and secret session, by decision of two thirds of those present the persons of royal blood possessing the conditions required by the present law, taking into account the supreme interest of the country, to be proposed to the Cortes, as King. If the person proposed is not accepted, the Government and the Council of the Kingdom can submit a second proposal, in accordance with the same procedure, in favour of another person of royal blood who also fulfils the legal conditions.

When in the opinion of those present there is none who fulfils these conditions, or the proposals made to the Cortes have not been accepted, they will propose to these, as Regent, in accordance with the same conditions, the person who for his prestige, capabilities and possible services to the nation should occupy this office. When making this proposal, they may indicate the length of time and conditions of the Regency and the Cortes must make a decision in respect to each of these. If the person proposed as Regent is not accepted by the Cortes, the Government and the Council of the Kingdom will have to make new proposals, following the same procedure until the Cortes have duly given their approval.

On the death of General Franco, 20 November 1975, Don Juan Carlos Borbón y Borbón (designated successor to General Franco) was sworn in as King of Spain. Born in 1938, he is the son of Don Juan de Borbón y Battenberg and Doña Maria de las Mercedes de Borbón y Orleans, and grandson of King Alfonso XIII and Queen Victoria Eugenia of Spain. In 1962 Juan Carlos married Princess Sophia, daughter of the late King Paul of the Hellenes and of Queen Frederica. There is a son and two daughters.

**Ministry**

*President of the Government:* Adolfo Suarez Gonzalez.
*First Deputy Prime Minister—Defence:* Don Manuel Gutierrez Mellado.
*Second Deputy Prime Minister—Economic Affairs:* Don Enrique Fuentes Quintana.
*Third Deputy Prime Minister—Political Affairs:* Don Fernando Abril Martorell.
*Minister of Foreign Affairs:* Don Marcelino Oreja.
*Minister of Justice:* Don Landelino Lavilla Alsina.

*Minister of the Treasury:* Don Francisco Fernandez Ordoñez.
*Minister of the Interior:* Don Rodolfo Martin Villa.
*Minister of Education:* Don Iñigo Cavero Lataillade.
*Minister of Industry and Power:* Don Alberto Oliart Sausol.
*Minister of Transport and Communications:* Don Jose Llado y Fernández-Urrutia.
*Minister of Agriculture:* Don Jose E. Martinez Genique.
*Minister of Commerce and Tourism:* Don Juan Antonio García Díez.
*Minister of Public Works and Town Planning:* Don Joaquin Garrigues Walker.
*Minister of Labour:* Don Manuel Jimenez de Parga.
*Minister of Culture and Welfare:* Don Pio Cabanillas Gallas.
*Minister for the Presidency:* Don Jose M. Otero Novas.
*Minister of Health and Social Security:* Don Enrique Sanchez de León.
*Minister co-opted for Relations with the Regions:* Don Manuel Clavero Arevalo.
*Minister co-opted for Relations with the Cortes:* Don Ignacio Camuñas Solis.

## LOCAL GOVERNMENT

The country is divided into 50 provinces, including the Balearic Islands and the Canaries. Each province has a Civil Governor, who is a delegate of the Central administration, and a *Diputación Provincial* (Provincial Council). This Council has one deputy for each *partido* (legal division) in the province. The deputy is elected by delegates of the various municipalities contained in the *partido*. There are 489 *partidos* and over 9,212 municipalities.

Each municipality has its own *Ayuntamiento* (Town Council) headed by an *Alcalde* (Mayor) who is nominated by the Government in the provincial capitals and by the Civil Governor in the other towns. The other councillors are elected, and their number varies with the size of the population. One-third of the councillors are elected by heads of households, one-third by the syndical organizations and the others are coopted by the first two groups from among the leading citizens of the municipality.

Both the Provincial and the Town Councils have their own budgets and a large measure of autonomy in expenditure and the means of covering it.

The Balearic Islands have the same administration as the mainland, but the two groups of the Canary Islands (Las Palmas and Santa Cruz de Tenerife) are each governed by a *Cabildo* (Chapter).

## LEGAL SYSTEM

The judicial organization is asf ollows: the *Tribunal Supremo* (Supreme High Court) situated in Madrid; 22 *Audiencias Territoriales* (Territorial High Courts) most of them covering several provinces, which decide in the second instance on sentences passed in civil matters; an *Audiencia Provincial* (Provincial High Court) for each province numbering 50, before which all criminal cases are tried; a *Juzgado de Primera Instancia* (Court of First Instance) for each *partido* (division) 467 in number; 256 *Juzgados Municipales* (Municipal Courts), 443 *Juzgados Comarcales* (District Courts) and 7,695 *Juzgados de Paz* (Courts of Peace). These last three groups deal with minor infractions of the law. There are 301 Judicial Districts.

The *Tribunal Supremo* contains six courts: the first is the court of cassation for civil and commercial actions; the second is the court of criminal appeal: the third, fourth and fifth deal with contentious administrative matters, and the sixth is the court of appeal in social matters.

The President of the *Tribunal Supremo* is appointed by the Government.

## AREA AND POPULATION

Spain covers an area of 490,774 sq. km. With the Balearic and Canary Islands the area is 503,061 sq. km.

The *Islas Baleares* (Balearic Islands) are a province of Spain. They are situated in the Mediterranean, off the east coast of Spain, opposite Valencia. They consist of four large and seven small islands. The four large islands are *Mallorca* (Majorca), *Menorca* (Minorca), *Ibiza* (Iviza) and *Formentora*. Their combined area is 5,014 sq. km.

The *Islas Canarias* (Canary Islands) are situated off the north-west coast of Africa, to the south of Casablanca. They are divided into two groups, each considered a province of Spain, named after their respective capitals *Las Palmas de Gran Canaria* and *Santa Cruz de Tenerife*. The first group contains Gran Canaria, Fuerteventura, Lanzarote and six islets; the second group consists of Tenerife, Palma, Gomera and Hierro. They cover a total area of 7,273 sq. km.

The population at mid-1974 was 35,109,000. The annual average percentage growth rate of the population for the period 1960–74 and for the period 1965–74 was 1·1. The population of the Balearic Islands is 468,342, and that of the Canaries 1,047,370. Ceuta has a population of 76,098 and Melilla 80,758.

In 1974, 30,346,000 tourists visited Spain; revenue from this source totalled 2,862,100 million dollars.

Vital statistics for 1974 were:

| | 1974* |
|---|---|
| Marriages | 266,449 |
| Births | 678,049 |
| Deaths | 294,567 |

* Provisional figures.

The population of the principal Provinces at 31 December 1973 was as follows:

| *Province* | *Population* | *Province* | *Population* |
|---|---|---|---|
| Alava | 220,722 | Madrid | 4,002,296 |
| Albacete | 344,328 | Málaga | 896,120 |
| Alicante | 982,951 | Murcia | 875,114 |
| Almeria | 395,462 | Navarra | 479,893 |
| Avila | 210,889 | Orense | 448,531 |
| Badajoz | 700,901 | Oviedo | 1,089,311 |
| Baleares | 557,434 | Palencia | 197,952 |
| Barcelona | 4,174,846 | Palmas (Las) | 600,297 |
| Burgos | 360,724 | Pontevedra | 815,165 |
| Cáceres | 469,836 | Salamanca | 380,816 |
| Cádiz | 916,429 | Santa Cruz de Tenerife | 611,683 |
| Castellón | 399,451 | Santander | 492,155 |
| Ciudad Real | 508,739 | Segovia | 161,992 |
| Córdoba | 742,727 | Sevilla | 1,375,401 |
| Coruña (La) | 1,067,600 | Soria | 114,649 |
| Guenca | 246,280 | Tarragona | 452,881 |
| Gerona | 428,789 | Teruel | 167,416 |
| Granada | 756,899 | Toledo | 480,271 |
| Guadaljara | 147,195 | Valencia | 1,837,304 |
| Guipúzcoa | 649,246 | Valladolid | 432,361 |
| Huelva | 416,342 | Vizcaya | 1,095,298 |
| Huesca | 221,099 | Zamora | 257,031 |
| Jaén | 676,680 | Zaragoza | 793,866 |
| León | 565,821 | Ceuta | 64,576 |
| Lérida | 347,241 | Melilla | 59,529 |
| Logroño | 239,300 | | |
| Lugo | 425,209 | | |

## CURRENCY

The unit of currency is the *peseta* of 100 *céntimos*. There are notes to the value of 100, 500 and 1,000 *pesetas*. There are nickel coins of 50, 25 and 5 *pesetas* and others made of an alloy of copper and aluminium valued at 1 *peseta*. Smaller denominations of 5, 10 and 50 *céntimos* are made of an alloy of aluminium, tin and copper.

Notes in circulation in 1973: 487,991 million *pesetas*.
Coins in circulation in 1973: 17,089 million *pesetas*.

## FINANCE

The following table gives some cost of living indices percentage increases from December 1975 to December 1976 taking as a base 1968 = 100:

| | *National aggregate* | *Aggregate for capital cities*[1] | *Aggregate for non-capital townships*[2] |
|---|---|---|---|
| General index | 19·8 | 19·2 | 20·2 |
| Food | 22·0 | 19·5 | 23·4 |
| Clothing and footwear | 21·9 | 23·0 | 21·2 |
| Housing | 10·5 | 10·1 | 11·0 |
| Household expenses | 16·3 | 21·0 | 13·3 |
| Sundries | 18·0 | 19·2 | 16·7 |

[1] The 'aggregate for capital cities' comprises the 50 provincial capitals and the non-capital townships with more than 50,000 inhabitants.

[2] The 'non-capital townships aggregate' comprises the non-capital townships with fewer than 50,000 inhabitants.

The GNP at market prices for 1974 was U.S. $ millions 87,250, and the GNP per capita at market prices was U.S. $2,490. The annual average percentage growth rate of the GNP per capita for the period 1960–74 was 5·8, and for the period 1965–74 was 5·4 [*See the note at the beginning of this section concerning GNP.*]

The net income received in 1974 was 570,538 million pesetas; payments made were 589,137 million pesetas.

## PRINCIPAL BANKS

**Banco de España.** (Governor, Mariano Navarro Rubio.) Established 1895; Sole Bank of Issue for Spain; Balance Sheet at 30 August 1969 showed assets, P.419,010,568,856; deposits, current and other accounts, P.13,673,886,873; Gold reserve, P.4,701,594,637; notes in circulation, P.234,904,856,983.

**Banco Central.** (Chairman, Alfonso Escamez López.) Established 1920; Balance Sheet at 31 December 1976 showed assets P.306,194,801,413; deposits and current accounts P.592,364,655,287. *Head Office:* Alcalá 49, Madrid, Spain. 1,200 Branches.

**Banco de Bilbao.** Chairman, J. A. S. Asiaín. Hon. Chairman, D. Gervario Colla. Established 1857; Balance Sheet at 31 December 1973 showed assets 502,195,807,990·29; deposits and current accounts P.219,686,475,627·93. *Head Office:* Gran Via, 12, Bilbao. 512 Branches and agencies.

**Banco del Comercio.** (Director, Ferando Martínez de Bedoyei. Established 1891; Balance Sheet at 31 December 1964 showed assets P.1,105,532,892; deposits and current accounts P.626,468,508. *Head Office:* Bilbao.

**Banco de Santander.** (President, D. Emilio Botin-S. de Sautuola y López.) Established 1857; Balance Sheet at 31 December 1974 showed assets P.389,713,012,785; deposits and current accounts P.205,766,616,028. *Head Office:* Paseo de Pereda 9–12, Santander. 320 Branches.

**Banco de Valencia.** (President, D. Joaquin Reig Rodriguez.) Established 1900; Balance Sheet at 31 December 1973 showed assets P.59,320,128,728·82; deposits and current accounts P.25,113,265,690·19. *Head Office:* Calle Pintor Sorolla No. 2, 4y 6, Valencia. 135 Branches.

**Banco Español de Crédito.** (President, José Maria Agiurre Gonzalo.) Established 1902; Balance Sheet at 31 December 1976 showed total resources Ptas. 1,007,606·72 m. deposits Ptas. 197,135,685,243. *Head Office:* Madrid. Branches throughout Spain.

**Banco Hispano Americano.** (President, Ignacio Herrer de Collantes.) Established 1900; Balance Sheet at 31 December 1964 showed assets P.116,254,677,000; deposits and current accounts P.73,563,078,000. *Head Office:* Plaza de Canalejas 1, Madrid. 380 Branches.

**Banco Internacional de Comercio.** (President and Chairman, Alejandro F. de Araoz y Marañon.) Established 1950; Assets as 31 December 1975, P.36,818 millions; deposits and current accounts P.15,772 millions. *Head Office:* Carrera de San Jerónimo, 28, Madrid 14. 23 Branches.

**Banca Jover.** Established 1737. (President, C. C. Jover; Chairman, A. G. Iguacel.) Assets as at 30 June 1975, Capital Ptas. 280.000, Capital Reserve Ptas. 221.000; deposits and current accounts Ptas. 5.000.000.000. *Head Office:* Via Layetana, 64 Barcelona 3. 17 Branches.

**Banco de Vizcaya, S.A.** Established 1901. (President, P. de C. Y Basabe; Chairman, M. M. de G. Y Landecho.) Assets as at 31 December 1974, P.513,637,358,243; deposits and current accounts, P.223,828,110,784. *Head Office:* Gran Vía, No. 1 Bilbao. 410 Branches.

**Société Générale de Banque.** (Subsidiary of the Société Générale pour favoriser le développement du Commerce et de l'Industrie en France—see France).

**Banco Popular Espanol.** (Chairman, Ferando Camacho Baños.) Established 1926; Balance Sheet at 31 December 1968 showed assets P.70,396,200,000; deposits and current accounts P.31,376,000,000. *Head Office:* Alcalá 26, Madrid. 163 Branches.

## PRODUCTION, INDUSTRY AND COMMERCE

The following table shows the volume of production for various industries for 1974–76, the figures shown for 1976 are however, provisional:

| *Product* | | 1974 | 1975 | 1976 |
|---|---|---|---|---|
| Mineral coal | (thousands of metric tons) | 13,221 | 14,036 | 14,680 |
| Iron ore | ,, | 9,010 | 8,617 | 7,980 |
| Steel, total | ,, | 11,473 | 11,137 | 10,920 |
| Artificial cement | ,, | 23,660 | 25,316 | 24,977 |
| Aluminium | ,, | 191 | 210 | 211 |
| Pure copper, total | ,, | 120 | 130 | 144 |
| Sulphuric acid | ,, | 2,919 | 3,624 | 3,726 |
| Calcium superphosphate | (thousands of metric tons of P.O.) | 385 | 448 | 376 |
| Nitrogenous fertilizers | (thousands of metric tons of nitrogen) | 718 | 731 | — |
| Crude oil in refineries | (thousands of metric tons) | 44,917 | 42,585 | 50,712 |
| Coke | (thousands of metric tons) | 4,329 | 4,860 | 4,423 |
| Ships launched over 100 GRT | (number) | 258 | 227 | — |
| Thousands GRT | | 1,434 | 1,666 | — |
| Motorcycles | (thousands of units) | 260 | 240 | 242 |
| Private cars | ,, | 707 | 697 | 753 |
| Lorries and vans | (thousands of units) | 110 | 95 | 91 |
| Electricity, total | (millions of kWh) | 80,855 | 81,875 | 90,220 |
| Electricity, hydro-electric | ,, | 31,347 | 26,040 | 22,110 |
| Electricity, thermo-nuclear | ,, | 49,508 | 55,835 | 68,110 |
| Preserved vegetables | (thousands of metric tons) | 804 | 707 | — |
| Preserved fish | ,, | 127 | 116 | 112 |
| Canned meat | ,, | 25 | 21 | 23 |
| Homogenized milk | ,, | 1,711 | 1,861 | 2,023 |
| Sugar | ,, | 751 | 549 | 795 |
| Beer | (thousands of hectolitres) | 15,483 | 16,626 | 17,130 |
| Textiles—cotton, viscose, wool and mixtures thereof | (thousands of metric tons) | 169 | 157 | 151 |
| Textiles—natural silk, rayon, synthetic fibres and mixtures thereof | (thousands of metric tons) | 32 | 31 | 32 |

**Agriculture.** Spain has a rich and varied agriculture, the main products being wheat, barley, maize, rye, onions, sugar-beet, beans and potatoes. There are also extensive vineyards and orange and olive groves.

## SPAIN

The following table gives some figures in connection with agricultural production for the years 1974, 1975, and 1976:

| | | 1974 | 1975 | 1976 |
|---|---|---|---|---|
| Area under cultivation (thousands of hectares) | | 46,792 | 46,865 | — |
| Total value of agricultural production (millions of pesetas) | | 807,813 | 520,807 | 561,079[1] |
| Cereals | | 63,777 | 120,990 | 115,223[1] |
| Fruit | | 67,711 | 81,586 | 77,157[1] |
| Vegetables | | 85,082 | 96,337 | 96,369[1] |
| Production (thousands of metric quintals) of: | | | | |
| Wheat | | 45,340 | 43,024 | 41,760[1] |
| Potatoes | | 56,930 | 53,378 | 56,330[1] |
| Sugar beet | | 39,900 | 63,365 | 97,000[1] |
| Grapes | | 58,596 | 52,021 | 40,780[1] |
| *Olive Oil* | | 3,340 | 4,554 | 3,910[1] |
| Number of tractors (thousands of units) | | 31,328 | 379 | 402 |
| Number of combine harvesters (thousands of units) | | 1,870 | 40 | 40 |
| Cattle | (thousands of head) | 4,438 | 4,335 | 4,384 |
| Sheep | ,, | 15,599 | 15,195 | 14,776 |
| Goats | ,, | 2,230 | 2,293 | 2,178 |
| Pigs | ,, | 8,671 | 8,662 | 9,248 |
| Meat production | (thousands of metric tons) | 1,942 | 1,889 | 2,008 |
| Value of meat | (millions of pesetas) | 167,674 | 188,957 | 216,222[1] |
| Milk production | (millions of litres) | 5,430 | 5,504 | 5,859 |
| Value of milk | (millions of pesetas) | 53,841 | 76,116 | 89,651[1] |
| Egg production | (thousands of dozens) | 710,200 | 846,100 | 902,300 |
| Value of eggs | (millions of pesetas) | 29,331 | 33,528 | 43,022[1] |

[1] Provisional Figures

**Forestry.** The forested area, including the Balearic and Canary Islands, covers over 26·8 million hectares (over 62 million acres).

**Fishing.** There were in 1974 16,749 fishing vessels, totalling 744,713 tons.

The principal catches were sardine, hake, cod and tunny. The total catch in 1976 was 362,000 tons valued at 76,320 million pesetas.

The chief centres of the fishing industry are Vigo, La Coruña, Pasajes, Gijón, Cádiz, Seville, Algeciras, Málaga, Huelva and Barcelona. The number of factories in 1970 was 531, producing 92,593 metric tons, the total produce in metric tons for 1971 was 94,450.

**Industry.** The production of electricity in 1974 (provisional figures) totalled 81,110 million kWh, water driven power stations contributed 30,680 kWh, and thermonuclear 50,430 kWh. Gas production was approximately 864·7 m. cu. m. in 1974.

The following vehicles were manufactured in 1974 (Provisional): cars, 707,750; lorries, 109,450; motor cycles, 260,440; tractors, 35,710, and special land vehicles 14,620.

Spain has an important textile industry, producing cotton, woollen and silk fabrics. The following list shows the production (in metric tons) in 1974:

| | 1974 (*Provisional figures*) |
|---|---|
| Wool yarn | 35,430 |
| Pure cotton yarn | 76,480 |
| Silk yarn | 25 |
| Pure cotton fabrics | 73,620 |
| Pure rayon and mixture woven fabrics | 21,210 |

**Mining.** The mineral wealth of the country is considerable. The amount of extracted silvinite in connection with potash production for 1975 was 4,705,000 metric tons. The money value of potassium chloride in 1975 was 2,769,000 pesetas.

The following table gives the quantity in varying units, of various substances (chiefly minerals), produced in 1975:

| *Mineral* | *Unit* | *Quantity* 1975 (*Provisional figures*) |
|---|---|---|
| *Coal Mining* | | |
| Coal | th. metric tons | 7,570 |
| Anthracite | ,, | 3,100 |
| Lignite | ,, | 3,360 |
| *Extraction of Minerals* | | |
| Iron pyrites | ,, | 2,845 |
| Iron ore | ,, | 8,630 |
| Zinc ore | metric tons | 171,780 |
| Manganese ore | ,, | N.A. |
| Wolfram ore | ,, | 680 |
| Tin ore | ,, | 1,290 |
| Lead ore | ,, | 93,010 |
| *Basic Metal Industries* | | |
| Iron (ingot) | th. metric tons | 6,860 |
| Steel | ,, | 11,100 |
| Ferromanganese | metric tons | 126,160 |
| *Basic Non-ferrous Metal Industries* | | |
| Semi-processed zinc | ,, | 133,900 |
| Blister copper | ,, | 116,360 |
| Refined copper | ,, | 116,130 |
| Semi-processed tin | ,, | 7,660 |
| Lead | ,, | 73,640 |
| Aluminium | ,, | 212,340 |
| Silver | | N.A. |
| Gold | kg | N.A. |
| *Other* | | |
| Refined sulphur | metric tons | 20,040 |
| Cement | th. metric tons | 21,750 |

**Commerce.** The value of the principal imports and exports is shown in the following table (in million pesetas):

| Commodity | 1973 Imports | 1973 Exports | 1974 Imports | 1974 Exports |
|---|---|---|---|---|
| Food, beverages and tobacco | 75,357 | 74,567 | 101,658 | 79,024 |
| Minerals (combustibles and lubricants) | 72,254 | 14,195 | 224,859 | 27,608 |
| Raw materials (except lubricants), oils and animal and vegetable fat | 87,733 | 22,950 | 127,468 | 32,409 |
| Manufactured Goods | 322,323 | 190,957 | 429,674 | 268,852 |
| Gold (bullion and money) | 3,376 | — | 5,027 | 78,200 |

The table below shows the quantity of types of wines exported in 1975:

| Commodity | Unit | 1975 |
|---|---|---|
| Sparkling wines | th. litres | 2,323 |
| Fortified wines | ,, | 85,253 |
| (Of these: Sherry comprised) | ,, | 71,058 |
| Wines with denomination of origin | ,, | 79,758 |
| Other white wines | ,, | 116,047 |
| Other wines | ,, | 197,760 |
| Export of Sherry to United Kingdom: | | |
| Quantity | ,, | 33,117 |
| Value (million Pesetas) | | 2,355 |

The following table shows the provisional trading figures for 1974 (value in million pesetas):

| Country | Imports 1974 | Exports 1974 |
|---|---|---|
| W. Germany | 99,681·3 | 45,146·6 |
| France | 75,546·8 | 51,497·2 |
| Italy | 47,204·8 | 22,530·3 |
| Netherlands | 23,553·8 | 19,719·7 |
| United Kingdom | 45,329·8 | 37,376·8 |
| Sweden | 20,146·4 | 5,487·7 |
| Switzerland | 18,344·2 | 8,979·5 |
| Belgium | 20,498·2 | 13,312·5 |
| U.S.A. | 137,369·5 | 47,866·2 |
| Japan | 20,090·9 | 6,103·5 |

## COMMUNICATIONS

**Railways and Roads.** The length of the railway lines in 1973 was 13,460 km., of which 3,383 km. were electrified. The normal gauge is the broad one of 1·67 metres, but about one-quarter of the track is on various narrow gauges, mostly of one metre.

Material in service include 134 steam locomotives, 393 electric, 715 diesel, 3,477 carriages, 628 goods wagons, and 684 railcars.

The length of roads in 1974 was 143,282 km., of which 26,027 km. were macadamised.

**Shipping.** In 1973, 97,704 vessels entered Spanish ports; the figure for outgoing vessels was 97,662. In 1973 the number of passengers entering Spanish ports was 3,355,665, the number of those leaving was 3,174,557. In 1972 there were 2,962 ships in the Spanish merchant navy.

The principal ports are Bilbao, Santander, Vigo, Barcelona, Cádiz, Seville and Las Palmas.

The following are the principal shipping lines:

**Compañia Trasatlántica Española S.A.** (President, Alnciranto D. Pascual Pery Junquere.) Share capital P.117,391,000; nine motor vessels, total tonnage 64,089 D.W.T.; *services operated:* to U.S.A., Central America, Mexico, Italy. *Head Office:* Paseo de Calvo Sotelo 4, Madrid.

**Empresa Nacional 'Elcano' de la Marina Mercante S.A.** Vessels 17, total tonnage 100,000 gross and four ships of 300,000 gross under construction; *services operated:* Spanish coastal, Mediterranean ports, North, South and Central America. *Head Office:* Miguel Angel 9, Madrid 10.

**Naviera Aznar S.A.** (Chairman Eduardo Aznar.) Share capital P.347,663,000; motor vessels 14; total tonnage 186,153 T.D.W.; *services operated:* United Kingdom, United Kingdom–Canaries. *Head Office:* Plaza de los Alfereces Provisionales 2 (Apartado 13), Bilbao. Telex 32052.

**Ybarra y Cia. S.A.** (Chairman, D. Luis Ybarra Ybarra, Count Ybarra.) Share capital (1969) P.200,000,000; vessels eight; total tonnage 60,000 gross; *services operated:* Italy, France, Portugal and Spain–Brazil, Uruguay and Argentina; Cruises. *Head Office:* Menendez Pelayo, 4 Apartado 15, Seville; *Cruises Office:* Victor Hugo, I-Madrid-14.

**Civil Aviation.** In 1966 there were 24 airports on the mainland and 13 in the Balearic Islands, the Canaries and the Colonies. In 1972, 276,712 aircraft landed at the Spanish airports and the same number quitted: 15,620,000 passengers and 101,107,000 metric tons of goods were brought in, and 15,679,000 passengers and 121,571,000 metric tons of goods were taken out.

**IBERIA—Líneas Aéreas de Espana** (Airlines of Spain*). (President and Chairman Manuel de Prado y Colón de Carvajal) Share capital P.5,000,000,000; *services operated: European services:* Amsterdam, Athens, Bruxelles, Budapest, Bordeaux, Copenhagen, Dublin, Düsseldorf, Frankfurt a. M., Geneva, Hamburg, Lisbon, London, Lyons, Marseille, Milan, Munich, Nice, Paris, Rome, Toulouse, Warsaw, Vienna and Zürich. *Asian services:* Beirut. *African services:* Abidjan, Algiers, Casablanca, Dahkla, Dakar, Johannesburg, Kinshasa, Lagos, Libreville, Malabo, Monrovia, Nouadhibou, and Tangier. North, Central and South American Services. Internal services. In 1975–76, 10,647,057 passengers were transported over 128,985,672 km. *Head Office:* Velázquez 130, Madrid 6.

* The name '*Airlines of Spain*' is registered.

**Posts, Telegraphs and Telephones.** In 1975, there were 12,505 Post Offices in Spain; postal revenue was 11,500 million pesetas; expenditure, 13,500 million pesetas.

The following table shows the (provisional) economic and other data of the telegraph and telephone system for 1975.

| | 1975* |
|---|---|
| No. of telegraph offices | 10,228 |
| Kilometers of telegraph cable | 36,675 |
| Revenue (millions of pesetas) | 2,271 |
| Expenditure (millions of pesetas) | 4,391 |
| Telephones (thousands) | 7,836 |

* Provisional figures.

## NEWSPAPERS

**Ya.** F. 1935. Morning. Catholic. Madrid.

**A.B.C.** F. 1905. Morning. Catholic and Monarchist. Madrid; office in Seville.

**Arriba.** F. 1939. Morning. Prensa y Radiodel Movimiento, Avenida Generalisimo 142, Madrid 16, Madrid.

**Informaciones.** F. 1921. Evening. Independent. San Roque 7, Madrid-13.

**Diario de Barcelona.** F. 1792. Oldest established paper in Europe after the London Times. Morning. Monarchical, Conservative. Muntaner 49, Barcelona.

**La Vanguardia.** F. 1881. Morning. Independent. Barcelona.

## EDUCATION

In Spain there are 32,759 first and second stage schools with 3,667,500 and 1,278,200 pupils respectively. High Schools number 3,011 with 1,012,900 pupils. The number of University colleges and faculties is 196 with 251,800 pupils.

## ATOMIC ENERGY

Work has already begun on Spain's first nuclear power plant, at Almonacid de Zorita, some 80 km. from Madrid. The first stage of the plant, to be completed by the autumn of 1967 at a cost of 1,700 m. pesetas, will have a capacity of 153,200 kW.; this will be raised later by 300,000 kW. The plant is to use Spanish uranium, to be enriched at U.S. diffusion plants.

General Electric of the U.S.A. has announced that it has been awarded the contract for construction of Spain's second nuclear power plant at Santa María de Garoña (Burgos) for NUCLENOR, a company formed by Iberduero and Electra de Viesgo. The official decision on the award was to be announced in September 1966 but Sr. José María Otero, head of the Nuclear Energy Council, stated recently that the contract. worth some 3,000 m. pesetas, would go to a U.S. bidder. The plant hould be in operation in 1967, with a capacity of 300,000 kW.

**RELIGION**

The Catholic religion is the established religion of the State. There are nine Archbishoprics—Toledo, Seville, Tarragona, Santiago, Valencia, Zaragoza, Granada, Burgos and Valladolid. There are 57 suffragan sees.

The Archbishop of Toledo is the Primate, and he is generally made a Cardinal. In 1952 there were three Cardinals—the Archbishops of Toledo, Seville and Santiago.

There is freedom of worship for other religions, though not in public. It is estimated that there are about 25,000 Protestants and 177 Protestant chapels and centres of worship.

## SPANISH SAHARA

(SAHARA ESPAÑOL AFRICA OCCIDENTAL ESPAÑOLA)

**Capital**—Aaiun.

The Spanish Sahara is 266,000 sq. kilometres in area. In 1974 had a population of 74,902. The principal towns with their population are Aaiun: 28,010; Villa Cisneros: 5,370; Smara: 7,280; Güera: 1,299.

In July 1974 the 'Yemaa General' of the Sahara accepted an antomous status for Spanish Sahara. There is a council of government with eight representatives elected by the 'Yemaa'. The establishment of this council constitutes a first step towards complete independence. The intention to achieve complete independence was announced by the Spanish government at the United Nations.

These are secondary schools in Aaiun and Villa Cisneros. There are, in addition 200 schools and professional training centers. There is a Centre for Arabic Studies in Aaiun.

There are two hospitals, one in Aaiun and one in Villa Cisneros. Also, there are several dispensaries and medical centres in all other towns and stations in the interior.

There are two broadcasting stations of 50 kW and 5 kW respectively.

A boat service exists between the Canary Islands and the, ports of Aaiun, Villa Cisneros, and Güera carrying both passengers and cargo. There are three airports Aaiun, Villa Cisneros, and Güera. The airport at Aaiun is an international port, the other two airports have direct connections with the Canary Islands and the interior only.

There is a great variety of local fish, including white sea bass, 'sama', and 'cherna'. These latter two species are a Mediterranean type of fish. The most valuable products are celphalopodic, and then lobster, crab, mussels, and prawns.

The territories' principal wealth is in its phosphate deposits. The estimated reserves are of the order of 1,500 million tons. In 1974 2·5 million tons were exported.

The Spanish suzerainty came to an end on 28 February 1976.

# Sri Lanka

(MEMBER OF THE COMMONWEALTH)

**Capital**—Colombo.

**President**—His Excellency Mr. W. Gopallawa.

**National Flag**: On a field dark crimson bordered gold, a lion passant gold, in its right paw a sword of the same; at the hoist two stripes pale-wise green and saffron, each $\frac{1}{7}$ the width of the flag without border.

**CONSTITUTION AND GOVERNMENT**

SRI LANKA (Ceylon), which had previously been administered as a British Crown Colony, was granted fully responsible status by the Ceylon Independence Act of 1947, which came into force on 4 February 1948. Parliament consisted of Her Majesty, represented by the Governor-General and two Chambers, the Senate and the House of Representatives. The Senate consisted of 30 members, 15 of whom were elected by the House of Representatives, the remaining 15 being appointed by the Governor-General, on the recommendation of the Prime Minister. Senators were elected for a term of six years, one-third retiring every second year.

There were 157 members of the House of Representatives, 151 of whom were elected by universal adult suffrage and six were appointed by the Governor-General.

The first general elections to the House of Representatives were held in the months of July, August and September, 1947 and the first session of Parliament was opened by H.R.H. The Duke of Gloucester on 10 February 1948.

The Senate was abolished on 2 October 1971.

After the general elections held in May 1970 the members of the House of Representatives constituted themselves into a Constituent Assembly to draft, adopt and enact a new Constitution for Sri Lanka.

On 22 May 1972 the new Constitution drafted by the Constituent Assembly was adopted and enacted and Sri Lanka. was declared a Free, Sovereign and Independent Republic.

The Republic of Sri Lanka is a unitary state, its Sovereignty is in the People and is inalienable and the Sovereignty of the People is exercised through a National State Assembly of elected representatives of the People.

The National State Assembly is the supreme instrument of State power of the Republic and exercises (a) the legislative power of the people; (b) the executive power of the people, including the defence of Sri Lanka, through the President, and the Cabinet of Ministers and (c) the judicial power of the people through the courts and other institutions created by law except in the case of matters relating to its powers and privileges, wherein the judicial power of the people may be exercised directly by the National State Assembly. The National State Assembly at present consists of 157 members. It is elected on a wide franchise, every citizen of Sri Lanka of the age of 18 years and over being entitled to vote.

The Prime Minister nominates the President of the Republic of Sri Lanka who is Head of the State, Head of the Executive and Commander-in-Chief of the Armed Forces.

The Executive consists of a Prime Minister and a Cabinet of Ministers charged with the direction and control of the Government of the Republic which shall be collectively responsible to the National State Assembly and answerable to the National State Assembly on all matters for which they are responsible.

The Prime Minister, appointed by the President, is the Head of the Cabinet of Ministers. The other Ministers of the Cabinet and the Deputy Ministers are appointed by the President on the recommendation of the Prime Minister.

**Council of Ministers**

*Prime Minister, Minister of Defence, Minister of Planning and Economic Affairs, Minister of Plan Implementation:* Hon. J. R. Jayawardene.
*Minister of Foreign Affairs:* Hon. A. C. S. Hameed.
*Minister of Irrigation Power and Highways:* Hon. Gamini Dissanayake.
*Minister of Trade:* Hon. Lalith Athulathmudali.
*Minister of Public Administration and Home Affairs:* Hon. Montague Jayawickreme.
*Minister of Shipping Aviation and Tourism:* Hon. Mrs. Wimala Kannangara.
*Minister of Education:* Hon. N. P. Wijeyeratne.
*Minister of Finance:* Hon. Ronnie De Mel.
*Minister of Labour:* Hon. Capt. C. P. J. Seneviratne.

*Minister of Industries and Scientific Affairs:* Hon. Cyril Mathew.
*Minister of Local Government, Housing and Construction:* Hon. R. Premadasa.
*Minister of Cultural Affairs:* Hon. E. L. B. Hurulle.
*Minister of Fisheries:* Hon. S. de S. Jayasinghe.
*Minister of Health:* Hon. Gamini Jayasooriya.
*Minister of Information and Broadcasting:* Hon. D. B. Wijetunge.
*Minister of Parliamentary Affairs and Sports:* Hon. M. Vincent Perera.
*Minister of Transport:* Hon. M. H. Mohamed.
*Minister of Agriculture and Lands:* Hon. E. L. Senenayake.
*Minister of Posts and Telecommunication:* Hon. D. Shelton Jayasinghe.
*Minister of Plantation Industries:* Hon. M. D. H. Jayawardene.
*Minister of Textile Industry:* Hon. Wijepala Mendis.
*Minister of Justice:* Hon. K. W. Dewanayagam.
*Minister of Social Services:* Hon. Asoka Karunaratne.
*Minister of Food and Co-operatives:* Hon. S. B. Herath.

## MINISTRY OF PUBLIC ADMINISTRATION, LOCAL GOVERNMENT, AND HOME AFFAIRS

The Ministry of Public Administration and Home Affairs is charged with the overall responsibility of the formulation of desirable policies, initiation of development programmes, and ensuring their effective implementation in the following areas:

*Public Administration*

1. Establishment services for all Ministries, and Departments and administering the Combined Services.
2. Consultancy services to, and management development of, the State Services.
3. Superannuation benefits to government employees.
4. Implementation of the official language policy within the framework of the Official Language Enactments.

*Home Affairs*

5. District Administration for co-ordination of activities and execution of development programmes for other Ministries and Departments at the district level.
6. Registration of Births, Marriages and Deaths and registration of deeds and preservation of such records.
7. Stimulate and develop the enthusiasm and efforts of rural people for the improvement of their social, economic and cultural conditions through the establishment of village organizations as Rural Development Societies.
8. Administering the legal enactments pertaining to Mosques and Muslim Charitable Trusts.

The main function of the Ministry is to direct, control and co-ordinate the programme of work of the following Departments, which are specifically in charge of the above mentioned areas—

1. Department of Pensions.
2. District Administration (viz., Kachcheries).
3. Department of Registrar General.
4. Department of Rural Developments.
5. Department of Mosques and Muslim Charitable Trusts.

## LEGAL SYSTEM

On 1 January 1974, the system of courts in the Republic of Sri Lanka established under the Courts Ordinance No. 1 of 1889, was replaced by a new system. The judicature consists of the Supreme Court, High Courts, District Courts and Magistrate's Courts. The High Courts, District Courts and Magistrates Courts are established for the Zones, districts and divisions respectively. The Judges of the Supreme Court and the High Courts are appointed by the President of the Republic. The age of retirement of the Judges of the Supreme Court is 63 years while that of the High Court Judges is 61 years. The District Judges and Magistrates are appointed by the Cabinet of Ministers on the recommendations of the Judicial Services Advisory Board.

Conciliation Boards Act No. 10 of 1958 empowers the Minister of Justice to form panels of conciliators consisting of not less than 12 persons for three year periods for every village area and other areas determined by him. Suitable persons are selected from these areas by advertisement in the Government Gazette. Conciliation Boards each consisting of not less than three persons are drawn from these panels. The purpose of these boards is to bring about an amicable settlement of disputes arising in these areas before parties go to formal Courts of Law. These boards apart from relieving the pressure on the formal Courts provide an acceptable way of settling disputes quickly and without any expenditure. Speedy settlement of disputes by these boards also naturally tends to bring down the incidence of crime. Statistics collected indicate that the Conciliation Boards are rendering a great service to the people.

In 1972 the Criminal Justice Commissions Act No. 14, 1972 was passed. Under this Act the President may establish a Criminal Justice Commission to try:

(i) offences in connection with, in the course of, or during, any rebellion or insurrection, or
(ii) offences in relation to currency or foreign exchange of such a scale and nature as to endanger the national economy or interest, or
(iii) widespread offences of destruction, damage or destroying of factories, industrial plant and other installations, whether public or private,

where in his opinion the practice and procedure of the ordinary courts are inadequate to administer criminal justice for the purpose of securing the trial and punishment of the persons who committed such offences. Membership of Criminal Justice Commission are confined to Judges of the Supreme Court.

*Supreme Court of the Republic of Sri Lanka:*

*Chief Justice:*
The Hon. Victor Tennekoon.

## AREA AND POPULATION

The following table shows the area and population by districts (Census 1971):

| | *Total land area including inland waters, sq. miles* | *Large inland waters sq. miles* | *Census of population 1971* |
|---|---|---|---|
| Sri Lanka | 25,332·0 | 369·8 | 12,689,897 |
| Colombo | 808·25 | 16·25 | 2,672,265 |
| Kalutara | 623·75 | 3·5 | 729,514 |
| Kandy | 914·0 | ·08 | 1,187,925 |
| Matale | 770·28 | — | 314,841 |
| Nuwara Eliya | 474·0 | — | 450,278 |
| Galle | 652·25 | 6·0 | 735,173 |
| Matara | 481·25 | — | 586,443 |
| Hambantota | 1,012·75 | 11·5 | 340,254 |
| Jaffna | 998·65 | 34·13 | 701,603 |
| Mannar | 964·0 | 6·5 | 77,780 |
| Vavuniya | 1,466·75 | 35·25 | 95,243 |
| Batticaloa | 1,016·65 | 65·1 | 256,721 |
| Amparai | 1,177·6 | 24·9 | 272,605 |
| Trincomalee | 1,048·0 | 37·14 | 188,245 |
| Kurunegala | 1,844·0 | 1·25 | 1,025,633 |
| Puttalam | 1,172·15 | 22·75 | 378,430 |
| Anuradhapura | 2,808·64 | 56·05 | 388,770 |
| Polonnruwa | 1,331·64 | 17·45 | 163,653 |
| Badulla | 1,089·57 | 1·5 | 615,405 |
| Moneragala | 2,785·32 | 30·5 | 193,020 |
| Ratnapura | 1,250·5 | — | 661,344 |
| Kegalle | 642·0 | — | 654,752 |

### Vital Statistics

| | 1971 | 1972 | 1973 | 1974 |
|---|---|---|---|---|
| Marriages | 86,095 | 90,311 | 93,162 | 91,730 |
| Births | 382,480 | 384,066 | 366,186 | 365,765 |
| Deaths | 97,209 | 103,918 | 100,678 | 119,581 |

The annual average percentage growth rate of the population for the period 1960–74 was 2·2, and for the period 1965–74 was 2·9.

## CURRENCY

The Central Bank of Ceylon is the sole currency issuing authority and issues both currency notes and coins. The standard unit of monetary value is the Sri Lanka Rupee, which has a par value of 0·149297 grams of fine gold and is divided into 100 cents.

Currency notes are issued in the denominations Rs. 100, Rs.50, Rs10, Rs.5, Rs.2, and coins are issued in the denominations Rs. 5, Rs.2, Rs.1, 50 cents, 25 cents, 10 cents, 5 cents, 2 cents and 1 cent. All denominations of notes and coins are legal tender for the payment of any amount.

## FINANCE

Budget figures for 1976 in million rupees were: Revenue Rs. 5749·9 million, Expenditure Rs. 7844·6 million (including Rs. 1072·7 million foreign aid).

The GNP at market prices for 1974 was U.S.$ millions 1,760 and the GNP per capita at market prices was U.S.$ 130.

The annual average percentage growth rate of the GNP per capita for the period 1960–74 was 2·1 and for the period 1965–74 was 2·0. [*See the note at the beginning of this section concerning GNP.*]

## PRINCIPAL BANKS

**Central Bank of Ceylon.** F. 1950. Governor: H. E. Tennekoon, MBE; Bank of Issue; Balance Sheet as at 31 December 1972 showed assets of Rs. 3,924·4 million; deposits amounted to Rs. 847·8 million; notes in circulation Rs. 1,359·1 million, *Head Office:* 34–36, Queen Street, Colombo 1.

**Bank of Ceylon.** *Central Office:* Bank of Ceylon Building, York Street, Colombo 1. Chairman, L. N. L. Perera.

**People's Bank.** G.C.S.U. Building, Colombo 2. (Chairman: Hector Abhayawardhana.)

**State Bank of India,** 16 Sir Baron Jayatilleke Mawatha, Colombo 1.

**National and Grindlays Bank, Limited,** 37 York Street, Colombo 1.

**The Chartered Bank,** 17 Queen Street, Colombo 1.

**Hatton National Bank Ltd.,** 16, Janadhipathi Mawatha, (Queen St.), P.O. Box 98 Colombo 1, Sri Lanka. Authorised capital, Rs. 10,000,000. Issued and Paid-up Capital, Rs. 2,700,000. Total Reserves, Rs. 5,265,467. Total Assets Rs. 304,973,811 (31 December 1975).

**Hongkong and Shanghai Banking Corporation, The.** Branch in Colombo. See Hong Kong.

**Commercial Bank of Ceylon Limited,** 57 Sir Baron Jayatilaka Mawatha, Colombo, 1. Branches: Kandy, Galle, Jaffna, Matara, Matale, Galewela, Kollupitiya, Wellawatte, Kotahena.

**Habib Bank Limited,** 163 Keyzer Street, Colombo 11.

**Indian Bank,** 48 Baillie Street, Colombo 1.

**Indian Overseas Bank,** 139 Main Street, Colombo 11.

## PRODUCTION, INDUSTRY AND COMMERCE

**Agriculture.** The following table shows the acreage of the principal crops and livestock in 1976:

| *Crop* | 1976 *Acres* (*Provisional*) | 1976 *Production* (*Provisional*) |
|---|---|---|
| Tea | 594,481 | 433,336,266 lbs |
| Rubber | 561,000 | 335,396,220 lbs |
| Coconut | 1,152,428 | 2,330,000,000 Nuts |

| *Livestock* | 1976 *Numbers* |
|---|---|
| Cattle | 1,743,754 |
| Buffaloes | 853,726 |
| Sheep | 29,669 |
| Pigs | 35,801 |
| Goats | 562,190 |
| Poultry | 5,699,675 |

The table below gives the provisional production figures and acreage for various crops for 1976.

| *Agriculture* | 1976 *Acres* | 1976 *Production Cwts.* |
|---|---|---|
| Cinnamon | 53,907 | 347,980 |
| Cardamon | 10,075 | 80,518 |
| Cocoa | 20,799 | 224,519 |
| Citronella | 10,573 | 57,536 |
| Tobacco | 32,901 | 743,220 |
| Arecanuts | 44,719 | 3,396,837 |

**Mines and Minerals.** Precious and semi-precious stones were the most important mineral commodity in 1976 and all the exports were handled by the State Gem Corporation. A large variety of precious and semi-precious stones were obtained from placer deposits in the South-west part of the island and the Matale District. Exports of gemstones in 1976 were valued at Rs. 287,147,710.

Almost the entire production of graphite is exported and the total export in 1976 amounted to 7,887 long tons valued at Rs. 19,130,636.

Ilmenite, rutile and zircon are recovered from an extensive beach sand deposit on the east coast. In 1976 the exports of ilmenite amounted to Rs. 52,259 long tons valued at Rs. 6,786,724. In addition 2,220 long tons of rutile valued at Rs. 4,373,916 were exported during the year.

The kaoline refinery produced 4,291 long tons of refined kaolin valued at Rs. 1,501,850. The greater portion of this was used by the local ceramic industry. Some of the production was used by the insecticide and paper industries.

3,148 long tons of feldspar valued at Rs. 377,760 and 825 long tons of quartz valued at Rs. 78,375 were produced. Part of the production was taken by the Ceramic Industry.

636,951 long tons of limestone valued at Rs. 9,846,243 and 56,402 long tons of clay valued at Rs. 930,633 were used in the manufacture of cement.

The experimental plant operated by the Geological Survey Department produced 10 long tons of zircon valued at Rs. 11,731 in 1976 during the course of processing heavy mineral sands.

**Public Sector Industries.** During the year 1975 increases in the value of production of Public Sector Industries were recorded in 10 of the 16 manufacturing Corporations. The total value of production increased from Rs. 2,616,160,321 in 1974 to Rs. 2,786,248,089 in 1975. The foreign exchange earnings were Rs. 429,862,921 in 1975 as against Rs. 392,242,554 earnings of 1974. The return on total capital employed for production in 1975 was 8·6 per cent.

There were 38,738 persons employed in these institutions.

**Fisheries.** Rs. 5,019,469 was earned as foreign exchange in 1976 by export of fish by the Fishing Corporation and Rs. 268,375 was earned as foreign exchange in 1976 by export of Tuna boats. Above earnings were inclusive of FEECs.

**Commerce.** The following table shows the imports and exports to and from principal countries for the year 1976:

| *Country* | *Imports* (*in thousand Rupees*) | *Exports* (*in thousand Rupees*) |
|---|---|---|
| United Kingdom | 275,155 | 446,548 |
| Australia | 272,531 | 129,227 |
| Canada | 106,261 | 116,972 |
| India | 181,142 | 2,001 |
| Pakistan | — | — |
| South Africa | 5,345 | 141,239 |
| Belgium | 50,440 | 10,424 |
| Burma | 231,046 | 1,695 |
| China | 56,194 | 481,427 |
| France | 293,846 | 55,828 |
| German Democratic Republic | 34,880 | 24,371 |
| German Federal Republic | 182,837 | 162,984 |
| Italy | 51,655 | 130,814 |
| Japan | 375,520 | 213,366 |
| Netherlands | 65,548 | 115,590 |
| Thailand | 171,909 | 2,745 |
| U.S.A. | 378,848 | 334,636 |
| Iran | 3,626 | 99,929 |

The following table shows the value of imports by major categories for 1976 in million rupees:

| | 1976 (*m. rupees*) |
|---|---|
| *Consumer goods* | |
| Food and drink | 1,534 |
| Textile (including clothing) | 49 |
| Other consumer goods | 149 |
| *Intermediate goods* | |
| (Fertilizers, petroleum products, coal, colouring materials, tea, paper, unmanufactured tobacco, etc.) | 2,259 |
| *Investment goods* | |
| (Building materials,machinery and equipment, etc.) | 643 |
| *Unclassified imports* | 54 |
| Total | 4,688 |

The following table shows the value of exports by commodities for 1976 in million rupees:

| | 1976 (*m. rupees*) |
|---|---|
| Tea | 2,100 |
| Rubber | 890 |
| Coconuts | 383 |
| Precious and Semi-precious stones | 261 |
| Other domestic exports | 1,167 |
| Bunkers—Domestic | 4,801 |
| Re-exports | 14 |
| Total | 4,815 |

## COMMUNICATIONS

**Railways.** The railways are owned and operated by Government. In September 1976 there were 954 route miles and a total track of 1,259·32 miles.

**Shipping.** In 1976 the tonnage of ships entering Sri Lanka ports was 10,061,343. Ships weighing 8,357,187 cleared these ports. Figures for sailing vessels and coastwise vessels are not included.

**Civil Aviation.** Civil air Services in Sri Lanka are operated by Air Ceylon, British Airways, Indian Airlines, KLM Royal Dutch Airlines, Pakistan International Airlines, Royal Nepal Airways Corporation, Singapore Airlines, Swissair, Aeroflot, Thai Airways International, UTA French Airlines.
Regular tourist charters are operated into Sri Lanka by: Balair, Condor, Scanair, Sterling, Maerskair, Helitours.

**Broadcasting.** The Sri Lanka Broadcasting Corporation was constituted under the Ceylon Broadcasting Act No. 37 of 1966 and came into being on 5 January 1967. The Broadcasting Service in Sri Lanka functioned earlier as a Government Department and had been in exstenice for forty two years at the time it became a Corporation. It was then known as "Radio Ceylon". The Corporation now comes under the Ministry of Information and Broadcasting and provides a public broadcasting system that covers all aspects of broadcasting that is customary to such an organization with a certain stress laid on those aspects that are relevant to a developing nation.

## NEWSPAPERS

**Dinamina.** F. 1909. Sinhala language daily. Circulation 84,715. The Associated Newspapers of Ceylon Ltd., Lake House, Colombo 1.

**Lankadipa.** F. 1947. Sinhala. Circulation 40,906. Times of Ceylon Ltd., No. 51, Bristol Street, Colombo.

**Davasa.** F. 1961. Sinhala. Circulation 70,000. Independent Newspapers Ltd., N. 5, Gunasena Mawaha, Colombo 12.

**Thinakaran.** F. 1932. Tamil. Circulation 27,842. The Associated Newspapers of Ceylon Ltd., Lake House, Colombo.

**Ceylon Daily News.** F. 1918. English daily. Circulation 46,095. The Associated Newspapers of Ceylon Ltd., Lake House, Colombo 1.

**Ceylon Daily Mirror.** F. 1961. English. Circulation 19,127. The Times of Ceylon, Ltd., No. 3, Bristol Street, Colombo.

**Daily Observer.** Evening English daily 4,722.

**Janata.** F. 1953. Sinhala evening daily. Circulation 6,747. The Associated Newspapers of Ceylon Ltd., Lake House, Colombo 1.

**Ceylon Observer.** F. 1834. English. Circulation 8,151. The Associated Newspapers of Ceylon Ltd., Lake House, Colombo.

**Times of Ceylon.** F. 1846. English. Circulation 9,500. The Times of Ceylon Ltd., No. 3, Bristol Street, Colombo.

**Sunday Times.** F. 1973. English. Circulation 42,000. The Times of Ceylon Ltd., No. 3, Bristol Street, Colombo.

**Savasa.** F. 1961. Sinhala. Circulation 25,000. Independent Newspapers Ltd. No. 5 Gunasena Mawatha Colombo 12.

**Mithran Daily.** F. 1964. Tamil. Circulation 14,000. Express Newspapers (Ceylon) Ltd., 185 Grandpass Road, Colombo 14.

**Mithran Varamalar.** F. 1972. Tamil. Circulation 13,000. Express Newspapers (Ceylon) Ltd., 185 Grandpass Road, Colombo.

**Silumina.** F. 1930. Sinhal Sunday newspaper. Circulation 262,689. The Associated Newspapers of Ceylon Ltd., Lake House, Colombo 1.

**Sri Lankadipa.** F. 1951. Sinhala. Circulation 109,472. Times of Ceylon Ltd., No. 31, Bristol Street, Colombo.

**Riviresa.** F. 1961. Sinhala. Circulation 195,000. Independent Newspapers Ltd., No. 5, Gunasena Mawatha, Colombo 12.

**Thinakaran Varamanjari.** F. 1948. Tamil Circulation 34,522. The Associated Newspapers of Ceylon Ltd., Lake House, Colombo.

**Observer Magazine.** Sunday paper. F. 1923. English. Circulation 68,290. The Associated Newspapers of Ceylon Ltd. Lake House, Colombo 1.

**Thinakaran.** F. 1932. Tamil language daily. Circulation 15,582. The Associated Newspapers of Ceylon Ltd., Lake House, Colombo 1.

**Times Weekender.** F. 1923. English. Circulation 31,171. Times of Ceylon Ltd., No. 3, Bristol Street, Colombo.

**Virakesari.** F. 1931. Weekly. Tamil. Circulation 31,000. Express Newspapers (Ceylon) Ltd., Grandpass Road, Colombo 14.

**Vaara Manjari.** Tamil Sunday Paper. Circulation 22,925.

**Mithran Weekly.** F. 1964. Tamil. Circulation 14,000. The Virakesari Ltd., Grandpass Road, Colombo 14.

## EDUCATION

The expenditure on primary and secondary education in 1976 was Rs. 692,684,000.
*Science Education:* The number of science teaching units was 1,068 in 1976.
*Training of Teachers:* There were 28 Teachers' Training Colleges with an enrolment of 5,147 in 1976. Staff total was 597.
*Technical Education:* There are 14 institutions for technical education. The total enrolment of full time and part time students was 6,970 in 1976.

## RELIGION

**About two-thirds of the inhabitants are Buddhists, there are over a million and a half Hindus and a substantial minority of Christians and Moslems.**

# The Democratic Republic of Sudan

**Capital**—Khartoum.

**President**—Major General Gaafar Mohamed El Nimieri.

**National Flag:** Fesse-wise, crimson, white and grey. Green triangle on the dexter side.

## HISTORY, CONSTITUTION AND GOVERNMENT

Little is known about the prehistoric periods in the Sudan; nevertheless, as far as is known, early Sudanese men apparently went from being hunters to settled farmers and then members of a centralized kingdom. Of these, the Kerma Kingdom stands as the first centralized power in the Sudan. It is dated approximately to 2000–1600 B.C. and sited in the rich Dongola region. This was a powerful kingdom which seems to have ruled a very large region. It had political and trade relations with Egypt. The Kerma Kingdom was destroyed by the first generation of the 18th Dynasty of the Kingdom of Egypt.

With the end of the occupation of the Egyptian Kingdom of Nubia in about the 12th Century B.C., Sudanese history is not recorded until the establishment of the Kushite Kingdom in the province of Napta in about 850–750 B.C. A Kushite family living in the region of el-Kurru in the 9th and early 8th centuries B.C. seems to have established military power through economic development and gold trade with tribes of the Eastern Desert. With its cultural and economic importance to Kush, Egypt was an obvious field for this new military power. So King Kashta and King Piankhy ruled Egypt for 57 years. But after a series of wars with the Assyrians, the Kushites were driven out of Egypt. So Kush had to develop an economy to maintain the Kingdom. As a result, the center of power began to shift South. By the 4th century B.C. the center of the Kushite was in Merowe.

A cultural evolution went side by side with the political evolution and the peak of Sudanese cultural development is thought to be during the period between the second century B.C. and the third century A.D. when the Kushites developed their own style of writing and arts.

The decline of the Kushite Kingdom in the third and fourth centuries A.D. which led to the collapse of the centralized power at Merowe, seem to have been caused by a decline in the calibre of the royal family and a shift of economic prosperity from the centre to the North due to the trade relations between the Romans in Egypt and the princes of lower Nubia. It was also due to the introduction of the water wheel in the North.

However, the collapse of the kingdom as military power did not mean the demise of the Kushite Culture which lingered in the Sudan until Christianity was introduced in the Sudan in 543 A.D. The Nubians gradually adopted Christianity while the Blemmys of the Eastern Dersert and Red Sea Hills stood as champions of paganism until the arrival of the Arabs.

During the 7th century and afterwards, waves of Arab tribes infiltrated the country bringing with them a new religion, Islam, and a new system of education through the Koranic Schools that spread in many remote villages. The Islamization of the country started gradually but effectively until it took its full place in 1502 A.D. when the first Moslem Monarchy was established by the Funj Sultans with its capital at Sennar. Christianity, having lost its contact with the Christian World, withered away in the 16th century.

The Funj Kingdom lasted for over three centuries until Mohamed Ali, ruler of Egypt, conquered the decadent Sultanate in 1820. Turko-Egyptian conquest established the Sudan as a single administrative and political unit under a Governor-General with Khartoum as its capital. The purpose of Mohamed Ali in conquering the Sudan was to furnish his army with men and gold for his depleted treasury. All endeavours to rule the country humanely failed and the Sudan rose in revolt under the leadership of Mohamed Ahmed El Mahdi. In 1885, the Mahdi's army stormed Khartoum and killed the last British Governor-General, Gordon. As a result, a theocratic state was founded. Six months after the liberation of Khartoum, the Mahdi died and his successor El Khalifa Abdullahi assumed power. But the odds against him were great as many European countries became interested in his domain. The scramble for Africa made the British hasten their occupation of the country in order to outpace the French. The well-equipped British and Egyptian forces routed the Sudanese forces in the Battle of Kerreri in 1898. The Sudan was put under Anglo-Egyptian rule (condominium). This agreement lasted until another one was signed in 1953 between the powers giving autonomy to the Sudan and granting its people the right of self-determination.

National independence was achieved in 1956. Soon thereafter it became apparent that the non-programmatic character of the political parties was a weakness. The two main parties, Umma and the Nationalist United Party (NUP), broke up into conflicting splinter groups which formed a shifting and unstable base for parliamentary government. Governments changed, but cabinets were slow to form, and when constituted, they were unwieldy coalitions. Parliamentary instability invited a military coup in November 1958. General Aboud's regime continued in power until 1964, when civilian rule was again restored after a popular uprising.

The May 1969 revolution brought General Nimeiri into power. A single party presidential system was instituted with the Sudanese Socialist Union (SSU) as a mass political party. The President is nominated by the SSU and approved by popular referendum for a term of six years. The President exercises the executive powers of government and is supreme commander of the armed forces. Ministers are appointed by him and are responsible to him. A Prime Minister is authorised by the Constitution of 1973.

Legislative power is formally vested in a 250 member Peoples Assembly, 25 of whom are appointed by the President, 125 are directly elected from geographical constituencies, 70 are selected by functional and occupational associations, and 30 are selected by Provincial Peoples Councils. All candidates must be approved by the SSU. Major legislative proposals are initiated by the President after having been approved by the Political Bureau of the SSU and are referred to functional committees before consideration by the full Assembly. Legislation may be enacted over a Presidential veto by a two-thirds majority of the Assembly.

Though the government has hitherto been highly centralised in Khartoum, under the provisions of the People's Local Government Act of 1971, Government operations in all fields other than foreign affairs, national defence and justice are to be decentralised to the 18 provinces. Among the delegated functions are education, public health, agriculture, community development, livestock, minor public works, housing, and social welfare. It is intended that a substantial number of officials now serving in Khartoum will gradually be assigned to the Provincial Governments while Ministry headquarters will retain control over policy, national priorities, standards of administration, review of performance, the execution of large development projects, and the management of public corporations.

A Provincial Commissioner, appointed by the President, is responsible for planning, integrating and directing the public services which are being devolved to the provinces. Civil servants from the national Ministries are seconded to the provinces and are administratively responsible to the Provincial Commissioner. In each province there is a People's Executive Council composed of representatives selected by local councils and occupational groups and of senior civil servants in the provincial government. The Council has a broad range of legislative powers over provincial and local administration. It reviews the consolidated provincial budget before it is submitted to Khartoum and approves the budgets of local authorities. It is empowered to propose major development projects and to recommend national policies to the President, the relevant Ministries and the People's Assembly.

The People's Executive Council in each province is enjoined to delegate powers over local social and economic services and to authorise taxing powers to People's Local Councils in towns, rural areas and villages. Members of the People's Local Councils, a quarter of whom must be women, are chosen by popular election. Civil servants have been posted in growing numbers by the Provincial Commissioners to serve the local councils.

The SSU has been assigned a major role in promoting the Government's development programmes, mobilising popular participation, and assisting and controlling public administration. The President of the Republic is Chairman of the SSU. He is assisted by a 17 member Political Bureau which he appoints with the approval of the 180 man Central Committee. The latter meets annually to debate and determine Party policy. National Party Congresses, with 1,500 delegates in attendance, meet every three years. SSU headquarters maintains a large General Secretariat which manages its day-to-day activities concerned with dissemination of information, Party organisation, and the development and evaluation of public policy. It also operates an Institute of Socialist Studies which trains party cadres.

At the Provincial level, the Provincial Commissioner is Secretary-General of the SSU, assisted by a Provincial Committee. The hierarchy of the SSU structures extends down to the village, neighbourhood and enterprise levels. These units are expected to carry the government's message to the grass roots and to reflect and convey local opinion to senior party officials. The basic units of the SSU in the rural and urban areas are elected by the active membership. Higher echelons of the Party Congresses and Committees are filled by indirect election.

The parallel structures of the SSU and the Government are intended to insure a close and continuous link between politics and administration. The Party is superordinate to Government. Major policies of Government are shaped by the SSU which is also responsible for guiding the administration at all levels in the execution of these policies. Civil servants are required to demonstrate a positive commitment to the objectives and policies of the SSU. At the local level, SSU cadres and members are expected to counteract the influence of traditional sectarian, ethnic and political groups, where these are disinclined to support the political and administrative authorities.

There is a strong emphasis in the SSU's platform on national unity. A major achievement of the Nimeiri government has been the rapprochement between the North and the South, ending the long and costly insurgency in the three southern provinces which started shortly after Independence. Attempts at military pacification were unsuccessful and led to heavy loss of lives and disruption of the South's economy and public services. After 1971 President Nimeiri assumed personal responsibility for achieving a political solution, and his efforts culminated in the Addis Ababa Accord of March 1972 which stilled the guns. Then began the difficult task of integrating the South into the political and economic life of the country, while permitting it to retain a large measure of regional autonomy. Under the provisions of the 1972 accord, the internal affairs of the southern provinces are administered by an autonomous Regional Government with its parallel structure of ministries, government agencies, and civil servants. Both the annual and the development budgets of the Southern Region are subsidized by the national Government. The theme of national unity also stresses the reduction and regulation of the ethnic, sectarian, and political cleavages which characterized public life in Sudan in the past.

#### Cabinet Ministers

*Minister of Defence and C-in-C.:* Lt. General Bashir Mohamed Ali.
*Minister of Interior:* Sayed A/Wahab Ibrahim.
*Minister of Foreign Affairs:* Dr. Mansour Khalid.
*Minister of Energy and Mining:* Major (Rtd) Mamoun Awad Abu Zaid.
*Minister of Youth and Sports:* Major (Rtd) Zein el Abdin Mohamed Ahmed A/gadir.
*Minister of Health:* General (Rtd) Khalid Hassan Abbass.
*Minister of Planning:* General (Rtd) Nasr ElDin Mustafa
*Minister of Finance and National Economy:* Sayed El Sharif El Khatim.
*Minister of Public Service and Administrative Reform:* Sayed Karamalla El Awad.
*Minister of Industry and Mining:* Sayed Abdel Rahman Abdalla.
*Minister of Transport and Communications:* Dr. Bashir Abbadi.
*Minister of Education:* Sayed Dafalla El Haj Yousif.
*Minister of Culture and Information:* Sayed Bona Malwal.
*Minister of Trade and Supply:* Sayed Haroon El Awad.
*Minister of Irrigation and Hydro-electric Power:* Sayed Saghayroon El Zein.
*Minister of Religious Affairs and Awkaf:* Dr. Awn El Sharif Gasim.
*Minister of Personal Affairs in Presidential Headquarters:* Dr. Baha El Din Mohamed Idris.
*Minister of Social Affairs:* Dr. Fatima Abdel Mahmoud.
*Minister of Building and Public Construction:* General (Rtd) Mustafa Osman.
*Minister of Agriculture, Food and Natural Resources:* Dr. Abdel Ahmed Abdalla.
*Minister of Co-operation:* Dr. Mohamed Hashim Awad.
*Attorney General:* Dr. Hassan Omer.

### LOCAL GOVERNMENT

The country is divided into nine Provinces and two Commissionerships. In each Province there is a Provincial Council of some 12–20 members representing local authorities in the Province.

The Provinces are sub-divided into a total of 46 districts, each in charge of a district Commissioner.

The Sudan is now divided into 84 Local Government Areas with Councils at varying degrees of development. A local authority may be the District Commissioner (27 areas) or a local Inspector (58 areas).

### LEGAL SYSTEM

Under the Self-Government Statute the Judiciary has become an independent department of state, directly and solely responsible to the Supreme Council of the Armed Forces.

Civil Justice is administered by the Chief Justice and Judges of the High Court, who are also members of the Court of Appeal, and by subordinate district judges. The religious law of Islam is administered by the Mohammedan Law Courts in matters of inheritance, marriage, divorce and family relations amongst the Muslim population. There are District and Provincial courts and a High Court at Khartoum presided over by the Grand Kadi. The first Juvenile Court in the Sudan was opened in June 1960.

Serious crimes are tried by Major Courts constituted under the code of Criminal Procedure and composed of a President and two members. In the Provinces in which circuits of the High Court extend, Major Courts are, as a rule, presided over by a judge of the High Court. In the other Provinces by the Provincial Judge. Decisions of a Major Court require confirmation by the Chief Justice, to whom there is a right of appeal.

Lesser crimes are tried by Minor Courts of three Magistrates and by Magistrates' Courts consisting of a single Magistrate or a Bench of lay magistrates. There also exist throughout the country Courts of Sheikhs or Chiefs with varying powers of limited jurisdiction. These administer civil and criminal justice in accordance with native custom and deal with offences against specific Ordinances, under the general supervision of the Sudan Government Authorities.

### AREA AND POPULATION

The Northern Sudan is predominantly Arab and Muslim. The main tribal divisions comprise (*a*) the Hadendoa, Bisharin and Bani 'Amer of the Red Sea Hills speaking their own Hamitic and Semitic languages; (*b*) the Berbinne (Nubian) tribes of the northern Nile valley, with remnants of their old language; (*c*) a central mass of 'Arab' tribes occupying the whole central belt of the Sudan, e.g. Kababish, Kawahla, Ja'alin, the various Baggara (cattle owning) tribes, etc.; (*d*) remains of earlier peoples such as the Nuba, Fur, Ingessana, etc., mostly with their own languages, although using also Arabic. The common language of the whole Northern Sudan is Arabic, of which there are considerable local dialect variations.

The Southern Sudan (south of about lat. 10°) was preserved from external influence in the early days by climatic and geographical difficulties and is inhabited by negroid peoples speaking a large number of separate languages and dialects, sometimes in very small units. They may be classified as follows: (*a*) Sudanic; various clusters of tribes west of the Nile, including the Azande (230,000) and Moru-Madi; (*b*) Nilotic; the peoples of the rivers and swamps, Dinka (820,000), Nuer (350,000), Shilluk-Acoli (200,000); (*c*) Nilo-Hamitic; the peoples of the southern Nile valley, Bari (100,000), Latuka, etc.

English or a very rudimentary Arabic serve as *lingua franca*. Many of the tribes have affinities more or less close, with tribes to be found in Abyssinia, Kenya, Uganda or the Belgian Congo, as the international boundary is nowhere an ethnic one.

The population at mid-1974 was 15,227,000. The annual average percentage growth rate of the population for the periods 1960–74 and 1965–74 was 2·2. Provinces and districts with areas and approximate population figures with chief towns:

| *Province* | *Area* | *Population* | *Chief Towns* |
|---|---|---|---|
| Bahr el Ghazal | 82,530 | 991,022 | Wau (8,009) |
| Blue Nile | 54,880 | 2,069,646 | Wad Medani (47,677)<br>Kosti (22,688)<br>Ed Dueim (12,319) |

| *Province* | *Area* | *Population* | *Chief Towns* |
|---|---|---|---|
| Darfur | 191,650 | 1,328,765 | El Fasher (26,161) |
| Equatoria | 76,495 | 903,503 | Juba (10,660) |
| Kassala | 131,528 | 941,039 | Kassala (40,612) Port Sudan (47,561) |
| Khartoum | 8,097 | 504,923 | Khartoum (93,103) Omdurman (113,686) Khartoum North (39,090) |
| Kordofan | 146,930 | 1,761,968 | El Obeid (52,372) En Nahud (16,498) |
| Northern | 184,200 | 873,059 | El Damer (5,454) Atbara (36,298) Berber (10,978) |
| Upper Nile | 91,190 | 888,611 | Shendi (10,868) Malakal (9,680) |
| Totals | 967,500 | 10,262,536 | |

## CURRENCY

The unit of currency is the Sudanese pound of 100 piastres or 1,000 milliemes.

## FINANCE

The GNP at market prices for 1974 was U.S. $ millions 3,460, and the GNP per capita at market prices was U.S. $230. The annual average percentage growth rate of the GNP per capita for the period 1960–74 was 1·7 and for the period 1965–74 was 4·3. [*See the note at the beginning of this section concerning GNP.*]
The Budget figures for 1971–72 are: Revenue, £S.189,000,000; Expenditure, £S.178,000,000.

The chief sources of revenue are:

1. Indirect taxation from customs duties on imported goods and royalties on products exported.
2. Profit on trading concerns (Sudan Railways, shares of cotton scheme profits, sugar monopoly, etc.).
3. Direct taxation.

## BANKING

The following are the principal banks in the Sudan:

**Bank of Sudan** (Khartoum).

**Agricultural Bank of Sudan.** F. 1957. Managing Director, Sayed Hammad Tewfik Hammad. Authorized Capital, £S.5,000,000 provided wholly by the Government. Khartoum.

**Sudan Commercial Bank** (Khartoum).

**State Bank for Foreign Trade.**

**El Nilein Bank.** Established 1964. (Acting Managing Director, Mahmoud Mustafa Oleim). Capital: LS.4,500,000; Reserves: LS.2,952,216. Total Resources: LS.165,824,995, as at 31 December 1976. *Head Office:* P.O. Box 466, Parliament Street, Khartoum.

**Omdurman National Bank.**

**People's Co-operative Bank.**

**The Arab Bank** (3 branches in the Sudan, 33 in other countries).

**Juba Commercial Bank.** Provides International Banking Services. Specializes in foreign trade with African countries and development financing in Southern Sudan. *Head Office:* P.O. Box 1186, Khartoum. Cable address: Jubank. Branches in Southern Sudan at Juba, Malakal and Wau.

**The Industrial Bank of the Sudan** (Khartoum).

## PRODUCTION, INDUSTRY AND COMMERCE

**Agriculture.** The annual rainfall in the Sudan ranges from less than 100 mm. on the Egyptian border to over 1,200 mm. in the south. Irrigation, essential to crop production in areas with under 400 mm. of rain, is now important on both Niles as far south as Lat. 12° (rainfall 600–1,000 mm.). The chief irrigated area is in the Gezira Scheme which, with the Managil Extension, has an area of 1·8 million acres. These are cropped annually in a canalized area of over one million acres, fed by gravity irrigation from the Sennar Dam. In addition the Sudan has some 400,000 acres watered by pump irrigation and an average of 170,000 acres cultivated by flood irrigation annually.

The most important export crop is cotton, mostly high quality long-staple, annual production of lint averaging 73,000 tons and of seed 140,000 tons. The staple food crop is millet, grown both on rain and irrigated cultivation. Sesame and groundnuts grown in the rainland areas of the central and southern Sudan are important for oil and food and provide surpluses for export. Crop production in the great clay plains is expanding with the provision of permanent water supplies and new roads.

Dates have been grown for centuries in the north along the Nile. Improved varieties and new packing methods make them a potential export. Citrus fruits and mangoes are being more widely grown. The Sudan produces 75 per cent of the world's gum arabic needs.

Latest estimated figures for animals are: cattle, 12,300,000; sheep, 10,300,000; goats, 7,200,000. Most camels and sheep are owned by nomad tribes in the vast grazing areas of the Sudan and an accurate census is not possible.

**Forestry.** Much of the Sudan is covered by acacia, but there are forests of more useful timber of little commercial use except for firewood and fuel. Timber is extracted from the southern tropical forests, and further north an extensive system of reservation and afforestation ensures supplies of building materials, railway sleepers and fuel for the towns. There are four groups of sawmills, The Blue Nile, Wau, Loka and Katire, with an annual output of 1,000,000 cubic feet. The chief forest product is gum arabic, the greater part of the world's needs of which come from the forests of Kordofan and Blue Nile Provinces. There are 2,664,546 acres of forest reserves.

## COMMUNICATIONS

**Railways.** The Sudan Railways system, which is owned and operated by the Sudan Government, extends from Wadi Halfa in the north and Port Sudan in the Red Sea, through Atbara, Khartoum and Sennar to Nyala in the west, and Aweil in the south. The system includes the Sennar–Haiya loop line and branches to Karima Roseires, opened during 1954–55. The gauge is 3 ft. 6 in. and the total route is 5,225 km. Further extensions are planned. In 1958 the line to the west was extended from Babanusa to Ed Duein and in 1959 to Nyala. Construction of the southwards extension from Babanusa on the new Nyala line to Wau, a distance of approximately 279 miles, began in April 1959.

The system now operates from Wadi Halfa in the north to Wau in the south, and from Port Sudan in the east to Nyala in the west. There are branch lines to Karima, El Obeid, and Roseires and an eastern route to the coast from Sennar via Haiya.

The steamer services cover some 2,500 miles and render efficient services for goods and passengers throughout the navigable reaches:

(*a*) From Khartoum to Juba on the White Nile (including the Sobat to Gambeila and the Bahr el Ghazal to Meshra and Wau).
(*b*) From Karima to Dongola and Kerma.
(*c*) From Wadi Halfa to Shellal in Egypt.

The ocean port at Port Sudan is administered by Sudan Railways.

**Civil Aviation—Sudan Airways** (General Manager: S/Mohammed El Amir); a state-operated corporation; *services operated:* Khartoum to Addis Ababa, Aden, Asmara, Athens, Beirut, Cairo, Entebbe, Fort Lamy, Jeddah, Nairobi, Rome, El Fasher, El Roseines, El Obeid, Geneina, Kassala, Khashm El Girba, Juba, London, Malakal, Nyala, Port Sudan, Tripoli, Wad Medani, Wau, Frankfurt, Abu Dahbi. *Head Office:* P.O. Box 253, Khartoum, Sudan. *Fleet:* 2 Boeing 707s, 2 Boeing 737s, 5 Fokker 27s, 2 Twin Otters.

The number of passengers carried in 1974–75 was 250,140.

**Telegraphs and Telephones.** There are 130 telephone exchanges 48 of which are connected to the internal trunk system which covers approximately ½ million sq. miles. This system is linked by three lines to Cairo to connect with the International services with the United Kingdom, Europe and the United States of America. There are also telephone services with Eritrea, Saudi Arabia and Japan. In 1964 the number of telephones was over 35,000. In all the large towns, exchanges are automatic; others are scheduled for conversion. Plans are being considered for the building of a new

Telephone Exchange Centre in Khartoum. The new Exchange is expected to cater for 20,000 telephone lines in the Khartoum Central area.

**Broadcasting.** The Sudan Broadcasting Service, with studios in Omdurman, was founded in 1940, and is now fitted with the most up-to-date equipment, by which programmes are transmitted for 65 hours a week.

## NEWSPAPERS

**El Rai El Amm.** F. 1945. Arabic. Khartoum. Independent. P.O. Box 424. Daily. Printed in Arabic. Editor, Fatih Tigani.

**Morning News.** F. 1954. English. P.O. Box 363. Khartoum.

**El Sudan El Gadid.** F. 1944. Arabic. P.O. Box 358, Khartoum. Daily. Editor, M. Nourani.

**El Sahafa.** F. 1961. Arabic. Daily Circulation 60,000. Founder: Abdel Rahman Mukhtar. Nationalized 1970. El Sahafa House. P.O. Box 1228, Khartoum.

**Al Ayam.** F. 1953. Arabic. P.O. Box 363, Khartoum. Daily. Editor, M. M. Salih.

**Sawt El Sudan.** P.O. Box 197, Khartoum.

**Al Adwaa.** Twice Weekly.

**Akhbar-Al-Sbaua.** Weekly.

**Al Hayat.** Weekly.

## EDUCATION

The system of education starts with a four-year course in elementary schools from which about 20 per cent of the pupils pass on to intermediate schools for a further four years. Secondary education up to School Certificate standard is provided by the government at Wadi Seidna (Khartoum Province), Hantoub (Blue Nile Province), Khor Taggat (Kordofan Province) and Rumbek (Bahr-el-Ghazal Province) where there are full boarding facilities and at Khartoum and Atbara day secondary schools. There are also three non-government secondary schools in Omdurman, one in Port Sudan and three community and denominational schools in Khartoum. A commercial secondary school is run under government auspices in Omdurman.

Technical education is provided for at intermediate technical schools at Omdurman, El Obeid, Wad Medani and Atbara, Port Sudan, Kosti and Nyala. The Khartoum Technical Institute gives a secondary course for four years in technical education. There are also post-secondary courses in building, civil and mechanical engineering, commercial subjects and art and handicrafts. The Khartoum Technical Institute runs evening classes in further education on a large variety of subjects.

The training of teachers is carried out at the Institutes of Education at Bakht-er-Ruda, Shendi, Dilling and Meridi. Bakht-er-Ruda is the parent institution which not only trains teachers up to the intermediate level but also prepares syllabuses and is the centre of the subject inspectorate.

The government system of education is supplemented by a large number of village schools run by local government councils for which the councils receive a 40 per cent grant from the Ministry. Local communities have also opened a number of schools mainly at the intermediate level, many of which are substantially subsidized by the government. In the southern provinces, Protestant and Catholic missionary bodies contribute widely in the spread of education. Government grants are paid to the missions. All non-government schools are inspected regularly by government inspectors and payment of grants is dependent upon standards attained.

The organization of girls' education follows much the same lines as the boys, although the number of schools is still considerably less. At the elementary level the girls' schools number half those of the boys, at the intermediate level one-quarter and at the secondary one-fifth. There are elementary teacher training centres in four provinces, and a student-teacher training system for girls with secondary education wishing to qualify for work at the intermediate level.

Night schools for women operate in Khartoum, Wad Medani and Atbara and the attendance is good. Practical subjects are taught but the women are primarily interested to acquire literacy. There are 207 sub-grade and 229 elementary schools for girls in the Northern Provinces and 25 non-government intermediate schools in the whole of Sudan.

In the Southern Provinces there are only 152 government elementary schools and 19 intermediate schools.

The Kitchener School of Medicine was opened in 1924 and grants diplomas in Medicine, Surgery and Obstetrics and Gynaecology.

By an ordinance of 1951 the Kitchener School of Medicine and the Gordon Memorial College were amalgamated and became the University College of Khartoum. It was raised to the status of an independent university in 1956 by an Act of Parliament. It is constitutionally independent of the Sudan Government and is governed by its own council of 35 members.

## RELIGION

No census of religions has yet been taken in the Sudan, but the population of North Sudan is almost entirely Moslem (Sunni), apart from a few small areas of pagans and a small Christian community, mostly in the towns. In Southern Sudan there are a certain number of Christians and Moslems, but the majority are pagans.

# Surinam

## (*Suriname*)

**Capital**—Paramaribo.

**President**—Dr. J. H. E. Ferrier.

### CONSTITUTION AND GOVERNMENT

Surinam is situated on the north coast of South America, between French Guiana and Guyana and bounded in the south by Brazil.

The first large scale colonization was made by Francis Willoughby, the 5th Baron Willoughby, the English Governor of Barbados, who sent an expedition to Surinam under Anthony Rowse, who became its first governor.

At the peace of Breda, in 1667 between England and the United Netherlands, Surinam was assigned to the Netherlands in exchange for the Colony of New Netherland in North America, and this was confirmed by the Treaty of Westminster of February 1674. Since then Surinam has been twice in the possession of England, from 1799 till 1802, when it was restored at the Peace of Amiens, and from 1804 to 1816, when it was returned according to the Convention of London of 31 August 1814, confirmed at the Peace of Paris of 20 November 1815, with the other Dutch colonies, except Berbice, Demerara, Essequibo and the Cape of Good Hope.

A new legal order was enacted by the Netherlands Surinam and the Netherlands Antilles which took effect on 29 December 1954 and was embodied in the Charter for the Kingdom of the Netherlands. By this, these countries were given management of their own affairs and are united with the Netherlands on a footing of equality for the protection of their common interests and the granting of mutual assistance.

On the 25 November, 1975 Surinam became an independent country.

### LEGAL SYSTEM

Throughout Surinam are in force Surinam laws, which are mainly concordant with Dutch laws. The Supreme Court of Justice, whose members are appointed by the Queen, sits at Paramaribo.

#### Government and Ministry

*Prime Minister and General Affairs:* Henk A. E. Arron.
*Finance:* Henk A. E. Arron.
*Justice and Police:* Mr. E. Hoost.
*Agriculture, Animal Husbandry and Fisheries.* Mr. W. Soemita.
*Development:* Mr. M. Cambridge.
*Interior Affairs:* Dr. C. Ooft.
*Public Works:* Mr. E. Karamat Ali.
*Education:* Mr. R. R. Veneziaan.
*Social Affairs:* Mr. S. Soeperman.
*Labour and Housing:* Mr. F. Freymersum.
*Economic Affairs:* Mr. Bruma.
*Public Health:* Mr. J. Brahim.
*Rural Development:* Mr. O. W. van Genderen.
*Minister Plenipotentiary in The Hague:* Mr. W. F. van Eer.

### AREA AND POPULATION

Surinam has a total area of 164,000 sq. kilometres.

The population at mid-1974 was 387,000. The annual average percentage growth rate of the population for the period 1960–74 was 2·7 and for the period 1965–74 was 2·2.

Distribution by nationalities by percentage shows Europeans and other minorities 8, Creoles 30, Hindostanis 35, Indonesians 15, Bush Negroes, 10, Amerindians two.

45·2 per cent of the population is under 15 years of age. The annual population increase is 3·15 per cent.

Population of the chief town Paramaribo is 105,000.

### CURRENCY

The unit of currency is the Surinam guilder (Sur. fl.). The rate of exchange is Sur. fl. 100 = Netherlands fl. 185.

### FINANCE

The provisional figures of revenue and expenditure for two years (in million Sur. fl.) are shown below:

| | 1972 | 1973 |
|---|---|---|
| Revenue | 183·2 | 234·6 |
| Expenditure | 222·5 | 288·9 |

The GNP at market prices for 1974 was U.S. $ million 460, and the GNP per capita at market prices was U.S. $1,180. The annual average percentage growth rate of the GNP per capita for the period 1960–74 was 3·6 and for the period 1965–74 was 2·2. [*See the note at the beginning of this section concerning GNP.*]

### PRODUCTION, INDUSTRY AND COMMERCE

Agriculture is carried on along the coastal belt and the rivers. Like the Dutch polders, in the coastal belt the soil is in many places muddy and is kept in condition by a system of ditches and dykes. The main agricultural products are rice, bananas, tropical fruit such as coconuts, sugar and coffee.

In real terms the average growth was—one half per cent. Exports in 1975 amounted to Sf 581·4 millions and imports were valued at Sf 631·1 millions. The main trading partners are the U.S.A. (minerals, consumer goods, fuels), the Netherlands (minerals, rice, machines, consumer goods) and Japan (consumer durables, light industrial equipment).

The most important economic sector is bauxite mining and processing. There are large deposits of bauxite which are worked by two foreign mining companies.

This sector's contribution to GDP amounted in 1975 Sf 179 millions. Exports in 1975 were valued at Sf 340·8 millions.

Agriculture is carried out along the coastal belt and the main rivers. In the coastal belt the soil is in most places muddy and is kept in condition by a system of ditches and dykes, the so called "polders". The main agricultural products are rice, bananas, sugar, palm oil and tropical fruits.

Agricultural output in 1975 was estimated at Sf 110·5 millions.

Almost 80 per cent of Surinam's area is covered with tropical forests which contain much valuable wood. Contribution to GDP is small; in 1975 only 1·6 per cent. Exports in 1973 amounted Sf 11·7 millions.

Other industrial activities include food products, cement and a chemical factory. Contributions from this sector amounted Sf 45 millions in 1975.

At the moment some important development plans are in the course of being realized, including the Kabalebo hydro-electric project, the Bakhuys railway project (which will link the Bakhuys bauxite deposits with the Apoera port) and some agricultural projects. Development investments in 1975 amounted to Sf 75·3 millions.

# The Kingdom of Swaziland

**Chief Town**—Mbabane.

**Head of State**—His Majesty King Sobhuza II.

## CONSTITUTION AND GOVERNMENT

SWAZILAND is bounded on the north, west and south by the Transvaal Province and on the east by Mozambique and Natal Province. Up to a hundred years ago the Swazis occupied the country just north of the Pongola River, but hostile neighbours forced them to turn north. By absorbing smaller clans and by linking the ruling Dlamini clan maritally with other clans, they occupied the territory now known as Swaziland.

The independence of the Swazis had been guaranteed in the Conventions of 1881 and 1884, entered into between the Government of Queen Victoria and the Government of the late South African Republic. In 1890 a provisional government was established, representative of the Swazi, the British and the South African Republican Governments. In 1894 the South African Republic was given powers of protection and administration without incorporation, and Swaziland was under this form of control until the outbreak of the Boer War in 1899. In 1902, after the conclusion of hostilities, a Special Commissioner took charge. Under an Order-in-Council dated 1 December 1906, the High Commissioner assumed control. Administration was in the hands of a Resident Commissioner, whose secretariat worked through District Commissioners and various departments. An Advisory Council was established in 1921 to advise the administration in purely European matters. The Council received statutory recognition in 1949. A constitution for Swaziland was established by the Swaziland Order in Council, 1963. It made provision for an Executive Council of eight members (four official and four unofficial) and a Legislative Council of four members, 24 elected members and up to three members nominated by Her Majesty's Commissioner. In August 1965, the number of unofficial members in the Executive Council was increased from four to six and in October 1966 to seven. Her Majesty's Commissioner, a post equivalent to the status of Governor, assented to legislation and was directly responsible to the Secretary of State.

On 25 April 1967, the Kingdom of Swaziland came into being under a new internal self-government constitution, which took effect on that day. Sobhuza II was recognized as King and Head of State, and the constitution established a Parliament partly elected by the people and partly appointed by the King. Under a special treaty, the Protected State Agreement, which also came into force 25 April 1967, Britain was responsible for defence, external affairs, internal security, the civil service and certain aspects of finance until Swaziland became fully independent, on 6 September 1968, under a constitution which varied only slightly from the 1967 constitution.

Parliament consists of a Senate and a House of Assembly. The House of Assembly has 24 elected members, and six Members nominated by the King. The Attorney-General is also a member but has no vote. The Senate has 12 members—six elected by the House of Assembly and six appointed by the King The second House of Assembly election was held on 16 and 17 May 1972 and the royalist Imbokodvo National Movement won 21 seats.

**Cabinet** (1977)

*Prime Minister and Minister Responsible for Foreign Affairs and Head of Government:* H. E. The Right Hon. Col Maphevu Dlamini.
*Deputy Prime Minister:* Hon. Zonke A. Khumalo.
*Minister for Agriculture:* Hon. A. Kuseni Hlophe.
*Minister for Justice:* Hon. Polycarp L. Dlamini.
*Ministsr of Finance and Economic Planning:* Hon. Robert P. Stephens.
*Minister of Works, Power and Communications:* Hon. Dr. Allen M. Nxumalo.
*Minister for Local Administration:* Hon. Prince Masitsela.
*Minister for Commerce and Co-operatives:* Hon. Prince Mfanasibili.
*Minister of Industry, Mines and Tourism:* Hon. Sishayi S. Nxumalo.
*Minister of Education and Health:* Hon. Dr. Percy S. P. Dlamini.
*Assistant Minister for Education and Health:* Hon. Elias S. Dhladhla.
*Minister of State for Foreign Affairs:* Hon. Mhlangana S. Matsebula.
*Minister of State for Establishments and Training:* Hon. Khanyakwezwe H. Dlamini.
*Assistant Minister for Local Administration:* Hon. Mndeni S. Shabalala.
*Assistant Minister in Deputy Prime Minister's Office:* Hon. Bhekimpi A. Dlamini.

## LEGAL SYSTEM

The constitution provides for a Court of Appeal consisting of a President and two Judges. The High Court of Swaziland has civil and criminal jurisdiction. It also has power to review the proceedings of all subordinate courts and hear appeals. There are subordinate courts of the First, Second and Third classes, presided over by professional magistrates and District Officers.

There are 14 Swazi Courts, two Courts of Appeal and a Higher Swazi Court of Appeal. Swazi Courts have civil and criminal jurisdiction, subject to the provisions of the Proclamation, in all matters in which the parties are Africans. Appeal in criminal cases lies from the courts of first instance to a Swazi Appeal Court, to the Higher Swazi Court of Appeal, to the Judicial Commissioner and thence, in certain cases, to the High Court of Swaziland. Appeals in certain civil cases may go direct from the Higher Swazi Appeal Court to the High Court.

## AREA AND POPULATION

The area of Swaziland is 6,704·6 square miles.

The population at mid-1974 was 478,000. The annual average percentage growth rate of the population for the period 1960–74 was 3·0 and for 1965–74 was 3·1.

## CURRENCY AND FINANCE

The unit of currency is the South African rand.

The GNP at market prices for 1974 was U.S. $ millions 190, and the GNP per capita at market prices was U.S. $390. The annual average percentage growth rate of the GNP per capita for the period 1960–74 was 6·7, and for the period 1965–74 was 6·0. [*See the note at the beginning of this section concerning GNP.*]

Revenue for the year 1971–72 amounted to an estimated SAR.17,241,000 and estimated expenditure to SAR. 16,505,000. The chief items of revenue are income tax, customs and excise, posts and telecommunications and licences.

## PRODUCTION, INDUSTRY AND COMMERCE

The principal exports during 1971 were SAR. 12,502,900, iron ore SAR. 12,178,400, woodpulp SAR. 9,567,000, and asbestos SAR. 5,904,100. Total exports were SAR. 56,100,500.

The imports for 1971 were SAR. 46,966,100.

The most important export minerals are iron ore and asbestos. In 1971, 2,312,400 metric tons and 38,100 metric tons valued at SAR. 12,178,400 and SAR. 5,904,100 respectively for iron ore and asbestos.

By an agreement with the Republic of South Africa Swaziland is dealt with for Customs purposes as part of the Republic and a proportion of the total collection is paid to the country annually depending on the value of her imports.

## COMMUNICATIONS

Work on a 137-mile railway line (3 ft. 6 in. gauge) was completed by the end of 1964. The line runs from the iron ore mine on the western border, through the centre of the country to Goba, where it connects with the Mozambique line to the port of Lourenco Marques. There are spur lines to the Matsapa industrial estate, just outside Manzini.

The Territory has its own postal and telegraph facilities.

There are 114 miles of tarred roads.

## EDUCATION

There are 420 schools, including 69 operated by the Government and 246 which are Government-aided, with a total of 80,500 pupils.

There are 71,500 pupils in 366 primary schools, and 9,000 pupils in 54 secondary schools.

# Sweden

## (SVERIGE)

**Capital**—Stockholm.

**Sovereign**—King Carl XVI Gustaf.

**National Flag:** Light blue, charged with a cross yellow, the upright one-third from the hoist.

### CONSTITUTION AND GOVERNMENT

It is laid down in the new constitution, which entered into force in 1975, that Sweden is a representative and parliamentary democracy. Parliament (the Riksdag) is declared to be the central organ of government. The executive power of the country is vested in the Government, which is responsible to Parliament. The King is Head of State, but he does not participate in the government of the country. Since 1971 Parliament has consisted of one chamber. It has 349 members, who are elected for a period of three years in direct, general elections. Every man and woman who has reached the age of 18 on the election day at the latest and who is not under wardship has the right to vote and to stand for election.

The manner of election to the Parliament is proportional. The country is divided into 28 constituencies. In these constituencies 310 members are elected. The remaining 39 seats constitute a nation-wide pool intended to give absolute proportionality to parties that receive at least four per cent of the votes. A party receiving less than four per cent of the votes in the country is, however, entitled to participate in the distribution of seats in a constituency, if it has obtained at least 12 per cent of the votes cast there.

Members of the *Riksdag* in 1977 received an annual salary of 88,860 kronor, annual compensation for expenses amounting to 3,600 kronor, and during sessions a monthly expense allowance of 2,160 kronor.

**Reigning Royal Family.** Lutheran.—The house of Bernadotte originated with Jean-Baptiste-Jules Bernadotte, a Marshal of the French Empire, who was elected Prince Royal of Sweden 21 August 1810 and adopted by King Carl XIII, of the old reigning house of Holstein-Gottorp, whom he succeeded 5 February 1818 as Carl XIV Johan, King of Sweden and Norway. King Oscar II renounced the crown of Norway in a letter addressed to the Norwegian Storting 26 October 1905. Succession is in the male line and the cadet members of the family bear the title prince or princess of Sweden, Royal Highness.

**H.M. CARL XVI GUSTAF** Folke Hubertus, King of Sweden; born at Haga Castle, 30 April 1946, only son of HRH Prince Gustaf Adolf, eldest son of King Gustaf VI Adolf, by his wife Princess Sibylla, elder daughter of HRH Karl Eduard, Duke of Saxe-Coburg-Gotha, Prince of GB and Ireland, 2nd Duke of Albany; acceded to the Throne on the death of his grandfather, 15 September 1973; married Stockholm (Storkyrkan) 19 June 1976, Silvia Renate Sommerlath, Queen of Sweden, born at Heidelberg 23 December 1943, daughter of Mr. Walther Sommerlath and Alice de Toledo-Sommerlath. Child: Princess VICTORIA Ingrid Alice Désirée, born at Stockholm, 14 July 1977.

Children of the late king, H.M. Gustaf VI Adolf: 1. The late Prince GUSTAF ADOLF Oscar Fredrik Arthur Edmund, Duke of Västerbotten; born at Stockholm, 22 April 1906; killed in an air accident at Copenhagen, 26 January 1947; married at Coburg, 20 October 1932, Princess Sibylla (born at Gotha, 18 January 1908, died at Stockholm 28 November 1972).

Children: 1. Princess MARGARETHA Désirée Victoria; born at Haga Caste, 31 October 1934; married at Gärdslösa church on Öland, 30 June 1964, Mr. John Kenneth Ambler (born 6 June 1924). Bears the title Princess Margaretha, Mrs. Ambler. 2. Princess BIRGITTA Ingeborg Alice; born at Haga Castle, 19 January 1937; married at Stockholm (civil marriage), 25 May and at Sigmaringen (religious ceremony), 30 May 1961, *Johann Georg* Leopold Eitel-Friedrich Meinrad Maria Hubertus Michael, Prince of Hohenzollern (born at Sigmaringen, 31 July 1932). 3. Princess DÉSIRÉE Elisabeth Sibylla; born at Haga Castle, 2 June 1938; married Stockholm, 5 June 1964, Baron Nils-August Otto Carl Niclas Silfverschiöld (born 31 May 1934). Bears the title Princess Désirée, Baroness Silverschiöld. 4. Princess CHRISTINA Louise Helena; born at Haga Castle, 3 August 1943; married Stockholm 15 June 1974, Mr. Tord Gösta Magnuson (born 7 Apr. 1941). Bears the title Princess Christina, Mrs Magnuson. 5. H. M. CARL XVI Gustaf Folke Hubertus; (see above).

2. SIGVARD Oscar Fredrik; born at Drottningholm Castle, 7 June 1907; renounced his titles and rights of succession to the throne of Sweden on his marriage 15 June 1934; created Count of Wisborg 2 July 1951. 3. Princess INGRID Victoria Sofia Louise Margareta; born at Stockholm, 28 March 1910; married at Stockholm, 24 May 1935, Frederik IX, King of Denmark, and has issue. 4. Prince BERTIL Gustaf Oscar Carl Eugen, Duke of Halland; born at Stockholm, 28 February 1912. 5. CARL JOHAN Arthur; born at Stockholm, 31 October 1916; renounced his titles and rights of succession to the throne of Sweden on his marriage 19 February 1946; created Count of Wisborg 2 July 1951.

**Ministry** (8 October 1976)

*Prime Minister:* Mr. Thorbjörn Fälldin (Cen.).
*Minister of Labour and Deputy Prime Minister:* Mr. Per Ahlmark (Lib.).
*Minister of Justice:* Mr. Sven Romanus (non-pol.).
*Minister for Foreign Affairs:* Ms. Karin Söder (Cen.).
*Minister for International Development Co-operation:* Mr. Ola Ullsten (Lib.).
*Minister of Defence:* Mr. Eric Krönmark (Cons.).
*Minister of Health and Social Affairs:* Mr. Rune Gustavsson (Cen.).
*Deputy Minister of Health and Social Affairs:* Ms. Ingegerd Troedsson (Cons.).
*Minister of Transport and Communications:* Mr. Bo Turesson (Cons.).
*Minister for Fiscal Affairs:* Mr. Ingemar Mundebo (Lib.).
*Minister for Economic Affairs:* Mr. Gösta Bohman (Cons.).
*Minister of Education and Cultural Affairs:* Mr. Jan-Erik Wikström (Lib.).
*Deputy Minister of Education and Cultural Affairs:* Ms. Britt Mogård (Cons.).
*Minister of Agriculture:* Mr. Anders Dahlgren (Cen.).
*Minister of Commerce:* Mr. Staffan Burenstam Linder (Cons.).
*Minister of Housing and Physical Planning:* Ms. Elvy Olsson (Cen.).
*Deputy Minister of Housing and Physical Planning:* Ms. Birgit Friggebo (Lib.).
*Minister of Industry:* Mr. Nils G. Åsling (Cen.).
*Minister for Energy:* Mr. Olof Johansson (Cen.).
*Minister of Local Government:* Mr. Johannes Antonsson (Cen.).

(Abbreviations: Cen. = Center Party, Lib. = Liberal Party, Cons. = Conservative Party).

**Parliament (Riksdagen) in 1977.**

*Speaker:* Henry Allard.

Representation of the Parties was as follows: Conservatives (Moderata samlingspartiet), 55; Centre Party (Centerpartiet), 86; Liberals (Folkpartiet), 39; Social Democrats (Arbetarepartiet-Social-demokraterna), 152; Communists (Vänsterpartiet kommunisterna), 17; Christian Democrat Union, nil; Communist Marxist-Leninist Association, nil.

### LOCAL GOVERNMENT

For purposes of general administration, the country is divided into 24 counties (*län*). At the head of each county administration is a Governor (*landshövding*) as official representative of the Crown and a board of ten members, five of whom are appointed by the king and five elected by the County Council.

Each county (except the County of Gotland) has its County Council (*landsting*), the members of which are elected for three years by universal suffrage. These councils meet annually to deal with local government matters and with public health and education. The communes of Göteborg, Malmö and Gotland have in this respect their separate administration.

**County Governors**

Stockholm: N. G. Helén.
Uppsala: R. H. L. Edenman.
Södermanland: M. H. Lemne.
Östergötland: P. A Eckerberg.

**Jönköping:** S. O. af Geijerstam.
**Kronoberg:** A. M. Kristensson.
**Kalmar:** E. A. Westerlind.
**Gotland:** G. E. Gustafsson.
**Blekinge:** E. C. Odhnoff.
**Kristianstad:** B. A. W. Petrí.
**Malmöhus:** N. J. Hörjel.
**Halland:** Y. Holmberg.
**Göteborgs och Bohus:** E. J. Huss.
**Älvsborg:** G. von Sydow.
**Skaraborg:** K. A. F. Frithiofson.
**Värmland:** B. O. Norling
**rebro:** H. S. Aronsson.
**Västmanland:** G. F. E. Cederwall.
**Kopparberg:** B. K. Olsson.
**Gävleborg:** H. Hagnell.
**Västernorrland:** B. A. F. Löfberg.
**Jämtland:** H. A. I. Pettersson.
**Västerbotten:** B. Lyberg.
**Norrbotten:** J. R. Lassinantti.

## LEGAL SYSTEM

The administration of justice is presided over by the Chancellor of Justice *Justitiekansler*), who is appointed by the Government. (The present Chancellor is S. I. Gullnäs, app. 1973.) There are two supreme courts of judicature for the whole kingdom.

**The Supreme Court** (Högsta domstolen) G. O. E. Petrén (Chmn.).

**The Supreme Administrative Court** (Regeringsrätten) C. V. Abjörnsson (Chmn.).

## AREA AND POPULATION

The area and population (31 December 1976) are shown below:

| *County* | *Population* | *Land area (sq. km.)* |
|---|---|---|
| Stockholm län | 1,500,868 | 6,487·9 |
| Uppsala län | 233,115 | 6,988·9 |
| Södermanlands län | 251,996 | 6,060·1 |
| Östergötlands län | 389,431 | 10,565·7 |
| Jönköpings län | 302,142 | 9,943·9 |
| Kronobergs län | 170,319 | 8,452,9 |
| Kalmar län | 240,969 | 11,171·6 |
| Gotlands län | 54,621 | 3,140·1 |
| Blekinge län | 154,962 | 2,918·9 |
| Kristianstads län | 273,941 | 6,053·9 |
| Malmöhus län | 739,682 | 4,928·9 |
| Hallands län | 222,985 | 5,454·4 |
| Göteborg and Bohus län | 714,374 | 5,112·1 |
| Älvsborgs län | 420,192 | 11,394·4 |
| Skaraborgs län | 264,286 | 7,937·7 |
| Värmlands län | 284,529 | 17,609·2 |
| Örebro län | 273,819 | 8,514·9 |
| Västmanlands län | 260,164 | 6,302·1 |
| Kopparbergs län | 283,350 | 28,344·4 |
| Gävleborgs län | 294,627 | 18,191·3 |
| Västernorrlands län | 268,237 | 21,786·7 |
| Jämtlands län | 133,752 | 49,916·6 |
| Västerbottens län | 237,705 | 55,432·2 |
| Norrbottens län | 266,113 | 98,906·3 |
| Total | 8,236,179 | 411,614·8 |

The four largest lakes in Sweden are:

| *Lake* | *Area (sq. km.)* |
|---|---|
| **Vänern** | **5,585** |
| **Vättern** | **1,912** |
| **Mälaren** | **1,140** |
| **Hjälmaren** | **484** |

The total area of Sweden (land and water) is **449,964 sq. km.**

The following table shows the vital statistics for two recent years:

| | 1976 | 1974 | 1975 |
|---|---|---|---|
| Marriages | 44,790 | 44,864 | 44,103 |
| Live Births | 98,228 | 109,874 | 103,632 |
| Deaths | 90,677 | 86,316 | 88,208 |

The annual average percentage growth rate of the population for the period 1960–74 was 0·7 and for the period 1965–74 was 0·6.

## CURRENCY

**The unit of currency is the Swedish krona of 100 öre. The national bank has issued notes of 5, 10, 50, 100, 1,000 and 10,000 kronor.**

## FINANCE

**In 1976–77, voted estimates of revenue and expenditure—were 95,512 million kronor and 103,070 million kronor. Net capital investments were 4,429 million kronor.**

Details of the 1977–78 Current Budget (in thousand kronor) according to voted estimates:

*Revenue*

| | |
|---|---|
| A. Current revenue | |
| I. Taxes | 101,676,152 |
| 1. Income and property tax | 45,365,000 |
| 2. Automobile duty | 4,830,000 |
| 3. Employer charge | 7,292,000 |
| 4. Customs and other duties | |
| a. Customs duty | 990,000 |
| b. Duties on spirits, wines and malt liquors | 5,527,000 |
| c. Added value tax | 28,998,500 |
| d. Tobacco duty | 2,,630,450 |
| e. Electricity duty | 4,116,000 |
| f. Others | 2,127,202 |
| II. Civil service fees, etc. | 2,298,151 |
| III. Other revenues | 1,093,560 |
| Total | 105,013,863 |
| B. Receipts from State capital funds | 6,544,041 |
| Grand Total | 111,557,904 |

**The G.N.P. at market prices for 1974 was U.S.$ million 59,100 and the G.N.P. per capita at market prices was U.S. $7,240. The annual average percentage growth rate of the G.N.P. per capita for the period 1960–74 was 3·2 and for the period 1965–74 was 2·8.** [*See the note at the beginning of this section concerning G.N.P.*]

*Expenditure*

| | |
|---|---|
| Current expenditure | |
| Royal Household and Establishment | 15,677 |
| Ministry of Justice | 4,459,196 |
| Ministry for Foreign Affairs | 3,958,444 |
| Ministry of Defence | 11,057,571 |
| Ministry of Health and Social Affairs | 34,702,233 |
| Ministry of Communications | 5,372,559 |
| Ministry of Economics | 331,649 |
| Ministry of Budget | 8,272,124 |
| Ministry of Education and Cultural Affairs | 15,267,762 |
| Ministry of Agriculture | 5,258,815 |
| Ministry of Commerce | 370,944 |
| Ministry of Labour Market | 6,064,674 |
| Ministry of Housing | 5,252,819 |
| Ministry of Industry | 1,369,090 |
| Ministry of Local Government | 1,671,370 |
| Unforeseen expenditure | 4,000,000 |
| Cost of the Riksdag, etc. | 178,404 |
| Total | 107,962,331 |
| Expenditure for State Capital Funds | 7,890,299 |
| Grand Total | 115,852,630 |

# SWEDEN

## PRINCIPAL BANKS

**Bohusbanken.** Established 1919. (President, Åke Gustavsson; Chairman, Sten Kjellman.)

**Götabanken.** Established 1848. (Chairman, Gösta Olson.) Balance Sheet at December 1976 showed assets Kr. 11,513,200,000; deposits and current accounts Kr. 7,572,100,000. *Head Office:* Östra Hamngatan 16, Göteborg. 191 Branches.

**Post-och Kreditbanken, PKbanken.** Established 1974. (Chairman, Arne Geijer.) Balance Sheet at 30 June 1977 showed assets Kr.47,869 million; deposits Kr.37,845 million. *Head Office:* Hamngatan 12, Box 7042, S-103 81 Stockholm. 140 Branches.

**Skandinaviska Enskilda Banken.** Established 1972 out of Skandinaviska Banken and Stockholms Enskilda Bank. (Chairman, Dr. L. E. Thunholm.) Balance Sheet at 31 December 1976 showed assets Skr.46,959 million; deposits Skr.24,200 million. *Head Office:* Kungsträdgardsgatan 8, Stockholm. *Central Offices:* Stockholm, Göteborg and Malmö. 375 Offices and Branches. *Representative Offices:* Athens (for Middle East), Madrid, Paris, Tokyo, São, Paulo. *Foreign Subsidiaries:* Scandinavian Securities Corporation, New York; Skandinaviska. Enskilda Banken (Luxembourg) S.A. Luxembourg. *Foreign Affiliates:* Banque Scandinave en Suisse, Geneva; Deutsche-Skandinavische Bank. A. G. Frankfurt am Main; Neue Bank A. G. Zurich; Scandiavian Bank Ltd., London; Ship Mortgage International Amsterdam.

**Skaraborgsbanken.** Established 1865. (President, Gösta Karlsson; Chairman, G. Ivar Virgin.) Assets: SKr. 2,165,698,642; deposits and current accounts: SKr.1,643,396,392. *Head Office:* Rädhusgatan 5, S-541 00 Skövde. 40 Branches.

**Sundsvallsbanken.** Established 1864. (President, Erik Ehn; Chairman, Gunnar Hellerot.) Assets: SKr.4,200,000; deposits and current accounts: SKr.2,870,000. *Head Office:* Kyrkogatan 15, Fack, 851 01 Sundsvall 1. 58 Branches.

**Svenska Handelsbanken.** Established 1871. (Chairman, Tore Browaldh.) Balance Sheet at 31 December 1976 showed assets Kr.41·8 billions; deposits and current accounts Kr.21·3 billions. *Head Office:* Arsenalgatan 11, S-102, Stockholm 24. 492 Branches.

**Sveriges Riksbank.** Established 1668. (Governor, Carl-Henrik Nordlander); Sole Bank of Issue for Sweden; capital paid up Kr.50,000,000 and Reserve Fund Kr.20,000,000 are owned by the State: Balance Sheet at 30 June 1977 showed assets Kr.32,836,506,431; deposits and current accounts, Kr.5,735,204,793; banknotes in circulation Kr.21,578,147,991 gold reserves Kr.1,128,137,102. *Head Office:* Stockholm. No. of Offices: 23.

**Wermlandsbanken.** Established 1832. (President, Sven Lönnqvist; Chairman, Erik Wästlund.) Balance Sheet at 31 December 1976 showed assets Skr.3,307·9 millions; deposits and current accounts SKr. 2,946·8 millions. *Head Office:* Tingvallagatan 13, Karlstad. 63 Branches.

## PRODUCTION, INDUSTRY AND COMMERCE

**Agriculture.** (Figures refer to holdings of more than 2 hectares of arable land.) Only about seven per cent of the land is cultivated. Nevertheless, Sweden is normally self-supporting in respect to agricultural products, but fertilizers and feed concentrates are imported to a certain extent. As much as 42 per cent of the farms have ten hectares or less of arable land.

The economically active population in agriculture is decreasing and was, in 1976, 6 per cent of the total active population.

The main crops in 1976 are given below:

| *Chief crops* | *Area (thousand hectares)* | *Yield (thousand, metric tons)* |
|---|---|---|
| Wheat | 398 | 1,765 |
| Winter Rye | 173 | 424 |
| Barley | 595 | 1,826 |
| Oats | 483 | 1,251 |
| Mixed Grain | 68 | 165 |
| Potatoes | 45 | 1,058 |
| Sugar-beet | 53 | 2,077 |
| Ley | 687 | 3,636 |
| Oleiferous plants | 148 | 881 |

In 1973 there were about 183,000 farm tractors and in 1976 the livestock numbered: cattle, 1,863,000; sheep, 389,000; pigs, 2,468,000.

**Forestry.** The forests of Sweden form one of the country's greatest natural assets. In 1973 forests covered an area of 23,473,000 hectares, i.e. roughly 57 per cent of the country's land area. Municipal and State ownership accounts for one-fourth of the forests, companies own another fourth, and farmers, the remaining half. In the felling seasons 1974–75 and 1975–76 respectively, 56·0 and 54·3 mill. cu. metres (solid volume) of wood were cut in Sweden. The sawmill, wood pulp and paper industries are all of great importance. The number of sawmills in 1973 was about 3,600, 530 of which were commercial sawmills, with 90 per cent of the total production of sawn hard- and soft-wood, that was about 10·7 mill. cu. metres in 1975. The wood pulp factories numbered 96 in 1973 and their total output amounted to 8·3 mill. tons (including dissolving pulp) (dry weight) in 1975 and 8·3 mill. tons (dry weight) in 1976. Sweden had in 1974 the world's second largest export of sawn soft wood and, as regards wood pulp, Sweden was the second greatest exporting country of the world.

**Mining.** Production of minerals and metals in tons for the years 1972, 1973, 1974, 1975 and 1976

| *Ores* | | 1972 | 1973 | 1974 | 1975 (Prel) | 1976 |
|---|---|---|---|---|---|---|
| Iron ore | | 33,979,184 | 34,727,244 | 36,152,545 | 30,866,969 | 29,861,766 |
| Silver and lead | | 108,038 | 106,741 | 104,404 | 100,154 | 114,237 |
| Copper | | 120,130 | 179,011 | 167,530 | 158,950 | 187,833 |
| Manganese | | — | — | — | — | — |
| Zinc | | 203,466 | 211,474 | 201,969 | 197,153 | 225,793 |
| Pyrites | | 486,480 | 450,047 | 425,016 | 413,595 | 404,433 |
| *Metals* | | | | | | |
| Pig iron | | 2,348,201 | 2,562,811 | 2,966,879 | 3,303,031 | 2,991,497 |
| Aluminium | | 76,620 | 81,659 | 82,480 | 77,393 | 82,517 |
| Lead | | 47,594 | 46,681 | 45,247 | 38,673 | 49,822 |
| Copper, electrolyte | | 51,596 | 59,491 | 59,908 | 56,221 | 62,867 |
| Silver | Kgs | 168,325 | 196,037 | 186,810 | 218,792 | 197,897 |
| Gold | Kgs | 3,916 | 3,799 | 3,701 | 13,419 | 4,598 |

The mining and metal industry accounts for a major part of the production. To a great extent, however, iron ore is exported. The rest is manufactured at home, mostly high-grade iron and steel, such as knives, razor blades, saws, ball-bearings, cream separators and motor cars.

**Industry.** In 1970, 40 per cent of the economically active population were engaged in construction, mining and quarrying, manufacturing, electricity, gas, water and sanitary services.

Owing to the lack of fossil fuel, import of oil, etc., is and will always be necessary. An important part of the energy production is accounted for by the hydroelectric plants.

There were 12,383 industrial establishments in Sweden in 1975. The most important industries are the manufacturing of machinery, vehicles, ships, high quality steel, sawn timber, pulp and paper products. Among specific mechanical products may be mentioned cars and lorries, aircraft, water turbines and steam turbines, refrigerators and freezing equipment, excavating machinery, machine tools, compressors, office machinery, ball bearings, electrical generators and motors and other high voltage equipment, telephone and radio equipment, electric and diesel-electric locomotives, tankers, ore-tankers and refrigerator vessels, etc.

The following table shows output of principal commodities for the years 1974–76 (in thousand tons):

| *Commodity* | 1974 | 1975 | 1976 |
|---|---|---|---|
| Milk | 2,961 | 3,023 | 3,107 |
| Butter | 43 | 42 | 40 |
| Meat | 437 | 433 | 450 |
| Pig iron and sponge iron | 3,176 | 3,484 | 3,139 |
| Steel ingots and castings | 5,989 | 5,611 | 5,146 |
| Finished steel | 4,313 | 3,934 | 3,601 |
| Pulp, sulphite and sulphate: of which | 9,745 | 8,419 | 8,378 |
| Mechanical pulp | 1,919 | 1,636 | 1,532 |
| Semi-chemical pulp | 407 | 292 | 331 |
| Paper and cardboard | 5,511 | 4,441 | 4,946 |
| Textile yarn | 25 | 22 | 20 |
| Woven fabrics | 46 | 39 | 42 |

The Swedish Gross Domestic Product rose to about Kr.284 billion in 1976. The increase in volume amounted to 1·5 per cent. In 1975 the volume increased by 0·5 per cent. The volume of exports increased by 3·9 per cent while the volume of import increased by 6·2 per cent in 1976.

| *Branch of Industry* | *Average No. of workers* 1975 | *Value of output (thousand kronor)* 1975 |
|---|---|---|
| Metal Ore mining | 10,406 | 2,996,203 |
| Other mining | 1,439 | 313,703 |
| Manufacture of food beverages and tobacco | 54,085 | 25,239,467 |
| Textile, wearing apparel and leather industries | 46,392 | 6,959,252 |
| Manufacture of wood and wood products inc. furniture | 62,968 | 14,278,262 |
| Manufacture of paper and paper products | 73,632 | 26,148,306 |
| Manufacture of chemicals and chemical, petroleum, coal, rubber and plastic products | 44,773 | 19,682,117 |
| Manufacture of non-metallic mineral products except products of coal and petroleum | 24,933 | 5,107,694 |
| Basic metal industries | 52,907 | 16,489,995 |
| Manufacture of fabricated metal products, machinery and equipment | 304,570 | 74,950,717 |
| Other manufacturing industries | 4,909 | 807,171 |

The increase in disposable income of households was about 13·2 per cent which corresponds to an increase in real terms of 2·9 per cent.

The total wages rose by 13·6 per cent in 1976. It is estimated that, of this increase, 10·4 per cent was the result of agreements under collective bargaining, while 2·7 per cent was due to wage drift.

Consumer prices rose by 9·8 per cent.

The following table shows the imports and exports by principal countries (in million kronor) for the year 1976:

| *Country* | *Imports* | *Exports* |
|---|---|---|
| Argentine | 87 | 141 |
| Australia | 332 | 958 |
| Belgium and Luxembourg | 2,683 | 2,397 |
| Brazil | 805 | 1,032 |
| Denmark | 5,861 | 7,827 |
| Finland | 4,768 | 5,163 |
| France | 3,341 | 4,394 |
| Germany (West) | 15,676 | 7,918 |
| Italy | 2,244 | 2,093 |
| Netherlands | 3,715 | 3,366 |
| Norway | 5,107 | 9,014 |
| Poland | 1,129 | 1,572 |
| Switzerland | 1,899 | 1,404 |
| U.S.S.R. | 2,069 | 1,225 |
| Union of South Africa | 171 | 421 |
| United Kingdom | 8,760 | 9,034 |
| United States of America | 5,597 | 3,682 |
| Venezuela | 597 | 411 |
| Canada | 503 | 1,082 |
| Chile | 92 | 46 |
| Hong Kong | 680 | 113 |
| Japan | 2,672 | 723 |
| Portugal | 681 | 574 |
| Spain | 697 | 1,161 |

**Commerce**

The following table shows imports and exports by products (in million kronor) for the year 1976:

| *Product* | *Imports* | *Exports* |
|---|---|---|
| Food and live animals chiefly food | 6,057 | 1,784 |
| Meat and meat preparations | 423 | 231 |
| Dairy products and birds' eggs | 127 | 69 |
| Cereals and cereal preparations | 295 | 837 |
| Vegetables and fruit | 1,752 | 141 |
| Coffee, tea, cocoa, spices, and manufactures thereof | 1,719 | 159 |
| Feeding stuff for animals (not including unmilled cereals) | 511 | 20 |
| Beverages and tobacco | 643 | 76 |
| Crude materials, inedible, except fuels | 3,559 | 12,450 |
| Hides, skins and furskins, raw | 243 | 238 |
| Crude rubber (including synthetic and reclaimed) | 229 | 48 |
| Cork and wood | 771 | 3,905 |
| Pulp and waste paper | 56 | 5,478 |
| Textile fibres (other than wool tops) and their wastes (not manufactured into yarn or fabric) | 169 | 113 |
| Crude fertilizers and crude minerals (excluding coal, petroleum and precious stones) | 546 | 130 |
| Metalliferous ores and metal scrap | 920 | 2,336 |
| Mineral fuels, lubricants and related materials | 14,707 | 1,351 |
| Coal, coke and briquettes | 925 | 27 |

| *Product* | *Imports* | *Exports* |
|---|---|---|
| Petroleum, petroleum products and related materials | 13,449 | 994 |
| Animal and vegetable oils, fats and waxes | 265 | 200 |
| Chemicals and related products, n.e.s. | 6,559 | 3,768 |
| Manufactured goods classified chiefly by material | 15,616 | 19,989 |
| Rubber manufactures, n.e.s. | 933 | 541 |
| Paper, paperboard, and articles of paper pulp, of paper or of paperboard | 845 | 6,892 |
| Textile yarn, fabrics, made-up articles, n.e.s., and related products | 3,154 | 1,135 |
| Non-metallic mineral manufactures, n.e.s. | 1,251 | 667 |
| Iron and steel | 4,357 | 5,442 |
| Non-ferrous metals | 2,093 | 1,290 |
| Manufactures of metal, n.e.s. | 2,222 | 2,957 |
| Machinery and transport equipment | 25,877 | 35,217 |
| Power generating machinery and equipment | 1,922 | 2,185 |
| Machinery specialized for particular industries | 2,972 | 4,086 |
| Metalworking machinery | 955 | 958 |
| General industrial machinery and equipment, n.e.s. and machine parts, n.e.s. | 4,376 | 5,653 |
| Office machines and automatic data processing equipment | 1,534 | 1,347 |
| Telecommunications and sound recording and reproducing apparatus and equipment | 1,910 | 3,347 |
| Electrical machinery, apparatus and appliances, n.e.s., and electrical parts thereof (including non-electrical counterparts, n.e.s., of electrical household type equipment) | 4,026 | 3,175 |
| Road vehicles (including air cushion vehicles) | 6,544 | 8,402 |
| Other transport equipment | 1,637 | 6,063 |
| Miscellaneous manufactured articles | 9,814 | 5,133 |
| Commodities and transactions not classified elsewhere in the SITC | 128 | 226 |

## COMMUNICATIONS

**Railways.** In 1976 Sweden had a total of 12,061 kilometres of track, of which 11,361 is State-owned. The railways in 1976 carried 79 million passengers and 63 million tons of freight. Total receipts of the state owned railways amounted to 4,093 million kronor in the budget year 1975–76.

**Shipping.** The Swedish Mercantile Marine at the end of 1976 comprised 562 vessels with a total gross tonnage of 7,008,000 (only vessels of over 100 tons are included). The chief ports are Stockholm and Göteborg. A total of 50,588 cargo vessels in foreign traffic entered and cleared all ports in 1976 with a net tonnage of 74,636,000. A total of 233,227 passenger ships and ferries in foreign traffic entered and cleared in 1976 with a net tonnage of 214,003.

**Johnson Line** (President Axel A. Johnson); motor vessels 28; total tonnage about 450,000 T.D.W.; *regular services operated: Brazil/River Plate*—Sweden, Baltic ports, Brazil/ River Plate; *North Pacific*—Scandinavia, Continent, U.K., North Pacific; *Caribbean/South Pacific*—Scandinavia, Baltic ports, Continent, Venezuela, Colombia, South Pacific; *Far East*—Far East, India, Pakistan, Middle East and vice versa. Johnson Line has a majority interest in Svea shipping group. (See Stockholm Rederi AB Svea below.) *Head Office:* Stureplan 3, Fack, S-103 80 Stockholm, Sweden. Telephone 08-220500, Telex 17100 johnson S.

**Swedish American Line.** (Managing Director, Ingemar Blennow); two passenger vessels of 49,404 gross reg. tons, two roll-on/roll-off cargo vessels, 22,500 T.D.W., one bulk carrier 26,885 T.D.W., one cargo vessel of 10,590 T.D.W.; *services operated:* Northern Europe to U.S.A., North Atlantic ports. *Head Office:* (Packhusplatsen 6) P.O. Box 2157, S-403 13 Göteborg 2, Sweden.

**Swedish East Asia Co. Ltd.** (Managing Director, Kristian von Sydow); vessels 13; total tonnage 534,655 T.D.W.; *services operated:* Europe–Far East, Indonesia, India, Pakistan, Bangladesh, Sri Lanka, Middle East, U.S.A., Far East, Australia, South East Asia. *Head Office:* Packhusplatsen 6, P.O. Box 2524, S-40317, Göteborg 2, Sweden.

**Rederiaktiebolaget Svenska Lloyd (Swedish Lloyd).** (Managing Director, Folke Kristensen); 13 vessels comprising: 2 combined passenger/cargo roll-on/roll-off vessels capacity 750 passengers, 200 motorcars, 100 20-foot container units each; 2 cargo vessels roll-on/roll-off capacity 200 20-foot container units each; 2 cargo ships, DW 5,800 tons each; 3 Wine-tankers—capacity 10,000–15,000 hectolitres each—all in partnership with the Swedish Orient Line; 1 OBC-carrier (ore, bulk, container)—DW abt. 24,000 tons—in partnership with Aug. Leffler & Son, Gothenburg; 3 Hovercrafts—in partnership with the Swedish American Line—operated by Hoverlloyd, London; *services operated:* Passenger: Gothenburg–London and v.v. Southampton–Bilbao and v.v. Ramsgate–Calais and v.v. (Hoverlloyd). Cargo: Gothenburg/ Halmstead–London and v.v. Gothenburg Halmstead–Grangemouth and v.v. Gothenburg–Hamburg and v.v. Sweden–Portugal, France, Spain, Morocco, various Mediterranean ports and v.v. Southampton–Bilbao and v.v. *Head Office:* Pack-huspl. 6, P.O. Box 2125, S-40313, Göteborg 2, Sweden. *U.K. Office* (Cargo): Swedish Lloyd Terminal, Tilbury Docks, Essex. *Office* (Passenger): 49 Charles Street, London W1X 8AE.

**Transatlantic S.S. Co. Ltd.** (Manager, Torkel Carlsson); vessels: 15 wholly owned and part ownership in 29 with subsidiary companies; total tonnage 569,365 T.D.W.; *services operated:* Sweden to North America, (A.C.L.), Sweden to Canary Islands, South Africa, East Africa, Australia, (Scan Austral), Sweden and Continent to West Africa, (SWAL and Scan-Lloyd), France, West African (Scadoa), and New Zealand (ScaNZeal). Pacific West Coast to Australia, (PAD), Scandinavia–Continent U.K. (Tor Line). *Head Office:* Packhusplatsen 3, Fack, S-403 10 Göteborg 2, Sweden.

**A.B. Transmarin** (Managing Director, Mats Olsson; Chairman, Hans Hök); vessels three, total tonnage 14,135 T.D.W.; *services operated:* regular line, Western Europe and London to Levant and LPG tanker trading. *Head Office:* Kungsgatan 2, S-252 21 Helsingborg, Sweden. Subsidiary company in Hamburg: six vessels, 30,075 T.D.W.

**Stockholms Rederi, AB Svea.** (Managing Director Curt Högberg; vessels 23 (with subsidiary companies); total tonnage 112,492 T.D.W. (tankers and cargo vessels); 59,053 gross tons (passenger gross tons (passenger vessels); *services operated:* Sweden–Finland, Denmark, Western Germany (passengers and lorries); Sweden–United Kingdom, Netherlands, Belgium (cargo); France–West African ports (cargo), tanker service. *Head Office:* P.O. Box 2065, S-103 12 Stockholm 2, Sweden.

**Gothon Lines.** (Manager, Stig Gorthon); vessels (11; total tonnage 173,380 T.D.W.; *services operated:* England, Sweden, Finland, Continent, U.S. East Coast; Canada. *Head Office:* Stortorget 2, S-252 23, Helsingborg, Sweden.

**Salén Shipping Cies.** (Manager, Sture Ödner); vessels 70 (with subsidiary companies); total tonnage 5,600,000 T.D.W. (including ships on order); *services operated:* Tanker, dry cargo, refrigerated and ferries. *Head Office:* P.O. Box 14018, S-104 40, Stockholm 14, Sweden.

**Granges Shipping (The Granges Co.).** President Ingemar Wahlström); vessels 19; total tonnage 1,265,000 T.D.W.; *services operated:* Iron ore transport Scandinavia–U.K./Continent and Lower Buchanan–Continent. Worldwide bulk, chemical and oil tramping. *Head Office:* Birger Jarlsgatan 52, P.O. Box 16330, S-10326, Stockholm, 16, Sweden.

**Wallenius Lines.** (Manager, John G. Kleberg); vessels 13; time chartered for long period 6; total tonnage 581,915 T.D.W.; *services operated:* Europe–N. America, N. America–Far East–Japan, Japan–Europe; cruises in the Caribbean; participating in Atlantic Container Line and Care Line admitted to the Japan–Europe Freight Conference. *Head Office:* P.O. Box 17086, S-10462, Stockholm, Sweden.

**Civil Aviation**

**SAS—Scandinavian Airlines System.** (President, Knut Hagrup); a consortium partnered by Danish, Norwegian and Swedish Airlines (DDL, DNL and ABA) in proportion 2:2:3 for the operation of joint traffic in and from Scandinavia to rest of Europe, North, Central and South America, Africa, Near and Far East. S.A.S. was the first carrier with service via the North Pole to Los Angeles and Tokyo. Passengers carried in fiscal year 1973–74; 6,325,000. *Head Office:* S-161 87 Stockholm-Bromma 10, Sweden. *Regional Offices:* At Kastrup Airport, Copenhagen, Denmark, Fornebu Airport, Oslo, Norway and Bromma Airport, Stockholm, Sweden.

**Telegraphs and Telephones.** Internal and external telegraphs and telephone services are State-owned. At the end of 1976 there were 5,673,427 telephones in use, corresponding to 689 telephones per 1,000 inhabitants.

**Broadcasting.** At the beginning of 1977 there were 100 State-owned sound broadcasting stations and 375 television stations. At the end of the first quarter of 1977 there were 3,018,280 combined radio and television fee payers; the radio fee payers exclusively numbered 214,715.

**NEWSPAPERS**

**Aftonbladet.** F. 1830. Evening. Social-Democratic. Circulation: 464,040 weekdays; 493,733 Sunday, Stockholm.

**Arbetet.** F. 1887. Morning. Social-Democratic. Circulation: 106,000 weekdays; 118,000 Sunday. Malmö.

**Dagen.** F. 1945. Morning. Religious—Non-Political. Circulation: 27,381 weekdays; except Monday. Stockholm.

**Dagens Nyheter.** F. 1864. Morning. Liberal. Circulation 435,000 weekdays; 529,000 Sunday. Stockholm.

**Expressen.** F. 1944. Evening. Liberal. Circulation 570,918 weekdays; 646,171 Sunday. Stockholm.

**Göteborgs Handels-och Sjöfarts-Tidning.** F. 1832. Liberal. Göteborg. Editor-in-Chief: Anders Bothén.

**Göteborgs-Posten.** F. 1858. Morning. Liberal. Circulation: 310,783 weekdays; 293,312 Sunday. Göteborg.

**Goteborgs-Tidningen.** F. 1902. Evening. Liberal. Circulation: 308,483 weekdays; 296,253 Sunday. Göteborg.

**Kvallsposten.** F. 1948. Evening. Independent Liberal. Circulation: 114,498 weekdays; 141,077 Sunday. Malmö.

**Skänska Dagbladet.** F. 1888. Morning. Centre Party. Circulation 31,644. Malmö.

**Svenska Dagbladet.** F. 1884. Morning. Conservative. Circulation: 175,957 weekdays; 180,887 Sunday. Stockholm.

**Sydsvenska Dagbladet Snällposten.** F. 1848. Morning. Independent Liberal. Circulation 115,000 weekdays; 148,000 Sunday. Malmö.

**ATOMIC ENERGY**

Sweden has been engaged in pure research work on atoms for many years. Fundamental research is sponsored by the Government. There are very well-equipped laboratories in nuclear physics, nuclear chemistry and other branches of science connected with the development of nuclear energy.

An organization in the form of a stock holding company, known as AB Atomenergi, was set up in 1947 to deal with applied research and development of atomic energy in Sweden. Industrial undertakings, public utilities and power production companies held 43 per cent of the stock and the balance of 57 per cent was held by the government. Costs were met by the government. In 1969 the government bought out the other shareholders.

Uranium, present in shale ore deposits, is Sweden's greatest energy reserve. A mill and extraction plant with a capacity of 120 tons of uranium per year was opened at Ranstad in 1965. Since 1969 the Ranstad mill is used solely for experimental work in a study of further development of the extraction process. The study has been enlarged to comprise the technical and economic possibilities for large-scale milling and for a more complex operation comprising the extraction of not only uranium but also aluminium, vanadium, molybdenum, fertilizer components such as nitrogen, phosphor and potassium as well as utilizing the energy content of the organic matters in the shale.

In 1954 the first nuclear research reactor (600 kW) was completed. It was housed underground in Stockholm. It was operated by AB Atomenergi but also used by the Royal Institute of Technology in Stockholm. In June 1970, the reactor was shut off and the operation at R1 was ended. Instead of R1, the R2 reactor at Studsvik is used.

The research station Studsvik on the Baltic coast has three reactors. KRITZ is a zero-energy reactor for reactor physical experiments and R2, a modified swimming pool type reactor is being used mainly for materials testing but also for neutron physics research and isotope production. The reactor has a power of 50,000 MW. R2 is supplied with a complementary reactor R2–0, delivered by the Swedish firm ASEA. This reactor is used for neutron physical experiments and neutron radiographic examinations. R2-0 can be operated at power levels up to 1,000 kW.

The research facilities also include a 5·5 MeV Van de Graaff generator, physical, thermal, hot metallurgy and chemistry laboratories, a radiation protection laboratory with a whole-body counter, a plant for waste disposal, etc. AB Atomenergi now employs a staff of about 1,000 persons. About 900 persons are working at Studsvik.

The company's efforts are being directed mainly towards supporting the Swedish nuclear power programme. Lately the company has considerably widened its R & D efforts on energy technique outside the nuclear field. AB Atomnergi is responsible for advising the authorities on matters concerning the nuclear energy and also co-operates with Swedish power utilities and with the reactor industry.

From the 1 January 1969 a company, ASEA-ATOM, formed by the Swedish Government and ASEA on a fifty/fifty basis operates in the world market on the production and sale of nuclear reactors, reactor components and nuclear fuel. The Company which has its head office in Västerås, in principle consists of ASEA's former nuclear energy department, AB Atomenergi's fuel element department and part of the latter company's reactor engineering department. ASEA-ATOM has a staff of about 1,300 people.

In 1973 Svensk Kärnbränsleförsörjning AB (the Swedish Nuclear Fuel Supply Company) was formed by the three Swedish nuclear power utilities, the State Power Board, Sydkraft AB and the Oskarshamn Power Group with the general purpose of planning and co-ordination of long-term policy of nuclear fuel supply for the total Swedish power system and executing contracts for nuclear materials and services.

Other Swedish firms act as subcontractors for certain components. For the purpose five large industries have formed AB Monitor with its head office in Göteborg, co-operating with Westinghouse Electric Corp. U.S.A. In 1973 Westinghouse acquired a majority interest in Monitor and the name of the company was changed to 'Westinghouse/Monitor AB'.

Sandvik AB specializes in fuel element cladding. Uddcomb Sweden AB with new workshops at Karlskrona in South Sweden was formed in 1969 by the Swedish Government (having 50 per cent of the shares), Uddeholm AB (25 per cent) and Combustion Engineering Inc., U.S.A. (25 per cent). In 1974 the Government acquired the shares owned by Uddeholm. The company specializes in heavy mechanical manufacture such as reactor pressure vessels, etc.

In July 1963, Sweden's first nuclear power plant, the Ågesta nuclear power station, was started by AB Atomenergi. The reactor was shut down once and for all in June 1974. It had then fulfilled its purpose of giving operational experience of a nuclear power station, being a training centre for reactor operators and being used for experiments with full scale nuclear reactor fuel. The ASEA company was the main contractor for Ågesta.

Private and municipal power undertakings form a group (OKG) for a joint project—the Oskarshamn Nuclear Power Station with a 440 MW boiling water reactor (BWR) using enriched uranium. The station was connected to the grid in 1971. A second 580 MW reactor unit also with ASEA-ATOM as main contractor was connected to the grid in 1975.

A third unit with a 1060 BWR was ordered in May 1976 from ASEA-ATOM. It is scheduled for commercial operation in 1982/83.

The State Power Board is building a 3,000 MW nuclear power station at Ringhals, on the west coast south of Göteborg. The first unit of 760 MW and a second unit of 820 MW were commissioned and started electricity production in the autumn 1974. A third and fourth unit of 900 MW each are planned for commissioning in 1977 and 1979 respectively. The first unit was ordered from ASEA-ATOM, the other three from Westinghouse Monitor AB.

The first unit was connected to the grid in May 1975, the other started commercial operation in 1977.

Sydkraft AB has built a nuclear power station at Barsebäck (near Malmö) with two reactor units each of 580 MW ordered from ASEA-ATOM. The first unit was connected to the grid in 1975, the second unit in 1977.

The State Power Board is erecting three reactor units at Forsmark on the Baltic 120 kilometers north of Stockholm. All three units are BWRs and ordered from ASEA-ATOM. The first and second units are each of 900 MW and are scheduled for commercial operation in 1978 and 1980 respectively. The third unit is of 1,050 MW and scheduled for commercial operation in 1982.

Nuclear power is expected to amount to about 7,400 MW in Sweden in 1980.

### EDUCATION AND RELIGION

Sweden has compulsory comprehensive schools within which all children from seven to sixteen years old receive general education. A new group of integrated upper secondary schools was introduced in 1971. They have four streams of three years duration, viz. liberal art, social sciences, economics and natural sciences and a four-year technical stream. There is also a group of upper secondary schools of two years' duration (into which most of the former vocational schools have been integrated). There are also special courses of variable length within the upper secondary school.

The parliament in 1975 decided to reorganize nearly all state supported education on third level. From the autumn semester 1977 the universities, those colleges and professional schools which by tradition are regarded as on university level, teachers colleges, colleges for nurses, colleges for professional musicians advanced art schools and several other types of state supported educations on third level are organized in a new institutional structure. Only the two largest towns, Stockholm and Gothenburg, will have more than one institution for third level education. In all other towns with education of this kind there will be but one institution for all types of third level education. Some important reasons for this re-structuring is to give the students a greater freedom to combine courses which to day do exist within different institutions. Further, the student shall also have better possibilities to participate in single courses without being admitted to a full programme covering several years. On the other hand no formal degrees will be awarded, instead every student shall have the right to get an official record, telling which courses he has passed, and whether the courses have been organized as a study programme (which might be unique for that very student). In addition, no border line will exist between university type and non-university type of education on third level.

# Switzerland

**Capital**—Berne.

**President of the Confederation**—Rudolf Gnagi.

**National Flag:** Red, with a white cross couped.

### CONSTITUTION AND GOVERNMENT

THE constitution of Switzerland has many unique features which distinguish the Swiss system of government from that of any other country. This resulted from the peculiar origin of the Republic and its development throughout the centuries. In August 1291, under the Holy Roman Empire, the three communities of Uri, Schwyz and Unterwalden formed an alliance in the defence of their independence by their combined forces. The alliance, known as the 'Everlasting League', established a complete and unconditional political, economic and military solidarity. The League had to struggle hard for existence, but it was greatly strengthened by the adhesion of Lucerene, Zürich, Berne, Glarus and Zug and in the 16th century Fribourg, Solothurn, Basle, Schaffhausen and Appenzell. In this form it remained for three centuries as the League of Thirteen Members. In 1648 the League was formally separated from the Empire by the Peace of Westphalia, although the Empire had for many years exercised no effective control.

When the French army occupied Switzerland in 1798, this meant the end of the 'Ancien Régime'. The Directory imposed on the country a single constitution moulded on the French, and the Helvetic Republic was formed. It dissolved in 1803 and a new Constitution called 'Act of Mediation' was given to Switzerland by Napoleon. In 1815 the Congress of Vienna recognized the independence of the Confederation, and the neutrality of Switzerland was guaranteed by Austria, Great Britain, Portugal, Prussia and Russia. A new Federal Constitution was adopted in 1848 which was in turn superseded by the constitution of 1874.

The supreme legislative authority is the Federal Assembly, of two chambers: the National Council (*Nationalrat*) and the Council of States (*Ständerat.*). The National Council is elected by the people. The number of Councillors used to vary according to the population, but growth of population has forced the government to set a maximum of 200 on the National Council seats. Each canton has at least one representative. The Council of States consists of 44 members, two sitting for each canton. Three cantons are divided into two half-cantons each—Unterwalden, by a very old tradition, into Obwalden and Nidwalden and Appenzell into Catholic Innerrhoden and Protestant Ausserrhoden and Basle, after the fierce conflict between town and country in the 1830s, into Basle City and Basle Country. Each one of these half-cantons is as independent a state as any canton, but in federal matters they have only half a vote and hence only one seat in the Council of States. This gives rise to a curious situation, since the Canton of Basle City with 235,000 inhabitants has only one vote, while the canton of Uri, with only 34,000 inhabitants has two votes.

The government is in the hands of the Federal Council, which is appointed every four years at the first session of the Federal Assembly after the election in autumn. It consists of seven members and they jointly govern the country. One of them in turn takes the chair for one year and is called the President of the Confederation. In choosing the Federal Council the various regions of the country, languages, religions and parties are taken into consideration. The President and Vice-President of the Confederation are elected by the Federal Assembly, but this is a mere matter of routine, as the former Vice-President invariably becomes President, being next on the list of the Federal Council, which is drawn up by an old-established rule. The President cannot dismiss his colleagues; there can be no Cabinet crises and no votes of censure. Neither the Parliamentary vote nor referendum can cause the Council to resign.

Two peculiar features of Swiss democracy are the 'referendum' and the 'initiative'. A bill approved by the Federal Assembly must, by the constitution, be submitted to the referendum. It comes into force only if no petition is made against it within 90 days. If a petition is submitted bearing the signature of no less than 30,000 citizens, a referendum is held and the final decision as to whether it shall become law rests with the people. Citizens have another means by which they can actively take part in the affairs of the country, namely by the 'initiative'. By this means the people, given the support of 50,000 signatures, can demand that the Federal Constitution shall be amended or totally or partially revised. Should the Federal Constitution be amended, not only is the consent of the majority of people required in every case, but a majority of the cantons must be obtained also. This 'double majority' is settled by first determining the majority of votes, and the proportion of votes for and against the motion in each separate canton. If there is a majority of votes as well as majority of cantons in favour of the motion, it then becomes law.

**Members of the Federal Council**

*Head of the Political Department:* Pierre Graber.
*Head of the Department of the Interior:* Hans Hurlimann.
*Head of the Military Department:* Rudolf Gnägi.
*Head of the Department of Justice and Police:* Kurt Furgler.
*Head of the Department of Finance and Customs:* Georges André Chevallaz.
*Head of the Department of Agriculture and Industry:* Ernst Brugger.
*Head of the Department of Transport, Communications and Energy:* Willi Ritschard.

**Parliament**

COUNCIL OF STATES (Ständerat)

*President for* 1976: Willi Wenk.

*Vice-President for* 1976: Hans Munz.

Party representation is as follows: Christian Democratic People's Party, 17; Radical-Democrats, 15; Social Democrats, five; Central Democrats, five; Liberal-Democrats, one; Independents, one.

**National Council (Nationalrat)**

*President for* 1976: Rudolf Etter.

*Vice-President for* 1976: Hans Wyer.

Party representation is as follows: Radical-Democrats, 47; Social Democrats, 55; Conservative-Catholic, 46; Central Democrats, 21; Independent, 11; Liberal-Democrat, nine; Republicans, four; Communists, four; National Action, two; Independent Socialists, one.

## LOCAL GOVERNMENT

Local government in Switzerland is based on the 3,063 communes, which have a large measure of self-government. Every Swiss has a home commune and within the commune every citizen has a share in the administration and is expected to play his part as an active member of the commune.

The cantons resemble the states of the U.S.A.; each has its own constitution, and its own legislative and executive bodies. They are, according to the constitution, sovereign in so far as their sovereign rights are not limited by the Federal constitution. There are a number of small cantons, as for instance Unterwalden, Appenzell and Glarus and in certain communes in Schwyz, in which a convocation of the citizens takes place annually in the form of a *Landsgemeinde* or folkmoot. At the appointed time the citizens assemble in the public place of the capital of the canton. They can take part in the discussion, decide by a show of hands which laws and financial measures are to be enacted, and elect the members of the government. Most cantons have given up this form of direct democracy but the citizen has still far-reaching rights to a direct participation in the life of the canton beyond the right to elect officials. In a number of cantons every law enacted by the Canton Council must be submitted to the people for approval. In other cantons the referendum may be brought into operation. This means that, if a sufficient number of signatures is collected by the citizens among themselves, they have the right to demand that a law approved by the Legislative Assembly be submitted to the vote of the people.

In the Cantons, the citizens can propose new laws by the right of the 'initiative'.

## LEGAL SYSTEM

The Federal Court, the supreme federal tribunal, has its seat at Lausanne. The Federal judges are elected by the Federal Assembly for a period of 6 years. This court, which has 4 divisions, is the supreme court of Switzerland. Its constitutional division is charged with the highly political duty of protecting the rights of the citizen, but it has no power to examine federal laws for their constitutionality.

*President of the Federal Court for* 1976: Pierre Cavin.

*Vice-President for* 1976: André Grisel.

## AREA AND POPULATION

The total area of the country is 41,288 sq. km.
The total population at mid-1974 was 6,440,000.
The annual average percentage growth rate of the population for the period 1960–74 was 1·2, and for the period 1965–74 was 1·1.

## CURRENCY

The unit of currency is the franc of 100 Rappen or centimes. There are in circulation bronze 1 and 2 centime pieces, nickel coins of 5, 10, 20 centimes and of ½ franc, 1, 2 and 5 francs. Notes are issued in values of 10 to 1,000 francs.

The National Bank has the exclusive right of banknote issue.

## FINANCE

Federal budget figures for 1975 were (in million francs); Revenue, 12,232, Expenditure, 13,541.

The GNP at market prices for 1974 was U.S. $ millions 50,680, and the GNP per capita at market prices was U.S.$7,870. The annual average percentage growth rate of the GNP per capita for the period 1960–74 was 2·9, and for the period 1965–74 was 2·9. [*See the note at the beginning of this section concerning GNP.*]

## PRINCIPAL BANKS

**Aargauische Kantonalbank.** Managers, Dr. Heinrich Bolliger, Hans Moser. Assets as at 31 December 1976, S.fr.2,324,696,427; deposits and current accounts S.fr. 1,999,614,793. *Head Office:* Bahnhofstrasse 58, CH 5001, Aarau.

**Bank Leumi Le-Israel (Switzerland).** Chairman, Mr. E. I. Japhet; Director, Dr F. Oppenheimer. Assets at 31 December 1976 S.fr.254,622,000; deposits and current accounts 210,279,000. *Head Office:* Claridenstrasse 34, 8002 Zurich. Branches: 1.

**Banque Commerciale de Sion, S.A.** Manager, Melchior Kuntschen; Chairman, Henm Dallèves. Assets as at 30 June 1976 S.fr.100,980,630; deposits and current accounts S.fr. 60,820,279. *Head Office:* Bank Commerciale de Sion, S.A., Rue de Lausanne 15, Sion, Switzerland.

**Banque Nationale Suisse.** Balance Sheet at 31 December 1973 showed assets S.fr.32,297,754,749; banknotes in circulation S.fr.18,296,224,170; gold reserves S.fr.11,892,732,280.

**Banque Populaire Suisse.** Chairman, Paul Chaudet. Assets 31 December 1976 S.fr.11,342,633,500; deposits and current accounts S.fr.9,576,677,297. *Head Office:* Bundesgasse 26, CH 3001 Bern. Branches 129.

**Crédit Suisse.** Balance Sheet at 31 March 1972 showed assets S.fr.32,016,747,070.

**Hentsch & Cie** (private bankers) 15 Corraterie, CH 1211, Geneve, 11, Switzerland.

**Pivot & Cie.** Managing Partner, Pierre Pivot; Holder of Procuration, Guy Burnier. *Head Office:* 60–62 rue du Stand, Geneva.

**Sarasin, A., et Cie.** Partners, Alfred Sarasin, Guy Sarasin, David von Wyss, Hans Edward Moppert, Beat Sarasin. *Head Office:* Freiestrasse 107, CH 4002, Basel, Switzerland.

**Swiss Bank Corporation.** Chairman, Prof. Dr. M. Staehelin. Balance Sheet at 31 December 1976 showed assets S.fr.52,757,094,000. *Head Office:* 1 Aeschenvorstadt, Basle.

**Swiss Volksbank.** Balance Sheet at 31 December 1976 showed assets of S.fr.11,342,633,500. *Head Office:* Bundesgasse 26, 3001 Berne.

**Union Bank of Switzerland.** Chairman, Dr. A. Schaefer. Balance Sheet at 31 December 1974 showed assets S.fr. 40,713,525,287. *Head Office:* Bahnhofstrasse 45, Zurich.

## NEWSPAPERS

There are over 460 newspapers. Some of the most influential are Neue Zürcher Zeitung (Zürich, Liberal-Democratic), Der Bund (Berne, Liberal-Democratic), National-Zeitung (Basle, Liberal-Democratic), Basler Nachrichten (Basle, Liberal-Conservative), Vaterland (Lucerne, Catholic-Conservative), A-Z (Zürich, Social-Democratic), Journal de Genève (Liberal-Conservative) and Gazette de Lausanne (Liberal-Conservative).

## PRODUCTION, INDUSTRY AND COMMERCE

**Agriculture.** In 1975 about 168,000 of the population were engaged in agriculture. Most of the holdings are medium-sized to small (1975):

27,429 have less than 1 hectare,
30,080 between 1 and 5 hectares,
24,580 between 5 and 10 hectares,
36,125 between 10 and 20 hectares,
14,069 between 20 and 50 hectares,
843 above 50 hectares,

Total 133,126 holdings.

The agricultural products are varied, but milk and milk products hold first place. Milk production in 1975 was 3·96 million quintals. Gross revenue from agriculture in 1975 is estimated at S.fr.6,292 million.

**Industry.** The metal-working and machine industry employs the greatest number of workers (390,000: 1971). Switzerland is noted for the manufacture of heavy electrical equipment, steam and diesel engines. An allied industry is watchmaking, the origins of which go back to the 16th century. In 1971, 69,430 persons, including commercial employees, were engaged in the watchmaking industry. The textile industry is next in importance. At the end of 1971, 117,500 workers were engaged in the textile, clothing and footwear industry. In 1971, the workers in the chemical industry numbered 66,700. During the present century, the chemical industry has become increasingly important, especially from the point of view of exports. About 25 per cent of the total exports consists of chemical products, chiefly medicines and aniline dyes.

**Commerce.** The following table shows the value of imports and exports by principal countries for the years 1974 and 1975 (in million francs):

| *Imports* | 1974 | 1975 |
|---|---|---|
| Austria | 2,109 | 1,489 |
| Finland | 277 | 189 |
| Ireland | 60 | 10 |
| Norway | 209 | 164 |
| Portugal | 194 | 157 |
| Sweden | 1,190 | 934 |
| Total | 4,040 | 2,943 |

| *Exports* | 1974 | 1975 |
|---|---|---|
| Belgium, Luxembourg | 1,459 | 1,110 |
| Denmark | 483 | 371 |
| France | 5,886 | 4,754 |
| Germany | 12,479 | 9,553 |
| Iceland | 74 | 63 |
| Italy | 3,930 | 3,386 |
| Netherlands | 1,760 | 1,376 |
| United Kingdom | 2,502 | 2,105 |
| Total | 28,573 | 22,718 |

## COMMUNICATIONS

**Railways.** The Swiss railways system extends over 4,990 kms. and is one of the densest in the world. Practically the whole of it is electrified. The Swiss Federal Railways are the largest railway undertaking in the country, and came into being as a result of the amalgamation of the most important railway companies in 1903. They are now under state ownership.

Traffic receipts in 1973 (estimated) were fr.3,129 millions. Expenses (estimated) were fr.3,127 millions.

**Roads.** The total length of roads is 61,620 kms. At the end of September 1975 there were 2,121,366 motor vehicles, of which 1,794,255 were private cars.

Boring under the Great St. Bernard Pass was completed early in 1962. The road tunnel is now open to traffic. The San Bernardino road tunnel was opened in 1967. In April 1970 the boring began under the St. Gotthard Pass.

**Shipping.** Although Switzerland has no coastline, a merchant marine was created by decree of the Swiss Government in 1941, the place of registration being Basle. Both passenger and cargo steamers ply on the Swiss lakes and communicate with the outside world by means of the Rhine, which brings Switzerland into direct contact with the sea. Entering traffic handled at Basle in 1975 totalled 7,859,531 tons.

In 1975 Switzerland had 27 seagoing vessels totalling 243,375 gross tons and belonging to 16 companies. The Rhine fleet consisted of 473 vessels of all kinds including barges.

**Civil Aviation.** In 1975, 9,255,422 passengers were carried. together with 255,992 met. tons of freight. 152,551,000 km, were flown.

**Swissair—Schweizerische Luftverkehr A.G.** (Chairman, F. Gugelmann, President, A. Baltensweiler); share capital S.fr.422,130,100; *services operated:* to principal capitals of Europe and to U.S.A., South America, Africa and to Near, Middle and Far East. *Head Office:* Balsberg, Kloten P.O. Box 8058, Zurich.

**Telephones.** The telephone system is a state monopoly administered by the Federal Posts. More than 5,242 million calls were made in 1975, amounting to about 820 calls per head of the population. The telephone system comprises over 2·0 million miles of cable. There are about 3,910,000 (1975) telephones in use.

**Broadcasting.** The Swiss broadcasting system is under the technical direction of the Postal Administration. It has four transmitters broadcasting in seven languages at Beromünster, Sottens, Monte Ceneri and Schwarzenburg, the latter being a short-wave station. The licence-holders at the end of 1975 were 2,075,000 for radio and 1,759,000 for television.

## EDUCATION

The Swiss primary and secondary schools are under the direction of the cantons and are financed by the State. Every child must attend school for 8 or 9 years. In 1973–74 about 573,742 boys and girls attended primary schools. Secondary schools have an attendance of 262,431 and the high schools of 85,638.

There were in all ten universities with a total of 48,628 students in 1973–74. There is a bill now pending to provide for Federal aid to cantonal universities. Of the universities, Basle is the oldest, having been founded in 1460. Zurich is the largest and Berne follows next. Both date back to the first half of the 19th century. Of the university students quite a large proportion are foreigners.

## ATOMIC ENERGY

The Swiss reactor centre at Würenlingen has operated under government direction since 1960, and has the following main research facilities: swimming-pool reactor SAPHIR, engineering test reactor DIORIT, subcritical assembly MINOR, a hot laboratory and assorted test laboratories for physics metallurgy and other sciences.

The Société Nationale pour l'Encouragement de la Technique Atomique Industrielle is developing a heavy-water moderated pressure tube reactor. Since 1965 a much larger reactor (300 tMW) has been under construction. It is scheduled to come into operation in 1971.

## RELIGION

There is no State religion The constitution has declared religious belief to be a private matter in which the State has no right to interfere but which has a right to the protection of the State against the domination of any other religious community. The State schools are open to all without prejudice to their freedom of conscience and creed; thus Switzerland is a country of absolute religious tolerance.

# Syrian Arab Republic

**Head of State**—Lieut.-Gen. Hafez al Hassad.

**National Flag:** A tricolour fesse-wise, red, white, black, the white charged with three stars five-pointed green.

## CONSTITUTION AND GOVERNMENT

THE new régime in Syria has been marked by a number of military *coups d'état*. Organized by Colonel Zaim the first *coup d'état* took place in March 1949. The new régime lasted only until August 1949 when Colonel Hinnawi led a second *coup*. Zaim was shot after a summary trial. There was a general election in November 1949.

In December 1949 Colonel Hinnawi, who had assumed the title of Commander-in-Chief, was himself removed from office by troops under the command of Lieut.-Col. Adib Shishakly. Throughout 1950 and 1951 Lieut.-Col. Shishakly tried to maintain Cabinet government and work through civilian ministers. The Constituent Assembly drew up the new Constitution which was passed in September 1950. In December 1951, however, Lieut.-Col. Shishakly carried out a second *coup d'état*, and ruled as dictator until February 1954.

In February 1954 the former President, Brigadier Shishakly, was overthrown by a revolt of Syrian Army commanders, and a new Government of 12 members was formed with Hashem Atassi as President. In June a 'neutral' caretaker Government of six members was formed. Elections took place in September, and the results were as follows: Independents, 67 seats; Nationalists, 18; People's Party, 27; Arab Socialist Regeneration Party, 16; Nomad Party, 9; Social Co-operatives, 2; Socialist Nationalists, 2; and Communists, 1.

On 28 September 1961, after a revolt of army officers, Syria seceded from the United Arab Republic. On 8 March 1963, a National Council of Revolution took over power. On 23 February 1966 this government was overthrown by the 'Provisional National Leadership'. The President, General M. A. Al-Hafez was replaced by Dr. Nureddin al-Atassi as head of State. In 1970 Ahmed Hatib was appointed head of State and Hafez Assad as head of Government.

The 1973 Arab-Israeli war commenced on 6 October 1973. The full effects of the subsequent cease-fire and peace negotiations have yet to be evaluated.

## LOCAL GOVERNMENT AND LEGAL SYSTEM

Syria is divided administratively into fourteen Mohafaza (province/county). Each Mohafaza is divided into districts, and the districts are further divided into smaller units called 'Nahia'. A Nahia contains a number of villages and a village is the smallest administrative unit. Each Mohafaza is headed by a Mohafaz (Governor), and a district is headed by a district. officer, and a Nahia is represented by a sub-district officer. The villages are represented by village headmen. The Mohafazat are: Damascus City, Damascus, Aleppo, Homs, Hama, Lattakia, Deir Ezzour, Idleb, Al Hasakeh, Al Rakka, Sweida, Dara, Tartous Quneitra.

## AREA AND POPULATION

Syria covers an area of about 71,800 sq. miles.

The population at mid-1974 was 7,177,000. The average annual percentage growth rate of the population for the periods 1960–74 and 1965–74 was 3·3.

The chief towns, with the estimated populations (1970), are: Aleppo, 670,230; Damascus, 836,668; Homs, 215,423; Hama, 137,421; Idlib, 34,515; Latakia, 125,716; Deir-ez-zor, 66,164; Al-Rakka, 37,151; Hasakeh, 32,746; Daria, 22,312; and Soueida, 29,524.

## CURRENCY

The unit of currency is the Syrian £ of 100 *piastres*.

## FINANCE

The Syrian budget for 1975 was 10·5 milliards £S. It is planned that a fourteen per cent increase in the GNP will be achieved. The main government expenditure is on defence, development (which amounts to sixty per cent of expenditure), and stabilisation of the prices of consumer goods.

The GNP at market prices for 1974 was U.S.$ millions 3,990, and the GNP per capita at market prices was U.S.$560. The annual average percentage growth rate of the GNP per capita for the period 1960–74 was 4·0, and for the period 1965–742. was 4·2 [*See the note at the beginning of this section concerning GNP.*]

## BANKING

The sole right of note issue is held by the Banque de Syrie et du Liban in virtue of an agreement made in 1937 and expiring in 1962. An agreement was reached between the Syrian Government and the Banque de Syrie et du Liban in January 1956 for the termination of the Bank's concession, and the transfer of the Institute of Issue to the official Central Bank of Syria, the constitution of which was drawn up in May 1956.

**Banque de Syrie et du Liban, S.A.**

**Commercial Bank of Syria, S.A.** *Head Office:* Moawiya Street P.O. Box 933, Damascus Telex: 11002.

**Central Bank of Syria.**

## PRODUCTION, INDUSTRY AND COMMERCE

**Agriculture.** Syria is mainly an agricultural country. The area under cultivation is estimated at over 6 million hectares, which is about one-fourth of the total area of the country.

The following table shows yield of the principal crops (thousand met. tons) for 1971:

| *Crop* | *Yield* |
|---|---|
| Wheat | 593 |
| Barley | 102 |
| Tobacco | 10·9 |
| Olives | 117 |
| Lentils | 23·7 |
| Millet | 12·5 |
| Sugar-beet | 151·4 |
| Maize | 16·8 |
| Onions | 97·6 |
| Cotton | 404·3 |

**Livestock.** A great many farmers are employed in cattle-breeding. Large numbers of live animals and great quantities of raw hides and skins are exported.

In 1968, livestock was numbered as follows: Sheep, 4,847,000; Goats, 779,000; Camels, 6,400; Horses, 63,000; Cattle, 273,000; Asses, 235,000; Mules, 65,000.

**Industry.** The following table shows production of some industrial items in 1971:

| *Industry* | 1971 |
|---|---|
| Wool fabrics (tons) | 1,300,000 |
| Cotton yarn (tons) | 23,400 |
| Cement (tons) | 91,000 |
| Sugar (tons) | 130,400 |
| Tobacco (tons) | 4,400 |
| Vegetable oil (tons) | 26,200 |

**Mining and Oil.** There is very little mining industry. The chief deposits under exploitation are bitumen and sodium chloride, but it is believed there are also deposits of lead, copper, chrome and other minerals.

In March 1965 the government nationalized all oil companies. Three of the nine companies were foreign—Socony Vacuum Oil, Esso Middle East and Shell. The nine companies have been put under the administration of the Syrian General Petroleum Organization.

## COMMUNICATIONS

**Railways and Roads.** There are railway lines linking Aleppo, Hama, Homs, Riyak (Lebanon) and Damascus, Aleppo and Mosul, Aleppo and Turkey, Homs via Tripoli (Lebanon) to Beirut (Lebanon) and between Damascus and Beirut via Riyak. There is also a railway between Damascus and Amman (Jordan) via Izra and Dera'a, and proposals are in hand to rebuild this railway as far as Jeddah (Saudi Arabia).

Branch lines link the railway from Dera'a to Himme, Dera'a to Busra Ash Sham and from Irza to Suweida.

Asphalted roads connect the main towns of Syria and there are asphalted roads between Damascus and the capitals of the neighbouring Arab States and with Turkey. Many of the secondary roads in the country are metalled.

A motor coach service operated by the Nairn Transport Company links the capitals of Lebanon, Syria and Iraq.

**Shipping.** The deep water harbour at Lattakia is now completed, and the bulk of the country's imports and exports pass through this port, although some still pass through the Lebanese port of Beirut. In 1962, a total of 3,127 ships entered Syrian ports carrying 1,229,650 tons of goods. 3,155 ships left carrying 24,381,916 tons of goods.

**Civil Aviation.** There is an International airport at Damascus, which is served by most of the world's leading airlines. Other airports are at Aleppo, Kamishli, Deir es Zor, Humeimim, and Palmyra. In 1962 4,320 flights landed at Damascus carrying 47,000 passengers, 4,357 left carrying 52,874 passengers.

An automatic telephone service is now operating in the principal towns.

There is a national broadcasting system, with transmitters at Aleppo, Damascus, and Homs. A television service has been operating in Damascus since 1960.

## NEWSPAPERS

There are two National Daily Newspapers in Damascus, and local papers in Homs, Hama, Aleppo and Lattakia.

**Al Ba'ath.** Morning. Damascus.

**Al Thawrah.** Morning. Damascus.

## EDUCATION AND RELIGION

Education is expanding rapidly. In 1966 there were 4,647 primary schools with 688,165 pupils, 581 secondary schools with 46,796 pupils; in addition there were 5,198 pupils in vocational schools.

There are at present two universities, one at Damascus and one at Aleppo with a total of 19,739 students. There are estimated to be 4,000 students at universities abroad, both in Europe and America.

The State Religion is Islam, but many different sects of Christianity are represented in quite large numbers throughout Syria.

# Taiwan

## (REPUBLIC OF CHINA)

**President**—Yen Chia-Kan.

**National Flag:** On a field of crimson, a sun white in a sky blue at the upper hoist.

### CONSTITUTION AND GOVERNMENT

THE Government of the Republic of China has its provisional seat in Taipei, Taiwan.

The Executive Yuan is the highest administrative organ of the country. At present the incumbents are:

*Prime Minister:* Chiang Ching-Kuo.
*Deputy Prime Minister:* Hsu Ching-chung.
*Minister of the Interior:* Chang Feng-shu.
*Minister of Foreign Affairs:* Shen Chang-huan.
*Minister of National Defence:* Kao Kuei-yuan.
*Minister of Finance:* Fei. W. H.
*Minister of Education:* Li Yuan-Su.
*Minister of Justice:* Wang Tao-yuan.
*Minister of Economic Affairs:* Sun Yun-suan.
*Minister of Communications:* Lin Chin-sheng.
*Chairman of Mongolian and Tibetan Affairs Commission:* Tsui Chui yien.
*Chairman of Overseas Chinese Affairs Commission:* Mao Sung-nien.
*Ministers without Portfolio:* George K. C. Yeh, Yu Kuo-hua, Henry Kao, S. K. Chow, Li Kwoh-ting, Li Teng-Hui, Chin Chuang-Huan.
*Director-General of Government Information Office:* Ding Mou-shih.

There are three political parties now functioning in Taiwan, namely the Kuomintang (or Nationalist Party), the Young China Party (or Youth Party), and the China Democratic Socialist Party. The Kuomintang holds the majority in the National Assembly, the Legislative and Control Yuans.

### LOCAL GOVERNMENT

Taiwan's legislative body is the Provincial Assembly. Its 72 members hold office for four years and are eligible for re-election. The Assembly is headed by a speaker and a deputy speaker. It meets for two months out of every six. A special session may be called by the governor or more than one-third of the members.

The policy making body of the Taiwan Provincial Government is the Provincial Government Council, which is composed of 18 members appointed by the National Government.

County and municipal governments have councils which handle affairs within their areas.

Taipei is a special city directly under the Executive Yuan and co-equal with Taiwan province.

### LEGAL SYSTEM

The Supreme Court is the highest tribunal in the three-level court system. Parties to a civil case in which less than 500 silver dollars are involved may not appeal to the Supreme Court. It exercises appellate jurisdiction only.

The Ministry of Justice is in charge of all administrative affairs concerning judicial and penal institutions. It selects judges and overseas courts and prison administration.

There are eleven district courts, which handle civil and criminal cases of the first instance.

The Taiwan Provincial High Court is located in Taipei and there are three branches at Tainan, Taichung and Haulien. The Amoy branch court of the Fukien Provincial High Court covers the Kinmen (Quemoy) district.

### AREA AND POPULATION

The island of Taiwan is 81 to 125 miles off the south China coast with an area of 13,892·5 square miles; or, including the Pescadores, a total of 13,961·7 square miles.

In February 1977, Taiwan had a population of 16,624,927 (not including foreign residents). About fifty-three per cent live in towns.

The chief cities are Taipei, the provisional capital, Taichung, Kaohsiung, Tainan, and Chilung (Keelung).

There are also two groups of islands along the mainland coast. The Kinmen (or Quemoy) islands are situated in the Amoy Bay along the coast of Fukien Province. Big Kinmen is 60 square miles in area and has a population of 59,687. To its northeast lie the 19 islands of the Matsu groups, one of them being only five nautical miles from the mainland. Besides the military, there are about 12,629 people there.

### CURRENCY

The New Taiwan dollar is the currency used in Taiwan. Its official rate of exchange has been pegged at a floating rate of that of the Pound Sterling or NT $38 = U.S. $1.00.

### FINANCE

In the fiscal year 1975 Revenue totalled NT$139,937 million, and Expenditure NT$134,164 million.

### BANKS

**Central Bank of China.** Reactivated July, 1961. Functions as regulator of the money market, management of foreign exchange, issue of currency and fiscal services for the government.

**The International Commercial Bank of China.** Foreign exchange bank with branch offices and agencies in New York, Chicago, Tokyo, Osaka, Bangkok and Panama. *Address:* 100 Chi Lim Road, Taipei.

**Bank of Communications.** Industrial bank specializing in financing for industry, including manufacturing, mining and transportation. Has branches in Saigon and Cholon.

**Central Trust of China.** Acts as government trading agency. Engaged in trust and insurance business.

**Hua Nan Commercial Bank, Ltd.** Established 1919. (President, H. A. Chen; Chairman, F. H. Chang.) Assets at 30 June 1977. NT$67,824,293,435; deposits NT$45,614,071,760; current accounts NT$20,845,640,947. *Head Office:* 33, Kaifeng Street, Sec. 1, Taipei, Taiwan. Number of branches, 113.

**Postal Remittances and Savings Bank.** Accepts savings deposits and makes domestic transfers.

**Bank of Taiwan.** Largest commercial bank. Fiscal agent of Taiwan Provincial Government. Acts as Central Bank agent in issuing New Taiwan Dollar notes. Has 41 branches in Taiwan.

### PRODUCTION, INDUSTRY AND COMMERCE

From 1953, six four-year plans were implemented. The first three plans increased real national income by 134·9 per cent and real per capita income by 59 per cent. The annual average growth of real national income has been 8·6 per cent, and of real per capita income 5·8 per cent.

The year of 1976 was to be the third year of the sixth four-year plan. Because of drastic economic changes at home and abroad, this plan was no longer practical. A Six-Year Economic Development Plan was drawn up for implementation beginning in 1976 and ending in 1981. The target of the Republic of China's annual economic growth rate is 5·8 per cent on the average. The per capita income will be increased from the projected US$ 700 in 1976 to US$ 1,344 in 1981.

The annual growth rate of agriculture is set at 2·5 per cent. The annual growth in the manufacturing industry is set at 9·5 per cent on the average. Its percentage in the domestic gross national product will rise from 35 per cent in 1975 to 39 per cent in 1981.

The average annual growth rate for power is set at 8·3 per cent and the annual business operation of transportation and telecommunications will be increased by 8·9 per cent on the average.

The annual trade expansion is planned at 12·2 per cent for exports and 10·6 per cent for imports.

The rise of domestic commodity prices will be kept under five per cent.

33·7 per cent of the people in Taiwan are farmers, and up until 1949 only one-third of them owned all the land they cultivated. All tenant farmers were paying rents ranging from 50 to 70 per cent of the main crop. A government land reform programme was initiated in 1949, and in 1963 tenant farmers who had purchased their land under the programme paid their last instalments.

From 1952 to 1969, unit yields of major crops increased by 17 to 155 per cent. About 2·7 million metric tons of rice were produced in 1976.

Fishing production reached 810,600 metric tons in 1976, as opposed to 121,697 in 1952. Fishing craft are being equipped with diesel engines.

Since 1953, logging has been carried out under a government forestry development programme. Production in 1974 was more than 823,732 cubic metres.

Industrial production has improved steadily. In 1975 private enterprise turned out about 81·3 per cent of total industrial production. American economic assistance ended in June 1965.

The following table shows some figures for industrial production for the year ending February 1977 (in metric tons):

| | |
|---|---|
| Electric power (million kWh) | 26,877 |
| Cotton fabric (thousand m) | 295,000 |
| Paper | 649,000 |
| Fertilizer | 1,634,000 |
| Cement | 8,749,000 |
| Sewing machines (sets) | 1,379,000 |
| Fluorescent lamps (units) | 19,917,000 |
| Shipbuilding (gross tons) | 172,000 |
| Coal | 3,236,000 |

Taiwan has 2,265,948·2 acres of arable land and 6,266,488 acres of forests. The principal agricultural products include sugar cane, rice, sweet potatoes, tea, bananas, pineapples, peanuts, soyabeans, jute and citrus fruits.

The following table shows the output of principal crops for the year ending February 1977 (in metric tons):

| | |
|---|---|
| Rice (brown) | 2,713,000 |
| Sweet potatoes | 1,851,000 |
| Wheat | 1,000 |
| Soyabeans | 53,000 |
| Groundnuts | 89,000 |
| Tea | 25,000 |
| Bananas | 213,000 |
| Pineapples | 279,000 |
| Sugar cane | 8,669,000 |
| Sugar | 779,000 |

Taiwan's foreign trade has been rapidly expanding. The trade deficit was U.S. $110 million in 1961. By 1963 there was a favourable balance of U.S. $20·7 million. In 1969, exports totalled U.S. $1,111 million and imports U.S. $1,205 million. In February 1977 exports totalled U.S. 8,080 million and imports U.S. $7,590 million.

The following table shows the trading figures for 1977 (in U.S. $ million):

| *Country* | *Imports* | *Exports* |
|---|---|---|
| U.S.A. | 1,797·6 | 3,038·7 |
| Japan | 2,451·5 | 1,094·7 |
| U.K. | 165·3 | 162·9 |
| Hong Kong | 101·4 | 610·4 |
| Singapore and Malaya | 143·5 | 267·6 |
| West Germany | 352·2 | 422·1 |

Textile products, metals and machinery are among Taiwan's leading exports. Others include sugar, rice, lumber, timber, bananas, ores, metals and machinery, chemicals, building materials, canned mushrooms, canned pineapples, tea and citronella oil.

Principal imports are ores, machinery, tools, raw cotton, vehicles, ships, wheat and cereals, beans and peas, crude and fuel oil, fertilizers and lumber.

## COMMUNICATIONS

Taiwan has a good railway system, and with completion of the east coast final link and a cross-island road will have an excellent highway network connecting all the important cities and towns of the province. The total length of railway is 5,600 kilometres. During 1976, the Taiwan railroads carried 143 million passengers, and 35 million metric tons of freight. The total length of highway is 17,172 kilometres. The Silo Bridge (which is 1·2 miles long) on the west side of Taiwan is the longest highway bridge of its kind in the Far East. An East–West cross-island highway of 180 miles through spectacular mountain scenery has been completed.

Kinmen and Matsu islands both maintain good highway systems for military purposes as well as for civilian transportation. Most of the roads have been constructed by the soldiers of the defence forces.

There are 9,443 postal offices and 584 telecommunication offices scattered over Taiwan, the Pescadores, Kinmen and Matsu.

There are 111 radio stations and three televisions stations.

Because of its strategic position, Taiwan depends largely on air transportation. China Airlines operates domestic and international scheduled and chartered flights. Far Eastern Air Transport makes domestic scheduled and chartered flights. Civil Air Transport operates Taipei–Hong Kong–Bangkok scheduled and chartered cargo flights. Fohsing Airlines operates international and domestic chartered cargo flights. Winner Airway Company and Taiwan Aviation Corporation operates domestic and overseas chartered flights. Yung Shing Air Transport operates helicopter passenger and agricultural chartered flights. Military flights are frequent between Taiwan and the off-shore islands. International airlines keep Taipei in close contact with all parts of the free world. On Taipei's recently-expanded airfield, the largest commercial aeroplanes land and take off daily.

As an island, Taiwan's ocean transportation is important also. The China Merchants Steam Navigation Co. and the Taiwan Navigation Co., together with other shipping companies, own 168 vessels of various descriptions with a total tonnage of 60,883,000.

## NEWSPAPERS

**Central Daily News.** 83 Chung-hsiao W. Road, Sec. 1, Taipei, Taiwan, Republic of China 100. Cir.: 520,000.

**Shin Sheng Daily News.** 127 Yenping S. Road, Taipei. Morning. Circulation 301,350.

**United Daily News.** 555 Chunghsiao East Road, Section 4, Taipei. Morning. Circulation 610,000.

**China Daily News.** 131 Sungkiang Road, Taipei. Cir.: 340,000.

**China Times.** 132 Tali Street, Taipei. Morning. Cir.: 500,000.

## EDUCATION

The following table shows the number of schools, teachers and pupils for the year 1977:

| | *Schools* | *Teachers* | *Pupils* |
|---|---|---|---|
| Pre-School | 778 | 3,716 | 121,373 |
| Primary | 2,378 | 64,974 | 2,341,413 |
| Secondary (inc. Vocational) | 987 | 62,392 | 1,539,150 |
| Higher | 101 | 14,548 | 299,414 |

# United Republic of Tanzania

(MEMBER OF THE COMMONWEALTH)

**Capital**—Dar-es-Salaam.

**President**—Mwalimu Julius K. Nyerere.

## CONSTITUTION AND GOVERNMENT

THE United Republic of Tanzania was formed by the Union of the former Republic of Tanganyika and the People's Republic of Zanzibar. The Articles of Union were signed on 22 April, 1964 by Mwalimu Julius K. Nyerere on behalf of the Government of the Republic of Tanganyika and the late Sheikh Abeid Amani Karume on behalf of the Government of the People's Republic of Zanzibar. The Articles of Union were subsequently approved and ratified by the Parliament of Tanganyika and the Revolutionary Council of Zanzibar. The union came into being officially with effect from 26 April, 1964. At the time of the Union the existing constitution of the Republic of Tanganyika was adapted to form an interim constitution of the United Republic. This constitution was repealed and replaced by the Interim Constitution of Tanzania enacted in 1965, the main provisions of which are:

(a) The Parliament and Executive of the United Republic has authority with respect to all Union matters in and for the United Republic and with respect to all other matters in and for Tanganyika. Union matters include External Affairs; Defence; Police; Emergency Powers; Citizenship; Immigration; External trade and borrowing; Income Tax, Corporation tax, customs and excise duties; the government and Public Service of the United Republic; Harbours, civil aviation, posts and telegraphs; currency, coinage, banking, foreign exchange; industrial licensing and statistics; Higher education; Mineral oil resources and certain other matters specified in Annex X to the Treaty for East African Co-operation.

(b) A separate Legislature and Executive for Zanzibar has exclusive authority within Zanzibar for matters other than those reserved to the Parliament and Executive of the United Republic. Administration of justice is an example of a matter which is not a Union consideration.

(c) There are two Vice-Presidents one of whom (being a person normally resident in Zanzibar) is also the head of the Executive in and for Zanzibar and is the principal assistant of the President of the United Republic in the discharge of his executive functions in relation to Zanzibar.

(d) The Parliament of the United Republic consists of the President and the National Assembly, but the President is not a member of the National Assembly. Members of the National Assembly include members appointed by the President from among the members of the Revolutionary Council of Zanzibar.

**Ministry** (October 1975)

*First Vice-President:* Ndugu Aboud Jumbe.
*Prime Minister and Second Vice-President:* Ndugu Rashidi Kawawa.
*Minister for Finance and Planning:* Ndugu Amir Jamal.
*Minister for Foreign Affairs:* Ndugu Ibrahim Kaduma.
*Minister for Home Affairs:* Ndkgu Ali Hassan Mwinyi.
*Minister for Defence and National Service:* Ndugu Edward Sokoine.
*Minister for Justice:* Ndugu Julie Manning (Miss).
*Minister for Agriculture:* Ndugu John Malecela.
*Minister for Industries:* Ndugu Cleopa Msuya.
*Minister for Commerce:* Ndugu Alphonce Rulegura.
*Minister for Water, Energy and Minerals:* Ndugu Wilbert Chagula.
*Minister for Manpower Development:* Ndugu Nicholas Kuhanga.
*Minister for Communications and Transport:* Ndugu Alfred Tandau.
*Minister for National Education:* Ndugu Isael Elinewinga.
*Minister for Health:* Ndugu Leader Stirling.
*Minister for National Culture and Youth:* Ndugu Mirisno Sarakikya.
*Minister for Information and Broadcasting:* Ndugu Daudi Mwakawago.
*Minister for Lands, Housing and Urban Development:* Ndugu Tabitha Siwale (Mrs).
*Minister for Natural Resources and Tourism:* Ndugu Solomon Ole-Saibull.
*Minister for Labour and Social Welfare:* Ndugu Crispin Tungaraza.
*Minister for Works:* Ndugu Louis Sazia.
*Minister for Capital Development:* Ndugu Hasnu Makame.
*Minister of State, President's Office:* Ndugu Peter Siyovelwa.
*Minister of State, 1st Vice-President's Office:* Ndugu Hassan Moyo.
*Minister of State, Prime Minister's Office:* Ndugu Hussein Shekilango.

**Junior Ministers**

*Prime Minister's Office:* Ndugu Ali Mchumo.
*Prime Minister's Office:* Ndugu Robert Ng'itu.
*Ministry of Defence and National Service:* Ndugu Seif Bakari.
*Ministry of Agriculture:* Ndugu Edward Barongo.
*Ministry of Foreign Affairs:* Nudugu Isaac Sepetu.
*Ministry of Industries:* Ndugu Chrysant Mzindakaya.
*Ministry of Health:* Ndugu Mustafa Nyang'anyi.
*Ministry of National Education:* Ndugu Nazar Nyoni.

## LEGAL SYSTEM

The laws of the United Republic of Tanzania consists of Acts of the Parliament of the United Republic, Subsidiary Legislation made in pursuance of those Acts and other laws in respect of which statutory provision has been made expressly applying or recognizing the application of those other laws. Of the latter the most important are Common Law, the Customary and Islamic Laws and Acts of the East African Community enacted with respect to certain matters specified in the Treaty for East African Co-operation signed on 6 June 1967 on behalf of the Governments of the United Republic of Tanzania, the Republic of Uganda and the Republic of Kenya.

The system of courts in and for Tanganyika comprise, in ascending order, the primary courts, the district courts and courts of resident magistrates, the High Court of the United Republic and the Court of Appeal for East Africa.

Under the Magistrates' Courts Act of 1963, a primary court has been established in every district and there are normally a number of places within the district where the primary court regularly holds its sittings. A primary court is presided over by a primary court magistrate who is appointed to that office by the Minister responsible for legal affairs. Every primary court magistrate must sit with two or more assessors, and all matters before the court are decided by the votes of a majority of the magistrate and the assessors present. In the event of an equality of votes the magistrate has a casting vote in addition to his deliberative vote. A primary court exercises jurisdiction in all proceedings of a civil nature where the law applicable is customary law or, subject to certain limitations, Islamic law, and in all other proceedings in respect of which jurisdiction is conferred on a primary court by law. The practice and procedure of primary courts are regulated by specially simplified rules made under the Magistrates' Courts Act. Similarly, there are special regulations prescribing rules of evidence in primary courts. In both civil and criminal proceedings an appeal lies from a primary court to the district court of the district for which the primary court has been established.

There has been established in every district a district court which exercises jurisdiction within the district in which it is established. In addition, the Magistrates' Courts Act empowers the Chief Justice, by order, to establish courts of resident magistrates which shall exercise jurisdiction in such areas as may be specified in the order. The Chief Justice has established resident magistrates' courts with jurisdiction generally co-extensive with a particular administrative region, that is, an area comprising normally three to four districts. According to the statutory definition, "district magistrate" includes a resident magistrate so that the distinction between a district court and resident magistrate's court lies in the difference in jurisdiction exercisable by these courts and more particularly in proceedings of a civil nature. For the purposes of civil procedure, every court of a resident magistrate and every district court is subordinate tothe High Court, and every district court is subordinate to the Court of the resident magistrate within the area of whose jurisdiction it is situated. Generally, a district court exercises original jurisdiction in all proceedings of a criminal nature in respect of which jurisdiction has been conferred on a district court by law, and in proceedings of a civil nature only when the court is held by a civil magistrate, that is, a resident magistrate or such other magistrate as the Chief Justice may appoint to be a civil magistrate. The pecuniary jurisdiction of a district court held by a civil magistrate is limited to Shs. 200,000/- in proceedings for the recovery of possession of immovable property and Shs. 20,000/- in other proceedings. A court of a resident magistrate exercises jurisdiction in all proceedings in respect of which jurisdiction has been conferred by law on a court of a resident magistrate or on a district court, or a district court held by a resident magistrate or a civil magistrate, in the exercise of its original jurisdiction. District and resident magistrates are appointed by the Judicial Service Commission. In the exercise of their original criminal jurisdiction the practice and procedure of district courts and courts of resident magistrates are regulated by the Penal Code and the Criminal Procedure Code. Original civil jurisdiction is exercised in accordance with the principles and provisions of the Civil Procedure Code.

Next in rank is the High Court of the United Republic. The Judges of the High Court are the Chief Justice appointed by the President and at least 15 puisne judges also appointed by the President after consultation with the Chief Justice. The High Court has full jurisdiction, Civil and criminal and has exclusive jurisdiction in questions as to the interpretation of the Constitution. It exercises jurisdiction in accordance with the laws with which district courts and courts of resident magistrates are required to exercise their jurisdiction. Appeals go to the High Court from the subordinate courts both in civil and criminal matters, and in respect of both the High Court has additional powers of review, exercisable either on application or on the court's own motion.

In cases other than questions relating to the interpretation of the Constitution appeals go from the High Court to the Court of Appeal for East Africa, this being one of the common institutions under the Treaty for East African Co-operation. This is the final appellate court in and for Tanganyika. In any appeal the court has, in addition to any other power, authority and jurisdiction conferred on it by law, whatever power, authority and jurisdiction is vested on the court from which the appeal is brought. Similarly, the law applicable is the law applicable to the case in the court from which the appeal is brought. The Court of Appeal has its own rules of appeal practice. The Court may sit either within or outside Tanganyika.

The Interim Constitution of Tanzania makes provision for the continuance or establishment of a High Court in and for Zanzibar or courts subordinate thereto. The High Court of Zanzibar shall have such jurisdiction as may be conferred on a High Court by or under any law in force in Zanzibar, and where jurisdiction is conferred on a High Court by law of the Parliament of the United Republic which applies to, or a law in force in Tanganyika which is extended to, Zanzibar, the jurisdiction of the High Court of Zanzibar shall be concurrent with that of the High Court of the United Republic.

### CURRENCY

The standard unit of currency in the United Republic is the Tanzania shilling (15·1473 shillings to the £ sterling). There are subsidiary coins of 50 cents (cupro-nickel) and 20 cents and 5 cents (bronze). There are also coins of 5, and 1 shilling denomination. Notes of higher value are in circulation.

## MAINLAND

### AREA AND POPULATION

The total area of the territory is 362,688 square miles including 19,982 square miles of water.

The population of mainland Tanzania in mid-1972 was 13,606,000. The percentage population growth rate for the period 1960–72 was 3·0, and for the period 1965–72 was 2·8.

### FINANCE

Revenue (recurrent and development) for 1976–77, and Expenditure (development and recurrent) for 1976–77 (in shs(T)) were 7,883 and 7,228 millions respectively.

All commercial banks were nationalized in February 1967 and now operate as branches of the National Bank of Commerce.

Early in 1964 the first five-year development plan was announced. Since this occurred before the ratification of the Article of Union it remained exclusive to Tanganyika. The plan envisaged the expenditure of £246 million, of which £102 million was to have been spent by the central Government on the improvement of public services, education and health. £116 million was earmarked for the development of the private sector of the economy with an emphasis on mining and industry.

The year 1969 witnessed the completion of this first Five Year Plan and the beginning of the Second Five Year Plan (1969–74). The total investment programme for the Second Five Year Plan reflects its dynamic development-oriented philosophy. Altogether, there is planned a total investment of shs. 8,085 million.

The 2nd Five-Year Development Plan ended in 1974 and the 3rd Five-Year Development Plan was delayed one year because of unfavourable economic conditions. It starts this financial year 1976/77 with an investment of shs. 3,470 millions for only 1976/77.

During the 1976/77 financial year Tanzania expects to receive grants and soft loans from a number of countries and international organizations which are ready to help her in her development endeavours. The countries and international organizations expected to help are: Sweden, Norway, West Germany, Holland, Denmark, Finland, Canada, U.S.A., The People's Republic of China, Cuba, USSR, Italy U.K., Romania, India, Japan, Mexico, the World Bank, the Nordic Co-operation Council, the Africa Development Bank, the UNDP, the Arab-Africa Development, and other voluntary agencies. Discussions are still under way with a number of other countries and international organizations for more financial help.

### PRODUCTION, INDUSTRY AND COMMERCE

The United Kingdom is by far the most important of Tanzania's trading partners. In 1974, Shs. 584·5 worth of goods were exported to U.K. and Shs. 403·8 imported from the U.K.

In recent years trade with non-traditional markets has increased, and agreements have been signed with several countries of the Soviet Bloc. Trade relations with China are stronger than any one of the other non-traditional countries. In 1969, for instance, exports to China amounted to T£3·85 million while imports were T£4 million. Imports are expected to increase under the agreement whereby local costs of the Tanzania–Zambia railway are to be offset by Zambian and Tanzanian purchases of Chinese goods.

The gross domestic product of Tanzania (Mainland) in 1968 was estimated at shs.6.869,000 at current factor cost.

Production is mainly agricultural. Tanzania is the second largest producer of sisal. Other main crops are coffee, cotton, tea, tobacco, oil seeds, sugar, maize, beans and pulses, rice, wheat, cashew nuts, copra and pyrethrum. The gross Domestic Product (GDP) for Tanzania as a whole in 1975 was shs. 16,534 millions. Minerals in order of importance—diamonds, gemstones, tin, ornamental stones (art stones and amethystine quartz), and salt. There are new discoveries of coal and iron ore in Southern Tanzania; copper, cobalt, nickel and tin in Western Tanzania. Prospecting for asbestos, bauxite and rare earth is going on, while gas in shallow depth has been found in large quantities in coastal areas. Deposits of pyrochlore are being developed and there is large scale prospecting in progress for radioactive minerals. Parts of the Territory are well stocked with cattle and hides and skins are an important export. There are extensive fisheries in operation on Lakes Tanganyika and Victoria and on the sea coast. Local forests contain substantial quantities of timber, both hard and soft woods, and there are considerable exports. Tanzania is the second largest exporter of beeswax in the world. It also exports large numbers of mangrove poles to the Persian Gulf area.

**Commerce**

The following table show exports for 1975:

| *Exports* | *(Shs. million)* 1975 | *Tonnage* 1975 |
|---|---|---|
| Sisal | 346·3 | 101,685 |
| Coffee | 302·8 | 62,416 |
| Cotton | 296·7 | 30,364 |
| Cashew nuts | 250·5 | 120,153 |
| Tobacco | 201·2 | 18,200 |
| Sugar | 114·5 | 30,615 |
| Tea | 69·05 | 9,637 |
| Pyrethrum | 32·5 | 5,000 |

The following table shows the value of imports for the period January–September 1975 in mill. shillings:

| *Imports* | *(Shs. million) Jan-Sept. 1975* |
|---|---|
| Mineral fuels | 759·8 |
| Food | 725·6 |
| Machinery | 716·0 |
| Transport equipment | 497·9 |
| Chemicals | 337·1 |
| Textiles | 117·3 |
| Misc. manuf. articles | 89·9 |
| Crude materials | 35·1 |
| Beverages and Tobacco | 2·9 |
| Others | 617·9 |

The following table shows Tanzania's trade position for 1975:

| | (*Shs. millions*) 1975 |
|---|---|
| Net Imports | 5,694 |
| Domestic Exports | 2,765 |
| Balance of trade | 2,929 |

The decade after the achievement of independence has seen the establishment and expansion of many industries within the manufacturing sector. Apart from the brewing, plastics, enamel ware, metal, and plywood industries, new industries have been established for the manufacture of motor-vehicle tyres, fertilizers, steel, soluble coffee, textiles, meerschaum pipes, leather, farm implements, sisal bags, and processing of cashew nuts. It is intended that the large cement plant in operation at Wazo Hill will, in 1973/74, produce 400,000 tons of cement.

Most of the large industrial firms belong to the state owned National Development Corporation. The National Development Corporation, which is the principal government investment institution for the development of the manufacturing and mining sector, has over forty operating groups and associate companies. Apart from the operating companies, it is starting several projects and about twenty projects are under evaluation.

The private sector, whose individual investment level is of the order of Shs.200,000/- has about 663 productive units each employing ten or more people. These remarks concerning private industry apply only to the industries registered under the National Industries (Licensing and Registration) Act 1967. The registered companies include those involved in the garment, aluminium, galvanised iron sheet, hydrogenised vegetable oil, and glass industries.

Studies are now being undertaken of the large deposits of iron ore, coal, and gold deposits in the Ruvuma, Iringa and Mbeya regions. Although no complete assessment of the local resources has been arrived at, gemstones are now being exploited in the Northern regions of Tanzania. In addition an oil refinery is now in operation at Dar es Salaam, (with a crude oil capacity of 775,000 tons per year), and many factories are projected for the processing of Tanzanian agricultural products. The second half of the sixties has also seen the establishment of several mills in the textile industry, mainly under the umbrella of the National Development Corporation.

In the industrial sector the 3rd Five-Year Development Plan, apart from putting emphasis on basic industries, aims at producing goods which will cater for basic consumer needs at prices which are within the reach of most consumers. The plan also puts emphasis on providing the industries with the necessary raw materials, meeting various equipment requirements and ensuring an efficient distribution network. It envisages the establishment of small workshops in factory premises to manufacture simple spare parts, like nuts and bolts. The plan puts greater emphasis on the establishment of industries which are directly productive in the short turn. This should enable the nation to increase her supply of commodities for local consumption and foreign exchange earnings.

## COMMUNICATIONS

Motor traffic is now possible over 25,000 miles of road during the dry season and at almost all times over 21,000 miles of road.

The East African Railways Corporation operate road services, lake steamer services and the railways. There is a main line from Dar-es-Salaam to Kigoma (783 miles) and other lines from Tabora to Mwanza (237 miles). Tanga to Moshi and Arusha (272 miles). There are also two other branch lines.

The 1,162-mile Tanzania-Zambia railway has been completed. It started trial operations last October and has since made a profit of some shs. 90 millions.

There are 53 airports and landing strips maintained or licensed by the government, of these, two are of international standard, and seven are capable of accommodating Fokker Friendship aircraft. Kilimanjaro, and Dar-es-Salaam airports are capable of accommodating the Boeing 747 jumbo-jet airliner.

The East African Airways Corporation provide regular and frequent services to all the more important towns within the territory, and the neighbouring countries of Kenya and Uganda. There is also a service to the U.K., India and Pakistan, Zambia and Malawi. Domestic charter services are operated by two companies. In 1975, 345,688 passengers passed through Dar-es-Salaam airport, and 92,335 passengers passed through Kilimanjaro International Airport.

Telegraph services are operated by the East African Posts and Telecommunications Corporation which is, among other institutions, administered by the East African community.

Radio Tanzania operates a high and a low power transmitter in Dar-es-Salaam, broadcasting daily in English and Swahili on both transmitters.

## EDUCATION

By November 1977 all school-age children will be at school. This has been resolved by the Party's National Executive Committee. The illiteracy rate has been reduced to 31 per cent during the four-year campaign that started in 1972. Education is free up to University level.

A University College was opened in Dar-es-Salaam in 1962 with faculties of Science, Law, Arts and Social Sciences, Medicine and Agriculture. Since 1970 it has been operating as an independent University of Dar-es-Salaam and has opened an Engineering faculty and two departments of Veterinary Science and Forestry. There are also departments of Development Studies, Institute of Education and Institute for Kiswahili Research.

## NEWSPAPERS

**The Daily News.** P.O. Box 9033, Dar-es-Salaam.

**Sunday News.** P.O. Box 9033, Dar-es-Salaam.

**Mzalendo.** F. 1972. P.O. Box 9221. Dar-es-Salaam.

**Uhuru.** F. 1972. P.O. Box 9221, Dar-es-Salaam.

## RELIGION

The majority of the inhabitants of the territory are pagans, but there is a large African Moslem minority to be found chiefly in the coastal areas and in the up-country settlements. Among the immigrant Indian population the majority ar Hindus, Sikhs and Moslems. Christians of all races number some 2,000,000.

## ZANZIBAR

### AREA AND POPULATION

The area of Zanzibar Island is 641 square miles and of Pemba 380 square miles.

The population of Zanzibar (as at 1967 census) is 354,360 (Zanzibar Island 190,117, Pemba Island 164,243). The Africans form a large majority of the population.

The population of the township of Zanzibar is 68,380.

### FINANCE

Since the five-year development plan for Tanganyika was drawn up before Union, Zanzibar had her own three-year plan, involving an expenditure of £23 million. Emphasis was placed on improving the island's education and health services. The plan also envisages diversification of the economy, which hitherto had been mainly dependent on the growing of cloves. Manufacturing and processing industries allied to Zanzibar's primarily agricultural economy were to be set up.

### PRODUCTION, INDUSTRY AND COMMERCE

Zanzibar is the main source of the world's supply of cloves, and nearly three-quarters of the total value of the territory's exports is derived from the export of cloves and clove stem oil. Second only to cloves is the copra industry comprising the production of coconuts, copra, coconut oil, coconut oil cake and soap. Other export crops are chillies, fresh fruit, tobacco, kapok and marine products (shells and beche-de-mer). The main local food crops are rice, maize, millet and cassava. Zanzibar is famed for its excellent fruit, including citrus and pineapples. There are some 47,000 head of cattle and hides and skins are exported. Fishing is also an important activity. The only industries are the distillation of clove oil, coconut oil expression, and the manufacture of soap and coir fibre products.

### COMMUNICATIONS

The port of Zanzibar is one of the finest in Africa and was, for a long time, the main centre of commerce between India, Arabia and the mainland. Its importance as a port of transhipment and distribution centre has, however, largely decreased owing to the opening up of coastal ports on the mainland to direct steamship traffic with Europe. Government steamers maintain regular weekly communications with Pemba and Dar-es-Salaam. An air service between Dar-es-Salaam and Nairobi via Zanzibar, Tanga, and Mombasa is operated by the East African Airways Corporation. There is a regular air service between Zanzibar and Pemba.

### NEWSPAPERS

**Official Government Gazette.** F. 1892. P.O. Box 61, Zanzibar.

### EDUCATION

There are inter-racial government schools and grant-aided schools, some run by Indian sects, and others by the missions. There were, in 1962, 74 government primary schools and 10 grant-aided schools, 12 government secondary schools, two for boys and one for girls (both inter-racial), and a rural middle school for boys and two teacher-training centres, one for men and one for women. There is no post-secondary education in Zanzibar but students go to East Africa (Makerere College), the United Kingdom, United States of America, Middle East, Communist Countries, Pakistan and India. Post-primary technical education is provided for certain pupils at the Mombasa Institute of Moslem Education. There is a Muslim Academy for the teaching of Islamic Law, Customs, Religion and Language. There is a (higher) post-secondary education in King George VI School. One Post-primary; Karimjee Trade School, six Independent Schools. Primary education became compulsory in 1965.

### RELIGION

Islam is the prominent religion, and embraces about 95 per cent of the population (about 252,000). Of the 14,000 or so non-Muslims, about 5,500 are Christians, 4,000 are Hindus, and there are small groups of Parsees, Buddhists and other sects.

# Thailand

(SIAM)

**Capital**—Bangkok.

**Sovereign**—King Bhumibol Adulyadej.

**National Flag:** Divided fess-wise, red, white, blue, white red, the blue stripe twice the width of each white or red.

### CONSTITUTION AND GOVERNMENT

Thailand is a constitutional Monarchy. Following the overthrow of the elected Government on 6 October 1976, a new constitution—the tenth since 1932—was promulgated on 22 October 1976. This provides for a phased return to full democracy over a period of 12 years. For the first four years legislative power will be exercised by an appointed National Administrative Reform Assembly. During the next four years power will be shared equally by an elected National Assembly and an appointed Senate. In the third four-year period the power of the National Assembly will be increased and that of the Senate reduced, as much as possible, until, if the people show they realize their duties towards the country under the democratic system of government, the Senate is dissolved.

Following disturbances at Thammasart University in Bangkok on 6 October 1976, power was seized by the National Administrative Reform Council (NARC), composed of high-ranking officers of all three armed forces. On 22 October the present government was appointed, with Mr. Tanin Kraivixien as Prime Minister, and the NARC became the Advisory Council to the Prime Minister (ACPM). Under the constitution, the cabinet and the ACPM jointly determine policies concerning national security, which the cabinet must then carry out. In November 1977 King Bhumibol installed General Kriangsak Chammanand as Prime Minister, thereby marking a return to normal. Under the terms of the new interim constitution General Kriangsak can be dismissed only by the chairman of the National Policy Council.

**Reigning Royal Family.** Buddhist.—The present dynasty descends from General Chao Phya Chakri, who in 1782 was proclaimed King under the title of Phra Baht Somdech Phra Buddha Yod Fa Chulalok. Succession is in the male line, according to the Kot Monthien Bal 'Law of the Land' on Succession as revised 11 November 1924.

**Phra Baht Somdech Phra Paramindra Maha BHUMIBOL ADULYADEJ** (H.M. King BHUMIBOL ADULYADEJ of Thailand); born at Cambridge, Mass., U.S.A., 5 December 1927, son of H.R.H. Prince Mahidol of Songkhla, Somdech Phra Mahitaladhibes Aduladejaviknom Phria Boromariajajanok (born 1 January 1892, died 24 September 1929); succeeded to the throne on the death of his brother, King Ananda Mahidol, 9 June 1946; married at Bangkok, 28 April 1950, Mom Rajwongse Ying SIRIKIT KITIYAKARA (born 12 August 1932), elder daughter of General H.H. Kromphra Prince Chandhaburi Narunat (formerly H.S.H. Prince Nakkhatra Mangala Kitiyakara).

Children: 1, Princess UBOL Ratana; born at Lausanne, 6 April 1951. 2. Crown Prince VAJIRALONGKORN; born at Bangkok, 28 July 1952. 3. Princess SIRINDHORN born at Bangkok, 2 April 1955. 4. Princess CHULABHORN Valai Laksana, born at Bangkok, 4 July 1957.

### LOCAL GOVERNMENT

The country is divided into 71 provinces or Changwads, each of which is sub-divided into districts or Amphurs. Each Changwad is governed by a Provincial Governor and each Amphur by a Nai Amphur, both being appointed by the Ministry of the Interior. Municipalities are governed by an elected Municipal Council and Provincial Governors can call upon the advice of an elected Provincial Council. Metropolitan Bangkok is governed by an elected Governor and Municipal Assembly.

**LEGAL SYSTEM**

Broadly speaking the Thai Legal system is that of 'Code' Law, consisting of the Criminal Code, the Land Code, the Revenue Code, the Civil and Commercial Code, the Criminal Procedure Code and the Civil Procedure Code.

The judicial courts in Thailand are:

The Dika Court, which is the court of the highest appeal;
The Court of Appeal;
The Criminal Court;
The Civil Courts;
The Bangkok District Court;
The Central Juvenile Court.

These are all in Bangkok.

There is a Changwad Court in every Changwad having judicial power over all criminal and civil cases of first instance in its jurisdiction.

Officers of the Dika Court:

*President:* Mr. Sutham Phatrakom.
*Vice-Presidents:* Mr. Ratana Sri-hrai-win.
Mr. Pra-poj Tri-ra-wat.
Mr. Sa-noh Kum-phi-ra-yos.

**AREA AND POPULATION**

Thailand has an area of 514,000 sq. km. The population of Thailand at mid-1974 was 40,780,000. The annual average percentage growth rate of the population for the periods 1960–74 was 3·1 and for the period 1964–74 was 3·1. The bulk of the population are Thais, but those in the north-east of the country are Thais of the branch known as Laos, the same as the people of the Kingdom of Laos. About 3 million are of Chinese origin but inter marriage is on a large scale and most of them have been assimilated, using their names and speaking Thai. The population of Bangkok, the capital with its twin city of Thonburi across the Chao Phya River, is estimated to be about 4·5 million.

**CURRENCY**

The unit of currency is the baht which is divided into 100 satangs. The open market rate of exchange, which is the rate at which almost all imports have to be financed, fluctuates according to market conditions, but for general purposes can be considered at July 1975 to be about baht 36 per £1 sterling. The following coins are at present minted: 5 baht and 1 baht (in silver), 50, 25, 10 and 5 satang in tin, 50, 25, 10 and 5 satang in bronze (actually a copper and aluminium alloy). Notes are printed in 100, 20, 10 and 5 baht denominations.

The GNP at market prices for 1974 was U.S.$ millions 12,670, and the GNP per capita at market prices was U.S.$310. The annual average percentage growth rate of the GNP per capita for the period 1960–74 was 4·6, and for the period 1965–74 was 4·3. [*See the note at the beginning of this section concerning GNP.*]

**FINANCE**

Estimated Revenues for the fiscal year 1978 is Baht 81,000 million.

**BANKS**

**Thai**

**The Bank of Asia for Industry & Commerce.** Bangkok.

**The Bank of Ayudhya, Ltd.** Bangkok.

**The Bank of Thailand.** Est. 1942. Governor, Dr. Sanoa Unakul; Depty. Gov., Abhijai Jaiwatana. Assets as at 31 December 1974, Bt.46,535,282,605·53; deposits and current accounts, Bt.15,149,220,202·07. *Head Office:* Bang Khun Prom Palace, Bangkok. Branches, 3.

**Krung Thai Bank Ltd.** Total assets as at 31 December 1975: Baht 8,707,220,144. *Head Office:* 260 Yawaraj Road, Bangkok. A network of more than 127 Branches throughout Thailand.

**The Siam City Bank Ltd.** Bangkok.

**The Thai Danu Bank Ltd.** P.O. Box 1101, Bangkok.

**The Thai Farmers Bank Ltd.** 143 Silom Road, Bangkok.

**The Union Bank of Bangkok Ltd.** Bangkok.

**Wang Lee Bank,** 1016 Rama IV Road, Bangkok 5. Cables: 'Wanleebank', Telex: Th2837.

**Thai Military Bank Ltd.** Mansion 2, Rajdamnern Avenue, Bangkok, 2

**Laemthong Bank Ltd.** Bangkok.

**Bangkok Metropolitan Bank Ltd.** Bangkok.

**Bangkok Bank of Commerce.** Bangkok.

**The Thai Development Bank.** Assets at 31 December 1973 Baht 2,823,381,616·94. *Head Office:* 20 Yukhon Road 2, Suanmali, Bangkok.

**The Siam Commercial Bank Ltd.** 1060 New Petchburi Road, Bangkok, P.O. Box 15, Bangkok.

**British**

**The Chartered Bank** Bangkok (two offices); also Bhuket.

**The Hongkong and Shanghai Banking Corporation.** 2 Branches in Bangkok. See Hong Kong.

**Mercantile Bank Ltd.** Bangkok.

**American**

**The Bank of America** NT & SA, G.P.O. Box 158. Bangkok.

**The Chase Manhattan Bank.** Bangkok.

**French**

**Banque de l'Indochine et de Suez.** 142, Wireless Road, P.O. Box 303. Bangkok. Telephone 2522111–9. Telex: TH2546. Cable: INDOSUEZ.

**Chinese**

**The International Commercial Bank of China.** Bangkok Branch, 95 Suapa Road, Bangkok.

**The Bank of Canton Ltd.** (Manager: C.Y. Sun). 1911 Silom Road, Bangkok 5.

**Four Seas Communications Bank Ltd.** Bangkok.

**Indian**

**Bharat Overseas Bank.** Bangkok.

**Japanese**

**The Mitsui Bank Ltd.** Bangkok.

**The Bank of Tokyo Ltd.** (Manager, Kiyohiko Wada.) 62 Thaniya Building, Silom Road, Bangkok.

**Malayan**

**United Malayan Banking Corporation Ltd.** Bangkok.

**PRODUCTION, INDUSTRY AND COMMERCE**

**Planning**

The First Development Plan (1962–66) achieved an annual growth rate of 7 per cent in Gross Domestic Product, the Second Plan (1967–71) aimed at an 8·5 per cent annual increase but achieved a 6·6 per cent increase. The Third Plan (1971–76) was initiated in October 1971, and aimed at an annual growth rate of seven per cent but achieved only a six per cent increase. The Fourth Plan (1977–1981) aims at a seven per cent increase in real GDP.

**Agriculture.** The output figures of Thailand's natural products are: (in 1974–75) rice (13 million tons), maize (2·5 million tons), sugar cane (14·5 million tons), tapioca roots (4 million tons), kenaf and jute (360,000 tons), rubber (380,000). Exports were: rice (940,000 tons), rubber (336,000 tons), maize (2·1 million tons), tapioca products (2·4 million tons), sugar (595,000 tons), jute and kenaf (157,000 tons).

**Mining.** Tin is a staple export of Thailand. Mineral resources comprise tin, wolfram, scheelite, antimony, lignite, copper, gold, iron, lead, manganese, molybdenum, rubies, sapphires, silver, zinc and zicons. By far the most important are tin and wolfram, but iron ore will be increasingly valuable for the new smelting industry. Other metallic and radioactive minerals consist of ilmenite sands and monazite and non-metallic includes kaolin, soapstone, marble and gypsum deposits, which have been worked since 1943.

# THAILAND

Production in 1975 of the main claims were: tin (metal) 22,402 tons, lignite 462,320 tons, fluorite 286,146 tons, gypsum 254,842 tons, marl 467,500 tons, iron ore 32,476 tons, antimony ore 7,370 tons.

**Industry.** International oil companies have been granted concessions to search for oil in the Gulf of Thailand and the Andaman Sea. Drilling has been centred in certain areas and gas and oil have been located. It is still too early to say whether these exist in commercial quantities. The major industries in Thailand include textile production, cement, iron and steel, paper, plastics and oil refining. A petrochemical complex will soon be established. Special privileges are granted to investors wishing to set up certain listed industries. The tourist industry has become an important factor in the Thai economy, probably second only to rice in terms of foreign exchange earnings.

Gross National Product by Industrial Origin (Million Baht) at current prices:

| | 1976 |
|---|---|
| Agriculture | 97,138 |
| Mining and quarrying | 3,964 |
| Manufacturing | 59,529 |
| Construction | 13,791 |
| Electricity and water supply | 3,499 |
| Communication and transportation | 20,689 |
| Wholesale and retail trade | 58,797 |
| Banking, insurance and real estate | 17,563 |
| Ownership of dwellings | 4,802 |
| Public administration and Defence | 14,255 |
| Services | 31,088 |
| Gross Domestic Product | 325,112 |

**Commerce.** Imports are mainly manufactured goods, especially machinery, vehicles and construction and household equipment. Exports are mainly agricultural products, especially rice and mineral materials. Some details are given below (million baht):

| *Imports* | 1976 (*Preliminary figures*) |
|---|---|
| Food | 2,249 |
| Beverage and Tobacco | 655 |
| Crude Materials | 5,225 |
| Mineral fuels and lubricants | 16,697 |
| Animal and vegetable oils and fats | 165 |
| Chemicals | 10,511 |
| Manufactured goods | 12,142 |
| Machinery | 21,435 |
| Misc. manufactured goods | 2,882 |
| Misc. transactions and commodities | 1,037 |
| | 73,178 |

| *Exports* | 1975 |
|---|---|
| Rice | 5,773 |
| Maize | 5,614 |
| Rubber | 3,451 |
| Tapioca products (cassava) | 4,589 |
| Sugar | 5,614 |
| Tin | 2,240 |
| Jute and Kenaf | 643 |

Source: Department of Customs.

The table below shows the imports and exports by main countries in 1976 (million baht):

| | *Exports* | *Imports* |
|---|---|---|
| Japan | 15,686 | 23,649 |
| U.S.A. | 6,098 | 9,739 |
| West Germany | 1,979 | 3,469 |
| Saudi Arabia | 778 | 5,538 |
| U.K. | 980 | 2,623 |
| Netherlands | 8,064 | 815 |
| Singapore | 4,114 | 1,836 |
| Hong Kong | 3,049 | 756 |

Source: Department of Customs.

## COMMUNICATIONS

**Roads.** In 1975 there were 11,507 km. of highways, 6,197 km. of provincial roads. The North-East Highway (158 km.) was finished in 1958; the East-West Highway (130 km.), in 1960 and the Nakorn Rajsima–Hongtsi Highway in 1965.

**Railways.** In 1972 the length of track open to traffic was 3,830 kilometres. Track is metre gauge. The State railway is being enlarged and modernized.

**Shipping.** Apart from some small harbours which can accommodate coastal and fishing vessels, Thailand's only port is Bangkok, which takes ocean-going vessels of up to 12,000 tons dead weight.

Consideration is being given to the construction of a new deep water port. As an interim measure berths at the naval base of Sattahip will probably be used for commercial purposes.

**Civil Aviation.** Bangkok has a modern airport (Don Muang), about fifteen miles from the city centre, which is served by a number of international airlines, including Air Ceylon, China Air Lines, East African, Korean Airlines, Pakistan International, Sabena, Air France, Air India International, Royal Air Lao, Alitalia, Air New Zealand, Air Vietnam, B.O.A.C., Civil Air Transport, Cathay Pacific Airways, Garuda Indonesian Airways, Japan Air Lines, K.L.M., Lufthansa, Malayan Airways, P.A.A., Q.A.N.T.A.S., Royal Air Cambodge, S.A.S., Swissair, T.W.A. and Union of Burma Airways. In early 1960 the former Thai Airways Company was reorganized and a new company, Thai Airways International, was formed, with S.A.S. participation, to take over international services, leaving Thai Airways Company to operate internal service and a few routes to neighbouring countries.

**Telephones.** Thailand has some 240,000 telephone lines throughout the country. Served by automatic exchanges in the capital and other large towns and manned exchanges in remoter districts. Modernization and expansion are taking place to meet the estimated requirement of 10 years time of 300,000 lines in the area of Bangkok and 70,000 in provincial areas.

**T.A.C.—Thai Airways Company Ltd.** (Chairman, Air Chief Marshal Boonchoo Chandrubeksa; Managing Director, Lt. Cdr. Prasong Suchiva.) Share capital 300 million baht, held by the Ministry of Communications. *Services operated:* internal to most parts of Thailand and to Penang, and Vientiane. *Head Office:* 6 Larnluang Road, Bangkok.

**THAI.—Thai Airways International Ltd.** (Chairman, Air Chief Marshal Kamol Thejatunga; President, Choo Suthichot Share capital 200 million baht, 70 per cent of the shares being held by T.A.C. and 30 per cent by S.A.S. This share co-operation will end on March 31, 1977. *Services operated:* Bangkok, Bali, Calcutta, Dacca, Delhi, Djakarta, Hong Kong, Kathmandu, Kuala Lumpur, Manila, Osaka, Penang, Phnom Penh, Rangoon, Saigon, Seoul, Singapore, Sydney, Taipei, Tokyo, and Copenhagen. *Head Office:* 1043 Phaholyothin Road, Bangkok.

## NEWSPAPERS

Nine daily newspapers are published in Thai in Bangkok alone, of which *Thai Rath*, *Daily News*, *Phim Thai* and *Siam Rath* have the biggest circulations. There are also five Chinese and three English language dailies.

Periodicals are published in all three languages.

## ATOMIC ENERGY

Under President Eisenhower's 'Atoms for Peace' programme a small 'swimming pool' type reactor was established and opened in 1961. The U.S.A. contributed half the cost of it. The Electricity Generating Authority of Thailand is considering seeking tenders for Thailands first nuclear power station.

### EDUCATION

Primary education is compulsory for children from the age of 7 to 14 and is free in the public and municipal schools.

The Chulalonghorn University was founded at Bangkok in 1917 and the Thammasat University in 1934. Other universities are the University of Medical Science, founded in 1888, and more recently the University of Agriculture and the University of Fine Arts, all in Bangkok. There is also a University at Chiang Mai in North Thailand. New universities have been set up in the North-East, at Khon Kaen, and in the South at Songkhla. An Open University was established in Bangkok in 1972.

### RELIGION

The great majority of the population (93·6 per cent) is Buddhist. In 1973 3·9 per cent of the population were Moslems, 0·6 per cent Christians, and 1·9 per cent other religions.

# Republic of Togo

**Capital**—Lomé.

**President**—General Gnassingbé Eyadéma.

**National Flag:** Parti of 5 fesse-wise, alternately green and yellow; a canton red charged with a star five-pointed white.

### CONSTITUTION AND GOVERNMENT

TOGO, which lies between Dahomey and Ghana, formed part of the German colony of Togoland which was surrendered to the Allies in August 1914. After 4 years of Anglo-French administration the territory was divided and placed under League of Nations Mandate, the western part being allotted to Great Britain and the largest eastern area to France. Both areas became United Nations Trust Territories in 1946. On 24 August 1956, French Togo became a Republic with limited autonomy within the French Union. The United Nations General Assembly voted on 14 November 1958, for the abolition of the Trusteeship on the establishment of complete independence. This was achieved on 27 April 1960.

The former Prime Minister, Sylvanus Olympio, was elected as President and a new Constitution adopted on 9 April 1961. On 13 January 1963, Olympio was assassinated by a group of army officers. The National Assembly was dissolved and the Constitution suspended by the provisional Government of Nicolas Grunitzky. Grunitzky became President on 10 May 1963, when a new Constitution and National Assembly came into force. Political difficulties led to the overthrow of Grunitzky himself by the army on 13 January 1967. Political activity was suspended by the National Reconciliation Committee which ran the country for 3 months until the Commander-in-Chief of the Togolese army, Lt. Colonel (later General) Gnassingbé Eyadéma named himself President on 14 April. In May 1967 it was agreed that all former political parties would cease their political activities. A Constitutional Committee was established to advise on the future constitution of the country, and on the eventual return to civilian rule. A single political party, the Rassemblement du Peuple Togolais, was formerly inaugurated in November 1970. General Eyadéma was confirmed as President by a referendum held in January 1972.

The territory is divided into four geographical regions: the maritime, the plateau, the central and the savanna. Each of these regions is divided into Administrative Districts of which there are 18 in the whole country.

Criminal justice is administered by a Court of Assize at Lomé and three Justices of the Peace. Civil cases are dealt with by a Court of First Instance at Lomé, a First Degree Tribunal seated at the chief town of each sub-district and a Second Degree Tribunal for each District.

### AREA AND POPULATION

Togo's area is 56,600 sq. km.

The population of the country (mid-1974) is 2,176,000, and that of Lomé, the capital 214,200.

The annual average percentage growth rate of the population for the period 1960–74 was 2·7, and for the period 1965–74 was also 2·7.

The population is divided into three basic ethnic groups: in the south, the Ewe, Mina and Ouatchi (550,000); in the central region, the Akposso-Adele (60,000); and in the north, the Kabre (600,000). There are, however, at least 27 different kinds of tribal groups. There also are about 2,000 Europeans in the country.

### FINANCE

The budget for the year 1975 was balanced at C.F.A. francs 30,514,684,000 which represents a massive increase of about 88 per cent over the preceding years budget due to increased revenue from the government-run phosphate-mining industry.

The GNP at market prices for 1974 was U.S.$ millions 550. and the GNP per capita at market prices was U.S.$250. The annual average percentage growth rate of the GNP per capita for the period 1960–74 was 4·4, and for the period 1965–74 was 2·8. [*See the note at the beginning of this section concerning GNP.*]

### PRODUCTION, INDUSTRY AND COMMERCE

Togo's economy is based principally on agriculture. The principal products are cocoa, coffee, palm oil, palm kernels, cotton and groundnuts. Vegetables, manioc, maize, yams and rice are grown for local consumption. The principal money earner is, however, phosphate, which through the five-fold increase in world prices accounted for 80 per cent of export earnings in 1974. Coffee and cocoa are the principal agricultural products exported which between them account for about 85 per cent of total exports.

In 1974, a total of more than 2·4 million tons of phosphates were exported, valued at C.F.A. francs 34,533 million.

The following table shows values of principal exports for 1973 and 1974 (million fr. C.F.A.):

| *Commodity* | 1973 | 1974 |
|---|---|---|
| Tapioca | 183 | 163 |
| Raw coffee | 1,789 | 1,970 |
| Groundnuts | — | — |
| Copra | 3 | 5 |
| Phosphates | 6,266 | 34,533 |
| Cocoa | 3,556 | 5,363 |
| Cotton, shelled | 274 | 357 |
| Cotton seeds | 36 | 53 |
| Palm kernels | 210 | 610 |
| Manioc | 8 | 139 |
| Total Exports | 12,325 | 45,174 |

# Tonga

(MEMBER OF THE COMMONWEALTH)

**Capital**—Nuku'alofa.

**Sovereign**—His Majesty King Taufa'ahau Tupou IV.

**National Flag**: Red with a white square canton, bearing a red cross centred in the canton.

## CONSTITUTION AND GOVERNMENT

Tonga is an independent, constitutional monarchy. Its constitution dates from 1875, with relatively little amendment, and is based on the British model, providing for a Government consisting of the Sovereign, a Privy Council and Cabinet, a Legislative Assembly and a Judiciary.

The chief executive body is the Privy Council, presided over by the Sovereign and comprising the Prime Minister and five other Ministers and the Governors of Vava'u and Ha'apai. The Privy Council advises the Sovereign on affairs of State and in intervals between meetings of the legislature makes ordinances which become law if confirmed by the next meeting of the legislature. Lesser executive decisions are taken by the Cabinet, which consists of the Privy Council members, presided over by the Prime Minister. The unicameral Legislative Assembly consists of a Speaker appointed by the Sovereign; the eight Privy Councillors, *ex officio*; seven nobles elected by their 33 hereditary peers and seven representatives elected by the people for a three-year-term.

## LOCAL GOVERNMENT

Town and district officers are elected by the people. Town officers represent the Central Government in a village and district officers have authority over a group of villages.

## LEGAL SYSTEM

Tongan courts consist of a Land Court, which hears all land claims; the Magistrates' Courts, which hear minor civil and criminal cases, and a Supreme Court, which exercises jurisdiction in major civil and criminal cases. The Privy Council, with the addition of the Chief Justice, sits as Court of Appeal. Judges are appointed by the Sovereign-in-Council.

## AREA AND POPULATION

The area of Tonga is 270 sq. miles (700 sq. km.) including inland waters. The largest inhabited islands are Tongatapu (99·2 sq. miles or 257 sq. km.), Vava'u (34·6 sq. miles or 89·7 sq. km.), 'Eua (33·7 sq. miles or 87·3 sq. km.) and Lifuka (4·6 sq. miles or 11·8 sq. km.).

The population at mid-1974 was 97,000. The annual average percentage growth rate of the population for the period 1960–74 was 3·3 and for the period 1965–74 was 3·0.

## CURRENCY AND FINANCE

The unit of currency is the pa'anga ($T), divided into 100 seniti. Tonga changed to decimal currency in April 197 and now uses its own coinage. As at June 1977 the rate of exchange was £1 sterling to $T 1·55.

The following table shows revenue and expenditure for the period 1974–77:

| | *Revenue* $T'000 | *Expenditure* $T'000 |
|---|---|---|
| 1974–75 | 5,530 | 4,772 |
| 1975–76 | 5,054 | 5,873 |
| 1976–77 | 6,261 | 6,789 |

The principal sources of recurrent revenue are Income tax, Import and export dues, port and service tax, commission charges and postal and philatelic revenue. Public debt as at 30 June 1976 amounted to T$1,798,000. The Bank of Tonga opened 1 July, 1974, and now carries out all trading bank and savings bank activities in the Kingdom.

## PRODUCTION, INDUSTRY AND COMMERCE

The economy of Tonga is based mainly on agriculture. In 1975–76 the Gross Domestic Product was T$25,000,000. Most people engage in agriculture and fishing. Principal exports are copra and bananas. The visible trade balance is normally in deficit: the size of this deficit being influenced by the world price of copra. Invisible earnings, chiefly Remittances from Abroad, and Tourism, have until recently more than off-set the invisible deficit. However, world economic conditions in the last few years have changed this pattern resulting in deficits on balance of payments. A Five Year Development Plan was inaugurated in 1975, financed largely by external aid, to stimulate local industry—mainly, import substitution. A commercial bank is already well established and a development bank, aided by the Asian Development Bank, is being established this year (1977).

The following table shows values of principal imports for 1975 and 1976 (T$):

| *Commodity* | 1975 | 1976 |
|---|---|---|
| Flour | 751,629 | 697,561 |
| Timber (dressed and undressed) | 844,204 | 597,634 |
| Diesoline | 293,534 | 494,493 |
| Road motor vehicles | 693,863 | 487,439 |
| Mutton etc. | 417,499 | 473,919 |
| Motor spirit and aviation gasoline | 279,334 | 439,378 |
| Meat in airtight containers | 384,030 | 439,133 |
| Beef | 478,380 | 386,614 |
| Cigarettes | 392,265 | 381,749 |
| Cement | 270,114 | 280,870 |
| Finished structural parts n.e.s. (of iron, steel, aluminium etc.) | 316,674 | 253,719 |
| Kerosene | — | 247,597 |
| Sugar | 246,825 | 247,521 |
| Electric power machinery and switchgear | — | 232,098 |
| Beer, ale, stout | 275,368 | 225,304 |
| Soaps, and other washing preparations | 202,607 | 187,920 |
| Machinery and appliances (other than electrical) | 260,497 | 175,393 |
| Paints, pigment, varnishes | — | 174,367 |
| All articles made of paper | 175,322 | 163,594 |
| Ships and boats | — | 159,224 |
| Textile fabrics, woven and other than cotton fabrics | 167,897 | 153,855 |
| Total | 6,450,042 | 6,899,382 |

The following table shows value of imports and exports by principal countries for 1976 in T$:

| *Country* | *Imports* 1976 | *Exports* 1976 |
|---|---|---|
| Netherlands | — | 994,521 |
| New Zealand | 4,665,803 | 981,995 |
| Australia | 2,599,551 | — |
| West Germany | — | 704,522 |
| United Kingdom | 1,271,391 | 203,291 |
| Japan | 686,980 | — |
| Fiji | 609,627 | 178,305 |
| Singapore | 584,099 | — |
| U.S.A. | 370,610 | — |
| Iran | 246,982 | — |
| Hong Kong | 204,547 | — |
| China (Mainland) | 79,211 | — |
| Switzerland | 42,025 | — |
| India | 28,008 | — |
| China (Taiwan) | 23,666 | — |
| Pakistan | 22,878 | — |

**Agriculture and Fishing.** Among the products grown for local consumption are yams, taro, cassava, groundnuts, sweet potatoes, vegetables, maize, tobacco, sugar-cane, avocado pears, pineapples, water melons, mangoes and citrus fruits. Since the growing of vanilla began in 1968, a quantity has been exported. A coconut rehabilitation scheme was started in 1965 to increase the production of copra; this is a ten-year project covering rehabilitation, clearance and replanting. After the record banana production of 1967–68, the plantations were severely damaged by storms and diseases and production fell to less than half. The Government is carrying out measures to control and eradicate such pests as banana scab moth and the coconut pest, the rhinoceros beetle. Because rats damage the majority of crops the Government began in 1970 a programme of rodent research and control.

Although there has been little commercial development of the fishing industry, the abundant supply of fish in Tongan waters is an important source of food. There is some deep sea fishing. Limited areas of forest on 'Eua and Vava'u supply timber for local use and consideration is being given to the development of forest resources. The major types of livestock are pigs, goats and poultry, but the number of heads of cattle kept are increasing, thereby reducing beef imports. Horses are kept for domestic use.

**Minerals.** Oil seepages were confirmed on 'Eua and Tongatapu in 1968. In 1970 a consortium of foreign oil companies was formed to carry out land and off-shore exploration but so far there have been no significant strikes. Otherwise no minerals have been discovered.

**Manufacturing.** Import replacement type industries are showing a recent modest growth and include roofing materials fencing, furniture, biscuits, lumber, baking, prefabrecated housing, pipe, soft drinks, meat processing and sandals. Export oriented industries are limited to desiccated coconut, coconut buttons and consumer charcoal. Handicraft items include tapa cloth, wood carvings, mats, baskets and shell jewellery.

**Tourism.** Tourism is relatively small, but growing. It experienced a 15 per cent annual growth during the recent world-wide recession. Modern accommodation is adequate and emphasis is being placed on transportation facilities.

## COMMUNICATIONS

**Roads.** At the end of 1971 there were 148 miles (237 km.) of sealed and gravel road on Tongatapu; 44 miles (70·4 km.) on Vava'u; 11 miles (17·6 km.) on Ha'apal and 9 miles (14·5 Km.) on 'Eua, as well as many miles of unsurfaced road and track. Excluding agricultural tractors etc., there were 1,652 registered motor vehicles.

**Ports.** Nuku'alofa and Neifu are the ports of call for regular passengers and cargo services from New Zealand via Fiji. At both these ports vessels can tie up at the wharf. At Pangai on Lifuka, which is a port of entry for copra collection, ships anchor about a mile from the jetty. The Pacific Navigation Company of Tonga, maintains regular inter-island and external services. Vessels of the Bank Line call every six weeks to load copra for Britain and the continent.

**Air.** Air Pacific (formerly Fiji Airways), in which Tonga has a 2 per cent interest, operates four services a week between Fiji and Tonga, one via Western Samoa. Polynesian Airlines also fly three services a week from Western Samoa to Tonga. The airport is at Fua'amotu, 14 miles (22·4 km.) from Nuku'alofa. An airstrip on Vava'u and 'Eua are now in use for flights to and from Nuku'alofa.

**Telecommunications.** A Government station at Nuku'alofa operates radio telegraph and radio telephone links with Suva and internally with 'Eua, Nomuka, Haafeva, Ha'apai, Vava'u, Niuatoputapu and Niuafo'ou. There is a manual telephone exchange in Nuku'alofa.

**Broadcasting.** A local broadcasting station (A3Z) was opened at Nuku'alofa in 1961. Known as the 'Call of the Friendly Islands', it is under the control of the Tonga Broadcasting Commission. Broadcasts in Tongan and English can be heard in New Zealand, Fiji, Norfolk Island, Western Samoa, Niue, the Gilbert and Ellice Islands and throughout the Kingdom of Tonga.

## EDUCATION

Education is compulsory for children between the ages of six and 14. Primary education is free but fees are payable at secondary schools. In 1971 there were 186 schools, 87 of which were run by Government and 99 by church 'missions'. Of the 26,871 pupils enrolled, 16,416 were at primary schools. Apart from three Government schools, the majority of post-primary education is provided by the missions. Several post-primary schools include agriculture and practical subjects in the curriculum. Five schools prepare candidates for the New Zealand School Certificate and the Tonga High School prepares candidates for the New Zealand University Entrance. A Government scholarship scheme provides for some Tongan students to receive higher education abroad, chiefly in Australia, New Zealand and Fiji; in 1970 approximately 150 students were in schools or under training overseas. H.M. King Taufa'ahau Tupou IV is the first Chancellor of the regional University of the South Pacific and Fiji.

# Trinidad and Tobago

(MEMBER OF THE COMMONWEALTH)

**Capital**—Port of Spain.

**President**—H. E. Sir Ellis Clarke, TC, GCMG.

**National Flag**: On a red field a Bend Dexter Sable bordered Silver.

## CONSTITUTION AND GOVERNMENT

THE Island of Trinidad lies seven miles to the eastward of Venezuela and is separated from South America by the Gulf of Paria, into which fall the northern mouths of the Orinoco. It was discovered by Columbus on 31 July 1498, but was not colonized by the Spanish until the middle of the sixteenth century. On 18 February 1797 it was captured from the Spaniards by a British expedition and was finally ceded to the Crown of Great Britain in 1802.

The Island of Tobago (formerly in the Windward Islands) amalgamated with Trinidad on 1 January 1889.

Trinidad and Tobago attained fully responsible status within the Commonwealth on 31 August, by virtue of the Trinidad and Tobago Independence Act, 1962. An Order made under the Act provides for a new Constitution for Trinidad and Tobago, with effect from that date, including provision for the executive government, the legislature, the judicature and the public service. The Constitution also contains provisions relating to citizenship of Trinidad and Tobago and fundamental rights and freedoms of the individual.

Parliament consists of the Senate and the House of Representatives. The House of Representatives is composed of 36 members elected by universal suffrage. The Senate consists of 24 members appointed by the Governor-General. Of these 13 are appointed on the advice of the Prime Minister, four on the advice of the Leader of the Opposition and seven on the advice of the Prime Minister after consultation by him with those religious, economic or social bodies or associations from which he considers that such Senators should be selected.

The Prime Minister presides over the Cabinet.

The life of Parliament is five years from the date of its first sitting following a General Election. Parliament may be prorogued or dissolved at any time by the Governor-General, acting in accordance with the advice of the Prime Minister. A General Election must be held within three months of a dissolution.

The following human rights and fundamental freedoms exist without discrimination by reason of race, origin, colour, religion or sex:

(*a*) the right of the individual to life, liberty, security of the person and enjoyment of property, and the right not to be deprived thereof except by due process of law; (*b*) the right of the individual to equality before the law and the protection of the law; (*c*) the right of the individual to respect for his private and family life; (*d*) the right of the individual to equality of treatment from any public authority in the exercise of any functions; (*e*) the right to join political parties and to express political views; (*f*) the right of a parent or guardian to provide a school of his own choice for the education of his child or ward; (*g*) freedom of movement; (*h*) freedom of conscience and religious belief and observance; (*i*) freedom of thought and expression; (*j*) freedom of association and assembly; and (*k*) freedom of the press.

Trinidad and Tobago is divided for administrative purpose into seven counties—the counties of St. George, Caroni, Victoria, St. Patrick, St. Andrew and St. Davis, Nariva and Mayaro and the island ward of Tobago. There is an elected County Council for each district.

The Peoples National Movement (P.N.M.) headed by Dr. the Rt. Hon. Eric Williams, won all of the 36 Seats in the Trinidad and Tobago General Elections on 24 May 1971 and formed the Government for the fourth successive term since it took Office in 1956. Two other political parties, and two Independents contested. The former D.L.P., merged with the newly formed A.C.D.C., did not contest.

It was the third General Election held in Trinidad and Tobago in which the electorate recorded their votes by machines and the first since the country attained Independence on 31 August 1962.

On 1 August 1976 Trinidad and Tobago became a republic under the new republican Constitution, the British Sovereign will be replaced as head of state by a president elected in secret ballot by members of both houses of parliament.

### Cabinet

*Prime Minister, Minister of External Affairs, Minister of West Indian Affairs:* Dr. the Rt. Hon. Eric Eustace Williams.
*Minister in charge of administration and operation of External Affairs, West Indian Affairs:* Hon. Dr. Cuthbert Joseph.
*Minister of Industry and Commerce:* Hon. Errol Mahabir.
*Minister of National Security:* Hon. Overand R. Padmore.
*Minister of Labour:* Hon. Hector McLean.
*Minister of Health and Local Government:* Hon. Kamaluddin Mohammed.
*Minister of Public Utilities:* Hon. Sham Mohammed.
*Minister of Agriculture, Land and Fisheries:* Lionel Robinson.
*Minister of Works:* Victor Campbell.
*Minister for Tobago Affairs:* Hon. W. Winchester.
*Minister of Finance:* G. Chambers.
*Minister without Portfolio and Special Adviser to the Prime Minister:* Dr. C. Joseph.
*Minister of Education and Culture:* Hon. Carlton Gomes.
*Minister of Legal Affairs, and Attorney-General:* Hon. Basil Pitt.
*Minister of Planning and Development and Minister of Housing:* Hon. Brensley Barrow.

## AREA AND POPULATION

Trinidad has an area of 1,864 sq. miles and Tobago 116 sq. miles.

The population of Trinidad and Tobago at mid-1974 was 1,070,000. The principal towns with population are: Port of Spain, 93,954; San Fernando, 39,830; Arima, 10,982.

The white population is chiefly English, Portuguese, French and Spanish. There is also a large number of East Indians (36 per cent at 1960 census).

The annual average percentage growth rate of the population for the period 1960–74 was 1·6 and for the period 1965–74 was 0·9.

## FINANCE

The unit of currency is the Trinidad and Tobago dollar. (T. & T. $4·8 = £1.)

| | 1971 | 1972 | 1973 |
|---|---|---|---|
| Revenue | $342,100,000 | $518,800,000 | $591,300,000 |
| Expenditure | $472,900,000 | $519,700,000 | $573,500,000 |

Under the customs tariff British goods enjoy a preference ranging from 50 per cent to 75 per cent or even higher on certain types of goods. There is an export duty on asphalt of $1·20 per ton (crude) and $1·66 per ton (refined).

The GNP at market prices for 1974 was U.S. $ millions 1,810. and the GNP per capita at market prices was U.S. $1,700. The annual average percentage growth rate of the GNP per capita for the period 1960–74 was 2·1 and for the period 1965–74 was 2·2. [*See the note at the beginning of this section concerning GNP.*]

## BANK

**Central Bank of Trinidad and Tobago.** (Governor and Chairman of Board, Victor E. Bruce.) *Head Office:* St. Vincent Street, Port-of-Spain, Trinidad and Tobago, West Indies.

Statement of Assets and Liabilities as at 30 June 1976.

| | |
|---|---|
| *Assets* | |
| Cash and Banks | 1,654,931,012 |
| Investments | 545,577,351 |
| Loans and Discounts | 231,643 |
| Other Assets | 185,386,209 |
| Total | 2,386,126,215 |
| *Liabilities* | |
| Deposits | 1,979,616,181 |
| Other Liabilities | 238,704,949 |
| Capital | 3,000,000 |
| Surplus Profits and Reserves | 164,805,085 |
| Total | 2,386,126,215 |

## PRODUCTION, INDUSTRY AND COMMERCE

The chief agricultural crops are sugar cane (102,000 acres), caco (80,000 acres), coconuts (40,000 acres) and citrus fruits (14,500 acres).

Attempts were made in the 1920s and 1930s to set up a dairy farming industry, but they met with little success due to lack of grazing grass. In 1953, however, the first plants of Pangola grass were introduced into Trinidad, and by 1959 it was established as a good pasture grass. As a result, interest in cattle is being revived and emphasis is being placed on the development of dairying. In addition, advances have been made in the knowledge of cattle management and a beef industry is emerging based on Pangola grass grazing.

The chief mineral products are asphalt, obtained from the asphalt lake at La Brea, petroleum and natural gas. In 1974, 81,574 long tons of asphalt were produced.

The value of the principal imports and exports during 1973 are shown below (million $):

| *Commodity* | *Imports* | *Exports* |
|---|---|---|
| Food | 154·0 | 85·2 |
| Beverages and tobacco | 11·3 | 10·8 |
| Crude materials | 19·6 | 6·7 |
| Mineral fuels, lubricants etc. | 789·5 | 1,131·3 |
| of which Processing Agreement | 761·7 | 678·8 |
| Animal and vegetable oils and fats | 11·1 | 0·4 |
| Chemicals | 84·2 | 75·9 |
| Manufactured goods | 213·1 | 21·6 |
| Machinery and transport equipment | 206·5 | 13·2 |
| Miscellaneous manufacturers | 61·8 | 26·6 |
| Miscellaneous transactions | 5·6 | 3·6 |
| Total | 1,556·8 | 1,375·3 |

## COMMUNICATIONS

The old railway of 109 miles in length has been recently replaced by road transport.

Government coastal steamers maintain regular services, ships called at Trinidad from Canadian, American and South American ports, Europe, South Africa and Australia. Over 6,000 ships enter the harbours of Trinidad and Tobago every year with a total net registered tonnage of approximately 23,000,000.

Regular air services are maintained by the following eight Airlines: British West Indian Airways, Ltd., Pan American World Airways Inc., Linea Aeropostal Venezolana, K.L.M. (Royal Dutch Airlines), Air France, Aerolineas Argentinas, B.O.A.C., Trans Canada Airlines. There are two International Airports, one at Piarco in Trinidad and one at Crown Point near Scarborough, the chief town of Tobago.

**BWIA—British West Indian Airways Limited.** (Chairman, D. Alleyne; Managing Director, S-E. Svanberg.) Share capital, paid up $2,700,000; *services operated:* Trinidad–Tobago – Guyana – Barbados – St. Lucia – Antigua – Puerto Rico – Jamaica – Miami – New York – Toronto – Guadeloupe – London. *Head Office:* Kent House, Long Circular Road, Maraval, P.O. Box, 604, Port of Spain, Trinidad.

## NEWSPAPERS

**Trinidad Guardian.** Est. 1917. Daily. 22 St. Vincent St., Port of Spain.

**Trinidad and Tobago Express.** 35 Independence Square, Port of Spain.

There are two daily, one evening, one Sunday, and five weekly newspapers.

## EDUCATION

The system of education is being reformed to co-ordinate more closely the interlocking levels—Primary, Post-Primary/Secondary and Higher. The system will provide for education of the pupils from five to 12 in Primary Schools—456 at present—and from 12 plus to 18 in a present total of 36 Government and Assisted Secondary Schools—Grammar, Modern and two Technical. There are also about 55 recognized Private Secondary Schools.

Figures for 1970–71 of a Primary and intermediate enrolment amount to 228,319.

The Government Polytechnic Institute was established in 1959. Four Science laboratories for the Institute are built and are in use.

Of the three training colleges for teachers, two are in Port of Spain. One is Government maintained, one Roman Catholic and one Presbyterian.

## RELIGION

Of the Christian population, the Roman Catholic and Anglican communities are by far the largest, having followings of 36 per cent and 21 per cent respectively of the total population of the country. The non-Christian element is almost entirely Hindu or Moslem.

# The Republic of Tunisia

**Capital**—Tunis.

**President of the Republic**—M. Habib Bourguiba.

**National Flag:** Red, on a white disk centred, a crescent and star five-pointed red.

## CONSTITUTION AND GOVERNMENT

TUNISIA was formerly a French Protectorate. The State was granted Home Rule in 1955, and Independence in 1956. The President is assisted by an Advisory Body, The Council of the Republic.

On 25 March 1956, the first general elections took place. These resulted in the return of the National Front who secured all the 98 seats of the (then) Constituent Assembly. On 8 April the Bourguiba Government was formed with M. Habib Bourguiba as Prime Minister. On 13 April, the Constituent Assembly adopted Article 1 of the new Tunisian Constitution which is as follows:

'Tunisia is a free, independent, and sovereign State, Islamic in religion and Arabic in language. Sovereignty, which will be defined in the new Constitution, rests legally with the Tunisian people. The State assures freedom of religious belief and protection of religious expression, in conformity with the spirit of the law.'

On 25 July 1957, the Tunisian National Assembly (so-called since the abolition of the Monarchy) unanimously decided to abolish the monarchy, to proclaim Tunisia a Republic and to appoint the Prime Minister, M. Habib Bourguiba, the Head of State and President of the Republic. The former Cabinet tendered its resignation collectively, and on 30 July a new Government was formed. M. Bourguiba was re-elected President in 1959, 1964, 1969, and 1974. In March 1975 M. Bourguiba's election as President for life was ratified by the National Assembly.

### Government (June 1975)

*Prime Minister:* Hédi Nouira.
*Minister délégué in the Prime Minister's office:* Mohamed Sayah.
*Secretary of State in the Prime Minister's office responsible for Information:* Mustapha Masmoudi.
*Minister of Justice:* Slaheddine Baly.
*Minister of Foreign Affairs:* Habib Chatti.
*Minister of the Interior:* Tahar Belkhodja.
*Minister of National Defence:* Abdallah Farhat.
*Minister of Finance:* Mohamed Fitouri.
*Minister of National Economy:* Abdelaziz Lasram.
*Minister of Agriculture:* Hassan Belkhodja.
*Minister of National Education:* Mohamed M'Zali.
*Minister of Public Health:* Mongi Kooli.
*Minister of Cultural Affairs:* Mahmoud Messadi.
*Minister of Transport and Communications:* Abdelhamid Sassi.
*Minister of Social Affairs:* Mohamed Ennaceur.
*Minister of Youth and Sport:* Fouad M'Bazaa.
*Minister of Equipment:* Lassaad Ben Osman.
*Secretary of State in the Prime Minister's office, responsible for the Plan:* Mustapha Zaanouni.
*Secretary of State to the Minister of Defence:* Ahmed Bennour.
*Secretary of State to the Minister of National Education:* Hedi Zghal.
*Secretary of State to the Minister for Foreign Affairs:* Brahim Turki.
*Secretary of State to the Minister of Equipment:* Larbi Mellakh.
*Secretary-General of the Government:* Moncef Belhadj Amor.

## LEGAL SYSTEM

In 1956 a number of reforms were made in the legal system which include a redisposition of the legal status of women. The most important is the abolition of polygamy which is now a criminal offence. Men polygamously married before the change in the law are exempt from its provisions.

The civil and criminal codes closely follow the French pattern but they have been supplemented by local legislation to suit the needs of the country. At the end of 1964 legislation was enacted to govern rights to real property.

## AREA AND POPULATION

The area of the country is 63,378 sq. miles. The number of Europeans in the country has increased rapidly over the past few years, and it is estimated that there are now about 40,000, living mainly in Tunis.

The population at mid-1974 was 5,460,000. The annual average percentage growth rate of the population for the period 1960–74 was 2·2 and for the period 1965–74 was 2·3.

The capital is Tunis with a population of 1,127,000. Other important towns and populations are Sfax, 482,000; Sousse, 586,000; Bizerta, 316,000, and the Moslem holy city of Kairouan, 302,000.

## CURRENCY AND FINANCE

The GNP at market prices for 1974 was U.S.$ millions 3,560, and the GNP per capita at market prices was U.S.$650. The annual average percentage growth rate of the GNP per capita for the period 1960–74 was 3·9, and for the period 1965–74 was 5·4. [*See the note at the beginning of this section concerning GNP.*]

The unit of currency is the dinar = 1,000 millines.

Attempts are also being made to encourage foreign investment in the country. The 1972 Investment Law, which gives benefits to companies manufacturing for export, has already attracted foreign investors mainly within the textile industry.

Although tourism suffered setbacks in 1973–74, 1975 was a record year for tourism with over a million visitors. However the upward trend from 1973 has levelled off and the 1976 figure is expected to be lower than the 1975 figure. However, crude oil exports remain the countries' principal foreign exchange earner.

## BANKS

**Banque Centrale de Tunisie.** (Governor, Mohamed Ghenima Mathari.) Est. 1958. Has the sole right to issue notes. *Head Office:* 7, Place de la Monnaie, Tunis. Branches in Bizerta, Sousse and Sfax.

**Société Tunisienne de Banque.** (President, M. Hassan Belkhodja.) Est. 1958. Société Anonyme; Capital 2,000,000 dinars; reserves 2,000,000 dinars. *Head office,* Avenue Habib Thameur, Tunis. Branches in Tunisia, France and Lebanon.

## PRODUCTION, INDUSTRY AND COMMERCE

Agriculture is of first importance in Tunisia. Although the interior is hot and dry all the year round, spring and autumn in the north are very mild and pleasant, and the winter normally brings rain. Olives, the production of olive oil, is the country's largest cash crop. Dates and wine are also important export earners. Vegetables are grown both for home consumption and for export.

The forest area in the north-west of the country is dense and includes oak, corkwood and pine trees. Many of the plains are thickly covered with esparto grass.

Fisheries are also important, especially in connection with tunny and sponges. Tunisian sponge production is the second highest in the whole of the Mediterranean.

Tunisia has some mineral wealth. Phosphates and iron ore are now the most important minerals. Lead and zinc are also found. Oil has recently been discovered, in relatively small quantities. Oil production in 1973 was in the region of four million tons which rose to five million tons in 1975 but dropped again in 1976 to 3·7 million tons due to a fall in pressure of the Asphalt field. During 1974 sizeable natural gas discoveries were made, mainly offshore, in the Gulf of Gabes.

Tunisian industry is based mainly on mining and agriculture. New industries are being developed, mainly to cover domestic demands for refined petroleum products, sugar textile, steel. Some light industries are also being developed Tourism is being developed rapidly and by 1966 had become the principle foreign exchange earner.

The principal commodities include phosphate of lime, iron ore, lead ore, zinc ore, refined lead, cement, lime, and electricity.

As far as overseas commerce is concerned the bulk of Tunisia's trade is still with France. The following table shows imports by continents for 1975 (in dinars):

| Continent | 1975 |
|---|---|
| Africa | 11,385,749 |
| America | 62,974,227 |
| Asia | 49,996,590 |
| Europe | 445,536,750 |
| Oceania | 1,928,982 |

The following table shows exports by continent for 1975:

| Continent | Value (in dinars) 1975 |
|---|---|
| Africa | 36,755,948 |
| America | 36,796,050 |
| Asia | 8,713,602 |
| Europe | 259,875,917 |

Total exports from Tunisia in 1975 amounted to 345,580,423 Tunisian Dinars. Imports totalled 572,814,710 dinars.

The following table shows the values for a selection of imports for 1974:

| Commodity | Value (in thousand dinars) 1974 |
|---|---|
| Cattle | 3,167 |
| Milk | 4,866 |
| Wheat and mixed wheat and rye | 17,949 |
| Soya bean oil | 15,562 |
| Sugar | 24,299 |
| Crude oil and petrol | 32,287 |
| Timber | 17,033 |
| Textiles | 17,056 |
| Chassis, bodies and trucks | 10,357 |

The following table gives the area given over to certain types of cereal production for the years 1972 and 1973:

| Crop | Th. of hectares 1972 | 1973 |
|---|---|---|
| Hard Wheat (which contains more protein than soft wheat) | 862 | 865 |
| Soft Wheat | 260 | 275 |
| Barley | 385 | 400 |

The following table shows the quantity produced, in millions of metric tonnes, of certain types of cereal for the years 1972 and 1973:

| Crop | millions of metric tons 1972 | 1973 |
|---|---|---|
| Hard Wheat (which contains more protein than soft wheat) | 652 | 490 |
| Soft Wheat | 262 | 200 |
| Barley | 236 | 210 |

The following table shows values of principal exports for 1974:

| Commodity | Value (in thousand dinars) 1974 |
|---|---|
| Olive oil | 70,335 |
| Phosphates and natural calcium | 46,847 |
| Crude petroleum oil | 136,904 |
| Phosphoric acid | 15,636 |
| Super phosphates | 33,845 |

## COMMUNICATIONS

There are approximately 1,900 km. of railway lines being operated by the Société National des Chemins de Fer Tunisiens (S.N.C.F.T.).

The Tunisian road network covers about 15,000 kilometres of which nearly 9,000 km. are paved.

Tunis-La Goulette is the main port. Other major ports are Sfax, Sousse and Bizerta.

**Tunis Air** is the principal airline (Director General: M. A. Zenaidi). Share capital nominal: 900,000 Tunisian Dinars. *Services operated:* Tunis–Paris, London, Nice, Marseilles, Algiers, Rome, Casablanca, Geneva, Luxembourg, Frankfurt, Djerba, Tripoli. *Head Office:* 47, Rue Ave Farhat Hached, Tunis.

## EDUCATION

With more than half her population under the age of 20, Tunisia is currently devoting about one-third of her ordinary government expenditure to education. For the 1973–4 scholastic year, there are 918,100 pupils in primary schools and 182,499 in secondary schools. The University of Tunis, with faculties of Arts, Theology, Science, Medicine, Law, Politics and Economics, and a number of other institutes and schools of higher studies, were estimated to have in 1973–4 a total enrolment of more than 12,000 students.

## RELIGION

The vast majority of the inhabitants are Moslems, and there is a Moslem university at Tunis. The Europeans are mostly Roman Catholic. The Greek Church has a few adherents and there is a small Jewish community.

# Turkey

(TÜRKIYE CÜMHURIYETI)

**Capital**—Ankara.

**Head of State**—President Fahri Korutürk.

**National Flag:** Red, charged towards the hoist with a crescent white, horns to the fly, and between them, a star of the same five-pointed.

## CONSTITUTION AND GOVERNMENT

TURKEY was proclaimed a Republic in 1923. The proclamation followed the Turkish 'War of Independence', waged by Mustafa Kemal against the Allied Forces of occupation. With the Allied victory of 1918, the old Ottoman Empire crumbled to pieces, and the objective of the Turkish resistance movement was to preserve that part of the Empire which was essentially Turkish. This was achieved at the signing of the Peace Treaty at Lausanne in July 1923. Mustafa Kemal became the Republic's first President, and a new Constitution was adopted the following year.

It introduced the first of the revolutionary changes, that, during the next ten years, were to sweep away all traces of the former Ottoman Code and bring Turkey into line with the Western Democracies. Religious affairs were separated from the State, schools were made co-educational, the fez and the veil were abolished, the Swiss civil code, adopted almost in its entirety, freed marriage, divorce and inheritance from Islamic law, and Turkish women achieved social equality with men. Other innovations included the introduction of an alphabet based on Latin characters in place of the Arabic script, and gave women the right to vote and to stand for election to the Grand National Assembly.

Under the 1924 Constitution the Grand National Assembly was chosen every four years at a general election and, following the introduction of a multi-party régime in 1945, Parliament evolved along the lines of a multi-party system. From the date of the first presidency of Mustafa Kemal (afterwards named 'Atatürk' or 'Father of the Turks') the Republican People's Party (R.P.P.) ruled uninterruptedly until the elections of 14 May 1950, when the Democratic Party (D.P.), which had been formed in 1945, was returned to power with an overwhelming majority. It retained power in the elections of 1954 and again in 1957, when its majority was substantially reduced.

Political tension between the D.P. and the main Opposition party, the P.R.P., greatly increased after 1957, the latter party accusing the Government of various irregularities in the 1957 elections and of generally adopting dictatorial policies incompatible with a democratic régime. Matters came to a head in the Spring of 1960 when the D.P. majority in the Grand National Assembly voted widespread powers (generally regarded as unconstitutional) for an Investigation Commission composed of 15 Government deputies, whose task was to investigate the 'illegal and subversive' activities of the Opposition and of certain sections of the Press. Martial law was proclaimed in the two main cities of Ankara and Istanbul on 28 April following anti-government student demonstrations, but these continued sporadically in both cities during May. On 27 May the Armed Forces intervened, overthrew the D.P. Government and assumed power through the Committee of National Unity (C.N.U.), a body consisting of 38 officers presided over by General Cemal Gürsel, as Head of State, Prime Minister and Commander-in-Chief. The C.N.U. replaced the Grand National Assembly as the supreme sovereign body under the terms of a law amending the 1924 Constitution. In January 1961 a Constituent Assembly, charged with the preparation of a new Constitution for the Republic, was set up consisting of a lower house of members nominated by various organizations and an upper house consisting of the C.N.U. The new Constitution was approved by the Turkish people in a referendum held on 9 July.

This provided for a 450-member National Assembly elected every four years and a 184-member Senate, of whose members 150 are elected for a six-year term, 15 are nominated by the President. The former members of the Committee of National Unity (18) and former Presidents of the Republic are *ex officio* members. The President is elected for a seven-year term. In 1971, having observed the need for a revision, the Parliament decided to amend the 1961 Constitution after ten years of implementation and consequently 35 Articles were amended and nine provisional Articles were added to the Constitution. In addition, in March 1973 five more articles were amended.

On 12 March 1971, Prime Minister Demirel found it necessary to submit the resignation of his Cabinet after the Chief of the General Staff and the Commanders of the Armed Forces presented a memorandum criticising his administration.

On 7 April 1971 Professor Nihat Erim's programme was approved in the National Assembly by an overwhelming majority of 321 in favour, and 46 against, with 3 abstentions. The resignation of 11 members of the cabinet led Professor Erim to form his second cabinet which received a vote of confidence with 301 for, 45 against and 3 abstentions, on 22 December 1971.

Professor Nihat Erim's Second Government resigned on 17 April 1972 when the Prime Minister announced that because of exhaustion he was unable to continue as Premier.

Two days later, President Cevdet Sunay asked Mr. Ferit Melen, the Minister of Defence in the outgoing Government, and Acting Prime Minister, to form the new Cabinet. The new Council of Ministers announced by Mr. Melen on 22 May 1972 once again included members from three of the main political parties in Turkey: eight Ministers from the Justice Party (JP), five from the Republican People's Party (RPP), and two from the National Reliance Party (NRP). One Minister was a Senator appointed by the President of the Republic and nine Ministers were appointed from outside Parliament. The Prime Minister himself was the Deputy Leader of the National Reliance Party.

The programme of the new government formed by Mr. Ferit Melen, who was Minister of Defence in the Erim Cabinet was approved in the National Assembly on 5 June 1972 by an overwhelming majority: 262 votes in favour and 4 against. There were 24 abstentions. Some Deputies were unable to attend the meeting because they had left Ankara in order to follow local elections held in various parts of the country.

Fourteen Ministers of the Second Erim Government retained their posts and three were given new Ministries.

The Melen cabinet decided to resign following the decision of the RPP to withdraw its members from the Cabinet, and presented its resignation to the newly elected President of the Republic (retired Admiral Fahri Korutürk), on 7 April 1973. The resignation was accepted on 10 April and Mr. Naim Talû, Minister of Commerce in the outgoing cabinet, was asked to form a new government on 10 April 1973. He received a vote of confidence from the National Assembly with 261 votes for, 94 against, and 2 abstentions, and transferred power to the new coalition government formed after the general elections held on 14 October 1973.

### Ministry

On 7 February 1974 the National Assembly approved the programme of the new Turkish Government formed on 25 January by Mr. Bülent Ecevit, leader of the Republican People's Party. The Government was a coalition between the Republican People's Party, which held 18 portfolios, and the National Salvation Party, which was represented by 7 Ministers.

235 members of the Assembly voted in favour of the Government, 136 against, while 2 members abstained. The vote in favour exceeded the maximum voting strength of the two coalition partners, of whom the Republican People's Party had 185 seats, and the National Salvation Party 48 in the 450-member Assembly.

As a result of disagreement between the two wings of the coalition government the RPP and the NSP the Ecevit, Government resigned on 18 October 1974 and a new government formed by Sadi Irmak Senator, from the Presidential quota, was unable to receive a vote of confidence from the National Assembly. However, this government continued to run the affairs of the State until a new coalition Government with the participation of the Justice Party, National Salvation Party, Republican Reliance Party, and the Nationalist Movement Party, was formed on 31 March 1975 under the premiership of Mr. Süleyman Demirel, Leader of the Justice Party.

### The Turkish Cabinet

*Prime Minister:* Bulent Ecevit.
*Deputy Prime Minister:* Orhan Eyoboglu.
*Deputy Prime Minister:* Turhan Feyzioglu.
*Deputy Prime Minister:* Faruk Sukan.
*Minister of State:* Hikmet Cetin.

*Minister of State:* Enver Akova.
*Minister of State:* Lutfu Dogan.
*Minister of State:* Salih Yildiz.
*Minister of State:* Alir Riza Septioglu.
*Minister of State:* Mustafa Kilic.
*Minister of State:* Ahmet Sener.
*Minister of Justice:* Mehmet Can.
*Minister of National Defence:* Hasan Esat Isik.
*Minister of Interior:* Irfan Ozaydinli.
*Minister of Foreign Affairs:* Gunduz Okcun.
*Minister of Finance:* Ziya Muezzinoglu.
*Minister of Education:* Necdet Ugur.
*Minister of Public Works:* Serafettin Elci.
*Minister of Trade:* Teoman Koprululer.
*Minister of Public Health:* Mete Tan.
*Minister of Customs and Monopolies:* Tuncay Mataraci.
*Minister of Transport and Communications:* Gunes Ongut.
*Minister of Agriculture:* Mehmet Yuceler.
*Minister of Labour:* Bahir Ersoy.
*Minister of Industry and Technology:* Orhan Alp.
*Minister of Management:* Kenan Bulutoglu.
*Minister of Energy and Natural Resources:* Deniz Baykai.
*Minister of Tourism and Information:* Alev Coskun.
*Minister of Housing and Reconstruction:* Ahmet Karaasian.
*Minister of Rural Affairs and Cooperatives:* Ali Topuz.
*Minister of Forestry:* Vecdi Ilhan.
*Minister of Youth and Sports:* Yuksel Cakmur.
*Minister of Social Security:* Hilmi Isguzar.
*Minister of Culture:* Ahmet Taner Kislali.
*Minister of Regional Administration:* Mahmut Ozdemir.

## LOCAL GOVERNMENT

The biggest administrative division in Turkey is the *il* (province). *Ils* are divided into *ilçe* and *ilçe* into *bucak*. A *bucak* is the union of a certain number of villages—the smallest administrative units—under one administrator.

The highest Administrative Officers in the *il, ilçe* and *bucak* are the *vali* (governors), the *Kaymakam,* and the *bucak müdürü,* respectively. Villages are administered by an elective Council of Elders consisting of five to 12 members according to the population of the village. The *muhtar,* who is the chairman of the Council of Elders, is at the same time representative of the central government.

The *vali* is the head of the central administrative organization within the *il,* and the chairman and executive organ of the Provincial Administrative Council.

Municipalities are a form of local government of which the authority and field of action are limited by the boundaries of the town or city concerned. Municipal government is conducted under the responsibility of the Municipal Council and Mayor elected by the people. The Mayor is assisted by a Permanent Committee, which is composed of members of the Municipal Council, and which is always in session.

In Turkey today, there are 67 *ils* subdivided into *ilçes* and *bucaks.* There were 1,367 municipalities and 35,997 villages and districts in 1971.

## LEGAL SYSTEM

The highest Turkish court is the Constitutional Court, set up in 1962 under the terms of the Constitution which was adopted in 1961. It sits in the capital and has powers to try members of the Government indicted before it and to review legislation. The Court of Cassation is composed of 24 chambers of which 15 are civil (commercial, bankruptcy, enforcement included) and 9 are penal (since May 1973). Each court chamber has a president and four member judges. All the members together constitute the Court of Cassation as a whole, which has its own president. The functions of the Court of Cassation are the hearing of appeals, whether by the public prosecutor or by the party concerned, against the decision of a lower court.

The State Security Courts formed after the amendment of the Constitution in 1973 are empowered to prosecute offences committed against the integrity and security of the state.

The central criminal courts are composed of a president and two member judges. Cases where the crime on trial is punishable by imprisonment exceeding five years, long-term imprisonment, hard labour, or by the death penalty, come within the jurisdiction of the central criminal courts.

The commercial courts are composed of a president and two member judges who pass judgment upon commercial matters and disputes arising therefrom.

The courts, of first instance are one-judge courts which handle cases outside the jurisdiction of the central criminal and commercial courts. The lowest courts are the courts of the Justices of the Peace which are also single-judge courts. They deal with cases of debt, up to 5,000 Turkish lira, alimony and peace matters. Criminal cases appertaining to public peace and order are instituted by the public prosecutor. In other instances, it is the parties concerned who bring action and follow it up before the court.

The newly instituted State Security Courts deal with cases concerning offenses against the integrity of the State, its territory, people, free democratic order, and the Republic, in addition to offenses directly related to the security of the State. Special judicial courts are set up by law to meet special needs. Among them are: press courts, foreign exchange courts, cadastral courts, land courts, labour courts and traffic courts.

## AREA AND POPULATION

The total area of European Turkey (Eastern Thrace) and Asiatic Turkey (Anatolia) is 296,185 sq. miles. European Turkey is by far the smallest part of the Republic covering only 9,500 sq. miles of the total. These figures do not include 3,708 sq. miles of lakes and marshes. The total length of the Republic's frontier is 1,633 miles, bordering on the following countries: U.S.S.R., 367 miles; Persia, 290 miles; Iraq, 235 miles; Syria, 490 miles; Greece, 127 miles; Bulgaria, 124 miles.

The population at mid-1974 was 39,167,000. The annual average percentage growth rate of the population for the period 1960–74 was 2·5 and for 1965–74 was 2·6. The population figures for major towns are approximately as follows: Istanbul, 2,247,630; Ankara, 1,208,791; Izmir, 520,686; Adana, 351,655; Bursa, 275,917.

In all, there are 20 cities and towns with over 100,000 population, and 20 with populations of 50,000 to 100,000.

The population is increasing at the rate of 2·6 per cent to 3 per cent a year.

## CURRENCY

The unit of currency is the Turkish Lira (pound) of 100 kurus. There are in circulation brass and copper coins of 1, 5 and 10 kurus, and cupro-nickel coins of 25, 50, 100, 250 and 500 kurus. Banknotes in circulation are issued by the Central Bank of Turkey.

## FINANCE

The GNP at market prices for 1974 was U.S.$ millions 29,460, and the GNP per capita at market prices was U.S.$750. The annual average percentage growth rate of the GNP per capita for the period 1960–74 was 3·9, and for the period 1965–74 was 4·3. [*See the note at the beginning of this section concerning GNP.*]

Budget figures for 1974 were: Expenditure, £T.81,657,576, 903 Revenue, £T.75,657,576,903.

The external debt, payable in foreign currencies $3,511 (including $857 millions representing the amount of unutilized credit), as of December 1973. In terms of Turkish Lira 3,638 million. The internal debt with respect to the General budget was £T.26,733, and with respect to the State Investment Bank, State Public Enterprises, and Municipalities was 9,299·4.

## PRINCIPAL BANKS

**Ziraat Bankasi.** (Chairman Davut Akça.) Est. 1930; Bank of Issue; All of the share capital is owned by the State; Balance Sheet at 31 December 1976 showed capital £T.1·5 billion, assets £T.80,964,985,203, deposits and current accounts £T.76,001,375,767, gold reserves £T.2,048,997,433; banknotes in circulation £T.40,937,692,355; deposits £T.36,927,307,768. *Head Office:* Ulus, Ankra. 878 Branches.

**Akbank T.A.Ş.** (Chairman, Bülent Yazici; Managing Director, Medenî Berk.) Est. 1948; capital £T.300,000,000; Balance Sheet at 31 December 1974 shows assets (including contra accounts), £T.28,996,829,095; deposits and current accounts £T.10,154,571,742. *Head Office:* Findikli, Istanbul. 450 Branches.

**Türkiye Cümhuriyet Ziraat Bankasi.** (Chairman, Davut Akça.) Est. 1863; All the share capital is owned by the State; Balance Sheet at 31 December 1975 showed capital £T.1·5 billion; assets £T.64,611,173,809; deposits and current accounts £T.60,179,440,135. *Head Office:* Bankalar Caddesi, 33 Ankara. 867 Branches.

**Etibank.** (General Manager, Nezihi Berkkam.) Est. 1935; All the share capital is owned by the State; Balance Sheet at 31 December 1973 showed total assets £T.9,490,719,703; profits £T.109,958,092. *Head Office:* Cihan Sokak 2, Sihhiye, Ankara. 73 Branches (banking) and 15 mining and industria establishments.

**Ottoman Bank.** (General Manager, J. Jeulin.) Est. 1863; Balance Sheet at 31 December 1971 showed assets £T.2,139,766,594; deposit, current and other accounts £T.1,547,025,689. *Head Office:* Bankalar Caddesi, Karaköy, Instanbul. 90 Branches.

**Pamukbank T.A.S.** (Chairman of the Board, Mehmet Emin Karamehmet.) Assets as at 31 December 1975 (including contra accounts totalling £T.2,531,938,544) £T.3,980,704,348; deposits and current accounts £T.1,100,947,729. *Head Office:* Pamukbank T.A.S., Istiklāl caddesi 261, P.O. Box 324, Galatasaray, Istanbul, Turkey. 100 Branches.

**Sümerbank.** (General Manager, Hizir Geylân.) Est. 1933; All the share capital is owned by the State; Balance Sheet at 31 December 1971 showed assets £T.5,665,413,072; current accounts £T.203,000,000. *Head Office:* Ulus Meydani 2, Ankara. 18 Branches.

**Türkiye Emlâk Kredi Bankasi A.O.** (Real Estate Credit Bank of Turkey.) (General Manager, MuzafferKemal Denizdöven); Est. 1926; 55 per cent of the share capital is owned by the State; Balance Sheet at 31 December 1975 showed total assets £T.22,176,386,954,730. *Head Office and Foreign Dept.* Ankara. *Representative Offices:* Munich and Berlin. 173 Branches.

**Turkiye İs Bankasi, A.S.** (General Manager, Cahit Kocaömer.) Est. 1924; Balance Sheet at 31 December 1975 showed assets £T.43,127,885,000; deposits and current accounts £T.22,498,855,000. *Head Office:* Ankara. *Foreign Dept.:* Istanbul. More than 700 branches. *Representative Offices:* Frankfurt-Main and London.

**Yapi ve Kredi Bankası A.S.** Est. 1944; (Chairman and Managing Director, Hayri Baran.) Capital £T.300,000,000; assets £T.22,578,970,721; deposit accounts £T.18,688,746,025; 31 December 1975. *Head Office:* P.O.B. 250, Beyoğlu, Istanbul. 524 Branches. *Representative's Offices:* Zurich, Switzerland; Frankfurt/Main, Germany; London, England.

## PRODUCTION, INDUSTRY AND COMMERCE

**Agriculture.** Agriculture, forestry and fishing accounts for roughly 40 per cent of Turkey's national income.

The following table gives land figures for 1973:

| *Land Use* | *thousands of hectares* 1973 |
|---|---|
| Crop area | 5·382 |
| Field and pastures | 21·765 |
| Orchards and gardens | 2·104 |
| Forests | 20·115 |
| Unsuitable for use | 13·600 |

Turkey is predominantly agricultural. Wheat ranks first among Turkish crops, and in recent years the acreage under wheat has steadily increased. Barley, oats, rye, corn, rice, millet are other important grain products. Cotton, citrus fruits and bananas are grown in the south. Tobacco is the most valuable export crop followed by cotton, nuts and raisins. Figs and raisins, filberts and walnuts are grown in wide area. Olives, olive oil, flax, hemp, sesame, spices, attar of roses are other valuable export items. Opium-poppy growing was banned after the 1972 season, however the growing was once again authorized on 1 July 1974 in six provinces and partially in another province.

Production of industrial timber in 1964 was 3,076,000 cubic metres.

The following table shows forestry production figures for 1972 and 1973.

| *Forest Product* | 1972 | 1973 |
|---|---|---|
| | *thousands cu. metres* | |
| Logs | 4,638 | 5,162 |
| Pit props and poles | 712 | 661 |
| Industrial timber | 370 | 457 |

The production of firewood for the years 1970 and 1971 was eight million tons for each year.

Turkey is a country of small farmholders and no individual or organization is permitted to hold more than 1,200 acres. The size of the individual farm varies according to the fertility of the soil. The average farm, however, has about 14 acres. Each village has in addition a good deal of common property which may include grazing and meadow land, forests, marshes and mountains.

Below is shown agricultural production (in thousand tons) for the years 1972 and 1973 (metric):

| *Crop* | 1972 | 1973 |
|---|---|---|
| Cereals | 18,761 | 13,602 |
| Pulses | 622 | 598 |
| Fresh fruit (citrus not inc.) | 5,588 | 5,601 |
| Tea (green leaves) | 252 | 297 |
| Tobacco | 176 | 130 |
| Olives | 740 | 1,019 |
| Sugar beet | 5,600 | 5,096 |
| Cotton | 520 | 543 |
| Potatoes | 2,000 | 2,200 |
| Sunflower seed | 465 | 560 |
| Hazelnuts | 180 | 190 |

**Livestock.** Livestock-raising is one of the outstanding Turkish occupations. Horses, cattle, water-buffalo, sheep and goats are the main animals. Both they and their products (mohair, hides, etc.) are exported in large quantities.

The following table gives the number of domestic animals in Turkey for the years 1970 and 1971.

*Domestic animal population (in thousands)*

| | 1970 | 1971 |
|---|---|---|
| Horses | 1,049 | 1,027 |
| Donkeys | 1,805 | 1,760 |
| Mules | 299 | 301 |
| Cattle | 12,756 | 12,653 |
| Sheep | 36,471 | 36,760 |
| Goats | 19,483 | 18,863 |
| Buffaloes | 1,117 | 1,026 |
| Camels | 31 | 29 |
| Domestic fowl | 34,280 | — |

The amount of foreign capital liable to authorization was £T.145,546,000 in 1972. The capital actually invested was 129 million in 1972. The total of authorized capital in the period 1951–72 is £T.2,512,000 and the total actually invested in the same period was £T.1,104,000.

**Mining and Industry.** Turkey has very rich mineral resources. The most abundant item is coal of good quality. For many years chromium has been second to coal. Next in importance are copper, iron, manganese, emery, mercury and sulphur. Besides these, there are nickel, tin, cobalt, phosphate, alabaster, platinum, alum, antimony, soda and zinc. Rather recent are the oilfields discovered in the south-east, which have now begun to provide some one-third of national requirements.

Petroleum prospecting is being vigorously pursued in Turkey. Prospecting is carried out by the Turkish Petroleum Corporation in which the State has a share, and by foreign private companies. There are three refineries in Turkey, at Batman, Izmit and Mersin. A fourth refinery is being built in Izmir in order to meet the country's increasing need for petroleum products.

A State organization known as 'Etibank', composed of various mining departments, was established in 1935 to deal with mine and power development.

Coal is produced from the Zonguldak-Ereğli coalfield, situated on the shores of the Black Sea, along with coke and briquettes made up from compressed coal dust.

The industries, except those locally connected with certain agricultural products or mines, are located around the larger cities where adequate transportation facilities are available. Therefore, only scattered plants are to be found in the mountainous eastern part of the country despite the fact that the mineral resources warrant more extensive manufacturing activity. Turkey has a world monopoly of one rare mineral product—meerschaum.

The Ottoman Empire was totally dependent upon imports of all types of industrial products. The industrialization programme of the Republic, however, aims at establishing essential industries with emphasis upon those for which Turkey is particularly well adapted such as copper manufacturing, iron and steel works, the textile industry, sugar refining, paper mills, and cement factories. A law for the encouragement of foreign capital investment was revised early in 1954. During the years (1967–70) $113 m. of foreign capital has entered Turkey.

The growth of Turkish industry and the accompanying expansion of commerce are best indicated by their increasing share in the national income. In 1942 they contributed less than 35 per cent to the nation's income. In 1950 they were providing nearly half the national wealth.

The following table shows production figures in thousand metric tons for 1972 and 1973:

| *Commodity* | 1972 | 1973 |
|---|---|---|
| Mining: | | |
| Chrome ore (sifted) | 650 | 559 |
| Iron ore | 1,954 | 2,545 |
| Coal | 7,870 | 7,850 |
| Lignite | 10,247 | 10,543 |
| Manganese | 15 | 15 |
| Crude petroleum | 3,410 | 3,511 |
| Manufactures: | | |
| Cement | 8,424 | 8,947 |
| Steel and ingots | 1,442 | 1,163 |
| Pig iron | 1,111 | 894 |
| Sugar | — | 873 |
| Cotton yarn | 53 | 250* |
| Cotton textiles | 226 | 1,060* |
| Woollen yarns | 4 | 39* |
| Woollen textiles | 4·705 | 37* |
| Petroleum products | 10·394 | 12,532 |
| Fertilizers | 1·059 | 1,212 |

* Estimated

**Commerce**

Value of Principal Imports—1972–1973

| | 1972 (*thousands of U.S. $*) | 1973 |
|---|---|---|
| Machinery | 517,000 | 652,723 |
| Base metals | 148 | 175 |
| Fuel | 155 | 218 |
| Chemicals and chemical products | 147 | 160 |
| Transport | 142 | 234 |
| Textiles | 52 | 52 |
| Vegetable, and animal oils | 21 | 4 |

Value of Principal Exports—19–1972

| | 1972 (*thousands of U.S. $*) | 1973 |
|---|---|---|
| Tobacco | 130,800 | 132,874 |
| Fruit (mainly sultanas, hazelnuts and figs) | 197,360 | 274,452 |
| Cotton | 191,300 | 305,842 |
| Minerals | 50,250 | — |
| Wool, hair, mohair | — | — |
| Livestock | 15,700 | 25,498 |
| Cereals | 36,200 | — |

Value of Imports and Exports by Principal Countries—1973

| *Country* | *Imports* (*thousands of U.S. $*) | *Exports* |
|---|---|---|
| West Germany | 437·4 | 221·2 |
| France | 133·5 | 72·7 |
| Netherlands | 99·6 | 41·0 |
| Italy | 170·2 | 115·4 |
| United Kingdom | 223·9 | 100·5 |
| Switzerland | 185·5 | 115·8 |
| U.S.A. | 185·4 | 130·8 |
| U.S.S.R. | 126·0 | 50·4 |

## COMMUNICATIONS

**Railways.** All railways in Turkey are owned by the State and are run by the Turkish State Railways Administration. Lines that were owned formerly by foreign companies were nationalized by the Republican Government. At the end of 1972 the total network consisted of 10,102 km. of track. The the years 1970, 1971, and 1972:

| | 1970 | 1971 | 1972 |
|---|---|---|---|
| Passenger/km. | 41,311 | 41,310 | 44,040 |
| Freight/km. | 17,442 | 18,100 | 19,750 |

**Shipping.** The Turkish merchant fleet consists of 322 vessels, and 46 passenger ferries, as well as 17 car ferries of above 300 tons; 65 of these are above 3,000 tons gross weight and 17 are passenger vessels.

The operation of the former State Seaways Administration was turned over in 1953 to the Maritime (Denizcilik) Bank, which operates in the form of an incorporated company and under the same competitive conditions as apply to any other shipowner.

In 1962 the Bank cargo carrying activities were transferred to a subsidiary, the Deniz Nakliyat, which operates 46 cargo vessels, and eight tankers totalling 693,010 gross weight. Passenger ferry activities are operated by Maritime Bank. Eleven cargo passenger lines are operated by the Bank, which also operates various port facilities, service salvage and pilot vessels.

**Civil Aviation.** The principal towns and cities of Turkey are linked together by the Turkish Airlines (Turk Hava Yollari), with a fleet of two DC-10 jets, and nine DC-9 jets, five Fellowships F-28 and three Boeing 707 (rented). Passengers carried in 1972 totalled 1,512,000 (both external and internal flights). Only Turkish aircraft are allowed to carry passengers and freight between Turkish towns and cities. External services are operated by Turkish Airlines and by foreign companies from Istanbul and Ankara to all parts of the world. The chief routes are operated by Pan American Airways, B.E.A., QANTAS, Scandinavian Airways, Lufthansa, Air France, K.L.M., Swissair, ElAl, Olympic Airways, Pia, Aeroflot, Alitalia, M.E.A., Cyprus Airways, J.A.T., Sabena, Iran Air and Tarom, Malev and Iberia.

**Posts, Telegraphs and Telephones.** Turkey had a total of 5,700 post offices or offices for the sale of stamps in 1970. There were, in 1971, 543,000 telephones. There are telegraphic and telephonic communications with all parts of the world.

**Broadcasting.** All radio and television broadcasting in Turkey is under exclusive control of the Turkish Radio and Television corporation. TRT has the following 7 main radio stations under operation: Ankara, (L.W.) 1,200 kW.; İstanbul, (M.W.) 1,200 kW. Antalya, (M.W.) 600 kW.; Mersin, (M.W.) 300 kW.; Diyarbakir, (M.W.) 300 kW.; İzmir, (M.W.) 200 kW. Erzurum, (L.W.) 200 kW.

Apart from these stations there are 9 small capacity local stations: Gaziantep, (M.W.) 2 kW.; Kars, (M.W.) 2 kW.; Van, (M.W.) 2 kW.; Trabzon, (M.W.) 2 kW.; Hakkari, (S.W.) 1 kW.; Ankara II, (M.W.) 2 kW.; Ankara III, (F.M.) 2 kW.; İstanbul II, (M.W.) 150 kW.; İzmir II, (M.W.) 2 kW.

The shortwave Service of TRT, "The Voice of Turkey" puts out programmes in English, French, German, Serbo-Croat, Bulgarian, Greek, Rumanian and Arabic on two different shortwave bands with transmitters of 250 kW. and 100 kW. capacity respectively.

# TURKEY

The television programmes originating in Ankara are distributed by the national radio-link system and retransmitted in İstanbul, Bursa, İzmir, Eskişehir, Edirne, Balikesir, Kirikkale, İzmit, Aydin, Düzce, Bolu, Afyon and Zonguldak. The national radio-link system is also linked to Eurovision and programmes from the latter are conveyed to the above mentioned cities from time to time. Seven regional television studios using packaged programmes are in operation in Erzurum, Trabzon, Diyarbakir, Hatay, Kayseri, Adana and Antalya.

## NEWSPAPERS

There is a flourishing Turkish language press centred mainly in Ankara and Istanbul. There is one French language daily and seven English language papers. The leading papers are:

*Ankara*

**Adalet.** Morning adily.

**Baris.** Morning daily.

**Zafer.** Morning daily.

*Istanbul*

**Akşam** Morning daily.

**Apoyevmatini.** Greek language daily.

**Cumhuriyet.** Morning daily.

**Dünya.** Morning daily.

**Günaydin.** Morning daily.

**Hürriyet.** Morning daily. Largest circulation.

**Jamanak.** Morning daily. Armenian language.

**Milliyet.** Morning daily. Circulation 200,000; Sundays, 250,000.

**Son Havadis.** Morning daily.

**Tercüman.** Morning daily.

*İzmir*

**Ekspres.** Morning daily.

**Yeni Asir.** Morning daily.

## EDUCATION AND RELIGION

Elementary education in Turkey is compulsory for children of both sexes between the ages of seven and 12 though places are only available to 83 per cent of children of primary school age. In 1968 primary school pupils numbered 4,900,000. In 1973 there were 5,292,553 pupils. Elementary schools in 1973 numbered 40,309.

Secondary education is in two stages, Middle Schools and Lycées. In 1973 there were 2,011 Middle Schools and 577 Lycées. In 1973 there were 930,125 Middle School students and 275,221 Lycée pupils. In 1973 there were 89 Teachers' Training Schools for Primary Schools.

There are eleven Universities, three in İstanbul (İstanbul, İstanbul Technical and Boğaziçi Universities) three in Ankara (Ankara, Hacettepe and Middle East Technical Universities), and one in each of the following cities: Izmir (Ege), Trabzon (Karadeniz Technical), Erzurum (Atatürk), Adana (Çukurova), and Diyarbakir. Five more Universities are to be founded in the following cities: Bursa, Konya (Selçuk), Samsum (19 Mayis), Elaziğ (Firat) and Malatya (Inönü).

İstanbul University has 13 Faculties, İstanbul Technical University 9, Boğazi University 4, Ankara University 12, Hacettepe University 9 Faculties. The Middle East Technical University, which has English as its official language and a number of foreign experts on its staff, has 4 Faculties, Atatürk University 7, Ege University 10, Çukurova and Diyarbakir Universities both have 2 and the Karadeniz Technical University has six Faculties. The number of students at Universities and Institutes of Higher Learning in 1973 was 168,818.

There is no state religion in Turkey, but Moslems form 99 per cent of the population.

## ATOMIC ENERGY

A governmental Atomic Energy Commission came into being officially on 19 March 1957 and meets in Ankara. A Committee for the Application of Nuclear Energy to Industry has also been constituted and this has its headquarters in the İstanbul Technical University. There is one American-designed research reactor outside İstanbul. The construction of an atomic energy plant is projected in the third five-year Plan (1973–77).

# Uganda

(MEMBER OF THE COMMONWEALTH)

**Capital**—Kampala.

**Head of State**—H.E. Field Marshal Idi Amin Dada.

**National Flag:** On a field parti of six horizontal black, yellow, red, black, yellow, red a white circle charged with a crested crane.

UGANDA became internally self-governing on 1 March 1962. In the general election which followed, the Democratic Party Government was defeated by the Uganda People's Congress alliance with the Kabaka Yekka movement. Dr. A. M. Obote, President of the Uganda People's Congress, took office as Prime Minister on 1 May 1962.

A further series of constitutional talks were held in London in June 1962 to pave the way for complete independence on 9 October 1962. Under the new constitution, known as 'The Constitution of Uganda (First Amendment) Act, 1962', Uganda became an Independent Sovereign State, on 9 October 1963. On that date, the Governor-General, who was the Queen's representative, was replaced by a Ugandan Head of State—the President.

On 15 April 1966 Dr. A. M. Obote, formerly Prime Minister of Uganda, was sworn in as President.

On Friday, 8 September 1967, a new Constitution was enacted by Parliament sitting as a Constituent Assembly. Under the new Constitution, the country became a Republic with an executive President who is Head of State, Head of Government and Commander-in-Chief of the Armed Forces. The Institutions of Kings and Constitutional Rulers were abolished. Under a new administrative structure introduced by President Amin, Uganda now consists of ten provinces, namely, Busoga, Central, Eastern, Karamoja, Nile, North Buganda, Northern, South Buganda, Southern, and Western Province.

The Parliament consisted of the President and a National Assembly of 82 elected members and nine specially elected members.

In January 1971 Dr. A. M. Obote and his government were replaced by the regime of Field-Marshal Idi Amin Dada, Military Head of State and Government and Commander-in-Chief of the Armed Forces, who appointed a Council of Ministers of the Military Government of the Second Republic of Uganda.

**Ministry** (as at 11 August 1975)

*President of the Second Republic of Uganda, Head of State:* H.E. Field Marshal Idi Amin Dada.
*Minister of Defence:* General A. Mustafa.
*Minister of State in the Office of the President:* Hon. P. Etiang.
*Minister of Provincial Administrations:* Hon. Brig. Moses Ali.
*Minister of Commerce:* Hon. Captain Noah Mohammed.
*Minister of Industry and Power:* Hon. Col. Sabuni.
*Minister of Agriculture and Forestry:* Hon. J. M. Byagagaire.
*Minister of Foreign Affairs:* Hon. Lt.-Col. Juma Oris.
*Minister of Labour:* Hon. L. Katagyira.
*Minister of Finance:* Hon. Oboth-Ofumbi (Acting).
*Minister of State for Finance:* Hon. M. S. Kiyingi.
*Minister of Information and Broadcasting:* Mr. Abd-el-Nasser.
*Minister of Education:* Hon. Brig. B. Kili.
*Minister of Culture and Community Development:* Hon. Maj.-Gen. F. Nyangweso.
*Minister of Co-operatives and Marketing:* Hon. M. Ramathan.
*Minister of Works and Housing:* Hon. Lt.-Col. S. Lukakamwa.
*Minister of Justice/Attorney General:* Hon. G. S. Lule.
*Minister of Public Service and Cabinet Affairs:* Hon. R. B. Nshekanabo.
*Minister of Transport and Communications:* Mrs. Hajati Kateregа.
*Minister of Health:* Hon. H. Kyemba.
*Minister of Tourism and Wildlife:* Hon. Lt.-Col. Onaah.
*Director of Planning and Economic Development:* Hon. I. K. Kabanda.
*Minister of Animal Resources:* Mr. Nsubuga H. Sik (Acting).

The qualifications for citizenship of Uganda are laid down. The Fundamental Rights of the Individual are given the fullest possible protection.

Uganda is an independent member of the Commonwealth lying astride the Equator in East Africa. It is bounded on the north by the Sudan, on the west by the Congo Republic, on the south by Tanzania, Rwanda and Burundi and on the east by Kenya.

The main commercial centres are Kampala and rapidly growing Jinja, Mbale and Masaka. Some Government offices are situated in Entebbe, the former capital.

Kiswahili is the national language while English is the official one used in schools, Government transactions, in courts of law, etc. This arrangement was reached after a nation-wide debate in 1973 to determine the country's national language. In addition to English and Kiswahili, each of the major 15 or so tribes in Uganda is identified by its own language or dialect.

## LEGAL SYSTEM

The laws of the country consist of Acts of Parliament, Ordinances, Rules, Regulations, Decrees, Orders and Notices made thereunder. The Constitution is the supreme law of the land. Civil and Criminal jurisdiction is exercised in conformity with such enactments and in conformity with Common law and the doctrines of equity.

However, some parts of the Constitution were suspended during the change of Government in 1971. A new Constitution will be introduced in due course.

## AREA AND POPULATION

The total land area of the country is 197,400 sq. km.

The population at mid-1974 was 11,186,000. This total was comprised of African, 9,456,466; Asian, 74,308; Arab, 3,238; European 9,533; Others, 5,302. Due to Government policy a large majority of the Asian population were deported from Uganda in 1972. The annual average percentage growth rate of the population for the period 1960–74 was 2·9, and for period 1965–74 was 3·1.

## FINANCE

The unit of currency is the Uganda shilling divided into 100 cents. In 1954 a new financial year was introduced to run from 1 July to 30 June. Previously the Financial Year was the same as the calendar year.

| | *In Million Shillings* 1971–72 | 1972–73 |
|---|---|---|
| Revenue | 1,436 | 1,525 |
| Expenditure | 1,374 | 1,430 |

The revenue is principally derived from export taxes on cotton and coffee, customs and excise duty, income tax and poll taxes.

The GNP at market prices for 1974 was U.S.$ millions 2,700, and the GNP per capita at market prices was U.S.$240. The annual average percentage growth rate of the GNP per capita for the period 1960–74 was 1·8, and for the period 1965–74 was 0·7, [*See the note at the beginning of this section concerning GNP.*]

## BANK

**Standard Bank Uganda Ltd.** (Chairman, N. A. Levick.) Assets as at 31 March 1977, Ug.shgs.289,627,771; deposits and current accounts, 2,64,729,340. *Head Office:* P.O. Box 311 Kampala, Uganda. One branch.

## PRODUCTION, INDUSTRY AND COMMERCE

Uganda is primarily an agricultural country and production is totally in the hands of Ugandans. Coffee and cotton are the most important crops. Tea and sugar are produced mainly on non-native estates but native production is increasing. Other export crops are tobacco, oilseeds and groundnuts. The principal native food crops are maize, plantains, millet, cassava and sweet potatoes. There is a large cattle population and hides and skins are an important export. The fishing industry on Lake Victoria and the other great lakes is growing in importance and quantities of fish are exported. Exploitable forests consist mainly of hard woods. Copper is the chief mineral export and quantities of tin and beryl are also mined. Tungsten production, previously an important item, is declining. Other minerals include gold, lead and bismuth. Large scale development of the substantial apatite pyrochlore deposits is planned.

Apart from industries processing the products of the country's natural resources secondary industry in Uganda is largely in the hands of companies associated with the Uganda Development Corporation. The largest is a textile mill at Jinja and the cement factory at Tororo. Other industries include building materials, gramophone records, containers and beer.

## EDUCATION

The education system in Uganda is arranged into three categories, primary (seven years), secondary (six years), and university (three to five years). Secondary schools offer a four-year course leading to the East African Certificate of Education, awarded by the East African Examinations Council. Since the abolition of the former Cambridge School Certificate in 1968, the standard has been carefully maintained.

There are more than 32 secondary schools offering a further two-year course leading to the "A" level, East African Advanced Certificate of Education. Secondary schools offer not only academic but also practical subjects like woodwork, metalwork, agriculture, commerce, home economics, etc. The object in diversifying the curriculum is to ensure that young people leaving school will be equipped, not only with academic knowledge and training, but also with practical skills.

In 1971, the school-leavers were as follows:

| | |
|---|---|
| Primary VII | 100,681 |
| Senior IV | 11,305 |
| Senior VI | 1,778 |
| Graduates | (about) 1,000 |

The number of schools in the country in 1971 was as follows:

| | |
|---|---|
| Primary | 2,888 |
| Secondary | 139 |
| Teacher training colleges | 27 |
| Technical | 5 |
| University | 1 |

Great efforts are being made to increase the output of trained teachers. Primary Training Colleges have a capacity of 3,500. Better rates of pay are attracting large numbers of boys and girls wishing to study for the profession. Of the 13,645 teachers in Uganda's schools, about 12,406 are African.

## COMMUNICATIONS

A system of all-weather main roads linking the principal administrative centres and having a road mileage of 2,989 is maintained by the Ministry of Works and Labour. There are also about 8,300 miles of good roads which are kept up by the Uganda Government and other local government bodies.

Railway and postal services are administered by the East African Community. The railway from Mombasa to Kampala has been extended to the Kasese near the western border. The northern rail from Soroti has now reached Pakmach.

Entebbe international airport is on the main trunk route through Africa, and air services link it to the main centres in Europe, Asia and other parts of Africa.

The Uganda Broadcasting Service of the Ministry of Information, Broadcasting and Tourism broadcasts daily in English and 14 vernacular languages. There is also a Television programme service operating in the evening.

## NEWSPAPERS

**Voice of Uganda.** Box 20081. Kampala.

**The People.** P.O. Box 20017, Kampala.

## RELIGION

There is no state religion in Uganda. Two religions are officially accepted by the Uganda Government: the Christian faith, which consists of the Protestant and Roman Catholic denominations, and the Islamic faith. There is also a small percentage of pagans.

# The United Arab Emirates

(FORMERLY THE TRUCIAL STATES)

**National Flag:** Twice as long as high, a red vertical stripe one quarter of the length of the flag near the staff, three horizontal stripes each one third of the height of the flag taking up the remainder of its area, green on top, white in the centre, black at the bottom.

## CONSTITUTION AND GOVERNMENT

The territory of the United Arab Emirates extends eastwards from the base of the Qatar peninsula to a point almost as far as the promontory of Musandam, and then turns inland to meet the sea again at Dibba in the Gulf of Oman. The Union is comprised of seven Emirates, from west to east these are: Abu Dhabi, Dubai, Sharjah, Ajman, Umm al Qaiwain, Ras al Khaimah and Fujairah.

Abu Dhabi is the temporary headquarters of a new Union (the constitution provides for the building of a new capital between Abu Dhabi and Dubai) and the Ruler of Abu Dhabi, Sheikh Zayed bin Sultan al Nahayan, as its first President. Other Ministers in the Union Government include:

*Prime Minister:* Sheikh Maktoum bin Rashid al-Maktoum.
*Deputy Prime Minister:* Sheikh Khalifa bin Zayed al-Nahyan.
*Minister of Finance and Industry:* Sheikh Hamdan bin Rashid al-Maktoum.
*Minister of Interior:* Sheikh Moubarak bin Mohammed al-Nahyan.
*Minister of Defence:* Sheikh Mohammed bin Rashid al-Maktoum.
*Minister of Foreign Affairs:* Sayyed Ahmed Khalifa al-Sweidi.
*Acting Minister of Agriculture and Fisheries:* Sayyed Saeed Salman.
*Minister of Communications:* Sayyed Mohammed Saeed al-Mulla.
*Minister of Education:* Sayyed Abdullah bin Omran Taryam.
*Minister of Health:* Sheikh Saif bin Mohammed al-Nahyan.
*Minister of Housing:* Sayyed Saeed Salman.
*Minister of Information and Tourism:* Sheikh Ahmed bin Hamad.
*Minister of Justice:* Sheikh Ahmed Sultan al-Qasimi.
*Minister of Employment and Labour:* Sheikh Mohammed bin Sultan al-Qasimi.
*Minister of Social Affairs:* Sheikh Abdulaziz bin Rashid al-Nuaimi.
*Minister of Planning:* Sayyed Mohammed Khalifa al-Kindi.
*Minister of Public Works:* Sheikh Hamdan bin Mohammed al-Nayhan.
*Minister of Electricity and Water:* Sheikh Abdullah bin Humaid al-Qasimi.
*Minister of Youth and Sports:* Sayyed Rashid bin Hamid.
*Minister of Economy and Trade:* Sheikh Sultan bin Ahmed al-Moualla.
*Minister of Petroleum:* Sayyed Mana' Saeed al-Oteiba.
*Minister of Islamic Affairs:* Sheikh Thani bin Essa bin Harib.
*Minister of State:* Sayyed Ahmed bin Sultan bin Soulayyem.
*Minister of State, Financial and Industrial Affairs:* Sayyed Mohammed Habroush.
*Minister of State, Supreme Council Affairs:* Sheikh Abdulla Kaed al-Qasimi.
*Minister of State, Foreign Affairs:* Sayyed Saif Saeed al-Ghobash.
*Minister of State, Information:* Sayyed Saeed al-Ghaith.
*Minister of State, Interior Affairs:* Sayyed Hamouda bin Ali.

### Rulers of the Member-Emirates

*Abu Dhabi:* Shaikh Zaid bin Sultan Al-Nihayyan.
*Dubai:* Shaikh Rashid bin Said al Maktoum.
*Sharjah:* Shaikh Sultan bin Mohamed al Qasimi.
*Ajman:* Shaikh Rashid bin Humaid al Naimi.
*Umm al-Qaiwain:* Shaikh Ahmed bin Rashid al Mualla, MBE.
*Ras al Khaimah:* Shaikh Saqr bin Muhammad al Qasimi.
*Fujairah:* Shaikh Mohammed bin Hamad al Sharqi.

British representation consists of twin Embassies in Abu Dhabi and Dubai, the Ambassador residing in Abu Dhabi.

Abu Dhabi is larger than all the other Emirates combined with approximately 25,000 of the total 32,000 square miles. Its revenue from oil has risen rapidly over the years since independence from Britain in 1971, partly because of increased production and partly because of the rise in oil prices. Production from the two major companies, Abu Dhabi Marine Areas and Abu Dhabi Petroleum Company, both partly owned by the Government-owned Abu Dhabi National Oil Company, totalled 66·7 million long tons in 1975 compared with 44·09 million long tons in 1971. A free health service operates both in Abu Dhabi and Al Ain, the other main town, as well as in the remoter regions and both primary and secondary education are also free. A large deep water harbour has recently been built and there is also an international airport. A larger airport is under consideration. The road network includes a four lane highway between Abu Dhabi and Al Ain, and a similar highway to Dubai and Sharjah.

## AREA AND POPULATION

The combined area of the Emirates is 32,000 sq. miles. The largest is Abu Dhabi with 25,000 sq. miles followed by Dubai, 1,500 sq. miles; Sharjah 1,000 sq. miles; Ras al Khaimah 650 sq. miles; Fujeirah 450 sq. miles; Umm al Qaiwain 300 sq. miles and Ajman 100 sq. miles. In 1974 the total population was estimated at 350,000 but the country's first census in December 1975 revealed a total of 655,937. Abu Dhabi had 235,662; Dubai 206,861; Sharjah 88,188; Ras al Khaimah 57,282; Fujeirah 26,498; Ajman 21,566 and Umm al Qaiwain 16,789. The remaining 629 lived in areas of contested ownership.

The annual average percentage growth rate of the population for the years 1960–74 was 13·4, and for the years 1965–74 was 17·1.

## CURRENCY

The UAE Dirham was introduced as legal currency replacing the Bahrain dinar in Abu Dhabi and the Qatar/Dubai riyal in other Emirates, the dirham being at par with the renamed Qatari riyal. In 1976 the currencies of Bahrain and the UAE were made freely transferrable as part of moves towards a Gulf monetary union. The dirham's value was initially fixed with the International Monetary Fund at a par value of 0·186621 grammes of gold effective from 1 February 1974; corresponding to 4·76190 dirhams per SDR unit (SDR 0·21 per dirham). The UAE Government also informed the IMF that it accepted the obligation of the Fund's article VIII by which it undertook to avoid imposing restrictions on payments and transfers for current international transactions or engaging in multiple currency practices or discriminatory currency arrangements without obtaining prior approval. It also became the 41st member of the Fund.

The value of the dirham has remained steady and has benefited from the Government's decision not to follow the lead of some other Gulf states in breaking its link with an SDR par value. Exchange rates:—June 1976: £1 Sterling = 6·825 DH. US$1 = 3·960 DH.

## FINANCE

The 1976–77 Federal budget was 3·423 million dirhams compared with 2·278 million in the previous year. Fifty per cent will be provided by the Emirate of Abu Dhabi. Major allocations included 386 million for communications; 327 million for water and electricity; 298 million for housing; and 281 million for education. The Abu Dhabi budget is 18,205 million dirhams. The 1975–76 figure was approximately one third less. 5,000 million dirhams are allocated for development; 4,500 million for overseas aid and 4,296 million for Abu Dhabi departments falling under the Federal Government. The 1975–76 budget was approximately one third less. Revenue is expected to be 18,401 million dirhams (approx. US$ 4,640 million).

## PRODUCTION, INDUSTRY AND COMMERCE

The UAE has emerged as a major trading nation in the years since the oil price increases in 1973–74. In 1975 Dubai, the main entrepot, imported goods worth 7,115 million dirhams compared with less than 4,500 million dirhams the previous year; while Abu Dhabi imported goods worth 3,569 million dirhams, more than 1,340 million dirhams greater in value than in 1974. Japan maintained its position as leading exporter to Dubai with goods worth 1,355 million; the United Kingdom exported goods worth 1,073 million and the United States 973 million. The major exporters to Abu Dhabi were the United Kingdom with a total of 839·6 million; the United States exported 557·5 million and West Germany 491·6 million worth of goods. Japan was in fourth place with goods worth 436,270,000 dirhams.

## UNITED ARAB EMIRATES

Trade with other Gulf states continued to play an important part particularly for Dubai. Kuwait's exports totalled 93 million dirhams in 1975 down from 161·9 million in 1974, but Saudi Arabia's exports to Dubai rose from 36 million to 65·8 million dirhams.

In the past few years, Abu Dhabi has completed the first stage of its own port Mina Zaid, and Mina Khaled has been built in Sharjah but Dubai continues to dominate the country's import trade, apart from Abu Dhabi's oil exports mainly from Das Island and the Jebel Dhanna land-based terminal. Lying on a natural deep-water creek Dubai, and its twin town of Deira have had a natural advantage enhanced by the opening of a new port—Mina Rashid—in 1972 with fifteen deep water berths. A contract for the construction of a further twenty-two berths was granted to a British company in 1976 which, when completed, will make Dubai the biggest port in the Middle East while a dry dock complex, designed to compete with that at Bahrain, is also in use. The picturesque water-taxi service across the creek has been largely rendered redundant with the building of two bridges and a tunnel, while a third bridge and a second tunnel are under construction.

The development of the port has been accompanied by the development of the town itself. It is now a major commercial and banking centre and most of the forty eight banks licensed for operation in the UAE have at least one branch in either Dubai or Deira.

Following a decision by the UAE Currency Board in mid-1976, it is soon expected to enter the offshore banking market as well as the local sector. Dubai's development has been enhanced by its position at the centre of the country's communications system. Connected by a four lane highway to Abu Dhabi and Sharjah it is also within easy reach, on metalled roads, of all the other Emirates the last of which, Fujeirah, was only connected by good roads to the rest of the country at the end of 1975.

Dubai also has an international airport while plans have recently been announced for the construction of a second together with a major industrial complex at Jebel Ali not far from the border with Abu Dhabi Emirate.

Another Emirate showing signs of rapid development is Sharjah not only on the west coast, near Dubai, but also in the eastern dependency of Khor Fakkan where a container port is being constructed. Ras al Khaimah in the north is primarily agricultural while the small Emirates of Umm al Qaiwain, Ajman and Fujeirah are still relatively underdeveloped although they are receiving some benefits from the federal government's development programme. Both Sharjah and Ras al Khaimah have international airports, and a new one at Sharjah, to replace that presently in use, is due to be opened in 1977.

The industrial sector has recently announced plans for a variety of schemes, including petro-chemical complexes in Dubai and Abu Dhabi and a steel rolling plant, a rope factory and two more cement factories to add to that recently opened at Al Ain in Abu Dhabi Emirate. Development is primarily co-ordinated on the federal level from the provisional capital in Abu Dhabi but each state within the UAE retains the right to initiate its own projects and to raise capital either at home or abroad, outside the framework of the federal budget.

The biggest producer is Abu Dhabi whose two major companies Abu Dhabi Marine Areas and Abu Dhabi Petroleum Company (ADMA and ADPC) produced a total of 66·71 million long tons of oil in 1975. ADMA production is down from a high point of 23·94 million long tons in 1973 but ADPC has continued to raise production from 37·56 million long tons in 1973 to 43·31 in 1974 and 46·50 in 1975. 60 per cent of each company is owned by the Abu Dhabi National Oil Company, representing the local government. The remaining 40 per cent of ADMA is owned by British Petroleum, Compagnie Francaise des Petroles and the Japan Oil Development Co. The 40 per cent balance in ADPC is owned by BP, Shell, Compagnie Francaise des Petroles, Standard Oil of New Jersey and Mobil.

A number of other companies, notably the Abu Dhabi Oil Company (Japan), Total Abu Bukhoosh and Sunningdale are exploiting smaller fields in which ADNOC has so far waived its right to a majority shareholding.

The Dubai Petroleum Company which was formerly owned by a consortium headed by Continental Oil (CONOCO) of the United States was taken over by the Dubai government in 1975. The former owners, who include Compagnie Francaise des Petroles, Hispanoil, Sun Oil of the USA and Deutsche Texaco Ltd, continue as operators. 1975 production was estimated at 12·04 million long tons compared with 11·42 million long tons in the previous year.

Sharjah became an oil producer in 1974 from a field near Abu Musa Island. The operating company, Crescent Petroleum, is dominated by Buttes Oil and Gas and also has Ashland, Shell, Kerr McGee, Cities Services and Juniper Petroleum as part owners. Production began at about 40,000 barrels a day but was reported by mid-1976 to have fallen to about 20,000 barrels a day.

Oil was discovered offshore in Ras al Khaimah by the Dutch company Vitol Explorations in July 1976. Preliminary tests showed a yield of 4,000 barrels a day. Drilling or geological surveys are also under way in the other three Emirates.

### COMMUNICATIONS

There are no railways in the UAE, but a sophisticated road network now links all of the Emirates and is being extended both to the Liwa oasis in southern Abu Dhabi and along the coast towards the border with Qatar in the West. A good telephone network exists, and direct dialling is now possible from Abu Dhabi, Dubai and Sharjah to Qatar and Bahrain while direct dialling was introduced in mid 1976 from London to Abu Dhabi, Al Ain and Dubai. A television service exists in Dubai and Abu Dhabi which is being extended by micro-wave to all of the other Emirates. A ground station was completed at Jebel Ali in Dubai in late 1975 connected to the Indian Ocean communications satellite, while plans have been announced for two more ground stations one in the extreme west of Abu Dhabi, which will be linked with the Atlantic satellite, and in Ras al Khaimah which will be on the Indian Ocean satellite.

The four international airports, at Abu Dhabi, Dubai, Sharjah and Ras al Khaimah are served by nearly twenty international airlines as well as the major freight contractors, while an air-taxi service was initiated in June 1976. Airstrips exist at Al Ain and in the oil fields, while construction of one is under way at Khor Fakkan in eastern Sharjah.

A number of shipping companies make regular calls to Emirates ports including the British India Steam Navigation Company, the British India Company, Holland Persian Gulf, DDG Hansa and Maersk Line. Most services are to Dubai although Abu Dhabi is now too becoming an important port of call.

### HEALTH SERVICE

There is a well-equipped medical service throughout the Emirates providing free treatment and advice on preventative medicine to all inhabitants of the country. Some of the local clinics were initially provided by the Kuwaiti Red Crescent and the Iranian Government, but most services are now the responsibility of the Federal Government.

### EDUCATION

Education at primary and secondary level is provided free throughout the country and plans for a UAE university have been announced. Students wishing to follow further education are currently sent abroad to other Arab countries, Europe or the United States at government expense. There are foreign community schools in Dubai and Abu Dhabi.

# Union of Soviet Socialist Republics

## (SOYUZ SOVIETSKIKH SOTSIALISTICHESKIKH RESPUBLIK)

**Capital**—Moscow.

**President of the Presidium of the Supreme Soviet of the U.S.S.R.**—Leonid Ilyich Brezhnev.

### CONSTITUTION AND GOVERNMENT

**National Flag:** Red, length to width 2 : 1; at the top of the hoist, a hammer and sickle gold under a star of five points gold-bordered red.

THE history of Russia is that of the peoples who inhabited the vast areas of Eastern Europe, Transcaucasus, Siberia, the Far East and Central Asia. The first States formed in these territories were in the Transcaucasus, Central Asia, and to the north of the Black Sea (the first millenium B.C.), the Bosporan Kingdom. In the second half of the ninth century, the Kievan Russ, the first feudal Russian state, was formed. In the struggle against the Tartar-Mongol hordes, the Kievan Russ was reduced to independent principalities. The hordes could not penetrate into Europe; but for three centuries the West Slav principalities remained under their yoke. At the end of the 15th century there was formed around the Muscovian principality the Russian centralized state which became the large multi-national Russian empire in the 16th–19th centuries.

The first Russian workers' revolutionary organizations were founded in the seventies of the last century. In 1883, Plekhanov created the Emancipation of Labour group; but the embryo of the future workers' party was founded by Lenin in 1895 with the title League of Struggle for the Emancipation of the Working Class; the first congress of the Russian Social Democratic Labour Party was held in 1898. At its second congress, in 1903, the party divided into bolsheviks and mensheviks. The revolutionary situation led to the 1905–07 revolution, which was suppressed by the Czarist forces; but from 1916 the situation was aggravated by the defeats of the Russian army, enormous military losses, and the economic problem. The year 1917 began with strikes and demonstrations in Petrograd (now Leningrad), and in February and March the strikes became general and took on a political character.

On 11 March (old calendar 26 February) the workers went over from political strikes to an armed uprising, gaining increasing support from the troops. On 15 March Czar Nicholas II was forced to abdicate. Dual power arose in the course of the February bourgeois-democratic revolution—on the one hand Soviets of Workers' and Soldiers' Deputies were set up all over the country (beginning with the Petrograd Soviet on 12 March), and on the other hand there was the Provisional Government headed by Prince G. E. Lvov, with A. F. Kerensky as one of its ministers, which was formed on 15 March. Kerensky later became head of the provisional government.

There was mounting dissatisfaction in the country and on 7 November the October Socialist Revolution was carried through. Power passed into the hands of the Revolutionary Military Committee, the organ of the Petrograd Soviet of Workers' and Soldiers' Deputies, and the Second All-Russia Congress of Soviets of Workers' and Soldiers' Deputies (9–11 November) proclaimed the establishment of Soviet power. The Congress immediately passed the Decree on Peace, proclaiming the Soviet Government's determination to conclude peace as soon as possible on just terms, and the Decree on Land, confiscating the big landowners' estates without compensation and transferring all the land to the people.

The Soviet government, The Soviet of Peoples' Commissars, under the chairmanship of V. I. Lenin, was also formed at the Second All-Russia Congress of Soviets. After Petrograd, Soviet power was established in Moscow and in all the principal cities and industrial centres of the country and by January–February 1918 in all Russia. Among the first measures undertaken by the Soviet government was a series of decrees and decisions on the equality and sovereignty of all nationalities in Russia and their right to free self-determination, including that of separation and the formation of independent states and the declaration on the rights of nationalities in Russia. The nationalization of the principal means of production, of banks, natural resources and means of communication was decreed. The Soviet government was obliged to sign a humiliating treaty with Germany in Brest–Litovsk on 3 March, 1918, but this was soon invalidated when revolution broke out in Germany.

The first Constitution of the Russian Socialist Federal Soviet Republic (R.S.F.S.R.) was adopted on 10 July 1918 by the fifth All-Russia Congress of Soviets.

The period from 1918 to 1922 saw the formation, with the R.S.F.S.R., of the Ukrainian S.S.R. (25 December 1917), of the Byelorussian S.S.R. (1 January 1919), of the Azerbaijan S.S.R. (28 April 1920), of the Armenian S.S.R. (29 November 1920), of the Georgian S.S.R. (25 February 1921). In 1922 these last three republics formed the Transcaucasian S.F.S.R.

In addition to this, a series of autonomous republics was formed inside the R.S.F.S.R.: the Turkestan A.S.S.R. (30 April 1918), the Tartar A.S.S.R. (27 May 1920), the Bashkir A.S.S.R. (23 March 1919), the Kazakh A.S.S.R. (26 August 1920) and others.

The Union or Soviet Socialist Republics was formed on 30 December 1922 through the amalgamation of the four Soviet Socialist Republics: the R.S.F.S.R., the Ukrainian S.S.R., the Byelorussian S.S.R. and the Transcaucasian S.F.S.R. The decision on the formation of the Union was adopted, together with its new Constitution, by the Central Executive Committee of the U.S.S.R. on 6 July 1923, and finally ratified in 1924. In 1924–25, as a result of the division of Central Asia into states according to nationalities, the Turkmen S.S.R. and the Uzbek S.S.R. were formed. In May 1925 they were accepted into the Union of Soviet Socialist Republics. The Tadjik A.S.S.R., formed in 1924, became a union republic in 1929. In December 1936 the Transcaucasian Federation was abolished and the Georgian, Armenian and Azerbaijan Soviet Socialist Republics, which had formed the Transcaucasian Federation became Union Republics. In that same year the Kazakh A.S.S.R., formerly a part of the R.S.F.S.R., and the Kirghiz A.S.S.R. (created on 1 February 1926), were also declared Union Republics within the U.S.S.R., as a result of which the overall number was now brought up to 11. In the three pre-war five-year plans, the U.S.S.R. built up its industrial base. During this same period, millions of peasant holdings were amalgamated into collectives—large-scale, mechanized collective farms.

After the aggression of Germany against Poland, on 17 September 1939 the Red Army entered the eastern regions of Western Ukraine and Western Byelorussia. Western Ukraine and Western Byelorussia were added to the Ukrainian S.S.R. and the Byelorussian S.S.R. On 31 March 1940 most of the territory ceded by Finland under the 1940 treaty which terminated the Soviet-Finnish war of 1939–40 joined the Karelian A.S.S.R. to form the Karelo-Finnish S.S.R. The other part of this territory, including the town of Viborg (Vippuri), was added to the R.S.F.S.R. On 2 August 1940 a large part of Bessarabia (seized from Soviet Russia in 1918), was returned by Rumania to the U.S.S.R., and together with the Moldavian A.S.S.R. (created 12 October 1924) went to form the Moldavian S.S.R. Northern Bukovina, and the regions of Khotin, Ismail and Akkerman were added to the Ukrainian S.S.R. The new Soviet-Romanian frontier was confirmed by the 1947 peace treaty. In 1940 Latvia, Lithuania and Estonia established Soviet Socialist Republics. In August 1940 the Latvian S.S.R., the Lithuanian S.S.R. and the Estonian S.S.R. were received into the U.S.S.R. In September 1956, at the request of the Supreme Soviet of the Karelo-Finnish S.S.R., the republic was transformed into the Karelian A.S.S.R. within the R.S.F.S.R. Since then the U.S.S.R. has consisted of 15 Union republics. The war between the Soviet Union and Germany lasted from 22 June 1941 until 9 May 1945. After the war, the three Great Powers agreed at Potsdam to integrate a part of East Prussia, including Königsberg, Tilsit and Insterburg, into the U.S.S.R. This territory was added to the R.S.F.S.R. and the abovementioned three towns were renamed Kaliningrad, Sovetsk and Cherniakhovsk respectively. By the 1947 peace treaty with Finland the ancient Russian province of Petsamo (Pechenga) was added to the territory of the R.S.F.S.R. In the Far East, after the defeat of Japan, the southern half of the island of Sakhalin (Karafuto) and the strategically important Kuril islands were added to the R.S.F.S.R. by mutual agreement with the allies.

The first Soviet Constitution (R.S.F.S.R.) was adopted in July 1918. In January 1924 the first Constitution of the U.S.S.R. was adopted at the 2nd All-union Congress of Soviets. It granted all nationalities in the Union the right of self-determination and abolished all national and national religious privileges and restrictions. In December 1936, the 8th All-Union Congress of Soviets adopted a new Constitution of the U.S.S.R., which proclaimed the victory of socialism in the U.S.S.R. and defined the state as one of workers and peasants, in which all power belonged to the working people of town and country, as represented by the Soviets of Working People's Deputies and all economic life was based on a socialist system of economy and on socialist ownership of the means of production.

The new Constitution adopted in October 1977 speaks of the creation of a developed socialist society in the U.S.S.R. and of the building of communism as the supreme aim of the Soviet state. It defines the state as being one of the whole people, with power belonging to the people and exercised by Soviets of People's Deputies. The leading and guiding force of Soviet society is defined as the Communist Party, all organizations of which must function within the framework of the Constitution.

The main trend is the extension of Soviet democracy. The Constitution sets out the basic rights, freedoms and duties of citizens, which have been amplified and added to. They include the right to work according to choice, to enjoy rest and leisure, maintenance in old age, sickness or disability or loss of breadwinner, free education, and freedom of speech, the press, assembly and meetings, street processions and demonstrations. Women and men have equal rights, as have all citizens, regardless of sex, race or nationality. Racial discrimination and propaganda are banned. New rights in the 1977 Constitution include the right to a free health service and health protection, to housing, and to participation in the management of state and public affairs and in nationwide discussion of draft laws. Citizens' rights must not be used to the detriment of society. Duties include safeguarding the interests of the state, helping to maintain public order, combating abuse of public property, conserving nature and protecting historic monuments. Universal military service is law.

The Constitution embodies the results of recent work to improve legislation and guarantees against bureaucracy and violations of rights.

It retains the basic features of the Federal structure, with its democratic dovetailing of the general interests of the multinational state and the particular interests of the constituent republics. The U.S.S.R. is a voluntary union of 15 equal Soviet Socialist Republics, namely: the Russian Soviet Federative Socialist Republic, the Ukrainian, Byelorussian, Uzbek, Kazakh, Georgian, Azerbaijan, Lithuanian, Moldavian, Latvian, Kirghiz, Tajik, Armenian, Turkmen and Estonian Soviet Socialist Republics. The sovereignty of the Union Republics is limited only in the spheres defined in Art. 73. Outside of these spheres each Union Republic exercises state authority independently.

The basis of the economic system remains socialist ownership of the means of production, with the combination of planned centralized management with the economic independence and initiative of enterprises. Socialist ownership takes the form of state property or collective farm and cooperative property. The land, its minerals, waters and forests are the exclusive property of the state, which also owns the basic means of production in industry, construction and agriculture, means of transport and communications, the banks, the property of state-run organizations and public utilities, and other state-run undertakings, most urban housing and other property necessary for state purposes. Citizens may own and inherit articles of everyday use, personal consumption and convenience, the implements and other objects of a small-holding, a house and earned savings.

This is the first constitution to include a chapter on "Foreign Policy", which lays it down that the Soviet state consistently pursues a policy of peace and advocates the strengthening of international security. Another chapter introduced for the first time is "Defence of the Socialist Homeland".

### The Supreme Soviet

The highest organ of state power is the Supreme Soviet. In the Soviet Union laws are enacted exclusively by the higher government bodies—the Supreme Soviet of the U.S.S.R. parliament which passes All-Union laws, and the Supreme Soviets of the Union and Autonomous Republics which pass effective laws in the republics concerned.

Apart from adopting and repealing the laws of the U.S.S.R., the Supreme Soviet takes decisions on the most important questions of Soviet external and internal policy, forms the leading bodies of the Soviet State, supervises the work of state bodies and officials. It elects the President of the Soviet Union; the Presidium of the U.S.S.R. Supreme Soviet; the Council of Ministers (the Soviet Government); the U.S.S.R. Supreme Court and appoints the Procurator-General. All the bodies are accountable and responsible to the Supreme Soviet.

The Supreme Soviet is elected every four years by all citizens of 18 years and over. There are two constituent Chambers, with equal rights: the Soviet of the Union and the Soviet of Nationalities.

The Soviet of the Union represents the common interest of all citizens, irrespective of their nationality. The Soviet of Nationalities represents the specific interests of each nationality living in the U.S.S.R. The two Chambers of the U.S.S.R. Supreme Soviet are vested with equal powers to initiate legislation, with equal terms of office, simultaneous beginning and end of sessions; and approval of both Chambers is required for a bill to be passed.

Whenever necessary, the Supreme Soviet appoints investigation and auditing committees to look into any question. The committees exercise systematic supervision over the work of ministries and departments and actively promote implementation of Supreme Soviet decisions.

Sessions, called twice a year, are the main form of the Supreme Soviet's work. They debate and decide important questions of domestic and foreign policy. The Supreme Soviet's Standing Committees function between sessions. They consider the most important questions before their submission to the next session.

The Presidium of the U.S.S.R. Supreme Soviet is a permanently functioning body. It is elected from among the Supreme Soviet deputies at a joint meeting of the Soviet of the Union and the Soviet of Nationalities. The Presidium is fully accountable to the Supreme Soviet.

The Presidium consists of a Chairman, 15 Vice-Chairmen (one from each Union Republic), a Secretary and 20 members. Meetings of the Presidium are called by the President approximately every two months.

The Presidium considers and settles all the main questions of state administration and supervises the work of bodies accountable to the Supreme Soviet. It reports to the regular sessions of the Supreme Soviet on the Decrees issued in the intervals between sessions.

The highest executive and administrative body in the country is the U.S.S.R. Council of Ministers, i.e. the Soviet Government.

The U.S.S.R. Council of Ministers consists of the Chairman, Vice-Chairmen, Ministers and Chairmen of the State Committees.

The Soviet Government is accountable to the Supreme Soviet and responsible to it, or, in the intervals between sessions of the Supreme Soviet, to the Presidium of the Supreme Soviet. The Government annually reports to the Supreme Soviet on the State Budget and on foreign policy. The Governments of the Union and Autonomous Republics also report to their respective Supreme Soviets on their budgets and state administration.

The U.S.S.R. Council of Ministers is charged with management of the national economy and cultural development, maintenance of law and order, protection of state interests and citizens' rights, the policy of the Armed Forces and general management of relations with foreign countries. It directs the work of ministries and departments, implements the national economic plan and ensures execution of the state budget.

### The Council of Ministers of the U.S.S.R.

*Chairman:* Alexei N. Kosygin.
*First Vice-Chairmen:* Kirill T. Mazurov, Nikolai Tikhonov.
*Vice-Chairmen:* Ivan K. Arkhipov, Nikolai K. Baibakov, Vladimir A. Kirillin, Mikhail A. Lesechko, Vladimir N. Novikov, Ignaty T. Novikov, Ziya N. Nuriev, Leonid V. Smirnov.
*Vice-Chairman and Chairman of the State Planning Committee:* Nikolai Baibakov.
*Vice-Chairman and Chairman of the State Building Committee:* Ignaty Novikov.
*Vice-Chairman and Chairman of the State Committee for Material and Technical Supply:* Nikolai Martynov.
*Vice-Chairman and Chairman of the State Committee for Science and Technology:* Vladimir Kirillin.
*Minister of Aircraft Industry:* Vasily Kasakov.
*Minister of the Automobile Industry:* Victor Polyakov.
*Minister of Foreign Trade:* Nikolai Patolichev.
*Minister of the Gas Industry:* Sabit Orudjev.
*Minister of Civil Aviation:* Boris Bugayev.
*Minister of Machine Building for the Light and Food Industries and Household Appliances:* Vasily Doyenin.
*Minister of Engineering:* Vyacheslav Bakhirev.
*Minister of the Medical Industry:* Afanasy Melnichenko.

*Minister of Merchant Marine:* Timofey Guzhenko.
*Minister of Defence Industry:* Sergei Zverev.
*Minister of General Engineering:* Sergei Afanasyev.
*Minister of Instrument-Making, Means of Automation and Control Systems:* Konstantin Rudnev.
*Minister of Justice:* Vladimir Terebilov.
*Minister of Railways:* Boris Beshchev.
*Minister of Radio Industry:* Pyotr Pleshakov.
*Minister of Medium Machine Building:* Efim Slavsky.
*Minister of Tool-Making Industry:* Anatoly Kostousov.
*Minister of Machine Building for Construction, Road Building and Municipal Services:* Efim Novoselov.
*Minister of Shipbuilding:* Mikhail Egorov.
*Minister of Transport Construction:* Ivan Sosnov.
*Minister of Tractor and Agricultural Machinery Industry:* Ivan Sinitsyn.
*Minister of Heavy and Transport Engineering:* Vladimir Zhigalin.
*Minister of the Electronic Industry:* Alexandr Shokin.
*Minister of the Chemical Industry:* Leonid Kostandov.
*Minister of Chemical and Oil Machine-Building:* Konstantin Brekhov.
*Minister of Oil-Extracting Industry:* Nikolai Maltsev.
*Minister for the Manufacture of Means of Communication:* Erlen Pervyshin.
*Minister for Machine Building for Livestock Farming and Fodder Production:* Konstantin Belyak
*Minister of Electro-Technical Industry:* Alexei Antonov.
*Minister of Power Engineering:* Victor Krotov.
*Minister of Pulp and Paper Industry:* Konstantin Galanshin.
*Minister of Higher and Secondary Specialized Education:* Vyacheslav Elyutin.
*Minister of Geology:* Yevgeni Kozlovsky.
*Minister of Public Health:* Boris Petrovsky
*Minister of Foreign Affairs:* Andrei Gromyko.
*Minister of Culture:* Pyotr Demichev.
*Minister of Light Industry:* Nikolai Tarasov.
*Minister of Timber and Wood Working Industries:* Nikolai Timofeyev.
*Minister of Melioration and Water Conservancy:* Evgeny Alekseevsky.
*Minister of Assembly and Special Construction Works:* Boris Bakin.
*Minister of Meat Packing and Dairy Industry:* Sergei Antonov.
*Minister of Oil-Refining and Petrochemical Industry:* Viktor Fedorov.
*Minister of Food Industry:* Voldemar Lein.
*Minister of Farm Produce Purchases:* Grigory S. Zolotukhin.
*Minister of Building Materials Industry:* Ivan Grishmanov.
*Minister of Fisheries:* Alexandr Ishkov.
*Minister of Communications:* Nikolai Talyzin.
*Minister of Defence:* Dimitry Ustinov.
*Minister of Agriculture:* Valentin Mesyats.
*Minister of Trade:* Alexandr Struyev.
*Minister of Coal Industry:* Boris Bratchenko.
*Minister of Finance:* Vasily Garbuzov.
*Minister of Non-Ferrous Metallurgy:* Pyotr Lomako.
*Minister of Ferrous Metallurgy:* Ivan Kazanets.
*Minister of Electric Power Development and Electrification:* Pyotr Neporozhny.
*Minister of the Interior:* Nikolai Shchelokov.
*Minister of Public Education:* Prof. Mikhail Prokofiev.
*Minister for the Construction of Heavy Industry Enterprises:* Nikolai Goldin.
*Minister of Industrial Construction:* Alexandr Tokarev.
*Minister of Construction:* Georgi Karavayev.
*Minister for Construction of Agricultural Enterprises:* Stepan Khitrov.
*Minister for the Construction of Enterprises for the Oil and Gas Industry:* Boris Shcherbina.
*Chairman of the All-Union Board for the Supply of Farm Machinery, Fuel and Fertilizers:* Alexandr Ezhevsky.
*Chairman of the State Committee for Foreign Economic Relations:* Semen Skachkov.
*Chairman of the State Committee for Forestry:* Georgy Vorobyov.
*Chairman of the State Committee for Inventions and Discoveries:* Yuri Maxarev.
*Chairman of the State Committee for Vocational Technical Training:* Alexandr Bulgakov.
*Chairman of the State Committee for Cinematography:* Filipp Ermash.
*Chairman of the State Committee for Publishing Houses, Printing and the Book Trade:* Boris Stukalin.
*Chairman of the State Security Committee:* Yury Andropov.
*Chairman of the People's Control Committee:* Alexei Shkolnikov.
*Chairman of the State Committee for Television and Radio:* Sergei Lapin.
*Chairman of the Administrative Board of the U.S.S.R. State Bank:* Nikolai Sveshnikov.
*Chief of the Central Statistical Board:* Vladimir Starovsky.

In addition all the Chairmen of the Councils of Ministers of the Union Republics are *ex officio* members of the Council of Ministers of the U.S.S.R., in accordance with article 70 of the Constitution of the U.S.S.R.

### Electoral System

All citizens who have reached the age of 18, irrespective of race or nationality, sex, creed, educational qualifications, domicile, social origin, property qualifications, and past activities, have the right to take part in the election of deputies, with the exception of persons certified as insane as prescribed by law. Every citizen of 21 or more is eligible for election to the Supreme Soviet of the U.S.S.R. (art. 96). Every citizen has one vote. Citizens serving in the U.S.S.R. armed forces have the same right to elect and be elected as other citizens. Candidates for election are nominated for each electoral district.

### The Soviets of Working People's Deputies

The Soviets of Working People's Deputies are the organs of state power in the country—the political foundation of the state. They represent all sections of the population, the working people engaged in various spheres of the material and intellectual life of society.

The deputies not only attend sessions to discuss and adopt legislation and take various decisions, but participate regularly in running state and public affairs.

They work in permanent commissions, propose questions for discussion at the Soviet sessions and examine applications and requests from constituents. Some 25 million people take part in the activities of the voluntary departments set up by the Soviets, and of street and house committees, volunteer militia, library and club boards, women's councils and other voluntary bodies.

### The Communist Party of the Soviet Union

The Communist Party is the sole political Party in the Soviet Union. By 1973 the Communist Party had 14,821,031 members and candidate members of whom 57·3 per cent are workers, 11·7 per cent collective farmers and 31·0 per cent employees. In 1971 approximately every eleventh citizen of the U.S.S.R. who had reached the age of 18 was a member of the Party.

The supreme organ of the Communist Party of the Soviet Union is the Party Congress which is convened by the Central Committee at least every four years. Congress elects a central committee which supervises all Party activities in between congresses and guides the work of the central state and public organizations through Party organizations in them. The Central Committee elects the Political Bureau of the C.P.S.U. Central Committee and Secretariat. The latest and Twenty-Fifth Congress of the C.P.S.U. was held in Spring 1976.

The guiding principle of the organizational structure of the C.P.S.U. is democratic centralism which signifies that the entire work of the Party is built on the basis of a single Programme and the Rules, which specify leadership from a single centre, strict Party discipline, and subordination of the minority to the majority, and of lower bodies to higher bodies.

Party members are accepted on an individual basis only. Membership is confined to working people accepting the Programme and charter of the Party, fulfilling Party decisions, paying Party dues and working in one of the Party organizations. A period of candidature is demanded before admission.

The C.P.S.U. gives guidance in all branches of the national economy, state administration, activity of state bodies and public organizations.

### The Politbureau of the C.P.S.U. Central Committee

*Members:* Leonid Brezhnev, Yuri Andropov, Victor Grishin, Andrei Gromyko, Andrei Kirilenko, Alexei Kosygin, Fyodor Kulakov, Dinmohammed Kunayev, Kiril Mazurov, Arrid Pelshe, Grigory Romanov, Vladimir Scherbitsky, Mikhail Suslov, Dimitry Ustinov.

*Alternate members:* Geidar Aliev, Konstantin Chernenko, Pyotr Demichev, Pyotr Masherov, Boris Ponomaryov, Sharaf Rashidov, Mikhail Solomentsev.

*Secretariat*
General Secretary: Leonid Brezhnev.

*Secretaries:* Vasily Dolgikh, Konstantin Chernenko, Ivan Kapitanov, Konstantin Katushev, Andrei Kirilenko, Fyodor Kulakov, Vasily Kuznetsov, Boris Ponomaryov, Yakov Ryabov, Mikhail Suslov.

*Chairman of the Central Auditing Commission:* G. F. Sizov.

### LOCAL GOVERNMENT

The 15 union republics of the U.S.S.R. are sovereign states. There are national autonomous states for smaller nationalities within the Union Republics. There are 20 Autonomous Republics, eight Autonomous Regions and ten National Areas in the U.S.S.R. All the union republics exercise state power independently in their own territories regarding all questions except those they have voluntarily transferred to the all-union organs of state power. Every union republic reserves the right of free secession from the U.S.S.R. Laws of the U.S.S.R. are of equal force on the territories of all the Union republics.

Territorial changes to a union republic cannot be made without its consent. Every union republic has the right to enter into direct relations with foreign powers, sign agreements and exchange diplomatic and consular representatives with them and also to take part in the work of international organizations. Every union republic has its own republican government and its own armed formations.

The Supreme Soviet of each union republic consists of a single chamber. It is the sole legislative organ of the republic. Deputies are elected for a term of four years, each union republic having the right to determine the total number and the proportion of the number of inhabitants represented by each deputy. Each Supreme Soviet elects its Presidium consisting of a President, Vice-Presidents, a secretary and a certain number of members. The Supreme Soviet of the Republic forms the republic's government, the Council of Ministers.

Autonomous republics likewise have their own constitutions. The supreme organ of state power and sole legislative organ of the Autonomous Repuplic is the Supreme Soviet of the A.S.S.R. The Supreme Soviet of an A.S.S.R. forms the government of the republic, its Council of Ministers. Numerically small nationalities form autonomous regions or national areas which form part of the Union Republics. Apart from the Autonomous Republics, Autonomous Regions and National Areas, the union republics are divided into administrative units: these are, regions, districts, towns and rural localities (villages, hamlets, stanitsas, kishlaks, auls). In addition, the R.S.F.S.R. has Territories. Matters of administration or territorial arrangement within the regions or Territories come within the competence of the Union republics. The organs of state power in the Territories, regions, autonomous regions, national areas, districts, towns and rural localities (stanitsas, villages, kishlaks and auls) are the Soviets of Working People's Deputies, established on democratic principles and elected by the population for a term of two years.

The executive and administrative organs of the Soviets of Working People's Deputies are executive committees elected by them.

### LEGAL SYSTEM

In the U.S.S.R. justice is administered by the Supreme Court of the U.S.S.R., the Supreme Courts of the Union Republics, the Supreme Courts of the Autonomous Republics, the Regional. Territorial, Town courts, the courts of the Autonomous Regions and National areas, the District (town) people's courts and by the Military tribunals. Cases in all courts are heard jointly: at the court of first instance—by a judge and two People's Assessors, at the courts of higher instances (in cases of appeals and objections)—by three members of the corresponding court. The People's Court is the basic link in the legal system of the U.S.S.R. It acts within the confines of its area (district, town, etc.). The overwhelming majority of civil and criminal cases are brought before it. Cases are heard by a judge and two People's Assessors who have all the rights of a judge when the Court is sitting. The judges of district (town) courts are elected by the citizens of the district (town) for a term of five years on the basis of universal, direct and equal suffrage, by secret ballot. The assessors are elected for a term of two years.

Regional and territorial courts, and the courts of autonomous regions and national areas, are elected by the corresponding Soviets of Working People's deputies for a period of five years.

The supreme court of an autonomous republic is elected by the Supreme Soviet of that republic for a term of five years.

The supreme court of the Union republic is the highest judicial organ of the Union republic. It is elected by the Supreme Soviet of the republic for a term of five years.

The Supreme Court of the U.S.S.R. is the highest judicial organ, it watches over the judicial activity of all the judicial organs of the U.S.S.R. and union republics. It is elected by the Supreme Soviet of the U.S.S.R. for a term of five years and consists of a Chairman, two Deputy-Chairmen, 13 members of the Supreme Court and 45 People's Assessors, and also the chairmen of the supreme courts of the Union republics who are members of the Supreme Court of the U.S.S.R. by virtue of their position. The Supreme Court of the U.S.S.R. consists of Plenary, Civil Session, Criminal and Military Collegiums. The Supreme Court can initiate legislation.

The constitution provides for the creation of special courts which can be set up on the initiative of the Supreme Soviet of the U.S.S.R.

Soviet judges are independent and answer only to their electors. Cases in all courts are heard with the participation of assessors. Legal proceedings are carried on in the language of the union or autonomous republic, or autonomous region, with provision for persons not in possession of that language. They are entitled to the services of an interpreter, and the right, through him, to address the court in their native language. The hearing of cases in all courts is open and the rights of the accused to defence are guaranteed.

The Procurator-General of the U.S.S.R. has supreme supervisory power to ensure execution of the law. The work of the Procurator's department is governed by the regulations of the Procurator Supervision of the U.S.S.R., adopted by the Presidium of the Supreme Soviet on 24 May 1955. The Procurator-General is appointed by the Supreme Soviet of the U.S.S.R. for seven years. He appoints the procurators of the Union republics, Autonomous republics, Territories, regions and autonomous regions, for a term of five years. The Procurators of the Union republics appoint regional, district and town procurators, for a term of five years, the appointment to be subsequently confirmed by the Procurator-General. The organs of the Procurator's office perform their functions independently of any local organs, and are subordi nate solely to the Procurator-General of the U.S.S.R.

***Procurator-General of the U.S.S.R.:*** R. A. Rudenko.
***Chairman of the Supreme Court of the U.S.S.R.:*** A. F. Gorkin.

### AREA AND POPULATION

The following table shows the area and population of the U.S.S.R. and the constituent (Union) republics:

| *Union Republics (with capitals)* | *Area (in thousand sq. km.)* | *Population 1.1.77 (in thousands)* |
|---|---|---|
| Azerbaijan S.S.R. (Baku) | 86·6 | 5,786 |
| Armenian S.S.R. (Yerevan) | 29·8 | 2,894 |
| Byelorussian S.S.R. (Minsk) | 207·6 | 9,426 |
| Estonian S.S.R. (Tallin) | 45·1 | 1,447 |
| Georgian S.S.R. (Tbilisi) | 69·7 | 4,999 |
| Kazakh S.S.R. (Alma-Ata) | 2,717·3 | 14,527 |
| Kirghiz S.S.R. (Frunze) | 198·5 | 3,451 |
| Latvian S.S.R. (Riga) | 63·7 | 2,521 |
| Lithuanian S.S.R. (Vilnius) | 65·2 | 3,336 |
| Moldavian S.S.R. (Kishinev) | 33·7 | 3,896 |
| Russian S.F.S.R. (Moscow) | 17,075·4 | 135,569 |
| Tadzhik S.S.R. (Dushanbe) | 143·1 | 3,589 |
| Turkmen S.S.R. (Ashkhabad) | 488·1 | 2,652 |
| Ukrainian S.S.R. (Kiev) | 603·7 | 49,343 |
| Uzbek S.S.R. (Tashkent) | 447·4 | 14,485 |
| Total | 22,274·9 | 257,912 |

* Total area of USSR includes areas of the White Sea (90,000 sq. km.) and Sea of Azor (37,300 sq. km.) not forming part of surrounding territories.

The urban population increased from 28·5 million in 1913 to 149·6 million by 1 January 1974.

The following table shows population figures for capitals of all the Union Republics and for cities with more than 500,000 inhabitants at 1 January 1977 (in thousands):

| | | | |
|---|---|---|---|
| Moscow | 7,819 | Ufa | 942 |
| Leningrad | 4,425 | Volgograd | 931 |
| Kiev | 2,079 | Rostov-on-Don | 921 |
| Tashkent | 1,689 | Alma-Ata | 871 |
| Baku | 1,435 | Saratov | 856 |
| Kharkov | 1,405 | Riga | 816 |
| Gorky | 1,319 | Voronezh | 779 |
| Novosibirsk | 1,304 | Zaporozh | 772 |
| Minsk | 1,230 | Krasnoyarsk | 769 |
| Kuibyshev | 1,204 | Lvov | 642 |
| Sverdlovsk | 1,187 | Krivoi Rog | 641 |
| Tbilisi | 1,042 | Yaroslavl | 584 |
| Odessa | 1,039 | Karaganda | 576 |
| Omsk | 1,026 | Krasnodar | 552 |
| Chelyabinsk | 1,007 | Novokuznetsk | 537 |
| Dnepropetrovsk | 995 | Izhevsk | 534 |
| Donetsk | 984 | Irkutsk | 532 |
| Perm | 972 | Vladivostok | 526 |
| Kazan | 970 | Khabarovsk | 524 |
| Yerevan | 956 | Barnaul | 522 |

## CURRENCY

The unit of currency is the rouble of 100 copeks; the gold content of the rouble is fixed at 0·987412 gr. There are in circulation bank notes issued by the State Bank of the U.S.S.R. in denominations of 100, 50, 25, and 10 roubles, State currency notes in denominations of 5, 3 and 1 roubles, and coins of 1 rouble, 50, 20, 15 and 10 copeks (copper-nickel alloy) and 1, 2, 3 and 5 copeks (copper-zinc alloy).

## FINANCE

Revenue and expenditure increased in 1975–1977 as shown below (in thousand million roubles):

| | 1975 | 1976 | 1977 |
|---|---|---|---|
| Planned revenue | 208·5 | 223·7 | 238·9 |
| Planned expenditure | 206·5 | 223·5 | 238·7 |

Actual figures for 1976 proved to be 232,200 million roubles (revenue) and 226,700 million roubles (expenditure).

The constant growth of revenue derives from increases in social production and thus in national income.

Receipts from the economy are planned at 217,000 million roubles. Revenue from income tax constitutes a minor part of the whole.

In the 1977 budget a total of 123,400 million roubles was allocated for financing the national economy, an increase of 4,900 million roubles on the 1976 figure.

A total of 83,854 million roubles was appropriated for social and cultural measures—including education, research, libraries, clubs, theatres, press, television, radio, health services, physical culture, pensions, etc.

Defence appropriations amounted to 17,230 million roubles, as against 17,430 million in 1976.

State administration, law courts and procurators' offices were allocated 2,031 million roubles for 1977.

The Union Republics have their own budgets, which receive funds from the U.S.S.R. state budget. Allocations from the central budget amount to 106,900 million roubles.

## BANKS

Immediately after the socialist revolution in November 1918 banking was declared a state monopoly, and this principle has since formed the basis of the whole of Soviet policy in this matter. By the end of 1917 all private commercial banks had been nationalized.

Under socialism banks are public property and all their activities are closely related to the economic policy of the Soviet state.

The central credit institution is *Gosbank* (the State Bank of the U.S.S.R.), the only bank of issue, the bank of credit for the national economy, and the country's clearing and monetary centre. Its statutory fund is fixed at 1,500 million roubles. In 1971, the Gosbank system consisted of 4,213 establishments. Credit investment by Gosbank in the national economy, in the form of short-term loans, amounted on 1 January 1971 to 108,175 million roubles. Credit investments in the industry are growing both absolutely and relatively. On 1 January 1971 short term industrial investments were 36,337 million roubles. In 1971 the total volume of long-term credits amounted to 18,057 million roubles (of which sum 10,296 million roubles were to collective farms). Gosbank fixes the exchange rate of the rouble. It has main offices in each of the Union Republics, 150 regional and town offices, nearly 4,000 smaller branches and over 78,700 savings banks throughout the Soviet Union.

An important part in the country's economy is also played by *Stroibank* of the U.S.S.R. (All-Union Bank for Financing Capital Investments). Stroibank finances capital investments for enterprises and for organizations in industry, transport, communications, construction, industry, commerce, education, housing and municipal economy and makes short-term loans to contract and construction organizations. Like *Gosbank*, *Stroibank* is directly subordinate to the Council of Ministers of the U.S.S.R. In January 1971 credit investments by Stroibank amounted to 7,985 million roubles (short-term loans) and 3,000 million roubles (long-term loans). It has over a thousand local branches.

The international payment turnover of the Soviet Union is served by *Vneshtorbank* (Bank for Foreign Trade of the U.S.S.R.), established in 1924. Capital and reserves—Roubles 438 million, number of foreign correspondent banks —1,414).

The Bank opens accounts in Soviet and foreign currency, accepts deposits from Soviet and foreign juridical and physical persons, finances the Soviet foreign trade by granting loans to Soviet foreign trade organizations, effects settlements for export and import transactions and non-commercial operations, grants/receives credits to/from foreign banks, handles operations with Promissory Notes and Bills of Exchange, buys and sells foreign currency, issues, sells and buys its Travellers Cheques, sells and cashes Travellers Cheques of State Bank of the U.S.S.R. and foreign banks, accepts for custody foreign currency, precious metals, securities, etc., and through its dealing staff is active in the field of foreign exchange and deposit transactions.

The Bank's Commercial Department is engaged in wholesale and retail selling to foreign juridical and physical persons of gold bars, gold and silver coins and other numismatic commodities, and retail sales of precious stones.

*Sberkassa* (Savings Bank): By the beginning of 1977 the U.S.S.R. had 80,100 savings banks, of which 24,300 were in towns and other urban centres and 55,800 in rural areas. The deposits of the population in savings banks increased, amounting to 103,000 million roubles at 1 January 1977. The total number of depositors was 113,101,000.

**Insurance.** Several types of insurance exist in the U.S.S.R.—state social insurance, state personal and property insurance.

State social insurance is universal, embracing all citizens, from the day they start work. Under this system they are guaranteed all types of maintenance when they grow old, fall ill or are temporarily disabled. The arrangements include free qualified medical aid to all citizens, without exception; a uniform system of grants and pensions; aid to families in the education and upkeep of children; a network of free state institutions for old and disabled persons who cannot live with their families for some reason or other; various means of training invalids so that they can do certain jobs, etc.

Personal insurance is effected by the U.S.S.R. State Insurance bodies. There are several forms of life insurance, with mixed insurance and accident insurance being the most widespread. The citizens who take out a mixed insurance policy are guaranteed payment in the following cases: if they survive until the time laid down in the policy, or if they are disabled as a result of an accident. If a person dies before the policy expires, the insurance is paid to the person or persons indicated in the policy.

Citizens of 16 years of age are insurable for 5, 10, 15 or 20 years, for a sum of 100 roubles or more. Insurance fees depend on the length of insurance, the age of the person and the sum assured.

Property insurance is also handled by the U.S.S.R. State Insurance agencies. This type of insurance covers domestic property, cars and other items of personal property, and houses, outhouses and animals belonging to citizens. When domestic property is insured, the policy may be made out for any sum not exceeding the actual value of the property. The policy can be made out for a time of up to one year. The same principles form the basis for insuring other types of personal property.

The agencies of the U.S.S.R. State Insurance also insure public property and the property of co-operative and public organizations against natural calamities. This is done at the expense of the insurance fund which is built up out of the fees paid by these organizations.

**Ninth and Tenth Five-Year Plans**

The main economic and social tasks of the Ninth Five-Year Plan (1971–75) were carried out. The Soviet economy developed at a high and stable rate, the national income rising by 28 per cent, i.e. by 76,000 million roubles. Total industrial production grew by 43 per cent.

Despite highly unfavourable weather, average annual agricultural output over the five years was 13 per cent more than over the previous five-year period.

More than 75 million people received wage increases, and 40 million more benefited from higher pensions, allowances and grants. Prices, rents, etc. remained unchanged. Nearly 13 million flats were completed.

The Main Guidelines for the Development of the U.S.S.R. Economy in 1976–1980, adopted at the Twenty-fifth Congress of the C.P.S.U. in spring 1976 envisage the chief task of industry during the Tenth Five-Year Plan to be to satisfy more fully the requirements of the economy and the population for high quality goods and ensure the technical re-equipment and intensification of all spheres of production.

The Draft sets the aim of increasing national income by 24–28 per cent over the five-year period, with real incomes per head of population rising by 20–22 per cent. Labour productivity in industry should rise by 30–40 per cent.

Industrial output is expected to go up by 35–39 per cent, including a 38–42 per cent rise in output of capital goods and a 30–32 per cent increase in output of consumer goods.

Annual output of fuel and power is expected to increase by 1980 as follows: electricity (thousand million kwh)—to 1,340–1,380; oil—to 620–640 million tonnes; natural gas—to 400–435 thousand million cubic metres; coal—to 790–810 million tonnes.

Increases in the production of some major types of raw and other materials are envisaged over the five years: steel—to 160–170 million tonnes per annum; chemical and petrochemical industry—by 60–65 per cent; plastics and synthetic resins—by 90–110 per cent; chemical fibres—to 1,450–1,500 thousand tonnes; wood pulp and paper industry—by 22–25 per cent; cement—to 143–146 million tonnes per annum.

In the engineering industry the following increases are envisaged by 1980: engineering and iron and steel industries—by 50–60 per cent; motor vehicles—to 2·1–2·2 million per annum; instruments used in automation—by 60–70 per cent; machines and equipment for light industry and the food industry—by 30–40 per cent; farm machinery (for crops and livestock)—to 5,000 million roubles per annum.

The following output levels are envisaged for consumer goods industries: light industry—by 26–28 per cent; furniture—by 40–50 per cent; fabrics—to 12·5–13·1 thousand million sq.m. per annum; food industry—by 26–28 per cent; meat and milk industry—by 20–22 per cent.

In agriculture average annual production figures are envisaged as increasing as follows by 1980: gross output—by 14–17 per cent; grain—to 215–220 million tonnes; raw cotton—to at least 9 million tonnes; meat (slaughter weight)—to 15–15·6 million tonnes; milk—to 94–96 million tonnes; eggs—to 58–61 thousand million; wool—to 511 thousand tonnes.

Transport operations should show the following increases over the five years: freight carried by all forms of transport—by 30 per cent; rail freight—by 22 per cent; road freight—by 42 per cent; marine freight—by about 30 per cent; river freight—by about 22 per cent. Passenger traffic on transport as a whole should increase by 23 per cent.

An extensive programme for social development and rises in living standards is proposed.

## AGRICULTURE, INDUSTRY AND COMMERCE

**Agriculture.** Whereas pre-1917 Russia was a backward, essentially agricultural country, the Soviet Union today is an industrial power with its agriculture organized on a large-scale basis.

Owing to the wide variety of climatic conditions and soils, a variety of crops is grown. Wheat is the main crop, but increasing areas are being sown with maize, cotton, sugar beet, flax, soya beans sunflower, tobacco, etc.

Climatic differences give rise to different problems. In the Baltic area, Byelorussia and the central part of the Russian Federation the main trouble is excessive moisture. To combat this, drainage is being carried out on a wide scale.

On the other hand, the Ukraine, the Volga areas and Kazakhstan—the country's main grain producers—suffer from lack of moisture. Once in three or four years, or even more frequently, extensive areas are hit by drought. Large irrigation works are being built to bring water to drought-affected land.

The bulk of the country's farmland is used by collective and state farms. Collective farms are voluntary co-operatives, to which the state grants the free use of land in perpetuity. Members of collective farms are paid according to the quality and quantity of their work. State farms are state-owned agricultural enterprises, manned by workers who receive fixed wages.

Collective and state farmers are given small household plots of land which they use for fruit, vegetable and grape-growing. Surplus produce from such individual plots and from collective farms may be sold at collective farm markets.

There is an increasing tendency to set up inter-collective farm enterprises with the resources of a number of farms to carry on specialized crop-growing or livestock-raising, or to engage in some auxiliary work such as construction, fruit and vegetable canning, etc.

At 1 January 1977 there were 27,700 collective farms, 19,617 state farms, and over 7,000 inter-collective farm enterprises.

In 1976 agriculture received 368,000 tractors (totalling 28 mln. h.p.), 98,000 grain harvesters, 11,000 maize harvesters, 12,000 potato diggers, 14,000 beet pullers, 8,000 cotton-picking machines, 54,000 milking machines and many others.

During the past few years the emphasis has been increasingly on intensification of farming, which involves big capital investments.

The following table shows the areas sown to the main crops (in million hectares):

| *Crop* | 1975 | 1976 |
|---|---|---|
| All cereal crops | 127·9 | 127·8 |
| Fodder crops | 65·6 | 66·3 |
| Industrial crops | 14·1 | 14·6 |
| Melon crops, potatoes and other vegetables | 10·1 | 9·2 |
| Total sown area | 217·7 | 217·9 |

The following table gives the gross harvest of the main crops:

| *Crop* | | 1975 | 1976 |
|---|---|---|---|
| Grain | (million tonnes) | 140 | 223·8 |
| Raw cotton | ,, | 7·9 | 8·3 |
| Sunflower | ,, | 5 | 5·3 |
| Flax fibre | (thousand tonnes) | 478 | 507·0 |
| Sugar beet | (million tonnes for refining) | 66·2 | 99·9 |
| Potatoes | (million tonnes) | 88·5 | 85·1 |

**Livestock.** The figures below give the head of productive livestock on the collective, state and individual farms (in millions, on 1 January):

| *Domestic livestock* | 1976 | 1977 |
|---|---|---|
| Cattle | 111 | 110·3 |
| of which, cows | 41·9 | 42·0 |
| Pigs | 57·8 | 63·0 |
| Sheep and goats | 146·9 | 145·4 |

Output of the main products of animal husbandry:

| *Product* | 1976 | 1977 |
|---|---|---|
| Meat, deadweight (million tonnes) | 15·2 | 13·4 |
| Milk (million tonnes) | 90·8 | 89·2 |
| Wool (thousand tonnes) | 463 | 432·8 |
| Eggs (thousand millions) | 57·7 | 55·6 |

**Forestry.** The total area covered by forests is 746,800,000 hectares, or 33 per cent of the country's territory. About 70 per cent of the timber supply is concentrated in the Northern and Eastern regions of the country, which abound in forests. There are big sawmills in Archangelsk, Leningrad, Volgograd, Astrakhan, Kremenchug, Igarka and other towns. In 1976 timber production (roundwood removals) was 306 million cubic metres.

**Mining.** The Soviet Union today ranks first in the world for the known reserves of many basic raw materials (iron and manganese ores, coal, copper, lead, zinc, wolfram, nickel, bauxites, mercury, apatite, mica, asbestos and potassium) and holds one of the first places for proved supplies of oil and gas.

A great deal of oil is extracted from the vast oilfields between the Volga and the Urals, from the Baku oilfields and also the oil deposits near Grozny and Maikop. West Siberia has now become the main oil producer, however, and in 1976–1980 is expected to reach an annual figure of 300–310 million tonnes, as against the 620–640 predicted for the country as a whole. Oil is also produced in the valley of the river Emba, in Central Asia, Western Siberia, Sakhalin and in the Western Ukraine and in some other parts. Total oil production in 1976 exceeded the 500 million tonne mark for the first time, increasing to 520 million tonnes.

Pig iron output rose from 66,200,000 in 1965 to 105 million tonnes in 1976. The rise in production is the result of the construction of new enterprises and the exploitation of new deposits of first-grade ores. In the last few years new deposits of iron ore have been discovered in Siberia, Kustanai Region (Kazakhistan), Belgorod, Kursk and other regions. The Soviet Union ranks first in the world in iron ore output. Production in 1976 reached 239 million tonnes.

There are vast resources of coal, mainly in Siberia, though the Donetz Basin (Donbas) was the most intensively worked before the war. The Donbas supplies coal for the metallurgical industry of the south as well as raw materials and fuel for the chemical industries and transport of the Ukraine. In spite of the tremendous devastation wrought in the Donbas during the war, this area has now been completely rehabilitated, and is once more the most highly mechanized and productive coalfield of the country. The coalfield near Moscow, too, has been rapidly restored. The Kuznetsk Basin is second in production in the U.S.S.R. The U.S.S.R. has the world's largest coal output. Production in 1976 reached 711 million tonnes.

**Industry.** The main branch of the U.S.S.R. economy. The foundation of Soviet industry is public ownership of the means of production. Thanks to the advantages of the socialist system, the U.S.S.R., rapidly wiped out its age-old backwardness in this sphere and in the volume of industrial production now holds first place in Europe and second in the world, next to the U.S.A.

The U.S.S.R. is at the top of the world's table in the output of iron ore, coke, coal, trunk-line diesel and electric locomotives, tractors (in sum-total units), harvesters, timber, cement, precast ferro-concrete structural elements, pane glass, woollen and cotton fabrics, sugar and fish. Soviet share in the world's industrial output is steadily growing. In 1917 it was less than 3 per cent, by 1937 it had increased to about 10 per cent, and in 1973 the U.S.S.R. accounted for about one-fifth of the world's gross industrial output. The number of factory and office workers in the national economy of the U.S.S.R. in 1974 amounted to 99,700,000.

The oil, coal, chemical, timber, pulp, woodworking, iron and steel, and nonferrous metal industries are under joint national and republican jurisdiction. Gross output of industrial production in 1975 amounted to 511,300 million roubles.

All industries using local raw materials exclusively are under the jurisdiction of the Union Republics.

Ministries of the U.S.S.R. exercise control of different branches of industry and are supervised by the U.S.S.R. Council of Ministers through its central planning agency *Gosplan*.

The U.S.S.R. State Planning Committee, *Gosplan*, which is responsible for elaborating the main trends and problems of economic development and for drafting economic plans and checking their implementation, generalizes the sectoral plans of the economy and refers them for consideration to the U.S.S.R. Council of Ministers, which submits the draft state plan for the approval of the U.S.S.R. Supreme Soviet. The drafts of republican economic plans are drawn up in the same way.

The following table shows industrial output:

| *Product* | *Unit* | 1975 | 1976 |
|---|---|---|---|
| Pig iron | million tonnes | 103·0 | 105·0 |
| Steel | ,, | 141·0 | 145·0 |
| Rolled stock | ,, | 115·0 | 121·0 |
| Coal | ,, | 701·0 | 712·0 |
| Oil | ,, | 491·0 | 520·0 |
| Gas | 1,000 million m$^3$ | 289·0 | 299·0 |
| Electric power | 1,000 million kWh | 1,038·0 | |
| Mineral fertiliser | in conventional units, million tonnes | 90·2 | 92·3 |
| Roundwood removal | million m$^3$ | 311·0 | 306·0 |
| Cement | million tonnes | 122·0 | 124·0 |
| Bricks | 1,000 million | 47·2 | 47·0 |
| Metal-cutting machine tools | thousands | 231·0 | 232·0 |
| Forge and press equipment | ,, | 50·0 | 51·9 |
| Blast furnace and steel smelting equipment | thousands tonnes | 187·0 | 192·0 |
| Rolling equipment | ,, | 132·0 | 146·0 |
| Chemical fibres | ,, | 955·0 | 1,020·0 |
| Turbines | million kW | 19·1 | 19·0 |
| Diesel locomotives | units | 1,375·0 | 1,455·0 |
| Electric locomotives | ,, | 395·0 | 410·0 |
| Mainline goods wagons | thousands | 69·9 | 71·9 |
| Cars and lorries | ,, | 1,897·0 | 1,955·0 |
| Tractors (phys. units) | ,, | 550·0 | 562·0 |
| Excavators | ,, | 39·0 | 40·4 |
| Paper and cardboard | thousands tonnes | 8,600·0 | 8,916·0 |

The table below gives the figures for some consumer goods:

| *Product* | *Unit* | 1975 | 1976 |
|---|---|---|---|
| Cotton fabrics | million m. | 6,635 | 6,775 |
| Woollen fabrics | ,, | 740 | 764 |
| Silk fabrics | ,, | 1,508 | 1,598 |
| Linen fabrics | ,, | 779 | 807 |
| Leather footwear | million prs. | 698 | 725 |
| Bicycles and mopeds | thousands | 5,007 | 5,072 |
| Motor cycles and motor scooters | ,, | 1,029 | 1,059 |
| Radio and TV sets | ,, | 15,400 | 15,503 |
| Domestic refrigerators | ,, | 5,600 | 5,834 |
| Domestic washing machines | ,, | 3,300 | 3,509 |
| Clocks and watches, domestic | millions | 55 | 58 |

The following table gives figures for the production of a number of commodities by the food industry:

| *Product* | *Unit* | 1975 | 1976 |
|---|---|---|---|
| Granulated sugar | million tonnes | 10·4 | 9·2 |
| Meat | ,, | 9·9 | 8·3 |
| Fish products | thousand million roubles | 3·8 | 4·5 |
| Butter | million tonnes | 1·2 | 1·3 |
| Vegetable Oil | ,, | 3·4 | 2·8 |
| Canned foods | thousand million standard tins | 14·5 | 14·5 |
| Bakery products | million tonnes | 3·2 | 3·4 |

**Commerce.** Commerce in the Soviet Union takes three forms: state, co-operative and collective farm trade. In 1975 State trade accounted for 70 per cent of the total, while co-operative and collective farm trade accounted for 30 per cent.

The following table shows comparative figures for the overall state and co-operative retail trade for some of the years between 1940–76 (in million roubles):

| | 1940 | 1958 | 1965 | 1970 | 1976 |
|---|---|---|---|---|---|
| Overall retail trade, including | 17·5 | 67·7 | 104·8 | 155·5 | 225·6 |
| State trade | 12·8 | 46·8 | 104·8 | 109·8 | 156·5 |
| Co-operative trade | 4·7 | 20·9 | 31·0 | 45·9 | 63·5 |

Soviet foreign trade increased from 50,700 million roubles in 1975 to 56,800 million roubles in 1976, with exports rising by 16·6 per cent during the year and imports by 7·7 per cent.

Trade with the socialist countries accounted for 31,600 million roubles, with the developed capitalist countries 18,700 million roubles and the developing countries 6,500 million roubles.

The following table shows the volume of the Soviet Union's foreign trade with its biggest trading partners in 1974 and 1976:

| *Countries* | 1974 (*million roubles*) | 1976 (*million roubles*) |
|---|---|---|
| Britain | 890 | 1,232 |
| Bulgaria | 2,904 | 4,500 |
| Cuba | 1,642 | 2,900 |
| Czechoslovakia | 3,029 | 4,500 |
| Egypt, Arab Republic | 728 | 531 |
| Federal Republic of Germany | 2,209 | 3,000 |
| Finland | 1,540 | 2,000 |
| France | 941 | 1,700 |
| German Democratic Republic | 4,315 | 6,000 |
| Hungary | 2,282 | 3,500 |
| India | 615 | 648 |
| Iraq | 536 | 714 |
| Italy | 1,137 | 1,800 |
| Japan | 1,683 | 2,100 |
| Poland | 3,584 | 5,200 |
| Romania | 1,191 | 1,600 |
| Sweden | 435 | 539 |
| U.S.A. | 742 | 2,200 |
| Yugoslavia | 1,240 | 1,800 |

The Soviet Union imports from the socialist countries industrial goods of popular consumption, fruit, vegetables, sugar, some types of raw materials, machines and equipment.

The Soviet Union's trade with the developing nations is acquiring an ever greater significance. The U.S.S.R. is increasing the purchase of traditional exports of these countries. In return, it supplies them with industrial manufactures. Forty-seven of these countries have signed agreements on trade and payments with the Soviet Union, and 35 countries on economic and technical co-operation.

Structure of Soviet exports and imports (including re-exports) in percentages:

| *Imports* | 1974 | 1976 |
|---|---|---|
| Machinery and equipment | 32·4 | 36·3 |
| Fuel and electricity | 3·5 | 3·6 |
| Metals (incl. ores, concentrates and metal items) | 13·6 | 10·8 |
| Chemical products, fertilizers and rubber | 6·3 | 4·3 |
| Timber, pulp, paper | 1·9 | 1·8 |
| Textiles | 4·1 | 2·3 |
| Foodstuffs | 17·1 | 22·8 |
| Consumer goods | 14·6 | 12·6 |

| *Exports* | 1974 | 1976 |
|---|---|---|
| Machinery and equipment | 19·2 | 19·4 |
| Fuel and electricity | 25·4 | 34·3 |
| Metals (including ores, concentrates and metal items) | 14·7 | 13·2 |
| Chemical products, fertilizers and rubber | 3·6 | 3·0 |
| Timber, pulp, paper | 6·9 | 5·3 |
| Textiles | 3·3 | 2·9 |
| Furs | 0·3 | 0·3 |
| Foodstuffs | 7·1 | 3·0 |
| Consumer goods | 3·9 | 3·0 |

## COMMUNICATIONS

The railways handle the bulk of Soviet freight and passenger traffic. Even at the present stage of development of other forms of freight transport, the railways account for about two-thirds of the total freight turnover.

In 1976 Soviet railways transported about 3,655 million tons of goods including 730·3 million tons of coal, 394·4 million tons of oil and oil products, and 130·1 million tons of grain and grain products.

Freight turnover was 3,295,100 million tonne-km and passenger turnover 315,000 million passenger km. (3,545 million passengers).

The railway network is over 138,500 km. in length (1,524 mm. gauge).

About 99 per cent of the line is served by electrical and diesel locomotives, which haul 95 per cent of all freight.

A new 3,200 km. line is under construction in the east of the Soviet Union—the Baikal–Amur line, which will run north of the Trans-Siberian railway, from Ust-Kut to Komsomolsk-on-Amur. This will play a large part in the development of a new large industrial region in Siberia and the Far East.

Main highways connect Moscow with Kiev, the Crimea, Leningrad, Minsk, Riga and Warsaw, the Caucasus, Kazakhstan, Alma-Ata, Frunze and Tashkent, and with parts of Siberia. The total length of roads is 1,398,000 km. of which 598,400 km. are hard surfaced.

Each Republic controls its own waterways; total length about 145,600 km. River transport has always been of great importance to the U.S.S.R. and in those areas where railway lines are few it is essential. The main inland waterway systems are those of the Volga, Dnieper, Don, Ob, Yenisei, Lena, Amur and Amu-Darya.

The length of the coastline of the U.S.S.R. is about 47,000 km. The Soviet Union has 17 shipping lines, each of which specializes in a particular shipping operation. The Soviet merchant marine numbers over 1,200 transport vessels which carry goods overseas. In 1976 the total tonnage of the Soviet merchant fleet (including fishing vessels) was 19,870,906 registered tonnes. It is one of the largest in the world.

All civil air services are operated by Aeroflot, which has regular flights to 76 countries. Twenty-six international airlines have reciprocal arrangements with Aeroflot.

Aeroflot has 3,000 domestic routes totalling over 650,000 km and connecting 3,500 towns. In 1976 Aeroflot handled 100 million passengers.

The supersonic liner TU-144 is now in regular passenger service between Moscow and Alma-Ata, covering the 3,300 km in under two hours. It had previously been carrying mail and cargo between the two cities for two years.

The first Soviet airbus, the 350-seater Il-86, has been undergoing trials and is expected to be in use by Aeroflot by the end of 1979.

**Post, Telegraph, Telephone, Broadcasting and Television.** By the end of 1976 the number of post, telegraph and telephone offices was 88,000, of which 63,000 were in rural areas. There were 61·6 million radios, 66·2 million rediffusion loudspeakers, 57·2 television sets and 18·6 million telephones.

## NEWSPAPERS

**Pravda.** Founded 1912. Organ of the Central Committee of the C.P.S.U. Daily. Ulitsa Pravdy, 24, Moscow.

**Izvestia.** Founded 1917. Six issues weekly. Newspaper of the Presidium of the Supreme Soviet of the U.S.S.R. Pushkinskaya Ploschad, 5, Moscow.

**Ekonomicheskaya Gazeta.** Founded 1918. (The former title 'Ekonomicheskaya Zhizn'.) Newspaper of the Central Committee of the C.P.S.U. Published weekly. Bumazhniy proyezd, 14, Moscow.

**Trud.** Founded 1921. Newspaper of the All-Union Central Council of Trade Unions. Six issues weekly. Ulitsa Gorkogo, 18b, Moscow.

**Selskaya Zhizn.** Founded 1918. Newspaper of the Central Committee of the C.P.S.U. Six issues weekly, 7·7 million copies per issue. Ulitsa Pravdy, 24, Moscow.

**Komsomolskaya Pravda.** Founded 1925. Six issues weekly. Central Committee of the Leninist Young Communist League of the Soviet Union. Ulitsa Pravdy, 24, Moscow.

**Krasnaya Zvezda.** Founded 1924. Newspaper of the Ministry of Defence of the U.S.S.R. Six issues weekly. Khoroshevskoye Chaussee, 38, Moscow.

**Moskovskaya Pravda.** Founded 1919. Newspaper of the Moscow City Committee of the C.P.S.U. and of the Moscow City Soviet of Working People's Deputies. Six issues weekly. Chistoprudny Bulvar, 8, Moscow.

**Vechernaya Moskva.** Founded 1923. Newspaper of the Moscow City Committee of the C.P.S.U. and the Moscow City Soviet of Working People's Deputies. Six issues weekly. Chistoprudny Bulvar, 8, Moscow.

**Sovietskaya Rossiya.** Founded 1955. Newspaper of the Central Committee of the C.P.S.U. and the Council of Ministers of the R.S.F.S.R. Ulitsa Pravdy, 24, Moscow.

The Soviet Press produces 7,863 newspapers and 5,966 periodicals. The most influential daily is *Pravda* which has a circulation of 9,600,000. It is an organ of the Central Committee of the Communist Party. More than 85,500 books and booklets were published in 1976, in a total printing exceeding 1,800 million copies. Newspapers are published in 58 languages of the peoples of the Soviet Union. The main news agency, *TASS*, plays an important role in distributing by radio or telegraph foreign and domestic news to newspapers throughout the republic; it also transmits *Pravda* editorials. The circulation figures for various newspapers are: Izvestia—8,352,000; Trud—8,352,000; Komsomolskaya Pravda—9,950,000; Selskaya Zhizn—8,125,000.

## HEALTH SERVICES

Public health is one of the most important responsibilities of the Soviet state. All medical aid and treatment are free, and the basic principle of the health service is prevention. The public undergo regular medical examinations, particular attention being paid to the detection of cancer, tuberculosis, hypertension, and diabetes, among other things.

All citizens are registered at polyclinics either near their homes or, if they work at a large plant, on the premises of their workplace. These may be likened to a combination of GP's surgery and hospital out-patient department as all specialists, physiotherapy, X-ray facilities, laboratories, etc., are under the same roof. There are separate clinics for children up to 15 years of age.

By the end of 1976 there were 3,077,000 beds in urban and rural civil hospitals, i.e. 119 beds per 10,000 of population. The number of civilian doctors totalled 862,000, or 33·4 per 10,000 of population.

In the past few years priority has been given to hospital building so that the widest possible practical use may be made of the latest scientific advances in medicine.

Emergency services are equipped with ambulances in which treatment can be given immediately by the ambulance medical team to patients suffering from heart attacks, shock, severe poisoning, burns, etc.

Mother and child welfare occupies a prominent place in the health service. Pregnant women are not allowed to do any heavy work or overtime, and are entitled to fully-paid leave for two months before birth and two months after—longer if birth is complicated. A mother may, of course, give up work entirely, but her job is kept open for her for a year. If she returns to it within that period she retains an unbroken work record, which is important for pension purposes. Working mothers of young babies are allowed time off to feed their babies and take additional rest, the time being paid for as working time. Over 12 million children attend nurseries and nursery schools.

The Soviet Union pioneered in the field of painless childbirth.

Help is given to many foreign countries to control infectious diseases, build hospitals and build up a national pharmaceutical industry. Here an important part is played by the U.S.S.R. Union of Red Cross and Red Crescent Societies.

The health service is backed up by a constant complex of social measures designed to improve living standards and working conditions, and to reduce such health hazards as environmental pollution.

## ATOMIC ENERGY

The world's first commercial atomic power station was put into operation in the Soviet Union in 1954. This is a 5,000 kW station at Obninsk, near Moscow, with a water-graphite reactor.

Its first few years of operation showed that there were realistic possibilities for improving energy parameters by increasing pressure and temperature of the heat-transfer agent and by producing saturated or super-heated steam inside the reactor.

The Novovoronezh and Beloyarsk atomic power stations have been operating successfully for 13 years, providing an impetus for the large-scale introduction of nuclear power generation in the U.S.S.R.

With the commissioning of the first generating sets of new atomic stations at Kursk (one million kW) and the Armenian plant (405,000 kW) and the fourth 12,000 kW set at the Bilibino Heat and Power Plant (in the Arctic Circle), the number of big atomic power stations in operation is brought up to nine.

In future large stations will be built only in the European part of the U.S.S.R., in areas most remote from economic sources of organic fuel.

Thermal neutron reactors of two types are used in Soviet atomic power stations: the vessel pressurized water reactor (VVER) and the channel graphite-water reactor (RBMK).

The main tendency in the technical improvement of atomic power stations is the enlargement of unit capacity of reactors and all equipment.

So far VVER reactors with a unit capacity of 440,000 kW have been set up at Soviet atomic power stations, and are also to be installed at the Chernobyl and Smolensk plants. A 1,500,000 reactor has been designed for the Ignalina station (Lithuania), now under construction.

In 1977 the first one million kW VVER reactors are being installed at the Novovoronezh station (no. 5 block) and at the South Ukrainian, Rovno and Kalinin plants.

One million kW RBMK reactors have been installed at the Leningrad and Kursk stations.

All the large atomic power stations are to be linked to the European part of the U.S.S.R. power grid, the total capacity of which will amount to about 160 million kilowatts by 1980.

Radiation safety, both for personnel and the environment, is ensured by strict adherence to safety regulations.

Emphasis will shift increasingly to the fast breeder reactor. One example already in operation is Shevchenko on the Caspian Sea. This is a 350 megawatt breeder which runs a 150 megawatt power station and also desalinates nearly 30 million gallons of sea water a day.

Work is also going ahead to develop thermonuclear power stations, and a thermonuclear reactor, the largest in the world, known as Tokamak-10, was put into operation at the Kurchatov Atomic Energy Institute in Moscow in June 1975. A new Tokamak unit, differing in important respects from Tokamak-10, has now been designed, which will retain deuterium plasura, heated up to 50 million degrees Centigrade, for more than a second.

It is planned to build a 12-mile ring accelerator-accumulator complex with an energy of 2,000–5,000 GEV at Protvino in the Moscow region, to work in a set with the already operating 76 GEV proton accelerator at Serpukhov.

In 1959 the nuclear-powered ice-breaker Lenin was commissioned. It has a virtually unlimited range of operation without need to refuel, and increased the navigation period on the Northern Sea Route by two months. Two of a new series of more powerful ice breakers, the Arctica and the Siberia, are now in service. In August 1977 the Arctica cut through to the North Pole, bringing considerably nearer the possibility of prolonging the navigation season on the traditional northern sea route and starting navigation in high latitudes of the Arctic.

The U.S.S.R. has helped set up national nuclear research centres in a number of countries, including East European socialist countries, China and the United Arab Republic. It has also helped other countries to build their first atomic power stations.

## SPACE RESEARCH

In 1949 the Soviet Union began probing the upper atmosphere and outer space, sending geophysical rockets with payloads ranging from hundreds of kilograms to several tonnes up to heights of 500 km and more.

On 4 October 1957 man broke away from terrestrial gravity for the first time when a Soviet rocket put the world's first artificial satellite, Sputnik-1, into orbit round the Earth, where it remained for 92 days, completing 1,400 orbits.

A heavier spaceship, of more advanced design, Sputnik-2, was launched on 3 November 1957. This was the first space experiment with a test animal, Laika, a Husky. The Sputnik-2 spent almost 160 days in orbit and made 2,370 circuits of the Earth. Sputnik-3, a still heavier space laboratory, was launched on 15 May 1958. It spent 691 days in orbit, circuiting the Earth 10,137 times and carrying out an extensive research programme.

A further victory over terrestrial gravity was achieved on 2 January 1959, when moon probe Luna-1 attained escape velocity and passed within 5–6,000 km of the Moon to settle in solar orbit to become the Sun's first artificial satellite.

*Investigation of the Moon:* The Soviet Union continued its programme of lunar research with the aid of automatic vehicles, which is less costly than manned expeditions and involves no risk to life.

Luna-2 spacecraft reached the Moon on 14 September 1959, the first man-made craft to do so. It left on the moon the Soviet state emblem and other tokens. Luna-3, launched 20 days later into lunar orbit, transmitted to Earth the first photographs of the far side of the Moon.

Subsequent lunar probes had more complex trajectories. They were first launched into terrestrial orbit and then accelerated to escape velocity on a course towards the Moon. The first ever successful soft landing on the Moon was accomplished on 3 February 1966 by Luna-9, which sent back panoramic photos of the lunar surface. This experiment proved wrong the idea that the lunar surface was dust. It was found to be hard, hummocky and rock-strewn, with craters ranging from tiny to large.

The first probe to collect hard rock samples from the Moon and deliver them to Earth was Luna-16, in September 1970. A little over a year later the Luna-20 soft landed on another part of the lunar surface to collect more rocks. Its return module arrived back on Earth with them on 25 February 1972.

Another stage of long-term research in lunar space opened in September 1971 with the launching of the Luna-19 probe, which orbited the Moon for over a year, making about 4,000 circuits. It studied the Moon's gravitational and magnetic fields, cosmic rays, micro-meteorites and interplanetary plasma, and transmitted a great amount of scientific data to Earth in 1,000 communications sessions. This research was later continued by Luna-22, put into lunar orbit on 2 June 1974.

The first moon rover, Lunokhod-1, a self-propelled laboratory controlled from the Earth, was landed on the Moon by Luna-17 on 17 November 1970. Over a period of ten-and-a-half months it travelled 10,540 metres in the Sea of Rains, exploring the terrain and photographing the lunar surface. When it stopped, it did so in such a position that the French laser reflector installed on it faced the Earth during lunar nights to facilitate further astronomical investigation.

On 16 January 1973 another self-propelled vehicle, Lunokhod-2, was landed on the Moon's surface by the Luna-21 probe. Lunokhod-2 incorporated several new technical innovations and improvements and carried additional instrumentation. It explored the Moon's surface for four months, continuing the programme started by the first moon rover.

Luna 24, launched in August 1976, soft-landed on the moon on 18 August in the S.E. area of the Sea of Crises. After drilling lunar soil to a depth of about 2 metres, it returned to earth on 22 August with samples of lunar rock.

*Manned Spaceflight:* Over 30 Soviet cosmonauts have orbited the Earth since Yuri Gagarin's historic flight in Vostok-1 on 12 April 1961.

Between 1961 and 1965 eight Vostok and Voskhod spaceships designed for solo and group flights took Soviet cosmonauts into space. The Vostok, a solo craft weighing 6·17 tons, incorporated an ejector seat for the pilot, who parachuted to Earth from a height of 7 kilometres. The Voskhod, on the other hand, was a heavier multi-seater with a soft-landing system, stand-by retro-engineandadditional instrumentation.

Subsequent Vostok pilots were Herman Titov (Vostok-2, 6 August 1961, 24 hours in orbit), Andrian Nikolayev (Vostok-3, 11 August 1962, four days), Pavel Popov (Vostok-4, 11 August 1962, three days). Nikolayev and Popov made the world's first group space flight, which featured the first television broadcast back to Earth from space.

Then came Valery Bykovsky (Vostok-5, 1 June 1963, five days) and Valentina Tereshkova, the first ever space woman (Vostok-6, 16 June 1963, almost three days) in twin flight.

Voskhod-1 was manned by Vladimir Komarov, Konstantin Feoktistov and Boris Yegorov (12 October 1964, 24 hours), who were the first cosmonauts to work without space suits. The Voskhod-2 crew were Pavel Belyaev and Alexei Leonov, who was the first man to walk in space, spending 20 minutes outside the spaceship wearing a pressurized suit.

In 1968 the first three of the Soyuz series were put into orbit. The Soyuz, weighing 6·45–6·65 tonnes, is an orbital module housing research equipment and serving as restroom for the crew, together with a re-entry module which doubles as crew cabin, and an instrument compartment with the main equipment and a two-engine vernier installation. It has an automatic docking system.

Soyuz-1 was piloted by Vladimir Komarov (25 October 1968, 3 days). Tragically the parachute system failed during descent and the pilot lost his life.

Soyuz-2 was put into orbit, unmanned, on 25 October 1968, and as it flew over the cosmodrome next day Georgi Beregovoi took off in Soyuz-3, which approached the other spaceship automatically. Beregovoi then took over manually and performed a series of manoeuvres before landing on 30 October.

Two more manned Soyuz craft, 4 and 5, launched in mid-January 1969, came together using automatic controls and docked manually. Two of the three-man crew of Soyuz-5 transferred to the other vehicle via open space, and the two craft undocked and continued separately.

Another series of Soyuz—6, 7 and 8—was launched in October 1969.

On 1 June 1970 Soyuz-9 was launched with a two-man crew which spent almost 18 days in a state of weightlessness, showing that man could withstand the stress of prolonged space travel.

Since 1971 the trend has been towards manned flights n long-life orbital research stations, the first Salyut orbital station having been launched in April of that year. It was in operation for nearly six months. The first stage of its work was a joint flight with Soyuz-10, which met and docked, and whose crew of three checked on-board systems to ensure suitable conditions for the arrival of subsequent expeditions. After Salyut had been in orbit for six weeks, another crew was brought to the station by Soyuz-11. The cosmonauts carried out medical and biological experiments and measurements, and tests to determine optimal conditions for cosmonauts to live and work in. Unfortunately the crew of the Soyuz-11—Georgi Dobrovolsky, Vladislav Volkov and Victor Patsayev died while returning to Earth.

The Salyut-2 orbital station was launched on 3 April 1973 for the purpose of perfecting the design, on-board systems and equipment, and conducting further research.

A test flight to confirm the reliability of the improved design and equipment of Soyuz was carried out by the Soyuz-12 (put into orbit on 27 September 1973 with a two-man crew). On 18 December 1973 the Soyuz-13, also with two men aboard, was launched on a flight to conduct astrophysical observations of stars in the ultra-violet band. For this purpose the craft was fitted with an Orion-2 complex, the telescope with camera attachment being fixed to the outside of the orbital module instead of the docking unit with which the Soyuz is normally equipped. The Soyuz-13 eight-day flight programme also included spectrazonal photography of sections of the Earth's surface and biological research to study, among other things, the breeding of micro-organisms in weightless conditions.

Salyut-3, differing in a number of design features from preceding stations, was put into terrestrial orbit on 25 June 1974. On July 3 the Soyuz-14 went into orbit and docked with the station the following day, returning to Earth with its crew after a 15-day research programme. Two other spaceships, Soyuz-15 and Soyuz-16, docked with the Salyut-3 (in August and December 1974). The crew of the latter tested various systems in connection with the Soyuz–Apollo flight which took place the following July.

A new orbital station, Salyut-4, was launched on 26 December 1974. Soyuz-17, launched 11 January 1975, docked with it next day, and the crew carried out a 30-day research programme, landing on February 9. Soyuz-18 docked with Salyut on 26 May and landed on 26 July, after 63 days in orbit.

The joint Soviet American space venture took place in July 1975. On 15 July the Soyuz-19 lifted off from Soviet territory and a few hours later the Apollo spaceship was launched from the U.S.A. Soviet and American crews cooperated successfully in docking and crew transfer operations and joint research experiments were undertaken. The Soyuz-19 landed on 21 July and the Apollo continued with an autonomous programme until 25 July.

An unmanned spaceship, Soyuz-20, launched on 17 November 1975, docked automatically with Salyut-3 on 9 November. It completed its programme and returned to the earth on 16 February 1976.

In June and August Salyut 5 (launched 22 June) and Soyuz 21 (launched 6 July) conducted a 48-day research programme undertaken in cooperation with scientists in the German Democratic Republic and returned to earth on 23 September 1976.

The Soyuz 23, manned by two Soviet cosmonauts and launched on 14 October to continue scientific research with Salyut 5, returned to earth on 16 October 1976. Manned spaceship Soyuz 24, launched on 7 February 1977, docked with Salyut 5 and its crew completed a two-week programme of research before returning to Earth on 23 February 1977.

On 9 October 1977 the Soyuz 25, with two cosmonauts aboard, made an unsuccessful attempt to dock with Salyut 6, launched on 29 September, and returned to Earth on 11 October.

*Planetary Research:* The Soviet research programme gives an important place to the study of the Earth's nearest neighbours—Venus and Mars.

The first Soviet space probes made flight to these planets more than a decade ago. Such flights have immeasurably increased man's knowledge about interplanetary space and physical conditions on the planets Venus and Mars.

The first direct measurements of the characteristics of Venus's atmosphere and the first tests of its chemical composition were made by the Soviet interplanetary probe Venus-4 in October 1967. This research was continued in subsequent years by Venus-5 to Venus-7. The stage of direct measurement of physical and chemical characteristics was completed by Venus-8 as it descended into the Venusian atmosphere to make the first soft landing on the daylight side of the planet on 22 July 1972.

Venus-9 and Venus-10 (launched 8 and 14 June 1975) both went into orbit round the planet to become its first two artificial satellites, and they landed descent modules in areas 2,300 km apart on 22 and 25 October the same year. Both transmitted panoramic views of the Venusian surface and scientific data via their parent craft. The photographs, unexpectedly, showed the surface to be rocky. The planned research programme was completed in March 1976, and scientific measurements are being made under an additional programme.

*Research in Near-Earth Space:* In the last few years the Soviet Union has been launching roughly one hundred space vehicles into space a year. The vast majority of these are artificial Earth satellites, among them automatic satellites of the Cosmos series, Molnia communications satellites, meteorological probes of the Meteor system, manned Soyuz spaceships and Salyut orbital stations. The scientific problems being tackled cover several areas of research: the investigation of the physical characteristics of near-Earth space, the properties of cosmic rays that reach our planet, the study of the atmosphere, radiation belts, ionosphere and magnetic field of the Earth and observation of solar radiation and activity. This basic research is closely interlinked with applied research in meteorology, communications, geodesy and navigation.

Cosmos satellites make up the most numerous section of Soviet space vehicles. Among other things they study the Earth's atmosphere, corpuscular fluxes and cosmic rays. They are used in the study of many problems of space medicine and biology and the solution of numerous problems connected with the design and construction of space vehicles.

Since 1969, 16 Intercosmos research satellites have been launched, which series is the joint responsibility of the Comecon countries. The Intercosmos programme also envisages joint manned spaceflight with cosmonauts from other Socialist countries, and the first trainees from those countries arrived in the Soviet Union in November 1976.

Sixteen satellites, four geophysical rockets and dozens of meteorological rockets had been launched under the Intercosmos programme by the end of 1976.

Prognoz artificial Earth satellites occupy a special place in solar research. There have been three so far, the last one having been launched in February 1973. Circling the Earth in a distant orbit, the Prognoz measure solar winds, the characteristics of solar X-rays, gamma-rays and radio emissions, doing so when the satellite is outside the Earth's magnetosphere. Its work helps scientists to get a better idea of Sun–Earth relationships and ultimately to lay the foundations for space weather forecasts. The individual Prognoz satellite weighs 845 kg.

Molnia communications satellites transmit television programmes, telephone calls, cables, telephoto images and other types of information. Orbital stations have been set up on the ground to receive Molnia relays and transmit them to the appropriate quarter.

Meteor satellites have been functioning for eight years gathering information about the Earth's cloud canopy, the snow and ice cover on light and dark sides of the Earth, the intensity of radiation emitted or reflected by the Earth–Atmosphere system, etc. The data they have obtained has considerably improved the accuracy of short and long term weather forecasts.

## EDUCATION

The Soviet educational system is a state system throughout, and education at all levels is free. Whereas under tsarism four out of five children had no opportunity to go to school, education is universal and compulsory in the Soviet Union. Ten years of general education (from seven to seventeen) is now the general rule and will soon be universal. In areas where Russian is not the predominant language, parents may choose whether to have their children educated in the local language or in Russian. Tuition is given in 51 languages in Soviet schools.

Pupils may continue at general secondary school to the end of their ten year education or may transfer to specialised secondary schools for vocational training at fifteen. In both cases they continue their general education to the same standard, and to make this possible the course at specialised schools usually lasts three years or more.

Higher education is open to any boy or girl, without privileges or restrictions dependent upon origin, nationality, sex or the social status or position of their parents. Competitive entrance examinations are held at all universities and colleges. Students receive grants and those from out of town are provided with hostel accommodation.

In the 1976–77 school year there were 159,000 general educational schools with a total of 46,500,000 pupils. The 4,600 specialised secondary schools had 4,600,000 pupils, and the 859 institutions of higher learning 4,950,000. There were 734,600 graduates from the latter.

There are wide opportunities for people who work to continue their education in various ways in their spare time. There are at present about three million students studying part time with universities and colleges, either at evening classes or by correspondence. Such students get additional paid examination leave each year, and in their final year have four months leave to prepare their graduation projects. They may also take further leave without pay.

The Soviet Union has a 100 per cent literacy rate as compared to approximately 25 per cent under tsarism. In the cases of non-Russian nationalities the rate was usually much lower before the Revolution—for example the Kirghiz 0·6 per cent, the Tajiks 0·5 per cent and the Uzbek 1·6 per cent. Forty-eight nationalities had no written language of their own.

**Libraries, Clubs, Museums.** By the end of 1976 there were 131,000 public libraries with a book stock of 1,575 million. There were 135,400 clubs and 1,323 museums.

**U.S.S.R. Academy of Sciences.** The general scientific direction of research into problems of the natural and social sciences is exercised by the U.S.S.R. Academy of Sciences, which celebrated its 250th anniversary in 1974. Composed of leading scientists in all fields throughout the Soviet Union, its main objectives are the development of fundamental research, the search for fundamentally new possibilities of achieving technical progress, and the comprehensive application of scientific achievements.

All administrative bodies of the Academy are elective.

The Academy has a Siberian branch at Akademgorodok, near Novosibirsk, and a Far Eastern branch at Vladivostock.

## RELIGION

All citizens are ensured freedom of conscience (freedom of religious worship and freedom to conduct anti-religious propaganda), guaranteed them by the Constitution of the U.S.S.R. It is stipulated by law that all religious associations in the Soviet Union enjoy equal rights and bear equal responsibilities. A decree issued by the Soviet Government of 23 January 1918, divorced the church from the State and school from the church.

The largest ecclesiastical organization is the Russian

Orthodox Church, headed by Patriarch Pimen, Metropolitan of Krutitsa and Kolomna (acting from the election in May 1971). The Patriarch has a Holy Synod of eight persons to assist him, five being permanent members, and three temporary (changed periodically): Metropolitans, Archbishops and Bishops. The Russian Orthodox Church also has dioceses (eparchies) in other countries. The Alexandrian, Antioch and Bulgarian Orthodox Churches also maintain representatives in the Soviet Union.

In addition to the Russian Orthodox Church, there are the Georgian Orthodox Church, whose head is Catholicos Yefrem II of All Georgia (residence in Tbilisi), and the Armenian-Gregorian Church, which, for ecclesiastical purposes, unites Armenians throughout the world. Its centre is in Echmiadzin (Armenian Soviet Socialist Republic). The head of the Armenian-Gregorian Church is Supreme Patriarch Vazgen I, Catholicos of All Armenians.

The ecclesiastic life of Moslems in the U.S.S.R. is directed by four territorial boards, each independent of the other: the Moslems of central Asia and Kazakhstan (Tashkent, chairman Mufti Ziyautdin Babakhanov); Moslems of the European part of the U.S.S.R. and Siberia (Ufa, chairman Mufti Shakir Hiyalitdinov); Moslems of North Caucasus and Daghestan (Buynaksk, chairman Mufti Mahomed Khadji Kurbanov); Moslems of Transcaucasia (Baku, chairman Suleyman-Zade).

Roman Catholics are mainly in the Western republics of the U.S.S.R., in the Latvian Soviet Socialist Republic and in the Lithuanian Soviet Socialist Republic, western regions of the Ukrainian Soviet Socialist Republic and Byelorussian Soviet Socialist Republic.

The Evangelical Lutheran Church has its communities principally in the Latvian and Estonian S.S. Republics.

The Church of the Old Believers is divided into three main sects, not connected with one another. The first is the Belokrinitsy hierarchy, headed by the Archbishop of Moscow and All Russia (Moscow). There is also a sect which does not recognize the ecclesiastical hierarchy, called 'bespopovtsy' (without priests). The third sect admits priests who have come over from the Greek Eastern Church (Kuibyshev).

The centre for the Evangelican Christian Baptists is the All-Union Council of Christian Baptists (Moscow).

Followers of Buddhism are found in several Autonomous Soviet Socialist Republics, in various regions, and in national areas of the Irkutsk and Chita regions. They are headed by the Ecclesiastical Board of Buddhists of the U.S.S.R. in the town of Ivolga, Buryat Autonomous S.S.R.

There is no central body for Judaism; the religious communities, with their synagogues, function independently of one another.

There are several other religious organizations in the U.S.S.R. with a few followers (Seventh Day Adventists, Methodists, Molokans and others). All the churches and religious associations, parishes, central religious boards, religious schools, publications, etc., are financed by the voluntary donations of the believers.

The Council for Religious Affairs under the U.S.S.R. Council of Ministers has been set up for the purpose of maintaining contact between the Soviet government and the heads of the religious organizations on questions concerning these organizations requiring solution by the Soviet government. Its chairman is V. A. Kuroedov.

# RUSSIAN SOVIET FEDERAL SOCIALIST REPUBLIC (R.S.F.S.R.)

(*Rossiiskaya Sovietskaya Federativnaya Sotsialisticheskaya Respublika*)

**Capital**—Moscow.

## AREA AND POPULATION

The R.S.F.S.R. is the largest of the constituent republics both in area and population of the Soviet Union and is composed of the greater part of the former Russian Empire. The Republic was formed on 7 November 1917.

The R.S.F.S.R. occupies over 76 per cent of the total area of the U.S.S.R. and covers 17,075,400 sq. km. Its population is 135,569,000 (1977). Because of the many nationalities of the R.S.F.S.R. there is a somewhat intricate system of administrative subdivisions. These are as follows:

16 Autonomous Soviet Socialist Republics:

| | |
|---|---|
| Bashkir A.S.S.R. | Daghestan A.S.S.R. |
| Buryat A.S.S.R. | Kabardino-Balkar A.S.S.R. |
| Checheno-Ingushia A.S.S.R. | Kalmyk A.S.S.R. |
| Chuvash A.S.S.R. | Karelian A.S.S.R. |
| Komi A.S.S.R. | Tatar A.S.S.R. |
| Mari A.S.S.R. | Tuva A.S.S.R. |
| Mordovan A.S.S.R. | Udmurt A.S.S.R. |
| North Ossetian A.S.S.R. | Yakut A.S.S.R. |

On 1 January 1977, principal cities and their populations were:

| | | | |
|---|---|---|---|
| Moscow | 7,819,000 | Perm | 972,000 |
| Leningrad | 4,425,000 | Kazan | 970,000 |
| Gorky | 1,319,000 | Ufa | 942,000 |
| Novosibirsk | 1,304,000 | Volograd | 931,000 |
| Kuibyshev | 1,204,000 | Rostov-on-Don | 921,000 |
| Sverdlovsk | 1,187,000 | Saratov | 856,000 |
| Omsk | 1,026,000 | Voronezh | 779,000 |
| Chelyabinsk | 1,007,000 | Krasnoyarsk | 769,000 |

In 1976 82 per cent of the population of the R.S.F.S.R. were Russians. In addition there are Tartars, Ukrainians, Chuvashi, Mordovians, Bashkirs, Jews, Byelorussians, Germans, peoples of Daghestan, Udmurts, Maris, Komis and Komi-Permyaks, Kazakhs, Armenians, Buryats, Ossetians, and others. The total number of nationalities living in the R.S.F.S.R. is over 60.

The Russian believers and some national minorities are Greek Orthodox; among members of the Turkic peoples the religion is Islam (Moslem), and among some of the Mongol peoples Buddhism (Lamaism) is partially practised. The Russian Orthodox Church has its Russian Patriarch in Moscow as well as two Metropolitans: one in Moscow, and the other in Leningrad.

**Supreme Soviet**

*Chairman:* V. A. Kotelnikov.
*Presidium President:* M. Yasnov.

**Council of Ministers**

*Chairman:* M. S. Solomenstev.

## FINANCE

The budget figure for 1976 was 54,299,459,000 roubles.

## PRODUCTION, INDUSTRY AND COMMERCE

**Industry.** The Russian Federation is the most economically developed of the Union Republics.

In the R.S.F.S.R. there are ten large economic zones: North-West, Central, Volga-Vyatka, Central-Black Earth, Volga, North Caucasus, Urals, West Siberia, East Siberia, Far East.

The average population density of the central zone is the highest in the U.S.S.R. (27·8 million) and the zone occupies 485·100 sq. km.

Recently the central zone has changed radically, not only as regards the structure of its economy, but also as regards the volume of industrial output.

Central area factories produce the most complex and advanced machine tools and instruments. Apparatus and instruments are made not only by specialized factories, but also by machine-building plants. Control, regulating and radiometering instruments and apparatus, computers and other instruments are among the items made.

Technological equipment for various industries is produced on a very big scale in the central zone. It accounts for about one-quarter of the country's entire production of equipment for the printing, cement, leather and footwear industries, one-half for the textile industry and two-thirds for the knitwear industries. It also produces equipment for the metallurgical, chemical, food, paper and pulp and other industries.

The Volga-Vyatsky economic zone occupies 263·3 thousand sq. km. with 8·3 million people. The leading place in the Volga-Vyatsky economic zone is held by those branches of the engineering and metal-working industries that are characterized by a high degree of labour consumption. This zone produces more automobiles, rivercraft and milling machines than any other zone in the R.S.F.S.R.

The Central Black-Earth zone occupies 167·7 thousand sq. km, with 7·9 million people.

Iron ore and non-ferrous metals are the zone's most

mportant industries. Here are found the world's biggest iron-ore deposits, the Kursk Magnetic Anomaly.

The Central Black-Earth zone has everything necessary for diversified engineering development. It is near the biggest Soviet coal and metallurgical base, the Donets basin, and has its own metallurgical industry and adequate labour reserves released from agriculture due to mechanization.

The North-West Zone occupies a vast strip of the European part of the R.S.F.S.R.—1,662·8 thousand sq. km. with 12·5 million people. The important engineering industries are represented by ship-building, the production of equipment for the power and electrical industries, electrical engineering machine-tool building, instrument-making, the production of machinery and equipment for the fuel and metallurgical industries.

The North-West economic zone has enormous timber resources, especially in the East. The rich timber resources contribute to the development of the zone's paper and pulp industry.

The Volga zone with over 18·7 million people occupies 680 thousand square kilometres.

Heavy industry, represented by power engineering, machine-building and instrument-making, oil, gas, and the chemical industries, predominates in the zone. At the same time the zone has become the Soviet Union's biggest salt producer and supplier of sulphuric acid and other products to the national economy.

The North Caucasus is a big industrial and agrarian area. It occupies 355·1 thousand sq. km. with 14·8 million people. Its production structure both in industry and in agriculture is highly diversified.

The Urals zone's exceptionally rich natural resources and its advantageous geographical position have contributed to its economic development. The Ural zone occupies 680·0 thousand sq. km. with 15·2 million people.

The Urals non-ferrous metal industry provides not only cheap, but high grade metals for the national economy. In addition it produces substantial quantities of copper, zinc, nickel, aluminium and magnesium.

Urals engineering is mainly concerned with mining, metallurgical and transport equipment power and electrical engineering. The manufacture of tractors, agricultural implements, machine tools and instruments is also of great importance.

There are large salt deposits in the Urals and other raw materials. The Urals accounts for about two-fifths of the national production of soda hash and over one-quarter of the mineral fertilizers. The timber and paper and pulp industries occupy an important place in the zone's economy. It is responsible for over one-fifth of Soviet paper production.

East and West Siberia are traditionally big suppliers of the most valuable minerals (gold, tin, nickel, mica, graphite fluorspar, etc.), timber and furs. Certain branches of engineering and the chemical industry have developed to a high level. Vast amounts of oil have been discovered in West Siberia, which is now the biggest supplier of oil in the Soviet Union. These zones, with 19·8 million people, occupy 6,550,000 sq. km. The Far East zone occupies 6,215,000 sq. km. and has 6,168 million people. New industrial zones are to be developed in the Far East and East Siberia along the route of the new Baikal–Amur railway under construction.

**Agriculture.** In January 1977 there were 12,682 collective farms and 11,321 state farms. The Republic is the biggest grain and livestock producer in the Soviet Union. The chief agricultural crops in the R.S.F.S.R. are grain and vegetables. The principal grain crops are spring and winter wheat, rye, oats, barley and buckwheat.

Potatoes and other vegetables are grown intensively everywhere, especially round the cities.

Big efforts are being made to advance agriculture in the non-Black Earth zones of the R.S.F.S.R.

### EDUCATION

In 1976–77, 22,105,000 children studied at 88,400 general education schools, 2,732,300 at specialised secondary schools and 2,905,700 at 483 higher educational establishments.

Apart from the chief institutions of the U.S.S.R. Academy of Sciences there are its Siberian and Far East branches, and a number of departments, the All-Union Agricultural Academy named after Lenin, the Academy of Medical Sciences of the U.S.S.R., the Art Academy of the U.S.S.R., the Academy of Pedagogical Sciences of the R.S.F.S.R. and other research institutions. In all, 2,709 research institutes employing 600,000 scientific workers function in the Republic.

In 1976 there were 54,292 books and booklets published, including 3,891 in national languages of the Soviet people.

# ARMENIAN SOVIET SOCIALIST REPUBLIC

## (*Armyanskaya Sovietskaya Sotsialisticheskaya Respublika*)

**Capital**—Yerevan.

### AREA AND POPULATION

The Armenian Soviet Socialist Republic was founded on 29 November 1920. From 1922–36 it formed part of the Transcaucasian Federation of Soviet Socialist Republics, together with Georgia and Azerbaidjan. It was proclaimed a constituent republic of the U.S.S.R. in 1936.

The Armenian S.S.R. is the southernmost of the Transcaucasian Republics and is bounded in the south by Iran and in the west by Turkey. The principal towns are Yerevan, Leninakan, Kirovakan, Echmiadzin, Kafan, Alaverdi, Octemberyan, Kajaran, Dilijan, Goris, Stepanavan, Artik, Kamo, Razdan.

The area of the Republic is 29,800 sq. km., and the population 2,900,000 (1977). Armenians formed over 88 per cent of the total at the time of the 1970 census, and the rest are Azerbaijanians, Russians, Kurds and others. The capital, Yerevan, has a population of over 956,000 (1977).

#### Supreme Soviet

*Chairman:* A. M. Gasparyan.
*Presidium President:* B. E. Sarkisov.

#### Council of Ministers

*Chairman:* G. A. Arzumanyan.

*First Secretary of the Central Committee of the Communist Party:* K. S. Demirchyan.

### FINANCE

The budget figure for 1976 was 1,187,416,000 roubles.

### PRODUCTION

**Industry.** This is developing rapidly. Among the most important sectors are the foodstuffs and the light industries, machine-building, metallurgy and the power industry. In the mountains of Armenia are copper and iron ore, pyrite, manganese, molybdenum, nepheline and tufa.

Armenia manufactures machine tools, ball bearings, electric locomotives, lorries, drilling equipment, agricultural machinery, electrical equipment and many other items.

The chemical industry based on pyrites, limestone and other raw materials is growing in importance. It produces fertilizers, toxic chemicals for agriculture and various synthetic materials.

Large power stations have been built on the Razdan, the Kura and some other rivers. Power generation at Armenian power stations costs considerably less than the average for the whole of the country. It has thus been possible to establish power-intensive industries such as aluminium, rubber, and ferro-alloys production.

The first section of an atomic power station (405,000 kW) went into operation early in 1977.

**Agriculture.** In January 1977 there were 371 collective farms and 384 state farms in the Republic.

Armenia is in the sub-tropical zone. Thanks to extensive irrigation projects the valleys give good harvests of many crops—wheat, maize, barley, sugar beet, cotton, grapes, and tobacco, as well as peaches, apricots, pomegranates and figs.

### EDUCATION, CULTURE AND SCIENCE

In the 1976–77 academic year 651,000 pupils studied in 1,600 general schools of all types; 53,700 students studied in 64 specialized secondary schools and 55,500 students in 12 institutions of high learning.

The Armenian Academy of Sciences, founded in 1943, had on 1 January 1976, a total of 2,714 research workers, among them 90 academicians or corresponding members.

In 1976 there were 1,165 books published including 812 in Armenian.

### NEWSPAPERS

**Kommunist.** Founded 1934. Six issues weekly in Russian.

**Sovietakan Aiastan (Soviet Armenia).** Founded 1920. Six issues weekly in Armenian.

**Avangard.** Founded 1923. Three issues weekly in Armenian.

**Komsomolets.** Founded 1938. Three issues weekly in Russian.

# AZERBAIJAN SOVIET SOCIALIST REPUBLIC

## (*Azerbaidjanskaya Sovietskaya Sotsialisticheskaya Respublika*)

**Capital**—Baku.

### AREA AND POPULATION

The Azerbaijan S.S.R. was formed on 28 April 1920, and became a Union Republic in 1936; from 1922 to 1936 it was part of the Transcaucasian Federation. The Azerbaijan S.S.R. comprises the Nakhichevan Autonomous S.S.R. and the Nagarno-Karabakh Autonomous Region. Over two-thirds of the population are Azerbaijanians, the remainder being Russians, Armenians and others (according to 1970 census).

The Republic covers an area of 86,600 sq. km., and has a population of 5,800,000. The capital, Baku, had in January 1977 a population of 1,435,000. The Republic occupies the eastern part of Transcaucasia, facing the Caspian Sea.

**Supreme Soviet**

*Chairman:* S. A. Rustamzade.
*Presidium President:* K. A. Khalilov.

**Council of Ministers**

*Chairman:* A. I. Ibragimov.

*First Secretary of the Central Committee of the Communist Party:* G. A. Aliev.

### FINANCE

The budget figure for 1976 was 1,653,871,000 roubles.

### PRODUCTION

**Industry.** The most important branches of Azerbaijan's economy are the oil and the gas industries.

Oil derricks have appeared in the basin of the Kura, in the foothills of the Greater Caucasus and extend into the open sea. The Republic also manufactures the machinery for oil-prospecting, extraction and refining. The chemical industry is developing on the basis of oil and gas and the refineries are putting out more than ninety different kinds of products. Azerbaijan is one of the oldest oil-producing areas of the world. Oil was first extracted in the middle of the nineteenth century.

At Karadag there is one of the Soviet Union's largest portland-cement plants. Azerbaijan holds first place in the Transcaucasia in carpet-making.

The food industry also plays an important role; most developed are the fishing, canning, wine-making, meat-packing, creamery, cheese-making, flour and cereal grinding and tobacco industries.

**Agriculture.** In January 1977 there were 779 collective farms and 546 state farms in the Republic. Agriculture in the Republic is very diversified due to favourable natural conditions: warm weather, variety of fertile soils, high rainfall in the west and an abundant water supply in the east. The trend is to specialize in growing valuable sub-tropical and other southern plants. Irrigation systems are continually extending the fertile area. A new breed of mountain fine-fleeced merino sheep has been produced. In coming years, agricultural production will be considerably expanded, both by increasing sown areas on irrigated and drained land, and better cultivation in general.

### EDUCATION, CULTURE AND SCIENCE

At the beginning of the 1976–77 academic year there were 4,600 general schools of all types with 1,618,000 pupils, 78 specialized secondary schools with a total of 76,300 students and 17 institutions of higher learning with a student body of 100,200.

The Azerbaijan Academy of Sciences, founded in 1945, had on 1 January 1976 a total of 4,185 research workers, including 95 academicians or corresponding members.

In 1975 there were 1,263 books published in the Republic including 798 in Azerbaijanian.

### NEWSPAPERS

**Bakinski Rabochi.** Founded 1906. Six issues weekly in Russian.

**Kommunist.** Founded 1919. Six issues weekly in Azerbaijanian.

**Azerbaijan Kanchlari (Youth of Azerbaijan).** Founded 1919. Six issues weekly in Azerbaijanian.

# BYELORUSSIAN SOVIET SOCIALIST REPUBLIC

## (*Byelorusskaya Sovietskaya Sotsialisticheskaya Respublika*)

**Capital**—Minsk.

### AREA AND POPULATION

Byelorussia lies in the western part of the European U.S.S.R. Was founded on 1 January 1919, and in 1939 Western Byelorussia was reunited with the Byelorussian S.S.R. The area of the Republic is 207,600 sq. km. and the population is 9,426,000. The capital, Minsk, has a population of 1,230,000 (1977). Over four-fifths of the population are Byelorussians, the remainder being Russians, Poles, Jews and Ukrainians according to the 1970 census.

**Supreme Soviet**
*Chairman:* E. I. Skurko.
*Presidium President:* F. A. Surganov.

**Council of Ministers**
*Chairman:* T. Y. Kiselyov.
*First Secretary of the Central Committee of the Communist Party:* P. M. Masherov.

### FINANCE

The budget figure for 1976 was 4,351,107 roubles.

### PRODUCTION

**Industry.** Electrical and mechanical engineering hold a leading place in the Byelorussian economy. The republic builds machine tools, motor vehicles, tractors and farm machinery. The machine-tool industry, which specializes in metal-cutting machines, is important for the entire engineering industry. The republic boasts the largest petrochemical complex in Europe. In the south of the Minsk region is the Soligorsk potassium combine.

**Agriculture.** In January 1977 there were 1,994 collective farms and 899 state farms in Byelorussia. Grain farming is the basis of the Republic's agriculture.

Rye, wheat, buckwheat, barley and oats are the most important crops. Flax, hemp, sugar beet and native brands of tobacco are also grown.

Potatoes are a traditional crop, taking up in different regions from 15 to 20 per cent of the entire sown area.
Further development of agriculture is through expanding dairy farming and pig breeding.

### EDUCATION, CULTURE AND SCIENCE

The Republic's 8,900 general schools of all types had 1,669,000 pupils in the 1976–77 academic year. There were 159,200 students in 133 specialized secondary schools, and 164,600 students in 31 institutions of higher learning.
The Academy of Sciences set up in 1928, had on 1 January 1976, 4,406 research workers, including 136 academicians or corresponding members.
In 1976 there were 3,000 books published in the Republic including about 480 in Byelorussian.

### NEWSPAPERS

**Sovietskaya Byelorussia.** Founded 1927. Six issues weekly in Russian.

**Zvjazda (The Star).** Founded 1917. Six copies weekly in Byelorussian.

**Chyrvonaya Zmena.** Founded 1921. Five issues weekly in Byelorussian.

**Znamya Yunosti (Banner of Youth).** Founded 1938. Five issues weekly in Russian.

## ESTONIAN SOVIET SOCIALIST REPUBLIC

## (*Estonskaya Sovietskaya Sotsialisticheskaya Respublika*)

**Capital**—Tallinn.

### AREA AND POPULATION

Estonia is the northernmost of the Baltic Republics, situated between the Finnish Gulf and the Gulf of Riga. Numerous islands in the Baltic Sea belong to the Republic. The Republic was formed on 21 July 1940 and joined the U.S.S.R. on 6 August 1940.
The area of the Republic is 45,100 sq. km., and the population is 1,447,000 (1977). The chief towns are Tallinn (population 415,000) and Tartu.

**Supreme Soviet**

*Chairman:* I. A. Lot.
*Presidium President:* A. Vader.

**Council of Ministers**

*Chairman:* V. I. Klauson.

*First Secretary of the Central Committee of the Communist Party:* I. G. Kebin.

### FINANCE

The budget figure was for 1976 was 854,193,000 roubles.

### PRODUCTION

**Industry.** The main industries of the Republic are machine building, instrument-making and metal-working. Estonia produces road-building machines, ditch-and-trench excavators, precision measuring instruments and equipment for oil, mining and chemical enterprises. It is also well known for its radio-engineering, furniture and fishing industries.
The Republic is rich in peat and shale and the shale-processing plant in Kokhtla-Jarve is the biggest in the world.
Estonia fishing trawlers and refrigerator ships work in the North Atlantic, the main catch being herring. The Republic has the biggest *per capita* fish catch and output of tinned fish in the country.

**Agriculture.** In January 1975 there were 211 collective farms and 153 state farms in Estonia. The main branches of agriculture are animal husbandry, including pig breeding.
Considerable areas of land are under barley, oats, maize, flax and potatoes.

### EDUCATION, CULTURE AND SCIENCE

In the 1976–77 academic year the 700 general schools of all types had 215,000 pupils. There were 24,600 students in 37 secondary vocational schools, and 24,100 students in six institutions of higher learning.
The Academy of Science, founded in 1946, had on 1 January 1976 909 research workers, including 41 full or corresponding members.
In 1976, 2,234 books were published (1,555 of them in Estonian).

### NEWSPAPERS

**Ravna Hääl (The Voice of the People).** Founded 1940. Six issues weekly in Estonian.

**Sovietskaya Estonia.** Founded 1940. Six issues weekly in Russian.

**Noorte Hääl** (The Voice of Youth). Founded 1940. Six issues weekly in Estonian.

## GEORGIAN SOVIET SOCIALIST REPUBLIC

## (*Gruzinskaya Sovietskaya Sotsialisticheskaya Respublika*)

**Capital**—Tbilisi.

### AREA AND POPULATION

Established on 25 February 1921. From 1922 to 1936 Georgia was part of the Transcaucasian Soviet Federal Socialist Republic. It became one of the constituent Republics of the U.S.S.R. in 1936.
The Georgian S.S.R. includes two Autonomous Republics: Abkhazia and Ajaria, and the South Ossetian Autonomous Region. For administrative purposes the Republic is divided into 45 districts and has 39 towns; these include Kutaisi, Batumi, Sukhumi, Rustavi, Poti, Gori and Tkvarcheli.
Georgians, a people of high and ancient culture, form about two-thirds of the population. The rest include Armenians, Russians, Azerbaijanians, Ossetinians and others.
The total area is 69,700 sq. km. and the total population is 4,999,000 (1977). The capital, Tbilisi, has a population of 1,042,000.

**Supreme Soviet**

*Chairman:* V. B. Abashidze.
*Presidium President:* P. G. Gilashvili.

**Council of Ministers**

*Chairman:* Z. A. Pataridze.

*First Secretary of the Central Committee of the Communist Party:* E. A. Shevardnadze.

### FINANCE

The budget figure for 1976 was 1,764,907,000 roubles.

### PRODUCTION

**Industry.** Georgia is a centre of the ore mining, hydropower, electrical-metallurgical, machine-tool, automobile, electrical and electronic engineering, instrument-making and other industries.
The Georgian S.S.R. possesses vast hydropower resources. The Transcaucasian, Adjaris-Tskhali, Chitakhevi, Khrami, Shaori, Tkibuli, Gumati and other hydroelectric stations have been built. Thermal power stations have been constructed at Tkvarcheli, Rustavi and other places.
The first metallurgical plant was built at Rustavi after

the war to supply metal to the engineering industry and pipes for the oil industry.

**Agriculture.** In January 1977 there were 729 collective farms and 382 state farms. Georgia's main crop is tea. In the last Five-Year Plan the Republic produced 1,155,000 tons of tea leaf, or 115,000 tons more than planned. The Republic also grows tangerines and lemons and is renowned for its grapes, wines, tobaccos, essential oils and mineral waters.

Animal husbandry is developing as more feed is grown and more use is made of the vast grazing lands. On the Georgian highlands and particularly near industrial centres, stock is raised for milk and meat, and in dry mountainous areas, for meat and wool.

### EDUCATION, CULTURE AND SCIENCE

The number of pupils in the 4,400 general schools of all types was 1,002,000 in the 1976–77 academic year; the 97 specialized secondary schools had 50,900 students, and the 19 institutions of higher learning had a student body of 84,200.

The Academy of Sciences, set up in 1941, had 5,128 research workers, including 113 full or corresponding members on 1 January 1976.

In 1976, there were 2,311 books published in the republic (1,508 in Georgian).

### NEWSPAPERS

**Kommunisti.** Founded 1920. Six issues weekly in Russian.

**Zarya Vostoka.** Founded 1922. Six issues weekly in Russian.

**Akhalgazdra Kommunisti (Young Communist).** Founded 1925. Three issues weekly in Georgian.

# KAZAKH SOVIET SOCIALIST REPUBLIC

## (*Kazakhskaya Sovietskaya Sotsialisticheskaya Respublika*)

**Capital**—Alma-Ata.

### AREA AND POPULATION

The Kazakh S.S.R. was formerly part of the R.S.F.S.R. but in December 1936 it was proclaimed a constituent republic of the U.S.S.R. It is bounded on the west by the Caspian Sea and the R.S.F.S.R., on the east by the People's Republic of China, on the north by the R.S.F.S.R. and on the south by Uzbekistan and Kirghizia.

The Republic's area is 2,717,300 sq. km. and the population 14,500,000 (1977). The population of Alma-Ata is 871,000. Kazakhs comprise about 30 per cent of the population and Russians and Ukrainians together about 51 per cent (according to the 1959 census).

**Supreme Soviet**

*Chairman:* M. E. Esenov.
*Presidium President:* S. B. Niyazbekov

**Council of Ministers**

*Chairman:* B. Ashimov.

*First Secretary of the Central Committee of the Communist Party:* D. A. Kunayev.

### FINANCE

The budget figure for 1976 was 6,721,354,000 roubles.

### PRODUCTION

**Industry.** The Kazakh economy combines a well-established heavy industry with food and light industries.

The heavy industry is made up of non-ferrous and ferrous metal production, the fuel and power industry, a rapidly developing chemical industry and mechanical engineering. The non-ferrous metal industry supplies the national economy with copper, zinc, lead, and other metals.

The Karaganda coal basin is the largest in the zone as regards size and output. Coal is also mined at other fields. Kazakhstan has established an oil industry in the Guryev and the Aktyubinsk regions. New oil fields found in the Mangyshlak Peninsula are now being actively exploited.

Large thermal power stations have been built in Petropavlovsk, Alma-Ata, Chimkent and other industrial centres.

The light and the foodstuffs industries are well supplied with raw materials. The meat industry is the most important of the foodstuffs industries.

Two four million kW stations are under construction at Ekibastuz and others of the same capacity in other parts of Kazakhstan. The atomic power station on the Mangyshlak peninsula has the world's first industrial fast-breeder reactor.

**Agriculture.** In January 1977 there were 421 collective farms and 1,984 state farms.

A 450-km canal takes the waters of Irtysh to Kazakhstan's arid steppes. The Republic is the country's third biggest producer of grain and meat and its second biggest producer of wool and astrakhan. Cotton, sugar beet, rice, sunflower, grape and other fruits are also grown.

Kazakhstan has a large number of livestock mainly consisting of sheep, cattle and horses. With its vast pastures on which grazing is possible all the year round, sheep-breeding has good prospects for the future.

### EDUCATION, CULTURE AND SCIENCE

In the 1976–77 academic year the Republic's 9,800 general schools of all types had 3,293,000 pupils. There were 210 specialized secondary schools with a total enrolment of 240,500, and 49 institutions of higher learning with 225,000 students.

The Academy of Sciences, set up in 1945, had on January 1 1976 a total of 3,583 research workers, including 111 full and corresponding members.

In 1976 there were 1,922 books published in the Republic, 660 of them in Kazakh.

### NEWSPAPERS

**Kazakhstanskaya Pravda.** Founded 1920. Six issues weekly in Russian.

**Sotsialistik Kazakhstan.** Founded 1919. Six issues weekly in Kazakh.

**Leninchil Zhas (Leninist Youth).** Founded 1921. Five issues weekly in Kazakh.

**Leninskaya Smena (Leninist Rising Generation).** Founded 1922. Five issues weekly in Russian.

# KIRGHIZ SOVIET SOCIALIST REPUBLIC

## (*Kirghizskaya Sovietskaya Sotsialisticheskaya Respublika*)

**Capital**—Frunze.

### AREA AND POPULATION

Kirghizia lies in the north-east of Central Asia, mainly on the Tien Shan and the Pamir Altai ranges. In the south-east it borders the People's Republic of China. The Republic includes the Osh Region. It is divided into 29 districts and has 15 towns including Frunze, Osh, Przhevalsk, Kzyl-Kia, Djalal-Abad and Tokmak. The Republic was established on 14 October 1924 as the Kara-Kirghiz (since May 1925—Kirghiz) autonomous region within the Russian Federation. On 1 February 1926 it became the Kirghiz Autonomous Republic and on 5 December 1936 it was proclaimed a constituent republic of the Soviet Union.

The Republic has an area of 198,500 sq. km., and had a population in 1977 of 3,372,000. The capital, Frunze, has a population of 512,000 (1977). The Kirghizians form about 40 per cent of the population; the rest are Russians, Ukrainians, Uzbeks and others (according to the 1959 census). Most of the population is concentrated in the valleys of the rivers,

Chu and Talas, and the Ferghana valley as well as in the Issyk-Kul valley.

**Supreme Soviet**

*Chairman:* B. Djamgertchinov.
*Presidium President:* T. K. Kulatov.

**Council of Ministers**

*Chairman:* A. S. Suyumbaev.

*First Secretary of the Central Committee of the Communist Party:* T. U. Usubaliev.

### FINANCE

The budget figure for 1976 was 1,154,745,000 roubles.

### PRODUCTION

**Industry.** The construction of roads and the introduction of air transport have assisted in the growth of industry. There are deposits of lead ore and oil and Kirghizia is one of the country's main suppliers of mercury and antimony. It has large non-ferrous metal, machine-building and instrument-making plants. Light industry and the oil, natural gas and food industries are developing rapidly.

**Agriculture.** In January 1976 there were 213 collective farms and 183 state farms in the Republic. The Kirghiz were formerly wandering herdsmen. They have now settled on the land, taken up agriculture and built up their own industry. Kirghizia produces wheat, cotton, tobacco, southern hemp, kenaf and essential-oil plants. Grape and fruit growing and silkworm breeding also have an important place in the economy.

The wealth of the Republic is in its cattle, fine-fleece sheep and horses.

### EDUCATION, CULTURE AND SCIENCE

The Republic's 1,800 general schools of all types had 854,000 pupils in the 1976–77 academic year; there were 45,400 students in 38 specialized secondary schools, and 51,500 students in nine institutions of higher learning. The Academy of Sciences, set up in 1954, had on 1 January 1976 a total of 1,405 research workers, including 47 full and corresponding members. In 1976 a total of 897 books were published, 416 of them in Kirghiz.

### NEWSPAPERS

**Sovietskaya Kirghizia.** Founded 1925. Six issues weekly in Russian.

**Soviettik Kyrghyzstan.** Founded 1924. Six issues weekly in Kirghizian.

**Leninchil Zhash.** Founded 1926. Three issues weekly in Kirghizian.

**Komsomolets Kirghizii.** Founded 1938. Three issues weekly in Russian.

# LATVIAN SOVIET SOCIALIST REPUBLIC

## (*Latviskaya Sovietskaya Sotsialisticheskaya Respublika*)

**Capital**—Riga.

### AREA AND POPULATION

The Latvian S.S.R. is situated on the Baltic coast, between the Estonian and Lithuanian S.S.R. For administrative purposes it is divided into 21 districts. Riga, the capital, is situated at the mouth of the Daugava River. On 5 August 1940 Latvia joined the Soviet Union as a constituent republic.

The area of the Republic is 63,700 sq. km., and the population is 2,499,000 (1977), Riga having a population of 816,000. Latvians form 62 per cent of the population, Russians 27 per cent; others include Byelorussians and Poles.

**Supreme Soviet**

*Chairman:* vacant
*Presidium President:* P. Y. Strautmanis.

**Council of Ministers**

*Chairman:* Y. Y. Ruben.

*First Secretary of the Central Committee of the Communist Party:* A. E. Voss.

### FINANCE

The budget figure for 1976 was 1,353,279,000 roubles.

### PRODUCTION

**Industry.** Latvia manufactures a quarter of the railway carriages produced in the U.S.S.R. for electric railway lines, all the diesel trains, one-fifth of the radio sets and one-sixth of household washing machines. It also produces steel, ferrous metals, mineral fertilizers, cement, fabrics, footwear and foodstuffs. Industrial output has increased rapidly in recent years, particularly in the engineering and metal-working industries.

**Agriculture.** In January 1977 there were 378 collective farms and 246 state farms in Latvia. Latvia is a maritime country and fishing plays a big part in its economy. There has been a considerable increase in the amount of fish caught and in the output of tinned fish (herring and sprat). The raising of livestock is important and there are a growing number of food factories, creameries and cheese factories. In many districts there are collective farms which raise poultry and keep bees. The Republic also has silver fox and mink farms.

### EDUCATION, CULTURE AND SCIENCE

At the beginning of the 1976–77 academic year there were 361,000 pupils in 1,100 general schools, 42,200 students in 54 specialized secondary schools and 46,300 students in ten institutions of higher learning.

The Academy of Sciences was set up in 1946. On 1 January 1976 it had 1,710 research workers, of whom 52 were full or corresponding members.

In 1976 there were 2,168 books published in the Republic including 1,095 in Lettish.

### NEWSPAPERS

**Sovietskaya Latvia.** Founded 1940. Six issues weekly in Russian.

**Tsinya (Struggle).** Founded 1904. Six issues weekly in Lettish.

**Radomju Jaunatre (Soviet Youth).** Founded 1944. Five issues weekly in Lettish.

**Sovietskaya Molodezh.** Founded 1945. Five issues weekly in Russian.

# LITHUANIAN SOVIET SOCIALIST REPUBLIC

## (*Litovskaya Sovietskaya Sotsialisticheskaya Respublika*)

**Capital**—Vilnius.

### AREA AND POPULATION

The Lithuanian S.S.R. is the southernmost and most densely populated of the three Baltic republics. Its area is 65,200 sq. km. and the population was 3,317,000 in 1977. 79 per cent of the population are Lithuanians, the rest being Russians Byelorussians, Poles, Jews and others (according to the 1959 census). The capital, Vilnius, with a population of 458,000 was founded in the tenth century. It is an important railway junction and contains a 16th-century university which is one of the oldest in Eastern Europe. Other major towns include: Kaunas, Klaipeda, Shauliay and Panevezhis.

**Supreme Soviet**

*Chairman:* A. S. Barkauskas.
*Presidium President:* M. Y. Shumauskas.

**Council of Ministers**

*Chairman:* U. A. Manjushis.

*First Secretary of the Central Committee of the Communist Party:* P. P. Grishkiavicius.

### FINANCE

The budget figure for 1976 was 2,047,738,000 roubles.

### PRODUCTION

**Industry.** Lithuania produces radio equipment, diesel engines, mineral fertilizers, fabrics, footwear, furniture, bicycles and handicrafts from wood, ceramics and amber. There is a modern fishing fleet.

**Agriculture.** In January 1977 there were 838 collective farms and 343 state farms. Over half the entire sown area is under food crops, including grain. Meadows and pastures make up about two-fifths of the agricultural land. Grain farming and sheep farming are being developed.

The breeding of stud-horses, sheep-farming and bee-keeping are being developed. The poultry farming industry is expanding. Dairy-farming is highly productive.

### EDUCATION, CULTURE AND SCIENCE

At the beginning of the 1976–77 academic year 600,000 pupils were studying at 2,700 general schools of all types, 69,600 at 76 specialized secondary schools and 64,900 students in 12 instutitions of higher learning.

The Academy of Sciences, set up in 1941, had a total of 1,469 research workers on 1 January 1976, of whom 40 were full or corresponding members.

In 1976 there were 1,476 books published in the Republic, including 1,155 in Lithuanian.

### NEWSPAPERS

**Sovietskaya Litva.** Founded 1944. Six issues weekly in Russian.

**Tiesa (Truth).** Founded 1917. Six issues weekly in Lithuanian.

**Komjaunimo Ties (Komsomol Pravda).** Founded 1919. Five issues weekly in Lithuanian.

**Czervoni Shtanda (Red Banner).** Founded 1953. Six issues weekly in Lithuanian.

# MOLDAVIAN SOVIET SOCIALIST REPUBLIC

## (*Moldavskaya Sovietskaya Sotsialisticheskaya Respublika*)

**Capital**—Kishinev.

### AREA AND POPULATION

The Moldavian S.S.R. is situated in the south-western corner of the U.S.S.R. and shares a common frontier with Romania along the Prut River in the west. Elsewhere it borders on the Ukrainian S.S.R. It was formed on 2 August 1940 by the union of the Moldavian Autonomous S.S.R., an autonomous republic within the Ukrainian S.S.R. and most of Bessarabia, returned to the U.S.S.R. by Romania on 28 June 1940. Principal towns are Kishinev, Beltsi, Tiraspol and Bendery.

The total area of the Repuouc is 33,700 sq. km. and the population 3,858,000. Accordinr to the 1970 census 65·4 per cent of the population are Moldavians and the rest are Ukrainians, Russians, Jews and others. Kishinev has a population of 489,000 (1977).

**Supreme Soviet**

*Chairman:* A. M. Lazarev.

*Presidium President:* K. F. Ilyashenko.

**Council of Ministers**

*Chairman:* S. K. Kozub.

*First Secretary of the Central Committee of the Communist Party:* I. I. Bodyul.

### FINANCE

The budget figure for 1976 was 1,263,700,000 roubles.

### PRODUCTION AND INDUSTRY

**Industry.** Moldavia manufactures electric motors, cables, tractors, cement, prefabricated concrete elements, washing machines, refrigerators and leather footwear.

**Agriculture.** In January 1977 there were 454 collective farms and 227 state farms.

Moldavia contributes a quarter of the grape crop in the Soviet Union, half of the rose oil and holds second place in tobacco production, after the Ukraine. In addition to grapes and fruit, the Republic grows high-grade winter wheat, maize, sunflowers and also hemp, soya beans and essential-oil plants. The growth of production of fruit, grapes, vegetables and sugar beet has led to greater development in the food industries. Thus, Moldavia is a big producer of grape wines and also makes large quantities of canned foods.

### EDUCATION

In the 1976–77 academic year the Republic's 2,100 general schools of all types had 800,000 pupils; there were 56,600 students in 46 specialized secondary schools, and 45,300 students in eight institutions of higher learning. The Academy of Sciences set up in 1961 had, on 1 January 1976, a total of 847 research workers, 39 of them full or corresponding members.

In 1976 there were 1,557 books published in the Republic including 574 in Moldavian.

### NEWSPAPERS

**Moldova Sotsialiste.** Founded 1927. Six issues weekly in Moldavian.

**Sovietskaya Moldavia.** Founded 1925. Six issues weekly in Russian.

**Tinerimya Moldovei (Youth of Moldavia).** Founded 1928; Three issues weekly in Moldavian.

# TADZHIK SOVIET SOCIALIST REPUBLIC

## (*Tadjikskaya Sovietskaya Sotsialisticheskaya Respublika*)

**Capital**—Dushanbe.

### AREA AND POPULATION

Tadzhikistan is situated in the south-east of Central Asia. It shares its eastern and southern frontiers with the People's Republic of China and Afghanistan respectively. In 1924, as a result of the national division of Central Asia, the Tadzhikistan Autonomous Republic was set up. Originally an Autonomous Republic within the Uzbek S.R.S. it became a constituent republic of the U.S.S.R. in December 1929. The Tadzhikistan S.S.R. includes the Gorny Badakhshan Autonomous Region. Most of the population is concentrated in the three valleys of Ferghana, Vakhsh and Ghissar.

The area of the Republic is 143,100 sq. km., and the population on 1 January 1977 was 3,600,000. 53·1 per cent of the population are Tajiks. There are also Uzbeks, Russians and others. The capital, Dushanbe, has a population of 460,000 (1977).

**Supreme Soviet**

*Chairman:* M. Mirshakarov.
*Presidium President:* M. Kholov.

**Council of Ministers**

*Chairman:* R. Nabiev.

*First Secretary of the Central Committee of the Communist Party:* D. R. Rasulov.

### FINANCE

The budget figure for 1976 was 1,024,048,000 roubles.

### PRODUCTION

**Industry.** Coal, oil, gas, ozocerite, lead, zinc, tungsten, bismuth, gold, silver, mountain crystal and building materials have been found in this area. Tadzhikistan has cotton gins, food factories, mining, metal-working, engineering, electrical engineering and chemical industries. The capital has factories manufacturing tractor and automobile spare parts, cotton gins, and silk reeling and woollen mills.

**Agriculture.** In January 1977 there were 209 collective farms and 168 state farms.

Apart from cotton, vegetables are grown under irrigation in a number of areas; hemp, kenaf, ground-nuts, sugar beet and essential-oil crops are cultivated. Rice, wheat and maize are the main grain crops.

Sheep-breeding is the most developed branch of animal husbandry.

Irrigation is the problem of Tadzhikistan. The old irrigation system has been radically reconstructed and many new canals and reservoirs built.

### EDUCATION

At the beginning of the 1976–77 academic year there were 956,000 pupils in 3,200 general schools of all types; 38,500 students in 38 specialized secondary schools, and 51,900 students in nine institutions of higher learning. The Academy of Sciences was set up in 1951 and on 1 January 1976 had 1,218 research workers, including 42 full or corresponding members.

In 1976 there were 784 books published in the Republic, including 369 in Tadzhik.

### NEWSPAPERS

**Kommunist Tadzhikistana.** Founded 1929. Six issues weekly in Russian.

**Tochikistoni Sovieti.** Founded 1925. Six issues weekly in Tadzhik.

**Komsomoli Tochikistoni.** Founded 1930. Three issues weekly in Tadzhik.

**Komsomolets Tadzhikistana.** Founded 1938. Three issues weekly in Russian.

# TURKMENIAN SOVIET SOCIALIST REPUBLIC

## (*Turkmenskaya Sovietskaya Sotsialisticheskaya Respublika*)

**Capital**—Ashkhabad.

### AREA AND POPULATION

Turkmenistan, the southernmost of the Central Asian republics, lies between the Amu Darya River and the Caspian Sea in a low plain with a fringe of mountains along its southern frontiers. In the south it borders on Iran and Afghanistan. The major towns are Ashkhabad, Krasnovodsk, Chardzhou, Mary, Nebit-Dag and Tashauz. Turkmenia is the hottest and most arid of the Central Asian republics. About 80 per cent of its territory consists of desert and is waterless. The Republic was formed on 27 October 1924.

The area of the Republic is 488,100 sq. km., and its population on 1 January 1977 was 2,600,000. The capital, Ashkhabad, had in 1977 a population of 302,000. The majority of the population are Turkmenians (61 per cent according to the 1970 census), the remainder being Russians, Uzbeks, Kazakhs, Tajiks and others. The capital, Ashakhabad, had a population of 266,000 in 1972.

**Supreme Soviet**

*Chairman:* B. Izkulies.
*Presidium President:* A. M. Klychev.

**Council of Ministers**
*Chairman:* B. Y. Yazkuliev.

*First Secretary of the Central Committee of the Communist Party:* M. N. Gapurov.

### FINANCE

The budget figure for 1976 was 820,999,000 roubles.

### PRODUCTION

**Industry.** Oil is the basic source of wealth in Turkmenistan. The chief oil deposits are found in Nebit-Dag, Cheleken, Okaren, Kamishidja, Barsa-gelmes and Kotun-Tepe.

Machine-building is the newest branch of heavy industry. Its output includes electrical engineering equipment, ventilators, centrifugal oil pumps, fittings for the oil and chemical industries, and bulldozers.

**Agriculture.** In January 1977 there were 338 collective farms and 58 state farms. The Great Kara-Kum Canal is now under construction. It supplies water for Ashkhabad and has already provided water for irrigating more than 160,000 hectares of desert land. Due to the climatic conditions, Turkmenia is able to grow large quantities of long-staple cotton.

Agricultural areas occupy almost half the territory of the Republic. Cotton-growing and sheep-breeding are the main branches of agriculture.

Turkmenia enjoys the world's highest cotton yields. Sowing and cultivation are fully mechanized, and 45 per cent of all packing is done by machine. New and valuable varieties of fine-staple cotton have been produced and are now cultivated on 80 per cent of all crop area.

### EDUCATION

In the 1976–77 academic year there were 700,000 pupils in 1,800 general schools of all types, 30,500 students in 30 specialized secondary schools, and 32,100 students in six institutions of higher learning. The Academy of Sciences was set up in 1951 and on 1 January 1976 had a total of 799 research workers, of whom 48 were full or corresponding members.

In 1976 there were 506 books published in the Republic, including 206 in Turkmenian.

### NEWSPAPERS

**Soviet Turkmenistani.** Founded 1920. Six issues weekly in Turkman.

**Turkmenskaya Iskra.** Founded 1924. Six issues weekly in Russian.

**Yash Kommunist (Young Communist).** Founded 1925. Three issues weekly in Turkmen.

**Komsomolets Turkmenistana.** Founded 1938. Three issues weekly in Russian.

# UKRAINIAN SOVIET SOCIALIST REPUBLIC

*(Ukrainskaya Sovietskaya Sotsialisticheskaya Respublika)*

**Capital**—Kiev.

## AREA AND POPULATION

The Ukraine lies in the south-west European U.S.S.R. It is bounded by Poland in the north-west and by Czechoslovakia, Hungary and Romania in the west. In the south it faces the Black and Azov Seas.

The Ukrainian Republic was formed on 25 December 1917.

The Ukraine occupies a total of 603,700 sq. km., and has a population of 49,300,000. According to the 1970 census, the majority of the population are Ukrainians (76·8 per cent). There are also Russians (16·9 per cent), Jews (2 per cent). Poles (0·9 per cent) and others. The capital, Kiev, had a population of 2,079,000 in 1977. The principal towns are Kiev, Kharkov, Donetsk, Dnepropetrovsk, Odessa, Zaporozhye, etc.

**Supreme Soviet**

*Chairman:* M. U. Beliy.
*Presidium President:* A. F. Vatchenko

**Council of Ministers**

*Chairman:* A. P. Lyashko.

*First Secretary of the Central Committee of the Communist Party:* V. V. Shcherbitsky.

## FINANCE

The budget figure for 1976 was 16,845,033,000 roubles.

## PRODUCTION

**Industry.** Engineering is the leading industrial branch and it produces mainly metal-cutting machine tools, electrical apparatus, radio and optical devices, automation appliances, cameras, medical equipment, agricultural machinery, river-craft, buses, motor-cycles.

The meat, buttermaking and canning industries are well developed; the latter produces mostly canned vegetables and fruit.

The fuel and power resources are coal which is widely used, natural gas, oil, peat and hydropower.

**Agriculture.** In January 1977 there were 7,235 collective farms and 2,087 state farms. The Ukraine is the second most productive agricultural area of the Soviet Union as the warm climate and black earth give high yields of diverse crops such as wheat, sugar beet, maize and sunflower. About a quarter of the industrial crops and more than a quarter of the meat and milk in the Soviet Union is produced in the Ukraine.

## EDUCATION

The Academy of Sciences set up in 1919, had on 1 January 1975, 11,625 research workers, of whom 296 were full or corresponding members.

In 1976 there were 9,110 books published in the Republic including 2,494 in Ukrainian.

## NEWSPAPERS

**Pravda Ukrainy.** Founded 1938. Six issues weekly in Russian.

**Rabochaya Gazeta.** Founded 1957. Six issues weekly in Russian.

**Radyanskaya Ukraina.** Founded 1919. Six issues weekly in Ukrainian.

**Silski Visti.** Founded 1939. Six weekly issues in Ukrainian.

# UZBEK SOVIET SOCIALIST REPUBLIC

*(Uzbekskaya Sovietskaya Sotsialisticheskaya Respublika)*

**Capital**—Tashkent.

## AREA AND POPULATION

Uzbekistan is situated in the heart of Soviet Central Asia and borders on Afghanistan in the south. Economically, it is one of the most developed Central Asian republics. The main towns are Tashkent, Samarkand, Andizhan, Ferghana. The greater part of Uzbekistan consists of hills and vast deserts. It is only the oases which are centres of habitation and economic life. The largest of them is the Ferghana Valley irrigated by waters of the Syr-Darya and Naryn Rivers. The Great Ferghana Canal (270 km.), completed in 1939, distributes the waters of the rivers Syr-Darya, Kara-Darya and Naryn in the southern part of the Ferghana Valley. The Tashkent, Zeravshan, Bukhara and Khorezm are the other big oases. They lie in the river valleys with excellent farming soil.

The Republic was proclaimed on 27 October 1924 and on 13 May 1925 it joined the U.S.S.R. as a constituent republic.

The area of the Republic is 447,400 sq. km. and the population is 14,090,000. The capital, Tashkent, had a population of 1,689,000 in 1977. The Uzbeks form about 62·2 per cent of the population and (according to the 1970 census) the rest is composed of Russians, Kazakhs, Tajiks and others.

**Supreme Soviet**

*Chairman:* B. Kh. Sirajdinov.
*Presidium President:* N. M. Machanov.

**Council of Ministers**

*Chairman:* N. D. Khudaiberdyev.

*First Secretary of the Central Committee of the Communist Party:* Sh. R. Rashidov.

## FINANCE

The budget figure for 1976 was 4,298,696,000 roubles.

## PRODUCTION

**Industry.** The heavy, chemical, power, non-ferrous metals, as well as large textile and food-processing industries play the leading part in Uzbekistan's economy.

Tashkent is the main machine-building centre. Numerous other industries occur in the Republic including chemical, building materials, food-processing, electrical generating and many others.

**Agriculture.** In January 1977 there were 947 collective farms and 626 state farms. The principal crop is cotton.

Apart from cotton, sugar beet, groundnuts, rice, wheat and maize are grown under irrigation in a number of areas.

## EDUCATION

The Academy of Sciences was set up in 1943 and had on 1 January 1976 a total of 3,562 research workers, of whom 103 are full or corresponding members.

In 1976 there were 1,980 books published in the Republic, including 897 in Uzbek.

## NEWSPAPERS

**Pravda Vostoka.** Founded 1917. Six issues weekly in Russian.

**Soviet Uzbekistoni.** Founded 1918. Six issues weekly in Uzbek.

**Esh Leninchil (Young Leninist).** Founded 1925. Five issues weekly in Uzbek.

**Komsomolets Uzbekistana.** Founded 1926. Five issues weekly in Russian.

# United Kingdom of Great Britain and Northern Ireland

**Capital**—London.

**Sovereign**—H.M. Queen Elizabeth II.

**National Flag:** (United Kingdom), The Union Jack; Dark blue charged with the White Cross of St. Andrew (for Scotland) and the Red Cross of St. Patrick (for Ireland), the colours counter-changed, surmounted by the Red Cross of St. George (for England) bordered white.

## CONSTITUTION AND GOVERNMENT

THERE is no single legal document setting forth and defining the British Constitution. It is always in fact described as unwritten and this feature has given to it a flexibility and power of development denied to any formal instrument. It is a structure based on a number of statutes, laws, traditions and customs assembled over a long period of time. These laws are not immutable, though some have remained for centuries. They are continually undergoing change and others are being added. One of the earliest, dating from 1215, is known as *Magna Carta*, which provides among other things for the equality of all men before the law. One of the latest was the Statute of Westminster, 1931, by which legislative autonomy was granted to the Dominions.

Britain is a constitutional monarchy in which the crown is hereditary. The Act of Settlement, 1701, secured the Protestant succession to the throne. When the Sovereign leaves the realm, Counsellors of State are appointed to carry out the chief official functions of the monarch, including the holding of Privy Councils and signing of Acts passed by Parliament. The normal procedure is to appoint as Counsellors of State the members of the Royal family of full age who are next in succession to the throne.

The legislative power resides in the Parliament, which consists of the Sovereign, the House of Lords and the House of Commons. The forerunner of Parliament was the Witan before the Norman conquest and the Great Council in Norman and Angevin times. At the end of the 13th century Edward I summoned to Westminster not only the magnates, but the knights of the shire and burgesses as representatives of the 'community of the realm'. Only occasionally now does the Sovereign preside over Parliament. Usually this is done at the opening of a new session, when the Sovereign, sitting on the throne in the House of Lords, addresses the members of both chambers.

The executive power belongs to the Sovereign, but it is entrusted to the Cabinet, which consists of the most important Ministers of the Crown, presided over by the Prime Minister. When it is known which Parliamentary party has a majority, or is able to command a majority of supporters, in a newly elected House of Commons, the Sovereign calls the leader of that Party to become Prime Minister and form a Government. The Prime Minister chooses the other ministers and these are then officially appointed by the Sovereign.

If the Góvernment is defeated in the House of Commons on what is considered a major issue, it must resign or else ask the Sovereign to dissolve Parliament and hold a new election. Ministers remain in office after Parliament is dissolved and until a new Ministry is appointed.

Parliament's main functions are law-making, authorizing taxation and public expenditure, and examining the actions of the Government. Most of this work is carried out, in both Houses, by a system of debates.

During their passage through Parliament measures relating to public policy are called 'Bills'. The great majority are Government Bills, introduced by a Minister; a few (known as Private Members' Bills) are sponsored by individual members on their own initiative, but not many of these become law.

Bills are introduced in either House, except for Money Bills which impose taxation, which can only be introduced in the House of Commons.

When the Bill is introduced it normally receives its formal 'first reading', after which it is printed and circulated to members. At the 'second reading' the Bill is debated and if it passes this stage it is sent to a Committee, when details are discussed and amendments generally made. Finally the Bill is given a 'third reading' by the House and if passed is then sent to the other House.

When a Bill has passed through all its Parliamentary stages, it receives royal assent. It then becomes an Act of Parliament and is the law of the land. Royal assent may be given by the Sovereign in person or, periodically, by Royal Commission, but is usually declared by their Speakers (presidents) to both Houses.

Normally a Bill is passed by both the House of Commons and the House of Lords. A Bill which originates in the House of Lords cannot become law unless it is passed by the House of Commons, whereas a Bill, passed in the Commons, can become law under certain circumstances even if rejected by the Lords. The Lords cannot reject a Money Bill and they can merely delay for one year any other Bill which they do not like. This was the result of the Parliament Acts of 1911 and 1949, restricting the power of the Lords, whose consent had, prior to 1911, been necessary for a Bill to become law.

All laws are theoretically the laws of the Sovereign, which the judges cannot question, and therefore Parliament is free to legislate as it wishes. It can make new laws and alter the old ones, but it follows that a subsequent Parliament can alter the laws made by its predecessor.

The members of the House of Commons (MPs) are elected by popular vote, representing the counties and borough constituencies. These members are delegates of the people, so that it is true to say that power ultimately resides in the people. The number of members elected at the last general election was in the House of Commons, 635.

The House of Commons elects is own Speaker. He presides over the debates but does not vote unless the voting is equal, in which case he gives the casting vote in accordance with rules which preclude an expression of opinion upon the merits of the question. In the absence of the Speaker his place is taken by one of his three deputies.

The House of Lords consists of the Lords 'spiritual and temporal'. The Lords Spiritual are the two Archbishops (Canterbury and York), the Bishops of London, Durham and Winchester, and 21 other bishops of the Church of England, according to their seniority as diocesan bishops. The Lords Temporal include peers by hereditary right, peers by virtue of their office (the Law lords), and Life peers created under the Life Peerages Act, 1958. Peerages are created by the Sovereign; about half have been created since 1920. Peerages can also be renounced for life under the Peerages Act 1963. In the full House of Lords there are some 1,000 potential members, though the actual numbers are cut to under 700 working members by a voluntary process of 'leave of absence'. The Speaker of the House is the Lord Chancellor.

The maximum statutory period for the duration of Parliament is five years, but Parliament is generally dissolved by proclamation before that period has fully elapsed.

The Ministers of the Crown Act, 1975, provides that 95 Ministers in receipt of salaries may sit and vote in the Commons, and nowadays the majority of Ministers sit in that House. There are, however, always some Ministers in the Lords to act as spokesmen for the Government in that House. There are at present 24 Cabinet Ministers and 66 other Ministers.

On 1 January 1973, when Britain acceded to the European Community, the provisions of the European Communities Act 1972 (passed by Parliament) applying the Treaty of Rome became operative. These provide for various types of Community legislation to have effect in Britain, including regulations, which take direct effect in member countries, and directives, which are binding as to the result achieved upon each member State to which they are addressed, but allow the national parliaments to choose the form and method of implementation. Under the Treaty of Rome the national parliaments delegate a number of their members to sit in the European Assembly. It is intended that these representatives shall be directly elected from 1978.

British membership of the Community was endorsed in June 1975 by a more than two-to-one majority in the first national referendum to be held in Britain. Some 67·2 per cent of those voting wanted Britain to remain in the Community, against 32·8 per cent who voted for withdrawal. Almost 65 per cent of those eligible to vote did so.

**Reigning Royal Family.** House of Windsor. Anglican. The Sovereign descends in the male line from, and represents, the old German House of Saxe-Coburg, and descends through Queen Victoria from the houses of Hanover and Brunswick-Lüneburg. As also through females from the Kings of Wessex, the Anglo-Saxon Kings of England, the Dukes of Normandy and the Norman Kings of England, the Tudor and Stewart Kings of England, the Stuart, Bruce and earlier Kings of Scotland, and the early Princes of Wales. By a royal proclamation, 17 July 1917, King George V abandoned all German styles and titles for himself and the Royal Family and adopted the house and family name of Windsor. Succession is in both male and female lines, in which case a daughter would take precedence over her father's brother and more distant male relatives. The members of the family have the title prince or princess of Great Britain and Ireland, Royal Highness, but this style was limited by King George V to children, and grandchildren of the sovereign in the male line and the eldest grandson of the Prince of Wales. In 1977 Queen Elizabeth II celebrated the Silver Jubilee of her reign.

**H.M. ELIZABETH II** Alexandra Mary, Queen of the United Kingdom of Great Britain and Northern Ireland and of her other Realms and Territories, Head of the Commonwealth, Defender of the Faith; born at 17 Bruton Street, London, 21 April 1926, elder daughter of King George VI (born 14 December 1895, died 6 February 1952); succeeded to the throne on the death of her father; married at Westminster Abbey, 20 November 1947, Lieut. Philip Mountbatten, RN (created Duke of Edinburgh, Earl of Merioneth, and Baron Greenwich, 19 November 1947; further created Prince of Great Britain, 22 February 1957) formerly Prince of Greece and Denmark (born at Corfu, 10 June 1921), only son of late Prince Andrew of Greece and Denmark.

Children: 1. Prince CHARLES Philip Arthur George, Prince of Wales, Duke of Cornwall; born at Buckingham Palace, 14 November 1948. 2. Princess ANNE Elizabeth Alice Louise; born at Clarence House, St. James's, 15 August 1950; married at Westminster Abbey, 14 November 1973, Capt. Mark Phillips. 3. Prince ANDREW Albert Christian Edward; born at Buckingham Palace, 19 February 1960. 4. Prince EDWARD Antony Richard Louis; born at Buckingham Palace, 10 March 1964.

Sister of the Queen: Princess MARGARET Rose; born at Glamis Castle, Scotland, 21 August 1930; married in Westminster Abbey on 6 May 1960 Antony Armstrong-Jones (created 1st Earl of Snowdon in 1961); issue: David, Viscount Linley born 3 November 1961 and Lady Sarah Armstrong-Jones born 1 May 1964.

Mother of the Queen: Queen ELIZABETH The Queen Mother, daughter of Claude George, 14th Earl of Strathmore and Kinghorne; born at St. Paul's Waldenbury, Hitchin, 4 August 1900; married to King George VI at Westminster Abbey, 26 April 1923.

Uncles and Aunt of the Queen: 1. EDWARD Albert Christian George Andrew Patrick David, Duke of Windsor (created 8 March 1937); born at White Lodge, Richmond Park, 23 June 1894; succeeded to the throne as King EDWARD VIII on the death of his father, King George V (born 3 June 1865, died 20 January 1936); abdicated in favour of his brother, the Duke of York, 11 December 1936; married at the Château de Candé, nr. Tours, 3 June 1937 (Bessie) Wallis (born at Monterey, Virginia, 19 June 1896), formerly wife of (1) late Capt. Earl Winfield Spencer, U.S.N., and (2) Ernest Aldrich Simpson, and daughter of Teakle Wallis Warfield. The Duke of Windsor died 29 May 1972. 2. Princess Victoria Alexandra Alice MARY (The Princess Royal); born at Sandringham, 25 April 1897; married at Westminster Abbey, 28 February 1922, Henry, Viscount Lascelles (later 6th Earl of Harewood), had issue; died 1965. He died at Harewood House, Leeds, 24 May 1947. 3. Prince HENRY William Frederick Albert, Duke of Gloucester, Earl of Ulster and Baron Culloden (created 31 March 1928); born at Sandringham, 31 March 1900, died 10 June 1974; married at Buckingham Palace, 6 November 1935, Lady Alice Montagu-Douglas-Scott (born at London 25 December 1901), daughter of John Charles, 7th Duke of Buccleuch and Queensberry.

Sons: 1. Prince WILLIAM Henry Andrew Frederick; born at Barnet, Herts, 18 December 1941, killed in a flying accident, 28 August 1972. 2. Prince RICHARD Alexander Walter George, Duke of Gloucester; born at Northampton, 26 August 1944; married Birgitte van Deurs at Barnwell Parish Church on 8 July 1972; issue: Alexander, Earl of Ulster born 24 October 1974.

The late Prince GEORGE Duke of Kent (4th son of King George V); born 20 December 1902; killed in a flying accident, 25 August 1942; married 29 November 1934, Princess Marina (born 13 December 1906, died September 1968), youngest daughter of Prince Nicholas of Greece and Denmark:

Sons: 1. Prince EDWARD George Nicholas Paul Patrick, 2nd Duke of Kent, Earl of St. Andrews and Baron Down-Patrick; born at London, 9 October 1935; married Katherine Worsley on 8 June 1961; issue: George, Earl of St. Andrews born 26 June 1962, Lady Helen Windsor born 28 April 1964 and Lord Nicholas Windsor born 25 July 1970. 2. Princess ALEXANDRA Helen Elizabeth Olga Christabel; born at London, 25 December 1936; married the Hon. Angus Ogilvy on 24 April 1963; issue: James born 29 February 1964 and Marina born 31 July 1966. 3. Prince MICHAEL George Charles Franklin; born at Iver, 4 July 1942.

First Cousin of King George V: Princess ALICE Mary Victoria Augusta Pauline; born at Windsor, 25 February 1883; married at Windsor, 10 February 1904, Alexander, Prince of Teck, later 1st Earl of Athlone (created 16 July 1917), and has issue. He died at Kensington Palace, 16 January 1957.

### Cabinet

*Prime Minister and First Lord of the Treasury:* Mr James Callaghan.
*Lord President of the Council and Leader of the House of Commons:* Mr Michael Foot.
*Lord Chancellor:* Lord Elwyn-Jones.
*Chancellor of the Exchequer:* Mr Denis Healey.
*Secretary of State for the Home Department:* Mr Merlyn Rees.
*Secretary of State for Foreign and Commonwealth Affairs:* Dr David Owen.
*Secretary of State for Education and Science and Paymaster General:* Mrs Shirley Williams.
*Secretary of State for Energy:* Mr Anthony Wedgwood Benn.
*Secretary of State for Industry:* Mr Eric Varley.
*Secretary of State for the Environment:* Mr Peter Shore.
*Secretary of State for Northern Ireland:* Mr Roy Mason.
*Secretary of State for Scotland:* Mr Bruce Millan.
*Secretary of State for Wales:* Mr John Morris, QC.
*Secretary of State for Defence:* Mr Frederick Mulley.
*Secretary of State for Employment:* Mr Albert Booth.
*Secretary of State for Social Services:* Mr David Ennals.
*Secretary of State for Trade:* Mr Edmund Dell.
*Lord Privy Seal and Leader of the House of Lords:* Lord Peart.
*Chief Secretary to the Treasury:* Mr. Joel Barnett.
*Minister of Agriculture, Fisheries and Food:* Mr John Silkin.
*Secretary of State for Prices and Consumer Protection:* Mr Roy Hattersley.
*Secretary of State for Transport:* Mr William Rodgers.
*Minister for Social Security:* Mr Stanley Orme.
*Chancellor of the Duchy of Lancaster:* Mr Harold Lever.

Parliamentary elections were held on 28 February 1974. The State of the Parties after the election was: Labour 301, Conservative 296, Liberal 14, United Ulster Unionists 10, Scottish Nationalists 7, Independent Labour 1, Protestant Unionists 1, Plaid Cymru 2, S.D.L.P. 1, Democratic Labour 1.

*Note:* For a chart showing the structure of the Foreign Office see chart immediately prior to States of the World.

## LOCAL GOVERNMENT

### England and Wales

Local Government in England and Wales was reorganized from 1 April 1974 under the Local Government Act 1972. As a result some 1,400 old counties, county boroughs, boroughs, urban districts and rural districts disappeared. In their place are 39 county councils in England and within these areas are 296 district councils. There are now also six metropolitan county councils within which are 36 metropolitan districts. Wales has eight county councils and 37 district councils.

The number of councillors as a result of reorganization in approximately 22,000.

Most of the previous services remain with local government but water supply was re-organized under regional water authorities although local government representatives serve on the committees of each water authority. Local authorities continue to be responsible for local servicing of sewage. Local authorities lost responsibility for those personal health services, administered before 1 April 1974, to the reorganized National Health Service. Several members of each area Health Authority and half the members of each community health council are nominated by local authorities.

Elections to the county councils took place for the first time in 1973 and these will now be held every four years, the councillors retiring together. Elections to county councils, including the Greater London Council, were held in May 1977. The district councils were elected for the first time in 1973. Further elections took place in 1976 and also will take place in 1979 and from then onwards in every fourth year.

However, provision has been made under the Act for councillors of a district to retire simultaneously or, alternatively, for a system of election of one-third to be elected each year, except in the year of county council elections.

The Greater London Council and the City of London were not affected by the 1974 reorganization. The City is an area of one square mile with its own time-honoured council and its own Lord Mayor. The Greater London Council was created by the London Government Act, 1963. It has under its jurisdiction an area of 117 square miles which is divided into 32 London boroughs each with its own mayor, aldermen and councillors.

The GLC is responsible for the main drainage system of London, the maintenance of 16 bridges over the Thames and some 20 or 30 other bridges, the Woolwich Ferry across the Thames, Blackwall Tunnel and the Thames embankments. It also has control of the fire brigade and the management of parks and open spaces.

The local administrative authorities in London are the Councils of the 32 boroughs and the Corporation of the City of London. They attend to local environmental health, consumer protection and housing services, personal social services, streets, baths, libraries and other local affairs. Some of the London boroughs have grouped together to administer weights and measures including the Food and Drugs Act. They are responsible singly for education except in the 12 inner London boroughs and the City of London which combine in the Inner London Education Authority. Although autonomous, the Authority is a special committee of the GLC, and members of the GLC as well as one representative from each of the inner London boroughs and of the Common Council of the City serve on it.

Aldermen throughout England disappeared under the new arrangements and there are only councillors. The aldermen in London were discontinued in 1977, save that the City of London will retain its aldermen.

The six new *metropolitan* county councils cover main centres of population and the big conurbations. These are Greater Manchester, Merseyside, South Yorkshire, Tyne and Wear, West Midlands and West Yorkshire. Unlike the *non-metropolitan* county councils these councils are not responsible for education, youth employment, personal social services or libraries; these functions are dealt with by the 36 *metropolitan district* councils.

However, all county councils are in charge of structure planning under town development although local plans are the responsibility of the new *district* councils. There are concurrent powers exercised by county and district councils in a number of instances. For example, this sharing of responsibility covers country parks, derelict land, conservation areas, museums and art galleries, physical training and recreation. Refuse disposal is a county function (except in Wales where the districts undertake it), but refuse collection (distinct from disposal) is a district service. Most housing matters come under the district councils while transportation in most aspects is a county responsibility, although district councils may claim maintenance powers for urban roads which are not trunk or classified roads. Environmental health, including food safety and hygiene, slaughterhouses, and communicable diseases, together with clean air and building regulations, markets and fairs and the making of bye-laws come under the new district councils. Important consumer protection activities, such as weights and measures, explosives, food and drugs are the responsibility of the trading standards departments of the new county councils. Police and fire are also the county council's responsibility.

The ministries mainly concerned with local government are the Department of the Environment, the Department of Health and Social Security, the Department of Education and Science, the Home Office, the Ministry of Agriculture and as regards consumer affairs, the Department of Prices and Consumer Protection, and as regards civil aviation, the Department of Trade.

Local authority Associations, formed to succeed the previous associations and to look after the collective districts of their members, are the Association of County Councils, which all county councils and the GLC are eligible to join, all the 47 non-metropolitan county councils in England and Wales are members of the Association; the Association of District Councils, representing the new non-metropolitan districts; and the Association of Metropolitan Authorities, representing all the metropolitan counties, the metropolitan districts, the Greater London Council, the London boroughs and the City of London.

The National Association of Parish Councils was renamed the National Association of Local Councils to represent the new parish councils in England and the community councils in Wales.

Certain other national bodies were reconstituted, including mportant ones like the Local Authorities Conditions of Service Advisory Board (LACSAB), the Local Authorities Management Services and Computer Committee (LAMSAC) and the Local Government Training Board.

**Scotland**

Under the new structure of local government which, in terms of the Local Government (Scotland) Act 1973, came into administrative effect on 16 May 1975, Scotland is for local government purposes divided into nine regions (within which are a total of 53 districts), and three islands areas covering respectively Orkney, Shetland and the Western Isles. This replaced the former local government structure of counties, large and small burghs, and districts.

Each of the local government areas has its own council. Councillors are elected for a period of four years, the next elections will take place in 1978. At present the term of office of district councillors is three years but after the next district council elections in 1980 their term of office will also be four years.

The Scottish police forces were reorganised from the same date, creating eight new forces, six directly linked with new regions and two amalgamations. At 31 March 1977 the actual total strength of police in Scotland was 11,494 men and 756 women.

## LEGAL SYSTEM

The supreme judicial authority and highest court of appeal for England, Wales, Scotland and Northern Ireland is the House of Lords. Sitting as a judicial body, the House of Lords consists of a minimum quorum of three members (though usually five attend) drawn from the Lord Chancellor, the Lords of Appeal in Ordinary and Peers who hold or have held high judicial office as defined by the Appellate Jurisdiction Act, 1876.

There is a Judicial Committee of the Privy Council which is the highest court of appeal for certain independent members of the Commonwealth and for the British dependencies, and has limited jurisdiction in certain matters (e.g. appeals by members of the medical and kindred professions against decisions of their disciplinary bodies) in Britain. Those who sit on the Committee hold or have held high judicial office in Britain or in the Commonwealth and are Privy Counsellors.

**England and Wales**

Below the House of Lords, there is for civil and criminal matters in England and Wales the Supreme Court of Judicature. It comprises the Court of Appeal, the High Court which has civil jurisdiction and the Crown Court which has a predominantly criminal jurisdiction. The Court of Appeal consists of a civil division, which hears appeals from the High Court and the County Courts, and a criminal division, which hears criminal appeals from the Crown Court.

The Civil Division of the Court of Appeal consists in practice of the Master of the Rolls and the Lords Justices of Appeal. The Lord Chancellor, its nominal head, very rarely sits there. In the Criminal Division, which is normally presided over by the Lord Chief Justice or a Lord Justice of Appeal, Judges of the Queen's Bench Division sit with Lords Justices.

The High Court has three divisions—Chancery, Queen's Bench, and Family. The Chancery Division is headed by the Lord Chancellor and has a Vice-Chancellor and ten judges. It deals (*inter alia*) with the construction of wills, settlements, trusts and mortgages. The Queen's Bench Division consists of the Lord Chief Justice, as president, and 43 judges. There is a separate Admiralty Court and Commercial Court within the Queen's Bench Division. The Family Division consists of the President and 16 other judges.

The High Court judges on circuit at first and second tier Crown Court Centres try the more serious criminal cases. At first tier centres they also try civil actions which fall within the competence of the Queen's Bench Division and defended divorce cases.

In addition to the High Court judges there are Circuit judges who normally sit in the Crown Court and the county courts, and Recorders, experienced members of the legal profession who undertake to sit as judges for a number of days each year.

The County Courts were established to provide local justice in minor civil matters. Their jurisdiction covers virtually the whole range of civil proceedings including divorce. Unless the parties consent, certain pecuniary limits are set to the competence of these courts, e.g. £2,000 in contract and tort, and Admiralty matters, (except in the nature of salvage, when the value of the goods salvaged may be £15,000). The parties can, however, agree to waive these limits. From County Courts an appeal lies to the Court of Appeal.

On the criminal side beneath the Crown Court there are the magistrates' courts for the trial of minor offences. These offences are, in general, dealt with by lay justices exercising summary jurisdiction. Justices of the Peace are appointed by the Lord Chancellor. In the case of graver offences, prisoners are sent for trial to the Crown Court. In London, and in some large towns the summary jurisdiction is exercised by legally qualified magistrates called stipendiaries. So many offences have been placed by statute within the competence of the justices and the stipendiaries that the limits of their jurisdiction are impossible to lay down. In the case of customs offences, for example, they may impose very heavy penalties. But in general, prison sentences of not more than six months may be imposed by magistrates and fines not exceeding £400 and prison sentences of not more than 12 months by stipendiaries.

The Crown Court hears appeals and commitals for sentence from the magistrates' courts and also tries more serious cases. Appeal may be made to the Criminal Division of the Court of Appeal.

The largest Crown Court for Greater London is the Central Criminal Court, which sits in the Old Bailey, a name which probably derives from the medieval latin 'balium', the wall defending an outer courtyard in the fortifications of the city.

At the Crown Court, all criminal trials are tried in open court by a judge and jury consisting of 12 persons.

Persons committed for trial whose means are insufficient to enable them to pay for legal assistance may, at the discretion of the committing justices or the court of trial, have free legal aid and have counsel and solicitor assigned to them for their defence. If the charge is murder legal aid must be granted.

Where the case raises a point of law of general importance, an appeal lies to the House of Lords with the leave of the Court of Appeal or, in military or naval jurisdiction of the Courts Martial Appeal Court. There remains the possibility of invoking the Royal Prerogative. This may be exercised on the advice of the Home Secretary, after full consideration of all the circumstances of the case.

In each county the Crown is represented by Her Majesty's Lord Lieutenant, who as Keeper of the Rolls, is the Chief Magistrate in the County. Assisted by an advisory committee, he recommends to the Lord Chancellor the names of persons for appointment as Justices of the Peace.

Each county has a sheriff who is responsible for several under-sheriffs. It is the duty of the under-sheriffs to issue High Court writs.

Another officer of the Crown is the Coroner, whose duty it is to inquire into cases of sudden death or death of a suspicious nature. He also adjudicates on questions of treasure trove.

### The House of Lords

*The Lord Chancellor*

Rt. Hon. Lord Elwyn-Jones, C.H.

*Lords of Appeal in Ordinary (in order of seniority)*

Rt. Hon. Lord Wilberforce. CMG, OBE.
Rt. Hon. Lord Diplock.
Rt. Hon. Viscount Dilhorne, DL.
Rt. Hon. Lord Simon of Glaisdale, DL.
Rt. Hon. Lord Salmon.
Rt. Hon. Lord Edmund-Davies.
Rt. Hon. Lord Fraser of Tullybelton.
Rt. Hon. Lord Russell of Killowen.
Rt. Hon. Lord Keith of Kinkel.

*Lords of Appeal*

Rt. Hon. Lord MacDermott, MC.
Rt. Hon. Lord Tucker.
Rt. Hon. Lord Denning (Master of the Rolls).
Rt. Hon. Lord Morris of Borth-y-Gest, CH, GBE, MC.
Rt. Hon. Lord Hodson, MC.
Rt. Hon. Lord Guest.
Rt. Hon. Lord Devlin.
Rt. Hon. Lord Pearce.
Rt. Hon. Lord Gardiner.
Rt. Hon. Lord Pearson, CBE.
Rt. Hon. Lord Hailsham of Saint Marylebone.
Rt. Hon. Lord Wheatley (Lord Justice Clerk).
Rt. Hon. Lord Cross of Chelsea.
Rt. Hon. Lord Widgery (Lord Chief Justice).
Rt. Hon. Lord Kilbrandon.

### Supreme Courts of Judicature

**Court of Appeal**

*Ex-Officio Judges:*

Rt. Hon. the Lord High Chancellor (President).
Rt. Hon. the Lord Chief Justice of England.
Rt. Hon. the Master of the Rolls.
Rt. Hon. the President of the Family Division.

*The Master of the Rolls:*

Rt. Hon. Lord Denning.

*Lords Justices of Appeal:*

Rt. Hon. Sir John Megaw, CBE, TD.
Rt. Hon. Sir Denys Burton Buckley, MBE.
Rt. Hon. Sir Edward Blanshard Stamp.
Rt. Hon. Sir John Frederick Eustace Stephenson.
Rt. Hon. Sir Alan Stewart Orr, OBE.
Rt. Hon. Sir Eustace Wentworth Roskill.
Rt. Hon. Sir Frederick Horace Lawton.
Rt. Hon. Sir Leslie George Scarman, OBE.
Rt. Hon. Sir Roger Fray Greenwood Ormrod.
Rt. Hon. Sir Patrick Reginald Evelyn Browne, OBE, TD.
Rt. Hon. Sir Geoffrey Dawson Lane, AFC.
Rt. Hon. Sir Reginald William Goff.
Rt. Hon. Sir Nigel Cyprian Bridge.
Rt. Hon. Sir Sebag Shaw.
Rt. Hon. Sir George Stanley Waller.
Rt. Hon. Sir James Roualeyn Hovell-Thurlow-Cumming Bruce.

### High Court of Justice

**Chancery Division**

*President:* The Rt. Hon. The Lord High Chancellor.

*Judges:* Hon. Sir Robert Edgar Megarry (The Vice-Chancellor).
Hon. Sir John Patrick Graham.
Hon. Sir Peter Harry Batson Woodroffe Foster, MBE, TD.
Hon. Sir John Norman Keates Whitford.
Hon. Sir John Anson Brightman.
Hon. Sir Ernest Irvine Goulding.
Hon. Sir Sydney William Templeman, MBE.
Hon. Sir Raymond Henry Walton.
Hon. Sir Peter Raymond Oliver.
Hon. Sir Michael John Fox.
Hon. Sir Christopher John Slade.
Hon. Sir Nicolas Christopher Henry Browne-Wilkinson.

**Queen's Bench Division**

*The Lord Chief Justice of England:*

Rt. Hon. Lord Widgery, PC, OBE, TD (President).

*Judges:* The Rt. Hon. Sir Aubrey Melford Steed Stevenson.
Hon. Sir Gerald Alfred Thesiger, MBE.
Hon. Sir Basil Edward Nield, CBE.
Hon. Sir Bernard Joseph Maxwell MacKenna.
Hon. Sir Alan Abraham Mocatta, OBE.
Hon. Sir John Thompson.
Hon. Sir Helenus Patrick Joseph Milmo.
Hon. Sir Joseph Donaldson Cantley, OBE.
Hon. Sir Hugh Eames Park.
Hon. Sir Ralph Vincent Cusack.
Hon. Sir Stephen Chapman.
Hon. Sir John Ramsay Willis.
Hon. Sir Graham Russell Swanwick, MBE.
Hon. Sir Patrick McCarthy O'Connor.
Hon. Sir John Francis Donaldson.
Hon. Sir John Robertson Dunn Crichton.
Hon. Sir Samuel Burgess Ridgway Cooke.
Hon. Sir Bernard Caulfield.
Hon. Sir Hiliary Gwynne Talbot.
Hon. Sir Edward Walter Eveleigh.
Hon. Sir William Lloyd Mars-Jones, MBE.
Hon. Sir Ralph Kilner Brown, OBE, TD.
Hon. Sir Philip Wien.
Hon. Sir Peter Henry Rowley Bristow.
Hon. Sir Hugh Harry Valentine Forbes.
Hon. Sir Desmond James Conrad Ackner.
Hon. Sir William Hugh Griffiths, MC.
Hon. Sir Robert Hugh Mais.
Hon. Sir Neil Lawson.
Hon. Sir David Powell Croom-Johnson, DSC, VRD.
Hon. Sir Tasker Watkins, VC.
Hon. Sir John Raymond Phillips, MC.
Hon. Sir Leslie Kenneth Edward Boreham.
Hon. Sir John Douglas May.

Hon. Sir Michael Robert Emanuel Kerr.
Hon. Sir Alfred William Michael Davies.
Hon. Sir John Dexter Stocker, MC, TD.
Hon. Sir Kenneth George Illtyd Jones.
Hon. Sir Peter Richard Pain.
Hon. Sir Kenneth Graham Jupp MC.
Hon. Sir Robert Lionel Archibald Goff.
Hon. Sir Gordon Slynn.
Hon. Sir Roger Jocelyn Parker.
Hon. Sir Ralph Brian Gibson.

**Family Division**

*President:* Rt. Hon. Sir George Gillespie Baker, OBE.

*Judges:* Hon. Sir Charles William Stanley Rees, TD.
Hon. Sir Reginald Withers Payne.
Hon. Sir Neville Major Ginner Faulks, MBE, TD.
Hon. Sir John Brinsmead Latey, MBE.
Hon. Dame Elizabeth Kathleen Lane, DBE.
Hon. Sir Henry Vivian Brandon, MC.
Hon. Sir Robin Horace Walford Dunn, MC.
Hon. Sir Alfred Kenneth Hollings, MC.
Hon. Sir John Lewis Arnold.
Hon. Sir Charles Trevor Reeve.
Hon. Sir Francis Brooks Purchas.
Hon. Sir Haydn Tudor Evans.
Hon. Dame Rose Heilbron, DBE.
Hon. Sir Stephen Brown.
Hon. Sir Brian Drex Bush.
Hon. Sir Alfred John Balcombe.

**Scotland.** The supreme civil court in Scotland is the Court of Session, from which there is no appeal except to the House of Lords.

It is divided into two Houses, the Inner with eight judges and the Outer with twelve. The Inner House has two Divisions with four judges in each. The judges of the Outer House sit in separate courts and from them appeals are sent to a Division of the Inner House.

The supreme criminal court is the High Court of Justiciary. It sits in Edinburgh and the circuit towns and consists of all the judges of the Court of Session. Its functions are generally limited to the trial of serious cases. It is the only competent court in cases of treason and murder.

The principal local courts are the Sheriff Courts with both civil and criminal jurisdiction. In civil matters these courts provide the advantage of justice locally administered and the saving of expense. There is no pecuniary limit to their jurisdiction. Appeals are taken to the Court of Session. The criminal jurisdiction of the Sheriff Courts extends only to crimes punishable with fine or imprisonment for two years or less.

Minor offences are dealt with by the District Courts.

COURT OF SESSION

**Inner House—First Division**

*Lord President of the Court of Session:* Rt. Hon. Lord Emslie, MBE.

*Judges:* Hon. Lord Cameron, Hon. Lord Johnston, Rt. Hon. Lord Avonside.

**Inner House—Second Division**

*Lord Justice Clerk:* Rt. Hon. Lord Wheatley.

*Judges:* Rt. Hon. Lord Hunter (seconded to Scottish Law Commission as Chairman), Hon. Lord Kissen, Hon. Lord Robertson.

**Outer House**

*Judges:* Hon. Lord Thomson.
Rt. Hon. Lord Stott.
Hon. Lord Dunpark.
Hon. Lord Grieve.
Hon. Lord Brand.
Hon. Lord Kincraig.
Hon. Lord Maxwell.
Hon. Lord McDonald.
Rt. Hon. Lord Wylie.
Hon. Lord Stewart.
Hon. Lord Ross.
Hon. Lord Allanbridge.
Hon. Lord Cowie.

*Principal Clerk of Session and Justiciary:* Ormond John Brown.

**High Court of Justiciary**

*Lord Justice General:* Rt. Hon. Lord Emslie, MBE.

*Lord Justice Clerk:* Rt. Hon. Lord Wheatley.

***Lords Commissioners of Justiciary:*** **All the other Judges.**

**CURRENCY**

The unit of currency is the (£) sterling of 100 pence. It was originally a pound weight of silver and was derived from the Roman libra (£) which itself denoted a weight of metal, its full name being libra pondo, a libra by weight, which in course of time became known as a pondo or pound. The word 'sterling', which is of uncertain origin, was applied in or before the 12th century to the fineness of English silver coin, but by the 17th century was officially recognized as denoting 'current money of England' (Proclamation of 11 November 1606). In 1971 the subsidiary units of coinage were re-established on a decimal basis (see below). The £.s.d. has been withdrawn from circulation except for the two shilling, one shilling and sixpence coins. The two shilling and one shilling equate exactly in size and value to the 10p and 5p units respectively. In January, 1973 it was decided that the 6d (2½p) coin should remain legal tender for at least another year, and in April 1977 it was stated in Parliament that there was no present intention of withdrawing the coin, although the position would be kept under review.

In 1976, the Royal Mint produced 1,567 million coins. Production is now entirely carried out at the Royal Mint's factory in Llantrisant, Wales. Tower Hill concentrated on the manufacture of sovereigns, coinage blanks, official and commercial medals and the production of embossing seals and revenue dies until the transfer of the remaining production operations at the end of October.

The following table shows the details of coinage produced during 1976:

| | |
|---|---|
| Sovereigns | 1,150,000 |
| 50p | 28,050,000 |
| 10p | 197,391,000 |
| 5p | 3,300,000 |
| 2p | 179,532,000 |
| 1p | 245,696,000 |
| ½p | 221,048,000 |
| U.K. Decimal Proof Coin | 1,660,636 |
| Maundy Money | 4,632 |
| Overseas Coin | 689,020,955 |
| Overseas Proof Coin | 927,739 |

Of the total coinage produced, nearly 44 per cent of the year's production was for overseas governments. In addition to their own production the Royal Mint arranged for some 414 million coins to be struck by sub-contractors working under Royal Mint supervision.

Countries and territories to which coins were supplied include:

Bahamas, Bahrain, Bermuda, Botswana, Brunei, Cayman Islands, Cyprus, Dominican Republic, Gambia, Ghana, Gibraltar, Guernsey, Guyana, Hong Kong, Iceland, Iraq, Irish Republic, Jamaica, Kenya, Kuwait, Malta, Malawi, Mauritius, Morocco, New Zealand, Oman, Papua New Guinea, People's Democratic Republic of Yemen, Philippines, Qatar, Saudi Arabia, Sierra Leone, Sri Lanka, Tanzania, Tunisia, Trinidad and Tobago, Tuvalu, United Arab Emirate, Yemen Arab Republic, and Zambia.

The output of medals for the year was 48,025. Three new designs were produced: the Bermuda Badge of Honour, and medals for the International Nickel Company and the Cement and Concrete Association. Among the seals manufactured were a number for various British Embassy posts and for Government Departments in this country. The public seal for Trinidad and Tobago was also produced.

Bank of England notes are currently in denominations of £1, £5, £10 and £20. Issue of an earlier series of notes of £10 and higher denominations ceased in 1943 and the Bank of England began to withdraw those in circulation. These notes, and also the old 10s and £1 notes (without the portrait of Her Majesty the Queen) and the old £5 notes (on white paper), ceased to be legal tender on various dates between 1945 and 1962. £5 notes of the later series (predominantly blue in colour and bearing a portrait of Britannia) were withdrawn in 1967, whilst the next series (the first £5 notes to bear the Royal Portrait) was withdrawn in 1973. A new series £5 note was introduced in 1971. Two series of £10 notes are currently in circulation, the series which re-introduced this denomination in 1964 and a new series introduced in 1975. The £20 note was re-introduced in 1970. Also in that year, ten shilling notes were withdrawn from circulation after the introduction of the 50p piece.

Under the Gold Standard Act, 1925, Banknotes were not redeemable in legal coin, but the Bank of England was obliged to sell gold in the form of bars at a fixed price. This provision was cancelled by the Gold Standard (Amendment) Act, 1931.

£1 notes are legal tender in Great Britain for the payment of any amount. Those of £5, £10 and £20 are legal tender only in England and Wales.

The Bank of England is the Government's banker and the central reserve bank of the country. It manages the National Debt and the note issue and administers the exchange control regulations; it also acts as banker for the principal British banks, a number of overseas commercial banks, and the majority of oversea's central banks. The profits of the two statutory departments of the Bank, the Issue Department (which undertakes the note issue function) and the Banking Department, are paid to H.M. Treasury, those of the Banking Department after agreed provision for the Bank's reserves and working capital.

Under the Bank of England Act, 1946, the capital stock amounting to £14,553,000 was transferred to the Treasury, stock-holders receiving in exchange a compensatory amount of 3 per cent Treasury Stock.

The total currency in circulation (Bank of England, Scottish and Irish notes and coins) in April 1977 amounted to £7,853 million, but the average amount with the public was estimated at £6,700 million. Another £20 million was held by the Bank of England, £344 million by the Scottish Banks, £42 million by the Banks of Northern Ireland and £747 million by the London Clearing Banks.

A decimal currency system was introduced on 15 February 1971, based on the £ as the major unit, divided into 100 new pence. Six new coins were introduced, viz. half new penny; one new penny; two new pence (which are bronze coins); five new pence; ten new pence; and fifty new pence (which are cupro-nickel coins). The five and ten new pence coins came into circulation in April 1968, and are completely interchangeable with shilling and two-shilling pieces. The sixpenny piece was re-denominated two and a half new pence in August 1971. The fifty new pence came into circulation in October 1969 to replace the ten shilling note. The bronze coins became legal tender on Decimalization Day. The halfpenny ceased to be legal tender in August 1969, the half-crown in January 1970, and both the penny and three-penny pieces in September 1971.

The 'Verdict of the Trial of the Pyx' is held annually by the Jury summoned by the Goldsmiths' Company to ensure that United Kingdom gold, silver and cupro-nickel coins have been produced to the standards of weight, diameter and composition prescribed by law. Once again coins produced for New Zealand were also presented for trial.

Enquiries on matters concerning the Royal Mint should normally be addressed to the Royal Mint (*Tel:* 01-488 3424, Ext. 244. Mr. Acres). After working hours enquiries will be dealt with by the Treasury Duty Press Officer (01-233 3415).

## FINANCE

The following table shows the value of receipts from Inland Revenue for 1976–77 (£ million):

| *Heads of Duty* | *Net Receipts* |
|---|---|
| Income Tax | 17,010 |
| Surtax | 62 |
| Corporation Tax | 2,654 |
| Capital Gains Tax | 323 |
| Estate Duty | 125 |
| Capital Transfer Tax | 260 |
| Stamp Duties | 271 |
| Development Land Tax | 1 |
| Total Inland Revenue | 20,706 |

The following table shows the value of receipts from Customs and Excise for 1976–77 (£ million):

| *Heads of Duty* | *Net Receipts* |
|---|---|
| Value added tax | 3,770 |
| Hydrocarbon Oil | 2,065 |
| Tobacco | 1,873 |
| Beer | 808 |
| Spirits<br>Wine and British Wine | 1,137 |
| Betting and Gaming | 284 |
| Car Tax | 218 |
| Protective Duties | 729 |
| Purchase Tax | 1 |
| Other Duties | 2 |
| Total Customs and Excise | 10,837 |

The following table shows (in £ million) the main details of the actual ordinary revenue and expenditure for 1975–76 and the estimated amounts for 1976–77 (£ million):

| *Expenditure* | 1975–76 | 1976–77 *Estimate* |
|---|---|---|
| Supply Services | 34,072 | 36,928 |
| Debt Interest | 964 | 1,770 |
| Payments to Northern Ireland | 576 | 631 |
| Payments to European Communities etc. | 382 | 568 |
| Other Expenditure | 53 | 18 |
| Total | 36,047 | 39,915 |
| Deficit met from National Loans Fund | 6,630 | 6,718 |
| Surplus transferred to National Loans Fund | — | — |

The following table shows details of Supply Services for 1975–76 (£ million):

| *Department* | 1975–76 |
|---|---|
| I. Defence | 5,270 |
| II. Overseas Services | 723 |
| III. Agriculture, Fisheries & Forestry | 1,146 |
| IV. Trade, Industry and Employment | 3,796 |
| VI. Roads and Transport | 1,358 |
| VII. Housing | 1,565 |
| VIII. Other Environmental Services | 314 |
| IX. Law, Order and Protective Services | 933 |
| X. Education and Libraries, Science and Arts | 1,285 |
| XI. Health and Personal Social Services | 4,768 |
| XII. Social Security | 3,472 |
| XIII. Other Public Services | 886 |
| XIV. Common Services | 838 |
| XV. Northern Ireland | 534 |
| XVII. Rate Support Grant, Financial Transactions, etc. | 7,184 |

The following table shows details of estimated Supply Services for 1976–77 (£ million):

| *Department* | 1976–77 |
|---|---|
| I. Defence | 5,604 |
| II. Overseas Services | 815 |
| III. Agriculture, Fisheries and Forestry | 856 |
| IV. Trade, Industry and Employment | 2,860 |
| VI. Roads and Transport | 1,247 |
| VII. Housing | 2,089 |
| VIII. Other Environmental Services | 337 |
| IX. Law, Order and Protective Services | 991 |
| X. Education and Libraries, Science and Arts | 1,406 |
| XI. Health and Personal Social Services | 4,907 |

*continued*

| *Department* | | 1976–77 |
|---|---|---|
| XII. | Social Security | 4,001 |
| XIII. | Other Public Services | 915 |
| XIV. | Common Services | 890 |
| XV. | Northern Ireland | 526 |
| XVII. | Rate Support Grant, Financial Transactions etc. | 7,124 |
| | Supplementary provision (net) | 60 |
| | Allowance for price changes | 2,300 |

The following table shows details of expenditure for Supply Services for the year 1976–77 (£ million):

| *Services* | | *Total* |
|---|---|---|
| I. | Defence | 6,118 |
| II. | Overseas Services | 844 |
| III. | Agriculture, Fisheries and Forestry | 844 |
| IV. | Trade, Industry and Employment | 3,086 |
| VI. | Roads and Transport | 1,292 |
| VII. | Housing | 2,139 |
| VIII. | Other Environmental Services | 243 |
| IX. | Law, Order and Protective Services | 1,066 |
| X. | Education and Libraries, Science and Arts | 1,514 |
| XI. | Health and Personal Social Services | 5,412 |
| XII. | Social Security | 4,225 |
| XIII. | Other Public Services | 962 |
| XIV. | Common Services | 953 |
| XV. | Northern Ireland | 557 |
| XVII. | Rate Support Grant, Financial Transactions, etc. | 7,737 |
| | Total Supply Services | 36,992 |

The following table shows details of Exchequer Receipts for 1975–76 and Budget Estimates for 1976–77 (£ million):

| *Revenue* | 1975–76 *Exchequer Receipts* | 1976–77 *Budget Estimate* |
|---|---|---|
| Inland Revenue | 18,159 | 20,700 |
| Customs and Excise | 9,176 | 10,425 |
| Motor Vehicle Duties | 781 | 835 |
| Selective Employment Tax | — | — |
| Miscellaneous Receipts | 2,196 | 1,237 |
| Total | 30,312 | 33,197 |

The position of the National Debt, excluding external debt arising out of World War I, was:

| | |
|---|---|
| 31 March 1975 | £46,405 million (provisional) |
| 31 March 1976 | £56,884 million (provisional) |

**BANKS**

**Alexanders Discount Company Limited.** (Chairman, John Patrick Riversdale Glyn.) Est. 1810; Balance Sheet at 31 December 1976 showed assets £9,213,557 (paid up capital and published revenues). *Head Office:* 1, St. Swithin's Lane, London, EC4N 8DN.

**Australia and New Zealand Banking Group Limited.** *Registered Office:* 71 Cornhill, London, EC3V 3PR. Branches: Australia, New Zealand, Fiji, Papua, New Guinea, British Solomon Islands Protectorate, New Hebrides.

**Bank of England.** (Governor Rt. Hon. Gordon Richardson. MBE). Est. 1694; Bank of Issue: State-owned; Return 13 July, 1977 showed notes issued (in circulation) £7,312,615,331; (Banking Department) £12,384,669 public and other deposits £1,904,464,781. *Head Office:* Threadneedle Street, London, EC2R 8AH. 8 Branches.

**Bank of London & South America Limited.** (Chairman, D. G. Mitchell.) Est. 1862; wholly owned subsidiary of Lloyds. *Head Office:* 40/66 Queen Victoria St., London, EC4P 4EL. Branches in South and Central America, Spain and Portugal.

**Bank of New Zealand** (branch), see New Zealand.

**Bank of Nova Scotia** (branch), see Canada.

**Bank of Scotland.** (Governor, Rt. Hon. Lord Clydesmuir, KT, CB, MBE, TD, LLD, DSc.) Est. 1695; Bank of Issue: Balance Sheet at 28 February 1977 showed assets £1,674,594,000; deposits and current accounts £1,379,416,000; bank notes in circulation £119,071,000. *Head Office:* The Mound, Edinburgh, EH1 1YZ, Scotland.

**Barclays Bank International Limited.** (Chairman, A. F. Tuke.) Est. 1836 as the Colonial Bank, incorporated with Anglo-Egyptian Bank Limited and National Bank of South Africa Limited in 1925; Balance Sheet at 31 March 1973 showed assets £4,203,657,000; current and other accounts, £3,925,237,000. *Head Office:* 54 Lombard Street, London, EC3P 3AH. 1,643 branches throughout Africa, Europe, Far East, U.S.A., W. Indies, and United Kingdom, etc., which include those of various subsidiary companies.

**Barclays Bank Limited.** (Chairman, Mr. Anthony F. Tuke.) Est. 1896 as Barclay & Co., Ltd., changed in 1917 to Barclays Bank Limited; Balance Sheet at 31 December 1976 showed assets £8,546,734,000 (Group, £19,320,053,000), deposits and current accounts £7,402,307,000 (Group, £17,254,206,000). *Head Office:* 54 Lombard Street, London, EC3P 3AH. Over 3,000 Branches.

**Baring Brothers & Co., Limited.** Est. 1763; Balance Sheet at 31 December 1976 showed total assets £285,687,951; deposits, current and other accounts £232,888,232; share capital (authorized) £5,550,000 (issued) £5,550,000. *Head Office:* 88 Leadenhall Street, London EC3A 3DT.

**The British Bank of the Middle East.** (Chairman, A. Macqueen.) Est. 1889; Balance Sheet at 31 December 1974 showed assets 1,052,131,971; current, deposit and other accounts £689,235,849. *Head Office:* 20 Abchurch Lane, London, EC4N 7AY.

**Banque Nationale de Paris Limited.** (formerly British and French Bank Ltd.). Member of the Banque Nationale de Paris Group. (Chairman, Sir Patrick Reilly, GCMG, OBE.) Est. 1867; Balance Sheet at 31 March 1974 showed assets £275,463,842; deposits, current and other accounts £228,634,515. *Head Office:* 8/13 King William Street, London, EC4P 4HS.

**Standard Chartered Bank Limited.** (Chairman: Rt. Hon. Lord Barber). At 31st March 1977 assets totalled £7,653,000,000, *Address:* 10, Clements Lane E.C.4. The Standard Chartered Group has more than 1,500 offices in sixty countries.

**Clydesdale Bank Limited.** (Chairman, Sir Robert Fairbairn, J.P.) Bank of Issue; Amalgamation 1 January 1950 of the Clydesdale Bank Limited and North of Scotland Bank Limited; Balance Sheet at 31 December 1975 showed assets £787,065,000; deposits and current accounts £635,082,000; Banknotes in circulation £45,208,000. *Head Office:* 30 St. Vincent Place, Glasgow, G1 2HL, Scotland. 367 Branches.

**Commonwealth Bank of Australia** (branches), London, see Australia.

**Co-operative Bank Limited** (formerly C.W.S. Ltd., Banking Department). Est. 1872; Balance Sheet total at 8 January 1977 showed £366,403,000; deposits, current and other accounts £322,467,000. *Head Office:* New Century House, Manchester M60 4EP.

## UNITED KINGDOM

**Coutts & Company.** (Chairman and Managing Director, David B. Money-Coutts.) Est. 1692; Balance Sheet at 31 December 1976 showed assets £727,484,000; current, deposits and other accounts £666,371,000. *Head Office:* 440 Strand, London, WC2R 0QS. *Temporary address during re-building:* 1 Suffolk Street, London, SW1Y 4HF. 10 Branches.

**Credit Lyonnais, S.A.** (branch) London, see France.

**English, Scottish and Australian Bank, Limited** now merged with the Australia and New Zealand Bank under the name Australia and New Zealand Banking Group Ltd.

**Grindlays Bank Limited.** (formerly National and Grindlays Bank). Associated with Lloyd's Bank Ltd. and Citibank N.A. Group Balance Sheet at 31 December 1976 showed advances £1,487 m; deposits, £2,368·4 m. *Head Office:* 23 Fenchurch Street, London EC3P 3ED; *West End Offices:* 13 St. James's Square, SW1 4LF. Over 200 Branches and offices in 35 countries.

**Hambros Limited.** (Chairman, J. O. Hambro.) Est. 1839; Balance Sheet at 31 March 1975; showed assets £1,073,963,000; current, deposit and other accounts £1,261,423,000. *Head Office:* 41 Bishopsgate, London, EC2P 2AA. 2 Branches.

**Hongkong and Shanghai Banking Corporation, The.** (Chairman: M. G. R. Sandberg); Est. 1865; Bank of Issue for Hong Kong; Balance Sheet at 31 December 1976 showed assets H.K.$39,939,000,000; deposits, current and other accounts, H.K.$25,514,000,000; notes in circulation H.K. $3,942,000,000. *Head Office:* 1 Queen's Road Central, Hongkong. *London Office:* 99 Bishopsgate, London EC2P 2LA and 123 Pall Mall, SW1 5YEA. *Manchester Office:* P.O. Box 347, Barlow House, 4 Minshull St., Manchester M60 2AP. *Jersey Office:* 3 Mulcaster St., St. Helier, Jersey, Channel Islands. 147 Branches in Hong Kong; The Hongkong and Shanghai Banking Corporation (Offshore Banking Unit) Bahrain; Branches also in Bandar Seri Begawan and 4 branches; Paris; Frankfurt and Hamburg; Jakarta and one branch; Osaka and Tokyo; Macao; Kuala Lumpur and 26 branches; Kota Kinabalu and five branches; Kuching and two branches; Amsterdam; Vila; Manila and Iloilo; Singapore and nine branches; Honiara; Colombo; Bangkok and one branch; Chicago, New York and Seattle.

**Lloyds Bank Limited.** (Chairman, Sir Jeremy Morse, KCMG.) Est. 1765; Balance Sheet at 31 December 1976 showed assets £5,409,871,000; deposits and current accounts £4,600,620,000. *Head Office:* 71 Lombard Street, London, EC3P 3BS. 2,409 Offices.

**Lloyds Bank International Limited.** (Chairman, Sir R. Verdon-Smith.) Est. 1971 through merger by Bank of London & South America Limited with Lloyds Bank Europe Limited, subsidiary of Lloyds Bank Ltd. Issued capital £39,801,919; Balance Sheet at 30 September 1973 showed assets £2,711,922,000; deposit and current accounts £2,581,016,000. *Head Office:* 40/66 Queen Victoria Street, London, EC4P 4EL. Branches in U.K., U.S.A., Switzerland, Netherlands, also branches and agents under subsidiary companies Bank of London and South America Limited, and Bank of London and Montreal Limited, in Belgium, France Portugal, Spain, West Germany, Central and South America, and the Bahamas.

**Mercantile Bank Limited.** 15 Gracechurch Street, London, EC3V 0DU.

**Midland Bank Limited.** (Chairman, The Rt. Hon. Lord Armstrong of Sanderstead, PC, GCB, MVO.) Est. 1836; Balance Sheet at 31 December 1976 showed assets £11,843,390,000; current and other accounts £10,441,104,000. *Head Office:* Poultry, London, EC2P 2BX. 3,750 Branches.

**National Bank of Australasia Limited** (branch), London, see Australia.

**National Bank of Egypt** (branch), London, see Egypt.

**National and Commercial Banking Group Limited.** (Chairman, Sir James Blair-Cunynghame, OBE, LLD, DSc.) Holding Company. Est. 25 March 1968. Balance Sheet at 30 September 1976 showed current liabilities and other accounts £3,370,255,000; assets £3,677,529,000. *Registered Office:* 36 St. Andrew Square, Edinburgh, EH2 2YB.

**National Provincial Bank Limited,** see under National Westminster Bank Ltd.

**National Westminster Bank Limited.** (Chairman, Mr. Robert Leigh-Pemberton, DL.) Est. 1968 as the result of the merger between National Provincial Bank Limited and Westminster Bank Limited. Consolidated Balance Sheet at 31 December 1976 showed assets of £17,070·044 m; deposits and current accounts £15,383·498 m. *Head Office:* 41 Lothbury, London, EC2P 2BP. 3,200 Branches.

**Ottoman Bank.** (Chairman, Mr. M. J. Babington Smith.) Est. 1863; Balance Sheet at 31 December 1976 showed assets £333,003,745 (sterling); deposit, current and other accounts £256,601,486 (sterling). *London Office:* 2/3 Philpot Lane, London, EC3M 8AQ. 93 Branches.

**Northern Bank Limited.** (Member of Midland Bank Group.) Est. 1824; Balance Sheet at 31 December 1974 showed assets £366,995,000; deposit, current and other accounts £312,639,000. *Head Office:* 16 Victoria Street, Belfast, 167 Branches and 93 Sub-Branches.

**The Royal Bank of Scotland Limited.** (Chairman, Sir Michael Herries, OBE, MC, LLD.) Bank of Issue, *Head Office:* 42 St. Andrew Square, Edinburgh, EH2 2YE, Scotland.

**Société Générale pour favoriser le développement du Commerce et de l'Industrie en France** (branch) London, see France.

**Standard and Chartered Banking Group Limited.** (Chairman, Rt. Hon. Anthony Barber TD, MP.) At 31 March 1973 assets totalled £4,578,901,000. There are 1,447 offices in the Standard Bank group.

**Standard Chartered Bank Limited.** (Chairman, Lord Barber.) Est. 1975. *Head Office:* 10 Clements Lane, London, EC4N 7AB.

**The Union Discount Company of London Limited.** (Chairman, A. J. O. Ritchie.) Est. 1885; Balance Sheet at 31 December 1976 showed assets £628,550,562; deposits, other liabilities and reserve for contingencies £613,114,055. *Office:* 78/80 Cornhill, London, EC3V 3NH.

**Westminster Bank Limited**—see under National Westminster Bank Limited.

**Williams & Glyn's Bank Limited.** (Chairman, Sir James Blair-Cunynghame OBE, LLD, DSc.) Established to merge the businesses of William Deacon's, Glyn, Mills and National Banks. Registered Office: 20 Birchin Lane, London, EC3P 3DP. 325 Branches.

**Yorkshire Bank Limited.** (General Manager, E. C. Muxlow.) Est. 1859; Balance Sheet at 31 December 1976 showed assets £385,399,863; due to depositors and other accounts £345,403,279. *Registered Office:* 2 Infirmary Street, Leeds. 186 Branches.

### AREA AND POPULATION

The area of England and Wales, Scotland and Northern Ireland is shown in the following table:

| | *sq. miles* | | |
|---|---|---|---|
| | *Total* | *Land* | *Inland* water* |
| United Kingdom | 94,250 | 93,066 | 1,184 |
| England | 50,383 | 50,095 | 270 |
| Wales | 8,018 | 7,969 | 49 |
| Scotland | 30,415 | 29,796 | 619 |
| Northern Ireland† | 5,452 | 5,206 | 246 |

* Excluding tidal water.

† Not including 6,492 acres (about 10·5 sq. miles) of tidal waters that are part of statutory areas in Northern Ireland.

The census figures of the United Kingdom for 1961 and 1971 are shown (in thousands) in the following table:

| | 1961 *Census* | 1971 *Census* |
|---|---|---|
| United Kingdom | 52,709 | 55,515 |
| Males | 25,481 | 26,952 |
| Females | 27,228 | 28,562 |
| England | 43,461 | 46,018 |
| Wales | 2,644 | 2,731 |
| Scotland | 5,179 | 5,229 |
| Northern Ireland | 1,425 | 1,536 |

The projected population of the United Kingdom in the year 1981 is 56·3 million, increasing to 58·2 million in 1991 and 59·9 million in 2001. Between 1861 and 1951 emigration from Scotland totalled 1,616,394.

The population of Greater London according to the census taken on the night of 25/26 April 1971 was 7,452,346. Greater London comprises the City (population 4,245) and the 32 London boroughs. The population of the same area in 1961 was 7,992,443.

The area of Greater London in 1971 was 390,294 acres. The area of the City was 677 acres.

The following table shows the estimated population of the new metropolitan and new non-metropolitan counties*:

PART I

METROPOLITAN COUNTIES

| *Name of county* | *Mid*-1976 *estimate* (*thousands*) |
|---|---|
| Greater Manchester | 2,684·1 |
| Merseyside | 1,578·0 |
| South Yorkshire | 1,318·3 |
| Tyne and Wear | 1,182·9 |
| West Midlands | 2,743·3 |
| West Yorkshire | 2,072·5 |

PART II

NON-METROPOLITAN COUNTIES

| *Name of county* | *Mid*-1976 *estimate* (*thousands*) |
|---|---|
| Avon | 920·2 |
| Bedfordshire | 491·7 |
| Berkshire | 659·0 |
| Buckinghamshire | 512·0 |
| Cambridgeshire | 563·0 |
| Cheshire | 916·4 |
| Cleveland | 567·9 |
| Cornwall and Isles of Scilly | 407·1 |
| Cumbria | 473·6 |
| Derbyshire | 887·6 |
| Devon | 942·1 |
| Dorset | 575·8 |
| Durham | 610·4 |
| East Sussex | 655·6 |
| Essex | 1,426·2 |
| Gloucestershire | 491·5 |
| Hampshire | 1,456·1 |
| Hereford and Worcester | 594·2 |
| Hertfordshire | 937·3 |
| Humberside | 848·6 |
| Isle of Wight | 111·3 |
| Kent | 1,448·1 |
| Lancashire | 1,375·5 |
| Leicestershire | 837·9 |
| Lincolnshire | 525·4 |

*continued*

| *Name of county* | *Mid*-1976 *estimate* (*thousands*) |
|---|---|
| Norfolk | 662·5 |
| Northamptonshire | 505·9 |
| Northumberland | 287·3 |
| North Yorkshire | 653·0 |
| Nottinghamshire | 977·5 |
| Oxfordshire | 541·8 |
| Salop | 359·0 |
| Somerset | 404·4 |
| Staffordshire | 997·6 |
| Suffolk | 577·6 |
| Surrey | 1,002·9 |
| Warwickshire | 471·0 |
| West Sussex | 623·4 |
| Wiltshire | 512·8 |
| Clwyd | 376·0 |
| Dyfed | 323·1 |
| Gwent | 439·6 |
| Gwynedd | 225·1 |
| Mid-Glamorgan | 540·4 |
| Powys | 101·5 |
| South Glamorgan | 389·2 |
| West Glamorgan | 371·9 |

Greater London comprises the City (677 acres) and the 32 London Boroughs (389,617 acres). Populations are shown below:

| | 1961 *Census* | 1971 *Census* | *Mid*-1976 *estimate* (*thousands*) |
|---|---|---|---|
| City of London | 4,767 | 4,245 | 6·8 |
| London Boroughs | | | |
| Barking | 177,092 | 160,800 | 153·8 |
| Barnet | 318,373 | 306,560 | 305·2 |
| Bexley | 209,893 | 217,076 | 213·5 |
| Brent | 295,899 | 280,657 | 256·5 |
| Bromley | 293,394 | 305,377 | 299·1 |
| Camden | 245,707 | 206,737 | 185·8 |
| Croydon | 323,927 | 333,870 | 330·6 |
| Ealing | 301,646 | 301,108 | 293·8 |
| Enfield | 273,857 | 268,004 | 260·9 |
| Greenwich | 229,810 | 217,664 | 207·2 |
| Hackney | 257,522 | 220,279 | 192·5 |
| Hammersmith | 222,124 | 187,195 | 170·0 |
| Haringey | 259,156 | 240,078 | 228·2 |
| Harrow | 209,083 | 203,215 | 200·2 |
| Havering | 245,598 | 247,696 | 239·2 |
| Hillingdon | 228,361 | 234,888 | 230·8 |
| Hounslow | 208,893 | 206,956 | 199·1 |
| Islington | 261,232 | 201,874 | 171·6 |
| Kensington and Chelsea | 218,528 | 188,227 | 161·4 |
| Kingston-upon-Thames | 146,010 | 140,525 | 135·6 |
| Lambeth | 341,624 | 307,516 | 290·3 |
| Lewisham | 290,582 | 268,474 | 237·3 |
| Merton | 189,013 | 177,324 | 169·4 |
| Newham | 265,388 | 237,390 | 228·9 |
| Redbridge | 250,080 | 239,889 | 231·6 |
| Richmond-on-Thames | 180,949 | 174,628 | 166·8 |
| Southwark | 313,413 | 262,138 | 224·9 |
| Sutton | 169,095 | 169,494 | 166·7 |
| Tower Hamlets | 205,682 | 165,776 | 146·1 |
| Waltham Forest | 248,591 | 234,680 | 223·7 |
| Wandsworth | 335,451 | 302,258 | 284·6 |
| Westminster | 271,703 | 239,748 | 216·1 |

From 16 May 1975, the existing local authorities in Scotland were reorganized to form 9 regions, which were sub-divided into districts, and 3 islands areas.

| | 1971 *Census* | *Mid*-1976 *estimate* |
|---|---|---|
| *Highland Region* | 175,473 | 186,460 |
| Caithness | 29,610 | 29,442 |
| Sutherland | 11,968 | 11,634 |
| Ross and Cromarty | 34,858 | 42,031 |
| Skye and Lochalsh | 9,725 | 9,777 |
| Lochaber | 19,192 | 19,601 |
| Inverness | 49,760 | 55,045 |
| Badenoch and Strathspey | 9,309 | 9,297 |
| Nairn | 11,051 | 9,633 |
| *Islands Areas* | | |
| Orkney | 17,077 | 17,748 |
| Shetland | 17,327 | 18,962 |
| Western Isles | 29,891 | 29,693 |
| *Grampian Region* | 438,629 | 453,829 |
| Moray | 75,659 | 81,046 |
| Banff and Buchan | 72,829 | 76,363 |
| Gordon | 44,979 | 50,976 |
| City of Aberdeen | 211,848 | 209,831 |
| Kincardine and Deeside | 33,315 | 35,613 |
| *Tayside Region* | 397,607 | 402,180 |
| Angus | 84,178 | 89,700 |
| City of Dundee | 197,371 | 194,420 |
| Perth and Kinross | 116,056 | 118,060 |
| *Fife Region* | 327,132 | 338,734 |
| Kirkcaldy | 145,027 | 148,537 |
| North East Fife | 61,645 | 65,170 |
| Dunfermline | 120,459 | 125,027 |
| *Lothian Region* | 745,624 | 755,293 |
| West Lothian | 111,849 | 124,304 |
| City of Edinburgh | 476,633 | 467,097 |
| Midlothian | 79,746 | 84,882 |
| East Lothian | 77,395 | 79,010 |
| *Central Region* | 263,025 | 270,056 |
| Clackmannan | 46,100 | 47,847 |
| Stirling | 76,443 | 79,042 |
| Falkirk | 140,485 | 143,167 |
| *Borders Region* | 98,476 | 99,917 |
| Tweeddale | 13,676 | 14,035 |
| Eltrick and Lauderdale | 32,421 | 32,498 |
| Roxburgh | 35,400 | 35,656 |
| Berwickshire | 16,980 | 17,728 |
| *Strathclyde Region* | 2,575,515 | 2,488,643 |
| Argyll and Bute | 65,142 | 65,615 |
| Dumbarton | 78,723 | 80,934 |
| Renfrew | 202,901 | 209,476 |
| Inverclyde | 109,365 | 104,116 |
| Clydebank | 58,835 | 55,902 |
| Bearsden and Milngavie | 35,926 | 38,022 |
| Glasgow City | 982,315 | 856,012 |
| Strathkelvin | 77,436 | 81,455 |
| Eastwood | 49,857 | 50,598 |
| Cumbernauld and Kilsyth | 45,617 | 56,268 |
| Monklands | 109,620 | 107,561 |
| Motherwell | 161,570 | 161,104 |
| Lanark | 53,524 | 55,049 |
| Hamilton | 104,359 | 107,178 |
| East Kilbride | 74,181 | 83,441 |
| Cunninghame | 125,865 | 133,296 |
| Kilmarnock and Loudoun | 81,005 | 82,520 |
| Kyle and Carnick | 110,458 | 112,458 |
| Cumnock and Doon Valley | 48,815 | 47,638 |
| *Dumfries and Galloway Region* | 143,189 | 143,585 |
| Wigtown | 29,938 | 29,845 |
| Stewartry | 22,192 | 22,419 |
| Nithsdale | 56,474 | 56,180 |
| Annandale and Eskdale | 34,583 | 35,141 |

At the 1971 Census, 38·2 million people in England and Wales lived in urban areas, and 10·6 million in rural areas. The figures for Scotland are 3·7 million and 1·5 million respectively.

The following table is the Life table for the period 1971–73:

| Age | *Males* | | *Females* | |
|---|---|---|---|---|
| | lx[1] | $\mathring{e}_x$[2] | lx[1] | $\mathring{e}_x$[2] |
| 0 | 10,000 | 68·8 | 10,000 | 75·1 |
| 5 | 9,772 | 65·4 | 9,821 | 71·4 |
| 10 | 9,751 | 60·5 | 9,807 | 66·5 |
| 15 | 9,733 | 55·6 | 9,796 | 61·6 |
| 20 | 9,689 | 50·9 | 9,776 | 56·7 |
| 25 | 9,639 | 46·1 | 9,755 | 51·8 |
| 30 | 9,594 | 41·3 | 9,731 | 47·0 |
| 35 | 9,540 | 36·6 | 9,696 | 42·1 |
| 40 | 9,460 | 31·8 | 9,640 | 37·3 |
| 45 | 9,319 | 27·3 | 9,541 | 32·7 |
| 50 | 9,065 | 23·0 | 9,372 | 28·2 |
| 55 | 8,651 | 19·0 | 9,122 | 24·0 |
| 60 | 7,993 | 15·3 | 8,752 | 19·9 |
| 65 | 7,017 | 12·1 | 8,213 | 16·0 |
| 70 | 5,660 | 9·4 | 7,404 | 12·5 |
| 75 | 4,023 | 7·2 | 6,199 | 9·4 |
| 80 | 2,377 | 5·5 | 4,538 | 7·0 |
| 85 | 1,084 | 4·0 | 2,675 | 5·0 |

[1]Column lx shows the numbers who would survive to exact age x out of 10,000 born who were subject to age specific mortality rates for 1971–73.

[2]Column $\mathring{e}_x$ is the 'expectation of life', that is, the average future life time which would be lived by a person aged exactly x if likewise subject to these mortality rates.

The following table shows the Age Specific Fertility rate or seven selected years for G.B.:

| Women aged | Births per 1,000 women | | | | | | |
|---|---|---|---|---|---|---|---|
| | 1961 | 1966 | 1971 | 1972 | 1973 | 1974 | 1975 |
| 15–19 | 37 | 48 | 51 | 48 | 44 | 41 | 37 |
| 20–24 | 173 | 177 | 155 | 142 | 132 | 124 | 115 |
| 25–29 | 178 | 175 | 155 | 143 | 136 | 130 | 124 |
| 30–34 | 104 | 98 | 78 | 70 | 64 | 60 | 59 |
| 35–39 | 49 | 46 | 33 | 29 | 25 | 22 | 20 |
| 40–44 | 14 | 12 | 8 | 7 | 6 | 5 | 5 |
| All ages 15–44 | 90·0 | 91·1 | 84·2 | 77·5 | 71·8 | 67·6 | 63·5 |

The following table shows death rates per 100,000 in each age group, for selected causes by sex for 1975*.

| | *Males* | *Females* |
|---|---|---|
| Ages under 1 year | | |
| Infective etc. diseases | 62 | 45 |
| of which respiratory tuberculosis | 0 | 0 |
| Pheumonia | 136 | 100 |
| Congenital anomalies | 392 | 378 |
| All non-motor vehicle accidents | 41 | 42 |
| Certain causes of perinatal mortality | 800 | 594 |
| All other causes | 324 | 236 |
| All causes | 1,754 | 1,395 |
| Ages 1–14 years | | |
| Infective etc. diseases | 2 | 2 |
| of which respiratory tuberculosis | — | — |
| Cancer, including leukaemia | 7 | 5 |
| Pneumonia | 2 | 2 |
| Congenital anomalities | 5 | 5 |

* Provisional.

*continued*

| | Male | Female |
|---|---|---|
| Motor vehicle accidents | 8 | 4 |
| All other accidents | 9 | 4 |
| All other causes | 11 | 9 |
| All causes | 44 | 30 |
| Ages 15–34 years | | |
| Infective etc. diseases | 1 | 1 |
| of which respiratory tuberculosis | 0 | 0 |
| Cancer, including leukaemia | 13 | 11 |
| Motor vehicle accidents | 27 | 6 |
| All other accidents | 17 | 5 |
| Suicide | 8 | 4 |
| All other causes | 31 | 22 |
| All causes | 97 | 49 |
| Ages 35–44 years | | |
| Infective etc. diseases | 2 | 2 |
| Cancer, including leukaemia | 43 | 68 |
| Motor vehicle accidents | 12 | 4 |
| All other accidents | 19 | 7 |
| Suicide | 11 | 7 |
| All other causes | 128 | 67 |
| All causes | 217 | 155 |
| Ages 45–64 years | | |
| Infective etc. diseases | 9 | 5 |
| of which respiratory buberculosis | 3 | 1 |
| Cancer, including leukaemia | 371 | 298 |
| of which lung | 166 | 45 |
| breast | 0 | 79 |
| uterus | — | 25 |
| Heart diseases | 560 | 174 |
| Cerebrovascular diseases | 90 | 71 |
| Bronchitis | 58 | 19 |
| Motor vehicle accidents | 15 | 6 |
| All other accidents | 25 | 14 |
| Suicide | 15 | 10 |
| All other causes | 177 | 131 |
| All causes | 1,316 | 726 |
| Ages 65–74 years | | |
| Infective etc. diseases | 25 | 10 |
| Cancer, including leukaemia | 1,327 | 656 |
| Heart diseases | 1,928 | 895 |
| Cerebrovascular diseases | 535 | 403 |
| Pneumonia | 263 | 153 |
| Bronchitis | 366 | 65 |
| All accidents, poisonings and violence | 75 | 57 |
| All other causes | 575 | 380 |
| All causes | 5,094 | 2,618 |

The following table gives the Death Analysis by cause and rate per 100,000, without regard to age, for 1975*:

| *Cause of death* | *Deaths* | *Rates* |
|---|---|---|
| Deaths from natural causes | 637,340 | 1,139 |
| Cholera | 1 | 0 |
| Typhoid fever | 1 | 0 |
| Bacillary dysentery and amoebiasis | 10 | 0 |
| Enteritis and other diarrhoeal diseases | 502 | 1 |
| Tuberculosis of respiratory system | 860 | 2 |
| Other tuberculosis, including late effects | 645 | 1 |
| Plague | — | — |
| Diphtheria | 1 | 0 |
| Whooping cough | 12 | 0 |
| Streptococcal sore throat and scarlet fever | 7 | 0 |
| Meningococcal infection | 189 | 0 |
| Acute poliomyelitis | 5 | 0 |
| Smallpox | — | — |
| Measles | 20 | 0 |
| Typhus and other rickettsioses | 1 | 0 |
| Malaria | 5 | 0 |
| Syphilis and its sequelae | 116 | 0 |
| All other infective and parasitic diseases | 1,170 | 2 |
| Malignant neoplasm of stomach | 13,549 | 24 |
| Malignant neoplasm of lung and bronchus | 37,157 | 66 |
| Malignant neoplasm of breast | 13,081 | 23 |
| Malignant neoplasm of uterus | 4,028 | 7 |
| Leukaemia | 3,594 | 6 |
| Other malignant neoplasms including neoplasms of lymphatic and haematopoietic tissue | 67,020 | 120 |
| Benign neoplasms and neoplasms of unspecified nature | 1,429 | 3 |
| Diabetes mellitus | 5,869 | 10 |
| Avitaminoses and other nutritional deficiency | 306 | 1 |
| Other endocrine, nutritional and metabolic diseases | 1,900 | 3 |
| Anaemias | 1,700 | 3 |
| Other diseases of blood and blood-forming organs | 313 | 1 |
| Mental disorders | 2,428 | 4 |
| Meningitis | 370 | 1 |
| Other diseases of nervous system and sense organs | 6,805 | 12 |
| Active rheumatic fever | 45 | 0 |
| Chronic rheumatic heart disease | 6,626 | 12 |
| Hypertensive disease | 8,952 | 16 |
| Ischaemic heart disease | 177,372 | 317 |
| Other forms of heart disease | 30,304 | 54 |
| Other diseases of circulatory system | 119,293 | 213 |
| Influenza | 1,692 | 3 |
| Pneumonia | 51,899 | 93 |
| Bronchitis, emphysema | 27,685 | 49 |
| Asthma | 1,315 | 2 |
| Other diseases of respiratory system | 6,563 | 12 |
| Peptic ulcer | 4,745 | 8 |
| Appendicitis | 328 | 1 |
| Intestinal obstruction and hernia | 2,690 | 5 |
| Cirrhosis of liver | 2,208 | 4 |
| Other diseases of digestive system | 6,962 | 12 |
| Nephritis and nephrosis | 3,451 | 6 |
| Hyperplasia of prostate | 1,083 | 2 |
| Other diseases of genito-urinary system | 4,443 | 8 |
| Abortion | 8 | 0 |
| Other complications of pregnancy, childbirth and puerperium | 78 | 0 |
| Diseases of skin and subcutaneous tissue | 455 | 1 |
| Diseases of musculo-skeletal system and connective tissue | 3,054 | 5 |
| Congenital anomalies | 4,407 | 8 |
| Birth injury, difficult labour and other anoxic and hypoxic conditions | 2,965 | 5 |
| Other causes of perinatal mortality | 1,996 | 4 |
| Symptoms and other ill-defined conditions | 3,627 | 6 |
| Deaths by violence | 25,137 | 45 |
| Motor vehicle accidents | 6,956 | 12 |
| All other accidents | 11,516 | 21 |
| Suicide and other self-inflicted injuries | 4,176 | 7 |
| All other external causes | 2,489 | 4 |

* Provisional

## UNITED KINGDOM

The following table shows the expectation of life for four separate periods for the U.K.:

| *Males* | | | | *Further number of years a person can expect to live* | *Females* | | | |
|---|---|---|---|---|---|---|---|---|
| 1959–61 | 1965–67 | 1970–72 | 1971–73 | | 1959–61 | 1965–67 | 1970–72 | 1971–73 |
| 67·9 | 68·5 | 68·7 | 68·8 | at birth | 73·6 | 74·6 | 75·0 | 75·1 |
| 64·9 | 65·2 | 65·3 | 65·4 | at age 5 | 70·4 | 71·1 | 71·4 | 71·4 |
| 60·1 | 60·4 | 60·5 | 60·5 | 10 | 65·5 | 66·2 | 66·5 | 66·5 |
| 50·4 | 50·8 | 50·8 | 50·9 | 20 | 55·7 | 56·4 | 56·6 | 56·7 |
| 40·9 | 41·2 | 41·3 | 41·3 | 30 | 46·0 | 46·7 | 46·9 | 47·0 |
| 31·5 | 31·7 | 31·8 | 31·8 | 40 | 36·4 | 37·1 | 37·3 | 37·3 |
| 22·6 | 22·9 | 22·9 | 23·0 | 50 | 27·3 | 28·0 | 28·2 | 28·2 |
| 15·1 | 15·2 | 15·2 | 15·3 | 60 | 18·9 | 19·6 | 19·8 | 19·9 |
| 9·3 | 9·5 | 9·4 | 9·4 | 70 | 11·6 | 12·3 | 12·4 | 12·5 |
| 5·3 | 5·4 | 5·4 | 5·5 | 80 | 6·3 | 6·8 | 6·9 | 7·0 |

The following table shows the Age Distribution of the estimated population of the U.K. at 30 June 1976 in thousands:

| | *De facto or home population* | | | | | | | | | | |
|---|---|---|---|---|---|---|---|---|---|---|---|
| | *United Kingdom* | | | *England and Wales* | | *Wales* | | *Scotland* | | *Northern Ireland* | |
| | *Total* | *Males* | *Females* | *Males* | *Females* | *Males* | *Females* | *Males* | *Females* | *Males* | *Females* |
| All ages | 55,927·6 | 27,218·5 | 28,709·1 | 23,953·3 | 25,231·1 | 1,343·7 | 1,423·1 | 2,503·6 | 2,701·5 | 761·6 | 776·5 |
| Years of age: | | | | | | | | | | | |
| 0–14 | 12,838·2 | 6,593·9 | 6,244·2 | 5,722·8 | 5,421·5 | 321·4 | 304·5 | 644·1 | 610·8 | 227·0 | 212·0 |
| 15–64 | 35,162·4 | 17,549·2 | 17,613·5 | 15,488·1 | 15,495·2 | 863·8 | 869·8 | 1594·5 | 1,657·2 | 466·1 | 460·9 |
| 65 and over | 7,927·1 | 3,075·4 | 4,851·6 | 2,742·4 | 4,314·4 | 159·0 | 248·8 | 264·6 | 4,033·5 | 68·5 | 103·6 |
| Under 5 | 3,738·9 | 1,924·8 | 1,814·1 | 1,671·2 | 1,575·7 | 95·4 | 89·1 | 183·8 | 173·9 | 69·8 | 64·5 |
| 5–9 | 4,446·2 | 2,282·4 | 2,163·7 | 1,981·6 | 1,879·4 | 110·5 | 105·3 | 223·6 | 211·5 | 77·2 | 72·8 |
| 10–14 | 4,653·1 | 2,386·7 | 2,266·4 | 2,070·0 | 1,966·4 | 115·5 | 110·1 | 236·7 | 225·3 | 80·0 | 74·7 |
| 15–19 | 4,235·7 | 2,168·0 | 2,067·7 | 1,876·0 | 1,789·5 | 105·5 | 102·2 | 219·4 | 211·0 | 72·6 | 67·2 |
| 20–24 | 3,871·0 | 1,978·2 | 1,892·8 | 1,727·8 | 1,652·6 | 94·8 | 91·7 | 189·1 | 186·1 | 61·3 | 54·1 |
| 25–29 | 4,194·8 | 2,115·5 | 2,079·4 | 1,872·5 | 1,843·0 | 100·0 | 99·0 | 189·4 | 187·3 | 53·6 | 49·1 |
| 30–34 | 3,588·3 | 1,816·1 | 1,772·2 | 1,609·4 | 1,568·9 | 87·2 | 84·6 | 156·7 | 155·7 | 50·0 | 47·6 |
| 35–39 | 3,209·2 | 1,624·0 | 1,585·3 | 1,437·1 | 1,394·1 | 78·7 | 75·8 | 144·6 | 149·6 | 42·3 | 41·6 |
| 40–44 | 3,127·4 | 1,576·9 | 1,550·5 | 1,394·4 | 1,360·3 | 77·1 | 75·0 | 143·3 | 149·5 | 39·2 | 40·7 |
| 45–49 | 3,255·8 | 1,618·5 | 1,637·3 | 1,433·4 | 1,439·6 | 82·0 | 82·4 | 146·3 | 155·6 | 38·8 | 42·1 |
| 50–54 | 3,426·1 | 1,684·7 | 1,741·4 | 1,496·8 | 1,539·5 | 86·4 | 89·3 | 149·0 | 160·0 | 38·9 | 41·9 |
| 55–59 | 3,145·7 | 1,510·7 | 1,635·0 | 1,343·8 | 1,446·4 | 78·3 | 85·3 | 130·5 | 150·2 | 36·4 | 38·4 |
| 60–64 | 3,108·4 | 1,456·6 | 1,651·9 | 1,296·9 | 1,461·3 | 73·8 | 84·5 | 126·7 | 152·4 | 33·0 | 38·2 |
| 65–69 | 2,838·5 | 1,265·7 | 1,572·8 | 1,127·0 | 1,392·4 | 64·1 | 81·3 | 111·1 | 145·0 | 27·6 | 35·4 |
| 70–74 | 2,240·6 | 916·3 | 1,324·3 | 817·1 | 1,174·0 | 47·9 | 69·3 | 79·2 | 121·2 | 20·0 | 29·1 |
| 75–79 | 1,493·5 | 517·8 | 975·7 | 461·4 | 867·3 | 27·8 | 50·3 | 43·7 | 87·0 | 12·7 | 21·4 |
| 80–84 | 830·5 | 246·7 | 583·7 | 220·9 | 522·8 | 12·8 | 29·1 | 20·1 | 49·6 | 5·7 | 11·2 |
| 85 and over | 524·0 | 128·9 | 395·1 | 116·0 | 357·8 | 6·4 | 18·8 | 10·4 | 30·8 | 2·5 | 6·5 |

The following table shows the persons marrying in 1975 by Age and Marital Condition:

| | *All Ages* | 16–17 | 18–20 | 21–24 | 25–34 | 35–44 | 45+ |
|---|---|---|---|---|---|---|---|
| All brides | 430,678 | 23,253 | 130,959 | 128,847 | 90,726 | 26,014 | 30,879 |
| All spinsters | 342,366 | 23,250 | 130,494 | 121,454 | 55,651 | 6,425 | 5,092 |
| All widows | 19,382 | 1 | 34 | 270 | 1,648 | 2,702 | 14,727 |
| All divorced women | 68,930 | 2 | 431 | 7,123 | 33,427 | 16,887 | 11,060 |
| All grooms | 430,678 | 3,582 | 63,811 | 152,241 | 136,947 | 33,764 | 40,333 |
| All bachelors | 339,883 | 3,582 | 63,774 | 149,508 | 105,866 | 11,176 | 5,977 |
| All widowers | 19,349 | — | 2 | 64 | 757 | 1,662 | 16,864 |
| All divorced men | 71,446 | — | 35 | 2,669 | 30,324 | 20,926 | 17,492 |

**Principal Vital Statistics for a selected eight years up to 1975.**

| | Unit | 1966 | 1969 | 1970 | 1971 | 1972 | 1973 | 1974 | 1975 |
|---|---|---|---|---|---|---|---|---|---|
| Estimated Population (mid year) | Thousands | 54,500 | 55,263 | 55,421 | 55,610 | 55,793 | 55,933 | 55,965 | 55,943 |
| Live births | Thousands | 980 | 920 | 904 | 902 | 834 | 780 | 737 | 698 |
| | Rate per 1,000 population | 18·0 | 16·6 | 16·3 | 16·2 | 14·9 | 13·9 | 13·2 | 12·5 |
| Deaths | Thousands | 644 | 660 | 655 | 645 | 674 | 670 | 667 | 662 |
| | Rate per 1,000 population | 11·8 | 11·9 | 11·8 | 11·6 | 12·1 | 12·0 | 11·9 | 11·8 |
| Natural Increase | Thousands | 336 | 261 | 249 | 257 | 160 | 110 | 70 | 35 |
| | Rate per 1,000 population | 6·2 | 4·7 | 4·5 | 4·6 | 2·9 | 2·0 | 1·2 | 0·6 |
| Marriages | Thousands | 437 | 452 | 471 | 459 | 480 | 454 | 436 | 431 |
| | Persons marrying per 1,000 population | 16·0 | 16·3 | 17·0 | 16·5 | 17·2 | 16·2 | 15·6 | 15·4 |
| Infant Mortality Rate per 1,000 live-births | | 19·6 | 18·6 | 18·5 | 17·9 | 17·5 | 17·2 | 16·8 | 16·0 |

## PRODUCTION, INDUSTRY AND COMMERCE

**Agriculture.** 1975–76 was an exceptional year. In spite of difficult conditions, the value of gross output of United Kingdom agriculture is expected to rise in 1975–76 by about 14 per cent, but net product at constant prices is forecast to fall by a similar percentage. Unfavourable weather had its biggest effect on arable production. The sowing season during last winter and spring was very difficult for farmers, so that more land was left fallow. Late plantings and the dry summer reduced yields well below normal levels. The cereals harvest was about 2·6 million tonnes below the 1974 crop. Potato yields have been very poor. The harvested area of sugar beet is a little larger than in 1974 but yields are again below average. These results have inevitably had an adverse effect on total net product of the industry. Favourable weather returned, however, in the autumn. A large area has been planted with winter wheat and the sown area appears generally to be in excellent condition. Given normal weather, the next cereal harvest should show a substantial recovery.

Many livestock farmers had problems in providing adequate fodder for their stock, particularly in the late spring. The hay harvest was small, although of good quality. Farmers made considerable and successful efforts to help themselves by moving hay and straw into the livestock areas. The open autumn has also been favourable and livestock generally went into the winter in very good condition. The dairy breeding herd at the June 1975 census was down but milk yields have continued to improve. Milk production has recently been running above last year's level and total production in 1975–76 is expected to be about the same as production in 1974–75. The beef breeding herd at June 1975 was unchanged but the September sample inquiry showed a small fall in England and Wales. Home-fed beef production in 1975–76 is forecast to be at a record level but may be lower next year. At June 1975 the sheep breeding flock in the hills was unchanged but the total breeding flock showed a small fall of one per cent. The pig breeding herd at June 1975, although nine per cent smaller than in June

The following table shows the estimated average yields of crops and livestock products (June–May years except 1977):

| | *Unit* | *Average of* 1964–65–1966–67 | 1971–72 (*e*) | 1972–73 | 1973–74 | 1974–75 | Jan. 1977–Dec. 1977 |
|---|---|---|---|---|---|---|---|
| *Crops* | | | | | | | |
| Wheat | tonnes/hectare | 4·05 | 4·39 | 4·24 | 4·36 | 4·97 | 4·92 |
| Barley | ,, ,, | 3·65 | 3·74 | 4·04 | 3·97 | 4·12 | 4·45 |
| Oats | ,, ,, | 3·00 | 3·76 | 3·98 | 3·84 | 3·77 | 4·15 |
| Potatoes | ,, ,, | 24·0 | 28·8 | 27·7 | 30·4 | 31·6 | 28·60 |
| Sugar (*a*) | ,, ,, | 5·9 | 6·9 | 5·7 | 6·1 | 3·6 | 5·8 |
| Oilseed rape | ,, ,, | — | 2·0 | 2·1 | 2·3 | 2·1 | 2·5 |
| Apples: | | | | | | | |
| Dessert (*b*) | ,, ,, | 11·1 | 13·6 | 8·7 | 12·6 | 9·2 | 7·2 |
| Culinary (*b*) | ,, ,, | 12·2 | 12·0 | 10·6 | 12·9 | 11·1 | 11·2 |
| Pears (*b*) | ,, ,, | 8·7 | 12·5 | 9·1 | 8·2 | 9·5 | 8·2 |
| Tomatoes (*b*) | ,, ,, | 89·9 | 105·9 | 109·8 | 117·8 | 123·1 | 133·9 |
| Cauliflowers (*b*) | ,, ,, | 20·1 | 19·6 | 20·7 | 21·1 | 19·9 | 20·4 |
| Hops | 100 kg./hectare | 15·0 | 16·3 | 13·9 | 15·4 | 15·5 | 1·23 |
| *Livestock products* | | | | | | | |
| Milk (*c*) | litres/cow | 3,565 | 3,942 | 4,037 | 3,925 | 3,989 | 4,407 |
| Eggs (*d*) | no./bird | 202·5 | 225·5 | 232·5 | 225·5 | 231·5 | 240·5 |

[a] Sugar-in-beet per crop hectare.

[b] Gross yields from cropped area.

[c] Yield per dairy type cow per annum.

[d] Eggs per paying bird.

[e] 366 days.

1974, was at much the same level as in April 1975, with an increase in gilts in pig. It is probable that a recovery in the pig breeding herd is now beginning. It is expected that poultrymeat production in 1975–76 will increase by about 2 or 3 per cent and that egg production will be almost unchanged. Poultrymeat production should increase again in 1976–77.

The aggregate net income of the agricultural industry at current prices is estimated to increase by about 7½ per cent in 1975–76. In real terms it will again have fallen. Aggregate cost increases since the 1975 Review are assessed at £455 million.

In the course of the year since the last Annual Review and the fixing of Community support prices for 1975–76 the Government have taken important steps to assist the industry. The Green Pound (the representative rate at which prices under the common agricultural policy are converted into sterling) was reduced in August and October by five per cent and 5·8 per cent respectively, the implementation of the changes being deferred for some products. These changes raised Community support prices for United Kingdom farmers by over 11 per cent in sterling terms. Moreover, they were reflected in increases in the guaranteed price for milk. The guaranteed price for milk for 1975–76 in relation to estimated production is now 8·148p per litre (37·04p a gallon), 0·504p per litre (2·29p a gallon) above the level of 7·644p per litre (34·75p a gallon) set at the 1975 Review. In addition, the new beef regime introduced following the renegotiation of the terms of entry into the European Community has restored stability of returns to beef fatteners. Breeders' and rearers' returns this autumn showed a recovery from the severely depressed levels of a year ago.

The following table shows the net income, net product and labour productivity (see footnotes), (June–May years), for 1964–76 for all commercially significant holdings:

| *Year* | *Net Income at current prices*[1] *£ million* | | *Adjusted Net Income*[2] *(£ million)* | *Net Product at constant prices*[3] | *Labour Productivity*[4] |
|---|---|---|---|---|---|
| | *Actual* | *3-year moving average* | | 1968–69—1971–72 = 100 | 1968–69—1971–72 = 100 |
| 1965–66 | 455 | — | 412 | — | 76 |
| 1966–67 | 479 | 485 | 457 | — | 80 |
| 1967–68 | 520 | 493 | 476 | — | 88 |
| 1968–69 | 481 | 520 | 425 | 91 | 87 |
| 1969–70 | 560 | 550 | 490 | 96 | 95 |
| 1970–71 | 610 | 618 | 482 | 102 | 104 |
| 1971–72 | 684 | 720 | 587 | 110 | 115 |
| 1972–73 | 866 | 942 | 711 | 112 | 117 |
| 1973–74 | 1,275 | 1,135 | 871 | 117 | 125 |
| 1974–75 | 1,263 (1,267*) | 1,298 | 798 | 119 | 132 |
| 1975–76 (forecast) | 1,357 (1,383*) | — | 950 | 102 | 120 |

* Adjusted to normal weather conditions.

[1] Net income is defined as the return to farmers and their wives for their manual and managerial labour and for the use of the occupiers' investment after provision has been made for depreciation. The occupiers' investment includes all tenant-type Physical assets in livestock, crops, machinery, etc. but excludes any financial assets and all landlord-type assets such as land and buildings. The estimates of aggregate net income include a profit in recent years of about £5 million on the production of food for consumption in the farm household. In other industries the corresponding sums are not treated as profit and are relatively much smaller (in many cases non-existent). These figures are not directly comparable with incomes in other sectors of the economy since farm income also includes elements of wages and changes in stock valuations as well as profits.

[2] This is net income at current prices, adjusted for those changes in works-in-progress and stocks which are ascribable to changes in costs.

[3] Net Product (Net Output) measures year-to-year changes in the value-added at constant prices by farmers, landowners and farmworkers, to all the goods and services purchased from outside the agricultural sector.

[4] Labour productivity is here defined as gross product per person engaged in agriculture. Gross product is gross output and all inputs other than depreciation, labour, net rent and interest. It is here measured at constant prices. In order to be consistent with national economic conventions, gross product as used in the calculation of labour productivity covers agricultural contractors as well as all commercially significant holdings. The total number of persons engaged in agriculture comprises the number of employees, employers and self-employed recorded in the annual June census taken by the Agricultural Departments. Prior to 1971, however, the trends in numbers of employers and employees were estimated respectively from the Population Censuses and the Department of Employment count of national insurance cards.

The following table gives some information on crop acreages and livestock numbers at June of each year:

| | *Average of 1964–66* | 1971 | 1972 | 1973 | 1974 |
|---|---|---|---|---|---|
| *A. Crop areas* ('000 hectares) | | | | | |
| *Total area* | 19,628 | 19,115 | 19,039 | 18,988 | 19,010 |
| of which: Wheat | 941 | 1,097 | 1,127 | 1,146 | 1,233 |
| Barley | 2,234 | 2,288 | 2,288 | 2,267 | 2,214 |
| Oats | 411 | 363 | 315 | 281 | 253 |
| Mixed corn | 31 | 55 | 61 | 51 | 42 |
| Rye | 7 | 6 | 6 | 5 | 5 |
| Maize | — | 1 | 2 | 1 | 1 |
| *Total cereals*[1] | 3,623 | 3,810 | 3,799 | 3,752 | 3,747 |
| Potatoes | 295 | 256 | 237 | 225 | 215 |

*continued*

| | *Average of* 1962–64 | 1971 | 1972 | 1973 | 1974 |
|---|---|---|---|---|---|
| Sugar beet | 181 | 190 | 190 | 194 | 195 |
| Oilseed rape | — | 5 | 7 | 14 | 25 |
| Hops | 8 | 7 | 7 | 7 | 7 |
| Vegetables grown in the open | 149 | 183 | 179 | 187 | 194 |
| Orchard fruit | 81 | 62 | 59 | 57 | 55 |
| Soft fruit[2] | 20 | 18 | 18 | 18 | 18 |
| Ornamentals[3] | 14 | 15 | 15 | 16 | 16 |
| *Total horticulture*[4] | 265 | 280 | 273 | 281 | 285 |
| *Total tillage*[5] | 4,809 | 4,912 | 4,865 | 4,818 | 4,838 |
| All grasses under five years old[6] | 2,663 | 2,314 | 2,357 | 2,346 | 2,316 |
| *Total arable* | 7,472 | 7,226 | 7,222 | 7,164 | 7,154 |
| All grasses five years old and over | 4,943 | 4,926 | 4,910 | 4,914 | 4,920 |
| Rough grazing [7] | 7,214 | 6,678 | 6,614 | 6,605 | 6,564 |
| Other land[8] | — | 285 | 294 | 305 | 372 |
| *B Livestock numbers* ('000 head) | | | | | |
| *Total cattle and calves* | 11,925 | 12,804 | 13,483 | 14,445 | 15,203 |
| of which: Dairy cows | 3,164 | 3,234 | 3,325 | 3,436 | 3,394 |
| Beef cows | 1,035 | 1,378 | 1,476 | 1,678 | 1,887 |
| Heifers in calf | 769 | 831 | 954 | 988 | 1,041 |
| *Total sheep and lambs* | 29,842 | 25,981 | 26,877 | 27,943 | 28,498 |
| of which: Ewes | 11,961 | 10,422 | 10,668 | 10,921 | 11,192 |
| Shearlings | 2,541 | 2,263 | 2,438 | 2,733 | 2,673 |
| *Total pigs* | 7,564 | 8,724 | 8,619 | 8,979 | 8,544 |
| of which: Sows for breeding | 746 | 862 | 832 | 859 | 783 |
| Gilts in pig | 144 | 121 | 128 | 156 | 107 |
| *Total poultry* | 118,486 | 139,016 | 140,045 | 144,079 | 139,672 |
| of which: Table fowls (incl. broilers) | 30,390 | 49,730 | 50,933 | 58,366 | 56,701 |
| Laying fowls | 51,760 | 53,705 | 53,831 | 51,766 | 49,924 |
| Growing pullets | 24,163 | 22,465 | 21,678 | 18,808 | 18,958 |

1 For threshing.
2 Includes small area of soft fruit grown under orchard trees in England and Wales.
3 Hardy nursery stock, bulbs and flowers.
4 Most of the difference between total horticultural area and the sum of individual sectors is made up by the glasshouse area.
5 Includes acreages of other crops and bare fallow not shown in the table.
6 Includes lucerne.
7 Includes common reugh grazings.
8 Returns of 'other land' were collected for the first time in England and Wales in June 1969. From June 1969 to June 1973 'other land' in Great Britain was collected as woodland and areas under roads, yards, buildings, etc., the use of which was ancillary to the farming of the land; in Northern Ireland it included land within agricultural holdings which was under bog, water, roads, buildings, etc., and waste land not used for agriculture. In June 1974 the definition was changed in England and Wales to include all other land forming part of the holding and in Scotland it was extended to include ponds and derelict land. The Northern Ireland definition is unchanged.

**Forestry.** Prior to the First World War, Great Britain had no national forest policy, her needs being met mainly by imports. Since that period the policy has been to make the country more self-supporting in meeting her timber requirements. About nine-tenths of all the timber and wood products used are currently imported at a cost of some £1,684 million in 1974.

Until 1919, Government activity was limited to the maintenance of a relatively small area of ancient forests in England, which had once been royal hunting grounds, and to a small amount of advisory, educational and experimental work.

The Forestry Commission was set up under the Forestry Act of 1919 and this and subsequent legislation (consolidated in the Forestry Act 1967) has placed responsibility on the Commission for extending the forest estate and encouraging economic management of private woodlands. The Commission was reorganized in 1965 in the light of its increasing importance as a timber producer. There is now a part-time Chairman and four executive Commissioners; one of these is the Director General and the others, respectively, are in charge of Administration and Finance; Forest and Estate Management; and Harvesting and Marketing. The remaining Commissioners are part-time and represent various interests —for example, those of the timber trade, trade unions, amenity interests and private forestry. Forest operations are controlled by 11 Conservators, five in England, four in Scotland, and two in Wales.

There are in Great Britain rather more than 1·8 million hectares of woodland, representing 8 per cent of the land surface. Included in this area are over 826,133 hectares of plantations formed by The Forestry Commission since 1919. The balance is in private ownership; over 500,000 hectares have been placed within various grant schemes operated by the Commission.

The planting programmes of the Forestry Commission are fixed by periodic reviews by the Government, and at present stand at about 55,000 acres per annum covering both afforestation and re-planting of felled areas. In carrying out this planting the Commission will pay special attention to upland areas, particularly in Scotland and Wales where there is need of diversification of employment and other social benefits which spring from forestry. The majority of new planting, i.e. re-afforestation will be in Scotland.

Production in 1975–76 was 1,559,000 cu. metres. This was double the 1960 volume which is expected to double by 1980, treble by A.D. 2000. By entering into long-term contracts for supplying timber the Commission actively encourages the establishment of new timber processing industries in Britain.

The Commission has seven parks totalling some 24,000 hectares open to the public who are welcome to all its forests where there are no lease-hold or sporting-right restrictions on the Commission, and provides many picnic sites, forest trails, interpretive and wild-life centres for general use. It retains a landscape architect to advise on planting and felling so that these may be done in such a way as to preserve the beauty of the countryside. In 1975 over one and a quarter million camper/nights were spent in the commission's twelve fully equipped camp sites and some 20 million visits were paid to the forests by the public. In 1973 the Commission opened its first log-cabins for short-let holidays at Strathyre Perthshire; the second will be opened in Kernow Forest, Cornwall, in April 1977 and other sites are planned.

The grant schemes referred to above, which have as their purpose the encouragement of systematic management, include the Dedication scheme Bases I and II, in which the owner undertook to put his woodlands permanently to timber production, and received a planting and management grant. In 1974 a new Basis (Basis III) of Dedication was commenced by Her Majesty's Government under which once-for-all grants will be given for forest providing employment in certain areas or satisfying environmental criteria in any area. A higher rate of grant under Basis III will be paid to woodland owners planting broad-leaved trees on a long rotation.

Research work and special investigations into forestry problems have been extended in Great Britain in recent years; the Forestry Commission maintains Forest Research Stations in Surrey and outside Edinburgh. At these seed-testing is carried out, together with work on forest genetics, pathology and entomology; much attention is also paid to studies of tree growth and timber yield. Investigations into potential fields of timber utilization are also given priority, while the development of forest machinery is regarded as being of considerable importance.

The Commission changed to metric measurement in all its operations in February 1971.

The Commission make grants for research on forestry problems, which is carried out by universities and other institutions qualified to undertake such work.

**Fishing.** The following table shows the numbers of fishing vessels owned and operated in Great Britain for the years 1971–76:

| | *Under* 40 *ft* | | | 40–79·9 *ft* | | |
|---|---|---|---|---|---|---|
| *Year* | *England and Wales* | *Scotland* | *GB* | *England and Wales* | *Scotland* | *GB* |
| 1971 | 2,116 | 1,524 | 3,640 | 718 | 972 | 1,690 |
| 1972 | 2,232 | 1,584 | 3,816 | 760 | 1,003 | 1,763 |
| 1973 | 2,410 | 1,515 | 3,925 | 832 | 1,049 | 1,881 |
| 1974 | 2,628 | 1,559 | 4,187 | 905 | 1,080 | 1,985 |
| 1975 | 2,483 | 1,505 | 3,988 | 945 | 1,067 | 2,012 |
| 1976 | 2,647 | 1,487 | 4,134 | 932 | 1,033 | 1,965 |

| | 80–139·9 *ft* | | | 140 *ft* or *over* | | |
|---|---|---|---|---|---|---|
| *Year* | *England and Wales* | *Scotland* | *GB* | *England and Wales* | *Scotland* | *GB* |
| 1971 | 205 | 121 | 326 | 161 | 3 | 164 |
| 1972 | 207 | 122 | 329 | 164 | 4 | 168 |
| 1973 | 206 | 120 | 326 | 164 | 4 | 168 |
| 1974 | 180 | 111 | 291 | 159 | 4 | 162 |
| 1975 | 165 | 102 | 267 | 128 | 4 | 132 |
| 1976 | 152 | 88 | 240 | 101 | 3 | 104 |

The following table shows the quantity of fish landed by variety and group for the years 1975 and 1976:

| | 1975 | | | 1976 | | |
|---|---|---|---|---|---|---|
| *Variety* | *England and Wales* | *Scotland* | *GB* | *England and Wales* | *Scotland* | *GB* |
| | tonnes | tonnes | tonnes | tonnes | tonnes | tonnes |
| Bream | 19 | — | 19 | 22 | — | 22 |
| Brill | 153 | 13 | 166 | 153 | 17 | 170 |
| Catfish | 3,453 | 461 | 3,914 | 2,605 | 483 | 3,258 |
| Cod | 194,921 | 46,556 | 241,477 | 163,978 | 47,141 | 211,119 |
| Conger Eels | 387 | 79 | 466 | 398 | 98 | 496 |
| Dabs, long rough | 286 | — | 286 | 80 | — | 80 |
| Dabs, other | 822 | 759 | 1,581 | 783 | 722 | 1,505 |
| Dogfish | 7,566 | 9,083 | 16,649 | 6,703 | 9,937 | 16,640 |
| Flounders/Flukes | 202 | 33 | 235 | 208 | 25 | 233 |
| Gurnards/Latchets | 612 | 67 | 679 | 790 | 40 | 830 |

| Variety | 1975 England and Wales | 1975 Scotland | 1975 GB | 1976 England and Wales | 1976 Scotland | 1976 GB |
|---|---|---|---|---|---|---|
| | tonnes | tonnes | tonnes | tonnes | tonnes | tonnes |
| Haddock | 39,632 | 72,834 | 112,466 | 36,618 | 90,846 | 127,464 |
| Hake | 465 | 1,830 | 2,295 | 450 | 1,249 | 1,699 |
| Halibut | 509 | 296 | 805 | 384 | 294 | 678 |
| Halibut, Greenland | 1,863 | — | 1,863 | 2,346 | — | 2,346 |
| Lemon Soles | 2,377 | 1,869 | 4,246 | 2,574 | 1,812 | 4,386 |
| Ling | 1,715 | 1,378 | 3,093 | 1,998 | 1,418 | 3,416 |
| Megrims | 152 | 599 | 751 | 136 | 589 | 725 |
| Monks or Anglers | 1,003 | 3,254 | 4,257 | 1,124 | 3,783 | 4,907 |
| Mullet, grey | 103 | — | 103 | 114 | — | 114 |
| Norway Pout | — | 33,228 | 33,228 | 72 | 25,389 | 25,461 |
| Plaice | 23,869 | 3,968 | 27,837 | 27,856 | 3,891 | 31,747 |
| Pollack (Lythe) | 447 | 402 | 849 | 563 | 448 | 1,011 |
| Redfish | 5,905 | 133 | 6,038 | 6,211 | 246 | 6,457 |
| Saithe | 16,835 | 17,668 | 34,503 | 19,356 | 21,019 | 40,375 |
| Skates and Rays | 3,807 | 2,891 | 6,698 | 3,649 | 3,115 | 6,764 |
| Soles | 1,144 | 20 | 1,164 | 1,260 | 21 | 1,281 |
| Torsk (Tusk) | 430 | 516 | 946 | 235 | 477 | 712 |
| Turbot | 544 | 86 | 630 | 669 | 94 | 763 |
| Whiting | 6,832 | 37,060 | 43,892 | 6,924 | 39,215 | 46,139 |
| Witches | 152 | 662 | 814 | 138 | 774 | 912 |
| Other Demersal | 2,990 | 13,276 | 16,266 | 2,841 | 18,751 | 21,592 |
| Fish Livers | 5,920 | — | 5,920 | 4,925 | 1 | 4,926 |
| Fish Roes | 379 | 482 | 861 | 500 | 492 | 992 |
| Total Demersal[1]: | 325,494 | 249,503 | 574,997 | 296,663 | 272,387 | 569,050 |
| Herring | 8,727 | 98,506 | 107,233 | 12,163 | 73,119 | 85,282 |
| Mackerel | 31,590 | 16,756 | 48,346 | 57,397 | 29,606 | 87,003 |
| Pilchards | 1,548 | — | 1,548 | 4,444 | — | 4,444 |
| Sprats | 36,354 | 22,354 | 58,708 | 53,169 | 36,571 | 89,740 |
| Whitebait | 204 | — | 204 | 192 | — | 192 |
| Other Pelagic | 448 | 469 | 917 | 2,060 | 1,658 | 3,718 |
| Total Pelagic[2]: | 78,871 | 138,085 | 216,956 | 129,425 | 140,954 | 270,379 |
| Total Demersal and Pelagic: | 404,365 | 387,588 | 791,953 | 426,088 | 413,341 | 839,429 |
| Oysters(b) | 487 | 1 | 488 | 925 | 27 | 952 |
| Crabs | 4,898 | 1.686 | 6,584 | 5,714 | 1,996 | 7,710 |
| Crawfish | 56 | — | 56 | 105 | — | 105 |
| Lobsters | 342 | 505 | 847 | 348 | 528 | 876 |
| Cockles | 16,382 | 2 | 16,384 | 18,524 | — | 18,524 |
| Escallops and Queens | 6,112 | 7,562 | 13,674 | 8,787 | 9,986 | 18,773 |
| Mussels | 6,209 | 706 | 6,915 | 6,701 | 749 | 7,450 |
| Nephrops | 1,156 | 8,218 | 9,374 | 1,734 | 10,905 | 12,639 |
| Periwinkles | 610 | 2,034 | 2,644 | 459 | 2,240 | 2,699 |
| Shrimps | 1,531 | 538 | 2,069 | 1,238 | 2,027 | 3,265 |
| Squids | 648 | 356 | 1,004 | 906 | 462 | 1,368 |
| Whelks | 3,146 | 2 | 3,148 | 3,229 | — | 3,229 |
| Other Shellfish | 196 | — | 196 | 207 | — | 207 |
| Total Shellfish: | 41,773 | 21,610 | 63,383 | 48,877 | 28,920 | 77,797 |
| Total All Fish: | 446,138 | 409,041 | 855,177 | 474,965 | 442,261 | 917,226 |

(a) Weight of oysters calculated on the basis of one tonne as equal to 15,748 oysters in England and Wales and 11,811 in Scotland.

[1] Demersal species are those species living on or near the seabed.

[2] Pelagic species are those species living mainly in coast waters, in shoals near the surface of the sea.

## UNITED KINGDOM

**The following table shows the number of fishermen in Great Britain for selected years from 1900 to 1976:**

| Year | *England and Wales* (a) | | *Scotland* (c) | | *Great Britain* | |
|---|---|---|---|---|---|---|
| | *Regularly Employed* | *Partially Employed* (b) | *Regularly Employed* | *Partially Employed* | *Regularly Employed* | *Partially Employed* |
| 1900 | 31,589 | 7,994 | 35,806 (d) | | 75,389 | |
| 1910 | 36,471 | 7,159 | 38,941 (d) | | 82,571 | |
| 1920 | 34,844 | 6,273 | 36,319 (d) | | 77,436 | |
| 1930 | 30,309 | 3,825 | 17,558 | 6,765 | 47,867 | 10,590 |
| 1938 | 26,062 | 2,949 | 12,976 | 4,939 | 39,038 | 7,888 |
| 1948 | 25,946 | 3,373 | 12,080 | 5,148 | 38,026 | 8,521 |
| 1951 | 23,705 | 3,685 | 10,934 | 3,597 | 34,639 | 7,282 |
| 1960 | 12,712 | 3,646 | 8,795 | 2,451 | 21,507 | 6,097 |
| 1961 | 13,241 | 3,864 | 8,671 | 2,199 | 21,912 | 6,063 |
| 1962 | 12,898 | 3,635 | 8,441 | 2,169 | 21,339 | 5,804 |
| 1963 | 12,145 | 3,506 | 8,289 | 2,238 | 20,434 | 5,744 |
| 1964 | 11,566 | 3,862 | 8 181 | 2 068 | 19 747 | 5,930 |
| 1965 | 11,064 | 4,045 | 8,057 | 2,088 | 19,121 | 6,133 |
| 1966 | 10,641 | 3,300 | 8,073 | 2,084 | 18,714 | 5,384 |
| 1967 | 10,110 | 3,076 | 8,057 | 1,847 | 18,167 | 4,923 |
| 1968 | 9,420 | 2,821 | 7,927 | 1,740 | 17,347 | 4,561 |
| 1969 | 9,291 | 2,527 | 7,696 | 1,524 | 16,987 | 4,051 |
| 1970 | 9,424 | 2,382 | 7,656 | 1,441 | 17,080 | 3,823 |
| 1971 | 9,454 | 2,479 | 7,897 | 1,435 | 17,351 | 3,914 |
| 1972 | 9,703 | 2,630 | 8,110 | 1,460 | 17,813 | 4,090 |
| 1973 | 10,199 | 2,830 | 8,311 | 1,336 | 18,510 | 4,166 |
| 1974 | 9,799 | 3,256 | 8,172 | 1,399 | 17,971 | 4,655 |
| 1975 | 9,016 | 3,447 | 7,507 | 1,341 | 16,523 | 4,788 |
| 1976 | 8,730 | 3,601 | 7,572 | 1,289 | 16,302 | 4,890 |

(a) Prior to 1952 figures were based on information supplied by the Registrar General of Shipping and Seamen. Since 1952 figures have been supplied by the District Fishery Officers of the Ministry ofAgriculture, Fisheries and Food.
(b) Since 1966 these figures exclude 'hobby fishermen' i.e. fishermen who did not fish commercially.
(c) Prior to 1961 Scottish figures were as at 30 November of each year.
(d) Separate figures not available.

### Oil and Natural Gas

*Oil production.* By the end of 1976, seven of the fourteen "commercial" fields were in production. Argyll and Forties had come into production during 1975. During 1976 Auk, Montrose, Beryl, Brent and Piper successively came on-stream. Each of these fields encountered some delays in start-up; Beryl was hindered by an accident to the offshore loading tower and Auk by damage to the platform; Piper was held up by piling operations in difficult seabed conditions, and Brent also suffered technical delays. Despite these difficulties, production was running at a rate of over half a million barrels per day (equal to 25 million tonnes a year) at the end of 1976. However, total production for the year was 12 million tonnes, rather than the 15–20 million tonnes envisaged in last year's Brown Book. The 12 million tonnes includes 400,000 tonnes of Natural Gas Liquids, and 100,000 tonnes of oil produced from landward areas.

The Flotta terminal in the Orkneys, built to receive oil from Piper and from Claymore when it starts producing later this year, was inaugurated by the Chairman of Occidental and the Secretary of State for Energy, on 11 January 1977. Work at the Sullom Voe terminal in the Shetlands, which will handle oil brought ashore from the Ninian and Brent pipeline systems, is going ahead with a view to bringing the first oil ashore in 1978. By the end of the decade half or more of the United Kingdom's oil production, from a total of seven fields, will be handled by Sullom Voe. Two more fields, Thistle and Claymore, are expected to come onstream in 1977 and the five remaining commercial fields should be brought into production during 1978–79.

Because of the geological and technical complexities involved and the need to apply the lessons on costs learned during the early 1970s, as well as the scale of managerial and other resources already committed by many operators to existing developments, the licensees are adopting a more deliberate approach to the appraisal of discoveries. As a result, development did not start on any new field in 1976, although it seems likely that work may start on several during the next year. Design contracts have already been let for the platform and topside facilities for Murchison.

All these factors, together with the increased estimate of production from Forties, which is now expected to produce at a peak rate of some 500,000 barrels per day from the end of 1977, are reflected in the latest forecasts of oil production for the next five years at Table 1. The rate of production will continue to increase during 1977 and total production for the year is expected to fall within the range of 40–45 million tonnes, equivalent to nearly half United Kingdom demand. The United Kingdom should achieve net self-sufficiency in oil by 1980, although the estimated range of production for that year is 5 million tonnes lower than last year's forecast, because of the longer period of appraisal before decisions are taken to develop new fields. Thereafter production during the early 1980s is still expected to lie within the range 100–150 million tonnes a year. But the uncertainties surrounding the number of fields which will be in production, both those already identified and those not yet found, make it unrealistic to attempt to estimate within narrower limits.

*Table 1 Forecast of United Kingdom Continental Shelf oil production*

| Year | 1977 | 1978 | 1979 | 1980 | 1981 |
|---|---|---|---|---|---|
| Forecast production (m. tonnes) | 40–45 | 60–70 | 80–95 | 90–110 | 100–120 |

*Oil reserves*

The possible total of reserves from fields in production or under development (directly comparable to last year's category of commercial fields) has increased from 1,170 million tonnes to 1,260 million tonnes. The estimates for other significant discoveries not yet fully appraised show a rise of 120 million tonnes reflecting both the new discoveries of 1976 which have entered this category and lower reserves estimates resulting from appraisal of some earlier finds. Together these figures represent the possible total from known discoveries which is up from the 2,290 million tonnes estimate in the 1976 Brown Book to 2,500 million tonnes. Table 2 shows that the likely range for the recoverable reserves from all the fields so far discovered is between 2,000 million tonnes (on the assumption that only the proven and probable reserves can be recovered) and 2,500 million tonnes (on the optimistic assumption that all the possible reserves are also recovered).

Future finds are necessarily much more speculative. A comprehensive analysis of all the available geophysical and geological data, the likely stratigraphy, petrophysical characteristics and success ratios has led to a revised estimate of the likely range of reserves of oil remaining to be discovered in the presently licensed area including that licensed in the 5th Round. This range is now believed to be 350–700 million tonnes. The range of all oil reserves in the licensed area therefore lies between 2,300 million tonnes and 3,200 million tonnes, the same range as that quoted in the 1976 report, although within that range there is now a shift in the balance between what has already been discovered and what is still to be found; also the range now relates to a larger area, i.e. that covered by 5th Round licenses as well as those in the 1st–4th Rounds.

Total estimated reserves remain in the range 3,000–4,500 million tonnes, taking account of areas designated but not yet licensed. The higher end of the range now includes an allowance for areas not yet designated but expected to fall to the United Kingdom when the dividing lines between the United Kingdom and other countries such as France, Norway and Ireland are fully determined.

Earlier estimates of reserves have therefore been broadly borne out by the results of exploration and development, but with some changes both in what we are reasonably sure will be developed (where the estimates are increased) and what may possibly be the ultimate total of our reserves (where the estimates are lower). Previous assumptions about the potential contribution of oil to United Kingdom indigenous energy supplies remain valid. But the width of the ranges quoted reflects the uncertainties which still exist. The amount of oil in the category of possible reserves is by definition especially uncertain. Further exploration and indeed further licensing will be necessary before the ranges can be narrowed.

*Table 2 Estimated oil reserves in United Kingdom licensed area (million tonnes)*

| | *Proven*[1] | *Probable* | *Possible* | *Possible total* |
|---|---|---|---|---|
| 1. Fields in production or under development | 1,070 | 110 | 80 | 1,260 |
| 2. Other significant discoveries not yet fully appraised | 310 | 460 | 470 | 1,240 |
| Total present discoveries | 1,380 | 570 | 550 | 2,500 |
| | 1,950 | | | |
| Expected discoveries present licences (including 5th round) | — | 350 | 350 | 700 |
| Total presently licensed areas (including 5th round) | 1,380 | 920 | 900 | 3,200 |
| | 2,300 | | | |

[1] The terms 'proven', 'probable' and 'possible' are given the internationally accepted meanings in this context of:

(i) Proven—those which on the available evidence are virtually certain to be technically and economically producible.
(ii) Probable—those which are estimated to have better than a 50 per cent chance of being technically and economically producible.
(iii) Possible—those which at present are estimated to have a significant but less than 50 per cent chance of being technically and economically producible.

*Gas production*

It is ten years since the first North Sea gas came ashore from the Southern Basin. Since then supplies by the gas industry to the country have increased four-fold. Last year 39·4 billion cubic metres of natural gas from the Continental Shelf was sold to the British Gas Corporation, accounting for about 98 per cent of the United Kingdom's gas requirements.

This year, for the first time, gas will be coming ashore from the Northern Basin for sale to British Gas. In the Autumn, gas under contract to British Gas from the U.K./Norwegian Frigg field should be delivered via the completed gas pipeline to St Fergus, and should be sufficient to build up to annual production rate of at least 15 billion cubic metres, or about 40 per cent of current supply.

Small quantities of gas from the Forties oil field will become available to British Gas this Spring, and when the Brent field gas pipeline system is completed, it will bring larger quantities of associated gas ashore.

Total reserves under contract to British Gas, including gas from the Norwegian part of the Frigg field, will support an average production rate of about 170 million cubic metres a day (6,000 mcfd) by the 1980s. Further contracts and discoveries are likely to prolong this level of gas production.

All North Sea oilfields produce associated gas in varying quantities. With the exception of the Brent field, no proven oil field in the United Kingdom sector has yet shown a sufficient quantity to justify a separate gas pipeline to shore. In some cases it may be possible and worthwhile to re-inject the gas into the reservoir provided that the geological formations are suitable. When the field is served by an oil pipeline it is possible to transport some gas dissolved in the oil. On most fields some associated gas is used for power generation on the platforms. But gas which cannot safely be recovered or conserved by any of these methods will have to be flared. Associated gas from the producing North Sea oilfields totalled around 860 million cubic metres in 1976. Of this, about 12 per cent was either sold or used at the field, and the remainder flared. Gas flaring is especially likely in the early stages of production in advance of the installation of offshore compression equipment, the commissioning of gas-driven utilities, or the completion of pipeline or onshore handling facilities. As development work is completed the percentage of gas used, transported or sold should increase. An example of this is the Brent field, where the commissioning of the re-injection compressors and utilities, the Sullom Voe terminal, and the gas pipeline to St Fergus will ultimately mean the full utilization of all associated gas.

Under model Clause 21 of the terms of the petroleum production licences the Secretary of States' approval is required for flaring or re-injection of gas. Applications to flare and/or re-inject gas must be made at least two years before flaring or injection is due to start. The aim is to minimize the wastage of gas. Consents have been issued, to ensure continued oil production, for the seven oilfields currently onstream. These consents are limited, in case circumstances change, with the exception of the Argyll and Auk fields where the Government is satisfied that the quantities of gas to be produced are too small for delivery to be practical.

*Gas reserves*

Remaining proven gas reserves at the end of 1976 were 809 billion cubic metres (28·6 trillion cubic feet), compared to last year's figure of 815 bcm (28·7 tcf). 1976 consumption of 39·4 bcm (1·4 tcf) was therefore largely offset by an increase of 33·4 bcm (1·2 tcf) in estimates, mainly of associated gas reserves in the northern North Sea. Taking the Southern Basin on its own, 1976 production was also partly offset by new discoveries, the net decrease in Southern Basin reserves being only 20 bcm (0·7 tcf); see Table 3.

The reserve figures do not include allowances for fields which, though significant discoveries, have not yet reached the development planning stage. No allowance is included for prospective reserves from future discoveries, which will undoubtedly be made in the northern North Sea and to a lesser extent in the southern North Sea.

The economics of the recovery and transportation of associated gas involves many factors. In September 1975 the Government commissioned Williams-Merz (consulting engineers) to produce a feasibility study examining whether there was a case for an economically viable gas-gathering system in the Northern Basin of the North Sea. Their report suggested that their preferred system could bring ashore up to 1,500 million cubic feet a day (or 40 million cubic metres a day) of methane, and 6 to 9 million tonnes a year of heavier gases. The Government considered the report and the many comments received from interested parties upon it, and decided that further extensive studies costing several million pounds were needed to establish the economic viability of such a system.

A joint public/private sector study company, Gas Gathering Pipelines (North Sea) Ltd, has therefore been set up by British Gas and BNOC with four private sector companies, to finance and be responsible for the further studies. Gas Gathering Pipelines Ltd. has been asked to submit an initial report by the end of 1977 and to update the information by March 1978. If the project proves viable Gas Gathering Pipelines Ltd. will recommend a suitable pipeline configuration for Government consideration.

*Table 3 Estimated United Kingdom Continental Shelf gas reserves (remaining in known discoveries at 31 December 1976)*

(Totals in billion cubic metres (figures in brackets trillion cubic feet)[1])

| | *Proven* | *Probable* | *Possible* | *Total* |
|---|---|---|---|---|
| *Southern Basin* | | | | |
| Fields under contract to British Gas | 462 (16·3) | 14 (0·5) | 25 (0·9) | 501 (17·7) |
| Other discoveries believed commercial but not yet under contract to BGC | 51 (1·8) | 65 (2·3) | — | 116 (4·1) |
| Other discoveries | — | 34 (1·2) | 40 (1·4) | 74 (2·6) |
| Total Southern Basin | 513 (18·1) | 113 (4·0) | 65 (2·3) | 691 (24·4) |
| *Northern Basin* | | | | |
| Fields under contract to British Gas | 178 (6·3) | — | 6 (0·2) | 184 (6·5) |
| Other significant finds[2] (gas and condensate) | 40 (1·4) | 102 (3·6) | 198 (7·0) | 340 (12·0) |
| Other associated gas with oil | 79 (2·8) | 56 (2·0) | 93 (3·3) | 228 (8·1) |
| Total Northern Basin | 297 (10·5) | 158 (5·6) | 297 (10·5) | 752 (26·6) |
| Total UK Continental Shelf | 809 (28·6) | 272 (9·6) | 362 (12·8) | 1,443 (51·0) |

1 The conversion factor assumed is 1 tcf ($10^{12}$ cubic feet) = $28·317 \times 10^9$ cubic metres.
2 Including reserves found in Liverpool Bay.

**Mining.** At the end of 1976 there were 241,024 wage-earners on colliery books, a decrease of 4,178 since December 1975. The average weekly output in 1976 was 2,313,000 tons (2,087,000 deep-mined and 226,000 opencast). Total production was as follows (in million tons):

| | 1974 | 1975 | 1976 |
|---|---|---|---|
| Deep-mined* | 98·4 | 115·5 | 108·5 |
| Opencast | 9·1 | 10·2 | 11·7 |
| Total | 107·5 | 125·7 | 120·2 |

* Excluding about 900,000 tons in 1975 and 1,600,000 tons in 1976, recovered and disposed of as in those years from dumps, ponds, etc.

Exports of coal in 1976 were 1·4 million tons. In 1975 they totalled 2·1 million tons.

In 1976, 76·6 million tons of coal were used by the electricity generating stations, 6·1 million tons by general manufacturers other than iron and steel and engineering trades, 9,000 tons by the gas works and 0·1 million tons by the railways. Domestic consumption amounted to 10·7 million tons (including miners' coal). The NCB are currently implementing 'Plan for Coal', a massive investment programme designed to achieve an annual output of at least135 million tons by 1985. Because of continuing exhaustion this means providing an additional 42 million tons of annual deep-mined capacity, and expanding opencast output from ten to 15 million tons p.a. Investment in 28 million tons of new deep-mined capacity has already been committed, including the Selby coalfield project. This received planning permission and financial approval in 1976, and is planned to produce ten million tons p.a. from about 1987 to well into the next century.

Production of non-metallic minerals at mines and quarries in 1975 and 1976 is shown in this table:

| *U.K. Production* *Mineral* | Thousand tonnes 1975 (*final*) | 1976 (*provisional*) |
|---|---|---|
| Chalk | 17,924 | 15,941 |
| Chert and flint | 362 | 322 |
| China Clay }<br>Potters' clay and ball clay } | 3,232 | 3,861 |
| Clay shale (including fuller's earth) | 28,004 | 26,228 |
| Fireclay | 1,606 | 1,513 |
| Gravel and Sand[1] | 110,060 | 101,814 |
| Industrial sand | 6,139 | 5,678 |
| Igneous Rock | 42,017 | 37,215 |
| Limestone and Dolomite | 95,213 | 89,364 |
| Sandstone (including silica stone and ganister) | 13,394 | 13,522 |
| Slate[2] | 547 | 295 |
| Calcspar | 19 | 16 |
| Fluorspar | 235 | 217 |
| Gypsum and Anhydrite | 3,479 | 3,350 |
| Rock Salt | 754 | 611 |
| Barytes | 52 | 50 |
| Other non-metalliferous minerals | 378 | 598 |

1 Not including marine dredged.
2 Slate figures include waste used for constructional fill, and powder and granules used in manufacturing.

The iron and steel production for 1974–76 is shown in the following table (in thousand tonnes):

| | 1974 | 1975 | 1976 |
|---|---|---|---|
| Iron ore | 3,602 | 4,490 | 4,582 |
| Pig iron | 13,902 | 12,131 | 13,835 |
| Ingots and castings[1] | 22,426 | 20,198 | 22,274 |

[1] The definition of ingots and castings changed slightly in 1976 therefore figures for individual years are not strictly comparable.

The total net deliveries of finished steel in 1976 were 19·4 million tonnes. There were 535 steel furnaces in existence at the end of 1974, 535 at the end of 1975, and 520 at the end of 1976.

**Commerce.** The following tables show the value in £ millions of exports and imports by countries for 1976 and some of 1977:

*Imports (£ millions)*

| | 1976 | | | 1977 | | | |
|---|---|---|---|---|---|---|---|
| | *2nd quarter* | *3rd quarter* | *4th quarter* | *1st quarter* | *2nd quarter* | *July* | *August* |
| *All countries: total* | 7,775·9 | 7,804·5 | 8,753·9 | 9,089·5 | 9,669·9 | 3,091·9 | 2,739·1 |
| *EEC: total* | 2,876·9 | 2,716·4 | 3,287·4 | 3,426·1 | 3,482·8 | 1,236·5 | 1,062·5 |
| Germany, Federal Republic | 654·0 | 678·7 | 819·4 | 882·6 | 835·0 | 328·1 | 266·3 |
| Netherlands | 609·5 | 547·8 | 683·7 | 676·0 | 635·3 | 194·9 | 189·8 |
| Belgium and Luxembourg | 307·5 | 328·2 | 403·9 | 311·0 | 429·1 | 154·8 | 101·9 |
| France | 637·7 | 458·6 | 543·8 | 613·5 | 688·0 | 237·3 | 205·6 |
| Italy | 259·7 | 285·9 | 320·6 | 360·6 | 383·1 | 150·9 | 124·7 |
| Denmark | 170·5 | 179·0 | 195·5 | 190·9 | 214·2 | 68·3 | 63·4 |
| Irish Republic | 238·1 | 237·4 | 320·6 | 291·4 | 298·2 | 102·2 | 110·7 |
| *Rest of Western Europe: total* | 1,071·9 | 1,173·7 | 1,333·7 | 1,286·0 | 1,634·4 | 405·6 | 317·3 |
| Finland | 134·8 | 145·7 | 160·5 | 153·6 | 154·0 | 45·2 | 46·2 |
| Sweden | 296·2 | 307·3 | 336·4 | 335·4 | 321·7 | 96·3 | 78·6 |
| Norway | 129·0 | 211·5 | 161·1 | 142·2 | 401·9 | 43·8 | 40·3 |
| Switzerland | 224·3 | 213·5 | 300·6 | 257·4 | 397·8 | 106·5 | 51·3 |
| Portugal | 47·2 | 50·8 | 52·1 | 63·5 | 56·6 | 20·0 | 18·2 |
| Austria | 53·5 | 58·2 | 71·5 | 69·8 | 64·4 | 22·5 | 18·6 |
| Spain | 92·4 | 82·6 | 104·0 | 119·0 | 100·7 | 27·9 | 26·6 |
| Greece | 16·9 | 17·5 | 16·1 | 20·1 | 27·5 | 10·7 | 6·5 |
| Turkey | 14·9 | 12·6 | 15·7 | 17·9 | 13·5 | 3·7 | 3·8 |
| Yugoslavia | 8·6 | 9·0 | 8·9 | 11·4 | 10·0 | 2·8 | 3·2 |
| Other countries | 54·3 | 65·0 | 106·9 | 95·7 | 86·2 | 26·3 | 23·9 |
| *North America: total* | 1,059·0 | 1,049·9 | 1,206·9 | 1,276·3 | 1,326·6 | 447·5 | 386·3 |
| Canada | 314·3 | 303·9 | 326·0 | 301·4 | 316·2 | 114·5 | 96·3 |
| United States | 741·8 | 741·2 | 876·0 | 969·5 | 1,002·2 | 328·7 | 285·5 |
| Other countries | 3·0 | 4·8 | 4·8 | 5·4 | 8·2 | 4·4 | 4·5 |
| *Other developed countries: total* | 526·4 | 567·2 | 585·5 | 636·6 | 749·6 | 220·2 | 195·2 |
| South Africa | 168·6 | 177·3 | 150·9 | 190·6 | 277·0 | 71·6 | 42·7 |
| Japan | 182·4 | 217·5 | 233·9 | 248·9 | 270·9 | 94·6 | 91·5 |
| Australia | 93·0 | 99·9 | 113·6 | 87·8 | 97·7 | 29·8 | 21·1 |
| New Zealand | 82·5 | 72·5 | 87·0 | 109·2 | 103·9 | 24·2 | 40·0 |
| *Oil exporting countries: total* | 998·9 | 1,106·1 | 1,127·8 | 1,064·6 | 1,001·0 | 270·3 | 278·8 |
| Algeria | 16·7 | 23·4 | 12·9 | 15·6 | 12·0 | 5·7 | 6·7 |
| Libya | 23·2 | 55·6 | 52·6 | 17·4 | 47·1 | 16·6 | 11·2 |
| Nigeria | 92·9 | 78·4 | 65·3 | 92·9 | 40·1 | 11·6 | 20·0 |
| Gabon | 5·3 | 1·7 | 1·6 | 1·4 | 0·6 | 0·3 | 0·1 |
| Saudi Arabia | 213·9 | 251·8 | 266·0 | 291·0 | 325·0 | 97·6 | 69·6 |
| Kuwait | 127·3 | 127·8 | 220·4 | 130·9 | 164·5 | 46·0 | 36·4 |
| Bahrain | 5·3 | 13·1 | 7·8 | 4·3 | 1·5 | 1·0 | 4·0 |
| Qatar | 80·4 | 58·5 | 35·3 | 58·0 | 19·0 | 9·0 | 5·3 |
| Abu Dhabi | 12·7 | 27·3 | 10·2 | 26·7 | 33·7 | 11·9 | 11·1 |
| Dubai | 44·3 | 31·0 | 25·2 | 27·0 | 25·5 | 3·8 | 17·9 |
| Sharjah, etc. | — | 0·2 | — | — | 0·2 | — | — |
| Oman | 9·5 | 9·5 | 5·3 | 8·7 | 2·4 | 0·5 | 0·6 |
| Iraq | 38·4 | 111·3 | 94·5 | 80·8 | 84·9 | 13·5 | 20·7 |
| Iran | 264·9 | 267·9 | 300·9 | 281·3 | 209·0 | 41·1 | 62·8 |
| Brunei | 0·1 | 0·1 | — | 2·8 | –2·6 | — | 1·2 |
| Indonesia | 4·9 | 7·6 | 6·1 | 5·3 | 6·4 | 2·3 | 2·3 |
| Trinidad and Tobago | 22·3 | 11·5 | 5·1 | 8·3 | 9·9 | 4·6 | 1·2 |
| Venezuela | 36·0 | 28·7 | 17·8 | 11·6 | 20·6 | 4·7 | 6·9 |
| Ecuador | 0·6 | 0·7 | 0·7 | 0·5 | 1·3 | 0·2 | 0·8 |
| *Other developing countries: total* | 926·1 | 902·6 | 929·5 | 1,100·6 | 1,123·4 | 386·9 | 366·9 |
| Egypt | 26·4 | 13·3 | 6·0 | 15·6 | 25·4 | 10·1 | 4·1 |
| Ghana | 18·5 | 22·2 | 20·7 | 40·1 | 31·9 | 5·4 | 26·6 |
| Kenya | 14·3 | 12·7 | 21·7 | 44·0 | 46·2 | 20·7 | 16·1 |
| Tanzania | 9·6 | 6·3 | 7·2 | 10·5 | 11·6 | 6·6 | 2·0 |
| Zambia | 16·2 | 14·7 | 25·1 | 23·6 | 24·6 | 10·4 | 5·8 |
| Cyprus | 38·7 | 8·6 | 8·9 | 15·2 | 42·5 | 6·4 | 3·6 |
| Lebanon | 2·1 | — | 0·8 | 1·3 | 2·5 | 1·0 | 0·6 |

## UNITED KINGDOM

*continued*

*Imports (£ millions)*

| | 1976 | | | 1977 | | | |
|---|---|---|---|---|---|---|---|
| | *2nd quarter* | *3rd quarter* | *4th quarter* | *1st quarter* | *2nd quarter* | *July* | *August* |
| Israel | 32·9 | 25·8 | 29·1 | 53·2 | 46·7 | 10·7 | 13·6 |
| Pakistan | 13·7 | 8·8 | 8·8 | 17·4 | 10·9 | 2·3 | 3·5 |
| India | 111·6 | 82·0 | 90·0 | 93·1 | 100·7 | 28·8 | 31·2 |
| Thailand | 8·1 | 6·3 | 6·4 | 10·2 | 8·0 | 3·4 | 2·4 |
| Malaysia | 40·5 | 40·5 | 44·5 | 66·4 | 53·6 | 20·5 | 19·7 |
| Singapore | 21·7 | 25·0 | 26·5 | 30·0 | 26·1 | 7·3 | 7·9 |
| Taiwan | 20·6 | 24·3 | 33·4 | 35·3 | 34·3 | 11·7 | 10·4 |
| Hong Kong | 115·2 | 109·6 | 113·7 | 129·5 | 106·5 | 38·4 | 34·8 |
| South Korea | 35·8 | 42·8 | 33·0 | 51·5 | 45·6 | 15·2 | 16·2 |
| Philippines | 7·3 | 13·5 | 9·0 | 10·7 | 10·5 | 5·7 | 3·2 |
| Jamaica | 15·2 | 21·7 | 11·3 | 13·1 | 22·5 | 10·8 | 9·7 |
| Mexico | 7·2 | 5·7 | 6·0 | 10·8 | 11·4 | 2·2 | 2·8 |
| Chile | 27·2 | 16·1 | 21·5 | 19·9 | 22·7 | 6·9 | 4·6 |
| Brazil | 63·1 | 71·8 | 64·2 | 89·6 | 73·2 | 33·7 | 23·9 |
| Argentina | 19·4 | 23·8 | 28·3 | 30·7 | 32·4 | 8·8 | 13·3 |
| Other countries | 260·9 | 306·9 | 313·6 | 289·0 | 333·5 | 120·0 | 110·7 |
| *Centrally planned economies: total* | 308·9 | 281·1 | 275·4 | 285·6 | 338·2 | 121·4 | 128·4 |
| Soviet Union | 196·9 | 163·9 | 146·8 | 146·9 | 206·1 | 65·2 | 87·3 |
| Poland | 37·6 | 39·5 | 39·9 | 42·3 | 35·5 | 14·0 | 12·7 |
| German Democratic Republic | 11·8 | 15·0 | 21·9 | 18·6 | 21·1 | 13·1 | 7·7 |
| Czechoslovakia | 18·2 | 16·8 | 18·6 | 22·7 | 22·7 | 7·1 | 6·1 |
| Romania | 14·7 | 13·8 | 10·5 | 14·4 | 14·9 | 4·7 | 3·7 |
| Other countries | 29·6 | 32·1 | 37·8 | 40·8 | 38·0 | 17·4 | 10·9 |
| *Low value trade* | 7·8 | 7·6 | 7·6 | 13·8 | 13·8 | 3·6 | 3·8 |

*Exports (£ millions)*

| | 1976 | | | 1977 | | | |
|---|---|---|---|---|---|---|---|
| *Countries* | *2nd quarter* | *3rd quarter* | *4th quarter* | *1st quarter* | *2nd quarter* | *July* | *August* |
| *All countries: total* | 6,393·1 | 6,259·7 | 7,298·6 | 7,674·3 | 8,362·3 | 2,862·4 | 2,660·7 |
| *EEC: total* | 2,276·3 | 2,205·9 | 2,686·1 | 2,827·8 | 3,073·4 | 980·7 | 927·4 |
| Germany, Federal Republic | 452·1 | 450·1 | 545·3 | 567·8 | 602·1 | 193·8 | 222·0 |
| Netherlands | 359·4 | 361·5 | 462·4 | 493·0 | 611·6 | 192·4 | 178·6 |
| Belgium and Luxembourg | 357·8 | 330·9 | 415·4 | 423·7 | 486·2 | 152·1 | 105·5 |
| France | 433·8 | 412·2 | 478·6 | 518·8 | 533·1 | 171·3 | 157·7 |
| Italy | 210·7 | 201·0 | 237·2 | 258·2 | 254·7 | 76·9 | 66·9 |
| Denmark | 152·3 | 155·1 | 184·4 | 197·9 | 196·2 | 60·7 | 69·6 |
| Irish Republic | 310·3 | 295·1 | 362·7 | 368·3 | 389·4 | 133·6 | 127·1 |
| *Rest of Western Europe: total* | 1,070·9 | 1,001·6 | 1,261·8 | 1,317·7 | 1,464·7 | 580·0 | 388·7 |
| Finland | 68·4 | 68·3 | 83·8 | 85·6 | 88·6 | 35·7 | 25·5 |
| Sweden | 254·2 | 235·0 | 333·1 | 319·6 | 309·5 | 92·3 | 89·7 |
| Norway | 119·3 | 105·2 | 145·3 | 139·9 | 151·6 | 198·3 | 43·1 |
| Switzerland | 246·4 | 234·8 | 285·0 | 335·4 | 418·0 | 88·9 | 89·2 |
| Portugal | 52·0 | 51·7 | 70·5 | 76·3 | 73·2 | 25·2 | 24·6 |
| Austria | 50·2 | 51·0 | 62·9 | 60·2 | 66·8 | 20·8 | 20·8 |
| Spain | 96·7 | 87·6 | 98·1 | 119·3 | 123·3 | 42·4 | 31·7 |
| Greece | 38·2 | 37·8 | 39·1 | 46·6 | 66·8 | 17·9 | 17·9 |
| Turkey | 51·4 | 60·0 | 55·9 | 59·2 | 69·4 | 23·6 | 12·4 |
| Yugoslavia | 27·4 | 35·2 | 39·9 | 35·9 | 53·1 | 13·3 | 11·1 |
| Other countries | 66·7 | 34·8 | 48·2 | 39·8 | 44·4 | 21·5 | 22·7 |
| *North America: total* | 777·5 | 795·4 | 843·5 | 881·1 | 945·8 | 323·7 | 337·3 |
| Canada | 161·6 | 150·2 | 170·7 | 163·1 | 181·1 | 61·4 | 59·2 |
| United States | 610·1 | 641·0 | 665·6 | 713·1 | 758·6 | 258·7 | 275·9 |
| Other countries | 5·7 | 4·1 | 7·2 | 4·9 | 6·2 | 3·6 | 2·2 |
| *Other developed countries: total* | 471·7 | 482·0 | 491·3 | 533·2 | 508·7 | 175·0 | 182·9 |
| South Africa | 166·7 | 155·5 | 142·9 | 147·4 | 145·4 | 48·3 | 49·6 |
| Japan | 86·0 | 87·2 | 103·1 | 117·9 | 110·6 | 39·7 | 39·4 |
| Australia | 151·9 | 177·9 | 184·0 | 198·4 | 182·3 | 58·8 | 69·4 |
| New Zealand | 67·0 | 61·4 | 61·3 | 69·5 | 70·4 | 28·2 | 24·5 |

*continued*

*Exports (£ millions)*

| | 1975 | | | 1976 | | | |
|---|---|---|---|---|---|---|---|
| | *2nd quarter* | *3rd quarter* | *4th quarter* | *1st quarter* | *2nd quarter* | *July* | *Augus* |
| *Oil exporting countries: total* | 763·2 | 781·3 | 917·8 | 983·0 | 1,069·9 | 368·5 | 379·3 |
| Algeria | 26·0 | 24·9 | 26·0 | 22·6 | 19·9 | 7·7 | 8·1 |
| Libya | 33·7 | 36·6 | 35·7 | 36·1 | 45·1 | 12·7 | 15·7 |
| Nigeria | 187·3 | 192·7 | 224·0 | 237·6 | 280·9 | 93·3 | 87·7 |
| Gabon | 1·1 | 0·9 | 1·1 | 1·2 | 2·0 | 0·5 | 0·4 |
| Saudi Arabia | 89·1 | 109·7 | 134·8 | 122·4 | 145·9 | 53·2 | 52·6 |
| Kuwait | 33·1 | 39·5 | 45·9 | 46·2 | 66·1 | 17·4 | 34·1 |
| Bahrain | 21·1 | 21·3 | 26·4 | 26·5 | 26·5 | 10·9 | 12·1 |
| Qatar | 24·5 | 19·2 | 23·9 | 24·8 | 33·2 | 9·8 | 9·0 |
| Abu Dhabi | 28·3 | 26·6 | 41·0 | 40·5 | 33·1 | 10·4 | 12·4 |
| Dubai | 46·6 | 44·9 | 57·8 | 70·3 | 62·7 | 22·2 | 25·9 |
| Sharjah, etc. | 1·2 | 2·3 | 4·7 | 11·3 | 17·5 | 8·5 | 5·0 |
| Oman | 23·8 | 21·8 | 30·5 | 46·9 | 37·4 | 14·0 | 13·4 |
| Iraq | 33·7 | 35·9 | 34·6 | 38·8 | 40·5 | 11·4 | 49·1 |
| Iran | 138·9 | 128·0 | 128·6 | 160·1 | 164·4 | 59·8 | 16·5 |
| Brunei | 3·9 | 3·3 | 3·6 | 3·4 | 2·9 | 1·8 | 1·4 |
| Indonesia | 21·4 | 18·2 | 24·2 | 24·9 | 17·6 | 7·0 | 6·7 |
| Trinidad and Tobago | 17·5 | 20·4 | 21·6 | 21·6 | 21·7 | 9·3 | 7·3 |
| Venezuela | 27·0 | 28·8 | 45·3 | 34·9 | 37·4 | 16·4 | 13·7 |
| Ecuador | 5·1 | 6·4 | 8·2 | 13·0 | 15·2 | 2·1 | 7·8 |
| *Other developing countries: total* | 830·1 | 805·0 | 897·5 | 906·7 | 1,028·6 | 343·8 | 371·3 |
| Egypt | 43·4 | 45·4 | 40·8 | 42·3 | 48·9 | 17·2 | 12·4 |
| Ghana | 16·9 | 23·0 | 21·5 | 22·2 | 17·5 | 9·5 | 12·4 |
| Kenya | 28·7 | 21·1 | 27·7 | 22·1 | 27·9 | 10·1 | 10·7 |
| Tanzania | 11·6 | 9·6 | 11·6 | 12·8 | 18·8 | 7·2 | 6·6 |
| Zambia | 17·2 | 16·1 | 16·9 | 19·0 | 21·5 | 7·7 | 6·7 |
| Cyprus | 9·5 | 12·5 | 19·3 | 20·8 | 18·6 | 7·3 | 6·3 |
| Lebanon | 2·6 | 2·4 | 2·2 | 6·2 | 13·0 | 3·4 | 4·9 |
| Israel | 71·9 | 51·5 | 68·0 | 51·9 | 73·9 | 26·9 | 17·0 |
| Pakistan | 18·5 | 25·7 | 26·9 | 26·7 | 36·5 | 8·0 | 5·6 |
| India | 50·7 | 52·5 | 59·0 | 65·4 | 70·1 | 23·6 | 19·6 |
| Thailand | 11·8 | 12·4 | 18·2 | 16·8 | 22·7 | 6·0 | 8·3 |
| Malaysia | 28·5 | 27·6 | 34·2 | 32·7 | 35·0 | 11·3 | 12·2 |
| Singapore | 39·7 | 40·0 | 47·9 | 44·6 | 48·5 | 15·3 | 16·9 |
| Taiwan | 13·6 | 12·8 | 14·6 | 11·6 | 14·8 | 4·7 | 5·3 |
| Hong Kong | 52·9 | 51·8 | 56·7 | 64·0 | 65·9 | 22·9 | 24·5 |
| South Korea | 14·9 | 12·4 | 15·9 | 21·3 | 15·2 | 5·5 | 5·0 |
| Philippines | 15·7 | 22·1 | 29·6 | 24·2 | 26·8 | 7·3 | 5·1 |
| Jamaica | 12·8 | 11·7 | 13·0 | 9·4 | 7·5 | 3·2 | 3·3 |
| Mexico | 36·0 | 23·1 | 24·9 | 17·4 | 20·1 | 5·8 | 4·7 |
| Chile | 5·1 | 17·3 | 7·6 | 6·6 | 14·6 | 3·9 | 2·5 |
| Brazil | 40·0 | 46·4 | 46·7 | 42·7 | 44·1 | 13·8 | 46·9 |
| Argentina | 16·3 | 15·3 | 16·7 | 19·8 | 27·7 | 9·5 | 27·6 |
| Other countries | 271·9 | 252·1 | 277·8 | 306·2 | 339·2 | 113·7 | 106·9 |
| *Centrally planned economies: total* | 189·1 | 175·2 | 186·4 | 201·2 | 246·9 | 82·6 | 66·4 |
| Soviet Union | 64·4 | 52·0 | 67·1 | 54·0 | 90·9 | 37·8 | 27·1 |
| Poland | 45·2 | 46·2 | 47·5 | 59·3 | 52·2 | 16·3 | 13·6 |
| German Democratic Republic | 13·4 | 13·4 | 10·4 | 17·5 | 18·0 | 2·8 | 2·6 |
| Czechoslovakia | 13·9 | 15·7 | 16·0 | 19·7 | 14·2 | 4·9 | 4·4 |
| Romania | 11·5 | 14·5 | 14·6 | 17·5 | 25·9 | 8·3 | 5·4 |
| Other countries | 40·6 | 33·3 | 30·7 | 33·1 | 45·7 | 11·4 | 13·3 |
| *Low value trade* | 14·4 | 13·2 | 14·2 | 23·6 | 24·2 | 8·1 | 7·4 |

*Employees in employment*

| Industry (Standard Industrial Classification 1968) | June 1976 | | | April 1977 | | | May 1977 | | | June 1977 | | |
|---|---|---|---|---|---|---|---|---|---|---|---|---|
| | Males | Females | Total | Males | Females | Total | Males | Females | Total | Males | Females | Total |
| *Total, Index of Production Industries* | *6,775·4* | *2,267·5* | *9,042·9* | *6,779·9* | *2,304·0* | *9,083·9* | *6,783·0* | *2,307·1* | *9,090·0* | *6,788·9* | *2,317·2* | *9,106·1* |
| *Total, all manufacturing industries* | *5,045·0* | *2,090·7* | *7,135·8* | *5,093·7* | *2,127·6* | *7,221·2* | *5,093·8* | *2,130·6* | *7,224·4* | *5,099·5* | *2,140·7* | *7,240·3* |
| Mining and quarrying | 328·1 | 13·9 | 342·0 | 328·6 | 13·9 | 342·5 | 329·2 | 13·9 | 343·1 | 329·0 | 13·9 | 342·9 |
| Coalmining | 285·7 | 9·7 | 295·4 | 286·2 | 9·7 | 295·9 | 286·8 | 9·7 | 296·5 | 286·6 | 9·7 | 296·3 |
| Food, drink and tobacco | 416·3 | 277·5 | 693·8 | 416·0 | 279·9 | 695·9 | 416·3 | 281·0 | 697·2 | 420·9 | 284·4 | 705·3 |
| Coal and petroleum products | 34·1 | 4·2 | 38·3 | 33·8 | 4·2 | 38·0 | 33·7 | 4·2 | 37·9 | 33·8 | 4·2 | 38·0 |
| Chemicals and allied industries | 304·0 | 119·5 | 423·5 | 308·3 | 121·3 | 429·7 | 308·3 | 121·9 | 430·2 | 308·1 | 122·4 | 430·5 |
| Metal manufacture | 419·9 | 53·5 | 473·4 | 426·5 | 54·2 | 480·7 | 425·4 | 54·4 | 479·7 | 425·9 | 54·3 | 480·2 |
| Mechanical engineering | 777·2 | 142·1 | 919·3 | 779·4 | 142·8 | 922·2 | 778·6 | 143·1 | 921·7 | 774·4 | 143·4 | 920·8 |
| Instrument engineering | 93·8 | 52·5 | 146·2 | 94·4 | 53·1 | 147·5 | 94·6 | 53·4 | 148·0 | 94·8 | 53·7 | 148·5 |
| Electrical engineering | 464·0 | 267·9 | 731·9 | 467·8 | 273·9 | 741·8 | 466·9 | 273·6 | 740·6 | 466·2 | 274·3 | 740·5 |
| Vehicles | 638·6 | 88·1 | 726·6 | 658·4 | 91·5 | 749·9 | 659·2 | 91·6 | 750·7 | 660·0 | 92·2 | 752·1 |
| Metal goods not elsewhere specified | 377·5 | 148·6 | 526·2 | 385·3 | 153·5 | 538·8 | 386·0 | 154·0 | 540·0 | 386·5 | 154·6 | 541·1 |
| Textiles | 265·4 | 220·8 | 486·2 | 267·4 | 223·2 | 490·5 | 267·5 | 223·1 | 490·6 | 267·2 | 224·9 | 492·1 |
| Leather, leather goods and fur | 23·3 | 18·4 | 41·7 | 23·2 | 18·6 | 41·8 | 23·2 | 18·6 | 41·8 | 23·1 | 18·5 | 41·6 |
| Clothing and footwear | 90·6 | 285·1 | 375·7 | 91·2 | 292·7 | 383·9 | 90·8 | 292·5 | 383·3 | 90·6 | 293·0 | 383·6 |
| Bricks, pottery, glass, cement, etc. | 201·9 | 59·6 | 261·6 | 201·2 | 61·4 | 262·6 | 202·2 | 61·8 | 264·0 | 203·0 | 62·1 | 265·2 |
| Timber, furniture, etc. | 208·9 | 50·4 | 259·3 | 207·8 | 50·0 | 257·8 | 207·8 | 49·6 | 257·4 | 207·9 | 49·9 | 257·8 |
| Paper, printing and publishing | 363·7 | 172·4 | 536·1 | 361·6 | 172·9 | 534·5 | 361·3 | 173·2 | 534·5 | 362·1 | 174·6 | 536·7 |
| Other manufacturing industries | 206·4 | 117·7 | 324·1 | 212·6 | 122·1 | 334·7 | 213·1 | 122·5 | 335·6 | 213·5 | 122·2 | 335·7 |
| Construction | 1,134·9 | 96·8 | 1,231·7 | 1,093·4 | 96·8 | 1,190·2 | 1,096·2 | 96·8 | 1,193·0 | 1,096·6 | 96·8 | 1,193·4 |
| Gas, electricity and water | 267·4 | 66·1 | 333·4 | 264·2 | 65·7 | 330·0 | 263·8 | 65·8 | 329·5 | 263·8 | 65·8 | 329·5 |

*Note* Although the estimates are given in hundreds, this does not imply that they are reliable to that degree of precision. They are shown in this way in order to give as much information as is available about the extent of the change from one month to the next.

The following tables show the value of exports (f.o.b.) and imports (c.i.f.) by commodity in 1975 and 1976 (in million £) (the numbers on the left hand side of the tables refer to the Section and Division code numbers of the *Standard International Trade Classification*).

| *Exports* | 1975 | 1976 | *Jan.–Aug.* 1977 *compared with Jan.–Aug.* 1976 |
|---|---|---|---|
| | | | *per cent* |
| **0. Food and live animals** | 884·1 | 1,034·2 | + 37 |
| 00. Live animals | 53·4 | 62·4 | + 46 |
| 01. Meat and meat preparations | 139·9 | 182·0 | + 23 |
| 02. Dairy products and eggs | 51·7 | 115·0 | + 5 |
| 03. Fish and fish preparations | 57·8 | 81·2 | + 32 |
| 04. Cereals and cereal preparations | 169·1 | 134·3 | + 30 |
| 05. Fruit and vegetables | 67·4 | 84·1 | + 44 |
| 06. Sugar, sugar preparations and honey | 162·0 | 128·7 | − 3 |
| 07. Coffee, cocoa preparations, tea and spices | 101·0 | 142·2 | +118 |
| 08 and 09. Other food and food preparations | 81·8 | 104·3 | + 44 |
| **1. Beverages and tobacco** | 543·5 | 658·3 | + 28 |
| 11. Beverages | 437·1 | 524·5 | + 28 |
| 12. Tobacco | 106·3 | 133·8 | + 26 |
| **2. Crude materials, inedible** | 533·9 | 739·5 | + 29 |
| 21. Hides, skins and furskins, undressed | 102·3 | 157·8 | + 11 |
| 23. Crude rubber (including synthetic and reclaimed) | 41·8 | 61·5 | + 33 |
| 26. Textile fibres, not manufactured and their waste | 184·5 | 260·3 | + 36 |
| 27. Crude fertilizers and minerals | 80·0 | 107·0 | + 28 |
| 28. Metalliferous ores and metal scrap | 86·1 | 99·5 | + 37 |
| Other crude materials | 39·3 | 53·3 | + 24 |
| **3. Mineral fuels, lubricants, etc.** | 813·5 | 1,254·5 | + 93 |
| 33. Petroleum and petroleum proudcts | 720·7 | 1,161·5 | + 98 |
| Coal, coke, gas and electric energy | 92·8 | 93·0 | + 31 |
| **4. Animal and vegetable oils and fats** | 27·0 | 36·2 | + 89 |
| **5. Chemicals** | 2,178·6 | 3,045·2 | + 32 |
| 51. Chemical elements and compounds | 653·4 | 1,045·3 | + 34 |
| 53. Dyeing, tanning and colouring materials | 201·4 | 282·1 | + 35 |
| 54. Medicinal and pharmaceutical products | 373·0 | 451·9 | + 25 |
| 55. Essential oils and perfume materials | 169·3 | 235·7 | + 44 |
| 58. Plastic materials and artificial resins | 354·5 | 531·5 | + 28 |
| All other | 427·0 | 498·6 | + 30 |
| **6. Manufactured goods classified chiefly by materials** | 4,267·8 | 5,788·4 | + 37 |
| 61. Leather manufactures and dressed furs | 98·8 | 148·3 | + 27 |
| 62. Rubber manufactures, not elsewhere specified | 221·0 | 299·6 | + 19 |
| 63. Wood and cork manufactures | 28·5 | 53·3 | + 78 |
| 64. Paper, paperboard and manufactures thereof | 205·8 | 278·2 | + 37 |
| 65. Textile yarn, fabrics and articles | 698·7 | 933·5 | + 32 |
| 66. Non-metallic mineral manufactures | 1,177·6 | 1,730·5 | + 54 |
| 67. Iron and steel | 681·9 | 823·4 | + 34 |
| 68. Non-ferrous metals | 539·1 | 721·3 | + 29 |
| 69. Other metal manufactures | 616·4 | 800·3 | + 28 |
| **7. Machinery and transport equipment** | 8,233·1 | 10,124·6 | + 24 |
| 71. Machinery other than electric | 4,251·9 | 5,056·1 | + 22 |
| 72. Electric machinery, apparatus and appliances | 1,530·2 | 2,003·9 | + 26 |
| 73. Transport equipment | 2,451·0 | 3,064·6 | + 24 |
| **8. Miscellaneous manufactured articles** | 1,779·7 | 2,379·5 | + 35 |
| 81. Sanitary, plumbing, heating and lighting fittings | 56·0 | 61·0 | + 57 |
| 82. Furniture | 98·4 | 142·3 | + 61 |
| 84. Clothing | 265·8 | 412·3 | + 51 |
| 85. Footwear | 52·9 | 68·2 | + 48 |
| 86. Professional, scientific and controlling instruments, photographic and optical goods, watches and clocks | 517·9 | 627·5 | + 24 |
| Other | 788·8 | 1,068·2 | + 30 |
| **5–8. Manufactured goods** | 16,459·2 | 21,337·7 | + 30 |
| **9. Commodities and transactions not classified according to kind** | 660·2 | 709·0 | + 8 |
| **Total United Kingdom exports** | 19,921·4 | 25,769·5 | + 32 |

## UNITED KINGDOM

| *Imports* | 1975 | 1976 | *Jan.–Aug.* 1977 *compared with Jan.–Aug.* 1976 |
|---|---|---|---|
| | | | *per cent* |
| **0. Food and live animals** | 3,920·7 | 4,495·4 | + 33 |
| 00. Live animals | 108·0 | 84·0 | + 18 |
| 01. Meat and meat preparations | 701·9 | 838·5 | + 29 |
| 02. Dairy products and eggs | 522·6 | 504·6 | − 5 |
| 03. Fish and fish preparations | 136·5 | 191·2 | + 40 |
| 04. Cereals and cereal preparations | 612·0 | 747·5 | + 23 |
| 05. Fruit and vegetables | 690·8 | 941·5 | + 22 |
| 06. Sugar, sugar preparations and honey | 631·6 | 428·8 | + 1 |
| 07. Coffee, cocoa and preparations, tea and spices | 321·6 | 493·1 | +130 |
| 08. Feeding stuffs for animals | 110·5 | 172·8 | + 47 |
| 09. Miscellaneous food preparations | 85·0 | 93·6 | + 86 |
| **1. Beverages and tobacco** | 414·1 | 487·9 | + 25 |
| 11. Beverages | 222·1 | 251·3 | + 31 |
| 12. Tobacco | 192·0 | 236·6 | + 18 |
| **2. Crude materials, inedible** | 2,039·6 | 3,017·4 | + 20 |
| 21. Hides, skins, and furskins, undressed | 106·7 | 171·6 | + 33 |
| 22. Oil seeds, oil nuts and oil kernels | 127·7 | 205·6 | + 73 |
| 23. Crude rubber (including synthetic and reclaimed) | 92·8 | 140·5 | + 29 |
| 24. Wood, lumber and cork | 362·2 | 585·2 | + 19 |
| 25. Pulp and waste paper | 357·8 | 463·3 | + 1 |
| 26. Textile fibres, not manufactured and their waste | 262·3 | 438·5 | + 19 |
| 27. Crude fertilizers and minerals | 155·7 | 195·3 | + 20 |
| 28. Metalliferous ores and metal scrap | 469·8 | 682·9 | + 14 |
| 29. Crude animal and vegetable materials | 104·6 | 134·4 | + 27 |
| **3. Mineral fuels, lubricants, etc.** | 4,300·8 | 5,645·1 | − 2 |
| 33. Petroleum and petroleum products | 4,159·7 | 5,511·7 | − 1 |
| **4. Animal and vegetable oils and fats** | 164·7 | 220·8 | + 53 |
| **5. Chemicals** | 1,410·8 | 1,999·4 | + 34 |
| 51. Chemical elements and compounds | 674·6 | 875·6 | + 36 |
| 55. Essential oils and perfume materials | 68·7 | 97·0 | + 47 |
| 58. Plastic materials and artificial resins | 262·0 | 462·6 | + 31 |
| All other | 405·5 | 564·2 | + 32 |
| **6. Manufactured goods classified by chiefly materials** | 4,725·7 | 6,044·9 | + 30 |
| 61. Leather, leather manufactures and dressed furs | 68·9 | 107·5 | + 47 |
| 62. Rubber manufactures | 97·2 | 130·5 | + 65 |
| 63. Wood and cork manufactures | 217·5 | 290·1 | + 20 |
| 64. Paper, paperboard and manufactures thereof | 621·8 | 826·1 | + 27 |
| 65. Textile yarn, fabrics and articles | 682·4 | 911·3 | + 28 |
| 66. Non-metallic mineral manufactures | 1,062·6 | 1,363·2 | + 54 |
| 67. Iron and steel | 823·9 | 965·7 | + 13 |
| 68. Non-ferrous metals | 819·2 | 1,035·3 | + 20 |
| 69. Other metal manufactures | 332·2 | 415·1 | + 23 |
| **7. Machinery and transport equipment** | 4,793·7 | 6,385·9 | + 37 |
| 71. Machinery other than electric | 2,568·5 | 3,254·5 | + 26 |
| 72. Electrical machinery, apparatus and appliances | 1,045·8 | 1,382·4 | + 37 |
| 73. Transport equipment | 1,179·4 | 1,749·0 | + 58 |
| **8. Miscellaneous manufactured articles** | 1,869·4 | 2,466·8 | + 30 |
| 82. Furniture | 92·0 | 122·5 | + 22 |
| 84. Clothing | 505·1 | 683·7 | + 16 |
| 85. Footwear | 123·3 | 165·5 | + 42 |
| 86. Professional, scientific and controlling instruments; photographic and optical goods | 446·8 | 574·3 | + 37 |
| Other | 702·2 | 920·7 | + 35 |
| **5–8. Manufactured goods** | 12,799·6 | 16,896·9 | + 33 |
| **9. Commodities and transactions not classified according to kind** | 489·0 | 411·3 | + 7 |
| **Total United Kingdom imports** | 24,128·4 | 31,154·7 | + 25 |

**Industry.** The table on p. 492 provides an industrial analysis of employees in employment in Great Britain for industries covered by the Index of Production at June 1976, for April, May and June 1977.

The term employees in employment (in the table) includes persons temporarily laid off but still on employers' payrolls and persons unable to work because of short-term sickness. Part-time workers are included and counted as full units.

For manufacturing industries, the returns rendered 1947 have been used to provide a ratio of change. For the remaining industries in the table, estimates of monthly changes have been provided by the nationalised industries and government departments concerned.

## COMMUNICATIONS

**Railways.** On 1 January 1948, in virtue of the Transport Act 1947, the four main-line railways of Great Britain and their associated lines, docks, steamships and hotels, together with the London Passenger Transport Board and most of the principal canal transport undertakings, passed to the ownership of the State. They were taken over by the British Transport Commission set up by the Transport Act.

The British Railways Board was constituted by the Transport Act, 1962 and took over some of the assets of the former British Transport Commission on 1 January 1963. The Board's duty is to provide railway services in Great Britain, some other ancilliary services and facilities including hotels and catering and cross-channel shipping, and hovercraft services.

Its Members are appointed by the Minister of Transport. The Railways Board was required by the Act to set up regional railway Boards to whom it delegated certain management and operational functions. The Board reserved to itself general direction of policy and financial control, industrial relations of a national character, design and manufacture of equipment and approval of major projects.

The Transport Act 1968 made a number of changes with regard to the Railways Board. The Board itself now consists of between ten and 16 members (including the Chairman and any Deputy or Vice-Chairman). The railways capital debt was written down from a figure of £1,562 millions (of which £705 million had already been suspended under the 1962 Act) to £300 million. The Minister of Transport was empowered to make specified grants to the Railways Board for the maintenance of unprofitable, but socially necessary passenger services. Grants were paid until 1973 to assist the Board while surplus track and signalling was eliminated. The Railway Board, together with certain other Boards, now enjoy extended powers as regards manufacturing for outside customers, hotel activities and the development of land. The Board are also affected by the establishment of the National Freight Corporation, who are obliged by statute to use rail to the maximum economic extent; the Board and the N.F.C. are further obliged to co-operate in the provision of freight transport services. The Act provided for the transfer to the N.F.C. of the Railways Board's collection and delivery vehicles and responsibility for the freightlines business.

The Railways Act 1974 introduced a new system of financial support in accordance with E.E.C. Regulations 1191/69 and 1192/69. As from 1 January 1975, the capital debt is reduced to £250m. Grants for unremunerative passenger services cease but the Secretary of State, who assumes authority to impose general obligations on the Board to operate passenger services, is empowered to pay compensation for provision of adequate transport services.

The Board has the power to fix its own charges. It has no common carrier obligations.

The total length of railway open for traffic in 1976 was 11,189 miles. Locomotives in use numbered 3,689 and passenger-carrying vehicles 17,111. Freight vehicles on British Railways totalled 187,000.

The number of passenger journeys in 1976 amounted to 708 million. Goods carried totalled 176·2 million tonnes.

Total receipts on British Rail in 1976 amounted to £1,243,711,000 made up as follows: passengers, £505,072,000; Government and local authority support, £319,092,000; freight, parcels and mail, £405,155,000; miscellaneous, £14,392,000. In addition receipts from shipping services amounted to £79,544,000.

British Rail's prototype high speed train, forerunner to the advanced passenger train, broke the world speed record for a diesel train in June 1973 by reaching a speed of 143 m.p.h. on a test run between York and Darlington.

The high speed train project has now successfully completed the development stage and complete fleet service—comprising a total of 73 high speed trains—will be progressively introduced in Western, Eastern and Scottish Regions.

The advanced passenger train project has now entered the prototype phase and three prototype electric advanced passenger trains are currently being built for trials between London and Glasgow.

The services, on London/Bristol and South Wales and London/Newcastle/Edinburgh routes are known as Inter-City 125 trains. With a normal maximum of 125 m.p.h. they are the fastest diesel trains in the world.

London Transport in January 1976 had in use 4,409 railway cars and 6,907 buses. The number of passenger journeys in 1975 totalled 2,056 million made up of 1,455 million bus and 601 million underground journeys. Receipts in 1975 were £187,800,000.

**Roads.** The total length of surfaced public roads in Great Britain in 1976 was 207,177 miles. Trunk roads and motorways, the main arteries for which the Secretary of State for the Environment, the Secretary of State for Wales and the Secretary of State for Scotland are fully responsible, were 9,704 miles in length. There were 20,649 miles of principal road and 176,824 miles of classified and unclassified road.

The number of vehicles with licences current during the quarter ended 30 September 1976 totalled 17,811,000 made up as follows: 14,029,000 private cars; 1,755,000 goods vehicles; 1,331,000 motor cycles and tricycles; 79,000 buses and coaches; 34,000 taxis and private hire cars. The remainder were tractors and vehicles exempt from licensing such as ambulances, fire appliances and road construction vehicles. During 1976, 7·797 billion passenger journeys were made in public service vehicles; 1,423 million of these being in vehicles of London Transport. Receipts totalled £1,037·1 million of which £128 million was taken by London Transport.

**Shipping.** Steam and motor merchant vessels on the United Kingdom register at 31 December 1976 numbered 7,114 made up as follows: 4,965 under 500 gross tons; 2,149 over 500 gross tons.

The following table shows the metric tonnage of cargo handled at specific British ports in 1974:

| *Ports* | *All Traffic Thousand Tonnes* | *Traffic other than fuels Thousand Tonnes* |
|---|---|---|
| *South East* | | |
| London | 56,499 | 19,221 |
| Medway | 27,132 | 1,757 |
| Dover | 2,764 | 2,567 |
| Shoreham | 2,069 | 937 |
| Southampton | 29,075 | 3,624 |
| Other ports | 3,223 | 2,727 |
| Total | 120,763 | 30,832 |
| *South West* | | |
| Teignmouth | 384 | 384 |
| Plymouth | 1,840 | 782 |
| Fowey | 1,170 | 1,170 |
| Par | 974 | 876 |
| Bristol | 6,013 | 3,008 |
| Other ports | 4,081 | 2,122 |
| Total | 14,462 | 8,342 |
| *Wales and Monmouthshire* | | |
| Newport | 4,583 | 4,047 |
| Cardiff | 3,384 | 2,059 |
| Port Talbot | 4,112 | 3,433 |
| Swansea | 7,118 | 860 |
| Milford Haven | 53,352 | 20 |
| Holyhead | 804 | 782 |
| Other ports | 3,089 | 2,097 |
| Total | 76,442 | 12,299 |
| *North West* | | |
| Liverpool | 27,255 | 11,104 |
| Manchester | 15,948 | 6,191 |
| Preston | 1,792 | 1,537 |
| Barrow | 69 | 68 |
| Other ports | 1,225 | 950 |
| Total | 46,289 | 19,850 |
| *Scotland* | | |
| *West Coast* | | |
| Ardrossan | 1,303 | 714 |
| Clyde | 16,826 | 5,803 |
| Other ports | 1,818 | 1,087 |
| Total | 19,947 | 7,603 |

*continued*

| *Ports* | *All Traffic Thousand Tonnes* | *Traffic other than fuels Thousand Tonnes* |
|---|---|---|
| *East Coast* | | |
| Aberdeen | 1,482 | 661 |
| Dundee | 1,060 | 204 |
| Forth | 10,308 | 4,254 |
| Other ports | 2,254 | 1,532 |
| Total | 15,104 | 6,651 |
| Total | 35,051 | 14,255 |
| *Northern East Coast* | | |
| Tyne | 5,821 | 2,408 |
| Tees and Hartlepool | 26,031 | 9,442 |
| Other ports | 4,527 | 960 |
| Total | 36,378 | 12,810 |
| *West Coast* | | |
| Whitehaven | 609 | 476 |
| Workington | 1,026 | 920 |
| Other ports | 105 | 105 |
| Total | 1,739 | 1,502 |
| Total | 38,118 | 14,312 |
| *Yorkshire and Humberside* | | |
| Hull | 5,601 | 4,282 |
| Goole | 1,563 | 948 |
| Grimsby | 893 | 850 |
| Immingham | 23,474 | 7,654 |
| Other ports | 7,502 | 3,025 |
| Total | 39,034 | 16,759 |
| *East Midlands* | | |
| Total (Boston) | 837 | 821 |
| *East Anglia* | | |
| King's Lynn | 887 | 518 |
| Great Yarmouth | 1,350 | 805 |
| Felixstowe | 3,380 | 3,152 |
| Ipswich | 2,107 | 936 |
| Harwich | 2,544 | 2,392 |
| Other ports | 703 | 560 |
| Total | 10,971 | 8,364 |
| *Total Seaports of Great Britain* | 381,966 | 126,833 |

The following are the principal shipping lines:

**Anchor Line**; (Chairman, W. G. Runciman); share capital £2,000,000; motor vessels 7; total tonnage 272,394 deadweight; *services operated:* United Kingdom–India and Pakistan; tramping. *Head Office:* 59 Waterloo Street, Glasgow, C.2.

**Bank Line Limited, The**; (Chairman, The Lord Inverforth share capital, paid up £5,517,769; motor vessels 27. Total tonnage 408,693 G.R.T. *Services Operated:* U.S.Gulf–Australia and New Zealand; Bay of Bengal–Africa and vice-versa; Bay of Bengal–Brazil and River Plate; Bay of Bengal–West Coast of South America; Far East–Africa and vice-versa; U.K., Continent–Pacific Islands; Papua New Guinea–North America and U.K., Continent; Solomons, Pacific Islands–U.K., Continent. *Head Office:* 19–21 Bury Street, London, EC3A 5AU.

**Ben Line Containers Limited**; (Chairman, M. F. Strachan); issued share capital £100,000; vessels 3; total tonnage 219,000 displacement; *services operated:* United Kingdom and North Continent–Japan, South Korea, Taiwan, P.I. Hong Kong–Singapore, West Malaysia; also over 12,000 B.L.C., I.S.O. containers in service between Europe and the Far East. *Head Office:* 29 Bernard Street, Edinburgh EH6 6R7, Scotland. Telephone 031-225 2622, Telex 72611.

**Ben Line Steamers Limited, The**; (Chairman, M. F. Strachan); issued share capital £272,795; vessels 18; total tonnage 260,000 deadweight; *services operated:* Liner services operated between United Kingdom and North Continent and the Far East including Japan and Indonesia. Also Charters and bulk carriers. *Head Office:* 29 Bernard Street, Edinburgh 6, Scotland. Telephone 031-225 2622, Telex 72611.

**Ben Line Ship Management Limited**; (Chairman, Sir F. D. D. Thomson, Bt.); issued share capital £5,000. World wide ship management services for tankers, RO/RO container ships, dry cargo vessels and bulk carriers of all sizes. *Head Office:* 29 Bernard Street, Edinburgh 6. Telephone 031-225 2622, Telex 72611.

**Bibby Line Limited**; motor vessels 21; total tonnage 688,500 gross; *services operated:* world-wide charters. *Head Office:* Norwich House, Water Street, Liverpool L2 8UW.

**The Blue Funnel Line** (see Ocean Transport and Trading Ltd., The).

**Blue Star Line**; (Chairman, E. H. Vestey); share capital £500,000; motor vessels 19 (owned), 4 (chartered); steam vessels 2 (owned), 1 (chartered); total vessels 26; total gross tonnage 266,089; *services operated:* United Kingdom to Brazil–Uruguay–Argentina, South Africa, Australia, New Zealand, North Pacific Coast. *Head Office:* 34–35 Leadenhall St., London, E.C.3.

**The Booth Steamship Co. Limited**; (Chairman, E. H. Vestey); share capital £1,800,000; motor vessels 11; total tonnage 30,336; *services operated:* United Kingdom–Continent–West Indies–North Brazil–New York–West Indies–Brazil–Peru. *Head Office:* Cunard Building, Liverpool L3 1EA.

**The British & Commonwealth Shipping Co. Limited**; (Chairman, Sir Nicholas Cayzer, Bt.); issued share capital £16,196,000. *Head Office:* 2 St. Mary Axe, London, EC3A 8BP. Principal subsidiary companies: The Clan Line Steamers Ltd., Houston Line Ltd., King Line Ltd., Scottish Lion Insurance Co. Ltd., Scottish Shire Line Ltd., Scottish Tanker Co. Ltd., The Union-Castle Mail S.S. Co. Ltd., British Air Transport (Holdings) Ltd., Air Holding Ltd., Anglo-Swedish Electric Welding Co. Ltd., BCA Travel Ltd., Beira Boating Co. Ltd., Bricomin Investments Ltd., Cayzer Irvine & Co. Ltd., International Liner Services Ltd., Meldrum Investment Trust, Ltd., Scottish Co-ordinated Investments Ltd., Sculthorpe Ltd., Airwork Services Ltd., Bristow Helicopter Group Ltd., British Island Airways Ltd., African Lands & Hotels Ltd., Cayzer Investments South Africa (Pty) Ltd., Cayzer Irvine South Africa (Pty) Ltd., Embankment Trust (Pty) Ltd., Vicbank Investments (Pty) Ltd.

**Cairn Line of Steamships Limited**; (Chairman, Captain O. O. Thomas); share capital. nominal £1,500,000. *Head Office:* Lloyd's Building, 14–19 Leadenhall Street, London, EC3V 1NP.

**CP Ships**; (Chairman, John D. Dakin) a subsidiary of Canadian Pacific Ltd.; 3 container vessels. *Services operated:* London–Rotterdam–Le Havre–Quebec. *Head Office:* 62–65 Trafalgar Square, London, WC2N 5EB. Telephone 01-930 5100.

**Charente Steam-Ship Co. Limited. Thos. & Jas. Harrison Ltd.** (Chairman, Mr. P. S. Wilson); motor vessels 27; total tonnage 232,869; *services operated:* to West Indies, Guyana, Surinam, Venezuela, Colombia, Mexico, Guatemala, British Honduras, Belize, U.S. Gulf Ports and South and East Africa including the Red Sea. *Head Office:* Mersey Chambers, Old Churchyard, Liverpool L2 8UF.

**City Line Limited**; (Chairman, D. E. Martin-Jenkins); share capital nominal £750,000; vessels 8; total tonnage 61,453 G.R.T.; *services operated:* Middle East, India and Pakistan. *Head Offie:* 75 Bothwell Street, Glasgow, C.2.

**The Clan Line Steamers Limited**; (Chairman, Sir Nicholas Cayzer, Bart.); issued share capital £3,750,000; *services operated:* United Kingdom–South and East Africa, Sri Lanka, India, Bangladesh. *Head Office:* Cayzer House, 2/4 St. Mary Axe, London, EC3A 8BP.

**The Cunard Steam-Ship Co. Limited**; (Chairman, V. C. Matthews); share capital, issued £15,500,000; subsidiaries include Cunard Line Ltd., Thos. & Jno, Brocklebank Ltd., Moss Tankers Ltd., Offshore Marine Ltd., Port Line Ltd., Transmeridian Air Cargo Ltd.; total ships (Group) at 30 June 1977, 66 and shares in six ships and 12 aircraft. *Head Office:* 1 Berkeley Street, London W1X 6NN.

**Currie Line Limited**; (Chairman, D. J. Haley); share capital £900,000; motor vessels 1; total tonnage 16,664 G.R.T.; *services operated:* United Kingdom–Germany, Holland, France, Belgium, Portugal and Scandinavia. *Head Office:* 16 Bernard Street, Leith, Edinburgh, EH6 6QA, Scotland.

**Elder Dempster Lines Limited** (see Ocean Transport and Trading Ltd.).

**Ellerman Lines Limited.** (Chairman, D. F. Martin-Jenkins, TD). Authorized and issued share capital £5,450.000. *Head*

*Office:* 12-20 Camomile Street, London EC3A 7EX Trading divisions:—

1. Ellerman City Liners (ECL). Shipping activities. *Divisional Head office:* 12-20 Camomile Street, London EC3A 7EX.
2. Ellerman Travel and Leisure (ETL). Travel activities. *Divisional Head office:* 75 Bothwell Street, Glasgow G2 6TT.
3. EWL (the transport division). Transport and warehousing activities. *Divisional Head office:* Commercial Road, Hull HU1 2SG.
4. J. W. Cameron and Co. Ltd. Brewing activities. *Divisional Head Office:* Lion Brewery, Hartlepool, Cleveland.

**Furness Withy & Co. Limited**; (Chairman, Sir James Steel); issued share capital £1,500,000 (Pref.), £26,803,054 (Ord.). Controls a group of shipping companies with combined fleets of nearly one million tons. Other interests include insurance, stevedoring, hotels and travel. *Head Office:* 105, Fenchurch Street, London EC3M 5HH.

**Fyffes' Line**; vessels 16; total tonnage 95,000 gross; *services operated:* U.K. to West Indies. *Head Office:* 15 Stratton Street, London, W1A 2LL.

**Houlder Brothers & Co. Limited**; (Chairman, John M. Houlder, MBE); share capital £1,600,000; ship managers for Houlder Line Ltd., Empire Transport Co. Ltd., Alexander Shipping Co. Ltd., Ore Carriers Ltd., Warwick Tanker Co. Ltd., South American Saint Line Ltd., Ocean Gas Transport Ltd., Vallum Shipping Co. Ltd., Pacific Maritime Services Ltd., Furness Withy Co. Ltd., and Wm. France Fenwick Co. Ltd., whose fleet comprises a total of 2 motor vessels and steam vessels; *services operated:* United Kingdom and Antwerp to Brazil and River Plate and regular services to South Africa. *Head Office:* 53 Leadenhall Street, London, EC3A 2BR.

**Johnston Warren Lines Limited**; (Chairman, John A. MacConochie, MBE); share capital £1,164,675; motor vessels 5; total tonnage 25,687 G.R.T.; *services operated:* Liverpool–St. John's–Halifax–Boston, Antwerp, Swansea and Liverpool–Greece, Turkey, Bulgaria and Rumania, Black Sea and Turkey–United Kingdom and Continent, Levant–Continent. *Head Office:* Pacific Buildings, 30 James Street, Liverpool.

**Lamport & Holt Line Limited**; (Chairman, E. H. Vestey); share capital £3,000,000; motor vessels 4; total tonnage 30,482 gross; *services operated:* West European ports–Brazil and River Plate, New York–Brazil. *Head Office:* Albion House, 30 James Street, Liverpool L2 7SY.

**Manchester Liners Limited; (Chairman, Robert B. Stoker)**; share capital £3,000,000; owned vessels 7; total tonnage 63,956 dwt; chartered vessels 2; tonnage 41,203 dwt; *services* Dublin to Montreal, Toronto, Hamilton, Detroit and Chicago calling at Dublin and Greenock. Dublin once a month and Greenock fortnightly. Manchester to Malta, Israel, Cyprus, Greece, Lebanon and Turkey. *Head Office:* Manchester Liners House, P.O. Box 189, Port of Manchester, Manchester M5 2XA.

**Ocean Transport and Trading Limited, The**; (Chairman, Sir J. Lindsay Alexander); *Address:* India Buildings, Water Street, Liverpool L2 0RB. Telephone: 051 236-9292. Cables: ODYSSEY. Telex: 629236.

*Operating Subsidiaries:*

**Blue Funnel Line Limited.** *Services:* U.K. and Continent to and from the Far East (Malaya, Singapore, Thailand, Sabah, Sarawak, Hong Kong, Korea, Philippines and Japan. Calling Sri Lanka homewards). U.K. and Continent to and from Indonesia. Australia to and from Singapore and Malaya. Gulf of Mexico and Atlantic Coast Ports of U.S.A. to Malaya, Singapore and Indonesia returning via Philippines, Hong Kong and Japan to Kingston (Ja.), Gulf and Atlantic Coast Ports of U.S.A. via Panama.

**Elder Dempster Lines Limited** (including Guinea Gulf Line Ltd.). *Services:* U.K. and Continent to and from Canary Islands and West Africa .U.S.A. and Canada to and from Canary Islands and West Africa, India, Bangladesh and Burma to West Africa.

**Glen Line Limited** (incorporating the Shire Line). *Services:* U.K. and Continent to and from the Far East (Singapore, Malaysia, Bangkok, Philippines, Sri Lanka, Manila and Japan).

**Nederlandsche Stoomvaart Maatschappij 'Oceaan' B.V.** Number of ships operated 3 (included in total of Blue Funnel Line ships). *Services:* U.K. and Continent to and from Indonesia.

**Principal Subsidiary Companies**

Ocean Fleets Ltd., Liverpool.
Straits Group Co. Ltd., Singapore.
Meyer & Co.'s Scheepvaart Mij. B.V., Amsterdam.
McGregor, Gow & Holland Ltd., London.
Roxburgh, Henderson & Co. Ltd., Glasgow.
McGregor Swire Air Charter, London.
Repcon (U.K.) Ltd., Liverpool.
Barnard Sons and Co. Ltd., St. Lucia.

**Pacific Steam Navigation Company, The** (Chairman, J. J. Gawne); *Services:* U.K.–Bermuda, Bahamas, Colombia, Ecuador, Peru and Chile. *Head Office:* Wheelwright House, 157 Regent Road, Liverpool L5 9YF.

**P. & O.—The Peninsular & Oriental Steam Navigation Co.**; (Chairman, The Earl of Inchcape); parent company of the P & O Group; authorised capital £150,000,000; 8 passenger ships, 65 cargo ships, 6 container ships, 3 bulk carriers, 7 oil/bulk/ore carriers, 9 tankers, 7 LPG carriers, 14 ferries, 7 offshore service vessels, 3 other ships; total ships 129 of 3·1m DWT; 16 ships on order (June 1977); *services operated:* cruising from Europe, Australia and North America; cargo liner services and bulk shipping world-wide; ferries U.K./Europe, Ireland, offshore oil support services in N. Sea and Australian waters; petroleum industry in N. America; road transport, freight forwarding, air freight (Pandair) and building construction (Bovis). *Head Office:* P & O Building, Leadenhall Street, London EC3V 4QL.

**Port Line Limited** (Chairman, W. B. Slater); share capital, nominal £17,900,000, issued £17,886,187; motor vessels 9. *Principal services operated:* United Kingdom–Australia, New Zealand, U.S.A.–Australia and New Zealand. *Head Office:* 1, Berkeley Street, London W1X 6NN.

**Royal Mail Lines Limited** (Chairman, J. J. Gawne); *services operated:* United Kingdom–Jamaica, Atlantic Colombia, Panama West Coast, Central America and Mexico. *Head Office:* Wheelwright House, 157 Regent Road, Liverpool, L5 9YF.

**Shaw Savill Line—Shaw Savill & Albion Co. Ltd.**; (Chairman, B. P. Shaw Esq.); share capital, nominal £6,200,000; motor vessels 16, steam vessels 1; 165,447 g.r.t.; *service operation:* United Kingdom–Continent–Australia–New Zealand; Australia–Caribbean Ports; New Zealand–Caribbean Ports; U.S. Gulf–New Zealand; U.S. Gulf–Australia. Middle Sea Trades (White Sea–Mediterranean), Motor Vessels, 5. 7,961. g.r.t. *Head Office:* Lloyd's Building, 14–19 Leadenhall Street, London, EC3V 1NP.

**Silver Line Limited** (Wholly owned subsidiary of Navcot Shipping (Holdings) Ltd.). (Chairman, R. G. Crawford): Managers of the Bishopsgate Shipping Co. Ltd., Silver Bulk Carriers Ltd., Silver Bulk Shipping Ltd., Silver Chemical Tankers Ltd., Silverdee Shipping Ltd., Silverness Shipping Ltd., Silverfleet Shipping Ltd., Silver Isle Navigation (Bermuda) Ltd., Silverfjord Shipping Co. Ltd., Alva Bay Shipping Co. Ltd., Alva Sea Shipping Co. Ltd., Alkor Shipping Co. Ltd., motor vessels 8 (owned) total tonnage 913,832; 16 (managed), total tonnage 701,428; Under construction 8 (managed), total tonnage 425,000. General Trading *Head Office:* 43 Fetter Lane, London EC4.

**South American Saint Line Limited, The**; (Chairman, John M. Houlder, MBE); share capital nominal £1,275,000; 53 Leadenhall Street, London EC3A 2BR.

**Thos. and Jno. Brocklebank Limited**; share capital £3,000,000; total ships at 30 June 1977; *services operated:* United Kingdom and Continent to Red Sea Ports, Seychelles, Sri Lanka, India and Bangladesh; Bangladesh, India and Sri Lanka to United Kingdom and Continent; Bangladesh, India and Ceylon to U.S. Gulf. *Registered Office:* Marble Arch House, 36 Edgware Road, London W2 2EL.

**Union-Castle Line**; (Chairman, Sir W. Nicholas Cayzer, Bt.); share capital, nominal £10,000,000, issued £10,000,000; *services operated:* United Kingdom and the Continent–South and East Africa (mail, passenger and cargo)–Mauritius. *Head Office:* 4 St. Mary Axe, London, EC3A 8BP.

**Civil Aviation.** Under powers derived from the Civil Aviation Act 1971, there is a Civil Aviation Authority which has responsibility for the regulation of the British air transport industry. Its functions include the licensing of air transport services by British operators, both state-owned and independent, and the regulation of the safety of civil aviation operations and of the airworthiness of the aircraft employed. The Authority also operates 8 aerodromes in the Scottish Highlands and Islands, and jointly with the Ministry of Defence, runs the National Air Traffic Services. The Department of Trade is responsible for international civil aviation relations, including the negotiation of Air Services Agreements with foreign countries and the licensing and control of public transport operations into the United Kingdom by foreign (including Commonwealth) operators.

There is a British Airways Board which exercises control over and has financial responsibility for British Airways and their subsidiaries as a group.

In accordance with the terms of the Airports Authority Act 1965 the British Airports Authority operates seven airports (the London Group, Prestwick, Edinburgh, Glasgow and Aberdeen); other airports are operated by local authorities and other bodies and agencies.

The Eurocontrol Convention, establishing an international organization to control air traffic conforming to ICAO procedures and flying in the upper airspace over the states concerned, came into force on 1 March 1963 following ratification by the six original member states: United Kingdom, Luxembourg, Belgium, France, Netherlands and the Federal Republic of Germany. The Republic of Ireland joined on 1 January 1965. A bilateral agreement has been concluded between the United Kingdom and Eurocontrol whereby the U.K. provides control of this air traffic in its upper airspace on Eurocontrol's behalf.

During the year ending 31 March 1976 British Airways carried 13,792,000 passengers on scheduled services who flew a total of 27,280 million passenger kilometres. Passengers carried on international services numbered 9,340,806 and flew 25,515 million passenger kilometres, and on domestic services 4,451,433 passengers, flying 1,765 million passenger kilometres, were carried. Total freight traffic amounted to 679 million tonne-kilometres and mail traffic to 128 million tonne-kilometres. Nearly all the freight and mail traffic was carried on international services. In the year ended 31 March 1976 British Airways made an operating surplus of 1·2 million. Taking into account the interest on capital borrowings, taxation, and losses on foreign currency, and capital borrowings the total loss for the year was 16·3 million.

Movements of aircraft including foreign planes, at civil airports in 1975 totalled 1,910,546, of which 700,504 were air transport movements. Passengers handled numbered 41,845,788. Commercial freight set down amounted to 277,401 tonnes, and freight picked up to 360,300 tonnes. Post Office mail handled at United Kingdom airports totalled 54,400 tonnes.

**British Airways (European Division)**; a state-owned Corporation; *services operated:* London to principal cities of Europe, and the Middle East, and internal in the U.K. *Head Office:* **Bealine House, Ruislip, Middlesex.**

**Posts, Telegraphs and Telephones.** Letters posted in the United Kingdom during the year ended 31 March 1977 totalled 9,457·8 million. Parcels numbered 152·3 million. Postal orders issued numbered 192,200,000 valued at £527·5 million.

Telegrams handled in the year ended 31 March 1977 totalled 18,649,000 of which 3,367,000 were inland and 15,282,000 foreign.

In March 1977 there were 22,076,000 private telephones. Public call offices in use at 31 March 1977 numbered 77,302.

**Broadcasting.** The British Broadcasting Corporation was set up by Royal Charter on 1 January 1927 as successor to the British Broadcasting Company. The Charter has been renewed from time to time; the present Charter expires on 31 July 1979. Under the Charter the BBC is responsible for public service broadcasting in sound and in television in the United Kingdom.

The Corporation is precluded from broadcasting commercial advertisements or sponsored programmes. The greater part of the money for operating the public service broadcasting in the United Kingdom is related to the sale of broadcast receiving licences costing £8 for combined radio and monochrome television, and £18 for combined radio, monochrome and colour television. The radio only licence has been abolished. At 31 March 1976 there were in force 9,148,732 monochrome television licences; and 8,639,252 colour television licences. The gross revenue from the sale of licences for the year to 31 March 1976 amounted to £234,108,000. After deductions for Post Office charges of £21,246,000 the income receivable by the Corporation for the year amounted to £212,862,000.

The BBC has extensive research and design facilities and its engineers have been responsible for many new and important developments in the field of broadcast engineering. The Corporation has received the Queen's Award to Industry on two occasions, firstly for work on the development of television standard converters (which enable television signals to be converted electronically from one system to another) and secondly for a system known as 'Sound in Syncs' which enables the sound component of a television programme to be distributed with the picture signal, thus saving the need for separate sound circuits.

The BBC has also introduced a new system for distributing its sound radio programmes throughout the country based on a technique known as Pulse Code Modulation; this provides for a number of programmes, in stereo if necessary, which can be conveyed over any required distance without loss of quality.

In 1972 the BBC proposed a new system, already in experimental use and called 'Ceefax', to enable television viewers to select any one of a number of pages of information, which then appears on the television screen. The information is transmitted as part of the picture signal but is separated from it and stored in the receiver. The service provides News Headlines, Sports Results, Weather Forecasts, Financial News, Programme Details and so on. The information can be continuously up-dated and is available whenever the viewer cares to select it.

After an experimental period the Home Office, in November 1976, gave permission for a full service. Mass production of teletext receivers began in 1977.

The BBC produces two television programmes—BBC-1 and BBC-2—both of which are transmitted on UHF (Ultra High Frequency) using the 625 line PAL colour system, which provides viewers with the option of black and white, or colour reception. The UHF service is already available to about 95 per cent of the population, and this coverage is being increased as rapidly as possible. BBC-1 is also transmitted on VHF using the 405 line system, which was the only system used for television broadcasting in the United Kingdom from 1936 until 1964. It is intended that the 405 line transmissions should be discontinued some time after 1980. The number of 405 line receivers is falling quite rapidly as the number of 625 line, and particularly colour, receivers increases.

BBC-2 is at present broadcast in all parts of the country without variation. BBC-1 on the other hand has provision for regional variations and this is extensively used, especially in Wales and Scotland, in order to provide special news and other programmes of local interest.

In Radio the BBC provides four complementary services, Radio 1 (the 'pop' network), Radio 2 (light music), Radio 3 (serious music plus programmes reflecting the arts) and Radio 4 (news, current affairs and other speech programmes). Most programmes are available on both VHF as well as long or medium waves but Radio 1 is normally available on medium wave only, although the programme is transmitted on the Radio 2 VHF network at times. In November 1967 the BBC began an experiment in local radio and there are now twenty BBC local radio stations covering all the main centres of population in England, and broadcasting on both VHF and medium wave. The BBC's external services are financed by a grant-in-aid and no part of their cost falls directly on the holders of wireless licences. News bulletins, talks and other varied programmes are broadcast in English and 39 other languages to audiences all over the world.

**Independent Broadcasting.** The Independent Television Authority (now the Independent Broadcasting Authority) was created by the Television Act 1954 to 'provide . . . television broadcasting services additional to those of the BBC and of high quality both as to transmission and as to the matter transmitted'. The Authority bases its policy on the Independent Broadcasting Authority Act, 1973. This Act was amended in 1974 to extend the life of the Authority to 1979. Authority members are appointed by the Home Secretary, and three must make their special interest the affairs of Scotland, Wales and Northern Ireland respectively.

The Authority at present consists of the Chairman, The Lady Plowden, DBE; Deputy Chairman, Mr. Christopher Bland; Walter Anderson, CBE; Dr. T. F. Carbery; Professor J. Ring; Mrs. Mary Warnock; A. J. R. Pursell; Professor Huw Morris-Jones; The Marchioness of Anglesey, CBE; Mrs. A. M. Coulson; W. J. Blease.

The Authority has an administrative staff, headed by the Director General, Sir Brian Young, and includes a group of technical experts responsible for future planning and the building of new transmitters.

The Authority does not provide programmes itself although empowered in exceptional circumstances to do so, but appoints a group of Programme Contractors for this purpose. The Authority itself has four main functions: to choose the programme companies; to plan, provide, and operate the transmitters; to supervise the programmes and their scheduling; and to control the advertising.

The programme contractors earn their revenues by the sale of advertising time; the rentals they pay to the Authority enable it to meet all its outgoings. Advertisers may only purchase short 'spot' periods. The advertisements must be 'clearly distinguishable as such and recognizably separate from the rest of the programme.' In no circumstances can the programme material itself be sponsored by an advertiser.

In order to preserve the national and international impartiality of news broadcasts a separate company, Independent Television News, was set up. This company is a non-profit-making organization supported by all the ITV programme contractors and supplies a common service to them all, though each contractor may, if he wishes, also produce a programme of local news. The arrangement for the gathering and editing of such local news is subject to the Authority's approval.

Independent Television started broadcasting on 22 September 1955 from its London station at Croydon, a 120 kW station serving about 12 million people. There are now about 50 VHF transmitters and more than 300 UHF transmitters covering all parts of the United Kingdom and Northern Ireland.

About 99 per cent of the people of the U.K. are within range of one or more of the IBA's transmitting stations. Additional relay stations are being built to improve or extend coverage. The duplicate ITV service on 625-lines in UHF which came into service in London, the Midlands and the North of England (Lancashire and Yorkshire) in November 1969, has now been extended in colour to all regions, with a population coverage of about 98 per cent. Colour has been introduced into this duplicate service. Under the Sound Broadcasting Act, 1972, the Authority was renamed 'The Independent Broadcasting Authority', and its functions extended to cover the provision of Independent Local Radio.

The Independent Local Radio Companies are appointed and controlled by the Independent Broadcasting Authority in the same way as the Independent Television Companies. They offer an alternative service of news, information and entertainment in the United Kingdom.

There are nineteen ILR stations now on the air: in London (2), Glasgow, Birmingham, Manchester, Tyne/Wear, Swansea, Liverpool, Edinburgh, Plymouth, Sheffield and Rotherham, Nottingham, Teesside, Belfast, Bradford, Ipswich, Portsmouth, Reading, and Wolverhampton.

Independent Radio News, a subsidiary of the London Broadcasting Company Ltd. (which operates the London News and Information Station) acts as a news agency for all other ILR companies, providing spoken and other live material, and a teleprinter service.

**Daily Express.** F.1900. 121–128 Fleet Street, London, E.C.4. Independent.

**Daily Mail.** F. 1896. Average Net Sale January–June, 1977, 1,829,380 copies. New Carmelite House, Carmelite Street, London EC4Y 0JA.

**Daily Mirror.** F. 1903. Holborn Circus, London, EC1P 1DQ. Independent Left.

**The Daily Telegraph.** F.1855. 135 Fleet Street, London, EC4P 4BL. Independent.

**Financial Times.** F.1888. Bracken House, Cannon Street, London, EC4P 4BY.

**The Guardian.** F. 1821. 119 Farringdon Road, London, EC1R 3ER. Independent.

**The Sun.** 30 Bouverie Street, London, E.C.4. F. 1969. Independent.

**The Times.** F.1785. New Printing House Square, Grays Inn Road, London, WC1X 8EZ. Independent.

## ATOMIC ENERGY

### United Kingdom Atomic Energy Authority

The Authority was created by Act of Parliament in 1954 to take over from the Ministry of Supply responsibility for the rapidly growing programme of research and development into all aspects of atomic energy. A public corporation with a structure akin to that of a big industrial organization was considered more appropriate than that of a Government Department in order to meet the need for closer contact and co-operation with industry and the widening applications of nuclear techniques.

The Authority has been, and remains, responsible for research and development on reactor systems suitable for the generation of electricity in U.K. conditions; this has included the construction of prototypes. For much of its history the Authority has also been responsible for the production and marketing of nuclear fuel and its reprocessing after use; the production and marketing of radioisotopes, together with the development of new applications, as well as production and research work associated with the military programme. The Authority, however, far from regarding the original structure as static, encouraged the changes which resulted in the formation of separate companies to market nuclear fuel and radioisotopes.

The expertise of the Authority's Production Group in manufacturing and reprocessing nuclear fuel had developed into a thirty million pound a year international business by 1970. The production and uses of radioisotopes, also largely pioneered in the U.K. by the Authority, was also yielding an income of several million pounds each year. At this stage, it was decided that these operations should be undertaken by separate commercial organizations and in 1971 British Nuclear Fuels Ltd. and The Radiochemical Centre, were set up. (See separate entries for BNFL and TRC.)

With the formation of these two companies and with weapons research passing to the Ministry of Defence, the Authority's role became four-fold. First, their stewardship on behalf of the Government in atomic affairs, generally; secondly, research into new reactor systems and safety and environmental matters; thirdly, continuing R & D support for Britain's nuclear industry and, fourthly, research using the Authority's special expertise and skills in areas outside the nuclear power field.

The Authority is managed by a board, of which the Chairman is Sir John Hill, and the Deputy Chairman Dr. Walter Marshall, C.B.E., F.R.S., and on which there are a number of other full and part-time members. The Authority, whose headquarters are in London, has the following organization:

**Northern Division.** The Northern Division of the Authority is centred on the Nuclear Power Development Establishment at Risley, near Warrington, Lancs., which was known formerly as the headquarters of the Reactor Group. This management unit is responsible for the design and development of nuclear reactors; it comprises a Nuclear Power Development Establishment at Dounreay, Thurso, Highland, and Nuclear Power Development Laboratories at Risley itself (formerly known as the Risley Engineering and Materials Laboratory); Springfields, Lancs., (formerly the Springfields Reactor Fuel Element Laboratories); and Windscale, Cumbria (formerly the Reactor Development Laboratories). The Atomic Energy Establishment at Winfrith, Dorset, continues under that name as an additional centre for reactor research and development work (outwith the Northern Division). Each of the sites named contributes to the work of the Authority as a consultant to the Electricity Boards, overseas organizations and the Nuclear Power Company, which was formed to build nuclear power stations. Staff at various sites are also engaged on research work outside the nuclear field, as authorized for example by Requirements Boards of the Department of Industry.

**Research.** The Atomic Energy Research Establishment at Harwell, Oxon., is the largest research laboratory of the Authority. About half of its effort is directly concerned with problems of reactor development and nuclear power generally, with particular reference to materials research; this is supported by a related programme of underlying research. The rest of the laboratory's work is divided about equally between work done for industry and for the public sector (including Government departments) in areas which are not necessarily related to nuclear energy. Most of this work is done on direct repayment, but a small effort is devoted to joint innovative projects with industrial firms.

Culham Laboratory (also Oxon) is the UKAEA centre for research in nuclear fusion and plasma physics and associated technology. The British fusion research programme is carried out in close collaboration with other countries in the European Economic Community. In addition, the Laboratory undertakes contract research in the fields of electrotechnology, laser applications, space technology, electrostatics and computing.

**Britain's nuclear power programme**

In October 1956, only three years after site construction started, Her Majesty the Queen performed the opening ceremony at Calder Hall, the world's first commercial-scale nuclear power station. In 1959 the Authority commissioned another four-reactor station at Chapelcross, Scotland.

Nuclear power stations based on the Calder Hall 'magnox' concept, but built for the generating boards by the British nuclear industry, now have an installed capacity of more than 5,000 MW(e). The first two, Berkeley (Gloucestershire) and Bradwell (Essex), started to produce, electricity in the summer of 1962 and the others, at Hinkley Point 'A' (Somerset), Trawsfynydd (Merionethshire), Dungeness 'A' (Kent), Sizewell (Suffolk), Oldbury-on-Severn (Gloucestershire), Hunterston (Ayrshire), and Wylfa (Anglesey), were all on load by 1971. At the end of 1976 the Magnox stations in the U.K. had produced about a quarter of the world's nuclear electricity and, in the year 1976–77, accounted for more than 12 per cent of all electricity generated in Great Britain.

Two of the five Advanced Gas-Cooled Reactor (AGR) stations being built in the U.K. began producing electricity in 1976. When all five are completed they will provide some 6,000 MW(e) of capacity. The Authority continues to develop both thermal and fast reactor systems to meet future energy needs.

**British Nuclear Fuels Limited.** A private limited company all the shares in which are currently owned by the Government. The Company manufactures uranium fuel elements and uranium hexafluoride at Springfields in Lancashire. The reprocessing of irradiated nuclear fuel and the manufacture of plutonium fuel elements is carried out at the Windscale factory in Cumbria. The Company operates a uranium enrichment plant at Capenhurst in Cheshire and nuclear power reactors at Calder Hall (Cumbria) and Chapelcross (Dumfriesshire). BNFL's Head Office and design offices are at Risley in Cheshire.

BNFL is the U.K. shareholder in the international nuclear companies: CENTEC, URENCO, United Reprocessors GmbH, and Nuclear Transport Ltd.

**The Radiochemical Centre Limited**

The Radiochemical Centre was established under public ownership in 1946 for the purpose of providing a reliable supply of radioactive products for use in medicine, science and industry.

From 1954–1971 the Centre was a trading establishment within the U.K.A.E.A. On 1 April 1971, The Radiochemical Centre Limited was registered as a company, the shares being at present wholly owned by the U.K.A.E.A.

The main laboratories and offices are situated at Amersham, where work with radioactive materials began for war-time purposes in 1940. There is also a Department at Harwell which organizes isotope production in the research reactors of the U.K.A.E.A.

The Company has subsidiaries in West Germany (Amersham Buchler GmbH and Co. KG), in the U.S.A. (Amersham/Searle Corp.).

**International Co-operation**

The UK continues to support the activities of the International Atomic Energy Agency (IAEA) and of the Nuclear Energy Agency of the OECD. The U.K. is also a participant in the joint NEA/IAEA and WHO/FAO food irradiation project based on Karlsruhe.

A contract has been signed between the European Atomic Energy Community (Euratom) and the U.K.A.E.A. to advance collaboration in research into controlled nuclear fusion and plasma physics.

U.K. collaboration in the nuclear field is maintained with countries of the Commonwealth, Europe, including the European Economic Community, Latin America, Japan, South Africa, the U.S.A. and the U.S.S.R.; through bilateral and other agreements for the exchange of information, attachment of personnel, visits and other reciprocal arrangements. This collaboration extends over a wide variety of topics, including thermal and fast reactor systems development, reactor safety, fuel enrichment and reprocessing, fusion research and other research and development.

## EDUCATION

### England and Wales

The educational system of England and Wales is governed by the Education Acts, 1944–76. The local administration of the Education Service under these acts is the responsibility of 105 local education authorities of which eight are in Wales. From 1 November 1970 primary and secondary education in Wales became the responsibility of the Secretary of State for Wales.

Education is compulsory for all children from the age of five years to 16 years.

There are three stages of education—*primary*, for children up to 11 years; *secondary*, from 11 to 16 years or, for those remaining at secondary schools, up to 18; and *higher and further education* which includes most other organized education or leisure time recreation for persons over compulsory school age.

Broadly speaking children attend *infants' schools* from five to seven, and *junior schools* from seven to 11, but in a growing number of cases (particularly those where secondary education has been organized on comprehensive lines) other systems, such as first schools and middle schools, have been introduced with breaks at various ages. There are also *nursery* schools and classes for children under 5 and provision is increasing.

Many children in maintained schools switch to secondary education at 11. In many areas, secondary education has been reorganized on comprehensive lines (with a variety of patterns) and children are admitted to these schools without reference to their ability or aptitude. In areas where this reorganization has yet to take place pupils transferring from primary to secondary schools take a selection test to determine whether they should receive their education in grammar, secondary modern or in one of the few remaining technical schools.

Further education is given in tertiary colleges, colleges of technology, technical colleges, agricultural establishments, art and commercial schools, evening institutes, etc.

30 polytechnics, as major centres within the further education system, have been established to complement the universities and colleges in the field of higher education. Some reorganization is taking place which will result in polytechnics and other colleges of higher and further education merging with colleges of education to form new combined institutions within the non-university education sector.

In January 1976 there were 631 nursery, 22,708 primary, 1,154 middle and 4,473 secondary schools maintained by the local education authorities, accommodating 8,999,089 full-time and 151,712 part-time pupils. About one-third of these schools were being directed by voluntary bodies, mainly religious. In addition 179 schools including 170 grammar schools received grants direct from central Government funds. As from September 1976 the grants being paid to the grammar schools are being phased out. There were also 1,614 special schools and hospital schools for handicapped children.

In November 1975 there were 7,900 establishments in England and Wales for further education (including 575 major establishments). Over 3,527,000 part-time students course and 412,000 full-time and sandwich-course students were enrolled at that date.

In January 1977 full-time teachers employed by local education authorities numbered 534,989, of whom 245,699 were men and 289,290 women.

In October 1975 there were 197 establishments offering initial teacher training courses. These included departments of education in 30 universities and 14 polytechnics.

### Scotland

The educational system of Scotland is governed by thg Education (Scotland) Act 1962. The general supervision of the national system of education, except for the universities, is the responsibility of the Secretary of State for Scotland acting through the Scottish Education Department. The duty of providing education locally rests with the education authorities.

There are three groups of schools in Scotland: education authority schools, grant-aided schools and independent/private schools. Education authority and grant-aided schools include nursery, primary and secondary schools of all types and also special schools for handicapped pupils. In session 1975/76 there were 3,640 education authority and grant-aided schools and departments of which 376 were nursery, 2,533 primary, 467 secondary and 264 special. The total number of pupils in education authority and grant-aided schools and departments (including special) was 1,076,178 (550,681 boys, 525,497 girls) of which 22,750 (11,570 boys, 11,180 girls) received nursery education. There were 28 grant-aided secondary schools conducted by bodies of managers who receive grants direct from the Scottish Education Department (but grants to the schools that elect not to join the public system of education will be phased out over six years beginning in 1976–77); 26 of these schools have primary departments; all, except one, charge fees. There were also 103 registered independent schools which are conducted by the proprietors without aid from public funds and include both preparatory schools for pupils up to about age 13 and schools for other pupils.

Education authorities are free to decide for themselves the form of secondary education best suited to their areas. At present all 12 Education Authorities have either implemented or are implementing a reorganization of secondary education on comprehensive lines. In session 1975–76 over 98 per cent of secondary pupils attended education authority schools which have a comprehensive intake to the first year. The majority of these schools provide a full range of courses appropriate to all levels of ability from first to sixth year, although a decreasing number offer only two-and four-year courses, on completion of which children may continue their secondary education at the nearest six-year comprehensive. There are also a few schools which are selective in that they admit only the less able pupils and which offer only non-certificate courses or courses leading to the Ordinary grade in the Scottish Certificate of Education examinations. Pupils from these schools wishing to continue their education to the Higher grade of the SCE may also transfer to the fifth and sixth year local comprehensive.

The first two years of secondary courses are, to an increasing extent, becoming an exploratory period during which the progress of each pupil is carefully observed and during which pupils are given experience of a wide variety of subjects so that they can find out where their particular aptitudes, abilities and interests lie. The content of any particular course is decided by the education authority in consultation with the teachers. In the first two years, courses normally include English, History, Geography, Mathematics, Science, Art, Music, Physical Education, Religious Education and courses of a practical nature such as Technical Education and Home Economics. In addition, as many pupils as staffing allows begin the study of a modern foreign language. During this period, some pupils may add a subject, usually a second foreign language (classical or modern). At the end of the second year, a preliminary decision is taken as to the subjects, if any, in which pupils will aim at presentation in the examinations on the Ordinary Grade of the Scottish Certificate of Education; these examinations are generally taken in the fourth year. Arrangements are sometimes made for pupils to combine the more demanding certificate courses in some subjects with less arduous ones in others. Though some selection of subjects may be necessary at this stage the general aim has been and still is to maintain a well balanced curriculum for all pupils, whether studying for an external examination or not. At the later stages of courses for pupils who intend to leave school at the statutory leaving age (16 years) some of the work done may have a vocational bias or be based on some centre of interest.

Pupils continuing at school to the 5th and 6th years and aiming at presentation at the Scottish Certificate of Education Higher Grade examinations may choose from a very wide range of subjects. The Certificate is awarded to those who obtain a suitable grading in at least one subject on the Ordinary or Higher Grade. In addition, pupils who remain at school for a 6th year can be presented in a limited range of subjects for the Certificate of Sixth Year Studies, an examination designed to prepare students for entry to higher education but not a formal requirement for such entry.

In session 1975–76, full-time qualified teachers employed by education authorities and other managers of grant-aided schools numbered 54,917, of whom 18,697 were men and 36,220 women. Teachers are trained at 10 colleges of education.

### Universities

In 1975–76 in England there were 33 universities, one university institute of Science and Technology (Manchester). There was the University of Wales comprising constituent colleges at Aberystwyth, Bangor, Cardiff, Swansea, Lampeter, the Welsh National School of Medicine, and the University of Wales Institute of Science and Technology. There were eight universities in Scotland and two in Northern Ireland.

The following table shows the number of full-time professors, readers, senior lecturers, lecturers and assistant lecturers, together with the number of students, at those universities in operation in 1975–76.

| *University or College* | *Total Students* | *Teaching staff wholly paid from general university funds* |
|---|---|---|
| Aston | 4,529 | 452 |
| Bath | 3,351 | 331 |
| Birmingham | 7,980 | 1,055 |
| Bradford | 4,175 | 493 |
| Bristol | 6,637 | 754 |
| Brunel | 2,375 | 268 |
| Cambridge | 10,849 | 1,089 |
| City | 2,202 | 302 |
| Durham | 4,192 | 392 |
| East Anglia | 3,472 | 325 |
| Essex | 2,294 | 246 |
| Exeter | 4,076 | 401 |
| Hull | 4,174 | 479 |
| Keele | 2,320 | 298 |
| Kent | 3,008 | 355 |
| Lancaster | 3,828 | 424 |
| Leeds | 9,480 | 1,076 |
| Leicester | 3,774 | 443 |
| Liverpool | 7,151 | 897 |
| London Graduate School of Business Studies | 194 | 32 |
| London University | 35,941 | 5,300 |
| Loughborough | 3,684 | 380 |
| Manchester Business School | 132 | 33 |
| Manchester | 10,381 | 1,407 |
| University of Manchester Institute of Science and Technology | 3,540 | 482 |
| Newcastle | 6,682 | 763 |
| Nottingham | 5,988 | 682 |
| Oxford | 11,591 | 1,299 |
| Reading | 5,329 | 612 |
| Salford | 3,968 | 476 |
| Sheffield | 7,121 | 856 |
| Southampton | 5,437 | 616 |
| Surrey | 2,770 | 311 |
| Sussex | 4,191 | 436 |
| Warwick | 3,944 | 345 |
| York | 2,814 | 276 |
| Total England | 203,574 | 24,386 |
| Aberystwyth U.C. | 2,974 | 376 |
| Bangor U.C. | 2,720 | 342 |
| Cardiff U.C. | 4,568 | 492 |
| St. David's, Lampeter | 536 | 62 |
| Swansea U.C. | 3,221 | 390 |
| Welsh National School of Medicine | 587 | 111 |
| University of Wales Institute of Science and Technology | 2,530 | 265 |
| Total Wales | 17,136 | 2,038 |
| Total England and Wales | 220,710 | 26,424 |
| Aberdeen | 5,325 | 699 |
| Dundee | 2,758 | 406 |
| Edinburgh | 9,337 | 1,127 |
| Glasgow | 9,241 | 1,210 |
| Heriot-Watt | 2,792 | 264 |
| St. Andrews | 3,037 | 321 |
| Stirling | 2,075 | 242 |
| Strathclyde | 5,983 | 688 |
| Total Scotland | 40,548 | 4,957 |
| Total Great Britain | 261,258 | 31,381 |
| Queen's, Belfast | 5,735 | 610 |
| Ulster, Coleraine | 1,721 | 217 |
| Total Northern Ireland | 7,456 | 827 |
| Total United Kingdom | 268,714 | 32,208 |

There were also 26,317 part-time students attending the above institutions at the time of the student count.

All these universities and institutions are self-governing. Those in England, Wales and Scotland receive Exchequer grants on the recommendation of the University Grants Committee; Queen's University, Belfast, and the New University of Ulster, Coleraine, receive grants from the Department of Education, Northern Ireland. Exchequer grants made to the institutions on the University Grants Committee's list in 1975–6 amounted to over £632 million.

**RELIGION**

There is complete freedom of religious belief and worship in the United Kingdom. There are four churches in communion with the See of Canterbury. These are the Church of England, the Church in Wales, the Church of Ireland and the Episcopal Church in Scotland.

**The Established Church of England,** which is Protestant, Catholic and Episcopal, is the official religion in England. It is the centre of that community of autonomous Christian Churches known as the Anglican Communion.

The Sovereign is, under God, the supreme Governor of the Church of England, with the statutory right to nominate archbishops and bishops. For ecclesiastical legislation there is a General Synod, consisting of bishops, clergy and laity. Measures passed by this Synod are submitted to the Ecclesiastical Committee, which consists of 15 members of the House of Lords and 15 members of the Commons. This Committee reports to Parliament on any new measure submitted to it. If both Houses of Parliament approve of the measure, it is submitted to the Sovereign for the Royal Assent, on receiving which it becomes law.

England is divided into two ecclesiastical provinces, Canterbury and York. Each province is divided into bishoprics under the archbishops of Canterbury and York, respectively, and has a Convocation.

The Province of Canterbury contains, besides the diocese of Canterbury, 28 bishoprics. They are London, Winchester, Bath and Wells, Birmingham, Bristol, Chelmsford, Chichester, Coventry, Derby, Ely, Exeter, Gloucester, Guildford, Hereford, Leicester, Lichfield, Lincoln, Norwich, Oxford, Peterborough, Portsmouth, Rochester, St. Albans, St. Edmundsbury and Ipswich, Salisbury, Southwark, Truro and Worcester.

The Province of York contains, besides the diocese of York, 13 other bishoprics—Durham, Blackburn, Bradford, Carlisle, Chester, Liverpool, Manchester, Newcastle, Ripon, Sheffield, Sodor and Man, Southwell and Wakefield. Nearly all of the dioceses in the provinces of Canterbury and York have assistant bishops and suffragan bishops.

In addition there are a number of bishoprics in the Commonwealth and other parts of the world under the ecclesiastical jurisdiction of the Archbishop of Canterbury.

Except for the diocese of Sodor and Man there is a cathedral in every diocese and this is the mother church of the diocese. The Church of England in each diocese is administratively divided into archdeaconries and rural deaneries.

The parishes are administratively arranged in 724 rural deaneries and 107 archdeaconries. According to the Government Census of Ecclesiastical Areas of 1961, there were 14,191 parishes in the Provinces of Canterbury and York which includes the Channel Islands, The Isle of Man and a small part of Wales in the counties of Radnorshire, Montgomeryshire and Monmouthshire. Owing to the continuing decline in the supply of ordained men for the ministry it is no longer possible for each of the smaller parishes to have an incumbent. Since 1961 a number of parishes have been joined together and some new ones created, so that at the 31 December 1976 there were 13,860 parishes, 10,675 benefices, 90 conventional districts, divided into 9,020 parochial livings. There were 17,185 parochial churches and about 2,500 extra-parochial churches and chapels.

In 1973 27,484,000 or 60 per cent of the population of the provinces of Canterbury and York (excluding persons born elsewhere) were baptized members of the Church of England and 9,304,000, or 20 per cent, were confirmed members. The Electoral Roll in 1973 contained 2,021,137 names of persons aged 17 years and over and there were 1,684,111 Easter communicants; 297,580 infant baptisms, i.e. 465 per 1,000 live births; and 96,379 confirmations, i.e. 16·7 per 1,000 population aged 12 to 20. The total number of marriages in England and Wales in 1972 was 426,241, of which 155,538 were solemnized according to the rites of the Church of England, i.e. 365 per 1,000 of all marriages.

**The Church in Wales** (i.e. the Anglican Church in Wales) was disestablished on 31 March 1920. When it was disestablished, property belonging to the Church in Wales was handed over for administration to a body representing the Church (called the Representative Body) and to certain other authorities including the University of Wales. This independent province of the Anglican Communion has six bishoprics: Llandaff, Bangor, St. Asaph, Monmouth, St. Davids and Swansea and Brecon.

The Province of Wales comprises an area of 5,164,111 acres and the population according to the census of 1971 numbered 2,686,665. There are 14 archdeaconries and 722 incumbencies in the Province.

**The Church of Scotland,** the Established Church in Scotland, is Presbyterian. In each parish there is a kirk (church) session, consisting of the minister and several elders, men or women, who are ordained for life to assist in the pastoral oversight of the Congretation. Parishes are grouped into presbyteries and these into synods. The presbyteries meet frequently and the synods twice yearly. There are 12 synods and 47 presbyteries in Scotland, one presbytery in England, one in Europe and one in Jerusalem.

There is a General Assembly of 1,298 members, half being ministers and half elders, elected by the presbyteries. The Assembly appoints a Moderator, who presides over its meetings. At this Assembly the Sovereign, when not present in person, is represented by the Lord High Commissioner.

At 31 December 1976 there were in the Church of Scotland 1,942 congregations with 1,020,403 members.

**The Episcopal Church in Scotland** (in communion with the Church of England) has seven bishoprics—Aberdeen and Orkney, Argyll and The Isles, Brechin, Edinburgh, Glasgow and Galloway, Moray, Ross and Caithness, and St. Andrews, Dunkeld and Dunblane. In 1977 there were 340 churches, 209 stipendary clergy, 163 non-stipendary clergy, and 76,300 members.

**Roman Catholic Religion.** Roman Catholics in England and Wales in 1974 were 4,156,038, and in Northern Ireland at 497,547 (1961 census). There are five Archbishoprics and 14 Bishoprics in England and Wales. The Archbishop of Westminister is generally made a Cardinal. There are two Archbishoprics and eight Bishoprics in Scotland. In Scotland in 1976 there were 814,100 Catholics, 1,181 priests, 1,215 nuns, 465 parishes, 14,467 baptisms and 6,569 marriages. Three new bishops have joined the hierarchy in 1977 and it now consists of a Cardinal, an archbishop and nine bishops. The Roman Catholics have approximately 4,980 secular priests and 3,710 churches and chapels in England and Wales. In 1974 there were 4,849 adult conversions, 87,284 Baptisms (up to seven years), and 40,675 marriages.

**The Jewish Community** in the United Kingdom comprises about 410,000 people.

For secular purposes the Jewish community's official representative organization, recognized in Parliamentary statutes, is the Board of Deputies of British Jews, founded in 1760. The main Synagogal institutions in the Metropolis are the United Synagogue (whose Ecclesiastical Head is Dr. I. Jacobovits, the Chief Rabbi of the United Hebrew Congregations of the Commonwealth); the Federation of Synagogues; the Union of Orthodox Hebrew Congregations; the Spanish and Portuguese Jews' Congregation; the Reform Synagogues of Great Britian; the Union of Liberal and Progressive Synagogues. Most of the provincial Synagogues are independent, but recognize the authority of the Chief Rabbi.

The total number of synagogues throughout the United Kingdom is about 300.

The Jewish community has established in London and provincial centres a number of Welfare organizations and other Institutions, as well as a number of day schools many of which are recognized by the Department of Education and Science.

**Other Religious Denominations** in the United Kingdom include: the Methodist Church, with about 1,150,000 full members and over 5,000 ministers; the Independent Methodists, with over 9,000 members and nearly 14,000 attending Sunday schools, 155 chapels and 331 ministers; the Congregational Union, with about 372,000 members and 2,600 ministers; the Baptists, with 338,000 members and about 2,000 ministers; the General Assembly of Unitarian and Free Christian Churches, with about 80,000 members, 339 chapels and 275 ministers; the Wesley Reform Union, with 6,300 members and about 13,000 Sunday-school scholars, 178 chapels, 20 ministers and over 300 lay preachers. In recent years there has been an increase of Hindus and Muslims resident in the United Kingdom.

# NORTHERN IRELAND

**Capital**—Belfast.

## GOVERNMENT

Northern Ireland comprises the counties of Antrim, Armagh, Down, Fermanagh, Londonderry and Tyrone, and the County Borough of Belfast. A subordinate Parliament and executive Government were established in Northern Ireland in 1921 by the Government of Ireland Act 1920. Under that Act twelve members, however, are returned by Northern Ireland constituencies to the United Kingdom House of Commons.

An Act was passed at Westminister on 30 March 1972 transferring for one year to a Secretary of State for Northern Ireland and the United Kingdom Parliament the legislative and executive powers formerly vested in the Northern Ireland Government and Parliament. This legislation was renewed for a further year.

The Northern Ireland Constitution Act 1973 abolished the Parliament of Northern Ireland and provides for the devolution of legislative powers to the Northern Ireland Assembly, established by the Northern Ireland Assembly Act 1973, and for the devolution of executive powers to the Northern Ireland Executive.

Devolution took place on 1 January 1974, but following the collapse of the Executive at the end of May 1974, the Assembly was prorogued for a limited period and the functions of the Executive became the responsibility of the Secretary of State for Northern Ireland.

The Northern Ireland Act 1974 provided for the Dissolution of the Northern Ireland Assembly and for the election and holding of a Constitutional Convention in Northern Ireland. The Assembly was dissolved on 27 March 1975 and the election of 78 members to the Constitutional Convention took place on 1 May 1975. The Convention after six months of deliberation submitted its report to the Secretary of State on 7 November. It was laid before Parliament on 20 November, and the government's views on the proposals contained in the report were made known by the Secretary of State during a House of Commons debate on 12 January 1976. Mr. Rees announced the government's intention to reconvene the Convention from 3 February to consider certain specific matters. These are set out in a letter to the Chairman of the Convention and published as a White Paper. As no further report was made, the Convention was dissolved on 5 March 1976. Direct Rule therefore continues in being under the terms of the Northern Ireland Act 1974.

## LOCAL GOVERNMENT

26 district councils are responsible for the provision of a wide range of local services including gas supply, street cleansing and sanitation, litter prevention, consumer protection, environmental health, miscellaneous licensing, the provision of recreational and cultural facilities, the promotion of tourist development schemes and the enforcement of the new building regulations. They have in addition a representative role in which they send forward representatives to sit as members of statutory bodies including the Housing Executive and the Area Boards for health and personal social services, education and libraries; and a consultative role under which government departments and the Housing Executive have a statutory obligation to consult them regarding the provision of the regional services for which these bodies are responsible.

## LEGAL SYSTEM

The Supreme Court of Judicature of Northern Ireland was established by the Government of Ireland Act, 1920. It consists of two Divisions—The Court of Appeal in Northern Ireland and The High Court of Justice in Northern Ireland. A Court of Criminal Appeal was established in Northern Ireland in 1930.

The Court of Appeal has four judges, namely, the Lord Chief Justice, who is president, and three Lords Justices of Appeal.

The High Court has five judges, namely the Lord Chief Justice, who is president, and four puisne judges.

Under the County Courts Act (N.I.) 1959 County Courts now exercise the original criminal and civil jurisdictions formerly exercised by Courts of Quarter sessions and Civil Bill Courts. At least four ordinary sittings of these Courts are held annually in each County Court division. The general civil jurisdiction of County Courts is limited to actions in which the amount claimed or the value of the specific chattels. claimed does not exceed £1,000. In certain cases these courts have wider powers. They also act as courts of appeal from the Resident Magistrates. These are the permanent judicial officers presiding over Courts of Summary Jurisdiction (Petty Sessions).

**Supreme Court of Judicature**

*Judges:* The Rt. Hon. Sir Robert Lowry (Lord Chief Justice).
The Rt. Hon. Lord Justice Jones.
The Rt. Hon. Lord Justice McGonigal.
The Rt. Hon. Lord Justice Gibson.
The Hon. Mr. Justice O'Donnell.
The Rt. Hon. Mr. Justice Kelly
The Hon. Mr. Justice MacDermott.
The Hon. Mr. Justice Murray.

**Police Services.** On 31 July 1976, there were 4,706 men and 402 women and 145 cadets in the Royal Ulster Constabulary which is a centralized police force.

## AREA AND POPULATION

Northern Ireland covers an area of 5,452 square miles. The population as enumerated at the Census taken on 25 April 1971 was 1,536,065 made up of 754,676 males and 781,389 females.

The following table shows the area and population of the counties and county boroughs as at 25 April 1971:

| *County or County Borough* | *Area in statute acres* — *Land* | *Water (Including tidal)* | *Population* |
|---|---|---|---|
| Antrim | 699,928 | 52,565 | 355,716 |
| Down | 604,518 | 4,899 | 311,876 |
| Armagh | 309,876 | 18,030 | 133,969 |
| Fermanagh | 413,810 | 43,580 | 50,255 |
| Tyrone | 775,184 | 31,734 | 139,073 |
| Londonderry (excluding County Borough) | 510,780 | 10,071 | 130,889 |
| Belfast County Borough | 15,815 | 2,237 | 362,082 |
| Londonderry County Borough | 2,182 | 399 | 52,205 |

## FINANCE

Taxation in Northern Ireland is largely imposed and collected by the United Kingdom Government. After deducting the cost of collection and of Northern Ireland's contributions to the European Economic Community the balance, known as the Attributed Share of Taxation, is paid over to the Northern Ireland Consolidated Fund. Northern Ireland's revenue is insufficient to meet its expenditure and is supplemented by a grand in aid from the United Kingdom Government.

| | 1976–77* | 1977–78** |
|---|---|---|
| | £ | £ |
| Public Income | 1,207,524,700 | 1,296,500,000 |
| Public Expenditure | 1,207,396,408 | 1,296,309,000 |

*Outturn **Estimate

## PRINCIPAL BANKS

**Ulster Bank Limited.** Est. 1836; Balance Sheet at 31 December 1976 showed assets £613,804,000; deposits and current accounts £518,979,000; banknotes in circulation £11,676,000. *Head Office:* 47 Donegall Place, Belfast BT1 5AU. 144 Branches.

**Northern Bank Limited.** (Member of Midland Bank Group). Est. 1824. Balance Sheet at 31 December 1976 showed assets £534,906,000; deposits and current accounts £478,940,000. *Head Office:* Donegall Square West, Belfast BT1 6JS. 170 Branches and 92 sub-Branches.

# NORTHERN IRELAND

## PRODUCTION, INDUSTRY AND COMMERCE

**Agriculture.** The area under crops (in 1,000 hectare) in June 1976 was as follows: Oats, 6·9; Barley, 49·8; other cereals, 2·1; Potatoes, 14·2; other root and green crops, 3·7; Hay, 266·7. There were approximately 1,548,000 head of cattle; 926,000 sheep; 12,109,000 fowl and 698,000 pigs at the same date.

**Mining.** In 1976 the total production of minerals was 19,214 thousand tons. This was made up from (figures are in 1,000 tons) basalt and igneous rock (other than granite), 8,642; sand and gravel, 3,887; limestone, 2,143; grit and conglomerate, 3,442; chalk, 598; clay and shale, 265; others (diatomite, flint, perlite, granite, sandstone and rock salt), 237.

**Industry.** Total employees in employment in manufacturing stood at 147,200 in mid-1976, majority of these workers being engaged in four main industries which are, in order of employment size:

(*a*) Engineering and metals: this industry, with a work-force of 45,200, includes major traditional activities such as shipbuilding and textile machinery manufacture, and an increasing amount of new production. The electrical and electronic industries are well represented, and there is also a long-established aircraft industry.

(*b*) Textiles: within this industry, which employs 33,300 workers, there have been dramatic changes, as the traditional linen trades have declined and carpet-making and man-made fibre production have developed. A major part of the United Kingdom man-made fibre industry is now located in Northern Ireland.

(*c*) Food, drink and tobacco: 23,200 workers are employed on a wide range of products, many of which use the output of local agriculture.

(*d*) Clothing and footwear: the main centres of this industry, with 17,700 workers, are Belfast and Londonderry. In the latter area there is a major concentration of shirt and pyjama manufacture.

Other manufacturing trades—including oil refining, chemicals, printing and box-making, cement, furniture, pottery, leather tanning and tyre manufacture—together employ 27,800 workers.

## RAILWAYS AND ROADS

The public sector of transport in Northern Ireland operates in competition with private transport and is owned, on behalf of the Government, by the Northern Ireland Transport Holding Company. Subsidiary companies, privately registered under the Companies Acts (NI), operate on a commercial basis the Belfast buses (Citybus Ltd.), the rural buses (Ulsterbus Ltd.), the railways (Northern Ireland Railways Co. Ltd.) and the largest road haulage concern (Northern Ireland Carriers Ltd.). With the exception of the road haulage company, which is half owned by the National Freight Corporation of Great Britain, all of the subsidiaries are wholly owned by the Holding Company.

The Railways Company operates over approximately 200 miles of track and recently completed work on a major scheme begun in 1972 comprising the re-commissioning of the Belfast Central Railway, thereby linking the Belfast–Bangor line to the main system, and replacing two former termini by a new central system. Road passenger services are operated under licence from the Department of the Environment (NI). In addition to the services provided by Citybus and Ulsterbus services are provided in some localities by private enterprise. Northern Ireland Carriers operates road freight services in open competition with some 1,800 privately owned licenced operators.

## SHIPPING

There are regular passenger and freight services from Belfast and Larne to various ports in Great Britain while freight services operate from Londonderry, Warrenpoint and Coleraine. The total number of ships using the principal ports in 1976 was 11,236.

## CIVIL AVIATION

Belfast (Aldergrove) Airport, which is the main civil airport for Northern Ireland, is managed by Northern Ireland Airports Ltd., a subsidiary of the Northern Ireland Transport Holding Company. The Airport handles about 1·1 million passengers and 11,000 tonnes of freight per annum, making it the sixth busiest airport in the United Kingdom. Following the extension of the main runway to 9,100 feet in the summer of 1972 the airport is capable of providing a direct trans-Atlantic or European service. Firm outline proposals for the development of the Airport's terminal facilities have also been agreed and work commenced in 1977.

## EDUCATION

Responsibility for the local administration of the education and library services in Northern Ireland rests with the five Education and Library Boards. The Boards are representative of locally elected district councillors, transferors of schools and maintained school authorities, teachers and other persons by reason of their interest in, or knowledge of the service administered by the Boards.

In 1975–76 there were 1,146 primary schools (including 36 nursery schools) with 213,130 pupils; 182 secondary (intermediate) schools with 102,586 pupils; 80 grammar schools with 54,921 pupils; and 30 special schools with 2,519 pupils. In 27 institutions of further education there were 10,459 full-time students, 567 block-release students, 25,393 part-time students on vocational courses, and a further 33,965 students on non-vocational courses.

At the Ulster College there were 2,277 full-time students, 235 block-release students and 2,251 part-time students in courses of vocational education and professional training mainly at the highest level, and 405 students in non-vocational courses.

Adult Education facilities provided by Queen's University (Department of Extra-Mural Studies), New University of Ulster (Institute of Continuing Education) and the Workers' Educational Association catered for 9,671 registered students.

Enrolments in the 3 general colleges of education totalled 2,270, and in four other teacher training establishments (including University departments and the Ulster College) 1,249 students.

Queen's University, Belfast, catered for 5,708 full-time students and the New University of Ulster, Coleraine, for 1,730 full-time students.

The financial assistance given from public funds depends on the class of management of the school. The entire cost of all types of schools managed by Education and Library Boards and known in general as 'controlled schools' is met from public funds. In the case of maintained schools, i.e. primary, secondary (intermediate) and special schools managed by committees, one-third of whose members are appointed by the Education and Library Boards, all day-to-day running costs are met from public funds and the voluntary trustees are required to meet only 15 per cent of building costs. Capital expenditure by voluntary grammar schools is grant-aided by the Department at the rate of 65 per cent, or 85 per cent in the case of schools which accept public representatives on their Governing Bodies. Day-to-day costs are largely met from public funds through direct Department grants and scholarships to pupils by the Education and Library Boards.

## NEWSPAPERS

**Belfast Telegraph.** F. 1870. Daily. Belfast, Circulation 163,571 (July–Dec. 1976).

**News Letter.** F. 1737. Morning. Belfast. Circulation 72,204.

**Irish News.** F. 1855. Daily. Belfast. Circulation 54,403.

**Sunday News.** F. 1965. Sunday. Belfast. Circulation 97,257.

## RELIGION

According to the report of the census of 1971 there were 477,921 Roman Catholics; 405,717 Presbyterians; 334,318 Church of Ireland; and 71,235 Methodists. Those belonging to other Churches and of no stated denomination numbered 230,449.

# ISLE OF MAN

**Capital**—Douglas.

**Lieut-Governor**—Sir John Warburton Paul GCMG, OBE, MC.

## CONSTITUTION AND GOVERNMENT

The Isle of Man is a small island in the Irish Sea, almost midway between England and Ireland. It is not bound by Acts of the United Kingdom Parliament, unless specially mentioned in them. It has its own Legislature called Tynwald consisting of the Legislative Council and the House of Keys. The word 'Keys' is possibly derived from the Scandinavian 'Keise', meaning 'chosen'.

The Legislative Council, consists of the Governor, the Bishop of Sodor, Southern Isles and Man, the Attorney-General, and eight members appointed by the House of Keys.

The House of Keys consists of 24 members, elected by the population, both male and female. The six *sheadings*, or divisions, return 13 of these members; the capital, Douglas, returns seven, Ramsey returns two, and Peel and Castletown send one member each to the House of Keys.

In 1946, by resolution of the Tynwald, an Executive Council was appointed to assist the Governor in matters of government. This Council consists of seven members, chosen from the House of Keys and from the Legislative Council.

The House of Keys is elected every five years. The present House was elected in November 1976. When Bills have been passed by both branches of the Legislature they are submitted for the Royal Assent.

## AREA AND POPULATION

The island is about 33 miles in length and about 13½ miles in width. It covers an area of 141,263 acres (221 sq. miles).

In 1976 the total resident population was 60,496, of whom 28,735 were male and 31,761 female. The population of the capital, Douglas, is 19,897.

## FINANCE

Customs and Excise duties, income tax and social security taxes are the principal sources of income. Social security benefits and taxes are similar to those paid in the United Kingdom. Standard rate of income tax is 21·25 per cent in the £ and personal allowances are usually higher than in the United Kingdom. There is no surtax, death duty or corporation tax.

The estimate of the Government's gross expenditure for 1977–78 is:

| | |
|---|---|
| Revenue Expenditure | £47,351,710 |
| Capital Expenditure | £10,631,170 |

Isle of Man banknotes are issued in denominations of £10, £5, £1 and 50p by the Government. Coins are also issued, in 1970 a crown, and in 1971—decimal coins ½p, 1p, 2p, 5p, 10p and 50p.

In 1972 a crown was issued to commemorate the Royal Silver wedding. In 1973 gold coins were issued in denominations of £5, £2, sovereign and half-sovereign, and a similar issue was made in 1974. In 1974 a crown depicting a Manx Cat and a crown commemorating the centenary of the birth of Sir Winston Churchill were issued. Another issue of the six decimal coins was made in 1975, and in 1976 a newly designed set of six coins was put into circulation. Two crowns were issued in 1976, commemorating the bi-centenary of American Independence and the centenary of the Douglas Horse Trams, and in 1977 two crowns were issued, to commemorate the Royal Silver Jubilee and for the Royal Silver Jubilee Appeal Fund.

## PRODUCTION, INDUSTRY AND COMMERCE

The traditional industries of agriculture and fishing now receive considerable Government support, employ relatively few, and directly contribute only 1½ per cent towards Manx National Income.

The Tourist industry as a whole provides 13½ per cent of National Income, and although an important employer of labour it is far less dominant than in the past.

Government policy has been to diversify the economy, and a variety of grants and loans being offered to industry satisfying certain environmental criteria has led to rapid growth in the manufacturing sector, which now accounts for 12½ per cent of National Income.

Banking, financial and professional services are excellent, and the financial sector, encouraged by low and stable rates of taxation, modern legislation and a pleasant environment within the Sterling Area has expanded to become one of the major reasons for the continued growth of National Income.

The Isle of Man is not a full member of the E.E.C., but imposes tariffs and levies in the same way as the United Kingdom, and participates in the principle of free trade within the Community. The Isle of Man does not contribute to E.E.C. funds and is not eligible for aid from these funds.

## COMMUNICATIONS

Daily sea and air services operate between the Island and various points in the United Kingdom and Eire. There are seven miles of steam railway still operating and 12 miles of double track for electric trams. The total length of road is approximately 450 miles. The Tourist Trophy and Manx Grand Prix Motor Cycle Races and various cycling and motor rallying events are held annually at various times of the Summer.

## EDUCATION

There are 36 primary schools, four comprehensive co-educational secondary schools and a college of further education. In addition, King William's College for boys and the Buchan School for girls, both situated in the South of the island, are public schools, the college being independent.

## NEWSPAPERS

**Isle of Man Examiner.** F. 1880. Weekly. Douglas.

**Isle of Man Weekly Times.** Weekly. Douglas.

**Manx Star.** Weekly. Douglas.

**Isle of Man Courier.** (incorporating Mona's Herald). Weekly. Douglas. Circulation 13,000. Webb-offset. Other publications 'What's on in the Isle of Man' (summer only). TT Special (June and September). Specially written newspapers for the international motorcycle race meetings.

**Peel City Guardian.** Weekly. Peel.

# CHANNEL ISLANDS

## CONSTITUTION AND GOVERNMENT

The Channel Islands are a group of small islands and islets off the north-west coast of France. The main islands are Jersey, Guernsey, Alderney and Sark. They are the only portions of the Dukedom of Normandy now belonging to the British Crown.

There are two representatives of the Sovereign in the islands, the Lieutenant-Governors of Jersey and of Guernsey and the other islands. These representatives are also Commanders-in-Chief.

The Sovereign appoints the Bailiffs of Jersey and Guernsey. These act as presidents of their parliaments, called the Assembly of the States, in which they have a right to speak and to vote. The Bailiffs also preside over the Royal Courts of Justice in Jersey and Guernsey.

## AREA AND POPULATION

The total area of the islands is 48,491 acres.

The area of the different islands and islets is as follows: Jersey, 28,717 acres; Guernsey, 16,062; Alderney, 1,962; Great Sark, 1,035; Little Sark, 239; Herm, 320; Jethou, 44; Brechou, 74; Lihou, 38.

The population (including visitors) of the different islands by the census of 1971 was as follows: Jersey, 63,345; Guernsey, 54,381; Alderney, 1,686; Sark, 590.

## THE CHANNEL ISLANDS

The official language is English. *Patois* is spoken by an increasingly small number of islanders.

### PRODUCTION, INDUSTRY AND COMMERCE

The main agricultural products are potatoes, tomatoes and flowers. Large quantities of early potatoes and tomatoes are sent to the English market.

The chief imports are foodstuffs, manufactured goods, building materials, and fossil fuels. The chief exports, besides those already mentioned, are grapes and other fruits, vegetables, flowers, and electronic equipment. Cattle are also exported.

Trade with the U.K. is regarded as internal trade.

### COMMUNICATIONS

British Rail operates a regular passenger shipping service between Jersey, Guernsey and England (Weymouth). Locally operated passenger shipping and hydrofoil services join the islands with France (St. Malo). Cargo vessels operate between Jersey, Guernsey, Portsmouth, Southampton, London and Liverpool. Alderney and Sark have privately operated services connecting them with Guernsey. Regular air links are maintained between Jersey, Guernsey and England—mainly through London and Southampton. A local air service connects Jersey, Guernsey and Alderney. The Postal and Telephone services are operated by the Insular Authorities and which are also responsible for telegraph and trunk telephone services.

## Jersey

**Chief Town**—St. Helier.

**Lieut.-Governor**—His Excellency, General Sir Desmond Fitzpatrick, GCB, DSO, MBE, MC.

**Flag**: A white field charged with a red saltire.

The parliament of the island is called 'The States of Jersey', members of which are elected by the population, male and female.

The States comprises the Bailiff, the Lieutenant-Governor, 12 Senators, the Constables of the 12 parishes of the Island, 28 Deputies, the Dean of Jersey, the Attorney-General and the Solicitor-General. They all have the right to speak in the Assembly, but only the 52 elected members (the Senators, Constables and Deputies) have the right to vote; the Bailiff has a casting vote.

Senators are elected by the electors of the whole Island for a term of six years, six retiring in every third year. The Constables are members of the States by virtue of their office, to which they are elected for a term of three years by the electors of the parish. If unable to attend a sitting of the States, they are represented by the next senior officer of their parish. Deputies are elected on a constituency basis for a term of three years. General elections for Senators and Deputies are held in every third year, the election for Senators being held in the month of November and the election for Deputies being held in the month of December.

Except in specific instances, enactments passed by the States require the sanction of Her Majesty in Council.

The administration of the Island's affairs is carried out by Committees of the States, which in many instances have powers very similar to those of Ministers in the United Kingdom Government.

Justice is administered by the Royal Court, consisting of the Bailiff and 12 Jurats (magistrates). There is a final appeal in certain cases to the Sovereign in Council. There is also a Court of Appeal, which consists of the Bailiff and two judges. Minor civil and criminal cases are dealt with by a stipendiary magistrate.

The area of Jersey is 28,717 acres and the population in 1976 was 74,470. Births in the year 1975 numbered 868 and deaths 965.

Revenue and expenditure for the year ending 31 January 1976 were as follows: revenue, £55,167,513; expenditure, £39,882,100. The public debt was £4,138,690.

3,836 vessels entered St. Helier in 1975. The number of terminal passengers by air was 1,401,038 in 1976. Total arrivals by sea were 427,790 and departures were 423,177.

There are 12,364 children receiving full-time primary and secondary education in the Island. The Education Committee acts as Governing Body to Victoria College, which is a Headmaster's Conference School, and of the Jersey College for Girls. In addition it administers seven secondary and 28 primary schools. There are local facilities for further and part-time education in a wide range of cultural and vocational subjects and a scheme of awards to students attending universities and other institutions of further education in the United Kingdom.

Jersey is a deanery of the diocese of Winchester. There are 12 rectories which are in the gift of the Crown. There are also Roman Catholic and Nonconformist churches.

### NEWSPAPERS

**Jersey Evening Post.** F. 1890. St. Saviour.

**Jersey Weekly Post.** F. 1910. St. Saviour.

## Guernsey and Dependencies

**Chief Town**—St. Peter Port.

**Lieut.-Governor**—H. E. Vice-Admiral Sir John Martin, KCB, DSC.

**Bailiff**—Sir J. H. Loveridge, CBE.

**Flag**: The Red Cross of St. George on a white background.

The Parliament of Guernsey is called the States of Deliberation. These were reconstituted under the Reform (Guernsey) Law of 1948, and as from January 1949 consisted of the following members: 12 *Conseillers*, elected for six years, (and six retiring every third year) by another official body called the States of Election, 33 People's Deputies, elected for three years by popular vote, and 10 *Douzaine* Representatives, elected by the parochial councils, called the parochial *douzaines* ('dozens'). Two Alderney representatives were added by the States of Guernsey (Representation of Alderney) Law, 1949.

The Bailiff is *ex officio* President of the States of Deliberation and has a casting vote in the States. The Lieut.-Governor and the Law Officers of the Crown also have a right to sit in the States but not to vote. Major legislation requires the sanction of the Sovereign in Privy Council, but subsidiary legislation is operated by Ordinance of the States.

The electoral body, known as the States of Election, which elects the *conseillers* and the magistrates (*jurats*), consists of over 100 members, 67 of whom are elected by the people. *Jurats* act as magistrates but also have other judicial functions. The other members are the Bailiff, the ten rectors of parishes, 12 *conseillers* and 12 magistrates.

There are administrative committees, which are appointed by the States of Deliberation.

Justice is administered by the Royal Court, consisting of the Bailiff, the jurats and certain Court officials. The Guernsey Court of Appeal hears appeals from the Royal Court in civil and criminal cases. Cases in the magistrates court are heard by a jurat sitting alone.

The Lieut.-Governor's jurisdiction includes not only Guernsey but also its dependencies, namely, Alderney, Sark and the remaining islets.

The area of Guernsey is 16,062 acres, and the population (including visitors) at the April 1976 census was 54,256. With Herm (118) and Jethou (7) the population was 54,381. In 1961 it was 45,066. Births registered in 1975 were 618 and deaths 632.

Budget figures for the year ending 31 December 1977 are: Revenue £23,416,461 (includes £738,410 for Alderney); Expenditure, £24,816,656 (includes £833,965 for Alderney).

Principal imports in 1976 totalled £80,000,000.

Principal exports totalled £40,000,000. (These are approximate figures.)

Ships entering the ports in 1976 totalled 3·2 million tons. Passengers arriving by sea were 105,723 in 1976.

Passengers arriving by air were 190,072 in 1976.

There are five schools providing education up to G.C.E. Advanced Level. Two, Elizabeth College for boys (734) and the Ladies College (508), are considered as equivalent to direct-grammar schools, a third is an independent convent school for girls (Blanchelande College, 270 pupils) whilst the other two are wholly maintained Grammar schools, one for boys (370) and one for girls (315). In addition there are five secondary modern schools, 18 primary schools, three special schools and four private schools.

Guernsey is a deanery of the diocese of Winchester. Besides ten rectories which are in the gift of the Crown, there are several other livings of the Church of England. There are also Roman Catholic and Nonconformist churches.

**Alderney**

This, the third largest of the Channel Islands, lies about 20 miles north-east of Guernsey. It has its own president and assembly, called the States, elected by popular vote. The President of the States is the head of the island.

The island covers an area of 1,962 acres and at 1971 had a population of 1,686. The chief town is St. Anne's.

*President of the States:* Mr. J. Kay-Mouat.

**Sark**

This small island lies about eight miles to the east of Guernsey. Its assembly is called the Chief Pleas. It consists of 40 tenants and 12 elected members. The president of the Chief Pleas is called the *Seneschal*. The head of the island is called the *Seigneur* or *La Dame*.

The area of Sark, including Great and Little Sark. Brechou, is 1,348 acres, and the population at 1971 was 500.

*Seigneur de Sercq:* Mr. Michael Beaumont.

*Seneschal:* B. A. Jones, MBE.

**NEWSPAPER**

**Evening Press.** F. 1897. Daily. St. Peter Port.

# British Colonies and Protectorates

## BERMUDA

**Capital**—Hamilton.

**Governor**—His Excellency Sir Edwin Leather.

The Bermudas are a group of some 150 small islands, roughly in the form of a fish-hook measuring about 22 miles in length and about one mile in average width. They are situated in the Western Atlantic Ocean about 570 miles ESE of Cape Hatteras in North Carolina. A 17th-century French cartographer gives the date of discovery as 1503. According to the Spanish navigator and historian Ferdinand d'Oviedo, who sailed close to the islands in 1515, they were discovered by Juan de Bermudez, after whom they were named. No steps were taken to form a settlement on the islands and they were still uninhabited when in 1609 Admiral George Somers' ship, the 'Sea Venture', while on a voyage with a fleet of eight other vessels, conveying a party of colonists to Virginia, was wrecked on one of the sunken reefs which surround the islands. The Virginia Company was granted an extension of their Charter by King James I so as to include the islands within their dominion but shortly afterwards they sold the islands for the sum of £2,000 to a new body of adventurers called 'The Governor and Company of the City of London for the Plantation of the Somers' Islands', as they were then known. The Government of the Colony passed to the Crown in 1684.

### CONSTITUTION AND GOVERNMENT

Responsible Government was provided by a new constitution introduced on 8 June 1968. The Governor, appointed by the Crown, retains responsibility for external affairs, defence, the police and internal security. The Cabinet and the Premier are appointed from the House of Assembly except that not less than one and not more than two Members must be appointed from the Legislative Council. The House is elected under universal adult suffrage on the basis of two Members from each of 20 constituencies. The Legislative Council consists of four Members appointed by the Governor on the advice of the Premier, two on the advice of the Opposition Leader and five appointed in the Governor's discretion.

### AREA AND POPULATION

The total area of the islands was estimated at 18·83 square miles until 1940; the present estimate is 19·34 square miles. This corresponds to the original area which has been increased by dredging to a total of 20·59 square miles. The largest island, 14 miles in length, includes the capital, Hamilton. There is communication between the islands by roads, bridges and causeways.

The total civil population was estimated at mid-1969 at 50,927. According to the 1960 census the working force totalled almost 20,000. The population of the city of Hamilton is 3,000.

### FINANCE

Revenue and expenditure estimate for 1972–73 are shown below:

| | |
|---|---|
| Revenue | $52,245,598·00 |
| Expenditure | $49,895,419·00 |

On 6 February 1970 the currency was decimalized and new notes were issued in denominations of $50, $20, $10, $5 and $1 together with cupro-nickel coinage of 50c, 25c, 10c and 5c and a bronze coin 1 cent. The parity of the Bermudian dollar with sterling was established at BD$2·40 and equal to £1.

### PRODUCTION AND COMMERCE

**Agriculture.** The area of arable land, always small, is steadily diminishing owing to encroachment by building development. Of 740 acres now remaining, some 300 acres are utilized for vegetable crops, 220 for fruit and 50 for flowers. The climate permits double cropping for most vegetables and four crops a year for beans. The value of the 1970 vegetable crop was $687,760. Bananas valued at $222,410, and citrus fruits valued at $72,000 were produced. Cut flowers valued at $15,000 were exported.

Dairy farming is the most important branch of agriculture. The value of produce in 1970 was: eggs, $1,307,580; milk, $479,694; poultry, $20,736; pork, $50,156; beef and veal, $50,000.

**Commerce.** The principal domestic exports in dollars are as follows:

| | 1 *April* 1970–31 *March* 1971 |
|---|---|
| Beauty preparations | 216,238·14 |
| Pharmaceuticals | 1,718·90 |
| Essences | 667,359·92 |
| Flowers (cut) | 19,227·42 |

The value of the tourist trade in 1970 was estimated to be about $72,800,000, an increase of about 12 per cent over 1969.

### COMMUNICATIONS

Until 1948 a narrow gauge railway was in operation on the island. Buses now operate regular services throughout the island. From 1908 to 1946 the use of motor vehicles with the exception of those operated in connection with certain essential services was prohibited. With the passing of the

Motor Car Act in 1946, the use of motor vehicles, subject to certain limitations on size and horsepower, became lawful. The importation of used private cars is prohibited except in the case of an owner who has owned a new car for not longer than six months.

Frequent regular direct or indirect seaborne passenger and cargo communication is maintained with all parts of the world. During 1970 a total of 873 ships visited the colony.

The colony is served by six scheduled international air carriers, as follows: B.O.A.C.; Eastern; Qantas; Air Canada; Pan American World Airways, and Delta Airlines with regular flights to the Americas, Europe, West Indies and Australia.

The privately owned Bermuda Telephone Company operates an internal telephone service with over 15,000 subscribers. Cable and Wireless Ltd. operates coaxial telegraph and telephone cables to the U.S.A., and thence, via Montreal and Canadian networks, to the Commonwealth and World systems. A second cable links Bermuda with Tortola and the rest of the Caribbean, and a third link, direct to Canada, was being laid in 1970. There are locally operated radio and television stations.

### NEWSPAPERS

**Royal Gazette.** F. 1828. Daily. Reid St., Hamilton.

**Mid-Ocean News.** F. 1911. Week-end. Reid Street, Hamilton.

**Bermuda Sun Weekly.** F. 1964. Week-end. Victoria Street, Hamilton. ABC Circulation 12,593.

### EDUCATION

The Minister of Education is advised by a Board consisting of 11 members appointed by the Governor. Free education was introduced on 1 May 1949, and attendance is now compulsory up to the age of 16 years.

### RELIGION

The 1960 census revealed that almost half of the population were members of the Church of England; approximately 5,000 were members of the African Methodist Episcopal Church and another 4,300 members of the Roman Catholic Church. Altogether, 21 denominations were represented.

## BELIZE (BRITISH HONDURAS)

**Capital**—Belmopan.

**Governor and Commander-in-Chief**—Peter Donovan McEntee, OBE.

### CONSTITUTION AND GOVERNMENT

Belize is a Colony on the east coast of Central America. The first authenticated settlement was made about 1638 by British adventurers attracted by the logwood, then enormously valuable, which grew plentifully in the area. For many years the settlers managed their own affairs and government in spite of repeated efforts by the Spaniards to eject them. Although the settlers repeatedly petitioned for Crown recognition and logwood was the backbone of Britain's woollen trade, it was not until 1765 official recognition, long dallied with, was granted to the extent of sending Admiral Sir William Burnaby to plan the Settlement's defence. While in the Settlement, Burnaby codified the 'Ancient Customs and Usages' created by the settlers, and granted them in the King's name. In 1786 the Crown appointed its first Superintendent over the Settlement. In 1798 the Settlers, although heavily outnumbered and underarmed, administered a crushing defeat to an invading Spanish Armada and ended Spanish armed attacks on the Settlement. An Executive Council was established in 1840 to assist the Superintendent, and in 1853 a Legislative Assembly with a Speaker was formally constituted. This Assembly, of 18 elected members, was abrogated and replaced by a Legislative Council on Crown Colony government lines in 1871 at the request of the people. On 12 May 1862 the Settlement was declared a Colony and the Superintendent was raised to the status of a Lieut.-Governor, under the Governor of Jamaica. With effect from 2 October 1884 the Colony was detached from Jamaica and the Lieut.-Governor raised to the status of a Governor (the rank and title of Commander-in-Chief had been granted officially in 1797). Although the composition of the Legislative varied through the ensuing years the principle of an unofficial majority was maintained.

More important changes in the Constitution were brought into effect by the introduction of a Ministerial system after the elections held in 1961. This was followed by the introduction of internal self-government with the Governor retaining responsibility for external affairs, defence, internal security and the public service on 1 January 1964. This Constitution, which is still in operation to-day, provides for a Cabinet presided over by the Premier and a bicameral system of Government consisting of an elected 18 member House of Representatives and a nominated eight m mber Senate. The term of office for the legislature is five years. Elections were last held in 1974 when the Peoples United Party, led by Mr G. C. Price, won 12 seats and the Opposition, United Democratic Party, led by Mr Dean Lindo, won six seats in the House of Representatives.

Belize became a full member of the Caribbean Economic Community on 1 May 1971 and has an LDC (Less Developed Country) status in the Association.

**Cabinet**

*Premier, Minister of Finance and Economic Development:* Hon. G. C. Price.
*Minister of Home Affairs and Health:* Hon. C. L. B. Rogers.
*Minister of Works:* Hon. F. H. Hunter.
*Minister of Trade and Industry:* Hon. S. A. Perdomo.
*Minister of Energy and Communications:* Hon. L. S. Sylvestre.
*Minister of Social Services, Labour and Local Government:* Hon. D. L. McKoy.
*Minister of Agriculture and Lands:* Hon. F. J. Marin.
*Attorney General:* Hon. A. Shoman.
*Minister of Education and Housing:* Hon. G. Pech

### AREA AND POPULATION

The area of the country is 8,867 square miles.

The population is 119,853. Belize City has an estimated population of 39,332 (second provisional figures at the 1970 census).

### CURRENCY

For many years Belize currency was tied to sterling at the rate of Belize $4·00 to £1·00. In May 1976 the peg was altered from sterling to the U.S.$ and the rate of exchange is now Belize $2·00 to U.S. $1·00. The rate against sterling fluctuates as the pound sterling moves in relation to the U.S. dollar. The Government issues all notes and coins. Notes have the values of $1·00, $2·00, $5·00, $10·00 and $20·00. The coins are 10, 25, and 50 cent pieces in silver, 5 cent pieces in mixed metal and 1 cent pieces in bronze.

### PRODUCTION AND INDUSTRY

Value of the chief items of exports for 1974 are shown in the following table:

| *Commodity* | $ |
|---|---|
| Sugar, unrefined | 57,222,000 |
| Citrus Products | 5,383,000 |
| Molasses | 1,198,000 |
| Timber | 4,274 |
| Fishery Products | 3,107,000 |
| Vegetables | 398,000 |
| Chicle | 888,000 |
| Clothing | 8,292,000 |

Domestic exports totalled $82,786,000 for 1974.

Sugar and citrus were the big contributions to the increase of domestic exports and also clothing.

In 1974, 33·70 per cent of imports came from the U.S.A. and 25·41 per cent from the U.K.

### FINANCE

Estimated budget figures for 1976 were: Revenue, $23,031,191 (capital), $38,546,819 (recurrent).

### BANKS

**Atlantic Bank** (Banco Atlantida).

**Bank of Nova Scotia.**

**Barclays Bank International Ltd.** Albert St., Belize City.

**Development Finance Corp.** *General Manager:* Mr. R. A. Fuller, P.O. Box 40, Belmopan, Belize, Central America.

**Royal Bank of Canada.** *Main Office:* Belize City, Belize. 7 Branches.

### COMMUNICATIONS

Prior to 1935, there were only 35 miles of roads in the country which were considered at that date to be suitable for motor traffic throughout the year. In 1975 there were about 1,344 miles of roads consisting of 184 miles of metal surface, 583 miles of improved dry weather roads, 269 miles of gravel and 308 miles of earth surface.

A modern telecommunications system using a mixture of microwave uhf and vhf radio links providing full automatic long distance telephone traffic was inaugurated in September 1973. $5·1 million was spent on the project and it links all the district towns and capitals to a building housing switching equipment in Belize city.

A massive programme of works has been put in train for the reconstruction and improvement of the Western and Northern Highways. By 1974 the greater portion of the Western Highway (Belize City–Belmopan) was completed.

TACA International Airlines maintain six air services, three southbound and three northbound, between New Orleans and San Salvador *via* Belize City each week. TACA also have seven return flights to Miami. A weekly air service from San Pedro Sula, Republic of Honduras, and a service, Belize–New Orleans–San Pedro Sula–Belize–New Orleans, is provided by SAHSA, a Pan American Airways affiliate *via* Puerto Barrios, Guatemala. TAN Airlines also of Honduras provide four flights weekly to and from Miami and San Pedro Sula *via* Belize City, and once a week to Mexico City, using Electra aircraft. Maya Airways based in Belize City continue to operate all domestic air services. The International Airport of Entry, Stanley Field, is located nine miles west of Belize City (Belize International Airport). Belize International Airport is undergoing massive expansion. A modern radar system and meteorological laboratory are now in use. Ships of the United Fruit Company (U.S.A.) and T. & J. Harrison (Liverpool) call at Belize City Harbour and Stann Creek Town with and for cargo. The Royal Netherlands Steamship Co. maintains a fortnightly service between Amsterdam and Belize City with cargo from Europe. The 'K' Line of Japan comes in monthly.

There is one radio station, Radio Belize, which is semi-commercial. It is operated by the Government.

### NEWSPAPERS

**The Belize Times.** Three times a week. Circulation 4,000.

**The Reporter.** Weekly. Circulation 6,600.

**The Beacon.** Weekly. Circulation 5,500.

**Amandalla.** Weekly. Circulation 2,000.

**The Belize Newsletter.** Weekly.

**The Liberal.** Weekly. 2,000.

**The New Belize.** Monthly.

The two last publications are published by the Government Information Service.

### EDUCATION

Primary education is compulsory throughout the country for children between the ages of six and 14. The schools are almost all denominational.

There are 167 primary schools (grant-aided and government) with a total enrolment of 31,192, and 12 privately run primary schools and two government special schools for physically and mentally retarded children.

Secondary schools number 20 with a total enrolment of 4,324. These include two government secondary schools and a Junior Secondary school also run by government. Junior Secondary Schools are to be established in all district towns. There are three post secondary institutions with an enrolment of 563. Private primary schools have a total enrolment of 830. Two secondary schools also offer adult education classes in addition to extra mural classes offered by the University of the West Indies.

There are at present two Vocational Training Centres, one in Belize City and one in Stann Creek Town.

# CAYMAN, TURKS AND CAICOS ISLANDS

### Cayman Islands

**Governor**—His Excellency, Mr. T. Russell, CBE.

The Cayman Islands consist of three islands, Grand Gayman, Little Cayman and Cayman Brac, which have a total area of about 100 square miles. The principal island, Grand Cayman, is about 178 miles from Jamaica. It is about 22 miles in length and from four to eight miles in breadth with an area of 76 square miles. The estimated population of the islands for 1976 was 14,028.

The principal industries are seafaring and tourism. Remittances from Caymanian seamen and a growing tourist trade are very important items in the economy. There are virtually no exports since Jamaica ceased to import the thatch rope formerly made in the islands and the Nicaraguan Government refused licences to fishermen to catch turtles round the Cays off Nicaragua. Exports from Cayman Turtle Farm Ltd were the only substantial outgoing items in 1976. The islands offering tax-haven facilities also contributed considerably to the economy.

There are nine Government Primary and five church-sponsored schools, two of which have a secondary department, and one government comprehensive school for all children over eleven plus. Enrolment in all schools in 1976 was 3,675.

Government revenue for 1976 was (Recurrent) CI$11,653,531 (Revised Estimates); Expenditure CI$10,420,103; Revenue (Capital) CI$2,899,025; Expenditure CI$3,076,141. The Caymans have an interest free Development Aid Loan of CI$1,980,654. Total imports in 1976 were estimated at CI$29,779,506 and exports at CI$550,476 (est.).

Under the latest Constitution which came into effect on the 22 August 1972, the composition of the Executive Council and the Legislative Assembly, also the qualification for candidates and voters was changed.

The Executive Council now consists of the Governor as Chairman, the Attorney-General, the Chief Secretary, the Financial Secretary (i.e. three official members) and 4 elected members who are now responsible for certain subjects i.e. Hon. Truman M. Bodden, Health Education and Social Services, Hon. G. Haig Bodden, Agriculture and Natural Resources, Hon. Charles L. Kirkconnell, Communications, Works and Local Administration, Hon. James M. Bodden, Tourism, Aviation and Trade.

There are no longer any nominated members either in the Executive Council or the Legislative Assembly.

The Legislative Assembly is comprised of 12 elected members and 3 official members with the Governor as President. Provision is made in the Constitution for the appointment of a Speaker if deemed desirable and the life of the House has been extended from 3 to 4 years.

The voting age has been lowered from 21 years to 18 years and in order to be placed on the Electoral Roll a person must be a British subject who has been resident in the islands for at least 5 years out of the 7 prior to registration.

Candidates must be over 21 years, have resided in the islands for 5 out of the 7 years immediately preceding the date of nomination, born in the islands or be domiciled in the islands at the date of nomination.

This Constitution is a considerable step forward and gives the elected representatives of the people much more say in the conduct of the affairs of the territory.

# BRITISH COLONIES AND PROTECTORATES

## Turks and Caicos Islands

**Governor**—His Excellency A. C. Watson.

The Turks and Caicos Islands are situated between 21°–72°–30° West, about 100 miles north of Haiti and 50 miles West of the Bahamas of which they are geographically an extension.

There are over 30 islands of which eight are inhabited, covering an estimated area of 192 square miles. The principal island is Grand Turk. The 1970 Census of population showed a total population of 5,675 (Grand Turk 2,500). The total population at the end of 1976 was estimated as 7,500. The most important industry is fishing, but tourism is of increasing importance, with over 7,055 visitors in 1976.

The Islands lie in the Trade Winds but have an excellent climate. The average temperature varies from 75°F–80°F in the winter and 85°F–90°F in the summer, humidity is generally low. Average rainfall is 21 inches per annum. Hurricanes are rare, the last occurring in 1960.

The 1976 Constitution provides for a Governor, a Legislative Council, a Supreme Court and a Court of Appeal. The Legislative Council consists of a Speaker, 11 Elected Members, three Appointed Members and three Official Members. The normal life of Legislative Council is four years.

A Chief Minister and three other Ministers are drawn from the Legislative Council and they with the Governor and the three Official Members constitute the Executive Council.

The following table shows Revenue and Expenditure for 1975 and 1976.

| | *1975* *U.S.$* | *1976* *U.S.$* |
|---|---|---|
| Revenue | 3,378,000 | 4,922,711 |
| Expenditure | 3,692,000 | 4,076,437 |

The following table shows the value of exports and imports for 1976:

| | *1976* *U.S.$* |
|---|---|
| Imports | 4,939,725 |
| Exports | 1,608,548 |

Education is free in the 14 Government Schools between the ages of seven and 14; there are also four private and three secondary schools. Average number on rolls in 1976 was 2,435 (Turks and Caicos High School and North Caicos Junior High 496; Pierson High School 129). Expenditure on Education at 31 December, 1976 was U.S. $669,296.

The principal airports are on the islands of Grand Turk, South Caicos and Providenciales. There is a direct shipping service to the U.S.A. (Miami). There is a three times weekly air service between Miami Florida and Grand Turk, and a Weekly air service between Nassau, Bahamas and South Caicos. An internal air service provides a twice daily service between the six inhabited islands. A comprehensive telephone and telex service is provided by Cable and Wireless (W.I.) Ltd.

# FALKLAND ISLANDS

**Governor**—J. R. W. Parker, OBE.

The Falkland Islands are situated in the South Atlantic Ocean about 480 miles north-east of Cape Horn. The numerous islands of which they are composed cover 4,700 square miles. South Georgia, 800 miles south-east of the Falklands and the South Sandwich group 470 miles south-east of South Georgia, are dependencies of the Falklands.

The Falklands were discovered by Davis in 1592. A small French settlement was made in 1764 but was taken over by Spain two years later. West Falkland was taken possession of by Captain Byron in 1765 in the name of the British Crown. The Islands have been definitively administered by the British since 1833. The Government is administered by a Governor aided by an Executive Council, over which he presides, composed of the Chief Secretary, the Financial Secretary, two nominated members, and two elected members, elected by the unofficial members of the legislature from among the elected members of the same body; and a Legislative Council composed of two *ex-officio* members, namely, the Chief Secretary and the Financial Secretary and six elected members. The last general election was held in 1977.

### AREA AND POPULATION

The area of the Islands is estimated at 4,700 square miles.

A provisional estimate of the population in 1976 was 1,896. The only town is Stanley, in East Falkland, with a population of slightly over 1,100. The population is predominantly of British descent.

### PRODUCTION AND COMMERCE

The economy depends on wool, and about half of the male population is employed in sheep farming. Some hides are also exported. In 1975–76 there were some 644,820 sheep in the Islands as well as 5,443 cattle and 1,642 horses.

Total imports in 1976 amounted to £1,525,771.

The budget figures for 1977–78 (estimated) are in pounds sterling:

| | |
|---|---|
| Ordinary Revenue | 1,408,000 |
| Ordinary Expenditure | 1,362,000 |

In June 1977 the Financial Secretary announced that £200,000 was to be transferred to the Colony's development fund, the largest amount ever. During 1977–78 an estimated £668,000 would be spent on development projects, of which some £153,000 would be from local funds and £515,000 from overseas aid.

The Grasslands Trials Unit, established in 1975, would for the third year running have its staff expanded by one officer in 1977–78.

### COMMUNICATIONS

There are no made-up roads in the island beyond the immediate vicinity of Stanley. There is a small internal air service. Communication between Stanley and the outside world is effected principally by a weekly air service provided by the Argentine development airline L.A.D.E. with F27 aircraft. A Falkland Islands Company charter vessel comes in from the United Kingdom four or five times a year carrying mail and general cargo. Communications with the ports in the Dependencies and the British Antarctic Territory is kept up when ice conditions allow by the Royal Research ships *John Biscoe* and *Bransfield,* and by ice patrol ship H.M.S. *Endurance.*

In 1976 the total tonnage of shipping entered and cleared was 126,741 in the Falkland Islands.

Over the last few years a comprehensive development scheme has provided extra concrete roads in Stanley, improved education facilities throughout the Colony, radio telephone services to many countries including the United Kingdom, New Zealand and Australia, and up-to-date telex and telecommunication facilities. Since 1 October 1974 these facilities have been managed by Cable and Wireless Ltd.

# GIBRALTAR

**Governor and Commander-in-Chief**—Marshal of the Royal Air Force Sir John Grandy, GCB, KBE, DSO.

## CONSTITUTION AND GOVERNMENT

Gibraltar was captured by British forces under Admiral Sir George Rooke in 1704 and was ceded by Spain to Great Britain by the Treaty of Utrecht in 1713.

Under the Gibraltar (Constitution) Order in Council, 1964, Gibraltar attained a large measure of internal self-government. In 1969, a revised constitution was introduced, going as far towards internal self-government as is consistent with the position of Her Majesty's Government under the Treaty of Utrecht. Responsibility for defined domestic matters devolves upon Ministers, while responsibility for matters concerned primarily with external affairs, defence, and internal security is retained by the Governor. Other residual matters are the responsibility of the Governor acting in consultation, as appropriate, with the Gibraltar Council.

There is a House of Assembly which consists of a Speaker, fifteen elected members, the Attorney-General and the Financial and Development Secretary.

Executive authority is exercised by the Governor, who is also Commander-in-Chief, but in the exercise of his functions the Governor is normally required to act in accordance with the advice of the Gibraltar Council which consists of the Chief Minister and four other Ministers, and the Deputy Fortress Commander, the Deputy Governor, the Attorney-General and the Financial and Development Secretary. The four Ministers on the Gibraltar Council are appointed by the Governor after consultation with the Chief Minister. There is a Council of Ministers presided over by the Chief Minister, which consists of not less than four nor more than eight Ministers.

The Deputy Governor performs the functions of the Governor during his absence or incapacity.

The Preamble to the Order in Council contains the following: 'Whereas Gibraltar is part of Her Majesty's Dominions and Her Majesty's Government have given assurances to the people of Gibraltar that Gibraltar will remain part of Her Majesty's Dominions unless and until an Act of Parliament otherwise provides, and furthermore that Her Majesty's Government will never enter into arrangements under which the people of Gibraltar would pass under the sovereignty of any other state against their freely and democratically expressed wishes.' This undertaking by the British Government defined and consolidated Gibraltar's relationship with Britain in accordance with the freely expressed wishes of the people of Gibraltar.

## AREA AND POPULATION

Gibraltar is $2\frac{3}{4}$ miles long and its greatest breadth is $\frac{3}{4}$ mile. As a result of reclamation work its area has been increased from $1\frac{7}{8}$ square miles to $2\frac{1}{4}$ square miles. The population according to the 1970 census was 26,833, and was estimated as 30,117 at 31 December 1976.

## FINANCE

Some budget figures for 1972 to 1976 were as follows:

| Revenue | *Recurrent* | *Capital* | *Total* |
|---|---|---|---|
| 1972–73 | £5,735,012 | £2,284,831 | £8,019,843 |
| 1973–74 | £6,906,250 | £3,373,063 | £10,279,313 |
| 1974–75 | £8,790,210 | £3,398,323 | £12,188,733 |
| 1975–76 | £11,807,045 | £1,658,658 | £13,465,703 |
| Expenditure | | | |
| 1974–75 | £8,653,078 | £3,193,350 | £11,896,428 |
| 1975–76 | £10,322,937 | £2,691,409 | £13,014,346 |

## BANKS

There are five banks including a branch of Barclays Bank International.

**Gibraltar Government Savings Bank.** At 31 March 1976, there were 12,199 depositors with savings of about £1,331,323.

## COMMERCE

Imports and exports for the two years 1975 and 1976 are shown below:

| | 1975 | 1976 |
|---|---|---|
| Imports | £27,027,401 | £32,415,906 |
| Exports | £1,384,463 | £1,825,450 |

The figures for exports are exclusive of petroleum and petroleum products.

## COMMUNICATIONS

There is a Car Ferry Service operated daily by Messrs. M. H. Bland & Co. Ltd. to and from Tangier.

A number of cruise ships call at Gibraltar each year allowing from four to 12 hours ashore.

The following air services are in operation to and from the United Kingdom and Gibraltar and Gibraltar–Morocco.

**British Airways:** Gibraltar–Madrid–London (one service weekly), Gibraltar–London direct (three services per week summer schedules, seven services per week winter schedules). All operated by Trident aircraft.

**British Caledonian:** Gibraltar–London, operated by BAC 1-11 aircraft. Three services per week summer schedules, two services per week winter schedules.

**Gibraltar Airways:** Gibraltar–Tangier–Gibraltar, operated by Vickers Viscount aircraft. Twice daily services, except Sundays.

**Royal Air Inter:** Gibraltar–Tangier–Gibaltar 3 flights weekly all flights operated by Fokker Friendship Aircraft.

## NEWSPAPERS

**Gibraltar Chronicle:** E. 1801. Daily, Sundays excepted. 2 Library Gdns.

**Gibraltar Evening Post:** Daily. 93–95 Irish Town.

**Vox:** Weekly. 1 Fountain Ramp.

**Gibraltar Who's Who:** P.O. Box 225. Gibraltar.

**Gibraltar Year Book:** P.O. Box 225, Gibraltar.

## EDUCATION

Free compulsory education is provided for all entitled children between the ages of five and fifteen, although children are allowed to enter school at the age of 4. The structure, which was changed in 1972, consists of first, middle and comprehensive schools with transfer ages at eight and twelve. In all there are seven first, four middle, one primary school (4–12) and two comprehensive schools. All first and middle schools are mixed but the comprehensives are single-sex. In addition, there is one private primary school. A new purpose-built Special School for Handicapped Children was opened in 1977. Technical education is available at the Gibraltar and Dockyard Technical College managed by the U.K. Ministry of Defence for which Government pays 50 per cent of all recurrent costs and scholarships are made available in Britain for university, teacher training and other forms of higher education. The enrolment at September 1976, was 4,395 including 50 at the Technical College.

# HONG KONG

**Governor**—Sir Crawford Murray MacLehose, GBE, KCMG, KCVO.

The Crown Colony of Hong Kong, consisting of a number of islands and a portion of the mainland on the south-eastern coast of China, is situated at the eastern side of the mouth of the Pearl River between 22° 9′ and 22° 37′ N. and 113° 52′ to 114° 30′ E.

The island of Hong Kong is 91 miles south-east of Canton and 40 miles east of the Portuguese province of Macao, and 70 nautical miles south of the Tropic of Cancer. The harbour (23 square miles water area) lies between the island and the mainland on which is situated Kowloon and New Kowloon, with a combined population of 2·3 million.

The island of Hong Kong is about 11 miles long and from two to five miles broad, with a total area of 29 square miles;

it lies close to the mainland, being separated at one point by a narrow strait (Lei Yue Mun), not more than 500–900 yards wide. It was first occupied by Great Britain in January 1841, and was formally ceded by the Treaty of Nanking in 1842; Kowloon was subsequently acquired by the Peking Convention of 1860, and the New Territories (a peninsula in the southern part of Kwangtung Province together with adjacent islands) by a 99 year lease signed 9 June 1898. The estimated population of Hong Kong at the end of 1976 was 4,477,600. About 98·5 per cent could be described as Chinese on the basis of language and place of origin.

### CONSTITUTION AND GOVERNMENT

The Government consists of a Governor, advised by an Executive Council, comprising six official and eight unofficial members, and by a Legislative Council presided over by the Governor and comprising 19 official and 22 unofficial members. There is also an Urban Council which has the power to make bye-laws in respect of certain matters relating to public health and sanitation.

The administrative functions of government are discharged by some 43 departments, all the officers of which are members of the Civil Service. Local administration in the New Territories is in the hands of the Secretary for the New Territories and District Officers.

### AREA AND POPULATION

The area of the territory, including recent reclamations, is 404 square miles, a large part of it being unproductive hill country, and the population is mainly crowded into the urban areas of Hong Kong Island, and of Kowloon and New Kowloon on the mainland.

The Hong Kong Housing Authority was created on 1st April 1973 to spearhead the ambitious housing programme to provide self-contained homes for an additional 1·8 million persons. During its first year of operation, the Authority offered accommodation to 67,000 persons who were formerly inadequately housed or who were cleared from Crown land required for development. The Authority has adopted a more generous allocation standard as well as improved the design and planning of public housing estates and their amenities. Flats being built are self-contained with water and electricity supplied. For flats in the earliest types of public housing estates which are not self-contained, a redevelopment programme has been drawn up to improve living conditions, reduce densities and incorporate essential facilities. At mid-1977 levels, rents charged in public housing estates varied from £2·95 to £68·40 per month which were approximately 12 per cent to 40 per cent of rents for similar accommodation in the private sector. By 31 December 1976, the total number of persons accommodated in Hong Kong's 61 public housing estates was over 1·86 million or some 43 per cent of the total population. In addition, the Hong Kong Housing Society, a government-subsidized non-profit-making private body provided homes for another 145,400 people to-date.

The tremendous growth of population and industry since 1945 has created a demand for land, and many major reclamation and land formation projects have been carried out. Since 1945 about 1,061·65 hectares have been reclaimed from the sea by the Government. These include 870·49 hectares in the New Territories and on the Kowloon peninsula, where the industrial suburb of Kwun Tong is now well established, and 191·16 hectares on Hong Kong Island. In the New Territories the new town of Tsuen Wan (incorporating Tsuen Wan, Kwai Chung and Tsing Yi) with an ultimate population of 860,000 is well advanced and already houses over half a million people. The expansion of the container terminal at Kwai Chung has now been completed and there are now seven births in operation. The construction of two further new towns at Sha Tin and Tuen Mun is now well under way and the development programmes envisage them being completed in about ten years' time with population capacities of 550,000 and 530,000 respectively. Extensive development and re-development of Crown land for all purposes is proceeding.

There are about 1,080 kilometres of Government-maintained roads in Hong Kong, with a total vehicle count of more than 188,000; this gives a vehicle density of more than 174 vehicles per kilometre, one of the highest in the world. A big programme of improvements and construction is underway, including the construction of two new road tunnels and 21 new grade-separated intersections or flyovers. Modern traffic management techniques now being introduced include the computerized control of some 80 traffic light signals in West Kowloon. Since 1972 Hong Kong Island and the Kowloon peninsula have been linked by a cross-harbour road tunnel. A Mass Transit Railway with 15 stations and 15·6 kilometres of railway is under construction. Work began in 1976 and the first section from Kowloon Bay to Shek Kip Mei is due to be opened in September 1979. Extension of this system to Tsuen Wan was announced in July 1977. The extended system, with 26 stations and 26·3 kilometres of railway, will be operational in 1982.

Until the second of three major post-war water schemes was completed in 1964, Hong Kong suffered continually from water shortages and restrictions were again imposed during the drought of 1967. In 1968, the third and largest scheme was commissioned. This involved the construction of a dam across the mouth of a sea inlet at Plover Cove to form a fresh-water lake of such size that available storage was trebled. To meet the continuing increase in demand, the dam was raised in 1973, increasing available storage by 25 per cent.

Apart from a brief period in the autumn of 1974, when water restrictions were necessary as a result of a particularly dry summer, full supply has been maintained since 1968. Water restrictions were again introduced in June, 1977 due to rainfall being below average in the preceding months.

In 1964 an agreement was reached with the Chinese authorities whereby Hong Kong agreed to purchase 68 million cubic metres of water each year. This agreement came into effect in March, 1965 and the agreed annual supply was increased to 84 million cubic metres in 1972 and to 109 million cubic metres in 1976, which represented about 25 per cent of the total supply that year.

By 1979 it is hoped to complete the even larger High Island Scheme, involving the conversion of another sea inlet, which will almost double the total available storage. High Island is the last potential big new reservoir for Hong Kong and future increases in demand for fresh water will have to be met by desalting sea-water. With this in mind, the Government decided to set up a $480 million desalination plant. Construction work at Lok On Pai near Castle Peak in the New Territories , began in 1973. The plant, by far the largest in the world, was commissioned in early 1975 and is capable of producing 181,800 cubic metres a day. The quality and purity of water supplied by the Waterworks is in accordance with recognized international standards.

### CURRENCY

The unit of currency is the Hong Kong dollar. It was allowed to float as from 26 November 1974. On 30 June 1977 the middle market rate for the U.S. dollar was about HK$4·67 = U.S.$1. Bank-notes (of denominations of $5 upwards) are issued by the Hongkong and Shanghai Banking Corporation, the Chartered Bank and the Mercantile Bank, Ltd, Their combined note issue was, at the end of June, 1977, HK$5,140 million. Subsidiary currency consisting of HK$5, HK$2, HK$1, 50-cents, 20-cents, 10-cents and 5-cents coins. 1-cent notes and HK$1,000 commemorative gold coin are issued by the Hong Kong Government and at the end of June, 1977 totalled HK$490 million.

### FINANCE

Actual figures for 1976–77 were: Total revenue and receipts $7,493·5 million; Expenditure, $6,590·9 million.

There is a separate tax on income fro many of the following sources: property ownership, employment, profit from any trade, business or profession, and interest on any loan on indebtedness. The standard rate of 15 per cent applies to everything but earnings, for which it is the maximum. For the fiscal year 1977–78, the standard rate of tax on profits of unincorporated businesses is 15 per cent, the standard rate of tax on profits of corporations is 17 per cent. An important source of revenue shared by the Government and the Urban Council is rates in the urban areas, which, for the fiscal year 1977–78, is 11½ per cent of rateable value (that is, 7½ per cent General rate plus four per cent Urban Council rate). Rates in the New Territories vary from 11 per cent to 5½ per cent.

### BANKING

The use of the word "bank" in Hong Kong is restricted to banks licensed under the Banking Ordinance and to representative offices of foreign banks. The ordinance provides for the supervision and inspection of banks by the Commissioner of Banking and obliges the banks to meet certain minimum requirements with respect to their capital and liquidity. At the end of 1976 there were 74 licensed banks with a total of 759 banking offices, and also 93 representative offices of foreign banks.

Bank deposits increased during 1976 by 21 per cent to HK$44,030 million at December 31. Loans and advances increased by 22 per cent to reach HK$42,735 million at the same date.

Finance companies owned by foreign banks and other non-bank financial institutions which take deposits from the public are now required to register under the Deposit-taking Companies Ordinance which came into effect on April 1, 1976. By the end of the year 179 companies had registered under the ordinance.

**Commercial Bank of Hong Kong, The, Ltd.** Chairman, Robin S. K. Loh; (Managing Director, Robin Y. H. Chan; Director Manager, Siao Er Yang; Deputy Manager and Manager of Foreign Dept, Tseng Yu-Pei.) Assets as at 31 December 1976, HK$543,122,511; deposits and current accounts, HK$268,954,928. *Head Office:* International Building, P.O. Box 824, Hong Kong. Telex: 73085 HX. 6 branches.

**Hong Kong and Shanghai Banking Corporation, The.** (Chairman: M. G. R. Sandberg); Est. 1865; Bank of Issue for Hong Kong; Balance Sheet at 31 December 1976 showed assets HK$39,939,000,000; deposits, current and other accounts, HK$25,514,000,000; notes in circulation HK $3,942,000,000. *Head Office:* 1 Queens Road Central, Hong Kong. *London Offices:* 99 Bishopsgate, EC2P 2LA and 123 Pall Mall, SW1 5YEA, *Manchester Office:* P.O. Box 347, Barlow House, 4 Minshull St., Manchester M60 2AP.

**Chartered Bank, The.** 75 branches in Hong Kong, Kowloon and New Territories. See United Kingdom.

**Mercantile Bank Limited.** (Chairman: G. M. Sayer.) Est. 1892; Bank of Issue for Hong Kong; Balance Sheet at 31 December 1976 showed assets £199,679,205; current and other accounts £119,262,713; notes in circulation £3,706,511. *Head Office:* 1 Queen's Road, Central, Hong Kong. 32 Branches. Share capital acquired by The Hong Kong and Shanghai Banking Corporation in 1959.

**Liu Chong Hing Bank Limited.** (Managing Director, Liu Lit-man, FIBA; Chairman, Ngan Shing-kwan, CBE, JP.) Est. 1948. Assets as at 31 December 1974, H.K.$802,888,356·00; deposits and current accounts, H.K.$540,550,521·00. *Head Office:* 24 Des Voeux Road, Central Hong Kong. 14 branches.

**Wing Lung Bank Ltd.** (General Manager, Jieh-Yee Wu; Chairman, Patrick P. K. Wu.) Est. 1933. Assets as at 31 December 1976, HK$1,287,610,637; deposits and current accounts, HK$956,094,279. *Head Office:* 45 Des Voeux Road, Central Hong Kong. 8 branches.

**The Bank of Canton, Ltd.** (Chairman, Huo Pao-Tsai; Vice-Chairman, R. P. Williamson; Chief Manager, R. C. Corteway.) Est. 1912. Assets, as at 31 December 1976, HK$ 1,607,479,240; deposits and current accounts, HK$ 1,147,068,498. *Head Office:* #6 Des Voeux Road, Central Hong Kong. Branches, 9 in Hong Kong, 5 elsewhere.

## COMMERCE

Hong Kong, which lies on the main sea and air routes of the Far East, is now established as an industrial territory producing light manufactured goods for export. Entrepôt trade declined as a result of political changes in China, of the Korean war, and of the restrictions on trade with China but now shows signs of regaining some of its former importance.

Imports for 1976 were valued at $43,293 million, of which those from China accounted for $7,761 million, largely foodstuffs for domestic consumption. Exports were valued at $32,629 million, and re-exports at $8,928 million, of which only $123 million worth went to China.

Imports from the United Kingdom were valued at $1,833 million in 1976, while exports to the United Kingdom amounted to $3,286 million and re-exports $116 million.

The most important items of domestic manufacture entering the export trade during 1976 were clothing ($14,288 million); electronic products ($3,971 million); textiles, other than clothing ($3,051 million); toys and dolls ($2,260 million); watches and clocks ($1,208 million); metal products ($844 million); travel goods, handbags and similar articles ($690 million) and jewellery and goldsmiths' and silversmiths' wares ($687 million).

The three main customers are the United States, The Federal Republic of Germany, and Britain, which absorbed between them 56·8 per cent of Hong Kong's exports.

## COMMUNICATIONS

**Railways.** The Hong Kong Government owns the section of the Kowloon-Canton Railway that runs for 22 miles as a single line from the tip of the Kowloon peninsula to Lo Wu on the Chinese frontier. Passengers travelling to China disembark at Lo Wu and walk across the frontier to board a Chinese train. Goods trains go right through.

The railway has made a profit continuously over the last 22 years and has recently begun to participate in the export of oil from the People's Republic of China. In the latter part of 1975 a new terminus opened in Kowloon for both freighter and passenger traffic. It is next to the Cross Harbour Tunnel and ferry services to Hong Kong Island. Double tracking of the railway between Kowloon and Shatin commenced in August 1975 and this will continue to Tai Po, some 14 miles from Kowloon. Construction of a new railway station at the proposed Shatin racecourse is due to be completed in 1978. A marshalling yard to facilitate the movement of freight from China will open in 1977 and work will commence in the same year on the construction of a new double track tunnel to $\frac{3}{8}$ miles at Beacon Hill.

Consultants have been appointed to provide recommendations for the modernization and expansion of the railway.

**Shipping.** Hong Kong possesses one of the most magnificent natural harbours in the world, with excellent facilities for handling all types of vessel and cargo. Extensive dockyard facilities are available including a floating dock capable of accommodating vessels up to 100,000 tons deadweight. The modern container terminal at Kwai Chung which commenced services in 1972 was completed in 1976, and has six berths with a total length of more than 7,000 running feet. In 1976 container throughput in the port was 1,029,056 T.E.U.'s (twenty-foot equivalent units); 7,071 ocean-going vessels with a total net tonnage of 36,604,396 entered the port, discharging and loading a total of 21,188,390 long tons of cargo.

Regular cargo liner services exist to every major port throughout the world, there being more than 170 shipping lines serving the port.

The Hong Kong Shipowners' Association represents 53 owners who own ships with a total deadweight of approximately 21 million tons. *Office:* Room 401 Hilton Hotel, 2 Queen's Road Central, Hong Kong.

**Airports.** Hong Kong International Airport, situated on the north shore of Kowloon Bay, is an important link on the main air routes of the Far East. It is regularly used by 28 scheduled airlines, and 18 non-scheduled passenger and 21 freight carriers, providing frequent services throughout the Far East to Europe, North America, Africa, Australia and New Zealand.

British Airways operates 19 outgoing passenger services per week, 10 to London, four to Australia and New Zealand, three to Japan, one to South Africa and one to East Africa. Cathay Pacific Airways Ltd., the Hong Kong based airline provides an average of 96 flights per week on Far East routes.

Hong Kong International Airport offers full operational facilities including an Instrument Landing System, Surveillance and Precision Approach Radars. During the year ending 31 March 1977, 50,151 civilian aircraft on international flights arrived and departed, carrying 4,558,048 passengers (including transit passengers), 164,862 metric tons of freight and 5,541 metric tons of mail.

**Broadcasting and Television.** Radio Television Hong Kong, the Government broadcasting station, provides a daily radio service in Chinese and English. Each service broadcasts on two channels, AM and FM, from 0600 to 0300 daily. The Hong Kong Commercial Broadcasting Co. provides daily one English and two Chinese services on the medium wave.

Commercial Television Ltd. (CTV) operates a single service in Chinese on CCIR 625-PAL, offering, apart from regular entertainment programmes and news and public affairs broadcasts, instructional programmes on a non-commercial basis on weekly evenings at prime time. Rediffusion Television Limited operates two commercial television services (English and Chinese) on CCIR 625 Line PAL System I. Television Broadcasts Ltd. also transmit two commercial television services on the CCIR 625 Line PAL System I, colour. The television service of RTHK provides documentary films, community involvement programmes, message-based social dramas and youth programmes which are transmitted by the three commercial television stations. The Educational Television Division (ETV) provides ETV programmes for 60 hours a week for transmission by the commercial stations which are viewed by about 482,000 primary and secondary school children and 12,000 teachers, not including the general public. Transmission of programmes made in colour for secondary schools began in September 1976.

**Satellite Earth Station.** Cable and Wireless owns and operates two 30-metre fully steerable dish-shaped antennae in Stanley, Hong Kong Island. They provide direct communication links to 25 countries via the Indian and Pacific Oceans. The station handles 310 voice channels, with additional facilities for expansion. It is mainly used for carrying international telephony and telegraph. Colour television can be trans mitted and received in either of the two line standards (625/50 PAL and 525/60 NTSC), and has been widely used for coverage of news, sporting events, beauty contests and musical programmes.

### HOUSING

The provision of public housing is the responsibility of the Hong Kong Housing Authority which is a statutory corporation. The Authority already houses almost 2 million people in 61 multi-storey estates and is currently building 18 new estates for another 250,000 people at a cost of HK$670 million. These estates are part of a long-term programme aimed at alleviating Hong Kong's housing shortage and includes the development of new towns, the redevelopment of unsatisfactory housing, and the resettlement of squatters. Also involved in this programme is the Hong Kong Housing Society, a Government-aided voluntary body which houses over 145,400 people and is currently planning an improvement scheme.

### PRESS

There are 333 publications produced in Hong Kong. Included among the 107 daily or weekly newspapers are four daily and two weekly English-language newspapers; the remainder are almost all in Chinese.

### EDUCATION

As at September 1976 there were 2,814 schools with 1,323,098 pupils, of whom 685,494 were receiving education financed wholly or in part by the Government, 239,787 boys (10,653 receiving technical vocational training) and 214,004 girls (3,471 in technical and vocational training) were in secondary classes. The Hong Kong Polytechnic, inaugurated in August 1972, has an enrolment of 21,638. The University of Hong Kong, opened in 1912, has a full-time residential strength of 4,005, in Faculties of Medicine, Engineering and Architecture, Arts, Science, Social Science and Law. There is also a Centre of Asian Studies and an extra-mural Department of Studies. The Chinese University of Hong Kong was inaugurated in October 1963 and has at present an enrolment of 4,087 students in three Faculties, namely Arts, Science, Social Science, and Business Administration.

## MAURITIUS

**Capital**—Port Louis.

**Governor**—Sir Ramon Osman, GCMG, CBE.

Mauritius is an island in the Indian Ocean, 500 miles off the east coast of Madagascar. It was discovered by the Portuguese early in the sixteenth century. In 1598 a Dutch Fleet landed on the island, to which its commander gave the name of Mauritius, in honour of the Stadtholder, Prince Maurice of Nassau, but it was not actually occupied until 1721. It was captured by British Forces in 1810 and British sovereignty was confirmed by the Treaty of Paris in 1814.

The executive authority is vested in Her Majesty. The Mauritius Independence Order, 1968, as amended by the Constitution of Mauritius (Amendment) Act, 1969, provides for a Cabinet which is composed of the Prime Minister and 20 other Ministers.

The Legislative Assembly, also provided for by the Mauritius Independence Order, 1968 consists of the Speaker, 62 elected members (including two for Rodrigues) and eight additional members. Mr. Speaker, who is deemed to be a member of the Legislative Assembly, and who was appointed by the Governor by Instruments under the Public Seal of the former Legislative Council, holds office as Speaker of the present Legislative Assembly and will do so until such time as by writing under his hand addressed to the Assembly he resigns his office. The next Speaker will be elected by the Legislative Assembly from amongst its members. Mr. Speaker is assisted by a Deputy-Speaker who is elected by the Assembly at the beginning of every Session. General Elections are usually held every five years on the universal adult suffrage basis. The island is divided into 20 electoral areas, or constituencies, and each constituency is entitled to elect three members of the Legislative Assembly. Rodrigues which is another constituency of Mauritius elects two members. The leader of the House is Dr. the Rt. Hon. Sir Seewoosagur Ramgoolam, Prime Minister, Minister of Defence and Internal Security, Minister of Reform Institutions, Information and Broadcasting, and Minister of Communications. The leader of the Opposition is the Honourable Aneerod Jugnanth.

### LEGAL SYSTEM

The laws of Mauritius are mainly based on the old French Codes—the Civil Code, the Penal Code, the Code of Commerce and the Code of Civil Procedure, to which a number of amendments have been made.

The Bankruptcy Law, the Law of Evidence and the Law of Criminal Procedure and Labour Laws are, however, to a great extent based on English Law.

The Courts exercising jurisdiction in Mauritius are the Supreme Court, the Intermediate Court, the District Court and the Industrial Court.

*Chief Justice:* William Henry Garrioch.

### AREA AND POPULATION

Mauritius has an area of approximately 720 square miles. It is 36 miles long and 29 miles wide.

The great increase in population during the last century has made Mauritius one of the most densely populated regions of the world. The population at June 1976 was 894,700.

### CURRENCY

The currency of the island is the rupee and cents of the rupee.

### FINANCE

Revenue and expenditure for two years are shown below:

| | 1975–76 | 1976–77 |
|---|---|---|
| | *Rs.* | *Rs.* (*Provisional*) |
| Revenue | 1,065,451,320 | 1,154,947,440 |
| Expenditure | 1,028,241,137 | 1,259,851,940 |

The Public Debt at 30 June 1976 amounted to Rs. 1,076,500,000 after deducting the value of Accumulated Sinking Funds.

### BANKS

**Mauritius Commercial Bank.** (General Manager: P. Louis Eynaud.) Est. 1838; Balance Sheet at 10 April 1972 showed assets Rs. 226,342,964; deposits and current accounts Rs. 210,686,423. *Head Office:* Port Louis, Mauritius. 13 Branches and Counter at Plaisance Airport.

**Development Bank of Mauritius.** Chaussée, Port Louis.

**Thailand Mercantile Bank Ltd.** Two branches in Bangkok.

**Barclays Bank International Ltd.** (Main Branch, Port Louis; 14 others in the Island and one in Rodrigues Island.)

**The Bank of Baroda Ltd.** (Branch, Port Louis.)

**Habib Bank Ltd.** (Branches, Curepipe and Port Louis.)

### PRODUCTION AND COMMERCE

Large-scale planting of sugar has reduced to some extent the native flora, but there are at present some 159,300 acres under forest, scrub areas, grassland and grazing lands and some excellent timber such as teak and other hardwoods is available for local consumption. The fertile, volcanic soils of Mauritius support extensive sugar plantations; and sugar accounts for about 92 per cent of the domestic exports. In 1976 the production of sugar was 689,932 metric tons. Molasses and rum are by-products of the sugar cane and production figures for the year 1975 were 129,432 metric tons and 28,437 hecto litres respectively. Besides sugar and its by-products, Mauritius also exports tea, copra, ginger, cattle-hides, aloe fibre bags and sacks and a number of other commodities.

Further, as a result of gradual industrialization, textile products, electronic products, paint, louvres, metal doors and windows, mirrors and glass-work, furniture, cigarettes, cotton thread, tap, plastic materials, floor polish, fibreglass goods, car batteries, shirts, footwear, groundnut oil, soap, chemical products, gloves and other manufactured products are now exported in appreciable quantities.

Balance of Visible Trade 1970–76 (June):

| *Year* | *Total Imports millions Rs.* | *Domestic Exports millions Rs.* | *Re-exports millions Rs.* | *Total Exports millions Rs.* |
|---|---|---|---|---|
| 1970 | 419·9 | 375·1 | 8·2 | 384·5 |
| 1971 | 461·6 | 354·7 | 6·0 | 361·7 |
| 1972 | 635·8 | 566·1 | 7·7 | 573·8 |
| 1973 | 915·8 | 736·8 | 11·6 | 748·4 |
| 1974 | 1,756·3 | 1,786·4 | 15·4 | 1,770·9 |
| 1975 | 1,996·3 | 1,818·0 | 20·9 | 1,838·9 |
| 1976 (June) | 1,180·4 | 552·1 | 16·2 | 568·3 |

### COMMUNICATIONS

**Roads.** There are 9½ miles of motorway, 351 miles of main roads, 369 miles of urban roads and 380 miles of rural roads. All the main roads and 656 miles of urban and rural roads have a bitumen surface. The Ministry of Works is responsible for the care of the motorway and of the main roads, the Municipalities for the urban roads and the District Councils for the rural roads.

**Shipping.** Port Louis is the only port and it can accommodate 11 ocean-going and six small vessels at any one time. During 1975 a total of 1,125 vessels entered the port, giving a total of 3,239,614 net tons.

**Civil Aviation.** Mauritius is served by the International Airport situated at Plaisance, at the South East of the Island. It is managed and operated by the Department of Civil Aviation of the Mauritius Government. There are no other airfields.

**Broadcasting.** Mauritius Broadcasting Corporation, which also operates a television service, was founded in 1964. The station operates on medium and short waves. There were 90,420 radio licence-holders and 40,790 television licence holders in December, 1975.

The earth communication satellite station is run by Cable and Wireless (Mauritius).

### EDUCATION

*Primary.* The 317* Government, Aided and non-aided private primary schools catered for 139,439 pupils.

* Including 113 preprimary schools with 1,621 pupils following Std. I. In addition, preprimary education was being provided by 281 females and male infant private schools, with an enrolment of 8,004 pupils.

*Secondary.* There were four Government, 13 grant-aided and *Junior Technical.* 781 pupils attended the three junior and two technical schools.

*Junior Technical.* 781 pupils attended the three junior and two technical schools.

*Secondary.* There were four Government, 102 grant-aided and 18 non-aided Secondary Schools where the enrolments were 3,459, 60,073, and 3,388 respectively.

*Teacher Training.* In 1976 there were 478 students in training for teachership.

*Small Scale Industries.* This section of the Ministry continues to provide training facilities at its five training centres in dressmaking, basketry, general handicrafts and leather works.

*The Trade Training Centre.* Full time Courses are organized at this institution in machine shop engineering, auto-mechanics, electrical maintenance, masonry and concrete works, plumbing and pipe fitting, welding and metal fabrication.

*Finance:* The recurrent expenditure incurred on education in 1970–71 was Rs 35·7 millions and the capital expenditure for the year 1970–71 was 3·1 millions.

### NEWSPAPERS

**Advance:** F. 1940. 5, Dumat St., Port Louis.

**Le Cernéen.** F. 1832. Lord Kitchener St., Port Louis. Port Louis.

**Le Mauricien:** F. 1908. St. Georges Street, Port Louis.

**L'Express:** F. 1963. Brown Sequard Street, Port Louis.

**The Star:** F. 1963. Daily morning paper. Circulation: over 12,000. 3 President John Kennedy Street, P.O. Box 201, Port Louis.

**L'Aube:** F. 1968. 4, Barracks St., Port Louis.

**L'Action:** F. 1969. Lord Kitchener St., Port Louis.

**The Nation.** French and English. *Director:* Prakash Ramlallah. F. 1971. Circulation: 8,000. Edith Cavell St., Port Louis.

**Le Militant:** F. 1971. 24, Bourbon St., Port Louis.

All the above are bilingual (English and French).

**China Times:** Chinese, 1953, Joseph Riviere St., Port Louis

**Chinese Daily News:** Chinese, 1932, R. Ollier St., Port Louis.

**New Chinese Commercial Paper.** F. 1956, 19 Joseph Rivier, St., Port Louis.

### RELIGION

At the 1972 Census there were 245,570 Roman Catholics, and 6,224 members of the Church of Scotland. The majority of the Indo-Mauritians are Hindus (421,707), the remainder, numbering 136,997, being Muslims.

### DEPENDENCIES

The dependencies of Mauritius consist of a number of islands scattered over the Indian Ocean. The most important is Rodriguez, situated 344 nautical miles from Mauritius. It has an area of 40 square miles and its population is estimated at about 26,000. It is administered by a Magistrate and Civil Commissioner under the Governor of Mauritius.

## ST. HELENA

**Capital**—Jamestown.

**Governor**—Sir Thomas Oates, CMG, OBE.

### CONSTITUTION AND GOVERNMENT

St. Helena is an island in the South Atlantic Ocean, 1,200 miles from the coast of Africa. It was discovered by the Portuguese Commander, Juan de Nova Castella, in May 1502, but no permanent settlement was made. It became a port of call for ships of various nations voyaging between the East Indies and Europe. On 5 May 1659, it was annexed and occupied by Captain John Dutton who was sent out by the East India Company for that purpose. A charter was issued to the East India Company for its possession by Charles II in December 1673 and it remained in the Company's possession until 22 April 1834, when it was brought under the direct government of the Crown by an Act of Parliament.

The government is administered by a Governor aided by a Legislative Council and an Executive Council.

### AREA AND POPULATION

St. Helena is 10½ miles long and 6½ miles broad, covering an area of 47 square miles. The population at 1971 was 5,056, of whom some 1,600 lived in Jamestown, the capital and the only town on the island.

### FINANCE

Revenue (including Grant in Aid and Development Aid funds) and Expenditure for 1971–72 were £954,709 and £853,255 respectively. Corresponding figures for 1970 were £522,421 and £548,308.

### PRODUCTION, INDUSTRY AND FINANCE

The main crops are flax, common and sweet potatoes and vegetables. At the end of 1965 the market price of hemp dropped considerably and production ceased in 1966.

Livestock numbers in 1971 were: cattle 821; sheep 1,407; goats 1,217; poultry 10,309; pigs 452.

Total imports in 1971 amounted to £403,832.

Imports from the United Kingdom totalled £261,124 in 1971. Exports to the United Kingdom totalled nil in 1971.

### COMMUNICATIONS

Steamers proceeding from England to the Cape and vice versa call at the island approximately once in three to four weeks in each direction. The total net tonnage of merchant shipping entered and cleared in 1971 was 178,097. There is a cable station on the island operated by Cable and Wireless Ltd., with direct connection with Cape Town and Ascension, thus linking the colony with all parts of the world through the Company's system.

## DEPENDENCIES

### ASCENSION

The island of Ascension is a dependency of St. Helena. It was taken possession of in 1815, and until 1922 it was under the supervision of the Admiralty which maintained a small naval station there. The island, which is 34 square miles in area, is a barren rocky peak of purely volcanic origin, and destitute of all vegetation except at the highest point. The population in 1971 was 1,231 of whom 674 were St. Helenians.

### TRISTAN DA CUNHA

Tristan da Cunha, Nightingale, Inaccessible and Gough islands were made dependencies of St. Helena by Letters Patent dated 12 January 1938. The islands, of which Tristan de Cunha is the principal, are situated midway between South America and South Africa. Tristan da Cunha itself is a volcano rising to 6,760 feet above sea level, with a crater lake near its summit. It was taken possession of by a military force during the residence of Napoleon at St. Helena. When the garrison was withdrawn in 1817, William Glass, a corporal of artillery, and his wife, elected to remain, and they were joined by two ex-Navy men, Alexander Cotton and John Mooney, and these, with certain shipwrecked sailors, became the founders of the present settlement.

In 1970 the Islanders numbered 276, nearly all of whom were born on the island. In October 1961, the entire population was evacuated by reason of a severe volcanic eruption. Most of the inhabitants returned in November 1963. The inhabitants had between them about 116 head of cattle, 760 sheep and a stock of poultry. Potatoes, which grow well. form a staple article of diet. The island is only visited occasionally by passing ships.

# SOUTHERN RHODESIA

**Capital**—Salisbury.

Rhodesia takes its name from Cecil John Rhodes (1853–1902) on whose initiative it was opened up for European settlement and development.

Apart from three Portuguese expeditions in the sixteenth century, little is known of the early history of Rhodesia. It is thought that Rhodesia was first settled during a great southward migration by peoples of Bantu stock (a linguistic classification) and that these were the ancestors of the tribes collectively known as the Mashona. The Zimbabwe ruins in Mashonaland were once (between the eleventh and fifteenth centuries) the centre of a well-organized African kingdom in contact with the commerce of the Indian Ocean.

Around 1830 the Matabele, a section of the Zulu nation led by Mzilikazi, entered Rhodesia from the south and occupied the south-west of the country. From this area, Matabeleland, they carried out frequent raids on the less warlike Mashona.

European contact with Rhodesia was renewed in 1851 by the missionary-explorer David Livingstone who reached the Victoria Falls in 1855. The first Christian mission to the Matabele was established by the London Missionary Society in 1861. The extension of British influence to the Rhodesias was mainly due to Cecil Rhodes, after whom they were named. In 1887 the High Commissioner at the Cape, acting on Rhodes's advice, sent the Assistant Commissioner in Bechuanaland to negotiate a treaty with Lobengula, the chief of the Matabele, and in 1888 Lobengula gave to Rhodes's emissaries the monopoly of the minerals in his kingdom. This concession—the 'Rudd Concession'—resulted in the formation of the British South Africa Company and the grant to it of a Royal Charter in 1889 to promote, under the supervision of the High Commissioner for South Africa, trade, commerce, civilization and good government in the area 'lying immediately to the north of British Bechuanaland and to the north and west of the South African Republic and to the west of the Portuguese Dominions'. Mashonaland was occupied by a Pioneer Column in 1890.

Renewed Matabele raids on the Mashona gave rise to the Matabele War in 1893. The war ended with the decisive defeat of the Matabele, the death of Lobengula in 1894, and the occupation of Matabeleland. The Matabeleland Order in Council of 1894 provided for the government of the whole of Southern Rhodesia. The northern part of the Company's area (later Northern Rhodesia) was already separately administered.

Southern Rhodesia was administered until 1923 by the British South Africa Company which concentrated on the development of gold-mining, agriculture and much-needed communications, including rail links with South Africa and Mozambique. Both Executive and Legislative Councils were set up in 1898; by 1907 there was a majority of elected members, representing settlers, on the Legislative Council. In 1920 the council passed a resolution requesting the establishment of responsible government 'forthwith'. The issue was put to the electorate as one of two choices: responsible government or entry into the Union of South Africa as the fifth province; at a referendum in 1922, 8,744 votes were cast for self-government and 5,989 for the alternative.

After the 1922 referendum Southern Rhodesia was formally annexed to His Majesty's Dominions as a colony on 12 September 1923; under the Southern Rhodesia Constitution Letters Patent, 1923, issued on 1 October 1923, the colony was granted full self-government with the exception that legislation affecting African interests, the Rhodesia Railways and certain other matters were reserved to the Secretary of State. Except for those concerning differential legislation affecting the African population, these reservations fell away in time so far as internal affairs were concerned. The British Government conducted formal international relations on behalf of Southern Rhodesia; Commonwealth relations, trade relations, and relations with Colonial territories in Africa were mainly conducted by the Southern Rhodesian Government directly.

For over ten years, from September 1953, Southern Rhodesia formed part, together with Northern Rhodesia (now Zambia) and Nyasaland (now Malawi), of the Federation of Rhodesia and Nyasaland. When the Federation was dissolved on 31 December 1963, the Southern Rhodesian Government resumed the powers which had been transferred to the Federal Government in 1953.

On 11 November 1965, the then Rhodesian Government under the leadership of Mr. Ian Smith unilaterally declared Rhodesia independent. Since that date, successive British Governments have tried to reach a settlement with those in power in Rhodesia. In March 1970 the regime introduced a republican constitution which provided for eventual progress to parity between the races, but expressly ruled out majority rule.

In 1971 agreement was reached between the British Government and the regime on proposals for a settlement which provided for eventual majority rule. The British Government had to be satisfied that these Proposals were acceptable as a basis for independence to the people of Rhodesia as a whole, and a Royal Commission under Lord Pearce reported that this condition was not met. The British Government accepted the Pearce Report and did not implement the Proposals. A new settlement initiative promoted by the Presidents of Botswana, Tanzania, Zambia, Mozambique and the Prime Minister of South Africa led to an agreement in Lusaka in December 1974 between the Rhodesian regime and the enlarged African National Council that they would start constitutional talks. The other principal movements—the Zimbabwe African People's Union (ZAPU), the Zimbabwe African Nationalist Union (ZANU) and the Front for the Liberation of Zimbabwe (FROLIZI)—had some days earlier joined together under the umbrella of the ANC led by Bishop Abel Muzorewa. In the first half of 1975 a series of meetings was held between Mr Smith and an African National Council delegation led by Bishop Muzorewa. These talks were unsuccessful despite a last minute attempt to bring the two sides together at a meeting held at the Victoria Falls in August 1975.

After this meeting no further discussions were held between Mr Smith and the African nationalist movements until December 1975 when Mr Smith held preliminary talks with an African delegation led by Mr Joshua Nkomo. As a result of these discussions, substantive constitutional talks were held between the two sides but these discussions were broken off in March 1976.

On 22 March 1976 the Foreign and Commonwealth Secretary, Mr James Callaghan, announced to the British Parliament the conditions under which Britain would agree to become involved in further constitutional discussions on Rhodesia. These were:

1. the acceptance of the principle of majority rule;
2. elections for majority rule to take place in 18 months to 2 years;
3. agreement that there would be no independence before majority rule (NIBMAR);
4. any negotiations should not be long drawn out.

Mr Callaghan also said that there would need to be assurances that the transition to majority rule and to an independent Rhodesia would not be thwarted and would be orderly.

In April 1976, Dr. Kissinger the U.S. Secretary of State, who remained in close consultation with the British Government, started a series of visits to African countries which included contacts with Mr Vorster and Mr Smith. On 24 September 1976, Mr Smith announced his acceptance of the Kissinger proposals including the introduction of majority rule within two years. There followed an inconclusive Constitutional Conference at Geneva, chaired by Mr Richard, from 28 October to 14 December 1976, and attended by representatives of the African Nationalist parties and the Smith regime. In January 1977, Mr Richard toured Africa to seek agreement between the parties but his revised proposals were rejected by Mr Smith on 24 January. A further Anglo-American initiative was launched in March 1977 and the British Secretary of State, Dr Owen, visited Rhodesia in April. Negotiations continued until 18 July, when Mr Smith, declaring himself sceptical of any chance of success for the current initiative, announced a General Election for 31 August 1977, and his intention to seek some form of internal settlement.

*'Prime Minister'*: Ian Douglas Smith; *'Deputy Prime Minister'* and *'Minister' of Finance:* David Colville Smith; *'Minister' of Commerce and Industry:* Desmond William Lardner-Burke; *'Minister' of Education:* Wilfred Denis Walker; *'Minister' of Internal Affairs:* George Rollo Hayman; *'Minister' of Lands and Natural Resources, 'Minister' of Mines* and *'Minister' of Water Development:* Bernard Horace Mussett; *'Minister' of Foreign Affairs* and *'Minister' of Information, Immigration and Tourism:* Pieter Kenyon Fleming and Voltelyn van der Byl; *'Minister' of Defence* and *'Minister' of Combined Operations:* Roger Tancred Robert Hawkins; *'Minister' of Transport and Power, 'Minister' of Roads and Road Traffic* and *'Minister' of Posts:* Air Marshall Archie Wilson; *'Minister' of Local Government and Housing:* William Michie Irvine; *'Minister' of Health, 'Minister' of Manpower, Industrial Relations and Social Affairs:* Rowan Cronje; *'Minister' of Agriculture:* Mark Henry Heathcote Partridge; *'Minister' of Justice* and *'Minister' of Law and Order:* Hilary Gwyn Squires; *'Minister' of Development in Mashonaland West and Central:* Vacant; *'Minister' of Development in Matabeleland North and South:* Vacant; *'Minister' of Development in Mashonaland East and Manicaland:* Tafirenykia Chibanda Mangwende; *'Minister' of Development in Midlands and Victoria:* Zefenia Charumbira; *Deputy 'Minister' African Agriculture:* Zephaniah Maybin Bafanah; *Deputy 'Minister', African Education:* Fani Mlingo; *Deputy 'Minister', Information, Immigration, Tourism and the Public Service:* Andre Holland; *Deputy 'Minister' Internal Affairs:* Alec Moseley; *Deputy 'Minister' combined Operations and Defence:* Esmond Micklem.

### AREA AND POPULATION

Rhodesia extends from the Zambesi River to the Limpopo River and from Botswana to Mozambique. It is entirely land-locked, its neighbours being Zambia on the north and north-west, Botswana on the south-west, the Republic of South Africa on the south, and Mozambique on the east and north-east. Part of the boundary to the north with Zambia runs through Lake Kariba which was formed by the damming of the Zambesi in the Kariba Gorge. This was completed in 1959. The lake is 175 miles long, up to 20 miles wide, and covers 2,000 square miles.

The area of Rhodesia is 150,820 square miles, which is about three times the size of England. Although Rhodesia lies within the tropics the climate is not typically tropical owing to the elevation of much of the country, particularly in the High Veld areas where the majority of the population live. Of the total area 21 per cent lies over 4,000 feet above sea-level.

At 31 December 1976 the total population was estimated to be 6·65 million comprising 6·34 million Africans, 273,000 Europeans and 32,100 Asians and persons of mixed races. The African population is composed mainly of the Mashona and Matabele and their related tribes. The official language is English but Shona and Sindebele are important vernaculars.

The annual average percentage growth rate of the population for the period 1960–71 was 3·3 and for the period 1965–71 was 3·5.

### PRODUCTION, INDUSTRY AND COMMERCE

Full economic and trade statistics were last published for the year ending December 1965. In that year the Rhodesian Gross Domestic Product was £R354·3 million of which agriculture made up £R67·3 million (19·2 per cent) and manufacturing industry £R6·66 million.

In agriculture, the most valuable single crop was tobacco, worth £R32·7 million, but important contributions were made by sugar at £R9·6 million, cattle and pig slaughterings £R10·7 million, grains £R7·3 million and dairy products £R2·5 million.

Rhodesia also produced a wide variety of minerals, notably asbestos, gold, chrome and copper. Total mineral production in 1965 was valued at nearly £R32 million and mineral exports were worth over £R30 million. Exports of asbestos were £R10·8 million, those of gold £R6·8 million, copper £R6·1 million and chrome £R3·8 million. Other minerals produced in Rhodesia include coal, lithium and iron ore.

Since 1966 the international community through the United Nations has imposed sanctions on Rhodesia. The patterns of industry and agricultural development have changed as a result with emphasis being placed on diversification of crops and the development of import substitution industries. Although the Rhodesians have been able to continue some trade, the country has suffered from acute balance of payments problems and has been denied access to the international money market. Agriculture, particularly the tobacco industry, has been badly affected by the restrictions on trade.

### COMMUNICATIONS

The principal airports are Salisbury, the centre of Rhodesia's internal and external civil air communications, and Woodvale which serves Bulawayo. All the main centres of population are served by Rhodesia Railways which are connected with the South African, Mozambique and (through Zambia) the Angolan railways. The total mileage of roads at the end of 1968 (including local authority roads) was 47,084 of which 2,983 were of bitumen standard. The Rhodesian Broadcasting Corporation operates a network of medium- and short-wave transmitters for sound broadcasts and provides television programmes in the Salisbury, Bulawayo, Gwelo and Umtali areas.

### RELIGION

Numerous Christian missions of various denominations are active throughout the country, but many Africans adhere to animistic and other traditional beliefs. There are small Muslim, Hindu and Jewish communities.

# PACIFIC DEPENDENT TERRITORIES

## TUVALU

**Her Majesty's Commissioner**—T. H. Layng.

The Colony, the former Ellice Islands, comprises the nine islands of Nanumea, Nanumanga, Nuitao, Nui, Vaitupu, Nukufeatu, Funafuti, Nukulaelae and Niulakita. They are spread over 0·5 million square miles of Ocean and have an aggregate land area of about 10 square miles. The present population is estimated to be about 8,000–9,000. Tuvaluans are Polynesian and there are few of other races in the territory.

Tuvalu, as the Ellice Islands, was until 1 October 1975, part of the then GEIC (see Gilbert Islands entry). On 1 October the Ellice Islands separated from the Gilberts to form a new colony called Tuvalu. The decision to do so was made by the islanders at a referendum held in 1974 and had the full agreement of the Gilbertese.

The headquarters of the Colony are on Funafuti, Local Government is carried out through the Island Councils established on each island.

The present constitution provides for a Cabinet of three Ministers including the Chief Minister who is elected by and from the eight elected members of the House of Assembly. The Financial Secretary and Attorney-General sit ex-officio in the Cabinet and the House of Assembly. The number of members of the House will be increased to 12 at the next general election.

Independence is expected in late 1978.

Tuvalu's only cash crop is copra. The colony at present receives budgetary aid from the U.K.

There are eight primary schools and one secondary school. Further education is taken outside the colony if required.

## GILBERT ISLANDS

**Governor**—J. H. Smith, CBE.

The colony consists of the following five geographical divisions:

1. **The Gilbert Group,** comprising the 16 islands of Makin, Butaritari, Marakei, Abaiang, Tarawa, Maiana, Abemama, Kuria, Aranuka, Nonouti, Tabiteuea, Beru, Nikunau, Onotoa, Tamana and Arorae.
2. **Ocean Island.**
3. **The Phoenix Group,** comprising the eight islands of Canton (Abariringa), Enderbury, McKean, Birnie, Phoenix Sydney (Manra), Hull (Orona) and Gardner (Nikumaroro).
4. **The Line Islands,** comprising the eight islands of Fanning, Washington, Christmas, Malden, Starbuck, Vastock, Caroline, and Flint.

The Gilbert Islands extend over 2,000,000 square miles of the Central Pacific Ocean but the aggregate land area is estimated to be only 264 square miles. The population at the census of 1973 was as follows:

Gilbert Islands, 47,714; Phoenix Islands, none; Line Islands, 1,472; Ocean Island, 2,314; Ships, 429, totalling 51,926. The Gilbertese are Micronesians. At the time of the census 2,240 were listed as other Indigenous (mixtures of either Micronesians or Polynesian with any third component, such as European, Chinese, etc.), and 546 Non-indigenous (Europeans, Asians, other non-Micronesians or non-Polynesians or any mixtures of these).

There are also small colonies of Gilbertese living in the Solomon Islands, Nauru, the New Hebrides and Fiji.

The Gilbert and Ellice Islands Colony was, until 1 January 1972, within the jurisdiction of the High Commissioner for the Western Pacific, whose headquarters were at Honiara in the Solomon Islands. By an Order-in-Council dated 27 October 1971, however, the Colony was withdrawn from that jurisdiction on 1 January 1972 and is now administered by its own governor. On the same day the Central and Southern Line Islands, previously administered by the High Commissioner for the Western Pacific were included within the boundaries of the Colony.

On 1 October 1975 the Ellice Islands separated from the Gilberts to form a separate colony named Tuvalu (q.v.). The remainder of the former GEIC was renamed the Gilbert Islands.

The headquarters of the Colony are at Tarawa in the Gilbert Islands and for administration purposes, the country is divided into 5 Districts—Northern Gilberts, Central Gilberts, Southern Gilberts, Ocean Island, and Line Islands. Each one is under the charge of a District Officer, responsible to the Office of the Chief Minister in Bairiki, Tarawa. The uninhabited Phoenix Island Group comes directly under the Chief Minister's Office.

There are 17 elected Island Councils, one Urban and one Town Council each presided over by an elected President. An Island Executive Officer is appointed as Clerk to each Council.

On 1 January 1977 the Gilbert Islands (Amendment) Order 1976 introduced internal Self-Government. This provides for not more than five, nor less than seven, Ministers. The House of Assembly has 21 elected members and one ex-officio member (the Attorney-General). The number of elected members will be increased to 36 at the next general election.

The main exports of the Colony are phosphate of lime (from Ocean Island) and copra. The phosphate deposits on Ocean Island are worked by the British Phosphate Commissioners. Exports of phosphate and copra for 1974 were 521,530 tons (worth $A 18,851,122) and 8,838 tons (worth $A 3,780,784) respectively. Equivalent figures for 1975 were 520,400 tons ($A 26,695,826) and 5,792 ($A 950,456) respectively.

In 1974 there were over 12,000 children attending 102 registered primary schools. The Government Secondary School had 427 pupils, 49 of whom took the examination for the Joint Cambridge Overseas School Certificate and General Certificate of Education. Another 344 pupils attended three church secondary schools. A Government Teacher Training College provides courses for primary school teachers and the Tarawa Technical Institute conducts commercial and technical courses for a wide range of students. The Marine Training School provides a one year course, with three intakes a year, for deck, engine room and catering staff destined for employment in merchant shipping overseas. The course includes four months sea-going on board T.S. Teraaka. The Gilbert Islands participates in the University of the South Pacific.

## SOLOMON ISLANDS

**Governor**—Sir Colin H. Allan KCMG, OBE.

The Solomon Islands consists of a double row of mountainous islands extending from Bougainville Straits to Mitre Island in the Santa Cruz Group for a distance of 900 miles, and north and south from the Ontong Java group to Rennell Island for a distance of 430 miles. The total land area of the protectorate is about 11,500 square miles.

A British Protectorate was proclaimed over the Southern Solomon Islands (Guadalcanal, Savo, Malaita, San Cristoval. the New Georgia Group and its dependencies) in 1893. In 1898 and 1899 the islands of the Santa Cruz group, including Utupua, Ticopia Vanikoro, the remote islands of Cherry and Mitre, Sikaiana, and the islands of Rennel and Bellona were added to the protectorate, and in 1900 the northern islands, namely Santa Ysabel, Choiseul, the islands of the Shortlands Group, south and south-east of the main island of Bougainville, and the atoll group of Ontong Java, were transferred under convention from Germany to Great Britain.

A full census was taken in the Solomon Islands in February 1976, and the provisional figure for the population is 197,000 mainly Melanesians. The growth rate is approximately 1·4 per cent.

Until 1960 the High Commissioner, who administered the Protectorate, was assisted by an Advisory Council. In that year nominated Executive and Legislative Councils were established and elected members were introduced in 1964. A revised constitution was introduced in 1967 and from then until its dissolution in March 1970 the Legislative Council consisted of three *ex-officio* members, 14 elected members and not more than 12 public service members.

In 1970, the Executive and Legislative Councils were replaced by a single Governing Council, with an elected majority for the first time, which combined both executive and legislative functions and exercises executive control through a series of functional committees.

In 1974 a new Constitution was introduced, and a new office of Governor of the Protectorate, replacing the High Commissioner was introduced. The Governing Council was replaced in its legislative capacity by the new Legislative Assembly whose 24 elected members chose a Chief Minister. He selected the Ministers who, together with ex-officio members, formed the Council of Ministers, which replaced the Governing Council in its executive capacity. Originally the Council of Ministers was composed of six Ministers and three *ex-officio* members, but in June 1975 the number of Ministers was increased to eight, to include a Minister of Finance and the number of *ex-officio* members dropped to two. The Constitution has recently been further amended to increase the number of ministers to 10 and to recognize the Opposition and Independent Groups.

Internal self-government was conferred on 2 January 1976. Under the revised Constitution, the Governor must act in accordance with the advice of the Council of Ministers except in his reserved subjects of defence, external affairs, and internal security. The Public Service has now been executivized. The Council of Ministers presided over by the Chief Minister is collectively responsible to the Legislative Assembly for the advice given to the Governor. The size of the Legislative Assembly has been increased from 24 to 38 elected members.

Independence is expected in mid-1978.

The economy of the Solomons is largely dependent on the copra industry. The greater part of the copra exported before the war was produced on coconut plantations owned and operated by Europeans. During the Japanese occupation the plantations were abandoned but production recovered in due course. More than half the total production now comes from Solomon Islanders' smallholdings. In 1975, 23,108 tons were produced. Timber, the second main export, is a rapidly expanding industry. In 1975, 229,000 cubic metres of timber were produced. Cocoa is slowly being developed as another cash crop: 122 tons being exported in 1975. Rice is being grown on the Guadalcanal plains and the country is fast approaching self-sufficiency in this crop. An export trade in spices is growing and over 40 tons was exported in 1974. Investigations into other crops continue. The cattle population in 1975 was 24,000. Following successful oil-palm trials, an 8,000 acre oil-palm plantation has been developed on Guadalcanal by the Commonwealth Development Corporation, with local participation. Milling is expected to start in the second quarter of 1976.

In April 1971 an agreement with Taiyo Fisheries Company of Japan, was concluded, providing for a fisheries survey of the Solomons waters with a view to development of a fishing industry. An agreement between the Territory and Taiyo was subsequently signed in September 1972. Fish catches in 1975 amounted to 7,160 tons of skipjack, of which 3,372 tons were shipped frozen and most of the rest processed into cans or arabushi (smoked).

Mineral exploration for copper, bauxite and nickel is being carried out by private interests and in May 1971 an agreement was reached between the Government and the Mitsui Mining and Smelting Company of Japan for the trial mining of bauxite on Rennell Island. No final decision has yet been taken about full scale operations.

The Solomons National Development Plan for 1975–79 provides for expenditure of some $A60 m with emphasis on productive investment in agriculture, forestry, and mineral resources, and the provision of trained manpower.

Total domestic exports in 1975 amounted to $A11·8 m. Imports (mainly manufactured goods, machinery, transport and equipment totalled $A22·3 m. The revised estimate of revenue for 1976 is $A18,247,370 (including British Development Aid of $A5,750,000; U.K. Grant-in-Aid of $A1,600,000).

## PITCAIRN ISLAND GROUP

**Governor**—Mr. Harold Smedley CMG, MBE(Mil), British High Commission, Wellington, New Zealand.

Pitcairn Island lies 25° 04′ S. and 130° 06′ W., about half way between Panama and New Zealand. The land is fertile but there is little surface water; agriculture is at the subsistence level and the economy is based on the sale of postage stamps and handicrafts.

Pitcairn was discovered by Cartaret in 1767 and in 1790 Fletcher Christian, finding it uninhabited, landed with nine of the 'Bounty' mutineers and 18 Tahitians of whom 12 were women. After ten years of strife and murder the small community settled down under the leadership of John Adams and its existence remained unknown until 1808. On two occasions the island was evacuated but each time people returned.

Pitcairn is a British colony by settlement and its constitutional history began in 1838 when a formal constitution was first introduced. In 1898 it came within the jurisdiction of the High Commissioner for the Western Pacific, and in 1952 administration was transferred to the Governor of Fiji. When Fiji became independent on 10 October 1970, and the Office of Governor lapsed, the governorship of the islands was transferred to the British High Commissioner in New Zealand. The Island has its own elected local government headed by the Island Magistrate.

The Islanders are almost all active members of the Seventh Day Adventist Church which is in charge of a resident minister from overseas. Compulsory primary education has been a feature of Pitcairn's life for almost one hundred and forty years and a Government school is conducted by a teacher seconded from the New Zealand Department of Education. There is no resident doctor but a Government dispensary is run by a qualified nurse who is usually the wife of the resident minister.

The population in June 1977 was 67.

Communication with the outside world is primarily dependent on a well-equipped Government radio station. Supplies are brought at tri-monthly intervals by scheduled cargo vessels. Other cargo vessels make unscheduled stopovers.

There are no facilities on the Island for visitors and immigration is controlled.

The remaining three islands of the Pitcairn Group—Henderson, Ducie and Oeno—are uninhabited.

*Commissioner:* R. J. Hicks, British Consulate General, Auckland, New Zealand.

*Island Magistrate:* Ivan Christian, Pitcairn Island.

## THE NEW HEBRIDES (ANGLO-FRENCH CONDOMINIUM)

The New Hebrides Islands were discovered by a Spanish explorer, de Quiros, in 1606. They were visited on a number of occasions during the next two centuries, and by 1887 a number of British and French missionaries, planters and traders had established themselves throughout the islands. In that year an Anglo-French Convention was signed, by which each nation agreed not to exercise separate control over the group and appointed a joint naval mission, charged with the protection, in the New Hebrides, of the lives and property of the subjects of France and England.

In February 1906 a conference of British and French officials took place in London and a draft convention was prepared to provide for the settlement of difficulties which had arisen from the absence of jurisdiction over the natives. A protocol, drawn up in London in 1914 to replace the Convention of 1906, was ratified on the 18 March 1922 and proclaimed in the New Hebrides in August 1923.

Administration is in the hands of British and French Resident Commissioners, subordinate to their respective High Commissioners. Each has a staff of national officers and there is, in addition, a Joint Administration: a mixed British and French staff working in departments under the joint control of the two Resident Commissioners. Following a Ministerial meeting in London, in November 1974, between the British and French Governments, it was agreed to create a Representative Assembly for the New Hebrides, elected by universal suffrage, to replace the old Advisory Council. The Assembly would have wider statutory powers to deal with issues and problems affecting the New Hebrides, and elections for the Assembly were held in November 1975. It was also agreed to create municipal councils for the towns of Vila and Santo and, eventually, community councils in the outlying islands.

### AREA AND POPULATION

The total area of the New Hebrides, to which are attached the Banks and Torres Islands, is about 5,700 square miles.

The total population, including persons under the jurisdiction of Britain and France at the time of the first census in May 1967 was 77,988, of whom 92·5 per cent were Melanesians; 1,631 were British subjects or under British jurisdiction. The population at 31 December 1975 was estimated to be 96,532.

### FINANCE

English sterling and French currency in the form of New Hebridean francs are both legal tender in the New Hebrides. Australian currency is officially recognized in substitution for sterling at current exchange rates. In 1975, Condominium revenue was 666,800,000 FNH, and recurrent expenditure 841,000,000 FNH. The national administration are financed largely from metropolitan funds, and development funds are provided from metropolitan sources.

In view of the absence of direct taxation (with the exception of an Added Value Tax on subdivided land sales) there has been growing interest in the New Hebrides as a finance centre.

The number of banks in Vila increased from one in early 1969 to 12 at the end of 1975, and there was a corresponding growth in other professions associated with the finance industry.

## PRODUCTION AND COMMERCE

Main subsistence crops are yams, taro, manioc, sweet potato, and breadfruit.

There is a plant for freezing fish on Santo. Chilled and frozen meat are exported from Santo, and there are meat canners at Santo and Vila.

Imports during 1975 were valued at 2,496,000,000 FNH. Principal items imported in 1973 included foodstuffs, timber and building supplies, motor vehicles, mineral fuels and agricultural machinery. The main food imports were rice, canned meat and fish, dairy products, frozen meat and fresh fruit and vegetables.

The sources of imports continue to be principally Australia, France and Japan which has become an important source, particularly for motor vehicles.

Substantial progress has been made in the Co-operative field since 1964; at the end of 1975 there were 190 operating societies with a membership of more than 11,000 adults and an estimated turnover of $A5,000,000.

There are about 400 miles of roads, 240 of these being seasonal earth motor tracks. Shipping services are maintained with Sydney, Australia, Noumea, New Caledonia, Marseilles via Panama Canal and San Francisco. There are daily flights to New Caledonia, thrice-weekly flights to Fiji, and once weekly to Nauru, with connections to Australia, Asia, Europe and the U.S.A.

## COMMUNICATIONS

Since July 1975, the New Hebrides have been participants in 'Peace Sat' programmes, using a former U.S. satellite launched in 1966, known as ATS 1 (Applications Technology Satellite) which is in fixed orbit over 155°W. This is used solely for educational purposes; the New Hebrides terminal is in the Teacher Training College, and the control centre is at the University of the South Pacific, Suva, Fiji. It is not narrowly educational—time is given to gerontology, social welfare, management training, architecture, nursing etc etc.

## EDUCATION

The first missionaries to reach the island, Williams and Harris of the London Missionary Society, were murdered in 1839. Frequent and persistent attempts were afterwards made by various mission bodies for the Christianizing of the natives, and half a century later mission stations existed in various parts. The chief bodies carrying on work in the New Hebrides are the Presbyterian Church, the Melanesian Missionary Society, the Seventh-Day Adventists, the Church of Christ and the Roman Catholic Church.

The Condominium Government has no education service as the British and French Education Departments each organize Primary and Secondary schools. However it does control Tagabe Agriculture School with alternate years of entry for Anglophones and Francophones. The Condominium makes an annual subsidy to each national Administration (in 1975 the subsidy to the British service was $388,500). The balance spent on the British education programme comes mainly from British aid funds. Education is not compulsory, but places at primary schools, many established in the past by missions, are now available for most children. District Education Committees supervise the mangement of most English-medium Primary schools. The S.D.A. church operates its school system quite separately. Secondary education is available at the British Government secondary school, (Forms I–V) opened in 1966, and the French Lyceé, both in Vila. Three other High Schools offer English-medium education to selected pupils throughout the New Hebrides. These schools are foundations of the Anglican and Presbyterian Churches and the Churches of Christ. They are subsidized by the British National Service and a fourth high school run by the S.D.A. church remains outside the system. There is limited secondary education at three French mission schools. In 1975 there were 125 British Primary schools with 9,551 pupils, 226 pupils were enrolled at the secondary school, and 512 at lower secondary schools (Forms I–III).

A British teacher training college, established with the aid of CD & W funds, had 56 students in 1975.

Scholarships from local and overseas funds enabled 118 New Hebridean students to follow courses of study overseas in 1975, in Australia, Britain, Fiji, New Zealand, Papua/New Guinea and the British Solomon Islands.

# United States of America

**Capital**—Washington, D.C.

**President**—James E. Carter, Jnr.

**National Flag:** Parti of 13 fesse-wise, countercharged red and white; on a canton blue extending to the lower edge of the fourth red stripe 50 five-pointed stars white.

## CONSTITUTION AND GOVERNMENT

THE United States of America is a federal union of 50 states or commonwealths. Its basic law is the Constitution, adopted in 1789, which prescribes the structure and method of national government and lists its rights and fields of authority, other rights and activities being reserved to the individual states. All government in America, therefore, has the dual character of both Federal and State Government.

The basic principle of all American government is the separation of the three branches: legislative, executive and judicial, with a system of checks and balances.

Supreme legislative power lies with Congress, which consists of a Senate and a House of Representatives. The Senate is composed of 100 members, two from each of the 50 states, who are elected for a term of six years. Senators were originally chosen by the State legislatures, but this procedure was changed by the 17th Amendment to the Constitution adopted in 1913, which made the election of Senators a function of the electorate. One-third of the Senate is elected every two years, thereby ensuring continuity. The House of Representatives, at the present time, consists of 435 members, the number representing each State being based on population, but every State, no matter how small, is entitled to at least one Representative. Members are elected by the electorate for two-year terms, all terms running for the same period.

Both Senators and Representatives must be residents of the State from which they are chosen. In addition, a Senator must be at least 30 years of age and must have been a citizen of the United States for at least nine years. A Representative must be at least 25 years of age and must have been a citizen for at least seven years.

One Resident Commissioner is elected to the House of Representatives from the Commonwealth of Puerto Rico. This Commissioner takes part in the discussions, serves on committees, but has no vote.

A delegate from the District of Columbia is elected by the qualified voters of the District, which is the capital of the United States. He likewise participates in debates and committee work but does not have a vote. He may, however, introduce legislation, as does the Resident Commissioner of Puerto Rico.

The work of preparing and considering legislation is done mainly by committees of both Houses of Congress. There are 17 standing committees in the Senate and 21 in the House of Representatives. In addition, there are special committees in each House and more than 20 congressional commissions and joint committees composed of Members of both Houses.

Included in the powers of Congress are the powers to assess and collect taxes, to regulate foreign and interstate commerce, to coin money, to establish post offices and post roads, to establish courts inferior to the Supreme Court, to declare war and to raise and maintain an army and navy.

Another power possessed by Congress is the right to propose amendments to the Constitution whenever two-thirds of both Houses shall consider it necessary. Should two-thirds of the State legislatures demand changes in the Constitution, it is the duty of Congress to call a constitutional convention. Proposed amendments, however, are not valid until ratified by the legislatures or by conventions of three-fourths of the States, as one or other mode of ratification may be proposed by Congress.

Under the Constitution, the Senate is granted certain powers not accorded to the House of Representatives. The Senate approves or disapproves major Presidential appointments by majority vote, and treaties must be ratified by a two-thirds vote. The President may call a special session of the Senate even when the House is not sitting. The House of Representatives is granted the sole right of originating all bills for the raising of revenue.

This method of granting different powers to the different Houses is part of the fundamental idea of 'checks and balances' that has always inspired American government to prevent the possibility of any one section obtaining too much power. The House of Representatives, for example, has the sole right of instituting impeachment proceedings against the President, Vice-President or other civil officers, but the Senate has the sole right of trying such impeachment. Senators and Representatives cannot be impeached, but each House may expel a Member by a two-thirds vote.

The Constitution also imposes prohibitions on Congress. No export duty can be imposed. Ports of one State cannot be given preference over those of another State. No title of nobility may be granted.

Twenty-six amendments have so far been added to the original Constitution of seven articles. The first ten amendments, known as the Bill of Rights, were added in a group in 1791. These establish the individual rights and freedoms to all people of the States, including freedom of speech, freedom of the press, freedom of worship, the right to peaceful assembly, the right to be secure in one's home against unreasonable searches and seizures, and the right of an accused person to a speedy trial by jury.

The eleventh amendment deprives the federal courts of jurisdiction over suits against States instituted by citizens of other states or foreign countries. The twelfth amendment defines the rather complicated method of electing the President and Vice-President, whereby the people elect 'electors' for the purpose. The thirteenth amendment abolished slavery.

The fourteenth and fifteenth defined citizenship and gave the vote to all male citizens, regardless of race, colour or previous condition of servitude. These were adopted in 1868 and 1870, and there were no more amendments until 1913, when the Federal Government, by the sixteenth amendment, at last gained the power to levy income tax. The seventeenth, as already mentioned, defined the procedure for the election of Senators. The eighteenth was the famous Prohibition Law, repealed by the twenty-first. The nineteenth gave the vote to women, and was adopted in 1920. The twentieth defines the terms of President and Vice-President, which 'shall end on the twentieth day of January', and also of the Senators and Representatives, which end 'at noon on the third day of January'. Prior to this amendment there was a lapse of four months between election and taking office. The twenty-second amendment, adopted in 1951, makes it impossible for any President to hold office for more than two terms. The twenty-third amendment, adopted in 1961, gives to the residents of the District of Columbia—the seat of government—the right to vote in the election of the President and Vice-President. The twenty-fourth amendment, adopted in 1964, provides that the right of citizens to vote in federal elections shall not be denied or abridged for failure to pay a poll tax or any other tax. The twenty-fifth amendment, adopted in 1967, provides for the office of Acting President in case of the inability of the President to discharge the powers and duties of his office. It also provides for the nomination by the President of a Vice-President when there is a vacancy in the office of Vice-President.

The twenty-sixth amendment, adopted in 1971, provides that the right of citizens, who are eighteen years of age or older, to vote shall not be abridged on account of age.

The President heads the executive branch of the government and is elected for a four-year term. He must be a native-born citizen of the United States at least 35 years old. His chief duties are to carry out the programme of the government as directed in the Constitution and in laws made by Congress. In addition, however, he recommends to Congress much major legislation and the amounts of money which should be appropriated to carry out government functions. He also has the right to veto legislation passed by Congress, although Congress in turn may enact legislation over his veto by a two-thirds majority vote. The President is also commander-in-chief of the armed forces. His cabinet is formed by the heads of the various executive departments, known as Secretaries, who are appointed by him for an indefinite term. Cabinet officers may not serve in the Congress while they hold posts in the Executive branch of the Government.

*President:* James Earl Carter Jr.
*Vice-President:* Walter Frederick Mondale.

**Cabinet**

*Secretary of State:* Cyrus R. Vance.
*Secretary of the Treasury:* W. Michael Blumenthal.
*Secretary of Defense:* Harold Brown.
*Attorney General:* Griffin B. Bell.
*Secretary of the Interior:* Cecil D. Andrus.
*Secretary of Agriculture:* Bob S. Bergland.

*Secretary of Commerce:* Juanita M. Kreps.
*Secretary of Labor:* F. Ray Marshall.
*Secretary of Health, Education, and Welfare:* Joseph A. Califano Jnr.
*Secretary of Housing and Urban Development:* Patricia Roberta Harris.
*Secretary of Transportation:* Brock Adams.
*Director of Office Management and Budget:* James McIntyre.
*Chairman of the Council of Economic Advisors:* Charles L. Schultze.
*Director of Central Intelligence:* Adm. Stansfield Turner.
*Permanent U.S. Representative to the United Nations:* Andrew J. Young.
*National Security Advisor:* Zbigniew Brzezinski.
*Energy Advisor:* James Schlesinger.

**House of Representatives.** The Ninety-fifth Congress of the United States is constituted as follows: Democrats, 289; Republicans, 145; Vacancies, 1.

**Senate.** Senators are elected for terms of six years, one-third retiring or seeking re-election every two years. Representation of the parties is as follows: Democrats, 62; Republicans, 38.

### LOCAL GOVERNMENT

State Government follows much the same pattern as Federal Government. Each State has its own Constitution and, with the exception of Nebraska, a two-chamber legislature. The States are entitled to make their own laws providing these do not conflict with the main Constitution. Within limits, however, there are many differences in detail. Most State legislatures meet every two years, but those of New York, New Jersey, Massachusetts, Rhode Island and South Carolina meet annually, while in Alabama the legislature meets only once every four years.

Each State has a Governor, elected by popular vote, and his term varies from two to four years. The State is entitled to its own police and militia, has authority over education, public works, roads and development, and has its own State courts and legal system. In every State except North Carolina the Governor has the power to veto acts of the legislature, but the latter may over-rule the veto if it can muster the required number of votes.

The States are subdivided into counties (parishes in Louisiana), townships, cities, villages and special areas, such as school districts, water-control districts and forest-preserve areas. Each of these political subdivisions has its own administration suitable for the type of area covered (urban or rural), but the administrations have no authority of their own. Authority flows only from the State. Counties administer State laws and have fairly wide powers in the fields of health, education, taxation and so on, besides being the electoral area for the election of State officials; towns and villages are more limited in their local government. Cities are usually governed under a charter from the State legislature, although many have recently been granted the privilege of framing their own charters within the State constitution. In all cases officials are elected, not appointed by the State.

### LEGAL SYSTEM

The United States judiciary consists of both State and Federal systems, the Federal system dealing purely with Federal matters except suits between citizens of different States. It consists of a Supreme Court created by Article III, section 1, of the Constitution, which provides that 'the Judicial Power of the United States shall be vested in one supreme Court, and in such inferior Courts as the Congress may from time to time ordain and establish'.

The Supreme Court comprises a Chief Justice and eight Associate Justices, who are appointed for life by the President with the advice and consent of the Senate. A Justice or Judge may, if he so desires retire at the age of 70 after serving for ten years as a Federal judge or at age 65 after 15 years service.

Below the Supreme Court are the Courts of Appeals and District Courts, still in the Federal System. The Courts of Appeals are intermediate appellate courts to relieve the Supreme Court of considering all appeals in cases originally decided by the Federal trial courts. The United States is divided into 11 judicial circuits, including the District of Columbia as a circuit, in each of which there is a United States Court of Appeals. Each of the 50 States is assigned to one of the circuits, and the territories are assigned variously to the first, third, fifth and ninth circuits. Each Court of Appeals has from three to 15 circuit judges, making 97 in all, depending upon the amount of work in the circuit.

The District Courts are the trial courts with general Federal jurisdiction. Each State has at least one District Court, while some of the larger States have as many as four. Altogether there are 93 District Courts in the 50 States, plus the one in the District of Columbia. In addition, the Commonwealth of Puerto Rico has a United States district court with limited jurisdiction corresponding to that of district courts in the various States. Each District Court has from one to 27 judges.

In addition, the Federal system has special courts as follows: the United States Court of Claims, the United States Court of Customs and Patent Appeals, the United States Customs Court, the United States Tax Court, the District Courts in the Canal Zone, Guam, and the Virgin Islands, and the Court of Military Appeals.

Each State has a system of courts which is independent of the Federal system. These Courts cover all State matters from civil disputes to crime. Cases may be taken on appeal from the highest State court to the Federal Supreme Court either (*a*) when it is claimed that the State has denied the appellant his federal constitutional rights, or (*b*) when the case is such that it comes under Federal jurisdiction because it involves a Federal question.

State courts consist of Justices' Courts, or Municipal Courts in large cities, for minor cases, of County Courts or other courts of original jurisdiction for the trial of more important cases, in some States of intermediate courts of appeals, and of a Supreme Court or highest court of appeals. The Municipal Court system of a city usually includes police courts, and a civil court. Many of the States also have special courts such as the Probate Court, Juvenile Court, Court of Domestic Relations and Courts of Small Claims.

State law varies in the various States on such matters as divorce, licensing, procedure and so on, but no State may make a law which conflicts with the Constitution.

**Supreme Court**

*Chief Justice:* Warren E. Burger.

**Court of Appeals** (For the District of Columbia Circuit)

*Chief Judge:* David L. Bazelon.

**Court of Customs and Patent Appeals**

*Chief Judge:* Howard T. Markey.

**Court of Claims**

*Chief Judge:* Wilson Cowen.

**Customs Court**

*Chief Judge:* Nils A. Boe.

### AREA AND POPULATION

The United States lies in the temperate zone of North America, covering an area of 3,615,122 sq. miles. This is the area of what is known as the 'continental' United States, which reaches from the Atlantic to the Pacific and from the borders of Canada to Mexico, plus Alaska and Hawaii. Including the Territories and Possessions, the total area is 3,628,062 sq. miles. The inhabitants of Puerto Rico, and the outlying areas of U.S. sovereignty or jurisdiction, together with members of the Armed Forces and other Americans abroad, numbered 4·7 million on 1 April 1970.

The continental United States is divided into 50 States and one district, the District of Columbia, which contains the Federal Capital, Washington. The original number of States at the time of the formation of the United States was 13, and the territory and population expanded as shown by the following two tables:

| *Census date* | *Gross area* | *Population* | *Population per sq. mile land* |
|---|---|---|---|
| 1790 | 888,811 | 3,929,214 | 4·5 |
| 1810 | 1,716,003 | 7,239,881 | 4·3 |
| 1830 | 1,788,006 | 12,866,020 | 7·4 |
| 1850 | 2,992,747 | 23,191,876 | 7·9 |
| 1870 | 3,022,387 | 38,558,371 | 13·0 |
| 1890 | 3,022,387 | 62,979,766 | 21·2 |
| 1910 | 3,022,387 | 92,228,496 | 31·0 |
| 1930 | 3,022,387 | 123,202,624 | 41·2 |
| 1950 | 3,022,387 | 151,325,798 | 50·7 |
| 1960 | 3,615,122 | 179,323,175 | 50·6 |
| 1970 | 3,615,122 | 203,235,298 | 57·5 |

| *Accession* | *Date* | *Gross Area (Land and water sq. miles)* |
|---|---|---|
| Total | — | 3,628,062* |
| Continental U.S. | — | 3,022,260 |
| Territory in 1790 (i) | — | 888,685 |
| Louisiana Purchase | 1803 | 827,192 |
| By Treaty with Spain: | | |
| Florida | 1819 | 58,560 |
| Other areas | 1819 | 13,443 |
| Texas | 1845 | 390,143 |
| Oregon | 1846 | 285,580 |
| Mexican Cession | 1848 | 529,017 |
| Gadsden Purchase | 1853 | 29,640 |
| Alaska | 1867 | 586,412 |
| Hawaii | 1898 | 6,450 |
| Puerto Rico | 1898 | 3,435 |
| Guam | 1899 | 212 |
| American Samoa | 1900 | 76 |
| Panama Canal Zone | 1904 | 553 |
| Virgin Islands of the U.S. | 1917 | 133 |

* Includes the Trust Territory of the Pacific Islands (8,489) and misc. other islands (42).

(i) Excludes that part of drainage basin of Red River of the North, south of 49th parallel, sometimes considered part of Louisiana Purchase.

Area and population of the individual States are shown below:

| | *Area in Sq. Mile* | | *Population* | |
|---|---|---|---|---|
| *Division and State* | *Gross* | *Inland Water** | *Census 1960* | *Census 1970* |
| **New England** | | | | |
| Maine | 33,215 | 2,295 | 969,265 | 993,663 |
| New Hampshire | 9,304 | 277 | 606,921 | 737,681 |
| Vermont | 9,609 | 342 | 389,881 | 444,732 |
| Massachu'ts | 8,257 | 431 | 5,148,578 | 5,689,170 |
| Rhode Island | 1,214 | 165 | 859,488 | 949,723 |
| Connecticut | 5,009 | 147 | 2,535,234 | 3,032,217 |
| **Total** | 66,608 | 3,657 | 10,509,367 | 11,847,186 |
| **Middle Atlantic** | | | | |
| New York | 49,576 | 1,745 | 16,782,304 | 18,241,266 |
| New Jersey | 7,836 | 315 | 6,066,782 | 7,168,164 |
| Pennsylvania | 45,333 | 367 | 11,319,366 | 11,793,909 |
| **Total** | 102,745 | 2,427 | 34,168,452 | 37,203,339 |
| **East North Central** | | | | |
| Ohio | 41,222 | 247 | 9,706,397 | 10,652,017 |
| Indiana | 36,291 | 194 | 4,662,498 | 5,193,669 |
| Illinois | 56,400 | 652 | 10,081,158 | 11,113,976 |
| Michigan | 58,216 | 1,399 | 7,823,194 | 8,875,083 |
| Wisconsin | 56,154 | 1,690 | 3,951,777 | 4,417,933 |
| **Total** | 248,283 | 4,182 | 36,225,024 | 40,252,678 |
| **West North Central** | | | | |
| Minnesota | 84,068 | 4,779 | 3,413,864 | 3,805,069 |
| Iowa | 56,290 | 349 | 2,757,537 | 2,825,041 |
| Missouri | 69,686 | 691 | 4,319,813 | 4,677,399 |
| N. Dakota | 70,665 | 1,392 | 632,446 | 617,761 |
| S. Dakota | 77,047 | 1,092 | 680,514 | 666,257 |
| Nebraska | 77,227 | 744 | 1,411,330 | 1,483,791 |
| Kansas | 82,264 | 477 | 2,178,611 | 2,249,071 |
| **Total** | 517,247 | 9,524 | 15,394,115 | 16,324,389 |

*continued*

| | *Area in Sq. Mile* | | *Population* | |
|---|---|---|---|---|
| *Division and State* | *Gross* | *Inland Water** | *Census 1960* | *Census 1970* |
| **South Atlantic** | | | | |
| Delaware | 2,057 | 75 | 446,292 | 548,104 |
| Maryland | 10,577 | 686 | 3,100,689 | 3,922,399 |
| District of Columbia | 67 | 6 | 763,956 | 756,510 |
| Virginia | 40,817 | 1,037 | 3,966,949 | 4,648,494 |
| W. Virginia | 24,181 | 111 | 1,860,421 | 1,744,237 |
| N. Carolina | 52,586 | 3,788 | 4,556,155 | 5,082,059 |
| S. Carolina | 31,055 | 830 | 2,382,594 | 2,590,516 |
| Georgia | 58,876 | 803 | 3,943,116 | 4,589,575 |
| Florida | 58,560 | 4,470 | 4,951,560 | 6,789,443 |
| **Total** | 278,776 | 11,806 | 25,971,732 | 30,671,337 |
| **East South Central** | | | | |
| Kentucky | 40,395 | 745 | 3,038,156 | 3,219,311 |
| Tennessee | 42,244 | 916 | 3,567,089 | 3,924,164 |
| Alabama | 51,609 | 901 | 3,266,740 | 3,444,165 |
| Mississippi | 47,716 | 420 | 2,178,141 | 2,216,912 |
| **Total** | 181,964 | 2,982 | 12,050,126 | 12,804,552 |
| **West South Central** | | | | |
| Arkansas | 53,104 | 1,159 | 1,786,272 | 1,923,295 |
| Louisiana | 48,523 | 3,593 | 3,257,022 | 3,643,180 |
| Oklahoma | 69,919 | 1,137 | 2,328,284 | 2,559,253 |
| Texas | 267,338 | 5,204 | 9,579,677 | 11,196,730 |
| **Total** | 438,884 | 11,093 | 16,951,255 | 19,322,458 |
| **Mountain** | | | | |
| Montana | 147,138 | 1,551 | 674,767 | 694,409 |
| Idaho | 83,557 | 880 | 667,191 | 713,008 |
| Wyoming | 97,914 | 711 | 330,066 | 332,416 |
| Colorado | 104,247 | 481 | 1,753,947 | 2,207,259 |
| New Mexico | 121,666 | 254 | 951,023 | 1,016,000 |
| Arizona | 113,909 | 492 | 1,302,161 | 1,772,482 |
| Utah | 84,916 | 2,820 | 890,627 | 1,059,273 |
| Nevada | 110,540 | 651 | 285,278 | 488,738 |
| **Total** | 863,887 | 7,840 | 6,855,060 | 8,283,585 |
| **Pacific** | | | | |
| Washington | 68,192 | 1,622 | 2,853,214 | 3,409,169 |
| Oregon | 96,981 | 797 | 1,768,687 | 2,091,385 |
| California | 158,693 | 2,332 | 15,717,204 | 19,953,134 |
| Alaska | 586,412 | 19,980 | 226,167 | 302,173 |
| Hawaii | 6,450 | 25 | 632,772 | 769,913 |
| **Total** | 916,728 | 24,756 | 21,198,044 | 26,525,774 |
| Puerto Rico | 3,435 | 14 | 2,349,544 | 2,712,033 |
| **Grand Total*** | 3,615,122 | 78,267 | 181,672,719 | 205,947,331 |

* Excluding areas of oceans and bays, the Gulf of Mexico, the Great Lakes, Long Island Sound, Puget Sound and the Straits of Juan de Fuca and Georgia.

There are 513 towns and cities with a population of more than 100,000. The following table shows cities and populations of 100,000 or more and the States in which they are located. Figures are taken from the 1970 census count:

| City | State | Population |
|---|---|---|
| Akron | Ohio | 275,425 |
| Albany | New York | 115,781 |
| Albuquerque | New Mexico | 243,751 |
| Alexandria | Virginia | 110,927 |
| Allentown | Pennsylvania | 109,871 |
| Amarillo | Texas | 127,010 |
| Anaheim | California | 166,408 |
| Ann Arbor | Michigan | 100,035 |
| Atlanta | Georgia | 495,039 |
| Austin | Texas | 253,539 |
| Baltimore | Maryland | 905,787 |
| Baton Rouge | Louisiana | 165,921 |
| Beaumont | Texas | 117,548 |
| Berkeley | California | 114,091 |
| Birmingham | Alabama | 300,910 |
| Boston | Massachusetts | 641,071 |
| Bridgeport | Connecticut | 156,542 |
| Buffalo | New York | 462,768 |
| Cambridge | Massachusetts | 100,361 |
| Camden | New Jersey | 102,551 |
| Canton | Ohio | 110,053 |
| Cedar Rapids | Iowa | 110,642 |
| Charlotte | North Carolina | 241,299 |
| Chattanooga | Tennessee | 119,923 |
| Chicago | Illinois | 3,369,357 |
| Cincinnati | Ohio | 453,514 |
| Cleveland | Ohio | 750,879 |
| Colorado Springs | Colorado | 135,060 |
| Columbia | South Carolina | 113,542 |
| Columbus | Georgia | 155,028 |
| Columbus | Ohio | 540,025 |
| Corpus Christi | Texas | 204,525 |
| Dallas | Texas | 844,401 |
| Dayton | Ohio | 242,917 |
| Dearborn | Michigan | 104,199 |
| Denver | Colorado | 514,678 |
| Des Moines | Iowa | 201,404 |
| Detroit | Michigan | 1,514,063 |
| Duluth | Minnesota | 100,578 |
| Elizabeth | New Jersey | 112,654 |
| El Paso | Texas | 322,261 |
| Erie | Pennsylvania | 129,265 |
| Evansville | Indiana | 138,764 |
| Flint | Michigan | 193,317 |
| Fort Lauderdale | Florida | 139,590 |
| Fort Wayne | Indiana | 178,021 |
| Fort Worth | Texas | 393,476 |
| Fremont | California | 100,869 |
| Fresno | California | 165,655 |
| Garden Grove | California | 121,155 |
| Gary | Indiana | 175,415 |
| Glendale | California | 132,664 |
| Grand Rapids | Michigan | 197,649 |
| Greensboro | North Carolina | 144,076 |
| Hammond | Indiana | 107,983 |
| Hampton | Virginia | 120,779 |
| Hartford | Connecticut | 158,017 |
| Hialeah | Florida | 102,452 |
| Hollywood | Florida | 106,873 |
| Honolulu | Hawaii | 324,871 |
| Houston | Texas | 1,233,535 |
| Huntington Beach | California | 115,960 |
| Huntsville | Alabama | 139,282 |
| Independence | Missouri | 111,630 |
| Indianapolis | Indiana | 746,428 |
| Jackson | Mississippi | 162,380 |
| Jacksonville | Florida | 528,865 |
| Jersey City | New Jersey | 260,350 |
| Kansas City | Kansas | 168,213 |
| Kansas City | Missouri | 507,330 |
| Knoxville | Tennessee | 174,587 |
| Lansing | Michigan | 131,403 |
| Las Vegas | Nevada | 125,787 |
| Lexington | Kentucky | 108,137 |
| Lincoln | Nebraska | 149,518 |
| Little Rock | Arkansas | 132,483 |
| Livonia | Michigan | 110,109 |
| Long Beach | California | 358,879 |
| Los Angeles | California | 2,811.801 |
| Louisville | Kentucky | 361,706 |
| Lubbock | Texas | 149,101 |
| Macon | Georgia | 122,423 |
| Madison | Wisconsin | 171,988 |
| Memphis | Tennessee | 623,988 |

*continued*

| City | State | Population |
|---|---|---|
| Miami | Florida | 334,859 |
| Milwaukee | Wisconsin | 717,372 |
| Minneapolis | Minnesota | 434,400 |
| Mobile | Alabama | 190,026 |
| Montgomery | Alabama | 140,102 |
| Nashville-Davidson | Tennessee | 447,877 |
| Newark | New Jersey | 381,930 |
| New Bedford | Massachusetts | 101,777 |
| New Haven | Connecticut | 137,707 |
| New Orleans | Louisiana | 593,471 |
| Newport News | Virginia | 138,177 |
| New York (City) | New York | 7,895,563 |
| Norfolk | Virginia | 307,951 |
| Oakland | California | 361,561 |
| Oklahoma City | Oklahoma | 368,164 |
| Omaha | Nebraska | 346,929 |
| Parma | Ohio | 100,216 |
| Pasadena | California | 112,951 |
| Paterson | New Jersey | 144,824 |
| Peoria | Illinois | 126,963 |
| Philadelphia | Pennsylvania | 1,949,996 |
| Phoenix | Arizona | 584,303 |
| Pittsburgh | Pennsylvania | 520,089 |
| Portland | Oregon | 379,967 |
| Portsmouth | Virginia | 110,963 |
| Providence | Rhode Island | 179,116 |
| Raleigh | North Carolina | 122,830 |
| Richmond | Virginia | 249,431 |
| Riverside | California | 140,089 |
| Rochester | New York | 295,011 |
| Rockford | Illinois | 147,370 |
| Sacramento | California | 257,105 |
| St. Louis | Missouri | 622,236 |
| St. Paul | Minnesota | 309,866 |
| St. Petersburg | Florida | 216,159 |
| Salt Lake City | Utah | 175,885 |
| San Antonio | Texas | 654,153 |
| San Bernardino | California | 106,869 |
| San Diego | California | 697,027 |
| San Francisco | California | 715,674 |
| San Jose | California | 459,913 |
| Santa Ana | California | 155,710 |
| Savannah | Georgia | 118,349 |
| Scranton | Pennsylvania | 102,696 |
| Seattle | Washington | 530,831 |
| Shreveport | Louisiana | 182,064 |
| South Bend | Indiana | 125,580 |
| Spokane | Washington | 170,516 |
| Springfield | Massachusetts | 163,905 |
| Springfield | Missouri | 120,096 |
| Stamford | Connecticut | 108,798 |
| Stockton | California | 109,963 |
| Syracuse | New York | 197,297 |
| Tacoma | Washington | 154,407 |
| Tampa | Florida | 277,714 |
| Toledo | Ohio | 383,062 |
| Topeka | Kansas | 125,011 |
| Torrance | California | 134,968 |
| Trenton | New Jersey | 104,786 |
| Tucson | Arizona | 262,933 |
| Tulsa | Oklahoma | 330,350 |
| Virginia Beach | Virginia | 172,106 |
| Warren | Michigan | 179,260 |
| Washington | District of Columbia | 756,510 |
| Waterbury | Connecticut | 108,033 |
| Wichita | Kansas | 276,554 |
| Winston-Salem | North Carolina | 133,683 |
| Worcester | Massachusetts | 176,572 |
| Yonkers | New York | 204,297 |
| Youngstown | Ohio | 140,909 |

The population of the United States has been estimated by the Bureau of the Census as follows: 1 July 1970—205 million, 1976—215 million to 213 million, 1980—220 million to 226 million.

**Vital Statistics**

The provisional vital statistics reported here monthly have been summarized for the year. These preliminary totals show fewer births, deaths, and marriages and more divorces in 1975 than in 1974.

*Births.* The number of births and the birth rate declined in 1975 despite an increase in the number of women in the childbearing ages. Births totalled 3,144,148 in 1975 for a birth rate of 14·8 births per 1,000 population. These data were less than one per cent lower than the final levels observed for 1974. The fertility rate continued to decline in 1975 to 66·7 births per 1,000 women 15–44 years of age, reaching an alltime low for the 4th consecutive year.

Between 1974 and 1975 the number of women in the childbearing ages (assumed to be 15–44 years) increased two per cent and, according to projections from the U.S. Bureau of the Census, it will increase another 10 per cent by 1980. The number of women at ages 20–29 years, where fertility rates are highest, is also projected to increase by this amount between 1975 and 1980. Unless there are further declines in the age-specific birth rates the projected changes in the number of young women will tend to raise the future number of births.

Provisional data by place of occurrence show that the number of births declined in five of the nine geographic divisions between 1974 and 1975 while the birth rate declined in all except the West North Central Division. The number of births declined in 28 States and the District of Columbia and the birth rate declined in all but 17 States.

*Vital Statistics of the United States*

| *Item* | Rate per 1,000 population | | | | | | |
|---|---|---|---|---|---|---|---|
| | 1975 | 1974 | 1973 | 1972 | 1971 | 1970 | 1969 |
| Births | 14·8 | 14·9 | 14·9 | 15·6 | 17·2 | 18·4 | 17·8 |
| Deaths | 8·9 | 9·2 | 9·4 | 9·4 | 9·3 | 9·5 | 9·5 |
| Natural increase | 5·9 | 5·8 | 5·5 | 6·2 | 7·9 | 8·9 | 8·3 |
| Marriages | 10·1 | 10·5 | 10·9 | 11·0 | 10·6 | 10·6 | 10·6 |
| Divorces | 4·9 | 4·6 | 4·4 | 4·1 | 3·7 | 3·5 | 3·2 |

*Natural Increase.* (The excess of births over deaths) resulted in the net addition of 1,239,000 persons to the population during 1975. The provisional rate of natural increase was 5·8 persons per 1,000 population compared with the final rate of 5·7 for 1974. The increase in this rate can be attributed entirely to the decline in the death rate.

*Table A: Live Births, Birth Rates, and Fertility Rates, by Month: United States, 1974 and 1975.*
(Rates on an annual basis. Birth rates per 1,000 population and fertility rates per 1,000 women aged 15–44 years. Data are provisional unless otherwise specified.)

| *Month* | *Number* | | *Birth rate* | | *Fertility rate* | |
|---|---|---|---|---|---|---|
| | 1975 | 1974 | 1975 | 1974 | 1975 | 1974 |
| January | 259,173 | 257,455 | 14·4 | 14·4 | 65·3 | 66·2 |
| February | 238,153 | 236,551 | 14·6 | 14·6 | 66·3 | 67·2 |
| March | 261,608 | 257,951 | 14·5 | 14·4 | 65·7 | 66·1 |
| April | 250,992 | 246,469 | 14·4 | 14·2 | 65·0 | 65·1 |
| May | 261,572 | 256,986 | 14·5 | 14·3 | 65·5 | 65·6 |
| June | 255,734 | 250,525 | 14·6 | 14·4 | 66.0 | 66·0 |
| July | 279,744 | 279,630 | 15·5 | 15·6 | 69·7 | 71·2 |
| August | 279,937 | 286,496 | 15·5 | 15·9 | 69·7 | 72·8 |
| September | 273,750 | 283,718 | 15·6 | 16·3 | 70·3 | 74·4 |
| October | 267,841 | 280,280 | 14·8 | 15·6 | 66·4 | 71·0 |
| November | 249,907 | 258,011 | 14·2 | 14·8 | 63·9 | 67·4 |
| December | 265,787 | 265,886 | 14·6 | 14·8 | 65·7 | 67·1 |
| Total | 3,144,198 | 3,159,957 | 14·8 | 14·9 | 66·7 | 68·4 |

During 1975 an estimated 1,892,879 deaths occurred in the United States. The provisional death rate was 8·9 per 1,000 population, a reduction of 3·3 per cent from the final rate for the previous year (9·2 per 1,000). This reduction occurred despite the influenza epidemic during the first quarter of 1975 and the continuing increase in the proportion of the total population in the older age groups. At ages 65 years and over the proportions were 9·9 per cent for 1970, 10·3 for 1974, and 10·5 per cent for 1975.

The usual pattern of the highest death rates occurring in the winter and the lowest in the summer was evident again in 1975. Only January and February 1975, during which the influenza epidemic occurred, had higher rates than the corresponding months for 1974.

*Major Causes of Death.* The 15 leading causes of death are ranked for 1975 in table B. Again for 1975 as for final data for 1974, deaths assigned to these causes accounted for about 88 percent of the total number of deaths. There were no changes in the rank of the leading causes between 1974 and 1975, except that Suicide and Bronchitis, emphysema, and asthma changed places, making Suicide the 10th leading cause. As explained below, this dropping in rank for Bronchitis, emphysema, and asthma is artifactual, resulting primarily from assignment of some deaths from emphysema to the new category Chronic obstructive lung disease.

The continued decline of the death rate observed for 1975 resulted from lower rates for most of the leading causes of death. Because of the large numbers of deaths they represent, major contributors to the decline were three of the four leading causes of death; Diseases of heart, Cerebrovascular diseases, and Accidents, most notably Motor vehicle accidents. Malignant neoplasms, the second leading cause of death, continued to be an exception. Both the unadjusted death rate and the age-adjusted death rate for Malignant neoplasms increased from 1974 to 1975 and were the highest ever recorded in the United States for these conditions. Of the major components of this category, the greatest increase was for Malignant neoplasms of the respiratory system. Other leading causes for which the death rate increased from 1974 to 1975 were Influenza and pneumonia, a result of the influenza epidemic during the first quarter of 1975, and Suicide.

*Diseases of heart.* Despite the influenza epidemic of 1975 and the increasing proportion of older persons in the population, the provisional total death rate for Diseases of heart (339·0 per 100,000) was 2·9 per cent lower than the 1974 final rate (349·2 per 100,000).

As measured by age-adjusted death rates. Diseases of heart declined an estimated 28 per cent between 1950 (307·6 deaths per 100,000) and 1975 (an estimated 222·5 deaths per 100,000). The drop in the death rate was steepest in recent years, amounting to 15 per cent between 1969 (262·3 deaths per 100,000) and 1975.

*Malignant neoplasms.* For Malignant neoplasms the estimated 1975 total death rate (174·4 per 100,000) was 2·3 per cent higher than the final rate for 1974 (170·5 per 100,000); and the 1975 age-adjusted death rate (132·7 deaths per 100,000) was 0·7 per cent higher than the final rate for 1974.

*Cerebrovascular diseases.* Between 1974 and 1975 the total death rate for these causes dropped 6·4 per cent—from 98·1 deaths per 100,000 to an estimated 91·8 for 1975.

*Accidents.* The highlight of the accident experience for 1975 is that the total death rate for Motor vehicle accidents fell 5·0 per cent (from 22·0 deaths per 100,000 for 1974 to an estimated 20·9 for 1975). This drop followed a decrease of 17·0 per cent between the rate for 1973 and 1974 (from 26·5 to 22·0 deaths per 100,000).

*Influenza and pneumonia.* From 1974 to 1975 the unadjusted and the age-adjusted death rates for influenza and pneumonia increased 4·2 and 1·2 per cent, respectively.

*Diabetes mellitus.* The unadjusted death rate for Diabetes mellitus for 1975 is 16·8 per 100,000; and the age-adjusted death rate for this cause is 11·8 deaths per 100,000. These rates are 5·1 and 5·6 per cent lower, respectively, than the corresponding unadjusted and adjusted rates for 1974 (based on final figures).

*Cirrhosis of liver.* Again for 1975, as for 1974 and 1973, Cirrhosis of liver ranked as the seventh leading cause of death.

*Arteriosclerosis.* The death rate for Arteriosclerosis dropped an estimated 10·5 per cent between 1974 and 1975—from 15·3 to 13·7 deaths per 100,000.

*Certain causes of mortality in early infancy.* The 1975 death rate for these causes (12·8 per 100,000 population) dropped from the sixth to the ninth leading cause between 1968 and 1975. Between 1974 and 1975 the estimated decrease for this rate was 5·9 per cent. The infant mortality rate for these causes (number of these deaths at ages under 1 year per 1,000 live births) decreased 5·5 per cent from 9·1 for 1974 to an estimated 8·6 for 1975.

*Suicide.* Suicide became the 10th leading cause in 1975. The estimated suicide rate (12·6 per 100,000) was 4·1 per cent higher than the rate in 1974. The age-adjusted rate for this cause increased 3·3 per cent, from 12·2 to 12·6 deaths per 100,000.

*Bronchitis, emphysema, and asthma.* The decrease of 6·3 per cent between 1974 and 1975 in the death rate for Bronchitis, emphysema, and asthma (ICDA Nos. 490–493), from 12·7 to 11·9 deaths per 100,000 is misleading. The probable stability of mortality from these causes between 1974 and 1975 has been obscured by the increasing frequency with which medical certifiers are entering the generalized term "chronic obstructive lung disease" on certificates instead of a more specific diagnosis of "Emphysema," "Bronchitis," or "Asthma." Chronic obstructive lung disease is, by international rules, assigned to the category "Other diseases of lung" (ICDA No. 519·2). The United States established a separate category (denoted by *519·3) to identify deaths assigned to Chronic obstructive lung disease, beginning with data year 1969. Effective with data for 1972 the title was changed to Chronic obstructive lung disease without mention of asthma, bronchitis, or emphysema. The following table shows separate death rates for each year of the period 1969–74 for these complementary categories and for their combinations.

The percentage of the combined death rates that are deaths attributed to Chronic obstructive lung disease without mention of asthma, bronchitis, or emphysema increased from 7·7 for 1969 to 34·9 for 1974. Separate death rates for this category are not available from provisional data.

*Homicide.* Both the unadjusted and the age-adjusted death rates for Homicide for 1975 (10·2 and 10·8 per 100,000 population) were the same as the corresponding rates for 1974. These rates are the highest annual rates for homicide victims recorded for the United States during 1933–75. (The year 1933 was the first year that the death-registration area included all 48 States and the District of Columbia.) In 1975, as for prior years, the age group 25–34 years had a markedly higher death rate for this cause (18·9 deaths per 100,000) than any other age group.

*Congenital anomalies.* For 1975 deaths at ages under 1 year assigned to Congenital anomalies (8,670) constituted about 60 per cent of the total number of 14,380 deaths assigned to this cause.

*Nephritis and nephrosis.* The death rate for this cause rises with age. For 1975 it increased from an estimated 0·6 per 100,000 at ages under 1 year to 31·6 for the age group 75–84 years.

*Peptic ulcer.* For 1975 the death rate for Peptic ulcer (3·2 per 100,000) continued the slow downturn observed for the period 1968–74, during which the rate decreased from 4·7 to 3·3 deaths per 100,000.

*Sex differentials for mortality by age.* The 1975 death rate for the male population (10·2 per 1,000) was 1·3 times the corresponding rate for the female population (7·8), which was about the same as the ratio for 1974. For both years the death rate was higher for males than for females in each age group and the mortality sex ratio varied widely by age with a major peak at ages 15–24 years (3·0).

The largest mortality sex differential occurred at ages 15–24 years for both the white and the other than white races. The ratio at these ages were 3·4 for 1975 and 2·8 for 1974 for the white population and 3·1 for 1975 and 2·9 for 1974 for the other than white population. A secondary peak in the ratio of the death rate for the white male population over the corresponding rate for the white female population occurred for the age group 55–64 years, with a ratio of 2·1 for 1975 and 1974.

*Colour differentials by age.* The 1975 death rate for persons other than white (8·4 per 1,000) was lower than the rate for white persons (9·1 per 1,000). The reverse was true for most of the age-specific rates; the rates were higher for persons other than white for each age group under 75 years. This anomaly reflects differences in the age composition of the two population groups. The population of races other than white is relatively young. For 1975 it had a median age of 23·7 years and only 7·2 percent of its total population was 65 years of age and over. For 1975 the white population had a median age of 29·6 years and 11·0 percent of its total population was 65 years of age and over.

Although there was some reduction between 1970 and 1975 in the greater mortality for persons of races other than white, for most age groups large mortality differentials continued through 1975. For the age groups under 75 years the mortality colour ratios for 1975 ranged from a low of 1·3 for the age group 65–74 years to 2·5 for the age group 25–34 years. The corresponding colour ratios for the age group 25–34 years were somewhat higher in 1970 (2·7) and 1974 (2·6). A decrease in the colour ratios occurred for both the male and female population.

Despite the persistence of higher age-specific rates, during the period 1970–75 general improvement was observed for the female population of races other than white: a decrease in the ratio of their mortality over that for the white female population occurred for every age group except under 1 year, for which the ratio was about the same. Improvement for the male population of races other than white was less pronounced, but a decrease in the ratio of their mortality over that for the white male population did occur for all age groups except 5–14 years and 55 years and over.

*Maternal and infant mortality.* In 1975 the deaths of an estimated 340 women were assigned to Complications of pregnancy, childbirth, and the puerperium. The provisional maternal mortality rate was 10·8 per 100,000 live births. The maternal mortality rates per 100,000 live births for 1950 and each of the last 16 years are as follows:

| Year | Rate | Year | Rate |
|---|---|---|---|
| 1975 | 12·8 | 1966 | 29·1 |
| 1974 | 14·6 | 1965 | 31·6 |
| 1973 | 15·2 | 1964 | 33·3 |
| 1972 | 18·8 | 1963 | 35·8 |
| 1971 | 18·8 | 1962 | 35·2 |
| 1970 | 21·5 | 1961 | 36·9 |
| 1969 | 22·2 | 1960 | 37·1 |
| 1968 | 24·5 | 1950 | 83·3 |
| 1967 | 28·0 | | |

*Table B.*

*Death Rates from* 15 *Leading Causes of Death: United States,* 1975

(Based on a ten per cent sample of deaths. Rates per 100,000 population.)

| *Rank* | *Cause of death* | *Death rate* | *Per cent of total deaths* |
|---|---|---|---|
| | All causes | 888·5 | 100·0 |
| 1 | Diseases of heart | 336·2 | 37·8 |
| 2 | Malignant neoplasms, including neoplasms of lymphatic and haematopoietic tissues | 171·7 | 19·3 |
| 3 | Cerebrovascular diseases | 91·1 | 10·3 |
| 4 | Accidents | 48·4 | 5·4 |
| 5 | Influenza and pneumonia | 26·1 | 2·9 |
| 6 | Diabetes mellitus | 16·5 | 1·9 |
| 7 | Cirrhosis of liver | 14·8 | 1·7 |
| 8 | Arteriosclerosis | 13·6 | 1·5 |
| 9 | Suicide | 12·7 | 1·4 |
| 10 | Certain causes of mortality in early infancy | 12·5 | 1·4 |
| 11 | Bronchitis, emphysema, and asthma | 12·0 | 1·3 |
| 12 | Homicide | 10·0 | 1·1 |
| 13 | Congenital anomalies | 6·2 | 0·7 |
| 14 | Nephritis and nephrosis | 3·8 | 0·4 |
| 15 | Peptic ulcer | 3·2 | 0·4 |
| ... | All other causes | 109·7 | 12·4 |

*Expectation of life.* The estimated expectation of life at birth in 1975 was 72·4 years for the total population, the highest life expectancy ever attained in the United States. Expectation of life is the average number of years that an infant could be expected to live if the age-specific death rates observed during the year of birth were to continue unchanged throughout his lifetime. Based on the respective annual age-specific death rates, the expectation of life at birth for each of the five years 1971–75, was as follows:

| | |
|---|---|
| 1975 | 72·5 |
| 1974 | 72·0 |
| 1973 | 71·3 |
| 1972 | 71·1 |
| 1971 | 71·1 |

*Table C.*

*Death Rates by Age: United States,* 1974 *and* 1975

(For 1975, based on a 10 per cent sample of deaths. Rates per 100,000 population in specified group.)

| *Age* | 1975 (*final*) | 1974 (*final*) | *Per cent difference* |
|---|---|---|---|
| All ages[1] | 888·5 | 915·1 | −2·1 |
| Under 1 year | 1,641·0 | 1,755·7 | −6·3 |
| 1–4 years | 70·8 | 73·9 | −1·8 |
| 5–14 years | 35·7 | 38·2 | −5·0 |
| 15–24 years | 118·9 | 121·7 | −1·9 |
| 25–34 years | 143·2 | 146·8 | −2·2 |
| 35–44 years | 266·8 | 278·6 | −3·1 |
| 45–54 years | 649·6 | 675·0 | −4·7 |
| 55–64 years | 1,495·5 | 1,549·2 | −3·0 |
| 65–74 years | 3,189·2 | 3,327·6 | −3·3 |
| 75–84 years | 7,359·2 | 7,654·8 | −2·7 |
| 85+ years | 15,187·9 | 16,532·8 | −7·4 |

[1] Figures for age not stated included in "All ages" but not distributed among age groups.

The following table shows Infant Mortality Rates, by Age and Selected Causes for the United States, 1971–75. This table is based on a ten per cent sample of deaths; for all other years based on final data, the Rates are per 1,000 live births:

*Table D.*

| *Age and cause of death* | 1975 (*est.*) | 1974 | 1973 | 1972 |
|---|---|---|---|---|
| Under 28 days | 11·8 | 12·3 | 13·0 | 13·6 |
| 28 days to 11 months | 4·3 | 4·4 | 4·8 | 4·8 |
| Certain gastrointestinal diseases | 0·3 | 0·2 | 0·2 | 0·2 |
| Influenza and pneumonia | 0·7 | 0·8 | 1·1 | 1·3 |
| Congenital anomalies | 2·8 | 2·7 | 2·9 | 2·9 |
| Birth injuries | 0·6 | 0·6 | 0·6 | 0·6 |
| Asphyxia of newborn, | | | | 2·1 |
| unspecified | 1·3 | 1·5 | 1·7 | 1·9 |
| Immaturity, unqualified | 1·4 | 1·5 | 1·7 | |
| Other diseases of early infancy | 5·4 | 5·5 | 5·6 | 5·8 |
| All other causes | 3·8 | 3·8 | 3·8 | 3·7 |
| Total, under 1 year | 16·1 | 16·7 | 17·7 | 18·5 |

The following table shows the estimated and projected population, by age and sex: 1950 to 2000.
*Table E.*

**In thousands.** Includes Armed Forces abroad. Projections are consistent with the 1 April, 1970 census. These projections were prepared using the "cohort-component" technique and assume a slight improvement in mortality, an annual net immigration of 400,000, and a completed cohort fertility rate (i.e., the average number of births per 1,000 women upon completion of childbearing) that will move gradually toward the following levels: Series C—2,800; Series D—2,500; Series E—2,100; Series F—1,800.

| *Year, Series, and Sex* | *Total, all ages* | *Under 5 years* | *5–9 years* | *10–14 years* | *15–19 years* | *20–24 years* | *25–29 years* | *30–34 years* | *35–39 years* | *40–44 years* | *45–54 years* | *55–64 years* | *65–74 years* | *75 years and over* | *Median age* |
|---|---|---|---|---|---|---|---|---|---|---|---|---|---|---|---|
| *Total* | | | | | | | | | | | | | | | |
| 1950 | 152,271 | 16,410 | 13,375 | 11,213 | 10,675 | 11,680 | 12,362 | 11,674 | 11,347 | 10,290 | 17,453 | 13,396 | 8,493 | 3,904 | 30·2 |
| 1960 | 180,671 | 20,337 | 18,812 | 16,923 | 13,455 | 11,124 | 10,939 | 11,979 | 12,542 | 11,680 | 20,573 | 15,627 | 11,055 | 5,624 | 29·4 |
| 1970 | 204,879 | 17,167 | 19,888 | 20,800 | 19,301 | 17,192 | 13,687 | 11,570 | 11,174 | 11,982 | 23,287 | 18,651 | 12,482 | 7,695 | 28·0 |
| 1972 | 208,837 | 17,242 | 18,702 | 20,804 | 20,101 | 18,219 | 15,045 | 12,308 | 11,125 | 11,648 | 23,591 | 19,104 | 12,845 | 8,104 | 28·1 |
| Per cent of total: | | | | | | | | | | | | | | | |
| 1950 | 100·0 | 10·8 | 8·8 | 7·4 | 7·0 | 7·7 | 8·1 | 7·7 | 7·5 | 6·8 | 11·5 | 8·8 | 5·6 | 2·6 | (x) |
| 1960 | 100·0 | 11·3 | 10·4 | 9·4 | 7·4 | 6·2 | 6·1 | 6·6 | 6·9 | 6·5 | 11·4 | 8·6 | 6·1 | 3·1 | (x) |
| 1970 | 100·0 | 8·4 | 9·7 | 10·2 | 9·4 | 8·4 | 6·7 | 5·6 | 5·5 | 5·8 | 11·4 | 9·1 | 6·1 | 3·8 | (x) |
| 1972 | 100·0 | 8·3 | 9·0 | 10·0 | 9·6 | 8·7 | 7·2 | 5·9 | 5·3 | 5·6 | 11·3 | 9·1 | 6·2 | 3·9 | (x) |
| Projections: | | | | | | | | | | | | | | | |
| 1975—C | 215,872 | 18,710 | 17,318 | 20,062 | 20,943 | 19,404 | 17,312 | 13,802 | 11,604 | 11,117 | 23,563 | 19,867 | 13,549 | 8,621 | 28·3 |
| D | 215,324 | 18,162 | | | | | | | | | | | | | 28·4 |
| E | 213,925 | 16,763 | | | | | | | | | | | | | 28·6 |
| F | 213,378 | 16,216 | | | | | | | | | | | | | 28·7 |
| 1980—C | 230,955 | 23,449 | 18,847 | 17,497 | 20,221 | 21,067 | 19,544 | 17,418 | 13,822 | 11,548 | 22,406 | 21,083 | 14,680 | 9,371 | 28·7 |
| D | 228,676 | 21,716 | 18,301 | | | | | | | | | | | | 29·0 |
| E | 224,132 | 18,566 | 16,907 | | | | | | | | | | | | 29·6 |
| F | 221,848 | 16,827 | 16,363 | | | | | | | | | | | | 29·8 |
| 1990—C | 266,238 | 27,149 | 26,893 | 23,745 | 19,194 | 17,823 | 20,501 | 21,290 | 19,615 | 17,287 | 24,617 | 20,357 | 16,769 | 10,999 | 29·5 |
| D | 258,692 | 24,368 | 24,396 | 22,021 | 18,650 | | | | | | | | | | 30·4 |
| E | 246,639 | 20,531 | 20,704 | 18,885 | 17,262 | | | | | | | | | | 31·8 |
| F | 239,084 | 17,752 | 18,201 | 17,154 | 16,719 | | | | | | | | | | 32·7 |
| 2000—C | 300,406 | 28,458 | 26,879 | 27,440 | 27,209 | 24,038 | 19,510 | 18,110 | 20,580 | 21,102 | 35,730 | 22,508 | 16,291 | 12,551 | 29·1 |
| D | 285,969 | 24,545 | 23,858 | 24,670 | 24,724 | 22,327 | 18,972 | | | | | | | | 31·1 |
| E | 264,435 | 19,152 | 19,694 | 20,849 | 21,048 | 19,216 | 17,599 | | | | | | | | 34·0 |
| F | 250,686 | 15,802 | 16,814 | 18,083 | 18,556 | 17,499 | 17,062 | | | | | | | | 35.8 |
| *Male* | | | | | | | | | | | | | | | |
| 1950 | 75,849 | 8,362 | 6,811 | 5,707 | 5,381 | 5,794 | 6,071 | 5,733 | 5,585 | 5,121 | 8,715 | 6,714 | 4,091 | 1,766 | 29·8 |
| 1960 | 89,319 | 10,336 | 9,566 | 8,602 | 6,809 | 5,563 | 5,425 | 5,902 | 6,140 | 5,733 | 10,139 | 7,560 | 5,134 | 2,411 | 28·5 |
| 1970 | 100,264 | 8,752 | 10,134 | 10,595 | 9,802 | 8,649 | 6,796 | 5,708 | 5,484 | 5,838 | 11,236 | 8,817 | 5,454 | 2,996 | 26·6 |
| 1972 | 102.051 | 8.803 | 9·526 | 10,600 | 10,226 | 9,178 | 7,482 | 6,080 | 5,456 | 5,686 | 11,355 | 8,990 | 5,584 | 3,087 | 26·8 |

| | | | | | | | | | | | | | | | |
|---|---|---|---|---|---|---|---|---|---|---|---|---|---|---|---|
| Projections: | | | | | | | | | | | | | | | |
| 1975—C | 105,372 | 9,564 | 8,823 | 10,218 | 10,652 | 9,806 | 8,661 | 6,829 | 5,704 | 5,426 | 11,327 | 9,293 | 5,875 | 3,195 | 27·1 |
| D | 105,092 | 9,284 | | | | | | | | | | | | | 27·2 |
| E | 104,377 | 8,569 | | | | | | | | | | | | | 27·4 |
| F | 104,097 | 8,289 | | | | | | | | | | | | | 27·5 |
| 1980—C | 112,726 | 11,983 | 9,627 | 8,910 | 10,284 | 10,666 | 9,831 | 8,690 | 6,819 | 5,649 | 10,781 | 9,776 | 6,329 | 3,381 | 27·5 |
| D | 111,562 | 11,098 | 9,348 | | | | | | | | | | | | 27·8 |
| E | 109,240 | 9,488 | 8,636 | | | | | | | | | | | | 28·4 |
| F | 108,073 | 8,599 | 8,358 | | | | | | | | | | | | 28·7 |
| 1990—C | 130,388 | 13,876 | 13,737 | 12,122 | 9,786 | 9,021 | 10,335 | 10,705 | 9,814 | 8,564 | 11,922 | 9,424 | 7,135 | 3,946 | 28·2 |
| D | 126,533 | 12,455 | 12,461 | 11,241 | 9,509 | | | | | | | | | | 29·2 |
| E | 120,376 | 10,494 | 10,575 | 9,640 | 8,800 | | | | | | | | | | 30·6 |
| F | 116,516 | 9,073 | 9,296 | 8,756 | 8,524 | | | | | | | | | | 31·5 |
| 2000—C | 147,804 | 14,548 | 13,732 | 14,012 | 13,873 | 12,210 | 9,866 | 9,107 | 10,326 | 10,544 | 17,558 | 10,523 | 6,965 | 4,538 | 27·8 |
| D | 140,433 | 12,547 | 12,188 | 12,597 | 12,608 | 11,339 | 9,592 | | | | | | | | 29·7 |
| E | 129,439 | 9,790 | 10,060 | 10,645 | 10,732 | 9,755 | 8,895 | | | | | | | | 32·7 |
| F | 122,423 | 8,078 | 8,589 | 9,232 | 9,461 | 8,881 | 8,622 | | | | | | | | 34·6 |
| *Female* | | | | | | | | | | | | | | | |
| 1950 | 76,422 | 8,048 | 6,564 | 5,506 | 5,294 | 5,886 | 6,291 | 5,942 | 5,762 | 5,169 | 8,738 | 6,682 | 4,402 | 2,139 | 30·5 |
| 1960 | 91,352 | 10,001 | 9,246 | 8,322 | 6,646 | 5,561 | 5,514 | 6,077 | 6,402 | 5,947 | 10,434 | 8,068 | 5,921 | 3,213 | 30·3 |
| 1970 | 104,615 | 8,415 | 9,754 | 10,205 | 9,499 | 8,543 | 6,891 | 5,862 | 5,390 | 6,143 | 12,051 | 9,834 | 7,028 | 4,699 | 29·3 |
| 1972 | 106,786 | 8,439 | 9,176 | 10,204 | 9,876 | 9,041 | 7,564 | 6,228 | 5,670 | 5,962 | 12,236 | 10,113 | 7,261 | 5,017 | 29·4 |
| Projections: | | | | | | | | | | | | | | | |
| 1975—C | 110,500 | 9,146 | 8,495 | 9,844 | 10,291 | 9,598 | 8,651 | 6,973 | 5,899 | 5,691 | 12,237 | 10,574 | 7,674 | 5,426 | 29·6 |
| D | 110,232 | 8,878 | | | | | | | | | | | | | 29·6 |
| E | 109,548 | 8,194 | | | | | | | | | | | | | 29·8 |
| F | 109,281 | 7,927 | | | | | | | | | | | | | 29·9 |
| 1980—C | 118,229 | 11,465 | 9,220 | 8,587 | 9,937 | 10,401 | 9,714 | 8,728 | 7,004 | 5,899 | 11,625 | 11,307 | 8,352 | 5,991 | 29·9 |
| D | 117,115 | 10,619 | 8,953 | | | | | | | | | | | | 30·2 |
| E | 114,893 | 9,078 | 8,271 | | | | | | | | | | | | 30·8 |
| F | 113,776 | 8,228 | 8,005 | | | | | | | | | | | | 31·2 |
| 1990—C | 135,849 | 13,273 | 13,156 | 11,623 | 9,407 | 8,801 | 10,165 | 10,585 | 9,801 | 8,723 | 12,695 | 10,934 | 9,635 | 7,052 | 30·7 |
| D | 132,159 | 11,913 | 11,935 | 10,780 | 9,141 | | | | | | | | | | 31·6 |
| E | 126,263 | 10,037 | 10,130 | 9,245 | 8,462 | | | | | | | | | | 33·0 |
| F | 122,568 | 8,679 | 8,905 | 8,398 | 8,196 | | | | | | | | | | 33·8 |
| 2000—C | 152,602 | 13,910 | 13,147 | 13,428 | 13,333 | 11,828 | 9,645 | 9,003 | 10,254 | 10,558 | 18,172 | 11,986 | 9,325 | 8,013 | 30·6 |
| D | 145,536 | 11,997 | 11,669 | 12,073 | 12,116 | 10,988 | 9,380 | | | | | | | | 32·5 |
| E | 134,991 | 9,361 | 9,633 | 10,204 | 10,316 | 9,461 | 8,704 | | | | | | | | 35·4 |
| F | 128,264 | 7,724 | 8,225 | 8,851 | 9,095 | 8,618 | 8,440 | | | | | | | | 37·0 |

x Not applicable.

# UNITED STATES OF AMERICA

## CURRENCY AND FINANCE

The par value of the dollar was raised from $38 to $42·22 per ounce of gold on 18 October 1973. This change was made in accordance with an amendment to the Par Value Modification Act that was proposed by the President on 12 February 1973 and was subsequently passed by the Congress. The par value of the dollar had been raised from $35 to $38 per ounce of gold on 8 May 1972. The former value had been in effect since 31 January 1934.

American currency is based on the decimal system with the dollar (100 cents) the primary unit of account. The coinage consists of pennies (one cent), nickels (five cents), dimes (10 cents), quarters (25 cents), half dollars (50 cents), and dollars. Paper currency is currently issued in denominations ranging from $1 to $100. Small amounts of higher denominations issued in the past are still in circulation. As of April 1976, 72 per cent of the money stock was in the form of demand deposits in commercial banks, 25 per cent was paper currency, and 3 per cent was coin.

The Federal Reserve System has been the central bank and has conducted monetary policy since its establishment in 1913. The system is headed by the Board of Governors, seven men appointed by the President of the United States for overlapping fourteen-year terms, and by the presidents of the twelve regional Federal Reserve Banks, whose appointments must be approved by the Board of Governors. The Federal Reserve carries out monetary policy primarily by buying and selling U.S. Government securities on the open market. In addition, it sets the reserve requirement ratios of those commercial banks that are members of the Federal Reserve System and the discount rate at which member banks can borrow from the Federal Reserve Banks.

As of June 1976, 5,775 of the 14,632 commercial banks in the Nation were members of the Federal Reserve System. The member banks owned 74 percent of the assets of all commercial banks. Member banks include all national banks and those qualified State banks wishing to join.

The table below shows budget receipts and outlays for fiscal years 1976 and 1977, in U.S. billions of dollars. The U.S. fiscal year has been shifted from a July-through-June basis to an October-through-September basis. Fiscal year 1976 covers 1 July, 1975 to 30 June, 1976. Fiscal year 1977 runs from 1 October, 1976 to 30 September, 1977.

The following table shows budget outlays for 1975 and 1976.

| *Description* | 1975 *actual* | 1976[1] *estimate* |
|---|---|---|
| *Receipts by source*: | | |
| Individual income taxes | 131·6 | 152·6 |
| Corporation income taxes | 41·4 | 53·1 |
| Social insurance taxes and contributions: | | |
| Employment taxes and contributions | 79·9 | 96·0 |
| Unemployment insurance | 8·1 | 10·0 |
| Contributions for other insurance and retirement | 4·8 | 5·1 |
| Excise taxes | 17·0 | 17·8 |
| Estate and gift taxes | 5·2 | 5·8 |
| Customs | 4·1 | 4·6 |
| Miscellaneous | 8·0 | 7·4 |
| Total receipts | 300·0 | 352·5 |
| *Outlay by function*: | | |
| National defence | 90·2 | 101·6 |
| International affairs | 4·5 | 7·1 |
| General science, space and technology | 4·2 | 4·5 |
| Natural resources, environment, and energy | 11·7 | 15·1 |
| Agriculture | 2·0 | 1·8 |
| Commerce and transportation | 17·2 | 16·4 |
| Community and regional development | 5·0 | 6·0 |
| Education, training, employment, and social services | 17·7 | 18·4 |
| Health | 33·6 | 36·5 |
| Income security | 126·9 | 136·2 |
| Veterans benefits and services | 18·4 | 17·8 |
| Law enforcement and justice | 3·3 | 3·4 |
| General government | 3·0 | 3·5 |

*continued*

| *Description* | 1975 *actual* | 1976[1] *estimate* |
|---|---|---|
| Revenue sharing and general purpose fiscal assistance | 7·1 | 7·4 |
| Interest | 35·5 | 40·2 |
| Allowance for civilian agency pay raises | — | 0·8 |
| Undistributed offsetting receipts: | | |
| Employer share, employee retirement | −4·2 | −4·5 |
| Interest received by trust funds | −7·8 | −8·3 |
| Rents and royalties on the Outer Continental Shelf | −2·7 | −4·0 |
| Total budget outlays | 365·6 | 400·0 |

[1] Based on the Mid-Session Review of the 1977 budget issued 16 July 1976.

## PRINCIPAL BANKS

**American National Bank and Trust Company of Chicago.** (Chairman, Allen P. Stults.) Est. 1928; Balance Sheet at 30 June 1974 showed assets $1,416,931,000; deposits and current accounts $1,319,834,000. *Head Office:* La Salle Street at Washington, Chicago 60690.

**American Security Bank.** (President, Donald L. MacGregor, Jr.) Est. 1935. Balance Sheet at 31 December 1976 showed assets $237,989,268; deposits $216,785,833; loans $131,700,606. *Head Office:* Honolulu. 13 Branches.

**American B and T Corporation, American Bank & Trust Company.** (President, Stanley Kreitman; Chairman of the Board, Saul Kagan.) Est. 1914; Balance Sheet at 31 December 1975 showed assets $284,260,949. *Head Office:* 645 Fifth Avenue, New York. 5 Branches.

**Bancal Tri-State Corporation.** (Chairman of the Board, President and Chief Executive Officer, C. E. Schmidt; Senior Vice-President, Secretary and Counsel, E. M. Carpenter SeniorVice-President and Controller, D. W. Ehlers.) Assets as at June 1977, $2,980,539,000; deposits and current accounts, $2,486,960,000. *Head Office:* 400 California Street, San Francisco, California 94104. 81 Offices.

**Bankers Trust Company.** (Chairman of the Board, Alfred Brittain III.) Est. 1903; Balance Sheet at 31 December 1973 showed assets 17,721,284; deposits $14,009,736. *Head Office:* 16 Wall Street, New York. 102 Branches.

**Bank of America National Trust and Savings Association.** (President, A. W. Clausen.) Est. 1904; Balance Sheet at 31 December 1974 showed assets $59,369,267,000; deposits and current accounts $51,192,118,000. *Head Office:* 555 California Street, San Francisco, California. Over 1,000 Branches.

**The National Bank of Georgia.** *Head Office:* Peachtree Street, Atlanta, Georgia 30303.

**Bank of Hawaii.** (Chairman and Chief Executive Officer, Clifton D. Terry.) Est. 1897. Balance Sheet at 30 June 1976 showed assets $1,229,898,583; deposits and current accounts $1,122,379,343. *Head Office:* Financial Plaza of the Pacific, Honolulu. 72 Branches.

**Bank of New York.** (President, Elliott Averett. Est. 1784; Balance Sheet at 31 December 1972 showed assets $2,718,461,000; deposits and current accounts $1,869,586,000 *Head Office:* 48 Wall Street, New York. 9 Branches.

**Bank of Virginia Company.** (President, S. Wayne Bazzle; Chairman, Frederick Deane, Jr.) Balance Sheet at 30 June 1975 showed assets $1,588,388,188; deposits and current accounts $1,160,822,708. *Head Office:* 7 North Eighth Street, Richmond, VA 23260. Branches, 16 affiliated banks and 130 branches in Virginia.

**Brown Brothers Harriman & Co.** Private Bankers. Est. 1818; Balance Sheet at 30 June 1977 showed assets $506,379,073; deposits $439,399,316. *Head Office:* 59 Wall Street, New York 10005. 3 Branches.

**Central Pacific Bank.** (President, Kazuo Ishii.) Est. 1954; Balance Sheet at 31 December 1972 showed assets $176,465,495; deposits $159,724,515. *Head Office:* Honolulu. 9 Branches.

**The Chartered Bank.** Branch, 76 William Street, New York 5. See United Kingdom.

**The Chase Manhattan Bank, N.A.** (Chairman, David Rockefeller; President, Willard Butcher.) Est. 1799; Balance Sheet at 29 June 1968 showed assets $16,342,251,954. *Head Office:* 1 Chase Manhattan Plaza, New York, N.Y. 10015. Over 140 Home Branches and over 1,300 Overseas Locations.

**Chemical Bank.** (Chairman, Donald C. Platten.) Est. 1824. Balance Sheet at 30 June 1976 showed assets $23,908,358,000; deposits $19,307,675,000. *Head Office:* 20 Pine Street. New York, N.Y. 10015. 277 Branches.

**City Bank of Honolulu.** (President, Koichi Itoh.) Est. 1959. Balance Sheet at 31 December 1966 showed assets $54,265,220; deposits and current accounts $44,899,810. *Head Office:* Honolulu. 3 Branches.

**Citytrust.** (President, E. Cortright Phillips; Chairman, Normal Schaff Jr.) Est. 1848. Balance Sheet as at 30 June 1977 showed assets $523,247,261; deposits $453,462,533. *Head Office:* 961 Main St., Bridgeport, Connecticut 06602. 30 Branches.

**City National Bank and Trust Company of Chicago.** Est. 1932; Merged into Continental Illinois National Bank in 1961.

**Cleveland Trust Company.** (President and C.E.O., M. Brock Weir.) Est. 1894; Balance Sheet at 30 June 1974 showed assets $3,637,096,077. *Head office:* 900 Euclid Avenue, Cleveland 44101. 80 Banking offices.

**Commerce Bank of Kansas City NA.** (President, P. V. Miller, Jr.; Chairman, James M. Kemper, Jr.) Est. 1865. Assets as at 31 December 1975, $733,000,000; deposits and current accounts, $675,000,000. (Part of Commerce Bancshares Inc., a holding company with 32 affiliates in Missouri.) *Head Office:* 922, Walnut, Kansas City, Missouri.

**Continental Illinois National Bank and Trust Company of Chicago.** (Chairman of the Board, Roger E. Anderson.) Est. 1857; Balance Sheet at 30 June 1974 showed total resources $18,380,854,000; total deposits $13,585,715,000. *Head Office:* 231 South La Salle Street, Chicago, Illinois, 60693.

**Discount Corporation of New York.** (President, Robert H. Bethke; Chairman, Charles E. Dunbar.) Est. 1918. Balance Sheet showed assets at 30 June 1976 $619,170,104; deposits and current accounts $529,181,014. *Head Office:* 58 Pine Street, New York, N.Y. 10005.

**Exchange Bancorporation Inc.** (President, Gordon W. Campbell; Chairman, William C. MacInnes.) Est. 1968. Balance Sheet as at 31 December 1974 showed assets $624,960,323; deposits as at 10 July 1975, $522,586,000. *Head Office:* Exchange National Bank of Tampa, P.O. Box 1809, 600 N. Fla. Ave, Tampa, Fla. 33601. Branches, 13 affiliate banks.

**First American National Bank of Nashville.** (President, T. Scott Fillebrown, Jr.; Chairman, Andrew B. Benedict, Jr.) Est. 1883. Balance Sheet at 31 March 1975 showed assets $1,567,718,814; deposits and current accounts $1,300,900. *Head Office:* First American National Bank, First American Center, Nashville, TN 37237. 30 Branches.

**The First Chicago Corporation.** (Chairman of Board, A. Robert Abboud.) Est. 1863; Balance Sheet at 30 June 1975 showed assets $18,780,000,000. *Head Office:* 1, First National Plaza, Chicago, Illinois, 60670. *London Branch:* 1 Royal Exchange Buildings, London E.C.3.

**First Federal Savings and Loan Association of Chicago.** (Chairman of the Board and Chief Executive Officer, E. Stanley Enlund.) Est. 1934. Balance Sheet at 30 June 1977 showed assets $2·31 billion (U.S.A.) *Head Office:* 1, South Dearborn, Chicago 60603.

**First National Bank of Atlanta, The.** (President, D. R. Riddle; Chairman, Thomas R. Williams.) Est. 1865. Balance Sheet at 30 June 1976 showed assets $2,268,013,000; liabilities $2,149,558,000 *Head Office:* Two Peachtree Street, N.W. Atlanta, Georgia, U.S.A. 30303. 53 branches in Augusta; 3 branches in Georgia; and London Representative Office Leith House, 47 Gresham Street, London, EC2V 7AY, England.

**First National Bank of Boston. (Chairman, Richard D. Hill.)** President, William L. Brown.) Est. 1784; Balance Sheet at 30 June 1976 showed assets $7,541,046,000. *Head Office.* 100 Federal Street, Boston. 39 Local Offices; Branch and representative offices in 25 major cities throughout the world.

**First National Bank in Menomonie, The.** (President, C. Talen; Chairman, C. Talen.) Est. 1879. Balance Sheet at 30 June 1975 showed assets $27,036,000·00; deposits and current accounts $24,660,000·00. *Head Office:* 200 Main Street, Menomonie, Wisconsin. 3 Branches.

**First National Bank of Minneapolis.** (President, George H. Dixon; Chairman, George H. Dixon.) Est. 1865. Balance Sheet at 31 December 1974 showed assets $1,891,900,000; deposits and current accounts $1,318,000,000. *Head Office:* 120 South 6th Street, Minneapolis, Minnesota 55402. 1Branch

**First American National Bank of Nashville.** (President, T. Scott Fillebrown, Jr.; Chairman, Andrew B. Benedict, Jr.) Est. 1883. Assets as at 31March1975, $1,567,718,814; deposits and current accounts as of 31 March 1975, $1,300,900. *Head office:* First American National Bank, First American Center, Nashville, TN 37237. Branches, 30.

**First Hawaiian Bank.** (President, John D. Bellinger.) Est. 1858. Balance Sheet at 30 June 1975 showed assets $1,000,869,666; deposits, $852,914,026.

**First Huntington National Bank, The.** (President and Chief Executive Officer, E. B. Enslow.) Est. 1872. Balance Sheet at 30 June 1976 showed assets $168,346,277; total deposits $156,368,503. *Head Office:* 1000 Fifth Avenue, Huntington, West Virginia, 25701.

**First National City Bank.** (Chairman, Walter B. Wriston.) Est. 1812; Balance Sheet at 30 June 1974 showed assets $53,546,000,000; deposits $41,467,000,000. *Headquarters:* 399 Park Avenue, New York. 240 United States and over 660 Overseas Branches and Offices.

**First Security National Bank & Trust Co.** (Chairman and President, Walter W. Hillenmeyer, Jr.) Est. 1865. Balance Sheet at 31 December 1974 showed assets $386,235,803; deposits $318,818,752. *Head Office:* 1, First Security Plaza, Lexington, KY 40507. 9 Branches.

**First Union National Bank of North Carolina** (the major subsidiary of First Union Corp., a one-bank holding company headquartered in Charlotte, N.C.). (President, Edward E. Crutchfield, Jr.; Chairman, Theodore B. Sumner, Jr.) Est. 1908. Balance Sheet at 31 December 1974 showed assets $1,874,868,000; deposits and current accounts $1,427,778,000. *Head Office:* Jefferson-First Union Plaza, Charlotte, North Carolina 28288. 182 Branches in 81 North Carolina cities and Nassau, Bahamas, also representative offices in Tokyo and London.

**Hawaii National Bank.** (President, Kan Jung Luke.) Est. 1960; Balance Sheet at 30 June 1972 showed assets $92,918,743; deposits and current accounts $85,430,807. *Head Office:* Honolulu. 9 Branches; Hilo, 1 Branch.

**Hibernia National Bank in New Orleans.** (President and Chairman, Martin C. Miler; Senior Vice-President and Manager, International Division, Gilbert H. Vorhoff.) Est. 1933. Balance Sheet at 31 December 1976 showed assets $707,777,000; deposits and current accounts $662,554,000. *Head Office:* 313 Carondelet Street, New Orleans, Louisiana, U.S.A. 70130. 15 Branches.

**Hongkong and Shanghai Banking Corporation, The.** Offices in Chicago, New York and Seattle. See Hong Kong.

**Hongkong Bank of California, The.** (Chairman, M. G. R. Sandberg.) Est. 1955. Balance Sheet at 30 June 1976 showed assets $151,940,036; deposits $132,966,598. *Head Office:* 180 Sansome Street, San Francisco. 8 Branches. Wholly-owned subsidiary of The Hongkong and Shanghai Banking Corporation. See Hong Kong.

**Indiana National Bank, The.** (President, John R. Benbow; Chairman, Thomas W. Binford.) Est. 1834. Balance Sheet at 31 December 1975 showed assets $1,813,965,000; deposits and current accounts $1,336,135,000. *Head Office:* One Indiana Square, Indianapolis, Indiana 46266. 53 Home Branches; 6 Foreign Offices and Affiliates.

**Irving Trust Company.** (Chairman of the Board, Gordon T. Wallis; President, Joseph A. Rice.) Est. 1851; Balance Sheet at 30 June 1974 showed assets $9,734,760,178; deposits $8,499,164,193. *Head Office:* 1 Wall Street, New York. 14 Branches.

**Liberty Bank.** (President, Lawrence S. L. Ching.) Est. 1922. Balance sheet at 1 December 1974 showed assets

$137,195,777; total deposits $119,279,413. *Head Office:* Honolulu, Hawaii. 8 Branches.

**Liberty National Bank and Trust Company.** (President, J. W. Phelps; Chairman, Frank B. Hower, Jr.; Vice-President, International Division, George A. Collin, Jr.) Est. 1935. Balance Sheet at 30 June 1975 showed capital $10,200,000; surplus, profits and reserves $21,113,110; deposits $475,763,179; Total resources $580,251,419. *Head Office:* 416 West Jefferson St., Louisville, Kentucky, U.S.A. 32 Branches.

**Lincoln First Bank of Rochester.** (President and Chief Operating Officer, Louis A. Langie, Jr.; Chairman and Chief Executive Officer, William B. Webber.) Est. 1920. Balance Sheet at 30 June 1977 showed assets $1,196,330,000; deposits and current accounts $1,987,675,000. *Head Office:* 1 Lincoln First Square, Rochester, New York 14643. 52 Branches.

**Manufacturers Bank, Los Angeles.** (President, Leonard Weil.) Est. 1962. Balance sheet at 30 June 1975 showed, assets as $289,310,000; deposits and current accounts, $260,455,000. *Head Office:* 135 East Ninth St., Los Angeles, California 90015. 7 Branches.

**Manufacturers Hanover Corporation.** (Chairman, Gabriel Hauge.) Balance Sheet at 30 June 1976 showed assets $28,797,196,000. *Head Office:* 350, Park Avenue, New York City 10022. 236 Branches in New York State.

**Marine Midland Bank, New York.** (President and Chief Exec. Officer, Charles F. Mansfield; Chairman, Edward W. Duffy.) Est. 1907; Balance Sheet at 30 June 1975 showed assets $6,798,662,000; deposits $5,604,503,000. *Head Office:* 140 Broadway, New York, N.Y. 10015. 29 Branches.

**Mellon Bank N.A.** (Chairman, James H. Higgins; President, Curtis E. Jones.) Est. 1902; Balance Sheet at 31 March 1976 showed assets $8,941,959,000. *Head Office:* Mellon Square, Pittsburgh 15230. 119 domestic, 1 London Branch, 1 Frankfurt Branch, 1 Tokyo Branch.

**Merchants National Bank.** (President, Thomas G. Barksdale; Chairman, M. E. Ward.) Est. 1886. Balance Sheet at 30 June 1975 showed assets $63,934,419·67. *Head Office:* 820 South Street, Vicksburg, Mississippi. 3 Branches.

**Merchants National Bank and Trust Company.** (President, Donald W. Tanselle; Chairman, Otto N. Frenzel, III.) Balance sheet at 31 December 1975, showed assets $941,203,485; deposits, $706,527,047. *Head Office:* 11 South Meridian Street, Indianapolis, Indiana 46204. Branches: 42 domestic; 1 (Nassau).

**Merchants National Bank & Trust Company of Syracuse, The.** (President and Chief Executive Officer, John W. Finlay; Chairman, Thomas W. Higgins.) Est. 1850. Balance Sheet at 30 June 1976 showed assets $286,921,547; total deposits $263,043,059. *Head Office:* 216–220 South Warren St., Syracuse, N.Y. 13201, U.S.A. Branches, 26 offices throughout Central N.Y. State; Subsidiary of Charter New York Corporation; London Correspondent, Irving Trust Company.

**Merchants National Bank of Mobile.** (President and Chief Executive Officer, Ken L. Lott.) Est. 1901. Balance Sheet at 30 June 1977 showed assets $473,869,679; deposits and current accounts $430,262,345. *Head Office:* 106 St. Francis Street, Mobile, Alabama 36602—P.O. Drawer 2527, Mobile 36622. 14 Branches.

**Morgan Guaranty Trust Company of New York.** (Chairman, Ellmore C. Patterson; President, Walter H. Page.) Formed through the merger of J. P. Morgan & Co. Incorporated and Guaranty Trust Company of New York on 24 April 1959; Balance Sheet at 30 June 1977 showed assets $29,450,527,000; deposits and current accounts $21,848,328,000. *Principal Offices:* 23 Wall Street, New York 10015.

**National Bank of Commerce.** (President and Chairman, Bruce E. Campbell, Jr.) Est. 1873. Balance Sheet at 31 December 1976 showed assets $542,833,000; deposits $362,433,684. *Head Office:* One Commerce Square, Memphis, Tennessee, 38150, U.S.A. 23 Branches.

**National Bank of Detroit.** (Chairman, Robert M. Surdam; President, Charles T. Fisher, III.) Est. 1933. Balance Sheet at 31 December 1974 showed assets $7,551,850,917; deposits $6,159,909,456. *Head Office:* Woodward at Fort Detroit, Michigan 48232, U.S.A. Branches: Detroit, 103; London, 1; Frankfurt, 1; Tokyo, 1; Makati, Philippines. 1.

**National Bank of Westchester.** *Head Office:* Tarry Town, N.Y.

**National City Bank, Cleveland, Ohio.** As at 31 December 1975, deposits $1,883,470,000; capital funds £188,699,000; total resources $2,645,225,000. *Head Office:* 623 Euclid Avenue, Cleveland, Ohio, 44101.

**New England Merchants National Bank.** (President, R. M. Macdougall; Chairman, M. C. Wheeler.) Est. 1831. Balance sheet at 31 December 1974, showed assets $1,296,750,000; deposits at 31 December 1974, $1,045,386,000. *Head Office:* Prudential Center, Boston, Massachusetts 02199. 16 Branches.

**Northeastern Bank of Pennslyvania.** *Administrative Office:* Scranton, Penna.

**Ohio National Bank** (Holding Co. name is BancOhio). (President, Brooks P. Julian.) Established 1888. Balance Sheet at 30 June 1977 showed assets: Ohio National Bank, $1,281,067,603; BancOhio, $2,976,424,000. *Head Office:* 55 East Broad Street, Columbus, Ohio, 43265. Branches: Ohio National Bank has 41 branches. Total number of offices of BancOhio Group in Ohio: 219.

**Pacific National Bank of Washington.** (Chairman, R. E. Bangert.) Est. 1970. Balance Sheet at 30 June 1977 showed assets $1,223,228,235; deposits and current accounts $974,726,534. *Head Office:* 1215 Fourth Avenue, Seattle, Washington 98161. 71 Branches in Washington State.

**Philadelphia National Bank.** (Chairman, G. Morris Dorrance, Jr.) Est. 1803; Balance Sheet at 30 June 1976 showed assets $3,929,500,000. *Head Office:* Broad and Chestnut Street, Philadelphia. 76 Branches.

**The Riggs National Bank.** (Chairman of the Board, Vincent C. Burke.) Est. 1836. Balance Sheet at 30 June 1977 showed assets $1,840,077,221; deposits $1,605,378,141. *Head Office:* 1503 Pennsylvania Avenue, N.W., Washington, D.C. 20077. 20 Branches, 2 facilities.

**Rhode Island Hospital Trust National Bank.** (President, Henry S. Woodbridge, Jr.; Chairman, Clarence H. Gifford, Jr.) Est. 1867. Assets $846,345,000; deposits and current accounts $688,770,000. *Head Office:* 1, Hospital Trust Plaza, Providence, Rhode Island 02903. 34 Branches.

**Seattle-First National Bank.** (Chairman and Chief Executive Officer, William M. Jenkins.) Est. 1870; Balance Sheet of the parent Company, Seafirst Corporation at 30 June 1977 showed assets $5,582,440,000; deposits $4,271,486,000. *Head Office:* 1001 Fourth Avenue, Seattle. 166 Offices.

**Seattle Trust and Savings Bank.** (President, Leonard F. Eshom; Chairman, Joseph Cebert Baillargeon.) Est. 1905. Balance Sheet at 30 June, 1975 showed assets $296,085,611; deposits and current accounts $234,502,039. *Head Office:* 804 Second Avenue, Seattle, Washington 98104. 24 Branches.

**Security Pacific National Bank, Los Angeles.** (Chairman, Frederick G. Larkin, Jr.; Vice-Chairman, William E. Siegel; President, Carl E. Hartnack.) Est. 1871; Balance Sheet at 30 June 1970 showed assets $6,958,959,946. *Head Office:* Sixth and Spring Streets, Los Angeles 90054. 404 Branches.

**Société Générale pour favoriser le développements du Commerce et de l'Industrie en France** (branch), see France.

**Trust Company of Georgia.** (Chairman, Augustus H. Sterne.) Est. 1891. Balance Sheet at 30 June, 1977 showed assets $1,870,553,000; deposits $1,387,155,000. *Head Office:* P. O. Drawer 4418, Atlanta, Georgia 30302. This is a bank holding.

**Union Bank and Trust Company, N.A.** (President, James W. Carpenter Chairman, E. J. Frey and Edward G. Williams.) Est. 1918. Balance Sheet at 31 December 1974 showed assets $412,304,250·00; deposits and current accounts $351,300,000·00. *Head Office:* 200 Ottawa, N.W., Grand Rapids, Michigan 49502. 27 Branches.

**Union Trust Company.** (President, Thomas F. Richardson, Executive Vice-Presidents, Eric R. Hansen, Edward G. Williams.) Est. 1889. Balance Sheet at 31 December 1976 showed assets $812,254,006; deposits and current accounts $705,054,846. *Head Office:* New Haven Executive Office, Corner Church and Elm Streets, New Haven, Conn., U.S.A. 53 Branches.

**Virgin Islands National Bank.** (President, Eduardo J. Corneiro; Chairman, Gordon M. Skeoch.) Balance sheet at 31 December 1974, showed assets as $142,285,850; deposits,

$127,504,172. *Head Office:* 80 Kronprindsens Gade, Charlotte Amalie, St. Thomas, U.S. Virgin Islands.

**Virginia National Bankshares.** (President, C. A. Cutchins, III; Chairman, W. Wright Harrison.) Est. 1972. As of 1977 Assets $2,084,152; deposits and current accounts $1,772,701. *Head Office:* 1 Commercial Place, Norfolk, Virginia 23510. 149 Branches.

**Wachovia Bank and Trust Company, N.A.** (Chairman, John F. Watlington, Jr.; President, John G. Medlin. Jr.) Est. 1879; Balance Sheet at 30 June 1974 showed assets $4,038,278,213; deposits $2,629,150,926. *Head Office:* Winston-Salem, North Carolina.

**Wells Fargo Bank.** (President, Richard P. Cooley.) Est. 1852; Balance Sheet at 30 June 1975 showed assets $11,257,071; deposits $9,381,768. *Head Office:* 464 California Street, San Francisco 94104.

## PRODUCTION, INDUSTRY AND COMMERCE

**Agriculture.** Nearly 50 per cent of the total land area of the United States consists of land in farms. Among the most important crops are wheat, corn, cotton, soybeans, citrus fruits and tobacco. Livestock and livestock products accounted for approximately one-half of the total cash farm incomes in 1976.

The total land area in farms in 1976 was 1,084,671,000 acres; the cropland harvested amounted to about 319 million acres. The crop area is larger than the combined areas of France, Germany and Italy. It is nearly one-third the combined area of India and Pakistan. During 1974 the United States shipped to other countries $22 billion worth of agricultural products.

The latest estimate for the number of farms is 2,785,780 for 1976; as at April 1976 the farm population numbered 8,253,000 or 4·4 per cent of the total population.

U.S. farm production in 1975 was still the second largest on record. Crop production for 1975 increased about 11 per cent over the previous year, with gains in all areas except vegetables and cotton. Output of livestock and livestock products was down slightly in 1975.

American farming is greatly mechanized. The number of farm tractors in use increased from 827,000 in 1929 to 4,263,000 at the beginning of 1975. Mechanical corn pickers increased from 110,000 in 1940 to 594,000 at the beginning of 1975. Virtually all farms have control station electrical service. There were only about 2,350,000 horses, mules, ponies, and burros on farms in 1971 and the numbers are decreasing. Few of these are used full time for farm work. Estimated cash receipts for the year 1975 from all farm crops were $45,053,000,000; the total receipts from all livestock and products amounted to $43,024,000,000. The result of these figures adds to a total from farm marketing in 1975 of $88,077,000,000.

Realized gross farm income totalled $96,668,000,000, or $34,420 per farm. Net income per farm averaged $8,637.

**Forestry.** Of the total 2·3 billion acres of land in the United States, 754 million acres, or one-third is forested. The most recent timber survey indicated that of this forested area, 500,000,000 acres are suitable and available for producing timber of commercial value on a sustained yield basis. About twenty seven per cent of all commercial forest land is in Federal, State, or municipal ownership.

There are more than 1,000 varieties of forest trees in the U.S., of which over 100 have commercial value. Species most used in the production of lumber, plywood, and wood pulp include Douglas fir, ponderosa pine, true firs, southern pines, redwood, white pine, oak, hemlock, gum, maple, spruce and cypress. Over 3/4 per cent of the annual wood harvest is softwood. Over two thirds of the annual roundwood softwood harvest is logs for manufacture into lumber, veneer for plywood, or for export. The remainder is pulpwood, fuelwood or used for various other products.

In the fiscal year 1974 trees were planted on a total of 1·58 million acres; total nursery production was over 1 billion seedlings. Of the acres planted 166,705 were direct seeded by hand or by plane. Seventy four per cent of all forest planting was on privately owned lands.

About 43,000 companies in the U.S. produce lumber and other wood products. Lumber production in 1975 was 32·6 billion board feet. Plywood production of 16·5 billion (U.S.) square feet in 1975. Pulp wood production was 74·6 million cords, and newsprint production reached 3·61 million tons. The southern pine forests yielded 447,590 barrels of turpentine and 1·1 million drums of resin in the crop year 1973.

The Forest Service of the U.S. Department of Agriculture protects and manages 187,000,000 acres of forest land in the National Forest System. This includes 154 National Forests, 19 National grasslands, 17 Land Utilization Projects, 25 Research and Experimental Areas, and 70 other research locations. National Forest resources—wood, water, range, wildlife, and recreation use—are managed in co-ordination with one another to meet present and future public demands both local and national. National Forest timber is sold to private companies by means of competitive bidding and is cut under Forest Service regulation and supervision. In the fiscal year 1976, some 10·3 billion board feet of timber were sold, and 9·6 billion board feet cut.

Scenery and recreation opportunities such as camping, swimming, boating, skiing, picnicking, hunting, fishing, etc. resulted in almost 199·9 million visitor days of recreation use during calender year 1976. The Forest Service have developed facilities that could accommodate 1,419 million people if fully occupied at one time.

As part of the continuing policy to assure a sustained yield of timber, 285,788 acres were planted or seeded to trees on National Forest land during the fiscal year 1976. An additional 441,036 acres of growing timber stands were improved by cultural treatment, and 60,456 acres were regenerated naturally.

Fifty State Foresters and the Forest Service co-operate in a number of programmes for better protection and management of non-Federal forest lands. In the fiscal year 1976. State forestry agencies distributed 506,464,000 tree seedlings for forest and windbarrier plantings, and State-employed foresters helped 104,471 woodland owners in the management of 4·1 million acres of privately-owned forest lands, with 333,657 thousand board feet of timber products harvested. Forest fire protection was provided on almost 726 million acres.

**Bureau of Land Management.** The Bureau of Land Management in the United States Department of the Interior is responsible for the management and conservation of the lands and natural resources on the remaining unreserved and unappropriated public domain lands.

The Bureau exclusively administers approximately 451 million acres of public domain lands, mostly in 11 Western States; about 276 million acres are in Alaska. BLM also manages the mineral resources on certain lands now in private ownership, in which the Federal Government has retained the mineral rights, and submerged lands on the Outer Continental Shelf.

The Bureau issues competitive and non-competitive leases for oil, gas, phosphate and other minerals, and grants patents to lands located under the General Mining Law.

In addition, the Bureau manages the mineral resources on federally owned lands of which the principal management responsibility rests with other agencies. An example of this is administration of the mining and mineral leasing laws in the National Forests of the Department of Agriculture.

Continuing an activity that dates back to the Ordinance of 1785, cadastral surveyors of the Bureau survey lands of the United States to determine property boundaries. These surveys provide legal descriptions for ownership and title purposes.

The activation of the BLM programme falls into eight principal categories: cadastral surveys, range, forestry minerals, recreation, wildlife, watershed, and lands.

During 1973 BLM surveyors made original surveys on nearly 1,838,181 acres, and re-surveyed over 1,596,823 acres.

Bureau range managers and conservation technicians work to conserve water, soil, and other resources in the management of western range lands, to provide browse for wild-life, and forage for livestock. They issue grazing permits in grazing districts established under the Taylor Grazing Act, and grazing leases on public lands outside of these districts. The protection of vital watershed areas, and fire prevention and suppression are also major parts of this programme.

BLM administers more than 23 million acres of commercial forest and lands in the continental United States and Alaska. Almost 2 million acres of these are the so-called Oregon and California Railroad grant lands in western Oregon. The BLM timber management programme includes: sustained yield and multiple use forest management; sale of mature timber; scientific cutting; protection from fire, disease, and insects; reforestation; and construction of access roads.

Another law (The Recreations & Public Purposes Act) authorizes States and local governments and non-profit organizations to obtain lands for recreational and other public purposes. There are also laws authorizing the with

## UNITED STATES OF AMERICA

The following table shows acreage, yield, and production for some crops for the years 1974–76:

| Crop and Unit | | *Acreage Harvested (In thousands)* | | | *Yield per Acres* | | | *Production (In thousands)* | | |
|---|---|---|---|---|---|---|---|---|---|---|
| | | 1974 | 1975 | 1976 | 1974 | 1975 | 1976 | 1974 | 1975 | 1976 |
| Corn for grain | Bu. | 65,357 | 67,222 | 71,085 | 71·4 | 86·2 | 87·4 | 4,663,631 | 5,797,048 | 6,216,032 |
| White corn (10 States) | Bu. | 611 | 631 | 513 | 64·3 | 67·2 | 77·2 | 39,295 | 42,646 | 39,597 |
| Corn silage | Ton | 10,623 | 9,673 | 11,190 | 10·4 | 167 | 10·4 | 110,537 | 112,835 | 116,199 |
| Corn forage | | 758 | 601 | 910 | | | | | | |
| Sorghum for grain | Bu. | 13,876 | 15,519 | 14,877 | 45·3 | 49·0 | 48·6 | 629,222 | 760,069 | 723,679 |
| Sorghum silage | Ton | 719 | 759 | 782 | 9·7 | 9·9 | 9·3 | 6,972 | 7,529 | 7,277 |
| Sorghum forage | | 2,179 | 1,612 | 1,919 | | | | | | |
| Oats | Bu. | 13,206 | 13,609 | 12,392 | 46·5 | 48·3 | 45·4 | 613,777 | 657,640 | 562,452 |
| Barley | ,, | 8,168 | 8,743 | 8,417 | 37·2 | 43·9 | 44·8 | 304,112 | 383,920 | 377,264 |
| All Wheat | ,, | 65,613 | 69,641 | 70,824 | 27·4 | 30·7 | 30·8 | 1,796,187 | 2,134,833 | 2,147,408 |
| Winter | ,, | 47,043 | 51,567 | 49,535 | 29·6 | 32·1 | 31·6 | 1,390,144 | 1,652,923 | 1,566,074 |
| Durum | ,, | 4,099 | 4,680 | 4,584 | 19·8 | 26·4 | 29·4 | 81,245 | 123,362 | 134,914 |
| Other Spring | ,, | 14,471 | 13,394 | 16,705 | 22·4 | 26·8 | 26·7 | 324,798 | 358,548 | 446,420 |
| Rice | Cwt. | 2,536·0 | 2,802·0 | 2,501·0 | 4,432 | 4,567 | 4,679 | 112,394 | 127,972 | 117,019 |
| Rye | Bu. | 897 | 814 | 804 | 21·5 | 22·0 | 20·7 | 19,293 | 17,875 | 16,667 |
| Soybeans for beans | ,, | 52,368 | 53,761 | 49,443 | 23·2 | 28·8 | 25·6 | 1,214,802 | 1,546,120 | 1,264,890 |
| Flaxseed | ,, | 1,673 | 1,520 | 954 | 8·1 | 9·9 | 7·7 | 13,541 | 15,019 | 7,356 |
| Peanuts harvested for nuts | Lb. | 1,472·1 | 1,504·0 | 1,511·5 | 2,491 | 2,565 | 2,471 | 3,667,604 | 3,857,122 | 3,735,435 |
| Popcorn | ,, | 188·7 | 224·2 | 210·1 | 2,036 | 2,240 | 2,863 | 384,200 | 542,668 | 601,610 |
| Cotton Lint | Bale | 12,566·6 | 8,796·0 | 10,899·0 | 441 | 453 | 465 | 11,540·1 | 8,301·6 | 10,556·6 |
| Cottonseed | Ton | | | | | | | 4,509·9 | 3,030·0 | 4,035·2 |
| Hay, all | ,, | 60,571 | 61,673 | 60,915 | 2·10 | 2·15 | 1·98 | 127,143 | 132,729 | 120,876 |
| Alfalfa hay | ,, | 26,817 | 21,092 | 26,556 | 2·78 | 2·87 | 2·63 | 74,672 | 77,826 | 69,911 |
| All other hay | ,, | 33,754 | 34,581 | 34,359 | 1·55 | 1·59 | 1·48 | 52,471 | 54,903 | 50,965 |
| Dry beans | Cwt. | 1,541·7 | 1,467·1 | 1,485·3 | 1,320 | 1,188 | 1,159 | 20,343 | 11,422 | 17,216 |
| Dry peas | ,, | 213·0 | 188·5 | 125·0 | 1,515 | 1,449 | 1,720 | 3,228 | 2,731 | 2,150 |
| Potatoes | | | | | | | | | | |
| Winter | ,, | 13·7 | 14·3 | 14·4 | 214 | 202 | 207 | 2,933 | 2,887 | 2,984 |
| Spring | ,, | 103·4 | 84·5 | 99·0 | 242 | 237 | 250 | 25,032 | 19,994 | 24,779 |
| Summer | ,, | 133·3 | 115·7 | 120·3 | 191 | 181 | 190 | 25,421 | 20,898 | 22,805 |
| Autumn | ,, | 1,140·4 | 1,047·3 | 1,140·4 | 253 | 264 | 266 | 288,674 | 276,055 | 302,818 |
| Total | ,, | 1,390·8 | 1,261·8 | 1,374·4 | 246 | 253 | 257 | 342,060 | 319,834 | 353,386 |
| Sweetpotatoes | ,, | 121·7 | 118·5 | 118·6 | 114 | 114 | 116 | 13,921 | 13,567 | 13,703 |
| Tobacco | Lb. | 962·6 | 1,086·4 | 1,042·6 | 2,067 | 2,008 | 2,032 | 1,989,728 | 2,181,775 | 2,118,560 |
| Sugarbeets | Ton | 1,212·6 | 1,516·6 | 1,480·5 | 18·2 | 19·6 | 19·9 | 22,123 | 29,704 | 29,427 |
| Sugarcane for sugar and seed | ,, | 734·1 | 774·0 | 759·5 | 33·8 | 36·9 | 37·9 | 24,812 | 28,523 | 28,790 |
| Maple Syrup | Gal. | | | | | | | | | |
| Peppermint for oil | Lb. | 61·0 | 68·1 | 72·2 | 54 | 55 | 51 | 3,302 | 3,753 | 3,700 |
| Spearmint for oil | ,, | 26·1 | 27·9 | 28·9 | 56 | 64 | 58 | 1,455 | 7,775 | 1,683 |
| Taro (HI) | ,, | 0·5 | 0·5 | 0·5 | 19,200 | 16,500 | 16,100 | 8,835 | 7,592 | 7,564 |
| Coffee | ,, | 2·5 | 2·0 | 2·0 | 620 | 930 | 1,000 | 1,540 | 1,860 | 2,020 |

The following table shows the production and value of principal vegetables and melons for the fresh market of the U.S. (including Hawaii) for 1974–76:

| Crop | *Production* | | | *Total Value* | | |
|---|---|---|---|---|---|---|
| | 1974 | 1975 | 1976 | 1974 | 1975 | 1976 |
| | 1,000 *cwt* | | | 1,000 *dollars* | | |
| *Vegetables* | | | | | | |
| Artichokes | 702 | 734 | 806 | 12,152 | 11,847 | 11,568 |
| Asparagus | 2,604 | 2,141 | 2,322 | 74,277 | 61,436 | 72,629 |
| Snap Beans | 2,923 | 3,179 | 3,027 | 54,439 | 62,303 | 61,146 |
| Broccoli | 3,933 | 3,940 | 4,044 | 55,912 | 59,444 | 63,761 |
| Brussels Sprouts | 656 | 696 | 490 | 12,169 | 12,205 | 9,530 |
| Cabbage | 19,118 | 19,797 | 18,770 | 86,689 | 104,120 | 95,853 |
| Carrots | 22,344 | 19,047 | 20,089 | 118,400 | 132,407 | 117,424 |
| Cauliflower | 3,033 | 2,998 | 3,218 | 39,594 | 45,504 | 52,575 |
| Celery | 16,476 | 15,826 | 16,722 | 93,956 | 118,122 | 137,374 |
| Sweet Corn | 13,000 | 13,566 | 13,951 | 101,940 | 114,606 | 114,849 |
| Cucumbers | 4,639 | 4,819 | 5,079 | 48,293 | 49,946 | 49,073 |
| Eggplant | 605 | 701 | 680 | 7,042 | 7,289 | 7,240 |
| Escarole | 1,123 | 1,092 | 1,072 | 12,157 | 13,195 | 14,990 |
| Garlic | 1,170 | 1,404 | 924 | 14,265 | 18,415 | 11,792 |
| Lettuce | 51,394 | 53,632 | 53,275 | 355,536 | 365,608 | 473,837 |
| Onions | 33,045 | 31,362 | 34,354 | 146,754 | 265,812 | 167,135 |
| Green Peppers | 5,231 | 5,106 | 5,152 | 76,021 | 84,892 | 88,149 |
| Spinach | 607 | 629 | 696 | 9,176 | 10,305 | 12,425 |
| Tomatoes | 19,968 | 20,976 | 21,492 | 345,241 | 390,985 | 425,887 |
| Total 19 Vegetables | 202,571 | 201,645 | 206,163 | 1,664,003 | 1,928,441 | 1,987,237 |
| *Melons* | | | | | | |
| Cantaloups | 9,730 | 9,787 | 9,853 | 97,180 | 102,356 | 108,075 |
| Honeydew Melons | 2,185 | 2,395 | 2,207 | 17,993 | 22,286 | 23,409 |
| Watermelons | 23,220 | 24,300 | 26,073 | 88,572 | 97,299 | 85,010 |
| Total Melons | 35,135 | 36,487 | 38,133 | 203,745 | 221,941 | 216,494 |
| Total 22 vegetables and melons | 237,706 | 238,127 | 244,296 | 1,867,748 | 2,150,382 | 2,203,731 |
| Strawberries (Total) | 5,337 | 5,420 | 5,711 | 152,759 | 165,046 | 187,610 |

The following table shows for field seeds, the acreage, yield, production, season average price, and value of production for the years 1974–76:

| Crop | *Acres Harvested* | | | *Yield per Acre* | | | *Production (Clean Seed)* | | |
|---|---|---|---|---|---|---|---|---|---|
| | 1974 | 1975 | 1976 | 1974 | 1975 | 1976 | 1974 | 1975 | 1976 |
| | *Acres* | | | *Pounds* | | | 1,000 *Pounds* | | |
| Alfalfa | 449,500 | 343,500 | 346,000 | 248 | 268 | 228 | 111,435 | 91,913 | 78,948 |
| Red Clover | 328,900 | 355,100 | 370,300 | 92 | 106 | 100 | 30,186 | 37,470 | 37,163 |
| Ladino Clover | 9,000 | 11,000 | 11,600 | 365 | 390 | 295 | 3,285 | 4,290 | 3,422 |
| Lespedeza | 67,000 | 77,800 | 66,100 | 186 | 218 | 191 | 12,495 | 16,939 | 12,630 |
| Timothy | 146,400 | 78,700 | 73,500 | 165 | 183 | 173 | 23,284 | 14,375 | 12,693 |
| Orchardgrass | 37,400 | 31,000 | 27,500 | 436 | 470 | 450 | 16,322 | 14,585 | 12,365 |
| Merion Ky. Bluegrass | 14,500 | 8,400 | 4,300 | 275 | 273 | 249 | 3,988 | 2,294 | 1,072 |
| Other Ky. Bluegrass | | | | | | | 54,553 | 35,633 | 33,101 |
| Chewing Fescue | 13,000 | 11,500 | 9,500 | 525 | 500 | 570 | 6,825 | 5,750 | 5,415 |
| Red Fescue | 15,000 | 13,000 | 11,000 | 460 | 450 | 500 | 6,900 | 5,850 | 5,500 |
| Tall Fescue | 418,000 | 462,500 | 377,000 | 253 | 264 | 230 | 105,895 | 122,125 | 86,635 |
| Bentgrass | 28,000 | 20,000 | 14,500 | 330 | 330 | 320 | 9,240 | 6,600 | 4,640 |
| Crimson Clover | 7,150 | 6,550 | 11,500 | 249 | 340 | 320 | 1,778 | 2,228 | 3,680 |
| Hairy Vetch | 24,500 | 28,400 | 27,000 | 176 | 241 | 251 | 4,310 | 6,841 | 6,765 |
| All Ryegrass | 190,000 | 180,000 | 166,000 | 1,150 | 1,260 | 1,180 | 218,500 | 226,800 | 195,940 |

drawal of certain lands from all forms of entry and appropriation—for defence purposes, for wild-life and recreation areas, national parks and national forests, and for other management uses.

Management of the recreation resource is one of the important functions of BLM. Visitor facilities and camp sites have already been constructed on the O & C lands in Oregon. During 1964, BLM received its first appropriation for recreational developments.

As a part of its lands function, the Bureau of Land Management is responsible for the custody and maintenance of the Nation's public land records. They describe the present status and past history of over a billion and a half acres of public and private lands.

BLM headquarters is located in Washington, D.C. There are state offices in Anchorage, Alaska; Salt Lake City, Utah; Denver, Colorado; Sacramento, California; Phoenix, Arizona; Boise, Idaho; Billings, Montana; Reno, Nevada; Santa Fe, New Mexico; Portland, Oregon; Cheyenne, Wyoming; and Silver Spring, Md.

**Fisheries.**

*U.S. Commercial Landings.* Commercial fishery landings at ports in the United States were a near-record 5·4 billion pounds (round weight), valued at a record $1·4 billion to the fishermen in 1976. The quantity landed was 11 per cent more than in 1975 and only four million pounds less than the 1962 record. The increase in quantity landed was due to increased landings of edible species and species for industrial purposes.

U.S. flag vessels also landed tuna and shrimp at ports outside the United States. These landings consisted of 174·3 million pounds of tuna valued at $50·0 million, landed principally in Puerto Rico, and 7·8 million pounds of shrimp valued at $15·1 million, landed at Caribbean ports.

Commercial landings in the United States of edible species were 2·8 billion pounds, valued at $1·3 billion, up 14 per cent in quantity and 40 per cent in value. The quantity landed was the largest since 1952 and considerably above the average for the previous five years. Record landings of two important species–tuna (486 million pounds) and shrimp (404 million pounds)–and improved landings of crabs (345 million pounds), salmon (309 million pounds), flounders (165 million pounds), and cod and other groundfish (157 million pounds) accounted for a large share of the increase.

Landings at U.S. ports of species used for reduction to fish meal and for other industrial purposes were 2·6 billion pounds valued at $89 million in 1976. This quantity, seven per cent greater than in 1975 and five per cent above the average for the previous five years, was short of the record amount landed in 1962. The value of the landings in 1976 was second to the record made in 1973. The increase in quantity was due to heavy landings of menhaden, which more than offset a decline in landings of anchovies.

*Marine Recreational Landings.* The most recent year that data is available is 1970. In that year, U.S. marine recreational fishermen caught an estimated 1·6 billion pounds of marine (saltwater) finfish, or about the same as the average amount of edible finfish landed by commercial fishermen in recent years.

*World Landings.* In 1975, world landings were 69,732 thousand metric tons (153·7 billion pounds), down one per cent from the 1974 production of 70,493 thousand metric tons (155·4 billion pounds). Japan, with 15 per cent of the total landings, continues to be the world leader in fishery landings, followed by the U.S.S.R. with 14 per cent. The Peoples Republic of China was third, with 10 per cent; followed by Peru, five per cent; and the United States, four per cent. The United States was in fifth place for the third consecutive year.

*Prices.* During 1976, U.S. exvessel prices (prices received by fishermen for their landings) moved upward in most months and were at, or near, record levels by the end of the year. The largest gains were for shellfish. The same upward movement was apparent in prices quoted at the wholesale level for fresh, frozen, and canned fishery products.

*Processed Products.* The total value of domestic production of processed fishery products (edible and industrial) was $3·2 billion in 1976, up 22 per cent over 1975. The value of edible products, which comprises almost 90 per cent of the total, was almost $2·9 billion, up 23 per cent in 1976. The value of all major categories of edible products increased, but the greatest increase was in the value of production of canned products, which reached $1·2 billion in 1976. The value of industrial products in 1976 was $377 million, up 16 per cent over 1975. Most of the increase in industrial items was in the value of the production of fish meal, oil, and solubles.

*Foreign Trade.* The value of U.S. imports of edible and industrial fishery products was a record $2,277 million in 1976, up 39 per cent over 1975. Imports of edible products reached 2,206 million pounds, valued at $1,861 million. Imports of all major categories increased–fillets, blocks, tuna for canning, lobsters, shrimp, canned sardines, canned tuna, and canned oysters. Imports of industrial products rose to a record $416 million.

Total U.S. exports of edible and industrial fishery products were valued at $382 million in 1976, up 25 per cent over 1975.

*Supply.* The U.S. supply of commercial fishery products (domestic landings plus imports, round weight equivalent) was 11·6 billion pounds in 1976-an increase of 14 per cent over 1975. Edible fish and shellfish accounted for 64 per cent of total supply. Imports provided 63 per cent of the edible products and 38 per cent of the supply of industrial products in 1976.

*Per Capita Consumption.* In 1976, U.S. consumption reached 12·9 pounds of edible meat per person, tying the record set in 1973. This was 0·7 pound more than the 12·2 pounds eaten in 1975.

The table below shows the commercial landings of fish for 1976(*1*).

| *Catch of Species* | 1976 | | |
|---|---|---|---|
| *Fish* | *Thousand pounds weight* | *Thousand dollars* | *Five year Average 1971–75 Thousand pounds weight* |
| Alewives: | | | |
| Atlantic and Gulf | 14,367 | 625 | 25,818 |
| Great Lakes | 39,845 | 477 | 35,452 |
| Anchovies | 257,073 | 5,676 | 220,339 |
| Bluefish | 10,387 | 1,091 | 9,216 |
| Bonito | 8,847 | 1,253 | 24,778 |
| Butterfish | 3,074 | 867 | 3,368 |
| Cod: | | | |
| Atlantic | 55,845 | 14,350 | 53,186 |
| Pacific | 11,944 | 1,527 | 9,169 |
| Croaker | 31,594 | 3,821 | 20,572 |
| Cusk | 2,831 | 504 | 2,588 |
| Flounders: | | | |
| Atlantic and Gulf: | | | |
| Blackback | 20,868 | 7,303 | 20,010 |
| Fluke | 23,714 | 10,696 | 10,313 |
| Yellowtail | 37,828 | 15,521 | 59,804 |
| Other | 24,179 | 8,282 | 21,412 |
| Pacific | 58,093 | 10,205 | 49,627 |
| Total | 164,682 | 52,007 | 161,166 |
| Groupers | 9,242 | 4,303 | 7,188 |
| Haddock | 12,761 | 5,551 | 13,198 |
| Hake: | | | |
| Pacific | 3,124 | 46 | 4,487 |
| Red | 4,972 | 417 | 2,681 |
| White | 9,081 | 1,208 | 6,865 |
| Halibut | 20,614 | 19,418 | 24,136 |
| Herring, sea: | | | |
| Atlantic | 110,524 | 4,363 | 75,075 |
| Pacific | 40,392 | 6,297 | 33,134 |
| Jack mackerel | 38,519 | 1,925 | 36,676 |
| Lingcod | 7,484 | 1,280 | (3) |
| Mackerel: | | | |
| Atlantic | 5,976 | 703 | 4,447 |
| King | 8,936 | 3,886 | 5,866 |
| Spanish | 14,077 | 3,208 | 10,467 |
| Menhaden: | | | |
| Atlantic | 801,698 | 23,212 | 704,592 |
| Gulf | 1,237,779 | 43,967 | 1,256,595 |
| Total | 2,039,477 | 67,179 | 1,961,187 |
| Mullet | 30,495 | 4,536 | 33,959 |
| Ocean perch: | | | |
| Atlantic | 32,139 | 4,395 | 49,201 |
| Pacific | 5,658 | 719 | 6,995 |
| Pollock | 24,284 | 3,250 | 15,740 |
| Rockfishes | 39,683 | 5,360 | 32,857 |
| Sablefish | 17,406 | 3,151 | (3) |
| Salmon, Pacific: | | | |
| Chinook or king | 34,511 | 51,422 | 30,287 |
| Chum or keta | 52,645 | 20,577 | 51,614 |
| Pink | 99,237 | 28,393 | 58,413 |
| Red or sockeye | 83,159 | 51,445 | 62,395 |
| Silver or coho | 39,690 | 44,659 | 34,023 |
| Total | 309,242 | 196,496 | 236,732 |
| Scup or porgy | 15,998 | 3,403 | 12,363 |
| Sea bass: | | | |
| Black | 4,296 | 1,528 | 3,822 |
| White | 949 | 617 | 842 |
| Sea trout: | | | |
| Gray | 20,881 | 2,619 | 15,355 |
| Spotted | 7,072 | 3,073 | 7,566 |
| White | 1,805 | 231 | 1,972 |
| Sharks | 7,252 | 629 | 1,195 |

*continued*

| *Catch of Species* | 1976 | | |
|---|---|---|---|
| *Fish* | *Thousand pounds weight* | *Thousand dollars* | *Five year Average 1971–75 Thousand pounds weight* |
| Snapper: | | | |
| Red | 9,216 | 8,024 | 8,689 |
| Other | 2,486 | 1,593 | 2,595 |
| Striped bass | 5,838 | 3,189 | 10,530 |
| Tuna: | | | |
| Albacore | 41,931 | 19,810 | 50,552 |
| Bigeye | 2,286 | 1,389 | (3) |
| Bluefin | 22,930 | 7,135 | 22,288 |
| Little | 78 | 18 | 44 |
| Skipjack | 142,132 | 39,593 | 71,391 |
| Yellowfin | 276,060 | 81,793 | 227,119 |
| Unclassified | 89 | 27 | 23 |
| Total | 485,506 | 149,765 | 371,417 |
| Warsaw | 190 | 53 | 196 |
| Whiting | 47,666 | 3,973 | 34,856 |
| Wolffish | 1,048 | 99 | 723 |
| Other | 355,233 | 57,642 | — |
| Total fish | 4,350,011 | 656,327 | — |
| *Shellfish et al.* | | | |
| Clams: | | | |
| Hard | 15,600 | 25,437 | 15,432 |
| Soft | 10,540 | 12,213 | 9,542 |
| Surf | 49,133 | 23,344 | 76,281 |
| Other | 5,728 | 1,715 | 1,476 |
| Total | 81,001 | 62,709 | 102,731 |
| Crabs: | | | |
| Blue, hard | 113,152 | 22,966 | 141,277 |
| Dungeness | 35,804 | 22,568 | 23,261 |
| King | 105,825 | 70,072 | 87,882 |
| Snow | 80,712 | 16,142 | 46,185 |
| Other | 9,317 | 5,207 | 7,516 |
| Total | 344,810 | 136,955 | 306,121 |
| Lobsters: | | | |
| American | 31,741 | 52,684 | 30,445 |
| Spiny | 4,889 | 7,491 | 10,619 |
| Oysters | 54,391 | 53,098 | 52,793 |
| Scallops: | | | |
| Bay | 2,131 | 4,682 | 1,873 |
| Calico | 2,261 | 1,582 | 1,102 |
| Sea | 19,840 | 35,061 | 7,202 |
| Shrimp: | | | |
| New England | 2,254 | 765 | 19,796 |
| South Atlantic | 26,121 | 35,014 | 26,561 |
| Gulf | 210,078 | 275,187 | 198,848 |
| Pacific | 165,114 | 20,379 | 129,047 |
| Other | 10 | 30 | 5 |
| Total | 403,577 | 331,375 | 374,257 |
| Squid | 28,838 | 2,102 | 24,655 |
| Other | 26,910 | 8,634 | — |
| Other | 26,910 | 8,634 | — |
| Total shellfish *et al.* | 1,000,389 | 696,373 | — |
| Grand total | 5,350,400 | 1,352,700 | — |

(1) Statistics on landings are shown in round weight for all items except univalve and bivalve mollusks such as clams, oysters, and scallops, which are shown in weight of meats excluding the shell.
*Note:* Data are preliminary. Data do not include landings by U.S. flag vessels at Puerto Rico or other ports outside the 50 States. Data do not include production of artificially cultivated fish and shellfish.

**Mining.** Coal, iron ore, copper, lead, zinc, silver, tungsten, gold and mercury are mined in the United States. Other essential minerals are also produced, including petroleum, natural gas, bauxite, sulphur, lime, salt, clays and slate.

Annual production of iron ore is about 79,000,000 tons, mine production of recoverable copper about 1,400,000 tons, of lead about 621,000 short tons and of zinc about 469,000 tons.

Coal is produced to the extent of 648,000,000 tons a year. More than 97 per cent of all bituminous coal mined underground is cut by mechanical cutters, and more than 97 per cent is loaded mechanically. Coal is produced in approximately half the 50 States.

Production of petroleum in 1975 was 3,056,779,000 (42 gallon) barrels and in 1974 it was 3,202,585,000. The production, refining and marketing of petroleum products such as gasoline, lubricating oil, fuel oil and kerosene is one of the largest industries in the country, employing over 1,000,000 people.

The following tables give details of mineral production in both the continental United States and the Territories and Possessions for 1975.

| *Mineral* | *Quantity* | *Value (thousand $)* |
|---|---|---|
| *Mineral fuels* | | |
| *Asphalt and related bitumens (native):* | | |
| Bituminous limestone and sandstone and gilsonite (short tons) | 1,901,715 | 19,838 |
| Carbon dioxide, natural (est.) (1,000 cu. ft.) | 1,070,024 | 279 |
| *Coal:* | | |
| Bituminous and lignite (1) (thousand short tons) | 648,438 | 12,472,486 |
| Pennsylvania anthracite (thousand short tons) | 6,203 | 198,481 |
| *Helium:* | | |
| Crude (1,000 cu. ft.) | 334 | 4,008 |
| Grade A (1,000 cu. ft.) | 745 | 19,915 |
| Natural gas (million cu. ft) | 20,108,661 | 8,945,062 |
| *Natural gas liquids:* | | |
| Petrol and cycle products (thousand gallons) | 151,872 | 878,698 |
| LP gases (thousand gallons) | 444,086 | 1,893,890 |
| Peat (short tons) | 746,000 | 12,294 |
| Petroleum (crude) (1,000 42-gallon barrels) | 3,056,779 | 23,116,059 |
| **Total mineral fuels** | — | 47,561,000 |
| *Non-metals (except fuels)* | | |
| Abrasive stone (2) (short tons) | 2,953 | 1,060 |
| Asbestos (short tons) | 98,654 | 14,220 |
| Barite (thousand short tons) | 1,287 | 20,673 |
| Boron minerals (thousand short tons) | 1,172 | 158,772 |
| Bromine (thousand pounds) | 407,163 | 113,126 |
| Calcium-magnesium chloride (short tons) | 594,400 | 29,047 |
| *Cement:* | | |
| Portland (thousand short tons) | 65,215 | 2,015,625 |
| Masonry (thousand short tons) | 2,868 | 111,801 |
| Natural and slag (thousand short tons) | (3) | (3) |
| Clays (thousand short tons) | 49,047 | 424,556 |
| Diatomite (short tons) | 573,000 | 45,812 |

*continued*

| *Mineral* | *Quantity* | *Value (thousand $)* |
|---|---|---|
| Emery (short tons) | 3,487 | — |
| Feldspar (short tons) | 684,898 | 11,893 |
| Fluorspar (short tons) | 139,913 | 10,888 |
| Garnet (abrasive) (short tons) | 17,204 | 1,690 |
| Gem stones (estimate) | NA | 13,900 |
| Gypsum (thousand short tons) | 9,751 | 44,654 |
| Lime (thousand short tons) | 19,133 | 523,805 |
| Magnesium compounds from sea water and brine (except for metals) short tons, MgO equivalent) | (3) | (3) |
| *Mica:* | | |
| Scrap (short tons) | 135,000 | 5,219 |
| Sheet (pounds) | 5,000 | 3 |
| Perlite (short tons) | 512,000 | 7,282 |
| Phosphate rock (thousand short tons) | 48,816 | 1,122,184 |
| Potassium salts (thousand short tons, $K_2O$ equivalent) | 2,501 | 223,098 |
| Pumice (thousand short tons) | 3,892 | 11,203 |
| Pyrites (thousand long tons) | 625 | 4,776 |
| Salt (thousand short tons) | 41,030 | 368,063 |
| Sand and gravel (thousand short tons) | 789,436 | 1,416,346 |
| Sodium carbonate (natural) (Short tons) | 4,328,000 | 182,620 |
| Sodium sulphate (natural) (short tons) | 667,000 | 27,667 |
| Stone (4) (thousand short tons) | 902,900 | 2,123,049 |
| *Sulphur:* | | |
| Frasch process mines (thousand long tons) | 6,077 | 304,843 |
| Other mines (long tons) | — | — |
| Talc, soapstone, and pyrophyllite (short tons) | 927,548 | 8,309 |
| Tripoli (short tons) | 80,562 | 565 |
| Vermiculite (thousand short tons) | 330 | 13,761 |
| Value of items that cannot be disclosed: Aplite, graphite, iodine, kyanite, lithium minerals, magnesite, greensand marl, olivine, staurolite, wollastonite, and values indicated by footnote (3) | — | 157,180 |
| **Total nonmetals** | — | 9,518,000 |
| *Metals* | | |
| Antimony ore and concentrate (short tons, antimony content) | 886 | 2,131 |
| Bauxite (thousand long tons, dried equivalent) | 1,772 | 25,083 |
| Beryllium concentrate (short tons, gross weight) | (5) | (5) |
| Copper (recoverable content of ores, etc.) (short tons) | 1,413,366 | 1,814,763 |
| Gold (recoverable content of ores, etc. (troy ounces) | 1,052,252 | 169,928 |
| Iron ore, usable (excl. byproduct iron sinter) (thousand long tons, gross wt.) | 75,695 | 1,620,599 |
| Lead (recoverable content of ores, etc. (short tons) | 621,464 | 267,230 |
| Manganese ore (35 per cent or more (Mn) (short tons, gross wt.) | — | — |
| Manganiferous ore (5 to 35 per cent Mn) (short tons, gross wt.) | 158,725 | 1,412 |
| Mercury (76-pound flasks) | 7,366 | 1,165 |
| Molybdenum (content of concentrate) (thousand pounds) | 105,170 | 259,328 |
| Nickel (content of ore and concentrate (short tons) | 16,987 | (5) |
| Rare-earth metal concentrates (short tons) | (5) | (5) |
| Silver (recoverable content of ores, etc.) (thousand troy ounces) | 34,938 | 154,424 |
| Tin (content of concentrate) (long tons) | (5) | 5) |

# UNITED STATES OF AMERICA

*continued*

| *Mineral* | *Quantity* | *Value (thousand$)* |
|---|---|---|
| *Titanium concentrate:* | | |
| Ilmenite (short tons, gross wt.) | 702,252 | 26,946 |
| Tungsten ore and concentrate (thousand pounds contained W) | 5,490 | 29,090 |
| Uranium (recoverable content $U_3O_8$) (thousand pounds) | 22,877 | 281,388 |
| Vanadium (recoverable in ore and concentrate) (short tons) | 4,743 | 49,329 |
| Zinc (recoverable content of ores, etc.) (short tons) | 469,355 | 366,097 |
| Value of items that cannot be disclosed: magnesium chloride for magnesium metal, manganiferous residuum, platinum-group metals (crude), zirconium concentrate, and values indicated by footnote (5) | — | 127,459 |
| **Total metals** | — | 5,196,000 |
| **Grand total mineral production** | — | 62,275,000 |

NA—Not available.

*Note:* Production as measured by mine shipments, sales, or marketable production (including consumption by producers).

(1) Includes small quantity of anthracite mined in States other than Pennsylvania.

(2) Grindstones, pulpstones, grinding pebbles, sharpening stones, and tube-mill liners.

(3) Figure withheld to avoid disclosing individual company confidential data; value included with 'Nonmetal items that cannot be disclosed'.

(4) Excludes abrasive stone, bituminous limestones, bituminous sandstone, and ground soapstone, all included elsewhere in table.

(5) Figure withheld to avoid disclosing individual company confidential data; value included with 'Metal items that cannot be disclosed'.

The chief copper States with production for 1975 (in short tons) are: Arizona, 813,211; Utah, 177,155. New Mexico, 146,263; Montana, 87,959.

The chief gold-producing States (figures for 1975 in troy ounces) are: South Dakota, 304,935; Nevada, 332,814; Utah, 189,620.

The silver-producing States (1975 figures in thousand troy ounces) are: Idaho, 13,868; Arizona, 6,286; Colorado, 3,366; Utah, 2,822.

The chief lead-producing States (1975 figures in short are: New York, 76,612; Missouri, 74,867; Tennessee, 83,293; Colorado, 48,460.

Coal is produced mainly in Kentucky West Virginia, and Pennsylvania, the latter State producing most of the anthracite. The chief coal States with 1975 production figures (in thousand short tons) are: Kentucky, 143,643; West Virginia, 109,283; Pennsylvania, 84,137; Illinois, 59,537.

The major natural gas producing States (1975 marketable production) in million cubic feet are: Texas, 7,485,764; Louisiana, 7,090,645; Oklahoma, 1,605,410; New Mexico, 1,217,430.

At the end of 1975 the United States had 500,333 oil wells in production. The following are the chief oil States and the number of wells in production in each: Texas, 160,603; Louisiana, 27,734; California, 41,029; Oklahoma, 71,576; Wyoming, 9,450; and New Mexico, 13,715. U.S. production per day per well was 16·8 barrels in 1975, only 199 wells producing 972 barrels per day while Pennsylvania with 32,095 wells produced 0·3 barrels per well per day. The average daily production per well in Texas remained unchanged from 1973 at 20·9 barrels per day; in Louisiana, 64·0 barrels; in California, 21·7 barrels; in Oklahoma, 6·2 barrels; in Wyoming, 41·1 barrels; in Kansas, 4·1 barrels; in New Mexico, 19·3 barrels.

**Industry.** The table shows the hours worked by person engaged in production by Industry in millions of persons for the years 1973–76[1]:

| | 1973 | 1974 | 1975 | 1976 |
|---|---|---|---|---|
| *Hours worked by persons engaged in production* | 165,472 | 165,480 | 160,749 | 165,840 |
| *Domestic industries* | 165,491 | 165,501 | 160,776 | 165,875 |
| Agriculture, forestry, and fisheries | 7,979 | 7,857, | 7,707 | 7,899 |
| Farms | 7,047 | 6,942 | 6,876 | 6,949 |
| Mining | 1,326 | 1,469 | 1,570 | 1,661 |
| Contract construction | 9,431 | 9,293 | 8,232 | 8,510 |
| Manufacturing | 39,537 | 38,731 | 35,071 | 36,805 |
| Nondurable goods | 16,047 | 15,582 | 14,556 | 15,285 |
| Durable goods | 23,490 | 23,149 | 20,515 | 21,520 |
| Transportation | 5,780 | 5,774 | 5,416 | 5,506 |
| Communication | 2,185 | 2,198 | 2,120 | 2,127 |
| Electric, gas and sanitary services | 1,424 | 1,430 | 1,401 | 1,413 |
| Wholesale and retail trade | 33,638 | 33,594 | 33,261 | 34,406 |
| Wholesale trade | 8,565 | 9,120 | 8,886 | 9,231 |
| Retail trade | 25,072 | 24,474 | 24,375 | 25,175 |
| Finance, insurance, and real estate | 7,948 | 8,121 | 8,185 | 8,408 |
| Services | 28,693 | 29,093 | 29,390 | 30,624 |
| Government and government enterprises | 27,550 | 27,941 | 28,423 | 28,516 |
| *Rest of the world* | –19 | –21 | –27 | –35 |

1. Persons engaged in production equals the number of employees on full-time schedules plus the number on part-time schedules plus active proprietors and partners of unincorporated enterprises. Unpaid family workers are excluded.

The following table shows the number of Full-Time Equivalent Employees by industry for 1973–76:

| | *(thousands)* 1973 | 1974 | 1975 | 1976 |
|---|---|---|---|---|
| All industries, total | 75,484 | 76,476 | 74,290 | 76,728 |
| Agriculture, forestry and fisheries | 1,332 | 1,405 | 1,411 | 1,555 |
| Mining | 624 | 684 | 733 | 757 |
| Contract construction | 3,915 | 3,831 | 3,345 | 3,345 |
| Manufacturing | 19,566 | 19,489 | 17,727 | 18,480 |
| Wholesale and retail trade | 14,288 | 14,574 | 15,509 | 15,178 |
| Finance, insurance and real estate | 3,866 | 3,980 | 4,000 | 4,108 |
| Transportation | 2,638 | 2,670 | 2,514 | 2,558 |
| Communications and public utilities | 1,822 | 1,860 | 1,823 | 1,822 |
| Services | 12,643 | 12,964 | 12,909 | 13,557 |
| Government | 14,586 | 15,039 | 15,332 | 15,385 |
| Addendum: | | | | |
| All private non-farm industries | 50,353 | 60,032 | 57,547 | 59,788 |

The tables below show the Gross National Product in billions of Current Dollars and billions of Constant 1972 Dollars (U.S. billion), for 1973–1976.[1]

| | *Current (U.S. billion)* 1973 | 1974 | 1975 | 1976 |
|---|---|---|---|---|
| Gross national product | 1,306·5 | 1,412·9 | 1,528·8 | 1,706·5 |
| Personal consumption expenditures | 809·9 | 889·6 | 980·4 | 1,094·0 |
| Durable goods | 123·7 | 122·0 | 132·9 | 158·9 |
| Non-durable goods | 333·8 | 376·3 | 409·3 | 442·7 |
| Services | 352·3 | 391·3 | 438·2 | 492·3 |

*continued*

| | *Current (U.S. billion)* | | | |
|---|---|---|---|---|
| | 1973 | 1974 | 1975 | 1976 |
| Gross private domestic investment | 220·0 | 214·6 | 189·1 | 243·3 |
| Fixed investment | 202·1 | 205·7 | 200·6 | 230·0 |
| Residential | 66·1 | 55·1 | 51·5 | 68·0 |
| Non-residential | 136·0 | 150·6 | 149·1 | 161·9 |
| Change in business inventories | 17·9 | 8·9 | −11·5 | 13·3 |
| Non-farm | 14·7 | 10·8 | −15·1 | 14·9 |
| Farm | 3·2 | −1·8 | 3·6 | −1·6 |
| Net exports of goods and services (GNP basis) | 7·1 | 6·0 | 20·4 | 7·8 |
| Exports | 101·6 | 137·9 | 147·3 | 162·9 |
| Imports | 94·4 | 131·9 | 126·9 | 155·1 |
| Government purchases of goods and services | 269·5 | 302·7 | 338·9 | 361·4 |
| Federal | 102·2 | 111·1 | 123·3 | 130·1 |
| State and local | 167·3 | 191·5 | 215·6 | 231·21 |

| | *Constant* 1972 $ (*U.S. billion*) | | | |
|---|---|---|---|---|
| | 1973 | 1974 | 1975 | 1976 |
| Gross national product | 1,235·0 | 1,217·8 | 1,202·1 | 1,274·7 |
| Personal consumption expenditures | 767·7 | 760·7 | 775·1 | 821·3 |
| Durable goods | 121·8 | 112·5 | 112·7 | 127·5 |
| Non-durable goods | 309·3 | 303·9 | 307·6 | 321·6 |
| Services | 336·5 | 344·3 | 354·8 | 372·2 |
| Gross private domestic investment | 207·2 | 183·6 | 141·6 | 173·0 |
| Fixed investment | 190·7 | 175·6 | 151·5 | 164·5 |
| Residential | 59·7 | 45·0 | 38·8 | 47·7 |
| Non-residential | 131·0 | 130·6 | 112·7 | 116·8 |
| Change in business inventories | 16·5 | 8·0 | −9·9 | 8·5 |
| Non-farm | 14·2 | 8·3 | −11·2 | 10·1 |
| Farm | 2·3 | −·3 | 1·2 | −1·6 |
| Net exports of goods and services (GNP basis) | 7·6 | 15·9 | 22·5 | 16·0 |
| Exports | 87·4 | 93·0 | 89·9 | 95·8 |
| Imports | 79·9 | 77·1 | 67·4 | 79·8 |
| Government purchases of goods and services | 252·5 | 257·7 | 263·0 | 264·4 |
| Federal | 96·6 | 95·8 | 96·7 | 96·5 |
| State and local | 155·9 | 161·8 | 166·3 | 167·9 |

[1] G.N.P. revised back to 1929.

**Commerce.** The following tables show the principal imports and exports for 1973–76:

| *Product* | 1973 million $ | 1974 million $ | 1975 million $ | 1976 million $ |
|---|---|---|---|---|
| Meat and preparations | 444 | 381 | 528 | 798 |
| Dairy produce and eggs | 56 | 67 | 134 | 128 |
| Grains | 8,945 | 10,331 | 11,643 | 10,911 |
| Vegetables | 307 | 391 | 406 | 559 |
| Beverages and Tobacco | 1,009 | 1,247 | 1,310 | 1,523 |
| Hides and skins | 377 | 339 | 296 | 522 |
| Soybeans | 2,757 | 3,537 | 2,865 | 3,315 |
| Synthetic rubber | 196 | 290 | 261 | 329 |
| Wood, rough | 824 | 744 | 751 | 945 |
| Wood, shaped | 474 | 468 | 413 | 563 |
| Textile fibres | 1,319 | 1,782 | 1,345 | 1,426 |

*continued*

| *Products* | 1973 million $ | 1974 million $ | 1975 million $ | 1976 million $ |
|---|---|---|---|---|
| Ores and scrap | 1,081 | 1,475 | 1,355 | 1,285 |
| Coal | 1,014 | 2,437 | 3,259 | 2,910 |
| Petroleum | 518 | 792 | 907 | 998 |
| Animal oils and fats | 337 | 563 | 341 | 421 |
| Chemicals | 5,748 | 8,822 | 8,705 | 9,958 |
| Machinery and transport equipment | 27,842 | 38,189 | 45,710 | 49,510 |
| Electrical apparatus | 5,031 | 7,019 | 7,587 | 9,278 |
| Other manufactured goods | 11,112 | 16,516 | 16,590 | 17,777 |
| Paper and manufactures | 919 | 1,522 | 1,448 | 1,624 |
| Metal manufactures | 3,469 | 5,725 | 5,661 | 5,180 |
| Textiles, other than clothing | 1,225 | 1,795 | 1,625 | 1,970 |
| Scientific Measuring and Controlling instruments | 524 | 679 | 786 | 855 |
| Other transactions | 1,844 | 2,587 | 3,162 | 2,749 |

*IMPORTS*

| *Product* | 1973 million $ | 1974 million $ | 1975 million $ | 1976 million $ |
|---|---|---|---|---|
| Cattle, other than for breeding | 192 | 107 | 76 | 158 |
| Meat and preparations | 1,668 | 1,344 | 1.140 | 1 446 |
| Fish | 1,387 | 1,499 | 1,355 | 1,854 |
| Fruits (fresh, only) | 411 | 444 | 458 | 556 |
| Vegetables | 409 | 388 | 355 | 425 |
| Sugar | 918 | 2,256 | 1,872 | 1,148 |
| Coffee | 1,689 | 1,638 | 1,674 | 2,859 |
| Cocoa | 279 | 431 | 434 | 555 |
| Tea | 69 | 79 | 88 | 96 |
| Spices | 78 | 110 | 99 | 104 |
| Alcoholic beverages | 996 | 1,028 | 1,032 | 1,172 |
| Tobacco | 215 | 291 | 383 | 446 |
| Hides and skins | 84 | 78 | 78 | 89 |
| Fur skins | 77 | 79 | 79 | 101 |
| Rubber | 413 | 599 | 442 | 620 |
| Wood shaped | 1,493 | 1,056 | 792 | 1,339 |
| Textile fibres | 236 | 225 | 175 | 249 |
| Industrial diamonds | 62 | 48 | 42 | 46 |
| Asbestos | 99 | 124 | 111 | 142 |
| Ores and scrap | 1,291 | 1,838 | 1,961 | 2,246 |
| Petroleum products | 7,549 | 24,210 | 24,766 | 31,755 |
| Natural gas | 493 | 866 | 1,435 | 2,015 |
| Animal and vegetable oils | 255 | 544 | 554 | 464 |
| Chemicals | 2,437 | 3,991 | 3,707 | 4,829 |
| Engines and parts | 1,156 | 1,190 | 1,299 | 1,682 |
| Agricultural machinery | 491 | 743 | 872 | 853 |
| Office machines | 905 | 1,020 | 1,067 | 1,353 |
| Metal working machinery | 188 | 305 | 368 | 366 |
| Textile and leather machinery | 625 | 609 | 521 | 641 |
| Electrical apparatus | 4,471 | 5,417 | 4,972 | 7,484 |
| Automobiles and parts | 9,400 | 10,861 | 10,672 | 14,064 |
| Leather and manufactures | 137 | 128 | 132 | 248 |
| Wood manufactures | 769 | 676 | 569 | 820 |
| Paper and manufactures | 1,457 | 1,831 | 1,664 | 2,103 |
| Glass and pottery | 521 | 528 | 523 | 644 |
| Diamonds, non-industrial | 827 | 775 | 730 | 1,019 |
| Metal and manufactures | 6,886 | 11,383 | 9,053 | 10,065 |
| Textiles, other than clothing | 1,568 | 1,629 | 1,234 | 1,653 |
| Clothing | 2,154 | 2,323 | 2,551 | 3,613 |
| Footwear | 1,079 | 1,153 | 1,301 | 1,725 |
| Scientific Measuring and Controlling instruments | 133 | 159 | 142 | 163 |

The following table shows imports and exports by principal countries for 1974 and 1975 (million $):

| Country | Imports 1975 | Imports 1976 | Exports 1975 | Exports 1976 |
|---|---|---|---|---|
| Canada | 22,151 | 26,827 | 21,744 | 24,109 |
| Mexico | 3,067 | 3,606 | 5,141 | 4,990 |
| Guatemala | 173 | 288 | 255 | 334 |
| El Salvador | 182 | 287 | 194 | 232 |
| Honduras | 145 | 216 | 151 | 162 |
| Nicaragua | 131 | 181 | 156 | 169 |
| Costa Rica | 179 | 235 | 212 | 255 |
| Panama Republic | 196 | 142 | 317 | 358 |
| Dominican Republic | 634 | 520 | 453 | 432 |
| Netherlands Antilles | 1,559 | 1,170 | 228 | 248 |
| Columbia | 596 | 657 | 643 | 703 |
| Venezuela | 3,625 | 3,576 | 2,243 | 2,628 |
| Ecuador | 463 | 539 | 410 | 416 |
| Peru | 398 | 378 | 896 | 573 |
| Bolivia | 89 | 113 | 138 | 133 |
| Chile | 138 | 222 | 533 | 508 |
| Brazil | 1,467 | 1,740 | 3,056 | 2,809 |
| Latin American Free Trade Assn. (inc. Paraguay and Uruguay) | 10,100 | 11,225 | 13,773 | 13,399 |
| Argentina | 215 | 310 | 628 | 544 |
| Sweden | 887 | — | 925 | 1,036 |
| Norway | 403 | — | 510 | 500 |
| Denmark | 464 | 565 | 445 | 444 |
| United Kingdom | 3,773 | 4,289 | 4,527 | 4,799 |
| Ireland | 178 | 206 | 190 | 280 |
| Netherlands | 1,089 | 1,094 | 4,194 | 4,645 |
| Belgium, Luxembourg | 1,199 | 1,131 | 2,417 | 2,991 |
| France | 2,164 | 2,541 | 3,031 | 3,449 |
| Germany (West) | 5,410 | 5,700 | 5,194 | 5,730 |
| Austria | 243 | 242 | 181 | 197 |
| Switzerland | 879 | 1,041 | 1,153 | 1,173 |
| Soviet Bloc in Europe | 731 | 867 | 2,787 | 3,502 |
| Spain | 836 | 919 | 2,164 | 2,021 |
| Italy | 2,457 | 2,544 | 2,867 | 3,068 |
| Yugoslavia | 261 | 387 | 328 | 298 |
| Greece | 110 | 146 | 450 | 591 |
| Turkey | 145 | 223 | 608 | 451 |
| Iran | 1,398 | 1,480 | 3,244 | 2,776 |
| Israel | 314 | 424 | 1,551 | 1,409 |
| Kuwait | 111 | 38 | 366 | 472 |
| Saudi Arabia | 2,623 | 5,213 | 1,502 | 2,774 |
| India | 549 | 710 | 1,290 | 1,135 |
| Pakistan | 49 | 70 | 372 | 394 |
| Thailand | 217 | 277 | 357 | 347 |
| Malaysia | 772 | 943 | 393 | 536 |
| Indonesia | 2,222 | 3,007 | 810 | 1,036 |
| Philippines | 757 | 888 | 832 | 819 |
| Korea (South) | 1,442 | 2,440 | 1,762 | 2,015 |
| Taiwan (Formosa) | 1,946 | 2,999 | 1,660 | 1,635 |
| Japan | 11,425 | 15,683 | 9,563 | 10,144 |
| Australia | 1,147 | 1,214 | 1,815 | 2,185 |
| New Zealand | 245 | 331 | 411 | 415 |

*continued*

| Country | Imports 1975 | Imports 1976 | Exports 1975 | Exports 1976 |
|---|---|---|---|---|
| Liberia | 96 | 98 | 90 | 85 |
| Congo (Zaire) | 67 | 190 | 188 | 99 |
| South Africa | 840 | 926 | 1,302 | 1,348 |

## COMMUNICATIONS

**Roads and Railways. The most widely-used means of transport in the United States is the privately-owned automobile. There is one automobile to every 2·1 people, and automobiles averaged 9,992 miles in 1973. In addition, it is possible to reach almost any city, town or village by motor bus.** There are some 1,000 bus companies. They operate about 20,100 buses and carry approximately 340 million passengers, some 25·6 thousand million passenger miles annually. The Official Bus Guide lists about 15,000 localities in the United States to which scheduled service is provided. Freight is also transported in great measure by motor truck. Motor vehicles in 1975 carried an estimated inter-city 443 billion ton-miles of freight. The individual States build and repair main roads within their borders, and also obtain funds for this purpose from the Federal Government. Design and maintenance standards for the major national highway systems are set by the Federal Government and administered by State highway departments. State and Federal gasoline taxes, State vehicle registration fees and general taxes provide the money for building and maintaining highways. The total length of roads between towns and cities (not counting urban roads) in 1975 was 3,198,596 miles. Of this only 227,255 miles were included in Federal highway systems. 710,797 miles were under State control and the rest, 2,260,544 miles, were under local control.

During 1975, $26,660,000,000 was spent on all roads and streets for the following purposes: capital outlay $14,261,000,000, maintenance $7,070,000,000 interest on highway debt $1,120,000,000, and $4,209,000,000 for State highway police and highway administrative costs.

The estimated total length of all railway track in 1974 was 326,000 miles. Railroads connect all the main towns or cities as well as providing, by connecting roads, several transcontinental routes. They are all of standard gauge except for 46 miles of narrow gauge in the west. In 1974 the railroads travelled 10,300 million passenger-miles and carried 859,700 million ton-miles of freight. Locomotives in service (electric, diesel-electric and others) numbered 28,355, passenger cars 6,230, and freight cars 1,720,573. The actual number of passengers carried was 274,186,000, bringing in a revenue of $460 million, the weight of freight carried was 2·732 billion tons and the revenue amounted to $15,783,725,000. Total revenue was $16,944,823,000 and total expenses $13,122,839,000.

Railways in the United States are, with a few exceptions, owned and managed by private companies, but the rates and fares charged are regulated by the Interstate Commerce Commission, a Federal Agency.

The following table shows the amount of cargo handled (in millions of short tons) by the top thirty U.S. waterborne commerce ports for the commercial year 1975.

| | Port | Total Cargo | Import/Export | Exports | Imports | Domestic | Draft (footage) |
|---|---|---|---|---|---|---|---|
| 1 | New York | 177·8 | 55·7 | 6·7 | 49·0 | 122·1 | 45 |
| 2 | New Orleans | 140·4 | 47·6 | 35·4 | 12·2 | 92·7 | 40 |
| 3 | Houston | 83·6 | 36·2 | 18·0 | 18·2 | 47·9 | 40 |
| 4 | Baton Rouge | 60·2 | 20·4 | 8·4 | 12·0 | 37·8 | 40 |
| 5 | Baltimore | 52·6 | 34·5 | 13·8 | 20·6 | 18·1 | 41 |
| 6 | Philadelphia | 52·0 | 33·5 | 5·1 | 28·4 | 18·5 | 40 |
| 7 | Norfolk | 49·7 | 38·3 | 31·9 | 6·4 | 11·3 | 47 |
| 8 | Chicago | 42·6 | 4·6 | 2·6 | 1·9 | 37·9 | 27 |
| 9 | Tampa | 39·8 | 16·7 | 12·7 | 4·0 | 23·0 | 36 |
| 10 | Corpus Christi | 35·4 | 18·2 | 5·2 | 13·0 | 17·2 | 40 |
| 11 | Duluth/Superior | 33·6 | 5·0 | 4·7 | 0·2 | 28·5 | 28 |
| 12 | Mobile | 32·4 | 13·3 | 5·4 | 7·9 | 19·1 | 40 |
| 13 | Los Angeles | 30·7 | 16·0 | 3·0 | 13·1 | 14·6 | 54 |
| 14 | Beaumont | 30·5 | 10·0 | 4·0 | 6·0 | 20·5 | 37 |
| 15 | Portland, ME | 27·5 | 23·1 | — | 23·1 | 4·4 | 48 |
| 16 | Paulsboro, NJ | 27·1 | 12·0 | — | 12·0 | 15·2 | 40 |
| 17 | Port Arthur | 26·6 | 10·3 | 2·1 | 8·1 | 16·2 | 38 |
| 18 | Long Beach | 26·5 | 17·1 | 5·6 | 11·5 | 9·3 | 55 |

*continued*

| | Port | Total Cargo | Import/ Export | Exports | Imports | Domestic | Draft |
|---|---|---|---|---|---|---|---|
| 19 | Detroit | 26·4 | 4·3 | 0·5 | 3·7 | 22·1 | 29 |
| 20 | Boston | 24·7 | 6·5 | 0·5 | 6·0 | 18·1 | 40 |
| 21 | Marcus Hook, PA | 24·4 | 12·5 | 0·2 | 12·3 | 11·9 | 40 |
| 22 | Texas City | 23·8 | 6·1 | 0·5 | 5·6 | 17·6 | 38 |
| 23 | Toledo | 23·6 | 7·6 | 6·4 | 1·2 | 16·0 | 28 |
| 24 | Pascagoula | 20·0 | 8·0 | 2·2 | 5·8 | 12·0 | 40 |
| 25 | Portland, OR | 19·6 | 8·5 | 6·5 | 2·0 | 11·0 | 40 |
| 26 | Conneaut, OH | 19·2 | 8·6 | 6·5 | 2·1 | 10·4 | 28 |
| 27 | Cleveland | 18·1 | 4·0 | 0·2 | 3·8 | 14·1 | 28 |
| 28 | Lake Charles | 17·4 | 5·6 | 1·1 | 4·5 | 9·7 | 36 |
| 29 | New Port News | 17·2 | 12·5 | 11·4 | 1·1 | 4·7 | 45 |
| 30 | Indiana Harbor | 17·1 | 1·9 | — | 1·9 | 15·2 | 27 |

Following are the principal shipping lines:

**U.S. Department of Commerce; Maritime Administration.** (R. J. Blackwell, Asst. Sec. of Commerce.) *Head Office:* 14th and E STS NW, Washington, D.C. 20235.

**Alcoa Steamship Co. Inc.** (President, G. C. Halstead.) Vessels operated, over 30; *Liner services operated:* United States Atlantic and Gulf Coast ports to the Caribbean and north coast of South America, also world-wide bulk carrier service. *Head Office:* Two Pennsylvania Plaza, New York, New York 10001.

**American Export Lines Inc.** (President, Laurence J. Buser.) Steam vessels 24; total tonnage 290,292 gross; *services operated:* U.S. Atlantic to Mediterranean; U.S. Atlantic to Red Sea, India, Pakistan; U.S. Atlantic to Far East; U.S. North Atlantic, United Kingdom, Europe. *Head Office:* 17 Battery Place, New York, New York 10004.

**American President Lines Limited.** (President, N. Scott.) Steam vessels 23; gross tonnage 397,733; *services operated:* Round-the-World (Westbound). Trans-Pacific, Atlantic/ Straits. *Head Office:* 1950 Franklin Street, Oakland, California 94612.

**Central Gulf Lines, Inc.**; (Chairman, N. F. Johnsen; Vice Chairman, N. W. Johnsen; President, E. F. Johnson); owned vessels 8; gross 191,725 tons. *Services operated:* U.S. Gulf-North Europe; U.S. Atlantic/Gulf-Southeast Asia. *Head Office:* International Trade Mart, 2 Canal Street, P.O. Box 53366, New Orleans, Louisiana 70153.

**Delta Steamship Lines Inc.** (formerly Mississippi Shipping Co. Inc.); (President, Capt. J. W. Clark); 11 vessels; total tonnage 166,619 d.w.t.; *services operated:* U.S. Gulf of Mexico to Caribbean, Central America, East Coast of South America and West Coast of Africa. *Head Office:* 1700 International Trade Mart, P.O. Box 50250, New Orleans, Louisiana 70150.

**Farrell Lines Incorporated**; (Chairman, James A. Farrell, Jr.; President and Chief Executive Officer, Thomas J. Smith); vessels 16; gross tonnage, 263,069 d.w.t., 282,000; *services operated:* Ports to Pacific, Australasia and South Pacific Islands. *Head Office:* One Whitehall Street, New York, N.Y. 10004.

**Lykes Brothers S.S. Company Incorporated**; (President, W. J. Amoss, Jr.); steam vessels 41; total tonnage 700,653 T.D.W.; *services operated:* U.S. Gulf to Mediterranean; U.S. Gulf to West Coast of South America; U.S. Gulf to Far East; U.S. Gulf to South and East Africa; Great Lakes to Mediterranean and Black Sea; U.S. Gulf to United Kingdom, Europe. *Head Office:* P.O. Box 53068. New Orleans, Louisiana 70153.

**Matson Navigation Company.** (President, R. J. Pfeiffer.) 15 vessels; *services operated:* Pacific Coast ports–Hawaii, Guam. *Head Office:* 100 Mission Street, San Francisco, California 94105.

**Moore-McCormack Lines Incorporated**; (President, Robert E. O'Brien); vessels 13, total displacement tonnage 281,687; *services operated:* U.S. Atlantic to East Coast South America; U.S. Atlantic to South and East Africa. *Head Office:* 2 Broadway, New York, N.Y. 10004.

**Pacific East Line Inc.** (President John I. Alioto.) Vessels 10; total tonnage 372,165 d.w.t.; *services operated:* U.S. West Coast to Orient and U.S. East Coast to Mid-East Gulf. *Head Office:* One Embarcadero Centre, San Francisco, California 94111.

**Prudential Grace Lines Incorporated** (President, A. T. De-Smedt); owned vessels 5; total gross tonnage 263,197; *service operated:* U.S. North Atlantic/Mediterranean. *Head Office:* One Whitehall Street, New York, New York 10004.

**Sea-Land Service, Incorporated**; (Chairman and Chief Executive Officer, Charles I. Hiltzheimer); owned vessels 3; demise chartered vessels 42; total deadweight 945,055 tons; *services operated:* U.S. Atlantic/Gulf United Kingdom, Continent; U.S. and Europe/Middle East; U.S. Atlantic/ Panama U.S. Gulf Atlantic and Pacific/Caribbean; U.S. Pacific/Far East; U.S. intercoastally and to Alaska. Head Office: P.O. Box 900, Edison, New Jersey 08817.

**States Steamship Company**; (President, J. R. Dant); Steam vessels 11; total tonnage 156,253 d.w.t.; *services operated:* U.S. Pacific to Far East. *Head Office:* 320 California Street, San Francisco, California 94104.

**United Fruit Company**; (President, Herbert C. Cornuelle); vessels owned, 15; total deadweight, 87,895 tons; *services operated:* U.S. North Atlantic, Gulf/Caribbean, West Coast Central America. *Head Office:* Prudential Center, Boston, Mass. 0219.

**United States Lines**; (President Ch. Executive Edward J. Heine, Jr.); *Services operated:* Tri Continent Container Service between Europe, the East and West Coasts of the U.S.A., Panama, Costa Rica, Hawaii, Guam and Far East and Southeast Asian ports. *Head Office:* One Broadway, New York, N.Y. 10904.

**Waterman Steamship Corporation**; (President, E. P. Walsh); steam vessels 19; total tonnage 322,225 F.D.W.; *services operated:* U.S. Gulf, to United Kingdom, Continental Europe, Scandinavian and Baltic Ports; U.S. Gulf, North Atlantic to Red Sea, Persian Gulf, India, Bangladesh; U.S. Gulf, North Atlantic to Far East. *Head Office:* 120 Wall Street, New York, N.Y. 10005.

**Civil Aviation.** The United States had 37 scheduled airlines operating 2,260 planes on domestic and overseas services at 31 December 1976. The number of revenue passengers carried in 1976 was 223,313,000. Express and freight carried totalled 4,890,074 ton miles.

There were 13,770 airports as at 31 December 1976.

As of December 1975 the Federal Aviation Administration was operating 423 airport traffic control towers.

As at December 1976, the FAA maintained 347 flight services providing weather, flight following, and other flight service to airmen.

The number of available seats per plane averaged 134 in domestic service and 230 in international service in 1976.

Following are the principal airlines:

**AAL—American Airlines Inc.** (Chairman and President Albert V. Casey); *services operated:* Bridgetown, Barbados; Hamilton, Bermuda; Toronto, Canada; Santo Domingo, Dominican Republic; Port-au-Prince, Haiti; Honolulu, Hawaii; Acapulco, Mexico City, Mexico; Aruba, Curacao,

Netherlands Antilles; San Juan, Puerto Rico; St. Croix, St. Thomas, Virgin Islands Kingston and Montego Bay; Jamaica, and Martinique and Guadeloupe in the French West Indies; Internal throughout U.S.A. *Head Office:* 633 Third Avenue, New York, 10017, N.Y.

**Allegheny Airlines Inc.** (Incorporating Lake Central Airlines Inc. and Mohawk Airlines Inc.) (President and Chief Executive Officer, Edwin I. Colodny.) The Company operates a route system connecting most of the large and intermediate size cities in the region bounded by Minneapolis–St. Paul, St. Louis and Memphis on the west, and Montreal, Boston, New York, Washington, and Norfolk on the east. The company is now the sixth largest domestic air carrier in terms of passengers carried. *Head Office:* National Airport, Washington, D.C. 20001.

**Aloha Airlines Inc.**; (President, Edward E. Swofford); *services operated:* internal throughout the Hawaiian Islands. *Head Office:* Honolulu International Airport, P.O. Box 30028, Honolulu, Hawaii, 96820.

**BNF—Braniff International**; (Chairman of the Board and Chief Executive Officer, Harding L. Lawrence); *services operated:* Commercial air passenger and cargo services in the U.S. between the East Coast and Southwest, Pacific Northwest and Southwest and throughout the Middle West and to Hawaii; via Dallas, Fort Worth, Houston and San Antonio gateways to Mexico City and Acapulco, and via the New York, Washington, D.C., Miami, Houston, Los Angeles and San Francisco gateways to South America including Panama, Bogota, Cali., Guayaquil, Quito, Lima, La Paz, Santiago, Sao Paulo, Rio de Janeiro, Asuncion and Buenos Aires. *Head Office:* Braniff Tower, Exchange Park, Dallas, Texas 75235.

**Caribair—Caribbean Atlantic Airlines Inc.**; *services operated:* Puerto Rico–Dominican Republic–U.S. Virgin Islands–St. Martin N.A.–St. Kitts–Antigua–Guadeloupe F.W.I.–Dominica–Martinique F.W.I.–St. Lucia–Barbados–St. Vincent–Grenada–Trinidad–Tobago–Miami–Kingston and Montego Bay–Haiti–Curaçao–Aruba–Caracas–Venezuela. *Head Office:* P.O. Box 6035, Loiza Station, Santurce, Puerto Rico.

**Continental Air Lines Inc.** (President, Robert F. Six); total assets as per unaudited comparative balance sheet 30 June 1974, $696,571,000; *services operated:* internal throughout the Mid-West and West, to Hawaii, and international from Hawaii to Okinawa. *Head Office:* Los Angeles International Airport, Los Angeles, California.

**DAL—Delta Air Lines** (Chairman, W. T. Beebe; President, David C. Garrett, Jr.) *services operated:* 90 cities in the U.S.A. and the Caribbean, Jamaica, Puerto Rico, Venezuela, Bahamas, Bermuda, Canada. Principal U.S. domestic cities served: Atlanta, Birmingham, Boston, Cincinnati, Chicago, Kansas City, Detroit, Memphis, St. Louis, New Orleans, Houston, Dallas and Miami, New York, Philadelphia, Baltimore, Washington D.C., Los Angeles, San Francisco, Las Vegas and San Diego. *General Office:* Hartsfield Atlanta International Airport, Atlanta, Georgia, 30320.

**EAL—Eastern Air Lines Inc.**; (President and Chief Executive Officer, Frank Borman); *services operated:* throughout the eastern half of U.S.A., Seattle, Wash., Portland, Ore., Omaha, Nebraska, Texas, Los Angeles, California, and to Puerto Rico, U.S. Virgin Islands, Bermuda, The Bahamas, Jamaica, Montreal, Ottawa and Toronto, Canada, Acapulco, islands in the Caribbean including Aniboy Curaçoa, Barbados, St. Lucia, Antigua, Martinique, St. Maurten, Sabad, Haiti, Dominican Republic and Mexico City. *Head Office:* Miami International Airport, Miami, Florida, 33148.

**Hawaiian Airlines Inc.**; (President, John H. Magoon, Jr.); share capital, paid up $4,753,659; *services operated:* between the major islands of the Hawaiian Group: Oahu, Molokai, Lanai, Maui, Hawaii, Kauai. *Head Office:* International Airport, P.O. Box 30008, Honolulu, Hawaii 96820.

**NAL—National Airlines**; *services operated:* New York–Miami–California, Miami–London international service—and internal. *Head Office:* P.O. Box 592055, Airport Mail Facility, Miami 33159, Florida.

**NCA—North Central Airlines**; (Chairman of the Board, H. N. Carr; President and Chief Executive Officer, Bernard Sweet); *services operated:* internal in the States of Illinois, Wisconsin, Massachusetts, Michigan, Minnesota, New York, North Dakota, Colorado, Missouri, Indiana, South Dakota, Iowa, Nebraska and Ohio. International to Thunder Bay, and Toronto (Ontario) and Winnipeg (Manitoba), Canada. *Head Office:* 7500 Northliner Drive, Minneapolis, Minnesota 55450.

**NWA—Northwest Orient Airlines**; (Chairman, Donald W. Nyrop); *services operated:* (1) New York/Newark–Philadelphia–Washington/Baltimore to Seattle Tacoma and Portland via Pittsburgh, Cleveland, Detroit, Chicago, Milwaukee, Madison, Rochester, Minneapolis–St. Paul and points in North Dakota, Montana and Spokane; (2) Boston to Milwaukee–Minneapolis/St. Paul; (3) Miami/Ft. Lauderdale–Tampa/St. Petersburg, Atlanta to Chicago, Milwaukee and Minneapolis; (4) Minneapolis–St. Paul to Los Angeles or San Francisco; (5) Minneapolis–St. Paul to Winnipeg, Canada; (6) Chicago–New Orleans; (7) New York–Chicago–Minneapolis–St Paul–Edmonton, Canada–Anchorage (8) Between the U.S. cities listed above in (1)–(3) and Japan, Korea, Okinawa, Taiwan, Hong Kong and the Philippines via Ancorage, Alaska; (9) Between the U.S. cities listed above in (1)–(4) and the Orient countries listed above in (8) via Honolulu and Hilo, Hawaii. *Head Office:* Minneapolis/St. Paul International Airport, St. Paul, Minn.

**PAA—Pan American World Airways Inc.** (Chairman, William T. Seawell); *services operated:* Round-the-World: U.S.A – United Kingdom – Germany – Iran – Pakistan – India – Thailand – Hong Kong – Japan.

U.S.A. – Europe: U.S.A. – United Kingdom – Belgium/ Netherlands/Norway/Sweden; U.S.A. – Germany – Czechoslovakia/Yogoslovia/Hungary/Syria/Turkey, U.S.A. – Italy – Turkey – Iran; U.S.A. – Spain; U.S.A. – Denmark – Russia/Poland.

U.S.A. – Africa: U.S.A. – Brazil – South Africa; U.S.A. – Senegal – Liberia – Ivory Coast – Benin – Cameroon; U.S.A. – Senegal – Liberia – Nigeria – Congo – Kenya – Tanzania; U.S.A. – Nigeria – Ghana.

U.S.A. – South America: U.S.A. – Venezuela – Trinidad; U.S.A. – Guatemala – El Salvador/Costa Rica – U.S.A. – Mexico – Guatemala – Nicaragua – Panama; U.S.A. – Puerto Rico/Dominica Republic/Haiti; U.S.A. – Guayana; U.S.A. – Brazil – Argentina – Uruguay.

U.S.A. – Asia: U.S.A. – Japan; U.S.A. – Japan – Hong Kong Thailand; U.S.A. – Hawaii – Guam – Japan – China – Hong Kong; U.S.A. – Hawaii – Guam – Philippines – Hong Kong; U.S.A. – Hawaii – Guam – Singapore.

U.S.A. – South Pacific: U.S.A. – Hawaii – American Samoa – Tahiti; U.S.A. – Hawaii – American Samoa/Fiji – New Zealand – Australia.

U.S.A. – Alaska.

**Piedmont Airlines—Piedmont Aviation Inc.**; *service operated:* internal throughout the Southern States. *Head Office:* Smith Reynolds Airport, Winston-Salem, N. Carolina.

**Texas International Airlines, Inc.**; *services operated:* internal throughout Arkansas, California, Colorado, Louisiana, Mississippi, New Mexico, Tennessee, Texas, Utah and the Republic of Mexico. *Head Office:* P.O. Box 60188, (8451 Lockheed), Houston, Texas 77060.

**TWA—Trans-World Airlines Inc.**; (President, Forwood C. Wiser, Jr.; Chairman, Charles C. Tillinghast, Jr.); *services operated:* between U.S. co-terminals New York, Chicago, Detroit, Philadelphia, Boston, Washington, Cleveland, St. Louis, Kansas City, Tulsa, Oklahoma City, Denver, Los Angeles and San Francisco; and Azores–Shannon–London–Paris–Frankfurt–Zurich–Geneva–Lisbon–Madrid–Algiers–Milan–Rome–Athens–Nairobi–Cairo–Tel Aviv–Dhahran–Bombay, Bangkok, Hong Kong, Okinawa, Taipei, Guam, Honolulu and internal. *Head Office:* 605 Third Avenue, New York, N.Y. 10016.

**UAL—United Air Lines, Inc.**: United Air Lines, Inc. is a wholly owned subsidiary of U.A.L. Inc. The airline is the largest in the United States and serves 118 cities on 19,249 miles of unduplicated routes from coast-to-coast, the length of the Atlantic and Pacific coasts and from California to Hawaii. *Head Office:* P.O. Box 66100, Chicago 60666, Illinois.

**WAL—Western Air Lines Inc.**; (Chairman, Arthur F. Kelly); share capital outstanding $12,655,000; *services operated:* internal throughout the Middle and Far Western States, Alaska Florida, Hawaii, Canada and Mexico. *Head Office:* P.O. Box 92005, World Way Postal Center, Los Angeles, California 90009.

**Postal Service.** On 1 July 1971, the U.S. Postal Service, an independent agency within the Executive Branch of the

Government, was established to replace the Post Office Department. The 1970 Postal Reorganization Act – creating the U.S. Postal Service contained four basic provisions considered necessary for postal reform: adequate financing authority; removal of the postal system from politics, assuring continuity of management; collective bargaining between postal management and employees; and setting of postal rates by an independent rate commission.

On 20 July 1971, the Postal Service signed a historic agreement with employee unions, the first labour contract in the history of the Federal Government to be achieved through the collective bargaining process. A second two-year agreement was reached in July of 1973 and a three-year agreement in August 1975.

A series of National Service Standards for the Postal Service have been implemented since 1970 to improve delivery time, including: (1) Overnight delivery of local area first-class mail; (2) Overnight delivery of airmail moving between major cities; (3) Second-day delivery of parcel post travelling up to 150 miles, with one day delivery time being added for each additional 400 miles.

Since reorganization, many of the shortcomings prompting postal reorganization have been overcome: (1) Delivery performance standards have been maintained despite an increase in mail volume and a decrease in postal employment; (2) Postal rates in the U.S. have been kept lower than anywhere else in the world, except Canada whose postal service is heavily subsidized; (3) A deteriorating and backward physical plant has been modernized and mechanized so that today the Postal Service is sorting 60 per cent of letters mechanically, compared to 25 per cent before reorganization; (4) Postal productivity has increased more than in any other comparable period in modern times. (5) Employee working conditions have been improved and employee compensation moved up to comparability with the private sector; (6) A total advancement-by-merit system has been implemented and postal employees who previously saw no future beyond the jobs they were in can now look forward to a postal career limited only by their own potential.

The statistics below are for Fiscal Year 1976. Income of the Postal Service for the Fiscal Year totalled $12,841 million; FY '76 appropriations were $1,645 million. The net loss for the year was $1,176 million.

Mail volume processed by the Postal Service during the 1976 Fiscal Year amounted (in terms of originating mail) to 89·7 billion[1] pieces. Special service transactions (involving money orders, registry, certified, insured, collect on delivery, and special delivery) numbered about 505 million. As of 30 June 1976 the Postal Service had a total of 678,949 employees, including substitute employees, more civilian personnel than any other non-military department of the Federal Government. There were 29,273 postmasters, 196,465 city carriers, 52,346 rural carriers, 298,530 postal clerks and mail handlers.

On 30 June 1976, the close of the Fiscal Year, there were 30,521 post offices and 9,871 classified and contract stations and branches and rural stations.

During Fiscal Year 1976 nearly 31·3 billion[1] stamps were issued to post offices for sale to customers. Revenues from money orders totalled $63 million for an estimated 178 million money orders issued.

[1] U.S. billion.

## NEWSPAPERS

**Atlanta Constitution.** Morning. Circulation 214,000. 72, Marietta St., N.W., Atlanta, Ga.

**Chicago News and Sun Times.** Sun Times circulation: 574,587 daily; 439,435 Saturday; 694,227 Sunday; Daily News circulation: 351,061 daily; 360,116 Saturday–Sunday. 401 N. Wabash Ave., Chicago, Illinois 60611.

**Chicago Tribune.** Circulation 757,117 daily; and 1,155,572 Sunday. 435 N. Michigan Ave., Chicago, Ill. 60611.

**Cleveland Plain Dealer.** Circulation 412,444 morning; 511,679 Sunday. 1801 Superior Ave., Cleveland, Ohio 44114.

**Courier-Journal and Louisville Times.** Circulation 227,463 morning; 173,165 evening; 361,996 Sunday. 525 W. Broadway, Louisville, Ky.

**Detroit Free Press.** Circulation 619,000 morning; 735,000 Sunday. 321 W. Lafayette Blvd., Detroit, Mich.

**Detroit News.** Circulation 653,698 evening; 847,461 Sunday. 615 Lafayette Blvd., Detroit, Mich. 48321.

**Los Angeles Herald-Examiner.** Circulation 503,000 evening; 510,000 Sunday. 1111 S. Broadway, Los Angeles, Calif.

**Los Angeles Times.** Circulation 1,020,479 morning; 1,289,183 Sunday. Times Mirror Square, Los Angeles, California, 90053.

**New York Daily News.** ABC Circulation figures for six months ending 31 March 1976, Daily 1,903,000; Sunday, 2,818,000. 220 E. 42nd St.

**New York Post.** Circulation 630,000 evening; 377,000 Saturday. 210 South Street, New York 10002, N.Y.

**Philadelphia Inquirer.** Circulation 411,938 morning; 861,600 Sunday. 400 N. Broad St., Philadelphia, Pa 19101.

**St. Louis Globe-Democrat.** Circulation 274,917 morning; 275,019 weekend. 12th Blvd. at Delmar St., St. Louis, Mo 63101.

**St. Louis Post-Dispatch.** 900 N. 12th Blvd., St. Louis, Mo., 63101. Circulation 270,000 daily; 450,000 Sunday.

**Wall Street Journal.** National (daily, except Saturdays, Sundays and holidays): 1,465,633 (including Eastern Edition, 583,603; Midwest Edition 450,487; Southwest Edition, 157,590; and Pacific Coast Edition, 273,953. 22 Cortlandt Street, New York, New York 10007. Tel. 212–285–5000.

(Above figures as of 31 March, 1976, as audited by ABC.)

**Washington Post.** Circulation 535,000 morning; 710,000 Sunday. 1150–50th L St., N.W., Washington, D.C. 20005.

## ENERGY

In the United States, energy—its shortages, rising costs, more efficient use, and development of new sources—is receiving considerable attention.

The Energy Reorganization Act of 1974 abolished the United States Atomic Energy Commission and established the Energy Research and Development Administration (ERDA), the Energy Resources Council (an inter-agency council) and the Nuclear Regulatory Commission (NRC) which assumed all nuclear licensing and regulatory activities. The Act became law in January 1975.

Creation of the Energy Research and Development Administration (ERDA) brought together the Federal energy research and development programmes formerly carried out by the Atomic Energy Commission, the Department of the Interior, the National Science Foundation, and the Environmental Protection Agency. These programmes include fossil energy, nuclear energy, solar, geothermal, and advanced energy systems, environment, health, and safety, conservation, and national security applications.

Working closely with other Government agencies, the industrial and university communities, and drawing heavily on the existing resources of its national laboratories, the Energy Research and Development Administration seeks to advance the state of energy technology and provide new or improved sources of energy that can be produced by the private sector in ways that are economically and environmentally acceptable. This agency (ERDA) is also developing more efficient energy conservation technologies to make better use of energy already available.

ERDA is structured to assure a balanced pursuit of all promising energy technologies. The agency's programmes are carried out principally under six Assistant Administrators responsible, respectively, for:

—fossil energy development including coal liquefaction and gasification, enhanced oil and gas recovery, oil shale, and magnetohydrodynamics;

—nuclear energy development including the breeder reactors, naval reactor development, space nuclear power, production of enriched uranium, and radiation waste management;

—solar, geothermal and advanced energy systems, including solar heating and cooling of buildings, solar electric magnetic confinement fusion, and basic physical research;

—conservation, including alternative automotive power systems, electrical transmission and storage, buildings and industry applications;

—environment and safety including biomedical research, operational safety, and waste management and transportation systems; and

—national security, including military applications, laser fusion, safeguards and international security.

## UNITED STATES OF AMERICA

The United States has a third of the world's coal, vast resources of oil shale, and substantial amounts of uranium. Between now and the year 2000, ERDA's essential task is to advance the state of energy technologies. During this period it is essential to develop these resources in a commercially feasible, safe and environmentally acceptable manner.

Beyond the year 2000, as non-renewable energy resources in the United States are depleted, ERDA's task becomes one of assuring that new energy options—solar electric, fusion and breeder reactors—are ready to take over. These advanced technologies require solutions to complex research and engineering problems on the frontiers of our scientific knowledge. Decades may be required but these research efforts must proceed at full speed now if the new options are to be available when needed early in the 21st century.

Most importantly ERDA's mission will be accomplished by the transfer of proven energy technologies to the private sector for widespread commercial application. ERDA is working with the public, the Congress and other Government agencies to overcome the many economic, political, social and even cultural barriers to bring these new energy technologies on line.

To facilitate this mission, ERDA has prepared a national plan for energy, research and development which is continually revised to reflect new information and changed conditions, and is issued in the updated form each year. The ERDA plan states priorities in research and development programmes and details on the Government's activities to bring them about.

### SPACE PROGRAMME

Since the United States National Aeronautics and Space Administration began in 1958 it has developed a basic space-vehicle technology, and realized the possibility of both manned and unmanned space flight. Space flight and technology have now reached a point analogous to that attained in aeronautics in 1927.

NASA's space programmes follow four main lines of development: 1. Manned Vehicles. 2. Unmanned, instrumented scientific spacecraft. 3. Applications technology satellites, and 4. Rocket boosters for the vehicles, spacecraft, and satellites.

So far as the line of development one is concerned, on 20 July 1969 the successful landing of Apollo XI astronauts, Armstrong and Aldrin demonstrated to a television audience of over one billion people throughout the world the feasibility of a dependable, reasonably safe, manned space flight beyond earth orbital limits. The following table gives a complete tabulation of all manned lunar landing space flights from July 1969 to April 1972.

The line of development, two i.e. unmanned scientific spacecraft includes the Mariner series involving unmanned flights to both Mars and Venus.

Mariner IV sent back the first photographs taken within 6,000 miles of the pock-marked Martian landscape, revealing in startling detail features hardly imagined for the Red Planet. These, together with data as its atmosphere caused scientists to revise some long-held theories and assumptions about Mars. More than three years later Mariner IV returned useful experimental data having travelled 1,300,000,000 miles. In July and August 1969, Mariners VI and VII flew by the Red Planet and sent back almost 200 photographs, ranging from full-disc portraits to overlapping high resolution close-ups. Mariner IX was launched towards Mars on 30 May 1971 and arrived 3 November 1971 to take more than 7,000 close-up pictures of the planet as it orbited Mars. Two other Mariners, II and V, transmitted much data about our nearest but most mysterious neighbour, Venus. Little about that cloud shrouded planet can be learned from Earth-based observation. Mariner V, however, revealed a weird, dense atmosphere largely carbon dioxide, which would produce strange, almost psychedelic optical effects in a human visitor. High temperatures of approximately 800°F also were recorded, although Venutian polar temperatures are thought to be considerably cooler.

Development number three is of great importance.

The emphasis that NASA places on the applications programmes can be measured by the recent establishment of an Office of Applications. This step has been taken to put together the many NASA activities dealing with the direct benefits to man and society of the new techniques and approaches that have resulted from space research and development.

The most significant among these are the Earth Observations Programmes which include meteorological and earth resources programmes and Communications Programmes. Both of these areas have produced operational space-based systems. Many other new operational applications will be forthcoming from research and development work, especially in the area of systematic monitoring and measurement of terrestrial phenomena. Later space manufacturing and space power generation will provide even more benefits to the U.S. and the world.

NASA's efforts in space applications affect almost every Federal department, their state and local counterparts, private enterprises, and the man in the street.

NASA's job is to be the catalyst, to do the experimentation, and lead the way toward understanding the rational use of these new space tools for the human good.

Space provides an opportunity for near realtime communications between any point on the surface of the globe and any other. It provides a vantage point from which we can effectively and efficiently observe the surface of the globe—its dynamic atmospheric envelope, its land masses, and the oceans which make up seven-tenths of its area.

Spacecraft will be used in conjunction with many othe kinds of platforms such as aircraft, buoys, balloons, and ground-based stations, to collect a wealth of data in the form of measurements, both direct and inferred.

This work will lead, in turn, to the development of models of the natural world. Such models are just beginning to emerge, but in limited forms and constrained scope. There are steps being taken in the development of a global atmospheric model which is expected to provide weather predictions on the order of two weeks or more into the future. There are theoretical models of oceanic circulation, but they are still very incomplete. The oceans, together with solar radiation, are the driving forces that shape the world's climate and weather and, as a result, affect the life of everyone.

The ability to communicate globally as well as to observe and measure the phenomena that affect our everyday life, rapidly, globally, and accurately, is one of the most important products of the space programme. NASA's communications and weather satellite development programmes have resulted in the first international space systems, providing global communications and weather services used by many nations. NASA continues to work on more advanced communications and meteorological satellites as well as Earth Resources Technology Satellites, LANDSATS. The Earth Resources Survey Programme is an experimental approach to remote sensing of the earth and oceans using ground-based, airborne and space capabilities. A new development in connection with satellites is the Space Shuttle.

The Space Shuttle will be a manned reusable space vehicle which will be used for a wide variety of space missions in Earth orbit.

The Space Shuttle will deploy in Earth orbit scientific and applications satellites of all types. Since it can carry payloads weighing up to 29,500 kilograms (65,000 pounds) it will replace most of the expendable launch vehicles currently used.

The Space Shuttle will also be able to retrieve satellites from Earth orbit and bring them back to Earth for repair and reuse. It can also be used to carry out manned missions in Earth orbit on which scientists and technicians conduct experiments in orbit or service unmanned satellites already in orbit.

The National Aeronautics and Space Administration plans to develop the Space Shuttle over the next six years. Test flights are to begin in 1976, manned orbital test flights in 1978, and the complete Space Shuttle vehicle is to be operational before 1980.

The Space Shuttle will provide the most effective and economical means for the United States to stabilize and advance its capabilities in space. It will reduce substantially the cost of space operations for all foreseeable civilian and defence needs in the decade of the 1980's. The Space Shuttle programme can be accomplished within a total annual NASA budget at the current \$3·4 billion level.

The Shuttle will consist of a manned reusable orbiter, mounted at launch 'piggy back' on a large expendable propellant tank and two recoverable and reusable solid propellant rockets. The orbiter will look like a delta-winged airplane, about the size of a DC-9 jet liner. It will be powered by three liquid rocket engines, piloted by a crew of four, two pilots, and two flight engineers, and have a cargo bay about 18 metres (60 feet) long and about 4·5 metres (15 feet) in diameter.

At launch, both the solid rockets and orbiter liquid rocket engines will ignite and burn simultaneously. When the complete vehicle attains an altitude of about 40 kilometers (approximately 25 statute miles) the solid rockets will be staged, and recovered in the ocean for reuse, and the orbiter

*N.A.S.A. Manned Space Flights*

| *Project* | *Date* | *Crew* | *Time in Space* | *Orbits/Revs* |
|---|---|---|---|---|
| Apollo 11 (Columbia, Eagle, Tranquility Base) | 16–24 July 1969 Recovery Ship—Hornet (P)** | Civilian Neil A. Armstrong<br>Air Force Lt. Col. Michael Collins<br>Air Force Col. Edwin E. Aldrin, Jr. | 195:18:35 | First lunar landing; Sea of Tranquility; 1 EVA 2 hrs. 31 min., 44 lbs. of lunar material |
| Apollo 12 (Yankee Clipper and Intrepid) | 14–24 Nov 1969 Recovery Ship—Hornet (P) | Navy Cmdr. Charles Conrad, Jr.<br>Navy Cmdr. Richard F. Gordon, Jr.<br>Navy Cmdr. Alan L. Bean | 244:36:25 | Second-lunar landing; Ocean of Storms; 2 EVAs total 7 hrs. 39 min., 75 lbs. lunar material |
| Apollo 13 (Odyssey and Aquarius) | 11–17 Apr 1970 Recovery Ship—Iwo Jima (P) | Navy Capt. James A. Lovell, Jr.<br>Civilian Fred W. Haise, Jr.<br>Civilian John L. Swigert, Jr. | 142:54:41 | Planned lunar landing aborted after service module oxygen tank rupture |
| Apollo 14 (Kitty Hawk and Antares) | 31 Jan–9 Feb 1971 Recovery Ship—New Orleans (P) | Navy Capt. Alan B. Shepard<br>Air Force Maj. Stuard A. Roosa<br>Navy Cmdr. Edgar D. Mitchell | 216:42:01 | Third lunar landing; Fra Mauro; 2 EVA's total 9 hrs. 25 min., returned 98 lbs. lunar material |
| Apollo 15 (Endeavour and Falcon) | 26 July–7 Aug 1971 Recovery Ship—Okinawa (P) | Air Force Col. David R. Scott<br>Air Force Lt. Col. James B. Irwin<br>Air Force Maj. Alfred M. Worden, Jr. | 295:12:00 | Fourth lunar landing: Hadley Apennine; 3 surface EVAs, totalling 18 hrs. 36 min., returned 173 lbs. samples |
| Apollo 16 (Casper and Orion) | 16–27 Apr 1972 Recovery Ship—Ticonderoga (P) | Navy Capt. John W. Young<br>Navy Lt. Cdr. Thos. K. Mattingly, II<br>Air Force Lt. Col. Charles M. Duke, Jr. | 265:51:06 | Fifth lunar landing; Descartes highlands 3 surface EVAs totalling 20 hrs. 14 min., returned 210 lbs. samples |
| Apollo 17 (America and Challenger) | 6–19 Dec 1972 Recovery Ship—Ticonderoga (P) | Navy Capt. Eugene A. Cernan.<br>Dr. Harrison H, Schmitt<br>Navy Cdr. Ronald E. Evans | 288:3:33 | Sixth lunar landing; Taurus–Littrow; 3 surface EVAs totalling 22 hrs. 5 min., returned with an estimated 258 lbs. samples. |

** P after recovery ship denotes Pacific Ocean.

*Launches for 1976*

| *Name* | *Launch Date* | *Vehicle* | *Range* | *Mission Remarks* |
|---|---|---|---|---|
| Helios-2 | Jan. 15 | Titan/Centaur | ETR | Scientific satellite to investigate the properties of interplanetary space close to the Sun. Cooperative with Germany. |
| CTS | Jan. 17 | Delta | ETR | Experimental high-powered communications satellite. Cooperative with Canada. |
| Intelsat IVA-F2 | Jan. 29 | Atlas/Centaur | ETR | Comsat communications satellite. |
| Marisat-1 | Feb. 19 | Delta | ETR | Comsat maritime communications satellite. |
| RCA-B | March 26 | Delta | ETR | Second RCA (Satcom) domestic communications satellite. |
| NATO-III-A | April 22 | Delta | ETR | Communications satellite for the North Atlantic Treaty Organization. |
| Lageos-1 | May 4 | Delta | WTR | To demonstrate space techniques that will contribute to the development and validation of predictive models for earthquake hazard alleviation, ocean surface conditions and ocean circulation. |
| Comstar-1 | May 13 | Atlas/Centaur | ETR | Domestic communications satellite for Comsat. |
| Air Force Test | May 22 | Scout | WTR | USAF scientific payload. |
| Marisat-B | June 9 | Delta | ETR | Second Comsat satellite to provide maritime satellite communications. |
| Relativity | June 17 | Scout | Wallops | Scientific probe to test the Einstein Theory |
| Indonesia-A (Palapa) | July 8 | Delta | ETR | Indonesian communications satellite 1. |
| Comstar-2 | July 22 | Atlas/Centaur | ETR | Second domestic communications satellite for Comsat. |
| NOAA-5 | July 29 | Delta | WTR | Operational meteorological satellite of the National Oceanic and Atmospheric Administration to provide day and night cloud cover imagery—reimbursable. |
| Navy Transit | Aug. 11 | Scout | WTR | Navy navigation satellite. |
| RCA-C | October | Delta | ETR | Third domestic communications satellite for RCA. |
| Marisat-C | December | Delta | ETR | Third Comsat satellite to provide maritime satellit communications service. |
| Intelsat-IVA-C | December | Atlas/Centaur | ETR | Third of a series of improved Intelsat satellites. |

## UNITED STATES OF AMERICA

The following table shows the launch record for 1977:

| *Name* | *Launch Date* | *Vehicle* | *Range* | *Mission Remarks* |
|---|---|---|---|---|
| NATO-3 B | Jan. 27 | Delta | ETR | Second communications satellite in synchronous orbit to perform communications relay for NATO. Reimbursable. |
| Palapa-2 | March 10 | Delta | ETR | Back-up satellite for Indonesian domestic communications network. Reimbursable. |
| GEOS/ESA | April 20 | Delta | ETR | ESA spacecraft to conduct scientific investigation of waves and particles in magnetosphere. Reimbursable. Failed to reach correct orbit. |
| Intelsat IVA-C | May 26 | Atlas/Cen. | ETR | Improved communications satellite for Comsat. Reimbursable. |
| GOES/NOAA | June 16 | Delta | ETR | Second operational satellite to provide continuous daytime and nighttime global cloud cover observations for NOAA. Reimbursable. |
| GMS-Japan | July 14 | Delta | ETR | Geosynchronous Meteorological Satellite. Japanese portion of global network of geostationary environmental satellites. Reimbursable. |
| HEAO-A | Aug. 12 | Atlas/Cen. | ETR | High Energy Astronomical Observatory to study energetic radiation from space. |
| SIRIO-I | Aug. 17 | Delta | ETR | Italian project to investigate radio propagation, trapped radiation flux, magnetic field intensity and variation, and the primary electron energy spectrum. Reimbursable. |
| Voyager 2 | Aug. 20 | Titan III Centaur | ETR | Jupiter and Saturn planetary systems and the interplanetary medium out to Saturn. |
| Voyager 1 | Sept. 5 | Titan III Centaur | ETR | Same as above. |
| OTS/ESA | Sept. 9 | Delta | ETR | Orbital Test Satellite. ESA experimental communications satellite. Reimbursable. Launch vehicle exploded. Investigation underway. |
| Navy Transit | Sept. 28 | Scout | WTR | Navy navigation satellite. Reimbursable. |
| Intelsat IVA-D | Sept. 29 | Atlas/Cen. | ETR | Follow-on series of improved communications satellites for Comsat. Launch vehicle exploded. |
| ISEE-A/B | Oct. 13 | Delta | ETR | NASA's international Sun-Earth explorer. |
| FLTSATCOM | Nov. | Atlas/Cen. | ETR | DOD fleet communications satellite. |
| Meteosat/ESA | Nov. 3 | Delta | ETR | ESA meteorological satellite. Reimbursable. |
| Intelsat IVA-E | Nov. 10 | Atlas/Cen. | ETR | Follow-on earlier Intelsats. |

and its propellant tank will continue into low Earth orbit. After the desired orbit is attained, the expendable propellant tank will be jettisoned by retrotrockets into the ocean. The orbiter with its crew and payload will remain in orbit to carry out its mission, normally about seven days, but when required as long as 30 days. When the mission is completed it will return to Earth and land like an aeroplane.

So far as development four is concerned the space agency early began developing the Saturn Programme in anticipation of the need to expand space flight capabilities beyond the capacities of military boosters available. As a result, America now has a booster capability ranging from the small Scout's 300 pounds-in-orbit to Saturn V's 290,000.

*The U.S./U.S.S.R. Rendezvous and Docking Agreement.* On 24 May 1972 the National Aeronautics and Space Administration released the text of an April 1972 agreement with the Academy of ciences of the U.S.S.R. on the organization, development, scheduling, and conduct of a test docking mission for manned spacecraft in 1975. The agreement will be the basis for implementing those sections of the space accord reached by the President this week in Moscow which relate to the test docking mission.

The April agreement builds on three previous agreements of October 1970, June 1971, and November–December 1971, on the design and flight testing of compatible rendezvous and docking systems. The April meeting was requested by NASA to satisfy management and operational considerations attaching to a joint mission prior to possible commitment at a government-to-government level.

Dr. George M. Low, Deputy Administrator, headed the NASA delegation which included Arnold W. Frutkin, Assistant Administrator for International Affairs, and Dr. Glynn Lunney, Special Assistant to the Apollo Programme Manager. The Soviet delegation was headed by Vice President of the Soviet Academy of Sciences, V. A. Kotelnikov, and included Academician B. N. Petrov, Drs. I. P. Rumyantsev, K. D. Bushuyev and others. Drs. Lunney and Bushuyev have been designated the Project Managers for the test mission.

During the April meeting, agreement was reached on such matters as regular and direct contact through frequent telephone and telex communications as well as visits; the requirement for and control of detailed formal documentation; joint reviews of designs and hardware at various stages of development; the requirement for joint tests of interconnecting systems; early participation in the joint preparations by flight operations specialists; the development of crew training and orientation plans; and the training in each country of the other country's flight crew and operations personnel.

Agreement was reached also on the requirement for and level of detail of project schedules, including early specification of development milestones and countdown and launch dates.

Agreement was reached as well on the principles of communications, command and control of the flight; the requirements for flight plans and mission rules for normal and contingency situations; the immediate transmission of flight television received in one country to the other's control centre; the level of reciprocal language familiarity; and the need to develop public information plans taking into account the obligations and practices of both sides.

Beyond the test mission, the accord announced in Moscow provides that future generations of manned spacecraft of both the United States and the Soviet Union will be capable of docking with each other. That capability will facilitate emergency assistance to astronauts in difficulty and will make possible the conduct of co-operative projects, with attendant economies. The U.S./U.S.S.R. rendezvous and docking was successfully accomplished on Thursday 17 July 1975 at 17.15 hours G.M.T., and undocked on Saturday 19 July 1975 at 16.26. Both spacecraft returned safely to earth.

The table on page 545 gives details of launches in 1976.

### EDUCATION

*Elementary and secondary education.* Systems of free public schools supported by taxation are established by law in each State and the District of Columbia. Attendance is now compulsory in every State and D. C., generally through ages seven and sixteen years of age. A few States extend the compulsory age to seventeen while one State specifies the compulsory age as thirteen. A few States begin the compulsory age at six. The effects of compulsory attendance may be observed in retention rates of pupils entering the fifth grade in the fall of 1967 and graduating from high school in 1975. 95·6 per cent entered the tenth grade, usually the last year of compulsory attendance; 87·0 per cent entered the eleventh grade; 77·5 per cent entered the twelfth grade; and 74·3 per cent graduated from high school.

There are two levels of free public education: (1) elementary, which may begin with nursery-kindergarten and extend through the eighth grade, and (2) secondary, which begins where elementary ends and extends through grade twelve. Grades seven and eight are reported in some instances at the secondary level, depending on the organization of the school of which they are a part. Each grade is equivalent to one school year.

There is no National control or direction of education except as influenced through special Federal aid programmes. State legislatures set minimum education requirement for communities within their borders, and community school boards are then free to establish educational programmes of a higher standard if they desire to do so and are willing to provide the additional funds needed for improvement.

As of the fall of 1975 there were 61,704 public schools with elementary grades only, 23,792 public schools with secondary grades only, 1,538 public schools with combined elementary and secondary grades, and 1,563 public special education schools for the handicapped. As of the fall of 1976, enrolment in public elementary schools was 25,437,000 while public secondary schools enrolled 18,956,000. Public elementary and secondary schools employed 2,208,000 classroom teachers as of the fall of 1976.

More than one child in ten (10·7 per cent) attended a nonpublic elementary and secondary school. Enrolment in 14,400 nonpublic elementary schools was estimated at 3,900,000 and in 3,800 nonpublic secondary schools at 1,400,000 as of the fall of 1976. Nonpublic elementary schools employed 175,000 classroom teachers and nonpublic secondary schools 92,000 classroom teachers as of the fall of 1976. Nonpublic schools are supported by church funds, by endowments, and by tuition fees. Pupils may and do transfer freely from nonpublic to public schools and vice versa.

An estimated $81,600,000,000 was expended on elementary and secondary education during the 1976–77 school year: $72,700,000,000 on public elementary and secondary schools; and $8,900,000,000 on nonpublic elementary and secondary schools. Included in the above figures were $6,300,000,000 for publicly controlled and $800,000,000 for nonpublicly controlled elementary and secondary schools. Current expenditures of publicly controlled elementary schools per pupil in average daily attendance was estimated at $1,530 for the school year 1966–67.

*Institutions of higher education.* The fall 1976 survey of enrollments covered 3,047 institutions classified as follows: 1,913 universities, colleges, and professional schools enrolling 7,161,151 degree and nondegree students and 1,134 two-year colleges enrolling 3,944,772 degree and nondegree students. Publicly controlled institutions of higher education enrolled 8,741,548 (78·7 per cent) of the students and privately controlled enrolled 2,364,375 (21·3 per cent).

Institutions of higher education employed 528,000 full-time-equivalent members of the instructional staff for resident courses as of fall 1976. 486,000 were instructors or above and 42,000 were junior instructors.

During the 1975–76 school year, 909,000 bachelor's degrees were conferred, including 425,000 to women; 58,690 first-professional degrees, including 9,270 to women; 316,000 master's degrees, including 143,000 to women; and 35,000 doctorates, including 8,000 to women.

An estimated $49,200,000,000 was expended by institutions of higher education during the 1976–77 school year; $33,500,000,000 by publicly controlled institutions and $15,700,000,000 by privately controlled. Included in the above figures were $5,500,000,000 for capital outlay, $3,800,000,000 by publicly controlled institutions and $1,700,000,000 by privately controlled.

## RELIGION

Church membership in the United States totalled 131,012,953 in 1976, and there are 34,839,384 children who attend Sunday schools.

Support of religious institutions is voluntary. The government gives no funds to churches. The separation of church and state is a cardinal American principle.

There are 333,114 (1976) churches altogether and a total of 223 religious sects or denominations. Religions of all peoples and all ages have found their way into the country and have built followings.

The principal religious organizations are Protestant, Roman Catholic and Jewish. The Roman Catholic baptized membership is 48,881,872 and Synagogue membership 6,115,000; the remaining 76,016,081 are in various Protestant, Eastern Orthodox and 'other religious groups', which include the Russian Orthodox, Greek Orthodox, Polish National Catholic, Serbian Eastern Orthodox, Buddhists of America, Ukrainian Orthodox, Syrian Antiochian Orthodox and small numbers of virtually every other religion known in the world.

The Constitution of the United States protects the freedom of each American to choose his or her own church and faith and to worship according to his own conscience. The First Amendment to the Constitution states:

'Congress shall make no law respecting an establishment of religion, or prohibiting the free exercise thereof'.

Voluntary religion prevails in the United States because there is no established Church and because the legal structure makes no provision for automatic membership in any religious group. The Constitution further provides that 'no religious test shall ever be required as a qualification to any office or trust under the United States'.

The same restriction is imposed upon the legislatures of the 50 States, both by similar provisions in the State Constitutions and by judicial opinions handed down during the years.

Theological training is given in a number of the larger universities and in many special theological schools. Enrolment for the 1974–75 academic year exceeded 36,810.

Courses of religious study for both young children and adults are provided in Protestant and Roman Catholic churches and in Jewish synagogues. Almost 35 million youths are reported to receive religious instruction, over 8,837,407 in the Catholic Church, and 26 million in Protestant Sunday Schools.

In about 2,000 American communities, school students are released from classes for a stated number of hours each week to receive voluntary religious instruction.

More than 70 Christian communions, including the Roman Catholic Church, contribute to the work of the American Bible Society, which is responsible for the distribution of Bibles in more than 1,500 different languages and dialects.

# District of Columbia

**Area** 68 sq. miles.

**Population** (1975 Census) 739,600.

**Government.** The District of Columbia is the seat of Government of the United States. The land was ceded by the State of Maryland as a site for the National Capital. Congress first met there in 1800. Legislation passed by Congress and signed by the President, 24 December 1973, effected a changeover from the former Presidential appointed Mayor-Commissioner and Nine-member City Council form of government to the current elected Mayor and elected 13-member City Council government. The new system went into operation 2 January 1975, and replaced the approximately seven and one-half year-old Presidential-appointed Mayor and Nine-member City Council form of government.

Local government is administered by the elected Mayor-13-member District of Columbia City Council. The Mayor—who is elected every four years—has the principal responsibility for carrying out the municipal programmes, providing City leadership and is the official spokesman for the District of Columbia. He is assisted by a City Administrator, who is appointed by the mayor.

The City Council, composed of a Chairman, four At-large members, and eight Ward members (one from each of the city's eight wards), serves on a staggered basis, from two to four years. The Council is the quasi-legislative, or rule-making, branch of the local government.

Legislation is enacted by the City Council; however, the legislation cannot take effect for 30 days, during which time either the Senate or the House may by concurrent resolution disapprove it. From 20 June 1874, until the passage of the 23rd Amendment to the U.S. Constitution was ratified on 3 April 1961, there was no suffrage in the District of Columbia except the election of delegates to the National Party Conventions nominating candidates for President and Vice-President. Under the 23rd Amendment to the Constitution, District residents are entitled to vote for the U.S. President.

On 22 April 1968, the President signed a bill into law whereby in November 1968 for the first time the citizens of the District of Columbia elected a nine-member Board of Education. The Board determines the entire public school programme of the District of Columbia. Heretofore members were appointed by the United States District Court judges of the District of Columbia.

On 22 September 1970, legislation was enacted authorizing the election of a non-voting delegate from the District of Columbia to the U.S. House of Representatives.

*Mayor:* Walter E. Washington.

*City Council:*

*Chairman:* Sterling Tucker.

**Finance.** Budget figures for the year ended 30 June 1975 were:

Revenue, $1,459,387,259; Expenditure, $1,357,982,315.

**Universities and Colleges.** Georgetown University; George Washington University; Howard University; American University; Catholic University of America; D. C. Teachers College; Federal City College; Washington Technical Institute.

# States

## ALABAMA

### (*Cotton State or Yellowhammer State*)

**Capital**—Montgomery.

**Area:** 51,609 sq. miles.

**Population:** (1970) 3,444,165. Chief cities and towns with populations: Birmingham, 301,510; Mobile, 190,026; Montgomery, 137,646; Huntsville, 140,077; Tuscaloosa, 65,773; Gadsden, 53,928.

**Entered the Union:** 14 December 1819.

**Governor:** Geo. C. Wallace.

**Legislature**

*Senate:* 35 members elected every four years.
*House of Representatives:* 105 members elected every four years.

**Supreme Court.** *Chief Justice:* C. C. "Bo" Torbert, and Associated Judges, all elected for a term of six years.

**Finance.** The cash brought forward from financial Year 1975 was $421,856,191·20.

**Production.** Cash receipts from farm marketings exceeded 1·6 billion in 1976. Livestock and poultry receipts, at $993 million, accounted for 61 per cent of this income and crops, at $625 million, 39 per cent.

Alabama's most valuable crop was soybeans followed by cotton, peanuts, corn and hay in that order.

Poultry made the largest contribution to receipts from farm marketings of livestock and poultry products followed by returns from cattle and calves. Other leading livestock enterprises were hogs and dairying. Generally, higher prices combined with increased marketings accounted for the increase in cash receipts from livestock.

**State Institutions of Higher Education 1976.** Students totalled 26,987 at the University of Alabama (including campuses at Birmingham and Huntsville), at Auburn University (including Montgomery campus) 21,065, at University of North Alabama, 4,298; at Jacksonville State University, 6,020; at Livingston State University, 1,390; at Troy State University (all campuses), 6,307; at University of Montevallo, 2,565; at University of South Alabama, 5,476; at Alabama Agricultural and Mechanical University, 4,085; at Alabama State University, 3,531; Athens State College, 804; at Junior Colleges, 32,557; at State Technical Colleges, 14,087.

## ALASKA

**Capital**—Juneau.

**Area:** 586,400 sq. miles.

**Population:** (July 1975) 404,634. Principal communities population are: Juneau, 19,200; Anchorage, 175,600; Fairbanks, 30,400.

**Established as a State of the Union:** 3 January 1959.

**Governor:** J. S. Hammond.

**Lieutenant Governor:** Lowell Thomas, Jr.

**Legislative Assembly** *Senate:* 20 members elected for four years. *House of Representatives:* 40 members elected for two years.

**High Court.** *State Supreme Court: Chief Justice:* Robert Boochever; *Associate Justices:* Edmond W. Burke, Roger G. Connor, Warren Matthews, Jay A. Rabinowitz.

**Production.** Alaska's total value of crop production in 1976 was $4,427,000. The total value of livestock production in 1976 was $4,598,000. The combined total of crop and livestock production in 1976 is $9,025,000. The 1976 salmon catch was 243,761,062 lbs., with a wholesale value of $103,768,708. The 1976 king crab catch was 105,904,617 lbs., with a total wholesale value of $68,015,914. Alaska's total shellfish catch for 1976 equalled 316,852,579 lbs., and the total miscellaneous groundfish catch equalled 37,184,000 lbs.

Oil production in 1976 was 67.008,789 barrels, with a total wellhead value of $318,787,532. Natural gas production in 1976 equalled 143,725,090,000 cubic feet of dry gas and 126,855,669,000 cubic feet of casing head gas. Their combined total wellhead value equalled $56,811,944.

**State Universities.** For the 1975–76 academic year, the main campus of the University of Alaska in Fairbanks enrolled 1,452 full-time students. The remaining campus extensions enrolled 3,617 full-time students. The full-time equivalency for the academic year was 11,029 FTE students, a number extrapolated from over 17,000 students. Sheldon Jackson Junior College and the Alaska Methodist University, both private institutions, enrolled 200 and 400 students respectively for the 1975–76 school year.

## ARIZONA

### (*Grand Canyon State*)

**Capital**—Phoenix.

**Area:** 113,956 sq. miles.

**Population:** (U.S. Census 1970) 1,770,900. Chief cities and towns with populations: Phoenix, 581,562; Tucson, 262,933; Scottsdale, 67,823; Tempe, 62,907; Mesa, 62,853.

**Entered the Union:** 14 February 1912.

**Governor:** Rau'l H. Castro (Democrat).

**Legislature**

*Senate:* 30 members elected every two years.

*House of Representatives:* 60 members elected every two years.

**Supreme Court.** *Chief Justice,* James D. Cameron and four additional Justices presently serving for terms of six years. Recommendations to be made by the Committee on Judicial Appointments for Governors appointment.

**Finance.** Estimated revenue for 1976–77, 1,309,776,300 including federal revenue from all sources.

**State Universities.** University of Arizona, 30,146 students for year 1976–77, Arizona State University, 34,366 students and Northern Arizona University, 11,700 students for year 1976–77.

## ARKANSAS

### (*The Land of Opportunity*)

**Capital**—Little Rock.

**Area:** 53,104 sq. miles.

**Population:** (Census of 1970) 1,923,295. Chief town with population: Little Rock and North Little Rock Metropolitan Area, 340,700.

**Entered the Union:** 15 June 1836.

**Governor:** David Pryor (Democrat).

**Legislature**

*Senate:* 35 members elected for four years.
*House of Representatives:* 100 members elected for two years.

**Supreme Court.** Chief Justice Carleton Harris and six Associate Justices, all elected for a term of eight years by popular vote.

**Finance.** For the year 1973–74: Total appropriation $2,560,556,395·05.

**Production.** Arkansas rates 14th among the States in cultivated area, with a total of over 7,353,000 acres. The largest source of farm income is cotton (1,435,000 bales in 1973). However, rice and soybeans are replacing cotton as major farm crops. The State has 18,216,700 acres of forest land; and lumber and paper industries are important. Annual mineral production is valued at about $24 1,179,000, with petroleum, natural gas and coal accounting for one-half of this figure. Arkansas supplies 97 per cent of the nation's domestic bauxite, and has the only diamond mines in North America.

**State University.** University of Arkansas. (11,134 students Autumn 1973) Arkansas State University (6,460 Autumn 1973 students).

## CALIFORNIA

### (*Golden State*)

**Capital**—Sacramento.

**Area:** 158,693 sq. miles.

**Population** 1976 (estimate) 21,520,000. Chief cities and towns with populations over 100,000: Anaheim, 196,300; Berkeley, 113,100; Fremont, 115,400; Fresno, 176,800; Garden Grove, 123,200; Glendale, 139,300; Huntington Beach, 151,500; Long Beach, 355,202; Los Angeles, 2,816,000; Oakland, 362,100; Pasadena, 113,800; Riverside, 154,500; Sacramento, 263,000; San Bernardino, 108,100; San Diego, 773,700; San Francisco, 667,700; San Jose, 557,000; Santa Ana, 179,500; Stockton, 118,500; Sunnyvale, 106,000; Torrance, 135,600.

**Entered the Union:** 9 September 1850.

**Governor:** Edmund G. Brown Jr. (Democrat).

**Legislature**

*Senate:* 40 members elected for four-year terms, half being elected every two years.
*Assembly:* 80 members elected for two years.

**Supreme Court.** Chief Justice Rose Elizabeth Bird, and six Associate Justices, all elected for a term of 12 years by popular vote.

**Finance.** Budget estimate figures for 1977–78 are: Revenue, $14,445,000,000; Expenditure, $13,911,000,000. Estimates for 1976–77 were: Revenue, $12,986,000,000; Expenditure, $12,913,000,000.

**Production.** Gold was the economic resource which led California's first development. From 1848 to 1975 inclusive, California's gold mines yielded an estimated $2·5 billion in treasure. However, petroleum has far outstripped the yellow metal as a source of new wealth. Since 1876, the first year of recorded production, over 16·6 billion barrels valued at $29·5 billion have been produced in the State. These figures do not include natural gas, and other oil industry mined products which have added many additional billions of dollars to the State. In 1975, 307 million barrels of petroleum, valued at $1·8 billion, were produced.

Agriculture is the number one resource base industry in the Golden State, and California again led the nation in agriculture in 1975, with cash receipts from farm marketings of $8·6 billion. Major commodity groupings in 1975, ranked in order of value, were: Cattle and calves, $1·1 billion; Milk and cream $997 million; Cotton lint, $481 million; Grapes, $479 million; Hay, $459 million; Tomatoes for processing, $454 million; Sugar beets, 232 million; Eggs, $351 million; Nursery products, $294 million; Rice, $256 million; Lettuce, $248 million; Cottonseed, $86 million; Almonds, $115 million; Oranges, $179 million; Wheat, $203 million; Potatoes, $127 million; Peaches, $136 million; Barley, $151 million; Tomatoes, Fresh, $112 million; Cut Flowers, $159 million; Strawberries, $112 million; and Corn, $11 million.

Fresno County leads the nation in agriculture, followed by Kern and Tulare Counties. California accounts for 12 out of the top 20 agricultural counties in the nation. Some 200 farm products are recognized, including field crops, fruit and nut crops, vegetables, seeds, flowers and ornamentals, livestock, and poultry products.

California leads the nation in the value of fishery products and leads all states in the fish industry employment, both season and year average. California is second to the leading states, Louisiana, in the quantity and Alaska in value of fish caught. In 1976, the California catch was 897 million pounds, valued at $185,647,000.

Principal manufacturing, ranked in order of the total "value added" by manufacturing, as reported by the U.S. Department of Commerce for 1973, were: transportation equipment, food and kindred products, electrical equipment and supplies, machinery, fabricated metal products, printing and publishing, chemicals and allied products, and lumber and wood products. These products combine for a cumulative total of $27·6 billion for California in 1973.

California also leads all states in human resources. It not only has more population and more people employed than any other state, it leads all states in the number of scientists and engineers, and leads all states in research and development activities.

**State University and the State Colleges.** University of California. (128,697 full-time and part-time students, including all branches.) California State Universities (303,734 students on 19 campuses according to fall 1976 estimates).

## COLORADO

### (*Centennial State*)

**Capital**—Denver.

**Area:** 104,247 sq. miles.

**Population** (Census of 1970) 2,209,596. Chief cities and towns with populations: Denver, 514,600; Colorado Springs, 140,500; Pueblo, 99,900; Lakewood, 92,700; Aurora, 76,400; Boulder, 66,800; Arvada, 49,700; Fort Collins, 43,300; Greeley, 38,900; Englewood, 33,600; Wheat Ridge, 29,700; North Glenn, 29,300; Littleton, 26,400; Longmont, 23,200; Grand Junction, 24,000.

**Entered the Union:** 1 August 1876.

**Governor:** Richard D. Lamm (Democrat).

**Legislature**

*Senate:* 35 members elected for four years, one-half retiring every two years.
*House of Representatives:* 65 members elected for two years.

**Supreme Court.** (1973). Chief Justice, Edward E. Pringle and six Associate Justices. Justices are appointed by the Governor for a term of ten years and may be retained by popular vote.

**Finance.** Budget figures for 1975–76 were: Revenue, $1,742,100,000; Expenditure, $1,832,600,000.

**Production.** Cattle and sheep raising are the most important branches of agriculture. There are (1975) 3,375,000 head of cattle and 990,000 sheep. The State's mineral resources are considerable. Colorado produces about 66 per cent of the world's supply of molybdenum. Other important minerals are coal, gold, silver and lead. There are 14,334,184 acres of forests. The Total Retail Sales for the fiscal year 1974–75 were: 13,915,124,000. The Bank Deposits in National and State Banks as of 1 January 1975 was $8,050,000,000 (est.).

**State Universities.** (Enrolment in the autumn of 1975.) University of Colorado, 33,004; (21,619 on the Boulder Campus); Colorado State University (Fort Collins), 16,809; University of North Colorado (Greeley), 10,829.

## CONNECTICUT

*(Constitution State)*

**Capital**—Hartford.

**Area:** 5,009 sq. miles.

**Population:** (Estimated 1976), 3,152,000. Chief cities and towns with populations: Hartford, 153,500; Bridgeport, 153,000; New Haven, 133,000; Waterbury, 113,900; Stamford, 108,500.

**One of the original 13 states of the Union** (9 January 1788).

**Governor:** Ella T. Grasso (Democrat).

**Legislature**

*Senate:* 36 members elected for two years.
*House of Representatives:* 151 members elected for two years.

**Supreme Court.** Chief Justice Charles S. House and five Associate Justices, all approved by the General Assembly on nomination by the Governor. Associate Justices serve for a term of eight years. All terms expire by limitation of age at 70.

**Finance.** Budget figures for 1975–76 were: Revenue, $3,135,000,000; Expenditure, $3,133,000,000.

**Production.** Manufacturing employment averaged 395,600 in 1975, approximately 31·9 per cent of the non-agricultural workers. The State is a leader of the nation in the production of aircraft engines, helicopters, submarines, ball bearings, cutlery, silverware, and copper rolling and drawing. Value added by manufacturing amounts to over $7,893 million annually. Retail trade volume in 1974 was $8,626,313. Connecticut ranks third among the 50 States in annual *per capita* income. The home offices of many large insurance companies are located in the State. Poultry, dairy products, nursery and forest products, tobacco and general farming are chief sources of agricultural income.

**State University.** The University of Connecticut (Storrs). In October 1975, number of students in credit courses, 23,049; in non-credit extension courses, 2,722; in summer session credit courses, 7,474; and in conferences and institutes, 38,431.

## DELAWARE

*(First State)*

**Capital**—Dover.

**Area:** 2,400 sq. miles.

**Population:** (Census of 1970) 548,104. Chief city with population: Wilmington, 80,386.

**One of the original 13 states of the Union** (7 December 1787); **first to ratify the U.S. Constitution, 7 December, 1787.**

**Governor:** Pierre S. duPont IV (Democrat).

**Legislature**

*Senate:* 21 members elected for four-year terms; one-half of Senate seats are contested in each general election.
*House of Representatives:* 41 members elected for two years.

**Supreme Court.** Chief Justice Daniel L. Hermann. The Chief Justice and two Associate Justices, all appointed by the Governor, with confirmation by the Senate, for twelve year terms.

**Finance.** Budget figures for the year ending June 1976 were: Revenue, $432,000,000; Expenditure, $438,800,000. Largest sources of State revenues are income taxes, both personal, and corporate, the Corporation Franchise Tax. There is no general sales taxes in Delaware.

**Production.** Delaware's three main industries are manufacturing, travel and recreation, and agriculture. Chief manufactured product: chemicals and chemical products.

**State University.** University of Delaware (Newark) 18,000 students for year 1976–77. There are also two other four-year institutions; three junior colleges: and a technical college with branches in all parts of the State.

## FLORIDA

*(Sunshine State)*

**Capital**—Tallahassee.

**Area:** 58,560 sq. miles including 4,424 sq. miles of inland water.

**Population:** (Florida Estimates of Population, 1 July 1975). Chief cities and towns with populations: Miami, 350,742; Miami Beach, 90,391; Jacksonville, 549,590; Tampa, 291,103; St. Petersburg, 242,611.

**Entered the Union:** 3 March 1845.

**Governor:** Reubin O'D. Askew (Democrat).

**Legislature**

*Senate:* Members are elected to serve four-year terms. Half of the senate members are elected every two years. Currently, on the basis of one senator for every 169,773 residents, the senate consists of 40 seats.
*House of Representatives:* Members are elected to two-year terms. On the basis of one House member for every 56,591 residents, the House now consists of 120 seats, all of which were up for election in November, 1974.

**Supreme Court.** Chief Justice Ben F. Overton, and six Associate Justices, all elected for a term of six years by popular vote.

**Finance.** Budget figures for the fiscal year ended 30 June 1975 were: Total Direct Revenue, State taxation was $4·34 billion. Other revenue amounted to $2·64 billion. Total Operating Expenses $3·14 billion.

**Production.** Tourism is one of Florida's largest industries—some 27 million people a year visit the State. Forestry is the main product in the State's northern region. 16·2 million acres of forests supply timber to ten pulp mills, which produce about $630,000,000 a year of paper products. There are 14 veneer plants with an estimated output of 136·6 m. board feet. Central Florida is the world's leading citrus-producing area—877,470 acres were planted in 1972 and 6,116,998 tons of citrus were picked with a total value of $693 million. Cape Kennedy is an important space centre. There are approximately 375,000 million employees in manufacturing and 730,000 in trade.

**State Universities.** (Autumn 1975.) University of Florida, 27,779 students; Florida State University, 22,381 students; University of South Florida, 22,781 students; Florida Atlantic University, 7,342 students; Florida Technological University, 10,545 students; Florida A and M University, 5,463 students; University of West Florida, 5,232 students; Florida International University, 10,673 students; University of North Florida, 4,307 students. There are 28 public community (junior) colleges in the state system and seventeen (major) accredited, degree granting independent colleges.

## GEORGIA

### (*Empire State of the South*)

**Capital**—Atlanta.

**Area: 58,876** sq. miles.

**Population:** (1970) 4,589,575. Chief cities and towns with populations: Atlanta, 496,973; Savannah, 118,349; Augusta, 59,864; Macon, 122,423; Columbus, 154,168; Albany, 72,623.

**One of the original 13 states of the Union** (2 January 1788).

**Governor:** George Busbee (Democrat).

**Legislature**

*Senate:* 56 members elected for two years.
*House of Representatives:* 180 members elected for two years.

**Supreme Court.** Chief Justice H. E. Nichols and six Associate Justices, all elected for a term of six years by popular vote.

**Finance.** Budget figures for the year ending 30 June 1976 were: Funds available, $3,214,678,810; Expenditures, $2,766,605,213; Excess $448,073,597.

**Production.** Georgia was basically an agricultural state until the decade of 1950–60 during which time industry became predominate. The state's top five industries, in rank order of 'Value Added by Manufacture' are: textiles, transportation equipment, food processing, apparel, paper and allied products. In 1973, these five industries employed 62·3 per cent of all industrial employees; Value Added by Manufacture was $6·8 billion; and new capital expenditures reached $669·6 million. Agriculture still contributes measurably to the State's economy. The number of farms in 1976 totalled 73,000 averaging 233 acres per farm. Total cash farm income in 1975 (excluding home consumption payments) was $2,218,929,000 of which $1,102,527,000 was derived from crops and $1,116,402,000 from livestock and poultry. Principal crops were peanuts, corn, tobacco, soybeans, and truck crops. In 1973 68 per cent of Georgia's total land area, some 25·3 million acres, was in forests. Dollar wise, in 1974, Georgia forests produced $2 billion in lumber and forests products. The State is first in production of kaolin, crushed and dimension granite, crushed and dimensioned marble; second in fuller's earth, rare earth concentration products, kyanite and zicron; third in scrap mica and bauxite; fourth in titanium and feldspar; and fifth in barite.

**State Universities.** University of Georgia (Athens)—enrolment 1976–77; 19,538, Georgia State University (Atlanta)—enrolment, 19,357 Georgia Institute of Technology (Atlanta): enrolment—8,338.

## HAWAII

**Capital—Honolulu.**

**Area: 6,424 sq. miles.**

**Population:** (mid-1974 estimate) 846,900.

**Admitted as a State of the Union:** 21 August 1959.

**Governor:** George R. Ariyoshi (Democrat).

**Legislature**

*Senate:* 25 members elected for four years (1974–78: 18 Democrats, 7 Republicans).
*House of Representatives:* 51 members elected for two years (1974–76: 37 Democrats, 15 Republicans).

**Supreme Court**

**Chief Justice William S. Richardson.**
Associate Justices: Bert T. Kobayashi, Thomas S. Ogata, Benjamin Menor, H. Baird Kidwell.

**Production and Commerce**

*Agriculture.* In 1974, there were 4,300 farms in Hawaii with a total land area of 2,300,000 acres. Crop sales in 1974 were valued at $516 million; livestock sales were valued at $58 million. Major crops (in 1974):

1. Sugar, $442 million
2. Pineapple, $41 million
3. Vegetables and melons, $10 million
4. Diversified agriculture (other than sugar and pineapple), $32 million.

In 1974, Hawaii produced 42 per cent of the fresh market vegetables consumed locally, 34 per cent of the fresh market fruits, 100 per cent of the milk, 35 per cent of the red meat, 18 per cent of the poultry, and 91 per cent of the eggs.

*Tourism.* Visitors staying overnight or longer in 1974 numbered 2,786,000. Visitor expenditures in that yea- amounted to $1·1 (U.S.) billion. Total units in hotels, apartr ment-hotels, motels, and rental cottages, in 1975, were 39,632. Occupancy rates averaged 82 per cent in Waikiki and 69·4 per cent on the Neighbor Islands.

*Foreign and Interstate Commerce.* Imports to Hawaii from foreign nations, in 1974, totaled $582 million; exports exceeded $73 million. Imports from the Mainland United States were in excess of $1·2 (U.S.) billion. Exports to the Mainland exceeded $350 million.

**Education.** In 1974, there were 225 public schools in Hawaii with 7,711 teachers and a total enrolment of 176,844. In addition, there were 120 private schools with a total enrolment of 34,858. Approximately 45,600 students were attending the colleges and universities in the State in 1974, 50 per cent attending the University of Hawaii Manoa Campus.

**Transportation.** There were 484,000 registered motor vehicles in Hawaii in 1974, and 509,000 licensed drivers. There are 3,600 miles of streets and highways in the State.

Most scheduled inter-island travel is by air and a recently initiated hydrofoil service. In 1974, the two scheduled airlines and a number of air taxis reported 5·2 million interisland passengers.

Transpacific travel, in 1974, included 6,000 surface passenger arrivals and 3·0 million air passengers. Overseas cargo amounted to 44,000 tons by air and 8·2 million tons by ship.

**Airlines**

**Aloha Airlines Inc.** (President, Edward E. Swofford); *services operated:* internal throughout the Hawaiian Islands. *Head Office:* International Airport, Honolulu, Hawaii 96820.

**State University.** University of Hawaii. In 1973–74 the main campus of the University had a total student enrolment of 22,272.

## IDAHO

### (*Gem State*)

**Capital**—Boise.

**Area: 83,557 sq. miles.**

**Population** (Census of 1970) 713,008. Chief cities and towns with populations: Greater Boise, 97,392; Pocatello, 40,036; Idaho Falls, 35,776.

**Entered the Union:** 3 July 1890.

**Governor:** John V. Evans (Democrat).

**Legislature**

*Senate:* 35 members elected for two years.
*House of Representatives:* 70 members elected for two years.

**Supreme Court.** Chief Justice, Henry F. McFadden and four Associate Justices, all elected for a term of six years by popular vote.

**Finance.** Planned State revenue and expenditure for 1975–76 is $726·03 million from the General Fund, and supplemental fund.

**Production.** Potatoes and wheat are the State's most important crops. In 1976 the value of production for potatoes was $247 million, sugar beets $73·256 million and wheat $171·0 million. Idaho has over 15·8 million acres of commercial forests, which produced $254·7 million in 1975 cash receipts. Zinc, antimony, lead, silver and phosphate are the State's most important minerals. In 1976 value of mining production was $219 million. Other production figures were: total farm and ranch receipts $1,326·0 million, value added by manufacturing $821 million, and tourism $358 million. In 1977 Idaho had a labour force of 392,600.

**State University.** University of Idaho in Moscow, 8,168 students; Idaho State University in Pocatello 9,843, and Boise State University, 11,193. All these education figures are for Spring, 1976.

# ILLINOIS

## (*Prairie State or Sucker State*)

**Capital**—Springfield.

**Area**: 56,400 sq. miles.

**Population**: The population estimates for 1 July 1975 are: Illinois, 11,206,393. Chief cities and towns with populations: Chicago, 3,099,300; Rockford, 145,400; Peoria, 125,900; Decatur, 89,600; Springfield, 87,400; East St. Louis, 57,900.

**Entered the Union**: 3 December 1818.

**Governor**: James R. Thompson (Republican).

**Secretary of State**: Alan J. Dixon (Democrat).

**Legislature**

*Senate:* 59 members elected for four years.
*House of Representatives:* 177 members elected for two years.
The State is divided into 102 counties.

**Supreme Court**

*Judges:* William G. Clark, James A. Dooley, Joseph H. Goldenhersh, Thomas J. Moran, Howard C. Ryan, Robert C. Underwood, Daniel P. Ward.

All elected for a term of ten years by popular vote. The Chief Justice, selected by fellow judges, serves for three years.

**Finance.** Budget figures for the year ending 30 June 1976 were: Revenue, $5,462,000,000; Expenditure, $5,580,000,000.

**Production.** In 1976 there were 122,000 farms with a total area of 29,100,000 acres. The average farm is 239 acres. In 1975 cash receipts from marketing were: Crops, $3,513,362,000, Livestock, $1,891,545,000; Total: $5,404,907,000. Production (1975): Maize, 1,242,360,000 bu.; Soybeans, 291,810,000 bu.; Oats, 26,460,000 bu.; and wheat, 67,470,000 bu. In January 1976 there were 244,000 milk cows. Livestock totals were: Cattle (1 January 1976), 3,400,000; Swine (1 December 1975), 5,600,000; Sheep (1 January 1977), 180,000. 1977 wool production (estimated) is 1,323,000 lbs. In 1974, 17,906 manufacturing establishments employed 1,413,334 workers earning $16,077,888,000. The value added by manufacture was $25,682,000,000. 57,031 retail establishments with total sales of $5,663,000,000 employed 711,456 people; 20,208 wholesale establishments with total sales of $11,498,000,000 employed 291,454 people; 54,326 selected service establishments with total receipts of $10,703,000,000 employed 726,894 people. Mineral production in 1973 was valued at $825,600,000. National forestry area under the U.S. Forest Service administration as of 1976 was 255,320 acres.

**State Universities.** Enrollment in Autumn 1976. University of Illinois, 58,342 (all campuses); Southern Illinois University, 32,190 (all campuses): Chicago State University, 6,118; Eastern Illinois University, 9,252; Governors State University, 3,800 (estimated); Illinois State University, 19,049; Northeastern State University, 9,130 (estimated) Northern Illinois University, 21,690; Sangamon State University, 3,307; and Western Illinois University, 13,604. There are 52 public junior colleges which had a total enrolment of 227,143.

# INDIANA

## (*Hoosier State*)

**Capital**—Indianapolis.

**Area** 36,097 sq. miles.

**Population:** (Census of 1970) 5,193,669. Chief cities and towns with populations (1970): Indianapolis, 744,624; Fort Wayne, 177,671; Gary, 175,415; Evansville, 138,764; South Bend, 125,580.

**Entered the Union:** 11 December 1816.

**Governor:** Otis R. Bowen, M.D.

**Legislature**

*Senate:* 50 members elected for four years.
*House of Representatives:* 100 members elected for two years.

**Supreme Court**

New constitutional amendment allows five non-partisan Judges including a Chief Justice. Judges are appointed for a two-year term, then voters can approve or reject an additional ten-year period.

**Production.** Indiana is a major manufacturing State with approximately 4 per cent of the nation's value added by manufacturing. Value added by manufacture was $14,280,400,000 in 1972. Manufacturing payroll was $6,911,100,000 in 1972, paid to 706,300 employees.

Indiana is a major agricultural producer. There are approximately 107,000 farms in the State; the average size of a farm is 164 acres. Farm income for 1973 was $2,103,138,000 from livestock, and livestock products were valued at $967,171,000, corn at $383,033,000, soyabeans at $334,226,000, hogs at $472,298,000, dairy products at $145,360,000 and poultry and eggs at $113,000,000.

In 1971 the value of mineral production was $281,565,000. The principal minerals in order of value were coal, cement, stone and sand and gravel.

**State Universities.** In the autumn of 1974 the enrolment figures were: Indiana University (including regional campuses), 70,286 students; Purdue University (including regional campuses), 38,368 students; Ball State University (Muncie), 18,524 students; Indiana State University (Terre Haute), 15,671 students; Vincennes University (Vincennes—2-year University), 3,091 students.

## IOWA

### (*Hawkeye State*)

**Capital**—Des Moines.

**Area:** 56,290 sq. miles including 294 sq. miles of water.

**Population:** (Census of 1970) 2,824,376. Chief cities and towns with populations: Ames, 39,504; Burlington, 32,366; Cedar Falls, 29,597; Ft. Dodge, 31,263; Iowa City, 46,850; Cedar Rapids, 110,642; Clinton, 34,719; Council Bluffs, 60,348; Davenport, 98,469; Des Moines, 200,587; Dubuque, 62,309; Mason City, 30,491; Ottumwa, 29,610; Sioux City, 85,295; Waterloo, 75,533.

**Entered the Union:** 28 December 1846.

**Governor:** Robert D. Ray (Republican).

**Legislature**

*Senate:* 50 members elected for four years, half returning every two years.
*House of Representatives:* 100 members elected for two years.

**Supreme Court**

*Judges:* C Edwin Moore, K. David Harris, Mark McCormick, W. Ward Reynoldson, M. L. Mason, Maurice E. Rawlings, Clay LeGrand, Harvey Uhlenhopp, Warren J. Rees.

Under a recently adopted constitutional provision there are eight judicial districts with 92 district judges, 14 full time magistrates, eight full substitute full time magistrates and 170 part time magistrates.

**Finance.** Budget figures for the year ending 30 June 1976 were: Revenue, $989,175,866 (act.).

**Production.** Over 95 per cent of the State's area is farmland —over 34·3 million acres. Cash farm income was $6·9 billion in 1976. The most important commercial mineral resources are limestone, sand and gravel, and gypsum. Principal industries are machinery manufacture, metal products, insurance and publishing. The following employment figures are appertaining to May 1975; Manufacturing Industries, 229,600; Non-manufacturing, 763,500; Agricultural, 154,000; Non-Agricultural by place of residence, 942,400; Non-Agricultural by place of work, 993,100; and all other agricultural workers, 134,500.

**State Universities.** University of Iowa, 22,393 students; Iowa State University, 21,831 students; University of Northern Iowa, 9,699 students. (1973–74 enrolment.)

## KANSAS

### (*Sunflower State*)

**Capital**—Topeka.

**Area:** 82,276 sq. miles.

**Population:** (1975) 2,327,400. Chief cities and towns with populations: Wichita, 265,400; Kansas City 174,100; Topeka, 141,000; Overland Park, 82,300; Hutchinson, 40,700; Lawrence, 46,300; Salina, 39,600; Leavenworth, 31,200; Prairie Village, 27,300; Manhattan, 30,200.

**Entered the Union:** 29 January 1861.

**Governor:** Robert F. Bennett (Republican).

**Legislature**

*Senate:* 40 members elected for four years.
*House of Representatives:* 125 members elected for two years.
**Supreme Court.** Chief Justice, Alfred G. Schroeder, six Associate Justices and two Commissioners. The Governor makes the appointment from a list of three nominees furnished by the Supreme Court nominating commission. After he has served one year in office he must be approved by the electorate vote at the next general election. Six years is then the term of office.

**Finance.** Budget figures for the year ended 30 June 1977 were: Revenue, $1,733,866,903; Expenditure, $1,722,962,933

**Production.** Kansas is predominantly agricultural. It leads the nation in wheat production (1976, 339 m. bushels), sorghum silage (2·5 m. tons) and sorghum forage (646,000 tons). There are 49 m. acres of farmland. In 1976 farm cash receipts were $3·5 billion. At the beginning of 1977 there were 6,400,000 cattle; 1,730 sheep; 1,850,000 hogs; 3,300,000 chickens. Coal, natural gas, and petroleum are the most important minerals. 1976 value of mineral production was $1·2 billion. Transportation equipment, food processing and petroleum refining are the most important industries. 1973 value added by manufacturing was $3,384,800,000.

**State Universities.** University of Kansas, 22,011 full-time students for year 1975. Kansas State University, 17,170 full-time students for year 1976. Wichita State University, 9,953 full-time students in 1976.

## KENTUCKY

### (*Blue Grass State*)

**Capital**—Frankfort.

**Area:** 40,395 sq. miles including 656 sq. miles of water.

**Population:** (Census of 1970) 3,219,311. Chief cities and towns with populations: (Census of 1970): Louisville, 361,472; Covington, 52,535; Lexington, 108,137; Owensboro, 50,329; Paducah, 31,627; Ashland, 29,245; Newport, 25,998; Bowling Green, 36,253.

**Entered the Union:** 1 June 1792.

**Governor:** Julian M. Carroll.

**Legislature**

*Senate:* 38 members elected for four years, one-half retiring every two years.
*House of Representatives:* 100 members elected for two years.
**Supreme Court** (Court of Appeals). Chief Justice, Scott Reed and six Associate Justices, all elected for staggered terms of eight years by popular vote.

**Finance.** Budget figures for the year ended 30 June 1976 were: Revenue, $2,338,697,785; Expenditure, $2,346,788,666.

**Production.** Harvested acreage of principal crops in Kentucky for 1976 totalled 4,739,000 acres, compared to 4,700,000 acres harvested in 1975. The largest acreage increase was in corn, up 19 per cent from 1975.

Kentucky's soybean production in 1976 totalled 28·4 million bushels, 12 per cent below the record high 32·4 million bushels in 1975. Harvested acreage of 1,070,000 was 11 per cent below the 1975 figure. The decrease in soybean acreage was due to an increase in corn acreage resulting from favorable spring weather which allowed farmers to plant corn early. Daviess County lead the state in soybean production.

Kentucky's 1976 corn crop was a record 138·72 million bushels, easily exceeding the previous record of 95·24 million bushels set in 1948. The 1976 crop was a 58 per cent increase over 1975. Kentucky's corn production was a substantial part of the increase for the United States. Union was the state's leading corn producing county.

Burley tobacco production was up 7 per cent in 1976, and burley acreage was up 2 per cent to 190,000 acres. Burley yield was 2,425 pounds per acre, compared to 2,320 pounds per acre in 1975. Increased acreage coupled with larger yields resulted in production of 460·8 million pounds.

Wheat production was down 6½ per cent from 1975's total of 11·97 million bushels. The decrease in production was due to both lower yields and less acreage harvested.

Value of production for Kentucky's 20 principal crops increased 21 per cent over 1975 to a record high $1,259,218 during 1976. Kentucky's ranking among states, based on total crop value, jumped from 19th in 1975 to 15th in 1976. Value of each of the four major crops—tobacco, corn, soybeans, and hay set a new value record in 1976.

Tobacco was the top crop, accounting for 45 per cent of the total value of all crops produced. Corn increased from 21·7 per cent to 25·9 per cent of the total value of all crops.

Coal is a major industry employing approximately 41,700 men and producing over 100 million tons annually. Coal, natural gas, petroleum, stone, sand and gravel are the most important mineral resources. Kentucky's forests cover some 11,713,000 acres, about 46 per cent of total land area. In 1976, non-agricultural employment averaged 1,276,900. Leading manufacturing industries are electrical equipment and supplies, wearing apparel, machinery (except electrical), food and kindred products and fabricated metal products.

**State Universities and Colleges.** In autumn 1976, the state supported system was made up of eight senior institutions and 13 community colleges, the latter being under the University of Kentucky. The total enrolment of students was 85,047. There are also 21 independent or private institutions where the enrolments for autumn 1976 were 16,006.

## LOUISIANA

### (*Pelican State*)

**Capital**—Baton Rouge.

**Area:** 50,820 sq. miles.

**Population:** (1970 Census) 3,641,709. Chief cities and towns with populations: New Orleans, 593,471; Shreveport, 182,064; Baton Rouge, 165,963; Lake Charles, 77,998; Lafayette, 68,908; Monroe, 56,374; Alexandria, 41,557.

**Entered the Union:** 30 April 1812.

**Governor:** Edwin W. Edwards. Term 1976–1980.

**Legislature**

*Senate:* 30 members elected for four years.
*House of Representatives:* 105 members elected for four years.

**Supreme Court.** Chief Justice, Joe W. Sanders and six Associate Justices. All are elected for a term of ten years by popular vote.

**Finance.** Estimated Budget figures for the year 1975–76 were: Revenue, $3,040,899,017; Expenditure, $3,022,477,690.

**Production.** Total value of agricultural and livestock production in 1975 was $1,083,592. The State leads in production of sugar cane, strawberries and sweet potatoes. Forests cover 47 per cent of the land. Income from forest production and allied manufacturing industries is about $1·9 billion (U.S.) a year. Louisiana leads the U.S. in the production of salt (12,313 million tons) and is second in sulphur (3,426,000 tons), second in crude petroleum with an annual yield of 657,638,000 barrels, and second in natural gas with 6,941,687 Mcf total production. The State is also the leading produ cer of aluminia and Southern pine plywood, and a major manufacturing centre for petroleum refining, petrochemicals, pulp, paper, carbon black, cargo vessels, offshore oil exploration and drilling equipment and aluminium. Louisiana marches supply most of the country's muskrat pelts, and the fishing industry is important, both fresh and salt-water.

**State University.** Louisiana State University. Total L.S.U, system (1975–76), 45,824; Alexandria, 1,261; Baton Rouge, 24,791; Eunice, 939; Medical Center, 1,967; U. of New Orleans, 13,705; Shreveport, 3,161.

## MAINE

### (*Pine Tree State*)

**Capital**—Augusta.

**Area:** 33,215 sq. miles land area, 2,175 sq. miles of inland water.

**Population:** (1970 Census) 993,663. Cities and towns with population over 15,000: Portland, 65,120; Lewiston, 41,780; Bangor, 33,170; Auburn, 24,150; South Portland, 23,270; Augusta, 21,950; Biddeford, 19,980; Waterville, 18,190; Brunswick, 16,200; Sanford, 15,810.

**Entered the Union:** 15 March 1820.

**Governor:** James Longley (Independent).

**Legislature**

*Senate:* 33 members elected for two years.
*House of Representatives:* 151 members elected for two years.

**Supreme Judicial Court.** Chief Justice, Armand A. Du Fresne, Jr. and five Associate Judges, 13 superior Court Judges, with such active justices as may be appointed. All appointed by the Governor with advice and consent of the Council for a term of seven years.

**Finance.** Budget figures (operating funds) for the year ending 30 June 1976 were: Revenue, $857,821,000; Expenditure, $876,900,000; Total Bonded Debt, $279,225,000.

**Production.** Approximately 27 per cent of employed persons in Maine are engaged in manufacturing industries, while only 3·5 per cent are engaged in agricultural activity. In May 1977 the total labour force was 482,600. Leading sources of employment are trade, services, government and manufacturing. Manufacturing production currently exceeds $3·8 billion. Statistical surveys show that tourist incomes for the year 1976, were: total tourist expenditure $378,700,000, and total tourism business generated $670,200,000.

**State Universities.** State University of Maine includes the main campus at Orono, branch campuses at Bangor, Portland-Gorham, Fort Kent, Farmington, Machias, Presque-Isle, and Augusta.

## MARYLAND

*(Old Line State or Free State)*

**Capital**—Annapolis.

**Area:** 12,303 sq. miles, including 703 sq. miles of inland water.

**Population:** (Census of 1970) 3,922,399. Chief cities and towns with populations: Annapolis, 29,592; Baltimore, 905,759; Cambridge, 11,595; Cumberland, 29,724; Frederick, 23,641; Hagerstown, 35,862; Salisbury, 15,252.

**One of the original 13 states of the Union** (28 April 1788).

**Governor:** Marvin Mandel.

**Lieutenant-Governor:** Blair Lee III. (Democrat).

**Secretary of State:** Fred. L. Wineland (Democrat).

**Legislature**

*Senate:* 47 members elected for four years.
*House of Delegates:* 141 members elected for four years.

**Court of Appeals.** Chief Justice Robert C. Murphy, and six Associate Justices, all elected for a term of 15 years by popular vote.

**Finance.** Budget figures for the year ending 30 June 1976 were: Revenue, $3,619,142,000; Expenditure, $3,504,293,000.

**Production.** The principal crops are tobacco, sweet potatoes, melons and truck-farm vegetables. Maryland cans about one-third of the nation's tomato supply. It also produces maize, wheat, poultry and livestock. Dairy products are the largest agricultural revenue-producers. The annual fish catch is about 69 million pounds, worth almost $14 million. Striped bass and oysters are most important. Fifty per cent of the State's area is forest area—about half the lumber yield is soft wood. Cement is the leading mineral product. Maryland is highly industrialized and produces steel products, missiles, nuclear equipment, instruments and electronic components.

**State University.** University of Maryland. 60,270 (first semester figure) students for the fall of 1976.

## MASSACHUSETTS

*(Bay State or Old Colony)*

**Capital**—Boston

**Area:** 8,257 sq. miles.

**Population:** 5,790,478. Chief cities with populations (State Census, 1975): Boston, 637,900; Worcester, 172,300; Springfield, 168,700; Cambridge, 102,000; New Bedford, 100,300; Fall River, 100,300; Brockton, 95,600; Quincy, 91,400; Newton, 89,100; Somerville, 80,500.

**One of the original 13 states of the Union** (6 February 1788).

**Governor:** Michael S. Dukakis (Democrat).

**Legislature**

*Senate:* 40 members elected every two years.
*House of Representatives:* 240 members elected every two years.

**Supreme Judicial Court.** Chief Justice Edward F. Hennessey and six Associate Justices. All are appointed by the Governor with advice and consent of the Executive Council.

**Finance.** Total expenditures for fiscal year 1976 (including Debt Retirement) $4,693,615,522. Total expenditures (without Debt Retirement) $4,273,682,522. State Revenue, including Bond Issue, $5,459,703,540. Revenue without Bond Issue, $4,349,703,540.

**Production.** The agricultural industry was valued at $218 million dollars and its principal income was from dairy and cattle. About 700,000 acres are devoted to agriculture. Cranberry production is the highest in the U.S.A. The main industries are machinery, electronics, leather goods, fishing and tourism.

**State Universities.** In the 1976–77 academic year, the Massachusetts Board of Higher Education estimated that a total of 366,045 students were enrolled full-time and part-time in institutions of higher learning of which 208,900 were in private (non-public) colleges and universities. The figures for full-time students for state support institutions are: the University of Massachusetts, 29,157; the University of Lowell, 6,821; Southeastern Massachusetts University, 4,785; the State Colleges, 32,995 and the Community Colleges, 28,448. A total of 55,000 students attend publically supported institutions on a part-time basis. There are 124 degree-granting institutions in the Commonwealth of Massachusetts.

## MICHIGAN

*(Wolverine State)*

**Capital**—Lansing.

**Area:** 56,817 sq. miles of land; 1,398 sq. miles of inland water and 38,575 sq. miles of Great Lakes water area.

**Population:** (1975 Census Bureau Estimates) State, 9,116,600; Detroit, 1,335,000; Grand Rapids, 187,900; Flint, 174,200; Warren, 172,700; Lansing, 126,800; Livonia, 114,800; Sterling Heights, 86,900; Dearborn, 98,900; Ann Arbor, 103,500; Saginaw, 86,200; St. Clair Shores, 85,934; Westland, 92,600; Kalamazoo, 79,500; Royal Oak, 79,100; Pontiac, 76,000.

**Entered the Union:** 26 January 1837.

**Governor:** William G. Milliken (Republican).

**Legislature**

*Senate:* 38 members.
*House of Representatives:* 110 members.

**Supreme Court.** Chief Justice Thomas G. Kavanagh and six Associate Justices, all elected for a term of eight years by popular vote.

**Finance.** Total combined general and special funds for Michigan State government for fiscal year 1975–76 was Total funds 7,913,592,024; total combined state operating expenditures $7,317,353,318.

**Production.** Automobile manufacturing is the State's most important industry, centred in Detroit. It employed an average of 327,900 people for the year 1975. Some 33·0 per cent of U.S. passenger cars for the model year 1975 were assembled in Michigan. The annual value of all manufactures in the State is over 23 billion (U.S.) or 6·7 per cent of the United States' total. Iron ore and cement are the most important minerals produced. There are 18,125,000 acres of forest land and 12,300,000 acres of farmland. Cash income from crops in 1975 was about $949,900,000 and from livestock $732,400,000.

**State Universities.** University of Michigan, 45,837 students for 1975. Michigan State University, 48,488 students for 1975. Wayne State University, 38,073 students for 1975.

## MINNESOTA

*(Gopher State)*

**Capital**—St. Paul.

**Area:** 84,068 sq. miles, including 4,059 sq. miles of water.

**Population:** (1976 Est.) 3,967,000. Chief cities and towns with populations: Minneapolis, 434,400; St. Paul, 309,980; Duluth, 100,578; Bloomington, 84,104; Rochester, 53,883; St. Louis Park, 48,883; Richfield, 47,231; Edina, 44,046; St. Cloud, 39,691.

**Entered the Union:** 11 May 1858.

**Governor:** Rudy Perpich (Democrat Farm Labor (DFL).)

**Legislature**

*Senate:* 67 members elected for four years.
*House of Representatives:* 135 members elected for two years.

**Supreme Court.** Chief Justice, Robert J. Sheran and eight Associate Justices, all elected for a term of six years by popular vote.

**Finance.** Financial report for year ending 30 June 1976: Total operating receipts, $3,601,778,924 and total operating disbursements, $3,389,554,666.

**Production.** In terms of the total U.S. farm production the following table gives the ranking of Minnesota farm products 1st. in Oats, timothy seed, wild rice, turkeys, butter, non-fat dry milk; 2nd. in flax seed, sugar beets, sweetcorn for processing, American cheese; 3rd. in rye, green peas for processing, milk cows, honey; 4th. in milk produced; 5th in barley, hay, and hogs; 6th. in corn for grain, wheat red clover, and cash farm income; 7th in number of farms In 1976 cash farm receipts were $3,852,300,000, – 0·1 per cent down from 1975. The 1976 total annual average non-agricultural employment figure was 1,514,200. The State supplies 63·0 (preliminary figure) per cent of U.S. iron ore shipments of which 79·9 per cent is taconite. Total mineral produced in 1976 was estimated at $1,179,468,000 (preliminary figure). Forestry producers value in 1975 was $486,637,000. Value added by manufacturing was estimated to be $6,704,100,000 in 1973.

**State University.** The following table gives details concerning the numbers and types of educational institutions together with the number of students enrolled for the academic year 1976–77:

| *Number* | *Type* | *No. of Students* |
|---|---|---|
| — | Univ. of Minnesota | 56,211 |
| 7 | State Universities | 37,188 |
| 18 | State Community Colleges | 27,253 |
| 33 | Vocational Technical Colleges | 27,745 |
| 4 | Private Junior Colleges | 1,609 |
| 23 | Private (4 year) Colleges | 33,493 |
| 9 | Private Professional Colleges | 2,910 |
| 29 | Private Trade Colleges | 5,712 |
| | Total enrollment | 192,121 |

## MISSISSIPPI

*(Magnolia State)*

**Capital**—Jackson.

**Area:** 47,716 sq. miles.

**Population:** (Rand McNally estimates) 1 January 1975 2,281,000. Chief cities and towns with populations: Jackson, 171,000; Hattiesburg, 40,300; Greenville, 44,000; Biloxi, 51,000; Gulfport, 43,600.

**Entered the Union:** 10 December 1817.

**Governor:** Charles C. ("Cliff") Finch (Democrat). Term 1976–80.

**Legislature**

*Senate:* 52 members elected for a term of four years.
*House of Representatives:* 122 members elected for four years.

**Supreme Court.** Chief Justice Robert Gill Gillespy and eight Associate Justices, all elected for a term of eight years by popular vote.

**Production.** Mississippi's major source of personal income is manufacturing. Within the State everything is made from apparel to nuclear submarines, from furniture to missile and satellite components. Total value of shipments for 1972 was $6,445,200,000. For the period 1 July 1975 to 30 June 1976 retail sales were $9,122,250,830 (U.S.) and wholesale sales were $2,770,281,154 (U.S.). The State ranks fourth in cash receipts from cotton lint. Forests contributed large quantities of raw material to furniture plants and paper mills in Mississippi and the rest of the southeast. Other important crops include corn, soybeans, wheat, rice, sweet potatoes. Cattle are increasingly important to the State's economy. The gross farm income for all agricultural commodities including Government subsidies for 1975 was $1,551,300,000.

**State Universities.** The Universitv of Mississippi, University, Mississippi; Mississippi State University; Mississippi State College, Mississippi; University of Southern Mississippi, Hattiesburg, Mississippi; Jackson State University; Mississippi University for Women; Delta State University; Alcorn University; Mississippi Valley State University.

## MISSOURI

*(Show-Me State)*

**Capital**—Jefferson City.

**Area:** 68,995 sq. miles.

**Population:** (Census of 1970) 4,677,983. Chief cities and towns with populations: St. Louis City, 622,236; Kansas City, 507,330; St. Joseph, 72,748; Springfield, 120,096; Jefferson City, 32,407.

**Entered the Union:** 10 August 1821.

**Governor:** Joseph Teasdale (Democrat).

**Legislature**

*Senate:* 34 members elected for four years, half elected every two years.
*House of Representatives:* 163 members to be elected for two years.

**Supreme Court.** Chief Justice Robert E. Seiler and six Associate Justices, all appointed for a term of 12 years by the Governor from nominees submitted by judicial commission under non-partisan court plan; succeeding terms subject to ballot of the people.

**Finance.** Budget figures as of July 1976 were: General Revenue, $1,140,026,891. All other Funds, $1,126,850,409; Total, $2,266,877,300.

**State University.** University of Missouri. In the fall of 1975 approximately 55,289 students were on four campuses.

## MONTANA

*(Treasure State)*

**Capital**—Helena.

**Area:** 147,138 sq. miles.

**Population:** (1970 Census) 694,409. Chief cities and towns with populations: Anaconda, 9,771; Billings, 61,581; Bozeman, 18,670; Butte, 23,368; Great Falls, 60,091; Havre, 10,558; Helena, 22,730; Missoula, 29,497.

**Entered the Union:** 8 November 1889.

**Governor:** Thomas L. Judge.

**Secretary of State:** Frank Murray.

**Legislature**
*Senate:* 50 members elected for four years, one-half at each biennial election.
*House of Representatives:* 100 members elected for two years.

**Supreme Court.** Chief Justice Paul G. Hatfield and four Associate Justices, all elected for a term of eight years by popular vote.

**Finance.** Budget figures for the fiscal year ending 1975 were: Operating Receipts, $873,452,693; Operating Disbursements, $812,058,862.

**State University System.** Six units. In 1975–76 there were 21,837 students.

## NEBRASKA

*(Cornhusker State)*

**Capital**—Lincoln.

**Area:** 77,227 sq. miles.

**Population:** (Estimated 1976) 1,553,000. Chief cities and towns with populations (1970); Omaha, 371,400; Lincoln, 163,100; Grand Island, 33,300; Hastings, 22,600; Fremont, 24,000; Bellevue, 21,000; North Platte, 21,900; Kearney, 19,300; Norfolk, 17,400; Columbus, 16,800; Scottsbluff, 12,700; Beatrice, 11,300.

**Entered the Union:** 1 March 1867.

**Governor:** J. J. Exon (Democrat).

**Legislature.** Single Chambered legislature consisting of 49 members elected on a non-partisan basis. All elected for a term of four years.

**Supreme Court.** Chief Justice Paul White and six Associate Justices, all elected for a term of six years by merit system.

**Finance.** The Budget appropriated for the 1976–77 fiscal year was $967,500,000.

**Production.** Agriculture is the primary source of income for the State of Nebraska. In 1976, Nebraska ranked fifth in cash receipts from farm marketing ($3,922,900,000). On 1 January 1977, there were 6,450,000 cattle and calves and 3,100,000 hogs and pigs on Nebraska farms. With 24,000,000 acres under cultivation (5,900,000 of them irrigated) Nebraska is a great wheat, corn, forage and livestock state, Oats, clover, wild hay, beans, sorghum grain, soybeans, popcorn, potatoes and sugar beets are also grown. In 1976 Nebraska ranked first in alfalfa meal (660,000 tons), Great Northern beans (1,275,000 bags) and wild hay (1,425,000 tons), and second in commercial cattle slaughter (5,010,000 lbs). Value of mineral production reached almost $126·5 million a year. Sand, gravel and petroleum are the most important minerals. There are 88,200 people working in manufacturing. The most important industries are food processing, electrical and other machinery, metal products, transportation equipment, chemicals, instruments and related equipment, rubber, and miscellaneous plastic products.

**State University.** University of Nebraska at Lincoln and Omaha. Approximately 39,226 students in 1976–77.

## NEVADA

*(Sagebrush State or Silver State or Battle Born State)*

**Capital**—Carson City.

**Area:** 110,540 sq. miles.

**Population:** (Estimated 1976) 628,480. Chief population centers: Clark County (Las Vegas area), 345,700; Washoe County (Reno area), 162,000; Carson City, 29,000.

**Entered the Union:** 31 October 1864.

**Governor:** Mike O'Callaghan (Democrat).

**Legislature**
*Senate:* 20 members elected for four-year 'staggered' terms.
*Assembly:* 40 members. Term two years.

**Supreme Court.** Chief Justice Cameron M. Batjer and four Associate Justices, all elected for a term of six years by popular vote.

**Finance.** General Fund figures for the year ending 30 June 1975 were: Revenue, $195,435,957; Appropriations, $188,272,126.

**Production.** There are some nine million acres of farmland, which in 1976 earned about $161 million from crops and livestock. Chief crops are hay, alfalfa seed, and potatoes. Nevada has extensive mineral resources. Copper, gold, silver, sand and gravel, stone, mercury, gypsum and barite are the most important minerals. 1976 value of mineral production was estimated at $211·2 million. Gross taxable gambling revenue for 1976 was $1·26 (U.S.) billion. Main industries are tourism, gambling warehousing and distribution, chemicals and minerals.

**State University.** University of Nevada (Las Vegas and Reno). 15,928 full-time students in autumn 1976. Community College enrolment for autumn 1976 was 16,004.

## NEW HAMPSHIRE

*(Granite State)*

**Capital**—Concord.

**Land Area:** 9,024 sq. miles.

**Population:** (Census of 1970) 737,681. Chief cities and towns with populations: Concord, 30,022; Manchester, 87,754; Nashua, 55,820; Portsmouth, 25,717; Dover, 20,850.

**One of the original 13 states of the Union** (21 June 1788).

**Governor:** Meldrim Thomson Jr. (Republican).

**Legislature**

*Senate:* 24 members elected for two years.
*House of Representatives:* Not less than 375 nor more than 400 representatives elected for two years.

**Supreme Court.** Chief Justice Frank R. Kenison and four Associate Justices, all appointed by the Governor and the Council and terminate their office at the age of 70.

**Finance.** Budget figures for year ending 30 June 1976 were: Revenue, $388,311,223; Expenditure, $417,292,116.

Although in the above figures the expenditure exceeds the revenue this is due to complicated budget transfers involving Federal funds and does not mean that New Hampshire operates at a deficit.

**Production.** 2,412 farms constitute 506·5 thousand acres of farm land. Cash receipts from crops and livestock in 1976 was $95 million. Chief products are milk, poultry and eggs, meat animals and cash crops. Leading industries are electronics, electrical machinery, paper and allied products, leather products, and machinery. Industry earns value added $1·5 (U.S.) billion a year. After manufacturing, tourism is the second biggest industry.

**State University and Colleges:** (1976–77 estimate). University of New Hampshire. 9,369 students, Keene State College, and Plymouth State College, have a combined enrolment of 6,119.

## NEW JERSEY

*(Garden State)*

**Capital**—Trenton.

**Area:** 8,204 sq. miles.

**Population:** (Official State Estimates, 1 July 1975) 7,431,750. Chief cities and towns with populations: Newark, 373,000; Jersey City, 256,000; Paterson, 147,000; Trenton, 106,000; Camden, 100,000; Elizabeth, 114,000.

**One of the original 13 states of the Union** (18 December 1787).

**Governor:** Brendan Byrne (Democratic). Term four years.

**Legislature**

*Senate:* 40 members elected for four years.
*General Assembly:* 80 members elected for two years.

**Supreme Court.** Chief Justice Richard J. Hughes, and six Associate Justices, all appointed by the Governor with Senate confirmation for a term of seven years.

**Finance.** Estimated budget figures for 1977–78 were: Revenue, $3,111,819,414; Expenditure, $3,065,624,245

**Production.** Chief sources of income based on cash receipts from sales at farm level (1975–76) are: crops $174,237,000; livestock and products, $101,406,000. Total $351,000,000*

* Includes Government payments.

**Rutgers. The State University.** 46,491 students (Undergraduate, 26,621; Graduate and Professional, 12,621; others, 6,925 for the year 1976–77.

## NEW MEXICO

*(Land of Enchantment)*

**Capital**—Santa Fé.

**Area:** 121,666 sq. miles, including 221 sq. miles of water.

**Population** (1976) 1,168,000. Chief cities and towns with populations: Albuquerque, 285,700; Santa Fé, 48,000; Las Cruces. 47,600; Roswell, 44,500; Clovis, 32,800; Hobbs 33,500; Alamogordo, 30,000; Farmington, 37,000; and Carlsbad, 30,600.

**Entered the Union:** 6 January 1912.

**Governor:** Jerry Apodaca (Democrat).

**Legislature**

*Senate:* 42 members elected for 4 years.
*House of Representatives:* 70 members elected for 2 years.

**Supreme Court:** Chief Justice and four Justices, all elected for a term of eight years by popular vote.

**Finance.** Budget figures for 1974–75 were: Revenue, $1,801,540,871; Expenditure, $1,773,214,728.

**Production.** Value of agricultural products in 1976 was $730 million. Livestock sales were $535 million. Mineral production in 1976 was $2,372 million. Fuel products accounted for $1,480 million. New Mexico is leading producer of uranium, perlite and potassium salts in U.S. The state is nationally recognized as a centre for technological research and development. About 30,500 people are employed in manufacturing. *Per capita* income in 1976 was $5,213; personal income, $5,467 million.

**State Universities:** Students for Autumn 1976—University of New Mexico, 22,687; New Mexico State University, 13,447; New Mexico Highlands University, 2,099; Western New Mexico University, 1,830; Eastern New Mexico University, 5,668; New Mexico Institute of Mining and Technology, 921.

## NEW YORK STATE

### (*Empire State*)

**Capital**—Albany.

**Area:** 49,576 sq. miles including 1,632 sq. miles of water.

**Population:** (Census of 1970) 18,241,266. Chief cities with populations: New York, 7,895,563; Buffalo, 462,768; Rochester, 295,011; Schenectady, 77,958; Syracuse, 197,297; Yonkers, 204,297; Albany, 115,781; Utica, 91,611; Binghamton, 64,123; Niagara Falls, 85,615; Troy, 62,918; Mount Vernon, 72,778; New Rochelle, 75,385.

**One of the original 13 states of the Union** (26 July 1788).

**Governor:** Hugh L. Carey (Democrat).

**Legislature**

*Senate:* 60 members elected every two years.
*Assembly:* 150 members elected every two years.

For Local Government purposes the State is divided into 62 counties.

**Court of Appeals.** Chief Justice Charles D. Breitel and six Associate Judges, all elected by popular vote.

**Finance.** Budget figures for the year ending 31 March 1977 were: Revenue, $11,095,055,109·67; Expenditure, $10,988,361,631·47.

**Production.** New York is the leading manufacturing State of the nation, ranking first in number of establishments, number of people employed, and variety of goods produced. Value added by manufacture totalled $33·6 (U.S.A.) billion in 1973. Printing and publishing, instruments, chemicals, apparel, machinery (except electrical), electrical equipment and food are the State's leading manufacturing industries. Agriculture in New York State is an important part of the nation's farming, with milk and dairy products accounting for over half the State's farm income. Cash receipts from farm marketing totalled over $1·5 billion (U.S.) in 1975. New York ranks second in income from dairy products and is an important producer of fresh fruits and vegetables, greenhouse and nursery products, eggs, poultry, cheese, and wines.

**State University. The State University of New York.**

## NORTH CAROLINA

### (*Tar Heel State*)

**Capital**—Raleigh.

**Area:** 52,712 sq. miles.

**Population:** (1975) 5,451,000. Chief cities and towns with populations: Charlotte, 272,270; Greensboro, 156,940; Winston-Salem, 143,620; Raleigh, 147,380; Durham, 105,560; Asheville, 60,900; Fayetteville, 60,750; High Point, 64,230; Wilmington, 52,870.

**One of the original 13 states of the Union** (21 November 1789).

**Governor:** James B. Hunt, Jr. (Democrat).

**Secretary of State:** Thad Eure.

**Legislature**

*Senate:* 50 members elected for two years.
*House of Representatives:* 120 members elected for two years.

**Supreme Court.** Chief Justice Susie Sharp and six Associate Justices, all elected for a term of eight years by popular vote.

**Finance.** Authorized budget figures for 1977–78 were: Revenue $3,977,000,000. The budget figures include general, highway, federal and other receipts.

**Production.** North Carolina's economy, once predominantly agricultural, is increasingly oriented to manufacturing. The State leads the U.S.A. in textiles, tobacco, household furniture and brick production. The State also is fourth in the nation in the production of commercial broiler chickens (315·6 million in 1976). Mineral production is important. North Carolina leads in lithium, feldspar and mica. The value of mineral production in 1976 was $160,000,000. Commercial fishing contributed $26,000,000 in 1976.

**State University.** The North Carolina University system is composed of sixteen units with a total enrolment of 104,786.

North Carolina has 57 community colleges and technical institutes, all public. In addition there are 38 private colleges (29 senior, 9 junior).

## NORTH DAKOTA

### (*Sioux State or Flickertail State*)

**Capital**—Bismarck.

**Area:** 70,665 sq. miles.

**Population:** (Census of 1970) 617,761. Chief cities and towns with populations: Bismarck, 34,703; Fargo, 55,815; Grand Forks, 40,060; Minot, 32,290; Jamestown, 15,385; Valley City, 7,843.

**Entered the Union:** 2 November 1889.

**Governor:** Arthur A. Link (Democrat). Term four years (1977–1980).

**Secretary of State:** Ben Meier.

**Legislature**

*Senate:* 50 members elected for four years.
*House of Representatives.* 100 members elected for two years.

The State is divided into 53 counties.

**Supreme Court.** Chief Justice Ralph J. Erickstad and four Associate Justices, all elected for a term of ten years by popular vote.

**Finance.** Budget figures for the year ending 30 June 1975 were: Revenue, $931,154,322·96; Expenditure $908,822,176·26.

**Production.** 92 per cent of the land is farm land. There are about 40,000 farms, producing $1,459,484,000 worth of crops and $538,739,000 of livestock products in 1976. North Dakota ranks first in production of hard spring wheat, durum wheat, flax, barley, rye and sunflowers. Principal minerals are lignite (reserves, 350,000 billion short tons), leonardite, petroleum, limestone and clays. Annual value of mineral production is $179·6 million.

**State University.** University of North Dakota, Grand Forks, 8,632 students for year 1975–76.

## OHIO

*(Buckeye State)*

**Capital**—Columbus.

**Area:** 41,000 sq. miles.

**Population:** (Census of 1970) 10,652,017. Chief cities and towns with populations: Cleveland, 750,879; Columbus, 540,025; Cincinnati, 453,514; Toledo, 383,062; Akron, 275,425; Dayton, 242,917; Youngstown, 140,880; Canton, 110,053.

**Entered the Union:** 1 March 1803.

**Governor:** James A. Rhodes.

**Legislature**

*Senate:* 33 members (four-year terms).
*House of Representatives:* 99 members elected for two years.
For Local Government purposes the State is divided into 88 counties.

**Supreme Court.** Chief Justice C. William O'Neill and six Associate Justices, all elected for a term of six years by popular vote.

**Finance.** Budget figures for the year ending 30 June 1976 were: All Funds Revenue, $5,780,562,000; All Funds Expenditure, $5,839,473,000.

**Production.** Seventy per cent of the State's land is agricultural. Main crops are corn, winter wheat, oats, soybeans and hay. Ohio leads the country in production of lime and iron alloys. Salt and coal are important mineral products, and the chemical industry produces many coke chemicals. Ohio is number three among the top ten manufacturing states in terms of value added. Its versatility is demonstrated by its substantially exceeding the U.S. average in transportation equipment, machinery, fabricated metal products, primary metal products, rubber and plastics, and stone, clay, and glass.

**State Universities.** There are twelve State Universities: Bowling Green State University; Central State University; Cleveland State University; Kent State University; Miami University; Ohio State University; Ohio University; Wright State University; University of Akron; University of Cincinnati; University of Toledo; and Youngstown State University.

## OKLAHOMA

*(Sooner State)*

**Capital**—Oklahoma City.

**Area:** 69,919 sq. miles.

**Population:** (Estimated by the Oklahoma Employment Security Commission, 1 July 1975) State: 2,712,000. Chief cities and towns: Altus, 25,300; Ardmore, 24,200; Bartlesville, 29,500; Bethany, 23,000; Del City, 29,500; Duncan, 21,300; Enid, 50,000; Lawton, 81,000; McAlister, 18,600; Midwest City, 56,500; Moore, 24,500; Muskogee, 39,400; Norman, 63,600; Oklahoma City, 368,700; Ponca City, 27,600; Sapulpa, 16,200; Shawnee, 30,700; Stillwater, 36,100; Tulsa, 348,800.

**Governor:** David Boren (Democrat).

**Entered the Union:** 16 November 1907.

**Legislature**

*Senate:* 48 members elected for four years (24 elected biennially).
*House of Representatives:* 101 members elected for two years.

**Supreme Court.** Chief Justice Ralph B. Hodges. Members are retained or removed by popular vote after each six-year term; if removed, a successor is appointed by the Governor from three nominees of a special judicial committee.

**Finance.** Budget figures for the year ending 30 June 1977 were: Revenue, $1,988,321,575; Expenditure, $2,006,775,453.

**Production.** Oklahoma is favoured with a long growing season, fertile soil, and rich mineral resources. A producing oil well, located on the Capitol grounds, is indicative of the importance of petroleum in the State's economy. During 1975, 40,831 persons were employed in petroleum, gas and coal mining with total wages of $599,447,374. Natural conditions in Oklahoma are extremely favourable for the production of livestock. There were 6,400,000 head of livestock as of 1 January 1975. Wheat is the largest cash crop followed by peanuts, cotton, hay, and grain sorghum. Income from farm marketing in 1975 was $1,944,309,000. 148,859 people, who earned $1,512,542,454, are employed in manufacturing industries, the most important of which are machinery, food processing, fabricated metal products, and transportation.

**State Universities.** University of Oklahoma, 20,010 students and Oklahoma State University (formerly A. and M. College), 21,129 and Central State University, 12,763 students for the Autumn of 1976.

Total enrolled in Autumn 1976 in all public institutions including Junior Colleges was 19,193.

## OREGON

*(Beaver State)*

**Capital**—Salem.

**Area:** 96,981 sq. miles.

**Population:** (estimated 1975) 2,241,700. Chief cities and towns with populations: Portland, 382,000; Salem, 80,000; Eugene, 96,600 Corvallis, 40,100; Medford, 34,900.

**Entered the Union:** 14 February 1859.

**Governor:** Robert W. Straub (Democrat). Term expires 1979.

**State Treasurer:** Clay Myers (Republican). Term expires 1981.

**Legislature**

*Senate:* 30 members elected for four years (half their number retiring every two years).
*House of Representatives:* 60 members elected for two years.

**Supreme Court.** Chief Justice Arno Denecke and six Associate Justices, all are elected for a term of six years by popular vote.

**Finance.** Estimated budget figures for 1977–79: $9,900,000.

**Production.** Of the total land area 61,641,600 acres in the State of Oregon, approximately 44·8 per cent is in forest land, 9·9 per cent is in agriculture, and 41·5 per cent is in grazing (1972 figures). In 1975, there were 32,500 farms with an average size of almost 600 acres. Cash farm receipts in 1975 totalled $1·07 billion with crops accounting for 60 per cent and livestock accounting for 40 per cent. Forest products, are, by far, Oregon's leading industry and accounts for nearly half of the State's 5,000 manufacturing establishments. The value of forest products in Oregon for 1975 exceeded $3 billion (U.S.). In the same year, the amount of all lumber produced in the State totalled 9·8 million board feet. Tourism is also an important industry. Tourist expenditures reached an estimated $600 million in 1975. Total employment in Oregon reached 968,000 in 1975. Total electrical capacity in 1976 was 7,723,000 kilowatts with total sales of 27·9 billion kilowatt hours and gross revenues of $477,414,847. The 7,723,000 kilowatts is inclusive of Bonneville, which serves part of Washington also. Total capacity generated in Oregon only was 6,660,000.

**State Universities.** (Autumn, 1976.) University of Oregon, located at Eugene, 17,384 students; Oregon State University at Corvallis, 16,500; University of Oregon Health Sciences Center, 2,000; Portland State University at Portland, 15,300.

Oregon College of Education, Monmouth, 3,371 students; Southern Oregon College, Ashland, 4,500; Eastern Oregon State College, La Grande, 1,400; Oregon Institute of Technology at Klamath Falls, 2,300.

## PENNSYLVANIA

*(Keystone State)*

**Capital**—Harrisburg.

**Area:** 45,333 sq. miles.

**Population:** (Census of 1970) 11,793,909. Chief cities and towns with populations: Philadelphia, 1,948,609; Pittsburgh, 520,117; Scranton, 103,564; Erie, 129,231; Reading, 87,643; Allentown, 109,527; Wilkes-Barre, 58,856; Harrisburg, 68,061; Bethlehem, 72,686; Altoona, 62,900; Chester, 56,331.

**One of the original 13 states of the Union** (12 December 1787).

**Governor:** Milton J. Shapp (Democrat).

**Secretary of the Commonwealth:** C. DeLores Tucker.

**Legislature**

*Senate:* 50 members elected for four years.
*House of Representatives:* 203 members elected for two years.

**Supreme Court.** Chief Justice Benjamin R. Jones and six Justices. Justices elected after 1 January 1969 serve a term of ten years. Those elected before that date serve a term of 21 years.

**Finance.** General Fund budget figures for 1974–75 were: Revenue, $4,579 million; Expenditure, 4,322 million.

**Production.** Farm acreage is about 10,008,000. Main crops are corn, wheat, hay, oats, barley/potatoes, mushrooms, tobacco grapes, greenhouse nursery products, and apples. Cash farm income in 1975 was almost $1,591,800,000. Pennsylvania supplies most of the nation's anthracite coal (5,628,741 tons, 1975). 1975 output of bituminous coal was 84,479,031 short tons. The State leads in iron and steel production. Pig iron production 1975, 17·6 million tons, Steel ingot production 1975, 25·8 million tons.

**State University.** Pennsylvania State University.

## RHODE ISLAND

*(The Ocean State)*

**Capital**—Providence.

**Area:** 1,214 sq. miles.

**Population:** (Census of 1970) 949,723. There are eight cities in the State and their populations are: Providence, 179,116; Warwick, 83,694; Pawtucket, 76,984; Cranston, 74,287; East Providence, 48,207; Woonsocket, 46,820; and Central Falls, 18,716. There are 31 towns, the greatest in population is North Kingstown, 29,793; the smallest, New Shoreham, 489.

**One of the original 13 states of the Union** (29 May 1790).

**Governor:** J. Joseph Garrahy (Democrat).

**Legislature**

*Senate:* 50 members elected for two years.
*House of Representatives:* 100 members elected for two years.

**Supreme Court.** Chief Justice Joseph A. Bevilacqua and four Associate Justices. All are elected for life or during good behaviour, by both houses of legislature in grand committee.

**Finance.** Budget figures for the year ending 30 June 1976 were: Revenue (including federal grants), $641,185,145; Expenditure, $651,190,158.

**Production.** In 1977 there were 700 farms (average size 98·1 acres). Value of farm products sold in 1975 was $27,300,000. Value of commercial fish catch, 1975, was $18,796,322. In 1976 there were 122,400 people employed in manufacturing, and value added by manufacture was $1,924,200 in 1975. Jewellery, textiles, and electronics are important industries.

**Universities.** Each year Rhode Island colleges and universities graduate over 6,000 students. Three public and eight private colleges provide enrolment for over 46,000 undergraduate and 6,000 graduate students. Rhode Island colleges offer extension and evening courses providing the opportunity for all to continue their education.

## SOUTH CAROLINA

*(Palmetto State)*

**Capital**—Columbia.

**Area:** 31,055 sq. miles.

**Population:** Provisional figures dated 1 July 1975: 2,818,000. Chief cities and towns with populations: Columbia, 370,700; Charleston, 371,600; Greenville–Spartanburg, 525,300.

**One of the original 13 states of the Union** (23 May 1788).

**Governor:** James B. Edwards (Republican).

**Legislature**

*Senate:* 46 members elected for four years.
*House of Representatives:* 124 members elected for two years.

**Supreme Court.** Chief Justice Woodrow Lewis and four Associate Justices, all elected by the General Assembly for a term of ten years.

**Finance.** Budget figures for 1976 were: Total receipts at the State Treasurer's Office, 1975–76, $2,295,522,514; Total disbursements, $2,391,085,111.

**Production.** South Carolina is a major producer of tobacco and soybeans. In 1976 the state had 47,000 farms. Mineral production in 1975 was valued at $106 million, and consisted principally of kaolin and other clays, sand and gravel, stone, cement, vermiculite, and minor non-metallic minerals. The major industries are textiles and related manufacturing, paper, chemicals and synthetic fibres and precision metal-working. In the year 1973 the value added by manufacturing in the State was $5.8 billion.

**Universities:** 33 colleges and Junior colleges. The University of South Carolina had an enrolment of 31,739 students in 1976.

## SOUTH DAKOTA

*(Sunshine State)*

**Capital**—Pierre.

**Area:** 77,047 sq. miles.

**Population:** (Census of 1970) 666,257. Chief cities and towns with populations: Aberdeen, 26,476; Huron, 14,210; Mitchell, 13,425; Rapid City, 43,836; Sioux Falls, 72,448; Watertown, 13,388; Yankton, 11,919; Brookings, 13,717; Pierre (Capital), 9,699.

**Entered the Union:** 2 November 1889.

**Governor:** Richard F. Kneip (Democrat).

**Legislature**

*Senate:* 35 members elected for two years.
*House of Representatives:* 70 members elected for two years.

**Supreme Court.** Chief Justice Francis Dunn, and four other judges, all elected for a term of eight years by popular vote.

**Finance.** Budget figures for the year ending 30 June 1975 were: Revenue, $416,852,271·35; Expenditure, $389,289,869·26.

**Production.** South Dakota ranks second in the production of oats, rye and flaxseed and ranks third in production of durham wheat. It ranks in the top ten states in the production of spring wheat, hay and barley. Value of crop production in 1975 was $977,004,000. The cash receipt from livestock production in 1975 was $1,327,200,000. There are 43,000 farms of an average size of 1,058 acres. The state leads the nation in gold production (almost 40 per cent of the nation's total). Other principal minerals are stone, sand and gravel. Chief industries are meat packing, metal fabrication and assembly, and electronics. The tourism industry grossed $300,000,000 in 1975.

**Universities and Colleges** (1974–75). Public Institutions: Black Hills State College, had 1,875 students; Dakota State College, 870; Northern State College, 2,369; S. Dakota School of Mines, 1,609; S. Dakota State University, 6,412; University of S. Dakota, Springfield, 805; University of South Dakota, 5,632; the total of students being 19,572. Enrolments in private colleges totalled 6,989 for 1975–76, making a grand total of 26,561 enrolments.

## TENNESSEE

*(Volunteer State)*

**Capital—Nashville.**

**Area:** 42,244 sq. miles.

**Population:** (Census of 1970) 3,924,164. Chief cities and towns with populations: Memphis, 623,530; Chattanooga 119,082; Knoxville, 174,587; Nashville, 448,003.

**Entered the Union:** 1 June 1796.

**Governor:** Ray Blanton (Democrat).

**Legislature**

*Senate:* 33 members elected for four years.
*House of Representatives:* 99 members elected for two years.

**Supreme Court.** Chief Justice Robert E. Cooper, and four Associate Justices, all confirmed for a term of eight years by popular vote.

**Finance.** Budget figures for the year ending 30 June 1975 were: Revenue, $2,037,298,000; Expenditure, $2,187,759,000.

**Production.** Total cash receipts from farm crops in 1975 was $514 million and from livestock, $581·7 million. Soybeans and tobacco are the most important crops. Forests cover over half the State and yielded over 161 million cubic ft. of timber in 1972. Tennessee is a leading producer of zinc, ball clay and pyrite. In 1974 value of mineral production was $376 million.

**State University.** University of Tennessee at Knoxville. The average enrolment was 28,001 students for 1975–76. The other state colleges have an enrolment of 75,697 for 1975–76 Ten community colleges had an average total enrolment of 18,626 students for 1975–76.

## TEXAS

*(Lone Star State)*

**Capital**—Austin.

**Area:** 267,339 sq. miles including 4,499 sq. miles of water.

**Population:** (Census of 1974), 12,050,000. Chief cities and towns with populations: Houston, 1,386,000; Dallas, 912,900; San Antonio, 761,100; Fort Worth, 401,800; El Paso, 391,700; Corpus Christi, 215,000; Lubbock, 167,700; Amarillo, 142,400; Beaumont, 119,100.

**Entered the Union:** 29 December 1845.

**Governor:** Dolph Briscoe (Democrat). Term four years.

**Legislature**

*Senate:* 31 members elected for a term of four years.
*House of Representatives:* 150 members elected for a term of two years.

**Supreme Court.** Chief Justice Joe Greenhill and eight Associate Justices, all elected for a term of six years by popular vote.

**Production.** Texas produces more cotton than any other state. Other important crops are pecans, sorghum, corn and winter wheat. Large, highly-mechanized farms predominate. The livestock industry is also important; beef stock numbers over ten million and there are over five million sheep. The value of mineral production is about one-fourth of the national total—over 4,000 million a year. Petroleum is the principal mineral. Chemical production, particularly petrochemicals, is the most important industry.

**State University.** University of Texas at Austin, 42,598 students enrolled for Fall Semester, and 39,192 for Spring Semester, of 1975–76.

## UTAH

*(Beehive State)*

**Capital**—Salt Lake City.

**Area:** 82,096 sq. miles (including 2,577 sq. miles of water).

**Population** (1973 Revenue Sharing estimates) 1,157,000. chief cities and towns with populations: Salt Lake City, 169,234; Ogden, 66,357; Provo, 55,654; Logan, 22,642; Orem, 32,743; Bountiful, 29,220.

**Entered the Union:** 4 January 1896.

**Governor:** Scott Matheson (Democrat). Term four years.

**Legislature**

*Senate:* 29 members elected for four years (in part renewed every two years).
*House of Representatives:* 75 members elected for two years.

**Supreme Court.** Chief Justice Henri Henriod and four Associate Justices, all are elected for a term of ten years by non-partisan ballot vote.

**Finance.** Actual figures for the fiscal year ending 30 June 1975 were: Revenue, $733,830,580; Expenditure, $762,528,251.

**Production.** 1975 production figures for main crops are listed in order of greatest sales dollar value:

| | |
|---|---|
| Corn (silage) | 1,440,000 tons |
| Hay | 1,670,000 tons |
| Wheat (spring and winter) | 7,164,000 bushels |
| Sugar beets | 354,000 tons |
| Barley | 8,100,000 bushels |
| Potatoes | 1,508,000 cwt. |
| Corn (grain) | 1,650,000 bushels |
| Apples | 24,500 tons |
| Alfalfa seed | 3,640,000 lbs. |
| Peaches | 8,000 tons |
| Dry beans | 63,000 cwt. |
| Sweet cherries | 2,800 tons |
| Sour cherries | 4,000 tons |
| Pears | 4,100 tons |
| Oats | 728,000 bushels |
| Apricots | 500 tons |

Principal minerals produced in 1975 were (in order of greatest dollar value):

| | |
|---|---|
| Petroleum (crude) | 39,854,000 42-gal. barrels |
| Copper (recoverable content of ores, etc.) | 180,515 short tons |
| Coal (bituminous) | 6,900,000 short tons |
| Natural Gas | 58,888 million cu. ft. |
| Gold (recoverable content of ores, etc.) | 188,275 troy ounces |
| Sand and Gravel | 11,463,000 short tons |
| Zinc (recoverable content of ores, etc.) | 18,850 short tons |
| Iron ore (usable) | 1,455,000 long tons |
| Silver (recoverable content of ores, etc.) | 2,733,000 troy ounces |
| Salt | 651,000 short tons |
| Stone | 2,669,000 short tons |
| Lead (recoverable content of ores, etc.) | 11,775 short tons |
| Lime | 159,000 short tons |

The five leading manufactures are: (by value added) primary metals, transportation equipment, food, fabricated metals and machinery, and stone, clay and glass products.

**State Universities** .(Autumn 1975):

| | *No. of Students* |
|---|---|
| Brigham Young University, Provo (private) | 27,218 |
| Westminister, Salt Lake City (private) | 1,052 |
| College of Eastern Utah, Price | 552 |
| Snow College, Ephraim | 897 |
| Dixie College, St. George | 1,174 |
| Southern Utah State College, Cedar City | 1,883 |
| Weber State College, Ogden | 9,458 |
| University of Utah, Salt Lake City | 22,180 |
| Utah State University, Logan | 9,113 |
| Utah Technical College, Salt Lake City | 6,047 |
| Utah Technical College, Provo | 3,434 |
| **Total Autumn 1975 enrolment** | 83,008 |

## VERMONT

*(Green Mountain State)*

**Capital**—Montpelier.

**Area:** 9,609 sq. miles including 333 sq. miles of water.

**Population:** (Census of 1970) 444,732. Barre, 10,209; Burlington, 38,633; Montpelier, 8,609; Newport, 4,664; Rutland, 19,293; So. Burlington, 10,032; St. Albans, 8,082; Vergennes, 2,242; Winooski, 7,309.

**Entered the Union:** 4 March 1791.

**Governor:** Richard Snelling (Republican).

**Legislature**

*Senate:* 30 members elected for two years.
*House of Representatives:* 150 members elected for two years.

**Finance.** Budget figures for the year ending 30 June 1975 were: Revenue, $334,503,039; Expenditure, $343,307,012.

**Production.** Estimated spending by tourists was $280 million in 1975.

**State University.** University of Vermont. About 8,287 (spring 1976) 8,600 (autumn, 1976) students. In 1955 the General Assembly declared the University of Vermont to be a State university. Its previous status was that of a private institution.

## VIRGINIA

*(Old Dominion)*

**Capital**—Richmond.

**Area:** 40,817 sq. miles.

**Population:** (1975 estimate) 4,967,000. Chief cities with populations (1973): Alexandria, 108,300; Charlottesville, 40,600; Chesapeake, 100,800; Danville, 47,000; Hampton, 126,800; Lynchburg, 53,600; Newport News, 136,400; Norfolk, 289,200; Portsmouth, 109,500; Richmond, 233,100; Roanoke, 88,900; Suffolk, 47,800; Virginia Beach, 209,200.

**One of the original 13 states of the Union** (26 June 1788).

**Governor:** Mills E. Godwin, Jr. (Republican). Term 1974–78.

**Secretary of the Commonwealth:** Mrs. Patricia Perkinson.

**Legislature**

*Senate:* 40 members elected for four years.
*House of Delegates* 100 members elected for two years.

**Supreme Court of Appeals.** Chief Justice and six Associate Justices. All elected for a term of 12 years by joint vote of both Houses of Assembly.

**Finance.** Budget figures for the year ending 30 June 1975 were: Revenue, $3,348,132,146; Expenditure, $3,339,574,100.

**Production.** Chief crops are tobacco, peanuts, soybeans, apples, corn and potatoes. Crop land acreage is about 2·9 million acres. About half of the State's cash receipts from farm marketings of more than $972 million annually comes from livestock and livestock products, principally dairy products, cattle and calves, poultry and hogs. Coal with an annual output of about 35 million tons, is the most important mineral. Shipbuilding, synthetic fibres and cigarettes are among the most important industries. Value added by manufactures in 1974 was 7,717,352,000 for all manufacturing industries.

**State Universities:** Virginia Commonwealth University (17,843 students); Virginia Polytechnic Institute and State University (18,477); University of Virginia (14,839 students); Old Dominion University (13,160 students); College of William and Mary (6,200); George Mason University (7,638).

## WASHINGTON

### (*Evergreen State*)

**Capital**—Olympia.

**Area:** 68,192 sq. miles.

**Population:** (State Estimate 1976) 3,571,591. Major cities: Seattle, 500,000; Spokane, 174,500; Tacoma, 156,000; Bellevue, 68,500; Everett, 51,700; Yakima, 51,100; Vancouver, 46,500; Bellingham, 43,160; Bremerton, 39,350; Longview, 29,830; Richland, 31,050; Renton, 27,150.

**Entered the Union:** 11 November 1889.

**Governor:** Dixy Lee Ray (Democrat).

**Secretary of State:** Bruce K. Chapman (Republican).

**Legislature**

*Senate:* 49 members elected for four years, half their number retiring every two years.
*House of Representatives:* 98 members elected for two years two from each legislative district.

**Supreme Court.** Chief Justice Charles Wright. Nine justices elected for six years, one third retiring every two years. Chief Justice chosen for two years from among incumbent full-term justices.

**Finance.** Estimated State Government Expenditures for the 1975–77 biennium are $6,498 million. Estimated Revenues for the 1975–77 biennium are $6,538.

**Production.** Manufacturing is the State's primary source of wealth; the most important branches are lumber, food processing, the aeroplane industry and paper. Total employment in 1976 was 1,386,000.

Farm production in 1976 was $1,969 million, including $1,116 million in field and seed crops, $214 million in fruits and berries. The amount of revenue from livestock in the State was $431 million for 1976.

Softwood lumber production in 1976 was 3,207 million board feet. Expansion is expected in lumber and wood products, metals, machinery production, and food processing.

**Trade.** Taxable retail sales in 1976 reached $16,529·6 million.

**State Universities.** The projected enrolments for 1977–78 for the University of Washington, Seattle is 33,539 students, and for Washington State University, Pullman, is 16,420 students.

## WEST VIRGINIA

### (*Mountain State*)

**Capital—Charleston.**

**Area: 24,282 sq. miles.**

**Population:** (Census of 1976) 1,744,237. Chief cities and towns with populations: Huntington, 74,300; Charleston, 71,500; Wheeling, 48,100.

**Entered the Union:** 20 June 1863.

**Governor:** John D. Rockefeller IV.

**Legislature**

*Senate:* 34 elected for four years.
*House of Delegates:* 100 members elected for two years.

**Supreme Court.** Chief Justice, Fred H. Caplan, and four Associated Justices, all elected for a term of 12 years.

**Finance.** Budget figures for the year ending 30 June 1977 were: Revenue, $661·9; Expenditures, $659·8.

**Production.** Bituminous Coal, Employment, 55,256; Production, (109,048,898); Natural Gas (million cu. ft.) 54,484,175.

**State University.** West Virginia University, more than 20,000 full and part-time students; Marshall University, with more than 11,000 full and part-time students, both figures based on enrolments of Fall Semester 1976.

## WISCONSIN

### (*Badger State*)

**Capital**—Madison.

**Area:** 54,464 sq. miles (land). 2,378 sq. miles of Lake Superior and 7,500 sq. miles of Lake Michigan.

**Population:** (Census of 1970) Total 4,417,933. Urban, 2,910,418; Rural, 1,507,313; Milwaukee, 717,372; Madison, 171,769; Racine, 95,162; Kenosha, 78,805; Green Bay, 87,809; La Crosse, 51,153; Sheboygan, 48,484; Oshkosh, 53,104; West Allis, 71,649; Superior, 32,237; Eau Claire, 44,619; Appleton, 56,377; Janesville, 46,426; Wauwatosa, 58,676.

**Entered the Union:** 29 May 1848.

**Acting Governor:** Martin J. Schreiber (Democrat).

**Secretary of State:** Douglas J. LaFollette (Democrat).

**Legislature**

*Senate:* 33 members elected for four years, one-half (16 or 17 alternately) being elected each two years.
*Assembly:* 99 members elected for two years.

The 1977 Wisconsin Legislature is controlled by the Democrats in both the Senate and the Assembly. Of the six elected constitutional officers, five are Democrats and one is non-partisan.

The 1977 Wisconsin Legislature strengthened the open meetings law; instituted an easy access voter registration system; provided for the compensation of crime victims and substitution of generic drugs for namebrands; revised the inheritance tax law, the rape law and the unemployment compensation law; established medical malpractice laws and a power plant siting law; and placed levy limitations on municipalities and counties and budget limitations on school districts.

**Supreme Court.** Chief Justice Bruce F. Beilfuss. Term expires January 1983. Six Associate Justices, all elected for a term of ten years by popular vote.

**Finance.** Budget figures for 1975–76 were: Revenue (all funds) $4,722,528,845; Expenditure (all funds), $5,153,845,689.

**Production.** Wisconsin ranks 12th in value added by manufacture; heavy industry is the major industrial group, followed by food processing, transportation equipment, electrical equipment, paper manufacturing and fabricated metals. Dairy products are the major source of farm income, and Wisconsin is first in the country in this respect. In 1975 the State ranked first in the number of dairy cows (1,796,000), and produced 16 per cent of the nation's total output of milk. The State ranks first in the amount of corn for silage, all hay, peas for processing, snap beans for processing, beets for canning, and cranberries. Sand, gravel, stone, copper and zinc are the chief mineral products.

**State University.** 1976–77: In the University of Wisconsin system, total student enrolment 1976–77) at its 13 four-year campuses and 17 centre system campuses was 143,282. Extension enrolment (1975–76) was 133,866.

## WYOMING

*(Equality State)*

**Capital**—Cheyenne.

**Area:** 97,914 sq. miles including 408 sq. miles of water.

**Population** (1975 Census, Estimate) 376,300. Chief cities and towns with populations: Cheyenne, 46,600; Casper, 41,100; Laramie, 23,400; Rock Springs, 17,700; Sheridan, 11,600.

**Entered the Union:** 10 July 1890 (44th State).

**Governor:** Ed Herschler (Democrat).

**Secretary of State:** Thyra Thomson.

**Legislature**

*Senate:* 30 members elected for four years, 15 retiring every two years.

*House of Representatives:* 62 members elected for two years.

**Supreme Court.** Chief Justice Rodney M. Guthrie and Justices Richard V. Thomas, John F. Raper, A. G. McClintock, and Robert R. Rose, Jr. When vacancies occur the Governor will appoint new Justices.

**Production.** The value of minerals produced in 1976 in millions of dollars was Oil, 894·1; Gas, 88·9, Coal, 124·7. The value of various other commercial items for 1976 in millions of dollars was crops, 181·1; Livestock, 180·3.

**Finance.** Cash receipts for the fiscal year 1977 were: 582,042,506·19; Expenditure, $444,333,153·63.

**State University.** University of Wyoming (Laramie). 8,726 students in 1976–77.

# United States Territories and Possessions

## GUAM

**Capital**—Agana.

**Governor:** Ricardo Jerome Bordallo.

**Area and Population.** Guam is the largest and southern island of the Marianas Archipelago, in 13° 26′ N. lat., 144° 43′ E. long. Magellan is said to have discovered the island in 1521; it was ceded by Spain to the U.S. by the Treaty of Paris (10 December 1898). The island was captured by the Japanese on 10 December 1941, and retaken by American forces from 21 July 1944. Guam is of great strategic importance; substantial naval and air force personnel occupy about one-third of the usable land. Its constitutional status is that of an 'unincorporated territory' of the U.S. Entry of U.S. citizens is unrestricted; foreign nationals are subject to normal regulations. The port is open to foreign vessels.

The length of Guam is 30 miles, the breadth from four to 10 miles, and the area about 210 sq. miles (450 sq. km). Agana, the seat of government is about eight miles from the anchorage in Apra Harbour. The census on 1 April 1970 showed a population of 84,996, an increase of 17,952 or 26·8 per cent since 1960; those of Guamanian ancestry numbered about 52,000; foreign-born, 13,484; density was 321 per sq. mile On 1 January 1970 transient residents connected with the military were estimated at 19,307. Estimated population, 1975, 105,400. The Malay strain is predominant. The native language is Chamorro; English is the official language and is taught in all schools.

**Government.** In 1949 the President transferred the administration of the island from the Navy Department (who held it from 1899) to the Interior Department. The transfer was completed by 1 August 1950, on the passage of the Organic Act, which conferred full citizenship on the Guamanians, who had previously been 'nationals' of the U.S.

The Governor and his staff constitute the executive arm of the government. The Legislature is unicameral. The latter's powers are similar to those of an American state legislature. Following the general election of November 1976, the Democratic Party won eight seats and the Republicans won 13. All adults 18 years of age or over, including women, are enfranchised.

**Trade.** Guam is the only American territory which is completely 'free trade'; excise duties are levied only upon imports of tobacco, liquid fuel and liquor. In the year ending 30 June 1976 imports were valued at $266·3m and accounted for 91 per cent of trade.

**Agriculture.** The major products of the island are maize, sweet potatoes, taro, cassava, bananas, and citrus and truck crops, including breadfruit, coconuts and sugar-cane. In 1970–71, 569 full-time and part-time farmers each held 500 acres under cultivation. Livestock included 605 carabao, 5,800 cattle, 900 goats, 8,750 hogs, 95 horses and 130,000 laying-hens. Commercial production of fruit and vegetables amounted to 2·4m. lb. ($2·3m.); fish caught, 201,000 lb. in 1974; egg production, 2·3m. dozen.

**Communications.** Four Commercial airlines (PANAM, Air Nauru, Air Pacific and Continental Air Micronesia) serve Guam; Island Aviation serves all Micronesia on a charter basis.

There are 183 miles of paved and 63 miles of improved roads. Overseas telephone and radio dispatch facilities are available. On 30 June 1975 there were over 22,055 telephones.

There is a commercial radio station, a commercial television station, a public broadcasting station, and a cable television station with three channels.

**Education.** Elementary education is compulsory. There were, in September 1976, 28 elementary schools, one school for handicapped children, five junior high schools, three senior high schools and one vocational-technical school for high school students and adults. There were 16,803 elementary school pupils, 6,460 junior high and 4,864 senior high school pupils, Department of Education staff, 2,400, including teachers, counsellors and administrators.

# CANAL ZONE

**Capital**—Balboa Heights.

**Area:** 648 sq. miles.

**Population:** (1970 Census) 44,198.

**Government.** The basic Treaty between the United States and Panama, which was signed on 18 November 1903, granted to the United States in perpetuity, the use, occupation and control of a zone five miles wide on each side of the canal, construction of which was to link the Atlantic and Pacific Oceans. In 1967 representatives of both countries met to negotiate new treaties which would replace the one currently in effect.

In February 1974 a joint statement was signed by Henry A. Kissinger, Secretary of State and by Juan Antonio Tack, Panamanian Minister of Foreign Affairs. This contained eight principles for the negotation of a new Panama Canal treaty. The wording of the principles indicated that the new treaty would abrogate the 1903 treaty and should have a fixed termination date.

The ending of United States jurisdiction over Panamanian territory should take place promptly but rights should be granted to the U.S.A. to use such land, water and airspace as might be necessary for the operation and defence of the canal. Benefits from the operation of the canal should be shared equitably and it was recognized that the canal was the principal resource of the Republic of Panama.

In addition, Panama should participate in the administration of the canal and should assume total responsibility for its operation when the treaty ended.

Panama should participate with the U.S.A. in the protection and defence of the canal. Any possible new projects for the enlargement of the waterway should be agreed between the two parties.

The civil government of the Canal Zone is administered by a governor appointed by the President of the United States. The Governor of the Canal Zone is also the President, *ex officio*, of the Panama Canal Company, a corporate agency of the United States Government. It is charged with the operation and maintenance of the Panama Canal.

In the year ending 30 June 1976, 12,280 ocean going ships paid tolls in the amount of $134,912,053 to the Panama Canal. These ships carried 117,395,409 long tons of cargo through the canal.

# AMERICAN SAMOA

**Capital**—Pago Pago.

**Governor:** Earl B. Ruth.

**Area:** The total area is about 76 sq. miles which includes seven islands as follows: Tutuila (the main island of about 42 sq. miles); Aunu'u; Swain's Island (an atoll 200 miles north of Tutuila); The Manu'a Group: Ofu, Olosega, Ta'u; Rose Island (uninhabited).

**Population:** (Preliminary census figures 25 September 1974) 29,191.

**Government.** Since 1951 the Government of American Samoa has been administered by the Department of the Interior. The Governor is appointed by the Secretary of the Interior with the approval of the President. Samoan District Governors who are High Chiefs direct the activities of local government. In April 1960 a Constitutional Convention conferred upon the Legislature law making authority and a constitutional form of Government effective from 17 October 1960. The Legislature is composed of two houses, the Senate of 15 members elected in accordance with Samoan custom from among the chiefs, and the House of Representatives composed of 17 members by universal suffrage and secret ballot. In 1970 a constitutional amendment was passed making members of the Legislature (House and Senate) serve on a full-time basis. It also requires that no member of the Legislature can be employed in the Executive Departments. The structure and election procedure was not changed. Also in 1970 the Legislature created the office of Delegate-at-Large to Washington. He was elected by popular vote. The delegate works in the capital but has no vote or status in Congress.

**Judiciary.** There are a High Court and five district courts. The High Court consists of three divisions: Appelate, Trial and Probate. All courts are courts of record.

**Development Programme.** The economic development programme for 1971 focused on strengthening the Territory's economic base by soliciting outside investment and encouraging local investment which would raise the Territory's income through exports and the expansion of tourist facilities and services to attract new income to the region. The programme also concentrated on local market related business development to raise income through substituting local production for imported goods and services.

Pacific Time Corporation, a division of Bulova Watch Company, became the first outside interest under our development programme to start operations in American Samoa during the latter part of 1971.

Other industries which have shown an active interest in establishing plants in American Samoa in order to take advantage of the territory's duty-free status and advantages under United States customs laws include jewellery, food processing, industrial gasses, furniture and additional clothing manufacturers.

Fiscal Year 1972 saw the start of construction on an 80-acres industrial-commercial park near the International Airport of Tafuna. It is financed by a $1 million grant from the Economic Development Administration and matching funds appropriated by the local Legislature.

This will finance such work as fill, grading, street, sewer, water, power and landscaping. Already more than 20 acres of the 55-acre industrial portion of the part have been committed to new manufacturing, wholesaling and warehousing operations.

The territory is continuing its efforts to attract light manufacturing industries.

**Production and Commerce.** Principal exports are fish, fish products, and Samoan handicraft work. Two canneries for tuna fish at Pago Pago employ about 1,000 Samoan processors and 4,000 Asian (Korean, Japanese, Nationalist Chinese) fishermen.

The following table shows the value of exports (detail) and imports for the Fiscal Year 1974:

| *Exports* | *Value* | *Imports* |
|---|---|---|
| Fish Meal | $138,478 | |
| Fish, Fresh | $2,421,275 | |
| Pet Food | $3,480,854 | |
| Shark Fins | $262,911 | |
| Tuna | $73,600,255 | |
| Jewellery | $88,219 | |
| Watches and clocks | $4,706,622 | |
| Wearing Apparel | $469,112 | |
| Total | $84,988,726 | $46,549,418 |

**Finance**

| | 1974 |
|---|---|
| Territorial Budget | 14,000,000 |
| Local Appropriations | 12,676,000 |
| Other Federal Appropriations | 4,889,000 |
| Total | 31,565,000 |

As regards agriculture, a concerted drive by the government is succeeding in encouraging commercial farming. Due to better methods of farming, the territory is now producing more agricultural products than before. Efforts are also being made by the Department of Agriculture to encourage local people to use modern farming techniques in farming their lands.

**Communications.** By air, weekly Pan American Clippers arrive from the continental United States via Honolulu or from Auckland, New Zealand, via Nandi, Fiji, and from Sydney (Australia), in less than 24 hours. Polynesian Airlines operate a daily schedule between American Samoa and Western Samoa. Air New Zealand offers weekly flights from New Zealand and Fiji to Samoa. In August 1970, American Airlines began serving American Samoa with one weekly flight from Honolulu to Auckland and plans were completed to increase service with flights to Sydney.

Pan Am recently added the 747 Jet to its South Pacific run with two scheduled flights a week via the U.S. West Coast, Honolulu, Auckland and New Zealand. Air New Zealand continues its weekly service and American Airlines has recently discontinued its run to Pago Pago.

By ship, monthly connections from New Zealand are available, and Matson luxury liners call at Pago Pago about every five weeks en route to the mainland. Freighters from the United States with limited accommodation also call from time to time.

The Pacific Far East Line serves the area with its Lash ships which call at Pago Pago twice a month from the U.S. West Coast, New Zealand and Australia. The Pacific Island Transport Line also call in monthly and many foreign luxury cruise ships make frequent calls to Pago Pago.

**Religion.** Approximately 62·6 per cent of the population is Christian Congregational Church (London Missionary Society), 19·23 per cent are Roman Catholic and 8·84 per cent Mormon. The remainder consists of smaller Protestant churches.

## VIRGIN ISLANDS OF THE UNITED STATES

**Capital**—Charlotte Amalie.

**Area:** The Virgin Islands group comprises the three principal Islands of St. Thomas (28 sq. miles), St. Croix (84 sq. miles), St. John (20 sq. miles) and about 50 smaller islands mostly uninhabited.

**Population:** (June 1975) 99,981. St. Thomas, 47,825; St. Croix, 49,647; St. John, 2,509.

The Islands were purchased from Denmark in 1916 for $25,000,000 and were proclaimed a United States Possession on 25 January 1917.

**Governor:** Cyril E. King.

**Lieutenant Governor:** Juan Luis.

**Legislation.** The Revised Organic Act of the Virgin Islands provides for a single legislative body, designated as the 'Legislature of the Virgin Islands', and composed of fifteen members known as senators. The Virgin Islands are divided into two legislative districts, as follows: The District of St. Thomas–St. John and the District of St. Croix. Seven senators are elected from each district and the other senator, who must be a bona fide resident of St. John, is elected at large from the Virgin Islands as a whole. Members of the Legislature are elected biennially, the franchise being vested in residents of the Virgin Islands (men and women) 18 years of age or over, who are citizens of the United States and able to read and write the English language.

The executive power of the Islands is vested in the Governor. The Governor and Lieutenant Governor are elected quadrennially, the franchise being vested in residents of the Virgin Islands (men and women) 18 years of age or over, who are citizens of the United States.

**Finance.** In Fiscal Year 1976 the operating revenues totalled $304,105,634 compared with $293,542,516 in 1975. Operating expenditures for Fiscal Year 1976 totalled $312,930,490 compared with $133,530,829 in 1975.

*Note:* A total of $146,830,603 in Investment Incentive Subsidies was paid to tax-exempt 'businesses' and individuals during the Fiscal Year 1976 compared with $133,530,829 for the same purpose during the Fiscal Year 1975.

**Production and Industry.** Chief industries of St. Croix are refining of crude oil, production of alumina, vegetable growing and the manufacture of rum. St. Thomas is the leading port in the Virgin Islands; its industries are servicing of ships, manufacture of rum and truck gardening, deep-sea fishing, handicrafts, and small manufacturing industries.

**Commerce.** Figures for 1976 indicate total imports increased to $2,680,742,421 an increase of 21per cent over the previous year. Foreign imports totalled $2,463,852,630 compared to $1,934,447,260 in 1975. Imports from the U.S. mainland and Puerto Rico for 1976 totalled $216,889,791 a decrease of $47,172,951 or 17·5 per cent.

Total exports increased in 1976 to $2,010,164,653 up 4 per cent. Exports to the U.S. mainland and Puerto Rico totalled $1,936,842,995 an increase of 3·5 per cent when compared to 1975. Exports to foreign countries increased 2 per cent to $73,321,658 from $62,333,191 in 1975.

Tourist expenditures were estimated to be $152,212,400 in Fiscal Year 1976.

**Shipping.** During the Fiscal Year 1976 740 cruise ships visited the Virgin Islands with 471,073 passengers on board.

**Banking.** United States currency became legal tender on 1 July 1934, succeeding that formerly issued by the National Bank of the Danish West Indies in the form of the franc valued at 19·3 cents, United States money. In June 1975, there were eight banks comprising a total of 34 main and branch offices. In addition to these banks, there were two financial institutions: First Federal Savings and Loan of Puerto Rico; Virgin Islands Title and Trust Company—operating three offices in the Virgin Islands.

**Education and Religion.** Education is compulsory for all children commencing their school education by attending an approved Kindergarten from the beginning of the school year nearest their fifth birthday and continue to attend until until the expiration of the school year nearest their sixteenth birthday.

In October 1976 there were 25,036 pupils in public schools and 6,694 in other schools.

The principal religious bodies in the islands are the Episcopal Church, Roman Catholic Church, Christian Mission, Hebrew Synagogue, Lutheran Church, Methodist Church, Moravian Church, Reformed Church of America, Salvation Army and Seventh Day Adventists.

# The Commonwealth of Puerto Rico

(ESTADO LIBRE ASOCIADO DE PUERTO RICO)

**Capital**—San Juan.

**Governor:** Rafael Hernández Colón

**Flag:** On a field of five horizontal stripes red and white countercharged a blue triangle at the hoist charged with a white star.

**Constitution and Government.** The Island of Puerto Rico was discovered by Christopher Columbus in 1493. During 400 years Spain ruled over Puerto Rico and imprinted in its people the Hispanic culture, the Spanish language and the Roman Catholic religion. In 1897 Spain granted to Puerto Rico a Charter of Autonomy establishing a system of self-government.

By the Treaty of Paris of 10 December 1898 ending the Spanish-American war, Spain ceded Puerto Rico to the United States. After two years of military government, the United States Congress passed the Foraker Organic Act establishing a civil government headed by a Governor appointed by the President, with a Legislative Assembly elected by the people. American citizenship was granted in 1917. In 1946 the President of the U.S. appointed the first Puerto Rican as Governor of the Island, and in 1947 the Congress granted authority to Puerto Ricans to elect their own Governor.

On 25 July 1952 the Commonwealth of Puerto Rico was established as a self-governing community, voluntarily associated to the U.S. by virtue of a compact freely entered into by the people of Puerto Rico and the United States. On that date a Constitution drafted and adopted by the Puerto Ricans was proclaimed. The Constitution provides for a republican government with separation of powers and separation of State and Church, and contains a Bill of Rights. Under the present status Puerto Ricans have retained the American citizenship. Free trade between Puerto Rico and the U.S. is continued and Puerto Ricans are exempted from payment of federal taxes. Defence and international affairs remain a U.S. responsibility. In a plebiscite held on 23 July 1967, 60·4 per cent of voters ratified the continuation of Commonwealth; 39 per cent voted for incorporation as a State of the United States and only 0·6 per cent favoured independence.

Puerto Rico is represented in the United States Congress by a Resident Commissioner elected by direct vote for a four-year term. He holds a seat with voice but no vote in the House of Representatives, but otherwise enjoys the same privileges and immunities as other Congressmen.

*Resident Commissioner:* Jaime Benitez.

The executive power is vested in a Governor elected by direct vote for a four-year term, and ten executive departments headed by Secretaries appointed by the Governor with the consent of the Senate: State, Justice, Treasury, Education, Health, Labour, Transportation and Public Works, Social Services, Agriculture, Housing, National Resources, Consumer Services and Addiction Services. There are 30 executive agencies and 26 public corporations. In case of temporary absence, disability or death of the Governor he is succeeded by the Secretary of State.

*Secretary of State:* Victor M. Pons, Jr.

The Legislative power is vested in a Legislative Assembly consisting of a Senate of 29 members and a House of Representatives of 54 members, elected by direct vote for a four-year term.

*President of the Senate:* Juan Cancel-Ríos.

*Speaker of the House of Representatives:* Luis E. Ramos-Yordán.

**The Judiciary.** The Judiciary is vested in a Supreme Court and other courts as may be established by law. The Supreme Court is composed of a Chief Justice and eight Associate Justices appointed by the Governor with the consent of the Senate. The lower Judiciary consists of Superior and District Courts and Justices of the Peace equally appointed.

*Chief Justice of the Supreme Court:* Pedro Pérez-Pimentel.

**Area and Population.** The total area of the Commonwealth of Puerto Rico, including adjacent islands under its jurisdiction, is 3,435 square miles. The population (as of June 1972) is 2,856,000. The population density is approximately 780 persons per square mile. Population increases at the rate of two per cent annually and life expectancy is estimated at 70 years.

Population of principal cities (1972): San Juan (metropolitan): 880,000; Bayamõn, 165,000; Mayaguez, 89,900; Arecibo, 77,000; Caguas, 101,000.

**Finance.** In 1971–72, U.S. payments to Puerto Rico were about $436·7 million.

**Banks.** In addition to the Puerto Rican, American and foreign commercial banks operating in the Island, there is a Central Government Development Bank which serves as fiscal agent of the Commonwealth and helps in financing Government-sponsored industrial development projects. The principal American banks operating in Puerto Rico are the First National City Bank of New York and the Chase Manhattan Bank. Principal Canadian banks are the Royal Bank of Canada and Bank of Nova Scotia. The principal Puerto Rican banks are:

**Banco de Ponce.** (President, Roberto de Jesús-Toro); Est. 1917. Balance Sheet at 30 June 1973 showed assets $546,407,215 and deposits, $498,980,773. *Head Office:* Ponce. 26 Branches in Puerto Rico, 9 in New York.

**Banco Credito y Ahorro Ponceño.** (President, Angel M. Rivera.) Est. 1895. Balance Sheet at 31 March 1973 showed deposits $653,119,018; total assets $311,018,729. *Head Office:* Ponce, 50 Branches in Puerto Rico and 1 in New York.

**Commonwealth Government Development Bank.** (President, Mariano Mier Tous.) Est. 1942. Balance Sheet at 30 June 1976 showed total deposits $631,827,227; capital fund and reserves $74,299,731. *Head Office:* San Juan.

**Banco Popular de Puerto Rico.** (President, Rafael Carrión, Jr.) Est. 1893; Balance Sheet at 31 March 1973 showed deposits $801,189,830; reserves $17,552,278; total assets $973,117,011. *Head Office:* Popular Center, Hato Rey, San Juan. 65 Branches in Puerto Rico and 7 in New York.

**Production and Commerce.** The economy of Puerto Rico, traditionally based on agriculture, is now predominantly industrial. In the last two decades a large-scale Government-sponsored industrialization programme has brought to the Island about 1,800 new manufacturing plants, creating more than 130,000 new direct jobs. Incentives to attract new industries include exemption from local taxes for a period ranging from ten to 17 years. In the fiscal year 1971–72 the net income from manufacturing amounted to $1,139 million, while the net income from agriculture was $306·8 million. The principal agricultural products are sugar cane, tobacco, coffee, pineapples, coconuts, bananas, oranges, lemons, limes, avocados and vegetables. The main industries are cane sugar, molasses, rum, cement, cigars, distilled spirits, clothing, footwear, textiles, furniture, electrical equipment, toys, cosmetics and canned products.

| Major Agricultural Products: | 1971–72 |
|---|---|
| Sugar Cane (million short tons) | 4·6 |
| Tobacco (thousand cwt.) | 51 |
| Coffee (thousand cwt.) | 340 |
| Molasses (million gallons) | 35·7 |

| Principal Industrial Products (million $): | 1971–72 |
|---|---|
| Food | 181·3 |
| Clothing | 166·9 |
| Metal | 192·4 |
| Chemicals | 115·4 |
| Tobacco | 41·8 |
| Textiles | 37·5 |
| Wood | 29·1 |

| Mining Production: | 1969–70 |
|---|---|
| Cement (million bbls.) | 9·5 |
| Sand, gravel (million short tons) | 16·8 |
| Stone (million short tons) | 7·4 |

The total value of mineral production was about $68·7 million.

Tourism is becoming a major industry; in the fiscal year 1971–72 over one million tourists spent an estimated $258·9 million in the country.

Net income in the fiscal year 1971–72 was $4,824 million; the per capital income being $1,713.

**Commerce.** For the year 1971–72 the imports and exports were: Imports: $3,707·8 million, 81 per cent from United States. Exports: $1,974·1 million, 88 per cent to United States.

**Communications.** There is no railway in Puerto Rico. Paved roads total about 6,050 miles. There are ten ports, of which the principal are San Juan, Ponce and Mayaguez. Internal and international air service is provided by more than ten local, American and foreign airlines. International airport is located in San Juan.

There are over 335,000 telephones. World-wide cable and radio systems connect Puerto Rico by telephone and cable with the United States, the Western Hemisphere and the rest of the world. There is a communication satellite (COMSAT) station in Cayey.

There are 68 radio stations of which three broadcast in English. There are 14 television stations, of which one broadcasts in English. There are 1·6 million radio sets and 421,011 television sets in use.

### NEWSPAPERS

**El Mundo.** F. 1919. San Juan, morning. daily and Sun., Spanish, independent. Circ. Daily, 114,310. Sun. (commenced 7 June 1970). 128,435.

**El Imparcial.** F. 1933. San Juan, morning, Spanish, independent. Average circulation 95,000.

**El Dia.** F. 1909. Ponce and San Juan, morning, daily except Sun., Spanish, independent. Circ. Mon.–Fri., 103,107, Sat. 98,000.

**The San Juan Star.** F. 1959. San Juan, daily, English, Scripps-Howard. Circ. Mon.–Sat., 56,000; Sun. 51,200.

**Education.** Education is free through pre-college level. In 1971–72 there were 712,581 students in public schools and 84,870 in private schools. For the same period, there were 82,709 students in the six campuses of the University of Puerto Rico and 33,215 in four private universities and one junior college. There were 23,758 teachers. About 33 per cent of the Government's annual budget is devoted to education. Illiteracy rate is 11 per cent. Public education is conducted in Spanish.

**Religion.** There is complete separation of State and Church, Eighty-five per cent of the population are Roman Catholics. the remainder belong to various Protestant denominations.

# Upper Volta

## (RÉPUBLIQUE DE HAUTE-VOLTA)

**Capital**—Ouagadougou.

**President**—Gen. Saugoulé Lamizana.

**National Flag**: A tricolour, fesse-wise black, white and red.

### CONSTITUTION AND GOVERNMENT

UPPER VOLTA, a former territory of the French West African Federation, became independent on 5 August 1960. The presidential constitution, with a single-chamber National Assembly, adopted by referendum on 27 November 1960, was suspended in January 1966 when the Army assumed power after popular demonstrations in Ouagadougou against the regime of the former President Yaméogo Maurice. In December 1966, after the political leaders had failed to agree on a common programme for a return to civil rule, the Army decided that it would retain power for four years. General Saugoulé Lamizana exercises the functions of President of the Republic; he reshaped his mixed civilian and military Government in April 1967. In February 1974, following disagreement among political leaders. President Lamizana suspended the constitution, dissolved the National Assembly, and set up a government of National Renewal. Upper Volta is a member of the 'Counseil de l'Entente'; in 1976, a Government Commission recommended the re-emergence of political parties, and a return to civilian rule, the 'Organisation Commune Africaine et Malagache' (OCAM) the OAU; the UN; the CEAO and ECOWAS.

### AREA AND POPULATION

The total area of the country is 274,122 sq. km.

The mid-1974 population was 5,760,000. The annual average percentage growth rate of the population for the period 1960–74 was 2·0 and for the period 1965–74 was 1·9. The population of the capital is 105,000.

### CURRENCY AND FINANCE

Unit of currency, the West African franc.
The budget for 1975 was: fr. CFA 15,064,000,000.

The GNP at market prices for 1974 was U.S. $ millions 520, and the GNP per capita at market prices was U.S. $90. The annual average percentage growth rate of the GNP per capita for the period 1960–74 was —0·1, and for the period 1965–74 was —0·5. [*See the note at the beginning of this section concerning GNP.*]

### PRODUCTION, INDUSTRY AND COMMERCE

Industry is still very much in its infancy and almost 95 per cent of the population is engaged in agriculture and animal husbandry. The three important cash crops are groundnuts, cotton and sesame; the main subsistence crops are sorghum, millet, maize, and rice. There are two and a half million head of cattle, and three and a half million sheep and goats. Exports of agricultural products and livestock normally form over half the total exports, but severe droughts in recent years have greatly reduced production.

The following table shows the output, for varying periods, of some agricultural crops in metric tonnes:

| *Commodity* | *metric tonnes* | *period* |
|---|---|---|
| Millet and Sorghum | 733,900 | Estimated for 1972–1973 |
| Rice | 31,800 | Estimated for 1972–1973 |
| Ground nuts | 62,900 | Estimated for 1972–1973 |
| Cotton seeds | 26,670 | Estimated for 1973–1974 |

*continued*

| *Commodity* | *metric tonnes* | *period* |
|---|---|---|
| Cotton seeds | 11,328 | 1st quarter of 1975 |
| Cotton fibre | 10,973 | 1st quarter of 1975 |
| Karité nuts | 4,875 | Estimated for 1972–1973 |
| Sesame | 5,300 | Estimated for 1972–1973 |
| Sugar cane | 62,000 | Estimated for 1974–1975 |

The following table shows the estimated numbers of animals of various kinds in 1974:

| *Kind* | *Head* |
|---|---|
| Cattle | 2,235,000 |
| Sheep and goats | 4,775,000 |
| Asses | 200,000 |
| Horses | 70,000 |
| Camels | 5,000 |
| Pigs | 150,000 |
| Poultry | 10,000,000 |

In 1973, the value of Upper Volta's imports from France was 8,493 million fr. CFA. In the same year, value of exports to France was 2,063 million fr. CFA. Imports from the Ivory Coast for 1972 were valued at 3,060 million fr. CFA, exports to the Ivory Coast at 2,458 million fr. CFA. Exports to Ghana were valued at 281 million fr. CFA. Total exports were valued at 5,141 millions fr. CFA, imports were valued at 15,312 millions fr. CFA.

The value of the main imports from France in 1973 in millions FF are shown below:

| *Commodity* | 1973 |
|---|---|
| Sugar | 8,067 |
| Pharmaceuticals | 8,446 |
| Tyres | 11,423 |
| Vehicles | 9,936 |
| Iron and Steel products | 19,975 |
| Machinery | 29,539 |

Manganese ore was discovered at Tambao in the north-east of the country. This deposit consists of an estimated 13 million metric tonnes of commercially useable ore. In addition, a chalk deposit of about 66 million metric tonnes was discovered at Tin Hrassan in 1965.

### COMMUNICATIONS

There are about 17,000 km. of roads, of which about 9,000 are all-weather. In 1973 there were 15,368 motor vehicles of all sorts in Upper Volta. 517 km. of the Abidjan–Ouagadougou railway are in Upper Volta. In 1972 the railway carried 2,595,512 passengers and 872,070 tons of freight. There are two airports, one at Onagadougou, and one at Bobo-Dioulasso.

### EDUCATION

In 1975 there were 700 primary schools with approximately 131,000 children, and 25 secondary schools with 10,400 pupils. In addition there are three training colleges with 338 pupils between them, and one University with 345 students.

# Uruguay

## (REPÚBLICA ORIENTAL DEL URUGUAY)

**Capital**—Montevideo.

**President**—Dr. Aparicio Méndez.

**National Flag:** Parti of g fesse-wise, alternately white and light blue; a canton white bearing a golden sun in splendour with sixteen rays.

### CONSTITUTION AND GOVERNMENT

URUGUAY became independent of Spanish rule on 25 May 1810, but was later invaded by Brazil. The inhabitants revolted against the Brazilians in 1825 and on 25 August declared their independence of all foreign powers, including Argentina, which was at war with Brazil over the possession of Uruguay. This war was finally settled by the mediation of the United Kingdom, and Uruguay was declared an Independent State in 1828. The first Constitution was adopted in 1830.

From 1 March 1952 to 28 February 1967 a collegiate system of government was in force. The powers formerly wielded by the President were transferred to a National Council of Government of nine members, six from the majority and three from the minority party.

As a result, however, of a referendum held in conjunction with the elections in November 1966, Presidential rule was restored. The Colorado Party won a majority in both Houses of Parliament and General Oscar Gestido was elected President. The new administration took office on 1 March 1967.

Under the present Constitution, the Executive Power is discharged by the President of the Republic acting with the appropriate Minister or Ministers or the full Council of Ministers (whom he appoints and has power to dismiss). The Constitution provides that there shall be 11 Ministries. The Legislature (General Assembly) consists of two houses: the Senate of 30 members and the House of Representatives of 99 members. The President, Vice-President and members of both Houses are elected together for a five-year term.

Since February 1973 the country has been governed by presidential rule with military support.

In September 1976 a new Government took over.

**Council of Ministers**

*President:* Dr. Aparicio Méndez.
*Minister of the Interior:* Gral. Hugo Linares Brum.
*Minister of Foreign Affairs:* Sr. Alejandro Reueira.
*Minister of Economy and Finance:* Cr. Valentin Arismendi.
*Minister of National Defence:* Dr. Walter Ravenna.
*Minister of Transport and Public Works:* Ing. Eduardo Sampson.
*Minister of Public Health:* Dr. Antonio Cañellas.
*Minister of Agriculture and Fishing:* Dr. Estanislao Valdés Otero.
*Minister of Justice:* Dr. Fernando Bayardo Bengoa.
*Minister of Industry and Energy:* Ing. Quim Luis Meyer.
*Minister of Education and Culture:* Dr. Daniel Darracq.
*Minister of Labour and Social Security:* Dr. José E. Etcheverry Stirling.
*Secretariat of Planning, Coordination and Decentralisation:* Brig. José D. Cardozo.

**Parliament.** Parliament was dissolved by Presidential decree on 27 June 1973.

### LEGAL SYSTEM

There is a Supreme Court of five judges elected by Parliament. It is the final court of appeal from the judgments of the three Appeal Courts, and has original jurisdiction in constitutional, international and admiralty cases. There are Civil, Commercial and Criminal Courts of First Instance in Montevideo, and a Departmental Court in each of the departments. Minor cases are heard by Justices of the Peace.

### AREA AND POPULATION

Uruguay covers an area of 72,172 sq. miles. Estimated population at mid-1974 was 2,754,000.

The annual average percentage growth rate of the population for the period 1960–74 was 0·5 and for the period 1965–74 was 0·4. The following table shows the area of each department and the population as estimated in the 1975 census.

| *Department (capital in brackets)* | *Area (in sq miles)* | *Population* |
|---|---|---|
| Artigas (Artigas) | 4,394 | 57,528 |
| Canelones (Canelones) | 1,834 | 313,858 |
| Cerro Largo (Melo) | 5,763 | 73,204 |
| Colonia (Colonia) | 2,193 | 110,820 |
| Durazno (Durazno) | 5,525 | 54.990 |
| Flores (Trinidad) | 1,744 | 24,684 |
| Florida (Florida) | 4,673 | 66,092 |
| Lavalleja (Minas) | 4,819 | 65,240 |
| Maldonado (Maldonado) | 1,587 | 75,607 |
| Montevideo (Montevideo City) | 256 | 1,229,748 |
| Paysandú (Paysandú) | 5,115 | 98,735 |
| Rio Negro (Fray Bentos) | 3,269 | 49,816 |
| Rivera (Rivera) | 3,793 | 79,330 |
| Rocha (Rocha) | 4,280 | 59,952 |
| Salto (Salto) | 4,865 | 100,407 |
| San José (San José) | 2,688 | 88,281 |
| Soriano (Mercedes) | 3,461 | 80,114 |
| Tacuarembó (Tacuarembó) | 8,122 | 84,829 |
| Treinta y Tres (Treinta y Tres) | 3,682 | 45,680 |

The chief towns with present estimated population are: Montevideo, 1,229,748; Salto, 57,958; Paysandú, 52,472; Las Piedras, 41,509; Rivera, 41,263.

### CURRENCY

The unit of currency is the Nuevo Peso (1,000 old pesos) of 100 centésimos. The actual circulation medium consists of paper notes issued by the Central Bank in denominations of 50, 100, 500, 1,000, 5,000 and 10,000 old pesos. (Some notes have been re-stamped N$5 and N$10). New notes in Nuevo Peso denominations will be in circulation by 1976. There are bronze and aluminium coins of 50, 20 and 10 old pesos.

In December 1964, the gold content of the peso was fixed at 0·059245 grammes of pure gold. The import rate of exchange at 21 June 1977 was UrN$8·04 per £1. Import surcharges of 10 to 225 per cent of the CIF value of goods are levied on some imports. The peso proceeds of some export exchange earnings are subject to retentions. After years of severe restrictions and periodical bans on imports, measures adopted in April–June 1975 have liberalised the import regime, eliminating import quotas and establishing a system of prior deposits of 35 per cent value of goods (sole exceptions are capital goods, imports under temporary admission, imports without exchange transactions and a restricted list of products related to the chemical and agricultural fields).

Notes in circulation at 31 December 1974, amounted to Ur$397,700 million (Ur$397,700,000).

### FINANCE

Revenue and expenditure for the years 1975–76 were as follows (in thousands of millions of Uruguayan pesos:

| | 1975 | 1976 |
|---|---|---|
| Revenue | 985·5 | 1,719·6 |
| Expenditure | 1,348·8 | 2,031·4 |

* Estimated.

The GNP at market prices for 1974 was U.S. $ millions 3,290, and the GNP per capita at market prices was U.S. $1,190. The annual average percentage growth rate of the GNP per capita for the period 1960–74 was 0·5, and for the period 1965–74 was 0·8. [*See the note at the beginning of this section concerning GNP.*]

### PRINCIPAL BANKS

**Banco de la República Oriental del Uruguay.** (President, Ing. Jorge Seré del Campo.) Est. 1896; All the share capital is owned by the State; Balance Sheet at 31 December 1971 showed assets Ur.$608,990,808,553; deposits and current accounts Ur.$240,607,845,120. *Head Office:* Calles Cerrito, Zabala, Solís y Piedras, Montevideo. 72 Branches and 6 Agencies.

## URUGUAY

**Banco Central de Uruguay.** (President, Carlos Ricci.) Est. 1 March 1967.

**Banco Comercial.** (General Managers, Mr. Yamandú D'Elia, Mr. H. Porteiro.) Est. 1857. Balance Sheet at 30 September 1976 showed assets N$399,812,198·21, deposits and current accounts N$323,237,335·20. *Head Office:* Cerrito 400, Montevideo. 19 Branches, 22 Agencies.

**Banco de Crédito.** *Head Office:* 18 de Julio y Médanos.

**Banco La Caja Obrera.** *Head Office:* 25 de Mayo y Treinta y Tres.

**Banco de Montevideo.** (President, Dr. Bernado Supervielle; General Manager, Carlos Langwagen). Est. 1941. Assets as at 30 June 1974. Ur. $42,636,531,340; deposits and liabilities, Ur. $41,404,175,409. *Head Office:* Ricón esq. Misiones, Montevideo, Uruguay. 3 Branches.

A number of foreign banks have branches in Montevideo, including the Bank of London and South America (Zabala 1500).

### PRODUCTION, INDUSTRY AND COMMERCE

**Agriculture.** Of the total area of the country, only 9 per cent is used for crop farming. About 60 per cent is suitable for grazing, and the wealth of the country chiefly comes from the stock-raising industry, particularly cattle and sheep. The greatest source of income at present is wool. According to the latest livestock census (1970) the livestock population of Uruguay consists basically of about 8·5 million cattle, 19·8 million sheep, 420,972 horses, and 400,000 pigs. However, in 1973 the number of cattle rose to 11 million. The poultry population is on the increase and is estimated to be in the region of six million.

Meat is the most important export. The incidence of meat exports to total exports for 1975 was 17·8 per cent.

The following table shows the value (in thousands of $ U.S.) of the exports of meat for the years 1974, 1975 and 1976.

| | 1974 | 1975 | 1976 |
|---|---|---|---|
| Total meat and by-products | 134,837 | 68,400 | 115,100 |

Exports of textiles in 1975 accounted for 27·9 per cent of the total for the year.

The 1975 wool clip was estimated at 55·3 thousand tons.

The harvests of principal crops in metric tons are shown in the following table for the years 1975 and 1976:

| Crop | 1975 | 1976 |
|---|---|---|
| | *(metric tons)* | |
| Wheat | 526,500 | 455,700 |
| Maize | 157,100 | 210,000 |
| Rice | 188,500 | 216,500 |
| Oats | 46,600 | 69,600 |

**Mining.** All minerals belong to the nation. Silver, copper, lead, manganese, gold, iron and lignite are found, but are not worked to any great extent as they are not found in sufficient quantity to make their production commercially practicable. Marble and granite are quarried.

**Industry.** Since World War II there has been a rapid growth of secondary industry. Estimates for 1960 showed gross industrial production at Ur.$5,798 million with 216,682 workers and employees. The edible foodstuffs industry is now the largest industry having supplanted both the textile and construction industries which previously had been the main source of employment in the country. Production of foodstuffs for local consumption and for limited exports is valued at Ur.$1,183 million with 24,201 workers and employees. The local textile industry, although having lost its preeminent position in the economy, nevertheless supplies the home market almost entirely and exchange surcharges on imported textiles continue to offer it adequate protection against foreign competition.

Industrial production also includes tyres, paper, plastics, cement, chemicals, paints, sugar, radio, glass and an ever-increasing variety of consumer goods. The metallurgical industry has also increased considerably in importance.

**Commerce.** Uruguay exports consist mainly of meat, wool, hides, skins, wheat and vegetable oils. She imports manufactured goods, fuel and raw materials for her secondary industries. Breeding of cattle and sheep forms the economic backbone of the country.

The following table shows the principal imports (in thousands of U.S. $) for 1975:

| *Commodity* | 1975 |
|---|---|
| Animal and Vegetable products | 37·3 |
| Foodstuff | 11·2 |
| Mineral products | 196·6 |
| Crude petroleum | 164·0 |
| Chemicals | 74·0 |
| Plastic, rubber, etc. | 25·5 |
| Metal and metal goods | 45·7 |
| Electrical machinery | 64·9 |
| Transport | 43·8 |

The principal exports (in thousand $ U.S.) are shown in the following table for 1975:

| *Commodity* | 1975 |
|---|---|
| Animals and byproducts | 97·2 |
| Vegetable products | 55·7 |
| Rice | 32·8 |
| Hides and leather goods | 52·8 |
| Textile goods | 105·2 |
| Shoes, etc. | 8·9 |
| Various non-specific industries | 64·0 |

The following tables show the value (in thousand $ U.S.) of imports and exports by principal countries for 1975 and 1976

| *Imports* | 1975[1] | 1976[2] |
|---|---|---|
| LAFTA | 160·4 | 209·9 |
| Argentina | 47·3 | 65·5 |
| Brazil | 71·9 | 90·3 |
| USA and Canada | 69·2 | 57·5 |
| Rest of America | 4·1 | 9·8 |
| EEC | 112·6 | 96·1 |
| Federal Germany | 47·1 | 40·9 |
| France | 9·8 | 9·7 |
| Holland | 8·7 | 6·4 |
| Italy | 15·2 | 11·4 |
| Belgium and Luxemburg | 8·1 | 5·4 |
| United Kingdom | 22·0 | 21·0 |
| EFTA | 18·9 | 19·1 |
| Rest of Western Europe | 10·4 | 8·0 |
| European Socialist countries | 8·3 | 10·2 |
| Middle East | 119·7 | 118·0 |
| Rest of world | 52·9 | 69·5 |
| Nigeria | 17·1 | 43·7 |

[1] Adjusted [2] Estimated

| *Exports* | 1975[1] | 1976[2] |
|---|---|---|
| LAFTA | 121·1 | 125·7 |
| Argentina | 29·6 | 25·1 |
| Brazil | 65·5 | 67·5 |
| USA and Canada | 27·2 | 63·0 |
| Rest of America | 0·3 | 4·9 |
| EEC | 130·5 | 188·8 |

*continued*

| *Exports* | 1975[1] | 1976[2] |
|---|---|---|
| Federal Germany | 46·1 | 66·9 |
| France | 10·3 | 20·6 |
| Holland | 27·8 | 40·8 |
| Italy | 19·4 | 29·5 |
| Belgium and Luxemburg | 7·7 | 8·7 |
| United Kingdom | 18·1 | 21·0 |
| EFTA | 10·6 | 21·7 |
| Rest of Western Europe | 27·6 | 23·1 |
| Spain | 11·8 | 23·1 |
| European Socialist countries | 28·9 | 17·8 |
| Middle East | 28·6 | 38·6 |
| Rest of world | 18·0 | 32·7 |

[1] Adjusted [2] Estimated

## COMMUNICATIONS

**Roads, Railways and Shipping.** There are over 4,000 miles of roads including a section of the Pan American Highway from Montevideo westwards to Colonia.

The total railway system open for traffic consists of about 3,000 km. of standard gauge. The railways all converge upon Montevideo, and were bought by the State from the original British Companies in 1948. There are 806 miles of navigable rivers and inland waterways.

Montevideo is the chief port, and there were, in 1974, eight merchant vessels and four tankers under the Uruguayan flag with a gross tonnage of 103,336. In 1974, 759 vessels cleared the port of which 56 were British.

**Civil Aviation.** PLUNA (Primeras Lineas Uruguayas de Navigación Aerea) flies five services to Buenos Aires, and two to Paraguay.

The principal capitals of the interior and a limited freight service are connected to Montevideo by TAMO another State owned airline, using principally military aircraft and personnel.

International air services to countries outside Latin America are run by Pan-American Airways, Air France, K.L.M.—Royal Dutch Airlines, Alitalia and S.A.S. (Scandinavian Airlines System), Lufthansa, Iberia, Lan Chile and Varigo.

**Telephones and Broadcasting.** There are about 4,455 miles of telegraph lines in operation. The Montevideo telephone system is controlled by the State, but the internal system is chiefly operated by a number of private companies.

There are 60 medium-wave and 10 short-wave broadcasting stations. These are owned and operated by com mercial broadcasting undertakings, except for three long-wave and four short-wave official State stations. The number of radio sets is estimated at 900,000. There are four television stations in Montevideo and ten small country stations. The number of receivers is estimated at 200,000.

## NEWSPAPERS

**Mundo Color.** F. 1976. Evening. Cuareim 1283, Montevideo.

**El Día.** F. 1886. Morning. Colorado Batllista (List 14). 18 de Julio 1297, Montevideo.

**El Diario.** F. 1922. Evening. Colorado Independiente. Bartolome Mitre 1275, Montevideo.

**La Mañana.** F. 1917. Morning. Colorado. Bartolome Mitre 1275, Montevideo.

**El País.** F. 1918. Morning. Blanco Cuareim 1287, Montevideo.

**El Diario Español.** F. 1905. Morning. Spanish community Cerrito 551. Montevideo.

## EDUCATION AND RELIGION

Primary education is free and compulsory for all children. Apart from private schools there were, in 1973, about 322,000 pupils in 2,362 state schools.

There is no state religion and all sects have complete liberty of worship. The majority of the inhabitants are Roman Catholic.

# Vatican City

## (STATO DELLA CITTÀ DEL VATICANO)

**Sovereign**—Pope Paul VI.

**National Flag:** Divided pale-wise yellow and white, the white bearing the crossed keys of St. Peter and a triple crown in silver and gold.

THE State of the City of the Vatican is the territory of the temporal sovereignty of the Holy See, the residence of the Pope, Bishop of Rome, Vicar of Jesus Christ, Supreme Pontiff of the Universal Church. The Papacy is the oldest monarchy in Europe but Vatican City is an entirely new State. It was established by the Lateran Treaty of 11 February 1929, signed in the Palace of the Lateran in Rome by Cardinal Pietro Gasparri, Papal Secretary of State, on behalf of Pope Pius XI, and by Benito Mussolini, Prime Minister of Italy, on behalf of King Victor Emmanuel III. Ratifications were exchanged on 7 June of the same year and all the treaty's provisions thereupon came into force.

No country outside Italy was involved in the treaty negotiations. Four days before the signing, however, the diplomatic corps accredited to the Holy See were invited to the Vatican and informed by Cardinal Gasparri that a treaty had been arranged, and on 9 March they went to the Vatican again to offer the Pope their congratulations. Great Britain was among the first States to recognize the Pope as a Sovereign of Vatican City.

Vatican City is an integral part of the Holy See but in some respects it is a distinct entity; and as a sovereign State it has some unique features. It deals with other States only in regard to its own internal affairs: with Italy for postal, travel, trade and economic facilities, and with other States for postal and economic matters. It has no parliament and no diplomatic corps of its own. The sovereignty of the Papal State belongs to the Holy See. All Papal envoys, both those with and those without diplomatic status, represent the Holy See; they are the representatives of the Pope as Supreme Pontiff of the Universal Church. All diplomatic missions 'at the Vatican'—there are 83 embassies and four legations—are in fact accredited to the Holy See. By virtue of the treaty the foreign envoys reside in Rome outside Vatican City, with all the normal diplomatic rights guaranteed to them even if their countries have no diplomatic relations with Italy. During the Second World War the envoys of the Allied nations were accommodated as the guests of the Pope in buildings on Vatican soil; but they have the right at any time, in peace or war, to travel across Italian territory to their own countries and back to Vatican City, just as the Holy See's diplomatic envoys and couriers of any nationality, as well as Church dignitaries, have the right to go to and from the City.

All the foreign envoys require for this is an endorsement on their passport by a Papal representative in their country of origin: this representative (as in the cases of the Apostolic Delegates in London and Washington) need not possess diplomatic status.

In the Lateran Treaty the Holy See declared that 'it wishes to remain and will remain extraneous to the temporal competitions between other States and to international congresses convened for such a purpose, unless the parties in the conflict unanimously appeal to its mission of peace'. The Holy See with Vatican City is thus a perpetual neutral, the Holy See, however, reserving 'the right in any case to the exercise of its moral and spiritual power', a right which enables the Pope in wartime to continue to speak freely and take whatever action he deems right and necessary to hasten the return of peace or to mitigate the severities of the conflict.

The Lateran Treaty, in spite of its importance, was regarded by Pope Pius XI as secondary, in regard to the religious welfare of Italy, to the Lateran Concordat which was negotiated and signed at the same time. The concordat, in the words of the Pope, 'gave Italy back to God and God back to Italy': its purpose was 'to regulate the status of Religion and of the Church in Italy'. In its chief provisions Italy recognized the Catholic faith as the religion of the State and guaranteed its free exercise, recognized the secrecy of sacramental confession, restored Catholic teaching in the State schools and recognized marriage as a sacrament and indissoluble. One of the principal concessions to Italy was the right to object to—but solely on political grounds—the appointments of bishops who were to govern dioceses in Italy, except the diocese of Rome and the dioceses of the six Cardinal Bishops, which are in the vicinity of Rome.

Vatican City covers an area of 108·3 acres. In the main it consists of the Vatican Palace and gardens, St. Peter's Basilica (the largest church in the world), a number of other separate churches and numerous other buildings housing, for example, the Vatican Polyglot Press, Vatican Radio, quarters of the Swiss Guard and other forces of the Holy See, and residences for members of the City's administration and of employees of the Holy See.

The Vatican Palace has been the constant residence of the Popes since 1870, when Pius IX, after the capture of Rome by the Piedmontese, was obliged to flee from the Quirinal Palace, which then became the residence of the King of Italy, and later, on the fall of the Italian monarchy, of the President of Italy. In the Vatican the Pope accommodates himself in a small apartment on an upper floor overlooking St. Peter's Square: it is composed of a study from which he directs the Universal Church, a private library, a small oratory where he celebrates his daily Mass, and a simply furnished bedroom.

The rest of the Palace, stately but not luxurious, might well be the envy of every other monarch and State, for it contains what in one respect at least is the world's greatest library, with its collection of 70,000 manuscripts, most of them irreplaceable, and every one open for study to recognized students of any religious faith or none, together with 770,000 printed books and 7,500 incunabula. Most of these works have also been microfilmed. In its buildings, sculptures and pictures, the Palace holds the greatest masterpieces of Michaelangelo, Raphael and many others of the world's most celebrated artists. The works of Michaelangelo are to be seen principally in the Sistine Chapel, where, normally, the Popes are elected by the Sacred College of Cardinals (The Lateran Treaty makes it clear that Papal elections may be held outside the Vatican.) An Audience Chamber, designed by Luigi Nervi and situated near St. Peter's Basilica, was opened in June 1971; it has a seating capacity of 6,300.

Vatican City, which had no more than 903 inhabitants in 1968 (520 with the status and title of Vatican citizens), originated in a territorial sense with the grants of lands to the Pope after the Peace of Constantine in the fourth century, and developed to the point where the Popes, through governors, ruled over territory—the States of the Church—covering more than 16,000 square miles with a total population of 3,000,000. Effective sovereignty over these possessions, after a series of seizures, finally came to an end in 1870, when the forces of King Victor Emmanuel entered Rome itself.

The seizure of the Eternal City, the City of the Popes, was the source of what became known as the Roman Question—the dispute between the Holy See and the Kingdom of Italy. Italy, while proclaiming certain immunities for the Pope, officially regarded him as an Italian citizen. Pius IX, the Pope reigning in 1870, refused to accept this position and, unwilling to place himself in the appearance of subjection by stepping upon the territory seized from him, became the 'Prisoner of the Vatican'. His successors, Leo XIII, St. Pius X, Benedict XV and Pius XI, each on his election made a formal official protest at their position and declined to appear in public outside St. Peter's. Italy made an ill-fated unilateral attempt to settle the dispute by enacting in 1871 the Law of Guarantees. This acknowledged the Pope's person as sacred and inviolable, offered him royal honours and protection, provided for extra-territorial rights for the Vatican and other Papal buildings, and set aside a yearly sum of 3,500,000 lire for the Pope. All this was refused, the Popes maintaining that their sovereignty depended upon divine right and not upon a civil concession.

In 1929, after negotiations between the Italian Government and the Holy See, the Lateran Treaty was signed.

The Lateran Treaty declared that the Law of Guarantees was abolished and the Roman Question settled permanently. The Treaty gave visible, tangible, territorial witness to the fact of the temporal sovereignty of the Pope and his independence of any state.

St. Peter's Square is part of the Papal State but the Holy See agreed that it shall normally be open to the public and policed by Italian police. The powers of these police cease at the foot of the steps leading to St. Peter's, and they must not mount them or enter the basilica unless invited to do so by the Vatican authorities. When special ceremonies are to be held in the square, they must, unless invited to remain, withdraw beyond the frontier—the line continuing from the outer side of the two arms of Bernini's colonnade which, as it were, embrace the piazza. Outstanding Papal ceremonies here since the treaty include the Coronation of Pope Paul VI (1963) and the closing ceremony of the Second Vatican Council (1965), the proclamation in 1950 of the dogma of the bodily assumption of the Mother of God, and the canonization of Pope Pius X in 1954.

In other articles, Italy agreed to assure the Vatican City of an adequate supply of water, to link the State railways with the Vatican railway, and to provide for the connection of the Papal State directly with other States by the telegraphic, telephonic, radio-telegraphic and postal services of Vatican City. Provision was also made for the circulation in Italy of land vehicles and aircraft belonging to Vatican City. Other aircraft are not allowed to fly over the City.

Italy undertook not to allow on land adjoining the Papal State the construction of buildings that would overlook Vatican City, and to demolish some that were already there.

Regarding the person of the Sovereign Pontiff as sacred and inviolable, Italy declared that attempts against his life and incitement to commit such attempts would be punishable by the same penalties as those prescribed for attempts against the person of the King of Italy.

The head of the Administration of Vatican City under Pope Pius XI was a layman, the Marquis Camillo Serafini. He continued in office under Pope Pius XII, but the Pope instituted a commission of five Cardinals, with an ecclesiastic as secretary and a layman with the title of special delegate. The Governor, hitherto subject only to the Pope, now came under the authority of this commission. Since the death of the Marquis Serafini in 1952, the office of Governor has been retained but has remained vacant. A Consultative Council of 30 appointed members (all lay persons with a lay President) was established in March 1968. There are four main Departments, all under the direction of laymen—one for the Vatican Art Galleries and Museum, another for technical services, the third for economic services, and the fourth for the health services. The commission has authority over Vatican Radio (situated at the top of the Vatican gardens) and the Vatican Observatory (at Castelgandolfo). Vatican Radio's Director at present is an Italian Jesuit. The Observatory's Director is the Rev. Patrick Treanor, S.J.

Vatican City has four law courts, for both civil and ecclesiastical cases: almost all the members of these are members of the Holy See's courts.

The law of the Papal State is (1) The Constitution; (2) Code of Civil Procedure of Vatican City State; (3) Canon law; (4) Laws enacted by the City's Administration. The Official bulletin is published as a supplement to the *Acta Apostolicae Sedis*, the Holy See's official bulletin. The *Osservatore Romano* is the official newspaper in so far as it publishes officially issued statements.

Vatican City has its own flag (yellow and white), coat-of-arms and seal. Each of these bears the crossed keys of St. Peter and the Papal triple crown. The seal bears the words 'Stato della Città del Vaticano'. It has its own passports, coinage and postage stamps. It has its own general stores. The motor registration letters are SCV (the Pope's car having SCV1). Vatican Radio's call sign is HVJ: its broadcasts always begin with the words 'Laudetur Jesus Christus' (Praised be Jesus Christ).

Vatican citizenship is normally granted by reason of employment by the Holy See. A citizen who ceases to be subject to the Holy See's sovereignty—a Swiss Guard, for example, at the end of his service—loses his citizenship. In such cases the Lateran Treaty provides that Italy shall then regard them as Italian citizens unless they possess citizenship of another country. Catholics are not subjects of the Pope as Sovereign of the State of Vatican City.

By virtue of the Lateran Treaty a number of buildings outside the Papal State are recognized as the property of the Holy See and have extra-territorial rights. The chief of these are the Basilica and Palace of the Lateran (the palace was the residence of the Popes for 1,000 years from the beginning of the fourth century: the original palace was the gift of the Emperor Constantine); the Basilica of St. Mary Major, the Basilica of St. Paul Outside-the-Walls, the Pope's summer residence at Castelgandolfo in the Alban Hills, and buildings which house offices of the Roman Curia, whose members—Cardinals, bishops, priests and some laymen—are the closest collaborators of the Pope in the government and administration of the Universal Church. Extra-territorial rights are enjoyed by any church in any part of Italy if and when the Pope is present at religious ceremonies taking place in them.

The Lateran Treaty was accompanied by a financial agreement. Italy agreed to pay the Holy See a sum computed at £8½ million and deliver Italian State bonds to the nominal value of £11 million.

For the spiritual and religious administration of Vatican City the Pope has a vicar-general (distinct from the Cardinal Vicar of Rome). He is always a member of the Augustinian Order (at present Bishop van Lierde, a Dutchman) and always bears the title of Bishop of Porfireone (a titular see without territory); he is also the Papal Sacristan, one of whose duties is to administer the Last Sacraments to a dying Pope. St. Peter's Basilica is outside his care, but his care does extend to other Papal properties which are outside Vatican City, principally the Papal residence at Castelgandolfo.

St. Peter's is not the Pope's cathedral. The title belongs to the Archbasilica of St. John Lateran, on the other side of Rome: it is this church of which a new Pope 'takes possession' soon after his election as Bishop of Rome. St. Peter's is not even the parish church of Vatican City: this title belongs to the very much smaller Church of St. Anne.

*Secretary of State:* His Eminence Jean Cardinal Villot. Appointed 2 May 1969.

### NEWSPAPER

**L'Osservatore Romano.** F. 1861. Italian. Daily. Semi-official organ of the Holy See. Religious matters and general news. Its editorial board and staff of about 20 reporters are directed by Raimondo Manzini. Weekly editions are published in French, English, Portuguese, German, and Spanish.

The official printing plant of Vatican City is the *Vatican Polyglot Press*, which has facilities for printing a great variety of material in about 30 languages.

### OTHER PUBLICATIONS

**Acta Apostolicae Sedis:** F. 1908. The only 'official commentary' of the Holy See, for the publication of its activities and the laws, decrees, and acts of congregations and tribunals of the Roman Curia.

**Annuario Pontificio:** The Yearbook of the Holy See, edited by the Vatican Secretariat of State and printed in Italian, with some portions in other languages. It covers the worldwide organization of the Church, lists members of the hierarchy, and includes a wide range of statistical information.

**L'Attività della Santa Sede:** Annual volume chronicling the activities of the Pope and of the various departments of the Holy See.

**L'Osservatore della Domenica:** Weekly Italian magazine.

### BROADCASTING

Radio-Vatican, designed by Guglielmo Marconi, the inventor of radio, was founded in 1931 and was supervised by Marconi until his death. One of the most powerful stations in Europe, it operates on international frequencies for 20 hours every day, including Sundays, in any of 32 languages. More than half its programmes are beamed to Iron Curtain countries. Its staff of 260 broadcasters and technicians is directed by Father Roberto Tucci, S.J.

# Venezuela

**Capital**—Caracas.

**Constitutional President**—Dr. Carlos Andrés Pérez.

**National Flag**: A tricolour fesse-wise, yellow, blue, red; on the blue stripe seven white stars five-pointed centred forming an arc.

## CONSTITUTION AND GOVERNMENT

VENEZUELA was discovered by Christopher Columbus on his third voyage to the New World in 1498. In the following year, Alonzo de Ojeda led an expedition along the coast, but no attempt at settlement was made until 1520. Caracas was founded in 1567, and ten years later became the capital of the colony. In 1718 the Vice-Royalty of New Granada was created to include what is now Venezuela, together with Colombia and Ecuador. The Province of Venezuela was made a separate Captaincy-General in 1777, with boundaries roughly approximating to those of the present Republic. In 1810, on the occupation of the Iberian Peninsula by Napoleon Bonaparte, who placed his brother Joseph on the throne of Spain, a revolt broke out in Venezuela, and a provisional government was formed. The leading spirit in the battle for independence was General Francisco de Miranda, the 'Precursor' as he is now called. It was, however, only after a long and desperate war that independence was finally won, under the leadership of Simón Bolívar. During the period 1821–1830, Venezuela constituted, together with the present Republics of Colombia and Ecuador, under the Presidency of Bolívar, one Republic under the name of the Republic of Colombia. In 1830 Venezuela withdrew from the Confederation and formed a separate Republic.

The country has since had various Constitutions. The one now in force was adopted on 23 January 1961. It provides for a presidential form of government, with a bicameral legislature, which has a term of five years.

Since independence Venezuela has had only intermittent periods of liberal government. However, the last dictator, Marcos Pérez Jiménez, was overthrown in January 1958, and in free elections held on 7 December 1958, the Acción Democrática Party (A.D.) secured a majority, followed in order by the Unión Republicana Democrática (U.R.D.), the Christian Socialist Party, Copei, and the Venezuelan Communist Party (P.C.V.). Sr. Rómulo Betancourt of A.D. was elected President of Venezuela. An initial coalition of the first three parties was formed but in November 1960 the U.R.D. left the Government. A.D. subsequently suffered two internal divisions: in 1960 the extreme left, Castroist wing of A.D., broke away and formed the Movimiento de Izquierda Revolucionaria (M.I.R.), and in 1961 a further section left the party and moved into opposition, with the current name of Partido Revolucionaria Nacionalista (P.R.N.). The years 1959–60 witnessed several unsuccessful attempts to restore military rule through a *coup d'état*; and from 1961 Sr. Betancourt's government was faced with a campaign of terrorism mounted by the P.C.V. and M.I.R. As a consequence, the political activities of the P.C.V. and the M.I.R. were suspended in August 1962. In September/October 1963, terrorism was made a crime of military subversion, and the leading members of the two extremist parties, including their congressional representatives, were arrested.

Nevertheless, Sr. Betancourt's Government survived its term, and in free national elections on 1 December 1963, A.D. retained a much reduced majority, followed in order by Copei, U.R.D. and independents. The P.C.V. and M.I.R. were not permitted to participate. Dr. Raúl Leoni of A.D. was elected as the new President of Venezuela and his Government was inaugurated on 11 March 1964. The formation of a coalition made up of A.D., U.R.D. and the Frente Nacional Democratico was announced in November 1964. On 15 March 1966, the Frente Nacional Democrático party withdrew from the coalition. The M.I.R. and P.R.N. parties were formally integrated on 17 December 1965. The new party is called Partido Revolucionario de Izquierda Nacionalista (P.R.I.N.).

In the elections of 1968 Dr. Rafael Caldera was elected by a narrow margin of votes over Dr. Gonzalo Barrios.

### Ministry

*President:* Sr. Carlos Andrés Pérez.
*Minister of State, Secretary General of the Presidency:* Dr. Carmelo Lauría Lesseur.
*Ministry of Internal Affairs:* Dr. Octavio Lepage.
*Ministry of Foreign Affairs:* Dr. Simón A. Consalvi.
*Ministry of Justice:* Dr. Juan Martín Echeverría.
*Ministry of the Environment:* Ing. José Arnoldo Gabaldón.
*Chancellor of the Exchequer:* Dr. Luis José Silva Luongo.
*Ministry of Development:* Dr. Luis Alvarez Domínguez.
*Ministry of Labour:* Dr. José Manzo González.
*Ministry of Energy and Mines:* Dr. Valentín Hernández.
*Ministry of Agriculture and Livestock:* Dr. Manuel Pinto Cohen.
*Ministry of Transport and Communications:* Dr. Jesús E. Vivas Casanova.
*Ministry of Education:* Dr. Carlos Rafael Silva.
*Ministry of Health and Social Security:* Dr. Antonio Parra León.
*Ministry of Defence:* General de División Fernando Paredes Bello.
*President of the Venezuelan Investment Fund:* Dr. Héctor Hurtado.
*Ministry of Information and Tourism:* Dr. Diego Arria.
*Ministry of Urban Development:* Dr. Roberto Padilla.

*Minister of State, Central Office of Co-ordination and Planning:* Dr. Lorenzo Azpurua Marturet.
*Minister of State for International Economic Affairs:* Dr. Manuel Pérez-Guerrero.
*Minister of State for Culture:* Dr. José Luis Salcedo Bastardo.
*President of the Supreme Court:* Dr. Martín Pérez Guevara.

## LOCAL GOVERNMENT

The Federal District, two Federal Territories and the 20 States which make up Venezuela have Governors and Legislative Assemblies.

## LEGAL SYSTEM

Supreme judicial power is vested in the Supreme Court which is divided into chambers for each main branch of law. Each chamber must have at least five judges all of whom must be over 30 years of age and University graduates in law. Judges are elected by a joint session of both chambers for a period of nine years, a third of whom are renewed every three years.

### Supreme Court

*President:* Dr. Martin Perez Guevara.

## AREA AND POPULATION

The area of the country is 363,500 sq. miles.

The estimated population at mid-1974 was 11,632,000. The states with capitals and approximate population are shown below:

| *State* | *Capital* | *Population of State Capitals* |
|---|---|---|
| D.F. | Caracas | 3,000,000 |
| Anzoátegui | Barcelona | 50,000 |
| Apure | San Fernando | 150,000 |
| Aragua | Maracay | 200,000 |
| Barinas | Barinas | 50,000 |
| Bolivar | Ciudad Bolivar | 100,000 |
| Carabobo | Valencia | 224,820 |
| Cojedes | San Carlos | 18,000 |
| Falcón | Coro | 45,506 |
| Guarico | San Juan | 45,000 |
| Lara | Barquisimeto | 270,000 |
| Mérida | Mérida | 80,000 |
| Miranda | Los Teques | 60,000 |
| Monagas | Maturín | 100,000 |
| Nueva Esparta | La Asunción | 6,000 |
| Portuguesa | Guanare | 28,000 |
| Sucre | Cumaná | 100,000 |
| Táchira | San Cristóbal | 195,000 |
| Trujillo | Trujillo | 71,223 |
| Yaracuy | San Felipe | 29,096 |
| Zulia | Maracaibo | 900,000 |
| T. Federal Amazonas | Puerto Ayacucho | 5,465 |
| Ter. Delta Amacuro | Tuccupita | 9,922 |
| Dep. Federales | | 861 |

The annual average percentage growth rate of the population for the period 1960–74 was 3·3 and for the period 1965–74 was 3·3.

## VITAL STATISTICS

| | 1968 |
|---|---|
| Births | 382,914 |
| Marriages | 55,345 |
| Deaths | 64,052 |

## CURRENCY

The unit of currency is the *bolívar* of 100 *centimos*. The following are coins in current circulation: 5, 12½, 25 and 50 centimos, 1 and 2 bolívars and there are banknotes of 10, 20, 50, 100 and 500 bolívars. The selling rate for foreign exchange for all purposes is Bs. 4·30 = U.S. $1. The rates for other currencies fluctuate according to their quotation against the U.S. dollar. Importers of wheat and skimmed powdered milk can obtain a subsidy of Bs. 1·15 per U.S. dollar.

## FINANCE

The principal source of government revenue consists of income tax and royalties paid by the petroleum companies.

The GNP at market prices for 1974 was U.S. $ millions 22,780. and the GNP per capita at market prices was U.S. $1,960. The annual average percentage growth rate of the GNP per capita for the period 1960–74 was 2·4, and for the period 1965–74 was 2·2. [*See the note at the beginning of this section concerning GNP.*]

The following table shows the foreign trade figures for some recent years:

*Foreign Trade*

| | *Exports* (*bn. bolivars*) | *Imports* (*bn. bolivars*) | *Export surplus* (*bn. bolivars*) |
|---|---|---|---|
| 1970 | 12·1 | 7·4 | 4·7 |
| 1971 | 14·8 | 8·3 | 6·6 |
| 1972 | 16·3 | 9·5 | 6·8 |
| 1973 | 23·6 | 10·9 | 13·0 |
| 1974 | 62·5 | 16·1 | 46·4 |
| 1975 (to end May) | 19·2 | 7·2 | 11·0 |

## PRINCIPAL BANKS

**Banco Central de Venezuela S.A.** (President, Dr. Benito Raul Losada.) Est. 1940; Sole Bank of Issue for Venezuela; Half the share capital is owned by the State; Balance Sheet at 31 May 1963 showed assets Bs. 5,559,939,938; deposits Bs. 1,453,303,170; gold reserve Bs. 1,341,496,390. *Head Office:* Esquina de Las Carmelitas, Caracas.

**Banco de Venezuela.** (President, Sr. Feliciano Pacanins.) Est. 1890; Balance Sheet at 28 February 1963 showed assets Bs. 971,351,279; deposits Bs. 613,269,125. *Head Office:* Sociedad a Traposos, Caracas. 65 Branches and Agencies.

**Banco Union.** *Head Office:* Chorro a Dr. Diaz 45–47, Caracas,

**Banco Nacional de Descuento.** *Head Office:* Conde A. Carmelitas, Caracas.

**Banco Venezolano de Crédito.** *Head Office:* Monjas a San Francisco 7, Caracas 101.

**Banco Mercantil y Agricola.** *Head Office:* Sociedad a San Francisco, Caracas.

**Foreign banks** operating in Venezuela include: The Royal Bank of Canada, The First National City Bank of New York, the Banco Holandés Unido and the Banco Francés e Italiano. The Bank of London and South America has merged with the Venezuelan Banco La Guaira to form the Banco La Guaira Internacional.

## PRODUCTION, INDUSTRY AND COMMERCE

**Agriculture.** Progress is being made in the introduction of modern methods and equipment, and recent years have seen notable efforts in many directions which should produce valuable dividends in coming years; the industry continues to receive encouragement and substantial financial assistance from the Government. The most important crops consist of: Rice, Corn, Beans, Cassava, Potatoes, Sesame, Cocoa, Coffee, Sugar cane, and Tobacco.

**Forestry.** Nearly half of Venezuela is covered with forests, but their resources have not yet been fully exploited. They contain many important cabinet woods such as cedar, mahogany, ceiba and jabillo. Rubber, divi-divi, mangrove bark, tonka beans, oil-bearing palm nuts and medicinal plants are also produced, and there is a substantial lumbering industry. The total production in 1968 in cubic metres was 475,500, compared to 287,495 in 1962.

**Fishing.** Sea fishing is plentiful and varied. There is a steadily growing merchant fishing fleet, which employs many people. The principal fishing areas are La Guaira, a region north of Caracas, the Paraguana peninsula and the Cariaco—Margarita Island—Carúpano area.

In 1968 the total catch of fresh fish was 124,585 metric tons. Production of salt fish was 6,914 metric tons and of canned fish 21,966 metric tons.

**Minerals.** Venezuela is the third largest producer of petroleum in the world. The average daily production of crude petroleum in 1973 was 3,347,039 barrels and 1974 was 3,120,906 barrels daily. The chief producing zones are the region of the Lake of Maracaibo and the East-Central Zone, Guarico-Monagas-Anzoategui, the Portuguesa-Barinas Zone. Large foreign oil companies own the concessions. A large part of the crude oil produced is shipped to Aruba and Curaçao in the Netherlands Antilles for refining. Some 90 per cent of total exports are petroleum. The production of iron ore rose from 15·6 million tons in 1964 to 16·7 million tons in 1968, an increase of 3·2 per cent.

The following table shows mineral production for 1970:

| | *Unit* | 1970 |
|---|---|---|
| Petroleum production | thousand $m^3$ | 215,177 |
| Natural Gas | million $m^3$ | 48,427 |
| Gold | kgs | — |
| Iron | thousand m.t. | — |
| Coal | thousand m.t. | — |
| Diamonds | thousand carats | — |
| Salt | thousand m.t. | 225 (est.) |

**Industry.** Apart from petroleum (including refining) and mining, Venezuela is in the process of an industrialization programme. Basic industries are being built up mainly by State organizations, and consist of a steelworks and a petrochemical complex. Manufacturing industry has also been encouraged by the government and receives protection. It includes vehicle assembly, components for motor vehicles, textiles, food products and drinks, glass, rubber, paper, cable, plastics, paints, cigarettes, sugar refining and leather.

## COMMUNICATIONS

**Roads and Railways.** Internal transport is almost entirely by the excellent network of roads or by air. Apart from special railway lines (e.g. those of the iron ore mining companies) there are only about 450 kilometres of railway of which the only lines of any importance are those from Caracas to Valencia (narrow gauge) and from Puerto Cabello to Barquisimeto (standard gauge).

There are 28,199 km. of paved roads. In December 1965 President Leoni inaugurated the 36 km. Valencia–Puerto Cabello motorway, which was built at a cost of 211 million bolivars.

**Shipping.** The chief ports are La Guaira, Maracaibo, Puerto Cabello and Guanta. The Venezuelan merchant fleet comprised, at the end of 1961, 93 ships distributed as follows: 16 tankers, nine for overseas freight, 39 for coastal freight, 13 ferries, six dredgers, five survey ships, five for transit of iron ore. The total tonnage is: net, 219,625; gross, 342,262.

**Cia. Anónima Venezolana de Navegación.** President, Dr. Alfonso Marquez Añez; 12 vessels, total tonnage 63,000.

*Services operated:* Venezuela–Caribbean Sea–U.S.A.–Canada–Europe. *Head Office:* Edificio Central, 2nd floor, Ave. General Urdaneta—Ibarras a Pelota, Caracas, Venezuela.

**Civil Aviation.** Regular air services operated by British Airways, Pan-American Airways, K.L.M., Air France, and B.W.I.A., Delta, Chicago and Southern Iberia, Alitalia, Avianca and Aerovias de Brazil, V.I.A.S.A. and L.A.V. connect Venezuela with the chief capitals of the world.

The chief Venezuelan airlines are as follows:

**AVENSA—Aerovias Venezolanas S.A.**; share capital Bs. 30,000,000; *services operated:* internal. *Head Office:* Apartado 943, Edeficio 29 Esq. El Chorro, Caracas.

**LAV—Línea Aeropostal Venezolana**; totally State owned; (President: Gen. Francisco Migliani A.); *services operated:* Caracas–Trinidad; Caracas–Curazao.

**V.I.A.S.A.**—Venezolana Internacional de Aviacion S.A.; 55 per cent State-owned, 45 per cent owned privately, has working arrangement with K.L.M., B.O.A.C., Alitalia, Air France, Iberia; ***services operated:*** **to Europe, U.S.A., the** Caribbean and Latin America and the Middle East. (President, Dr. Oscar Machado Zuloaga.) *Address:* Edf. Seguros, Caracas, Marrón a Dr. Paúl, Caracas. P.O. Box 6857, Caracas.

**Posts, Telegraphs and Telephones.** There is a State telegraph system with 691 telegraph offices and 75 radio telegraph stations in the national territory. Additional overseas telegraphic services are operated by All-American Cables.

The telephone systems in Venezuela are operated by Compañia Anónima Nacional Teléfonos de Venezuela, a national company which is state owned. An extensive programme of telephone development is now taking place in Caracas and will in due course be extended to the interior. There is a submarine telephone cable link with the United States.

**Broadcasting.** There is one Government-run radio station and about 80 commercial stations.

There are four television stations, one government owned and three privately owned. Several of these stations have relay transmitters in other parts of the country.

## NEWSPAPERS

**Caracas**

**El Nacional.** F. 1943. Morning. Independent. Puente Nuevo a Puerto Escondido.

**El Universal.** F. 1908. Morning. Independent. Principal a Conde.

**El Mundo.** F. 1958. Evening. Independent. Puente La Trinidad.

**Ultimas Noticias.** F. 1941. Morning. Independent. Puente La Trinidad a Panteón.

**La Religión.** F. 1890. Morning. Catholic. Torre a Gradillas.

**The Daily Journal.** F. 1945. Morning. English language. Apartado 1408, San Ramón a Crucecita 65, Caracas.

**La Verdad.** F. 1965. Morning. Independent. Calle Real de Quebrada Honda No. 30–32, P.O. Box 1089, Caracas.

**Panorama.** F. 1914. Independent. Calle 96 Ciencias No. 3–55, Maracaibo.

**La Columna.** F. 1924. Morning. Catholic. Calle 95 No. 7–11 Maracaibo.

**Critica.** F. 1966. Morning. Independent. Maracaibo.

**Valencia**

**El Carabobeno.** F. 1933. Morning. Independent. Avenida Urdaneta.

## EDUCATION AND RELIGION

Elementary education is free and, from the age of seven to the completion of the primary grade, compulsory. In the 1969–70 school year Venezuela had 10,916 primary schools, of which 1,046 were private, with a total of 1,699,456 pupils of which 229,330 were private, and 1,043 secondary schools, of which 567 were private, with a total of 446,080 pupils. There are 14 universities in Venezuela, amongst which are included the Simón Bolívar (public), and four private ones in Caracas, namely Metropolitana and Instituto de Estudios Superiores de Administración. The number of university students totalled 72,649 of which 64,200 attended official universities and 8,449 private universities.

Roman Catholicism is the prevailing religion, but there s complete religious toleration.

# The Socialist Republic of Vietnam

**Capital**—Hanoi.

**President**—Ton Duc Thang.

**Flag**: On a red field, a star five-pointed centred gold.

## CONSTITUTION AND GOVERNMENT

The Socialist Republic of Vietnam was proclaimed on 2 July 1976 by the first National Assembly of deputies elected from both north and south. This declaration formally concluded the struggle to create a united, independent Vietnam under communist rule which had gone on for more than 40 years.

Before 1954, Vietnam was part of French-ruled Indochina. Tonkin in the north, Annam in the centre and Cochinchina in the south came under French control in 1884, 1886 and 1862 respectively. During the 1920s and 1930s, resistance to French rule developed steadily; the nationalist cause was divided between the Vietnamese communists, led by Ho Chi Minh and various anti-communist groups inspired by the Chinese nationalist movement. Of these, the most important was the Vietnam Quoc Dan Dang (Nationalist Party of Vietnam) founded in 1927. French efforts to suppress the nationalists forced many leaders of all political colours into jail or exile in China.

The Second World War and Japan's occupation of French Indochina gave the nationalists a new opportunity. In 1941, the Indochinese Communist Party (founded in 1930) at a conference in China called on all Vietnamese political parties to combine against the Japanese. The Viet Minh—an abbreviation of "Vietnam Doc Lap Dong Minh Hoi" (Vietnamese Independence League) was formed under Ho Chi Minh's leadership. Viet Minh guerrilla groups began operations, with the French rather than the Japanese as their chief target, and began to establish a political network.

In March 1945, the Japanese ousted the French civil and military authorities and encouraged the Emperor Bao Dai to proclaim Vietnam's independence under Japanese protection. In fact no effective government could be established for Japanese control was already disintegrating in the cities and almost non-existent in the countryside. In the north, this political vacuum was filled by the well organized Viet Minh who refused to support Bao Dai. On 15 August, Japan surrendered to the Allies and on 29 August, 2,000 men of the Viet Minh army led by General Giap marched into Hanoi. Boa Dai abdicated handing over his symbols of office to Ho Chi Minh who became first President of the Viet Minh's provisional government. On 2 September, he proclaimed Vietnam's independence and issued a declaration creating the Democratic Republic of Vietnam.

In the south, Viet Minh influence was weaker. British and French troops arrived in Saigon in September and the French re-established control in Cochinchina. Negotiations between Ho Chi Minh's government and France followed and in March 1946 an agreement was signed by which Vietnam was recognized as a "free state with its own government, parliament, army and finance." Further negotiations to clarify Vietnam's future relationship with France broke down and after December 1946, there was open warfare between the Viet Minh forces on one side and the French with the various Vietnamese groups supporting them on the other. Aware of the need to develop a non-communist nationalist alternative to the Viet Minh, France began negotiations with Bao Dai. These culminated in March 1949 with the Elysée Agreement which gave Vietnam a form of independence. In January 1950, Bao Dai was installed as Head of State: the fighting, however, continued.

In 1954, the war was ended by the Geneva Ceasefire Agreement. The two opposing armies were to be regrouped on either side of the 17th parallel, separated by a demilitarized zone. The Geneva Conference also issued a final declaration from which the United States and Bao Dai's government dissociated themselves, calling for countrywide elections in 1956 to reunite Vietnam. French withdrawal began and in 1955, the southern part of the country was declared a republic under the presidency of Ngo Dinh Diem.

In the north, Ho Chi Minh's government led by the Lao Dong (Workers') Party turned its attention to developing the economy and to reconstructing society on communist principles. When, however, it became clear that there would be no elections to reunite the country, pro-communists and other opponents of President Diem in the south began, with northern support, to organize guerrilla warfare against the government. In 1960, the National Liberation Front of South Vietnam (NLFSV) was founded. The rapid decline of security in the countryside led the South Vietnamese government to request special help from the United States. U.S. military aid was stepped up, the number of American military advisers grew steadily and in 1962 the Military Assistance Command (Vietnam) was established to provide South Vietnam's army with operational training and U.S. logistical support.

On 1 November 1963, Ngo Dinh Diem's government was overthrown in a military coup. A period of great political instability followed whilst in the countryside the government's position deteriorated rapidly in spite of increasing U.S. military help. By early 1965, the United States was bombing targets in both North and South Vietnam and the first American combat troops had landed in the south. North Vietnam, meanwhile, continued to step up its own commitment of troops and supplies to the southern battlefields.

In 1967, a more stable government was established in the south under the presidency of Lt. Gen. Nguyen Van Thieu. However, in January 1968, countrywide attacks by NLFSV and North Vietnamese forces brought the war into Saigon and demonstrated that the military initiative still lay with the communist side. By mid-1968, American forces in South Vietnam had reached a peak of 545,000.

On 3 April 1968, North Vietnam agreed to meet U.S. representatives in Paris and in October, the U.S. suspended its bombing in the north. Nine months later, in January 1969, peace talks began in Paris between representatives of North Vietnam, the United States, the NLFSV—later to be represented by the Provisional Revolutionary Government of South Vietnam (PRG) formed in June 1969—and South Vietnam. In the summer of the same year, the United States began withdrawing its troops, announcing that in future its military aid would be concentrated on building up the southern army to replace the departing U.S. divisions. In the autumn, President Ho Chi Minh died; his death in no way diminished North Vietnam's willingness to continue the struggle, the fighting continued and the peace talks made little headway.

In March 1972, a major offensive by North Vietnamese and NLFSV forces brought heavy casualties to both sides and was followed by a resumption of American bombing in the north and a blockade of northern ports. Finally on 27 January 1973, an agreement to end the Vietnam war was signed in Paris by representatives of the four sides. The agreement provided for a ceasefire and the withdrawal of all foreign troops. A final settlement was to be reached through political and military discussions between the two Vietnamese sides.

In the eighteen months that followed the ceasefire was frequently broken and talks between the South Vietnamese government and the PRG were eventually suspended. Early in 1975, North Vietnamese and NLFSV forces launched successful attacks in the Central Highlands forcing South Vietnamese government troops to retreat to the coast. Further southern withdrawals followed and by the end of March the cities of Hue and Da Nang were in communist hands. By the end of April, Saigon itself was surrounded and President Thieu had resigned and left the country. On 30 April, the new southern government ordered its troops to stop fighting and NLFSV and North Vietnamese forces entered the city, bringing the war to an end.

In November 1975, a political consultative conference on national reunification was held in Saigon and preparations began for nationwide elections. These were held in April 1976 and reports said 95 per cent of the population voted. The new National Assembly of 488 seats—243 of them in the south—met from 24 June–23 July and decided on the name, the flag, anthem and national emblem of the united state of Vietnam. Hanoi was declared the capital of the new state and Saigon was renamed Ho Chi Minh City. A commission to draft a new constitution was set up. Pending its decisions, the North Vietnamese constitution was adopted.

## GOVERNMENT AND CONSTITUTION

In December 1976, the ruling communist party—the Vietnamese Workers' Party (VWP)—held its fourth Congress, the first since 1960. A new party constitution was adopted and a new Central Committee of 138 members elected. The Politbureau was enlarged to 14 members with three alternate members. In 1977, the VWP had 1·5 million members.

# THE SOCIALIST REPUBLIC OF VIETNAM

In September 1977, Vietnam was admitted to membership of the United Nations.

**Vietnamese Workers' Party Politbureau**

Le Duan—Secretary General
Truong Chinh
Pham Van Dong
Pham Hung
Le Duc Tho
Vo Nguyen Giap
Nguyen Duy Trinh
Le Thanh Nghi
Tran Quoc Hoan
Van Tien Dung
Le Van Luong
Nguyen Van Linh
Vo Chi Cong
Chu Huy Man
Alternate members—To Huu, Vo Van Kiet, Do Muoi

**Members of the Government (1976)**

*President:* Ton Duc Thang.
*Vice-Presidents:* Nguyen Luong Bang, Nguyen Huu Tho.

**Council of Ministers**

*Prime Minister:* Pham Van Dong.
*Vice-Premiers:* Pham Hung, Huynh Tan Phat, Vo Nguyen Giap Nguyen Duy Trinh, Le Thanh Nghi, Vo Chi Cong, Do Muoi.
*Minister of the Interior:* Tran Quoc Hoan.
*Minister of Foreign Affairs:* Nguyen Duy Trinh.
*Minister of National Defence:* Vo Nguyen Giap.
*Chairman of the State Planning Commission:* Le Thanh Nghi.
*Minister, Vice-Chairman of the State Planning Commission:* Nguyen Huu Mai.
*Minister of Agriculture:* Yo Chi Cong.
*Minister in Charge of Agricultural Science and Technology:* Nghiem Xuan Yem.
*Minister of Forestry:* Hoang Van Chieu.
*Minister of Water Conservancy:* Nguyen Thanh Binh.
*Minister of Engineering and Metallurgy:* Nguyen Con.
*Minister of Construction:* Do Muoi.
*Minister of Communications and Transport:* Phan Trong Tue.
*Minister of Light Industry:* Tran Huu Doc.
*Minister of Food and Foodstuffs:* Ngo Minh Loan.
*Minister of Maritime Products:* Nguyen Quang Lam.
*Minister of Home Trade:* Hoang Quoc Thinh.
*Minister for Foreign Trade:* Dang Viet Chau.
*Minister of Finance:* Hoang Anh
*Director General of State Bank:* Tran Duong.
*Chairman of the State Commission for Prices:* To Duy.
*Minister of Labour:* Nguyen Tho Chan.
*Minister of Material Supplies:* Tran Sam.
*Chairman of the Central Commission of Nationalties:* Vu Lap.
*Chairman of the State Commission for Science and Technology:* Tran Quynh.
*Minister of Culture:* Nguyen Van Hieu.
*Minister of Higher and Secondary Vocational Education:* Nguyen Dinh Tu.
*Minister of Education:* Mrs Nguyen Thi Binh.
*Minister of Public Health:* Vu Van Can.
*Minister of War Invalid and Social Affairs:* Duong Quoc Chinh.
*Minister in Charge of Da River Project:* Ha Ke Tan.
*Minister in Charge of Oil and Gas:* Dinh Duc Thien.
*Chairman of Government Inspection Commission:* Tran Nam Trung.
*Minister in Charge of Culture and Education at the Premier's Office:* Tran Quang Huy.
*Minister at the Premier's Office:* Dang Thi.
*Minister in Charge of Premier's Office:* Phan My.

**National Defence Council**

*Chairman:* Ton Duc Thang.
*Vice Chairman:* Pham Van Dong.
*Members:* Le Duan, Truong Chinh, Pham Hung, General Vo Nguyen Giap, Nguyen Duy Trinh, Le Thanh Nghi, Tran Quoc Hoan, General Van Tien Dung.

**Standing Committee of the National Assembly**

*Chairman:* Truong Chinh.
*Vice-Chairmen:* Hoang Van Hoan, Xuan Thuy, Phan Van Dan, Mrs Nguyen Thi Thap, Lt. Gen. Chu Van Tan, Nguyen Xien, Tran Dang Khoa, Nguyen Xuan Yem.
*General Secretary:* Xuan Thuy.

## AREA AND POPULATION

The Socialist Republic of Vietnam covers an area of 329,600 square kilometres. It is bounded on the west by Cambodia and Laos and on the north by China. To the east is the South China Sea. Vietnam has a 3,300 km. coastline.

In 1977, the population was 49 million with an annual growth rate of three per cent, Hanoi the capital, has a population of 1,443,500, while the largest town, Ho Chi Minh City—formerly Saigon—had 3,460,500 inhabitants at the end of 1976. In northern Vietnam, where two thirds of the land area is mountainous, most of the population is concentrated in the lowlands and particularly in the rich rice-growing area of the Red River delta where population densities are among the highest in the world. In southern Vietnam, the most populous region is the fertile Mekong delta.

The mountain areas of Vietnam are sparsely inhabited, mainly by nomadic tribespeople, numbering around two million. Two large areas in the northern mountains have been designated tribal autonomous regions. The government is anxious to settle the tribal groups in one place and, more urgently, to bring about a more equal distribution of population throughout the country. In the north, a campaign to move people from the overcrowded lowlands to the empty highlands began as long ago as 1960. In the south, as soon as the war ended in May 1975, the new government began to resettle people from the cities, particularly Ho Chi Minh City and Da Nang. Those who have left—many originally refugees from the war—are reported to have returned to their villages or gone to open up new agricultural areas. By mid-1977 more than 700,000 people had left Ho Chi Minh City and there were plans for a smimilar number to leave before 1979.

The Republic is divided for administrative purposes into 35 provinces and three municipalities—Hanoi, Ho Chi Minh City and Haiphong.

## CURRENCY AND FINANCE

Before the end of the war, North Vietnam's unit of currency was the dong, officially valued in 1975 at 5·13 to the £ sterling, while the South Vietnamese unit of currency was the piastre valued in the same year at approximately 1625 to the £ sterling. In May 1975, all banks in South Vietnam were closed by the new government. In June the Vietnam National Bank resumed operations and in September a new currency was introduced in the south, one new piastre replacing 500 old piastres. The North Vietnamese dong circulated freely at par with the new piastre. Strict controls were imposed on bank accounts to reduce the amount of currency in circulation. In October, all private financial institutions, including foreign banks, were ordered to close.

Since the end of the war, Vietnam has joined the IMF, the World Bank and the Asian Development Bank. It has also begun to seek medium and short term commercial loans to finance economic development.

In January 1977, the National Assembly approved a budget for that year of US $3,315 million.

In October 1977, the dong was valued at an official rate of 4·4 to the pound sterling.

## PRODUCTION, INDUSTRY AND COMMERCE

The political reunification of North and South Vietnam, also united two very different but potentially complementary economies. In the north, the communist government had stressed the development of centralized heavy industry while at the same time striving for intensive agricultural production. However a shortage of cultivable land and a large population meant that even in a good year the north could barely expect to be self-sufficient in rice, the staple crop. Industrial production was severely damaged by air raids and the war also brought serious distribution problems. As a result the north was heavily dependent on the Soviet Union and China for foodstuffs, fuel, fertilizers, vehicles, consumer goods and industrial equipment to replace installations destroyed by bombing.

The south's wartime economy was equally dependent on the outside world, particularly the United States, for raw materials, finance, spare parts, consumer goods and fuel. Although the south is potentially a rice exporting region with large areas of fertile agricultural land, the war drove farmers into the cities and into the service industries which flourished as a result of the American presence. In 1960, agriculture accounted for 46 per cent of South Vietnam's GNP, industry for 17 per cent and service industries for 37 per cent. By 1970, the service industries accounted for 65 per cent of the GNP and agriculture and industry shared the remaining 35 per cent. The American withdrawal and the end of the war left 3·5 million unemployed, 700,000 in Ho Chi Minh City.

In 1976, the Vietnamese government announced a new five year plan which placed heavy emphasis on agricultural development in order to raise living standards rapidly and make the most of southern resources. 30 per cent of the investment outlay for these five years was earmarked for agriculture and of 35 per cent allocated to industry, a large part was to be channelled into the production of agricultural equipment. The government has said that heavy industry must back up agriculture more effectively and that co-ordination between industry and agriculture at the local level must be developed, to that local industry can provide the farmers with power, machinery and chemicals and process farm products.

## AGRICULTURE

Vietnam has some five million hectares of farmland and several million hectares of potentially cultivable land. In both north and south, rice is the principal food crop. Other crops include maize, rubber, timber, sugar, tea, peanuts, ute, cotton, tobacco and fruit.

The economy of Vietnam is still primarily agricultural with 60 per cent of the work force employed on the land. In spite of attempts in both north and south to mechanize agriculture, only about 10 per cent of farming in the north and 17 per cent in the south were mechanized when the war ended in 1975. The average rice yield throughout Vietnam is 3·2 tons per hectare, but the potential yield, particularly in the fertile Mekong Delta, is considerably more.

In the north, agricultural production is collectivized with 95 per cent of the work force organized into around 23,000 co-operatives which the government has begun to consolidate into larger units farming from 500 to 800 hectares. There are also over 100 large state farms employing over 70,000 people and the government had begun, before 1975, to develop specialized agricultural regions as a step towards large scale production. In its efforts to feed a large population from a relatively small rice-growing area, Hanoi had also begun to grow new high yield rice strains and invested much capital and labour in irrigation projects to make double cropping possible in many areas and protect the capital and the Red River delta from flooding.

After Vietnam was united in 1975, Hanoi began to apply its experience in intensive cultivation, irrigation and double cropping to the south. Southern Vietnam has more than three million hectares of cultivated land, of which 84·5 per cent is used to grow rice. There are some two million hectares of riceland in the Mekong Delta which is among the richest rice producing areas in the world. Once a rice exporting country, South Vietnam's production declined during the war to a point where rice imports were necessary and in 1976, production in the delta averaged only two tons per hectare. Land was privately owned or rented and production generally on a small scale. The re-organization of farmers into co-operatives began slowly after 1975, but by 1977 the government was saying that it must be speeded up so that by 1979 co-operativization in the south would be basically complete.

With some two million hectares in the south lying fallow as a result of the war, land reclamation is high on Hanoi's list of priorities. Several hundred thousand people—many of them originally refugees—are reported to have left southern cities to develop new economic regions in the mountains and foothills or to cultivate land fought over for years. By 1980, the government plans to have settled four million workers from the crowded areas of north and south in new, specialized agricultural areas and to increase cultivated land throughout the country by one million hectares.

At present, however, Vietnamese agriculture is still handicapped by shortages of fertilizer, insecticides, fuel, tools, building materials and draught animals. It also suffered greatly in 1977 from the weather—severe cold in the north at the beginning of the year was followed by prolonged drought in both north and south. The winter-spring rice crop, vegetables and subsidiary starch crops were badly damaged while planting for the autumn rice crop, the most important of the year, was severely set back. As a result, Vietnam may have a rice deficit of more than one million tons in 1977 and the government has called for strict economies in the use of rice and is attempting to prevent hoarding and to induce farmers—particularly in the south—to sell more grain to the state.

The importance of growing industrial crops is also being stressed and with the end of the war the chief obstacle to exploiting such crops as rubber, sugar, timber, coffee and tea has been removed. In May 1975, 90 per cent of the rubber plantations in the south were French-owned and most had been heavily damaged. Production of dry rubber in 1974 was 20,830 tons. There were 24,000 hectares of sugar cane in the south in 1974, and 12,000 hectares of tobacco. In the north, jute, tea, sugar, rushes, cotton, peanuts, rubber and tobacco are grown.

Vietnam has more than 15 million hectares of forests containing many types of valuable timber. Marine products are another potentially valuable resource—in the second half of 1975, in spite of transportation and other difficulties, 1,200 tons of frozen shrimp were exported by southern Vietnam.

## INDUSTRY

Heavy industry is principally concentrated in the north of the country where since 1954, the government has stressed the development of such key sectors as electrical power, iron and steel, engineering and chemicals. There are also important coal deposits in the north, including the Quang Yen coal field near Haiphong, producing high grade anthracite, which is the largest in South East Asia. By 1965 a number of heavy industrial enterprises had been built and industrial districts in Haiphong (cement, ship building and canning), Thai Nguyen (iron and steel), Viet Tri (paper and chemicals) and Nam Dinh (textiles) had been set up or expanded. In 1965, the north had more than a thousand industrial enterprises of which 200 were completely modern. 88 were in Hanoi which had become the industrial centre of the country.

From 1965 until 1972, production was severely disrupted by air raids and in spite of strenuous efforts to protect industry, many factories and their equipment were destroyed. By 1972, production was largely dependent on small scale local industry and handicrafts. When the war ended in the north in 1973, the government began to rebuild urgently with the help of large quantities of foreign aid.

By the end of 1975, the government's first aim—to restore production to pre-war levels with priority going to power, steel, coal, cement, chemicals and engineering—had been largely accomplished. Progress was greater, however, in centrally administered industries than in the regions, where factories had failed to meet their targets. Until 1975, south Vietnam's industrial development was based on light industry, particularly textiles (225 million metres a year), consumer goods, food processing and the production of beverages. There are also a substantial number of machine repair and assembly shops, producing vehicles, sewing machines, radios, televisions and other consumer goods, but relying for the most part on imported parts. Industry in southern Vietnam is principally concentrated round Ho Chi Minh City and has benefitted from the installation of modern machinery. It has depended, however, on imported raw materials and in mid-1975 only two-thirds of 10,000 industrial units were functioning because these were in short supply. The government is emphasizing the need to produce more raw materials locally, and by 1977 it was reported that 400 privately owned factories and 14,000 small industrial enterprises and handicraft workshops in Ho Chi Minh City had resumed production.

A new five year plan, announced in 1976, shifted emphasis from the development of heavy industry to agriculture. It was underlined that industry must support agriculture more effectively and that more consumer goods must be produced, not only in order to raise living standards but to provide an incentive for farmers. In 1976, 70 per cent of all consumer goods were still produced in small handicraft workshops which were responsible for 36 per cent of the industrial output value of the whole country. There are plans for 36 new factories to be built in Hanoi over the next five years producing consumer goods such as electric fans, refrigerators, clocks, sewing machines, bicycle spare parts and processed foods. The production of electric power and building materials are also given priority in the new plan; power stations are to be enlarged and new ones built, especially in the central highlands. The Thai Nguyen steelworks are being restructured and expanded to reach an annual capacity of 250,000 tons. Major cement works are being enlarged and smaller plants, each with an annual output of a few thousand tons have been built by 28 cities and provinces to serve local needs.

At the end of the war, while taking control of certain major enterprises such as the Vietnam Iron Rolling Co. and some foreign owned companies, the government said that privately owned manufacturing businesses in the south would be encouraged to re-open under state supervision and with more worker control. By 1977, however, the government had said that private industry must be brought more rapidly under state control though it emphasized that this should should not be done without thorough preparation or at the expense of efficiency. At the same time, Hanoi is anxious to stimulate foreign investment in industrial projects in southern Vietnam, encouraging France and Japan to maintain their participation in existing factories and seeking new investment from western countries. In 1977 an investment code was drafted providing a 10–15 year guarantee against the nationalization of any joint Vietnamese and foreign ventures.

Vietnam is also negotiating with foreign oil companies to explore and exploit oil deposits off the south Vietnamese coast. The Delta offshore area is considered to have the best prospects for commercial oil in the South China Sea.

### COMMERCE

Vietnam's principal exports are coal, rubber, tea, rice, raw silk, timber, tropical foodstuffs, shrimps and handicrafts. As a result of the war all exports and particularly rubber and timber declined drastically, while rice had to be imported. During the war, throughout Vietnam, imports far exceeded exports: food, fuel, consumer goods, machinery, metals, building materials and fertilizers were imported, while the south in particular relied on imported raw materials for its industry. In 1973, southern exports totalled U.S. $60 million while imports stood at U.S. $715 million. The north published no figures, but repeatedly stressed the need to improve both the quality and quantity of good sold abroad. Northern exports in 1975 were estimated at approximately U.S. $400 million.

Before reunification, the north's chief trading partners were the U.S.S.R., China and other countries in the socialist bloc, which provided extensive military and economic aid. The south relied chiefly on the United States. Other countries trading with both parts of Vietnam included Japan, France, Singapore and Hong Kong.

Since the end of the war, Hanoi has stressed the importance of stepping up exports and reducing imports by producing more raw materials at home. In 1976, Vietnam's overall trade deficit was more than US $700 million. The socialist bloc countries remained important trading partners and between 1975 and 1977, communist aid and credits reached an estimated US $2,400 million. Hanoi is also anxious, however, to develop trade with the west and to import modern equipment and technology from countries outside the socialist bloc. Since 1975, trade with Japan in particular has expanded rapidly. Exports to Japan rose from US $39·6 million in 1975 to US $49 million in 1976. Imports from Japan, worth US $78·8 million in 1975 rose to US $168 million in 1976.

### COMMUNICATIONS

All land communications, thoughout Vietnam, suffered damage during the war. In the south, however, foreign aid and the needs of the American army helped to establish a well developed communications network, including extensive port facilities, roads modernized to reasonably high standards and airports throughout the country. In the north, roads, railways and bridges were heavily damaged by air raids between 1965 and 1972 while ports and waterways were mined.

In 1973, the north had approximately 15,000 kms. of motor road and the south nearly 21,000 kms. of road, including nearly 10,000 kms. of paved or asphalt roadway. By the end of 1975, the government said all main roads had been re-opened and work begun on new roads to open up the mountain areas and serve the new economic regions. A road linking Thanh Hoa in northern Vietnam with Sam Neua in Laos was opened in 1975. Work began in 1976 on a 1,518 kilometre asphalted road running from northern Vietnam across the central highlands to the south-east.

Vietnam's railway system was originally developed by the French with the most important line running south for 1,700 kms. to link Hanoi with Saigon. This line was severed at the 17th parallel by the division between north and south and in the south most of the route fell into disuse as a result of sabotage and lack of security. At the end of 1976, after 18 months of repair work, the entire route was re-opened. By June 1977 a daily train service between Hanoi and Ho Chi Minh City was in operation. In north Vietnam there are also railways linking Hanoi with Haiphong (102 kms.), Lao Cai, and Lang Son, both on the Chinese border. A 72 km. spur also runs from the Lang Son line near Hanoi to Thai Nguyen. By the end of 1975, the capacity of all main lines in the north had been restored to pre-war levels.

Vietnam's main ports are Haiphong in the north, and Ho Chi Minh City, Da Nang and Cam Ranh in the south. Passenger shipping between Haiphong and Ho Chi Minh City began in July 1975. There are approximately 13,000 km. of navigable waterways throughout Vietnam.

The main airports are Hanoi, Ho Chi Minh City (the largest), Da Nang, Hue, Can Tho, Qui Nhon, and Nha Trang. Domestic flights between Hanoi, Da Nang and Ho Chi Minh City began in 1975. The Vietnamese airline flies to Moscow, Peking, Berlin and Vientiane. There are also fortnightly flights to Cambodia.

In 1975 cable and mail links between north and south Vietnam were restored.

### BROADCASTING

The national radio service broadcasts daily on short and medium waves in Vietnamese, French, English, Chinese, Thai Lao, Khmer, Indonesian, Malay, Japanese and Korean.

### NEWSPAPERS

**Nhan Dan (The People)**: leading northern daily and official organ of the Lao Dong Party.

**Quan Doi Nhan Dan (People's Army)**: daily. Army paper.

**Tap Chi Cong San**: monthly. Party theoretical journal.

**Dai Doan Ket (Great Unity)**: Weekly.

**Hanoi Moi (New Hanoi)**: newspaper for the capital.

**Saigon Giao Phong (Saigon Liberation)**: southern daily.

### EDUCATION AND RELIGION

In 1974–75 school year Vietnam had a general school enrolment of over nine million pupils, with 5,248,055 in the north and approximately four million in the south. There were 165,200 general school teachers in the north and 96,000 in the south. At the end of the war, 15 per cent of elementary pupils and 45 per cent of high school pupils in the south were at private schools and by 1976, steps had been taken to merge these into the state system.

A new educational system was introduced in the south in the 1974–75 school year with a revised "revolutionary" curriculum and new text books. Southern teachers have attended professional and political re-education courses and additional teachers have been recruited from the north. In northern Vietnam, where practical as well as classroom work is emphasized in both schools and colleges, a programme for rebuilding and modernizing schools began in 1974.

In the north there were 37 universities and 192 professional secondary schools in 1973 with 115,600 students in the 1973–74 school year. Many students were also studying in the U.S.S.R., China and other countries. The principal southern universities are in Ho Chi Minh City, Hue, Da Lat and Can Tho and before the end of the war there were also a number of privately run universities and colleges. The new government has said that teaching in certain faculties such as law and letters will be reappraised and students guided away from purely academic courses to vocational and professional training.

There is no state religion. The population is mainly Buddhist. There are about four million Christians, mostly Roman Catholics.

# West Indies

(BRITISH AND COMMONWEALTH TERRITORIES IN THE EAST CARIBBEAN, WEST INDIES ASSOCIATED STATES, INDEPENDENT STATES)

## *BRITISH AND COMMONWEALTH TERRITORIES IN THE EAST CARIBBEAN*

The Islands in the East Caribbean presently or formerly administered by the UK fall geographically into two groups and were administered as two separate units until 1960. The Leeward Islands group consists of Antigua, with Barbuda and Redonda; St. Christopher, Nevis and Anguilla; Montserrat; and the British Virgin Islands. The second group is known as the Windward Islands and consits of Dominica, St. Lucia, St. Vincent and Grenada, together with smaller islands known as the Grenadines which lie between St. Vincent and Grenada, those to the north forming part of St. Vincent and those to the south forming part of Grenada. Although the administrative groupings of the Leeward and Windward Islands were dissolved in 1956 and separate colonies established, they continued to be administered by two Governors until 1960 when these offices were abolished. The Queen's representative was subsequently an Administrator in each colony.

In 1958 the Federation of the West Indies was formed comprising almost all the Caribbean Islands which were at that time dependencies of Britain. The federation was dissolved in 1962 following the withdrawal of Jamaica and Trinidad and Tobago which then proceeded to Independence.

## *WEST INDIES ASSOCIATED STATES*

### *General Introduction*

The West Indies Associated States, set up under the West Indies Act of 1967, at present comprise Antigua, Dominica, St. Lucia, St. Vincent and St. Kitts-Nevis-Anguilla. Grenada, formerly an Associated State, became Indepenent in 1974.

Following the dissolution of the West Indies Federation and the failure of their proposed federation of the "Little Eight" of the Eastern Caribbean, Associated Statehood provided a means of constitutional advance for these small islands without going as far as sovereign independence.

The Associated States have full internal autonomy. The British Government retain responsibility for matters relating to defence and external affairs, but have delegated responsibility in certain areas, particularly regional affairs and trade. Each State has the right and ability (subject to certain safeguards) to advance unilaterally to full independence. The United Kingdom also may terminate the association by Order in Council under the West Indies Act.

The constitutions of all the States except Antigua provide for the exercise of government through a Parliament comprising The Queen and an elected House of Assembly. Parliament in Antigua comprises The Queen, an appointed Senate and an elected House of Representatives. Executive Government is exercised in each state through a cabinet presided over by a Premier. The Queen is represented by a *Governor* in each State.

### ST. KITTS-NEVIS-ANGUILLA

The islands were discovered by Columbus in 1493. St. Kitts (St. Christopher) was the first Island in the West Indies to be colonized by the British. The three islands were united by Federal Act in 1882. Anguilla is formally a part of the Associated State of St. Kitts-Nevis-Anguilla but has a separate Constitution and Ministerial form of government under HM Commissioner as provided for in the Anguilla (Constitution) Order 1976. In 1974 the estimated population of St. Kitts-Nevis-Anguilla was 46,000, and the estimated per capita GNP was $500. The figures for revenue and expenditure during 1975 were estimated at EC$36,968,863 to produce a deficit of $6,752,227. Imports for St. Kitts and Nevis in 1973, amounted to $30,300,000 and exports to $12,000,000. In 1974, 26,100 tons of sugar were exported.

### ANTIGUA

Antigua was discovered in 1493 by Christopher Columbus who named it after a church in Seville called Santa Maria de la Antigua. Sugar was for many years the dominant crop but a for a number of reasons it was discontinued in 1972. Considerable agricultural development is in hand to replace sugar, including livestock, sea island cotton, improved vegetable and fruit production. Tourism is an important feature of the economy. In 1974 the estimated population was 71,000, and the estimated per capita GNP was $540. Revenue and expenditure in 1975 were estimated to balance at EC$44,221,381.

### DOMINICA

Dominica is situated between the French islands of Guadeloupe and Martinique, being about 30 miles away from each. It has an area of approximately 290 sq. miles and the estimated population was 80,705 in 1975. The chief town, Roseau (population approximately 16,800) is a port of registry. The other town is Portsmouth to the north-west of the island in Prince Rupert's Bay. Estimated figures for recurrent revenue and expenditure for 1975 were 17,013,320 and 20,391,780. Considerable areas of the island are at the present uncultivated and total production is much below what it can be. An intensive major road programme has now been embarked on and as this programme proceeds much valuable land will be brought under cultivation. The estimated banana exports for 1975 valued $14,407,117. The total estimated value of imports for 1975 is $45,036,386.

### ST. LUCIA

St. Lucia is situated 24 miles to the south of Martinique and 24 miles to the north-east of St. Vincent. It is 27 miles in length and 14 miles in breadth and has an area of 238 sq. miles. The population and per capita GNP were estimated at 108,000 and $530 respectively. The chief town, Castries (population 47,000) has an excellent harbour and airport. It is a port of registry. The town of Vieux Fort at the southern end of the island also has a deep water harbour, good berthing facilities and also an excellent airfield. The estimated budget figures for 1975 were: Revenue $29,056,378 and Expenditure $34,237,093. The chief products were bananas, coconuts, spices, cocoa and fruit. In 1975 export agriculture earned $19,122,000 of which bananas accounted for $17,539,000. The total estimated value of imports for 1975 is $100,425,000. The economy is now being diversified and tourism developed.

### ST. VINCENT

St. Vincent is situated 24 miles to the south-west of St. Lucia and 100 miles west of Barbados. It is 18 miles in length and 11 miles in breadth and covers an area of 150 sq. miles. The State includes, in addition to the main island of St. Vincent, a number of the Grenadine group of islands to the south, the principal one of which is Bequia. The estimated population in 1975 was 100,249. About 23,645 of these lived in the capital, Kingstown. The estimated per capita GNP was $340. Revenue and expenditure in 1975 were estimated at $40,131,816 to produce a deficit of $3,300,000.

## *DEPENDENT TERRITORIES OF THE UK*

Both the British Virgin Islands and Montserrat have constitutions which provide a measure of local autonomy just short of internal self-government but with a full Ministerial system. The Governor in each case is appointed by the Crown and remains responsible for defence and internal security, external affairs, the civil service and administration of the courts but is normally bound to act in accordance with the advice of the Executive Council.

### BRITISH VIRGIN ISLANDS

The Virgin Islands were discovered in 1493 by Columbus who named them after St. Ursula and her 11,000 virgins. They are an archipelago adjacent to Puerto Rico and the American Virgin Islands. There are 36 islands and islets of which 11 are inhabited, the largest being Tortola, Virgin Gorda, Anegada and Jost Van Dykes. The capital is Road Town, Tortola, with a population in 1974 of 3,400. The major industry is tourism, in particular yacht chartering, which contributes considerably to the territory's gross national output. Exports in 1973 amounted to US $98,402

The estimated figures for Revenue and Expenditure in 1977 are US $6,698,700 and US $7,157,573 respectively. Capital expenditure in 1977 is estimated at US $2,027,044.

### MONTSERRAT

The island was discovered by Columbus in 1493 and named by him after a famous mountain in Spain. It is situated 27 miles west of Antigua and is about 11 miles in length and 17 miles in breadth. Agriculture, which a decade ago contributed 41 per cent to the GDP, amounted only to 15·2 per cent in 1972. Taken together tourism and construction are now the main industries, tourism being closely related to real estate construction. Considerable effort is being made to redevelop the agricultural industry. Imports for 1974 were $15,297,600. Value of the main domestic exports for 1974 amounted to $259,200. The estimated figures for revenue and expenditure in 1977 are $6,500,000 and $8,512,000 respectively.

*INDEPENDENT STATE*

### GRENADA

Grenada, the most southerly of the Windward group, lies 68 miles south-west of St. Vincent and about 90 miles north of Trinidad. In February 1974, Grenada became an independent monarchy within the Commonwealth. The Governor General is Her Majesty's Representative. The Cabinet consists of the Prime Minister, the other Ministers, and the Attorney-General. The Legislature consists of Her Majesty, a Senate and a House of Representatives. The principal town, St. George's is a port of registry for shipping. The other towns are Gouyave (or Charlottetown), Victoria (or Grand Pauve), Sauteura, Grandville (or La Baye) and Hillsborough or Carriacou. About two per cent of the population is European, the remainder being African or mixed descent. The estimated Revenue figures for 1974 were: local EC$22,219,980; development aid EC$117,000; other aids, EC$10,000. Cocoa and nutmegs, the principle crops grown in Grenada, occupy some 22,000 acres of the best agricultural land and account for the major proportion of the territory's revenue. Other crops grown, in order of importance, are coconuts (3,700 acres), sugar-cane (1,600 acres), citrus (1,000 acres), cotton (1,100 acres), in addition to small scattered cultivations of cloves, vanilla and coffee. All nutmegs and mace produced in the territory are marketed through a single agency, the Grenada Co-operative Nutmeg Association, and the principal market is at present the USA. A cocoa Industry Improvement Scheme, financed partly by Colonial Development and Welfare Funds and partly by a tax of one per cent per lb on all cocoa exported from the territory, has been initiated with the object of replanting 10,000 acres of the existing old and uneconomic cocoa cultivations with selected high-yielding clones. Colonial Development and Welfare Funds have also been provided for other phases of agricultural development in the territory, notably Fisheries, Land Settlement, Small Scale Agriculture and a special scheme for the Agricultural Development of Carriacou.

# Western Samoa

(MEMBER OF THE COMMONWEALTH)

**Capital**—Apia.

**Head of State**—H.H. Maleitoa Tanumafili II, CBE.

**National Flag**: On a red field, a canton blue charged with five stars five-pointed white.

Western Samoa, which had been, since 1920, administered by New Zealand, first under League of Nations Mandate and later under a United Nations Trusteeship Agreement, attained full independence as from 1 January 1962.

A plebiscite was held under the supervision of the United Nations on ninth May 1960, on the basis of universal adult suffrage, and Samoan people voted overwhelmingly for independence. The United Nations approved that the 1946 Trusteeship Agreement cease on 1st January 1962, and Western Samoa emerged as a fully Independent State.

The Western Samoa Parliament consists of the Head of State and a Legislative Assembly of forty-seven members, forty-five of whom are elected by territorial constituencies in a franchise limited to matais (heads of extended families); the remaining two members are elected by the part-Samoan and European community by numerical suffrage. Executive government is carried out by a Cabinet consisting of a Prime Minister who holds the confidence of a majority in the Legislative Assembly and who selects eight other ministers. National elections are held after every three years.

### AREA AND POPULATION

Western Samoa is the larger and westerly part of the Samoan archipelago whose geographic position is some 1,900 miles north-west of New Zealand, 2,600 miles south-west of Hawaii and 800 miles east of Fiji. The Western Samoa group comprises the two large islands of Savaii and Upolu together with seven other smaller islands of which only Manono and Apolima are inhabited. The total area of the islands is 2,785 square kilometres (1,075·15 sq. miles). Rugged high country forms the core of the main islands with mountains rising to some 3,600 feet on Upolu and 6,100 feet on Savai'i.

The population of Western Samoa at mid-1974 was 157,000.

The average annual percentage growth rate of the population for the period 1960–74 was 2·5, and for the period 1965–74 was 2·4.

### CURRENCY AND FINANCE

Western Samoa has had a decimal currency since 10 July 1967. The exchange rate (mid-point rate) as at 31 December 1976 was 0·8000 WS tala (dollar) per US dollar.

Total government budgeted expenditure (in thousands of tala) for 1976 were: WS$14,043·8. The major items of the budget (in thousands of tala) in 1976 were Development expenditure, 4,209·6; Education, 2,205·7; Health, 1,946·1; Public Works, 1,826·9; Treasury, 1,620·6; Customs, 1,244·2.

Government receipts (in thousands of tala) were estimated WS$16,255.0 in 1976 the major sources were: Customs, 7,988·0; Inland Revenue, 2,890·0; Treasury, 1,832·0; Public Works, 1,337·0; Post Office, 714·7.

The GNP at market prices for 1974 was U.S. $ millions 50, and the GNP per capita at market prices was U.S. $300. The annual average percentage growth rate of the GNP per capita for the period 1960–74 was 0·9 and for the period 1965–74 was 1·3. [*See the note at the beginning of this section concerning GNP*].

### COMMERCE

Western Samoa's trade deficit in 1976 was WS$(000) 18,180. The value of imports for 1976 was WS $(000) 23,627 and of exports WS $(000) 5,447.

The following table shows the value in WS $(000) of exports from the named countries to Western Samoa in 1976:

| | |
|---|---|
| New Zealand | 6,544 |
| Australia | 4,719 |
| Other Pacific island countries | 2,824 |
| Japan | 3,622 |
| United Kingdom | 950 |

The following table shows the value in WS $(000) of exports from Western Samoa to the named countries in 1976:

| | |
|---|---|
| Netherlands | 346 |
| New Zealand | 1,987 |
| West Germany | 1,907 |
| Australia | 206 |

The following table shows the value in WS $(000) of principal type exports for 1976:

| | |
|---|---|
| Copra | 1,893·8 |
| Cocoa | 2,230·6 |
| Timber | 446·7 |
| Bananas | 144·4 |

### EDUCATION

In 1976, there were 32,878 pupils attending primary schools. 7,618 in intermediate schools and 8,258 in secondary schools. There were 1,322 teachers teaching in primary and intermediate schools and 418 in secondary, vocational schools, and the Teachers' Training College.

# People's Democratic Republic of Yemen

**Capital—Aden.**

## AREA AND POPULATION

THE Republic covers an area of approximately 130,000 square miles.

The population at mid-1974 was 1,632,000. The annual average percentage growth rate of the population for the period 1960–74 was 3·1 and for the period 1965–74 was 2·9.

## FINANCE

The unit of currency is the dinar, which is equal to the pound sterling. It is issued in denominations of 10 dinars, 5 dinars, 1 dinar, 500 fils and 250 fils notes, and 50 fils, 25 fils, 5 fils and 1 fils coins.

The GNP at market prices for 1974 was U.S. $millions 360, and the GNP per capita at market prices was U.S.$220. The annual average percentage growth rate of the GNP per capita for the period 1960–74 was n.a., and for the period 1965–74 was −4·3. [*See the note at the beginning of this section concerning GNP.*]

## PRODUCTION

Agriculture is the main occupation of the inhabitants of the Republic, excluding Aden and some of the Islands. This is largely of a subsistence nature, sorghum, sesame and millets being the chief crops, with wheat and barley widely grown at the higher elevations.

Of increasing importance, however, are the cash crops which have been developed since the Second World War, by far the most important of which is the Abyan long-staple cotton, which is now the country's major export. 1965 estimates for cotton lint yield were 36,694 bales; and for cotton seed, 13,105 tons. 1964–65 value of cotton sales was £608,072.

Owing to paucity of rainfall, cultivation is largely confined to fertile valleys and flood plains on silt, built up and irrigated in the traditional manner. Of recent years, however, these traditional methods have been augmented and replaced by the use of modern earth-moving machinery and pumps. Irrigation schemes, designed to replace some of the more important traditional structures with permanent installations, are now being undertaken.

Nearly all the fruit and vegetables grown are sold through the Central Wholesale Produce Market in Aden, through which pass annually some 30,000 tons of locally produced fruits and vegetables worth up to £500,000 annually. The fishing industry landed a catch of 16,540 tons in 1965.

The co-operative movement was initiated in 1956, and the first society formed that year. Today there are 65 co-operative societies marketing agricultural and fisheries products, while the Ministry of Agriculture and Agrarian Reform supervises the school savings societies.

A new power house, costing £250,000 has been opened at Ja'ar in the Abyan area. Zara, Kukheiras, Dhala and Beihan all have small power stations with an output of 30 kilowatts. At present a new generator of 69 kilowatts is being installed at Habban, which is the biggest town in the Republic after Aden and Lahej. Lahej is supplied by high-power cable from the British Petroleum power station in Little Aden and the Aden Electricity Corporation.

## COMMUNICATIONS

The automatic telephone system of Aden is integrated with a manual switchboard at Ashaab, the Administrative Capital, to provide service to about 4,700 subscribers.

Radio telephone services are available with London (with extensions to Europe and America), Kenya, Somaliland, Bahrain and Addis Ababa.

There is no inland public telegraph service. World-wide external telegraph services are operated by Cable and Wireless Ltd., which also operate wireless telegraph services to Mukalla, Seiyun and Meifaa'h and to Kamaran.

**Civil Aviation.** Eleven airlines operate scheduled services into the Republic: BASCO (Brothers' Air Service Company), Air-India, East-African Airways, Ethiopian Airlines, Middle East Airlines, United Arab Airlines, Sudan Airways, Air Djibouti, Somali Airlines, Kuwait Airways, Yemen Airlines.

Some air traffic figures for 1967 are: passenger arrivals, 40,234; passenger departures, 49,690; movements of aircraft, 6,157; freight (kilo): inwards, 683,548; outwards, 1,043,168; in transit, 14,159.

**Roads.** A system of undeveloped but motorable roads suitable for heavy lorries and vehicles of the land-rover type, links the principal towns and villages outside Aden. Surfaces vary widely, from tarmac, as yet only in short stretches in the Abyan and Lahej areas relatively close to Aden, to open desert in the north towards Beihan.

## EDUCATION

The Educational system consists of six years of primary, three years of intermediate and three years of secondary schooling. The Ministry of Education is responsible for 366 Government Primary Schools, 57 Intermediate Schools, 11 Secondary Schools, and a technical Institute in Maalla, State of Aden. In addition, there are aided and non-aided schools; 16 primary, 14 intermediate and 18 secondary. There are six teacher training centres (three for men and three for women), and there are evening Adult Education classes.

## HEALTH

At present the Ministry of Health comprises three divisions—one provides service for the treatment and cure of disease, another deals with School Health, and the third with Port Health.

The curative services are based on a hospital, the Al-Gamhoria Hospital (Republic), at Khormaksar, 14 rural hospitals, six general dispensaries, and about 90 health units, the latter being auxiliaries of the rural hospitals. The total number of beds available is 900, of which 495, including those for tuberculosis patients, are provided at Al-Gamhoria Hospital (Republic). Specialist facilities are based on the Al-Gamhoria hospital. This hospital has established the Aden Nursing Training School, for both men and women, which provides a three year course in nursing, with opportunities for further courses in midwifery, and for overseas scholarships, to suitable candidates.

# Yemen Arab Republic

**Capital—Sana'a.**

THE Yemen Arab Republic lies in the south-west of the Arabian peninsula with frontiers on Saudi Arabia and the Red Sea.

## AREA AND POPULATION

The total area of the Yemen Arab Republic is about 75,000 sq. miles.

The population of the Yemen Arab Republic at mid-1974 was 6,379,000. The annual average percentage growth rate of the population for the period 1960–74 was 2·4 and for the period 1965–74 was 2·4.

The principal towns with their populations are: Sana'a 150,000, Hodeida 100,000, Taiz 120,000, Yarim 20,000. Ibb 80,000, Albeida 50,000, Thamer 25,000, Radae 20,000, Hajja 20,000.

## CURRENCY AND FINANCE

The GNP at market prices for 1974 was U.S.$millions 1,160. and the GNP per capita at market prices was U.S.$180. The annual average percentage growth rate of GNP per capita for the period 1960–74 was n.a. and for the period 1965–74 was n.a. [*See the note at the beginning of this section concerning GNP.*]

The unit of currency is the Riyal, divided into 40 buqsha. 1 American dollar is equal to four Riyals. The main sources of Government revenue are the tithe on crops, the tax on capital and a poll tax. However, it is in the coffee crop that the principal wealth of the country lies, and coffee, together with hides, skins and salt, are the most important exports.

The country encourages foreign investment. The 1964 Act regarding foreign capital investment has given the right of foreign investors to transfer their capital profits to any country of their choice.

## PRODUCTION, INDUSTRY AND COMMERCE

The territory has greater fertility than the rest of the peninsula and exports a great deal of food to other Arabian countries, including coffee, raisins and dates. Coffee is also exported to Europe via Hodeida. Hides and skins are also exported.

Besides barley, wheat and millet, large quantities of strawberries, mangoes, pomegranates and grapes (about 24 varieties) and a great abundance of vegetables are produced. Although of an elementary kind, there is an intensive and well-developed system of agriculture.

As yet there has been little industrial development, but there are two textile plants, a cigarette factory and a cement factory now in operation, and there are also schemes for the erection of many other factories to make the country more self-sustaining. There are two Yemeni Banks; however, because of the country's open-door policy and the peace agreement with Saudi Arabia and the normalisation of relations with all countries, many foreign banks, such as the British Bank of the Middle East and the United Bank, the Habeeb Bank, the Arab Bank and the Bank of Indo-China have all opened branches throughout the country. The 1962 Revolution re-initiated a programme in which major improvements are proposed in all spheres of the economy, but further technical assistance will be needed to bring industrial progress to this land.

The Yemen Arab Republic encourages tourism and has expanded the construction of hotels catering for the tourist trade.

The principal imports are textiles, sugar and glass.

Hodeida is the chief port. Mocha, Lohiya, and Saleef are the smaller ports. Sana'a, an ancient walled city, is the largest town. The climate of the inland highlands is the most temperate in the peninsula; the rainfall is heavy, reaching as high as 32 in. in certain parts. There is a wireless station at Sana'a.

## RELIGION

The religion is Islam and the two main sects are the Zaida and the Shafi. Education is mainly Koranic in nature, but after 1962 in addition primary and secondary schools are now being expanded, and scholarships are granted by the Government to promising students who are selected to complete their studies abroad.

# Yugoslavia

## (SOCIJALISTIČKA FEDERATIVNA REPUBLIKA JUGOSLAVIJA)

**Capital**—Belgrade.

**President of the Socialist Federal Republic of Yugoslavia**—Marshal Josip Broz Tito.

**National Flag**: a tricolour fesse-wise, blue, white, red; a star five-pointed red gold-bordered centred.

### CONSTITUTION AND GOVERNMENT

During the victorious four-year struggle of the National Liberation Army of Yugoslavia, under the command of Marshal Josip Broz Tito, against the occupying forces of the Axis powers, the elected representatives of all the nations of Yugoslavia at the II Session of the Anti-Fascist Council of the National Liberation of Yugoslavia, held in Jajce, Bosnia on 29 November 1943, made the decision to establish the new state community of Yugoslavia, on federal principles. Following the general election held in the liberated country on 11 November 1945, the Constitutional Assembly approved a Declaration, on 29 November 1945, naming the state 'The Federal People's Republic of Yugoslavia' composed of six republics: Bosnia and Herzegovina, Croatia, Macedonia, Montenegro, Slovenia and Serbia, as well as the autonomous province of Vojvodina and the autonomous region of Kosovo and Metohija as part of the Republic of Serbia.

The Peace Treaty with Italy, signed in Paris on 10 February 1947, stipulated the cession to Yugoslavia of the greater part of the Italian provinces of Venezia Giulia, Istria and the Slovenian Littoral, Zadar and several islands along the Yugoslav coast. Ethnically Croatian and Slovenian, these territories, liberated during the war by the forces of the National Liberation Army of Yugoslavia, were given to Italy after World War I.

The Constitutional Law in 1953 began the system of self-management actually begun in 1950, as the basis of the entire economic, social and political system of Yugoslavia. The Constitution passed on 7 April 1963 enshrined the right of the working people to self-management in a constitution and also changed the name of the country to 'The Socialist Federal Republic of Yugoslavia', composed of six socialist republics and two socialist autonomous provinces—of Vojvodina and Kosovo—as constituent parts of Serbia.

Amendments made to that Constitution in 1967, 1968 and especially in 1971 consolidated the leading role of the working class in society, and established new relations between the Federation and the constituent republics and provinces on the basis of full equality. These amendments led to the constitutional reform which was completed with the new Constitution being accepted on 21 February 1974, succeeded by the proclamation of respective constitutions of the socialist republics and socialist autonomous provinces.

The new Constitution proceeds from the given facts of economic and political developments, and is adaptable to new circumstances and change in social relations.

The SFR of Yugoslavia is a federal state community of voluntarily united nations and their socialist republics and socialist provinces; it is also a socialist self-managing democratic community of working people and citizens, and of nations and nationalities having equal rights. The socialist republics are states which are self-managing democratic communities. The socialist autonomous provinces are self-managing Socio-political communities. Federal decisions are made with the equal participation and responsibility of the republics and autonomous provinces.

The social system is based on freely associated labour and self-management by the working people in all spheres of public affairs. The basis of the social system is social ownership. Workers can exercise their socio-economic rights. The joint income is distributed independently according to criteria which they have jointly established. Decisions are made at meetings of workers, through referenda. These meetings elect workers' councils and delegations which will take part in political decision-making. The workers' council is the most important part of business management. It also defines the business policy, the plan of work, and the development of the organization. It takes care that workers are kept informed on all matters.

Workers in education, public health, science, social welfare, etc., associate in self-managing communities, which make their own decisions on financing etc.

There are also associations which decide on such matters as the improvement of the environment, child and social welfare education, sports, consumer protection, public utilities and similar things.

Farmers working with their own labour and material are guaranteed the right to make use of the results of their labour, and to enjoy the same status and rights as workers in associated labour. They may, if they wish, pool their labour and resources thus forming agricultural co-operatives, or they may have a common enterprise with associated labour. In this latter case they also have the right to help manage the association on an equal footing with the workers.

Freedom of independent labour with privately-owned labour and materials is guaranteed in other work such as crafts.

Territorial defence is organized uniformally throughout the country. The units of the army are created by the communal assemblies of republics and provinces, from conscripts, and volunteers.

The political structure is delegational. The delegates are drawn from communal assemblies, provinces, the republics, and the Federation. The delegates do not leave their employment during their term of office. The term of office lasts for four years. At the elections, held in 1974, 51,254 delegations, with 839,561 members were elected.

Every citizen over the age of 18 has the vote. The maximum working week is 42 hours. There is freedom of religious worship.

The Assembly of the SFR of Yugoslavia has two chambers: the Federal Chamber consisting of 30 delegates from each of the six republics and 20 delegates from each of the two provinces, 220 delegates in all; the Chamber of Republics and Provinces consists of 12 delegates from each Assembly of the Republic and eight from each Assembly of the Province, 58 in all. These retain their membership of the assemblies to which they have been elected. The term of delegate lasts four years. The President of the SFRY Assembly at May 1974 was Gligorov Kiro, the Vice-Presidents were Cvetković Marijan, Dapčević Peko, Hasani Sinan, Kolak Rudi, and Pešiš Branko. The President of the Federal Chamber is Kekić Danilo, and of the Chamber of the Republics and Provinces Polič Zoran.

The SFRY Presidency represents the SFRY at home and abroad. The Presidency is composed of a member from each Republic, and autonomous Province elected by the respective assemblies for a tenure of five years. The president of the LCY is a member of the presidency by virtue of his office. The Presidency of the SFRY elects a president and a Vice-President from among its members for a tenure of one year. In view of the historical role of Josip Broz Tito in the National Liberation War, Socialist Revolution, and creation and development of the SFRY and in line with the expressed will of the working people and citizens, nations and nationalities of Yugoslavia, the SFRY Assembly elected Josip Broz Tito President of the Republic for an unlimited term of office.

The Federal Executive Council is the executive body of the SFRY Assembly. The President of the Federal Executive Council is elected by both chambers of the SFRY Assembly at the proposal of the SFRY Presidency, and the members of the Council at the proposal of the candidate for the president of the Federal Executive Council. Each republic is represented in the Council by at least three members and each autonomous province by at least two members. The President of the Federal Executive Council is Djuranović Veselin; the Vice Presidents are: Ćulafić Dobroslav, Minić Miloš, Šefer Dr. Berislav and Vratuša Dr. Anton. There are 28 members out of whom 18 are members by virtue of their offices as federal secretaries and chairmen of federal committees.

### POLITICAL ORGANIZATIONS

**The League of Communists of Yugoslavia**

The first Congress of the Communist Party of Yugoslavia was held in April 1919, shortly after the establishment of the new state of the South Slavs, the Kingdom of the Serbs, Croats and Slovenes.

A year later, the second, Vukovar Congress, was held at which the former name of the Party was changed to that of the Communist Party of Yugoslavia, and its Programme and Statutes adopted.

The success of the Communists at the parliamentary and local elections held in November 1920, on which occasion 59

Communist deputies, out of a total of 300 deputies, were elected. Their growing influence provoked the hostility of the ruling circles, which culminated in a Government decree passed in December 1920, under which the Communist Party was outlawed.

When the Second World War broke out, the Communist Party of Yugoslavia had 12,000 members, together with some 30,000 members of the Communist Youth League. At the end of the war, in spite of heavy losses, it had a membership of 141,066.

At the Fifth Congress held in July 1948, which was also the first post-war congress, the Communist Party numbered 468,175 members.

The most important document adopted by the Seventh Congress, held in April 1958, was the new Programme of the League of Communists of Yugoslavia.

The Eighth Congress of the League was held in Belgrade in December 1964. Congress accepted the new statute of the League of Communists of Yugoslavia.

The Tenth Congress of the League of Communists of Yugoslavia was held in Belgrade from 27 May to 30 May 1974. This Congress unanimously elected Josip Broz Tito as President of the League of Communists of Yugoslavia with unlimited tenure. The Central Committee of the LCY has 165 members.

**Presidium of the Central Committee of the League of Communists of Yugoslavia**

*President:* Broz Josip Tito

*Members:*

| | |
|---|---|
| Albreht, Roman | Mesihović, Munir |
| Bakarić, Dr. Vladimir | Mijatović, Cvijetin |
| Balint, Imre | Milatović, Veljko |
| Baltić, Milutin | Minić, Miloš |
| Bilić, Jure | Popović, Dušan |
| Ćulafić, Dobroslav | Popović, Mirko |
| Dolanc, Stane | Ravnik, Miha |
| Doronjski, Stevan | Ristić, Dušan |
| Dugonjić, Rato | Smole, Jože |
| Gligorov, Kiro | Srzentić, Vojislav |
| Grličkov, Aleksandar | Stambolić, Petar |
| Hodža, Fadilj | Stavrev, Dragoljub |
| Kardelj, Edvard | Špiljak, Mika |
| Koliševski, Lazar | Šukrija, Ali |
| Kukoč, Ivan | Vidić, Dobrivoje |
| Kurtović, Todo | Vrhovec, Josip |
| Ljubičić, Nikola | Vujadinović, Jovan |
| Markovski, Krste | Žarković, Vidoje |

**Presidency of the Socialist Federative Republic of Yugoslavia**

*President:* Josip Broz Tito.

*Vice President:* Doronjski Stevan.

*Members:*

Cvijetin, Mijatović (Bosnia-Herzegovina)
Dr. Vladimir, Bakarić (Croatia)
Lazar, Koliševski (Macedonia)
Vidoje, Žarković (Montenegro)
Petar, Stambolić (Serbia)
Edvard, Kardelj (Slovenia)
Fadilj, Hodža (Kosovo)
Stevan, Doronjski (Vojvodina)

*Secretary General:* Kuhar Slavko

**Executive Bureau of the Presidium of the Central Commitee of the League of Communists of Yugoslavia**

*Secretary:* Stane Dolanc
*Secretaries in the Executive Committee:* Jure Bilić, Todo Kurtović, Mirko Popović and Dr. Aleksandar Grličkov.

*Members:*

| | |
|---|---|
| Ivan, Kukoč | Dragoljub, Stavrev |
| Munir, Mesihović | Ali, Šurkija |
| Dušan, Popović | Dobrivoje, Vidić. |

**Presidents of Central and Provincial Committees and the Secretary of the Conferences Committee in the Yugoslav People's Army.** These, by their functions, are also members of the Presidium:

| | |
|---|---|
| Alimpić, Dušan | Popit, France |
| Bakali, Mahmut | Srzentić, Vojislav |
| Čemerski, Angel | Šarac, Džemil |
| Mikulić, Branko | Vlaškalić, Dr. Tihomir |
| Planinc, Milka | |

**The Socialist Alliance of the Working People of Yugoslavia**

This organization grew up from the People's Front of Yugoslavia which had come into being during the National Liberation War as a nationwide political organization. It was given its present name at the IVth Congress in February 1953. The Socialist Alliance had 8,582,000 members in 1974.

The President of the Federal Conference of the SAWP is Petrović Dušan who was elected on 14 June 1974, the Vice-Presidents are: Džunov Risto and Cetinić Marin; the Secretary is Rožić Marijan. The Presidency has 40 members, and comprises four members from each republic, three from each province, presidents of republican and provincial Conferences and representatives of socio-political organizations in the Federation as well as of the Yugoslav People's Army.

## LEGAL SYSTEM

The structure of the judicial system in Yugoslavia is set out in the Constitution of 1963 which states that judicial functions are to be discharged within a uniform system and that the jurisdiction of the courts shall be established and altered only by law. In general, court proceedings are conducted in public. Exceptionally the public may be excluded to preserve professional secrets, public order or morals. Court proceedings are also in the national language of the region in which the court is situated. Citizens who do not know the language in which the proceedings are being conducted may use their own language.

The judicial system consists of courts of general jurisdiction, i.e. communal courts, district courts, republican supreme courts, and supreme courts of autonomous provinces which decide on appeals against the decisions of country courts, the Federal Court, and courts of specialized jurisdiction. Economic cases and other legal matters of concern to the economy are heard by economic courts, and criminal offences committed by military persons in any way connected with service in the army are heard by military courts. Some other courts decide specific disputes brought to them by working people. These other Courts are of several types: courts of associated labour, courts of arbitration, conciliation councils, select courts, and other kinds of self-management courts.

Judges are elected or dismissed by the Assembly of the particular Republic and lay judges are elected or dismissed by the assembly of the particular district or town.

The Constitutional Court of Yugoslavia decides on the questions of consistency of the laws with the Constitution.

*President of the Constitutional Court of Yugoslavia:* Nikola Sekulić.

Number of members: 13.

The Federal Court of Yugoslavia is the highest organ of justice in Yugoslavia.

*President of the Federal Court of Yugoslavia:* Pero Korobar.

Number of members: 24.

There is also an Office of the Public Prosecutor.

*Federal Public Prosecutor:* Vuko Gozze-Gučetić.

The Office of Public Attorney represents proprietary interests of the Federation, republics, districts and communities.

*Federal Attorney-General:* Drago Dragojević.

The Federal Social Attorney of Self-Management carries out his function within the framework of federal rights and duties.

*Social Attorney of Self-Management:* Momčilo Milovanović.

Matters concerning the improvements and functioning of the judiciary system are controlled by the Federal Council for the Judiciary.

*President:* Fira, Aleksandar.

## AREA AND POPULATION

The table at bottom of page 589 shows the basic population structure of Yugoslavia according to the 1971 Census in thousands, and the area of Yugoslavia, its Republics and Provinces.

| | | SFRY | Bosnia & Herze-govina | Monte-negro | Croatia | Mace-donia | Slov-enia | Serbia | | | |
|---|---|---|---|---|---|---|---|---|---|---|---|
| | | | | | | | | all | Restrict. territ. | Vojvo-dina | Kosovo |
| *Population* | | | | | | | | | | | |
| According to national structure: | | | | | | | | | | | |
| Montenegrins | | 509 | 13 | 356 | 10 | 3 | 2 | 125 | 57 | 36 | 32 |
| Croats | | 4,527 | 772 | 9 | 3,514 | 4 | 43 | 185 | 38 | 139 | 8 |
| Macedonians | | 1,195 | 2 | 1 | 5 | 1,142 | 2 | 43 | 25 | 17 | 1 |
| Moslems (in national sense) | | 1,730 | 1,483 | 70 | 19 | 1 | 3 | 154 | 125 | 3 | 26 |
| Slovenes | | 1,678 | 4 | 1 | 32 | 1 | 1,624 | 16 | 11 | 4 | 1 |
| Serbs | | 8,143 | 1,393 | 39 | 627 | 46 | 21 | 6,017 | 4,700 | 1,089 | 228 |
| Albanians | | 1,309 | 4 | 35 | 4 | 280 | 1 | 985 | 66 | 3 | 916 |
| Bulgarians | | 59 | — | 1 | 1 | 3 | — | 54 | 50 | 4 | — |
| Czechs | | 24 | 1 | — | 19 | — | — | 4 | 1 | 3 | — |
| Italians | | 22 | 1 | — | 17 | — | 3 | 1 | — | — | — |
| Hungarians | | 477 | 1 | — | 36 | — | 10 | 430 | 6 | 424 | — |
| Romanians | | 58 | — | — | 1 | — | — | 57 | 4 | 53 | — |
| Ruthenians | | 25 | — | — | 4 | — | — | 20 | — | 20 | — |
| Slovaks | | 84 | — | — | 7 | — | — | 77 | 4 | 73 | — |
| Turks | | 128 | 1 | 1 | — | 109 | — | 18 | 6 | — | 12 |
| Others | | 167 | 9 | 1 | 13 | 50 | 3 | 91 | 51 | 24 | 16 |
| Undeclared nationally | | 33 | 8 | 1 | 16 | 1 | 3 | 4 | 3 | 1 | — |
| "Yugoslavs" | | 273 | 44 | 11 | 84 | 3 | 7 | 124 | 76 | 47 | 1 |
| Regional belonging | | 15 | — | 1 | — | 1 | 3 | 10 | 5 | 5 | — |
| Unknown | | 67 | 10 | 3 | 19 | 2 | 3 | 30 | 22 | 6 | 2 |
| According to age and sex: | | | | | | | | | | | |
| Total | all | 20,523 | 3,746 | 530 | 4,426 | 1,647 | 1,727 | 8,447 | 5,250 | 1,953 | 1,244 |
| | females | 10,446 | 1,912 | 270 | 2,287 | 813 | 891 | 4,273 | 2,665 | 1,001 | 607 |
| 0–34 | all | 12,053 | 2,536 | 344 | 2,367 | 1,091 | 961 | 4,751 | 2,825 | 1,021 | 914 |
| | females | 5,914 | 1,258 | 170 | 1,157 | 533 | 466 | 2,330 | 1,385 | 503 | 441 |
| 35 and over | all | 8,470 | 1,210 | 186 | 2,059 | 686 | 766 | 3,696 | 2,425 | 922 | 330 |
| | females | 4,532 | 654 | 100 | 1,130 | 280 | 425 | 1,943 | 1,280 | 498 | 166 |
| According to economic activity | | | | | | | | | | | |
| Economically active | | 8,890 | 1,374 | 174 | 2,016 | 630 | 837 | 3,859 | 2,703 | 833 | 323 |
| Receiving personal income (pensions, etc.) | | 1,241 | 149 | 35 | 367 | 55 | 195 | 440 | 258 | 156 | 26 |
| Dependents | | 10,392 | 2,223 | 321 | 2,044 | 961 | 696 | 4,147 | 2,289 | 895 | 963 |
| *Area* in square kilometres | | 255,804 | 51,129 | 13,812 | 56,538 | 25,713 | 20,251 | 88,361 | 55,968 | 21,506 | 10,887 |

## CURRENCY AND FINANCE

The unit of currency is the dinar, of 100 paras. Par value is set at 43·3330226 mg. of fine gold as at the end of October 1975. The US dollar equals 17·83 dinars.

There are coins of metal alloys of 1, 2, 5 and 10 dinars and 5, 10, 20 and 50 paras. Notes are of 10, 20, 50, 100, 500 and 1,000 dinars. In 1976 currency circulation, notes and coins amounted to D,46,353 million in December of that year. Federal Budget figures for 1976 were: Revenue D.59,944 million; Expenditure D.59,944 million.

## NATIONAL BANK

**The National Bank of Yugoslavia.** Est. 1883. (Governor, Bogoev, Dr. Ksente); Sole Bank of Issue. *Head Office:* Bulevar Revolucije 15, Belgrade, six Republican National Banks in the capitals of the Socialist Republics.

Specialized banks, such as the Yugoslav Investment Bank, the Agricultural Bank, the Yugoslav Bank for Foreign Trade and seventeen other authorized commercial banks are in charge of financing investments, foreign and internal trade, and promoting production.

## PRODUCTION, INDUSTRY AND COMMERCE

**Agriculture.** In 1976, the country had produced 5·99 million tons of wheat, whereas the wheat output in 1953 had amounted to only 2·8 million tons. Similarly, the production of maize increased from 3·8 million tons in 1953, to 9·1 million tons in 1976. (The maize output in 1975 has amounted to 9·4 million tons.)

Agriculture has been mechanized to a considerable extent, modern methods of land tillage have been introduced and production co-operation between the socialist sector and private farmers extended. In 1976 there were 226,000 tractors.

Before the war 75 per cent of the total population depended on agriculture for their living; now only 38·2 per cent of the inhabitants are engaged in agriculture, although the total population has grown by 5·5 million.

The following table shows the output and area of various crops for 1975 and 1976:

| *Crop* | | 1975 | 1976 |
|---|---|---|---|
| *Area* | (thousand hectares) | | |
| Wheat | ,, | 1,621 | 1,727 |
| Rye | ,, | 84 | 77 |
| Maize | ,, | 2,382 | 2,385 |
| Hemp | ,, | 9 | 8 |
| Tobacco | ,, | 63 | 69 |
| Sugar beet | ,, | 109 | 108 |
| Potatoes | ,, | 314 | 308 |
| *Productive trees* | (thousands) | | |
| Plum trees | ,, | 73,604 | 73,138 |
| Apple trees | ,, | 19,396 | 20,060 |
| Vines | (millions) | 1,450 | 1,412 |
| *Production* | (thousand tons) | | |
| Wheat | ,, | 4,404 | 5,979 |
| Rye | ,, | 98 | 105 |
| Maize | ,, | 9,389 | 9,106 |
| Hemp | ,, | 52 | 56 |
| Tobacco | ,, | 70 | 75 |
| Sugar beet | ,, | 4,213 | 4,711 |
| Potatoes | ,, | 2,394 | 2,828 |
| Plums | ,, | 950 | 562 |
| Apples | ,, | 370 | 486 |
| Grapes | ,, | 1,029 | 1,204 |
| *Yield per hectare* | (quintals) | | |
| Wheat | ,, | 27 | 35 |
| Rye | ,, | 12 | 14 |
| Maize | ,, | 40 | 39 |
| Hemp | ,, | 58 | 74 |
| Tobacco | ,, | 12 | 11 |
| Sugar beet | ,, | 392 | 442 |
| Potatoes | ,, | 75 | 91 |
| | (kilograms per tree) | | |
| Plums | ,, | 13 | 8 |
| Apples | ,, | 19 | 24 |

# YUGOSLAVIA

**Livestock.** In 1976 there were 5,755,000 cattle, 7,831,000 sheep, 7,831,000 pigs and 54,764,000 poultry.

**Forestry.** The forested area covers 9,040,000 hectares. Cut timber production in 1976 amounted to 18,492,000 cubic metres.

**Industry.** Industrial production has increased twelvefold in the post-war period. The increased tempo of industrial activity is shown by the fact that although the number of persons employed in industry and mining rose from 300,000 in 1939 to 1,757,000 in 1974, i.e. six times, productivity grew by more than five times.

The following table gives the output figures of some main industrial products and materials in 1975 and 1976:

| *Product* | | 1975 | 1976 |
|---|---|---|---|
| *Machinery production* | | | |
| Machinery for industry | (thousand tons) | 131 | 138 |
| Machinery for construction | ,, | 35 | 38 |
| Machinery for agriculture | ,, | 69 | 59 |
| Tractors | number | 33,207 | 42,246 |
| Trucks | ,, | 14,847 | 17,471 |
| Waggons, freight | ,, | 3,333 | 3,321 |
| Rotating machines | (MW) | 3,724 | 2,952 |
| Power transformers | 1,000 kVA | 7,897 | 9,815 |
| *Materials production* | | | |
| Electric energy | mill. kWh | 40,040 | 43,573 |
| Coal | (thousand tons) | 35,537 | 36,845 |
| Coke | ,, | 1,351 | 1,786 |
| Crude petroleum production | ,, | 3,692 | 3,880 |
| Petroleum processing | ,, | 10,888 | 11,724 |
| Iron ore | ,, | 5,239 | 4,259 |
| Pig iron | ,, | 2,000 | 1,918 |
| Steel | ,, | 2,916 | 2,715 |
| Rolled goods | ,, | 2,359 | 2,440 |
| Extruded goods | ,, | 286 | 276 |
| Electrolytic copper[1] | ,, | 138 | 136 |
| Lead | ,, | 126 | 111 |
| Zinc | ,, | 89 | 95 |
| Aluminium | ,, | 168 | 198 |
| Mercury | (tons) | 584 | 431 |
| Rolled copper goods | (thousand tons) | 114 | 150 |
| Rolled aluminium goods | ,, | 112 | 131 |
| Ferro-alloys | ,, | 196 | 200 |
| Refractory material | ,, | 334 | 297 |
| Flat glass | (mill. sq. m.) | 21 | 22 |
| Castings | (thousand tons) | 513 | 518 |
| Insulated conductors | ,, | 134 | 122 |
| Sulphuric acid | ,, | 935 | 904 |
| Calcined soda | ,, | 147 | 137 |
| Manufactured fertilizers[2] | ,, | 2,196 | 2,056 |
| Plastics | ,, | 160 | 205 |
| Man-made fibres | ,, | 64 | 65 |
| Bricks | (millions) | 3,331 | 3,342 |
| Roofing tiles | ,, | 356 | 322 |
| Cement | (thousand tons) | 7,066 | 7,621 |
| Sawn conifers | (thousand cu. m.) | 2,161 | 2,183 |
| Sawn non-conifers | ,, | 1,320 | 1,436 |
| Veneer | ,, | 207 | 235 |
| Plywood | ,, | 126 | 121 |
| Particle boards | ,, | 413 | 484 |
| Woodpulp | (thousand tons) | 88 | 100 |
| Cellulose | ,, | 439 | 395 |
| Paper | ,, | 634 | 696 |
| Cardboard and paste-board | ,, | 120 | 114 |
| Cotton yarn | ,, | 107 | 117 |
| Woollen yarn | ,, | 42 | 44 |
| Sole leather | ,, | 3 | 4 |
| Upper leather | (mill. sq. m.) | 17 | 17 |
| Tyres, automobile | (thousands) | 5,110 | 5,644 |
| Tobacco, fermented | (thousand tons) | 59 | 77 |
| *Production of consumer goods* | | | |
| Blown glass | (thousand tons) | 306 | 271 |
| Ceramics, household use | (tons) | 11 | 12 |
| Automobiles | (thousands) | 183 | 195 |
| Motorcycles | (number) | 78 | 58 |
| Bicycles | (thousands) | 373 | 296 |
| Radio-sets | ,, | 140 | 109 |
| Television sets | ,, | 425 | 402 |
| Thermic apparatus | (tons) | 58 | 55 |

*continued*

| *Product* | | 1975 | 1976 |
|---|---|---|---|
| Washing machines, textile | (thousands) | 216 | 336 |
| Soap[3] | (thousand tons) | 184 | 177 |
| Furniture | (thousand suites) | 413 | 432 |
| Cotton fabrics[4] | (mill. sq. m.) | 376 | 385 |
| Woollen fabrics[4] | ,, | 66 | 667 |
| Rayon fabrics | ,, | 39 | 36 |
| Knitwear | (thousand tons) | 25 | 26 |
| Hosiery | (mill. pairs) | 179 | 155 |
| Ready-made underwear | (mill. sq. m.) | 118 | 125 |
| Ready-made outerwear | ,, | 92 | 100 |
| Leather footwear | (mill. pairs) | 48 | 49 |
| Rubber footwear[5] | ,, | 22 | 20 |
| Sugar | (thousand tons) | 525 | 577 |
| Tinned vegetable | ,, | 111 | 113 |
| Tinned meat | ,, | 73 | 81 |
| Tinned fish | ,, | 31 | 28 |
| Edible oil | ,, | 175 | 176 |
| Sweets and chocolate | ,, | 79 | 89 |
| Beer | (thousand hl.) | 8,454 | 8,685 |
| Cigarettes | (thousand tons) | 41 | 42 |

[1] Including the production of secondary electrolytic copper.
[2] Includes production of nitrogenous and phosphorus fertilisers.
[3] Soap and detergents.
[4] Including fabrics of artificial (cellulosic) fibre.
[5] Including footwear made of plastic material.

The following table shows exports and imports by principal countries in million dinars:

| | *Exports* | | *Imports* | |
|---|---|---|---|---|
| | 1975 | 1976 | 1975 | 1976 |
| Total (*Europe*): | 51,379 | 62,130 | 98,840 | 95,971 |
| Austria | 1,273 | 1,711 | 5,384 | 4,219 |
| Belgium | 415 | 588 | 1,693 | 1,670 |
| Bulgaria | 934 | 1,086 | 1,126 | 1,208 |
| Czechoslovakia | 4,154 | 3,923 | 5,409 | 5,559 |
| Denmark | 214 | 317 | 715 | 593 |
| Fed. Rep. of Germany | 5,369 | 7,242 | 24,436 | 20,956 |
| France | 1,478 | 2,161 | 5,962 | 5,410 |
| German Dem. Rep. | 3,217 | 3,281 | 3,798 | 3,716 |
| Greece | 697 | 1,441 | 1,301 | 858 |
| Hungary | 1,469 | 1,519 | 1,933 | 2,140 |
| Italy | 6,323 | 10,132 | 14,722 | 12,927 |
| Netherlands | 930 | 1,075 | 2,022 | 2,106 |
| Norway | 172 | 120 | 464 | 298 |
| Poland | 3,090 | 3,418 | 3,385 | 3,338 |
| Romania | 1,740 | 1,853 | 1,972 | 3,530 |
| Spain | 120 | 247 | 734 | 460 |
| Sweden | 406 | 540 | 1,911 | 1,667 |
| Switzerland | 680 | 761 | 3,468 | 2,644 |
| United Kingdom | 1,070 | 1,005 | 4,036 | 5,142 |
| U.S.S.R. | 17,211 | 19,411 | 13,712 | 17,034 |
| Other countries | 417 | 299 | 607 | 496 |
| Total (*Asia*): | 6,716 | 7,992 | 13,769 | 12,519 |
| Bangladesh | 73 | 66 | 137 | 70 |
| China, P.R. of | 211 | 195 | 315 | 297 |
| India | 2,057 | 2,168 | 793 | 915 |
| Iran | 265 | 405 | 1,056 | 106 |
| Iraq | 2,038 | 1,758 | 6,610 | 7,615 |
| Israel | 219 | 247 | 263 | 256 |
| Japan | 147 | 210 | 3,091 | 1,582 |
| Korea, D.P.R. of | 330 | 191 | 157 | 214 |
| Malaysia | 22 | 100 | 419 | 482 |
| Pakistan | 149 | 230 | 211 | 72 |
| Turkey | 301 | 416 | 155 | 166 |
| Other countries | 707 | 1,907 | 490 | 705 |
| Total (*Africa*): | 4,927 | 5,217 | 5,710 | 4,381 |

*continued*

| | *Exports* | | *Imports* | |
|---|---|---|---|---|
| | 1975 | 1976 | 1975 | 1976 |
| Algeria | 47 | 253 | 345 | 14 |
| Egypt | 856 | 1,234 | 328 | 358 |
| Ghana | 134 | 235 | 495 | 297 |
| Guinea | 67 | 10 | 183 | 63 |
| Libyan Arab Rep. | 1,044 | 1,119 | 747 | 769 |
| Morocco | 108 | 234 | 1,040 | 767 |
| Nigeria | 308 | 1,115 | 6 | 9 |
| Sudan | 54 | 140 | 381 | 427 |
| Tunisia | 204 | 323 | 170 | 118 |
| Zambia | 260 | 124 | 676 | 601 |
| Other countries | 1,845 | 430 | 1,339 | 958 |
| Total (*North and Central Amer.*): | 5,661 | 6,619 | 8,742 | 8,080 |
| Canada | 306 | 309 | 964 | 338 |
| Cuba | 103 | 98 | 244 | 1,082 |
| U.S.A. | 4,498 | 6,001 | 7,096 | 6,286 |
| Other countries | 754 | 211 | 438 | 374 |
| Total (*South America*): | 437 | 764 | 2,708 | 3,279 |
| Argentina | 45 | 27 | 91 | 99 |
| Brazil | 204 | 479 | 1,437 | 2,103 |
| Chile | 10 | 2 | 574 | 380 |
| Colombia | 39 | 48 | 61 | 83 |
| Equador | 38 | 115 | 290 | 346 |
| Peru | 70 | 36 | 167 | 225 |
| Other countries | 31 | 57 | 88 | 43 |
| Total (*Oceania*): | 108 | 205 | 1,075 | 1,005 |
| Australia | 90 | 110 | 896 | 724 |
| New Zealand | 12 | 83 | 179 | 280 |
| Other countries | 6 | 12 | — | 1 |
| Total | 69,228 | 82,927 | 130,844 | 125,235 |

**Commerce.** The following table shows (in thousands of tons) the amounts of imports for various goods:

| *Commodity* | 1975 | 1976 |
|---|---|---|
| Wheat | — | 862 |
| Rice | 5·3 | 10·0 |
| Tropical fruit | 210 | 238 |
| Sugar | 92 | 299 |
| Coffee | 46 | 37 |
| Raw hide, big | 22 | 27 |
| Oil seeds | 12 | 27 |
| Rubber (natural and synthetic) | 77 | 74 |
| Cellulose | 102 | 116 |
| Wool | 18 | 17 |
| Cotton | 85 | 103 |
| Fibres, natural and synthetic | 34 | 32 |
| Fertilizers (natural and manufactured) | 1,310 | 1,403 |
| Coal | 2,310 | 2,755 |
| Coke | 499 | 170 |
| Crude petroleum | 7,398 | 8,293 |
| Organic synthetic dyes | 3·1 | 3·6 |
| Plastic materials | 161 | 161 |
| Tyres and tubes (for transport vehicles) | 26 | 18 |
| Yarns, synthetic and artificial fibres | 20 | 17 |
| Fabrics, synthetic and artificial fibres | 4·5 | 8·3 |
| Pig and scrap iron | 449 | 482 |
| Rolled and extruded steel | 414 | 190 |
| Sheets and plates | 546 | 409 |
| Wire | 196 | 155 |
| Pipes and fittings | 103 | 118 |
| Machines excluding electrical | 414 | 379 |
| Electrical machines, appar. and equip. | 117 | 112 |
| Electrical apparatus for household use | 9·2 | 7·1 |
| Cars and buses | 30 | 41 |
| Trucks | 18 | 17 |

**The following table shows (in thousands of tons) the amounts of exports for various goods:**

| *Commodity* | 1975 | 1976 |
|---|---|---|
| Big livestock | 18 | 12 |
| Horses | 48 | 41 |
| Meat, fresh | 58 | 66 |
| Canned meat | 21 | 25 |
| Canned fish | 11 | 16 |
| Fresh fruit | 33 | 20 |
| Prunes | 15 | 4·6 |
| Hops | 3·8 | 2·9 |
| Wine | 59 | 73 |
| Tobacco | 25 | 25 |
| Fuelwood and pulp wood | 366 | 477 |
| Sawn timber | 555 | 963 |
| Cellulose | 35 | 40 |
| Magnesite | 70 | 35 |
| Bauxite | 1,283 | 1,024 |
| Plastic materials | 34 | 31 |
| Veneer | 16 | 19 |
| Cotton fabrics | 6·6 | 12·9 |
| Ferro-alloys | 65 | 88 |
| Rolled and extruded steel products | 167 | 215 |
| Pipes and fittings | 170 | 246 |
| Copper and alloy products | 81 | 99 |
| Aluminium and alloy products | 124 | 134* |
| Lead and lead products | 63 | 49 |
| Zinc and zinc products | 59 | 53* |
| Machines, parts and equipment (excluding electrical) | 95 | 128 |
| Electrical machines, equip. and apparatus | 110 | 122 |
| Cables and wire | 53 | 55 |
| Rail and road vehicles and parts | 119 | 137 |
| Ships | 251 | 224 |
| Furniture and parts thereof | 77 | 108 |
| Outerwear | 11 | 12·8 |
| Footwear | 20·1 | 22·5 |

* Data for 11 months.

## COMMUNICATIONS

Yugoslavia exploited in 1976 a railway network of 9,967 kilometres with 3,648 passenger cars, 51,228 freight cars and 1,605 locomotives. In 1976 the railways carried over 126 million passengers and over 74 million tons of freight. In recent years, work has begun on the electrification of certain main railway lines, 2·65 thousand km. have been electrified. Modern diesel and electric trains connect Belgrade with Ljubljana, Rijeka, Split, Zagreb, Sarajevo, Skopje and other towns.

The modern highway system in Yugoslavia is steadily expanding. There were 101,607 kilometres of road, including 41,018 kilometres concrete road in 1976.

In 1976, there were 1,735,141 automobiles, 21,029 buses, and 152,356 lorries. Public motor transport enterprises carried a total of 933 million passengers. Simultaneously, 11,175 million kilometre tons of freight were transported in 1976.

Traffic in the seaports increased from 2,100,000 tons in 1939 to 22,945,000 tons in 1976. The number of passengers has quadrupled, the total amounting to more than 11 million in 1976. Yugoslav passenger planes transported 12,700 passengers in 1939 and 4,594,000 in 1976. The Yugoslav Aerotransport—JAT—maintains 47 airliners.

At the end of 1976 there were 1,431,000 telephones in operation. There were 189 broadcasting stations and 4,526,000 wireless sets in use. There were eight television stations and 3,463,000 television sets in operation in 1976.

A telecommunications earth (satellite) station for inter-continental, telephone, telegraph and television communications has been in operation since 1974.

## NEWSPAPERS

**Politika**: Belgrade, circulation (1976) 272,000.

**Borba**: Belgrade, circulation 60,000.

**Vjesnik**: Zagreb, circulation 88,000.

**Delo**: (in Slovenian), Ljubljana, circulation 93,000.

**Oslobodjenje**: Sarajevo, circulation 79,000.

**Nova Makedonija:** (in Macedonian), Skopje, circulation 26,000.

**Pobjeda:** Titograd, circulation 13,000.

**Rilindja:** (in Albanian), Priština, circulation 19,000.

**Magyar Szó:** (in Hungarian), Novi Sad, circulation 32,000.

**Dnevnik:** Novi Sad, circulation 29,000.

*Evening Papers:*

**Večernje novosti:** Belgrade, circulation 341,000.

**Politika Ekspres:** Belgrade, circulation 226,000.

**Večernji list.** Zagreb, circulation 242,000.

## EDUCATION AND RELIGION

In the period 1947/48–1975/76, the network of educational institutions was considerably expanded. 2,554 new schools were opened, comprising 978 elementary, 1,328 secondary, and 248 schools of higher education. In 1975/76 there were 13,442 primary schools with 2,856,453 pupils and 130,977 teachers; 792 schools for skilled workers with 247,315 pupils and 3,016 teachers; 836 technical and other vocational schools with 266,462 pupils and 5,506 teachers; 80 teacher training and art schools with 13,680 pupils and 2,329 teachers; 459 General Secondary schools with 211,919 pupils and 9,827 teachers; and 1,964 other schools with 198,812 pupils and 11,181 teachers.

Higher education has developed rapidly, as regards both number of schools and students enrolled. The largest increase was recorded by advanced vocational schools, their number increasing from nine in 1947/48 to 131 in 1975/76; the number of pupils attending these schools rose in the same period from 3,000 to 119,218 in 1977.

There were 180 faculties and high schools in the winter semester for 1976/77 with 285,055 students and 16,428 teaching staff (including collaborators in teaching).

The Church is separated from the State, and all denominations recognized by law enjoy equal rights.

The churches with numerous adherents are the Serbian Orthodox Church, the Roman Catholic Church, the Islamic Religious Community, and the Macedonian Orthodox Church, though there are other smaller religious groups.

# Zaire

**Capital—Kinshasa.**

**President—Joseph Mobutu.**

**National Flag:** Vert, on a bezant a dexter forearm **sable, the** hand grasping a flaming torch proper.

## CONSTITUTION AND GOVERNMENT

IN June 1960, the former Belgian Congo became an independent Republic. As a result of the elections the distribution of the seats in the Congolese Chamber was on 8 June, announced as follows: The National Congress Movement (Lumumba wing), 41; The National Congress Movement (Kalonji wing), 8; National Progressive Party, 22; African Solidarity Party, 13; Bakango Association, 12; Cerea, 10; Balubakat, 7; Others, 24.

The provincial legislature provides for the election of 14 senators including tribal leaders for each province, the Provinces being Kinshasa, Province of Bandundu, Equatorial Province, Kasai Occidental, Kasai Oriental, Katanga, Kivu, Kongo Central and Oriental Province.

As representative of the largest party, M. Patrice Lumumba was charged with the task of forming the future government, and on 23 June he did, in fact, nominate a Cabinet of 27 members and ten Secretaries of State. M. Joseph Kasavubu, elected Head of State on 24 June, offered to collaborate in the formation of the government.

On 30 June independence was proclaimed. During the independence ceremony, President Kasavubu received the credentials of diplomatic representatives including those of the United Kingdom, U.S.A., the Soviet Union, France, India, Pakistan, Ceylon and Ghana.

After the murder of M. Patrice Lumumba in February 1961, a confused situation developed. Until 1962 there were grave civil and military disorders amounting to civil war. This was due mainly to the régime set up in the Katanga Province where M. Tshombe was President. The policy was to make Katanga independent, or at least to give it autonomous status. Lubumbashi was the headquarters of the Katanga régime.

M. Antoine Gizenga was head of the Lumumbist régime. The Lumumbists did not seek autonomy for any part of the Congo but sought to implement the policies of what was the Lumumbist wing of the National Congress movement which was substantially the largest party in the Congolese Chamber in 1960. The headquarters of the movement were at Kisangani.

In an endeavour to reconcile differences a round-table conference met at Tananarive (Madagascar) but this was not attended by M. Gizenga. The conference was followed by another at Coquilhaville. This abruptly concluded with the arrest and detention of President Tshombe of Katanga. The President was, however, later released and returned to Lubumbashi.

In 1963 the President suspended the constitution until new elections could be held. Tshombe was appointed Prime Minister in July 1964. Elections were held in March 1965.

In November 1965 Major General Joseph Mobutu deposed Kasavubu, proclaimed himself President and suspended presidential elections.

A new Constitution was drawn up which established a Presidential régime, the President of the Republic being constituted head of the executive. The Constitution provides for a single Chamber and has reduced the number of Provinces to eight. The town of Kinshasa has autonomous status. In addition, the Constitution provides for the creation of two political parties.

## AREA AND POPULATION

The Congo has an area of 2,345,409 sq. kilometres.

The population of the country at mid-1974 was 24,071,000. The annual average percentage growth rate of the population for the period 1960–74 was 2·7, and for the period 1965–74 was 2·7. The dopulation is distributed roughly as follows: Kinshasa, 1,225,700; Province of Bandundu, 2,100,000; Equatorial Province, 1,700,000; Kasai Occidental, 1,600,000; Kasai Oriental, 1,717,000; Kivu, 2,168,000; Province du Bas daire, 1,067,000; Province du Shaba, 1,853,000; Province Zu Haut Zaire, 2,400,000.

These are the latest figures available. Owing to the movements of Europeans and of African refugees both within the country and without, these figures only approximate the population figure.

## FINANCE

The general budgetary activities are almost entirely those of implementing the budget of the Republic. Other residual activities include the balance of some cash or accountable operations which do not depend on the implementation of the Budget, under the heading 'extra-budgetary and accountable balance'. Up till 1970 only domestic resources were involved in these operations: ordinary receipts, fiscal or non fiscal, and recourse to the home money market which was almost entirely limited to advances by monetary bodies. This is why the result of those operations resulted practically in the variation of the credits of only the monetary system at the Treasury. Since 1971, the Government has provided, for the general support of the budget, the mobilization of loans from foreign capital markets. General budgetary activities are not only concerned with public domestic debt but extend also to foreign debts.

These activities, which in 1969 had left a surplus of 3·9 million zaires, in 1970 left a deficit of 13·7 million zaires which was expressed in an increase in Treasury financing. In the first half of 1971 this deficit rose to the 41·2 million zaire mark; the result has been an increase both in debts to the domestic financial system and commitments abroad.

The GNP at market prices for 1974 was U.S. $ millions 3,530, and the GNP per capita at market prices was U.S. $150. The annual average percentage growth rate of the GNP for the period 1960–74 was 2·6, and for the period 1965–74 was 2·9. [*See the note at the beginning of this section concerning GNP.*]

## CURRENCY

The unit of currency is now the Zaire. This replaces 1,000 Congolese francs and is divided into 100 Makuta. Each Likuta (plural Makuta) is divided into 100 Sengi. Banknotes are in denominations of 5 Zaire, 1 Zaire, 50, 20 and 10 Makuta.

## PRINCIPAL BANKS

**Banque du Zaire.** (Governor, J. Sambwa.)—Association de droit public (Governor, Martin). Est. 1951; Bank of issue; Balance Sheet at 31 December 1959 showed assets millions fr. 9,685 notes and coin issued millions fr. 6,315 gold assets millions fr. 2,112. *Head Office:* Kinshasa P.B. 27. *European Office:* 54, rue de Namur, Brussels (Belgium).

**Union Zairoise de Banque.**—Société congolaise par actions á responsabilité limitée (Président, Vicomte Paul van Zeeland). Est. 1929 as a Société Anonyme January 1949 transformed into a Limited Congolese Company. Balance Sheet at 31 December 1969 showed assets Z.15,301,826; deposits and current accounts Z.800,000. *Head Office:* Coin avenues Ministre Rubbens et des Aviateurs-Kinshasa. *Secretarial Office:* 3, rue de Namur, 1000 Brussels. 7 Branches.

**Banque Commerciale Zairoise.** (Chairman, Bokana w'Ondangela.) Est. 1909. Balance Sheet at 31 December 1976, Capital and Reserves Z.11,815,505; Assets Z.178,817,060; Deposits and Current accounts Z.2,820,000. *Head Office:* Boulevard du 30 Juin, Kinshasa.

**Banque du Peuple.** (Président, N'Sele Ekofo Anyenga.) Est. December 1947. At 31 March 1972 assets 35,815,279 Zaires; deposits and current accounts 27,000,335 Zaires. *Head Office* 4 rue d'Egmont, Brussels. 2 Branches.

**Barclays Bank Zaire.**—(S.C.P.A.A.L.). Founded December 1901. Nominal capital fr. 40,040,000. *Registered Office:* Brussels, 61 Avenue Louis G.

## PRODUCTION, INDUSTRY AND COMMERCE

**Agriculture.** Agriculture plays an important part in the economy of the Congo. It can provide all the food for the native population with a substantial surplus. Up to 1959 agricultural products supplied raw materials to the local industries. and accounted for 51 per cent in weight, and 35 per cent in value of the country's total exports. Chief agricultural exports are oils and fats, timber, cotton, coffee, rubber, bananas and manioc.

## ZAIRE

**Commerce.** The statistics in the table below, showing export tonnage and value for various commodities for the year 1971 should be treated with caution, quarterly exports being variable and dependent on seasonal harvests as well as on the movement of commodity prices on the world market.

| | *Tons* | *Value in thousands of Zaire* |
|---|---|---|
| Wood | 13,242 | 424 |
| Cocoa | 1,787 | 202 |
| Coffee | 15,928 | 5,585 |
| Tea | 2,000 | 325 |
| India-rubber | 11,647 | 1,577 |
| Copal | 77 | 2 |
| Urena-punga fibre | 278 | — |
| Rauwalfia bark | 137 | 53 |
| Palm oil | 33,107 | 3,557 |
| Palm kernel oil | 11,991 | 1,354 |
| Cottonseed oil | — | 642 |
| Cotton | 1,756 | 491 |
| Palm kernel cakes | 20,509 | 465 |
| Cotton cakes | 693 | 198 |
| Ivory | 20 | — |
| Gold | 1·5 | 791 |
| Silver | — | 377 |
| Copper | 98,885 | 52,621 |
| Zinc | 16,621 | 2,126 |
| Tin | 450 | 645 |
| Cobalt | 895 | 8,428 |
| Cassiterite | 757 | 1,481 |
| Germanium | 324 | 481 |
| Manganese | 90,000 | 384 |
| Zinc alloy | 4,771 | — |
| Wolfram | 96 | 176 |
| Diamonds (carats) | 3,013,641 | 3,478 |
| Petrol products | 61,086 | 143 |
| Electric energy million kWh. | 79 | — |
| Cement | 4 | 53 |
| Glycerine | 163 | 75 |
| Sundries | 5,000·5 | 1,685 |
| Total (tonnage) | 392,226 | 87,819 |

### COMMUNICATIONS

Activity in the field of transport, measured in units of traffic, that is, in ton/kilometres and traveller/kilometres, rose by 7·2 per cent in 1970 and only by 3 per cent in the first half of 1971. These figures, which are lower than the growth rate of general economic activity, are only valid for the large transport bodies for which traffic statistics are available. It is probable that the sector as a whole has made greater strides forward in view of the development of private road transport enterprises and the increase of transport laid on by farming and industrial organizations for their own use.

The condition of the roads, never very satisfactory, has deteriorated as a result of the internal disorders. The traffic on the Congo river, however, traditionally a most important means of transport, has been in the circumstances well maintained. At least up to the end of 1961, the transport organization ONATRA increased its overall river traffic. In September 1960, up-river traffic was 23,457 metric tons and down-river traffic 42,744 tons. The corresponding figures for 1961 were 35,106 and 33,384 metric tons.

Air transport is being maintained and even developed. Towards the end of 1961, SABENA supplied three reconditioned DC6 planes to Air Congo. These are being used for Entebbe–Nairobi and Lagos flights, the transport is to be extended to Dar-es-Salaam, Luanda and Lagos.

There are four daily newspapers, *Salongo*, *Elima*, *Zaire*, and *Masano*.

### EDUCATION AND RELIGION

Before independence, primary education was chiefly in the hands of Catholic and Protestant missionaries. Primary and secondary schools educated over a million native children. There is one National University divided into three campuses, the campus of Kuishasa, the campus of Lubumbashi and the campus of Kisangami.

The religion of the Congo is mainly idol and fetish worship, but there is a substantial native Christian population. There are between three and four million Catholics and about eight hundred thousand Protestants.

# Zambia

(MEMBER OF THE COMMONWEALTH)

**Capital**—Lusaka.

**President**—H.E. Dr. Kenneth D. Kaunda.

**National Flag:** Green background with orange eagle in flight over a rectangular block of three vertical stripes in red, black and orange.

### CONSTITUTION AND GOVERNMENT

ZAMBIA was placed under the direct administration of the British Government in 1924. During the previous 24 years it had been administered separately as north-western and north-eastern Rhodesia and later in 1911, as Northern Rhodesia, by the British South Africa Company. In 1948 the African people were granted their first part in the country's government—two members appointed to the Legislative Council. European settlers had been given a limited voice in the territory's administration in 1918 when an Advisory Council of five elected members was formed. Various constitutional adjustments were made between 1948 and 1959. The electorate under the 1962 constitution was made more representative, introducing direct adult suffrage. A general election in October produced the country's first African Government.

From 1953 to 1963 Northern Rhodesia formed part of the Federation of Rhodesia and Nyasaland. The federation was completely broken up on 31 December 1963.

Late in January 1964, Northern Rhodesia went to the polls under self-governing constitution for the first time. Franchise was based upon universal adult suffrage. Dr. Kaunda's United National Independence Party won 55 of the 65 main roll seats, the African National Congress filling the remaining ten. The National Progress Party secured all ten reserved seats. Dr. Kaunda was installed as the first Prime Minister of Northern Rhodesia.

After the election Dr. Kaunda led a delegation to the London Independence Conference to urge his case for full independence without another election. With the approval of the British Government, Northern Rhodesia, on 24 October 1964, became the Republic of Zambia within the Commonwealth

The President is Head of State and Commander-in-Chief of the armed forces. He must be a citizen of the Republic and a qualified voter. Thirty years is the minimum age for election and the election takes place at the same time as the election of members to the National Assembly. The President normally remains in office until the next presidential election result is known, but the constitution does provide for his removal in special circumstances.

The Vice-President, M. M. Chona, is principal assistant to the President as well as Leader of the National Assembly.

The President may assign portfolios to a maximum of 16 ministers. The Cabinet comprises the President as Chairman, the Vice-President and Ministers.

#### Ministry

*Prime Minister:* The Rt. Hon. E. H. K. Mudenda.
*Minister of Information and Broadcasting:* Hon. Unia Mwila.
*Minister of Foreign Affairs:* Hon. Dr. Siteke Mwale.
*Minister of Home Affairs:* Hon. Aaron Milner.
*Minister of Finance:* Hon. John Mwanakatwe.
*Minister of Rural Development:* Hon. Paul Lusaka.
*Minister of Development Planning:* Hon. Peter Matoka.
*Minister of Power, Transport and Communications:* Hon. James Mapoma.
*Minister of Legal Affairs and Attorney General's Chamber:* Hon. Maiza Chona.
*Minister of Labour and Social Services:* Hon. Hyden Banda.
*Minister of Education:* Hon. Professor Lameck Goma.
*Minister of Commerce:* Hon. Dr. Mutumba Bull.
*Minister of Health:* Hon. Clement Mwananshiku.
*Minister of Local Govt. and Housing:* Hon. Alexander Chikwanda.
*Minister of Lands, Natural Resources and Tourism:* Hon. Safelino Mulenga.
*Minister of Mines and Industry:* Hon. Ackson Soko.

Subject to the President's powers as Head of State, the Cabinet is responsible for the making of government policy.

Parliament consists of the President and a National Assembly of 125 elected members. The President has the power to nominate up to ten additional members. The President is not a member of the National Assembly but can address it any time he wishes.

The normal life of Parliament is five years. Parliament has law-making powers, subject to the assent of the President. It has power to alter the constitution, provided that the proposed amendment has the support of two-thirds of all members at the second and third readings of the Bill proposing the amendment.

The 27-member House of Chiefs is a constitutional instrument whose functions are mainly advisory, but it examines legislation and debates other matters referred to it by the President.

### LOCAL GOVERNMENT

There is a Department of Local Government, three City Councils, six Municipal Councils, 22 Management Boards and a large number of District and Rural Councils. Elections are held once a year, one-third of the Council retiring every year. There are Cabinet Ministers in charge of each of the eight Provinces. The Senior Civil Servant in each Province is the Permanent Secretary.

### LEGAL SYSTEM

The court system includes the Court of Appeal, the High Court and the subordinate and local courts. All have civil and criminal jurisdiction. The High Court exercises the same powers as the British High Court of Justice, subject to the High Court Ordinance of Zambia.

The Court of Appeal is presided over by the Chief Justice and the Justice of Appeal. The Court always sits with a three-man bench; the third member is one of the Puisne Judges of the High Court. The Court of Appeal is at Lusaka, where three High Court Justices are stationed. Two Puisne Judges are at Ndola.

There are four classes of subordinate courts. All criminal cases tried by subordinate courts are subject to review by the High Court.

### AREA AND POPULATION

Zambia's area is 290,586 square miles.

The population of Zambia at mid-1974, was 4,781,000. The annual average percentage population growth rate for the periods 1960–74 and 1965–74 was 2·9. The main cities are Lusaka, the capital (238,200), Kitwe (179,300), Ndola (150,800), Mufulira (101,200), Chingola (92,800), Luanshya (90,400), Kabwe (67,200) and Livingstone (43,000).

### THE ECONOMY

Since Independence, the Zambian economy has forged ahead, making notable advances on several fronts. The achievements have indeed been remarkable considering the various challenges thrown before the country since Independence. The Unilateral Declaration of Independence (UDI) by the rebel regime in Rhodesia in 1965 caused considerable disruption to Zambia's trade routes and accentuated its already disadvantageous position as a land-locked country, but also provided added stimulus to the nation's efforts towards diversification, self-reliance and a reorientation of its trade and commerce from the rebel south to the friendly north.

The second challenge the nation had to face was the emergence of inflationary pressures arising from the upsurge in domestic demand—a natural development in the immediate post-Independence period. In meeting the demand, the nation's enlarged import bill caused a balance of payments deficit in 1968 for the first time since 1962.

Thirdly, the restrictive budget of 1969, designed to arrest the boom and inflation, caused a cut-back in Government expenditure which in turn arrested the growth of investment and of the economy in general. Fourthly, the Mufulira Mine disaster, towards the end of 1970, caused a drop in copper output while prices of this mineral declined steeply from about the middle of 1970 till about the end of December, 1972; these two factors acted adversely on the resources position of the Government and thus reduced the amount of money available for investment and economic development.

The balance of payments situation also deteriorated as a result of fall in exports of copper, on the one hand, and an increase in import bill as well as invisible payments on the other. Hardly had the Government extricated itself from this situation through a series of corrective measures than the nation had to face fresh challenges such as the border closure by the rebel regime in Rhodesia in January, 1973, the worsening international economic situation, which was further accentuated by the oil crisis, giving rise to world-wide economic recession and inflation. In the wake of border closure, the nation's efforts had to be diverted for contingency planning. This, coupled with various constraints like transport bottlenecks, material and manpower constraints, hampered the orderly implementation of the Second National Development Plan and caused a futher slowing down of overall economic growth.

The impact of these factors was reflected in the overall growth rate of the economy since Independence. Aided by the initial boom conditions in copper, the country's gross domestic product, in real terms (at 1965 prices), rose spectacularly at an annual rate of 10·3 per cent during the period 1965–69.

Largely because of the Mufulira Mine disaster and a fall in copper prices which affected Government revenues and investment, the rate of growth of gross domestic product was halved to an annual rate of 5·0 per cent during 1970–72. During 1973 and 1974, copper revenues rose substantially as a result of buoyancy in copper prices but because of the various constraints referred to earlier, economic activity was on a low key during 1973 and 1974, the annual rate of growth being less than 1 per cent during this period.

The structure of the gross domestic product indicates continued dependence of the economy on copper as a main source of income. Mining, predominantly copper, accounted for nearly 40 per cent of the total GDP in 1974. However, during the past ten years or so, its share in the total has fluctuated between a low of about 40 per cent to a high of 53 per cent in 1969. Copper also accounted for 94 per cent of the country's export earnings during 1973, with other minerals—zinc, lead and cobalt—accounting for only 4 per cent.

The degree of the importance of copper to the national economy depends upon the degree of fluctuations in copper prices, which in turn is largely influenced by the trends in world demand for this metal. This the need for diversification of the economy. A measure of success was achieved as may be seen from the fact that the share of manufacturing in GDP increased steadily from about seven per cent in1965 to about 13 per cent in 1974.

As regards the other sectors of the economy, the nation doubled its output of energy and power and made spectacular advances in transport and communications. The construction sector made notable advance up to 1969, after which because of the 1969 restrictive budget, and the emergence of shortage of building materials,the activity slackened. The only sector to show less than expected promise was the agricultural sector: concerted efforts are being made to accelerate activity of this sector. Diversification of the economy is a long-term process. In the meantime, Zambia has initiated some measures to ensure a degree of stability in copper prices.

Firstly, a metal Marketing Corporation was established in 1974 as a result of the Economic Reforms with the responsibility of marketing copper and other metals. Secondly, as a member of CIPEC, Zambia, along with the other members of this organization, has effected a cut in exports of copper in an endeavour to maintain prices by influencing the supply side. Finally, by virtue of its membership of this organization, which is expanding by the addition of new members, Zambia and other members will be able to strengthen their world position in respect of copper.

The economic achievements of Zambia, since Independence, have been the result of the country embarking upon a process of planned development. After two short-term plans the First National Development Plan was launched in June 1966, with the main objective of securing rapid and sustained development in all areas of the economy.

The Plan was scheduled to run up to December, 1970, but was extended up to December, 1971, so as to consolidate the gains achieved already. Meanwhile, a much more comprehensive plan—the Second National Development Plan, 1972–76—was in the process of formulation and was launched in January, 1972.

The First National Development Plan was successfully mplemented, the achievements both in financial, as well as in physical terms, having exceeded or at least approximated the targets. In terms of physical achievements, the manufacturing sector witnessed a phenomenal growth, the annual rate of growth exceeding the planned rate by three per cent. The programme of industrialization resulted in the establishment of several new industries—sugar, textiles, milling, nitrogenous fertilizers, fruit canning, metal fabrication—and expansion of existing ones—cement and brewery. In power and electricity the nation is poised for attaining self-sufficiency (and is even likely to become a net exporter of electricity), whereas in 1964 50 per cent of the energy requirements were met by imports.

The Second National Development Plan seeks to carry further the main objectives embodied in the First National Development Plan. Briefly, it is aimed at further diversification of the economy, rapid development of the rural economy and spread of rural industrialization, and expansion in education and training so as to achieve rapid Zambianization. The Plan envisaged a total investment outlay of K1,956 million over the Plan period 1972–76, of which K1,271 million is the public sector outlay and K685 million the private sector outlay; however because of inflation and other factors the costs went up considerably.

As in the case of the First National Development Plan, the implementation of the Second National Development Plan was hampered by a number of external factors such as the worsening international monetary and economic situation, the Rhodesia border closure which created temporary shortages and the adverse agricultural performance during 1973. Though the country has succeeded in overcoming the situation created by the border closure, with assistance from friendly countries, and succeeded in developing alternative trade routes, the rerouting exercise accentuated the inflationary situation; the Plan outlays during 1972 and 1973 were below the levels postulated in the Plan.

Aided by a spurt in copper prices and, therefore, Government revenues and with a view to stimulating the economy, the Minister of Planning and Finance introduced an expansionary budget for 1974, the main features of which were a step up in Government capital expenditure and provision of a number of tax incentives. However, because of the transport bottlenecks and shortages, the actual outlay once again turned out to be below the level provided. With a view to making up for the shortfall, the budget for 1975 has once again provided for a steep increase in capital expenditure.

Zambia, like all the developing nations, is feeling the bite of the oil crisis and the worldwide economic recession. Copper, the mainstay, is no longer buoyant but is facing a slump in demand. Secondly, the impact of imported inflation is also affecting the economy severely causing considerable hardship to the common man. The challenge can be met only by concerted steps towards self-reliance and self-sufficiency in food and in other essential commodities. Government has been sparing no pains in providing all incentives to the people to become self-reliant and to promote food production. It is up to the people to respond to Government's initiative and to work hard towards the objective of becoming self-reliant.

Another major challenge is the problem of unemployment. The target of employment creation embodied in the SNDP is far from being fulfilled. To meet this situation, the Plan is laying great emphasis on projects which are labour intensive. The Rural Reconstruction Programme, under the auspices of the Zambia National Service could, if implemented successfully, go a long way in solving the problem of unemployment.

The GNP at market prices for 1974 was U.S. $2,470 million, and the GNP *per capita* at market prices was U.S.$520. The annual average percentage growth rate of the GNP *per capita* for the period 1960–74 was 2·3, and for the period 1965–74 was 1·0. [*See the note at the beginning of this section concerning GNP.*]

## PRODUCTION, INDUSTRY AND COMMERCE

**Agriculture and Livestock.** About three-quarters of the people of Zambia derive a living from agriculture. The agricultural industry stands second only to copper mining in importance in the national economy.

The broad aim of agricultural development is for self-sufficiency in the basic foods which constitute a balanced nutritive diet and, where possible, a surplus production of certain crops for re-distribution within the country and for export. Increased production of both crops and livestock is planned through state projects and from the small- and large-scale farmers and farm co-operatives.

Whilst aiming for self-sufficiency in crop and livestock production, one of the main considerations affecting agricultural policy is the need to improve the way of life of the rural communities so as to reduce the disparity between rural and urban communities and the flow of people from the agricultural districts to the towns.

In 1965, a total of 263,000 tonnes of maize was bought

by marketing organizations and, apart from the poor growing season of 1969–70, this total has been exceeded every year, culminating in a mammoth crop of over 616,000 tonnes in 1972. A poor rainy season had an adverse effect on the 1972–73 crop but even so more than 386,000 tonnes were bought in 1973. An excess of rain in the 1973–74 season has made growing conditions difficult but production went up to 565,000 tonnes. Maize is the staple food of Zambia's people.

The raising of poultry is now the second most important agricultural activity, following maize. The remarkable transformation in production is shown in the following figures:

| | 1964 | 1974 |
|---|---|---|
| Day-old-chicks | 25,000 | 8,750,000 |
| Eggs | 17,000,000 | 134,000,000 |
| Table birds | 65,000 | 7,250,000 |

In this period the value of marketed poultry products rose from K1,100,000 to K12,120,000—though the 1974 figure no longer includes the value of local sales of day-old-chicks, which forms the major part of the hatcheries' business. In 1973 exports of day-old chicks were up to 1,350,000, compared with 135,000 in 1967, the year when exports were first made. Principal customers were Uganda, Tanzania and Zaire.

In 1974 the raw sugar factory at the Nakambala Sugar Estates produced 64,550 tonnes of raw sugar from 570,000 tonnes of crushed cane. This, together with opening stock held over and 16,000 tonnes of raw sugar imported from Swaziland, was refined into 80,000 tonnes. The Zambia Sugar Company's original estimate of 80,000 tonnes of raw sugar from Nakambala had to be reduced to 66,000, as a result of adverse climatic conditions, particularly the heavy rain which caused flowering in the cane. It was the longest harvesting season experienced at Nakambala, lasting 256 days from 9 April to 20 December.

Estimates for the 1975 crop are 97,000 tonnes of raw sugar from 810,000 tonnes of cane produced at Nakambala and by private farmers in the district, a 50 per cent increase. To cope with the additional cane the ZSC is spending K750,000 to extend the capacity of the raw sugar factoryat Nakambala.

Further expansion is also taking place at the Ndola Sugar Refinery. This will bring the annual capacity to 75,000 tonnes from the present 60,000 tonnes at a cost of K300,000

An ambitious five-year scheme which will turn Zambia into a sugar exporting country has already been started. It involves increasing the capacity of the raw sugar factory at Nakambala from 100,000 tonnes to 150,000 per year at an estimated capital cost of K21 million. The cane growing area will in turn be extended to 12,150 hectares through the development of a further 4,050 hectares which will include the contribution from local cane farmers.

At Ndola the ZSC's refinery will be raised to an annual capacity of 100,000 tonnes of refined sugar per year, costing an estimated K650,000 in capital expenditure.

The project will ensure continued self-sufficiency in sugar for Zambia and during the last three years of the development scheme the sugar company plans to have a surplus of between 10,000 and 20,000 tonnes available for export. If the price of sugar remains at its current high level on the open market this should mean a considerable earning in foreign exchange.

The company's products include treacle, syrup and jams in addition to white and brown sugar.

Virginia flue-cured and Burley tobaccos are grown to supply the local cigarette manufacturing industry and there is a surplus for export. In 1974, 6,201 tonnes of Virginia tobacco sold for K6,118,000, while 430 tonnes of Burley realised K379,000. Production of Virginia, which has a good export potential, is being boosted by small-farmer schemes run under Government auspices. There were only twenty-eight farmers involved in these schemes in 1967 but the number has now reached 2,025.

In 1964–65 the total area under cotton was 2,468 hectares, of which almost exactly half was grown by small-scale farmers. Production was 2,273 tonnes. In 1972 production of 8,376 tonnes off 12,038 hectares was entirely by small-scale farmers. Production was as high as 12,053 tonnes in 1971, but declined to 4,090 tonnes in 1973, due both to the difficult season and the more attractive price offered for maize. The price offered for cotton has now been raised to promote production. The two ginneries in Lusaka and Chipata provide the raw materials for the textile factory at Kafue.

The country has a total beef cattle population of about 1,500,000. Commercial farmers own 200,000 and their annual "take-off" for slaughter is 17 per cent. The majority of the herd is owned by those who in the past regarded their animals more as an asset and a status symbol than as a commercial venture and consequently annual take-off was low, but showed a marked improvement in 1973. Total sales were 103,900 head as against 72,443 in 1972 and 47,000 in 1968. There is considerable scope for expansion of the beef industry and Zambia, which at present imports beef, could become a major exporter.

The Dairy Produce Board supplies milk and milk products along the line of rail with the exception of the Choma and Livingstone areas, which have their own organizations. The commissioning in 1973 of a new factory in Lusaka, producing ultra-heat-treated milk which is capable of remaining fresh without refrigeration for at least three weeks, has greatly extended the Board's potential market. With the increased demand for milk since Independence there is now a shortage and the Government has established State dairies near the line of the railway and in the rural areas to boost supplies and to assist in the development of livestock generally. To meet the shortfall the DPB sells at a lower price, fortified milk, made from imported ingredients. In 1974 the DPB bought 12,818,000 litres and sold 24,075,000 litres of fortified and 12,043,000 of fresh milk.

Imports are controlled through the National Agricultural Marketing Board which has now become a major wholesale agency for fruit and vegetables. Production of these commodities in Zambia in 1973 was: fruit 5,500 tonnes; and vegetables 20,000 tonnes. Producers are being encouraged to diversify and to improve techniques to avert seasonal shortfalls. To supply the growing demand for citrus and other fruit budlings, fourteen fruit nurseries have been established and in 1973 produced 50,000 trees. Pineapple production is concentrated in the Mwinilunga district where there is a cannery which also processes tomatoes and guavas. Strawberries (42 tonnes) and melons (402 tonnes) were exported to Britain and Holland by a Lusaka farmer in 1973.

Coffee production in 1973 was 14·5 tonnes. Government policy is to increase production on a small-scale farmer basis.

Zambia's requirements of edible cooking oil were 13,000 tonnes in 1973 and this is expected to increase to more than 16,000 tonnes in 1976. Most of this has been met by imports but the Government is now actively encouraging the production of sunflowers, soyabeans and groundnuts to avoid unnecessary reliance on imports.

## COMMUNICATIONS

**Roads.** Since independence, land-locked Zambia has undergone a major revolution in the field of communications. As the functioning of the nation's economy is almost entirely dependent on transport routes to the sea it is vital that Zambia be allowed to develop her full potential without the fear of outside interference with her imports and exports and it is to this end that the Government's policy has been directed.

Under colonial administration the early development of communications tied Zambia firmly to southern Africa and roads, railways, air routes and telecommunications were historically developed with that region. With the coming of independence and the immediate upsurge in the nation's economy, Zambia's lines of communication were quickly shown to be inadequate and, when Rhodesia made her unilateral declaration of independence in November 1965, the pressing need for development and a reliable route to the sea suddenly became urgent. This need for a reliable route was further demonstrated when Rhodesia closed her border with Zambia in 1973 in an attempt at economic blackmail.

The Great North Road, connecting Kapiri Mposhi (mid-way between Lusaka and the Copperbelt) to the port of Dar-es-Salaam on the Tanzania coast, has now been tarred throughout the 809 km which fall within Zambia. Tanzania has been responsible for tarring the remainder of the route.

The Great East Road from Lusaka to Chipata and thence to the Malawi border, a distance of 586 km, has now been completely tarred, providing a good second route for imports and exports via Salima on the Malawi railway system.

A tarred road 185 km in length has been completed along part of the southern border of Zambia between Livingstone and Sesheke. This road will soon be connected via Kazungula on the Zambezi River with a greatly improved road which the Botswana Government is constructing between Kazungula and Francistown.

Internally, Mongu is now connected to Lusaka by a tarred road (583 km) and Solwezi is connected to the Copperbelt through Chingola by a 173 km tarred road.

A 90 km tarred road linking Mansa to Chembe on the

Luapula River has been completed. Negotiations are taking place with the Zaire Government regarding improvement of the 68 km of road passing through the 'Pedicle' between Chembe and Mokambo and construction of a major bridge across the Luapula River at Chembe.

It is also planned to tar the 211 km stretch of road between Kasama and Mpika. Meanwhile Kasama is now being served by the new Tanzania/Zambia railway line. Zambia now has nearly 3,650 km of tarred Class I roads as against 1,280 km at Independence.

**Railways.** Construction of the 1,860 km railway linking Zambia with Dar-es-Salaam started in 1970 at the Tanzanian end and by August 1973 the line had already crossed into Zambia. Built and financed on generous terms by the People's Republic of China, work on the line is now two years ahead of schedule and went into operation in 1975. China has given an interest-free loan of K286,600,000 which will be repaid by Zambia and Tanzania on a 50 per cent per country basis over a 30-year period commencing in 1983. This line will obviously become Zambia's main transport route and will speed up the development of the areas through which it passes.

The line will connect with Zambia's existing rail system at Kapiri Mposhi. This was developed as an extension of the South Africa system and runs through Zambia from Livingstone in the south to the Zaire border in the north-west, serving the lead and zinc mine at Kabwe and the Copperbelt mines.

**Civil Aviation.** There are some 125 aerodromes in Zambia. fifty of which are Government-owned: the remainder being mainly minor aerodromes operated for specific purposes by the private sector.

The principal aerodrome is the Lusaka International Airport, which was commissioned in July 1967, and is rated as being one of the most advanced of its kind in Africa, capable of handling the most sophisticated types of aircraft likely to be introduced on world air routes in the foreseeable future. Passenger movements through the airport in 1973 totalled some 305,000 whilst the rapidly expanding air freight centre handled over 20,000 tonnes of goods.

Seven international airlines—Air Malawi, Alitalia, British Airways, British Caledonian Airways, East African Airways, UTA French Airlines and Zambia Airways—operate services through Lusaka and provide a broad coverage of connections to most parts of the world.

There are regional airports at Ndola and Livingstone, and secondary aerodromes at Mongu, Solwezi, Mansa, Kasama, Chipata and at certain other towns of importance, carrying regular scheduled air services which provide essential links with Lusaka and other parts of the country.

The national airline, Zambia Airways Corporation, wa formed in 1967 and during its initial development period has established a gradually expanding network on both international and domestic routes. In 1973 these services covered nineteen domestic centres and foreign cities in Botswana, Britain, Cyprus, Italy, Kenya, Malawi, Mauritius and Tanzania. The airline's fleet consisted of one DC-8, two BAC 1-11s and four HS-748 aircraft.

A number of charter companies, based mainly in Lusaka and on the Copperbelt, operate a variety of light aircraft for air taxi purposes and, in most cases, provide a maintenance service for these aircraft.

The Government operated Zambia Air Services Training Institute is the country's air 'college', offering courses in flying training to professional pilot licence standards, air traffic control, telecommunications, engineering and operations, aircraft engineering and rescue/fire operations. In addition, there are a number of flying clubs providing private pilot licence instruction and recreational flying.

The number of aircraft registered in Zambia exceed 200 and range from light single-engined aeroplanes to a four-jet-engined DC-5.

**Posts, Telegraphs and Telephones.** Post offices operate at 200 towns and villages throughout Zambia offering all normal postal services. International air mail services operate to all parts of the world.

An automatic telephone service is provided in most of the larger towns with manual exchanges at some of the smaller centres, and an international service operates in thirteen major centres.

Ordinary and urgent telegrams are accepted for transmission within Zambia and an international telegraph service is also provided to all parts of the world.

An automatic telex service operates in the larger towns with connections to most parts of the world.

**Education.** Since 1964 the Ministry of Education has carried out one of the most ambitious programmes of expansion ever undertaken on the African continent and this has already led to a complete transformation of the educational scene. Primary school enrolments were up from 378,417 in 1964 to 810,739 in 1973. The number of pupils starting primary school each year is approaching that of the seven-year age group although rapid population increases and massive internal migration are providing serious challenges to achieving the target of universal primary education.

At secondary level progress has been, if anything, even more spectacular, with an increase from 13,871 to 65,764 in 1974, and by the start of the 1975 school year there were 119 secondary schools in Zambia. Prior to Independence most secondary schools had been sited in or near the major centres of population. The policy since then has been to ensure that opportunities for secondary education should be as widely spread as possible and now every district has at least one secondary school.

Great progress has been made in providing a curriculum suitable for Zambia and the basic structure and teaching materials for the seven-year Zambia Primary Course are now virtually complete. There is still more work to be done on developing the secondary school curriculum as well as practical subject training for the upper primary school, and this will be a continuous process so that it keeps pace with the needs and aspirations of a fast-changing society. The Ministry's Curriculum Development Centre also publishes *Orbit*, a magazine for Zambian youth which vividly presents science and technology, history, public affairs and sport to an ever-increasing readership. The seven main Zambian languages are taught and four of them, Tonga, Lozi, Bemba and Nyanja, can be taken at School Certificate level.

Pupils write the Grade VII composite examination at the end of their primary course and the results of this examination both determine who will proceed to secondary school and provide a school-leaving qualification. In 1974, 95,000 candidates wrote the examination, of whom 22 per cent were offered places in Form I of the secondary school. A second examination is written at Form III level on the basis of which roughly half the candidates are given the change to complete the secondary school course. The Cambridge Overseas School Certificate examination is written after five years of secondary school. Various overseas examinations, including the University of London GCE are also administered to external students.

The University of Zambia, which admitted its first students 1966, had an enrolment of 2,600 full-time students in 1974, housed in fine modern buildings on the outskirts of Lusaka. The first twenty-seven graduates were capped in early 1969 and 284 students graduated in 1973–74. The schools at the University are: Humanities and Social Sciences, Natural Sciences, Education, Law, Engineering, Mining, Agricultural Sciences and Medicine.

The Department of Technical Education and Vocational Training is concerned with training for occupational competence in Zambia. As recently as 1968 only about 300 Zambians were in formal technical education training, either in Zambia or abroad. Now almost 4,000 are enrolled in Departmental training programmes. In addition, 5,000 people are doing part-time courses. By the end of 1976 full-time enrolment is expected to exceed 8,000. The Department also assists with the training programmes of individual firms and industries.

Adult education has also been expanded. Before Independence classes for adults were confined to the major centres of population. Now they are available in all parts of the country and enrolments exceed 53,000. The academic subjects offered run from the beginners' level to GCE 'O'-level and it is also possible to take courses in typewriting, shorthand, book-keeping, commerce, banking, office practice, secretarial work, shopkeeping and librarianship.

The Correspondence Course Unit in Luanshya provides correspondence education in academic subjects to those who have already passed Grade VII. It is intended soon to offer commercial, technical, agricultural and management subjects.

The Ministry has an Educational Broadcasting and Television Service and there are plans to expand it for use in adult education. Some of its programmes have been specially designed for those who leave school at Grade VII and Form III levels to assist them in coping with the difficulties they are likely to encounter.

In addition, teaching was provided for 126 physically handicapped students in 1974 and 166 deaf students in special schools and units. In the same year 378 blind students were at primary school, fifty-four at secondary school, five at a teacher training college and one at University.

Due to the expansion of teacher training facilities in

Zambia the Ministry of Education has now stopped recruiting primary school teachers from abroad. There are eight primary school teacher training colleges and one National In-Service Training College. The colleges in Kitwe, Livingstone and Mongu are being expanded and new colleges are under construction at Mansa and Solwezi. To supply tutors for these colleges a number of carefully selected primary school teachers with good qualifications and experience are undergoing a two-year course at the University's Institute of Education, leading to a diploma in teacher education.

Increasing numbers of secondary school teachers are now qualifying at the country's training establishments. Output from the University was 91 in 1974 as against ten in 1970 with 210 from Nkrumah Teachers College (sixty-seven in 1970) and twenty-four from the Natural Resources Development College (six in 1972). The Copperbelt Teachers College opened in 1974 with 150 students. It specializes in mathematics, science and homecraft and doubled its enrolment in 1975. The Technical and Vocational Teachers College opened that year at Luanshya with an initial enrolment of 180 which increased to 320 in 1976.

At present only 26·5 per cent of the staff of the University of Zambia are Zambians but a vigorous staff development programme is under way and it is hoped that by 1978 more than half of the academic posts will be filled by Zambians.

The rapid expansion and increasing complexity of the education system has required a rise in recurrent expenditure by the Ministry of Education from K14·36 million in 1964–65 to an estimated K71·6 million in 1975.

# A

**AALTO, Erkki Tauno,** MSc. Building Entrepeneur. *B.* 1904. *Educ.* Institute of Technology (MSc). *M.* 1932, Aune Mirjam Pulkki. *S.* Erkki Juhani. *Daus.* Mirja Sinikka and Riitta Liisa. *Career:* Asst. Supt. Ahvenkoski Power Station construction 1930–31; Consulting Designer 1930–34; Assoc. Engineer, Central Board of Road & Waterways Construction 1932; Chief Designer and Asst. Supt. Rouhiala Power Station construction 1934–36; Head, Dept. of Construction, Yhtyneet Paperitehtaat Oy Paper Mills 1937–43; Man. Dir. of Pohjolan Voima Power Stations and of its subsidiary companies, Lapin Voimajohto Oy (Chmn. 1949–54), Ouko Oy, and Hava Oy (Chmn. 1950–57) 1943–56; Gen. Man. (and Chmn. Fuel Bureau), Finnish State Railways 1956–67; Chmn. or Bd. mem.: Jokoinen-Forssa Railway Co. 1597–67; Pohjolan Liikenne 1957–67; Viipurin Linja-auto Oy 1957–67; Ajokki Oy 1957–67; Matkaravinto Oy 1957–67; Chmn. (Man. Dir. 1955), Atomienergia Oy 1955–67; member, Administrative Council, Tarmo Insurance Co. 1947–67; Bd. Mem., Finnish Tourist Assoc. 1958–67; Ministry of Transportation 1957–67; Mem., Espoo City Council 1977–. *Member:* Assn. Power Station Constructors; Construction Industry Assn.; Finnish Water Power Assn.; Kemi Chamber of Commerce; Central Chamber of Commerce; Foundation for Productivity Research (Bd. Mem.), and several State committees. Has participated in the design and construction of (among other undertakings) 14 water power stations in Finland. *Awards:* Cross of Liberty 4th Class; Knight 1st Class Order of the White Rose; Knight Comdr. 1st Class, Order of the Lion (both of Finland); Cmdr. Order of the Crown (Belgium) and of St. Olav (Norway). *Publications:* articles in technical reviews, on Finland's water power resources, power stations and their exploitation. *Address:* Italinnake 8, 02160 Espoo 61, Finland.

**AAMUNDSEN, Carl Nicolai Ring.** Norwegian naval architect. *B.* 28 June 1894. *Educ.* Univ. of Glasgow (BSc, LLD). *M.* 1921, Birgit Aamundsen. *Career:* With A/S Burmeister & Wain's Maskin- og Skibsbyggeri 1909–15; Asst. Dir., A/S Akers mek. Verksted 1920–32, Man. Dir. 1932–58; Vice-Chmn. Bd. of Dirs. 1958–64; Pres. Norwegian Shipbuilders Assn. 1940–55, and Fed. of Employers of the Iron Industry of Norway 1955–58; Mem. of Bd., Norway Employers' Assn. 1933–65; Norwegian Veritas 1936–65; Oslo Sparebank 1940–64, and of other companies and associations. *Awards:* Gov. Fondation Européenne de la Culture; War Medal 1940–45; Knight, Order of Dannebrog (Denmark); Knight, Order of St. Olav (Norway); His Majesty's Gold Medal of Merit; Chevalier, Legion of Honour (France); Officer, Order of Orange Nassau (Netherlands); Grand Comdr., Order of the Sun and the Lion (Iran). Hon. Corresponding; Fellow, Royal Institution of Naval Architects. *Address:* Hambros Alle 4, Hellerup, Copenhagen.

**ABAYOMI, Sir Kofo,** MD, ChB, DTM & H, FRSA. Yoruba eye specialist; Rhodes Scholar in Ophthalmology. *B.* 1896. *Educ.* Methodist Boys' High School, Lagos; Edinburgh Univ.; Moorfields Eye Hospital, London; DOMS 1941. *M.* 1932, Oyinkan Morenikeji, MBE, *S.* 3. *Dau.* 1. *Career:* Consultant Oculist, School Clinic; served with ambulance in Cameroons in World War I; Government Dispenser 1917–22; Mem. of Privy Council, Nigeria 1947–60; Chief Onashokum of Oyo (since 1949); Chief Baba Isale of Lagos (since 1952); Mem. Legislative Council 1938–41; Executive Council 1949; Univ. College Council 1947–60; Chmn., Bd. Man., Univ. Teaching Hospital, Ibadan; Chmn. Lagos Executive Development Bd.; Hon. LLD, Mount Allison Univ., Canada, and of Ibadan; Chmn., Bd. of Trustees, Glover Memorial Hall, Ibadan; Dir., Nigeria Branch, Barclays Bank, D.C.O., I.C.I., Nigerian Rediffusion Co., P.L. Co. Ltd., P.Z. & Co. Ltd., Nigerian Univ. Pensions Management Co. Ltd., Nigerian Life & Pensions Consultants Ltd., and Phoenix Assurance Co., Nigeria; Vice-Chmn., Bd. of Dir., Bata Shoe Co. (Nigeria). Clubs: Metropolitan Lagos; Dining Ikoyi. *Address:* P.O. Box 300, Lagos, Nigeria.

**ABBETT, Robert William.** American. Consulting engineer to various National, State, County and City Governments; industrial corporations and other agencies. *B.* 1902. *Educ.* Univ. of Missouri School of Mines (BS in CE 1927; CE 1933); Yale Univ. (MS n CE 1932). *M.* 1953, Ruth Virginia Bloomer. *S.* Robert William, Jr. *Career:* Surveyor, designer and engineer on construction of railroads, municipal projects, bridges and buildings for various private and governmental agencies 1923–29; Instructor, Dept. of Civil Engineering, Yale Univ. 1929–33; Assoc. Prof. of Civil Engineering, Union Coll. 1933–38; Associate, Parsons, Klapp, Brinckerhoff & Douglas, and Waddell & Hardesty, N.Y.C. 1938–40; Asst. Prof. of Civil Engineering, Columbia Univ. 1940–41; Lieut. to Commander, Civil Engineer Corps, U.S.N.R. (technical specialist on waterfront structures) 1941–45; Partner, Tippetts-Abbett-McCarthy-Stratton, consulting engineers in the U.S. and 30 other countries, on major engineering projects in the fields of highways, railroads, bridges, water resources development and harbour work; also on major mineral development projects, in U.S., Quebec, Venezuela, Africa and Australia 1945–. *Member:* Amer. Inst. of Consulting Engineers; Amer. Socy. of Civil Engineers; Socy. of Sigma Xi; Amer. Concrete Inst.; Amer. Railway Engineering Assn. *Publications:* Engineering Contracts and Specifications, 4th edn. 1963; Editor-in-Chief, Amer. Civil Engineering Practice, 1957; miscellaneous articles in technical journals and magazines. DSc, Gettysburg Coll. 1953. *Clubs:* Explorers, Yale, Univ. (N.Y.C.); Army & Navy (Washington, D.C.). *Address:* 2 Sutton Place South, New York City, 10022; and *office* 345 Park Avenue, New York City 10022, U.S.A.

**ABBOTT, Charles Homer.** *B.* 1909. *Educ.* Yale Univ. (BA) and St. Lawrence Univ. (LLB). *M.* 1940, Jane Millikin. *S.* Edwin Hunt, John Millikin, and Fred Hardy. *Dau.* Betsy. *Career:* Sales dept., National Distillers Prod. Corp. 1933–42; Field Operations Officer, Fuel Rationing Div., O.P.A. 1942–43; Administrator in charge, Price Boards O.P.A. 1946–47; Special Representative, Great Lakes Steel Corp. 1947–49; With General Plywood Corp. District Mgr. 1949–50, Sales Mgr. 1950–52, Vice-Pres. Sales 1952–56, Gen. Mgr. Panel & Door div., Atlas Plywood Co. 1956–58; Vice-Pres. Marketing, Stylon Corp. 1958–62; With Samson Ocean Systems Inc., Dir. since 1962, Pres. 1963–75, Chmn since 1975. *Member:* Phi Delta Theta; Phi Delta Phi. *Clubs:* Yale (N.Y.C.). *Address:* 156 Ridgeway Road, Weston, Mass. 02193; and *office* 99 High Street, Boston, Mass. 02110, U.S.A.

**ABBOTT, Stuart Evelyn,** OBE. British banker. *B.* 21 Aug. 1910. *Educ.* Rugby School; Balliol Coll., Oxford; BA (Oxon.), MA (Cantab.); Fellow and Bursar of Trinity Hall. *M.* 1936, Jocelyn E. O. Niemeyer. *S.* 3. *Career:* Entered Indian Civil Service, Punjab 1934; Secy. to the Premier 1939–44; Deputy Commissioner 1944–46; Secy. to the Gov. 1946–57; Dir. and Mem. of London Committee, Ottoman Bank since 1949. *Address:* The Ottoman Bank, 2/3 Philpot Lane, London, EC3M 8AQ.

**ABDEL-HAMID, El Sayed Nabih,** Egyptian. *B.* 1911. *Educ.* Military Academy and Staff College, Cairo. *M.* 1938, Doria d. Hamdi. *S.* 6. *Career:* Military career to rank of Major-General. Joined Ministry of Foreign Affairs 1955; Ambassador to Ghana, 1958–62; Secy. of Ministry, Cairo, 1962–64; Ambassador of the United Arab Republic to Australia 1964–68. *Awards:* Recipient Grand Order of Merit 1st Class; Order of Rising Sun (Japan); DSO; MSc; p.s.c.; Dip. Pol. Sc. *Clubs:* Heliopolis, Armed Forces (Cairo). *Address:* Ministry of Foreign Affairs, Cairo, Egypt.

**ABDULAH, Frank Owen.** Trinidad & Tobago Diplomat. *B.* 1928. *Educ.* Queen's Royal Coll., Port of Spain, Trinidad; Magdalen Coll., Oxford. *M.* 1954, Norma Miller. *Daus.* 4. *Career:* Graduate Master, Ministry of Education 1953–57; Asst. Superintendent of Police 1957–60; Asst. Sec., Fed. Govt. of the West Indies 1960–62; Asst. Sec., Ministry of External Affairs 1962–63; 2nd Sec., Trinidad & Tobago High Comm., Kingston 1963–64; 1st Sec,. Trinidad & Tobago High Comm., London 1964–68; Counsellor, Trinidad & Tobago High Comm., Ottawa 1968–70; Dep. Perm. Rep., Trinidad & Tobago Mission to the UN, New York 1970–73; Perm. Sec., Ministry of External Affairs 1973–75; Perm. Rep., Trinidad & Tobago Mission to the UN, New

York since 1975. *Address:* Trinidad & Tobago Mission to the UN, 801 Second Avenue, New York, N.Y. 10017, U.S.A.

**ABDULLA, Rahmatalla.** Sudanese diplomat. *B.* 1922. *Educ.* Trinity College, Cambridge (MA). *M.* 1954, F. I. Allam. *S.* Mohannad, Tarig, and Amir. *Dau.* Aliya. *Career:* With Min. of Education 1944–53; Social Development Officer, and Asst. Gen. Man. of The Sudan Giezra Bd. 1953–56. First Ambassador to India 1956–60, and to Nigeria 1960–61. Min. of National Education 1964–65; Deputy Under-Secy., Min. of Foreign Affairs 1965–68. Ambassador of the Sudan to France, 1968–70, (second term) and concurrently to the Netherlands, Switzerland and Spain. Ambassador to Zaire 1970–71; Sudan Perm. Rep. to U.N. and Representative at Security Council 1972–74. *Publications:* Black Sultanate in the Sudan (Amara and Gammaa). *Club:* Rotary (New Delhi). *Address:* c/o Ministry of Foreign Affairs, Khartoum, Sudan.

**ABENDROTH, Wolfgang,** Dr. jur. German judge and university professor. *B.* 1906. *M.* 1946, Lisa Hoermeyer, Dr. phil. *S.* Ulrich. *Daus.* Elisabeth, Barbara. *Career:* Gerichtsreferendar 1930; political prisoner 1937–45; Regierungsrat, Brandenburg Min. of Justice 1947; Oberjustizrat of German Legal Administration of the Soviet Zone of Occupation 1947; Teacher, Univ. of Halle 1947; Professor, Univ. of Leipzig 1948; Ordinary Professor, Univ. of Jena 1948; Ordinary Professor, Hochschule für Arbeit, Politik und Wirtschaft, Wilhelmshaven since 1948, Rector 1949–51; Judge, State High Court, Bremen 1949–64. Head, Verwaltungs-Akademie, Oldenburg 1949–51; Ordinary Professor, Univ. of Marburg/Lahn since 1950. *Publications:* Die völkerrechtliche Stellung der B- und C-Mandate (1936); Die Haftung der Reichs, Preussens und der Gebietskörperschaften des öffentlichen Rechts für vor der Kapitulation entstandene Verbindlichkeiten (1947); Die deutschen Gewerkschaften (1954); Bürokratischer Verwaltungsstaat und soziale Demokratie (1955); Auftstieg und Krise der deutschen Sozialdemokratie (1964, 3rd ed. 1973, Jap. & Span. editions 1970); Sozialgeschicte der europaischer Arbeiterbewegung (1965, 9th edition (1974); English, French, Spanish, Italian Slovene, Greek and Japanese editions (1973); Das Grundgesetz der Bundesrepublik Deutschland (1966, 3rd edition 1973); Antagonistische Gesellschaft und politische Demokratie (1967, 3rd edition 1973); Einfuhrung in Die Politische Wissenschaft (1968 4th edition 1974); Arbeiterklasse Verfassung und Staat (1975). *Address:* Neuhauss Strasse 5, Frankfurt/M, Federal Republic of Germany.

**ABESS, Leonard L.** *B.* 1904. *Educ.* N.Y. Univ. (Certified Public Accountant—CPA). *M.* 1936, Bertha Ungar. *S.* Leonard, Jr. *Daus.* Linda (Ellis) and Marcella (Gans). *Career:* Practised as a Public Accountant 1925–55. Former Chmn. Florida State Board of Accountancy; Chmn. Bd. City National Bank Corporation; Dir. Ryder Systems Inc.; Past President, Dade County Community Chest; Past-Pres., Mt. Sinai Hospital. Trustee, Univ. of Miami Biscayne Coll. Miami; Recipient of Awards by National Conference of Christians and Jews, and the Anti-Defamation League; Dr. of Humanities (Hon. Biscayne). *Members:* Amer. Inst. of Cert. Public Accountants; Florida Inst. of C.P.A.s (Past Pres.); Amer. Accounting Soc. Democrat. *Clubs:* Miami, Standard (Miami); Rotary (Miami Beach); Harmonie N.Y.C.); Bankers Club (Miami). *Address:* 5255 Collins Avenue, Miami Beach, Fla.; and *office* 25 West Flagler St., Miami, Fla., U.S.A.

**ABINGER, The Rt. Hon. Lord James Richard,** MA. British. Politician and company director. *B.* 1914. *Educ.* Cambridge Univ. *M.* 1957, Isla Rivett Carnac. *S.* 2. *Career:* Serving Officer, Army 1935–47; Mem. House of Lords since 1947. *Clubs:* Carlton; Royal Automobile. *Address:* Clees Hall, Bures, Suffolk; and *office* 1c Portman Mansions, Chiltern St, London W1.

**ABLAHAT, Newton André.** American. *B.* 1914. *Educ.* Northwestern Univ. (BS); graduate degree work, Chicago, Colorado, Johns Hopkins, Syracuse and American Universities. *M.* 1947, Ella May Cason. *S.* Roger Haydon. *Career:* Economist and Economic Intelligence Officer, U.S. Govt. 1943–46; Owner, Trans-World Assoc. 1946–50; Man. Marketing and Merchandise Res. and Policy Dir. Spiegel Inc. 1946; Consultant Asst. Branch Chief, Bureau of Labor Statistics 1950; Senior Ops, Analyst, Johns Hopkins Univ. 1953; Head Ops. Research Group, G.E.C. 1956; Operations Research Consultant, Haskins & Sells 1958; Consulting Management Scientist G.E.C. 1959: Man. Plans Apparatenindustrie Defense Electronics N.V. 1961; Consultant, General Electric Co. 1962–67; Consultant, U.S. Dept. of Transportation 1967; Vice-Pres. Corporate Planning, Investors Diversified Services Inc. (Minneapolis, Minn.) since July 1967. *Publications:* many books on research, the credit system, analysis, accountancy, operations and other subjects. Recipient, Special Commendation for Outstanding Service, from U.S. Ambassador to China. *Member:* Operations Research Socy. of America (Certificate of Service Award; member Nominating Cttee. Chmm. Membership Cttee; Finance Cttee); Inst. of Management Science; Amer. Economic Assn.; Amer. Statistical Assn.; Washington Operations Research Council; Bd. Dirs. Twin Cities Citizen League; Pres. Bd. Dirs., North American Soc. of Corp. Planners (Minn.); Soc. of Long Range Planning. Shriner. *Club:* Minneapolis Athletic. *Address:* 5200 Chantrey Road, Edina, Minn. 55436; and *office* Investors Diversified Services Inc. IDS Tower, Minneapolis, Minn. 55402, U.S.A.

**ABLON, Arnold Norman.** American. Certified public accountant, investments. *B.* 1921. *Educ.* Louisiana State Univ. (BS *summa cum laude*, 1941); Northwestern Univ. (MBA 1942). *M.* 1962, Carol Sarbin. *S.* William Neal, Robert Jack. *Daus.* Jane Ellen, Elizabeth Jane. *Career:* Lecturer in Accounting, Northwestern Univ. 1942; Captain, U.S. Army (served 1942–45); Lecturer in Accounting, Southern Methodist Univ. 1946–47; with Peat, Marwick, Mitchell & Co. 1947–48; Auditor, Levine's Department Stores 1948–49; Senior Partner, Arnold N. Ablon & Co., C.P.A.s 1949—. Member, Bd. Dir.: Ablon Enterprises, Inc.; Greenhill Sch.; June Shelton Sch.; Special Care Sch.; Temple Emanu-El; First Continental Enterprises, Inc.; partner, Troth and Ablon Investments, Dallas. *Member:* American Institute of Certified Public Accountants, National Assn. of Accountants, Texas Society of C.P.A.s. Mason (Shriner). *Clubs:* Dallas Athletic; Variety International, Columbion, Dallas. *Address:* 9129 Clearlake, Dallas, Texas, U.S.A.; and *office* 1620 Rep. Nat. Bank Building, Dallas, Texas 75201.

**ABRAHAM, John Milton.** American. *B.* 1904. *Educ.* Univ. of Chicago (BS); Fellow, Royal Soc. of Arts (England). *M.* 1929, Esther Kelso. *S.* John K. *Dau.* Bonnie Jean (Le May). *Career:* Vice-Pres., Coronet Instructional Films (a division of Esquire Ltd.); Sen. Vice-Pres. and Dir., Esquire Inc.; Pres., Coronet Films Ltd. (Canada). Publisher of Esquire and Gentleman's Quarterly magazines; Pres. Esquire Educ. Group, producers and distributors of educational films and material for classroom use; formerly Fin. Controller, Balaban & Katz Corp. (principal subsidiary of Paramount Pictures). Republican. Mem. Sigma Alpha Epsilon Fraternity. *Clubs:* Executives, Interfraternity (Chicago). *Address:* 1331 Braeburn Road, Flossmoor, Ill., U.S.A.

**ABRAHAM, William I.** American. Economist and statistician. *B.* 1919. *Educ.* Columbia Univ. (PhD Econ.), Univ. of Chicago (MBA Stats.) and Univ. of Pennsylvania (AB Maths.). *M.* 1945, Janet Elizabeth Margaret Abraham. *S.* Stephen Benjamin, Roger Douglas, Charles Raymond. *Dau.* Susan Edith. *Career:* Served in World War II (U.S. Army Signal Intelligence) 1943–45; Consultant: United Nations, Organ. of Amer. States; Agency for Int'l. Develop., Ford Foundation, National Planning Assn., Harvard Univ. Development Advisory Service; U.N. Secretariat 1946–61; representative at 3rd Regional Conf. of Asian Statisticians, New Delhi 1954; U.N. Latin American National Accounts Seminar, Rio de Janeiro 1959, etc; National Income Adviser to Govt. of the Philippines, Manila 1952; Adviser on National Income Statistics, U.N. Economic Comm. for Latin America, Santiago (Chile) 1956; Economic or Statistical Adviser to Govts. of Ireland 1960, Indonesia 1962, Thailand 1963, Panama 1965, Brazil 1966, Malaysia 1968–69; Prof. of Economic Graduate School of Arts and Sciences, New York Univ; Development Adviser, Center for International Affairs, Harvard University. *Publications:* The National Income of the Philippines and its Distribution (Central Bank of the Philippines) (1952); National Income and Economic Accounting (Prentice-Hall) (1969); various arts. on natl. income and related subjects; Editor or contributor to various U.N. publications on national income, *e.g.*, Methods of National Income Estimation (U.N.) (1954). *Member:* Int. Assn. for Research in Income and Wealth; Amer. Economic Assn.; Amer. Statistical Assn.; Conf. on Research in Income and Wealth. *Address:* Yekom Consultants, 77 North Saba Avenue, Tehran 14, Iran.

**ABRAHAMS, Basil George.** British (Rhodesian citizen) chartered valuation surveyor. *B.* 23 April 1908. *Educ.* London (FRICS, FIARB, FEI); Com. of Oaths; mem., Rent-Appeal Bd. of Rhodesia. *M.* 1941, Evelyn Mary Steele. *S.* Patrick Simon, David George. *Career:* With Territorial Army and R. W. Africa Frontier Force (served in U.K., Africa and Far East 1938–45). Chmn. Indus. Council for the

Banking Undertaking in Rhodesia. Past Pres. and Hon. Examiner, Inst. of Auctioneers, Estate Agents and Valuers of Rhodesia; qualified and practised in London prior to 1936. *Member:* Estate Agents Council (Chmn.); Road Compensation Bd., Planning Appeal Bd., Rhodesia. *Clubs:* Salisbury Blantyre Sports. *Address* P.O. Box A300, Avonale, Salisbury, Rhodesia; and *office* P.O. Box 441 Blantyre, Malawi.

**ABRAHAMSON, Abraham Eliezer.** British (Rhodesian citizen). *B.* 1922. *Educ.* Milton School, Bulawayo, and Univ. of Cape Town (BA). *M.* 1946, Anita Pearl Rabinovitz. *S.* Lawrence Paul, Martin Julian. *Dau.* Irene Etta (Salomon). *Career:* Pres.: Bulawayo Chamber of Industries 1951–53; Federation of Rhodesian Industries 1953–54; Assn. of Rhodesian and Nyasaland Industries (1st Pres.) 1957–58; Pres. Rhodesian Jewish Bd. of Deputies 1956–58; M.P., Bulawayo East 1953–65 when did not contest Gen. Election; Min. of the Treasury, Local Govt. and Housing, Jan.–Feb. 1958. Min. of Labour, Social Welfare and Housing 1958–62. Pres., Central Africa Jewish Bd. Deputies since 1963. *Publications:* articles on industrial development, labour and employment. *Clubs:* Parkview. *Address:* P.O. Box 791, Bulawayo, Rhodesia.

**ABRAM, David Edwin.** American *B.* 1912. *Educ.* Drake Univ. (BComSc). *M.* 1935, Marguerite Hartley. *S.* Theodore David. *Daus.* Barbara (Marksbery), Catherine Lynn (Crowley). *Career:* Exec. V.-Pres. U.S. National Bank of Oregon since 1944. *Member:* Amer. Bankers Assn.; Oregon Bankers Association. Republican. *Clubs:* The Arlington; University. *Address:* 4310 S.W. Fairview Circus, Portland, Ore. 97221; and *office* Box 4412, Portland, Ore. 97208, U.S.A.

**ABRAMS, George J.** American. *B.* 1918. *Educ.* New York Univ. (BSc *magna cum laude*, 1947; MBA 1949). *M.* 1941, Mary Sablom. *Dau.* Adèle. *Career:* Pres., Hudnut-Du Barry Div., Warner Lambert Corp. 1959–60; Vice-Pres. Advertising, Reylon Inc. 1955–59, and Vice-Pres., Sales and Advertising, Block Drug Co. Inc. 1947–55; Vice-Pres., Dir. Corporate Development, J. B. Williams Co. Inc. 1960–62. Pres., Maradd Products Inc. 1962–65; Senr. Vice-Pres., William Esty Co. 1965–67; Bd. of Dir. U.S.O. 1964—; Cardinals Cttee. for the Laity 1965—; Pres. Cole Fischer Ragow Inc. 1969–27; Pres. George J. Abrams and Associates since 1971; Exec. Vice-Pres., Reach McGlinton Co.; Exec. Vice-Pres. Bd. of Dirs., N.Y. Univ. Grad. School of Business Administration, 1967; Assoc, Prof., Graduate Schools of Bus. Admin. Pace Univ. & Montclair State Univ. *Awards:* Achievement Award Advertising Club, Washington, D.C. 1958; Outstanding Young Advertising Man of the Year, N.Y.C. 1954; Management Award of Alpha Delta Sigma, N.Y.C. 1955; Free Enterprise Assn. Award 1963. *Member:* Assn. of Nat. Advertisers (Ed. of Dir. 1956–59), and Advertising Club of N.J. (Bd. of Gov. 1954–55). Nat. Bd. of Gov., U.S.O. *Publications:* How I made a Million Dollars with Ideas; The Guilt of Michael Pagett; That man; contributions to Printer's Ink, Markets of America, The Advertiser, etc. *Club:* Pinnacle (N.Y.C.); Curzon (London, England). *Address:* 22 Dalewood Road, W. Caldwell, N.Y., N.Y.C., U.S.A.

**ABRAMS, Talbert.** American photogrammetrist, scientific consultant and manufacturer of scientific instruments. *B.* 1895. *Educ.* U.S.N. Aeronautical School; Hon. Dr. Eng. 1961; Hon. DSc 1952. *M.* 1923, Leota Fry. *Career:* Vice-Pres., Michigan Post Amer. Ordnance Assn. 1959–62, 1965–68; Dir., Amer. Congress on Surveying and Mapping 1960–62; Defence Orientation Conf. Assn., Wash., D.C. *Member:* Atomic Energy Cttee., Nat. Assn. of Mfg., 1958–62; Financial Cttee., Photo Optical Instrumentation Eng., L.A.; Commissioner, Air Pollution Control Bd., State of Michigan; Scientific Consultant, T.I.I.C. Mission, Europe 1945; U.S.A.F., Alaska 1948; "Operation Frigid" trip through Russia 1956; first man to make round trip, Paris–New York, on Pan American's Jets 1958; Argentine–Antarctic Expedition 1959; first man around the world, Pan Amer. inaugural jet service, 10 Oct. 1959 (flying time 42 hours 26 min.—68 hours elapsed time); Oper. Deep Freeze 1963–64, 1966–67, Antarctica and the S. Pole; Inaugural Jet Passenger Services, U.S.–Russia, 15–16 July 1968; Defence Orientation-W. Pacific & S.E. Asia, 1968. Previously with U.S. Air Mail Service, U.S.A.F. (R), and Aviation Section, U.S. Marine Corps. Chmn. of Bd., Abrams Aerial Survey Corp; Pres., Airlandia; Inc., Aerial Explorers Corp.; Talbert & Leota Abrams Foundation Inc.; Dir., Bank of Lansing; Photogrammetry Inc.; Washington Apartments, Inc. *Awards:* Order of the Arctic Realm, U.S.A.F. Civilian Service Award, U.S. Army 1951; Antarctic Service Award; U.S.N.; Centennial Award, Michigan State Univ.; Prominent Citizens Award, City of Lansing; Award of Merit, Michigan Assn. of Professions; Order of Magellan, Circumnavigators Club, N.Y. Hon. member: Tau Beta Pi, Pi Tau Sigma, Chi Epsilon, Eugene Field Soc. of Authors, Amer. Soc. of Civ. Engrs. Fellow, Amer. Geographic Soc. *Publication:* Essentials of Aerial Surveying and Photo Interpretation. *Member:* Detroit Soc. of Engrs., Amer. Military Engrs. Hon. Life Member: Soc. of Professional Engrs.; Amer. Soc. of Photogrammetry; Michigan Soc. of Engrs.; Australian Inst. of Cartographers. Life Member Biscayne Bay Lodge, 124 F & AM, Miami. *Clubs:* Explorers (N.Y.C.); Wings (N.Y.C.); Quiet Birdmen (Detroit); Lansing Rotary; Lansing Engineers; Circumnavigators; OXS. Lived, worked and travelled in 96 countries. *Address:* 1310 Cambridge Road, Lansing, Mich.; and *office* Abrams Aerial Survey Corp., 124 North Larch Street, Lansing, Mich., U.S.A.

**ABS, Hermann J.** Company Chmn. *B.* 1901. *Career:* Hon. Pres. of Deutsche Bank AG.; Chmn. of Supervisory Board and Hon. Chmn. of Supervisory Board of several companies. *Address:* Deutsche Bank, Aktiengesellschaft, Frankfurt/Main, F.R. Germany.

**ABU NOWAR, Ma'an.** Jordanian diplomat. *B.* 1928. *Educ.* London University. *M.* 1959, Vivian Richards (dec'd). *S.* 2. *Daus.* 7. *Career:* joined Jordan Arab Army 1943, Col. Commd. 7th Infantry Regt. 1956; Commander 1st Inf. Brigade 1957–63; Counsellor Jordan Embassy London 1963; Dir. Jordan Civil Defence 1964–67; Public Security 1967–69; Asst. Chief of Staff, General Affairs 1969–72; Minister, Culture and Information, 1972; Ambassador to United Kingdom 1973–77. *Award:* Star of Jordan First Class. *Address:* c/o Ministry of Foreign Affairs, Amman, Jordan.

**ABUSHADI, Mohamed Mahmoud,** PHD, BCOM., ACIP. Egyptian banker. *B.* 1913. *Educ.* Cairo Univ., Chartered Inst. of Patent Agents; Amer. Univ. Washington DC. U.S.A. *M.* 1947, Colleen Althea Bennett. *S.* Farid Karim. *Dau.* Farida Sonya. *Career:* Controller-Gen. Insurance Dept. Ministry Finance 1949–52; Dir.-Gen. Govt. Insurance Provident Funds 1953; Chmn. Man. Dir., Development & Popular Housing Co. 1954–55; Sub-Gov. National Bank Egypt 1955–60, Man. Dir. 1961–66, Chmn. 1967–70. Chmn., Social Insurance Org. 1956–57; Chmn. & Man. Dir., Cairo Insurance Co. 1956–57; Man. Dir., Cairo Bank, 1956–57. Chmn., Union De Banques Arabes Et Francaise since 1970; UBAF Ltd. since 1972. *Awards:* Order of Republic 2nd Class; Order of Merit 1st Class. *Publications:* The Art of Central Banking & its Application in Egypt (1952); Central Banking in Egypt (1952). *Address:* 52, Avenue Foch, Paris 16°, France.

**ACHEAMPONG, General I. K.** Ghanaian Statesman. *B.* 1931. *Education:* St Peter's Catholic School, Kumasi; Cath. School, Ejura; Central College of Commerce Agona Swedru; Mons Officer Cadet School, UK; General Staff College, Fort Leavenworth, U.S.A. *M.* Faustina Aboagye. *S.* 3. *Daus.* 4. *Career:* Prin. Western Commercial Inst. Achiase 1949–50; Vice-Prin. Central Coll of Commerce 1950–51; Instructor, Kumasi Comm. Inst 1951–52; Commissioned into the Army of Ghana 1959; Commanding Officer 6th Battalion 1966–67; Chmn. Western Regional Cotte of Admin. 1967–69; Commanding Officer 5th Battalion 1969–71; Brigade Commander 1st Infantry Brigade 1972; Head of State since 1972, and Chmn. of Supreme Military Council. *Decorations:* Companion of Star of Ghana (1976). *Address:* PO Box 1627, The Castle, Accra, Ghana; and *home:* Burma Camp, Accra, Ghana.

**ACHTER, Viktor,** Dr. jur. German lawyer, university professor and business executive. *B.* 1905. *Educ.* Barrister 1927; Dr. jur. 1928; Called Bar Cologne 1931, Habilitation 1948; Extra-Ordinary Prof. Univ. Cologne 1952—. *M.* 1933, Lotte Höpp. *S.* 2. *Dau.* 1. *Career:* Founded the firm of Viktor Achter & Co. 1959. Pres., Chamber of Industry & Commerce, Mönchengladbach; Advisory Bd., Deutsche Bank A.G., and Gerling-Konzern; Mem. Bd. of Trustees, Arts Assn. for Rhineland and Westphalia, Dusseldorf; Hon-Pres. Arts-Club for Rhinelands & Westphalia. *Publications:* Birth of Punishment (1950); About the Source of God's Peaces (1956); many articles in journals, etc. *Awards:* Knight Ordo Equestris S. Sepulcri Hierosolymitani and Papal Order of Gregory; Commander with Star of Order of Knighthood of Holy Grave of Jerusalem; Grosses Verdienstkreuz des Verdienstordens der Bundes-republik Deutschland. *Club:* Rotary Mönchengladbach-Niers (foundation president). *Address:* 4050 Monchengladbach 1, Zum Bunten Garten 20, Germany; and *office* 4060 Viersen 11, Albertstr. 4, Germany.

**ACKERLIND, Erik.** American electronics consultant. *B.* 1910. *Educ.* Polytechnic Inst. of Brooklyn (BEE *cum laude* 1932); Columbia Univ. (MSEE 1934); Dr. of EE Polytechnic Inst. of Brooklyn 1937. *M.* 1944, Florence R. Jason. *S.* Edmund. *Career:* Shellac Research Fellow, Polytechnic Inst. of Brooklyn 1934–37; Electronics Engineer, Hazeltine Service Corp., Little Neck, N.Y. 1939–41; Sub-Section Head, Naval Research Laboratory, Washington, D.C. 1941–46; Section Head, Northrop Aircraft Co., Hawthorne, Calif. 1946–49; Group Supervisor, Jet Propulsion Laboratory, Pasadena, Calif. 1949–51; Tech. Dir., Ackerlind Corp., Lomita, California 1951–53; Manager, Systems Engineering, Radio Corp. of America, Los Angeles, Calif. 1953–57; Mathematics Instructor, Univ. Extension, Univ. of California, Los Angeles 1948–49; Assoc. Prof. of Engineering, Sacramento State Coll. 1957–59; Electronics Consultant since 1957. *Publications:* Paper on testing of shellac varnish films (Transactions of the Electro-Chemical Society); two joint papers on detection of signals in noise (Transactions of the Professional Group on Information Theory, Inst. of Radio Engineers). Holder of 6 U.S. patents. *Member:* Inst. Electrical and Electronic Engineers; American Inst. of Aeronautics and Astronautics. *Address:* P.O. Box 976, Bellingham, Washington 98225, U.S.A.

**ACKERMAN, Leopold II.** American. Former Democratic National Committeeman for Arizona (elected June 1964). *B.* 1921. *Educ.* Principia School (St. Louis), Governor Dummer Acad. (Mass.), and Harvard Univ. (ABGovt. 1947). *M.* (1) Leslie Rogers, (2) 1962, Mrs. Celia Meyer. *S.* Byron, Carl, Douglas, Paul. *Daus.* Mary Lee, Elizabeth. *Career:* Pres.: Lee Ackerman Investment Co. Inc., Diamond Valley Inc., and West Coast Investment Co., Yavapai Hotels Corp. and Western Growth Capital Inc.; Pilot, Pan-American Airways 1942; free-lance publicity, promotion for Boston Globe, and writing for N.Y. Times 1945–47; Vice-Pres., King, Ackerman, Deckard & Burch (advertising) 1948–52; Former Pres. of Western Equities Inc. (on Amer. Stock Exchange) *Awards:* Citation for Valor in Africa; 2 battle Stars 1942–45; Alumni Achievement Award (Governor Dummer Acad. 1961); Silver Heart Award (County and State Heart Assn. 1960); Bronze Plaque Award (Ariz. Socy. for Crippled Children 1960); Citation from Maricopa County Bd. of Supervisors 1960. *Publications:* Young Millionaires of Phoenix (1961); Shift in Leadership: Will the West take over? (1961) (Saturday Evening Post); Sweet Success (1960) (television film). *Clubs:* Cloud, Phoenix Press, American Legion. *Address:* 6130 East Camelback Road, Phoenix, Ariz. 85018, U.S.A.

**ACKLEY, H. Gardner.** American. *B.* 1915. *Educ.* A. B. Western Mich. Univ. 1936; MA 1937, PhD 1940, Univ. of Mich. *M.* 1937, Bonnie Lowry. *S.* David Albert, Donald Gardner. *Career:* Instructor in Econ., Ohio State Univ. 1939–40; Univ. of Michigan 1940–41; Asst. Prof. 1946–47; Assoc. Prof. 1947–52; Prof. 1952–68; Chmn., Dept. 1954—61. U.S. Govt. Economist, Office Price Admin., 1941–43, 1944–46, Office Strategic Services 1943–44; Economic Adviser, Asst. Dir. Office Price Stabil. 1951–52; Member Bd. Editors, Amer. Econ. Rev. 1953–56; Univ.-Nat. Bureau Cttee. for Econ. Research 1954–56; Dir. Social Science Res. Council 1959–61; Fulbright Res. Scholar, Italy 1956–57; Ford Foundation Faculty Res. Fellow (Italy) 1961–62. Mem., Council Economic Advisers 1962–68, Chmn., 1964–68; Ambassador to Italy 1968–69; Henry Carter Adams Prof. of Poliicalt Economy, Univ. of Michigan since 1969; Non-resident staff mem.,Brookings Inst. since 1975; Dir. National Bureau Econ. Research since 1971; Dir. Joint Council Econ. Education since 1971; Dir. Banco di Roma (Chicago) since 1973; Columnist on economy Dun's Review since 1970. *Awards:* Cavaliere del Gran Croce, Ordine della Merita, Repubblica d'Italia 1969; Fellow, Amer. Acad. of Arts & Sciences; Mem., Amer. Philosophical Soc.; LLD, Western Mich. Univ. 1964; LLD, Kalamazoo Coll. 1967; Distinguished faculty achievement award, Univ. of Mich. 1976. *Publications:* Macroeconomic Theory (1961); Un Modello Econometrico Dello Sviluppo Italiano Nel Dopoguerra (1963); Stemming World Inflation (1971). Many articles, reviews, reports, symposia, etc. Vice-Pres., Amer. Econ. Assn. 1962; Mich. Acad. of Arts & Sciences. Democratic. *Clubs:* National Economist (Washington, D.C.). *Address:* 907 Berkshire Road, Ann Arbor, Mich. 48104; and *office* Dept. of Economics Univ. of Mich., Ann Arbor 48109, U.S.A.

**ACREE, Jr., John Thomas.** American. Chmn. of Board Lincoln Income Life Insurance Co., Louisville, Ky. *B.* 1909. *Educ.* Oklahoma City University (Graduated AB *magna cum laude*). *M.* 1970, Mary M. Turner. *S.* John T. III, Edwin Linnell. *Dau.* Laura Diana Hager. *Career:* Pres., Inst. of Home Office Underwriters 1950–51; Pres., Life Insurers Conference 1958–59; Executive Committee, Insurance Economics Soc. 1959–62; Kentucky State Vice-Pres., American Life Convention 1959–68; Bd. of Dir., Oklahoma Industrial Finance Corp. 1959–60; Pres., Old Kentucky Home Council, Boy Scouts of America 1957–60; Pres., Better Business Bureau 1959–60; Louisville Goodwill Industries of Kentucky, Kentucky Chamber of Commerce; member, National Assn. of Life Underwriters; Chmn., Bd. of Trustees, Lexington Theological Seminary Amer. Humanics Foundation, Louisville 1968–71; Dir.: Lousiville Central Area Community Chest; Louisville Chamber of Commerce 1959–60; Gen. Campaign Chmn., United Appeal 1962; International Center, Univ. of Louisville; United Cerebral Palsy (Louisville), Liberty National Bank & Trust Co., Louisville. Pres., Life Insurers Conference; Trustee, Kentucky Independent Coll. Foundation; Region 4 Chmn., Boy Scouts of America 1969–71, Pres., Kentucky Chamber of Commerce 1970–71. Bd. of Governors Kosair Shrine Hospital. *Member:* Crescent Hill Lodge F. & A.M.; Rotarian; 33rd degree Mason and Shriner; Elder, Beargrass Christian Church. *Clubs:* Pendennis; President, Louisville Auto., 1967–69. Scottish Rite Choir; Kentucky Colonel. *Address:* Rail Splitter Farm, Rt. 1, Box 470, La Grange, Ky. 40031, U.S.A.; and *office* 6100 Dutchman's Lane, Louisville, Ky. 40205, U.S.A.

**ADAIR, Charles Wallace, Jr.** American diplomat. *B.* 1914. *Educ.* Univ. of Wisconsin (AB); Amer. Inst. of Banking, N.Y.C.; George Washington Univ.; Princeton Univ.; Nat. War Coll. *M.* 1947, Caroline Lee Marshall. *S.* Marshall Porter. *Daus.* Caroline Lee, Sarah Torrence. *Career:* NATO Advisor, Bureau of European Affairs, Depart. of State, 1952–54; Counsellor for Economic Affairs, American Embassy Brussels 1954–56; U.S. Commissioner, Tripartite Comm. for Restitution of Monetary Gold, Brussels 1954–56; Chief, Trade Agreements Division, and Dir., Office of International Finance, Dept. of State, 1956–59; Chmn., Colombo Plan Officials Meeting, Seattle 1958; Deputy Asst. Secy. of State for Economic Affairs 1959–61; Deputy Secy. Gen., Organization for Economic Cooperation & Development, Paris 1961–63; Min.-Counsellor, Embassy, Buenos Aires, 1963–65; Ambassador to Panama 1965–69 to Uruguay since 1969. *Clubs:* University, Washington; Royal Bombay Yacht (India). *Address:* Stuart, Florida, U.S.A.; and American Embassy, Panama, R.P.

**ADAM, Sir Alistair (Alexander Duncan Grant) (Hon. Mr. Justice Adam).** Former Justice of the Supreme Court of Victoria. *B.* Greenock, Scotland, 1902. *Educ.* Scotch Coll. and Melbourne Univ.; Final Honour Scholarship, Law; MA; LLM. *M.* 1930, Nora Laver. *S.* Ralph. *Daus.* Judith, Jill. *Career:* Lecturer on Real Property, Melbourne Univ. 1932–51; practised at Victoria Bar 1928–57; Q.C. 1950; Judge of the Supreme Court May 1957–75. *Member:* Council of the Univ. of Melbourne 1958–69. *Publications:* various articles in legal journals. Council, National Museum of Victoria. *Club:* Australian. *Address:* 39, Walsh Street, Bolwyn, Victoria; and Supreme Court, Melbourne, Vic., Australia.

**ADAM, Kenneth,** CBE, MA (Cantab.), FRSA, FAMS. British. *B.* 1908. *Educ.* Nottingham School and St. John's Coll., Cambridge (Snr. Scholar and Prizeman). *M.* 1932, Ruth Augusta King. *S.* 3. *Dau.* 1. *Career:* Reporter, Leader Writer, Dramatic Critic, Manchester Guardian 1930–34; Home News Editor, B.B.C. 1934–36; Chief Correspondent, The Star 1936–40; Press and Public Relations Officer, B.O.A.C. 1940–41; Dir. of Publicity and Editor, Supplementary Publications, B.B.C. 1941–50; Controller, Light Programme, B.B.C. 1950–54; Gen. Mgr. (Joint) Hulton Press 1954–56; Controller of Programmes, B.B.C. Television 1956–61; Dir. of Television, B.B.C. 1961–69; Visiting Prof. of Communications, Temple Univ., Philadelphia 1969—; Danforth Travelling Fellow, U.S.A. 1970–71; Visiting Lect. Syracuse Univ. N.Y. since 1972. *Address:* 19 Old Court House, London W.8; and Tomlinson Hall, Temple Univ., Philadelphia, Pa. 19113, U.S.A.

**ADAMS, Alva B.** Executive. *B.* 1915. *Educ.* Univ. of Virginia (BS Degree). *M.* 1945, Loretta Kissel. *S.* Alva B., Jr. *Dau.* Loretta. *Career:* Lieut., U.S. Coast Guard 1942–45. Chmn. Bd., The Pueblo Bank & Trust Co. Pres., The Holmes Hardware Co. and The Holmes Realty Co. Vice-Pres., Fifth & Court Street Co. (these companies are established in Pueblo, Colo.). Co-owner, Radio Station K.C.R.T., Trinidad, Colo. Chmn. Colorado State Bd. of Education. *Award:* Citizen-of-the-Year Award (Adams State College). *Member:* Colorado Bankers' Assn.; Rocky Mountain Distributors;

Chamber of Commerce; Colorado Tax Equalization Committee. Shriner. Elk. Democrat. *Clubs:* Pueblo Golf; Garden of the Gods. *Address: office* The Pueblo Bank & Trust Co., Pueblo, Colo., U.S.A.

**ADAMS, Brock.** American Lawyer & Politician. *B.* 1927. *Educ.* Univ. of Washington - BS (Econ.), Summa Cum Laude Graduate; Harvard Law Sch. - Juris Doctor. *M.* 1952, Mary Elizabeth Scott. *S.* 2. *Daus.* 2. *Career:* U.S. Navy 1944–46; Attorney, Little, LeSourd, Palmer, Scott & Clemens 1952; Partner, LeSourd, Patten & Adams 1961; U.S. District Attorney for Western Washington 1961–64; Mem., U.S. House of Reps. 1964–77; U.S. Sec. of Transportation since 1977. *Member:* Phi Beta Kappa. *Address:* Department of Transportation, Washington, D.C. 20590, U.S.A.

**ADAMS, Bruce Leslie.** Australian. *B.* 1927. *Educ.* Scotch Coll., Melbourne: AASA (Prov.). *M.* 1955, Gwenneth Mary Cocks. *S.* Robert Leslie, Andrew George. *Daus.* Catherine Mary, Janet Gwen. *Career:* With Commonwealth Bank of Australia 1944, and 1947–50. With R.A.N.R. 1945–46. Mgr. and Secy., Australian Canned Fruits Bd. since 1960. *Member:* Australian Socy. of Accountants. *Clubs:* Melbourne Cricket; Royal Automobile (of Victoria). *Address:* 36 The Avenue, Blackburn, Vic.; and *office* 100 Exhibition Street, Melbourne, Vic., Australia.

**ADAMS, Charles Francis.** American. Commander, Order of Merit, Italian Republic. *B.* 1910. *Educ.* Harvard Coll. (AB). *M.* 1934, Margaret Stockton (Dec.). *S.* Timothy. *Daus.* Abigail (Manny), Alison (Robinson). (2) 1973, Beatrice D. Penati. *Career:* Partner, Paine Webber, Jackson & Curtis 1938–47; With U.S. Navy 1940–46; With Raytheon Co.: Exec. Vice-Pres. 1947–48, Pres. 1948–60 and 1962–64; Chmn. 1960–62 and 1964–75. Dir: The Gillette Co., Pan American World Airways; Liberty Mutual Insurance Co; Liberty Mutual Fire Insurance Co., A. C. Cossor Ltd. *Awards:* LLD Bates Coll.; DBA Northeastern Univ. Fellow, Amer. Acad. of Arts and Sciences. *Member:* Trustee, Equitable Life Mortgage and Realty Inc.; Chmn. Bd. Woods Hole Oceanographic Institution. *Clubs:* Somerset, The Brook; New York Yacht; Cruising Club of America. *Address:* Dedham Street, Dover, Mass. 02030; and *office* Raytheon Co., 141 Spring Street, Lexington, Mass. 02173, U.S.A.

**ADAMS, Donald Croxton.** *B.* 1914. *Educ.* Yale Univ. (BA 1935). *M.* 1938, Nancy Jane Downer. *S.* Peter Webster, David Huntington. *Career:* With Addressograph-Multigraph Corp.: Trainee 1935–37; Export Corrst. 1937–38; Asst. Export Mgr. 1938–44; Export Mgr. 1944–45; Treas. 1955–59, Admin. Vice-Pres., Treasury, Addressograph-Multigraph Corp. 1965—. Treas.-Dir.: Varityper Corp. 1956—; Buckeye Ribbon & Carbon Co. 1957—; Addressograph-Multigraph of Canada Ltd. 1955—; Emeloid Co. Inc. 1960—; Electronic Image Systems Corp. 1967—. Dir., Hill-Acme Co. 1965—; Corporate Services since 1969. *Member:* Treasurers Club, Cleveland; Amer. Management Assn.; National Assn. of Manufacturers. Republican. *Clubs:* Union; Mayfield Country. *Address: office* 1200 Babbitt Road, Cleveland, Ohio, U.S.A.

**ADAMS, James Frederick,** PhD. Prof. of Psychology and Educational Psychology. *B.* 1927. *Educ.* Univ. of California (BA 1950); Temple Univ. (EdM 1951); Washington State Univ. (PhD 1959). *Career:* Staff, Testing Bureau, Temple Univ. 1951–52; Asst. Prof. of Psychology, Whitworth Coll., Spokane, Wash. 1952–55; Teaching and Research Asst., Wash. State Univ., Pullman, Wash. 1955–57; Research Associate, Miami Univ., Oxford, Ohio 1957–59. Prof. of Psychology, Temple Univ. 1959—; Visiting Prof. of Psychology, Univ. of Puerto Rico, San Juan, Puerto Rico 1963–64; Visiting Prof. Catholic Univ. of Puerto Rico 1971–72. *Publications:* Problems in Counseling (1962); Counseling and Guidance: a Summary View (1965); Understanding Adolescence (1968, 2nd ed. 1973, 3rd ed. 1976); Human Behaviour in a Changing Society (1973); 60 articles in Journal of General Psychology; Audio-Visual Instruction; Improving College and University Teaching; Junior College Journal; Educational and Psychological Measurement; American Phychologist; Harvard Educational Review; Journal of Psychology; Journal of Educational Psychology; Personnel Guidance Journal; School & Society; Journal of Genetic Psychology; Journal of the History Behavioural Sciences. *Member:* Sigma Xi; Psi Chi; Amer. Psychological Assn.; Amer. Personnel & Guidance Assn.; National Vocational Guidance Assn.; American Assn. for Advancement of Science. *Address:* Dept. of Psychology, Temple Univ. Philadelphia, Pa., U.S.A.

**ADAMS, John Bertram,** CMG, FRS. British scientist. *B.* 1920. *Educ.* Eltham Coll., London; Univ. of Geneva (DSc h.c. 1960); Birmingham Univ. (DSc h.c. 1961); Univ. of Surrey (DSc h.c. 1966); MA Oxford Univ. 1967; Röntgen Prize, Univ. of Giessen 1960; Duddell Medal, Physical Socy. 1961; Leverhulme Medal, Royal Soc. 1972; Faraday Medal, Inst. of Electrical Engrs., London 1977; Kelvin Lecturer, Inst. of Elec. Engineers 1962; Guthrie Lecturer, Physical Socy. 1965; Mond Lecturer, Manchester Univ. 1967. *M.* 1943, Renie Warburton. *S.* Christopher John. *Daus.* Josephine, Katherine. *Career:* In Research Laboratory, Siemens Telecommunications Research Establishment, Swanage and Malvern 1940–45; Atomic Energy Establishment, Harwell 1945–53; European Organisation for Nuclear Research (CERN), Geneva 1953 (Dir. of Proton Synchroton Div. 1954–60; Dir-Gen. 1960–61); Dir., Culham Laboratory (U.K.A.E.A.), Culham, Abingdon, Berks., 1960–67; Controller, Min. of Technology 1965–66. Member for Research, U.K. Atomic Energy Authority 1966–69; Dir.-Gen. of the CERN 300 Gev Programme 1969–75; Executive Director-General, CERN since 1976. *Publications:* Contributor to Nature, Nuovo Cimento, etc. Fellow, Inst. of Elec. Engrs. and of Wolfson Coll., Oxford. *Address:* Champ Rosset, Founex (Vaud), Switzerland; and *office* European Organization for Nuclear Research (CERN), 1211 Genève 23, Switzerland.

**ADAMS, John McLauchlan,** OBE. *B.* 1914. *Educ.* R.A.N. College 1928–31, and R.N. College, Greenwich 1934–35. *M.* 1946, Evelyn Margaret Bryant. *S.* 2. *Career:* With Royal Australian Navy 1928–61; Qualified Anti-submarine specialization 1939. War Service: Atlantic Escort Forces 1939–42; Eastern Fleet Destroyers 1943–45. Captain, Royal Australian Navy (Retd.). State Civil Defence Officer, Victoria, 1961–73. *Club:* Naval & Military (Melbourne). *Address:* 15 Constance Street, Hawthorn East, Victoria, 3123, Australia.

**ADAMS, Joseph Elkan.** *B.* 1913. *Educ.* Carnegie Inst. of Tech. (BSME). *M.* 1940. Eleanor Ture. *S.* Stephen Eric. *Dau.* Gail M. *Career:* With White Motor Corp.: Vice-Pres. Manufacturing 1956–59; Gen. Mgr. Manufacturing 1955; Dir., Purchasing & Planning 1950–55; and Material Control 1945–50; Gen. Mgr., International Molded Plastics 1938–41; Asst. to Pres., Garland Co. 1934–38. Executive Vice-Pres., White Motor Corp. 1959–71; Member Bd. of Dirs. 1969–72; Chmn of Board Flo-York Inc. since 1973; UP Roulston & Co. Investments since 1974; J. E. Adams, Consultant & Investor since 1975; Chmn., General Computer Corp. since 1977. *Publications:* The Human Element—Catalyst in Proper Planning for a Diversified Assembly Operation, Mar. 1954 (Socy. of Automotive Engrs.); America's Answer to Foreign Competition (Mar. 1960, Socy. of Automotive Engrs.). *Member:* Pi Tau Sigma; Pi Delta Epsilon; Socy. of Automotive Engrs.; Council on World Affairs. Republican. *Clubs:* Mid-Day; Musical Arts Assn.; Cleveland City; Republic; Oakwood; Clevelander; Sharon. *Address:* 3031 Manchester Rd., Shaker Heights 22, Ohio.

**ADAMS, Kenneth Galt.** British. *B.* 1920. *Career:* Comino Fellow, St. George's House, Windsor Castle; Former Co. Dir. Proprietors of Hay's Wharf Ltd. and other Companies. Fellow, British Inst. Management; Inst. Directors; Inst. Work Study; Member, Chartered Inst. of Transport; Vice Chmn. Archbishops' Council for Evangelism; Member: Industrial Cttee. Bd. for Social Responsibility (C. of E.); Dept. of Employment, Services Re-Settlement Cttee. *Clubs:* Army & Navy. *Address:* 7 Datchet Road, Windsor and *office:* St. George's House, Windsor Castle.

**ADAMS, Kenneth Stanley.** American. *B.* 1899. *M.* 1946, Dorothy Glynn Stephens. *S.* Kenneth Stanley, Jr., Stephen Stanley, Kenneth Glenn, Gary Clark. *Daus.* Mary Louise, Stephanie Lyn, Lisa Ann. *Career:* With Phillips Petroleum Co.: warehouse clerk 1920–22; then successively assistant operations mgr., prod. dept.; asst. to clerk, accounting div. 1922–27; Asst. Secy. 1927; Asst. Secy. and Treas. 192–832; Asst. to Pres. 1932–35; Dir. and member Exec. Cttee. 1935–64; Treasurer and Asst. to Pres. 1935–38; Exec. Vice-Pres. 1938; Pres. 1938–51. Chmn., Emeritus 1951—, and Chmn. of Finance Committee 1964 of Phillips Petroleum Co. Retired as employee in 1964. LLD Drury Coll. 1955, and Oklahoma Baptist Univ. 1959. Member and Dir.: Amer. Petroleum Inst.; Mid-Continent Oil & Gas Association. *Member:* Sigma Chi; Mason (33°); Shriner; Jester. *Clubs:* Hillcrest Country (Bartlesville, Okla.); Cherokee Yacht (Afton,

Okla.). *Address:* Drawer A, Bartlesville, Oklahoma 74003, U.S.A.

**ADAMS, Kirkwood Floyd.** American. *B.* 1904. *Educ.* McGuires Univ. School; Virginia Military Inst.; Univ. of Virginia (BS in Comm. and Science); Management Course, American Management Assn. *M.* 1947, Sarah Anne Chaney. *S.* Kirkwood Floyd, Jr. *Daus.* Anne S., Margaret L. *Career:* Clerk, C & O Railway 1925–26. With Albemarle Paper Mfg. Co. 1926–28, Specialty Sales 1928–39, Production Sales Co-ordinator 1939–42, Production Mgr. 1942–45, Resident Mgr., Halifax Paper Co. Inc. 1945–48, Vice-Pres. and Div. Mgr. 1948–56. Dir.: Pulp and Paper Foundation, N.C. State Coll. 1962—, and Roanoke River Basin Assn. 1946. Executive Vice-Pres. 1956—, and Dir. 1946—, Halifax Paper Co. Inc. Vice-Pres. 1950—, and Dir. 1948—, The Albemarle Paper Manufacturing Co. Dir.: Seaboard Manufacturing Co. 1951—; Raymond Bag Co. 1954—. Member, Bd. of Mgrs., The Planters National Bank & Trust Co., Roanoke Rapids, N.C. 1962—. Trustee, Roanoke Rapids Library. Pres.: N.C. Traffic League 1962—. *Member:* Forest Policy Cttee., American Paper and Pulp Assn. 1955—; Roanoke Rapids Planning Comm. 1960—. Technical Assn. of Pulp & Paper Industry; Amer. Management Assn.; Roanoke Rapids Chamber of Comm.; Steering Cttee., Roanoke River Studies; Amer. Forestry Assn.; Alpha Kappa Psi; Phi Kappa Psi; Sons of American Revolution; Newcomen Socy. of N. America. Democrat. *Address:* 240 White Avenue, Roanoke Rapids, N.C. 27870, U.S.A.; and *office* Halifax Paper Co. Inc., Roanoke Rapids, N.C., U.S.A.

**ADAMS, Sir Maurice Edward,** KBE. British civil engineer. *B.* 1901. *Educ.* Bristol; member, Inst. of Civil Engineers. *M.* 1924, Hilda May Williams. *S.* 1. *Dau.* 1. *Career:* Midshipman Royal Naval Reserve during World War I; entered Admiralty as Asst. Civil Engineer 1927; served in H.M. Dockyards at Devonport, Malta and Portsmouth; promoted Civil Engineer 1935; served in this rank at Trincomalee, Aden and Portsmouth; promoted to Superintending Civil Engineer (L.G.) 1939; at Admiralty 1939–41 (promoted to Higher Grade 1940); served at Singapore 1941 until evacuation; Simonstown 1942–43; promoted Asst. Civil Engineer-in-Chief 1943; served in Eastern Theatre 1943–45 and Admiralty 1945–46; promoted Deputy Civil Engineer-in-Chief 1946; resigned to join firm of Balfour, Beatty & Co. Ltd., Public Works Contractors, Oct. 1949; re-entered Admiralty service as Civil Engineer-in-Chief 1954–59; Civil Engineer-in-Chief, Admiralty, London, since 1954. Company director; Consultant, Brian Colquhoun & Partners. *Clubs:* Caledonian; RAC. *Address:* 12 Melville Lane, Willingdon, Eastbourne, Sussex.

**ADAMS, Philip.** American. *B.* 1905. *Educ.* Pomona Coll. (Claremont, Calif.), and Hastings Coll. of the Law of the Univ. of California (JD 1938). *M* (1) 1933, Alice Rahman. *S.* Stephen. *Daus.* Judith, Deborah, Kate. (2) 1968, Elaine M. Anderson. *Career:* Attorney-at-Law; Admitted to the Bar: California 1938, and U.S. Supreme Court 1942. In general law practice in San Francisco since 1938. Pres., Bd. of Trustees, Graduate Theological Union, Berkeley 1963—. Trustee, Church Divinity School of the Pacific 1951—. Chancellor, Diocese of California 1960—. Dir.: Americans for Democratic Action (Natl.), United Cerebral Palsy Assn. (Natl.), and Assn. for Mental Health of San Francisco. *Publications:* Adoption Practice in California (Univ. of Calif. Press, 1956). LLD *honoris causa*, Church Divinity School of Pacific 1965. *Member:* Socy. of Genealogists, London; Hon. Old Boy, Sir Thomas Adams Grammar School (Wem, Salop); Amer. Acad. of Political and Social Science; San Francisco Symphony Assn.; Amer. Bar Assn.; Amer. Civil Liberties Union. Democrat. *Clubs:* Commonwealth. *Address:* 2170 Jackson Street, San Francisco 15; and *office* 220 Montgomery Street, San Francisco Calif., U.S.A.

**ADAMS, Phillip Rennell,** QC, LLM. Australian. *Educ.* Aquinas Coll. (Perth) and Univ. of Western Australia (LLB (Hons.) 1934; LLM 1953). *M.* (1) 1935, Hazel Marion Hatfield (dec'd). *S.* 2. *Daus.* 2. (2) 1974, Gertrude Elaine Paxton. *Career:* Served in World War II, in New Guinea and the Pacific Islands, as Brigade Major of the 14th Australian Infantry Brigade and as Gen. Staff Officer. Former Visiting Lecturer in Real Property at Univ. of Western Australia. Counsel to Govt. of Fiji to Advise on revision of Property Laws 1966–68; Dir. of several public companies. Pres. Law Socy. of Western Australia 1962–64. Chmn. of Cttee. to review State Liquor Laws, Western Australia 1969; Chmn. Cttee. to review State Mining Laws 1970; Chmn. Bd. of Enquiry to review liquor laws, NTA 1973; Chmn. Royal Commission into State Gambling Laws 1974; Hon. Consul for Fed. Rep. of Germany since 1972; Pro-Chanc. Murdock Univ.; Dept. Chmn. Environmental Protection Authority; Mem., Parliamentary & Judicial Salaries Tribunal. *Publications:* Company Directors in Australia. Australian Tax Planning (*Butterworths*, Sydney). *Club:* Weld (Perth). *Address:* 34 The Esplanade, Peppermint Grove, W.A.; and *office* Bar Chambers, 524 Hay Street, Perth, W.A., Australia.

**ADAMS, Russell Baird.** American consultant. *B.* 1910. *Educ.* Elliott Business Coll. (Wheeling, West Va.); Bethany Coll.; Univ. of Kentucky. *M.* 1935, Frances Esther Nordin. *S.* Russell Baird, Jr., Richard Alan, David Anthony. *Dau.* Marilyn (Felter). *Career:* Various positions in Office of Chief Inspector, Post Office Dept. 1930–36; Post Office Inspector 1936; transferred to Economic Bureau, Civil Aeronautics Authority (now Civil Aeronautics Bd.) 1939; Dir., Economic Bureau 1945; Member of Bd. 1948; Representative, Inter-departmental Advisory Cttee. on Surplus Aircraft Disposal 1944–46; Technical Adviser U.S. Delegation, International Civil Aviation Conf., Chicago 1944; Adviser, U.S. Delegation, First Interim Assembly, International Civil Aviation Organization (ICAO), Montreal 1946; member, U.S. Section, Cttee. on International Technical Aerial Legal Experts 1946; Chmn., Economic Div., Air Co-ordinating Cttee. 1946–50; Alternate Representative, Civil Aeronautics Bd. on Air Co-ordinating Cttee. 1946–50; member, ICAO Panel of Air Co-ordinating Cttee. 1947–50; Alternate Delegate, U.S. Delegation, First Assembly, ICAO, Montreal 1947; Delegate, U.S. Delegation, Comm. on Multilateral Agreement on Commercial Air Rights in International Air Transport, Geneva 1947; Chmn. of following U.S. Delegations: Second Assembly ICAO, Geneva 1948, signing on behalf of U.S. in accordance with powers given by the President, Convention of International Recognition of Rights in Aircraft 1948; U.S.-Peru bilateral air transport negotiations 1948; U.S.-Canada bilateral air transport negotiations, May–June 1949; Fourth Assembly, ICAO, Montreal 1950; U.S.-Philippines bilateral air transport negotiations 1950; U.S.-France bilateral air transport negotiations, Feb. 1951, and U.S.-Netherlands bilateral air transport negotiations, May 1951; transferred to Dept. of State, Jan. 1951; Special Asst. to Secy. of State, Jan.–July 1951; Vice Pres. Pan American World Airways Inc. 1951–72; Member Bd. Govs. National Aviation Club 1956–72; Secy. International Club of Washington. *Awards:* Grand Official of Merit, Sovereign Order of Vera Cruz (Brazil) 1959. Democrat. *Address:* 9120 Harrington Drive, Potomac, Md. 20854, U.S.A.

**ADAMS, Samuel Clifford, Jr.** American. *B.* 1920. *Educ.* Fisk Univ., Nashville, Tenn. (MA); Univ. of Chicago (PhD Sociology); Post Doctoral, Univ. of London (LSE & School of Oriental & African Studies); Syracuse Univ. (Maxwell School of Public Administration). *M.* 1958, Evelyn Baker. *Career:* Social Science Res. Asst., Cttee. of Education, Training & Res. in Race Relations, Univ. of Chicago 1950–51; Dir., Marion Co-operative Center, Amer. Missionary Association, Lincoln School, Marion, Alabama, 1947–50; U.S. Army 1944–46. Education Adviser, U.S. Special Tech. & Economic Mission to Indo-China 1952–54; Chief, Education & Community Development Divs., USOM to Cambodia 1954–57; Chief Educ. Adviser, USAID, Nigeria 1958–60; I.C.A. Representative, American Embassy, Bamako 1961–62; Dir., USAID Mission to Republic of Mali 1962–64; U.S. Delegation, Fifth Special Session, U.N. General Assembly 1967; Dir., USAID Mission to Morocco 1965–68; Ambassador to Niger 1968; Asst. Administrator, Bureau for Africa Agency for International Development, Dept. of State, Washington, D.C. 1969. Pres., Samuel C. Adams, Jr. & Co. International since 1975. *Awards:* Alaouite Decoration (King of Morocco) 1968; John Hay Whitney Foundation Opportunity Fellow 1951–52. *Address:* 3226 North MacGregor Way, Houston, Texas; and *office* 2716 Wichita Street, Houston, Texas 77004, U.S.A.

**ADAMS, Thomas Boylston.** *B.* 1910. *Educ.* Harvard Coll. (Class of 1933; Hon. Phi Beta Kappa). *M.* 1940, Ramelle Cochrane. *S.* John, Peter, Douglas, Henry. *Dau.* Ramelle. *Career:* Editorial writer, Boston Herald 1932–35; Executive, Waltham Watch Co. 1935–41; Officer, U.S. Army Air Corps 1941–46; Vice-Pres. and Dir., Sheraton Corp. of America 1946–63; Pres., Adams Securities Co. 1964–68; Elected delegate, Democratic National Convention 1972. Fellow and Treas., Amer. Acad. of Arts and Sciences; member of Faculty, Peabody Museum, Harvard Univ.; Pres., Massachusetts Historical Socy.; Trustee: Adams Manuscript

Trust, Boston Athenaeum and Neurosciences Research Foundation. Candidate for Democratic nomination, U.S. Senate for Massachusetts 1966. *Publications:* various papers in Proceedings of The Massachusetts Historical Socy. *Clubs:* Somerset, Tavern (Boston); Cohasset Yacht. *Address:* Concord Road, Lincoln, Mass.; and *office* 15 State Street, Boston, Mass., U.S.A.

**ADAMSEN, Jorgen.** Danish Diplomat. *B.* 1920 *Educ:* Copenhagen Univ.—Master of Law. *M.* 1953 Aase Christensen. *S.* 2. *Career:* Sec. of Embassy, Washington D.C. 1953–56; Counsellor of Embassy, Moscow 1960–64; Ambassador to Finland since 1974. *Address:* Danish Embassy, Georgsgatan 9, SF 00120 Helsingfors 12, Finland.

**ADAMSON, Alfred Victor.** Australian chartered accountant in private practise since 1935; *B.* 1906. *Educ.* Unley High School and Univ. of Adelaide; AUA (Commerce); FCA. *M.* (1) 1931, Norma M. Treleaven (*d.* 1962); (2) 1963, Lottie M. Pocklington (*d.* 1966); (3) 1967, Gweneth E. Nelson. *S.* Malcolm S. *Daus.* Barbara E. Lee, Margaret G. Arthur. *Career:* Senior partner in firm of Adamson, Penhall & Co. 1941–63; Private Consultant since 1963; Chmn. and Man. Dir., Argo Investments Ltd. 1946—; Chmn., Elder's Trustee & Executor Co. Ltd.; Co-op. Building Socy. of South Australia; Argo Investments Ltd.; Quarry Industries Ltd; Dir. of several other public companies; Chmn., Taxation Cttee. of Adelaide Chamber of Commerce 1949–64; Member, Commonwealth Valuation Bd. 1955–73; and of S.A. Council of Inst. of Chartered Accountants in Australia 1956–58, and Fed. Taxpayers Assn. of Australia 1958–60. *Publication:* Valuation of company shares and businesses (Law Book Co. of Australia, 1948–54–66–74). *Member:* Congregational Ins. Co. of Australia (Chmn.), and Bd of Govs., Parkin Trust. *Clubs:* Adelaide; Stock Exchange. *Address:* 16 Auburn Avenue, Myrtle Bank, Adelaide, S.A.; and *office* 23 King William Street, Adelaide, S.A., Australia.

**ADARKAR, Bhaskar Namdeo.** Indian banker. *B.* 1910. *Educ.* Wilson Coll., Bombay; and Gonville and Caius Coll., Cambridge. *M.* Sarala Wagle. *S.* 2. *Dau.* 1. *Career:* Deputy Economic Adviser, Govt. of India 1945–49; Member Indian Tariff Bd. 1949 and 1950–52; Indian Tariff Comm. 1952–57; I.M.F. 1957–61; Min. of Embassy, Washington 1958–61; Additional Secy.: Min. of Economic and Defence Coordination Feb.–Aug. 1963; Min. of Finance, Dept. of Coordination 1963; Min of Finance, Dept. of Economic Affairs 1963; Dep. Gov. Reserve Bank of India 1965–70; Gov. 1970; Chmn. Central Bank of India 1971–74; Chmn. Maharashtra State Road Transport Corp. since 1974. *Publications:* Indian Tariff Policy; Devaluation of the Rupee; The Gold Problem; History of the Indian Tariff. *Address:* Goolestan, New Cuffe Parade, Colaba, Bombay 5; and *office* Maharashtra State Road Transport Corp., Bombay Central, India

**ADDIS, Sir John Mansfield,** KCMG. *B.* 1914. *Educ.* Bonn, Oxford and Harvard Univs. *Career:* British Diplomatic Service 1938–74; served in China 1947–50 and 1954–57; Ambassador to Laos 1960–62; and to the Philippines 1963–70; Senior Civilian Instructor at the Royal Coll. of Defence Studies, London, 1970–72; Ambassador to China 1972–74; Sen. Research Fellow, Wolfson Coll. Oxford since 1975. *Member:* Oriental Ceramic Socy. (Pres. 1974); Royal Horticultural Society. *Club:* Boodle's. *Address:* Woodside Frant, Tunbridge Wells, England.

**ADDISON, Edward Norman.** British. *B.* 1918 *M.* 1945, Patricia Saint. *Daus.* 2. *Career:* Chmn & Man. Dir. Addison Tool Co. Ltd.; Chmn. Channel Tool Distributors Ltd., Pressbend Ltd.; Addison Tool (Sales) Co. Ltd. *Address:* Fernacres, Fulmer, Buckinghamshire, SL3 6JW; and *office* Westfields Road, London, W3 ORE.

**ADEANE, Col. Sir Robert Philip Wyndham,** OBE. British. *B.* 1905. *Educ.* Eton and Trinity Coll., Cambridge. *M.* (1) 1929, Joyce Violet Burnett (dissolved 1946); (2) 1947, Mrs. Kathleen Higgins; (3) 1971, Mrs. Elizabeth Jane Cator. *S.* 3. *Dau.* 1. *Career:* Served with R.A. in World War II (Lt.-Col. 1941; Temp. Col. 1943); Dir.: Colonial Securities Trust Co. Ltd., Ruberoid Co. Ltd., Decca Ltd. Trustee Tate Gallery 1955–62. *Clubs:* Brooks's; Bath; Beefsteak. *Address:* Loudham Hall, Wickham Market, Suffolk.

**ADEBO, Simeon Olaosebikan,** Nigerian Statesman, CMG, BA, LLB. *B.* 1913. *Educ:* Abeokuta Grammar School; King's Coll., Lagos; Univ. of London; Barrister-at-Law (Gray's Inn). *M.* 1941, Regina Abimbola Majekodunmi. *S.* 3. *Dau.* 1. *Career:* Registrar of the Church of the Province of West Africa (Anglican Communion) until 1962; Permanent Representative of Nigeria at the United Nations in N.Y. and Commissioner-Gen. for Economic Affairs in Washington 1962–67; Executive Dir., U.N. Inst. for Training and Research, and Under-Sec.-Gen., U.N. from 1968–72; Chmn. National Universities Commission of Nigeria since 1975. *Awards:* 11 honorary degrees. *Publication:* Report on the Nigerianisation of the Nigerian Public Service (in collaboration with Sir Sydney Phillipson), (1952). *Address:* Fowotade House, Oke-Ilewo Road, PO Box 139, Abeokuta, Nigeria.

**ADEREMI, Sir Adesoji Tadeniawo,** PC, KCMG, KBE, the Oni of Ife, Nigeria; *B.* 1889. *Educ.* C.M.S. School, Ife. *M.* Several children. *Career:* Joined staff of government railway construction 1909; Civil Service 1910; resigned and commenced trading, and engaged in motor transport business 1921; founded Oduduwa Coll. (first secondary school for boys in Ife Div.) 1932; Member House of Assembly, Western Nigeria 1946; M.L.C. Nigeria 1947; Member House of Representatives 1951–54; Central Min. without Portfolio 1951–55. Member Nigeria Cocoa Marketing Bd. 1947; led delegation to Coronation of Queen Elizabeth II 1953; Delegate to Conference for revision of Nigerian Constitution: London 1953, Lagos 1954, and London 1957 and 1958; P.C. (Western Nigeria) 1954; Pres., House of Chiefs 1954–60; Natural Ruler and Gov. of Western Region of Nigeria (Gov. 1960–63); Chmn., Council of Obas & Chiefs, Western Nigeria, since 1966. *Address:* The Afin (Palace), Ife, Nigeria.

**ADERMANN, Rt. Hon. Sir Charles Frederick,** PC, KBE. *B.* 1896. *M.* 1926, Mildred Turner. *S.* Albert Evan, Charles Neville. *Daus.* Nellie Viola, Mildred Joy. *Career:* Dairy Farmer; Chmn., Queensland Peanut Marketing Bd. for 24½ years until retirement in 1952; Chmn., Kingaroy Shire Council 1939–46 .Member House of Representatives (Maranoa, Qld. 1943–49) for Fisher, Qld. 1949–72 (Ret'd); Chmn. of Committees 1950–58; Chmn., South Burnett Broadcasting Co. *Member:* Australian Country Party, Dep. Leader, Dec. 1963 to Dec. 1966; Min. of State for Primary Industry 1958–67. Created Knight Commander 1971. *Address:* Box 182, Kingaroy, Qld. 4610, Australia.

**ADETORO, Dr. Joseph Eyitayo.** Nigerian University Lecturer. *B.* 1933. *Educ.* London BA; Oxford (Dip.Ed.); Birmingham (M.Ed); Alberta Ph.D. *M.* Francisca Bamideleayo. *S.* 1. *Daus.* 6. *Career:* Vice-Princ. Memorial College Igbajo; Lect. (Grade II) Univ of Lagos 1965–68, Sen. Lecturer 1968–75; Federal Commissioner for Health 1967–70; Fed. Commissioner for Agriculture and Natural Resources 1970; Federal Commissioner for Industries 1970–74; Sen. Lecturer, Univ. of Lagos since 1975. Chmn.—Abee Engineering & Construction Co. Ltd.; Medal Brothers Co. Ltd.; Town & Gown Press, *Fellow.* RGS, RMet.S, College of Preceptors, Intercontinental Biographical Assoc. *Member:* Assoc. Univ. Teachers of Nigeria; Nigerian Inst. of Management; British Inst. of Management. *Decorations:* Commander St J, Bal. of MOPA, Olu Ko Hi of Okeyao. *Publications:* The Handbook of Education in Nigeria; A National Bureau of Ideas; An Introduction to Philosophy and Education; The Indigenisation SAGA; Geography and Social Studies textbooks (for schools). *Clubs:* Metropolitan Club; Island Club; Nigerian Country Club. *Address:* 1 Eyitayo Adetoro Street, Igbari-Akoka, Lagos, Nigeria; & *office* 4 Adenuga Kajero Street, P.M.B. 1073, Yaba, Lagos, Nigeria.

**ADEVA, Manuel Aurelio.** Philippine diplomat; (Retired). *B.* 1901. *Educ.* Philippine Law School, Manila (LLB) and School of Law, New York Univ. (LLM); Graduate, U.S. State Dept. Foreign Affairs Service Programme. *M.* 1932, Araceli Villongco Dizon. *Daus.* Aurora Fé, Manuela Hope. *Career:* Philippine Secy., Cttee. on Friendly Relations Among Foreign Students in the U.S.A. 1930–38; Asst., Office of the Resident Commissioner of the Philippines, Washington, D.C. 1938–46; Technical Adviser, Philippine Delegation to U.N. Conf. of International Organizations, San Francisco, April–May 1945, and to Philippine Delegation, Far Eastern Advisory Comm., Washington, Oct.–Dec. 1945; Consul San Francisco, Nov. 1946, and New York Dec. 1946–Feb. 1948; Foreign Affairs Officer Class 1, Dec. 1948; First Secy. and Consul-Gen. Nanking Apr. 1948–Sept. 1949; Chargé d'Affaires a.i. and Consul-Gen. (with personal rank of Minister Oct. 1950) Taipei, Formosa March 1950; Min. of Career, Nov. 1952; Min. to the Repub. of China, Taipei 1953–56; Council Representative of the Philippines to SEATO 1956–58; Ambassador to Thailand 1956–58 (concurrently Min. to Burma); Special Envoy to inauguration of the Republic of Pakistan, Karachi Mar. 1956; Member of Delegation to 2nd and 4th Council of Ministers meetings, SEATO, Karachi

1956, and Manila 1958; Chief of Mission (Class III) Oct. 1956, (Class II) Aug. 1958; (Class I) Jan. 1962; Ambassador to Japan 1958–62; Ambassador to Italy 1962–66; concurrently to Turkey 1963–66 and to Greece 1964–66. *Member:* Philippine Panel, Philippine-Japan Treaty Negotiations, Tokyo 1960, State Visit of President Diosdado Macapagal to Italy, July 6–7 1962. *Address:* 7553 Pomelo Drive, Canoga Park, Calif. 91304, U.S.A.

**ADHIN, Dr. Jnan Hansdev,** BA Hons. Surinamer Jurist, Educationist, Lecturer and Politician. *B.* 1927. *Educ.* Bachelor of Arts, Panjab Univ., New Delhi Coll.; LLM (Master at Law); MSc Sociology and MEd, Master of Education, State Univ., Utrecht; MSc Anthropology, Municipal Univ., Amsterdam; Dr. Economics, (cum laude); State Univ., Groningen. *M.* 1948, Esha Damayanti. *S.* Shyam Maheshdatt, Rakesh Shivadatt. *Daus.* Vidya Satyavati, Shanti Dharmavati, Nirmala Sarasvati, Kanta Shilavati. *Career:* Editor, Nieuwe West-Indische Gids since 1959; Senior Lect. in Legal Philosophy, Govt. Law Coll. since 1961 and Faculty of Law Univ. of Surinam since 1968; in Philosophy, Pedagogics and Sociology, Govt. Educational Coll., Surinam since 1962; M.P. (Parlement van Suriname) since 1963; Min. of Justice and Police 1964–67 and since 1969; Editor, Surinaams Juristenblad since 1969; Minister of Education 1971–72; Senior Lect. in Socio-Econ. Problems of Devel. Counties, Faculty of Socio-Econ. Studies, Univ. of Surinam since 1975; *Awards:* Knight in the Order of the Nederlandse Leeuw, 1968; Commander in the Order of Oranje Nassau, 1974; Hon Title of Vidya Nidhi, 1975; Medal "Pro Mundi Beneficio", 1975; Medal "For Service to the Community", 1975. *Member:* Socy. Scientific Workers; Surinam Jurists Assn.; Foundation for Scientific Research in the Tropics; International Law Assn.; World Peace Through Law Centre Geneva; Socy. of Educationists; Surinam Socy. of Economists. *Publications:* A Hindi-Dutch Dictionary (1953); Development Planning in Surinam in Historical Perspective (1961); Design of a Romanized Spelling of Surinam Hindustani (1963); Romanized Spelling of Sarnami Hindustani (1964); Origin and Development of Asian Marriage Law (1969); Dutch for Surinam Schools (1972); One Hundred Years of Law Development (1973); One Hundred Years of Educational Development (1973); The Hindu Marriage (1976). Numerous articles on various topics in several papers and learned journals. Numerous lectures for universities, colleges, associations and other institutions in Surinam, India, Guyana, Trinidad, Puerto Rico, Jamaica and the Netherlands. *Clubs:* Rotary, Paramaribo; Golf. *Address:* Anand Nivas, Zorg en Hoop, Soelastraat 2, Paramaribo-Z, Surinam; and *office* Lim A Postraat 6, Paramaribo, Surinam.

**ADIV, Dov.** Israeli. *B.* 1922. *Educ.* Ben Shemen H.S. (Agric.). *M.* 1948, Ellen Asch. *S.* 1. *Dau.* 1. *Career:* Instrument Engineer, Anglo-Iranian Co., Abadan 1941–46; Representative, Jewish Agency, Teheran 1946–48; Mgr., Near East Air Transport 1948–52; Representative for Far East of El Al Israel Airlines 1952–58; Commercial Mgr. for the Americas for El Al 1958–62, Mgr. (Israel) for El Al Israel Airlines 1962–67; System Sales Mgr. 1967–69; Dir., Marketing Div. for El Al Israel Airlines Ltd.; Gen. Mgr. for Canada & the Far East, Montreal, Quebec 1976. *Address:* Ben Gurion Airport, Israel.

**ADKINSON, Burton Wilbur.** American geographer. *B.* 1909. *Educ.* Univ. of Washington (BA, MA); Clark Univ. (PhD). *M.* 1942, Margaret L. Klock. *Daus.* Karen Louise, Margaret Jane. *Career:* Teacher, public schools, Washington State 1929–39; Regional Research Asst., Office of the Geographer, State Dept. 1942–43; Research Assoc. and Asst. Dir., Bd. of Geographic Names 1943–44; Asst. Chief, Map Intelligence Section, Office of Strategic Services 1944–45. With Library of Congress: Asst. Chief, Map Division 1945–47 (Chief 1947–48); Asst. Dir., Reference Dept. 1948–49 (Dir. 1949–57); Head, Office of Science Information Service, National Science Foundation 1957–71; Dir. American Geographical Socy. 1971–73; Private Consultant since 1973. *Publications:* The Alpine Glacial History and Post-Glacial Adjustments of a Section of the Cabinet Mountains, Montana; Library of Congress Maps Program; Maps; Facilities of the Library of Congress—Their use in Studying the History of Nutrition; Cartography in the Seventeenth International Geographical Congress; Current Status of Scientific Information Activities in the U.S. Government (pub. in Nachrichten für Dokumentation); chapter contributed to Documentation in Action. *Member:* Amer. Geographical Socy.; Amer. Assn. for the Advancement of Science (Fellow); Assn. of Amer. Geographers; Special Libraries Assn. (Pres. 1959–60); Amer. Documentation Inst.; Internatl. Fed. for Documentation (Press. 1963–65). *Club:* Cosmost (Washington). *Address:* 5907 Welborn Drive, Washington, D.C. 20016, U.S.A.

**ADLER, Carleton David.** American investment counselor. *B.* 1925. *Educ.* Amherst Coll., Harvard Univ., Clark Univ., Kenyon Coll., and Babson Inst. of Business Administration (BSc 1952). *M.* 1954, Jean Frances Hannigan. *S.* Sailing David. *Dau.* Oona Ann. *Career:* Financial Statistician, Boston (Mass.) Insce. Co. 1952–54; Editor-Analyst, Arthur Wiesenberger & Co., N.Y.C. (Members N.Y. Stock Exchange) 1954–56; Investment Analyst, unlisted securities, Hirsch & Co. N.Y.C. (members N.Y. Stock Exchange) 1956–57. Dir. of Research, Plymouth Securities Corp., N.Y.C. 1957–58; Owner, Carleton & Co., Boston, Mass. (members Natl. Assn. of Securities Dealers) 1958–61; Investment Counsellor, Babson's Reports Inc., Wellesley Hills, Mass. 1963—. *Publications:* The Carleton Investment Report (Lexington, Mass. 1961–63); Associate Editor, Investment Companies (pub. Arthur Wiesenberger & Co. N.Y.C.). *Member:* Financial Analysts Federation; Boston Socy. of Security Analysts. *Address:* 98 Robert Best Road, Sudbury. Mass. 01776; and *office* 370 Washington Street, Wellesley Hills, Mass. 02181, U.S.A.

**ADLEY, Robert James,** MP. British politician. *B.* 1935. *Educ.* Falconbury and Uppingham. *M.* 1961, Jane Elizabeth Pople. *S.* Simon Henry, Rupert George. *Career:* Lived and worked in Malaya, Singapore and Thailand, established Pearl & Dean (Thailand) Ltd. 1956–58; Sales Dir. May Fair Hotel 1960–64; Former Dir. joint company Holiday Inns and Great Universal Stores; European Marketing Dir. Commonwealth Holiday Inns of Canada Ltd. since 1970; Vice-Chmn. Parly. Tourism Cttee.; Vice-Chmn. Conservative Wessex Members Group: Founder and First Chmn. Brunel Socy.: Gov., S.S. Great Britain Project; Vice-Chmn. Parly. Transport Cttee.; Chmn. British–Jordanian Parly. Group; Vice Chmn. All Party British Chinese Parliamentary Group. *Member,* National Council, British Hotels, Restaurants and Caterers' Assn. *Publications:* Hotels, The Case for Aid (1966); A Policy for Tourism (1977). *Clubs:* Carlton (London); Royal Lymington Yacht (Lymington). *Address:* Woodend House, Ridgeway Lane, Lymington, Hants.; and *office* 182 King Henry's Road, Swiss Cottage, London, N.W.3.

**ADUKO, Louis Antoine, BA, MA.** Ambassador of the Ivory Coast in U.K. *M.* (2) 1963, Marcelle Nahas. *S.* 4. *Daus.* 3. *Career:* Chef de Service du Personnel; Ministère de l'Educ. Nationale; Chef de Service des Bourses Ministère de l'Educ. Nationale; Deputy Dir. Charge African Affairs; Ministry Affairs Etrang; Dir. Political Affairs; Ministère des Affairs Etrangères; Ambassador Resident, Chmn. of National Border Commission; Ambassador Extra. and Plenipotentiary of the Republic of Ivory Coast in United Kingdom. *Address:* The Embassy of The Ivory Coast, 2 Upper Belgrave Street, London, S.W.1.

**AEPLI, Hans.** Dr. rer. pol.; Dir. of Swiss National Bank. *B.* 21 Mar. 1913. *Educ.* Handels-Hochschule, St. Gall (dipl. Kaufmann) and Univ. of Berne (Dr. rer. pol.). *M.* 1947, Renata Piantini. *S.* 2. *Dau.* 1. *Career:* previously Chief of Section of Swiss Finance Administration (until June 1954). *Publication:* Die schweiz. Aussenhandelspolitik von der Abwertung des Schweizerfrankens bis zum Kriegsbeginn (1936–39). *Address:* Seidenhofstrasse 14, Lucerne, Switzerland.

**AFRICA, Augusto, T.,** Philippine Customs Collector. *B.* 1927. *Educ.* Zamboanga City Schools; Univ. of Philippines, AB, LL.B. *M.* 1953, Celina Ramos. *Daus.* 2. *Career:* Admitted to Philippine Bar 1935; Govt. service Law Division, Manila Customhouse, legal asst, Chief Appraiser, Deputy Collector of Customs, currently Collector of Customs. *Chmn.* Bureau of Customs Embroidery Board. *Mem:* Sigma Rho, Phi Kappa (both U.P.). *Clubs:* Baguio Country; Filipino; Army and Navy. *Address:* 2 Atok St., Quezon City; and *office* Manila Customhouse, Port Area, Manila, Philippines.

**AFSHAR, Amir Aslan.** Iranian diplomat. *B.* 1922. *Educ.* Univ. of Berlin, Greifswald, Vienna, Geneva. Doctorate, Political Science, Univ. of Vienna; Hon. PhD Univ. of Utah. *M.* 1950, Camilla Saed. *S.* Mohammad. *Dau.* Fatima. *Career:* With Min. of Foreign Affairs, Tehran, Iran since 1948; Attaché Imperial Embassy of Iran, The Hague, Netherlands 1950–54; Toured U.S. Eisenhower Exchange Fellowship Program 1955–56; Dep., 19th, 20th Session, Iranian National Assembly (MAJLIS) 1956–64; Delegate U.N. Gen. Assembly 1957–60; Min. Extraordinary & Plenipotentiary 1962;

Ambassador, Iran to Austria 1967–69; Rep. Outer Space Conference, Vienna 1968; Unesco Conference Vienna and Roads & Traffic Conference 1968; Chmn. Bd. of Govs., Atomic Energy Agency 1968–69; Ambassador of Iran to the U.S.A. 1969–73, and accredited to Mexico 1970–73; Ambassador to German Federal Rep. since 1973; Rep. Int. Telecommunication Satelite Conference Washington 1971. *Awards:* Order of Homayoun, First and Second Grade; Medal of Farhang Second Grade (Educational); Persian; Order of House of Orange Nassau (Grand Officer, Commdr. and Officer) Holland; Order of Gross Kreuz, First Grade (Cordon), Bundesverdienst Kreuz (Gold & Silver) Austria; Order, Comndr. de la Legion d'Honneur, France; Order of Grand Officer, Thailand; Order of Ehren Kreuz, Grand Officer, Order of Ehren Kreuz Comndr., Germany. *Publications:* Study of the Constitution of the German Third Reich; Study about the Administrative Law of the German Third Reich; The Possibilities of the Expansion of the Iranian Economy (all in German); The Fall of the Third Reich; Ways and Means of Iran's Participation in International Organizations; God Created The World, The Dutch Built Holland (all in Persian); Report on America (in English). *Clubs:* Metropolitan International; Tehran (Iran); Redocote, American (Bonn). *Address* and *office* Kölner Str. 133–137, 53 Bonn Bad Godesberg, Federal Republic of Germany.

**AFSHAR, Amir Khosrow,** KCMG. Iranian diplomat. *B.* 1920. *Educ.* American Coll., Tehran (Diploma); Univ. of Geneva (BA); Faculty of Law, Paris Univ. *M.* Parvine Nikpour. *S.* Allahyar. *Daus.* Iran, Soundabeh. *Career:* First Secy., Imperial Iranian Embassy, Washington 1947–48, and Permanent Delegation, Iran to U.N. 1948–50; Head, U.N. Dept. Min., Foreign Affairs, Tehran 1950–51; Head, Third Political Dept. Min. Foreign Affairs, Tehran 1951–53, and Fourth Pol. Dept. 1953; Chargé d'Affaires, London 1953–54; Min. Plenipotentiary, Imperial Iranian Embassy, London 1954–57; Dir. Gen., Political Affairs, M.F.O., Tehran 1958–59; Political and Parliamentary Under-Secy., M.F.O., Tehran 1959–61; H.I.M's Ambassador to Germany 1961–63; to France 1963–66; Dep., Acting Foreign Min. 1967–69; H.I.M's Ambassador to the Court of St. James's 1969–74. *Address:* Ministry of Foreign Affairs, Tehran, Iran.

**AFUHS, Georg.** *B.* 1909. Retired Austrian diplomat. *Educ.* High School, Univ., Faculty of Law (LLD). *M.* 1947, Hedwig Hoinig. *Daus.* 4. *Career:* Entered Civil Service (Head of Finance Office Korneuberg) 1932; in Denmark, and later in charge of the repatriation of Austrian prisoners-of-war 1940–46; in Foreign Office since 1946; Secy. of Legation, Paris 1947, and Brussels 1948, and later in the year in Political Dept., Federal Chancellery; Head of Liaison Office, Munich 1950–51; Federal Chancellery 1955–56; Min. at The Hague 1956–58 (Ambassador 1958–62); in Austrian Foreign Office 1962–75. *Address:* Michaelerstrasse, 19–23, Vienna 18, Austria.

**AGAR, Herbert,** PhD. American author and publisher. *B.* 1897. *Educ.* Columbia Univ. (AB); Princeton Univ. (MA, PhD). *M.* 1945, Barbara Lutyens Wallace. *Career:* served in World War I (U.S. Naval Reserve) 1917–18; London correspondent for Louisville (Kentucky) Courier-Journal 1930–34; editor of same newspaper 1939–42; U.S. Naval Reserve 1942–43; Special Asst. to U.S. Ambassador at the Court of St. James's 1943–45; Counsellor for Public Affairs, U.S. Embassy in London 1945; Dir., British Div., U.S. Office of War Information 1943–45; Dir., Rupert Hart-Davis Ltd., publishers 1953–64, and T. W. W. Ltd., 1957–68. *Publications:* Milton and Plato (1928); Bread and Circuses (1930); The Defeat of Baudelaire (trans.) (1932); The People's Choice (1933); Land of the Free (1935); Pursuit of Happiness (1938); A Time for Greatness (1942); The Price of Union (1950); Declaration of Faith (1952); Abraham Lincoln (1952); The Unquiet Years, U.S.A. 1945–55 (1957); The Saving Remnant (1960); The Perils of Democracy (1965); Britain Alone (1973), etc. *Address:* Beechwood, Petworth, Sussex.

**AGATHER, Niels Victor.** American. Associated with Bruno Pagliai Group since 1958. *B.* 1912. *Educ.* Georgetown Univ. (BS) and Harvard Business School (MBA). *M.* Josephine O'Connor. *S.* Victor, Jr., John. *Daus.* Merrilee, Anne. *Career:* Exec. Vice-Pres.: La Consolidada México 1946–58; Shields & Co., New York. *Clubs:* University, Bankers, Acapulco Yacht, and Chapultepec Golf. *Address:* Monte Libano No. 865, México 10, D.F.; and (*office*) Paris No. 15 (1st Floor), México 4, D.F., México.

**AGNEW, James Broughton.** British. *B.* 1906. *Educ.* Sydney Boys' High School. *M.* 1932, Ada Winifred Burgess. *S.* 2. *Career:* Gen. Mgr., N.S.W. Fresh Food & Ice Co. Ltd. 1941–52; Finance Mgr., Commonwealth Hostels Ltd. 1953; Gen. Mgr., Rex Hotels Pty. Ltd. 1954–61. Finance Mgr. and Alternate Dir., Hooker Corporation Ltd., June 1961–71; T. M. Burke Pty. Ltd., Preuds Pty. Ltd., and subsidiaries Jan. 1963—, and Hooker Pastoral Co. Pty. Ltd. 1964—. *Member:* Associate, Inst. of Chartered Accountants in Australia (A.C.A.); Associate (Senior) Australian Socy. of Accountants (A.A.S.A. Senr.). *Clubs:* Australian Golf; Double Bay Bowling. *Address:* 7A 13 Bellevue Road, Bellevue Hill, Sydney; and *office* c/o Hooker Corp. Ltd., Wingello House, Angel Place, Sydney, N.S.W., Australia.

**AGNEW, Peter Graeme,** MBE. Publisher and printer. *B.* 1914. *Educ.* Stowe School and Trinity Coll., Cambridge. *M.* 1937, Diana Mary Hervey. *S.* Ian Hervey, James Philip. *Daus.* Penelope Mary, Diana Nicola. Dep. Chmn., Bradbury Agnew & Co. Ltd, since 1969. *Address:* 23–27, Tudor Street, London, E.C.4.

**AGNEW, Spiro Theodore.** *B.* 1918. *Educ.* student, Johns Hopkins, LLB.U. Baltimore. *M.* 1942, Elinor Isabel Judefind. *S.* 1. *Daus.* 3. *Career:* Formerly engaged in Private Practice Law, Baltimore; Served as Officer AUS 1941–45, 51; Chmn., Baltimore County Bd. Appeals 1958–61; Baltimore County Chief Exec. 1962–66; Governor of Maryland 1967–68; Vice-Pres. U.S. 1969–73; with Pathlite Inc., Crofton, Md. since 1974. *Member:* Maryland, Baltimore Bar Associations. *Award:* Bronze Star. Republican. *Address:* Towson, Md. 21212, U.S.A.

**AHIDJO, Ahmadou.** President, United Republic of Cameroon & National Pres. Cameroon National Union. *B.* 1924. *Educ.* Ecole Supérieure, Yaoundé (Diploma). *M.* Germaine. *S.* 1. *Daus.* 3. *Career:* Civil Servant 1942–46; elected to the first Cameroon Representative Assembly 1947; re-elected to the Territorial Assembly 1952; Councillor in the French Union 1953 (Assembly Secy. 1954); Pres. Legislative Assembly, Cameroon 1957; Deputy Prime Minister responsible Home Affairs, independent government of Cameroon 1957; Prime Minister 1958; President, Republic 1960; President Federal Republic of Cameroon 1961; Pres. United Republic of Cameroon 1972. *Awards:* Grand Master Order of Valour (Cameroon); Grand Cross, Legion of Honour (France); holder of numerous foreign decorations; Dr. Hon. Causa: Univs. of Montreal, Duquesne, Pittsburg and New York. *Publications:* Contribution à la Construction Nationale; Nation et Developpement dans l'Unité et la Justice. *Address:* Presidency of the Republic, Post Box 1085, Yaoundé, UR of Cameroon.

**AHLBERG, Claes Axel Hakon.** Swedish professor and practising architect. *B.* 1891. *Educ.* Royal Inst. of Technology, Stockholm; Royal Acad. of Fine Arts. *M.* 1925, Ellen Nisser (*d.* 1959); (2) 1965, Elisabet Waldenström. *Career:* Hon. corresponding member, Royal Inst. of British Architects (RIBA), American Inst. of Architects (AIA), Architectural Assn., London (AA), Royal Academy of Fine Arts, Copenhagen, and Société centrale des Architectes, Paris. Founder and Editor of the magazine Byggmästaren 1922–24; Founder and Pres., Swedish Inst. of Architects (SAR) 1936–45; Hon. Pres. since 1945. Past Pres. of the Royal Academy of Fine Arts, Stockholm 1954–62. *Publications:* Modern Swedish Architecture (1924); Architect Gunnar Asplund (1943). *Awards:* Comdr., Order of Vasa; Comdr. 1st Class Order of the North Star; King Gustav's 90th Year Memorial; Cmdr., Order to St. Olav (Norway); Order of White Rose, 1st Class (Finland). *Address:* St. Paulsgatan 1, 11647 Stockholm.

**AHLÉN, Gosta Mauritz.** Former Swedish company director. *B.* 9 Aug. 1904. *M.* 1927, Gunhild Hörberg. *Daus.* Karin Kerstin, Inger. *Career:* Man. Dir., Tempo AB 1933–69; Ahlén & Holm AB 1939–69; Mem. of Bd.: Ahlén & Holm AB 1929–76; Svenska Handelsbanken 1941–75. *Awards:* Comdr. 1st Class, Order of Vasa; Knight, Order of North Star; Order of Finnish Lion. *Address:* Stigbergsgatan 35, Stockholm.

**AHMAD, Mr. Justice Muhammad Basheer,** MA, MLitt. MPHistS, FRHistS (London), CSP. Judge, High Court, Nigeria; Pakistan Constitutional lawyer and historian, *Educ.* Muslim Univ. of Aligarh (MA); School of Oriental Studies, London; Fitzwilliam House, Cambridge (MLitt). *M.* 1955, Rafia. *S.* Harris. *Dau.* Maleeha. *Career:* Entered I.C.S. as Assv. Magistrate in U.P., India 1928; Judge of Court of Session and Appeal 1934; served in U.P.; Mem. Meerut Riot Enquiry Cttee. 1940; Secy., Pakistan Constituent Assembly 1947; Secy./Mem., Pakistan Delegation to Commonwealth Parliamentary Conf., London (1948), Sydney (1950), Ottawa (1952) and to Inter-Parliamentary Union Conference, Rome 1948; Constitutional Adviser to Constituent Assembly 1947–52; Chmn., Delimitation Bd., Bahawalpur 1951, and Delimitation Authority, Khairpur 1952; attended Coronation, London 1953; Secy., Pakistan Parliamentary Deleg., Stockholm (1952), Vienna (1954), London (1957) and Rio de Janeiro (1958); Secy., Min. of Information and Broadcasting, Govt. of Pakistan 1954–56; Advisor, deputation to U.S. Congress, and Turkish National Assembly 1956; Secy., National Assembly of Pakistan 1956; Secy. to Govt. of Pakistan, Mins. of Education and Rehabilitation 1958. *Publications:* The Problem of Rural Uplift in India (1933); The Administration of Justice in Medieval India (1941); The Influence of Muslim Culture in India (1928); The Meaning & Scope of Law among Muslim Peoples (1940); Judicial System of the Moghul Empire (1961); Select Constitutions of the World (vols. I–IV). *Address:* 20/C Annexe, VI-P.E.C.H.S., Ltd., Karachi, Pakistan.

**AHMED, Jamal Mohamed.** Sudanese diplomat. *B.* 1917. *Educ.* Univ. Coll. Exeter (BA 1946) and Balliol Coll. Oxford (BLitt 1954). *M.* 1937, Fatima. *S.* 4. *Daus.* 3. *Career:* Ambassador to Iraq 1956–59, to Ethiopia 1959–64; Sudan Permanent Delegate to the U.N. 1964–65; Ambassador to the United Kingdom 1965–67; Permanent Under-Secy., Min. of Foreign Affairs 1967–69. Ambassador to the Court of St. James's 1969–74. *Member:* Editorial Bd., Modern Journal of African History. *Awards:* Decorated by King of Iraq, King of Jordan, Emperor of Ethiopia, and President of Syria. *Publications:* The Intellectual Origins of Egyptian Nati onal ism (1960); translated the Federalist Papers, and Africa Rediscovered into Arabic; adviser to Hiwar magazine, Beirut. *Address:* c/o Ministry of Foreign Affairs, Khartoum, Sudan.

**AHO, Lauri (Emil).** Finnish politician and journalist. *B.* 1901. *Educ.* MA & PhD (hc 1973) Helsinki. *M.* 1931, Sisko Heikkilä (*d.* 1967). *S.* Matti Lauri, Eero Lauri Yrjänä and Antti Lauri Henrikki. *Career:* Dir., K. J. Gummerus Publishing Co. 1931–34; Political Ed., newspaper Uusi Suomi 1934–40, Editor-in-Chief 1940–56; First Mayor of Helsinki 1956–68; Central Cttee. of Conservative Party 1936–56; Chmn Helsinki City Council 1953–56; Vice Chmn. Administrative Council, Kansallis-Osake-Pankki. *Member:* Conservative Party; Pres., Assn. of Finnish Cities 1958–67; Int. Press Inst. *Awards:* Grand Officer, Order of the Lion (Finland); Cross of Liberty, 4th Class with swords; Memorial Medals of the War of 1939–40 (with swords), and of the War of 1941–45; Decoration of Assn. of Finnish Cities; Great Golden Decoration with Star of Order of Merit (Austria); Grand Officer of the following Orders: Dannebrog (Denmark), the Falcon (Iceland), St. Olav (Norway), and Order of the Tunisian Republic; Great Cross of Merit, with Star, Order of Merit (Fed. Germany); Comdr.: Order of Merit (Hungary), of Polonia Restituta (Poland), of Merit (France) and of North Star of Sweden; Helsinki Medal; Golden Decoration of Finnish Travel Association. *Address:* Kaartintorpantie 6 A 6, Helskinki, Finland.

**AHOUA, Timothee N'Guetta.** Ambassador of the Ivory Coast to the United States and Canada. *B.* 1931. *Educ.* Univ. of Paris (Bachelor in Public Laws Political Science); Nat. School of French Magistracy; Inst. of Overseas Higher Studies, Univ. of Paris. *M.* 1965, Germaine Rochemont. *S.* Philippe. *Career:* First Counsellor, Embassy of the Ivory Coast in Washington, Jan. 1964–May 1965; Ambassador to Morocco July–Sept. 1965; Cmdr. of the National Order of the Ivory Coast; Parti Democratique de la Cote d'Ivoire. *Club:* International, Washington. *Address:* 5111 Broad Branch Rd. N.W., Washington D.C. 20008, U.S.A.; and *office* 2424 Massachusetts Avenue N.W., Washington D.C. 20008.

**AIGNER, Dr. Heinrich.** German politician. *B.* 1924. *Education:* Schools in Amberg and Munich; studied law at Erlangen; junior barrister, assessor, took degree of Dr. Jur. (LL.D.). *M.* Elisabeth Furtner. *S.* 2. *dau.* 1. *Career:* Bavarian Ministry of Agriculture 1954–57; Govt. Councillor; Member of German Federal Council (Bundestag) since 1957; Member of European Parlt since 1961. *Vice-Pres.* German foundation, Berlin. *Curator:* German–Brazilian Society. *Member:* Bd. of Central Agency of Catholic Church for aid to developing countries; German–Latin American Parly. Group, German–Israeli Parly. Group; German–Soviet Parly. Group; German–British Parly. Group; German–French Parly. Group. *Decorations:* Bavarian Order of Merit; Rio Branco Order (Brazil); Cross of Commander of the Order of Gregory (Vatican). *Publications:* Thesis, Research into Abortion based on the Legal Records of the Provincial Court Dt. of Amberg 1925–50; Address in favour of a European Audit Office (1973). *Address:* 8450 Amberg, Kaiser-Wilhelm-Ring 14 F.R.G. and *office:* 5300 Bonn, Bundeshaus, Federal Republic of Germany.

**AIKEN, Frank.** Tánaiste. *B.* Feb. 1898. *Educ.* Christian Brothers Schools. *M.* 1934, Maud Davin. *S.* Proinsias, Lochlann. *Dau.* Aedamar. *Career:* Joined Irish Volunteers 1913; appointed Captain, Irish Republican Army 1918; Commandant, Camlough Battalion 1919; Vice-Brig., Newry Brigade 1920; Commandant, 4th Northern Div., Irish Republican Army 1921; Chief of Staff, Irish Republican Army 1923; Secy., Camlough Branch, Gaelic League 1914; Secy., Sinn Féin Organization, S. Armagh 1917; elected on local and County Councils 1920; member for County Louth (Fianna Fáil) Dáil Eireann since 1923; Min. for Defence 1932–39; Min. for Co-ordination and Defensive Measures Oct. 1939–45; Min. for Finance 1945; Minister, External Affairs 1951–54, 1969; Deputy Prime Minister Govt. Ireland 1965–69; Retd. member Government. *Address:* Dun Gaoithe, Sandyford, Co. Dublin, Ireland.

**AIKENS, Thomas, MLA, JP**; *B.* 1900. *Educ.* Charters Towers High School. *M.* 1921, Margaret Ann Myers. *Dau.* 1. *Career:* Councillor and Deputy Chmn., Cloncurry Shire Council 1924–30; Alderman and Deputy Mayor, Townsville City Council 1936–49. Member of the Legislative Assembly of Queensland for Townsville S., since 1944. For varying periods was a prominent member and official of the Australian Railways Union. *Member:* North Queensland Party. *Address:* 30 Soule Street, Hermit Park, Townsville, N. Qld., Australia.

**AIKMAN, Barry Thomson,** DFC. British. *B.* 1913. *Educ.* Stowe Sch.; Worcester Coll., Oxford. *M.* 1936, Joyce Carter. *S.* 1. *Daus.* 2. *Career:* Chmn. Barry Aikman Travel Ltd.; Aikman (London) Ltd.; Tour Vouchers Ltd.; Dir. Alta Holidays Ltd.; Dir. & Gen. Man. Lancashire Aircraft Corp. Ltd. 1945–47; Chmn. & Man. Dir. Aquila Airways Ltd., 1948–56; Royal Air Force; Hurlingham. *Address:* 105 Rivermead Court, London, SW6; and *office* Silver City House, 62 Brompton Rd., London, SW3.

**AIRD, Hon. John Black,** OC, QC, LLD, BA. Canadian Barrister & Solicitor. *B.* 1923. *Educ.* Upper Canada Coll., Trinity Coll. – BA; Osgoode Hall; Read law with Wilton & Edison. *M.* 1944, Lucille Jane Housser. *S.* 1. *Daus.* 3. *Career:* Lieut. RCNVR 1942–45; with Wilson & Edison 1949–53; Partner, Edison, Aird & Berlis 1953–74, Aird, Zimmerman & Berlis since 1974; appointed Queen's Counsel 1960; Mem., Senate of Canada 1964–74; Chmn. Canadian Section of Canada–United States Perm. Joint Bd. on Defence 1971; Mem. Cttee. of Nine March–Oct. 1973; Chmn. Inst. for Research on Public Policy 1974. Chmn of the Bd. & Dir., Algoma Central Railway. Vice-Chmn. of the Bd. & Dir., Reed Shaw Osler Ltd. *Director:* All Canadian–American Investments Ltd.; AMAX, Inc.; The Bank of Nova Scotia; Canada Tungsten Mining Corp. Ltd.; Consolidated–Bathurst Ltd.; Domglas Ltd.; Economic Investment Trust Ltd.; Famous Players Ltd.; The Molson Companies Ltd.; The National Life Assurance Co. of Canada; Petro–Canada; Rolland Paper Co. Ltd. *Member:* Hon. Pres., The Naval Officers' Assocs. of Canada; Bd. of Govs., Lester B. Pearson Coll. of the Pacific; Nat. Adv. Bd., Canadian Mental Health Assoc. Trustee, The Hospital for Sick Children. Chancellor, Wilfred Laurier Univ., 1977. *Awards:* Officer of the Order of Canada, 1976; Doctor of Laws (h.c.), Wilfred Laurier Univ., 1975. *Clubs:* York; Toronto; Toronto Golf; Granite. *Address:* 2 Glenallan Road, Toronto, Ontario M4N 1G7, Canada.

**AIREY, Arthur Wilson,** JP. British. *B.* 1906. *Educ.* Fremantle Boys' School, and Christian Brothers Coll., Fremantle. *M.* 1930, Ida Amy Viles. *S.* 3. *Daus.* 3. *Career:* Entered service of National Bank of Australasia Ltd. 1922; various positions therein until appointed Acctnt. of Branch Dept., Perth; resigned Aug. 1945 to enter Rural & Industries Bank as Branch Inspector; Secy, later Deputy Chmn. Commissioners Rural & Industries Bank, West Australia 1945–71. *Address:* 8 Buntine Road, Webley Downs, West Australia.

**AITCHISON, Donald Leslie Judson.** Australian. *B.* 1915. *Educ.* Diploma in Commerce (AUA), Univ. of Adelaide. *M.* Dorothy Olive Turner. *S.* Anthony Donald, Wayne Gordon. *Daus.* Heather Dorothy (Duff), Junesse Vivien (Cramond). *Career:* Officer S. Aust. Public Service 1933–57. Dep. Commonwealth Statistician in South Australia 1959–77. *Member:* S. Aust. Public Service Board 1949–57, and S. Aust. Superannuation Fund Board 1949–57; Pres., Public Service Fed. of Australia 1955–57. *Club:* Public Service. *Address:* 49 Inverness Avenue, St. Georges, SA 5064, Australia.

**AITCHISON, Dr. Gordon Douglas.** Australian. *B.* 1918. *Educ.* Univ. of Adelaide (BE & ME); Univ. of Melbourne (PhD). *M.* 1945, Joyce Chadfield Stephens. *S.* John Leslie. *Dau.* Anne Selby (Allwood). *Career:* Officer-in-Charge, Soil Mechanics Section, Commonwealth Scientific & Industrial Res. Organization, 1958–67; Chief, Div. of Soil Mechanics, Commonwealth Scientific & Industrial Res. Organization 1967–70. Chief Div. of Applied Geomechanics, Commonwealth Scientific & Industrial Research Organization since 1970. *Awards:* Fellow, Inst. of Engineering, Australia. *Publications:* About sixty papers on soil physics, geomechanics and terrain evaluation for engineering. *Clubs:* Wallaby; R.A.C.V.; Kingston Heath Golf. *Address: office:* C.S.I.R.O., Div. of Applied Geomechanics, Kinnoul Grove, Syndal, Victoria, Australia.

**AITKEN, Charles Ronald,** CBE. Australian. *B.* 1907. *M.* 1932, Ada Jane Irwin. *S.* 2. *Career:* Formerly Man. Dir., The South Australian Brewing Co. Ltd., Adelaide; Past Chmn., Liquor Industry Council of S.A.; Fellow, Australian Socy. of Accountants; Fellow Chartered Inst. of Secys.; Fellow, Australian Inst. of Management; Pres. and Life Mem., Amateur Athletic Union of Australia; Life Mem. and Past Pres., S.A. Olympic Council; Chmn. Australian, Commonwealth Games Assn. (S.A. Div.); Pres. and Life Mem., S.A. Amateur Athletic Assn.; Life Mem., Victorian Amateur Athletic Assn.; Past-Pres. Commonwealth Club of Adelaide; Mem. S.A. Sports Advisory Council; served in World War II in A.I.F. with R.A.O.C., with rank of Major. *Address:* 21 Orange Grove, Kensington Park, S.A., Australia.

**AITKEN, Sir (John William) Max, Bt,** DSO, DFC. British. *B.* 15 Feb. 1910. *Educ.* Westminster School; Pembroke Coll., Cambridge. *M.* (1) 1939, Cynthia Monteith (marriage diss.); (2) 1946, Jane Kenyon-Slaney (marriage diss.). *Daus.* Kirsty Jane, Lynda Mary; (3) 1951, Violet de Trafford. *S.* Maxwell William Humphrey. *Dau.* Laura. *Career:* Joined Auxiliary Air Force 1935; served in World War II in R.A.F., Day Fighter Pilot during Battle of Britain, commanded Night Fighter Squadron (Group Captain, despatches) 1935–45; M.P. (Cons.) for Holborn July 1945–50; former Chmn.: Beaverbrook Newspapers Ltd. (publishers of Daily Express, Sunday Express, Scottish Daily Express, Scottish Sunday Express, Evening Standard (London), Evening Citizen (Glasgow)), Associated Television Ltd. *Address:* The Garden House, Cherkley, Leatherhead, Surrey.

**AITKEN, Sir Robert Stevenson.** British. *B.* 1901. *Educ.* MD (New Zealand); DPhil (Oxon); FRCP (London); FRACP; Hon. FRCP Edin.; Hon. FDSRCS (Eng.); Hon. DCL (Oxon.); Hon. DSc (Sydney, Liverpool); Hon. LLD (Dalhousie, McGill, Melbourne, Punjab, Pennsylvania, Aberdeen, Newfoundland, Leicester, Birmingham, Otago). *M.* 1929, Margaret Kane. *S.* 1. *Daus.* 2. *Career:* Reader in Medicine, Univ. of London 1935–38; Regius Prof. of Medicine, Univ. of Aberdeen 1939–48; Vice-Chancellor, Univ. of Otago (New Zealand) 1948–53; Vice-Chancellor, Univ. of Birmingham 1953–68. Dep. Chmn., University Grants Committee 1968–73. *Publications:* papers and articles in medical journals. *Address:* 6 Hintlesham Avenue, Birmingham 15.

**AKÇAL, Erol Yilmaz.** Turkish politician. *B.* 1931. *Education:* Faculty of Law, Ankara, BA, MA; City College of New York (Int. Relations). *Career:* Foreign Trade Dept. 1957–61; Deputy of Rise (Turkey) 1961–73; Member, Council of Europe since 1963; Vice-Chmn. Budget Cttee 1963–69; Vice-Chmn. Council of Europe 1968–71; Chmn. Budget Cttee 1969–71; Minister of Tourism and Information 1971–73; Asst-Prof. Academy of Economy and Commerce 1973–75; Private business 1975–77. *Publications:* Tourism Industry (1974); various newspaper articles. *Club:* YPO, Lions. *Address:* Halaskargazi cad. No. 198/16, Maya apt, Osmanbey, Istanbul, Turkey; & *office* Densan A. S., Findikli, Bilezik Sok. Güneş Han No 3/3, Istanbul, Turkey.

**AKE, Siméon.** *B.* 1932. *Educ.* Faculty of Law Dakar (Lic. en D); Grenoble (Diplomé in Higher Studies of Public Law). *M.* Anne Maud Bonful. 6 children. *Career:* Chief of Cabinet, Ministry of Public Affairs 1959–61; First Counsellor, Ivory Coast Permanent Mission to U.N. 1961–63, and to the 16th and 17th Sessions of the General Assembly; Dir. of Protocol, Ministry of Foreign Affairs Apr. 1963–Mar. 1964; Ambassador of the Republic of the Ivory Coast to U.K., Sweden, Denmark and Norway Apr. 1964–July 1966. Ambassador Extraordinary and Plenipotentiary, Permanent Representative of the Ivory Coast to the U.N. since 1966. *Award:* Decorated Officer of the National Order. *Address:* Permanent Mission of Ivory Coast to the U.N., 46 East 74th Street, New York, N.Y., 10021, U.S.A.

**AKERS, Anthony Boyce.** American diplomat and lawyer. *B.* 1914. *Educ.* Univ. of Texas (BA 1936) and Columbia Univ. (LLB 1949). *M.* 1942, Jane Pope. *Daus.* Andra (Frazier), Ellery Jane. *Career:* Instructor, Public Schools, Texas 1936–37, California 1938–39; U.S.N.R. Mdn. School, Northwestern Univ. 1941, and Notre Dame Univ. 1945; Admitted to New York Bar 1950, District of Columbia Bar and to Practice at Supreme Court of U.S.A. 1953; engaged in private practice, N.Y.C. 1950—; of Counsel Cabell, Martin, Hammer and Gallo since 1967; Dep. Asst. Secy., then Dep. Under-Secy., international negotiations, Office of the Secy. of the Air Force 1951–53; Dir., N.Y. State Dept. of Commerce for N.Y.C. 1955–58; Chmn., N.Y.C. Community Mental Health Bd. 1957–58; Democratic candidate for Congress 1954–56–58 (N.Y. 17th Congressional District); Chmn., N.Y. Citizens for Kennedy-Johnson 1960; Ambassador of the United States to New Zealand, July 1961–Oct. 1963. *Member:* American Delegation to ANZUS Conferences, Australia 1962, and New Zealand 1963; Conference of American Ambassadors in the Far East, Baguio, Philippine Islands Mar. 1962; Latin American Representative, Inter-American Trade and Cultural Center 1966; Served to Lieut.-Comdr. U.S. Navy 1940–46; Pres. Landfall Development Co. since 1972. Council on Foreign Relations; Bd. of Trustees, Freedom House; Assn. of Bar of City of N.Y.; Federal Bar Council; Bar Assn. of District of Columbia. Democrat. *Awards:* Silver Star Medal with Gold Star. *Address:* 102 North Fifth Avenue, Wilmington, North Carolina 28401; and *office* 555 Madison Ave., N.Y.C., 10022, U.S.A.

**AKHUND, Iqbal Ahmed,** Pakistan diplomat. *B.* 1924. *Education.* Bombay Univ., MA (Degree in Econs & Polit. Science). *M.* 1955 Yolanda Gombert. *S.* 3. *Dau.* 1. *Career:* Private Secy. to For. Min. 1956–58; Dir.-Gen. Ministry for For. Affairs 1966–68; Ambass. to Egypt 1968–71, to Yugoslavia 1971–72; Perm. Rep. to U.N. (of Pakistan) since 1972; Pres. of U.N. Economic and Social Council 1975.; Chmn., Security Council Cttee. on Sanctions against Southern Rhodesia 1976; Chmn., Group of 77 1976–77. *Address:* 8 East 65th Street, New York, N.Y. 10021, U.S.A.

**AKIN, William M.** American. *B.* 1896. *Educ.* Harvard Univ.; Hon. DEng., Univ. of Missouri School of Mines 1953. *M.* 1918, Rosalind Bigelow. *S.* Paul B., Thomas. *Career:* U.S. Navy 1917–19; with Laclede Steel Co. since 1919. Hon. Chmn. and Dir., Laclede Steel Co. 1937—; Dir.: St. Louis Union Trust 1947—; Wagner Electric 1959–66; Washington Univ. 1948—; American Iron & Steel Inst. 1947–67. *Member:* many societies and clubs; Pres., Assn. Harvard Clubs 1948–49. *Address:* Equitable Building, 10 Broadway, St. Louis, Mo., U.S.A.

**AKNER, Erik Birger.** Swedish. *B.* 1920. *Educ.* Royal Inst. of Technology. *M.* 1949, Brita Kristina. *S.* 3. *Career:* Asst. Man. Dir. AB Gotlands Kraftverk, 1957–59; Chief Engineer, AB Skandinaviska Elverk, 1959–62; Man. Dir. AB Gotlands Kraftverk & Voxnan Projekt AB 1962–71 and Gullspångs Kraft AB 1971. *Clubs:* Rotary; Masons. *Address:* Olaigatan 55, 70361 Örebro, Sweden; and *office* Stubbengatan 2, 703 44 Örebro, Sweden.

**AKRAWI, Matta.** Iraqi educationist. *B.* 9 Dec. 1901. *Educ.* American Univ. of Beirut (BA Hon.); Columbia Univ., New York (MA, PhD). *M.* 1936, Najla Tannous. *S.* Sabah, Amin. *Career:* Instructor in Education, Primary Teachers' Coll., Baghdad 1924–25; Principal of the Coll. 1929–33; Dir. of Primary Educ. and Research, Min. of Educ., Baghdad 1934–35; Dir. of Educ., Kirkuk and Hillah areas 1935–37; Prof. of Educ. and Dean, Higher Teachers' Coll., Baghdad 1937–46; *Member:* American Cncl. on Educ. Comm. for Survey of Educ. in the Arab States 1945–47; Dir.-Gen. of Higher Educ., Min. of Educ., Baghdad 1946–50; Head, Education Clearing House, UNESCO 1949–51; Head, Div. of the Extension of School Educ., UNESCO 1952; Dep.-Dir., Dept. of Educ. for Extension of School Educ. 1953–57; Pres., Univ. of Baghdad 1957–58; Expert for Organization of Educ. in Sudan 1958–59; Dir., UNESCO Office, N.Y. 1959–61; Dir. of Research, UNESCO-IAU study on the role of institutions of higher education in the development of countries in S.E. Asia 1961–62; Prof. of Educ., American Univ. of Beirut 1963–71; Int. Adv. Cttee. of the World Book Encyclopedia International 1963–67; Int. Cttee. for planning King Abdul-

Aziz Univ. in Jiddah 1966; Visiting Prof. of Educ., Univ. of Kuwait 1969–70; Director, Survey of Experiments, Researches and Innovations on the Teaching of Arabic to Arabs since 1974; Adviser UNICEF programme' aid to education in Sudan 1970; represented Iraq and, later, UNESCO in many conferences; participated in international expert committees and meetings on educational subjects. *Awards:* Teachers Coll. (Columbia Univ.) Medal of Distinguished Service; Order of the Cedar, 'Chevalier' Class, Republic of Lebanon. *Publications:* many books and articles in Arabic and English on varied subjects, but dealing chiefly with education. *Address:* American Univ. of Beirut, Beirut, Lebanon.

**AKWEI, Richard Maximilian.** Ghanaian diplomat. *B.* 1923. *Educ.* Achimota Coll., Ghana; Christ Church, Oxford (BA); London Univ.; Inst. of Educ. *M.* 1956, Josephine Akosua Aphram. *S.* Richard Adote, Adotei. *Dau.* Adjeley Abla. *Career:* Admin. Officer and Magistrate to Gold Coast 1952–56; Cadet Diplomat, U.K. High Comm., Ottawa 1956–57; First Secy., Ghana Embassy, Washington 1957–60; Dir., W. and E. European Depts., Min. of Foreign Affairs, Accra 1960–62; Prin. Secy. of Min. 1963; Ghana Ambassador to Mexico 1964–65; Ambassador and Perm. Representative to U.N. European Office, Geneva, Ambassador to Switzerland and Representative IAEA, Vienna 1965–67; Ambassador Extraordinary and Plenipotentiary, Permanent Representative to Ghana to the U.N. 1967–72; Ambassador to People's Republic of China since 1972. *Address:* Ghanaian Embassy, 35 San Li Tung, Pekin, People's Republic of China.

**ALAM, Hon. Anthony Alexander.** Australian parliamentarian. *B.* 1898. *Educ.* Del la Salle Coll., Armidale. *M.* 1924, Therese Anthony. *Career:* Member of Legislative Council of New South Wales 1925–59, and since 1963; Government Representative, Kuring Chase Trust, N.S.W. 1954; Governing Dir., Mala Building Co. 1949; Dir., Alam Stores Pty. Ltd. 1939, Governing Dir. 1955. *Awards:* Chevalier, Legion of Honour; Commander, Etoile Noir; Grand Officer, Nechan Iftakar; Grand Cross Orders of St. Mark and Torsina; Grand Officer, Order of Phoenix; Coronation and Silver Jubilee Medals. *Club:* Parliamentary Bowling. *Address:* 69 Bradley's Head Road, Mosman, N.S.W. 2088, Australia.

**AL-BAKR, Ahmed Hassan.** *B.* 1914. *Educ.* Teachers' Coll.; Military Acad. *Career:* Member Military Court July 1958; detained in military prison Oct. 1958 and placed on retired list Apr. 1959. Pres. of the Republic of Iraq; Chmn., Revolutionary Command Council; Gen.-Secy. of Regional Leadership Socialist Arab Baath Party since 1968. *Address:* Presidential Palace, Baghdad, Iraq.

**ALBERS, O. G.** South African Ambassador in Paraguay. *Address:* South African Embassy, Asuncion, Paraguay.

**ALBERT, Sir Alexis Francois,** Kt. CMG, OStJ, VRD. Australian executive. *B.* 1904. *Educ.* Knox Coll.; St. Paul's Coll. (Univ. of Sydney); BEc. *M.* 1934, Elsa K. R. Lundgren (*Dec.*). *S.* 3. *Career:* with Royal Australian Naval Reserve 1918–49; Retired Lieut.-Cmdr.; Hon. ADC to Governors of New South Wales 1937–57; Chmn., J. Albert & Son. Pty. Ltd., Sydney 1933—. Underwriting Member, Lloyds of London 1944–74; Dir., Australasian Performing Right Assn. 1946–76; Amalgamated Television Services Pty. Ltd. 1954—; Pres., Royal Blind Socy. of N.S.W.; Fellow of the Council of St. Paul's Coll., Univ. of Sydney; Council National Heart Foundation of Australia, N.S.W. Div. *Clubs:* Australian; Union; Royal Sydney Golf; Royal Sydney Yacht Squadron (Commodore 1971–75); New York Yacht; Naval & Military (London). *Address:* 25 Coolong Road, Vaucluse, N.S.W. 2030; and *office* 139 King Street, Sydney, N.S.W. 2000, Australia.

**ALBERTI, Jules.** Advertising executive. *B.* 1903. *Educ.* Chicago. *M.* Maybelle Ross. *Career:* Producer, Chicago radio stations 1921–35; New York radio stations 1935–42; National co-ordinator of talent, War Bond Div. U.S. Treas. Dept., Washington 1942–43; National Dir., Radio Advertising, 20th Century-Fox 1943–45; Founder, Pres., Endorsements Int. Ltd. 1945; Consultant and National Co-ordinator of Special Projects, U.S. Navy 1957; National Co-ordinator, U.S. Merchant Marine Div., Dept. of Comm. 1957–58. *Awards:* Bronze Applause Medallion; United States Treasury Dept. Citation; American Heritage Foundation, Citation; Meritorious Public Service Citation, U.S. Navy; Meritorious Award, Navy League; Caballero Comendador de Gracia Magistral, Orden Militar del ss Salvadory y Santa Brigada de Suecia, 1974. *Publications:* A Primer of Testimonial Advertising (1950, Revised 1955); articles on advertising for professional Journals. *Clubs:* Sales Executives Club; Friars; Conference, Personal Managers. *Address:* 300 East 57th Street, New York, N.Y. 10022, U.S.A.; and *office* 111 West 57th Street, New York, N.Y. 10019, U.S.A.

**ALBERTSEN, Kristian.** Danish politican. *B.* 1917. *Education.* Trade degree 1935. *M.* 1948, Mette. *Career:* Cons. at Social-democratic newspaper 1941–63; member city council Frederiksberg 1947–64; Member of Parliament since 1960; Member European Parliament 1973–76; Member of Board of Royal Danish Hypotekbank; Member of Nordisk Råd (Council), Chmn. of Justice Commission. *Chairman:* Danish Assoc. for elderly people. *Publication:* Pensionist in Denmark. *Address:* Johs V. Jensens Alle 46, 2500 Valby, Denmark; and Å Boulevard 56, Copenhagen N 2200, Denmark.

**ALBERTSON, Fred (Woodward).** American lawyer and engineer; radio and communications legal counsel for radio, television, telegraph, telephone and broadcasting companies and stations since 1935. *B.* 1908. *Educ.* Univ. of Michigan (AB 1931, JD 1934). *M.* 1942, Catherine Frances Dolan. *S.* Fred Woodward, Jr. *Dau.* Helen Dolan. *Career:* Licensed radio operator since 1924; engineered construction and operation of several radio broadcast and radio telegraph stations 1925–27; radio equipped and handled communications with several remote meteorological expeditions and stations for Univ. of Michigan 1927–34; Admitted to Michigan Bar 1934, District of Columbia Bar 1935 and Supreme Court of the United States 1940; Partner, Dow, Lohnes & Albertson (specializing in communications, radio and air law), Washington D.C., since 1944. Member, Bd. of Trustees and Dir., Delta Theta Phi Foundation 1945–46; Registered Professional Electrical-Communications Engineer in the District of Columbia; Senior Member, Inst. of Electrical & Electronics Engineers (Chmn., Washington, D.C., Section 1946–47; Bd. of Editors of Proceedings of I.R.E. 1946–54); Member, Broadcast Pioneers; Pres., American Federal Communications Bar Assn. 1953–54. *Member:* American Bar Assn. (House of Delegates 1953–54; Chmn. Standing Cttee. on Communications 1957–58); Fellow, American Bar Foundation. Amateur Radio W4BD. *Address:* 310 Harbor Drive, Key Biscayne, Florida 33149, U.S.A.; *office* 1225 Connecticut Avenue, Washington, D.C., 20036, U.S.A.

**ALBERTZ, Heinrich.** German ecclesiastic and politician. *B.* Jan. 1915. *M.* 1939, Ilse Schall. *S.* Rainer. *Daus.* Ilse-Sibylle, Regine. *Career:* Pastor in Upper Silesia 1942; Min. for Refugees, Lower Saxony 1948; Senate Dir. of Culture, Berlin 1955; Chief of Senate Office 1959–61; Senator of the Interior, Berlin 1961–63; Bürgermeister and Senator for Public Order and Security, Berlin 1963. *Member:* (S.P.D.), Lower Saxon Landtag since 1947; Bundesrat since 1949; Min. of Social Affairs, Land Lower Saxony since 1951; (S.P.D.) of Abgeordnetenhaus Berlin and Bundesrat 1963 (retd.). *Address:* Roland. 6B, Berlin 38, Federal Republic of Germany.

**ALBIG, Reed Harrison.** American. *B.* 1906. *Educ.* McKeesport High School; Gettysburg Coll.; Amherst Coll. (AB 1926); graduate work at Harvard. *M.* 1940, Helen Spaide. *Career:* Began working in 1924 as messenger and clerk (summertime) for National Bank of McKeesport (Dir. 1928, Vice-Pres. 1929, Executive Vice-Pres. 1932, Pres. 1937—); Pres., McKeesport National Bank 1937—; Dir., G. C. Murphy Co.; Member, Advisory Cttee. to Office Comptroller Currency. developed and expanded installment loan dept.; initiated FHA (Federal Housing Administration) mortgage financing to help residential development; and the re-sale of such mortgages to mortgage investors; devised programme for general book-keeping by the use of one machine (adopted by Burroughs Corp.); Dir., Spaide Shirt Co. (Pres. 1945–47); Pres., Independent Bankers Assn. 1961; Dir. and Past Pres., McKeesport Chamber of Commerce; served as Dir. of Y.M.C.A., McKeesport Hospital, Community Fund, and McKeesport Community Development Council; First Pres., Mon Yough Conf. on Community Developments; Dir., Passavant Hospital. *Member:* Hampton Township School District Authority; served as Lieut., U.S. Naval Reserve 1943–45. *Address:* McKeesport National Bank, McKeesport, Pa., U.S.A.

**ALBION, Robert Greenhaigh.** Professor of history and author. *B.* 1896. *Educ.* Bowdoin (AB 1918); Harvard (PhD 1924); LittD. Bowdoin 1948; LittD. Southampton Coll. 1970; L.H.D. Univ. of Meine 1971. *M.* 1923, Jennie B. Pope (*Dec.* 1976). *Career:* Served in World War I (2nd Lieut. Inf.) 1917–

18; At Princeton Univ. 1922–49; Instructor to professor of history; Asst. Dean of faculty; Dir. of summer session; historian of naval administration, Navy Dept. 1943–50; Gardiner Prof. of Oceanic History & Affairs, Harvard Univ. 1949–63, Emeritus 1963; Dir., Munson Inst. of Maritime History 1955—; Harvard-Navy Polaris Programme 1963–73; Pres., Maine Historical Socy. 1963–70, Overseer Beth Marine Museum since 1974. *Award:* Presidential Certificate of Merit 1948. *Publications:* (in collab. with wife): Forests & Sea Power (1926); Intro. to Military History (1929); History of England and the British Empire (1937); Square Riggers on Schedule (1938); The Rise of New York Port (1939); Sea Lanes in Wartime (1942); Maritime & Naval History—a Bibliography (1955); Seaports South of Sahara (1959); Forrestal and the Navy (1962); New England and the Sea (1972); Five Centuries of Famous Ships (1977). Republican. *Address:* Harvard Faculty Club, Cambridge, Mass. 02138.

**ALBISTON, Harold Edward,** CBE. Australian. *B.* 1897. *Educ.* Univ. of Melbourne (Doctor of Veterinary Science). *M.* 1923, Hazel Ruve Hattam. *S.* 2. *Daus.* 2. *Career:* At Univ. of Melbourne: Caroline Kay Scholar 1920; Walter and Eliza Hall Fellow 1921–22; Lecturer, Veterinary Pathology and Bacteriology 1923–29; Dir., Veterinary Research Inst. 1929–63. Pres., Veterinary Bd. of Victoria 1960–62. Research Veterinarian, Dept. of Health, Commonwealth of Australia 1963–67. *Publications:* Diseases of Domestic Animals in Australia (6 vols); Editor, Australian Veterinary Journal 1939–62; articles in scientific journals. *Fellow:* Australian Veterinary Assn.; Hon/Austr. Coll. Fellow Vet. Scs; Gilruth Prize Winner. *Member:* Zoological Bd. of Victoria. *Address:* 11 Nicholson Street, North Balwyn, Vic., Australia.

**ALBRECHT, Karl.** Dr. rer. pol. German political economist. *B.* 1902. *Educ.* Schiller Realgymnasium (Berlin-Charlottenburg); Univs. Berlin and Jena (studies of political science). *M.* 1925, Katharina Bardorf. *Daus.* 2. *Career:* At Emil Busch A.G. Optical Industries, Rathenow 1924–34; Mgr. of industrial organizations 1934–43; Mgr., Dept. of Foreign Administration, Reichsgruppe 1943–45; freelancing in political economics, and Asst. to Ministry of Economics at Bayern and Württemberg-Hohenzollern 1945–49; Dep. Mgr., Bundes Ministry for Affairs (concerning the Marshall Plan) 1949–53; Man.-Dir. Chamber of Commerce and Industry 1952–71; C. Rudolf Poensgen Foundation for the Training for Advanced Management, Düsseldorf 1956–1971; Kuratoriumsmitgl. Ifo-Institut, München 1950–75; Stllv. Vorsitzer d. Aufsichtsrates der W. H. Jones & Co. GmbH. Dusseldorf. *Publications:* A Chance for the Middle Class (1959); Present Problems of the Young Leaders in Economics (1961); Risks and Chances in the Common Market (1957); Problems & Methods of the Economic Integration (1951); Wirtschaftspraxis und Wirtschaftspolitik gestern—heute—morgen (1964); Planifikateure beim Werk (1964); Um die Freiheit der Entscheidung (1965); Das Menschlichehinter dem Wunder (1970); numerous articles in trade, political, financial and economic journals. *Clubs:* Industrial; Rotary (Düsseldorf). *Address:* Eitelstrasse 68, Düsseldorf-Rath, Federal Republic of Germany.

**ALBRECHT, Ralph Gerhart.** American lawyer. *B.* 1896. *Educ.* Univ. of Pennsylvania (AB); Harvard Univ. (JD 1923); *M.* 1936, Aillinn Leffingwell. *S.* Peter Leffingwell. *Career:* Admitted to Bar of N.Y. 1924, and U.S. Supreme Court 1927; Associate Counsel for American claimants in sabotage cases (Black Tom and Kingsland explosions) before Mixed Claims Comn., U.S.-Germany 1924–40, resulting in awards totalling $50 million; Special Dep. Atty. Gen., New York 1926; Senior partner, Peaslee, Albrecht & McMahon (general practice, specializing in foreign causes and international law) 1933–60; Counsel to firm 1961—; Special Asst. to U.S. Atty Gen. 1945; Member, U.S. War Crimes Comm., and exec. trial Counsel to Mr. Justice Robert H. Jackson in prosecution of major Nazi war criminals before the International Military Tribunal, Nuremberg 1945–46; prosecuted Hermann Goering; Counsel to German steel, coal and chemical industries in de-cartelization proceedings before Allied High Comm. for Germany 1950–53; Member, Republican County Cttee., N.Y. County 1933–35; Harvard Overseers' Visiting Cttee. to Faculty of Germanic Languages and Literatures; Apprentice Seaman, U.S. Naval Reserve Force 1918; Comdr. U.S.N.R. on active duty 1941–45; Naval Observer, American Embassy, London 1942; letter of commendation from Chief of Naval Operations; Asst. Dir. O.S.S. (War Crimes). *Member:* Mason; Republican; American Socy. Int. Law: Chmn., Manley O. Hudson Medal Cttee; International Law Assn; World Peace through Law Center Geneva Cttee. in Settlement and Mediation of Disputes. *Publications:* translated from German, Stappert's Forms of Securities and Methods of Transfer according to German Law, for Cahiers de Droit Comparé, Paris; collaborated with Prof. Walter B. Pitkin on studies for vocational guidance on recent school and college graduates and with Peter Markham (pseud.), author of America Next. *Clubs:* University; Harvard; Pilgrims of U.S. Squadron A. *Address:* 520 East 86th Street, New York City 10028; and *office* 501 Fifth Avenue, New York City 10017, U.S.A.

**ALBRIGHT, William Beaumont.** British company director. *B.* 26 Dec. 1907. *Educ.* Charterhouse, Faraday House Engineering Coll., London. *M.* (1) 1932, Evelyn May Bromley (dec'd 1974). (2) 1974, Hilary Anne Heyes. *Career:* Dir., Albright & Wilson Ltd. 1937; Man.-Dir. 1942–56; Scottish Chemicals Ltd. *Address:* Highclere, Woodnorton, nr. Evesham, Worcs.; and *office* Albright & Wilson Ltd., Oldbury, Birmingham.

**ALCOCK, Norman Zinkan,** PhD. Canadian physicist. *B.* 1918. *Educ.* Queen's Univ., Kingston, Ont. (BSc Elec. Eng.); Caltech (MS Elec. Eng.); McGill (PhD Physics). *M.* 1948, Patricia Christian Sinclair (Hunter). *S.* Stephen, Christopher, David. *Dau.* Nancy. *Career:* Commissioned R.C.A.F. 1942; Scientific Officer: National Research Council, Ottawa 1941, and T.R.E., Great Malvern, England 1943; Research Physicist: McGill Univ. 1945, and Atomic Energy of Canada 1947; Vice-Pres. & Dir., Isotope Products Ltd. 1950; Dir. of Engineering, Canadian Curtiss-Wright Ltd. 1958; self-employed on Peace Research Promotion 1959—; Pres. & Dir., Canadian Peace Research Inst., Ontario since 1961. *Publications:* The Bridge of Reason (1961): The Emperor's New Clothes; The War Disease; The Logic of Love. Many Canadian and U.S. Patents. *Address:* 244 Lakewood Drive, Oakville, Ont., Canada.

**ALDER, Keith Frederick.** Australian metallurgist. *B.* 1921. *Educ.* BSc and MSc (Melbourne). *M.* 1947, Pauline Mary Robertson. *S.* Andrew, Robert, Graeme. *Career:* Metallurgist, Ammunition Factory, Footscray, Vic. 1945–46; Lecturer in Metallurgy, Newcastle (N.S.W.) Technical Coll. 1946–48; Senior Scientific Officer, British Ministry of Supply, A.R.E., Woolwich 1949–50; Lecturer in Metallurgy, Newcastle (N.S.W.) Univ. Coll. 1951; Senior Lecturer in Physical Metallurgy, Univ. of Melbourne 1952–53; with Australian Atomic Energy Comm. 1954—; (attached A.E.R.E., Harwell (U.K.) 1954–57; Head of Metallurgy Section 1955; Dep. Dir. 1960). Member, Australian Atomic Energy Comm. 1968–75; and Dir., A.A.E.C. Research Establishment, Lucas Heights, N.S.W. 1962–70; Head Nuclear Science and Technology Branch since 1974. *Publications:* author of papers on ultrasonics, electronic instrumentation, beryllium metallurgy, welding and corrosion in reactor technology, liquid metal and gas-cooled reactors. *Member:* Fellow, Institution of Metallurgists, London; Inst. of Radio and Electronic Engineers (Australia); Australian Inst. of Mining and Metallurgy. *Address:* 60 Kuring-gai Avenue, Turramurra, N.S.W.; and *office* A.A.E.C. Research Establishment, Lucas Heights, via Sutherland, N.S.W., Australia.

**ALDINGTON, Rt. Hon. Lord( Toby Austin Richard William Low),** PC., KCMG, CBE, DSO, TD, DL. British banker, industrialist and politician. *B.* 25 May 1914. *Educ.* Winchester Coll.; Oxford Univ. (New Coll.), (BA, 2nd Class Hons. Law, MA). *M.* 1947, Araminta MacMichael. *S.* 1. *Daus.* 2. *Career:* Barrister (Middle Temple) 1939; served in the World War II (with K.R.R.C.; Greece, Western Desert, Tunisia; on Staff 8th Army 1943; Brig. Gen. Staff 5th Corps 1944–45); elected M.P. (Blackpool N.) 1945–62; Dir., Grindlays Bank Ltd. 1946–51; Parliamentary Secy., Ministry of Supply 1951–54 Min. of State, Bd. of Trade 1954–57; Chmn., Grindlays Bank Ltd. 1963–76; Port of London Authority 1971–77; Sun Alliance & London Insurance Co. Ltd.; Westland Aircraft Ltd.; National Nuclear Corp.; Dep. Chmn., The General Electric Co. Ltd. Dir. Lloyds Bank Ltd., Citicorp (U.S.A.); Dep. Chmn. Conservative Party Organization 1959–63. Hon. Fellow, New Coll., Oxford (1976); Fellow, Winchester Coll., Chmn., Management Cttee., Inst. of Neurology, Chmn. General Advisory Council of BBC since 1971. *Awards:* Croix de Guerre avec palme (France); Commander. Legion of Merit (U.S.A.). *Address:* 21d Cadogan Gardens, London, S.W.1; and Knoll Farm, Aldington, Kent.

**ALDINGTON, John Norman.** British executive. *B.* 1905. *Educ.* Balshaws Grammar School, Leyland; Harris Inst., Preston (BSc, PhD, FRIC, FInstP, FIEE). *M.* 1930, Edna Entwisle. *S.* 1. *Career:* Joined Siemens Electric Lamps of Supplies Ltd. 1923 (Head of Laboratories 1935; Dir. &

Research 1948; Dir. of the firm 1948); Dir., Alfred Graham & Co. Ltd. 1950; Man. Dir., Siemens Bros. & Co. Ltd. 1955; Chmn., The London Electric Wire Co. & Smith Ltd. 1960–67; Telephone Cables Ltd. 1961–67; Vice-Chmn., A.E.I. Ltd. 1965–67 (Dir. 1955–67; Man. Dir. 1963–67); Dir. Royal Worcester Ltd., Deputy Chmn., Chmn. 1974. *Publications:* The High Current Density Mercury Vapor Arc (1944) (thesis, London Univ. Library); numerous papers, particularly on light sources and kindred devices, and on high current discharges and xenon gas arc. *Member:* Fellow and Past Pres., Illuminating Eng. Socy.; Leon Gaster Memorial Award I.E.S. 1944 and 1945; Crompton Award, I.E.E. 1949; Gold Medal, IES, 1969; Chmn. of Light Sources Secretariat, Internatl. Comm. on Illumination 1945–54; member of various B.S.I. Committees; Part-time Lecturer, Harris Inst., Preston 1928–38; Gov., Preston Grammar School 1950–55; J.P.; Duchy of Lancaster 1953–55. M.R.I. 1958. *Club:* Athenaeum (London). *Address:* White Oaks, 39 Forest Drive, Keston, Kent.

**ALDRICH, Hulbert Stratton.** American. *B.* 1907. *Educ.* Phillips Andover Acad.; Yale Coll. (PhB 1930). *M.* 1934, Amy W. Durfee. *Daus.* Ann Hazard, Jane Stratton. *Career:* Joined The New York Trust Co. Sept. 1930; successively Asst. Treas., Vice-Pres. and Pres.; Vice-Chmn. and Dir., Chemical Bank 1959–72; Chmn. Hill Samuel Inc.; Dir.: National Distillers & Chemical Corp.; Charles T. Wilson Co.; Hill Samuel Group Limited; Member Ad. Cttee. to Bd. of Chemical New York Corp.; Int. Adv. Bd. of Chemical Bank; Chmn. Commonwealth Fund; International Business Machine World Trade Corp.; Ametek Inc.; Empire Savings Bank; Harvey Hubbell, Inc.; Peter Paul, Inc.; Geo. W. Rogers Construction Corp.; Trustee, Presbyterian Hospital. *Clubs:* Union; The Links; The River; The Yale; The Century; The Sky (all of N.Y.C.); Links Golf. *Address:* 1088 Park Avenue, New York City, U.S.A.

**ALDRICH, Malcolm P.** American banker. *B.* 1 Oct. 1900. *Educ.* Yale (AB). *M.* 1925, Ella F. Buffington. *S.* 1. *Daus.* 2. *Career:* Hon. Chmn., The Commonwealth Fund, N.Y.C.; Dir.: Southern Pacific Co., Equitable Life Assurance Socy., American Electric Power Co.; Trustee, American Museum of Natural History, N.Y.C., Metropolitan Museum of Art, Presbyterian Hospital. *Address:* 1 East 75th Street, New York, N.Y., U.S.A.

**ALDRIDGE, Albert Ernest, Jr.** *B.* 1912. *Educ.* Temple Univ. (BSc in Journalism and Business); Charles Norris Price School (Post graduate advertising and merchandise). *M.* 1938, Doris J. Haimerl. *Dau.* Constance Barbara. *Career:* Asst. Advertising Mgr., E. F. Houghton Co. 1935–37; Sales Promotion Mgr., Sun Oil Co. 1937–44 (Gen. Advertising Mgr. 1944–46). Pres., A. E. Aldridge Assoc. Advertising Agency, Jenkintown, Pa. 1946—, and of First Advertising Agency Group. Dir.: Abington Library (also Trustee), and Rydal Meadowbrook Civic Association. *Awards:* Associated Business Paper Award for Excellent Advertising; Topper Award (National Industrial Advertisers); First Advertising Agency Group Award for Advertising Excellence. *Member:* Eastern Industrial Advertisers Assn.; National Industrial Advertisers Assn.; Amer. Marketing Assn.; National Business Publications Assn.; Abington Library Assn.; Rotary International (Dir.); Ocean City Civic Assn. (Pres.); Ocean City Chamber of Commerce. *Clubs:* Ocean City Yacht; Poor Richard; Suburban Public Relations. *Address:* P.O. Box 125, Ocean City, N.J.; and *office* 709 Garden City Parkway, Ocean City, N.J., U.S.A.

**ALEXANDER, Alfred Elroy.** Pres.: Crestwave Offshore Services, Inc.; Crestwave International Bd. of Dirs., Texas Gas Transmission; Trustee, Grandison Land Co.; Pres., Tuberculosis Assn. of Greater New Orleans; Bd. of Trustees of Rayne Memorial Methodist Church. *Member:* A.I.M.E.; Natural Gas Men's Assn. of Houston; Sigma Alpha Epsilon; American Assn. of Oilwell Drilling Contractors (Pres., New Orleans Chapter); Adjuster Mason (32°, Shriner). *Clubs:* Petroleum; Country; Plimsoll (all of New Orleans); Houston. *Address:* 25 Versailles Boulevard, New Orleans 1403, La. 70125; and *office* International Trade Mart Building, New Orleans, Louisiana 70130, U.S.A.

**ALEXANDER, Sir Charles Gundry,** MA, AIMarE. British company director. *B.* 1923. *Educ.* Bishops Stortford Coll.; St. John's Coll., Cambridge (MA). *M.* 1944, Mary Neale. *S.* 1. *Dau.* 1. *Career:* Served in World War II, Royal Navy 1943–46; Furness-Houlder (Insurance) Ltd.; Houlder Bros. & Co. Ltd. 1948—; Ore Carriers Ltd. 1951—; Furness-Houlder Insurance Ltd.; Ocean Gas Transport; Bergl Australia (London) Ltd.; Houlder Marine Drilling Co. Ltd.; Lytcott Holdings Ltd.; Pacific Maritime Services Ltd.; Compugraphics International Ltd.; Furness Houlder (Reinsurance Services) Ltd.; Port Glaud Development Co. Ltd.; Vallum Shipping Co. Ltd.; Chmn. Alexander Shipping Co. Ltd.; Inner London Regional Board, Nat. Westminster Bank Ltd. *Address:* 53 Leadenhall Street, London, E.C.3.

**ALEXANDER, Herbert M.** American publisher. *B.* 1910. *Educ.* New York Univ. (BA *magna cum laude* with hons. 1931). *M.* 1942, Greta Maren Hinterauer. *S.* Thomas P. *Career:* U.S. Air Force (Master Sgt. to 2nd Lieut.) 1942–46; Copy Chief, Norman Warren & Co. 1939–42; Editor, N.Y. Graphic Socy. 1936–39; Social Worker; Publishers' Traveller 1932–36. Executive Vice-Pres., Washington Square Press 1959—; Vice-Pres. and Dir., Simon & Schuster Inc. 1966—. Publisher, Pocket Book Div., and Trident Press. Editor-in-Chief (1948–66), Vice-Pres. (1953–66) and Dir. (1959–66), Pocket Books Inc.; Pres., Trident Press 1963. *Publications:* short stories, articles, and translations from French and Italian; contributor to newspapers and periodicals. *Member:* Pi Lambda Phi; Phi Beta Kappa, Democrat. *Club:* Player's. *Address:* 280 Riverside Drive, New York, N.Y., U.S.A.

**ALEXANDER, Stanley Walter,** MBE. British. *B.* 1895. *Educ.* Roan School (Greenwich). *M.* 1919, Doris Emily Kibble. *S.* 2. *Career:* Entered service of Lord Beaverbrook 1910 and in 1919 joined the Daily Express; became Financial Editor of it, and of Sunday Express and Evening Standard; contested City of London as Free Trade candidate 1945 and Ilford 1951; Editor, City Press 1946, and acquired it in 1951 and conducted campaign for sound money, free trade, and against coercion of the people by the State; until recently Chmn., Alexander Publications Ltd. (which published the City Press, the City of London newspaper); Pres. of the Cobden Club; Pres., Free Trade League; Governor Cripplegate Foundation. Liveryman of Worshipful Company of Tallow Chandlers; Member Council Kipling Society. *Publications:* The Price we Pay; Save the Pound—Save the People. *Clubs:* Reform; City Livery; Cobden. *Address:* 44 Speed House, London, E.C.2.

**ALEXANDRAKIS, Menelas D.** Greek Diplomat. *B.* 1915. *Educ.* Degree in Political Sciences, Univ. of Athens; Graduate work at the Inst. for Int'l Law in Paris and the Int'l Law Academy at the Hague and in economics at the LSE. *M.* 1956, Nicole Contomichalos. *S.* 2. *Career:* Attaché at the Min. for Foreign Affairs 1945; promoted to rank of Second Secretary of Embassy 1947; at the Greek Embassy in Washington D.C. 1948–52; Promoted to First Secretary of Embassy 1949; Acting Consul General in San Francisco 1949; Min. for Foreign Affairs 1952–53 & 1955–56; Consul of Greece in Alexandria 1953–55; Mem. of Greek Delegation to NATO 1956–60; Promoted to rank of Counsellor at Embassy 1959; at NATO Defence School 1960–61; Min. Foreign Affairs 1961–64; Promoted to rank of Minister Plenipotentiary 1964; Ambassador to Cyprus 1964–70; Min. for Foreign Affairs 1970–71; Ambassador to Austria 1971–74; Ambassador to the U.S.A. since 1974. *Decorations:* Cross of the Order of Distinguished War Services; Grand Commander of the Order of Phoenix; Knight Commander of the Order of George 1; Grand Cross of the Order of Merit of the Fed. Rep. of Germany; Commander of the Order of Merit of the Rep. of Italy; Grand Cross of the Rep. of Austria. *Publications:* The Dissolution of Parliament, Paris 1937 (French); For Freedom and Justice, 1967 (Greek). *Club:* Cosmos Club, Washington D.C. *Address:* 2221 Massachusetts Avenue N.W., Washington D.C. 20008, U.S.A.

**ALGER, Frederick Moulton, Jr.** *B.* 3 Aug. 1907. *Educ.* Milton Acad., Mass.; Phillips Acad., Andover, Mass.; Harvard Univ. *M* .(1) 1929, Suzette de Marigny Dewey (*d.* 1963); (2) Katherine Sutton Topping. *S.* Frederick M. III, David Dewey. *Dau.* Suzette (Howard). *Career:* Asst. to American Financial Adviser of the Polish Government in Warsaw in late 1920's; Secy.-Treas., Vice-Pres., and Pres. successively of The Allen Corp. (Industrial Ventilating Equipment) 1930–46; Asst. Treas. and Trustee, Jennings Memorial Hospital 1934; Trustee since 1934; Dir., The First of Michigan Corp. (investment banking) 1936–46; First Pres., Wayne County Republican Precinct Organization in Michigan 1935; Republican nominee for Representative in Congress 1936; Cmdr. U.S.N.R. in World War II; Secy. of State for Michigan 1946–52; Republican Candidate for Gov. of Michigan 1952; U.S. Ambassador Ex. and Plen. to Belgium 1953–57. *Address:* 1349 Free Press Building, Detroit, Mich., U.S.A.

**ALGER, Philip Langdon.** American retired Engineer and writer. *B.* 1894. *Educ.* St. John's Coll., Md. (BS 1912, MA

1915); Mass. Inst. of Technology (BS 1915); Union Coll. (MS 1920). *M.* (1) Catharine E. Jackson (*d.* 1945); (2) 1946, Helen Jackson Hubbell (dec'd 1974). *S.* John R. M., Andrew. *Daus.* Augusta J. (Prince, Jr.), Anne V. (Ehrlich). *Career:* Lieut., Ordnance Dept., U.S.A. 1917–19; Major, Ordnance Reserve Corps. 1920–42; Instructor, Mass. Inst. of Technology 1915–17; with Gen. Elect. Co., Schenectady, N.Y. 1919–59; Consulting Engineer, G.E.A.C. Motor Dept. 1950–59; Professional Engineer, New York State; Consulting Prof. of Electrical Engineering, Rensselaer Polytechnic Inst., Troy, N.Y. 1958–70. *Publications:* about 100 technical articles in Transactions of American Inst. of Electrical Engineers; The Nature of Polyphase Induction Machines (John Wiley & Sons 1951); Mathematics for Science & Engineering (McGraw-Hill 1957, 2nd edition 1969); Induction Machines (Gordon & Breach, Science Publishers, N.Y. 1965; Enlarged & updated edition 1970); joint author, Ethical Problems in Engineering (Wiley, N.Y. 1965); Editor, The Life and Times of Gabriel Kron (1969); Co-compiler of Steinmetz—The Philosopher (Mohawk Development Service, Inc., Schenectady 1965); The Human Side of Engineering (1972); Tales of My Life and Family (1974). *Member:* Republican; Hon. Dr. Sc. (Univ. of Colorado 1968); Fellow: I.E.E.E. (Recipient of Lamme Medal for 1958), A.S.M.E., A.S.Q.C., A.A.A.S. Mem.: I.E.E. (British); National Municipal League; Amer. Ordnance Assn.; N.S.P.E.; Newcomen Socy.; Amer. Legion. Socy. of the Cincinnati, Amer. Mathematical Socy.; Technology Club of Eastern New York; Eminent member of Eta Kappa Nu and Tau Beta Pi; Unitarian. *Address:* 1758 Wendell Avenue, Schenectady, N.Y. 12308, U.S.A.

**ALHEGELAN, Sheikh Faisal.** Saudi Arabian Diplomat. *B.* 1929. *Educ.* Faculty of Law, Fouad Univ., Cairo. *M.* 1961, Nouha Tarazi. *S.* 3. *Career:* Ministry of Foreign Affairs, Jeddah 1952–54; Saudi Arabian Embassy, Washington, D.C. 1954–58; Chief of Protocol, Jeddah 1958–60; Political Adviser to the King 1960–61; Ambassador to Spain 1961–68; Ambassador to Venezuela, concurrently to Argentina 1968–75; Ambassador to Denmark 1975–76; Ambassador to the U.K. since 1976. *Decorations.* Order of King Abdulaziz (Saudi Arabia); Gran Cruz Isobella Catholica (Spain); Gran Cordon, Orden Del Libertador (Venezuela); Grande Oficial, Orden Riobranco (Brazil). *Address:* 24 Kensington Palace Gardens, London W.8; & *office* 30 Belgrave Square, London S.W.1.

**ALHOLM, Bjorn-Olof Georg.** Finnish Diplomat. *B.* 1925. *Education:* Univ. Helsinki, MA (Polit. and Econ. Sciences). *M.* 1958 Anneli Wallasvaara. *S.* 2. *Career:* Ministry of Foreign Affairs, Helsinki 1948–49; Attaché Finnish Consulate, Frankfurt/Main 1949–51; Attaché Finnish Embassy, Washington 1951–54; First Secy. Perm. Mission to UN, New York 1956–59; First Secy, Finish Embassy Brussels 1960–61; Chief of Bureau, Ministry For. Affairs, Helsinki 1961–63; Counsellor Finnish Embassy Moscow 1963–66; Ambassador, to Bucharest 1966–68; Amb. to Berne 1968–70; Amb. to Moscow 1970–74; Amb. to Bonn since 1974; Vice-Chmn., Finnish Delegation to UN's Gen. Assembly 1966, 1968–69; Chmn., Finnish Delegation to Conf. Non-Nuclear Nations, Geneva 1968. *Decorations:* Comdr. Lion (Finland); Comdr. Leopold II (Belgium); Medal of Freedom 1st and 2nd class (Finland); Grand Cross 2nd Class of the Order of Merit (Fed. Rep. of Germany). *Address:* Büchelstrasse 53, 5300 Bonn-Bad Godesberg; and *office* Finnish Embassy, Am Aennchenplatz, 5300 Bonn-Bad Godesberg, Federal Republic of Germany.

**ALIREZA, Sheikh Ali Abdullah.** Saudi Arabian diplomat. *B.* 12 May 1921. *Educ.* Falah Schools, Mecca; Victoria Coll., Alexandria, Egypt; studied petroleum engineering and business engineering, Berkeley, California. *M.* 1943, Huguette Misk. *Children:* Hamida, Faisal, Tarik, Nadia, Ghassan. *Career:* Business Mgr., Haji Abdullah Alireza & Co. 1934, now Man. Dir.; Member, Saudi Arabian Delegation to U.N. Conference on International Organization, San Francisco 1945; Technical Adviser to Saudi Arabian Delegation to U.N. Conference, London 1946; Financial Adviser to H.E. Shaikh Abdullah Sulaiman; Finance Min.; Member, Saudi Arabian Economic Delegation to U.S. 1946; Alternate Representative to U.N. Conference, New York 1946; Liaison Officer between H.M. King Abdel Aziz Al Saud and Anglo-American Inquiry Cttee. on Palestine 1946; Councillor First Class with Prince Saud Al Saud, Crown Prince of Saudi Arabia during State Visit to U.S., U.K. and Egypt 1947: Adviser to H.R.H. Prince Faisal Al Saud, Saudi Arabian Min. of Foreign Affairs, summer 1947; appointed Min. Plenipotentiary and full Delegate to U.N.O.; Min. without Portfolio; Member: Official Delegation headed by H.R.H. Prince Faisal to Greece 1953; Delegation that represented H.M. the King of Saudi Arabia at the Coronation of H.M. Queen Elizabeth II 1953; appointed Min. of State and Delegate to Asian African Conference at Bandung 1955; Member of Delegation headed by Crown Prince Faisal to India and Pakistan 1955; Official Delegation, Governor of Mecca Province to Lebanon 1972; Appointed Royal Decree member Bd. Dirs. Saudi Arabian Monetary Agency (The Central Bank Saudi Arabia) 1972; Ambassador to the U.S.A. since 1975. *Awards:* Holder, Grand Order and Sash of the Phoenix; Grand Order and Sash, Cedar of Lebanon; Grand Cross of the Merito Civil (Spanish Government); Holder, the Grand Cross of Leopold II (Belg.). *Address:* Embassy of Saudi Arabia, 1520 Eighteenth Street, N.W., Washington, D.C. 20036, U.S.A.

**ALISON, Michael James Hugh,** MP. British Politician. *B.* 1926. *Educ.* Eton; Wadham Coll., Oxford—MA (Hons.). *M.* 1958, S.M. Haigh. *S.* 2. *Dau.* 1. *Career:* Conservative MP for Barkston Ash since 1964; Parlia. Under-Sec. of State, Dept. of Health & Social Security 1970–74; Official Opposition Spokesman, Home Office Affairs since 1975. *Address:* Moat Hall, Ouseburn, York; & House of Commons, London SW1A 10AA.

**AL-KHALIFAH, H.H. Shaikh Isa bin Sulman,** Amir of State of Bahrain since 1961. *B.* 1933. *S.* Hamad, Rashid, Abdulla, Mohamed. Succeeded his father, Shaikh Sulman bin Hamad Al-Khalifah, KCMG, KCIE. *Address:* The Palace, Rafaa, Bahrain, Arabian Gulf.

**ALLAN, George Urquhart,** CBE, AFC, AFRAeS. British executive. *B.* 1900. *M.* 1944, Barbara Millbourn. *Dau.* Barbara Urquhart. *Career:* With Royal Flying Corps 1917; Royal Air Force 1921; Australian National Airways 1930; Qantas Empire Airways 1934; Royal Australian Air Force 1939–45; with Qantas Empire Airways Ltd.: Technical Mgr. 1945; Asst. Gen. Mgr. 1951; Dep. Chief Executive 1959–61; Chmn., Fiji Airways Ltd. since 1961. Councillor of The Royal Flying Doctor Service of Australia. *Clubs:* Elanora Country (Narrabeen, N.S.W.); N.S.W. Rod Fishers Socy.; American National. *Address:* 808 Barrenjoey Road, Palm Beach, N.S.W.; and *office* 70 Hunter Street, Sydney, N.S.W., Australia.

**ALLAN, William Norman.** Canadian executive. *B.* 1925. *Educ.* Victoria Coll.; Univ. Toronto (BA); Univ. of Toronto Graduate School of Business Admin. (MCom). *Career:* Economist Govt. of Ontario Treasury (Economic Survey) 1949–52 Consulting Economist and Tax Consultant 1952–57; Exec. Asst. to the Min. of Finance for Canada 1957–61; Pres. and Man. Dir.: Great Lakes Commercial & Holding Corp. Ltd., and of Fiscal Investments Ltd.; Vice-Pres. and Dir., Reserve Acceptance Co. Ltd.; Chmn., Economic Realty Corp., Transprovincial Financial Corp. Ltd.; Vice-Pres., Founding Dir. Laurier Life Insurance Co.; Dir., Miller Fluid Engineering Co. Ltd.; Pres. T.B.C. Investment Association; Chmn. of Board, Great North Uranium & Energy Resources Inc. *Member:* Royal Humane Socy. (Life Gov.); Inst. Commercial & Industrial Managers (Fellow); Board of Trade of Metrop. Toronto; St. Andrew's Socy. of Toronto; Canad. Economics Assn.; Canadian Political Science Assn.; National Trust for Scotland; Kappa Sigma Fraternity; Alumni Assn. of Toronto; Bd. of Trade Club, Metropolitan Toronto; 32° Mason (Scottish Rite) and Shriner. *Awards:* Life Fellow; Roy. Economic Socy. (London, Eng.), and Acad. of Political Science, Columbia Univ. *Clubs:* Albany (Toronto); University (Ottawa); Kensington Fishing—The Gatineau (Quebec); Sommerville Recreation Country (Vict.). *Address:* 157 Golfdale Road, Toronto, Ontario M4N 2CI; and *office* Suite 410, 44 Eglinton Ave West, Toronto, Ontario, M4R 1A1, Canada.

**ALLAUN, Frank,** BCom, ACA, MP. British. *B.* 1913. *Educ.* Manchester Grammar School; External BCom degree, London Univ. *M.* 1941, Lilian Ball. *S.* David. *Dau.* Ruth Carolyn. *Career:* Newspaper Reporter 1945–55; M.P., Labour Salford East since 1955; Nat. Exec. of Labour Party since 1967; Nat. Chmn. Labour Action for Peace; Vice-Pres., Public Health Inspectors Association. *Publications:* No Place Like Home; Heartbreak Housing; End the H-Bomb Race; The Wasted £30 Billions. *Address:* 1 South Drive, Manchester 21; and *office* House of Commons, London, S.W.1.

**ALLEBAUGH, Frank Irving.** American advertising executive (ret'd); lecturer, writer. *B.* 1915. *Educ.* Denver Univ.; Univ. of Colorado. *M.* 1936, Pearl Elizabeth Murray. *Daus.* Judy Marie (Viner), Kathi D. (McCulley). *Career:* With U.S.

Govt. Public Relations 1935–43; Engineering Writer, E.I. Du Pont Co. 1943–44; Advertising Mgr. (Ind.), The Gates Rubber Co. 1944–54; joined Galen E. Brovles Co. in 1954; has lectured at Denver Univ., Univ. of Colorado, and Denver Public Schools; Chmn. Bd., Broyles, Allebaugh & Davis Inc. (Advertising Agency), Denver, Colo. *Member:* Bus. & Prof. Adv. Assoc. (Past Natl. Vice-Pres., Past Pres. Denver Chapter, Past International Dir.); Denver Chamber of Commerce; Past Chmn. and Regional Gov., National Cttee. on Business Media; American Assn. of Advertising Agencies; Elected member, Internat. Platform Assn.; Bd. of Trustees, Rocky Mountain Hosp., Denver, Col. U.S.A. *Clubs:* Press; Athletic (Denver). *Address:* 9315 E Center, Denver, Colo. 80231, U.S.A.; and *office* 31 Denver Technological Center, Englewood, Col. 80231, U.S.A.

**ALLEN, Antony William**, FCA. British. *B.* 1926. *Educ.* Haileybury & Imperial Services Coll. *M.* 1953, Hazel Mary King, *S.* 2. *Daus.* 2. *Career:* Partner, Gilbert Allen & Co. Dir. Municipal Properties Ltd.; Gilbertall Property Co. Ltd.; Allen & Norris Ltd.; Housing & Land Development Corp. Ltd. *Address:* West Wind, Wadhurst, Sussex; and *office* Gilbert House, River Walk, Tonbridge, Kent.

**ALLEN, C. A.**, MVO. Australian Consul-General in Toronto. *Address:* P.O. Box 69. Commerce Court Postal Station, Toronto, Canada.

**ALLEN, Sir Douglas Albert Vivian**, GCB. British. *B.* 1917. *Educ.* London School of Economics; London Univ. BSc (Econ.). *M.* 1941, Sybil Eileen Allegro. *S.* John Douglas, Richard Anthony. *Dau.* Rosamund Sybil. *Career:* Entered Board of Trade 1939; Royal Artillery 1940–45; Cabinet Office 1947; Asst. Secy. Treasury 1949–58; Min. of Health Under Secy. 1958–60; Under Secy. and later Deputy-Secy. Treasury 1960–64; Deputy Secy. and later Perm. Secy. Dept. Economic Affairs 1964–68; Permanent Secy., Treasury, U.K. 1968–74; Perm. Secy. Civil Service Dept. Head, Home Civil Service since 1974; Fellow (Hon.) London School of Economics; Roy. Statistical Socy; R. Econ. Socy.; RSA; BIM. *Decorations:* CB (1963), KCB (1967), GCB (1973). DSc (Hon.), Southampton. *Club:* Reform (London). *Address:* 9 Manor Way, South Croydon, Surrey; and *office* Civil Service Dept., Whitehall, London, S.W.1.

**ALLEN, Edward George, Jr.** American. *B.* 1919. *Educ.* Harvard Univ., Business School (Adv. Management Program). *M.* 1943, Eleanor Bauer. *Dau.* Julia Nottingham. *Career:* Asst. Publicity Dir., Philadelphia Orchestra 1937–40; Sales Promotion Mgr., Stonhard Co., Philadelphia 1940–41. Vice-Pres., Dir., Buttenheim Pub. Co., New York City 1946–67; Vice-Pres. and Publisher Jewelers' Circular—Keystone (Chilton Co., Philadelphia); President Allen-Pacific Co. (Pacif. Goldsmith and Pacif. Stationer). *Award:* Bronze Star Medal. *Member:* Ex-Members Assn. of Squadron "A" (N.Y.C.). *Clubs:* Overseas Press. *Address:* 46 Barbaree Way, Tiburon, Calif. 94920, U.S.A.; and *office:* 41 Sutter St. San Francisco, Cal. 94104, U.S.A.

**ALLEN, Gabriel.** American geologist. *B.* 1900. *Educ.* New York City School System; elected to N.Y. Academy of Sciences. *M.* 1922, Minnie Christina Waver. *Dau.* Louisa F. (Dean). *Career:* Formerly: feature photographer, New York Evening World; designed one of the original sound on film (optical) recorders; adviser to several financial corporations; volunteered and served in World War II (Inf. Res. Officer); Pres.: Ocean Water Pipeline Corp.; 50 States Mining & Exploration Corp. *Award:* Croix de Guerre, W.W. II. *Member:* Royal Photograph Socy.; Socy. of Photographic Scientists & Engineers; Assn. for Applied Solar Energy; Pres., Assn. Advanced Sanitary Systems; Socy. of Sulurians; Founder, Allen Research. Founder, The American Home Party. *Address:* 1215 North Lake Way, Palm Beach, Fla., U.S.A.

**ALLEN, George Cyril**, CBE, FBA. British. Emeritus Prof. of Political Economy. *B.* 1900. *Educ.* King Henry VIII School, Coventry; Univ. of Birmingham (MCom., PhD). *M.* 1929, Eleanora Cameron McKinlay Shanks, (D. 1972). *Career:* Part-time Member of U.K. Monopolies Comm. 1950–62; Lecturer, Nagoya Commercial Coll., Japan 1922–25; Lecturer and Research Fellow, Faculty of Commerce, Univ. of Birmingham 1925–29; Prof. Economics and Commerce, Univ. Coll., Hull 1929–33; Brunner Prof. Economic Science, Univ. of Liverpool 1933–47; Tempy. Asst. Secy. Bd. of Trade 1940–44; Tempy. Counsellor, Foreign Office 1945–46; Prof. of Political Economy, Univ. of London 1947–67; Hon. Fellow School Oriental and African Studies, London Univ.; Academic Planning Bd. Cttee. New Univ. of Ulster 1965–77; Trustee, Inst. of Economic Affairs. *Publications:* Modern Japan and Its Problems (1928); The Industrial Development of Birmingham and the Black Country (1929); British Industries and their Organization (1933—5th Ed. 1970); (part author), The Industrialization of Japan and Manchukuo (1940); A Short Economic History of Japan (1946; 3rd Ed., 1972); Western Enterprise in Far Eastern Economic Development (in collaboration) (1954); Western Enterprise in Indonesia and Malaya (in collaboration) (1957); The Structure of Industry in Britain (1961; 3rd edn. 1970); Japan's Economic Expansion (1965); Japan as a Market and Source of Supply (1967); Monopoly and Restrictive Practices (1968); The British Disease (1976). *Award:* Order of the Rising Sun, 3rd Class (Japan). *Club:* Reform. *Address:* Flat 15, Ritchie Court, 380 Banbury Road, Oxford.

**ALLEN, George Howard.** American publishing executive. *B.* 1914. *Educ.* Univ. of Massachusetts (BS 1936, LlD 1968, Hon.); Harvard (MBA 1938). *M.* 1940, Virginia Russell. *S.* Russell Lawton. *Career:* Asst. to Pres., Nat. Theatre Supply Co. 1938–40; Res. Man., Radio Station WOR, 1941; Asst. Dir., Promotion and Research (same radio station) 1942–43; Radio Consultant U.S. Treas. Dept. 1943–45; Gen.-Mgr., Secy., Co-operative Analysis of Broadcasting, N.Y.C. 1944–46; N.E. Sales Mgr., N.Y. Herald Tribune 1946 (Promotion Mgr. 1947–50); Dir., Sales Promotion, McCall's 1950–57; Vice-Pres., Mass Market Publications, Inc. 1953–54 (Pres. 1954–55, Dir. 1953–55); Publisher, Better Living Magazine 1956; Better Homes & Gardens and Successful Farming magazines 1964–66; Vice-Pres., Man. Dir., Meredith Corp. 1962–66, Asst. to Pres., Meredith Corp. 1960–62; Exec. Vice-Pres. and Publisher Magazine Div., Fawcett Publications, Inc., New York since 1966; Snr. Vice-Pres., CBS Publications; Publisher, Woman's Day Mag. *Award:* Leadership Award, Amer. Legion 1932; Young Advertising Man of the Year citation (by Assn. of Advertising Men and Women of N.Y.) 1956; Achievement Award, Washington (D.C.) Ad. Club 1956; Bell Ringer Award, Salt Lake City Ad. Club 1957; Silver Anvil Award (Pub. Relations Socy. of America) 1956; Gold Medal Award, Freedoms Found. 1956–59; Public Relations News Citation 1957; Management Man of the Year, Iowa National Management Assn. 1963; Hon. LLD Univ. Mass. 1967; Vice-Pres., Mass Market Publrs., Inc. 1953–54 (Pres., 1954–55, Dir., 1953–55). *Member:* Amer. Marketing Assn. (Pres., N.Y. 1946–47); Nat. Assn. of Manufacturers (Dir.); Amer. Statistical Assn.; Advertising Research Found. (Dir.); Magazine Publs. Assn. (Dir.); U.S. Chamber of Commerce, etc. *Clubs:* Harvard; Economic (all N.Y.); International (Chicago); Canadian. *Address:* 112 Pear Tree Point Road, Darien, Conn.; and *office* 1515 Broadway, New York, N.Y. 10036, U.S.A.

**ALLEN, Gordon Ainslie.** Canadian. *B.* 1922. *Educ.* Univs. of Western Ontario (BA Hons., Chem. and Physics 1943); Rochester (PhD Chem. 1949). *M.* 1954, Jean McLennan Weatherup. *S.* John Gordon. *Daus.* Margaret Jean, Susan Louise. *Career:* With Fraser Companies Ltd.: Co-ordinator of Commercial Development 1962–65; Exec. Staff Asst. 1958–62; Asst. Dir. of Research 1953–57; Chemist: Pulp and Paper Research Inst. of Canada 1950–53, and L'Air Liquide Socy. 1944–46. Dir. of Research and Development. The Great Lakes Paper Co. Ltd. since 1965; Dir. of Enviromental services since 1974. *Award:* Post-Doctoral Fellowship, Natl. Research Council of Canada 1949–50. *Member:* Chem. Inst. of Canada; Amer. Chem. Socy.; Socy. of the Sigma Xi; Technical Section, Canadian Pulp & Paper Assn. and Tech. Assn. of the Pulp and Paper Industry. *Publications:* The Mercury Photosensitized Reactions of Isobutene (with H. E. Gunning) (1948); Turbulent Diffusion in Fourdrinier Machines (with S. G. Mason, A. A. Robertson, and C. W. E. Walker) (1954); The Preparation of Radio-actively-Labelled Pulp Fibres (with A. Rezanowich and S. G. Mason) (1958). *Address:* 622 Rosewood Crescent, Thunder Bay, Ont. Canada P7E 2R7; and *office* The Great Lakes Paper Co. Ltd., Thunder Bay, Ont., Canada P7C 4W3.

**ALLEN, Harold Norman Gwynne**, CBE, MA, DSc. *B.* 1912. *Educ.* Westminster School; Trinity Coll., Cambridge (BA 1933, MA 1936). *M.* 1938, Marjorie Ellen Brown. *S.* David Gwynne. *Daus.* Wendy Simone, Corinne Marjorie, Patricia Jane. *Career:* With W. H. Allen: Asst. Works Mgr. 1937–40; Installation and Ser. Mgr. 1940–43; Dir. 1943; Engineering Dir. 1945; Jt. Man. Dir. 1952; Dep. Chmn. 1962–70; Pres., The Inst. of Mech. Engrs. 1965–66; Former Chmn., W. H. Allen Sons & Co. Ltd., Bedford; Former Dir., Bellis & Morcom Ltd., Birmingham; Former Deputy Chmn. and Executive Dir., Amalgamated Power Engineers Ltd.;

Pro-Chancellor Cranfield Inst. of Technology 1970–75. *Member:* Executive Bd., British Standards Institution 1970–75. *Member:* Fellow: Inst. of Civil Engineers, Instn. of Mech. Engineers, Instn. of Marine Engineers, Instn. of Production Engineers; Royal Instn. of Naval Architects. *Publications:* Epicyclic Gears (Inst. Marine Engineers 1953); Epicyclic Gears (Engr. Inst. of Canada 1961); Gas Turbines (South African Inst. of Mech. Engineers 1953); A Portrait of Tomorrow's Engineer. *Clubs:* United Oxford & Cambridge (London); Island Sailing (Cowes, I.o.W.). *Address:* Gwylfa Bontddu, Dolgellau, Gwynedd, Wales.

**ALLEN, James Lawrence,** OBE. Australian. *B.* 1913. *Educ.* Adelaide Univ. (BA-Hons Classics), and London Univ. (Education Diploma). *M.* 1939, Marion Stanley Kelly. *S.* Robin Stuart, Christopher Howard, Richard Lincoln. *Daus.* Elphine Elizabeth, Rosalie Helen. *Career:* Prof. of English, Christian Coll., Bankura, West Bengal 1937–41; Intelligence Corps, Indian Army (Burma Theatre) 1942–44; Indian Civil Service (Bengal Cadre) 1945–46; with Australian Foreign Service: New Delhi 1946–47 and 1960–62; Washington 1953–55, Manila 1956–57; Dir., Colombo Plan Bureau, Ceylon 1964–65; Deputy High Commissioner East Pakistan 1969–70; High Commissioner Bangladesh 1972–73. *Address:* 11 Wickham Crescent, Red Hill, Canberra, A.C.T., Australia.

**ALLEN, Joseph Henry.** American. *B.* 1916. *Educ.* Kenyon Coll., Gambier, Ohio (AB). *M.* 1941, Eleanor Clark. *S.* David Clark. *Daus.* Elisabeth (Adams), Melinda. *Career:* With McGraw-Hill Publishing Co.; Magazine Salesman 1938–40; Editor and Advertising Salesman, Chicago Office 1940–42; Served as Lieutenant U.S.N.R. 1942–45. Returned McGraw-Hill, Advertising Salesman, Chicago Office 1945–49; Branch Manager, Dallas Office 1949–51; Div. Manager, Los Angeles Office 1951–55; Vice-Pres., Marketing 1955–63; Senior Vice-Pres., Operations 1963–66; Pres., McGraw-Hill Publications Co., New York, Jan. 1966–70; Group Vice-Pres. McGraw-Hill Inc. New York 1970–71; Group Pres. Dir. since 1966; Dir., The Adv. Council and F and M Schaefer Corp.; Sen. Vice-pres. United Technologies Corp. since 1974. *Clubs:* The University (N.Y.C.); Wee Burn Country (Darien, Conn.). *Address:* 29 Tokeneke Trail, Darien, Conn. 06820; and *office* United Technologies Bldg., Hartford, Conn. 06101, U.S.A.

**ALLEN, Kingsley Anketell.** Australian. *B.* 1923. *Educ.* Geelong Grammar School (Corio, Vic.). *M.* 1958, Susanna Hogg. *S.* Roderick Kingsley, Mathew Curzon. *Daus.* Rosita, Jennifer. *Career:* In R.A.A.F. (Instructor in Air photography 1943–45); in Service 1941–45; Chmn. of Dirs., Kingsway Stores Pty. Ltd., Melbourne 1948—; Vice-Pres., Australian Wholesale Softgoods Vederation, Canberra A.C.T. 1955–57, President 1957–59: Chairman, Softgoods Section of Melbourne Chamber of Commerce 1959–61; Pres. Melbourne Chamber of Commerce 1969–71; Member Melbourne Underground Rail Loop Authority since 1971; Snr. Cons. Management Div., J. R. Waite & Associates, Management Consultants; Mem. Bd. of Marine Board of Victoria; Premier of Victoria's Cttee to inquire into status of women. *Clubs:* Athenaeum, Metropolitan Golf, Peninsula Country Golf, Canadian Bay, VRC, Royal Automobile (Victoria); Royal Victoria Aero. *Address:* 17 Millicent Avenue, Toorak, Melbourne; and *office* 21 Murphy Street, South Yarra, Melbourne, Vic., Australia.

**ALLEN, Hon. Percy Benjamin,** QSO, JP. New Zealand Company Director. *B.* 1913. *Educ.* Rotorua High School. *M.* 1939, Peggy Donaldson, *S.* Raymond John. *Dau.* June. *Career:* Mem., N.Z. National Party; Minister of Works 1963–72, and Minister of Police, 1963–69 & 1972; Minister of Electricity 1969–72; Member of Parliament for the Bay of Plenty 1957–75;. Chairman of National Roads Board 1963–72; National Water Authority, 1968–72; N.Z. Gas Council, 1969–72; Opposition Spokesman on Works 1972–75. *Decoration:* Queen's Service Order. *Clubs:* R.S.A. *Address:* 1 Halberg Crescent, Whakatane, New Zealand.

**ALLEN, Sir Peter (Christopher).** Kt, MA, BSc (Oxon). British. *B.* 1905. *Educ.* Harrow School and Trinity Coll. Oxford Univ. (MA; BSc); Hon. DTech. (Loughborough). *M.* (1) 1931, Violet Sylvester Wingate-Saul (*D.* 1951); *Daus.* 2; (2) 1952, Consuelo Maria Linares Rivas. *Career:* Joined Brunner, Mond & Co. 1928; Chmn., Plastics Div. of I.C.I. 1948–51 (Man. Dir. 1942–48); Dir., British Nylon Spinners Ltd. 1954–58. Pres.: Plastics Inst. 1950–52, and of Canadian Indust. Ltd. 1959–62. Dir.: Royal Trust Co., Canada 1961–64; Vice-Pres., Manufacturing Chemists .,Assn U.S.A. 1961–62 (Dir., 1959–62); Pres. and Chmn., I.C.I. of Canada Ltd. 1961–68; Chmn., Imperial Chemical Industries Ltd. 1968–71; Dir., Bank of Montreal, 1968—; Pres., Univ. of Manchester Institute of Science and Technology 1968–71; Vice-Pres., Institute of Manpower Studies 1968—; BACIE 1969; Dir., British Insulated Callenders Cables since 1971. Mem., Export Cncl. for Europe 1962–65; Chmn., Bd. of Canadian Industries Ltd. 1962–68; Mem. & Vice-Chmn., Cncl. of Assn. of British Chemical Manufacturers 1963–65; Pres., British Plastics Federation 1963–65. *Member:* Iron & Steel Holding & Realisation Agency 1963–67; N.E.D.C. for the Chemical Industry 1964–67; B.N.E.C., 1964–67; Chmn., 1970–71; Overseas Development Institute Cncl. 1963–64; Chmn., Cttee. for Exports to Canada 1964–67; Commonwealth Export Cncl. 1964–67; Gov., Nat. Coll. of Rubber Technology 1964–68; Mem., Cncl. of Canadian Chamber of Commerce in G.B. Inc. 1964–68; Cncl. of C.B.I. 1965–67; Pres., Chemical Industries Assn. Ltd. 1965–67; Member of Court of the British Shippers Council 1968–71; Mem. and Vice-Chmn., Board of Directors of Societé de Chimie Industrielle 1968–71; Mem., Industrial Policy Group, 1969–71; Gov., Harrow School, 1969; Fellow, Institute Directors, 1969—; Trustee, Civic Trust, 1970—; British Industry Roads Campaign, 1970–72; Mem., Council of Industry for Management Education, 1970–71. Hon. Mem., Institution of Chemical Engineers; Fellow, British Institute of Management; Hon. Fellow, Trinity College, Oxford. *Publications:* The Railways of the Isle of Wight (1928); Locomotives of Many Lands (1954); On the Old Lines (1957); Narrow Gauge Railways of Europe (with P. B. Whitehouse) (1959); Steam on the Sierra (with R. A. Wheeler) (1960); Round the World on the Narrow Gauge (with P. B. Whitehouse) (1966); The Curve of Earth's Shoulder (with Consuelo Allen) (1966); Rails in the Isle of Wight (with A. B. Macleod) (1967); Famous Fairways (1968). *Clubs:* Junior Carlton, Mount Royal (Montreal); Royal & Ancient, Royal Cinque Ports, Rye, Royal St George's, Augusta National; Pine Valley (New Jersey); Oxford & Cambridge Golfing Socy. *Address:* Telham Hill House, nr. Battle, East Sussex.

**ALLEN, Robert E.** Advertising executive. *B.* 1913. *Educ.* Temple Univ., Philadelphia (BSC) and Columbia Univ., New York City (graduate work). *M.* 1935, Dorothy Nelson. *Dau.* Patricia Ann. *Career:* Formerly: Vice-Pres. and Man., Fuller & Smith & Ross; Marketing and Sales Promotion, Pennzoil Co.; Chmn., Fuller & Smith & Ross Inc.; 1967–77; Dir., 1955–66; Chmn., Committee got Improving Advertising, and of A.N.A.A.A.A.A. Ethics Cttee.; Exec. Cttee. N.O.A.B.; Dir., Advertising Council; Former Dir., Amer. Assn. of Advertising Agencies; N.O.A.B.; Freedoms Foundation; Reeves Industries Inc.; Gov., New Rochelle Hospital. *Member:* Sigma Delta Chi; Pennsylvania Society. Trustee, Presbyterian Church; Order of St. John Queen of England 1969. *Clubs:* Canadian, Larchmont Yacht, Winged Foot Golf (N.Y.); Duquesne (Pittsburgh); Union (Cleveland); Seaview Country (Absecon, N.J.); University (N.Y.C.), Mid-America Club (Chicago, Ill.). *Address:* 200 Barnard Road, New Rochelle, N.Y.; and *office:* 666 Fifth Avenue, New York City, U.S.A.

**ALLEN, Samuel Carson Fitzwilliam.** British. *B.* 1904. *Educ.* Eton College. *M.* (1) 1937, Barbara Welford Dixon (*D.* 1952); (2) 1953, Patricia Beatrice Eden Neate. *S.* (by 1st marriage) David Michael Richard Cecil and Robin Richard. *Career:* Entered David Allen & Sons Ltd. 1920; Dir., David Allen & Sons Ltd. 1925–70; Joint Man. Dir. 1930–64; Deputy Chmn. Mills & Allen Ltd. 1964–72, (now Mills & Allen (Holdings Ltd.), Chmn. since 1972; Dir. Mills & Allen International Ltd.; Dir. News International Ltd.; Dir. Leonard Ripley and Co. Ltd.; Chmn. Universal Poster Agency Ltd. *Member:* of the Council, British Poster Advertising Association (Pres. 1948–49, 1959–61 and 1973–75); Rep. British National Section, Fédération Europêene de la Publicité Extérieuré, Chmn. 1961–66; Member, Council and Exec. Cttee. The Advertising Assn. 1961–69 and since 1971; Council, Confederation of British Industry 1972–75. *Clubs:* Carlton and Turf. *Address:* Lathbury Park, Newport Pagnell, Bucks.; and *office* 17 New Burlington Street, London, W1X 1FF.

**ALLIBONE, Thomas Edward,** CBE, FRS, FIEE, FInstP, FAmIEE. *B.* 1903. *Educ.* Sheffield University. (Linley Scholar PhD, DSc 1937); Cambridge Univ. Wollaston Scholar; Senior Exhibitioner, Cavendish Laboratory, Cambridge (PhD); Hon. DSc Reading; Hon. DEng Sheffield; Hon. DSc City University. *M.* 1931, Dorothy Margery Boulden. *Daus.* 2. *Career:* In charge, High Voltage Laboratory, Metropolitan-Vickers Manchester 1930–46; Mem.,

British Government Mission on Atomic Energy, Berkeley (California) and Oakridge (Tenn.) 1944–45; Dir., Research Laboratory, Associated Electrical Industries, Aldermaston, and Director for Research and Education, A.E.I. (Woolwich) Ltd. 1946–63; Mem., I.E.E. Council 1937–40, 1946–49 and 1950–53, and of Committee on Law of Copyright 1951–52; Vice-Pres., Institute of Physics 1948–52; Mem. of Council, Elec. Res. Assn. 1948–64 (Chmn. Research Committee); Nuclear Adv. Cttee., Min. of Power: Adv. Council, Royal Military Coll.; Trustee, British Museum 1968–75; Mem., Exec. Cttee. of Board, National Physical Laboratory 1952–60; Council of British Non-Ferrous Research Assn. 1953–58; Council, Physical Socy.; Pres., Inst. of Information Sciences 1966–68; Council, Southern Electricity Board; Gov. Downe House 1959–69; Chmn. Bd. Govs., Reading Tech. College 1953–69. Chief Scientist, Central Electricity Generating Board, Oct. 1 1963–70; British research scientist; External Professor, Electrical Engineering Leeds University, 1967—; Visiting Professor in Physics, City University since 1971. Lord of the Manor of Aldermaston. *Awards:* Freeman City of London 1967. *Publications:* Release and Use of Atomic Energy (book) (1961); The Royal Society and its Dining Clubs; Rutherford, the Father of Nuclear Energy; papers on high voltage and transient electrical phenomena, and thermonuclear reactions. *Address:* York Cottage, Lovel Road, Winkfield, Windsor, Berks.

**ALLISON, Don Alden.** American investment broker and furniture executive. *B.* 1907. *Educ.* Univ. of California, Los Angeles (EE); Univ. of Southern California; Navigator, U.S. P.S. *M.* 1940, Mildred Evelyn Sallee. *S.* Don. Jr. *Dau.* Sallie Irene. *Career:* Mem., Institute of Navigation 1948—; Mem., U.S. Sharp Cup Team; Staff Commodore, Hollywood Yacht Club, American Power Boat Assn.; (Pres., Western Region 1942); Commander, U.S. Power Squadron, Los Angeles; Past Pres., Tuna Club, Catalina; Previously: Junior Partner, Brown-Collins Company 1929–30; Vice-Pres., House of Chesterfield 1931–32; Pres., Don Allison Company. Los Angeles 1932—. USC Oceanographic Associates; International Oceanographic Foundation. *Publications:* Many articles on navigation, boating, racing, furniture and furnishing. Republican. *Clubs:* The Tuna; Southern California Tuna; Hollywood Yacht; Sertoma; Los Angeles Athletic; Long Beach Yacht; Bel Air Guild; Delta Sigma Phi; National League. *Address:* 9398 Monte Leon Lane, Beverly Hills, Calif., U.S.A.

**ALLISON, James.** British. *B.* 1934. *Educ.* Forfar Academy and Aberdeen University (BSc Agric.). *M.* 1957, Margo Duthie. *S.* James Duthie, Graeme Fotheringham. *Career:* Man. Dir., Allisons Freightlines Ltd. Oct. 1965–71; Tayfreight Ltd. since 1971. *Member:* Institute of Directors. *Address:* Netherby House, Glamis Road, Forfar; and *office* 40–42 Perrie Street, Lochee, Dundee, Scotland.

**ALLISON, Lindsay Rowand.** Australian. *B.* 1916. *Educ.* Univ. of West Australia (BSc) and Univ. of Melbourne (Dip. App. Chemistry). *M.* 1944, Audrey Margaret Pritchard. *S.* Ronald Lindsay. *Dau.* Josine Louise. *Career:* Development Superintendent, Commonwealth Fertilisers & Chemicals Ltd. 1945–49 (Man., Chemical Division 1949–60); Dir., George Shirleys Pty. Ltd. 1957–58. Technical Mgr., Imperial Chemical Industries of Australia and New Zealand Ltd. 1962—. *Member:* Royal Australian Chemical Inst. (Fellow; Hon. General Treasurer; Councillor 1956–63); Socy. of Chemical Industry of Victoria; Lawn Tennis Assn. of Victoria (Councillor 1949–56); Melbourne Univ. Business Administration Assn. *Address:* 287 Belmore Road, Melbourne, 3104; and *office* 1 Nicholson Street, Melbourne, C.1, Vic., Australia.

**ALLON, Yigal.** Israeli Soldier and Politician. *B.* 1918. *Educ* Kadourie Agricultural School; St. Antony's Coll., Oxford; Hebrew Univ., Jerusalem. *Married. S.* 1. *Dau.* 1. *Career:* Founder Member of Kibbutz Ginossar 1937; Joined Haganah 1931, Founder Member of Palmah (Haganah's Striking Force) 1941 and its Commander 1945–48; Special Duties with Allied Forces in Syria and Lebanon 1941–42; Major-General in War of Independence from 1948; Member of Knesset since 1954; Minister of Labour 1961–67; Deputy P.M. and Min. of Immigrant Absorption 1967–69; Deputy P.M. and Min. of Education and Culture 1969–74; Deputy P.M. and Min. for Foreign Affairs 1974–77. Member of Cabinet Cttee. for Defence; one of the Leaders of the Labour Party and the Labour-Mapam Alignment; Member of the Secretariat of the Kibbutz Meuhad Movement; State visits and lecture tours in Middle East, U.S.A., Europe, U.S.S.R., Africa, India, Australia, Canada. *Publications:* Campaigns of the Palmah; Curtain of Sand; The Making of Israel's Army; Shield of David; Three Wars and One Peace; My Father's House; various essays and articles on political, military, educational and cultural subjects in Hebrew, Yiddish, Arabic and English. *Address:* Kibbutz Ginossar, Israel; and *office* Knesset, Jerusalem, Israel.

**ALLOO, Roger Charles Henri.** Belgian. *B.* 1920. *Educ.* LLD, BSc in the Faculty of Commerce and Finance, Univ. of Louvain. *M.* 1946, Marie José Van Haren. *S.* Michel. *Daus.* Nicole, Marie Christine, Isabelle. *Career:* Executive Dir., Head of International Division, Société Générale de Banque. Chmn. Banque Belge Limited, London; Banque Belge pour l'Etranger Brussels; Banque Européenne pour l'Amérique Latine "BEAL", Brussels; Vice-Chmn. European-Arab Bank; Banque Generale du Luxembourg; Dir. Banque Belge (France)—Chairman of Directorate; European-American Banking Corporation, New York; European–American Bank & Trust Cy, New York; European–American Finance (Bermuda) Ltd., Hamilton; Banque Européenne de Crédit "BEC", Brussels; Société géné rale Libano Européenne de Banque, Beirut; European-Asian Bank; Euro–Pacific Finance Corp., Melbourne; ASEA, Brussels (Vice Chmn. for Belgium); STAL–LAVAL (Benelux), Antwerp (Chmn. for Belgium); Association pour la Coordination du Financement à Moyen Terme des Exportations Belges "Créditexport", Brussels; Délégué Général, Ligue Européenne de Coopération Economique. *Publications:* Various articles on Finance and Economics. *Clubs:* Marks' (London). Cercle Gaulois and American Common Market both of Brussels. *Address:* 20, Avenue de la Faisanderie, 1150 Brussels and *office* 3 Montagne du Parc, 1000 Brussels 1.

**ALLUM, Robert Wilfred,** QSM, JP. *B.* 1916. *Educ.* Auckland Grammar School. *M.* 1944, Betty Barbara Blower. *S.* J. L. R. and C. W. *Career:* Prior to 1939, lived and worked in Australia, England and Switzerland. At the outbreak of World War II, enlisted in the U.K. and served 5½ years in U.K., France and Middle East (including Greece and Crete); invalided home to N.Z. by hospital ship (5 war service medals). Past Pres., Royal New Zealand Honorary Justice of the Peace Federation; Mem., Wellington Hospital Board 1953–68; Patron, New Settlers Assn. 1950–69. Charter Pres., Lions Club of Karori, Wellington, 1969. *Clubs:* Wellesley, Savage, Bowling, C.T. & W.A., Star Boating, Racing (all of Wellington); West End Rowing (Auckland). *Address:* 140 Messines Road, Karori, Wellington, N.Z.

**AL-MAHDI, Mohammed Sadiq.** Iraqi economist. *B.* 1934. *Education.* Univ. Baghdad, BA Econ, (1955); Univ. Penn. (USA) MA, Econ, (1959) Ph.D.Econ (1965). *M.* 1969, (Mrs.) Widad A K Kammouna. *Career:* Economist, Commercial Bank of Iraq 1954–57; Sen. Economist, Min. of Industry Baghdad 1959–61, Ministry of Oil, 1966–67; Head, Econs Dept. Iraq National Oil Co. 1967–71; Chief, Econs. Dept. OPEC, Vienna 1971–73; Head Econs Dept. INOC and Ministry of Oil, Baghdad since 1973. *Member:* Assn. of Iraqi Economists, Baghdad. *Publications:* Middle East Oil Industry (Ph.D Thesis 1968); various articles in Arabic and English on oil economics. *Address:* c/o Ministry of Oil, Baghdad, Iraq.

**ALPORT, Rt. Hon. Lord,** PC, TD, DL (Cuthbert James McCal Alport). *B.* 1912. *Educ.* Haileybury and Pembroke Coll. Cambridge (MA); Barrister-at-Law (Middle Temple). *M.* 1945, Rachel Cecilia Bingham. *S.* 1. *Daus.* 2. *Career:* Served in World War II (Coy. Comdr. R.W.F. 1940; War Office 1940; Staff Course, Camberley 1941; H.Q.E. Africa Comd. 1942; Coy. Comdr. K.A.R. 1943, G.S.O.1, E. Africa Comd. 1944–45); Hon. Lieut.-Col.; Dir., Conservative Political Centre 1945; Member, Parliament (Con.) Colchester Div. of Essex 1950–61; Chmn., Joint East and Central African Board 1953; Asst. Postmaster General 1955–57; Under-Secy. of State, Commonwealth Relations Office 1957–59; Minister of State 1959–61; British High Commissioner in the Federation of Rhodesia & Nyasaland 1961–63; A Deputy Speaker House of Lords since 1971. *Member:* Council of Europe 1964–65; Master, Skinners Company; Special Representative to Rhodesia, June–July 1967; High Steward of Colchester 1967; Pro Chancellor City University 1972; An Adviser to Home Secy. 1974. *Publications:* Kingdoms in Partnership (1937) Hope in Africa (1952). *Address:* The Cross House, Layer de la Haye, Colchester, Essex.

**ALS, Robert.** Hon. Minister Plenipotentiary & Chambellan e.s.e. de S.A.R. le Grand Duc de Luxembourg. *B.* 1897.

*Educ.* Docteur en droit. *M.* 1924, Yvonne Alice Neuman. *S.* Georges. *Dau.* Sonia. *Career:* Lawyer, 1921; Dep. State Prosecutor, 1929; Judge of District Tribunal, 1932; Advocat-General in High Court of Justice 1936; expatriated by the Germans 1941; State Attorney 1944; Min. of the Interior 1945; Mem., Council of State 1946; Min. Plenipotentiary: in Belgium, 1947 in France 1952; Ambassador to France 1955. *Awards:* Grand Officer: Order of Adolphe of Nassau; of the Couronne de Chêne; Grand Cross of the Lion of Finland; Grand Cordon of the Order of Leopold; Grand Cross of the Legion of Honour. *Address:* 9A. Bd. Joseph II, Luxembourg.

**AL-SABAH, Shaikh Saud Nasir.** Kuwaiti Diplomat. *B.* 1944. *Educ.* Gray's Inn—Barrister-at-Law. *M.* Shaikha Awatif Al-Sabah. *S.* 2. *Daus.* 2. *Career:* Joined Legal Dept., Ministry of Foreign Affairs; Representative of Kuwait, 6th Cttee. of the U.N. General Assembly 1969–74; Rep. of Kuwait to Seabed Cttee. of the U.N. 1969–73; Vice-Chmn. of Kuwaiti Delegation to Conference of the Law of the Sea 1974–75; Rep. of the Delegation to the Conference of the Law of Treaties; Ambassador of Kuwait to the U.K., Norway, Sweden and Denmark since 1975. *Address:* 11A Belgrave Square, London SW1; and *office* Embassy of the State of Kuwait, 46 Queen's Gate, London SW7.

**ALSAÇ, Orhan.** Turkish architect. *B.* 1914. *Educ.* Faculty of Architecture, Technische Hochschule, Munich. *M.* 1938, Nezihe Dikerman. *S.* Üstün. Ongun, Aydin, Engin. *Career:* Prof. of Architecture; Mem. and Pres., High Committee for the Conservation of Antiquities and Old Monuments; Architect, Min. of Public Works 1941; Dir., Technical Committee, Town Planning Dept., of Min. of Public Works 1948; Vice-Pres. of the Buildings and Town Planning Dept. 1951, Pres. 1954; Teacher, Foremen's School, Ankara 1948–51; Specialist Mem., Reconstruction Committee of Ankara 1949–58; Teacher, Technical School, Ankara 1951–53; Adviser, Min. of Public Works 1958; Gen. Dir. Housing Dept., Min. of Reconstruction & Settlement 1959; Asst. Under-Secy., Min. of Reconstruction & Settlement 1960; Trustee, M.E.T.U. 1960; Under-Secy., Min. of Public Works 1960. Asst. Pres. (in charge of campus development) Middle East Technical Univ. Ankara 1962–73; Pres. Construction Office, TIS Bank Society Ankara 1973–75; Member of Acad. Staff, Academy of Archit. and Eng. Ankara since 1975; Dir. School of Architecture & Engineering, Ankara since 1975. *Publications:* Our Laws Pertaining to Reconstruction together With a Comparison with those of Other Countries; Table for Reckoning Wooden Construction (translation); various articles and lectures. *Address:* Yesilyurd Sokak No. 13, Kavaklidere, Ankara, Turkey.

**AL-SAID, Tarik,** Omani Diplomat. *B.* 1923. *Educ.* Turkey and Germany. *M.* 1965, Helen Lucy Bromm. (By previous marriages); *S.* 7. *Daus.* 2. *Career:* Army Officer 1941–45; Administrator of Municipalities 1945–57; Liaison Officer and later Director of Civil and Military Operations Jabal Akhdar War 1957–59; Self-Exile & Businessman 1962–66; Political Leader in Exile of Anti-Sultan Front 1966–70; Prime Minister under new Sultan 1970–71; Personal Advisor of H.M. Sultan Qaboos bin Said 1972; Chmn. Bd. of Governors, Central Bank of Oman since 1975. *Awards:* Order of Oman, 1st Class; Order of Renaissance (Oman), 1st Class; Order of Imperial Iran, 1st Class; Order of Italy, 1st Class. *Clubs:* Curzon House Club & Associated Clubs; Clermont; Casanova etc. *Address:* PO Box 202, Muscat, Sultanate of Oman; and Leuchtturmweg 21, 2000 Hamburg 56, West Germany; and 47 Grosvenor Square, London.

**ALSDORF, James William.** American executive. *B.* 1913. *Educ.* Wharton School of Finance and Commerce, Univ. of Pennsylvania. *M.* (1) 1935, Barbara Brach (div. 1950), and (2) 1952, Marilynn Markham. *S.* Gregg, Jeffery, James. *Dau.* Lynne. *Career:* Past Pres., Treasurer, Dir., Cory Corp. (manufacturers), Chicago; Pres. and Dir., Cory A. G., Zürich (also officer and Dir. of subsidiary companies and divisions); Pres. and Dir., Cory Coffee Service Plan Inc., Cory Sales Corp. (both in Chicago); Dir. and Treasurer: Cory Coffee Service Plan, Toronto; Pres., Dir., Mitchell Mfg. Co. and subsidiaries, Chicago; The A. J. Alsdorf Corp., exporters and international merchants, Chicago; Condor Motors Inc., Chicago; Alsdorf Foundation. Dir.: L. A. Darling Co., Bronson, Mich.; Currently Pres. Dir. The A. J. Alsdorf Corp.; Chmn. Bd. Dir. Cory Food Services Inc. (both Chicago); Pres. Dir. Cory AG. Zurich Switzerland and its subsidiary Cory Kaffee Serviceplan; Dir., Chmn. of the Exec Cttee., Vice-Pres. and Sec., Grindmaster of Kentucky, Inc.; Dir., Hyatt International Corp., Chicago. *Member:* Vice-Pres. and Dir., Sarah Siddons Socy. of Chicago; Bd. of Trustees, Menninger Foundation, Topeka, Kansas; Chmn., Trustee, Life Gov., Exec. Cttee., Major Benefactor, Art Inst., Chicago. Mem., Nat. Cttee. Univ. Art Museum, Univ. of Calif. Advisory Council, Univ. Art Gallery, Univ. Notre Dame; Subscribing member, American Craftsmen's Council New York; Contributing Mem., Trustee Com., Amer. Assn. of Museums, Archaeological Institute; Housewares Mfg. Assn. Chicago; The Renaissance Socy. Chicago; Ordre des Compagnons du Beaujolais; Chicago Horticultural Socy.; Oriental Ceramics Society (London); Univ. Library Council N.W. Univ. Library; Centennial Cttee. Friends of Chicago Public Library; Amer. National Geographic Socy;. Newcomen Socy. Princeton; General Alumni. Board, Univ. Pennsylvania; Northwestern Univ. Associates; Newberry Library Assn.; The Asia Socy.-Inc.; Chinese Art Socy. of America; Sigma Chi (Significant Sig Award, 1975); Pres. Dir. Alsdorf Foundation, Chicago; Life Trustee Indianapolis Museum of Art Indianapolis; Opus Man., Ravinia Festival Assn.; Gov. member, The Orchestral Assn.; Visiting Cttee. Div. of Humanities, Univ. Chicago; Life member, The Antiquarian Socy. Chicago; Patron member, Friends of Art. Northwestern Univ.; Life member, Field Museum, Natural History; Life Gov. Chicago Historical Society. *Clubs:* Sunset Ridge Country (Northbrook, Ill.); Arlington Post & Paddock (Dir.) (Exec. Cttee.); The Arts, The Executive of Chicago, Tavern, Casino, Zorine's, Chicago Club (Chicago). *Address:* 301 Woodley Road, Winnetka, Ill. 60093, U.S.A.; and *office* 3200 West Peterson Avenue, Chicago 60659, Ill., U.S.A.

**ALSHAMY, Ahmed Mohammed.** Yemeni Min. of State and diplomat. Min. of Foreign Affairs for the Yemen. *B.* 1924. *Educ.* Arabic Literature, Sana. *M.* 1942, Mrs. Abdul Rahman Alshamy. *Career:* Private Secy. to Crown Prince of Yemen 1952; Chargé d'Affaires, Cairo 1953–55; Yemen Representative in the Arab League 1953–55; Yemen Min. at the Supreme Council of the United Arab States 1958–60; Min. Extraordinary and Plenipotentiary to Court of St. James's, 1961. For. Min. of Royalist during Civil War in Yemen 1962–68; Member of Repub. Council 1969–70; Ambassador in London 1971; Ambassador in Paris 1973; Currently Ambassador at Large. *Publications:* A book of Arabic Poetry; Lectures on the History of Yemen. *Address:* Embassy of the Yemen, 41 South Street, W.1.

**ALTER, Gerald Leslie.** American realtor. *B.* 1910. *Educ.* Completed grade and high schools. *M.* 1939, Margaret A. Davis. *S.* John Edward. *Dau.* Judith Ann (*D.*). *Career:* Dir., Torrance Optimist 1948; Bd. of Dirs., Harbor Area United Way 1968–69; Former Dir. Harbor United Way; Torrance–Lomita Board of Realtors; Pres., Darpco, Inc.; Alter Realty, Inc.; Alter Insurance Agency Inc., Alter Realty & Insurance, Leads, Inc., and Alter Insurance & Property Management; Past Dir. California Real Estate Assn; Chmn. Planning & Zoning Cttee. Calif. Real Estate Assn. 1972; Pres., Remco-Real Estate Mangt. Co.; Member Planning Commission City Torrance; American Legion; Past Dir. Torrance Chamber of Commerce; California Real Estate Association Republican. *Clubs:* Torrance Rotary; Los Angeles Transportation; OX-5 Club of America (Pioneer Airman). *Address:* 2305 Torrance Boulevard, Torrance, Calif., 90501, U.S.A.

**ALTMAN, Irving B.** American bank executive. *B.* 1901. *Educ.* New York Univ. (AB). *M.* 1930, Hazel M. Sammett. *Career:* Executive, Chase National Bank, New York 1929–34; Editor and Publisher, Dynamic America (monthly magazine) (1935–41); Radio Special Events Commentator 1935–42; Candidate for Congress 1940; Vice-Pres., The Merchants Bank of New York 1945–64; Field Counsellor, Mutual Security Agency, Washington 1949—; Exec. Vice Pres. & Dir. Freedom National Bank of N.Y. since 1964; Independent in politics; Mem., B.Nai B'rith; American Academy of Political Science, Columbia Univ.; Academy of Political & Social Science. Univ. of Pennsylvania; American Inst. of Management; National Planning Assn., Washington, D.C.; Treasurer, Syracuse Univ. Parents' Association. *Publications:* The People's Money (1935); Contributer to various economic and sociological journals. *Club:* Economic (New York). *Address:* 41 Peck Avenue, Rye, N.Y., U.S.A.

**ALVAREZ de TOLEDO, José M.G.** Argentinian. *B.* 1921. *Educ.* Univ. of Buenos Aires (Lawyer). *M.* 1945, Enriqueta de Anchorena. *S.* 4 *Daus.* 2. *Career:* Chief of Cabinet, Ministry of External Relations 1957; Chargé d'Affaires in the Fed. Republic of Germany 1959; Min. in Czechoslovakia 1960–61; Under Secy., Ministry of External Relations 1962; Dir. of the National Ceremonial 1963; Ambassador in

Switzerland 1963–64; in Rumania 1964–65; in S. Africa 1965–66; in Uruguay, 1967–69; Under Secy. Min. of External Relations 1969–71; Perm. Del. to U.N.E.S.C.O. 1971–72; Ambassador in Brazil 1972–75; Dir. of Foreign Service Inst. since 1976. *Member:* Accadémie Diplomatique Internationale. *Awards:* Medalla de Oro de bachiller, Champagnat Coll. 1939; Grand Cross of Merit (Fed. Germany); Order of Merit (Repub. of Italy); Order of Malta; Grand Cross of Leopold II of Belgium; Grand Cross Order of Merit (Repub. of Peru); Grand Cross of the Cruzeiro do Sul (Brazil). *Club:* Jockey (Buenos Aires). *Address:* Ministry of Foreign Affairs, Buenos Aires, Argentina.

**ALYEA, Ethan Davidson.** American lawyer. *B.* 1896. *Educ.* Princeton Univ. (A.B. 1916, M.A. 1917); Edinburgh Univ.; Harvard Law School (Note Editor, Harvard Law Review; LLB); Phi Beta Kappa. *M.* 1923, Dorothy Collins. *S.* Ethan Davidson, Jr. *Dau.* Jane (Cooney). *Career:* Trustee: Montclair Public Library 1947–57, Adult School of Montclair, and Montclair Community Chest; Formerly Pres., Montclair Adult School and of Council of Social Agencies of Montclair Trustee and Vice-Pres., Montclair, Art Museum; Chmn. Cttee. on International Trade & Investment of American Bar Assn.; Partner, Dewey, Ballantine, Bushby, Palmer & Wood, N.Y.C. Dir.: The Royal Bank of Canada Trust Co.; The Fairbanks Co.; and Cintas Foundation Inc. (Pres.); *Member:* American and N.Y. State Bar Assns.; Assn. of Bar of City of N.Y.; N.Y. County Lawyers Assn.; Huguenot Society. *Publications:* Publications in Law Reviews of Harvard and the International Bar Assn. *Clubs:* Univ.; Downtown Assn. *Address:* 77 Highland Avenue, Montclair, N.J.; and *office* 140, Broadway Street, New York City 5, U.S.A.

**ALVES DE SOUZA, Carlos.** Retired Brazilian Diplomat. *B.* 1901. *Education.* Colegio Paula Freitas, Rio de Janeiro, Diploma; Braz. Naval Academy, Lieut.; Polytech. School Brasil. *M.* 1923, Clelia Bernardes. *S.* 1. *Dau.* 1. *Career:* Diplomatic Secretary for Brazil in several countries, including Montevideo, Uruguay, Paris, Vienna, and Head of Passport & Immigration Services Braz. F/O (1931–34) all between 1924–38; Secy. and later Counsellor Brazilian Embassy in Mexico 1935–37; Head of Political and Diplomatic Division in Braz. F/O 1938–39; Diplomatic Minister to Yugoslavia 1939–41; Head of Personnel Service Braz. F/O 1942–43; Head of Admin. 1943—45; Brazilian Ambassador in Cuba 1945–49; Brazilian Ambassador in Rome 1950–56; Brazilian Ambassador in Paris 1956–64; Brazilian Ambassador to Court of St. James 1964–66 (retired from dipl. service); Has acted additionally as Chargé d'Affaires in Montevideo, Paris, Vienna, Budapest and Mexico, Ambassador for special Missions for Inauguration of Govts. of Cuba and Italy. *Delegate:* Head of Brazil Delegations for Latin-Am. Econ. Conf. (1949); Migrations Conf. in Naples, Geneva and Brussels (1951–52); Civilisation & Peace Conf. in Florence (1953–54), Conf. of FAO, Rome 1955. *Decorations:* Awards and Gold Medal Brazilian Navy; Gold Metal (Civil & Military 50 years service); Grand Crosses: Corona (Italy) and Legion d'Honneur (France); Carlos Manuel de Cespedes (Cuba); Baron Rio Branco (Brasil); Boyacá 1st Class (Colombia); Condor de los Andes (Bolivia). *Clubs:* Jockey (France); Circola della Caccia (Rome); Jockey, Gavea and Golf (both of R. de Janeiro); Golf (Belgrade) Yacht, Country (both Havana). *Address:* Avenida Vieira Scuto, 50, Rio de Janeiro, Brazil.

**ALZHEIMER, Dr. Alois.,** DSO (Bavaria). *B.* 1901. *Educ.* Legal studies; appointed Judge 1927. *M.* 1933, Hilde Schiedermair. *Dau.* 1. *Career:* In Legal Branch, Bavarian Government 1927–29. With Münchener Rück since 1929; Hon. Pres.: Münchener Rückversicherungs-Gesellschaft, Munich; Berlinische Lebensversicherung-A.G., Wiesbaden; Karlsruher Lebensversicherung-A.G., Karlsruhe; Hamburg-Mannheimer Versicherungs-A.G., Hamburg; Hermes Kreditversicherungs-A.G., Hamburg. *Publications:* various on the subject of international reinsurance. *Member* of several institutions for aid to art and science. *Address:* Storistr. 1, D-8100 Garmisch-Partenkirchen; and *office* Königistr. 107, Munich, Germany.

**AMAN, Richard.** Swiss diplomat. *B.* 1914. *Educ.* Universities of Zürich and Paris (Dr jur). *M.* 1948, Gabrielle Veillon. *Career:* Entered Political Dept. 1944; Attaché, Brussels 1946, Commercial Attaché, Warsaw 1951; First Secy., Paris 1954, Counsellor, Tokyo 1956; Chief of Swiss Delegation at Neutral Nations Supervisory Comm., Korea 1958; Chief of Protocol, Berne 1958; Ambassador of Switzerland to Thailand, Burma and Malaysia, Jan. 1963–68. Ambassador of Switzerland to Hungary 1969–73, and to Ireland since 1973. *Club:* Grasshopper (Zürich). *Address:* The Swiss Embassy, Dublin, Ireland.

**AMBLER, Frederick Norman,** OBE, SBStJ, JP. New Zealand. *B.* 1894. *M.* 1917, Helen Becquet Skelton. *S.* Norman Godfray. *Dau.* Margaret Phyllis. *Career:* Dep. Mayor of Auckland 1958–62; Chmn. of Dirs., Ambler & Co. Ltd., manufacturers, Auckland; City Councillor of Auckland (30 years); Mem., Harbour Bridge Authority. Past Pres.: Manufacturers Assn.; Kindergarten Assn.; Past. Chmn., St. John Ambulance Assn.; Past Rangatira, Savage Club. Patron, Old Contemptibles Assn. *Address:* 1 Hona Avenue, Mt. Eden, Auckland, N.2; and *office* 54 Wellesley Street, Auckland, New Zealand.

**AMBRIDGE, Douglas White,** CBE, BSc, LLD. *B.* 1898. *Educ.* Lower Canada Coll. (Montreal); McGill Univ. (Montreal); BSc. *M.* 1924, Jessie Louise Barlow. *Daus.* Mrs. N. B. Bell, Mrs. J. M. G. Scott, Shirley, Charlotte. *Career:* Served in World War I (three years overseas with C.F.A., 2nd Div. C.E.F.; commissioned); joined Abitibi Power & Paper Co., Ltd. as control engineer at Iroquois Falls, 1923; Gen. Supt. Anglo-Canadian Pulp & Paper Mills Ltd. 1927–36; later Asst. Gen. Mgr., Anglo-Newfoundland Development Co.; joined Ontario Paper Co., Thorold, Ontario, as assistant to the president (and later Asst. Gen. Mgr.) 1936; V.P. & Asst. Gen. Mgr. 1943; during 1937 was closely connected with construction of the company's plant at Baie Comeau, Que.; in World War II was called to Ottawa as Director Shipbuilding Branch, Dept. of Munitions & Supply 1941; Dir. (and subsequently Vice-Pres.) Polymer Corp. 1942; directed construction of the synthetic rubber properties at Sarnia, Ont.; Dir.-Gen. of Shipbuilding, Dept. of Munitions & Supply 1943–44; Pres., Polymer Corp. 1945; Pres. & Gen. Mgr., Abitibi Power & Paper Co., Ltd. 1946–63. Hon. Chmn. Abitibi Paper Co. Ltd.; Hon. Dir. Canada Malting Co. Ltd. *Awards:* Insignia of Commander, Order of the British Empire 1946; resigned as Pres. of Polymer 1947; left Bd. of the Corp. 1950; Gen. Chmn., Building Fund for new Canadian Nat. Inst. for the Blind Centre, Toronto 1954–55; Chmn., Ontario Heart Foundation 1955–59; Pres., Canadian Heart Foundation, 1963 and 1964. *Member:* McGill Graduates Society, Toronto. *Clubs:* York: Mount Royal. *Address:* 19, Wychwood Park, Toronto, 4, Ont., Canada M6G 2V5.

**AMEEN, Einar Louis.** Swedish. Kt.-Comdr. Order of Vasa (Sweden). *B.* 1901. *Educ.* Royal Inst. of Technology, Stockholm (MSc). *M.* 1928, Elsa Margareta Wahlqvist. *S.* Louis. *Daus.* Kerstin Utterström, Jeanette Söderberg, Birgitta Cederberg. *Career:* Control Engr.: Norsk Staal A.S., Trondheim 1926; Specialist and Co-ordinator in the manufacture of stainless steel, Uddeholms A.B. Hagfors Ironworks 1926–40; Works Mgr., Söderfors Bruks, Stora Kopparbergs Bergslags A.B. 1940–47; Pres., Surahammars Bruks A.B. 1947–66 retired 1966; Former Chmn. Korrosions Institutet Stockholm; Mem., Ingeniörsvetenskapsakademien, Stockholm; Hon. Mem., Iron and Steel Institute of Japan. Former Member of the Board of Jernkontoret. *Publications:* various papers concerning iron and steel, e.g. Investigations concerning dimensional variations of steel during hardening and annealing (1937); Manufacture of sponge iron according to the Wiberg-Södenfors Method (1938); Electric Power in Swedish Iron and Steel Industry (1953); The Iron and Steel Industry of Japan (1967). *Address:* Sysslomansgatan 16, 75223 Uppsala, Sweden.

**AMERASINGHE, Hamilton Shirley.** Sri Lankan diplomat. *B.* 1913. *Educ.* Univ. of London, B.A. (Hons.) in Western Classics. *Career:* Entered Ceylon Civil Service 1937, served in various judicial and administrative capacities; Resident Manager, Gal Oya Development Board 1950–52; Counsellor, Embassy of Ceylon in Washington, D.C., 1953–55; Controller of Establishments, General Treasury, Ceylon 1955–57; Controller of Finance, Supply and Cadre, General Treasury, Ceylon 1958; Perm. Sec. to Ministry of Nationalized Services and Road Transport and Chmn. of the Port (Cargo) Corp. 1958; Sec. to the Treasury and Perm. Sec. to Ministry of Finance, Official Mem., Monetary Bd. of Central Bank of Ceylon and Alt. Gov. for Ceylon in the International Bank for Reconstruction and Development, 1961–63; High Commissioner for Ceylon in India and concurrently Ambassador to Nepal and Afghanistan 1963–67; Perm. Rep. to the UN since 1967; Chmn. of numerous UN committees, including Ad Hoc Cttee. on Peaceful Uses of the Sea-Bed, 1968; Standing Cttee. on Peaceful Uses of the Sea-Bed, 1969; Ad Hoc. Cttee on the Indian Ocean, 1973, etc.; Ambassador to Brazil (concurrent accreditation) since 1973; Pres., Third

UN Conf. on Law of the Sea 1973; Pres., Thirty-first Regular Session of the General Assembly of the UN 1976. *Address:* 1155 Park Avenue, Apt. 5SW, New York, N.Y. 10028; and *office:* 630 Third Avenue, New York, N.Y. 10017, U.S.A.

**AMERY, (Harold) Julian.** British politician. *B.* 1919. *Educ.* Eton and Balliol College, Oxford. *M.* 1950, Catherine. *S.* 1. *Daus.* 3. *Career:* War Correspondent in Spanish Civil War 1938–39; Attaché British Legation in Belgrade, and on special missions in Bulgaria, Turkey, Romania and Middle East 1939–40; Sergeant in R.A.F. 1940–41; Commissioned and transf. to Army in 1941; on active service in Egypt, Palestine and Adriatic 1941–42; Liaison Officer to Albanian Resistance Movement 1944; served on staff of General Carton de Wiart, V.C.; Mr. Churchill's personal representative with Generalissimo Chiang Kai-shek 1945; Contested Preston North unsuccessfully for Conservatives 1945, but successfully in 1950–51–55–59–64; Delegate to Consultative Assembly of Council of Europe 1950–53 and 1956; Mem., Round Table Conference on Malta 1955; Under-Secy. of State: for War Jan. 1957–Dec. 1958; for Colonies 1958–1960; Secy. of State for Air 1960–1962; Minister of Aviation 1962–64; Mem. of Parliament for Brighton, 1969—; Min. of Public Building and Works, 1970; Housing and Construction, 1970–72; Foreign & Commonwealth Office, 1972–74; Knight Commander, Order of the Phoenix. *Publications:* Sons of the Eagle (1948); The Life of Joseph Chamberlain (Vol. IV) (1950) Vol. V & VI (1969); Approach March (1973). Conservative. *Clubs:* White's; Beefsteak; Carlton; Buck's. *Address:* 112 Eaton Square, London, S.W.1.; and Forest Farm House, Chelwood Gate, Nr. Haywoods Heath, Sussex.

**AMES, Edward Carder.** *B.* 1906. *Educ.* University of Chicago (PhB *cum laude* 1926); Harvard Univ. (AM 1928). *M.* 1929, Mary Helen Cornwall. *S.* Daniel G., Geoffrey C. *Dau.* Stephanie. *Career:* Mem.: Toledo Board of Education 1945–53 (elected 1945, re-elected 1949; Pres. 1947, 1950); Pres., Rotary Club of Toledo 1951–52; Mem., U.S. Chamber of Commerce Committee on Education 1951–59; Instructor, Ohio Wesleyan Univ. 1927–29; Editorial Staff, Toledo Times 1930–34; Asst. Prof., Univ. of Toledo 1934–38; Exec. Mgr., Toledo Hospital Service Assn. 1938–40; radio newscaster, WSPD Toledo 1935–40; Asst. to Pres. and Public Relations Dir., Owens-Corning Fiberglas Corp., Toledo 1940–53; P.R.D., Calumet & Hecla Inc., Chicago 1953–54. Vice-Pres., Public Relations. Administrative Div., Owens-Illinois Inc., Toledo, Ohio 1954–71; Pres.: State Board of Education of Ohio 1968–69; (elected Mem. 1957; re-elected 1959, 1965 & 1967; Vice-Pres. 1966–67); National Industrial Conference Board; Council of Executives on Company Contributions 1957–71; Public Relations Seminar 1959–71; Glass Container Manufacturers Inst. (Vice-Chmn. Public Affairs Cttee. 1968, Chmn. 1969–70); Mem., Ohio Advisory Council for Vocational Education 1975–78. *Publications:* English in Business and Engineering (Prentice-Hall, 1936); Dr. of Humanics, Salem Coll., W.Va. 1961; Univ. of Chicago Alumni Citation for Distinguished Service 1951; LLD Univ. of Toledo 1973 Distinguished Service Award 1939; Toledo Junior Chamber of Commerce; Ohio Governor's Award, 1969. *Member:* Phi Beta Kappa; P.R. Socy. of America. Republican. *Clubs:* Univ. (Chicago); Toledo, Harvard, Hermits, Rotary (Toledo). *Address:* 4315 Northmoor Road, Toledo 43615, Ohio, U.S.A.

**AMES, Eugene Leroy,** petroleum production. Pres., Gilcrease Oil Co. 1946–62; Dir., National Bank of Commerce, San Antonio. *B.* 1903. *Educ.* Univ. of Oklahoma (LLB 1927). *M.* 1931, Mary Johnston. *S.* Eugene L. Jr., George J. *Clubs:* Country, Petroleum (both of San Antonio). *Address:* 333 Morningside Drive, San Antonio; and (*office*) P.O. Box 2708, San Antonio, Tex., U.S.A.

**AMES, John Brewer.** *B.* 1922. *Educ.* Auburn Univ. (BS 1946). *M.* 1950, Mae Hackney. *S.* John B. II, David, James H. *Dau.* Elizabeth A. Laurie. *Career:* With U.S. Army (Field Artillery) 1941–46; Ames Bag & Packaging Corp.: Successively Sales Mgr., Vice-Pres., Pres. 1946–61; Pres. 1951–71, Bd. Chmn. since 1971. *Member:* T.M.B.A.; Red Cross; Chamber of Commerce; Packaging Institute; Fibre Can & Tube Association. *Clubs:* Rotary; University (Cleveland, Ohio); Selma Country. *Address:* Valley Road, Marion Ala., 36756; and *office* Ames Bag & Packaging Corp., S. Washington Street, Marion, Ala., 36756, U.S.A.

**AMES, John Dawes.** American citizen. Investment banker. *B.* 1904. *Educ.* Princeton Univ. (AB 1928). *M.* 1949, Constance Hasler. *S.* John D., Jr., William S. *Dau.* Knowlton (Reynders, Jr.). *Career:* Served in World War II (Lt.-Col.; Amer. & Italian Bronze Stars); Limited Partner, Bacon, Whipple & Co., Chicago 1953—; Publisher, Chicago Jnl. of Commerce 1928–53, Mem., Exec. Cttee., U.S. Golf Assn., June 1946–Jan. 1960 (Pres. 1958 and 1959); First U.S. Co-Chmn., World Amateur Golf Council, organized May 1958; biennial play for Eisenhower Trophy; Alumni Trustee, Region III of Princeton Univ. 1946–50; Fin. Cttee. Chmn., National Citizens for Eisenhower for 1956; Chmn., Community Fund of Chicago 1947; Dir., Children's Memorial Hospital, Chicago; Mem. Adv. Board, Chicago Council, Boy Scouts of America; Governing Mem., Glenwood School for Boys, Chicago. *Member:* Newcomen Socy. in North America; Republican. Pres., United States Senior Golf Assn., 1969–70. *Clubs:* Pine Valley; The Links N.Y.; Onwentsia, Old Elm, Commercial (Chicago); The Chicago; Augusta National Golf; R. & A. of St. Andrews; Hon. Company of Edinburgh Golfers. *Address:* 600 Washington Road, Lake Forest, Ill.; and *office* 135 South LaSalle Street, Chicago 3, Ill., U.S.A.

**AMIES, Jack Lowell,** CBE, ED. British. Chartered Accountant and Company director. *B.* 1913. *Educ.* Brisbane; FASA; FCA. *M.* 1940, Mary Isabell Wetherell. *S.* Peter Lowell. *Dau.* Helen. *Career:* Served in Australian Imp. Forces 1939–45, U.K. Egypt, Palestine, Syria and New Guinea; Cmnd. Officer 1942–52 9th and 15th Bns.; G.S.O.I. (CMF) H.Q. Northern Command 1952–54; Brigadier, Cmdg. 7 Inf. Bde. 1954–58; Hon. Colonel, Royal Queensland Regt. 1967–73; Dir., National Bank of Aust. Ltd., The City Mutual Life Assurance Soc. Ltd., Aust. Inst. of Management Ltd., Aust. Fixed Trusts (Qld.) Ltd., R. M. Gow & Co. Ltd., Hyne & Son Pty. Ltd., Medical Benefits Fund of Aust. Ltd., Roneo Vickers Pty. Ltd. Group, The Read Press Pty. Ltd. and previously a Dir. of a number of other Public Companies. *Member:* The Metropolitan Transit Authority (Qld.) 1976—; Qld. Cttee. Australian Broadcasting Commission 1956–62; Mem. Bd. of Faculty of Commerce, Univ. of Qld. 1959–69; Pres.: United Service Inst. of Queensland 1961–65, and R.A.C., Queensland 1965–67, United Service Club 1950–51, Aust. Inst. of Management 1970–72; Chmn., Qld. Cttee. Services Canteens Trust Fund 1953–72, Qld. Inst. Technology 1971–73, State Registrar Aust. Soc. of Accountants & Aust. Inst. Cost Accountants 1953–59. *Clubs:* Queensland; Brisbane; United Services; Union Club. Sydney. *Address:* 56 Eighth Avenue, St. Lucia, Brisbane; and *office* 379 Queen Street, Brisbane, Qld., Australia.

**AMIN, Samir.** Egyptian Professor and Economist. *B.* 1931. *Education.* University of Paris, Ph.D. (Econ.). *Career:* Adviser, Economic Development Org. Cairo 1957–60; Adviser and Governor of Mali, Bamaka 1960–63; Professor IDEP (UN) Dakar 1963–66; Professor, Univs. of Poitiers, Dakar and Paris 1966–70; Director, IDEP (UN) Dakar since 1970. *Publications:* Many books including Le Dèveloppement Inegal (1973); La Crise de l'Imperialisme (1975). *Address:* IDEP, B.P. 3186, Dakar, Senegal.

**AMIN DADA, Field-Marshal Al-Hajji Idi.** Head of State of Uganda. *B.* 1925. *Career:* Joined King's African Rifles 1946; Corporal 1949, Major 1963, Col. 1964; Dep. Commander of the Army 1964; Commander of Army and Air Force 1966–70; Brig.-Gen. 1967, Maj.-Gen. 1968; leader of military coup which deposed President Obote, Jan. 1971; Pres., C-in-C of the Armed Forces and Minister of Defence since 1971, President for Life since 1976. *Address:* Office of the Head of State, Kampala, Uganda.

**AMODIO, John Julius, The Marquis de,** OBE, MA, FRGS. British. *Educ.* Stowe School and Oxford (MA). *M.* 1948, Countess-Princess Anne de La Rochefoucauld. *Career:* Founder and Captain of Fencing at Stowe School; Fencing Half-Blue, Oxford 1930 (Captain 1933); with Lapland Expedition 1937; Pilot Officer R.A.F.V.R. 1940; Squadron-Leader Normandy (Dispatches) 1944; Asst. to British Air Attaché at Embassy, Paris 1946; Life Vice-Pres., R.A.F. Assn., London, 1962, and Pres., R.A.F. Assn. European Central Council 1967; Pres.: Société des Courses and Societe du Concours Hippique Mansle (France); Vice-Pres. and Permanent Delegate of "Europa Nostra" and of the I.B.I. (Historical Castles Inst.) at the Council of Europe Strasbourg; Grande Chancellor, Principauté de Franc Pineau at Cognac (France) 1957—. *Awards:* Chev. Legion of Honour; Kt.-Cmdr. Order of the Holy Sepulchre; Cmdr. Order of White Eagle (with Swords); Hon. Citizen of Dallas (Texas); Fellow of the Royal Geographical Socy.; Hon. Fellow, Ancient Monuments Socy.; mem. of the Société d'Archéologie Française; Fellow British Interplanetary Society. *Publications:* After the Destroyer; Les Defences et Souterrains du Château de Verteuil; translated 'Collector's Choice' (by

Ethel Le Vane and J. Paul Getty) under the French title of 'Vingt Mille Lieues dans les Musées' and 'Johannes Mercator' into English. *Clubs:* Commonwealth, Geneva; R.A.F. (London); R.A.F. Yacht (Hamble); Vincent's (Oxford); Jockey (Paris); Cercle de l'Union, and Cercle Interallié (Paris). *Address:* Celigny, Switzerland; 93 rue de l'Université, Paris; Château de Verteuil (Charente) France; and Dar Richlieu, Agadir Morocco; *office* 43 Grove Park Road, London, W.4.

**AMORY, Viscount** (of Tiverton; Derick Heathcoat Amory), KG, PC, GCMG. *B.* 1899. *Educ.* Eton; Christ Church, Oxford, LLD Exeter Univ. and McGill. *Career:* Served World War II: M.P. (Cons.) for Tiverton (Devon) 1945–60; Min. of Pensions 1951–53; Min. of State, B.O.T. 1953–54; Min. of Agric. and Fisheries July 1954; Min. of Agric. and Fisheries and Min. of Food Oct. 1954; Min. of Agric., Fisheries and Food 1955–58; Chancellor of the Exchequer 1958–60; Chmn., Medical Research Council 1960–61 and 1965–69; D.L. Devon); British High Commissioner in Canada 1961–63; Chancellor Exeter University since 1972; Hon. DCL, Oxford Univ. *Address:* 150 Marsham Court, London, S.W.1.; and The Wooden House, Chevithorne, Tiverton, Devon.

**AMRAM, Philip Werner.** American Attorney-at-Law. *B.* 1900. *Educ.* Univ. of Pennsylvania (AB 1920, LLB 1927); Pennsylvania State College (BSA 1922). *M.* 1924, Emilie S. Weyl. *S.* David Werner III. *Dau.* Mariana A. Fitzpatrick. *Career:* Practised law in Philadelphia 1927–42; Teacher, Univ. of Pennsylvania Law School 1929–42; Government Service 1942–45; Special Asst. to Attorney-General of the U.S. and Special Adviser to Alien Property Custodian 1943–45; practised law in Washington since 1945. *Member:* Procedural Rules Committee, Supreme Court of Pennsylvania 1938— (Chmn. 1958—) and Chmn. Advisory Cttee., U.S. Comm. on International Rules of Civil Procedure 1957–63. Mem. of U.S. Deleg. to the Hague Conf. on Private Interntl. Law, 1956–60–64–68–72–76, Chmn. 1972; Vice-Chmn., State Dept. Advisory Cttee. on International Private Law. *Member:* American Law Inst.; and local, national and international bar assns. and legal societies. *Award:* Officer Legion of Honour; Commander Ordre des Palmes Academiques. *Publications:* Amram's Pennsylvania Common Pleas Practice (7 editions); Goodrich-Amram Pennsylvania Procedural Rules Service (annually since 1938); numerous articles in legal periodicals and law reviews. *Address:* 2601–31st Street, N.W., Washington, D.C. 20008; *office* 1150 Connecticut Ave., N.W., Washington, D.C. 20036; and Loveladies, N.J. 08008, U.S.A.

**AMSTUTZ, Eduard.** Swiss engineer; Dr. hc ETH. Lausanne. *B.* 18 Nov. 1903. *Educ.* Public and Grammar Schools and Swiss Fed. Inst. of Technology, Zürich (Dipl. Mech. Engr.). *M.* 1952, Johanna Tschannen. *S.* 2. *Dau.* 1. *Career:* Asst., Swiss Fed. Inst. of Technology 1927–28; with Escher Wyss & Co., Zürich 1928–30 and Kraftwerke Oberhasli 1930–32; Fed. Office of Civil Aviation, Berne 1932–37; Prof. for Aircraft Structures and Design, Swiss Fed. Inst. of Technology 1937–49; Pres., Swiss Fed. Laboratories for Testing Materials and Research 1949–69; Vice-Chmn of Bd., Swissair 1947–73. *Address:* Susenbergstrasse 169, 8044 Zürich, Switzerland.

**AMUNDSEN, Gunnar.** Norwegian; Hon. Consul-General, Republic of S. Africa. *B.* 1907. *Educ.* Gymnasium and School of Commerce, Oslo; language courses in England and France. *M.* 1933, Margrethe Lund. *S.* Gunnar, Ivar. *Dau.* Unni Margrethe. *Career:* Estb. his own business as importer of wines, spirits and fresh fruits 1935. Mem. of Cttee., Andresens Bank A/S, Oslo since 1953. *Awards:* Life Saving Medal, Norsk Seskab til Skibbrudnes Redning, 1925; King George VI of England Commendation for valour in war services in Norway during World War II 1950. 'Orden Nacional' Al Mérito en el Grado de Caballero de la Republica del Ecuador, 1970; Commander of the Order of Good Hope of the Republic of South Africa. Conservative. *Address:* Meltzersgt 4, P.O.B. 2540 Solli, Oslo 2, Norway.

**AMUNDSEN, Gunnar Lund.** Norwegian. Senior Research Fellow. *B.* 1934. *Educ.* Dipl. Business Admin. Lausanne; PhD. London; Dr. Phil. Strasbourg. *M.* 1962, Stefi Elisabeth Alder. *Career:* Marketing Dir. Oslo 1962–64; Research Fellow, Strasbourg 1965–67; Sen. Research Fellow, Norwegian Research Council 1968–71; Dir. Research Projects since 1971. *Awards:* Order of Merit (milit.), Serv. Milit. Volontaires, Mérito Académico, Al Mérito del Ecuador, Lee Silver Medal 1963; King's College Silver Medal 1965. *Publications:* nine books on the theory of growth, international trade and the theory of economic integration. *Address:* Majorstuveien 31, Oslo 3, Norway.

**ANDERSEN, A. Bogh.** Danish Diplomat. *Address:* Danish Embassy, Boite Postale 203, Rabat, Morocco.

**ANDERSEN, C. B.** Danish banker. *B.* 1913. *M.* 1939, Agnete Marie Jensen. *S.* Mogens. *Dau.* Bodil. *Career:* Joined Handelsbank at Aarhus Branch 1930; Holder of Procuration, Aarhus 1954; Dept. Mgr., Aarhus 1958; Secy. to Management, Head Office, Copenhagen 1960; Asst. Gen. Mgr. 1961, Managing Dir. 1962; Kjøbenhavns Handelsbank 1962—; Mem. of Bd. The Negotiation Union of Danish Banks 1962–68; Mem., Universitets Samvirket (Univ. Assn.) Aarhus 1954 (Treasurer 1954–60); Chmn. of various univ. building cttees. 1956–60; Mem. of Bd.: Student Hostels of Aarhus Univ. 1954–60; Aarhus Theatre 1956–60, and Aarhus Art Gallery 1958–60; Denmark-America Foundation 1962, and Danish Red Cross 1964–68; City of Aarhus Honorary Prize 1953; Mem. of the Bd. of Representatives of Information Council of Trades and Industries 1964–69; Mem.: Adv. Council for the Rationalization of Government Administration 1965–67; Institut International d'Etudes Bancaires 1965–74; Bd. of Dir., Fed. of Danish Banks 1966; Mem. Bd. & Cttee. The Danish Museum of Decorative Art 1968; Ship Credit Fund of Denmark 1969. *Member:* Finance Councils Cttee. Academy of Applied Science 1971; Mem. Bd. Gammel Estrup Manor House Museum of Jutland 1971; Foreningen Norden (Nordic Association) 1972–74; Selskabet for Bygnings-og Landskabskultur (Soc. for Bldg. & Landscape Culture) 1974. *Award:* Knight, Order of Dannebrog, 1st Degree. *Address:* Duevej 16, Copenhagen F, Denmark.

**ANDERSEN, Elmer L.** *B.* 1909. *Educ.* Muskegon Junior Coll., and Univ. of Minnesota (BBA 1931). *M.* 1932, Eleanor A. Johnson. *S.* Anthony L., Julian L. *Dau.* Emily E. *Career:* Sales Rep., E. H. Sheldon Co., Muskegon, Mich. 1928–34; Advertising and Sales Production Mgr., H. B. Fuller Co., St. Paul, Minn. 1934–37 (Sales Mgr. 1937–41, Pres. 1941–71); Mem. of the State Senate of Minnesota 1949–59; Gov. of the State of Minnesota 1961–63; Regent, Univ. of Minnesota 1967–75; Pres. Bush Foundation 1970–72; Chmn. of Bd. Regents Univ. of Minnesota 1971–75; Chmn. H. B. Fuller Co. since 1971; Dir. Assn. Gov. Boards of Colls & Univs, 1974–75; Dir., Council on Foundations 1974–77; Pres., The Bush Foundation; Publisher, Princeton Union-Eagle; Dir., Univ. of Minnesota Foundation. *Member:* Council on Post-secondary Accreditation; Minnesota Historical Soc. Exec. Council; Voyageurs National Park Assn.; Governor's Voyageurs National Park Advisory Comm. *Award:* Received Univ. of Minnesota Outstanding Achievement Award 1959; LLD Macalester Coll. 1965; Dr. Humane Letters, Carleton Coll. 1972; Order of the Lion (Finland); Award of Merit, Izaak Walton League; Silver Beaver and Silver Antelope Award, Boy Scouts of America; Minneapolis Junior Chamber Conservation Award; AAA Service to Motoring Award; Alpha Kappa Psi Award, Twin Cities Alumni Chapter; Taconite Award, Amer. Inst. of Mining Engineers (Minnesota Chapter) 1976. Republican. *Club:* St Paul Rotary (Past-Pres. and District Gov. of Rotary International) Grolier; New York City. *Address:* 2230 West Hoyt Avenue, St. Paul, Mn. 55108, U.S.A.

**ANDERSEN, Hans Georg.** Icelandic diplomat. *B.* 1919. *Education.* University of Iceland, LL B; Harvard Law Sch. LL M. *M.* 1946, Astridur Helgadottir. *S.* 1. *D.* 1. *Career:* Legal Adviser, Minister of Foreign Affairs 1946–54; Ambassador to NATO 1954–1962; Icelandic Ambassador in Sweden 1962–63; Icelandic Ambassador in Norway 1963–69; Legal Adviser, Ministry for Foreign Affairs 1969–76; Ambassador to U.S.A. since 1976. *Decorations:* Cmdr. with Star, Order of the Falcon (Iceland); Grand Cross of St Olav (Norway); Gr. Cross Order of Merit (Italy); Cmdr. (with star) Order of Leopold (Belgium). *Address:* Embassy of Iceland, 2022 Connecticut Avenue, Washington D.C., U.S.A.

**ANDERSEN, Hermann Rudolf,** Dr. rer. pol.; German politician. *B.* 21 May 1901. *Educ.* Kiel Freiburg i. Br., Göttingen. *M.* 1931, Gertrud Eversz. *S.* Norman Jess, Jan Holger. *Daus.* Ute Maria, Heidi Felicitas. *Career:* Partner and Mgr., Gebrüder Andersen 1925–50; Partner, Maschinenfabrik Wihl. G. Schroeder Nachfolger G.m.b.H., Lübeck 1948–67; Min. of Economy and Transport, Land Schleswig-Holstein 1950–52; Mgr., Fachverband Dampf-Kessel, Behalter- und Rohrleitungsbau, Düsseldorf, 1955–66. *Publication:* Die Privatgüterwagen auf den deutschen Eisenbahnen. *Address:* 34 Steuben-Str., Wiesbaden, Germany.

**ANDERSEN, K. B.** Danish Politician. *B.* 1914. *Education.* M. Economics. *M.* 1943, Grethe Trock. *S.* 4. *Career:* Danmarks Radio 1940–50 Teacher Krogerup Folk High School,

1946–50; Headmaster Workers' Folk High School, Roskilde 1950–57; Headmaster, Scandinavian Folk High School, Geneva 1953 and 1958; Adviser, Prison Education Dept. 1957–64; Mem. Danish Nat. Comm for UNESCO 1949–70; Member Folketing 1957–70 and since 1973; Minister of Education 1964–68; Mem. Nordic Council 1962–64, 1968–70 and 1973–75; Gen. Secy. Social Democratic Pary of Denmark 1970–71; Minister for Foreign Affairs 1971–73 and since 1975. *Member:* Rask Orsted Foundation 1957–64. *Publications:* Co-Editor Verdens Gang 1953–58; (with J. O. Krag) Kamp og Fornyelse. *Address:* Urbansgade 2, Copenhagen Ø, DK 2100, Denmark; and *office:* Ministry of Foreign Affairs, Christiansborg Castle, 1218 Copenhagen, Denmark.

**ANDERSON, Arthur Brayton**, OBE, MB, ChB, FACMA; Australian medical practitioner. *B.* 1905. *Educ.* Brookfield School and Univ. of Liverpool (MB, ChB). *M.* 1930, Doris Howlett. *S.* John Brayton. *Dau.* Enid. *Career:* Asst. Medical Supt., Bootham Park, York (Eng.) 1929; Medical Officer, Mental Hospitals Dept., West Australia 1930–36; Dept. Medical Officer, Repatriation Dept., West Australia 1936–39; Medical Supt.: Repatriation General Hospital, Hobart (Tasmania) 1946, and Repatriation General Hospital, Adelaide, S.A. 1947–59; Hon. Consultant-Psychiatrist, Children's Hospital, Perth, W.A. 1937–46; with R.A.A.F.: Sqdn. Medical Officer, No. 25 Sqdn. 1939; Comdg. Officer, No. 2 R.A.A.F. Hospital 1940–41; Principal Medical Officer, Western Area 1942–43; Consulting Psychiatrist 1943–46; Rank: Wing-Commander; Dir. (Medical Services) Dept. of Repatriation, New South Wales Jan. 1959–70. *Publications:* One Hundred and Twenty Consecutive Autopsies on the Insane; Medical Examination for Air Crew; A Case of Anaphylactoid Purpura Following Penicillin. *Club:* Imperial Services (Sydney). *Address:* 25 Carunta Str., Wattle Park, South Australia, 5066.

**ANDERSON, Sir Colin Skelton**, KB 1950, KBE 1969. *B.* 1904. *Educ.* Eton, Trinity Coll. Oxford. *M.* Morna Campbell MacCormick. *Daus.* Catriona Garrett (Williams), Rose Ferlina Garrett (Carver). *Career:* Dir. Orient SN Co. Ltd. 1950–69; Midland Bank Ltd. 1953–74; Marine Insurance Co. Ltd. 1950–70; Australia and New Zealand Bank Ltd. 1951–70; P. & OSN Co. 1960–69; Royal Opera House Covent Garden 1961–73; Pres. British Employers' Confederation 1956–58; Seamen's Hospital Socy. 1962—; Chamber of Shipping of the United Kingdom 1949–50; Design and Industry Assn. 1950–53; Chmn., National Assn. of Port Employers 1947–48 and 1950–54; International Chamber of Shipping 1949–63; Council of Royal Coll. of Art 1952–56; Ministry of Transport Advisory Cttee. on Traffic Signs for Motor Roads 1957–60; Ministry of Education Cttee. on Grants to Students 1958–60; Contemporary Art Socy. 1956–60; Chmn. of Trustees, The Tate Gallery 1960–67; (Vice-Chmn. 1953–59); Gray Dawes Westray & Co. Ltd. 1960–69; Anderson Green & Co. Ltd.; Royal Fine Art Comm. 1968–76; Sea Transport Comm. of Internal Chamber of Commerce 1965–71; Mem., Design Panel of British Transport Comm. 1962–76; *Awards:* Officer, Order of Orange-Nassau (Netherlands) 1948; F.R.S.A. 1953; Provost, Royal Coll. of Art 1967; Hon. Des. RCA; Hon. ARIBA 1953; Hon. Fellow, Trinity Coll., Oxford 1963; Hon. LLD, Aberdeen University 1963; Hon. FRIBA 1971. *Address:* Le Val House, St. Brelade, Jersey, Channel Islands.

**ANDERSON, Dillon.** American. *B.* 1906. *Educ.* Univ. of Oklahoma (BS 1928) and Yale University (LLB 1929). *M.* 1931, Lena Carter Carroll. *Daus.* Susan, Lena, Elizabeth. *Career:* Associated with present firm (formerly known as Baker, Botts, Andrews & Garwood) since 1929; served in World War II (U.S. Army; honourably discharged as Colonel; awarded Legion of Merit 1944) 1942–45; served as Special Asst. to the Pres. of the United States for National Security Affairs Apr. 1955–Sept. 1956; Partner in law firm of Baker and Botts 1940—; Dir.: Westinghouse Electric Corp., Monsanto Co., Federated Dept. Stores Inc.; U.S. Plywood-Champion Papers Inc.; Trustee: Carnegie Endowment for International Peace; The Brookings Instn; Mem., U.S. Delegation to Summit Conference, Geneva, July 1955. *Publications:* I and Claudie: Claudie's Kinfolks (both published by Little, Brown & Co.); The Billingsley Papers (pub. Simon & Schuster Inc.). Independent Democrat. *Address* and *office:* One Shell Plaza, Houston, Texas, U.S.A.

**ANDERSON, Donald**, MP. British Politician & Barrister. *B.* 1939. *Educ.* Swansea Grammar School; Univ. Coll.. Swansea. *M.* 1963, Dr. Dorothy Anderson. *S.* 3. *Career:* H.M. Foreign Service 1960–64; Lecturer, Univ. of Wales 1964—66; M.P. for Monmouth 1966–70; Barrister since 1969; M.P. for Swansea East since 1974. *Address:* c/o House of Commons, London SW1.

**ANDERSON, Donald Sutherland.** Canadian banker. *B.* 1913. *Educ.* Public and High Schools, Winnipeg. *M.* 1941, Margaret Richmond Stoddart. *S.* Ian Sutherland, Robert James. *Dau.* Jocelyn (Green). *Career:* Entered service of the Royal Bank of Canada in Winnipeg 1930; transferred to Head Office 1941 after war service appointed Senior Asst. Mgr., Winnipeg Main Branch 1947; Mgr., 3rd Street West Branch, Calgary 1949; Mgr., Calgary Branch 1951; Mgr., Toronto Main Branch 1952; Asst. Gen. Mgr., Head Office Montreal 1957; Asst. Gen. Mgr. 1958; Gen. Mgr. 1961, Ont.; Dir. and Vice-Pres. 1964; Snr. Vice-Pres. 1970; Chmn., Canada Realties Ltd.; Other Directorships include: Markborough Properties Ltd.; Canadian Cablesystems Ltd.; Slough Estates (Canada) Ltd.; Denison Mines Ltd.; CN Tower Ltd.; Crum & Forster of Canada Ltd.; Herald Insurance Co.; Inglis Ltd.; Algonquin Mercantile Corp.; Hardee Farms International; The Continental Group of Canada Ltd.; The Empire Club Foundation; National Life Assurance Co. of Canada; etc. Trustee, Toronto General Hospital; Mem. Adv. Bd., United Community Fund of Greater Toronto; Past Pres., Bd. of Trade of Metropolitan Toronto; Mem. Nat. Adv. Bd., Boys' and Girls' Clubs of Canada; Mem. Bd. of Hon. Govs., Canadian Assoc. for Retarded Children. *Clubs:* Toronto, The York, Rosedale Golf, Mount Royal (Montreal); Ranchmen's (Calgary); Manitoba (Winnipeg); Lost Tree, Jupiter Hills (Fla.); Ristigouche Salmon Club (Matapedia). *Address:* 42 Arjay Crescent, Willowdale, Ont., Canada.

**ANDERSON, Sir Edward Arthur**, JP. *B.* 1908. *Educ.* Middlesbrough High School and South Shields Engineering School; Assoc. IEE. *M.* 1937, Elsa French. *Career:* Mem., Middlesbrough Borough Council 1945–55; Chmn., Middlesbrough Conservative Assn. 1947–60; Dir.: A. Anderson & Son (Electrical Engineers) Ltd. *Club:* Cleveland (Middlesborough). *Address:* Spring Lodge, Guisborough, Cleveland.

**ANDERSON, George David**, CMG, BA. British diplomat. *B.* 1913. *Educ.* King Edward VII Grammar School, Kings Lynn; Emmanuel Coll. Cambridge. *M.* 1950, Audrey Rowena Money. *Dau.* 1. *Career:* National Assn. of Boys Clubs 1934–37; MacGregor & Co. Ltd. Rangoon 1938–40; Service, British Army India, Burma (Lieut-Colonel) 1940–46; H.M. Treasury 1946; British High Commission Delhi and Calcutta First Secy. 1947–51; Commonwealth Relations Office London 1951–56; British Embassy Dublin 1957–60; Whitehall London 1961; British High Comm. Colombo Ceylon (Dep. High Comm.) 1961–66; Head of Chancery, British High Comm. Lagos 1967–69; British High Commissioner in Botswana 1969–73 (retd.). *Member:* Commonwealth Socy.; Royal African Society. *Address:* National and Grindlays Bank, 13 St. James's Square, London, SW1Y 4LF.

**ANDERSON, Harold David**, OBE, Australian diplomat. *B.* 1923. *Education.* St Peter's College, Adelaide, Univs. of Adelaide and Melbourne, BA. *M.* 1952, Annabel Bessie Johnson. *Daus.* 2. *Career:* 3rd Secy. Australian Embassy Paris 1947–49; Karachi 1949–50; Australian Consul, New Caledonia 1950–53; Dept of Foreign Affairs 1953–55; Chargé d'Affaires, Phnom-Penn 1955–57; First Secy. Tokyo 1957–58; Branch Head and Asst.-Secy. Canberra 1959–62; Ambassador Saigon 1964–66; Asst.-Secy. Canberra 1966–68; Australian Observer to Viet-nam Peace Negotiations (Paris) 1968–70; First Asst.-Secy. Canberra 1970–73; Australian Ambassador, Paris since 1973. *Decoration:* Order of the British Empire. *Club:* Racing Club of France. *Address:* 13 rue Las Cases (Paris) and *office:* Australian Embassy 64/66 Ave. d'Iena, Paris.

**ANDERSON, James Donald.** American. *B.* 1909. *Educ.* Univ. of Wyoming. *M.* Rhea Wadsworth. *Daus.* 2. *Career:* Senior Vice-Pres. Production & Dir. Marathon Oil Co.; Vice-Pres. & Dir. Marathon Oil Co.; various previous appointments with Marathon Oil Co. since 1936. *Member* Masonic Lodges; American Petroleum Inst.; American Inst. of Mining, Metallurgical & Petroleum Engineers; Mem. Bd. of Mans., Rose-Hulman Inst. *Address:* 120 Beechmont Drive, Findlay, Ohio, U.S.A.; and *office* 539 Main St., Findlay, Ohio, U.S.A.

**ANDERSON, Sir John Muir**, CMG; Australian. *B.* 1914. *Educ.* Brighton Grammar School and Melbourne Univ. Commerce). *M.* 1949, Audrey Drayton Jamieson. *S.* Roderick Weir. *Dau.* Kim Olivia. *Career:* Asst. Gen. Mgr., Preservene Pty. Ltd. 1932–42 and 1946–51; served 2/6th

Australian Commando Coy. 1942–44; officer, 1st Australian Parachute Bn. 1944–46; established John M. Anderson & Co. 1952; Proprietor of John M. Anderson & Co. Pty. Ltd.; agents, importers and manufacturers; Victoria Insurance Co. Ltd. 1965—; Man. Dir., King Oscar Fine Foods Pty. Ltd. 1966—; Pres., Liberal & Country Party of Victoria 1952–56, Treasurer 1956–61; Commissioner, State Savings Bank of Victoria June 1962—; Commissioner, Melb. Harbour Trust 1972; Chmn. Comms. of State Savings Bank 1967; Trustee, Melbourne Exhibition (Chmn. 1967). *Award:* Coronation Medal. *Address:* 25 Cosham Street, Brighton, Vic., Australia.

**ANDERSON, John Stuart.** British. *B.* 1908. *Educ.* Univ. of London and Imperial Coll. of Science; PhD. *M.* 1935, Joan Taylor. *S.* 1. *Daus.* 3. *Career:* Senior Lecturer, Univ. of Melbourne 1938–47; Deputy Chief Scientific Officer, Atomic Energy Research Establishment, Harwell 1947–53; Prof. of Inorganic Chemistry and Head of the Chemistry Dept., Univ. of Melbourne 1954–59; Dir., National Chemical Laboratory, D.S.I.R. 1959–63; Prof. of Inorganic Chemistry, Oxford Univ. 1963–75; Fellow of St. Catherine's College, Oxford; Hon. Professorial Fellow, Univ. Coll. of Wales, Aberystwyth 1975. *Publications:* numerous papers, etc., in scientific journals; MSc (Melbourne); MA (Oxford); Fellow, Royal Socy.; Fellow, Australian Academy of Science. *Member:* Chemical Socy. of London; Faraday Socy.; Royal Australian Chemical Inst. *Address:* Edward Davies Chemical Laboratories, Aberystwyth.

**ANDERSON, Nils, Jr.** Merchant and executive. *B.* 1914. *Educ.* Lawrenceville and Loomis Schools, Williams Coll. (BA 1937), Colorado School of Mines, and George Washington Univ. Law School. *M.* 1938, Jean Derby Ferris. *S.* Nils III, Derby Ferris, Stephens Massie, Ward Reynolds. *Career:* with Koppers Co. summers 1933–37; Bakelite Corp. 1937–41; War Production Bd. 1941–45, (Chief Adhesives United 1942; Chief, Plastics Branch 1944–45; Government Presiding Officer of eight adhesives and plastics industry advisory committees, and chemical division adviser to Dept. of Agriculture; Combined Raw Materials Bd., Stock Pile and Shipping Branch during World War II); Vice-Pres., Casein Co. of America 1945, subsequently Chemical Division of The Borden Company until 1950; Dir. of American and South American companies during this time; Chmn. of Bd., Debevoise-Anderson Co. 1965— (Pres. 1950–58). Author of technical articles on adhesives and plastics. *Member:* Socy. of War of 1812; Socy. of Colonial Wars; Pilgrims Socy.; Alpha Delta Phi; AIME; Amer. Socy. of Mechanical Engineers; Amer. Iron & Steel Inst.; Mem. of U.S. Trade Mission to Romania and Poland 1965. *Clubs:* Pinnacle, Univ. Links, Williams (N.Y.C.); Country, Pequot Yacht (Fairfield); Duquesne (Pittsburgh); Rolling Rock (Ligonier, Pa.); Travellers (Paris). *Address:* 1100 Pequot Road, Southport, Conn.; and *office* P.O. Box 511, Southport, Conn. 06490, U.S.A.

**ANDERSON, O. Kelley.** *B.* 1907. *Educ.* Univ. of Iowa (BA) and Harvard Graduate School of Business Administration (MBA). *M.* 1933, Alma U. Weichel. *S.* O. Kelley, Jr. *Career:* Pres. & Trustee, Consolidated Investment Trust 1935–50; Pres., Dir. and a founder of Boston Fund Inc. 1939–50 (now Vance, Sanders Investors Fund, Inc.); Pres. & Dir. of New England Mutual Life Insurance Co. 1951–66; Chmn. & Dir. 1966–71; Managing General Partner, Vance Sanders Exchange Fund; Dir. of various industrial companies, including Gillette Co.; Boston Edison Co.; Ritz-Carlton Hotel Co.; Trustee, Century Shares Trust, Provident Instn. for Savings in the Town of Boston, Consolidated Investment Trust; Dir.: investment companies, Vance, Sanders Income Fund Inc.; Capital Exchange Fund Inc.; Depositors Fund of Boston Inc.; Diversification Fund. Inc.; Exchange Fund of Boston Inc.; Fiduciary Exchange Leverage Fund of Boston Inc.; Second Fiduciary Exchange Fund Inc.; Chmn. Exec. Cttee., Real Estate Investment Trust of America; Fellow, Amer. Acad. of Arts & Sciences; Honorary Trustee, Cttee. for Economic Development. *Address:* 68 Beacon Street, Boston, Mass.; and *office* 294 Washington Street, Mass. U.S.A.

**ANDERSON, Peter Hamilton.** South African. *B.* 1912. *Educ.* Malvern Coll., England. *M.* 1942, Cynthia Dudley Stock. *S.* Peter Robin Guildford. *Dau.* Jenifer Nola. *Career:* former Chmn. Rand Mines Ltd.; Pres. Chamber of Mines of South Africa; Chmn. Harvey & Russell (Pty.) Ltd.; Dir. Argus Printing & Publishing Co.; S.A. Eagle Insurance Co.; Chmn. South African Inst. for Medical Research, S.A. National Tuberculosis Assoc., National Kidney Foundation, Roedean Trust. *Member:* Witwatersrand Council of Education. *Clubs:* Country; Rand (both of Johannesburg). *Address:* 45 Valley Road, Parktown, Johannesburg, South Africa.

**ANDERSON, Robert Orville.** *B.* 1917. *Educ.* Univ. of Chicago (BA 1939). *M.* 1939, Barbara Phelps. *S.* Robert Bruce, William Phelps. *Daus.* Katherine, Julia, Maria, Barbara, Beverley. *Career:* owner, Lincoln County Livestock Co., Roswell, N.M.; Chmn. of the Bd. and Dir., Atlantic Richfield Co. *Member:* National Petroleum Council, Washington, D.C.; Trustee, Univ. of Chicago; Chmn., Aspen (Colo.) Inst. for Humanistic Activities; Chmn., Lovelace Foundation, Albuquerque, N.M. *Clubs:* Roswell Country; California (Los Angeles). *Address* and *office* Lincoln County Livestock Co., P.O. Box 1000, Rosewell, N.M. 88201, U.S.A.

**ANDERSON, Robert William Charles,** OBE, FAIM. *B.* 1911. *M.* 1936, Lilian Clarke. *S.* 2. *Daus.* 2. *Career:* Dir-Gen. Australia–Japan Business Co-op. Cttee; Pacific Basin Economic Council; Australia–Korea Business Co-op Cttee; Dir. Cementrazzo Ltd Sydney 1932–40; Tariff Off. Chamber of Mftrs. NSW 1942–51; Asst. Dir. ACMA 1951–57; Attended GATT Session Geneva as Adviser 1954; Dir.-Gen. Assoc. Chambers of Mftrs. of Australia, Canberra 1957–72 (retired); Attended ILO Conferences, Geneva 1959–71; Adviser to C'wealth Govt. Internat. Common Market Conf. (London and Brussels) 1962. *Director:* (Man) Austr. Export Promotions Pty Ltd.; Canberra TV Holdings Ltd.; *Chairman:* Anderson Holdings Pty Ltd.; Handshake Holdings Pty Ltd.; Nord Industries Pty Ltd. *Member:* Australian Tariff Advisory Cttee; Immigration Advisory Cttee; Executive International Org. of Employers Geneva. *Award:* Order of Sacred Treasure (Japanese) 1971. *Publications:* Canberra Letter, History of ACMA. *Clubs:* Commonwealth (Canb.); Canberra; Royal Canberra Golf; Rotary; Tattersalls (Sydney). *Address:* 17 Couvreur Street, Garran, ACT 2605, Australia.

**ANDERSON, Walter Stratton, Jr.** American. *B.* 1912. *Educ.* Harvard Univ. (BS 1933) and Univ. of Chicago. *M.* 1944. Mary McIntire Betts. *S.* Thomas Stratton. *Dau.* Virginia Randolph. *Career:* American Foreign Service Officer, Dept. of State (with diplomatic and consular assignments at Le Havre, Johannesburg, Lagos, Accra, Lima, London, Rangoon, Oslo and Washington) 1937–62; Secy., Center for International Affairs, Harvard Univ. 1962–63; Vice-Pres., General Telephone & Electronics International Inc. since 1963. *Member:* Amer. Foreign Service Assn.; DACOR Inc.; Armed Forces Communications and Electronics Assn. *Club:* International (Washington). *Address:* 5310 Albemarle Street, Washington, D.C. 20016; and *office* Suite 900, 1120 Connecticut Avenue, N.W., Washington, D.C. 20036, U.S.A.

**ANDERSON, Wendell Richard.** U.S. Senator. *B.* 1933. *Educ.* St. Paul public schools; Univ. of Minnesota, BA; Univ. of Minnesota Law Sch., JD. *M.* Mary McKee. *S.* 1. *Daus.* 2. *Career:* Lawyer, admitted to the bar 1960 and commenced practice in St. Paul; served in U.S. Army 1959–63; mem., Minnesota House of Reps. 1959–63, Minnesota Senate 1963–71; Governor of Minnesota 1971–76; appointed to U.S. Senate Dec. 1976. *Member:* U.S. Olympic hockey team 1956; U.S. National hockey team 1955, 1957; Chmn., Democratic Governors' Conf. 1974–75; Chmn., Platform Cttee., Democratic National Convention 1976. *Address:* Senate Office Building, Washington, D.C. 20510, U.S.A.

**ANDERSSEN, Friedrich Gustav,** PhD. South African. Research physiologist and biochemist; Company Dir. *B.* 1901. *Educ.* PhD. *M.* 1928, Marjorie Thorburn Black. *S.* Gustav Friedrich. *Dau.* Sandra Majorie. *Career:* Research Physiologist 1927–63; Dir. of Horticulture for Repub. of South Africa 1931–63. *Publications:* contributions to Journal of Plant Physiology, Journal of Pomology & Horticultural Science, and other media; various scientific reports on research. *Clubs:* Pretoria; Pretoria Country. *Address:* 47 Julius Jeppe Street, Waterkloof, Pretoria, South Africa.

**ANDERSSON, Sven Olof Morgan.** Swedish politician. *B.* 1910 *Career:* Member of Parliament 1940–44 and since 1948; Party Secy. to Swedish Social-Democratic Labour Party; Minister without Portfolio 1948–51; Min. of Communications 1951–57; Min. of Defence 1957–73; Min. of Foreign Affairs 1973–76; Mem. of Parliament 1976. *Address:* Strandvagen 55, S-115 23 Stockholm, Sweden.

**ANDREADIS, Stratis G.** Greek Banker. *Educ.* Univ. of Athens (Graduate Faculty of Law); Univ. of Paris (Political Science Degree), Dr. of Law, Dip. Advanced Studies Polit. Economy & Public Law. *Career:* Called to Bar, Athens 1927; Prof. of Admin. Law, Univ. of Salonica 1939; Prof. of Admin. Law,

Athens Grad. School of Economics & Business Sciences 1939–69; Prof. Emeritus since 1969; Rector of Athens Graduate School of Economics & Business Sciences (1943–44, 1956–57, 1960–61, 1964–65, 1965–66, 1967–68); Correspondent Member of Academy of Moral & Political Sciences (Inst. of France) 1972. President and Chmn. Commercial Bank of Greece; Ionian and Popular Bank of Greece. Chmn. Investment Bank; Bank of Piraeus; Bank of Attica; Commercial Bank of the Near East Ltd. London; Bank Commerciale de Grèce, Paris; Griesche Handelsbank, Frankfurt; Hellenic Electric Railways (also Fin-Admin. Man.); The Phoenix, Greek General Insurance Co.; General Insurance Co. of Greece, S.A.; Phosphoric Fertilizers Industry Ltd.; Andreadis (U.K.) Ltd. (Shipping) London; Eleusis Shipyards, S.A.; Greek Juice Processing and Canning Industry Ltd.; Ioniki Hotel Enterprises Ltd.; Hellenic General Enterprises Co.; Greek Industry for Sacks and Plastic Products Co. Ltd.; Hellenic Mutual Fund Mgmt. Co. S.A. President and Chairman of numerous Associations both national and international. *Awards:* Knight-Comm. Order of George I; Knight-Comm. Order of Phoenix; Grand Cross of Merit with Star of Federal Republic of Germany; Grand Official of Order of Merit of Italian Republic; Officer of Legion of Honour; Officer of Order of Leopold (Belgium); Archon Megas Ritor (Dignitary of Ecumenical Patriarchate); Cross of St. Mark; Golden Cross (Mt. Athos); Grand Commander Order of Knights of Greek Patriarchate of Jerusalem. *Publications:* Contributions in Greek to several legal works; numerous monographs and studies. *Address:* Commercial Bank of Greece, Athens.

**ANDREASSEN, Reidar.** Norwegian textile agent since 1923. *B.* 1905. *Educ.* Grammar and Commercial Schools. *Address:* Huitfeldtsgt 8b, Oslo 2, (P.O. Box 2505), Norway.

**ANDREOTTI, Giulio.** Italian politician. *B.* 1919. *Educ.* Graduated in Law. *M. Children.* 4. *Career:* Journalist and Editor Azione Fucina; Pres. Italian Catholic Univ. Federation 1942; Member, National Council, Christian Democrats Naples Conference 1944; Deputy to Constituent Assembly, of Rome, 1946; Under Secy. of State, Secy. Council of Ministers 1947–54; Min. Interior, Fanfani Cabinet 1954; Min. Finance 1955–58; Minister of the Treasury, Min. Defence 1958–66; Ministry of Industry 1966–68; President Christian Democratic Parly. Group, House of Deputies, later President of the Council of Ministers; Minister of Defence 1974; Minister of the Budget and Economic Planning for Extraordinary Projects in the South; Prime Minister 1976. *Publications:* Many books and essays. *Address:* Camera Dei Deputati, Rome, Italy.

**ANDRESEN, Dr. Karl N.,** Dr.-Ing. German. *B.* 1911. *Educ.* Study of electrical engineering; Graduated Dr.-Ing. 1941. *M.* 1937, Annie Vollstedt. *S.* Hans Uwe, Jürgen, Peter. *Member:* I.C.D.C.; Max-Planck-Gesellschaft; Fachverband Kabel und isolierte Drähte; Verband der Metallindustriellen Nidersachsens. Chmn. of the Executive Bd.; President of Kabel- und Metallwerke Gutehoffnungshütte Aktiengesellschaft since 1967; Council of BNF Metals Technology Centre; Intern. Wrought Copper Council. *Address:* Feldweg, 33, 3002 Bissendorf, West Germany; and (*office*) Postfach 260, 3000 Hanover, West Germany.

**ANDRESEN, Rudolf Kristian.** Norwegian Diplomat. *B.* 1914. *Educ.* Naval Officer. *M.* 1942, Thelma May Andresen. *Career:* Various naval appointments 1939–40, 1945–48 (War Service in Royal Norwegian Navy 1940–45); Commander 1948; Commodore 1951; Aide-de-Camp to HM the King 1951; Dep. Commander of Royal Norwegian Navy and Commander of Allied Naval Forces in Norway 1953; Rear-Admiral 1953; Chief of Naval District Western Norway 1959–60; Ret'd from Navy 1964; Dir. of the *Dragon* atomreactor project in Great Britain 1960–62; Sec.-Gen., Norwegian Development Aid 1962–68; Dir., Norwegian Agency for International Development 1968–75; Ambassador to Kenya, Madagascar and Ethiopia since 1975. *Decorations:* St. Olav's Medal with oak leaves, King Haakon VII Commemoration Medal in Gold, King Haakon VII Jubilee Medal 1955, King Haakon VII Commemoration Medal 1972, War Medal and other Norwegian distinctions from World War II (Norway); Officer of the Order of the British Empire, 1939–45 Star, Atlantic Star, Africa Star with Cluster (U.K.); Officer Order of Dannebrog (Denmark); Officer Order of Falcon (Iceland); Commodore 1st Class Order of the Sword (Sweden); Commodore Order of Merit (Korea); Commodore Order of the Southern Cross (Brazil). *Address:* Royal Norwegian Embassy, P.O. Box 46363, Nairobi, Kenya.

**ANDREW, Arthur Julian.** Canadian diplomat. *B.* 1915. *Educ.* Dalhousie Univ. (BA and MA); King's Coll. DDL (hc). *M.* 1940, Joyce Mowbray Sircom. *Daus.* Stephanie, Victoria. *Career:* Canadian Press, Halifax, N.S. 1937–39; Joined Canadian Army 1939 (Lieut.); served on Atlantic Coast, United Kingdom, Italy and North-western Europe; discharged 1946 (Captain); joined External Affairs Dept. as F.S.O. 1947; Second Secy., Bonn Apr. 1950; First Secy. Oct. 1951; Chargé d'Affaires a.i., Vienna Jan. 1953; Ottawa Sept. 1954; Chargé d'Affaires, Prague July 1957; Ottawa June 1960; Ambassador to Israel and concurrently High Commissioner to Cyprus Aug. 1962–65; Ambassador to Sweden 1965–69; Dir. Gen. Bureau, Asian and Pacific Affairs 1970–74; Asst. Under Secy. of State for External Affairs 1974–75; Ambassador to Athens since 1976. *Publications:* Defence by Other Means. *Address:* Canadian Embassy, I. Ghennadiou V, Athens 140, Greece.

**ANDREW, Rev. Sir (George) Herbert,** KCMG, CB. *B.* 1910. *Educ.* Oxford Univ. (MA). *M.* 1936, Irene Jones. *S.* John Oliver, Stephen Leon. *Daus.* Christine Mary, Linden Margaret. *Career:* Asst. Examiner, Patent Office 1931; Asst. Secy., Board of Trade 1945, Under-Secy., 1952, Second Secy. 1955; Dep. Secy., Min. of Education, 1963; British civil servant; Permanent Under Secy. of State, Dept. of Education and Science 1963–70; Asst. Curate, Edenbridge, Kent since 1976. *Address:* 18 Stangrove Road, Edenbridge, Kent TN8 5HT.

**ANDREWS, Christopher E.** British. *B.* 1917. *Educ.* Bablake Sch. Coventry. *M.* 1943, Joyce E. Watts. *Dau.* 1. *Career:* Vice-Pres. & Dir. British Leyland Motors Inc.; Sales Exec., Standard-Triumph International Ltd. 1954–58; Export Sales Man. 1959–61; Export Comm. Man. 1962–63; Pres. Standard Triumph Motor Co. Inc. 1963–66; Vice-Pres. & Dir. Leyland Motor Corp. of Nth America, 1967–68. *Club:* New York Athletic. *Address:* 240 Central Park South, New York, N.Y. 10019, U.S.A.; and *office* 600 Willowtree Road, Leonia, NJ. 07605.

**ANDREWS, Rt. Hon. John Lawson Ormrod,** PC, K.C.B., DL. *B.* 1903. *Educ.* Shrewsbury. *M.* 1928, Marjorie Elaine Maynard James. *S.* 3. *Dau.* 1. *Career:* Chmn. and Man. Dir., John Andrews & Co., Ltd., flax spinners, Comber; M.P. (U.) Mid-Down, Northern Ireland Parliament 1953–64; Min. of Health and Local Government 1957–61; Min. of Commerce 1961–63; of Finance 1963–64; Min. of Senate, Northern Ireland 1964–72. *Address:* Maxwell Court, Comber, Co. Down, Northern Ireland.

**ANDREWS, Kenneth Edwin,** MBE. Australian. *B.* 1911. *Educ.* Canterbury High School; Sydney Technical Coll. (ASTC Chem. Eng.); Sydney Univ., BE (Hons.). *M.* 1936, Evelyn Slocombe. *S.* Brian, Dr. Colin, Malcolm. *Career:* Asst. to City Engineer, Sydney City Council 1946–49; various senior construction engineering appointments, Snowy Mountains Hydro-electric Authority 1950–60; Chief Engineer, Major Contracts, Snowy Mountains Hydro-electric Authority, July 1960–70; Asst. Dir., Snowy Mountains Engineering Corp. 1970–76; Civil Engineering Consultant since 1976. *Publications:* various technical papers on tunnelling and contract administration; Fellow, Instn. of Engineers (Australia); Fellow, Inst. of Arbitrators, Australia. *Member:* Royal Australian Planning Inst. *Address:* 12 Mawson Street, Cooma, N.S.W. 2630, Australia.

**ANDREWS, Mark Edwin.** American business executive, lawyer and teacher. *B.* 1903. *Educ.* Lawrenceville School (Dipl. *cum laude*) and Princeton Univ. (AB *cum laude*, 1927); LLD., Texas Coll. of Law 1934. *M.* (1) 1928, Marguerite McLellan (*d.*), (2) 1948, Lavoné Dickensheets. *S.* Mark Edwin, III. *Dau.* Marguerite McLellan. *Career:* Served in World War II (Capt., U.S. Navy) 1942–49; Asst. Secy., U.S.N., 1947–49; Pres.: Andrews-Loop & Co. (since 1928), M. E. Andrews, Inc. 1951 and Ancon Oil & Gas Co. 1957. *Awards:* Legion of Merit, U.S.N., 1946. *Publications:* Law v. Equity in the Merchant of Venice (1936); Buying a Navy (1946); Wildcatters Handbook (1952). *Clubs:* Houston; Houston Country; River; Links; Kildare St. (Dublin) (all of N.Y.C.); Fishers Island Country; Bayou, Houston. *Address:* 8 Shadder Way, Houston, and (*office*) 1000 Bank of the Southwest Building, Houston, Tex., U.S.A. (Summer residence, Fishers Island, New York) and Knappogue Castle, Quin, Co. Clare, Ireland.

**ANDREWS, William Charles,** OBE. Australian. *B.* 1908. *Educ.* Chartered Civil Engineer; Registered Surveyor; Registered Town and Country Planner. *M.* 1937, Lurline

Patricia Ross. *S.* William Michael Charles. *Daus.* Elizabeth Patricia, Lurline Helen. *Career:* Shire Engineer, Shire of Tenterfield 1936–46 (*ex* War Service in R.A.A.F.); Senior Planning Officer, Cumberland County 1946–50; City Engineer, City Planner, City of Parramatta 1950–58; Associate Commissioner, National Capital Development Comm., Canberra, 1958–72; Commissioner 1972–74; Consultant, Urban Planning and Development since 1974. *Fellow:* Inst. of Surveyors, Australia; Instn. of Engineers, Australia; Royal Socy. of Health, London; Australian Planning Institute. *Publications:* Sub-divisions and Traffic Planning; Airfield Stabilization; various technical articles. *Clubs:* Rotary; Air Force Association. *Address:* 75 National Circuit, Deakin, Canberra, A.C.T.

**ANGER, Per Johan Valentin.** Swedish Diplomat. *B.* 1913. *Education.* Stockholm; Uppsala, Bachelor of Law. *M.* 1943, Elena Wikstrom. *Career:* Swedish Foreign Service Stockholm 1941–42, Budapest 1942–5, Cairo and Addis Ababa 1946–48, Cairo and Stockholm 1948–53, Paris 1953–55, Vienna & Stockholm 1955–61, San Francisco & Stockholm 1961–70; Swedish Ambassador in Australia (Canberra) 1970–75, in Canada (Ottawa) since 1976. *Clubs:* Commonwealth (Canberra); Australian Pioneers (Sydney). *Address:* Royal Swedish Embassy, Ottawa, Canada.

**ANGERS, François-Albert.** Canadian. *Educ.* MSc (Commerce), BSc. Montreal: Diploma, Ecole Libre des Sciences Politiques, Paris. *M.* 1935, Gisèle Le Myre. *S.* Simon-Luc, René, Pierre-Yves. *Daus.* Françoise, Denise. *Career:* Prof. in Economics, Montreal Univ.; H.E.C. since 1937; Mem. Bd. of Dirs., La Solidarité, Société Nationale de Fiducie; Dir.: L'Actualité Economique, 1938–48; Head Dir. Institut d'Economie Appliquée à l'Ecole H.E.C. 1945–69; *Publications:* Introduction to The Economic Science (5th edn.; Fides, Montreal); Essay on Centralisation (Montreal); Social Security and Constitutional Problems (Quebec); Taxing and the Federal System (Quebec); The Financial Institutions and Bank of Canada's Control (Quebec); La Co-opération (de la réalité a la théorie économique; Pres., Société Canadienne de Science Economique 1968–71; Ligue d'Action Nationale. *Address:* 882 Victoria Street, St. Lambert, Montreal, P.Q., Canada.

**ANGERVO, Tauno Pietari.** Finnish. Jur. Lic.; Insurance Director. *B.* 1908. *Educ.* Jur Lic. *M.* 1935, Kaario Maire Mielikki. *S.* 2. *Daus.* 2. *Career:* Dir., Helsingin Suomalainen Säästöpankki 1934–40; Gen.-Mgr.: Postisäästopankki 1940–43; Finnish Insurance Cos. Assn. 1943–45; Man.-Dir. (1949–73) and Chmn. (1961—) Bd. Dirs. of Insurance Companies Vakuutusosakeyhtiö Pohjola, Tapaturmavakuutusosakeyhtiö Kullervo, Jälleenvakuutusosakeyhtiö Osmo; Member, Supervisory Bd., Kansallis-Osake-Pankki 1953—; Chmn., Bd. Dirs., Kajaani Oy 1956—; Chmn., Supervisory Bd., Oulu Oy 1973—; Vice-Chmn., Rauma-Repola Oy 1960—; Member, Supervisory Bd., Kauppiaitten Keskinäinen Vakuutusyhtiö 1960—; Chmn., Bd. Dirs., newspaper Uusi Suomi 1964—; Chmn., Supervisory Bd., Huhtamäki-Yhtymä 1974—; Vice-Chmn., Bd. Dirs., Eläkevakuutusosakeyhtiö Ilmarinen 1962–74; Chmn., Bd. Dirs., Keskeytysvakuutusosakeyhtiö Otso 1962—; Member, Supervisory Bd., Perusyhtymä Oy 1962—; Chmn., Bd. Dirs., Eurooppalainen Tavara- ja Matkatavaravakuutus Oy 1974—; Vice-Chmn., Supervisory Bd., Yhtyneet Paperitehtaat Oy 1974. Member, Bd. Dirs., Yrittäjäin Vakuutus keskinäinen yhtiö 1971—; *Member:* various State Cttees., administrative organs of various institutes, foundations, insurance and other assns., e.g., Finnish Cultural Foundation, Univs. of Helsinki and Turku, Internat. Chamber of Commerce, etc. *Publications:* articles on insurance and banking in professional journals. *Address:* Kartanontie 4, Helsinki 33.

**ANGLISS, Albert Reginald.** Australian. *B.* 1915. *Educ.* Melbourne Church of England Grammar School. *M.* 1939, Mary Jean Isobel Godley. *S.* Peter Ross. *Daus.* Janet Godley (Launder), Margaret Susan (Reid). *Career:* Man.-Dir., Jilpanger Pastoral Co. Pty. Ltd. 1937–49; Private Secy. and Com. Dir. 1949—; Chmn. of Trustees of estate of the late Sir William Charles Angliss and The William Angliss Charitable Trusts (Victoria and Queensland). Chmn. of Dirs., Investors Pty. Ltd., and of Clifton Brick Holdings Ltd. Group. Dir. Queensland Stations Ltd., Duke's & Orr's Dry Docks Ltd. (all since 1950). Member, Inst. of Directors (Australia). *Clubs:* Athenaeum; Royal Automobile of Victoria. *Address:* 18 Bates Street, East Malvern, Vic.; and *office* 500 Collins Street, Melbourne, Victoria, Australia.

**ANGUS, Edmund Graham,** CBE, MC, TD, DL, KStJ. Retired British company director. *B.* June 1889. *Educ.* Felsted School. *M.* 1922, Bridget Spencer (*Dec.* 1973). *S.* 3 (eldest officially presumed killed at Anzio; 2nd son decd.). *Dau.* 1. *Career:* Pres.: (Chmn. 1933–64), George Angus & Co. Ltd. and Newcastle upon Tyne Permanent Building Socy.; Pres., Newcastle & Gateshead Incorporated Chamber of Commerce 1951–55; Chmn., Venerable Order of St. John of Jerusalem, Council for Northumberland (relinquished 1954); served in World War I (France, MC) 1915–18; after war continedd to serve in Territorial Army (T.D. 1922); in Home Guard A.A. Group 1942–44; Army Cadet Force Commandant for Northumberland 1946–50. *Address:* Ravenstone, Corbridge, Northumberland.

**ANGUS, Melvyn Graham.** Canadian shipping director. *B.* 1911. *Educ.* Univ. of Toronto (BCom). *M.* 1936, Ada M. Hutchison. *S.* 1. *Daus.* 2. *Career:* Pres., Lunham & Moore Ltd. and Associated Companies, Montreal; Dir. and Past Pres., Canadian Shipowners Ass.; Dir., National Trust Co. Ltd.; Dir. Commercial Union Assurance Co. of Canada. Chmn. Montreal General Hospital Foundation; previously: with the Dominion Mortgage & Investments Assn., Toronto (Asst. Secy.-Treas. 1935) 1932–36; with brother in Angus & Co., Members Toronto and Montreal Stock Exchanges 1936–41; Dir., Clarke Ruse Aircraft Ltd., Nova Scotia 1941–45. *Clubs:* Mount Royal; St. James's; University; Mt. Bruno Country (Montreal); National (Toronto). *Address:* 699 Aberdeen Ave., Westmount, Que.; country residence, Hermitage Club Grounds, Lake Memphremagog, Quebec, Canada.

**ANKER, Christian Peder.** Norwegian. *B.* 1917. *Educ.* Oslo Commercial Coll. *M.* 1944, Sissel. *S.* 1. *Dau.* 1. *Career:* Dir., A/S Schreiner & Co.; Former Chmn. A/S Thunes-Eureka A/S Mesna Bruk; A/S Staal & Jern, A/S Andr; Gronneberg; A/S Schreiner & Co.; Sarpsborg; Chmn., Reps. Norvegia Insurance Co., Pallas Ins. Co., Norkreditt; Mem,. Cttee. Reps. A/S Atlantica and A/S Arcadia (Leif Höegh & Co.); Former Chmn. Bd. Norwegian Steel Merchant Assn;. Chmn., The Socy. of Welfare of Oslo Town; Former Chmn., A/S Moss Verft & Dokk; A/S Heramb Støperi & Mek Verksted; Royal Norwegian Yacht Club (Bd. Dirs.); Former Member Finance Cttee. & Cttee. Rep. Oslo Conservative Party; Former member Oslo Municipal Tax Committee; Mem., Cttee. Representatives Christiania Bank of Kreditkasse. *Club:* Royal Norwegian Yacht (Former mem., Bd. of Dirs.). *Address:* Holmenkollveien 135, Holmenkollen, Oslo 3, Norway; and *office* Marcus Thranesgt. 2, Oslo 4, Norway.

**ANNAN, The Rt. Hon. Lord (Noel Gilroy),** OBE, MA. British University administrator. *B.* 1916. *Educ.* Stowe School; Kings Coll., Cambridge (MA). *M.* 1950, Gabriele Ullstein. *Daus.* Amanda Lucy, Juliet Louise. *Career:* Served in War Office, War Cabinet Offices 1940–44; G.S.O.1, Political Div. of British Control Comm. 1945–46, France and Germany 1944–46; Asst. Tutor, King's Coll., Cambridge 1947, Fellow 1944–56; Univ. Lecturer in Politics, Cambridge 1948–66; Provost, King's Coll., Cambridge 1956–66; Provost, Univ. Coll., London since 1966. *Member:* Fellow Royal Historical Socy.; Trustee, British Museum. *Awards:* Commander, Royal Order, King George I of the Hellenes (Greece); Hon. DLitt, York Univ., Toronto; DUniv, Univ. of Essex. *Publications:* Leslie Stephen (1951); The Intellectual Aristocracy (1956); Kipling's Place in the History of Ideas (1964); The Curious Strength of Positivism in English Political Thought (1959); Roxburgh of Stowe (1965); articles in Victorian Studies and periodicals. *Address:* 10 Hanover Terrace, Regent's Park, London NW1 4RJ; and *office* University College, Gower Street, London, WC1E 6BT.

**ANNENBERG, Walter Hubert.** *B.* 1908. *Educ.* Milwaukee Univ. School; The Peddie School; Wharton School, Univ. of Pennsylvania; Hon. Degree Temple Univ. 1951; Hon. DHL, Penna. Military Coll. 1954, and Albert Einstein Coll. of Medicine; Hon. LLD, La Salle Coll. 1957; Dr. of Laws Degree, Univ. of Penna. 1966, and Dropsie Coll. 1968; Hon. LLD, Univ. of Southern California; LHD, Pennsylvania Coll. of Pediatric Medicine. *M.* 1951, Leonore Cohn. *Dau.* Wallis (by previous marriage). *Career:* Former Commander U.S. Naval Reserve. American Ambassador to the Court of St. James's 1969—. Stockholder and Dir., Triangle Publications Inc., Philadelphia, Pennsylvania. This company operates: T.V. Guide, weekly national magazine; Seventeen Magazine, monthly service; Daily Racing Form, daily newspapers, records recognized officially with thoroughbred racing in United States, Canada and Mexico; Pres., The M. L. Annenberg Foundation. The Annenberg Fund, Inc.

(charitable organizations), and Founder and Pres., The Annenberg School of Communications; Donor, Walter H. Annenberg Library and The Masters' House at the Peddie School, N.J.; Life Trustee, Univ. of Penn. Founder and Member, Bd. of Trustees, Eisenhower Exchange Fellowships Inc.; Trustee-at-large, Foundation for Independent Colleges, Inc.; Trustee Emeritus: Peddie School, Eisenhower Medical Centre; Trustee, Dermatology Foundation; Founder and Member, Bd. of Overseers of the Albert Einstein Coll. of Medicine, N.Y.C.; Founding Member, Business Cttee. for the Arts, Inc.; Dir., 1976 Bicentennial Observance Cttee., Philadelphia; Life Fellow, The Pennsylvania Acad. of Fine Arts; Member: Bd. of Corporators, The Peddie School; Bd. of Govs., Acad. of Food Marketing, St. Joseph's Coll.; Bd. of Trustees, United Fund, Philadelphia area; Phi Sigma Delta Fraternity; English-Speaking Union; Sigma Delta Chi Professional Journalistic Socy; American Newspaper Publishers Assn.; National Press Club; Overseas Press Club; International Press Inst.; Inter-American Press Assn. *Member:* Cum Laude Socy. (The Peddie School); The Friars Senior Socy. (Univ. of Penna.) *Awards:* Russell H. Conwell Award for outstanding citizenship, by Temple Univ.; Commonwealth of Pennsylvania Award for Excellence in Journalism; Samuel S. Fels Medal Award (1968); Humanitarian Award, Fed. of Jewish Agencies; Pennsylvania Meritorious Service Medal; "Man of the Year" Award (Delaware Valley Cncl.) 1964; Officer, French Legion of Honor; Cmdr., Order of the Crown of Italy; Cmdr., Order of Merit of the Italian Republic; Cmdr., Order of the Lion of Finland, Knight Commander, Order of the British Empire (1976). *Clubs:* Midday; Rittenhouse; Racquet; Faculty (Univ. of Pennsylvania); Hillcrest Country (Beverly Hills); Tamarisk Country (Palm Springs); Lyford Cay (Nassau, Bahamas); Century Country, White Plains and Lamb's (New York); Honorary Bencher Middle Temple, London; Turf; Whites; Buck's, (London); Swinley Forest Golf, Ascot. *Address:* 250 King of Prussia Rd, Radnor, Pennsylvania, U.S.A.

**ANNINO CAVALIERATO, Phedon.** *B.* 1912. *Educ.* Degree of Political Sciences of the Univ. of Athens. *M.* 1941, Maria Cantounias. *Career:* Attaché, Foreign Office, Athens 1936; Vice-Consul, Mansoura (Egypt) 1939; Second Secy. of Legation, Cairo 1942; First Secy.: Greek Embassy, Ankara 1944, and Moscow 1947; Head of Trade Affairs Dept., Ministry of Foreign Affairs, Athens 1948; Counsellor of Embassy, Washington 1950; Member, Greek Delegation to U.N. General Assembly, N.Y. 1957; Chief of Cabinet, Min. of For. Affairs, Athens 1958; Head of Western European Affairs 1959; Ambassador to Australia 1961–63; Dir.-Gen., Min. For. Affairs 1963–64; Ambassador to Bulgaria 1964; Under-Secy. State 1967; Head of Eastern European Affairs since 1967. *Awards:* Commander, Royal Order of George I, the Phoenix, etc. *Address:* Ministry for Foreign Affairs, Athens, Greece.

**ANSELL, Graham Keith.** New Zealand Diplomat. *B.* 1931. *Educ.* Victoria Univ. of Wellington, BA (Hons.). *M.* 1953, Mary Diana Wilson. *S.* 3. *Dau.* 1. *Career:* Dept. of Industries and Commerce, Wellington 1948–51; Dept. of External Affairs, Wellington 1951–56; 3rd, then 2nd Sec., N.Z. High Commission, Ottawa 1956–59; Asst., then Acting Head, FCOSOC Div., Min. of Foreign Affairs 1959–62; Dep. N.Z. High Commissioner, Apia 1962–64; Dep. N.Z. High Commissioner, Canberra 1964–68; Head, Economic Div., Min. of Foreign Affairs 1968–71; Minister, N.Z. Embassy, Tokyo 1971–73; N.Z. High Commissioner to Fiji and Nauru 1973–76; N.Z. Ambassador to Belgium, Luxembourg, Denmark and the European Communities since 1977. *Clubs:* University Club, Wellington; Chateau St. Anne, Brussels. *Address:* Avenue Mostinck 16, 1150 Woluwe St. Pierre, Brussels; and *office:* New Zealand Embassy, Boulevard du Regent 47–48, 1000 Brussels, Belgium.

**ANSETT, Sir Reginald,** KBE. Australian director and aviator. *B.* 1909. *Educ.* Swinburne Technical Coll., Melbourne. *M.* 1944, Joan McA. Adams. *Career:* Chmn. and Man.-Dir.: Ansett Transport Industries Ltd.; Ansett Hotels Pty. Ltd.; Austarama Television Pty. Ltd.; Universal Telecasters (Qld.) Ltd.: Ansett Brewarrana Holdings Pty. Ltd; Ansett Niugini Enterprises Ltd.; Transport Industries Ins. Co. Ltd.; Sist Constructions Pty. Ltd.; Ansett Transport Industries (Operations) Pty. Ltd. Company trade names, Ansett Airlines of Australia, Ansett Airlines of South Australia, Ansett Airlines of New South Wales, Ansett Pioneer, Ansett Freight Express, Aviation Engineering Supplies, N.I.C. Instrument Co., MacRobertson Miller Airlines Services, Ansett Motors, Provincial Motors; Mildura Bus Lines; Ansair, Ansett General Aviation; Ansett Television Films; Wridgways Australia; Albury Border Transport; P.E. Power (Wagga); Pyrometric Service and Supplies; Cooper Airmotive Australia; Dir. Diners Club Ltd., Dir. Biro Bic (Australia) Pty. Ltd.; Dir. Associated Securities Ltd. *Clubs:* Mornington Racing (Chmn.); Victoria Racing; Victoria Amateur Turf; Moonee Valley Racing; Victorian. *Address:* 489 Swanston Street, Melbourne, Vic., and 'Gunyong Valley', Mount Eliza, Vic., Australia.

**ANSIAUX, Baron (Hubert Jacques Nicolas).** Belgian banker. *B.* 1908. *Educ.* Free Univ. of Brussels. *M.* 1938, Mayer-Astruc Genevieve Myrian-Alice. *S.* 1. *Dau.* 1. *Career:* Hon. Governor National Bank Belgium, Dir., 1941–54; Deputy Governor 1954–57; Governor 1957–71; Mem. of Bd. of Bank for International Settlements 1957. Canadian Imperial Bank of Commerce Toronto 1971 and Petrofina Brussels 1972; Chmn. Intra-European Payments Cttee of OEEC 1947–55; Mem. European Payments Union Mngn. Board 1950–55; Chmn. Cttee of Central Banks Governors of EEC 1967–71; Gov. for Belgium International Monetary Fund 1957–71; Mem. of Gen. Motors Europ. Advisory Council, London since 1974. *Awards:* Grand Officer, Order of Leopold, 1970; Grand Officer, Order of the Crown, 1961 (both Belgium); Grand Cross, Order of Orange Nassau 1971 (Netherlands); Grand Cross Order de Merite du Grand-Duché de Luxembourg, 1971; Grand Officer Order of Civil and Military Merit of Adolf of Nassau, 1562; Grand Officer of the Oak Crown, 1963 (all Luxembourg); Grand Officer Order of Merit, 1956 (Syria); Commander Royal Order of St. Olav, 1950 (Norway); Commander Order of Merit, 1953 (Italy); Grand Officer Royal Order of George I, 1966 (Greece); Commander Legion of Honour, 1966 (France); MBE; Medal of Freedom with Silver Palm (U.S.A.); Knight Commander of Most Exalted Order of White Elephant, 1969 (Thailand). *Address:* Le Bois Tranquille, Dreve Pittoresque 109, 1180 Brussels, Belgium.

**ANTHONY, Rt. Hon. John Douglas,** MHR (Richmond, Sept. 1957—). *B.* 1929. *Educ.* Queensland Diploma of Agriculture. *M.* 1957, Margot Budd. *S.* Dugald, Larry. *Dau.* Jane. *Career:* Min. for the Interior Mar. 1964–67; Minister Primary Industry 1967–71; Leader Aust. Country Party since 1971 (called Nat. Country Party of Australia since 1975); Deputy Prime Minister, Minister for Trade and Industry 1971–72; Dep. Prime Minister, Minister for National Resources & Overseas Trade 1975—. *Address:* "Sunny Meadows", Murwillumbah, N.S.W.; and Parliament House, Canberra, A.C.T., Australia.

**ANTHONY, Julian Danford.** *B.* 1907. *Educ.* Wesleyan Univ. (AB 1928); Northeastern Univ. (LLB 1943). *M.* 1932, Eleanor Hopkins. *S.* J. Danford, Jr., Stephen H., Cushman D. *Dau.* Caroline (Smith). *Career:* With Old Colony Corp., Boston 1928–30; Asst. Treas., Massachusetts General Trust 1930–31; with Columbian National Life Insurance Co. 1931 (name changed June 1960 to Hartford Life Insurance Co.): Asst. Treas. 1934–44, Vice-Pres. 1945–47, Pres. 1947–67; Dir. and former Pres.: Hartford Life Insurance Co., Hartford, Conn.; Dir., New England Merchants National Bank 1948—; Trustee, Wesleyan Univ., Andover Newton Theological School (and Vice-Chmn. of Bd.); Trustee Children's Hospital Medical Center, and Newton Wellesley Hospital; Pres., Mass. Congregational Fund; Dir and Treas., Greater Boston Y.M.C.A.; Trustee, National Board of Y.M.C.A.s. *Address:* 45 Devon Road, Newton Centre, Mass.; and *office* 2 Center Plaza, Boston, Mass., U.S.A.

**ANTONIOZZI, Dario,** Italian Member of Parliament. *B.* 1923. *M.* 1950. *S.* 3. *Career:* Member of Parliament since 1953; Under-Secretary of State 1958–72; Member of the European Parliament since 1972; Vice-Secretary of the National Christian Democrats since 1975; Vice-President of the Partito Popolore Europeo since 1976. *Address:* Camera dei Deputati, 00100 Rome, Italy.

**ANUTA, Michael J(oseph).** American lawyer. *B.* 1902. LLD Alma (Michigan) Coll. *M.* 1921, Marianne Mildred Strelec. *S.* Michael John, Karl Frederic. *Daus.* Mary Hope (Milidonis), Nancy Ellen (Beauchamp), Janet Grace (Lloyd John Dalquist). *Career:* Partner, Law Office Anuta, Minerman and Redpath; Admitted to Michigan Bar 1929; Interstate Commerce Comm., 1929; U.S. Supreme Court 1932; Prosecuting Attorney, Menominee County 1939–48; Circuit Court Commissioner 1950–54; Municipal Judge, City of Menominee 1959–68; Pres., Nicolet Area Council, Boy Scouts of America 1945–46 (awarded Silver Beaver 1941, Silver Antelope 1967); Lieut.-Col. Michigan Wing, Civil Air Patrol

(Retired); Menominee Rotary Club (Pres. 1934–35); Gov. District 622 Rotary International 1963–64. *Member:* American Bar Assn., Michigan State Bar Assn., Menominee County Bar Assn. (Pres. 1957–61); Mich. Prosecuting Attorneys Assn. (Pres. 1946); Moderator, Lake Superior Presbytery 1945–46; Lay Delegate to World Presbyterian Alliance 1954; Moderator, Synod of Michigan, Presbyterian Church in U.S.A. 1953–54; Mason 33° (Shriner); Order of Purple Cross, 1976. *Address:* RA 655, Westland, Menominee, Michigan 49858; and *office* 960 First Street, Menominee, Mich., U.S.A.

**APODACA, Jerry.** American State Governor. *B.* 1934. *Education:* Univ. of New Mexico, BSc. *M.* 1956, Clara Melendres Apodaca. *S.* 2. *Daus.* 3. *Career:* History teacher and football and track coach, Valley High School (Albuquerque) 1957–60; Owner Jerry Apodaca Ins. Agency, and Realty, also Pres., Family Shoe Store of N.M. since 1960. New Mexico State Senator, rep. Dona Ana Cnty 1966–74; Governor of New Mexico 1974. *Address:* Governor's Residence, Mansion Dr., Sante Fe, New Mexico 87501; and *office:* Governor's Office, Executive-Legislative Building, Santa Fe, New Mexico 87503.

**APPLETON, Clarence Norman.** Canadian. *B.* 1895. *Educ.* Fellow, Chartered Inst. of Secretaries. *M.* 1948, Lulu Capner (*Dec.* 1976). *Career:* with Massey-Harris Co. Ltd. and Massey-Harris-Ferguson Ltd. 1910–56; Dir.: Chmn., Bd. of Governors, Queensway General Hospital, Toronto 1956–71, Hon. Chmn. since 1972; Chmn., Canadian Manufacturers Assn., Ontario Div. 1953–54. *Member:* Chartered Inst. of Secretaries. *Clubs:* National; St. George's Golf & Country (both of Toronto). *Address:* 52 Ridgevalley Crescent, Islington, M9A 3J6, Ont., Canada.

**APPLEY, Lawrence A.** American. *B.* 1904. *Educ.* Ohio Wesleyan Univ. (BA 1927). *M.* 1927, Ruth Wilson (*Dec.*). *Daus.* Ruth Ann Cohen, Judith Schatz. *Career:* Educational Dir., Mobil Oil Co. Inc., for Domestic and Foreign Operations 1930–41; Vice-Pres. i/c of Personnel, and Dir. of Vick Chemical Co. (now Richardson-Merrell, 1941–46; Vice-Pres. and Dir., Montgomery Ward & Co. 1946–48; Chmn. Bd., American Management Assn. 1968–74, (Pres. 1948–68), Chmn. Emeritus since 1974. *Awards:* Medal of Merit by the President of the United States 1946; LLD Colgate, St. Lawrence, and Ohio Wesleyan Univs.; and Bethany Coll.; LitD, Bryant Coll. 1970; Henry Laurence Gantt Memorial Medal 1963; Taylor Key Award 1961; Human Relations Medal of the Socy. for the Advancement of Management 1952; "Man of the Year" Award (Foreign Trade Socy. of CCNY) 1964. The Horatio Alger Award 1971. *Member:* New York Personnel Management Assn. (Life Member); Socy. for the Advancement of Management; New York Personnel Management Assn. (Life Member); Socy. for the Advancement of Management; Amer. Socy. for Mech. Engrs.; International Acad. of Management (Fellow); Pres. and Dir., American Morgan Horse Assn. 1970–75. *Publications:* Management the Simple Way (1943); Management in Action (1956); The Management Evolution (1963); Values in Management (1969); A Manager's Heritage (1970); Formula for Success. *Address:* Box 125, West Lake Moraine Road, Hamilton 13346 N.Y.; and *office* Box 88, Hamilton, N.Y., U.S.A.

**APPLEYARD, Raymond Kenelm.** British Scientist. *B.* 1922. *Educ.* Rugby & Cambridge (BA 1943, MA 1944, PhD 1949). *M.* 1947. Joan Greenwood. *S.* 1. *Daus.* 2. *Career:* Instructor, Yale Univ. 1949–51; Fellow, Rockefeller Foundation 1951–53; Research Officer, Atomic Energy of Canada Ltd., 1953–56; Secretary, U.N. Scientific Cttee. on Effects of Atomic Radiation 1956–61; Director, Biology Div. of EURATOM 1961–73; Exec. Sec., European Molecular Biology Org. 1965–73 & Sec., European Molecular Biology Conference 1969–73; Dir.-Gen. for Scientific & Technical Information & Information Management, Commission of the European Communities since 1973. *Publications:* Articles in Nature, Jnl. of General Microbiology, Genetics etc. *Clubs:* The Athenaeum, London; Chateau Ste. Anne, Brussels. *Address:* 5a Avenue Grand Air, 1640 St Genesius-Rode, Belgium; & 72 Boulevard Napoleon, Luxemburg; and *office* Bâtiment Jean Monnet, Rue Alcide de Gasperi, Plateau du Kirchberg, Luxemburg.

**ARANA OSORIO, Brig.-General Carlos Manuel.** Ex-President of Guatamala. *B.* 1918. *Education:* Polytechnic School, cadet trooper. *M.* Alida Espana Esquivel. *S.* 2. *Daus.* 3. *Career:* Army, commissioned 1939; 2nd Lieut (infantry) 1939; Lieut. 1942; Captain 1945; Major 1949; Lieut-Colonel 1952; (various positions as Master of Roads, Asst Secy, Asst Engineer, Dir. of Polytechnic School, and in command of infantry regiment); Colonel (infantry), Dir. of Polytech. School, 1st under-secy. Min. Nat. Defence, Attaché Nat. Defence, Military Attaché to Guatemala Embassy (USA), Hgtrs. Gen Justo Rufino Barrios Military Zone, Commander Gen. Aguilar Santa Maria Military Zone, Commander Capitan General Rafael Carrera Military Brigade Zacapa, all between 1955–68; Ambassador Extr. and Plenipotentiary of Guatamala in Nicaragua 1968–69; Constitutional President of Guatamala and General Officer commanding Army 1970–74. Brigadier-General since 1973. *Member:* Numerous commissions in Uruguay, Mexico and USA; Supreme Court of Justice (military member). *Decorations:* Several medals between 1952 and 1967, Diploma (Corps of Defenders of Mexican Rep.); Foreign Chains, Cordons Crosses and awards from Panama, Nicaragua, Chinese Republic, El Salvador, Honduras, Sweden, Malta; Grand Chain of Quetzal Order, Grand Chain, Order of Antonio Jose de Irissari and Grand Cross, gold badge, of the Order of the Five Volcanoes (all Guatamala). *Address:* 11 Avenida 19–49, Zona 14, Guatemala City, Guatemala.

**ARANYOS, Alexander Sandor.** International Operations Executive. *B.* 1909. *Educ.* Degree in Commercial Engineering; *cum laude* Graduate, School of Commerce, Univ. of Prague *M.* 1937, Gertrude Reisman. *S.* 1. *Dau.* 1. *Career:* Coburg mining and foundry company, Bratislava, Czechoslovakia 1933–40; Administrative Asst. to Pres. and Export Mgr.; Mgr. Import Div. Gen. Motors Distributors, Republic of Panama 1940–41; Mgr.. Latin Amer. Div Van Raalte Co. N.Y.C. 1945–53; Fruehauf Corp., Detroit 1953—; Vice-Pres., International Operations 1956—; Pres. and Dir., Fruehauf International Ltd. 1957—; Chmn. 1976—; Bd. Dir. Fruehauf Corp. 1973—; Administrative Council Viaturas FNV-Fruehauf S.A., Sao Paulo; Dir., Fruehauf Trailers (Australasia) Pty. Ltd.; Fruehauf Finance Corp. Pt. Ltd. Melbourne; (Austr.); Crane Fruehauf Ltd., Hayes, Middlesex, England; Fruehauf France, S.A. Ris-Orangis, France; Fruehauf de Mexico, S.A. Coacalco, Mexico; Nippon Fruehauf Co. Ltd., Tokyo, Japan; NETAM, N.V. Nederlandsche Tank Apparaten- en Machine-fabriek, Rotterdam, Netherlands; Henred-Fruehauf Trailers (Pty.) Ltd., Johannesburg, Rep. of S. Africa; Fruehauf S.A. Madrid, Spain; Forss-Parator AB, Huskvarna, Sweden; Chmn. RenTco Europe B.V., Netherlands; Assoc.-Dir., Clyde Industries Ltd., Sydney, Australia. *Member:* Research Inst. of Amer.; Amer. Inst. of Management; Detroit Bd. of Commerce; Regional Export Expansion Council, U.S. Dept. of Commerce 1970–73; Chamber Commerce U.S. Int. Cttee.; World Trade Club of Detroit; International Executives Assn. N.Y. *Clubs:* Rotary (NY); Rockefeller Center Luncheon (N.Y.C.); Detroit Athletic. *Address:* 2 Bridle Lane, Sands Point, N.Y. 11050, and *office* 10900 Harper Avenue, Detroit, Mich. 48232, and 30 Rockefeller Plaza, New York, N.Y. 10020, U.S.A.

**ARBUTHNOT, Sir John Sinclair-Wemyss, Bt, MBE, TD.** *B.* 1912. *Educ.* Eton; Trinity Coll., Cambridge (BA Hons. in Natural Sciences 1933, MA 1938). *M.* 1943, Margaret Jean Duff. *S.* 2. *Daus.* 3. *Career:* Worked in the Tea Industry; Conservative Candidate: Don Valley Div. of Yorkshire 1934–35, Dunbartonshire 1936–44, and Dover Div. of Kent 1945–50; served in World War II (Major R.A.); Dep. Inspector of Shell; M.P. (Dover 1950–64); Member, Church Assembly (C. of E.) 1955–70; General Synod member 1970–75; panel of Chmn. 1970–72; Chmn., The Folkestone and District Water Co. and Dir., Ecclesiastical Insurance Office Ltd.; Mem., Exec. Council, Water Companies Association 1976—; A Church Commissioner for England 1965–77; Vice-Chmn., Assets Cttee. 1968–77; National Vice-Pres., Trustee Savings Banks Assn. 1961–66; Chmn. of Cttees. and Temporary Chmn. of the House of Commons 1958–64; Second Church Estates Commissioner 1962–64; Chmn., Archbishop of Canterbury's Comm. on reorganization of diocesan boundaries in S.E. England 1965–67; Member of Public Accounts Cttee. 1955–64; P.P.S. Min. of Pensions 1952–55, and. Min. of Health 1956–57; Member of Parly. Delegations to West Africa 1956, to U.S.A. 1957, to Zanzibar, Mauritius and Madagascar 1961; Leader of Parly. Delegation to Bulgaria 1963; Joint Hon.-Secy. Assn. of British Chambers of Commerce 1953–59; Member, Standing Cttee. of the Ross Inst. 1951–62. *Fellow:* Royal Commonwealth Society. *Club:* Carlton. *Address:* Poulton Manor Ash, Canterbury, CT3 2HW and 7 Fairholt Street, London, SW7 1EG.

**ARCAINI, Dr. Giuseppe.** Italian executive. *B.* 1901. *M.* Giannina Ghisalberti. *S.* 3. *Daus.* 3. *Career:* Previously Under-Secy. of State to the Treasury; Dir.-Gen., dell'**Istituto di Credito delle Casse di Risparmio Italiane (Credit**

Inst. for Italian Savings Banks); Counsellor of Administration, Istituto di Credito per le Imprese di Pubblica Utilità (Credit Inst. for Public Utility Companies), Consorzio di Credito per le Opere Pubbliche (Credit Trust for Public Works); Finsider, and Metanodotti Factory SNAM; AGIP; Pres. Assn. Bancario Italiana. *Awards:* Knight, Order of St. Agatha (San Marino); Cavaliere Gr. Cr. al Merito della Republica, Christian Democrat. *Publications:* Aspetti tecnici ed umani della funzione del dirigente bancario (Technical and human aspects of the work of a bank manager). *Address:* Via San Bassiano, 8, Lodi (Milan); and *office* 15 Via San Basilio, Rome, Italy.

**ARCHAMBAULT, Bennett.** American industrial executive. *Educ.* Massachusetts Inst. of Technology (BSC). *M.* 1948, Margaret Henrietta Morgan. *S.* Steven Bennett. *Daus.* Suzanne Morgan, Michele Lorraine. *Career:* Vice-Pres. and Gen.-Man., The M. W. Kellogg Co. to June 1954; in charge of activities in European Theatre of Operations, U.S. Office of Scientific Research and Development 1942–45; Chmn. Bd. and Pres., Stewart-Warner Corp.; Chmn. Bd., Stewart-Warner Corp. of Canada Ltd., Stewart-Warner Ltd.; Pres. Thor Power Tool Co.; Dir. American Motorists Insurance Co., Lumbermen's Mutual Casualty Co.; Harris Bankcorp Inc.; Kemper Corp. Inc.; Trans Union Corp.; Federal Kemper Insurance Co.; Harris Trust & Savings Bank; American Manufacturers Mutual Ins. Co.; Medal of Merit (U.S.A.); His Majesty's Medal for Service in the Cause of Freedom (U.K.); Trustee, Illinois Inst. of Technology; Museum of Science and Industry; Trustee, IIT Research Institute; Mem. Advisory Board Illinois Mfrs. Assn.; Member, Corporation Development Cttee Massachusetts Inst. of Technology; Dir., Chicago Chapter, Amer. Defense Preparedness Association; Dir.: The Employers' Assn. of Greater Chicago; Former Mem., Exec. Cttee, Nat. Assn. of Manufacturers; Republican. *Member:* Socy. of Automotive Engineers; Research Socy. of America; The Newcomen Socy. in North America. *Clubs:* Chicago: The Chicago; Westmoreland Country; Saddle & Cycle; The Racquet; Executives'; The Commercial Club of Chicago; Metropolitan; Economic. *Address:* 1826 West Diversey Parkway, Chicago, Ill. 60614, U.S.A.

**ARCHER, Peter Kingsley,** PC, QC, BA, LLM, MP. British. Politician, Advocate. *B.* 1926. *Educ.* Wednesbury High School; London School of Economics; Univ. Coll., London. *M.* 1954, Margaret Irene Smith. *S.* John Kingsley. *Career:* Practising Barrister since 1954; Vice-Chmn., Amnesty International (Brit. Section), 1965, Chmn. 1971–74; M.P. for Rowley Regis and Tipton 1966–74, & for Warley West since 1974; Parly. Private Secy. to Attorney General 1967–70; Chmn.. Parly. Group for World Government 1970–74; Chmn., Socy. of Labour Lawyers 1971–74; Privy Councillor; Bencher, Grays Inn; Solictor-General since 1974. *Publications:* Social Welfare and The Citizen (1967); The Queen's Courts (1956); Communism and the Law (1963); Freedom At Stake (1966); Human Rights (1969); (Joint Author) Purpose in Socialism (1973). *Address:* 44 Clements Road, Chorleywood, Herts.; and *office* House of Commons, London, S.W.1.

**ARCHIBALD, Arnold Adams.** American steel executive (ret.). *B.* 1905. *Educ.* Massachusetts Inst. of Technology (BSc). *M.* 1937, Clara West Butler. *S.* Lewis Edgar II, Roger Williams, John Baird. *Career:* With Jones & Laughlin Steel Corp. 1935–70; with War Production Bd., Washington, D.C. 1942–44 and 1945; with Civilian Production Administration, Washington 1946–47; Vice-Pres., Jones & Laughlin Steel Corp. 1954–65; Administrative Vice-Pres. 1965–70. *Member:* American Iron & Steel Inst. *Clubs:* Duquesne (Pittsburgh, Pa.); Union (Cleveland, O.). *Address:* 1327 Coraopolis Heights Road, Coraopolis, Pa., U.S.A.

**ARCHIBALD, Frederick Ratcliffe.** American consulting metallurgist. *B.* 1905. *Educ.* Queen's (MA Chem.); Professional Engineer, Ontario. *M.* 1928, Doris P. Kindree. *Daus.* Doreen (Messenger), Ruth (Laffey). *Career:* Research Chemist to Dir. of Research, Ventures Ltd. and Assoc. Companies 1934–42; Chief Engr., Metal Hydrides Inc. 1942–44; Tech. Dir., Ancor Corp. 1944–47; Chemical Engr., Oliver Iron Mining Co. 1947–50; Chief Metallurgist to Vice-Pres., Metallurgy and Research, Falconbridge Nickel Mines Ltd. 1951–70; Consultant since 1971. *Publications:* various technical publications and patents in Canada and U.S.A. *Member:* Canadian Inst. Min. and Met.; Inst. Min. and Met. (London); Amer. Inst. Min. and Met. Engrs.: Amer. Chemical Socy. *Clubs:* Engineers, Toronto; Moorings Golf and Country Club, Naples, Fla. *Address:* P.O. Box 8117, Naples, Florida 33941, U.S.A.

**ARCHIBALD, Paul A.** American. *B.* 1911. *Educ.* Massachusetts Inst. of Technology and Colorado School of Mines (EMet. 1935). *M.* 1934, Ellamay Gaddis. *S.* Robert T. *Daus.* Janice A. (Goss), Carol A. *Career:* Metallurgist: U.S.Steel Corp. 1935–37, and Denver & Rio Grande Western Railroad 1937–41; Research Metallurgist, Standard Steel Works 1941–49; Chief Metallurgist, Standard Steel Div., Baldwin-Lima-Hamilton Corp., Burnham, Pa. since 1949. *Publications:* technical papers on metallurgy of forgings and castings for railway, heavy machinery, marine and aerospace. *Member:* Tau Beta Pi; Sigma Gamma Epsilon; Scabbard and Blade; Amer. Socy. for Testing Metals (Dir. 1958–61); Amer. Socy. for Metals; British Iron & Steel Inst.; Iron & Steel Inst. of Japan; Amer. Socy. of Mechanical Engineers; Amer. Inst. of Mining & Petroleum Engineers; Amer. Ordnance Assn.; Socy. of Automotive Engineers; Masonic Orders. *Clubs:* Lewistown Country; Engineers (of Western Penna.); Elks. *Address:* Church Hill Manor, Reedsville, Pa.; and *office* Standard Steel Division, Baldwin-Lima-Hamilton Corp., Burnham, Pa., U.S.A.

**ARCHIBALD, Raymond Douglas.** Canadian Barrister & Solicitor. *B.* 1921. *Educ.* BA; LLB; read law with Estey, Moxon & Schmidt of Saskatoon; called to Bar of Saskatchewan 1945. *M.* 1945, Jocelyn Fallis Yule. *S.* 1. *Dau.* 2. *Career:* Manufacturer's agent in Saskatchewan (summers) 1939–41; served in World War II (Calgary Tank Regt. and Canadian Grenadier Guards as Lieut., wounded in action at Falaise 1944); Secy., Dominion Textile Co. Ltd. 1951; Vice-Pres. Gen Mgr., Caldwell Linen Mills Ltd. 1960; Partner, firm of Lang, Michener, Cranston, Farquharson & Wright, Toronto since 1976; Member of the Duke of Edinburgh's Study Conference, Oxford 1956; Law Socy. of Saskatchewan; Law Socy. of Upper Canada. *Address:* Box 10, First Canadian Place, Toronto, Canada M5X 1A2.

**ARCULUS, Ronald.** CMG, BA. British diplomat. *B.* 1923. *Educ.* Solihull; Exeter Coll.; Oxford (BA). *M.* 1953, Sheila Mary Faux. *S.* 1. *Dau.* 1. *Career:* Capt. 4th Queen's Own Hussars (now Queen's Royal Irish) 1942–45; Joined HM Diplomatic Service Foreign Office 1947; San Francisco 1948; La Paz 1950; F.O. 1951; Ankara 1953; F.O. 1957; Washington 1961; Counsellor 1965; New York 1965–68; Imperial Defence College 1969; F.C.O. 1970; Minister (Economic), Paris 1973; Ambassador and Leader UK Delegation to Conference on the Law of the Sea, 1977. *Awards:* Companion, Order of St. Michael & St. George. *Club:* Cavalry. *Address:* c/o Lloyds Bank Limited, Cox's & King's Branch, Guards and Cavalry Section, 6 Pall Mall, London, S.W.1.

**ARENA, Andrea.** Italian Doctor of Law and Doctor of Economics and Commerce. *B.* 1905. *M.* 1927, Concettina Lo Cascio. *Career:* Marine and Commercial lawyer; Staff Prof. in Commercial Law, Univ. of Palermo; Member of the Comm. which arranged the 1942 Navigation Code; former Mgr.. Banco di Sicilia. *Publications:* 120+ publications on marine and commercial law. *Clubs:* Rotary (Palermo); Borsa (Messina); Unione (Palermo). *Address:* Largo Abeti 10, Palermo and Via Francesco Crispi 8, Messina, Italy.

**ARENBERG, Gerald S.** American. *B.* 1930. *Educ.* National Law Enforcement Acad. (BS); Philathia Coll., London, Ontario, Canada (Hon. LLD). *Career:* Chief of Police, Golf, Illinois 1955–60; Dir., Police Hall of Fame 1960–66; Editor, Valor Magazine; Editor-in-Chief, Police Times Magazine; Trustee, National Law Enforcement Academy 1966—; Executive Dir.: American Federation of Police 1966—; World Police Congress since 1968. *Member:* American Assn. of Criminology; American Fed. of Police; World Police Congress; American Secy. of Assn. Executives; Internat. Police Association. *Awards:* Distinguished Service Medal, State of Illinois; Grand Cross, Panama Foundation; Knight, Order of Constantine; Honour Awards, Amer. Assn. of Criminology. *Address:* 1100 NE 125th St., North Miami, Fla. 33161, U.S.A.

**ARENSBERG, Conrad M.** American anthropologist-sociologist. *B.* 1910. *Educ.* Harvard Coll. (BA 1931); Harvard Univ. (PhD, Social Anthropology). *M.* 1935, Margaret Jacklin Walsh. *S.* Cornelius Wright. *Daus.* Emily Maynadier, Margaret Farrell. *Career:* Junior Fellow, Harvard Univ. 1934–37; Asst. Prof., Dept. of Economics and Social Science; Member (research), Industrial Relations Section, Massachusetts Inst. of Technology 1937–40; Assoc. Prof., Chmn., Dept. of Sociology and Anthropology, Brooklyn Coll. 1940–42; U.S. Army 1942–46; Assoc. Prof., Chmn., Dept. of Sociology, Barnard Coll., Columbia Univ. 1946–53; Prof., Dept. of Anthropology 1953— (Chmn. 1956–59); Dir. for Research, Unesco Inst. for the Social Sciences, Cologne 1950–

52. Prof. of Anthropology, Columbia Univ., N.Y. since 1953 (teaching: Old World Europe, Middle Eastern, Indian ethnology; community studies method and contributions to social and cultural anthropology, cultural universals and comparative social structure, comparative institutions, applied anthropology). *Publications:* The Irish Countryman (1937); American Communities (1955); The Community Study Method (1953); Trade and Markets in the Early Empires—Economics in History and in Theory (with Karl Polanyi and Harry W. Pearson) (1957); Measuring Human Relations (with Eliot D. Chapple) (1940); Family and Community in Ireland (with Solon T. Kimball) (1940); Behaviour and Organization—Industrial Studies (in Social Psychology at the Cross Roads; ed. John Rohrer and Muzafer Sherif) (1952); Plant Sociology—Discoveries and Real Problems (with Geoffrey Tootel, in Common Frontiers of the Social Sciences; ed. Mirra Komarovsky) (1957); Industrial Human Relations Research (editor, contributor, with Barkin, Chalmers, Worthy) (1957); The Determination of Morale (with Douglas McGregor) (1942); Introducing Social Change (with Arthue Niehoff) (1964); Culture and Community (with Solon T. Kimball) (1965). *Clubs:* St. Botolph (Boston); Harvard (N.Y.C.). *Address:* Compton, Trappe, Md.; and 456 Schermerhorn Hall, Columbia Univ., New York City 27, U.S.A.

**ARFA, Hassan.** Iranian Army General, politician and diplomat; *B.* 1895. *Educ.* Military Colls. in Turkey, Switzerland and France; Ecole Supérieure de Guerre, Paris. *Career:* Commissioned 1914; Platoon Comdr. 1914; Squadron Comdr. 1920; Cavalry Group Comdr. 1925; Military Attaché in London 1926; Comdr. 1st Guards Cavalry Regt. 1931; Aide-de-Camp to the late Reza Shah 1931; Comdr., Military Acad. 1932; Inspector-Gen. of Cavalry 1936; Lecturer on tactics at staff coll. 1936; Dep. Chief of Staff 1942; Aide-de-Camp to H.M. Mohammed Reza Shah 1942; Chief, Intelligence Dept. of the Army 1942; Comdr., Teheran Training Centre 1942; Comdr. 1st Army Div. 1942; Gov. of roads, railways and ports 1943; Chief of Staff, Iranian Army 1943–46; retired 1947; Leader of Asiatic Group 1947; Leader of National Movement Party 1951; Min. of Communications 1951; Ambassador to Turkey 1958–61; accredited to Greece 1958–59; Ambassador to Pakistan 1961–63; accredited to Ceylon 1962; Vice-Pres., Iran-Pakistan Cultural Association 1971. *Awards:* Order of Homayun (1st Class); Order of Rastakhiz (1st Class); Royal Order of Phoenix (1st Class); several military medals. *Publications:* Under Five Shahs; The Kurds; numerous military manuals and articles in military magazines. *Address:* Larak, Niaveran, Teheran, Iran.

**ARGALL, George O., Jr.** Mining Engineer. *B.* 1913. *Educ.* Colorado School of Mines (BS Eng. of Mines). *M.* 1940, Patricia Haley. *Dau.* Joan. *Career:* Mine Supt., Highland Mary Mines Inc., Silverton, Colo. 1937; Engineer Open Pit Foreman, Mine shift boss, U.S. Vanadium Corp. Bishop, Calif. 1938–40; Mine Foreman, U.S. Vanadium Corp. Rifle, Colo. 1941; Supervising Engineer, Reconstruction Finance Corp. 1942–44; Lieut., Civil Engineers Corps., U.S. Naval Reserve (service in U.S. and S. Korea) 1944–46; Supervising Engineer, Recon. Finance Corp., Denver 1946–47; Consulting Engineer, Denver, Colo. 1948–49; Editor, Mining World 1950–63, World Mining 1950—; Publisher since 1974. *Member*, Alumni Advisory Council to Bd. of Trustees of Colorado School of Mines 1961—. *Publications:* Occurrence and Production of Vanadium; Industrial Minerals of Colorado; numerous articles to technical journals. *Member:* Mining & Metallurgical Socy. of America; Colorado Mining Assn.; Nevada Mining Assn.; Northwest Mining Assn., AIME. *Address:* (European *office*) 123a chaussée de Charlreoi, Brussels 6, Belgium; (Headquarter *office*) 500 Howard Street, San Francisco, California, U.S.A.

**ARIK, Haluk N.** Turkish mechanical and aeronautical engineer. *B.* 1917. *Educ.* MS in Mechanical Engineering; BS in Aeronautical Engineering. *M.* Rabia Arik. *S.* Pinar. *Dau.* Deniz. *Career:* Asst. Gen. Dir., Turkish State Airlines 1953–54; Chief, Factories Div., Maintenance Directorate, Turkish Air Force 1951–53; Dir., Civil Aviation Dept., Ministry of Communications, Turkey; Min. of Communications since 1971. *Publications:* several technical articles; an official report on jet engines and aircraft. *Address:* 98 Serdar Street, Yenimahalle, Ankara; and *office* Min. of Communications, Ankara, Turkey.

**ARKELL, Capt. Sir (Thomas) Noël, DL.** Joint Man.-Dir., J. Arkell & Sons Ltd. (Brewers, Swindon, Wilts.); Member, Bath Bd. of Royal Insurance Co., Ltd. *B.* Dec. 25th 1893. *Educ.* Bradfield Coll., Berks. *M.* 1919, Olive Arscott Quick. *S.* James William, MC and Bar (killed in action in Indonesia 1946), Peter, Anthony Graham. *Daus.* Pamela (McGrath), Anne Elizabeth (Goodrich), Rosemary (Johnston). *Career:* High Sheriff of Wiltshire (1953); Mem., Nat. Exec. of Conservative Party 1933–38; Knighted 1937; Chmn., Swindon Conservative Assn. 1927–53; Past Chmn., Wessex Area Assn.; joined 4th Btn. Wiltshire Regt. (T.F.) 1912, served in World War I (wounded three times) 1914–18. *Address:* Hillcrest, Highworth, Wilts.

**ARLING, Leonard Swenson,** MD. *B.* 1910. *Educ.* Univ. of Minnesota (BS 1933, MB 1934, MD 1936); Harvard (MD 1969). *M.* 1938, Marion Arline Schroeder. *S.* Bryan Jeremy. *Daus.* Heather Marion (Greenagel), Pamela Jill (Simmons). *Career:* In medical practice, Minneapolis 1936–44; limited to Occupational Medical Services since 1944 with founding of the Northwest Industrial Clinic; Pres., The Northwest Industrial Clinic, Minneapolis, Minn. 1944—; Secy., Industrial Medical Assn. of America 1957–61; Medical Dir., Twin-City Assembly Plant, Ford Div., Ford Motor Co.; staff appointments at the Swedish Hospital (Past Chief of Staff), Minneapolis, and Mid-way Hospital, St. Paul; Member, Governor's Advisory Cttee. on Employment of the Handicapped 1948–55, and of the Bd. of the United Hospital Fund of Minneapolis and Hennepin County; Regional Consultant, R.R. Retirement Board 1947—; Member, Bd. of Dirs. of Junior Achievement of Minneapolis and Hennepin County 1964—. *Member:* Minnesota Acad. of Occupational Medicine & Surgery (Secy. 1961–62, Vice, Pres. 1963, Pres. 1969); Bd. of Dirs. and Exec. Cttee.. Hennepin County Unit of Amer. Cancer Socy. (Pres-1964–65); Hennepin County Medical Socy.; Minnesota State Medical Assn.; A.M.A.; Central States Socy. of Industrial Medicine & Surgery (Past Pres.); Minneapolis Chamber of Commerce (Educ. Cttee., Legislative Action Cttee., Industrial Cttee.; Chmn. Health Section); American-Swedish Inst.; Photographic Socy. of America; Citizens' League of Greater Minneapolis. *Publication:* Recent Experiments in Small Plants Medical Services, Industrial Clinics and Occupational Medicine (archives of Environmental Health 5–66 Vol. 12 A.M.A.). *Clubs:* Minneapolis, Probus (Minneapolis); Midway (St. Paul). *Address:* 2310 East 43rd Street, Minneapolis 55406 Minn., U.S.A.; winter home, Dickey Cay, Man-o-War, Abaco, Bahamas.

**ARLIOTIS, Charles.** Greek banker. *B.* 1895. *M.* Lily Vlachopoulos. *Career:* Entered National Bank of Greece 1916; Secy.-Gen., National Mortgage Bank of Greece 1927, Economic Counsellor 1942, Dep. Gov. 1945–51; Gov. 1951–71, Hon. Gov. 1971; Chmn., Public Power Corp. 1962–63; Member of Bd. of many important Greek companies; former Min. of Economic Co-ordination; Member, Patronage Cttee., European Federation of Savings and Loan Institutions for Construction, Brussels. *Address:* Rigillis 18, Athens.

**ARMAND, Louis Francois.** French. *B.* 1905. *Educ.* Ecole Polytechnique; Ecole Nationale Superieure des Mines de Paris. *M.* 1928, Genevieve Gazel. *S.* Maurice, Joseph. *Daus.* Jeannine (Mme du Pre de Saint-Maur), France Marie (Mme Lefebvre de Ladonchamps). *Career:* Dir-Gen., SNCF 1949–55, Pres. 1955–57; Pres. du Bureau Industriel Africain 1953–58; Comm. Europeenne de l'Energie Atomique (EURATOM) 1958–59 and Houille, res du Bassin de Lorraine 1959–64; Secy.-Gen., l'Union Internationale des Chemins de fer 1961—; Pres., Assn. Française de Normalisation, and Cie d'Assurance La Protectrice; Administrator: Union de Banques, Petrofina, Compagnie Internationale des Wagons-Lits et du Tourisme, etc. *Awards:* Grand Officier Legion d'Honneur; Companion de la Liberation; KBE, Medal of Freedom (U.S.A.). *Publications:* Plaidoyer pour l'Avenir (in collaboration with Michel Drancourt) 1961; Simples Propos (1968); Le Pari Europeen (with Michel Drancourt Propos Ferroviaires (1970). *Member:* l'Institut (Académie des Sciences Morales et Politiques); l'Académie Française. *Address:* 30 Avenue de Villiers, Paris 17 ème; and *office* 14 rue Jean Rey, Paris 15 ème.

**ARMBRECHT, William H.** American lawyer and business executive. *B.* 1 Nov. 1908. *Educ.* Univ. of Alabama (LLB). *M.* 1927, Katherine Little. *S.* William H. III, Conrad P. *Daus.* Katherine, Anna Bell, Clara. *Career:* Admitted to Alabama Bar 1932: since practised in Mobile; partner, Armbrecht, Jackson, DeMouy, Crowe. Holmes & Reeves; Dir., The First National Bank of Mobile; Dir. First Bancgroup-Ala., Inc.; Dir. Southern Industries, Inc.; Grand Hotel Co.; Diamondhead Corp.; Bd. of Regents Spring Hill College. *Member:* American, Alabama, Mobile (Pres. 1954) Bar Assns.; Chamber of Commerce (Vice-Pres.-Dir.); Alabama Chamber of Commerce; Dauphin Island Property

Owners' Assn. (Dir.); Phi Delta Phi; Tau Omega; Episcopalian (Trustee). *Clubs:* Lakewood Country (Point Clear, Ala.); Country; Athelstan; Propeller; Kiwanis Bienville; Int'l. Trade (Mobile); Lunch (N.Y.C.). *Address:* 112 Pinebrook Dr. W., Spring Hill, Ala.; and *office* Merchants Nat. Bank, Bank Building, Mobile, Ala. 36601, U.S.A.

**ARMBRUSTER, John H.** American realtor. *B.* 1895. *M.* 1919, Eleanor L. Doepke. *Daus.* Priscilla, Elizabeth, Alice, Joan. *Career:* Dir.: Better Business Bureau, and William Woods College. Member: Metropolitan Y.M.C.A. Dir.: International Y.M.C.A.; U.S. Junior Chamber of Commerce (Hon. Vice-Pres.); Junior Chamber International (Senator and Historian); Exec. Bd., St. Louis Council, Boy Scouts of America; Clayton Rotary Past Pres.; St. Louis County Real Estate Board Past Pres.; St. Louis Chapter, American Inst. of Appraisers Past Pres.; Order of Kentucky Colonels, Editor, Elder Statesman; Trustee, Jaycee War Memorial Fund, Central Inst. for the Deaf. *Clubs* St. Louis; Clayton, Missouri Athletic; Wydown. *Address:* 710 S. Hanley Road, Apt. 19c, St. Louis, Mo. 63105, U.S.A.; and *office* 8944 St. Charles Road, St Louis, Mo 63114, U.S.A.

**ARMENTEROS, S. Jose,** Grand Cross of Place Plata. Dominican. *B.* 1915. *Educ.* Escuelas Pias de Sarria, Barcelona. *M.* 1937, Dolores Malla de Armenteros. *Daus.* 3. *Career:* Pres. & Treas., Jose Armenteros & Co. C. por A., Metropolitan Armenteros C. por A.; Pres., Industrias de Asbesto Cemento C. por A.; Assoc., Pro-Bienentar Social, Inc., Maplima S.A.; Vice-Pres., Sidomovil C. por A. 1965–71; Sec., Jose Armenteros, Hijos & Co. C. por A. 1945–71; Vice-Pres., Comision National Desacollo 1966–72; Junta Pro Faro de Colon; Pres., Centro Recreativo Espanol, Inc. 1938–43; Member Finance Cttee. Banco Central de la Republica Dominicana, 1954–56, 1958–60; Dir., Banco de Reservas de la Republica Dominicana 1952–56; Banco Agricola de la Republica Dominicana 1954–56; Min. de Industria Comercio 1956–58; First Vice-Pres., Finance Cttee. Banco Central de la Republica Dominicana 1956–57; Pres., Banco de Reservas de la Republica Dominicana 1956–57; Banco Agricola e Industrial de la Republica Dominicana 1956–57; First Vice-Pres., Soc. Automotiva, C. por A. 1959–61; Member Admin. Council, Fabrica Dominicana de Cemento 1960–62; First Vice-Pres. Banco de Reservas de la Republica Dominicana 1963–65; Fabrica Dominicana de Cemento 1965. *Clubs:* Santo Domingo Yacht; Mem., Santo Domingo Chamber of Commerce; Assoc. de Industrias; Fundacion de Desarollo de la Rep. Dominicana. *Address:* Bolivar Ave, 117. Santo Domingo City, Dominican Rep.; and *office* San Martin Ave. 122, Santo Dominigo City.

**ARMINJON, Henri Marie Jean.** *B.* 24 June 1906. *Educ.* École des Hautes Études Commerciales. *M.* 1933. Thérèse Neyrand de Baudreville. *S.* Charles, Jean-Louis, Patrick, Bernard, Gérard. *Daus.* Christiane (Vicomtesse Gérard de Meaux), Odile (Mme. de Charsonville), Geneviève (Comtesse Xavier de Longevialle), Ghislaine (Mme. François de Conigliano), Huguette (S. A. Princesse Murat de Chasseloup-Laubat), Anne, (Mme. Yves Vlieghe). *Career:* Hon. Chmn., Société Lyonnaise de Dépôts; Administrator, Credit Industriel et Commercial; Banque Régionale de l'Ain S.A., and Banque Pasche S.A. à Genève. *Awards:* Officier de la Légion d'Honneur; Commandeur dans l'Ordre National du Merite; Commandeur du Mérité de la Republique Italienne. *Address:* Le Val des Chênes, 69260 Charbonnières les Bains, France.

**ARMISTEAD, Moss William III.** Corporation executive. Press. & Dir., Landmark Communications, Inc. Norfolk; formerly Vice-Pres., Virginia State Chamber of Commerce, and Pres., Roanoke Chamber of Commerce; Reporter and Utility Editor, The Roanoke Times 1936–47; Exec. Secy. to Governor William M. Tuck of Virginia and Secy. of the Commonwealth 1946–47; Assoc. Publisher 1947–51, Vice-Pres. 1951–54, Times-World Corp.; Press. Times-World Corp. (publishers, The Roanoke Times, The Roanoke World News 1954–73; *Award:* Freedom Foundation Award for Editorial Writing. *Member:* Sigma Delta Chi; Alpha Kappa Psi; American Newspaper Publishers Assn. (Dir.); Chmn., Southern Newspaper Publishers Assn.; Hon. Doctor of Law Degree, Washington & Lee Univ. 1967. *Clubs:* Norfok Yacht & Country; Shenandoah (Roanoke). *Address:* 7310 Ruthven Road, Norfolk, Va 23505; and *office* 150 W. Brambleton Avenue, Norfolk, Va. 23501, U.S.A.

**ARMOUR, Laurance Hearne, Jr.** American. *B.* 1923. *Educ.* Princeton (BA 1945). *M.* 1954, Margot Boyd Kelly. *S.* Laurance H., III, Steven Shelby. *Dau.* Margot Brooks. *Career:* Dir., La Salle National Bank, Chicago; Dir., Episcopal Charities; Northwestern Memorial Hospital; Goodwill Industries. *Clubs:* Chicago; Owentsia; Post & Paddock; Princeton; Racquet; Shoreacres; The Travellers; Chicago and New York Yacht Clubs; Mid-Ocean Club, Tuckers Town, Bermuda; Royal Bermuda Yacht; Royal Hamilton Amateur Dinghy. *Address:* 930 Rosemary Road, Lake Forest, Ill. 60045; and *office* 135 South LaSalle Street, Chicago, Ill. 60603, U.S.A.

**ARMOUTI, Mohammad Nazzal.** Jordanian. Legal Advocate. *B.* 1924. *Educ.* License in Law, Syrian Univ. 1946; Damascus S.A.R.; Dipl. in Public Admin., Exeter Univ. U.K. 1959. *M.* 1949, Su'ad Omar Khalil Ma'ani. *S.* Mazin, Sultan, Nazzal, Omar. *Daus.* Intissar, Maissoun, Alia, Zein, Sabah. *Career:* Chief Clerk, Chief Justice Dept. 1947; Secy.-Gen., Ministry of Interior 1948; Secy.-Gen., Parliaments (both Houses of Senates and Representatives) 1950; Inspector-Gen., Income Tax Dept. 1952; Legal Adviser, Min. of Finance 1954; Gov. of the following governates respectively: Irbid, Ma'an, Hebron, Karak, Nablus and Salt 1955–61; Under-Secy., Min. of Interior 1961; Minister of Interior 1964–66; Ambassador to Libya, Tunisia, and Algeria 1965, to Kuwait 1967–71; Chmn. RAFIA Industrial Co.; Chmn. Almuzare' National Co.; Bd. mem. National Bank of Jordan. Other Appointments: Pres. Nat. Economic Dev. Company (NEDCO); Chmn., The Arab International Hotels Co. (AIHC); Chmn. Arab Dev. & Investment Co.; Chmn., Bd. of Trustees of the Arab College; Chmn., Jordan & Gulf Bank; Pres., Jordan Univ. Friends Assoc.; Vice-Chmn., Royal Soc. for the Conservation of Nature; Pres., Drilling & Exploration Petroleum Services Co. *Awards:* Jordanian 1st Rank Estiklal (Independence) also 1st rank Kawkab (Star); Syrian 1st Rank Istihkak; Grand Cross, Solver Knights Organization (Papal); Grand Decoration of Holy Sepulchre (Greek Orthodox). *Publication:* Citizen Guide (dealing with Jordan constitution, election law and by-laws, etc.). *Clubs:* Hussein Sports; King Hussein; Royal Automobile Cars. *Address:* P.O. Box 357, Amman, Jordan.

**ARMSEY, James William.** American Foundation executive. *B.* 1917. *Educ.* Univ. of Illinois (BA, MA); LLD, Alaska Methodist Univ. 1965; New York Univ. LHD (1975); Univ. of Notre Dame, LLD (1976). *M.* 1941, Beth Louise Loveless. *Career:* Mgr., Public Inform. Office, Chicago Professional Colleges, Univ. of Illinois 1946–47; Public Relations Dir., Illinois Inst. of Tech., Chicago 1947–52; and Armour Research Foundation of Illinois Inst. of Technology 1949–52; Program Officer in Charge, Special Projects in Education and Research, Ford Foundation Jan. 1967–71; International Div. Education and Research Div., Program Advisor 1971–75; Consultant since 1975; Editor, Illinois Technical Engineer, 1947–49; Asst. to the Chancellor of New York Univ., N.Y.C. 1952–56; Asst. to the Press., Ford Foundation, N.Y.C. 1956–58 (Assoc. Program Dir., Education Div. 1958–60; Program Dir., Special Program in Education 1960–64; Dir., Special Programs 1964–67. *Clubs:* University (N.Y.C.). *Address:* 11 Washington Mews, New York City 3; and *office* 320 E.43 St., New York City, 10017, U.S.A.

**ARMSTRONG OF SANDERSTEAD, LORD** (William), PC, GCB, MVO. British. *B.* 1915. *Educ.* Bec. School (London); Exeter Coll., Oxford. MA. *M.* 1942, Gwendoline Enid Bennett. *S.* 1. *Dau.* 1. *Career:* Civil Service—Board of Education, Cabinet Office, Treasury 1938–68; Permanent Sec. to Civil Ser. Dept. & Head of Civil Service 1968–74; President Manpower Soc. 1970–73; Member Council Manchester Business School 1970–74; Chmn. Coll. Council, Mansfield Coll., Oxford, and a Member Governing Council Oxford Centre for Management Studies; Hon. Fellow Exeter Coll., Oxford 1963, and Visiting Fellow of Nuffield Coll., Oxford 1964–72. Hon. Fellow of Institution of Civil Engineers 1973; Director and Deputy Chmn. Midland Bank Limited 1974–75; Chairman, Midland Bank 1975—; Chmn., Midland & International Banks Ltd. 1976—; Dep. Chmn., Cttee. of London Clearing Bankers 1976—; Dir., Shell Transport & Trading Co. Ltd. 1976—; Hon. Liveryman of Salters' Company 1974; Trustee, Wellcome Trust 1974; Trustee, Civic Trust 1975—. *Awards:* Hon. DCL Oxford 1971; Hon. Degree Open University 1974; Hon. D.Litt. City University 1974; Hon. Degree Cranfield Institute of Technology 1975; Hon. Degree Heriot-Watt University 1975; Hon. Degree Sheffield University 1975; cr. MVO (4th class) 1945; CB (civil) 1957; KCB (civil) 1963; GCB (civil) 1968; PC 1973; Life Peer 1975. *Address:* 143 Whitehall Court, London, SW1A 2EP.

**ARMSTRONG, Alexander Ewan.** *B.* 1916. *Educ.* The Scots Coll., Sydney (Matriculation). *M.* (1) 1945, Marjorie

A. Goodhew; (2) 1963, Margaret Rose Cleary. *Daus.* Mary, Margaret. *Career:* After matriculation personally managed family pastoral properties until 1955; since then engaged in commercial and real estate development enterprises in Sydney; Chmn., A. E. Armstrong Pty. Ltd.; George Armstrong & Son Pty. Ltd.; Dir. of Pastoral Companies. *Clubs:* R.M.Y.C. (Sydney); Commonwealth (Canberra). *Address:* No. 5 Coolong Road, Vaucluse, N.S.W.; and *office* Floor 11, 183 Macquarie Street, Sydney, N.S.W., Australia; P.O. Box 2616, Sydney 2001.

**ARMSTRONG, Ernest.** MP. British politician. *B.* 1915. *Educ.* Wolsingham Grammar School; Leeds Teachers Training College. *M.* 1941, Hannah Lamb. *S.* 1. *Dau.* 1. *Career:* Teacher 1937–40; R.A.F. (Admin. Officer) 1940–46; Teacher 1946–52; Headmaster 1952–64; Member of Parliament Durham N.W. since 1964; Government Whip 1967–70; Parly. Under Secy., Education and Science 1974–75; Parly. Under-Secy., Dept of Environment since 1975. *Member:* Nat. Union of Teachers. *Address:* Penny Well, Witton-Le-Wear, Durham.

**ARMSTRONG, J. Sinclair.** American. *B.* 1915. *Educ.* Harvard Coll. (AB 1938); Harvard Law School (JD 1941). By previous marriage: *S.* James S., Stephen H., Robert S. *Daus.* Katherine C., Elisabeth S. *Career:* Mem. Illinois and N.Y. Bars; Assoc., law firm of Isham, Lincoln & Beale, Chicago 1941–45, and 1946–50, Mem. 1950–53; Lt. (j.g.) U.S.N.R., Office of Gen. Counsel, Navy Dept., Washington 1945–46. Member, Securities Exchange Comm., Washington (Chmn. 1955–57) 1953–57, and of President's Conf. on Administrative Procedure 1953–54; Asst. Secy. of the Navy (Financial Management) and Comptroller, Dept. of the Navy 1957–59; Exec. Vice-Pres., United States Trust Co. of New York 1959—; Dir.: Royal Globe Life Ins. Co. of N.Y.; Rexham Corp.; Va Chemicals Inc. *Member:* Amer. Law Inst., Amer. Bar Assn.; Amer. Socy. of Corporate Secretaries; Kappa Beta Phi (Wall Street Chapter); Navy League of U.S.; Assn. of Bar of City of N.Y., Bond Club of N.Y.; Legal Club of Chicago. Trustee: The (Episcopal) Church Pension Fund; Diocesan (N.Y.) Investment Trust; The Gunnery School, Pres.; New York Univ. Medical Center; The Samuel Rubin Fdn. (N.Y.); St. Andrew's Soc. (N.Y.), Past Pres., Mem. Standing Cttee.; Mem., Huguenot Soc. of Amer.; St. Nicholas Soc. (N.Y.); Soc. of Colonial Wars. *Publications:* The Blue Sky Laws (1958); Congress and the Securities and Exchange Commission (1959); Financial Management in the Navy, 1950–1960 (1960). *Clubs:* Metropolitan (Washington); Century; Down Town; Harvard; Pilgrims of U.S., N.Y. Yacht (all N.Y.C.); Chevy Chase (Md.). *Address:* 333 West 70th St., New York, N.Y. 10023; U.S.A.; and *office* 45 Wall Street, New York, N.Y. 10005, U.S.A.

**ARMSTRONG, Lawrence Alfred.** Australian. *B.* 1927. *Educ.* St. Andrew's Coll.; Sydney Univ. (BA). *M.* 1951, Mary Paul. *Daus.* Susan Mary, Jan Patricia. *Career:* With Dept. of Trade and Customs 1950; Commonwealth Treasury 1951–53; Secy. to the Commonwealth Treas. 1953–58; Mgr., Customs Traffic and Government Services Dept., Ford Motor Co. of Australia Ltd. Mar. 1966–68; Public Relations Mgr. of Ford Motor Co. of Australia 1968–69; Mgr., Public Relations and Adv., Alcan Australia Ltd. 1969–75; Dir., Oil Industry Secretariat since 1976. Former Secy., Aust. Automobile Chamber of Commerce; Gen. Secy., Victorian Auto. Chamber of Commerce; Secy., National Automobile Dealers Association. *Club:* Australian Jockey; North Sydney Leagues; South Melbourne Cricket. *Address:* 21 Burwood Road, Hawthorn, Vic., Australia.

**ARMSTRONG, Terence Philip La Grange.** South African company director. *B.* 1911. *Educ.* Durban High School. *M.* 1935, Doreen Bouch. *Daus.* 3. *Career:* Owned own motor business, Durban 1929–32; free-lance journalist and traveller 1932–33; Pres., South African Motor Trade Assn. 1950–51; elected member of the Inst. of the Motor Industry (M.I.M.I.) of Great Britain (S.A. Region) Jan. 1954; Chmn. Bd., Garden City Motors (Pty.) Ltd. *Award:* Freeman of the City of London. *Club:* (Steward) Pietermaltzburg Turf; Rand; Johannesburg Country; Victoria, Country, (Pieterm). *Address:* P.O. Box 13, Hilton, Natal, South Africa.

**ARNALL, Ellis Gibbs.** American. *B.* 1907. *Educ.* Univ. of the South (BA, DCL); Univ. of Georgia (LLB); Bryant Coll. (LLD); Piedmont Coll. (LLD). *M.* 1935, Mildred DeLaney Slemons. *S.* Alvan. *Dau.* Alice. *Career:* Senior Partner, Arnall, Golden & Gregory, Attorneys-at-Law, Fulton Federal Building, Atlanta, Ga.; Attorney-Gen. of Georgia 1939–42; Gov. of Georgia 1942–47; Pres., Dixie Life Insurance Co. 1946–55; Socy. of Independent Motion Picture Producers 1948–65; Independent Film Producers Export Corp. 1954–65; Dir., Simmons Plating Works, The Rushton Co., Alterman Foods, First National Bank, since 1950; U.S. Office Price Stabilization 1952; Columbus National Life Insurance Co. 1955–57; Chmn. Bd.: Coastal States Life Insurance Co., since 1957; National Assn. of Life Companies, since 1955; Atlanta Americana Motor Hotel Corp. since 1962: Member, U.S. National Comm. for U.N.E.S.C.O. 1949–52; U.S. Delegation, Paris Conference for U.N.E.S.C.O. 1949; U.S. Comm. for U.N.E.S.C.O. 1963–69; Trustee, Univ. of the South 1950–56; Trustee, Mercer Univ. 1963–74; Commissioner, Franklin D. Roosevelt Warm Springs Memorial Comm. 1970—. *Publications:* The Shore Dimly Seen (1946); What the People Want (1948). Democrat. *Address:* 213 Jackson Street, Newnan, Ga., U.S.A.

**ARNESEN, K. Martin.** Norwegian. *B.* 1931. *Educ.* Comm. Certificates England, France, Insurance & Reinsurance; Study Admin. A.F.F. several European countries. *M.* 1960, Anne-Marie Sviland. *S.* 3. *Career:* joined F/A Dovre and F/A Arne 1956, Reins Superintendent 1959, Manager 1967, Dir. 1968, Man. Dir. since 1972. Member Bds. various Industrial, Financial and Insurance Companies. *Address:* Glassverkveien 3, 1322 Hovik, Norway.

**ARNOLD, Dick McRae.** Retired Australian banking executive. *B.* 1910. *Educ.* Perth Modern School; Univ. of London; Univ. of Western Australia (BA 1947); FASA, FAIM, ACIS, ABIA. *M.* 1933, Essie Millicent Byers. *S.* 1. *Dau.* 1. *Career:* Joined Western Australian Bank 1925 (absorbed by Bank of N.S.W. 1927); Supervisor, Bank of N.S. W. Savings Bank1957–59; Chief Man. for W. Aust. 1960–62; for N.Z. 1962–67. Asst. Gen. Mgr. 1968–73; Gen. Mgr. 1973–75; Chmn. Bank of Tonga 1971–75; Chmn. International Marketing Inst. of Australia 1970–73; Advisory Council Y.W.C.A. Sydney, since 1971; Dir. Barclays Australia Ltd. since 1975; Dir. Walden Properties Ltd since 1975; Dir., Aust. National Industries Ltd. since 1975; Dir., Associated Securities Ltd. since 1975. War Service, Air raid Warden, London 1939–42; Flying Officer (Navigator), R.A.A.F. 1943–45. *Clubs:* Australian Sydney; Wellington Golf; Pymble Golf. *Address:* 26 Cowan Rd., St. Ives NSW 2075 Australia.

**ARNOLD, Hans.** German Diplomat. *B.* 1923. *Education.* Univ. of Munich; Georgetown Univ. Washington (Post-Grad. studies). *M.* 1954, Karin von Egloffstein. *Daus.* 3. *Career:* German Embassy Paris 1952–55; Foreign Office Bonn 1955–57; German Embassy Washington 1957–61; Foreign Office Bonn 1961–68; Ambassador to the Netherlands 1968–72; Head, Cultural Dept. Foreign Office 1972–77; Ambassador to Italy since 1977. *Publications:* Cultural Export as Policy?—Aspects of German Foreign Cultural Policy (in German). *Address:* German Embassy, Via Po 25c, Rome, Italy.

**ARNOLD, Vere Arbuthnot,** CBE, MC, TD, DL, JP. British merchant. *B.* 1902. *Educ.* Haileybury Coll.; Jesus Coll., Cambridge (BA). *M.* 1928, Joan Kathleen Tully. *S.* Vere Hugo Cholmondeley. *Dau.* Heather Virginia. *Career:* Pres., Liverpool Corn Trade Assn. Ltd. 1947–48, and 1951–52; High Sheriff of Cheshire 1958; Chmn., Ross T. Smyth & Co. Ltd. 1957—; Chmn., Liverpool Grain Storage & Transit Co. Ltd.; Chmn., Alexander Silos Ltd.; Dir., D. T. Russell & Baird (Ireland) Ltd.; Justice of the Peace. *Club:* Army and Navy. *Address:* Ardmore, Great Barrow, Cheshire; and *office* The Corn Exchange, Liverpool 2.

**ARNOLD, Victor Henry.** British actuary. *B.* 1914. Fellow, Inst. of Actuaries, London (F.I.A.); Assoc. Australian Insur. Inst. (A.A.I.I.); Assoc. Socy. of Actuaries, Chicago (A.S.A.). *M.* 1938, Barbara June Jessie Lloyd. *Daus.* 3. *Career:* Government Actuary and Statist, State of Victoria, Australia 1954–73; also appointed Dep. Commonwealth Statistician 1958–73; Chmn., Premiums Cttee., 3rd Party Insurance 1961–73; Chmn. Superannuation Board of Victoria since 1965; Chmn. Motor Accidents Board of Victoria since 1973; Member of Cttee. of Inquiry into Activities of Housing Comm. 1955; Chmn., Bd. of Inquiry into Industrial Accidents 1958; Pres., Actuarial Socy. of Australia and N.Z. 1960; qualified as Fellow, Inst. of Actuaries, Western Australia 1948. *Address:* 35 Spring Street, Melbourne, Victoria, Australia.

**ARNON, Michael.** Israeli official. *B.* 10 Apr. 1925. *Educ.* Balfour Gymnasium, Tel Aviv; London Univ. (Dipl. Int. Affairs). *M.* Hadara Strod. *S.* 1. *Dau.* 1. *Career:* Member,

Editorial Staff, The Palestine Post 1945–48; served in Israeli Defence Army 1948–49; Press Officer, Ministry of Foreign Affairs 1949–51; Press Attaché, Embassy of Israel, London 1951–54; Dir., Israel Government Press Office, Jerusalem 1955–56; Press and Information Counsellor, Washington 1956–61; Dir., Information Div., Ministry for Foreign Affairs 1961–62; Ambassador to Ghana 1962–65; Consul-Gen., New York 1965–68; Secy. to the Government of Israel, Jerusalem 1968–74; Pres. and Chief Executive Officer, Development Corporation for Israel, N.Y., U.S.A. since 1974. *Address:* 2 Haportazim Street, Jerusalem, Israel.

**ARNOW, Leslie Earle.** American. Scientific Consulant. *B.* 1909. *Educ.* Univs. of Florida (PhG, BS) and Minnesota (PhD, MB, MD). *M* 1933, Jennie McLemore Martin. *S.* Peter Leslie. *Career:* At Univ. of Minnesota; Grad. Asst. in physiological chemistry and biophysics 1931–34; instructor in physiological chemistry 1934–40; Asst. Prof. of physiological chemistry 1940–42; Merck & Co. Inc.: Dir. of biochemical research, Sharp & Dohme Inc. 1942–44; Dir. of Research 1944–53; Vice-Pres. and Dir. of Research, Sharp & Dohme Div. of Merck & Co. 1953–56; Vice-Pres., Merck Sharp & Dohme Research Laboratories and Executive Dir., Merck Inst. for Therapeutic Research 1956–58; Pres.: Warner-Lambert Res. Inst. 1958–65; Warner-Lambert Res. Inst. of Canada Ltd. 1964–65; Vice-Pres., Warner-Lambert Co. 1958–65; Sen. Scientific Consultant, Warner-Lambert Research Inst. 1965–74. *Publications:* Introduction to Physiological and Pathological Chemistry (9th edn.); Introduction to Laboratory Chemistry; Introduction to Organic and Biological Chemistry (with H. C. Reitz); Health in a Bottle; Food Power. *Awards:* Centennial Award, Univ. of Florida 1953; Outstanding Achievement, Univ. of Minnesota 1955; Philadelphia Science Council 1958; Fellow: Amer. Assn. for Advancement of Science, and of N.Y. Acad. of Sciences. *Member:* Amer. Medical Assn.; American Society for Clinical Pharmacology & Therapeutics; Amer. Chemical Socy.; Amer. Socy. of Biological Chemists; Socy. for Experimental Biology & Medicine; Nutrition Today Society. *Address:* 14 Fairfield Drive, Convent, N.J. 07961, U.S.A.

**ARPAIA, Anthony F.** American lawyer. *B.* 1897. *Educ.* Yale Coll. (BA 1921); Yale Law School (LLB 1923). *M.* 1940, Charlotte Bergen. *Dau.* Judith A. (Sedgeman). *Career:* Associated with Chadbourne, Hunt, Jaeckel & Brown (engaged in practice of corporate, finance and public utility law), New York City 1923–25; with Wirth & Picard, Berlin (American attorney in charge, engaged in practice of private international law, representing American interests in Central and Eastern Europe) 1925–27; General practice of law, New Haven, Conn. 1927–42; Judge, Town Court of East Haven, Conn. 1931–33; Dir., New Haven O.P.A. Defence Rental Area 1942–43; Chief Attorney, Connecticut, Office of Price Administration 1943 (State Dir. 1943–45); Vice-Pres. and Gen. Counsel, The Adley Express Co. 1945–51; Practice of law (specializing in corporate, estate planning and tax law), New Haven 1951–52; Chmn., Interstate Commerce Comm. Jan.–Dec. 1956; Vice-Pres., International Services, Railway Express Agency 1960–65; Executive Consultant to Railway Express Agency, N.Y.C. 1960—; Commissioner, Interstate Commerce Comm. July 1952–Mar. 1960; Conducted Pilot Study on Mass Transit for New York, Connecticut & New Jersey Area 1961, the Report to the Senate leading to Mass Transit Act of 1963; presided at plenary sessions of International Standards Org. (T.C. 104) at Hamburg (1964), The Hague (1965), Moscow (1967); participated in and addressed numerous seminars, conferences and similar meetings on transportation all over the world. *Publications:* numerous articles on transporation and its economics in legal periodicals. *Address:* 4153, 57th Street North, St. Petersburg, Florida 33709, U.S.A.

**ARRANDALE, Dr. Roy S.** *B.* 1911. *Educ.* Univ. of Illinois (BS Chm. Eng. 1933); Carnegie Inst. of Technology (MS in Phys. Chem. 1934); Yale Univ. (PhD in Eng. 1939). *M.* 1939, Eleanor M. Reynolds. *S.* Thomas. *Dau.* Adele. *Career:* Process Engr., Standard Oil Development Co. (now Esso Res. & Engineering Co.) 1938–41; joined Thatcher Glass Mfg. Co. 1941; Senior Vice-Pres., Research & Engineering, Thatcher Glass Mfg. Co., Div. of Dart Industries 1954–76; Consultant to the Company since 1976; Member, Bd. Dirs.: Ceramic Assn. of New York; New York State Electric & Gas Corp.; Marine Midland Bank—Southern; Capabilities, Inc.; Arnot Ogden Memorial Hospital. *Publications:* Furnace Design and Glass Melting; Some Critical Points of Glass Furnace Design (1954); Air Pollution Control in Glass Melting (1958); Fuels & Combustion, Furnace Technology Sections of *Handbook of the Glass Industry. Awards:* Bronze Tablet, Univ. of Illinois 1933; Knight of St. Patrick Award for Alfred Univ. 1956; Phoenix Award (Glass Man of the Year) 1976; Toledo Award 1977. *Member:* Sigma Xi; Sigma Tau; Phi Lambda Upsilon; Omega Chi Epsilon. *Clubs:* Elmira; Torch; Illini (N.Y.). *Address:* 1720 West Church Street, Elmira, N.Y.; and *office* Thatcher Glass Manufacturing Co. Inc., P.O. Box 265, Elmira, N.Y., U.S.A.

**ARROW, Kenneth J.** American University Professor. *B.* 1921 *Educ.* City Coll. (BS Soc. Sc. 1940); Columbia Univ. (MA 1941, PhD 1951). *M.* 1947, Selma Schweitzer. *S.* David, Andrew. *Career:* Capt. (weather officer), U.S. Army 1942–46; Research Assoc., Cowles Comm. for Research in Economics 1947–49; Prof. of Economics, Statistics and Operations Research, Stanford Univ. 1949–68; Prof. of Economics Harvard Univ. 1968–74; James Bryant Conant Univ. Prof., Harvard Univ. since 1974. *Publications:* Social Choice and Individual Values (1951, 2nd edn. 1963); Mathematical Studies in the Theory of Inventory and Production (with S. Karlin and H. Scarf) (1958); Studies in Linear and Non-Linear Programming (with L. Hurwicz and H. Uzawa) (1959); A Time Series Analysis of Interindustry Demands (with M. Hoffenberg) (1959); Public Investment and Optimal Fiscal Policy (1971); General Competitive Analysis (1972); The Limits of Organization (1974); numerous articles in various journals. *Awards:* John Bates Clark Medal, Amer. Economic Assn. 1957; Fellow, Amer. Acad. of Arts & Sciences, Econometric Socy., Amer. Statistical Assn., Inst. of Mathematical Statistics, & Amer. Economic Assn.; Hon. LLD, Univ. of Chicago 1967; Hon. Doctor, Social and Economic Sciences, Univ. of Vienna 1971; Hon. DSC. City Univ. N.Y. 1972; Nobel (Memorial) Award, Economic Science 1972; Hon. LLD. Columbia Univ. 1973; Hon. Dr. Soc. Scs. Yale 1974; Hon. Dr. Univ. Rene Descartes (1974); Hon. Ph.D. Hebrew Univ. of Jerusalem 1975; Hon. Dr. Pol., Univ. of Helsinki 1976. *Member:* Nat. Acad. of Sciences; Amer Philosophical Society; Finnish Acad. of Science; British Acad. *Address:* Room 404, 1737 Cambridge Street, Harvard Univ., Cambridge, Mass. 02138, U.S.A.

**ARTHINGTON-DAVY, Humphrey Augustine,** MVO, OBE, British dipomat. B. 1920. *Educ.* Eastbourne Coll.; Trinity Coll. Cambridge. *Career:* with Indian Army 1941–46; Indian Political Service 1946–47; Civil Service of Pakistan 1947–56; H.M. Diplomatic Service 1957—; British Representative in the Maldives 1959–65; Deputy High Commissioner, Botswana 1966–68, Mauritius 1968–70, Tonga and Samoa 1970–73; British High Commissioner Tonga and Western Samoa 1973–77. *Club:* Naval & Miltary S.W.1. *Address:* c/o Foreign & Commonwealth Office, London, S.W.1.

**ARTHUR, Sir Geoffrey (George),** KCMG. *B.* 1920. *Educ.* MA (Oxon.). *M.* 1946, Margaret Woodcock. *Career:* Served in: Embassies Baghdad 1948–50, and Ankara 1950–53; Foreign Office, London 1953–55; Bonn 1956–58; Cairo (Counsellor) 1959–63; Foreign Office 1963; British Ambassador to Kuwait May 1967–68; Asst. Under-Secy. of State, Foreign & Commonwealth Office Nov. 1968–70; Political Resident in the Persian Gulf 1970–72; Visiting Fellow, St. Antony's Coll. Oxford 1972–73; Deputy Under Secy. of State, Foreign and Commonwealth Office 1973–75; Master of Pembroke Coll. Oxford & Dir., British Bank of the Middle East since 1975. *Club:* United University; Beefsteak (London). *Address:* Pembroke College, Oxford, OX1 1DW.

**ARTHUR, Henry Bradford,** Professor of Agriculture and Business Administration. *B.* 1904. *Educ.* Union Coll. (AB); Harvard Univ. (MA, PhD (Econ.)). *M.* 1931, Charlotte Beals. *S.* H. Bradford, Jr. *Dau.* Janice A. McCoy. *Career:* Instructor economics, Harvard 1930–32; Research in Div. of Research and Planning, N.R.A., Washington 1933; Cttee. of Govt. Statistics & Information Services 1933–34; Consumers Div., Natl. Emergency Cncl. 1934–35; Asst. Dir., Div. of Research, W.P.A. 1935–36; Lecturer, Amer. Univ. 1935–36; in Commercial Research Dept., Swift & Co. 1936–39; elected Economist 1939–60; Dir. of Security, Mutual Casualty Co. 1939–60; Consultant to House of Representatives Cttee. on post-war economic policy 1944–46; Consultant on Rationing, O.P.A. 1942–43; Chief, Program Review Div., European Office of E.C.A., Paris 1948–49; Industry member WSB 1950–51; Member, E.C.A. Evaluation Mission to Denmark 1953; Visiting Prof., Salzburg Seminar in American Studies 1966; George M. Moffett Prof. of Agriculture and Business Emer., and Prof. Emer., Graduate School of Business Administration, Harvard University *Publications:* Wholesale Price Work of the U.S. Bureau of Labor Statistics (thesis) (1935); Contrib.: Turning the Searchlight on Farm Policy (1952); Theory in Marketing (1964); Dynamics of Adjustment in the Broiler Industry (with B. F. Tobin) (1964); Inventory Profits in the Business Cycle (1938); Tropical Agribusiness Structures and Adjustments—Bananas (1968); Commodity Futures as a Management Tool (1971); The Nature of Commodity Futures as an Economic & Business Instrument (1973); Fallstudien Zum Agribusiness Nach der Harvard Case Method (1975). *Award:* Hon. LLD, Union Coll. *Member:* Amer. Econ. Assn.; Amer. Stat. Assn. (Fellow, former Vice-Pres.); Amer. Agric. Econ. Assn.; Amer. Mktg. Assn.; Conf. of Business Economists; Phi Beta Kappa. *Club:* Cosmos (Washington). *Address:* 28 Tyler Road, Belmont, Mass.; and *office* Soldiers Field, Boston Mass., U.S.A.

**ARTHUR, James Stanley,** CMG. British Diplomat. *B.* 1923. *Educ.* Trinity Academy, Edinburgh; Liverpool Univ., BSc. *M.* 1950, Marion North. *S.* 2. *Daus.* 2. *Career:* Scientific Civil Service 1944–46; Asst. Principal, Scottish Education Dept. 1946; Min. of Education/Dept. of Educ. & Science 1947–66; Private Sec. to Parly. Sec. 1948–50; Principal Private Sec. to Minister 1960–62; Counsellor, Foreign Office 1966; Counsellor, Nairobi 1967–70; Dep. High Commissioner, Malta 1970–73; British High Commissioner, Fiji since 1974. *Decorations:* Companion of the Most Distinguished Order of St. Michael and St. George, 1977. *Clubs:* Travellers'; Royal Commonwealth Soc. *Address:* c/o Foreign & Commonwealth Office, London S.W.1.

**ARUP, Sir Ove Nyquist,** CBE. British. Senior Partner: Ove Arup and Partners Consulting Engineers 1949—, and Arup Associates 1963—. *B.* 1895. *Educ.* Preparatory School, Hamburg; Public School Soro, Denmark; Univ. of Copenhagen; Royal Technical Coll., Copenhagen (MSc). *M.* 1925, Ruth Samuel Sorensen. *S.* Jens Mand. *Daus.* Anja Liengaard, Karin Perry. *Career:* Chief Designer, Christiani & Nielsen 1925–34; Dir. and Chief Designer, J. L. Kier & Co. Ltd. 1934–38; Dir., Arup & Arup Ltd. 1938–46; Guest Lecturer at Harvard Univ. 1955. Member. Akadamiet for de Tekniske Videnskaber 1956; Vice-Pres., Inst. of Civil Engineers 1969–71; now Fellow Inst. Civil Eng. *Member:* Dansk Ingeniørforening, Inst. of Civil Engineers, Inst. of Structural Engineers; Architectural Assn.; Assn. of Consulting Engineers; Concrete Socy., etc. *Awards:* Commander 1st Class, Order of Dannebrog 1975; Roy., Gold Medal, Inst. of British Architects 1966; Hon. DSc, Univ. of Durham 1967; East Anglia Univ. 1968; Heriot-Watt Univ. 1976; Gold Medal, Inst. Struct. Eng. 1973; Hon. Doctorate of Danmarks Tekniske Hojskole Lyngby, 1974. *Publications:* Design, Cost, Construction and Relative Safety of Trench, Surface, Bombproof and other Air Raid Shelters (1939); London Shelter Problem (1940); Safe Housing in War Time (1941); Memorandum on Box Frame Construction (1944); various contributions to technical journals. *Clubs:* Athenaeum; Danish. *Address:* 6 Fitzroy Park, Highgate, London, N.6; and *office* 13 Fitzroy Street, London, W.1.

**ARVONEN, Veli Taari.** Finnish building consultant. *Educ.* Technical School. *Career:* Man. Dir., Chmn. Bd. of Dirs., Arvonen Oy, Building Contractors 1934–69; Bd., Sampo Mutual Insurance Co. 1957–69; Chmn. Bd. Dirs., Keramia Oy 1961–69; Bd. Dirs., Travel Bureau Area 1966—, Chmn. 1970; Bd. Admin., Finnish Contractors Ltd. 1966–69; Man. Dir., Economic Building Consultance since 1969. *Member:* Bd., Finnish Building Industry Assn. 1947—; Finnish Building Employers Assn. 1950–69; Turku Chamber Commerce; Bd. Admin., Huhtamaki Oy, Turku Fair Assn.; Finnair Oy 1962—, Chmn. since 1967. *Address:* Finnair, Mannerheimintie 102, 00250, Helsinki 25.

**ASANO, Kaisaku,** BS, MBA. Japanese. *B.* 1926. *Educ.* Tohoku Univ. (BS Mech. Eng.); Harvard Graduate Sch. of Business Admin. (MBA). *M.* 1956, Hosomi Michiko. *S.* 1. *Dau.* 1. *Career:* Exec. Man. Dir., Kayaba Industry Co. Ltd.: Dir., KYB Corp. of America; Dir. Japan Indust. Robot Assoc.; Dir., Nihon Koki Co. Ltd.; Kayaba Engineering & Service Co. Ltd.; Dir., Japan Cttee. for Economic Development. *Address:* 4-1-19 Komazawa, Setgayku, Tokyo, 154; and *office* World Trade Center Bldg., 2-4-1 Hamamatsucho, Minatoku, Tokyo, 105, Japan.

**ASBRINK, Per Valfrid.** *B.* 1912. *Educ.* Univ. of Stockholm; pol. mag. *M.* (1) 1939, Erika Richter; (2) 1970, Karin Winberg. *Career:* Swedish Co-op. Union and Wholesale Socy. 1934–38; Exec. Officer, Central Assn. for Soc. Research (CSA) and ed. of Social Yearbk. 1938–42; Secy., Finance Dept. and Chancellery of the City of Stockholm 1943–45: Secy., Comm. Education and Adviser to Ministry of Education 1946–47, and to Ministry of Communications 1949–50; Under-Secy., Ministry of Communications 1951–55; Gov., Bank of Sweden 1955–73; Exec. Dir. International Monetary Fund since 1973. *Address:* Intern. Monetary Fund, Washington, D.C. 20431, USA.

**ASH, Roy L.,** MBA. American. *B.* 1918. *Educ.* Harvard Univ. Graduate Sch. of Business Admin. (MBA). *M.* 1943, Lila Hornbek. *S.* 3. *Daus.* 2. *Career:* Co-Founder Litton Industries Inc. 1953, Dir. 1953–72, Pres. 1961–72; Bd. of Dirs., Bank of America NT & SA 1964–72; Bank America Corp. 1968–72, 1976—: Global Marine Inc. 1965–72, 1975—; Pacific Mutual Life Ins. Co. 1967–72; Daniel, Mann, Johnson & Mendenhall 1976—; J. C. Schumacher & Co. 1976—; Chmn. of the Bd. & Chief Exec. Officer, Addressograph Multigraph Corp. 1976—. Cabinet Mem. in Nixon and Ford Administrations; Asst. to the Pres. of the US and Dir. Office of Management and Budget 1973–75. Chmn., Presidents Advisory Council, Exec. Organization 1969–71; Trustee, Cttee. Economic Development 1970–72, 1975—; Pres., Los Angeles World Affairs Council 1970–72 (Dir. 1968–72); Trustee, Federal City Council 1972—; Trustee, Roy L. & Lila M. Ash Foundation. *Club:* Harvard. *Address:* 655 Funchal Rd., Los Angeles, Calif. 90024, U.S.A.; and *office* 1901 Ave. of the Stars Suite 1620, Los Angeles, Calif. 90067, U.S.A.

**ASHBOLT, Anthony Alfred.** Man. Dir., Webster Ltd., Hobart, since 1957 & Chmn. since 1969. *B.* 1921. *Educ.* Geelong Grammar School; Trinity Coll., Univ. of Melbourne. *M.* 1951, Diana Ottaway *S.* Andrew, Robert, Nicholas. *Career:* Overseas Service, Second A.I.F.; President of Hobart Chamber of Commerce, 1958–59; Vice President of Associated Chambers of Commerce of Australia, 1959–60; Member of the Council of the Royal Agricultural Society of Tasmania; President of the Kennel Control Council of Tasmania; Member of the Australia/Japan Business Co-operation Committee; Member of the Australian Government Trade Development Council; Member of the Auctioneers & Estate Agents Council of Tasmania; Member of the Federal Council of the Australian Institute of Directors; Member of the general committee of the Savings Bank of Tasmania; Director: Richardson's Meat Industries Ltd.; Consolidated Forest Owners Pty Ltd; Ceilcote Pty Ltd. *Clubs:* Tasmanian, Launceston. *Address:* 534 Sandy Bay Road, Hobart, Tasmania; *office* 60 Liverpool Street, Hobart, Tasmania.

**ASHBURTON, 6th Baron, Sir (Alexander Francis St. Vincent Baring),** KG, KCVO, KtStJ, JP, CA. *B.* 1898. *Educ.* Eton & Sandhurst. *M.* 1924, Hon. Doris Mary Therese Harcourt. *S.* 2. *Career:* Lieut., Royal Scots Greys, 1917–23; Flt.-Lieut., A.A.F. 1939; Group-Capt. 1944; Member, London Cttee., Hong Kong & Shanghai Banking Corp. 1935–39; Man.-Dir., Baring Brothers & Co. Ltd. 1928–62; Dir. 1962–68; Dir., Alliance Assurance 1932–68; Pressed Steel Co. Ltd. 1944–66. County Councillor Hampshire 1945–55; Trustee, King George's Jubilee Trust 1949–68; Treas. King Edward VII Hospital Fund for London 1955–64; Vice-Lieut. of Hampshire 1951–60; Member, Hampshire & I.O.W. Territorial Assn. 1951–60; Pres. 1960–67; J.P., Hampshire 1951—; County Alderman 1955–74; Lord Lieut. & Custos Rotolorum. of Hampshire & the Isle of Wight 1960–73; Receiver-Gen. to the Duchy of Cornwall 1961—; Trustee, St. Cross Hospital, Winchester 1961—; Chantrey Bequest 1963, High Steward of Winchester 1967—; Chmn., Hampshire Police Authority 1967–71; Pres., Eastern Wessex Territorial Assn. 1968. *Address:* Itchen Stoke House, Alresford, Hampshire.

**ASHBY, Philip Clark.** Pharmacist, pharmaceutical chemist. *B.* 1898. *Educ.* Univ. of Oklahoma (Pharm. Chem. 1922); Oklahoma City Univ. (Chem.). *M.* 1938, Ethel Ferne Gordanier. *Career:* Military Service, U.S.N.R. 1918–22; Tech. Sgt. 159 Hosp. Co.; 120 Med. Reg., Oklahoma National Guard 1926–29; Amer. Legion, 51 yr.; Mem. Bio-Chemist, Univ. of Oklahoma Medical Center 1922–25; State Chemist, Oklahoma State Bd. of Health 1925–27; Chief Chemist, Balyeat Hay Fever & Asthma Clinic 1927–32; Co-founder, Ashby Chem. Co. Inc. 1929–46; Vice-Pres. and Consultant, Allergy Laboratories Inc. 1951— (Dir. of Laboratories 1932). *Member:* (Life) Phi Delta Chi, and Lambda Chi Alpha (Charter Member, Univ. of Oklahoma Chapter), and Univ. of Oklahoma Assn. Charter Member (and Class Rep. of 1922) Univ. of Okla. Alumni Development Fund; Sigma Gamma Nu (Hon. Chemistry Fraternity); Shriners Hospital for Children, Permanent Contributing; Amer. Chemical Socy.; Amer. Assn. for Advancement of Science; Oklahoma Pharmaceutical Assn.; Nat. Adv. Bd. of American Security Council; Higher Educ. Alumni Council of Oklahoma; The

Statesman's Club of Oklahoma. *Awards:* Citation, Univ. of Okla.; Alumni Dev. Fund 1964; David Ross Boyd Council Award, 1975; Hon Alum Club and Golden Diploma for 50 years service (Okla.); Other 50 year awards. Republican. *Clubs:* Oklahoma City Scottish Rite; India Temple Shriners; O.U. Touchdown; Cimarron; Shriners' Hospitals; 100 Million Dollar; Century; Hon. Member, Noble; The Statesman's Club of Oklahoma. *Address:* 110 West 11th Street, Watonga, Okla, 73772, U.S.A.

**ASHE, Derick Rosslyn,** CMG. British diplomat. *B.* 1919. *Educ.* Bradfield Coll.; Trinity Coll. Oxford. *M.* 1957, Rissa Guinness Parker. *S.* Dominick James Alexander. *Dau.* Victoria Jane Roberta. *Career:* H.M. Forces 1940–46; 2nd Secy., Berlin & Frankfurt/Main 1947–49; Foreign Office, London 1949–50; Private Secy. to Permanent Under-Secy. of State for German Affairs 1950–53; First Secy., La Paz, Bolivia 1953–55; Foreign Office, London 1955–57; First Secy., (Information) Madrid 1957–61; Foreign Office London 1961–62; Counsellor & Head of Chancery, Addis Ababa 1962–64, Havana 1964–66; Head, Security Dept., Foreign Office London 1966–69; Minister Tokyo 1969–71; Ambassador Bucharest 1972–75; Ambassador Buenos Aires 1975–77; Ambassador & Alt. Leader, UK Perm. Delegation to the Conference of the Cttee. on Disarmament, Geneva since 1977. *Awards:* Companion of the Order St. Michael & St. George; Knight Order of Orange Nassau, Netherlands, with Swords. Mentioned in Dispatches. *Clubs:* Travellers' and Beefsteak (London). *Address:* 37–39 Rue de Vermont, 1202 Geneva, Switzerland.

**ASHENHEIM, The Honourable Leslie Erle.** Jamaican. *B.* 1899. *Educ.* Jamaica Coll., Kingston; Wadham Coll., Oxford Univ. (MA). *M.* (1) 1925, Rita Valerie Brandon; (2) 1944, Helene Vivienne Myers. *S.* Jack Douglas, Bryan Lewis. *Dau.* Jill Rosemary (Andrews). *Career:* Admitted Solicitor of Supreme Court of Jamaica 1925; Member of the Privy Council of Jamaica; Dir.: Bank of Jamaica; Chmn.: Gleaner Co. Ltd.; Insurance Co. of Jamaica Ltd.; Crown Continental Merchant Bank (Ja.) Ltd.; Jamaica Permanent Bldg. Socy.; Past Pres.: Jamaica Lawn Tennis Assn.; Past-Pres., Incorporated Law Socy. of Jamaica. *Member:* Gen. Legal Council; Council of Legal Education; Fellow, Inst. of Dir., London. *Clubs:* Jamaica; Liguanea; St. Andrew; Kingston Cricket; R.A.C., London. *Address:* 12 Seaview Avenue, Kingston 10; and *office* 32 Duke Street, Kingston, Jamaica.

**ASHFORTH, Henry Adams.** American. *B.* 1901. *Educ.* St. Paul's School (Concord, N.H.); Yale Univ. *M.* (1) 1925, Elizabeth Milbank Anderson (*D.* 1930); (2) 1931, Mariana T. Richardson (*Div.* 1951). *S.* Henry A., Jr., Alden B. *Daus.* Eleanor (Harvey), Marna (Geoffroy). (3) 1954, Elsi L. Madden. Stepchildren: Michael, Peter and Christina Madden. *Career:* Chmn. Bd. & Dir., Albert B. Ashforth Inc.; Pres. & Dir., Albert B. Ashforth Ltd.; The 415 Fifth Avenue Co. Inc.; Pecksland Realty Corp.; Ashforth Properties Inc.; Commercial Management Corp.; Vice-Pres. & Dir., Greenwich Plaza Inc.; Gen. Partner, Ashforth Todd & Co.; Dir., University Properties Inc.; The Bank of New York; Trustee, The Bowery Savings Bank; Assoc. Dir., Union Trust Co.; Dir., New York Assn. for the Blind (The Lighthouse); The East Side Assn. Inc.; Selective Amer. Realty Fund HV; Vice-Pres. & Dir., 5 East 71st Street Inc.; Hon. Chmn. Judson Health Center. *Member:* Holland Lodge F. & A. M. No. 8; St. George's Socy.; English-Speaking Union; Newcomen Socy. of England; National Inst. of Social Sciences; International Real Estate Federation (American Chapter). *Clubs:* Union; Links; Yale; Down Town (all of N.Y.C.); Round Hill (Greenwich, Conn.). *Address:* 79, Pecksland Road, Greenwich, Conn.; and *office* 12 East 44th Street, New York City 10017, U.S.A.

**ASHIOTIS, Costas A.,** MBE. High Commissioner of Cyprus. *Address:* Cyprus High Commission, 93 Park Street, London W.1.

**ASHLEY, Maurice Percy.** *B.* 1907. *Educ.* New Coll., Oxford (BA, DPh). *M.* 1935, Phyllis Griffiths. *S.* 1. *Dau.* 1. *Career:* Editor, The Listener 1958–67; Research Fellow, Loughborough Univ. of Technology 1967–70. *Publications:* England in the Seventeenth Century; Charles II the Man and the Statesman; General Monck. *Club:* Reform. *Address:* 34 Wood Lane, Ruislip, Middlesex, HA4 6EX.

**ASHTAL, Abdalla Saleh.** Yemeni Diplomat. *B.* 1940. *Educ.* Menelik Sec. School (Addis Ababa); American Univ. of Beirut, BBA; New York Univ. MA (Polit. Science). *M.* 1973, Vivian Eshoo. *Career:* Assist. Dir. of Yemeni Bank (Sanaa Branch) for Reconstr. and Development 1966–67; Mem. Supreme People's Council and Editor of Ash-Arara (wkly pub.) 1967–68; Mem. Gen Command of People's Democratic Republic of Yemen 1968–72; Sen. Counsellor to Perm. Mission of PDRY to UN 1970–73; Ambassador and Permanent Rep. of PDRY to UN since 1973; Advisor of PDRY for Int'l Monetary Fund Cttee. 1972; Non-Resident Ambassador of PDRY to Canada since 1974, and to Mexico since 1975. *Address:* 413 East 51st Street, New York, N.Y. 10022, U.S.A.

**ASHTON HILL, Norman.** MBE, TD, LLB. British. *B.* 1918. *Educ.* Old Hall Prep. Sch. Wellington; Uppingham Sch.; Birmingham Univ. (LLB Hons.). *M.* 1971, Ireina Hilda Marie. *S.* 1. *Daus.* 2. (by former marriage). *Career:* Principal Partner, Ashton Hill & Co.; Commissioner for Oaths; Dir.: Morgan Housing Co. Ltd. & group: Bonser Engineering Ltd.: North Midland Construction Co.; Chmn., Radio Trent Ltd.; Chmn., Air Transport Cttee.; Vice-Pres., Association of British Chamber of Commerce; Mem. Law Soc.; Nottinghamshire Law Soc.; Royal Aeronautical Soc.; Exec. Cttee. (Vice-Chmn.) N.S.P.C.C.; Vice-Consul for Norway in Nottinghamshire; Chmn., Air Transport British National Cttee. International Chamber of Commerce. *Address:* Old Manor House, Gregory St. Lenton, Nottingham; and *office* Pearl Assurance House, Friar Lane, Nottingham.

**ASHWORTH, Sir Herbert.** British. *B.* 1910. *Educ.* Burnley Grammar School; London Univ. (LLB, BSc Econ.). *M.* 1936, Barbara Helen Mary Henderson. *S.* 2. *Dau.* 1. *Career:* Gen.-Mgr.: Portman Building Socy. 1938–50; Co-operative Permanent Building Socy. 1950–61; Dir. and Gen.-Mgr., Hallmark Securities Ltd. 1961–66; Chmn., Housing Corp. 1968–73; Chmn., Nationwide Building Socy. 1970—; Dir., The Builder Ltd. since 1975; Chmn. Orbit General Housing Assoc. since 1977; Chmn. Surrey, E. Sussex & W. Sussex Agricultural Wages Cttee. since 1974. *Member:* Building Societies Inst. (Pres. 1947–49); Metropolitan Assn. of Building Societies (Vice-Pres.); Inst. of Directors; Building Societies Assoc. (Vice-Pres.). *Publications:* Housing in (Great Britain (1951); Building Society Work Explained (15 edn. 1977); Housing Standards. *Address:* 8 Tracery, Park Road, Banstead, Surrey; and *office* Nationwide Building Society, New Oxford House, High Holborn, London WC1V 6PW.

**ASHWORTH, Gerald Lawrence.** British. *B.* 1927. *Educ.* Nazareth House Orphanage, Widnes; Sharmans Cross Sch., Shirley, Solihull; Birmingham Coll. of Technology. *M.* 1947, Sheila. *Dau.* 1. *Career:* Dir., Stonhard-Tremco Ltd.; formerly Contracts Man., Stonhard Co. 1955; Man., New Construction Div. 1960. *Clubs:* Mem. Inst. of Marketing; Faculty Building. *Address:* Ravensdale, St. Catherine's Rd., Hayling Island, Hants.; and *office* St. Georges Road, London S.W.19.

**ASKEW, Reubin O'Donovan.** American attorney and politician. *B.* 1928. *Education:* Florida State Univ., BS; Denver Univ.; Univ of Florida LL B. *M.* 1956, Donna Lou Harper. *S.* 1. *Dau.* 1. *Career:* Assist.-solicitor Escambia County 1956–58; Member House of Representatives 1958–62; State Senator 1962–70; Governor of State of Florida since 1971 (re-elected in 1975). *Awards:* Hon. Degrees, Notre Dame, Stetson Univ, Rollins College, Eckerd College, Florida Southern College; Conversationist of the Year, Florida Audobon Socy. (1973); Nat. Wm. Booth (S.A.), (1973); Herbett H. Lehman Ethics Medal (1972); Nat. Wildlife Fed. Spec. Award (1972); Man of the Year, Fla. Country Music Foundation (1972); Hall of Fame Award, convention-planning (1972); Profile in Courage, John F. Kennedy Lodge Wash. DC (1972). *Clubs:* Scottish and York Rite Mason; Rotary (Presbyt.). *Address:* Mansion, North Adams Street, Tallahassee, Fla., U.S.A.; and *office* State Capitol Building, Tallahassee, Fla., U.S.A.

**ASKIN, Hon. Sir Robert William,** GCMG. Former Australian Premier of New South Wales. *B.* 1909. *Educ.* Sydney Technical High School. *M.* 1937, Mollie Underhill. *Career:* Leader of the Opposition in N.S.W. Parliament 1959–65; Premier and Treas. of New South Wales 13 May 1965–75 (Ret'd). *Award:* Hon. DLitt. (Univ. of N.S.W.); Grand Officer, Order of Cedar (Lebanon). *Member:* Liberal Party, *Club:* University (Sydney). *Address:* Bower Street, Manly. N.S.W.; and *office* TNT Building, Redfern, Sydney, N.S.W., Australia.

**ASKIN, Simon.** American business executive. *B.* 1910. *Educ.* Lehigh Univ. (BS Bus. Admin. 1932). *M.* 1939, Lucille Bunin. *S.* Neil Zachary. *Dau.* Glenn Nairn. *Career:* Vice-Chmn.

Bd. and Dir., Tenneco Inc.; Chmn. and Dir., Butler Chemicals Ltd.; Dir.: J. I. Case, Co.; Heyden Newport Export Corp.; Nuodex International Inc.; Nuodex Italiana, S.p.A.; Vice-Pres. and Dir., Resinera del Tigre S. de R.L. de C.V. and Newport Mexicana, S.A. de C.V.; Dir.: Nuodex Products of Canada Ltd.; Nuodex France S.A.R.L.; Nuodex Ltd. (England); Salicilatos de Mexico S.A.; N.V. Transicol (Netherlands); Nuodex Australia (Pty.) Ltd.; British Bewoid Co. Ltd.; Cal/Ink Chemical Co. (also Member Exec. Cttee.); Packaging Corp. of America; Petro-Tex Chemical Co. S.A.; Ferdinand Dobler (France); Butler Malros Ltd. (England). *Member:* Synthetic Organic Chemical Mfrs. Assn. (past Gov.); Mfg. Chemists Assn.; Socy. of the Chemical Industry; Newcomen Socy. of N. America; Council of Amer. Ordnance Assn. (Member-at-Large); Inst. of Directors, England (Fellow); Pi Lambda Phi. *Clubs:* Chemists'; Pinnacle. *Address:* 200 East 57th Street, New York, N.Y. 10022; and *office* 280 Park Avenue, New York 10017.

**ASKVIG, Kristen.** Norwegian. *B.* 1917. *Educ.* Cranleigh Sch. Surrey; Cambridge Univ.; Oslo Commercial Coll. *M.* 1945, Jorunn Marie Holter. *S.* 2. *Dau.* 1. *Career:* served to Lt. Comdr. Royal Norwegian Naval Reserve, World War II; Dep. Chmn. & Man. Dir., Norsk Braendselolje A/S; Dir., Bjölsen Valsemöle A/S; Moss Aktiemoeller; A/S Epa; A/S Auronor; A/S Vinmonopolet; Andresens Bank A/S; Norinvest A/S; Chmn. Norwegian Inst. Petroleum; Chmn. Supply Service A/S; Ret'd. *Awards:* Norwegian and British decorations; Commander, Order of the British Empire. *Address:* Holmenveien 38 B, Oslo 3, Norway.

**ASPLUND, John M.** Owner, John M. Asplund Co. *B.* 1913. *Educ.* High School; Univ. of Minnesota. *M.* 1942, Ida Moberg. *S.* John Edward, Larry Curtis, David Ronald. *Dau.* Karen Sue. *Career:* Owner: John M. Asplund Trucking Co., Minneapolis, Minn. 1934–40, and Arrow Tire Co., Minneapolis 1941–43; Manufacturer's Agent 1943–46, (maintenance, supplies, equipment), Anchorage, Alaska 1946—; Chmn. of the Bd., Asplund Supply Inc., Anchorage, Alaska 1970—; Partner, Products Big John (manufacturers), Mexico City, D.F.; Pres.: Far North Oil Co., and Spenard Public Utility District; Member, School Bd., Anchorage Independent School District; Chmn., Borough Formation Cttee. (and past Vice-Pres.), Anchorage Chamber of Commerce 1955–57, and of Economic Advisory Cttee. 1956–57; Vice-Pres., Anchorage Independent School District, Anchorage, Alaska 1963—; Chmn., Greater Anchorage Area Borough. *Member:* National Sanitary Supply Assn.; International Platform Assn.; National Assn. of County Administrators; Bd. Dirs., San Francisco Western Opera Theatre; Elected Bd. Dirs., The National Assn. of Counties 1971; Conservative. *Address:* 4001 North Wood Drive, Anchorage Alaska; and 1360-85th, N.E., Bellevue, Washington; and *office* 4005 Spenard Road, Anchorage, Alaska; and 1167 Andover Park West, Seatte, Wash., U.S.A.

**ASTON, Hon. Sir William John,** KCMG, Korean Order of Distinguished Service Merit, JP. British. *B.* 1916. *Educ.* Randwick Boys' High School, Assn. of Accountants (Diploma). *M.* 1942, Beatrice Delaney Burrett. *S.* Raymond William. *Daus.* Anne Ethel, Margaret Lillian. *Career:* Lieut., A.I.F.; Mayor of Waverley 1952–53; Pres., Bronte R.S.L. 1948; Liberal M.P. for Phillip, 1955–61 and 1963–72; Former Speaker, House of Representatives 1967–73; Chmn., Government Parties Immigration Cttee. 1958–61; Mem., Joint Parliamentary Cttee. on Foreign Affairs 1959–61, and 1964–66; Dep. Government Whip 1959–61, and 1963–64; Chief Government Whip 1964–67; Trustee, Parliamentary Retiring Allowances 1964–67; Mem., and Dep. Chmn., Joint Select Cttee. on the New and Permanent Parliament House 1965–72; Chmn., House of Representatives Standing Orders Cttee.; Chmn., Joint House Cttee.; Chmn., Library Cttee. 1967–72; Chmn., Joint Cttee. on Broadcasting of Parliamentary Proceedings 1967–72; Joint Chmn., Inter-Parliamentary Union (Chmn. of Australian Branch), and Commonweatlh Parliamentary Assn. (Australian Branch) 1967–72; Australian Delegate, Asian Peoples Anti-Communist Conference, Taipei 1960; Mem., Parliamentary Delegation to S.E. Asia 1964; Leader, Australian Delegation to Inter-Parliamentary Union Conf., Ottawa 1965; represented Australian Parliament at Opening of new Parliament Building, Zambia 1967; Convenor and Chmn., First Conf. of Australian Presiding Officers and Clerks at Table 1968; Represented Australian Parliament at State Funeral of Israeli Prime Minister Eshkol 1968; Represented Australian Parliament at I.P.U. Symposium, Geneva 1968; Conference of Comm. Presiding Officers, Ottawa 1969; Attended 2nd Conf. Comm. Presiding Officers, New Delhi 1971; Opened Aust. House Mt./Scopus Univ. Israel 1971; Led Aust. Parly. Del. Turkey, Yugoslavia, England 1971; Council, Europe Strasbourg 1971. *Clubs:* Royal Automobile; Waverley Bowling. *Address:* 55 Olola Avenue, Vaucluse, N.S.W. 2030, Australia.

**ASTOR, Hon. (Francis) David (Langhorne).** British journalist. *B.* 1912. *Educ.* Eton; Balliol Coll., Oxford. *M.* (1) 1945, Melanie Hauser. *Dau.* 1; (2) 1952, Bridget Aphra Wreford. *S.* 2. *Daus.* 3. *Career:* Yorkshire Post 1936; served in World War II (Royal Marines; Croix de Guerre) 1940–45; Foreign Editor of the Observer 1946–48; Editor of the Observer 1948–75. *Address:* 9 Cavendish Avenue, St. John's Wood, London, N.W.8.

**ASTOR, Rt. Hon. Lord of HEVER, 2nd Baron (Gavin Astor).** British. *B.* 1918. *Educ.* Eton; New Coll., Oxford. *M.* 1945, Lady Irene Haig. *S.* John Jacob, Philip. *Daus.* Bridget, Louise, Sarah. *Career:* With the Life Guards 1940–46; Chmn., Times Publishing Co. Ltd. 1959–66; Co-Chief Proprietor of The Times 1962–66; Life Pres., Times Newspapers Ltd. 1967; Dir., Alliance Assurance Co. 1954—; Chmn. of Council of Commonwealth Press Union 1959, Pres. since 1972; Chmn., Royal Commonwealth Socy. 1972–75; Lord Lieut. of Kent 1972. *Address:* Hever Castle, Edenbridge, Kent.

**ASTOR, Hon. Hugh Waldorf,** JP. British. *B.* 1920. *Educ.* Eton Coll.; Oxford Univ. *M.* 1950, Emily Lucy Kinloch. *S.* 2. *Daus.* 3. *Career:* Joined staff of The Times 1947 (Dir. 1956, Dep. Chmn. 1959); resigned Feb. 1967 on completion of merger of The Times with The Sunday Times; Chmn., The Times Bookshop 1960–67 (resigned owing to the merger stated above); Dir., Hutchinson Ltd. 1959—; Hambros Ltd. Oct. 1960—; Winterbottom Trust Ltd. 1961—; Phoenix Assurance Co. Ltd. Nov. 1962—; Dep.-Chmn., Olympia Ltd. 1968–73, Dep/Chmn. (merger); 1971–73 Chmn. and Dir.: Times Trust, T.P.C. (Holdings) Ltd., T.P.C. (Investments) Ltd., T.P.C. (Participation) Ltd.; Chmn., Council Trust Houses Forte Ltd. since 1971; Gov. and Dep.-Chmn.: Middlesex Hospital Mar. 1962–74, and Bradfield Coll. July 1962—; Gov., Gresham's School; Trust Houses Forte Ltd. since 1962 mem. of council, Chmn. since 1971. High Sheriff of Berkshire 1963; RNLI Life Gov. 1973. *Member:* The Pilgrims; Fishmongers Company (Prime Warden 1976–77); Governor R.N.L.I. 1952–64. *Clubs:* Royal Yacht Squadron; Pratt's; Brooks's; Buck's; Royal Southern Yacht; Royal Aero. *Address:* 14 Culross Street, London, W.I.

**ASTRUP HOEL, Nils.** Norwegian business executive. *B.* 1899. *Educ.* Graduate in Political Economy (1920) and Law (1926). *M.* 1931, Astrid Johanna Arnesen. *Award:* Knight of the Order of St. Olav, 1st Class. *Career:* Correspondent, Centralbanken for Norge 1921–22; Secy., A/S Freia Chocoladefabrik 1922–24; Secy., Finance Dept. 1927–28; Secy. Bd., A/S Hafslund 1928–33 (Sub-Mgr. 1933–36); Man. Dir., A/S Hafslund 1936–66 (retd.); Member Bd.: A/S Hafslund 1947, and Glommens & Laagens Brukseierforening 1938. *Publications:* Press articles on juridical and economic subjects. *Address:* Slemdalsveien 37, Oslo; P.O. Box 5010, Oslo, 3.

**ATCHLEY, Dana Winslow, Jr.,** BS. American. *B.* 1917. *Educ.* Harvard Univ. (BS). *M.* 1954, Barbara Standish Payne. *S.* 1. *Daus.* 7. *Career:* Sales Man., Tracerlab, Inc. 1947–50; Dir.: Engineering, 1950–51; Technical Co-ordinator, United Paramount Theatres 1951–52; Chmn. Bd. of Dirs. & Chief Exec. Officer, Microwave Associates Inc. Senior. *Member:* Inst. Electrical & Electronic Engineers; Amer. Radio Relay League; Visiting Cttee. Bd. Overseers Harvard Coll. Harvard Medical School, School Dental Medicine. *Clubs:* St. Botolph; Appalachian Mountain; New York Yacht; Exec. Cttee. Yacht Racing Union; Massachusetts Bay; Marblehead Frostbite Sailing; Edgartown Yacht; Radio Club America. *Address:* Concord Rd., Lincoln, Mass., U.S.A.; and *office* Burlington, Massachusetts.

**ATHERTON, Thomas Geoffrey Fenton,** MA, CEng, MIEE, FBIM, GradIMechE. British. *B.* 1929. *Educ.* Giggleswick Sch.; Clare Coll., Cambridge (MA). *M.* Ann Morgan. *S.* 1. *Dau.* 1. *Career:* Chmn. Dorman Smith Switchgear Ltd.; Dorman Smith Holdings Ltd.; Dorman Smith Fuses Ltd.; Dorman Smith Controlgear Ltd.; Dorman Smith Traffic Products Ltd. *Address:* Arragon House, Santon, Isle of Man; and *office* Preston, Lancs.

**ATKIN, Stacy,** BEcon. British. *B.* 1905. *Educ.* Fort St. Boys High Sch.; Sydney Univ. (BEcon). *M.* 1933, Peggy Edna St. Ledger. *S.* 2. *Dau.* 1. *Career:* Asst. Gen. Mgr. M.L.C. Assurance Co. Ltd.; Dir. M.L.C. Nominees Ltd.; M.L.C.

Nominees (Vic.) Ltd.; M.L.C. Custodian Pty. Ltd.; M.L.C. Fire & General Insurance Co. Pty. Ltd.; M.L.C. New Zealand Fire & General Insurance Co. Pty, Ltd.; formerly Mgr. Superannuation Dept. M.L.C. Assurance Co. Ltd. 1947–61; Mem. Economics Soc. of N.S.W.; Treas, Anglican Church of Australia; Archbishop of Sydney's Commn.; Chmn., Church of England Superannuation Fund, Chmn. Finance and Loans Board, Financial Adv. Property Admin. Board, Chmn. Invest. Trust, Chmn. finance Cttee., Treasurer Car finance & Ins. Board, Anglican Diocese of Sydney. *Address:* 30 Stanley Rd., Epping, N.S.W. 2121, Australia; and *office* 275 George Street, Sydney, N.S.W., Australia.

**ATKINSON, Basil Grose.** Australian. *B.* 1924. *M.* 1947 Margaret Shirley Geddes. *S.* 3. *Dau.* 1. *Career:* On literary staff, The West Australian 1940–54; Pilot, Royal Australian Air Force 1942–46; Mgr., San Francisco Office, Australian National Travel Assn. 1956–57; Gen. Mgr., Australian Nat. Travel Assn. and Man. Editor, Walkabout magazine 1957–67; Dir., Coates Building Ltd., Melbourne 1960–74; Pres., International Union of Official Travel Organizations 1963–65; Gen. Mgr., Australian Tourist Comm. 1967–74; Dir.-Gen. of Tourism for Bahamas 1974–76; Exec. Dir., Confederation of Western Australian Industry since 1976. Vice-Pres., Pacific Area Travel Assn. 1973–74. *Awards:* Australian Kemsley Empire Journalist 1952–53; Perth (W.A.) Newspaper Proprietors Prize Award 1947; Comdr. of Royal Order of Phoenix 1966. *Clubs:* Naval & Military; Royal King's Park Tennis. *Address:* 15 Fairbairn Street, Mosman Park, W.A. 6012, Australia.

**ATKINSON, Colin George,** J.P. Australian. *B.* 1915. *Educ.* BCom.; LLB; Dipl. Pub. Admin., AASA, ACIS, Justice of Peace. *M.* 1942, Gwenyth Margaret Lloyd. *S.* 2. *Daus.* 2. *Career:* In Tax Dept. 1934–38; Postmaster-General's Dept. 1938–39; Accountant, Dept. of Civil Aviation, Perth 1947–49; Asst. Public Service Inspector, Canberra 1949–51; Senior Inspector, Dept. of Social Services, Melbourne 1951–56; Dir. of Social Security, South Australia and Northern Territory 1956–64; Dir. of Soc. Security for Queensland 1964—. *Awards:* Efficiency Medal; Coronation Medal; LLB Queensland 1973. *Clubs:* Tattersalls; Brisbane Golf. *Address:* 136 Marshall Lane, Kenmore, Queensland; and *office* Australian Govt. Centre, 295 Ann Street, Brisbane, Australia.

**ATKINSON, John Dunstan.** New Zealand executive. *B.* 1909. *Educ.* Wanganui Collegiate School; Massy Agricultural Coll. (MAgrSc—1st Hons.). *M.* 1934, Ethel Mary Thorp. *S.* 2. *Career:* Appointed to Plant Diseases Div. 1932; worked on physiological diseases of fruit (discovered boron deficiency of apples) 1935; served with artillery of 2nd N.Z.E.F. in Egypt and Italy 1940–46 (substantive Major, M.I.D.); returned to Plant Diseases Div. 1946; Dir., Plant Diseases Div., N.Z. Dept. of Scientific and Industrial Research May 1948—; Council Member, Auckland Inst. and Museum 1960—. *Publications:* 75 scientific papers, mainly in N.Z. journals; Diseases of Tree Fruits in New Zealand. *Award:* DSc 1972; Fellow, Royal Socy. of N.Z.; Fellow, N.Z. Inst. of Agricultural Science. *Clubs:* Northern; Officers' (Auckland). *Address:* 28 Asquith Avenue, Mt. Albert, Auckland; and *office* Plant Diseases Div., Private Bag, Auckland, New Zealand.

**ATKINSON, Robert William,** CEng. FIMechE. FIProdE. FInstM. British. *B.* 1922. *Educ.* Southend High Sch. *M.* 1946. *S.* 2. *Daus.* 2. *Career:* Sen. Exec., Molins Machine Co. 1955–64; Gen. Works Mgr., Rank Taylor Hobson 1964–65; Gen. Mgr., R. & J. Beck Ltd. 1965–67; Man. Dir., Machinery Div., Klinger Manufacturing Co. Ltd.; Consultant 1967–68; Chmn., John Bolding & Sons Ltd.; Chmn., Dir., Dent & Hellyer Ltd.; Chmn., Automated Printed Circuits Ltd.; Dir., Intermeasure Ltd.; Chief Exec., Spencer (Banbury) Ltd. *Address:* Highfield House, Hurstbourne Tarrant, Andover, Hants. SP11 0AH.

**ATSUMI, Takeo.** Japanese. *B.* 1919. *Educ.* Graduated from the course of Politics, the Dept. of Laws, Tokyo Imperial Univ. in 1943 (LLB). *M.* 1948, Itsuko Kajima. *S.* 2. *Dau.* 1. *Career:* Pres., Kajima Corporation since 1966; Pres,. East-West Development Corp. since 1973; Pres. Japan Federation of Constr. Contractors since 1975; Pres. Overseas Constr. Assn. of Japan since 1975; Pres. Intern. Federation of Asian and West Pacific Contractors Assns. 1973–74; Pres. Confederation of Intern. Contractors Assns. since 1976. *Club:* Rotary Club. *Address:* 3-3-16 Sekiguchi, Bunkyo-ku, Tokyo, Japan; and *office* 1-2-7 Motoakasaka, Minato-ku, Tokyo.

**AT-TAZI, Abdeladi.** Moroccan diplomat. *B.* 1921. *Educ.* Univ. of Karaouyune, Fez. *Career:* Prof. Emeritus at Karaouyune and later at the Univ. Mohammed-V; Officer at the Ministry of National Education; Gen. Secy., Co-ordinating body between UNESCO and Arab Countries; Member, Acad. of Baghdad; Ambassador to Iraq 1962–66; to Libya 1967–68 to Iraq 1968. *Address:* Ministry of Foreign Affairs, Rabat, Morocco.

**ATWOOD, John Leland.** Senior consultant. *B.* 1904. *Educ.* Plainview (Texas) public schools; Hardin-Simmons Univ. (AB 1926); Univ. of Texas (BS Civ. Eng. 1928). *Awards:* Hon. Doctor Degrees from Stevens Inst. of Technology 1955, and Carnegie-Mellon Univ. 1965; Pepperdine Univ. 1967; Clark Univ. 1969; Wayland Baptist Coll. 1968; Distinguished Engin. Grad. Univ. of Texas 1960; Dist. Alumni, Hardin-Simmons Univ. 1970; President's Certificate of Merit for war contributions 1948; Commander of Merit of Republic of Italy for aviation contributions 1955. *Career:* Began as junior airplane engineer with Army Air Corps, Wright Field, Dayton, Ohio 1928; Design Engineer, Douglas Aircraft Co. 1930; Chief Engineer and Vice-Pres., North American Aviation Inc. 1934, Pres. 1948; Chief Exec. Officer 1960, Chmn. Bd. 1962; North Amer. Aviation Inc. merged with Rockwell Standard Co. 1967: Pres. Chief Exec. Officer, North American Rockwell Corp. 1967–70; Senior Consultant since 1970 (name changed Rockwell International 1973); Dir., Cyprus Mines Corp. since 1971; Hon. Fellow. Amer. Inst. Aeronautics and Astronautics Pres. 1954–55); former Dir., California State Chamber of Commerce, Los Angeles Chamber of Commerce, Equitable Life Assurance Socy.; Pacific Indemnity Co.; Rockwell Intl.; Times Mirror Co.; American Management Assn., and Atomic Industrial Forum; Chmn., Nat. Advisory Cttee. for Aeronautics 1958–59; Dir., Los Angeles World Affairs Council 1965; Automobile Club, Southern California 1969. *Address:* 2230 East Imperial Highway, El Segundo, Calif., U.S.A.

**AUDETTE, Louis de la Chesnaye,** OC (Canada), QC, BA, LPh, LLB. Canadian public service (Retd.). *B.* 1907. *Educ.* Univ. of Ottawa (BA, LPh); Univ. of Montreal (LLB). Unmarried. *Career:* Called to Bar of Province of Quebec 1931; created Q.C. 1953; practised with Audette & O'Brien, Montreal 1931–39; served in World War II with R.C.N. 1939–45; commanding ships in North Atlantic and Mediterranean; mentioned in despatches; Commander RCN(R), (retd.); First Secy., Dept. of External Affairs 1945–47; Commissioner, Canadian Maritime Comm. 1947–54 (Chmn. 1954–59); Dir.: Export Development Corp. 1946–71; Crown Assets Disposal Corp. 1953–59; Park Steamship Co. Ltd. 1948–59 (Pres. 1954–59); Member, Northwest Territories Council 1947–59, and Court Martial Appeal Bd. 1951–59; Chmn., Tariff Bd. 1959–72; Chmn., Preparatory Cttee. 1954–59 and Pres., First Assembly (London 1959) of Intergovernmental Maritime Consultative Organizations; Pres., Canadian Club of Ottawa 1953–54, and Ottawa Philharmonic Orchestra 1955–59; Administrator, Maritime Pollution Claims Fund since 1973. *Club:* Cercle Universitaire. *Address:* 451 Besserer Street, Ottawa, Ont., Canada KIN 6C2.

**AUDLAND, Christopher John.** CMG. British. Official of the European Communities. *B.* 1926. *Educ.* Winchester College. *M.* 1955, Maura Daphne Sullivan. *S.* 2. *Dau.* 1. *Career:* service British Army, rising to Captain Royal Artillery 1944–48; British Foreign, later Diplomatic Service 1948; Foreign Office London 1948–49; (British element) Control Commission for Germany 1949–52; Vice Consul, Strasbourg, Deputy to the British Perm. Rep. to Council of Europe 1952–55; British Embassy Washington 1955–58; Foreign Office London 1959–61; Member, UK Del. negotiations, Member States, European Communities 1961–63; Head, Chancery British Embassy, Buenos Aires 1963–67; Common Market Dept. Commonwealth Office, London 1967; Head, Science & Technology Dept. Foreign Office 1968–70; Counsellor (Head of Chancery) Bonn, Deputy Leader, UK Del. Four Power negotiations Berlin 1970–73; Deputy Secy. General Commission of the European Communities since 1973. *Award:* Companion, Order of St. Michael & St. George. *Club:* United Oxford and Cambridge University. *Address:* Avenue des Lauriers 5, 1150 Brussels, Belgium; and *office* Commission of the European Communities, Rue de la Loi 200, 1040 Brussels.

**AUERBACH, Benjamin.** American radio (electronics) engineer. *B.* 1917. *Educ.* Univ. of Chicago; Illinois Inst. of Technology; Roosevelt Coll. (Chicago); Rutgers Univ. *Career:* Successively Production Supervisor and Asst. Engineer, Olson Mfg. Co. (now Olson Radio Warehouse), and Asst. Engineer, Electronic Engineering Co., Akron, Ohio 1936–42; Inspector-in-Charge, War and Navy Depts., Wright Field, Dayton 1942–44; Radio Engineer, Belmont Radio Corp., Chicago (designed and processed special export packing for army and navy heavy electronic equipment) 1944–46; Chief Engineer, Music-Auer Industries, Chicago (designed and manufactured radio-phonographic combinations) 1946; Resident Chief Engineer, Belmont Radio Corp. (division of Raytheon Corp.) 1946–47; with Radio Corp. of America (Camden, N.J., plant) 1947–73; successively foreman in charge of color TV prototype Dept. MFG., First Color TV for consumer market, and quality control engineer; in latter post assigned to environmental testing of government equipment and represented the government for its acceptance; also assigned to Quality Engineering Laboratory to evaluate materials to conform with government and company specifications; Eng. in charge of Electronic Prototype Dept. with R & D section, for Langston Co., Div. of Molins Machine Co. of Gt. Britain (NJ) since 1974. *Member:* Inst. of Electronic & Electrical Engineers; Ind. Mgmt. Council of Camden, American Radio Relay League (Radio Amateur Station K2POY); Y.M.C.A. American Assoc. of Retired Persons; Life Mem., Nat. Rifle Assoc. of America; the Conservative Caucus; Cttee. for Survival of a Free Congress. Republican. *Address:* 161 Watergate, Maple Shade, N.J. 08052, U.S.A.

**AULD, Hon. James Alexander Charles.** Canadian. *B.* 1921. *M.* 1946, Nancy Eleanor Gilmour. *S.* James Alan Gilmour. *Dau.* Alexandra Christine Gilmour. *Career:* Min. of Transport for Province of Ontario 1962; Min. of Tourism and Information, and Min. of Public Records and Archives, Province of Ontario, Canada Aug. 1963–71; Min. of Public Works 1971; Min. of the Environment 1972–74; Min. of Colls. & Univs. since 1974; Chmn. of Management Board of Cabinet since 1975. LID Univ. Dundee (Scotland) 1974. Progressive Conservative. *Clubs:* Canadian Legion; Royal Canadian Military Inst., Albany; Brockville Yacht. *Address:* 173 Hartley Street, Brockville, Ont.; and *office* Parliament Buildings, Queen's Park, Toronto, Ont., Canada.

**AULD, Kenneth Charles, J.P.** Australian Chartered Secy. *B.* 1907. *Educ.* Brisbane Grammar School; Fellow of Chartered Inst. of Secretaries; Fellow, Australian Socy. of Accountants. *M.* 1936, Margaret Elizabeth Mathers. *S.* Kelvin. *Dau.* Jeanette. *Career:* Gen. Secy. of The Presbyterian Church of Australia, in New South Wales (retired 10 Nov. 1973); for more than thirty years engaged in accounting, secretaryship and management of various companies in New South Wales and Queensland; Hon. Directorships: The Presbyterian Foundation & The Scottish Hospital (also Hon. Treas.); Elected as a Corporate Trustee, Presbyterian Church (N.S.W. & A.C.T.) May 1977; Past Queensland Pres. and Australasian Councillor of The Australasian Inst. of Secretaries; Past Queensland Vice-Pres. of The Commonwealth Inst. of Accountants; Past Councillor and Treasurer, Queensland Div. of The Australasian Inst. of Cost Accountants; Past Pres. (twice), Queensland Dais of The Australian Rostrum (appointed first Freeman of The Rostrum in Queensland); Past Pres., Brisbane Grammar School O.B. Union (N.S.W. Group). *Clubs:* Manly Bowling; New South Wales Bowlers. *Address:* Lindisfarne, 623 Great Western Highway, Faulconbridge, New South Wales 2776, Australia.

**AULT, Phillip H.** *B.* 1914, U.S.A. Editor and writer. *Educ.* De Pauw Univ. (AB). *M.* 1943, Karoline Byberg. *S.* Frank, Bruce. *Dau.* Ingrid. *Career:* United Press correspondent and editor 1938–48; Chief of Bureau, London 1944–45; War Correspondent in Iceland and North Africa 1941–43; Editorial Dir., Los Angeles Mirror-News 1948–57; Exec. Editor Associated Desert Newspapers, Indio, California 1958–67; Associate Editor, South Bend Tribune, South Bend. *Publications:* This is the Desert; News Around the Clock; How to Live in California; Home Book of Western Humor; Wonders of the Mosquito World; These are the Great Lakes; Wires West; "All Aboard!"; co-authors Reporting the News; Introduction to Mass Communications; Springboard to Berlin. *Address:* 3025 Woodridge Avenue, South Bend, Indiana 46626, U.S.A.

**AURA, Teuvo Ensio.** Finnish Statesman & Lord Mayor of Helsinki. *B.* 1912. *Educ.* Univ. of Helsinki. (UM). *M.* (1) 1939, Kaino Kelo Kivekas. (*D.* 1960). (2) 1976, Sirkka Wiik. *S.* Jalo Ensio, Matti Ilmari. *Dau.* Pirkko Tuulikki. *Career:* With Bd. of Supply 1940–41, Chmn. 1942; Dir. Post Office Savings Bank 1942–43; Dir. Gen. 1943–68; Lord Mayor of Helsinki 1968—; Min. of Commerce and Industry 1950–51, 1953–54 and 1957; Min. of Justice 1951; Prime Minister of Finland 1970–72. *Member:* (Pres.) Helsinki City Cncl. 1957–68; Chmn., Economic Cncl. 1946–47 and 1951–56; Mem., Joint Delegation of Credit Inst. 1949–68; Mem., Finance Bd. 1953; Member of Administration Bd. of Amer-Tupakka Oy 1961–73; Helsinki Chamber of Commerce 1958—; Mutual Life Insurance Co., Salama 1950–71; Insurance Company Pohjola 1955—; Administration Bd. of Rauma-Repola Oy. 1952—; Chmn. of Administration Bd. of Aluma Oy. 1957—; Chmn., Admin. Bd. of Industrialization Fund 1958–68; Chmn. of Administration Bd. of IBM Finland 1968—; Savo Oy 1969–76; The Finnish Fair Corp. 1972—; L. M. Ericsson (Finland) since 1975. *Address:* Aleksanterinkatu 14, Helsinki; and Kaupunginkanslia, Pohjoisesplanadi 11–13. 00170 Helsinki 17, Finland.

**AURNER, Robert Ray.** American consultant, corporate executive, author, educator. *B.* 1898. *Educ.* Univ. of Iowa (AB *summa cum laude* 1919, AM 1920, PhD 1922). *M.* 1921, Kathryn Dayton. *S.* Robert R. II. *Career:* member Officers Training Command, U.S. Naval Reserve Force 1919; State Commissioner, Wisconsin Library Certification Bd. 1931–38; Pres., Aurner & Associates, Corporate Counsel 1938—; Vice-Pres.: Pacific Futures Inc. 1962–72; Vice-Pres. and Mem. Bd. Dirs., Scott, Incorporated, Management Consultant Div., 1947—; Mem., Bd. Dirs., Carmel Savings and Loan Assn., Carmel, California 1960–71; Mem., Bd. Dirs., Mem., Exec. Cttee., Chmn. of the Finance Cttee., and Chmn. of the Cttee. on Memorials, The Carmel Foundation Inc. 1954—; Dir. SAE Corp. Evanston, Ill. 1943–53 (Pres., Chmn. of Board 1951–53); Trustee Levere Memorial Foundation (Chicago) 1943–53 (Pres., Chmn. of Bd. 1951–53); Mem. Nat. Advisory counsel, Atlantic Union, Inc. since 1949; Advisory Gov. and Mem. Bd., Monterey Fund for Education 1965—; Mem. Bd. and Chmn. of the Cttee. on Endowments, York School, Monterey 1966–69; Mem. of Faculty and Administrative Staff, Univ. of Wisconsin 1925–48; Ranking Research Prof. of Business Administration 1930–48; Visiting Prof. of Business Management, Univ. of Pittsburgh 1934, 1936, 1939; Administrative Consultant, International Cellucotton Products Co. 1947–52, and Fox River Paper Corp. 1947–60; Consultant: U.S. Naval Post-graduate School 1957–62; Dept. of Navy, Dept. of Defense; Allis Chalmers Corp., Milwaukee; Jahn & Ollier Corp., Morris Schenker Roth. Inc., First National Bank of Chicago, Wisconsin Div. of Vital Statistics; Dean, Coll. of Commerce, Biarritz American Univ. (Biarritz) 1945–46; Attached U.S. Army U.S.F.E.T., I. and E.Div. Field Grade, Rank Colonel 1945–46; Selected Mem., Univ. of Wisconsin Lecture Bureau 1930–48; Special Lecturer, Netherlands School of Economics, Rotterdam 1945; Guest Lecturer, Management Div., U.S. Naval Post-graduate School, Monterey, Calif.; Visiting Research Prof., The Huntington Library, San Marino, Calif. 1941; Special Mission Dept. of Defense, European Theatre of Operations 1945–46; Selected Hon. Fellow, Amer. Business Communication Assn. 1961. *Award:* Distinguished Service Award, with gold medal and citation, Sigma Alpha Epsilon Natl. Fraternity 1967. U.S. State Dept. Special Representative, Dutch-American Conference, The Hague 1945. *Publications:* Henry Fielding, Lucianist (1920); A History of the Structure of the English Sentence, from Caxton to Macaulay (1922); Pioneer in Prose, William Caxton (1924); Effective Communication in Business with Management Emphasis (Eight Edns. 1936–78); Effective English for Business Communication (Seven Edns. 1933–77); American Business Practice (4 vols.), co-author and contr. editor; American Encyclopaedia of the Social Sciences (contr. editor); Practical English for Colleges (Six edns 1945–77), etc. Winner of Championship Gold Medal, The Northern Oratorical League, Big Ten Univ. Group in 1919 intercollegiate competition. *Member:* Amer. Business Communication Assn. (Pres. 1940); Amer. Marketing Assn. (Vice-Pres. 1931); Phi Beta Kappa; Delta Sigma Rho; Alpha Kappa Psi; Sigma Alpha Epsilon (Natl. Pres. 1951–53, Mem. Supreme Council 1943–53). *Clubs:* Continental (Chicago); Highlands; Decemvir; Convivium (Carmel); The Group (Pebble Beach Calif.); Statesman's (Los Angeles). *Address:* San Antonio & Inspiration Avenues, Carmel-by-the-Sea, Calif. 93921; and *office* P.O. Box 3434, Carmel, Calif. 93921, U.S.A.

**AUSLANDER, George.** Retired American banker. *B.* 1904. *Educ.* Pratt Inst. Brooklyn (Architect and Mechanical Engineer). *M.* 1935, Evelyn Foster Steiner. *Daus.* June Foster, Diane Evelyn. *Career:* Mayor, Hewlett Harbor, L.I., N.Y.; Chmn. Bd., Valley National Bank of L.I. 1949, and of Public Service Heat & Power Co. 1945; Pres., National Combustion Co. Inc., N.Y.C.; Chmn., Finance Cttee., Congressional Life Insurance Co., N.Y.C. Republican. *Member:* Amer. Bankers' Assn.; Amer. Inst. of Banking; N.Y. State Bankers' Assn.;

Nassau Clearing House Assn. *Clubs:* Metropolitan (N.Y.C.) Lake Placid (N.Y.); Lawrence Beach (Atlantic Beach, N.Y.); Cherry Valley Golf (Garden City); Rockville Links (Rockville Center). *Address:* (Winter) 235 Eden Road, Palm Beach, Florida 33480; (Summer) Prospect Hill, Box 808, Montauk, N.Y. 11954, U.S.A.

**AUSTAD, Harold Iver,** MBE, CBE. New Zealand. *B.* 1900. *Educ.* Victoria Univ. Coll. (BCom), FCA (N.Z.). *M.* 1931, Ruth Allison Grenside. *S.* Warren Iver (MD). *Dau.* Pauline Allison. *Career:* With Public Works Dept. 1919–20; Engaged in advertising and publicity since 1920; Chmn., J. Ilott Ltd., Wellington N.Z.; Mgr., N.Z. Olympic Team to Rome 1960; Pres.: N.Z. Olympic Assn. 1960–77 (Life Member); Commonwealth Games Assn. 1960–77, Wellington Rugby Football Union 1956 and 1961; Assn. of N.Z. Advertising Agencies 1950–55, 1970; N.Z. Amateur Athletic Assn. 1941–42 (Chmn. 1936–63, Life Mem.; Mem. Lottery Bd. of Control. *Clubs:* Wellington Rotary; Wellesley (Pres. 1972–77); Miramar Golf; Athletic Rugby Football (Life Mem.). *Address:* 274 Oriental Parade, Wellington; and *office* c/o J. IlottLtd., P.O. Box 1491, Wellington, New Zealand.

**AUSTEN, William John,** OBE. AM. Inst. W. (Lond.), FAI, Ex, FAIM. Australian executive. *B.* 1910. *Educ.* Cleveland Street High School, Sydney. *Career:* Chmn. Dirs., William Austen & Associates Pty Ltd.; National Chmn., Australian Metal Trades Export Group; Mem., Aust. Manufactures Export Council since 1960, Pres. 1963–65; Foundation Chmn., Aust. Inst. of Export (N.S.W. Div.) 1964–65; Nat. Pres. since 1971; Mem., Export Devel. Council 1965; Export Awards Cttee. 1964–65; Dir., Lincoln Electric Co. (Aust.) Pty. Ltd. since 1948; Distragen Pty. Ltd. since 1961: Leader Australian Trade Mission to Middle East 1964; Leader Australian Survey Mission, South East Europe 1971. *Clubs:* Rotary; R.A.C.A.; American. *Address:* Shirley Road, Wollstonecraft, N.S.W. 2065, Australia.

**AUSTIN, Allan Stewart.** American. *B.* 1905. *Educ.* Sheffield Scientific School (BSc); Yale Univ. (1927). *M.* 1947, Winifred Nienhouse. *S.* Richard C., James W. *Career:* Chmn., The Austin Co., & Austin International Corp. 1963—. Trustee: Hiram Coll., Hiram, Ohio 1965—; Lake Erie Coll., Painesville, Ohio 1966—; Cleveland Inst. of Music 1957—. *Publications* and articles: Religion in Russia Today (1931); Communism Builds Its City of Utopia (1931); Data on Design and Construction at Autostroy Plant and Workers' City, Monograph; New Frontiers for North American Business (1961). *Member:* President's Assn. of The American Management Assn. Republican. *Clubs:* Kirtland Country (Ohio); Union (Cleveland); Yale (New York); Gulf Stream (Golf); Delray Beach (Florida); Delray Beach Yacht (Florida); Club de Golf (Sotograude, Spain). *Address:* 2731 Sherbrooke Road, Shaker Heights, Ohio, 44122; and *office* 3560 Mayfield Road, Cleveland, Ohio, 44121, U.S.A.

**AUSTIN, Harry G.** BS, MBA. American Construction Engineering director. *B.* 1917. *Educ.* Texas A. & M. Univ. (BS, (ElectEng)); Harvard Univ. (MBA). *M.* 1940, Elizabeth Ann Heard. *Daus.* 3. *Career:* Exec. Vice-Pres. Construction, and Dir., Brown & Root Inc.; Dir. Bank of Harris County; Atlas Travel Inc.; NUS Corp.; Wiley Coll. Marshall, Texas. *Member:* Nat. Socy. of Professional Engineers; Inst. of Electrical & Electronic Engineers; Houston Engineering & Scientific Socy.; Cttee. on Foreign Relations; Mem., Advisory Board, Salvation Army, Houston. *Award:* Dr. of Humanities, Wiley College. *Clubs:* Houston Country; Petroleum; Ramada. *Address:* 267 Pine Hollow Lane, Houston, Texas 77056, U.S.A.; and *office* P.O. Box 3, Houston, Texas 77001.

**AUSTIN, James B.** American research administrator. *B.* 1904. *Educ.* Lehigh Univ. (Chemical Engineer 1925); Yale Univ. (PhD 1928). *M.* 1930, Janet Evans. *S.* Peter A. *Dau.* Winifred M. *Career:* With U.S. Steel Corp.; Vice-Pres., Research 1956–68; Asst. Vice-Pres. 1955–56; Dir. of Research 1946–55; Admin. Vice-Pres. 1958–68; Hon. DSc, Lehigh Univ. 1962; Elected Trustee, Mt. Holyoke Coll., South Hadley, Mass. 1962; Hon. Mem. The Metals Socy. London 1974; Pres., America Inst. Mining Metallurgical & Petroleum Engineers 1973. *Member:* Nat. Acad. of Engineering; Hon. Mem., Iron & Steel Inst. of Japan. *Clubs:* Century Association (N.Y.C.); Duquesne (Pittsburgh); University (Pittsburgh); *Publications:* The Flow of Heat in Metal (Pub.: Amer. Soc. for Metals) (1941); many papers in scientific and technical journals. *Address:* 114 Buckingham Road, Pittsburgh 15, Pa., U.S.A.

**AUSTIN, Peter Roger.** Canadian. Professional engineer. *B* 1909. *Educ.* Queen's Univ., Kingston, Ont. (BSC Elec. Eng.). *M.* 1940, Margaret Johannsen. *S.* Peter John, Erik Andrew, Christopher Roger. *Daus.* Karen, Nancy. *Career:* Dir. and Vice-Pres., Planning, Imperial Tobacco Products Ltd., Montreal, P.Q. *Publication:* Two Mayors of Early Hamilton. *Address:* 4385 boulevard de Maisonneuve, Westmount, P.Q., Canada.

**AUSTIN, Robert Winthrop.** American lawyer and educator. *B.* 1908. *Educ.* Dartmouth Coll. (AB *cum laude*); Harvard Univ. (LLB); Hon. LLD, Hanover Coll. 1964. *M.* 1933, Mary L. Carpenter. *S.* Lewis. *Daus.* Linda, Jane, Mary King. *Career:* Assoc., Breed, Abbott & Morgan (law firm), New York City 1932 (partner 1944–46); Vice-Pres., Dir. and Secy., Penick & Ford Ltd., Inc., New York City 1946–51; Charles Edward Wilson Prof. of Business Administration, Prof., Harvard Graduate School of Business Administration 1967—; specialist in anti-trust, food and drug, pricing, advertising, distribution problems; Dir., Warren Pumps Inc. (Warren, Mass.); McCord Corp., Detroit; Sperry & Hutchison Co., N.Y.C. *Member:* American Bar Assn., and New York State Bar Assn. (Mem., Legislative Cttee.; Past Chmn., Food and Drug Law Cttee.; Anti-trust Cttee.; and Cttee. on Federal Trade Comm. Act); Delta Kappa Epsilon. *Address:* Harvard University Graduate School of Business Administration, Boston, Mass. 02163, U.S.A.

**AUSTIN, Roy Bailey,** Dip. CAM. British. *B.* 1928. *Educ.* Marling School. *M.* 1950, Margaret Blanche Brittain. *Daus.* 2. *Career:* Chmn.: Austin Hubbard Ltd.; Dir., Hubbard, Buck Inc.; Aston Broadlands Ltd.; Florista; Broadcast Exchange and Mart Ltd. *Address:* Ahwahnee, Manor Road, Brixham, Devon; and *office* 78 Tor Hill Road, Torquay TQ2 5RY.

**AVEROFF-TOSSIZZA, Evangelos.** Greek Politician. *B.* 1910. *Educ.* Univ. of Lausanne (Economics). *Career:* Commenced career as journalist in Switzerland and Greece. Active in the resistance movement 1939–45; imprisoned in Northern Italy, but escaped and continued the resistance until the end of the war; Elected Member of Parliament 1946 (National Radical Union); successively Min. of Supply, and Min. of National Economy and Commerce. Former Min. of Foreign Affairs in the Greek Government 1956–62; Active in resistance against Greek dictatorship 1967–74, and twice imprisoned; Min. of National Defense since 1974. *Publications:* Author of Literary Works and many texts on Political and Economic Subjects. *Address:* 33 Pentelis Street, Kifissia, Athens; and Ministry of National Defense, Athens, Greece.

**AVERY, Eric Nugent,** CBE. British business executive. *B.* 1907. *Educ.* Sedbergh School; St. John's Coll., Cambridge (MA); Princeton Univ.; Davison Scholar. *M.* 1944, Freda Connolly. *S.* Eric Anthony Nugent. *Daus.* Edwina Jane Nugent, Perdita Ann Nugent. *Career:* With Shell Co. of China Ltd. 1930–39; with Royal Dutch Shell Group 1930–58; in London, China and Australia 1939–55; when Chmn. of Shell companies in Australia was engaged in Marketing Refining Petrochemicals Exploration; Consul for Brazil, Melbourne 1967; Member Bd. of Management, Alfred Hospital since 1958; Chmn. Man. Dir., Assoc. Australian Resources N.L.; Chmn., Mines Administration Ltd.; CompAir Australasia, Glanvill, Holland; Dir., Jennings Industries Ltd.; Dun & Bradstreet Pty. Ltd. *Awards:* Shanghai Defence Medal (1937); Coronation Medal (1953). *Address:* 711 Toorak Road, Melbourne 3144; and *office* 411 Collins Street, Melbourne 3000, Vic., Australia.

**AVERY, Henry.** American. *B.* 1919. *Educ.* M.I.T. (BSc Chem. Eng. 1941). *M.* 1947, Mary Ruth Halverson. *S.* Eric. Halverson. *Daus.* Cynthia Gail, Deborah Lee, Sarah Ann. *Career:* Development Engr., G. L. Cabot Co., Boston 1946–51; Gen. Mgr., Industrial Chemicals Div., Pittsburgh Coke & Chemical Co. 1951–60; Exec. Vice-Pres. and Dir., Pittsburgh Chemical Co. 1960–66; Group V.P. 1966–69; served to Major A.U.S., World War II (Legion of Merit, U.S.; Medal of Valor (Italy); Civilian Aide to Secy. of Army for Western Penna. 1966; Vice-Pres., Plastics USS Chemicals Div., U.S. Steel Corp. 1969—. *Member* Penna. Advisory Council, Small Business Administration; Regional Export Expansion Cncl., Dept. of Commerce; M.I.T. Educational Counsellors, Western Penna. and Scholarship Cttee. (Chmn.); Mfg. Chemists Assn. (alternate Dir.); Commercial Development Assn. (Pres. Elect.); American Defense Preparedness Assn. (Pres. Pgh. Chapter), Nat. Bd. Dirs. & Exec. Cttee. 1976; M.I.T. Alumni Assn.; Greater Pittsburgh C. of C. (Chmn. Bd., Past Pres., Chmn., Econ. Development Cncl.); S.A.R.; Mayflower Descendants. *Decorations:* Commander, Military Order of the World Wars. *Publications:* Ordnance section, U.S. Military Encyclopaedia (1945). *Clubs:* University; Duquesne (Pittsburgh). *Address:* 2681 Cedarvue Drive, Pittsburgh, Pa. 15241; and *office* 600 Grant Street, Pittsburgh, Pa. 15230, U.S.A.

**AVERY, Wallace E.** Executive. *B.* 1905. *Educ.* Univ. of California (BSc 1930, LLB 1933). *M.* 1933, Viola Rohrs. *S.* John Wallace. *Daus.* Susan Irene, Sara Eleanor. *Career:* Oil business, California 1933–42; Asst. Chief Counsel, Petroleum Administration for War 1942–45; Attorney, Asst. Gen. Mgr., Industrial & Public Relations Dept., Texaco, New York 1945–54; Asst. Secy. 1954–56; Secy. 1956–61; Vice-Pres., Texaco, Los Angeles since 1961. Member of the Bars of State of California and the U.S. Supreme Court. *Clubs:* Cloud (N.Y.C.); California (Los Angeles). *Address:* 688 Canterbury Road, San Marino, Calif.; and *office* 3350 Wilshire Boulevard, Los Angeles 5, Calif., U.S.A.

**AVIDAR, Yoseph.** Israeli diplomat and soldier. *B.* 1906. *M.* 1932, Yemima Tschernowitz. *Daus.* 2. *Career:* Mem., Chief Command 1937–48; Dir., Military Industry 1945–46; Dep. Chief, Gen. Staff 1946–47; Quartermaster Gen., I.D.F. 1948–49; Brigadier Gen. Commander, Northern Command 1949–52; Commander, Central Command 1952–53; Head Gen. Staff branch 1954–55; Ambassador of Israel to U.S.S.R. 1955–58; Dir. Gen., Min. of Labour 1959–60; Ambassador of Israel to Argentina 1961–65; Dir., Govt. Corp. Authority 1966–68; Comptroller of the Histadrut 1968–71; Russian Studies Hebrew Univ. Jerusalem 1971–73, BA; Post-Grad. Student, Russian Studies since 1973. *Address:* 5 Mevo Yoram, Jerusalem, Israel.

**AVILA, Charles Francis.** American Corporate Director. *B.* 1906. *Educ.* Harvard Engineering and Business Schools (BS). *M.* 1934, Elizabeth McLean. *S.* Donald F. *Dau.* Carolyn L. (Quinn). *Career:* Pres.: Boston Edison Co. 1960–67, Electric Cncl. of New England 1964 and 1965; Chm., Electric Research Cncl. 1965–67; Pres., Edison Electric Inst. 1967–68; Chmn. Bd., Boston Edison Co. 1967–71 (now retired); Dir.: Liberty Mutual Fire Insurance Co., National Shawmut Bank of Boston and Shawmut Corporation; Raytheon Co., Liberty Mutual Insurance Co.; Charles T. Main, Inc.; Member, Harvard Univ. Overseers Cttee. to visit Dept. of Maths. *Awards:* Hon. LLD, Univ. of Mass.; IEEE Edison Medal 1968. *Member:* Socy. of Harvard Engnrs. and Scientists; Nat. Acad. of Engineering; Senior member, The Conference Board, Inc.; Fellow, Inst. Electrical and Electronic Engineers. *Clubs:* Commercial; Harvard; Beacon Society; Beach (Swampscott). *Address:* 272 Atlantic Avenue, Swampscott, Mass. 01907, U.S.A.

**AVINERI, Prof. Schlomo.** Israeli Political Scientist. *B.* 1933. *Educ.* BA cum laude, Hebrew Univ., Jerusalem 1956; MA cum summa laude, 1960; PhD, 1964. *M.* 1957, Dvora Nadler. *Dau.* 1. *Career:* Visiting Prof., Yale Univ. 1966–67; Prof. of Political Science, Hebrew Univ. since 1969; Fellow, Center for the Humanities, Wesleyan Univ. 1970–71; Research Fellow, Australian National Univ. 1971; Visiting Prof., Cornell Univ. 1973; Dean, Faculty of Social Sciences, Hebrew Univ. 1975–76; Dir. Gen., Min. for Foreign Affairs, Jerusalem since 1976. *Member:* Israel Political Science Assoc.; American Political Science Assoc.; Int'l. Hegel-Gesellschaft. *Awards:* Rubin Prize for Book on Marx. *Publications:* The Social & Political Thought of Karl Marx (Cambridge, 1968); Israel & the Palestinians (N.Y., 1971); Hegel's Theory of the Modern State (Cambridge, 1972). *Address:* 50 Harlap Street, Jerusalem, Israel; and *offices* Ministry of Foreign Affairs, Jerusalem; and Dept. of Political Science, Hebrew University, Jerusalem.

**AVNER, Gershon.** Israeli civil servant. *B.* 1919. *Educ.* Hebrew Secondary School, Haifa; Oxford Univ. *M.* 1950, Yael Vogel. *Career:* Political Dept., Jewish Agency for Palestine 1942–48; Dir., West European Dept., Ministry for Foreign Affairs 1948–52; Chargé d'Affaires, Legation Budapest and Sofia 1952–53; Counsellor, Israel Embassy in London 1953–57; Dir., U.S. Div., Min. for Foreign Affairs 1958–61; Ambassador to Norway 1962–63, to Canada 1963–67; Asst. Dir.-Gen. for European Affairs, Ministry for Foreign Affairs, Jerusalem 1967–71; Dir. Office, Israel Commissioner for Complaints from the Public (Ombudsman) 1971–74; Secretary to the Cabinet of Israel since 1974. *Address:* Prime Minister's Office, Jerusalem.

**AWOLOWO, Chief Obafemi.** Leader of Yoruba people. Ashiwaju of Ijebu Remo, Losi of Ikenne, Lisa of Ijeun, Apesin of Oshogbo, Odole of Ife, Ajagunla of Ado Ekiti, Odofin of Owo and Obon Ik an Isong of Ibibioland: Nigeria statesman and politician. *B.* 1909. *Educ.* London Univ. (BComs Hons.); Inner Temple (LLB, BL Hons.): LLD, DSc (Econ.), DLitt. *M.* 1937, Hannah Idown Dideolu. *S.* 2. *Daus.* 3. *Career:* Teacher 1928–29; Stenographer 1930–34; Newspaper Reporter 1934–35; engaged in motor transport and produce buying 1936–44; Solicitor and Advocate, Supreme Court of Nigeria 1947–51; Min. of Local Government and Leader of Government Business, Western Nigeria 1952–54; Co-founder and First Gen. Secy. of Egbe Omo Oduduwa; Founder and Fed. Pres. of the Action Group of Nigeria—the party in power in Western Nigeria 1952–62, and in Opposition both in the House of Representatives and in the Eastern and Northern Houses of Assembly 1954–65; Premier in the Government of Western Nigeria 1954–59; Leader of the Opposition in the Federal Parliament 1960–63; Pres., Amateur Athletic Assn. of Nigeria 1960–63. Chancellor of Univ. of Ife, Nigeria 1967–75; Vice-Pres., Federal Executive Cncl. and i/c Ministry of Finance 1967–71; Chancellor, Ahmadu Bello Univ., Zaria 1975—. *Publications:* Path to Nigerian Freedom; 'Awo'—an Autobiography of Chief O. Awolowo; Thoughts on Nigerian Constitution; My Early Life; The People's Republic; Strategy and Tactics of the People's Republic of Nigeria; various pamphlets. *Address:* P.O. Box 136, Ibadan, Nigeria.

**AWTRY, Col. John H.** (U.S. Army; retd.). Lawyer and insurance executive. *B.* 1897. *Educ.* Univ. of Texas School of Law (LLB, Doctor of Jurisprudence degree). *M.* 1922, Nell Catherine Jacoby. *Dau.* Nell Catherine (Gilchrist, now deceased). *Career:* Retired as full Colonel in the Army of the U.S. for disability incurred in line of duty in World War II and Korea; awarded Bronze Star Medal for meritorious achievement in ground operations against the enemy and for participation in planning the invasion of Europe 1944, and three battle campaigns across France to Germany; served continuously Sept. 1942–Mar. 1953. Awarded the Legion of Merit on an order of the President of the U.S. 'for Exceptionally Meritorious Conduct in the Performance of Outstanding Services' Jan. 1945–Jan. 1946, while on duty in the Office of the Judge Advocate General, U.S. Army, Washington, D.C. Lawyer (member of the Bar) from 1921, admitted to practice in all the Courts of Texas, U.S. Supreme Court, U.S. Court Military Appeals, U.S. Court of Claims. President and Counsel and member of Board of Directors of several insurance firms doing nationwide business 1927–42. *Publications:* judicial decisions while member of Armed Services Board of Contract Appeals, Dept. of Defense (pub. Commercial Clearing House). Mem.: Natl. Exchange Club (Pres. 1933–34 and 1934–35; Plaque certifying that his name is placed in Court of Honor of the Natl. Exchange Club 1966); Texas Exchange Clubs (Past Pres.); Dallas Exchange Club (Past Pres., and Life Mem.); Texas Socy. of Washington, D.C.; Texas Socy. of N.Y.; Ex-Students Assn. of Univ. of Texas; Federal Grand Jury Assn. (Southern District, New York); Military Order of World Wars; Order of Lafayette: Leisure Worlder of the Month, June 1977; Judge Advocate Assn. Mason (320 Scottish Rite; Royal Arch.). Mem.: American, Texas, Dallas and Federal Bar Assns. *Member:* The Shrine Masonic; Lambda Chi Alpha Fraternity; N.Y. Chamber of Commerce; Baptist Church; 12th U.S. Army Group Assn. (Life Mem.); Assn. of U.S. Army; Retd. Officers Assn.; Disabled Officers Assn. Ordered promoted to rank of full Colonel by direct and specific order of the President of the U.S.; Pres., National Civic Club; Life Mem., Town Club, Scarsdale, N.Y. *Clubs:* Bankers of America; Downton Athletic; Drug & Chemical (all of N.Y.); Dallas (Tex.) Athletic; Army & Navy (Washington D.C.); Town (Scarsdale, N.Y.); Scarsdale Golf; National Sojourners; High Twelve; Leisure World Shrine; Marine Corps Air Station Officers, El Toro (Cal.); *Address:* 3337–2A Punta Alta, Rossmoor Leisure World, PO Box 2833, Laguna Hills, California 92653, U.S.A.

**AXSTER, Heinrich.** German lawyer. *B.* 1910. *Educ.* Universities of Lausanne, Munich, Berlin and Kiel. *M.* 1959, Hilde Trappmann. *Career:* Lawyer at Berlin 1934–39; German Navy 1939–46; Lawyer at Pforzheim 1947—; Syndic German Jewelry & Silverware Industry 1947—. *Member:* D.W.B., and F.D.P. *Address:* Otto Braun Strasse 3 Pforzheim-Sonnenhof; and *office* Industriehaus, Pforzheim, Germany.

**AYER, Sir Alfred (Jules).** Professor of Logic Univ. of Oxford. *B.* 1910. *Educ.* Eton Coll. (scholar); Christ Church, Oxford (scholar). *M.* (1) 1932, Grace Isabel Reneé Lees. *S.* 1. *Dau.* 1. (2) 1960, Alberta Constance Chapman (Dee Wells). *S.* 1. *Career:* Lecturer, Philosophy at Christ Church 1932–35; Research Student 1935–44; Fellow of Wadham Coll. Oxford 1944–46; Hon. Fellow, 1957; Dean 1945–46; Grote Professor of the Philosophy of Mind and Logic, Univ. of London 1946–59; Wykeham Professor of Logic, Univ. of Oxford since 1959. *Awards:* Fellow, New Coll. Oxford; Hon. member, Amer. Acad. of Art and Sciences; Dr hc Univ. of Brussels; Hon D Litt East Anglia; Knighted 1970; Fellow, British Academy. *Publications:* Language Truth and Logic (1936, revised 1946); The Foundations of Empirical Knowledge (1940); Thinking and Meaning (Inaugural Lecture) 1947; The Concept of a Person and Other Essays (1963); The Origins of Pragmatism (1968); Metaphysics and Common Sense (1969); Russell & Moore (1971); Probability and Evidence (1972); Russell (1972); The Central Questions of Philosophy (1974); Philosophical Essays (1954); Problem of Knowledge (1956). *Address:* New College, Oxford; and 10 Regent's Park Terrace, N.W.1.

**AYER, Hazen H.** Investment counsel. *B.* 1902. *Educ.* University of Maine (AB); Hon. LLD. 1965. *M.* 1935, Catharine Winsor. *Daus.* Nancy, Catherine and Cynthia. *Career:* President, Lumber Mutual Fire Insurance Co. 1945–48, Univ. of Maine General Alumni Assn. 1946–48; President, Standish Ayer & Wood Inc. 1946–65; now Chmn. of Board; Prudential Fund of Boston 1950—. Director: Lumber Mutual Fire Insurance Co. 1944—, Suffolk Franklin Savings Bank 1948—, Federal Kemper Life Insurance Co. 1960—; Kemper Co. Inc.; Fidelity Life Assn.; Pres., Investment Counsel Assn. of America 1958–60. *Awards:* Alumni Service Award, University of Maine, and Hon. LLD, 1965. *Member:* Mass. Advisory Cncl. on Educ. Phi Kappa Sigma. Mason. *Clubs:* Winchester Country; Downtown, Badminton & Tennis (Boston). *Address:* 69 Yale Street, Winchester, Mass.; and *office* 50 Congress Street, Boston 9, Mass., U.S.A.

**AYERS, Lorenz Kneedler.** American executive. *B.* 1891. *Educ.* Lafayette Coll. (BS). *M.* (1) 1919, Anna Spackman (dec'd) *Daus.* Helen A. Detchon and Barbara A. Herbst. (2) Frances A. Campbell 1972. *Career:* Manager, C. K. Williams & Co. 1913–17; Lieut., Air Corps, World War I, 1917–19; Pres., Geo. S. Mepham Corp. 1919–48, and C. K. Williams & Co. 1948–62; Consultant, Chas. Pfizer & Co. Inc. Dir., Chas. Pfizer & Co., and Area Dir., American Mutual Liability Insurance Co. *Member:* Phi Gamma Delta. Republican. *Clubs:* Noonday; Racquet; Bellerive Country; St. Louis; Missouri Athletic; Union League; University; Bogey; Chemists. *Address:* 900 South Hanley Road, St. Louis, Mo. 63105; and *office* 2001 Lynch Avenue, East St. Louis, Ill., U.S.A.

**AYLESTONE, Lord (Herbert William Bowden),** PC, CH, CBE. *B.* 1905. *Educ.* Grammar School. *M.* 1928, Louise Grace Brown. *Dau.* 1. *Career:* Pres., Leicester Labour Party 1938; Member Parliament (Lab.) S. Leicester 1945–50; S.W. Div. Leicester 1950–67; Parliamentary Private Secy. to Postmaster-General 1947–49; Asst. Govt. Whip 1949–50; a Lord Commissioner of the Treasury 1950–51; Dep. Chief Opposition Whip 1951–55; Chief Opposition Whip 1955–64; Lord Pres. of the Council and Leader of the House of Commons Oct. 1964–Aug. 1966. Commonwealth Secy. Aug. 1966–67; Chmn., Independent Broadcasting Authority 1967–75. *Address:* Oamaru, 47 The Avenue, Worcester Park, Surrey.

**AYLESWORTH, John Bell,** QC. Canadian judge. *B.* 24 Dec. 1898. *Educ.* Queen's Univ. (BA); Osgoode Hall. *M.* 1927, Aileen Miriam Drake. *Daus.* Mary Fairfield, Catherine Bristol, Elizabeth Hope, Aileen Miriam. *Career:* Called to the Bar, Toronto 1923; King's Counsel 1935; Mem., Court of Appeal, Ontario 1946–72; Consultant since 1972. *Address:* Court of Appeal for Ontario, Toronto, Canada.

**AYRE, Lewis Haldane Miller.** Canadian. *B.* 1914. *Educ.* Mostyn House Sch., Cheshire; Wrekin Coll., Shropshire. *M.* 1939, Olga Rogers Crosbie. *S.* 1. *Dau.* 1. *Career:* Chmn. Ayre & Sons Ltd.: Chmn.: Holiday Lanes Ltd.; Job Brothers; Northlantic Fisheries; Nfld. Telephone Co., Ayre's Ltd., Blue Buoy Foods Ltd.; Dir.: Jannock Corp.; Bank of Nova Scotia; Colonial Cordage; Dominion Stores; Robinson-Blackmore Ltd.; Newfoundland & Labrador Hydro; Advisory Board Canada Permanent Trust Co.; Hollinger Mines Ltd., Labrador Mining & Exploration Co. Ltd. *Clubs:* Canadian, New York; Toronto; Montreal. *Address:* 26 King's Bridge Rd., St. John's, Newfoundland, Canada.

**AZIKIWE, Rt. Hon. Nnamdi,** PC, MA, MSc, LLD, DLitt. *B.* 16 Nov. 1904. *Educ.* Howard Univ., Wash., D.C., Lincoln Univ., Chester County, Pa.; Univ. of Pennsylvania. *M.* 1936, Flora Ogbenyeanu Ogoegbunam. *S.* 3. *Dau.* 1. *Career:* Instructor in Pol. Science, Lincoln Univ. 1931–34; Editor-in-Chief, African Morning Post, Accra 1934–37, and of West African Pilot, Lagos 1937–47; Man. Dir., Zik Enterprises, Ltd. 1937–53; Mem., Legislative Council of Nigeria 1947–51; Mem., Western House of Assembly 1952–53; Mem. of Eastern House of Assembly 1954–59; Mem., House of Representatives 1954; Min. of Local Government, Eastern Region 1954; Mem., Brooke Arbitration Tribunal 1944, Cameroon Arbitration Tribunal 1948, Lagos Rent Assessment Board 1941–42; Nat. Pres., National Council of Nigeria and Cameroons 1946–60; Foot Nigerianization Comm. 1948; Chmn., African Continental Bank, Ltd. 1948–53; Mem. of Eastern Region Privy Council 1954; Premier, Eastern Nigeria Oct. 1954–Dec. 1959; Min. of Internal Affairs 1954–57; Pres. Exec. Council, Govnt. Eastern Nigeria 1957–59; Pres. of the Senate 1960; Gov.-Gen. of Nigeria 1960–63; Field Marshall Nigerian Army 1960–66; Admiral Nigerian Navy 1960–66; President Fed. Republic Nigeria 1963–66. Doctor Civil Law, Univ. Liberia 1969; Chancellor, Univ. Lagos since 1972. *Publications:* A Critique of Polygyny (1931); The practice of Forced Labour (1932); Anthropology and the Problem of Race (1933); Syllabus for African History (1933); Mythology in Onitsha Society (1933); Theories on the Origins of the State (1933); Liberia in World Politics (1934); Renascent Africa (1937); Land Tenure in Northern Nigeria (1942); Political Blueprint of Nigeria (1943); Economic Reconstruction of Nigeria (1943); Our Struggle for Freedom (1955); Economic Rehabilitation of Eastern Nigeria (1956). *Address:* Onuiyi Haven, P.O. Box 7, Nsukka, Nigeria.

# B

**BABBERGER, Carl William.** American consulting engineer. Owner of Paragon Services. *B.* 1909. *Educ.* Stanford Univ. (AB 1932, ME 1934, Gen. Sec. Teaching Credential 1935). *M.* 1953, Enid Kathleen Ayres. *Career:* Professional Engineer of California and Colorado; Dir., Professional Engineers of Colorado and of Professional Land Surveyors of Colorado; Research Engineer, National Aeronautics and Space Admin. 1936–39; Chief of Research and Aerodynamics, Hughes Aircraft 1939–56; Consulting Engineer since 1956. *Publications:* contributor to Klemin's International Handbook for Airplane Designers; articles in technical journals. *Member:* American Inst. of Aeronautics and Astronautics; American Men of Science; American Congress on Surveying and Mapping; National Socy. of Professional Engineers; Sigma Xi; Tau Beta Pi. *Address:* P.O. Box 286, Canon City, Colo. 81212, U.S.A.

**BABCOCK, Donald Eric.** American. *B.* 1907. *Educ.* Ohio State Univ. (AB 1931, MA 1933, PhD 1935). *M.* 1936, Leah Brink. *Daus.* Beverly Jean (Deerhake). Shirley Ruth (Griebe), Eileen Kay (Thurnauer). *Career:* Asst., Dept. of Chemistry, Ohio State Univ. 1931–35; Physical Chemist, Republic Steel Corp. 1935–38; Industrial Fellow, Mellon Inst. 1938–40; Research Metallurgist, Pittsburgh Steel Corp. 1938–40; Research Mgr., Owens-Corning Fiberglas Co. 1940–42; Asst. to Dir., Ohio State Univ. Research Foundation 1942–43; Asst. Chief Metallurgist 1943–47, Research Engineer, Republic Steel Corp. 1947–52; Asst. Prof. of Chemistry, Youngstown Univ. 1944–48; Consultant to the R-N Corp. 1957—; Technical and Research Consultant, Republic Steel Corp. 1958—; Advisor U.S. State Dept. 1968—; Technical Advisor Republic Steel Corp. since 1968. *Publications:* numerous articles in technical journals and magazines on blast furnace operations and control, iron and steel metallurgy, electro-organic reductions, welding, and the R-N direct iron process. Republican. *Member:* Amer. Inst. of Mining Engineers; Amer. Chemical Socy.; Amer. Socy. of Metals; Amer. Inst. of Chemical Engineers; Army Ordnance

Assn.; Amer. Iron & Steel Inst. (awarded Inst. Medal for 1949). *Address:* 29611 W. Oakland Road, Bay Village, Ohio 44140, U.S.A.

**BABINGTON SMITH, Michael James**, CBE. British banker. *B.* 20 Mar. 1901. *Educ.* Eton; Trinity Coll., Cambridge. *M.* 1943, Jean Meade. *S.* 1. *Daus.* 2. *Career:* Entered Glyn Mills & Co. 1923; served in World War II, Middle East and N.W. Europe 1939–45; S.H.A.E.F. 1943–45 (Brigadier); Dep. Chmn. Glyn Mills & Co. 1946–63; Chmn., London Cttee., Ottoman Bank; Dir., Bank of England 1949–69, Compagnie Financière de Suez 1958–73, and Bank of International Settlements 1965–73. *Address:* Flat 6, 20 Embankment Gardens, London, S.W.3.

**BABSON, Arthur Clifford**. American business executive. *B.* 1909. *Educ.* Univ. of Oregon (BSc). *M.* 1946, Margery Tindle Grey. *S.* John Pell, Robert Grey. *Career:* With Union Terminal Cold Storage Co., Jersey City 1932–36; Lieut.-Comdr., U.S. Navy 1941–46; Formerly Dir. of Gamwell Co., Eagle Signal Co., and Rockwood Sprinkler Co.; (Presently) Vice-Pres., Babson's Reports Inc. (Investment Advisers to Corp. and Private Investors); Dir.: Home Insurance Co. (Mem. of Exec. Cttee.), Sierra Pacific Power Co. (mem. of Finance Cttee.), and Cape Ann Bank and Trust Co. (Mem. of Fiduciary Cttee.); City Investing Co. (Mem. Exec. Cttee.); Gen. Develop. Corp. (Mem. Finance Cttee.). *Member:* Pilgrims Socy. of U.S.A., Navy League, and Chi Psi; Chmn., Town of Sherborn Bd. of Selectmen (1964–70). *Address:* Meeting House Hill, Sherborn, Mass.; and *office* Babson's Reports Inc., Wellesley Hills, Mass., U.S.A.

**BACH, Otto**. German politician. *B.* 22 Dec. 1899. *Married.* Pres. of the Berlin House of Representatives 1961–67; until 1932 writer, lecturer in economic and social politics, Dept. Head of Berlin Branch Office of International Labour Office; Mem. of Secretariat, International Labour Office 1933–40; Mem. of Cttee., German Chamber of Commerce in Paris 1941–44; City Councillor, Berlin; Chmn., Political Economic Cttee. of S.P.D.; Mem. Bd. Dirs., Inst. für Wirtschaftsforschung 1946–47; Dir., Elektrowerke A.G. 1950–53; Senator for Social Affairs, Berlin Dir. Radio, Free Berlin 1954–57; Hon. Pres., Society for United Nations, Berlin; Hon.-Pres., Europa-Union Berlin; Chmn., Burgermeister-Reuter-Stifburg; Pres., Int. Rescue Cttee. e.V.; Vice-Pres., Deutsche Weltwirtschaftliche Gessellschaft; Vice-Pres., Steubken-Schurz-Gesellschaft; Chmn., Lessing-Hochschule; Pres., Europaische Akademie Berlin. *Address:* Marinesteig 36, Berlin 38, Schlachtensee, Germany.

**BACHENHEIMER, Ralph James**. Executive. *B.* 1928. *Educ.* University of Zurich, Switzerland; and Columbia University, N.Y. *M.* 1958, Clare C. Conway. *Daus.* Lisa Clare and Cara Conway. *Career:* Former President Indian Head Yarn Co. Has held various executive positions with Iselin-Jefferson Co. Past Vice-President, Director and Member of Executive Committee of the New York Board of Trade; Past Chmn. Standard Brands Ltd.; Past Vice-Pres. Int. Standard Brands; Vice-Pres. Genesco Inc.; Bd, of Governors Genesco Inc.; Dir. Delmar; former Vice-Pres., Dir., Exec. Cttee.; N.Y. Bd. Trade, past Chmn. Textile Section; Nat. Panel Arbitrators; past Chmn. Am. Arbitration Assn. Jr, C of C of N.Y.C. *Clubs:* Vets. 7th Regt. *Address:* Genesco Inc., 111 Seventh Ave. N,, Nashville, Tennesse 3702, U.S.A. 1113 Chickering Park Drive, Nashville, Tennessee 37215, U.S.A.

**BACHMANN, Hans Ulrich**. Swiss professor of economics. *B.* 1 Aug. 1898. *Educ.* Universities of Zürich, Montpellier, Paris, Berlin and Oxford. *M.* 1923, Emmy Tanner. *Career:* Secretary-General, European Aluminium Cartel, 1926; Secretary (1931) and Managing Secretary-General (1940), Aluminium World Cartel; Managing Director of various aluminium companies; Chmn. Benninger Eng. Co. Ltd, Uzwil; Professor of Economics, St. Gall School of Economics and Business Administration 1946—. Director, Swiss Institute for International Economics 1943–72; Co-editor of Aussenwirtschaft (economic quarterly) since 1946; Chairman, Swiss Government Commission of the Swiss Cheese Industry 1953–56; Economic Adviser to Philippine Govt. (U.N. Technical Assistance) 1956–57 and 1959; to Zaire 1960; to Ceylon 1962; to Iran 1964; to Peru 1969; to Zambia 1972; Pres., Benninger Engng. Co. Uzwil 1959—. *Publications:* Anglo-Saxon Monetary Plans (1943); Anglo-Saxon Plans for the Post War Economy (1944); The Conventions of Bretton Woods (1945); Swiss Agricultural Policy and Foreign Trade (1948); The World Trade Charter and Switzerland (1948); Western European Economic Union or Economic Co-operation? (1950); The Reform of the Swiss Milk Industry (1953); The Financing of Exports (1954); The British Exchange Control (1954); The Swiss Agricultural Programme (1956); Europe, a Political and Economic Analysis (1955); Problems of a European Free Trade Area (1958); A Free Trade Area of the 'Other Six'? (1959); The External Relations of Less-Developed Countries, a Manual of Economic Policies (1968); A European Monetary Union (1969 and 1970); A North Oceanic Monetary Co-operation (1974); numerous contributions to journals on economics. *Address:* Dierauerstrasse 15, St. Gallen 9000, Switzerland.

**BACK, Frank Gerard**. American scientist, inventor, author, lecturer and pioneer in the fields of design and engineering of photographic optical equipment. *B.* Vienna. *Educ.* Technische Hoschschule and the Univ. of Vienna (ME; DSc). Until 1939, an engineering consultant in Vienna, Paris and New York. Established the Research and Development Laboratory in New York City. In 1945 became President of Zoomar Inc., manufacturers of high precision optics. He has made major contributions to the progress of television, motion picture and still photography. He holds over 50 U.S. and European patents, and has written books and articles for technical publications. He is a member of the Society of American Military Engineers and the Society of Motion Picture and Television Engineers. *Awards:* Gold Medal Annual Award of Television Broadcasters Assn., 1947; Fellowship of the Royal Photographic Society, 1949, and Photographic Society of America, 1952; Friedrich Voigtlander Gold Medal Award, Vienna 1960; and Fellowship of the Society of Photographic Scientists and Engineers, 1961; Fellowship of Motion Picture & Television Engineers (recipient of their Progress Medal, 1962); Fellowship of the Optical Society of America 1966. *Address:* 1 Frost Creek Drive, Locust Valley, L.I., N.Y.; and *office* Zoomar Inc., 55 Sea Cliff Avenue, Glen Cove, L.I., N.Y., U.S.A.

**BACKE, Per Møystad**. Norwegian industralist. Chmn. and Chief Exec. Officer of A/S Norcem, Oslo, since 1968 and Chmn. and Board Member of a number of industrial and Financial Companies. *B.* 1914. *Educ.* Univ. of Oslo. *M.* 1939, Jacqueline Helliesen. *S.* Erik. *Daus.* Hege, Une. *Career:* Barrister and Assistant Judge, Oslo 1939–44; Secy., Royal Norwegian Legation, Stockholm 1944–45; Man. Dir., Norwegian Airlines 1946–48; Pres., Scandavian Airlines, Overseas Div, 1949–51; Exec. Vice-Pres., SAS, Stockholm 1951–55; Dir., Peter Møller, Oslo 1955–57; Norwegian Representive, Free Trade Area Negotiations, Paris 1957–59; Pres., A/S Dalen Portland-Cementfabrik, 1959–68. *Address:* A/S Norcem, Oslo, Norway.

**BACKER, Jan Loennecken**. Norwegian merchant and shipowner. *B.* 1906. *Educ.* Matriculation degree; Commercial School. *M.* 1931, Inger Ebbesen. *S.* Dan and Gunnar. *Daus.* Harriet and Rita. *Career:* Commercial experience in England, Germany, Spain and Portugal. Owner and President, Backers Rederi A/S (shipowners) and Halfdan Backer A/S, timber merchants; shipbrokers and sales agents. Founder and ex-Pres., Norwegian Trawler Owners Assn.; ex-President, Norwegian Union of Codfish Exporters; Kristiansund Union of Trade and Industry; Chmn., Local Y.M.C.A. and congregation. Ex-Pres. (and member of World Committee), Norwegian Y.M.C.A.: Ex-Pres., Rotary Club of Kristiansund Consul for West Germany. *Publications:* The Trawler Question in Norwegian Fisheries. Christian-Conservative. *Address:* 6500 Kristiansund, Norway.

**BACKER-GRØNDAHL, Fridtjof Jan**. Norwegian music publisher. *B.* 1914. *M.* 1941, Lilian Treider. *Daus.* Helen and Lilian. *Career:* Man. Dir. of Norsk Musikforlag A/S. President, Scandinavian Music Publishers' Association 1952–64; Chairman, Norwegian Music Dealers' Association 1951–62; Vice-Pres., Music Section of the International Publishers' Association 1959–64; Chmn. Norwegian Music Publishers Assoc. 1973. *Address:* Norsk Musikforlag A/S, Karl Johansgate 39, Oslo.

**BACON, Rt. Hon. Baroness Alice**, PC, CBE. British politician. *Educ.* Normanton Girls' High School; Stockwell Training College; Diploma in Publ. Admin. (London). *Career:* Member of Parliament for Leeds, 1945–70; Chmn., Labour Party, 1950–51; Member, National Exec. Cttee., Labour Party, 1941–70. Minister of State, Home Office, 1964–67. Minister of State, Department of Education & Science 1967–70. *Address:* 53 Snydale Road, Normanton, Yorkshire; and *office* House of Lord, London, S.W.1.

**BACON, Sir Edmund Castell**, Bt, KG, KBE, TD. British banker. *B.* 18 Mar. 1903. *Educ.* Eton; Trinity College, Cambridge. *M.* 1936, Priscilla Dora Ponsonby. *S.* 1. *Daus.* 4.

*Career:* Served in World War II, Suffolk Yeomanry (Lt.-Col.) 1940–45; Lord Lieutenant for Norfolk 1949—; Dir., Lloyds Bank 1949–73; Chairman British Sugar Corp. 1957–68. *Address:* Raveningham Hall, Norwich.

**BADER, I. Walton.** American lawyer. *B.* 1922. *Educ.* New York Univ. (AB Chem 1942; LLB 1948). *M.* 1972, Betty Sands. *Career:* Member of the Bar of the Supreme Court of the United States, 1953—, and of New York State Bar 1948—. Counsel, Global Invention Foundation 1963—. Patent Counsel, Albert Einstein College of Medicine 1958—, Swingline Inc. (and subsidiaries) 1957–72, and Yeshiva Univ. 1965—. Examiner, Fed. Trade Commission 1950–51; Counsel N.Y. State Rent Commission 1953–59; Trustee, and General Counsel, Heart Disease Research Fdn. 1963—; Secy. Trade Mark Service Corp. 1953–58; Gen. Counsel Independent Investor Protective League since 1971. Recipient Pacific Medal 1945. *Member:* Bar of the Supreme Court, United States; American and New York State Bar Associations; Westchester & Brooklyn Bar Assocs. New York Patent Law Association; National Democratic Club; New York University Club; Democratic Party (Local Campaign Manager 1964). *Address:* 40 Morrow Avenue, Scarsdale, New York 10583; and *office* 270 Madison Avenue, New York City, N.Y. 10016; and 65 Court Street, White Plains, NY 10601, U.S.A.

**BADGER, Edward Joseph.** Australian. *B.* 1922. *Educ.* University of Sydney (LLB). *M.* 1944, Joyce F. Pasley. *S.* David. *Dau.* Marilyn. *Career:* Principal Legal Officer, Sydney 1956–64; Assistant Deputy Crown Solicitor, Sydney 1964; Deputy Commonwealth Crown Solicitor, Queensland, Dec. 1964—. Member Queensland Law Society. *Clubs:* Keperra Golf; Theatre Organ Society. *Address:* 3 Niven Street, Stafford Heights, Brisbane, Qld.; and *office* 247 Adelaide Street, Brisbane, Qld., Australia.

**BADHAM, Douglas George,** CBE, JP, DL, FCA. British company director. *B.* 1914. *Educ.* Leys School, Cambridge; qualified as Chartered Accountant in 1937. *M.* 1939, Doreen Spencer Phillips. *Daus.* 2. *Career:* Exec. Dir., Powell Duffryn Group 1938–69; Chmn., Hamell (West) Ltd.; Powell Duffryn Wagon Co. Ltd.; Minton, Treharne & Davies Ltd.; Dir., Pearl Paints Ltd.; Chmn., Development Corp. for Wales; Chmn., South Wales Advisory Cttee. of the Forestry Commisson 1973–75 (Mem. of Advisory Cttee. 1946–75); Dir., Economic Forestry (Wales) Ltd.; Part-time member Telecommunications Board, Wales and the Marches; part-time member British Gas Corp. *Member:* Welsh Council. Chmn., Industry & Planning Panel (Welsh Council); Chmn., National Health Service Staff Adv. Cttee. Wales 1972–75; British Railways (Western) Adv. Bd.; Magistrate, County of Glamorgan; Dep. Lieutenant for Mid Glamorgan since 1975; High Sheriff for Mid Glamorgan 1976. *Member:* Advisory Cttee. for Wales, Nature Conservancy Council; Council of Univ. of Wales Inst. of Science and Technology. *Clubs:* Cardiff; County (Cardiff); R.A.C. (London). *Address:* Plas Watford, Caerphilly, Glam.

**BADIAN, Alan Maurice,** BCom, CA, FCIS. Retired Canadian business executive. *B.* 1900. *Educ.* Sale High School, Cheshire, England; Montreal High School; McGill University (BCom); Chartered Accountant (CA); Chartered Secretary (FCIS). *M.* 1934, Katherine Frances Hole. *S.* 2. Dir. Judo Investments Ltd. *Address:* 25 Northcote Road, Hampstead. Montreal, Que., Canada H3X 1P9.

**BAER, Albert Max.** American. *B.* 1905. *Educ.* Coll. of the City of New York; New York Univ.; Columbia Univ. *M.* 1930, Helene Gilbert (*dec.*). *Daus.* Mrs. John E. Kaufman and Mrs. Miles J. Schwartz. *Career:* Chairman of the Board, & Chief Exec. Officer, Imperial Knife Associated Cos. Inc.; Chmn. of the Board. Director: Ulster Knife Co.; Chairman of the Board, Director: Imperial International Corp., Richards of Sheffield England Inc.; Imperial Metal Box Corp; Director: S. A. Durol (France), J. A. Henckels-Imperial GmbH. Imperial Plating Co. Wallace Mfg Co.; Director, Treasurer: Vulcan Safety Razor Corp. *Awards:* St John's Univ. DCS; LLD. Hofstra Univ.; Purkyne Medal, Czech. Socy. of Cardiology Owl Award; Columbia Univ., International Cardiology Fdn. Gold Heart. Trustee: Japan Scholarship Foundation; Gold Heart Award, American Heart Assn. *Member:* St. John's Univ. Adv. Cncl.; Adv. Cncl. Sch. of General Studies, Columbia Univ.; Internatl. Cardiology Fdn. (Hon. Pres.); Amer. Heart Assn. Past Secy.; Greek & Spanish Cardiology Socs. *Clubs:* English Speaking Union; Harmonie; St. George Socy.; Nippon; Century Country; Independent Lodge 185 F & AM. *Address:* 45 East 85th Street, New York, N.Y. 10028; and *office* 1776 Broadway, New York, N.Y. 10019.

**BAEZ, Porfirio Herrera.** Dominican Diplomat. Amabassador of the Dominican Republic to the Court of St. James, concurrently to Portugal 1966–75; Ambassador to Italy since 1975. *Address:* Dominican Embassy, Rome, Italy.

**BAGNALL, Frank Colin,** CBE, MA. British. *B.* 1909. *Educ.* Repton; Brasenose College, Oxford; Dept. of Business Admin., London School of Economics. *M.* (1) 1941, Rona Rooker Roberts. *S.* 1. *Dau.* 1. (2) Christine Bagnall. *Career:* Mng. Director, British Nylon Spinners 1945–64; Chmn., Wales Business Training Cttee. 1946–49; Member Cncl., British Inst. of Management 1949–52; Dir., Oxford Univ. Business Summer School 1954; Member, Govt. Cttee. of Enquiry into Electricity Supply Industry 1954–55; Chmn. S.W. Reg. Cncl. F.B.I. 1956–57; Member, Air Transport Licensing Bd. 1960–64; Chmn., Man-Made Fibres Producers Cttee. 1961–65; Chmn., British Man-Made Fibres Fedn. 1963–65; Pres., Textile Inst. 1964–65. Commercial Director, Imperial Chemical Industries Ltd. 1965–70 and Finance Director 1967–68; Director, African Explosive & Chemical Industries Ltd. 1965–70. President, University College of South Wales & Monmouthshire 1962–68; Governor, Ashridge College, 1958–69. Vice-President, British Man-Made Fibres Fedn, 1965–69. *Awards:* Hon. LLD (Univ. of Wales). 1969; Comp T.I.; O. St. J. *Clubs:* Boodle's. *Address:* Vermont, Northview Road, Budleigh Salterton, Devon.

**BAGRIT, Sir Leon.** *B.* 1902. *Educ.* St. Olave's and London University. *M.* 1926, Stella Feldman. *Daus.* 2. *Career:* After various posts in engineering industry, organized first company in Europe devoted to automation; Chmn., Elliott-Automation Ltd. 1963— (Deputy Chairman from its formation ,1957–62). Director: Technology Investments Ltd. 1963–69; Director, Royal Opera House, Covent Garden 1962–69; Founder and Chmn., Friends of Covent Garden. *Member:* Council of Dept. for Scientific & Industrial Research 1963–65; Minister's Adv. Council on Technology, Ministry of Technology; Council of Royal Coll. of Art 1960–63; The Royal Institution; Advisory Council of the Science Museum 1967–72; Advisory Council, Victoria & Albert Museum. *Awards:* Fellow, Royal Society of Arts; Companion, Instn. of Electrical Engineers; Reith Lecturer 1964. R.S.A. Gold Albert Medal 1965; Ambassador Award 1965; DSc (Reading); Doctor, Univ. of Surrey. Pres., British Technion Society. *Publication:* The Age of Automation. *Club:* Devonshire (London). *Address:* Upper Terrace House, Hampstead, London, N.W.3.

**BAHNER, Hermann Friedrich Alban.** German manufacturer. *B.* 1912. *Educ.* State Grammar School, Chemnitz; Technical High School, Munich; Diploma (business). *M.* 1937, Madeleine Eichler. *S.* 3. *Career:* Apprentice in stocking knitting 1930; Export Merchant in Sweden and Switzerland 1934; Manager, Louis Bahner Elbeo Werke Oberlungwitz. Managing Part-Owner, Elbeo Werke, Augsburg-Mannheim 1946—; Complementaire at Bahner K.G.; Augsburg 1938—. *Club:* Rotary. *Address:* Hofer Strasse 10, Augsburg, Germany.

**BAHR, Egon.** German politician. *B.* 1922. *Education.* H.S. Cert; training for indust. business and admin. *M.* 1945, Dorothea Grob. *S.* 1. *Dau.* 1. *Career:* Journalist since 1945; Chief Commentator at Berlin Radio station (RIAS) and head of RIAS office at Bonn; During 1959 attached to Germany Embassy, Accra (Ghana) as represent. and press attaché of GFR; Head of Press and Info. office of Land, Berlin, 1960–66; Ambassador, FO Bonn, and Minist Dir. Planning Staff F.O. 1967–69; State Secy. Fed. Chancellery 1969–72 (Comm. of GFR in Berlin); M.P. since 1972; Fed. Min. without Portfolio, Fed. Chancellery 1972–74; Fed. Min. for Economic Co-operation 1974–76; Sec.-Gen. SPD since 1976; Mem. SPD since 1956; Mem. of Governing Council of Deutschlandfunk. *Address:* Ollenhauerstrasse 1, 5300 Bonn, Federal Republic of Germany.

**BAILAR, John Christian, Jr.** American professor, lecturer chemistry. *B.* 1904. *Educ.* Univ. of Colorado (BA 1924; MA 1925) and Univ. of Michigan (PhD 1928). *M.* (1) 1931, Florence L. Catherwood (*Dec.* 1975). (2) 1976, Katharine R. Ross. *S.* John C. III, Benjamin Franklin, *Career:* Prof. of Inorganic Chemistry, Univ. of Illinois 1943—(mem. of staff of the Univ. since 1928; National Lecturer Sigma Xi 1970–71; Visiting Professor at Univ. of Colorado (1962); Univ. of Arizona (1970); Univ. of Wyoming (1970); Univ. of Sao Paulo

(1972); Kyushu, Japan (1974); Colorado Coll. (1976); Univ. Guanajuato (1976). *Member:* Amer. Chemical Socy. (Pres. 1959); Treas. Int. Union, Pure & Applied Chemistry 1963–71. *Awards.* Hon. ScD.; Univ. of Buffalo, 1959, and Univ. of Colorado, 1959; Hon. ScD. Lehigh Univ. 1973; Scientific Apparatus Makers Award in Chemical Education 1961; Priestley Medal (Amer. Chem. Socy.) 1964; Frank P. Dwyer Medal; Chem. Socy. of N.S. Wales 1965; Gold Medal, Swiss Chem. Socy. 1966; Manufacturing Chemists Assoc. Award in the Teaching of Chemistry 1968; Midwest Award 1971; A.C.S., Achievement, Advancement of Inorganic Chemistry 1972. *Publications:* General Chemistry for Colleges; Essentials of Chemistry (both with Prof. B. S. Hopkins); Univ. Chemistry (with Therald Moeller and Jacob Kleinberg) 1965, Editor; Volume IV of Inorganic Syntheses, and of the ACS Monograph, Chemistry of the Co-ordination Compounds; many articles in technical and professional journals. *Address:* 304 West Pennsylvania Avenue, Urbana, Ill.; and *office* Univ. of Illinois, Urbana, Ill. 61801.

**BAILEY, Sir Donald Coleman,** OBE, JP. *B.* 1901. *Educ.* The Leys School and Sheffield Univ. (DEng); CEng, FIStructE, MICE. *M.* 1933, Phyllis Andrew (D. 1972). *S.* Richard Henry. *Career:* Dean, Royal Military Coll. of Science, Shrivenham, nr. Swindon, Wilts. to Oct. 1966; Hon. Fellow, Inst. of Welding; Hon. Mem., Inst. of Royal Engineers; Commander, Order of Orange-Nassau (Netherlands). *Address:* 14 Viking Close, Southbourne, Bournemouth.

**BAILEY, J. Edward.** American business executive. *B.* 6 April 1902. *Educ.* Kaigler's Business Coll., Macon, Ga. Baltimore Coll. of Commerce; Univ. of Maryland. *M.* 1924, Florence E. Miles. *S.* J. Edward, R. Clifton. *Career:* Served World War I in U.S. Navy; associated with the Hooper-Holmes Bureau, Inc., International Research Bureau, Basking Ridge, N.J. since 1923; Inspector, Baltimore branch office 1923–24; Mgr., Richmond, Va. Branch Office 1924–25; Asst. Mgr., Baltimore Branch Office 1925–28, Mgr. 1928–29; Assoc. Supervisor, Southern Div. 1928–29; Mgr., Philadelphia Branch Office 1930–31; Mgr., Los Angeles 1931–37; Virginia State Mgr. 1937–39; S.E. Div. Supervisor (1940–52), Middle Atlantic Div. Supervisor, Richmond, Va. 1952–59; retired; Mem., Civitan International (Vice-Pres.) 1943–45, Pres.-elect 1945–46, International Pres. 1946–47; Mem., International Executive Bd. 1943–50; Mem. of International Council 1951—. *Member:* American Arbitration Assn. since 1944; Assoc. Mem., Amer. Inst. of Management since 1954; Southern Inst. of Management; Mem. of Bd.: West End (Va.) Civitan Club, April 1959—, Chesapeake Civitan International Foundation for Aid to the Mentally Retarded 1957—. *Address:* 3319 Kensington Avenue, Richmond 21, Va. 23221, U.S.A.

**BAILEY, John Everett Creighton,** CBE. British. *B.* 1905 *Educ.* Brentwood School. *M.* 1928, Hilda Anne Jones. *S.* 1. *Daus.* 4. *Career:* Chmn. Man. Dir., Baird & Tatlock Group of Companies 1941–69; Chmn. Brit. Sc. Inst. Research Assn. 1952–64 (Pres. 1964–71); First Companion SIRA Inst.; Dir. Derbyshire Stone Ltd. 1959–69; Tarmac Derby Ltd. 1969–70; G. D. Searle & Co. 1969–70 and other Companies; Exec. Chmn. Difco Laboratories (U.K.) Ltd. Special member Prices and Incomes Board; Mem., Admiralty Chemical Adv. Panel 1940–50; Pres., Scientific Instrument Manufacturers' Assn. 1945–50; Chmn., British Laboratory Ware Assn. 1950–52; Mem.: Grand Cncl., F.B.I. (1945–58), Bd. of Trade Exhibitions Adv. Cttee. (1957—) and Census of Production Adv. Cttee. 1960–68; Second Master, Company of Scientific Instrument Makers 1957–58; Liveryman, later Assistant, Worshipful Co. of Needlemakers; Freeman of City of London *Member:* Inst. of Export; M.R.I.; F.B.I.M. *Clubs:* Athenaeum. *Address:* The Haven, Paternoster Row, Ottery St Mary, Devon; and 72 Melton Court, South Kensington, London, S.W.7.

**BAILEY, Leonard Alec.** FPS, DSc, JP, Hon. FRCS, Ed. Hon. FRCSI, Hon. FRCS (Eng.), Hon. FRCOG. British. *B.* 1910. *Educ.* Cardiff High School; Univ. of Wales; Univ. Coll., London. *M.* 1936, Audrey Margaret Colley. *S.* 1. *Dau.* 1. *Career:* Vice-Pres. Dir.: Johnson & Johnson International New Brunswick, New Jersey, U.S.A.; Commercial Mgr., ICI (Plastics) Ltd. 1939–41; Hospital Sales Mgr., Johnson & Johnson (Gt. Britain) Ltd. 1945–47; Sales Dir., Ethicon Ltd. 1947–51, Man. Dir. 1951–72. *Member:* Court Heriot-Watt University. *Clubs:* Royal Burgess Golfing Socy. *Address:* 21 Oswald Court, Oswald Road, Edinburgh EH9 2HY; and *office* P.O. Box 408, Bankhead Avenue, Edinburgh EH11 4HE.

**BAILEY, Ronald William.** Retired British diplomat. *B.* 1917. *Educ.* Cambridge Univ. (MA). *M.* 1946, Joan Hassall Gray. *S.* Nigel. *Dau.* Rowena. *Career:* Entered Foreign Service 1939; served: Beirut 1939–41 and 1949–52; Alexandria 1941–45; Cairo 1945–48; Foreign Office 1948–49; Washington 1952–57; Khartoum 1957–60: Chargé d'Affaires, Taiz 1960–62; Consul-Gen., Gothenburg, 1963–65; Min., Baghdad 1965–67; H.M. Ambassador to Bolivia 1967–71; to Morocco 1971–75 (retired); Vice-Pres., Soc. for the Protection of Animals in North Africa 1975–; Chmn. British-Moroccan Soc. 1976–. *Member:* Royal Inst. of International Affairs (London); Royal Soc. for Asian Affairs. *Clubs:* Athenaeum; Oriental. *Address:* Redwood, Tennyson's Lane, Haslemere, Surrey, GU27 3AF.

**BAILEY-TART, Wilfred Bailey.** Retired Journalist. *B.* 1906. *Educ.* BScAgr; HDA (Dipl. Agriculture, Hawkesbury Agricultural Coll., Richmond, N.S.W.). *M.* 1935, Mary Ethel de la Force. *S.* 1. *Daus.* 2. *Career:* Field Chemist, C.S.I.R. Station at Griffith 1927; Sydney Univ. 1928–31; on Literary Staff, Sydney Morning Herald 1932–38; Public Relations Officer, Dept. of Defence 1938–40; Asst. Dir. of Public Relations, R.A.A.F. 1940–41; Staff Officer, Publicity and History, R.A.A.F. overseas (H.Q. London) 1941–44; Editor, Daily Examiner, Grafton, N.S.W. 1944–60; Public Relations Consultant 1960–64; Agric. Editor, Sydney Morning Herald 1964–72. *Publications:* various, including History of Grafton and Agricultural Developments. *Clubs:* Journalists' (Sydney). *Address:* Manar, 42 Macleay Street, Potts Point, Sydney, N.S.W., Australia.

**BAILLIEU, John Madden.** *B.* 1912. *Educ.* Oxford Univ. (MA); Barrister-at-Law, Inner Temple, London, and Melbourne, Australia. *M.* 1938, Elizabeth Darling. *S.* Antony, Charles. *Dau.* Joanna. *Career:* Served in World War II, Major, Australian Imperial Forces; artillery; 1940–45; Partner, E. L. & C. Baillieu, Melbourne; Dir.: Carlton & United Breweries Ltd., Massey-Ferguson Holdings (Australia) Ltd.; Dalgety Australia Ltd.; Colonial Mutual Fire Insurance Co. Ltd. *Address:* Messrs. E. L. & C. Baillieu, (Level 7, 459 Collins St), Melbourne and Box No 48, Collins St P.O. Melbourne, Vic. 3000; and *home* 729 Orrong Road, Toorak, Vic., Australia.

**BAILLIEU, Marshal Lawrence.** Australian business executive. *B.* 1902. *Educ.* BA (Hons.) Cantab. *M.* 1930, Nancy Elizabeth Willsallen. *S.* 2. *Dau.* 1. Chmn.: North Broken Hill Ltd., Melbourne; The Broken Hill Associated Smelters Pty. Ltd., Melbourne; Metal Manufacturers Ltd.; on the Boards of Associated Pulp and Paper Mills Ltd.; Electrolytic Zinc Co. of Australasia Pty. Ltd.; Dunlop Rubber Co. *Club:* Melbourne. *Address:* Minta, Beaconsfield, Vic.; and *office* 360 Collins Street, Melbourne, Vic., Australia.

**BAIN, Margaret Anne,** MP. Scottish Politician. *B.* 1945. *Educ.* Glasgow Univ. MA; Strathclyde Univ. BA (Hons.). *M.* 1968, Donald S. Bain. *Career:* Asst. Teacher, Cumbernauld High 1968, Our Lady's High, Cumbernauld 1969–72; Head of Remedial Education. St. Modan's, Stirling 1972–74; MP (SNP) for East Dunbartonshire since 1974. *Member:* General Teaching Council, Scotland; Educational Inst. of Scotland; Assoc. of Scottish Nationalist Trade Unionists. *Address:* 60 West High Street, Kirkintilloch, Glasgow; and *office* House of Commons, London SW1A 0AA.

**BAIRD, Robert Breckenridge II.** American importer of and dealer in natural rubber; *B.* 1923. *Educ.* Lehigh Univ. (BS); Mount Union College, Alliance, O. (BA); Denver Univ. (MBS). *M.* 1946, Esther Madelyn Steere. *S.* Robert Lyle II, William Torrey IV, David, Andrew Hunt. *Daus.* Margaret Moran, Barbara Irene, Camille Rieder, Esther Steere (Jr.), Mary Elizabeth, Belinda Torrey, Cynthia Louise, Catherine Mowry. *Career:* Grandson of one of the founders, became associated with Baird Rubber on March 1, 1948; upon release from military service in 1946, joined the Acme-Hamilton Manufacturing Corp. of Trenton, N.J.; at the time of his resignation of this concern he was acting secy. and asst. to the gen. mgr. of the Acme Rubber Manufacturing Co., a div. of the parent firm; appointed Secy. and a Dir. of Baird Rubber 1948; Vice-Pres. 1952; Pres. & Dir., Robert B. Baird & Co. Inc., Jan. 1962—; Pres. & Dir., Polyesther Corp. and Ridgebreck Corp. Trustee, Polytechnic Preparatory Country Day School. Republican. *Member:* Amer. Chemical Socy.; Rubber Trade Assn.; N.Y. Commodity Exchange, N.Y. *Clubs:* India House; Whitehall; Princeton (N.Y.); Shinnecock Golf and Yacht (2); N.Y. Yacht; Quoque Field; Salmagundi; Quoque Beach. *Address:* Quoque Street, Quoque, L.I., N.Y., U.S.A.

**BAIZLEY, Hon. W. Obie.** Canadian. *B.* 1917. *Educ.* Dr. & Philosopher of Chiropractic. *M.* 1939, Jessie MacDonald. *S.* Donald, Brian. *Dau.* Brenda. *Career:* Manitoba Ministry of Labour 1963–68; Manitoba Min. of Municipal Affairs and Commissioner of Northern Affairs 1968. *Member:* Manitoba Chiropractors' Assn.; Progressive-Conservative Party. *Clubs:* Kinsmen; Canadian Legion. *Address:* 333 Legislative Building, Winnipeg, Manitoba, Canada.

**BAKEN, René A. J.** Belgian industrialist. *B.* 26 July 1892. *M.* 1919, Jehanne Dutordoir. *Daus.* Maryse (Theunissen), Nicole (Didier). *Career:* Pres., Federation Nationale des Chambres de Commerce et d'Industrie (1956); Hon. Pres., Chambre de Commerce de Bruxelles since 1947; former Consul-General for Honduras; Hon. Vice-Pres., Tribunal of Commerce; Pres., Internat. Amateur Cinematograph Union (U.N.I.C.A.); Vice-Pres., Royal Automobile Club of Belgium; Vice-Pres., International Fair, Brussels. *Awards:* Officer, Ordre de Léopold; Officer, Ordre de la Couronne; Comdr., Ordre de Léopold II; Croix de Guerre; Chevalier de la Légion d'Honneur; Citoyen d'Honneur de New Orléans (U.S.); Comdr. Ordre Phenix Grèce. *Address:* 98 Avenue Montjoie, Brussels.

**BAKER, Geoffrey Hunter.** CMG, MA. Retired British diplomat. *B.* 1916. *Educ.* Haberdashers Askes Hampstead School; Royal Masonic School; Gonville & Caius Coll. Cambridge. *M.* 1963, Anita Wägeler. *Dau.* 1. *Career:* H.M. Vice Consul, Hamburg 1938–39; Danzig July–Spt. 1939; Bergen 1939–40; Basra Mar.–July 1942; Second Secy. Jedda 1942–45; Foreign Office London 1945–47; First Secy. Rangoon 1947–51; Tehran 1951–52; F.O. London 1953–54; NATO Defence Coll. Paris Feb.–July 1954; Consul General Hanoi 1954–56; U.K. Del. UN New York 1956–57; Cabinet Office London 1957–60; UK Del. EFTA Geneva 1960–66; Consul. Gen. Munich 1966–71; H.M. Consul General Zagreb 1971–74 (retired). *Awards:* Companion, Order St. Michael & St. George; Master of Arts; Order of Merit, Bavaria. *Clubs:* United Oxford & Cambridge University; Pall Mall London; Cambridge Univ. Cruising. *Address:* 10 Leigh Road, Highfield, Southampton SO2 1EF.

**BAKER, Sir Ivor,** CBE, DL, JP, MA. FIMechE, FIProdE; FBIM. British. *B.* 1908. *Educ.* Bootham School, York; King's Coll. Cambridge (MA Eng); Harvard Graduate School of Business Admin. *M.* 1935, Josephine Baker Harley. *S.* 3. *Dau.* 1. *Career:* Lloyds Bank Ltd.; Chmn., Lloyds Bank Ltd. Eastern Reg. Board; various appointments with Baker Perkins 1931–75; Member of Board of Peterborough Development Corp. since 1968; Fellow British Inst. of Management. *Address:* 29 Westwood Park Road, Peterborough.

**BAKER, Lord** (Life Peer, cr. 1977; John Fleetwood Baker, Kt. 1961), OBE, FRS. British engineering prof. *B.* 19 March 1901. *Educ.* Rossall School and Clare Coll., Cambridge (MA, ScD); DSc. Wales; Hon. DSc, Leeds, Edinburgh, Aston, Manchester, Leicester, Salford, Cranfield, Lancaster; Hon. DEng, Liverpool; Hon. LLD, Glasgow; Hon. DA, Ghent; Hon. ARIBA, Hon. F.I.Mech.E. *M.* 1928, Fiona M.M. Walker. *Daus.* Joanna MacAlister, Dinah *Career:* Tech. Officer, Steel Structures Research Cttee. 1931–36; Prof. of Civil Engineering, Univ. of Bristol 1933–43; Scientific Adviser and Head of Design and Development Section, Ministry of Home Security, A.R.P. Dept. 1939–43; Prof. of Mechanical Sciences and Head of Dept. of Engineering, Univ. of Cambridge 1943–68; Vice-Pres., Inst. Civil Eng. 1969–71; Pres., Welding Ins. 1971–73; British Association 1975–76; Dir., I.D.C. Group Ltd. *Publications:* Differential Equations of Engineering Science (1929); Analysis of Engineering Structures (1936); The Steel Skeleton (Vol. I, 1954; Vol. II, 1956); Plastic Design of Frames (1969); various scientific and technical papers on theory of structures. *Address:* 100 Long Road, Cambridge.

**BAKER, John Victor T.** New Zealand Independent Consultant in Management and Economic Statistics. *B.* 1913. *Educ.* MA; MCom (Hons.); Fellow, Chartered Accountant (N.Z.); Diploma in Public Administration. *M.* 1938, Betty Agnes Erica Sargisson. *S.* Leslie, Edric, Bruce, John. *Daus.* Hilda, Hilary. *Career:* Senior Research Officer, Dept. of Labour, N.Z., 1946–50; Divisional Dir., Dept. of Statistics 1950–54; Lecturer (part-time) in Statistics at Victoria Univ. of Wellington 1953–66; Dep. Government Statistician 1955–58; Government Statistician 1958–69; has represented New Zealand at many international statistical conferences. including: U.N. Statistical Comm., 5th and 6th Conferences of British Commonwealth Statisticians (Chmn. 1960) ECAFE Seminar on Basic Statistics (Chmn.) 1962, World Population Conference, Belgrade 1965. *Member:* Economic Socy. of Australia and New Zealand; International Statistical Inst.; Past Pres., N.Z. Statistical Assn.; N.Z. Assn. of Economists; N.Z. Chess Assn. *Publication:* War Economy (N.Z. Official War History Volume). *Club:* Rotary (Paraparaumu). *Address:* Main Road North, Paraparaumu, New Zealand.

**BAKER, Kenneth Wilfred,** MP; Industrial Consultant. *B.* 3 Nov. 1934. *Educ.* St. Paul's School; Magdalen Coll., Oxford. *M.* 1963, Mary Elizabeth Gray-Muir. *S.* 1. *Daus.* 2. *Career:* Nat. Service, Lieut. Gunners, N. Africa, Artillery Inst. to Libyan Army 1953–55; Secy. of Union, Oxford 1955–58; Twickenham Borough Council 1960–62; Contested Poplar 1964, Acton 1966; MP, Acton 1968–70; Public Accounts Cttee. 1969–70; P.P.S. to the Min. of State, Dept. of Employment 1970; Member of Parliament, Conservative, St. Marylebone since 1970; Parly. Secy. Civil Service Department 1972–74; P.P.S. to the Leader of the Opposition 1974–75; Mem., Exec. of 1922 Cttee., 1975. *Clubs:* Carlton. *Address:* House of Commons, London, S.W.1.

**BAKER, Norman Lee.** American. Pres./Editor-in-Chief, Space Publications Inc. 1960—. *B.* 1926. *Educ.* BSc, Aeronautical Engineering. *M.* 1960, Lois Shanner. *S.* Gary Kale, Alan Dale. *Daus.* Mary Ellen King, Syntha Eleanor. *Publications:* Defense Space Business Daily (Defense Space Daily), Space Business Week (Space Week), Space Log, and Who's Who in Space; Soviet Aerospace. *Awards:* Order of the Silver Slide Rule; Bausch & Lomb Award; Space Pioneers Award. *Member:* National Space Club; Amer. Assn. for Advancement of Science; Amer. Inst. of Aeronautics & Astronautics; Air Force Assn.; Amer. Astronautical Socy.; Amer. Ordnance Assn.; The Air Force Historical Foundation; National Trust for Historic Preservation; East Tennessee Historical Society; AIAA History Committee. *Club:* National Press (Washington). *Address:* Rose Hill, Deleplane, Va, U.S.A. and *office* 1341 G Street N.W., Washington D.C. 20005, U.S.A.

**BAKER, Ralph Douglas.** Canadian. *B.* 1898. *Educ.* U.S. Naval Acad., Annapolis, Md. (Graduated and Commissioned Ensign U.S. Navy, June 1919). *M.* (1) 1931, Nan Virginia Ober. (2) 1976, Wilma Hetherington Young. *S.* Robert Whittington. *Dau.* Looe Adele (Dewar). *Career:* in U.S. Navy 1916–22; Standard Oil Co. of Calif. In various capacities 1922–38; with Standard Oil. Co. of British Columbia (Mgr. of marketing 1938–41; Vice-Pres. and Dir. 1941–43; Pres. and Man. Dir. 1943–63), retd. 1963; became a Canadian. citizen 1964; Hon. Dir.: Crown Zellerbach Canada Ltd.; Hon. Dir., Labatt Breweries of BC Ltd.; Past Dir. and Chmn., Park Royal Shopping Centres Ltd.; Past Dir. and Chmn., Brit. Pacific Properties Ltd.; Past Chmn. Bd. of Trustees, Vancouver Gen. Hospital; Hon. Member, Bd. of Governors, Leon and Thea Koerner Foundation; Member Past-Chmn., Adv. Bd. of Salvation Army; Past-Pres., Vancouver Bd. of Trade and Vancouver Merchants Exchange Ltd.; British Columbia Chamber of Commerce; Pacific Northwest Trade Assn.; Community Chests and Councils of Greater Vancouver. *Clubs:* Vancouver; Shaughnessy Golf & Country. *Address:* 1401 2077 Nelson Street, Vancouver, B.C., Canada V6G 2Y2.

**BAKER, William George.** Australian. *B.* 1902. *Educ.* Broken Hill High School and Univ. of Sydney (DScEng 1932; BEng (Mech. and Elec.) Hons. Cl 1 and Univ. Medal 1923; BSc Hons Cl 1 and Univ. Medal, Mathematics and Hons. Cl 2 —Physics (1921). *M.* 1927, Doris Vera Gilbert McRoberts. *S.* 2. *Career:* Officer, Radio Research Bd. (Aust.) 1927–32; Engineer, Amalgamated Wireless (A/sia) 1931–53; sent to R.C.A. Radiotron Co., Harrison, N.J., U.S.A., Nov. 1931–March 1932; Dir., Inospheric Prediction Service, Dept. of the Interior, Commonwealth of Australia 1953—; Chmn., International Working Party VI/3 of the International Radio Consultative Cttee. (C.C.I.R.) 1962. *Publications:* Refraction of Short Radio Waves in the Upper Atmosphere (with C. W. Rice) (1926); The Limiting Polarization of Radio Waves Travelling obliquely to the Earth's Magnetic Field (with A. L. Green) (1933); Studies in the Propagation of Radio Waves in an Isotropic Ionosphere (1938); Electric Currents in the Ionosphere: I. The Conductivity (with D. F. Martyn); II. The Atmospheric Dynamo; III. A paper by Martyn 1953. *Awards:* Deas-Thomson Scholarship for Physics 1920; Peter Nicol Russell Medal (Post-grad. Research) 1924; W. & E. Hall Travelling Fellowship 1924–27. *Member:* Inst. Engineers (Assoc.); Australian Delegate to meeting of C.C.I.R. (1 Warsaw; 4 Geneva, 1 Oslo), and 3rd Antarctic Conf. (I.G.Y.), Paris, 1956; Mem., Interdepartmental Telecommunications Adv. Cttee. 1953–67. *Address:* 14 Rothwell Crescent, Lane Cove, N.S.W., Australia.

**BAKEWELL, Robert Donald,** CMG, JP. Australian. *B.* 1899. *Educ.* Kyre (now Scotch) Coll., Adelaide (Dux and Captain of the School). *M.* 1929, Ydonea Dale. *Dau.* Patricia. *Career:* Chmn., Australian Woolgrowers Council 1949–54; Pres.: Graziers Fed. Council of Australia 1948–49, and of Graziers Assn. of Victoria 1943–46; Mem., Australian Wool Realization Comm. 1945–59; Vice-Pres., Chamber of Agriculture of Victoria 1946–48; Man. Dir., Farnley Grazing Pty. Ltd. 1935–73; Life Mem., Australian Woolgrowers and Graziers Council 1954; Mem., Australian Wool Industry Conference 1963; Trustee, Graziers Assn. of Victoria. *Clubs:* Australian (Melbourne); Adelaide; Benalla; Rotary. *Address:* P.O. Box 82, Benalla, Vic., Australia.

**BAKWIN, Edward M.** American. *B.* 1928. *Educ.* Hamilton Coll. (BA) and Univ. of Chicago (MBA). *Career:* Pres., West Central Assn. 1963–65; Chmn., Management conference, Univ. of Chicago 1967; Chmn. of the Bd. (Man. Dir.) 1967—, and Pres., 1962—, The Mid City National Bank of Chicago; Director: West Central Assn. of Chicago 1962; Darling Deleware, Inc. 1970—; St. Louis National Stockyards Co.; Oklahoma National Stockyards Co.; Chmn. Bd., Darling Delaware Inc. since 1972. *Member:* Advisory Bd., Univ. of Chicago; Young Presidents Organization; American Bankers Association. *Publications:* New Concepts in the Preparation and Use of Financial Statements. *Clubs:* The Mid-America. *Address:* 175 East Delaware, Chicago, Ill. 60611; and *office* 801 West Madison Street, Chicago, Ill. 60607, U.S.A.

**BĂLĂCEANU, Petre.** Rumanian diplomat and univ. prof. *B.* 1906. *Educ.* Commercial Academy of Bucharest. *M.* Maria Ioana. *Daus.* Voica, Ilinca. *Career:* Official, National Bank of Rumania 1928–41; Industrial Mgr. 1941–47; Mem. of the Rumanian Parliament 1946–48; Economic Councillor at Legation in Washington 1947; En. Ex. and Min. Plen. in Argentina 1947–48; Vice-Pres., Rumanian State Planning Cttee. 1948–53; Pres. of the State Bank and First Dep. of the Min. of Finance 1953–57; En. Ex. & Min. Plen. in United Kingdom 1957–61; Envoy Ex. and Min. Plen. of the Socialist Republic of Rumania to the U.S.A. Dec. 1961–64, Ambassador 1964–67. *Awards:* Star of the Rumanian People's Republic; Order of Labour; The Medal of Liberation from the Fascist Yoke, etc.; Mem., Rumanian Communist Party. *Address:* c/o Ministry of Foreign Affairs, Bucharest, Socialist Republic of Rumania.

**BALAGUER, Dr. Joaquín.** President of the Dominican Republic. *B.* 1907. *Educ.* Univ. of Santo Domingo—Licenciate in Law; Univ. of Paris (Sorbonne)—Doctorate in Law. *Career:* Prof. at the Escuela Normal of Santiago & Goverment Lawyer on the Land Tribunal, 1930; Sec. of the Dominican Legation in Madrid 1932–35; Under-Sec. of State of the Presidency 1936; Under Sec. of State for Foreign Affairs 1937; Prof. at the Faculty of Law 1937; Envoy Ex. & Plen. in Colombia & Venezuela 1940; Ambassador Counsellor at the Dept. of Foreign Affairs 1944; Envoy Extraordinary & Minister Plenipotentiary, Colombia 1945; Amb. Ex & Plen. in Honduras 1947, & Mexico 1947; Sec. for Education & Fine Arts 1949; Sec. of State for Foreign Affairs 1953; Sec. for Education 1955; Sec. of the Presidency 1956; Vice-Pres. of the Dominican Republic 1957–60; Pres. of the Dominican Republic 1960–62 and since 1966 (re-elected 1970, 1974). *Address:* Office of the President, Santo Domingo, Dominican Republic.

**BALANCY, Pierre Guy Girald,** CBE. Citizen of Mauritius. Ambassador to the U.S.A. High Commissioner to Canada, 1970—. *B.* 1924. *Educ.* Royal Coll. (Port Louis); Bhujoharry's Coll. *M.* 1947, Marie Thérèse. *S.* 2. *Dau.* 3. *Career:* Mem.: Action Sociale 1959–60; Cttee. of Dir., Le Centre Culturel Français 1957–62; Mauritius Legislative Assembly 1963–68; Municipal Counsellor 1963–64; Parliamentary Secy., Ministry of Education and Cultural Affairs 1964–65; Min. of Information, Post and Telegraphs 1965–67; Min. of Works 1967–68; Founder and Editor-in-Chief, L'Express 1963–64; Permanent Representative at the U.N. 1968–69; Secy., Cercle Littéraire de Port Louis 1962. *Clubs:* Cercle Remy Ollier; Racing c. de Maurice. *Address:* 3911 Bradley Lane, Chevy Chase, Md. 20015, U.S.A.

**BALCON, Sir Michael (Elias),** DLitt (Hon.) Birmingham. British independent film producer. *B.* 1896. *Educ.* George Dixon School, Birmingham. *M.* Aileen Leatherman, MBE. *S.* Jonathan Michael Henry. *Dau.* Jill Angela. *Career:* Dir. of Production for Gaumont-British Picture Corp. Ltd. 1931–36; Producer for M.G.M. 1936–38; Executive Producer, Ealing Films Ltd. 1938–59; independent production 1959—; Chmn., British Lion Films Ltd. 1964–65; Consultant, Border Television Ltd. Founder and Dir., Gainsborough Pictures Ltd.; *Awards:* 1st Class Order of St. Olav (Norway); Chevalier, Order of Arts & Letters (France); Hon. D.Litt. (Sussex Univ.); a Senior Fellow, Royal Coll. of Art; Hon. Fellow, British Kinematograph Socy.; Gov. British Film Inst. 1963–71, Chmn. Production Bd. from inception to 1971. *Clubs:* MCC; Garrick. *Deceased 17th October 1977.*

**BALDOCCHI, Archie.** American inventor, boatbuilder. *B.* 1913. *M.* 1941. *S.* 1. *Dau.* 1. *Career:* F. C. Boatbuilding & Production Consultant; Pilot Fuerza Area Salvador; Dir.: Cemento de el Salvador, S.A.; Phelps Dodge Corp. of Central America; Productos de Cafe, S.A. Beech Aircraft Corp. Dealer; Cotton Grower. *Clubs:* Bohemian, San Francisco; Warbirds of America; Intl. Mustang Pilots Association. *Address:* Colonia Duenas 525, San Salvador, El Salvador. C.A.; and *office* Edificio Rivas Cierra, Calle Arce 707, San Salvador, El Salvador, C.A.

**BALDOCK, Leonard Noel.** Canadian. *B.* 1924. *Educ.* Sr. Matric; 2 years coll.; 3 years CPA; APA 1963. *M.* (1) 1946, Pauline Joyce Ritchie (*dec.*). *S.* Wayne Noel, Brent Carey, Darrell Ritchie. *Daus.* Pamela Mary, Lloralee Irene; (2) 1969, Eleanor Rose Whelpton. *Career:* Accountant and Office Mgr., Standard Machine & Tool Co. 1948–53; Secy.-Treasurer, Rotofinish (Canada) Ltd. 1950–53; Cost Accountant, Ford Company of Canada 1947–48; Public Accountant 1945–47; Observer, Royal Canadian Air Force 1943–45; Accountant, G. G. McKeough Ltd. 1940–42; Controller, Toledo Scale Division since 1971; Asst. Secy. & Treasurer, Reliance Electric Ltd. since 1971. Treasurer (Jan. 1955), Asst. Secy. and Dir. (March 1955), Secy. (1964), Toledo Scale Co. of Canada, Ltd. *Awards:* Holder of Order of St. John (1973), Atlantic Star 1939–45 Medal, Canadian War Medal, C.V.S.M. and Clasp, and Coronation Medal 1953, and Canadian Forces Dec. (1969); National Pres., Royal Canadian Air Force Assn. (elected 20 May 1960, re-elected 1961); Senior Reserve Adviser Windsor Area (Colonel) 1962; Lecturer, Univ. of Windsor 1962. *Address:* 665 Bartlet Drive, Windsor N9G 1V1, Ont., Canada.

**BALDWIN, Oliver Hazard Perry.** *B.* 1904. *Educ.* Harvard Univ. (AB 1927) and Rutgers Univ. Grad. School of Banking 1943. *M.* 1929, Elizabeth S. Webb. *S.* Oliver Hazard Perry, Jr., Roger Conant. *Dau.* Jean (Ritchie, Jr.). *Career:* Mgr., T. Hogan Sons Inc. (Port Stevedores) 1927–30; Asst. Cashier, Natl. Shawmut Bank, Boston 1930–44; Vice-Pres., First Natl. Bank, Akron, Ohio 1944–46; Pres., Wilmington office and Senior Vice-Pres., Farmers Bank of State of Delaware 1946–59; Pres. 1959–70; Chmn. and Chief Executive Officer of Farmers Bank of the State of Delaware 1959–71; Dir.: Mulco Products Inc. 1953—, Kent Real Estate Corp. (also Pres.) 1959–66, Rollins International Inc., Dover Builders Inc., Chesapeake Utilities Inc., Contnl. American Life Insce. Co., and Newark Real Estate & Insce. Co.; Pres.: Wilmington Clearing House Assn. 1950–52 and 1962–64; Wilmington Gen. Hosp. (also Bd. Dirs. and Exec. Cttee.) 1952–55; Delaware State Chamber of Commerce (Bd. Dir. 1955–66; Exec. Fin. 1955–65; Vice-Pres., 1956–61; Pres. 1962–64. *Member:* Delaware Bankers Assn. (Pres. 1958–59); Amer. Bankers Assn. (Vice-Pres. Del. Exec. Cncl. 1961–64); Legislative Rel. Cttee. 1964–70; Robert Morris Assn.; Financial Public Relations Assn. (Dir. 1950–53); Newcomen Socy. *Clubs:* Harvard (N.Y.C.), Wilmington, Wilmington Country, Wilmington Rotary; Thursday (Boston). *Address:* 1002 Berkeley Road, Wilmington, Del.; and Canaan Street, Canaan, N.H.; and *office* 10th Market Streets, Wilmington, Del. 19899, U.S.A.

**BALDWIN, Paul Clay.** American. *B.* 1914. *Educ.* Syracuse Univ. (BS 1936) and Inst. of Paper Chemistry (MS 1938; PhD 1940). *M.* 1972, Doris W. Trainer. *S.* Paul Clay, Jr., Robert F. *Dau.* Barbara F. *Career:* All previous employment with Scott Paper Co.: Lab. Asst., Tech. Dir., Production Supervisor 1940–46; Gen. Plant Mgr. 1946–51; Asst. Vice-Pres. 1951–53; Vice-Pres. 1953–57; Vice-Pres. Manfg., Engrg. and Research 1957–60 (Exec. Vice-Pres. 1960–68); Vice-Chmn. 1969—, and Dir. 1955—, Scott Paper Co., Philadelphia; Dir.: Bowater-Scott Aust. Ltd.; Bowater-Scott

Corp. Ltd.; Papeles Scott de Colombia, S.A.; Bouton-Brochard Scott; Scott Benelux, S.A.; Scott Paper Co. de Costa Rica, S.A.; Tawain Scott Paper Corp.; Thai-Scott Paper Co. Ltd.; Dir. Vice-Chmn. Burgo Scott, S.P.A.; Gurelo-Scott, S.A.; Dir. Vice-Pres. Celulosa Jujuy, S.A.; Compania Industrial de San Cristobal, S.A.; Scott Paper Philippines Inc.; Dir. Exec. Vice-Pres., Sanyo Scott Co. Ltd.; Dir. Exec. Cttee., Scott Paper Ltd.; Former Bd. Dirs. Exec. Cttee., Amer. Paper Inst. Inc.; Chmn. Bd. Brunswick Pulp & Paper Co.; Syracuse Univ. Research Corp.; Trustee Syracuse Univ. *Member:* Syracuse Univ. Corporate Advisory Council; Tau Beta Pi; Phi Kappa Psi; Alpha Chi Sigma; PIMA; TAPPI. *Awards:* PIMA, Man of the Year 1969; Univ. Maine Pulp & Paper Foundation 1972; Hon. Doctor of Science Lawrence Univ. 1972. *Clubs:* Union League (Phila.); The Pennsylvania Socy.; Rose Tree Fox Hunting; United Hunts Racing Assn.; Amer. Foxhound Assn. *Address:* 1300 S. Leopard Rd, Berwyn, Pa. 19312, U.S.A. and *office* Scott Paper Co., Philadelphia, Pa. 19113, U.S.A.

**BALDWIN, Ralph B(elknap).** American. Pres., Oliver Machinery Co., Grand Rapids, Mich. *B.* 1912. *Educ.* Univ. of Michigan (BSc 1934, MSc 1935, PhD Astrophysics 1937). *M.* 1940, Lois Virginia Johnston. *S.* M. Dana II, Bruce Belknap. *Dau.* Pamela. *Career:* Asst. Instructor, Astronomy Dept., Univ. of Michigan 1935–36; Asst., Astronomy Dept., Univ. of Pennsylvania 1937–38; Instructor, Dept. of Astronomy, Northwestern Univ., Chicago 1938–42; Lecturer, Adler Planetarium, Chicago 1940–42; Senior Physicist in Applied Physics Lab. of Johns Hopkins Univ. 1942–46; Dir.: Employers' Assn. of Grand Rapids; National Assn. of Manufacturers 1963–65; Pres., Woodworking Machinery Manufacturers' Assn. 1964–68; Chmn. Bd., Int. Woodworking Machinery & Furniture Supply Fair 1968–70, Dir. since 1970. *Awards:* Presidential Certificate of Merit, U.S. Naval Bureau of Ordnance Award, and U.S. Army Chief of Ordnance Award (all for participation in development of the proximity fuse, the No. 2 secret weapon in World War II); Distinguished Alumnus Award, Univ. of Michigan (1967); Hon. LLD, Univ. of Michigan (1975); Fellow, Amer. Assn. for Advancement of Science; Amer. Geophysical Union. *Member:* Amer. Astronomical Socy.; Meteoritical Society. Republican. *Publications:* The Face of the Moon (1949); The Measure of the Moon (1963); The Moon—A Fundamental Survey (1965); numerous articles for tech. publications. *Clubs:* Peninsular (Grand Rapids); Univ. Grand Rapids Yacht; Grand Rapids Rotary; Kent Country. *Address:* 3110 Manhattan Lane, S.E., Grand Rapids, Mich. 49506; and *office* 445 Sixth Street N.W., Grand Rapids, Mich. 49504, U.S.A.

**BALENTINE, Conrad James.** American. *B.* 1917. *Educ.* Princeton Univ. (BScEE). *M.* 1947, Margaret Hollohan. *Daus.* Catherine, Anne. *Career:* With Franklin Electric Co. Inc.: Vice-Pres., Engineering 1961; Vice-Pres., Engineering & Manufacturing 1961; Exec. Vice-Pres. 1963; Mgr., power circuit breaker engineering, G.E. Co., Phila., Pa. 1950–61; Pres. and Chief Exec. Officer, Franklin Electric Co. Inc. (Bluffton, Ind.); Pres.: Franklin Electric of Canada Ltd. (Strathroy, Ont.); and Franklin Electric Europa GmbH (Wittlich, Germany); Chmn. of the Bd., Chief Exec. Officer, Battle Creek Packaging Machines Inc., Michigan; J. B. Dove, Inc. Pennsylvania; Chmn. of the Bd., Pres., Exact Weight Scale Co. Ohio; Mem. Bd., Nobility Homes, Ocala, Fla.; Indiana Mfg. Association. Chmn. of Board Programmed Power Inc., Menlo Park Calif.; Dir. Caylor-Nickel Medical Res. Found., Dir. Lincoln Nat. Bank & Trust Co.; Dir. Blufton Junior Achievement. Owner of three patents. Registered Professional Engineer—Pennsylvania; Dir. Indiana State Chamber of Commerce Indianpolis, Ind. U.S.A. *Member:* Amer. Inst. of Electrical & Electronic Engrs.; Amer. Standards Assn.; Amer. Inst. of Management; Amer. Management Assn.; Newcomen Socy. of N. America; Indiana Manufacturers Assn.; Princeton Univ. Engineering Association, Amer. Gear Mfg. Assn.; N.E.M.A. *Publications:* seven technical papers published in A.I.E.E.E. *Clubs:* Fort Wayne Country: Parlor City Country (Bluffton); Summit. *Address:* R.R. 4, Fackler Road, Bluffton, Ind.; and *office* 400 East Spring Street, Bluffton, Ind., U.S.A.

**BALERNO, The Rt. Hon. Lord Alick Drummond Buchanan Smith,** KB, CBE, MA, MS, DSc. British. Peer of the Realm. *B.* 1898. *Educ.* Univ. of Aberdeen (MA, BSc); Iowa State Univ. (MS). *M.* 1926, Mary Kathleen Smith (*D.* 1947). *S.* 4. *Daus.* 1. *Career:* Lecturer Animal Genetics Univ. of Edinburgh 1926–61; Lt. Colonel Comnd. Battalion Gordon Highlanders 1936–42; Brigadier, Dir., Selection of Personnel War Office 1942–45. *Member:* Royal Socy. of Edinburgh. *Awards:* Distinguished Alumnus, Iowa State Univ.; Hon. Associate, Royal Coll. of Veterinary Surgeons; DSc, Heriot Watt Univ. *Publications:* Scientific papers on animal breeding. *Clubs:* Caledonian; Royal Automobile (London); New (Edinburgh); Royal Northern (Aberdeen). *Address:* Balerno, Midlothian, EH14 7JD.

**BALFOUR, Earl of, (Gerald Arthur James),** JP. British. *B.* 1925. *Educ.* Eton and H.M.S. Conway. *M.* 1956, Natasha Georgina Anton. *Career:* Farmer and Land Owner; Merchant Navy 1944–54; Bruntons of Musselburgh Ltd. 1955–59; Representative, Building Industry 1959–68; Master Mariner; 4th Earl of Balfour. *Member:* Assn. of International Cape Horners. *Clubs:* R.N.V.R. (Scotland); English Speaking Union; Naval & Military. *Address:* Whittingehame, Haddington, Scotland; and *office* Whittingehame Estate Office.

**BALFOUR, St. Clair,** DSC, LLD(Hon.). Canadian publisher. *B.* 30 April 1910. *Educ.* Trinity Coll., Toronto (BA). *M.* 1933, Helen Gifford Staunton. *S.* St. Clair. *Dau.* Elizabeth Staunton. *Career:* Chmn. Southam Press. Ltd.; Pres., Balfours Ltd.; Chedoke Sesurities Ltd.; Dir.: Southam Business Publications Ltd.; Southam Printing Ltd.; Southam Press (Ontario) Ltd.; Past Pres., Canadian Heart Foundation; Vice-Chmn. C'wealth Press Union. *Award:* Hon. LLD, Univ. of Western Ontario 1976. *Address:* 17 Ardwold Gate, Toronto, Ont. M5R 2W1, Canada; and *office:* 801, 321 Bloor St. East. Toronto M4W 1H3.

**BALFOUR-PAUL, Hugh Glencairn,** CMG. British. Dir.-Gen., The Middle East Assn. *B.* 1917. *Educ.* Sedbergh; Magdalen College, Oxford. *M.* (1) 1950, Margaret Clare Oglivy (*D.* 1971). *S.* 1. *Daus.* 3. (2) 1974, Janet Alison Scott. *Career:* served war 1939–45; Sudan Defence and Political Service, Blue Nile 1946–54; Joined Foreign Office, Santiago, Beirut, Dubai, Bahrein, St. Antony's Coll. Oxford 1955–69; Ambassador to Iraq 1969–71, to Jordan 1972–75, and to Tunisia 1975–77. *Club:* Travellers. *Address:* 20 Essex Villas, London W8 7BN; and *office* The Middle East Association, 33 Bury Street, St. James's, London SW1Y 6AX.

**BALL, George Wildman.** American investment banker. *B.* 1909. *Educ.* Northwestern Univ. (BA 1930; JD 1933). *M.* 1932, Ruth Murdoch. *S.* John Colin, Douglas Bleakly. *Career:* Gen. Counsels Office, Treasury Dept., Washington, D.C. 1933–35; Admitted to Illinois Bar, 1934, D.C. Bar 1946; Assoc. Gen. Counsel, Lend-Lease Admin. 1942–44; Dir., U.S. Strategic Bombing Survey, London 1944–45; Gen. Counsel, French Supply Council, Washington 1945–46; Founding Partner of international law firm of Cleary, Gottlieb, Steen & Ball 1946–61; Under-Secy. of State for Economic Affairs 1961; Under-Secy. of State 1961–66; of Counsel, Cleary, Gottlieb, Steen & Hamilton, attorneys 1966–68; Chmn., Lehman Bros. International 1966–68; Sr. Partner, Lehman Bros. since 1969. U.S. Permanent Representative to the U.N. 1968. *Awards:* Legion of Honor (France); Grand Cross Order of the Crown (Belgium); Medal of Freedom (U.S.). Trustee: American Assembly, Columbia Univ. *Address:* 1 William St., New York, N.Y. 10004, U.S.A.

**BALL, Stuart Scoble.** American lawyer. *B.* 1904. *Educ.* Northwestern Univ. (BA, MA, JD). *M.* (1) 1930, Marion Wolcott Watrous (*d*). *S.* Stuart Scoble. *Daus.* Marion W., (Tramel), Eleanor W. (Hausheer); (2) 1969, Bernice Beckman Wilson. *Career:* Admitted to Illinois and Iowa Bars 1927; Mem., firm of Parrish, Cohen, Guthrie & Watters, Des Moines, Ia. 1927–32; Asst. Secy., Montgomery Ward & Co., Chicago 1932–33 (Secy. 1933–49; Vice-Pres. 1949; Pres. 1949–52; Dir. 1950–52); Partner, Sidley & Austin, Chicago since 1953; Mem., Bd. of Dir., John Sexton & Co. 1957–68. *Member:* Order of Coif; American, Illinois and Chicago Bar Associations; American College of Trial Lawyers; Chicago Assn. Commerce & Industry Dir. 1946–70; Pres. Orchestral Assn. Chicago; Trustee Wesley Mem. Hospital Associated Stationers, Chicago, Dir. 1956–64, Chmn. Bd. 1957–58; Chmn., Selection Cttee. Cook C. Hospital Gov. Cttee. 1969—; Republican. *Clubs:* Economic (Pres. 1952–53), Commercial, Chicago, Glen View, Univ. *Address:* 1419 Sheridan Road, Wilmette, Ill.; and *office* One First National Plaza, Chicago, Ill., U.S.A.

**BALLANTRAE, Lord. (Sir Bernard Edward Fergusson),** KT, GCMG, GCVO, DSO, OBE. British. *B.* 1911. *Educ.* Eton; Sandhurst. *M.* 1950, Laura Margaret Grenfell. *S.* 1. *Career:* Joined Army (The Black Watch) 1931. Served in Palestine 1937–38, Middle East 1941, India 1942, Burma 1943–44. Commanded 16th Infantry Brigade 1943–44. Director, Combined Operations 1945–46. Palestine Police 1947. Held various appointments as Brigadier until retiring in 1958 to write books; Governor-General and Commander-in-Chief of New Zealand 1962–67; Chmn., British Council 1972–76; Chancellor, St. Andrew's Univ.; Colonel, Black Watch 1969–76. *Awards:* DCL, DLitt., LLD, FRSL. International Observer Team, Nigeria, 1968–69. *Publications:* Eton Portrait (1937); Beyond the Chindwin (1945); Lowland Soldier (1945); The Wild Green Earth (1946); The Black Watch & The King's Enemies (1950; Rupert of the Rhine (1952); The Rare Adventure (1954); The Watery Maze (1961); Wavell (1961); Return to Burma (1962); The Trumpet in the Hall (1970); Captain John Niven (1972). *Clubs:* White's (London); New (Edinburgh). *Address:* Auchairne, Ballantrae, Ayrshire.

**BALLANTYNE, Kenneth Rex Hunter.** British. *B.* 1919. *Educ.* Melbourne Univ. (Matric.). *M.* 1952, Joan Margaret Lowe. *Career:* Dir., Best & Co. Pty. Ltd. 1946–57; Man., Publicity Dept., Philips Electrical Industries Pty. Ltd. 1957–58; Aust. Govt. Dir. of Trade Publicity (U.K.) 1958–61; Joint Man. Dir., U.S.P. Benson (N.S.W.) Pty. Ltd. 1961–67; Dir., U.S.P. Holdings Pty. Ltd. since 1966; Dep. Man. Dir., Compton Advertising Australia Pty. Ltd. 1967–71; Man. Dir., Ballantyne Advertising Pty Ltd. 1971–76; Dir., Talbot Evans Pty. Ltd. since 1976. *Award:* Fellow, Advertising Inst. of Australia. *Clubs:* Imperial Service, Royal Sydney Yacht Squadron; Southport Golf; Bonnie Doon Golf. *Address:* 351, Edgecliff Road, Edgecliff, N.S.W. 2027; and *office* 9–11 Grosvenor Street, Neutral Bay, N.S.W., Australia.

**BALLANTYNE, Walter Robert,** JP. British. *B.* 1905. *Educ.* George Heriots School (Edinburgh) Edinburgh Univ. (BL) and London Univ. (LLB). *M.* 1933, Charlotte Howden Fort Smith. *Dau.* Elizabeth Ann Fort. *Career:* Entered the service of the Bank in Edinburgh 1920; Asst. Secy. 1947; Dep. Man. in London 1950; Asst. Gen. Mgr. 1952; Joint Gen. Mgr 1953; Sole Gen. Mgr 1955; Dir.: Glyn Mills & Co. 1953–65, Williams Deacon's Bank Ltd. 1953–65, and Scottish Agricultural Securities Corp. Ltd. 1953–65; Dir.: Royal Bank of Scotland 1960–70 (Gen. Mgr. 1953–65); Chmn., Scottish Mutual Assurance Socy.; Ailsa Investment Trust Ltd.; Dir., Alva Investment Trust Ltd. (directorships dating from 1965); Scottish Advisory Bd., Abbey National Building Society 1968—; Dir., Noble Grossart Ltd. 1970—; Noble Grossart Investments Ltd. 1970—; Cosmas Developments Ltd., Chmn. since 1972; Pres., Scottish Economic Society 1972–75; Hon. Pres. Scottish Youth Hostels Assn. (Chmn. 1958–75); Chmn., Scottish Assn. of Boy's Clubs 1969–73; Chmn. North Merchiston Clubs, Edinburgh. *Publication:* (jointly with George Home) Recovery of Advances. *Clubs:* New (Edinburgh); Royal Scottish Automobile (Glasgow); Royal & Ancient Golf (St. Andrews); Royal Burgess Golfing Society. *Address:* 4 Ross Road, Edinburgh EH16 5QN.

**BALLARD, John Oman.** Australian. *B.* 1924. *Educ.* Jesus Coll., Cambridge (MA): Barrister-at-Law, Middle Temple, London; Barrister and Solicitor, Victoria, Australia. *M.* 1949, Sylvia Jocelyn Smith. *S.* John William. *Daus.* Sylvia Jane, Melissa Mary, Priscilla Isobel. *Career:* H.M. Overseas Civil Service 1950–63; successively Crown Counsel in Tanganyika and Cyprus, and Asst. Attorney-General in North Borneo; *Member:* Inter-governmental Cttee. on Malaysia; Asst. Secy. then First Asst. Secy., Dept. External Territories 1963–71; Order of Kinabalu (Sabah, Malaysia) Dep. Secy., Dept. of Interior, Commonwealth of Australia 1971–73; First Asst. Secy., Attorney General's Dept. 1973–76; Compensation Tribunal since 1976. *Club:* Canberra Yacht. *Address:* 'Biggins', Sutton, N.S.W. 2581, Australia; and *office*, Commonwealth Employees Compensation Tribunal, P.O. Box 260, Woden, A.C.T., Australia.

**BALOGH, Rt. Hon. Lord (Thomas).** British. *B.* 1905. *Educ.* Gymnasium of Budapest Univ. Drerpol; Oxford, MA; Universities of Berlin and Harvard. *M.* (1) 1945, Penelope Tower. *S.* Stephen, Christopher. *Dau.* Tessa; (2) 1970, Catherine Cole. *Stepdaus.* Sophia, Tirril, Cecilia, Emma. *Career:* Hungarian General Credit Bank 1922–27; Fellow, Royal Hungarian Coll., Berlin 1927–28 and Rockefeller Foundation 1928–30; Scientific Asst. of Finance, Mem., Secy. of State for India's Council, London 1930–31; Temp. Mem. League of Nations Secretariat 1931–32; Economic Adviser in the City of London 1932–38; Research Assoc., Nat. Inst. of Economic Research 1938–44; Lect. since 1939; Fellow, Balliol Coll., Oxford 1945–73; Special Lect. and Reader Economics, Oxford Univ. 1945–73; Economic Adv. to the Cabinet; Special Asst., Prime Minister 1964–68; Economic Adv. to various Governments, United Nations Organisation (UNDP FAO) OECD since 1945; Chmn., Fabian Socy. 1970; Minister of State, Dept. of Energy 1974–75; Dep. Chmn., British Nat. Oil Corp.; Fellow, Woodrow Wilson Center, Smithsonian Inst., Washington D.C. *Publications:* The Dollar Crisis (1949): Financial Organisation (1946); Unequal Partners (1964); Economics of Poverty (1966); Planning for Progress (1966); Labour and Inflation (1970); International Monetary Reform (1973). *Club:* Reform. *Address:* The Cottage, Christmas Common, Watlington, Oxon.; and *office* Queen Elizabeth House, Oxford; and British National Oil Corp., Stornoway House, Cleveland Row, St. James', London S.W.1.

**BAMBERG, Harold Rolf.** CBE. British. *B.* 1923. *M.* 1956, June Winifred Clarke. *S.* 2. *Daus.* 3. *Career:* Chmn. Bamberg Group Ltd.; Mitchell Cotts Airfreight (UK) Ltd.; Eagle Aircraft Services Ltd; Protection of Persons & Property Ltd; Integrity Finance Ltd; Eagle Flying Services Ltd; Aeronautical & Commercial Instrumentation Ltd. *Club:* Royal Aero. *Address:* Harewood Park, Sunninghill, Ascot, Berks; and *office* Leavesden Airport, Watford WD2 7BY.

**BAMFORD, Allan Edmund,** ED. Australian banker. *B.* 1910. *Educ.* Wesley Coll. (Melbourne, Victoria). *M.* 1942, Elaine Helen Vial. *Daus.* Shirley Irene, Katharine June. *Career:* Joined Commercial Banking Co. of Sydney in Melbourne 1927; attached London Office 1937–39; Asst. Mgr. Melbourne 1951–53; Mgr. Brisbane 1953–56, and Melbourne 1956–61: Asst. Chief Inspector, Head Office, Sydney 1961–63, Chief Inspector 1963–65; Senior Chief Inspector 1965–68; Chief Mgr. Victoria 1968–73; Asst. Gen. Mgr. 1971–73; Vice-Pres. Bankers Inst. of Australasia 1953–54; Principal, Bankers Administrative Staff Coll. 1956; Commissioned Lieut., C.M.F. 1933; A.I.F. 1939–45 (Middle East, Greece, New Guinea); Capt. 1939, Major 1941, Lieut-Col. 1942; p.s.c.; Retired List 1960. *Publications:* Some Aspects of the Legal Relationship between Banker and Customer (1954). *Awards:* Fellow: Inst. of Bankers, London; Inst. Chartered Secretaries and Administrators; Bankers Inst. of Australasia (Hon. Life Mem.); Aust Socy. of Accountants; Aust. Inst. of Management. *Member:* Council of United Service Instn. Victoria 1947–53 and 1957–61; N.S.W. 1961–68; Victoria 1968—; Vice-Pres. 1970—. *Clubs:* Athenaeum, Naval & Military, Melbourne Cricket (Melbourne); Union (Sydney). *Address:* 2 Adelaide Street, Armadale, Victoria 3143, Australia.

**BANDA, H. E. Ngwazi Dr. H. Kamuzu,** BSc., MB, Ch.B, PhD, MD, LRCSE. President of Malawi, *B.* 1906. *Educ.* Mission Schools, Meharry Medical Coll. Nashville, MD; Univ of Glasgow, Edinburgh. *Career:* Practised medicine Liverpool & Tyneside during World War II, & in London 1945–53; Practised medicine in Ghana 1954–58, Returned to Nyasaland (now Malawi) to head Congress Party & lead country to Inde; pence 1958. Detained during State of Emergency 1959–60e Min. of Nat. Resources & Local Govt 1951–63; Prim- Minister of Malawi 1963–66; Chancellor Univ. of Malawi since 1965; Elected President 1966; Elected Life President 1971. *Address:* State House, Box 40, Zomba, Malawi.

**BANDARANAIKE, Hon. (Mrs.) Sirimavo,** R.D. First Prime Minister, Sri-Lanka 1972–77. *B.* 1916; eldest dau. of the late Dissawa Barnes Ratwatte (Ratemahatmaya of the Ratnapura District). *Educ.* Ratnapura High School and St. Bridgets Convent, Colombo. *M.* 1940 Hon. S. W. R. D. Bandaranaike (who was at that time Min. of Health); *Career:* Mrs. Bandaranaike has had an active interest in politics and social service for the past 20 years; She assisted her husband (who was Prime Minister of Ceylon, 1956–59) in his political career, and was one of the leading figures in the Island-wide development of the Lanka Mahila Samitiya as Treasurer, Vice-Pres. and Pres.; when her husband was assassinated in 1959 she was unanimously elected Patron of Sri Lanka (Ceylon) Freedom Party, and in May 1960 its President; appointed Prime Min. and Min. of Defence and External Affairs July 1960, and Mem. of the Senate Aug. 1960; since then has led delegations to several conferences, such as the Commonwealth Prime Ministers Conf. in London 1961, 1964 and Singapore 1971 in Ottawa 1973 and Jamaica 1975; and the Conf. of non-aligned nations in Belgrade Sept. 1961; in Nov. 1962, she initiated the move to call for a conference at Colombo to discuss Sino-Indian border dispute; following this the Conference of the non-aligned nations was held at Colombo Dec. 1962, with delegates from Burma, Cambodia Ghana, Indonesia, U.A.R. and Ceylon; in Dec. 1962 she left for India and China on a mandate from the Colombo Conf. to clarify the proposals of this conference; in 1964 she led a delegation to the Conference of non-aligned nations in Cairo, in Lusaka 1970 and in Algiers 1973; elected M.P. for her husband's constituency, and Leader of the Opposition 1965; Min. Defence & External Affairs of Planning and Employment 1970; Addressed U.N. Gen. Assembly 1971; State Visits to France 1970; U.S.A., Canada and Britain 1971; Peoples Republic of China 1972, India, Maldives, Pakistan, West Germany, Romania, Yugoslavia, Iran, USSR 1974; Iraq and Guyana 1975 and Indonesia, Thailand and Burma 1976; Addressed ILO Conference, Geneva and U.N. Women's International Year Conf. at Mexico City 1975; First Prime Minister Republic of Sri Lanka 1972–77. *Address:* Rosmead Place, Colombo 7, Sri-Lanka.

**BANERJI, Shirshir Kumar.** Indian diplomat and administrator. *B.* 1913. *Educ.* Univ. of Allahabad (BA) and New Coll., Oxford. *M.* 1939, Gauri Chatterjee. *S.* Ranjan, Rohit. *Daus.* Ratna, Rupa. *Career:* Joined Indian Civil Service 1937; Dep. Commissioner, Khandwa, Balaghat, Nagpur, Akola (Central Provinces) until 1946; Joint Secy. and later Secy., Civil Supplies, Central Provinces Government 1946–47; First Secy. and later Chargé d'Affaires, Embassy of India, Teheran 1947–49; Dep. Secy., Ministry of External Affairs, New Delhi 1949–51; Dep. High Commissioner (with rank of Min. from 1952) for India in Pakistan, Lahore 1951–54; Consul-General, San Francisco 1954–56; Delegate to 10th Anniversary Session of U.N., San Francisco, June 1955; Chmn., U.N. Visiting Mission to British and French Togolands 1955; En. Ex. and Min. Plen. to Syria 1956, Ambassador 1957–58; High Commissioner for India to Malaya 1958–59; Joint Secy., Min. of External Affairs, New Delhi April 1960–March 1961, Chief of Protocol, and Controller General of Emigration; Min. of External Affairs, New Delhi March 1961–Jan. 1964; Additional Secy. and Chief Foreign Service Inspector Jan.–Oct. 1964; Ambassador at Bonn 1964–67; Tokyo 1967–70; Secy. Ministry External Affairs New Delhi 1970–72; Lieutenant Governor of Goa, Daman and Diu since 1972. *Address:* Lieutenant Governor, Goa, Daman and Diu, Panaji India.

**BANG, Thor.** Norwegian banker. *B.* 1925. *Educ.* Univ. of Oslo (Grad. Econ. 1947; Law 1951). *M.* 1952, Idah Fredriksen. *Career:* With Assn. of Mechanical Industries 1942–44; Norwegian Legation, Stockholm (Refugee Office) 1944–46; Central Bureau of Statistics 1946–47; Norwegian Shipowners Assn. 1947–58; Dep. Man. Dir., Den norske Creditbank since 1958; Dir., Norwegian Polytechnic Socy. 1952–60, Chmn., 1966–68; Chmn., Norwegian Bankers' Employers' Fed. 1964–67. *Publications:* various articles on general economic policy, shipping, and taxation. *Address:* Den norske Creditbank, Kirkegaten 21, Oslo, Norway.

**BANK, William Julius.** American. *B.* 1913. *Educ.* Univ. of Virginia; Univ. of Iowa; Purdue Univ.; Univ. of Richmond. *M.* 1935, Esther Sawney Kaplan. *S.* 3. *Career:* Pres. and Owner Jonbil Mfg. Co.; Blue Jeans Corp.; formerly Exec. Vice-Pres. Blue Ridge Mfrs. Inc.; Imperial Shirt Corp.; Vice-Pres. Blue Ridge Mfrs. Inc. 1942–49; Exec. Vice-Pres. H. D. Boskond Co. 1958–59; Mem. of Inter American Commn. Cttee.; Mem. American Management Assoc.; American Socy. of Personnel Administrations; Socy. for Advancement of Management; Nat. Academy of Sciences. Technical Advisory Cttee. Amer. Apparel Mfrs. Assoc.; Pres. Apparel Research. Foundation; Mem .United Inventors & Scientists of America; Dir., American Apparel Mfrs. Association. *Address:* 60 Ward Drive, New Rochelle, N.Y., U.S.A.: and *office* 350 5th Avenue, N.Y.C. N.Y.

**BANKS, Lord, (Desmond Anderson Harvie),** CBE. British politician and insurance broker. *B.* 1918. *Education:* University Coll. School, Hampstead. *M.* 1948, Barbara Wells. *S.* 2. *Career:* Hon. Secy. Liberal Candidates Assn. 1947–52; Lib. Parly. Candidate, Harrow (1950), St Ives (1955), S. W. Herts (1959); Chmn. Lib. Party Exec. 1961–63 and 1969–70; President Liberal Party 1968–69; Dir. of Policy Promotion (Lib. Party) 1972–74; Pres. Liberal European Action Group since 1972; Hon. Treas. Lib. Summer School since 1972; Vice-Chmn., Lib. Party Standing Ctee. since 1973; Dep. Liberal Whip, House of Lords since 1977; Liberal Spokesman for Social Services since 1977; Dir. Tweddle French & Co. Ltd. (Life and Pensions Consultants) Ltd. since 1973. *Member:* Chartered Ins. Inst.; Clyde River Steamer Club; Harrow Caledonian Socy.; (Assoc) D'Oyly Carte Trust Ltd.; Europe Movement-Exec Cttee of Brit. Council; Elder, United Reformed Church. *Decoration:* Commander of Order of Brit. Empire. *Publication:* Clyde Steamers (1947); numerous political pamphlets. *Club:* Nat. Liberal. *Address:* 58 The Ridgeway, Kenton, Harrow, Mddx HA3 0LL; and *office* Ibex House, Minories, EC3N 1DY.

**BANKS, J. Eugene.** American investment economist. *B.* 1908. *Educ.* Washington Univ., St. Louis, Mo. (BS 1930). *M.* 1956, Barbara Hall Vietor. *Step-dau.* Diana Vietor Mundy. *Career:* Lieut.-Cmdr. U.S.C.G.R. 1942–45; Investment Analyst, Merrill Lynch, Pierce, Fenner & Beane 1938–42; Mgr., Private Investment Funds 1931–38; Analyst, Boatman's National Bank, St. Louis 1930–31; Partner, Brown Brothers Harriman & Co., Private Bankers, 59 Wall Street, New York City. *Member:* Military Order of the World Wars; N.Y.; American Economic Assn.; Socy. of Security Analysts; Trustee: Trinity Church Assn.; Teachers' Coll., Columbia Univ. *Publication:* Institutional Investment Guides; contributions in financial field. *Clubs:* Univ., Down Town (both of N.Y.C.); The Pilgrims. *Address:* 880 Fifth Avenue, New York City 10021; and *office* 59 Wall Street, New York City, N.Y. 10005, U.S.A.

**BANKS, John Vallery.** Structural engineer. *B.* 1917. *Educ.* BSc Civil Engineering. *M.* 1938, Beatrice J. Fisher. *Daus.* Jan, Catherine, Becky, Elizabeth. *Career:* Design Engr. Shasta Dam, Calif. 1938–40; Capt., U.S. Army Corps of Engineers 1940–45; Chief Engr., Kaiser Frazer Assembly Plant, Long Beach 1946; Vice-Pres., Manufacturing, Kaiser Frazer Corp., Willow Run., Mich. 1946–53; Vice-Pres., Manufacturing, Willys Motors Inc. 1953–56; Asst. Gen. Mgr., Fabric Div., Kaiser Steel, Los Angeles 1956–61; Pres., National Steel & Shipbuilding Co., San Diego, Calif. since 1961, and Vice Chmn. of the Board since 1976. *Member:* Structural Engineers of Southern California; National Management Assn.; Socy. of Naval Architects & Marine Engineers; Amer. Bureau of Shipping. Republican. *Publications:* Production Line Steps Up Girder Welding (1958); Computer Solves Layout Problem (1961); A Specialized Exhaust System (1961). *Clubs:* Propeller (of S.U.); San Diego Yacht. *Address:* 6041 Camino de la Costa, La Jolla, Calif.; and *office* NASSCO, 28th & Harbour Drive, San Diego, Calif., U.S.A.

**BANKS, Robert George.** MP. *B.* 1937. *Educ.* Haileybury. *M.* 1967, Diana Margaret Payne Crawfurd. *S.* 4. *Dau.* 1. *Career:* Lt Comdr. RNR; Joint Founder/Dir., Antocks Lairn Ltd. 1963–67; Partner, Breckland Securities, Investment Company: MP (Cons.) for Harrogate, N. Yorks since 1974; Jt. Sec., Conservative Party Defence Cttee.; Vice-Chmn. Parly. Horticulture Cttee.; Sec., All-Party Tourism Group; Mem., Council of Europe & Western European Union since 1977. *Address:* Bretteston Hall, Stanstead, Sudbury, Suffolk; and Cow Myers, Galphay, Ripon, Yorks.

**BANKS, Talcott Miner.** American lawyer. *B.* 1905. *Educ.* Williams Coll. (BA 1928) and Harvard Law School (LLB 1931). *M.* (1) 1935, Kathleen Hall (*d.* 1966). *S.* Ridgway Macy, Oliver Talcott. *Dau.* Helen Macy; (2) 1967, Ann S. M. Banks (*D.* 1970) (3) 1973, Elisa C. Brooks. *Career:* Pres., National Intercollegiate Lawn Tennis Assn. 1927–28; Mem. Editorial Staff, Time Magazine 1930; admitted to the Bar 1931; General Counsel, Bd. of Investigation & Research, Washington, D.C. 1941–44; Trustee: Williams Coll., Williamstown, Mass. 1961–75; Dir., Comstock & Wescott Inc., Cambridge, Mass. 1957—; Pres. & Trustee, Sterling & Francine Clark Art Inst., Williamstown 1964—; Mem. Metropolitan Opera Assn., N.Y.C. Partner, Palmer & Dodge, Boston 1945—; Pres., The Fessenden School, West Newton, Mass. 1956–67; Boston Opera Assn., 1956–68; Boston Symphony Orchestra since 1968. *Member:* American Bar Assn. (Chmn. Sp. Cttee. on Securities, Laws and Regulations 1940–42); Massachusetts and Boston Bar Assns.; American Law Inst.; American Judicatures Socy.; Phi Beta Kappa; Kappa Alpha. *Publications:* articles in legal research journals and magazines. *Clubs:* Univ. (N.Y.C.); Somerset. St. Botolph (Pres. 1949–53); Cruising Club of America; American Alpine; Agawam Hunt (Prov.); Dunes (Narragansett). *Address:* Bedford Road, Lincoln, Mass. 01773; and *office* One Beacon St., Boston, Mass. 02108, U.S.A.

**BANWELL, Sir Harold.** *B.* 1900. *Educ.* Tankerton Coll., Kent. *M.* 1924, Kate Mary Bull. *S.* 2. *Daus.* 3. *Career:* Solicitor (admitted 1922, articled to Town Clerk of Canterbury); Asst. Solicitor, West Hartlepool County Borough Council, Cumberland County Council, and Sheffield City Council; Dep. Town Clerk, Norwich City Council 1929–32; Town Clerk, Lincoln City Council 1932–41; Clerk of the County Council of Lincoln—parts of Kesteven—1941–44; Secy., The Assn. of Municipal Corps. 1944–62; Mem.: Gen. Advisory Council, B.B.C. 1961–64; Exec. Council Royal Inst. Public Admin. 1961–64; Chmn., National Citizens Advice

Bureau, Council of the National Council of Social Service 1961–71; Chmn. of Council, Congregational Union of England & Wales 1962–66; Member, Nat. Incomes Comm. 1962–65; Advisory Council on Commonwealth Immigration 1962–64; Chmn. Cttee. on Placing & Management of Contracts for Building & Civil Engineering Work 1964; Chmn. of the Congregational Church in England & Wales 1966–69. *Member:* Parliamentary Boundary Comm. of England 1963–74; Departmental Cttee. on the Fire Service 1967–70; Dep. Chmn. of Comm. for New Towns 1964–71; Alderman Lincoln City Council 1967–74. *Award:* Created Kt 1955; Hon. LL.D. Nottingham 1972. *Address:* 2 Vicars' Court, Lincoln.

**BANZER SUAREZ, General Hugo.** President of the Republic of Bolivia and Commander in Chief of the Armed Forces. *B.* 1926. *Educ.* Colegio "Obispo Santiesteban", Santa Cruz; Colegio Nacional "Florida", Santa Cruz; Colegio Militar de la Nación, "Cnl. Gualberto Villarroel", La Paz; Colegio Militar de la Nación Argentina; Post-Grad.; Escuela de Aplicación de Armas Bolivia (Alumno Abanderado); Escuela de las Américas de Zona del Canal de Panamá (Alumno de Honor); Escuela Blindada de las Estados Unidos de Norte-América; Escuela de Altos Estudios Militares, la Paz. *M.* Yolanda Prada. *S.* 4. *Career:* Head of Army Intelligence Dept.; Commander of Army Military College (Bolivia); Military Attaché, USA; Chief of General Staff and Temporary Divisional Commander; Minister of Education and Culture 1964–66; Pres. of the Republic since 1971 and Commander in Chief of the Armed Forces. *Decorations:* Gold Medal of the Mayorality of the City of Sucre; Gold Medal of Retired Master; Naval Award of Merit; Air Award of Merit; "Lanza Warriors"; Condor of the Andes (National Decoration of Bolivia); Hon. Dr. of Inca Garcilazo de la Vega, Univ. of Peru; Award of Military Merit of USA Army; National Decorations of Argentina, Panama, Venezuela, Colombo, Ecuador, Peru, Brazil, Uruguay and Paraguay. *Address:* Palacio de Gobierno, La Paz, Bolivia.

**BARADI, Dr. Mauro Obtinalla.** Philippine Lawyer, Diplomat, Statesman, Freedom Advocate, Humanitarian, Author, Educator, Orator & Scholar. *Educ.* College of Law (Philippine Law Sch.), National Univ., Manila—LLB; National Univ., Washington, D.C.—AB, MA, MPL, SJD. *M.* 1935, Eden Guevara. *S.* 2. *Daus.* 2. *Career:* Admitted to Philippine Bar 1925; U.S. Supreme Court, D.C. & U.S. Court of Appeals, D.C. Circuit 1929; U.S. District Court, D.C. 1933; U.S. Court of Customs & Patent Appeals 1940; Adviser, Phil. Resident Comm., Washington D.C. 1929–34; Law Prof. & Pres. Villamor Colleges, Manila 1934–38 & 1946–50; Phil. Delegate to 7th World Federation of Educ. Assns., Tokyo 1937; Acting Dean, Abad Santos Law Sch. 1934–41, 1946–53; Mem. Phil. Educ. Mission Abroad 1938–39; Publicity Officer, Phil. Res. Comm. Office, Wash. D.C. 1940; Asst., Exec. Office, Malacañang 1941; Sec. & Adviser to Min. of Educ., Health & Pub. Welfare 1942–44; Editor. *The Cabletow* (Manila) 1945–55; Editor (for Phil. Bodies), *Far Eastern Freemason* (Manila) 1949–53; Legal Counsel, Phil. Senate 1952; Special Attorney, Comm. on Investigation (Blue Ribbon Comm.) 1952–54; Special Attorney, Comm. on Foreign Relations 1954–55; Phil. Rep. & Chmn., U.N. Advisory Council for Italian Somaliland 1956–60; Minister, Phil. Mission to the U.N., N.Y. 1960; Phil. Chief of Mission to Africa (South of Sahara) 1962; Phil. Amb to Nigeria, Cameroon, Ghana, Liberia & Sierra Leone 1963–65; Mem. Phil. Delegation to 2nd Afro-Asian Conf., Algiers 1965; International Law Consultant Mem. since 1966; Delegate, Phil. Constitutional Convention 1971; Mem., Phil. Delegation to Egypt 1975; Phil. Amb. to Kenya, East Africa; Special Adviser of Phil. Delegation to 30th session of UN Gen. Assembly, NY 1975; Phil. Perm. Rep. to UN Environment programme (UNEP) 1975; Co-Chmn., Phil. Delegation, 4th Session, UNEP Governing Council & Mem., Phil. Delegation, 4th Conf. of the UNCTAD 1976; Vice-Chmn., Phil. Delegation, 19th session of the Gen. Conf. of UNESCO 1976; Co-Chmn., Phil. delegation. 5th session of UNEP Governing Council 1977; First Phil. Amb. to Somalia & Ethiopia 1977. *Awards:* LLD, DP, DH (hon. causa); 23 gold medals for excellence in oratory; African Chiefs of Diplomatic Mission's (in Nairobi) testimonial for "outstanding services rendered on the continent of Africa"; numerous citations, gold medals, golden cups & silver plaques from: Boy Scouts, Chambers of Commerce, Community Chests, Diplomatic Corps, Eloy Alfaro International Foundation (Grand Cross), Grand Lodges & Supreme Councils (Freemasonry) & "Recognized as one of the world leaders of the Craft (Freemasonry)" by the American Lodge of Research, F. & A.M., Jan.–Dec. 1957; International Assns., Clubs & organisations incl. Christian Endeavor, DeMolay, Kiwanis, Knights of Columbus, Knights of Rizal, etc. *Publications:* The Influence of the US Constitution in the Philippines (1930); Radio Laws of the Philippines (1931); Life's Message to Youth (1932); The Philippine Charter of Liberty (co-author) (1933); American & Filipino Relations (3 vols, compilation) (1929–33); Questions of Privilege (compilation) (1934); The Constitutional Convention, Its Powers & Limitations (1935); Philippine Mining & Mining Laws (in collaboration) (1936); The Commonwealth & the Filipino Youth (1937); Masonic Personalities (1952); Man as a Mason (1953); Freemasonry in the Philippines Today (1954); Freemasons & Freemasonry (1956); many essays & articles. *Address:* Villa Eden, 338 Amang Rodriguez Avenue. Mangahan, Pasig, Metro Manila; & *Law Office* Don Pablo Building, 114 Amorsolo Street, Makati, Metro Manila, Philippines.

**BARAKAT, Gamal Eldin,** OM (Egypt), OM (Syria). Egyptian diplomat. *B.* 1921. *Educ.* Cairo Univ. (LLB); Dip. Inter. Law Academy, The Hague; Oxford Univ. (BLitt). *M.* 1955, Anbar Elham. *S.* 1. *Dau.* 2. *Career:* Egyptian Embassy, London 1950–52; Foreign Ministry, Cairo 1953–55; Consul General Aleppo 1955–58; Councillor, Washington 1958–60; Head of Foreign Office Training Dept., Cairo 1961–63; Ambassador to Uganda 1964–68; to Burundi 1968, to Finland 1968–73; Asst. to the President's Advisor, Nat. Security Cairo since 1973. *Awards:* Order of the Republic (ARE); Great Cross of the Lion (Finland). *Address:* Heliopolis, Cairo, ARE; and *office* Abdin Palace, Cairo, Egypt.

**BARBARA, (Miss) Agatha.** Maltese. *B.* 1923. *Educ.* Government Secondary School. *Career:* engaged in teaching 1943–47; entered politics 1947; on granting of the new Constitution in 1947, became the first woman M.P. in Malta; has held the seat since then; Min. of Education 1955–58; Min. of Education and Culture 1971–74; Min. of Labour, Employment and Welfare since 1974; Mem. of the Malta Labour Party. *Address:* 7 Graces Street, Zabbar, Malta, G.C.

**BARBER, The Rt. Hon. Lord (Anthony Perrinot Lysberg),** PC, TD, LLB, MN, British politician. *B.* 4 July 1920. *Educ.* Retford Grammar School; Oriel Coll. Oxford (Hon. Fellow); Law Degree with 1st Class Hons. while P.O. War. *M.* 1950, Jean Patricia Asquith. *Daus.* 2. *Career:* War Service 1939–45; Barrister-at-Law, Inner Temple since 1948; M.P. Doncaster 1951–64; P.P.S. to Under Secy. of State for Air 1952–55; Asst. Whip 1955–57; A Lord Commissioner of the Treasury 1957–58; Parly. Private Secy. to the Prime Minister 1958–59; Economic Secy. to the Treasury 1959–62 and Financial Secy. 1962–63; Min. of Health and Mem. of the Cabinet 1963–64; Mem. of Parliament Conservative for Altrincham and Sale 1965–70; Chancellor of the Duchy of Lancaster 1970; Chancellor of the Exchequer 1970–74; Chmn. Standard Chartered Bank Ltd. 1974, and Dir. of other companies. *Award:* Created Life Baron (UK) 1975. *Clubs:* Carlton. *Address:* c/o Standard Chartered Bank Ltd., 10 Clements Lane, London, E.C.4.

**BARBER, Frank Elliott, Jr.** Lawyer. *B.* 1912. *Educ.* Norwich Univ. (BS 1934) and Harvard Law School (LLB 1937). *M.* (1) 1938, Jeanne Freund (*div.* 1946) and (2) 1949, Frances Fairbrother. *S.* Frank Elliott III, Hugh Willard. *Daus.* Susan Elizabeth (Newton), Allison Frances. *Career:* Town Counsel, Brattleboro 1941–43, and 1945–47; State Senator 1947–49; Judge, Brattleboro Municipal Court 1947–49; Representative, State General Assembly 1951–53; Attorney General, State of Vermont 1953–55. Chmn., Vermont Liquor Control Bd. 1959–63. *Publications:* Attorney General's Biennial Report 1954 and 1956. *Award:* Breast order of Yun Hui with ribbon, National Government of the Republic of China, 1946. *Member:* American, Vermont and Windham County Bar Assns; Insurance Section of American Bar Assn., and Amer. Trial Lawyers Assn. Republican. Mason (including Shrine); B.P.O. Elks. *Clubs:* American Legion, V.F.W.; Brattleboro Country. *Address:* 16 Linden Street, Brattleboro, Vt.; and *office* 29 High Street, Brattleboro, Vt., U.S.A.

**BARBER, Jess Stavely.** American. *B.* 1901. *Educ.* New York Univ. (BCS 1925). *M.* 1924, Muriel V. Kozlay. *S.* Jess Stavely, Jr. *Dau.* Patricia Ann. *Career:* Secy., Treasurer, Dir., Eastern States Corp., Baltimore 1949—; Asst. Treasurer and Asst. Secy., St. Regis Paper Co., N.Y.C. 1956–65; Secy., Northwestern Pulp & Power Corp., Hinton, Alta, Canada 1950–62, and St. Paul Pulp & Paper Co., Tacoma. Wash. 1959–62. *Member:* Commerce & Industry Assn. (N.Y.C.).

*Clubs:* Presbyterian (S. Orange, N.J.); The Squires (Maplewood, N.J.). *Address:* 1921 Field Road, Sarasota, Fla.; and *office* 10 Light Street, Baltimore, Md.; also 150 East 42nd Street, New York, N.Y., U.S.A.

**BARBER**, John Rowlinson, Australian business consultant. *B.* 1895. *Educ.* St. Brendan's (Annandale, N.S.W.). *M.* 1925, Dorothea Beatrice O'Dee. *Dau.* Dorothea Elizabeth. *Career:* With Colonial Mutual Fire Co. & Central Insurance Co. 1912–15; The Chamber of Manufactures Insurance Ltd. 1915–61. Chartered Secy.; formerly Gen. Mgr. & Secy., The Chamber of Manufactures Insurance Ltd. 1955–61; Pres., Council of Fire & Accident Underwriters of Australia 1959–60, and The Australian Insce. Inst. 1961–62; Dir.: Accountants Publishing Co. Ltd. 1953–73; Famua (Victoria) Ltd. 1956–61; Australian Aviation Underwriting Pool Pty. Ltd. 1960–62; Mem., Faculty of Economics & Commerce, Univ. of Melbourne 1954–70; Mem., Bd. of Management, The Occupational Therapy School of Victoria 1948–66. *Publications:* Modern Business Practice, 1st Edition (Pitman); Editor 8th Aust. & N.Z. edition, Principles & Practice of Auditing (Pitman); with J. Alan McKie, Workers' Compensation & Allied Subjects (Australian Insurance Inst.); numerous articles and papers in technical journals. *Member:* Australian Insurance Inst. (Fellow); Australian Socy. of Accountants (Fellow); Chartered Inst. of Secretaries (Assoc.). *Clubs:* Athenaeum; M.C.C. *Address:* 10 Lambert Road, North Caulfield, Vic. 3161, Australia.

**BARBER**, Joseph. American administrator, author and editor. *B.* 1909. *Educ.* Phillips Academy (Andover); Harvard Univ. (AB); Columbia Univ. (BS). *M.* 1936, Eileen Paradis. *Career:* Berlin Correspondent, Universal Service 1933–34; Man. Editor, Atlantic Monthly 1935–38; Public Relations Counsel, Honolulu, Hawaii 1938–40; Assoc. Editor, Washington Post 1941–43; War service with U.S. Navy (Lieut. j.g. to Lieut.-Comdr. U.S.N.R.) 1943–46; Dir. of the branches (Committees on Foreign Relations) of the Council on Foreign Relations in 33 American cities 1946–63. *Publications:* Hawaii-Restless Rampart (1941); Good Fences Make Good Neighbours—Why the United States Provokes Canadians (1958); These are the Committees (1964); Political Handbook of the World (co-ed. with Walter H. Mallory) (1953); Editor of pamphlet series published by Council on Foreign Relations: American Policy Toward Germany (1947); The Marshall Plan as American Policy (1948); Military Co-operation with Western Europe (1949); American Policy Toward China (1950); The Containment of Soviet Expansion (1951); Foreign Aid & the National Interest (1952); Foreign Trade and U.S. Tariff Policy (1953); Diplomacy and the Communist Challenge (1954); Alliances and American Security (1960); Red China and Our U.N. Policy (1961); Atlantic Unity and the American Interest (1963). *Clubs:* Century, Harvard (N.Y.C.); St. Botolph (Boston). *Address:* 16 East 84th Street, New York City 28; and Fortune's Rocks, Biddeford, Me., U.S.A.

**BARBOUR**, Walworth. American diplomat. *B.* 1908. *Educ.* Harvard Univ. (AB 1930). *Career:* Vice-Consul Naples 1931; Athens 1933; Third Secy. Baghdad 1936; Sofia 1939; Second Secy. Sofia 1941; Cairo 1941; Baghdad and Cairo 1942; Second Secy. near Govt. of Greece and of Yugoslavia (both established in Egypt) 1943; Athens 1944; Asst. Chief, Div. of Southern European Affairs, Dept. of State, Washington, D.C. 1945; Chief of South-east European Affairs 1947; Counsellor (with rank of Min.) Moscow 1949; Dir., Office of Eastern European Affairs 1951; Dep. Asst. Secy. of State for European Affairs 1954; American Min. and Dep. Chief of Mission, London 1955–61; Ambassador of U.S. to Israel 1961–73. *Address:* 14 Grapevine Road, Gloucester, Mass. 01930, U.S.A.

**BARCHOFF**, Herbert. American executive. *B.* 1915. *Educ.* New York Univ. (BS 1935; JD 1938); recipient of the Eliot Shepard Scholarship, N.Y. Univ. Law School. *M.* 1963, Lilyan Blum. *S.* Michael Blum, Jared Blum. *Career:* Editor, N.Y. Univ. Law Quarterly Review 1938; drew up basic plan for Copper Recovery Corp. 1942; Businessmen's Group, President's Council of Economic Advisors 1952; National Advisor to Small Business Administration 1954; Pres.: Eastern Rolling Mills Inc. 1954—, Tubotron Inc. 1959–72; Citizens' Advisory Cttee. on Foreign Trade to the Senate Banking and Currency Cttee.; Pres., Copper & Brass Warehouse Assn. 1955–56; Mem., Conference to Plan a Strategy for Peace 1961, and American Assembly Arms Control 1961; Dir., YPO, N.Y. Chapter 1961; Member, Small Business Advisory Cttee., The National Democratic Platform Cttee. 1956; Arden House Conference 1961; Guest Lecturer: Columbia Univ.; Fairleigh Dickinson; Pace Coll.; Seminar Leader, Conf. at Bogota, Colombia, programme on Alliance for Progress; Conf. Mem., Columbia Univ. Amer. Assembly 'Uses of the Sea' 1968. *Member:* Amer. Management Assn. (initiated and chaired programme for 'Manage mentof the Smaller Co.'); Exec. Cttee. Action Cttee. for International Development; National Assn. of Independent Business (Pres. 1955); Young Presidents' Organization (Vice-Chmn. 1959); National Planning Assn. Nat. Chmn. Trades-Industries Anti-Defamation League Appeal, Vice-Chmn., N.Y. Board Anti-Defamation League, and Amer. rep. Canadian-Amer. Assembly on Nuclear Weapons (all 1967); Nat. Commissioner, Anti-Defamation League of B'nai B'rith 1968; Dir., United Cerebral Palsy; Chmn. Cttee. for Release of Copper Stockpile since 1974 (Vice Chmn. 1973–74); Pres. Copper Industry Action Cttee. since 1974; Pres., American Copper Council since 1974. *Awards:* Human Rights Award (Anti-Defamation League of B'nai B'rith). *Member:* Hon. Legal Socy.; Theta Sigma Lambda. *Publications:* Small Business—America's Bulwark (1952); Neutralizing the Tariff Barrier (1954); Democapic Management (1959); Maximizing Productivity (1963); Author and Publisher, monthly copper letter called "Sticking My Neck Out". *Address:* Eastern Rolling Mills Inc., 1122 East 180th Street, New York City 10460, U.S.A.

**BARCLAY**, Alexander P. H. Canadian. *B.* 1913. *Educ.* BA (Chem. Phys.) and MSc (Communication and Phys.). *M.* 1938, H. Eileen MacLaurin. *S.* William Alexander. *Dau.* Susan Eileen. *Career:* Dir.: Electronics Industries Assn. 1963–65, and Canadian Region, Inst. of Radio Engineers (now I.E.E.E.) 1960–62; Chmn., Toronto Section, Inst. of Radio Engineers (now I.E.E.E.) 1956–57; Eng. Mgr., Canada Post Office. *Member:* Ontario Assn. of Professional Engineers; Inst. of Electrical and Electronics Engineers. *Clubs:* Ottawa Hunt Golf; Carlton Rideau Yacht & Golf. *Address:* 2951 Riverside Dr. 403 Ottawa, K1V 8W6 Ont. Can; and *office:* Sir Alexander Campbell Bldg., Confederation Hts, Ottawa, K1A OB1 Ont. Canada.

**BARCLAY**, Hartley Wade. Editor & Publisher, Product Planning and Sales Development, & Publisher, OEM Newsletter since 1970; Owner, The Management Research Inst.; Aeronautical Pilot & Instr.; Corporate Dir. of Research, Analysis & Programming Corp.; Certified Manufacturing Engineer. *B.* 1903. *Educ.* Ohio Wesleyan Univ. (AB 1924); Aeronautics-Liberty Air Academy; special courses at Univ. of Florida, Wisconsin, Minnesota; Penn State Purdue; and Massachusetts; Lecturer, Army Industrial Coll. 1936–39; Regist. Corresp. Pentagon Dept. of Defense 1965; McConnell Prize, Ohio Wesleyan Univ. 1924; Public Service Citation, N.Y. Chapter, Professional Engineers; Citation Engineers Jt. Council. *M.* (1) 1924, Marjorie K. Witley (*Dec.*). *M.* (2) 1927, Lois Beveridge Wilson. *S.* Hartley W., James Crawford. *Career:* Eastern Vice-Pres. Engineering, Nova-Chrome Inc.; Aeronautical Consultant, town of Rye, N.Y. Publisher, Tide Magazine 1956–59; Industrial Advertising Mgr., The New York Times 1952–56 (Business Writer 1946–52); Corp. Consultant, General Motors Corp. and others 1944–46; Editorial Dir., Conover Mast Corp., N.Y. 1932–42; Assoc. Editor, Electrical Trades Publishing Co., Chicago 1929–31; Resident Representative: Reading Steel Casting Co. 1927–29 The Lunkenheimer Co. 1925–27, Advisor to the Select Joint Legis. Comm. on the state's economy. Republican. *Member:* American Defense Preparedness Assn. (Life); Life Member Soc. of Mfg. Engs.; Newcomen Socy.; Board member: Amer. Inst. of Industrial Engineers; Overseas Engineers Club, London, Eng. (Pres.); Order of Washington; The President's Cttee. for Employment of the Physically Handicapped; Chmn., Long Range Planning Cttee. Technical Socys., Council N.Y.C.; Hon. Mem. US Army 25th Infantry and 101st Airborne Divn.; Ambassador, North American Defense Command (NORAD). *Award:* Washington Medal Engineer. *Club:* Philia. P.A.; Special Rep. Engineers Inc. Newark, N.J.; Phi Gamma Delta; Sigma Delta Chi; Pi Delta Epsilon; Descendants of the Signers of the Magna Carta. *Publications:* Ford Production Methods (Harpe & Bros.); How Your Business Can Help Win the War (Simon & Schuster); The Foundation Survey (The Management Research Inst.); Labor's Stake in American Industry (Atlantic Monthly); Contributor, Manchester Union Leader. *Clubs:* National Press (Washington); Tri-State. *Address:* Who Torok Estate, King Street, Port Chester, N.Y., U.S.A.

**BARGUES**, Robert Isaac. French colonial administrator. *B.* 21 Oct. 1900. *Educ.* École Nationale de la France d'Outre Mer. *M.* 1931, Simone Mouchoux. *Dau.* Annie (Nocca). *Career:* District Commissioner, French West Africa 1924: Inspector of Colonies (West and Equatorial Africa, West Indies, Indo-China, French settlements in India) 1932; member for financial affairs and Colonial Secretary, French West Africa 1948; High Commissioner in Madagascar Jan. 1950; Representative of France on the Trusteeship Council of U.N. 1955; Gen. Manager, Ministry of Overseas France 1959; Counsellor of State 1961. *Address:* Villa Vera, 41 Avenue de Vallauris, 06400 Cannes, France.

**BARIBEAU, Lt.-Col. Hervé**, ED. French-Canadian industrialist and manufacturer of woodware and chemicals. *B.* 1900. *Educ.* Levis College (Prov. of Quebec). *M.* 1926, Cecile Couillard-Desprès. *S.* 3. *Dau.* 1. *Career:* awarded Certificate of Merit by H.E.C. Association of Montreal; Chairman of the Board, Paquet Inc.; Unique Assurance; Baribeau & Sons Inc.; Unigesco Inc.; Standard Woodenware Ltd., Inter-Quebec Publicité Ltée.; Industries Baribeau Inc., Gosford Lumbar Ltd., Pres., Radio Saguenay., Vice-Pres., Union Canadienne Insurance Co. Director, Tele-Capital Ltée; Fonderie Ste-Croix Ltd.; Quebec Aviation Inc.; Tapis Rouge Aéro-Service Inc.; St. Augustine Hospital. President, Levis School Board, 1953–62; Past President, Canadian Red Cross Campaign, Quebec District Community Chest, and Quebec Rotary Club; served in World War II (O.C. B. Co. 36 Inf. Bn. 1944–45; Lt.-Col. and O.C. Levis Regt. until Nov. 1945) 1939–45; actively engaged in welfare and social work both in the city and district of Levis; is a Progressive Conservative. *Clubs:* Rotary de Québec; de la Garriron. *Address:* 13 Place Baribeau, Levis, P.Q., and *office* 381 St. Laurent Street, Levis, P.Q., Canada.

**BARKE, (James) Allen.** British. *B.* 1903. *Educ.* Birley Street Central School, and Manchester College of Technology. *M.* (1) 1937, Doris Bayne (*d.* 1952). *S.* David and Harry. *Dau.* Marian; and (2) 1953, Marguerite Sutcliffe (*née* Williams); stepdaughter, Marguerite. *Career:* Gained general engineering experience with Mather & Platt 1922–32. Joined Ford Motor Co. 1932; successively Buyer, Purchase Dept. 1939; Chief Buyer (Tractors) 1947; Manager, Leamington Foundry 1948; Exec. Director and General Manager, Briggs Motor Bodies Ltd. 1953; Director, Product Divisions 1959; Asst. Managing Director 1961; Chief Exec. Officer and Man. Dir. 1963. Vice-Chairman, Ford Motor Company Ltd. 1965–71; Director, The De la Rue Co. 1971–73; Falcon Engineering Ltd. Brentwood since 1972. *Club:* Royal Automobile; Oriental. *Address:* Thirlstone, Mill Green, Ingatestone, Essex; and *office* Falcon Eng. Ltd., Wash Road, Hutton, Brentwood, Essex.

**BARKER, Sir Alwyn (Bowman)**, Kt. CMG, BSc, BE. Australian. Chartered engineer. *B.* 1900. *Educ.* St. Peter's College, Adelaide; Geelong C. of E. Grammar School; Univ. of Adelaide. *M.* 1926, Isabel B. Lucas. *Dau.* 1. *Career:* With British Thomson-Houston Co., Ltd., England, 1923–24; Hudson Motor Car Co., Detroit, 1925; Prod. Man., Holden's Motor Body Builders Ltd., Adelaide, 1925–30; Works Manager, Kelvinator Australia Ltd. 1931–40; General Mgr., Chrysler Australia Ltd. 1940–52; Managing Director, Kelvinator Australia Ltd. 1952–67; Chairman, Kelvinator Australia Ltd.; Tecalemit (Australasia) Pty. Ltd.: Member Bd. F. H. Faulding & Co. Ltd.; Santos Ltd.; Wormald (S.A.) Pty. Ltd. Lecturer in Industrial Engineering, Univ. of Adelaide, 1929–54; Member Faculty of Engineering 1938–68; Chmn., Municipal Tramways Trust (Adelaide), 1953–68; Chmn., Industrial Development Advisory Council. (S.A.); 1968–70. Member, Industrial Research & Development Adv. Cttee 1968–70; Manufacturing Industries Advisory Council 1958–72; Chmn., Adelaide Electrolysis Investigating Cttee.; Deputy Chmn., Aust. Mineral Foundation. *Awards:* Hon. Fellow, Aust. Inst. of Management; Fellow, Int. Academy of Management; Inst. of Engineers; Inst. of Production Engineers; John Storey Memorial; Jack Finlay National. *Club:* Adelaide. *Address:* 51 Hackney Road, Hackney, Adelaide, S.A., Australia 5069 and *office* G.P.O. Box 1347, Adelaide, South Australia, 5001.

**BARKER, George Llewellyn**, JP, MNZIT. *B.* 1909. *Educ.* Timaru Boys' High School. *M.* 1937, Gail Hamilton Borum. *Career:* Joined Union S.S. Co., Timaru 1925; at sea as Purser 1927–34; served at Rotorua, Wellington, Sydney, Vancouver and San Francisco; with Army overseas 1940–43. Deputy Mayor, Lower Hutt 1959–62. President: British Epilepsy Assn., Wellington 1957–63, Lower Hutt Justices of the Peace Assn. 1961–63, Lower Hutt Businessmen's Assn. 1958–59. Executive Member: Marriage Guidance 1960–64, St. John Ambulance Brigade 1962–63, H.V. Youth Advisory Board 1959–63, Hutt Park Committee 1959–62, Taita Board College Governors 1959–62. Established La Fayette Imp. Co. Ltd. 1972, Chmn. of Dirs. since 1974. *Member:* Wellington Harbor Board 1959–71; Patron, Lower Hutt Municipal Band 1961—; Hutt Valley Chamber of Commerce & Industry; Businessmen's Assn.; N.Z. Travel Agent's Assn. (Pres. 1964–66); Returned Services Assn.; Founders & Early Settlers' Assn. Stood against Labor Prime Minister Nash at 1960 elections and reduced his majority by half; also stood unsuccessfully for Mayor of Lower Hutt against Labor Mayor Dowse 1962. *Clubs:* Hutt Rotary; Patron Hutt Valley & Eastern Bays Travel Club. *Address:* 16 Pharazyn Street, Lower Hutt, New Zealand.

**BARKER, Robert Rankin.** American business executive. *B.* 1915. *Educ.* Harvard Univ. (AB *Magna cum laude* 1936). *M.* 1942, Elizabeth Van Dyke Shelly. *S.* James Robertson, William Benjamin. *Daus.* Ann Shelly, Margaret Welch. *Career:* Investment and Credit Analysis and Investment Advisory Depts. J. P. Morgan & Co. 1936–49; William A. M. Burden & Co. 1949–54 (when he became partner); Special Assistant to Assistant Secretary of Commerce for Air, Washington 1942–43; Officer, U.S. Naval Reserve (resigned as Lieutenant) 1943–46; General Partner, William A. M. Burden & Co. 1954—; Trustee & Public Mem., Hudson Institute, Inc.; Amer. Museum of Natural History (and Mem. Finance Cttee.); Trustee Amer. Farm School (and Mem. Investment Cttee.); Chmn., Advisory Cttee. on Endowment Management of Ford Found. Formerly Trustee: Amer. Geographical Soc.; Silvermine Guild of Artists; New Caanan Country School (also Pres.); New Canaan Library. *Member:* Cncl. Foreign Relations, Center for Inter-Amer. Relations Inc., N.Y. Soc. Security Analysts. Phi Beta Kappa; Harvard Univ. Visiting Committees on University Resources, Computing Center. *Clubs:* University, Harvard, The Brook, Hemisphere (all of New York); Country, New Canaan. *Address:* 809 Oenoke Road, New Canaan, Conn. 06840 and *office* 630 Fifth Avenue, New York, N.Y. 1002 U.S.A.

**BARKER, W. Gardner.** American business executive—food industry. *B.* 1913. *Educ.* Harvard University (AB 1935); Stanford University Graduate School of Business (special study courses); Massachusetts Inst. of Technology (MS 1937). *M.* 1935, Milda Allen. *S.* W. Gardner, Jr. and Bruce Allen. *Daus.* Sue Barker Gray and Elizabeth Barker Zubersky. *Career:* Dir. of New Products, Pepsodent Div. of Lever Bros. Co., Chicago 1948–49; Exec. Vice-Pres. and Director, Simoniz Co., Chicago 1950–56; Vice-Pres., New Products, Thomas J. Lipton Inc. 1956 (Exec. Vice-Pres., and Dir. 1957–58). Pres., Dir. and Chief Exec. Officer, Thomas J. Lipton Inc., Englewood Cliffs, N.J., Jan. 1959—: Chmn. Bd., Thomas J. Lipton Ltd. (Canada); Dir.: Constitution Exchange Fund, Inc.; Chmn. of Tea Council. *Member:* The Conference Bd.; The Cruising Club of America; The Presidents; Amer. Marketing Assn.: Amer. Management Assn.; Member, English-Speaking Union; Trustee: Consumer Research Institute (G.M.A.); Nutrition Fdn. *Clubs:* Sales Executive; New York Yacht; Indian Harbor Yacht; Eastern Yacht· The Brook; The Harvard (Boston); The University (Chicago); Economic (New York); Royal Thames Yacht (London), etc. *Address:* Andrews Road, Greenwich, Conn., and *office* 800 Sylvan Ave., Englewood Cliffs, N.J., U.S.A.

**BARKSHIRE, Robert Hugh**, CBE. British. *B.* 1909. *Educ.* King's School, Bruton. *M.* 1934, Emily Blunt. *S.* 1. *Career:* Bank of England 1927–55; Private Secretary to the Governor (Lord Cobbold) 1949–53; Assistant Chief Cashier 1953; Secretary to Committee of London Clearing Bankers, British Bankers' Association, Bankers' Clearing House and Foreign Exchange Committee and member of various Inter-bank Committees 1955–70, Consultant 1970–72; Hon. Secy. to Meetings of Officers of European Bankers' Associations 1959–72; General Commissioner of Income Tax for the City of London sice 1969; Governor of the National Institute of Economic and Social Research since 1970. *Awards:* Freeman of the City of London; Fellow, Inst. of Bankers. *Clubs:* Gresham; Hurlingham; Royal Wimbledon Golf. *Address:* 22 Clareville Court, Clareville Grove, London, S.W.7.

**BARLOW Dr. Erasmus Darwin.** British. *B.* 1915. *Educ.* Marlborough College; Trinity College Cambridge (MA, MB, BChir.); Univ. College Hospital, London. *M.* 1938, Brigit Ursula Hope Black. *S.* 1. *Daus.* 2. *Career:* House Physician, Univ. College Hospital 1942; Medical Res. Council Staff 1942–48; Psychiatric Registrar, South-West Metropolitan Regional Hospital Board 1949–51; Senior Lecturer. Dept. Psychological Medicine and Consultant

Psychiatrist, St. Thomas's Hosp. Med. Sch., London 1951–66. Dir. Group Investors Ltd. 1956—; Cambridge Instrument Co. Ltd. 1958–74; Chmn., Electronic Instruments Ltd., Richmond, Surrey 1962–70; Chmn. Cambridge Instrument Co. Ltd. 1963–70; Dep. Chmn., George Kent Ltd. 1968–74; Chmn. Scientific and Medical Instruments Ltd. (CSI and CML) 1974–75; Dep. Chmn., The Cambridge Instrument Co. 1975—. *Member:* Royal Soc. of Medicine; Royal Coll. of Psychiatrists. *Publications:* Slow recovery from ischaemia in human nerves (jointly); Effects on blood pressure of ventricular asystole during Stokes-Adams attacks and acetylcholine injections (jointly); The Dangers of Health; Mechanism of acute hypotension from fear of nausea (jointly); Compulsive water drinking (jointly). *Clubs:* Savile, Athenaeum (London). *Address:* 4 Downshire Hill, Hampstead, London, NW3 1BG and *office* The Cambridge Instrument Co. Ltd., Melbourne, Royston, Herts. SG8 6EJ.

**BARLOW, Professor Harold Everard Monteagle.** British. *B.* 1899. *Educ.* London Univ.; BSc(Eng.); PhD (Science). Hon. DSc Heriot Watt Edinburgh, 1971; Hon. D. Eng. Sheffield, 1973. *M.* 1931, Janet Hastings Eastwood. *S.* 3. *Dau.* 1. *Career:* Sub-Lieut. R.N.V.R. 1916–18; East Surrey Ironworks Ltd. 1923; Barlow & Young Ltd. 1923–24; Academic Staff, Univ. College, London 1924–67. Superintendent, Radio Dept., Royal Aircraft Establishment, Farnborough, 1939–45. Professor of Electrical Engineering, University College, London, 1945–67. Now Emeritus. Member, B.B.C. Scientific Advisory Committee; Fellow, Royal Socy., London. Faraday Medal 1967; Dellinger Gold Medal, International Union of Radio Science 1969; Harold Hartley Silver Medal, Inst. of Measurement and Control 1973; Mervin J. Kelly Award of IEEE (USA) 1975; Fellow I.E.E.E. (U.S.A.) 1956—; Hon. Fellow I.E.R.E. 1971; Hon. Mem. Inst. of Electronics & Communications Engs. of Japan 1973; FE 1976; Member, Cncl. of I.E.E. London 1955–58; Chairman, British Nat. Cttee. of Internat. Radio Union (U.R.S.I.) 1967–73. *Publications:* Microwaves and Waveguides (Constable) (1950); Microwave Measurements (with Prof. A. L. Cullen) (Constable) (1952); Surface Waves (with Dr. J. Brown) (Oxford Press) (1961); many scientific papers. *Club:* Athenaeum (London). *Address:* 13 Hookfield, Epsom, Surrey; and *office* University College, Gower Street, London, W.C.1.

**BARLOW, Joel.** American lawyer. *B.* 1908. *Educ.* Alma College (AB 1929, LLD 1973); The George Washington University (LLB 1935); Norwich University (LLD 1963). *M.* 1936, Eleanor Livingston Poe. *Dau.* Eleanor (Poe), Jae Barlow (Roosevelt) and Grace Barlow (Schneider). *Career:* Admitted to Washington bar 1934; Partner, Covington & Burling 1934—; Trustee, The George Washington University 1974, Alma College 1963–64), Norwich University 1958–63; Prof. Law, Columbus Univ. 1937, The George Washington University Law School; Director, The Madeira School 1958–68, National Cathedral Beauvoir School 1945–50, the Tax Council, Chamber of Commerce of the United States 1955–67; President and director, Tax Institute of America. *Member:* American Bar Foundation (Fellow); Bar Assn. of the City of New York, Bar Assn. of D.C.; Order of the Coif. *Clubs:* Chevy Chase; Metropolitan; Country Club of Florida; Ocean Club of Florida. *Address:* Watergate South, 700 New Hampshire Avenue, N.W., Washington, D.C. 20037; and *office* 888 Sixteenth Street, N.W., Washington, D.C. 20006, U.S.A.

**BARNARD, A(lfred) J(ames), Jr.,** PhD. U.S.A. Chemist and editor. *B.* 1920. *Educ.* Tufts College (BS in Chem. *magna cum laude* 1942), Harvard Univ. (MA 1944), and Lehigh Univ. (PhD 1950). *M.* 1958, Frances Longacre. *S.* Alfred David. *Career:* Junior Chemist, Godfrey L. Cabot Co., Boston, Mass. 1942–43; Austin Teaching Fellow, Harvard Univ. 1942–44; Medical Dept., U.S. Army (Bronze Star and Combat Medical Award) 1944–46; Research Div., J. T. Baker Chemical Co. 1947–48; scientific literature consultant 1948–50; Associate, M.G. Mulinos, M.D. and W. F. Greenwald, Consultants, N.Y.C. 1950–51; J. T. Baker Chemical Co. 1951— (various managerial posts; Dir., Analytical Services 1970–74; Asst. Dir. of Research since 1974); Editor, Chemist-Analyst, 1951–67. Co-Editor, Chelates in Analytical Chemistry, 1963—; Microchemical Journal (Advisory Bd. 1963–73; Editorial Bd. 1973—); International Micro-chemical Symposia (Gen. Secy. 1961, 1965; Organizing Cttee. 1973); Plenary Lecturer, Summer Insts. for College Chemistry Teaching (U.S.A.) and Summer Inst. for High School Science-Technology Programs (U.S.A.), 1966; Co-dir. and lecturer, High Purity Chemicals program. Center for Professional Advancement, 1970. *Member:* American Chemical Society (Secretary, Lehigh Valley Section, 1958; Co-Chmn. for anal., chemistry, Middle Atlantic Regional Meeting, 1966; Sub-cttee. on Chemical Nomenclature for Laboratory Use Chemicals 1967–73); Amer. Microchemical Socy. (mem. Exec. Board 1964–65); Amer. Socy. for Quality Control; Socy. for Applied Spectroscopy; Socy. Environmental Geochemistry and Health; Phil Beta Kappa. *Publications:* over 70 contributions to monographs and technical journals, on analytical chemistry, chemical reagents, high-purity chemicals, computer management of chemical information etc.; 2 Vol. text-book on analyt. chem. *Address:* 576 Pine Top Trail, Bethlehem, Pa. 18017; and *office* c/o J. T. Baker Chemical Co., Phillipsburg, N.J. 08865, U.S.A.

**BARNES, Sir Denis Charles,** KCB. British. Permanent-Secretary, Department of Employment 1966–74; Chmn. Manpower Services Comm. since 1974. *B.* 1914. *Educ.* Oxford University (BA). *M.* 1938, Patricia Abercrombie. *Club:* Savile (London). *Address:* 170 Gloucester Place, London, N.W.1.; and *office* 8 St. James's Square, London, S.W.1.

**BARNES, Sir (Ernest) John (Ward),** KCMG, MBE. British diplomat (Ret'd). *B.* 1917. *Educ.* Dragon School, Oxford; Winchester Coll,; Trinity Coll. Cambridge. *M.* Cynthia Stewart. *S.* 2. *Daus.* 3. *Career:* served Royal Artillery (Lt. Col.) 1939–46; H.M. Diplomatic Service 1946–77; H.M. Ambassador to Israel 1969–72 and to the Netherlands 1972–77. *Awards:* Knight Commander of St. Michael & St. George; Member Military Division, Order of British Empire; United States Bronze Star. *Address:* Hampton Lodge, Hurstpierpoint, Sussex.

**BARNES, George Elton.** *B.* 1900. *Educ.* Hamilton University, Mason City, Iowa. *M.* 1922, Florence Herrcke. *Dau.* Ruth Adele. *Career:* With LaSalle National Bank, LaSalle, Ill. 1918–30; Partner, Wayne Hummer & Co., Member of New York Stock Exchange 1931—; Chmn. of Board, Mid-West Stock Exchange 1956–58; Dir., Illinois State Chamber Commerce 1964–70; Dir., LaSalle Extension Univ. (1951–61); Suburban Trust & Savings Bank 1950–74; Chmn. of Budget Finance Cttee., Oak Park & River Forest Community Chest 1941–49 (Pres. 1950–51); member, National Budget Cttee., Community Chests Councils of America 1956–60; Corporate Large Gifts Div., Chicago Community Fund 1946; Vice-Pres., Governor, Natl. Assn. of Stock Exchange Firms 1942–46; Governor, Chmn. of Exec. Cttee., Chicago Stock Exchange 1946; Pres., Chicago Tennis Assn. 1947–48; Pres. U.S. Lawn Tennis Assn. 1960–61 (Member, Exec. Cttee.); Natl. Chmn., Sponsors Cttee. 1955 Davis Cup; Pres. Natl. Tennis Educational Found. Inc. 1961–66; Chicago Press Club 'Sportsman of the Year', 1961. *Publications:* Pay-as-you-go; Corporate Federal Tax Plans. *Clubs:* Oak Park Country, River Forest Tennis, Tavern, Fort Lauderdale Country; Yacht, Tower, (both Ft Lauderdale), Bankers, Executives. *Address:* 1005 Bonnie Brae Avenue, River Forest, Ill.; and *office* Wayne Hummer & Co., 105 W. Adams Street, Chicago, Ill., U.S.A.

**BARNES, Leo.** Professor and economist. *B.* 1910. *Educ.* (City College of New York (BSS 1931)); Brown University (AM 1933); PhD, New School for Social Research 1948. *M.* 1932, Regina Rosiny. *S.* Peter Franklin. *Dau.* Valeria Berta. *Career:* Director of Economic Research, Research Inst. of America, 1943–46; Lecturer, Rutgers 1947. Chief Economist, Prentice-Hall Inc. 1946–62; Lecturer New School for Social Research 1948–63; Vice-Pres., Medical Securities Fund 1962; Prof. Dept. of Finance and Investments, Hofstra University since 1965; Visiting Prof. of Economics, City University of New York 1963–65. *Member:* Phi Beta Kappa; Amer. Economics Assn.; Amer. Statistical Assn. National Assn. of Business Economists; Amer. Assn. of Univ. Professors. *Publications:* Handbook of Wealth Management (1977); Your Investments (annual editions 1954–68); Your Buying Guide to Mutual Funds and Investment Companies (annual editions 1956–60); Handbook for Business Forecasting (1950); An Experiment That Failed (1948); numerous articles in various periodicals. *Address:* 473 West End Avenue, New York, N.Y. 10024, U.S.A.

**BARNETSON of CROWBOROUGH, Lord William Denholm** (Barnetson), MA, FInstD. British. *B.* 1917. *Educ.* Roy. High School, Edinburgh Univ. (MA). *M.* 1940, Joan Fairley Davidson. *S.* 1. *Daus.* 3. *Career:* Chmn. & Man. Dir. United Newspapers Ltd.; United Newspaper Publications Ltd.; Chmn. Reuters Ltd.; Observer Ltd.; Bradbury Agnew & Co. Ltd.; Sheffield Newspapers Ltd.; Northampton Mercury Co. Ltd.; Northampton Independent Ltd.; Burnley Express

Printing Co. Ltd.; Nelson Leader & Colne Times Ltd.; London Newspaper Services Ltd.; Dir., Drayton Consolidated Trust; British Electric Traction Co.; Hill Samuel Group Ltd.; Earls Court & Olympia Ltd.; Castle Publishing Co. Ltd.; Country & Sporting Publications Ltd.; Herbert C. Hill Ltd.; Argus Press Holdings Ltd.; Yorkshire Post Newspapers Ltd.; Leader Writer, Edinburgh Evening News 1948–53; Editor 1954–61, Gen. Man. 1956–61; Mem. Council, Commonwealth Press Union; Pres. Advertising Assoc.; U.K. Cttee., International Press Inst.; Inst. of Journalists. *Awards:* Knighted 1972; Created Life Peer 1975. *Clubs:* Beefsteak; Press, London. *Address:* Broom, Chillies Lane, Crowborough, Sussex; and *office* 23–27 Tudor Street, London, EC4Y 0HR.

**BARNETT, J. Allen, Jr.** *B.* 1908. *Educ.* Taft School (Watertown, Conn.) and Princeton Univ. (BA 1931). *M.* (1) 1933, Jane Dodge, and (2) 1949, Harriet Brownell Pope. *S.* George Pope, Peter Pope and Guy Pope. *Daus.* Val Pope, Fayal, and Lucy. *Career:* With N.Y. Herald-Tribune 1931–38; Benton & Bowles (advertising) 1938–40; Vice-Pres., Sherman & Marquette (advertising) 1940–43; Vice-Pres. in Charge of Advertising, Pepsodent Div., Lever Bros. Co. 1945–49; Director and Vice-Pres. Advertising Lever Bros. Co. 1949–56; Vice-Pres., Rexall Drug Co. 1956–59; Senior Vice-Pres. and Director, Purex Corp. Ltd. 1959—; Dir., Pope & Talbot Lumber Co. Portland Ore since 1971. Republican. *Clubs:* Cottage (Princeton); University (N.Y.C.); Bel-Air C.C. (Los Angeles); Santa Monica Beach. *Address: office* Purex Corp., 5101 N. Clark Avenue, Lakewood Calif., U.S.A.

**BARNETT, Rt. Hon. Joel**, PC, FACCA, JP, MP. British politician. *B.* 1923. *Educ.* Elementary School, Grammar School, Corresp. Course to qualify as Accountant. *M.* 1949, Lilian Stella Goldstone. *Dau.* Erica Hazel. *Career:* Member, Prestwich Borough Council, Lancashire, 1956–59; Member of Parliament, Labour for Heywood & Royton, Lancs. since 1964; Chmn. Parly. Labour Party Economic & Finance Group, 1967–70; Opposition Front Bench Spokesman in Parliament on Treasury Affairs 1970–74; Member, Expenditure Cttee. House of Commons since 1971; Chief Secy. to Treasury since 1974; Created Privy Councillor 1975; Appointed to the Cabinet, Feb. 1977. *Address:* Prenda Mia, 10 Park Lane, Whitefield, Lancashire; and *office* Flat 92, 24 John Islip Street, London, S.W.1.

**BARNETT, (Nicolas) Guy.** MP. British Politician. *B.* 1928. *Educ.* Highgate School; St. Edmund Hall, Oxford. *M.* 1967, Daphne Anne Hortin. *S.* 1. *Dau.* 1. *Career:* Teacher, Queen Elizabeth Grammar School 1953–59 & Friends School Kamusinga Kenya 1960–61; VSO Staff 1966–69; Chief Educ. Officer, Commonwealth Inst. 1969–71; MP (Labour) for South Dorset 1962–64; Mem. of European Parliament 1975–76; Parliamentary Under Sec., Dept. of the Environment since 1976. Member, Royal Commonwealth Society. *Publication:* By the Lake. *Club:* Royal Commonwealth. *Address:* 32 Westcombe Park Road, London S.E.3; and *office* 32 Woolwich Road, London, S.E.10.

**BARNHARDT, William H.** American. *B.* 1903. *Educ.* N.C. State Coll. School of Textiles (BE 1923). *M.* 1927, Margaret McLaughlin. *S.* William M., Charles F. (dec'd) and John David. *Dau.* Nancy (Thomas). *Career:* President, Treasurer and Director of the following firms: Amer. Realty Corp., Barnhardt Brothers Co., Barnhardt Elastic Corp., Barnhardt International Corp., American Textile Corp., Tryon Processing Co. (Tryon, N.C.), and Novelty Yarns Corp. (all Charlotte NC); Chmn. of Board and Director, Southern Webbing Mills Inc. (Greensboro, N.C.). Treasurer and Director: providence Acre Inc.; Providence Associates; Riverview Acres Inc., Carolinas Corp.; Univ. Heights Inc.; Univ. Plantation; Dir.: N. Carolina Natl. Bank, Standard Bonded Warehouse Co., Airlie Inc. (Spartanburg, S.C.), Dan River Mills Inc. (Danville, Va.); Vice-Pres., Dir., Sharon Corp., Charlotte, N.C. *Member:* King of Caraousel 1955; Chmn., Foundation Univ. North Carolina, Charlotte 1963–66; Former Deacon & Elder, Myers Park Presbyterian Church (Vice Moderator 1965); Former mem. Bd. of Trustees, and Chairman of Finance Committee of Johnson C. Smith University; Life Member, Board of Trustees, Charlotte Country Day School; Former mem. Board of Trustees and Chairman of Fin. Committee, Crossnore School; former member Bd. of Trustees, Barber-Scotia Coll.; Governing Council, Royal Fraternity. Phi Kappa Phi; Newcomen Society of North America. Trustee and Treasurer of Greater Charlotte Founda- Socy. of the Knights of Carrousel; Pi Kappa Phi Hon. Fraternity; Newcomen Society of North America; Former Trustee and Treasurer of Greater Charlotte Foundation. Former Vice-President of United Community Services and Chairman of Capital Funds Board; Pres. of Charlotte YMCA 1952–53, Mem. of Building Cttee YMCA, 25 years Mem. of Exec. Cttee of Interstate YMCA; Mem. Regional Cttee. Boy Scouts of America; Mem. Adv. Council—Mecklenburg Council, Boy Scouts of America; Mem. Bd. of Trustees, Exec. Cttee and Chmn. of Finance Cttee QC Charlotte NC 1946–75; various exec and campaign cttees directorships. *Awards:* Silver Beaver (1947) and Silver Antelope (1949) Awards from Boy Scouts of Amer.; Algernon Sydney Sullivan Award from Queens Coll. 1953; and Service Youth Award, YMCA 1954. National Conference of Christians and Jews Award 1966; Man of the South (1973); Many Buildings Named in Honor including Barnhardt Hall, Queen's Coll.; Barnhardt Building; Barnhardt-Dowd Chapel. *Clubs:* Quail Hollow Country, Charlotte Country (Former Vice-Pres.), Charlotte City (Former Vice-Pres.), Executives (Pres. 1956), Textile (Charlotte); New York Athletic, Metropolitan (N.Y.C.); Carolina Yarn Assn. (Former Pres.); Travelers Century. Admiral, N. Carolina Navy; Hon. Colonel, State of Alabama. *Address:* 3600 NCNB Plaza, Charlotte, NC 28280, U.S.A.

**BARNUM, Jerome**, SC.D. American. *B.* 1910. *Educ.* Yale Univ., Univ. of Cincinnati, and New York Univ. *M.* 1939, Virginia Law. *S.* Jerome, Andrew and Bruce. *Daus.* Elizabeth Andrea Forbis. *Career:* Adjunct Prof., N.Y. Univ. 1946–53; Member, Advisory Cttee., Systems and Procedures Inst., The Management Inst., N.Y. Univ. 1947–54; Management Analyst, U.S. Dept. of Defense 1942–45; Asst. to Pres., Sterling Products International 1940–41; Management Analyst and Market Researcher 1935–40; Manager, The Barston Co. 1932–35. President, Jerome Barnum Associates, Management Consultants, N.Y. 1949—. Director: Academy of Management Arts & Sciences 1953—, Directed Energy Institute 1951—, Energio Dirigida S.A., Mexico 1954—, Instituto Internacional de Energia Dirigida A.C. Pres., JBA; Man. Dir. Experience Compression Lab. 1959; Chmn. Experience Compression Inst. 1975—, and Barnum Photographic Products Co., Los Angeles. *Member:* Amer. Inst. for Engineering Education: Amer. Sociological Assn.; Amer. Socy. for Training and Development; Council for International Progress in Management; Comité International de l'Organisation Scientifique; Sales Executive Club; International Platform Assn. Republican. *Publications:* Experience Compression; Directed Energy; numerous articles in scientific, technical and administrative journals. Honours: N.Y. University Citation for achievements in Human Relations and Work Simplification (conferred by Engineering Coll. and Div. of General Education); National Management Assn. Gold Medal for Leadership; 2 Citations & Certificates of Cooperation, U.S. Dept. of State; 2 Resolutions & Hon. Lifetime memberships, Florida Inst. of Park Personnel; Hon. Mem. of the Faculty, Air Univ., Air Force Inst. of Technology, Civil Engineering Sch.; Colonel, State of Kentucky; Certificate, The Federal Govt. Accountants Assn.; Applause Award, Sales Exec. Club; U.S. Air Force Geographic Scientiaeque Confinia Penetramus; Medal, Tennessee Technological Univ.; Cup, Virginia Poly. Inst.; Certificate, Florida Keys Community Coll.; 7 Certificates, Amer. Inst. of Industrial Engineers; 9 Certificates, Soc. for the Advancement of Management; 8 Certificates, National Assn. of Accountants; 3 Certificates, Financial Execs. Inst.; Mem. of Presidents' Council & Fellow; Amer. Inst. of Management; Achievement Plaque, Florida Dept. of Offender Rehabilitation; Hon. SC.D.; Society for Advancement of Management Citation; Founders Award, American Inst. Industrial Engineers. *Club:* N.Y. Univ. Faculty. *Address:* 423 Westchester Ave., White Plains, New York 10604, U.S.A.

**BARR, Stringfellow**, American academic (Ret'd). *B.* 1897. *Educ.* Univ. of Virginia (BA; MA); BA, MA Oxon; Diploma, Univ. of Paris; studied at Univ. of Ghent. *M.* 1921, Gladys Baldwin. *Career:* Asst. Prof. 1924–27, Assoc. Prof. 1927–30, and Prof. 1930–37, of Modern History, Univ. of Virginia; Visiting Prof., Liberal Arts, Univ. of Chicago 1936–37; Pres., St. John's College, Annapolis, Md., and member of Board of Visitors and Governors 1937–46; Pres., Foundation for World Government 1948–55; Visiting Prof., Political Science, Univ. of Virginia 1951–53; Professor of Humanities, Rutgers University, Newark, N.J. 1955–64; Senior Fellow of the Center for the Study of Democratic Institutions, Santa Barbara, Calif., 1966–69. Advisory Editor, Virginia Quarterly Review 1926–30, 1934–37; Editor 1930–34; Adv. Ed. Britannica Great Books 1944–46. Sergeant. U.S. Army 1917–19. *Publications:* Mazzini—Portrait of an Exile; The Pilgrimage of Western Man; Let's Join the Human Race; Citizen of the World; Copydog in India; The Kitchen Garden Book; Purely Academic; The Will of Zeus (1961); Three Worlds of Man (1963); The Mask of Jove (1967). Rhodes Scholar 1917. Phi Beta Kappa 1917; The Raven Society. Democrat. Recipient, the Waite Award for Literature (Nat. Inst. of Arts and Letters). *Address:* Box 365, Ridge Road, Kingston, N.J. 08528, U.S.A.

**BARRACLOUGH, Garth Wilson Egerton,** OBE. Australian. *B.* 1910. *Educ.* Newington College, Stanmore, N.S.W. *M.* 1936, Beatrice Amy Poate. *S.* Ian Hugh Egerton. *Daus.* Jocelyn Gai and Lyndall Patricia. *Career:* Man. Director: Edible Oil Industries Pty. Ltd. 1947–48, and J. Kitchen & Sons Pty. Ltd. 1949. President, Philippine Refining Co. Inc., Manila 1950–57; Man. Director, Unilever Australia Pty. Ltd., Sydney 1957–60; Chmn., Unilever Australia Pty. Ltd., Sydney, 1960–72; Chmn., Arnotts Ltd.; Dep. Chmn., MLC Ltd.; Dep. Chmn., EMI (Australia) Ltd.; Dir: Mim. Holdings Ltd.; Tooheys Ltd.; Doulton Australia Ltd.; Australian Finance & Investment Co. Ltd. *Member:* Australian Institute of Management (Fellow); Fellow Australian Society of Accountants; Austr. Inst. of Directors. *Clubs:* Rotary, Australian, Royal Sydney Yacht Squadron, Sydney Amateur Sailing. *Address:* 57 Cremorne Road, Cremorne, N.S.W.; *office* P.O. Box 410, Neutral Bay Junction, NSW 2089, Australia.

**BARRACLOUGH, Henry,** CVO. British shipowner. *B.* 10 Aug. 1894. *Educ.* Giggleswick. *M.* 1922, Ethel Mary Dix. *S.* Geoffrey, David. *Career:* Chairman Prince of Wales Dry Dock Co. Swansea Ltd. 1944–65; Treasury Director, Silver Line Ltd. 1940, Chairman 1948–59, Managing Director 1949–59; Director, Dene Shipping Co. Ltd. since foundation 1942, Chairman 1942–66, retd. Directorship 1970; Chmn., the 'Cutty Sark' Society. *Member:* General Committee, Lloyd's Register of Shipping since 1946. Deputy Chairman 1949–50; member of Lloyd's since 1949. *Address:* Bix Manor, Henley-on-Thames, Oxon., and Cotehow, Martindale, Penrith.

**BARRAN, Sir David Haven.** British. *B.* 1912. *Educ.* Winchester Coll.; Trinity Coll., Cambridge (BA). *M.* 1944, Jane Lechmere Macaskie. *S.* Tristram C., Julian M., Marius P. and Adrian S. *Daus.* Francesca, Lalage and Calista. *Career:* Pres., Asiatic Petroleum Corp. 1958–61; Dir., Shell Transport & Trading 1961; Deputy Chmn. and Man. Dir. 1964; Chmn. 1967. Managing Director, Royal Dutch Shell Group of Cos. 1961–72; Chairman and Managing Director, Shell Transport & Trading Ltd. 1967–72; Chmn. Shell Oil Co. 1971–72; Dep. Chmn., Midland Bank 1976—; Chmn., Administrative Staff Coll., Henley 1971–76. *Club:* River (New York). *Address:* 36 Kensington Square, London, W.8.; and Brent Eleigh Hall, Suffolk; and *office* Shell Centre, London, S.E.1.

**BARRAND, Harry P., Jr.** American banker. *B.* 1922. *Educ.* Yale University (BA). *M.* 1948, Helen Stukenorg. *S.* Keith Frederick, Stephen Ayres, and David Charles. *Dau.* Katherine Drayton. *Career:* Served as Yeoman 2nd Class USNR 1942–63; with U.S. Marine Corps Reserve: 2nd Lieut. 1943–45, 1st Lieut. 1945–51; Captain 1951–56. The Hanover Bank, 1946; Asst. Mgr. Fgn. Dept. 1951–53; European Rep. 1953–56; Vice-Pres. 1956–58; Vice-Pres. charge Foreign Dept. 1958–61; Sen. Vice-Pres. Foreign Dept. Manfs. Hanover Trust 1961–63; Exec. Vice-Pres. charge Int. Div. 1963–66; Banking Dept. 1966–70; Franklin National Bank; Exec. Vice-Pres. charge Int. Operations 1970–74; Vice-Chmn., WFC Corp., Coral Gables, Fla.; N.Y. Rep., Union de Bancos, Panama, Ajman Arab Bank, U.A.E. 1975—; Trustee, Westminster Sch., Simsbury, Conn., Bd. Dirs., U.S. Austrian C.C., Internat Center, N.Y., Musa Alami Foundation. *Member:* Mexican C.C.; Japan Soc.; Council on Foreign Relations. *Clubs:* Yale; Church; American (London); Elka Park (Dir.); India House. *Address:* 227 Fairmount Road, Ridgewood, N.J. 07450; and *office* 277 Park Avenue, Suite 1406, New York, N.Y. 10017, U.S.A.

**BARRATT, Sidney Edgar,** MBE. Australian production engineer. *B.* 1904. *M.* 1928, Beatrice Emma Weale. *S.* 1. *Dau.* 1. *Career:* Dir. (Mfg) 1947–55; Asst. to Man. Dir. A.E.I. Pty Ltd. 1956–65; Dir. Gen. Mgr. Hard Metals Pty Ltd. 1965–67; Senior Partner SEACAM Associates since 1970. Chmn. Inst. of Production Engineers Sydney Section 1944–45, Australian Council 1945; Australian Pres. 1966–68; Member N.S.W. Tech. Educ. Adv. Council 1952–74; Councillor Chamber of Mfcts. N.S.W. 1952–67, Metal Trades Employers Assn. (Pres. 1955–57); Member Electrical Industry Advisory Cttee. 1953–67; Pres. Federal Council, Electrical Manufacturers 1952; Aust. Metal Industries Association 1965–67; Councillor Univ. N.S.W. since 1965; Member Exec. Cttee. Standards Assn. of Australia since 1967; Industrial Relations Society (Pres. 1967–69); Chmn. N.S.W. Inst. of Technology 1969–73; Chancellor 1974; Chmn. NSW Council Tech. and F.Ed. 1975; Fellow Aust. Inst Mgmt, Inst of Production Engineers, Associate Plastics Inst. of Australia. *Awards:* Jack Finlay Medal 1963; Hon. Fellowship, Sydney Technical College; MBE 1974. *Address:* 82 Pentecost Avenue, St. Ives, N.S.W., Australia.

**BARRE, Raymond.** French Economist & Politician. *B.* 1924. *Educ.* Faculté de Droit, Paris; Inst. d'Etudes Politiques, Paris. *Career:* Prof., Inst. des Hautes Etudes, Tunis 1951–54; Prof., Faculté de Droit et des Sciences Economiques, Caen 1954–63; Prof., Inst. d'Etudes Politiques, Paris 1961; Faculté de Droit et de Sciences Economiques, Paris 1962; Dir. du Cabinet to Minister of Industry 1959–62; Mem., Cttee. of Experts (Comité Lorain) studying financing of investments in France 1963–64; Vice-Pres. of European Commission, responsible for Economic & Financial Affairs 1967–73; Mem., Gen. Council, Banque de France 1973—; appointed Minister for Foreign Trade, then Prime Minister 1976. *Address:* 6 Rue de Bagatelle, 92 Neuilly-sur-Seine, France.

**BARRETT, Sir Arthur George.** Australian. *B.* 1895. *Educ.* Melbourne Church of England Grammar School. *M.* 1922, Jean Beatrice Mair. *Daus.* 2. Member, Adelaide City Council 1931–53; Lord Mayor of Adelaide 1937–41. *Address:* 210 Stanley Street, North Adelaide, S.A., Australia.

**BARRETT, Charles Sanborn.** American metallurgist and crystallographer. *B.* 1902. *Educ.* Univ. of South Dakota (BS 1925) and Univ. of Chicago (PhD 1928). *M.* 1928, Dorothy A. Adams. *Dau.* Marjorie A. *Career:* At Metallurgy Dept., Naval Research Laboratory 1928–32; Metallurgy Dept. and Metal Research Laboratory, Carnegie Institute of Technology 1932–46; Visiting Professor, Univ. of Birmingham (England) 1951–52, Univ. of Denver 1961, and Stanford Univ. 1963; George Eastman Visiting Professor, Oxford 1965–66. Editor, Metal Section of Structure Reports for International Union of Crystallography 1949–51. Professor, James Franck Institute, University of Chicago 1946–71, emeritus, 1971; Professor and Senior Research Engineer, University of Denver, since 1970. *Publications:* Structure of Metals (McGraw-Hill Book Co.) 1943, 1952, 1966; numerous technical papers on physical metallurgy and crystallogrphy. *Awards:* Clamer Medal; Mathewson Medal (1934–44–51); Heyn Medal; Sauveur Medal; Hume-Rothery Award; Honda Medal; Howe Medal. *Member:* Amer. Physical Socy. (Fellow); Amer. Inst. for Mining and Metallurgical Engineers; Metallurgical Society (Fellow 1964); Amer. Socy. for Metals (Fellow and Hon. Member); Inst. of Metals (London); Amer. Crystallographic Assn.; Nat. Acad. of Sciences 1967; Hon. Mem., Japan Inst. of Metals. *Address:* Metallurgy Division, Denver Research Inst., University of Denver, Denver, Colo. 80210, U.S.A.

**BARRETT, Hon. David.** PC, BA. Canadian. *B.* 1930. *Educ.* Seattle Univ. (BA); St. Louis Univ. (Master of Social Work). *M.* 1953, Shirley Hackman. *S.* 2. *Dau.* 1. *Career:* worked in child welfare, prisons and as Probation Officer, advocated changes in social services; Elected Member, The Legislative Assembly for Dewdney 1960; Re-elected 1963; Elected to Redistributed Riding of Coquitlam 1966, 1969 and 1972; Elected New Democratic Party Leader 1970; Premier & Minister of Finance 1972–75. *Address:* Legislative Buildings, Victoria, British Columbia, Canada.

**BARRETT, Edward Ware.** Educator and editor. *B.* 3 July 1910. *Educ.* Princeton University; School Public & Internat. Affairs; Student Univ. Dijon, France; Doctor Laws (hon.), Bard College. *M.* 1939, Mason Daniel. *Daus.* Margo Mason, Lisa Lewis. *Career:* Reporting and editing for various news organizations 1933–42; Dir. Overseas Operations U.S. Office of War Inf. 1942–46; Editorial Dir. Newsweek 1946–50; Asst. Secy. State, Public Affairs 1950–52; Exec. Vice-Pres. Hill and Knowlton Inc. 1953–56; Dean Graduate School, Journalism, Columbia Univ. 1956–68; Dir. Communications Inst. Academy, Educational Development since 1969; Dir. Foreign Policy Assn., Dir. Radio Free Europe; Trustee Franklin Savings Bank; Dir. Public Affairs Press; Atlantic Council. *Member:* President's Study Commission Int. Radio Broadcasting 1972–74. *Publication:* Truth is Our Weapon; Journalists in Action; This is Our Challenge (editor). *Address:* Hawkwood Lane, Greenwich, Conn., U.S.A.; and *office* 680 Fifth Avenue, New York, N.Y. 10019, U.S.A.

**BARRETT, Leslie Charles,** QC. Canadian. General Manager and General Counsel, The Toronto Dominion Bank. *B.* 1913. *Educ.* Barrister-at-Law, Osgoode Hall. *M.* 1942, Jean Bronson. *S.* David and Stephen. *Career:* Formerly: Inspector, Foreign Exchange Control Board of Canada; Solicitor for Commodity Prices Stabilization Corp.; Captain, Royal Canadian Army Service Corps. *Member:* Law Socy. of Upper Canada; Canadian Bar Assn.; Lawyers' Club of Toronto; Assn. of Canadian General Counsel; Phi Delta Phi Legal fraternity). *Clubs:* University (Toronto); Toronto Cricket, Curling & Skating; Georgina Lodge AF & AM (Scottish Rite); Moore Sovereign Consistory; International Alumni Assn. *Address:* 3 Eastview Crescent, Toronto M5M 2W4, Ont.; and *office* The Toronto-Dominion Centre, Toronto M5K 1A2, Ont., Canada.

**BARRETT, Robert Tullius Tupper.** American banker. *B.* 1900. *Educ.* Univ. of Virginia (BA). *M.* 1923, Marie Thorpe. *S.* 3. *Dau.* 1. *Career:* Manager, Paris Office, Guaranty Trust Co. of N.Y. (now Morgan Guaranty Trust Co.) 1937–48; Vice-Pres., European Offices, Guaranty Trust Co. of N.Y. (now Morgan Guaranty Trust Co.) 1948–65. Served in World War II; first as Lt.-Col. and subsequently as Colonel, General Staff Corps, Army of U.S., participating in North African, Sicilian, Italian mainland, Normandy and Northern Europe campaigns. *Awards:* Chevalier, Legion of Honour; Croix de Guerre; Liberation Medal (all of France); Commander, Crown of Italy; Bronze Star (U.S.). *Clubs:* Metropolitan (Washington); St. James' (London); American (London); Travellers (Paris); Cercle Interallie (Paris); Automobile Club de France; St. Cloud Country, Fontainbleau Golf; American (Paris). *Address:* 18 Quai d'Orleans, Paris.

**BARRETT, Stephen Jeremy,** BA, MA. British diplomat. *B.* 1931. *Educ.* Westminster School, London; Christ Church, Oxford. *M.* 1958, Alison Mary Irvine. *S.* 3. *Career:* with Foreign Office 1955–57; Third later Second Secretary, Political Office, Middle East Forces, Cyprus 1957–59; Deputy Political Adviser, British Military Government Berlin 1959–62; First Secy. Foreign Office 1962–65; Head of Chancery British Embassy, Helsinki 1965–68; Foreign & Commonwealth Office 1968–72; Counsellor and Head of Chancery British Embassy Prague 1972–1974; Head of SW European Dept., Foreign and C'wealth Office 1974–75; Principal Private Secy. to Foreign and C'wealth Secy. 1975; Head of Science & Technology Dept., FCO since 1976. *Club:* Travellers (London); Hurlingham. *Address:* 7 St. Aubyn's Avenue, Wimbledon, London, SW19 7BL; and *office* c/o Foreign & Commonwealth Office, King Charles Street, London, S.W.1.

**BARRETT-LENNARD, Sir Thomas Richard Fiennes, Bt.,** OBE, KStJ. *B.* 1898. *Educ.* Clare Coll., Cambridge (MA). *M.* 1922. Finora. *Dau.* of Hon. J. D. Fitz-Gerald. *Career:* Vice-Pres., Norwich Union Life Insce. Society; Vice-Chmn., Norwich Union Fire Insurance Society Ltd.; Chairman, East Anglian Trustee Savings Bank; Dir., Scottish Union and National Insurance Co.; Maritime Insurance Co. Ltd. (Ret.). Conservative. *Club:* Leander. *Address:* Swallowfield Park, Reading.

**BARRIE, Sir Walter,** Kt 1958. Chmn. of Lloyd's 1953, 1954, 1957, 1958; Dir.: Jos. W. Hobbs Ltd., Westminster Bank Ltd. 1958–68, Ulster Bank 1964–72. *B.* 1901. *Educ.* Coleraine; Merchiston Castle, Edinburgh; Gonville & Caius Coll., Cambridge. *M.* 1927, Noele Margaret Furness (*Dec.* 1968). *S.* 2. *Career:* Entered Lloyd's 1926; first served on Cttee. of Lloyd's 1946; Dep. Chmn. of Lloyd's 1951, 1952. Lloyd's Gold Medal 1958. Pres., Insurance Inst. of London 1955–56; Vice-Pres., Chartered Insurance Inst. 1957, 1958, 1959, Dep. Pres. 1961, Pres. 1962–63. *Club:* City of London. *Address:* Compton Elms, Pinkneys Green, Maidenhead, Berks SL6 6NR.

**BARRINGER, Brandon.** American chartered financial Analyst. *B.* 1899. *Educ.* Haverford School (1916); Princeton Univ. (AB 1921); Phi Beta Kappa; Jefferson (DSc Hon. 1968). *M.* (1) 1945, Sonia Converse (*D.* 1964). *Daus.* Carla Sonia, (Rabinowitz), Elizabeth Brandon (Fentress), Felicity Anne (Taubman); (2) 1967, Diana Johnson Richardson. *Career:* With First Pennsylvanian Banking & Trust Co. 1921–49, Vice-Pres., trust investments 1933–49; Dir., Lehigh Valley R.R. 1938–42; Fleischmann's Vienna Model Baking Co., Philadelphia 1948–61; Treas. and Dir., The Curtis Publishing Co., Philadelphia, Pa., 1948–62; Dir., Curtis Circulation Co., Philadelphia 1949–62; Dir. Bryn Mawr Group Inc. 1949–73; New York & Pennsylvania Co., Inc., New York, N.Y. 1950–62; Bantam Books, Inc., New York 1957–61; Keystone Reader's Service, Inc., Bryn Mawr, Pa. 1957–62; President East Texas Iron Co. 1963–75; Cass County Iron Co. since 1975; Barringer Crater Co. 1963–77. *Member:* Finance Committee, Wellington Fund 1929–59. Captain to Colonel in Army Air Forces (1942–45), acting as Deputy Chief, Statistical Control, HQ AAF; awarded U.S. Legion of Merit. Trustee, Thomas Jefferson University; Academy of Natural Sciences, Philadelphia. Manager: Univ. Museum and Franklin Institute; Governor, Nature Conservancy 1968–75; Nat. Mental Health Assn. (Secy. 1951–62); member, Cttee. of Seventy 1950—. Fellow, Meteoritical Society; American Assn. Advancement of Science. *Publications:* articles on meteoritics and archaeology; The Wethered Book. *Clubs:* Princeton, Philadelphia, Wilderness, University Barge, Mill Dam (Philadelphia); Campus, Nassau (Princeton). *Address:* 550 Maplewood Road, Wayne Pa 19087, U.S.A.; and *office* 2106 Two Girard Plaza., Philadelphia, Pa. 19102, U.S.A.

**BARROS-CONTI, Oscar.** Peruvian diplomat. *B.* 1910. *Educ.* Lic. en Droit, Paris; Lic. en Lettres, Madrid. *M.* Doña Dora Quiroga-Aramayo. *S.* 3. *Career:* Third Secy., Paris 1936, London 1937, Brussels 1939. Second Secy., Paraguay (later Chargé d'Affaires); Head, European Section, Foreign Office 1945; Consul-Generale: Guayaquil 1946, and India 1949; Head, Boundaries Section 1961; Consul-General 1st Class, Bolivia 1953, Caracas 1959. Head, Political Section, Foreign Office 1961; Minister Plen., Director for Economics Studies 1962; Min. Plen., Alternate Delegate for Peru at U.N. 1963; Minister, Chargé d'Affaires, Haiti 1965–68. Ambassador in Ethiopia, 1967; Dir. General of Migrations, Peruvian Foreign Office, 1969; Ambassador in Sweden and Norway since 1971. *Awards:* Coronation Medal King George V; Chevalier, Order of Leopold 1st (Belgium); Comdr., Order of Merit (Paraguay); Grand Cross of the Brilliant Star of Taiwan. *Address:* Embassy of Peru, 111, Karlavägen, Stockholm 115 26, Sweden.

**BARROW, Rt. Hon. Errol Walton.** Barbadian. Prime Minister of Barbados 1966–76. *B.* 1920. *Educ.* Harrison College (Barbados), London School of Economics, Univ. of London, and Lincoln's Inn; Barrister-at-Law. *M.* 1945, Carolyn Plaskett. *S.* David O'Neal. *Dau.* Lesley. Hon. LLD McGill Univ.; LLD Univ. Sussex. Liveryman of Guild of Air Pilots and Air Navigators. Chairman Democratic Labour Party. *Clubs:* Barbados Light Aeroplane; Barbados Cruising. *Address:* Paradise Beach, St. Michael, Barbados, West Indies.

**BARRY, Aaron Wessels.** American. President, Barry Laboratories Inc. *B.* 1907. *Educ.* Wayne Univ. (1929) and Albion Coll. (1931). *M.* 1936, Irma Mary Jeffery. *S.* Jeffery Wessels and John Carl. *Dau.* Mary Elizabeth. *Publications:* Handbook of Allergy for Physician: Allergy Testing: a Manual for the Nurse Assistant. *Member:* Pharmaceutical Manufacturers Association (Public Relations Section); Wayne County Medical Society; Board of Children's Center of Wayne County; American Chemical Society; Alpha Tau Omega. *Clubs:* Lighthouse Point Yacht & Tennis. *Address:* 2360 N.E. 28th Street, Lighthouse Point, Fla. 33064, U.S.A.

**BARRY, Paul Thomas.** Australian executive. Managing Director, Barry & Roberts Ltd., Brisbane 1938—. President, Retailers' Association of Queensland 1951–56. *B.* 1914. *Educ.* Nudgee College, Brisbane. *M.* 1948, Evelyn Courtney. *S.* 4. *Dau.* 1. *Address:* 209 Moons Lane, Brookfield, Qld. 4069; and 126 Adelaide Street, Clayfield, Brisbane, Qld., Australia.

**BARSCH, Paul (Otto).** German advertising consultant. *B.* 1910. *M.* 1938, Maria Schachler. *S.* 1. *Career:* Head of advertising department and propagandist with Rudolf Mosse (publishers), Berlin and Presse Anzeigen & Verlags Ges., Berlin 1930–33; Head of publicity department, Universal Verlag W. Vobach & Co., Leipzig 1933–39; Managing Partner, Webeagentur, Berlin, Frankfurt 1945—; Owner, Paul O. Barsch (book and periodical publishers) Berlin 1945—; member, Committee for Sale, Promotion and Advertising, Chamber of Commerce & Industry, Berlin 1956—, Trade Committee for Advertising, Zentral Ausschuss der Werbewirtschaft e.V., Godesberg 1960—and I.A.A. (N.Y.). *Club:* Potsdamer Yacht (Berlin-Wannsee). *Address:* Bismarchallee, 34B, Berlin 33, and *office* Werbeagentur, Kurfürstendamm 182, Berlin 15, Germany; and Kennedyallee 86, Frankfurt, Germany.

**BARTELS, Charles Kwanina,** Flt.-Lieut., RAF (Ret'd), DFC, BSc (Journ.), FIBA. Journalist and Public Relations Consultant. *B.* 1927. *Education:* Ennitonia High School, Port Harcourt; Dennis Memorial Gr. Sch. Nigeria; School of Mod. Langs. and Journalism, Regent St. Poly. London; Columbia Univ., U.S.A.; Dip. Journ., BSc. (Journ.) FIBA.

Divorced. *S.* 1. *Dau.* 1. *Career:* Reporter, sub-editor and later acting-editor local papers until 1944; RAF (U.K.) Navigator 1945, Fl.-Lieut. 1947 (demobbed 1952); held various positions as Clerical Officer (Min. of Transport), compiler and Editorial Asst. 1952–57; Higher Exec. Officer and Foreign Service Officer (Information Attaché), Ghana High Commn., London 1957–63; held various editorial positions 1966–70; Editor-in-Chief "Who's Who" in Ghana and "Who's Who" in West Africa since 1970. *Clubs:* Playboy (London); Napoleon; Rivera Beach; Ghana Assn. of Writers. *Address:* 44 Sobukwe Rd., "Woana-Nye-Woana" House, P.O. Box 4446, Accra S4, Ghana; and "Who's Who" Villa, 6A South Street, CFC Estate, Dome, Nsawam Rd., Accra, Ghana.

**BARTH, Alan.** *B.* 1906. *Educ.* Yale Univ. (PhB 1929). *M.* 1939, Adrienne Mayer. *S.* Andrew Charles. *Dau.* Flora Wolf. *Career:* Reporter, Beaumont (Tex.) Enterprise, 1930–37; Editorial Writer, Beaumont Journal 1937–38; Washington Correspondent, McClure Newspaper Syndicate 1938–41; Editorial Assistant to the Secretary of the Treasury 1941–42; Editor of Reports, Office of War Information 1942–43; Editorial Writer, The Washington Post, April 1943–72; Professor of Journalism, Univ. of Montana 1958; Visiting Professor of Political Science, Univ. of California 1958–59. *Awards:* American Newspaper Guild Award, 1948; Sigma Delta Chi Award, 1947; Sidney Hillman Award, 1951; Oliver Wendell Holmes Bill of Rights Award, 1964. *Member:* National Committee of Amer. Civil Liberties Union, and Administrative Council of National Civil Liberties Clearing House. *Publications:* The Loyalty of Free Men (Viking Press, 1951); Government by Investigation (Viking Press, 1955); The Price of Liberty (Viking Press, Sept. 1961); Prophets with Honour (1974). *Honours:* Nieman Fellow, Harvard Univ. 1948–49. *Club:* National Press (Washington). *Address:* 3520 Rodman Street, N.W., Washington, D.C. 20008, U.S.A.

**BARTHOLOMÉE, Albert Ph.** Officer, Order of Leopold, and Order of the Crown (Belgium). *B.* 1909. *M.* 1934, Promial Anglo-Belge 1960–68; Manager S.A. Usines Destrée Andrée B. Richard. *S.* Pierre. *Daus.* Marinette and Sylvie. *Career:* Manager, S.A. Usines Destrée (Reckitt & Colman) until 1955; Partner, Usines Blanckaert until 1960; Manager, Promial Anglo-Belge 1960–68. Manager, S.A. Usines Destrée (Reckitt & Colman) 1968—. *Clubs:* Directeurs Commerciaux (Director); Mars et Mercure. *Address:* Chantecler, Tervuren; and *office* 40 rue Delaunoy, Brussels 8.

**BARTHOLOMEW, Frank Harmon.** *B.* 1898. *Educ.* Oregon State University (LLD). *M.* 1922, Antonia Luise Patzelt. *Career:* Chief of United Press war correspondents in World War II (Pacific); Chinese civil war; Korean war; and war in Indo-China; Chmn. emeritus and Dir. United Press International; Dir. San Francisco Federal Savings & Loan Assn.; Bd. Govs. Balboa Club; Proprietor Buena Vista Vineyards, Vice-Pres., Hacienda Wine Cellars, Sonoma, Cal. *Member:* Fellow of Sigma Delta Chi (international journalistic fraternity); Kappa Alpha Tau; American Legion. *Awards:* Omar N. Bradley Medal; Veterans of Foreign Wars; Nat. Citation. Combat reporting; Gold Star Mothers. *Clubs:* World Trade (San Francisco); Foreign Correspondents (Tokyo); Bohemian Press (San Francisco); Balboa; Mazatlan, Mexico. *Address:* United Press International, Grosvenor Plaza, San Francisco, Cal.; and (home) Glenbrook, Nevada, U.S.A.

**BARTLETT, Henry Frôncis,** CMG, OBE. Foundation Director. *B.* 1916. *Educ.* St. Paul's School; Queen's Coll. Oxford; Univ. of California (Commonwealth Fellow). *M.* 1940, A. D. Roy. *Career:* with Ministry of Information 1940–45; British Embassy Paris 1944–47; Vice Consul Lyons, 1948–49; Information Policy Dept. Foreign Office 1949–50; Vice Consul Szezecin 1950; Second later First Secy. British Embassy Warsaw 1951–53; United Nations Dept. For. Office 1953–55; First Secy. (Comm.) Caracas 1955–60, (Information) Mexico City 1960–63; H.M. Consul Khorramshahr 1964–67; Deputy High Commissioner Brisbane 1967–69; Counsellor British Embassy, Manila 1969–72; Ambassador to Paraguay 1972–75; Exec. Officer. Utah Foundation since 1976; Trustee, Queensland Art Gallery since 1977. *Award:* Companion of the Order of St. Michael and St George. Officer, Order of the British Empire. *Address:* c/o Utah Foundation, P.O. Box 1297, Brisbane, Australia 4001.

**BARTLETT, Norman.** Australian journalist and writer; *B.* 1908. *Educ.* University of Western Australia (BA Hons.; Dip. J.); Australian National Univ. (PhD 1977). *M.* 1932, Evelyn Ida Elliot. Short story writer and author of several books for children. *Career:* Began journalism in Perth, W.A. 1925; Editorial writer, West Australian 1933–40; Sunday Telegraph, Sydney 1940–41; Intelligence Officer, R.A.A.F., Fighter Sector, Townsville, N. Queensland 1941–42; R.A.A.F. Public Relations Correspondent, New Guinea, Great Britain, France and Germany 1942–45; Daily Telegraph, Sydney 1945–46; Commonwealth Department of Information, Canberra 1947–50; Leader Writer and Literary Editor, Daily Telegraph, Sydney 1951–53; Publications Editor, Australian War Memorial 1953–54; Press Attaché, Australian Embassy, Bangkok 1955–59. Information Attaché, Australian High Commission, New Delhi 1961–63; delegate to Commonwealth Education Conference, New Delhi, 1962; Australian Rep., U.N. Seminar on Freedom of Communications, New Delhi, 1962; Information Counsellor, Australian Embassy, Tokyo 1965–67; Liaison Officer Australia House, London 1969–72. *Publications:* The Pearl Seekers, London 1954; Island Victory (novel), Sydney 1955; Land of the Lotus Eaters, London 1959; Royal Visit, Australia, 1969; The Gold Seekers, London, 1965; Editor: With the Australians in Korea, Canberra 1954; Australia at Arms, Canberra 1955; Pictorial History of Australia at War 1939–45 (with Charles Meeking), Canberra 1958; Australia & America through Two Hundred Years, Sydney, 1976; contributor to Australian Quarterly, Meanjin and other periodicals. *Member:* Western Australian Historical Socy. (Secy. 1935–39); The Siam Socy., Bangkok (Life Member); Australian Socy. of Authors. *Clubs:* Imperial Service (Sydney); National Press Club (Canberra). *Address:* 31 Scott Street, Narrabundah, ACT 2604, Australia.

**BARTON, Leon Samuel Clay, Jr.,** American Architect, Planner, Lecturer. *B.* 1906. *Educ.* Clemson Univ. (B.S. in Architecture 1928), postgrad. N.Y.U., Atelier Morgan, N.Y. Med. Coll. & Columbia Univ. *M.* 1941, Barbara Alice Mosher (*dec.*). *Dau.* 1. *Career:* Designer, Draftsman, Engineering Div., E. R. Squibb & Sons 1928–35, Dir. Master Planning & Asst. to Chief Exec. Engr. 1944–47; Partner Barton & Pilafian, Architects & Engrs., consultants to Iranian Govt. 1935–38; principle Leon S. Barton 1939–41; Chief Architect & Head of Dept., Robert & Co. Inc. 1941–44; Naval Architect, Shipbldg. Div., Bethlehem Steel Co. 1944; Project Architect for Shreve Lamb & Harmon 1947–48; Associated with The Vitro Corp. (formerly Kellex Corp.); Chief Architect, Nuclear Energy Projects for U.S. AEC 1948–54; snr. partner, Barton & Pruitt & Associates 1954–75; Chmn. of Bd. & Pres. Walton Resilient Floors Inc. 1968–75. Corp. Member A.I.A. *Member:* N.Y. Chapter A.I.A. 1946–76; Corp. Mem. N.Y. State Assn. of Architects 1946–76; Am. Arbitration Assn. & nat. panel or Arbitrators 1971–76. *Awards:* First Hon. Mention Nat. W.G.N. Broadcasting Theater Competition 1934; Grand Prize Int'l. Teheran Stock Exchange (Bourse) Competition 1935; First Hon. Mention Prix de Rome Archel. Competition 1935; Cert. of Merit for Loyal & Efficient Services in W.W.11 Defense Projects, Robert & Co. Inc. 1934. *Address:* 537 North Country Road, Saint James, N.Y. 11780, U.S.A.; and *office:* 101 Park Avenue, New York City, N.Y. 10017, U.S.A.

**BARTON, William Hickson.** Canadian Diplomat. *B.* 1917. *Educ.* Univ. of British Columbia—BA. *M.* 1947. Jeanie Robinson. *S.* 1. *Career:* Canadian Army 1940–46; Joined Defence Research Bd. of Canada 1946, Sec. 1950–52 & Sec., Nat. Aeronautical Research Cttee. 1950–52; Sec., Canadian Section, Perm. Joint Bd. on Defence 1952; joined Dept. of External Affairs 1954; Counsellor, Canadian Embassy, Vienna 1956; Alt. Gov. for Canada to Internat. Atomic Energy Agency 1957; Dept of External Affairs, Ottawa 1959; Minister, Canadian Mission to UN 1961–64; Dir.-Gen., UN Bureau in Ottawa 1964–70; Asst. Under-Sec. of State for External Affairs 1970–72; Ambassador & Perm, Rep. in Geneva 1972–76; Ambassador & Perm. Rep. to the UN, New York since 1976. *Address:* 550 Park Avenue, New York, N.Y. 10021 and *office* Permanent Mission of Canada to the UN, 866 UN Plaza, Suite 250, New York, N.Y. 10017, U.S.A.

**BARTON, William L.** Lt.-Cdr. USNR (Retd.). *B.* 1908. *Educ.* Carnegie Inst. of Technology; Columbia Univ. (BS 1934); Graduate School of Banking, Rutgers Univ.: Advanced Management, Dartmouth College. *M.* 1946, Helen Bazzle, R.N. (formerly Lt.-Cdr. U.S. Navy Nurse Corps); *S.* Jeffrey Preston. *Career:* Management Consultant, Office of Quartermaster-General, Washington, D.C. 1940–42; City of New York Dept. of Purchase 1934–41. Senior Vice-President, General Services East River Savings Bank, New York (1962— (formerly Vice-Pres. and other official designations since 1941). *Publications:* How they Handle their Personnel (Management Publishing Corp., 1956); various articles in management and trade journals, including Present Day Banking, 1957. *Former Member:* Governor Rockefeller's Business Advisory Committee on Management Improvement; N.Y. Chapter, Amer. Inst. of Banking (Past Pres.; member Bd. Trustees); Peter Minuit Post, Amer. Legion; Military Order of World Wars; Reserve Officers Assn.; Commerce & Industry Assn. of N.Y.; Savings Banks Assn. of N.Y.; National Assn. of Mutual Savings Banks. *Clubs:* Officers (West Point Army Mess, West Point, N.Y.); New York Athletic (N.Y.A.C.); Officers (N.Y. Naval Shipyard, Brooklyn, N.Y.). *Address:* 26 Cortlandt Street, New York City 10007, U.S.A.

**BARUCH, Eduard.** Management consultant executive. *B.* 1907. *Educ.* Rhenania College, Switzerland; Columbia College, N.Y.C., and Columbia University Law School. *M.* 1934, Dorothy Hurd. *S.* Hurd. *Career:* Trust Officer, Irving Trust Co., N.Y.C. 1933–39; Sales Executive Bankers Life Co., Des Moines, Ia. 1939–42; Vice-Pres., i/c Sales, James H. Rhodes & Co., 1942–47; National Sales Manager, Vending Div., Pepsi-Cola Co. 1947–49; Vice-Pres., Heli-Coil Corp. 1949–55 (Exec. Vice-Pres. 1955–56); President, 1956–70; Corporation Consultant since 1970; Dir. Risdon Manft. Co. Naugatuck; Data Control Corp.; Dir. and Chmn. Exec. Ctte. John L. Schwab Associates Fairfield, Conn.: Dir. North East Bancorp Inc., New Haven, Conn.; Union Trust Co., Stamford, Conn.; Barden Corp., Danbury; N.B.I. Mortgage Co., New Haven; New England Council; Trustee, Member Board of Managers, Danbury Hospital. *Member:* Society of Automotive Engineers, Psi Upsilon, Phi Delta Phi. Mason. Shriner. *Clubs:* Columbia University, Wings (N.Y.C.); Ridgewood Country; Tower; Lago Mar Beach and Tennis, Coral Ridge Yacht (Ft. Lauderdale (Fla.)). *Address:* 16 Lake Drive, Candlewood Point, New Milford, Conn.; Harbor Beach, Ft. Lauderdale, Florida and *office* Suite 11 City Trust Building, Danbury, Conn., U.S.A.

**BARUCH, Jordan Jay.** Engineer, executive. *B.* 1923. *Educ.* MIT (BS 1947; MS 1948; ScD 1950). *M.* 1944, Rhoda Wasserman. *S.* Lawrence. *Daus.* Roberta Sara and Marjory Jean. *Career:* Vice-President, Bolt Beranek & Newman Inc. 1953–66; Lecturer in instrumentation, Massachusetts Institute of Technology 1953–70; General Manager, Medinet Dept., General Electric Co. 1966–68. President, EDUCOM, 1968–70; Lecturer, Harvard Business School 1970–74; Prof. of Busin. Admin. & Eng. Dartmouth Coll. 1974–77; Asst. Sec. of Commerce for Science & Technology 1977—. Contributor to Journal of Acoustical Society, Review of Scientific Instruments, Electronics, and Circulation Research. *Fellow:* N.Y. Academy of Science, Institute of Electrical & Electric Engineers, American Academy of Arts & Sciences, and Acoustical Society of America. Honor Award, Eta Kappa Nu. *Member:* Nat Acad. Engineers; American Institute of Physics; American Hospital Association. *Address:* 3025 Ordway Street N.W., Washington, D.C. 20008 and *office* U.S. Department of Commerce, Washington, D.C. 20230 ,U.S.A.

**BARWICK, E. T.** American textile manufacturer (carpets and rugs). *B.* 1913. *Educ.* Univ. of North Carolina (BS Com.). *M.* 1944, Anne M. McDougall. *S.* E. T. Jr. *Daus.* Nancy, Avis and Beverly. *Career:* Floor Covering Buyer, Sears Roebuck & Co. 1936–48; Chairman, President and Founder, E. T. Barwick Mills Inc. 1949—; Chairman & President, Monarch Rug Mills 1954—. Republican. *Clubs:* Metropolitan (New York); Lyford Cay, (B.W.I.); Capital City, Cherokee Town & Country, Peachtree Golf(Atlanta, Ga.). *Address:* 50 Valley Road, Atlanta. Ga.; and *office* E. T. Barwick Industries Inc. 5025 New Peachtree Road, Chamblee, Ga. 30341, U.S.A.

**BARWICK, Rt. Hon. Sir Garfield Edward John,** BA, LLB. LLD.; *B.* 1903. *Educ.* Fort Street High School and University of Sydney (Univ. Medal and Dalley Prize 1926). *M.* 1929, Norma M. Symons. *S.* Ross. *Dau.* Diane. *Career:* Admitted to N.S.W. Bar. 1927, K.C. 1941; Victorian Bar 1945, K.C. 1945; Queensland Bar 1958, Q.C. 1958. Practised extensively in all jurisdictions—Supreme Court, High Court of Australia and Privy Council. M.H.R. for Paramatta 1958–64; Commonwealth Attorney General 1958–64; Actg. Minister for External Affairs March–April and Aug.–Nov. 1959, and April–June 1960; Min. External Affairs 1961–64; Leader, Australian Delegation to United Nations, 1960, 1962–63–64; Chief Justice of Australia 1964—; Chancellor Macquarie Univ. Sydney, N.S.W. since 1967; Pres., N.S.W. Bar Assn. 1950–52 and 1955–56 and of Law Council of Australia 1952–54; Pres. Austr. Inst. of Internat. Affairs since 1972; Pres. Aust. Conservation Foundation 1965–71, Vice-Pres. 1971–73; Judge Ad Hoc International Court of Justice, 1973 and 1974. *Award:* LLD (Hon. Syd.) 1972. *Clubs:* Australian (Sydney), Melbourne (Melbourne), and Royal Sydney Yacht Squadron. *Address:* Mundroola, George Street, Careel Bay, N.S.W.; and High Court of Australia, Taylor Square, Sydney, Australia.

**BASELGA, Mariano M.** Spanish diplomat. Consul General of Spain in Bayonne (France). *B.* 1924. *Educ.* Licencié en Droit and in Philosophy and Letters. *M.* 1955, Paquita Calvo *S.* 2. *Daus.* 2. *Career:* Professor Adjoint, Faculty of Law, Univ. of Saragossa 1947–49; entered Diplomatic School 1952; Ministry of Foreign Affairs 1954; Secretary, Port-au-Prince 1956. Consul Adjoint, Algiers 1958; First Secretary, The Hague, 1960. First Secretary, Luxemburg 1965–67; Director of Telecommunications, Ministry of Foreign Affairs, 1967; Cultural Counsellor, Spanish Embassy, Bruxelles 1969; Minister Plenipotentiary 1976. *Publications:* En torno a la paz de Valençay 1813; Algunos aspectos de la Republica negra de Haiti, Chevalier, Order of Isabel la Catolica, and of Civil Merit (Spain); Officer, Order of Honour and Merit (Haiti); Order of Orange Nassau (Netherlands); Order of La Couronne de Chêne (Luxembourg); Commander, Order of Isabel la Catolica (Spain); Commander, Order of Leopold (Belgium). *Address:* Residence du Parc, 64100 Bayonne, France.

**BASLINI, Antonio.** Deputy of the Italian Parliament. President and Managing Director, Industrie Chimiche dr Baslini S.p.A. *B.* 1926. *Educ.* Univ. of Milan (Graduated Doctor in Chemistry). *M.* 1955, Gloria Carnelutti. *Daus.* Angelica, Antonia and Argenta. Member of Italian Liberal Party. *Club:* Rotary (Milano Est). *Address:* Via Serbelloni 10, Milan; and *office* Via Serbelloni 12, Milan, Italy.

**BASMACI, Ferid.** Turkish banker. *B.* 1911. *Educ.* Faculty of Economics & Commerce, Istanbul, Turkey. *M.* 1937, Faize. *Daus.* 2. *Career:* Treasurer, Türkiye Is Bankasii 1953–58; Vice-Pres., 1958–60; Manager, Galata Branch, 1960–66; Senior Vice-Pres., 1966–67; President, Türkiye is Bankasi A.S., 1967—; Chairman: Industrial Development Bank of Turkey, 1969—; Sinai Yatirim ve kredi Bankasi, 1967—; Türkiye Maden Bankasi, 1969—. *Address:* Vali Dr. Resit Caddesi 74/3, Cankaya, Ankara; and *office* Türkiye Is Bankas, A.S., Ulus, Ankara, Turkey.

**BASNYAT, Shri Upendra Bahadur.** Nepalese diplomat. *B.* 1919. *Educ.* Calcutta University. *M. S.* 2. *Career:* Commissioned in the Royal Nepalese Army, Lieut. 1940; Adjutant, Nepalese Contingent Second World War; Lieut. Col. Military Attaché, Royal Nepalese Embassy, New Delhi; Liaison Officer, Gorkha Rifles, Indian Army 1951–56; Foreign Service Nepal 1957; Consul Gen. Lhasa 1958–61; Deputy Royal Nepalese Embassy, Peking 1961–65; His Majesty's Ambassador to Pakistan 1965; concurrently accredited to Iran and Turkey; Ambassador to the Court of St. Jame's 1969–73. *Awards:* Prasiddha Prabal Gorkha Dakshin Bahu; Long Service Medal; War Service Medal; Defence Medal; Coronation Medal. *Address:* Royal Nepalese Ministry of Foreign Affairs (Ambassadorial Division), Kathmandu, Nepal.

**BASS, Harry Godfrey Mitchell,** CMG. Retired British diplomat. *B.* 1914. *Educ.* Marlborough Coll., Gonville & Caius Coll., Cambridge; and St. John's Coll., Oxford; MA (Cantab.), BA (Oxon.). *M.* 1948. Monica Mary Burroughs. *S.* Peter George Burroughs and Andrew Stephen Burroughs. *Dau.* Gillian Susan Burroughs. *Career:* Assistant Keeper, British Museum 1939; at Admiralty 1940; Dominions Office 1946; Office of U.K. High Commission; Canberra 1948 and Calcutta 1954. Deputy High Commissioner, Office of U.K. High Commission: Salisbury (S. Rhodesia) 1959; Cape Town 1961; Minister, British Embassy, Pretoria, Cape Town, 1961; Deputy U.K. High Commissioner, Ibadan, 1965–67; High Commissioner, Lesotho 1970–73 (Retired 1973); Chapter Clerk, St George's Chapel, Windsor Castle 1974–77. *Awards:* Companion of St Michael & St George, 1972; Jubilee Medal, 1977. *Address:* Tyler's Mead, Dereham Rd, Reepham, Norfolk, NR10 4LA.

**BASS, Robert Ness.** American. *B.* 1917. *Educ.* Bowdoin Coll. (AB 1940); Harvard Univ. School of Business Administration (MBA 1942). *M.* 1948, Martha W. Lord. *S.* John R. II, Peter L., and Robert N., Jr. *Daus.* Ann. Elisabeth and Mary Lord. *Career:* Lieut. U.S.N.R. 1941–46 (Bureau of Ordnance liaison with British Admiralty Div. of Lend-Lease). Director 1946—, Treasurer 1963—, President 1969—, Chmn. Bd. 1972—; G. H. Bass & Co., Wilton, Maine. Director, Union Mutual Life Insurance Co., Portland, Me. 1962—, President 1950–62, Chairman of Board 1962—.

Sugarloaf Mountain Corp., Kingfield, Me. Treasurer 1959–65; Pres. 1970–73, Ski Industries of America; Chmn. Bd. since 1973; Board Member 1955–65; now Director, Depositors Trust Co. and Depositors Corp.; Augusta, Me. Member Advisory Bd., Liberty Mutual Life Insurance Co., Boston, Mass., 1968. *Member:* Newcomen Soc. Overseer, Bowdoin College, Brunswick 1964. *Clubs:* DKE, Boothbay Harbor Yacht; Dir. and Treasurer, Megantic (one) Fish & Game. *Address* and *office:* G. H. Bass & Co., Wilton, Me 04294, U.S.A.

**BASSETT, John White Hughes.** Canadian broadcaster. *B.* 1915. *Educ.* Bishop's Univ. (BA). *M.* 1938, Moira Bradley; 1967, Isabel Gordon. *S.* 4. *Daus.* 2. *Career:* Dir., CTV Television Network Ltd.; Chmn., Baton Broadcasting Inc. (TV); Inland Publishing Co. Ltd.; CKLW-Radio Windsor; CFGO Radio, Ottawa: CFOC-TV and Radio, Saskatoon, Saskatchewan; CFTO-TV Ltd., Toronto; C. F. Haughton Ltd.; Dir. HM Tennant (England). *Member:* Governing Council of Univ. of Toronto. *Address:* Suite 1206, 101 Richmond Street, W., Toronto, Ont. M5H 1T1, Canada.

**BASSON, Jacob Daniel Duplessis.** South African politician. *B.* 1918. *Education.* University of Stellenbosch, BA (Law). *M.* 1947, Clare Strauss. *Daus.* 2. *Career:* Polit. Secy. in Cape Province 1939–41; Polit. Journalist and mem. Parly. Press Gallery, Cape Town, 1943; Polit. Secy. S.W. Africa 1947–50; MP for Namib, S.W. Africa 1950–61, Parly. Whip for 3 years; MP for Bezuidenhout const. Johannesburg, United Party (Official Opposition) since 1961, Shadow Minister for Foreign Affairs. *Member:* SA Inst. of International Affairs; Africa Institute. *Address:* Villa Milano, Federick Crescent, Tamboerskloof, Cape Town, SA; and *office* Box 66123, Broadway, 2020 Johannesburg; or House of Assembly, Cape Town, Republic of South Africa.

**BASTYAN, Lieut.-Gen. Sir Edric (Montague),** KCMG, KCVO, KBE, CB, KStJ. *B.* 1903. *M.* 1944, Victoria Eugénie Helen Bett. *S.* 1. *Career:* Second Lieut. Sherwood Foresters 1923; Captain West Yorks Regt. 1935, and Royal Irish Fusiliers 1937; Major 1940; Temp. Lt.-Col. 1941; Temp. Brigadier 1942; Actg. Maj.-Gen. Colonel 1944; 1945; Maj.-Gen. (with seniority 1946), 1948. Served in Palestine 1938–39 (despatches), World War II, in Africa, Italy and SEAC (despatches, OBE., CBE., CB); Maj.-Gen. i/c Administration Allied Land Forces, BAOR; employed on special duties, War Office 1949; Chief of Staff, Eastern Command 1949–50; Dir. of Staff Duties, W.O. 1950–52; Commander 53rd (Welsh) Infantry Div. (T.A.) and Mid-West District 1952–55; Vice Adjutant General, W.O. 1955–57; Lieut.-Gen. 1957; Commander, British Forces, Hong-Kong 1957–60. Hon. Air Commodore R.A.A.F.; Assoc. Mem., Royal South Aust. Soc. of Arts; Governor of South Australia, 1961–68; Governor of Tasmania 1968–74. *Clubs:* The Adelaide Club. *Address:* Flat 42, 52 Brougham Place, North Adelaide, SA 5006, Australia.

**BATEMAN, Dupuy, Jr.** American. *B.* 1904. *Educ.* Rice Univ. (Houston, Texas). *M.* Nancy Gay. *S.* George Rotan and Dupuy III. *Daus.* Sally (Goodhue) and Elizabeth (Ellerbee). *Career:* Officer of various subsidiaries of Anderson, Clayton & Co. 1927–45. Director, Member Executive Committee and Executive Vice-President, Anderson, Clayton & Co., Houston 1958–65 (Dir. and Vice-Pres. 1945–58). Partner, Anderson, Clayton & Fleming, N.Y.C. 1945–65; Partner, Golightly & Bateman, Houston 1965; Vice-President and Assistant to President, Rockwell-Standard Corp., Pittsburgh, Pa. 1965–67. Vice-Pres., North American Rockwell Corporation, 1967–68. Senr. Vice-President Director and Member Exec. Committee, North American Rockwell Corp. (now Rockwell International Corp.); El Segundo, Calif., 1968–71; Advisory Dir. and Consultant since 1971; Dir. Envirotech Corp. Member, Standing Liturgical Commission, Protestant Episcopal Church 1960—; Exec. Council, Chmn. Programme Budget Cttee. of General Convention Episcopal Church since 1970; Pre-Pres. Historical Soc. (Episc. Ch.) since 1974. *Clubs:* Houston Country; (Houston); Duquesne; Oakmont Country; (Pittsburgh, Pa.); Rolling Rock (Ligonier, Pa.); *Address:* 418 Emerson Street, Pittsburgh, Pa. 15206; and *office* Rockwell International Corp., 600 Grant Street, Pittsburgh, Pa. 15219.

**BATEMAN, Sir Ralph Melton,** KBE, MA, DSc, FCIS. British Co. Dir. *B.* 1910. *Educ.* Epsom Coll.; Univ. Coll., Oxford, MA. *M.* 1935, Barbara Yvonne Litton. *S.* 2. *Daus.* 2. *Career:* Joined Turner and Newall Group 1931; Held Directorships in many of the firm's subsidiary and assoc. cos. (home and overseas) since 1942; Appointed to Board of Turner and Newall 1957–59, Deputy Chmn. 1959, Chmn. 1967–76; Chmn., Stothert & Pitt Ltd., Bath; Dir., Rea Brothers Ltd., London. *Fellow:* Chartered Inst. of Secretaries; BIM; RSA. Past Pres. and Vice-Pres., Confederation of British Industry. *Member:* Council of University Coll. at Buckingham (Chmn.); Court of Univ. of Manchester; Governors of Ashridge Coll. of Mgmt. (Vice-Pres.); National Inst. of Economic and Social Research (Governor). *Decoration:* Knight Commander of Most excellent order of BE: Doctor of Science (*hon. causa*) Univ. of Salford. *Address:* Highfield, Withinlee Road, Prestbury, Cheshire.

**BATES, Alfred,** MP. British Politican. *B.* 1944. *Educ.* Univ. of Manchester—BSc; Corpus Christi Coll., Cambridge Univ. *Career:* Lecturer in Mathematics, De La Salle Coll. of Education, Manchester 1967–74; MP (Lab.) for Bebington and Ellesmere Port since 1974; Government Whip since 1976. *Member:* National Union of Teachers; Mathematical Assoc. *Address:* 5 Dunbar Close, Little Sutton, South Wirral and *office* House of Commons, London, SW1A 0AA.

**BATES, Sir John (David),** CBE, VRD, Kt. 1969. *B* 1904. *Educ.* Plymouth. Devon (England). *M.* 1930, Phyllis H. Müller. *S.* 1. *Career:* Joined Orient Line as Assistant Purser 1925; transferred to shore staff in Australia 1929; served Brisbane, Melbourne and Sydney; joined R.A.N.V.R. 1932; Commander 1946–57; Navy Office, Melbourne 1939–40; N.L.O. London 1940–43; Deputy Director, Far Eastern Liaison Office (Propaganda Warfare) Brisbane, Morotai Borneo 1943–45; General Manager in Australia, British Orient Line 1954–60; Deputy Chairman, P. & O. Orient Lines of Australia Pty. Ltd. 1960–67; Director, Perpetuel Trustee Company Ltd. 1967—; Chairman, Australian Tourist Commission 1967–69; Australian Consul General, New York 1970–73; Chairman, Honorary Board of Australian National Travel Association 1956–67; member, Export Development Council 1959–66; Federal President, Navy League of Australia, 1950–56: Trustee, Art Gallery of N.S.W. 1962–70. *Address:* 11 Grosvenor Street, Wahroonga, N.S.W. 2076, Australia.

**BATES, Philip Knight.** American corporation executive. *B.* 1902. *Educ.* Massachusetts Institute of Technology (BS 1924; PhD 1929). *M.* 1929, Eleanor Johnson. *S.* Charles Johnson, Philip Knight, Jr., and Bradford. *Career.* Head. Bacteriological Laboratory, Frigidaire Corp., Dayton, Ohio 1929–32; Bacteriologist, Rexall Drug Co., Boston 1936–40; (Director, Product Development Dept. 1941–49); Research Associate, M.I.T. 1924–27, 1933–35: Teaching Asst., Tufts Medical & Dental School, Boston 1924–26; Instructor, Boston. Univ. School of Medicine 1944–46; Pres., Riker Laboratories Inc., Los Angeles 1949–52; General Mgr. Research Laboratories of Carnation Co. 1952–67. Editor Journal of Agricultural and Food Chemistry (A.C.S.) since 1965. *Member:* Inst. Food Technologists (Pres. 1954–55); Amer. Chemical Socy.; Frasch Foundation Awards (Chmn. 1958—); Socy. Amer. Bacteriologists (now Amer. Socy. of Microbiology); Pharmaceutical Manufactures Assn. (Vice-Pres. 1950–51); N.Y. Acad. of Sciences. Member A.A.A.S. *Clubs:* Chemists (N.Y.C.); The Beach (Santa Monica). *Address:* 633 Seventeenth Street, Santa Monica, Calif., U.S.A. 90402.

**BATES, Sidney Henry James.** Lawyer and investment company executive. *B.* 1903. *M.* Frieda Anna Inglin. *S.* Jameson R. *Dau.* Lynda. *Career:* Admitted Solicitor of the Supreme Court 1930; Senior Partner, Bates, Son & Braby, London (and Leigh-on-Sea and Southend-on-Sea). Southend-on-Sea & District Law Society (Past-Pres.). Rotarian (Past Founder-Pres., Leigh-on-Sea). Squadron Leader R.A.F.V.R. 1940–46; Past Mayor, Southend-on-Sea, 1949–50. *Address:* 55 Abbotsbury Close, London, W.14; and *office* Temple Chambers, Temple Avenue, London, EC4Y.

**BATLINER, Dr. Gerard.** Lawyer. *B.* 1928. *Educ.* Kollegium Maria-Hilf (Switzerland) and Universities of Zürich, Fribourg, Paris, and Freiburg. *M.* 1965, Christina Negele. *Career:* Practised law in the County Court of Liechtenstein 1954–55. Attorney at Law, Vaduz 1956–61; Vice-President, Progressive Burgher Party 1958–62. Vice-Mayor of Eschen 1960–62; Head of Government, Principality of Liechtenstein 1962–70; Pres., Liechtenstein Parliament and Pres. of Parly. Cttee. for Foreign Affairs and of Cttee. for Financial Affairs since 1974; Observer to Consult. Assembly of Council of Europe since 1974. *Awards:* Grand Cross, Liechtenstein Order of Merit, 1970; Furstlicher Justizrat. LLD University of Fribourg. *Address:* Eschen, Liechenstein; and *office* Vaduz, Liechtenstein.

**BATSFORD, Sir Brian (Caldwell Cook).** *B.* 1910. *Educ:* Repton School. *M.* 1945, Joan Cunliffe. *Daus.* Georgina and Sophia. *Career:* Lectured in Canada under auspices of Canadian Nat. Council of Edn. 1935, 1937; and in Scandinavia and Baltic States for British Council 1940. Hon. Secy., Empire Youth Sunday Committee 1938; Chairman, Youth City Committee of Enquiry 1939. Served in R.A.F. 1941–46. Contested Chelmsford Div. of Essex for National Government 1945. Chairman, B. T. Batsford Ltd., Book Publishers, 1951–74; Member of Parliament Con. Ealing South 1958–74; Parliamentary Private Secy. to Minister of Works 1959–60. Asst. Government Whip 1962–64; Opposition Dep. Chief Whip 1964–67; Alderman, Greater London Council 1967–70; Conservative Parliamentary Representative on G.L.C. 1967–70; Chmn., Royal Socy. of Arts 1973–74, Vice-Pres. 1975; Fellow, Society of Industrial Artists 1971; Pres., London Appreciation Socy.; Member, Post Office Stamp Advisory Cttee.; Governor, Repton School 1973. *Award:* Kt. Bachelor. *Clubs:* Carlton, Pratt's, M.C.C. (London). *Address:* The Manor, Wyke Champflower, Bruton, Somerset; and D5 Albany, Piccadilly, London W.1.

**BATTEN, John Henry III.** American manufacturing executive. *B.* 1912. *Educ.* Phillips Acad., Andover, Mass.; Yale Univ. (BA); Univ. of Wisconsin (Ext. Div.—Cert. Mech. Engr.). *M.* 1938, Katherine Vernet Smith. *S.* Edmund Peter Smith and Michael Ellsworth. *Dau.* Linda Vernet (Barrington). *Career:* Chmn. and Chief Exec. Officer, Twin Disc Incorporated, Racine, Wis.; Director: Twin Disc International S.A. (Nivelles, Belgium), British Twin Disc Ltd. (Rochester, Eng.); Twin Disc Pacific (Pty.) Ltd., Aust. Niigata Converter Co. Ltd. (Tokyo), American Bank & Trust Co. (Racine), Employers' Mutuals of Wausau, Gliddings & Lewis Machine Tool Co. (Fond du Lac), Walker Forge (Racine), Racine Commercial Airport Corp. (and Chmn.), NAM. Republican. *Clubs:* University (Chicago); University (Milwaukee); Racine Country; Somerset. *Address:* 3030 Michigan Boulevard, Racine, Wis.; and *office* 1328 Racine Street, Racine, Wis., U.S.A.

**BATTLE, William Cullen.** *B.* 1920. *Educ.* University of Virginia (BA 1941; LLB 1947). *M.* 1953, Frances Barry Webb. *S.* William Cullen, Jr. and Robert Webb. *Dau.* Jane Tavernor. *Career:* Attorney, Charleston Group of Companies, Columbia Gas System 1947–51; Attorney, Partner, Perkins, Battle and Minor (now McGuire, Woods & Battle) 1951–62; Ambassador of the United States of America to the Commonwealth of Australia since 1962. Awarded the Silver Star, Democrat. Member of various clubs. *Address:* American Embassy, Canberra, A.C.T., Australia.

**BATTY, Sir William (Bradshaw),** TD., FIMI. British. *B.* 1913. *Educ.* Hulme Grammar Sch. Manchester. *M.* 1946, Jean Ella Brice. *S.* 1. *Dau.* 1. *Career:* Chmn., Ford Motor Co. Ltd.; Chmn., Ford Motor Credit Co. Ltd.; Chmn. Automotive Finance Co. Ltd.; Dir., Henry Ford & Son Ltd.; Ford Lusitana SARL, Portugal; Gen. Group Man. Tractor Group 1961–63; Dir. Tractor Group 1963–64; Car & Truck Group (1964); Man. Dir. Ford Motor Co. Ltd. 1968–73; Pres. Socy. of Motor Manufacturers and Traders Ltd. 1975–76; Mem., Engineering Industries Council since 1975. Hon. LLD, Manchester 1976. *Clubs:* R.A.C.; Thorndon Park Golf; Royal Western Yacht. Mem. American Chamber of Commerce (L.K.). *Address:* Glenhaven Cottage, Riverside Road West, Newton Ferrers, South Devon.

**BAUGHMAN, Ernest Theodore.** American. *B.* 1915. *Educ.* University of Minnesota (BS 1939; MS 1941). *M.* 1941, Esther M. Bajari. *Daus.* Carol, Verna and Francine. *Career:* Instructor, University of Minnesota 1940–41; Economist, Council of Farmer Co-operatives 1941–42; U.S. Navy 1943–5. With Federal Reserve Bank of Chicago: Economist 1946–52; Asst. Vice-Pres. 1952–58; Vice-Pres. 1959–68; Sr. Vice-Pres., 1969–70; First Vice-Pres. 1971–74; President, Federal Reserve Bank of Dallas, since 1974; Lecturer, Graduate School of Banking since 1950; Director of Research, Federal Reserve Bank of Chicago 1961–70. First Vice-President, Federal Reserve Bank of Chicago, 1970. Editor, Business Conditions, Federal Reserve Bank of Chicago. *Member:* Amer. Economic Assn.; Amer. Finance Assn.; Amer. Farm Economics Assn.; Bd. Trustee, Farm Foundation 1971. *Address:* 3714 Northview, Dallas, Texas, 95229, U.S.A. *office* 400 S. Akard St,. Dallas, Texas, 75222, U.S.A.

**BAUM, John P(inson).** American woollen textile manufacturer. Vice-President, Derby Co., and Nyanza Inc., Lawrence, Mass. *B.* 1902. *Educ.* Georgia Inst. of Technology (BS 1924) and Georgia Technical Evening School of Commerce (BS 1927). *M.* 1936, Martha Miller Bowen. *S.* John P., Jr. *Daus.* Martha Lucille, Mary Anna, and Marjorie Bowen. *Career:* Engineering department, Georgia Marble Co., Tate, Ga. 1924–25; Asst. Mgr., Textile Engineering Dept., Robert & Co., Atlanta, Ga. 1925–31; Sales Engineer, General Electric Vapor Lamp Co. 1931–32; Asst. Mgr. Pepperell Mfg. Co., Opelika, Ala. 1932–40; U.S. Army Q.M. General Office, Washington (discharged as Colonel) 1940–45; Vice-Chmn. and Director, J.P. Stevens & Co., Milledgeville, Ga. 1945–67. Director, Derby Co., Lawrence, Mass. 1956–61; Director, Merchants & Farmers Bank, Milledgeville, Ga., 1955–61. Recipient Legion of Merit, U.S. Army. Phi Kappa Phi; ANAK Senior (Hon. Societies); GA. Tech. Alumni, Dist. Service Award; Mason. *Clubs:* University (N.Y.C.); Capital City, Commerce (Atlanta); Milledgeville Country; Rotary. *Address:* 1921 Briarciff Rd, Milledgeville, Ga.; and *office* P.O. Box 654, Milledgeville, Ga., U.S.A.

**BAUMANN, Gérard Michel.** French. *B.* 1927. *Educ.* Baccalaureat Math. Elem.; Milling Technician Degree, Ecole de Meunerie, Paris. *M.* 1958, Arlette Alexandre. *S.* Marc and Thierry. *Career:* Entered Grands Moulins de Strasbourg 1951, and Fonde de Pouvoirs 1954; Director, Grands Moulins de Strasbourg S.A. Jan. 1958—. Administrator, Eurexpan (Paris), Somatra S.A. Marseille and Costimex S.A. Strasbourg (Paris). *Clubs:* State Français, Stade Français, Alpin Français. *Address:* 61 Avenue d'Iena, Paris 16.

**BAUMANN, John Hilary.** British. *B.* 1916. *Educ.* King's Sch., Canterbury; Handelschochsch, St. Gallen. *M.* 1949, Rosemary Eileen. *S.* 1. *Dau.* 1. *Career:* Chmn. Morganite Intl. Ltd.. *Member:* Inst. Directors; Council London Chamber Commerce & Industry. *Address:* 72 March Court, London SW15 6LD; and *office* 5 Grosvenor Gdns., London, S.W.1.

**BAUMANN, Paul.** American consulting civil and structural engineer. *B.* Berne, Switzerland 30 Jan. 1892. *Educ.* Federal Inst. of Technology, Zürich (Dipl. Ing.). *M.* 1924, Miriam M. May from Bristol, England. *S.* 2. *Career:* Engaged on military engineering on roads, fortifications and flood control work with Swiss Engineers 1914–18; with Bernese Power Co. on power development of the Alps 1918–19; Engineer with Fargo Engineering Co., Jackson, Mich. 1920; Chief Design Engineer, Paradise Verde Irrigation District, Arizona 1921; Chief Engineer, Arrowhead Lake Co., California 1922–25; Chief Design Engineer, Quinton Code & Hill, Leeds & Barnard, Consulting Engineers, Los Angeles 1926–34; Assistant Chief Engineer, L.A.C.F.C.D. 1934–59; member Board of Consultants, Taiwan Power Co. Nov. 1958—. Chairman and Member, Boards of Consultants, California State Dept. of Water Resources on Safety of Dams and Evaluation of Design and Construction, California Water Project, City of Los Angeles Dept. of Water and Power and U.S. Corps of Engrs. on dams & channels. Hon. Member Chi Epsilon, the National Honour Fraternity of Civil Engineering in U.S.A. *Publications:* Analysis of Sheet-Pile Bulkheads (which won James Laurie Prize A.S.C.E. 1936); Design and Construction of San Gabriel Dam No. 1 (Thomas Fitch Rowland Prize, A.S.C.E. 1943); Ground-Water Movement Controlled Through Spreading; The Function and Design of Check Dams; Debris Problems in Flood Control; Ground-Water Phenomena Related to Basin Recharge; Performance of San Gabriel No. 1 and No. 2 Rock fill Dams; Practical Aspects of Weather Modification; Use of Prepacked Aggregate Concrete in Major Dam Construction; Earthfill Overflow Dams in Flood Control; The Significance of Pre-stress in Embankment Dams; Experiments with Fresh-Water Barrier to Prevent Sea-Water Intrusion; Limit of Height Criteria for Loose-Dumped Rockfill Dams; Technical Development in Ground Water Recharge (Vol. 2, Advances in Hydroscience). *Address:* 756 Auburn Avenue, Sierra Madre, Calif., 91024, U.S.A.

**BAUMER, Edward Ferdinand.** Financial Marketing Consultant. *B.* 1913. *Educ.* Rutgers University (AB 1934; LLB 1937; JD 1970). *M.* 1940, Elizabeth Theresa Karl. *S.* Edward Karl and Richard Eaton. *Dau.* Jane Elizabeth. *Career:* Admitted to Bar of State of New Jersey as Attorney-at-Law 1937. Served in World War II (1st Lieut. to Lieut.Col.; Legion of Merit) 1940–46; Brigadier General U.S. Army (Ret'd). Served in various management positions with Prudential Insurance Co. of America 1934–55 (late post as Director of Advertising and Public Relations, Western Home Office, Los Angeles 1946–55); Vice-Pres., McCann-Erickson Inc., Vice-Pres. and Director, Communications Counselors Inc. 1955–59; Vice-Pres., Union Bank 1959–61; Vice-Pres., Great Western Financial Corp., Los Angeles, Calif. 1961–65; President, E. F. Baumer & Co., Western Financial Advertising Agency, and Western Financial Publications, 3810 Wilshire Boulevard, Los Angeles, Calif.; Member, President's Assn. (American Management Assn.). *Member:* The Sales & Marketing Executives International 1961—; Public Relations Society of America 1949—; and American Bar Association 1938—; Past Western Regional Vice-Pres., Public Relations Society of America 1953–54 (member, National Board of Directors 1953–55). *Publications:* contributions to various management publications, including Pension World. Republican. *Clubs:* California (Los Angeles); Los Angeles Tennis; Annandale Golf (Pasadena, Calif.). *Address:* 521 Bradford St., Pasadena, Calif., U.S.A.

**BAUMGARTNER, André Frederic.** Swiss advocate. *B.* 20 Aug. 1907. *Educ.* University of Lausanne (lic. et D. en D.). *M.* 1936, Helene Cosandey. *S.* 1. *Daus.* 2. *Career:* President, Swiss Ski Federation, 1948–52; Deputy (radical), Grand Council of Vaudois, 1949–53; member, Central Committee, Swiss Football and Athletic Association, 1952; Director, Association of Industries Vaudoises, 1957–67; Bâtonnier de l'Ordre des advocate Vaudois 1970–72. *Publications:* La Communauté héréditaire dans le procès civil (1936); La vérité sur le prétendu drame Paderewski (1948). *Address:* Place Bel-Air 1, Lausanne, Switzerland.

**BAUMGARTNER, Wilfrid,** LLD. Member, Institut de France. *B.* 21 May 1902. *M.* Christiane Mercier. *S.* Eric. *Daus.* Sylvie (Mme. Henri Hartung), Florence. *Career:* Inspector of Finance 1925; Chef du Cabinet of the Minister of Finance 1930; Asst. Dir., Mouvement Général des Fonds, Ministry of Finance 1930–34, Deputy Director 1934–36, Director 1935–36; Chairman and General Manager, Crédit National 1936; member of Board, Banque de France 1936–49; Governor, Banque de France 1949–60; Minister of Finance 1960–62; Chmn. of Board, Rhône Poulenc S.A. 1964–73. Grand Croix de la Légion d'Honneur. *Address:* 98 Rue de Grenelle, Paris, 7e.; and *office* 22 Avenue Montaigne, Paris 8e, France.

**BAUS, Herbert M(ichael).** American public relations counsellor. *B.* 1914. *Educ.* Univ. of California, Los Angeles (AB). *M.* 1952, Helene M. Walther. *Career:* Publicity Director, Los Angeles Chamber of Commerce, Junior Chamber of Commerce 1937–42; Promotion Director, Secretary, General Manager, Downtown Business Men's Assn., Los Angeles 1942–43; Reporter, Washington Post, Los Angeles Times, Los Angeles Herald-Express 1933–37; Public Relations Counsel, Los Angeles 1946. Partner, Baus & Ross (political campaign managers) 1947—. Previously Instructor, Univ. of Southern California; Public Relations Officer, A.T.S.C., N.Y.C., Special Events Officer, HQ U.S.A.A.F., Washington. Author: Publicity, How to Plan, Produce and Place It, 1942; Public Relations at Work, 1948; Tested Public Relations Procedure, 1948; Publicity in Action, 1954; Politics Battle Plan, 1968. *Member:* Los Angeles Chamber of Commerce; Public Relations Society of America (past Natl. Director); Lambda Chi Alpha. *Clubs:* Jonathan: Greater Los Angeles Press. *Address: office* 2796 West Eighth Street, Los Angeles, Calif. 90005, U.S.A.

**BAVERSTOCK, Donald Leighton.** British. *B.* 1924. *Educ.* Canton High School Cardiff and Christ Church Oxford (MA Modern History). *M.* 1957, Gillian Darrell Waters. *S.* Glyndwr and Owain. *Daus.* Sian and Sara. *Career:* Served with RAF 1943–46; History Master Wellington Coll., 1949; Producer B.B.C. Overseas Service, 1950–54; B.B.C. Television, 1954–57; Editor Tonight Programme, 1957–61; Asst. Controller B.B.C. Television, 1961–63; Chief of Programmes B.B.C. TV (2), 1963–65; Partner Jay Baverstock Milne & Co., 1965–67. Director of Programmes, Yorkshire Television 1967–73; Man. Dir., Granada Video Ltd. 1974–75; Exec. Prod., TV, B.B.C. Manchester since 1975. *Club:* Savile. *Address:* Low Hall, Middleton, Ilkley, Yorkshire.

**BAXTER, Prof. Alexander Duncan,** MEng., FIMechE, FRAeS, FInstPet. British Chartered Engineer, Research Consultant. *B.* 1908. *Educ.* Liverpool University (BEng 1st Cl. Hons.). *M.* 1933, Florence Kathleen McClean. *S.* 1. *Daus.* 2. *Career:* Executive Director (Engineering) De Havilland Engine Co. Ltd., 1958–63; Professor and Head of Department of Aircraft Propulsion, College of Aeronautics, Cranfield 1950–57; Deputy Principal 1954–57; Consultant to aero engine firms; member of various Government scientific committees; previously Supt., Rocket Propulsion Dept., Royal Aircraft Establishment, Westcott 1947–50; Principal Scientific Officer, R.A.E. Farnborough 1944–47; same post but concerned with gas turbines and jet propulsion 1937–44; Technical Officer, R.A.E., on piston engines 1935–37; Research Engineer, Inst. of Automobile Engineers 1934–35; Post-graduate pupil with Daimler Co., Coventry 1930–34 Senior Technical Executive, Bristol Siddeley Engines, 1962–70; (now Rolls Royce). Fellow, Inst. of Petroleum; Fellow, British Interplanetary Soc.; Member of Court, Cranfield Institute of Technology, Bristol University; Fellow and Member, Council Royal Aeronautical Society, 1953–70; (Vice-President 1962; President 1966–67); Board Member, Council of Engineering Institutions 1962–70. *Publications:* Various technical reports and papers in Government R. & M. papers, journals of professional institutes, and scientific publications. *Address:* Glebe Cottage, Pucklechurch, Glos. BS17 3PN.

**BAXTER, Raymond George,** CBE. Australian industrial consultant. *B.* 1902. *M.* 1945, Diana M. F. Armit. *S.* Christopher, Michael, Paul and Nicholas. *Career:* Consultant to leading Australian and overseas industrial concerns 1929–38; Adviser to Australian National Insurance Commission 1938–39; Director, Industrial Welfare, Commonwealth Department of Labour and National Service 1940–45; Government Adviser, I.L.O. Industrial Committees (iron and steel, engineering), U.K. and U.S.A. 1946. Chairman of Directors, Baxter Baird & Co. Pty. Ltd., Corporate Counsel; Member of Board, Commonwealth Banking Corporation and Papua & New Guinea Development Bank (P.N.G.); Chmn. Commonwealth Hostels Ltd. Principal, Raymond Baxter & Co., Industrial Consultants. *Publications:* The Role of the Company Director. Fellow, Australian Institute of Management (Pres. Melbourne Div. 1960–63). *Member:* Australian Inst. of Political Science; Economic Socy.; Pres. Australian-American Assn.; Chmn. Business Archives Council. *Clubs:* Savage, Constitutional (Pres. 1955), Rotary, Royal Automobile (all of Melbourne). *Address:* Collins House, 360 Collins Street, Melbourne, Vic. 3000, Australia.

**BAYER, Prof. Dr. h.c. mult. Otto.** German. *B.* 1902. *Educ.* Abitur, Frankfurt/Main; studies in Chemistry, Univ. of Frankfurt/ Main 1921–24. *M.* Eleonore Stellisch. *Career:* Private Asst. to J. von Braun 1924–27; entered IG Farbenindustrie AG 1927 (Prokurist 1934, Director 1939); Hon. Prof. for Technical Chemistry, Univ. of Cologne 1944—; Board Member (Head of Research) Farbenfabriken Bayer AG, Leverkusen 1951, Chmn. of Bd. 1964–74. *Publications:* numerous publications and holder of 400 German patents; inventor of Di-isocyanat-Poly Additions Process. Corresponding Member: Acad. for Science and Literature, Mainz; Kuratoriums Chmn., "Fonds der Chemie" (1950–1964); Assoc. Founder and honorary member, Gesellschaft Deutscher Chemiker (mem. Exec. Cttee. for several years); Rhein-Westfälische Akad. der Wissensch, Dusseldorf, 1952; Senator of the Max Planck-Society 1962–72; Hon. member, The Chemists' Club, New York. *Awards:* Baeyer Medal, Gauss-Weber (University of Göttingen), Duisberg Medal. Siemens-Ring and Otto N. Witt Medal, Goodyear Medal 1975. Six hon. Dr. degrees. *Address:* Haus am Eifgen, 5093 Burscheid, Germany.

**BAYLEY, George Wyrill,** OBE, ERD. British shipowner. *B.* 28 October 1915. *Educ.* St. Bede's, Hornsea; Durham School. *M.* 1941, Denise Margaret Alison Blockley. *S.* 2. *Career:* Joined Ellerman's Wilson Line, Ltd. 1933; served World War II, Royal Engrs. (Lieut-Col.) 1939–45; Managing Director, Ellerman's Wilson Line. Ltd. 1950—; Chairman, Antwerp Steamship Co., Ltd. 1959—; McMasters (Haulage) Ltd.; Svea Line (U.K.) Ltd.; Director, Associated Humber Lines Ltd. 1959—; Robb, Caledon (Shipbuilders) Ltd.; Ellerman Lines Ltd. 1966—; England-Sweden Line Ltd. 1965—; Chmn., EWL, Transport Div. Ellerman Lines Ltd. since 1973. *Address:* Applegarth, 24 Eastgate, Hornsea, North Humberside HU18 1DP.

**BAYULKEN, Umit Haluk.** Turkish Diplomat. *B.* 1921. *Educ.* Lycée of Haydarpasa, Istanbul (Graduated 1938–39) and Faculty of Political Science, Univ. of Ankara (Grad. 1942–43). *M.* Valihe Salci. *S.* Orhan. *Dau.* Handan. *Career:* Joined Ministry of Foreign Affairs as Third Secretary 1944; Vice-Consul, Frankfurt/Main July 1947; First Secy. of Legation at Bonn Mission, then Embassy Sept. 1950; Director Middle East Section, Min. of Foreign Affairs Oct. 1951; Adviser to Turkish Delegation at 7th Session of U.N. Gen. Assembly, Sept.–Dec. 1952; First Secy. of Legation at Turkish Permanent Mission to U.N., New York, Sept. 1953; First Secy. of Embassy, March 1954; promoted Counsellor, Turkish Permanent Mission to U.N. Aug. 1957; Turkish Representative at London Joint Committee on Cyprus 1959–60; Dir.-General, Policy Planning Group, Ankara 1960–63; Min. Plen. 1963; Deputy Secy.-General for Political Affairs 1963; First

Class Min. Plen. 1964; Secy.-General with rank of Ambassador 1964–66; Leader of Turkish Delegation at Meeting of Foreign Ministers for Second Afro-Asian Conf., Algiers, June 1965, and of the Delegation which paid an official visit to the U.A.R., March 1966; Member of Turkish Delegation to U.N. General Assembly meetings 1952–65, and of other conferences. Ambassador of Turkey to the Court of St. James's 1966–July 1969. Ambassador of Turkey to Malta, 1968–69; Permanent Representative of Turkey to the United Nations 1969–71: Minister of Foreign Affairs of Turkey 1971–74; Sec.-Gen., Cen. Treaty Org. 1975; Appointed to the President of the Republic's Office, Presidential Sec.-Gen. July 1977. Lecturer, Faculty of Political Sciences, University of Ankara, on International Disputes; Honorary Governor, School of Oriental and African Studies, London; Hon. Member, Mexican Academy of International Law. *Awards:* Order of Isabel la Catolica (Spain); Grand Cross, Order of Merit (Germany); G.C.V.O.; Pakistan, Sitara, Pakistan; Afghanistan Sirdar Ali; Star of the First Order (Jordon); Tunisia —1973; United Arab Republic—1973 *Publications:* numerous lectures, articles, studies and essays on subject of minorities, on Cyprus and on international relations and disputes, including: The Cyprus Question and the UN (1975); Collective Security & Defence Organizations in Changing World Conditions (1976). *Clubs:* Travellers, Hurlingham, St. James's, R.A.C., A.A. *Address:* Cumhurbaskanligi, Genel Sekreteri, Cankaya-Ankara, Turkey.

**BAZELON, David Lionel.** American judge. *B.* 3 Sept. 1909. *Educ.* Northwestern University (BSL). *M.* 1936, Miriam M. Kellner. *S.* James A., Richard Lee. *Career:* In law practice since 1932; Private Practice 1933–35; Asst. United States Attorney for Northern District of Illinois 1935–40; senior member, firm of Gottlieb and Schwartz 1940–46; Assistant Attorney-General, U.S. Lands Division 1946–47, Office of Alien Property 1947–49; Circuit Judge 1949—; Chief Judge 1962—; Lecturer in Law, University of Pennsylvania Law School 1957–58; Sloan Visiting Professor in Psychiatry, Johns Hopkins Univ. School of Medicine 1964—; Clinical Prof. of Psychiatry (Socio-legal Aspects), George Washington Univ. 1966—. *Member:* Menninger Foundation, Topeka, Kansas, 1961; President's Panel on Mental Retardation 1961–62; Member, U.S. Mission on Mental Health to USSR 1967; Bd. of Directors, Orthopsychiatric Assn. (President-Elect. 1968–69); Joint Commission on Mental Health of Children Inc. (Board Directors); Salk Inst. for Biological Studies (Bd. Trustees); Model School Div., D.C. Public Schools (Chmn. Adv. Cttee. 1964–66); Public Health Service, Nat. Advisory Mental Health Cncl. 1967—; Chmn. Adv. Bd. Boston Univ. Center for Law & Health Sciences, 1970. *Awards:* Isaac Ray Award from the American Psychiatric Association 1960; Hon. LLD Colby Coll. 1966; Boston Univ. Law School 1969; Albert Einstein Coll. of Medicine, Yestuva Univ. 1972; N. Western Univ. 1974; Univ. of Southern California 1977. Fellow Academy of Arts & Sciences, Boston, Mass. 1970. *Address: office* U.S. Court of Appeals, Washington, D.C., U.S.A.

**BAZY, Pierre.** French. *B.* 1919. *Educ.* BA (Law); BA, Ecole des Sciences Politiques. *M.* 1946, Angèle Luquet. *S.* Jean-Louis, Laurent and Dominique. *Career:* Envoy to the Bank of France 1944–45; and to the French Embassy in Argentina 1946–47; Director and then Director-General (Asst.) Banque Hoskier 1947–61. Administrator of the Insurance Companies: Chmn. Populaire Vie. General Manager, Banque Worms. *Club:* St. Cloud Country. *Address:* 17 rue de Constantine, Paris 7e; and *office* 45 Boulevard Haussmann, Paris 9e.

**BAZZI, Fausto.** Commander, Order of Merit of the Italian Republic. Industrialist. *B.* 1909 (*S.* of Capt. Carlo B—. Military Gold Medal 1916). *Educ.* Senior High School. Catering School Diploma. *Career:* Pres. Vikitalia S.p.A. associated with Viking Engineering Co. Ltd. President: S.I.A.M., Hotel du Lac et du Parc, Riva del Garda 1955. *Clubs:* Diners'. *Address:* Fausto Bazzi, Via Visconti di Modrone n 19, Italy.

**BEACH, Earl Francis.** Canadian; Professor of Economics, *B.* 1912. *Educ.* Queens Univ., Kingston, Ont. (BA); Harvard Univ., Cambridge, Mass. (AM, PhD). *M.* 1938, Katharine MacAdam. *S.* Charles. *Dau.* Elizabeth. *Career:* Professor of Economics McGill Univ. since 1940. *Member:* Canadian Political Science Assn.; American Economic Assn.; Econometric Society: Royal Economic Society; American Statistical Association. *Publications:* Economic Models (Wiley, N.Y. 1957); articles and reviews in professional journals. *Address:* McGill University, Montreal P.Q., Canada.

**BEADLE, Rt. Hon. Sir Thomas Hugh William;** PC, CMG, OBE, QC, GCOGPh. Southern Rhodesian judge. *B.* 6 Feb. 1905. *Educ.* Avondale School; Salisbury Boys High School; Diocesan Coll., Rondesbosch; Univ. of Cape Town (BA, LLB); Oxford Univ. (BCL); Hon. Fellow, Queens Coll., Oxford. *M.* 1934, Leonie Barry (*D.* 1953). *M.* (2) 1954, Olive S. Jackson. *Daus.* 2. *Career:* M.P. (United Party) for Bulawayo North 1939, 1946 and 1948; Captain, Gold Coast Regiment 1939–40; Parliament Secretary to Prime Minister 1940; Major, D.J.A.G., Southern Rhodesia 1942–46; Vice-President, United Party 1945; Minister of Internal Affairs, Justice, Health and Education 1946–50; Judge High Court, Southern Rhodesia since 1950; (Chief Justice 1961—). Chairman, Rhodesia Soc. for Blind and Physically Unfit; President, S. Rhodesian Nat. Hunters Assn. and of S. Rhodesian National Anglers Union; St. Giles Rehabilitation Centre, Salisbury; member, S. Rhodesian National Park Board; Chairman, S. Rhodesian Boy Scout Council. *Address:* Box 579, High Court, Bulawayo, Southern Rhodesia.

**BEADLE, Walter J.** American business executive (retired). *B.* 24 Feb. 1896. *Educ.* Massachusetts Institute of Technology (SB 1917). *M.* 1922, Christine S. Spofford. *S.* Spofford Jay. *Daus.* Sarah Spofford (Wolff), and Elizabeth Ocumpaugh (Herrmann); served as 2nd Lieut., Infantry, U.S. Army, in World War I. *Career:* with National Aniline & Chemical Co., 1917 and 1920; traffic engineer, Philadelphia Rapid Transit Co. 1921–24 (transportation manager 1925–27); joined E. I. du Pont de Nemours & Co. 1928; Asst.-Director Development Dept. 1929–41; Asst.-Treasurer 1942–46; Treasurer 1946–48; member Exec. Cttee. 1948–58; Vice-Pres. 1946–58, Director 1946–75; Director, Philadelphia National Bank 1950–70; Trustee, University of Delaware 1951–71; Life Member, Corporation, Massachusetts Institute of Technology, Cambridge, Mass. 1951—; Trustee, National Industrial Conference Board 1958–64. *Address:* Kendal at Longwood, Box 217, Kennett Square, Penna; 19348, U.S.A.

**BEALE, The Hon. Sir Howard,** KBE, QC. Australian Barrister-at-Law, Diplomat, and Company Director. *B.* 1898. *Educ.* Univ. of Sydney (BA; LLB). *M.* 1927, Margery Ellen Wood. *S.* Julian. *Career:* Called to N.S.W. Bar and High Court of Australia 1925 and practised until appointed to Cabinet 1949. Served as officer in Royal Australian Navy 1942–45. Liberal M.P. for Parramatta 1946–58. Member, Commonwealth Parliamentary Public Works Committee 1947–49; Australian Delegate, International Bar Congress, The Hague 1948; K.C. 1950; Appointed Cabinet Minister in Menzies Government 1949; Minister for Information and Minister of Transport 1949–50; Minister for Supply and Defence Production and Minister in Charge of Australian Aluminium Production Commission and of Australian Atomic Energy Commission 1950–58; Member: Australian Defence Council, Cabinet Cttee. on Uranium and Atomic Energy 1950–58; Acting Minister for Immigration 1951–52, 1953 and 1954; for National Development 1952–53; for Air 1952; and for Defence 1957. Ambassador to U.S.A. 1957–64. Australian Delegate Anzus Council, Washington 1958 and 1959 and Canberra 1962. Leader, Australian Delegation to Colombo Plan Conference, Seattle 1958; Deputy Leader, Australian Delegation to U.N., New York 1959; Deputy Leader and later leader, Australian Delegation to Antarctic Conference, Washington 1959; Australian Delegate to SEATO Conference, Washington 1959 and 1960; Alternate Governor of International Monetary Fund 1960, 1962 and 1964; Leader, Australian Delegation, World Food Congress, Washington 1963; Hon. LLD, Kent University, Ohio 1959; Honorary DHLit; Nebraska Wesleyan Univ. 1962; Hon. LLD Marquette Univ. 1969; Woodward Lecturer, Yale Univ. 1960; Regents' Vis. Professor: Univ. of Calif. 1966 and Marquette Univ., Wis., 1967 and 1969. Cr. KBE 1961. Dean of the British Commonwealth Diplomatic Corps in Washington 1961–64. Director: Occidental Mining Corp.; Oil Basins Ltd. (Chmn.); Weeks Petroleum Ltd. (Chmn.); Engelhard Industries Ltd.; Seltrust Iron Ore Pty. Ltd.; Pacific Australia (LNG) Pty. Ltd.; Pres., Arts Council of Australia 1964–66; Former Minister of State and Member Commonwealth Parliament. *Clubs:* Union; Australasian Pioneers' (Pres. 1964–66). *Address:* 1/4 Marathon Road, Darling Point, 2027, Sydney, N.S.W., Australia.

**BEALE, Hon. Jack Gordon.** Australian. *B.* 1917. *Educ.* Univ. of N.S.W. (ME) and Sydney Technical College (ASTC Mech. Eng.-Hons.). *M.* 1958, Stephanie Toth-Dobrzanski. *S.* 2. *Career:* Member, Legislative Assembly, New South Wales 1942–73; Consulting Engineer (own practice) 1943–65 (in civil, mechanical, agricultural and production engineering);

Chmn. The Water Research Foundation, Australia 1955—; Minister for Conservation, State of New South Wales, May 1965–71; Minister for Environment Control 1971–73; International Consultant (own practice) since 1973, in Environment, Conservation, Resources, Engineering, Planning & Management; Sen. Adviser to UN Environment Pgme since 1974. *Member:* Instn. of Engineers of Australia; Amer. Socy. of Civil Engineers; Amer. Socy. of Mechanical Engineers; Amer. Socy. of Agricultural Engineers. Member Liberal Party of Australia. *Address:* 95 Elizabeth Bay Rd. Elizabeth Bay, Sydney, NSW 2011. Australia.

**BEALE, Richard Christopher.** British. *B.* 1935. *Educ.* Downside School 1949–53. *M* 1962, Anne Patricia Bride. *S.* Giles William Kirwan. *Daus.* Camilla Frances and Sarah Louise. *Career:* Director, Key Markets Ltd. Ilford, Essex 1959—; Man. Dir., David Greig Division; Chairman, Green's Stores Trust Ltd. *Member:* Institute of Grocery Distribution; Institute of Directors; British Inst. of Management. *Club:* City Livery Conservative. *Address:* Magdalen Laver Hall, Ongar, Essex; and *office* Key Markets Ltd., Hope Farm, 320 New North Road, Ilford, Essex.

**BEALE, Sir William Francis, OBE.** British company director. *B.* 1908. *Educ.* Downside School; Pembroke College, Cambridge (MA). *M.* 1934, Deva Zaloudek. *S.* 1. *Dau.* 1. Director: Randalls Group Ltd., NCR Co. Ltd. *Address:* The Grange, All Cannings, Devizes, Wilts.

**BEALE, Wilson Thomas Moore.** American foreign service officer. *B.* 1909. *Educ.* Princeton Univ. (AB 1931); Univ. of Pennsylvania (MBA 1933); London School of Economics 1933–35; National War College 1948–49. *M.* 1944, Rita Williams (*Div.* 1969). *Career:* Economist, U.S. Tariff Commission 1936–42: Lieut.-Commander (Overseas), United States Navy 1942–45; Department of State 1946–67. Successively Minister for Economic Affairs, American Embassy, London; Dep. Asst. Secy. of State for Administration, Washington, D.C. Retired American Ambassador to Jamaica; Administrator, Washington Cathedral Foundation, 1969–73. *Club:* University, Washington, D.C. *Address:* Route 2 Box 314, Martinsburg West Va, 25401, U.S.A.

**BEAM, Jacob D.** American diplomat. *B.* 1908. *Educ.* Princeton Univ. (BA). *M.* Margaret Glassford. *S.* Jacob Alexander. *Career:* Deputy Asst. Secretary of State for European Affairs, 1953–57; Asst. Dir., U.S. Arms Control and Disarmament Agency, 1962–66; Ambassador: to Warsaw, 1957–62; to Czechoslovakia 1966–69, to the Soviet Union 1969–73. *Member:* Inter-Telecomm. Union Plenipot. Conf. Malaga. *Address:* 3129 "O" Street, N.W. Washington, D.C., 2007 and c/o Department of State, Washington, D.C. 20521, U.S.A.

**BEAN, Sir Edgar (Layton), CMG.** British barrister and solicitor. *B.* 1893. *Educ.* Universities of Adelaide (BA 1913) and Oxford (MA 1922). *M.* 1926, Constance Mary Greenlees. *S.* 2. *Career:* Parliamentary Draftsman, South Australia 1926–58; Chairman, Teachers Salaries Board 1946–64; Police Appeal Board 1951–67; previously Chairman, Local Government Commission 1929–34; member, South Australian Public Service Board 1942–51; Chairman, Education Enquiry Committee 1944–46; Director, Southern Television Corp. Ltd. 1959–70; News Ltd. 1960–70. *Publication:* South Australian Statutes 1837–1936 (with notes). *Address:* 51 Godfrey Terrace, Leabrook, South Australia.

**BEAN, Walter Alexander, CBE, ED, CD.** Canadian executive. *B.* 1908. *Educ.* Univ. of Toronto (BComm). *M.* 1934, Eleanore E. Fearman (Dec.). *S.* Douglas A. and W. Donald. *Career:* Various offices, Waterloo Trust & Savings Co. 1930–71, merged with Canada Trust Co.; Dir. Dominion Electrohome Industries Ltd. 1956—; Mutual Life Assurance Co. of Canada 1958—; Chmn. Economical Mutual Ins. Co. 1961—. Deputy Chairman. Vice-President and Director, The Canada Trust Co. and The Huron and Erie Mortgage Corp. 1968—; Chmn., Missisquoi & Rouville Ins. Co.; Central Ontario Television Co. since 1972; Chmn., Perth Ins. Co. 1973; Dir. Oxford Development Group Ltd. 1975. *Member:* Trust Companies Assn. of Canada (Past Pres.); Conservative. *Clubs:* Toronto, Muskoka Lakes; Westmount Golf; Rotary. *Address:* 238 Stanley Drive, Waterloo, Ont.; and *office* 305 King Street West, Kitchener, Ont., Canada.

**BEANE, Alpheus C.** American investment banker. *B.* 1910. *Educ.* Yale Univ. (BSc 1931). *M.* (1) 1938, Jean A. Tedger (*Div.* 1956), and (2) 1956, Elizabeth M. Geren. *S.* Alpheus C. Jr. *Daus.* Mary C. and Marian E. *Career:* General Partner, Fenner & Beane 1931–41, and Merril Lynch Pierce Fenner & Beane 1941–58; Served to Major USAAF 1942–45; Directing Partner, Chairman of Board, Chief Executive Officer, J. R. Williston & Beane 1958–63; Vice-Pres. and Dir. Walston and Co. 1963–64; Gen. Partner and Mem. Exec. Cttee Reynolds and Co. 1965–71; Vice-Pres. and Mem. Exec. Cttee. Reynolds Securities Inc. since 1971; Board of Managers, New York Cocoa Exchange 1958–60; Pres. Commodity Club, NY, 1952–53; Gov. Wool Assn. NY, Cotton Exchange 1952–53. *Member:* Bd. Govs. Am. Stock Exchange 1938–42; *Clubs:* Stock Exchange Lunch; Round Hill; Yale. *Address: office* 120 Broadway, New York, U.S.A.

**BEARD, Geoffrey Grinsell.** Retired Industrialist. *B.* 1904. *Educ.* Merchiston Castle School, Edinburgh (Scotland) and The Univ. of Strathclyde (BSc Hons); Glasgow, Scotland *M.* 1930, Gwedoline Amy Love. *Daus.* Marjorie Mary, Marcia May, and Madeline Macdonald. *Career:* Research Engineer, Ministry of Mines, London 1926–27; successively Engineer, Manager of Proposal Dept., Vice-President, Executive Vice-President, President, United Engineering & Foundry Co. 1927–64; Director, Continental Steel Co., Kokomo, Inc. 1950–55; Pittsburgh National Bank 1955–70; Sundstrand Corp., Rockford, Ill., 1965–69; Vice-Pres., Machinery & Allied Products Inst., U.S.A., 1959–69; Chairman: United Engineering & Foundry Co., Pittsburgh, Pa. since 1950, Chmn. 1964–69; Adamson United Co., Akron, O. 1959—; Stedman Foundry & Machine Co., Autora, Inc. 1959–69; and Unefcan Ltd., Toronto 1962–69; Wean United, Inc., Warren, Ohio since 1968; Director, Pittsburgh Regional Planning Assoc., Vice-Pres. Health Research & Services Foundation. U.S.A. Trustee, Episcopal Diocese of Pittsburgh, Pa.; Pres. Amer. Ordnance Assn. (Ptsbg. Chapter). Recipient, Montgomery Neilson Gold Medal (Royal College of Science & Technology), and James Reilly Medal (West of Scotland Iron & Steel Institute); Fellow American Soc. of Mechanical Engineers. Republican. *Clubs:* Merchistonian (Edinburgh). *Address:* 107 Driving Tee Circle, South Yarmouth, Mass 02664, U.S.A.; *office* 948 Fort Duquesne Boulevard, Pittsburgh 22, Pa., U.S.A.

**BEARDSLEY, J. Hartness.** American. *B.* 1914. *Educ.* Dartmouth College (BA). *M.* 1937, Margaret Whitcomb. *S.* Christopher, William and Anthony. *Dau.* Anne Katherine. *Career:* Pres. Bryant Chucking Grinder Co., Springfield, Vt. 1955–59. Director, Rock of Ages Corporation (Barre, Vt. and Stanstead, Quebec) 1960–69; Pres. Gen. Mgr. Twin Falls Power Co. Ltd., St. John's Nfld. 1960–66; Dir. Pres. and Gen. Mgr. Bowater Power Co. Ltd. 1966–75; Pres. Bowater Power Co. Ltd. 1975–77; Pres. and Gen. Man. Bowaters Newfoundland Ltd., Corner Brook, Newfoundland; Dir. Bowater Incorporated, Old Greenwich, Connecticut 1972–77. *Member:* Engineering Inst. of Canada; Dir., Canadian Electrical Assn.; Dir., International Grenfell Association for Newfoundland. Newfoundland. Arctic Inst. of North America. *Club:* University (Montreal). *Address:* Blue Hill, Maine, 04614, U.S.A.

**BEARDSLEY, Walter Raper.** American drugs and chemical expert. *B.* 1905. *Educ.* Princeton Univ. (BS in Politics, Hons. 1928). *M.* 1929, Mariory Buchanan. *S.* Robert B. *Career:* Vice-Pres. 1933–47, Pres. 1947–61, Miles Laboratories Inc. Three and a half years with U.S.A.F. 1942–45 (rank of Lieut.-Colonel at end of service); Dir. Miles Laboratories Inc., Elkhardt. Ind. since 1933. Chmn. of Board 1961–73, Chmn., Finance Cttee. 1973–76, Director Emeritus, First National Bank; Dir., Truth Publishing Co.; President, Board of Trustees, Elkhart General Hospital. Republican National Committeeman from Indiana 1961–68; Art Gallery Advisory Council; University of Notre Dame. National Chmn. Republican Congressional Boosters Club. Washington 1971–74; Benjamin Franklin Fellow, Royal Society of Arts, London, England; The Indiana Academy. *Clubs:* Elcona Country, (Elkhart); Princeton (Chicago); Sky, University (both N.Y.C.); Capitol Hill (Washington, D.C.). *Address:* 2233 Greenleaf Boulevard, Elkhart, Ind.; and *office* Miles Laboratories Inc., 1127 Myrtle Street, Elkhart, Ind., U.S.A.

**BEARSTED, Viscount (Marcus Richard Samuel).** British banker. *B.* 1909. *Educ.* Eton; New College, Oxford. *M.* (1) 1947, Elizabeth Heather Firmston-Williams (*m. diss.* 1966); *Dau.* 1. *M.* (2) 1968, Jean Agnew Somerville (née Wallace). *Career:* Served in World War II in Warwickshire Yeomanry (Major) in Middle East and Italy; Chairman (1946–66) and director, Hill, Samuel Group Ltd. (on merger with Philip Hill, Higginson, Erlangers Ltd. on 1 Apr. 1965); Chmn., Samuel Properties Ltd. and sub co's. 1961; Chmn., Hill Samuel & Co. (Jersey) Ltd. 1962; Chmn. Negit S.A. 1970; Director, Sun, Alliance & London Insurance Group 1949—; Lloyds Bank Ltd. 1963—; and other companies. *Address:*

Upton House, Banbury, Oxon. OX15 6HT; and 1 Eaton Close, London, S.W.1.

**BEATTIE, Corrie Pool,** CBE. *B.* 1918. *Educ.* Beckenham School England. *M.* 1956, Louise Grace Beckett. *Daus.* 3. *Career:* in British Army, India England, Burma World War II; arrived Thailand 1947; Chmn. Loxley (Bangkok) Ltd. 1962; Chmn. Castrol (Thailand) Ltd. 1972; Chmn. Thanakorn Aluminium (Loxley-Comalco) Ltd. 1974. Former member Royal Thai Air Force Flying Club. *Clubs:* Royal Automobile (London); Royal Bangkok Sports; Royal Varuna Yacht. *Address:* Loxley Building, 304 Suapa Road, G.P.O. Box 214 Bangkok 1, Thailand.

**BEATTIE, John Robert.** Canadian banker and economist. *B.* 1910. *Educ.* University of Manitoba (BA); Oxford University (BA Hons). *M.* (1) 1937, Katharine Ellen McIntyre (*D.* 1960), (2) 1964, Mary Angus Rogers. *Daus.* Peggy, Joan, Barbara, Elisabeth. *Career:* With Manufacturers Life Insurance Co. 1933; joined Bank of Canada 1935 (Deputy Chief, Research Department 1940; Chief 1944; Executive Assistant to Governors 1950); Senior Deputy Governor since 1955–72; Retired 1972, Economical and Financial Consultant since 1972. *Address:* RR 2 Mountain, Ontario, Canada.

**BEATTIE, Robert Wilson.** British. *B.* 1928. *Educ.* Alsop High Sch.; Liverpool Tech. Coll. *M.* 1955, Maureen. *Daus.* 2. *Career:* Head of Physics Laboratories, Automatic Telephones & Electric Co. Ltd. 1960–63; Exec. Dir. Telephone Mfg. Co. Ltd. 1964–65; Man. Dir. Electrosil Ltd. 1965–70; Chmn. Miniature Electronic Components Ltd. 1968–70; Chmn. Common Metals Ltd.; Armead Eng. Ltd.; R. W. Beattie and Co. *Address:* Springfield, Lower Dicker, Hailsham, Sussex BN27 4BT.

**BEATTY, A. Chester.** British company director. *B.* 17 Oct. 1907. *Educ.* Eton; Trin. College, Cambridge (MA). *M.* (1) 1933, Pamela Belas (marriage dissolved 1936). *Dau.* Sarah; (2) 1937, Enid Groome (marriage dissolved 1950), (3) 1953, Helen Casalis de Pury. *Career:* Joined Selection Trust Group of Companies, London 1931; served as Managing Director of Selection Trust Ltd. 1937–50; Chairman since 1950; Chairman, Vice-Chairman or Director of other companies in Selection Trust Group and associated companies. *Address:* Owley, Wittersham, Kent.

**BEATTY, William Harrison, Jr.** American. *B.* 1917. *Educ.* Indiana University. *M.* 1945, Emily Louise Rydeen. *S.* William III and Charles. *Dau.* Anna. *Career:* Commander U.S. Naval Reserve 1951. Vice-President: Area Exec. for Africa, Chase Manhattan Bank 1960–73, and of Chase Manhattan Overseas Banking Corp. 1960–73; Special Consultant on Africa in London since 1973. *Awards:* Grand Commander, Order of Star of Africa (Liberia); Commander, National Order, Ivory Coast. *Member:* American Society of Naval Engineers; Episcopalian; Democrat; President, African Affairs Society Ltd.; Vice-President, African American Chamber of Commerce and Nigerian American Chamber of Commerce; Army, Navy Club (Washington). *Clubs:* British Luncheon (N.Y.C.); Camp Fire Club of America; American Club, London. *Address:* 2903 Buckingham Road, Durham, North Carolina 27707, U.S.A.

**BEAUDET, Guy.** Canadian. Pres., Guy Beaudet & Associés Inc. since 1976 *B.* 1911. *Educ.* Bachelor of Arts; Bachelor in Applied Sciences; Professional Engineer. *M.* 1940, Andrée Leblond de Brumath. *S.* Alain. *Dau.* Marie-Christine. *Career:* Managing Engineer, City of Thetford Mines 1938–41; with Royal Canadian Engineers overseas 1941–45 Manager, Central Mortgage and Housing Corp., Montreal 1946; Asst. Director, Port of Montreal 1947–54, Port Manager 1954–71; Member National Harbours Board 1971–73, Vice Chmn. 1973–76; Pres., Guy Beaudet & Associés Inc. since 1976. *Member:* Corporation of Professional Engineers of Quebec; Engineering Inst. of Canada (Life mem.); Canadian Military Engineers Assn. (Life mem.); Association des diplomés de Polytechnique; Amer. Assn. of Port Authorities. (Pres. 1968); International Assn. of Ports & Harbours. *Clubs:* Naval Officers (Montreal); Grunt (Life mem.), Montreal. *Address:* 635 Powell Avenue, Town of Mount Royal, P.Q.; and *office* Guy Beandet & Associés Inc., Consultants, Lavalin Group, 1130 Sherbrooke St. West. Montreal H3A 2R5, P.Q., Canada.

**BEAULIEU, Paul André,** Q.C. Canadian diplomat. *B.* 1913. *Educ.* Univ. of Montreal (BA, LLL 1936). *M.* 1942, Simone Aubry. *S.* Louis Emery. *Dau.* Marie Simone. *Career:* Member of the Bar 1937; practised law with Beaulieu, Gouin, Tellier and Bourdon, Montreal 1938–40: joined Dept. of External Affairs as Third Secretary 1940; Third Secretary, Washington, Apr. 1944; Second Secretary, Oct. 1944; Second Secretary, Paris, Sept. 1945; Created Q.C. 1947. Consul, Boston, Mar. 1949; Ottawa, Oct. 1951; Counsellor, London, July 1954; Chargé d'Affaires a.i., Lebanon, Apr. 1958. Ambassador to Lebanon 1958–64, and Iraq, 1961–64; Ambassador to Brazil 1964; Assoc. Permanent Rep. and Ambassador, United Nations (New York) 1967; Ambassador to France 1968, and to Portugal 1970. *Publications:* Jacques Rivière; Katherine Mansfield contributor of articles to various periodicals in Canada and in France. Fellow, Royal Society of Canada. *Club:* Cercle Universitaire (Ottawa). *Address:* c/o Department of External Affairs, Ottawa, Canada.

**BEAULNE, Yvon.** Canadian foreign service officer. *B.* 1919. *Educ.* BA—Licentiate in Philosophy. *M.* 1946, Therese Pratte. *S.* François, Pierre, Leonard and Gilles. *Dau.* Louise. *Career:* With Canadian Army 1942–46. In Canadian Diplomatic Service: served in Rome 1949–52; Buenos Aires 1956–59; Cuba 1960; Ambassador to Brazil, Sept. 1967. Ambassador of Canada to Venezuela, Dec. 1961–64; Minister at Washington 1964. Ambassador and Permanent Representive of Canada to the United Nations 1969–72; Asst. Sec. of State 1972–74; Dir.-Gen., Bureau of African & Middle Eastern Affairs, Dept. of Ext. Affairs 1974–76; Perm. Delegate to UNESCO, since 1976. *Address:* Permanent Delegation of Canada to UNESCO, 1 rue Miollis, Paris XVe, France.

**BEAUMONT, Sir Richard Ashton,** KCMG, OBE. British Dir. General Middle East Association. *B.* 1912. *Educ.* Repton and Oriel College, Oxford (BA). *M.* 1942, Alou Camran. *Dau.* Carolyn Anne. *Career:* H.M. Consular Service 1936; served with H.M. Forces 1940–45; Foreign Office 1945–46 and 1949–50; Embassy, Caracas, Venezuela 1950–53; Embassy, Baghdad 1953–57; Imperial Defence College 1958; Head of Arabian Dept., Foreign Office 1959–61; Ambassador to Morocco 1961–65; Ambassador to Iraq 1965–67; Deputy Under Secretary, Foreign Office 1967–69; Ambassador to Egypt 1969–73. *Club:* Oxford & Cambridge (London). *Address:* Middle East Association, 33 Bury Street, St. James's, London, S.W.1 and 14 Cadogan Square, S.W.1.

**BEAUMONT OF WHITLEY, The Rt. Hon. Lord Timothy Wentworth,** MA. British politician and journalist. *B.* 1928, *Educ.* Gordonstoun; Christ Church, Oxford Master of (Arts). *M.* 1955, Mary Rose Wauchope. *S.* Hubert Wentworth and Alaric Charles Blackett. *Daus.* Atlanta Armstrong and Ariadne Grace. *Career:* Joint Hon. Treas. Liberal Party Organization, 1962–63; Chmn. Lib. Publications Dept. 1963–64; Head Lib. Party Organization 1965–66; Chmn. Lib. Organising Cttee. 1966–67; Chmn. Liberal Party, 1967–68 and President, 1969–70; Liberal spokesman, Education, 1971–73; Editor New Outlook 1972–74; Chmn. Gen. Election Cttee. 1974; Lib. Mem. Parly. Assemblies Council of Europe and W. European Union since 1975, Leader Liberal Delegation since 1977. *Clubs:* Beefsteak; National Liberal. *Address:* 1 Hampstead Square, London, N.W.3.

**BEAUPAIN, Jacques.** Belgian company director. *B.* 1909. *Educ.* Civil Engineer. *M.* 1934, Louise Delrez. *Daus.* 3. *Career:* Man. Dir., Establissements Beaupain, Liège, since 1938. Decorations include the 1940 Campaign and the Red Cross. *Publications:* of various publications concerning mining engineering. *Member:* Association of Engineers of Liège; Royal Society of Engineers and Industrialists, Brussels. *Club:* Cercle Gaulois (Brussels). *Address:* 111 Avenue Franklin Roosevelt, Brussels 5; and *office* 105 Rue de Serbie, Liège, Belgium.

**BEAUPERE, Louis Henri,** D. en D. Franch banker. *B.* 23 Dec. 1901. *M.* 1930, Madeleine Biosse Duplan. *S.* Dominique. *Daus.* Marie-Ange, Bernadette. *Career:* Dir.-Gen. (Hon.), Société Générale pour favoriser le Développement du Commerce et de l'Idustrie en France; Officer de la Légion d'Honneur; Croix de Guerre. *Address:* 15, rue Albéric Magnard, **Paris 16.**

**BEAUREPAIRE, Ian Francis,** CMG. Australian. Lord Mayor of Melbourne 1965–67. *B.* 1922. *Educ.* Scotch College (Melbourne) and Royal Melbourne Institute of Technology (Diploma of Industrial Management). *M.* 1946, Beryl E. Bedggood. *S.* 2. *Career:* World War II: R.A.A.F. Flying Officer. Mng. Director, Beaurepaire Tyre Service Pty. Ltd. 1953–55; General Manager, The Olympic Tyre & Rubber Co. Pty. Ltd. 1955–61: Member Melbourne City Council 1956–75. Chairman and Chief Executive, Olympic Consolidated Industries Ltd. 1959—; Member: Management Committee, Royal

Victorian Eye & Ear Hospital 1966— and of Exhibition Trustees 1967–75; Fellow Australian Institute of Management. *Clubs:* Melbourne, Athenaeum, Naval & Military, Peninsula Country Golf. *Address:* 124 Powlett Street, East Melbourne, Victoria, 3002; and *office* P.O. Box 1, West Footscray, Vic. 3012, Australia.

**BECH-BRUUN, Helge (Eli).** Danish lawyer. *B.* 1901. *M.* Lis Møller. *Daus.* 3. *Career:* Barrister at the Supreme Court of Justice. Member, Board of Directors: Scandinavian Airlines System, The East Asiatic Company's Holding Co. Ltd. A/S Kampsax; Chmn. Bd. Dirs.: A/S Kjøbenhavns Handelsbank, and Assurance-Compagniet BALTICA A/S.; A/S Datsun, Denmark; A/S S. Dyrup & Co. A/S Codan Gummi; A/S SAAB–SCANIA, Denmark; A/S ATLAS-COPCO, Denmark. *Address:* 2 Kirkevej, Rungsted Kyst, Denmark; and *office* 3 Nr. Farimagsgade, Copenhagen K.

**BECHERER, Robert Charles.** Machinery manufacturing executive *B.* 1902. *Educ.* Purdue Univ. (BS in Chem. Eng. 1923). *M.* 1930, Nell R. Norton. *Daus.* Nell J. (Smith) and Marjorie E. (Sterrett, Jr.). *Career:* With Link-Belt Co. 1923—. Vice-Pres. and Gen. Manager, Ewart Plant, Indianapolis 1949–51, Exec. President 1952–65; Chairman of the Board & Director, Link-Belt Co., Chicago, Mar. 1965—. Chairman of Board & Director of all Link-Belt Divisions and subsidiaries: Detroit Power Screw-driver Co., Detroit; Link-Belt Speeder Corp., Cedar Rapids, Ia.; Link-Belt Ltd., Toronto; Syntron Co., Homer City, Pa.; Link-Belt S.A., Geneva, Switzerland; Link-Belt Africa Ltd., Johannesburg; Link-Belt Mexicana S.A. de C.V., Mexico City. Director, Continental Illinois National Bank & Trust Co., Chicago; Hon. D. Eng., Purdue Univ., and Rose Polytechnic Inst. *Member:* Illinois Manufacturers Assn.; Exec. Cttee., Illinois Inst. of Technology, Machinery and Allied Products Inst. Republican. *Clubs:* Chicago, University, Mid-America, Westmoreland Country; Delta Tau Delta; Phi Lambda Upsilon; Tau Beta Pi. *Address:* 750 Sheridan Road, Winnetka, Ill.; and *office* 1700 Prudential Plaza, Chicago 1, Ill., U.S.A.

**BECHTEL, Stephen Davison.** American engineer-constructor. *B.* 1900. *Educ.* University of California; Hon. LLD, University of California (1954) and Loyola University (1958); Hon. D. Engrg., Univ. of the Pacific (1966); Beta Theta Pi. *M.* 1923, Laura Adaline Peart. *S.* Stephen Davison, Jr. *Dau.* Barbara (Davies, Jr.). *Career:* Registered professional engineer (State of Calif.). Served in World War I (20th Engineers, U.S. Army in France). In general construction business with father. Warren A. Bechtel; Vice-Pres., W. A. Bechtel Co. 1925–36; 1st Vice-Pres., Dir., Six Companies Inc. (constructors of Hoover Dam) 1931–35; co-organizer and Dir., Bechtel-McCone Corp. 1937–46. During World War II was Chmn., California Shipbuilding Corp. (Wilmington, Calif.) and Dir., Marinship Corp. (Sausalito, Calif.); Senior Director, Bechtel Corp.; President and Director, Lakeside Corp. Director: Industrial Indemnity Co., Southern Pacific Co., and Canadian Bechtel Ltd. *Member:* Pres. Eisenhower's Advisory Committee on a National Highway Programme 1954–55; Business Advisory Council for Dept. of Commerce 1950–60 (Chmn. 1958–59); The Business Council 1961— (Graduate Member); Directors Advisory Council and International Council, Morgan Guaranty Trust Co. of N.Y.; Senior Member, National Industrial Conference Board; Chmn. (1961–63) and Trustee, San Francisco Bay Area Council 1946—; Dir., Stanford Research Institute 1949—; Member: World Affairs Council of Northern California; Calif. Institute of Technology Associates. Achievement Award of Building Industry Conference Board, San Francisco 1951; The Moles Award for Outstanding Achievement in Construction 1952; Alumni Association Award, Alumnus of the Year 1952, Univ. of Calif.; Order of the Cedar (Lebanon) 1956; Forbes Magazine Award (one of America's Fifty Foremost Business Leaders) 1957; National Defence Transportation Award 1960; John Fritz Medal and Certificate 1961; Golden Beaver Award for Management, 1963. *Member:* Amer. Society of Civil Engineers; Society of Amer. Military Engineers; Amer. Petroleum Inst.; Consulting Constructors' Council of America; The Beavers; The Moles; Society of Naval Architects and Marine Engineers. Mason (32°), Shriner, Methodist, Republican. *Clubs:* San Francisco: Bohemian; Pacific-Union; Stock Exchange, Commonwealth; Engineers'. New York City: Brook; Links; Pinnacle; River; Fifth Avenue; Cloud; Sky; Blind Brook (Port Chester, N.Y.); California (Los Angeles); Claremont Country (Oakland); Cypress Point (Monterey Penin., Calif.). *Address:* 155 Sansome Street, San Francisco, Calif. 94104, U.S.A.

**BECK, Robert George.** Canadian business executive. *B.* 1904. *Educ.* McGill Univ. (Bachelor of Applied Science in Mechanical Engineering—Hons.) 1927. *M.* 1933, Marian Courtice. *S.* Arthur. *Daus.* Sybil and Jennifer. *Career:* With Miehle Printing Press & Manufacturing Co., Chicago 1927–30; Sales Engineer, Direct Control Valve Co., Milwaukee 1930–31; Estimates Engineer, Dominion Engineering Co., Montreal 1931; Supervisor, Canadian Industries Ltd., Shawinigan, Que. 1931; Manager, Nylon Division of C-I-L 1945 (Vice-Pres. 1948, Director 1949); on division of C-I-L into two new companies in 1954, he became Vice-Pres. and Dir., of one of these, Du Pont of Canada, and in 1960 was named Exec. Vice-Pres. President and Chief Executive Officer, Du Pont of Canada Ltd. Apr. 1965–69 (Dir. since 1949). *Address:* Tandalla Farm, R.R.I. Inverary, Ont. K0H 1X0; and *office* Box 660, Montreal, P.Q., Canada, H3C 2V1.

**BECK, Baron Rudolph Rolf.** British industrialist. *B.* 1914. *Educ.* Engineering Degrees. Chemistry and Mechanical Engineering Universities of Geneva, Switzerland, Vienna and Austria. *M.* 1944, Elizabeth Leslie Brenchley. *S.* Stephen Rolf. *Career:* Represented Automotive Div. Skoda Works various continental countries, United Kingdom 1937–39; Formed Slip Products Ltd. Chmn. Man. Dir. 1939; Min. War Transport, Adv. Capacity Gas Producer Research 1940–42; Formed & Managing Dir. Slip Products & Engineering Co. Ltd. 1946, Slip Trading & Shipping Co. Ltd. 1947, Slip Auto Sales & Eng. 1948, Prospect Garage 1948, Slip Estates 1957, Slip International Ltd. Molyslip 1961, and Holdings 1964, Molyslip Chemicals Ltd. 1967, Molytex Ltd. 1968, Beck Chemicals Ltd. 1969, Slip Trading & Shipping (Export) Ltd. 1970, Molytex International 1970. *Member:* Socy. Motor Manuf. & Traders; Brit. Amer. Chamber, Commerce Brit. Swedish, Brit Swiss and Institute of Directors. *Clubs:* Union Interalliee (Paris); Scottish Royal Automobile; Royal Automobile; Hurlingham; Harwich Yacht; West Mersey. *Address:* Layham Hall, Hadleigh, Suffolk; and *office* Slip Works, Hatfield Road, St. Albans, Herts.

**BECKER, Aharon.** Member of Knesset (Israeli Parliament). *B.* 1906. *M.* 1930, Cyla Selzer. *S.* 1. *Daus.* 2. *Career:* Went from Russia to Israel 1924; member of Kibbutz 1925; building worker 1926–28; Secretary, Ramat Gan Labour Council 1929–32; Secretary, Union of Textile Workers 1933–34; *Member:* Executive of Labour Council, of Tel-Aviv 1934–43; Managing Director, Industrial Dept., Co-operative Wholesale Society 1943–47; Head of Supply Mission, Ministry of Defence 1948–49; Head of Trade Union Dept. and Member of Exec. Bureau, General Fed. of Labour in Israel 1949–61; Secretary-General of Histadrut (General Federation of Labour in Israel) 1961–69. Member, Governing Body of I.L.O. Member, Secretariat of Israel Labour Party and of Council of Directors, Bank of Israel. *Publications:* Under Labour Government in England (1953); Labour Israel, 1949–69. Numerous articles in the Hebrew and British press; various booklets and publications on economic and labour problems. *Address:* 66, Keren Kayemet Blvd., Tel-Aviv, Israel.

**BECKER, Alex.** French industrialist. *B.* 1924. *Educ.* St. Etienne Coll. (Strasbourg); Coll. of Provence (Marseille) and Univ. of Geneva (Bachelier). *M.* 1965, Michèle Gerdolle. *S.* Jacques and Stanislas. *Daus.* Marie Christine and Isabella. *Career:* Manager, Grands Moulins de la Ganzau 1947–59; President-Director-General, Grands Moulins Becker S.A. (capital N.F. 5,000,000) since 1959; Administrator, Société de Navigation Le Rhin since 1950; Administrateur de l'Association Nationale de la Meunerie Francaise 1973; Pres. des Syndicats de Meuniers Region Alsace 1973. *Address:* La Ganzau, Strasbourg-Neuhof, Bas Rhin; and *office* Grands Moulins Becker Strasbourg-Neuhof, Bas Rhin, France.

**BECKER, Sir (Jack) Ellerton,** FAA. Fellow, Australian ;ademy of Science (by special election. Only seventh ustralian non-scientist ever elected) 1961. *B.* 1904. *Educ.* Unley High School, Adelaide Institute of Technology, and Univ. of Adelaide. *M.* 1928, Gladys Sarah Duggan. *Career:* Founder and Principal, Adelaide College of Music (30 teachers and 5,000 students) 1930–40. Organized Music League of South Australia and directed large scale theatrical productions in capital cities of Australia 1935–40. Associated with C.S.I.R.O. scientists in major discoveries in soil and pasture improvement and new pasture species 1942–55. Engaged in scientific research and management in sheep and cattle farming 1955–69. In recognition of services, the main auditorium of Australian Academy of Science Building in Canberra named Becker Hall, 1962. Formed private company in England and took over Lord Brocket's property and sheep and cattle studs in Hereford, 1962; Chairman, Managing Director. Smithfield Pastoral Co. Pty. Ltd.,

South Australia 1955—, Brewarrana Pty. Ltd., N.S.W. 1962—, Aldersend Ltd., Herefordshire, England 1962—. Stud Stock (International) Pty. Ltd., and Castle Bend Pty. Ltd., N.S.W. 1964—. Retd. as Managing Director but remained as Chairman 1968. Created Knight 1962. Elected to Council of Australian Academy of Science 1965, and served until 1968; Fellow (elected) Intercontinental Biographical Assn. 1974; Fellow (elected) Intern. Inst. of Community Service 1975. *Member:* The Imperial Socy. of Knights Bachelor, London. *Address:* Blue Highway, Point Shares, Pembroke, Bermuda.

**BECKER, Léon.** French industrialist. *B.* 1919. *Educ.* Institut d'Enseignement Commercial Supérieur, Strasbourg. *M.* 1946, Huguette Vix. *S.* Guy and Humphrey. *Dau.* Anne. *Career:* Administrator-Director-General, Fabrique Alsacienne de Levûre et Alcools (FALA), Strasbourg 1951; Former Turkish Republic Consul General. *Member:* Radical Republican and Radical Socialist parties. Member, Rotary Club (Strasbourg). *Address:* 15 rue Daniel Hirtz, Strasbourg; and *office* Fala B.P. 189, Strasbourg 67,000, France.

**BECKET, Lt.-Col. Ralph Wilson,** Q.C., Barrister and Solicitor. *B.* 1909. *Educ.* McGill Univ.; BA; BCL. *M.* 1938, Mary Evelyn MacKenzie. *S.* Wilson. *Daus.* Heather and Joanna. *Career:* Manager, Prince Edward Island Trust Company 1936–39; Canadian Army (Infantry-Para.); U.S. Silver Star. Member, Montgomery McMichael, Common, Howard, Forsyth & Ker 1945–50; Vice-President and General Counsel, Canadian International Paper Company 1950–75; General Counsel Imperial Trust Co. *Address:* 3497 Walkley Ave., Montreal, Canada H4B 2K2.

**BECKLER, David.** American science administration executive. *B.* 1918. *Educ.* Univ. of Rochester, BS (Chem. Eng.); George Washington Univ. JD; *M.* 1943, Harriet R. Levy. *S.* 2. *Dau.* 1. *Career:* Patent Agent, Pennie, Davis, Marvin and Edmonds 1939–42; Tech. Aide, Office of Scientific Res. and Devel. 1942–45; Deputy Tech. Historian, Operations Crossroads (Bikini) 1946–47; Physical Sc. Administrator, Research and Devel. Bd., Office of Secy. of Defense 1947–52; Asst. Dir., Office of Indust. Develop; U.S. Atomic Energy Commission 1952–53; Exec. Officer, Sc. Advisory Cttee, Office of Defense Mobilisation 1953–57, President's Sc. Advisory Cttee. (U.S.) since 1957; Asst. to Spec. Asst. to Pres. for Science and Technology 1957–73; Asst. to Pres. National Acad. of Sciences 1973–76; Dir. for Science, Technology & Industry, Org. for Economic Development & Cooperation. *Address:* 21 Rue Spontini, Paris 75116, France.

**BEDDIE, Brian Dugan.** *B.* 1920. *Educ.* Sydney C. of E. Grammar School, Univ. of Sydney (BA) and Univ. of London (PhD) 1961. *Career*: Third Secretary, Australian Dept. of External Affairs 1945–48; Lecturer in Political Science, Canberra University College 1948–54. Editor, Australian Outlook 1959–60; Professor of Political Science, A.N.U. 1966–69; Prof. of Government, Faculty of Military Studies, Univ. of N.S.W. 1970—, and Dean of the Faculty of Military Studies 1971–72. Author of articles in various learned journals. *Member:* Australian Inst. of International Affairs; Australian Political Science Assn.; Australian Assn. of Philosophy. *Address:* Dept. of Government, R.M.C., Duntroon, A.C.T., Australia.

**BEDDY, James Patrick.** Irish. Consultant, The Industrial Credit Co. Ltd. *B.* 1900. *Educ.* National Univ. of Ireland and Univ. College, Dublin (MComm; DEconSc). *Career:* Inspector of Taxes 1927–33; Secy., The Industrial Credit Co. 1933–49, Director 1949–52, Chmn. Man. Dir. 1952–72; Lecturer in Commerce, Univ. Coll. 1936–51.Chmn.: An Foras Tinoscal 1952–65, and The Industrial Development Authority 1949–65. Chmn., Commission on Emigration and Other Population Problems 1948–54, and of Cttee. of Inquiry into Internal Transport 1956–57. (Mem., Tribunal of Inquiry 1939). Member, Industrial Research Cttee. of Institute for Industrial Research and Standards 1946–60. *Publications:* Profits, Theoretical and Practical Aspects, (1940); various pamphlets and articles of economic interest. Hon. LLD Dublin. *Member:* Statistical & Social Inquiry Socy. of Ireland (Past Council Member and Pres. 1954–56), Royal Irish Academy, and Economic and Social Research Institute (Council Mem.). *Clubs:* Royal Irish Yacht (Dun Laoghaire). *Address:* 15 Spencer Villas, Glenageary, Co. Dublin, Eire.

**BEDFORD, Clay Patrick.** Director, Educational Facilities Laboratories Inc., N.Y.C. *B.* 1903. *Educ.* Rensselaer Polytechnic Inst., Troy, N.Y. (CEng). *M.* 1928, Catherine Ann Bermingham. *S.* Clay Patrick, Jr. and Peter B. *Dau.* Ann (Wallace). *Career:* With Kaiser and affiliated companies in heavy construction, shipbuilding, automobile, and aircraft manufacturing 1925–75; Assistant to Secretary of Defense, Jan.–May 1952, and to Dir. of Defense Mobilization, June 1951–Jan. 1952. Formerly Pres., Kaiser Aerospace Electronics Corp. & Dir., Kaiser Industries Corp,; Honorary Trustee Rensselaer Poly. Inst.; Former Governor U.S. Seniors Golf Assn., Calif. *Member:* Board of Directors, American Graduate School of International Management; Civil Engineers Society; Alpha Tau Omega. *Clubs:* Claremont Country (Oakland, Calif.); Paradise Valley (Scottsdale, Ariz.); R. & A. Golf (St. Andrews). *Address:* 5223 East Palo Verde Pl. Scottsdale, Arizona, U.S.A.

**BEDFORD, The Rt. Hon. The Duke of, John (Robert Russell).** British Peer of the Realm. *B.* 1917. *M.* 1960, Madame Nicole Milinaire. *S.* The Marquess of Tavistock; Lord Rudolf Russell; Lord Francis Russell. *Publications:* A Silver Plated Spoon; Book of Snobs; The Flying Duchess; How to Run a Stately Home. *Clubs:* Brooks's; Pratt's. *Address:* Villa San Carlo, 22 Boulevard des Moulins, Monte Carlo.

**BEDIÉ, Konan.** Politician. *B.* 1934. *Educ.* University o Poitiers, France (Lic.-en-D.; Certificate of Aptitude in the Profession of Advocate; Diplomé, Higher Studies in Economic and Political Sciences). *M.* 1958, Henriette Koizan. *S.* 2. *Daus.* 2. *Career:* Previously Asst. Director: Caisse de Sécurité de Côte d'Ivoire, Abidjan 1959–60; Caisse de Compensation et des Prestations Familiales; Counsellor in the French Embassy at Washington, May–Aug. 1960; Chargé d'Affaires, Embassy of the Ivory Coast at Washington Aug. 1960–Jan. 1961; Ambassador of the Ivory Coast in U.S.A., 1961–65; Ambassador of the Ivory Coast for Canada (residing in Washington) 1963–65; Member of the Ivory Coast Delegation to the General Assemblies of U.N.O., 1960–65; Ministry of Financial and Economic Affairs 1966–68, Minister 1968–70. *Member:* Convention of Yaoundé (1969); Pres. annual assembly of BIRD and FMI 1974; Pres. Joint Cttees. since 1974. *Decoration:* Commander, National Order of the Ivory Coast. *Address:* Abidjan, Ivory Coast.

**BEEBY, Dr. Clarence Edward,** CMG. *B.* 16 June 1902. *Educ.* Univ. of New Zealand (MA); Univ. College, London; Univ. of Manchester (PhD); Hon. LLD (Otago); Hon. LittD (Wellington). *M.* 1926, Beatrice Newnham. *S.* Christopher David. *Dau.* Helen (Leckie). *Career:* Lecturer in Philosophy and Education, Canterbury Univ. Coll., Univ. of N.Z. 1923–34; Dir., New Zealand Cncl. for Educational Res. 1934–38; Asst. Director of Education, Education Department 1938–40; Director of Education 1940–60; Chairman, Unesco Evaluation Panel for Functional Literary Projects, 1967–72; Educational Consultant, New Zealand Council for Educational Research, Wellington, 1969 New Zealand Ambassador to France 1960–63; Research Associate, Centre for Studies in Education and Development, Harvard Univ., 1963–67; Commonwealth Visiting Professor, Univ. of London, 1967–68; Educational Consultant in Papua and New Guinea for Australian Govt., 1969; Educational Consultant to Ford Foundation. Indonesian Dept. of Education since 1970; UNDP Consultant on Malaysian Education 1976; Leader of New Zealand Delegations to General Conference of U.N.E.S.C.O. during the period 1946–62; and to the Commonwealth Education Conference 1959; Assistant Director-General, U.N.E.S.C.O., Paris 1948–49; Honorary Counsellor of U.N.E.S.C.O. 1950—(Member Exec. Bd. 1960–63, Chmn. 1962–63). *Publications:* The Intermediate Schools of New Zealand; The Quality of Education in Developing Countries; Entrance to the University (with W. Thomas and M. H. Oram); Qualitative Aspects of Educational Planning, 1969. *Address:* 73 Barnard Street, Wellington, New Zealand.

**BEECHING, Lord (Richard Beeching),** PhD. *B.* 1913. *Educ.* Maidstone Grammar School, and Imperial College of Science & Technology, London; ARCS, BSc, 1st Class Hons; DIC, PhD, Hon LLD, London; Fellow Imperial Coll. London; Hon DSc (Nat. Univ. of Ireland). *M.* 1938, Ella Margaret Tiley. *Career:* With Mond Nickel Co. Ltd. 1937; Armaments Design Dept., Ministry of Supply 1943; Deputy Chief Engineer of Armaments Design 1946. Joined I.C.I. 1948, Director 1957–61, Vice-Pres. I.C.I. Canada Ltd. 1953; Chmn., Metals Div. I.C.I. 1955; Chairman, British Transport Commission 1961–62; Chmn., British Railways Board 1963 (resigned 31 May 1965; returned to Directorship of I.C.I.). Dep. Chmn., I.C.I. Jan. 1966–68; Director, Lloyds Bank, 1965; Chmn. Redland Ltd. 1970–77; Furness Withy & Co. Ltd. 1973–75; Chmn., Royal Commission on The Admin. of Justice through Assizes & Quarter Sessions 1966–69; First Pres. Inst. Work Study Practitioners 1967–72; Pres. Royal

Socy. Prevention of Accidents 1968–73; Member, Top Salaries Review Body 1971–75. *Publications:* Electron Diffraction, 1936; contributions to technical and professional journals. CIMechE, FInstP, and FCIT. *Address:* Little Manor, East Grinstead, Sussex.

**BEECROFT, Eric Armour.** Canadian. Professor of Political Science, Univ. of Western Ontario. *B.* 1903. *Educ.* Univ. of Toronto (BA; MA); Yale Univ. (PhD). *M.* 1952, Ann Granger. *S.* Douglas. *Career:* Lecturer, Instructor and Asst. Prof. of Political Science, Univ. of Calif. 1931–41; Secy., International Economic Studies, Natl. Planning Assn. 1941–42; Chief, Far Eastern Div., U.S. Board of Economic Warfare 1942–43; Special Representative in India for U.S. Foreign Economic Administration 1943–45; Special Asst. to the Secretary of the Interior (U.S.A.) 1945–47; Loan Officer, International Bank for Reconstruction & Development 1947–54 (serving on bank missions to Philippines 1948 and 1949; India 1949; Ceylon 1949 and 1951; Pakistan 1951, Ethiopia 1950–52); National Director, Community Planning Association of Canada, and Editor, Community Planning Review 1954–60. Dir. Urban Planning, Canad. Fed. of Mayors & Municipalities 1960–65. Member: Canadian Council on Urban Research (Chmn. of Board 1965–68); Canad. Political Science Assn.; Canad. Economic Assn.; Socy. for International Development; Canad. Public Admin.; Amer. Economic Assn.; Amer. Socy. of Planning Officials; Internat. Fed. for Housing and Planning (Gov. Board 1958–66); Internat. Union of Local Authorities (Exec. Cttee. 1970–71); Fellow, Royal Socy. of Arts (U.K.). *Clubs:* Rideau (Ottawa), Cosmos (Washington). *Address:* Univ. of Western Canada, London, Ont., Canada.

**BEER, Stafford,** MBA, FSS, FREconS. British. *B.* 1926. *Educ.* Whitgift Sch.; London Univ. *M.* (1) 1947, Cynthia Hannaway. *S.* 4. *Dau.* 1. (2) 1968, Sallie Steadman Child. *S.* 1. *Daus.* 2. *Career:* Man. Operational Research and Production Controller, S. Fox Co. Ltd. 1949–56; Head of Operational Research & Cybernetics, United Steel 1956–61; Man. Dir. SIGMA Science in General Management Ltd.; Dir. Metra International 1961–66; Dev. Dir. International Publishing Corp.; Dir. International Data Highways Ltd. 1966–69; Scientific Dir., Project Cybersyn, Chile 1971–73; International Consultant; Professor, Manchester Business School since 1969; Professor, Wharton School, Pennsylvania Univ. since 1972; Pres. Operational Research Socy. (U.K.) 1970–71; Socy. General Systems Research (U.S.A.) 1971–72. *Publications:* Cybernetics & Management (1959 & 1967); Decision and Control (1966); Lanchester Prize; Management Science (1967); Brain of the Firm (1972); Designing Freedom (1974); Platform for Change (1975); Transit (Poems) (1977); Heart of the Firm (1978). *Clubs:* Athenaeum. *Address:* Cwarel Isaf, Pont Creuddyn, Lampeter, Dyfed, Wales.

**BEEVOR, John Grosvenor,** OBE (Mil.). British. *B.* 1905. *Educ.* Winchester and Oxford; BA First Class Honours in Moderations (Classics) and Literae Humaniores (Greats). *M.* (1) 1933, Carinthia Waterfield (*Dis.* 1956); *S.* 3; (2) 1957, Mary Christine Grepe. *Career:* Partner, Slaughter & May, Solicitors, London, 1931–53; Managing Director, Commonwealth Development Finance Co., London 1954–56; Adviser to British Delegation to the Marshall Plan Conf., Paris, 1947—. Vice-Pres. Int. Finance Corp., Washington, D.C. 1956–64. Chmn., National Commercial Development Capital Ltd.; Dir.: Lafarge Org. Ltd.; Lafarge SA (Paris); National Commercial Development Capital Ltd.; Overseas Development Institute. *Clubs:* R.A.C. (London); Royal St. George's (Sandwich). *Address:* 51 Eaton Square, London, S.W.1.

**BEFFA, Harvey Arthur.** American. *B.* 1900. *M.* 1922, Henrietta Stahl. *S.* Harvey Jr. and Daniel. *Daus.* Mary Etta and Helen. *Career:* In his father's demolition and building supply business 1915–32. Past Imperial Potentate, Shrine of North America (1952); Chairman Emeritus, St. Louis Unit of Shriners Hospitals for Crippled Children (Chmn., National Board of Trustees). Chairman, Executive Committee, Falstaff Brewing Corporation, St. Louis, Mo.; Member, Board of Directors, Mercantile-Commerce National Bank of St. Louis. Member: Master Brewers Assn. of America; Chamber of Commerce of Metropolitan St. Louis; Normandy (Mo.) Presbyterian Church. Republican. *Clubs:* St. Louis Advertising; Glen Echo Country; Missouri Athletic. *Address:* 5 Lucas Lane, Normandy, Mo.; and *office* 5050 Oakland Avenue, St. Louis 63166, Mo., U.S.A.

**BEGGS, James Montgomery,** BS, MBA. American. Government Official. *B.* 1926. *Educ.* U.S. Naval Academy, (Bachelor of Science); Harvard Graduate, School of Business Administration. *M.* 1953, Mary Elizabeth Harrison. *S.* James Harrison and Charles Montgomery. *Daus.* Maureen Elizabeth, Kathleen Louise and Teresa Lynn. *Career:* Lieutenant Commander, USNR (Retd) 1947–54; Westinghouse Electric Corporation, Gen. Manager Underwater Div. 1955–60; Systems Operations, 1960–63; Vice-Pres. Surface Div. 1965–67; Chief Corporate Officer, Purchases & Traffic since 1968; NASA, Associate Administrator, Advanced Research & Technology, 1968–69; Under Secy. Dept. of Transportation 1969–73; Man. Dir. Summa Corp. 1973–74; Exec. Vice-Pres. General Dynamics since 1974; Dir., Con Rail. *Awards:* Hon. LLD, Washington & Jefferson Univ.; Hon. Dr. of Engineering Management, Embry Riddle Univ. *Member:* American Inst. Aeronautics & Astronautics; American Socy; Sigma Tau (Hon. Engineering Society). *Address:* 32 Woodoaks Trail, St Louis, Mo. 63124; and *office* Pierre Laclede Center, St Louis, Mo. 63105, U.S.A.

**BEGIN, Hon. J. D.** Canadian. Mayor of the City of Lac Etchemin, 1967—. *B.* 1900. *Educ.* BA. *M.* 1937, Madeleine Perron. *S.* Michel, Bruno, Maurice. *Daus.* Nicole, Odette, Suzanne and Helene. *Career:* Elected Deputy for Dorchester 1935; re-elected 1936–39–44–48–52–56–60; Minister of Colonization, Province of Quebec, 1944–60; Gen. Organizer, Nat. Union Party, Province of Quebec, 1940–60. Chmn. of the Bd., Les Presses Lithographiques Inc., L'Imprimerie Dorchester Inc.; Les Journaux Assoc. Inc.; La Voix du Sud; L'Aiglon, La Voix Nouvelle, Compelec Inc.; Pres. Caisse d'Entraide Economique de Dorchester et Bellechasse, Fondation J. D. Bégin, Cie Personnelle Nigeb Inc.; Begin Aviation Engineering and many others; Commander: Ordre du Mérite Agricole, and Ordre du Mérite du Defricheur; Coronation Medal. *Member:* National Geographic Society; Life member Société des Timbres de Noel de Quebec; member Int. Platform Assn.; Canadian Owners & Pilot Association; *Clubs:* Renaissance; Golf St. Georges; Nautique Lac Etchemin; Aero Club du Lac Etchemin; Country of Miami. *Address:* Lac Etchemin, Comté Dorchester, Province de Quebec, Canada.

**BEGIN, Menahem.** Israeli Politician. *B.* 1913. *Educ.* Mizrachi Hebrew Sch.; Polish Gymnasium; Univ. of Warsaw—Law degree. *M.* Aliza Arnold. *S.* 1. *Daus.* 2. *Career:* Joined Betar (Zionist Youth Movement) in Poland 1929, Head of Organization Dept. 1932, Head of Betar 1939; arrested, imprisoned in Siberia 1940–41; assumed command of Irgun Zva'i Leumi (National Military Org.), Palestine 1943; Founded Herut Movement 1948; mem. of Knesset since 1949; Minister without Portfolio, Govt. of National Unity 1967–70; Jt. Chmn., Likud Party since 1973; Prime Minister since 1977. *Publications:* The Revolt; White Nights; numerous articles. *Address:* 1 Rosenbaum Street, Tel-Aviv, Israel.

**BEGTRUP, Madame Bodil Gertrud.** Danish diplomat. *B.* 12 Nov. 1903. *Educ.* University of Copenhagen (MA). *M.* 1948, L. B. Bolt-Jorgensen (*dec.*). *Career:* Vice-President, National Council of Danish Women 1931, Pres. 1946; Member, Danish Delegation of League of Nations 1938, to United Nations 1946–52; Member, United Nations' Commission on Status of Women, Pres. 1946–47; En. Ex. and Min. Plen. to Iceland 1949; Ambassador 1955–56; at Foreign Office, Copenhagen 1956–59; Ambassador to Switzerland, 1959–68; to Portugal 1968–73; World Population conference (Bucharest) 1974; Doctor h.c., Smith College, U.S.A. *Address:* Strandvejen 16B$^{I}$, Copenhagen Ø, Denmark.

**BEHLEN, Walter Dietrich.** American inventor and manufacturer. Chmn. of Board, Behlen Manufacturing Co. 1964—. *B.* 1905. *Educ.* Columbus, Neb., Public Schools. *M.* 1940, Ruby Mae Cumming. *S.* Kent Walter. *Dau.* Mary Ann. *Career:* An illness interrupted the start of his high school education; four-and-a-half years later he returned to high school while working at night or half-days for the Union Pacific Railroad and the Railway Express Agency; after graduation he worked for the Railway Express Agency and in his spare time began a small manufacturing business in his home garage, making products needed by customers he served on his Express Agency route. He resigned his position with the Express Agency, and in 1941 devoted full time to his manufacturing venture. By 1946, the business outgrew several buildings and a new plant of 40,000 sq. ft. was erected; this plant was expanded several times, and a new plant was built, and this, too, has expanded to 830,000 sq. ft. Behlen employs a staff of 1,100 with an annual payroll exceeding $5 million; sales in the past 5 years have ranged from $25 to $45 million. Time magazine has referred to him as the Corn Belt Edison. His development is a sheet metal stressed skin design for a roof and ceiling system capable of a 1000-ft. clear span. *Honours:* DSc, Midland Coll., Freemont, Neb.; DEng Univ. of Nebraska;

Dr. of Humane Letters, Doane Coll., Crete Nebraska. Republican. *Address:* 2555 Pershing Road, Columbus, Neb., U.S.A.

**BEHRENS, Karl Christian,** Dr.oec. German. *B.* 1907. *Educ.* D.oec. o. Prof. *M.* 1953, Christa B. Küter. *S.* 1. *Dau.* 1. *Career:* Export & Import business in Hamburg 1923–27; study at Königsberg; proprietor of a private commercial school and Public Accountant 1933–45; Assistant, Berlin Univ. 1946–48; Reader Hamburg Univ. 1948–50; Asst. Prof., Free Univ., 1950–51, Ord. Prof. 1951. Professor of Economics, Free University, Berlin; Director, Institute for Market & Consumer Research, and Director of Economics Records. *Publications:* The lowering of the economic margin (1949); Goods Traffic (1956); Export business (1957); Market Research (1960); Demoscopic Market Research (1961); Dynamics in Marketing (1962); Modern Distribution (1962); Absatzwerbung (1963); The Location of Business (1961); The Location of Trading Enterprises (1965); Fundamentals of Trading Enterprise (1966); Handbuch der Webrung (1969); Handbuch der Markl forschung. Co-operative Advertising in small business. *Member:* Assn. of High School Teachers in Economics; Society for Social Policies; Rencontres de St. Gall; American Marketing Assn. *Address:* Irmgardstrasse 9, Berlin-Zehlendorf, Germany.

**BEITH, Alan James.** MP. British. *B.* 1943. *Educ.* King's School, Macclesfield; Balliol & Nuffield Colleges, Oxford—BLitt, MA (Oxon). *M.* 1965, Barbara Jean Ward. *S.* 1. *Career:* Lecturer, Dept. of Politics, Univ. of Newcastle-upon-Tyne 1966–73: Member of Parliament for Berwick-upon-Tweed since 1973; Liberal Chief Whip since 1976. *Member:* Parly. Assemblies of the Council of Europe & The Western European Union; Royal Inst. of Public Admin.; Political Studies Assoc.; Assoc. of Councillors (Jt. Chmn.). *Publications:* Chapter in "The British General Election of 1964", ed. Butler & King 1965; Articles in Public Admin. Bulletin, Government Chronicle, Policy & Politics, New Society etc. *Clubs:* National Liberal; Union Society (Oxford); Shilbottle Working Men's (Alnwick). *Address:* c/o House of Commons, London, S.W.1.

**BEITH, Sir John,** KCMG. British diplomat. *B.* 1914. *Educ.* Eton and King's Coll. Cambridge. *M.* 1949, Diana Gregory-Hood *née* Gilmour. *S.* 1 and 1 stepson. *Daus.* 1 and 1 step daughter. *Career:* Foreign Office 1937–40; Athens, Third Secy. 1940–41; Second Secy. Buenos Aires 1041—45; Foreign Office 1945–49; Head of U.K. Perm. Del. to U.N. Geneva 1950–53; Head of Chancery Prague 1953–54; Counsellor and Head of Chancery Paris 1954–59; Head, Levant Dept. 1959–61; Head, N. & E. African Dept. Foreign Office 1961–63; Ambassador to Israel 1963–65; Asst. Secy.-Gen. NATO 1966–67; Asst. Under-Secy. of State F.O. 1967–69; Ambassador to Belgium 1969–74. *Awards:* Knight Commander St. Michael and St. George. *Clubs:* Whites. *Address:* Dean Farm House, Sparsholt, Hants.

**BELCHER, Ronald Harry,** CMG. Retired British civil servant. *B.* 1916. *Educ.* Christ's Hospital (Horsham); Jesus College, Cambridge; Brasenose College, Oxford; BA (Hons. Classics). Cantab. 1937; Dipl. Class. Arch. Cantab. 1938; BA Oxon. 1938. *M.* 1948, Hildegarde Hellyer-Jones. *S.* Nicholas John. *Career:* Indian Civil Service, Punjab 1939–48; Commonwealth Relations Office 1948; seconded to Foreign Office for services in Embassy, Washington 1951–53; Private Secretary to Secretary of State for Commonwealth Relations 1954. Deputy High Commissioner for U.K. in South Africa 1956–59; in India 1961–65: Overseas Development Administration, 1965–76. *Club:* Royal Commonwealth Society. *Address:* Fieldview, Lower Road, Fetcham, Surrey.

**BELEN, Frederick Christopher.** American. *B.* 1913. *Educ.* Michigan State University (BA 1937) and George Washington University (JD 1942). *M.* 1943, Opal Marie Sheets. *S.* Frederick Christopher, Jr. *Career:* Asst. Postmaster-General, Bureau of Operations, U.S. Post Office, apptd. by Pres. Kennedy 1961–64. Counsel and Chief Counsel, House Committee on Post Office and Civil Service, House of Representatives 1946–61. Deputy Postmaster-General, U.S. Post Office Dept., 1964–69; Attorney, Private Law Practice, since 1969; Hon. LLD Michigan State Univ. 1967; National Business Publications Silver Scroll for outstanding contributions to improve mail service and postal efficiency 1964; Michigan State Univ. Inter-fraternity Council Alumnus Award for outstanding achievement in field of public service 1964, and Distinguished Alumni Award 1963; Recipient, Benjamin Franklin Award for exceptional leadership 1963. Admitted to practice before Michigan, District of Columbia and U.S. Supreme Court Bars. *Member:* State Bar for Michigan, and Federal Bar Assn. *Publications:* of various Congressional Reports and Studies, and postal articles. *Clubs:* National Democratic (Past President); Michigan State Socy. (Past President); Grand Isle (La.) Tarpon Rodeo & Gulf & Bay (Sarasota, Fla.). *Address:* 2658 North Upshur Street, Arlington, Va. 22207; and *office.* Suite 900, 1776 K St. NW, 20006, U.S.A.

**BELFRAGE, Leif Axel Lorentz,** GBE, Grand Cross, Order of the North Star. Swedish diplomat. *B.* 1910. *Educ.* Stockholm Univ. (LLD 1933). *M.* 1937, Greta Jering. *S.* 1. *Daus.* 3. *Career:* Ministry of Commerce, Stockholm, 1937; Director: Swedish Clearing Office, 1940; Swedish Trade Commission, 1943–45; Head of Section, Commercial Dept., Swedish Foreign Ministry, 1945; Commercial Cnclor., Swedish Embassy, Washington, 1946; Head, Commercial Dept. Foreign Ministry, Stockholm, 1949–53; Dep. Under-Secy. of State 1953–56; Permanent Under-Secy. of State, Foreign Ministry, 1956–67; Ambassador to the Court of St. James's, 1967–72; Ambassador Perm. Rep. to the OECD Paris 1972–76. *Address:* Sturegatan 14, 11436 Stockholm, Sweden.

**BELGRAVE, James Hamed Dacre.** former British official. *B.* 22 Apr. 1929. *Educ.* Bedford; American University of Beirut; School of Oriental and African Studies, London University. *Career:* Palestine Police 1947–48; Bahrain Petroleum Co. 1953–55; Dir. of Public Relations & Broadcasting, Government of Bahrain 1955–59. Dir., Harcourt Kitchin & Partners 1960–62; Dir., East. West Group Ltd., Arabconsult, Gulf Financial Services, Marshalls (Bahrain) Ltd., Gulf Publishing Co. *Publication:* Welcome to Bahrain. *Address:* P.O. Box 551, Bahrain, Arabian Gulf.

**BELL, Hon. David E.** *B.* 1919. *Educ.* Pomona College, Claremont, Calif. and Harvard Univ. (MA Econ.). *Career:* Served in World War II as a Marine Corps Officer. Commenced in the Government Service before the war in the Budget Bureau during the Roosevelt administration, and returned to that office after his discharge from military service in 1945; transferred to the White House in 1947, to work on presidential messages and other legislative and executive matters; appointed in 1951 one of President Truman's administrative assistants. In the presidential election campaign of 1952, he was a member of the research staff of the Democratic candidate, Mr. Adlai Stevenson. In 1953 he was given a Rockefeller Public Service award and returned to Harvard for advanced study. In 1954 he headed a Harvard Mission, financed by the Ford Foundation, to help the Pakistan Govt. with its development planning. In the autumn of 1957 he became Lecturer in Economics at Harvard and Research Associate in the Graduate School of Public Administration, of which he became Secretary in 1959; Director U.S. Bureau of the Budget, 1961–62; Administrator, Agency for International Development, U.S. Government, 1962–66; Vice-President, The Ford Foundation, New York, 1966–69. Executive Vice-President, The Ford Foundation since 1969. *Address:* The Ford Foundation, 320 East 43rd Street, New York, N.Y. 10017, U.S.A.

**BELL, Davitt Stranahan.** American steel manufacturer. *B.* 1905. *Educ.* Lehigh Univ. (Mech. Eng.). *M.* 1931, Marian Whieldon. *S.* Frank B. II and Michael D. *Dau.* Margaret W. (Woodwell), and Susan R. (McIntosh). *Career:* President, Edgewater Steel Co. 1942–67. Asst. to Pres., Edgewater Steel Co. 1937–42 (Engineer 1928–37); Engineer. Weirton Steel Co. 1926–28; Chairman of the Board, Edgewater Corp., Pittsburgh, Pa. 1967—; Director, Dravo Corp., Pittsburgh. *Member:* Amer. Socy. of Mech. Engineers. Republican. *Clubs:* Duquesne, Oakmont Country; Pittsburgh Golf; Rolling Rock. *Address:* B311 Woodland Manor 5903 Fifth Avenue, Pittsburgh, Pa 15232, and *office* Oakmont, Pa, 15139, Pa., U.S.A.

**BELL, Douglas Maurice,** CBE. British. *B.* 1914. *Educ.* The Edinburgh Academy and St. Andrews University (BSc with Hons. Chemistry). *M.* 1947, Elizabeth Mary Edelsten. *S.* Benjamin. *Daus.* Janet and Margaret. *Career:* Chemist, War Dept., Woolwich Arsenal 1936. With I.C.I.: Dyestuffs Division 1937–42; Regional Sales Manager 1946–53; Director, Billingham Division 1953 (Managing Director 1955–57); Managing Director, Heavy Organic Chemicals Division 1957–61. Chief Executive I.C.I. (Europa) Ltd. 1965–72; Dir. BTP Tioxide Ltd.; Tioxide Aust. Pty. Ltd.; Tioxide Canada Ltd.; Tioxide S.A.; Titanio S.A. Chmn. Chief, Exec. Tioxide Group Ltd. since 1973. *Member:* (Council) Chemical Industry Assn.; Socy. of Chemical Industry (Pres.); Fellow, British Inst. of Management; Fellow, Royal Society of Arts. *Awards:* Commendador de Numero de la Ordur del

Merito Civil (Spain); Commandeur d'Ordre de Leopold II (Belgium). *Clubs:* West Sussex Golf; Anglo-Belgian. *Address:* Stocks Cottage, Church Street, West Chiltington, Sussex; and *office* Tioxide Group Ltd., 10 Stratton Street, London, W.1.

**BELL, Elliott V.** American. *B.* 1902. *Educ.* Columbia Univ. (AB 1925); Hon. LLD Bard College (1950) and St. Lawrence Univ. (1954); Hon. DCS Pace Coll. (1956). *M.* 1927, Amelia Lange. *Dau.* Nancy Melissa (Hoving). *Career:* Financial Writer: New York Herald Tribune 1929, and New York Times 1929–39 (Member Editorial Board 1941–42); Economic Adviser to Thomas E. Dewey 1939–40; Research Consultant to Wendell L. Willkie 1940; Superintendent, Banks of the State of New York 1943–49; Trustee: Roger Williams Strau Memorial Foundation. Director Emeritus, Council on Foreign Relations. *Publications:* We Saw it Happen (with other *N.Y.* Times correspondents) 1938. *Member:* New York Financial Writers Assn. (First Pres. 1938–39). *Clubs:* Century Assn.; University; Angler's (N.Y.). *Address:* 200 East 66th Street, New York 10021, N.Y.; Quaker Hill, Pawling, N.Y. 12564.

**BELL, Frank Coffman.** American engineer (automatic navigation equipment). Consultant 1961—. *B.* 1911. *Educ.* Harvard College (ABMath 1933) and State of California (ME 1949). *M.* 1941, Doris Elizabeth Kistler. *S.* Gordon Arnold II. *Career:* Engineer ('Constellation' control system and wing design, helicopter design, compressible air flow study), Lockheed Aircraft Corp. 1940–46; Engineer, Project Engineer, Chief of Guidance Development, Northrop Aircraft Inc. (invented and developed 'Snark' missile guidance) 1946–50; Civilian member and Technical Consultant, sub-panels and working groups on self-contained long distance navigation systems, Committee on guided missiles, Research and Development Board, U.S. National Military Establishment 1947–50; Research Physicist, member of the technical staff, Hughes Aircraft Co. Missile Guidance Laboratories 1950–52; System Engineer, Fighter Aircraft Inertial Autonavigator XN-5, Missile and Control Equipment, Electro-Mechanical Engineering Department, North American Aviation Inc. 1952–55; Research Engineer, Electronic Equipments Division, Guidance Systems Laboratory, Litton Industries, Beverly Hills, Calif. 1955–61. *Publications:* The Geometric Basis of Celestial Navigation, 1947; Celestial Navigation of Guided Missiles, 1947; Differential-Geometric Theory of Line-of-Sight Navigation, 1952; Schuler's Principle and Inertial Navigation (Ann. N.Y. Acad. Sci.) 1969. *Member:* Institute of Navigation (U.S.); Royal Institute of Navigation; Phi Beta Kappa. *Club:* Harvard (of Southern California). *Address:* 4518 Sylmar Avenue, Sherman Oaks, Calif., U.S.A.

**BELL, Sir (George) Raymond,** KCMG, CB. British financial executive. *B.* 1916. *Educ.* Bradford Grammar Sch.; St. John's Coll., Cambridge (Scholar). *M.* 1944, Joan Elizabeth Coltham. *S.* 2. *Daus.* 2. *Career:* Entered Civil Service, Asst. Principal 1938; Ministry of Health 1938; transferred Treasury 1939; war service, Royal Navy (Lieut. RNVR) 1941–44; Principal, Civil Service 1945; Asst. Sec. 1951; Under-Sec. 1960; Dep. Sec. 1966; Dep Sec., HM Treasury 1966–72. Sec. (Finance), Office of HM High Commissioner for the UK in Canada 1945–48; Counsellor, UK Perm. Del. to OEEC/NATO, Paris 1953–56; Principal Private Sec. to Chancellor of the Exchequer 1958–60; mem., UK Del. to Brussels Conference 1961–62, & 1970–72; Vice-Chmn., European Investment Bank since 1973. *Decorations:* Knight Commander of St. Michael & St. George, 1973; Companion of the Bath, 1967. *Address:* European Investment Bank, 2 Place de Metz, Luxembourg.

**BELL, Harold Felix,** PhD (Lond.); Australian economist. *B.* 1921. *Educ.* Melbourne University (BA; MCom) and London School of Economics (PhD). Served as Lieut. (Sp.) in Royal Australian Naval Volunteer Reserve 1942–46; London House 1950–52; Pres., N.S.W. Branch of Economic Society of Australia and New Zealand 1956–57; Economist to Australian Mutual Provident Society 1953—. Member Development Corp. of N.S.W. 1966—, and Universities Board (N.S.W.) 1967—. Chairman, Australian National Committee of International Chamber of Commerce 1963–64; Executive of Constitutional Association of Australia 1954—. Member of Executive of Australian Institute of International Affairs (N.S.W. Branch) 1960—; Executive of Australian Society of Security Analysts 1960–64. Trustee, Committee of Economic Development, Australia. *Publications:* include numerous articles on institutional investment and economic and financial problems of Australian development. Associate Australian Society of Accountants; Fellow, Incorporated Australian Insurance Institute. *Clubs:* University, Royal Sydney Yacht Squadron (Sydney); American National; London House Fellowship. *Address:* 30 Plunkett Road, Mosman, N.S.W.; and *office* Box 4134, G.P.O., Sydney, N.S.W., Australia.

**BELL, James Dunbar.** American diplomat. *B.* 1911. *Educ.* Univ. of New Mexico (BA); Univ. of Chicago (MA; PhD). *M.* 1961, Stephanie Ann Matuzie. *S.* James D. Jr., Christopher J., Jefferson M. *Daus.* Diane Elizabeth, Stephanie Susan. *Career:* Reporter, *Albuquerque Journal,* 1934–35; Statistician, State of New Mexico, 1936–37; Instructor, Gary College, 1939–41; Labour Attaché, U.S. Embassy, Bogota, 1944–46; Assistant Professor, Hamilton College, 1946–47; Political Officer: U.S. Embassy, Santiago, 1947–50; Manila, 1950–53; Deputy Director, Philippine & South-east Asian Affairs, Dept. of State, 1953–57; Deputy Chief of Mission, U.S. Embassy, Djakarta, 1957–59; Ambassador to Malaysia, 1964–69; In Residence Univ. of California Santa Cruz, Lect. Merrell Coll. since 1969; Acting Dir. Center for S. Pacific Studies, Univ. Calif., Santa Cruz (1973–74). *Address:* Univ. of California, Santa Cruz, U.S.A.

**BELL, Ronald McMillan,** Q.C., M.P. (Con. Beaconsfield). *B.* 1914. *Educ.* Cardiff High School and Magdalen Coll. Oxford (BA 1936, MA 1940). *M.* 1954, Elizabeth Audrey Gossell. *S.* Andrew and Robert. *Daus.* Fiona and Lucinda. *Career:* Member of Consultative Assembly of the Council of Europe 1952–54 and 1963–66. *Publication:* Treatise on Crown Law. *Address:* First House, West Witheridge, Beaconsfield, Bucks.; and *office* 2 Mitre Court Buildings, Temple, London, E.C.4.

**BELLAN, Pierre-Jean.** French. *B.* 1912. *Educ.* Faculty de Paris (Dr. en Droit). *M.* 1938, Marie-Henriette Lavigne. *S.* Jean-Claude. *Dau.* Marie-Christine. *Career:* Insurance Broker 1931—; Member of Ministerial Cabinets 1946–49; President, Editorial Committee, Diplomatic Conference, Geneva (2nd Convention), for the revision of its conventions 1949; Member, Editorial Committee of the review *Le Particulier*; Paris Judge President de Chambre Honoraire of the Tribunal of Commerce: Administrator, Cie. d'Assurances L'URBAINEVIE 1947–65. Chairman, Société Générale pour les Assurances et le Contentieux; Insurance Broker Company. *Publications:* Technical and juridical articles. *Club:* Racing Club de France. *Address:* 5 Blvd. Richard Wallace, 92200 Neuilly, France; and *office* 120 Avenue des Champs Elysée, Paris 8.

**BELLEMARE, Hon. Maurice.** French-Canadian. *B.* 1912. *M.* 1939, Blanche Martel. *Career:* Brakeman with Canadian Pacific Railway. Deputy for Champlain 1944–70. Minister of Labour 1966–70. Member: Chamber of Commerce; Pres. of Quebec; Workmen's Compensation Commission, 1970–72. Acting Leader Union nat, party since 1974; National Assembly for Johnson (by-election) 1974, re-elected 1976. *Club:* Cap Curling. *Address:* Cap-de-la-Madeleine, P.O. Box 68, P.Q., Canada.

**BELLOWS, Everett Hollis.** American. *B.* 1913. *Educ.* The George Wash. Univ. (AB; MA). *M.* 1939, Edna Walter. *Dau.* Joanna Christine. *Career:* Chief of Exec. Recruit and Placement (1939–41) in former Fed. Sec. Agency, and as a Personnel Director in the Office for Emergency Management 1941–43; Executive Officer, Office of Foreign Service, Dept. of State 1946–48; Deputy Exec. Asst., Office of the U.S. Special Representative for Europe in the Marshall Plan 1948–50; Asst. to Admin. of the Economic Co-operation Administration 1950–51; Dir., Productivity and Technical Assistance Div., Office of U.S. Special Representative for Europe 1951–53; Asst. to Exec. Vice-Pres., Olin Mathieson Chem. Corp. 1954, Dir. of Personnel 1959, Vice-Pres., Corporate Services Feb. 1962; Vice-President, Olin Corp. 1962—. Const. U.S. Dept. of State 1963—; Chairman, Advisory Board, Center for the Behavioral Sciences, The George Washington University 1961–66; Corporator, Leslie College, Cambridge, Mass. 1964—; Trustee, The George Washington University 1970—. Member, Advisory Committee, School of Business, Manhattan College, New York 1965–68; School of Government and Business Admin., George Washington University 1968—. Lieut. j.g., U.S.N.R. 1943–46. *Clubs:* Cosmos (Washington); Washington Golf & Country. *Address:* 3701 N. 27th Street, Arlington, Va., 22207; and *office* 1730 K St. N.W., Washington, D.C. 20006.

**BELLWINKEL, Carl,** Dr. jur. German executive. *B.* 1904. *Educ.* High School of Economics, Berlin (Diploma as Businessman); Univ. of Leipzig (Dr. jur.). *M.* 1941. Traudl Kaup

(Dr. phil.). *Daus.* 3. *Career:* Deutsche Treuhand AG (Economics Examination Society) 1928–34; Works Director, Rütgerswerke AG, Rauxel 1934–40 (Manager 1940–41, member Board of Directors 1941–47); Chairman, Board of Directors, Rütgerswerke AG 1948—; Deputy Chairman: Phenolcheme, Gladbeck, and Sigmi Eleutrographit GMBH; Member, Supervisory Council: Chemische Fabrik AG, Frankfurt; Silesia Verein Chemischer Fabriken, Frankfurt; Bakelite Ges., Letmathe, Sauerland; German Gold & Silver Institutes, Frankfurt; Graphitwerke Kropfmühl AG, Munich; Hartmann & Braun AG, Frankfurt. Director, Landeszentralbank Hessen, Frankfurt; President; Association of the Chemical Industries, Frankfurt. *Member:* Frankfurt Society for Trade, Industry & Science. *Club:* Rotary (Frankfurt). *Address:* Niddablick 40, Frankfurt/Main-Ginnheim; and *office* Mainzer Landstr. 195–217, Frankfurt/Main, Germany.

**BELMORE, Frederick Martin.** American. *B.* 1915. *Educ.* Univ. of Virginia (BSc Chem., and BSc Chem. Engg.). *M.* 1937, Charlotte Lee Munn. *S.* Frederick Martin Jr. and Page Randolph. *Dau.* Charlotte Lee. *Career:* Dir. of Production, U.S. Atomic Energy Commission, N.Y. 1945–55; Asst. to Pres., Mallinckroot Chemical Works 1955–60; Vice-President 1960–63; Pres. and Chmn. of the Board, The Matheson Co. Inc., East Rutherford, N.J. 1963–67. Director, York Research Corporation, Stamford, Conn., 1965—; President and Dir. Will Ross Inc. Milwaukee, Wis. since 1967; Dir. Marine Corp. since 1971. Decoration for Exceptional Civil Service U.S. War Dept. 1946. *Member:* Amer. Chemical Socy.; Amer. Nuclear Socy.; Inst. of Chemical Engineers. *Clubs:* Phi Beta Kappa; Tau Beta Pi; Milwaukee Country; Milwaukee Hunt; Milwaukee. *Address:* 7275 N. River Road, Milwaukee, Wis.; and 4285 N. Port Washington Road, Milwaukee, Wis., U.S.A.

**BELSCHNER, Herman Godfrey (Geoff), ED, DVSc, HDA FACVSc.** British veterinary surgeon. *B.* 1895. *Educ.* Hawkesbury Agricultural Coll. (HDA) and Univ. of Sydney (BVSc 1922, DVSc 1936). *M.* 1926, Dorothy Jean Kimber. *Dau.* 1. *Career:* Appointed first graduate Inspector of Stock 1922; Govt. Veterinary Surgeon 1924; first District Vet. Officer, Western District 1925; Senior Vet. Officer 1937; Deputy Chief Div. of Animal Husbandry 1942; Chief 1953; retired to take up university appointment as Senior Lecturer in Animal Management at Univ. of Sydney (9 years) 1955. External Lecturer on Sheep Diseases, Univ. of N.S.W. for 20 years; Veterinarian to The Land Newspaper Ltd., Sydney 1955–74. Gilruth Prize for meritorious service to veterinary science in Australia 1960. War service: Asst. Dir. of Vet. Services to 1st Cavalry Div. N.S.W.; rank of Major, subsequently promoted to Lt.-Col.; when the Division was mechanized (1942) was withdrawn from the Army to assist in drive for food production; placed on R. of O. with rank of Lt.-Col. *Publications:* Sheep Management and Diseases, 1950 (9th ed. completely revised, enlarged and reset 1971, revised 1976); Cattle Diseases (1967) and (1974); Pig Diseases (1968, revised 1976); and (1972); Horse Diseases (1974); various scientific papers. Member Australian Veterinary Assn.; Life member, Aust. Coll. of Veterinary Scientists. *Address:* 9 Fletcher Avenue, Miranda, N.S.W., Australia.

**BELTRAN, Dr. Washington.** *B.* 1914. *Educ.* Graduated as lawyer. *M.* 1943, Esther Storace Arrosa; six children. *Career:* Joined editorial staff of *El Pais*, May 1939 (Deputy Head of the newspaper May 1949; Co-Director 1961). Elected to Chamber of Representatives for the Partido Nacional (National Party) 1947 (re-elected Deputy for Montevideo 1960). He set up a new political grouping within his own party, but gave up his seat 1954; but in the same year re-elected for the third time. Visited U.S.A. 1957; elected Senator and presided over the Social Security Commission; elected National Councillor Govt. of Uruguay 1962 (and Pres. of the Cttees. of the Exec. for Land, Public Health, Education and Social Security); in Mar. 1965, became Pres. of the National Council, a post he held for one year, during which he visited Buenos Aires to deliver a speech to the Argentinian Congress; in 1966, he went as President of the Uruguayan delegation to recognize the government of Dr. Lleras Restrepo; Elected Sentor 1966; re-elected 1971; participated in Int'l. Congress of Paris on situation of the Jews in the Middle East 1974; following Government invitations, visited Republic of Nationalist China (Taiwan), South Korea & the U.S., 1975. Past Mem. of the Directorate and Presently of the Convention of the Partido Nacional. *Address:* Director Newspaper *El Pais*, Curreim 1287, p.3, Montevideo, Uruguay.

**BELTZ, Charles Robert.** American aeronautical and refrigeration engineer. *B.* 1913. *Educ.* Cornell Univ. (ME); Univ. of Pittsburgh (BS in Aero.). *M.* 1935, Amy Ferguson. *S.* 3. *Daus.* 3. *Career:* President, National Aeronautic Assn. (Detroit Chapter); Dir., Aero Club of Michigan; Chmn., Inst. of Aeronautical Sciences; Pres. (past), Air Conditioning Inst. Formerly: Engineer Crane Co.; Aero. Design Engr., Stout Sky Craft Corp.; Gen. Mgr., Stout Engineering Labs. Inc.; Project Engr. Chrysler Corp., Century Motors Corp., Cycle Weld Labs. Inc.; Project Mgr., Experimental Flight Controls, Fairchild Engineering & Airplane Corp., Roosevelt Field Corp.; Field Engineer, Chrysler Corp. Airtemp Div.; President, Charles R. Beltz & Co.; Beltemp Inc. and Beltz Engineering Laboratories. *Member:* E.S.D.; A.S.H.R.A.E.; N.Y. Acad. of Science; F.A.I.; I.P.M.S.; P.S.G.; Detroit Museum of Art Founders Soc. *Clubs:* Economic (Detroit); Grosse Pointe Yacht; University, Curling (Detroit); Lost Lake Woods. *Address:* 500 Lakehead, Grosse Pointe, Mich. 48230, U.S.A.

**BEN ABBES TAARJI, Bachir.** *B.* 1918. *Educ.* Baccalaureat; Licence en Droit (Faculté de Paris); Licence es Lettres (Sorbonne). *M.* 1950, Khadija Benchakroune. *S.* Hicham. *Daus.* Houria, Hinde, Dounia. *Career:* Advocate at the Bars of Marrakesh (1947—) and Casablanca (1952—); Dir. of the Cabinet of the Sûreté Nationale, May 1956–June 1957; Governor of City of Marrakesh, June 1957–May 1958; Minister of Labour and Social Affairs, May–Dec. 1958; Ambassador, 1959–62; Mayor of the City of Marrakesh, 1969; Deputy of Marrakesh 1970; *Member:* Constitutional Court 1971; Governor of Province of Marrakesh May–Nov. 1972; Min. of Justice 1972–74. Member of Istiqlal Party. *Address:* 10 Place Mohamed V, Casablanca, Morocco.

**BENDETSEN, Karl Robin, JSD.** *B.* 1907. *Educ.* Leland Stanford University (AB 1929, JSD 1932). *M.* (1) 1939 (Div.). *S.* Brookes McIntosh. *Dau.* Anna Martha. (2) 1972, Gladys Ponton de Arce Johnson. *Career:* Chief Executive Officer, Champion International Corporation. Director: Westinghouse Electric Corp., New York Stock Exchange. Law practice 1932–40; Served in active military service, as Colonel, General Staff Corps., U.S. Army 1940–46. Management Counsel 1946–47; Special Counsel to Secretary of Defense 1948; Asst. Secy. and Under Secy. of Army (U.S.) 1948–52; Chmn. of Board, Panama Canal Co. 1950; Director-General, U.S. Railroads 1950–52. Joined Champion Paper & Fibre Co. (now Champion International Corporation) 1952; Special Representative West Germany and Philippine Governments, rank Ambassador, 1956; Chmn., Advisory cncl. to Secy. of Defense 1962; Vice-Chmn., Defense Manpower Commission 1974–76. *Awards:* DSM (Oak-Leaf Cluster), Silver Star, Legion of Merit (2 Oak-Leaf Clusters), Bronze Star (3 Clusters) and V device; Medal of Freedom, Distinguished Civilian Service Award (U.S.); de Croix Guerre with palm, Officer, Legion of Honour (France); Order of British Empire. *Member:* Wash., Oregon, California, San Francisco, Ohio, New York, District of Columbia Court of Appeals, Supreme Court U.S.A. and American Bar Assns.; Theta Delta Chi; Cincinnati Council on World Affairs (Dir.); Assn. of U.S. Army. *Clubs:* Bohemian, Pacific-Union (S. Francisco); Houston Country, Bayou, Tejas, Petroleum (Houston); Metropolitan, The Brook, Links (N.Y.C.); The George Towne, F. Street (Wash. DC). *Address:* 2918 Garfield Terrace N.W., Washington, D.C. 20008, U.S.A.

**BENEDEK, Martin Henry.** Industrialist. *B.* 1904. *Educ.* Public Schools, N.Y.C. *M.* 1935, Leonore Friedman. *S.* Warren Donald, A. Richard, and Barry Paul. *Career:* Pioneer in development of components in the electronics industry; inventor and developer of electronic devices. Founder; Albert Einstein Coll. of Medicine; Long Island Univ. Benedek Fellowship Fund. Chmn. Finance Comm., General Instrument Corporation 1955—. *Address:* 900 Fifth Ave., New York, N.Y. 10021; *office* 1775 Broadway, New York, N.Y. 10019.

**BENEDICT, Manson.** American nuclear engineer. *B.* 1907. *Educ.* Cornell Univ. (BChem 1928) and Massachusetts Inst. of Tech. (MS 1932; PhD 1935). *M.* 1935, Marjorie Oliver Allen. *Daus.* Mary Hannah (Sauer) and Marjorie Alice (Cohn). *Career:* Scientific Dir., Nat. Res. Corp. 1951–57; Tech. Asst. to Gen. Mgr., U.S. Atomic Energy Commission 1951–52; Dir. of Process Develop. Hydrocarbon Research Inc. 1946–51; in charge of Process Development, Kellex Corp. 1943–46; Research Chemist, M. W. Kellogg Co. 1938–43; Research Associate in Geophysics, Harvard Univ. 1936–37; National Research Fellow in Chemistry, Harvard 1935–36; member,

General Advisory Committee, U.S. Atomic Energy Commission 1958–68. (Chmn. 1962–64). Dir., Nuclear Science & Engineering Corpn. 1955–66; National Research Corp. 1962–67; Professor of Nuclear Engineering, Massachusetts Institute of Technology 1951–70, Institute Professor 1970–73, Emeritus Professor since 1973 (Head, Dept. of Nuclear Engineering 1958–71); Dir. Atomic Industrial Forum 1966–72. *Awards:* Fermi, U.S. Atomic Energy Commission 1972; founders, Nat. Acad. of Engineering 1976; National Medal of Science 1976. *Publications:* Nuclear Chem. Engnrg. (with T. H. Pigford); Engnrg. Dev. in the Gaseous Diffn. Process (with C. Williams). *Clubs:* Cosmos (Washington); Weston Golf; Country Club of Naples (Florida). *Address:* 25 Byron Road, Weston, Mass.; and *office* Massachusetts Institute of Technology, Cambridge, Mass., U.S.A.

**BENGE, Eugene Jackson.** President, Benge Associates (management consultants), Haverford, Pa. *B.* 1896. *Educ.* College (BS) plus one year fellowship in Applied Psychology for which no degree was granted; holds certificate in Accounting. *M.* 1953, Grace Griffith. *Career:* Industrial relations manager 1920–25 and 1930–38; Consultant 1926–29; and (self) 1939—. *Publications:* of 18 books in the field of management and personal development; including How to Become a Successful Executive; Cutting Clerical Costs; Office Administration; Salesmanship; Manpower in Marketing; The Right Career for You; Overcoming the Skilled Labor Shortage; Job Evaluation and Merit Rating; How to Manage for Tomorrow; Elements of Management Practice; You, Triumphant!—Now and Tomorrow!; and many contributions to management and other journals. *Member:* Socy. for Advancement of Management (Vice-Pres. for international affairs; received the Society's Industrial Incentive Award; is also a Fellow Vice-Pres. and Life Member); Council for International Progress in Management the U.S. affiliate of C.I.O.S.; Seminar leader, Long Range Planning, in Norway, Italy, Guatemala, Canada, South Africa, Sweden, England and U.S.A. *Address:* 0–4 Crowfields Lane, Crowfields, Asheville, N.C. 28803, U.S.A.

**BENIDICKSON, Hon. William Moore,** PC. Canadian Senator. *B.* 1911. Icelandic descent. *Educ.* Univ. of Manitoba (BA; LLB 1936). *M.* 1948, Agnes Richardson. *S.* 2 *Dau.* 1. *Career:* Barrister, Kenora 1935–39. Served in World War II (R.C.A.F.; attained rank of Acting Wing Commander) 1939–45. First elected to the House of Commons 1945; re-elected at General Elections 1949–53–57–58–62–63; Senator for Kenora-Rainy River, Ontario. Parliamentary Asst. to Minister of Transport 1951–53, and Minister of Finance 1951–57. Minister of Mines and Technical Surveys in the Canadian Federal Government, 1963–65. Former Hon. Solicitor for Kenora Trades & Labour Council. *Member:* A.F. & A.M.; Canadian Legion (life-member); Knight of the Order of the Falcon of Iceland. *Clubs:* Manitoba (Winnipeg). *Address:* 151 Mariposa, Rockcliffe, Ottawa, Ont.; and The Senate, Ottawa, Ont., Canada.

**BENJAMIN, Curtis G.** American book publisher. *B.* 1901. *Educ.* Universities of Kentucky (Hon. LLD 1957), Chicago, and Arizona (AB 1927; Hon. DLitt 1961). *M.* 1931, Norma Olson. *S.* John Lucien. *Dau.* Linda Baird (Smith). *Career:* President, McGraw-Hill Book Co. 1946–60; Chairman 1961–66, Member, Board of Directors of McGraw-Hill Publishing Co., McGraw-Hill International Corp., McGraw-Hill Publishing Co. Ltd., London, and McGraw-Hill Co. of Canada, Toronto; McGraw-Hill Book Co. of Australia Pty. Ltd.; The F. W. Dodge Corp., New York. Officer and Director, Franklin Publications Inc., N.Y.C. President, American Book Publishers Council 1958–60; Chmn., Government Advisory Committee, International Book Programs 1962–63. *Member:* Sigma Chi; Phi Kappa Phi; Sigma Delta Chi. Democrat. *Clubs:* University (New York); American (London). *Address:* Kellogg Hill Road, Weston, Conn., U.S.A.; and *office* c/o McGraw-Hill, 1221 Ave. of the Americas, Kellogg Hill Rd., Weston, Conn., U.S.A.

**BENJAMIN, Edward Bernard.** *B.* 1897. *Educ.* Harvard University (BA *magna cum laude,* 1918). *M.* 1921, Blanche Sterberger. *S.* Edward Bernard, Jr., William Mente Sternberger, and Jonathan Sterberger. *Career:* Vice-Pres., E. V. Benjamin Co. Inc. 1919–29 (Pres. 1930–47); President, Bay Chemical Co. 1938–47, and Myles Salt Co. 1940–47; Director, Whitney National Bank 1925–65; Pres. and Director, Starmount Co. 1930–68; member, Export Advisory Commission, U.S. Department of Commerce 1946; President and Director, Benjamin Minerals Inc. 1947—, and Friendly Center Inc. 1953–68. *Member:* Directors' Citizens' Cttee.; Duke Cancer Research Center. *Publications:* The Larger Liberalism (book); numerous articles on religion, sociology, economics, music and yachting for leading national magazines. Hon. DHL, University of Rochester, 1960. Past President, Cultural Attractions Fund for Greater New Orleans; Hon. Pres., Community Concert Assn. of New Orleans; Vice-Pres. & Director, New Orleans Opera House Association. Member, Chambers of Commerce of New Orleans, Greensboro, and New York. *Clubs:* Round Table; Petroleum and Southern Yacht of New Orleans; Merchants & Manufacturers (Greensboro); Bankers, Turf & Field of New York; New Orleans Country, Greensboro Country and Saratoga Golf; Lansdowne; Royal Thames Yacht (London, Eng.). *Address:* 383 Walnut Street, New Orleans 18; and *office* Whitney Building, New Orleans, La., U.S.A.

**BENJAMIN, Robert Saul.** American corporation executive; Attorney at Law. *B.* 1909. *Educ.* City College of the City of New York; Fordham Law School (JD); 1971, Brandeis Univ. Hon. Degree, Doctor of Humane Letters. *M.* 1949, Jean Kortright. *S.* Jonathan Adam. *Dau.* Margret Lisa, Taylor. *Career:* Recipient Legion of Merit, U.S. Army. Formerly, Director, Universal Pictures Corp., and Pathé Industries (now known as Amer. Corp.); Senior Partner, Phillips, Nizer, Benjamin, Krim & Ballon (law firm) since 1936. Chmn. of Bd. United Artists Corp. 1952–69, Co-Chmn. 1969–74 Chmn. Finance Cttee. since 1974; Director, Trans-America Corp. 1967—; Director, Urban League of Greater New York 1958—; Trustee, America-Israel Cultural Foundation Inc. 1958–68 and Hon. Trustee 1968—; Fellow 1960–67, Trustee 1967—, and Vice-Chmn. Board of Trustees 1969—, Brandeis University; Resident Member, Council of Foreign Relations 1967—; appointed by President Johnson, Director, Corporation for Public Broadcasting, 1968 and Chmn. since 1974; National Chmn. of the U.S. Committee for the United Nations 1961–64; Director, 1961–64, and National Chairman 1963–64; Amer. Assn. for U.N. President 1965–69, and Chmn. Bd. of Govnrs., 1969–73; Co-Chmn. Dir. Member Bd. Governors 1973, Chmn. 1974–75, Chmn. Bd. of Governors since 1975; United Nations Assn. of the U.S.A. Finance Chairman, Democratic Advisory Council of the Democratic National Cttee. 1958–60; Trustee & Treasurer, Carnegie Hall Corp. 1960–68; Hon. Trustee, 1968—; Chmn. National Citizens Commn. for Interntl. Co-operation Year 1965. Member, Exec. Cttee. for the Citizens' Cttee. for International Development 1961. Elected to N.Y. State Electoral College as an Elector for President Kennedy and Vice-President Johnson, 1960. Member, U.S. Delegation, 22nd U.N. General Assembly. *Address:* Dock Lane, Kings Point, L.I., N.Y. 11024; and *office* 729 Seventh Avenue, New York City 10019, U.S.A.

**BENN, Anthony Wedgwood,** MP. *B.* 1925. *M.* 1949. *Children* 4. Wartime R.A.F. pilot; Worked for BBC 1949; Elected Member of Parliament (Labour) Bristol S.E. 1950; Founder member, Movement for Colonial Freedom 1954; Rejected peerage 1960. Chmn. Fabian Society 1964; Postmaster General 1964; Minister of Technology 1966, Aviation 1967 and Power 1969; Chmn. of the Labour Party 1971; Opposition spokesman on Trade and Industry 1971–74; Secretary of State for Industry 1974–75; Sec. of State for Energy since 1975. Author of various political pamphlets. *Address:* House of Commons, London, SW1A 0AA.

**BENN, Edward Glanvill.** British. *B.* 1905. *Educ.* Harrow and Clare College, Cambridge. *M.* 1931, Beatrice Catherine Newbald. *S.* James Glanvill. *Dau.* Elizabeth. *Career:* Chairman, Benn Bros. Ltd., 1944—; The Exchange Telegraph Co. Ltd., 1969–72; Director, Ernest Benn Ltd.; Vice-President, Newspaper Press Fund, 1965; Honorary Treasurer, Commonwealth Press Union, 1967; Court Member, Worshipful Co., Stationers & Newspaper Makers, 1969; Trustee, N.A.B.S., 1955; Vice-Pres., Periodical Pub. Assoc., 1970. *Club:* The Reform. *Address:* 27 Lennox Gardens, London, SW1X ODE; and *office* Benn Brothers Ltd., 25 New Street Square, London, EC4A 3JA.

**BENNETT, Sir Charles Moihi,** DSO. New Zealand civil servant and diplomat. *B.* 1913. *Educ.* University of New Zealand and Exeter College, Oxford; MA; DipEd; Dip. Soc. Sci. *M. S.* 1. *Dau.* 1. *Career:* Is a member of a distinguished Maori family and has had a notable career as a soldier, scholar, public servant and sportsman. Entered the N.Z. Army as a private at the outbreak of war in 1939, and rose to the rank of Lieut.-Col. to command the Maori Battalion in Nov. 1942 (he was at that time the youngest battalion commander in the 2nd N.Z. Expeditionary Force). At the battle of Tebaga Gap against the Germans in North Africa—where he won the DSO—the Maori Battalion under his command was awarded 11 decorations, including the first

Victoria Cross ever won by a Maori soldier. He was severely wounded at the battle of Takrouna in April 1943. He has served in the Departments of Education, Broadcasting, Internal Affairs and Maori Affairs; was Director of Maori Welfare for N.Z.; was a member of the Parole Board, the Ngarimu Scholarship Fund Board, and the State Literary Fund Advisory Committee. High Commissioner, Malay 1959–63. Assistant Secretary, Department of Maori Affairs, Wellington 1963–69. National Vice-President of the N.Z. Labour Party, 1970–73; President 1973–75; Re-elected (for 3rd term) 1975. *Member:* N.Z. Prison Parole Board since 1974; Bd. of Dirs. Bank of N.Z. since 1974. *Awards:* Hon Dr. Laws, Canterbury Univ. (N.Z.) 1974; Created Knight Bachelor 1975. *Address:* MaKetu, Bay of Plenty, New Zealand.

**BENNETT, Colin James,** BA, LLB. Australian Barrister-at-Law. *B.* 1919. *Educ.* BA; LLB. *M.* 1942, Eileen Jocumsen. *S.* Christy, Walter and Colin (*D.*). *Daus.* Mary, Judith, Bridget, Anne (*D.*) and Imelda. *Career:* Nudgee College studies 1933–37; Queensland University 1938–42; Law Clerk 1941; House and Mathematics Master, Brisbane Grammar School 1942; active service with Royal Australian Air Force 1943–45; Crown Solicitor, Commonwealth Crown Solicitor's Office 1945–48; private practice of Barrister 1948—; Alderman. Brisbane City Council, Dec. 1949–May 1961 Member of Legislative Assembly, Queensland Parliament, May 1960–72. Member, Independent; Chmn., Univ. Student Council 1971–72; Hibernian Australasian Catholic Benefit Society; Southern Suburbs Football (Life member) and Cricket Clubs; South Brisbane Bowling. Past Pres. Nudgee Coll. O.B. Assn.; City Pastime Amateur Swimming Club; Johnsonian Club; Past Pres. Old Leonian Association. *Address:* 20 Paradise Street, Highgate Hill, Brisbane; and Inns of Court, 107 North Quay, Brisbane, Queensland 4000, Australia.

**BENNETT, Sir Frederic Mackarness,** M.P. *B.* 1918. *Educ.* Westminster School. *M.* 1945, Marion Patricia. *Career:* Served in Royal Artillery 1939–45. (Con.) Torbay (formerly Torquay) 1955—; Chmn. C'wealth Parl. Assn.; Exec. Cttee. General Council 1971–73 (Formerly Treasurer & Financial Adviser); Maj. R.A. (Retd.); Advisor International Affairs Kleinwort Benson Limited (London), Gulf Shipping & Faircloughs; Chairman: Commercial Union Assurance Co., Ltd., West End Board; Arawak Trust Co. (Caymans) Ltd.; Gulf Banking Corp. (Grand Cayman); BCCI Finance Limited Hong Kong; Dir.: Kleinwort, Benson Europe S.A.; Commercial Union Assurance Co., Ltd., Exeter Board; Arawak Trust Co. (Bahamas) Ltd.; Squibb A.S. (Denmark); Squibb Europe S.A., (France) Eubonia Services Isle of Man; Gibraltar Building Society. Member of the Council of Europe and The Western European Union. *Member:* Association Pour L'Etude des Problemes de L'Europe; Pakistan Socy.; Anglo-Turkish Socy. (President). *Awards:* Commander, Order of Phoenix (Greece); Star of Pakistan (1st Class). *Club:* Carlton (London). *Address:* The Hall, Aberangell, Nr. Machynlleth, Mont., Wales; and Kingswear Castle, South Devon.

**BENNETT, George Edward.** American. *B.* 1920. *Educ.* De Pauw Univ. (AB Chem. 1942) and Purdue Univ. (PhD, Organic Chemistry, 1947). *M.* 1943. *S.* Edward Alan. *Career:* With Monsanto: Research Chemist 1946–51; Research Group Leader 1951–54; Asst. Manager, Technical Recruitment 1954–59; Administrative Manager 1960–61; Personnel Manager 1961–63. Manager of Personnel, International Division, Monsanto Co. 1963–69; Personnel Dir. Latin America since 1969. *Publications:* three publications and nine patents in chemical fields. *Member:* Amer. Chemical Socy.; Amer. Management Assn.; Research Socy. of America. *Address:* 727 Twin Fawns Drive, Frontenac, Mo. 63131; and *office* 800 N. Lindbergh Boulevard, St. Louis, Mo. 63166, U.S.A.

**BENNETT, George F.** American investment manager. *B.* 1911. *Educ.* Harvard College (AB *cum laude* 1933). *M.* 1935, Helen Frances Brigham. *S.* Peter C., George F., Jr., and Robert B. *Career:* President & Director: State Street Investment Corp., and Federal Street Fund Inc. (both of Boston); Partner, State Street Research & Management Co., Boston. Director: Middle South Utilities Inc., N.Y.C.; New England Electric System, Boston; Commonwealth Oil Refining Inc., Puerto Rico; John Hancock Mutual Life Insurance Co., Boston; Ford Motor Co. Detroit; Florida Power & Light Co. Miami; Hewlett-Packard Co. Palo-Alto. Treasurer, Harvard University, Cambridge, Mass. Trustee, Committee for Economic Development. Republican. *Clubs:* Harvard Links, (N.Y.C.); Union (Boston); Cohasset Golf; Hingham Yacht. *Address :* 712 Main Street, Hingham, Mass.; and *office* 140 Federal Street, Boston 10, Mass., U.S.A.

**BENNETT, Hon. Gordon Lockhart.** Canadian. *B.* 1912. *Educ.* MSc., DCL (Acadia). *M.* 1937, Doris Lulu Bernard. *Dau.* 1. *Career:* Professor of Chemistry, Prince of Wales Coll., Charlottetown, Prince Edward I. 1939–66 (Registar 1959–66). Member of Provincial Government of Prince Edward Island. Legislative Assembly 1966–74, Minister of Education 1966–72, President, Executive Council of the Government 1966–74; Minister of Justice 1970–74; Lieut.-Gov. of the Province of Prince Edward Island since 1974. *Publications:* articles of various kinds relating to education. Past Pres. Canadian Club, Prince Edward I; Past Pres., Dominion Curling Assn., Mem. of Canadian Curling Hall of Fame; Past Gr. Master, Masons, Prince Edward I. Liberal. *Address:* Government House, Charlottetown, Prince Edward Island.

**BENNETT, John M., Jr.** Major General, U.S.A.F.R. (Silver Star, DFC, Legion of Merit, Bronze Star, Air Medal, Croix de Guerre with Palm). Rancher, banker. *B.* 1908. *Educ.* Phillips Academy, Andover, Mass. (Graduated), Princeton University, and University of Texas (BSc 1931). *M.* 1946, Eleanor Catherine Freeborn. *S.* Davis G. and John M. IV. *Daus.* Carolyn and Eleanor. *Career:* Commanded 100th Bomber Group stationed in England during World War II. Chairman of the Board; National Bank of Commerce 1953–76; Yoakum National Bank, Yoakum, Tex. 1950—; Dir.: Texas & Southwestern Cattle Raisers Association. *Publication:* Letters From England. Republican. *Clubs:* Country, Argyle (San Antonio); Army-Navy (Washington, D.C.). *Address:* 238 W. Craig Pl., San Antonio, Tex. 78205; and *office* 2111 National Bank of Commerce Building, San Antonio 78205, Tex., U.S.A.

**BENNETT, Joseph Bentley, Jr.** Retired American book publishing executive. *B.* 1906. *Educ.* William & Mary Coll.; University of Richmond; New York Univ. (Management Institute —graduate courses). *M.* (1) 1929, Marguerite Blount Holmes (*Dec.* 1976). (2) 1977, Anabelle Lee Pennybaker. *S.* Joseph Bentley III. *Career:* College Representative, The Macmillan Co. 1930–43; Assoc. Science Editor, College Dept. 1943–45; Science Editor 1945–47; Asst. Manager and Managing Editor, College Dept. 1947–48; elected to Board of Directors 1947; Asst. Gen. Mgr. 1948–51; General Manager 1951; Asst. Secy. 1952–59; Vice-President 1958. Vice-President, Secretary and General Manager, The Macmillan Co. 1959–62; Secretary & Director, Collier-Macmillan Canada Ltd. 1959–62; Vice-Pres. and Dir., Riverside (N.J.) Distribution Center 1962–64; Vice-Pres. Administration, N.Y. 1964; transferred to parent corporation, Crowell, Collier & Macmillan, as Director of Corporate Services, and Director of Relocation Project, Jan. 1965. Director of Corporate Facilities Planning, Aug. 1967. Asst. Vice-Pres. and Director, Facilities Planning, 1968. Vice-President and Director, Facilities Planning, Crowell, Collier & Macmillan 1968–70. *Publication:* Automatic Technique in Book Warehousing and Shipping (pub. American Inst. of Electrical Engineers). Republican. *Clubs:* Palm Beach Yacht Club, The Little Club (Florida). *Address:* 2 Barefoot Lane, Hypoluxo Island, Lantana, Florida.

**BENNETT, Lewis,** BDSc., LDS., FAIA. Australian commerical broadcasting executive. *B.* 1910. *Educ.* Brisbane Grammar School and Univ. of Queensland. *M.* 1936, Isabel Dalgleish. *Dau.* 1. *Career:* Production Manager, 2UE 1936; Manager 2TM 1936; Production Mgr. 3KZ 1939; Gen. Mgr. 5KA 1948; Man. Dir. Nilsen's Broadcasting Service (Station 3UZ) Melbourne, since 1950. *Member:* Federal Council, Broadcasting Fed. 1953–76; Chmn. Sporting, Engineering Research Cttees.; Founder and Chmn. Aust. Radio Adv. Bureau 1959–68; Pres. Fed. Aust. Commercial Broadcasters 1959–60; Chmn. Federal Broadcasting Cttee. Royal Tour 1954, Olympic Games 1955–56; Member Governing Council, Reference Bd. Aust. Inst. Advertising 1960–73; Deputy Chmn. Citizens Cttee. Victorian Red Cross Socy. 1951–55; Pres. Melbourne Rotary 1961–62; Secy. and Dir. Representation Services Australia. *Clubs:* Melbourne Rotary, Royal Automobile (Vic.), Victoria Racing, Victoria Amateur Turf, Kelvin Moonee Valley Racing. *Address:* 17 Stawell Street, Windsor, Melbourne, Victoria 3181, Australia.

**BENNETT, Nigel Jack,** DFC (& Bar), FCA, FBIM. British. *B.* 1913. *Educ.* King Edward VI Sch., Southampton; Fellow Brit. Inst. Mgnt. *M.* 1941, Mary Isobel Cain. *Career:* Chmn. Tecalemit Ltd.; Dir. British Filters Ltd., British Gas and Oil Burners Ltd., Industrial & Domestic Heaters Ltd. Tecalemit

(Australasia) Pty. Ltd., Tecalemit India Ltd. *Club:* Bath; Temple Golf. *Address: office* Tecalemit Ltd., Maidenhead, Berks., SL6 3AQ.

**BENNETT, Dr. Reginald,** VRD, MA, BM, BCh, LMSSA. DPM, MP, Grand Officer of the Order of Merit of the Italian Republic. British politician and businessman. *B.* 1911, *Educ.* Winchester & New Coll. Oxford. *M.* 1947, Henrietta Crane. *S.* 1. *Daus.* 3. *Career:* War Service, Naval Surgeon & Psychiatrist; Fleet Air Arm Pilot; Member, Parliament, Conservative, Gosport & Fareham 1950–74, Fareham 1974—; Psychiatrist, various Hospitals & Clinics prior to 1953; Parliamentary Private Secy. various Cabinet Ministers 1951–63; Chmn., Parly. Scientific Cttee. 1959–62; Chmn., Catering Sub-Cttee. House of Commons 1970–74, and 1976—; Chmn., Anglo Italian Parly. Group since 1971; Chmn., Amateur Yacht Research Society since 1972; Chmn., Downland Housing Soc. 1976; Vice-Pres., Franco British Group; Pres., Brit. Launderers Research Assn. 1962–77; Vice-Pres. of Trustees, Paddle Steamer "Tattershall Castle" Trust, 1976; Trustee, H.M.S. "Cavalier" Trust. *Member:* Council, International Inst. for Human Nutrition Vice-Pres., Club Oenologique 1973. *Awards:* Chevalier du Tastevin; Cmmandeur du Médoc; Galant de la Verte Marennes; Chevalier de Bretvin (Muscadet); Chevalier de St Etienne (Alsace); Hon. Citizen of Atlanta. *Publications:* Articles on Psychiatry, Criminology, Politics; Wine and Yacht Racing. *Clubs:* Whites; many Yacht. *Address:* House of Commons, London, S.W.1.

**BENNETT, Robert Royce.** American. Engineering and Management Consultant. *B.* 1926. *Educ.* California Inst. of Technology (BS 1945, MS 1947, PhD 1949). *M.* 1950, Margaret Stewart Keyes. *S.* Philip Keyes. *Daus.* Susan Keyes and Laurie Ann. *Career:* Vice-Pres. TRW Systems 1954–65; Member of Technical Staff, Hughes Aircraft Co. 1949–54; Eng. Mangt. Consultant (own Business) since 1965. *Member:* Accoustical Socy. of America; Inst. of Electrical and Electronic Engineers. Republican. *Address:* 6280 Willamette, Eugene, Ore. 97401, U.S.A.

**BENNETT, William Tapley, Jr.** American Diplomat. *B.* 1917. *Educ.* Univ. of Georgia—AB; George Washington Univ.—JD; Indiana State Univ.—DCL (Hon.). *M.* 1945, Margaret Rutherfurd White. *S.* 2. *Daus.* 3. *Career:* Dep. Dir., South American Affairs, Dept. of State 1951–54; Asst. to Under-Sec. of State, Washington D.C. 1955–57; Counsellor, U.S. Embassy, Austria 1957–60; Counsellor, U.S. Embassy, Italy 1960–61; Minister, U.S. Embassy, Greece 1961–64; Amb. Ex. & Plen. to Dominican Republic 1964–66, to Portugal 1966–69; State Dept. Rep. to Air University 1969–71; Amb. Ex. & Plen., Dep. U.S. Rep. to UN 1971–77; Amb. Ex. & Plen., U.S. Rep to NATO since 1977. *Address:* OTAN-NATO, 1110 Brussels, Belgium.

**BENSON, Hon. Edgar John,** PC, FCA. Canadian politician and accountant. *B.* 1923. *Educ.* Queen's Univ., Kingston, Ont. (BComm). *M.* Marie Louise Van Laar (Nymegan). *S.* Robert, Paul, Peter. *Dau.* Nancy. *Career:* Chartered Acct., Leonard Macpherson & Co. Kingston 1952–64; Asst. Professor of Commerce, Queen's Univ. 1952–62; elected Member of Parliament for Riding of Kingston 1963 and 1965. Parliamentary Secy. to Min. of Finance 1963–64; Minister of National Revenue 1964; Vice-Chmn. Treasury Board 1965–68; Minister of Finance 1968–72; Min. of National Defence 1972; Pres., Canadian Transport Commission since 1972. *Address:* 44 Strathcona Crescent, Kingston, Ontario; and 5115 Centre Block, House of Commons, Ottawa 4, Canada.

**BENSON, Sir Henry Alexander,** GBE. *B.* 1909. *Educ.* Johannesburg, S. Africa. *M.* 1939, Anne Virginia Macleod. *S.* 2. *Dau.* 1. *Career:* Partner, Coopers & Lybrand, Chartered Accountants, London 1934–75; Commissioned Grenadier Guards 1940–45; Director, Royal Ordnance Factories 1943–44. Director, Finance for Industry Ltd. since 1974; Member of Council, Institute of Chartered Accountants in England and Wales 1956–75; President, 1966. Member of Tribunal under Prevention of Fraud (Investments) Act (1939), 1957–74; Member of various Government committees and working parties. Director, Hudson's Bay Co. 1953 (Dep. Governor 1955; retired 1962). Appointed by Minister of Power to enquire into methods adopted by London Electricity Board for disposal of scrap cable and into allegations regarding these matters 1958. Appointed to investigate and report on position of railways in N. Ireland 1961. Chmn. of London Committee appointed by the three Produce Boards and the four shipping lines engaged in N.Z. trade to report on possibility of introducing economies in the shipping and ancillary services connected with export of meat, dairy produce and fruit, 1962; Joint Commissioner to report on the proposed formation of a National Industrial Organisation 1963. Apptd. Independent Chmn. of British Iron & Steel Fed. Development Co-ordinating Cttee. to consider all aspects of iron and steel industry. Apptd. by Minister of Ag. Fisheries and Food an independent member of the Permanent Joint Hops Cttee. 1967. Appointed by Nat. Trust as Chmn. of an Advisory Cttee. to review the management, organization and responsibilities of the Nat. Trust 1967; also by Joint Turf Authorities as Chmn. of the Racing Industry Cttee. of Inquiry which is to make a detailed study of the whole of the financial structure and requirements of the racing industry 1967; Independent member, Royal Dockyards Policy Board, 1971– 75; Cttee., enquire administration & organization of Ministry of Defence, 1969–71; Vice-Pres., Union Européenne des Experts Comptables Economiques et financiers, 1969; Member CBI Company Affairs Cttee. 1972–73; Chmn., Int. Accounting Standards Cttee. since 1973; Appointed Adviser to Governor of Bank of England on finance for Industry since 1975; Chmn., Royal Commission on Legal Services 1976—. *Publications:* The Future Role of the Accountant in Practice (1958). *Fellow:* Institute Chartered Accountants in England and Wales. *Clubs:* Brooks's; Jockey; Royal Yacht Sqdn. *Address:* 9 Durward House, 31 Kensington Court, London, W8 5BH.

**BENT, James Edward.** *B.* 1905. *Educ.* Trinity College, Hartford. *M.* 1936, Frances P. Williams. *Career:* Asst. Mgr., Aetna Leasing Corp., Denver, Colo. 1928–29; Securities Salesman, R. C. Buell & Co., Hartford 1929–30; Asst. Foreman, U.S. Rubber Co., Naugatuck, Conn. 1930–31; Sales Mgr., Page Steel & Wire Co., Hartford office 1931–32; Pres. and Chmn. of Board, Bent & Bent Inc. (Real Estate and Insurance Agency) 1932–63 (left active employment of this firm in 1946, to assume full-time responsibility of the Hartford Federal Savings & Loan Assn.); Chairman and Chief Executive Officer Hartford Federal Savings & Loan Assn., Jan. 1962—; Chairman of the Board and President, JEB Corp. President, Hartford Homes, Inc.; Member, Committee for Hartford; also Hospital Council of Greater Hartford; Advisor, Greater Hartford Community Ambassador Project. *Member:* Neighbourhood Planning Associates; Director. Urban League of Greater Hartford; Trustee, Connecticut Public Expenditure Council; Director, Hartford Times International Travel Club; Trustee, The Open Hearth Association; Director, Greater Hartford Housing Development Fund, Inc.; Security Insurance Company of Hartford; New Amsterdam Casualty Company; United States Casualty Company; The Connecticut Indemnity Company; Security-Connecticut Life Insurance Company; The Fire and Casualty Insurance Company of Connecticut; National Federal Home Loan Bank Board Committee on Emergency Preparedness; Underground Record Protection Cooperative Trust; President, Greater Hartford Chamber of Commerce 1963–65 and Hartford Homes Inc. 1959—; Past Pres., National League of Insured Savings Associations; New England Conference of Savings & Loans Assns. and Co-operative Banks; Director and Past Pres., Federal Savings League of New England; Past Director, Federal Home Loan Bank of Boston; served two terms on Federal Savings and Loan Advisory Council. *Publication:* A Report on Housing and Home Financing in Guatemala (including a Study and Recommended Methods for Providing Better Homes and Easier Home Financing)—prepared under the authority of the International Co-operation Administration, Washington, D.C., July 1960. *Clubs:* Rotary; Hartford; University; Hartford Golf; Tunxis; Oasis; Officers Club of Connecticut. *Address:* 343 North Steele Road, West Hartford 17, Conn.; and *office* 50 State Street, Hartford 1, Conn., U.S.A.

**BENTHALL, Sir (Arthur) Paul,** KBE. British company director (ret.). *B* 25 Jan. 1902. *Educ.* Eton; Christ Church, Oxford. *M.* 1932, Mary Lucy Pringle. *S.* 4. *Career:* Former Chmn., Amalgamated Metal Corp. Ltd.; Bird & Co. (London), Ltd.; Dir., Chartered Bank: Fellow of Linnean Society, *Publication:* The Trees of Calcutta and its Neighbourhood. *Address:* Benthall Hall, Broseley, Salop.

**BENTINCK van SCHOONHETEN, Baron Oswald François.** Netherlands diplomat. *B.* 1909. *M.* Meta van der Slooten, LLD. *S.* Hendrik Volkier and Willem Oswald. *Career:* Netherlands Indies Commercial Bank in the Netherlands and the Far East 1933–42; Netherlands East Indies Army and prisoner of war in Burma and Siam 1942–45; Ministry of Foreign Affairs 1946–47; Consul Montreal 1947–50; Ministry of Foreign Affairs 1950–52; Counsellor of Embassy Caracas 1952–56; Consul-General Munich 1957–59; Minister to New Zealand 1959–63; Ambassador to Czechoslovakia 1964–66;

to Israel 1967–71; Ireland 1971 until retirement. *Address:* Apartado Postal 221, Altea, Alicante, Spain.

**BENTSEN, Lloyd.** American Senator. *B.* 1921. *Educ.* Univ. of Texas, Univ. of Texas Sch. of Law—LLB. *M.* 1943, Beryl Ann Longino. *S.* 2. *Dau.* 1. *Career:* U.S. Army Air Corps during W.W.II, rising to Colonel in the Air Force Reserve; County Judge of Hidalgo County, Texas 1946–48; mem., U.S. House of Reps. 1948–54; entered business, becoming Pres. of Lincoln Consolidated & Dir. of a number of major corporations; U.S. Senator from Texas since 1970, re-elected 1976; Chmn., Transportation Sub-Cttee., Sub-Cttee. on Economic Growth & Sub-Cttee. on Private Pension Plans; mem. Standing Cttees. on Finance, & Environment & Public Works, & Joint Economic Cttee. Democrat. *Decorations:* Distinguished Flying Cross; Air Medal with three oak leaf clusters. *Address:* 115 Senate Office Building, Washington, D.C. 20510, U.S.A.

**BENTSUR, Shmuel.** Israeli diplomat. *B.* 1906. *Educ.* Cluj (Rumania) Academy of Commerce and Political Economy. *M.* 1930, Sara Weinstein. *S.* 1. *Career:* Consul, Budapest 1948–49; Consul and First Secretary, Budapest 1949–50; Chargé d'Affaires e.p. Budapest 1950–52; Chargé d'Affaires e.p. Sofia 1952; Director-Adjoint, Eastern European Division, Ministry of Foreign Affairs, Jerusalem 1952–53; Director, 1953–56; Minister to Austria 1956–58; Deputy Director General, Ministry of Foreign Affairs, Jerusalem 1958–62; Ambassador to Switzerland 1962–67. Inspector General of the Foreign Service, Ministry of Foreign Affairs, Jerusalem, 1967. *Member:* Labor Party. *Address:* Ministry of Foreign Affairs, Jerusalem, Israel.

**BENYON, William Richard,** MP. British Politician. *B.* 1930. *Educ.* Royal Naval Coll., Dartmouth. *M.* 1957, Elizabeth Ann Hallifax. *S.* 2. *Daus.* 3. *Career:* With Royal Navy until 1956; Courtaulds Ltd. 1956–64; MP (Cons.) for Buckingham since 1970. *Clubs:* Whites; Boodles; Pratts. *Address:* Englefield House, Theale, Reading; and *office* House of Commons, London SW1A 0AA.

**BERANEK, Leo Leroy.** Scientist, administrator. *B.* 1914. *Educ.* Cornell Coll., Iowa (BA 1936) and Harvard Univ. (MS 1937; DSc 1940). *M.* 1941, Phyllis Knight. *S.* James Knight and Thomas Haynes. *Career:* At Harvard Univ.: Instructor on Applied Physics 1940–41; Asst. Prof. of Applied Physics 1941–43; Dir. of Research of Sound 1943–45; Director of Electro-Acoustics and Systems Laboratories 1945–46. At M.I.T.: Assoc. Prof. Communication Engineering 1947–58; Technical Director, Acoustics Laboratory 1947–53; Dir. Bolt Beranek & Newman Inc., Cambridge, MA 1953— (Pres. 1943–69); Lecturer, Massachusetts Inst. of Technology (M.I.T.) 1958—; Chmn. Bd. Mueller-BBN GmbH, Munich 1962—; Pres. Inst. of Noise Control Engineering, Washington, D.C.; Dir. Pres. and Chief Exec. Officer of Boston Broadcasters Inc. operates Comm. TV. Channel 5, Boston. *Publications:* books: Sound Control in Airplanes (with others) (1944); Acoustic Measurements (1949); Acoustics (1954); Noise Reduction (with others) (1960); Music, Acoustics and Architecture (1962); Noise and Vibration Control; papers total over 100 in acoustics, psychoacoustics, electrical and audio communications. *Awards:* Phi Beta Kappa; Sigma Xi; Eta Kappa Nu; John Simon Guggenheim Fellowship 1946–47; United States Civilian Award of Merit 1947; Alumni Citation, Cornell, 1953; Biennial Award of Acoustical Socy. of America. 1944; Wallace Clement Sabine Award from the same Society, 1961; Gold Medal from the same Society, 1975; Abe Lincoln Television Award, 1976; Silver Commemorative Medal, Groupement des Acousticiens de Langue Française, 1966; Gold Medal, Audio Engineering Society 1971. *Fellow:* Amer. Acad. of Arts & Sciences; National Acad. of Engineering; Acoustical Socy. of America (Pres. 1954–55), Amer. Physical Socy., Inst. of Electrical and Electronic Engineers (Chmn. Professional Group on Audio 1950–51), Audio Engineering Socy. (President 1967–68); A.A.A.S. and Institute of Noise Control Engineering. Member, Groupement des Acousticiens de Langue Française. Chairman, Acoustical Standards Board, American Standards Assn. 1955–69. *Clubs:* Winchester (Mass.) Country; M.I.T. Faculty. *Address:* 7 Ledgewood Road, Winchester, Mass.; and *office* 5 TV Place, Needham, Mass., U.S.A.

**BÉRARD-ANDERSEN, Pierre.** Norwegian. *B.* 1901. *Educ.* College and Commercial High School, Oslo. *M.* 1932, Louisette Peraut. *S.* Jan, René, Pierre. *Career:* Manager, K. Andersen & Co. S/A (shipbrokers, charterers and forwarding agents), Fredrikstad; French Consular Agent for Fredrikstad and Sarpsborg. Commander, Order of Black Star; Chevalier of the Legion d'Honneur (France); Chevalier of the Orders of Leopold and the Crown (Belgium). *Address:* Bydalen Allee 10, Fredrikstad, Norway.

**BERCHTOLD, Walter,** Dr. jur., Dr. oecho. Swiss airline executive. *B.* 1 Oct. 1906. *M.* 1936, Berta Boller. *S.* Walter. *Dau.* Marianne. District Court, Winterthur June–Nov. 1930. *Career:* Practical Operation Service of Swiss Federal Railways in various parts of the country 1930–32; with Personnel Department and Secretariat-General, Swiss Federal Railways, Berne 1933–38; Financial Editor, Neue Zurcher Zeitung, Zürich 1938–45; District Manager, Swiss Federal Railways, Zürich 1945–50; Managing Director and President, Swiss-air (Swiss Air Transport Company Ltd.) since May 1950; Pres., Swiss Churchill Foundation. *Awards:* Gold medal Swiss Foundation; Pro Aero, Merits in Aviation. *Address:* Zollikerstrasse 10, Zollikon, Zurich, Switzerland.

**BERESFORD, Anthony de la Poer,** TD. British. *B.* 1915. *Educ.* Imperial Service Coll. *M.* 1939, E. Mary Canning. *S.* 2. *Career:* Dir. of Mfg. H. J. Heinz Co. Ltd., 1956–61; Dir. Sales & Marketing 1961–63; Dep. Man. Dir., 1963–64; Man. Dir., 1964–69; Vice-Chmn. 1969–74; Pres. Food Manufacturers Federation 1970–73; Chmn. British Nutrition Foundation 1975–76. *Member:* Royal Socy. Protection of Birds; Food Science & Technology Bd.; Bd., John Lyon & Orley Farm Schools, Liveryman Skinners Co. *Address:* Toll-Gate Cottage, London Road, Harrow on the Hill, Middx.; and *office* Hayes Park, Hayes, Middx.

**BERESFORD, Donald Charles de la Poer.** Australian. *B.* 1933. *Educ.* St. Peter's College, University of Adelaide. *M.* 1962, Ruth Tisdall. *S.* 1. *Dau.* 1. *Career:* Journalist (Adelaide Advertiser, Straits Times, Australian Broadcasting Commission, London) 1949–59. Public Relations Officer, Commonwealth Department of Social Services, Melbourne 1960–61. Manager, New York office, Australian National Travel Assn. 1961–64. Manager, U.K. and Europe Australian Tourist Commission 1964–68; Dir. Marketing, Australian Tourist Commission 1968–74; Asst. Gen. Man., Australian Tourist Commission 1974–77; Dir. of Tourism, New South Wales 1977. *Address:* N.S.W. Department of Tourism, 95 York Street, Sydney 2000, Australia.

**BERESFORD-STOOKE, Sir George,** KCMG. British administrator. *B.* 3 Jan. 1897. *Educ.* Fulneck School, Yorks.; King Edward's School, Bath. *M.* 1931, Creenagh Richards. *S.* 1. *Dau.* 1. *Career:* Served in World War I, Royal Navy 1914–19; Colonial Service, Sarawak 1920, Kenya 1925, Mauritius 1933, Kenya 1936, Zanzibar 1940, Northern Rhodesia 1942; Chief Secretary Nigeria 1945; Governor and C.-in-C., Sierra Leone 1948; Crown Agent for the Colonies 1953–55; Overseas Commissioner, Boy Scouts Assn., 1954–61; Gentleman Usher of the Blue Rod 1959–72; Vice-Chmn., Int. African Institute 1954–74. *Address:* Little Rydon, Hillfarrance, nr. Taunton, Somerset.

**BERG, Kristofer.** Norwegian. *B.* 1920. *Educ.* Harvard Bus. Sch. (MBA); Hartford Univ. Conn. (BS Eng); Norges Handelshøiskole (Siv.øk). *M.* 1947, Alice Graham. *S.* 1. *Daus.* 2. *Career:* Emhart Mfg. Co. Millipore Filter Corp. (USA) 1951–60; A/S Christiania Glasmagasin 1961–68; Man. Dir. 1964–68; Prof. Dir. Norwegian and Foreign Cos. since 1968. *Address:* Øvre Ullern Terasse 78, Oslo 3, Norway.

**BERGENHEIM, Holger Georg Edvard.** Finnish. Counsellor of Commerce. *B.* 1907. *M.* (1) 1931, Märta Cecilia Söderberg; (2) 1935, Stella Graf-Findeisen; (3) 1947, Doris Margareta Sophy Grünn (*dec.*). *S.* Kenneth, Christian and Torsten. *Daus.* Estelle, Brita Maria. *Career:* Military degree Captain 1941; Counsellor of Commerce 1962. Hon. Chairman of Board: Fedn. of Techno-Chemical Industries, and Society of Medicine Importers. Chairman of the Board of Directors: Oy Diaco Ab 1959—; Oy Epeko Ab 1966—; Oy Hoechst Fennica Ab 1961—; Oy Mallasjuoma since 1971. Managing Director: Epeco Ab, Sweden, 1967—, and Medicin-import Ab 1946—. Member of the Board: Assn. of Finnish Industries 1958—, and Oy Mainos-TV-Reklam Ab. Commercial TV, 1959—, Oy Mallasjuoma, 1969—. *Address:* Fabriksgatan 21 B, 46 Helsinki 15; and *office* Myntgatan 1 A, Helsinki 16.

**BERGESEN, Sigval.** d.y. Norwegian shipowner. *B.* 1893. *Educ.* Oslo Commercial Coll. *M.* 1945, Nanki de Fekete. *S.* Berge Sigval. *Daus.* Helene Sophie (Denstad), Ingerid, Charlotte (Bergesen). *Career:* Joined Sigval Bergesen, Stavanger, 1916; Partner and Head of Shipowning Dept. 1918–35; founded Sig. Bergesen d.y. & Co. 1935; Co-Director, A. P. Møller, Copenhagen, and of Odense Staalskibsvaerft,

Odense, 1934–39; Sen. Partner, Sig. Bergesen d.y. & Co. (Bergesen d.y. concern), Oslo and Stavanger, shipowners, insurance brokers and Lloyd's agents; Chairman of Board and Managing Director, A/S Sig Bergesen d.y. & Co., Skibsaktieselskapet Snefonn; Skipsaksjeseeskapet Bergehus A/S Sigmalm, A/S Siganka; Chmn. of Bd., Teknisk Bureau A/S, Rydberg & Petterson A/S; Underwriting Member Lloyd's since 1968; member of Bd. of Dirs., Norwegian Shipowners/ Assn. *Awards:* Commander, Order of St. Olav; Commander, Order of Dannebrog; Les Palmes d'Officier de l'Instr. Publique (France); Knights Cross, Order of the Redeemer (Greece); Royal Order of George 1; Médaille de l'Alliance Française. *Clubs:* Det Norske Selskab; Det Stavangerske Klubselskab; Royal Norwegian Automobile; Oslo Golf; Kongelig Norsk Seilforening. *Address:* Huk Avenue 15, Bygdoy, Oslo 2; and *office* 'Bergehus', Drammensveien 106, Oslo 2, Norway.

**BERGHIANU**, Maxim. Romanian economist and politician. *B.* 1925. *Educ.* Economic Sciences and Planning Institute, Bucharest. *M.* Silvia Popovici. *Daus.* 2. *Career:* member Union Communist Youth 1944; Romanian Comm. Party 1945—; First Secy., Comm. Party Cttee., Brasov Region 1955–59; Cluj Region 1963–65; Alt. member, Central Cttee., R.C.P. 1955—; Deputy to Grand Nat. Assembly 1957—; Alt. member, Exec. Cttee., Central Cttee. R.C.P. 1965, member 1966—; Member, Defence Council Romania since 1969. Hero of Socialist Labour 1971. *Address:* Central Committee of the Romanian Communist Party, Bucharest, Romania.

**BERGH-JACOBSEN**, Jacob Stein. Norwegian. *B.* 1918. *M.* 1946, Sissel Asper. *S.* 2. *Dau.* 1. *Career:* Dep. Man. Dir. Christiania Bank og Kreditkasse; Dir., Heimdal, Eksportfinans, Elektrofabrikken: Gjensidige, Invest-Man, Securus, CBK International S.A.; The Norwegian Export Council; Laboremus, Lorentzens Skibs A/S; Norema, Mustad Industrier A/S. *Address:* Åmotveien 2, Oslo 8, Norway; and *office* Stortorvet 7, Oslo 1.

**BERGLAND**, Sverre. Norwegian shipowner. *B.* 1900. *Educ.* Student 1921; Oslo University (LLB 1926); Called to the Bar 1927. *M.* 1934, Helene Klaveness Rasmussen. *S.* Aslak, Odd and Johan. *Dau.* Helene. *Career:* Barrister at the Supreme Court of Norway since 1938; Director: Hvalfangeraktieselskapet 'Rhosshavet' since 1949, and Hvalfangertaktieselskapet 'Vestfold' since 1947; Chairman, The Whaling Employers' Association (and its Negotiation Committee) since 1946; Chairman, Hvalfangernes Assuranceforening's Committee since 1955; member of Board, Tønsberg Sjøforsikringsselskap since 1954; member of various other organizations and associations. *Address:* Sandefjord, Norway.

**BERGQUIST**, Laurence Carl. American. International Oil Executive (Ret.). Comdr. USNR (Ret.); Legion of Merit (Combat V). *B.* 1905. *Educ.* Columbia University (MA Pol. Sc. and University of North Dakota (BSc Indus. Eng.); Graduate of U.S. Navy School of Military Government. *M.* 1931, Lillian V. Rasmussen. *Daus.* Karen Christina (Sincere, Jr.) and Kirsten Marea (Brundage). *Career:* Director, Standard-Vacuum Sales Co., Indonesia 1950–53; Assistant to Manager for S.E. Asia, Standard-Vacuum Oil Co., N.Y. Hq. 1946–50. President and General Manager, Iricon Agency Ltd. 1962–70 (Vice-Pres. and Asst. General Manager 1956–60, Exec. Vice-President 1960–62). Director: Iranian Oil Participants Ltd. 1960–70, and Iranian Oil Services (Holdings) Ltd. 1960–70 Sr. Military Government Officer on staff of Commander Marshalls-Gilbert Area 1944–45. District Mgr., Standard-Vacuum Oil Co. (various posts in Singapore and Malaya) 1932–41. Elected to Sigma Tau (hon. engineering fraternity), and to Blue Key (hon. service fraternity). *Member:* Amer. Chamber of Commerce (U.K.) (Director): 1960–70. American Society in London (Chmn. 1965); British-American Associates (mem. Exec. Cttee.); 1960–70. Graduate Faculties Alumni, Columbia Univ.; Tau Kappa Epsilon (collegiate social); The Pilgrims of the United States; Navy League, U.S. (Life member). *Clubs:* American in London (President, 1970); Commonwealth (California). *Address:* One Las Olas Circle—Apt 1101, Ft. Lauderdale, Florida, U.S.A.

**BERINSON**, Zvi. Israeli judge. *B.* 1907. *Educ.* Scots College, Palestine (Sc. Dip.), Jesus College, Cambridge (BA); Barrister-at-Law, Gray's Inn, London; Israeli Advocate. *M.* 1931, Hana Wolf. *S.* Haim. *Dau.* Ilana. *Career:* Teacher, Scots Coll., Safad, Palestine 1929–31; Legal Adviser and Head of Municipal Dept., General Federation of Labour 1935–49; Director-General, Ministry of Labour 1949–53; Chairman: The Socy. for Rehabilitation of Offenders in Jerusalem; Head, Israeli Deleg. to Int. Labour Conference 1949–53, 1958–59; Judge of the Supreme Court of Israel since Dec. 1953. Lecturer on Labour Law and Social Insurance, Hebrew Univ., Jerusalem 1952–71; Chairman, League of Societies for Rehabilitation of Offenders; Bd. Mem. Int. Prisoners Aid Assn.; Hon. Pres. Public Council for the Prevention of Noise and Air Pollution in Israel. Chairman, Israel Opera Council. *Address:* Supreme Court, Jerusalem, Israel.

**BERKMAN**, Jack Neville. American attorney-at-law and executive. *B.* London, England 1905. *Educ.* Univ. of Michigan (AB 1926); Harvard Law School (JD 1929). *M.* (1) 1933, Sybiel B. Altman (*d.* 27 May 1964). *S.* Myles P. Monroe E., and Stephen L.; (2) 1970, Lillian Rojtman. *Career:* Vice-Chmn. Bd. and Chmn. of Exec. Cttee. Dir. Rust Craft Greeting Cards, Inc.; Vice-Chmn. Bd. and Dir. Rust Craft Broadcasting Co.; Pres., Radio Buffalo, Inc.; Rust Craft Broadcasting of Pennsylvania Inc., of New York Inc. and of Tennessee Inc.; Dir., Rustcraft Ltd. (Toronto), Friendship House Ltd. (Toronto), Volland Ltd. (Canada), Associated American Artists (N.Y.), Rust Craft Greeting Cards (U.K.) Ltd., England; Dir. Emeritus Union Bancshares Co.; Dir. Emeritus Union Savings Bank & Trust Co. (both Ohio). *Member:* Radio & Television Executive Socy. (N.Y.). American Bar Association, Ohio State Bar Association, American Judicature Society, International Bar Association. Member Emeritus, Retina Foundation Development Board (Boston) and Member, Bd. Governors of the Technion, Haifa, Israel. Trustee, Sybiel B. Berkman Fd. *Publications:* Playing God (a play); short stories and articles. *Clubs:* Harvard (N.Y.C.); Harvard-Yale-Princeton (Pittsburgh); Broadcasters (Washington); Variety; Steubenville Country; Harmonie (N.Y.), Friars (N.Y.). *Address:* 22E 64th Street, New York, N.Y.; and *office* 680 Fifth Avenue, 11th Floor, New York, N.Y. 10019, U.S.A.

**BERNALD**, Eugene. American industrialist and communications executive. *B.* 1908. *Educ.* Columbia University, N.Y.C. *Career:* Advisor on broadcasting and communications to governments of Ceylon, Goa, Maldive Islands, Congo, Nigeria, Iraq, Colombia, Peru, Venezuela, Haiti and Nationalist China. Pres. of Pabco Inc., N.Y.C. Trustee of the following: Asia Foundation, N.Y.C.; and Inter-Relaciones S.A. Caracas; Union des Anciens Combattants de Elizabethville, Lubumbashi, Kinshasa (Congo); Adv. Committee, Operation Crossroads Africa Inc., N.Y.C.; International Broadcasters Society, Bussum, Netherlands; Chmn. Radio Industry Cttee., American Korean Foundation, N.Y.C.; Advisor on Minority Groups, Presidential Elections 1956–60–64, Republican National Cttee., Washington, D.C. Director: Pan American Broadcasting Co., N.Y.C.; Trans-African Development Corp., Lagos, Nigeria; Radio America West Indies Inc., St. Croix, Virgin Islands; Radio Anchorage Inc., Alaska; South Eastern Alaska Broadcasters Inc., Juneau. *Publications:* Primer of International Broadcasting (1938); Economics of Broadcasting (1940); Broadcasting Overseas (1948); Reaching Minority Groups (1952); Communications for Under-developed Countries (1960). *Address:* 83 Somerstown Road, Ossining, N.Y. 10562; and *office* 275 Madison Ave., New York, N.Y. 10016, U.S.A.

**BERNARD**, Robert. French banker (retired); Chevalier, Legion of Honour. Chartered Accountant. *B.* 1904. *M.* 1934, Marcelle Pihet. *S.* Philippe. *Dau.* Laurence. *Career:* Branch Manager, Banque de L'Indochine: Shanghai 1949–50, Tangiers 1951–52, Haiphong (Vietnam) 1953–54, and Dhahran (Saudi Arabia) 1956–57, Hong Kong, May 1957–63. *Address:* 69 Rue de la Faisanderie, Paris 16e, France.

**BERNER**, Endre (Qvie). Norwegian professor of chemistry. *B.* 24 Sept. 1893. *Educ.* State University of Technology, Trondheim (Dr. tech. 1926); studied organic chemistry at Munich and Birmingham. *M.* (1) 1922, Nathalia Weidemann (*d.* 1930) and (2) 1935, Erna Gay. *S.* Endre, Frederik W. *Daus.* Anne Karine, Agot. *Career:* Asst. (1918–22) and Lecturer (1922–33) in Organic Chemistry, State University of Technology; Pres. Norwegian Chem. Socy. 1947–51 (Hon. Member 1966); Hon. Foreign Mem., Socy. of Chem. Industry 1951; mem., Acad. of Science, Oslo; Royal Norwegian Soc. Scis.; Ingeniørsvetenskapskademien 1945; Royal Socy. of Arts 1957; Professor of Chemistry, University of Oslo, 1934–61; Vice-Pres. International Union of Pure and Applied Chemistry 1951–55. *Awards:* Order of St. Olav 1969. *Publications:* Textbook in Organic Chemistry (in Norwegian) (1952); scientific papers in Chemical Journals. *Address:* Gyldenløvesgt. 13, Oslo 2, Norway.

**BERNHEIM**, Daniel Marc. Advertising executive. *B.* 1924. *Educ.* University of Alabama (graduated from University of Newark). *M.* 1949, Frances Reinfeld (*Dec.* 1977). *S.* Lewis Andrew and Anthony Paul. *Dau.* Adelyn B. Firtel. *Career:* Chmn. of the Board of Reach, McClinton & Company Inc.; Chmn. Exec. Cttee., Renfield Importers Ltd., Newark, N.J; Pres. Bernheim Importers Inc., Newark, N.J. *Member:* Advertising Club of N.J. *Clubs:* Mountain Ridge Country, etc. *Address:* Elm Court, Campbell Rd., RDI, Far Hills, New Jersey; and *office* Reach, McClinton & Co. Inc., 69 Washington Street, Newark, N.J., U.S.A.

**BERNITT, Elmer William.** American. *B.* 1910. *Educ.* Univ. of Detroit (BME). *M.* 1938, Betty Thomas. *Daus.* Lois (Cardell) and Kathryn (Gadwell). *Career:* Vice-Pres., Automotive Manufacturing 1954–65; Vice-President, Automotive Safety & Quality Assurance since 1965. *Member:* Socy. of Automotive Engineers (SAE); National Socy. of Professional Engineers; Director, First National Bank of Kenosha, Wis.; and of American Management Assn. Mason; Shriner; Elk. *Clubs:* Detroit Athletic; St. Clair River Country. *Address:* 4385 Clark Drive, St. Clair, Mich. 48079; and *office* 14250 Plymouth Road, Detroit, Mich. 48232, U.S.A.

**BERNS, Robert.** Pres. & Dir.: Pullman Vacuum Cleaner Corp. 1946—, Marvel Industries Inc. 1947—, and Accordian Hose Corp. 1947—. Vice-President, Purex Corp. Ltd. 1967. *B.* 1925. *Educ.* Boston University (AB 1948) and Columbia University (MBA 1950). *M.* 1952, Norma Hartman. *S.* Bruce and Louis. *Daus.* Alison and Elizabeth. *Club:* University. *Address:* 21 Overlook Park, Newton Centre 59, Mass.; and *office* 129, Medford Street, Malden, Mass., U.S.A.

**BERNSTEIN Bertrand Leon,** Hon. LLD. South African. *B.* 1907. *Educ.* Univ. of the Witwatersrand; BA (Hons.): LLB. *M.* (1) 1937, Barbara Leon (*D.* 1968). (2) 1971, Beatrice Smithers. *Career:* Pres., S.A. Chamber of Mines 1955–56 (Vice-Pres. 1953–54 and 1954–55); Chmn., S.A. Inst. for Medical Research 1953–60; Man. Director, Anglo-Transvaal Consolidated Investment Co. Ltd. 1949–67; Syndic Member, Witwatersrand Education Council 1951—; Chmn. Anglo-Transvaal Consolidated Investment Co. Ltd. 1970–73; Chancellor Univ. of Witwatersrand since 1975; Chairman and Director of several goldmining and industrial companies. Exec. Member, S.A. Federated Chamber of Industries 1947; South African Chamber of Mines 1951–68. Chairman, Governing Council, Univ. of the Witwatersrand 1958–68; Trustee, Jan Smuts Memorial Foundation 1958–68; S.A. Wild Life Foundation. *Publications:* The Tide Turned at Alamein (war memoirs); Tomorrow is Another Day (historical novel). *Member:* Inst. of Directors: Royal Society of Arts (Fellow); Ornithological Socy. of S.A.; English Academy of Southern Africa. *Clubs:* Rand; Johannesburg Country; Inanda; Fly Fishers. *Address:* 44 Smits Road, Dunkeld, Johannesburg; and *office* P.O. Box 62379 Marshalltown, Transvaal, South Africa.

**BERNSTEIN, Cyrus.** Lt.-Col. (retd.) U.S. Army Reserve; Bronze Star Medal, Purple Heart, and Médaille de la France Liberée. *B.* 1912. *Educ.* N.Y. Univ. (BS in Bus. Admin. 1933) and City Coll. of N.Y. (Certificate in Retailing 1934). *M.* 1941, Lucia N. Augustine. *S.* Robert Alan and Bruce Carl. *Career:* Managing Editor, Towse Publishing Co. Inc. 1933–35 and Rosenthal & Smythe Inc. 1935–38; Managing Editor, home furnishing group 1938–41; Editor and Asst. Publisher, Toys Novelties Magazine 1956–60; Vice-President, Who's Who in Advertising Inc., Jan. 1963–65, and Who's Who in Retailing Inc., Jan. 1963–65. Vice-President, Secretary and Director, Haire Publishing Co., N.Y.C. 1968–69; Associate Publisher, Executive Business Media, Inc. Lynbrook, N.Y. 1970–75; Editor & Publishing Consultant, United Technical Publications Div. of Cox Broadcasting Corp., Garden City, N.Y. since 1975. *Publications:* Dictionary of Home Furnishing Terms (with Esther Skaar Hansen); Marketing Toys; contributor to Encyclopedia Americana. *Award:* Industrial Marketing First Award Plaque for Editorial Achievement, 1957; N.Y. State Conspicuous Service Cross with Cluster. *Member:* American Business Press; American Socy. of Business Press Editors; National Guard Assn. of U.S.; Militia Assn. of N.Y.; Rainbow Div. Officers Club; Alumni Assn. of N.Y. Univ. *Address:* 37 Peter Lane, New Hyde Park, N.Y.; and *office* 245 Stewart Avenue, Garden City, N.Y. 11530, U.S.A.

**BERRICK, Bernard Samuel.** *B.* 1927. *Educ.* King's College, London University. *M.* 1957, Barbara Brodie. *S.* Louis Emmanuel Max and Steven Isaac. *Career:* In R.A.F. 1948; Solicitor 1952; Joint Managing Director, London & Provincial Shop Centres (Holdings) Ltd. Member Law Society. *Club:* Guard's Polo. *Address:* 28 South Street, W.1.

**BERRY, Hon. Anthony George,** MA, CSt.J, MP. British. Politician and Banker. *B.* 1925. *Educ.* Eton College; Christ Church, Oxford. *M.* (1) 1954, Hon. Mary Roche. (2) 1966, Sarah Clifford-Turner. *S.* Edward, George. *Daus.* Alexandra, Antonia, Joanna and Sasha. *Career:* Dir.. Kemsley Newspapers Ltd. 1954–59; Managing Dir., Western Mail Echo Ltd. 1955–59; Justice of the Peace since 1960; High Sheriff of Glamorgan, 1961–62; Member of Parliament, Conservative for Southgate 1964—; Dep. Chmn., Leopold Joseph & Sons 1963—; Parly. Private Secy. to Minister of Housing 1970, to Secy. of State for the Environment 1970–72; to Secy. State for Trade and Industry 1972–74; Vice-Chmn. (Transport), Conservative Mem. Environment Cttee.; Opposition whip since 1975. *Clubs:* Whites; Portland. *Address:* 98 Ebury Mews, London, S.W.1; Warbrook House, Eversley, Hampshire; and *office* House of Commons, London, S.W.1.

**BERRY, Keehn W.** American banker. *B.* 12 Dec. 1894. *Educ.* University of Missouri (AB, LLB). *M.* 1920, Mary Lois Brown. *S.* Keehn W. *Dau.* Mary Ellen. Chairman of the Board, Whitney National Bank of New Orleans. *Address:* c/o Whitney National Bank of New Orleans, New Orleans, Louisiana 70161, U.S.A.

**BERTE, Alain Alfred.** Belgian sales manager and Univ. lecturer. Head of Commercial Division, Solvay & Cie.; Lecturer at the Brussels Advanced Institute of Commerce; Member of Examination Boards for Commercial Schools. *B.* 1914. *Educ.* Licentiate Comm. Sciences. *M.* 1955, Marcelle Blanche Everaerts. Officer, Order of the Crown; Knight, Order of Leopold; Croix de Guerre 1940–45, Prisoner's Medal; Commemorative Medal 1940–45. *Club:* National Association of Reserve Officers. *Address:* 9–11 Avenue Ernstine, Brussels 5; and *office* 33 rue Prince Albert, Brussels 5, Belgium.

**BERTELSEN, Hans.** Danish diplomat. *B.* 5 Feb. 1906. *Educ.* Univ. of Copenhagen (Law Degree with a First). *M.* Kirsten Boserup. *Dau.* 1. *Career:* Entered Danish Foreign Service 1931, to which he has since belonged; in the past 26 years he has served in all sections of the Foreign Min. (political, legal, administrative and economic sections); Chief of Section, Economic Div. (and in capacity of Chmn. negotiated agreements with France, Belgium, Netherlands, Indonesia, Norway, Sweden and Finland) 1949–54; Secy., Danish Delegation to League of Nations Assembly 1932–33; Secy., Legation, Brussels, 1937–38; Secy., Danish Trade Delegation, London, during first six months of World War II; Secy., Legation, Rome 1940–42; Head, Labour Office of Danish Consulate-Gen., Hamburg 1942–44 (arrested by Gestapo Apr. 1944 and imprisoned until end of war); Secy., Legation, Stockholm, May–Oct. 1945; Counsellor, Embassy, Washington 1946–49 (in this capacity represented Denmark in Working Group constructing Atlantic Pact Organisation); Amb. to Mexico, Costa Rica, Cuba, Dominican Republic, El Salvador, Guatemala, Haiti, Honduras, Nicaragua and Panama, Mar. 1954–59; Ambassador to the Chinese People's Republic, Aug. 1959–May 1962; Head of Dept., Foreign Office 1964. Ambassador to Lebanon, Syria, Jordan, Saudi Arabia, Kuwait and Cyprus 1967–69; Ambassador to Morocco, Senegal and Guinea 1969–73 (retired). *Awards:* Cdr., Order of Dannebrog (Denmark); Kt., Order of Leopold (Belgium); Kt., Order of Oak-Crown (Luxembourg); Cdr., Legion of Honour (France); Cdr., Order of North Star (Sweden); Grand Officer, Order of Orange Nassau (Netherlands); Grand Officer of Moroccan Order of Alaouitis; Senegal National Order of the Lion; Grand Cross of the Aztec (Mexico); Grand Cross of the Order of Independence (Jordan); Grand Cross of the Order of the Cedar (Lebanon); *Address:* Royal Danish Embassy, 5 Avenue de Marrakech, B.P. 203, Rabat, Morocco.

**BERTHOD, Alfred-Georges.** *B.* 4 July 1903. *Educ.* Lausanne (Lic. Sc. Economiques). *M.* 1929, Jeanne Nicolas. *Career:* Antwerp 1924, Catania 1927, Lille 1927, Lyon 1928, Strasbourg 1936; Consul. Lyon 1938; Consul-General Bordeaux (doyen of the Consular Corps) 1946–68. Former Swiss consular official; Lecturer and Author. *Member:* National Academie des Sciences, Belles-Lettres & Arts of Bordeaux; Hon. Citizen of Bordeaux; Academie de Stanislas, Nancy. *Award:* Chevalier de la Legion d'Honneur. *Address:* 20 r du Clos Ch., Vevey, Switzerland.

**BERTHOIN, Georges-Paul.** French. *B.* 1925. *Educ.* Licencié ès lettres; Licencié en droit. *M.* 1950, Ann White Whittlesey. *Daus.* Ariane, Christine, Diane and Paola. *M.* 1965, Pamela Jenkins. *S.* Jean-Paul, Jean. Médaille Militaire; Croix de

Guerre; Médaille de la Resistance avec Rosette. *Career:* At Harvard and McGill Universities 1947–48; Attaché in the Cabinet of the Ministry of Finance, Paris 1948–50; Director of the Cabinet of the Prefecture of Metz 1950–52; Private Secretary to the President of the High Authority of the European Coal and Steel Community 1952–55; Counsellor for Information 1955–56; Acting Chief Representative Jan.–May 1958; Acting Chief Representative, Commission, European Communities, 1967–68; Deputy and Special Advisor 1968–71; Chief Representative in the United Kingdom of the Commission of the Eureopean Communities 1971–73; Hon. Dir., General European Commission since 1973; Exec. Cttee. Mem., then European Chmn. of the Trilateral Commission (North America-Japan-Western Europe). *Address:* 96 Bis, Rue de Longchamp, 92200 Neuilly, France.

**BERTHOIN, Jean.** French politician and statesman. *B.* 1895. Chef du Cabinet of Resident General, Tunis (Sous-préfet and Préfet) 1920; Dir. of M. Sarraut's office, became in 1934, Director of the *Sûreté*, and subsequently Inspector-General of the Algerian Administrative Service; later Secretary-General, Ministry of the Interior (1939), Treasurer-General of the Department of Isère (1940) and of The Seine (1947). Senator of Isère 1948; Secretary of State (Interior) 1950; Minister of National Education in the Mendès-France Cabinet 1954, and in the Edgar Faure Cabinet; Minister of National Education in the de Gaulle Cabinet 1958; Minister of the Interior in the Debré Cabinet, Jan.–Apr. 1959. Awards: Grand Croix, Legion of Honour; Croix de Guerre (1944–18 and 1939–45); Resistance Medal. *Address:* Senat, Palais du Luxembourg, Paris.

**BERTHY, Charles John,** Royal Hungarian Knight's Cross, DSC, DSMS, DSMB, BS. American. *B.* 1921. *Educ.* Royal Hungarian Military Academy (BS, 1942); Ohio State Univ. (1965). *M.* 1944, Erika Ann Kocziha. *S.* 3. *Dau.* 1. *Career:* Vice-Pres. Gen. Mgr. International Div.; Dir. Corporate Planning, Ledex, Inc.; Senior Analyst, American Radiator & Standard Sanitary Corpn., 1956. *Member:* Management Policy Council Exec. Cttee.; Requirements Cttee. Government Products Div. Electronics Industries Assn.; Exec. Cttee. International Business Council; Membership & Scope Cttee. and Chmn. Trade Assn. Liaison of EIA; Regional Export Expansion Council of the Secy. Commerce U.S.A. Chmn. District Council, Southern Ohio; Amer. Defense Preparedness Assn.; U.S. Air Force Assn.; U.S. Naval Institute; Assn. of Corporate Planners; Past Chmn. World Trade Cttee. Dayton Area Chamber Commerce. *Address:* 6180 Southampton Dr., Dayton, Ohio, 45459; and *office* 123 Webster St., Dayton, Ohio 45401. U.S.A.

**BERTRAM, Richard.** German executive. *B.* 1904. *Educ.* Gymnasium. *M.* 1938. Lore Proebst. *S.* 2. *Dau.* 1. *Career:* Managing Director, Hapag-Lloyd AG. Member, Board of Directors: Alte Leipziger Lebensversicherungsgesellschaft, AG., Frankfurt/M. Securitas Bremer Allgemeine Versicherungs-Ges., Bremen; Deutsches Reisbüro GmbH, Frankfurt; Gilde-Versicherung AG, Düsseldorf. *Clubs:* Rotary; Bremen. *Address* and *office:* Hapag-Lloyd AG, Ballindamm 25, Hamburg 1, and Gustav-Deetjen-Allee 2/6, Bremen, Germany.

**BESANCON, Frits.** Dutch aeronautical engineer. *B.* 21 Nov. 1908. *Educ.* University of Delft. *Career:* Joined K.L.M. Royal Dutch Airlines 1934, later U.S. Technical Representative; served World War II, Netherlands East Indies Air Force 1942–45; Vice-President (Production Directorate), K.L.M. Royal Dutch Airlines 1949, Executive Vice-President 1951; Deputy President, K.L.M. Royal Dutch Airlines, since 1965. *Awards:* Knight, Order of the Lion (Netherlands); Commander First Class, Order of Civil Merits (Spain); Ward of Sikatuna, Rank of Maginoo (Philippines). *Address:* c/o K.L.M. Royal Dutch Airlines (home department), P.O. Box 7700, Schiphol Airport, Netherlands.

**BESSBOROUGH, The Rt. Hon. The Earl, Frederick Edward Neuflize Ponsonby,** DL, OStJ, MA. Chevalier Legion d'Honour. British. *B.* 1913. *Educ.* Eton; Trinity Coll., Cambridge. *M.* 1948, Mary Munn. *Dau.* Lady Charlotte Petsopoulos. *Career:* Secy. League of Nations High Comm. for Refugees 1936–39; Served War 1939–44 (Major 1942); Second and later First Secy. British Embassy, Paris 1944–49; with Robert Benson, Lonsdale Merchant Bankers; Dir. ATV and other Companies 1950–63; Parly. Secy. for Science 1963; Joint Parly. Under-Secy. for Education and Science 1964; Conservative Spokesman, House of Lords for Science, Technology, Power, Foreign & Commonwealth Affairs & Overseas Aid 1964–70; Deputy Chmn., Metrication Board 1969–70; Minister of State (Aviation), Ministry of Technology, June–Oct. 1970; Chmn. Cttee. of Enquiry into the Research Associations 1971–73; Member of European Parliament since 1973, Vice-Pres., 1973–76, and Deputy Leader, European Conservative Group, 1973–77; Pres., Chichester Festival Theatre Trust; Chmn. of Governors, Dulwich College 1972–73. *Clubs:* Turf & Garrick. *Address:* Stansted Park, Rowlands Castle, Hampshire.

**BESSE, Ralph M.** Lawyer-partner, Squire, Sanders & Dempsey. *B.* 1905. *Educ.* Heidelberg College (AB); University of Michigan Law School (JD); LLD Baldwin-Wallace College, Oberlin College, Case Institute of Technology; LHD Heidelberg College, Wilberforce University; Dr. of Law, Cleveland-Marshall Law School, Cleveland. *M.* 1934, Augusta Woodward Mitchell. *S.* William T. and Robert A. *Dau.* Jean E. (Minehart). *Career:* With Squire, Sanders & Dempsey 1929–48 (Ptnr. 1940–48); joined Cleveland Electric Illuminating Co. 1948; Vice-Pres. 1948–53, Exec. Vice-Pres. 1953–60; President 1960–67; Chairman of the Board and Chief Executive Officer, The Cleveland Electric Illuminating Co. 1967–70. Member of Board: American Airlines; Cleveland Trust Co.; Acme Cleveland Corporation; Tremco Mfg. Co.; National Machinery Co. Chmn. Bd.; District Chief, Cleveland Ordnance District 1948; Cleveland Community Chest (Vice-Pres., 1957, Pres. 1960); Vice-Pres., Friends of the Cleveland Public Library 1958; Chmn., Steering Cttee., United Negro College Fund 1958; Vice-Pres., Educational Res. Council of Cleveland 1959—; President, Cleveland Commission on Higher Education 1957–71. Member of Board: Council on World Affairs 1936; Heidelberg Coll. 1949; United Appeal of Cleveland 1958; Univ. School 1958; Ohio Electric Utility Institute 1954; American Management Assoc. 1958; Ursuline Coll. 1963; Case Western Reserve Univ. 1970 (Chmn. of Bd. 1971); Carnegie Commission, Higher Education 1967. *Member:* American, Cleveland, and Ohio Bar Assns.; Court of Nisi Prius; Newcomen Society. *Clubs:* Canterbury Golf; The Fifty; Union. *Address:* Box 5000 Illuminating Building, Cleveland 1, Ohio 44101, U.S.A.

**BESSO, Joseph M.** Canadian industrialist and investment banker. *B.* 1901. *Educ.* PhD Sciences in Economics and Finance; BSc in Textile Engineering Schools and Universities in Greece and Belgium. *M.* Margaret Daisy Kategno. *S.* Marc and John-Peter. *Dau.* Maryse-Astrid. *Career:* Consul-General of Thailand. Chairman, International Textile and Investment Besso Group (founded in Corfu in 1848); President: Inter-American Investment Corp. Ltd., Doric Textile Mills Ltd., and Doric Fabrics Ltd. President: Canadian Silk and Synthetic Textiles Assn. Inc., Canadian Nat. Delegate; Vice-Pres. Internat. Silk Assn.; Dir., Canadian Cncl. Internat. Chamber of Commerce and University of Montreal; *Awards:* Grand Comdr., Order of the Phoenix of Greece; Knight Commander: Royal Order of King George; and of Most Noble Order of the Crown of Thailand. *Address:* 57 Belvedere Road, Westmount H3Y 1P7, P.Q.; and *office* Canadian Imperial Bank of Commerce Building, 1155 Dorchester Boulevard West, Montreal H3B 2J2, P.Q., Canada.

**BEST, Charles Herbert,** CC, CH, CBE, FRS, FRSC, FRCP (C), FRCP. Canadian professor of medical research; Rtd. 1967. *B.* 1899. *Educ.* MA, MD (Toronto), DSc (Chicago, London, Oxford, Laval, Maine, Northwestern, Laurentian); Doctor *hon. causa* (Paris); ScD (Cantab.); Doctor Med. *hon. causa* (Amsterdam, Louvain, Liège); Doct. Med. H.C. Central Univ., Venezuela; Aristotelian Univ., Thessaloniki; Dr. Med. h.c. Univ. Ottawa 1972; PhD. h.c. Hebrew Univ. of Jerusalem 1971; LLD (Dalhousie, Queen's, Melbourne, Edinburgh, Toronto); Hon. DMed. Freie Univ., Berlin 1966, Zagreb 1976. *Career:* co-discoverer of Insulin with Sir Frederick Banting 1921; Scientific Director, International Health Div., Rockefeller Foundation 1941–43; Chmn. of Board of Scientific Directors 1943; member, Advisory Med. Board of Ontario Cancer Treatment and Research Foundation 1944; served in World War I with Canad. Field Artillery and Tank Corps 1918–19; initiated Canadian Serum Project for securing dried human serum for military use 1939; on active service in World War II with Royal Canadian Navy (as Director, R.C.N. Medical Research Div. and holding rank as Surgeon Captain) 1941–46. *Member:* Metabolic Diseases Study section of National Institutes of Health of the U.S. Public Health Service 1946–53; Research Defence Board, Department of National Defence, Canada 1946. Hon. Pres., Int. Diabetes Fed.; The Amer. Diabetes Assn.; The Can. Diabetes Assn.; Vice-Pres., The British Diabetic Assn.; President, 19th International Physiological Congress 1953 and of International Union of Physiological Societies 1953; Mem. of Pontifical Acad. of Sciences 1955; Professor of Physiology and Head of the Dept. 1929–65; Professor and Graduate

Lectr. 1965—; and Dir. and Prof. in the Banting and Best Dept. of Med. Research, Univ. of Toronto 1941–67; Director-Emeritus 1967—; Honorary Consultant 1973 & of Connaught Laboratories, University of Toronto, since 1941. *Publications:* co-author with F. G. Banting of the original publication on Insulin. 'The Internal Secretion of the Pancreas' 1922; co-author, with N. B. Taylor, of an advanced text-book on Physiology, 'The Physiological Basis of Medical Practice', and two elementary texts on Physiology, 'The Human Body' and 'The Living Body'; Selected Papers of Charles. H. Best 1963. *M.* 1924, Margaret Hooper Mahon. *S.* Charles Alexander, Henry Bruce Macleod. *Address:* 105 Woodlawn Ave. West, Toronto, Ont. M4V 1G6, Canada; and *office* Charles H. Best Inst., 112 College St, Toronto, Ont. M5G 1L6, Canada.

**BEST**, N. J. South African Diplomat. *B.* 1919. *Educ.* Witwatersrand Univ. BA. *M.* 1950, Evelyn Melville Aitken. *S.* 1. *Daus.* 2. *Career:* Active Military Service 1940–46; various Diplomatic Appointments 1946–68; South African Minister, Paris 1968–70; Under-Sec. of Foreign Affairs, Pretoria 1970–73; South African Ambassador to Canada, Ottawa since 1973. *Address:* 5 Rideau Gate, Ottawa, Ontario, Canada; and *office*: 15 Sussex Drive, Ottawa, Canada.

**BESWICK, The Rt. Hon. Lord.** PC. British. *B.* 1912. *M.* 1935, Dora. *S.* Frank J. *Daus.* Patricia Anne. *Career:* Royal Air Force, 1939–45; Member of Parliament for Uxbridge Division, 1945–59; Delegate, United Nations, 1946; U.K. Observer Atomic Tests Bikini, 1946; P.P.S. Under. Secy. State for Air, 1946–50; Parly. Secy. Ministry, Civil Aviation, 1950–51; Dir., Derby Aviation Ltd. 1951–57; Chmn. Labour Party, Aviation Cttee. 1952–59; Life Peerage 1964; Lord in Waiting 1964–65; Under Secy. of State, Commonwealth Office 1965–67; Govt. Chief Whip, House of Lords 1967–70; Captain, Hon. Corps., Gentlemen at Arms. 1967–70; Privy Council 1968. Opposition Chief Whip, House of Lords 1970–74; Special Adviser, Chmn., British Aircraft Corp. 1970–74: Minister of State, Dept. of Industry 1974–75; Chmn. British Aerospace 1975–77; Justice of the Peace; Vice-Pres., British Air Line Pilots Association; Companion, Royal Aeronautical Soc. *Publications:* Plan for the Aircraft Industry (1955). *Address:* House of Lords, London, S.W.1.

**BETHELL, Alan Francis.** *B.* 1923. *Educ.* Eastcote Lane Grammar School, and Harrow Tech. (both in England). *M.* 1961, Linda Florence Harvey. *Career:* Engineering student-apprentice, Standard Triumph Motor Co. Ltd. 1939–42; Warrant Officer, British Army in Far East 1942–47; Engineering Division, Standard Triumph Motor Co. 1947–49; Special Export Executive, Standard Triumph Motors Ltd. 1949–54; West Coast Manager, Standard Triumph Motor Co. Inc., U.S.A. 1954–56 (Exec. Vice-Pres. 1957; Director and President 1958–61). Director of Sales-Automotive Export, American Motors Corp., Detroit, 1961—. 1966, Gen. Sales Manager Feb. 1968—, Vice-President Marketing, International Division, 1970—; Gen. Marketing Manager, Eaton Corp.—Industrial Truck Div. 1971—; Dir., Marketing Materials Handling Group 1973–75; Group Vice-Pres., Eaton Materials Handling Group 1975—. *Clubs:* New York Athletic, Detroit Yacht; Cleveland Racquet; Mentor Harbor Yachting. *Address:* 31076 Park Lane Drive, Pepper Pike, Ohio 44124, U.S.A.; and *office* 100 Erieview Plaza, Cleveland, Ohio 44114, U.S.A.

**BETT, Frank Lincoln.** Australian senior principal research officer. *B.* 1926. *Educ.* Bachelor, Metallurgical Engineering (Final Honours) and Master, Engineering Science (First-Class Honours). *M.* 1955, Maisie Lorraine Male. *S.* Michael Gordon and Ian Macgregor. *Dau.* Jennifer Julienne. *Career:* Research Officer: Broken Hill Associated Smelters 1949–50, University of Melbourne 1951–55, and Australian Atomic Energy Commission 1956. Atomic Energy Attaché, Australian Embassy, Washington 1963–67; Attached to Prime Minister's Dept. 1967–69; Head, Technical Policy Section Aust. Atomic Energy Commission, then Dir., Safeguards Office, AAEC; Dir., Australian Safeguards Office. *Publications:* Papers published by Institution of Mining & Metallurgy 1956, Second Geneva Conference 1957, Australian Welding Institute 1958, Atomic Eenergy in Australia 1962; and several external A.A.E.E. reports. *Member:* Australasian Inst. of Mining and Metallurgy; Australian Welding Inst. *Address:* 70 Liverpool Road, Enfield, N.S.W. 2136, Australia and c/o Australian Atomic Energy Commission, Cliffbrook, 45 Beach Street, Coogee N.S.W. 2034, Australia.

**BETTENDORF, Harry J.** American publisher, Chicago, Ill., U.S.A. *B.* 1909. *Educ.* East Aurora (Ill.) High School (Grad.). *M.* 1935, Helen Muzik. *S.* Paul J. *Career:* With Magazines for Industry Inc. 1968–73, which acquired Bettendorf Publications Inc., as Publications Director (President 1951–68); Vice-President and Co-publisher 1941–50; Editor 1937–40. Secretary and Statistician, National Container Association 1934–37; Chmn., Bettendorf Systems Inc. 1970–74. *Member:* Fédération Européenne de Fabricant de Carton Ondulé; Amer. Forestry Assn.; Socy. of Packaging & Handling Engineers (honorary life); Technical Assn. of the Pulp & Paper Industry. *Awards:* Corrugated Containers Div. TAPPI 1971; FEFCO, Fibre Box Assn. and American Paper Inst. 1972; Paperboard Packaging Counsel 1973; Est. (1975) Bettendorf Prize for TAPPI Corrugated Containers Div. *Publications:* Paperboard and Paperboard Containers—A History (1947); The Wastepaper Industry (1945); What's Wrong with Paperboard Packaging and How to Right What's Wrong (1961); The Pridham Case —or How Packaging Got Out of the Woods (1964); The Corrugated Container Industry (1971). *Clubs:* Executives, Union League, Tower (Chicago); Survivors (Finnish). *Address:* 309 North East Avenue, Oak Park, Ill. 60302, U.S.A.

**BEVINS, Rt. Hon. John Reginald**, PC. British. *B.* 1908. *Educ.* Dovedale Road School, Liverpool; Liverpool Collegiate School. *M.* 1933, Mary Leonora Jones. *S.* Nicholas, Anthony & Stephen. *Career:* P.P.S. to Minister of Housing & Local Govnt., 1951–53; Parl. Sec., Ministry of Works, 1953–57; Ministry of Housing & Local Government, 1957–59; Postmaster Gen., 1959–64. *Publications:* The Greasy Pole (1965). *Address:* 37 Queens Drive, Liverpool, L18 2DT.

**BEYER, Otto N. M.** Norwegian; Managing The Director, Norwegian Salvage Company. *B.* 1908. *Educ.* Matric. (1927); Military Academy (Lieut. 1928); Commercial College (1929); holder of Average Adjuster's certificate (1930). *M.* 1935, Haldis Allers Tresselt. *Daus.* Elizabeth and Unni. *Career:* Employed with Bergen shipping firm 1929–30; with Average Adjusters in London and Hamburg 1930–32; joined The Norwegian Salvage Co. 1932; manager of branch firm in Trondheim 1935; Asst. Manager, Head Office 1939; has held present position since 1945. *Address:* Norsk Bjergningsco. A/S, Bergen, Norway.

**BEYER, Raymond Herman.** Admiral USTN, USNN; scientist, engineer, author. *B.* 1902. *Educ.* Keystone Inst. (Reading, Pa.) BSME; American School of Aviation (Chicago) AE. *M.* 1964, Regina H. Friedrich. *S.* Roy R. and Jeffrey S. *Dau.* Laura T. *Career:* With Dodge Corp. 1923–25; Westinghouse Electric Co. 1925–26; U.S. Airlines 1926–27; Bendix Aviation Corp. 1927–30; Rockne Motors 1930–32; Chevrolet Motors 1932–35; Works Progress Administrator 1935–38; Glenn L. Martin Co. 1938–40; Peerless of America 1940–45; Armour Research Foundation of Illinois Inst. of Technology 1945–52; General Dynamics 1952–57; Chance Vought 1957–59; Stanley Aviation Corp. 1959–62; Wheelabrater Corp. (Mishawaka, Ind.) 1966–68 (Consultant 1968—); Hercules Powder Co. 1962–64; Finder, Joint Engineers Council, Manpower Commission, 1945—; Consultant since 1964. *Publications:* Five papers on Gravitics; Private Flying; How to Handle Ideas; Value of a Patent. Early Bird—flew first airplane in Indiana. Designed first successful amphibian airplane, first airplane wheel and brake for balloon tyres: first directional aerial for radio; first airport floodlight for landing airplanes; gasoline segregator, walk around oxygen regulator, mechanical torpedo exploder, method for impregnating bamboo with plastic, recoilless 65 mm rifle for airplanes, launcher for airplanes, revolver type rifle for airplanes, container for A-bombs, ejection Sac-seat for B-58 bomber, ballistic cable cutter, ballistic quick disconnect for airplane capsules and space craft, and 134 patents of a secret nature. *Member:* A.I.A.A. (Associate Fellow); Amer. Ordnance Assn.; Amer. Socy. of Military Engineers; charter member of Fort Worth (Texas) Post. Republican. *Club:* Lodge No. 45 F. & M. *Address:* Route No. 2, Box 120, C/o Regina Cambria, New Carlisle, Indiana, U.S.A.

**BEZAZIAN, Paul D.** American business executive. *B.* 1906. Oberlin College (BA 1927). *M.* 1933, Florence Bell. *S.* John Paul and Harold A. *Dau.* Paulette F. *Career:* Investment Securities Salesman 1927–31; then successively sales manager of credit firm, partner Bezazian & Sutherland (food manufacturing), and partner and manager Bezazian Brothers (floor coverings, Chicago), 1937–40. Managing Partner and Treasurer: Burton Browne Advertising, Chicago (since 1941); Aero Needle Co. Chicago 1943; Milline Publishing Co., Chicago (1948); Chmn. of the Board and Chmn. of Exec. Cttee: Gaslight Club Inc. Chicago since 1975. *Publications:*

Strikes—Towards a Total Answer (Univ. of Detroit Journal of Urban Law, Vol. 45, No. 2, Winter 1967). *Club:* Lake Shore (Chicago). *Address:* One E. Huron St., Chicago Ill., 60611, U.S.A.

**BEZENCON, Marcel.** *B.* 1 May 1907. *Educ.* Universities of Lausanne and Vienna (L. ès L.). *M.* 1933, Marthe Droguet. *S.* Jean-Jaques. *Dau.* Michèle. *Career:* Pres., Theatre of Lausanne; member, Editorial Staff of Feuille d'Avis de Lausanne (1932–39); Director, Studio of Lausanne (1939–50). Director-General, Swiss Broadcasting Corpn. 1950–72; Promoter of Eurovision; Pres., E.B.U. Television Programme Cttee, 1954–69; Pres. EBU-European Broadcasting Union 1971–72. *Address:* 16, chemin de Renens, Château de Valency, CH-1000 Lausanne, Switzerland.

**BHABHA, Cooverji Hormusji,** JP. Indian company director. *B.* 22 July 1910. *Educ.* St. Xavier's Coll. (MA); Sydenham Coll. of Commerce, Bombay (BComm); Fellow and Lecturer in Banking Law and Practice, Sydenham College of Commerce, Bombay 1932–33; Chairman, United Carbon Co. Ltd. Chmn., Kelvinator of India Ltd. Trustee, 'Commerce'. Chairman Dir. Spencer & Co., Ltd. Dir. The Tata Power Co. Ltd., Swadeshi Mills Co. Ltd., Investment Corpn. of India Ltd. Justice of Peace; Commerce Member, Interim Indian Government, Sept. 1946; Member for Works, Mines and Power, Indian Government Nov. 1946; Minister of Commerce, Indian Government 1947–48; Leader, Indian Delegation to International World Trade Conference, Havana and Vice-President of Conference 1947. *Address:* c/o 'Commerce'. Maneck Mahal, Veer Nariman Rd., Churchgate, Bombay, India.

**BHAKDI, Luang Dithakar.** Thai diplomat. *B.* 10 June 1906. *Educ.* King's College, Bangkok; Law School, Bangkok; Middle Temple, London. *M.* 1942. Saiyude Gengradomying. *S.* 2. *Daus.* 2. *Career:* Clerk, Foreign Office 1925, Assistant Chief of Section 1928, Chief of Section 1929; Attaché, London 1931; Secretary of Legation, London 1934; Secretary of Legation, Washington 1935, Chargé d'Affaires 1945; transferred to Foreign Office 1947; En. Ex. and Min. Plen. to Switzerland 1948–52; Dir.-Gen. of Asian and African Affairs, Foreign Office 1953–54; Min. Plen. to Egypt 1955; Amb. Ex. & Plen. to U.A.R., and concurrently Min. Plen. to Lebanon 1958–60; Director General of Protocol Dept., Foreign Office 1961–63; Ambassador to Benelux and concurrently to E.E.C. 1963–66. *Address:* 1715 Terd Tai Road, Thonburi-Bangkok, Thailand.

**BHANDARY, Bharat Raj.** *B.* 1924. *Educ.* Calcutta Univ. (BSc); Allahabad Univ. (MA). *M.* 1945, Kalpana Joshi. *S.* 1. *Daus.* 3. *Career:* Deputy Secretary, Ministry of Foreign Affairs, Kathmandu until 1956; First Secretary, Royal Nepalese Embassy, New Delhi, 1956–61; and London 1961–64; Chargé d'Affaires, Royal Nepalese Embassy, Karachi, 1964–65. Nepalese. Ambassador Extraordinary and Plenipotentiary of the Kingdom of Nepal to Japan, Sept. 1965–69. Concurrently to Australia and to New Zealand, Mar. 1966–69; and Indonesia 1968–69; Foreign Secretary, Ministry of Foreign Affairs, Kathmandu, 1970–72; Royal Nepalese Ambassador to Burma since 1972—, concurrently to Thailand, Laos and Malaysia since 1973. *Awards:* Suprashidha Prabal Gorkha; Dakshinabahu (1st Class). *Address:* 8/370, Wotu Tole, Kathmandu, Nepal; and Royal Nepalese Embassy, No. 16, Natmauk Yeiktha, Park Avenue, Rangoon, Burma.

**BHARGAVA, Vashishtha.** Indian judge. *B.* 5 Feb. 1906. *Educ.* University of Allahabad (MSc). *M.* 1925, Vishnu Kumari Bhargava. *S.* Kapil, Dhruva, Ashok. *Career:* Joint Magistrate 1930–35; Civil and Sessions Judge 1936–37; District and Sessions Judge 1937–47; Additional Commissioner for Food and Civil Supplies, U.P. Government 1947–48, Legal Remembrancer and Judicial Secretary 1948–49; Puisne Judge High Court, Allahabad 1949–66, Chief Justice High Court Allahabad, Feb.–July 1966; Judge Supreme Court of India 1966–71; Chmn. Sugar Industry Enquiry Commission 1971–74. *Address:* A16/3 Vasant Vihar, New Delhi 110057, India.

**BHUTTO, Zulfika Ali.** Prime Minister of Pakistan 1973–77. *B.* 1928. *Educ.* University of California (BA (Hons.) Pol. Sc. 1960); Christ Church, Oxford University (MA Hons. in Jurisprudence 1952); Barrister-at-Law (Lincoln's Inn) 1953. *M.* 1951, Nusrat Ispahani. *S.* 2. *Daus.* 2. *Career:* Elected unopposed Member of the National Assembly of Pakistan Mar. 1962—. Ministerial posts: Commerce 1958–60; Information, National Reconstruction and Minority Affairs 1960; Fuel, Power and Natural Resources, and Kashmir Affairs (with portfolio of Minister of Works) 1960; Industries and Natural Resources (added portfolio of External Affairs 1963) 1962. Leader of Delegations: U.N. Gen. Asembly (1957–59–60–63–64–65); Afro-Asian Conf. Jakarta, Apr. 1964, and Bandung Conf. Apr. 1965; U.N. Conf. Law of the Sea, Geneva, Feb. 1958. Missions: India (Press Code) Apr. 1960; U.S.S.R. Dec. 1960; India (Kashmir dispute) Nov. 1962–63; Peking, Mar. 1963; Teheran, May 1963; Burma, Jan. 1964; Pres. de Gaulle, Jan. 1964; Moscow, Jan. 1965; Foreign Ministers Conf., Algiers, July 1965; Summit Conf., Cairo, July 1965. With Pres. Ayub Khan: Ankara, June 1964; Commonwealth Prime Ministers Conf., London: Peking, Feb.–Mar. 1965: State visits to U.S.S.R., Apr. 1965. Hilal-i-Pakistan. Secretary-General, Pakistan Muslim League, Mar. 1965; Chairman, Pakistan People's Party, 1967; Deputy Prime Minister and Foreign Minister 1971; President & Chief Martial Law Administrator of Pakistan 1971–73; Prime Minister 1973–77. *Member:* West Pakistan Social Welfare Council; Pres., Abadgar Assn.; Pakistan Islamic Council, International Affairs; Chmn. Bd. Governors, Pakistan Admin. Staff Coll.; Former Secy.-Gen., Pakistan Muslim League. *Awards:* Hilal-i-Pakistan; Nishan-i Hamayun, First Class; Order of the Republic of Indonesia; Gran Cruz de la Orden Del Libertador General San Martin, Argentine Civil Award; Orders of: Nishan-i-Hamayun (1st Cl.), Iran; Order of the Republic (Indonesia). Pres., Abadgar Assn., Larkana District; Chmn. Bd. Governors, Pakistan Administrative Staff Coll., Lahore. *Publication:* Myth of Independence (1968). *Address:* Al-Murtaza, Larkana, Pakistan.

**BIANCHI, Eric A.** American. *B.* 1906. *Educ.* Massachusetts Inst. of Technology (BS in ME). *M.* 1931, Katherine Denison. *S.* David Webster. Vice-Pres. 1956–60, Pres. 1960–64, Mason Neilan Div., Worthing Corp. *Member:* Fluid Control Inst. (Past Pres.); S.A.M.A. (Past Chmn. Recorder Controller Section); Instrument Socy. of America. Vice-President, Planning, Worthington Corp. 1965–68; Director of Planning, Studebaker, Worthington, Inc. since 1968. *Clubs:* Echo Lake Country; Dedham Country & Polo; Bald Peak Colony. *Address:* 10 Euclid Avenue, Summit, N.J. 07901; and 530 Fifth Ave., New York, N.Y. 10036.

**BIBBY, Dause L.** American office equipment industry executive. *B.* 1911. *Educ.* Texas A. & M. Coll.; Univ. of Texas (BBA 1933). *M.* 1937, Virginia Martin. *S.* Douglas. *Daus.* Carolyn and Martha. *Career:* with International Business Machines Corporation 1934–55 (successively Salesman 1934–37; Manager, Sales Office 1937–41; Asst. to Vice-Pres. 1941–43); Resident Manager (Poughkeepsie, N.Y. Plant) 1943–46; Exec. Asst. (Endicott, N.Y. Plant) 1946; General Manager (Poughkeepsie) 1946–49; Vice-President 1949–55; Exec. Vice-Pres. & Dir., Daystrom Inc. 1956–59; President, Remington-Rand 1960–63; Vice-Pres., Sperry Rand Corp. since 1963; Pres., Stromberg-Carlson Corp. 1964–74; Chmn. & Chief Exec. 1974–76 (Ret'd). *Member:* Society for Advancement of Management (Past Chairman of Board and Past President); Economic Club of N.Y.; Board of Advisors to the XIII International Management Congress in 1963; National Adv. Council, Society for Advancement of Management; Nat. Corp.; Nat. Cttee., Univ. Texas Dev. Bd.; Cttee., Industrial Mgt. Council; Bd. Trustees Rochester Chamber of Commerce. *Clubs:* University (N.Y.C.); Country Club Rochester. *Address:* 26 Broadway, Rochester, N.Y.; and *office* 100 Carlson Road, Rochester, N.Y. 14603, U.S.A.

**BICKFORD, Edward Davidson.** American. *B.* 1909. *Educ.* Yale Univ. *M.* 1937, Ann Watson. *S.* Edward W. and Peter W. *Daus.* Mary Ann (Patton), Patricia (Greenough) and Susan (Thomas III, Dec.). *Career:* With Bethlehem Steel Corp.: Manager of Sales, Cleveland, Jan. 1955; Asst. Gen. Mgr. of Sales, Bethlehem, May 1956; Asst. Vice-Pres., Bethlehem, June 1963; Vice-Pres., Sales, 1963–70; Dir. Oct. 1963–74, Bethlehem Steel Corporation; Dir: Ogden, Thompson Steel; Chmn. COMPUS (A.I.S.I. Com. to Promote the Use of Steel 1966–68; Senior Vice-Pres., Commercial 1970–74. *Member:* American Iron and Steel Institute. *Clubs:* The Brook, Yale (all of N.Y.C.); Saucon Valley Country; The Steel Division. *Address:* Saucon Valley Road, R.D. No 4, Bethlehem, Pa. 18015; and *office* One Bethlehem Plaza, Bethlehem Pa. 18018, U.S.A.

**BIDDLE, Eric Harbeson.** American administrator. *B.* 27 Apr. 1898. *Educ.* Philadelphia Public Schools; University of Pennsylvania and Oxford. *M.* Janet Mayo. *S.* Eric, Jr.,

John, Maurice. *Career:* served World War I in U.S. Army and Royal Air Force 1917–19. Executive Vice-President, U.S. Committee for the care of European children, organizing transportation, reception, and care of European children to the United States 1940–41; Head, Mission to the U.K. to study British War Administration 1941–42; Head of Special Mission to Great Britain, Executive Office of the President, Bureau of the Budget 1942–47; Special Assistant to the Secretary-General of U.N. 1946; Chairman, advisory Group of Experts on Administrative, Personnel and Budgetary Questions, U.N. 1945–46. Acting Chief, Economic Co-operation Administration Mission to Korea 1948–49; Special Assistant to Director, Bureau of German Affairs, Department of State Sept.–Dec. 1949; Consultant on Civil Defence Planning, Executive Office of the President, National Security Resources Board 1949–50; Consultant to Director of Administration, Economic Co-operation Administration, Congressional Presentation of Mutual Security Programme Mar. 1951; Director, Middle East Planning Staff, Economic Co-operation Administration, Programme Planning for Middle East and Dependent Overseas Territories of European countries of Mutual Security Administration, June 1951; Consultant to Assistant Director for Europe, M.S.A., Jan. 1952; Consultant to Chief of M.S.A. Mission to China and Far East Programme Div. 1952; Special Consultant to Executive Chairman, Technical Assistance Board (U.N.), field studies in various countries in S. and S.E. Asia, 1952; H.Q. studies T.A.B. 1952–53; Consultant to Publisher, The New York Times 1955; Dir., Porter International Co. 1957–65; Vice-Pres., U.S. Leasing Corp. 1958–61; Pres., Biddle Associates Inc. since 1961; Mem., Washington Inst. of Foreign Affairs. *Clubs:* Cosmos (Washington, D.C.),; The Athenaeum (London). *Address:* 1200 N. Nash Street, Arlington, Va. 22209; and *office* 1730 Rhode Is. Ave. NW, Washington, D.C. 20036, U.S.A.

**BIENECK, Dr.-Ing. E.h. Edmund A.** *B.* 1900. Deputy Chmn. Supervisory Bd. Didier Werke AG, Wiesbaden. Chairman of honour of Administrative Council, Didier SA, Lugones, Spain; Dep. Chairman, Magnesitas Navarras SA, San Sebastian 1972—. Chairman, Supervisory Council, Nederlandsche Ovenbouw Maatschappji NV, Nom, Zeist, Holland. Hon. President of Administrative Council, Didier-Société Industrielle de Produits Céramiques, Paris. Hon. Chmn. of Administrative Council, Rhein Chamotte und Dinas Werke, Bad Godesberg Mehlem; President of Honour; Federal Association of Stones & Earths Industry, Wiesbaden; Member of Honour of Board, Bavarian Industrial Federation of the Industry (Munich); Hon. Chmn., Refractory Industry Federation, Bonn.; President of Honour, European Federation of Producers of Refractory Products, Zurich; Export Committee of the German Economy (Eastern Section), Cologne. Vice-Pres., Chamber of Commerce and Industry, Wiesbaden. *Awards:* German Distinguished Service Order 1953; Grand Cross for Distinguished Service (German); Grand Cross, Order of Merit (Spain) 1960; Honorary Freeman of the Rheinisch-Westfalische Technische Hochschule, Aachen. Star of the Grand Cross of Federal Republic (Germany). *Address:* Hildastrasse 21, Wiesbaden; and *office* Lessingstrasse 16, Wiesbaden, Germany.

**BIERING, H. A.** Danish Diplomat. *B.* 1920. *Educ.* Univ. of Copenhagen-Master of Law. *M.* 1950, Annette Hänschell. *S.* 2. *Career:* Ministry of Foreign Affairs, Copenhagen 1945; Military Mission in Berlin 1949; Foreign Ministry, Copenhagen 1950; Embassy in Paris 1951; Foreign Ministry, Copenhagen 1954; Consul, London 1959; Ambassador, Accra, Ghana and also accredited to Liberia and the Ivory Coast 1961; Ambassador; New Delhi and also accredited to Sri Lanka, Nepal and Bangladesh 1967; Head of Dept., Foreign Ministry 1973; Ambassador, Dar-es-Salem and also accredited to Zambia, Botswana, Mozambique, Lesotho and Angola 1975–77; Ambassador, Warsaw since 1977. *Address:* Ambasade Dunska, Slaroscinska 5, 02-516 Warsaw, Poland.

**BIFFEN, William John,** MP. *B.* 1930. *Educ.* Cambridge University (1st Class History). Unmarried. *Career:* Member of Parliament, Cons. for Oswestry since 1961; Executive Member of 1922 Committee 1966—; Member Public Accounts Committee 1964–67; Select Cttee. on Nationalized Industries 1971–74. *Club:* Birmingham Club. *Address:* House of Commons, London, S.W.1.

**BIGGS-DAVISON, John Alec,** MP. British Politician. *B.* 1918. *Educ.* Scholar at Clifton Coll.; Exhibitioner at Magdalen Coll., Oxford—MA. *M.* 1948, Pamela Mary Hodder-Williams. *S.* 2. *Daus.* 4. *Career:* Commissioned in Royal Marines 1939; Indian Civil Service (last British Officer appointed to Punjab Commission) 1942; Forward Liaison Officer, Cox's Bazaar 1943–44; Political Asst. & Commandant Border Military Police & later Dep. Commissioner Dera Ghazi Khan 1946–48; Conservative Research Dept. 1950–55; MP (Cons.) for Chigwell 1955–70, & for Epping Forest since 1974. *Publications:* George Wyndham (1951); Tory Lives (1952); The Walls of Europe (1962); Portuguese Guinea (1970); Africa—Hope Deferred (1972); The Hand is Red (1975); contributor to many British & Continental periodicals. *Address:* 35 Hereford Square, London, S.W.7; and *office* House of Commons, London SW1A 0AA.

**BILBY, Kenneth W.** American business executive. *B.* 1918. *Educ.* Univ. of Arizona (BA 1941). *M.* 1948, Helen Owen Meeker. *S.* Kenneth Mansfield and Robert Bryan. *Daus.* Barbara Windsor and Marguerite Mansfield. *Career:* Foreign correspondent in Europe and Middle East for New York Herald Tribune 1947–50; public relations representative to RCA Victor, Camden, N.J. 1950–54; Vice-Pres., public relations, and Exec. Vice-Pres., National Broadcasting Co. (NBC) 1954–60; Exec. Vice-Pres., Public Affairs, RCA Corp. since 1962. Served to Lt.-Col., Army of the U.S. in World War II (Decorated Silver Star, Bronze Star, Legion of Merit, and Croix de Guerre). Member Board of Directors, World Press Institute. *Member:* Phi Delta Theta. *Publications:* New Star in the Near East, (1950). *Clubs:* Apawamis (Rye, N.Y.); Winged Foot Golf (Mamaroneck, N.Y.); Lake Placid (N.Y.); Burning Tree (Bethesda, Md.). *Address* and *office:* 30 Rockefeller Plaza, New York City 10020, U.S.A.

**BILLIG, Franklin Anthony.** American. *B.* 1923. *Educ.* Univ. of S. Calif. (BA Organic Chemistry, 1954). *M.* 1957, Tetsuko Morinaga. *Dau.* Patricia Ann Kikuko. *Career:* Senior Research Chemist, American Potash & Chemical Corp., Whittier Research Laboratory 1954–64. Principal Laboratory Mgr. & Safety Officer, Department of Chemistry, University of Southern California, Los Angeles 1964—. *Publications:* Quarterly Reports on Sulfur Compounds (1966); Advances in Chemistry (1959, 1961); Intra-Science Chemistry Reports; owner of several U.S. patents. *Member:* Sigma XI. *Fellow:* Amer. Inst. of Chemists; Amer. Assn. for Advancement of Science; The Chemical Socy. (London); Amer. Chemical Socy.; N.Y. Acad. of Science. *Address.* 12722 South Spindlewood Drive, La Mirada, Calif. 90638; and *office* Department of Chemistry, University of Southern California, Los Angeles, Calif. 90007, U.S.A.

**BILLINGS, Bruce Hadley.** American. *B.* 1915. *Educ.* Phillips Exeter Acad.; Harvard Univ. (AB 1936; AM 1937); and Johns Hopkins Univ. (PhD-Physics 1943). *M.* 1938, Sarah Winslow. *S.* Bruce Randolph and Peter Fayssoux. *Daus.* Sally Frances (Dooley) and Jane Winslow. *Career:* Teacher, Amer. Community School, Beirut (Lebanon) 1937–40; Physicist, Johns Hopkins Univ. 1940–41, and Polaroid Corp. 1941–47; Dir. of Research, Baird-Atomic Inc. 1947–63 (Exec. Vice-Pres. 1955–63); Assoc. Journal Editor, Optical Socy. of America 1956—; Dir., Ealing Corp. 1960–66; Asst. Dir., Defense Research & Engineering, U.S. Dept. of Defense 1959–60; Assoc. Editor, Amer. Inst. of Physics Handbook 1956—; Dir., Diffraction Ltd. 1960—; WIN Corporated 1966—; Vice-Pres., & Gen. Mgr., Laboratory Operations, Aerospace Corp. 1963–68; Special Asst. to American Ambassador, Teipei Taiwan for Science & Technology, U.S. Foreign Service 1968–73; Vice-Pres., Corp. Planning Aer. Corp. 1973–74; Vice-Pres., Washington Office, Aero. Corp. 1974—. *Member:* Radiology Safety Section, Atomic Bomb Test Bikini 1946; U.S.A. National Committee for International Commission of Optics 1963–66; National Acad. Adv. Committee for the Bureau of Standards; U.S. Air Force, Scientific Adv. Board 1962—; Vice-Pres., Int. Commission of Optics 1973—; U.S. Rep., U.N. Adv. Cttee., Consult. U.S. Arms Control and Disarmament Agency since 1974; Application, Science & Technology to Development 1973—. *Awards:* Fellow, Amer. Acad. Arts & Sciences; Optical Socy. of America, Pres. 1971; Amer. Physical Socy.; Acoustical Socy. of America; Hon. PhD. China Academy; Chinese Government Order of Brilliant Star. *Clubs:* St. Botolph, Boston Yacht (Boston, Mass.). *Address:* The Aerospace Corporation, 955 L'Enfant Plaza, S.W., Washington D.C. 20024, U.S.A.

**BILOFSKY, Maxwell Monroe.** American executive. *B.* 1901. *Educ.* College. *M.* Betty E. Keller. *Dau.* Frances Joan. President: Industrial Electronics Corp., Magno-Tronic Corp.,

Crown Starter Co. Inc., Secnarf Realty Co. Inc.; Gold Seal Radio Tube & Electronics Corp. Member of the New York Stock Exchange. Republican. *Member:* Pennsylvania Society New York Chamber of Commerce; Monmouth County Historical Assn.; N.Z. Chamber of Commerce. National Republican. *Clubs:* Shrine; Downtown. *Address: office* 295 Halsey Street Newark, N.J., U.S.A.

**BILTON, Roland Fisher.** Industrialist. *B.* 1904. *Educ.* Hymers College, Hull. *M.* 1928, Sybil Rose Dixon. *S.* Peter Frederick and Richard Charles Dixon. *Career:* Second Lieutenant, East Yorks. Regiment 1927, Captain 1932; served in World War II (France and Western Desert) 1939–45; Lieut.-Col. 1944; Sector Comdr., E.R. Yorks. Home Guard 1953. Justice of the Peace, East Riding of Yorkshire 1950; Deputy Lieutenant, E.R. of Yorkshire and Hull 1960; Director: Bilton Properties Ltd., Black Mill Ltd. *Club:* Army & Navy. *Address:* Rolston Hall, Hornsea, Yorks.; and 73 Cromwell Road, London S.W.7.

**BINGHAM, Barry,** CBE; Commander, Legion of Honour (France); American journalist. *B.* 1906. *Educ.:* Harvard Univ. (AB). *M.* 1931, Mary Caperton. *S.* Barry. *Daus.* Sallie and Eleanor. *Career:* Officer, U.S. Naval Reserve 1941–45; Public Information Officer, U.S. Naval Forces, Europe 1943–44; Chief, Mission to France, Economic Cooperation Admin. (Marshall Plan) 1949–50; Pres., Courier-Journal & Louisville Times 1937–62; Editor and Publisher, Courier-Journal and Louisville Times 1962–71; Chmn. of the Board 1971—; President, WHAS Inc. 1946–71; Chmn. of the Board 1971—; Trustee: Rockefeller Foundation 1958—, Asia Foundation 1957—, and Berea College 1937—. *Publications:* articles in Atlantic Monthly, Reader's Digest, Reporter, etc. Hon. LLD, Centre College, Kenyon College, Univ. of Kentucky; LittD Univ. of Louisville; DHL, Univ. of Cincinnati. Dir., American Press Inst. Chairman, International Press Inst. Chmn. of the Bd., English Speaking Union of the U.S. Department. *Clubs:* Century (N.Y.C.); Pendennis, River Valley, Louisville Country (all of Louisville). *Address:* Glenview, Ky.; and *office* 525 W. Broadway, Louisville 2, Ky., U.S.A.

**BINNS, Kenneth Johnstone,** CMG. Government Financial Adviser. *B.* 1912. *Educ.:* Melbourne C. of E. Grammar School, Univ. of Melbourne (MA; BCom) and Harvard Univ.; Fellow, Commonwealth Fund of New York. *M.* 1940, Nancy H. Mackenzie. *Career:* Bank of New South Wales 1934–35; Commonwealth Grants Commission 1936–38; Ian Potter & Co. 1939–41; Tasmanian Treasury 1942–76; Under Treasurer and State Commissioner of Taxes, Govt. of Tasmania, 1952–76; Dep. Chmn.; State Grants Commission; Tasmanian Government Insurance Office; State Library Board; Superannuation Board, 1976—. With I.M.F. as Advisor to Minister of Finance, Indonesia, 1968. Fiscal Review Commissioner in Nigeria 1964. *Publications:* Social Credit in Alberta (1947); Federal-State Financial Relations, Canada and Australia, (1948); articles in Economic Record. *Clubs:* Athenaeum, Tasmanian (Hobart). *Address:* 3 Ellington Road, Sandy Bay, Hobart, Tasmania.

**BIOBAKU, Saburi Oladeni,** CMG, MA, PhD. *B.* 1918. *Educ.:* Government Coll., Ibadan; Higer Coll., Yaba; Univ. Coll., Exeter; Trinity Coll., Cambridge. *M.* 1949, Muhabat Folasade Agusto. *S.* 1. *Career:* Registrar, Univ. Coll., Ibadan 1953–57. Secretary to Premier and Executive Council Western Nigeria 1957–61; Pro-Vice-Chancellor, Univ. of Ife 1961–65; Director, Yoruba Historical Research Scheme; Vice-Chancellor, Univ. of Lagos, Nigeria 1965–72; Chmn., Management Consultant Services Ltd., Lagos since 1972. *Publications:* The Origin of the Yorubas (1955); The Egba and their Neighbours (1957). *Address:* P.O. Box 7741, Lagos, Nigeria.

**BIRCH, Arthur John Richard,** OBE. Australian. *B.* 1908. *Educ.* State School; High School; Business Admin. College; Fellow, Inst. of Sales & Business Management (FSBM). *M.* 1938, Lorna M. Wyeth. *Daus.* 2. *Career:* Sales Administrator until 1936; in his 38 years' service with the Chamber of Commerce successively editor of its monthly journal, Assistant Secretary, Sydney Chamber of Commerce, Secretary of Export Development Group of N.S.W., and Federal Secretary of Australian Exporters Federation. Secretary Sydney Chamber of Commerce, Inc. 1952–63. Director, Sydney Chamber of Commerce, Inc. 1963. *Address:* 36 Bimburra Avenue, St. Ives, N.S.W., Australia.

**BIRD, George William Terence,** BSc, ARCS., FBIM. British. *B.* 1914. *Educ.* Prescot Grammar Sch.; Imperial Coll. London Univ. (BSc). *M.* 1942, Hylda O. Craven. *Dau.* 1. *Career:* Exec. Vice Chmn. Pilkington Bros. Ltd.; Dir. Pilkington Bros. (Canada) Ltd., Pilkington Bros. (South Africa) (Pty.) Ltd., Hindusthan-Pilkington Glass Works Ltd., Vidrieria Argentina S.A., Pilkington A.C.I. Ltd. *Address:* 21 Grange Drive, Eccleston Hill, St. Helens, Merseyside; and *office* Prescot Rd., St. Helens, Merseyside.

**BIRD, John Commons.** American attorney-at-law. *B.* 1922. *Educ.* Dartmouth College (AB 1943); College of Law, Univ. of Cincinnati (LLB 1948). *M.* 1948, Irene Elizabeth Grogloth. *S.* John Traill and Bruce Mackay. *Dau.* Elizabeth Anne. *Career:* Member of the Bar of the States of Kentucky, Ohio and Pennsylvania. Lieut. in U.S.N.R. (active duty 1943–46; Commanding Officer of L.S.M. 156; honourable discharge 1952). Attorney, U.S. Steel Corp., Pittsburgh, Pa. 1948–52; Attorney & Asst. Secy., U.S. Steel Homes, Inc., New Albany, Inc. 1952–57; Secretary and Patent Officer, U.S. Steel Homes, Inc. (in 1956 U.S. Steel Homes merged with U.S. Steel Corp., and became Steel Homes Div., U.S. Steel Corp.); Attorney and Asst. Secy., U.S. Steel Corp., Pittsburgh, Pa., 1958–66; Sen. Gen. Attorney, Southern Area, U.S. Steel Corp., Fairfield, Ala.; Secy. Birmingham Forest Products Inc.; Attorney & Asst. Secretary, U.S. Steel Corporation (specializing in Labour Law, collective bargaining, administration of labour agreements, and acting as Company advocate in labour arbitration). *Member:* Delta Upsilon; Phi Delta Phi (legal fraternity); American Bar Assn.; Allegheny County, Pennsylvania Bar Assn.; State of Kentucky Bar Assn.; Birmingham & Alabama Bar Assn. *Clubs:* The Downtown Club; Dartmouth Club (Western Pa.); Kiwanis. *Address:* 3125 Guilford Road, Mountain Brook, Ala. 35223, U.S.A.

**BIRD, John Frederick,** CBE, MC, TD, BSc, FIEE. British. *B.* 1914. *Educ.* Newcastle Royal Grammar Sch.; Durham Univ. (BSc). *M.* 1947, Joan Clark. *S.* 1. *Daus.* 3. *Career:* Eng. in charge Testing & Certification, A. Reyrolle & Co. Ltd. 1949–55; Manager, A. Reyrolle & Co. (Rhodesia) Ltd. 1955–60; Overseas Man. & Dir. 1965–69. *Member:* Fellow Inst. Electrical Engineers. *Clubs:* East India, Devonshire, Sports & Public Schools (London). *Address:* 17 Radcliffe Road, Bamburgh, Northumberland.

**BIRGI, Muharrem Nuri.** Turkish ambassador (Ret.). *B.* 1908. *Educ.* School of Political Sciences, Paris (Dipl.) and Faculty of Law, Geneva. *Career:* entered Ministry of Foreign Affairs 1932; First Secretary of Embassy, Warsaw 1935–39; Paris (Vichy) 1941; Counsellor of Legation, Madrid until 1944; at Central Administration; Director-General Adjoint, First Political Department (1944), Dept. of International Affairs (1945), Dept. of Co-ordination (1946), Dept. of Consular Affairs (1946), Second Political Dept. (1950), Secretary-General Adjoint, Ministry of Foreign Affairs (1951), Under-Secretary of State (1952); Secretary-General (with rank of Ambassador) 1954; participated in various diplomatic conferences, notably the General Assembly of the U.N. (1946–49–50); represented Turkey at the drafting of the Tripartite Balkan Alliance Treaty, Athens 1954; actively engaged in a number of political agreements, including the Turco-Greek-Yugoslav Treaty of Friendship (1953), The Turco-Pakistani Treaty of Collaboration (1954) and the Baghdad Pact (1955); Secretary-General, Ministry for Foreign Affairs until 1957; Ambassador of Turkey to the Court of St. James's 1957–60; Permanent Representative to NATO 1960–72. *Address:* Toprakli Sokak, 11 Salacak, Uskudar, Istanbul, Turkey.

**BIRK, The Rt. Hon. Baroness, Alma,** BSc, JP, Life Peer. British politician. *Educ.* South Hampstead High School (Hon. Economics before going to Univ.); London School of Economics; London University. Bachelor of Science in Economics, Hons. *M.* Ellis Birk. *S.* 1. *Dau.* 1. *Career:* Journalist; Justice of the Peace. Governor, London School, Economics; Chmn. Health Education Council 1969–72; Member Exec. Council Christians & Jews since 1971; Baroness in Waiting 1974; Parly. Under Secy. of State, Dept. of the Environment since 1974. *Address:* 13 Hanover Terrace, Regents Park, London, N.W.1.

**BIRNIE, Joseph Earle.** American banker. *B.* 30 Nov. 1903. *Educ.* Washington and Lee University. *M.* 1941, Octavia Norfleet Riley. *Dau.* Ada Lea. *Career:* Past National President, Consumer Bankers Association 1945–47; Chairman and Chief Exec. Officer, The Natl. Bank of Georgia 1938; Dir., Georgia International Life Assurance Corp. Trustee, Washington and Lee Univ. *Member:* The Society of the Cincinnati, Society of Colonial Wars in Virginia. *Address:* 3130 Habersham Road, N.W. Atlanta, Georgia, U.S.A.

**BISCAYART, Michel.** American. *B.* 1901. *Educ.* French BS, Ingénieur des Arts & Manufactures degree from Ecole Centrale (Paris); MBA Harvard Graduate School of Business Admin. *M.* 1938, Madeleine Agraz de Aguilar. *S.* Michel V. and Marc. K. *Career:* Trainee, Norton Co., Worcester, Mass. 1928–30; Sales Engineer, Sales Mgr., Asst. General Mgr., Cie. Norton, Paris 1930–45; Regional Mgr. Europe, Norton International 1945–58; President, E. W. Bliss Co. (Paris), 1959—. Professor, Centre Perfectionnement Administration des Affaires, H.E.C., C.N.A.M., etc., Paris. *Publications:* Marketing, Precis de Vente (Ed. Dunod, Paris), Le Management (E.M.E.). *Member:* St. Ouen Manufacturers Assn. (Hon. Pres.). *Club:* Harvard (of France). *Address:* 90 *bis* Chaussée de l'Etang, St. Mandé 94; and *office* 54 Boulevard Victor Hugo, St. Ouen 93, France.

**BISDEE, Colin Edward,** FRAS; British. Owner (and erector) Astronomical and Geophysical Observatory, on Mount Nelson, Hobart, Tasmania. *B.* 1899. *Educ.* Hutchins School, Hobart; and City & Guilds Institute, London (Full Technology Diploma in Electrical Engineering). Unmarried. *Career:* Electrical engineering in U.S.A., Europe and Australia 1919–39; Engineering war work, Ministry of Munitions, Australia 1940–45. His observatory now occupies his full time. *Publications:* engineering papers before various scientific bodies. *Life Member:* Royal Society of Tasmania; Tasmania Club; Astronomical Society of Tasmania. *Address:* Tasmanian Club, Macquarie Street, Hobart; and *office* 53 Collins Street, Hobart, Tasmania.

**BISHOP, Rt. Hon. Edward Stanley,** JP, MP, TEng (CEI), AMRASeS, MIED. British. *B.* 1920. *Educ.* Bristol University. *M.* 1945, Winifred Mary Bryant. *Daus.* Anne, Mary, Frances and Ursula. *Career:* Aero Nautical Design Engineer, British Aircraft Corp. 1938–64; Magistrate (JP) since 1957; Member of Parliament Labour, for Newark Notts. since 1964; U.K. Delegate, North Atlantic Assembly, Brussels 1966–73, Chmn. of the Economic Cttee. 1970–73; Opposition spokesman, Trade & Industry 1971–74; Parly-Secy., Min. of Agric, Fisheries and Food since 1974. later Min. of State; Second Church Estates Commissioner 1974. Privy Councillor, June 1977. *Member:* Institution, Engineering Designers and Royal Aeronautical Society. Fellow Ancient Monuments Society. *Address:* House of Commons, London, S.W.1.

**BISHOP, George Horace.** Australian. *B.* 1906. *Educ.* Sydney Technical College (Dipl. Metallurgy with Credit). *M.* 1931, Marian Maude Watkins. *S.* David Kingsley and Stephen Kingsley. *Career:* Manager, Newcastle Steel Works 1956–59; Gen. Mgr., The Broken Hill Pty. Co. Ltd., Newcastle 1959–63; Gen. Mgr., Distribution and Services, The Broken Hill Proprietary Co. Ltd., Melbourne, C.1. 1963–68; Board Dir. Noske Industries Ltd.; Pyrox Ltd. and Tennent New York Pty. Ltd. 1968–74. *Member:* Australian Inst. of Mining & Metallurgy; Australian Inst. of Metals. *Clubs:* The Australian (Melbourne); Metropolitan Golf; Frankston Golf Ltd. *Address:* Culverkeys, 12 Beach Rd, Beaumaris, Victoria 3193, Aust.

**BISHOP, Sir George Sidney,** CB, OBE. *B.* 1913. *Educ.* London School of Economics (Univ. of London); BSc (Econ.). *M.* 1961, Una C. C. Padel. *Dau.* Prudence. *Career:* In British Civil Service 1940–61; P.P.S., Minister of Food 1945–49; Under-Secy. Ministry of Agriculture, Fisheries & Food 1949–59; Deputy Secy. 1959–61; Chairman, International Sugar Council 1957; Vice-Chairman, International Wheat Council 1959; Chmn., West India Cttee. 1969–71, Pres. since 1977; Governor, Nat. Inst. for Economic & Social Research since 1968; Member of Panel for Civil Service Manpower Review 1968–70; Tropical Products Inst. Advisory Cttee.; CBI Council; Chmn., Industry Co-op Programme Exec. Cttee. of Food & Agric. Organisation of UN; Chmn., Overseas Development Inst. Ltd.; Royal Commission on the Press 1974–77; Chmn., Booker McConnell Ltd. since 1972; Dir., Barclay's Bank Intern. Ltd. 1972; Dir., Barclay's Bank Ltd. since 1974; Dir., Agricultural Mortgage Co. Ltd. since 1973; Dir., Rank Hovis McDougall Ltd. since 1976. *Clubs:* Reform; MCC; Club Alpin Français. *Address:* Brenva, Eghams Wood Road, Beaconsfield, Bucks.; 15 West Eaton Place, London, SW1X 8LT; and *office* Bucklersbury House, Cannon Street, London, E.C.4.

**BISHOP, Sir Harold,** CBE. British chartered electrical engineer and chartered mechanical engineer. *B.* 29 Oct. 1900. *Educ.* Alleyn's School; City & Guilds Coll.; BSc (Eng.)· FCGI, Fellow, Imperial Coll. of Science and Technology. *M*; 1925, Madge Adeline Vaus. *S.* 1 (*D*). *Daus.* 2. *Career:* Engineer, H.M. Office of Works 1920–22; Engineer, Marconi's Wireless Telegraph Co. Ltd. 1922–23; joined British Broadcasting Company (later Corporation) 1923; successivel, Senior Superintendent Engineer 1923–29, Assistant Chief Engineer 1929–43, Chief Engineer 1943–52, Director of Engineering 1952–63; Director Chemring Ltd.; Pres., Institution of Electrical Engineers 1953–54; Assn. of Supervising Electrical Engineers 1956–58, and Royal Television Socy. 1961–62; Hon. Fellow of Instn. of Electrical Engineers. *Fellow:* Instn. of Mechanical Engineers and Fellow of Institute of Electrical & Electronics Engineers. *Address:* Carbis, Harborough Hill, Pulborough, Sussex.

**BISHOP, Warner Bader.** Business executive. *B.* 1918. *Educ.* Dartmouth Coll. (A.B. 1941); Amos Tuck Sch. (M.B.A. 1942); Harvard Business Sch. (28th AMP, 1955). *M.* (1) 1944, Katharine Sue White. *Daus.* Susan K. Judith T., Katherine W., and Jennifer A. (2) 1967, Barrie Osborn. *Children:* Brooks & Wilder. *Career:* Vice-Pres., Archer-Daniels Midland Co. 1955–59; Pres., Federal Foundry Supply Co. 1957–59; various executive posts in Archer-Daniels Midland Co. 1946—. U.S. Naval Reserve 1942–46. President and Director, Basic Incorporated 1961–63; Pres. Union Savings Assn. 1963–74, Chmn. since 1970; Chmn. Transohio Finan. Corp. since 1974; Past Director & Member, Exec. Committee Twin Industries Corp.; Past Director, Acorn Chemical Co. *Member:* of Corporation, Fenn College 1962—; Vice-Pres., Dolomitic Refractories Association 1961—. Director: Cleveland Area Heart Society 1959—, Ohio State Heart Society 1961—, and Council on High Blood Pressure 1960—. *Publications:* Common Sense in the Core Room: Which Core Process? (articles in Foundry Magazine, 1951, 1957). Past Member: Amer. Inst. of Mining & Metallurgical Engineers; Amer. Foundrymen's Socy.; Refractories Inst. *Clubs:* Chagrin Valley Hunt; Tavern; Union (all of Cleveland, Ohio); Racquet & Tennis (New York). *Address:* The Chesterfield, 1801 E 12th, Cleve, Ohio 44114; 79 E 79th Street, NY 10021; and *office* One Penton Plaza, Cleveland, Ohio 44114, U.S.A.

**BISSELL, Claude Thomas.** CC. British. University Professor. *B.* 1916. *Educ.* Univ. of Toronto (BA 1936; MA 1937); Cornell Univ. (PhD 1940); Hon. Degrees: DLitt, Manitoba 1958; LLD, McGill 1958, Queen's 1959, New Brunswick 1959, Carleton 1960, Montreal 1960, St. Lawrence 1962, Michigan 1963, British Columbia 1962, Columbia 1965. Hon. Dr. Letters. Fellow, Royal Society of Canada 1957; D. ès L., Laval 1966. *M.* 1945, Christina Flora Gray. *Dau.* Deirdre MacFarlane. *Career:* Instructor in English Cornell 1938–41; Lecturer in English, Univ. of Toronto 1941–47; Asst. Prof. (1947–51), Associate Prof. (1951–56), Asst. to Pres. (1948–52), Vice-Pres. (1952–56), Prof. of English 1962—, Univ. of Toronto; Dean in Residence, Univ. Coll., Univ. of Toronto 1946–56; Pres., Carleton Univ. 1956–58. Served in World War II (Canadian Infantry Corps and Argyll and Sutherland Highlanders of Canada in N.W. European campaign; discharged with rank of Captain (1942–46); President Univ. of Toronto 1958–71; Chmn., The Canada Council 1960–62. Pres. Natl. Conf. of Candian Universities and Colleges 1962–63; Chmn. Canadian Universities Foundation 1962–63; Pres. World Universities Service of Canada 1962–63. Visiting Professor in Canadian Studies, Wm. Lyon MacKenzie King Endowment, Harvard Univ., 1967–68. LLD, York Univ., Prince of Wales College, & Univ. of Windsor; D.Litt. Univ. of Western Ontario (1971), Univ. of Lethbridge (1972); LLD, St Andrews Univ. (1972); D.Litt., Leeds Univ. (1976), Univ. of Toronto (1977); Chmn. Carnegie Foundation for the Advancement of Teaching, 1966; Hon. Mem. American Academy of Arts & Sciences, 1968. *Awards:* Companions of the Order of Canada 1971. *Publications:* Editor, Univ. Coll.: A portrait 1853–1953, (1953); Canada's Crisis in Higher Education, 1957; Our Living Tradition, 1957; Editor, Great Canadian Writing—A Century of Imagination, 1966; The Strength of the University, 1968; Half Way up Parnassus; A Personal Account of the Univ. of Toronto, 1952–71. various articles on Canadian and English literature in Canadian and American journals. Member, United Church of Canada. *Clubs:* Arts & Letters, University, York (all of Toronto); Rideau, Cercle Universitaire (Ottawa). *Address:* 229 Erskine Avenue, Toronto 5, Ont., Canada.

**BITSIOS, Dimitri.** Greek Diplomat. *B.* 1915. *Educ:* Athens Univ., Graduate in Law & Political & Economic Sciences. *M.* Angela Kyriazopoulou. *S.* 1. *Dau.* 1. *Career:* Entered Diplomatic Service 1939, served in Cairo, London and New York; Head of Economic Section and 4th Political Dept., Ministry of Foreign Affairs; Mem. of Delegation of Greece to UN 1956–61; Perm. Rep. of Greece to UN 1961–65; Head of 1st Political Dept., Ministry of Foreign Affairs; Private

Sec. to H.M. the King of the Hellenes 1966; Perm. Rep. of Greece to UN 1967–72 (Resigned); Under-Sec. of State for Foreign Affairs July 1974; Minister of Foreign Affairs 1974–77. *Decorations:* Knight Commander of the Order of the Phoenix; Distinguished Service Medal; various Foreign Decorations. *Publications:* Egypt & the Middle East; Greek Diplomatic History; Cyprus, the Vulnerable Republic. *Address:* Papanastassiou 57, Psychico; and *office* Zalocosta 2, Athens Greece.

**BITTEL, Hans Otto.** German film producer. *B.* 1912. *Educ.* Berlin Univ. (editorial and journalistic courses). *M.* Eva Füllgraf. *S.* Jörg. *Career:* Associated with W. Girardet, publishers, Essen; Asst. Publisher, Essener Allgemeine Zeitung 1935; with Ullstein Verlag, publishers, Berlin 1938; Axel Springer Verlag, Hamburg 1948; Manager-Director William Wilkens Advertising Agency, Hamburg 1950; co-owner William Wilkens. 1956–59; owner, Marken Film GmbH, Hamburg, 1959—. Owner TV Studio GmbH, Wedel 1965—. *Club:* Norddeutscher Reiterverein. *Address:* Schulauer Moorweg 23, Wedel/Holst, Hamburg, Germany.

**BITTEL, Lester Robert.** American publisher. *B.* 1918. *Educ.* Lehigh Univ. (BSc Industrial Engineering); MBA, Madison Coll. 1974. *M.* 1973, Muriel Albers Walcutt. *Daus.* Bethel Leslie, Martha Gilbert and Amy Helen. *Career:* Formerly Training Director, Koppers Co. Inc.; Pittsburgh; Director, Information Services, McGraw-Hill Publications Inc.; Assoc. Prof., Sch. of Business, James Madison Univ. *Publications:* Management by Exception (1964); What Every Supervisor Should Know, 3rd Ed. (1973); Practical Automation (co-author) (1957); Handbook for Training and Development (co-editor) (1967); Nine Master Keys of Management (1972); Improving Supervisory Performance (1976); Management Games for Supervisors (1977); (all titles published by McGraw-Hill). *Member:* Acad. of Mgmt.; Amer. Socy. of Mechanical Engineers; Socy. for Advancement of Management; Amer. Socy. for Training and Development. *Club:* Overseas Press. *Address:* 106 Breezewood Terrace, Bridgewater, Va. 22812; and *office* James Madison University, Harrisonburg, Va. 22801, U.S.A.

**BITTLESTONE, Robert.** British banker. *B.* 1910. *M.* June P. M. Richardson. *S.* Robert Gavin Alexander. *Daus.* Pamela Jill and Caroline Mary. *Career:* Accountancy training until 1935; with English Transcontinental 1935—; Managing Director, English Transcontinental Ltd., Merchant Bankers, 2 London Wall Buildings, London, E.C.2. Dir. Bell Fruit (Financial) Ltd.; English Transcontinental Ltd. & Subsideries; E. T. Realisation Ltd.; Leisure Incentive Vouchers Ltd.; London Residences Ltd.; New Guarantee Trust of Jersey Ltd.; Newspaper Colour Co. Ltd.; Speedtyping Ltd.; Transcontinental Banking Corp. Ltd.; United Automatics Ltd.; United Industries and Developments Ltd.; Transfilm Ltd.; Pan American Banking Corp. Ltd.; Cheshire Commercial Finance Ltd.; Associate, Chartered Inst. of Secretaries (ACIS); Fellow, Institute of Directors. Conservative. *Club:* Junior Army & Navy (London). *Address:* Whinfold, Hascombe, nr. Godalming, Surrey; and *office:* 2 London Wall Buildings, London, E.C.2.

**BIXBY, Harold Glenn.** American executive. *B.* 1903. *Educ.* University of Michigan( AB 1927). *M.* 1929, Pauline Summy; *S.* Richard Glenn. *Dau.* Mary Louise (Bartlett). *Career:* Started with Ex-Cell-O in accounting department, 1928; successively Assistant Secretary, Controller, Secretary and Treas., 1937; Vice-President and Treasurer 1947; President and General Manager 1951; Chairman of the Board and Director, Ex-Cell-O Corp. Detroit 1951–1973: Dir. & Chmn. Exec. Cttee since 1973; Chmn. Secy. and Dir. of Pure Sealed Dairy Inc.; Director: Michigan Chrome & Chemical Co., Detrex Chemical Industries Inc.; Dir. and Pres., Bixby Industries Inc.; Dir., Karmazin Product Corp. Republican. *Award:* Hon. Dr. of Laws, Univ. of Michigan (1972). *Clubs:* Detroit; Detroit Golf; Detroit Athletic. *Address:* 18510 Bretton Drive, Detroit, Mich. 48223, U.S.A.

**BIZOT, Henry.** French banker. *B.* 1901. *Educ.* Lic. es lettres et en droit. *M.* 1926, Guillemette Law de Lauriston Boubers. *S.* 4. *Dau.* Madame de la Rivière. *Career:* Formerly Inspector of Finances, Government of France. President D'Honneur Chmn., Banque Nationale de Paris. *Award:* Comdr. Legion of Honour; Croix de Guerre. *Address:* 70, rue Boissière, Paris 16; and *office* 2/18 Boulevard des Italiens, Paris.

**BJARNASON, Sigurdur.** Icelandic politician. *B.* 1915. *Educ.* Graduated in law from Univ. of Iceland, 1941; postgraduate studies in International & Company Law at Cambridge. *M.* 1956, Olöf Pálsdóttir. *S.* 1. *Dau.* 1. *Career:* Editor of a weekly newspaper 1942–47; political editor, Morgunbladid 1947–56, Editor in Chief 1956–70; member of Icelandic Parliament (Althing) 1942–70; Pres. of Lower House of the Althing 1949–56, 1963–70; Chmn., Cttee. of Foreign Affairs of the Parliament 1963–70; Pres., Municipal Council of Isfajördur 1946–50; mem., Council of the State Radio of Iceland 1947–70, Chmn. 1959, Vice-Chmn. 1960–70; Ambassador to Denmark 1970–76, to Turkey 1970–76, to China 1973–76, to Ireland since 1970, to Great Britain, Netherlands & Nigeria since 1976. *Member:* Pres. Icelandic Section of Society for Inter-Scandinavian Understanding 1965–70; mem., Nordic Council 1952–59, 1963–70 (Vice-Pres. 1952–56 & 1959, Pres. 1965 & 1970); Delegate of Iceland to General Assembly of UN 1960, 1961 & 1962; mem., Cultural Cttee. of the Nordic Countries 1954–70; mem. of an Icelandic Cttee. on territorial rights 1957–58. *Decorations:* Commander with Star of the Order of the Icelandic Falcon, 1950; Honorary emblem of the Foundation of the Icelandic Republic, 1944; Commander of the Finnish Lion, 1958; Commander of the Swedish Order of the Vasa, 1958; Grand Cross of the Danish Order of Dannebrog, 1970. *Address:* Icelandic Embassy, 1 Eaton Terrace, London SW1W 8EY.

**BJELKE-PETERSEN, Hon. Johannes.** MLA. British. *B.* 1911. *Educ.* Taabinga Valley School, Correspondence Courses and Private Studies. *M.* 1952, Florence Isabel Gilmour. *S.* 1. *Daus.* 3. *Career:* Minister for Works and Housing, Queensland Govt., 1963–68; Premier of Queensland and Minister for State Development of Queensland, since 1968. Member Legislative Assembly of Queensland, Electoral district of Barambah, 1947. Australian Country Party. *Address:* Bethany, Kingaroy, Q. 4610; and *office:* Premiers Department, George Street, Brisbane, Queensland 4000, Australia.

**BJERCKE, Alf Richard,** Com. Order of the Tunisian Republic, Officer Star of Ethiopia, Hon. Consul General of Tunisia. Norwegian. *B.* 1921. *Educ.* Frogner School, Massachusetts Inst. of Tech. *M.* 1946, Berit Blikstad. *S.* 2. *Daus.* 2. *Career:* Served with Royal Norwegian Air Force 1941–44; Major (Reserve); with Alf Bjercke A/S Oslo 1945—, Partner 1950—, Vice Chmn. 1966–69, Chmn. since 1969; with Addis Ababa Nat. Chem. Ind. Ltd. 1966—; Chmn. Norwater Norske Vannkilder A/S; Vice Chmn. Dir., Oplandske Dampskibsselskab; Dir. Norwegian Shipping Trade Journal; Alf Bjercke AB, Gothenberg; Alf Bjercke A/S Copenhagen; Bjerckes Handelsselskap; Akershus Broiler Co.; Trondhjems Farvehandel A/S; Chilinvest A/S, Ostlandets Skoleskib; Chmn., ABC Produkter A/S since 1972; Scanpump A/S since 1972; Dir., A/S Jotungruppen since 1972; Bd. Dir. Mosvold Overseas Trading Co. *Member:* Exec. Cttee. Norwegian Unido Council; Norwegian Arbitration Bd. Competitive Questions; Chmn., Socy. Protection Ancient Towns; Socy. Reconstrn. Old Christiania; Member Bd. Norwegian Assn.; Chmn. Fin. Comm. World Wild Life Fund, Norway; Bd. Dir. Norwegian Industries Assn.; Norway Athletics Association; Bd. Oslo Conservative Party 1974—; Camp. Cttee. Nat. Cons. Party 1974—; V. Chmn. Scan-Yachting Ltd. Oslo; Norw. Rep. Opsail 1976; Norw. Sail Training Assn.; Bd. Dir. Oslo Reserve Officers Assn.; M6. Commission III CIOR (Int. Conf. of Reserve Officiers). *Award:* Knight of St Olav's Order (Norw.) 1968. *Clubs:* Rotary (Past Pres.); Oslo Business Mens. *Address:* President Harbitz Gt. 14, Oslo 2; and *office* 104 Brobekkvein, Rislökka, Oslo 5, Norway.

**BJÖRNSSON, Henrik Sv.** Icelandic diplomat. *B.* 1914. *Educ.* University of Iceland (Law degree). *M.* 1941, Groa Torfhildur. *S.* Sveinn. *Daus.* Gudny and Helga. *Career:* Secretary, Danish Min of Foreign Affairs 1939–40; Icelandic Foreign Ministry 1940–42; First Secy., at Washington 1942–44; First Secy., Oslo 1947–49; Counsellor, Paris 1950–52; Secy. to President of Iceland 1952–56; Permanent Under-Secy., Ministry of Foreign Affairs 1956–60; Ambassador to Court of St. James's, concurrently the Netherlands, and Minister to Spain and Portugal 1961–65; Permanent Rep. to NATO and Ambassador to Belgium and EEC 1965–67; Ambassador of Iceland 1965–76, to France, Luxembourg, Yugoslavia, and Permanent Representative to OECD, UNESCO; Ambassador to the Arab Republic of Egypt and Ethiopia, concurrently 1971–76; Perm. Under-Sec., Ministry for Foreign Affairs since 1976. *Awards:* Commander with Star, Order of the Falcon (Iceland); Grand Cross of Lejon (Finland); Orange-Nassau (Netherlands); Ordre de la Couronne (Belgium); Merite (France); KBE and various other foreign decorations. *Address:* Ministry for Foreign Affairs, Reykjavik, Iceland.

**BLACHE-FRASER, Louis Nathaniel,** HBM. CMG. Trinidadian. *B.* 1904. *Educ.* Queen's Royal Coll., Trinidad. *M.* 1941,

Gwenyth Kent. *S.* 2. *Dau.* 1. *Career:* Financial Secy.: Trinidad and Tobago, 1953–56, and Government of the West Indies (now defunct) 1956–61; Chmn., West Indies Public Service Commission (now defunct) 1961–62; Assistant Secretary, Alstons Ltd. 1962–66. Secretary, 1966–70; Dir.: Central Bank of Trinidad and Tobago 1964—, Trinidad Building and Loan Assn. 1965—; Chmn. Ins. Brokers (WI) Ltd. 1976—; Dir., Furness Withy & Co. Ltd.; Geo. Wimpey (Caribbean) Ltd.; T. and T. National Insurance Board; Past President, Trinidad Chamber of Commerce. *Clubs:* Queen's Park Cricket; Harvard. *Address: office* 1–5 Cummins Lane, Port-of-Spain, Trinidad.

**BLACK, Charles A.** American consulting engineer. *B.* 1920. *Educ.* Univ. of Florida (BC Eng.). *M.* Elizabeth Beck. *S.* 2. *Dau.* 1. *Career:* Principal and Member of the Board, Black, Crow and Eidsness Inc., Consulting Engineers. Pres., Black Laboratories, Inc. 1947—; Vice-Pres., Black & Associates Land Planning & Eng. Co. 1951—; Principal and Board Member, Aerial Photogrammics Inc. 1947—. *Publications:* technical papers presented at national conventions of Amer. Water Works Assn. and published in journals. Recipient of a number of citations and awards. *Member:* Amer. Water Works Association, President-elect, 1970–71; Pres. AWWA 1971–72; Hon. Mem. 1975; Dipl. American Acad. of Environ. Engineers; Royal Society of Health (GB) American Society of Civil Engineers, Consulting Engineers Council, etc. *Clubs:* University; Racquet; Elk, etc. *Address:* 2941 N.W. 21st Avenue, Gainesville, Fla.; and *office:* 700 S.E. 3rd Street, Gainesville, Fla., U.S.A.

**BLACK, Sir Cyril Wilson,** JP, DL. British chartered surveyor. *B.* 8 April 1902. *Educ.* King's College School. *M.* 1930, Dorothy Joyce Birkett. *S.* 1. *Daus.* 2. *Career:* first elected Member of Parliament (C) for Wimbledon 1950; re-elected 1951–56–59—64–66; Alderman and Chmn. (1956–59) Surrey County Council; Mayor of Wimbledon 1945–47; Alderman, London Borough of Merton; Mayor of Merton 1966–67. *Address:* 'Rosewall', 21 Calonne Road, Wimbledon, London, S.W. 19.

**BLACK, Eugene Robert.** American. *B.* 1898. *Educ.* Univ. of Georgia (BA). *M.* 1930, Susette Heath. *S.* Eugene Robert and (by former marriage) William Heath. *Dau.* Elizabeth (Campbell). *Career:* Joined Harris, Forbes & Co., Atlanta 1918; associated with Harris, Forbes Corp., Atlanta 1919–33 Asst. Vice-Pres. 1933. Entered Chase National Bank, N.Y.C. 1933, Second Vice-Pres. 1933, Vice-Pres. 1937–47. Exec. Director for the U.S.A., Internat. Bank for Reconstruction and Development 1947–49; Senior Vice-Pres., Chase National Bank March-June 1949; Pres., International Bank for Reconstruction & Development (July 1949–Dec. 1962); Chase Manhatten Bank 1963–70; Dir. and Consultant, Boise Cascade Corp.; The Chase Manhatten Bank, 1970—Consultant American Express Co.; Trust Co. of Georgia; The New York Times, Cummins Engine Co. Inc.; International Telephone & Telegraph Co.; Chmn. Bd, Howmet Corporation; Dir., Hartford Fire Insurance Co. & Hartford Accident & Indemnity Co.; Chase International Investment Corp.; Chmn. Bd. Dirs., Blackwell Land Co. Inc.; Dir. Warner Communications Corporate Property Investors; Member Adv. Bd., Colonial Fund Inc.; Colonial Growth Shares Inc.; Colonial Income Fund; Trustee Amer. Shakespeare Festival (also Pres.), the Bowery Savings Bank, Johns Hopkins University, The Population Council, and The Atlantic Council. *Address:* 178 Columbia Heights, Brooklyn 1, N.Y.; and *office* 65 Broadway, New York, N.Y. 10006, U.S.A.

**BLACKALL, Frederick Steele III,** machinery executive. *B.* 1925. *Educ.* Yale Univ. (BEng.—Mechanical 1947) and Harvard Univ. (MBA 1949). *M.* 1947, Patricia Hancock. *S.* Frederick Steele IV and Grenville White. *Dau.* Holly Hancock Applegate. *Career:* Entire career with Taft-Pierce. Successively Assistant Superindendent, Small Tool Div. 1949–51; Assistant Superintendent Contract Serv. Div. and Advertising Manager 1951–53; Vice-Pres. and Asst. General Manager 1953–58; Exec. Vice-Pres. 1959–60; Pres. 1960–62; Pres. and Treas. 1963—. President and Treasurer, The Taft-Peirce Mfg., Co., Woonsocket, R. I. Vice-Pres. American National Standard Institute 1967–70; Director: Woonsocket Branch, R.I. Hospital Trust Co. 1954—, National Machine Tool Builders' Assn. 1966–69; Member, Yale Univ. Alumni Board 1961–66, and Southeastern Advisory Board, Liberty Mutual Insurance Co.; Mem. Exec. Council, Yale Science and Eng. Assoc. Trustee, Woonsocket Hospital. *Member:* Amer. Socy. of Mech. Engrs.; Pi Tau Sigma; Amer. Socy. of Quality Control; Socy. of Manufacturing Engineers (Certified Manufacturing Engineer). *Clubs:* Yale (R.I.); Yale (N.Y.C.); Harvard (R.I.); Hope; Agawam Hunt (Providence, R.I.). *Address:* Old Wrentham Road, Cumberland, R.I.; and *office* The Taft-Peirce Mfg. Co., 32 Mechanic Avenue, Woonsocket, R.I., U.S.A.

**BLACKBURN, James Edward, Jr.** American publisher and consultant. *B.* 1902. *Educ.* Rensselaer Polytechnic Institute (Mechanical Engineer). *M.* 1926, Harriet Nash. *Daus.* Joan B. Duys and Nancy B. Dale. Awarded Alfred Fox Demers Medal. Vice-Pres. and Dir., McGraw-Hill International 1947–56, McGraw-Hill Pub. Co. 1938–56; President, Blackburn Publications Inc. 1956–61; Partner, Blackburn-Flynn (publishers) since 1961. Consultant, Lockwood Trade Journal Co.; ex-Trustee, Village of Dering Habor. *Clubs:* Glen Ridge Country; Engineers; Overseas Press; Gardiners Bay Country; N.Y. Academy of Sciences. *Address:* 40 Elston Road, Upper Montclair, N.J., U.S.A. (Summer Address: Luckifours, Shelter Island, N.Y.).

**BLACKIE, William.** American. *B.* 1906. *Educ.* Chart. Accountant of Scotland; Cert. Public Accountant, Ill., and Wis. *M.* 1934, Florence M. Hewens. *S.* Bruce L. Blackie. *Career:* With Caterpillar Tractor Co.: Controller, 1939–44, Vice-Pres., 1944–54, Exec. Vice-Pres., 1954–62, Pres., 1962–66. Chairman of the Board and Chief Executive Officer, Caterpillar Tractor Co. 1966–72; Director: Caterpillar Tractor Co. 1958—; Shell Oil Co. 1964–77, Ampex Corp, 1969—; Sen. Partner Lehman Bros. San Francisco; Chmn. and Dir., Marconaflo Inc. 1974—. *Awards:* Hon. LLD Bradley Univ., Peoria; Hon. LLD Monmouth Coll.; Hon. D. Business Administration, S. Dakata School of Mines and Tech.; Captain Robert Dollar Mem. Award (Nat. Foreign Trade Cncl. 1967) and Mississippi Valley World Trade Conf. Award 1962; Officer Order of the Crown (Belgium) 1968; Man of the Year in Mid-America World Trade Award, Mid-America World Trade Conference, Chicago 1971; Leffingwell Award, Admin Mgt. Society 1972; Business Hall of Fame 1977. *Member:* Nat. Assn. Accountants, Amer. Inst.; Certified Public Accountants. *Clubs:* Pacific-Union; Union League (Chicago). *Address:* 1 Bush Street, San Francisco, Cal. 94104, U.S.A.

**BLACKSTONE, Peter Leonard,** TD, MA, CEng, FICE, FIEE. British. *B.* 1913. *Educ.* Oundle School; Cambridge Univ. (MA 1st Class Hons., Mech Sc). *M.* 1939, Mary Pauline. *S.* 2. *Daus.* 2. *Career:* Dir., Yarrow & Co. Ltd.; Dir., Y-ARD Ltd.; Head, Hydro-Electric Dept., Merz & McLellan, 1950–58; Head, Economics Planning Dept., 1958–64; *Clubs:* Naval & Military, Royal Northern Yacht. *Address:* Clarinish, Rhu, Dunbartonshire, Scotland; and *office* Charing Cross Tower, Glasgow G2 4PP.

**BLACKWELL, Sir Basil Henry,** MA, JP. British bookseller and publisher. *B.* 1889. *Educ.* Oxford Univ. (MA). *M.* 1914, Marion Christine Soans. *S.* 2. *Daus.* 3. Officier d'Académie. *Awards:* Hon Fellow of Merton College, Oxford. Hon. LLD, Manchester; Hon. Freeman City of Oxford; Hon. Mem. of Stationers Co. *Address:* Osse Field, Appleton, Abingdon, Oxon.

**BLACKWELL, John Kenneth,** CBE. British diplomat (Ret.). *B.* 1914. *Educ.* Downing Coll. Cambridge. *M.* 1951, Joan Hilary Field. *S.* 2. *Dau.* 1. *Career:* Vice Consul Peking 1938–1940; Kunming 1940–41, Lourencomarques 1942, Beira 1942–1945; Second Secretary (Commercial) Copenhagen 1946–47; Consul Canton 1947–50; Foreign Office 1950–52; Consul Recife 1952–56, Basle 1956–57; First Secy. and Head, Chancery Seoul 1957–59; Foreign Office 1959–61; U.K. Delegation to the European Communities Brussels 1961–62; Consul General Hanoi 1962–64, Lille 1965–69; Senior British Trade Commissioner Hong Kong 1969–72; H.M. Ambassador, San Jose, Costa Rica 1972–74. *Award:* Commander Order of the British Empire. *Member:* Royal Commonwealth Society. *Address:* Oakley Hay, Vincent Road, Selsey, Sussex.

**BLACKWELL, Richard John Neal,** FASA. Australian. *B.* 1909. *Educ.* Haselor, Winnington, and Scotch Colleges; Fellow, Australian Socy. of Accountants. *M.* 1939, Edna Agnes Dawson. *S.* 1. *Career:* Joined Bank of N.S.W. in Melbourne 1924; various positions in London, England, Branch of the Bank 1936–46; Asst. Manager, International Div., Head Office, Sydney 1946–50 (Chief Manager 1950–54); State Manager: Relieving Div. 1954–57, City Div. 1957–60, Head Office, Sydney; Chief Manager for Victoria 1960–63; for N.S.W. 1963–64; Asst. General Manager, Bank of New South Wales 1964–71; General Manager 1971–1974. *Clubs:* Australian, Royal Brighton Yacht (Melbourne); Union,

Middle Harbour Yacht (Sydney). *Address:* 6 High St., Beaumaris, Victoria, Australia 3193.

**BLACKWOOD, George Douglas.** *B.* 1909. *Educ.* Eton; Clare College, Cambridge. *M.* 1936, Phyllis Marion Caulcutt. *S.* 1. *Dau.* 1. *Career:* Commissioned R.A.F. 1932–38; rejoined 1939; formed first Czech Fighter Squadron 1940–41; Battle of Britain (despatches); commanded Czech Wing of R.A.F. 2nd T.A.F. 1944 (despatches); retired 1945; Editor of *Blackwood's Magazine*, and Managing Director of William Blackwood & Sons Ltd., publishers and printers, 1948–76, Chmn. since 1976. *Awards:* Czech War Cross 1940; Czech Military Medal 1st Cl. 1944. *Address:* Airhouse, Oxton, Lauder, Berwickshire.

**BLACKWOOD, Sir Robert (Rutherford).** Australian executive *B.* 1906. *Educ.* Melbourne C. of E. Grammar School, and Melbourne Univ.; BEE, MCE, Hon. LLD, FIE, Aust. *M.* 1932, Hazel Lavinia McLeod. *S.* Robert Andrew. *Dau.* Janet Lesley. *Career:* Testing officer 1928–30, and Lecturer in Agricultural Engineering, Melbourne Univ. 1930–33. Technical Manager, Dunlop Rubber Australia Ltd. 1933–46, General Manager 1948–66. Professor of Mechanical Engineering, Univ. of Melbourne 1947. Chairman, Interim Council, Monash Univ. 1958–61, Chancellor 1961–68. Chmn. of Dirs., Dunlop Australia Ltd.; Dir., Humes Ltd. Council Member, Univ. of Melbourne 1951–63; Trustee, National Museum of Victoria 1964–71; Pres. National Museum, Victoria Council since 1971; Pres. Royal Socy. of Victoria 1973–74. *Publications:* articles and technical papers, Monash University—the First Ten Years (1968); Beautiful Bali (1970). Fellow: Inst. Engrs., Australia; Soc. of Automotive Engrs. of America (Foreign Member). *Clubs:* Melbourne, Athenaeum. *Address:* 8 Huntingfield Road, Melbourne, Victoria 3186, Australia.

**BLADEN, Vincent Wheeler.** Canadian economist; Dean Emeritus University of Toronto. *B.* 1900. *Educ.* Oxford University (MA Oxon); LLD, Univ. of West Ont.; Carleton McGill, York & Toronto Univs.; DLitt Acadia Univ.; DScSoc Laval Univ. *M.* 1929, Margaret Landon Briggs. *Daus.* Sarah, Katharine and Norah. *Career:* Member of Staff of Dept. of Political Economy since 1921; Editor, Canadian Journal of Economics and Political Science 1935–47; Dir., Inst. of Industrial Relations 1946–50; and of Institute of Business Administration 1950–53; Chm. Department of Political Economy 1953–59. Royal Commission to inquire into the Canadian Automotive Industry 1960–61. Chmn. Commission on Financing of Higher Education in Canada 1964–65; and of Adjustment Assistant Board 1965–70; Professor of Political Economy 1940–70 and Dean of the Faculty of Arts & Sciences 1959–66, Professor Emeritus since 1970; Hon. Lectr. Scarborough Coll. since 1970; University of Toronto. *Awards:* Officer, Order of Canada, 1976. *Publication:* Introduction to Political Economy; Adam Smith to Maynard Keynes; Financing the Performing Arts in Canada. *Member:* Royal Society of Canada (Pres. Section II, 1958–59); Canadian Political Science Association (Pres. 1947–48). *Clubs:* York (Toronto). *Address:* 400 Walmer Road, Toronto, Ont., Canada M5P 2X7.

**BLAIR, Sir Alastair Campbell,** KCVO, TD, JP. British. *B.* 1908. *Educ.* Cargilfield; Charterhouse; Clare College, Cambridge (BA); Edinburgh Univ. (Thow Scholarship, Scots Law; LLB, Dist.). *M.* 1933 Catriona Hatchard Orr. *S.* 4. *Career:* Writer to the Signet, 1932. Partner, Dundas & Wilson, C.S., Edinburgh; Director: Bank of Scotland; Scottish Widows Fund & Life Assurance Society; British Assets Trust Ltd. (Chmn.); Tullis Russell & Co. Ltd., and other companies. Secretary, Queen's Body Guard for Scotland, Royal Company of Archers, 1946–59; Lieutenant 1974; Purse Bearer to Lord High Commissioner to General Assembly of Church of Scotland, 1961–69; Chairman, Scout Association of Edinburgh Area, 1964—. *Member:* Law Society of Scotland. *Club:* New (Edinburgh). *Address:* 14 Ainslie Place, Edinburgh; and *office:* 25 Charlotte Square, Edinburgh.

**BLAIR-CUNYNGHAME, Sir James Ogilvy,** OBE, LLD, DSc. British. *B.* 1913. *Educ.* Sedbergh School and King's Coll., Cambridge (MA): unmarried. *Career:* With Unilever Ltd. 1935–39; teaching in Economics Faculty, Cambridge 1938; elected Fellow St. Catharine's Coll. 1939. Royal Artillery and Intelligence, Mediterranean and Europe 1939–45, Lt. Col. 1944. Foreign Office 1946–47; Chief Personnel Officer, B.O.A.C. 1947–55; Dir.-Gen. of Staff, Natl. Coal Board 1955–57; Full-time Member of Coal Board 1957–59; Joined Royal Bank of Scotland 1960 (Dep. Chmn. 1961, Chmn. 1965–68 & 1970–76); Chmn.: National and Commercial Banking Group Ltd. since 1968; Williams & Glyn's Bank Ltd. since 1976. Dir.: The Royal Bank of Scotland Ltd.; Provincial Insurance Co. Ltd.; Scottish Mortgage & Trust Co. Ltd. *Governor:* Sedbergh School; London School of Economics. *Member:* Council Industrial Soc.; Council Edinburgh Festival Soc.; Council of Industry for Mgmt. Education; Exec. Cttee. Scottish Council Dev. & Ind.; Fellow, British Inst. of Management; Fellow, Inst. of Bankers; Pay Board 1973–74; Companion Inst. of Personnel Management; Scottish Economic Council 1965–75; Gov. Bd. British Transport Staff Coll. 1963–73; Scottish Rly Bd. 1963–65; Scottish Bus. Sch. Council 1972–76. *Publications:* various articles on aspects of personnel management. *Clubs:* New, Scottish Arts (Edinburgh); Savile, Flyfishers (London). *Address:* Broomfield, Moniaive, Thornhill, Dumfriesshire; and *office* National and Commercial Banking Group Ltd., 36 St. Andrew Square, Edinburgh, EH2 2YB.

**BLAISE, Henry.** Belgian. *B.* 1905. *Educ.* Univ. of Brussels (ScD in engineering 1927). *M.* 1927, Adrienne Dupont. *Daus.* Thérèse (Velge), Claudine (Glorieux), Nicole (van der Rest), and Kathleen (Harvey). *Career:* Hon. Counsellor Sté. Générale de Belgique; Chmn., Mines, Minerais & Métaux, Brussels; Dir., Usines Emile Henricot Belgium; Brunswick Mining & Smelting Corp. (Toronto), Hon. Dir., Sté Générale des Minerais, Brussels. *Decorations:* Chevalier, Ordre de la Couronne; Chevalier, Ordre de Léopold. *Address:* 28 Avenue de l'Horizon, Woluwe St. Pierre-Brussels 1150, Belgium.

**BLAKE, Francis,** SB, MBA, LLB, JD. American. *B.* 1909. *Educ.* Harvard Univ. (SB); Harvard Business School (MBA); Northeastern Univ. Law School (LLB), JD. *M.* 1936, Caroline Amory Hunnewell. *S.* 2. *Daus.* 2. *Career:* Dir. Irish Intercontinental Bank Ltd. Dublin; Founder/Dir., Aries Fund, N.V.; Dir., European Marketing Systems Ltd. (London); Pres./Dir., Scorpio Sales Co. Ltd. (Nassau); Exec. Vice-Pres. Dir., Investment Counsel, John P. Chase Inc., 1954–61; Vice-Chmn. & Dir., Allied Research & Service Corp. 1956–61; Vice-Pres. & European Representative Documat Inc. 1962–65; Principal, Francis Blake & Associates, Investment Advisory Services (London); Senior Vice-Pres. & Dir., Lowell Blake & Associates, Inc., Boston, Mass. *Member:* Boston Bar Assn.; Massachusetts Bar Assn.; American Bar Assn.; Boston Security Analyst Society; Financial Analysts Fed. (U.S.). *Clubs:* Boodles; American Club, London; Somerset; Country Club, Longwood Cricket, Boston; The Brook, N.Y. *Address:* Strawberry Hill Street, Dover, Mass. 02030, U.S.A., and London *office* Byron House, 7 St. James' Street, London, S.W.1.

**BLAKENEY, Frederick Joseph,** CBE. Australian diplomat; *B.* 1913. *Educ.* Sydney Univ.; BA (Hons.). *M.* 1943, Marjorie Grosmont Martin. *Dau.* Sally Martin. *Career:* A.M.F. 1940–42; R.A.A.F. (navigator) 1942–45. Joined Australian Dept. of External Affairs, Canberra, June 1946; 2nd Secy. Paris 1947; 1st Secy. Moscow 1949 (Chargé d'Affaires 1950–51); Counsellor, Dept. of External Affairs 1952–53; Counsellor, Washington 1953–56. Asst. Secretary (S. & .SE. Asia) Dept. of External Affairs 1959–62; Minister to Vietnam 1957–59, to Cambodia 1957 and to Laos 1957–59. Ambassador to the Federal Republic of Germany 1962–68, to the Soviet Union 1968–71; First Asst. Secy. (Defence) Dept. Foreign Affairs 1972–74; Ambassador to the Netherlands 1974–77; Ambassador, Perm. Rep. to the Office of the UN at Geneva since 1977. Has attended various international conferences. *Address:* c/o Department of Foreign Affairs, Canberra, ACT, Australia.

**BLAKENHAM, Rt. Hon. Viscount** (John Hugh Hare), PC, OBE, DL, VMH. *B.* 1911. *Educ.* Eton. *M.* 1934, Hon. Beryl Nancy Pearson. *S.* 1. *Daus.* 2. *Career:* Served in World War II (N. Africa and Italy; despatches; OBE; U.S. Legion of Merit) 1939–45. Alderman, L.C.C. 1937–52; Chmn. London Municipal Society 1947–52; a Vice-Chmn. Conservative Party Organisation 1952–55. M.P. (Con.) Woodbridge Div. of Suffolk 1945–50, and Sudbury and Woodbridge Div. 1950–63; Minister of State, Colonial Affairs 1955–56; Sec. of State for War 1956–58; Minister of Agriculture 1958–60; of Labour 1960–63; Chancellor of Duchy of Lancaster. Deputy Leader of the House of Lords, 1963–64; Chmn. of the Conservative Party Organization 1963–65. Chairman, Toynbee Hall Council 1966—. Chairman of Governors of Peabody Trust, 1967—; Treasurer, Royal Horticultural Society since 1970. *Address:* 10 Holland Park, London W11 3TH.

**BLAKER, Peter Allan Renshaw,** MA, BA, MP. British. politician. *B.* 1922. *Educ.* Shrewsbury; Trinity Coll. Toronto; New Coll. Oxford. *M.* 1953, Jennifer Dixon. *S.* 1. *Daus.* 2. *Career:* with Argyll and Sutherland Highlanders of Canada,

1942–46; Admitted, Solicitor 1948; Called to Bar, Lincoln's Inn, 1952; H.M. Foreign Service, 1953–64; Member of Parliament, Conservative for Blackpool South since 1964; Opposition Whip, 1966–67; Parly. Private Secy. to Chancellor of the Exchequer 1970–72; Parly. Under Secy. of State for Defence 1972–74; Parly. Under-Secy. of State, Foreign and C'wealth Off. 1974. *Clubs:* Travellers'. *Address:* 14 Egerton Terrace, London, S.W.3.

**BLALOCK, John V.** American. *B.* 1921. *Educ.* Duke Univ., Durham, N.C. (BA English) Harvard Business Sch. (Advanced Mgmt.) *M.* 1947, Kathleen Glymph. *S.* Barry Vernon. *Dau.* Kathleen Annetta. *Career:* Reporter, Book Review Editor, Feature Writer, Promotion Editor, Asst. City Editor, Sunday Editor, Editorial Writer, Durham Morning Herald 1942–48; Asst. to Director of Public Relations, Seaboard Air line Railroad 1948–49; Advertising and Public Relations Manager (and later Asst. Vice-Pres.), Liberty Life Insurance Co., Greenville, S.C. 1949–61. Director of Corporate Relations, Brown & Williamson Industries Inc., Louisville, Ky. since 1961. Recipient: 21 national awards in advertising and public relations, and of George Washington Honor Medals, Freedoms Foundation 1951 and 1953. *Member:* Public Relations Socy. of America. *Club:* Hurstbourne Country; Jefferson; Filson. *Address:* 4907 Clovernook Road, Riverwood, Louisville, Ky.; and *office* 2000 Citizens' Plaza, Louisville 40202 Ky., U.S.A.

**BLANCHET, André (René).** French journalist. *B.* 1918. *Educ.* Licencié-es-Lettres. *Member:* Académie des Sciences d'outremer (elected July 1960). *Career:* Chargé de conférences a'Institut des hautes études d'outremer 1952–64; Collaborator, *Le Monde* 1946–65; Professor, Institute of Political Studies, Univ. of Paris 1959–64; Head African News, French Television 1965–71; Editor, Informations d'outremer (1975). *Publications:* Au pays des balilla jaunes, 1947, and L'itineraire des partis africains depuis Bamako, 1958. *Member:* Société des Gens de lettres de France; Association française de science politique; Société des africanistes Français. *Address:* 17 bis, rue Campagne-Première, Paris, 14; and *office* Sedoric, 14 boulevard Montmartre Paris, 2c.

**BLANCO VILLALTA, Jorge G.,** Argentine diplomat; *b.* 9 Feb. 1909; *Educ.* in Hungary, Argentina, Mexico and Norway; *M.* 1946, Manuela Fernandez Reyna; Vice-Consul in charge of the Consulate-General, Istanbul 1933–35; later withdrew from diplomatic affairs to devote himself to literature; re-entered Diplomatic Service as First Secretary of Embassy 1946; Head of the Division for United Nations Affairs and Head of Liaison between the Ministry and the National Congress 1947; Secretary-General of the Argentine Delegation to the 2nd and 3rd Sessions of the General Assembly of the United Nations 1947–48; Counsellor of Embassy 1948; Director of the Department of Intellectual Co-operation in the Ministry 1949; Professor of the School of Diplomacy and the School of International Politics 1949–50; attached to the Presidencia de la Nacion 1949–52; Counsellor of Embassy attached to the Ministry of Foreign Affairs 1952–55; Retired in 1955 for political reasons; Resumed 1973; Ambassador on Special Mission to 50th Anniversary of Republic of Turkey; Dir. of Dept. of Asia and Oceania; Professor of Protocol at the Inst, of For. Service of the Ministry of Foreign Affairs; Dr. Gen of Politics and Currently Ambassador in Turkey. *Decorations:* Officer Royal Order of the Phoenix (Greece); Grand Cross of the Order to Diplomatic Merit of Rep. of Korea; Bintang Djaya Utama (Indonesia). *Publications:* The Diplomats, Art and Literature of the Turks; Tupiguaraniés Myths. *Address:* Las Heras 4095, Buenos Aires, Argentine.

**BLAND, Sir Henry Armand,** CBE. Australian. *B.* 1909. *Educ.* LLB Sydney (Hons.). *M.* 1933, Rosamund Nickal. *Daus.* Janet Meredith Graham, and Lesley Armand Ho. *Career:* Official Secretary and Acting Agent-General for New South Wales in London 1939–41. Secretary, Dept. of Labour & National Service, 1952–68. Secretary, Department of Defence, Commonwealth of Australia, 1968–70; Dep. Chmn, Blue Circle Southern Cement Ltd.; Dir., Australia Mining & Smelting Ltd.; Tubemakers of Aust. Ltd.; P. Rowe Pty. Ltd; Associated National Ins. Co Ltd. Bd. of Enquiry into Victorian Land Transport System, 1971; Chmn. Commonwealth Cttee on Administrative Discretions 1972–73; Bd. of Enqiry, Victorian Public Service 1973–75; Chmn., Commonwealth Administrative Review Cttee. 1975–76; Chmn., Australian Broadcasting Commission 1976. *Club:* Athenaeum (Melbourne). *Address:* 4/1 Monaro Road, Kooyong, Victoria, Australia.

**BLAND, William Graham.** Australian newspaper executive. *B.* 1918. *Educ.* University of Melbourne (BCom); Fellow, Chartered Institute of Secretaries; Associate, Australian Society of Accountants. *M.* 1950, Janet Richardson Morrison. *S.* Ian William. *Daus.* Elizabeth and Jane Meredith. *Career:* Flying Officer (Pilot) R.A.A.F. 1942–45; Asst. Secretary, David Syme & Co. Ltd., The Age newspaper 1948–56; Industrial Officer, David Syme & Co. Ltd. 1951–56; Display Advertising Manager 1956–63; Deputy General Manager 1963–65. Chairman, Australian Newspapers Council Advertising Board 1962, 1963, 1964; Chmn. Newspaper Publishers' Assn. of Melbourne 1977; Business Manager, The Age, Melbourne since 1965. *Clubs:* Naval & Military; Woodlands Golf. *Address:* 27 Beach Road, Beaumaris, Vic.; and *office:* The Age, 250 Spencer Street, Melbourne, Vic., Australia.

**BLANKE, John Herman Diedrich.** German editor and writer. *B.* 1895. *Educ.* Westmar College, LeMars, Iowa (BA 1921); post-graduate studies, Univ. of Chicago. *M.* (1) 1923, Frances E. Munday (*D.* 1946), and (2) 1954, Clara H. Seitz. *S.* George Robert. *Daus.* Mary Jane, Helen Louise and Ruth Marie. *Career:* Proof reader and copywriter, advertising dept., Technical Publishing Co., Chicago 1923–28; freelance translator and writer on technical and engineering topics for various periodicals since 1927; President, Village of Barrington, Ill., 1961–69. General consultant in Municipal Affairs, 1969. Technical Editor. The International Engineer (monthly journal of The International Union of Operating Engineers, Washington 6, D.C.), 1930–63; Member, Village Board of Trustees, Barrington, Ill. 1934–61. Barrington Historical Society; Honorary Member Barrington Chamber of Commerce; *Member:* Legislative Policy Cttee. Ill Municipal League 1967–69. *Publications:* Bridge for Mackinac Straits Rivals the World's Greatest (The International Engineer, June 1955); Burning Gas in Modern Power Boilers (Power Engineering, March 1951; 12 pages, reprinted); Incinerator Manual (Power Engineering—reprint 1960); articles in professional and general periodicals; Columnist in Free Press, Barrington area weekly newspaper; What's in My Basket in Barrington (1971). *Member:* Western Soc. of Engineers (Chicago), American Newspaper Press Guild (general press section, Chicago Local), The International Platform Association (Cleveland Heights, Ohio); and Natural History Society of Barrington. Pres., Northwestern Municipal Conference 1964. *Address:* 533 Summit Street, Post Office Box 88, Barrington, Ill., 60010, U.S.A.

**BLANKENHORN, Herbert,** GCVO (1965); German diplomat. *B.* 15 Dec. 1904. *Educ.* Karlsruhe Gymnasium; Barrister 1929; Grad. Diplomatic-Consular Ex. 1931. *M.* 1944, Gisela Krug. *S.* 2. *Daus.* 2. *Career:* entered diplomatic service 1929; served successively at Athens, Washington, Helsinki and Berne 1932–43; Protocol Div., Foreign Office, Berlin 1943–45; Genl. Secy., Zone Council in Br. Zone, Hamburg 1946–48; Private Secretary to Pres. Adenauer 1948–49; Chief, Liaison Div., Fed. Chancellery and Allied High Commission 1949: Ministerial-Director, Political Div., 1950; Ambassador, Representative of Federal German Republic in N.A.T.O. 1955–58; Ambassador to France, Nov. 1958–Nov. 1963; to Italy, Nov. 1963–March 1965; to Great Britain, 1965–70; Member Exec. Bd. U.N.E.S.C.O. 1970–76; Special Consultant to Dir.-Gen. of U.N.E.S.C.O. *Address:* 7847 Badenweiler, Hintere AU 2, Germany.

**BLASCHKE, Edwin H.,** BS. American. *B.* 1913. *Educ.* Univ. of Texas (BS Civil Eng.). *M.* 1940, Ruth Wynne Hightower. *S.* 1. *Career:* Group Vice-Pres., Brown & Root Inc.; Project Engineer, Foundation Co. of New York, 1940–44; Fellow, American Soc. of Civil Engineers; Mem. Texas & Nat. Socs. of Professional Engineers; Houston Engineering Scientific Soc; Texas State Board for Registration for Prof. Engs. *Clubs:* Tau Beta Pi; Chi Epsilon; Petroleum Club of Houston. *Address:* 1524 Park Drive, Channelview, Texas, 77530, U.S.A.; and *office* P.O. Box 3, Houston, Texas 77001.

**BLASIUS, Donald Charles,** BS. American. *B.* 1929. *Educ.* Northwestern Univ. (BS BusAdmin.). *M.* 1952, Carle Forslew. *S.* 1. *Dau.* 1. *Career:* Pres. The Tappan Co, Mansfield, Ohio; formerly Sen. Vice-Pres. & Gen. Man., Agricultural Equipment Div., J. I. Case Co.; Vice-Pres. & Gen. Man., McCulloch Corp.; Dir., F.I.E.I. Marketing & Management Council; Wisconsin Agri-Business Council; Trustee, Village of North Bay Wisconsin; Past Pres. & Dir., Power Saw Mfrs. Assn. *Member:* American Management Assn.; American Marketing Association *Address:* 1200 Millsboro

Road, Mansfield, Ohio 44906; and *office* Box 606, Tappan Park, Mansfield, Ohio 44901, U.S.A.

**BLAUSTEN, Cyril.** *B.* 1916. *M.* 1944, Norma Marion Cinnamon. *S.* Richard, Douglas, Simon, Peter. *Career:* Underwriting Member of Lloyds of London. Dir.: New Islington and Hackney Housing Assoc., and J.B.G. Housing Socy. Fellow, Zoological Society of London; Freeman of the City of London; Liveryman of the Worshipful Company of Glaziers and Painters of Glass. Commissioner of Taxes. Justice of the Peace. Fellow, Surveyors and Valuers Assn.; Member, Royal Society of Health; Vice-Pres. Jewish Welfare Board; Vice-Pres., Maccabi Association, London. *Clubs:* City Livery, United University, M.C.C. *Address:* 5 Linnell Close Meadway, London, N.W.11; and *office* 52 Brook Street, Grosvenor Square, London, W.1.

**BLEICKEN, Gerhard David.** American Company Chmn. *B.* 1913. *Educ.* Gettysburg Coll.; Boston University College of Liberal Arts; Boston University Law School J.D. (*cum laude*); D.C.S. Hon. Suffolk Univ.; M.I.T. School of Industrial Management; Aspen Inst. Humanistic Studies; Naval Air Training School, Quonset Point: Industrial College of the Armed Forces, Washington, D.C.; Hon. LHD Northeastern Univ. 1977; Hon. LLD Boston Coll. 1977. *M.* (1) Ellene T. Maihot. *S.* Kurt Douglas, Eric Vaughn and Carl Weeman. *M.* (2) Ann Mudge Meacham. *S.* David Holt and Neil Gerhard. *Career:* Mem., Massachusetts and U.S. Supreme Bars. General Practice 1938–39; Lt., USNR 1943–46; Chmn. Bd. Chief Exec. Officer and Dir., John Hancock Mutual Life Insurance Co.; Chmn. of the Bd., Life Insurance Assn. of Massachusetts; Dir.: World Affairs Council; The First National Bank of Boston; First National Boston Corp; Arthur D. Little Inc.; UN Assoc. of the U.S.A.; Trustee, Boston Univ.; Tax Foundation Inc.; Boston Urban Foundation; Chmn., Boston Univ. Medical Centre Trustee Cncl. Mem. of Presidents Commission on Personnel Interchange. *Member:* Bd. Visitors UCLA Graduate School of Mgmt. and of National Acad. of Sciences Adv. Cttee., to Dept. of Defense 1954–69; The Bostonian Socy.; American Battle Monuments Commission; Executive Committee of Massachusetts Committee Catholics, Protestants and Jews; Conference Bd. Economic Club of New York; Boston Symph. Orch., Board of Overseers; Benjamin Franklin Fellow Royal Society of Arts, London; Adv. Council, International Club; Trustee, Boston Museum of Science; Program Advisory Cttee, office of Emergency Preparedness, Office of the President 1958–73. *Awards:* Distinguished Service Award (Presidential); Dist. Community Service Award (Brandeis Univ.): Dist Service Citation (Dept. of Defense); Medal of Merit (Treasury Dept.); Mass. Inst. of Technology Corporate Leadership Award, 1976; Commander's Cross of the Order of Merit of the Fed. Republic of Germany, 1976; Boston Coll. Presidential Bicentennial Award, 1976. *Publications:* The Role of Non-Military Defense in American Foreign and Defense Policy, (1959); Apathy & Defense, (1960); Corporate Contributions to Charities, (1957). *Member:* Amer. Law Inst. *Clubs:* St. Botolph; Commercial; Algonquin (Boston); Wianno (Wianno, Mass.); Univ. (Boston). *Address:* 18 Wood Road, Sherborn, Mass. 01770; and *office* John Hancock Place, Boston, Mass., 02117.

**BLEIER, Richard M.** American. *B.* 1913. *Educ.* Cornell Univ. (BS in Admin. Eng. 1935) and Bordentown Military Institute. *M.* 1938, Jeanette Guinzburg. *S.* Richard J., Steven Randolph, and Ralph Kleinert. *Career:* With American Machinery & Foundry Co.: Engineer and Service Depts. 1935–40, 1940–41; Plant Engineer 1945–49, Asst. to President 1950–54, Vice-President 1954–62; President, I.B. Kleinert Rubber Co., 1962–67, Chmn. of the Bd. 1967–69. President of New Castle Water Co., Chappaque, N.Y. Military Service: five years as Major (wartime), Army Anti-Aircraft Service, Pacific and European Theatre. Member Board of Governors: American Jewish Cttee. (Chmn. Westchester Div. of N.Y. Chapter), Speakers Bureau, Trustee, N.Y. Fed. of Jewish Philanthropies (Chmn. of Notions Div.). Vice-Pres. member, Board of Directors: Federation Employment and Guidance Service, N.Y.C.; Sec. US International Tempest (Olympic Yacht) Association, 1975—; Past President: Temple Beth El of Northern Westchester 1954–56; Town Club of New Castle, N.Y. (civic) 1950; National Notions Assn. 1960. *Address:* 715 King Street, Chappaqua, N.Y.; U.S.A.

**BLICK, John Henry Penn, JP.** British executive. *B.* 1913. *Educ.* Canterbury (N.S.W.) High School. *M.* 1935, Mavis Myrtle Ball. *S.* Ross Albert Penn and Anthony John Penn. *Dau.* Diana Claire. *Career:* Sapper Volunteer Defence Corps 1942–45; Steward Royal Agricultural Socy. N.S.W. 1948–54; Member, N.S.W. Council Lib. Party of Aust. 1949–59; Pres. Ashfield State Electorate Conf. of Liberal Party of Australia 1953–58 (Pres. Evans Federal Electorate, same Party 1958–59); Manager, Fruit & Vegetable Section, Producers' Co-operative Distributing Society 1954–72; Export Promotion Dir. Golden Mile Orchard Pty. Ltd. (QL) since 1973, Secretary, N.S.W. Fruitgrowers' Central Council 1955–75; N.S.W. Citrus Growers' Council 1956–73; N.S.W. Fruit Shippers' Association 1955–70. *Member*, Australian Fruit Export Planning Committee 1962–70; Govt. appointee: N.S.W. Lemon Marketing Board 1963—; Fruit Industry Sugar Concession Committee 1963–75; Co-operative Adv. Council 1966–74; Australian Trade Mission to U.K. and N. Europe 1967; Representative of fruit industry, Sydney City Council Fruit & Vegetable Markets Advisory Committee 1956–68 (Chmn. 1967–68); Advisory Cttee., New Sydney Markets Authority. N.S.W. Representative, Australian Citrus Growers Federation 1958–73; Australian Apple & Pear Shippers' Association 1956–70; Chairman Agenda Cttee., N.S.W. Council, Liberal Party of Australia 1958–59–60–61; Chmn. Aust. Overseas Citrus Exporters Assn .1969–Secretary, N.S.W. Fruitgrowers' Central Council 1955–75; 72, Sec. 1975—; Hon. Sec. Chair., Horticulture Est. Cttee. Univ. Sydney; Secy. O'Land Exporters Cttee. 1968. *Clubs:* Bowlers' (N.S.W.); Masonic, N.S.W.; Western Suburbs District Cricket, Sydney (Vice-Pres. 1952–60). *Address:* MS 208, Gilston via Nerrang, Queensland 4211, Australia.

**BLICKWEDE, Donald Johnson.** American. Vice-President and Director of Research. *B.* 1920. *Educ.* Wayne Univ. (BS Chem. Eng.), Stevens Inst. of Technology (Grad. Studies), and M.I.T. (ScD Physical Metallurgy). *M.* 1943, Meredith Lloyd. *S.* Jon. *Dau.* Karen. *Career:* Previously: Metallurgist, Curtiss-Wright Corp. 1943–45; Chief, Naval Temp. Alloys Branch, Naval Research Labs 1948–49. With Bethlehem Steel Corp.: Asst. Division Head 1953, Dir. of Applications, Research 1961, Mgr. of Research 1963, Vice-President Research 1964. *Publications:* papers on aluminium alloys, transformations in steels and steel mill processes. Hons.: Bardley Stoughton Award, 1964; Campbell Memorial Lecture, 1968 Metal Congress. *Member:* Amer. Iron & Steel Inst.; Amer. Socy. for Metals; Amer. Inst. of Metallurgical Engineers; British Metallurgical Socy.; Assn. of Iron & Steel Engineers; Japan Iron & Steel Fed.; Industrial Research Inst. (Pres.). Republican. *Club:* Saucon Valley Country. *Address:* RD 4, Bethelehem, Pa. 18015; and *office* Homer Research Laboratories, Bethlehem Steel Corporation, Bethlehem, Pa. 18016, U.S.A.

**BLISS, Robert Landers.** American Public relations executive; consultant. *B.* 1907. *Educ.* Cornell Univ. BA 1930; graduate work. *M.* 1942, Friede Smidt. *S.* John Smidt. *Dau.* Friede Sherwood (Brayton). *Career:* Assistant to Chief, Press Bureau, J. Walter Thompson, N.Y.C. 1938; Asst. to Publisher, PM newspaper 1940; U.S. Army Air Corps (2nd Lieut. to Major) 1942–46; Director of Public Relations, National Association of Insurance Agents, N.Y.C. 1947–49; Executive Vice-Pres., Public Relations Society of America 1949–56; Pres., Robert L. Bliss Incorporated, N.Y.C. (public relations counsel) 1956–77; Bliss & Smith, Inc. 1977—; Republican Town Chmn., New Canaan, Conn., 1951–62; State Senator, 26th Dist., Conn., 1963–68; Conn. Transport Authority 1975. *Publications:* numerous articles and speeches on public relations, political participation, history, etc. *Awards:* Presidential Citation, Public Relations Socy. of America; Medal, Italian Public Relations Assn. (2nd World Congress on Public Relations, Venice 1961. Was General Rapporteur at the Congress). *Member:* Public Relations Socy. of America (Pres. N.Y. Chapter 1962); Founding Council Member, International Public Relations Assn., London 1955 (Vice-Pres. 1963–65; President 1965–68; and Cncl. Member); Programme Chmn., III World Congress on Public Relations, Montreal, Canada, Nov. 1964; Pres. IV World Congress, Public Relations Rio de Janeiro 1967. Founding Charter Member, Nat. Socy. of State Legislators, 1st Vice-Pres. (1963). Republican (Member, State Central Committee, Connecticut 1954–56; active in all national campaigns since 1936; and in all Connecticut state and local campaigns since 1948). *Clubs:* University, (N.Y.C.); Woodway (Darien, Conn.); Psi Upsilon Fraternity. *Address:* 162 Park Street, New Canaan, Conn. 06840; and *office* 51 Locust Avenue, New Canaan, Conn. 06840, U.S.A.

**BLOCK, Frank.** American. *B.* 1914. *Educ.* Western Military Academy (Alton, Ill.), Washington University, St. Louis. *M.* 1941, Jean Rauh. *S.* Frank. *Daus.* Elsie Block Wilkens and Jean Block Bessmer. *Career:* With World Color Press 1933–39; Olian Advertising Co. (Vice-Vres.) 1939–42; Secy.,

Amer. Industries Salvage Cttee. 1942–43; Dir.: War Activities Cttee. of Pulpwood Consuming Industries 1943–45, and Conservation Cttee. of Waste-Paper Consuming Industries 1943–45; Dir., U.S. Pulpwood Council 1946; Pres., Frank Block & Associates 1946. Winner, P.R.S.A. award for agriculture; Federal Aviation Administration Award of Merit 1976. *Member:* Edgewood Children's Center, Webster Groves, Mo. (Dir.); Child Welfare League of America, N.Y.C. (Dir.); International Institute (Dir.); Lakeside Centre for Boys (Dir.); Exec. Committee, St. Louis Educational Television Commission (Dir. and Member): Missouri–St. Louis Metropolitan Airport Authority; Public Relations Socy. of America; Amer. Assn. of Advertising Agencies; Missouri Pilots Assn.; Greater St. Louis Flight Instructors Assn. *Clubs:* Media Westwood Country. *Address:* 9721 Litzsinger Road, St. Louis 63124, Mo.; and *office* Chase Hotel, St. Louis 63108, Mo., U.S.A.

**BLOOMFIELD, Hon. Sir John Stoughton,** QC, FRSA. Australian Barrister-at-Law. *B.* 1901. *Educ.* Bach. of Laws (Melbourne). *M.* 1931, Beatrice Madge Taylor. *S.* Peter John Stoughton. *Dau.* Joan Madge Greig. *Career:* Solicitor 1927–40; A.I.F. 1940–45; Middle East and New Guinea. Lt. Col. R.A.A., now retired. Barrister since 1945; M.L.A. 1953–70; Minister of Labour & Industry and of Electrical Undertakings 1955–56. Minister of Education, State of Victoria, 1956–67. Member of Liberal Party. *Clubs:* Melbourne, Naval & Military (Melbourne). *Address:* 25 Mercer Road, Armadale, Victoria 3143 Australia.

**BLOOMFIELD, Maj. Louis Mortimer,** KStJ, QC, PhD, DCL, LLD. Canadian lawyer; specialist in international law. *B.* 1906. *Educ.* McGill Univ. (BA); Univ. of Montreal (LLM *cum laude*); admitted to Bar of Province of Quebec 1930; created QC 1948. *Career:* Member of Council, Internatl. Law Assn., London (Eng.) Hon. (Pres., Canadian Branch); Hon. Pres., Can. Socy. of Int. Law; Charter Patron, Int. Bar. Assn. Member: Canadian Bar Assn., Bar of Province of Quebec. Vice-Chmn. and Dir., Credit Suisse (Canada) Ltd.; President and Director, Heineken's Breweries (Canada) Ltd.; Vice-Pres., Reddy Memorial Hospital; Life Governor, Jeanne d'Arc Hospital; Member: Board of Govns., Weizmann Institute of Science, Rehovoth, Israel; Loyola College Development Bd.; Pres., Quebec Cncl., Order of the Hospital of St. John of Jerusalem; Vice-Pres., World Wildlife Fund (Canada); KStJ 1965; LLD (St. Francis Xavier Univ.); PhD Hebrew Univ. of Jerusalem; DCL St. Thomas Univ.; appointed to National Capital Commission Ottawa 1963; Hon. Consul General of Liberia. Montreal. *Publications:* The British Honduras-Guatemala Dispute (Carswell, Toronto 1953); Egypt, Israel and the Gulf of Aqaba in International Law (Carswell, Toronto 1957); Grundung und Aufbau kanadischer Aktiengesellschaften (Hamburg, 1960); La Convention de Varsovie dans une optique canadienne (Montreal, 1961); (co-author Boundary Waters Problems of Canada and the United States (Carswell, Toronto, 1958); Crimes Against Internationally Protected Persons (Praeger, N.Y. 1975); etc. *Club:* St. Denis. *Address:* 3 Westmount Square, Westmount, Que.; and *office* 1010 Beaver Hall Hill (Room 406), Montreal 1, Que., Canada.

**BLOOMINGDALE, Alfred S.** American corporation executive, *B.* 1916. *Educ.* Graduate of Brown University 1938. *M.* 1946, Betty Lee Newling. *S.* Lee Geoffrey and Robert Russell. *Dau.* Elisabeth Lee. *Career:* Assistant Merchandise Manager, Bloomingdale Bros., N.Y. City 1938–46; Motion Picture Executive 1946–50; Vice-Pres. Diners Club 1950–55; Pres. 1955–68; Chmn. of Board and Dir. 1964–69; Consultant, Diners Club since 1970. Director, Lyman G. Realty Co. and B. Bros. Realty Co. (both of N.Y. City); Beneficial Standard Corp. Los Angeles; President, Alfred Bloomingdale Enterprises. Inc. 1970—; Pres. and Dir. Marina Bay Club Ltd. since 1972; Chmn of Bd. Quadrox Corp. since 1974; Surfside 6 Floating Homes Inc. since 1970; Emeritus Brown University; Trustee, Loyola Marymount College and Bd. of Regents St. John's Hospital, Santa Mon. Ca.); Papal Knight Commander in the Order of Saint Gregory. *Address:* 1888 Century Park East, Suite 1018, Los Angeles, Calif. 90067; and (residence) 131 Delfern Drive, Los Angeles, Calif., 90024, U.S.A.

**BLOTT, John Arthur.** British. *B.* 1911. *Educ.* Malvern College (Worcestershire). *M.* 1947, Cecilia Elena Ridgway. *S.* James. *Dau.* Susan. *Career:* With Anciens Establissements George Whitechurch Ltd., Limoges, Haute Vienne, France 1929; Managing Director Société des Tannins Corses, Ponte Leccia, Corsica 1930–53. Director, Barrow Hepburn & Gale 1945–66; Chmn. Helmets Ltd. since 1962. *Member:* Institute of Directors; Institute of General Managers. *Club:* Durban. *Address:* Saybridge, Blackmore, Ingatestone, Essex.

**BLOUGH, Roger M.** Business executive and lawyer *B.* 1904. *Educ.* Susquehanna University (AB 1925) and Yale Law School (JD 1931). *M.* 1928, Helen Martha, Decker. *Daus.* (twin) Jane E. (French) and Judith A. (Wentz). *Career:* Engaged in general practice of law with White & Case, N.Y. City 1931–42; General Solicitor, U.S. Steel Corp. of Delaware 1942–51; Executive Vice-President law and Secretary, U.S. Steel Co. 1951; Vice-Chairman, Director, U.S. Steel Corp. 1952 and General Counsel 1953–55. Chairman, Board of Directors, Chief Executive Officer and Member of Executive Committee, U.S. Steel Corporation 1955–69. Dir. member Exec. Cttee. and Finance Cttee. U.S. Steel Corp. 1952–76 Trustee, U.S. Steel Foundation. Partner, White & Case 1969–75. Director, Campbell Soup Co., Commercial Union Corp., Carling National Breweries Inc., Susquehanna Univ. The Presbyterian Hospital, City of New York. *Publication:* Free Man and the Corporation, (1959); Hon. LLD: Susquehanna, Baylor, Washington & Jefferson, Washington, Akron; and Syracuse Univs. and Dickinson School of Law; and Rollins, Trinity, Roanoke, Gettysburg, Wartburg and Allegheny Colls.; DHumLitt Pace Coll. and Wagner Coll.; DCS Univ. of Pittsburgh and Wagner Coll.; DCL Univ. of the South and Bucknell Univ. Director & Founding Member, The Business Cttee. for the Arts. Dir. The Commonwealth Fund. Chmn. Bd. of Dirs. Council for Financial Aid to Education; Construction Users Anti-Inflation Roundtable. Fellow & Pres. Institute of Judicial Administration. Trustee, Lifetime Councillor, The Conference Board. Trustee & member, Exec. Cttee. United States Council, International Chamber of Commerce. Trustee & Chmn. Finance Cttee. Hawley Library Assn. Trustee, Grand Central Art Galleries. Hon Trustree Cttee. Economic Development. Fellow. Timothy Dwight Coll. Yale Univ. Hon. Member, Yale Law School Assn. Exec. Cttee.; Japan Iron & Steel Federation. Council Member, Pennsylvania Socy. (former Pres.). Chmn. Emeritus, Gen. MacArthur National Advisory Bd. National Football Foundation & Hall of Fame. *Member:* Amer. Iron & Steel Inst. (Hon. Vice Pres.); The Business Council (Former Chmn.); Life Member. Academy, Political Science; Metropolitan Museum of Art. Fellow, Amer. Bar Foundation. *Clubs:* Blooming Grove Hunting & Fishing (Penna); the Links; The Board Room, Recess; (N.Y.C.); Skytop; Cotton Bay (Bahamas); Pine Valley Golf. *Address:* Blooming Grove, Hawley, Pa., 18428, and *office* 300 Keystone Street, Hawley, Pa. 18428, U.S.A.

**BLOUIN, Georges Henri.** Canadian diplomat. *B.* 1921. *Education.* Collége Sainte-Marie Montreal, BA (1944); Univ Montreal LLB (1948). *M.* 1948, Denise Angers, *S.* 1. *Dau.* 1. *Career.* Second Secy. Canadian Embassy, New Delhi 1951–53; Consul in San Francisco, USA 1955–58; Counsellor Canad. Embassy, Athens 1961–63; Brussels 1963–65; Ambass. to Cameroon (also accredited to Gabon, Chad and C. African Rep.) 1965–67; Minister, Canadian Embassy, Washington 1967–70; Dir.-Gen. of Personnel, Ottawa 1970–73; Spec. Adviser to the Under-Sec. of State for External Affairs 1972–73; Canadian Ambassador in Spain 1973–77 *Address:* Department of External Affairs, Ottawa, Ont., Canada.

**BLOUNT, Winton M.** American. *B.* 1921. *Educ.* Staunton Military Academy, Virginia; Univ. of Alabama. *M.* 1942, Mary Katherine Archibald. *S.* Winton M. III. Thomas A., S. Roberts, Joseph W. *Dau.* Katherine. *Career:* President: Alabama Road Builders Association, 1954; Alabama State Chamber of Commerce, 1963–65; Chamber of Commerce of the U.S., 1968; Postmaster General of U.S.A., 1969–71; Chmn. of Bd. and Pres. Blount Inc. Trustee, Univ, of Alabama; Former Dir. Southern Research Institute; Former Chmn. Exec. Cttee. & Treas., Young Presidents Org.; Dir. Union Camp Corp NYC; Dir. Interfinancial Inc. Atlanta, GA; Dir, Ring Around Products, Montgomery, Ala.; Dir., Munford Inc., Atlanta, GA. *Clubs:* Montgomery, Ala.; Country; Chevy Chase Country; Chevy Chase Md.; River; New York City; Marco Polo, N.Y.; Rotary; Washington; Capitol Hill. *Address:* Wynfield, Vaughn. Road, Rt. 10, Box 43, Montgomery, Alabama 36111; and *office* 4520 Executive Park, Box 949, Montgomery, Alabama 36102.

**BLUM, Edgar Eric.** F Inst. FF. British. *B.* 1921. *Educ.* Cranleigh School. *M.* 1948, Anita. *S.* 1. *Dau.* 1. *Career:* Dir., Adolf Blum & Popper Ltd.: Bluship Ltd. *Member:* Baltic Shipping Exchange. *Address:* 18 Foscote Road, London, N.W.4; and *office* City Gate House, 39/45 Finsbury Square, London E.C.2.

**BLUNDELL, Sir Edward Denis,** GCMG, GCVO, KBE, OBE(Mil), Kt. St. John. New Zealand. *B.* 1907. *Educ.* Waitaki Boys High School, and Cambridge (BA Cantab.). Called to the Bar (Gray's Inn) 1929. *M.* 1945, June Daphne Halligan. *S.* Richard Denis. *Dau.* Sally Daphne. *Career:* with N.Z. Div. in Greece, Crete, W. Desert Italy 1939–44; Senior Partner in Bell, Gully & Co. Barristers and Solicitors Wellington N.Z. 1961–72; Chairman, Dalgety & N.Z. Loan Ltd. (Local Board) July 1967–68. Formerly Dir.: N.Z. Shipping Co. Ltd. (Local Board), N.Z. Breweries Ltd., Rheem (N.Z.) Ltd., Blundell Bros. Ltd., Bank of N.Z. Finance Ltd., Alliance Assurance Co. (Local Board). High Commissioner for New Zealand to Britain 1968–72; Ambassador of New Zealand to Ireland 1968–72; Governor Gen. N.Z. 1972–77. Pres., N.Z. Cricket Council 1959–62. Chmn. Royal Commission on Parliamentary Salaries 1961–64–67. Pres., N.Z. Law Society 1962–68; Vice-Pres., Law Assn. for Asia and Western Pacific 1966–68; (former) Pres., 'Birthright' (N.Z.) Inc. *Clubs:* Wellington, Wellesley (both in Wellington). *Address:* c/o Government House, Wellington, N.Z.

**BLUNDELL, Sir Michael,** KBE. Kenya citizen. *B.* 1907. *Educ.:* Wellington Coll. *M.* 1946, Geraldine Lötte Robarts. *Dau.* 1. *Career:* Farmer in Kenya 1925—. Second Lieut. R.E. 1940, Major 1940. Lt. Col. 1941, Colonel 1944. Commissioner for European Settlement 1946–47; Member of Legislative Council 1948; elected Member of the Legislative Council of Kenya, Rift Valley constituency 1948–63; Chairman, Pyrethrum Board of Kenya, 1949–54. Leader, New Kenya Group 1959–63; Leader, European Members 1952; Minister on Emergency War Council 1954; Minister of Agriculture 1955–59, and 1961–62. Chairman: E. A. Breweries Ltd. 1964–77, and Egerton Agricultural College 1962–72; Director, Barclays Bank (DCO) Kenya Ltd. 1968. *Publication:* So Rough a Wind (1964). *Clubs:* Muthaiga (Nairobi); Brook's. *Address:* Box 30181, Nairobi, Kenya.

**BLUNT, Sir Anthony Frederick,** KCVO, FBA, FSA, FRIBA. *B.* 1907. *Educ.:* Marlborough College; Trinity College, Cambridge: MA and DPh (Cantab.). Fellow, Trinity Coll. 1932–36; Hon. Fellow 1967. *Career:* on Staff of Warburg Inst. London 1937–39. Reader of Hist. of Art., Univ. of London, and Deputy Director of Courtauld Institute 1939; War Service (in France) 1939–40; War Office (1940–45); Surveyor of the Pictures of King George VI, 1945–52; Dir. Courtauld Inst. of Art & Professor of History of Art, Univ. of London 1947–74; Surveyor of The Queen's Pictures 1952–72; Adviser on The Queen's Pictures and Drawings since 1972. *Awards:* Cmdr. Legion of Honour and Order of Orange-Nassau; Hon. D.Litt. Bristol, Durham, Oxon; Docteur és Lettres Paris. *Publications:* Artistic Theory in Italy (1940) (2nd edit. 1956); François Mansart (1941); French Drawings at Windsor Castle (1945); Rouault's Miserere (1951); Poussin's Golden Calf (1951); (with Walter Friedlaender) The Drawings of Nicolas Poussin (1939–74); Art and Architecture in France 1500–1700 (1953, second edn. 1970). The drawings of G. B. Castiglione and Stefano della Bella at Windsor Castle (1954); The Venetian Drawings at Windsor Castle (1957); Philibert de l'Orme (1958); The Art of William Blake (1960); (with H. L. Cooke) The Roman Drawings at Windsor Castle (1960); (with Phoebe Pool) Picasso: The formative years (1962); Poussin: Lettres et propos sur l'art (1964); Seurat (1965); Nicholas Poussin (The Masters) (1965); The Paintings of Nicolas Poussin. A Critical Catalogue (1966); Nicolas Poussin, 2 vols. (1967); Sicilian Baroque (1968); Picasso's Guernica (1969); Supplements for the Catalogue of Italian & French Drawings at Windsor Castle (1973); Neapolitan Baroque and Rococo Architecture (1975). Articles in the Burlington Magazine, The Journal of the Warburg and Courtauld Institutes, etc. *Address:* 45 Portsea Hall, Portsea Place, London, W.2.

**BLYDENSTEIN, William John Harry.** Dutch banker. *B.* 3 April 1904. *Educ.* University of Amsterdam. *Career:* Partner, B. W. Blydenstein & Co., London 1936–47; Director, Clive Discount Co. 1947–54; Director, De Twentsche Bank N.V. General Bank of the Netherlands N.V. Amsterdam 1948–71. *Address:* 14 Chemin de Fantaisie, Pully Lausanne, Switzerland.

**BLYER, Lee L.** American executive. *B.* 1910. *Educ.* Engineering (BS; ChE). *M.* 1935, Betty G. Bernheiser (*Dec.* 1964). *M.* 1965, Evelyn G. Mancini. *S.* Lee L., Jr. *Dau.* Nancy Louise. *Career:* With DuPont Co. 1934–45, and Compo Chemical Co. (Vice-Pres.) 1945–54; Pres. Howe & French Inc. 1960–61; Ambroid Co. since 1964. *Member:* Sigma Xi F.A.I.C., New York Acad. of Science, Amer. Assn. for Advancement of Science, National Paint, Varnish & Lacquer Assn. (Past Vice-Pres. and Dir.), Hobby Industry Assn. (Past Pres. and Dir.) and Chemical Club of New England. Republican. *Publications:* numerous magazine articles on adhesives. *Clubs:* Massapoag Yacht; Sharon Fish & Game; Sharon Tennis; Sharon Country; Princeton (N.Y.C.); Downtown (Boston); World Trade Center. Member, Boston R.I. Rubber Groups. *Address:* 45 Chestnut Street, Sharon, Mass. 02067; and *office* 612 Montello Street, Brockton Mass. 02401, U.S.A.

**BLYTON, Neville Manning,** OBE, FAMI, FAIEx, FInstDA. British. *B* 1922. *M.* 1948, Eunice Phyllis. *Career:* Dir. Gen. Mgr. Export H. C. Sleigh Ltd.; Dir., Meatpak (Vic) Pty. Ltd.; Dir., H. C. Sleigh Resources Ltd. since 1977; Chmn. Dirs., Northern Woodchips; Northern Forest Investments Pty. Ltd.; Mgr., N.S.W. Merchandise Div. H. C. Sleigh Ltd. 1942–56; Dir., White Industries Ltd.; Dir., Warkworth Mining Ltd.; Pres., Australia-China Business Co-operation Cttee. since 1976; Fellow, Institute of Dirs.; Fellow, Australian Marketing Inst.; Australian Inst. of Export; Pres., Australian Chambers of Commerce Export Council 1963–65; Pres. Aust. Chamber of Commerce 1971–73; Mem. Export Development Council 1962–69; Pres., Melbourne Chamber of Commerce 1967–69; Consul for Belgium with Jurisdiction in State of Victoria Australia since 1973. *Clubs:* Australia Club, Melbourne; Royal Automobile Club of Victoria; Rotary Club of Melbourne. *Address:* 48 Lansell Road, Toorak, 3142, Victoria, Australia; and *office* 160 Queen Street, Melbourne, 3000 Victoria, Australia.

**BOARDMAN, Thomas Gray,** MC, TD, DL. British Politician and Solicitor. *B.* 1919. *Educ.* Bromsgrove. *M.* 1948, Deirdre. *S.* 2. *Dau.* 1. *Career:* Served Northants Yeomanry, 1939–45; Solicitor, since 1947; Commanded Northants Yeomanry 1956; Member of Parliament for Leicester South West 1967–74, and Leicester South Feb.–Oct. 1974; Minister for Industry 1972–74; Chief Secy. to Treasury Jan.–March, 1974; Dir., The Steetley Co. since 1975; Deputy Lieutenant Northamptonshire; Pres., the Assn. of British Chambers of Commerce 1977—. *Clubs:* Cavalry. *Address:* The Manor House, Welford, Northants; and 29 Tufton Court, Tufton Street, London, S.W.1.

**BOCH-GALHAU, Luitwin von.** German executive. *B.* 1906. *Educ.* K. G. Engineer's Diploma. *M.* 1935, Beatrice Dodd. *S.* 4. *Dau.* 1. Manager of Villeroy & Boch 1932–72. Chmn. Bd., Villeroy & Boch, Keramische Werke (ceramics), 6642 Mettlach (Saar) 1932—. *Address:* Haus Gangolf, 6642 Mettlach/Saar; and *office* Villeroy & Boch, Generaldirektion, 6642 Mettlach/Saar, Germany.

**BOCKETT, Herbert Leslie,** CMG. *B.* 1905. *M.* 1932, Olive Ramsay. *Daus.* Annette and Diane. *Career:* Entered Government Public Service 1921; Accountant, N.Z. Unemployment Board 1934; Assistant Director: Social Security Dept. 1939 and National Service Dept. 1940; Director of Employment 1946; Secretary of Labour and Director of Employment in the Government of New Zealand, 1947–64; Chmn. Workers' Compensation Board 1960. *Address:* 189, The Parade, Island Bay, Wellington, New Zealand.

**BOCKSRUTH, Marc Isidore Valentin.** Belgian publicity agent and counsellor. *B.* 1911. *Educ.* Humanities. *M.* 1946, Marguerite Vandenberghe; Director-Proprietor 1935—, President, S.A. Protor, Brussels. *Awards:* Captain-Commandant Honorary. Officer, Order of the Crown; Chevalier, Order of Leopold; Chevalier, Order of the Crown; Commemorative Medal of the War 1940–45; Medal of the Resistance; Commemorative Medal, H.M. King Albert Ier; Medal of Prisoner of War; Medal Volontary of War. Liberal. *Club:* Publicity (Brussels). *Address:* Avenue De La Forêt, 1050 Brussels, Belgium.

**BODDINGTON, Lewis,** CBE. British. *B.* 1907. *Educ.* Univ. College of South Wales and City of Cardiff Tech. College; Joint Diploma in Engineering; FIMechE; Sir Edward Nicholl Scholar; FRAeS. *M.* 1936, Morfydd Murray. *Career:* Pupil Engineer, Fraser & Chalmers Engineering Works 1928–31. Asst. to Major H. N. Wyllie 1931–36; R.A.E. 1936; Head of Catapult Section 1938; Supt. of Design Offices 1942–45; Supt. of Naval Aircraft Dept. 1945–51; Asst. Dir., R. and D.N. and Development (R.N.) Min. of Supply 1953–59; Dir.-Gen., Aircraft Research & Development (R.A.F.), Ministry of Air 1959–60; Techn. Director (Development), Westland Aircraft Ltd. 1960–62. Director, 1961–70. Asst. Man. Dir., 1962–67. *Awards:* Medal of Freedom (Bronze Palm), U.S.A.; Bronze Medal Royal Aeronautical Socy. *Address:* 7, Pine House, Lingwood Close, Southampton.

**BODENSIEK, Karl Heinz.** German writer. *B.* 1906. *Educ.* Universities of Köln and Bonn; editor (unpaid) Koblenzer General Anzeiger. *M.* 1936, Lotte Wirths. *S.* 1. *Career:* Journalist on various newspapers, e.g. Kölnische Zeitung, Stadt Anzeiger, Der Mittag, Frankfurter Zeitung, Die Hilfe, etc. Writer, journalist, Head of press section and literary department, Rhineland Assn. for Tourist Trade, Bad Godesberg 1937–69. Editor of the Press Information Service, "Das Schöne Rheinland". Leader of the cultural section; Later, Chief Editor "Rheinland in Wort und Bild" Deputy Manager and Press Officer Rheinland Tourist Association, Bonn-Bad Godesberg. *Publications:* Books: The Stage Picture, A Summer Novel; About Romain Rolland; With Goethe to the Rhein; Who Laughs is a Better Man; The Walk into the Christmas Woods; The Sure and Realistic Mystery Mirror; also a report on the extraordinary life of Peter Michel Dito; Das vergnügliche Kursbuch, Eifel and the Ardennes (in German and French); In den gläsernen Fluten der Zeit; Landschaften; Zeit und Leben; Die Welt ist in Dir (Poems); Romantischer Rhein; Das Siebengebirge; Bergisch Land; Der Niederhein; Eifel, Emmerich; Co-editor, Scenery Along the Rhine; With a Happy Face; associated with various collections of works, newspapers and travelogues, 'Der Rhein—Herzstrom Europas'; Features for Broadcasting, etc. 1973 Literaturpreis des Künstlervereins Malkasteu, Düsseldorf. *Member:* Association of German Tourism Journalists VDRJ; Society of Tourism in Germany VDKF. *Clubs:* Die Kogge. *Address:* Nachtigallenstrasse 18, D-5300 Bonn-Bad Godesberg, Germany.

**BODINE, Albert George.** American. *B.* 1914. *Educ.* Univ. of California, and California Inst. of Technology. *M.* 1939, Anna Thomsen (*Dec.*). *S.* Albert Jonathan. *Dau.* Linda Anne. *Career:* Chief Engineer, American Liquid Gas Co. 1937–39; Project Manager, Hughes Aircraft Co. 1939–41; President, Bodine Soundrive Co. 1941—; Director, Soundrive Engine Co. 1946—; Chairman of Board, Soundrill Corp. 1949— (these concerns are located in Los Angeles, Calif.); Lecturer, Univ. of Calif.; Governor, Chapman Coll., Orange, Calif. *Member:* Planning Council, Amer. Management Assn.; Calif. Inst. of Technology Alumni Assn.; Amer. Socy. of Mechanical Engineers; Amer. Inst. of Physics; Socy. of Automotive Engineers. Republican. Presbyterian. *Publications:* 200 patents and numerous technical articles. *Address:* 13180 Mulholland Drive, Beverly Hills, Calif.; and *office* 7877 Woodley Avenue, Loss Angeles, Calif., 91406 U.S.A.

**BODSON, Victor Hubert Joseph,** D en D. Luxembourg politician; Attorney at Law. *B.* 24 March 1902. *Educ.* Athénée de Luxembourg; Universities of Strasbourg, Algiers and Montpellier. *M.* Aline Krancher. *S.* Léon, Robert. *Daus.* Andrée, Marie-Thérèse, Sonia. *Career:* Member, Chamber of Dep. 1934–61; Communal Coun. 1934–40; Minister of Justice, of Transport and of Public Works 1940–47 and 1951–59; Vice-President, Chamber of Deputies 1937–40 and 1948–51 and 1959–61; Member of the State Council 1961–64; Pres., Chamber of Deputies 1964–67, and Hon. Pres. since 1967; Member of Commission of European Communities 1967–70. *Awards:* Grand Croix, Couronne de Chêne; Grand Cross Adolph Nassau; Grand Cordon, Couronne (Belgium); Chevalier. Al Merito of Italian Republic; Grand Cross, Falcon (Iceland); Grand Cordon, Orange-Nassau (Netherlands); Grand Croix, Legion of Honour (France); Commander, Order of the British Empire; Medal for Freedom with Silver Palm (U.S.A.); Das grosse Verdienstkreuz mit Stern und Schulterband (Germany); Grand Cordon, Olaf, Norway; Grand Cross, Merit (Austria); Grand Cross Republic of Tunis. *Address:* Villa Malpaartes, Mondorf-les-Bains, Grand Duchy of Luxembourg.

**BODY, Richard Bernard Frank Stewart.** MP. British Politician. *B.* 1927. *Educ.* Reading School; Middle Temple. *M.* 1959, Marion Graham. *S.* 1. *Dau.* 1. *Career:* Barrister 1949–70; Farmer 1950–76; MP for Billericay 1955–59, MP for Holland with Boston since 1966; Chmn., Open Seas Forum 1970; Jt. Chmn. of Council, Get Britain Out Referendum Campaign 1975. *Publications:* (Jointly) Destiny or Delusion, 1971; (Jointly) Freedom & Stability in the Free World. *Club:* Carlton. *Address:* Jewell's Farm, Standford Dingley, Reading, Berks.

**BOEL, Niels.** Danish Ambassador to Romania and Bulgaria. *Address:* c/o Danish Ministry of Foreign Affairs, Christiansborg, Copenhagen, Denmark.

**BOELAERTS, Albert Louis Marie.** Belgian diplomat. *B.* 31 Dec. 1914. *Education:* M.Econ.; M.Sc.Pol.Dipl.; Professor 1947. *M.* Francine Madeleine Marie Vanderstichelen. *Career:* Institut. Superieur des Sciences Administratives, Antwerp 1941–45; entered Ministry of Foreign Affairs, May 1945 and Ministry of External Commerce Sept. 1945; Attaché of Legation, Luxembourg July 1947; Attache of Embassy, The Hague Oct. 1947–April 1950; Secretary of Legation, Helsinki 1952–55; First Sec., Min. of For. Affs. and External Commerce since Dec. 1955; Asst. Chief of Cabinet of Minister of Trade, July–Nov. 1958; Counsellor. Nov. 1958; Consul-Gen., Cape Town, Jan. 1959–63; Chicago 1963–67; Ambassador in S. Africa in Botswana, Lesotho, 1968–71; in Swaziland, 1970–71; Min. Plenipot., Ministry for. Affairs 1971–74, Ambassador in Santiago (Chile) since 1974. *Awards:* Commander, Order of Leopold; Order of the Crown; Order of Holy Sepulchre; Knight, 1st C., Order of Finnish Lion; Knight, Order of Orange-Nassau; Civil Cross (1st class). *Address:* Ministerie des Affaires Entrempères, 2 rue du Quatre Bras, Brussels, Belgium and; Embassy of Belgium, Casillo 292V. Santiago de Chile.

**BOERMA, Addeke Hendrik.** Dutch. Former United Nations Official. *B.* 1912. *Educ.* Graduated Agricultural Univ. of Wageningen (Netherlands) 1934, Specializing in Horticulture and Agricultural Economics. *M.* 1935, (1) Maretta Postuma (2) 1953, Dinah Johnston. *Daus.* 5. *Career:* Entered Govt. Service Officer in Charge preparation, distribution & management of food, in case of war, 1938–40; Min. of Agriculture Dutch Food Supply, 1940–41; Dir., Crop Marketing Board, Dutch Purchasing Office, Agricultural Produce, 1942–44; Govt. Commissioner, Food & Agric. in liberated Holland, 1944–45; Acting Dir. Gen. of Food, 1945–46; Govt. Comm., Foreign Agricultural Relations, 1946–48. Member, Netherlands Preparatory Comm., study Lord Boyd Orr's proposals World Food Board. Representative Agric. Cttee. Benelux, Raporteur Agric. Cttee. Preparatory Commission, Marshall Plan, Chmn. European Seed Conference. Member Netherlands FAO Council; FAO Advisory Panel, Economics & Statistics, FAO Regional Rep., Europe, 1948–51; Dir., Economics Div., FAO 1951–58; Head Program & Budgetary Service FAO, 1958–62. Exec. Dir., World Food Program, FAO. Un., 1962–68. Director-General, Food and Agriculture Organization, of the United Nations, 1968–75. Hon. Doctor, Michigan Univ., 1968, Central Coll. Iowa, 1969, Agricultural Univ. of Wageningen, The Netherlands 1970; Doctor Honoris Causa Faculté des Sciences Agronomiques de Gembloux Belgique 1971; Agricultural Sciences, Univ. of Agric. Sciences, Keszthely, Hungary 1972; Agric. Sciences, Univ. Bologna, Italy 1973; Agric. Sciences, Univ. of Athens, Greece 1973; Dr. Hon. Causa, Sciences de l'agriculture et de l'alimentation, Laval Univ. Quebec 1975; Sciences de l'Agriculture et de l'Alimentation, Leuven, Belgium 1976. *Awards:* The Netherlands, 1948; Comdr. Order of Leopold II Belgium, 1948; Officier, Order Merite Agricole, France, 1948; Commandeur, Order of the Lion, The Netherlands 1976; Cavaliere di Gran Croce, Italy 1976; Wateler Peace Prize, Carnegie Foundation, The Hague 1976. *Address:* La Pergola, via Erodoto 11, Casal Palocco, Rome, Italy.

**BOGDAN, Corneliu.** Romanian Diplomat. *B.* 1921. *Education:* Graduate of Inst. of Economic Sciences (International Relations) Bucharest; *M.* 1949, Emilia Milco. *Daus.* 3. *Career:* Romanian Ministry of Foreign Affairs 1948–49; Dir. Western Dept. 1949–51; Counsellor Romanian Legation, Washington 1951–53; Deputy-Dir. Western Dept. 1953–55; Director Press Dept 1955–61; Dir. Western Europe 1961–66; (Deputy-Rep. Security Council 1962); Dir. Western Europe and North America 1966–67; Romanian Ambassador to USA 1967–76. *Decorations:* Star of Socialist Republic of Romania IIIrd Class; Tudor Vladimiresco IInd Class; Order of August 23rd IIIrd Class; and other awards. *Clubs:* International (Wash. DC). *Address:* c/o Ministry of Foreign Affairs, Bucharest, Romania.

**BOHLMANN, Hans Heinrich.** American. *B.* 1906. *Educ.* Amer. Inst. of Banking (in co-operation with Columbia Univ.), New York (winner Alexander Gilbert Prize for highest scholastic average 1929). *M.* 1935, Margaret G. Williams. *Career:* Various posts with Chase National Bank 1926–29; American Express Co. (in Shanghai, Hong Kong, Berlin and Munich) 1929–37; Firestone Tire & Rubber Co., Akron, Ohio, 1937–40; Seamless Rubber Co., New Haven, Conn. 1940–64. President, Conintrade Co., North Haven, Conn. Jan. 1964—. Appointed by U.S. Secretary of Commerce as Chairman of the Connecticut Regional Export Expansion Council, March 1963–June 1965. Member Combination Export Managers Assoc. of Connecticut (Pres. 1967–72). Member Connecticut Gov. Meskill's Presidential Conference on Exporting 1972. Elected to the International Registry of Who's Who Geneva. 1968; Named 'Community Leader of America' 1969.

Invited by Pres.-Elect Richard M. Nixon to assist in program of suggesting individuals who could make significant contributions to U.S.A., 1968. Member of various conferences called by U.S. Dept. of Commerce, namely: Washington Conference on Magnuson-Adams Bill 1965; White House Conference (by invitation of Pres. Kennedy) 1963; Conference on National Planning for Export Expansion, Washington 1960; Export Trade Promotion Conference (rubber industry) 1960; Task Force (dealing with Soviet trade proposals) 1958; Trade Mission to S.E. Asia 1957; World Trade Advisory Committee of U.S. Department of Commerce, Washington 1957–61; New England Regional Export Expansion Council 1960–63, and Connecticut Regional Export Expansion Council 1963—. Chmn., Foreign Trade Committee, Greater New Haven C. of C. 1944–45. *Member:* Speakers Bureau, Manufacturers Association of Connecticut Inc. (Past Chairman Foreign Trade Committee) to 1967; International Platform Assn., Cleveland, Ohio, 1967—. *Publications:* many articles and speeches on international trade. *Address:* Bubbling Well Farm, North Haven, Conn. 06473; and 222 Rimmon Road, North Haven, Conn. 06473, U.S.A.

**BOHON, Ellis G(ray).** American Certified Public Accountant, Management Consultant and Tax Adviser. *B.* 1902. *Educ.* Central YMCA Coll. Chicago; Westminster Coll., Fulton, Mo.; Walton School of Commerce and Northwestern Univ., Chicago; Knox Coll., Galesburg, Ill. (BS *cum laude* 1924); Univ. of Illinois (CPA degree 1935); Chicago Board of Trade Grain Institute. *M.* 1939, Joyce L. Finlayson. *S.* Walter Duncan and Ellis Gray II. *Career:* Attorney of the Tax Court of U.S.A.; Enrolled Agent, U.S. Treasury Dept.; CPA Illinois, Indiana, Iowa, Missouri and Kentucky. Former lecturer, Amer. Inst. of Banking, Walton School of Com., Illinois Inst. of Technology, and Lake Forest (Ill.) College. Proprietor, Ellis G. Bohon, CPAs 1936; member, Advisory Council of Jones Commercial High School 1958–66; Adviser, Lakes Chapter, Order of DeMolary 1959–62. *Member:* Amer. Accounting Assn.; Natl. Assn. of Accountants; Amer. Inst. of C.P.A.s; Amer. Inst of Laundering; Accounting Research Assn.; Midwest Business Administration Assn. Amer. Arbitration Assn. Multistate Tax Compact Panelist, SCORE; Kentucky Historical Socy.; Illinois and Iowa Socs. of C.P.A.s; Phi Delta Theta. Mason (Shriner). *Publication:* Hedging. *Clubs:* The Monroe Club, Union League (Chicago). *Address:* 523 East North Avenue. Lake Bluff, Ill. 60044 and *office* 140 South Dearbon Street, Chicago 60603, Ill., U.S.A.

**BOISDE, Raymond Paul Léon Victor,** L en D. French diplomat. Deputy M.P. (Cher 1951), company director and engineer. *B.* 15 August, 1899. *M.* 1921, Edmée Robineau. *Dau.* Geneviève. *Career:* Manager, Compagnie Lincrusta Walton 1921–27, Ets. Marechal, Lyon 1927–30; Con. Eng., Société Commerciale Titax 1930–36; Prés-Adjoint, Fédération Nationale des Industries de Lingerie since 1936; Deputy Chairman, Fédération Nationale de l'Habillement nouveauté et Accessoires 1938; member of Committee Conseil National du Patronat Français, Conseil National du Commerce, Confédération Générale des Petites et Moyennes Entreprises; Secretary of State for Commerce (Laniel Cabinet) since July 1953; Vice-Chmn Finance Commission of the National Assembly; Professeur Hon. d'Organisation Scientifique du Travail au Conservatoire National des Arts et Métiers 1954; President de l'Association Européenne des Organisations Nationales des Commerçants détaillants en Textile 1958. President du Conseil Régional de la Règion Centre. *Awards:* Chevalier de la Légion d'Honneur; Commandeur du Mérite Commercial; Commandeur du Mérite Social; Chevalier du Mérite Agricole. *Publications:* Commerce et Lois Sociales; Paysans de l'Avenir; Economie Organisée; Commerce et Corporation; Controle et Fixation des Prix; Réalisme Economique et Social; Technique de l'Organisation Professionnelle; Interférences techniques et politiques; L'Organisation de la Baisse; Libéralisme Actif, Le Rendezvous des Continents (Albin Michel), La Modernisation de la Politique (Plon); Technocratie et Démocratie (Plon); Lumières et Ombres Chinoises (Sedes), Mirages du Tiers Monde and other works. *Address:* 18 Rue des Bons-Enfants, Paris 1er, France.

**BOISSIER-PALUN, Léon Louis**, KBE. Diplomat. *B.* 1916. *Educ.* Lycée Faidherbe (Senegal) and University of Bordeaux (Lic. en Droit). *M.* 1944, Armelle A. Massard. *S.* Georges. *Career:* Defence Counsel, Court of Appeal, French West Africa; High Counsellor, Pt. Grand Council 1952–57; Minister of Economic Affairs, responsible for inter-territorial relations 1957; Administrator, Institute of Banking for the Issue of Currency of French West Africa and Togoland. Pt. Commission for Economic Affairs and the Planning of the Senegalese Legislative Assembly. Delegate to Federal Assembly of Mali. Member, Senate of Communauté (President of Commission for Legislation and Constitution of the Assembly 1959–61). Municipal Councillor, Dakar; Ambassador of Senegal to the Court of St. James 1960–66, concurrently to Vienna, Oslo, Stockholm and Copenhagen 1961–66, and to Switzerland 1964–66; President, Economic and Social Council, Dakar 1964–72; Amb. to France 1966. Deputy, Senegalese Legislative Assembly. *Awards:* Grand Cross, National Order of Senegal; Commander, Legion of Honour, KBE; Commander Black Star of the Star of Africa (Liberia); Comdr. National Order of Ivory Coast. *Address:* Ile de Gorée, Dakar, Senegal.

**BOÎTEUX, Marcel Paul.** French. *B.* 1922. *Educ.* Ecole Normale Supérieure; Professor in Mathematics; Diploma, Inst. d'Etudes Politiques. *M.* 1946, Juliette Barraud. *S.* Jean-Paul. *Daus.* Catherine and Martine. *Career:* Chairman, Comité Consultatif de la Recherche Scientifique et Technique 1966–67. Lecturer in Economics at the Ecole Nationale des Ponts et Chaussées 1963–67. General Director, Electricité de France 1967—. *Awards:* Légion d'Honneur War Cross (1939–45). Pres. Econometric Socy. 1959, European section of the Inst. of Management Science (Tims) 1962. International Federation of Operational Research Societies (IFORS) 1965–66. *Member:* Int. Statistical Inst. (ISI); Assn. Francaise de Science Economique; Société Française des Electriciens (SFE) etc. Club du Bois de Boulogne. *Address: office* 2 rue Louis Murat, Paris 8, France.

**BOKASSA, Marshal Jean Bédel.** Central African Empire Army Officer & Politician. *B.* 1921. *Career:* Comdr-in-Chief, Army of the Central African Empire since 1963; President 1966–77, crowned Emperor, Dec. 1977. *Decorations:* Legion d'Honneur; Croix de Guerre; Marshal of the Central African Republic 1974. *Address:* Office of the Emperor, Bangui, Central African Empire.

**BOKMAN, Karl Rudolf,** KBE. Swedish shipowner. *B.* 10 May 1895. *Educ.* State Grammar School. *M.* Marianne Blix. *Dau.* Christina. *Career:* Man. Dir., Swedish Lloyd Steamship Co. 1931–61; Member Bd. of Försäkr AB Atlantica 1931–67; Eriksbergs Mek. Verkstads AB 1931–68; Göteborgs Bogserings-Barnings AB 1939–70; Bergn. o. dykeri AB Neptun 1943–71; Svensk Interkontinental Lufttrafik AB (Sila) 1943—; Angfartygs AB Tirfing 1957–67; Vice-Chmn., Skandinaviska Banken 1957–66; Sveriges Angfartygs Assn. Forening 1958–60; Gothenburg Chamber of Commerce 1962–66; Chmn., Swedish Shipowners Assn. 1948–51; Nora Bergslags Jarnvags AB 1949–71; Lloyd's Register, Shipping Swedish Cttee. 1957—; Swedish Lloyd Steamship Co. 1961–69; International Paint (Sweden) Ltd. 1967—; Park Avenue Hotel since 1971; Chmn., Anglo-Swedish Socy. 1940–50, Sjofartsintresserades Fund since 1967. *Address:* Rederi AB Svenska Lloyd, Skeppsbron 5–6, Gothenburg, Sweden.

**BOLAND, Frederick Henry.** Irish diplomat. *B.* 11 Jan. 1904. *Educ.* Trinity College, Dublin; King's Inns, Dublin (BA, LLB, LLD); Rockefeller Research Fellow at Harvard, Chicago and North Carolina Universities. *M.* Frances Kelly. *S.* Fergal. *Daus.* Jane, Nessa, Mella, Eavan. *Career:* member of Irish Delegations to Conference on Operation of Dominion Legislation 1929, Commonwealth Economic Conference at Ottawa 1932, Meetings of League of Nations Council and Assembly, Commonwealth Conference on Nationality in London 1947, Committee on European Economic Co-operation, Paris 1947, Diplomatic Conference on Council of Europe, London 1949; Secretary, Department of External Affairs to, 1950; Amb. Ex. and Plen. to Court of St. James's 1950–56; Permanent Representative to U.N., New York 1956–63 (President, General Assembly 1960–61). Chancellor, Dublin University 1964—. Dir., Arthur Guinness Son & Co.; Chairman, National Industrial Economic Council. *Address:* 60 Ailesbury Rd., Dublin, Eire.

**BOLAND, Ronald Raymond.** Australian. *B.* 1911. *Educ.* Pulteney Grammar School, Adelaide. *M.* 1939, Thelma Jean Warren. *S.* Warren Desmond and Richard Ronald. *Career:* Joined News Ltd., Adelaide, Dec. 1926 (then reporter, sports writer, sub-editor of The News); Editor, Adelaide Sunday Mail 1951–60. Managing Director and Managing Editor, Western Press, Perth 1956–60. Worked in China and Far East 1934, Fleet Street (London) 1938, and U.S.A. and Britain on newspaper missions 1955. Managing Director Editor, The News Ltd. Adelaide Pty. Ltd. (publishers of The News: Adelaide's evening newspaper; circulation 175,000 June 1977). *Club:* Adelaide Rotary. *Address:* 256 East Terrace, Adelaide, S.A.; and *office* News Ltd., 116 North Terrace, Adelaide, S.A. Australia.

**BOLDT, David.** Canadian. *B.* 1918. *Educ.* Public & High School; Agricultural Course, Univ. of Sask., Electrical Course, Univ. of Sask. *M.* 1945, Anne Ens. *Daus.* Linda Anna, Betty Lou, and Dale Margaret. *Career:* Elected to Sask. Legislature, 1960, 1964–67 and 1971. Minister of Social Welfare & Rehabilitation 1964; Chairman, Sask. Govt. Insurance Office, 1965–70; Saskatchewan Minister of Highways and Transportation 1966–71; Minister in Charge of Highway Traffic Board, 1970–71; President Canadian Good Roads Association, 1969. Liberal. *Address:* House of Assembly, Regina, Saskatchewan, Canada.

**BOLGERT, Jean.** French bank director. *B.* 31 March 1893. *M.* 1931. *S.* 1. *Daus.* 2. Hon. General Manager, Banque de France; Commander of the Legion of Honour. *Address:* 15 Rue Lakanal, 75015 Paris, France.

**BÖLKOW, Ludwig,** Dr. Ing. German aeronautical engineer. *B.* 1912. *Educ.* Berlin Inst. of Technology, Dipl. Ing.; Technische Univ., Stuttgart. *M.* Annerose Marsmann. *S.* Ludwig. *Dau.* Elke. *Career:* Engineer, Messerschmitt Co. 1939–45, Independent Enterpriser 1948–56; Founder Bölkow Entwicklungen KG 1956 (later Bölkow GmbH); Shareholder & Chmn. of the Corporate Management, Messerschmitt-Bölkow-Blohm GmbH, Ottobrunn; Deputy-Chmn., Supervisory Board, Deutsche Airbus GmbH, München; Pres., Fed. German Aerospace Industries Assn. (BDLI); Vice-Pres., AECMA, NATO Industrial Advisory Group (NIAG), & EUROSPACE, Paris; Dep. Chmn., PANAVIA Aircraft GmbH Munich; Mem. of the Presidency, Bundesverband der Deutschen Industrie e.V. (BDI); Mem. Bd. of Dirs., AIRBUS Industrie, Paris; Chmn. Bd. of Shareholders, EUROMISSILE, Paris; Mem. of Bd., Eurosat, Geneva; Mem. of Cttee., Deutsches Museum, Munich. *Awards:* Order of Merit, State of Bavaria; VDI Award (German Engs.); Gold Diesel Medal; Ludwig-Prandtl Ring (German Aerospace Medal); Pionierkette der Windrose; Werner-von-Siemens Ring of Honour; Grand Cross of Merit of the Order of Merit of the Fed. Republic of Germany; Hermann Oberth Gold Pin; Dr.-Ing. (h.c.), Tech, Univ. of Stuttgart. *Member:* A.I.A.A., Club der Luftfahrt e.V., D.G.L.R. Deutsches Atomforum e.V., V.D.I., Royal Aero Club. *Address:* Messerschmitt-Bölkow-Blohm GmbH, P.O. Box 80 1109, 8000 Munich 80, Federal Republic of Germany.

**BOLT, Richard Henry.** Scientist, engineer, administrator. *B.* 1911. *Educ.* University of California; AB (Architecture); MA (Physics); PhD (Physics). *M.* 1933, Katherine Mary Smith. *S.* Richard Eugene. *Daus.* Beatrice (Scribner); Deborah (Zieses). *Career:* National Research Council Fellow, M.I.T. 1939–40; Associate (Physics), Univ. of Illinois, 1940–41; Technical Dir., Defense Research Project, M.I.T. 1941–43; Scientific Liaison Officer, Office of Scientific Research & Development, London, England 1943–44; Chief Technical Aide, National Defense Research Cttee., N.Y. 1944–45; Dir. of Acoustics Laboratory, M.I.T. 1946–57, Prof. of Acoustics 1954–63; Principal Consultant, Biophysics and Biphysical Chemistry Study Section, National Institutes of Health 1957–60; Associate Director National Science Foundation 1960–63; Lecturer, Massachusetts Institute of Technology 1964–69; Emeritus Chairman, Board of Directors. Bolt, Beranek & Newman Inc. *Publications:* Sonics (with T. F. Hueter) 1955; Biophysical Science and Its Relation to Medical Research 1959; Report on the Study Program in Biophysical Science, Boulder, Colo., 1958 Dec. 1959; Investing in Scientific Progress and Profiles of Manpower in Science and Technology 1961. Pres., Acoustical Soc. of America 1949–50; President, International Commission on Acoustics 1951–57; Chairman, Armed Forces-National Research Council Cttee. on Hearing and Bio-Acoustics, 1953–55. *Club:* Cosmos (Washington, D.C.). *Address: office.* Bolt, Beranek & Newman, Inc., 50, Moulton Street, Cambridge, Mass. 02138, U.S.A.

**BOLTE, Hon. Sir Henry (Edward),** GCMG, MP. *B.* 1908. *Educ.* Skipton State Sch.; C. of E. Grammar School, Ballarat. *M.* 1934, Edith L. *Dau.* of late D. F. M. Elder; Leader, Lib. and Country (now Lib.) Party of Victoria since 1953; member of Legislative Assembly for Hampden, Victoria, since 1947; Minister for Water Supply and Mines, 1948–50; Minister for Soil Conservation 1949–50, and 1955–61. Premier/Treasurer, Victoria, Australia, 1955–72 (sixth continuous term). Awarded LLD (hon.) by Universities of Melbourne and Monash, Vic. *Address:* 'Kialla', Meredith, Vic., 3333, Australia.

**BOLTON, Sir George Lewis French,** KCMG. British banker. *B.* 1900. *M.* 1928, May Howcroft. *S.* 1. *Daus.* 2. *Career:* United Kingdom Executive Dir., Internat. Monetary Fund 1946–52, and Alternate Governor 1952–57; Chmn., Bank of London & South America 1957–70; Chmn., Commonwealth Development Finance Co. Ltd.; Dir. Canadian Pacific Steamships Ltd.; Intercontinental Banking Services Ltd.; Pres., Alexander Fund 1967; Chmn., London United Investments Ltd.; Chmn., Australian Urban Investments Ltd.; Deputy Chmn., Lonrho Ltd.; Dir., Lloyds Bank Int. Ltd.; President, Bank of London & South America Ltd. *Address:* Pollards Cross, Hempstead, nr. Saffron Walden, Essex.

**BOLTON, Rt. Hon. Lord Richard William Algar,** JP British. *B.* 1929. *Educ.* Eton; Cambridge Univ. (BA). *M.* 1951 Christine Weld-Forrester. *S.* 2. *Dau.* 1. *Career:* Chmn. Waterers Group; Dir., Yorkshire Life; Fellow Land Agents Society; Royal Society of Arts; Timber Growers Association; Chartered Landowners Assn.; Chmn., Yorkshire Agricultural Society. *Clubs:* Whites; Central African; Deep Sea Fishing. *Address:* Bolton Hall, Leyburn, Yorkshire; and *office* Estate Office, Wensley, Leyburn, Yorkshire.

**BOMAN, Johan E.** Swedish. *B.* 1914. *Educ.* Royal Inst. of Technology (Mining Engineer 1939). *M.* 1940, Margareta Lewald. *S.* 1. *Dau.* 1. *Career:* Various positions with the Boliden Mining Co. 1940–45, the Uddeholms AB and Zinkgruvor 1946–50; Sandvik Steel Inc., Salt Lake City and San Francisco 1951–53; General Superintendent, Falu Mine of Stora Kopparbergs Bergslags AB 1953–61; Managing Director, Swedish Mining Association since 1962; numerous mandates and positions on cttees. and institutes, within government and industry, connected with mineral industries and resources. *Address:* Belestigen 9, 18264 Djursholm 2, Sweden.

**BOMBASSEI FRASCANI de VETTOR, Giorgio.** Italian diplomat. *B.* 1910. *Educ.* Univ. of Florence (LLD) and Istituto Cesare Alfieri, Florence (Econ Pol and Soc Sciences). *M.* 1940, Eli Tramontani. *S.* Ranieri. *Career:* Entered Italian Diplomatic Service 1933; served in Egypt, U.S.A., France, Ceylon, U.S.S.R., Switzerland, Brazil. Deputy Director-General: of International Co-operation 1951–52, and of Political Affairs 1956. Permanent Representative to the Council of Europe 1957–61. Ambassador to Luxembourg 1961–67. Perm. member of the Italian Delegation to the Special Council of Ministers of C.E.C.A.,Oct. 1961–65; Ambassador to Holland 1965–67. Permanent Representative to the European Communities 1967–76; Vice-Chmn., European Investment Bank since June 1976. *Clubs:* Circolo della Caccia, Circolo del Golf (Rome). *Address:* European Investment Bank, 2 Place de Metz, Luxembourg.

**BONALLACK, Sir Richard Frank,** CBE. British. *B.* 1904. *Educ.* Haileybury. *M.* 1930, Evelyn. *S.* 2. *Dau.* 1. *Career:* Chmn., Bonallack Group of Companies 1953–71; Chmn. Freight Bonallack Ltd. 1971–74, Pres. since 1974. *Address:* 4 The Willows, Thorpe Bay, Essex.

**BONAR, Sir Herbert Vernon,** CBE. British. *B.* 1907. *Educ.* Fettes Coll., Edinburgh and Brasenose Coll. Oxford (BA 1929). *M.* 1935, Marjory East. *S.* George, Christopher and Ronald Jonathan. *Career:* Jute Controller, Ministry of Supply 1942–46; The Low & Bonar Group Ltd. 1949-74 (retired); Dir., The First Scottish American Trust Co. Ltd.; The Northern American Trust Co. Ltd.; LLD St. Andrews University 1955; LLD, Birmingham 1974. *Clubs:* Eastern (Dundee); Blair Gowrie Golf; Panmure Golf. *Address:* St. Kitts, 24 Albany Road, Broughty Ferry, Dundee.

**BONAR, James Charles.** Canadian Transportation Executive. *B.* 1906. *Educ.* Faculty of Letters, Université de Montreal; Doctor of Social, Economic and Political Sciences (DPSc). Honoris causa. Fellow, The Chartered Institute of Secretaries of Joint Stock Companies and other Public Bodies F.C.I.S.); Knight of Sov. & Military Order of Malta; *M.* 1944, Andrée Beaubien. *S.* 3. *Daus.* 2. *Career:* with Canadian Pacific Railway Co. (now Canadian Pacific Ltd.) in Traffic Dept.; subsequently Advertising Supervisor, Secretary of Educational Committee, Chief of Office of Chairman and President of C.P.R.; appointed an officer of C.P.R.; Co. with title of Asst. Secretary, 1 June 1946; and (in 1956 and again in 1964) was also appointed Secretary of C.P.R. subsidiary companies; Archivist, June 1965–70. Chmn., Prov. of Quebec Branch, The Chartered Inst. of Secretaries and Administrators; Chmn., Canadian Adv. Coun. and Counr. of world organization. Gen. Chairman 1956–57 Combined Appeals for the Blind; at request of Canadian educational authorities (and with concurrence of Sir Edward Beatty) headed educational programme for Canadian Army, Navy, Air Force, Mercantile Marine in Military District No. 4, and later headed educational programme in Prov. of Quebec for veterans of World Wars I and II conducted by Canadian Legion of British Empire Service League. Chmn. and Pres., Business Archives Cncl. of Canada 1968–73. *Member:* Socy. Amer. Archivists; Canadian Hist. Assn. Past Pres., Canadian Railway Club. *Awards:* Cert. of Merit, Canadian Leg. of Brit. Empire Service League etc. *Publications:* The Dominion of Canada (co-author); Montreal and the Inauguration of Trans-Canada Transportation; Canadian Pacific Railway Company and its contributions to Canada (T/S); British Columbia and the Highway to the Far East; The Centenary of Sir William Van Horne; Canada Greets Kittery; Canada Upon the Seas; Committee Chairman and co-author of Survey of Canadian Political Parties; Survey of Civil Service in Canada. Former director and life member, Canadian Authors' Association. *Clubs:* St. James's (Montreal); Royal and Ancient Golf Club of St. Andrews (Scotland); Newcomen Socy. of N. America (Hon.). *Address:* 599 Lansdowne Avenue, Westmount, Que. H3Y 2V7, Canada.

**BOND, Christopher Samuel.** American attorney and politician. *B.* 1939. *Educated:* Princeton Univ. School of International Affairs, Hons. degree; Univ. of Virginia School of Law, Degree. *M.* 1967, Carolyn Ann Reid. *Career:* Clerk to Chief Justice, Court of Appeals, Atlanta, 1963–64; Covington and Burling Law firm, Wash. DC 1965–67; Private Law Practice, Mexico, Missouri, 1968; Chief Counsel, Consumer Protection Divn. Attorney, General's Office, State of Missouri, 1969–70; State Auditor, Missouri 1971–73; Governor, State of Missouri, 1973–77; Pres., Great Plains Legal Foundation, Kansas City, Mo. *Chairman:* Republican Governors' Ass. 1974–75; Exec. Cttee., National Governors' Conference 1974–76; Chmn., Mid-Western Governors' Conf. (1976) *Member:* Omicron Delta Kappa; Order of the Coif (legal); Missouri Bar Assn.; US Supreme Court Bar; *Decorations:* Hon. Dr. of Laws, Westminer Coll. (Fulton, Mo.) and William Jewell Coll. (Liberty, Mo.); Hon. Dr. of Laws, Drury Coll., Springfield, Missouri 1976. *Clubs:* Sunrise Optimists (Jefferson City Mo.). *Address:* 1243 West 59th Street, Kansas City, Mo. 64137; and *office* Suite 1022, 127 West 10th Street, Kansas City, Mo. 64105, U.S.A.

**BOND, Eric Ernest,** MBE. Australian. *B.* 1918. *Educ.* Diploma, Applied Chemistry (ARMTC). *M.* 1952, Patricia Mary Carter. *Daus.* 2. *Career:* Cereal Chemist, Victorian Dept. of Agriculture 1938–40; Chief Chemist, Brunton & Co. Pty. Ltd. 1940–47; Director of Research, Bread Research Institute of Australia 1947—; Officer-in-charge, C.S.I.R.O. Wheat Research Unit since 1957. Fellow, Royal Australian Chemical Inst. *Member:* American Assn. of Cereal Chemists; American Socy. of Bakery Engineers. President, International Association for Cereal Chemistry, 1970–72. *Award:* Farrer Medal, distinguished service Agric. Science 1971. *Fellow:* Australia Inst. Food Science and Technology. *Club:* Royal Automobile (Australia). *Address:* 2 Mycumbene Avenue, East Lindfield, N.S.W.; and *office* Bread Research Institute of Australia, Private Bag, P.O., North Ryde, N.S.W., Australia.

**BONDURANT, Arthur P.** American. *B.* 1907. *Educ.* Washington & Lee Univ. (BS); Graduate of Advanced Mngmt. Program, Harvard, of Harvard Business School; Graduate work at Yale. *M.* 1963, Elizabeth Kelley. *Daus.* Mary Chiles and Mary Ward Hillerich (stepdaughter). *Career:* Lieut.-Col. U.S.A.F. in World War II (Legion of Merit). Engaged in Sales Promotion, Reynolds Metals Co., New York 1929–34. First Vice-President, Glenmore Distilleries, Louisville, Ky 1967; Consultant Dir. Glenmore Distilleries Co.; Hillerich & Bradsby. *Member:* Advertising Club of Louisville; Washington & Lee Alumni Assn. *Clubs:* Tuscon National Golf (Arizona); Pendennis, Country (Louisville); Harvard Business. *Address:* 504 Ridgewood Road, Louisville, Ky. 40207, U.S.A.

**BONGO, Omar.** Gabonais. *B.* 1935. *Educ.* Diploma, Technical College of Brazzaville (commercial section). *M.* 1959, Josephine Kama. *S.* Alain. *Dau.* Albertine Philiberte. *Career:* Deputy- Dir. and later Dir. of the Presidents Dept, 1962: Head, Ministry of Information & Tourism, 1963; Head, Ministry of National Defence 1964–65; Vice-President of the Government, 1966; Vice-President of the Republic, 1967. President & Head of Government, Republic of Gabon, 1967—: Secretary General, Democratic Party of Gabon, 1968—. President, OAU 1977–78. *Awards:* 18 foreign and Gabonese awards including: Grand Chancellor, Order of the Equatorial Star; Grand Cross; Order of the Ivory Coast and the Niger; Grand Cordon, Order of the Leopard; Grand Cross, Order of Nationalist China; Order of Merit (France); Grand Cross of French Order of Légion d'Honneur; Grand Cross of the Central African Order of Merit; National Order of Value of Cameroon; National Order of Mono of Togo; Order of Saint Michael and Saint George (Gt. Britain); Great Collar of the Sovereign Order of Malta. *Club:* Rotary. *Address:* Palais Renovation. P.O. Box 546, Libreville, Gabon.

**BONILLA SOSA, Salvador,** AB, MD. Salvadorean. Chem. Co. Exec. *B.* 1913. *Educ.* Univ. of Cincinnati (BS); Univ. of Havana (MD). *M.* 1953, Vilma Mathe-Sol. *S.* 2. *Daus.* 2. *Career:* Part Time Prof. Xavier U. Cincinnati 1936–39, Habana U. Med. School 1947–53; Supr. Wm. S. Morrell Co. 1940–47; Med. Dir. Sales Mgr., Lederle Labs. 1947–52; Gen. Mgr. Med. Dir., Caribbean Area Pfizer Corp. 1952–59; Pres. Bocamps. Int. 1952, Comercial Interamericana S.A. 1959–66; Pres. Chmn., Bd. Corp. Bonima S.A. 1963–66; Pres., Funasa El Salvador 1961–70, Guatemala 1962; Pres. Chmn., Bd. Proquimia S.A. since 1967; Vice-Pres., Industrias Baturro S.A. Panama since 1970; *President:* of other cos, including La Esmaralda SA (El Salvador) and Petroquimica Centro-Americana SA (El. Salvador); Instituto Salvadoreño de Cultura Hispánica y; (Vice-Pres.), Pro Arte El Salvador; Comite Nacional d'Ecologia (El Salv.); Cosejo Superior Orquesta Sinfónica de la Habana; M. Circulo Bellas Artes; Ateneo Habana; Pres., Federación Salvadoreño Yate; Dir., Central Amer. & Caribbean Yacht Racing Union; Nat. Olympic Cttee.; Member Assn. Industriales; Pan Amer. Medical Assn.; Secy., Pan Amer. Cancer Citoly Assn. Exec. Cttee. *Awards:* Cruz del Mérito Comercial; Orden de Finlay; Orden de la Cruz Roja, Gran Cruz Orden S.S.S. Brigada de Suecia; Commendador Orden. Mérito Civil de España. *Clubs:* Rotary; Club Déportivo Int.; American Club Salvadoreño. *Address:* Apto. 01–84 San Salvador, El Salvador; and *office* 27 ASy, P. Palomo, Col Flor Blanca, San Salvador, El Salvador.

**BONINO, Angelo.** Italian industrialist. *B.* 1905. *Educ.* professional and technical schools. *M.* 1931, Annetta Robazza. *S.* Giancarlo. *Career:* Commenced his activities as an employee in the textile industry; est. his own business in 1933. Proprietor, Filatura Angelo Bonino, Biella. *Member:* Management Council of the Unione Industriale Biellese, Biella since 1946; Council Associzaione Lauiera Hal; Titular member of l'Institut Internationale d'Etudes des Classes Moyennes, Brussels since 1962; Grande Ufficiale, Order of Merit of the Italian Rep. *Address:* Via Piero Gobetti, 4, Biella; and *office* Post Bos 248, Biella, Italy.

**BONNER, Robert William,** QC, BA, LLB, CD. Canadian barrister and solicitor; Chmn. British Columbia Hydro & Power Authority. *B.* 1920. *Educ.* University of British Columbia (BA Economic and Political Science 1942) and Faculty of Law (LLB 1948). *M.* 1942, Barbara. *S.* Robert York. *Daus.* Barbara Carolyn and Elizabeth Louise. *Career:* Read law with J. A. Clark, QC, Vancouver; called to Bar of B.C. July 1948; before entering B.C. Government practised law with firm of Clark, Wilson, White, Clark & Maguire, Vancouver; served in World War II (Seaforth Highlanders of Canada in Canada, U.K., N. Africa, Sicily and Italy; wounded in action; retired with rank of Major) 1942–45; Lieut.-Col. Univ. of British Columbia Contingent, C.O.T.C. 1946–53; concurrently with office of Attorney-General (1952–68) was Minister of Education of B.C. Oct. 1953–Apr. 1954, and Minister of Industrial Development, Trade and Commerce of B.C. 1957–64; Minister of Commercial Transport B.C. 1964–68; Dir. and member, Exec. Cttee. MacMillan, Bloedel Ltd.. Vancouver 1968–74; Chmn. Bd. 1973–74; Dir., Canadian Cablesystems Ltd. 1969—; International Nickel Co. since 1973; Dir. J. Henry Schroder and Co. Ltd. since 1975; Dir. Montreal Trust Co. since 1976; Chmn. B. C. Hydro since 1976; Member (Social Credit) for Columbia Riding 1952; re-elected for Vancouver-Point Grey Riding 1953; re-elected to same constituency Sept. 1956; Sept. 1960 and Sept. 1963, re-elected for Cariboo Riding Nov. 1966–69. *Address:* 5679 Newton Wynd, Vancouver B.C.; and *office* 1055 West Georgia St., Vancouver B.C., Canada.

**BONNET, Christian Charles Auguste.** French politician. *B.* 1921. *Educ.* D.-en-D.; Diplomé, School of Political Sciences. *M.* 1943, Christiane Mertian. *S.* Denis, Eric and Rémi. *Dau.* Marie-Christine de Penanster and Sophie. *Career:* Deputy for Morbihan in the National Assembly (elected 1956, re-elected 1958, 1962, 1967, 1968 and 1973, (Mayor of Carnac); Member of Commission on Finances; Counsellor-General of the canton Belle-Ile en Mer 1958; Sec. d'Etat aupres du Ministre de l'Amenagement du Territoire, de l'Equipment, du Logement et du Tourisme 1972. Minister of Agriculture 1974–77; Minister of the Interior since 1977. *Member:* Independent Republican Party. *Address:* 12 Rue Cimarosa, Paris 16e; and Kerlescan, Carnac, Morbihan, France.

**BONNIN, James Arthur,** MD. Australian medical practitioner (Haematologist). *B.* 1920. *Educ.* MB, BS Adelaide 1946; MD Adelaide 1955; FRACP 1971; FRCPA 1971, *M.* 1955, Heather Birt McDonald. *S.* 1. *Daus.* 2. *Career:* R.M.O., Adelaide Hospital 1946; Captain A.A.M.C., 130 Australian General Hospital, B.C.O.F., Japan 1947–48; Pathology Registrar, Royal Adelaide Hospital 1948–49; Clinical Pathologist, Inst. of Medical & Veterinary Science 1949. Hon. Consulting Physician in Haematology, Adelaide Children's Hospital 1957. Senior Clinical Pathologist 1958; Hon. Consulting Haematologist, Royal Adelaide Hospital 1958; Part-time Lecturer, Univ. of Adelaide 1958; Director, Institute of Medical & Veterinary Science since 1962, *Publications:* articles and papers in medical journals. chiefly concerning work on the bleeding diseases. Fellow. Asian-Pacific Division, International Socy. of Haematology, *Member:* Haematology Socy. of Australia (elected Pres. 1967); Fellow Royal College of Pathologists of Australia; Royal Australasian College of Physicians; Fellow, Australian Coll. of Medical Administrators; Australian Medical Association. *Clubs:* Naval, Military & Air Force (South Australia); Royal Adelaide Golf. *Address:* 4 Salisbury Terrace Collinswood, S.A.; and *office* Institute of Medical & Veterinary Science, Frome Road, Adelaide, S.A., Australia.

**BONNYCASTLE, Lawrence Christopher.** Canadian executive. *B.* 1907. *Educ.* University of Manitoba (BA 1929) and Oxford University (BA jurisprudence); Fellow, Society of Actuaries. *M.* 1934, Mary F. Andrews. *S.* John Christopher, Michael Kurt and Stephen Rodney. *Career:* Treasurer, Northern Life Assurance Co. of Canada 1938–40, and John Labatt Ltd. 1940–48 (Vice-Pres. and Asst. General Manager 1948–49); General Manager, National Life Assurance Co. of Canada 1949–52; President, Canadian Corporate Management Co. Ltd. 1963–72, Vice-Chmn. since 1972; Dir., Harlequin Enterprises Ltd.; Eldorado Nuclear Ltd. *Address:* 9 Wychwood Park, Toronto, Ont., Canada.

**BONS, Jacob,** DEcon. Dutch. *B.* 1919. *Educ.* Municipal Univ. of Amsterdam (DEcon). *M.* E. D. de Levita. *S.* 2. *Dau.* 1. *Career:* Chmn. Chief Exec. KBB (N.V. Koninklijke Bijenkorf Beheer); Economic Adviser Bakkenist, Spits & Co. Auditors, 1948–57. *Address:* Nieuwe Blaricummerweg 14, Huizen, post Bussum, Netherlands; and *office* Zwaansvliet 5, Amsterdam 11, Netherlands.

**BONVOISIN, Baron.** Belgian. *B.* 1903. *Educ.* Collège St. François Xavier, Verviers; Université de Liège (Doctor of Laws); Princeton University (MA); Harvard University. *M.* 1933, Elisabeth Galopin. *S.* 2. *Daus.* 2. *Career:* Hon. chmn. Sté. Générale de Banque European Am. Banking Corp., European Am. Bank and Trust Co., Banque Belge Ltd., Belgian Bank (Far East), Banque Commerciale Zaïroise; Banque Italo-Belge, Cie Immobilière de Belgique, Crédit Foncier de Belgique, Credit Foncier International, Dir. Agence Maritime Internationale; Extraordinary Professor Emeritus, Univ. of Louvain. *Awards:* Grand Off: ordre Equestre de St. Sépulcre. Cdr: ordre Equestre de St Grégoire le Grand, ordre Nat. Cruzeiro do Sul (Brésil), ordre Au Mérite de la République Italienne. Officer: ordre de Léopold, ordre Royal du Lion, ordre du Cèdre du Liban. Chev. ordre de la Couronne (military). Médaille Commémorative de la Guerre 1940–45 ordre de Leopold II. *Address:* Blvd. St. Michel 30, 1040 Brussels, Belgium; *office* Montagne du Parc 3, 1000 Brussels, Belgium.

**BOOHER, Edward E.** American book publisher. *B.* 1911. *Educ.* Antioch College (AB). *M.* 1939, Selena Read Knight, *Div.* 1961. *S.* David Knight and Bruce Edward. *Dau.* Carol Read. *M.* 1961, Agnes M. Whitaker. *Career:* With McGraw-Hill Inc. in various capacities since 1936; Chmn. President 1960–68, Executive Vice-President 1954–60), McGraw-Hill Book Company, 1963–70; Pres., Books & Education Services Group, McGraw-Hill Inc. since 1970; Woodrow Wilson Fellow. Past President: New York Academy of Public Education. The American Textbook Publishers Institute, American Book Publishers Council; Member: Bd. of Higher Educ. of State of N.J.; Trustee, The Asia Society; Director, Fidelity Union Trust Co.; Trustee, Univ. of Negev; Gov., Yale Univ. Press. *Member:* American Society for Engineering Education; Chmn. International Group of Scientific Technical and Medical Publishers Association; Advisory Board, The Partisan Review; Vis. Cttee. of Harvard Graduate School of Education; Nat. Council on Educ. Research. *Address:* 121 Avenue of the Americas, New York, N.Y. 10020, U.S.A.

**BÖÖK, Klas Erik.** Swedish diplomat. *B.* 10 Mar. 1909. *M.* 1933, Aina Hakon-Pettersson. *S.* Ole, Kim, Peter. *Daus.* Annika, Susanne. *Career:* Joined Bank of Sweden 1936, Head of Statistical Section 1940, Assistant Manager, Foreign Exchange Office 1940 (member of Board 1947), Manager 1943, Deputy Governor 1944; Head of Commercial Section, Ministry of Foreign Affairs and En. Ex. and Min. Plen. 1947–48; member of Board, Foreign Capital Control Office 1945–51, Vice-Chairman, Export Credits Guarantee Board 1947–51; Chairman, Foreign Exchange Board 1948–51; Governor, Bank of Sweden 1948–51; Director, Post Office Savings Bank 1949–51; Member of Board, Bank for International Settlements 1949–51; Governor, International Bank for Reconstruction Development, 1951–52, and International Monetary Fund 1951; Minister to Canada 1951–55; Ambassador to China 1955–61; to India, Nepal and Ceylon 1961–65; to Switzerland 1965–72; Ministry of Foreign Affairs since 1972. *Awards:* Commander: 1st Cl., Order of North Star; 2nd Cl., Order of Dannebrog (Denmark); 1st Cl., Order of White Rose (Finland); Order of St. Olav (Norway). *Address:* Flacke Bjär, Lya, 260 97 0 Karup, Sweden.

**BOOKER, Malcolm Richard,** BA, FRAI. Australian official. *B.* 1915. *Educ.* Sydney University. *M.* 1951, Roxana Tayler. *S.* 1. *Dau.* 3. *Career:* Private Secy. to Attorney-General and Minister for the Navy 1940–41; 2nd Secy. Australian Legation, Chungking 1943–44; Political Secy., Australian Military Mission, Berlin 1945–47; 1st Secy., Manila 1950–52; Chargé d'Affaires, Rangoon 1952–53; Minister, Embassy, Washington 1958–60; Ambassador to Thailand June 1960–63. Deputy Secy., Dept. of Territories 1963–64; First Asst. Secy., Department of External Affairs 1964–70; Australian Ambassador to Italy 1970–74; Australian Ambassador to Yugoslavia, Rumania and Bulgaria 1974–76. *Publication:* The Last Domino (1976). *Address:* c/o Ministry of External Affairs, Canberra, A.C.T., Australia.

**BOON, Constant Emmanuel.** Belgian. *B.* 1911. *Educ.* Agronomic engineering. *M.* 1940, M. T. J. Robeyns. *S.* 5. *Daus.* 3. *Career:* Regent, Belgian National Bank 1961–76. Member, Central Economic Council. Professor Extraordinary, Catholic University of Leuven. President, Belgische Boerenbond since 1964. *Address:* Huttelaan 32, 3030 Heverlee, Belgium; and *office* Minderbroedersstraat 8, 3000 Leuven, Belgium.

**BOOTH, Albert,** MP. British Politician. *B.* 1928. *M.* 1957, Joan Amis. *S.* 3. *Career:* Labour MP for Barrow-in-Furness since 1966; Minister of State, Dept. of Employment 1974–76; Sec. of State since 1976. *Address:* House of Commons, London SW1A 0AA.

**BOOTH, Charles Stephen,** CBE. Canadian lawyer. *B.* 27 Jan. 1897. *Educ.* University of Manitoba (LLB). *M.* 1944, Zoë A. G. Young. *Dau.* Sandra. *Career:* Practised Law, Winnipeg 1924–40; M.P. (Lib.) Winnipeg North 1940–45; served World War II, 1st Canadian Corps and Military H.Q., London 1940–45; Secretary and Legal Adviser to Air Transport Board, Canada 1946–47; Senior Canadian Representative, I.C.A.O. 1947–54, also Canadian member of Legal Committee; Pres. Canadian Branch, In. Law Ass. 1952–53; Chmn. U.N. Joint Staff Pensions Board 1953; Senior Assistant Dep. Minister of Transport Sept. 1954 to Dec. 1965. President, I.C.A.O. Assembly 1955 and 1965. Adviser on bi-lateral air agreements to Govt. of Jamaica 1967–69. *Address:* 10 Birch Avenue, Rockcliffe, Ottawa.

**BOOTHBY, Lord (of Buchan and Rattray Head) (Sir Robert John Graham Boothby),** K.B.E. British Member of Parliament 1924–58. *B.* 12 Feb. 1900. *Educ.* Eton; Oxford (MA). *Career:* Parl. Sec. Min. of Food 1940; member of Consultative Assembly of Council of Europe 1949–57; Radner Lecturer, Columbia Univ., New York 1960; Rector of St. Andrews Univ. 1958–61; Hon LLD St. Andrews 1959; Hon. Burgess of the Burghs of Peterhead, Fraserburgh, Turriff and Rosehearty. Officier, Légion d'Honneur. *Publications:* The New Economy; I Fight to Live; My Yesterday, Your Tomorrow. *Address:* 1 Eaton Square, London, S.W.1.

**BOPP, Karl Richard.** American central banker. *B.* 1906. *Educ.* Univ. of Missouri (ABEcon. and BSBus Admin. 1928; MA 1929; PhD 1931). *M.* 1931, Ruth Callies. *S.* Karl Richard, Jr. *Dau.* Joanna Ruth (Bear). *Career:* Asst. Prof. 1931–37, Assoc. Prof. Economics and Finance. Univ. of Missouri

1937–41; Vice-Pres. i/c Research, Fed. Res. Bank of Philadelphia 1947–58 (Dir. of Research 1941–47); Lecturer on Finance, Wharton School of Finance & Commerce, Univ. of Pennsylvania 1946–58; On faculties of Grad. School of Banking, Rutgers Univ. 1950–58; School of Banking, Univ. of Wisconsin 1954–58; School of Banking of the South, Louisiana State Univ. 1955; Pres. Fed. Reserve of Philadelphia 1958–70; Technical Secy., Bretton Woods Monetary Conf. 1944; Chmn. Staff Cttee., Fed. Reserve System on Uniform Reserve Requirements for Member Banks 1947–48. Fellowships: Social Science Research Council 1932–33; John Simon Guggenheim Memorial Foundation 1939–40. Hon. LLD, Temple Univ. 1960, Univ. of Missouri 1961 and Cedar Crest College 1964. Trustee Emeritus Temple University; Dir. Atlantic City Electric Co. *Publications:* The Agencies of Federal Reserve Policy, (1935); Hjalmar Schacht; Central Banker, (1939); The Government and the Bank of France, (1941); Central Banking at the Cross-roads, (1944); The Bank of England, (1945); Nationalization of the Bank of England and the Bank of France, (1946); Three Decades of Federal Reserve Policy, (1947); Re-appraisal of Commercial Bank Reserve Requirements, (1948); Bank of France Policy—Brief Survey of Instruments, 1800–1914, (1952); Reichsbank Operations—1876–1914 (published in German only). (1953); Central Banking Objectives, Guides & Measures, (1954); The Rediscovery of Monetary Policy—Some Problems of Application, (1955). Director: Amer. Acad. of Political & Social Science. *Member:* American Philosophical Socy. (Secy. 1965–68); Amer. Economic Assn.; Amer. Statistical Assn. *Clubs:* Sunday Breakfast (Chmn. of Meetings 1963–66); Cosmos (Washington, D.C.). *Address:* 851 Angel Wing Drive, Sanibel, Florida 33957, U.S.A.

**BORCH, Otto Rose.** Danish diplomat. *B.* 1921. *Educ.* Copenhagen Univ. (Master of Law 1948). *M.* Astrid Lundbye. *Daus.* 2. *Career:* Joined Danish Foreign Service, 1948; Secretary of Embassy in Bonn, 1954; Head of Section (Political Affairs), Min. of Foreign Affairs, Copenhagen, 1959 & Head of the Dept., 1961; Deputy Perm. Rep., Minister Counsellor, Danish Perm. Representation to NATO, Paris, 1964; Ambassador, Perm. Rep. of Denmark to UN, 1967; Under Sec. of State for Political Affairs, Copenhagen 1974; Ambassador of Denmark to the U.S. since 1976. *Address:* 3200 Whitehaven Street N.W., Washington, D.C. 20008, U.S.A.

**BORDEN, Henry, OC, CMG, QC, LLD, DCL.** Canadian lawyer. *B.* Halifax, N.S. 1901. *Educ.* King's College School, Windsor, NS; McGill Univ. (BA Pol. Sc and Econ.); Dalhousie Law School; Rhodes Scholarship from Nova Scotia; Exeter College, Oxford (BA). *M.* 1929, Jean Creelman MacRae. *S.* 3. *Daus.* 2. *Career:* With Royal Bank of Canada 1921–22; Called to Bar (Lincoln's Inn) 1927, and to the Bars of Nova Scotia & Ontario 1927; King's Counsel 1938; Senior Member, Borden, Elliot, Kelley & Palmer 1936–46; General Counsel, Dept. of Munitions & Supply, Ottawa 1939–42; Chairman—Wartime Industries Control Board. Ottawa and Co-ordinator of Controls, Dept. of Munitions & Supply, Sept. 1942–Dec. 1943; Pres., Brazilian Light & Power Co. Ltd. 1946–63; Chairman, 1963–65; Hon. Director: BRASCAN Ltd., Toronto; Director: Canadian Investment Fund Ltd., Canadian Fund Inc., I.B.M. Canada Ltd.; Huron & Erie Mortgage Corp.; Dir. Emeritus, Canadian Imp. Bank of Commerce; Massey-Ferguson Ltd.; Past Chmn. Bd. of Governors, University of Toronto; Chairman, Royal Commission on Energy 1957–59; Dir. and Member Exec. Cttee. and Past President, Royal Agricultural Winter Fair. Formerly lecturer, Corporation Law, Osgoode Hall Law School; Past Pres. Canadian Club of Toronto; Past Pres. Lawyers Club of Toronto. *Decorations:* Companion of St. Michael & St. George (1943); Canadian Centennial Medal (1967); Order of Canada (1969); Created Grand Officer of the Nat. Order of the Southern Cross (Brazil) (1962). *Publications:* (joint author with Fraser) Handbook of Canadian Companies (1931); Editor, Robert Laird Borden —His Memoirs (1938); Letters to Limbo (1971). *Clubs:* York: Toronto; Phi Kappa Pi Fraternity. *Address:* Tannery Hill Farm, R.R. No. 2, King, Ont. L0G 1K0, Canada.

**BORDER, L. H., MVO.** Australian diplomat. *B.* 1920. *Educ.* Univ. of Sydney (BA). *M.* 1956, Margaret Fae Gerrand. *S.* 1. *Daus.* 3. *Career:* Australian Ambassador to Burma 1963–65, to S. Vietnam 1966–68; High Commissioner in Pakistan & concurrently Ambassador to Afghanistan 1968–70; Dep. Sec., Dept. of Foreign Affairs, Canberra 1971–75; Ambassador to the Federal Republic of Germany since 1975. *Decorations:* Member of the Victorian Order. *Address:* Australian Embassy, Kolnestrasse 107, 53 Bonn-Bad Godesberg 1, Bonn, Germany.

**BORG OLIVIER, Hon. Giorgio.** Knight Grand Cross of St. Sylvester. *B.* 1911. *Educ.* Lyceum and Royal University of Malta (LLD 1937; Hon. DLitt). *M.* 1943, Alexandra Mattei. *S.* Alexander and Peter. *Dau.* Angela. *Career:* Notary Public 1939; Member Council of Government 1939; Member Legislative Assembly and Deputy Leader of the Opposition 1947; Minister of Works and Reconstruction and Education 1950; Leader Nationalist Party 1950–77; Prime Minister 1950–55; Leader of Opposition 1955–58; Prime Minister and Minister of Economic Planning and Finance 1962–71; Minister of Commonwealth & Foreign Affairs 1965–72. Successfully concluded Malta Independence talks with the British Government 1964. *Member:* La Valette National Philharmonic Society. *Club:* Casino Maltese. *Address:* House of Representatives, Valletta, Malta.

**BORLAND, David Morton.** British. *B.* 1911. *Educ.* Glasgow Academy; Brasenose College, Oxford (BA). *M.* 1947, Nessa Claire Helwig. *S.* 1. *Dau.* 1. *Career:* Royal Marines (Lt.-Col.), 1940–46; Sales Manager, J. S. Fry & Sons Ltd., 1946–48 (Sales Dir. & a Man. Dir. 1948); Man. Dir.: British Cocoa & Chocolate Co. Ltd., 1959; Cadbury Bros. Ltd., 1963; Sales & Mktg. Dir. Confectionery Div. Cadbury Bros. Ltd., 1967. Chairman, Confectionery Group, Cadbury Schweppes Ltd., 1969–75. Director, Cadbury Schweppes Ltd., 1969–76. *Member:* Council, Bristol University & Careers Advisory Board, 1962; Bristol University Finance Committee, 1967. *Club:* Bath. *Address:* 1 Hollymead Lane, Bristol 9.

**BORN, Maynard Robert.** American engineering executive. *B.* 1907. *Educ.* Stanford University (AB 1929; Electrical Engineer 1930); American Management Assn. *M.* 1937, Bernice Olivia Rendahl. *S.* Robert Maynard. *Career:* Test Engineer, General Electric Co. 1930–31; Asst. Efficiency Engineer, Pacific Gas & Electric Co. 1931–36; Mechanical & Electrical Engineer, Standard Oil Co. of Calif. 1936–41; Chief Electrical Works & Project Engineer, Columbia-Geneva Steel Division, U.S. Steel Corp. 1941–45; Chief Engineer, Project Engineer, Shell Oil and Shell Chemical Cos. 1945–50; Chief Engine Test Facility, Arnold Engineering Development Center, U.S.A.F. 1950–51; Manager, Industrial and Governmental Projects Div., The Fluor Corp. 1951–54; Chief Project Engineer, Pacific Proving Grounds 1954–56, and Chief Engineer, Petroleum & Chemical Div. 1956–58, Holmes & Narver Inc.; Assistant Vice-President, Holmes & Narver Inc. 1958–60; Project Manager Peach Bottom Atomic Power Station 1960–64; Asst. to V.P. 1964–69; Special Applications and Senior Staff Member Gulf General Atomic Inc. 1969–73; Engineering Consultant. Contributor to technical publications. Republican. *Member:* Sigma XI; Fellow Amer. Socy. Mechanical Engineers. *Address:* 12897 Elmfield Lane, Poway, Ca. 92064, U.S.A.

**BORTEN, Per.** Norwegian. *B.* 1913. *Educ.* Norwegian Agricultural University. *Career:* since 1946 in charge of the technical section of the agricultural administration in Sør-Trøndelag). Entered politics in 1945; became Chairman of the municipal council of Flå in the same year; in 1948 he became Chmn. of the provincial council of Sør-Trøndelag. Member of the Storting (parliament) from Sør-Trøndelag for the Agrarian (later Centre) Party 1950— (Chairman of the Party 1955–67, and parliamentary leader 1957–65); Deputy Chairman of the state-owned Housing Bank 1955–65; Chairman of the Council of the United Life Insurance Companies of Norway (Norske forenede livsforsikringsselskaper) 1959—; Prime Minister of Norway 1965–71. Mem. of the Council of the Farmers Bank (Bønderness Bank) 1956–65. He took part in the founding of the Rural Youth League, 1945–47. *Address:* Storting, Oslo, Norway.

**BORTHWICK, A. H.** High Commissioner Sri Lanka. *Address:* Australian High Commission, 3 Cambridge Place, Colombo, Sri Lanka.

**BOSHOFF, Hon. Mr. Justice Wessel Groenewald.** Deputy Judge President of the Supreme Court of South Africa (Transvaal Provincial Divison). *B.* 1916. *Educ.* University of Pretoria (BA; LLB). *M.* 1943, Elizabeth Johanna Louw. *S.* Ben, Jan and Wessel. *Daus.* Annette and Susan. *Career:* Clerk in Civil Service (Public Service Commission) 1937–38; Public Prosecutor, Department of Justice, 1938–41; enrolled and admitted as an Advocate of the Supreme Court of S.A. (Transvaal Provincial Div.) July 1940; practised until elevated to the Bench; appointed Queen's Counsel June 1955;

Judge of the Supreme Court since 1957; Acting Judge President Nov. 1976–Jan. 1977 and May–Dec. 1977. *Address:* Judges' Chambers, Palace of Justice, Pretoria, South Africa.

**BOSQUET, Jean Paul Emile.** Belgian engineer. *B.* 1907. *Educ.* Civil Engineer; Dr. special in mechanics 1934. *M.* 1932, Denyse de Thoran. *S.* Alain, Thierry and Yves. *Career:* Assistant, Univ. of Brussels 1930–37; Engineer in naval dockyard of S.A. Cockerill, Hoboken, Antwerp 1937–41; Extraordinary Professor (acoustics and electro-acoustics; studies and projects relating to chemical plants), Univ. of Brussels 1937—; Engineer-Manager, UCB 1941—. Chairman of the Board, Ranney International S.A. *Publications:* some 45 books and articles, concerning variations, acoustics, launching of large vessels, fluid dynamics, heating, electro dynamics & biographies. *Decorations:* Grand Officer, Order of Leopold II. Member of several engineers' associations and scientific societies. *Address:* Avenue Fond' Roy 70, 1180 Brussels; and *office* Av. F. D. Roosevelt 50, 1050, Brussels, Belgium.

**BOSSOM, Hon. Sir Clive,** Bt, K St. J. British. *B.* 1918. *Educ.* Eton. *M.* 1951, Lady Barbara North. *S.* Bruce, Andrew and James. *Dau.* Arabella. *Career:* Regular Soldier, The Buffs, 1939–48; Member, Kent County Council, 1949–52; Conservative Party Candidate 1951, Faversham Div. Kent, 1955; Member of Parliament for Leominster 1959–74. *Chairman:* Europ. Assistance Ltd.; Royal Automobile Club; RAC Motor Sports Council; Pres. Industrial Fire Protection Assn. of G.B.; Vice-Pres., Anglo-Belgian Union, Vice-Pres., Federation Internationale de L'Automobile. *Director:* Vosper Thornycroft Ltd.; Northern Star Ins. Co.; Anglo Eastern Bank Ltd. *Member:* Joint Cttee. Order of St. John & British Red Cross; Chmn. Ex-Service War Disabled Help Dept. A Liveryman of Grocers; Pavoirs; Needlemakers Companies: *Awards:* Fellow. Royal Society of Arts. Commander of the Order of Leopold (Belgium); Order of Homayoon 3rd Class (Iran). *Clubs:* RAC; The Carlton; M.C.C. *Address:* 3 Eaton Mansions, London, S.W.1.

**BOT, Theodorus Hendrikus.** Netherlands diplomat. *B.* 1911. *Education:* Gymnasium; Univ of Utrecht, Jur Sciences. *M.* 1936, Elisabeth W. van Hal. *S.* 2. *Daus.* 5. *Career.* With East Asiatic Affairs Bureau, Djakarta 1936–42; Japanese P. of war Burma 1942–45; Political Adviser Djakarta 1946–50; Dep. Secy. Gen. Netherlands Indonesian Union 1950–54; Dir. Western Co-operation, Min. of For.-Affairs, The Hague, 1954–59; Parly. Secy. for Interior 1959–63; Min. of Educ. Arts and Sciences 1963–65; Min. without portfolio for devel. countries 1956–67; Netherlands Ambassador in Canada 1968–73; Netherlands Ambassador in Austria since 1973. *Awards:* Knight Commander, Order of Netherlands Lion; Comm. of St. Gregory (Holy See); Knight Grand Cross St. Olav of Norway, Merit (Luxembourg); Crown (Thailand); Republic of Tunisia; San Carlos of Colombia; Knight Commander, Sun of Peru. *Publications:* various articles in political magazines. *Address:* A-1030 Vienna, Jacquingasse 8–10, Austria; and *office* Royal Netherlands Embassy, A-1020 Vienna, Unt Donaustr 13–15, Austria.

**BOTHA, Johan Samuel Frederick.** South African diplomat. *B.* 1919. *Educ.* BAEcon. *M.* 1949. Teresa Monica Robbins. *S.* 3. *Dau.* 1. *Career:* In South African Army 1940–46. South African Embassy Washington 1950–54; S.A. High Commissioner's Office, Ottawa 1954–57; S.A. Permanent Representative to U.N., New York 1957–58; Counsellor for Ministry. Pretoria 1959–62; Consul-General, Tokyo 1962–64; Minister South African Embassy Washington 1964–67; Deputy Secy. Foreign Affairs, Pretoria 1967–71; Ambassador to U.S.A. 1971–75; presently attached to S.A. Ministry, Pretoria. *Address:* 357 StrubenKop, Lynnwood, Pretoria and Dept. of Foreign Affairs, Union Buildings, Pretoria, South Africa.

**BOTHA, Matthys Izak.** South African diplomat. *B.* 1913. *Educ.* Selborne College and University of Pretoria (BA; LLB). *M.* 1940, Hester le Roux Bosman. *S.* Matthys Johannes and Gerhard. *Career:* Dept. of Finance, Pretoria 1931–44; transferred to External Affairs Dept. 1944; South African Embassy, Washington 1944–51; S.A. Permanent Mission to U.N., N.Y. 1951–54; Asst. Secy., Head of Political Div., Dept. of External Affairs, Pretoria 1955–58; Minister to Switzerland 1959–60; Minister of S. Africa in London 1960–62. Ambassador to the U.N. New York, 1962–70 and to Canada 1970–73; Non resident Ambassador to Costa Rica, and El Salvador 1973–74, and to Panama 1973–76; Ambassador in Italy 1973–77, in the U.K. since 1977. Delegate to various sessions at U.N., to several specialized agencies and other nternational conferences. *Address:* South African Embassy, Trafalgar Square, London WC2N 5DP.

**BOTHA, Hon. Michiel Coenraad.** South African. *B.* 1912. *Educ.* Matriculation, BA degree, Higher Education Diploma and BEd. *M.* Lorraine Anna Gouws. *S.* 5. *Daus.* 2. *Career:* Various appointments in primary and High schools in the Transvaal, and lecturer in Afrikaans at the Technical College, Pretoria 1934–43; Asst. Secy., Afrikaanse Taal- en Kulturvereniging (S.A.R. & H.), then National Chief Secy. and editor of the Society's periodical Die Taalgenoot 1943; Elected Member of Parliament for Roodepoort (National Party) 1953; appointed Deputy Minister of Bantu Administration and Development 1960, and Minister of Bantu Administration and Development and of Bantu Education 1966–77. *Address:* P.O. Box 384, Pretoria, South Africa.

**BOTHA, Hon. Pieter Willem,** MP. Minister of Defence, Republic of South Africa; MP for George. *Educ.* Bethlehem and Univ. of Orange Free State, Bloemfontein. *M.* 1943, A. E. Rossouw. *S.* 2. *Daus.* 3. *Address:* P.O. Box 47, Cape Town; and 8th Floor, Voortrekkergedenkgebou, 224 Visagie Street, Pretoria, Republic of South Africa.

**BOTHA, Roelof Frederik.** South African Politician. *B.* 1932. *Educ.* Univ. of Pretoria—BA, LLB. *M.* 1953, Helena Susanna Bosman. *S.* 2. *Daus.* 2. *Career:* Joined S.A. Dept. of Foreign Affairs 1953; Served in S.A. Legation, Stockholm 1956 & S.A. Embassy, Cologne 1960; Transferred to Africa Div., Dept. of Foreign Affairs 1963; Member of S.A. Legal Team in S.W. Africa Case at Int'l. Court of Justice 1963–66 & represented S.A. Gov. as Agent there 1965–66; Appointed Legal Adviser of Dept. of Foreign Affairs 1966; Mem. of S.A. Delegation to 21st, 22nd, 23rd, 24th, 26th, 28th & 29th sessions of U.N. General Assembly in 1966, '67, '68, '69, '71, '73 & '74 respectively; Promoted to Under-Sec. in Dept. of Foreign Affairs 1968 & Head of S.W. Africa & U.N. Sections in Dept.; National Party M.P. for Wonderboom 1970; Mem. of S.A. Legal Team in advisory proceedings of Int'l. Court of Justice on S.W. Africa 1970–71; served on a number of select cttees. of S.A. Parliament, incl. Cttee. on Public Accounts 1970–74; Sec. of Foreign Affairs Study Group of National Party's M.P.'s 1974; S.A. Perm. Rep. & Amb. Extraordinary & Plenipotentiary to the U.N. 1974: Advocate of Supreme Court of S.A.; Amb. to the U.S. 1975; Appointed Minister of Foreign Affairs, April 1977; National Party M.P. for Westdene, May 1977. *Address:* Ministry of Foreign Affairs, Pretoria, South Africa.

**BOTTOMLEY, Rt. Hon. Arthur George,** PC, OBE, MP (Lab., Teeside, Middlesbrough). *B.* 1907. *M.* 1936, Bessie Ellen Wiles. *Career:* Parliamentary Under-Secretary of State for Dominions 1946–47; Secretary for Overseas Trade 1947-51; Secretary of State for Commonwealth Relations 1964–66. Minister of Overseas Development 1966–67. *Address:* 19 Lichfield Road, Woodford Green, Essex.

**BOTTOMLEY, Sir James Reginald Alfred,** KCMG. British diplomat. *B.* 1920. *Educ.* King's Coll. School Wimbledon; Trinity Coll. Cambridge. *M.* 1941, Barbara Evelyn Vardon. *S.* 2. *Daus.* 2. *Career:* Served with Inns of Court Regiment RAC 1940–46; Dominions Office 1946–48; Pretoria 1948–50; Commonwealth Relations Office 1951–53; Karachi 1953–55; Washington 1955–59; UK Mission to United Nations 1959; Head, Economic Policy Dept. Commonwealth Relations Office 1959–61; Head, Common Market Dept. CRO 1961–63; Deputy High Comm. Kuala Lumpur 1963–67; Asst. Under Secy. of State Commonwealth Office, Later Foreign & Commonwealth Office 1967–70; Deputy Under Secy. of State Foreign & Commonwealth Office 1970–72; Ambassador to South Africa 1973–76; Perm. Rep. at Geneva since 1976. *Award:* Knight Commander of St. Michael and St. George. *Address:* Chiltern Rise, Aldbury, Tring. Hertfordshire; and *office* United Kingdom Mission, 37–39 Rue De Vermont, Geneva, Switzerland.

**BOTTOMLEY, Peter James,** MP. British Industrial Economist. *B.* 1944. *Educ.* Trinity Coll., Cambridge—BA (Econ.). *M.* 1967, Virginia Garnett, JP, BA, MSc. *S.* 1. *Dau.* 1. *Career:* Lorry Driver 1966; Salesman 1967–68; Industrial Relations Officer 1969; Marketing Manager 1970–71; Industrial Consultant 1972–73; Managing Director 1974–75; Conservative M.P. for Woolwich West since 1975. *Member:* Chmn. British Union of Family Organizations; Vice-Pres., Conservative Trade Unionists National Advisory Cttee; Transport & General Workers Union. *Address:* 2 St. Barnabas Villas, London SW8 2EH; and House of Commons, London SW1A 0AA.

**BOTTS, Guy Warren.** Lawyer and corporation executive. *B.* 1914. *Educ.* Univ. of Florida (LLB 1937); admitted to Florida Bar JD. 1937. *M.* 1939, Edith M. Huddleston. *S.* William. *Dau.* Edith (Cockrel). *Career:* Chmn. Bd. Barnett Banks, Florida Inc; Chmn. Bd. Chmn. Exec. Cttee. Barnett Bank, Jacksonville, N.A.; Chmn. Bd. Barnett-Winston Co.; Member Exec. Cttee. Dir. at Large, National Bank Americard Inc.; Member Exec. Cttee. Assn. Registered Bank Holding Companies; Dir. Barnett Mortgage Advisers Inc.; Barnett Mortgage Co.; Florida Publishing Co.; Argyle Southern Co., Jacksonville, Florida; Jacksonville Branch, Federal Reserve Bank, Atlanta. Chief Exec. Officer and Director, Barnett National Bank of Jacksonville; Title Officer, Title Insurance Co. of Minnesota. Inc., Council Tool Co., Argyle Southern Co. *Member:* Governing Council Amer. Bankers Assn; Trustee, Barnett-Winston Investment Trust; Trustee, Barnett Mortgage Trust. Member: Bd. Trustees, Jacksonville Univ.; Bd. Dirs., Florida Council of 100; Exec. Bd., Boys Home Assn; Jacksonville Cttee. 100; Mayor's Adv. Council of Employment; Adv. Cttee. Technical Education, Jacksonville Area Chamber of Commerce; Bd. Dirs., Downtown Development Council; Planning & Renewal Cttee.; Downtown Dev. Council; Jacksonville Area Chamber of Commerce; American, Florida and Jacksonville (Past Pres.) Bar Associations; Amer. Judicature Socy; Amer. Law Inst.; Phi Eta Sigma; Phi Alpha Delta; Alpha Kappa Psi; Delta Tau Delta. *Publications:* British Statutes in Force in Florida; Banks; Banking Section of Florida Law & Practice. *Clubs:* Florida Yacht; Ponte Vedre; (Dir. & Pres.); Meninak; Timuquana Country; The River; Newcomen Society. *Address:* 100 Laura St. Jacksonville, Fla. 32202, USA and 3013 Doctor's Lake Drive, Orange Park, Florida 32073, U.S.A.

**BOUCHAYER, Jean.** French. *B.* 1893. *Educ.* Bachelor of Science and Letters. *M.* 1918, Marcelle Valerien Perrin. *S.* Robert and François. *Daus.* Renée Delasus and Nicole Constant. Chairman (Hon.) Establissement Bouchayer et Vialler; Chairman (Hon.) Caisse d'Epargne de Grenoble (savings bank); Comite Grenoblois d'Aide au logement (housing committee) *Decoration:* Officer, Legion of Honour (France) and Nat. Order of Merit. *Address:* 157 Avenue de l'Eygala, 38 La Tronche (Isère), France.

**BOUCHON (Albert Adolphe) Antoine.** French. *B.* 1905. *Educ.* School of Higher Commercial Studies (BSc; Lic. en droit). *M.* 1934, Solange Charoy. *Daus.* Nadine (Corbel), Anne (Droulers). Marie-Odile (Servel de Cosmi) Catherine (Ctesse de Haut de Sigy) and Béatrice (Ferri). Officier, Legion of Honour. President d'Honneur, Générale Sucrière 1973, also President Sucreries & Raffineries Bouchon & Pajot, Paris, April 1959—; President Credit Sucrier et Alimentaire 1974. *Clubs:* Automobile Club de France. *Address:* 132, Avenue de Malakoff, Paris 75116 and Chateau de Bigards 27550 Nassandres, and *office* 25 Avenue Franklin D. Roosevelt, Paris 75008, France.

**BOULADOUX, Maurice.** French, Counsellor of State 1964—; Hon. Chairman CFDT (CFTC) 1961—; Administrator, Crédit Lyonnais 1961—. Administrator Banque Francaise du commere extérieur 1967—. Chairman and Director-General, Société Immobilière MTC 1961—. International appointments: Chairman, CMT 1961—; member, Economic Cttee. of the Common Mkt. 1958—; Vice-Pres. since 1970. *B.* 1907. *M.* 1927, Marcelle Müntz-Berger. *S.* Michel and Jean. Secy. 1936–47, General Secy. 1947–53, Chmn. 1953–61 CFTC. *Member:* Conseil Economique et Social Français 1947–57, and of Administrative Council of BIT (Geneva) 1960–63. *Publications:* many articles and reviews on trade union topics. Cmdr., Legion of Honour, Comdr. of Mérite National; Comdr., Economique Nationale; Médaille d Or des Syndicats Professionals; Officier de l'Ordre de la Courronne de Belgique; Commandier de l'Ordre du Grand Duché de Luxembourg (1974). *Address:* 98 *bis* rue St. Prix, St. Leu La Forêt (Val d'Oise), France; and *office* 26 rue de Montholon Paris IX, France.

**BOULTON, Capt. Albert Norman,** MBE, VRD, BCom, AAUQ. *B.* 1904. *Educ.* Brentwood Grammar School and University of Brisbane (Bachelor of Commerce; Associate in Accountancy, Queensland). *M.* 1956, Sophie Burns. *Career:* Examiner of Masters and Mates, Sydney 1935, and Brisbane 1936; Commanding Officer, H.M.A.S. *Fremantle* 1942–46; Deputy Director of Lighthouses and Navigation, Western Australia 1946, and Victoria 1953; Principal Nautical and Ship Surveyor 1955; Chmn., Marine Council 1959–64; Delegate to Safety at Sea Conv., London 1960; Leader of Aust. Delegation to Pollution of Sea by Oil Conf., London 1962. Deputy Master, Company of Master Mariners 1939, and 1963; President: Legacy, Fremantle 1948, and Rotary, Fremantle 1953; Chairman, Mission to Seamen 1954; Director of Navigation, Commonwealth of Australia 1959–64. Director, R. W. Miller & Co. Ltd. 1965–67 Director, Royal Humane Socy. of Australia 1965–71; Chairman Committee of Advice (Manning), Dept.; Shipping and Transport 1967—69. *Member:* State Executive of Returned Soldiers & Sailors Assn. 1950—53; President, Navy League 1959 and 1963. *Clubs:* Naval & Military, Savage (Melbourne); Barwon Heads Golf (Victoria). *Address:* The Avenue, Ocean Grove, Vic., Australia.

**BOUMEDIENNE, Houari.** Head of State of Algeria. *B.* 1927. *Educ.* Islamic Inst., Constantine, & Cairo. *Career:* Former teacher, Guelma; Commander of Wilaya 1955–57; Chief of Staff of the FLN 1960–62; Minister of Defence since 1962; First Dep. Premier 1963–65; Pres. of the Council of the Revolution & of the Council of Ministers since 1965. *Address:* Office of the Council of the Revolution, Algiers, Algeria.

**BOURASSA, Robert.** Canadian. Prime Minister of Quebec 1970–76. *B.* 1933. *Educ.* Jean-de-Brébeuf Coll. (BA); Graduated Law Faculty, Univ. of Montreal; Political and Economic Science Oxford England (Masters Degree); Public Finance & Corporate Law, Harvard University. *M.* 1958, Andrée Simard. *S.* 1. *Dau.* 1. *Career:* Fiscal Adviser, Dept. Nat. Revenue, taught Economics & Public Finance, Ottawa Univ. 1960–63; Secy. Dir. of Research, Belanger Commission on Public Finance 1963–65; Member, Nat. Assembly for Mercier 1966–76; President Political Commission; Member Party's Stragegy Cttee.; Leader Quebec Liberal Party 1970–77; Prime Minister of Quebec 1970–76; Minister of Finance May–Nov. 1970; Minister of Inter-Governmental Affairs 1971–72. *Address:* c/o National Assembly, Quebec City, P.Q., Canada.

**BOURASSA, Yves Gustave.** Canadian advertising company executive. *B.* 1910. *Educ.* Université de Montreal (BA 1930). *M.* 1937, Marcelle Landreau. *Daus.* Liette Ferron and Danièle. *Career:* Announcer, program Dir. Radio Station CKAC 1932–40; served Canadian Army Lieut. to Lieut.-colonel 1940–45; with Spitzer & Mills Advt. 1945–46; Founder, Mgr. French Adv. Services 1946–49; Dir. Vice-Pres. Partner, Walsh Advertising Co. 1949–60; Sen. Vice-Pres. Manager, French Services McCann-Erickson (Canada) Ltd. 1960–63; Commissaires Gén. des Fêtes du Canada Francais 1963–64; Pres., Bourassa, Gagnon et Associés Ltee 1964–67; Sen. Vice-Pres., BCP Advertising Ltd. 1967–72; Chmn. Communicators Group Inc. Member, Provincial Council, St. John Ambulance; Montreal Chamber, Commerce. *Awards:* Knight Commander Military and Hospitaller Order of St. Lazarus; Named member Order of British Empire; Offi, Order of St. John of Jerusalem; Guest Lect. Univ. de Montreal. *Clubs:* Saint-Denis (Montreal, Quebec). *Address:* 428 Strathcona Drive, Mount Royal, Quebec; and *office* 1010 Ste-Catherine W. Montreal, Quebec, H3B 1G3, Canada.

**BOURDEILLETTE, Jean Adolphe.** L. ès L., L. en D.; French diplomat. *B.* 24 Oct. 1901. *M.* 1926, Antoinette Bourdeillette. *Dau.* Anne. *Career:* Assistant Consul Nov. 1925; Résidence Générale, Tunis Dec. 1925; Clerk to General Secretariat of Conference of Ambassadors Dec. 1928; Third Secretary, Vienna 1930; Clerk to Central Administration 1931; member. French Delegation to Stresa Conference 1932; Consul. Nuremberg 1933, Frankfurt-am-Main 1938, Genoa 1939; Chief of Section Central Administration 1942; relieved of post by Vichy Govt. 1943; First Counsellor, Vatican City 1944; Ambassador to Venezuela 1949–52; to Denmark 1952–58; Central Administration 1958; Ambassador to Israel 1959–65. Cmdr. de la Légion d'Honneur. *Publications:* Simulacres; Les étoiles dans la main; Reliques des Songes; La Pierre et L'anémone; Saison des Ombres; Pour Israël. *Address:* Brantöme (Dordogne), France.

**BOURDET, Claude.** French journalist. *B.* 1909. *Educ.* Collége de Normandie; Lycée Hoche (Special Mathematics); Ecole Polytechnique Fédérale de Zürich (grad. Ingénieur Diplômé). *M.* 1935, Ida Adamoff. *S.* Nicolas and Louis. *Dau.* Catherine. Member, Order of the Liberation; returned other awards (Legion of Honour) to the President in 1955, as a protest against the rearmament of Germany. Laboratory work 1935; Asst. to Minister of National Economy 1936; Artillery Lieut. 1939; commenced underground activity autumn of 1940; member, Executive Combat underground movement 1942, and of the National Council of the Resistance 1943; arrested by Gestapo and deported to Oranienburg and Buchenwald

1944; returned to France and became Vice Pres., Natl. Consultative Assembly 1945; Director-General, Radiodiffusion française 1945; Editor and Publisher, Combat daily paper 1947–50; Dir. France-Observateur 1950–1963 (resigned) Elected member, Paris Town Council 1959–71; foreign editor, Temoignage Chrétien, wkly. mag. since 1967. *Chairman:* Movement for Disarmament, Peace and Liberty. *Member:* Nat. Exec. United Socialist Party; International Confederation for Disarmament and Peace (one of Presidents); United Socialist Party. *Publications:* Le schisme yougoslave, (1950), Les Chemins de l'Unite (1964); A qui appartient Paris? (1972); L'aventure incertaine (1975); L'Europe Truquée (1977). *Club:* French Alpine. *Address:* 47 Avenue d'Iéna, Paris 75116, France.

**BOURGUIBA, Habib.** Tunisian. Life President of Tunisia. *B.* 1903. *Educ.* Sadiki College, Carnot Lyceum (Tunis), Sorbonne (Law Deg.), and Ecole des Sciences Politiques (Diploma). *Career:* As a student in Paris, he sympathized with the Destour movement (the only Tunisian opposition to French rule), but he split with the movement, which was composed of intellectuals cut off from the people, and (in March 1934) formed the Neo-Destour Party (to inspire national awareness) open to all young men from all classes of Tunisian society. He was arrested and placed in a concentration camp. 1934–36; re-arrested and imprisoned without trial 1938–43; escaped and reached Cairo, where, with other nationalists he set up an office to further the cause of N. African nationalism. Went to Paris with a programme of reforms to discuss with the French Government April 1950. When the Tunisian Government appealed to U.N. (14 Jan 1952) he was again arrested after delivering speeches in N. Tunisia; the people rose in revolt, and he was sent to a concentration camp in the Sahara, later placed in solitary confinement on the Isle of La Gallite, and in May 1954, sent to Croix Island (off the coast of Brittany); later he was transferred to the Château of la Ferté. Successful negotiations led the French Gov. to grant home-rule to a Nationalist-sponsored cabinet, and he returned home on 1 June 1955, The National Day of Victory. The independence of Tunisia was proclaimed on 20 March 1956, and some days later M. Bourguiba was elected Chmn. of the Constituent Assembly 9 April 1956; Pres. of Tunisia since 1957. Elected by universal suffrage 1959, 1964, 1969; Elected President for Life 1975. *Publications:* Le Destour et la France (1937), and La Tunisie et la France (1954), some 1,000 speeches and lectures in French, Arabic and English. *Address:* Presidency of the Republic, Carthage, Tunisia.

**BOURGUIBA, Habib, Jr.** Tunisian. *B.* 1927. *Educ.* Elementary Diploma in Arabic, Diploma for completed prog. at Sadiki College (first part of Baccalaureat Moderne: mathematics and spoken languages; second part Philosophy; Graduated from Law School, Paris-Grenoble). *M.* 1954. *Children* 3. *Career:* Collaborated with the national liberation movement, especially during 1951–54; Lawyer in training at Tunis 1954–56; participated in the setting up of the Dept. of Foreign Affairs. Counsellor of Embassy, Washington July 1956–Sept. 1957; represented Tunisian Govt. at the ceremonies following independence of Federation of Malaya; Ambassador to Rome, 1957–58, Paris 1958–61 and Washington, Ottawa and Mexico 1961–63, Secy. of State for Foreign Affairs 1964–70; represented Tunis at the sub-committee for Laos of the Security Council of U.N., Sept. 1959; the Congo (Léopoldville), 1960, Argentine 1963, Indonesia and Malaysia 1967; member, Tunisian delegation at XV Session of U.N., Sept.–Dec. 1960; attended the Rambouillet talks between President de Gaulle and President Bourguiba. Elected Member of Parliament, Nov. 1964. Secretary General of the Presidency of the Republic 1963–64; special missions to, Dakar, New Delhi, Middle East and Morocco; Minister of Justice June–Oct. 1970, Resigned from Public Office for health reasons; Pres., Banque de Devéloppement Economique de Tunisie (Formerly Société Nationale d'Investissement) since 1971. Member of the Council of the Republic; Deputy Mayor of Monastin. *Awards:* Grand Cordon, Order of the Republic (Tunisia); Cordon, Order of Independence. *Address:* Banque de Devéloppement Economique de Tunisie, Tunis, Tunisia.

**BOURKE, Sir Paget John,** SC. Judge. *B.* 1906. *Educ.* Mount St. Mary's College, Chesterfield; Trinity College, Dublin (Mod. BA; LLB). *M.* 1936, Susan Dorothy Killeen. *S.* 3. *Dau.* 1. *Career:* Barrister-at-Law, King's Inns 1928; Legal Adviser and Crown Prosecutor, Seychelles 1933; Chief Magistrate, Palestine 1936; Relieving President of District Court 1941; President 1945; Judge of Supreme Court of Kenya 1946; Gray's Inn, 1957; Chief Justice, Sierra Leone 1955–57; Chief Justice, Cyprus 1957–60; Acting Chief Justice, Gibraltar, Oct.–Nov., 1968. Judge of Court of Appeal for Bahamas and Bermuda 1965—, also British Honduras 1968—. President 1970–75 (retired as President); Judge of Court of Appeal for Gibraltar since 1970. *Publication:* Digest of Cases, Seychelles 1870–1933. *Address:* 9 Barnacoille Park, Dalkey, Co. Dublin, Eire.

**BOURN, James.** British Diplomat (Ret'd). *B.* 1917. *Educ.* Queen Elizabeth Grammar School, Darlington. *M.* 1944, Isobel Mackenzie. *S.* 1. *Career:* Assist. Insp. Min. of Health 1936–39; War Service 1939–46; Min. of Nat. Ins. 1946–47; Colonial Office 1947–61; Commonwealth Relations Office 1961–63; First Secy. Brit. High Commission Tanganyika 1963–64; Deputy High Commissioner Zanzibar 1964–65; Malawi 1966–70; Brit. Ambassador Somalia 1970–73; Brit. Consul-General, Istanbul 1973–75. *Address:* c/o Lloyds Bank, 46 Victoria Street, London SW1.

**BOURNE, Stafford.** British. *B.* 1900. *Educ.* Rugby School and Corpus Christi, Cambridge (MA); and in France. *M.* 1940, Magdalene Jane Leeson. *S.* Edward Leeson Stafford. *Dau.* Virginia Claire Stafford. *Career:* with Bourne & Hollingsworth Ltd. Co. Founder and First President of the Oxford Street Association (1958–68), War of 1939–45, Admiralty Ferry Crews. Life Pres. of Bourne & Hollingsworth Ltd., Chairman 1938–72. *Clubs:* United Oxford & Cambridge Univ.; Royal Cruising. *Address:* Drokes, Beaulieu, nr. Brockenhurst, Hants.; and *office* Bourne & Hollingsworth Ltd., Oxford Street, London, W.1.

**BOURSEAU, Marcel.** French. *B.* 1907. *Educ.* LLD. *M.* 1950, Yvonne Gardon. *Daus.* Christine, Françoise, Martine and Michelle. *Career:* Chmn., National Union of the French Hotel Industry 1948—. Director, Caisse Centrale de Crédit Hôtelier 1951—; Chmn. of International Hotel Association. *Publications:* Traité pratique de l'Industrie hôtelière, (1955); L'Equipement Hôtelier (1966); La Gestion Hôtelière 1974). *Address:* 68 Boulevard de Courcelles, Paris 17; and *office* 22 rue d'Anjou, Paris 8, France.

**BOUVIER, John André, Jr.** American. Attorney General Counsel, Patterson & Maloney, Lawyers. *B.* 1903. *Educ.* Davidson Coll., Univ. of Florida (AB, LLB, JD 1968), and Northwestern Univ. (MBA). *M.* 1928, Helen Schaefer. *S.* John A. III and Thomas Richardson. *Dau.* Helen Elizabeth (Richards). *Career:* Dir. Farquhar Mach. Co. 1938–50; Pres., Prosperity Co. 1954–56; Vice-Chmn. Ward Industries Corp. 1956–58; Pres., Prosperity Exporting Corp. (plant in Brussels) 1954–58; Consultant, Ward Industries Corp. 1958–59; Pres. and Chmn. of Board, Pantex Mfg. Corp. (plant in Winschoten, Holland); Pres., Pantex of Canada 1959–60; President: West Kingsway Inc., East Kingsway Inc., South Kingsway Inc. (all 1950—), Knaust Bros. Inc. 1961–65; K-B Products Corp., 1961–65; Iron Mountain Atomic Storage Corp. 1961–65; Farm Industries Inc. 1961–65. Secretary: Knight Manor No. 1 Inc. and No. 2 Inc. 1948—, 50th Street Heights Inc. 1948—, South Central Manor Inc. 1948—, and Karen Garden Inc.; Pres. and Dir. Dade Frutkoff Inc.; National Leasing Inc.; Dir. Landmark Banking Corp.; Ocean First National Bank. Chmn. Trustee First Presbyterian Church. F. Lauderdale, Fla. Director and Vice-Chairman, National Parkinson Foundation; Chmn., Exec. Committee, The Permutit Co. 1955–57; Dade County Zoning & Planning Boards 1948–56; Syracuse Govt. Research Bureau 1955–58. Trustee, Windham College, Putney, Vermont. *Publications:* Legal Aspects of Municipal Ownership (monograph); What's Wrong With Home Financing? (research report); A Synopsis of the Federal Home Loan Bank Act (a series of articles). *Member:* Dade County, Florida and American Bar Associations; American Judicature Socy.; Washington Lawyers Club: Acad. of Political Science; Field Commr. Boy Scouts of America (Dade County). Mason; Shriner; B.P.O. Elks; Dir. Boys Club. *Clubs:* Sigma Chi Fraternity; Miami Beach Rod & Reel; Ponte Vedra; Rotary; Tower; Admiral's; *Address:* 2756 N.E. 17th Street, Fort Lauderdale, Fla. 33305; and *office* 6888 N.W. 7th Avenue, Miami, Fla., U.S.A. (Also an office in Kenann Building, Fort Lauderdale.)

**BOVELL, The Hon. Sir (William) Stewart,** JP. *B.* 1906. *Career:* Banking 1924–40, Commissioned Active Service, Royal Australian Air Force 1940–45; Former Member, Legislative Assembly of Western Australia for Vasse 1947–71. Minister for Lands, Forests and Immigration 1959–71. Agent General for Western Australia 1971–75. Member, Liberal Party of Australia. *Address:* 24 West Street, Busselton, W.A. 6280, Australia.

**BOW, Malcolm Norman.** *B.* 1918. *Educ.* Univ. of British Columbia (BA 1948), Univ. of Alberta, and Acad. of International Law (Diploma). *M.* 1945, Betty Roberts. *S.* Paul (*Dec'd.*), Michael and Neil. *Dau.* Jane. *Career:* with Canadian Army (discharged Major) 1940–46; Vancouver Daily Province 1946–49; Vice Consul, N.Y.C. 1950–53; Dept. External Affairs 1953–56; First Secy. Madrid 1956–59; Chargé d'Affaires 1958–59; Dept. External Affairs, Ottawa 1960; Counsellor, Chargé d'Affairs Havana 1961; Special Asst. to Secy. of State for External Affairs 1962–64; Canadian Ambassador to Czechoslovakia, June 1964–68; and concurrently to Hungary, April 1965–July 1968; Dir., Arms Control and Disarmament Division 1968–71; Dir. Latin American Division, Dept. of External Affairs, Ottawa. 1971–73; Canadian Ambassador to Cuba 1973–75, and concurrently to Haiti 1974–75; Dir.-Gen. of Security & Intelligence, Ottawa 1975–76. *Member:* Professional Association, Foreign Service Officers; Canadian Inst. for International Affairs; U.N. Assn. *Club:* Rockcliffe Lawn Tennis (Ottawa). *Address:* 161 Manor Ave., Rockcliffe Park, Ottawa, Ont. and *office* LB Peterson Bldg., Sussex Drive, Ottawa, Canada.

**BOWATER, Sir Noël Vansittart,** Bt, GBE, MC. *B.* 1892. *Educ.* Rugby. *M.* 1921, Constance Heiton Bett. *S.* 1. *Daus.* 2. *Career:* Commissioned Territorial Force Royal Artillery 1913; served in France 1915–19 (MC); Sheriff of City of London 1948–49; Lord Mayor 1953–54; Gov. of Hon. The Irish Soc. 1961–63; Master of The Worshipful Co. of Vintners 1954–55; K.St.J.; Kt. Cmdr. Order of the North Star (Sweden), and of the Order of Menelik II (Ethiopia). *Clubs:* City Livery, United Wards, St. James', Guildhall. *Address:* Conifers, Old Avenue, St. George's Hill, Weybridge, Surrey.

**BOWEN, Charles Corbin.** American management consultant. *B.* 1897. *Educ.* Univ of California (BS); Harvard University (MBA). *M.* 1928, Mildred Virginia Moore. *Dau.* Jane Bowen Ericson. *Career:* Special Representative in Europe, U.S. Department of Agriculture 1923–24; Export Manager, Sun Maid Raisin Growers, Fresno, Calif. 1924–25; Head, Research Department, Tucker, Hunter Dulin & Co., Los Angeles 1925–28; Chief, California State Bureau of Commerce, Sacramento 1929–30; Vice-President and Director, American Trust Co., affiliates, San Francisco 1931–33; Executive Vice-President, Bishop Trust Co., Honolulu 1935–37; Assistant to Director, Reconstruction Finance Corp., Washington, D.C. 1934. (C.P.A.) and Management Consultant, Charles C. Bowen & Co., San Francisco 1938—; Director, President, Portland (Ore.) Transit Co. 1946—; President, Treasurer and Director, Rose City Transit Co., Portland; Pres. and Director: Pacific Associates, Inc., San Francisco; President, Treas., Dir., Landport Co. Inc., Portland, Ore.; Exec. Vice-Pres. & Dir., Empire Factors, San Francisco; Dir., American Transit Assn., Washington, D.C. *Clubs:* Harvard, Pinnacle (N.Y.C.); California (Los Angeles); Arlington; Multnomah (Portland); Olympic; Merchants Exchange (San Francisco); Capitol Hill (Washington). *Address:* 662 Russ Building, San Francisco 94104, Calif., U.S.A.

**BOWEN, Otis Ray,** MD. American physician and politician. *B.* 1918. *Education:* Indiana Univ., AB. (Chem) 1939; Indiana Univ School of Medicine, MD, 1942. *M.* 1939, Elizabeth Steinmann. *S.* 3. *Dau.* 1. *Career:* War Service 1st Lieut US Army Medical Corps, later Captain, 1942–46; General Practice of Medicine 1946–72; Marshall County (Indiana) Coroner 1952–56; Indiana State Representative 1957–73; Governor of Indiana since 1973. *Member:* American Med. Assn.; Ind. State Med. Assn.; Alpha Omega Alpha, Phi Beta Pi; Delta Chi; American Academy of Gen. Practitioners; Bremen Chamber of Commerce; Kiwanis; American Legion, Veterans of Foreign Wars; American Farm Bureau; Indiana Mental Health Assn.; Indiana Univ. Alumni Assn.; Trudeau Socy. *Decorations:* Dr. Benjamin Rush Award (Am. Med. Assn.); Ind. Public Health Assn. Merit Award, 1971; Ind. Univ. School of Medicine Alumnus of Year, 1971; Hon. LLD: Butler Univ., Indiana Univ., Valparaiso Univ., Anderson Coll., Vincennes Univ., Tri-State Univ., Calumet Coll., Univ. of Evansville, Indiana State Univ., Rose-Hulman Inst. *Address* and *office:* State Capitol, Indianopolis, Indiana 46204, U.S.A.

**BOWEN, William Albert.** American management consultant. *B.* 1919. *Educ.* Butler Univ. (AB) and Harvard (MBS). *M.* 1947, Virginia Phillips. *Daus.* 2 *Career:* US Navy (Lt.) 1941–46; With Rhode Island Hospital Trust Co. (from clerk to Vice-President) 1947–62; Director, Retail Trade Board of Providence 1955–62; Pres. Planations Bank RI 1962–68; On purchase by Old Stone Trust Co. and Old Stone Savings Bank became Vice-Pres. of both banks (Gen. Admin. and Ops.) 1965–69; Pres. Bank of Milwaukee and Trust Co. 1969–71; Pres. Whitefish Bay Bank and Trust Co. (Milwauk) 1969–71; Vice-Pres. Inland Financial Corp. 1969–71; Pres. and Chief Exec. Off. Calumet Nat. Bank, Hammond (Ind) 1971–73; Pres. and Chief Exec. Off. Continental Bank of Cleveland 1973–75; Resigned and became self-employed Mgmt. Consultant since 1975. Mayor's Voluntary O.P.S. Supervisory Board 1949; Eastern States Exposition Commission for R.I. 1951; Chmn., Warwick Citizens Committee for Public Schools 1953–54; Dir., National Conf. of Christians & Jews 1950— (Treas. 1951–57), R.I. Community Chests Inc. (General Campaign Chairman 9154, Director 1955); Director, United Fund of R.I. Inc. 1955–62. *Member:* Corporation, Providence T.B. League, Providence Building Sanitary and Educational Assn., Hospital Service. *Director* Am. R.I. (Treas. 1951) heart associations, (Sr. Adviser Jr. Achievement, R.I., 1950, Dir. 1951, V.P. 1955,); Dir. R.I. Philharmonic Orchestra, 1950–57, Chmn. 1951; *Member:* Providence Jr. C. of C. (V.P. 1949, Dir. 1948–51, Pres. 1950); C. of C. (Vice Chmn. Membership Com. 1954, Mem, Adv. Com. Conv. Bur.); Harvard Bus. School Assn. (Chmn. Alumna R.I. 1950–56); Treas. Bristol Art Museum, 1963; Pres., R.I. Bankers Assn. 1967–68, Narragansett Council Boy Scouts of America 1965–71; Dist. Chmn. Calumet Council; Dir. Downtown Hammond Council; St. Margaret Hospital Citizens Board; Vice Chmn. Bd. of Jr. Achievement of Hammond-East Chicago. *Clubs:* Canterbury Gold Club, Inc; Cleveland Athletic Club; Cleveland Racquet Club; Cleveland Wine and Food Society; Clevelander Club; Fork and Fiddle; Mid-Day Clambake Club of Newport, Rhode Island; Harvard Club of NYC; University Clubs of Chicago & Milwaukee; Columbia Club of Indianapolis. *Address:* 6674 Gates Mills Boulevard, Gates Mills, Ohio 44040, U.S.A.

**BOWER, Marvin.** American management consultant. *B.* 1903. *Educ.* Brown University (PhB); Harvard Law School (LLB); Harvard Business School (MBA). *M.* 1927, Helen M. McLaughlin. *S.* Peter H., Richard H. and James M. *Career:* Lawyer, Jones, Day, Cockley & Reavis, Cleveland, O. 1930–33. Associated with McKinsey & Co. Inc. since 1933; Managing Director 1950–67; McKinsey & Co. Inc. Sept. 1950—; Chmn., McKinsey Foundation for Management Research Inc. Aug. 1952—. Member, Massachusetts and Ohio Bars. *Publications:* Development of Executive Leadership; The Will to Manage (1966). *Member:* Committee for Economic Development (Trustee, Harvard Business School (Member Visiting Cttee.)). *Clubs:* Sky; University; Blind Brook (N.Y.C.). *Address:* 44 Greenfield Avenue, Bronxville, N.Y.; and *office* 245 Park Ave., New York, N.Y., 10017, U.S.A.

**BOWES, Frederick, Jr.** American. *B.* 1908. *Educ.* Dartmouth Coll. (AB); Harvard Univ. Graduate School of Business Admin (AMP). *M.* 1940, Priscilla Herron. *S.* 2. *Career:* Ret'd. Vice-Pres., International Operations, Pitney-Bowes Inc.; 2nd Dir. of its British, Canadian, German & French subsidiaries; *Clubs:* Country Club of New Canaan; Past Pres., Public Relations Socy. of America; Mem. International Public Relations Association. *Address:* 130 Ramhorne Rd., New Canaan, Connecticut, U.S.A.; and *office* 69 Walnut Street, Stamford, Conn., U.S.A.

**BOWES, Harold Leslie,** KCMG, CBE. British. *B.* 1893. *M.* (1) *S.* 2. *Dau.* 1. (2) Catherine Roberts. *Dau.* 1. *Career:* Joined Royal Mail Steam Company 1911, Chmn., and Managing Director of Royal Mail Lines and the Pacific Steam Navigation Company; Director: Rea Brothers Ltd., Ocean Wilsons (Holdings) Ltd.; Vice-President, Anglo-Chilean Society. Vice-President: Anglo Peruvian Society; Anglo Brazilian Society and of Hispanic & Luso-Brazilian Councils; Liveryman & Prime Warden (1964–65) of the Court of Assistants, Worshipful Company of Shipwrights, Member of Committee of Canning Club, Member of Executive Committee, Anglo-Portuguese Society, Member of Council and Past President, City Livery Club, Member of Council Brazilian Chamber of Commerce & Economic Affairs in Great Britiain 1968—, Hon. Vice-President, British Ship Adoption Socy. 1968—. Chmn., of British Chamber of Commerce in Chile, Maritime and Ports Chamber, British Nat., Service Committee in Valparaiso which organized local war effort and also of British Patriotic Fund, Chief Industrial Security Officer for Chile (unpaid) under Sir Connop Gutherie's leadership from N.Y. Mem., Council of Central Chamber of Commerce in Chile, Governor, City of Liverpool College of Commerce 1958–60, Chmn., Port of Liverpool Stevedoring Co., Ltd., 1958–65, Liverpool Chamber of Commerce 1957–58, Hispanic & Luso-Brazilian Councils 1965–66. In 1941 organized Chilean British Cultural Society in Valparaiso in collaboration with British Council. *Clubs:* Canning, City Livery. *Address:* 7 Chester Row, London, SW1 W 9JF; and Kings House, 36–37 King St., London, E.C.2.

**BOWKER, Sir (Reginald) James**, GBE, KCMG. British. *B.* 1901. *Educ.* Oxford Univ. (BA). *M.* 1947, Elsa Elizabeth Gued. *Career:* Ambassador to: Burma 1948–50, Turkey 1954–58, Austria 1958–61; Asst. Under-Secretary of State, Foreign Office 1950–53; Asst. Managing Director, Arthur Guinness Son & Co. (Park Royal) 1962–66. Member London Committee, Ottoman Bank since 1961. *Club:* Brooks's. *Address:* 3 West Eaton Place, London, SW1X 8LU.

**BOWLES, Hon. Chester.** American. *B.* 1901. *Educ.* Choate School; Yale (BS). *M.* 1934, Dorothy Stebbins. *S.* Chester, Samuel. *Daus.* Barbara, Cynthia, Sally. *Career:* Employed by Springfield Republican 1924–25; with George Batten Co. 1925–29; established Benton & Bowles Inc., New York 1929, Chmn. of the Board 1936—41; Connecticut State Director, Office of Price Administration 1942–43; appointed Prise Administrator 1943; and Director Office of Economic Stabilization Feb. 1946, resigned July 1946; member of War Production Board and Petroleum Council for War 1943–46; Chmn. of Econ. Stabilization Board 1946; Delegate from Connecticut to Democratic National Convention June 1940, 1948–56; Delegate to UNESCO Conference, Paris Nov.–Dec. 1946; Special Assistant to Secretary-General U.N. 1946–47; Chmn., International Children's Fund 1947–48; Member Democratic Adv. Council on Foreign Affairs; Trustee, Woodrow Wilson, Franklin D. Roosevelt, Rockefeller Foundations; Dir., Inst. of International Education. Inst of African-American Relations, and Fund for Peaceful Atomic Development. Chubb Fellow, Yale 1957; Fellow, Silliman Coll. at Yale; Franklin Delano Roosevelt Award for Fight Against Racial Discrimination 1950; Roosevelt Coll. Award for Outstanding Public Service, Gov. of the State of Connecticut 1949–51; Ambassador to India and Nepal 1951–53; Delegate and Chairman, Platform Committee, Democratic Convention 1960; Under Secy. of State 1960–61; President's Special Adviser on African, Asian and Latin-American Affairs 1961–63; Ambassador to India 1963–69. Member of Congress to the U.S. (2nd District, Connecticut). Member, Connecticut State Grange; Council of Foreign Relations of New York. *Publications:* Tomorrow Without Fear; Ambassador's Report (1954); New Dimensions of Peace (1955); American Politics in a Revolutionary World (1956); Africa's Challenge to America. (1956); Ideas, People, Peace (1958); The Coming Political Breakthrough (1959); Promises to Keep (1971). *Address:* Hayden's Point, Essex, Conn., U.S.A.

**BOWLES, Hon. Richard Spink.** Canadian. *B.* 1912. *Educ.* Univ. of Manitoba (BA 1933) and Manitoba Law School (LLB 1937). *M.* 1940, Frances Arnett. *S.* Sheldon, Kingsley and William. *Dau.* Maryann. *Career:* Called to Manitoba Bar 1937; in practice in Winnipeg since 1940; Senior Partner in law firm of Bowles, Pybus, Chornous, Smith & Green 1947—. Chairman, Winnipeg Board of Parks and Recreation 1955–56. Lieutenant-Governor of Manitoba, 1965–70; Chancellor Univ. of Manitoba 1974–77. LLD.: Lincoln College (Univ.) 1967, University of Manitoba 1968, Univ. of Winnipeg 1968. *Publications:* various articles on law. *Member:* Manitoba Bar Assn. (Pres. 1961); Law Society of Manitoba (Pres. 1964); Canadian Bar Assn. *Address:* 1928 Wellington Crescent, Winnipeg, Man., Canada.

**BOWMAN, Dean Orlando.** American economist. *B.* 1909. *Educ.* Purdue Univ. (BS 1933; MS 1934); University of Michigan (PhD 1941). *M.* 1936, Fate Thomas. *Dau.* Ann Pennington. *Career:* The University of Michigan and Purdue University, Teaching Fellow & Instructor Economics, 1937–42; Office of Price Administration, Midwest Exect., 1942–46; U.S. Dept. of State (various positions) 1946–49; U.S. Dept. of Commerce (various positions) 1949–53; Dir., Long Range Planning, Crown-Zellerbach 1953–60; Vice-President Autonetics (Division of North Amer. Rockwell Corp.), 1960–70. Director, Management Programs and Professor of Business Economics, Graduate School of Business Administration, The University of Michigan, 1970–73: Dean, School of Business Admin. State Univ., Long Beach 1973–77, Emeritus 1977—. *Publications:* Public Control of Labor Relations (Macmillan) 1942. Numerous Articles and Monographs. *Awards:* Two Commendations, World War II; Gold Medal Award for Public Service, U.S. Dept. of Commerce. *Member:* Amer. Economic Assn.; Consultant to AID, Dept. of State. *Address:* 862 Glenwood Circle, Fullerton, Calif.; and *office* School of Business Admin., Calif. State University, Long Beach, California, U.S.A.

**BOWMAN, Sir James**, Bt, KBE, DCL, JP. *B.* 8 March 1898. *M.* 1923, Jean Brooks. *S.* 1. *Dau.* 1. *Career:* General Secretary, Northumberland Miners' Assn. (later National Union of Mineworkers, Northumberland Area) 1935–49; Vice-President, National Union of Mineworkers 1938–49; member, General Council, T.U.C. 1945–49; Chairman, National Coal Board Northern (N. & C.) Division 1950–55; Deputy Chairman, National Coal Board Feb. 1955–56, Chairman 1956–61; former member, National Miners' Welfare Joint Council; D.S.I.R.; Royal Commission on the Press. *Address:* "Woodlands", Killingworth Station, Forest Hall, Newcastle-on-Tyne.

**BOYD, Alan Stephenson.** American. *B.* 1922. *Educ.* Univ. of Virginia (LLB). *M.* 1943, Flavil Townsend. *S.* 1. *Career:* Chairman 1961–65, Member 1959–61, Civil Aeronautics Board. Member Florida Railroad and Public Utilities Commission 1958–59 (Chmn. 1957–58). Under Secy. of Commerce for Transportation, 1965; Secretary of Transportation; 1966–69; Vice-Chmn. Illinois Central Gulf Railroad. *Member:* Virginia and Florida Bar Associations. Democrat. *Publications:* Streets, Roads and Bridges in Florida (Harrison Co. 1955). *Clubs:* Metropolitan, Burning Tree (both in Washington, D.C.), Chicago C.; Glen View (Chicago). *Address:* 999 N. Lake Shore Drive, Chicago, Ill. 60611; and *office* 233 No. Michigan Ave., Chicago Ill. 60601, U.S.A.

**BOYD, Hugh Alexander.** British. *B.* 1907. *Educ.* Ballycastle High School and Queen's Univ., Belfast, BA 1927, HDipEd 1928, MA 1933; Trinity Coll., Dublin, MLitt 1950; Fellow, Society of Antiq. Scot. *M.* 1939, Margaret Boyd McClure (BA, DipEd). *S.* 2. *Dau.* 1. *Career:* Vice-Principal, Ballycastle High School 1957–72, Member of Staff 1929–72 (retd.). *Member:* General Synod of the Church of Ireland and of the Senatus Academicus, Univ. of Dublin. Standing Committee of Convocation, Queen's Univ., Belfast; Advisory Member. Library and Ecclesiastical Records Cttee., Rep. Church Body, Dublin. *Publications:* A History of the Church of Ireland in Ramoan Parish (1930); A History of the Church of Ireland in Dunluce Parish (1937); A History of Rathlin Island (1947); Old Ballycastle and Marconi and Ballycastle (1968). Vice-Pres., Queen's Univ. Assoc. 1961–65, Pres. 1976–77. *Address:* Mowbray House, Ballycastle, Co. Antrim BT54 6BH, Northern Ireland.

**BOYD, James.** American mining engineer. *B.* 20 Dec. 1904. *Educ.* California Inst. of Tech. (BS); Colorado Sch. of Mines (DS). *M.* 1932, Ruth R. Brown. *S.* James Brown, Harry Bruce, Douglas Cane, Hudson. *Career:* Field Engineer, Radiore Co., Geophysics 1927–29; Instructor in Geology, Colorado Sch. of Mines 1929–34; Secy. and Mgr. B. E. Moritz Instrument Co. Denver (Electronics) 1931–40; Asst. Prof. of Mineralogy 1934–37; Associate Professor, Economic Geology 1938–41; served World War II, entered as Captain Aug. 1941, Major Feb. 1942, Lt.-Colonel Aug. 1942, Colonel Sept. 1943; Chief, Metals Section, Office of Under-Secretary of War 1941; Chief, Office Liaison & Coordination A.S.F.; Army Representative, W.P.B. Program Adjustment Committee; Alternate member, Requirements Committee and other offices 1942–44; Executive Officer to Director of Material A.S.F. 1944–45; Director, Industry Div., Office of Military Government for Germany 1945–46; Chief, Industry Branch G-4 SHAEF 1945; Dean, Faculty 1946–47; Special Assistant to Secy. of Interior on mineral mattes 1947; Director, U.S. Bureau of Mines 1947–51; Administrator, Defence Minerals Admin. Dept. of the Interior 1950–51; Exploration Manager, Kennecott Copper Corp. 1951–55; Vice-Pres. 1955–60; Pres., Copper Range Co., 1960–70; Chmn. since 1970. Director, White Pine Copper Co. Director: Copper Range Co.; Detroit Edison Co.; Felmont Oil; Exec. Dir. National Commission on Materials Policy 1971–73; Pres., Materials Associates since 1973; Chmn., Materials Advisory Panel to Office of Technology Assessment since 1974. *Address:* 700 N. Hampshire Avenue N.W. Washington D.C. 20037. U.S.A.

**BOYD, Leonard Louis.** South African company director. *B.* 26 July 1911. *Educ.* St. Charles Coll., Pietermaritzburg; Associate, Chartered Inst. of Secretaries (A.C.I.S.); Certified Assoc., Inst. of Bankers; Fellow, Inst. of Administration and Commerce (F.I.A.C.); Associate Institute of Valuers (SA). *M.* 1936, Anne Mosewicz. *S.* 8. *Dau.* 1. *Career:* Managing Director, Boshoff & Boyd Ltd., and Chairman of associated companies; Chmn., Natal Provincial Concl. (Govt. of Natal) 1949–58; Member of Executive (Natal Cabinet) 1958–59.

Chmn., Finance Cttee., Durban City Cncl. 1951–54; Mayor of Durban 1947–49; Pres., Municipal Executive of S. Africa 1950–52; Natal Leader, Progressive Party of South Africa 1959–73. *Address:* 100 Ridge Road, Durban, South Africa.

**BOYD, William.** Canadian professor of pathology. *B.* Portsoy, Scotland. *Educ.* University of Edinburgh (MB, ChB; MD (Gold Medal), CC; FRCP (Edin.), FRCS (Edin.), Diploma in Psychiatry); FRCP (London); LLD (Queen's, Sask.); MD (Oslo); DSc (Manitoba); FRCS (Canada); FICS. *Career:* Medical Officer, Borough Asylum, Derby, England 1909–12; Pathologist: Winwick Asylum, Warrington, England 1912–13, Royal Wolverhampton Hosp. 1913–14; Professor of Pathology, Univ. of Manitoba 1915–37 and Univ. of Toronto 1937–51: Capt., 3rd Field Ambulance, 46th Div. Imperial Forces 1914–15; Professor Emeritus of Pathology, University of Toronto. *Publications:* With a Field Ambulance at Ypres (1917); The Physiology and Pathology of the Cerebrospinal Fluid; Pathology for the Surgeon; Pathology for the Physician; Text-Book of Pathology; Introduction to the Study of Disease; The Spontaneous Regression of Cancer. *Address:* 40 Arjay Crescent, Willowdale, Ont., Canada M2L 1C7.

**BOYD, William, Jr.** American. *B.* 1915. *Educ.* Yale Univ. (BA). *M.* 1954, Harriet Ann Willets. *Dau.* Lucy Spencer. *Career:* With Gulf Oil Corp. 1938–54 (U.S. Naval Officer 1941–46); Consultant to President, Westinghouse Air Brake Co. 1954–56; Wm. Boyd, Jr. and Associates, Management Consultants, 1956–58. Manager of International Banking, Pittsburgh National Bank 1962–71, Senior Vice-Pres. since 1968; Executive Vice Pres. and Dir., Pittsburgh International Finance Corp. 1964–71. *Award:* Knight, Order of Leopold II (Belgium) 1963. *Clubs:* Duquesne (Pittsburgh); India House (N.Y.C.); Royal Ocean Racing (London). *Address:* Woodland Road, Sewickley, Pa.; and *office* Pittsburgh National Bank, Fifth Ave. & Wood St., Pittsburgh, Pa. 15222, U.S.A.

**BOYD OF MERTON, Rt. Hon. Viscount,** CH (Alan Tindal Lennox-Boyd). *B.* 1904. *Educ.* Sherborne School and Christ Church, Oxford (MA); President, Oxford Union 1926. *M.* 1938, Lady Patricia Guinness. *S.* 3. *Career:* Conservative MP for Mid-Bedfordshire 1931–60. Party Secy. to Minister of Labour 1938–39, to Ministry of Home Security 1939, to Ministry of Food 1939–40. In R.N.V.R. in World War II 1940–43; Parly. Secy. to Ministry of Aircraft Production 1943–45; Minister of State for the Colonies 1951–52; Minister of Transport and Civil Aviation 1952–54; Secretary of State for the Colonies 1954–59. Managing Director, Arthur Guinness, Son & Co. Ltd. 1961–67; Vice-Chmn. 1967—, Awarded Messel medal 1966. *Clubs:* Carlton, Pratt's, Buck's (London); Royal Yacht Squadron. *Address:* Iveagh House, Ormond Yard, St. James's, London, S.W.1; and Ince Castle, Saltash, Cornwall.

**BOYD-CARPENTER, The Rt. Hon. Lord (John Archibald),** PC. British statesman. *B.* 2 June 1908. *Educ.* Stowe Sch.; Balliol Coll., Oxford (BA); Dipl. Econ.; Pres. Oxford Union 1930; Harmsworth Law Scholar; called to Bar (Middle Temple) 1934. *M.* 1937, Margaret Hall. *S.* 1. *Daus.* 2. *Career:* Practised S.E. Circuit 1934–39; Served in World War II (Scots Guards, and with A.M.G. in Italy); MP (Con.) for Kingston-upon-Thames 1945–72; Financial Secy. to the Treasury 1951–54; Min. of Transport and Civ. Aviation 1954–55; of Pensions and National Insce. 1955–62; Chief Secretary to the Treasury & Paymaster General 1962–64. Opposition Front Bench spokesman on Housing and Land 1964–66; Chairman, Orion Insurance Co. 1969–72; Chairman, C.L.R.P. Investment Trust 1970–72; and Director of other companies. Elected Chmn., Public Accounts Cttee. 1964–70; Chmn., Civil Aviation Authority 1972–77; Chmn., Rugby Portland Cement Co. since 1976. Privy Councillor 1954; Created Life Peer 1972; Appointed High Steward, Kingston-upon-Thames 1973; Deputy Lieutenant, Greater London 1973. *Address:* 12 Eaton Terrace, London, S.W.1.

**BOYDEN, Harold James,** M.P. British Politician. *B.* 1910. *Educ.* London Univ., BA, BSc (Econ). *M.* 1935, Emily Pemberton. *Career:* RAF 1940–46; Admiralty, Chief Training Officer 1946–47; Dir. of Extra-Mural Studies, Durham Univ. 1947–59; M.P. (Lab.) for Bishop Auckland since 1959; Parly. Under-Sec. of State, Dept. of Education & Science 1964–65; Parly. Sec., Ministry of Public Building & Works 1965–67; Army Minister, Min. of Defence 1967–69; Delegate, Council of Europe & Western European Union 1970–73; Chmn., Expenditure Cttee., House of Commons since 1974. *Member:* Fabian Society. Fellow of King's Coll., London. *Address:* Appledown, The Avenue, Kingston nr. Lewes, Sussex BN7 3LL; and *office* House of Commons, London SW1A 0AA.

**BOYE, Thore (Albert).** Norwegian Diplomat. *B.* 1912. *Educ.* Univ. of Oslo. *M.* 1945, Augusta Sofie Siem. *S.* 2. *Career:* Sec., Norwegian Foreign Ministry 1938, Norwegian Consulate, Marseille 1939, Norwegian Finance Ministry, London 1940–41; Chief of Div., Norwegian Defence Ministry, London 1942–45; Commercial Counsellor, Norwegian Embassy, Brussels & Norwegian Delegate, Interallied Reparation Agency, Brussels 1946–48; Chief Sec., North European Regional Planning Group, NATO, London 1950–51; Dep. Dir.-Gen. Econ. Affairs, Norwegian Foreign Ministry, Oslo 1952; Dir.-Gen. Political Affairs, Norwegian Foreign Ministry 1953–55; Exec. Vice-Pres., Scandinavian Airlines System, Stockholm 1956–61; Ambassador to Rome and Athens 1962–65; Sec.-Gen., Norwegian Foreign Ministry 1966–72; Ambassador to Madrid sinse 1973. *Decorations:* Various National and Foreign Awards. *Address:* c/o Foreign Ministry, Oslo, Norway.

**BOYESEN, Jens.** Norwegian diplomat. *B.* 1920. *Education:* Oslo Univ., Law Degree, *M.* 1955, Erle. *Career:* Resistance Activities 1940–45; State Secy. Foreign Affairs 1951–54; State Secy. Defence 1954–55; Norwegian Ambassador to NATO and OECD 1955–64; State Secy. Foreign Affairs 1964–65; Fellow of Norwegian Defence Research Inst. 1967; Norwegian Permanent Rep. to International Organisations, Geneva 1968–73; Norwegian Ambassador to Belgium and EEC 1973–77; Norwegian Ambassador to the OECD, Paris since 1977. *Address:* 109 Ave. Henri Martin, Paris 16, France.

**BOYLE of Handsworth, Lord (Edward Charles Gurney),** PC, *B.* 1923. *Educ.* Eton and Christ Church, Oxford (Scholar). Unmarried. *Career:* Member, Oxford Union Debating team U.S.A. Oct. 1947–Feb. 1948; Pres., Oxford Union Socy. 1948; Member Parliament (Unionist) Handsworth 1950–70; P.P.S. to Under-Secy. for Air 1951–52, Parliamentary Secy., Ministry of Defence 1952–53, and Ministry of Supply 1954–55; Econ. Secy. to Treasury 1955–56 (Financial Secy. 1959–62); Minister of Education 1962–64; Minister of State for Education and Science April–Oct. 1964; Spokesman on Home Office affairs in Sir Alec Douglas-Home's Consultative Committee, Oct. 1964; Front Bench Spokesman on Education and Science, Feb. 1965–Oct. 1969; created Life Peer 1970; Chancellor of Leeds Univ. since 1970. *Clubs:* Carlton, Pratt's (London). *Address:* The Vice-Chancellor's Lodge, Grosvenor Road, Leeds LS6 2DZ.

**BOYLE, Henry Russell,** TD, JP, CEng, FIMarE, ARINA, FICS, RIIA, Officer in Order of Oranje Nassau. British. *B.* 1908. *Educ.* Glasgow Academy; Victoria U.C. *M.* 1947, Thelma Dorothy West. *S.* 1. *Dau.* 2. *Career:* War Service. Field Art. 1939–45; Chmn. & Man. Dir., Keller Bryant & Co, Ltd.; Man. Dir., Keller Shipping Co. Ltd., C. S. Gobey & Co. Ltd.; Mem. Baltic Exchange; Councillor, Lond. Boro. of St. Pancras 1948–52. *Clubs:* Athenaeum; Brooks's. *Address:* Wood House, Hadley Common, Barnet, Herts.; and *office* Cereal House, 58 Mark Lane, London EC3R 7LB.

**BRACKENREG, John,** OBE, FRSA (Lond.). British *B.* 1905. *Educ.* Technical High School, Perth, and The Julian Ashton Art School, Sydney. *M.* 1942, Eleanor F. Simpson. *S.* 2. *Daus.* 3. *Career:* Director of Private Art Galleries, Perth 1933–38, and Sydney 1938–41. Served in World War II (A.I.F. Survey Co.) 1942–45. Dir. Artarmon Galleries. Sydney, N.S.W.; Dir. & Editor, Australian Artist Editions & The Legend Press Pty. Ltd., Sydney, Life Member, Gallery Society of N.S.W. *Address:* 479 Pacific Highway, Artarmon, N.S.W., Australia.

**BRADDOCK, Lyall Arthur.** Australian. *B.* 1912. *Educ.* Univ. of Adelaide (B.Ec. and AUA; Associate of Commerce). *M.* 1935, Edna Agnes Jose. *S.* 3. *Career:* Head, School of Accountancy, South Australian Institute of Technology 1945–71. Chairman, South Australian Board of Advanced Education 1972–76 (Ret'd). *Fellow:* Australian Socy. of Accountants. *Trustee* of Savings Bank of South Australia. *Chairman* Finance and Budget Cttee., Conference of Churches of Christ, S. Australia. (formerly) *Member* Commission on Advanced Education. *Publications:* numerous articles and lectures in prof. Journals. *Address:* 27 Rowland Road, Magill, S.A. 5072, Australia.

**BRADFIELD, Frederick.** British. *B.* 1922. *Educ.* Handels Academy, Vienna. *M.* 1949, Susi Sara Neuwirth. *S.* Michael

Steven. *Dau.* Cheryl Lois. *Career:* Army Service (India, Ceylon, Burma, Malaya, Singapore) 1941–46; with family business 1946–48; established business as above. *Member,* Guild of Freemen of the City of London; Lloyds; Hospital Plan Insurance Services (partner). *Address:* 50 The Bishops Avenue, Highgate, London, N.2; and *office* 44 Baker Street, London, W.1.

**BRADFIELD, Keith Noel Everal,** OBE. Australian engineer. *B.* 25 Dec. 1910. *Educ.* University of Sydney (BSc, BEng.); New College, Oxford (DPhil.); Rhodes Scholar (N.S.W.) 1935. *M.* 1938, Enid Jeannette Lawrie. *S.* Peter John, James Lawrie. *Career:* Civil Engineer, Department of Civil Aviation, Australia 1939, Chief Airport Engineer 1945; Vice-President, Council of I.C.A.O. 1949, Australian Representative 1947–52; British West Indies Civil Aviation Commission 1960; First Assistant Director-General, Dept. of Civil Aviation, Australia, 1963–68; Australian Representative on Council of I.C.A.O., 1968–72; Civil Aviation Adviser to Papua New Guinea Government since 1973. *Address:* 13/4 Hilltop Crescent, Fairlight, N.S.W. 2094, Australia.

**BRADFIELD, Thomas Michael.** British. *B.* 1930. *Educ.* Merchant Taylors' School. *M.* 1955, Mavis Ann Briggs. *S.* Nicholas Edward, Peter Michael, Simon Christian. *Dau.* Julie Victoria. *Career:* National Servise 1949; Commissioned, R.A.S.C. 1949; Transferred to Territorial Army, 1950; resigned from latter 1954. Director, Bishops Stores Ltd. (multiple grocers and provision merchants), and Bishops Food Stores Ltd. *Clubs:* Moor Park Golf; Old Merchant Taylors. *Address:* Loudham's Barn, Burton's Lane, Little Chalfont, Amersham, Bucks.

**BRADFORD, Ralph.** Business organization consultant; Management Consultant, Chamber of Commerce of the U.S. *B.* 1892. *Educ.* Bay View Coll., portland, Texas, Baylor Univ., Waco, Tex. *M.* 1925, Hazel Munger. *S.* Ralph G. *Career:* U.S. Army 1917–19; newspaper work 1920–21; salesman 1922–24; Manager, Chamber of Commerce of Corpus Christi, Tex. 1924–29; Asst. Manager 1929–33, Manager 1933–39, Commercial Organization Dept., Chamber of Commerce of U.S.; Secretary 1939–42, Gen. Mgr. and Secretary 1942–47, Exec. Vice-Pres. 1947–50, International Vice-Pres. 1950–57, Chamber of Commerce of U.S. Lecturer, Houston Univ., Stanford Univ. and Univ. of N. Carolina 1957–58. Director: Washington Loan & Trust Co. 1944–54, International Bank 1956–60. Hon. Director, Riggs National Bank 1954–63 (Advisory Director 1963–67). Member of Council, International C. of C. 1950–57 active in Inter-Amer. Council 1947–56. Visiting lect. to colleges in New York, Penny., Virginia & North Carolina 1964–66. *Publications:* The Purple Robe (1929); The White Way (1931); In the Image of Man (1932); Brief Interludes (1933); After the Passage of Winter (1934); Three Men of Persia (1935); A Legend of the River People (1937); Reprieve (1940); A Bit of Christmas (1941); Along the Way, (1949); One there was in Palestine (1949); Heritage (1950); Bright Star (1953); Prologue for Tomorrow (1956); The Stolen Fire (1970); many newspaper and magazine articles incl. reg. contr. to the Freeman. *Awards:* Hon. LLD, Elon (NC) College 1950; Hon. Life Membership, American C. of C. Executives 1950; American Socy. of Association Executives 1957; National Assn. Esecutives Club 1962; Medal of Honor, Amer. C. of C. in France, 1954. Honor Certificate, Freedoms Foundation 1960. Independent. *Address:* 1755 S.E. Seventh Street, Ocala, Florida, U.S.A.

**BRADLEY, Phillips.** *B* 1894. *Educ.* Harvard (AB); University of London (PhD). *M.* 1918, Rebecca Pickering. *S.* Edward, John Pickering, Wendell Phillips. *Dau.* Helen Pickering (Henry). *M.* 1952, Anne Saba Parmalee. *Career:* Teacher of Political Science, Amherst, Wellesley, Vassar, Queens Colleges, University of Illinois 1949–50; Director of Education and Research, New York State Joint Legislative Cttee. on Industrial and Labor Conditions, 1941–45; Director of Extension, Secretary, and Professor, New York School of Industrial and Labor Relations, Cornell Univ. 1945–46; Dir., Institute of Labour and Industrial Relations and Professor of Political Science, University of Illinois 1946–50; Professor of Political Science, Maxwell Graduate School, Syracuse Univ. 1950–60 (now Emeritus); President, N.Y. State Conf. A.A.U.P. 1955–57; Professor, Indian School of International Studies, Delhi Univ., 1957–59; Attaché of Embassy, Public Affairs Officer, U.S. Information Service, Kathmandu, 1959–61; Consul, Chief Cultural Affairs Officer, USIS, Bombay, 1961–64; Visiting Professor, Grinnell College (Iowa) 1964–65; Berea College (Ky.) 1965–67; Lewis M. Stevens Professor of Public Affairs, Lincoln Univ. (Pa.) 1967–70; Visiting Professor Maine Maritime Academy 1971–72; Dir. of Admissions, Walden University 1975–76; Member, Maine Human Rights Commission since 1972. *Publications:* Can We Stay Out of War?—American Isolation Reconsidered; Editor, Tocqueville, A. de: Democracy in America. *Address:* 185 Cypress Way, Apt. A-102, Naples, Fla. 33940, U.S.A.

**BRADWELL, Eric.** Senior Editorial Representative, and Dramatic Critic, Napier office of Hawkes Bay Herald-Tribune. *B.* 1908. *Educ.* in England. *M.* 1943, Ngaire Dorothy Murphy. *S.* John Kester. *Dau.* Zoe Vanessa. *Career:* Chief copywriter and special feature writer, New Zealand National Broadcasting Service 1939–42; member, N.Z. War Publicity Committee 1941–42; Served in Royal N.Z. Air Force 1942–46; Dramatic Critic, The Times (N.Z.) 1953–63 (Manager, Feilding Branch 1955–63). *Publications:* Four one-act plays (G. Allen & Unwin, London); Play Production for Amateurs (G. Allen & Unwin); Clay—a play (National Magazines, N.Z.); other works in collected editions; numerous radio plays and documentaries. Twice winner of Radio Record Cup for best N.Z. play, 1933, 1935. *Member:* N.Z. Playwrights Assn. (Inaugural Pres.); British Guild of Drama Adjudicators; P.E.N. (N.Z. Branch). *Address:* 51 Shakespeare Road, Napier, N.Z.; and *office* Herald-Tribune Office, Dalton Street, Napier, New Zealand.

**BRADY, James Harry.** American industrialist, management consultant, author. *B.* 1925. *Educ.* American Univ.; Grad. Fork Union Military Acad.; and Washington Coll. of Law; unmarried. *Career:* Noted as writer, war correspondent, and White House correspondent and columnist; also lecturer; specialized in economics and psychology. Holder of several patents in fields of automation, particularly in grain handling industry. Columnist writing monthly *Washington Newsletter* for business publications. Owner, James H. Brady Enterprises; officer and director of a number of corporations in the U.S.A. *Member:* Variety International. Mason. Elk. Chmn. Bd. of Trustees, Serene Manor Medical Center. Member of Bd. Development Cumberland Coll. Williamsburg, Kentucky. *Clubs:* National Press (Washington); Deane Hill Country (Knoxville, Tenn.); Lancaster County Riding (Lancaster, Pa.). *Address* and *office:* The National Press Club, Washington 4, D.C., U.S.A.

**BRAHAM, Stephen Walter.** British. *B.* 1932. *Educ.* Isleworth Grammar School. *M.* 1952, June E. McIlwraith. *S.* 1. *Dau.* 1 *Career:* Chmn., Stephen W. Braham Ltd.; Owner, Stephen Walter (Retail Stamp Dealers); Mem. A.S.D.A.; B.P.A.; P.T.S. *Address:* 14 St. Mary's Cres., Osterley, Isleworth, Middx.; and *office* Kingsley House, 109 Kingsley Road, Hounslow, Middx. 7W3 4AL.

**BRAHIMI, Lakhdar.** Ambassador of Algeria to the Court of St. James's. *B.* 1934. *Educ.* Faculté de Droit & Institut des Sciences Politiques Algiers and Paris. *S.* 2. *Dau.* 1. *Career:* Student Leader 1953–56; Perm. Rep. F.L.N. and later Provisional Govt. Algeria in S.E. Asia 1956–61; Gen. Secretariat Ministry of External Affairs 1961–63; Ambassador to Arab Republic of Egypt and Sudan; Perm. Rep. to Arab League; Ambassador to U.K. since 1971. *Address:* 16 Hanover Terrace, London, N.W.1.; and *office* Algerian Embassy, 6 Hyde Park Gate, London, S.W.7.

**BRAIN, Christopher Langdon,** Baron Brain of Eynsham, MA, BA. British. Works Manager. *B.* 1926. *Educ.* Leighton Park School; Oxford University. *M.* 1953, Susan Mary Morris. *Daus.* 3. *Career:* Various management positions in U.K. and France with Ilford Ltd., 1951–69; Chmn. Rhone Alps regional Council British Chamber of Commerce France 1968; Senior Consultant, McLintock Mann and Whinney Murray 1970–73; Kiernan & Co. Inc. (U.K.) Ltd. 1973–75; Avalon Leather Board Ltd. 1976—. *Address:* 6 Bowling Green, Street, Somerset BA16 0AH.

**BRAINE, Sir Bernard Richard.** MP. British politician. *B.* 1914. *Educ.* Grammar School. *M.* 1935, Kathleen Mary Faun. *S.* Richard Laurence, Michael Rodney and Timothy Brendan. *Career:* Served in Army in Africa, N.W. Europe and S.E. Asia 1940–46, last appt. on Staff of Admiral Mountbatten; Lieut. Col.; Member of Parliament, Billericay 1950–55 and South East Essex since 1955; Parly. Sec. Ministry, Pensions Nat. Insurance, 1960–61; Under Sec. of State, Commonwealth Relations, 1961–62; Parly. Sec. Ministry of Health, 1962–64; Leader, Brit. Parly. Mission to India 1963; to Mauritius 1971; to Germany 1973; Deputy Chmn. Commonwealth Parly. Assn. U.K. Branch, 1964–65, 1970–74, Treasurer since 1974; A Governor, Commonwealth Inst. since 1965; Opposition Front Bench spokesman, Foreign,

Commonwealth Affairs & Overseas Aid, 1967–70; Chmn., Parly. Select Cttee. Overseas Aid 1970–71; Select Cttee. Overseas Development 1973–74; Chmn. Socy. for International Development (UK Chapter); *Chairman:* Anglo-German Parly. Group; National Council on Alcoholism 1973; SOS Childrens Villages. *Awards:* Knight Bachelor 1972; Commander of the Order of St. John of Jerusalem; Grand Cross of the German Order of Merit. Fellow, Royal Society of Arts; Assoc. Institute of Development Studies, Sussex University. *Clubs:* Carlton. *Address:* Kings Wood, Rayleigh, Essex; and *office* House of Commons, London S.W.1.

**BRAND, Hon. Sir David,** KCMG, WA. Australian. *B.* 1 Aug. 1912. *Educ.* Mullewa School. *M.* 1944, Doris McNeill. *S.* 2. *Dau.* 1. *Career:* Joined A.I.F. 1939; served Middle East, 1939–42; Volunteer Defence Force 1942; W.A. Legislative Assembly member for Greenough, 1945–75 (Ret'd.); Junior Minister for Housing, Local Government, and Forests, 1949; Minister for Works, Water Supply and Electricity 1950–Feb. 1953; (Leader Opposition 1957–59). Premier, Treasurer and Minister for Tourists 1959–71; Leader of Opposition 1971–72. *Club:* West Australian (Perth). *Address:* 24 Ednah Street, Como, Western Australia.

**BRAND, Perry Lewis.** American advertising executive. *B.* 1922. *Educ.* Beloit (Wis.) College, Northwestern Univ. (BS 1943) and Butler Univ.; PhD Colorado State. *M.* 1951 Cornelia Kellogg Sheldon (*Dec.*). *S.* Gerald Sheldon. *Daus.* Cornelia Kellogg, Pamela and Susan. *Career:* Served as Major USAAF 1942–46 (Korean Conflict; member USAF Res. and N.G. Policy Cttee., 10th AF. Decorated D.F.C., Air Medal with 2 oak leaf clusters, Presidential Citation, Commendation Medal, 4 Battle Stars). Sales and merchandising S & W Fine Foods Inc., Chicago 1946–52; former Vice-Pres., Campbell-Mithum Inc.; former Vice-Pres. and Chmn. Plans Bd., Clinton E. Frank; Named one of four outstanding young men in Chicago (by Chicago Junior Association of Commerce & Industry, 1957); Senior Vice-President, Chairman of Plans Board, Griswold-Eshleman, 1965–69; Vice-President, Polaris Corp. 1964—. Member, Board of Directors, Chef Pet Foods 1964—. Director, Midland Financial Corporation; President, Brand Advertising Inc. since 1970; Dir., Washington Park YMCA, Evanston YMCA; Chicago Aviation Cttee., VP Chmn., Plans Bd. Campbell-Mithun. Beta Theta Pi; Member of Chicago Commission on Economic Affairs, President of Illinois Y.M.C.A.s and Director. *Clubs:* Tavern (Chicago); Northbrook Sports; Old Willow; Les Ambassadeurs (London). *Address:* 915 Locust Road, Wilmette, Ill., U.S.A.

**BRAND, Walter J.** American executive. *B.* 1901. *Educ.* Univ. of Wisconsin and De Paul Univ. (Chicago). *M.* 1933, Mildred Koch (of Milwaukee). *S.* Walter J., Jr. *Daus.* Virginia M. and Dorothy A. *Career:* Sales Representative, Edgar Ricker & Co., Milwaukee 1921–27; Vice-Pres., Bank of Sheboygan 1927–35; Pres. Walter J. Brand & Co. Inc. Sheboygan, Wis. since 1935. *Member:* St. Vincent de Paul Socy., Holy Name Socy. Republican. *Clubs:* Univ. of Wisconsin Alumni; Rotary. *Address:* 511 Park Avenue, Sheboygan, Wis. 53081 and 648 Lake Shore Drive, Elk Hart Lake, Wis. 53020; and *office* 511 Park Avenue, Sheboygan, Wis. 53081, U.S.A.

**BRANDES, Rudolf.** German executive. *B.* 1906. *Educ.* DPhil. *M.* 1933, Katharina Fischer. *S.* Michael. *Dau.* Katrin. *Career:* Assistant, Zoological Gardens, Dresden 1932–34; with Coca-Cola GmbH: Sales Representative 1934–36, Advertising Manager 1937, Confidential Clerk 1939, Marketing Dir. 1965, Stellvertr Gesch. Fuhrer 1967; Gesch. Fuhrer, Coca-Cola GmbH 1969–71; Man. Dir., Pro Plaket e.V., Gemeinnütziger Verein für Förderung des Deutschen Plakat Museum; President B.D.W. (Assn. of German Advertising Practitioners and Managers) 1957–65; member of Board, ZAW (Central Committee of the Advertising Industry) 1958–67. Vice-Pres., International Federation of Advertising Managers Associations 1961—. *Member:* B.D.W., Wirtschaftvereiningung Werbung. *Club:* Rotary (Essen-Mitte). *Address:* Heidehang 21, D 4300 Essen-Stadtwald, Essen, Germany.

**BRANDT, Willy.** Former Chancellor, Federal Republic of Germany. *B.* 1913. *Educ.* Reform Real Gymnasium (passed final exam., Abitur). *Married. S.* 3. *Career:* Joined the Socialist Youth movement, and when not 17 years old became a member of the Social Democratic Party of Germany; worked temporarily as commercial employee of a shipping agent; also engaged in journalism. When after 30 Jan. 1933 his arrest by the Gestapo was threatened, he went to Norway, where he studied history and continued as a journalist, while maintaining connections with the German resistance group. Became Scandinavian newspaper correspondent and representative of a Norwegian charitable organization in Republican Spain 1937. At the outbreak of World War II he was one of the three secretaries of the Volkshilfe supported by the Norwegian trade unions. When the Norwegian forces surrendered, in May 1940, his friends gave him a uniform so that he be taken prisoner as a Norwegian soldier and thus escape the Gestapo (the Hitler régime had already deprived him of his German citizenship). After his release he went to Stockholm, where the Norwegian government granted him Norwegian citizenship; whilst there he continued his support of the Norwegian and German resistance. After the war he was Scandinavian Press Correspondent in Germany and, for a time, Press Attaché to the Norwegian Mission in Berlin. In the autumn of 1947 resumed his political work in Germany; the Schleswig-Holstein Land government restored his citizenship, and in 1948–49 he represented the Board of the Social Democratic party in Berlin; from 1950–51 he was chief editor of the Berliner Stadtblatt. Member, German Bundestag 1949–57. Has been a member of the Berlin House of Representatives since 1950 (Pres. 1955; Governing Mayor 1957; elected President of Deutscher Bundesrat 1957 and President of the Deutscher Städtetag 1958–63; in 1959 he was again re-elected Governing Mayor of Berlin); Chmn. S.P.D. 1964—. In Dec. 1966 he was appointed Vice-Chancellor and Foreign Minister; Chancellor of Germany 1969–74; Signed treaties with Soviet Union and Poland 1970. *Awards:* Nobel Peace Prize 1971. He has been one of the friends of Ernst Reuter, who was his teacher in the broadest sense of the word; he wrote a biography of Reuter. *Other Publications:* My Road to Berlin (1960); The Ordeal of Coexistence (1962) and Meetings with Kennedy (1964); Schriften Während der Emigration (1966); Policy of Peace in Europe (1968); Der Wille zum Frieden (1971); Über den Tag hinaus (1974); Begegnungen und Einsichten (1976). *Address:* Bundeshaus, Bonn, Germany.

**BRANIGAN, Sir Patrick Francis,** Kt.-Bach. (1954), QC, JP British colonial administrator (retd.). *B.* 30 Aug. 1906. *Educ.* Newbridge Coll. & Trinity Coll., Dublin University (BA); Downing College, Cambrdge. *M.* 1935, Ruth Prudence Avent. *S.* Patrick Mark Clinton. *Dau.* Susan Clare. *Career:* practised at the Irish Bar 1928–30; Assistant District Commissioner, Kenya 1931; Crown Counsel, Tanganyika 1934; Solicitor-General, N. Rhodesia 1938; Chairman, N. Rhodesia Manpower Committee 1939–41; Chairman, Conciliation Board on Copperbelt Strike 1940; member, N. Rhodesia Arbitration Tribunal 1940–45; Chairman of N. Rhodesia Electricity Board, and of Road Services Board 1939–45; Legal Secretary to Malta Government 1946–48 and periodically Acting Lieutenant-Governor of Malta; Chairman, War Damage Commission, Malta 1946–48; Attorney-General for the Gold Coast 1948–54; Minister of Justice 1951–54; member, Industrial Disputes Tribunal for Great Britain 1955–59; Chairman, commission of enquiry into industrial unrest on Copperbelt (N. Rhodesia) 1956; J.P. (Devon) 1955; Dep. Chmn., Devon Quarter Sessions 1956–71; Recorder, Crown Court 1972–75; Chmn., Agricultural Land Tribunal for S.W. Area of England; Chmn. of a Pensions Appeal Tribunal; Chmn., Mental Health Review Tribunal for S.W. Area of England and Medical Appeal Tribunal (Nat. Insce.) for S.W. Area, also Kt. Cdr., Order of St. Gregory. *Address:* Willhayne, Colyton, Devon.

**BRANSON, Colin William,** AM. Australian executive officer. *B.* 1913. *Educ.* King's Coll. and Univs. of Adelaide and Melbourne. (BEc Dip. Comm.); AASA Senior; FAIM; JP. *M.* 1939, Gwen Hilma Peek. *S.* Bryan. *Daus.* Judith, Pamela, Margaret and Helen. *Career:* School Teacher 1932–35 and 1938–39; Aust. Council for Edu. Research 1936–37; State Government Service 1939–44; Secretary, S.A. Industries Advisory Committee 1944–48; Chmn., South Australian Industries Advisory Cttee. 1949–67. Deputy Director, Dept. of Industrial Development 1949–52; Regional Director, Dept. of National Development 1953–55; General Secretary, South Australian Chamber of Manufactures, Inc. 1956–65, Gen. Mgr. 1965–72; Gen. Mgr. Chamber of Commerce and Industry, South Australia Inc. since 1973; Vice-Pres., Baptist Union of Australia 1956–68. Pres. Gen. 1968–71; President, Adelaide Benevolent and Strangers Friend Society since 1967; Treas., British & Foreign Bible Soc. (S.A. Auxiliary) 1961–69, Chmn. 1969–76, Pres. since 1977; Councillor, Industrial Design Council, Aust. 1965–75; Member of Council, Australian Inst. of Management (Adelaide Div.) 1949–75; Councillor, Corporation of City of Burnside, 1967–71, Alderman 1971–77; Deputy Chmn. King's Coll. 1963–73. *Awards:* Justice of the Peace 1962; Member of the Order of

Australia 1977. *Publications:* The Migration Programme and its Implications to Industry and the Government; Expansion of Secondary Industry in South Australia Creates New Opportunities. Liberal. *Clubs:* Public Schools (Inc.); Commerce; Commonwealth. *Address:* 37 Crompton Drive, Wattle Park, 5066 S.A.; and *office* Chamber of Commerce and Industry, South Australia Inc., 12 Pirie Street, Adelaide, 5000, Australia.

**BRASSEUR, Maurice Paul.** Belgian professor, politician, industrialist. *B.* 1909. *Educ.* Lic. Sup. Comm. and Consular Sc. *M.* Edmée Renaux. *S.* 2. *Daus.* 2. *Career:* Mayor of Loveral 1941–65; Vice Pres. of House of Representatives 1949–61; Minister of the Interior 1950–52; Minister, Foreign Trade and Technical Assistance 1961–65; Governor, Province of Luxembourg since 1965; has acted as President of economic missions to Central America and the Antilles; and undertook numerous missions to Africa, America and Asia. *Publications:* reports on missions, and many studies on periodicals dealing with economic and political problems. *Awards:* Croix de Guerre (Belgium); Grand Cordon, Order of Aztec; Order of Merit (Haiti); Grand Officer, Order of Christofer Colon; and Grand Cross; Order of Leopold (Belgium); Merit (Italy); and by other countries; decorated for activity in the resistance movement 1940–45. *Member:* Christian Social Party (P.S.C.). *Address:* Palais Provincial, Arlon, Belgium.

**BRASSEY, The Hon. Peter Esmé.** JP. British. *B.* 1907. *Educ.* MA (Cantab.). *M.* 1944, Lady Romayne Cecil. *S.* Henry Charles and Richard Edwin. *Dau.* Rowena Jane (Feilden). *Career:* Barrister-at-Law 1930. Chairman, Southend Waterworks Co. 1954–70. Deputy Chmn., The Essex Water Co. 1969–70; Member of Water Resources Bd. 1970–74. Lt.-Col. Northants Yeomanry 1945; Member of the Inner Temple and Midland Circuit; Lord Lieutenant County of Cambridgeshire. *Club:* Carlton. *Address:* The Close House, Barnack, Stamford, Lincs.

**BRAT, Pierre Jean Marie.** Belgian. *B.* 1903. *Educ.* Higher commercial studies and accountancy. *M.* Julia De Ceulaerde. *S.* Henri. *Dau.* Annie. *Career:* Previously: Managing Director of Codep, Brussels 1936–54. Director Caisse Générale d'Epargne et de Retraite (General Savings and Superannuation Fund), Brussels, 1954–57. Honored. Director, Banque Nationale de Belgique 1969—. *Awards:* Medal of the Resistance 1940–45; Commander, Order of the Crown (Belgium); Grand Officer, Order of Leopold II; Commander Order Oranje Nassau. *Address:* Lange Lozanastrast no 233, 2000 Antwerpen, Belgium.

**BRATT, Dr. (Björn Axel) Eyvind.** *B.* 1907. *Educ.* Univ of Uppsala (PhD). *M.* 1939, Carin Robbert. *S.* Carl Johan and Carl Gustaf. *Dau.* Amy. *Career:* Entered Swedish Foreign Service 1934; Consul, New York 1946; Chief of Section, Ministry of Foreign Affairs, Stockholm 1947–51; Consul-General, Berlin 1951–53; Minister to Ethiopia 1953–59; and to South Africa 1959–63; Ambassador to Iran 1963–67; Ambassador of Sweden to Ireland 1967–73. *Awards:* Knight Commander of the Swedish North Star; Grand Cross of Menelik (Ethiopia). *Publications:* The small state in the history of political ideas; Arrcadia Ethiopica (poetry); A travelogue from Iran & Afghanistan and translations of Russian poetry (Esenin). *Address:* Ballymadun, Ashbourne, Co. Meath, Ireland.

**BRATTELI, Trygve Martin.** Norwegian Politician. *B.* 1910. *Educ.* Public elementary School, *M.* 1946, Randi Helene Larssen. *S.* 1. *Daus.* 2. *Career:* Editor Socialist newspaper Folkets Frihet 1934; Arbeider-Ungdommen; Secy. Labour League of Youth 1934–40; Vice Chmn., Norwegian Labour Party 1945–65; Chmn., 1965–75; Chmn., Defence Cttee. 1946; Finance Cttee. 1950–51; Member of Parliament 1950—: Minister, Finance 1951–55. 1956–60; Minister, Communications 1960–64; Member, Nordic Council 1956—; Electoral Cttee. 1964–71; Chmn., Labour Parly. Group 1964–71 and since 1976; Prime Minister 1971–72 and 1973–75. *Address:* Ullevålsveien 58, Oslo 4, Norway; and *office* Stortinget, Oslo 1, Norway.

**BRAUN-BLANQUET, Dr. Josias,** *B.* 1884. *Educ.:* Univs. of Montpellier; Federal Polytechnic School, Zurich; Dr. hon. causa, Univ. of Algiers; Univ. of Uppsala; Agric. High School Vienna and Univ. of Rennes. *M.* 1915, Gabrielle Blanquet. *Dau.* 1. *Career:* Director, International Mediterranean and Alpin Geobotany Station 1930—. Member of numerous scientific bodies throughout the World including The British Ecological Society and la Società Italiana di Fitosociologia; Hon. member numerous botanic Societies. *Awards:* Chevalier, Légion d'Honneur, Officer de l'Ouissam Alaouite; Mem. d'Honneur de l'Accademia Italiana di Scienze Forestali. *Publications:* Plant Sociology (textbook) and numerous works dealing with plant sociology and other aspects of botany. Former Tech. Dir., of vegetation unities of France. *Address:* Rue du Pioch de Boutonnet, Montpellier, Hérault, France.

**BRAWNER, Alexander Harrison, Jr.** American banker. *B.* 1923. *Educ.* Menlo School & Coll. (BA); Princeton University. *M.* 1948, Ann Lowry. *S.* William Harrison, Brandon Lowry, James Coleman. *Dau.* Caroline Ann. *Career:* with W. P. Fuller & Co., San Francisco 1947–61, Int. Manager 1953–61; Man. Dir. Fuller & Co. S.A., Switzerland 1961–63; Head North Amer. Div. Bank of America N.T. & S.A., San Francisco 1963–70; Pres. & Chief Exec. Officer Bank of America, New York 1970–74; Pres. Bank of California Intern. N.Y, since 1974, *Member:* Dir. Internat. Exec. Serv. Corps.; Bus. Council for Internat. Understand; Trustee U.S. Council, Int. Chamber of Commerce; Menlo School & Coll. *Clubs:* Pacific Union; Burlingame Country; Menlo Circus; Apawamis; The River Club (New York). *Address:* 5 Chester Drive, Rye, New York; and *office* 2 Wall St., New York, N.Y., U.S.A.

**BRAY, Denis Campbell,** CMG, CVO. Hong Kong Commissioner in London. *B.* 1926. *Educ.* Kingswood School; Jesus Coll., Cambridge, MA; BSc (Econ) (Hons) (London). *M.* Marjorie Elizabeth Bottomley. *S.* 1 (*Dec.*). *Daus.* 4. *Career:* Hong Kong Administrative Service 1950; District Commissioner, New Territories, Hong Kong 1971; Secretary for Home Affairs 1973; Hong Kong Commissioner in London since 1977. *Decorations:* Companion, Order of St. Michael and St. George, 1977; Commander, Royal Victorian Order 1975. *Clubs:* Royal Ocean Racing; Leander; London Rowing; Royal Hong Kong Yacht; Royal Hong Kong Jockey; Hong Kong Club. *Address:* 31 Astell Street, London SW3; and *office* Hong Kong Government Office, 6 Grafton Street, London W1.

**BRAY, Dr. Jeremy William,** MP. *B.* 1930. *Educ.* Jesus College, Cambridge (MA; PhD); Choate Fellow, Harvard Univ. *M.* 1953, Elizabeth Trowell. *Daus.* 4. *Career:* M.P. (Labour) Middlesborough West 1962–70; Chairman, Estimates Committee Enquiry into Civil Service Recruitment 1964–65, and into Government Statistical Services 1965–66; Parliamentary Secy. Ministry of Power 1966–67; Joint Parliamentary Secretary, Ministry of Technology 1967–69; Personnel Dir., Mullard Ltd. 1970–73; Snr. Res. Fellow, Univ. Strathclyde 1974; Chmn., Fabian Society 1971; Vice-Chmn., Christian Aid 1972; MP Motherwell and Wishaw since 1974; Vis. Research Professor, Univ. of Strathclyde since 1975. *Publications:* The Politics of the Environment; 'Decision in Government'; pamphlets and articles on economic planning and automatic control. *Address:* House of Commons, London SW1A 0AA.

**BRAY, Sir Theodor,** CBE. Australian. *B.* 1905. *Educ.* State Schools and Adelaide Univ. *M.* 1931, Rosalie Trengove. *S.* 3. *Daus.* 2. *Career:* Successively Sub-editor, Asst. Editor and Chief Sub of Argus, Melbourne; and Chief Sub-editor, Courier-Mail. Editor-in-Chief, The Courier-Mail and The Sunday Mail, Brisbane, Qld. Joint Managing Director, Queensland Newspapers Pty. Ltd. 1953–70; Newspaper Dir. since 1970. Member Austn. Council Arts 1969–73; Chancellor Griffith Univ. *Clubs:* Johnsonian, Queensland, Brisbane. *Address:* 210 Clarence Road, Indooroopilly, Brisbane, Qld.; and *office* The Courier-Mail, Brisbane, Qld., Australia.

**BRAY, Thomas Leslie.** *B.* 1906. *Educ.* Sydney C. of E. Grammar School, Sydney. *M.* 1932, Josephine Craddock Benson. *S.* Thomas Michael Leslie. *Daus.* Josephine Laurie and Suezette Mary. *Career:* Lieut. 1932, Capt. 1936, Major 1939, 6th Light Horse, C.M.F.; Lieut.-Col., 2/11 Armoured Car Regt. 1944. Chairman of Directors, Lachlan Guarantee Ltd. 1958—; The Farmers & Graziers Co-op Co. Ltd. 1962—; Mactaggarts F. & G. Wool Selling Co-op. Ltd. Director, T. H. Bray Pty. Ltd. 1958—; John W. Lees Pty, Ltd. since 1968; Member of Executive. Graziers' Association of N.S.W. 1949–60, 1963–65. *Clubs:* The Australian; Royal Automobile (N.S.W.); Imperial Service. *Address:* Waugan Park, Eugowra, N.S.W.; and *office* 3 Spring Street, Sydney, N.S.W., Australia.

**BRAYMAN, Harold.** American. Public Relations Consultant. *B.* 1900. *Educ.* Cornell Univ. (BA 1920); LLD (Hon.) Gettysburg College. *M.* 1930, Martha Wood. *S.* Harold Halliday and Walter Witherspoon. *Career:* Teacher of

English and History, Fort Lee, N.J., High School 1920–22; Reporter, Albany, New York Evening Journal 1922–24; Asst. Legislative Correspondent (1924–26) and Legislative Correspondent (1926–28), N.Y. Evening Post; Washington (D.C.) Correspondent: N.Y. Evening Post (1928–33), Philadelphia Evening Ledger (1934–40), and Houston Chronicle and other newspapers 1940–42; Director, Public Relations Department, E. I. du Pont de Nemours & Co. 1944–65; Asst. Dir. 1942–44. *Awards:* the highest citation of the Public Relations Society of America for 'distinguished service in the advancement of public relations' 1963. Also named 'Public Relations Professional of 1963' by the Public Relations News. Received award for public relations leadership from the American Academy of Achievement, 1965 Vice-Pres. 1966–74. *Member:* Board of Visitors, School of Public Communications, Boston Univ. 1951–72; Chmn. 1961–72; sponsoring cttee. of the annual Public Relations Seminar 1952–61; Chmn., Public Relations Advisory Cttee., Manufacturing Chemists Assn. 1951–53; Ctee.; on Taxation of Chamber of Commerce of U.S. 1954–60. Chmn., Cornell Univ. Council 1961–63. Trustee, Foundation for Public Relations Research & Edu., 1956–62; Chmn. Adv. Cncl., Graduate School of Business and Public Admin., Cornell Univ. 1960–65. Corporate executive in residence, The American University (Washington, D.C.) 1968. Trustee Gettysburg College 1969—, Board of Directors: Continental American Life Insurance Co., Wilmington Country Club 1953–65 and Trustee, Wilmington Medical Center. *Publications:* Corporate Management in a World of Politics (1967); Developing a Philosophy for Business Action (1969); Lincoln Club of Delaware, A History (in collab. with A. O. H. Grier) 1970; The President Speaks Off the Record—Grover Cleveland to Gerald Ford (1976); writer of syndicated columns: The Daily Mirror of Washington (1937–40) and Washington Preview (1940–42); editor of Public Relations Journal (organ of Public Relations Socy. of America) during 1956. *Clubs:* Wilmington Country; Greenville Country; Wilmington; Du Pont Country; Wilmington Rotary; University (N.Y.); Gridiron (Pres. 1941), National Press (Pres. 1938), Overseas Writers (Washington, D.C.). *Address:* Greenville, Wilmington, Del. 19807; and *office* 1250 Wilmington Trust Building, Wilmington Del. 19801, U.S.A.

**BRAYNEN, Sir Alvin Rudolph,** Kt, JP. Bahamian Diplomat. *B.* 1904. *Educ.* Public Schools in the Bahamas. *M.* 1969, Lady Ena E. Braynen, née Elden. By former marriage: *S.* 1. *Dau.* 1. *Career:* Headmaster, Public Schools at Bimini & Tarpum Bay 1923–25; in Business 1925; Founded own Petroleum Business 1930, Representing Sinclair Oil Co. until 1965 when he sold franchise; Remained as their consultant until 1970, when he took on a consultancy agreement with Shell Bahamas Ltd., which he still holds. Entered Parliament 1935 representing Cat Island until 1942, changed to constituency of Harbour Island and when that was divided remained as the Representative of a section of it until 1972; served on many Public Boards, incl. Agriculture, Health, Education etc.; Chmn. of Boards of Education, Works, Prisons & Traffic 1952–58; Deputy Speaker of Parliament 1949–53; 1963–66; Speaker 1967–72; Mem. of the Exec. Council 1953–58; has served as Chairman or Dep. Chairman of many official committees; Delegate from the Bahamas at both 1963 & 1968 Parliamentary Conferences held in London; Chmn. of Exec. Standing Cttee. of Conference of Commonwealth Caribbean Parliaments 1970—72; appointed First High Commissioner in London, 1973 (Ret'd., 1977). Justice of the Peace of the Bahamas; organized present Chamber of Commerce and was its First Exec. Secretary; organized Nassau Mutual Aid Assoc. and was its First President; First Pres. of Kiwanis Club (Montague Branch); Awarded Knighthood in 1975. *Address:* Shirley Slope, P.O.B. N42, Nassau, Bahamas.

**BRÄZAO, Eduardo,** GCVO, Hon. LLD. Portuguese diplomat. *Educ.* Faculty of Law, University of Lisbon; Hon. LLD Univ. of St. John's, Newfoundland. *M. S.* 3. *Career:* Former Secy. of Embassy: Vatican, Madrid; Consul, Hong Kong; Chargé d'Affaires, Dublin; Chief of Protocol; National Secy. of Information and Culture; Ambassador in Rome 1958–63; in Canada 1963–66; in Belgium and Grand Duchy of Luxembourg 1966–68; Ambassador in Vatican 1968. *Awards:* Cmdr. Ord. Public Instruction and Officer Milit. Ord., S. Tiago da Espada of Portugal. Port. Red Cross; Grand Cross of Merit, Italy; Grand Cross, St. Sepulchre; Grand Cross Merit of Malta; Grand Cross Leopold II, Belgium; Grand Cross Piana (Holy See); Grand Cross SS. Mauricio and Lazaro (Saboia); Grand Officer of Orange-Nassau (Netherlands); Grand Officer, Al merito (Chile); Knight of Malta; Grand Officer, Order of St. Gregory (Holy See); Cmdr., Order of the Crown of Italy, Order of Alfonso X (Spain), Order of Cross of the South (Brazil), Order of George I (Greece); Member, Portuguese Academy of History and Correspondent of Royal Academy of History, Madrid. *Publications:* several books on diplomatic history. *Address:* Ministry of Foreign Affairs, Lisbon, Portugal.

**BREARLEY, Sir Norman,** Kt, CBE, DSO, MC, AFC, FRAeS. British. *B.* 1890. *Educ.* State and private schools, Geelong; technical education, Perth, W. Australia. *M.* 1917, Violet C. Stubbs. *S.* 1. *Dau.* 1. *Career:* Served in World War I (with R.F.C. and R.A.F.; fighter pilot; retired with rank of Major) 1914–18; founder of West Australian Airways Ltd.; first air mail contractors to the Federal Govt. of Australia 1921–36; served in World War II (with R.A.A.F. in various commands; retired with rank of Group-Captain). State Chairman, Services Canteens Trust Fund; and Director of several companies. *Club:* Weld (Perth). *Address:* 6 Esplanade, Peppermint Grove, W.A. 6011, Australia.

**BRECKWOLDT, Wilhelm.** German industrial executive. *B.* 1905. *Educ.* High School, trained in import & export trade, Hamburg. *Career:* Started original firm 1927; Launched 2 establishments, New Guinea 1931; Additional companies Alster Studios. Hamburg-Ohlstedt: Atlantik Film Kopierwerk; Hamburg-Ohlstedt; 5 travel-agencies: Holk & Co.; Stöber K'G; Wibro Keramik; Breckwoldt K'G; Itzehoe and Bad Segeberg (all Hamburg), since 1946; International Hotel-Chain BOLOLO SA. 1971; Launched 31 subsidiaries of Breckwoldt & Co. in all parts of the world; Consul General Sierra Leone since 1965. Deputy Bd. Chmn. GEBEKA; Adv. Bd. Gerling-Konzern. *Clubs:* Lions (Prec.); Skal (Hamburg). *Address:* Spaldingstr. 70, Hamburg 1, Germany.

**BREITENMOSER, Theodor H.** Swiss. *B.* 1929. *Educ.* St. Gall Business School; Univs. of Zurich & Lausanne. *Career:* Man. Dir., A. C. Nielsen Co., Mexico; Vice-Chmn. Custodian AG; Man. Dir., STAFCO, Paris, 1962–63; Vice-Pres., A. C. Nielsen Co. Chicago. *Clubs:* Mundet Tennis; Bellavista Golf; University; Club de Industriales; Mexico; Mem. Esomar. *Address:* Rio Escondido 17, Lomas Hipodromo, Mexico 10, D.F.; and *office* Presidente Masaryk 8, Mexico 5, D.F.

**BRELSFORD, William Vernon.** Company Director. *B.* 1907. *Educ.* Oxford University (BA Hons.). *M.* 1933, Wilma Morton. *Daus.* 2. *Career:* Appointed Colonial Service, N. Rhodesia 1930; seconded to establish Rhodes-Livingstone Institute and Museum as Secretary-Curator 1937–38; Acting Information Officer 1945; Acting Director of Information 1948; awarded Wellcome Research Medal for Research in Bangweulu area 1948; Officer i/c, Kasama Development area 1949; member, Whitley Council 1950–53; promoted Director of Information 1951; First President of N. Rhodesia Society and Editor of N.R. Journal 1950–65. Director of Federal Information Services, Fed. of Rhodesia & Nyasaland 1953–60; H.M. Overseas Service (Ret.). M.P. Rhodesia 1962–65; Editor Rhodesiana since 1967; Bd. of Govs., Rhodesia Broadcasting Corp. 1977—. *Publications:* Handbook to Rhodes-Livingstone Museum (1938); Succession of Bemba Chiefs (1944); Fishermen of Bangweulu Swamps (1946); African Dances (1949); The Story of the Northern Rhodesia Regiment (1954); The Tribes of Northern Rhodesia (1957); Generation of Men (1965); The Tribes of Zambia (1968); numerous articles in journals of learned societies and in magazines and newspapers on a wide variety of subjects. *Clubs:* Salisbury; Royal Anthropological Institute. *Address:* Box H.G. 221, Highlands, Salisbury, Rhodesia.

**BREMKAMP, Hugo,** Dr. German. *B.* 1900. *Educ.* Dr. jur. *M.* 1926, Hanni Adolphs. *S.* Dieter (MD), Detlev and Volker. *Career:* Formerly: Area Director, Hamburg-Bremer Feuer-Versicherungs Ges., Düsseldorf (Deputy Member of the Board, Hamburg 1934, Member of the Board 1938; Member of the Board, Hamburg-Bremer-Rückversicherungs AG 1954; Chairman of the Board, and General Director: Hamburg-Bremer-Feuer-Vers. Ges., and Hamburg-Bremer-Rückversicherungs AG 1955. Mitglied d. Aufscichtsrates; Hamburg-Mannheimer Sachversicherungsaktien-Gesellschaft. *Address:* Hamburg 60, Uberseering 45, Federal Republic of Germany.

**BRENCHLEY, Thomas Frank,** CMG. British diplomat (Ret'd.); Dep. Sec.-Gen., Joint Arab-British Chamber of Commerce since 1976. *B.* 1918. *Educ.* Oxford University (MA). *M.* 1946, Edith Helen Helfand. *Dau.* 3. *Career:* Counsellor, Khartoum, 1960–63; Chargé d'Affaires, Jedda, 1963; Counsellor, Foreign Office, 1963–67; Assistant Under

Secretary of State, Foreign Office, 1967–68; Ambassador to Norway, 1968–72; to Poland 1972–74; Dep. Secy. Cabinet Office 1975–76. *Clubs:* Travellers. *Address:* 15 Cadogan Sq., London SW1.

**BRENNAN, Keith G.** Australian Diplomat. *B.* 1915. *Educ.* St. Patrick's Coll., East Melbourne; Melbourne Univ.—LLB. *M.* 1945, Suzanne White. *S.* 3. *Daus.* 2. *Career:* Australian Consulate-General and Mission to UN, New York 1950–54; Dept. of Foreign Affairs, Canberra 1954–58; Counsellor, Australian Embassy, Tokyo 1959–61; Management Services Div. 1962–70 and Head, Int'l. Legal Div. 1970–71. Dept. of Foreign Affairs. Canberra; Ambassador to Ireland 1972–74; to Switzerland since 1974; Leader Australian Delegation to UN Conference on the Law of the Sea since 1976. *Address:* Egelbergstrasse 10, 3006 Berne, Switzerland; and *office* Australian Embassy, 29 Alpenstrasse, Berne, Switzerland.

**BRENNAN, William Joseph, Jr.** American. *B.* 1906. *Educ.* Univ. of Pennsylvania, Wharton School of Business (BS 1928) and Harvard Univ. (LLB 1931). *M.* 1928, Marjorie Leonard. *S.* William J. III and Hugh Leonard. *Dau.* Nancy. *Career:* Member New Jersey Superior Court 1949; New Jersey Supreme Court 1952; Associate Justice of the United States Supreme Court, Oct. 16 1956—; member National Historical Publications Commission, Oct. 14, 1966—. *Awards:* Legion of Merit; LLD Univ. of Penna, Wesleyan, St. John's New York, Rutgers, George Washington Univ., and Jewish Theological Seminary of America, Harvard Univ. 1968, Notre Dame Univ. 1968; D.C.L.: New York Univ. and Colgate; S.J.D. Suffolk Univ. *Member:* Amer. Judicature Socy. (Chmn.); Amer. Bar Assn.; New Jersey State Bar; Inst. of Judicial Administration. *Address:* United States Supereme Court, Washington, D.C. 20543, U.S.A.

**BRENT, John Elford,** BA, Hon. LLD. Canadian. *B.* 1908. *Educ.* Waterloo Coll., Univ. of Western Ontario, (BA (Business Admin.). *M.* 1938, Paula Mary Tillmann. *S.* 3. *Dau.* 1. *Career:* Various appointments with I.B.M. since 1931; Dir., Dominion Insurance Corp., Toronto; National Life Assurance Co. of Canada; Science Research Associates (Canada) Ltd.; Toronto-Dominion Bank; all Toronto; Chmn. Bd. & Dir. I.B.M. Canada Ltd., Toronto. *Member:* Bd. Governors Canadian Export Assn.; Massey Hall; Member Toronto Redevelopment Adv. Council; Vice-Pres. member Bd. Trustees, Toronto Western Hospital; Advisory Bd. International Business, Chemical Bank; Chmn. Advisory Cttee. Univ. Western Ontario School of Business Administration, London, Ontario; Exec. Council Canadian Manufacturers Assn.; Dir., Canadian Council Christians and Jews; Canadian Exec. Service Overseas; Canadian Council Int. Chamber Commerce; Canadian Chamber Commerce; Vice-Pres. & Dir. Univ. Western Ontario Foundation New York; Toronto Symphony; Bd. Trustees United Community Fund Greater Toronto: Member, Newcomen Socy. North America. *Clubs:* Canadian, New York; Canadian Club, Toronto, (Pres. 1972–73); Empire Club of Canada; York, Toronto; Granite, Toronto; Rosedale Golf; Seigniory (Montebello); Mount Royal (Montreal); Caledon Mountain Trout (Inglewood) *Address:* 61 Old Forest Hill Rd., Toronto, Ont., Canada; and *office* P.O. Box 15, Toronto Dominion Centre, Toronto, Ont. M5K 1B1, Canada.

**BRESLIN, Cormac, TD.** Irish. Merchant and Politician. *B.* 1902. *Educ.* St. Eunan's Coll. County Donegal. *M.* 1931, Antoinette Eugenie Willman. *S.* 8. *Daus.* 2. *Career:* Member, Dáil Eireann, Donegal constituency since 1937; Chmn. Donegal County Council 1940–59; Dep. Chmn. Dáil Eireann, 1951–67 Chmn. 1967–73; Chmn, Civil Service Commission, Local Appointments Commn. since 1967; Chmn. Irish Parly. Assn. Irish Group, Inter-Parly. Union, since 1967. *Address:* Glenside, Bunbeg. Letterkenny, County Donegal; and *office* Leinster House, Kildare Street, Dublin 2, Eire.

**BRÉTON, Jean Jacques Guillaume.** French publicity executive. *B.* 1905. *Educ.* Lic. ès Lettres; Bachelier. *M.* Kathleen Emma Turner. *S.* Guillaume. *Dau.* Francine (Mme. Jean Gauthier). *Career:* Founder, Publi-Télé-France Volt-Publicité; de PLAS-TROOST, S.J.B. Lieut. (Res.); Croix de Guerre 1939–40. *Clubs:* Royal Automobile (Great Britain); Deauville Yacht. *Address:* 22 Square Alboni, 75016 Paris; and *office* 216 Rue de Rivoli, 75001 Paris, France.

**BREWER, Hon. George T.** Liberian. *B.* 1903. *Educ.* Cuttington College and Liberia College (BA and Cert. of Law). *S.* 4. *Daus.* 4. *Career:* Clerk in Dept. of State, Monrovia; Chief Clerk, Department of Public Instruction; Commissioner for the Commonwealth District of the City of Harper 1935; Superintendant, Maryland County 1944–52; first Liberian Ambassador to Haiti 1952; Ambassador to Spain 1956–59; and to the Court of St. James's 1959–64. Ambassador to Sierra Leone 1966. Representative at numerous international conferences, including Delegation to Bi-centenary Celebrations of Haiti, and the Delegation to the U.N. General Assembly 1955, 1957 and 1969. *Awards:* Officer, Commander, Knight Commander and Grand Band of the Humane Order of African Redemption, Commander and Grand Commander of the Star of Africa and Knight Grand Commander of the Order of Pioneers (Liberia); Grand Cross of Civil Merit (Spain); Grand Cross of Haiti; Knight Grand Cross, Royal Victorian Order (U.K.). *Address:* c/o Dept. of State, Monrovia, Liberia.

**BREWER, Herbert Richard Wright.** Liberian lawyer and diplomat. *B.* 1931. *Educ.* BA, LLB, JD. *M.* 1958, Elizabeth Woods. *S.* 2. *Dau.* 1. *Career:* Legal Officer, Min. of Foreign Affairs, Monrovia, 1959–61; Counsellor, Min. of Foreign Affairs, Monrovia, 1961–72; Dep. Min. of Labour, Youth & Sports, Monrovia, 1972–74; Amb. to the Court of St. James since 1974 and concurrently to the Holy See and the Sovereign Military Order of Malta since 1976. *Member:* Phi Alpha Delta Law Fraternity (U.S.A.). *Awards:* Grand Commander, Star of Africa (Liberia); Grand Commander of the Polar Star (Sweden); Grand Commander of the Order of Tunisia; Commander of the Yugoslav Flag; Commander of the Cedar of Lebanon; Commander of the Order of Mono (Togo); Commander's Cross of the Order of Merit of the Fed. Rep. of Germany; Honour of Merit & Commander of the Islamic Rep. of Mauritania; Commander of the Order of the Central African Rep. etc., etc., *Clubs:* "Go-Getters Inc." (Liberia); Omicon Delta Kappa Fraternity; YMCA & Lions International. *Address:* Coombe Hill House, 176 Coombe Lane West, Kingston-upon-Thames, Surrey; and *office* 21 Prince's Gate, London SW7.

**BREZHNEV, Leonid Ilyich.** Soviet statesman. *B* in the Ukraine 1906. *Educ.* Secondary School for Land Organization and Land Reclamation. *Career:* Land surveyor in Kursk, and later Chief of a District Land Department and Deputy Chief of the Urals Regional Land Development 1927–30; served in the Red Army 1935–36. Graduated from the Dnieprodzerzhinsk Metallurgical Institute and appointed engineer at metallurgical works there 1935; Director of a specialized secondary school at Dnieprodzerzhinsk 1937–38. Successively Chief of a Department, 1938, Secretary 1939–41, and First Secretary 1947–50, Dniepropetrovsk Regional Party Committee of the Ukraine 1938–50. During war of 1941–45 carried out political work in the Army in the Field. First Secretary, Zaporozhye Regional Part of the Ukraine 1946–47, and of the Central Committee of the Communist Party of Moldavia 1950–52; elected Member of the C.P.S.U. Central Committee and Alternate Member of the Presidium 1952; Secretary, C.P.S.U. Central Cttee. 1952–53; Deputy Chief of the Central Political Department of the Soviet Army and Navy 1953–54; Second Secretary of the Central Committee of the C.P. of Kazakhstan, Feb. 1954 (First Secy. Aug. 1954). Member, Alternate Member and Secretary of C.P.S.U. Central Committee, Feb. 1956 (Member of the Presidium, June 1957). General Secretary Presidium of the C.P.S.U. Central Committee; Chairman of the Presidium of the Supreme Soviet of the U.S.S.R. 1960–64 and since 1977. *Awards:* Hero of Socialist Labour. Given rank of Maj.-General 1943, and Lieut.-General 1953; and in 1961 the title of Hero of Socialist Labour for outstanding services in development of rocket engineering and Hero of the Soviet Union in 1966. Is also Deputy to the Supreme Soviets of the U.S.S.R. and the R.S.F.S.R. Orders of Lenin (4), Red Banner (2), Patriotic War (1st Cl.), Bogan Khmelnitski, Red Star, Karl Marx Gold Medal (Soviet Acad, of Sciences), and medals of the U.S.S.R.; U.N. Peace Gold Medal 1977. *Address:* The Kremlin, Moscow, U.S.S.R.

**BRICKER, George W(alter), Jr.** American. Management consultant & lawyer, Chatham, Mass., U.S.A. *B.* 1902. *Educ.* Massachusetts Institute of Technology (BS); Harvard Univ. (MBA); Northeastern Univ. (JD). *M.* 1930, Elizabeth Cooper Jack. *Daus.* Jacqueline (Lewicki) and Elizabeth Louise (Johnson). *Career:* Public Accountant, H.C. Hopson & Co. Inc., N.Y.C. 1925–29; Public Utility Consultant, O'Hare-Lewis, Boston 1929–36; Law practice, Boston 1933–35; Management Consultant, Robert Heller & Associates Inc., Cleveland 1936–52; Celanese Corp. of America, N.Y.C. 1952–63 (Vice-Pres. 1952–58); Consultant 1958–63). Principal, C. W. Robinson & Co. Inc. New York 1964–72: Investment Advisory Centre of Pakistan, Marketing Advisor, 1965–66, Chief Technical Advisor 1966–67. UN Technical Assistance Expert in Yugoslavia 1973; IESC Tech. Advisor in Brazil 1974; Publisher, Bricker's International Directory of University Sponsored Executive Development Programs annually since 1969. Republican. *Member:* Society for Advancement of Management; North American Socy. for Corporate Planning; Newcomen Society in North America. *Clubs:* Harvard (N.Y.C.); Sind (Karachi); Harvard (Boston). *Address:* 216 Forest Beach Road, South Chatham, Mass. 02659, U.S.A.

**BRIDGES, Robert Lysle.** *B.* 1909. *Educ.* University of California (BA 1930; LLB 1933). *M.* 1930, Alice Marian Rodenberger. *S.* David Manning and James Robert. *Dau.* Linda Lee. *Career:* Partner, law firm of Thelen, Marrin, Johnson & Bridges, San Francisco. Director: Trans-Mountain Oil Pipe Line Co., Vancouver; Alpac Construction & Surveys Ltd., Vancouver; Canadian Industrial Corp., Toronto; Wells Fargo Bank, Wells Fargo & Co., San Francisco; Crum and Forster, New York. Dir. Industrial Indemnity, S.F. *Clubs:* California (Los Angeles); World Trade, Commonwealth, The Pacific Union, Stock Exchange (all of San Francisco); Links N.Y.C.3; Claremont Country (Oakland, Calif.). *Address:* 3972 Happy Valley Road, Lafayette, Calif.; and *office* 111 Sutter Street, San Francisco, 4, Calif., U.S.A.

**BRIDGFORTH, Robert Moore, Jr.** American Research Specialist. *B.* 1918. *Educ.* Iowa State Univ., BS (Chemical Technology); Massachusetts Inst. of Technology, SM (Physical Chemistry). *M.* 1943, Florence Jarnberg. *S.* 1. *Dau.* 1. *Career:* Research & Instructing Staff, Mass. Inst. of Technology 1940–48; Head, Dept. of Physics, Emory & Henry College 1949–51; Chief, Propulsion Systems Section, Systems Management Office, The Boeing Company 1951–60; Chmn. of the Board & Chief Exec. Officer, Rocket Research Corp. (New Rockcor, Inc.) 1960–69; Chmn. of the Board & Chief Exec. Officer, Explosives Corp. of America 1966–69. Fellow, British Interplanetary Soc.; Assoc. Fellow, American Inst. of Aeronautics & Astronautics; Member: American Astronautical Soc. (Dir.-at-Large 1959–66); American Rocket Soc. (Pres., Pacific North West Section 1955); Reticuloendothelial Soc.; Tissue Culture Assn. *Decorations:* Naval Ordnance Development Award. *Publications:* New Approach to Ultimate Chemical Propellant for Space Propulsion; Patents & Articles on Thermodynamics & Rocket Propellants. *Address:* 4325 87th Avenue, S.E., Mercer Island, Washington, D.C. 98040, U.S.A.

**BRIDLE, Paul Augustus.** Canadian diplomat. *B.* 1914. *Educ.* Univ. of Toronto (BA). *M.* 1942, Helen Joan Hilborn *Dau.* 1. *Career:* Previously: with Toronto Daily Star 1937; Master, Upper Canada College, Toronto 1937–40; at Bedford School, England 1938–39; Dept. of National War Services 1940–41. Joined R.C.N.V.R. (Sub-Lieut.) 1941; served in North Atlantic, Mediterranean and Newfoundland; discharged (Lieutenant) 1945. Entered Dept. of External Affairs, Aug. 1945; Third Secretary, St. John's (Nfld.), Sept. 1945; Ottawa Aug. 1946; Second Secretary, St. John's, May 1948 (Actg. High Commissioner, May–Oct. 1948); First Secretary, New Delhi, June 1949; Ottawa, June 1952; Canadian Commissioner I.C.S.C. in Laos, Sept. 1955; Counsellor, Delegation to N.A.C. and O.E.E.C., Paris, Jan. 1957; Minister-Counsellor, June 1957; Imperial Defence College, London 1960; Deputy to Canadian Representative at Conference on Laos, Geneva 1961; Ambassador to Turkey, 1961–62; Canadian Commissioner on the International Commission in Laos, Oct. 1962–Apr. 1964; Head U.S.A. Division Dept. External Affairs 1964–66; Head Latin American Div. 1966–70; Leave of Absence 1970–71. Historical Div. 1971. Retired Dec. 1975. *Address:* c/o Mail Room, Department of External Affairs, Ottawa, Canada.

**BRIERE, François,** Officer of the Legion of Honour (France). Commad. l'Ordre National de Merite. *B.* 1902. *Educ.* Paris University (Graduate in Law, History and Geography); Graduate, Ecole des Sciences Politiques. *M.* 1933, Melle Sosnowska. *Dau.* Mme Hilmi. *Career:* Served in Warsaw, Dublin, Washington, and Rio de Janeiro. Consul, Boston 1937–43; Consul-General, Chicago 1951–54. Member, French delegations to several international conferences. Member, Secretariat of U.N.O. 1946–47. Ambassador in Afghanistan 1954–57, Malaya 1958–60, Philippines 1960–63, Australia 1963–67. *Address:* Residence Negresco, Nice, France.

**BRIERLEY, Philip Reginald.** British engineer. *B.* 1906. *Educ.* St. Paul's School and King's College, London University; BSc (Eng.) Hons.: Diploma in Engineering; Fellow of King's College (FKC). *M.* 1931, Blanche Marie Frey. *Daus.* 2. *Career:* Joined Anglo-Swiss Screw Co. Ltd. 1927; Director 1935; (retd.), Chairman, Anglo-Swiss Holdings Ltd., West Drayton, Middx., 1962–71; Member of Technical Committees of British Standards Institution (BSI); Chairman, Screw Manufacturers' Association 1962; Income Tax Commissioner, Uxbridge. *Publications:* Papers on 'Small Screw Threads' read at and published following National Physical Laboratory Symposium on Engineering Dimensional Metrology in 1953 and the International Congress on Chronometry, Paris 1954. *Address:* 'Two Parishes', Longbottom Lane, Jordans, Bucks.

**BRIERS, Jan.** Belgian broadcasting executive. *B.* 1919. *Educ.* MA Classic Philology; Agrégé High Secondary Education; DPhilol; special degree, History of Music. *M.* 1953, Somonne Van den Broeck. *S.* Jan and Tom. *Dau.* Anne. *Career:* Radio announcer in a Canadian Army Scout Car at Nijmegen 1944; Radio Officer at H.Q. 2nd British Army Corps in Germany, and War Correspondent of the British Forces Network, and of the B.B.C. 1945; Radio Commentator 1945–53. Director, 2nd Programme; Founder and Secretary, Festival of Flanders; Professor, University of Ghent and Brussels. *Publications:* 1000 editorials on classical music; 250 press editorials on radio and television. *Address:* Aan de Bocht 2, Ghent; and *office* Brt. A. Reyerslann 52–1040, Brussels, Belgium.

**BRIGGS, John Danforth.** American. *B.* 1920. *Educ.* M.I.T. (BS Metallurgy, 1942). *M.* 1943, Agatha Crane Robb. *S.* 2. *Dau.* 1. *Career:* Previously: Mgr. Commercial Research & Industrial Development Nov. 1957; Mgr. Research & Planning 1964; Vice-President (Planning), Bethlehem Steel Corp. June 1967—. *Clubs:* Bethlehem; Saucon Valley Country (both of Bethlehem). *Address:* 2512 Center Street, Bethlehem, Pa. 18017, U.S.A.

**BRIGGS, Robert Peter.** *B.* 1903. *Educ.* Univ. of Michigan (AB 1925; MBA 1928). *M.* 1925 Maxine Corliss. *S.* 1. *Dau.* 1. *Career:* Professor of Business Administration, Kansas Wesleyan Univ. 1925–27. From junior accountant to partner, C.P.A. firm Paton & Ross, F. E. Ross & Co. and Briggs & Icerman 1927–45; Certified Public Accountant, Michigan 1933. Instructor in Economics, Univ. of Michigan 1927–35; Assistant Professor of Economics and Accounting 1935–40; Associate Professor 1940–44 (Assistant to President, Standard Steel Spring Co., Madison, Ill., Apr. 1944–June 1945—on leave from University of Michigan); Professor of Accounting and Vice-President 1945–51; Member Board of Directors, Consumers Power Co., Jackson, Mich. 1951–75, (Financial Vice-Pres. 1951–52, Exec. Vice-Pres. 1952–68); Chmn., Federal Reserve Bank of Chicago 1961–64; Pres., Michigan State Chamber of Commerce 1959–61; Member, Board of Regents, Univ. of Michigan 1964–68; State Commissioner, Financial Institutions 1968–73; Pres., Conference State Bank Supervisors 1972; Member, Bd. of Directors, Federal Home Loan Bank of Indianopolis since 1975. *Awards:* (Honorary) LLD West Mich. Univ. (1965) and Univ. of Mich. (1969). *Address:* Box 758, Elk Rapids, Michigan 49629.

**BRIGHAM, Francis Gorham, Jr.** *B.* 1915. *Educ.* Harvard Univ. (BA; MBA). *M.* 1941, Hester Amy Bull. *S.* Francis Gorham III, Dana S., and William McK. *Dau.* Lorena S. (Faerber). *Career:* Staff Accountant, Lybrand Ross Bros. & Montgomery 1939–40; First Lieut. to Lieut.-Col. U.S. Army (Office, Chief of Staff) 1940–46; awarded Legion of Merit, Col. USAR (Retd.); Treas. and Secy. Saco-Lowell Shops 1946–60; Financial Vice-Pres. Treas. & Dir. EPSCO Inc. 1960–62. Vice-Pres., Boston Safe Deposit & Trust Co.; Pres. & Trustee, Hospitals Laundry Assn. Inc. Trustee, Children's Hospital Medical Centre, New England Deaconess Hospital, and Newton-Wellesley Hospital; Director, Peter Gray Corp.; Treas. and Trustee, Joslin Diabetes Foundation Inc. Trustee St. Elizabeth's Hospital; Founder and Trustee, The Carroll School; Corporator, Boston Five Cents Savings Bank, and Affiliated Hospital Center Inc. *Member:* Amer. Assn. of Ind. Management of New England (Treas.); Financial Executives Inst. Boston; Socy. of the Mayflower Descendants; Socy. of the Cincinnati; Socy. of Colonial Wars; The Order of Founders and Patriots of America. *Clubs:* The Country, Down Town, Harvard; (Boston) Army & Navy Country (Washington). *Address:* 37 Perkins St., West Newton, Mass. 02165; ahd *office* One Boston Place, Boston, Mass. 02106, U.S.A.

**BRIGHOUSE, Gilbert.** Professor of Psychology. *B.* 1906. *Educ.* St. Bedes School (England); Hymers College, Hull (Eng.); Univ. of Oregon; Univ. of Chicago (BA and MA);

Univ. of Iowa (DPh). *M.* 1951, Janice Pheatt. *S.* Jeb. *Daus.* Beverly, Shirley, Nancy, Geralda and Ann. *Career:* Consultant in Industrial Psychology, various corporations; Prof. Psychology, Occidental Coll. 1942–71, Professor Emeritus since 1971; Senior Staff Asst. Jet Propulsion Laboratory, Calif. Inst. of Technology since 1971. *Publications:* On Industrial Psychology; Management; The Physically Handicapped. Fellow, Amer. Psychological Assn.; Past pres. Southern California Psychological Assn. Republicans. *Clubs:* Twilight; The Odd Group; Acad. of Magical Acts. *Address:* 1039 Laguna Road, Pasadena, Calif., 91105, U.S.A.

**BRIGHT, Dr. Willard M(ead).** American chemist and business executive. *B.* 1914. *Educ.* Harvard Univ. (AM, PhD); Univ. of Toledo (BS, MS). *M.* 1944, Martha Norris Land. *S.* Willard Mead. *Career:* Teaching Fellow; University of Toledo 1936–37 and Pittsburgh 1937–38; Austin Teaching Fellow and Tutor in Chemistry, Harvard Univ. 1938–42; Chemist Asst. Lab. Dir., The Kendal Co. 1942–52; Research Dir., Lever Bros. 1952–54; Dir. of Research and Development, Lever Bros. Co. 1954–60; Vice-Pres., Lever Bros. Co. 1960–64 (Member, Bd. of Directors 1962–64). Chmn. Bd. of Directors, W. H. Norris Lumber Co. 1957–64; Vice-Pres. & Dir., R. J. Reynolds Tobacco Co. 1964–68; formerly Dir., Penick & Ford Ltd.; R. J. Reynolds Foods Inc.; Filmco Inc.; Lane Services Co.; Senior Vice-Pres. & Dir., Warner-Lambert Pharmaceutical Co., 1968–70. President, Chief Executive Officer and Director, The Kendall Co. 1970–73; Dir., Colgate Palmolive Co. 1972–73; First National Boston Corp.; First National Bank of Boston 1970—; Liberty Mutual Insurance Co. since 1972; Pres. and Dir., Curtiss-Wright Corp. 1974; Dir., Lynch Corp. Dorr. Oliver Inc. 1974; Industrial Research Inst. Dir. 1962–69, Pres. 1967–68; Pres. Boehringer Mannheim Corp. since 1975; Dir. City Stores Co. since 1975; Dir. Furman Lumber Co. since 1975. Outstanding Alumni Award, Univ. of Toledo 1960. *Publications:* journal articles and patents on physical chemistry, adhesives, soaps and detergents, business mgmt. *Clubs:* Chemists' (N.Y.C.), University (N.Y.C.), and Forsyth Country (Winston-Salem); Commercial; Harvard; Down Town (All Boston); The Country (Brookline). *Address:* 1500 Palisades Ave., Fort Lee, New Jersey 07024, U.S.A.

**BRIGHTSEN, Ronald Armund.** *B.* 1925. *Educ.* Wagner College, University of Michigan and Massachusetts, Institute of Technology (BS, MS). *M.* 1955, Martha Vockley. *S.* Gordon. *Daus.* April Lee, Beverly and Laura. *Career:* Analytical Chemist, Oak Ridge 1945; Radio Chemist, Tracerlab 1948–49; Senior Scientist, Westinghouse 1950–54. President and Director (1954–66), Nuclear Science & Engineering Corp; President, Panatomics Inc. 1966—. Advisory Committee Axe Science Corp., 1955–70; Chairman, Advanced Technology Consultants Corp., 1968—; Director Nuclear Surveillance & Auditing Corp., 1968—; Chmn. Motor Home Rentals Inc. since 1971. *Member:* Sigma Xi; American Nuclear Socy.; Newcomen Socy.; New York Academy of Sciences; United World Federalists; Fed. of American Scientists. *Clubs:* Univ. of Michigan; M.I.T. of Western Pennsylvania; University, Duquesne. *Address:* 1725 Washington Road, Pittsburg, Pa., 15241, U.S.A.

**BRILEJ, Joza.** Yugoslav diplomat and lawyer. *B.* 1910. *Educ.* Univ. of Ljubljana. *M.* 1932, Marta Brilej. *S.* Joza. *Dau.* Tatjana. *Career:* Barrister until 1941; Colonel, National Liberation Army until 1945. Head, Political Dept., Ministry of Foreign Affairs until 1950. Deputy to Yugoslav Representative at Special Commission for Palestine, U.N. 1947; Delegate to Conference of the Interparliamentary Union; Ambassador to U.K. 1950; Asst. Foreign Minister 1949—; Counsellor of State for Foreign Affairs 1953; correspondent of International Academy of Diplomacy. Former Amb. and Permanent Representative to U.N.; Under-Secretary, Secretariat for Foreign Affairs; Amb. to United Arab Repub., Cairo 1961–63. Elected Member of the Federal Parliament June 1963—; member of the Federal Executive Council (Inner Cabinet) and Chairman of the Committee for Foreign Economic Relations; Vice-pres. of parlt. of Socialist Republic of Slovenia 1967–74; Pres. of Const. Court of Socialist Republic of Slovenia since 1974. *Awards:* of following Orders: Bravery; Brotherhood and Unity (1st Cl.); Merit for the People (2nd Cl.); Labour (1st Cl.); Flag (Albania); Polonia Restituta; Cross of Grunewald (Poland); and Partisan Star (1st and 2nd Cl.); Medal in Memory of War of Liberation. *Address:*Constitutional Court of Socialist Republic of Slovenia, Beethovnova lo, Ljubljana, Yugoslavia.

**BRILLANT de BOISBRILLANT, Jacques,** KM, KJLJ, Corporation executive and Sociologist. *Educ.* BA St. Joseph Univ. (Moncton) 1946 and Lic. in Political and Social Sciences, Univ. of Louvain, Belgium, 1951. *M.* 1956, Louise Casgrain. *S.* Jules, Jean, and Stéphane. *Career:* Director Québec-Téléphone 1952–70, Vice-Pres. 1956–62, Pres. 1962–67, Chmn. of the Bd. 1967–70; Pres and Founder Lover St. Laurence Radio and Television Inc. 1952–68; Dir. Administration and Trust Co. 1955–70; Formerly Dir. The Provincial Bank of Canada; Alliance Mutual Life Insurance Co.; Anglo Canadian Telephone Co; Canadian Breweries Ltd. *Award:* Knight Honour and Devotion of the Order of Malta. *Address:* Europa-Residence, Place des Moulins, Monte-Carlo, Monaco.

**BRILLIANDE, Robert.** American. *B.* 1909. *Educ.* Univ. of Hawaii (BA and Sc. 1935). *M.* 1938, Irvine Tewksbury Baptiste. *S.* 4. *Dau.* 1. *Career:* Editor and Publisher Waikiki Pictorial News (weekly) 1934–36. Pres. International Monetary Finance Socy. of Hawaii 1969–70; Vice-Pres., National Assn. of Life Insurance Companies; Founder, President and Chairman, Financial Security Life Insurance Co. Ltd. Pres. and Treas.: Brilliande Insurance Agency Ltd., Reliable Investment Corp. Ltd., and Hawaii Underwriting Co. Ltd. Benefactor, Honolulu Community Theatre Socy. Founded and organized 16th Section, U.S. Lawn Tennis Assn. (USLTA); Founder and first Pres., Hawaii Lawn Tennis Assn.; served on Exec. Cttee. and now on USLTA Natl. Junior Tennis Development Cttee.; recently appointed by USLTA as Hawaii's first Life Umpire. Is an active member of many cultural, civic, commercial and sports Int'l Platform Assn. (the first American to win honours in Natl. Tarpon Tournament, Mexico 1953). Mason (32°). *Member:* Million Dollar Round Table (1st Life Member); Natl. Assn. Life Underwriters in Hawaii; Insce. Accounting & Statistical Assn.; Amer. Risk & Insce. Assn. and several others; Honolulu Chamber of Commerce; Amer. Management Assn.; Amer. Presidents Assn.; Pi Delta Phi (Life Member); East African Professional Hunters Assn. (Hon. Life Member); African Socy. of Denmark (in Denmark) (Hon. Life Member). *Clubs:* Automobile Advertising, Cricket; Honolulu Press; Adventureres (Honolulu); Hickham Rod & Gun; Sailfish & Tarpon (Mexico); l'Alliance Francaise; Athletic (Wakiki); Aloha Skeet & Trap Club (Hon. Life Member), etc. *Address:* 3671B Diamond Head Road, Honolulu; and *office* 864 South Beretania Road, Honolulu, Hawaii.

**BRIME, Gunnar Arnold,** MEcon. Swedish. *B.* 1911. *M.* 1940, Elsa Bjorklund. *S.* 1. *Daus.* 3. *Career:* Pres. Svenska AB Iver Lee; Dir., SE-Banken; AB Dixie Cup; Berlingska Boktryckeriet, Lund; Exec. Vice-Pres. AB Akerlund & Rausing 1948–66. *Address:* Kavlingevagen 38, Lund, Sweden.

**BRIMELOW, Baron** cr. 1976 (Life Peer), of Tyldesley, Lancashire; **Thomas Brimelow,** GCMG, OBE. *B.* 1915. *Educ.* BA (Oxon.). *M.* 1945, Jean E. Cull. *Daus.* Alison Jane and Elizabeth Anne. *Career:* Head of Northern Dept., Foreign Office 1956; Counsellor, Washington 1960; Minister, Moscow 1963; Ambassador, Warsaw 1966; Deputy Under-Secretary of State, Foreign and Commonwealth Office 1969–73; Perm. Under-Secy. State and Head Diplomatic Service 1973–75; Member of European Parliament 1977. *Club:* Athenaeum. *Address:* 12 West Hill Court, Millfield Lane, London, N6 6JJ.

**BRINCH, Christian Nicolay Keyser.** Norwegian civil servant. *B.* 15 Aug. 1905. *Educ.* Commercial School and University, Oslo; Wadham College, Oxford. *M.* 1943, Berit Bjerke. *S.* Christian Nicolay. *Daus.* Kari Elisabeth, Anne Berit. *Career:* Secretary, Ministry of Finance 1930, Chief of Section 1937, Director 1945–48; Director, Finance Ministry of Norwegian Government in exile in London 1941–45; Financial Counsellor, Norwegian Embassy, London 1945; Chairman, Shipping Exchange Committee 1946–55; Secretary-General, Ministry of Commerce and Shipping 1955–75; Chairman, Persil-fabrikken A/S 1949–67; Alternate Governor for Norway, International Monetary Fund 1950–64, World Bank 1964–75; Deputy Chairman, Oslo Arts and Crafts Museum 1961–69. *Address:* 8 Sophus Lies Gate, Oslo, Norway.

**BRINTON, Sir Tatton,** OStJ, DL, MA. British. *B.* 1916 *Educ.* Eton Coll. Caius Coll. Cambridge; Vienna and Paris. *M.* (1) 1938, Mary E. Fahnestock (*D.* 1960). (2) 1961, Mrs. Irene Borthwick. *S.* 4. *Dau.* 1. *Career:* With Brintons Ltd. 1938–39; Army (XIIth Lancers, France, Egypt, Italy); Dir. Brintons Ltd. 1941—; Chmn. since 1968; Member of Parliament for Kidderminster 1964–74; Joint Treasurer, Conservative Party 1966–74; President Federation British Carpet Mfrs. 1974–75; Pres. British Carpet Mfrs. Assn.

1976. Member Government Cttee. on Aid to Political Parties 1975–76. *Clubs:* Carlton Bath. *Address:* Kyrewood House, Tenbury Wells, Worcs.; and *office* Brintons Ltd., Kidderminster, Worcs.

**BRISING, Lars (Harald).** Swedish. *B.* 1915. *Educ.* Royal Swedish Univ. of Technology, Stockholm (MSc Aeronautics 1938), and Royal Swedish Airforce (Pilot course for technicians 1936). *M.* (1) 1942, Maja-Brita Frödell. *S.* Dad H. *Daus.* Louise and Anneli. (2) 1977, Ylfva Nisser. *Career:* Inspection Engr., Royal Swedish Air Board 1938–39; Project Engr., Aeronautical Dept., AB Götaverken 1939; Group Leader Flight Testing, Saab Linköping 1939–41; Section Leader, J22 Development 1941–43. Saab Linköping: Technical Chief, Flight Testing 1943–45, Head of Project Office 1945, Chief Designer Jet Aircraft 1946–49; Chief Engineer, Design Department 1949–52; Vice-Pres. Engineering (Technical Director), Saab Aircraft Co., Linköping, 1954–65. Maj.-Gen.(E), RSAF 1965–68. Chief, RSAF Material Administration 1967–68; Director General, Swedish National Development Co. 1968–75; Maj.-Gen. (Eng.), Royal Swedish Air Force Res., Stockholm 1968—; Member, Bd. Stansaab Elektronik AB, Stockholm 1971–75; Contributor to Swedish technical journals. *Awards:* Thulin Medal in gold (Swedish Socy. of Aeronautics, 1961); John Ericsson Medal (American Socy. of Swedish Engineers, 1966); Fellow, Amer. Inst. of Aeronautics and Astronautics, 1956; Dr. Eng. hc 1974. *Member:* Royal Swedish Acad. of Engineering Sciences and Royal Swedish Acad. of Military Science. Senior Service Consultants 1976—; Chairman, Swedish Aeronautical Council 1965–67. *Address:* Johannisberg, Djurgården, S-11525, Stockholm, Sweden.

**BRITTAN, Leon,** MP. British politician and barrister. *B.* 1939. *Educ.* Haberdashers' Aske's School; Trinity Coll., Cambridge (MA); Yale Univ. *Career:* Pres., Cambridge Union 1960; Chmn., Bow Group 1964–65; Editor, Crossbow 1966–68; Member of Parliament (Conservative) for Cleveland and Whitby since 1974: Vice-Chmn., Conservative Party Employment Cttee. 1975–76; Opposition Dep. Spokesman on Devolution & House of Commons Affairs since 1976. *Publications:* Infancy & The Law; contributor to the Conservative Opportunity. *Clubs:* Carlton, M.C.C. *Address:* 20 Kensington Park Gardens, London W.11; and Lease Rigg Farm, Grosmont, Whitby, N. Yorkshire.

**BROADHURST, Air Chief Marshal Sir Harry,** GCB, KBE, DSO & bar, DFC & bar, AFC, Order Legion of Merit, U.S.A., Order of Orange Nassau. British. *B.* 1905. *M.* 1946, Jane Elizabeth Townley. *Dau.* 1. *Career:* Dep. Man. Dir., Hawker Siddeley Aviation Ltd.; Dir.: Hawker Siddeley Group Ltd. 1968–76; Pres. SBAC 1974–75. *Clubs:* Royal Thames Yacht; R.A.F. *Address:* Lock's End House, Birdham, Chichester, Sussex.

**BROADSTON, James Andrew.** American engineer. *B.* 1909. *Educ.* Univ. of Cincinnati (Mech. Eng. Degree); MSc Business Admin. San Fernando Valley State Coll. (now State Univ.). *M.* 1936, Elizabeth Jeannette Herrnstein. *S.* Donald Andrew. *Daus.* Susan B. Nichparenko and Loanne Koykka. *Career:* With Rockwell International 1936–70. Manager, Propulsion Field Laboratory 1951–57; Director, Logistics Div., Rocketdyne 1957–70. Experimental Group Leader, Aerophysics Laboratory 1951–53, Propulsion Group Leader 1948–51; Group Leader, Facilities Design, Aerophysics Dept. 1947–48; Design Group Engineer, Hydraulics and Armament, Engineering Dept. 1944–47; Asst. Engineer and Design Supervisor 1943–44; Chief Structures Test Engineer 1936–43; Chief Engineer, Rearwin Airplanes Inc. 1935–36; Design Engineer, Aeronautical Corp. of America 1934–35; Founder and Chief Engineer, Surface Checking Gage Co. 1944—. Fellow of Amer. Assn. for Advancement of Science, Amer. Socy. for Quality Control and Instrument Socy. of Amer. Associate Fellow, Amer. Inst. of Aeronautics & Astronautics. *Publications:* Control of Surface Quality (eleven editions 1944–77); Measurement and Designation of Surface Quality; Surface Finish Requirements in Design; Surface Roughness Measurement. Articles: Engineering Design Simplification; Designation of Surface Finish; Measuring and Designating Surface Finish; Surface Finish Standardization; Range of Surface Roughness and Drawing Symbols; Erosive Effects of Gun Blast; Horse Sense Produces Horsepower; Catalytic Heaters—Safe or Not?; Virtue Notagraph System of Music Notation; many subsequent mag. publications, etc. Registered Mechanical Engineer (State of California). *Address:* 19111 Sprague Street, Tarzana, Calif., U.S.A.

**BROCKLEHURST, George James,** CBE. New Zealand. *B.* 1906. *Educ.* Christchurch Boys High School and Canterbury University (BCom); is a chartered accountant. *M.* 1932, Elizabeth Stewart. *S.* Richard and David. *Dau.* Jane. *Career:* Accountant, various commercial organizations 1927–36; Administrative Officer, various Govt. departments 1936–44; overseas with N.Z. Air Force, Solomon Islands area, with rank of Flight Lieut. 1944–45; various administrative positions, Social Security Dept. 1946–63. On assignment to International Labour Office, Geneva, as social security expert in Singapore 1955–56; similar assignment in Trinidad and Tobago 1958; Chmn. N.Z. Social Security Commission, Permanent Head Social Security Dept. N.Z. Secy. War Pensions, Dir. Rehabilitation 1963–71; High Commissioner of Cook Islands 1972–75. *Member:* N.Z. Society of Accountants; Returned Servicemen's Association. *Award:* Commander of the Order of the British Empire 1975. *Publications:* Growth and Development of Social Security in New Zealand. *Clubs:* Civil Service. *Address:* 22 Platina Street, Remuera, Auckland, New Zealand.

**BROCKWAY, Archibald Fenner, Baron of Eton and Slough.** British. Author and Politician. *B.* 1888. *Educ.* School for the Sons of Missionaries, Blackheath. *M.* 1946, Edith Violet King. *S.* Christopher. *Daus.* Audrey, Joan and Olive (by previous marriage). *Career:* Editor, Labour Leader 1911–1915; Secy. British Cttee. of Indian National Congress 1920–21; Joint Secy. Prison System Enquiry Cttee. 1921–22; Chmn. War Resisters International 1922–24; Organizing Secy. Independent Labour Party, 1924–26; Editor, New Leader, 1926–29; Labour Member of Parliament, East Leyton, 1929–31; Chmn. Independent Labour Party, 1931–33; Editor, New Leader & Political Secy. I.L.P. 1933–46; Labour MP Eton & Slough, 1950–64; Appointed Life Peer, 1964; Chmn. Movement for Colonial Freedom, 1964–69; Pres. of 'Liberation' incorporating M.C.F. since 1969. *Member:* National Union Journalists. *Publications:* Sixteen books including, English Prisons Today; Socialism Over Sixty Years; Inside the Left; Bermondsey Story; African Socialism; Outside the Right; Red Liner; The Colonial Revolution; Towards Tomorrow (Autobiography). *Address:* 67 Southway. London, N20 8DE; and *office* House of Lords, London, S.W.1,

**BRODEN, Edwin Rauch.** American business executive, *B.* 1904. *Educ.* Carnegie Institute of Technology. *M.* 1935. Estelle Gill (*Div.*). *M.* Helen Lee Trumpy. *S.* Ronald Edwin., *Dau.* Gretchen Ann (Bartholomew). *Career:* Exec. Vice-Pres SKF Industries Inc. 1955; Exec. Vice-Pres., Carborundum Co., Niagara Falls, N.Y. 1950 (Vice-Pres. in Charge Operations 1947); Blaw-Knox Co.: successively Asst. Chief Engineer (Pittsburgh) 1936, Asst. Div. Manager (Pittsburgh) 1941, Division Manager (York, Pa.) 1944. Industrial Engineer, United Natural Gas Co., Oil City, Pa. 1931; Chmn. Bd. 1957–70; and Pres. 1956–68 SKF Industries Inc., Philadelphia; Owner, Delta Lok Company; mem. Advisory Cttee. Eutectic + Castolin Inst. Life Trustee Carnegie Mellon Univ.; Chmn. Bd. of Trustees Spring Garden College; Chmn. American Swedish Historical Foundation; Vice-Chmn., American Council for Co-ordinated Action. Republican. *Clubs:* Union League, Engineers (Philadelphia); Duquesne, Philadelphia Country; N.Y. Yacht. *Address:* 799 Harrison Road, Ithan, Pennsylvania 19085, U.S.A.

**BRODSKY, Michel,** Chev. lég. d'honneur, Croix de Guerre, Licencié ès Sciences, Docteur en Droit. French. *B.* 1917. *M.* 1940, Geneviève Pontramier. *S.* 1. *Dau.* 1. *Career:* Pres. Dir. Gen., PEC-Engineering; Administrateur Dir. Gen., Infratome. *Address:* 4 Rue Duguay Trouin à St.-Germain en Laye, Yvelines 78, France; and *office* Paris, 10 Av. George V, France.

**BROEKER, Bernard Dreher.** American. *B.* 1909. *Educ.* Univ. of Notre Dame (AB 1930) and Harvard Law School (J.D. *cum laude* 1933). *M.* 1961, Frances W. Mills. *S.* Bernard Dreher, Jr. *Dau.* Katherine A. Cundey. *Career:* Vice-Chmn. Finance Cttee. 1 July 1965–30 Jan. 1967; Secretary of the Corporation 25 Apr. 1957–1 July 1965. General Counsel (1 July 1963–70) and Chairman of Finance Committee. 1967–70 Executive Vice-Pres. 1970–74, Bethlehem Steel Corporation (Director of the Corp. 1957–65, and 1 Feb. 1967—). Counsel to Law Firm, Kolb, Holland & Taylor since 1974; Dir: Brinco Ltd. Montreal, since 1969. *Member:* American Bar Assn.; American Law Inst.; Assn. General Counsel; Amer. Socy. International Law; Am. Judicature Society. *Clubs:* Harvard (N.Y.C.); Bethlehem, Saucon Valley Country (Bethlehem, Pa.). *Address:* Weyhill Crescent, R.D.4, Bethlehem, Pa. 18015; and *office* 561 E. Market St. and 437 Main St., Bethlehem, Pa. 18018, U.S.A.

**BROGGINI, Adrian J.,** B.S. American. *B.* 1912. *Educ.* Univ. of Michigan (BS Chem.Eng). *M.* 1934, Virginia Reutter. *Daus.* 3. *Career:* Chmn., & Dir. Badger Co. Inc.; Dir., Badger America Inc.; Badger Ltd., Badger N.V. & other Badger Co. subsidiaries; Vice-Pres., E. B. Badger & Sons Co. 1949; Reg. Professional Engr. Mass. *Clubs:* Brae Burn Country; Hague C.C.; Bald Peak Colony; Univ. Club, N.Y.C.; Algonquin Club Boston; The Beach Club, Lost Tree C.C., Palm Beach, Fla.; Mem. American Petr. Inst.; A.I.C.H.E.; Tau Beta Pi. *Address:* 126 Woodlawn Ave., Wellesley Hills, Mass., U.S.A.; and *office* 1 Broadway, Cambridge, Mass., U.S.A.

**BROINOWSKI, John Herbert,** CMG, FCA. Australian. *B.* 1911. *Educ.* Sydney Church of England Grammar School. *M.* 1939, Jean Kater. *S.* 1. *Career:* Chmn., Sims Consolidated Ltd.; Hoyts Theatres Ltd.; Formfit Ltd., Aquila Steel Ltd; Dep. Chmn. Schroder Darling Holdings Ltd.; Dir., Peko-Wallsend Ltd.; Senior Partner, J. H. Broinowski & Storey, Chartered Accountants, 1945–56. *Clubs:* Australian, Sydney; Union, Sydney; Royal Sydney Golf; Commonwealth, Canberra; Pres., N.S.W. Soc. for Crippled Children 1969–77; Pres., Australian Council for Rehabilitation of Disabled, 1964–68; Vice-Pres. Rehabilitation International 1966–72. *Address:* 1c Wentworth Place, Point Piper, Sydney, Australia; and *office* 15 Bent Street, Sydney, Australia.

**BROMS, Karl Gustaf Arne.** Swedish. *B.* 1917. *Educ.* Military Univ.; Univ. of Commerce, Stockholm. *M.* 1942, Carola Toren. *S.* 1. *Daus.* 3. *Career:* Man. Dir., Swedevelop; Export Dir., Bolinder-Munktell 1960–65; Product Mgr., Bahco 1953–59. *Address:* Moelna Gard, Lidingo, Sweden; and *office* Riddargatan 30, Stockhoom.

**BRONFMAN, Gerald,** Officer, U.S. Legion of Merit, BComm. Canadian. *B.* 1911. *Educ.* McGill Univ. (BComm). *M.* 1941, Marjorie Meta. *S.* 1. *Daus.* 3. *Career:* Pres. Gerin Ltd.; Gerbro Corp.; Kensington Industries Inc.; Dir. Dominion Dairies Ltd.; Roslyn Developments Ltd.; Stressteel Corp. *Member:* Senate Stratford Shakespearean Festival Foundation; Chmn. Finance Advisory Cttee. of Montreal Volunteer Cttee.; Trustee, Montreal Museum of Fine Arts; Trustee YM-YWHA; Hon. Vice-Pres. Quebec Div. Canadian Red Cross Socy.; Nat. Council Joint Distribution Cttee.; Gov. Montreal Children's Hospital; Mount Sinai Hospital; Jewish General Hospital; Dir. Canadian Council, Christains and Jews; Mem., Advisory Council, Air Cadet League of Canada; Member: Montreal Amateur Athletic Association; McGill Graduates Socy.; Pi Lambda Phi; Mu Sigma; B'na'i B'rith. *Clubs:* Montefiore, St. Denis; Greystone Curling; Elm Ridge Country. *Address:* 475 Roslyn Ave., Westmount, Montreal, 217, P.Q. H3Y 2T6, Canada; and *office* 1245 Sherbrooke St. W., Suite 1700, Montreal 109, P.Q. H3G 1H4, Canada.

**BROOK, Sir Robin,** CMG, OBE. British banker. *B.* 1908. *Educ.* Eton; King's College, Cambridge. *M.* 1937, Helen Knewstub. *Daus.* Sarah, Diana. *Career:* Director, Bank of England 1946–49; Deputy Chmn., Colonial Development Corp. 1949–53; Chairman, Ionian Bank Ltd.; Leda Investment Trust, Carclo Ltd.; Director, Dimplex Ltd.; Deputy Chairman, United City Merchants; Director, B.P. 1970–73; President, London Chamber of Commerce 1969–72; Assn. of British Chambers of Commerce 1972–74; Assn. of Chambers of Commerce of EEC 1974–76; High Sheriff of London 1950; President, St. Bartholomew's Hospital Medical College; Vice-Chmn., City & East London Area Health Authority; Chmn. Sports Council since 1975; Council & Management Cttee., King Edward's Fund; mem. cttee. Invisible Exports 1969–75; Council & Finance Cttee. of City University; Master, Haberdashers Company 1966. *Address:* 31 Acacia Road, London NW8 6NS.

**BROOKE OF CUMNOR, Rt. Hon. Lord,** PC, CH. British politician. *B.* 1903. *Educ.* Balliol Coll., Oxford (MA). *M.* 1933, Barbara, Baroness Brooke of Ystradfellte. *S.* 2. *Daus.* 2. *Career:* Member of Parliament (Con.) West Lewisham 1938–45; Hampstead 1950–66; Financial Sec. to the Treasury 1954–57; Minister of Housing and Local Government and Minister for Welsh Affairs 1957–61; Chief Secretary to the Treasury and Paymaster-General 1961–62; Home Secy 1962–64; Chmn., Joint Select Cttee. on Delegated Legislation 1971–73. Member of London County Council 1945–55. *Address:* The Glebe House, Mildenhall, Marlborough, Wilts.

**BROOKE, John.** British tea merchant. *B.* 7 Mar. 1912. *M.* 1936, Bridget May. *S.* 2. *Dau.* 1. *Career:* Joined Brooke Bond & Co. Ltd. 1930; Chairman of the Company, now Brooke Bond Liebig Ltd., 1952–72. *Address:* 10 Parsonage Lane, Market Lavington, Devizes, Wilts. and 24 Lords View, St. John's Wood Road, Regents Park, London, N.W.8.

**BROOKE, John Balmain,** OBE. New Zealand. *B.* 1907. *Educ.* Auckland Grammar School and Auckland and Canterbury University Colleges BE (Civil); MIMechE; MNZIE; MRINA; C Eng. *M.* 1936, Elsie Maud Hunt. *S.* Donald Ernest and Robert Allan. *Dau.* Judith Mary. *Career:* Instructor in Mechanical Engineering, Seddon Memorial Technical College 1930–40; Senior Engineer, Dominion Physical Laboratory 1941–45; Dir., Auckland Industrial Development Div. Dept. of Scientific and Industrial Research 1945–71; Chmn. of Dirs. & Naval Architect, Salthouse Bros., Ship, Yacht and Boat Builders, 1971–77. *Publications:* The Manufacture of Gauges & Precision Tools in N.Z. (1947); More Research—Or Stagnation (1960); Scientific Services for N.Z. Industry (1960); Science in Industry (1961); New Zealand's Finest Investment—Creativity (1962); Science and Productivity (1964); Brains are the Nation's Richest raw Material (1966); Technical Innovation more important than Capital (1967); Scientific Assistance in Japan's Small Scale Industries (1968); The Organization of Research for Industry (1970). *Clubs:* Royal N.Z. Yacht Squadron. *Address:* 7 Old Lake Road, Devonport, Auckland, 9 and *office* Rame Rd, Greenhithe, Auckland, New Zealand.

**BROOKE, Hon. Peter Leonard,** MA, MBA, MP. British management consultant. *B.* 1934. *Educ.* Marlborough Coll.; Balliol Coll., Oxford (MA); Harvard Business School (MBA). *M.* 1964, Joan Margaret Smith. *S.* 4. *Career:* Chmn., Spencer Stuart & Associates; Dir., Ecole St. Georges S.A.; MP (Cons.) for the City of London & Westminster South since 1977. *Clubs:* Brooks's; I. Zingari; Harvard Business School Club of London; M.C.C.; City Livery. *Address:* 110A Ashley Gardens, London SW1; and *office* Brook House, Park Lane W.1.

**BROOKES, Edgar Harry.** Hon and Rev. Emeritus Professor of History and Political Science, Univ of Natal, S.A. *B.* 1897. *Educ.* University of South Africa (MA, DLitt), Hon, LLD, Cape Town, Rhodes and Queen's, Ontario, Hon. LittD, Natal. *M.* 1927, Heidi Geneviève Bourquin. *S.* 3. *Daus.* 2. *Career:* Delegate of South Africa, Assembly of League of Nations 1927; Principal Adams College 1933–45; Delegate to U.N.E.S.C.O. 1947; Senator, Parliament of South Africa, representing Africans of Natal and Zululand 1937–52; member. Social and Economic Planning Council 1943–51. *Publications:* History of Native Policy in South Africa; Native Education in South Africa; The Colour Problems of South Africa; The Bantu in South African Life; The House of Bread and other Poems; South Africa in a Changing World (with J. B. Macaulay); Civil Liberty in the Union of South Africa; The Commonwealth To-day; The City of God & the Politics of Crisis; Power, Law, Right and Love—A Study in Political Values; The City of God and The City of Man in South Africa (with A. Vandenbosch); A History of Natal (with C. B. Webb); A History of the University of Natal; Apartheid—a Documentary Study; White Rule in South Africa 1830–1910; A South African Pilgrimage (1977). *Address:* 4 Chapter Close, 6 Taunton Road, Pietermaritzburg 3201, South Africa.

**BROOKES, Baron** cr. 1975 (Life Peer), of West Bromwich; **Raymond Percival Brookes,** Kt 1971. British Company Director. *B.* 1909. *M.* 1937. Florence Edna Sharman. *S.* 1. *Career:* Life Pres. of Guest, Keen & Nettlefolds Ltd. 1975; Chmn. & Chief Exec. of GKN 1965–74; Dir.: BHP-GKN Holdings Ltd.; GKN Australia Ltd.; Dir. Plessey Co. Ltd. 1974; Dir. AMF Inc. 1976. Mem. of Royal Ordnance Factories Board 1960–67; Part-time mem. of Board of British Steel Corp. 1967–68; First Pres., British Mechanical Engineering Confederation 1968–70; Mem., British National Export Council 1969–71; Court of Governors, Univ. of Birmingham 1966–75; Mem. of Council of Soc. of Motor Mfrs. & Traders 1969–76; Mem. of Exec. Comm. of Soc. of Motor Mfrs. & Traders 1970–76; Pres. of Soc. of Motor Mfrs. & Traders 1974–75; Pres., Motor Industry Research Assn. 1973–75; Mem. Council of UK-South Africa Trade Assn. 1967–74; Vice-Pres., Engineering Employers Federation 1967–75; Mem. Council, Confederation of British Industry 1968–76; Mem., Industrial Development Advisory Board 1972–75; Mem. of Wilberforce Court of Inquiry into the Electrical Industry Dispute 1971. *Address:* Mallards, Santon, Isle of Man.

**BROOKES, Wilfred Deakin**, CBE, DSO, AEA. British. *B.* 1906. *Educ.* Melbourne Church of England Grammar School; Melbourne Univ. *M.* 1928, Betty Heal (Dec.). *S.* 1. *Career:* Chmn., Associated Pulp & Paper Mills Ltd. & subsidiaries, Electrolytic Refining & Smelting Co. of Aust. Ltd.; Colonial Mutual Life Assurance Soc. Ltd.; Dir., Western Mining Corp. Ltd. & Assoc. Cos.; BH South Ltd.; Alcoa Aust. Ltd.; North Broken Hill Ltd.; Copper Producers Assoc. Aust. Inc.; Pres., Institute of Public Affairs. *Clubs:* Melbourne; Australian. *Address:* 20 Heyington Pl., Toorak, Victoria, Australia; and *office* 459 Collins St., Melbourne, Australia.

**BROOKS, David William.** American. *B.* 1901. *Educ.* Univ. of Georgia (BSc Agric. 1922, MS 1923). *M.* 1930, Ruth McMurray. *S.* David William, Jr. *Dau.* Nancy Ruth. *Career:* Chmn. of Bd. Gold Kist Inc. formerly The Cotton Producers Assn., Atlanta, Ga. Gen. Mgr. 1933–68. Member of Board, National Council of Farmer Co-operatives (Pres. 1951–52), Washington D.C. 1943–68; and of Foundation for American Agriculture, Washington, D.C. 1960—; Trustee, Amer. Inst. of Co-operation, Washington, D.C. 1946–69; Chmn. of Board, Cotton States Mutual Ins. Co., Atlanta (Pres. 1947–59) 1959—, and Cotton States Life & Health Ins. Co., Atlanta (Pres. 1955–59) 1959—; member, N.Y. Cotton Exchange 1948–69; Trustee, Reinhardt College (Waleska, Ga.) 1954—, Emory Univ., Atlanta, and Wesleyan College (Macon, Ga.). Chmn., Emory Univ. Cttee of 100, Atlanta 1958; member, New Orleans Cotton Exch. 1957–69; Vice-Pres., National Cotton Council, Memphis, Tenn. 1958–69; member, Board of Gov., Agricultural Hall of Fame, Kansas City 1958—; Chmn., Official Board, St. Mark Methodist Church, Atlanta 1958–60; member of Board, National Peanut Council, Washington, D.C. 1959–61, and Board of Agricultural Missions Inc., New York 1959–67. Taught in Agronomy Div., Univ. of Georgia 1922–25; Field Superviser, Georgia Cotton Growers Co-operative Assn. 1925–33; Chmn., Bd. of Trustees, Lovett School, Atlanta 1949; member: Pres. Truman's National Advisory Board on Mobilization Policy 1951–53, and Pres. Eisenhower's National Agricultural Advisory Commission 1953–56. Member, Governing Board, National Council of Churches Apr. 1960–72; member of Board, Consol. Equities Corp., Atlanta 1960–69; Director, Farmers' Chemical Association, Chattanooga, Tenn. 1960–73; Elected to Agric. Hall of Fame, 1972; Member, Pres. Johnson's Advisory Committee on National Agriculture 1964–65, National Advisory Commission on Rural Poverty 1966–67 and on Trade Negotiations 1964–67. LLD. Emory University 1964. *Publications:* numerous articles on cotton and other subjects; writes monthly column in Association's paper, Gold Kist News. Fraternities: Alpha, Zeta; Phi Kappa Phi. *Clubs:* Capital City; Kiwanis (Atlanta). *Address:* 2374 Dellwood Drive, N.W., Atlanta 30305; and *office* 244 Perimeter Center Parkway, N.E., P.O. Box 2210, Atlanta 30301, Ga., U.S.A.

**BROOKS, Lindsay Davis.** Australian insurance executive. *B.* 1908. *Educ.* Clifton Hill State School and West Melbourne Technical School. *M.* 1939, Ivy May Gole. *S.* 1. *Dau.* 1. *Career:* With Royal Insurance Co. Ltd. until 1934; Chief Clerk, Bankers' & Traders' Insurance Co. 1934–41; Insurance Underwriter. Victorian Wheatgrowers' Corp. 1941–49. Managing Director, Australian Natives' Assn. Insce. Co. Ltd., Melbourne since 1949. *Clubs:* Collingwood Cricket; Melbourne Cricket; Royal Automobile (Victoria); Kew Golf. *Address:* 2/9 Citron Avenue, North Balwyn, Vic.; and *office* 28/32 Elizabeth Street, Melbourne, 3000 Vic., Australia.

**BROOKS, Ronald Clifton**, OBE, MC. British merchant. *B.* Mar. 1899. *Educ.* Haileybury College and Trinity College, Cambridge (BA). *M.* 1928, Iris Winifred Payne. *S.* Robert Anthony and John Brinsley. *Dau.* Belinda Jane. *Career:* served in World War I (Queen's Royal (R.W.S.) Regt.; MC); served in World War II (Brigadier; D.A.G., S.H.A.E.F.; awarded OBE, Legion of Merit, and Chevalier, Legion of Honour); joined firm of Robert Brooks & Co., Adelaide House, London Bridge, E.C.4 1923; Chairman of The International Tea Committee 1948–66; President of The Ceylon Association in London 1949 and 1950. Chmn., Commercial Union Assurance Co. Ltd. 1959–72.; director of other companies. *Address:* Crosby House, 36–37 Great St. Helens, London, E.C.3.

**BROSIO, Dr. Manlio.** Italian diplomat and parliamentarian. *B.* 1897. *Educ.* Turin University (LLD). *Career:* served World War I Italian Army; joined Liberal Party; Member, National Liberation Committee during German Occupation, World War II; appointed Secretary-General, Liberal Party 1943; Minister without Porfolio 1944–45; Vice-President, Council of Ministers 1945; Minister of Defence 1945–46; Amb. Ex. and Plen. to U.S.S.R. 1947–51; Amb. Ex. and Plen. to the Court of St. James's 1952–54; to U.S.A. 1955–61; to France 1961–64. Secretary-General of N.A.T.O. 1964–71; Senator of the Republic 1972–76. Member Liberal Party. *Address:* Corso Umberto 29 bis. Turin 10128, Italy.

**BROSIO, Valentino.** Italian publicist, moving picture producer and professor. *B.* 1903. *Educ.* Dr. jur. *M.* 1940, Caterina Cicchelli. *Career:* Commander of the Italian Republic. Newspaperman since 1946; producer and director of films; author of historical and artistic subjects; Pres. of Cinecittà, and Associazione Direttori di Cineproduzioni 1950–56. *Publications:* Francesco II Gonzaga; Monaco di Baviera; La Cabala delle Curiosità; Manuale del Produttore di Film; Porcellane e majoliche dell'800; Mobili dell'800; Ambienti dell'800; Oggetti dell'800; Lo Stile Liberty; I Mobile Italiano; Veilleuses dell' 800; Regalita di Torino; Torino 'Nell 800; etc. *Address:* Corso Vittorio Emanuele 141, Rome, Italy 00186.

**BROUGHTON, Sir Alfred Davies Devonsher**, Kt OStJ, MA, MB, MP. British politician and physician. *B.* 1902. *Educ.* Rossall School; Downing Coll. Cambridge; The London Hospital. *M.* (1) 1930, Dorothy Parry Jones. *S.* 1. *Dau.* 1. (2) 1967, Joyce Denton. *Career:* Member of Parliament for Batley & Morley since 1949; U.K. Delegate to Council of Europe and W.E.U. 1956–58; Opposition Whip, 1960–64; Member, Speaker's Panel of Chairman 1964–76; Hon. Treas. Commonwealth Parly. Association, 1969–70. *Awards:* Deputy Lieut. of West Yorkshire; Hon. Freeman, Borough of Morley 1972; Borough of Batley 1973. *Address:* Stockwell Shay Farm, Batley, Yorkshire; and *office* House of Commons, London, S.W.1.

**BROUWER, Luitzen Egbertus Jan**, Petroleum Co. Executive. *B.* 1910. *Educ.* Delft Univ. (Mining Engineer). *M.* 1938, Maria F. Rueb. *Career:* with Royal Dutch/Shell Group 1931—; served as geologist in Germany, Indonesia and Egypt; military service 1940–46; assignments in U.S.A. and Netherlands 1946–51, co-ordinator for exploration and production in 1951. General Managing Director Iranian Oil Exploration & Producing Co., Iranian Oil Refining Co. 1954. Man. Dir. Royal Dutch Petr. and Shell Petr. Comp. 1956; Pres. Royal Dutch Petroleum Co. Ltd., 1965–71; Dir. since 1971; Prin. Dir. Shell Petroleum N.V.; Man. Dir. The Shell Petroleum Co. Ltd. 1956–71; Chmn., Shell Canada Dir., Shell Oil Co. 1965–71; Member Bd. of Dirs. Shell Petroleum Co. Ltd. 1971–72; Chmn. of Bd., Boskalis Westminster, member Bd., Algemene Bank, Netherlands, all since 1972; Member Bd. of Dirs. Nedlloyd since 1971. *Awards:* Knight Order of Netherlands Lion; Officer Order of Orange-Nassau; Commander Order of Orange-Nassau; Officer in the Légion d'Honneur. *Address:* Shell Internationale Petroleum Maatschappij B.V., POB 162, The Hague, Netherlands and *office* Royal Dutch Petroleum Co., Carel van Bylandtlaan 30 The Hague, Netherlands.

**BROUWERS, Henri Marie Joseph.** Belgian brewer. *B.* 1910. *Educ.* Ecole d'Ergologie de Belgique. *M.* 1935, Yvonne Leblanc. *Dau.* Anne-Marie (Mme. Robert Destexhe). *Career:* Administrative President, Brasserie de Liège S.A. since 1948; Pres., Association Liègeoise de l'Industrie et du Négoce des Bières, Eaux et Limonades (ALINBEL); First Pres., Liège Chamber of Commerce & Industry. Juge au Tribunal de Commerce de Liège. *Clubs:* Mars et Mercure. *Address:* La Nayle, Milmort, Liège; and *office* Rue de la Limite 6, Liège, Belgium.

**BROWALDH, Tore.** Doctor of Technology. Hon. Causa. Swedish banker. *B.* 1917. *Educ.* Stockholm Univ. (LLM, 1940; BAEcon. 1942). *M.* 1942, Eva Gunnel Ericson. *S.* Dag, Lars-Gunnar, and Mikael. *Dau.* Suzanne. *Career:* Assistant to Prof. Gunnar Myrdal during latter's government mission to study American Post-war Planning 1943; Financial Attaché, Swedish Legation, Washington 1943; Asst. Secy. Royal Committee of Post-war Economic Planning 1944–45; Admin. Secy., Industrial Institute for Economic & Social Research 1944–45; Secy. to Board of Management, Svenska Handelsbanken 1946–49. Director, Economic, Social, Cultural and Refugee Dept. in the Secretariat-General of Council of Europe, Strasbourg 1949–51; Exec. Vice-Pres., Confederation of Swedish Employers 1951–54. Chairman, Svenska Handelsbanken 1955—; Member of the Bd. of the Swedish Bankers Association (Chmn. 1958–61). Member of the Boards of Swedish IBM (Chmn.), Industri-varden (Chairman), Svenska Cellulosa AB (Chairman), Swedish Esso (Chairman), NK-Ahlens (Chairman), Skandia, Volvo

AB, Swedish Unilever AB, Gränges Essem (Chmn.). *Awards:* St. Erik Medal; Cmdr. First Class, Order of Vasa. Member of the Boards of Dag Hammarskjold Foundation, Warship *Vasa* Foundation, and Museum of Far Eastern Antiquities (Chmn.); Nobel Foundation (Dept. Chmn.): Govt. Economic Planning Commission; Govt. Bd. for Industrial Policy and Govt. Scientific Research Adv. Bd. *Member:* Socy. of Scientists and Members of Parliament; Exec. Cttee of Swedish Red Cross 1952–61; U.N. Cttee. of Eminent Person or Multinational Corporations. One of the founders of the Industrial Council for Social and Economic Studies. *Address:* Skeppargatan 66, Stockholm; and *office* Arsenalsgatan 11, Stockholm, Sweden.

**BROWN, Alastair Alexander Anderson,** BSc, CEng, FIEE FIMechE, FRAS, MBIM. British. *B.* 1925. *Educ.* Allan Glen School, Glasgow; Royal Tech. Coll., Glasgow; Heriot-Watt Coll., Edinburgh; Paisley Tech. Coll. *M.* 1955, Mary Teresa MacMorrow. *S.* 1. *Dau.* 2. *Career:* Former Man. Dir., Kollsman Instrument Ltd; formerly Chief Eng. Smiths Aviation Div. Basingstoke; Asst. Chief Eng., Kelvin & Hughes Basingstoke 1956–61; Man. Dir., Fairey Engineering Ltd. *Clubs:* Royal Aero. *Address:* Hawthorn 59 Meadow Drive, Prestbury Cheshire and *office* P.O. Box 41, Crossley Road, Heaton Chapel, Stockport, Cheshire.

**BROWN, Sir Allen Stanley,** CBE. Australian civil servant. *B.* 1911. *Educ.* MA; LLM. *M.* 1936, Hilda May Wilke. *S.* 1. *Daus.* 2. *Career:* Secretary to the Australian Cabinet and the Prime Minister's Department 1949–58. Ambassador to Japan 1965–70; Australian Commissioner to British Phosphate Commis. Christmas Island Phosphate Commission. Deputy High Commissioner in the United Kingdom 1959–65. *Club:* Melbourne. *Address:* Phosphate House, 515 Collins St., Melbourne 3000, Australia.

**BROWN, Bruce Macdonald.** New Zealand Diplomat. *B.* 1930. *Educ.* Victoria Univ. of Wellington, MA (Hons). *M.* 1953, Edith Irene Raynor. *S.* 2. *Dau.* 1. *Career:* Dir., N.Z. Inst. of International Affairs 1969–71; Dep. N.Z. High Commissioner, Canberra 1972–74; N.Z. Ambassador to Iran since 1975 and to Pakistan since 1976. *Member:* International Inst. for Strategic Studies; N.Z. Inst. of International Affairs. *Publications:* The Rise of New Zealand Labour (1962); The United Nations (1966); (Editor) New Zealand in the Pacific (1970); (Editor) Asia and the Pacific in the 1970s (1971). *Clubs:* Imperial Country Club, Tehran; University Club, Wellington. *Address:* New Zealand Residence, Ave. Zafaranich, Shirkouh Street No. 3, Tehran; and *office* New Zealand Embassy, P.O. Box 128, Tehran, Iran.

**BROWN, Sir David,** KB, CEng., FIMechE, AFRAeS. British company director. *B.* 1904. *Educ.* Rossall; Private Tutor in Engineering; Huddersfield Technical College. *M.* (1) 1926, Daisie Muriel Firth (*Diss.*); (2) 1955, Marjorie Deans. *S.* 1. *Dau.* 1. Chairman: David Brown Holdings Ltd. & Vosper Ltd. & David Brown-Vosper (Offshore) Ltd.; Dir., David Brown Gear Industries Ltd.; Underwriting Member of Lloyds. Past Member, Board of Governors, Huddersfield Royal Infirmary; Council of Huddersfield Chamber of Commerce; British National Export Council, 1965–67. *Clubs:* Guards; Polo; Ham Polo; Pres., British Racing Drivers; Royal Automobile; Club International des Anciens Pilots de Grand Prix. *Address:* Chequers Manor, Cadmore End, nr. High Wycombe, Bucks; and *office* David Brown Holdings, 32 Curzon Street, London W1Y 8BH.

**BROWN, David Alexander.** British scientist. *B.* 1916. *Educ.* PhD (London); DIC, MSc (N.Z.). *M.* 1945, Rina Patricia Robertson. *S.* David and Roger. *Dau.* Caroline. *Career:* Geologist, New Zealand Geological Survey 1936–38, and N.Z. Oil Exploration Ltd. 1938–40; Lieutenant (A), Fleet Air Arm 1940–45; Imperial Coll. of Science 1945–48; Senr. Geologist, N.Z. Geological Survey 1948–50; Senr. Lect. in Geology, Univ. of Otago (Dunedin, N.Z.) 1950–56; Reader, same Univ. 1956–59. Professor of Geology, Australian National University 1959—; Dean of Students 1966–67. Dean of Science 1967–69. *Publications:* 6 books and 27 papers on fossil and recent polyzoa palaeontology, and regional geology; 4 major translations of Russian Geological Monographs. *Member:* Geological Socy.; Royal Geographical Socy.; President, Geological Socy. of Australia; Geological Socy. of N.Z.; Fellow Geological Socy. of America; Geologists' Assn.; Paleontological Socy. of America; Palaeontological Assn.; Hakluvt Socy.; Geol. Socy. Aust. 1961. Editor, Journal of Geo. Socy. of Australia; Pres. Section C ANZAAS, 1968. *Address:* 17 Crace Street, Weetangera, A.C.T., 2614 and Geology Dept., Australian National University, Canberra, A.C.T., Australia. (Postal code 2600).

**BROWN, Fred Elmore.** American. Legion of Merit. *B.* 1913. *Educ.* Univ. of Oklahoma (BS) and Harvard (MBA). *M.* 1941, Margaret Ann Gillham (*Dec.*). *S.* Frederick Elmore. *Career:* Second Lieut.-Col., Field Artillery, and Chief, Fiscal Control Branch, Office of the Quarter-master-Gen., U.S. Army 1942–46. Partner, J. & W. Seligman & Co. (investment), New York City 1955—. Chmn.: Tri-Continental Corp. 1959—, Broad Street Investing Corp. 1959—, National Investors Corp. 1959—, Union Capital Fund, Inc. 1969—. Union Income Fund Inc. since 1959, Chmn., Union Service Corp. 1960—, Union Data Service Centre, Inc. 1966—, Union Cash Management, Inc. 1976—; and Director: Mutual Benefit Life Insurance Co. 1964—; Trustee: Coll. Retirement Equities Fund 1960—, Morristown Memorial Hosp., and Vassar Coll.; Vice-Chmn. Association of Publicly-Traded Investment Companies; Governor Investment Company Institute. Advisory Council, Centre for the Study of Financial Institutions, Law School, Univ. of Pennsylvania. *Awards:* Award of Honour 1961, Beta Gamma Sigma Alumini; and 50th Anniversary National Award, same fraternity 1963. *Member:* N.Y. Society Security Analysts; Beta Theta Pi; Delta Sigma Pi; Beta Gamma Sigma. *Clubs:* Downtown Assn. N.Y.C.; Morristown, N.J.; Lake Placid (Lake Placid, N.Y.); Somerset Hills Country Club, Bernardsville, N.J. *Address:* Van Beuren Road, Morristown, N.J.; and *office* One Bankers Trust Plaza, New York City 10006, U.S.A.

**BROWN, George Arthur,** OJ, CMG (Jamaica). Jamaican. *Educ.* St. Simon's College, Jamaica and London School of Economics. *M.* 1964, Leila Leonie. *Daus.* 2. (*S.* 1, *Dau.* 1 by previous marriage). *Career:* With Income Tax Dept., Jamaica 1941; Ministry of Finance 1954; Dir., Central Planning Unit 1957; Financial Secretary, Jamaica 1962; Governor, Bank of Jamaica, July 1967—. *Clubs:* Jamaica; Kingston. *Address:* 'Long Acres', 9 Norbrook Road, Kingston 8, Jamaica; and *office* P.O. Box 621, Kingston, Jamaica.

**BROWN, George Bosworth.** American teacher and research biochemist. *B.* 1914. *Educ.* Illinois Wesleyan Univ. (BS 1934; Hon. DSc 1960) and Univ. of Illinois (MS 1936; PhD 1938). *M.* 1940, Katherine Matthews. Fellow to Assoc. Prof., Cornell Univ. Med. Coll. 1938–51. *Career:* with Sloan-Kettering Institute of Cornell University Medical College since 1946 (Member 1948—, Vice-President 1966); Consultant, U.S. Public Health Service 1949–54, 1963–67; member, Panels Committee on Growth, National Research Council 1949–51, and 1954; Professor of Biochemistry, Sloan-Kettering Div., Cornell University Medical College 1951—; Head, Nucleoprotein Div., Sloan-Kettering Institute for Cancer Research 1946—; Consultant to Chemotherapy National Service Center 1957–60. National Science Foundation 1958–60; Travelling Fellow, Rockefeller Foundation 1949; a U.S. Delegate to Atoms for Peace 1955; a Lacey-Zarubin exchange delegate to Russia 1959; Fulbright Fellow, Australia 1965. Trustee, Gordon Research Confs. 1956–59, and 1970–73. Chmn. 1959 (Member-at-Large 1954–56). *Publications:* too many to list, but all in professional journals; field of research is nucleic acids and proteins. Republican. *Member:* Amer. Socy. of Biological Chemists; Biochemical Socy. (London); Amer. Chemical Socy.; Harvey Socy.; Amer. Assn. for Advancement of Science; Amer. Assn. Cancer Research; Phi Kappa Phi; Sigma Xi. *Address:* 800 Grove Street, Mamaroneck, N.Y.; and *office* Sloan-Kettering Institute for Cancer Research, 145 Boston Post Rd., Rye, N.Y., U.S.A.

**BROWN, George H.** American. Administrator; Educator; Consultant. *B.* 1910. *Educ.* Univ. of Chicago (PhD Econs.); Harvard Univ. (MBA Marketing); Oberlin Coll. (BA Pre-Medicine). *M.* 1931, Catherine Smith (*Dec.* 1962). *Dau.* Ann C. *Career:* Professor, Univ. of Chicago 1938–54; Sales Mgr., Mallinckrodt Chem. Works 1931–37; Professorial Lecturer 1937–38; Consultant (part-time) to General Mills Inc., Toni Co., and Armour & Co. 1949–54; Editorship, Henry Holt & Co. 1952–55; Director of Marketing Research, Ford Motor Co. 1954–69; Dir. Bureau of the Census, U.S. Dept. of Commerce 1969–73; Secy. The Conference Board since 1973; Consultant, U.S. General Accounting Office. *Publications:* Readings in Marketing (1955); Readings in Price Policies (with J. E. Jeuck and Peter Peterson) (1952); What Economists Should Know About Marketing (1951): An Analysis of Brand Loyalties for Selected Commodities (1952); Measuring Consumer Attitude Towards Products (1950). *Member:* Amer. Marketing Assn. (National Pres. 1951–52); Amer. Statistical Assn. (Fellow). Trustee: Marketing Sciences Inst.,

Cambridge Mass 1962–69; Foundation for Research in Social Sciences, Ann Arbor, Mich. 1962–69. *Clubs:* Cosmos (Washington D.C.); River; Metropolitan Opera (N.Y.). *Address:* Apt. 14B, 870 United Nations Plaza, New York, 10017; and *office* The Conference Board, 845 3rd Avenue, New York, N.Y. 10022, U.S.A.

**BROWN, Harold.** American. *B.* 1927. *Educ.* Columbia University (BA 1945; MA 1946; PhD (Physics) 1949). *M.* 1953, Colene D. McDowell. *Daus.* 2 *Career:* Lecturer in Physics, Columbia Univ., 1947–48, Stevens Inst. of Tech. 1949–50, Univ. of California (Berkeley) 1951–2; Research Scientist, Univ. of Calif. (E. O. Lawrence) Radiation Lab. Berkely 1950–2. At Univ. of Calif. Radiation Lab. Berkely and Livermore 1952–61, (Dep. Dir. 1959–60 and Dir. 1960 Livermore); Mem. Polaris Steering Comm. 1956–58; Air Force Science Adv. Bd. Consultant 1957; Missiles Consultant to the Secy. of Defense 1958–61; panel Consultant to the Pres. Science Advis. Comm. 1958–60; Mem. 1961, Advisor to U.S. Delegation, Conf. to Experts on Detection of Nuclear Tests 1958; Senior Scientific Advisor to Conf. on Discontinuance of Nuclear Weapons Tests 1958–9; Mem. Adv. Council Peace Research Institute 1961–62; Director, Defense Research and Engineering, Dept. of Defense 1961–65; Secretary of the United States Air Force, Oct. 1965–69; Pres. California Inst of Technology 1969–Jan. 1977; Secretary of Defence since Jan. 1977. *Publications:* articles on scientific and defense subjects in Scientific American, Bulletin of the Atomic Scientific, Physics Today, NATO'S Fifteen Nations Foreign Affairs. Recipient: U.S. Navy Distinguished Public Service Award 1961, Columbia Univ. Medal of Excellence 1963, DEng Stevens Institute of Technology 1964, HonLLD Long Island Univ. 1966, Univ. of California, Los Angeles 1969, Occidental College, Los Angeles 1969, Gettysburg Coll. Pa. 1967; ScD Univ. of Rochester, N.Y. 1975, Brown Univ., Providence, R.I. 1977. *Member:* Amer. Physical Society, National Academy Engineering, New York Academy of Sciences, Sigma Xi, Phi Beta Kappa. Fellow: Amer. Academy of Arts and Sciences 1969, Amer. Astronautical Socy. 1969. *Clubs:* Army-Navy Country (Alexandria, Virginia), Cosmos (Wash. D.C.); The Athenaeum, (London); Bohemian, (San Fran., California). *Address:* Department of Defence, Washington, D.C. 20301, U.S.A.

**BROWN, Harold James.** Australian. *B.* 1911. *Educ.* Univ. of Sydney; BSc; BE (1st Cl. Hons., Univ. Medal); ME (1st Cl. Hons., Univ. Medal). *M.* 1936, Hazel Merlyn Dahl Helm. *S.* Andrew James and Quentin Robert. *Daus.* Suzanne and Trudy Louise. *Career:* At Research Lab., Amalgamated Wireless Asia Ltd. 1935–37; Hydroelectric Commission of Tasmania 1937–39; Radiophysics Lab., Commonwealth Scientific and Research Organization 1939–45; Communications Supt., Australian National Airways 1945–47; Professor of Electrical Engineering (and Dean of Faculty of Engineering), Univ. of N.S.W. 1947–51; Controller of Guided Weapons, Dept. of Supply, Australia 1951–58; Technical Director, Rola Pty. Ltd., Melbourne 1958–61. Technical Director, Philips Industries Holdings Ltd., Australia 1961—. *Publications:* Numerous technical articles. *Fellow:* Inst. of Engineers, Aust.; Inst. of Radio & Electronic Engineers of Aust. (Fellow); Councillor, Canberra College of Advanced Education; Chairman, of Visiting Committee Electrical Engineering School, Univ. of N.S.W.; Chmn., Engineering Course Assessment Cttee.; N.S.W. Advanced Education Bd.; Member, Engineering Advisory Cttee.; Chmn., Electronic & Electrical Sector Cttee., Metric Conversion Bd., Australia; Chmn., Aust. Council on Awards in Advanced Education. *Address:* 39C Boronia Av., Cheltenham, Sydney, N.S.W.; and *office* Philips Industries Holdings Ltd., 99 York St., Sydney, N.S.W., Australia.

**BROWN, Sir John Gilbert Newton,** CBE, MA. *B.* 1916. *Educ.* Lancing Coll. and Hertford Coll., Oxford (MA Zoology); Fellow Hertford Coll., Oxford. *M.* 1946, Virginia. *Dau.* of Darcy and Dorothy Braddell. *S.* 1. *Daus.* 2. *Career:* At Bombay Branch, Oxford Univ. Press 1937–40; Comm'd. Royal Artillery 1941; served with 5th Field Regt. 1941–46; captured by the Japanese at fall of Singapore 1942; Prisoner-of-War, Malaya, Formosa and Japan 1942–45; returned to O.U.P. 1946; Sales Manager 1949–56; Publisher of the Oxford University Press, Oct. 1956—; President, Publishers Association, Apr. 1963–65. *Member* of Council 1955—, Pres. 1963–65 Publishers' Assn.; Member, Bd. British Library 1973; Exec. Brit. Council. *Club:* Garrick. *Address:* Milton Lodge, Great Milton, Oxon.; and *office* Oxford University Press, Walton Street, Oxford.

**BROWN, Katharine Kennedy.** American politician. *Educ.* Dana Hall. *M.* 1921, Kleon Thaw Brown (*dec.*). *Career:* Member, Montgomery County, Ohio, Republican Executive Committee 1920–21, 1926–48, 1949–54–58–64–66–68–70–72; Member, Republican State Central and Executive Committees of Ohio 1929–54–58–64–66–68–70–72; Member, Exec. Committee, Republican National Committee 1942–52; Delegate-at-large from Ohio to Republican National Conventions 1932, 1944, 1948–52–56–60–64–68; Member, Advisory Board, National Federation Republican Women's Clubs 1940–64–68–70; Pres., Ohio Federation Republican Women's Organization 1940–72; Regent, Jonathon Dayton Chapter, D.A.R.; Chairman, Dayton Circle Colonial Dames of America.; Vice-President, Ohio Yellow Cab Co., Dayton, Ohio; Vice-Chairman, Republican National Committee 1944–52; Vice-Chairman, Robert A. Taft Memorial Foundation; Republican National Committeewoman for Ohio 1932–68. Presbyterian. *Address:* 'Duncarrick', Dayton, Ohio, U.S.A.

**BROWN, Kenneth Harold,** OBE, QC. Canadian advocate; partner in law firm of Lafleur & Brown, Montreal. *B.* 1908. *Educ.* McGill Univ. (BA); Oxford Univ. (BA, BCL). *M.* 1934, Agnes Morton. *S.* 1. *Dau.* 1. *Career:* Called to Bar (Inner Temple, London) 1932; Admitted to Bar, Province of Quebec 1933; practised as advocate in Montreal since 1933, except for war service; commissioned Lieut., R.C.A. 1941; served in Canada, U.K. and North. West Europe (successively in 7th Canadian L.A.A. Regt. H.Q., 1st Canadian A.A. Bde., H.Q. 4th Canadian Armd. Div., and H.Q. First Canadian Army) 1941–45; discharged with rank of Lieut.-Col. (General List) 1945; awarded OBE, (Miltary Div.) 1945. *Address:* 4300 de Maisonneuve West, Montreal, and *office* 800 Victoria Square, Montreal, Que., Canada.

**BROWN, Kenneth Stanley.** Australian. *B.* 1913. *Educ.* Melbourne C. of E. Grammar School, and Melbourne University (BEE). *M.* 1946. Miriam Morley. *S.* Alexander. *Career:* Technical Dir. (1962–77) and Mem. of Board of Dirs. (1975), Standard Telephones and Cables Pty. Ltd., Sydney; Dir., Austral Standard Cables Pty. Ltd., Melbourne (1975). *Member:* Institution of Electrical Engineers (London); Institution of Engineers, Australia. *Fellow:* Institution of Radio and Electronic Engineers, Australia (Past President). *Club:* Royal Automobile Club of Australia. *Address:* 'Rothenfels', 424 Old Northern Road (P.O. Box 109), Castle Hill, N.S.W. 2154; and *office* Box 525, G.P.O. Sydney, N.S.W., Australia.

**BROWN, Leland Scott.** American. *B.* 1908. *Educ.* Northwestern Univ. (BS 1930). *M.* 1939, Mary Murray Mahony. *S.* Morgan S. *Dau.* 1. *Career:* Senior Vice-Pres., Citibank, N.A., N.Y.C., 1953–68; Dir. LIN. Broadcasting Corp., New York, N.Y.; Republican. *Clubs:* University (N.Y.C.). *Address:* Baldwin Road, R.D. No. 2, Mt. Kisco, N.Y., U.S.A.

**BROWN, Mervyn,** CMG, OBE. British Diplomat. *B.* 1923. *Educ.* Ryhope Grammar School, Sunderland; St. John's Coll., Oxford (M.A.). *M.* 1949, Elizabeth Gittings. *Career:* Third Sec., Buenos Aires 1950–53; Second Sec. New York 1953–56; First Sec., Foreign Office 1956–59; Singapore 1959–60; Vientiane 1960–63; Foreign Office 1963–67; H.M. Ambassador, Tananarive 1967–70; Inspector, Diplomatic Service 1970–72; Head of Communication Dept., Foreign & Cwth. Office 1973–74; Asst. Under-Sec. (Dir. of Communications) 1974; British High Commissioner, Dar es Salam and concurrently H.M. Amb. to Tananarive since 1975. *Awards:* Companion of the Order of St. Michael & St. George, 1975; Officer of the Order of the British Empire, 1963. *Clubs:* Travellers Club; Hurlingham Club; Royal Commonwealth Socy. *Address* and *office:* British High Commission, P.O. Box 9200, Dar Es Salaam, Tanzania.

**BROWN, Sir Raymond Frederick,** OBE, CompIEE, FIERE. British. *B.* 19 July 1920. *Educ.* Morden Terrace L.C.C. School; S.E. London Tech. Coll.; Morley College. *M.* (2) Carol Jacquelin Elizabeth. *S.* 2. *Daus.* 2. *Career:* Joined Redifon eng. apprentice 1934; Sales Man., Communications Div. Plessey Ltd. 1949–50; formerly Chmn. Man. Dir., Racal Electronics Ltd. (Jt. founder 1950); Head of Defence Sales, Min. Technology-Defence 1966–69; Chmn. Man. Dir., Muirhead Ltd.; Chmn. Racecourse Technical Services Ltd.; Consultant Adviser Commercial Policy, & Exports to Secy. of State, Dept. Health & Social Security 1969–72; Brit. Overseas Trade Bd. Working Group. Innovation & Exports 1972–74; Adviser to NEDO "to promote export of equipments purchased by Nationalised Industries"; Past-Pres. Electronic Eng. Assoc.; Member, Liveryman-Scriveners Co.; Member, Soc. of Pilgrims. *Clubs:* Life Member, Guards Polo; Sunningdale Golf; City Livery; Travellers; Swinley Forest Golf; Canada; Australia. *Address:* Westcroft Park, Windesham Road, Chobham, Surrey GU24 8SN; and 12 Hill Street, London, W.1.

**BROWN, Ted W.** American state official. *B.* 19 Apr. 1906. *Educ.* Springfield City Schools; Springfield High School; Wittenberg College. *M.* 1926, Florence Mitchell. *Daus.* Marilyn (Bruning), Barbara Larkins), Sherrie (Rogers). *Career:* County Recorder, Clark County, Ohio 1932–36; worked with Bureau Motor Vehicles (Ohio) 1939–45; operated own business 1945–50; Secretary of State for Ohio since 1951. Past Pres., Nat. Assn. of Secretaries of State. *Publications:* Ohio Laws; National, State and County Roster; Ohio Capitols; Evolution of the Ballot with Digest of Party Functions; The American Flag and History of the Ohio Flag; Republican. *Address:* 6036 Dublin Road, Dublin, Ohio 43017; and *office* 14th Floor, State Office Tower, 30E Broad Street, Columbus, Ohio 43216, U.S.A.

**BROWN, William Anthony Bartlett,** MA, FIMechE. British. *B.* 1925. *Educ.* Beaumont Coll., Merton Coll., Oxford (MA Eng). *M.* 1950, Angela M. McKnight. *S.* 1. *Career:* Chmn. & Man. Dir., Rose Forgrove Ltd.; Dir. Baker Perkins Holdings Ltd.; John Waddington Ltd.; FRSA; Fellow, British Inst. of Management. *Member:* Royal Yachting Assoc. *Address:* The Brownberries, Brownberrie Lane, Horsforth, Leeds; and *office* Seacroft, Leeds, LS14 2AN.

**BROWN, Dr. William Byron.** American physicist. *B.* 1894. *Educ.* Univ. of Calif. (AB 1916); Ohio State Univ. (PhD 1922). *M.* 1919, Katharine Van Dyne. *S.* William Byron (*dec.*). *Daus.* Mary Adelaide, Katharine Belle and Frances Ann. *M.* Ruth Elizabeth Cleveland, 1967. *Career:* Physicist, Nat. Bureau of Standards 1917–20; Missionary, Judson Coll., Rangoon, Burma 1922–23; Prof., Emory and Henry Coll. 1925–32; Aeronautical Research Scientist, National Advisory Committee for Aeronautics 1941–52; Engineering Specialist, Northrop Corp. 1952—; Prof. Calif., Baptist Coll. since 1971. *Publications:* Some 23 publications, including Design of Fins for Air-Cooled Engines (1920); Mathematical Equations for Heat Conduction in the Fins of Air-Cooled Engines (1922); Thermal Conductivities of Some Metals and Alloys in the Solid and Liquid States (1923); Extension of Boundary-Layer Heat-Transfer Theory to Cooled Turbine Blades (1950); Exact Solutions of the Laminar Boundary-Layer Equations for a Porous Plate with Variable Fluid Properties and Pressure Gradient in the Main Stream (1951); A stability criterion for 3-dimensional laminar boundary layers; exact Solution of the Stability Equations for Laminar Boundary Layers in Comprehensible Flow (1961). Phi Beta Kappa; Sigma Xi. *Address:* 2832 Washington Avenue, Santa Monica, Calif., U.S.A.

**BROWNE, Sir (Edward) Humphrey,** CBE. British. *B.* 1911. *Educ.* Repton; Magdalene College, Cambridge (BA 1931; MA 1943); Birmingham University (Joint Mining Degree). *M.* 1934, Barbara Stone (*D.* 1970). *S.* .2. *Career:* Previously: Manager, Chanters Colliery; Director and Chief Mining Engineer, Manchester Collieries Ltd. 1943–46; Production Director, North Western Divisional Coal Board 1947–48; Chief Mining Engineer (Reconstruction and Planning), National Coal Board 1948–49; Director-General of Production, N.C.B. 1949–55; Chairman, West Midlands Division, N.C.B. 1955–60. Deputy Chairman, National Coal Board 1960–67; Dir., Bestobell 1969—; Chairman, John Thompson Ltd. 1967–70; Deputy Chmn., Woodhall Duckham Group 1967–71; Chmn., 1971–73; Haden Carrier Ltd. 1973—; Pro-Chancellor Keele Univ. 1971–75; Chmn., British Transport Docks Board 1971—; Bestobell Ltd. since 1973; Pres., British Coal Utilization Research Assn. 1963–68; Member, Bd. Commonwealth Development Corp. 1969–72. Holder of the Institution of Mining Engineers Medal. Fellow, Institute of Mining Engineers (Pres. 1957–58); Fellow, Chartered Inst. of Transport, 1976; Pres., Inst. of Freight Forwarders, 1976. *Club:* Brooks's (London). *Address:* 31, Dorset House, Gloucester Place, London, NW1 5AD, and Beckbury Hall, Shifnal, Shropshire; and *office* British Transport Docks Board, Melbury House, London, N.W.1.

**BROWNELL, Hon. Herbert.** *B.* 20 Feb. 1904. *Educ.* Grade and High Schools, Lincoln, Nebraska, the University of Nebraska (BA) and Yale Law School (LLB). *M.* 1934, Doris McCarter. *S.* Thomas McCarter, James Barker. *Daus.* Joan, Ann. *Career:* Began practice of law in 1927, first with Root, Clark, Buckner, Howland & Ballantine, and later (1929) with Lord, Day & Lord; Attorney-General, U.S.A. 1953–57. *Member:* Of the American, New York State, and the City of New York Bar Associations; U.S. Member, Permanent Hague Court of Arbitration. *Address:* 25 Broadway, New York City 4, U.S.A.

**BRUCE OF DONINGTON, Lord.** (Donald William Trevor). British Chartered Accountant, Economist. *B.* 1912. *Education:* Grammar-School, Donington (Lincs). *M.* 1939, Jane Letitia Butcher. *S.* 1. *Daus.* 2. *Career:* In business as Chartered Accountant 1938–39; Served at home and in France with R. Signals (Major) 1939–45; MP (labour) North Portsmouth and PPS to Rt. Hon. Aneurin Bevan 1945–50; Member of Min. of Health Delegation to Sweden and Denmark since 1946; Member of House of Commons Select Cttee on Public Accounts 1948–50; Resumed Practice as Chartered Accountant 1950; Created Life Baron 1974; Member of European Parlt. 1975. *Fellow* of Inst. of Chartered Accountants in England and Wales. *Publications:* Contributions to several Journals. *Club:* Reform. *Address:* Pinecroft, Heronsgate, Rickmansworth, Herts and *office* 24/27 Thayer Street, London W.1.

**BRUCE, David K. E.** American government official. *B.* 1898. *Educ.* Princeton Univ. and Univs. of Virginia and Maryland. *M.* (1) Ailsa Mellon (*D.*). *Dau.* Audrey (*D.*); (2) Evangeline Bell. *S.* David Surtees and Nicholas Cabell. *Dau.* Alexandra. *Career:* Served World War I in U.S. Army 1917–20 and World War II 1942–45; admitted to Maryland Bar 1921 and practised in Baltimore 1921–25; Member, Maryland House of Delegates 1924–26, Virginia House of Delegates 1939–42; Vice-Consul, U.S. Foreign Service, Rome 1926–28; engaged in business and farming 1928–40; with Office of Strategic Services 1941–45; Director, E.T.O. 1943–45; Chief Representative in Great Britain for American Red Cross 1940; Assistant Secretary of Commerce 1947–48; Chief, Economic Co-operation Administration to France May 1948–49; Amb. Ex. and Plen. to France 1949–52; Under-Secretary of State, 1952–53; U.S. Observer in Europe, Feb. 1953–Jan. 1955; Amb. Ex. & Plen. to Federal Republic of Germany, 1957–59; to Court of St. James's, Mar. 1961–69; U.S. Rep. to the Viet-Nam Peace Talks, Paris 1970–71; Chief U.S. Liaison Office, Peking, China 1973–74; U.S. Perm. Rep. to NATO, Brussels 1974–76. *Publication:* Revolution to Reconstruction. Deceased 5th December 1977.

**BRUCE-GARDYNE, John.** BA. British politician. *B.* 1930. *Educ.* Winchester Coll.; Magdalen Coll., Oxford (BA Hons.). *M.* 1959, Sarah Maitland. *S.* Thomas and Adam. *Dau.* Roselle. *Career:* With H.M. Foreign Service, 3rd Secy. London & Bulgaria, 1953–56; Financial Times Correspondent, Paris, 1957–60; Financial Times, London, 1960–61; Foreign Editor, The Statist, London, 1961–64; Member of Parliament for South Angus 1964–74; Parly. Private Secy. to Secy. of State for Scotland 1970–72; Vice-Chmn., Conservative Party Finance Cttee. 1972–74. *Club:* Garrick. *Address:* 13 Kelso Place, London, W.8.

**BRUCHÉSI, Jean.** Canadian diplomat. *B.* 1901. *Educ.* Univ. of Montreal (BA; LLM; Dr. Pol. Sc.) and Univ. of Paris (M. Pol. Sc.). *M.* 1930, Berthe Denis. *Daus.* Anne (married) and Nicole (married). Awarded many prizes and distinctions by Canadian cultural societies, including the Royal Society of Canada; Laureate of the Académie Française and of the Académie des Sciences morales et politiques (France); LLD (h.c.), Univ. of Caen, Univ. of Manitoba, Laval Univ., and Univ. of Bordeaux. *Career:* Lecturer in general history, Faculty of Letters, Univ. of Montreal 1927–37; Prof. of Political Science 1929–37, of Economic Policy 1931–37 and of Foreign Policy 1929–58, Faculty of Social Sciences, Economics and Politics, Univ. of Montreal; Prof. of Canadian History, Externat Classique Saint-Sulpice, Montreal 1930–37, and at the Marguerite-Bourgeoys Coll., Montreal 1932–59; Prof. of Canadian Economic History, High School of Commerce, Laval Univ. 1943–52; Lecturer, Faculty of Letters, Univ. of Paris 1948 and at Institute of Political Studies, Paris 1948. Under-Secretary of State and Deputy Registrar of Province of Quebec 1937–59. Ambassador to Spain 1959–64, and Morocco 1962–64; Ambassador to Argentina, Uruguay and Paraguay 1964–67; Research Fellow, History, Univ. Ottawa 1969–71. *Awards:* Knight, Legion of Honour (France); Officer, Order of Honour & Merit (Haiti); Comdr. Order Merite Culturel (Monaco); Knight Grand Cross, St. Gregory the Great (Vatican); Knight Grand Cross, Isabel (Spain). *Publications:* Chief Editor, La Revue Moderne, Montreal 1930–35 and l'Action Universitaire, 1934–37; contributor to French-language newspapers on foreign politics 1928–35, to French and English-language magazines, to the Memoirs of Royal Society of Canada, the Cahiers des Dix, World Book Encyclopedia, Encyclopedia Canadiana and Encyclopedia Americana. Author of 22 books and some

40 pamphlets on literature, international politics, Canadian history and education. His most important books are: Aux Marches de l'Europe; l'Epopée Canadienne; Rappels; Histoire du Canada; Le Chemin des Ecoliers; Canada, réalités d'hier et d'aujourd'hui (trans. to English); Le Canada (trans. to Eng.); Voyages . . . Mirages; Souvenirs à Vaincre and Souvenirs d'Ambassade (1959–72). *Address:* Apt. 903, 2 Square Westmount, Boul. de Maisonneuve, Montreal PQ, Canada, H32 2S4.

**BRUGGER, Ernst.** Swiss Politician. *B.* 1914. *Educ.* Univs of Zurich, London and Paris. *M.* 1937., Eleanora Ringer. *S.* 5. *Career:* Sec. School teacher Gossau 1936; cantonal councillor 1947–59; mem of cantonal govt. Zurich, 1959–70; Dir. of Interior and Justice Depts 1959–67; Dir. of Public Economy Dept. 1967–69; Federal Councillor, head of Ministry of Public Economy, Berne since 1970. *Address:* Egelberstr. 17, 3000 Berne, and *office:* Ministry of Public Economy, 3003 Berne, Switzerland.

**BRUN de PONTET, Dr. André.** Kt. of Malta; American. *B.* 1905. *Educ.* Univ. of Paris (PhD; LLD); Univ. of Madrid (LLD); Museum of Man, Institute of Ethnology, Paris; Mission for Columbia Univ. (Middle-East Research Project). *M.* 1937, Janine Meyer. *S.* Ariel. *Dau.* Joëlle (Lee Gatling II). *Career:* With Morgan & Co., Paris 1925–28; Barrister-at-Law, Court of Appeal, Paris 1928–31; Manager, Louis Dreyfus Bank, Paris 1931–40; Called to the Colours 1940–45; Pres., Central-Louisiana, New Orleans 1945–48; Chmn. of Board, Centra-Latina, Mexico 1946–49. Member, New York Stock Exchange, May 1947—; Director: Papeteries de Gascogne (France), Gaillard-Maroc (Casablanca), Motels Côte d'Azur (France); Financial Counsellor to the Government of Monaco since 1956. *Publications:* La Mejora et la Quotité Disponible, 1930; Revue du Liban, 1928–32; Périple d'Hammon, 1929; New Orleans—Foreign Trade Zone, 1942; Mika, 1947; Mission to the Druzes, 1950; The Canary Islands Story. *Member:* Int. Bar Assn.; Int. Law Assn.; N.Y. Acad. of Sciences; Amer. Anthropological Assn.; Amer. Ethnological Assn.; Athenée Louisianais (New Orleans), etc. *Clubs:* Umanak (Greenland) Explorers (N.Y.C.); Cercle Interallie, France Libre (Paris); Yachting (Monaco); Fins Becs (Cannes); American (Paris); University (Paris). *Address:* 23 rue Raynouard, Paris XVI, France; and 3705 33rd Place N.W., Washington, D.C., U.S.A.; and Palais Ruscino, Monaco.

**BRUNET, Jean Pierre.** French Diplomat. *B.* 1920. *Educ.* Lycée St. Louis, Paris; Ecole Navale, Brest; Grand Concours du Ministère des Affaires Etrangères. *M.* 1970, Geneviève Didry. *Dau.* 1. *Career:* Naval Officer, Free French Forces 1940–45; Second Sec., French Embassy London 1946–48; Economic Dept., French Foreign Ministry 1948–61; Deputy Head of Mission to the European Communities 1961–64; Head of Economic Cooperation Section 1964–66 and Head of Economic Dept. 1966–75, French Foreign Ministry; Ambassador to Japan 1975–77, to the Federal Republic of Germany since 1977. *Award:* Commander of the Legion of Honour. *Address:* Embassy of France, Bonn, Federal Republic of Germany.

**BRUNET, Meade.** *B.* 1894. American Engineer. *Educ.* Union Coll., Schenectady, N.Y. (BEng). LLD. *M.* 1925, Edythe Redman. *S.* Stuart. *Dau.* Sally (Beyen). *Career:* Production Clerk, General Electric Co. (Schenectady) and Sperry Gyroscope Co. 1915–17; Commercial Engineer, Electric Public Utility Dept. 1919–22; various positions with Radio Corp. of America 1922–46; Vice-Pres. & Man. Dir., RCA International Div. 1946–57; Vice-Pres., Staff, RCA 1957–66. Author of History of the 56th Engineers in the First World War. Recipient: Victory Medal (World War I); Officer, Cruzeiro do Sul (Brazil); Officer, Order of Merit (Chile); Former Dir.: National Foreign Trade Council, 1950–66, and Pan American Socy of the U.S.; Senior Trustee, U.S. Council; International Chamber of Commerce; Adv. Board, Inst. of World Affairs, and A.I.E.S.E.C.; Committee on World Trade Arbitration; Amer. Arbitration Association; School of World Business & International Development, San Francisco State College; Natl. Assn. of Manufacturers 1962–63; U.S. Business Industry Advisory Council to OECD 1963–67; Inst. of Radio Engineers (Life Member); Amer. Socy. of Naval Engineers; Acad. of Political Science (Life Member); Hon. life member Conference Natural Organizations; Chmn., Board of Trustees (1963–69) and Acting Pres. (Feb.–July 1965), Union Coll., Schenectady; Board of Governors, Union University (Acting Chancellor Feb.–July 1965). *Clubs:* Army & Navy (Washington); Somerset Hills Country (Bernardsville, N.J.); University (N.Y.C.); Sigma Phi; Sigma Xi; Tau Beta Pi. *Address:* Millsdale Farm, Washington Corners, Mendham, N.J., U.S.A.

**BRUNNER, Dr. Guido.** German Diplomat and Politician. *B.* 1930. *Educ.* Bergzabern, Munich; German School, Madrid; Studied Law and Economics at Universities of Munich (Dr. of Law), Heidelberg and Madrid (Licentiate of Law). *M.* 1958, Christa Speidel. *Career:* Diplomatic Service 1955–74; Foreign Minister's Office 1956; Office of the Sec. of State for Foreign Affairs 1958–60; Office of the German Observer to the UN, New York 1960–68; Dept. of Scientific & Technological Relations, Ministry for Foreign Affairs 1968–70; Press Spokesman of Min. for Foreign Affairs 1970–72; Head of Planning Staff in Min. for Foreign Affairs and Amb. and Head of Del. of Fed. Rep. of Germany to Conference for Security & Cooperation in Europe, Helsinki/Geneva 1972–74; Mem. of the Commission of the European Communities since 1974, Commissioner for Energy, Research, Science & Education since 1977. Free Democratic Party (FDP). *Publications:* Bipolarität und Sicherheit, 1965; Friedenssicherungsaktionen der Vereinten Nationen, 1968; Articles in Vierteljahreshefte für Zeitgeschichte, Aussenpolitik, and Europa Archiv. *Address:* 200 rue de la Loi, 1049 Brussels, Belgium.

**BRUNNING, Carl.** Advertising agent. *B.* 1908. *Educ.* Secondary School. *M.* 1933, Eileen Fry. *S.* Geoffrey Bernard. *Career:* Has a wide experience in printing, publishing and advertising. Served in World War II; six years in Royal Navy; Lieut.Cmdr. (mentioned in Despatches three times) 1939–45; Life Pres., The Brunning Group Ltd., June 1962—. Director, Readicut International Ltd., July 1957; Chmn., Seamaster Ltd., June 1961. Dir. Societe Rochefortoise, SA. *Publication:* Rock Climbing & Mountaineering. *Clubs:* United Services. *Address:* Venn House, Dunmow, Essex; and *office* Brunning House, 100 Whitechapel Road, London, E.1.

**BRUNO, Harry.** American. *B.* London, Eng. 1893. *Educ.* Portland Prep. Coll., London and Montclair (N.J.) High School. *M.* (1) 1930, Nydia, *dau.* late Baron J. de Sosnowski of Poland (Dec.). (2) 1972, Evelyn Denny Witten. *Career:* Founder member, Sales Executive Club (N.Y.C.); founder member Wings Club (N.Y.C.). member, Board Directors, Rockfeller Center Luncheon Club (N.Y.C.) 1940–50; Chmn. and Past Cmdr. Air Service Post 501, American Legion; Public Relations Advisor to War Savings Staff of N.Y. State (1942–45) and to War Activities Council, Advertising Club of N.Y. (1943–44); Special consultant to Sec. Air Force (1949–57); Chmn., Public Relations Adv. Cttee. of U.S. Air Force (1949–54), Civil Defense of N.Y.C. (1950–55) and Aviation Writers Assn. (1948–51); member, Advisory Public Relations Cttee. of U.N. 1947–50; Chairman of the Board, H. A. Bruno & Associates, Inc., public relations counsel, N.Y.C. Ret. 1969. President, Lotos Club (N.Y.C.) 1951–62, Hon. Pres. 1962—. President Emeritus 1966—; Life member, New York Athletic Club; Pres., Adventurers Club (N.Y.C.) 1948; Chmn., N. Atlantic Div. Early Birds (pilots who flew before 1916) 1953; member, Bd. Governors, and Exec. Cttee., Flight Safety Found., N.Y. 1954—; charter member, Airplane Owners and Pilots Assn.; one of the founders (and member Exec. Cttee.), the Quiet Birdmen 1921—; member Adv. Cttee., Harmon Int. Trophies 1950—; built and flew world's smallest monoplane glider 1910; designed, constructed and flew man-carrying gliders 1911; as pilot at age of 17 admitted to U.S. Aeronautical Reserve 1910; served in World War I with British R.F.C. in Canada; made first circumnavigation of Great Lakes in a flying boat and received Glidden Trophy 1921. Trustee, Air Force Hist. Socy. Washington, D.C. *Awards:* Dipl. of Honor, Int. League of Aviators, 1930; Distinguished Service Award, Sales Executives Club; William McGough Memorial Award; Award of Merit, American Legion 1950; Cross of Lorraine (France) 1951; General William Mitchell Medal 1951; Exceptional Service Award, U.S.A.F. 1953; Elder Statesman of Aviation Nat. Aeronautic Assn. U.S.A. 1962; Air Force Assoc. citation 1966; USAFA 'Hap' Arnold Award 1968; Aviation Space Writers Assn. citation 1970; Amer. Legion Air Service Post Award 1973; Hon. Life mem. Wings Club. *Publications:* One book on public relations and two on aviation, the latest being Wings over America (the inside story of American aviation, with introduction by Maj. A. P. de Seversky) 1942, and 1944; many articles in national periodicals. *Clubs:* Sky, New York Yacht, Overseas Press, Automobile, Banshees, Natl. Fed. Sales Exec. (N.Y.); Air Force Assn. (Washington); Anglers (Key Largo, Fla.); Gypsy Trail (Carmel, N.Y.); Navy League of U.S.; Socy. of Silurians; Broadcast Pioneers; Int. Socy. Aviation Writers; Amer. Geographical Socy. (Fellow); Aviation Space Writers

Assn. *Address:* 'Green Chimneys', 4 Fairview Avenue, Montauk, N.Y. 11954, U.S.A.

**BRYAN, Sir Andrew Meikle,** DSc, LLD. British mining engineer. *B.* 1 March 1893. *Educ.* Hamilton Academy; Glasgow University (BSc). *M.* 1922, Henrietta Begg. *S.* John Gordon. *Career:* Served World War I 1915–18; H.M. Junior Inspector of Mines 1920; Senior rank 1926; Dixon Professor of Mining, University of Glasgow and Royal Technical College, Glasgow 1932–40; General Manager, Shotts Iron Co. Ltd. 1940, Director 1942, Managing Director 1944–47; Director, Associated Coal Owners Ltd.; Deputy Director of Mining Supplies, Mines Department 1939–40; also Chairman of the Coal Industry Joint Fuel Efficiency Committee, and Group Production Director (Scottish Region) 1944 and 1945; H.M. Chief Inspector of Mines, Great Britain 1947–51; has been External Examiner in Mining Engineering to the Universities of Leeds, Sheffield, Wales and London; Member of Council, Mining Institute of Scotland (Past-President); Institution of Mining Engineers (President 1950 and 1951); National Association of Colliery Managers (Past-Pres.); Chmn. of Mining Qualifications Board, 1962–70. Member of Safety in Mines Research (Advisory) Bd. of Min. of Power 1947–67; member, for Staff, National Coal Board 1951–57; Hon. Fellow Institution of Mining and Metallurgy, Inst. of Mining Eng., and Natl. Assn. of Colliery Managers; Fellow Imperial Coll. of Science and Technology; FRSE; FICE; FIMinE; FIMM; CEng; FInstFuel; Founder Mem., Fellowship of Engineering, 1976. *Publications:* St. George's Coalfield, Newfoundland; The Evolution of Health and Safety in Mines (1975); papers on mining subjects in Transactions of Institution of Mining Engineers; National Association of Colliery Managers and Association of Mining, Electrical and Mechanical Engineers; Official Reports on Mining Disasters at Burngrange Oil Shale Mine; Whitehaven (William) Colliery; Ingham Colliery; Knockshinnoch Castle Colliery; and Cresswell Colliery. *Address:* National Coal Board, Hobart House, Grosvenor Place, London, S.W.1.

**BRYAN, Leslie Aulls.** American transportation economist. *B.* 1900. *Educ.* BS; MS; PhD; JD; ScD; Brewer Award; Arents Medal; Tissandier Diploma; Distinguished Service Medal, CAP; Silver Beaver and Silver Antelope Awards, Boy Scouts of America; Distinguished Public Service Award, Federal Aviation Agency; Award of Merit, Air Training Command. USAF; Good Citizenship Medal, Sons of the American Revolution. *M.* 1931, Gertrude C. Gelder. *S.* Leslie A., Jr. and George G. *Career:* Instructor to Franklin Professor of Transportation, Syracuse University 1925–46; President, Seneca Flying School 1943–46; Director of Aviation, New York State 1945; Board of Aeronautical Advisors, State of Illinois 1949–69; sometime consultant to U.S. Air Force, Armed Forces Institute, Federal Aviation Agency, U.S. Department of Commerce, Federal Civil Defence Administration etc.; Director, Institute of Aviation and Professor of Management, University of Illinois 1946–68, Emeritus 1968; member, President Kennedy's Committee on National Aviation Goals 1961. *Publications:* Aerial Transportation (1924); Industrial Traffic Management (1929); Principles of Water Transportation (1939); Air Transportation (1949); Traffic Management in Industry (1952); Fundamentals of Aviation and Space Technology (1959); revised edition (1968); also many monographs and articles. *Clubs:* Alpha Delta Sigma, Alpha Eta Rho, Alpha Phi Omega, Alpha Kappa Psi, Beta Gamma Sigma, Kappa Phi Kappa, Phi Delta Phi, Phi Kappa Alpha, Phi Kappa Phi, Pi Gamma Mu, Delta Nu Alpha, Sigma Alpha Tau, Tau Omega, Zeta Psi; Army and Navy; Champaign Country; Rotary. *Address:* 34 Fields East, Champaign, Ill., 61820, U.S.A.

**BRYAN, Wright.** American newspaper editor and university officer. *B.* 1905. *Educ.* Clemson College (BS and Hon Doctor of Letters); University of Missouri School of Journalism; Hon LLD, College of Wooster. *M.* 1932, Ellen Hillyer Newell. *S.* William Wright, Jr. *Daus.* Ellen Newell and Mary Lane. Recipient Medal of Freedom (U.S.A.). *Career:* Reporter (1924) and sports editor (1926) Greenville (S.C.) Piedmont; Reporter, City Editor, Managing Editor, Associate Editor, Atlanta Journal 1927–45 (Editor 1945–53). War Correspondent, Atlanta Journal and National Broadcasting Company (European Theatre) 1943–45. Editor, Cleveland Plain Dealer, Cleveland, Ohio, Jan. 1954–1963; Dir. and Overseer, Sweet Briar Coll. 1957–70; Dir. The Associated Press 1961–63; Vice-Pres. for Development, Clemson Univ. 1964–70. *Member:* Amer. Society of Newspaper Editors (Past Pres.); Sigma Delta Chi. *Clubs:* Piedmont Driving, Capital City, Nine O'Clocks (Atlanta); Overseas Press (N.Y.C.); Poinsett (Greenville, S.C.). *Address:* P.O. Box 470, Clemson, S.C. 29631, U.S.A.

**BRYCE, Robert Broughton.** Canadian Civil Servant. *B.* 1910. *Educ.* University of Toronto (BAScEng); Cambridge University (MAEcon); Harvard University (Post-Grad economics). *M.* 1937, Frances Robinson. *S.* Robert Charles and Alexander David. *Dau.* Marjory. *Career:* Economist, Sun Life Assurance Co., Montreal 1937–38; joined Department of Finance 1938; Secretary to Government's Economic Advisory Cttee. during World War II; First Canadian Director, International Bank, Washington 1946; Assistant Deputy Minister of Finance and Secretary to the Treasury Board 1947; Secretary to the Cabinet 1954; Deputy Minister of Finance 1963–70; Economic Adviser to the Prime Minister, 1970–71; Exec. Dir., International Monetary Fund 1971; Chmn. Royal Comm. on Corporate Concentration 1975. *Address:* 14 Monkland Avenue, Ottawa, Ont K1S 1Y9, Canada.

**BRYCESON, Michael Antony.** British. *B.* 1925. *Educ.* St. Paul's School. *M.* 1964, Pamela Ann Bennett. *S.* 2. *Career:* Partner, Kenneth Brown Baker Baker, 1955–69; Chmn. London & Midland Industrials Ltd. 1969–73; Principal, Michael Bryceson and Co. Solicitors; Hon. Vice-Pres., Anglo-Texan Soc.; Founder Member Council and Hon. Treasurer of Justice; Vice-Pres., European-Atlantic Group. *Clubs:* Royal Ocean Racing; Royal Thames Yacht; Boodles. *Address:* 34A Pembroke Square, London W8 6PD; and *office* 26 Bedford Row, London WC1R 4HE.

**BRYDEN, William,** CBE, BA, MSc, (N.Z.), PhD (Edin.), Hon. DSc. Tasmania FRSEd.; *B.* 1904. *M.* 1933, Muriel MacLaren (of Edinburgh). *S.* 3. *Career:* Lecturer, University, Christchurch, N.Z. 1930–40; Warden and Senior Lecturer, University of Melbourne 1935–40; Principal, Knox College, Sydney 1940–52; Director, Tasmanian Museum and Art Gallery, Hobart 1953–72; Chmn., National Parks & Wildlife Service; Tasmanian Div. Duke of Edinburgh Award Scheme. *Publications:* Numerous scientific and art journals. *Fellow:* Royal Society of Edinburgh, Royal Soc. of Tasmania (Life). *Clubs:* University; Tasmanian. *Address:* Summerless Road, Kingston, Tasmania, Australia.

**BRYDON, Adam Howie,** DFC (and Bar). Australian. *B.* 1921. *Educ.* The Armidale School (Armidale, N.S.W.). *M.* (1) 1954, Lois Stevens (*m.* dissolved), and (2) 1966, Lesley Ann Barker (*m.* dissolved), and (3) 1975, Jocelyn May Peters. *Dau.* Susan. *Career:* R.A.A.F. (Sqdn. Ldr., C.O. 78 Fighter Sqdn.) 1939–46; Prop. Brydon Motors (motor traders) 1948–55; Gen. Mgr. and Dir., Diners Club Pty. Ltd. 1956–60, and Cumberland Newspapers Pty. Ltd. 1960–62 (Managing Dir. 1962–64); Advertising Director, Mirror Newspapers Ltd. 1964–65, General Manager 1965–69; Group General Manager and Dir., News Ltd. of Australia, 1969–70; Director, Mirror Newspapers Ltd. and subsidiaries 1961–70; Chairman, Cumberland Newspapers Pty. Ltd. and subsidiaries 1964–70; Dep. Gen. Mgr., The Herald and Weekly Times Ltd. 1970–77; Chmn., Argus and Australasian Ltd. 1974–77; Vice-Pres. (Operations), New York Post 1977—. *Clubs:* Royal Brighton Yacht, Cruising Yacht, Naval & Military (all Australia). *Address:* 180 East End Avenue, New York, N.Y. 10028; and *office* New York Post Corp., 210 South Street, New York, N.Y. 10002, U.S.A.

**BRYK, Petri (Baldur).** Finnish chemical and metallurgical engineer; PhD *h.c.* ScDhc. *B.* 13 Dec. 1913. *M.* 1943, Liisa Maria Simula. *S.* Petri Juhani. *Dau.* Eeva Maria. *Career:* Managing Dir., Outokumpu Copper Mines Inc. (Outokumpu Oy) 1953–72; previously Metallurgist of the Company 1938–49 and Chief Metallurgist 1949–53. *Awards:* Commander First Class Order of the Lion (Finland); Commander First Class Order of Finlands White Rose, Liberty Cross 2nd Class. Medal for Civic Merits (Finland). *Address:* Jt. Kaivopuisto 3A, Helsinki, Finland.

**BUCHANAN, Alfred Edgar,** DSO. Captain, RAN (retd.); MID; Bronze Star (U.S.). Commonwealth (of Australia). *B.* 1903. *Educ.* Naval College, Jervis Bay. *M.* 1941, Norma Selby Shields Simpson. *S.* Peter, Robert. *Dau.* Susan. *Career:* Permanent Australian Navy 1917–48. At Dept. of Defence: Commonwealth War Book Office; Asst. Secretary: Intelligence and Administration. Director of Civil Defence, July 1961–67. *Clubs:* Naval & Military (Melbourne). *Address:* 27 Rest Drive, Flinders, Victoria, Australia.

**BUCHANAN, Richard,** JP, MP. British politician and engineer. *B.* 1914. *Educ.* St. Mungo's Academy, Royal Tech. Coll. (now Univ. of Strathclyde). *M.* (1) 1938, Margaret

McManus (*d.* 1963). *S.* 6. *Daus.* 2. (2) 1971, Helen Duggan. *Career:* Councillor & Magistrate, City of Glasgow 1949–64; Justice of the Peace 1952; Treas., City of Glasgow 1959–64; Pres., Scottish Central Library Assn. 1962–63; Hon. Life Pres. 1969; Chmn., Scottish Library 1964–74; Chmn., Advisory Council, Nat. Library of Scotland; Dir., Glasgow Citizens Theatre since 1959. Member: Parliament, Glasgow Springburn since 1964; Secy., Scottish Labour Members 1966–74; P.P.S. to Chief Secy. to Treasury 1968–70. *Club:* St. Mungo's Centenary. *Address:* 103 Oakwood Court, London, W.14 and *office* House of Commons, London, S.W.1.

**BUCHANAN-SMITH, Alick Laidlaw,** MA, MP. British. *B.* 1932. *Educ.* Cambridge. *M.* 1956, Janet Lawrie. *S.* James. *Daus.* Jean, Margaret and Fenella. *Career:* Member of Parliament, Conservative, North Angus & Mearns since 1964; Parly. Under-Secy. Scottish Office 1970–74. *Address:* House of Cockburn, Balerno, Midlothian.

**BUENCAMINO, Delfin.** Filipino. *B.* 1897. *Educ.* Jose Rizal Coll. (BCS; MBA; New York Univ. LLB); Far Eastern Univ. *M.* Salud Jakosalem. *S.* 3. *Daus.* 5. *Career:* Pres., Delsa Buencamino Inc., Philippine Institute of Banking; Chmn. Board of Dirs.; Chmn., Peroxide (Philippines) Inc.; Dir. & Financial Adviser Riverside Mills Corp.; Dir., Comimercial Bank & Trust Co., Manila; formerly Chmn., Rehabilitation Finance; Mem. Monetary Board, Central Bank; Vice-Pres. Philippine National Bank; Exec. Vice-Pres., Talisay Silay Sugar Central & Maao Sugar Central; Bacolod Sugar Central; Chmn. Pres. Eastman Chemical Industries; Chmn. Polystyrene. *Clubs:* Filipino; Inc; Valley Golf & Country; Philippine Columbian Assoc.; Wack-Wack Golf & Country (proprietary Mem. of all); Baguio Country; International, New York. *Address:* 44 Scout Borromeo, Quezon City, Philippines.

**BULL, William Frederick.** Canadian. *B.* 1903. *Educ.* Univ. of Toronto (BCom 1928). *M.* 1930, Marjorie Ruth Eoll. *S.* Roger and John. *Daus.* Frederica (Fleming) and Susan Lees. *Career:* Joined Dept. of Trade and Commerce, March 1929; Junior Trade Commissioner, Ottawa, March 1929; Asst. Trade Commissioner, New York, Sept. 1929; Trade Commissioner, Trinidad, July 1931 and Auckland, N.Z., Jan. 1937; Asst. Chief, Export Permit Branch, Ottawa, Jan. 1942; Commercial Attaché, Washington, March 1943; Director, Export Div. Ottawa, Aug. 1945 and Commodities Branch, Ottawa, March 1947; Asst. Deputy Minister, Ottawa, Sept. 1950; Deputy Minister, March 1951; Canadian Ambassador to Japan 1957–63; Ambassador to the Netherlands 1963–65. *Clubs:* Royal Ottawa Golf; Five Lakes Fishing. *Address:* 307 Faircrest Road, Ottawa, Ont. Canada.

**BULLEN, John Deacon.** British. *B.* 1924. *Educ.* Stockport Grammar School; Manchester Univ. *M.* 1946, Kathleen M. Preston. *Dau.* 1. *Career:* Man. Dir., British La Bour Pump Co. Ltd.; Dir., Metallic Construction Co. Ltd. 1947–53; Man. Dir., Northide Ltd. 1953–55; Chmn. & Man. Dir., Deacon Bullen Ltd. 1955–63; Chmn., Ludlow Industries (U.K.) Ltd.; Exec. Vice-Pres., Katy Industries Inc.; Dir., General & Engineering Industries Ltd.; Bach-Simpson (U.K.) Ltd. *Club:* Harpenden Golf. *Address:* Davylands, The Warren, West Common, Harpenden, Herts.; and *office* Dennington Estate, Wellingborough, Northants.

**BULLOCK, Alan John.** British. Director of Public Affairs, Chrysler United Kingdom Ltd.; Dir; Public Relations, Chrysler International S.A. *B.* 1924. *Educ.* Bromsgrove School. *M.* 1950, Jean Peters. *Daus.* Sally and Francesca. *Career:* Reporter, Redditch Indicator and Alcester Chronicle 1939–41; Military Service 1941–46; Chief Reporter, Evesham Standard 1946–47; Reporter, Evening News & Times 1947–48; Feature Writer, Evening Despatch 1948–49; Night News Editor, Birmingham Gazette 1949–51, and Westminster Press Group 1951–52. Senior Account Executive, Sidney Barton Ltd. 1952–54; Chief PRO Rootes Group 1954–61; Managing Director, Sidney Barton Ltd. 1961–63; Managing Director, Bullock & Turner Ltd. 1963–66. Fellow, Inst. Public Relations. *Member:* Transport Trust (Life); International Public Relations Assn.; National Union of Journalists. Institute of Directors; Foreign Press Assn.; British Horse Socy.; British Show Jumping Assn.; Surrey Union Hunt. *Clubs:* Royal Automobile; Press. *Address:* Shellwood Mill, Leigh, Surrey; and *office* Chrysler United Kingdom Ltd., Halkin House, Halkin Street, London, S.W.1.

**BULLOCK, H. W.,** Australian Ambassador to Argentina, concurrently to Paraguay and Uruguay. *Address:* Australian Embassy, Buenos Aires, Argentina.

**BULLOCK, Hugh,** GBE, Associate Knight of Grace, CStJ. American investment banker. *B.* 2 June 1898. *Educ.* Williams College (AB); Civilian Aide to Secretary of the Army, for First Army Area 1952–53; LLD (hon) Hamilton College 1954, and Williams College 1957. *M.* 1933, Marie Leontine Graves. *Daus.* Florence Eno, Fair Alice (McCormick). *Career:* Served in World War I as 2nd Lieut. in the Infantry; served in World War II as Lieut-Col.; Pres., The Pilgrims of the United States; Governor, Investment Bankers Association of America 1953–55; Pres., National Inst. of Social Sciences 1950–53; Pres., Calvin Bullock Forum; Chmn. and Chief Ex. Officer, Calvin Bullock Ltd.; Pres. and Dir., Bullock Fund Ltd., Canadian Fund Inc., Canadian Investment Fund Ltd., Carriers & General Corp., Dividend Shares Inc.; Dir. and Chmn. of the Board, Nation-Wide Securities Co., U.S. Elec. Light & Power Shares Inc.; member, Eastern Regional Cttee., Marshall Scholarship 1955–58; Trustee and member Exec. Cttee., The Roosevelt Hospital; Trustee, Estate and Property of the Diocesan Convention of N.Y.; Trustee, Williams College. Appointed Hon. Kt. Cmdr. of the Order of the British Empire by H.M. the Queen (Oct. 1957); elected Fellow, Royal Society of Arts, 1958; Hon. Kt. Comdr. Order of George I (Greece). *Address:* 1 Wall Street, New York 5, N.Y., U.S.A.

**BULLUS, Sir Eric Edward.** British director and journalist. *B.* 1906. *Educ.* Leeds Modern School; University of Leeds. *M.* 1949, Joan. *Daus.* Jane and Jennifer. *Career:* Journalist, Yorkshire Post, Leeds & London 1923–46; Diocesan Reader Ripon, London, St. Albans & Canterbury since 1929. *Member:* Leeds City Council, 1930–40; Royal Air Force, Air Ministry & SEAC India, Ceylon 1940–45; Harrow Urban District Council 1947–50; Member Parliament, Wembley North 1950–74; Parly. Private Secy. Minister, Overseas Trade, Aviation and to Secy. of State for Defence, 1953–64; Member, House of Laity, Church Assembly 1960–70; of Council, Westfield Coll. Univ. of London 1963–70. *Publications:* History of Parish of Meanwood; History of Leeds Modern School; History of Church in Delhi; History of Lords and Commons Cricket. *Club:* M.C.C. *Address:* Westway, Herne Bay, Kent.

**BUNGE-MEYER, Lars Ingemar.** Swedish. President, Svenska PR-byrån AB (The Swedish PR Counsel Inc.), public relations consultants. *B.* 1925. *M.* 1947, Gunnel Margareta Lindecrantz. *S.* Lars Christer and Lars Peter. *Career:* P.R.O. Swedish Air Lines 1946–47; Correspondent to all Stockholm daily newspapers, Stockholm International Airport 1947–56! P.R. consultant for international clients in Sweden 1951–56; present position since 1956. *Publications:* numerous articles on tourism, television and public relations. *Member:* Swedish Publicists Club; Swedish Public Relations Assn.; Public Relations Society of America. *Address:* Karlavägen 26, 11431 Stockholm; and *office* Gyllenstiernsgatan 14, 11526 Stock holm, Sweden.

**BUNNING, Gavin MacRae.** Australian. *B.* 1910. *Educ.* Scotch College, West Australia. *M.* 1938, Margaret Dorothy Law. *S.* Gavin Law. *Dau.* Susan. *Career:* Director: Peters Ice Cream (W.A.) Ltd since 1951; Dep.-Chmn. since 1956; Chmn. since 1975. The British Petroleum Co. of Australia Ltd. 1964—, Vickers Australia Ltd. 1965—. and Australian Industry Development Corporation since 1971; Bunning Timber Holdings Ltd.—Dep. Chmn. W. A. Chip & Pulp Co. Pty. Ltd. Fellow A.S.A. *Club:* Weld (Perth). *Address:* 41 McNeil Street, Peppermint Grove, W.A.; and *office* G.P.O. Box R.1276, Perth, 6001, W.A., Australia.

**BUNTING, Sir (Edward) John,** KBE, BA. Australian civi servant. *B.* 1918. *Educ.* Trinity Grammar School, Trinity Coll., Univ. of Melbourne; BA (Hons). *M.* 1942, Peggy MacGruer. *S.* 3. *Career:* Assistant Sec. Prime Minister's Dept. Canberra, 1949–53; Official Sec., Office of the High Commissioner for Australia, London 1953–55; Deputy Sec., Prime Minister's Dept., Canberra 1955–58. Secretary, Prime Minister's Dept. Canberra 1959–68. Secy Dept. of Cabinet Office 1968–71; Secy to Dept. of the Prime Minister and Cabinet Canberra 1971–75; Secy to Australian Cabinet 1959–75; Australian High Commissioner in London 1975–77. *Clubs:* Commonwealth (Canberra); Athenaeum (Melbourne); Melbourne Cricket; Royal Canberra Golf; Garrick; Hon. Member, Beefsteak, Traveller's, Oriental. *Address:* 8 Arnhem Place, Red Hill, A.C.T. 2603, Australia.

**BUNZL, Gustav George.** British. *B.* 1915. *Educ.* Vienna Technical School; Manchester Univ. *M.* 1937. Hanna Fischer. *S.* 2. *Daus.* 2. *Career:* Chmn., Bunzl Pulp & Paper Ltd.; Dir., Fisco Ltd.; Filtrona International Corp.; Ectona

Fibres Ltd.; Overseas Marketing Corp. Ltd.; Chmn., Wycombe Marsh Paper Mills Ltd.; Mem., British Overseas Trade Board/European Trade Council; CBI Overseas Cttee. *Clubs:* R.A.C.; Roehampton; Crockfords; Curzon. *Address:* 22 Parkside Gardens, London, S.W.19; and *office* 21 Chiswell Street, London, E.C.1.

**BUNZL, Viktor,** BSc (Eng.). Austrian executive. *B.* 1917. *Educ.* BSc (Engineering) London University. *M.* 1944, Dina Engelberg. *S.* John Michael. *Dau.* Katharine Elisabeth. *Career:* Teacher at Acton Technical College, London 1943–46; Technical Dir. Bunzl & Biach. *Member:* Technical Assn. of the Pulp & Paper Industry (New York); British Paper & Board Makers' Assn. *Address:* Ortmann 50, N. Öe., Austria.

**BURBRIDGE, Kenneth Joseph,** MA, BCL, PhD. Canadian diplomat. *B.* 1911. *Educ.* St. Thomas Univ. and St. Francis Xavier Univ. (BA; MA) 1936; Univ. of New Brunswick (BCL) 1939; Univ. of Ottawa (PhD) 1942. *M.* 1943, Marion Catherine Smith. *S.* John Kenneth. *Dau.* Sheila Marie. *Career:* In private practice of Law, St. John, N.B. 1939–41; various positions in public service of Canada, including: Legal Counsel, Dept. of Munitions & Supply, Ottawa 1941–43; Chief Legal Adviser to National Selective Service, Mobilization, Dept. of Labour, Ottawa 1943–44; Legal Adviser, Unemployment Insurance Commission, Ottawa 1945; Counsellor, Secy. of State Dir. War; Legal Adviser, Dept. of External Affairs; Claims Branch Dept. Secy of State Ottaway 1945–47; Counsel for Canada before International Joint Commission; Canadian delegate to Inter-Allied Reparations Agency, Brussels 1947; Canadian Adviser to Allied Conf. on German Industrial Property Rights, Neuchatel; Canadian Observer at Council of Europe, Strasbourg; Special Adviser to Canadian delegation to U.N. 1952–53; Deputy Permanent Representative to NATO and O.E.E.C., Paris 1954–57; Consul-General, Seattle, Wash. 1957–63; Delegate to Colombo Plan Conf., Seattle 1958; High Commissioner for Canada in New Zealand 1963–67; Head of the U.S. Division of the Department of External Affairs, Ottawa 1967–70; Conf. on International Combined Transport, London 1970; Del. Int. Conference unlawful Interference with Civil Aviation 1971; Special Advisor on International Policy, Canadian Transport Commission. *Member:* Canadian and New Brunswick Bar Assns.; American Assn. of U.N.; World Affairs Council; English-Speaking Union; International Law Assn. (Dir., Canadian Branch); Canadian Inst. of Foreign Affairs. *Clubs:* Rideau, Royal Golf (Ottawa). *Address:* 930 Sadler Crescent, Ottawa K2B 5H7, Canada.

**BURCHETT, Paul James.** American mechanical engineer. *B.* 1915. *Educ.* Los Angeles State University (BA) Registered Mechanical Engineer. *M.* Doreen A. *S.* Jay Nelson. *Career:* Engineering Draftsman, Bowllus Sail-planes, Vultee (Convair) Aircraft Corp., North American Aviation Inc. 1935–37; Design Engineer, Group Engineer, Asst. Engineering Manager Field Engineer, Liaison Engineer, Lockheed Aircraft 1937–59; Assistant Professor, Pasedena City College 1940—. Field Engineer, Technical Representative, Douglas Aircraft Corp. and U.S. Air Force W.W.2; Design Engineer and Design Checker, California Institute of Technology; General Tire and Rubber Inc. (Aero-Jet Div.) at short intervals. *Member:* National Education Assn.; United States Professional Tennis Assn.; Vice-Pres. Newport Beach Travel Inc.; Pres,. Sports Educational Devices Co.; Editor, Law Reform Review. *Publications:* That's How The Tennis Ball Bounces; The Anatomy of The Tennis Lob; Trigonometry Simplified; numerous technical manuals; originator and holder of several U.S. patents. Nat. Vice-Pres., U.S. Divorce Reform Inc. *Clubs:* Newport Harbor Racquet Inc.; Balboa Bay; Elks. *Address:* P.O. Box 274, Corona Del Mar, Calif., U.S.A. and *office* 4570 Campus Drive, Suite 9a, Newport Beach, Calif. 92660, U.S.A.

**BURCKHARDT, Helmuth.** German. Mining Engineer and Bergassessor. *B.* 1903. *Educ.* Tech. High Sch., Berlin. *M.* Luise von Poser und Gross-Naedlitz. *S.* 2. *Daus.* 3. *Career:* Technical Assistant: mining administration of Fürst von Pless at Waldenburg (Silesia) 1928–30, Administration Board of Mansfeld AG, Eisleben 1930; Works Director Eschweiler Bergwerks-Verein, Kohlscheid 1933, and Mine Director 1935. Mine Director and Member administration Board, Eschweiler Bergwerks-Verein 1938–44 and 1949–50. Army Service and Russian P.o.W. 1944–49. Gen. Manager and Chmn. of Board of Eschweiler Bergwerks-Verein 1951–65; Hon. Pres. Exec. Board of the Coal Producers' Association of the Aachen District. Member of Presidium of the Federal Association of German Industry (BDI), and Hon. President of the Board of Wirtschaftsvereinigung Bergbau. Chairman: Supervisory Boards of Eschweiler Berwerks-Verein, and Felten & Guilleaume Carlswerk AG, Cologne. *Member:* Study Group of the Coal Producers' Assn. of Western Europe, Brussels. *Publications:* numerous articles on management, power and mining. *Club:* Rotary. *Address* Roermonder Strasse 67, 5120 Herzogenrath-Kohlscheid, Germany.

**BURDEN, William Armistead Moale.** Financier and Government Official. *B.* 1906. *Educ.* Harvard College (AB *cum laude* 1927); Clarkson College of Technology, DSc (Hon) 1953, Hon DLLD, Fairleigh Univ. 1965, Doctor of Laws (Hon) Johns Hopkins Univ. 1970. *M.* 1931, Margaret Livingston Partridge. *S.* William A. M. (*Dec.*), Robert Livingston (*Dec.*), Hamilton Twombly, Ordway Partridge. *Career:* Analyst of aviation financing, Brown Bros., Harriman & Co., N.Y.C. 1928–32; In charge of aviation financial research, Scudder, Stevens and Clark, N Y.C. 1932–39; Vice-Pres., Natl. Aviation Corp. 1939–41; Vice-Pres., Defense Supplies Corp., Washington, D.C., in charge of Division of Amer. Republics Aviation 1941–42; Special Aviation Asst. to Sec. of Commerce 1942–43; Member, N.A.C.A. 1942–47; Assistant Secretary of Commerce for Air 1943–47; U.S. Delegate, International Civil Aviation Conference, Chicago 1944; Chairman, U.S. Delegation, Interim Assembly Provisional International Civil Aviation Organisation, Montreal 1946; Aviation Consultant, Smith, Barney & Co. 1947–49; Partner, William A. M. Burden & Co. 1949—; Special Asst. for Research and Development to the Sec. of Air Force 1950–52; Member, National Aeronautics & Space Council 1958–59; U.S. Ambassador to Belgium 1959–61; Member, U.S. Citizens Commission on NATO 1961–62. Chairman of Board, Institute for Defense Analyses. Trustee, Columbia University. Hon. Life Gov., N.Y. Hospital. Director: The Aerospace Corp.; Atlantic Institute; Columbia Broadcasting System Inc.; Dir. Emeritus, American Metal Climax, Inc.; Trustee (Past Pres.), Museum of Modern Art; Hon. Dir., Council on Foreign Relations. *Awards:* Legion of Honour, France; Commander, Cruzeiro do Sul, Brazil (1958); Commander, Order of Merit, Federal Republic of Germany (1958); Grand Officer, El Sol del Peru (1959); Grand Cordon, Order of Leopold of Belgium (1961); Commander, Order of Merit, Republic of Italy (1961); Associate Commander (Brother), Order of St. John (1962); Grand Officer, Legion of Honour, France (1970). *Publication:* The Struggle for Airways in Latin America. *Clubs:* Brook, Century, Links, Racquet & Tennis, River (New York); Somerset (Boston); Metropolitan (Washington, D.C.); White's, Buck's (London); Travellers (Paris); *Address:* 630 Fifth Avenue, New York N.Y. 10020, U.S.A.

**BURESCH, Dr. Eugen F.** *B.* 1915. *Educ.* Univ. of Vienna Law School, and School of Political Sciences, Paris (grad. 1938). *M.* 1961, Edda Grieshofer. *S.* Matthew and Karl. *Daus.* Alexandra, Michaela and Gabriele. *Career:* During period 1938–39: in Research Section, Comité International du Bois, Brussels (now part of FAO), then partner in Compagnie Française pour le Commerce Exterieur, Paris. Joined Austrian Diplomatic Service 1946, as First Secretary of Embassy, Rome; in Political Department, Foreign Office, Vienna 1949, First Secretary, London 1950–51; Dir., Austrian Information Service, New York 1952–55; Chargé d'Affaires, Teheran 1955, Minister 1958, Amb. 1960 (and concurrently to Kabul); Amb. to Canada 1960–64. Head of Austrian negotiating delegation with European Communities, Brussels and Luxembourg. 1965–68; Ambassador, Permanent Rep. of Austria to U.N. in Geneva 1968–72; Ambassador to Mexico and Central American States 1972–76; Head of Economic Section, Federal Ministry for Foreign Affairs since 1977. *Club:* Theresianisten, Vienna. *Address:* Federal Ministry for Foreign Affairs, Ballhausplatz 2, Vienna, Austria.

**BURGER, Warren Earl.** Chief Justice of the United States. *B.* 1907. *Educ.* University of Minnesota, St. Paul College of Law (now Mitchell Coll. of Law) (LLB, magna cumlaude); LLD, N.Y. Univ. School of Law 1970. *M.* 1933, Elvera Stromberg. *S.* Wade Allan. *Dau.* Margaret Elizabeth. *Career:* Admitted to Bar of Minnesota 1931; Mem. Faculty, Mitchell Coll. of Law 1931–48; Partner in Faricy, Burger, Moore & Costello 1935–53; Asst. Attorney-General of the U.S. 1953–56; Judge, U.S. Court of Appeals, Washington, D.C. 1956–69; Chief Justice since 1969; Past. Lectr., Law Schools in U.S. and Europe; Hon. Master of the Bench of the Middle Temple 1969; Pres., Bentham Club, Univ. Coll. London 1972–73; Chanc. and Regent, Smithsonian Inst., Washington, D.C.; Chmn. & Trustee, National Gallery of Art; Hon. Chmn.,

Inst. of Judicial Administration; Chmn., A.B.A. Proj. Standards for Crim. Justice; Trustee Emeritus, Macalester Coll., St. Paul, Minn.; Mayo Foundation, Rochester, Minn. *Publications:* articles Legal and Prof. journals. *Address:* Supreme Court Building, Washington, D.C. 20543, U.S.A.

**BURLETON, Eric Norman,** FRSA, FIPA, MCAM. British. *B.* 1923. *Educ.* Pelham Grammar School. *M.* 1953, Pamela Boughton. *S.* 2. *Career:* Jt. Man. Dir., Armstrong-Warden Ltd., 1960–62; Smith Wardeh Ltd. 1962–65; Dir. Stowe & Bowden (Holdings) Ltd. 1965–71; Man. Dir. L.P.A. Ltd. 1967–73; Dir. Royds (London) Ltd.; Vice-Chmn. Royds International Ltd. since 1973; Fellow, Inst. of Practitioners in Advertising. *Club:* R.A.F. *Address:* Malista, Sutton Pl., Abinger Hammer, Surrey; and *office* Royds Ltd., Mandeville place, London, W.1.

**BURLINSON, John Joseph, Jr.,** BSc, MA. American. *B.* 1930. *Educ.:* Fordham Univ. (BS Coll. of Arts & Sciences, MA Graduate School). *M.* 1954, Martha Marie Quigley. *S.* 1. *Daus.* 2. *Career:* Dir. of Sales Henry Regnery Publishing Co. 1962–63; Vice-Pres., Quigley Publishing Co. 1964–69; Dir., Inter Corporate Promotions, National Screen Service Corp. 1970—; Dir. Administration National Theatre Supply 1972–74; Gen. Man. National Theatre Supply since 1974; Exec. Sec. & Treas., Theatre Equipment & Supply Manufeacturers Assn.; Secy. Dir., Motion Picture Pioneers; Vice-Pres., Theatre Equipment Association; Chmn., TEA Convention Cttee.; Vice-Chmn., NY Catholic Charities—Motion Picture Div. *Clubs:* Winged Foot Golf; Skytop. *Address:* 29 Rockwood Drive, Larchmont, New York, U.S.A.

**BURMAN, Sir (John) Charles,** DL, JP; British. *B.* 1908. *Educ.* Rugby School. *M.* 1936, Ursula Hesketh-Wright (JP). *S.* John Hesketh (MB, FRCS) and Michael Charles (TD). *Daus.* Elizabeth Ursula (Landale) and Rosanne Margaret (Corben). *Career:* Chmn.: Tarmac Ltd. 1961–71; and South Staffordshire Waterworks Company 1959—. Dep. Chmn., Birmid-Qualcast Ltd. 1967–73, and other companies. Chmn., Birmingham Conservative Assn. 1936–72. Life Governor, Univ. of Birmingham. KStJ. Lord Mayor of Birmingham 1947–49; High Sheriff of Warwickshire 1958. *Member:* Government Committee on Administrative Tribunals 1955; Royal Commission on the Police 1960. *Club:* Birmingham Club. *Address:* Packwood Hall, Hockley Heath, Warwickshire, and *office* South Staffordshire Waterworks Co., Birmingham 15.

**BURMAN, Sir Stephen (France),** CBE, Hon LLD, MA. British. *B.* 1904. *Educ.* Oundle. *M.* 1931, Joan Margaret Rogers. *S.* 2. (1 Dec.). *Career:* Former Director Midland Bank Ltd.; former dir. Imperial Chemical Industries Ltd., Imperial Metal Industries Ltd., Joseph Lucas (Industries) Ltd., Member (formerly Chairman) United Birmingham Hospitals. Pro-Chancellor, Birmingham University 1955–66. *Member:* Midlands Electricity Board 1948–65, Council (former Pres.) of Birmingham Chamber of Commerce, and Royal Commission on Civil Service 1953–56. *Address:* 12 Cherry Hill Road, Barnt Green, Birmingham, B45 8LJ.

**BURMESTER, Harry Frederick.** American. *B.* 1903. *Educ* College of the Pacific and University of California. *M.* (1) 1924. Edna Jensen (dec'd). *Dau.* Maren (Houghton), (2) 1975, Margarete F. Allen. *Career:* R. G. Dun & Co., Oakland, California 1922–24; East Bay National Bank, Oakland 1924–28; Assistant Cashier and Secy., General Finance Committee, Bank of America N.T. and S.A., San Francisco 1928–33; Assistant Conservator and Special Deputy Superintendent of Banks of State of Ohio in liquidation of the Union Trust Co., Cleveland, Ohio 1933–38; Vice-Pres., Union Commerce Bank, Cleveland 1938–43; Senior Vice-Pres. 1943–56, Pres., 1956–68; Honorary Director, Union Commerce Bank, Cleveland, Ohio 1956—. Director: S.I.F. Co., Cleveland 1950—; Hon LLD, Baldwin-Wallace Coll., and Hon DSc Fenn Coll.; Hon DSc Cleveland State University. *Member:* Ancient Accepted Scottish Rite 33°. *Clubs:* The Union; Pepper Pike; The 50. *Address:* 13415 Shaker Boulevard, Cleveland 20, Ohio; and *office* 925 Euclid Avenue, Cleveland 44115, Ohio, U.S.A.

**BURNE, Sir Lewis Charles,** CBE, FAIB; British master builder and contractor. *B.* 1898. *Educ.* Xavier College, Melbourne. *M.* 1922, Florence Mary Stafford, *S.* 2. *Daus.* 2. *Career:* In World War I with Australian Flying Corps.; President, Old Xavierians Association, Victoria 1938–39; Pres., Master Builders' Association, Victoria 1941–44: Pres. Master Builders' Federation of Australia 1947; Foundation Member and Fellow, Australian Institute of Builders (F.A.I.B.); Pres., Victorian Employers Federation 1948–50, 1953–61, and Australian Council of Employers Federations 1957–58; President, Royal Melbourne Institute of Technology 1961; Chairman of Directors, Federation Insurance Ltd., Victoria 1956–73; Australian Employers Delegate to International Labour Organization 1950–52–55–56–57–60; Australian Employers Representative on the Asian Advisory Committee of I.L.O. 1951–66; Employer Member at the Governing Body meetings I.L.O. 1950–52–55–56–57, and Member of the Governing Body, I.L.O. 1957–66. *Address:* 20 Rockingham Street, Kew, Vic., Australia.

**BURNET, Sir (Frank) Macfarlane,** OM, FRS. Australian. *B.* 1899. *Educ.* MD (Melbourne), PhD (London). *M.* 1928, Edith Linda Druce (dec'd). *M.* 1976, Hazel Gertrude Jenkin. *S.* Ian Druce. *Daus.* Mrs. Elizabeth Dexter and Mrs. Deborah Giddy. *Career:* Beit Fellow 1926–27; Asst. Dir., Hall Inst. 1929–44. Director of Walter & Eliza Hall Institute for Medical Research, Melbourne, and Professor of Experimental Medicine, Melbourne University 1944–65. Nobel Prize for Medicine (shared) 1960. *Publications:* Natural History of Infectious Disease, (1940), (1953), (1962), (1972); Virus as Organism, (1945); Viruses and Man, (1953); Principles of Animal Virology, (1955), (1960); Clonal Selection Theory of Immunity, (1959); Integrity of the Body; (Autobiography) Changing Patterns, (1968); Cellular Immunology (1969); Dominant Mammal (1970); Genes, Dreams and Realities (1971); Autoimmunity and Autoimmune Disease (1972); Intrinsic Mutagenesis (1974). Many technical papers. *Member:* Royal Society (Fellow); Australian Academy of Sciences (Fellow); National Academy of Science, U.S.A. (Foreign member); Royal Swedish Academy of Science; American Philosophical Society; American Academy of Arts & Sciences. *Address:* 48 Monomeath Avenue, Canterbury, Victoria 3126; and *office* Department of Microbiology, Melbourne University, Parkville, Vic. 3052, Australia.

**BURNETT, John Mitchell,** CBE; Australian. *B.* 1903. *M.* 1942, Phyllis Heather Steele. *Daus.* Judith and Robyn. *Career:* Managing Director, E.M.I. (Australia) Ltd. Oct. 1950–70. Chairman of the company since March 1953. President, Chamber of Manufactures of N.S.W. 1958; Senior Vice-President 1958, President 1959, Associated Chambers of Manufactures of Australia; Pres. Association of Australian Record Manufacturers 1956–72; Associate, Institute of Chartered Accountants in Australia. *Fellow:* Australian Institute of Management, and of Institute of Directors. *Clubs:* Australian; Union. *Address:* 9 Kylie Avenue, Killara, N.S.W.; and *office* 301 Castlereagh Street, Sydney, N.S.W., Australia.

**BURNHAM, Linden Forbes Sampson,** OE, SC, MP. Guyanese politician. Prime Minister of Guyana. *B.* 1923. *Educ.* British Guiana; London Univ. BA, Bach Laws; Gray's Inn. *M.* (1) 1951, Sheila Bernice Lataste. *Daus.* 3; (2) 1967, Viola Victorine Harper. *Daus.* 2. *Career:* Pres. West Indian Student's Union London 1947–48; Delegate, Int. Union Students' Congress 1947–48; Co-founder, Chmn. People's Progressive Party 1949; Elected Georgetown Town Council 1952–56; Pres. Guyana Labour Union 1963–65; Minister, Education P.P.P. Government 1953; Founder, Leader People's National Congress 1957; Leader Parly. Opposition 1957–64; Mayor of Georgetown 1959 and 1964; Premier, British Guiana 1964; Prime Minister of Guyana since 1966: Re-elected Prime Minister 1968, 1973. *Member:* The Bar Assn. of Guyana (Pres. 1959). *Awards:* British Guiana Scholarship 1942; Best Speaker's Cup, London Univ. 1947; Queen's Counsel 1960; Senior Counsel 1966; Order of Excellence of Guyana 1973. *Publications:* A Destiny To Mould. *Clubs:* Pres. Guyana chess Assn.; Malteenoes Sports; Guyana Sports; Cosmos Sports; Non Pariel Park Tennis; Patron Guyana Motor Racing. *Address:* The Residence Vlissengen Road, Georgetown, Guyana; and, Office of the Prime Minister, Public Buildings, Georgetown, Guyana.

**BURNS, Charles Fowler Williams.** Canadian. *B.* 1907. *Educ.* Upper Canada Coll., Trinity Coll. School, and Univ. of Toronto. *M.* 1934, Janet Mary Wilson. *S.* Herbert Michael. *Daus.* Joan Harrison, and Janet Mary Cairine. *Career:* Floor Member, Campbell Stratton 1926–28; Investment Dealer, R. A. Daly & Co. 1931–32; Wing-Commander, R.C.A.F. 1941–46; Hon. Chmn., Burns Fry Ltd. *Director:* Crown Life Ins. Co.; chmn. (1946); All-Canadian-American Investments Ltd. (1955); Algoma Central Rly (1959); Baton Broadcasting Inc. (1971); Denison Mines Ltd. (1967); Lake Ontario

Cement Ltd. (1965); Royal Agric. Winter Fair (also past pres. and mem. of exec. cttee). *Member:* Bd. of Trustees, Sunnybrook Hosp. (vice-chmn. since 1966); Jockey Club of Canada Ltd. *Trustee:* Ontario Jockey Club Ltd. 1952; *Chmn.* (past) and Dir.-Emeritus, Toronto Redevelopment Adv. Council 1961–73. *Member:* Zeta Psi; A.F. & A.M. (Harcourt Lodge). Liberal. *Clubs:* The Toronto, The York, Halifax; St. Andrews Club, Gulf-stream Bath & Tennis Club, of Delray Beach, Florida. *Address:* Kingfield Farms, King. Ont LOG 1KO; and *office* P.O. Box No. 39, Toronto Dominion Centre, Toronto M5K 1C8, Ont., Canada.

**BURNS, John L.** American business executive. *B.* 1908. *Educ.* Northeastern Univ. (Degree in EE 1930); Harvard Univ. (MS 1931; DSc 1934); Hon DSc, Northeastern Univ. 1957. *M.* 1937, Beryl Spinney. *S.* John Spinney. *Dau.* Lara Lawrence. *Career:* While student at Northeastern and Harvard, employed by Western Electric Co. 1927–30, and Dewey & Almy Chemical Co. 1930–32; spent one year on the Faculty of Lehigh as Asst. Prof. of metallurgy, and joined Republic Steel Corp. in 1934 and rose to become Supt. of the Wire Division. In 1941 became partner and Vice-Chmn. of the Exec. Cttee. of Booz, Allen & Hamilton, Management Consultants; President, Radio Corp. of America March 1957–62; Pres. John L. Burns and Co. 1962–65; Vice Chmn. and Dir. Cities Service Co. June 1965–Dec. 1965; Chmn. 1966–68; President John L. Burns and Co. since 1968. Director: Babcock & Wilcox Co. E. F. MacDonald Co.; Kearney & Trecker Corp.; Thomas J. Lipton, Inc.; Studebaker Worthington, Inc.; Turner Construction Co.; UMC Industries, Incorporated. *Clubs:* Blind Brook (Portchester, N.Y.); Economic, Sky (N.Y.C.); Round Hill (Greenwich); Seminole and Island. *Address:* 81 Doubling Rd., Greenwich, 06830 Conn.; and *office* 200 Park Ave., New York 10017, U.S.A.

**BURNS, Malcolm McRae,** KBE, New Zealand. *B.* 1910. *Educ.* Univ. of New Zealand (MSc—1st Cl Hons 1932; Senior and Post-graduate Scholar): PhD (Aberdeen). *M.* 1936, Ruth Alvina Waugh. *S.* 1. *Daus.* 2. *Career:* Principal, Lincoln College, University of Canterbury 1952–74. Chairman, Council of Scientific & Industrial Research 1959–63; Chmn. National Environment Council, 1969–70; Member, Natural Development Council 1970–74. Member, International Advisory Committee on Natural Sciences Programme of UNESCO 1962–63. N.Z. Representative, Harkness Fellowships of Commonwealth Fund, N.Y.C. 1961–76. Occasional Adviser. Department of External Affairs, N.Z. 1957–65. Commonwealth Fund Fellow, Cornell Univ. 1934; Plant Physiologist, D.S.I.R. 1936–37; Senior Lecturer and Tutor, Lincoln Agric. College, N.Z. 1937–48; Director, N.Z. Fertiliser Manuf. Research Assn.; Chairman, N.Z. Vice-Chancellors Comm. 1967–68, member of Council of Assoc. Commonwealth Universities; Pres., Royal Soc. of N.Z. 1974–77; Trustee, Norman Kirk Memorial Fund, and various others. *Member:* Council National Museums since 1974; Sc. Research Distribution Cttee since 1975; Beech Forest Man. and Util. Coun. since 1974. *Publications:* various research papers. *Fellow:* N.Z. Inst of Chemistry, Royal Socy. of N.Z., N.Z. Inst. Agr. Sci. Amer. Assn. Advancement of Science. *Address:* 7 Royds Street, Christchurch 1, New Zealand.

**BURNSHAW, Stanley (Alfred).** American author and publisher. *B.* 1906. *Educ.* Univ. of Pittsburgh (AB 1925); Cornell Univ. (MA 1932); additional graduate study Univs. of Poitiers and Paris and New York and Columbia Univs. *M.* 1942, Lydia Powsner. *Daus.* Valerie (Razavi) and Amy (Blumberg). *Career:* Advertising, Blaw-Knox Steel Co., Pittsburgh 1925–27; Advertising, N.Y.C. 1928–32; Assoc. Editor and Drama Critic, New Masses Weekly 1933–36; Vice-Pres., Cordon Co., Publishers 1936–39; Founder, Pres., Editor-in-Chief, The Dryden Press, Publishers 1939–58; Vice-Pres. and Editorial Advisor, Holt, Rinehart & Winston 1958–68; Assoc. Director, Grad. Inst. of Book Publishing N.Y. Univ., and Lecturer in World Literature 1958–62; Board of Directors, Amer. Inst. of Graphic Arts 1960–62. *Publications:* André Spire and His Poetry (1933); The Iron Land (1936); The Bridge (1945); The Sunless Sea (1948); (1949); Early and Late Testament (1952); The Poem Itself (1960); Varieties of Literary Experience (1962); Caged in an Animal's Mind (1963); The Modern Hebrew Poem Itself (1965); The Seamless Web (1970); In the Terrified Radiance (1972); Mirages: Travel Notes in the Promised Land (1977); (The foregoing are books; has also contributed essays in The Sewanee Review, Poetry, and other journals). *Member:* Bd. of Judges, Nat. Book Award 1967; Awards Adv. Cttee. Nat. Book Cttee. 1967–72. *Awards:* awards several times from American Institute of Graphic Arts; Literary, National Inst. of Arts & Letters U.S.A. 1971. *Address:* 95–B Heritage Village, Southbury, Conn. 06488, U.S.A.

**BURNTWOOD, Lord (of Burntwood).** British. *B.* 1910. *Educ.* Haileybury College. *M.* 1950, Flavia Blois. *Dau.* Harriet. *Career:* Vice-Chamberlain to the Household 1945–46; Lord Commissioner of the Treasury 1946–50; Parly. Secy. Ministry of Aviation 1966; Ministry of Health 1967; Parly. Under Secy. of State (Health) Ministry Social Services 1968; Pres., British Japanese Parliamentary Group. *Member:* Union of Shop, Distributive & Allied Workers; Labour Party. Created Baron 1970. *Address:* Flat 2, 37 Chester Way, London, S.E.11; and House of Lords, London, S.W.1.

**BURROUGHS, Ronald Arthur,** CMG. British company Director. *B.* 1917. *Educ.* St. John's Leatherhead; Trinity Coll., Cambridge. *M.* (1) 1947, Jean Valerie McQuillen (Diss.). *Daus.* 2. (2) 1971, Audrey Cunha. *Career:* with Foreign Office 1946–47; Second Secretary, Rio de Janeiro 1947–49; Vice Consul, Acting Consul General Marseilles 1949; First Secy. Cairo 1950–53; Foreign Office 1953–55; National Defence Coll. Canada 1955–56; First Secy. (Information) Vienna 1956–59; Counsellor, Foreign Office 1959–62, Rio de Janeiro 1962–64; Lisbon 1964–67; Aden 1967–68; Asst. Under-Secy. of State Foreign Office 1968–70; U.K. Representative, Northern Ireland 1970–71; Ambassador to Algiers 1971–74. *Award:* Companion The Order of St. Michael and St. George. *Club:* Travellers. *Address:* The Post House, Graffham, Nr. Petworth, Sussex.

**BURROWS. Sir Bernard Alexander Brocas,** GCMG. British. *B.* 1910. *Educ.* Eton and Trinity College, Oxford (BA). *M.* 1944, Ines Walker. *S.* 1. *Dau.* 1. *Career:* Entered Foreign Service 1934, served at Embassy, Cairo 1938–45; at Foreign Office 1945–50; Counsellor, Embassy, Washington 1950–53; Political Resident, Persian Gulf 1953–58; Ambassador to Ankara 1958–63; Deputy Under Secretary, Foreign Office 1963–66; U.K. Permanent Representative to NATO 1966–70. Retired from Foreign Service 1970; Consultant (Dir.-Gen. 1973–76), Federal Trust for Education & Research. *Address:* Steep Farm, Petersfield, Hants.

**BURTICA, Cornel.** Romanian Politician & engineer. *B.* 1931. *Educ.* Polytechnical Institute Bucharest. *Career:* Asst. Professor 1956–62; various positions Union of Students Assn. of Romania and Union Communist Youth; Counsellor to S.R.R. Embassy France; Ambassador of Romania to Italy, Morocco and Malta, Minister Foreign Trade 1969–72; Member Central Cttee. of R.C.P. since 1969; Secy. to C.C. of R.C.P.; member Exec. Pol. Cttee. 1972; Pres. Nat. Council Romanian Radio, T.V. since 1972. *Award:* Order of the Star of S.R. of Romania, 2nd. Class. *Address:* Embassy of SR of Romania, 4 Palace Green, London W8, and Central Committee of the Romanian Communist Party, Bucharest, Romania.

**BURTON, John Wear.** *B.* 1915. *Educ.* Univ. of Sydney (BA); London Univ. (PhD Econ); DSc Int Rel. *Career:* Permanent Head, Dept. of External Affairs 1945–50; Aust. High Com. in Ceylon 1951; Visiting Research Fellow, Aust. Natl. Univ. 1960–63. Reader in International Relations, Univ. Coll., London; Dir., Centre for the Analysis of Conflict. *Publications:* The Alternative (1954); Peace Theory (1962); International Relations: A General Theory (1965); Systems, States, Diplomacy & Rules, (1968); Conflict & Communication, (1969); World Society (1972). *Address:* 4-8 Endsleigh Gardens, London, W.C.1.

**BURTON TAYLOR, Sir Alvin.** Kt. Australian executive. *B.* 1912. *Educ.* Sydney C. of E. Grammar School. *M.* 1949, Joan Toole. *S.* Nicholas, Timothy. *Daus.* Belinda, Jane. *Career:* With Allard Way & Hardie 1930–37; Asst. Gen. Mgr. and Gen. Mgr. Rheem Australia Pty. Ltd. 1937–57. Man. Dir. Email Ltd. 1957–74; C'wealth Banking Corp. 1959–75. *Chairman:* P. & O. Australia Ltd., Bishopsgate Insurance Australia Ltd., Country Television Services Ltd., Demag Industrial Equipment Pty. Ltd., Pirelli Cables Aust. Ltd., Slumberland (Aust.) Pty. Ltd.; *Director:* Email Ltd., Formica Plastics Pty. Ltd., International Combusion Australia Ltd., Nat. Heart Foundation of Australia, NSW Division, & O'Connell Street Associates Pty. Ltd. *Awards:* Created Kt. 1972. Fellow, Inst. Chartered Accountants, Aust.; Life Governor. Aust. Inst. of Management. *Clubs:* The Union; Royal Sydney Yacht Squadron; Elanora Country. *Address:* Unit 6, 50–58 Upper Pitt St., Kirribilli, N.S.W. 2061. and *office* 6th Floor, 16 O'Connell St., Sydney, Australia.

**BURY, Leslie Harry Ernest,** MP (Wentworth, Sydney, Dec. 1956). *B.* 1913. *Educ.* Queens' College, Cambridge Univ. (MA). *M.* 1940, Anne H. S. Weigall. *S.* 4. *Career:* went to United States 1951; with investment department, Provident Mutual Insurance Co. London 1934–35; Bank of New South Wales, Australia 1935–45; in charge economic relations Australian Dept. of External Affairs 1945–46; with Dept. Post-War Reconstruction 1947: member, Australian trade and financial missions, Dept. of Treasury 1948–51. Alternate Exec. Director, International Bank for Reconstruction and Development and International Monetary Fund 1951–53; Director: Legal and General Assurance Socy. Ltd., and Lend-Lease Corporation Ltd., Exec. Dir. for Australia and South Africa 1953–56, returned to Australia and elected to House of Representatives 1956; Minister for Air and Minister Assisting the Treasurer Dec. 1961 (resigned 1962); Minister for Housing 1963–66. Minister for Labour and National Service 1966–69; Treasurer, 1969–71; Minister for Foreign Affairs 1971 (Resigned); Retired from C'wealth Parlt. 1974. *Member:* Assoc. Bankers' Inst. of Australia; Fellow Australian Society of Accountants. *Address:* 85 Vaucluse Road, Vaucluse, N.S.W., Australia.

**BUSCK-NIELSEN, Torben.** Danish diplomat. *B.* 1913. *Educ.* Copenhagen Univ. (LLD). *M.* 1939, Marie-Rose Poulsen de Baerdemaecker. *S.* Allan. *Dau.* Anne. *Career:* Entered Ministry of Foreign Affairs 1938; Secretary, Legation, Paris 1944; London 1948; Chief of Section, Ministry of Foreign Affairs 1952; Counsellor, Stockholm 1955. Ambassador to Tokyo and Seoul 1959–67. Ambassador to Cairo 1967. Ambassador to Bucharest 1969–74; Amb. in Berne since 1974. *Awards:* Commdr. Danish Order of Danebrog: Knight Grand Cross of the Order of the Rising Sun of Japan; Knight Comdr. of St. Olav's Order of Norway; Comdr. of the Royal Victoria Order, the North Star of Sweden and Korean Order of Diplomatic Merit; Romanian Order & Tudor Wladimirescü (First Class). Hon. Dr. of Law, Kuniuk Univ., Korea. *Address:* Danish Embassy 51 Pourtalesstrasse, Berne, Switzerland.

**BUSHELL, John Christopher Wyndowe,** CMG. British diplomat. *B.* 1919. *Educ.* Winchester Coll.; Clare Coll. Cambridge. *M.* Theodora Senior. *Stepson* 1. *Stepdau.* 1. *S.* 1. *Career:* Served with Royal Air Force 1939–45; Joined Diplomatic Service 1945; Posts include Moscow, Rome, NATO, Paris and Brussels 1945–70; Deputy Commandant, British Military Govt. Berlin 1970; H.M. Ambassador, Saigon 1974–75; H.M. Amb., Islamabad since 1976. *Award:* Companion, Order of St. Michael and St. George. *Clubs:* Travellers; Pall Mall (London). *Address:* c/o Foreign & Commonwealth Office, Downing Street, London, S.W.1.

**BUSIGNIES, Henri.** *B.* 1905. *Educ.* Degree in Electrical Engineering, Paris 1926; Hon DSc, NCE, Newark, N.J. 1958. *M.* 1931, Cécile Phaeton. *Dau.* Monique (Honeck). *Career:* Research Development Engineer, Les Laboratoires, Le Matériel Téléphonique, Paris Laboratories of I.T.T. 1928–35; Departmental Head 1935–38; Head, project on Direction Finders, radar, instrument landing, receivers, antennae 1938–41; Laboratory Head, Fed. Telecom. Laboratories, I.T.T. Corp., Nutley, N.J. 1941–46; Director 1946–48; Technical Director 1948–54; Exec. Vice-Pres. 1954–56; Pres. 1956; Pres., I.T.T. Laboratories Div. 1958–60; Director, I.S.E. Corp., N.Y.; Vice-Pres., General Technical Dir., I.T.T. 1960—, (Senior Vice-Pres. 1965; Chief Scientist, 1967). Holder of 134 Patents. Senior Vice-President and Chief Scientist, International Telephone & Telegraph Corporation 1960—. Hon. Dr. of Engineering, Polytechnic Institute of Brooklyn, 1970; Dir. Amer. Optical Corporation. *Awards:* Lakhovsky Award of the Radio Club of France 1926; Cert. of Commendation for Outstanding Service, U.S.N. 1947; Presidential Certificate of Merit 1948. *Fellow:* I.E.E.E. (Recipient, Pioneer Award 1959); David Sarnoff Award of I.E.E.E., 1964; International Communications Award I.E.E.E., 1970; Industrial Research Inst. Medal 1971; Armstrong Medal, Radio Club of America 1975. Member, Natl. Acad. of Engineering. *Club:* Alliance Française Montclair (N.Y.). *Address:* 71 Melrose Place, Montclair, N.J.; and *office* International Telephone & Telegraph Corporation, 320 Park Avenue, New York City 22, U.S.A.

**BUSSCHAU, William John.** South African company director. *B.* 1908. *Educ.* Univ. of Natal and Oxford Univ. (DPhil). *M.* 1941, Joan Pringle. *S.* Godfrey and Andrew. *Dau.* Lynne. *Career:* Former Chairman, Executive Council, South African Inst. of International Affairs 1950–58; Pres., Transvaal and Orange Free State Chamber of Mines 1959–60. Director: Consolidated Gold Fields Ltd., S.A. Mutual Life Insurance Socy., Standard Bank of S.A. Ltd. Chairman, Gold Fields of South Africa Ltd. 1959–66; Director, South African Reserve Bank 1959–66; Chmn., National Committee of International Chamber of Commerce 1958–69. Vice-Chmn., Commission of Monetary Policy of I.C.C. 1959—. Appointed Chancellor Rhodes Univ., April 1966. *Publications:* The Theory of Gold Supply; The Development of Secondary Industries in Northern Rhodesia; The Measure of Gold; Gold and International Liquidity; The Glamour of Gold. *Address:* 9 Murray Street, Waverley, Johannesburg, Republic of South Africa.

**BUSSE, Ellis Earl.** American banker. *B.* 1909. *Educ.* Univ. of Chicago. *M.* 1940, Janet Moore Williams. *S.* Howard Williams. *Career:* With Packers Commission Company 1933–36; Glidden Company 1937; National Lead Company 1938–50. Chairman, The Continental Bank, Cleveland, Ohio since 1956; Director: The Mau-Sherwood Supply Company, Cleveland. *Address:* 19850 Marchmont Road, Shaker Heights 22, O., U.S.A.

**BUTENSCHÖN, Barthold A.** Norwegian publisher. *B.* 1904. *Educ.* University of Oslo (Economics). *M.* 1936, Ragnhild Jakhelln (sculptress). *S.* Hans, Peter Henrik and Nils. *Dau.* Kristin. *Career:* Senior Partner, Dreyers Forlag, B. A. Butenschön A/S & Co., & Bjerke Bruk. *Member:* Chmn., Bd. of Dirs., Nydalens Compagnie; Bd. of Dirs., Frogner Trykkerier A/S; Chmn., Bd. of Representatives, Forsikringsselskabet Viking. *Awards:* Knight Order of St. Olav, 1st Class (Norway). *Publication:* Symmetallism (George Allen & Unwin 1936). *Address:* Bjerke, 1830, Ytre Enebakk, Norway.

**BUTLAND, Sir Jack Richard,** KBE. New Zealand. *Educ.* Hokitika (N.Z.) High School. *M.* Gretta May Taylor (died 1962). *S.* 2. *Dau.* 1. *M.* (2) Joan Melville Bull. *Career:* Founder and Chairman: J. R. Butland Pty. Ltd. 1922—, New Zealand Cheese Ltd. 1926—, Butland Tobacco Ltd. 1936—, and Butland Industries Ltd. 1949—. Chairman: Rothmans (New Zealand) Ltd. 1956—. New Zealand Honey Control Board (1933–38), and New Zealand Packing Corp. (1953–60). Director: Rothmans Industries Ltd., New Zealand; and Dairy Industries (Jamaica) Ltd. President, The Food Bank of New Zealand. Hon. LLD Univ. of Auckland 1967; KBE (Civil) 1966. *Address:* 542 Remuera Road, Remuera, Auckland, New Zealand; and *office* J. R. Butland Pty. Ltd., Queen Street, Auckland, New Zealand.

**BUTLER, Hon. Adam Courtauld,** BA, MP. British. *B.* 1931. *Educ.* Eton Coll. Pembroke Coll. Cambridge. Economics & History. *M.* 1955, Felicity M.-St. Aubyn. *S.* Sam and Edward. *Dau.* Alexandra. *Career:* National Service 2nd Lieut. Kings Royal Rifle Corps. 1949–51; Camb. University, 1951–54; ADC to Gov. General of Canada, 1954–55; With Courtaulds Ltd. 1955–73; Dir. Aristoc Ltd. 1966–73; Member of Parliament, Conservative, Bosworth since 1970; Dir., Kayser Bondor Ltd. 1971–73; Dir. Capital and Counties Property Co. Ltd. since 1973; PPS to Rt. Hon. J. Godber, Foreign Office and Ministry of Agriculure 1971–74; Asst. Govt. Whip 1974; Opposition Whip 1974–75; PPS to Leader of the Opposition, 1975—. *Member:* National Farmers Union. *Address:* The Old Rectory, Lighthorne, Nr. Warwick; and *office* House of Commons, London, S.W.1.

**BUTLER, Albert Louis, Jr.** American executive. *B.* 1918. *Educ.* Woodberry Forest School and Princeton University (AB). *M.* 1941, Elizabeth Bahnson. *S.* David B. and R. Christian. *Dau.* 1. *Career:* President, Treasurer and Director, Arista Co., Winston-Salem, N.C.; Director: Wachovia Bank & Trust Co., W-S; US Filter Corps NY, Hayes-Albion Corp. Jackson, Mich, Southern Bdcstg Co. W-S. NC. Standard Savings & Loan Association, W-S, R. J. Reynolds Industries, Inc. W-S; Trustee, Northwestern Mutual Life Insurance Co., Milwaukee, Wis. *Clubs:* Princeton (N.Y.); Ivy; Rotary. *Address:* 2850 Galsworthy Drive, Winston-Salem, N.C.; and *office* 437 Goldfloss Street, Winston-Salem, N.C., U.S.A.

**BUTLER, Esmond Unwin,** CVO. Canadian. *B.* 1922. *Educ.* Univ. of Toronto (BA) and Univ. of Geneva (Lic ès sc pol). *M.* 1960, Georgiana North. *S.* 1. *Dau.* 1. *Career:* Asst. Press Secy. to H.M. the Queen, London 1958–59; Asst. to the Secretary to the Governor-General of Canada (Rt. Hon. Vincent Massey) 1955–58; Information Officer, Dept. of National Health and Welfare, Ottawa 1954, and Dept. of Trade and Commerce 1953; Asst. Secy.-Gen., Union of Official Travel Organizations, Geneva 1951–52; Journalist. United Press, Geneva 1949–50.

Secretary to the Governor General of Canada, Nov. 1959—. Secretary-General of Order of Canada, April 1967, and of Order of Military Merit 1972. *Award:* Commander of the Victorian Order 1972; Commander-Brother, Order of St. John of Jerusalem. *Address:* Rideau Cottage, Government House, Ottawa KIA OAI, Ont., Canada.

**BUTLER, Hon. Michael.** American. *B.* 26 Nov. 1926. *Career:* Chmn., Natoma Productions, Inc.; World Producer of Hair; Michael Butler Associates; Co-Producer of Lenny; Director, Butler Paper Corp.; International Sports Core; Former Vice-President, Butler Company. Director: J. W. Butler Paper Co. of Chicago, Butler Paper Co., Butler Engineering & Construction (also Exec. Vice-Pres.), Butler Overseas (also Exec. Vice-Pres.), Basic Investment Corp., Intrafi, Overseas Bank Ltd.; Oak Brook Utility; Drake Oak Brook Hotel, Oak Brook Landscaping Co., Ondine Inc.; Chmn., Talisman Co.; Land developments: Oak Brook, Sugarbush, and Talisman. Coal Washeries in India: Dugda I and II, and Petherdi; Formerly Civic Chancellor, Lincoln Acad. of Illinois; Organization of Economic Development; Pres., Illinois Sports Council; (Commissioner), Chicago Regional Port District. Special Advisor on India and Middle East affairs to Senator John F. Kennedy. *Awards:* Order of the Sword and Cutlass; Order of Lincoln; Order of Colonial Wars. *Member:* Chicago Historical Socy.; English-Speaking Union; Chicago Natural History Museum; Oceanographic Inst. *Clubs:* Chicago; Oak Brook Polo (Governor); Racquet & Tennis, Explorers, Knickerbocker (all in N.Y.C.); Talisman Corinthian Yacht, Port Antonio (Vice-Commodore); U.K., Guards Polo. *Address:* Natoma, Oak Brook, Ill., U.S.A. and *office* 11614 West Pico Blvd., Los Angeles, Ca. 90064, U.S.A.

**BUTLER, Sir Milo Boughton.** GCMG, GCVO, JP. Governor of the Bahamas. *Address:* The Residence of the Governor, Nassau, The Bahama Islands.

**BUTLER OF SAFFRON WALDEN, Lord** (Richard Austen Butler), KG, PC, CH, *B.* 9 Dec. 1902. *Educ.* Marlborough; Penbroke College, Cambridge (MA). *M.* (1) 1926, Sydney Courtauld (*D.* 1954). *S.* 3. *Dau.* 1. (2) 1959, Mollie, widow of Augustine Courtauld. *Career:* M.P. (Cons.) for Saffron Walden 1929–65; Under-Secretary of State, India Office 1932–37; Parliamentary Secretary, Ministry of Labour 1937–38; Under-Secretary of State for Foreign Affairs 1938–41; Minister of Education 1941–45; Minister of Labour June–July 1945; Chairman of Council, National Union of Conservative Associations 1945 (President 1956); Chancellor of the Exchequer Oct. 1951–Dec. 1955 and Home Secretary 1957–62 (also Lord Privy Seal Dec. 1955–Oct. 1959). Chairman of the Conservative Party, Oct. 1959–Oct. 1961. Leader of the House of Commons Dec. 1955–Oct. 1961. In charge of Central African Affairs Mar. 1962–Oct. 1963. First Secretary of State, also Deputy Prime Minister 1962–64. Secretary of State for Foreign Affairs Oct. 1963–64. Master of Trinity College, Cambridge since 1965; Chmn. Home Office Cttee. Mentally Abnormal Offenders1972–75. *Address:* 142 Whitehall Court, London, S.W.1; and the Master's Lodge, Trinity College, Cambridge.

**BUTLER, Richard Edmund.** Australian International Official. *B.* 1926. *Educ.* Diploma, Public Administration; Qualified Public Accountant. *M.* 1951, Patricia Carmel Kelly. *S.* 3. *Daus.* 2. Australian Post Office-Telegraph Messenger, Technician in training, Admin. Officer Posts 1941–55; Chief Industrial Officer, 1955–60; Exec. Officer, Deputy Asst. Dir.-Gen. (Ministerial & External Relations) 1960–68; (Appointed in absentia Secretary of Newly Established Australian Telecommunications Commission—TELECOM—1975); Elected International Official—Deputy Sec.-Gen. Int'l. Telecommunication Union (ITU), U.N. Specialized Agency for Telecommunications, 1968; Re-elected by Plenipotentiary Conference of all member Governments 1973. Chmn., ITU (Tripartite) Staff Pension Cttee.; Conference Programme Exec. Cttee. of Int'l. Conference on Computer Communication, ICCC 1974; Member, UN Joint Staff Pension Bd.; Bd. of Governors, ICCC; UN Inter-organization Bd. (Management System Devlpt.). *Member:* AASA; RIPA (fellow); CTA (Melbourne); Royal Commonwealth Socy.; Royal Overseas League (London). *Address:* 222B route d'Hermance, 1246 Corsier (Geneva), Switzerland; and *office* ITU, Place des Nations, 1211 Geneva 20, Switzerland.

**BUTLER, Thomas Clifton.** *B.* 1900. *Educ.* Troy Conference Academy. *M.* 1927 Helen V. Woods. *S.* Robert C. and Norman W. *Career:* Trustee Amer. Freedom from Hunger Foundation, Inc. Acad. of Food Marketing, St. Joseph's College, Philadelphia. Director N.J. State Chambers of Commerce; Director of Finance World Food Congress, Washington, D.C., 1963. Brotherhood Award Nat. Conference of Christians and Jews (1960) and mem. Bd. of Trustees; Marymount Coll. Tarrytown, N.Y. Chmn. Bd. of Trustees; Hospital Service Plan (Blue Cross) of N.J.; Bd. of Trustees of N.J. Citizens Transportations Council. Joined Grand Union Co. in 1918, Ass. Sec., 1928, Comptroller, 1930, Treas., 1936, Dir., 1948, Vice-Pres.— Treas., 1958. Chairman and Chief Exec. Officer, 1966. President and chief Exec. Officer, 1960; Chmn. Emeritus 1974; Director First National Bank of New Jersey; Member of Board of Managers, Bloomfield Savings Bank, Bloomfield N.J. *Awards:* Human Relations Award, Amer. Jewish Cttee. (1965), Freedoms Foundations at Valley Forge George Washington Honor Medal Award, 1967. *Club:* Serra and Mercier Clubs. *Address:* 565 Ridgewood Ave., Glen Ridge, N.J. and *office* 100 Broadway East Paterson, N.J., U.S.A.

**BUTTERFIELD, Alexander P.,** MS. American. *B.* 1926. *Educ.* UCLA, Univ. of Maryland (BS); George Washington Univ. (MS, International Affairs); National War Coll. *M.* Charlotte Mary Maguire. *Children* 3. *Career:* Served in U.S. Air Force as fighter-pilot; Mem. U.S. Air Force Europe Formation Aerobatic Team ("Skyblazers"); Operations Officer, Air Defense Squadron; Asst. Prof. at U.S. Air Force Academy; Senior Aide to Commander-in-chief Pacific Air Forces, Commander of fighter squadron Okinawa, Commander Photo-Recon Task Force, S.E. Asia; Senior U.S. Military Representative in Australia, retiring with rank of Colonel 1949–69; Deputy-Assistant to the President and Secy. to Cabinet White House, 1969–73; Administrator of Federal Aviation Administration 1973–75; Independent Management Consultant 1975–76; Exec. Vice-Pres., International Air Service Co. Ltd. of Burlingame, Calif. since 1977. *Member:* Nat. Armed Forces Museum Advisory Bd. (Smithsonian Inst.); Center for the Study of the Presidency; National Soc. of Literature & the Arts; Amer. Soc. for Public Administration; Academy of Political Science. *Publications:* various articles to professoinal Journals. *Awards:* Legion of Merit; DFC; Bronze Star; 4 air medals, and numerous campaign, service and commendation medals. *Address:* 3 Brent Court, Menlo Park, Ca. 94025, U.S.A.

**BUTTIGIEG, Dr. Anton.** Maltese Lawyer and Politician. *B.* 1912. *Educ.* Malta Univ., BA, LLD. *M.* (1) 1944, Carmen Bezzina. (2) 1953, Connie Scicluna. (3) 1975, Margery Patterson. *S.* 2. *Dau.* 1. *Career:* Notary Public 1939–41; Advocate 1941–71; Police Inspector 1942–44; Law Reporter and Leader Writer for *Times of Malta* 1944–48; Acting Magistrate 1955; Editor, *Voice of Malta* 1959–66; Member of Parliament 1955–76; Pres., Malta Labour Party 1959–61, Dep. Leader 1962–76; Del. to Malta Constitutional Conferences, London 1958–64; Rep. to Consultative Assembly, Council of Europe 1967–71; Vice-Pres. 1967–68; Dep. Prime Minister 1971–76; Minister of Justice and Parly. Affairs 1971–76; Pres. of the Republic of Malta since 1976. *Member:* Acad. of the Maltese Language. *Awards:* 1st Prize for Poetry, Govt. of Malta, 1971; Guze' Muscat Azzopardi Prize for Poetry, 1972; Silver Plaque for Poetry, Circolo Culturale Rhegium Julii of Reggio Calabria, 1975. *Publications:* Lyric Poetry: Mill-Gallerija ta' Zghoziti (1945); Finali bil-Lejl (1949); Qasba mar-Rih (1968); Fl-Arena (1970); Humerous Poetry: Ejjew nidhku ftit (1963); Ejjew nidhku ftit iehor (1966); Haikus and Tankas: Il-Muza bil-Kimono (1968); Ballati Maltin (1973); Il Mare di Malta (1974); Il-Ghanja tas-Sittin (1975). *Club:* St. Cajetan Band Club, Hamrun, Malta. *Address:* The Palace, San Anton; and *office* The Palace, Valletta, Malta.

**BUTTROSE, Brig. Alfred William,** DSO (and Bar), ED. *B.* 1912. *Educ.* Glenelg Public School and Thebarton Technical High School, S.A. *M.* 1935, Rhona M. Barrett. *S.* 3. *Dau.* 1. *Career:* Australian Army 27th Inf. Bn. 1933: Capt. A.I.F. 1939–45; England, Western Desert and Syria; Owen Stanleys Aitape-Wewak 2/5 & 2/33 Bns. Lt.-Col. Res. of Officers 1948; Brig. 1952; Cmd. H.Q. Group W. Command 1950–53; Comndr. 13th Inf. Bde. W.A. 1953–56, Aust. Military Forces; Retired 1967; Western Aust. Manager for Elder Smith Goldsbrough Mort Ltd. 1963—. Chmn., Trustees Anglican Diocese of Perth; Member W.A. Post Secondary Education Commission; Governor W.A. Arthritis & Rheumatism Foundation. *Clubs:* Weld, West Australian; Perth Rotary. *Address:* 9 Birdwood Parade, Dalkeith, W.A. 6009; and *office* 111–113 St. George's Terrace, Perth, W.A. 6001 Australia.

**BYERS, Rt. Hon., Lord (Frank Byers),** PC, OBE. British company director and politician. *B.* 1915. *Educ.* Westminster School, Christ Church. Oxford (MA) and Milton

Academy, Mass., U.S.A. (Exchange Scholar). *M.* 1939, Joan Elizabeth Oliver. *S.* 1. *Daus.* 3. *Career:* Chmn., Company Pensions Information Centre; Pres., O.U. Liberal Club 1937; served in World War II (enlisted 1939; com. 1940; served M.E.F., C.M.F. 1940–44; G.S.O.1. 8th Army 1943; served N.W. Europe 1944–45; G.S.O.1.H.Q., 21st Army Group); despatches thrice; Chevalier, Legion of Honour; Croix de Guerre with palms; M.P. (Lib.) North Dorset 1945–50; Liberal Chief Whip 1946–50: Chairman of the Liberal Party, April 1965–67. Leader of Liberal Peers 1967—. A Deputy Lieut. of Surrey. *Address:* Hunters Hill, Blindley Heath, Surrey.

**BYERS, Buckley Morris.** American. *B.* 1917. *Educ.* Yale Univ. (BA 1940). *M.* 1940, Rosamond Murray. *S.* Buckley Morris, Jr., Joseph Murray and Christopher Farrell. *Career:* Served in World War II (U.S. Naval Intelligence; overseas in four major invasions in European and Pacific Theatres; released to inactive duty as Lieut.; recipient of Presidential citation and individual commendation). With A. M. Byers Co.; successively Engineering Service Dept.; Sales Engineer, Washington, D.C. (office); Asst. Manager, N.Y. Division; Export Manager; Asst. Manager Steel Sales; Gen. Manager, Wrought Iron Sales; Vice-Pres. in charge of Sales; President 1957–62 and Director (1948–70), A. M. Byers Co., Pittsburgh, Pa.; President, Byers McManus Associates Inc. 1965—. Vice-President and Special Assistant to the President, Blaw-Knox Co., Pittsburgh 1962–65; Former member, Republican National Finance Committee. Trustee, Sewickley (Pa.) Valley Hospital. Republican. *Clubs:* Duquesne, Rolling Rock (Governor), Allegheny C.C. (all of Pittsburgh); Racquet & Tennis (New York) Capitol Hill; F Street Club; Carlton; International, Metropolitan (Washington, D.C.). *Address:* 5208 Upton Terrace, N.W., D.C.; and *office* 35 Wisconsin Circle, N.W., Washington, D.C. 20015, U.S.A.

**BYLANDT, Count Willem Frederik Lodewijk.** Netherlands diplomat. *B.* 1896. *Educ.* Univ. of Leyden (grad. in Law). M.(1) 1936, Emilia Corradi. (2) 1975, Cornelia Countess Van Limburg Stirum. *Career:* Entered diplomatic service 1923; Attaché, Legation London 1923; Ministry for Foreign Affairs. The Hague 1924–26; Secretary of Legation, Peking 1926–29; Ministry of Foreign Affairs, The Hague, 1929–32; Secretary, later Counsellor of Legation, Paris 1932; Chargé d'Affaires, Cairo 1937–40; Secretary-General, Ministry for Foreign Affairs Netherlands Government in London 1940–45; Political Adviser to the Lieut.-Governor, Batavia 1945–46; En. Ex. and Min. Plen. Rome 1947–52; High Commissioner for Netherlands Government, Djakarta 1952–56; Ambassador to Rome 1958–62. *Clubs:* Haagse (The Hague). *Address:* Claire Fontaine Avenue St. Exupery, Grasse, France.

**BYLER, William Henry. American industrial chemist and** executive. *B.* 1904. *Educ.* Central Missouri State Coll. (AB; BS 1927) and Missouri Univ. (MA 1931; PhD 1937). *M.* 1929, Thelma Tyson. *Career:* Dir. of Research U.S. Radium Corp. 1939–51; Asst. Biochemist, N.Y. State Dept. of Health 1938–39; Research Chemist, General Electric Co. 1937–38; Graduate Asst., Univ. of Missouri 1935–37; Prof. Chemistry and Physics, Hannibal-Lagrange College 1931–35. Vice-Pres. 1951—, and Dir. 1956—, Senior Vice-Pres 1968–70, Consultant since 1971. U.S. Radium Corp. *Publications:* (Co-Author) Pigment Handbook; & articles in Journal of Amer. Chemical Socy., Review of Scientific Instruments, Journal of Physical Chemistry, Journal of the Optical Socy. of Amer., Journal of Electro-Chemical Socy., Cathode Press. Non-Destructive Testing. *Member:* Sigma Xi; A.A.A.S.; Amer. Inst. of Chemists; Amer. Chemical Society; Amer. Electrochemical Socy.; Amer. Physical Society. *Address:* 690 Osceola Ave 608, Winter Park, Florida 32789, U.S.A.

**BYRAM, Stanley Harold.** American; *B.* 1908. *Educ.* DePauw University (AB); HonDLitt, Lincoln Memorial Univ.; HonD of Humane Letters, Lincoln College. *M.* (1) 1929, Edith Funston, and (2) 1969, Sarah B. Schnaiter. *Daus.* Beverly L. and Barbara J. *Career:* Delegate Methodist Jurisdictional Conference, Methodist General Conf. 1952; Chmn., Area Publicity Comm. 1951–53; Area Fin. Comm. 1949–52; Nat. Crusade for Christ 1948–52; Delegate, Ecumenical Conference, Oxford (England) 1951; Mem., Ind. Conf. Methodist Advance Programme 1952–56; Vice-Chmn., Special Projects Comm. 1952–56. Chairman, Indiana Conference Building Programme 1952–54; Pres., Rector Scholarship Alumni Association 1953; Lay Delegate, Indiana Conference 1940–55; Vice-Chmn., Commission on World Service and Finance 1952–56; Chmn., Cttee. on Nominations 1950–55; Chmn., Bloomington District Trustees 1948–54; Bloomington District Lay Leader 1948–52; member, bd. of Conference Claimants 1948–52; President, DePauw Beta Student Aid Fund, Inc. 1953–60; Chairman, Planning and Needs Committee, Greater DePauw Programme 1952–56; Chmn., Board of Trustees, Lincoln Memorial University 1940–73; DePauw Bequests Committee 1952–62; Member Indiana State Office Bldg. Comm. 1971—; Member of Board Metrop. YMCA (Ind.) 1973–77; Chmn. Morgan County YMCA 1974–77; Trustee, YMCA Foundation of Greater Indianapolis since 1974. *Member:* National Association of Manufacturers 1938–62; National Chamber of Commerce 1942–60; Natl. Small Business Men's Association 1942–53; Indiana Mfgs. Assoc. 1936–70 (Dir. 1938–42 and 1968–70); Manuscript Society 1950—; Chicago Historical Society 1946—; Abraham Lincoln Association 1938—; Civil War Round Table 1943—; Socy. of American Historians Inc. (Founder); American Fisheries Society 1948—; Chairman, Indiana Republican Finance Campaign 1960; Vice-Chmn. and mem. Exec. Cttee., Republican Citizens' Finance Cttee. of Indiana 1958–66 and Secretary since 1974; Chmn., Republican Citizens Finance Cttee. 7th District 1958–61; Treas., Indiana Republican Central Cttee. 1961–66; Chmn. Republican Finance Cttee. 1960–63; Delegate Republican National Conventions; member, National Republican Finance Committee 1958–66. 32 deg. Mason. Indiana Society, Chicago; New York Southern Society. *Awards:* Algernon Sidney Award; Rector Alumni Association Achievement Award; Council of the Sagamores of the Wabash; Beta Theta Pi; Pres., Delta Chapter 1927–28. *Publications:* various pamphlets and brochures. Republican. *Clubs:* Columbia, (of Indianapolis); Hillsboro; Pompano Beach Fla. *Address:* P.O. Box 364 Martinsville, Ind., 46151 U.S.A.

**BYRNE, Hon. Murray Lewis**, CMG, LLB, MLC. Australian barrister and solicitor. *B.* 1928. *Educ.* St. Patrick's College, Ballarat; Newman College, Univ. of Melbourne (LLB Pol Sc). *M.* 1951, Adele Hildora Coutts. *S.* Andrew Murray and David Donald. *Daus.* Jane Elizabeth, Ann Maria, Adele, Virginia, Carolyn and Rosemary. *Career:* Member of the Legislative Council for Ballarat Province, Victoria 1958— (the youngest member ever elected to the Council), Deputy Leader of the Upper House 1971, Leader 1973–76; Minister of Public Works, 1970–73; Minister, State Development & Decentralization, Tourism and Immigration 1973–76; Full-Time Legal Practice in Family Business of Byrne, Jones & Torney, Barristers & Solicitors, since 1976. *Decorations:* Companion of St. Michael and St. George, 1977; Total Community Development Award 1975. *Address:* 217 Wendouree Parade, Ballarat, Vic.; and *office* 38 Lydiard Street South, Ballarat 3350, Australia.

# C

**CABLE, Sir James Eric**, KCVO, CMG. British Diplomat. *B.* 1920. *Educ.* Stowe; Corpus Christi Coll., Cambridge; PhD (1973). *M.* 1954, Viveca Hollmerus. *S.* 1. *Career:* Served in HM Forces 1941–46 (Major, Royal Signals); joined HM Foreign Service 1947; Vice-Consul, Batavia (later Djakarta) 1949; 2nd Sec. 1950; 2nd Sec., HM Embassy, Helsinki 1952; Foreign Office 1953; 1st Sec. (Commercial), HM Legation, Budapest 1956; 1st Sec. and Consul, HM Embassy, Quito 1959; Foreign Office 1961; Counsellor, Head of S.E. Asia Dept., Foreign Office 1963; Counsellor, HM Embassy, Beirut 1966; Counsellor (Research Assoc.), Inst. of Strategic Studies 1969; Head of Western Organisations Dept., FCO 1970; Head of Planning Staff, FCO 1971; Asst. Under-Sec. of State 1972; HM Ambassador, Helsinki since 1975. *Member:* International Inst. for Strategic Studies. *Decorations:* Knight Commander of the Royal Victorian Order, 1976; Companion of the Order of St. Michael and St. George, 1967. *Publications:* Gunboat Diplomacy (1971). *Clubs:* Athenaeum; RAC. *Address:* British Embassy, Uudenmaank 16–20, 00210 Helsinki 12, Finland.

**CABOT, John Moors.** American diplomat. *B.* 1901. *Educ.* Harvard (AB); Brasenose College, Oxford (BLitt); Hon LLD Tufts Univ. 1956; Hon DFS Suffolk Univ. 1966. *M.* 1932, Elizabeth Lewis. *S.* John G. L. Lewis Pickering. *Daus.* Marjorie Moors (Enriquez), Elizabeth Tracy (von Wentzel). *Career:* U.S. Foreign Service Officer since 1926; Vice-Consul, Callao-Lima 1927–28; Third Secy., Dominican Republic 1929–31, Mexico 1931–32; Third Secy. and Second Secy., Rio de Janeiro 1932–35; Second Secy., The Hague 1935–38; Secretary, Stockholm 1938–39, Guatemala 1939–41; Department of State, Assistant Chief, Division of American Republics 1942; Chief, Division of Caribbean and Central American Affairs 1944; Counsellor of Embassy, Buenos Aires, Argentina 1945–46, Belgrade, Yugoslavia 1947; Consul-General, Shanghai 1948; appointed Career Minister 1948; En. Ex. and Min. Plen. to Finland 1950; Technical Officer, U.S. Delegations, Dumbarton Oaks, Mexico City and San Francisco Conferences; Asst.-Secretary of State for Inter-American Affairs 1953; Chief U.S. Delegate, Third Extraordinary Session of Inter-American Economic and Social Council, Caracas 1953; Delegate, Tenth International Conference of American States, Caracas 1954; Ambassador to Sweden 1954; to Colombia 1957; to Brazil 1959; to Poland 1962. Dpty. Commandant, Nat. War Coll. 1965, Rtd. 1966. Lecturer, Tufts Univ. and Pres., Pan-American Socy. of New England, 1967–68. *Award:* Grand Cross of the Order of the Cruzeiro Do Sul, Brazil. *Publications:* The Racial Conflict in Transylvania (1926); Towards our Common American Destiny (1954). *Address:* 1610 28th Street, N.W., Washington, D.C., U.S.A.

**CABOT. Paul Codman.** American banker. *B.* 1898. *Educ.* Harvard College (AB); Harvard Business School (MBA). *M.* 1924, Virginia Converse. *S.* Paul C., Edmund C., Frederick C. *Daus.* Virginia C. (Wood), Elizabeth M. (Minot). *Career:* Served World War I, 2nd Lieut. Field Artillery; with First National Bank of Boston 1923–24; Treas., State Street Investment Corp. 1924–34; Pres. 1934–58; Chmn. of the Board, 1958. Partner, State Street Research and Management Co. since 1928 Dir., Salvage Division, War Production Board 1941–42; Treas., Harvard Univ. 1948–65; Inc. Member Advisory Council, Morgan Guaranty Trust Co.; Chmn. & Dir. Federal Street Fund. Hon. Member, Business Council, Trustee, Eastern Gas & Fuel Assn. *Address:* 225 Franklin Street, Boston, Mass. 02110, U.S.A.

**CABRAL, Luis de Almeida.** President of the Council of State of Guinea-Bissau. *B.* 1931. *Educ.* Primary Sch. at Praia and Secondary Sch. at Sao Vicente, Cape Verde Islands. *M.* 1958, Lucette Andrade Cabral. *S.* 4. *Dau.* 1. *Career:* Accountant with GOUVEIA, associated company of Uniao Fabril, Bissau 1953–60; with his brother, the late Amilcar Cabral and Aristides Pereira (now Pres. of the Cape Verde Republic), founded the African Party of Independence for Guinea-Bissau & the Cape Veree Islands (PAIGC) as an under ground movement, 1956; underground political activity at Bissau within the Party framework 1956–60; self-exile 1960; Founder & First Sec.-Gen., National Union of the Workers of Guinea-Bissau (UNTG) 1961; elected to War Council (Staff) after the outbreak of the armed struggle, 1963; elected member of the Permanent Secretariat of the Exec. Cttee. for the Struggle 1971, entrusted with national reconstruction of the liberated areas; up to the Proclamation of the Republic (24 Sept. 1973), assumed direction of the struggle on the north front, with the inner core of the War Council; elected deputy to the National Popular Assembly by the Bissau constituency 1972; elected Asst. Gen. Sec. by the Second Congress of the PAIGC, July 1973; elected Pres. of the Council of State (Head of State) by the National Popular Assembly on the Proclamation of the Republic, Sept. 1973. First Vice-Pres. of the Organisation of African Unity. *Awards:* Decorations from Republic of Guinea, Senegal, Liberia & Yugoslavia.*Address:* Palais de la Republique, Bissau, Republic of Guinea- Bissau.

**CACCIA, Lord (Harold Anthony Caccia),** GCMG, GCVO. British diplomat. *B.* 1905. *Educ.* Eton; Trinity College, Oxford; Laming Travelling Fellow of Queen's Coll., Oxford. Hon. Fellow Trinity Coll. Oxford and Queens Coll. Oxford; Hon. DLitt, City Univ. *M.* 1932, Anne Catherine Barstow. *S.* 1. *Daus.* 2. *Career:* Entered Foreign Service 1929; transferred to British Legation, Peking 1932, Second Sectetary 1934; Foreign Office 1935, Assistant Private Secretary to Secretary of State 1936; British Legation, Athens 1939, First Secretary 1940; Foreign Office 1941; seconded for service with Resident Minister, North Africa 1943 and appointed Vice-President, Political Section, Allied Control Commission, Italy; Political Adviser, G.O.C.-in-C. Land Forces, Greece 1944; Minister local rank, British Embassy, Athens 1945; transferred to Foreign Office Sept. 1945, Asst. Under-Sec. of State 1946, Dep. Under-Sec. 1949; En. Ex. and Min. Plen. to Austria until 1949, High Commissioner since Aug. 1950, and Ambassador 1951–54; Dep. Under-Secretary, Foreign Office, Feb. 1954; Ambassador to U.S.A. 1956–61; Permanent Under-Secretary of State and Head of The Diplomatic Service, Foreign Office, 1962–65, Provost of Eton Coll. 1965–77. Lord Prior, O. St. J.; Chmn. Standard Telephone & Cables Ltd.; Dir. Orion Bank, Prudential Assurance Co. Foreign & Colonial Investment Co. *Address:* Abernant, Builta-Wells, Powys, Wales; and 1 Chester Place, Regent's Park, London, N.W.1.

**CADBURY, Sir Adrian,** Kt. 1977. Chmn., Cadbury-Schweppes. *B.* 1929. *Educ.* Eton; King's College Cambridge. *M.* 1926, Gillian Mary Skepper. *S.* 2. *Dau.* 1. *Career:* Personnel Dir. Cadbury Bros. Ltd. 1958–65; Chmn. British Cocoa and Chocolate Co. Ltd. (later called Cadbury Group Ltd.) parent company of Cadbury Bros. Ltd. 1965–69; Dep. Chmn. and Man. Dir. Cadbury Schweppes (on merging Cadbury Group Ltd. with Schweppes Ltd.) 1969–73; Dep. Chmn. Cadbury Schweppes Ltd. 1973–74; Chmn. Cadbury-Schweppes Ltd. since 1975; Dir., Bank of England since 1970; Non-Exec. Dir., IBM UK Holdings Ltd. since 1975; Chmn., Economic Policy Cttee. of the CBI since 1974. *Fellow:* BIM 1967. *Member:* President's Cttee., Advertising Assn. 1965; Council of Industrial Society 1964; Inst. of Personnel Mgmt., 1960; Council of Industry for Mgmt. Educ. 1967. *Publications:* Nuffield Memorial Lecture: Need for Technological Change (1969); Organisation and the Personnel Manager (1970); Stockton Lecture: Participation in UK Management (1975). *Clubs:* Boodle's; Hawks (Cambridge); Leander (Henley). *Address:* Rising Sun House, Baker's Lane, Knowle, Solihull, W. Midlands B93 8PT; and *office* Cadbury Scwheppes Ltd., Bournville, Birmingham B30 2LU.

**CADBURY, George Woodall.** Canadian. Chairman Emeritus of Governing Body International Planned Parenthood Federation & Chmn. Exec. Cttee., Conservation Council of Ontario. *B.* 1907. *Educ.* Cambridge University (MA); Economics Tripos; Wharton School, University of Pennsylvania. *M.* 1935. Mary Barbara Pearce. *Daus.* Lyndall Elizabeth (Boal), Caroline Ann (Woodroffe). *Career:* Managing Director, British Canners Ltd. 1929–35; Marketing Controller and Managing Director, Alfred Bird & Sons Ltd. 1935–45; Deputy Director, Material Production, Ministry of Aircraft Production and British Air Commission (U.S.A.) 1941–45; Chairman, Economic Advisory and Planning Board, Province of Saskatchewan 1946–51; Chief Industrial Executive, Province of Saskatchewan 1946–51; Director, Technical Assistance Administration, United Nations 1951–54; United Nations Advisor to Govts. of Ceylon, Burma, Indonesia, Jamaica and Barbados 1954–60. Special Representative I.P.P.F. 1960—, Vice-Chmn. of G.B. 1963–69, Chmn. of G.B. 1969–75; New Democratic Party of Canada, Pres. Ontario 1961–66; Member Federal Council 1961–71; Federal Treas. 1965–69; Trustee, Bournville Village Trust, and of Youth Hostels Trust of Great Britain. Resident, Toynbee Hall 1929–35; Meetings Cttee. Royal Inst. of, International Affairs 1931–35. Secy. and Founding Member, W. Midland Group for Post-war Reconstruction & Planning 1939–41; Bd. mem., League for Industrial Democracy (New York); Mem. Council of Minority Rights Group (London); Mem. International Advisory Council of the Population Inst. (Washington D.C.). *Address:* 35 Brentwood Road, Oakville, Ont., L6J 4B7, Canada.

**CADBURY, Laurence John,** OBE, LLD (Hons). *B.* 1889. *Educ.* Leighton Park School; Trinity Coll., Cambridge (Economics Tripos). *M.* 1925, Joyce Matthews. *S.* 4 (1 *Dec.*). *Daus.* 2 (1 Dec.). *Career:* Served with Friends' Ambulance Unit in France in World War I (Mons Star; Croix de Guerre) 1914–19. Managing Director, Cadbury Bros. Ltd. and associated companies 1919–59; Chairman, Cadbury Bros. Ltd. 1944–59, and of J. S. Fry & Sons Ltd. 1952–59; Nation Proprietory Co. Ltd.; Chmn. & Dir. Daily News Ltd. 1930–76, E.M.B. Ltd.; Chmn., Bournville Village Trust. Treas., Population Investigation Cttee. 1936–76; Head of Economic Section, Mission to Moscow 1941; High Sheriff of County of London 1947–48 and 1959–60; Director, Bank of England 1936–61; Tyne-Tees Television 1959–67. LLD Hons B'ham Univ. 1970. *Publications:* This Question of Population; numerous contributions to the Press and periodicals on economic and demographic subjects. *Clubs:* Athanaeum; Oxford & Cambridge. *Address:* The Davids, Northfield, Birmingham 31.

**CADBURY, Michael Hotham.** British. *B.* 1915. *Educ.* Leighton Park School, Reading; and at Univ. in Germany. *M.* 1939, M. Heather Chambers. *S.* 2. *Dau.* 1. *Career:* Director, Cadbury Bros. Ltd. 1953–75; and Friends Provident Life Office 1955–75;. Governor, Leighton Park School, Reading 1954—. Vice President: Office International du Cacao et du Chocolat 1961–75; Cocoa, Chocolate & Confectionery Alliance (Pres. 1966–68); High Sheriff, West Midlands Metrop. County 1974–75. *Member:* National Trust Midland Centre (President); Nat. Trust Regional Cttee; Scout Assn. (B'ham County Commissioner.). *Address:* 54 Ramsden Close, Selly Oak, Birmingham 29.

**CADBURY, Peter Egbert,** MA (Cantab.), ARAeS. British. *B.* 1918. *Educ.* Leighton Park School; Trinity Coll. Cambridge. Hon. Degree Economics & Law BA 1939; MA 1945; Called to Bar 1946. Inner Temple. *M.* (1) 1947 M. Eugenie Benedicta. Diss. 1968. *S.* Justin. *Dau.* Felicity. (2) 1970, Jennifer Morgan Jones. *S.* Joel. *Career:* Served in Fleet Air Arm 1940 until released to Ministry of Aircraft Production, 1942, as Research and Experimental Test Pilot. Stood as Liberal candidate for Stroud (Glos.) 1945; Chmn. Man. Dir. Keith Prowse & Co. Ltd. (Ticket Agents, Travel Agents) Chmn. 1954–69; Alfred Hays Ltd.; Ashton & Mitchell; T.T.M. Holdings, Chmn. 1955–68; Chmn. Man. Dir. Westward Television Ltd. since 1960. *Member:* London Travel Committee 1958–60. *Award:* Freeman, City of London, 1948. *Clubs:* Garrick, Bath, M.C.C. (London); 40; Royal West of England Yacht; Royal Motor Y.C.; Hawks and others. Founder Member 1001 Trust for Wildlife. *Address:* Preston House, Preston Candover, Nr. Basingstoke, Hants.; and *office* Sloane Square House, Sloane Square, London, S.W.1.

**CADWALLADER, Sir John.** Australian miller and company director. *B.* 1902. *Educ.* Sydney Church of England Grammar School. *M.* 1935, Helen Sheila Moxham. *S.* John Robert and David Alistair. *Dau.* Helen Janet. *Career:* Chairman: Allied Mills Ltd. and its subsidiaries; President, Bank of New South Wales. *Address:* 27 Marian Street, Killara, Sydney, N.S.W.; and *office* c/o Allied Mills Ltd., Smith Street, Summer Hill, Sydney, N.S.W., Australia.

**CAESAR, Otto Paul.** German Assistant Judge (retired). *B.* 1906. *Educ.* High Legal State Examination, Berlin 1935 (Assistant Judge). *M.* 1943, Friederike von Reinersdorff. *Daus.* Alix, Renate and Christiane. *Career:* Chmn. of the Managing Bd., Rheinmetall Berlin AG Berlin; Rheinmetall GmbH, Düsseldorf; Member, Supervisory Board, Eisen und Metall A.G., Gelsenkirchen; A.G. Kühnle, Kopp & Kausch, Frankenthal/Pfalz; Member, Advisory Board; Tornado GmbH, Lintorf; Benz & Hilgers GmbH; Aviatest GmbH, Düsseldorf; Rheinmetall Schmiede-und Presswerk Trier GmbH, Trier; Dresdner Bank A.G. (Beirat Rheinland). Member, Industrieund Handelskammer 20 Düsseldorf, Vollversammlung. *Club:* Industry (Düsseldorf). *Address:* Düsseldorf-Meererbüsch An den Linden 26; and *office* Ulmenstrasse 125, Düsseldorf, Germany.

**CAETANO, Professor Marcello José das Neves Alves.** Portugese Professor and Politician. *Career:* President of Council of Ministers until 1974. Head of Inst. of Comparative Law, Brazil, since 1974. *Address:* Inst of Comparative Law, Gama Filho University, Rua Miguel Vitorino 623, Rio de Janeiro, Brazil.

**CAHILL, Arthur Ripley.** American. *B.* 1907. *Educ.* Univ. of Chicago (PhBEcon 1931). *M.* 1934, Jeanette Smith. *S.* Douglas R. and Steven M. *Dau.* Susan S. *Career:* With Brunswick Corp. Skokie Ill. 1960–72, Vice-pres. Finance, Director 1961–72; Retired 1972; International Minerals & Chemical Corp., Skokie, Ill. 1953–60, Vice-Pres. Finance & Dir.; Montgomery Ward & Co., Chicago 1941–52 (joined Company as Asst. Treas., elected Vice-Pres. and Treas. 1949). Prior to 1941 with Federal Reserve Bank and Harris Trust & Savings Bank both in Chicago. Business Consult. since 1972. Director: Bradshow-Praeger & Co., Chicago; People's Bank & Trust Co. Branson, Mo.; Silver Dollar City Inc. Branson Mo.; Sherwood Medical Industries Inc. Skokie, Ill. Bd. of Trustees, School of the Ozarks, Point Leckout, Mo. *Member:* Economics, Executives' and Commonwealth Clubs of Chicago. *Clubs:* University (Chicago); Oak Park (Ill.) Country Hickory Hills Country, Springfield Mo. *Address:* Woodleigh Drive, P.O. Box 1124, Branson, Mo. 65616, U.S.A.

**CAIN, Sir Edward Thomas,** CBE. Australian. *B.* 1916. *Educ.* University of Queensland (BA, LLB). *M.* 1942, Marcia Yvonne Parbery.· *S* Edward Norman. *Dau.* Patricia Margaret. *Career:* Second Commissioner of Taxation, Australia 1959–64; Commissioner of Taxation in the Commonwealth of Australia 1964–76. *Award:* Knight Bachelor, 1972. *Clubs:* Commonwealth (Canberra); Royal Canberra Golf. *Address:* 99 Buxton Street, Deakin, Canberra, Australia.

**CAINE, Sir Sydney,** KCMG. British. *B.* 1902. *Educ.* London School of Economics (BSc Econ 1922). *M.* (1) 1925, Muriel Harris (*D.* 1962), (2) 1965, Doris Winifred Folkard (*D.* 1973) and (3) 1975, Elizabeth Crane Bowyer. *S.* Michael. *Career:* Deputy Under-Secy. of State, Colonial Office 1957; Third Secy., Treasury 1948; Vice-Chancellor, University of Malaya 1952. Director, London School of Economics 1957–67. Deputy Chairman, Independent Television Authority 1960–67. Chairman, Governing Board, International Institute of Educational Planning (Paris) 1963–70. *Publications:* History of the Foundation of the London School of Economics (1963); British Universities: Purpose and Prospects (1969). *Awards:* LLD (Malaya); Grand Officer of Orange-Nassau (Netherlands); Order of Dannebrog (Denmark). *Member:* Royal Economic Socy. *Club:* Reform. *Address:* Buckland House, Tarn Road, Hindhead, Surrey.

**CAINE, Walter Eugene.** American. *B.* 1908. *Educ.* BS, also Master, Business Administration. *M.* 1932, Jeanette C. Wenborne. *S.* Stephen Howard, Edward Arthur and Martin Squier. *Career:* Associate Dir., Electric Power Survey, Twentieth Century Fund, 1939–40; Chief, Negotiations Section, Office of War Utilities, War Production Board, 1942; Assistant Chief, Division of Rates & Research, Federal Power Commn. 1940–44; Dir., Bureau of Statistics, Amer. Gas Assn., 1944–48; Consultant, President's Materials Policy Comm., 1950–51; Dir., Gas Planning Division, Petroleum Admin. for Defense, 1951–52; Gas Industry Advisory Cncl., U.S. Dept. of the Interior, 1954–57; Vice-President, Corporate Services Division, Texas Eastern Transmission Corp. 1967–72. Member: Military Petroleum Advisory Bd. 1957–61; Future Requirements Cttee., Univ. of Denver, 1965–73; Vice-Chmn., 1970–71, Chmn. 1972–73; National Council, National Planning Assoc., 1969–74; Regional Exec. National Alliance of Businessmen 1972–74. Bd. mem. Houston Council on Human Relations. *Publications:* Electric Power and Government Policy, Twentieth Cent. fund (1948). *Member:* Newcomen Socy. of N. America; Amer. Economic Assn.; N.Y. Socy of Security Analysts. *Clubs:* Cosmos (Washington D.C.); Sky (N.Y.C.); Houston (Texas); Sheveport (La.). *Address:* 426 Westminster Drive, Houston, Texas 77024, U.S.A.

**CAIRNCROSS, Sir Alexander Kirkland,** KCMG. British. *B.* 1911. *Educ.* Glasgow (MA) and Cambridge (PhD). *M.* 1943. Mary Frances Glynn. *S.* 3. *Daus.* 2. *Career:* Professor of Applied Economics, Univ. of Glasgow 1951–61; Director, Economic Development Institute, Washington 1955–56; Economic Adviser to H.M. Government 1961–64. Head of Government Economic Service 1964–69. Master, St. Peter's Coll., Oxford, since 1969. *Awards:* LLD (Glasgow and Mount Allison, Sackville, N.B.), LittD (Reading), LLD (Exeter), DLitt (Heriot Watt); DSc. Econ. Univ. of Wales; Hon. Degrees Queens Belfast 1972, Stirling 1973. Vice-Pres.: Royal Economic Socy.; Pres. GPDST; Vice-Pres. Scott, Economic Society. LSE (Court of Governors); British Academy; National Inst. of Economic & Social Research (Council). Pres., British Assoc. for Advancement of Science 1970–71; Chancellor, Univ. of Glasgow since 1972. Hon. Foreign Mem. American Academy of Arts & Sciences. *Publications:* Introduction to Economics; Home & Foreign Investment 1870–1913; Monetary Policy in a Mixed Economy; Factors in Economic Development; Essays in Economic Management; Inflation, Growth and International Finance. *Club:* United Oxford and Cambridge University. *Address:* The Master's Lodgings, St. Peter's College, Oxford.

**CAIRNS, Rear-Admiral Earl (David Charles Cairns),** GCVO, CB, DL (Suffolk). *B.* 1909. *Educ.* Royal Naval College, Dartmouth. *M.* 1936, Barbara Jeanne Harrison Burgess. *S.* Simon Dallas (Viscount Garmoyle) and Hon. Hugh Andrew David. *Dau.* Lady Elisabeth Olive. *Career:* Served in World War II (despatches) 1939–45. Deputy Director, Signal Dept., Admiralty 1950; Commanded 7th Frigate Sqdn. 1952; H.M.S. Ganges 1953–54; Student Imperial Defence College 1955; Commanded H.M.S. Superb 1956–57; Pres. Royal Naval College, Greenwich 1958–61; Her Majesty's Marshal of the Diplomatic Corps 1962–71; Prime Warden, The Fishmongers Co. 1972; Dir., Brixton Estate Ltd.; Chmn. of Governors of Greshams School; Governor of Nuffield Nursing Homes Trust; Pres., The Navy League. *Club:* Turf (London). *Address:* Clopton Hall, nr. Woodbridge, Suffolk (Tel. 047.335 248).

**CAIRNS, Rt. Hon. Sir David Arnold Scott.** *B.* 1902. *Educ.* Bede School, Sunderland and Pembroke College, Cambridge (Scholar; MA, LLB); BSc London. *M.* 1932, Irene Cathery Phillips. *S.* 1. *Daus.* 2. *Career:* Called to the Bar (Middle Temple) 1926; K.C. 1947; Liberal candidate, Epsom Div. 1947; Chairman, Liberal Party Trade Union Commission 1948–49; member, Leatherhead Urban District Council 1948–54; knighted 1955; Chairman, Monopolies and Restrictive Practices Commission 1954–56; Chmn., Statutory Committee of Pharmaceutical Society of Great Britain 1952–60; Recorder of Sunderland 1957–60; Bencher, Middle Temple 1958; Chmn., Exec. Cttee. of Justise (British Section of Int. Commission of Jurists) 1959–60; Chairman, Committee on Aircraft Accident Investigation 1960; one of H.M. Judges of High Court of Justice (Probate, Divorce & Admiralty Division) 1960–70. Chairman, Advisory Cttee. on Rhodesian Travel Restrictions, 1968–70; Lord Justice of Appeal 1970–77; Privy Councillor 1970; Hon. Fellow, Pembroke Coll., Cambridge. *Address:* Applecroft, Ashstead, Surrey.

**CAKOBAU, Ratu Sir George Kadavulevu,** GCMG, GCVO, OBE, KStJ. Fijian. Governor General of Fiji. *B.* 1911. *Educ.* Queen Victoria School, Fiji; Newington Coll. Australia; Wanganui Technical Coll. New Zealand. *M.* Adi Lealea. *S.* Balekiwai. *S.* 3. *Dau.* 1. *Career:* Military service, Captain in Fiji Military Forces 1939–45; Member, Great Council of Chiefs 1938–72; Legislative Council 1951–70; Minister, Fijan Affairs & Local Government 1970–71; Minister without Portfolio 1971–72; Governor General Fiji since 1973. *Awards:* Knight Grand Cross, Most Distinguished Order, St. Michael & St. George; Officer , Most Excellent Order, British Empire; Knight, Order of St. John. *Address:* Government House, Suva, Fiji.

**CALDECOTE, Viscount,** DSC **(Robert Andrew Inskip).** British Engineer. *B.* 1917. *Educ.* Eton College and King's College, Cambridge (MA); Hon. DSc., Cranfield Inst. Technology; MRINA, FIMechE, FIEE, President: A.I.C.M.A. (1966-68); S.B.A.C. (1965–66). *M.* 1942, Jean Hamilton. *S.* Piers J. H. Inskip. *Daus.* Serena (Armit), Antonia (Rowlandson). *Career:* Served in R.N.V.R. 1939–45; Royal Corps of Naval Constructors 1945–47; Assistant Manager, Vickers-Armstrongs Ltd., Naval Yard, Walker-on-Tyne, 1947–48; Fellow, King's College, Cambridge, and lecturer in Univ. Eng. Dept. 1948–55. Member, U.K. delegation to the U.N. 1953. Dir., English Electric Co., 1953–69; British Aircraft Corp. 1960–69; Vice-Pres., Eurospace 1961–68; Chmn. E.D.C. for the Movement of Exports 1965–72; Pres., Parly. and Scientific Cttee. 1966–69; Director: Cincinnati Milacron, 1969–75; Consolidated Gold Fields, 1969—; Lloyds Bank 1975—; Legal & General Assurance Co. 1976; Exec. Dir., Delta Metal Co., 1969–72, Chmn. since 1972; Member Review Bd. Govt. Contracts 1969–76; Chmn., Export Council for Europe 1970–71; Chmn., Design Council since 1972; President, Dean Close School; Governor, St. Lawrence College; Member, Conservative Party. *Member:* Church Pastoral-Aid Society (Treasurer) and Church Society (Treasurer). *Clubs:* Pratts; Royal Ocean Racing; Boodles; Royal Yacht Squadron. *Address:* Orchard Cottage, South Harting, Petersfield, Hants.; and *office* Delta Metal Co. Ltd., 1 Kingsway, London, WC2B 6XF.

**CALDERA, Dr. Rafael.** Former President of Venezuela. *B.* 1916. *Educ.* Universidad Central de Venezuela, Dr. Polit Sciences. *M.* 1941, Alicia Pietri. *S.* 3. *Daus.* 3. *Career:* Professor, Labor Laws & Sociology, UCV 1942–74; Prof. Labor Law & Sociology, Univ. Andres Bello 1953–74; Diputado (Congressman) 1941–44 & 1946–48; President de la Camara (Speaker) 1959–62, Presidente de la Republica 1969–74; Senador vitalicio since 1974. *Awards:* Dr. h.c. Universidad Lima (Peru); ND Univ. Indiana; Univ. di Perugia; Univ. de los Andes (Venez); Univ. del Zulia (Venez); Univ. Santa Maria, Caracas (Venez). Univ. S. Marcos (Lima, Peru); Cath Univ. Quito (Ecuador); Univ. S. Bolivar (Caracas, Ven.); Hon. Prof. UCV, Caracas, 1975. *Address:* Quinta Tinajero, 2a, Calle Cachimbo, Los Chorros, Caracas; and *office* Ave. Urdaneta, 33–2 Caracas, Venezuela.

**CALDWELL, John Tyler.** (retired) American educational administrator. *B.* 1911. *Educ.* Mississippi State Coll. (BS 1932); Duke Univ. (AM 1936); Princeton Univ. (PhD 1939) and Columbia Univ. (MA 1945). *M.* (1) 1947, Catherine Wadsworth Zeek (*D.* 1961), (2) 1963, Carol Schroeder Erskine. *S.* Andrew Morton and Charles Franklin. *Daus.* Alice Beaulieu, Helen Tyler, Carol Case Erskine Rosen and Melanie Erskine Johnston. *Career:* Rosenwald Fellow, Princeton 1937–39; Instructor to Associate Professor in Political Science, Vanderbilt Univ. 1939–47; U.S. Navy 1942–45; Lieut. Comdr. President: Alabama Coll., 1947–52, and Univ. of Arkanas 1952–59; Consultant to Ford Foundation 1954; Chancellor, North Carolina State Univ. Raleigh 1959–75; Pres., Triangle Universities Center for Advanced Studies, 1975—. *Awards:* Hon. LLD: College of the Ozarks 1955, Wake Forest College 1960, Duke Univ. 1965, Univ. of Maryland 1970 and N. Carolina State Univ. 1975, Univ. of Arkansas 1976. *Member:* American Political Science Assn.; Southern Political Science Assn.; Amer. Soc. for Public Admin.; Trustee, Educational Testing Service. Former Member: U.S. National Commission for U.N.E.S.C.O.; Former member Bd. of Visitors, Air Univ. Maxwell Air Force Base. Member, Bd. of Dirs., Overseas Development Council; Trustee, National Humanities Center 1976—; Trustee, Princeton Univ. 1976—. *Club:* Rotary. *Address:* 3070 Granville Drive, Raleigh, N.C.; and *office* North Carolina State University, Raleigh, N.C., U.S.A.

**CALLAGHAN, Sir Allan Robert,** Kt, CMG. Australian agricultural consultant. *B.* 1903. *Educ.* Univ. of Sydney (BSc Agr); BSc (Oxon), DPhil (Oxon). *M.* 1928, Zillah May Sampson (*D.* 1964). *M.* (2) 1965, Doreen W. R. Draper. *S.* 3 (1 *Dec.*). *Dau.* 1. *Career:* Rhodes Scholar for N.S.W. 1925; Plant Breeder, N.S.W. Dept. of Agri. 1928–32; Principal, Roseworthy Agric. Coll. S. Australia 1932–49; Asst. Dir. (Rural Industries), Commonwealth Dept. of War Organisation of Industry 1942–43. Chairman: Crown Lands Development Committee (S. Aust.) 1942–45, and of Land Development Executive (S. Aust.) 1945–51; Chairman, Washington Consultative Sub-committee on Surplus Disposal 1962; Director of Agriculture (Permanent Head), Dept. of Agriculture, S. Australia 1949–59; Commercial Counsellor, Australian Embassy, Washington D.C. 1959–65; Chairman, Australian Wheat Board 1965–71. *Publications:* The Wheat Industry of Australia (with A. J. Millington; 486 pp., illustrated); numerous publications on agric. (agronomy and husbandry). *Awards:* Farrer Medal (for distinguished service to Aust. agric.). Fellow: Aust. Inst. of Agricultural Science (Pres.); Australian-New Zealand Assn. for Advancement of Science. *Address:* 2 Villanova, 45 Coolangatta Rd., Kirra, Queensland 4225, Australia.

**CALLAGHAN, Sir Bede Bertrand,** Kt. 1976, CBE 1968. Australian banker. *B.* 1912. *Educ.* Newcastle (N.S.W.) High School. *M.* 1940, Mary T. Brewer. *Daus.* Mary, Margaret and Kathryn. *Career:* Member of Boards of Exec. Dirs.: International Monetary Fund, and International Bank for Reconstruction and Development 1954–59; General Manager, Commonwealth Development Bank of Australia, Sept. 1959–65; Man. Dir., Commonwealth Banking Corp. 1965–76; Chmn., Aust. Admin. Staff Coll. 1969–76; Australian European Finance Corp. Ltd. 1971–76. Mem. Council Univ. of Newcastle 1966, Deputy Chancellor 1973–77, Chancellor 1977—; Chmn., Foreign Investment Review Bd. 1976—. *Address:* 69 Darnley Street, Gordon, N.S.W. Australia.

**CALLAGHAN, Rt. Hon. (Leonard) James,** PC, MP. *B.* 1912. *Educ.* Portsmouth Northern Secondary School. *M.* 1938, Audrey Elizabeth Moulton. *S.* 1. *Daus.* 2. *Career:* Entered Civil Service as Tax Officer 1929; Asst. Secretary Inland Revenue Staff Fed. 1936–47. Served in R.N. during World War II; Member of Parliament S. Cardiff 1945–50, and S.E. Cardiff 1950—. Parliamentary Secy., Ministry of Transport 1947–50; Chmn. Cttee. on Road Safety 1948–50; Parl. Secy. and Financial Secy., Admiralty 1950–51; Delegate to Council of Europe, Strasburg 1948–50 and 1954; Exec. Cttee. Labour Party 1957–67; Treasurer of Labour Party 1967–76; Consultant to Police Federations in England, Wales and Scotland 1955–64; Chancellor of the Exchequer of the U.K. 1964–67; Secretary of State for The Home Department 1967–70; Chmn. Labour Party 1973–74; Secy. of State for Foreign & Commonwealth Affairs 1974–76; Prime Minister & First Lord of the Treasury & Leader of the Labour Party since 1976; Hon. Master of the Bench of the Inner Temple 1976; Hon. LLD, Univ. of Wales 1976. Hon. Life Fellow, Nuffield Coll., Oxford; Hon. Freeman City of Cardiff, 1975; Pres., U.K. Pilots' Assn. 1963–76; Hon. Pres. Int. Maritime Pilots Association 1971–76. *Address:* 10 Downing St., London S.W.1; & House of Commons, London, S.W.1.

**CALLAHAN, North.** American author and educator; former Colonel of the U.S. Army. *B.* 1908. *Educ.* Univ. of Tennessee (AB and LHD); Columbia University (AM); New York University (PhD). *M.* 1939, Jennie Waugh. *S.* North, Jr. *Dau.* Mary Alice. *Career:* Educator, Tennessee Schools 1930–34; Educational Adviser, U.S. Government 1934–37;

Newspaper writer 1937–40; Army Officer, U.S.A. 1940–45; Educational Public Relations Counsellor 1945–50; College Professor 1950—; Associate Professor of History, New York Univ. 1957–62; Professor of History 1962–73; Professor Emeritus since 1973. *Publications:* Books: The Army, (1941); The Armed Forces as a Career, (1957); Smoky Mountain Country, (1952); Henry Knox; General Washington's General (1958); Daniel Morgan, Ranger of the Revolution, (1961); Royal Raiders: the Tories of The American Revolution (1963); Flight from the Republic, (1967); A Biography, Carl Sandburg, (1970); George Washington, Soldier and Man, (1972). Wrote a syndicated newspaper column; contributions to scholarly journals, magazines and encyclopedias. Independent politically. *Member:* Sigma Delta Chi; Thera Tau Alpha; Alpha Hon. Socy., etc. *Address:* 25 South Germantown Rd., Chattanooga, Tenn. 37411 and New York University, New York City 10003, U.S.A.

**CALLAHAN, Roy Haney.** American. *B.* 1904. *Educ.* Univ. of Michigan (AB, JD) and Southern Methodist Univ. (LLM). *M.* 1952, Monita Chaney. *S.* Roy H., Jr. and Michael C. *Dau.* Monita. Recipient: Bronze Star; Air Medal; Presidential Citation 3 stars; Philippine Liberation; Pacific, American and Asian Campaigns; 3 stars. *Career:* Rear-Admiral USNR; Special Asst. to Secy of Navy; 1945–48 (from time to time). Naval Aviator (various line, command, staff, administrative and executive duties) 1929–31 and 1940–46; active attorney 1931–40 and 1950–56; Asst. Commissioner, Marine and Aviation, N.Y. City 1946; Corporate office 1946–49 and 1956—. Executive Assistant to Vice-President, Eastern Air Lines Inc. 1961–69; Director: Airlines Terminal Corp. 1962; Bradley Facilities 1963—; Exec. Vice-Pres., Airline Facilities Corp. of America since 1969; Member of Bar, U.S. Supreme Court, Court of Appeal, 2nd, 3rd, 4th, 5th and 8th circuits, and courts of last resort in New York, Michigan and Texas. *Publications:* Corporate Mortgage Handbook—Under Texas Law; A Neglected Airline Market; Robinson Patman Act—a Study; National Policy for Aviation; Survival and Rescue in the Everglades; Airport for Future Aircraft, a planning Guide; Impact of the Next Two Aircraft Generations and Airport Design. *Member:* American, New York State, Dallas, Fort Worth and Texas Bar Associations; and Bar Assoc. of City of New York. Mason. *Clubs:* University; New York Athletic; Cipango. *Address:* 1 Old Easton Turnpike, Weston, Conn.; and *office* P.O. Box 2088 G.C.S., New York City, U.S.A.

**CALLARD, Sir Jack (Eric John).** British. *B.* 1913. *Educ.* Queen's Coll., Taunton, and Cambridge University (MA); Hon. DSc (Cranfield). *M.* 1938, Pauline Mary Pengelly. *Daus.* 3. *Career:* Division Chmn., I.C.I. Ltd. Paints Div. 1959–64; Joined I.C.I. Main Bd. 1964; Chmn., I.C.I. Europa Ltd. 1965–67; Dir., Midland Bank Ltd. since 1971; Chmn., Imperial Chemical Industries Ltd. 1971–75; *Director:* Commercial Union Assurance Co. 1975—; British Home Stores 1974—, Chmn. 1975—; Equity Capital for Industry 1976—; Ferguson Industrial Holdings 1974—. *Member:* Royal Institution of Great Britain; Hon. Fellow, Inst. Mech. Engineers; Fellow, British Institute of Management; Royal Society of Arts; Manchester Business School Assn.; Vice-Pres., Industrial Participation Association; Trustee Civic Trust; Governor, London Graduate School, Business studies. *Address:* Crookwalts Cottage, Dockray, nr. Penrith, Cumbria.

**CALLAWAY, Hon. Howard H.** *B.* 1927. *Educ.* U.S. Military Acad. (BSc). *M.* 1949, Elizabeth Walton. *S.* Howard, Jr., Edward, and Ralph. *Daus.* Betsy and Virginia. *Career:* Pres., Interfinancial Inc. Atlanta Georgia; Chmn., Finance Cttee. Garden Services Inc. (Pine Mountain, Ga.); Chairman, Board of Trustees, Freedoms Foundation at Valley Forge (Valley Forge, Pa.); Civilian Aide to Secy of the U.S. Army; Secy to U.S. Army 1973–75; Chmn., President Ford Cttee. 1975–76; Chmn., Interfinancial Inc., Atlanta, Ga. 1976; Pres., Crested Butte Development Corp., Crested Butte, Colorado 1977. Republican. Former International President, Young Presidents' Organization, Inc. (N.Y.C.). *Address:* Pine Mountain, Georgia, U.S.A.

**CALLINAN, Sir Bernard James,** Kt. 1977, CBE, DSO, MC. Australian. *B.* 1913. *Educ.* University of Melbourne (BCE; Diploma of Town and Regional Planning). *M.* 1943, Naomi Marian Cullinan. *S.* 5. *Career:* With Australian Imperial Forces 1940–46; Consulting Engineers, Gutteridge, Haskins & Davey, 1948—, Senior Partner 1964–71, Chmn. Man. Dir. since 1971; Commissioner, State Electricity Commission of Victoria 1963—; Director, Lower Yarra Crossing Authority 1965, Deputy Chmn. since 1971; British Petroleum Company of Australia 1969—; Councillor La Trobe University 1964–72; First Deputy Chancellor, 1967–70. Member, Royal Commission, Inquiry Aust. Post Office 1973; Commissioner, Australian Atomic Energy Comm. since 1976. *Awards:* P.N. Russell Memorial Medal. *Fellow:* Institution of Civil Engineers (London), and The Institution of Engineers (Australia), Pres. 1971. American Socy. of Civil Engineers. *Clubs:* Melbourne; Australian, Naval & Military; Melbourne Cricket; Rotary. *Address:* 'Belulic', 111 Sackville Street, Kew, Vic.; and *office* 380 Lonsdale Street, Melbourne, Vic. 3000, Australia.

**CAMARA, Sikhé.** *B.* 1921. *Educ.* Lic. en Droit; Diploma of Higher Studies for Doctorat; Certificate in History, Paris. *M.* Awa Camara. *S.* 2. *Dau.* 3. Previously Ambassador to Yugoslavia (1961–65, and to the U.S.S.R. 1965–67. Prior to appointment to the Diplomatic Corps, was Attorney-General of the Republic of Guinea. Was a barriester prior to the Independence of Guniea. Ambassador of Guinea to the Federal Republic of Germany, May 1957, and other West European countries. *Member:* Democratic Party of Guinea. *Address:* Ministry of Foreign Affairs, Conakry, Republic of Guinea.

**CAMERON, Allen.** American. *B.* 1911. *Educ.* Public Schools. *M.* 1944, Ruth Isabel Trankler. *Daus.* Suzanne Elizabeth and Laurie Ellen. *Career:* With U.S. Navy 1930–34; various American merchant marine vessels from Able Seamen to Master 1934–44; Asst. Port Captain to Vice-Pres. and General Mgr., Pacific Tankers, Inc. 1944–49; Vice-Pres., Nat. Bulk Carriers, Inc. 1959–68; Vice-Pres. and Dir., Lebanese International Airways; Dir. Air Ventures, Inc.; Vice-Pres. and Dir.: Joshua Hendy Corp. 1944–59; Trans World Carriers, Inc., 1950–59; Pres. Rogers, Slade & Hill Inc. 1961–71; Pres. Buckfield Corp. since 1972. *Member:* N.E. Coast Marine Engrs.; Council, Amer. Master Mariners; Amer. Petroleum Institute. *Clubs:* Union League, N.Y.; Greenwich Country; Bohemian; Circumnavigators. *Address* and *office:* 300 Broad Street, Stamford, Conn. 06901, U.S.A.

**CAMERON, Marshal of the Royal Air Force Sir Neil,** GCB, CBE, DSO, DFC. British. *B.* 1920. *Educ.* Perth Academy. *M.* 1947, Patricia Louise Asprey. *S.* 1. *Dau.* 1. *Career:* Programme Evaluation Group, Ministry of Defence 1966–68; Asst. Chief of Defence Staff, Min. of Defence 1968–70; Senior Air Staff Officer, Air Support Command 1970–72; Dep. Commander, HQ RAF Germany 1972–73; Air Officer Commanding, No. 46 Group 1973–74; Air Member for Personnel 1974–76; Chief of the Air Staff 1976–77; Chief of the Defence Staff since 1977. *Decorations:* Knight Grand Cross of the Order of the Bath, 1976; Commander of the Order of the British Empire, 1967; Companion of the Distinguished Service Order, 1945; Distinguished Flying Cross, 1944; Air Efficiency Award. *Publications:* Articles in Defence Journals. *Club:* Royal Air Force. *Address:* c/o Ministry of Defence, Whitehall, London SW1.

**CAMERON, Dr. R. J.** Australian diplomat. *B.* 1923. *Educ.* Univ. of Adelaide-M.Econ.; Harvard Univ.-PhD. *M.* 1951, Dorothy Olive Lober. *S.* 2. *Dau.* 1. *Career:* Lecturer in Economics, Canberra 1949–51; Economist, World Bank, Washington 1954–56; various positions in Dept. of the Treasury, Canberra 1956–73; Perm. Rep. of Australia to the OECD 1973–76; Australian Statistician since 1977. *Address:* Australian Bureau of Statistics, Cameron Offices, Belconnen, A.C.T. 2617, Australia.

**CAMILLERI, Sir Luigi,** LLD. *B.* Victoria (Gozo, Malta) 1892. *Educ.* Gozo Seminary and Royal Univ. of Malta (LLD 1913). *M.* 1914, Erminia Cali. *S.* Joseph M. (LLD, MP) Edwin A. (Lt.-Col. RMA), Antoine, Rev. Edward (SJ), and Louis A. (BSc MD). *Daus.* Evelyn (Zammit Maenpel), Myriam (Vassallo) and Margaret. *Career:* Consular Agent for France in Gozo 1919–24; Member Maltese Legislative Assembly 1921–24; Magistrate 1924–30; H. M. Judicial Bench (Malta) 1930–52; Chief Justice and President of H.M. Court of Appeal 1952–57; Representative of Graduates on Council, Royal University of Malta 1933–36; Examiner in Roman, Civil and Criminal Law at this Univ. 1933–70. Member, Judicial Service Commission 1959–63; Pres., Malta Medical Council 1958–68. Silver Jubilee Medal 1953; Coronation Medals 1937 and 1953; Knight Sovereign Military Order of Malta 1952; Knight Bach, 1954. *Club:* Casino Maltese. *Address:* 27 Victoria Avenue, Sliema, Malta.

**CAMP, Ehney Addison, Jr.** American. *B.* 1907. *Educ.* Univ. of Alabama (BS). *M.* 1933, Mildred Tillman. *S.* Ehney Addison III. *Daus.* Mrs. Patricia Camp (Faulkner) and Mary Eugenia (Boulware). *Career:* With Sterne, Agee &

Leach 1928–30; Bankers Mortgage Bond Co. 1930–32; Director 1943—, Exec. Vice-President, Liberty National Life Insurance Co. 1960–73. Director, American Cast Iron Pipe Co.; Trustee, Univ. of Alabama. *Member:* Phi Beta Kappa; Beta Gamma Sigma; Omicron Delta Kappa; Sigma Nu. *Clubs:* Kiwanis; Mountain Brook; Birmingham Country; Relay House; The Club; Alabama Academy of Honor. *Address:* 3232 East Briarcliff Road, Birmingham Ala. 35223, U.S.A.

**CAMPBELL of Croy, Lord (Gordon Thomas Calthrop),** MC, PC. British. *B.* 1921. *Educ.* Wellington College and hospital. *M.* 1949, Nicola Madan. *S.* 2. *Dau.* 1. *Career:* Served in World War II in 15th Scottish Div. (Major 1942, M.C. and Bar). Wounded and disabled 1945. In Diplomatic Service 1946–57; U.K. Mission to U.N., New York 1949–52; Cabinet Office, London 1954–56. Embassy Vienna 1956–57; MP for Moray & Nairn 1959–74; Lord Commissioner of the Treasury 1962–63; Parliamentary Under-Secretary of State for Scotland 1963–64; Secy. of State for Scotland 1970–4; created Life Peer 1974. *Club:* Brooks's (London). *Address:* Holme Rose, Nairnshire, Scotland.

**CAMPBELL, Alan Douglas.** Australian. *B.* 1920. *M.* 1951, Frances Hunter Evans. *S.* Gordon. *Daus.* Felicity, Elizabeth, Vanessa. *Career:* Gen. Manager McIlwraith McEacharn Ltd.; Chmn., Petterson & Co. Pty. Ltd.; Past Vice Chmn. Aust. Northbound Shipping Conference. *Member:* Australasian Steamship Owners' Federation; Aust. Japan Business Cooperation Committee. *Address:* 49 Tannock Street, North Balwyn, Vic. Australia.

**CAMPBELL, Sir Alan Hugh,** KCMG. British diplomat. *B.* 1919. *Educ.* Sherborne School; Caius Coll. Cambridge. *M.* 1947, Margaret Jean Taylor. *Daus.* 3. *Career:* British Ambassador to Ethiopia 1969–72; Asst. Under Secretary of State, Foreign & Commonwealth Office, London 1972–74; Deputy Under-Secretary of State 1974–76: Ambassador to Italy since 1976. *Award:* Knight Commander, Order of St. Michael and St. George. *Address:* British Embassy, Via XX Settembre 80a, Rome, Italy.

**CAMPBELL, Hon. Alexander Bradshaw,** PC, MLA, BA-LLB, LLD (Hon.). Canadian Provincial premier. *B.* 1933. *Educ.* BA; LLB, Dalhousie Univ. LLB; McGill Univ. LLD. *M.* 1961, Marilyn Ruth Gilmour. *S.* Blair Alexander, Graham Melville. *Dau.* Heather K. *Career:* P.E.I. Bar 1959; mem. P.E.I. Legis. Assembly 1965; Queen's Counsel 1966; Premier Prince Edward Is. since 1966; Min. of Justice and Attorney-General, 1966–69 and since 1974; Minister of Development 1969–72; Ministry, Agriculture 1972–74; Member, Privy Council 1967—; Chairman, Planning & Policy Board since 1970. *Member:* P.E.I. Law Society former Vice-Pres. Young Liberal Assn. *Address:* 330 Beaver Street, Summerside, P.E.I., Canada; and *office* P.O. Box 2000, Charlottetown, P.E.I., Canada.

**CAMPBELL, Alistair Matheson.** MA. FIA. FSA. *B.* Scotland 1905. *Educ.* Inverness Royal Academy (Scotland); University of Aberdeen (MA 1927; First Class Hons. in Maths.); Research Scholar in Maths. 1928. *M.* 1948, Barbara Isabel Hampson Alexander. *S.* Michael Alexander. *Daus.* Catherine, Barbara and Jill. *Career:* Actuarial Dept. Sun Life 1928; Asst. Actuary 1934; on loan to Foreign Exchange Control Board, Ottawa 1939–40; Actuary 1946; Vice-President and Actuary 1950; Director and Exec. Vice-President 1956; President 1962; Chairman 1970. Pres.: Canadian Assn of Actuaries 1947–48; and Canadian Life Insurance Assn. 1957–58. Chairman & Director, Sun Life Assurance Co. of Canada; Dir. Sun Life Assurance Co. of Canada (U.K.) Ltd.; Sun life Assurance Co. of Canada (U.S.); Director and Chairman, Executive Cttee. Canadian Enterprise Development Corp. Ltd.; Director and mem. Exec. Cttee.; Asbestos Corp. Ltd., Canadian Pacific Investments Ltd.; Royal Trust Co.; The Steel Co. of Canada Ltd. Director, Royal Trust Co. Mortgage Corp.; Royal Trust Corp. of Canada; Canadian Industries Ltd.; Digital Equipment of Canada, Ltd.; Textron Inc.; Textron Canada Ltd.; Provincial Vice-Pres. (Quebec), American Life Convention 1962–73 and mem. Exec. Cttee. 1965; Director, Life Insurance Assn. of America 1968–71; Former Dir. Canada Safety Council. *Fellow:* Inst. of Actuaries (Gt. Britain) and Socy. of Actuaries; Vice-Pres., Quebec Div. Canadian Red Cross Socy. 1950–53; awarded Canadian Red Cross Hon. Membership 1956; Hon. Governor Quebec Provincial Div. Canadian Red Cross Socy, 1975. *Clubs:* Mount Royal; University (both Montreal); Country (Ottawa); Royal Ottawa Golf. *Address:* 1700 McGregor Avenue, Montreal H3H 1B4, Quebec; and *office* Sun Life Building, Montreal H3B 2V9, P.Q., Canada.

**CAMPBELL, Arnold Everitt.** New Zealand citizen. *B.* 1906. *Educ.* Univ. of New Zealand (MA; Diploma in Education). *M.* 1934, Louise Annie Combs. *S.* Peter Frank. *Daus.* Jane Mabel and Margaret Louise. *Career:* Librarian and Asst. Lecturer in History, Wellington Teachers' Coll. 1926; Primary school teacher 1927–29; Asst. Lecturer in Education, then Lecturer, Victoria Univ. Coll., Wellington 1929–38; Asst. Secy., N.Z. Educational Inst. and editor of *National Education* 1934–35; Dir., N.Z. Council for Educational Research 1939–52; Chief Inspector of Primary Schools 1952–57, Asst. Dir. of Education 1958–59, Dept. of Education. C.M.G. 1966. Director General of Education 1960–66,. Department of Education, Wellington. Chairman, N.Z, National Commission for UNESCO 1960–66. Dep. Chairman. Board of Trustees, Maori Education Foundation 1962–66. *Publications:* Educating New Zealand, (1941); The Feilding Community Centre, (1945); The Control of Post-Primary Schools, (1948); Modern Trends in Education (Editor), (1938). *Address:* 13 Pitt Street, Wellington, 1, New Zealand.

**CAMPBELL, Arthur Grant.** Canadian diplomat. *Educ.* McGill Univ. BA 1938; Colombia Univ. Post-grad. studies (1951). *M.* 1940, Carol Wright. *S.* 1. *Career:* Asst. to Secy. Canadian Chamber of Commerce 1938–41; Canadian Army (Artillery) UK, Italy, N.W. Europe 1941–46; UN Secretariat 1946–56; Dept. External Affairs, Ottawa 1956–60; Counsellor 10 nation Conference on Disarmament, Geneva 1960; Counsellor New Delhi 1960–63; Head C'wealth Div. Ottawa 1963–67; Min.-Counsellor, 18 nation Disarmament Conference Geneva 1967–69; Min. Bonn 1969–72; Ambassador to S. Africa and High Commissioner to Botswana, Lesotho and Swaziland 1972–76; Ambassador to Norway and Iceland since 1977. *Decorations:* Despatches (1945). *Address:* Bygdoynesveien 15, Oslo 3; and *office* Postuttak, Oslo 1, Norway.

**CAMPBELL, Sir Clifford Clarence,** GCMG, GCVO. Jamaican. *B.* 1892. *Educ.* Petersfield and Mico Training Coll., Jamaica. *M.* 1920, Alice Esthephene Jolly. *S.* 2. *Daus.* 2. *Career:* Headmaster, Fullersfield Government School 1916–18, and Friendship Elementary School 1918–28; Principal, Grange Hill Government School 1928–44. Member (Jamaica Labour Party) for Westmoreland Western, House of Representatives 1944–49; Chairman, House Committee on Education 1945–49; First Vice-Pres., Elected Members Association 1945, re-elected 1949; Speaker of the House of Representatives 1950; Senator and President of the Senate 1962; Governor-General 1962–73. *Awards:* Created G.C.M.G. by H.M. The Queen 1962. Chief Scout for Jamaica; patron of numerous charitable and other organisations in Jamaica. Hon. Member: Trelawny, Jamaica, Ex-Services, Caymanas Golf and Country, Liguanea, Kingston Cricket, St. Andrew, Police Officers and Rotary Clubs. *Address:* King's House, Kingston 10, Jamaica, West Indies.

**CAMPBELL, Brig.-Gen. Colin Alexander,** DSO, OBE. Consulting mining engineer. *B.* 1901. *Educ.* Queen's University. *M.* 1923, Vera M. Smith. *S.* Archie K. and Donald R. *Daus.* Meryl (Yule) and June (Perry). *Career:* Engaged in mining 1921–34; Consulting practice 1934–37 and since 1946; elected to House of Commons of Canada (for Frontenac-Addington, Ontario) 1934; re-elected 1935; resigned and unsuccessfully contested Addington Provincial general election 1937; elected by acclamation, Sault Ste. Marie by-election Nov. 1937; Minister of Public Works 1937. Enlisted as 2nd Lieut. with Royal Canadian Engineers 1939; appointed 1st Lieut. and later in England promoted to Captain, and subsequently Major, Lieut.-Col. and Brigadier; served as Chief Engr., 1st Canadian Corps in Italy and Holland. Hon. Col. 2nd Field Engineer Regt. RCE (M) OBE 1943; MID 1944; DSO 1945; Legion of Merit (U.S.A.) 1945; President & General Manager, Amos Mines Ltd.; Vice-Pres. & Director, Bardyke Mines Ltd., Associated Senior Executives of Canada. *Address:* 269 Rayners Road, Keswick, Ontario; and *office* Suite 1204, 67 Yonge St., Toronto, Ont., Canada.

**CAMPBELL, Hon. Daniel Robert John.** Canadian. *B.* 1926. *Educ.* Univ. of British Columbia (BA 1954). *M.* Kathleen Jean Jensen. *S.* Patrick Michael and Mark William. *Daus.* Susan Joan and Shannon Jean. *Career:* Member Legislative Assembly of British Columbia 1956—; Minister of Municipal Affairs 1964, and Minister of Social Welfare 1966—, Province of British Columbia. *Address:* *office* Parliament Buildings, Victoria, B.C., Canada.

**CAMPBELL, Donald.** British. *B.* 1920. *Educ.* John Sch., Glasgow; Stow Coll. of Engineering. *M.* 1941, E. C. McGill. *S.* 1. *Dau.* 1. *Career:* Man. Dir. Bonney Forge Ltd.; *Chairman:* Laird Forge Ltd.; Barr Thomson Ltd.; Francis Caird Ltd.; T. Porter (Pipework) Ltd.; Taylor-Bonney International Ltd. *Director:* Jader Srl; Bonney Forge Italia SpA; Bonney Forge Vertriebs GmbH. *Member:* British Inst. Management; Inst. Directors; Fellow, Inst. Petroleum. *Club:* Nat. Liberal. *Address:* 138 Bank St., Irvine, Ayrshire, Scotland; and *office* Irvine, Ayrshire.

**CAMPBELL, Frederick Hugh.** British. *B.* 1908. *Educ.* Codrington Public School; Sydney Technical College. *M.* 1941, Jean Steele. *Daus.* 2. *Career:* Organiser, Electrical Trades Union of Australia 1941–46; Asst. Secy. E.T.U.A. 1946–48; Secy. N.S.W. Branch 1948–60, Vice-Pres. 1953–58, Pres. 1958–60. Member, Electricity Commn. of N.S.W. 1950—. Pres., N.S.W. Branch Aust. Labour Party 1955–60; Chmn. Electricity Authority of N.S.W. since 1960. *Clubs:* City Tattersalls; Coast Golf; Hurstville Bowling; Sydney Turf. *Address:* 50 Miller Street, North Sydney, Australia.

**CAMPBELL, Howard Edward.** Canadian Consul. *B.* 1920. *Educ.* Univ. of Calfornia (Associate in Arts) and McGill Univ. (BCom). *M.* 1945, Jean Joy Irving. *S.* 5. *Daus.* 2. *Career:* Commercial Counsellor, Bonn. Aug.-Oct. 1961; Trade Commissioner, Kingston (Jamaica) Aug. 1955–July 1961, and Johannesburg S.A. Nov. 1951–July 1955; Asst. Trade Commissioner and Vice-Consul, N.Y.C. Jan. 1948–Oct. 1951. Cdn. Consul Dusseldorf 1961–66. Asst-Dir. (Persennel) Trade Comm. Service Ottawa 1966–68; Insp. Trade Comm. (Ottawa) 1968–69; Comm. Couns. Berne 1969–74; Can. Consul. Philadelph. since 1974. Flying Officer, R.C.A.F. (Pathfinder Sqdn. 405) 1943–45. *Address:* 3 Parkway, suite 1310, Philadelphia, Penn. U.S.A. 19102.

**CAMPBELL, Ian,** CEng, MIMechE, JP, MP. British politician and Chartered Engineer. *B.* 1926. *M.* 1950, Mary Millar. *S.* 2. *Daus.* 3. *Career:* Electrical Power Engineer with South of Scotland Electricity Board; Member of Parliament for Dumbarton West. *Member:* I.Mech.E. Assn. *Address:* 20 Mc. Gregor Drive Dumbarton and *office* House of Commons, London S.W.1.

**CAMPBELL, Ian Edwin.** British executive. *B.* 1920. *Educ.* Neutral Bay Intermediate High School. *M.* 1948, Joan Norma Stubbs. *S.* Stuart Victor and Barton Charles. *Career:* Joined Oversea Shipping Reps. Assn. as Clerk 1937; Secretary, Space Allotment Cttee. 1940–41; joined Australian Imperial Forces (served in New Guinea with Water Transport Group and Australian Docks Operating Company; rank of Sgt.) 1942–46; Chairman, Space Allotment Cttee. 1948–50; Asst. Secretary, Oversea Shipping Reps. Assn. 1950–57; Acting Secretary of the Association 1957; concurrently Actg. Secy. of the Australian & New Zealand Passenger Conf. Secretary: Oversea Shipping Representatives' Association 1958–72, Exec. Dir. since 1973; Australian & New Zealand Passenger Conference 1958—, Trans Tasman Passenger Conference 1960–75; Joint Hon. Secretary, Australian Oversea Transport Association 1965—. Commissioner of the Peace, State of New South Wales, Feb. 1963, and Secretary, Australian Passenger Agency Cttee 1963–72. Member, Chartered Institute of Transport since 1971. *Clubs:* Balgowlah Golf; Cricketers (N.S.W.); Balgowlah-Seaforth Returned Servicemen's, Australian; Manly Golf. *Address:* 28 Bluegum Crescent, Frenchs Forest, N.S.W.; and *office* Oversea Shipping Representatives' Association, 50 Young Street, Sydney, N.S.W., Australia.

**CAMPBELL, Sir John Johnston.** British company director. *B.* 1897. *Educ.* Stewarton Secondary School. *M.* 1927, Margaret Fullarton Brown (*Dec.*). *S.* William John. *Dau.* Agnes Nicol (Barham). *Career:* Served in World War I (Royal Scots Fusiliers; in Palestine, France and Germany) 1916–19. Joined Clydesdale Bank 1913; London Manager 1944; General Manager 1946–58. President, Institute of Bankers 1953–55; Director: Clydesdale Bank Ltd. 1958–75; Chairman of Committee, Scottish Bank General Managers 1955–57; member of Restrictive Practices Court 1958–61. *Address:* 22 Saffrons Court, Compton Place Road, Eastbourne, East Sussex.

**CAMPBELL, Keith Oliver.** Australian professor. *B.* 1920. *Educ.* BScAgr. (Sydney); MA, PhD (Chicago); MPA (Harvard). *M.* 1949 Christiana McFadyen. *S.* William. *Daus.* Catherine and Margaret. *Career:* Economics Research Officer, N.S.W. Dept. of Agriculture 1943–49 (Principal Economics Research Officer 1950–51); Reader in Agricultural Economics, Univ. of Sydney 1951–56. Professor of Agricultural Economics, University of Sydney 1956—. Dean Faculty of Agriculture, 1968–71. *Member:* Royal Economic Socy.; Royal Inst. of Public Administration; American Agricultural Economics Assn.; Agricultural Economics Socy.; Australian Inst. of Agricultural Science; International Assn. of Agricultural Economists; Academy of the Social Sciences in Australia; Aust. Agricultural Economic Society. *Publications:* Agricultural Marketing and Prices (1973); numerous articles in professional journals. *Clubs:* University of Sydney Staff. *Address:* 188 Beecroft Road, Cheltenham, N.S.W.; and Department of Agricultural Economics, University of Sydney, Sydney 2006, N.S.W., Australia.

**CAMPBELL, Hon. Robin Dudley.** British company director. *B.* 1921. *Educ.* Eton, and Trinity College, Cambridge (interrupted by war service with Scots Guards 1940–46, wounded). *M.* 1954, Cecilia Barbara Leslie. *Daus.* Lenore Robina Cecilia and Zephyrine Alexandra. *Career:* With Forbes Forbes Campbell & Co. Ltd., Bombay 1946–60, (Director 1948—; Deputy Chairman 1953—. The family company and oldest company in India, dating from 1767; is now controlled by House of Tata; Was Director of several Indian companies—public and private—including Gokak Mills Ltd., Indian Vegetable Product Ltd., Bombay Safe Deposit Ltd., Man. Dir. Balfour Williamson and Co. Ltd. and several of its subsid, cos (England and o'seas) 1962–76; Man. Dir., Baltic Investments (London) Ltd. 1976—. *Member:* Institute of Directors; Institute of Export; Chairman, British Export Houses Assoc. 1966–67; Member of Court 1972–74; Adv. Council. Export Credit Guarantee Dept. (ECGD) 1972–76. *Clubs:* Guards (London); Willingdon (Bombay). *Address:* Sharp's Place, Boughbeech, Edenbridge, Kent; and *office* 85 Jermyn Street, London SW1.

**CAMPBELL, Ross,** DSC. Canadian. *B.* 1918. *Educ.* University of Toronto Schools, and University of Toronto (Trinity College) Faculty of Law (BA 1940). *M.* 1945, Penelope Grantham-Hill. *S.* 2. *Career:* Served RCN 1940–45 (Distinguished Service Cross 1944); former diplomat: joined Dept. of External Affairs, Canada 1945; Third Sec., Oslo 1946–47; Second Sec., Copenhagen 1947–50; European Div., Ottawa 1950–52; First Sec. Ankara 1952–56; Head of Middle East Div., Ottawa 1957–59; Special Asst. to Sec. of State for External Affairs 1959–62; Asst. Under-Sec. of State for External Affairs 1962–64; Advisor to Canadian Delegations to UN Gen. Assemblies 1958–63, and to North Atlantic Council 1959–64; Ambassador to Yugoslavia 1964–67, concurrently to Algeria 1965–67; Amb. & Perm. Rep. to NATO 1967–72 (Paris May 1967, Brussels Oct. 1967); Amb. to Japan 1973–75, and concurrently to Republic of Korea 1973–74; appointed Chmn. of the Board, Atomic Energy of Canada Ltd. 1976. *Address:* Atomic Energy of Canada Ltd., 275 Slater, Ottawa K1A OS4, Canada.

**CAMPBELL OF ESKAN, Lord** (John Middleton Campbell). *B.* 1912. *Educ.* Eton and Exeter Coll., Oxford. *M.* (1) 1938, Barbara Noel Arden Roffey (*Div.* 1948), and (2) 1949, Phyllis Jacqueline Gilmour Boyd. *S.* John Charles Middleton and Peter Mark Middleton. *Daus.* Rosalind Leonora Middleton and Agneta Joanna Middleton (Agnew). *Career:* Chairman: Milton Keynes Development Corp., Commonwealth Sugar Exporters Association; President: Booker McConnell Ltd.; Dir., Commonwealth Development Corp. Trustee, Runnymede Trust; Trustee, Chequers Trust; Hon. Doct. Open Univ. (1973); Hon. Fellow Exeter Coll., Oxford (1973). *Clubs:* Beefsteak; M.C.C.; All-England Lawn Tennis; Georgetown (Guyana). *Address:* 15 Eaton Square, London SW1W 9DD; and Crocker End House, Nettlebed, Oxfordshire.

**CAMPBELL-JOHNSON, Alan,** CIE, OBE, Officer, Legion of Merit (U.S.); British. *B.* 1913. *Educ.* Westminster School and Christ Church, Oxford (BA Hons Mod Hist; MA 1956). *M.* 1938, Imogen Fay Dunlap. *S.* Keith (*Dec.*). *Dau.* Virginia. *Career:* Asst. to Manager, Public Relations Dept., London Press Exchange 1937; in independent public relations practice 1948—. R.A.F. 1941–46; on staff of Lord Mountbatten 1942–48, first as Air P.R.O., Hq., Chief of Combined Operations; then O.C. Inter-Allied Record Section, Hq. Supreme Allied-Commander, S.E. Asia; finally Press Attache to Viceroy during transfer of power in India 1947–48; Chmn. and Mng. Dir., Campbell-Johnson Ltd. 1953—. *Publications:* Growing Opinions (edited), (1935); Peace Offering, (1936); Anthony Eden (biog.), (1938); revised and republished (1955); Viscount Halifax (biog.), (1941); Mission with Mountbatten, (1951, with Foreword by Lord Mountbatten 1972). Fellow and Past Pres., Inst. Public Relations. Fellow Royal Socy. of

Arts. *Member:* Royal Inst., and Royal Inst. Interntl. Affairs. Member Liberal Party (contested Gen. Elections 1945 and 1950; Hon. Political Secy. to Lord Thurso (then Sir Archibald Sinclair, Leader of the Parliamentary Liberal Party) 1937–40. *Clubs:* Brooks's; National Liberal; Marylebone Cricket. *Address:* 21 Ashley Gardens, Ambrosden Av., London. SWIP 1QD; and *office* 16 Bolton Street, London, W1Y 8HX.

**CAMPOS, Roberto de Oliveira,** Brazilian statesman and writer. *B.* 1917. *Educ.* Catholic seminaries of Guaxupé and Belo Horizonte in Brazil, Philosophy (1934) Theology (1937); George Washington Univ., Washington D.C., MA (Econ); Post-grad. studies in Columbia Univ. N.Y.C.; Dr (hon causa) New York Univ. *Career:* Prof. Money, Banking and Business Cycles, School of Economics, Univ. of Brasil, 1956–61; Econ. Counsellor of Brazil/United States Econ. Dev. Comm. 1951–53; Dir. Gen. Man. and Pres. of National Economic Dev. Bank 1952–55–59; Secy-Gen. of Nat. Devel. Council 1965–69; Roving Ambassador for financial negotiations in W. Europe 1961; Amb. of Brazil to U.S.A. 1961–63; Min. of State for Planning and Co-ordination 1964–67; mem. of Inter-American Cttee. for the Alliance for Progress (rep. Brazil, Eucador & Haiti) 1964-67; Pres. of CICYP 1968–70; mem. of Board of Govs. of Intern. Dev. Research Centre; men. of Board of Dirs. of Resources for the Future (inc. U.S.A.). *Publications:* numerous articles and the following books: Ensaios de História Econômica e Sociologia; Economia, Planejamento e Nacionalismo; A Moeda, o Govêrno e o Tempo; A Técnica e o Riso; Reflections on Latin American Development; Do outro lado da cerca; Temas e Sistemas; Ensaios contra a maré; Política Econômica e Mitos Políticos; (Co-author): Trends in International Trade (GATT report); Partners in Progress (Report of the Pearson Committee of the World Bank); A Nova Economia Brasileira. *Address:* c/o Chancery, 32 Green St., London W1Y 4AT.

**CAMUS, Quirico Serra, Jr.** Filipino. *B.* 1928. *Educ.* Harvard Graduate School of Business Administration (MBA) and University of the East (BBA); Certified Public Accountant. *M.* 1954, Milagros la O. *S.* José Vicente; Francisco Javier and and Rafael Quirico. *Daus.* Cecile Marie, Lis Anne and Maria Milagros. *Career:* General Manager, Philippine Portland Cement Co. 1954–56; Vice Pres. Credit Mgr. Philippine Bank of Commerce 1956–61; Exec. Vice-Pres.: First Acceptance & Investment Corp., First Nationwide Credit Corp., and First Nationwide Assurance Corp. 1961–66; Partner, Sycip, Gorres Velayo & Co. 1966–72; Pres. Atlantic, Gulf & Pacific Co. of Manila Inc.; Philippines Economic Socy.; Harvard Business School Assn. of the Philippines; *Publications:* various articles. *Clubs:* Golf & Country; Harvard Club of the Philippines; Baguio Country; Polo and Rotary (both Manila); Manila Golf and Ctry. *Address:* 21 Antares, Bel-Air, Makati, Rizal; and *office* 131 Ayala Avenue, Makati, Rizal, Philippines.

**CANALI, Paolo.** Italian diplomat. *B.* 1911. *Educ.* Rome Univ. (degree Econ.). *Career:* Assist. to Prime Minister (De Gasperi 1944–53; Consul-general of Italy in Montreal 1958–66; Italian Ambassador in Ireland 1966–71; Italian Ambassador in Australia since 1971. *Publ.* De Gasperi nella Politica estera Italiana (1953); Il Paese dai tre oceani (1971). *Clubs:* University (Montreal); Commonwealth (Canberra). *Address:* Italian Embassy, Canberra, Australia; and 19 Via N. Piccinni, Rome, Italy.

**CANAVAN, Dennis Andrew,** MP. Scottish politician. *B.* 1942. *Educ.* St. Columba's High School, Cowdenbeath; Edinburgh Univ., BSc. (Hons.), Dip. Ed. *M.* 1964, Elnor Stewart. *S.* 3. *Dau.* 1. *Career:* Head of Maths Dept., St. Modan's High School, Stirling 1970–74; Asst. Headmaster, Holy Rood High School, Edinburgh 1974; District Councillor 1973–74; Agent for West Stirlingshire Constituency Labour Party 1972–74; Labour Group Leader, Stirling District Council 1974; Labour Member of Parliament for West Stirlingshire since 1974; Convener, Education Sub.-Cttee. of Scottish Parly. Labour Group; Parly. Spokesman for Scottish Spina Bifida Assn. and Scottish Cttee. on Mobility for the Disabled. *Member:* Educational Inst, of Scotland; Socialist Educational Assoc.; Fabian Socy.; Inter-Parliamentary Union; Commonwealth Parliamentary Assoc. Scottish Universities' Football Internationalist 1966–67, 1967–68. *Publications:* Articles on education and politics in various newspapers and journals. *Club:* Bannockburn Miners' Welfare Club, Bannockburn. *Address:* 15 Margaret Road, Bannockburn, Stirlingshire; & House of Commons, London S.W.1.

**CANDAU, Dr. M. G.** Brazilian International Civil Servant. *B.* 1911. *Educ.* M.D. School of Medicine, State of Rio de Janeiro; special training in public health at Univ. of Brazil and at Johns Hopkins Univ., Baltimore, U.S.A.; Hon LLD, Univ. of Michigan, Johns Hopkins Univ., Baltimore, Univ. of Edinburgh, Queen's Univ. (Belfast), Seoul Univ. and Royal Univ. of Malta; Hon. Doctor of Medicine, Univ. of Geneva; Karolinska Institute Stockholm; Doctor h.c. Univ. of Brazil Univ. of San Paulo Univ. of Bordeaux, Charles Univ. Prague, Univ. Abidjan, Ivory Coast. Inst. Medicine and Pharmacy, Bucharest, Romania; Semmelweis Univ. of Medicine, Budapest; Hon. Doctor of Science, Bates Coll., Maine, U.S.A., Univ. of Ibadan Nigeria; Cambridge University. Awarded Mary Kingsley Medal 1966. Entered public health service of Brazil 1934; in charge of various health services in the State of Rio de Janeiro, ultimately becoming Assistant Director of the State Dept. of Health 1934–43; participated in the eradication campaign undertaken by the Brazilian Govt. in co-operation with the Rockefeller Found against the mosquito *A. gambiae* which coming from Africa had invaded the north-east of the country 1939; successively Dir. of Div., Asst. Superintendent and Superintendent of the Serviço Especial de Saude Publica (a co-operative health service established by the Brazilian Govt. together with the Institute of Inter-American Affairs) 1943–50. Joined staff of WHO at Geneva as Director of the Division of Organisation of Health Services 1950; appointed Asst. Director-General in charge of advisory services in the same year. Moved to Washington to Asst. Dir. of the Pan American Sanitary Bureau (which is also the Regional Office of WHO for the Americas) 1952; Dir. Gen of WHO 1953–73; Dir-Gen. Emeritus since 1973. *Publications:* various scientific papers on a wide range of subjects. Hon. Mem. Internatl. Dental Federation. Hon. Fellow: American Public Health Association; American College of Dentists; Natl. Acad. of Medicine, Peru; Peruvian Public Health Assn.; Royal Acad. of Medicine, Ireland; Royal Socy. of Medicine, London; Royal Socy. for the Promotion of Health, Great Britain; and (foreign) Argentine Medical Assn., Algerian Medical Society. Fellow, Royal Coll. of Physicians. London: Foreign Member, U.S.S.R. Acad of Medical Science; Foreign Correspondent Member, Natl. Acad. of Medicine, Paris. Bronfman Prize for Public Health Achievement, American Public Health Assn.; 'Eduardo Liceaga' medal for eminent services to public health by the Government of Mexico; gold medal of Roy. Socy. for the Promotion of Health, London, 1966. Moinho Santista Prize (São Paulo, Brazil); Sesquicentennial Award Univ. Michigan (U.S.A.) both 1967; Commonwealth of Massachusetts Dept. of Health Centennial Award, 1969; Jo Baptiste Morgagni Int. Prize Scientific Achievement, Assoc. Artistic Letteraria Inc., Florence, Italy, 1970; Harben Gold Medal, Royal Inst. of Public Health and Hygiene, London 1973; Geraldo Paula Sonza Medal, Public Health Assn. of São Paulo, Brazil 1974; Léon Bernard Medal and Prize, World Health Assembly 1974. *Address:* World Health Organization, Avenue Appia, 1211 Geneva 27, Switzerland.

**CANDLER, John Slaughter, II.** Colonel, U.S.A.R. (Retd.). Attorney-at-Law. *B.* 1908. *Educ.* Univ. of Georgia (AB *magna cum laude*); J.D. Emory Univ. *M.* 1933, Dorothy Bruce Warthen. *S.* John Slaughter, Jr. *Dau.* Dorothy Warthen (Hamilton). *Career:* Engaged in general practice of law in Atlanta, Ga. 1931—. Served in U.S. Army (including duty in Asiatic-Pacific Theatre) 1941–46; Army Commendation Ribbon with Pendant. Part-Time Univ. Instructor of Mathematics 1928–29, and of Law 1931–34; occasional lecturer in Law. Partner, Candler, Cox Andrews & Hansen. Dir.: Propane Gas Service Inc., Sungas Inc., Leon Propane Inc., Equipment Sales Co., Inc., Georgia Motor Club, Inc., The D.M. Weatherly Co. and others. Member of Chapter (Vestry) of St. Phillip, Episcopal Diocese of Atlanta 1953–56; senior warden of St. Philip's 1955; Episcopal Lay-Reader since 1972; Trustee, The Lovett School 1953–59; Cathedral Board of Trustees Epis. Dioc. of Atlanta 1957–68; Georgia Student Educational Fund 1950—; Northside Atlanta Kiwanis Foundation 1959— (Chmn. 1962—), and Kappa Alpha Scholarship Fund 1955— (President, 1970–72). Fellow, American College of Probate Counsel (Regent 1968–74); International Acad. of Law and Sciences; Post-commander, American Legion 1949–50; State President, Reserve Officers Association of U.S. 1946; Deputy Asst. Attorney-General of Georgia 1950–68. President, Atlanta Estate Planning Council 1963–64. *Member:* National Tax Assn.—Tax Institute of America, (TIA Advisory Council 1969–72); USO Council of Greater Atlanta 1969—; Exec. Cttee. 1970— (Pres. 1974–75); American and Atlanta Bar Associations; Amer. Judicature Socy.; State Bar of Georgia (Chmn., Section of Fiduciary Law 1964–65);

Lawyers' Club of Atlanta; Newcomen Society; International Platform Assn.; American Socy. for Literature and the Arts; Smithsonian Inst.; English-Speaking Union; Kiwanis; U.S. Power Squadrons; Military Order of World Wars; Phi Beta Kappa; Phi Kappa Phi; Kappa Alpha Order; Phi Delta Phi; Sigma Delta Chi; Sphinx; Gridiron; Masons and others. *Clubs:* Piedmont Driving; Capital City; The Oglethorpe (Savannah); The Commerce; Army & Navy (Washington D.C.); Officers' (Fort McPherson); Peachtree Racket. *Address:* 413 Manor Ridge Drive, N.W., Atlanta, Ga. 30305; and *office* 2400 Gas Light Tower, Atlanta, Ga. 30303, U.S.A.

**CANHAM, Erwin Dain.** *B.* 1904. *Educ.* Bates Coll. (BA 1925) and Oxford Univ. (BA, MA 1929). *M.* 1930, Thelma Whitman Hart. *Dau.* Carolyn (Shale Paul) and Elizabeth (Lyle Davis). *M.* (2) 1968, Patience M. Daltry. *Career:* With the Christian Science Monitor: Reporter 1925–26; Geneva Correspondent 1930–32; Chief of the Monitor Washington Bureau 1932–39; General News Editor, Boston 1939–42; Managing Editor 1942–45. Editor. 1945–64; Editor in Chief 1964–74; Editor Emeritus since 1974; CBE 1964; Dir. Keystone Custodian Funds, Inc. Chmn., National Manpower Council 1952–65; Dir. John Hancock Mutual Life Insurance Co. 1956—; Chmn. Federal Reserve Bank of Boston 1959–68; Dir. Datran Transmission Co.) since 1971. Trustee: Twentieth Century Fund 1951—, Boston Public Library 1956–74; Bates Coll., Wellesley Coll. 1961—; Chmn. Simmons College. *Publications:* Awakening: The World at Mid-Century, (1951); New Frontiers for Freedom, (1954); Commitment to Freedom, (1954); Commitment to Freedom. The Story of The Christian Science Monitor, (1958); Man's Great Future (edited). *Address:* 242 Beacon Street, Boston, Mass. 02116, U.S.A.

**CANNON, Curtis W.** American. *B.* 1911. *Educ.* Univ. of Oklahoma (BS). *M.* 1936, Lucile Curran. *S.* Douglas W., Gary C. *Daus.* Kristin L. and Carolyn Ann. *Career:* Pres., Frontier Chemical Co. 1950–57; Dir. and Vice-Pres., Union Chemical & Materials Corp. 1954–56. President: Climax Chemical Co., and Northwestern Rock Products Inc. 1961–65. Director, Edna Gladney Children's Home. Former director, Manufacturing Chemists Assn. of U.S.A., and of Fourth National Bank, Wichita, Kansas. Member of original committee of American businessmen to visit the Soviet Union. Holder of U.S. Patents—heavy chemical manufacturing, oil refining and refrigeration publications. *Member:* Crime Commission, Wichita; Amer. Chemical Socy.; Amer. Assn. for Advancement of Science, Republican. Sigma Tau; citation, Oxford Univ.; Colonel Aide-de-Camp, New Mexico Governor's Office; Hon. Dep. Sheriff, Sedgwick County, Kansas. *Clubs:* New York Athletic; Midland Petroleum; Denver; Wichita; Dallas Petroleum; Wichita Country; Boulder Country; Metropolitan; NYC. *Address:* Silver Springs, P.O. Box 437 Cloudcroft, New Mexico 88317 and *office* Climax Chemical Company, P.O. Box 1595 Hobbs, New Mexico 88240.

**CANT, Benjamin Revett.** British. *B.* 1920. *Educ.* Ewell Castle Surrey; R.A.F. Sch. of Technical Training, Halton. *M.* (1) 1948, Joan Miller (D.). *Daus.* 3. (2) 1972, Phyllis Thane. S.1. *Dau.* 1. *Career:* Works Man. J. & H. Mclaren 1955–57; Dir. Gen. Mgr. Nat. Gas. & Oil Engine Co. 1957–59; Man. Dir. Hamworthy Engineering Ltd. 1959–63; Dir. (Planning) Ransome Hoffmann Pollard Ltd.; Rubery Owen Holdings Ltd.; Brown Bayley Steels Ltd.; Flight Refueling Ltd. Present Appointments: Chmn. R.H.P. Bearings (Aust.) Ltd.; Chmn. Rubery-Owen Holdings (Aust.) Ltd. & Rubery Owen-Kemsley Ltd.; Chmn. Courtaulds Hilton Ltd.; Dep. Chmn., Tecalemit (Australia) Pty. Ltd.; Dir., Taubmans Industries Ltd. *Member:* British Int. Management. *Clubs:* Imp. Services Sydney. *Address:* The School House, Cobbora 2854, Australia and *office* 27 Flinders Lane, Melbourne 3000, Australia.

**CANTERBURY, Archbishop of,** Most Rev. and Rt. Hon. (Frederick) Donald Coggan, PC, MA, DD. British. *B.* 1909. *Educ.* Merchant Taylors' School; St. John's Cambridge; Wycliffe Hall Oxford. *M.* 1935, Jean Braithwaite Strain. *Daus.* 2. *Career:* Asst. Lecturer in Semitic Languages and Literature, Manchester Univ. 1931–34; Ordained Deacon 1934, Priest 1935; Curate St. Mary's Islington 1934–37; Professor New Testament, Wycliffe Coll., Toronto 1937–44; Principal, London Coll. of Divinity 1944–56; Bishop of Bradford 1956–61; Archbishop of York 1961–74; Elected Archbishop of Canterbury 1974. *Awards:* Hon. DD (Cambridge, Leeds, Aberdeen, Huron, Tokyo, Saskatoon, Hull, Manchester, Liverpool, Moravian Theological Seminary); D.Hum. (Princeton); DLitt. (Lancaster); LLD (Liverpool); STD (New York); DCL (Canterbury); D.Univ.(York). *Publications:* A People's Heritage (1944); The Ministry of the Word (1945); The Glory of God (1950); Stewards of Grace (1958); Five Makers of the New Testament (1962); Christian Priorities (1963); The Prayers of the New Testament (1967); Sinews of Faith (1969); Word and World (1971); Convictions (1975). *Club:* Athenaeum (London). *Address:* Lambeth Palace, London, SE1 7JU; and The Old Palace, Canterbury, Kent.

**CAPE, Donald Paul Montagu Stewart,** CMG. British Diplomat. *B.* 1923. *Educ.* Oxford Univ., BA (Hons). *M* 1948, Cathune Johnston. *S.* 4. *Dau.* 1. *Career:* 3rd Sec., Belgrade 1946–49, H.M. Foreign Office 1949–51; 2nd Sec., Lisbon 1951–54; 1st Sec., Singapore 1955–57, Foreign Office 1957–60, Bogotá 1960–62, Holy See 1962–67; Counsellor, Foreign and Commonwealth Office 1968–70, Washington 1970–73, Brasilia 1973–75; H.M. Ambassador, Vientiane since 1976. *Decorations:* Commander of the Order of St. Michael and St. George, 1977. *Address:* Hilltop, Wonersh, Guildford, Surrey; and *office* British Embassy, Vientiane, Laos.

**CAPEL-JONES, Deryck.** American. *B.* 1914. *Educ.* Cranleigh Sch., England. *M.* 1949, Fredrica Toren. *S.* 1. *Career:* Pres. & Dir. Mitchell Cotts & Co. Inc., Vice-Pres., John Holt & Co. Inc. 1948–54; Exec. Vice-Pres. Knight, Smith & Co. Inc., 1955–56; Dir. Brit.-Am. Chamber of Commerce. Tin Assoc. of U.S.A. Metropol. Club. N.Y.C. *Address:* Redding Rd., RFDI, Weston, Conn, 06880, U.S.A.; and *office* 230 Park Avenue, New York, N.Y. 10017, U.S.A.

**CAPON, Frank Samuel.** Retired Canadian chemical industry executive. *B.* 1915. *Educ.* Royal Liberty School (Romford, Eng.); Chartered Accountant (Canada). *M.* 1940, Marjorie O'Connell. *Daus.* Gail Frances and Susan Mary. *Career:* Accountant in Training, Riddell, Stead, Graham & Hutchinson, Chartered Accountants, Montreal 1930–38; successively, Clerk 1938–44, Asst. Treasurer 1944–47, and Treasurer 1947–54, Canadian Industries Ltd.; Secretary and Treasurer 1954–57, Director and Treasurer 1957–60, and Director and Vice-President 1960–70. DuPont of Canada Ltd.; Dir., Genstar Ltd.; Dir., Dennison Manufacturing Company of Canada Ltd. (Board Chmn.); Dir. Consumers' Glass Co. Ltd.; Union Miniere Canada Ltd. (Board Chmn.) *Member:* Inst. of Chartered Accountants of Quebec; President, Canadian Institute of Chartered Accountants, 1971–72, and Financial Executives Institute (formerly Controllers Institute of America) (Pres. 1960–61; Board Chmn. 1961–62). *Clubs:* Mount Bruno Country; Ashburn Golf (Halifax). *Address:* 3033 Sherbrooke St. W. (Apt. 704), Montreal, P.Q., Canada H3Z 1A3.

**CAPRILES AYALA, Carlos.** Venezuelan. *B.* 1923. *Educ.* BSc and BHumanities. *M.* Evangelina Méndez. *S.* Axel. *Dau.* Ruth. *Publications:* regular contributions to the journals of the Capriles chain: El Mundo, and Ultimas Noticias; and the reviews Elite and Páginas. Director of the newspapers Critica (Maracaibo, Venezuela). Vice-Pres. of Publicaciones Capriles (a chain of three newspapers and three reviews). Caracas; Ambassador in Spain 1969–72; Delegate Oficina de Educacions Ibero Americano (O.E.I.). *Hon. Member:* Associations of Journalists of Colombia and Bolivia. *Awards:* Gran Cruz Orden del Libertador (Venezuela); de Ysabel La Católica (Spain); de la Hispanidad (Spain). *Address:* Altamira, Urb. Country Club, Quinta Puerto de Hierro, Caracas, Venezuela; and *office* Torre de la Prensa, Plaza del Pantcón, Caracas, Venezuela.

**CARADON, Lord** (Hugh Mackintosh Foot), GCMG, KCVO, OBE, PC. *B.* 1907. *Educ.* Leighton Park School; St. John's College, Cambridge (BA). *M.* 1935, Sylvia Tod. *S.* Paul Mackintosh, Oliver Isaac, Benjamin Arthur. *Dau.* Sarah Dingle. *Career:* Administrative Officer, Palestine Government 1929–37; attached to the Colonial Office 1938–39; Assistant British Resident, Trans-Jordan 1939–42; British Military Administration, Cyrenaica 1943; Colonial Secretary, Cyprus 1943–45; Acting Governor, Cyprus 1944; Colonial Secretary, Jamaica 1945–47; Acting Governor, Jamaica Aug. 1945–Jan. 1946; Chief Secretary to the Government of Nigeria 1947–50; Acting Governor, Nigeria 1949 and 1950; Captain-General and Governor-in-Chief, Jamaica 1951–57; Governor of Cyprus 1957–60; Ambassador and Adviser in the U.K. Mission to the U.N. 1961–62, and U.K. Consultant to U.N. Special Fund 1963–64; Min. of State & U.K. Representative at the U.N. 1964–70. *Address:* Trematon Castle, Saltash, Cornwall.

**CARDEN, Derrick Charles,** CMG. British Diplomat. *B.* 1921. *Educ.* Marlborough Coll.; Christ Church, Oxford, MA. *M.*

1952, Elizabeth Anne Russell. *S.* 2. *Daus.* 2. *Career:* Military Service 1941–43; Sudan Political Service 1943–54; entered British Diplomatic Service 1954; Political Agent, Qatar 1955–58; 1st Secretary, Tripoli 1958–62; 1st Sec., Foreign and Commonwealth Office 1962–64; 1st Sec. and Head of Chancery, Cairo 1965; Consul-General, Muscat 1965–69; Dir., Middle East Centre for Arab Studies 1969–73; Ambassador, Sana'a 1973–76; Visiting Fellow, Inst. of Development Studies, Sussex Univ. 1977; Ambassador, Khartoum since 1977. *Decorations:* Companion of St. Michael and St. George. *Clubs:* Vincents; Royal Commonwealth Soc. *Address:* Wistaria Cottage, Castle Street, Portchester, Hants.; and *office* Foreign and Commonwealth Office, London SW1.

**CARDIN, Hon. Lucien,** PC. Canadian. *B.* 1919. *Educ.* Loyola College (BA) and Univ. of Montreal (LLB). *M.* 1950, Marcelle Petitclere. *S.* 3. *Dau.* 1. *Career:* Minister of Public Works Feb. 1965; Assoc. Minister of National Defence Apr. 1963; Parliamentary Asst. to Hon. Lester B. Pearson, then Secy. of State for External Affairs 1956. Served with Royal Canadian Navy 1942–45 (commissioned early in 1942, placed on Retired List Oct. 1945; promoted to rank of Lt.-Comdr., Aug. 1951). Member of Bar of Province of Quebec; M.P. for Richelieu-Vercheres 1952— (re-elected 1953–57–58–62–63); Minister of Public Works 1965, of Justice 1965–67; Mem., Immigration Appeal Bd. 1970–72; Asst. Chmn., Income Tax Revision Bd. since 1972. Liberal. *Clubs:* Richelieu; Reform; Sorel Golf. *Address; office* Parliament Buildings, Ottawa, Ont., Canada.

**CARDINALI, Gino,** Prof. Dott., Gr. Uff. Italian. *B.* 1913. *Educ.* L. Bocconi Univ. of Commerce, Milan (Degree) and Ca Foscari Venezia (MA Econ), Libera Docenza. *M.* 1959 Enrica Ranco. *S.* Andrea. *Dau.* Daniela-Nadina. *Career:* Secy. Jesi Savings Bank 1937; Asst. Dir. Vercelli Savings Bank 1951, Director-General 1955; on staff of L. Bocconi Univ. of Technical Banking, 1957; Co-Director, Trieste Savings Bank 1959, Director-General 1961; occupied Chair of Technical and Professional Banking, Univ. of Trieste 1960. Dir. General Banca Popolare di Novara 1964; Professor University di Tecnica Bancaria e Professionale, Libero Professionistra. *Member* Order of Doctors of Commerce (Trieste); Regional Inst. of Science, Letters and Arts (Ancona); A.C.I.E. (Belo Horizonte); Acad. Nationale Ragioneria (Bologna); Acad. of Cenacolo Triestino; Pres. A.L.U.T. (Trieste). *Publications:* The Overseas Banks; The Growth of Banking Adminisrattion in Connection with Investment Pools; The Fundamental Characteristics of the English Banking System; Problems and Aspects of the Credit Market in the last quarter of a century (4 vols.); Fundamental Characteristics of the English Stock Market; Life Insurance in the English Market; a further 50 studies on minor subjects. Awarded several honorary degrees; recipient Order of Merit of the Republic; Major of Artillery (three times awarded Croce di Guerra). *Clubs:* Rotary, Panathlon. *Address:* Salita Contovello 3, Trieste; and *office* Via Crispi 3, Trieste, Italy.

**CARDON de LICHTBUER, Pierre.** Belgian technical engineer. Directeur gérant, E.R.E.A., (transformer and rectifier manufacturers), Wynegem, Antwerp 1933—. *B.* 1904. *Educ.* High Technical School. *M.* (1) 1934, n. de Vos (*D.* 1953), and (2) 1956, n. Salles. *S.* Roger. *Member:* F.I.B. (Brussels). *Clubs:* Automobile (Antwerp). *Address:* 15a, Dennenlaan, Antwerp, Belgium.

**CARDOSO, Mario.** Congolese. *B.* 1933. *Educ.* Univ. of Louvain (Degree in Psychology). *M.* 1959, Charlotte Mujinga. *S.* 2. *Daus.* 3. *Career:* Permanent Representative to U.N., New York 1960–62; Chargé d'Affaires, Embassy, Washington 1962–65, Ambassador of the Democratic Republic of the Congo to the Court of St. James, London 1966–68 and to Morocco 1968–69; Minister for Education 1969–70. Director, Co-operation Internationale, Ministry for Foreign Affairs, Kinshasa 1970. Commander, Order of Leopard. *Club:* Anglo-Belgian. *Address:* Ministere des Affaires Etrangères, Kinshasa, Zaire.

**CARGILL, James Nelson.** American advertising executive. *B.* 1914. *Educ.* Virginia Polytechnic Inst. (BS, Architecture). *M.* 1939, Frances Virginia McDaniel. *S.* James Nelson, Jr. *Daus.* Nancy Virginia, Sally Page, Anne Barksdale. *Career:* Served in World War II (Lt.-Col., U.S. Army; with Commercial Credit Corp. 1937–40, and Richmond Oil Equipment 1946–49; Chairman, Cargill, Wilson & Acree Inc., Richmond, Va. 1950—; Past Member of Board: Richmond Chamber of Commerce; American Red Cross; Board of Governors, United Givers Fund. National Director, American Association of Advertising Agencies; Vice Pres., V.P.I. Alumni Assn. *Awards:* Legion of Merit; Bronze Star; 5 Battle Stars; Croix de Guerre (France); Croix de Guerre (Belgium)) 1940–46. *Clubs:* Rotunda (Board Member); Sales Executives; Kiwanis. *Address:* Box 236F., Deltaville, Va., U.S.A.

**CARLEN, Raymond N.** American. *B.* 1919. *Educ.* University of Illinois (BS in Metallurgical Engineering) and Univ. of Chicago Exec. Program (MS in Business Admin.). *M.* 1946, Jean Lovejoy. *Daus.* Cynthia Jean and Susan Joy. *Career:* Chmn., J. T. Ryerson & Son Inc. (Executive Vice-President 1964–68, Pres. 1968–76). Dir.: Pecker Plada Ltd., Tel Aviv 1964—, Ryerson (Holland) N.V., Amsterdam 1962—, Inland Steel Co., 1969–76, and Snr. Vice-Pres. since 1976, Joseph T. Ryerson & Son Inc., 1955, American National Bank & Trust Co. of Chicago 1969—, Hinsdale Federal Savings and Loan 1962—. Recipient Leadership Award (National Management Assn.). *Member:* Newcomen Socy. in N. America; Steel Division, National Assn. of Aluminium Distributors; Chicago Assn. of Commerce & Industry; Steel Service Center Inst.; Illinois State Chamber of Commerce. *Clubs:* Chicago Golf; Chicago; Economic (Chicago); Executive Program Hinsdale Golf; Commercial Club of Chicago. *Address:* 6 Oak Brook Club Drive, S305, Oak Brook, Illinois 60521, U.S.A.; and *office* P.O. Box 8000-A, Chicago, Ill. 60603, U.S.A.

**CARLISLE, Mark,** QC, MP. *B.* 1929 *Educ.* Radley Coll.; Manchester Univ., LLB (Hons.) Manchester. *M.* 1959, Sandra Joyce Des Voeux. *Dau.* 1. *Career:* called to the Bar, Gray's Inn 1953; Member, Parliament (Con.) Runcorn since 1964; Joint Hon. Secy. Cons. Home Affairs Cttee. 1965–69; Member, Home Office Adv. Council on the Penal System 1966–70: Cons. Front Bench Spokesman on Home Affairs 1969–70; QC 1971; Parly. Under-Secy. of State Home Office 1970–72; Minister of State Home Office 1972–74. *Address:* House of Commons, London SW1A 0AA.

**CARLSEN, Reidar.** Norwegian politician. *B.* 1908. *M.* 1932, Erna Carlsen. *S.* 3. *Dau.* 1. *Career:* Under-Secretary of State for Fisheries 1945–46, Minister 1946–51; Dir., Utbyggingsfondet for Nord-Norge 1952–61; Dir., Distriktenes Utbyggingsfond 1961—. MP (Lab.) Nordland 1945–61. *Address:* Sofienberggt 61, Oslo, Norway.

**CARLSON, John Swink.** Attorney-at-law and executive. *B.* 1911. *Educ.* Univ. of Colorado (AB 1932) and Harvard (LLB 1936); admitted to Bar of State of Oklahoma 1937, and to the Bar of the Supreme Court of the U.S. 1958. *M.* Barbara C. Spencer. *S.* John Swink, Jr. and Thomas George (*Dec.*). *Daus.* Lucie Pamela, Ann Brockenbrough and Virginia Charles. *Career:* On Legal Staff, Shell Oil Co. 1936–37; Legal Associate, law firm of Yancey & Spillers 1937–39; Legal Counsellor, Chapman, Barnard & McFarlin (oil, cattle and investment interests) 1939–42; Gen. Counsel, Seismograph Service Corp., Tulsa 1942–49; private law practice 1949–51; Gen. Counsel, Oklahoma Natural Gas Co. 1951–61; Snr. Partner, Carlson, Lupardus, Matthews, Holliman & Huffman 1951–61; Secy., Dir., Gen. Counsel, Exploration Consultants Inc. 1951–65; and Hayward-Wolff Research Corp. 1951; Dir., Secy. and Gen. Counsel Canadian Geophysical Measurements Corp. and Venezuelan Geophysical Measurements Corp. 1954–65; Sen. Vice-Pres. Gen., Counsel & Dir. Century Geophysical Corp. 1957–70; Pres. & Dir. Petroleum Research Corp. 1957–66; Vice-Pres., Secy., Dir., Gen. Counsel Enterprises & Businesses Inc. 1959–65; Chmn. Bd., Gen. Counsel Community Merchandisers Inc. 1959–65; Secy., Dir., Hemisphere Construction Co. 1960–65; Secy., Dir., Western Hemisphere Trade & Credit Corp. 1960–65; Pres.' Gen. Counsel & Dir. Western Petroleum Co. Inc. 1960–65; Vice-Pres., Secy., Dir. Gen., Counsel Jameson Corp. 1961–64; Head of the Legal firm of John S. Carlson 1961—; Chmn. Bd. and Pres., T'Oil Inc. 1962; Pres. Dir. and General Counsel, Oil Enterprises Inc. 1965—; Vice-Pres., General Counsel Digital Resources Corp. since 1972; Counsel to App. Devices Corp. since 1973; Editor, Compendium of Laws Relating to Problems of Men in the Armed Forces 1943. Republican. *Clubs:* The Tulsa, Harvard (Pres. 1949–50 and 1950–51)—all of Tusla. *Address:* 60 Plant Avenue, Hauppauge, New York, 11787, U.S.A.; and 1706 Devonshire Road, Windsor Village, Hauppauge, N.Y. 11787, U.S.A.

**CARLSON, Le Roy Theodore Sheridan.** American business executive. *B.* 1916. *Educ.* Tilden Technical High School; University of Chicago (BBA 1938); Harvard Graduate School of Business Administration (MBA 1941). *M.* 1945, Margaret Elizabeth Deffenbaugh. *S.* Le Roy Theodore, Jr. and Walter Carl Deffenbaugh. *Daus.* Prudence Elizabeth, Letitia Greta. *Career:* Sales Manager, Mid-west, McCall Corp., News Week

Inc. 1933–40; Accountant, U.S. Army Ordnance 1941–42; Asst. Treasurer, General Motors Overseas Corp. (in Persia and India) 1942–45; Administrative Asst. to Gen. Mgr. Merchandise Mart., Chicago 1946–49; with new products development division, Acme Steel Co. 1949–51; Ensign, U.S.N.R. 1945–46. President: Suttle Co. (since 1949); Co-Chmn. Telephones Inc. 1955–66, Merged with Continental Tel. Corp. 1966; Pres. Chmn. Bd. of Telephone & Data Systems, Inc. since 1968. *Publications:* various papers on business subjects. Republican. *Address:* 2 Milburn Park, Evanston, Ill.; and *office* 79 W. Monroe Street, Chicago 3, U.S.A.

**CARLSSON, Per (Gunnar).** Swedish shipowner. *B.* 1912. *Educ.* Bachelor of Laws. *M.* 1936, Anna Lisa Frick. *S.* Peter and Fabian. *Dau.* Elisabeth. *Career:* Chmn., Transatlantic, Transpacific S.S. Co; Secretary, Swedish Maritime Committee 1939; Director, A.B. Volvo, Skandinaviska Enskilda Banken A.B.; Chmn. Investment A.B. Asken; Trans.-Ex S.S. Co. Transmark S.S. Co., *Awards:* Comdr. Order of Vasa (Sweden), and Order of St. Olav (Norway); Knight-Cmdr., Dannebrog Order (Denmark). *Address:* Translantic S.S. Co., Gothenburg, Sweden.

**CARLYON, Norman Dean,** CBE, OBE. Australian. *B.* 1903. *Educ.* Geelong Grammar School, Victoria. *M.* 1935, Enid Murdoch. *S.* Norman Murdoch. *Dau.* Barbara Caroline Murdoch. Retired. Military Assistant to C in C Australian Military Forces, Field Marshal Sir Thomas Blamey 1940–44; Chairman, Housing Cttee., Olympic Games Melbourne, 1956; Chairman, Corps. of Commissionaries (Victoria) Ltd. 1949–73. *Clubs:* Melbourne Rotary; Victoria Racing; Victoria Amateur Turf; Moonee Valley Racing; Metropolitan Golf. *Address:* Unit 11, Clarendon, 58 Clarendon Street, East Melbourne, Australia.

**CARLYON, Thomas Symington,** CMG, OBE (Mil). Australian. *B.* 1902. *Educ.* Geelong Grammar School, Corio, Vic. *M.* 1950, Marie Pichoir de Launay. *S.* Thomas Scott. *Dau.* Margaret Scott (Low)—both by previous marriage. *Career:* Hotel training, Bellevue Stratford, Philadelphia, U.S.A. 1923–25. General Manager: Ushers Hotel, Sydney 1930–37; Menzies Hotel, Melbourne 1937–38; Australia Hotel, Sydney 1938–46. Served in R.A.A.F. (Squadron Leader), Pacific Area 1940–45; Man. Dir., T. S. Carlyon & Co. Pty. Ltd., Melbourne; operating hotel and catering organizations in Victoria, Australia. *Member:* Housing and Catering Committee, Olympic Games 1956; co-opted by Immigration Department for World Tour to secure personnel for Olympic Village, Heidelberg. Member Liberal Country Party. *Clubs:* Victoria Racing, Moonee Valley Racing, Metropolitan Golf, Melbourne Cricket. *Address:* Shipley, 77 Caroline Street, South Yarra, Vic., Australia.

**CARMICHAEL, Donald Scott.** *B.* 1912. *Educ.* Lakewood (Ohio) Elementary and High Schools; Harvard College (AB 1935); Harvard Law School; University of Michigan Law School (LLB 1942). *M.* 1940, Mary Glenn Dickinson. *Daus.* Mary Brooke and Pamela Hastings. *Career:* With City Law Dept., Cleveland 1938–40 (also Instructor in Constitutional Law, John Marshall Law School, Cleveland, in the same period); Admitted to Ohio Bar 1942; Chief, Re-negotiation Branch, Cleveland Ordnance District, War Dept. 1942–46; private practice of law, Cleveland Jan.–Nov. 1946; Assistant Secretary and Company Counsel, Diamond Alkali Co. (manufacturers of basic chemicals) 1946–48 (Secretary 1948–57; Secretary and General Counsel 1957–58); Vice-Pres.-Gen. Counsel, The Stouffer Corp. 1959–60; Exec. Vice Pres. and Chief Admin. Officer Stouffer Foods Corp. (food industry) 1960–64; Counsellor at Law 1964–71; Pres. Schrafft's Div. Pet Inc. 1971–75; Pres. Sportservice Corp. since 1975; Founder and Officer, Cleveland Metropolitan Services Commission (to study and recommend an approach to the problems of metropolitan government in the Greater Cleveland area); First Vice-Chairman, Cuyahoga County Chartered Commission (an elected commission to draw a Home Rule Charter for Cuyahoga County, Greater Cleveland) Nov. 1958–July 1959; Chairman, Governor's Advisory Committee on Industrial and Economic Development, Nov. 1959—; Chairman, Metropolitan Transit Co-ordinating Committee, Jan. 1960; member Cuyahoga County Democratic Executive Committee, 1958— (Delegate to Natl. Convention, Los Angeles 1960 and Atlantic City 1964). *Clubs:* Buffalo, Country Club, of Buffalo; Crag Burn, East Aurora, N.Y.; Union, Harvard (past Pres.), City, Fifty (all of Cleveland); Harvard (N.Y.C.); Chagrin Valley, Hunt Gates Mills, Ohio. *Address:* 38 Muirfield Road, Crag Burn, East Aurora, N.Y. 14052; and *office* 700 Delaware Avenue, Buffalo, N.Y. 14209, U.S.A.

**CARNE, Ian Hamilton.** Australian. *B.* 1915. *Educ.* Adelaide. University (S. Australia); BachEng; Diploma of Applied Science; Fellow, S. Australian School of Mines. *M.* 1943, Mary Steel Scott. *S.* David and Brian. *Dau.* Frances. *Career:* Successively Technical Officer 1939–51, American Representative 1951–55; Executive Assistant to Chief General Manager 1955–59, Manager, Overseas Division 1959–61; Executive Officer, Operations and Distribution 1961–64; Gen. Mgr. Western Australian Operations 1964–72; Gen. Mgr. Minerals Western Aust. 1972—; The Broken Hill Proprietary Co. Ltd.; General Manager, Dampier Mining Co. Ltd., 1965—; Chmn., The Structural Engineering Co. (W.A.) Pty. Ltd. 1965; Dir., Orbital Engine Co. Pty. Ltd. since 1972.; Dir. Western Australian Mining Engineering Services Pty Ltd. since 1973; Dir., Texada Mines Pty. Ltd. 1976. *Member:* Advisory Board in Engineering Univ. Western Aust. 1972; Member Graylands Teacher-Coll. Board. Deputy member, environmental Protection Council 1972; Energy Advisory Council 1976. Amer. Int. of Mining, Metallurgical & Petroleum Engineers. Council of The Australasian Inst. of Mining & Metallurgy, Melbourne. *Publications:* The Manufacture of Tungsten Powder and Ferro Silicon at the Works of The Broken Hill Proprietary Co. Ltd., Newcastle (published by the Australasian Inst. of Mining & Metallurgy). *Clubs:* Weld Koolyanobbing; Melville Bowling. *Address:* 108 Burke Drive, Attadale, W. Australia 6156; and *office* Leath Road, Kwinana, Western Australia (P.O. Box 160 Kwinana, WA 6167) Australia.

**CARNEY, Robert Forrest.** Chevalier, Legion of Honour (France). American lawyer and business executive. *B.* 1905. *Educ.* Univ. of Wisconsin (PhB 1927) and Harvard (LLD 1930). *M.* 1946, Lucille Kelly. *S.* (by former marriage) Michael Kerwin and Robert McShane. *Career:* Senior Partner, Carney, Crowell & Liebman, Chicago 1945–51 (now Sidley & Austin); Dir., Foote, Cone & Belding Communications Inc. 1951–74; Chairman of Finance Committee, Foote, Cone & Belding 1967–70; Chairman of Board 1951–67. *Member:* Wisconsin and Illinois Bars, and Chicago Bar Association. *Clubs:* Brook, Racquet & Tennis (N.Y.C.); National Golf Links of America; Shinnecock Hills Golf, Southampton (Long Island); Bath & Tennis; Everglades, Seminole. *Address:* Captain's Neck Lane, Southampton, L.I. 11968, U.S.A and 161 Woodbridge Rd., Palm Beach, Fla 33480, U.S.A.

**CARNEY, W. R.** Trade Commissioner, *Address:* Australian Govt. Trade Commission, Guiness Towers (Suite 500) 1055 West Hastings St. Vancouver 1BC, Canada.

**CARNICERO, Jorge.** American aeronautical engineer. *B.* 1921. *Educ.* Univ. of Buenos Aires; Rensselaer Polytechnic Institute; Pan American Airways (complete airline training course); Fellow, Institute of Interntl. Educ. Rensselaer Polytech. Inst.; Tech. *Member:* IAS; Assoc. Fellow Royal Aeronautical Society. *M.* 1946, Jacqueline Joanne Damman. *S.* Jorge Jay. *Dau.* 1. *Career:* Chief Engineer, Dodero Airlines, Argentine 1945; in charge of conversion of Sunderland Flying Boats on behalf of Dodero Airlines at Short & Harland, England 1945–46; Chief Engineer, Flota Aérea Mercante Argentina 1946; Vice Pres., Air Carrier Service Corp., Washington 1947–55; Chmn. Bd. Dir., Air Carrier Service Corp., Washington 1955—; Chmn. Bd. and Dir., Dynalectron Corp. (formerly California Eastern Aviation) Washington, D.C. since 1955. *Director:* Huyck Corp., Connecticut; Hydrocarbon Research Inc., New York; Airtech Service Inc., Florida; Hart Electric Inc., Florida; PAC ORD, California; Round Hill Development Ltd., Jamaica; Continental Honduras Inc., Honduras; Dir. Pres., Trans-American Aeronautical Corp., Delaware; ANECO Co., Georgia; Dir. Chmn. Bd., Servair Inc., Mass.; Dynalectron International Inc., Delaware; Fleetwood Insurance Co., Bermuda; AFB Contractors Inc., California; Solar Insulators Inc., Texas; Gulf Telephone & Electronics Inc., Texas. *Address:* 1313 Dolley Madison Blvd., McLean, Virginia 22101, U.S.A.

**CARNWATH, Sir Andrew Hunter,** KCVO (1975) DL. British Co. Dir. *B.* 1909. *Educ.* Eton (King's Scholar). *M.* (1) 1939, Kathleen Marianne Armstrong (*Dec.* 1968). *S.* 5. *Dau.* 1. (2) 1973, Joan Gertrude Wetherell-Pepper. *Career:* Joined Baring Bros. & Co. 1928 (uninterrupted service with them until 1974, except for service with the R.A.F. (Coastal Cmd. Intelligence 1939–45)). A Managing Director of Baring Brothers & Co. Ltd., Jan. 1955–74; Chmn. 1961—, and Dir. 1960—, Save & Prosper Group Ltd.; Director: Equity & Law Life Assurance Society Ltd. 1955—, Scottish Agricultural Industries Ltd., 1969–75, Great Portland Estates

Ltd., 1977—; Chmn., London Multinational Bank Ltd. 1971–74; Member, Central Bd. of Finance of the Church of Eng. and Chmn. of its investment Man. Cttee. 1960–74; Chairman, Chelmsford Diocesan Bd. of Finance 1966–75. Governor, King Edward's Hospital Fund for London since 1976 (Mem. of Council 1962–74; Treas. 1965–74). Trustee, Imperial War Graves Endowment Fund 1963–74 (Chmn. 1964–74). Joined Royal Commission for the Exhibition of 1851 in 1964. Member, Council of The Friends of the Tate Gallery 1962—. (Treas. 1965—). High Sheriff of Essex 1965–66. Governor of Felsted School; Pres. Saffron Walden Constituency Conservative Assn. (resigned 1977); President of the Inst. of Bankers (1970–72); Essex County Councillor 1973–77; Treasurer, Essex Univ.; Victoria League; British and Foreign Schools Soc.; Assistant Musicians Company since 1973. *Clubs:* Athenaeum; Essex. *Address:* Coachmans Cottage, Barnes, London SW13; and *office* 88 Leadenhall St., London, EC3A 3DT.

**CAROLIN, Charles A.** American (Irish ancestry). *B.* 1915. *Educ.* Catholic Central High School, Detroit; Assumption Coll., Windsor, Ont.; Detroit Business Inst. *M.* 1938, Helen E. Zawada. *S.* Charles R. *Dau.* Linda Lee Anne. *Career:* Pres.: Nat. Foundry Assn. 1961–62, and Nat. Castings Cncl. 1963; Dir.: Non-Ferrous Founders' Socy. (Past), Amer. Foundrymen's Socy (Past—1958–61), Boys' Cttee. of Detroit; Chmn., Amer. Red Cross, Berkley, Mich. Chapter (Past); Trustee, Foundary Educational Foundation. Appreciation Award (Amer. Foundrymen's Socy. 1967), Cert. of Co-operation (U.S. Dept. of State 1962), Herman Award (Nat. Foundry Assn., 2 years). *Member:* Engineering Socy. of Detroit, etc. *Clubs:* Oakland Hills Country; Lost Lake Woods Assn. *Address:* 4013 Fairline Drive, Birmingham, Mich.; and *office* 3633 Military Avenue, Detroit, Mich., U.S.A.

**CAROUR, Roger.** French Co. Dir. *Career:* former Assistant Director, Ministry of Finances; Director, Mercantile Marine Section, Ministère des Travaux Publics et des Transports 1945–47; Préfet 1948; Vice-Pres. de la Comp. General-Maritime; Vice-Pres. de la comp. General Transatlantique; former President Compagnie des Messageries Maritimes; Dir.-gen. Soc. Fonciére et Financiére Agache-Willot. *Awards:* Commander, Legion of Honour; Comdr. Mérite Maritime; Royal Order of Greece. *Address:* S.F.A.W., 5 Rue de Babylone, 75007 Paris; and 9 bis Route de la Croix, Le Vesinet (Les Yvelines), France.

**CARPENTIER, Michel André Georges.** Director-General Environment and Consumer Protection—Dept. EEC. *B.* 1930. *Educ.* Graduate of the Ecole des Hautes Etudes Commerciales, Paris; Graduate of the Inst. of Polit. Science, Paris; Faculty of Law, Paris; Graduate in law and economic sciences. *M.* 1956, Annick Puget. *S.* 4. *Career:* Assist. to Directorate-Gen. of Admin. and Finance, French Commissariat for Atomic Energy 1957–59; Administrator and later Div. Chief EURATOM 1959–67; Chief of Industrial Policy Div., with Directorate General for Indust. Tech. and Scient. Affairs 1968–71; and head of Envir. Questions Divs. 1971–72; Dir. of Environment and Consumer Protection Dept. since 1973; Director-General of Environment and Consumer Protection Dept. since 1977; President Board of Adm. Europ. Foundat. for the Improvement of Living and Working Conditions, 1975–77. *Award:* Elizabeth Haub Prize, Univ. Brussels (outstanding achievements environmental law). *Publications:* Une Politique de l'Environnement en Europe (Speech at IBC Ltd. London, 1972); Communauté et Qualité de la Vie; Les Communautés Européennes et l'Environnement (1974); L'Action des Communautés Européennes en Matière d'Environnement (Report of Bruges Speech, 1974); La Problématique de l'Environnement (Report of Speech at Namur, 1974); Implications internationales des politiques d'environnement (Speech at Paris, 1976). *Address:* 254 Drève Richelle, Waterloo, Belgium; and *office:* 200 Rue de la Loi, 1040 Brussels, Belgium.

**CARR, Clive Emsley Bracewell Lascelles.** British newspaper director. *B.* 1934. *Educ.* Radley College; Trinity College, Cambridge (BA). *M.* 1970, Isabel Pearce. *Career:* Director: News International Limited, Park Lane Hotel Ltd. (Chmn. and Man. Dir.), David & Charles (Holdings) Ltd. (Dep. Chmn.), Business and Finance Publishers (Scotland) Ltd. (Chmn.). *Address:* 3 Smith Terrace, London, S.W.3.

**CARR, James Henry Brownlow.** British. *B.* 1913. *Educ.* Beecroft (N.S.W.) Grammar School. *M.* 1943, Audrey R. B. Matthews. *S.* 1. *Daus.* 3. *Career:* Served in World War II (1 Australian Armoured Division, A.I.F.) 1941–43. Chairman of Directors: J. H. B. Carr Pty. Ltd., Mulgowrie Pty. Ltd., and General Manager, Funny Hill Pastoral Co. Director, Bideford, Lynmouth, Barnstaple Martinhoe, Torrington, all Pty. Ltd., Brownlow Investments Pty. Ltd.; N.S. Wales Bd. Colonial Mutual Life Assn. Socy. Ltd. since 1972. *Member:* Agricultural Socy. of N.S.W.; Cttee. Aust. Jockey Club 1955—; Vice-Chmn. 1969–74, Chmn. since 1974. *Clubs:* Union (Sydney); Royal Sydney Yacht Squadron; Royal Sydney Golf. *Address:* Funny Hill, Binda, N.S.W., Australia.

**CARR, Lord,** cr. 1975 (Life Peer), of Hadley; **The Rt. Hon. (Leonard) Robert,** PC, MP. *B.* 1916. *Educ.* Westminster School and Gonville and Caius College, Cambridge (BA Nat. Science Honours 1938; MA 1942). *M.* 1943, Joan Kathleen Twining. *S.* 1 (*Dec.* 1965). *Daus.*, 2. *Career:* Joined John Dale 1938 (Dir. 1948–55, Chmn. 1958–63, and 1965–74. Deputy Chmn. and Joint Managing Director, Metal Closures Group Ltd. 1960–63, and 1965–70; London Advisory Bd., Norwich Union Insurance Group 1965–70, and 1974–76. Dir., S. Hoffnung & Co.; Securicor Ltd.; S.G.B. Group Ltd.; Prudential Assurance Co. Ltd.; Member of Parliament for Mitcham 1950–74, and for Sutton, Carshalton 1974–75, Parly. Private Secy. to Foreign Secy. 1951–55, to Prime Minister 1955; Parly. Secy. Ministry of Labour 1955–58; Secy. for Technical Cooperation 1963–64; Secy. of State for Employment 1970–72; Lord Pres. of the Council; Leader House of Commons 1972; Home Secretary 1972–74; Opposition Spokesman on Economic & Treasury Affairs 1974–75; created Life Peer, Dec. 1975. *Publications:* One Nation (1950); Change is our Ally (1954); The Responsible Society (1958); One Europe (1965). Fellow, Inst. of Metallurgists. *Club:* Brooks's. *Address:* Monkenholt, Hadley Green, Barnet, Herts.

**CARR, Sir William Emsley.** British. President, News International Ltd. *B.* 1912. *Educ.* Clifton College and Trinity College, Cambridge (BA). *M.* 1938, Jean Mary Forsyth. *S.* William Forsyth Emsley. *Dau.* Sarah. *Career:* Served in World War II (Major, Royal Artillery) 1939–45. *Clubs:* Bucks, Hamilton; Royal & Ancient Golf (St. Andrews). *Deceased 14th November 1977.*

**CARRICK, John Leslie.** Australian. *B.* 1918. *Educ.* Univ. of Sydney (BEcon). *M.* 1951, Diana Margaret Hunter. *Daus.* 3. *Career:* At University 1936–39, War Service 1940–45. Reserve Officer 1946–47. General Secretary, N.S.W. Div. of Liberal Party of Australia 1948–71; Senator for New South Wales, Australian Senate since 1971; Federal Minister for Urban & Regional Development and Federal Min. for Housing & Construction, Nov.–Dec. 1975; Federal Min. for Education and Min. assisting the Prime Minister in Federal Affairs since Dec. 1975. *Clubs:* Australian; Tattersalls (Sydney). *Address:* 8 Montah Avenue, Killara, N.S.W.; and *office* Parliament House, Canberra A.C.T., Australia.

**CARRINGTON, Lord, 6th Baron** (Peter Alexander Rupert Carrington), PC, KCMG, MC. *B.* 1919. *Educ.* Eton; Royal Military College, Sandhurst. *M.* 1942, Iona, *Dau.* of Sir Francis McClean. *S.* Rupert Francis John. *Daus.* Alexandra and Virginia. *Career:* Served in World War II (N.W. Europe; Grenadier Guards; MC); Conservative Whip in House of Lords 1947–51; Parliamentary Secy.: Min. of Agric. (1951–54) and Min. of Defence (1954–56); High Comm. for the U.K. in Australia 1956–59; First Lord of the Admiralty, Oct. 1959–63. Minister Without Portfolio, The Foreign Office, and Leader of the House of Lords 1963–64. Leader of the Opposition in the House of Lords, Oct. 1964–70; Deputy Chmn., ANZ Bank 1965–67. Chairman, Australia and New Zealand Bank Ltd. 1967–70; Director, British Metal Corp. 1965–68; Barclays Bank Ltd. 1967–70; Hambros Bank Ltd. 1967–70; Schweppes Ltd., 1968–69; Cadbury-Schweppes Ltd. 1969–70; Amalgamated Metal Corporation, 1969–70. Secretary of State for Defence 1970–74: Minister for Aviation Supply 1971–74; Sec. of State for Energy, Jan.–Feb. 1974; Chmn., Conservative Party 1972–74; Dir., Cadbury-Schweppes Ltd. since 1974; Leader of the Opposition in the House of Lords since 1974; Dir., Rio Tinto-Zinc Corp. Ltd. since 1974; Dir., Barclays Bank Ltd. since 1974 and Barclays Bank International since 1975. Fellow of Eton 1966. *Clubs:* Turf; Beefsteak; Pratt's; White's; Carlton. *Address:* The Manor House, Bledlow, nr. Aylesbury, Bucks.

**CARROLL, Albert.** American financial company executive, *B.* 1914. *Educ.* University of Pennsylvania (BSEcon 1936). *M.* 1942. Rhoda Freudenthal. *S.* David William. *Dau.* Barbara Jean. *Career:* Served as 1st Lieut., U.S.A.A.F. 1943–45; Advertising Copywriter, N. W. Ayer & Son 1936–40;

Advertising Dir., Merck & Co. Inc., Rahway, N.J. 1940–55; Vice-Pres.; professional marketing div., Benton & Bowles Inc., New York City 1955–57; Vick Interntl. 1957–60; Lever Brothers Co., New York City 1960–68; Pres. Schmid Laboratories Inc. 1968–75; Pres. Med. Funding Corp. Trustee, Hartsdale Board of Education; Volunteer Co-ordinator, Advertising Council, National Blood Program 1952; Beta Gamma Sigma, Pi Gamma Mu. *Member:* Association of National Advertisers (Chairman Chemical group 1953); Business Publications Audit (Dir. 1952–55); Pharmaceutical Advertising Club (Dir. 1953–55). *Clubs:* American Marketing Association; Marketing Executive. *Address:* 7 Maplewood Road, Hartsdale, N.Y., 10530; and *office* 400 Old Hook Rd., Westwood, N.J. U.S.A.

**CARROLL, Donal Shemus Allingham.** Irish. *B.* 1927. *Educ.* Glenstal Priory School, and Trinity College, Dublin. *M.* 1951, Monica Moran. *S.* Jonathan. *Dau.* Jane. *Career:* Articled to Stokes Bros. & Pim (Chartered Accountants), Dublin 1947–52; Joined P. J. Carroll & Co. (cigarette and tobacco manufacturers) 1952, Director 1955. Elected Director, Bank of Ireland 1956, Deputy Governor 1962; Chairman & Managing Director, P. J. Carroll & Co. Ltd. 1960–70. Governor, Bank of Ireland 1964–70; Chairman, Irish Banks Standing Committee 1964–70; Chmn. Lloyds & Bolsa International Bank Ltd. (London 1971–73); Carreras Rothmans, Ltd., London; Dir., Rothmans International (London); Dunlop (Holdings) Ltd.; Bank of Ireland, Central Bank of Ireland; Chmn., P. J. Carroll & Co. Ltd., Iceland. *Member:* Inst. of Chartered Accountants in Ireland (FCA); Irish Management Inst. Hon. LLD, University of Dublin 1969. *Clubs:* Kildare Street (Dublin); Royal Irish Yacht (Dunlaoghaire, Co. Dublin); Brooks's, London. *Address:* P. J. Carroll & Co. Ltd., Grand Parade, Dublin 6, Eire.

**CARROLL, Hon. John Benson.** Canadian. *B.* 1921. *Educ.* Univ. of Manitoba (BCom). *M.* 1949, Hope Christianson. *S.* Peter and John. *Daus.* Sally and Catherine. *Career:* Minister of Public Utilities 1958–61; of Labour 1959–63; Provincial Secretary 1959–63; Minister of Welfare, Provinces of Manitoba 1963. Progressive Conservative. *Address: office* Room 302 Legislative Building, Winnipeg 1, Man., Canada.

**CARS, Ernest,** CEng, FIMechE, FIProdE. British. *B.* 1923. *Educ.* Duryfalls Sch., Hornchurch; S. E. Essex Tech. Coll. *M.* 1947, Joyce Kathleen May. *S.* 1. *Dau.* 1. *Career:* Chmn. & Man. Dir., Moss Engineering Group Ltd.; Chmn., Moss Gear Co. Ltd.; Jackson Bros. (Milton) Ltd.; Holbrook Engineering Co. (Accrington) Ltd.; The Moss Gear Co. (Accrington) Ltd.; Stevens & Bullivant Ltd.; Automatic Dryers Ltd.; The Moss Engineering Group Services Ltd.; Welded Presswork Ltd.; Wallwin (Pumps) Ltd.; Wallwin Foundries Ltd.; Electrical Systems Ltd.; William E. Farrer Ltd.; The Standard Pavement Co. Ltd.; Sewage Treatment Plant Advisory Services Ltd.; J. & T. Engineering Ltd.; Div. Man., F. Perkins Ltd. 1949–55; Works Dir., Turner Mfg. Co. Ltd. 1955–58. *Address:* 25 Ladywood Rd., Four Oaks, Sutton Coldfield; and *office* Tyburn, Birmingham 24.

**CARSTENS, Prof. Dr. Karl.** German Politician. *B.* 1914. *Educ.* Univs. of Frankfurt, Dijon, Munich, Königsberg, Hamburg & Yale—Dr. of Laws (Hamburg), LLM (Yale). *M.* 1944, Veronica Prior. *Career:* Lawyer, Bremen 1945–49; Rep. of Free Hanseatic City of Bremen in Bonn 1949–54; Rep. of Fed. Republic of Germany to Council of Europe, Strasbourg 1954–55; Prof., Cologne Univ. since 1950 and Prof. of Constitutional & International Law since 1960; Foreign Office, Bonn 1955–60; Sec. of State, Foreign Office 1960–66; Sec. of State, Ministry of Defence 1966–67; Head of Chancellor's Office, Bonn 1968–69; Dir. Research Inst. German Foreign Policy Assoc. 1969–72; Leader of Parliamentary Opposition 1973–76; Pres. German Bundestag 1976. *Decorations:* Numerous, incl. Bundesverdienstkreuz; Légion d'Honneur; Order of St. Michael and St. George; etc. *Publications:* Grundgedanken der Amerikanischen Verfassung und ihre Verwirklichung (1954); Das Recht des Europarats (1956); Politische Führung-Erfahrungen im Dienst Der Bundesregierung (1971). *Address:* 5309 Meckenheim, Dechant-Kreiten-Strasse 43, West Germany; and 5300 Bonn, Bundeshaus, West Germany.

**CARTER, Edward Robert Erskine.** Canadian. *B.* 1923. *Educ.* University of New Brunswick (BCL) and Oxford University (BCL). *M.* 1947, Verna Andrews. *S.* Erskine and Christopher. *Daus.* Jennifer and Sandra. *Career:* Dir., Hambro Canada Ltd.; Gibraltar Pari Mutuel Inc.; Chmn. and Dir., Advocate Mines Ltd.; Foodex Systems Ltd.; Bank of Montreal; Hambros Ltd.; Westroc Instries Ltd.; Sun Alliance Insurance Co. *Address* and *office:* Suite 1104, Royal Trust Tower, Toronto-Dominion Centre, M5K 1H6 Ont.

**CARTER, Emmett Finley.** American. *B.* 1901. *Educ.* The Rice Institute (BScEE, with Distinction). *M.* 1925, Charlotte Reid. *S.* Everett F. *Dau.* Caryl (Mezey). *Career:* Radio transmitter, receiver and television development, General Electric Co., Schenectady, N.Y. 1922–29; Director, radio engineering division, United Research Corp. 1929–32; Div. Eng., Hygrade Sylvania Corp., Emporium, Pa. 1932–41; Dir. Industrial Relations, Sylvania Electric Products Inc., N.Y.C. 1941–45; Vice-Pres. in charge of Ind. Relations 1945; Vice-Pres. in charge of Eng. 1946–53; Vice-Pres. & Technical Dir. 1953–54; Manager, Research Operations, Stanford Research Institute 1954–56, Dir. 1956–59; Pres. 1959–63. Senior Management Counselor 1963–65. President 1960, Director 1957–62, San Francisco Post, Regional Vice-Pres., Amer. Ordnance Ass. 1963–64; Dir. URS Corp. 1965–70; Ati-Itek 1966–70; Research Counsellor 1965—. Member, U.S. Department of Commerce Panel on Science & Technological Development. New Management Centre, 1970—. *Member:* Research & Development Adv. Council to Chief Signal Officer 1954–62; Trustee 1959–65, Vice-Pres. 1963–65, World Affairs Council of No. Calif.; President, Board of Trustees, Silver Bay Assn. (Y.M.C.A.) 1948–54; Member, Governor's Business Advisory Council 1961–66; Director, Management & Economics Research Inc. 1965–68. 20 patents. Outstanding Civilian Service Medal U.S. Army 1963; I.E.E.E. Founder's Medal 1969. Recipient, The Founders Award (I.E.E.E.), 1969. Member: A.I.E.E. (Life Member); Institute of Electrical and Electronics Engineers (Fellow) 1963—. Registered Professional Engineer. Radio Amateur K6GT. *Clubs:* University, Palo Alto; Standford Univ. Faculty; Commonwealth of Calif. *Address:* 137 Ash Lane, Portola Valley, Calif. 94025, U.S.A.

**CARTER, Harry Havilland.** Canadian Ambassador to Republic of South Africa. *B.* 1918. *Educ.* Univ. of Toronto (BA 1938, MA 1940). *M.* 1948, Pamela Christine Price. *Daus.* Vivien P. and Valerie I. *Career:* Served with Canadian Artillery (England, France, Belgium, Netherlands) 1940–45, discharged with rank of Captain. Joined Canadian Dept. of External Affairs, Jan. 1945; served in Washington, New York, The Hague, and New Delhi. Head, U.S. Div., Dept. of External Affairs 1961–64; Ambassador to Finland 1964–69; to Republic of South Africa since 1969; Canadian High Commissioner to Botswana, Lesotho and Swaziland. *Address:* P.O. Box 683, Cape Town, South Africa; and *office* P.O. Box 26006, Pretoria, South Africa.

**CARTER, (Jimmy) James Earl, Jr.** American politician. *B.* 1924. *Educ.* Georgia Tech. Coll.; US Naval Acad. *M.* Rosalynn Smith. *S.* 3. *Dau.* 1. *Career:* Served with US Navy until 1953; Peanut Farmer, Plains, Georgia since 1954; State Senator 1962–66; Governor of Georgia 1970–74; inaugurated as 38th President of the U.S.A., Jan. 1977. *Address:* The White House, Washington, D.C., U.S.A.

**CARTER, James R.** *B.* 1907. *Educ.* Harvard Coll. and Harvard Graduate School of Business Administration. *M.* 1954, Placidia White (2nd wife) 1954. *S.* James R. III. *Dau.* Anne S. (Snyder) Jr.). *Career:* With Townsend, Anthony & Tyson, stockbrokers 1930–32; American Paper & Pulp Assoc. 1933–34; Nashua Corp. 1934—. U.S. Army Air Force (Lieut.Col.) 1942–46. Chmn. 1969, President 1957—and Director 1948—, Nashua Corp., Nashua, N.H.; Director 1959—, Nashua Canada Ltd., Peterborough, Ont., Canada; Cabot Corp. (Boston) 1972—, Director, Nashua Copycat Ltd., London (England) 1963— (Chmn. of the Board 1966—). *Member:* Chmn. Hungarian U.S. Economic Council Wash D.C., since 1975; Chmn. Bd. of Visitors of Whittlemore Sch. of Business and Economics (Univ. of N. Hampshire) Durham NH since 1974; Trustee, Socy. for the Protection of NH Forests, Concord NH since 1974. *Member:* Sons of Colonial Wars; American Management Association. *Clubs:* Unions (Boston), Brook. *Address:* Powersbridge, Peterborough, N.H.; and *office* 44 Franklin Street, Nashua, N.H., U.S.A.

**CARTER, Sir John G.,** KB, QC. Guyanese Diplomat. *B.* 1919. *Educ.* Queen's Coll. Guyana; Univ. of London and Middle Temple. *M.* 1959, Sara Lou Carter. *S.* 2. *Career:* Barrister-at-Law Supreme Court of Guyana 1945–66; Ambassador of Guyana to U.S.A., High Commissioner to Canada 1966–70; Ambassador to the United Nations 1966–67, 1968–70; Vice Pres. United Nations 1968; High Commissioner to the United Kingdom 1970–76; Ambassador of Guyana to China since 1976. *Awards:* BA; LLB Univ. of London; Caccigue's Crown of Honour Guyana. *Address:* Embassy of Guyana,

No. 1 Hsui Hsueh Tung Chieh, Chien Kuo Men Wai, People's Republic of China.

**CARTER, Peers Lee,** CMG. British diplomat (Ret'd); free-lance interpreter. *B.* 1916. *Educ.* Radley College; Christ Church, Oxford (MA). *M.* 1940, Joan Eleanor Lovegrove. *S.* Peers Michael Somerville. *Career:* Vice-Consul, Amsterdam, 1939; Army 1940 (with French under General Leclerc in Africa and with S.O.E. in Southern Europe); 2nd (later 1st) Secretary, Baghdad, 1945–49; Head of Chancery, Commissioner-General's Office, Singapore, 1951; Counsellor, Washington, 1958; detached to U.N. New York, 1961; Head, Permanent Mission to U.N., Geneva, 1961–63; Inspector (later Chief Inspector), Diplomatic Service Establishments, 1963–68; Ambassador to Afghanistan 1968–72; Ministerial Interpreter and Assistant Under-Secy. of State, London. *Member:* International Assn. of Conference Interpreters (AIIC). *Award:* Sardar-e A'ala. *Clubs:* Special Forces; Travellers. *Address:* Holgate, Balcombe, Sussex.

**CARTER, Richard H.** American. President: Fostoria Corporation, and Tri-County Financial Corporation. *B.* 1920. *Educ.* Yale University (BS 1942). *M.* 1942, Ann Fuhrer. *S.* Richard H., Jr. *Dau.* Cynthia Ann. *Member:* Young Presidents' Organization; Mid-West Executive Council (N.I.C.B.); Business Leadership Advisory Council. *Club:* Rotary. *Address:* 512 Mount Vernon Drive, Fostoria, Ohio 44830; and *office* Fostoria Corporation, Fostoria, Ohio 44830, U.S.A.

**CARTER, Thomas,** MC. *B.* 1915. *Educ.* Bishop's Univ. (BA) and Univ. of London (MSc Econ.). *M.* (1) 1954, Marie-Louise Pattin (dec'd). *Dau.* Monique. (2) 1974, Alice Landwehr Clejan. *Career:* Served with Canadian Army 1940–45; entered Canadian Foreign Service 1945; served at Ottawa, Brussels, Rome, Warsaw, Saigon, London; High Commisioner, Lagos 1960–64; Ambassador, Cairo 1967–70; Ambassador, The Hague 1972–76; Ambassador, Vienna since 1976. *Address:* c/o Dept. of External Affairs, Ottawa, Canada.

**CARTER, Maj.-Gen. William A.** *B.* 1907. *Educ.* Mississippi State University, U.S. Military Academy, The Engineer School, Education Equivalent to Army War College and National War College, University of California. *M.* (1) 1934, Katherine Munson (*M.* dissolved). *Daus.* 2; *M.* 1962, Sara Croft Smith. *Career:* Commissioned 2nd Lieut. June 1930; 1st Lieut. 1935; Captain 1940, Major 1942; Lt.-Col. 1942; Colonel 1943; Brig. Gen. 1953; Maj.-Gen. 1957; Engineer Exec. Officer, H.Q., II U.S. Corps, North Africa 1942; Engineer, H.Q., II U.S. Corps, North Africa 1943; Engineer, H.Q., First U.S. Army, European Theater Operations 1944; Exec. Officer and Member, Engineer Board, Fort Belvoir, Va. 1945–46; Exec. Officer, Engineer Research and Development Laboratory 1947; Army Engineer, Third U.S. Army 1948–51; Chief, Construction Branch, Service Div., later Chief, Service Div.; later Director of Installations, Office of the Deputy Chief of Staff for Logistics, Washington, D.C. 1951–55; Engineer, H.Q. Army Forces Far East and Eighth U.S. Army, later Asst. Chief of Staff, G4, H.Q. Army Forces Far East and Eighth U.S. Army 1955–57; Division Engineer, U.S. Army Engineer Div., Lower Mississippi Valley, and President of the Mississippi River Commission 1957–60. Governor of Canal Zone and President of Panama Canal Company 1960–62; Project Analysis Div., Inter-American Development Bank, Washington, D.C.; Dir. Rio Parana Study Group Rio de Janeiro 1972–74; Consulting Eng. since 1974. *Awards:* Distinguished Service Medal, Legion of Merit, Bronze Star (U.S.); Croix de Guerre with palm, Legion of Honour (France); Couronne de Chene (Luxembourg). *Member:* American Society of Civil Engineers; Society of American Military Engineers; Internat. Commission on Large Dams. *Address:* 311 N. Underwood St., Falls Church, Va. 22046, U.S.A.

**CARTLAND, Sir George (Barrington),** Kt. CMG, KStJ. *B.* 1912. *Educ.* Manchester Univ. and Hertford Coll., Oxford. *M.* 1937, Dorothy Rayton. *S.* 2. *Career:* Served in British Civil Service in Gold Coast 1935–44; Colonial Office 1944–49; Secretary, London African Conference 1948; in Uganda: Administrative Secretary 1949; Secretary for Social Services & Local Government 1952, Minister for Social Services 1955, Minister for Education and Labour 1958 Chief Secretary 1960; Deputy Governor, Uganda 1961. Registrar, Univ. of Birmingham 1963–67. Vice-Chancellor. Univ. of Tasmania 1968—; Pres. Council of St. John in Tasmania since 1969. *Clubs:* Athenaeum; Royal Commonwealth Society; Tasmanian; Royal Yacht, Tasmania. *Address:* The University of Tasmania, Box 252C Hobart, Tasmania, Australia.

**CARTWRIGHT, William Frederick,** DL, OStJ. British engineer. *B.* 1906. *Educ.* Dragon School, Oxford; Rugby School. *M.* 1937, Sally Chrystobel Ware. *S.* Nigel John Frederick and Peter Aubrey. *Dau.* Lucy. *Career:* Chief Mechanical Engineer's Pupil at Great Western Railway, Swindon Works 1925; with Guest, Keen & Nettlefolds Ltd. 1929; study of Continental Practice in iron and steel works at Hoesch Koln A.G., Dortmund; August Thyssen Hutte, Duisburg; A.R.B.E.D. Esch, Luxembourg, and de Wendelet Cie., Hayange, France, late 1930; Asst. Works Manager, Guest Keen Baldwins Iron & Steel Co. Ltd., Port Talbot Works 1931 (Technical Asst. to Managing Director 1935, Director and Chief Eng. 1940); Director and General Manager, Margam and Port Talbot Works 1943; when Steel Company of Wales formed made Director of Company and General Manager of the Steel Division 1947; Assistant Managing Director 1954; Managing Director 1962. Group Managing Director, British Steel Corp., 1967–70; Director: Davy-International Ltd., British Steel Corp., (International) Ltd.; Harlech T.V. Ltd., Lloyds Bank Ltd., Deputy Chmn. British Steel Corporation 1970–72. *Publications:* many papers given to various learned bodies and technical journals. *Member:* Inst. of Mechanical Engineers, Iron and Steel Inst. (Pres. 1960). *Awards:* Bessemer Gold Medal, 1958; Federico Giolitti Steel Medal, 1960; Hon. LLD Wales, 1968. *Clubs:* Royal Ocean Racing; Royal Yacht Squadron; Royal Lymington Y.C.; Cardiff Business. *Address:* Castle-upon-Alun, St. Bride's Major, Bridgend, Glam.; and *office* British Steel Corp., 33 Grosvenor Place, London, S.W.1.

**CARUANA, The Hon. Dr. Carmelo,** Maltese Politician. *B.* 1916. *Educ.* Malta Lyceum 1928–36; Royal Malta University 1936–43 (BA 1939, LLD 1943). *M.* 1948, Pauline Zammit. *Dau.* Mary Fatima. *Career:* Elected to Malta Legislative Assembly in Nationalist Party Interests 1947; Minister of Industry and Commerce; Minister of Posts and Agriculture; Acting Prime Minister; Minister of Agriculture, Power and Communications; Min. Public Buildings & Works; Shadow Minister of Agriculture 1972–75. *Awards:* Civil Defence Medal; Coronation Medal. *Member:* Nationalist Part Exec.; Catholic Social Guild. *Address:* 77 Tarxien Street, Tarxien, Malta, G.C.

**CARVEL, Elbert N.** American business executive. *B.* 1910. *Educ.* Baltimore Polytechnic Institute (Grad.); University of Baltimore (LLB). *M.* 1932, Ann Hall Valliant. *S.* 1. *Daus.* 3. *Career:* Lieut.-Governor of Delaware 1945–49; Governor 1949–53, 1961–65; President, Delaware Pardon Board 1945–49; Delegate to Democratic Natnl. Convention 1948–52–56–60–64; Co-Nominator of Democratic Candidate for President (Adlai E. Stevenson) 1952; Chmn., Democratic State Committee of Delaware 1946–54–56; Democratic Candidate for U.S. Senate 1958 and 1964; Chmn. Bd., Valliant Fertilizer Co. Laurel, Del., Chmn. of Bd., Milford Fertilizer Co., Milford, Del. 1959—. Dir. Peoples Bank & Trust Co., Wilmington Del. 1957–75, Chmn, 1975. Chmn. Bd., Fischer Enterprises 1970–75; Chmn., Delmarva Ecumenical Agency 1971–72; Vice-Chmn., Bd. Trustees Univ. Delaware 1972—; Mem. Bd. Dirs., Central Shore Commodities Inc. 1976—; Dir., Beneficial Corp. 1975—; Mem., Governor's Judicial Screening Cttee. 1977—; Delegate from Delaware to BiCentennial Congress 1977. *Awards:* Commander, Order of Orange-Nassau (Netherlands) 1951; Vrooman Award, Community Service, Crime Prevention, Rehabilitation of Offenders, 1965; Good Citizenship Medal, Sons of the American Revolution 1967; Silver Beaver Boy Scouts of America, 1970, Vice-Pres., Delaware Safety Council. Chairman: Delaware Constitution Revision Commission, Church Club of Delaware, Delaware, Milford and Lewes Historical Societies; Sussex County Archaeological and Historical Society. Member Diocesan Council of Episcopal Church of Delaware, 1947–51, 1953–56–57–60, 1966–69. Delegate to General Convention of the Episcopal Church 1946, 1952. *Address:* Box 111, Laurel, Del., U.S.A.

**CARVER, Field-Marshal Lord,** GCB, CBE, DSO and Bar, MC. British Army Officer. *B.* 1915. *Educ.* Winchester Coll.; Royal Military Coll., Sandhurst. *M.* 1947, Edith Lowry-Corry. *S.* 2. *Daus.* 2. *Career:* Commander, 4th Armoured Brigade 1944–45; Chief of Staff, East Africa 1955–56; Director, Army Plans 1958–59; Commander, 6th Infantry Brigade 1960–62; G.O.C. 3rd Division 1962–64; Director, Army Staff Duties 1964–66; Commander, Far East Land Forces 1966; C. in C. Far East 1967–69; G.O.C. in C. Southern Command 1969–71; Chief of the General Staff 1971–73; Chief of the Defence Staff 1973–76; Created Life Peer, 1977; Resident Commissioner-Designate, Rhodesia 1977. *Decorations:* Knight Grand Cross Order of Bath; Commander of Order of British Empire; Companion of Distinguished

Service Order (& Bar); Military Cross; mentioned in Despatches (3 times). *Publications:* Second to none: History of Royal Scots Greys (1954); El Alamein (1962); Tobruk (1964); (Ed.) The War Lords (1976). *Club:* Anglo-Belgian. *Address:* Shackleford Old Rectory, Godalming, Surrey.

**CARY, Charles Oswald.** American. Government and corporation executive. *B.* 1917. *Educ.* Massachusetts Institute of Technology (Aero.) and Northeastern University School of Business (Management); Associate Fellow, American Inst. of Aeronautics and Astronautics. *M.* 1948, Jean M. Cochran. *S.* Peter C. and Charles P. *Daus.* Jean S., Anne O. and Elizabeth J. *Career:* Supt. of Operations and General Traffic Mgr., Alaska Airlines 1943–44; Executive Asst. to Chairman, Civil Aeronautics Board 1944–46; Specialist Asst. to Assistant Secretary of the Navy for Air 1946–48; Exec. Secy., the President's Air Co-ordinating Committee 1949–54. *Member:* U.S. Delegation to First Assembly of Provisional International Civil Aviation Organization 1946; U.S. Delegations to Assemblies of I.C.A.O. 1947–51–53; Civil Transport Aircraft Evaluation and Development Board 1948–49; Gen. Secy., National Security Resources Board, Air Transport Mobilization Survey 1950–51; Deputy Administrator. Defence Air Transporation Admin. 1951–54; Dir. of Sales, Curtiss Wright Corporation, Electronics Div. 1954–63; Consultant to Federal Aviation Administrator 1963; Vice-President, Hazeltine Corp. 1963–65. Asst. Administrator for International Aviation Affairs, Federal Aviation Administration 1965—. *Publications:* articles in various aviation and professional journals. *Member:* Academy of Political Science. *Clubs:* Wings (N.Y.); University (Washington, D.C.); Congressional Country (Md.). *Address:* 7703 Arrowwood Court, Bethesda, Md., 20034, U.S.A.

**CASALE, Renato.** Italian Industrialist. *B.* 1921. *Educ.* Physicist. *M.* 1946, Maria Teresa Casale Piazzoni. *S.* 2. *Daus.* 2. *Career:* Member, Board of Directors and of the Executive Board: Ammonia Casale S.A., Lugano, and of Panammonia S.A., Panama 1950—; Pres. Ital Elettronica S.p.A. Rome since 1959. *Address* and *office:* Via Ignazio Pettinengo 72, Rome Italy.

**CASEY, Eugene Bernard.** Comdr. U.S.N. (Retd.). *B.* 1904. *Educ.* Penna. State University and Georgetown University Law School. *M.* 1955, Betty Brown. *S.* Eugene Stokes and Douglas Robert. *Daus.* Virginia, Nancy, Betsey and Margaret Rose. *Career:* Decorated military medals for service and action in North Atlantic, Far East, and raids on Tokyo, Comdr. U.S.N.R. 1944–46; Exec. Assistant to Presidents Roosevelt and Truman 1941–53. Engaged in mechanical engineering, construction and housing projects since 1927; farming and ranching in Maryland 1933, and in Wisconsin, Minnesota, Virginia and N. and S. Dakota since 1943. Governor, Farm Credit Administration 1940–41. Pres. and Dir., Casey Engineering and Construction Co. and allied firms. Dir.: Financial General Corp., International Bank of Washington, D.C., and National Mortgage and Investment Corp., Atlantic City Racing Assn., Bowie Racing Assn., and Canadian Dredging & Drydock Corp; Wheelabrator Frye Corp., Gilbraltar Corp.; Recipient of Patrick Henry Memorial Assn. award for restoring last home, law office, grounds and grave of America's great patriot. *Member:* Lambda Sigma; Delta Upsilon; Amer. Socy. Mech. Engineers; Navy League; Amer. Legion; Newcomen Socy. of N. Amer. Socy. Military Engineers; Amer. Farm Bureau. *Clubs:* National Press, Winchester Golf, Washington Country, Maryland Jockey. *Address:* Springsbury Farms, Berryville, Va.; and *office* One West Deer Park Drive, Gaithersburg, Mid., U.S.A.

**CASPARI, Professor Fritz.** German Diplomat. *B.* 1914. *Educ.* Gymnasium Heidelberg; Univs. of Heidelberg, Oxford (Rhodes Scholar), Hamburg, BLitt., Dr. phil., Dip of Econ and Polit. Sc. *M.* 1944. Elita Galdos Walker. *S.* 2. *Dau.* 2. *Career:* Assist. Prof. Southwestern Univ. Memphis, Tenn. U.S.A., 1936–37; Inst. and Tutor, Scripps Coll. Claremont, Calif. 1939–42, Newberry Library, Chicago 1943–46; Inst. and Asst. Prof. (History) Univ. of Chicago 1946–54; Hon. Professor Univ. of Köln 1955; Foreign Office, Bonn, in charge of British, Irish and C'wealth Affairs 1954–58; Counsellor, Embassy of Federal Republic of Germany in London 1958–63; Counsellor and Minister, Office of German Observer to UN New York 1963–68; Asst. Under Secy. of State, Foreign Office, Bonn 1968–69 (in charge of Latin-Am., African and Asian affairs); Deputy Under-Secy. of State and Deputy Head, Federal President's Office, Bonn 1969–74; Ambass. of Federal Republic of Germany in Portugal since 1974. *Member:* Renaissance Socy. of America; Deutsche Gesellschaft für Auswärtige Politik. *Awards:* Grand Cross, Federal Order of Merit (Fed. Rep. of Germany); Knights Grand Cross, Order of St. Sylvester (Holy See); Libertador (Venezuela); San Carlos (Columbia); Merito Nacional (Ecuador); Grand Officer Orange-Nassau (Netherlands); Dannebrog (Denmark); Northern Star (Sweden); Adolph of Nassau (Luxemburg); Couronne (Belgium); St. Olav (Norway); Rising Sun (Japan); Order of Merit (Italy); Aztec Eagle (Mexico); Commander's Cross Malaysia and Romania; KCVO (UK, GB and Ireland); and others. Hon. Fell. of St. Johns Coll. Oxford. *Publications:* Humanism and the Social Order in Tudor England (1954); various articles in field of intellectual history. *Clubs:* Boodles (London), Gremio Literario (Lisbon), Swiss Alpine. *Address:* Rua Dom Constantino de Bragança 29, Restelo-Lisboa 3, Portugal; and *office* Embassy of Federal Republic of Germany, Caixa Postal 1046, Lisboa 1, Portugal.

**CASS, A. Carl.** American professor & international consulting engineer. *Educ.* Dr. Eng. School of Engineering, Fed. Univ., State of Rio de Janeiro 1965; Hon. DSc, Univ. of Nuevo Leon, Mexico 1958; Purdue Univ. (B. in Civil Eng.); Metallurgy and Geodetic Surveying, Rennsselaer Polytechnic Inst.; Higher Mathematics and Astronomy, Canisius College (Buffalo, N.Y.); cited for outstanding work in mathematics. *Career:* Registered Professional Engineer in District of Columbia; On steel production with Lackawanna Steel Co. and chemical converter supervisor with National Aniline & Chemical Co. 1928; Wickwire Spencer Steel Co. and Acme Steel Co. 1929; Asst. to Vice-Pres. i/c Operations, Erie R.R. 1930–31; Engineer, Bureau of Railroad Valuation, Interstate Commerce Commission 1931–33; Senior Engr., Coast and Geodetic Svy., U.S. Dept. of Commerce 1933–35; in general construction business for self 1935–37; Engineer, Reconstruction Finance Corp. 1938–41; Regional (metallurgical) Engr., Defense Plant Corp. 1941–48; Engr. (metallurgical) Export-Import Bank of the United States 1948–51; Chief, Engineering Div., Export-Import Bank of United States since 1951; present post embraces supervision of design, construction and operation of development and industrial projects in 200 countries, including extensive field investigations. Fellow, Amer. Socy. of Civil Engineers, Hon. Member, Instituto Latinoamericano del Fierro y El Acero (ILAFA). *Awards:* Citation from Italian Government 1968, with order, Commendatore dell'Ordine Al Merito della República Italiana. *Publications:* Technical Assistance & International Co. operation, (1954); Opportunities for Engineers Abroad, (1955); Latin American Iron & Steel Industries, (1962). Eximbank's Assistance in the Financing of Dams, (1967); El Desarrollo de la Industria Siderugica Latinoamericana, (1967); Export-Import Bank and its Relationship in the Development of an Iron and Steel Industry, (1968); Eximbank Financial Assistance to Latin America (1970); Eximbank and its Relationship to the Development of the Latin American Highway System and El Eximbank y su Relacion con el Desarrollo de la Industria Siderurgica Latinoamericana (1971); Proyectos Ferromineros par las Industrias de Manana (1972); World Dams Today (1977). *Address:* 37 Nicholson Street, N.W., Washington, D.C., 20011; and *office* Equibank N.A., Oliver Plaza, Pittsburgh, Pa. 15222, U.S.A.

**CASSELL, Frank Hyde.** American. *B.* 1916. *Educ.* Wabash Coll. (AB 1939) and Univ. of Chicago Graduate School of Business Administration. *M.* 1940, Marguerite Ellen Fletcher. *S.* Frank Allan, Thomas Watts and Christopher Bernard. *Career:* Chairman Governor's Committee on Unemployment, Illinois 1963 and 1964; Asst. to Pres., Inland Steel Co., Chicago, 1958–68. President, Frank H. Cassell and Associates Inc. Consultants, 1968—. Professor of Industrial Relations, Graduate School of Management. Northwestern Univ., Evanston, Ill., 1968—; Director, U.S. Employment Service 1966 and 1967—; Member, Board of Directors, F. W. Means Corp. since 1975; Member National Science Foundation Panel on Manpower since 1975. *Member:* Industrial Relations Research Association; Chicago Urban League; American Economic Association; Industrial Relations Association of Chicago (Past Pres.). *Publications:* The Public Employment Service: Organisation in Change (1968); (with Weber and Ginsburg) Public Private Manpower Policies (1969); Collective Bargaining in the Public Sector (1975); publications in the fields of labour-management relations, manpower, corporate social policy. *Clubs:* University (Chicago); International (Washington). *Address:* 128 Church Road, Winnetka, Ill.; and *office* 230 N. Michigan Ave. Chicago, Ill., 60601, U.S.A.

**CASTIELLA y MAIZ, Fernando Maria.** *B.* 1907. *Educ.* Univs. of Madrid, Sorbonne, Cambridge, Geneva and The Hague;

elected Pres. of Internatl. Studies Assn., Paris. *M.* 1942, Soledad Quijano. *S.* Fernando. *Daus.* Soledad, Begoña, and Christina. *Career:* Founder (and 1st Dean 1944), Faculty of Political & Economic Science, Univ. of Madrid. Attended Gen. Assembly of L.N. 1930, and Disarmament Conf. 1932. Prof. of Int. Law, Univ. of La Laguna (Canary Is.) 1935–39; Chair of History of Int. Law, Univ. of Madrid 1939; Member, Permanent Court of International Arbitration 1939—; Dir., Inst. of Political Studies 1943–48; Professor, Higher Studies of International Law, Univ. of Madrid 1944—; Amb. to Peru 1948–51 and to Holy See 1951; Minister for Foreign Affairs of Spain 1957–70. Shortly after proclamation of the Spanish Republic was arrested for his public defence of the Monarchy; and at the outbreak of the Civil War he had to seek asylum in the Norwegian Legation; he escaped later (disguised as a militiaman) to the National Zone and joined the Nationalist forces, and eventually reached the rank of captain. In 1941 he volunteered for the Blue Div. as a private and saw action on the Volchof front. As Minister for Foreign Affairs, his policy is the full incorporation of Spain into Europe and the maintenance of Spain's traditional friendship with Hispano-America and the Arab world. The results of his efforts are seen in the provement of relations with France, the United Kingdom, and Germany, and in the dual-nationality agreements with Chile, Peru, Nicaragua, Guatemala, Bolivia and Ecuador, his conversations with Pres. Eisenhower and Secretary of State Herter, his official visit to Washington, his visits to General Nasser (with consequent closer contact between the U.A.R. and Western worlds), the Cintra Conf. with the Moroccan Foreign Minister (for the return of the former Protectorate Zone, and the settlement regarding the Spanish Protectorate in that country), and Spain's official admission into the I.F.C., 1960, renewal of Hispano-U.S. Defensive Agreement (26.9.63) and his interviews with President Kennedy (9.10.63), with Secretary of State Dean Rusk in New York (23.4.64) and with M. Couve de Murville, French Foreign Minister, in Madrid (29.5.64). In May 1966 headed Spanish Del. which opened conversations in London with British Government about Gibraltar. In Mar. 1968 was awarded Dag Hammarskjöld Prize for Diplomatic Merit. *Publications:* with José María de Areilza, he was jointly awarded the National Prize for Literature in 1941, for their book Spanish Claims (a study of Spain's historical rights); The Consultative Function of the International Permanent Court of Justice, (1931); The International Problem in the Mind of the Pope, (1945); The Spanish Foreign Policy, (1960). *Address:* Faculty of Law, Univ. of Madrid. Spain.

**CASTLE, Rt. Hon. (Mrs.) Barbara Anne,** PC, MP. *B.* 1911. *Educ.* Bradford Girls Grammar School and St. Hugh's College, Oxford (BA Oxon). *M.* 1944, Edward Cyril Castle. *Career:* Member of Parliament (Lab.) for Blackburn 1945—. Minister of Overseas Development Oct. 1964–Dec. 1965; Minister of Transport Jan. 1966–Mar. 1968; First Secretary of State and Secretary of State for Employment and Productivity 1968–70; Secy. of State for Social Services 1974–76. Hon. Fellow, St. Hugh's College. *Member:* National Union of Journalists. *Address:* House of Commons, London, S.W.1.

**CASTRO, Raul H.** American lawyer & diplomat. *B.* 1916. *Educ.* Northern Arizona University (BA); University of Arizona (LLB). *M.* 1947, Patricia M. Norris. *Daus.* Mary Pat, Beth. *Career:* Spanish instructor, Univ. of Arizona, 1949; Deputy District Attorney in Arizona, 1952–54; District Attorney 1954–59; Judge: Juvenile Court, 1959–62; Superior Court, 1962–64; Ambassador to El Salvador, 1964–68 to Bolivia 1968–70; Private Law Practice, Tucson 1968–75; Gov. of Arizona since 1975. Outstanding naturalized Citizen Award, Pima Bar Assoc.; Oustanding Public Service Award, Univ. of Arizona. *Member:* American Bar Assoc.; American Judiciary Society; National Council of Juvenile Court Judges Assoc.; American International Law Society. Hon. LLD Northern Arizona University. *Address:* State Capitol, Tucson, Arizona, U.S.A.

**CASTRO RUZ, Fidel,** D-en-D. Cuban Politician. *B.* 1927. *Educ.* Havana University. *M.* 1948, Mirta Díaz Balart. *S.* Fidel. *Career:* With two other partners, established a law practice 1950; prospective candidate of the Partido del Pueblo Cubano (Ortodoxo) for a parliamentary seat in the elections banned by Batista, June 1952; led the attack on the Moncado barracks (in Santiago de Cuba); sentenced to 15 years' imprisonment (served for two years, of which seven months were spent in solitary confinement) 1953; in exile in U.S. and Mexico; organized the 26th July movement 1955; landed in Oriente Province to begin the armed fight in the Sierra Maestra, Nov. 1956; won the victory over Batista, who fled to the Dominican Republic, Jan. 1959: Prime Minister since 1959, Head of State, Pres. of Council of State and Council of Ministers since 1976. *Address:* Palacio del Gobierno, Havana, Cuba.

**CATCHPOLE, George Parkin.** Certified Accountant. *B.* 1885. *Educ.* City Grammar Sch., Sheffield. *Career:* Served with BEF France 1915–18; Dir., The Engineering Centre Ltd. 1947–54; Chairman. Osborne Saul Ltd. 1948–76, Fairstands Ltd. 1949–76, Leisure Centre Ltd. 1950–76, Pleasure Centre Ltd. 1950–76, Anglo-European Exhibitions Ltd. 1958–76, Notabilia Ltd. 1960–76, Patent Investments & Royalties Ltd. 1962–76, Country & Coastal Properties Ltd. 1962–76. *Member:* of CNCL. Certified Accountants 1908–10, Faculty of Insurance 1912–15, London County Insurance Committee 1913–19, Faculty of Arts 1921–32, Council of Park Lane Group 1950; President, Relation Arts Centre 1960; Vice-President: Certified & Corporate Accountants Benevolent Association 1961; Film Critic, Daily Dispatch 1927–29, literary pseudonym 'Hermes'; Delegate to International Conventions and Conferences at Berlin, Brussels, New York, Paris and Zurich; London Correspondent, Sheffield Guardian 1910–11; Editor of Insurance Magazine 1912–15 and The Orbit 1922–32; Impressario, Productions & Concert Parties: Merry Monks; Carnation Concert Co. "34 Varieties", "Fanfare"; Musicals: "The Rajah's Ruby"; Pantomimes: "Cinderella", "Babes in the Wood"; Dir., Park Lane Theatre & Faculty of Arts Theatre, London; Palace Court Theatre, Bournemouth and Theatre Royal, Eastbourne. *Fellow:* Association of Certified Accountants, Assn. of International Accountants, Chartered Institute of Directors, Royal Horticultural Socy., and the Building Centre 1950–64. Member, British Institute of Management. *Address:* Badgers Mount, Cranborne Avenue, The Meads, Eastbourne, Sussex BN20 7TS; and *offices* 12 Bolton Street, Piccadilly, London W1Y 8AU; 1 Woodbury Park Road, Tunbridge Wells, Kent; and 16 The Avenue, Eastbourne, Sussex BN27 3YD.

**CATHERWOOD, Sir Frederick.** British. *B.* 1925. *Educ.* Shrewsbury and Clare Coll., Cambridge. *M.* 1954, Elizabeth Lloyd-Jones. *S.* Christopher Martyn Stuart and Jonathan. *Dau.* Bethan Jane. *Career:* With Richard Costain Ltd.: Secy. and Controller 1954–55, Chief Executive 1955–60, Asst. Mng. Dir. 1960–62, Mng. Dir. 1962–64, The British Aluminium Co. Ltd. Chief Industrial Adviser, Dept. of Economic Affairs 1964–66. Director-General of the National Economic Development Council 1 May 1966–71; Managing Dir., John Laing & Son Ltd. 1971–74; Vice-Pres., British Inst. Mgmt.; Chmn. British O'seas Trade Board since 1975; Chmn., Mallinson Denny Ltd. *Director:* John Laing and Sons Ltd.; Goodyear Tyre (GB) Ltd. *Publications:* The Christian in the Industrial Society; The Christian Citizen; A Better Way. Fellow: Institute of Chartered Accountants; Pres., Fellowship of Independent Evangelical Churches. *Clubs:* Oxford and Cambridge. *Address:* 25 Woodville Gardens, London, W.5.; and *office* 1 Victoria Street, London, S.W.1.

**CATLIN, Sir George Edward Gordon,** FWAAS. British political scientist. *B.* 1896. *Educ.* MA Oxon, triple prizeman; PhD Cornell. *M.* (1) 1925, Vera Brittain (D.). *S.* John. *Dau.* Shirley (Williams). (2) 1971, Delinda Gates. *Career:* co-operater with C. E. Merriam and Harold Lasswell in the reconstruction of contemporary Political Science; Co-author of the proposal (pre-1939) for an Atlantic Community; Draftsman of the International Declaration in support of Indian Independence. *Member:* American, Canadian & British Political Science Assn.; International etc. Sociological Association; Mem., FCO Liaison Cttee., American Bicentennial. *Awards:* Commander, Grand Cross, Order of Merit, German Federal Republic; Vice-Pres. World Academy of Arts & Sciences. *Publications:* Political Science, Encyclopaedia Britannica. *Clubs:* Pilgrims; United Service. *Address:* Corner Cottage, Allum Green, Lyndhurst, Hants.

**CATTO, Lord** (of Cairncatto) **Stephen Gordon Catto.** *B.* 1923. *Educ.* Eton; Cambridge University. *M.* (1) 1948, Josephine Innes Packer (marriage diss. 1965). *M.* (2) 1966, Margaret Forrest. *Career:* Served with R.A.F.V.R. 1943–47; Chmn., Morgan Grenfell & Co. Ltd.; Chmn., Australian Mutual Provident Socy. (London Board), and Yule Catto & Co. Ltd.; The General Electric Company Ltd., News International Ltd. and other companies. Member, London Adv. Cttee. Hongkong & Shanghai Banking Corporation. *Member:* Advisory Council Export Credits Guarantee Dept., Board of Trade June 1959–65. Part-time member, London Transport Board Dec. 1962–68. *Clubs:* Oriental (London) and Melbourne (Australia). *Address:* Morgan Grenfell & Co. Ltd., 23 Great Winchester Street, London, EC2P 2AX.

**CAVAN, Roger Hamilton Struthers.** British executive. *B.* 1907. *M.* 1936, Cecile Thornton. *Career:* Manager, London Office of the Bank 1949–54; Chief Manager for Victoria 1954–60; Chief Inspector, Head Office 1960–61; Asst. General Manager 1961–62; General Manager, Commercial Banking Co. of Sydney Ltd., Sydney 1962–70. Chairman, Association of Australasian Banks in London 1954 and of Australian Bankers Assn. 1966–67. *Clubs:* Union, Australian (Melbourne). *Address:* 34/1 Lauderdale Avenue, Fairlight, N.S.W. 2094, Australia.

**CAVENDISH-BENTINCK, Victor Frederick William,** CMG. *B.* 1897. *Educ.* Wellington College. *M.* Kathleen Barry. *S.* 1. *Dau.* 1. *Career:* Second Lieut. Grenadier Guards 1918. Entered the Diplomatic Service 1919. Attended the Lusanne and Locarno Conferences and held posts in Paris, The Hague, Athens and Santiago, and in the Foreign Office. Chmn. Joint Intelligence Sub-Committee of the Chiefs of Staff and Adviser to the Dir. of Plans 1939–45. Ambassador to Poland 1945–47; retired 1947. *President:* of British Nuclear Forum; Bayer (U.K.) Ltd.; Nukem Nuklear-Chemie und Metallurgie GmbH; *Clubs:* Beefsteak; Turf. *Address:* 21 Carlyle Sq., London, S.W.3.

**CAVERS, David Farquhar.** American lawyer. *B.* 1902. *Educ.* Univ. of Pennsylvania (BS in Econ. 1923) and Harvard Univ. (LLB 1926). *M.* 1931, Lelia Yeaman. *S.* David F., Jr. *Career:* Instructor, Harvard Law School 1929–30; Asst. Prof.: West Virginia Univ. College of Law 1930–31, and Duke Univ. School of Law 1931–32 (Prof. 1932–45); Editor, Law & Contemporary Problems 1933–43; Asst. Gen. Counsel, U.S. Office of Price Administration 1943–45 (Assoc. Gen. Counsel 1945–46); Assoc. Dean, Harvard Law School 1951–58; Fessenden Professor of Law, Law School of Harvard University 1951–69; Emeritus 1969—; (Professor of Law 1945—); President & Chairman, Board of Trustees, Walter E. Meyer Research Institute of Law 1958–69; Pres. Council on Law-Related Studies since 1969. Fellow, Center for Advanced Study in the Behavioral Sciences 1958–59; LLD, Chuo University, Japan 1964; U.S. Del. 12th Session, Hague Conference, Private International Law 1972–73. *Publications:* Electric Power Regulation in Latin America (with J. R. Nelson), (1959); The Choice-of-Law Process, 1965; Contemporary Conflicts Law in American Perspective Hague, Academy for Private International Law (1970); numerous contributions to learned and other periodicals. *Member:* Amer. Acad. of Arts & Science (Fellow); Amer. Bar Assn.; Amer. Socy. of Intl. Law; Amer. Assn. for the Comparative Study of Laws; Japanese-Amer. Socy. for Legal Studies (Dir.). *Address:* 986 Memorial Drive, Cambridge, Mass.; and *office* Harvard Law School, Cambridge, Mass., 02138 U.S.A.

**CAYCE, Eldred A.** American. *B.* 1900. *Educ.* Univ. of Missouri, Kansas City (LLB); admitted to the Missouri Bar, 1936. *M.* 1923, Amanda Thomasson. *Daus.* Amanda Ruth (Lane, Seattle, Wash.) and Martha Susan (Golden, St. Louis, Mo.). *Career:* Exec. President, A. & E. Company, St. Louis (investments); Director of Ralston Purina Company, St. Louis. Director and Vice-President: Bethesda General Hospital, Bethesda Dilworth Home, Bethesda Townhouse, Vocational Counselling and Rehabilitation Services Inc. (all of St. Louis). Regional Chairman, Abilene Christian College Design for Development Program, Abilene, Texas. Recipient, Certificate of Service Award, by U.S. Dept. of Agriculture during World War II. *Member:* St. Louis Merchants Exchange (past pres.); National Grain Trade Council, Washington, D.C. (past Chmn.). President and Director, Wallace Foundation, Little Rock, Ark. Member, Missouri Bar Assn. *Clubs:* University, Old Warson Country (both of St. Louis); Tennessee Society of St. Louis (Past Pres.). *Address* and *office* 5100 Oakland Avenue, St. Louis, Missouri 63110, U.S.A.

**CAYZER, Sir (William) Nicholas,** Bt. British shipowner. *B.* 1910. *Educ.* Eton and Cambridge University. *M.* 1935, Betty Williams. *Daus.* Nichola, Elizabeth. *Career:* Director, African Lands & Hotels Ltd.; Air Holdings Ltd.; Airwork Services Ltd.; Alliance Assurance Co. Ltd.; Battle Farm Lands Ltd.; Bricomin Investments Ltd.; British Air Transport (Holdings) Ltd.; British & Commonwealth (Group Management) Ltd.; The British & Commonwealth Shipping Co. Ltd.; British & Commonwealth Shipping Co. (Aviation) Ltd.; British and C'wealth Shipping Co. (Hotel and Travel Enterprises) Ltd.; British Commonwealth Investment Co. Ltd.; British & South American Steam Navigation Co. Ltd.; Broadford Finance Co. Ltd.; Caledonia Investments Ltd.; The Caledonia Stevedoring Co. Ltd.; Cayzer, Irvine & Co. Ltd.; Cayzer, Irvine (Group Finance) Ltd.; Cayzer, Irvine (Investments) Ltd.; Cayzer, Irvine (Ins. Mgmt.) Ltd.; Cayzer Ltd.; Cayzer, Steel Bowater Holdings Ltd.; The Cayzer Trust Co. Ltd.; C.I. Investments Ltd.; Clanair Ltd.; Clan Line Investments Ltd.; The Clan Line Steamers Ltd.; H.P. Cooper Ltd.; Crewkerne Investments Ltd.; Dock & Airport Services Ltd.; English & Scottish Investors Ltd.; Gartmore (Finance) Ltd.; Gartmore Investment Ltd.; Gartmore Securities Ltd.; Hector Whaling Ltd.; Houston Line Ltd.; Huntley Cook & Co. Ltd.; Huntley & Sparks (Lands) Ltd.; International Shipping Information Services Ltd.; King Line Ltd.; London-American Maritime Trading Co. Ltd.; London & Gartmore Trust Ltd.; London & Southampton Stevedoring Co. Ltd.; Maniford Travel Ltd.; Meldrum Investment Trust Ltd.; North British Hire Purchase Ltd.; Overseas Containers Holdings Ltd.; Paragon (Construction) Ltd.; Pearson Lands Ltd.; Pearson Spinning Co. Ltd.; Redhill Aerodrome (Holdings) Ltd.; Redhill Flying Club Ltd.; St. Mary Axe Holdings Ltd.; Scottan Investments Ltd.; The Scottish Lion Insurance Co. Ltd.; Scottish Lion Insurance (Holdings) Ltd.; Scottish Lion Insurance (Investments) Ltd.; The Scottish Shire Line Ltd.; The Scottish Tanker Co. Ltd.; Sea Lion (Group Management) Ltd.; Sea Lion Investments Ltd.; Seapool Ltd.; Sterling Industries Ltd.; Travel Savings Ltd.; Travel Savings (I) Ltd.; Travel Savings (XII) Ltd.; Turnbull, Martin & Co. Ltd.; Union-Castle Investments Ltd.; The Union-Castle Mail Steamship Co. Ltd.; Universal Dampers (Lands) Ltd.; Urquhart Engineering Co. Ltd.; William Herbert Ltd.; President, Chamber of Shipping of the U.K. 1959, Institute of Marine Engineers 1963–64; Chairman, General Council of British Shipping 1959. *Address:* 2 St. Mary Axe, London, E.C.3.

**CAZALET-KEIR (Mrs.) Thelma,** CBE. *M.* 1939, David Edwin Keir, MBE, MA (*Dec.*, 1969). *Career:* Member, London County Council for E. Islington 1925–31; Alderman, County of London 1931; MP (Nat. Cons.) for E. Islington 1931–45; Parliamentary Private Secy. to Parliamentary Secretary to Bd. of Education 1937–40; Parliamentary Secretary to Ministry of Education, May 1945; member, Committee of Enquiry into conditions in Women's Services 1942; of Committee on Equal Compensation (Civil Injuries) 1943; Chmn., London Area Women's. Advisory Committee, Conservative & Unionist Associations 1943–46, and Chmn. of Equal Pay Campaign Committee. Former member Cost of Living Committee; Arts Council of Great Britain 1940–49; Exectuve Committee of Contemporary Art Society; Transport Users Consultative Committee for London 1950–52; Governor of British Broadcasting Corporation 1956–62 (appointment renewed 1960). *Member:* Royal United Kingdom Beneficient Assn.; Former Pres., The Fawcett Society. *Publications:* From the Wings (1967); Editor, Homage to P. G. Wodehouse. *Address:* 90 Eaton Square, London, S.W.1.

**CEAUSESCU, Nicolae.** President of the Socialist Republic of Romania. *B.* 1918. Member, Union of Communist Youth 1933— (Secretary 1944–45), and of the R.C.P. 1933—; numerous appts. in RCP (CC) and ministerial posts 1945–65; Secretary-General of R.C.P. 1965—; President of the State Council of the Socialist Republic of Romania 1967; Pres. of Socialist Unity Front, 1968; Gen. Secy. Romanian Communist Party 1969; Chmn. High Council of Econ. and Social Devel. 1973; Pres. Socialist Rep. of Romania since 1974. *Awards:* Hero of Socialist Labour 1964; Dr. (hon causa) Bucharest University and other countries. *Publications:* Collections of selected texts, translated and published in 13 other languages. *Address:* Central Committee of the Romanian Communist Party, Bucharest, Romania.

**CHADWICK, Sir Albert Edward,** CMG, MSM. Australian. *B.* 1897. *Educ.* Tungamah State Sch.; Univ. High Sch. Melbourne. *M.* 1924, Thelma Marea Crawley. *S.* 1. *Dau.* 1. *Career:* Former Dir. Gas & Fuel Corp. of Victoria; Former Dir. Leighton Contractors Ltd.; Lubricants Man. Shell Co. of Australia Ltd. 1935; joined Metropolitan Gas Co. as Controller of Gas Sales 1935; Gen. Man. Gas & Fuel Corp. of Victoria 1960–63, Chmn. 1964–71; Chmn. Overseas Telecommunications Comm. of Australia, 1963–68. *Clubs:* Athenaeum; Melbourne Cricket (Pres.); Victoria Amateur Turf; Riversdale Golf. *Address:* 413 Torak Rd., Vic., 3142, Australia.

**CHAFFEY, William Adolphus,** MLA. (Tamworth, N.S.W. 10 Aug. 1940—). *B.* 1915. *Educ.* The King's School, Parramatta, N.S.W. (Intermediate Certificate 1930), and Hawkesbury Agricultural College, Richmond, N.S.W. (Hons. Diploma 1933). *M.* 1946, Patricia Ann Egerton-Warburton. *S.* David Frank Egerton. *Daus.* Mary Ann and Elizabeth

Patricia. *Career:* Vice-Pres. Royal Agricultural Socy., N.S.W.; Member Exec. Committee, Commonwealth Parliamentary Association (N.S.W. Branch); Councillor and Past Pres., Hawkesbury Agricultural College Old Boys Union. Member Australian Country Party, N.S.W. (Acting Leader Aug.–Dec. 1962; Deputy Leader Apr. 1959–68); Minister of Agriculture, State of New South Wales, 13 May 1965–68; Member Executives Council, N.S.W. 13 May 1965–68. *Award:* U.S. Bronze Star Medal; twice mentioned in Despatches; Major 12/16 Hunter River Lancers (Retd.). *Clubs:* Agriculture; Rugby Union; Tamworth Bowling; Imperial Services; Tamworth; Tamworth Returned Services League of Australia. *Address:* 119 Fitzroy Street, Tamworth, N.S.W. 2340, Australia.

**CHAGLA, Hon. Mahomedali Currim,** BA (Oxon.). Bar.-at-Law; *B.* 1900. *M.* Meher-un-nissa Dharsi Jivraj (*D.* 29.11. 1961). *S.* 2. *Dau.* 1. *Educ.* St. Xavier's High School and College, Bombay; Lincoln College, Oxford; graduated at Oxford in Honours, School of Modern History 1922; President, Oxford Asiatic Society 1921, Oxford Indian Majlis 1922. *Career:* called to the Bar, Inner Temple 1922. Prof. of Constitutional Law, Government Law College, Bombay 1927–30; Honorary Secretary, Bar Council, High Court of Judicature, Bombay 1933–41; Puisne Judge, High Court, Bombay 1941–47; Delegate to U.N.O. to fight the cause of Indians in South Africa 1946; Vice-Chancellor, Bombay Univ. 1947; Fellow, Bombay Univ.; Chief Justice, High Court, Bombay 1947–58; Mem. Law Commission 1955–58. Governor of Bombay Oct–Dec. 1956; Ad Hoc Judge, International Court of Justice, The Hague 1957–60; Chairman, Life Insurance Corporation Enquiry Commission 1958; Ambassador of India in U.S.A., Mexico and Cuba 1958–61; Member, Sikh Grievances Enquiry Commission, Sept.–Oct. 1961. High Commissioner in U.K. 1961–63; Minister of Educaiton of India 1963–66; Leader, Indian Delegation to Security Council Debate on Kashmir Feb. and May 1964, and of Indian Deleg. to Commonwealth Education Conf., Ottawa 1964; Leader, Indian Deleg. to General Conf. of Unesco, Paris, Oct. 1964; to UN General Assembly 1967; Minister, External Affairs 1966–67. Hon. Fellow, Lincoln Coll., Oxford; Hon. LLD: Univs. of Hartford, Temple (Philadelphia), Boston, Leningrad, Panjab and Benares. *Publications:* The Indian Constitution; Law, Liberty & Life; The Individual and the State; An Ambassador Speaks; Education & The Nation; Roses in December (Autobiog.). *Address:* Pallonji Mansion, New Cuffe Parade, Bombay, India.

**CHAKRAVARTY, Birendra Narayan,** OBE. Indian diplomat. *B.* 20 Dec. 1904. *Educ.* Presidency Coll. Calcutta Univ.; University Coll. London; School of Oriental Studies, London. *M.* 1931, Indira Sanyal. *S.* Subrata. *Dau.* Anita. *Career:* joined Indian Civil Service 1929; held various appointments in Bengal districts and Bengal Secretariat; Finance Secretary, Bengal Government Nov. 1944; Secretary to Governor of West Bengal Aug. 1947; Counsellor and Charge d'Affaires Embassy, Nanking Feb. 1948; Head of Indian Liaison Mission, Tokyo (with personal rank of Minister) June 1948–49; Joint Secretary, Ministry of External Affairs 1949–May 1951; Secretary, Commonwealth Relations, Ministry of External Affairs May 1951–Jan. 1952; Amb. Ex. and Plen. to the Netherlands 1952–54; Senior Alternate Chairman, Neutral Nations Repatriation Commission in Korea, Aug.–Dec. 1953; Acting High Commissioner for India in London, Aug.–Nov. 1954; High Commissioner for India in Ceylon 1955–56; Special Secretary, Ministry of External Affairs, 1956–60; High Commissioner for India in Canada 1960–62; Permanent Representative of India to the U.N., New York Aug. 1962–65, Governor, Haryana since 1967. *Publications:* India Speaks to America (1965); Governor Speaks (Vol. I 1970, Vol. II 1971). *Address:* Haryana Raj Bhavan, Chandigarh, India.

**CHALFONT, Rt. Hon. Lord,** PC, OBE, MC (Alun Arthur Gwynne-Jones). British. *B.* 1919. *M.* 1948, Mona Mitchell, MB, ChB. *Career:* Officer (Lt.-Col.) in the British Army until 1961, qual. as Russian Interpreter 1951; Defence Correspondent The Times 1961–64; Minister of State Foreign and Commonwealth Office 1964–70; Consultant on Foreign Affairs to BBC Television; UK Permanent Representative, WEU 1969; Dir., IBM U.K. Ltd. 1973—; IBM U.K. Holdings Ltd. since 1973. *Member:* European Advisory Council; IBM; St. David's Theatre Trust; Pres., Hispanic & Luso-Brazilian Councils. *Publications:* The Sword and the Spirit (1963). *Clubs:* Garrick, M.C.C., City Livery. *Address:* House of Lords, London, S.W.1.; and 65 Ashley Gardens, London, S.W.1.

**CHALK, Hon. Sir Gordon,** KBE, LLD. Australian company director. *B.* 1913. *Educ.* Gatton State High School. *M.* 1937, Ellen Clare Grant. *S.* Gregory. *Dau.* Meredith. *Career:* Formerly Queensland Sales Manager for Toowoomba Foundry Pty. Ltd.; also Taxation Agent. Elected Queensland Parliament 1947; Minister Transport 1957–65; Dep. Premier and Treasurer, Queensland (Country Party–Liberal Party Coalition Govt.) 1965–76; Ret'd. 1976; now Dir. several Australian Financial and Engineering companies. *Clubs:* Tattersall's (Queensland); Rotary International. *Address:* 277 Indooroopilly Road, Indooroopilly, Brisbane, Australia.

**CHALKER, Hon. James Ronald.** Canadian. Minister of Public Works, Province of Newfoundland. *B.* 1912. *Educ.* Bishop Field Coll., St. John's; and St. Andrews Coll., Aurora, Ont. *M.* 1937, Margaret L. Butt. *S.* Richard George and Timothy James. *Dau.* Margaret Jill. *Career:* Previously Minister of Health, of Education, and of Economic Development. Liberal. *Clubs:* Royal Newfoundland Yacht; Masonic. *Address:* 101 Forest Road, St. John's, Nfld; and *office* Confederation Building, St. John's, Nfld., Canada.

**CHALKER (Mrs) Lynda,** MP. British politician and statistician. *B.* 1942. *Educ.* Roedean; Heidelberg Univ.; Westfield Coll., London Univ. and Central Poly. *Divorced. Career:* Statistical Asst., Kodak Ltd. 1962–63; Unilever Ltd., Research Bureau-Statistician 1963–67 and Deputy Chief Statistician 1967–69; Deputy Market Research Mgr., Shell Mex & BP Ltd 1969–72; Louis Harris International Inc., Chief Exec. Int'l Div. 1972–Feb. '74, and Advisor Feb. '74–Dec. '74; MP for Wallasey since 1974; Shadow Spokeswoman on Social Services 1976. *Member:* Fellow, Royal Statistical Socy.; Full Member of Market Research Socy. and its Parliamentary Advisor; Mem., Inst. of Statisticians. *Publications:* (jointly) Police in Retreat (1967); (jointly) Set the Party Free (1969). *Address:* c/o House of Commons London SW1A 0AA.

**CHALLIS, Reuben Lionel Grover.** New Zealand government official. *B.* 12 Mar. 1916. Commissioned, Royal New Zealand Naval Volunteer Reserve, Seconded to R.N. and Squadron Radar Officer (D.) to British E. Fleet 1942–45; Executive Officer, United Nations Relief and Rehabilitation Admin. in China, and Dep. Liaison Officer, Chinese National Govt. in Nanking 1946–47; attached to New Zealand Legation Washington as N.Z. Official to Far E. Commission 1947; Head, New Zealand Government Reparations and Trade Mission in Occupied Japan 1947–51; Head, N.Z. Diplomatic Mission in Japan 1951–52; Chargé d'Affaires for N.Z. in Japan 1952–56; Chargé d'Affaires, Embassy. Thailand 1956–58; Acting New Zealand member. SEATO Council Representatives 1958; Acting High Commissioner for New Zealand in India 1958–60; Consul-General of N.Z. for Western U.S.A. 1960–63. Commissioner for New Zealand in Singapore and Borneo Territories 1963–64; Commissioner for N.Z. in Hong Kong and concurrently Minister of N.Z. to the Philippines 1965–68; Ambassador to Indonesia 1968. *Address:* c/o Ministry of Foreign Affairs, Auckland, New Zealand.

**CHALMERS, Bruce.** Metallurgist. *B.* 1907. *Educ.* BSc, PhD, DSc (all of London, Eng.). *M.* 1938, Gladys Ema Arnouts. *S.* Stephen P. *Daus.* Carol A., Jane H., Alison F., and Heather C. *Career:* Prof., Univ. of Toronto 1948–53; Head of Metallurgy Dept., Atomic Energy Research Establishment, Harwell 1946–48, and of Metallurgy Dept., Farnborough 1944–46; Physicist, Tin Research Int. 1938–44; Lecturer, Univ. of London 1932–38; Gordon McKay Professor of Metallurgy, Harvard University 1953—; Master, John Winthrop House, Harvard Univ. 1964-74. *Publications:* Principles of Solidification, (1964); Energy, (1963); Physical Metallurgy, (1959); Structure and Mechanical Properties of Metals, (1951); Physical Examination of Metals, (1939). Editor: Progress in Metal Physics 1949–62; Progress in Materials Science 1962—, and of *Acta Metallurgica* 1953–74. *Awards:* Acta Metallurgica Gold Medal 1975; A. M. (Harvard); Sauveur Award (Amer. Socy. for Metals) 1960. Clamer Medal, Franklin Inst. 1964. *Member:* (Hon.) Japan Inst. of Metals (1974); Nat. Academy of Sciences 1975. Hon. Member, Sté. Française de Metallurgy 1964; Fellow, Met. Sec. of AIME 1964. Fellow, Amer. Acad. of Arts & Sciences. *Member:* Amer. Socy. for Metals: The Inst. of Metals (Hon) Indian Inst. of Metals 1973. *Club:* Harvard (Boston). *Address:* 498 Sippewissett Rd. Falmouth, Mass., U.S.A.

**CHALMERS, Floyd Sherman,** OC, LLD, LittD, BFA. Canadian publisher. *B.* 1898. *M.* 1921, Jean Alberta Boxall. *S.* Wallace G. *Dau.* Margaret Joan. *Career:* Journalist 1917–25; Editor, Financial Post (Canada) 1925–42; Exec. Vice-

Pres., Maclean-Hunter Ltd. 1942–52, Pres., 1952–64, Chmn., 1964–69; Dir., Maclean-Hunter Ltd., Toronto since 1934; Macmillan Co. (Canada); Pres., Stratford Shakespearean Festival of Canada 1965–67; Pres., Canadian Opera Company 1957–61; Periodical Assn. of Canada 1947–49. Chancellor, York University (Toronto) 1968–73. Fellow, International Institute of Arts and Letters; Freeman, City of London 1957; Liveryman, Worshipful Company of Stationers and Newspapermakers, London; LLD (*honoris causa*) Univ. of Western Ontario 1962, Waterloo Lutheran Univ. 1963; LittD (hc) Trent Univ. 1968; BFA (hc) York Univ. 1973; Officer Order of Canada 1967; Can. Centennial Medal 1967; Diplome d'Honneur, Canadian Conf. of Arts 1974; News Hall of Fame of Canada 1975 *Address:* Apt. 4611, 44 Charles St. W., Toronto M4Y 1R8, Canada.

**CHAMBERLAIN, (Miss) Betty.** American. *B.* 1908. *Educ.* Smith Coll., Northampton, Mass. (AB) and Sorbonne, Paris (Lic. ès lettres studies; graduate). *Career:* Dir. of Publicity & Community Development, Brooklyn Museum, N.T. 1956–59; Man. Editor, Art News (monthly) 1954–56; Dir. of Publicity, Museum of Modern Art 1948–54; Production Head, editing, etc., Magazine of Art 1945–48; (also conducted surveys of museums and their communities; edited MSS for Columbia Univ. King's Crown Press, etc.); war work, Washington (war graphics, shipyard labor relations, etc.) 1942–45; wrote art section, Time magazine 1940–42. President, Betty Chamberlain Associates 1959—. Director of free non-profit and tax deductible clearing house for art information, The Art Information Center Inc., 1959—. *Member:* Civil Liberties Union; Eastern Co-operative Assn.; Amer. Museum Assn.; Adv. Bd., Museum of Amer. Folk Arts, N.Y. Democrat (elected member, Democratic Town Cttee., Justice of the Peace, Cornwall Conn.). *Publications:* The Artist's Guide to His Market (1970, revised and enlarged 1975); and various articles on art subjects in numerous periodicals; monthly column, Lincoln Center and Carnegie Hall Programmes; American Artist. *Address:* Cornwall Bridge, Conn. 06754 and 342 E 65 St. New York City 10021 and *office* 189 Lexington Ave., New York City 10016, U.S.A.

**CHAMBERLAIN, Edward Edinborough.** British. *B.* 1906. *Educ.* Victoria University Coll., University of N.Z. (BSc 1928, MSc 1929, DSc 1938). *M.* 1941, Geraldine Laura Sandford Baylis. *S.* Geoffrey Edward. *Career:* Asst. Mycologist, Plant Research Station, Palmerston North, N.Z. 1928; Mycologist, Plant Diseases Div., Auckland 1936 (Asst. Director 1943). Director, Plant Diseases Div., D.S.I.R., New Zealand Govt. 1957–68. Division, Contract to, D.S.I.R. 1970–71. Dir. Agricultural Div. Wattie Industries Ltd. since 1971; Dir. of Agric. Research Div. 1971–74; Retired 1974. *Publications:* Plant Virus Diseases in N.Z., (1954); 116 scientific papers dealing mainly with plant virus diseases. *Member:* Royal Socy. of N.Z. (Fellow; Member, National Cttee. for Biological Sciences); N.Z. Microbiological Socy. (Pres. 1962–64). *Address:* Scott Road, Tamaterau, RD4 Whangarli, New Zealand.

**CHAMBERLAINE, G. Harry.** *B.* 1900. *Educ.* Dartmouth Coll. (BA); Tuck Graduate School (MCS). *M.* 1923, Helen B. Pickard. *Daus.* Diane (Lucas, Jr.) and Janice (Pierce). *Career:* Account Executive, N. W. Ayer & Son, 1922–27; Vice-President and Director of Advertising of Good Housekeeping 1927–58; publisher of Science Digest, and Popular Mechanics (with editions in France, Australia, Denmark Sweden, Brazil, Netherlands, and Latin America) 1959–61; VP. Research-Marketing Hearst Magazines 1961–66. *Member:* Phi Beta Kappa; Beta Theta Pi; Sphinx Socy.; Bd. Trustees, Rye Library; Pres. Rye Assn. for the Handicapped. *Clubs:* Apawamis (Rye, N.Y.); Manursing Island. *Address:* 17 Highland Park Place, Rye, N.Y., 10580, U.S.A.

**CHAMBERS, Hon. Mr. Justice David Montagu.** Australian. *B.* 1916. *Educ.* Hutchins School, Hobart, and University of Tasmania (LLB). *M.* 1949, Mary Sweetingham. *Daus.* 2. *Career:* Admitted to Bar 1939; Crown Prosecutor 1946; Crown Solicitor 1951; Solicitor-General and Queen's Counsel 1956; Justice of the Supreme Court of Tasmania 1968; Chancellor of the Diocese of Tasmania 1969—. President National Union of Austalian University Students 1939; Service with Australian Military Forces 1941–46; Church Advocate for Church of England in Tasmania 1948–69. *Address:* 340 Davey Street, Hobart, Tasmania, Australia.

**CHAMBERS, Harold Joseph Ashbridge,** MASc, P. Eng. Canadian management consultant. *B.* 1902. *M.* 1927, Madeline Agnes Detlor-Milne. *S.* Thomas Frederick and Peter Milne. *Dau.* Edith May (Sellers). *Career:* Chief Designing Engineer, The Canadian Bridge Co. Ltd. 1924–39; Chief Engineer, The Hamilton Bridge Co. Ltd. 1939–42; General Manager, later Vice-President and General Manager of the company, 1942–45; President: Standard Machine & Tool Co. Ltd. 1946–57, Modern Tool Works Ltd. 1955–57, Standard Modern Tool Co. Ltd. 1955–57; Dir. Cybernetics Ltd. 1950, (Pres. 1950–71); Trojan Securities 1957–63; Viceroy Manufacturing Co. Ltd. 1958–73; Pres. 1960–64, Fluid Power Ltd. Chmn. 1964–73; Chmn. of Board: A. R. Williams Machinery Co. Ltd., A. R. Williams Western Ltd., and Pacific Tractor & Equipment Co. Ltd. 1955–57; Vice-Pres. & Dir., Trojan Securities Ltd. 1958–63; Special Consultant, Clare Brothers 1968–69 (President 1961–68); Pres., H. J. A. Chambers & Associates Ltd. since 1972. *Address:* Donridge, 7095 Bayview Avenue, Thornhill, Ont., Canada.

**CHAMBERS, Sir Stanley Paul,** KBE, CB, CIE. British company director. *B.* 1904. *Educ.* City of London Coll., London Sch. of Econ. (London Univ.); BCom. 1928, MSc (Econ.) 1934. *M.* 1955, Edith Pollack. *Daus.* Naomi Katherine and Sarah Penelope. *Career:* Member, Indian Income Tax Enquiry Cttee. 1935–36; Income Tax Adviser to the Government of India 1937–40; Secy. and Com., Board of Inland Revenue 1942–47; Chief of Finance Division, Control Commission for Germany, British Element 1945–47; Member of Committee appointed to review the organization of Customs and Excise, Oct. 1951–Sept. 1953; Member, Committee on Departmental Records, June 1952–July 1954; Chairman, Committee of Enquiry into London Transport, Apr. 1953–Jan. 1955; Member, National Coal Board 1956–60; Dir., 1947–60; Chairman, I.C.I. Ltd. 1960–68; Chairman, Royal Insurance Co. Ltd., Liverpool & London Insurance Co. Ltd., and London & Lancashire Co. Ltd. 1968–74; Director, National Westminster Bank Ltd. 1968–74; President, National Institute of Economic & Social Research, Dec. 1955–62; Advertising Assn. 1968–70; Inst. of Directors 1964–68, British Shippers' Council 1963–68. Treasurer, Open University, 1969–75; Pro-Chancellor Univ. of Kent, Canterbury 1971—; Report on Organisation, British Medical Assn. 1972. *Clubs:* Athenaeum, Reform. *Address:* 1A Frognal Gardens, Hampstead, N.W.3.

**CHAMPION, Walter,** Dr rer pol. Swiss. Corporation Secretary and Editor 1940. *B.* 1902. *Educ.* Univs. of Berne and Lausanne. *M.* 1933, Lucie Dietschi. *Daus.* Esther and Delphine. *Career:* Professor at the Grammar Schools of Burgdorf and Berne 1925–28; Lawyer, Secy. to Canton Police and Education Depts., Solothurn 1928–31; Board Secy., Verb andost-schweiz. landwirtschaftl. Genossenschaften (VOLG) Winterthur 1931–40; Secy. and Editor, Genossenschafter VOLG 1940–67. *Publications:* various articles on co-operative systems. Member of several professional organizations. *Address:* St. Georgenstrasse 10, Winterthur, Switzerland.

**CHAMPLIN, Malcolm McGregor,** NC, American Statesman, Judge and Capt. (USNR). *B.* 1911. *Educ.* U.S. Naval Academy, Annapolis (BS 1934); University of California Law School (D.J. 1939). *M.* (1) 1944, Betty Mee (*Div.*) and (2) 1955, Virginia Pearson. *S.* William Bradford. *Daus.* Sarah Jane and Mimi Lizette. *Career:* Admitted to California Bar 1940; associated with firm of Fitzgerald, Abbott & Beardsley (Oakland) 1940; Special Agent with F.B.I., Department of Justice, Washington, D.C., 1941; continued with the Department until ordered to duty with U.S. Navy for the period, 1941–45; graduated at U.S. Naval War College, Newport, R.I. 1944; served in Bataan, Corregidor, Aleutian Islands and the Pacific and Asiatic Waters; awarded the Navy's highest decoration, the Navy Cross, for heroism in the Philippines; in addition to service ribbons, has received the Army's Silver Star awarded him by General Jonathan Wainwright in the Bataan campaign; after the war, resumed his association with Fitzgerald, Abbott & Bearsley until 1947; was for eight years Director of the Ventura Coastal Lemon Co., Inc., and for five years a Vice-Pres. and a Dir. of Ventura Processors, Ventura County, Calif.; in 1947 organized and later became senior partner in Stark & Chaplin (1947–67). Judge of the Municipal Court, Oakland-Piedmont Judicial District since 1967; elected for a six year term Nov. 1970, without opposition, re-elected Nov. 1976, again without opposition. Delegate to Republican National Convention (which nominated Richard Nixon for President), Chicago 1960. Delegate to Republican Convention 1964. Nominated by Republican Party in Primary Election as candidate for Congress, U.S. House of Representatives, Seventh District of California. *Member:* State Bar of California, American and Alameda County Bar Assocs.; Phi Delta Phi legal frat., American Legion, American Legion Service Club. Reserve

Officers' Association; takes an active interest in American Legion affairs; successively Post Commander, District Commander and State Commander; unanimously elected to represent the State of California as its National Executive Committeeman. *Clubs:* Commonwealth (San Francisco). Mason. Scottish Rite Oakland Bodies KCCH. Republican. *Address:* 485 Ellita Avenue, Oakland, Calif., U.S.A.

**CHAN, Keng-howe, Harry,** Singapore diplomat. *B.* 1926 *Educ:* BA (Hons.); AIBA; Post-grad. courses at Oxford; Stanford Univ. (Calif); International Manpower Inst. Washington. *M.* 1954, Geraldine Wee. *S.* 1. *Dau.* 1. *Career:* Singapore Admin. Service as Asst-Secy. Min. of Comm. and Works; Princ. Asst. Secy., Min. Commerce and Industry; Dep. Secy. Treasury and Education; Secy. Public Service Comm.; Ag. Perm. Secy. and concurrently ASEAN Secy-Gen. Min. of Foreign Affairs, 1950–1969; Ambassador to Cambodia 1969–72; High Commissioner to New Zealand since 1974. *Member:* Singapore Inst. of Mgmt. (founder); Inst. of Business Admin. (Assoc.). *Clubs:* Singapore Island Country; Wellington; Wellington Golf. *Address:* 16 Hurman Street, Karori, Wellington 5, New Zealand; and *office* Singapore High Commission, Molesworth House, 101 Molesworth St, Wellington, New Zealand.

**CHANCE, Francis Gano.** *B.* 1905. *Educ.* Central Coll. and Univ. of Mo. (AB and BS Chem. Eng. 1929). *M.* 1930, Anna Lee Toalson. *S.* Phillip Gano and John Hardin. *Career:* Chairman of the Board, A. B. Chanse Co. 1949— (Asst. Gen. Mgr. 1931; Pres. 1939–60). Member Bd. of Directors: Missouri (Mo.) State Chamber of Commerce 1941— (Pres. 1944–46), Associated Industries of Mo. 1941–62 (Pres. 1954–56), and Mo. Public Expenditure Survey 1958— (also Vice-Pres.). *Trustee:* Chance Foundation, and Centralia Chamber of Commerce; Board Member, Southern States Industrial Council 1957—; N.A.M. (Bd. mem. 1953–60); Amer. Progress Foundation (Bd. mem.). Member, Alpha Chi Sigma, and Alpha Tau Omega (Chmn. Natl. Foundation Bd. 1957—). Baptist: Industry Chmn. National Bible Week 1953–65; Chmn. of Bd., Centralia Library 1963–65. *Awards:* Life Hon. Membership, Junior C. of C. 1964. Honor Certificate Award (Freedoms Found. 1963); Award for Community Progress (Centralia C. of C. 1951); Distinguished service in engineering (Univ. of Missouri 1955); Medal of Recognition (Culver-Stockton Coll. 1952); Citation of Appreciation (Boone County Fair 1954); Certificate of Merit (Mo. State C. of C. 1955). *Clubs:* Missouri Athletic, Noon Day, Discussion (St. Louis); Kiva (Phoenix); Centralia Country, Mexico Country; Marco Polo (N.Y.C.); Rotary (Centralia). *Address:* 950 S. Jefferson Street, Route 1, Centralia, Missouri 65240; and *office* 210 North Allen, Centralia, Missouri, U.S.A.

**CHANCE, Sir (William) Hugh (Stobart),** CBE, DL. British. *B.* 1896. *Educ.* MA (Cantab.); Hon. A.C.T. B'ham. *M.* 1961. *S.* 2. *Daus.* 3. *Career:* For many years Director (and for some years Chairman) of Chance Bros. Ltd., Glass Manufacturers and Lighthouse Engineers; also Director (and for some years Chairman) of Fibreglass Ltd. Retired since Dec. 1964. Recipient Parsons Memorial Medal. *Club:* Leander. *Address:* The Clock House, Birlingham, Pershore, Worcestershire.

**CHAND, Khub.** Indian Consultant for International Development and Business Relations. *B.* 16 Dec. 1911. *Educ.* University of Delhi (BA); Oriel College, Oxford. *M.* 1948, Nirmal née Singh. *Career:* Assistant Magistrate and Collector, United Provinces 1935–36, Joint Magistrate 1936–38; Additional District Magistrate, Cawnpore 1938–39; Under-Secretary, Department of Defence and Secretary, Indian Soldiers Board, India 1939–43; District Magistrate, Azamgarh 1943–45; Regional Food Controller, United Provinces 1945–47 Deputy Sec., Ministry of Defence 1947–48; Head of Indian Military Mission (with rank of Major-General), Berlin 1948–50; concurrently Head of Indian Mission (with rank of Minister) Allied High Commission for Germany, Bonn 1949–50; Deputy High Commissioner in Pakistan Sept. 1950, Acting High Commissioner 1950–52; Envoy. Ex. and Min. Plen. to Iraq 1952–55 and concurrently to Jordan 1954–55; Joint Secretary, Min. of External Affairs 1955–57; Ambassador to Italy 1957–60; concurrently Minister to Albania; High Commissioner for India in Ghana, 1960–62, concurrently Commissioner in Nigeria, Ambassador to Liberia, Guinea and Mali, and High Commissioner in Sierra Leone; Ambassador of India to Sweden 1962–66; concurrently accredited as Ambassador to Finland. Leader of Indian delegation to Economic and Social Cncl. of U.N. 1966; Representative of India on ad hoc Cttee. of U.N. Narcotics Commission 1966; Ambassador of India to Lebanon: concurrently accredited as Ambassador to Kuwait and Jordan and High Commissioner in Cyprus 1966–67; Ambassador to the Federal Republic of Germany, Bonn. 1967–70. Member Exec. Board 1972, and Vice-Pres. Indian Council of World Affairs, 1974; Pres., Indo-German Society 1976. *Address:* 1/8A, Shanti Niketan, New Delhi 21, India.

**CHANEY, Frederick Charles,** CBE, AFC. British. *B.* 1914. *M.* 1938, Mavis M. Bond. *S.* 4. *Daus.* 3. *Career:* Government Whip 1962–63. Minister for the Navy (Australian) March 1964–66. Administrator of Northern Territory Australia, 1970–73. Member of the Liberal Party. *Address:* 14 Nanhoa Street, Mt. Lawley, W.A., Australia.

**CHANNING, James Gregory.** Canadian. *B.* 1913. *Educ.* St. Bonaventure's Coll. and Memorial Coll. of Newfoundland. *M.* 1941, Mary S. Murphy. *S.* Robert. *Daus.* Elizabeth Ann and Catherine. *Career:* Clerk, Office of Secy. of Commission of Government 1934; Registrar, Dept. of Natural Resources 1935, Asst. Secretary, 1946; Secy. Nfld. Deleg. to Ottawa to finalize terms of union with Canada 1948; Asst. Deputy Min. of Finance 1949; Clerk of Exec. Cncl. and Deputy Min. of Provincial Affairs 1956; Supt. of Insurance 1956; Clerk of Executive Council and Deputy Minister, Office of Premier, Newfoundland since 1968; Head, NFD Public Service 1968. *Awards:* Member of Order of Canada; Queen Elizabeth II Coronation, and Canada Centennial medals. Member, Fedn. of Insurance Counsel. *Club:* Knights of Columbus. *Address:* 131 Elizabeth Avenue, St. John's; and *office* Confederation Building, St. John's, Newfoundland.

**CHANNON, Henry Paul Guinness,** MP. *B.* 1935. *Educ.* Eton and Christ Church Oxford. *M.* 1963, Mrs. J. Guinness (née Wyndham). *S.* Henry. *Daus.* Olivia Gwendolen Violet and Georgia Honor Margrethe. *Career:* Member of Parliament for Southend West Cons since 1959; P.P.S. to Hon. R.A. Butler (when he was Home Secretary and later Foreign Secretary) 1960–64; Junior Opposition Spokesman on Public Buildings and Works 1965–66, and on Arts and Amenities 1967–70. Joint Parly. Secy., Ministry of Housing & Local Government in 1970; Joint Parly. Under-Secy. Department of Environment 1970–72, Minister of State, Northern Ireland 1972; Minister for Housing and Construction 1972–74; Opposition Spokesman, Prices & Consumer Protection 1974; and the Environment 1974–75. *Clubs:* Bucks, Whites (both London). *Address:* 96 Cheyne Walk, London, S.W.1. and Kelvedon Hall, Brentwood, Essex.

**CHANTREN, Georges François.** *B.* 1922. *Educ.* Classics Athénée de Saint-Gilles; Diploma National Advt. Institute. *M.* Children 2. *Career:* Political prisoner Buchenwald Concentration Camp 1944–45; Free Lance Advertising 1945–47; Adv. Mgr. Tech. Dir. SA Vanypeco Advertising 1948–52; Adviser Brussels Int. Trade Fair, Press & Publications Dept. 1952–58; Founder and Dir. of the review *Présence de Bruxelles* 1950–71; Head Public Relations Socy. Brussels International & 58 World Exhibition 1954–56; Gen. Mgr. Brussels Int. Fair since 1958; Past Pres. Belgian Central Office for Congresses & Technical Advisory Cttee. Fairs & Shows; Commission, Union Int. Fairs (U.F.I.) & Int. Chamber of Commerce 1962–63; Gen. Mgr. A.S.B.L. Le Centenaire, Grands Palais since 1962; Secy. Gen. Union European Community Capitals since 1962; Member Managerial Cttee. Union Int. Fairs, Paris since 1962; Administrator Fed. Belgian Chamber of Commerce since 1971; Administrator Tourist Inf. Brussels; Vice-Pres., Union of International Fairs (U.F.I.) since 1977. *Awards:* Knight Order of the Crown; Knight Order of Leopold II; Croix de Guerre 1940–45 with Palm; Political Prisoner Cross (2 stars); Medal of the Resistance; Commemorative Medal 1940–45 (2 crossed swords); Officer Order of Merit, Grand Duchy of Luxembourg; Officer Order King George, Greece; Officer Order of the British Empire; Knight Order of Merit, Italian Republic; Officer, Order of la Couronne de Chêne, Luxembourg. *Address:* Vire Vent, Linkebeek, Belgium; and *office* Palais du Centenaire, Brussels.

**CHAPDELAINE, Jean.** *B.* 1914. *Educ.* St. Marie Coll., Montreal (BA 1933); Hertford College, Oxford (Rhodes Scholar) 1934–37; MA. *M.* 1941. Rita Laframboise. *S.* Antoine. *Daus.* Claude and Annick. *Career:* Third Secretary Ottawa 1937, and Washington 1940; First Secretary, Paris 1946; Chargé d'Affaires, Dublin 1950; Counsellor, Bonn 1950; Asst. Under-Sec. of State, Ottawa 1954; Ambassador of Canada to Sweden and Minister to Finland 1956–59; Ambassador to: Brazil 1959–63; United Arab Republic 1964–65. Delegate-General of Quebec in France 1965. *Clubs:* Cercle Universitaire (Ottawa); Garnison (Quebec); Club de Golf; St. Nom la Brelèche (France). *Address:* c/o Ministère des

Affaires Intergouvernementales, Hôtel du Gouvernement, Québec, Canada.

**CHAPMAN, Albert Kinkade.** American. *B.* 1890. *Educ.* Ohio State University (BA 1912; MA 1913; LLD 1956); Princeton University (PhD 1916); DSc Clarkson 1965. *M.* 1916, Ercil Howard. *Daus.* Ercil H. (Haywood Hawks, Jr.) and Elizabeth (Hanson). *Career:* Engaged in physiological optics research, Clark University (Worcester, Mass.) 1916–17; First Lieut. in Science and research Division, U.S. Signal Corps, later First Lieut. and Captain (development work in aerial phtography), U.S. Air Corps 1917–19; with Eastman Kodak Company 1919–66 (organized and headed photographic equipment development department 1919–21); Assistant to Vice-President in charge of manufacturing 1922–29; Production Manager 1930–41; Dir. 1943–66; Pres. 1952–60; Vice Chmn. Bd. Dirs. 1960–62, Chmn. Exec. Cttee. 1961–66; Chmn. Bd. Dirs. 1962–66; Dir. Eastman Gelatine Corp. 1930–66; Canadian Kodak Co. Ltd. 1931–66; Kodak Ltd. 1959–66. *Member,* Advisory Committee to Board, Lincoln First Bank of Rochester; Honorary Trustee: Univ. of Rochester, Rochester Inst. of Technology; Honorary Trustee, International Museum of Photography at George Eastman House; Board of Managers, Eastman School of Music, Rochester Memorial Art Gallery. Honours: Chevalier, Legion of Honour (France) 1955; Phi Beta Kappa; Sigma Xi. Republican. *Address:* 810 Allens Creek Road, Rochester, N.Y. 14618, and *office* 343 State Street, Rochester, N.Y. 14650, U.S.A.

**CHAPMAN, Dave.** American industrial designer. *B.* 1909. *Educ.* Armour Institute of Technology (now Illinois Inst. of Tech.); BSc Architecture 1932. *M.* 1939, Eileen Ryan. *Daus.* Nancy Eileen and Carol Elisabeth. *Career:* Member of Design Staff of the Century of Progress Exposition, Chicago 1932–33; Product Design Director, Bureau of Design, Montgomery Ward & Co. 1933–36; opened independent design office 1936; President and Chmn. of the Board, Dave Chapman Design Inc. and Design Research Inc. (estab. 1955); Director (elected 1950), American Society of Industrial Designers. *Awards:* Design Award Medal of the Industrial Designers' Inst. 1954 and 1960; numerous design citations from various sources. *Member:* Amer. Society of Industrial Designers (Fellow; Pres. 1950–51) Sons of the American Revolution; Benjamin Franklin Fellow, Royal Society of Arts and Letters (Fellow); Chicago Natural History Museum Assoc. Member); Art Institute of Chicago (Life member), Chicago Historical Society (Life member); Consultant and Lecturer to Tech. Center, Northwestern Univ., Ill. *Clubs:* Yacht, Tavern (both of Chicago). New York Yacht. *Address:* 3240 Lake Shore Drive, Chicago, Ill., U.S.A.

**CHAPMAN, Douglas K.** American. *B.* 1928. *Educ.* Univ. of Toronto. *M.* 1950, Doreen E. Lowe, *S.* 1, *Daus.* 2. *Career:* Pres. Acco International Inc. Chicago; Pres. & Dir. Acco Canadian Co. Ltd.; Pres. W. E. Prior Loose Leaf Ltd. Toronto; Dir. Acco Co. Ltd., London, Acco Nederland, BV. Utrecht, Acco Mexicana, S.A. de C.V., Acco France S.A.R.L., Acco International, GmbH; Vice-Pres. & Dir. Cel-U-Dex de Mexico; Dir. Acco Jamaica Ltd.; Dir. Vice Pres. C.A. Acco Mfg. Venezuela; Chmn., Mfrs. Div., National Office Products Assoc., Washington D.C. *Clubs:* Scarboro Golf & Country; Past Pres. Stationery & Office Equipment Guild of Canada; Northshore Country Club, Chicago; Mid-America Club; Metropolitan Club; Mission Hills C.C. *Address:* 175 Dickens Rd. Northfield, Ill; and *office* 770 S. Acco Plaza, Wheeling, Il. 60090, U.S.A.

**CHAPMAN, Sir Robert Macgowan** (commonly known as Robin), Bt, CBE, TD. British. *B.* 1911. *Educ.* Marlborough and Corpus Christi College, Cambridge; MA (Cantab.). *M.* 1941, Barbara May Tonks. *S.* David Robert Macgowan and Peter Stuart. *Dau.* Elizabeth Mary. *Career:* Territorial Army Service 1933–51; Lt.-Col. 1948; Honorary Colonel 1963–75. Chartered Accountant 1938; Dir. George Angus & Co. Ltd. 1952–73; Manchester Dry Docks Co. Ltd. 1963–71 and of other companies. Chairman, Northern Area Conservative Council 1953–56. Member, Conservative National Executive Committee 1953–69; President, Jarrow Conservative Association 1962 (Chmn. 1957–59). D.L. Co. Durham 1952; J.P. 1946. President, Northern Society of Chartered Accountants 1958. High Sheriff, Co. Durham 1960; Vice Lord Lieut., County of Tyne and Wear 1974. *Award:* Boy Scouts Silver Acorn. *Clubs:* Junior Carlton; Hawks. *Address* Cherry Tree House, Cleadon, Sunderland; and *office* Barring-Street, South Shields.

**CHAPMAN-ANDREWS, Sir Edwin Arthur,** KCMG, OBE. British diplomat. *B.* 9 Sept. 1903. *Educ.* University College, London (BA, Fellow 1952); University of Paris; Sorbonne; St. John's College, Cambridge (Oriental Languages). *M.* 1931, Sadie Barbara Nixon. *S.* David, John. *Daus.* Charlotte, Harriet. *Career:* Levant Consular Service 1926; Vice-Consul. Port Said, Cairo, Suez 1928, Addis Ababa 1929; Foreign Office 1931; Kirkuk (Iraq) and Rowanduz (Iraq) 1932–34; Acting Consul, Harar (Ethiopia) 1934–36; Foreign Office 1936–37; Assistant Oriental Secretary (1st Secretary), British Embassy, Cairo 1937–39; Royal Sussex Regt., Political Liaison Officer to H.I.M. The Emperor Haile Selassie 1940–42; Foreign Office 1942–46; Inspector, Foreign Service Establishments abroad 1946–47; H.M. Minister, British Embassy, Cairo Oct. 1947–June 1951; En. Ex. and Min. Plen. to the Lebanon June 1951–52 (Ambassador since Oct. 1952); Amb. Ex. & Plen. to the Sudan 1956–61; retired Apr. 1961. Director: Massey-Ferguson (Export) Ltd., and of other companies. *Member:* College Cttee., Univ. College, London; Cncl.: London Chamber of Commerce; Royal Albert Hall; Anglo-Arab Assoc.; Lord Kitchener National Memorial Fund. *Awards:* Order of Star of Ethiopia; K. St. J.; Kt. St. Gregory the Great (Papal). *Clubs:* Athenaeum, Oriental. *Address:* 2 The Leys, Brim Hill, London N2 0HE.

**CHARARA, Mohamed.** Saudian Diplomat. *B.* 1924. *Educ.* Farouk Univ., Alexandria—LLB; Univ. of Rome. *M.* 1953, Anna Ruscisce. *S.* 1. *Career:* Ministry of Foreign Affairs, Jeddah 1949–51; Attaché & Sec., Saudi Arabian Legation, Rome 1951–58; Counsellor, Embassy of Saudi Arabia, Tokyo 1958–61; Chargé d'Affaires a.i., Embassy of Saudi Arabia, Tokyo 1958–60; nominated Plenipotentiary Minister 1963, & Ambassador 1964; Chief of Western Section, Min. of Foreign Affairs, Jeddah 1961–65; Mem., Saudi Delegation to UN Sessions of 1955, '57, '60, & Saudi Delegation to Non Alignment Conference, Belgrade 1961 & Cairo 1964; Ambassador Ex. & Plen., Perm. Delegate to European H.Q. of UN & specialized Organisations in Geneva, 1965–72; Amb. Ex. & Plen. to Belgium since 1972; Amb. & Head of Saudi Mission to the EEC since 1973; Pres. of Saudi Delegation to Economic Cooperation Conference of Developing Countries of Group 77, Mexico 1976. *Decorations:* Decoration of King Abdulaziz, 1972 (Saudi Arabia); Grand Officer de l'Ordre de Leopold II, 1976 (Belgium). *Clubs:* Islamic & Cultural Center, Brussels (Pres.); Club Euro-Arabe, Brussels (Pres.); International Club, Geneva; Royal Golf Club, Belgium; Cercle Royal Gaulois, Belgium; Cercle des Nations, Belgium. *Address:* 69 avenue F. Roosevelt, 1050 Brussels; and *office* 45 avenue F. Roosevelt, 1050 Brussels, Belgium.

**CHARLES, George J,** Lt.-Col. USAFR. Attorney and Counsellor-at-Law. *B.* Canada. *Educ.* Univ. of Pennsylvania (BA Hons.) and George Washington Univ. Law School (Juris Doctor with Hons.). *M.* Helen Clara Chigges. *S.* James. *Daus.* Deborah, Mary, and Constance. *Career:* Served with U.S.A.A.F. in World War II, in Africa, Italy, and Germany (Decorated Bronze Star, Army Commendation Medal, Occupation Medal, and Victory Medal); Gold Cross, George I of Greece. Press and Information Officer, Royal Greek Embassy, Washington, D.C. 1950–57; Press Aide to King and Queen of Greece on Royal Tour of U.S. 1953; Attorney & Counsellor-at-Law Washington since 1953. Pres., Bd. of Trustees, Saint Sophia Cathedral 1963–64–65–66–67–68. *Member:* District of Columbia and Maryland Bars; Admitted before the U.S. Supreme Court. Greek Orthodox Arch-diocesan Council; Archon of Ecumenical Patriarchate; American and District of Columbia Bar Assns.; Phi Delta Phi; Amer. Legion. *Clubs:* National Lawyers', Athenaeum (Past Pres.) (Washington), Bethesda Country. *Address:* 7604 Carter Court, Bethesda 34, Md.; and *office* Suite 318, 1250 Connecticut Avenue N.W., Washington, D.C., U.S.A.

**CHARPENTIER, Fulgence,** MBE. *B.* 1897. *Educ.* Terrebonne College, Joliette College, and Laval University (BA); also Law School, Osgoode Hall, Toronto. *M.* (1) 1921, Florence Gagnon, (2) 1934, Louise Dionne. *S.* Georges, Pierre, Jean, Jacques. *Daus.* Claire, Louise. *Career:* Editor, Le Droit, Ottawa 1922–24; Parl. Corres., La Presse 1924–26; Sec. to Secretary of State 1926–30; Alderman, City of Ottawa 1928–29; Controller 1930–34; Chief, Votes and Proceedings, House of Commons 1935–39; Chief Press Censor 1939–44; Dir. of Censorship 1944–46; 1st Sec. Dept. External Affairs 1947; Press and Cultural Attaché, Canadian Embassy, Paris 1948–53; Chargé d'Affaires, Embassy, Montevideo 1953–56; Secretariat, E.C.O.S.O.C., London 1946; Canadian Adviser U.N. General Assembly, Paris 1948; Delegate U.N.E.S.C.O. Confce., Paris, 1949, and Gen. Assembly, U.N. 1950 and 1952, Paris; delegate U.N.E.S.C.O. 8th General Conf., Montevideo; appointed Chargé d'Affaires, Montevideo, Uruguay March 1953, Rio de Janeiro 1956–57; Port au Prince 1957–60.

Canadian Ambassador, Yaoundé (Cameroun); Gabon (Libreville); Congo (Brazzaville); Chad (Fort-Lamy); Central African Republic (Bangui) 1962; Retired from the Civil Service 1966; Pres. Alliance Francaise, Bailli national Chaine des Rôtisseurs, editorialist Le Droit; Assistant to Commissioner General, 1967 World Exhibition, Montreal, May 1966—. *Awards:* Order of the British Empire (M.B.E.), holds King's Coronation Medal; Canada Centennial Medal and foreign decorations. *Publications:* Contributions on historical, literary and economic subjects to La Presse, Le Devoir, Le Soleil, London Times, etc. *Address:* 42 Southern Drive, Ottawa, Canada.

**CHARPENTIER, Pierre J. E.** Canadian Diplomat. *B.* 1925. *Educ.* Univ of Montreal—LL.L (Law); Oxford Univ.—MA. *M.* 1952, Marion Tantot. *S.* 1. *Daus.* 2. *Career:* Ambassador to Peru & Bolivia 1970–73; Head of Latin American Division, Dept. of External Affairs, Ottawa 1973–76; Ambassador to Algeria since 1976. *Member:* Rhodes Scholars Soc.; Chaine des Rôtisseurs, Paris; Chevaliers du Tastevin, Beune, France; Quebec Bar. *Address:* Canadian Embassy, P.O. Box 225, Alger Gare, Algiers, Algeria.

**CHARRIN, Paul J. D.** American consultant. *B.* 1901. *Educ.* University of Paris (BA, S, LLB) and Paris School of Mines (MS). *M.* 1935, Gilberte Denise Moullière. *S.* Jack R. and Pierre H. *Dau.* Monique. *Career:* Eng.-Geophy. to Gen. Manager-Operations, Société de Prospection Électrique, Paris 1926–36; Vice-Pres., Schlumberger Well Surveying Corp., Houston 1936–45; Pres. Universal Exploration Co., Houston 1945–49; Pres. Pan Geo Atlas Corp., Houston 1946–65 (Chmn. of the Board 1966–68). Special Consultant to the Petroleum & Mining Group, Dresser Industries, Inc. 1968–70. *Publications:* Les Méthodes Géophysiques et les Recherches Minières (with Prof. Geoffroy 1933); Radiation Logging and its Applications in the Oil Fields (with J. H. Russell 1962); many technical articles. *Member:* Amer. Assn. of Petroleum Geologists; Socy. of Exploration Geophysicists; Amer. Inst. of Mining and Metallurgical Engineers; Assn. Française des Techniciens du Pétrole; Sté. des Ingénieurs Civils de France. *Decoration:* Chevalier, Ordre National du Merite (France). *Clubs:* Houston; Warwick; L'Alliance Française de Houston. *Address:* 11902 Cobblestone Drive, Houston, Tex. 77024; and *office* Suite 419, 3130 Southwest Freeway, Houston, Tex. 77098, U.S.A.

**CHASE, John Peirce.** American. *B.* 1906. *Educ.* Milton (Mass.) Academy; Phillips-Exeter (NH) Academy; Harvard (AB *magna cum laude* 1928); Hon. DComSc (Suffolk Univ.). *M.* Gisele Parenty. *S.* George Wigglesworth, John Peirce, Jr., Willard Parenty. *Daus.* Barbara Harwood, Anna Lanier, Sarah Flynn, Laura Dennison Crocker, Louise Elizabeth (Campbell). *Career:* Research analyst. Lee Higginson Co., Boston, Mass, 1928; Head, research and statistical dept., Lee Higginson Trust Co. 1929–32; Pres. 1932–58, Treas. 1932–76, Dir. 1932, John P. Chase Inc. investment council, now Phoenix Investment Counsel of Boston, Inc., Chmn. Bd. 1959—; Dir. Treas. Robert B. Brigham Hospital 1932 and 1948; Assoc. Admin. Dir., National Defense Research Cttee., Office of Scientific Res. and Development, serving overseas with the assimilated rank of Colonel 1944–45; Trustee, Member Exec. Cttee. Consolidated Investment Trust 1947—; Chmn. Bd. Trustees Shareholders' Trust of Boston 1948—; Chmn. Bd. Trustees, The Chase Fund of Boston 1958—; Treas. and Member Exec. Committee & Dir., Center for Blood Research, Inc. (formerly Protein Foundation, Inc.) 1972—; Trustees of Reservations, Member of Corporation 1964—; Suffolk Franklin Savings Bank, Incorporator 1938—; Chairman of Board and Director: Income and Capital Shares Inc., 1966—; Chmn. Bd. Dirs. Chase Frontier Capital Fund of Boston 1968—; Chmn. of Bd. & Dir., Chase Special Fund of Boston Inc., 1969—. Director: Continental Investment Corp., 1969; Vice-President and Director Community Broadcasting of Boston Inc. 1969—; Dir. & Chmn. of Exec. Cttee., Technicare Corp. 1960 & 1971 (formerly Boston Capital Corp.); Chmn. Bd. Dirs. Chase Convertible Fund of Boston Inc. since 1971. Chairman, Adv. Council, Coll. of Business Admin. 1967—, and Trustee, Suffolk Univ. 1965—; Woods Hole Oceanographic Inst., Member of Corp. 1960—. Trustee 1966–74, 1975—, Chmn. of Finance & Retirement Cttees. 1975—; Director and Member of Executive Committee, Japan Fund, 1962—; Dir., Asia Management Corp. 1974—; Affiliated Hospitals Center, Inc.: Trustee Member Finance Cttee. & Development Cttee. 1975—; Member of Corp., Massachusetts General Hospital 1947—. *Award:* Purple Heart and President's Certificate of Merit. Independent Republican. *Clubs:* Harvard (Boston); The Country; Dedham Country and Polo; Owl; Boston Madison Square Garden (Gov. and Secy. 1929—); Harvard Varsity (Treas. 1939—). *Address:* The Chase Building, 535 Boylston Street, Boston, Mass. 02116, U.S.A.

**CHASE, Morris.** American Certified public Accountant and Economist. *B.* 1918. *Educ.* College of the City of New York (BBA); Univ. of Paris. *M.* 1942, Claire Perintz. *Daus.* Sylvia and Viviane. *Career:* Deputy Controller, U.S. Marshall Plan Mission to France 1949; Controller & Acting Finance Officer, U.S. Special Tech. & Economic Aid Missions to Vietnam, Cambodia and Laos 1950; Controller, U.S. Economic Aid Mission to Yugoslavia 1951; Int. Economist, Office of U.S.; Rep. to European Regional Organizations, Paris 1952–54; Assistant to International Board of Auditors for NATO (Infra) 1954–56; Chairman, International Board of Auditors for NATO Infrastructure Accounts June 1957–60 (Controller, 1961); U.S. Member of the Board Nov. 1956; Chairman, NATO Payments and Progress Cttee. 1961–68, and Head NATO Infrastructure (Defense Installations) Directorate. Consultant to NADGECO (NATO Air Defense Ground Environment Co.) and NATO Satellite Communications Consortium since 1969. *Member:* Amer. Inst. of Certified Public Accountants; Beta Gamma Sigma. *Address:* N.A.T.O., Evere, Brussels, Belgium.

**CHASE, W. Howard.** International management consultant. *B.* 1910. *Educ.* Iowa State College; State University of Iowa (Sanxey Prize Winner); attended London School of Economics and Harvard University; Phi Beta Kappa. *M.* 1935, Elizabeth Coykendall. *S.* Thomas. *Daus.* Anne and Alison. *Career:* Housing Dir., Iowa State Planning Bd. 1933–34; Instructor, International Relations, Harvard and Radcliffe 1934–36; Guest Prof., Drake Univ. 1936–38; editorial writer, Register and Tribune, Des Moines 1936–38; Asst. to Pres., Amer. Retail Fed., Washington 1938–40; editor, Whaley Eaton letters 1941; Dir. of Public Services, General Mills, Minneapolis 1941–45; Dir. of Public Relations, General Foods 1945–52; Partner, Selvage, Lee & Chase 1952–55; Vice-President and General Executive, McCann-Erickson Inc. 1955–59; President Communications Counsellors Inc. 1955–59; Chairman, Howard Chase Associates Inc., and Chairman of the Council for The Management of Change Inc. Corp. 1964—; Vice President, Public Affairs and Asst. Chmn. American Can Company since 1971; Prof., Univ. of Connecticut 1975—; Publisher, *Corporate Public Issues* 1976—. Adviser to State Department of San Francisco U.N. Conf. 1945; Exec. Chmn., Minnesota U.N. Cttee. Elected by U.S. Junior Chamber of Commerce as one of ten outstanding men of 1943; founding member, Grocery Manufacturers of America P.R. Advisory Cttee.; First Chmn., Joint ANA-4A Cttee. on Better Understanding of our Economic System 1946–47; Chmn. of Advertising and Selling Gold Medal Advertising Awards Cttee. 1948; founding member of P.R.S.A. (served as its first Exec. Cttee. Chmn. 1948; Chmn. of its 1949 Annual Awards Committee; awarded citation in public relations by P.R.S.A.). Consultant to Secretary of Commerce in organizing National Production Authority 1950; Asst. to Director, Office of Defense Mobilization 1951; Chmn. for Convention Arrangements, Special Events for National Citizens for Eisenhower 1952; Pres., P.R.S.A. 1956. Former Trustee of Wellesley College, Sarah Lawrence College, and of Town Hall, N.Y. Hon.PhD (Econ.) Dong Guk University, Seoul, Korea, 1968; Election of Bd. Amer. Arthritis Foundation 1971. *Member:* Policy Cttee., Chamber of Comm. of the U.S. Exec. Reserve, USIA; Amer. Academy of Asian Studies (Trustee); Mannes Coll. of Music; Commission on Survey of Dentistry of American Council on Education; member, Advisory Cncl. U.S. National Insts. of Health; Cncl. on Foreign Relations; British Institute of Public Relations (Overseas Associate); International Public Relations Council; Canadian Public Relations Society. *Clubs:* Harvard (N.Y.C.); Metropolitan (Washington, D.C.). *Address:* 333 Mayapple Road, North Stamford, Conn., U.S.A.

**CHASTON, Col. Alfred John,** OBE, MC, CStJ, TD. DL. British company director and engineer. *B.* 1916. *Educ.* Monmouth School. *M.* 1940, Syvil Eveline Byers. *S.* 2. *Daus.* 2. *Career:* Joined Austin Motor Co. 1932 and family business 1936; joined 2nd Bn. Monmouth Regt. T.A. 1936, served with this Bn. throughout World War II; Commanded 1950–53 (M.C. Europe 1944; T.D. 1946); O.B.E. 1954; appointed D.L. 1954; C. St. J. 1968. Man. Director: Howell's Group Garages Ltd., Cardiff since 1965. Appointed Chmn. Wales TAVR Assoc. 1975. *Address:* Tynewydd, St. Brides-super-Ely, Glamorgan, Wales.

**CHATAWAY, Rt. Hon. Christopher John,** PC. *B.* 1931. *Educ.* Sherborne School, Magdalen Coll., Oxford. Hon.

Degree PPE. *M.* 1959, Anna Lett. *S.* 2. *Dau* 1. *Career:* Member, Parliament (Con.) Chichester 1969–74. Alderman GLC 1967–70; Minister, Posts and Telecommunications 1970–72; Minister, Industrial Development 1972–74; Man. Dir., Orion Bank Ltd.; Dir., Fisons; British Electric Traction Co.; Allied Investments; Dorchester Hotel Ltd. *Address:* 40 Addison Road, London W14.

**CHATILLON, Claude Charles Edouard.** Canadian Diplomat. *B.* 1917. *Educ.* Univ. of Ottawa—BA, BPH, LPH. *M.* 1948, Simone Boutin. *S.* 1. *Daus.* 2. *Career:* Vice-Consul, New York 1946; 2nd Sec., New Delhi, Feb. 1950; Asst. Chief of Protocol, Ottawa, March 1950; 2nd Sec., Paris 1953; 1st Sec., Paris 1955; Nat. Defence Coll., Kingston, Ontario 1956; Direction de l'Information, Ottawa 1957; Consul, Seattle 1959; Consul, Boston 1962; Counsellor, Madrid & Rabat 1965; Directeur de la Politique consulaire, Ottawa 1972; Ambassador to Cameroon, Chad & the Central African Empire since 1975. *Member:* Association des Anciens de l'Université d'Ottawa; Association du Royal 22ème Régiment. *Clubs:* Rockcliffe Tennis Club (Ottawa); Golf Club de Yaoundé. *Address:* B.P. 572, Yaoundé, United Republic of Cameroon.

**CHATT, Prof. Joseph,** Hon. DSc (East Anglia). British professor of Chemistry. *B.* 1914. *Educ.* Emmanuel Coll., Cambridge. *M.* 1947, Ethel Williams. *S.* Joseph. *Dau.* Elizabeth Mary. *Career:* Research Chemist, Woolwich Arsenal 1941–42; Deputy Chief Chemist, later Chief Chemist, Peter Spence & Son Ltd., Widnes 1942–46; I.C.I. Research Fellow, Imperial Coll., London 1946–47; Head of Inorganic Chemistry Dept., Butterwick, later Akers Research Laboratories, I.C.I. Ltd. 1947–60; Heavy Organic Chemicals Div., I.C.I. 1960–62; Dir. Unit of Nitrogen Fixation, Agricultural Research Council since 1963; Professor of Chemistry, Univ. of Sussex since 1965. *Publications:* research papers in scientific journals, mainly in the Journal of the Chemical Society. *Member:* Royal Society; Chemical Society; American Chemical Society; Royal Inst. of Chemistry. *Address:* 28 Tongdean Avenue, Hove, Sussex BN3 6TN; and *office* Unit of Nitrogen Fixation, Univ. of Sussex, Brighton, East Sussex BN1 9QJ.

**CHATTERJEE, Dwarka Nath.** Indian diplomat. *B.* 1914. *Educ.* Calcutta Univ. (BA 1st Cl. Hons. History), King's Coll., London (until entry into the Indian Military Acad. on declaration of war); Staff Coll., Quetta 1945. *M.* (1) 1940, Hon. Geeta Sinha (dau. of Lord Sinha), and (2) 1950, Odette Leonie Brausch (Grand Duchy of Luxembourg). *S.* 1. *Daus.* 5. *Career:* Major, Royal Indian Artillery (various staff appointments and regimental command) 1946–48. Joined Indian Foreign Service 1948; First Secy., Embassy, Paris 1948–49; P.P.S., High Commission of India, London Aug. 1949–May 1954; Dep. Secy. Min. of External Affairs in 1954–55; Dep. High Commissioner, Karachi 1955–58; Consul General Geneva May 1958–Jan. 1959; Minister, Washington 1959–62 Ambassador in Leopoldville 1962–65. High Commr. for India in Canberra 1965–67; Acting High Commr. for India in the U.K. 1967–68; Deputy High Commr. for India in the U.K. 1968–69; Ambassador to France since 1969. Member, Indian Council of World Affairs, New Delhi. *Clubs:* Calcutta. *Address:* Embassy of India, 15 Rue Alfred Dehodencq, Paris 16e, France.

**CHAUVEL, Jean.** French diplomat. Grand Croix, Lég. d'Honneur. GCVO, GCMG. *B.* 16 April 1897. *M.* Mdlle. de Warzée d'Hermalle. *S.* 2. *Daus.* 2. *Career:* Entered diplomatic service 1921; served at Peking (1924–27), Beirut, Paris and Vienna (1936–38); resigned 1942 and went underground: became representative for Foreign Affairs, in occupied France, of the French Committee of National Liberation; escaped to Algiers and appointed Sec.-General, Commissariat for Foreign Affairs, a post which he retained on the return of the French Provisional Government to Paris; promoted Ambassador and became, in 1949, permanent French representative at U.N., New York; Ambassador to Berne (1952) and played a prominent part at the Geneva Conf. (June–July 1954); later Amb. to Vienna, Amb. Ex. and Plen. to the Court of St. James's 1955–62; Ministère des Affaires Etrangères, Paris. *Address:* 123 rue de la Tour, Paris XVIa, France.

**CHAVANON, Christian,** D. en D. *B.* 1913. *Educ.* Docteur en Droit. *M.* 1941 Marguerite Enselme. *S.* Yves. *Dau.* Anne. *Career:* Advocate of the Court and later Master of Claims. Council of State; Secrétaire Général à l'Information then Directeur Général de la Radio-diffusion Télévision Française. Président du Comité de la concurrence au Commissariat Général du Plan. Président Honoraire de la Confédération de la Publicité Française. Président Honneur de l'Agence Havas; Pres. de la section des finances du Conseil d'Etat 1973; Adminstrateur Délégué de la Cie. Luxembourgeoise de Télédiffusion (RTL) 1975. *Publications:* Essai sur la nature et le régime juridique des services publics industriels et commerciaux (1939); Les fonctionnaires et la fonction publique (1950); le fait publicitaire et les valeurs etablies (1967); various articles and notes; delivered a course of lectures on the conduct of public affairs under various regimes at the National School of Administration, et Cours de droit public économique à l'Institut d'Etudes Politiques de Paris. *Address:* 18 Boulevard Maillot, Neuilly-sur-Seine (Seine), France.

**CHAVEZ, Dr. Juan R.** President of the Senate of Paraguay. *Address:* Office of the President of the Senate, Congress Building, Asuncion, Paraguay.

**CHEATHAM, John McGee.** American textile manufacturer. *B.* 1913. *Educ.* Darlington Schools and Furman Univ. *M.* 1939, Elizabeth Mathis. *S.* John M. Jr.; Harvey M.; Jackson K. *Daus.* Elizabeth M. *Career:* Past Pres., Amer. Cotton Manufacturers Institute Inc., Member, Trustee, Georgia Baptist Foundation Inc. Trainee, Rushton Cotton Mills 1933–36; Junior Salesman, Woodward, Baldwin & Co., N.Y.C. 1936–37; Asst. to Pres., Dundee Mills Inc. 1937–42 (Vice-Pres. 1942–43); Junior Officer, U.S. Navy 1944–46; Vice-Pres., Dundee Mills Inc. 1946–50, Pres. 1950; Pres. & Treas. The Hartwell Mills; Rushton Cotton Mills Div.; Dir. Trust Co. of Atlanta, Ga. *Member:* Kappa Alpha Order: New York Southern Society. *Clubs:* Griffin Rotary; Griffin Elks; Satilla River; Capital City. *Address: office* Dundee Mills Inc., Griffin, Ga., U.S.A.

**CHECCHI, Vincent V.** American. *B.* 1918. *Educ.* Univ. of Maine (AB); George Washington Univ. (MA); Harvard Univ. *M.* 1941, Mary Elizabeth Pate. *S.* Vincent. *Daus.* Mary Jane, Dina (Davis). *Career:* Statistician-economist, WPB, 1941–45; Dep. Dir. Requirements Branch, Allied Military Govt. in Italy, 1945–46; Program co-ordination UNRRA Italy, then Asst. to Chief of Mission in China, 1946–47; loan officer, IBRD, 1947; Dir. China Economic Branch, later Dir. East-West Branch, ECA, 1947–49; spl. representative in Philippines, ECA, 1950–51; Economic Editor, Reporter Magazine, 1951. President and Chairman of the Board, Checchi and Co. 1951—; Director: Trans-Philippines Investment Corp., Investment Development Corp., Checchi-Pacific Corp., 1960—, and Nelson Associates Inc. since 1962. *Publication:* Honduras: A Problem in Economic Development (1959) (co-author). *Address: office* 1730 Rhode Island Avenue, N.W., Washington, D.C. 20037, U.S.A.

**CHEGWIDDEN, Sir Thomas (Sidney),** CB, CVO, MA (Oxon). British. *B.* 1895. *Educ.* Plymouth College; Maidstone Grammar School; Worcester College, Oxford (Math. Scholar); RMA Woolwich. *M.* (1) 1919, Kathleen Muriel Breeds. *Dau.* 1. (2) 1934, Beryl Sinclair Nicholson. *Career:* Past President: Association of Rhodesian and Nyasaland Industries; Life Patron, Rhodesian College of Music. Fellow, Rhodesian Institute of Management. Entered Min. of Labour, London 1919; Asst. Private Sec. to several Ministers of Labour; Principal Private Sec. to Mr. Oliver Stanley and Mr. Ernest Brown; Under-Sec. Min. of Supply 1941–42, and Min. of Production 1942–46; Civilian Director of Studies, Imperial Defence Coll. 1946–47; Chairman, Public Services Board, S. Rhodesia 1947–53, and Interim Federal Public Service Commission, Fed. of Rhodesia & Nyasaland 1953–55. Chevalier, Legion of Honour 1956. *Publication:* The Employment Exchange Service of Great Britain (with G. Myrddin Evans). *Address:* Barclays Bank International Ltd., Oceanic House, Cockspur Street, London SW1Y 5BG.

**CHELLI, Zouhir,** Tunisian diplomat. *B.* 1930. *Educ.* Sadiki and Sousse Colleges (Tunisia) & Univ. of London. *M.* 1954, Lilia Tounsi. *S.* 2. *Dau.* 1. *Career:* Chief of Division, Ministry of Foreign Affairs 1956–60; Chief of Cabinet of the Secretary of State and Information 1958; Deputy Permanent Representative of Tunis at the Security Council and U.N.O., New York 1960–62. Ambassador of Tunisia to Switzerland, May 1962, and concurrently to Austria, Nov. 1965. Permanent Representative of Tunis at the European office of U.N.O. at Geneva 1962–66; Amb. to Spain 1967–70; Advisor to Min. of Foreign Affairs, Tunis 1970–72; Amb. to Syria 1973–74, to Iraq 1974–76, to Czechoslovakia since 1976. *Address:* c/o Ministry of Foreign Affairs, Tunis, Tunisia.

**CHEN, Chih-Mai.** Ambassador of the Republic of China. *B.* 1908. *Educ.* Tsing Hua Coll., Peiping, China; Ohio State

Univ. (AB 1928); Columbia Univ. (PhD 1933). *Career:* Prof. of History and Government, National Tsing Hua Univ. Peiping 1933–37; Senior Secretary, Executive Yuan (Cabinet) 1938–44; Counsellor, Washington 1944–50 (Minister 1950–55); Ambassador to: the Philippines 1955–59; Australia 1959–66: Japan 1966–69; the Holy See since 1969. *Address:* Chinese Embassy, Via Tolmino, 31, Rome 00198, Italy.

**CHEN, Chih-ping.** Chinese. National Policy Adviser to the President of the Republic of China. *B.* 1907. *Educ.* National Central Univ., Nanking, BA 1927; China Academy Hon. LLD and Mexican Academy of International Law, Hon. LLD. *M.* Lilleo Jungchieh Wong. *S.* Shih-piao, Shih-ven, Shih-yu, Shih-ta, Shih-hsiung, Shih-tso. *Career:* Chief Political Dept. of Hanchow Public Safety Bureau, 1928; Deputy Chief Pol. Dept., East Route Army Headquarters, 1928–29; Professor, National Honan Univ., 1930–33; Dean, Shanghai Police Training Academy, 1933–35; Councillor, National Military Council, 1934–43; Director, South-West Transportation Administration, Singapore, 1937–38; Dir. Gen. China-Burma, Transportation Admin. Rangoon, Burma, 1938–42; concur. Rep. of Exec. Yuan, Burma 1940–42; Chief Representative, China Supplies, China-Burma India Theatres, Calcutta, 1942–43; Consul General, Republic of China to India 1943–46; First Minister, to the Philippines, 1946–49; Member, Pres. Chiang's Entourage to the Baguio Conference 1949; First Ambassador to the Philippines, 1949–54; to Iraq 1956–58; to Jordan, 1957–59; to the Arab Union, 1958; to Libya, 1959–65; Ambassador to Mexico 1965–71; Delegate to Sessions of the General Assembly of U.N. 1965, 67, 68, 69, 70 and 71; National Policy Adviser since 1972. *Member:* Central Adv. Cttee. Kuomintang. *Publications:* 'The Arabs Yesterday and Today' (English and Chinese). *Awards:* Order of Victory (China); First Class Order of the Star (Jordan); Grand Cordon, Order of Propitious Clouds (China); Special Grand Cordon, Order of Brilliant Star (China); First Class Order of Sikatuna (Philippine Civil); First Class Order of Rafidain (Iraqui Civil); Order of King Faisal of Iraq (Iraq); First Class Order of Independence (Libya) and many others. Member of the Central Advisory Cttee., Kuomintang, 1969. *Address:* Ministry of Foreign Affairs, Taipei, Taiwan Republic of China.

**CHENEY, Reynolds Smith.** *B.* 1910. *Educ.* Millsaps Coll., Jackson (BA) and Jackson Schl. of Law (LLB). *M.* 1934, Winifred Tunstall Green. *S.* Reynolds S. II (Rev.) and William Garner. *Dau.* Winifred Calhoon (Barron). *Career:* Lieut. U.S.N.R. 1943–52. Partner in law firm of Green, Cheney Jones, Hughes, McKibben & Stack, of Jackson, Miss; Director, Mississippi Cottonseed Products Co., Jackson 1961—; The Merchants Co. since 1971; Chancellor of Diocese of Mississippi, 1966—. Member of Standing Cttee. of Episcopal Diocese of Mississippi 1948–65. Founder and Trustee of St. Andrew's Episcopal Day Sch. 1947–56 and 1961–69. Deputy to General Convention of Episcopal Church in U.S.A. 1958–61–64–67–69–70–73–76. Bd. of Directors, Jackson Y.M.C.A. 1938–58; Dir. 1953–59, Pres. 1958, Family Service Assn.; Bd. of Governors, Jackson Symphony Orchestra Assn. 1951–54. Fellow, American College of Probate Counsel. *Member:* Mississippi Cttee. Newcomen Society in North America; Knight Commander of Kappa Alpha Order. Omicron Delta Kappa; Sigma Delta Kappa; American Judicature Society; American, Mississippi State and Hinds Country Bar Association. *Club:* Capital City, Petroleum, Jackson (Charter Member). *Address:* 800 Electric Building, Jackson, Miss., U.S.A.

**CHEYSSON, Claude.** French politician. *B.* 1920. *Educ:* Graduated from Ecole Polytech. and Ecol nationale d'administration, Paris. *M.* 1969, Daniele Schwarz. *S.* 3. *Dau.* 2. *Career:* Tank Officer in Free French Forces 1943–45; Liaison Officer to German authorities, Bonn 1948–52; Political adviser of Prime Minister of Viet Nam, Saigon 1952–53; Personal adviser of French Prime Minister, Paris 1954–55; Personal Adviser of French Minister for Morocco, Tunisia and Paris 1956, Secy.-Gen. of Commission for Technical co-op. in Africa 1957–62; Dir.-Gen. of Sahara Authority, Algiers 1962-66; Ambassador of France in Djakarta (Indonesia) 1966–69; Pres. of Entreprise miniére et chimique, Paris 1970–73; European Commissioner for development (Brussels) since 1973. *Member:* Board of Le Monde (daily) Paris, since 1969. Dr. Soc. Sc. (h.c.) Univ. of Louvain. *Decorations:* Officer, French Leg. of Honour; French War Cross (5 citations); Grand Officer of National orders of Cameroun, Lebanon, Niger, Chad, Togo, Tunisia, Upper Volta; Commander of National Orders of Centrafrican Rep., Indonesia and Mali. *Address:* 200 rue de la Loi, Brussels 1040, Belgium and (home) 15 av. de la Faisanderie, Brussels 1050, Belgium.

**CHIANG YUN-TIEN.** Chinese professor and statesman. *B.* 1904. *Educ.* Cheng Chi University, Shanghai (BA). *M.* 1931, Daisy Young. *S.* 5. *Daus.* 6. *Career:* University Professor 1936–45; Chief Editor of Renaissance Weekly 1938–40; member of Standing Committee, Democratic League 1945–46; Delegate to the People's Assembly 1946–47; Minister without portfolio, National Government 1947–48; member of Standing Committee and Director of Organisation Department, Democratic Socialist Party 1949–52; Minister without portfolio 1950–54; High Adviser to President since 1954; Consultant to H.R.A.F. China Project, Stanford Univ., U.S.A. 1955; Research at Harvard 1958; Lecturer in U.S.A. 1964–66. Vice-Chmn., Democratic Socialist Party. Member, Assn. for Asian Studies, U.S.A. *Publications:* Socialism and Democracy; The New Analysis of Political Theory; Political Ideal and Practice 1963; War against Slavery, 1965; My View of International Problems, 1966. *Address:* House 15, Lane 58, 1st Section, South New Life Road, Taipei, R.O.C.

**CHICHESTER-CLARK, Sir Robert,** BA. British management consultant and company director. *B.* 1928. *Educ.* Royal Naval Coll.; Magdalene Coll., Cambridge. *M.* (1) 1953, Jane Helen Goddard (Diss.). *S.* 1. *Daus.* 2. (2) 1974, Caroline Bull. *S.* 2. *Career:* Member, Parliament Londonderry 1955–74; Parly. Private Secy., Financial Secy. Treasury 1958; Asst. Whip, Lord Commissioner, The Treasury 1958–61; Comptroller, Royal Household 1961–64; Opposition Spokesman, Public Building & Works, The Arts & Northern Ireland 1964–70; Minister of State, Dept. of Employment 1972–74. Hon. Fellow, Inst. Works Managers. *Club:* Carlton. *Address:* Carlton Club, St. James Street, London, S.W.1.

**CHILD, Arthur James Edward,** MA, BCom, FCIS. Canadian. *B.* 1910. *Educ.* Queen's, Toronto, Laval and Harvard Univs. *M.* 1955, Mary Gordon. *Career:* Until 1960 Vice-Pres. and Dir. Canada Packers Ltd.; until April 1966 Pres. and Dir. Intercontinental Packers Ltd.; Pres. and Chief Executive Officer Burns Foods Ltd.; Pres., Canadian Dressed Meats Ltd., Ajex Investments Ltd., Jamat Inc.; Chairman: Scott National Co. Ltd., Palm Dairies Ltd., Burns Meats Ltd.; Vice-Chmn., Canbra Foods Ltd.; *Director:* Dominion Bridge Co. Ltd.; LaVerendrye Management Corp. Ltd.; Allendale Mutual Insurance Co.; Stafford Foods Ltd.; Alberta Gas Trunk Line Co. Ltd.; Alberta Gas Chemicals Ltd.; Revelstoke Companies Ltd.; Montreal Trust Co.; Newsco Investments Ltd.; Canada Life Assurance Co.; WAGI International S.p.A.; Quebecair Ltd.; Canoe Cove MFG Ltd.; Grove Value & Regulator Co.; Intnl. Inst. Pres. of Internal Auditors 1948–49; Treasurer and Dir. Canadian Authors Assn. 1950–52; Chmn., Canada West Foundation; Dir. Canadian Life Assurance Co. *Publications:* Economics and Politics in U.S. Banking; Internal Control; Contributor to professional journals. *Clubs:* University, Royal Canadian Yacht; Royal Canadian Military Institute (Toronto); St. James's (Montreal); Vancouver (Vancouver); Golf & Country (Calgary); Harvard (Boston); Ranchman's. *Address:* 1320 Baldwin Cres. S.W., Calgary, Alberta, T2P 2M7, Canada.

**CHILDS, James H., Jr.** American shoe sales executive. *B.* 1913. *Educ.* College BA; Graduate, Yale. *M.* 1941, Elizabeth D. Littell. *S.* Walton. *Dau.* Helen A. *Career:* Treasurer, H. Childs & Co. 1945–48. Pres. & Dir., Childs Corporation, Keystone Shoe Stores Inc., Fort Pitt Shoe Stores Inc., and Southern Shoe Stores Inc.; Director, Volume Footwear Retailers Association. *Member:* Young Presidents' Organizations. *Clubs:* Duquesne; Allegheny Country; H-Y-P. *Address:* 217 Edgeworth Lane, Sewickley, Pa.; and *office* 2406 Woodmere Drive, Pittsburgh, Pennsylvania 15205, U.S.A.

**CHILDS, John F.** American financial analyst. *B.* 1909. *Educ.* Trinity College, Hartford, Conn. (BS 1931; MS 1932); Harvard Business School (MBA 1933); Fordham Law School (LLB 1946). *M.* 1950, Mary E. Cardozo. *Dau.* Susan E. *Career:* Member of the New York Bar. Before World War II, he was for five years financial analyst with an investment banking firm. During the war he served at sea and in the air as Lieutenant-Commander, U.S.N.R.; with Irving Trust 1945–74, became Sen. Vice-Pres. Irving Trust. He is well known in financial and corporate circles as the originator and conductor of the Irving Trust seminars on financial policy for top executives of utility, industrial, retailing and banking corporations; Vice-Pres. Kidder Peabody and Co. Inc. (N.Y.). Past Dir., American Management Assoc.; The Atomic Industrial Forum 1967–70; Past Dir. Florida Power Corp. Lecturer, Trustee, The Lenox (girls') School 1961–65, New York. *Publications:* Long-Term Financing (Prentice-Hall Inc.

1961); Profit Goals and Capital Management (Prentice-Hall 1968); Navy Gun Crew (for children); A Practical; Introduction to Public Utility Analysis; Earnings Per Share and Management Decisions (1971). Encyclopaedia of Long Term Financing and Capital Management (1976). *Clubs:* Pine Valley Golf. *Address:* 15 Washington Place, New York City 30 and *office* c/o Kidder Peabody & Co., 10 Hanover Square, New York City 10005, U.S.A.

**CHILDS, Thomas Warren,** CBE. American financier overseas projects. *B.* 1906. *Educ.* Princeton Univ. (BSc Eng. *summa cum laude* 1928), Oxford Univ. (Rhodes Scholar; BCL, MA, BA 1928–31), and Yale Univ. (JSD 1932). *M.* 1934, Isabel Lockward. *S.* Thomas W., Jr., Henry C. and William A. P. *Career:* Practised law with Sullican & Cromwell, N.Y.C. 1932–40 (in Paris 1937–38). General Counsel to British Supply Council in North Amer., and Exec. Asst. to the Minister resident in the U.S. 1940–45. With Lazard Fréres 1945–48; China Industries; American Metal Climax Inc., N.Y.C. 1948–62. Chairman, International Nickel Ltd., London. Vice-Pres., International Nickel Co. of Canada 1963–68; Chmn., International Nickel Projects Ltd. Bermuda since 1969. Dir. Bank of N.T. Butterfield and Sons Ltd. (Bermuda); Schroders (Bermuda) Ltd.; Aegis Indemnity Ltd. (Bermuda) since 1971. Republican. *Member:* Pilgrim English-Speaking Union. *Clubs:* Brooks's (London); Royal Bermuda Yacht. *Address:* Stancombe, Paget West, Bermuda; and *office* P.O. Box 1560, Hamilton, Bermuda.

**CHILES, Harrell Edmond.** American petroleum engineer. *B.* 1910. *Educ.* Wentworth Military Academy, Lexington, Mo. and University of Oklahoma (BS in Petroleum Engineering 1934). *M.* (1) 1935. *S.* Jerry Edmonds. *Dau.* Carol Ann. (2) 1974, Frances Hafer. *Career:* Engineer, Reed Roller Bit Co., Houston, Texas 1934–39; organized The Western Co. April 1939; President, The Western Co., Fort Worth, Texas, April 1939— (Mr. Chiles is the president and Chairman—oil well servicing— which has grown from three employees to approx. 2000 employees, operating in Texas, Oklahoma, Kanas, New Mexico, Colorado, Wyoming; Presidents' Professional Association, New York 1961—; Advisory Committee, YMCA, City of Fort Worth 1961—; Chief Executives Forum, New York 1961—; Civil Service Commission, Fort Worth 1961—; Chamber of Commerce, Fort Worth. Named 'Engineer of the Year', Permian Basin Chapter, Texas Socy. Prof. Engineers 1953; Pres., Young Presidents' Organization, N.Y. 1954–55; Dir., American Management Assn. 1954–57; Director, Fort Worth Chamber of Commerce, 1970. Sigma Tau (hon. engineering fraternity), Pi Epsilon Tau (eng. frat.), Sigma Iota Epsilon (prof. management), and Sigma Alpha Epsilon (social); Engineer of the Year, Fort Worth Chapter, Texas Socy. of Prof. Engineers 1976. *Clubs:* Shady Oaks C.C., Fort Worth (Fort Worth); Pine Valley C.C. (Clementon, N.J.); Bel Air (Calif.) C.C.; Paradise Valley C.C. (Phoenix, Ariz.). *Address:* 1300 Shady Oaks Lane, Fort Worth 76107; and *office* P.O. Box 186, Fort Worth, Tex. 76101, U.S.A.

**CHIN, Peel Shik.** Korean diplomat. Ambassador to Federal Republic of Germany. *B.* 14 Nov. 1923. *Educ.* Seoul National Univ. Political Science, BA. *M.* 1949, Duke Kyung Lee. *S.* Byung Jik; Byung Kyu. *Daus.* Yeon, Hi,; Jean. *Career:* Vice Consul San Francisco, U.S.A., 1952–54; Consul, Korean Consulate Gen. Los Angeles 1954–55; Chief Asian Section, Political Affairs Bureau Foreign Ministry, Seoul 1955–57; Counsellor, Korean Diplomatic Mission Tokyo 1957–60; Dir. Economic Bureau, Foreign Min. Seoul 1960–61; Political Affairs Bureau, Min. Foreign Affairs 1962–63; Perm. Rep. International Organizations in Europe, Geneva, Switzerland 1963–64; Consul Gen. Hong Kong 1965–66; Ambassador, Republic of Chile 1966–67; Deputy Min. Foreign Min. Seoul 1967–69; Ambassador to Canada 1970–74; Ambassador to Federal Republic of Germany since 1974. *Member:* Political Science Assn.; Assn. of International Law Korea. *Awards:* Order, Distinguished Diplomatic Service (Korea); Distinguished Service Cross (Peru); Distinguished Service Cross (Ethiopia); Distinguished Service (Thailand); Distinguished Service Cross (Tunisia). *Publications:* Essay on American Policy on China during 1945–49. *Address:* Adenaueralle 124, Bonn, Federal Republic of Germany.

**CHIOMENTI, Pasquale.** Italian advocate. *B.* 1914. *Educ.* Univ. of Rome (LLD). *M.* Donata Vassalli. *S.* Filippo, Carlo. *Career:* Chairman, Italcable S.p.A.; Société Financière pour les Telecommunications et l'Ectronique SA; Metra Industria S.p.A.; Vice-Chmn., SIRTI, S.p.A.; Dir. IFI Instituto Finanziario Industriale S.p.A.; STET Society Finanziaria Telefonica p.A.; Fiat, S.p.A. *Address:* Viale Bruno Buozzi 98, Rome, Italy.

**CHIPP, Donald Leslie,** MP. *B.* 1925. *Educ.* BCom. *M.* 1951, Monica Teresa Lalor. *S.* Gregory Shane and John Leslie. *Daus.* Deborah Marilyn and Melissa Maree. *Career:* Accountant, Raleigh Engineer Co. Pty. Ltd. 1949–59; State Registrar, Australian Society of Accountants 1947–54; Private Accountancy Practice; Chief Executive Officer, Olympic Civic Committee, 1954–56; Director, Victoria Promotion Committee. Minister of State for the Navy and Minister in Charge of Tourist Activities 1967–68. (Federal Parliament of Australia; representing Hotham Dec. 1960–77; Liberal). Minister for Customs and Excise, 1969–72; Governing Director, Donald L. Chipp & Co. Pty. Ltd., management consultants: Minister Assisting, Minister National Development and Dep. Leader 1971; Leader, House of Reps. Aug–Nov. 1972; Shadow minister for Social Services 1972–75; Minister for Health, Minister for Social Security, Minister for Repatriation & Compensation in the Caretaker Govt. Nov.–Dec. 1975; resigned from Liberal Party & founded new political party, Australian Democrats, March 1977; elected to Senate, Dec. 1977. *Address:* 60 Bluff Road, Black Rock, Vic., Australia.

**CHIRAC, Jacques.** French politician. *B.* 1932. *Educ.* Ecole Nationale d'Adminstration. *Career:* Head of Dept., Secr.-Gen. of Govt. 1962; Head of Dept., Private Office of M. Pompidou 1962–65; Counsellor, Cour des Comptes 1965–67; Sec. of State for Employment Problems 1967–68; Sec. of State for Economy & Finance 1968–71; Minister for Parl. Relations 1971–72, for Agriculture & Rural Development 1972–74, of the Interior 1974; Prime Minister 1974–76. Sec.-Gen., Union des Démocrates pour la République 1975–76; Pres., Rassemblement des Francais pour la République since 1976; Mayor of Paris since 1977. *Address:* 57 Rue Boissière, Paris 16e, France.

**CHISHOLM, Sir Henry,** CBE, MA, FCA. British company director. *B.* 1900. *Educ.* Westminster School (Scholar); Christ Church, Oxford (Scholar). *M.* (1) 1925, Eve Hyde-Thomson. *S.* 1. (2) 1940, Audrey Hughes (née Lamb). *S.* 2. (3) 1956, Margaret Grace Crofton-Atkins (née Brantom). *Career:* Manager, Paris Office, Barton Mayhew & Co., Chartered Accountants 1927–32; Partner, Chisholm, Hanke & Co., Financial Consultants, London 1932–38; Overseas Mills Liaison Officer, Bowater Group 1938–44; Director, Bowater-Lloyd (Newfoundland) Ltd., London 1940–44; member and Chairman of Departmental Committees on Organization of Naval Supply Services, Admiralty 1942–45; Director and Financial Controller, The Metal Box Co. Ltd. 1945–46; Joint Managing Director, A. C. Cossor Ltd. 1947–60; Chmn., Cossor (Canada) Ltd. 1948–60; Corby Development Corp. (New Town) 1950–56; Ada (Halifax) Ltd. 1961–73; Member Monopolies Commission 1966–69. Chmn. Whitley Council for New Towns, Staffs, 1962–75. Mem. Advisory Council, Industrial States Ltd., Nova Scotia 1968–75; Director Philips Electronic Holdings Ltd. *Address:* Scotts Grove House, Chobham, Woking, Surrey.

**CHISHOLM, John Richard Harrison.** British. Editor & Examiner in Gemmology (ret'd Solicitor). *B.* 1905. *Educ.* Westminster School and Christ Church Oxford (BA 1929; MA 1943); FGA 1950. *M.* Marie-Louise Garduit. *S.* 3. *Career:* Solicitor 1932–74; Asst. Secy., Equity & Law Life Assurance Society 1940–44; Solicitor, 1945–69; Director: Union Cinemas Subsidiary Properties Ltd. 1938–41; Middlesex Brick Co. Ltd. 1940–41 (Joint Receiver 1941–47); London & District Cinemas Ltd. 1943–47; London & Coastal Oil Wharves Ltd. (alternate) 1947–50; Guildhall Property Co. Ltd. 1946–63; Guildhall Development Co. Ltd. 1946–63; Freehold Building & Land Development Co. Ltd. and Equity & Estate Investment Ltd. 1963–69; Retired from practice as Solicitor 1974. Examiner, Gemmological Association of Great Britain 1955—. Editor, The Journal of Gemmology since 1973. *Publications:* Articles in The Journal of Gemmology. *Member:* Law Society; Life Assurance Legal Society (past Chairman), Justice. *Clubs:* Elstree Aero; Elstree Flying. *Address:* Highfield House, Theobald Street, Radlett, Herts WD7 7LT.

**CHLIAPNIKOV, Guerman E.** Soviet Diplomat. *B.* 1929. *Educ.* State Foreign Affairs Institute, Moscow and Foreign Ministry's College for Diplomats. *M.* Zaira M. Chliapnikova. *S.* 1. *Dau.* 1. *Career:* Joined USSR Foreign Ministry, 1952; Diplomatic posts in the People's Republic of China, People's Republic of Mongolia, New Zealand, Republic of Bolivia and the Foreign Ministry; Soviet Ambassador to Ecuador since 1975. *Awards:* Decorations from the Governments of the USSR, People's Republic of Mongolia and the Republic of Bolivia. *Address:* Embassy of the Union of Soviet Socialist Republics, Calle Reina Victoria 462 y Roca, Quito, Ecuador.

**CHODRON DE COURCEL, Geoffroy,** GCVO, MC. *B.* 1912. *Educ.* Stanislas College, Paris; Univ. degrees: Docteur en Droit, Licencié ès Lettres, Diplômé de l'Ecole des Sciences Politiques. *M.* 1954, Martine Hallade. *S.* Jean and Antoine. *Career:* Attaché, Warsaw 1937–38; Secretary, Athens 1938–39; Army of the Levant 1939; joined Free French Forces June 1940; Chief, Cabinet of General de Gaulle (London) 1940–41; Captain, 1st Spahis Marocains in Egypt, Libya and Tunisia 1941–43; Deputy Director, Cabinet of General de Gaulle, Algiers 1943–44; member, Council of the Order of the Liberation 1944; Regional Commissioner of the French Republic in the Liberated Territories 1944, and afterwards in charge of Alsace and Lorraine at the Ministry of the Interior; Counsellor 1946; Deputy Director, Central and North European Sections, Ministry of Foreign Affairs 1945–47; First Counsellor, Rome 1947–50, Minister Plenipotentiary 1951; Director, Bilateral Trade Agreements Section, Ministry of Foreign Affairs 1951–53; Director of African and Middle East Affairs, Ministry of Foreign Affairs 1953–54; Director-General, Political and Economic Affairs, Ministry of Moroccan and Tunisian Affairs 1954; Permanent Secretary to National Defence 1955–58; Ambassador, Permanent Representative at NATO 1958; Secretary-General, Presidence of the Republic 1959–62. Ambassador of France to the Court of St. James's 1962–72. Ambassador of France 1965; Secy. Gen. Ministry, Foreign Affairs 1973–76. *Awards:* Grand Officer, Legion of Honour; Companion of the Liberation; Croix de Guerre (1939–45); Military Cross. *Address:* 7 rue de Medicis, 75006 Paris, France.

**CHOI, Duk-Shin.** *B.* 1914. *Educ.* Central Military Academy, China; U.S. Army General School and Infantry School. *M.* Mi Ryung Ryu. *S.* 2. *Daus.* 3. *Career:* At age of 7 exiled with parents to China 1921; joined Chinese army and fought throughout the war in China-Burma-India theatre, and later joined the U.S. General Stilwell's forces in Burma and fought from Ledo (India) to Lashio (Burma) 1937–45; after V-J day, participated in receiving the surrender of Japanese army in Canton 1945; returned to Korea as 2nd Lieut. in the Korean army 1946; promoted to Lieut.-General and retired April 1956; commanded regiment, brigade, division and army corps; Korean army representative in UNCHQ and at the Panmunjon talks 1953; walked out on May 25, 1953, when U.N.C. gave up hope over the P.O.W. issue; member, Korean delegation at 7th Special and 8th U.N. General Assemblies Aug.–Nov. 1953; visited Free China as military member of President Rhee's party Nov. 1953; accompanied the President to U.S. as Deputy Chief of Staff for planning and research in respect of R.O.K. army, July 1954; made frequent visits to S.E. Asian countries 1953–54; established diplomatic relations with Vietnam 1955. First Korean Ambassador to Vietnam Apr. 1956–Sept. 1961; Chief, Korean deleg. to 14th Conf. of ECAFE, Kuala Lumpur March 1958; member, Korean delegation to 13th U.N. Gen. Assembly Sept. 1958. First Korean non-resident envoy to Thailand Feb. 1959; For. Minister 1961–63; led deleg. to 1961 and 1962 sessions of U.N. Gen. Assembly; resigned as Ministry of Foreign Affairs and accredited Ambassador to Bonn 1963–67; Governor of the Republic of Korea in International Atomic Energy Agency in Wien 1965–67. April 1967 elected Supreme Leader of Korean Chondo-gyo Church, the only religion native to Korea. *Publications:* Memoir of Anti-Japanese war in China-India-Burma theatre (in Korean); Secret Records of Panmunjon Truce Talks (in Korean) (Chinese translation completed; English translation pending); Japan Inside Out by Dr. Syngman Rhee (trans. from English to Korean). *Address:* Ministry of Foreign Affairs, Seoul, Korea.

**CHOISY, Eric.** Swiss. *B.* 1897. *Educ.* Engineer (Doctorate *honoris causa*). *M.* 1924, Alix Necker. *S.* 1. *Daus.* 2. *Career:* Pres. Geneva Industrial Services 1941. Chairman: Swiss Assn. of Engineers and Architects 1949. President, S.A. Grande Dixence 1950—. Deputy of the Council of States 1963-71. The European Atomic Forum 1963, and Federal Commission for Hydraulic and Power Economy 1964. Pres., Industrial Council, Polytechnic School of Lausanne 1965. Hon. Pres., European Federation of National Associations of Engineers (FEANI). Pres., World Federation of Engineering Organizations. Liberal. *Club:* Rotary. *Address:* Satigny, near Geneva, Switzerland; and *office* Grande Dixence S.A., Sion (Valais), Switzerland.

**CHONA, Hon. M. Mainza,** SC, MP. Zambian politician, diplomat and lawyer *B.* 1930. *Educ.* Chona Out School, Monze; Chikuni Mission, Chisekesi; Munali Training Centre, Lusaka; Grays Inn, London. *M.* 1953, Yolanta Chimbamu Chona. *S.* 2. *Daus.* 5. *Career:* Minister of Justice 1964; Min. of Home Affairs 1964–66; Min. of Presidential Affairs 1966–67; Min. without Portfolio 1967–69; Min. for Central Province 1969; Min. without Portfolio 1969; Min. of Provincial & Local Government 1969; Amb. to USA 1969–70; Vice-Pres. of the Republic 1970–73; Prime Minister 1973–75; Min. of Legal Affairs and Attorney-General 1975; Prime Minister for second time since July 1977. *Member:* Law Assoc. of Zambia; Int'l. African Law Assoc. *Awards:* Margaret Wrong Medal for Novel, 1956; Dignity of State Counsel (equivalent of QC), 1975. *Publication:* Kabuca Uleta Tunji. *Address:* 362 Independence Avenue, Lusaka, Zambia.

**CHOPRA, Surendranath.** Indian diplomat. *B.* 1916. *Educ.* MA; BSc (Hons.). *M.* 1940, Kamla Sarin. *Daus.* 3. *Career:* Consul-General for India in Madagascar 1955–58; Director, Indian Ministry of External Affairs 1961–65; High Commissioner in New Zealand 1965. *Address:* c/o Ministry of External Affairs, New Dehli, India.

**CHOUDHURY, Humayun Rasheed.** Bengali Diplomat. *B.* 1928. *Educ.* Aligarh Univ., India—BSc; London Inst. of World Affairs—Diploma in International Affairs; Fletcher Sch. of Law & Diplomacy, Cambridge, Mass.—MA & Graduate Certificate of Honour. *M.* 1947, Mehjabeen Banoo. *S.* 1. *Dau.* 1. *Career:* Pakistan Foreign Service: 3rd Sec., Rome 1955–59, Baghdad 1959–61; 3rd, 2nd, then 1st Sec., Paris 1961–64; Dir., Pakistan Ministry of Foreign Affairs, Islamabad 1964–67; Chargé d'Affaires, Embassy of Pakistan, Lisbon 1967–69, & Djakarta 1969–71; joined Bangladesh Liberation Movement & appointed Chief of Mission, New Delhi 1971–72; first Bangladesh Ambassador Ex. & Plen. to Federal Republic of Germany, Austria, Switzerland & Holy See & Perm. Rep. to International Atomic Energy Agency & UN Industrial Development Org. 1972–76; first Bangladesh Ambassador Ex. & Plen. to Kingdom of Saudi Arabia, concurrently to Sultanate of Oman, Hashemite Kingdom of Jordan, & Perm. Rep. to the Organisation of Islamic Conference since 1976. *Member:* Inner Temple, London; Fletcher School Alumni; Vice-Pres., Foreign Service Assoc. of Bangladesh. *Publications:* Several articles on various aspects of International Diplomacy & on Bangladesh. *Clubs:* Golfe Club do Estoril (Portugal); Senayon Club of Djakarta (Indonesia). *Address:* Embassy of Bangladesh, P.O. Box 6215, Jeddah, Saudi Arabia.

**CHOW SHU-KAI.** *B.* 1913. *Educ.* National Univ., Nanking and Univ. of London. *Career:* Attaché Chinese Embassy London 1941–43; Vice-Consul Manchester, England 1944–45; Secy. to Minister, Ministry of Foreign Affairs (MFA) 1946–47; Visiting Prof. of International Relations, Univ. of Nanking 1946–47; Dep. Dir., Information Dept. MFA 1947–49; Counsellor of Embassy, Philippines 1950–52 (Minister and Chargé d'Affaires 1953–55); Chief Delegate; U.N. Economic Commission for Asia and Far East 1953, and Pacific Regional Conf. ICAO 1953; Vice Minister MFA 1956–60; Chmn. of Overseas Chinese Affairs 1960–62; Special Envoy, Independence Celebrations: Madagascar 1960, and Malta 1964; Representative to U.N. Gen. Assembly 1961–64. Ambassador to Spain 1963–65; Ambassador to U.S.A. 1965–71; Minister, Foreign Affairs of the Republic of China 1971–72; Minister without portfolio, Exec. Yuan since 1972. *Address:* Executive Yuan (Cabinet), Republic of China, Taipei, Taiwan.

**CHOWDHURY, Justice Abu Sayeed,** Hon. DL. Bangalese diplomat, politician and jurist. *B.* 1921. *Educ.* Calcutta Univ.; Lincoln's Inn, Barrister-at-Law. *M.* 1948, Begum Khurshid. *S.* 2. *Dau.* 1. *Career:* Advocate-General (former East Pakistan) 1960–61; Judge Dacca High Court 1961–72; Chmn., Central Board development Bengali 1963–68; Vice-Chancellor, Dacca and Judge, Dacca High Court 1969–72; Chancellor, Univs. Dacca, Rajshahi and Chittagong 1972–73; President, Peoples' Republic of Bangladesh 1972–73; Special Rep. of Govt. Bangladesh with cabinet rank since 1973; Gen.-Secy. Presidency Coll. Union 1941–42; Pres., Brit. branch All India Muslim Students' Federation 1946. *Award:* Deshikottama (Indian degree). *Clubs:* Royal Overseas League; Royal C'wealth. Soc.; Rotary (Dacca). *Address:* Rosendale, 103 Mymensingh Rd., Dacca, Bangladesh; and *office* Bangladesh Mission, 7 Rue Veyrassat, Geneva, Switzerland.

**CHRISTENSEN, Hans Peter.** Danish technical doctor. *B.* 1886. *Educ.* Danish Naval College and the Technical High School, Charlottenburg (Naval Architect and Marine Engineer). *M.* 1916, Karen Sofie Jensen. *S.* Jørgen. *Career:* Naval Architect, Royal Dockyard 1911 (Sub-Manager 1917–19); Managing Director, Nakskov Shipyard 1919–25: Managing Director, Helsingør Shipyard and Engine Works 1925–63; Chairman of the following: Former (Pres.), Board of Directors, Danish Steelworks. Past member, Board of Dirs., Danish Air Lines; Past member, Board of Dirs., Danish National Bank; Former Vice-Pres., Danish Atomic Energy Commission; Past Pres., Academy of Technical Science (Dr. techn. h.c. 1954); Past President, Federation of Danish Industry; Danish Committee of Lloyd's Register of Shipping. *Awards:* Kt., Order of St. Olav (Norway); Grand Cross (Denmark) Grand Cross, Crown of Rumania; Order of the White Rose (Finland); Cmdr., Order of North Star (Sweden); Officer, Legion of Honour (France). Awarded the Tietgen Prize 1959. *Publications:* Several papers on aerodynamics, shipbuilding, marine engineering and economy. *Address:* Strandvei 42, 3000 Helsingor, Denmark.

**CHRISTENSEN, Jens.** Danish Diplomat. *B.* 1921. *Educ.* Univ. of Copenhagen—M.Pol.Sc. *M.* 1950, Tove Jessen. *S.* 1. *Daus.* 2. *Career:* Entered Danish Foreign Service 1945; OECD Delegation, Paris 1949–52; NATO Delegation, Paris, 1952; Chargé d'Affaires a.i. & Counsellor of Legation, Vienna 1957–60; Asst. Head, Economic-Political Dept., Ministry of Foreign Affairs 1960–61; Dep. Under-Sec. 1961–64; Under-Sec. & Head of the Economic-Political Dept. 1964–71; Head of the Secretariat for European Integration 1966–72; Ambassador Ex. & Plen. 1967; Sec. of State for Foreign Economic Affairs 1971–77; Ambassador of Denmark to the UK since 1977. *Decorations:* Commander (first class), Order of the Dannebrog; Knight Grand Cross: Order of the Icelandic Falcon, Norwegian Order of St. Olav, Swedish Order of the Northern Star; & others. *Address:* 2 Hans Street, London SW1; & *office* Danish Embassy, 55 Sloane Street, London SW1X 9SR.

**CHRISTESEN, Clement Byrne,** OBE, DLitt, FAHA. *B.* 1911. *Educ.* King's College, Univ. of Queensland. *M.* 1942, Nina Maximoff. *Career:* Literary critic, poet, short story writer, painter, radio and television commentator; editor (and founder, 1940) of the Australian literary journal Meanjin Quarterly. Lockie Fellow, Univ. of Melbourne, Vice-Pres. Australian Society of Authors, Fellowship of Aust. Writers, P.E.N. (Melb. Centre). Member U.N.E.S.C.O. Arts Committee; represented Australian, U.K., U.S.A. and U.S.S.R. verse and short story anthologies; FAHA. *Awards:* Australian Literature Socy. gold medal; Britannica Aust. Award for Humanities; D.Litt. *Publications:* Australian Heritage (1949); Coast to Coast (1954); On Native Grounds (1968); The Gallery on Eastern Hill (1970); The Hand of Memory (1971). *Address:* Stanhope House, Eltham, Victoria, Australia.

**CHRISTIANI, Alex(ander) Oldenburg.** Danish. *B.* 1910. *Educ.* Univ. of Copenhagen (BSc) and Cambridge (MSc). *M.* 1969, Hanne Germark. *Career:* Engineer with Rendel Palmer & Tritton, London 1937–38; Chief Engineer, French Christiani & Nielsen S.A.F., Paris 1938–42, Pres. and Manager 1942–45; Partner in Christiani & Nielsen, Copenhagen 1946–58; Managing Director of the company after its transformation into a limited company 1958—; Managing Director, Christiani & Nielsen A/S, Civil Engineers, Copenhagen. *Member:* Institution of Civil Engineers, London; Dansk Ingeniørforening, Copenhagen. *Club:* United Oxford & Cambridge (London). *Address:* Bernstorffsvej 33A, Copenhagen, Hellerup; and *office* Christiani & Nielsen A/S, 41 Vester Farimagsgade, Copenhagen V, Denmark.

**CHRISTIANSEN, Aksel.** Danish Diplomat. *Address:* Calle de Serrano 63, Madrid 6, Spain.

**CHRISTIANSON, Lloyd F.** American. *B.* 1914. *Educ.* Kansas Univ. (BS and Prof. Degs.). *M.* 1935, Sergie A. Danneberg. *S.* 3. *Dau.* 1. *Career:* Captain, U.S. Army Signal Corps 1942–46; Petroleum Engr., U.S. Dept. of the Interior, Bureau of Mines, Petroleum and Natural Gas Division, Petroleum Experimental Station, Bartlesville, Okla. 1935–42; President & Chief Executive Officer, Electronics Associates Inc., West Long Branch, N.J. 1945–70. Former Director: NJ National Corporation and its subsidiary, New Jersey National Bank, Trenton, N.J.; Dir., The Howard Savings Inst. (Board of Managers). Trustee, Monmouth College, W. Long Branch. *Member:* Fort Monmouth Adv. Cttee., Armed Forces Communications Assn.; New Jersey Council of Economic Development; Theta Tau. *Address:* 99 Rumson Road, N.J. 07760, U.S.A.

**CHRISTIE, Walter Henry John,** CSI, CIE, OBE. British Consultant development banking. *B.* 1905. *Educ.* Eton (King's Scholar) and King's College, Cambridge (MA). *M.* 1934, Elizabeth Louise Stapleton. S. David Campbell and Robert Douglas. *Daus.* Valentine Clare and Serena Louise. *Career:* In Indian Civil Service 1928–47; Joint Private Secretary to Viceroy of India 1947; Vice-Chmn., British India Corp. Ltd. 1952–59; Chairman, Upper India Chamber of Commerce 1956; Controller of Operations, Commonwealth Development Finance Co. Ltd. 1959–68; Adviser, East African Development Bank 1969–70. *Club:* East India & Sports (London). *Address:* 'Quarry Ridge', Oxted, Surrey.

**CHRISTIENSEN, Hans J.** Danish diplomat. *Address:* Staroscinska 5, Warsaw 12, Poland.

**CHRISTOFAS, Kenneth Cavendish,** CMG, MBE. British diplomat. *B.* 1917. *Educ.* Merchant Taylors' School and University Coll., London (BA & Fellow of the College). *M.* 1948, Jessica Laura Sparshott. *Daus.* 2. *Career:* War Service (Lieutenant-Colonel) 1939–45; Foreign Office and posts abroad (Rio de Janeiro, Rome, Brussels, Lagos) 1946–69; Minister and Deputy Head of UK Delegation to the European Communities 1969–72, Acting Head Mar.–Oct. 1971; Cabinet Office (on secondment) 1972–73; Dir.-Gen., Secretariat of the Council of Ministers of the European Communities, Brussels. *Member:* Royal Inst. of Int'l Affairs, London. *Awards:* Companion of the Most Distinguished Order of St. Michael & St. George; Member of the Most Excellent Order of the British Empire; Order of Polonia Restituta (Poland). *Clubs:* East India; Sports & Public Schools (London); Cercle Royal Gaulois (Brussels). *Address:* 3 The Ridge, Bolsover Road, Eastbourne, Sussex BN2O 7JE; and *office* Rue de la Loi 170, 1040 Brussels.

**CHRISTOFFERSEN, Torgeir.** Swedish. Knight of the Order of Vasa. *B.* 1915. *Educ.* BL, BCom. *M.* 1941, Ane-Margrethe Sörensen. *S.* Terje. *Dau.* Sigrun. *Career:* Man. Dir. Rederiaktiebolaget Svenska Lloyd, 1967–72; Chairman: Hoverlloyd Ltd., 1968–72. *Clubs:* Gothenburg Golf; Royal Gothenburg Yacht; Ashridge Golf. *Address:* The Beguine, Ashridge Golf Club Road, L. Gaddesden, Herts.

**CHRYSTAL, Albert Francis.** American steamship company executive. *B.* 1899. *Educ.* Columbia Univ. (AB 1923; LLB 1925). *M.* (1) 1935, Jean Perley (D.). *Dau.* Joan Margaret (D). (2) 1973, Dorothy Donovan. *Career:* Practised Law 1927–36; with Moore-McCormack Lines; Asst. Avc. 1936–55; Sec. 1955–61; Vice-Pres., 1944–64; Practising Law 1964—; Vice-President, Moore-McCormack Lines Inc. 1944–64 (Counsel 1944–64). *Member:* International Law Assn.; New York County Bar Assn.; New York State Bar Assn.; Martime Law Assn.; Y.M.C.A. (member Bd. of Managers Seamen's House). *Clubs:* Downtown Athletic (N.Y.C.); National Propeller. *Address:* 30 Sutton Place, New York City 10022.

**CHUKS-ADOPHY, Chief.** *B.* 1920. *Educ.* Govt. Training Coll. (Umuahia, Nigeria); King's Coll. (Lagos); Univ. of London (Inst. of World Affairs). *M.* 1961 Norma Audrey Coy. *S.* 1. *Daus.* 2. *Career:* In Nigerian Civil Service 1939–44; Freelance journalist for many years (regular contributor to the ZIK group of newspapers throughout Nigeria, e.g. West African Pilot, Eastern Nigeria Guardian, Nigerian Spokesman, the Comet under the late Duse Mohammed Ali) and later under the Zikpress Ltd., Eastern Nigerian Sentinel; occasional contributor to West African Review, West Africa, Nigerian Daily Times, Eastern Nigerian Advertiser, etc. *Publications:* What Africa Wants; Marriage: An International Problem; Three Wise Men of Eastern Nigeria, etc. (The World Digest). Degrees: FRSA 1948; FRGS 1949; FRAI (Anthropological) 1949; FREconS 1955. Secy.-Gen., African National & Cultural Bureau Cttee.; Cttee. member Movement for Colonial Freedom. *Member:* Inst. of World Affairs, Inst. of Journalists (London), Diplomatic Press Corps. Elected Life-Fellow of the Internat. Inst. of Arts & Letters (Switzerland) 1962. P.R.O. Eastern Nigeria Office, London 1956–63; Nigerian Federal Govt. Service 1963—. Press Secretary to the President of the Rep. of Nigeria 1963–66; Seconded Nigerian Foreign Service Oct. 1966. *Clubs:* several press clubs; Foundation Member, Vic-Lex Circle, Lagos; Ikoyi Club. *Address:* c/o Federal Ministry of Information, Ikoyi Rd., Lagos, Nigeria.

**CHUNG, Arthur.** President of the Republic of Guyana. *B.* 1918. *Educ.* Modern High School, Georgetown; Middle Temple, London. *M.* 1954, Doreen Pamela Ng-See-Quan. *S.* 1. *Dau.* 1. *Career:* Land Surveyor 1940; resident in UK 1946–48, Asst. Legal Examiner, UK Inland Revenue Dept. 1947; returned to Guyana 1948, Magistrate 1954, Senior Magistrate 1960; Registrar of Deeds of the Supreme Court 1961; Judge of the Supreme Court 1962–70; First Pres. of the Republic of Guyana, 1970, re-elected 1976. *Address:* Office of the President, Georgetown, Guyana.

**CHUNG, Il-Yung.** Korean Diplomat. *B.* 1926. *Educ.* Seoul National Univ. (BA); London School of Economics and Political Science; Univ. of Geneva (Dr. es sciences politiques (major in Internat. Law)). *M.* 1948, Jin Kang Seo. *Daus.* 3. *Career:* Asst. Professor, Law School, Seoul Nat. Univ. 1960–62. Expert, Korean Deleg. to Korea-Japan Overall Talks, Tokyo, 1960–61; Consultant to Foreign Minister, Seoul, 1961–62; Minister, Korean Embassy, Paris, 1962–63; Vice-Min., Foreign Affairs, Seoul, 1963–64; Ambassador, Chief of Korean Permanent Mission, Geneva, 1964–66; Ambassador to Switzerland 1966–71. *Publications:* Legal Problems Involved in the Corfu Channel Incident, (1959); Geneva; Interim Measures of Protection in the Practice of International Courts (1962); Seoul Law Journal; and a number of essays on International Law and Politics. *Address:* Ministry of Foreign Affairs, Seoul, Korea.

**CHUNG, Kyung Cho,** LLD, DLit. Korean scholar, Statesman, world traveller, writer, educator, linguist. *B.* 1921. *Educ.* Waseda University, Tokyo; Seoul National Univ.; Faculty of Political Science, Columbia Univ., N.Y.; Grad. School of Arts and Science, New York Univ.; Monterey Inst. of Foreign Studies. *Career:* Faculty Mem., U.S. Army Language School, 1951 (Supervisor, Korean Language Dept., 1958); Professor, Korean Language Dept., United States Defence Language Institute, 1965—; Faculty, Monterey Inst. of Foreign Studies, U.S.A. 1973–74; Hartnell College U.S.A. since 1974; Advisor, American-Korean Foundation, 1967; Hon. Professor, Kunkuk Univ., 1968; Director, Pan-Asian Foundation 1969; Treasurer, Dir., Korean Research Cncl., 1970—; Editor, Korean Research Bulletin, 1970—. *Publications:* Korea Tomorrow, (1957); New Korea, (1962); 'Seoul', (1964); Hankuk Naeil (1965); Sae Hankuk, (1969); Korea, The Third Republic (1971); Korean Unification (N.Y. Times) (1972). *Member:* American Association of University. Professors; American Academy of Political & Social Science; American Association of Asian Studies, American-Korean Foundation; Pan-Asia Foundation. *Address:* 25845 South Carmel Hills Drive, Route 3, Box 339, Carmel, Calif, 93921, U.S.A.; and *office* Presidio of Monterey, California, 93940, U.S.A.

**CHURCH, Ian Berkeley,** FCIB. British. *B.* 1927. *Educ.* Stowe Sch. *M.* 1956, Elizabeth Messel. *S.* 1. *Dau.* 1. *Career:* Vice-Chmn. & Dir. Church & Co. Ltd. later Chmn; Dir. Church & Co. (Canada) Ltd., Chandler Henderson Financial Services Ltd., Babers Ltd. (Jersey). *Clubs:* Bucks; Underwriting Mem. Lloyds. *Address:* 12 Cranley Mews, London, S.W.7; and *office* Church & Co. Ltd., St. James, Northampton NN5 5JB.

**CHURCHILL, Winston Spencer,** MP. British politician, author & journalist. *B.* 1940. *Educ.* Eton & Christ Church Coll., Oxford. *M.* 1964, Minnie d'Erlanger. *S.* 2. *Daus.* 2. *Career:* Correspondent Yemen, Congo & Angola 1963, Borneo & Vietnam 1966, Middle East War 1967, Democratic Convention in Chicago 1968, Czechoslovakia 1968, Nigeria & Middle East 1969; introduced daily BBC current affairs programe "This Time of Day" 1964–65; Roving correspondent for *The Times* 1969–70; Special correspondent for the *London Observer* in China 1972; Conservative MP for Stretford, Lancs. since 1970; Parly. Private Secy. to Min. of Housing 1970–73, to Min. of State at Foreign & Commonwealth Office 1973–74; Secy. of Conservative Party Foreign Affairs Cttee. 1974–76; Conservative Party Frontbench Spokesman on Defence since 1976. Hon. Fellow of Churchill Coll., Cambridge 1969; Gov., English-Speaking Union 1975; Trustee, Winston Churchill Memorial Trust 1968; Trustee, National Benevolent Fund for the Aged 1974. *Publications:* First Journey (1964); (with Randolph Churchill) The Six Day War (1967). *Clubs:* White's; Bucks; Foreign Affairs Club; St. James's Club, Manchester. *Address:* House of Commons, London SW1A 0AA.

**CHURCHMAN, John Wilfred.** Canadian civil servant. *B.* 1914. *Educ.* Saskatoon Normal School; University of Saskatchewan. *M.* 1941, Olive Violet Fredell. *S.* Gregory Lane. *Daus.* Jennifer Lea, Rhonda Claire. *Career:* Schoolteacher and principal 1934–41; served in World War II in R.C.A.F. 1942–45; Chief Clerk, Saskatchewan Civil Service 1946, Executive Assistant 1947; Assistant Deputy Minister, Saskatchewan Department of Natural Resources 1948–52; Deputy Minister 1953–65; Director, Saskatchewan Government Airways 1949–54. Saskatchewan Forest Products Corporation 1949–54, Saskatchewan Anti-Tuberculosis League 1950–65, 1976—; Saskatchewan Marketing Services 1952–54; Saskatchewan Fur Marketing Service 1958–62, 1972–74; Canadian Forestry Association Apr. 1958—; Member, South Saskatchewan River Development Commission 1958–65; Dir. of Development, Indian Affairs Branch, Dept. of Citizenship & Immigration, Ottawa 1965–66; Dir. of Indian Affairs, Dept. of Indian Affairs & Northern Development, Ottawa 1966–68; Dir. of Operations & Dir. of Community Affairs 1969–70; Dir. of Research & Liaison 1970–72; Dep. Minister, Dept. of Northern Saskatchewan 1972–74; Dir., North-Sask Electric 1972–74 (ret'd.). *Address:* 3418 25th Avenue, Regina, Sask., Canada.

**CIGRANG, Marcel Jean Pierre.** Belgian company director and shipowner. *B.* 1912. *Educ.* Latin High School; Higher Inst. of Commerce, Antwerp. *M.* 1949, Bertha Wilhelmina Parent. *Career:* Dir.: Ets. Cigrang Frères S.A.; Cie. Belge d'Affrètements Cobelfret N.V.; U.B.E.M., S.A. Exmar S.A. *Award:* Knight, Order of Maritime Merit (France); Chevalier, Ordre de Léopold II (Belgium), Officer Order of Oak Crown (Luxembourg); Officer of the Leopold Order. *Clubs:* Cercle Royal, La Concorde, Philotaxe, Royal Yacht (Belgium). *Address:* Mechelsesteenweg 150, B-2000 Antwerpen, Belgium.

**CIOFFARI, Vincenzo.** American. *B.* 1905. *Educ.* Cornell Univ. (AB 1927; AM 1928) and Columbia Univ. (PhD 1935). *M.* 1937, Angelina Grimaldi. *S.* Vincent Grimaldi. Assoc. Prof., State Univ. of Iowa 1943–44. *Career:* Lecturer, Hunter Coll. of City of New York 1938–42, 1945–46; Lecturer, Coll., of New Rochelle 1931–35. Special Consultant, Editorial Staff, U.S. Armed Forces Inst. 1943; Consultant, Joint Brazil-U.S. Commission, Rio de Janeiro 1945; Head, Modern Language Dept., D. C. Heath & Co. 1946–67. Professor Roman Languages, Boston University, 1967–71; President, Dante Society of America 1967–73 (Vice-Pres. 1963–67); National Chairman for Dante Centenary Celebrations in U.S.A. 1965—. *Publications:* Fortune and Fate from Democritus to St. Thomas Aquinas; The Conception of Fortune and Fate in the Works of Dante; Fourteenth Century Dante Commentators; Beginning Italian Grammar; Guido da Pesa's Commentary on Dante's Inferno; *Member:* Phi Beta Kappa; Phi Kappa Phi; Phi Sigma Iota. Recipient National Achievement Award of the Fed. of Modern Language Teachers Assn. ('Hall of Fame'); one of the first five recipients of a free trip to Italy (1934) as one of the best teachers of Italian. *Member:* Modern Language Assn.; Medieval Acad.; Linguistic Socy.; Dante Socy. of America; Scoietà Dantesca Italiana (Hon. Life Member); Amer. Assn. of Teachers of Italian; Amer. Assoc. of Univ. Professors (AAUP). *Clubs:* Harvard Faculty; Cornell (N.Y.C.). *Address:* 45 Amherst Road, Waban, Mass.; and *office* 718 Commonwealth Avenue, Boston, Mass., U.S.A.

**CITRINE, Lord,** of Wembley (created 1946) (Sir Walter McLennan Citrine, PC, GBE). *B.* 1887. *M.* 1913, Doris Helen Slade. *S.* 2. *Career:* Asst. Sec., Electrical Trades Union 1920–23; Asst. Sec. T.U.C. 1924–25; Gen. Sec., Trades Union Congress 1926–46; President, Int. Fed. of Trade Unions 1928–45; Director, later Vice-Chairman, *Daily Herald* 1929–46; Member of Royal Commission on W. Indies 1938; Trustee of Imperial Relations Trust, Lord Nuffield's Fund for the Forces 1939–46; Member of Treasury Consultative Council 1940–46; Chairman, Production Cttee. on Regional Boards (Munitions) 1942; Chairman, Miners' Welfare Commission 1946–47; Member of National Coal Board 1946–47; Chairman, Central Electricity Authority 1947–57; Part-time Member: Electricity Council 1958–62, and Atomic Energy Authority 1958–62 President, British Electrical Development Association 1948–52, and of Electrical Research Association 1950–52 and 1956–57; Companion of the Institution of Electrical Engineers; Pres. (1955) and Member of Directing Cttee., Union Internationale des Producteurs et Distributeurs d'Energie Electrique; Hon. LLD, Manchester. *Publications:* A.B.C. of Chairmanship; I Search for Truth in Russia; My Finnish Diary; My American Diary; The Trade Union Movement of Great Britain; British Trade Unions; Labour and the Community; Men and Work; Two Careers. *Address:* Gorse Cottage, Berry Head, Brixham, S. Devon.

**CIUTI, Corrado,** Cav. Gr. Croce of Merit, Repubblica Italiana, DSc. Italian. *B.* 1904. *M.* 1959, Margherita de'Vecchi. *Career:* Chmn. Acciaierie di Piombino, AIFO-Appl. Ind. FIAT-OM, SRM Hydromekanik AB; Hon. Chmn. F.I. Magneti Marelli; Board Mem. La Rimascente. *Clubs:* Rotary. *Address:* Via Cappuccio, 14 Milan, Italy; and *office* Via Guastalla 2, Milan.

**CLAGUE, Colonel Sir Douglas,** CBE, MC, QPM, CPM, TD, JP. British. *B.* 1917. *M.* 1947, Margaret Isolin Cowley. *S.* Jonathan David. *Daus.* Isolin Jane and Penelope Ann. *Career:* With Royal Artillery, World War II 1939–47. *Member:* Governor's Executive Council, Hongkong 1962–74; Chairman, Hutchison Group of Companies 1952—. Director,

Property, Commodity, Financial, Industrial and Commercial Companies. *Clubs:* Hongkong; Steward Hong Kong Jockey. *Address:* 26 Middle Gap Road, Hong Kong.

**CLANCY, Patrick Nevill**, MA. British. *B.* 1925. *Educ.* Blundell's School; Oxford Univ.; Harvard Business School, AMP. *M.* 1954, Geraldine Nicholas. *S.* 1. *Dau.* 1. *Career:* merchanting Manager Tootal Ltd. 1950–64; Man. Dir. Blackstaff Ltd. & Subsidiary Comp. 1964–67; Joint Man. Dir. Arthur Sanderson & Sons Ltd.; Man. Dir. Sanderson Fabrics; Chmn. B.S.T. Silks Ltd.; William E. Rees & Co. Ltd.; Dir. Dawes & Co. Ltd.; Man. Dir. Bradfield Brett Holdings Ltd.; Dir. Wall Paper Manufacturers Ltd. *Member:* Inst. of Directors. *Clubs:* R.A.C.; Harvard Business. *Address: office* Hundred Acres, Uxbridge, Middlesex.

**CLAPHAM, Sir Michael John Sinclair**, KBE (1973). British. *B.* 1912. *Educ.* Marlborough and King's College, Cambridge (MA). *M.* 1935, The Hon. Elisabeth Russell Rea. *S.* 3. *Dau.* 1. *Career:* Director Metals Div. 1945, Joint Managing Director 1952, and Chmn. Metals Div. I.C.I. Ltd. 1959–60; Director, I.C.I. (India) Private Ltd. 1961–68. Deputy Chairman: Imperial Chemical Industries Ltd. 1968–74, Imperial Chemical Industries of Australia and New Zealand Ltd. 1961–74; Lloyds Bank Ltd. since 1971, Deputy Chmn. 1974; Imperial Metal Industries Ltd. 1962–70, Chmn. 1974; Chmn. BPM Holdings since 1974; Grindlays Holdings Ltd. since 1975; Life Governor, Birmingham University 1955—. *Member:* Council for National Academic Awards 1964—, Chmn. 1971, Industrial Reorganization Corp. 1969–71; Court of London Univ. since 1969; Pres., Confederation of British Industry 1972–74; Vice-Pres. since 1974. *Publications:* Printing 1400–1730 (in The History of Technology) 1957; various articles on printing, personnel management and education; Multinational Enterprises and Nation States (1975). *Address:* 26 Hill Street, London, W.1.; and *office* c/o Lloyds Bank, 71 Lombard St., London EC3.

**CLAPP, Eugene Howard II.** American financier. *B.* 1913. *Educ.* Lafayette Coll. (BS). *M.* 1943, Maud Millicent Greenwell. *S.* Eugene H. III. *Dau.* Candace M. *Career:* With W. T. Grant Co. 1937–38; Penobscot Chemical Fibre Co. 1938 (Treas. 1946–50). Served in World War II (O.S.S.) 1942–46. President and Director Penobscot Capital Investment Co. 1946—; Penobscot Co. 1950–67; Pine Tree Land Co. since 1969; Dir. Fidelity Funds 1975; Treas. & Dir. King Spruce Co; Dir. La Primera Americana SA Compañia e Seguros; Roxbury Home for the Aged; Associated Industries of Massachusetts; American Mutual Liability Insurance Co.; Arkwright Boston Mfr. Mutual Insurance Co.; A.M. Life Insurance Co.; Republican. Vice-Chmn., Bd. of Trustees of Lafayette Coll.; Trustee, Newton Wellesley Hospital and Children's Hospital. *Clubs:* The Country; Ponte Vedra; Nantucket Yacht; Mayflower Socy. *Address:* 78 Arnold Road, Wellesley Hills, Mass.; and *office* 10 High Street, Boston, Mass. 02110. U.S.A.

**CLARIZIO, Most Rev. Emmanuel.** *B.* 1911. *Educ.* Licence in Philosophy and Theology, and Doctorate in Law. *Career:* Tit. Archibishop of Anzio, Pro-Pres. of Pontifical Commission Migrations and Tourism; Apostolic Inter. Nuncio, Pakistan; Nuncio, The Dominican Republic; Pro Nuncio in Canada. *Address:* Piazza S. Calisto, 16, Citta' del Vaticano.

**CLARK, Col. Charles Willoughby**, DSO, OBE, MC, DL. British. *B.* 1888. *Educ.* Atherstone Grammar School; apprentice engineer, Alfred Herbert Ltd. 1903. *S.* Charles Willoughby, LLB (Solicitor-at-Law, Notary Public). *Dau.* 1 (*b.* 1921; died as result of war service Nov. 1944). *Career:* Served in World War I in France (D.S.O., M.C.; twice mentioned in dispatches), World War II (O.B.E.); Chairman, Manufacturers' Section of the Machine Tool Trades Association for 10 years until 1957; Former, President, Alfred Herbert Ltd., Coventry 1966—, (Director 1934—). Chmn., Coventry Conservative Association 1945–48; Pres., Coventry Chamber of Commerce 1951–53; Fellow: Inst. of Directors and of Royal Commonwealth Socy.; member, Inst. of Export; Freeman and Liveryman of the City of London; Hon. President, Coventry Branch of the British Limbless Ex-Servicemen's Association 1951—; Deputy Lieut. Warwickshire 1965; Freemason (Past Master, London Warwickshire Lodge, London Rank). *Club:* Royal Automobile (London). *Address:* 41 Regency House, Newbold Terrace, Leamington Spa., Warwickshire.

**CLARK, Brig. Donald McGillivray**, QC. Canadian barrister and solicitor. *B.* 1915. *Educ.* Royal Military Coll. (Diploma of graduation); B.C. Law School. *M.* 1941, Joan Napier Ross. *S.* Donald Ross and Campbell McGillivray. *Dau.* Sally Joan. *Career:* Served in World War II (with Seaforth Highlanders of Canada in Italy, France and Holland, & on staff. Senior Partner in law firm of Clark, Wilson, & Co. (1700–1750 W. Pender Street, Vancouver, B.C.); Director and Vice-Pres.; Silver Standard Mines Ltd. (since 1948); Dir. and Sec., Bank of British Columbia; Trustee, BBC Realty Investors; Gov., Canadian Tax Foundation 1954–56, 1972–74; Dir., Vancouver Foundation, Children's Hospital. *Address:* 475 Howe Street, Vancouver 1, B.C., Canada.

**CLARK, Capt. Sir George Anthony**, Bt, DL. British. *B.* 1914. *Educ.* Canford, England. *M.* 1949, Nancy Catherine. *Dau.* of G. W. M. Clark of Co. Londonderry. *Dau.* Elizabeth Frances Catherine. *Career:* Commissioned (S.R.) The Black Watch 1939; Member, Senate of Northern Ireland Parliament 1951–69. *Clubs:* Bath (London). *Address:* Tullygirvan House, Ballygowan, Newtownards, Co. Down, Northern Ireland.

**CLARK, George Evans.** *B.* 1905. *Educ.* Princeton Univ. (BS). *M.* 1940, Margery Jarvis. *S.* George E., Jr. *Dau.* Margery Jarvis (Peters). *Career:* With Tri-Continental Corp., New York City 1930–37; Joined The Adams Express Co. 1937 (Treasurer 1939, Asst. to President 1940, Vice-Pres. 1941, Exec. Vice-Pres. 1943, President 1948–70, (retired) also Dir. and Chmn. of Board until 1970. President: American International Corp. 1948, Petroleum Corp. of American 1944, now Dir. *Clubs:* The Kittansett; Beverly Yacht; Sippican Tennis (Mass.); Princeton (New York City); Riomar Golf; Riomar Bay Yacht; John's Island Golf (all Fla.); Nassau (New Jersey). *Address:* 510 River Drive, Vero Beach, Florida, 32960; and 163 Allens Point Road, Marion, Mass., 02738.

**CLARK, George Roberts.** American. *B.* 1910. *Educ.* St. Paul's School, Concord, N.H.; Harvard College (BA 1932); Harvard Business School (MBA 1934). *M.* 1937, May D. Howe. *Career:* Was Exec. Vice-Pres., Corn Exchange National Bank & Trust Co. at time of merger—Jan. 1951—with Girard Trust Co. Vice-Chairman, Girard Trust Bank, Philadelphia, 1960–74 (also former director); Director, General Coal Co., Whitehall Cement Manufacturing Co., Westmoreland Coal Co.; Vice-Chmn. Bd. of Academy of Natural Sciences. *Address:* 519 Auburn Avenue, Chestnut Hill, Pa., U.S.A.; and *office* Nineteenth and the Parkway, Philadelphia, Penn. 19103, U.S.A.

**CLARK, Harry Edmund.** Canadian. *B* .1911. *Educ.* Dip. Com. *Career:* President, Overseas Chemicals Co. Ltd. Secretary-Treasurer, Consolidated Warehouses Corp. *Club:* Toastmasters (Pres. 1966–67); Montefior. *Address:* 3555 Cote des Neiges Road, Montreal; and *office* 2485 St. Patrick Street, Montreal, P.Q., H3K 1B3 Canada.

**CLARK, Sir John Allen.** British. *B.* 1926. *Educ.* Harrow. Cambridge. *M.* (1) 1952, Deirdre Kathleen (*diss.*) *S.* 1. *Dau.* 1. (2) Olivia Pratt. *S.* 2. *Dau.* 1. *Career:* Received early industrial training with Metropolitan Vickers and Ford Motor Co; spent over a year in U.S.A., studying the electronics industry. Served War of 1939–45; commissioned RNVR. Asst. to Gen. Manager, Plessey International Ltd., 1949; Dir. and Gen. Man. Plessey (Ireland) Ltd. and Wireless Telephone Co. Ltd., 1950; appointed to main board, The Plessey Co. Ltd. 1953; Gen. Man. Plessey Components Group 1957; Man. Dir. (1962–70) and Dep. Chm. (1967–70) The Plessey Co. Ltd.; Dir. ICI Ltd. 1968, & Banque Nationale de Paris 1976. Pres. Telecommunication Engineering and Manufacturing Assoc., 1964–68 and 1971–73; Vice President: Inst. of Works Managers; Engineering Employers' Fedn. Mem., Nat. Defence Industries Council. CompIEE; FIM. *Award:* Order of Henry the Navigator, Portugal 1973. *Clubs:* Bath. *Address:* The Plessey Co. Ltd., Millbank Tower, London SW1.

**CLARK, LeRoy Vincent.** American chemical engineer, explosives engineer and plant manager. *B.* 1902. *Educ.* Grove City (Pa.) College (BS Chem. Eng.); West Virginia Univ.; McGill Univ., and Univ. of Pittsburgh; Reg. Professional Eng. (Commonwealth of Pennsylvania). *M.* 1933, Winsome Nancy Robinson. *Daus.* Barbara Ann (Davis) and Sara Winsome (Polakov). *Career:* Demonstrator, West Virginia Univ. (Morgantown) 1925–26, and McGill Univ. 1926–27; Bacteriologist, Borden Farm Products Ltd., Montreal 1927; Chemist, Grasselli Powder Co., New Castle 1927–28, and E. I. duPont de Nemours & Co., Gibbstown, N.J. 1928–29; Special Investigator, Western Cartridge Co., East Alton, Ill. 1929–30; Asst. Physical Chemist, U.S. Bureau of Mines 1930–34; Fellow, Mellon Inst., Univ. of Pittsburgh 1934–36; Research

Explosives Engineer, Explosives Department, American Cyanamid and Chemical Corp., Latrobe (Pa.) 1936–41; Assistant Director of Research, Explosives Department, American Cyanamid Co., New Castle 1941–47. Plant Manager (1947–60), Manager of Explosives Research and Development, American Cyanamid Company, New Castle, Pa. 1960–66; Dept. of Labor and Industry, Commonwealth of Pennsylvania 1966; Acting Chief, Div. of Quarries and Explosives, Dept. of Environmental Resources, Commonwealth of Pennsylvania 1971–73; Supervising Inspector since 1973. *Publications:* Absorbents for Liquid Oxygen Explosives—Their Relation to Sensitiveness to Impact and Other Properties of L.O.X. 1932; Diazodinitrophenol, A Detonating Explosive 1933; Analogs of Tetryl-Trinitrophenylnitraminoethyl Nitrate (Pentryl) 1933; Analogs of Tetryl-Hexanitrodiphenylaminoethyl Nitrate 1934; Effect of Low Temperatures on Brisance of Explosives 1933; Unterwasser-Explosionen; Torpedo Wirkung 1932; To Tamp or Not to Tamp (with I. E. Tiffany) 1931). Holds patents on explosives, blasting methods, manufacturing equipment, absorbents for liquid oxygen explosives, etc. Fellow, American Association for the Advancement of Science; American Institute of Chemists; Amer. Inst. of Chemical Engineers; Pennsylvania Socy. for Professional Engineers; Amer. Chemical Socy.; member, Exec. Cncl., Lawrence County (Pa.) Boy Scouts of America. *Address:* 203 East Garfield Avenue, New Castle, Pa., 16105, U.S.A.

**CLARK, Sir Lindesay** AC, KBE, CMG, MC; DEngHon.; British mining engineer. *B.* 1896. *Educ.* C. E. Grammar School Launceston, Tasmania, Univ. of Tasmania (BSc 1915), and Melbourne Univ. (MME 1923; Hon. DEng. 1961). *M.* 1922, Barbara Jane Crosby Walch. *S.* 1. *Daus.* 2. *Career:* Prior to 1934 Consultant & Managing Director of Gold Mines of Australia Ltd.; Western Mining Corpn. Ltd., Dir. 1934— (Managing Dir. 1934–62; Chmn. 1952–74); Central Norseman Gold Corp. N.L., Dir. 1935–74 (Chmn. 1952–74); Gold Mines of Kalgoorlie (Aust.) Ltd., Dir. 1948–74 (Chmn. 1952–74); BH South Ltd., Dir 1944— (Chmn. 1956–74); Broken Hill Associated Smelters Ltd., Dir 1944–67; North Broken Hill Ltd., Dir 1953–71; Alcoa of Australia Ltd., Chmn. 1961–70 Deputy Chmn. 1970–72; Beach Petroleum N. L., Dir. 1964–72. *Award:* Companion of the Order of Australia. *Member:* Executive Committee, Australian Mining Industry Council, 1967–73; Councillor, Chamber of Mines of Victoria (Australia) (Inc.); Former Councillor, Chamber of Mines of Western Australia, Inc., resigned 1971. Australiasian Inst. of Mining & Metallurgy (Past Pres.) Hon. Mem. since 1973; Canadian Inst. of Mining & Metallurgy; Inst. of Mining & Metallurgy (London) Hon. Mem. since 1971; Inst. of Mining & Metallurgy (S.A.); Amer. Inst. of Mining, Metallurgical & Petroleum Engineers. *Clubs:* Melbourne, Australian (Melbourne); Tasmanian (Hobart); Weld (Perth, W.A.). *Address:* 8 Moralla Road, Kooyong, Melbourne, Vic.; and *office* 459 Collins Street, Melbourne, Vic., 3000 Australia.

**CLARK, Michael W.** British. *B.* 1927. *Educ.* Harrow. *M.* 1955, Shirley MacPhadyen (Dec'd) *S.* Matthew Craig (stepson) and Ducan Allen. *Daus.* Marion Ann and Miranda. *Career:* Appointed Exec. Dir., The Plessey Co. Ltd. 1951; appointed to the main board of the Company 1953; Deputy Man. Dir. 1962, Man. Dir. 1970–75, Dep. Chmn. and dep. Chief Exec. since 1976; Member of Council, National Electronics Council, Inst. of Directors, BIM. *Member:* Econ. Dev. Cttee. for Electronics Industry; Comp. IEE & IERE; Court of Essex University. *Club:* Boodle's. *Address:* The Plessey Company Ltd., Millbank Tower, Millbank, London, SW1P 4QP.

**CLARK, William Donaldson.** British. *B.* 1916. *Educ.* Oundle School and Oriel Coll., Oxford (MA; 1st Class Hons. Mod. Hist.). *Career:* Commonwealth Fellow and Lecturer in Humanities Univ. Chicago 1938–40; with Ministry of Information and British Information, Chicago 1941–44; Diplomatic Correspondent, Observer 1950–55; Public Relations Adviser to Prime Minister 1955–56; Director, Overseas Development Institute 1960—; Director, Information and Public Affairs World Bank 1968, Dir. External Relations 1973, Vice-Pres. External Relations 1974. *Publications:* Less than Kin (a study of Anglo-American Relations), (1957); What is the Commonwealth? (1958); Number 10 (a political novel) (1968); Special Relationship (1968). *Clubs:* Athenaeum, Savile (London). *Address:* 3407 Rodman Street, N.W., Washington, D.C. 20008, U.S.A.; The Mill, Cuxham, Oxford; and *office* World Bank, 1818 H. Street, N.W., Washington, D.C. 20433, U.S.A.

**CLARK, William Holbrook.** American. *B.* 1914. *Educ.* Yale Univ.; Harvard Univ. Law Sch. (LLB). *M.* 1942, Rosemary Dudley Clark. *S.* 1. *Daus.* 2. *Career:* Chmn. and a Dir. of William H. Clark Associates, Inc.; formerly Principal, Price Waterhouse & Co., N.Y. *Clubs:* Field and Round Hill Greenwich (Conn.); Yale (of N.Y.). *Address:* Dewart Rd., Greenwich, Conn., U.S.A.; and *office* 292 Madison Ave., New York, New York 10017.

**CLARKE, Sir Ellis (Emmanuel Innocent),** TC 1969, GCMG 1972 (CMG 1960), Kt 1963. President of Trinidad & Tobago since 1976. *B.* 1917. *Educ.* St. Mary's Coll., Trinidad (Jerningham Gold Medal); London Univ. (LLB 1940); Gray's Inn. *M.* 1952 Eyrmyntrude Hagley. *S.* 1. *Dau.* 1. *Career:* Private Practice at Bar of Trinidad & Tobago 1941–54; Solicitor-Gen., Oct. 1954; Dep. Colonial Sec., Dec. 1956; Attorney-Gen. 1957–62; Trinidad & Tobago Perm. Rep. to UN 1962–66; Ambassador to USA 1962–73, to Mexico 1966–73; Rep. on Council of OAS 1967–73. Chmn. of Bd., British West Indian Airways 1968–72; Governor-Gen. & C.-in-C. of Trinidad & Tobago 1973–76. K St. J 1973. *Clubs:* Queen's Park Cricket (Port of Spain); Arima Race Trinidad Turf (Trinidad); Tobago Golf (Pres. 1969–75). *Address:* President's House, Port of Spain, Trinidad.

**CLARKE, Sir Frederick Joseph.** British. Governor of St. Lucia, 1967–73. *B.* 1912. *Educ.* School of Medicine, Edinburgh (LRCP). *M.* 1944, Phyllis Lunn. *S.* Roderick James. *Daus.* Charlotte Jennifer and Barbara Janice. *Career:* Speaker, Legislative Council, St. Lucia, July 1964; Chief Medical Officer, St. Lucia, Aug. 1961; District Medical Officer, St. Lucia, Apr. 1946. *Member:* British Medical Assn.; West India Committee; St. John Ambulance Brigade; Chief Scout, St. Lucia. *Clubs:* St. Lucia Cricket Assn.; St. Lucia Yacht; Press Assn. (St. Lucia). *Address:* P.O .Box 391, Castries, St. Lucia, West Indies.

**CLARKE, Sir (Henry) Ashley,** GCMG, GCVO. British diplomat. *B.* 1903. *Educ.* Repton; Pembroke College, Cambridge; Hon. Doctor of Political Science, Genoa University 1956; Hon. Fellow of Pembroke College 1962; Hon. Fellow Royal Academy of Music. *M.* (1) 1937, Virginia Bell (marriage diss. 1960). (2) 1962, Frances Molyneux. *Career:* Entered Diplomatic Service 1925; served at Budapest, Warsaw, Constantinople, Tokyo; Counsellor, with local rank of Min. Plen., Lisbon 1944; Minister at Paris, 1946; Assistant Under-Secretary of State (Administration), Foreign Office 1949, Deputy Under-Secretary of State (Administration) 1950; Ambassador to Italy 1953–62. Governor: B.B.C. and National Theatre Board 1962–67; and British Inst. of Recorded Sound 1964–67. Member, Council of British School in Rome since 1963. Chairman, Royal Academy of Dancing 1964–69, Member, Committee of Management Royal Acad. of Music 1967–73; General Board, Assicurazioni Generali of Trieste 1964; London Advisor, Banca Commerciale Italiana 1962–71; Trustees, D'Oyly Carte Opera Trust; Chmn., Italian Art and Archives Rescue Fund 1966–69; Mem., Adv. Council Victoria and Albert Museum 1969–73; Vice Chmn. Venice in Peril Fund since 1969; Secretary General, Europa Nostra, 1969–70; Kt. Grand Cross, Order Al Merito della Repubblica; Kt. Grand Cross, Order of St. Gregory the Great; Premio Torta for restoration in Venice 1974. *Address:* Fondamenta Bonlini, 1113, Dorsoduro, 30123, Venice, Italy.

**CLARKE, John G.** American. Realtor and contractor. *B.* 1913. *Educ.* Univ. of Oregon (BS 1940) and George Peabody Coll. (MA 1942). *M.* 1944 Jeanne McCormack, *S.* George, John and James. *Dau.* Candace. *Career:* Public School Principal 1933–40; War Production Training Instructor 1940–45; Realtor, self-employed, 1945—; Pres. The Guaranty Co. Inc. since 1956. Omega Tau Rho; Phi Kappa Delta; Kappa Delta Phi. *Member:* Socy. of Real Estate Appraisers; Portland Board of Realtors; Investment Real Estate Exchange; Masonic Lodge. *Address:* 409 N.E. 150th Place, Portland, Ore; & 1507 S.E. 122nd Avenue, Portland, Ore., U.S.A.

**CLARKE, Kenneth Charles,** OBE, MC. Australian. *B.* 1916. *Educ.* FISM; Graduate, Royal Military Staff College, Duntroon; PSC, BM 17 Aust. Inf. Bde. *M.* 1944, Jean Lillian Miles. *S.* 1. *Daus.* 2. *Career:* Director, Australian Motor Industries Ltd. 1958–62; Deputy General Manager, Standard Motor Products 1948–54; Dir., Japan, International Wool Secretariat, 1962–67; Regional Dir. Asia International Wool Secretariat 1972, Man. Dir. 1973–75; Dir., Dalgety Japan Ltd. since 1976. *Member:* Australian Society in Japan; Institute of Sales Management. *Award:* Order Rising Sun Japan 1972. *Clubs:* Legacy (Pres. 1961), Naval & Military (Melbourne); Tokyo Tennis. *Address:*

International Wool Secretariat, Wool House, Carlton Gardens, London.

**CLARKE, Kenneth Harry, BA, LLB, MP.** British politician and Barrister. *B.* 1940. *Educ.* Nottingham High School; Gonville and Caius Coll. Cambridge. *M.* 1964, Gillian Mary Edwards. *S.* Kenneth Bruce. *Dau.* Esther Susan. *Career:* President, Cambridge Union, 1963; Chmn. Federation of Conservative Students, 1963–64; Member, Parliament Rushcliffe Div. of Nottinghamshire since 1970; Parly. Private Secy. The Solicitor General 1971–72; Government Whip 1972–74; Lord Commissioner of Treasury 1974: Cons. Shadow Spokesman on Health & Social Security 1974–76, on Industry since 1976. *Publications:* Various Pamphlets, Bow Group. *Address:* House of Commons, London, S.W.1.

**CLARKE, Sir Rupert William John,** Bt, MBE (Mil.), MA (Oxon). Australian grazier and company director. *B.* 1919. *Educ.* Eton College and Magdalen College, Oxford; MA (Oxon.). *M.* 1947, Kathleen Grant Hay. *S.* Rupert Grant Alexander, Ernest William Grant (*D.* 1961) and Peter R. J. *Dau.* Vanessa Margaret. *Career:* Served in Scots Guards, France 1940, Commissioned Irish Guards 1940 (mentioned in despatches); 2nd Lieut., 1st Bn. 1940–41; A.D.C. to C.-in-C., Burma Army 1942; P.A. to C.-in-C. Middle East 1942–43, and to C.-in-C. Allied Armies in Italy 1943–44; served (Major) 3rd Bn. Irish Guards, Germany 1945–46. Consul-General for Monaco. Chmn.: Cadbury Schweppes (Australia) Ltd., United Distillers Pty. Ltd., Victory Re-insurance Co. of Aust. Ltd., Bain Dawes Australia Ltd., King Ranch Australia Pty. Ltd., and Dir., National Bank of Australasia, Deltec International, Capel National Fund, Conzine Riotinto of Australia, Austiran Ltd., Cadbury Schweppes Ltd. (U.K.). *Member:* Royal Agricultural Society of Victoria (Councillor); Royal Humane Society of Australasia (Director); Victorian Amateur Turf Club, Chmn. 1972. *Clubs:* Melbourne Australian, Athenaeum (Melbourne); Union (Sydney); Queensland (Brisbane) Guards', Lansdowne (London). *Address:* Bolinda Vale, Clarkefield, Vic.; Richmond House, 56 Avoca Street, Melbourne. 3141; A.M.P. Tower, 535 Bourke Street, Melbourne 300 Vic., Australia.

**CLARKE, William Malpas.** British. *B.* 1922. *Educ.* Manchester University (BA, Hons. Econ.). *M.* (1) 1946, Margaret Braithwaite. *Daus.* Deborah and Pamela; (2) 1973, Faith Elizabeth Dawson. *Career:* Editorial Staff, Manchester Guardian, 1948–55; City Editor, The Times, 1957–63; and Financial and Industrial Editor 1963–66. The Director, Committee on Invisible Exports since 1968, Dir.-Gen. and Dep. Chmn. 1976; Dep. Chmn., City Communications Organisation 1976; Director: Grindlays Bank since 1966; U.K. Provident Institution since 1967; Cincinnati, Milacron Ltd. since 1968; Euromoney Publications since 1968; Trade Indemnity Ltd. since 1971; Swiss Reinsurance (U.K.) Ltd. 1977. Cncl. Mem. Royal Inst. of International Affairs since 1967. *Publications:* The City's Invisible Earnings (1958); The City in the World Economy (1965) and (Penguin 1967); Private Enterprise in Developing Countries (1966); Britain's Invisible Earnings (1967: Director of Studies); The World's Money (1970). *Club:* Reform. *Address:* 37 Park Vista, Greenwich, London, S.E.10; and *office* Committee on Invisible Exports, 7th Floor, Stock Exchange, London EC2.

**CLARKSON, John Bowes.** Australian. *B.* 1921. *Educ.* C. of E. Grammar School. *M.* 1951, Elizabeth Joan Vance. *Daus.* Janelle, Camilla, and Yolande. *Career:* Served in World War II—Lieut., 2nd 17th Aust. Infantry Battalion 1941–46. Vice-Chairman, Alcan Australia Ltd. 1970, Chmn. Man. Dir. since 1972; Chairman, Alcan New Zealand Ltd.; Director, Queensland Aluminia Ltd.; Borg Warner (Aust.) Ltd; Brambles Industries Ltd.; Dep. Chmn., Export Payments Insurance Corp. Chmn. Industry Cttee. for the Development of Offsets to Overseas Procurements; Dir. Heart Foundation; Council of the Univ. of New South Wales; Council, N.S.W. Inst. of Technology. *Clubs:* Royal Sydney Yacht Squadron; Royal Sydney Golf; Australian Club; Union; American (all Sydney). *Address: office* c/o Alcan Australia Ltd.; Suite 2800, Australia Square, Sydney, N.S.W., Australia.

**CLASEN, Andrew Joseph,** GCVO, FIC, Dr Ing., ARSM, BSc. Luxembourg diplomat. *B.* 5 Sept. 1906. *Educ.* Beaumont College; Oxford Univ.; Imperial College, London; Aix-la-Chapelle. *M.* 1944, Joan Luke. *S.* 1. *Dau.* 1. *Career:* Acting Secretary-General, Ministry of Foreign Affairs 1941–44; En. Ex. and Min. Plen. to the Court of St. James's 1944–55; Amb. Ex. and Plen. 1955–72. *Awards:* Grand Cross, Ordre d'Adolphe de Nassau; Cmdeur., Ordre de la Couronne de Chene; Grand Cross, Order of Orange-Nassau; Grand Cross, Islandic Falcon; Grand Officer Ordre de la Republique Tunisienne. *Club:* Turf. *Address* The Manor House, Rotherfield, Sussex.

**CLAY, Douglas Mark.** Australian advertising. *B.* 1921. *Educ.* Randwick High School. *M.* 1949, Muriel E. Lord. *Daus.* Stephanie, Kathryn and Charmian. *Career:* Executive with various advertising agencies 1937–41. Lieut., Royal Australian Artillery 1941–45. Executive, advertising agencies 1945–51; Executive, McClelland Advertising Co. Pty. Ltd. 1951–52, Became NAS Sydney Pty. Ltd. (Director 1952–56). Managing Dir. 1956–70, Chairman 1970. Chairman, NAS (Australia) Pty. Ltd. 1959–70. Chairman, N.S.W. Div. Australian Assn. of Advertising Agencies, 1961–63; Director, Murray Evans Advertising Pty. Ltd. since 1971. Member Commonwealth Advertising Council, 1967–71. *Clubs:* Elanora Golf; American National; Tattersall's. *Address: office* 5 Young Street, Neutral Bay, N.S.W., Australia.

**CLAY, Lucius DuBignon.** General, U.S. Army (Retd.). *B.* 1897. *Educ.* U.S. Military Academy, West Point, N.Y. (BS). *M.* 1918, Marjorie McKeown. *S.* Major Gen. Lucius D. Clay, Jr., U.S.A.F.; and Gen. Frank B. Clay, U.S. Army. *Career:* With U.S. Army, advancing through grades to General in 1947, retired May 1949. Chmn. of the Board, Continental Can Co. Inc. 1950–62; Senior Partner, Lehman Brothers (investment banking) 1963–73; Chmn. of the Board, Federal National Mortgage Assn. Director, Chase International Investment Corp., Chmn. Bd. Radio Free Europe; Trustee, Presbyterian Hospital at Columbia Presbyterian Medical Center, Tuskegee Institute. Chairman, Republican National Finance Committee, June 1965–68. *Publications:* Decision in Germany, (1950); Germany and the Fight for Freedom (collection of his Godkin Lectures at Harvard Univ.). *Awards:* 24 Hon. Degrees from Universities in U.S.A., including 18 LLD. Distinguished Service Medal (2 Oak Leaf Clusters), Legion of Merit, Bronze Star (all from U.S.); Hon. Knight Comdr. Order of the British Empire, Légion d'Honneur, and numerous other decorations and awards. Republican. *Clubs:* Blind Brook, Links, Pinnacle University (N.Y.C.); Eastward Ho! (Chatham, Mass.); Bohemian Grove (Calif.). *Address:* 633 Third Avenue, New York, N.Y. 10017, U.S.A.

**CLAYSON, Sir Eric (Maurice),** DL, FCA. British company director. *B.* 1908. *Educ.* Woodbridge School. *M.* 1933, Pauline Audrey Wright. *S.* John Edward, Charles Harry. *Career:* Chairman, The Birmingham Post & Mail Group 1957–74; Director, The Press Association Ltd. 1959–66, Reuters Ltd 1964–66, Assoc. Television Ltd. 1964–74; Sun Alliance and London Assurance Group 1965–76; ATV Network Ltd. since 1966. Member, West Midland Region Economic Planning Council, 1965–68. Chmn., Birmingham Publicity Assn. 1947–48 (President 1948–49); President, West Midlands Newspaper Society 1949–50; President, The Newspaper Socy. 1951–52 (Hon. Treas. 1956–60); Member of Council, Birmingham Chamber of Commerce since 1951 (Vice-President, 1953–54; President, 1955); Chairman, Exec. Cttee. British Industries Fair 1956–57; Pres., Incorporated Sales Managers' Assn. (Birmingham Branch) 1953–54. Member, The Press Council 1953–72; B.B.C. Midland Regional Adv. Council 1954–57; Vice-Pres., Fédération Internationale des Editeurs de Journaux et Publications 1954–67; Life Gov., Birmingham Univ. since 1956; member of council 1959–70; member, Midlands Regular Forces Resettlement Cttee. 1958–70; Chmn. 1961–70; Governor, Royal Shakespeare Theatre, Stratford-upon-Avon 1963—, and Mem. Exec. Council to 1975; Pres., Radio Industries Club of the Midlands, 1959–61; Midland Counties Golf Association 1960–62, Vice-Pres., Professional Golfers Association since 1960; Pres., Birmingham and Midland Inst. 1967–68. Dep. Lieutenant, County of West Midlands 1975—. *Address:* The Poor's Piece, Linthurst Road, Barnt Green, Birmingham.

**CLEARY, Frederick Ernest,** MBE. British Chartered Surveyor. *B.* 1905. *Educ.* Dame Alice Owen School. *M.* 1929. *Daus.* Pauline Margaret and Patricia Anne. *Career:* Chmn. Haslemere & Estates of various property companies; President: City & Metropolitan Building Society (37 Ludgate Hill, E.C.4); Metropolitan & Public Gardens Association; Director. South British Insurance Company. *Publications*: Beauty and the Borough; The Flowering City. *Clubs*: City Livery; M.C.C. (London). *Address:* 33 Grosvenor Square, London, W.1.

**CLEAVER, Richard,** JP. (1961), MHR (1955–69). Australian company director. *B.* 1917. *Educ.* Fellow, Chartered Institute of Secretaries. *M.* 1942, Mavis A. Painter. *S.* Colin Richard,

Geoffrey Owen, Peter Murray and Brian Barry. *Career:* Credit Officer, Shell Co. of Australia 1938–47; Accountant, Rheem Australia Pty. Ltd. 1947–49; Sales Manager, Mortlock Bros. Ltd. 1949–55. Commissioned Officer, Royal Australian Artillery 1941–46 (Rank of Major at date of discharge). Director, Norwich Union Fire Society since 1956. *Member:* Federal Joint Parly. Cttee. of Public Accounts 1958–61 (Chmn. 1964–69). Federal Parliament Foreign Affairs Cttee, 1962–63; Royal Commonwealth Society; Commonwealth Parly. Assn.; Liberal Party, Australia. Founder and Chmn. Swan Cottage Homes. 'Ningana' Home for the Frail; Aust. Italian Assn. of W.A.; Nat. Pres. Aust. Christian Endeavour Union Inc.; Vice-Pres., Overseas Del. World Freedom League; Australasian Inst. of Accountants. *Address:* 18 Ridge Street, South Perth, W.A., Australia.

**CLEGG, Sir Cuthbert Barwick,** TD. British banker. *B.* 9 Aug. 1904. *Educ.* Charterhouse; Trinity College, Oxford (MA). *M.* 1930, Helen Margaret Jefferson. *S.* Richard Ninian Barwick. *Career:* President, British Employers' Confederation, 1950–52. Member, Economic Planning Board 1949–53. President, The United Kingdom Textile Manufacturers' Assoc. 1961–69; Pres. Institute of Bankers 1968–69. Chairman, Martins Bank Ltd. 1964–69. Director: Barclays Bank Ltd. 1968–75; Halifax Building Socy. 1960–76; Pres., The Cotton, Silk & Man-Made Fibres Res. Assn. 1962–67. Mem., Cotton Industry Working Party 1946 and Cotton Manufacturing Commn. 1947–49; Anglo-Amer. Cncl. on Productivity 1948–52; British Productivity Council 1952–54; Chmn., U.K. Cotton Textile Mission to India, Hong Kong and Pakistan 1957. Pres. Overseas Bankers Club 1966–67. *Address:* Willow Cottage, Arkholme, Carnforth Lancashire.

**CLEGG, Walter,** MP. British solicitor. *B.* 1920. *Educ.* Bury Grammar School; Arnold School; Blackpool & Manchester Univ. Law School. *M.* 1951, Elise Hargreaves. *Career:* Appointed, Solicitor, 1947; Member of Parliament for North Fylde since 1966; Opposition Whip 1969–70; Govt. Whip and Lord Commissioner of the Treasury 1970–71; Vice Chamberlain, H.M. Household 1972–73; Comptroller, H.M. Household 1973–74; Vice-Chmn. Assn. of Conservative Clubs 1969–72, Pres. 1977; elected member of Exec. of 1922 Cttee. (1975), Treasurer, 1976. *Clubs:* Carlton. *Address:* Beech House, Raikes Road, Little Thornton, Nr. Blackpool, Lancs.

**CLEMENTI di SAN MICHELE, Count Raffaele.** Italian diplomat. *B.* 1905. *Educ.* Univ. of Padua (Doctor of Law). *M.* 1941, Elena Solaro del Borgo. *Dau.* Carla. *Career:* Entered Italian Foreign Service 1934; Ministry of Foreign Affairs, Rome 1934–37; 3rd Secretary of Legation, Budapest 1937–40; Ministry of Foreign Affairs 1940–42; 2nd Secy. of Embassy to the Holy See 1942–43; 2nd Secretary of Embassy, Madrid 1943–44; Consul, Seville (Spain) 1944–45; Ministry of Foreign Affairs 1945–47; Asst. Consul-General, Tangiers (Morocco) 1947–51; 1st Secretary of Embassy, Stockholm 1951–53; Counsellor of Embassy, Teheran 1953–56; Ministry of Foreign Affairs 1956–60, Minister Plenipotentiary; Ambassador to Ghana 1960–62. Ambassador of the Republic of Italy to Panama, July 1962–67; Ambassador to Oslo (Norway) 1967–70. *Club:* Circolo della Caccia (Rome). *Address:* Via Appia Antica 230, Rome.

**CLENDENIN, Robert James.** American lawyer. *B.* 1904. *Educ.* Leland Stanford Univ. (AB with distinction); Univ. of Michigan Law Sch. (*Dr. juris*). *M.* 1941, Louise Velde. *S.* Robert James, Jr., John Velde, William Harvey & Thomas Mills. *Career:* Law Clerk to Judge of Illinois Appellate Court 1933–35; Assistant, U.S. Attorney, Southern District of Illinois 1935–39; Referee in Bankruptcy, Southern District of Illinois 1939–53. Officer, U.S. Navy in World War II 1943–45; Captain, U.S.N.R. (Ret'd.). Secretary and Treasurer, National Association of Referees in Bankruptcy 1949–61; Director and Chmn. Bd., Monmouth Trust & Savings Bank since 1939; Dir. and Pres., Edward Arthur Mellinger Foundation 1959—; Mem. Exec. Cttee., US Naval Academy Foundation. *Member:* Illinois, Peoria County, Warren County, Chicago, Federal and American Bar Associations; member, American Judicature Society. *Awards:* Alumni Service Award, Culver Military Academy; Hon. Degree Doctor of Humanities LHD conferred by the Coll. of the Ozarks, 1971. *Publications:* Associate Editor: Michigan Law Review (1929–30) and Journal of National Association of Referees in Bankruptcy 1949–53. *Clubs:* University Club of Chicago; Creve Coeur Club of Peoria; Army & Navy (Washington). *Address:* 1111 E. Euclid Avenue, Monmouth, Ill.; and *office* 1205 First National Bank Building, Peoria, Ill. 61462, U.S.A.

**CLIBBORN, Donovan Harold,** CMG, MA. (Ret'd.). British diplomat. *B.* 1917. *Educ.* County High School, Ilford; St. Edmund Hall, Oxford; Laming Travelling Fellow, The Queen's Coll. Oxford. *M.* (1) 1940, Margaret Mercedes Edwige Nelson (*D.* 1966). *S.* 1. *Daus.* 2 (2) 1973, Marina Victoria Ondiviela. *Career:* Probationer, Vice Consul Genoa Italy 1939–40; Army Service (Major 1944) 1940–45; 2nd Secy. Foreign Office 1945–46; H.M. Vice Consul Los Angeles U.S.A. 1946–48; 1st Secy. Foreign Office 1948–50; High Commission, Madras India 1950–52 (Information) Rio De Janeiro, Brazil 1952–56; (Commercial) Madrid Spain 1956–60; H.M. Consul (Commercial) Milan Italy 1960–63; Counsellor (Economic) Tehran, Iran 1963–64; Rio De Janeiro Brazil 1964–66; H.M. Consul-Gen. Barcelona Spain 1966–71; H.M. Ambassador, San Salvador, El Salvador 1971–75. *Address:* Paseo del Dr. Moragas 188, Atico 1A, Santa María de Barberá, Prov. Barcelona, Spain.

**CLIFFORD, Henry Hoblitzelle.** American investment counselor. *B.* 1910. *Educ.* Yale University (BA 1932). *M.* 1933, Lucetta Rathbone Andrews. *S.* Arthur Morton II. *Dau.* Sara Dwight (White). *Career:* With A. M. Clifford 1933–39; Partner A. M. Clifford Assocs. 1939–56; Proprietor Clifford Assocs. 1956–73; Partner Clifford Assocs. since 1973; Governor and past Pres. Investment Counselors' Association of Southern California. *Member:* Investment Counsel, Assn. of America. Dir. Pasadena Foundation for Medical Research; *Member:* Rancheros Visitadores, Los Caballeros (Pres. 1966–68); Desert Caballeros (Arizona); Vaqueros del Desierto; Los Angeles Westerners (pas Sheriff; Zamorano, Roxburghe & Grolier (Book) Clubs. *Publications:* various papers and booklets on investments and correlated subjects; also articles on Western U.S. history. *Clubs:* California; Valley Hunt; Yale. *Address:* 1048 Armada Drive, Pasadena, Calif., 91103; and *office* 523 West Sixth Street, Los Angeles 90014, U.S.A.

**CLINCH, John J., Jr.** American Associate Judge. Attorney-at-Law. *B.* 1914. *Educ.* University of Illinois College of Commerce (BS 1939), and Univ. of Illinois Coll. of Law (JD 1941). *M.* 1944, LaVerne I. Hoerner. *Daus.* Ellen Thomas (Gary), and Marcia Ann (Charles). *Career:* Served U.S. Army W.W. II 1941–44; Admitted to Illinois Bar 1941; Candidate for States Attorney 1948 and 1952; Hearings Referee, Division of Motor Carriers, State of Illinois, 1949–53; Joint Member of the Board (representative of Illinois), U.S. Interstate Commerce Commission Motor Bureau, 1949–53; Vice-Chmn., La Salle County Democratic Central Committee 1956–60; City Attorney, Peru, Ill., 1957–61; Candidate for Judge 13th Illinois Judicial Circuit, 1957; Member, La Salle County Board of Tax Review 1960–64. Special Asst. Illinois Attorney General 1966–67; Magistrate, Circuit Court Thirteenth Illinois Judicial Circuit 1967–71; Candidate for Justice Illinois Appellate Court 3rd District 1968; Associate Judge, Circuit Court Thirteenth Illinois Judical Circuit since 1971. *Member:* La Salle County (Past-Pres. 1967); La Salle-Peru-Oglesby-Spring Valley (Past-Pres. 1954) Illinois State, and Amer. Bar Assn.; Amer. Judicature Soc.; Nat. Coll. of Probate Judges; Phi Alpha Delta; Democratic Party; Knights of Columbus (Past Grand Knight). *Club:* Elks; Jolaelma Kennel. *Address:* 2409 Tenth Street, Peru, Ill., U.S.A.; and *office* 809 Peoria Street, Peru, Illinois, U.S.A.

**CLITHEROE, Lord,** PC (Sir Ralph Assheton); Lord Lieut of Lancashire (Ret'd. 1976); High Steward of Westminster. *B.* 1901. *Educ.* Eton; Christ Church Oxford (MA). *M.* 1924, Hon. Sylvia Benita Frances Hotham. *S.* 2. *Dau.* 1. *Career:* Called to the Bar, Inner Temple 1925; member of London Stock Exchange 1927–39; JP (Lancs.) 1934; MP (Cons.) Rushcliffe Division of Notts 1934–45; Parliamentary Private Secretary to Rt. Hon. W. Ormsby Gore, First Commissioner of Works and Secretary of State for the Colonies 1936–38; Royal Commission on West Indies 1938–39; Parliamentary Secretary, Ministry of Labour and National Service 1939–42, Ministry of Supply 1942; Financial Secretary to the Treasury 1942–44; Chairman, Cons. and Unionist Party Organization 1944–46; MP (Cons.) City of London 1945–50, Blackburn West 1950–55; Chmn. Public Accounts Cttee. 1948–50. Chmn. Select Committee on Nationalized Industries 1951–53; Former Dir. National Westminster Bank; Tube Investments Ltd.; Coutts & Co.; London & North Eastern Rly. Co. and other companies; Former Chmn. Borax Holdings Ltd.; Mercantile Investment Trust Ltd. *Address:* Downham Hall, Clitheroe, Lancs. and 17 Chelsea Park Gardens, London, S.W.3.

**CLOAKE, John Cecil,** CMG. British Diplomat. *B.* 1924. *Educ:* King's College Sch., Wimbledon; Peterhouse, Cambridge—MA. *M.* 1956, Margaret Thomure Morris. *S.* 1. *Career:* Army,

Royal Engineers 1943–46; entered HM Diplomatic Service 1948; 3rd Sec., British Embassy, Baghdad 1949–51; 2nd Sec., British Legation, Saigon 1951–54; Foreign Office 1954–58 (Private Sec. to Perm. Under-Sec. 1956–57, & to Parly. Under-Sec. 1957–58); Commercial Consul, New York 1958–62; 1st Sec., British Embassy, Moscow 1962–63; F.O. & D.S.A.O. 1963–68 (Counsellor 1967); Commercial Counsellor, British Embassy, Tehran, 1968–72; Visiting Fellow, London School of Economics 1972–73; Head of Trade Relations & Exports Dept., F.C.O. 1973–76; HM Ambassador, Bulgaria since 1976. *Decorations:* Companion, Order of St. Michael & St. George, 1977. *Club:* Travellers' (London). *Address:* c/o Foreign & Commonwealth Office, King Charles Street, London SW1A 2AH.

**CLORE, Sir Charles.** British company director. *B.* 1904. *M.* 1943, Francine Rachel Halphen (*Dis.*). *S.* 1. *Dau.* 1. *Career:* Chairman: Sears Holdings Ltd., British Shoe Corp. Ltd., Sears Engineering Ltd., Princes Investments Ltd., The Bentley Engineering Group Ltd., Taylor & Lodge Ltd., B.S.C. Footwear Ltd., Sears Industries Inc., Lewis's Investment Trust Ltd., Selfridge's Ltd., Mappin & Webb Ltd., Scottish Motor Traction Co. Ltd., Kaye & Stewart Ltd. Director of several other companies. Created Kt. 1971. *Address:* 22 Park Street, Park Lane, London W1Y 4AE.

**CLOUGH, John Alan,** CBE, MC. British. *B.* 1924. *Educ.* Marlborough and Leeds University. *M.* 1961, Mary Cowan Catherwood. *S.* Christopher and Andrew. *Daus.* Amanda, Joanna and Annabel. *Career:* Director: Smith (Allerton) Ltd.; Jeremiah Ambler Ltd.; Robert Clough (Kly.) Holdings Ltd.; Christopher Waud Ltd.; Croften Yarns Ltd.; Jeremiah Ambler (Ulster) Ltd.; Robert Clough (Kly.) Ltd.; Keighley Fleece Mills Co. Ltd.; Stork Brothers Ltd. Deputy Chmn. & Chief Exec., British Mohair Spinners Ltd. Chmn., Wool Textile Delegation 1969–72; President, British Textile Confederation 1974–77; past-Mayor, The Merchants of the the Staple of England; Chmn., Wool Industries Research Association 1967–69. *Member:* The Merchants of the Company of the Staple of England; Worsted Spinners Federation; The Wool Textile Delegation; Pres., Comitextil Brussels 1975–77. Companion of the Textile Inst. 1975. *Club:* Boodles. *Address:* British Mohair Spinners Ltd.; Midland Mills, Bradford, Yorkshire.

**CLYNE, John Valentine.** Lawyer (ret.), corporation executive. *B.* 1902. *Educ.* University of British Columbia (BA); post-grad. studies, London School of Economics, Kings Coll., London. *M.* 1927, Betty V.A. Somerset. *S.* 1. *Dau.* 1. *Career:* Former Chairman, Canadian Maritime Commission; ex-Pres., Park Steamship Co., Ltd.; Representative, Canadian Sub-Cttee., UN and Nato dealing with shipping; Chmn., Preparatory Cttee., Inter-Governmental Maritime Consultative Organization, Lake Success; Justice, Supreme Court of British Columbia; Royal Commissioner (3 times); Whatshan Power House Disaster 1954; Milk Industry Inquiry 1954–55; Expropriations 1961; Former Director, Canada Trust Co.; MacMillan Bloedel Ltd (Retired as Chmn. 1973); Board Member, National Industrial Conference Board, Canada, 1961–73; NICB (US) 1962–73; Fellow, Foundation for Legal Research; Dir. C. D. Howe Research Institute. *Award:* Companion, Order of Canada (1972). *Address:* 3738 Angus Drive, Vancouver, British Columbia V6J 4H5; and *office* 1075 West Georgia Street, Vancouver, B.C., V6E 3R9, Canada.

**COBBOLD, Rt. Hon. Lord** (Cameron Fromanteel Cobbold), KG, PC, GCVO. British banker. *B.* 1904. *Educ.* Eton and King's Coll., Cambridge; Hon. LLD McGill Univ.; Hon. DSc (Econ) Univ. of London. *M.* 1930, Lady Margaret Hermione Millicent Bulwer-Lytton. *S.* 2. *Dau.* 1. *Career:* Adviser to Bank of England 1935–38; Exec. Director 1938–45; Dep. Governor 1945–49; Governor 1949–61. Director, Bank for International Settlements 1949–61. Lord Chamberlain of H.M. Household 1963–71; Former Director Hudson's Bay Co.; former Director: British Petroleum Ltd., Guardian Royal Exchange Assnce., Chmn., Bd. of Governors, Middlesex Hosp. 1963–74; Permanent Lord-in-Waiting to the Queen since 1971; Former Chmn., Italian International Bank; Vice-Pres. British Heart Foundation; One of H.M. Lieutenants for the City of London; Deputy Lieut. County of Hertford. *Address,* Lake House, Knebworth, Herts.

**COBDEN, Harry Alexander.** American engineer. *B.* 1904. *Educ.* University of California (BS; MS 1930; LLB 1933) and Stanford University (graduate study in engineering and chemistry). *M.* 1937, Mary Margaret Ryan. *S.* Richard Henry and John Edward. *Dau.* Maria Elena. *Career:* Chief, Building and Safety, Berkeley 1940–48; with Great Lakes Steel Corporation 1948–58; served as 2nd Lieut., U.S. Army Certified Chemist (U.S. Certificate No. 393); Licenced General Contractor, California. Director and Vice-President, Manco Pacific Co., Berkeley, Calif.; Mother Lode Foundation. *Member:* Structural Engineers of Calif.; International Fire Chiefs Assn.; National Fire Protection Assn. (Fire Protection Engineer Cert. 1065); Certified Chemists' Asn.; Amer. Public Health Assn.; Los Angeles, Oakland and Calif. State Chambers of Commerce; Socy. of Calif. Pioneers; Native Sons of the Golden West; E. Clampus Vitus; Pi Kappa Alpha; Phi Alpha Delta (Legal). Recipient, Order of Merit (Zero), Socy. of Trial Lawyers (Calif.). Democratic Delegate to state and national convention 1932–36–40–44–48–52. Sacramento Elks Lodge; Save the Redwood League. *Publications:* Articles to professional journals. Co-inventor: Nelson Steel Process, and Iron Oxide method of sewage treatment. Roman Catholic. *Address:* 2149 Claremont Road, Carmichael, Calif.; 95608, U.S.A.

**COBEY, Ralph.** American industrialist. *B.* 1909. *Educ.* Carnegie Inst. of Tech. (Mech Engrn); Hon. DSc Findlay Coll. 1958. *M.* 1944, Hortense Kohn. *Daus.* Minnie and Susanne Yetta. *Career:* With Armed Forces World War II (U.S.A.F. 1942–46; Korea 1951); Charge of Army Tank Production and Facilities, Washington, D.C. 1940–42; Represented Northern Ohio Industry at Industrial Safety Conf., Washington D.C. 1956 & 1958; Mem., Governor's Advisory Council on Economics, State of Ohio 1957–58; Mem. (Republican) original Ohio Expositions Commission 1961; Chmn., Commerce & Industry Cttee. 1966; Mem., Ohio Expositions Comm. 1964; Mem. Presidents Kennedy & Johnson's Tax Cttee. 1962–66; Exec. Advisory Council, Nat. Register of Prominent Americans; Pres., Friends of the Land Int'l. 1958–59; Mem., Gov. Gilligan's Citizens' Task Force on Environmental Protection 1971–72. *President:* Eagle Crusher Co. Inc. 1954—, Perfection-Cobey Co. 1965–70, Perfection Steel Body Co. 1945–65, Philips-Davies Co. 1965–70, Cobey Co. 1950–70, World-Wide Investment Co., Crawford County Land Co., Marion County Land Co., Galion Corp. 1972, Daybrook Hydraulic Co. 1973, Diamond Iron Works 1975, Austin-Western Crusher Co. 1975, Scoopmobile Co. 1976; Pres. & Chmn. of Bd., Imco Inc., Crestline, Ohio; Mem. Bd. of Dirs., The First National Bank, Galion, Ohio. *Member:* Board of Overseers, Jewish Theological Seminary of America; pioneered and instituted weekly non-denominational Chapel Services in plant facilities and offices. Philanthropic activities: Chmn., Special Gifts Cttee., Natl. Conf. of Christians and Jews; Pres. and Founder, Harry Cobey Foundation. Trustee: Hillel Foundation (Ohio State Univ.); Galion City Hosp. Found. Bd.; Chmn. and Founder, Minnie Cobey Memorial Library. Member, Natl. Council, The American Jewish Committee. Founder Chmn., Bd. of Trustees, Louis Bromfield Malabar Farm Foundation; Chmn. Malaber Advisory Council 1972; Bd. Mem., Mary Elizabeth Smith Foundn., Marion, Ohio. Area Chmn. United States Savings Bond Program; member, Nat. and Local Assns. 4-H Clubs Future Farmers of America; U.S. Chamber of Commerce; Taxation, Foreign Affairs & Labor Relations; Nat. and Ohio Assn. of Manufacturers; Cttee. Mem., Radio Free Europe; Chmn., Long Range Planning Cttee., Johnny Appleseed Area B.S.A.; Mem., Bd. of Dirs., Johnny Appleseed Area Council, Boy Scouts of America; Mem., Ohio Republican Finance Cttee.; Hon. Mem., Galion Community Center; President's Advisory Council for Development, Ashland Coll., Ohio; Chmn., Community Heart Fund Campaign 1971 & 1972: Pres. and Special Gifts Chmn., Heart Fund, Crawford County 1972, '73, '74, '75, '76, '77; Dep. Sheriff, Morrow County, Ohio 1974–77. *Awards:* Defense Dept. commendation for contribution to B-29 Bomber Program, W.W.II O.P.M. Dollar-a-Year Man (apptd. by Pres. Roosevelt), Washington; 1969 Wisdom of honor of the Wisdom Encyclopedia; Alumni Merit. Award (Alumni Assoc. of Carnegie Mellon Univ. 1974). Mason, 32nd Degree, and Shrine. *Address:* R. F. D., Galion, Ohio; and *office* Rt. 2, Box 72, Galion, Ohio, U.S.A.

**COBLER, Walter W.** German Consul General of Iceland. *B.* 1908. *Educ.* Gymnasium. *M.* 1945, Liselotte Freese. *S.* Christian-Michael and Andreas-Bernd. *Dau.* Sabine. *Career:* Attended Gymnasium until 1926; apprenticeship as an industrial businessman until 1929; industrial businessman with AEG until 1930. Managing Assoc., and owner, Turbon-Werke, Berlin and Strücklingen (air-conditioning and ventilation systems, established 1907) 1931—; Member of the Bd. of Management, Berliner Bank AG. Präsident der Industrie- und Handelskammer zu Berlin (member of the Council of the Chamber for Industry and Commerce, Berlin); Mitglied des Vorstandes des Wema (Chairman of WEMA);

Geschäftsführender Gesellschafter der Turbon-Werke, Berlin u. Strücklingen (Managing Associate, Turbon-Werke, Berlin and Strücklingen). Presidential Member, des Bundes der Deutschen Industrie, Köln; des Deutschen Industrie- und Handelstages, Bonn; Member Committee of Landeszentralbank Berlin; Mitglied des Beirates der Landeszentralbank Berlin; Mitglied des Aufsichtstrates Bergmann Kabel-Werke AG—; Pres. of Board of Dirs. Berliner Aluminium Gesellschaft mbH and Co.; Member of Board of Dirs. Grundstucksges and Gedachtnisk. AG; Member of the Aufsichtrates der Aktiengesell. fur Haus und Grundbesitz, Berlin (West); Pres. of Board of Dirs. of Berliner Industriebank AG. *Publications:* Fachbeiträge über Klimat- und Lufttechnische Anlagen (technical treatises on air-conditioning and ventilating). *Clubs:* Golf- und Land-club (Berlin-Wannsee); Berliner Hockey; Lions (Berlin). *Address:* Im Dol 49, Berlin-Dahlem; and *office* Alt-Reinickendorf 28/29, Berlin-Reinickendorf, Germany.

**COCHRAN, Alexander McKie,** DFC, Lt.-Col. AFRES (Ret'd). American. *B.* 1923. *Educ.* Randolph-Macon Academy & Virginia Military Institute. *M.* 1948, Katharine S. Mason. *S.* 1. *Dau.* 1. *Career:* On active service with U.S.A.A.F. 1942–46 (2 Distinguished Flying Crosses & 5 Air Medals); was attached to H.Q. TAC as a mem. of the A.F. Reserve (AFRES); Pres., Northeastern Associates (mosquito control, equipment & consultants, specialists in thermal aerosols & high-pressure cleaners) 1946–76; Pres., Eagle Point Corp. (insecticide dispensing equipment, mechanical aerosols, high pressure sprayers) since 1977. *Publications:* Numerous technical papers in the field. Conservative. *Address:* Route 2, Box 98A, Heathsville, Virginia 22473, U.S.A.

**COCHRAN, Lloyd See.** American manufacturing executive and lecturer. *B.* 1901. *Educ.* University of Pennsylvania (BE Econ). *M.* 1924, Dorothy Tomlinson. *S.* James W. and Robert E. *Dau.* Dorothy M. (Gleason). *Career:* Secretary-Treasurer, Niagara Cotton Co. 1926; Director of Sales, Lockport Cotton Batting Co. 1932. Vice-Pres., Dir. Marketing, Lockport Mills Inc., 1947–67. President, Lloyd Cochran Associates. Sales Counsel, The Stearns & Foster Co., Cincinnati, Ohio. *Publications:* Technical, trade and sales articles. *Member:* American National Red Cross (Regional Chairman 1952–54; Vice-Chairman, National Fund, 1955–62); National Sales Executives (Dir., Buffalo Chapter 1959–67); N.Y. State League for Nursing (Dir.-Treas. 1957); National Interfraternity Conference (Dir.-Secy. 1958; Trustee Research Council 1954–55; National Pres. 1954–55, of Conference, and Vice-Chmn. and Secy.); Y.W.C.A. (Chmn., Bd. of Trustees 1942–67); West N.Y. District Golf Association (Vice-Pres. 1945); National Assn. of Batting Manufacturers (Vice-Pres.; Chmn., Legislative Cttee. 1936; Chmn., National Code Authority 1933–35); International Assn. of Basket Ball Officials (Pres. 1955–56); The Newcomen Socy.; American Scientific Affiliation; Alpha Sigma Phi (National Pres. 1948–52); Hon. Delta Beta Xi, and Phi Kappa Beta. Mason 33° (District Deputy Grand Master 1959; Chmn. of Trustees 1946–66); Dir., Masonic Foundation for Medical Research and Human Welfare; Grand Lodge Committee on Youth; Dir., Masonic Youth Foundation; Sir Kt. of the Red Cross of Constantine, Puissant Sovereign; Deputy Grand Master, F. & A.M., State of N.Y., Most Wise Master Niag. Lodge F. & A.M.; Grand Master of Masons in the State of New York 1972, '73, '74; Grand Representative in the Province of Ontario near the Grand Lodge of New York; President, Lay Ministers Council, N.Y.; Jnr. Grand Warden, Deputy Grand Master F. & A.M. (N.Y.); President, American Baptist Men, N.Y.; Executive Vice-President N.Y. State Baptist Men. Board of Managers Baptist Convention (N.Y.); Board of Directors, N.Y. State Council of Churches; Shriner; Jesters; Grand Master of Masons, State of New York 1972, 73 and 74. *Clubs:* Wings; University; International; Town & Country (Past Pres.). *Address:* 515 S. Locust Street, Lockport, N.Y. 14094, U.S.A.

**COCHRANE, Andrew R.** American. *B.* 1908. *Educ.* Mercersburg Academy (Regent) and Washington & Jefferson College (BA; also Trustee of College). *M.* 1938, Dorothy Lott. *Daus.* Eleanor B., Christine A., and Dorothy Louise. *Career:* Pres. and Treas., Home Quality Laundry Co. Inc. 1931–42; Vice-Pres.-Secy., Federated Steel Corp. 1946–54; President and Treasurer, Pittsburgh Metals Fabricating Co. Inc. 1955—; Pearson Manufacturing Co. Inc. 1956—; Arch Engineering Co. Inc. 1958—; Pres. & Treas. Dir., Crest Contracting Co., Wise Machine Co.; Vice Pres. & Dir., Wright Bearings Inc.; Treas. & Dir. Fox. Chapel Authority; Trustee, Lincoln Mutual Savings Bank. *Director:* Duquesne Slag Products Co.; Don S. Grove Co.; Couplesign Inc.; Pittsburgh Abrasive and Supply Co. *Clubs:* Duquesne; University, Fox Chapel Golf (all of Pittsburgh). *Address:* 251 Fairview Road, Pittsburgh, Pa. 15238; and *office* 550 Butler Street, Pittsburgh, Pa. 15223, U.S.A.

**COCHRANE, Sir Desmond Oriel Alastair George Weston,** Bt. Irish diplomat. *B.* 1918. *Educ.* Eton. *M.* 1946, Yvonne Sursock. *S.* Henry Mark Sursock, Alfred Marie Stanislas Sursock, Roderick Inigo Marie Sursock. *Dau.* Isabelle Elsa Sursock. *Career:* Commissioned Lancashire Fusiliers 1939; Northern Command Staff 1940; War Office (Staff Captain A.G. 12) 1942; GHQ M.E.F. (Staff Captain M.S.) 1943; Military Secretary to G.O.C. 9th Army 1944; Hon. Consul-General of Ireland to the Lebanon and Syria. *Address:* c/o Marc Cochrane, Woodbrook, Brey, Co. Wicklow, Ireland.

**COCHRANE, Prof. Donald,** CBE 1974. Australian. *B.* 1917. *Educ.* Univ. of Melbourne (BCom) and Clare Coll., Cambridge (PhD). *M.* 1946, Margaret Schofield (pianist). *S.* Andrew Donald. *Dau.* Fiona Margaret. *Career:* Senior Lecturer, Univ. of Melbourne 1949–54; Economist, Dept. of Economic Affairs, United Nations, New York 1951–52; Professor of Commerce, Univ. of Melbourne 1955–61; Professor of Economics and Dean of Faculty of Economics and Politics, Monash University 1961—; Chmn. State Savings Bank of Victoria 1961—. Member, Commonwealth Bureau of Roads 1966–74; Mem., Defence Business Board 1968–76. *Member:* Commonwealth Export Development Council 1961–66; Australian Research Grants Cttee. 1965–68; Chmn., Cttee. of Inquiry into Australian Labour Market Training 1974. *Clubs:* Melbourne, Peninsula Golf; Green Acres Golf. *Address:* 10 Carnsworth Avenue, Kew, Vic. 3101; and *office* Monash University, Clayton, Vic., Australia.

**COCKBURN, Sir Robert,** KBE, CB. American Congressional Medal for Merit: British civil servant. Fellow, Churchill College, Cambridge 1969–76. *B.* 1909. *Educ.* Southern Secondary School and Municipal Coll., Portsmouth; and London Univ. (BSc 1928; MSc 1935; PhD 1939), MA Cantab. *M.* 1935, Phyllis Hoyland. *Daus.* 2. *Career:* Research in communications, Royal Aircraft Establishment, Farnborough, 1937–39; in radar at Telecommunications Research Establishment, Malvern 1939–45; in atomic energy at Atomic Energy Research Establishment, Harwell 1945–48; Scientific Adviser to the Air Ministry 1948–53; Principal Director of Scientific Research (Guided Weapons and Electronics) 1954–55, Deputy Controller of Electronics 1955–56, and Controller of Guided Weapons and Electronics 1956–59, Ministry of Supply; Chief Scientist, Ministry of Aviation, 1959; Director Royal Aircraft Establishment, Farnborough 1964–69; Chmn. National Computing Centre 1970–77; Television Adv. Cttee. 1972—; BBC Engineering Cttee. since 1973. *Publications:* Various scientific papers. *Member:* FInstP; MIEE; Hon. FRAeS. *Club:* Athenaeum (London). *Address:* 21 Fitzroy Road, Fleet, Hants; and *office* Churchill College, Cambridge.

**COCKE, Erle, Jr.** Business consultant. *B.* 1921. *Educ.* University of Georgia (AB), Harvard Business School (MBA), Mercer University (LLD), Missouri Valley College (HLD). *M.* 1955, Madelyn Alice Grotnes. *Daus.* Elise Carol, Jennifer Aline and Carolyn Laurine. *Career:* U.S. Army. B/Gen. Georgia Nat. Guard 1941–47; Asst. Gen. Mgr., Cinderella Foods, Dawson, 1946–47; Exec. Dir., Dept. of Commerce, State of Ga. 1947–48; Gen. Indsl. Agt. Central of Ga. Rly. Co. 1948–50; Asst. to Pres., Delta Air Lines 1950–52; Vice-Pres. 1952–61; Alt. Exec. Dir., International Bank for Reconstruction and Development, Washington, (World Bank); Rep. U.S., operational Boards, Cttees., Senior full-time U.S. official admin. of the World Bank 1961–64; Vice-Pres. Peruvian Airlines, Democratic Candidate for Congress 1964–66; Member special mission U.S. House of Rep. Armed Services Cttee. Dominican Republic, South Vietnam, Thailand and Laos; Chmn. Bd. Counsel for Int. Finance Tanner Johnson McInarnay & Cocke Inc. 1973–74; Business consultant, governmental & leglislative affairs, International Financing 1973. *Awards:* Silver Star, Purple Heart, Bronze Star, French Croix de Guerre; and other decorations from Italy, Spain, Cuba, Mexico, China and Philippines. National Commander, The American Legion 1950–51; Special Consultant, military manpower, training installations 1951–53; Nat. Bd. Govs. Amer. Nat. Red Cross 1954–60; Member Bd. Dirs. State Mutual Insurance Co. 1954—; Trustee Missouri Valley Coll. 1960—; Pres. Harvard Business School Club 1969–70, Chmn. 1970–71. U.S. Delegate to 14th General Assembly of U.N.; Co-Chairman, Committee for International Economic Growth 1958;. Democrat. *Clubs:* Army-Navy (Washington); Capital City, Piedmont Driving (Atlanta); National Aviation, National Capitol Democratic

(Washington). *Address:* 1629 K Street, N.W. Washington, D.C. 20006; 5116 Cammack Drive, N.W. Washington, D.C. 20016 and P.O. Box 388, Dawson, Georgia 31742, U.S.A.

**COCKERAM, Eric Paul**, JP, MP. British politician and company chairman. *B.* 1924. *Educ.* The Leys, Cambridge. *M.* 1949, Frances Irving. *S.* 2. *Daus.* 2. *Career:* Captain, The Gloucestershire Regt. 1942–45; Chmn. and Dir., Watson Prickard Ltd. since 1946; Chmn. Liverpool Exec. Council, N.H.S. 1960–70; Parly. Private Secy. to Minister for Industry 1971–72; to Minister for Post & Telecommunications 1972; to Chancellor of the Exchequer since 1972. Member, Bd. of Governors, United L'pool. Hospitals since 1964. *Member:* Menswear Assn. of Britain (Chmn. 1964–65); L'pool Cttee. Institute, Direstors; Select Cttee. Corporation Tax. *Awards:* Freeman of the City Springfield, Illinois and The City of London. *Clubs:* Carlton; R.A.C.; Lyceum (Liverpool). *Address:* Fairway Lodge, Links Hey Road, Caldy, Wirral, Cheshire L48 1NB; and *office* The House of Commons, London, S.W.1.

**COCKERELL, Sir Christopher (Sydney)**, Kt, 1969, CBE, MA. British. *B.* 1910. *Educ.* Gresham's and Peterhouse, Camb. (MA); Pupil, W. H. Allen & Sons, Bedford 1931–33. *M.* 1937, Margaret Elinor Belsham. *Daus.* 2. *Career:* Engaged in Radio Research, Camb., 1933–35, airborne and navigational equipment, research and development, Marconi Co. Ltd. 1935–50; Inventor of and engaged on hovercraft 1953—; Consultant (hovercraft), Min. of Supply 1957–58; Consultant, Hovercraft Development Ltd. 1958–70; (Dir. 1958–66); Chmn., Ripplecraft Co. Ltd. 1950—; Mem., Min. Technology's Adv. Cttee. for Hovercraft 1968–70, Consultant, British Hovercraft Corp. since 1973; Pres., International Air Cushion Engineering Socy. (formed 1969); Pres., The United Kingdom Hovercraft Society since 1972; Fellow of the Royal Society 1967; Trustee, National Portrait Gallery 1967—. *Awards:* F.R.S.A. 1960–70; Hon. Fellow, Swedish Socy. Aeronautics 1963; Hon. Fellow Socy. Engineers 1966; Hon. Fellow, Manchester Inst. Sc. & Techn. 1967; Hon. Mem., Southampton Chamber of Commerce 1967; Hon. DSc. Leicester 1967; Hon. Dr. RCA 1968; Hon. Fellow, Downing College, Cambridge 1969; Viva Shield, Worshipful Co. of Carmen 1961; R.A.C. Diamond Jubilee Trophy 1962; Thulin Medal, Swedish Socy. of Aeronautics 1963; Howard N. Potts Medal, Franklin Inst. 1965; Albert Medal of the R.S.A. 1966; Churchill Medal Socy. Engineers 1966; Royal Medal of the Royal Society 1966; Mitchell Memorial Medal, Stoke-on-Trent Assn. Engineers 1967; Columbus Prize of Genoa 1968; Elmer A. Sperry Award 1968; John Scott Award, City of Philadelphia 1968; Gold Medal, Calais Chamber of Commerce 1969; Bluebird Trophy 1969; Hon., member, Calais Chamber of Commerce; Hon. Freeman, Borough of Ramsgate 1971; Hon. DSc. Heriot-Watt Univ., Edinburgh, London Univ. 1975; Hon. Fellow Peterhouse, Cambridge 1974. *Address:* 16 Prospect Place, Hythe, Southampton SO4 6AU.

**COCKROFT, John Hoyle**, MP. British Politician. *B.* 1934. *Educ.* Local Primary Sch.; Tre-Arddur House; Oundle; St. John's Coll., Cambridge—Senior Major Scholar (History), Tripos Honours (History & Econ.). *M.* 1971, Tessa Shepley. *Daus.* 2. *Career:* 2nd Lieutenant, Royal Artillery 1953–55; Feature Writer, Financial Times and Investment Analyst 1959–61; Economic Adviser with Guest Keen & Nettlefolds 1962–67: Seconded to Treasury. Public Enterprises Div. as Temporary Principal 1965–66; Economic Leader Writer on Daily Telegraph 1967–74; Conservative MP for Nantwich, Cheshire since 1974; Select Cttee. on Nationalised Industries 1975; Scottish Grand Cttee. 1975; Standing Cttee. on Statutory Instruments 1976–77; Iron & Steel (Amendment) Bill Standing Cttee. 1976; Methodist Church Bill 1976. *Publications:* Why England Sleeps (1971); co-author of a history of Guest Keen & Nettlefolds. *Club:* Farmers'. *Address:* The Cottages, Great Gransden, Cambs.; and House of Commons, London, SW1A 0AA.

**COE, Henry Eugene III.** American Commercial Banker—Vice-Pres. & Division Exec. of Mining & Metals Division. *B.* 1925. *Educ.* Yale Univ. (BA 1946). *M.* 1947, Nancy Bell Wesson. *S.* John Taylor Johnston. *Daus.* Nancy Bell, Elice James, Cynthia Wesson and Alexandra Colles. *Career:* Salesman, Little, Brown & Co. 1947–50; Dir. of Sales, Farrar-Straus & Co. 1950–54; Chase Manhattan Bank 1954; Vice-President, Chase Manhattan Bank 1964—; Pres. & Dir., Improved N.Y. Properties Corp. 1962—; Dir.: Niagara Fire Insurance Co. 1954–65, and Fidelity & Casualty Co. of New York 1956–65; Treasurer, Incorporated Village of Lawrence 1957-66. *Member:* Robert Morris Assn.; Socy. of the Cincinnati (State of Conn.); AIME. Republican. *Clubs:* Rockaway Hunting; Cedarhurst Yacht; Lawrence Beach; Union; Rolling Rock; Clove Valley Rod & Gun. *Address:* 200 Sage Avenue, Lawrence, N.Y.; and *office* 1 Chase Manhattan, Plaza, New York, N.Y., U.S.A.

**COGAN, David (Harold).** American. *B.* 1909. *Educ.* Northeastern Univ. (BS). *M.* 1957, Martha Sharp. *S.* Bruce M. *Career:* Vice-President, Dir., Hytron Radio & Electronic Co. 1931–54; Pres., Dir., Air King Products Corp. 1946–54; Vice-Pres., Dir., Columbia Broadcasting System Inc, 1951–54; Pres., Dir., CBS—Columbia, Inc. 1951–54; Chmn.. Pres., Dir., VLN Corporation 1957–74; Premier Microwave 1963—; Chmn. Phaostron Instrument and Electronic Co. 1966–69; Dir. Hampshire-Designers Inc. since 1972. *Member:* Amer. Management Assn.; Chmn. Pres. The Colonial Press Inc 1967–74; Chmn. Amer. Council Nationalities Service. *Club:* Stamford Yacht. *Address:* 1 Rogers Road, Stamford, Conn. 06902; and *office* 18 East 80th Street, New York, N.Y. 10021.

**COGGAN, Bernard F. ('Sandy').** Executive aerospace industries. *B.* 1918. *Educ.* Michigan State Univ. (MA Electronic Engineering); graduate: U.S. Air Force War College, and U.S. Naval War College; Dr. Humane Letters 1974; Mach. 2 Jet Pilot. *M.* 1940, Bonita C. Creagan. *S.* Barry Braun. *Dau.* Sandra Bee. *Career:* Executive, General Motors Corp. 1939–52; Vice-Pres. and Gen. Mgr., General Dynamics Corp. 1952–60; Director of Navau Corp. Pres., San Diego International Development Corp., and Investment Trusts (both domestic and foreign) 1960—; Vice-Pres., operations, Douglas Aircraft Corp.; Fluidgencies Inc. (fluids control co.), and Video Corp. (electronics); Vice-Pres. North American Rockwell Corp. Special Consultant, Dept. of Defense U.S. since 1963. Asst. to Pres., North American Aviation Inc. 1967—; Consulting Executive: Bendix Corp., and General Dynamics Corp. Senior L.M.I. Consultant to Dept. of Defense, Chmn. of Board Douglas Aircraft of Canada, Senr. Inter-Regional Adviser, U.N. (N.Y.) 1966; Dir., Michigan State Univ. Coll. of Engineering; President Economic Development Corporation, 1971; Pres. and Chmn. Bd. Patent Development Corporation; Pres. & Chmn. Mission Park Corporation since 1973; Chmn and Chief Exec. Officer EZ-8 Motels Inc. 1975; Pres., Piranaha Products Inc. *Member:* San Diego City Harbor Commission; San Diego City School Board (Pres.); San Diego City Industrial Commission (Chairman); Director, Los Angeles Chamber of Commerce; California Nuclear Energy Commission; San Diego Chamber of Commerce; U.S. Naval Weapon Systems Advisory Board; American Rocket Society (Senior Member); National Kt. of the Holy Sepulchre; National Dir., Electronic Industries Assn.; Chairman of the Board, American Ordinance Assoc., President, National Security Industries Assoc. Member, Dept. of Commerce Export Committee; Nat'l. Socy. of Professional Engineers. *Publications:* Moon-Mind and Mysteries; Management of the Future; The Meaning of Man; Man's Mud Ball; Why an Iron Curtain?; Our Communist Competition. *Awards:* Outstanding Management Man of 1960 (National Management Assn.); Outstanding Graduate of 1960 (Michigan State Univ.); National Ordinance Assn.; Amer. Red Cross (National Vice-Chmn.); Engineering Award 1961; Tau Beta Pi (National Engineering Honorary); Outstanding Management Man of the Year 1972; Professional Ind. Achievement 1972; Honorary Doctorate Nat. Univ. 1974. *Club:* Ambassadors; Wilshire Country Club; Washington Aviation; Koni Kai; Cuyamaca. *Address:* 6436 Camino de la Costa, La Jolla, 92037 U.S.A.; and *office* 6160 Mission Gorge Rd., San Diego, Calif. 92171, U.S.A.

**COGHILL, Calvin Edward.** American public accountant. *B.* 1906. *Educ.* Virginia Mechanics Inst. (Business). *M.* 1926, Marjorie Harding. *S.* Thomas Ellis and Donald Edward. *Career:* Previously Senior Accountant with Ernst & Ernst. Dir., Reynolds Metals Co., Richmond, Va. 1961–76. Certified Public Accountant, State of Virginia. *Member:* Virginia Socy. of Public Accountants; Financial Executives Inst. *Clubs:* Country (of Virginia), Commonwealth, Deep Run Hunt (all in Richmond); Metropolitan (Washington). *Address:* 'Krafton', River Road and Herndon Road, Richmond 29, Va., U.S.A.

**COGHLAN, Patrick Boyle Lake**, JP, FCIS. British company director. *B.* 1907. *Educ.* Rugby; Pembroke College, Cambridge (MA). *M.* 1936, Rosemary Norma Ailsa Snelling (*Dec.*). *S.* Timothy Boyle Lake. *Daus.* Sally Lake, Anne Louise Lake. *Career:* Served in World War II with R.A.F. 1940–44. Chairman: Bacolet Estates Ltd., Buccoo Developments (Tobago) Ltd., Chapman, Lowry & Puttick, Ltd., Kulim

(Malaysia) Berhad, Mount Irvine Bay Hotel Ltd., Mount Irvine Developments Ltd., Plantations & General Investment Trust Ltd., Tobago Estates Agency Ltd., Tropical & Eastern Produce Co. Ltd., Ulu Tiram Manufacturing Co. (Malaysia) Sdn. Berhad; Director: Gordon Grant & Co. (Tobago) Ltd.; Minister Bay Hotel Ltd. *Address:* Three Quays, Tower Hill, London, E.C.3.

**COHEN, Sir Edward**, LLB. Australian solicitor. *Educ.* Scotch College, Melbourne, and Ormond College, University of Melbourne (LLB); Exhibitioner, Greek and Roman History. *M.* 1939, Meryl D. Fink. *S.* Adrian. *Career:* Australian Blue (Athletics and Hockey); served with 2/12 Fd. Regt. 9th Div. Arty. A.I.F. 1940–45 (Captain 1942); Partner, Pavey, Wilson Cohen & Carter, Melbourne. Former member Faculty of Law, Melbourne University, Council of Legal Education and Board of Examiners. Chairman: E Z Industries Ltd., Electrolytic Zinc Co. of Australasia Ltd., Commercial Union Assurance Co. of Australia Ltd., Commercial Union Properties Pty. Ltd., Derwent Metals Pty. Ltd., Emu Bay Railway Co. Ltd., CUB Fibre Containers Pty. Ltd., Carlton & United Breweries Ltd., and Northern Australian Breweries Ltd. Director: Associated Pulp & Paper Mills Ltd., Herald & Weekly Times Ltd., and other companies. Chairman Pensions Committee Melbourne Legacy from February 1959. Former member, Council and President Law Institute of Victoria, 1965–66. *Clubs:* Naval & Miliary; Victoria Racing; Royal Automobile, etc. *Address:* 19 Russell Street, Toorak, Vic.; and *office* 390 Lonsdale Street, Melbourne, Vic., Australia.

**COHEN, Geoffrey**, LLB. Australian executive. *B.* 1908. *Educ.* Adwalton Scotch Coll. and Melbourne Univ. *M.* (1) 1930, Lorna Wenzel. *Daus.* 2. *M.* (2) 1955, Elizabeth Merryweather. *Career:* Partner law firm of Pavey, Wilson, Cohen & Carter 1931. Commissioned Aust. Military Forces 1933; private air pilot's certificate 1938, commercial certificate 1944; active duty A.M.F. 1939; Aust. Imperial Forces Oct. 1939; Staff Capt. Aust. O/S Base; M.E. Jan. 1940 (D.A.A. and Q.M.G. Aug. 1940); D.A.Q.M.G. 1st Aust. Corps Aug.–Nov. 1940; C.O. A.I.F. (M.E.) K.S. 1940–42; D.A.Q.M.G. HQ Allied Land Forces, S.W.P.A., Maj., May 1942–44; Res. of Officers, Maj. 1944. Chairman of Directors of numerous companies in Eastern States before removing to Perth 1951. Chairman, The Swan Brewery Co. Ltd., and director of many other companies in the brewing, hotel, radio, television and insurance spheres. Past-Pres. Chamber of Manufactures; Austr. Tourist Commission; Council Aust. Nat. Gallery; currently Fellow and/or Council Member of various institutes and associations in the professional service and manufacturing spheres. *Address:* 18 Esplanade, Peppermint Grove, W.A.; and 15 Mount Street, Perth, W.A., Australia.

**COHEN, Maurice**, OBE. Australian solicitor and company director. *B.* 1915. *Educ.* Melbourne Univ. (LLM). *M.* 1941, Thelma Libow. *Daus.* 2. *Career:* Commissioner for taking Affidavits: High Court, all Australian States, Papua-New Guinea, and New Zealand. Pres., Melbourne High School Council 1958–61, Melbourne High School Old Boys' Assn. 1953–55, and Hillel Foundation Victoria 1960–64. Mem. Bd. Governors, Hebrew Univ., Jerusalem 1969–71; Exec. Member of several Jewish organizations since 1935. *Member:* Australian Inst. of International Affairs; United Services Inst. and Graduates Union. *Clubs:* Royal Automobile Victoria; Cranbourne Country. *Address:* 56 Kooyong Road, Caulfield, Vic.; and *office* 400 Lonsdale Street, Melbourne, Vic.. Australia.

**COHEN, Sir Rex Arthur Louis**, KBE. British. *B.* 1906. *Educ.* Rugby School and Trinity Coll., Cambridge (BA). *M.* 1932, Nina Alice Castello. Dir. Tribune Investment Trust. *Award:* Officer, Order of Orange Nassau (Netherlands). *Address:* Ruckmans Farm, Oakwood Hill, Dorking, Surrey.

**COHEN, Stanley**. British politician. *B.* 1927. *Educ.* Elementary School. *M.* 1954, Brenda Patricia Rafferty. *S.* 3. *Dau.* 1. *Career:* Employed, Tailoring Industry 1941–45; Royal Navy 1945–47; Tailoring Industry 1947–52; Clerical Officer British Rail 1952–70; Member Leeds City Council 1953–71; Member of Parliament for Leeds since 1970; PPS to Min. of State, Dept. of Educ. & Science since 1976. *Clubs:* Irish Centre Leeds; Crossgates Recreational. *Address: office* House of Commons, London, S.W.1.

**COHEN, Wilbur Joseph**. American Dean, School of Education Univ. Mich., U.S.A. *B.* 1913. *Educ.* Univ. of Wisconsin (PhB 1934). *M.* 1938, Eloise Bittel. *S.* 3. *Career:* Asst. Secy. for Legislation, Dept. of Health, Education and Welfare 1961–65; Under Secy., 1965–68, Secy. 1968–69; Professor of Education since 1969. Chmn., Pres. Kennedy's Task Force on Health and Social Security 1960; Prof. of Public Welfare Admin., School of Social Work, University of Michigan 1956–; Dir., Div. of Res. and Statistics, Social Security Admin. 1953–56 (Technical Advisor to Commissioner for Social Security 1935–52); Asst. to Exec. Dir., Pres. Roosevelt's Cabinet Cttee. on Economic Security 1934–35. *Publications:* Retirement Policies in Social Security; Social Security, Programs, Problems and Policies; Income and Welfare in the United States; Readings in Social Security. LHD Adelphi Coll.; LLD Univ. of Wisconsin, Yeshiva, Brandeis, Detroit, Kenyon, Louisville; Cleveland State, Ohio State. Mich. State. *Member:* National Association Social Workers; American Public Welfare Association; American Economic Association; Industrial Relations Research Association; Phi Kappa Phi; Artus; Bd. of Governors, Univ. of Haifa. Democrat; National Academy of Sciences, National Inst. of Medicine. *Club:* National Democratic. *Address:* School of Education, The Univ. of Michigan, Ann Arbor, Michigan, 48104, U.S.A.

**COKE, Gerald Edward**, CBE, Hon. FRAM, DL, JP. British merchant banker (retired). *B.* 1907. *Educ:* Eton; New Coll., Oxford (MA). *M.* 1939, Patricia, eldest dau. of Hon. Sir Alexander Cadogan. *S.* John Alexander, Michael Gerald (*Dec.*) and David Edward. *Dau.* Lavinia May. *Career:* (Former) Director: Rio Tinto-Zinc Corp. Ltd., S. G. Warburg & Co., UK Provident Inst. and other companies; Treas., Bridewell Royal Hospital (King Edwards School, Witley) 1946–72; Chairman, Glyndebourne Arts Trust 1955–75; a Governor of the BBC 1961–66; JP, Hants. *Club:* Brooks's. *Address:* Jenkyn Place, Bentley, Hants. (Tel. Bentley 3118.)

**COLBAN, Erik**. Norwegian diplomat. *B.* 1912. *Educ.* University of Oslo, Dr. Juris (Dr. of Law). *M.* 1949, *S.* 1. *Daus.* 4. *Career* Secy. Ministry of Foreign Affairs 1938–46; Secy. of Norwegian legation, the Hague 1946–47; Chief of Division, Ministry of Foreign Affairs 1947–52; Counsellor of Norwegian Embassy, Stockholm 1952–59; Consul-General Cape Town 1959–63; Ambassador, Buenos Aires, Asuncion and Montevideo 1963–68; Dir.-Gen. Ministry of Foreign Affairs 1968-73; Norwegian Ambassador, Berne since 1973. *Member:* International Law Assn. (Norwegion Section). *Decorations:* Comdr. Norwegian Order of St. Olav; Grand Cross Argentinian Order of Mayo Al Merito; Comdr. Finnish Order of the Lion; Comdr. (1st Class) Swedish Order Polar Star. *Publications:* Stortinget og Utenrikspolitikken (The Norwegian Parliament and Foreign Affairs.) *Address:* 90 Kirchenfeldstrasse, CH 3005 Berne; and *office* 29 Dufourstrasse, CH-3005, Berne, Switzerland.

**COLE, Lord (George James Cole)**, GBE (1973). British. Commander, Order of Orange Nassau, 1963. *B.* 1906. *Educ.* Raffles Institution Singapore. *M.* 1940, Ruth Harpham. *S.* Jonathan Dare. *Dau.* Juliet Anthea. *Career:* Joint Managing Director, The United Africa Co. Ltd. 1952–55 (Director 1945–63); Chairman, Palm Line 1952–55. Chairman, Unilever Ltd., 1960–70; Vice-Chairman, Unilever N.V., 1960–70; Director: Finance Corp. for Industry Ltd. 1965–73; Chmn., Rolls Royce (1971) Ltd. 1971–73. *Member:* Chmn., Leverhulme Trust; Civic Trust (Trustee); Chmn., Advertising Association 1970–73; Member, International Advisory Cttee. Chase Manhattan Bank 1965–73; Council Royal Inst. International Affairs; Vice-Pres., United Kingdom South Africa Trade Assn.; Member Cttee. into the Governanse of the Univ. of London 1970–72; Past Dep. Chmn., The Lond. Grad. School of Business Studies (Gov. Body); Government Advisory Committee on the appointment of Advertising Agents (Chairman) 1962–70. *Clubs:* Athenaeum; Travellers'; Hurlingham. *Address:* 50 Victoria Road, Kensington, London, W.8.

**COLE, Claude Neville David**, LBE, JP. British (Welsh). *B.* 1928. *Educ.* Royal Masonic School; Harvard Business School. *M.* 1950, Alma Gwlithyn Williams. *S.* Robert David. *Dau.* Deborah Gwlithyn. *Career:* Journalist, Merthyr Express; South Wales Echo; Daily Graphic (Manchester); Daily Sketch (London). Welsh Editor, Empire News 1954–56; Editor, Western Mail (National Daily of Wales) 1956–59, Man. Dir., Western Mail & Echo Ltd., 1960–67; Man. Dir., Newcastle Chronicle and Journal Ltd.; Celtic Press Ltd., Press Consul. tancy Services Ltd. since 1965; Dir., Press Association Ltd. since 1972, Chmn. 1976–78; Trustee, Visnews Ltd.; Asst. Man. Dir. and Editorial Dir., Thomson Regional Newspapers Ltd.; Man. Dir. and Chief Exec. Thomson Regional Newspapers Ltd.; Dir., Welsh National Opera Co. Ltd. since 1964. *Member:* Court and Cncl., Univ. of Wales. Former member, Council of Welsh National School of Medicine; Governing Body, Cardiff College of Music and Drama; Council of Industrial Association of Wales; Welsh Hospitals Board; Council of Social Services for Wales. Chairman, Working Party, Welsh Tourist Board; Cardiff New Theatre Trust; Pres., Tenovus Charities. *Clubs:* East India & Public Schools; Lansdowne; Cardiff and County. *Publications:* This and Other Worlds; Meeting Places & Other Poems; The Practice of Journalism; numerous papers and articles. *Address:* 71 Ashley Gardens, Westminster, London, S.W.1. and *office* Greater London House, Hampstead Road, London, N.W.1.

**COLE, Sir David (Lee)** KCMG, MC. *B.* 1920. *Educ.* Cheltenham College and Sidney Sussex College, Cambridge (MA with First Class Hons. in History). *M.* 1945, Dorothy Patton. *S.* David. *Career:* First Secretary: U.K. Mission to U.N., New York 1948–51, and British High Commn., New Delhi 1953–56; Principal Private Sec. to Secretary of State for Commonwealth Relations 1957–60; Head of Personnel Dept., Commonwealth Office 1961–63; British Deputy High Commissioner in Ghana 1963–64; British High Commissioner in Malawi 1964–67; Minister (Political) British High Commission in India, 1967–70; Asst. Under-Secy. State Foreign & C'wealth. Office 1970–73; British Ambassador to Thailand since 1973. *Club:* Travellers' (London). *Address:* c/o Foreign and Commonwealth Office, London, S.W.1.

**COLE, Desmond Thorne,** MA. South African. *B.* 1922. *Educ.* MA (Rand.), *cum laude,* 1952. *M.* 1967, Naureen Adele Lambert. *S.* 2 (by previous marriage). *Career:* Served in World War II (in East Africa, Egypt, Western Desert to Tunis with British 8th Army; Actg. Captain, commissioned 1942) 1940–46; released to Reserve of Officers with rank of WS/Lieut. Lecturer in Bantu Languages 1949; Professor of Bantu Languages, University of the Witwatersrand July 1954—; Editor, African Studies (quarterly journal, Witwatersrand University Press); Visiting Research Professor in African Linguistics, Georgetown Univ., Washington, D.C., 1961–62; Visiting professor in African Linguistics at Univ. of Calif., Los Angeles, Jan.–June 1966; and at Duquesne Univ., Pittsburgh, Pa., June–Aug. 1966. *Publications:* An Introduction to Tswana Grammar (1955); Bantu Linguistic Studies in South Africa (1957); A Course in Tswana, (1962); Some Features of Ganda Linguistic Structure, (1965); various articles in academic and technical journals. Fellow, African Studies Assn., U.S.A. 1961–70. *Member:* International Organization for Succulent Plant Research; Royal Society of South Africa; Linguistic Society of America; International Linguistic Association; International Phonetic Association; International African Institute, etc. *Address:* Department of African Languages, University of the Witwatersrand, 2001 Johannesburg, South Africa.

**COLE, Fred Carrington.** President, Council on Library Resources Inc. 1967—. *B.* 1912. *Educ.* Louisiana State Univ. (AB 1934, MA 1936, PhD 1941). *M.* 1937, Lois Ferguson. *S.* Fred Carrington, Jr., Robert Grey and Taylor Morris. *Dau.* Caroline. *Career:* Member, Board of Directors, American Council on Education; Chmn., Commission on Education, and International Affairs, American Council on Education. Member, Ford Scholarship Board, Ford Motor Co. Fund 1964; Chmn. and member, Board of Trustees, College Entrance Examination Board 1962—. Director, Council on Library Resources Inc. 1963—; Chmn., Dept. of Army Historical Advisory Committee 1963—; Member, Research Adv. Council of Education, Dept. of Health, Education and Welfare 1963—. Successively research asst. instructor in history and editorial associate of Journal of Southern History (managing editor 1941–42), Louisiana State Univ. 1936–42. Active duty with U.S.N.R. 1942–46. Co-editor, Southern Biography Series 1938–42; Assoc. Prof. of History, Tulane Univ. 1946–47 (Prof. 1947–59. Dean, Coll. of Arts and Sciences 1947–55, Academic Vice-Pres. 1954–59); Pres. of Washington and Lee Univ., 1959–67; Special Consultant to Ford Foundation 1954–55; Assoc. Editor, Mississippi Valley History Review 1946–53. *Publications:* International Relations in Institutions of Higher Learnings in the South. Hon. LLD, Union College 1961, Washington & Lee Univ. 1968; special commendation from Surgeon-General U.S.N. 1945. *Member:* Southern American and Mississippi Valley Historical Associations; Academy of Political Science; Chmn., Council Nominating Committee, Phi Beta Kappa; Phil Kappa Phi: Pi Sigma Alpha; Omicron Delta Kappa; Sigma Chi. *Club:* Century (N.Y.C.); Cosmos (Washington D.C.). *Address:* 3900 Watson Pl. NW, Wash., D.C., U.S.A.

**COLE, George Francis.** British. *B.* 1918. *Educ.* Manchester Grammar Sch. *Career:* Founder Chmn., The National Exhibition Centre Ltd; 1970–75; Dir., Clarkson Head Harris Ltd.; Chmn. Crane's Screw (Holdings) Ltd., James Cooke & Son Ltd.; Past Pres., Birmingham Chamber of Commerce. Fellow, British Inst. of Management & Life Gov., Birmingham Univ.; Liveryman & Freeman, City of London. *Address:* 27 Garnet Court, Sceptre Park, Chelmscote Road, Olton, Solihull, West Midlands B92 8DA; and *office* Wellington Mills, Floodgate St. Birmingham B5 5SH.

**COLE, Thomas Frederick Cooper,** QC. Canadian barrister, solicitor and notary public; Director and officer of miscellaneous companies. *B.* 1917. *Educ.* University Coll., Univ. of Toronto (BA 1938); Osgoode Hall Law School (Barrister-at-law 1941). *M.* 1946, Marianne Elizabeth Marks. *S.* 1. *Dau.* 1. *Career:* With Legal Dept., Wartime Housing Ltd. 1941–43; Roberts, Osborne, Archibald & Seagram 1943–45; Roberts, Archibald, Seagram & Cole 1946–67; Strathy, Archibald, Seagram & Cole 1968–77; Strathy, Archibald & Seagram 1977—. *Member:* Law Socy. of Upper Canada; Canadian Bar Assn.; County of York Law Assn.; International Bar Association; Board of Trade of Metropolitan Toronto; Phi Delta Theta. *Publication:* Mining Law of Canada (Amer. Inst. of Mining Law). *Clubs:* Lawyers; Badminton & Racquet (Toronto); Cuckoo Valley Fishing; Beaver Winter. *Address:* 219 Inglewood Drive, Toronto, Ont.; and *office* Box 438, Commerce Court Postal Station, Toronto, Ont. M5L 1J3, Canada.

**COLEFAX, Peter.** American. *B.* 1903. *Educ.* Eton College and Christ Church Coll., Oxford Univ. (MA). Dir., Kerr-McGee Corp.; Investment Company of America; New Perspective Fund Inc.; Pres., Santa Barbara Museum of Art. *Address:* 1636 Moore Road, Santa Barbara, Calif. 93108, U.S.A.

**COLEMAN, Donald Richard,** MP. British politician and Lord Commissioner of HM Treasury since 1974. *B.* 1925. *Educ:* Cadoxton Boys' School, Cardiff Technical College. *M.* 1966, Margaret Elizabeth Morgan. *S.* 1. *Dau.* 1. *Career:* Labour MP for Neath since 1964; Parliamentary Private Secretary to Min. of State for Wales (later Secy. of State for Wales) 1967–70; Opposition Whip 1970–74. *Address:* House of Commons, London, S.W.1.

**COLEMAN, Raymond W.** Professor Emeritus, Univ. of Illinois. *B.* 1901. *Educ.* BBA; MBA; PhD. *M.* 1927, Essie Bee Pumphrey. *S.* Ellsworth Pumphrey and Bruce Pumphrey. *Career:* Asst. Prof. and Associate Prof., Management Engineering, Carnegie Inst. of Technology 1929–42; With A.A.F. (Captain 1942, Lieutenant-Col. 1946); Chief Ext. Service U.S. Dept. Commerce 1946–48; Dir., Bureau of Business Research, West Virginia Univ. 1948–56; Consultant, United States Dept. Commerce, Small Bus. Administration 1949—; Dean, College of Commerce, West Virginia Univ. 1952–61; Ford Foundation Scholar 1961–62; Dean, College of Business Admin., Univ. of Illinois 1963–66; Professor, Economics and Management 1966–69; Past President, West Virginia Tax Institute; Member, Board of Trustees, Joint Council on Economic Education 1958–61. *Publications:* Pledged Revenue for Government Bonds (1936); Elements of Accounting (1941); Government Bonds and the Balanced Budget (1941); The Role of Accounting in Management (1948); Bureaus of Business and Economic Research—A Survey of Objectives (1958); Our Changing American Economy (1963); Contr. to Business Topics, Mich. State Univ. (1968) and Contr. to La Revista Internazionale di Economiche e Commerciali (1970). *Member:* Beta Gamma Sigma; Beta Alpha Psi; Alpha Kappa Psi. *Address:* 4117 Schwalbe Drive, Sarasota, Florida 33580 U.S.A.

**COLES, Sir Edgar Barton.** Australian company director. *B.* 1899. *Educ.* Scotch College (Launceston, Tasmania); Associate of Australian Society of Accountants. *M.* 1927, Mabel Irene Johnston. *S.* Robert Barton. *Daus.* Lois Irene and Jennifer Anne Eldridge. *Career:* With G. J. Coles & Co. Ltd.; Secretary 1921–34, Director since 1930, Managing Director 1940–44, Sole Managing Director 1944–61, Controlling Man. Dir. 1961–67, Chmn. 1963–68. President: Retail Traders Assoc. of Victoria 1946–48 and 1951–54; and Australian Council of Retailers 1952–54. Member, Council of Royal Agricultural Socy. of Victoria 1957—. *Clubs:* Athenaeum, Victoria Racing (Melbourne); Victoria Amateur Turf; Melbourne Cricket; Peninsula Country Golf; Lawn Tennis Assn. of Victoria. *Address:* Hendra, Mount Eliza, Vic.; and *office* 282 Lt. Collins Street, Melbourne, Vic., Australia.

**COLIN, André,** D. en D. French politician. *B.* 1910. *M.* 1950, Marguerite Laurent. *S.* Pierre, Paul. *Daus.* Anne-Marie, Françoise. *Career:* Secretary of State, Presidency of the Council, in charge of information, Bidault Cabinet 1946; Minister of Merchant Marine, Queuille Cabinet 1948–49;

Secretary of State for the Interior, Bidault Cabinet 1950, Pleven Cabinet, Aug. 1951, and Faure Cabinet, Jan. 1952; Sec. of State for Interior in René Mayer Cabinet, Jan. 1953; Deputy for Finistère since 1945; Minister for Overseas France, May 1958; Senator for Finistère, Apr. 1959—; National President, M.R.P., May 1959–May 1963; President, Popular Republican Group and Democratic Centre at Senate 1963; Member, European Parliament since 1964; President of the Commission on Foreign Affairs of Defence and the armed forces since 1973; Pres., General Council of Finistère since 1964; Pres., Regional Council of Brittany 1976. *Awards:* Croix de Guerre; Chevalier de la Légion d'Honneur; Médaille de la Résistance avec rosette. *Address:* 11 Place Vauban, Paris 7e, and 10 Rue Voltaire, Brest.

**COLIN, Ralph Frederick.** American Attorney-at-Law; Counsel to Rosenman Colin Freund Lewis & Cohen. (575 Madison Avenue, N.Y.C.). *B.* 1900. *Educ.* N.Y. Public Schools; Townsend Harris Hall; College of the City of New York (BA 1919); Columbia Univ. Law School (LLB 1921). *M.* 1931, Georgia Talmey. *S.* Ralph Frederick, Jr. *Dau.* Pamela Talmey (Lady Harlech). *Career:* Director and Gen. Counsel, Columbia Broadcasting System Inc. 1927–70; Rotary Electric Steel Co. 1943–57; Jonas & Naumburg Corp. 1931–59; Columbia Artists Management Inc., Parke-Bernet Galleries Inc. 1959–64; Director, Alfred A. Knopf Inc. (1938–66); Calvert Petroleum Co. 1957–61. *Member:* Association of the Bar of the City of New York (Vice-Pres. 1958–59). County Lawyers Assn., New York State Bar Assn., American Bar Association, Administrative Vice-President and General Counsel, Art Dealers Assn. of America, Inc.; Trustee and Vice-Pres., Museum of Modern Art, N.Y. 1954–69; Trustee, Amer. Fed. of Arts 1946–56; member, Visiting Cttee., for the Department of Fine Arts and the Fogg Museum, Harvard University 1951–66–67–74; Member Advisory Cttee., The Arts Center Program, Columbia Univ.; Member, Board of Visitors to School of Law, Columbia Univ. 1961—. *Publications:* The Priority of the United States in the Payment of its Claims Against a Bankrupt (Columbia Law Review Apr. 1924); An Analysis of the 1926 Amendments of the Bankruptcy Act (Columbia Law Review, Nov. 1926); Why Upset Price, an Argument for Reorganization By Decree (Illinois Law Review, June 1933). *Address:* 941 Park Avenue, New York 10028; and *office* 575 Madison Avenue, New York 10022, N.Y., U.S.A.

**COLLADO, Emilio Gabriel.** American. *B.* 1910. *Educ.* MIT, SB; Harvard Univ., AM, PhD. *M.* (1) 1932, Janet Gilbert (*Dec.*). *S.* Emilio Gabriel III. *Dau.* Lisa. (2) 1972, Maria Elvira Tanco. *Career:* With Standard Oil Co. (N.J.) (now EXXON Corp.). Assistant Treasurer 1949–54; Treasurer 1954–60; Director 1960—; Vice-President 1962–66. Executive Vice-President and Director 1966–75 (Ret'd.); Director: Discount Corp. of New York 1961—Member Bd. Dir., Morgan Guaranty Trust Co. of New York & J. P. Morgan & Co. Inc.; Pres., Adela Investment Co. S.A. 1976—. *Member:* Council of the Americas; Board of Visitors, Fletcher School of Law and Diplomacy of Tufts Univ.; Member Bd. Dirs., Academy of Political Science; Member and Dir.: National Bureau of Economic Research, American Economic Association; Trustee and Member. Cttee. Economic Development; Chmn. Center, Inter-Amer. Relations; Dir., Atlantic Cncl. of the U.S. Atlantic Inst. & Spanish Inst. USA-BIAC; Trustee Hispanic Socy. of America; *Awards:* Hon. LLD New Mexico State Univ. 1957; Hon. LLD Lond Island Univ. 1973. *Publications:* Foreign Affairs, July 1963, article: Economic Development Through Private Enterprise. *Clubs:* University (NYC); Metropolitan, International (Washington); Piping Rock, Racquet and Tennis, River (N.Y.). *Address: office* 1 Rockefeller Plaza, New York, N.Y. 10020, U.S.A.

**COLLIN, Fernand Jozef Maria Fanny.** Belgian banker and university professor. *B.* 1897. *Educ.* University of Louvain (LLD, L en Ph). *M.* (1) 1928, Madeleine Casters (*Dec.* 1961), (2) Maria BelleKens. *S.* Fernand, Paul. *Daus.* Myriam, Rita, Lydia. *Career:* Lawyer, Antwerp 1923–38; Lecturer, Univ. of Louvain 1925; Professor, Univ. of Louvain 1927–68; member, Conseil Supérieur de l'Education physique et des sports 1930–40; Royal Commissary to middle classes 1937; Chmn., Central Social Section, Belgian Banking Association 1939–45; Dean of Faculty of Law and member of Rectorial Council 1945–48; Chairman of Board, Kredietbank, Brussels 1938–73; Member, Managing Committee, Institut de Réescompte et de Garantie 1940–63; Chairman Banque Diamantaire Anversoise 1964–68; Continental Foods since 1968; Director, Gevaert Photo Products since 1952; Chmn., High Council of the Family 1952–59; Chmn., Benelux Committee 1959–66, Cardiol Foundation Princess Liliane 1961–73, Business Managers Training Center, University of Louvain 1962–71. *Awards:* Grand Officer Ordre de la Couronne; Grand Officer, Ordre Leopold II; Commander, Ordre de la Couronne; Commander, Ordre de Léopold; Commander, Order of Orange Nassau; Commander, Order Al Merito della Republica (Italy); Comdeur, Ordre Grand-Ducal de la Couronne de Chêne; Commander, Order S. Gregory the Great; Grand Officer, Ordre de Merit du G D de Luxembourg. *Publications:* Enrico Ferri et l'Avant-Projet du code pénal italien de 1921; Verslagbetreffende den Ambachts—en handeldrijvenden Middenstand; Strafrecht; Strafwetboek—Wetboek van Strafvordering en Bijvoegsel (with H. Bekaert); The Use of a Currency of Account in International Loans. *Address:* 196 Mechelse steenweg, Antwerp, Belgium.

**COLLINS, Arthur Andrews.** *B.* 1909. *Educ.* Amherst (Mass.) College, Coe College, and State Univ. of Iowa (special classes). Dr. Science (Hon.) Coe Coll., 1954; Dr. Eng. (Hon.) Poly. Inst. Brooklyn 1968, S.M.U. 1970; Dr. Sc. (Hon.) Mount Mercy Coll. 1974. *M.* (1) 1930, Margaret Van Dyke (*D.* 1955), (2) 1957, Mary Margaret Meis. *S.* Michael, Alan and David. *Dau.* Susan. *Career:* President & Chairman of the Board, Collins Radio Co. (which he founded in 1931). Pioneer in the development of high frequency radio communication; inventor of various radio electronic devices and circuitary; automatic tuned multi-channel radio equipment; data transmission equipment and systems; propagation and reception. Bd. Trustees Coe Coll. 1945–51; Graduate Research Center, Southwest 1962–69; Herbert Hoover Foundation 1965. *Awards:* DSc Coe College; Secy. Navy's Distinguished Public Service Citation; Fellow Inst. of Radio Engineers; Fellow I.E.E.E. *Publication:* Telecommunications—a Time for Innovation, 1973. *Address:* 13731 Danvers Drive, Dallas, Texas, 75240; and *office* 13601 Preston Rd., Suite 509W, Texas, 75240, U.S.A.

**COLLINS, Charles J.** *B.* 1894. *Educ.* BA; Hon. MA. *M.* 1919, Hazel Beatrice Wharton. *Daus.* Ann Wharton (Husted) and Josephine Spencer (Penberthy). *Career:* Second Lieut. Regular Army U.S.A. 1917 (resigned as Major 1919; served with VIII and IV French Armies, and I and II American Armies, France). Investment Analyst, E. E. MacCrone & Co. 1919–23 (Partner 1923–63); Chmn. and Dir. Investment Counsel 1930–59; Trustee, Investment Co. of America 1927–32; Editor and Publisher, Investment Letters Inc. 1934–62. Director: American Midland Co. 1930–63, American Industries Corp. 1929–33, 1955–63; Investment Research Corp. 1927–32, American Industries Securities Corp. 1930–33. Member N.Y. Stock Exchange 1929–30. Pres. Detroit Financial Analysts Socy. 1952; Trustee Virginia Military Institute Lexington Va. *Publications:* Fortune's Before You; The Coming Battle for World Sovereignty; contributions to various publications. Independent. *Clubs:* Detroit; Detroit Country. *Address:* 858 Lochmoor Blvd., Grosse Pointe Woods Mich. 48236, U.S.A.

**COLLINS, Galen F.** American. *B.* 1927. *Educ.* Purdue Univ. (BS Pharm, MS, PhD Pharm Chem). *M.* 1956, Ann Elizabeth Averitt. *S.* Galen Robert and Scott Franklin. *Dau.* Amelia Lynn. *Career:* Chief, Norwich Products Development, Norwich Pharmacal Co. 1960–63; Head, Ames Pharmac. Research Section, Miles Laboratories Inc., Elkart, Ind. 1959–60; Asst. to Dir., Miles-Ames Pharmaceutical Research Lab., Miles Labs. Inc. 1958–59, Research Pharmaceutical Chemist 1953–58. Director, Research Division, The S. E. Massengill Co., Bristol, Tenn. 1967 (Manager 1963–67). Contributor to various journals. Owner of several U.S. patents. *Member:* Sigma Xi; Phi Lambda Upsilon; Rho Chi. *Fellow.* Amer. Inst. of Chemists, and Amer. Association for Advancement of Science. *Member:* Amer. Pharmaceutical Assn.; Amer. Inst. of Management; Amer. Chemical Socy.; Assoc. Clinical Chemists; Assoc. Clinical Scientists. *Clubs:* Elks; Coral Gable County. *Address:* V.P. Scientific Director, Dade Div. American Hospital Supply Corp, P.O. Box 672, Miami, Florida and 10800 S.W. 6th Avenue, Miami, Florida, U.S.A.

**COLLINS, Henry Edward,** CBE. British consulting mining engineer. *B.* 1903. *Educ.* Univ. of Sheffield; MEng. FInst-MinE, Chartered Engineer. *M.* 1934, Cecilia Harris. (*D.* 1975). *Career:* Sen. Lect. in Mining, Univ. of Sheffield 1935–39; Manager, Rossington Main Colliery 1939–42; Agent, Markham Main Colliery 1942–44; Chief Mining Agent, Doncaster Amalgamated Collieries Ltd. 1944–45; Dir. of Coal Production, Control Commission for Germany 1945–47; British Chairman, Coal Control Group, Control Commission for Germany, 1947–50; Production Director, Durham Division, N.C.B., 1950–56; Director-General of Reconstruction, N.C.B. 1956–57. Board Member for Production, N.C.B. 1957—67; Member, Govt. Cttee. on Coal Derivatives 1959–60, Chmn.; N.C.B. Opencast Exec. 1961–67, N.C.B. Brickworks Exec. 1962–67 and Whittlesea Central Brick Co. Ltd. 1967; Dir. Omnia Concrete Sales Ltd., and Bradley's (Concrete) Ltd. 1966–67. Former Member Advisory Council, Research and Development, Ministry of Power; Mining Qualifications Board Member, Safety in Mines Advisory Board. *Publications:* various papers on mining engineering and allied subjects to professional societies. *Club:* Athenaeum. *Address:* 22 West Side, London, SW19 4UF.

**COLLINS, Norman Richard.** British author. *B.* 1907. *Educ.* William Ellis School (London). *M.* 1931, Sarah Helen Martin. *S.* 1. *Daus.* 2. *Career:* At Oxford Univ. Press 1926–29; Asst. Literary Editor, News Chronicle 1929–33; Deputy Chairman, Victor Gollancz Ltd. (publishers) 1934–41; Controller, Light Programme, B.B.C. 1946–47; late Gen. Overseas Service Director, B.B.C.; Controller of Television, B.B.C. 1947–50 (resigned); Governor, British Film Institute 1949–51. President: Pitman Fellowship 1957; Radio Industries Club 1950; Regent Advertising Club 1959–66; Vice-Pres., Council for Nature, 1963–66. Governor: Sadlers Wells Foundation; Atlantic Institute 1964–69; Chmn., Central Sch. of Speech & Drama; General Commissioner for Income Tax 1967—; Chmn., Age Action Year 1976; Deputy Chairman, Associated Television Ltd. *Publications:* The Facts of Fiction (1932); Penang Appointment (1934); The Three Friends (1935); Trinity Town (1936); Flames Coming out of the Top (1937); Love in Our Time (1937); 'I Shall Not Want' (1940); Anna (1942); London Belongs to Me (1945); Black Ivory (1947); Children of the Archbishop (1951); The Bat that Flits (1952); The Bond Street Story (1958); The Governor's Lady (1969); The Captain's Lamp (play). Conservative. *Clubs:* Turf; M.C.C. *Address:* Mulberry House, Church Row, London, N.W.3.

**COLLINS, Peter Blumfeld.** British journalist. *B.* 1909. *Educ.* Sherborne School; Royal College of Science (Imperial College); ARCS; BSc (Entomology). *M.* (1) 1934, Gloria Welby Fisher, and (2) 1948, Leonora Dorf. *S.* 2. *Daus.* 3. *Career:* Reporter, Daily Express, London 1933; Writer and Editor, Amalgamated Press 1934–39; served in World War II (Royal Corps of Signals and Reconnaissance Corps; later with Control Commission, and finally O.C. No. 1 British Army Newspaper Unit; released as Major) 1939–46; Agricultural Officer, British Council, and editor of British Agricultural Bulletin 1947–50; Agricultural Officer, Festival of Britain 1950–51; joined F.A.O. 1951 as Chief Editor, becoming in 1952 Senior Information Officer and, in 1956, Chief, Reports Section. *Publications:* Household Pests (Pitman, 1936); Millions Still Go Hungry (for F.A.O., 1957); British Trees (Sunday Times, 1959); Fertilizers (Overseas Development Instit., 1963); articles, chiefly on agriculture, forestry and tropical diseases, and on F.A.O. and other international bodies in many publications; considerable broadcasting on scientific subjects. Science Correspondent, The Sunday Times (London) 1958–60; Special Information Officer attached to U.N. Special Fund 1960–61; Adviser on Scientific Publicity, Fed. Govt. of Nigeria 1961–62; Editor, U.N. Conference on Science and Technology 1963; Consultant, U.N. and its Specialized Agencies, 1964–72. Editor, Lower Indus Report, 1965; Consultant, Office of National Development and Planning, Govt. of Zambia, 1966; Consultant, UN Conference on the Human Environment 1971, and to UN/CESI since 1973; Geneva Correspondent, Nature, since 1974. *Address:* 5 Umbria Street, London, S.W.15.

**COLLINS, Samuel Vernon.** American. Managing Director, Southern Diamond Corp. Ltd. Director: Argus Oil Exploration Pty. Ltd.; Collins Consultants Pty. Ltd.; Collins Submarine Pipelines Ltd. (London); Collins Submarine Pipelines Africa Pty. Ltd.; Collins Submarine Pipelines S.W.A. Pty. Ltd.; Capetex Engineering Works Pty. Ltd.; Colprop Pty. Ltd.; Dolphin Marine Craft Pty. Ltd.; Die Veld Waterboor Maatskappy (Edms.) Bpk.; Establishment Collins International; Heerengracht Craft Pty. Ltd.; Marine Diamond Corp. Ltd.; Marine Terminals Pty. Ltd.; Mercor Trading Co. Pty. Ltd.; Mercury Travel Pty. Ltd.; Natal Farm Service Centre Pty. Ltd.; Savic Enterprises Pty. Ltd.; Sea Diamond Corp. Pty. Ltd.; Sea Outfalls Pty. Ltd.; South Carbonade Pty. Ltd.; Stag Brewery Ltd.; Taltex Engineering Pty. Ltd.; Vaalcol Explorations & Development Co. Pty. Ltd.; Viking Marine Craft Corp. Ltd.; Western Off-Shore Diamond Corp. Ltd.; Western Explorations Pty. Ltd. Sole Owner Collins Construction Co. (Port Lavaca, Texas). Life Member, American Underwater Socy. *Member:* S.W.A. Diamond Board. Hon. Attorney-General, Louisiana, and Hon. Asst. Attorney-General, Texas. Deputy Sheriff, Calhoun County, Texas. *Address:* 6th Floor, Barclays Bank Building, Heerengracht, Cape Town, South Africa.

**COLLINS, Hon. Mr. Justice Wilfred Herbert.** Judge of the Supreme Court. *B.* 1909. *Educ.* Sydney University (LLB). *M.* 1937, Margaret Agnes Simpson. *S.* 2. *Daus.* 3. *Career:* Called to Bar 1932; with Australian Imperial Forces 1942–45; member of N.S.W. Bar Council 1951–55; Judge, Supreme Court, New South Wales since 1955. Chairman Electoral Districts Commission 1957; Member, Archives Authority of N.S.W. 1961–73, Royal Commission on Petroleum 1973–76. *Clubs:* University; Tattersall's. *Address:* Judges' Chambers, Supreme Court, Sydney, N.S.W., Australia.

**COLLINS, William Howes.** Capt. U.S.N.R. (retd.). *B.* 1908. *Educ.* Williams Coll. (BA); Univ. of Grenoble (Dipl. 1924); Univ. of Heidelberg (Dipl. 1928); Indust. Coll. of Armed Forces 1949. *M.* 1935, Dorothy Jane Walker. *S.* William W. and Kent Howes. *Dau.* Derfla Jean. *Career:* Assistant to District Intelligence Officer, 4th Naval Dist. 1941–46; Dir. of Advertising (P.R.) Staff of President, Junior Board of Directors, member Sales Committee, Chairman, Employee Communications Advisory Committee, Dravo Corporation 1947–55 (similar positions with subsidiaries); Manager, Advertising and Sales Promotion, Standard Vacuum Oil Co., White Plains, New York, 1955–61. Manager, Advertising and Market Research, Mobil Petroleum Co. Inc. 1962–64; Pres. and Chmn. Intercontinental Associates Inc. since 1964. Appointed, by Secretary of State, Adviser to U.S. Delegation, Fifth Int. Conf. on Public Affairs, Geneva. Member, U.S. Trade Development Mission to Brazil 1967. Appointed by U.S. Secretary of Commerce as member of Regional Export Expansion Council. National Defense Executive Reserve Emeritus. *Member:* Beta Theta Pi; Naval Order of U.S.; Newcomen Socy. in N. America; Pennsylvania Consistory A.A.S.R.; Pennsylvania Socy.; Phi Beta Kappa Alumni of N.Y. (Life); Phi Beta Kappa Assoc. (Life); Public Relations Socy. of America; Sons of the American Revolution; Sons of the Revolution; U.S. Naval Institute; Order of Founders & Patriots; Soc. of Mayflower Descendants. Mason. *Clubs:* Williams (N.Y.); Victory (London); Old Lyme Country Club. *Address:* Kentwill, Essex, Conn. 06426, U.S.A.; and *office* Intercontinental Associates Inc., P.O. Box 396, Essex Conn. 06426, U.S.A.

**COLLIS, Richard John.** British. *B.* 1904. *M.* 1957, Marjorie Ridpath. *S.* John R. *Dau.* Patricia Anne (Brazier). *Career:* Chairman: Ridpath Bros. Ltd. 1962, Bamford Bros. Ltd. 1962, Lard Packers Ltd. 1960, Redriff Refinery Ltd. since 1964. *Member:* Anglo-Yugoslav Trade Council, and Joint Consultative Council for the Meat Trade in the U.K. New Zealand & Australian Agents Assn. 1953–64; Dir. Imported Meat Trade Association 1943; Chmn. Cttee. of the London Provision Exchange 1943–47. *Clubs:* City Livery; Australia; Canada: Royal Commonwealth; Moor Park Golf. *Address: office* Ridpath Bros. Ltd., 43 Shoe Lane, London, E.C.4.

**COLLYER, John Lyon.** American industrialist. *B.* 1893. *Educ.* Cornell Univ. (ME); Hon. Degrees from Mount Holyoke Coll., Ohio State Univ., New York Univ., Marietta Coll., Univ. of Akron and Coll. of Wooster. *M.* 1930, Georgia Forman. *Dau.* Georgia (Rea), and (*stepchildren*) Deborah (Shepard), Gilbert. *Career:* Member, Directors Advisory Committee, Morgan Guaranty Trust Co. of New York 1963—. Director: Automotive Old Timers; Hon. Trustee, Cttee. for Economic Development; Trustee: Alfred P. Sloan Fdn. 1949–66 (now Trustee Adv. Cttee.), Industr. Relations Counsellors 1957–65 (now Hon. Trustee). Successively Foreman, Personnel Dir. and Gen. Supt., Bethlehem Shipbuilding Corp. 1917–23; Vice-Pres., Dunlop Tyre & Rubber Co., Buffalo, N.Y. 1923–29; Works Dir., Dir. of Manufacture, Dir., Man. Dir., Dunlop Rubber Co., Fort Dunlop, England 1929–39; Dir.: Morgan Guaranty Trust Co. of N.Y. 1946–63; Eastman Kodak Co., 1959–69. Pres. and Chief Exec. Officer 1939–50, Pres., Chmn. and Chief Exec. Officer 1950–54, Chairman and Chief Exec. Officer 1954–58, Chairman 1958–60, The B.F. Goodrich Co. (Director 1939–64). Trustee, Cornell University 1941–65 (Chmn. 1953–59); Trustee Emeritus 1965—; Presidential Councillor, Cornell University. Industry Adviser to U.S. State Dept. in rubber meeting with representatives of Great Britain, France, Netherlands, etc. 1945–53; Special Director of Rubber Programmes, War Production Board, Mar.–July 1945; member. Business Council, U.S. Dept. of Commerce 1942— (Chmn. 1947–48). Awarded Medal for Merit by President for exceptionally meritorious conduct in the performance of outstanding service to U.S. in connection with development and production of synthetic rubber throughout the period of emergency and as special director Rubber Programs, War Board, 21 Mar.–18 July 1945. Chevalier, Legion of Honour (France). *Address:* 9016 Sandfly Lane, Vero Beach, Florida 32960, U.S.A.

**COLQUHOUN, Thomas Talbot,** MBE. Australian. *B.* 1904. *Educ.* Melbourne Univ. (MSc). *M.* 1931, Madge Kathleen Lindsay. *S.* Lindsay Talbot. *Dau.* Athalie Madge. *Career:* Lecturer in Botany and Zoology, Univ. of Adelaide, S.A. 1929–35; Plant Pathologist, Waite Agricultural Research Inst., Adelaide 1936–45; Deputy Director, War Service Land Settlement, South Australia 1946–53; Commonwealth Director of War Service Land Settlement, July 1953–69. Land Settlement Consultant to Department of Agriculture, 1969—. *Publications:* various botanical papers in scientific journals. MSc *ad cundem graduum*, Adelaide Univ. Fellow & Past Pres., Aust. Inst. of Agricultural Science. *Club:* Canberra Bowling. *Address:* 51 Melbourne Avenue, Forrest, Canberra; and *office* Department of Agriculture, Canberra, A.C.T., Australia.

**COLVILLE, Sir John Rupert,** CB, CVO. British banker. *B.* 1915. *Educ.* Harrow and Cambridge (First Class Honours History). *M.* 1948, Lady Margaret Egerton. *S.* 2. *Dau.* 1. *Career:* Asst. Private Secy. to Mr. Neville Chamberlain 1939–40; to Mr. Winston Churchill 1940–41 and 1943–45; to Mr. Clement Attlee 1945. Served in World War II (Pilot, R.A.F.V.R.) 1939–45. Counsellor, Foreign Service 1951; Private Secy. to Princess Elizabeth 1947–49; First Secy., British Embassy, Lisbon 1949–51; Joint Principal Private Secy. to the Prime Minister 1951–55. Director (since 1955): Hill, Samuel & Co. Ltd., Coutts & Co., Grindlay's Bank Ltd., Ottoman Bank (Dep. Chmn.); BASF (UK) Ltd.; Provident Life Assurance; Chmn. Eucalyptus Pulp Mills Ltd. & Thames Valley Broadcasting Ltd. *Publications:* Men of Valour (1972); Footprints in Time (1976); The New Elizabethans (1977). Officer, Legion of Honour (France). *Clubs:* White's; Pratts. *Address:* The Old Rectory, Stratfield Saye, Reading, Berks.; and *office* 100 Wood St., London EC2.

**COLVILLE OF CULROSS, Viscount (John Mark Alexander Colville).** *B.* 1933. *Educ.* Rugby; New Coll. Oxford (MA). *M.* 1958, Mary Elizabeth Webb-Bowen (diss. 1973). *S.* 4. (2) Margaret Birgitta, Vicountess Davidson, née Norton. *Career:* Lieut. Grenadier Guards Reserve; Barrister-at-law, Lincoln's Inn 1960; Minister of State, Home Office 1972–74. *Member:* Royal Company, Archers (Queen's Body Guard for Scotland). *Address:* Worlingham Hall, Beccles, Suffolk, and Fawsyde Kinneff, Inverbervie, Kincardineshire, Scotland.

**COLVIN, John Horace Ragnar,** CMG. British diplomat. *B.* 1922. *Educ.* Royal Naval Coll. Dartmouth; London Univ. School of Slavonic Studies. *M.* (1) 1948, Anne Manifold; (2) 1967, Moranna Cazenove. *S.* Mark, David. *Daus.* Zoë, Joanna. *Career:* Royal Navy 1935–49; H.M. Diplomatic Service since 1949, Oslo, Vienna, Kuala Lumpur; Consul-General, Hanoi 1965–67; Ambassador to Mongolia 1970–74. *Award:* Companion of the Order of St. Michael and St. George. *Clubs:* St. James. *Address:* The Old Parsonage, Pamber Heath, Basingstoke, Hants.; and *office* Foreign and Commonwealth Office, King Charles Street, London, S.W.1.

**COMANS, Charles Kennedy,** CBE, QC. Australian barrister and solicitor. *B.* 1914. *Educ.* St. Kevin's Christian Brothers College, Melbourne; and Univ. of Melbourne (LLM). *M.* 1944, Nancy Louisa Button. *S.* Michael, Charles Peter and Philip. *Dau.* Leigh. *Career:* Clerk, Taxation Dept., Canberra 1936; Lecturer (part-time) in law subjects, Canberra University College 1938–40 and 1945–48; various legal positions in Attorney-General's Dept. 1938–49; First Assistant Parliamentary Draftsman, 1949–70; Second Parliamentary Counsel 1970–72; First Parly. Counsel 1972–77; Consultant to Attorney-General since Feb. 1977. *Publications:* legal periodicals, including Australian Law Journal, Federal Law Review and Canadian Bar Review. John Madden Exhibitioner and Jessie Leggatt scholarship at Melbourne University. *Clubs:* Royal Canberra Golf; Canberra Wine & Food. *Address:* 21 Tasmania Circle, Forrest, Canberra, A.C.T., Australia.

**COMBE, Gordon Desmond,** MC. Australian. *B.* 1917. *Educ.* AASA and ACIS. *M.* 1940, Margaret Eley. *S.* 1. *Daus.* 4. *Career:* Bank Officer, State Bank of S.A. 1934–39; Officer of Parliament, S.A. 1940–72. With 2/43rd Australian Infantry Battalion 1940–45 (Commissioned 1941; twice wounded; Military Cross 1943); Grad. L.H.Q. Jnr. Staff School 1944; Bn. Adjutant (Capt.) 1944–45. Clerk of the House of Assembly, Parliament of South Australia (S.A.), 1953–72; Ombudsman for South Australia since 1972. *Publications:* Responsible Government in South Australia (1957); The Parliament of South Australia (1961); The second 43rd (1972). *Clubs:* Kooyonga Golf, Legacy. *Address;* 98 Penang Avenue, Edwardston, Ombudsman's Office, 50 Grenfell St., Adelaide, S.A., Australia.

**COMBS, Sir Willis (Ide).** KCVO, CMG. Retired diplomat. *B.* 1916. *Educ.* Victoria Univ. College N.Z.; St John's Coll. Cambridge. *M.* 1942, Grace Willis. *Daus.* 2. *Career:* with British Embassy, Paris 1947–51; Rio de Janeiro 1951–52, Peking 1953–55; Foreign Office 1956–59; Baghdad 1959–62; Rangoon 1965–67; Foreign and Commonwealth Office 1968–70; Ambassador to Indonesia 1970–75. *Award:* Knight Commander Royal Victorian Order; Companion St. Michael and St. George. *Address:* Sunset, Wadhurst Park, Wadhurst, Sussex.

**COMINOS, Achilles Z.,** Dr RER, Pol. Greek economist. *B.* 1911. *Educ.* Athens State Coll. Economic & Commercial Science; Berlin Univ. Doctor Diploma (1938). *M.* 1951, Betty Hellen Papastratos. *Dau.* Mina. *Career:* Asst. Secy., Velca Spinning Co., Piracus, Greece 1928–30; Analyst, UNRRA, assigned short periods, Ministry of Supply, Min. Finance 1945–46; Gen. Economic Advisor, Ministry, Co-ordination, Delegation OEEC, Paris, asst. head for Financial Affairs; Member Exec. Cttee., Supreme Board Economic Planning 1946–53; Ec. Advisor, member Bd., Papastratos Cigarette Mfg. Co. Ltd., Greek Delegate Cttee. International Cooperation, Development Southern Europe, Economic Commission for Europe 1953–55; Member, Permanent ministerial Cttee. attracting foreign investment to Greece 1953–74; Chmn. Bd., Greek Line Shipping, Dexion (Hellans) Ltd., Colgate Palmolive Ltd. 1968; Chmn., Interministerial Comm. European Cooperation, 1965–7 & 1972–74; Bd. Centre of Planning & Economic Research; Governor, National Bank of Greece; Chmn., Union, Greek Banks, ETHNIKI Insurance Co., National Bank Investment, Industrial Development, Hellenic, Hull & Aircraft Ins. Co., National Bank Foundation; Member Bd., Royal Research Inst., Nat. Gallery, Royal Welfare Fund; Central Cttee., Economic Development Programme, Alternate Governor for Greece Int. Bank 1968–71. *Member:* Econometric Socy. and Greek Socy. for Economics. *Awards:* Commander, Royal Order of the Phoenix; Royal Order of George I. Gold Cross. *Publications:* Die Waehrungs und Kreditpolik Der Bank von Griechenland (1940); The Necessity To Coordinate The Greek Money Market (1941); The Tools of Control Money and Capital-Markets (1940); Economic Development (1960); Weak Points of the Greek Economy (1964). *Address:* 1 Marasli Street, Athens (140), Greece.

**COMMINS, Thomas Vincent.** Irish Diplomat. *B.* 1913. *Educ.* Rockwell College, Univ. College, Dublin. *Career:* Entered Civil Service 1933; served in Departments of Argriculture, Industry and Commerce, and External Affairs; Commercial Attaché Embassy, Washington 1946–48; Counsellor, Dept. of External Affairs 1948–54; Counsellor, Embassy, Paris 1954–55; Chargé d'Affairs en titre, Lisbon 1955–59; Minister to Argentine 1959–60; Ambassador to Italy 1960–62; Ambassador to The Holy See 1962–66; Ambassador to France 1966–70 to The Holy See 1970–74; Dep. Secy., Dept. of For. Affairs Dublin 1974–77 (ret'd). *Address:* 12 Fairbrook Lawn, Ballyboden Road, Rathfarnham, W. Dublin, Ireland.

**COMMON, Frank B., Jr.,** QC. Canadian lawyer. *B.* 1920. *Educ.* Roslyn Avenue School and Westmount P.Q. High School (prep. and matric.), Royal Military College of Canada, Kingston, Ontario (eng.; grad. with diploma) and McGill Univ. *M.* 1946, Katharine Ruth Laws. *S.* 2 (1 dec'd). *Daus.* 5 *Career:* Served in World War II (Royal Canadian Engineers, in Canada, England and N.W. Europe; Mentioned in Dispatches); Senior Partner in firm of Ogilvy, Cope, Porteous, Montgomery Renault Clarke and Kirkpatrick (Montreal) Chmn. Fin. Cttee. and Dir., Gleneagles Investment Co. Ltd. Chairman and Director; Chmn. Exec. Ctee. Montreal Refrigerating Storage Ltd. Peterson, Howell & Heather (Canada) Ltd., PHH Leasing of Canada Ltd., Canadian Lease Management Ltd. PHH Aviation Ltd; Director: The Royal Bank of Canada, Trizec Corp. Ltd.; Place Viger Warehouse Ltd.; Peterson, Howel. & Heather Inc.; PHH Management Services Ltd. (U.K.); Canadian Salt Co. Ltd.; Canadian Rock Salt Co. Ltd.; Morton Industries of Canada Ltd.; Selco Mining Co. Ltd.; Artald Investments Ltd.; Ralston-Purina of Canada Ltd. (also Secy.), CIBA GEIGY Canada Ltd.; N. Amer. Car (Canada) Ltd.; Covent Canada Corp. Ltd (also

Chmn.); Covent North American Properties Ltd.; Beneficial Finance Co. of Canada; Priory Investment Co. Ltd.; Dep. Chmn. Dir. Cadbury-Schweppes Powell Ltd.; Canadian Adv. Bd. Sun Alliance & London Insurance Group. Assistant Secretary; Morton Chemical of Canada Ltd. *Member:* Canadian Tax Foundation (and Panel Member at various meetings), Public Relations Committee, Montreal Bar; First and Second Commonwealth and Empire Law Conferences (London 1955, Ottawa 1960); Formerly Chairman of Board, Life Governor and member of Board of Management, Douglas Hospital (1,650-bed public and private mental hospital); Past Pres., member of Exec. Cttee., Bd. of Management Canadian Red Cross (Quebec Provincial Div.); Hon. Mem., Canadian Red Cross 1964. Founder and Pres., Canadian Fdn. for Educational Development; Governor, Montreal Symphony Orchestra; Campaign Chairman, First Campaign in Greater Montreal of Combined Health Appeal and Red Cross; former Dir., Graduate Socy. of McGill Alma Mater; former member, City Council of Westmount (Commissioner of Finance and Public Works). *Clubs:* Mount Royal, Mt. Bruno Country, Montreal Indoor Tennis, (all in and around Montreal); The Brook (N.Y.C.); Bayou (Louisiana). *Address:* Apt. B101 3940 Cote Des Neiges Road, Montreal H3H 1W2 P.Q., and *office* 700 Place Ville Marie, Montreal, P.Q., H3B 1Z7, Canada.

**COMMON, Gilbert Andrew.** British. *B.* 1930. *Educ.* Winchester and Wadham College, Oxford (MA). *M.* 1956, Ann Chrisp. *Daus.* Fiona Joy, Kirsten Elizabeth, Catrina Mary and Shuna Ann Louise. *Career:* At Winchester 1944–48 then 18 months Nat. Service. Commissioned in the Royal Artillery, Wadham Coll., Oxford 1951–54. Joined Common Bros. Ltd., Exchange Bldgs., Newcastle-upon-Tyne 1955. Director: Hindustan Steam Shipping Co. Ltd. 1958—, Northumbrian Shipping Co. Ltd. 1958—, Home Line Ltd. 1959—, Burnside Shipping Co. Ltd. 1962—, Common Brothers, Ltd. 1956—, Common Brothers Shipping Services Ltd. Common Brothers Guarantee Co. Ltd. 1959—, Risdons (Sunderland) Ltd. 1963—, North of England P & I Assoc. Ltd. 1959—, United Shipowners Freight Demurrage and Protective Assoc. Ltd. 1959—, South Docks Supply Co. Ltd. 1958—, Hopemount Shipping Co. Ltd. 1966; Common Bros. (Travel Agency) Ltd., 1969—; E. C. Wigg Ltd.; Common Brothers Insurance Services Ltd.; Common Brothers (Middle East) Services Ltd.; Common Brothers (Bermuda) Ltd. (Alternate); First Stratton Shipping Co. Ltd. 1970—; Horncastle Investments Ltd.; Joint Man. Dir. Common Bros. Ltd. Common Brothers USA Ltd. *Address:* Foulmartlaw, Whalton, Morpeth, Northumberland; and *office* Bamburgh House, Market Street, Newcastle upon Tyne.

**COMMON, John Walford.** British. Shipowner/Shipmanager. *B.* 1920. *Educ.* Emmanuel College (MA). *M.* Violet Irene Morris. *Career:* Deputy Chmn. Common Bros. Ltd.; Director of Common Brothers (Management) Ltd., Northumbrian Shipping Co., Home Line Ltd., South Docks Supply Co., Risdons (Sunderland) Ltd., Burnside Shipping Co. Ltd., Hindustan Steam Shipping Co. Ltd., North Shipping Co. Ltd., Common Brothers Guarantee Co. Ltd., Hopemount Shipping Co. Ltd. Former Chairman, Missions to Seamen (Tyne and Blyth Stations); E. C. Wigg Ltd.; Common Brothers (Travel and Agency Ltd.); Common Brothers Shipping Services Ltd.; First Stratton Shipping Co. Ltd.; Chmn. and Dir. Sir Joseph W. Isherwood & Co. Ltd. Former Chmn., North of England Shipowners Assn.; Pres. The North East Coast Inst. of Engineers & Shipbuilders 1973. Director, North of England Protecting & Indemnity Association Ltd.; Sun Alliance Assurance Co. Ltd.; Part-time member on Board of Port of Tyne Authority 1977–80. *Address:* Stable House, Farnley, Corbridge, Northumberland; and *office* Bamburgh House, Market Street, Newcastle upon Tyne NE1 6JU.

**COMPTON, Sir Edmund Gerald,** GCB, KBE, MA. British civil servant. *B.* 1906. *Educ.* Rugby School (Scholar); New College Oxford (Scholar); 1st Cl., Literae Humaniores 1929, MA. *M.* 1934, Betty Tresyllian Williams. *S.* 1. *Daus.* 4. Entered Civil Service 1929; Colonial Office 1930; Treasury 1931–58; Compt. and Aud. Gen. 1958–66; Parliamentary Commissioner ('Ombudsman') 1967–71; Chmn. Local Government Boundaries Commission since 1972; Chmn. of Governing Body, Royal Academy of Music since 1974. *Society:* Bach Choir. *Clubs:* Athenaeum; Boodles. *Address:* 53 Evelyn Gardens, London, S.W.7.

**COMPTON, Randolph Parker.** *B.* 1892. *Educ.* Smith Academy 1911; Princeton (LLB 1915); war industrial training, Harvard Business School. *M.* 1917, Dorothy Danforth. *S.* W. Danforth (Dec.), James Randolph and John Parker (*Dec.*). *Dau.* Ann (Stephens). *Career:* Vice-Pres. i/c New York Office William R. Compton Co. 1919–29; Compton Co. sold to Chatham Phoenix National Bank 1929; operated municipal bond company in own name, N.Y.C. 1929–34; Vice-Pres. i/c municipal bond dept., Lazard Freres & Co., N.Y.C. 1934–41; Vice-Pres. i/c municipal bond dept., Union Securities Corp., N.Y.C. 1941–43; Corporation Relations Manager, Republic Aviation Co. Ltd., Farmingdale, L.I., N.Y. 1942–44. Chmn. of Board of Trustees, Fund for Peace, N.Y.C. 1967. Vice-President, Kidder, Peabody & Co., Inc., investment bankers, New York City 1945. *Clubs:* Recess (N.Y.C.); Elm (Princeton); Fox Meadow Tennis, Manursing Island (Scarsdale); Princeton (N.Y.C.). *Address: office* Kidder, Peabody & Co., 10 Hanover Square, New York City, U.S.A.

**COMPTON, Walter Ames,** MD. American Health Care Industry Exec. *B.* 1911. *Educ.* Princeton Univ. (AB Chem 1933) and Harvard Medical School MD Med. 1937). *M.* 1935, Phoebe Emerson. *S.* Walter Ames, Jr. and Gordon. *Daus.* Cynthia (Mosher), Joan, and Phoebe (Moores). *Career:* Joined Miles Labs. as Medical and Research Director 1938; Vice-Pres. Medical and Research Div. 1946; Exec. Vice-Pres. 1961, Pres. 1964, Chmn. and Chief Exec. Officer 1973—. Director, Miles Laboratories Inc., Elkhart, Ind., and First National Bank, Elkhart, Ind. *Member:* Amer. Medical Assn.; Indiana State Medical Assn.; Elkhart County Medical Socy.; Amer. Assn. for Advancement of Science; New York Acad. of Sciences; Royal Socy. of Medicine; Royal Socy. of Health; Bd. Trustees Royal Socy. Med. Foundation; Adv. Council, South Bend Center, Medical Education; Japan Socy.: Adv. Council, Goshen College; Adv. Council, School of Science of Notre Dame Univ.; Univ. of Chicago's Council for the Biological Sciences & the Pritzker School of Medicine; Corporate visiting Cttee. for the School of Medicine of Tufts Univ.; Chmn. Elkhart Conference. *Address:* 2225 Greenleaf Boulevard Elkhart, Inc.; and *office* Miles Laboratories Inc., 1127 Myrtle Street, Elkhart, Ind., U.S.A.

**CONDE, Javier.** Ambassador of Spain. *B.* 1908. *Educ.* Doctor of Law; Professor of the Faculty of Law, Madrid. *M.* 1945, Maria Jesus Saro. *S.* 4. *Daus.* 2. *Career:* Ambassador in the Philippines 1956, and in Uruguay 1959; formerly Director of the Institute of Political Studies of Madrid. Is a Professor of the Faculty of Law in the University of Madrid; Ambassador of Spain in Canada 1964, Bonn Germany 1971. *Member:* Academy of Sciences, Ethics and Politics (Madrid); The Academy of Political Sciences (Paris); and Political Science Association (U.S.); Doctor *honoris causa* (Univ. of Buenos Aires). *Publications:* Introduccion al Derecho Politico; Teoria y Sistema de las Formas Politicas; El Hombre Animal Politico; Escritos y Fragmentos Politicos (1974). Editor and Director of the review *Clavileño* (Hispanismo). Decorated Order of Sikatuna (Philippines); Instruccion Publica (Portugal); Cisneros, Carlos III. and Isabel la Catolica (Spain). *Address:* c/o Ministry of Foreign Affairs, Madrid, Spain.

**CONNAUGHTON, James Francis.** American manufacturing executive. *B.* 1915. *Educ.* University of Cincinnati (BSc 1937); Doctor of Commercial Science (Duquesne University). *M.* 1938, Sue Graham. *S.* James Francis, Thomas Alfred and Stephen Graham. *Dau.* Mary Jane. *Career:* President and Director, Wheelabrator Corp., Mishawaka, Inc. 1958–72; Chmn. Wheelabrator International 1972–74; Exec Vice-Pres. Gladding Corp. 1975; First Bank & Trust Co.; South Bend, Indiana. *Member:* Advisory Council, Arts and Letters, University of Notre Dame, La Lumiere Prep. School, La Porte, (all of Indiana). Roman Catholic. *Clubs:* Metropolitan, New York; Chicago; Union League (Philadelphia); Detroit Athletic. *Address:* 1515 E. Jefferson Boulevard, South Bend, Ind.; and *office* 400 South Byrkit Street, Mishawaka, Ind., U.S.A.

**CONNELL, John William.** Australian consulting engineer *B.* 1913. *Educ.* Royal Melbourne Inst. of Technology; C.Eng.; FIStructE. FIE Aust; MASCE, FAIB FRSH, MCons EAust. *M.* 1938. Merlyn Gladys Sharpe. *S.* John. *Daus.* Helen and Barbara. *Career:* Commonwealth Military Forces (part-time) 1931–40; Australian Imperial Forces 1940–45, service in 15th Aust. Inf. Brig.; rank, Major, Principal, John Connell & Associates, Consulting Engineers, Melbourne, Canberra, Adelaide, Perth and Darwin; Connell and Hagenbach, Sydney and Brisbane; Partner Mott, Hay and Anderson (London); Group Princ. John Connell Group of Consultants; Member Faculty of Engineering; Univ. of Melbourne, Former Pres. Building Industry Congress of Victoria. Elder. Presbyterian Church of Victoria. *Member:* Royal Socy. of

Victoria; Proprietor, Althill Poll Hereford Stud; Vice-Pres. Ivanhoe Grammar Sch. Council. *Clubs:* Athenaeum (Melbourne); Naval & Military (Melbourne); RACV (Melbourne); Sciences Club (Melbourne); Kingston Heath Golf; *Address:* 'Barecroft', 531 The Boulevard, East Ivanhoe, Vic. 3079; and *office* 60 Albert Rd., S. Melbourne, Vic. 3205, Australia.

**CONNELLAN, Edward John,** OBE. Australian Pastoralist. *B.* 1912. *Educ.* St. Xavier College and Univ. of Melbourne· *M.* 1940, Evelyn Mary Bell. *S.* Roger Damian (*Dec.* 1977), Christopher Anthony. *Dau.* Cynthia Mary (*D.* 1942). *Career:* Took up aviation 1934. Made aerial survey of Northern Territory to locate areas for pastoral development 1935–38; commissioned R.A.A.F. Reserve and carried out Army co-operation flying, World War II 1939–45; founded and operated Connellan Airways 1939, now Chairman & Advisor, Connair Pty. Ltd. formerly Connellan Airways Pty. Ltd. (formed in 1951 name changed 1970); Owner, Narwietooma cattle station, Central Australia. *Address:* Narwietooma Station, via Alice Springs, Central Australia.

**CONNELLY, John H.** President, Pacific Air Lines 1939—. *B.* 1903. *Educ.* New York Univ. *M.* 1943, Dorothy Martin. *S.* Scott. *Clubs:* Burlingame Country; Newport Harbor Yacht; National Aviation. *Address: office* Pacific Air Lines, San Francisco, Calif., U.S.A.

**CONNOLLY, Hon. John Joseph,** PC, OBE, QC, PhD, LLD. Kt. Comdr. (with Star) Order of St. Gregory the Great. Summoned to the Senate June 1953. President, General Cncl. Commonwealth Parliamentary Assn. 1965–66. *B.* 1906. *Educ.* University of Ottawa; Queen's University; University of Notre Dame, Indiana; and University of Montreal (PhD, LLD, BA, PhB, PhL and LLB). *M.* 1938, Ida Bernadette Jones. *S.* 2. *Career:* Past-Pres. National Liberal Federation of Canada 1961–63; Exec. Asst. to Minister of National Defence for Naval Services 1941–45; Professor of Philosophy, Univ. of Notre Dame 1928–31. Counsel to law firm of Honeywell, Wotherspoon. Minister without Portfolio and Leader of the Government in the Senate of Canada, 1964–68. *Clubs:* Rideau; Royal Ottawa; Cercle Universitaire (all of Ottawa). *Address:* 281 Roger Road, Ottawa; and *office* The Senate, Parliament Buildings, Ottawa, Ont. Canada.

**CONNOLLY, Sir Willis Henry,** CBE, Hon. Monesh, DEng Hon. D.Ed (V.I.C.), BEE, BCom, FIEAust, MIEEE (U.S.A.), FAIM. Australian Electrical Engineer. *B.* 1901. *Educ.* Benalla High Sch., Melbourne Univ. (BEE; BCom). *M.* 1927, Mary M. Clark. *S.* 1. *Dau.* 1. *Career:* with S.E.C. of Victoria: Engineer, various departments 1921–37; Engineer & Man., Electricity Supply Dept. 1937-49; Asst. to Gen. Man. 1949–51; Asst. Gen. Man. 1951–56. Chmn. of The State Electricity Commission of Victoria Australia, Sept. 1956–71; Chmn. Australian National Cttee. World Energy Conference, since 1958. Hon. Pres. World Energy Conference. *Awards:* Kernot Medal; Australasia Engineer Award; Peter Nicol Russell Medal. Hon. member Australasian Inst. Mining and Metallurgy; *Clubs:* Australian; Melbourne; Rotary (Melbourne). *Address:* 16 Monkstadt Street, St. Kilda, Vic.; and *office* 15–27 William Street, Melbourne, Vic., Australia.

**CONNOR, George John.** Australian. Economist, City Planner and Development Consultant. *B.* 1913. *Educ.* Univ. of Melbourne (BCom); Univ. of California (Berkeley) 1954–55 Post-graduate research scholar; awarded U.S. Smith-Mundt-Fulbright Scholarship in City Planning, 1954. *M.* 1940, Mona Jean Rogerson. *S.* Peter Henry. *Dau.* Susan Felicity. *Career:* War Service—1939–45: Lt.-Cmdr. R.A.N.R. (including 4 years as Staff Officer to C.-in-C. South West Pacific, General Douglas MacArthur, U.S.A.); Legion of Merit (U.S.); VRD (R.A.N.); 1939–45 Star and Medal; Pacific Star; Australian Service Medal. Member first Australian Trade Mission to Japan 1947; Economist and Sociologist, Melbourne, and Metropolitan Board of Works (for preparation of Melbourne Master Plan) 1950–54; Principal, George J. Connor & Associates Pty. Ltd. 1955—. Economic adviser to leading commercial, industrial and financial organizations and civic authorities on planning and urban developments in Australia and New Zealand cities; Australian representative, International Industrial Development Conference, San Francisco, Oct. 1957; Dir. Interplan Pty. Ltd. International Planning Consortiom. Preparation, Strategy Plan for The Inner City of Melbourne 1973. *Publications:* Surveys and Analysis, Melbourne and Metropolitan Planning Scheme, (1954); articles and reports for Australian newspapers and technical journals. Melbourne University Blue for Baseball. Member Royal Australian Planning Institute. *Clubs:* Naval & Military (Melbourne); Melbourne Cricket; Lawn Tennis Assn. of Victoria. *Address:* 25 Wrixon Street, Kew, Vic.; and *office* Marland House, 570 Bourke Street, Melbourne 3000, Vic., Australia.

**CONNOR, Hon. John Thomas.** American. *B.* 1914. *Educ.* Syracuse Univ. (AB *magna cum laude* 1936) and Harvard Law School (JD 1939). *M.* 1940, Mary O'Boyle. *S.* John Thomas and Geoffrey. *Dau.* Lisa Forrestal. *Career:* Associated with Cravath, de Gersdorff, Swaine & Wood, New York City 1939–42; General Counsel, O.S.R.D., Washington, D.C. 1942–44. Air Combat Intelligence Officer, U.S. Marine Corps 1944–45. Counsel to Office of Naval Research and Special Assistant to Navy Secretary James Forrestal 1945–47. With Merck & Co.: General Attorney 1947, Secretary 1947–50, Vice-Pres. 1950–55, Pres. 1955–65. Incorporator and Director, Communications Satellite Corp. 1963–64. Secretary of Commerce of the United States, Jan. 1965–Jan. 1967. Allied Chemical Corp., Dir. since 1967, Pres. 1967–68, Chief Exec. Officer since 1968, Chmn. of the Bd. since 1969; Member, Board of Directors: General Motors Corp., Chase Manhatten Bank, Warner-Lambert Co. *Awards:* Presidential Certificate of Merit (U.S.) 1948; N.J. Brotherhood Award, National Conf. of Christians and Jews, 1959; Jefferson Medal, N.J. Patent Law Assn. 1962; N.J. Business Statesman of the Year 1964; Harvard Business Club Award 1965; Anti-Defamation League New Jersey, 1966; C. Walter Nichols Award; New York Univ. 1968. Phi Beta Kappa (and Associates), Phi Kappa Phi, Phi Kappa Alpha Beta Gamma Sigma (Hon. Member), Phi Kappa Psi. *Member:* Business Council, Washington, D.C.; Council on Foreign Relations, Conference Board; Council, Financial Aid to Education. *Publications:* articles relating to pharmaceutical industry, research, medicine, patents, etc. *Clubs:* Morris County Golf (N.J.); Metropolitan; (Washington, D.C.); Chevy Chase; Harvard, Links (N.Y.C.): Oyster Harbors (Mass.); Pinnacle (N.Y.C.). *Address:* P.O. Box 3000R, Morristown, N.J., U.S.A.

**CONNOR, Ralph.** American chemist. *B.* 1907. *Educ.* Univ. of Illinois (BS 1929); Univ. of Wisconsin (PhD Organic Chemistry 1932). *M.* 1931, Margaret Raef. *S.* Stephen R. Hon. DSc Philadelphia College of Pharmacy & Science, and Univ. of Pennsylvania; Hon. LLD Lehigh Univ. 1966; DSc (Hon.) Polytechnic Inst. of Brooklyn 1967; Vice-President and Director, Rohm & Haas Co. 1948–73; member, Executive Committee 1949–73, Chmn. 1970—73; Chairman of Board 1960–70; Chairman Board of Directors, American Chemical Society 1956–58. Technical Advisory Panel on Chemical and Biological Warfare, Dept. of Defense 1954–61; International Union of Pure & Applied Chemistry (U.S. National Committee) 1951–58; Associate Trustee, University of Pennsylvania 1958—; Bd. of Directors, Ursinus College since 1971. *Awards:* King's Medal for Service in Cause of Freedom (Eng.); Medal for Merit (U.S.A.); Gold Medal, Amer. Inst. of Chemists, 1963; Chemistry Industry Medal, Socy. of Chemical Industry, 1965; Priestly Medal, Amer. Chem. Socy. 1967; Chemical Pioneer Award (AIC) 1968; The, Outstanding Civilian Service Medal, Dept. of the Army. 1970—Illini Achievement Award Univ. Illi 1971. Naval Ordnance Dev. Award. Instr. of Organic Chem., Cornell Univ. 1932–35; Asst. Prof. Organic Chemistry, Univ. of Pennsylvania 1935–38 (Assoc. Prof. 1938–45); Technical Aide, Section Chief and Divisional Chief Division of Explosives, Office of Scientific Research & Development 1941–45; Assoc. Director of Research, Rohm & Haas Co., and Resinous Products & Chemical Co. 1945–48. *Publications:* Brief Course in Organic Chemistry (with Fuson, Price and Snyder, 1947). *Member:* Amer. Chemical Socy.; Alpha Chi Sigma; Phi Kappa Phi; Theta Chi; Phi Eta Sigma; Sigma Xi; Phi Lambda Upsilon. Hon. Membership: Phi Lambda Upsilon, 1969. *Clubs:* Manufacturers' Golf & Country; Mink Pond. *Address:* 234 North Bent Road, Wyncote, Pa., 19095, U.S.A.

**CONROY, Jack (John Wesley).** American author, critic, editor, encyclopaedist and folklorist. *B.* 1899. *Educ.* University of Missouri; John Simon Guggenheim Fellowship in Creative Writing, 1935; James L. Dow Award, 1966. *M.* 1922, Gladys Kelly. *S.* Thomas Vernon (*D.*) and John Wesley Jr. *Dau.* Margaret Jean (*D.*). *Career:* Editor: The Rebel Poet, 1931–32, The Anvil, 1933–37, The New Anvil, 1939–41; Assoc. Ed., Nelson's Encyclopedia, 1943–47, Universal World Reference Encyclopedia, 1943–47; Literary Ed.: Chicago Defender (1946–47), Chicago Globe (1950) & The Foolkiller (1975—); Senior Editor, New Standard Encyclopedia 1947–66; Director of Standard Information Service (1949); Creative Writing Instructor, Columbia College, 1962–66. *Awards:* Literary Times, 1967; Louis M. Rabinowitz Foundation grant. *Publications:* Editor, Unrest (anthologies of verse with Ralph Cheyney) 1929–30–31; novels: The Disinherited (1933, reissued 1963), and A World to Win (1935); juveniles with Arna Bontemps: The Fast Sooner Hound (1942); Slappy Hooper, the Wonderful Sign Painter (1946), and Sam Patch, the High, Wide and Handsome Jumper (1951); They Seek a City (study of Negro migration, Arna Bontemps) (1945); ed., Midland Humor; a Harvest of Fun and Folklore (1947); Anyplace but Here (with Arna Bontemps, 1966); Writers in Revolt: The Anvil Anthology (with Curt Johnson) (1973). *Award:* Hon. LHD. Univ. of Missouri. *Address:* 701 Fisk Avenue, Moberly, Missouri, 65270, U.S.A.

**CONSTANTINE, Sir Theodore,** CBE, DL, TD. British company director. *B.* 1910. *Educ.* Acton College. *M.* 1935, Sylvia Mary Legge-Pointing. *S.* Roy. *Dau.* Jill Diane. *Career:* Dir. Wickgate Estates 1963—; Chmn. Anscon Ltd. since 1966. *Member:* Nat. Exec. Cttee. Conservative Party 1956—; Chmn., National Union of Conservative Party, 1967–68; Deputy Lieut, and Sheriff of Greater London, 1968. *Clubs:* Carlton; Royal Automobile. *Address:* Hunters Beck, Stanmore, Middlesex; and *office* 128 Park Lane, London, W.1.

**CONWAY, H. McKinley, Jr.** American publisher. *B.* 1920. *Educ.* Georgia Inst. of Technology, Atlanta (BSGE; BAE Aero. Eng.). *M.* 1942, Rebecca Kellam. *Daus* Linda and Laura. *Career:* State Senate 1963–64 and 19.67–68; Past Chmn., Georgia Science and Technology Commn. Past Chmn., Local Govt. Commission, DeKalb County, Ga.; member and Past Chmn., DeKalb County Planning Commission. Asst. to Director, Nat. Aeronautics and Space Administration (then N.A.C.A.), Washington, D.C. 1942–44; Engineering Officer, U.S. Navy (testing experimental aircraft) 1944–46; Research Engineer, Ames Aeronautical Laboratory, Calif. 1946–48; Director, Southern Assn. of Science and Industry, Atlanta 1949–54. President, Conway Research Inc., Atlanta, Ga. since 1954. *Publications:* Principles of High Speed Flight (textbook), (1947); some 25 scientific papers 1944–48; Editor, Journal of Southern Research (1949); currently Editor and Publisher: Industrial Development, Manufacturers Record, Site Selection Handbook, Area Development Guide, The Weather Handbook; author of several hundred magazine articles. Fellow, Amer. Association for Advancement of Science; Dir. Industrial Development Research Council. *Member:* Urban Land Institute; Amer. Socy. of Planning Officials; and Amer. Industrial Development Council; U.S. Trade and Industrial Development Mission to Burma 1962; Consultant, U.S. Dept. of State, Alliance for Progress Programme, Latin America. *Address:* Peachtree Air Terminal, Atlanta, Ga. 30341, U.S.A.

**CONWAY, Harry Donald.** Professor of Applied Mechanics, *B.* 1917. *Educ.* London Univ. (BSc, PhD, DSc Eng.) and Cambridge Univ. (MA. ScD.). *M.* 1946, Dorothy D. Conway (*Dec.* 1976). *S.* Geoffrey S. and Peter S. *Career:* Scientific Officer, Eng. Div., Natl. Physical Lab., Teddington, Eng. 1942–45; Demonstrator in Eng., Cambridge University and Asst. Dir. of Studies, St. Catharines Coll., Cambridge 1946–47; Professor, Cornell Univ. 1948—; Guggenheim Fellow and Visiting Prof., Imperial Coll., London (on leave from Cornell) 1953–54; Julius F. Stone Visiting Research Prof., Ohio Univ. (on leave from Cornell) 1958–59; National Science Foundation Senior Postdoctoral Fellow and Visiting Prof., Imperial Coll. (on leave from Cornell). *Award:* Hon. D.Sc. *Publications:* numerous publications in Applied Mechanics (elasticity, vibrations, plates and shells, etc.) in scientific and technical journals. Whitworth Scholar 1941. *Address:* Thurston Hall, Cornell University, Ithaca, N.Y., U.S.A.

**CONWAY, Hugh Graham,** CBE. British. *B.* 1914. *Educ.* Cambridge Univ. (MA). *M.* 1937, Eva Gordon Simpson. *S.* 2. Chief Engineer: Messier Aircraft Equipment Ltd., Warrington 1938–45, and Aviation Div., Dunlop Rubber Co. Ltd. 1945–47; Technical Dir., British Messier Ltd. 1947–53; Deputy Mng. Dir. and Chief Engineer, Short Bros. and Harland Ltd. 1954–64. Managing Director, Bristol Engine Division of Rolls Royce Ltd. 1964–70; Dir. Rolls Royce (1971) Ltd. 1971; Gp. Mgr. Dir., Gas Turbines, Rolls-Royce Ltd. 1970–71; Mem., Decimal Currency Bd. 1967–71; Dep. Chmn., Design Council 1972–76. Fellow, Royal Aeronautical Socy.; Institution of Mechanical Engineers. *Publications:* several technical books. *Clubs:* Unit. Serv.; Royal Aero. *Address:* 33 Sussex Square, Hyde Park, London, W.2.

**CONYBEARE, Dr. Charles Eric Bruce.** MSc. PhD. Canadian geologist. *B.* 1917. *Educ.* Univ. of Alberta 1938–41; Queen's Univ.; Univ. Alberta 1946–47; Washington State University. *M.* 1965, Jean Louise. *S.* 3. *Dau.* 1. *Career:* with Royal Canadian Corps of Signals, Major European Theatre of Operations 1941–45; Geological Survey, Canada and Eldorado Mining 1946–49; Asst. Prof. Univ. Manitoba 1949–50; Geologist, U.S. Geological Survey, Ghana 1950–52; Research geologist, Shell Oil Co. Canada and U.S.A. 1952–61; Supervisory geologist, Petroleum Exploration Branch, Bureau, Mineral Resources Aust. 1961–64; Senior Lect. Dept. Geology Aust. National Univ. 1964–71; Distinguished Lect. Univ. Oklahoma, Visiting Prof. Colorado School, Mines 1970—; Reader in Petroleum Geology Australian Nat. Univ. since 1972. *Member:* Geological Socy. of Aust; Amer. Assn. Petroleum Geologists; Aust. N. Zealand Assn. Advancement of Science *Awards:* Canadian Efficiency Medal; Stillwell, Geological Socy. of Australia; Fellow Geological Socy. of America. *Publications:* contributions to five books, geology, natural resources; Articles Encyclopaedia Britannica; Scientific papers on petroleum and economic geology. *Club:* Canberra Alpine. *Address:* 22 Scarborough Street, Red Hill, Canberra, A.C.T. 2603 Australia and *office* Department of Geology, Australian National University, Canberra, A.C.T.

**CONZEN, Willibald Hermann.** Pharmaceutical company executive. *B.* 1913. *Educ.* abitur degree, Kaiserin Augusta Gymnasium, Koblenz 1931. *M.* Salome Bruwer, 1951. *S.* Vincent. *Daus.* Elizabeth, Suzanne. *Career:* Went to United States 1952, naturalized 1959. With Schering A.G., Berlin 1931–38; Scherag (Pty.) Ltd., Johannesburg 1938–52; (General Manager 1941–52). With Schering Corp., U.S.A., Bloomfield, New Jersey 1952—; General Manager: International Div. 1952–62; Schering Laboratories Div. 1962–65; Vice-Pres .1959–65; Senior Vice-Pres. 1965–66; Pres. 1966–72, Chmn. Bd. 1972–75; President & Chief Exec. Officer Schering-Plough Corp. 1971–76; Chmn. of the Board & Chief Exec. Officer 1976—. *Clubs:* Montclair Golf (Montclair, N.J.), Essex (Newark, N.J.), Union League (N.Y.C.). *Address:* 130 Lloyd Road, Montclair, New Jersey; *office* Galloping Hill Road, Kenilworth New Jersey, 07033 U.S.A.

**COOK, David C., III.** American publisher and editor. *B.* 1912. *Educ.* Mesa (Ariz.) Ranch School; Occidental College, Los Angeles; University of Chicago (PhB 1934); Lit.D. Judson College 1965. *M.* Betty M. *S.* Bruce L. and Gregory D. *Daus.* Margaret Anne, Martha L., and Rebecca. *Career:* Chmn. of the Board and Editor-in-Chief, David C. Cook Publishing Co. (founded by grandfather 1875); President, David C. Cook Foundation. Trustee: First Methodist Church; Conference Point Camp; Laubach Literacy and Judson College, Elgin, Illinois. Publisher of Sunday School curriculum materials; general educational materials, preschool & junior; & religious trade books. *Address:* 850 North Grove Avenue, Elgin, Ill. 60120, U.S.A.

**COOK, Donald Clarence.** American. *B.* 1909. *Educ.* University of Michigan (AB 1932, MBA 1935) and George Washington University Law School (JD 1939, LLM 1940) CPA (Maryland) 1941. *M.* 1943, Winifred V. Carlsen. *S.* Nicholas Bryant, *Career:* Admitted to practice before all courts of the State of Michigan, Court of Appeals of the District of Columbia, and the Supreme Court of the U.S. With Securities and Exchange Commission (successively Financial Examiner, Registration Div.; Utilities Analyst, Public Utilities Div.; and Asst. Director, Public Utilities Div.) 1935–45; Special Counsel to U.S. House of Representatives Committee on Naval Affairs 1943–45; Exec. Asst. to Attorney General of the U.S. 1945–46; Director, Office of Alien Property (successor to the Alien Property Custodian), U.S. Dept. of Justice 1946–47; Partner in Washington law firm of Cook and Berger 1947–49; successively Commissioner, Vice-Chmn. and Chairman, Securities and Exchange Commission 1949–53; Chief Counsel of the Preparedness Investigating Sub-committee of the Senate Armed Services Committee 1950–52. Joined American Electric Power Service Corp. as Vice-Pres. and Asst. to the President 1953; Exec. Vice-Pres. (Legal, Finance and Accounting) 1954; Director of parent company (American Electric Power Co.) Jan. 1960; member of parent company's Exec. Committee Oct. 1960; Vice-Pres. of parent company Apr. 1961; Chairman of the Board & President, American Electric Power Co. (remaining a Director and member of Executive Committee). President, Director and Chief Executive Officer, since Dec. 1961, of the following subsidiaries: American Electric Power Service Corp., Appalachian Power Co., Beech Bottom Power Co. Inc., Cardinal Operating Co., Central Appalachian Coal Co., Central Coal Co., Central Ohio Coal Co., Central Operating Co., Franklin Real Estate Co., Indiana & Michigan Electric Co., Indiana Franklin Realty Inc., Kanawha Valley Power Co., Kentucky Power Co., Kingsport Power Co., Michigan Power Co., Ohio Power Co., South Bend Manufacturing Co., Twin Branch Railroad Co.,

West Virginia Power Co., Wheeling Electric Co. since 1972; Chmn. Bd.: AEP Service Corp.; Trustee Center for Advanced Study in the Behavioral Sciences, Stanford, Calif.; Past Dir. Edison Electric Inst. *Member:* Amer. and Michigan Bar Assns.; Amer. Accounting Assn.; Amer. Inst. of Certified Public Accountants; Amer. Judicature Socy.; Theta Xi; Phi Delta Phi; Hon. member, Beta Gamma Sigma. *Publications:* numerous articles on legal, financial and accounting subjects. Democrat. *Clubs:* Harbor View, University; Mining; Univ. of Michigan (all of N.Y.C.); National Capital Democratic Metropolitan; Geo. Wash.; Natl. Capital Democratic (all Washington D.C.); Univ. of Mich. Presidents Club, Ann. Arbor, Mich. *Address: office* American Electric Power Co., 2 Broadway, New York City 10004, U.S.A.

**COOK, Thomas I.** Professor of Political Theory, *B.* 1907. *Educ.* Dover Coll., England; London School of Economics (BSc econ.); Columbia Univ. (PhD). *M.* (1) 1930, Anne Peloubet (*Dec.* 1965). *Daus.* 2. *Career:* Instructor in Economics, Acadia (N.S.) Univ. 1929–30, and in Government, Columbia Univ. 1930–36; Asst. Prof. in Political Science, Univ. of California (Los Angeles) 1936–39; Assoc. and Full Prof. in Political Sciences, Univ. of Washington 1939–49; Visiting Prof., Social Sciences, Univ. of Chicago 1948–49; Visiting Prof. in Political Science, The Johns Hopkins Univ. 1949–50; Full Prof. Political Science, Johns Hopkins Univ. 1950—, Chmn. of Dept. 1961–64; H.Y. Benedict Prof. Univ. of Texas, El Paso since 1966. Asst. Director, Wage Stabilization Bd., 12th Regional War Labor Board 1942–44; Public Member, 4th Regional Wage Stabilization Board, Richmond, Va. *Publications:* History of Political Philosophy from Plato to Burke; John Locke, Two Treatises of Government; Power Through Purpose; Democracy versus Communist Activity; numerous articles in professional journals. *Member:* Amer. Political Science Assn.; Amer. Socy. of Political & Legal Philosophy; Southern Political Science Assn.; Western Political Science Ann. *Address:* Political Science Dept., Univ. of Texas, El Paso, Tex., U.S.A.

**COOK, Sir William Richard Joseph,** KCB, FRS. British scientist. *B.* 1905. *Educ.* Trowbridge High Sch. and Bristol Univ. *M.* 1929, Grace Purnell. *Dau.* 1. *M.* 1939, Gladys Allen. *S.* 1. *Dau.* 1. *Career:* Entered Civil Service 1928; in Research Establishments of War Office and Ministry of Supply 1928–47; Director of Physical Research, Admiralty 1947–50: Chief of Royal Naval Scientific Service 1950–54: Deputy Director, Atomic Weapons Research Establishment, Aldermaston 1954–58; Member, Atomic Energy Authority; Dev. Engineering and Production 1958; Development and Engineering 1959; For Reactors 1960–64; Deputy Chief-Scientific Adviser. Min. of Defence 1964–67; Chief Adviser Projects and Research 1968–70; Dir. Buck & Hickman Ltd. since 1970; Dir. Rolls-Royce (1971) Ltd. 1971–76; Chmn. Marconi Marine Ltd. 1971–75; Dir. GEC-Marconi Electronics Ltd. since 1972. *Club:* Athenaeum. *Address:* Adbury Springs, Newbury, Berks.

**COOK, Winfield Clinton.** American sales executive. *B.* 1908. *Educ.* Dickinson Co., (AB 1932); Universities of Pennsylvania and Maryland (graduate work). *M.* 1933, Isabelle Killian. *S.* Thomas and Roger. *Daus.* Barbara, Nancy. Knight of the Sauna (Finland). *Career:* President, Vita Craft Pa. Sales Inc. 1948–59; Fine Arts Accept. Co. 1954–57; Director: Ridgewood China Co., Fine Arts Sterling Co., and Edwin Development Co. 1948–59; Pres. and Chmn. of Board, National Association of Direct Selling Companies 1955–57; Pres. Pennsylvania Junior Chamber of Commerce 1942; National Dir, U.S. Junior Chamber of Commerce 1942; National Chmn., New Clubs National Sales Exec. 1957–58; speaker on Operation Enterprise (covered 100,000 miles in Europe, Asia, South Pacific, Russia and South America) 1952–54–55–57, President: Homec Inc. 1962—; Edwin Development Co. 1960—; Dir., Homestead Ocean City, N.J. *Member:* Penna. Socy., Penna. Historical Socy. Trustee, Dickinson College.: Doctor, Human Letters Combs Coll. of Music. Republican; Kentucky Colonel 1974. *Publications:* articles in trade journals. Dir. Suburban General Hospital. *Clubs:* Sales Managers (Philadelphia); Exhausted Roosters; Seaview C.C.; Ocean City Yacht; J.C.I. Senator; U.S. Power Squadron; Leigh Valley; Clipper; Ambassadors; Chamber of Commerce; National Sales Exec; American Management; National Small Business; American Management; High Twelve (Pres.); Union League (Philadelphia, Pa.); Manatee Repub. Exec. (Chmn.); Mason; 32 deg. Shriner. *Address:* 4235 Gulf of Mexico Drive, Sarasota, Fla., U.S.A.

**COOKE, Jack Kent.** American business executive. *M.* 1934, Barbara Jean Carnegie. *Career:* joined Northern Broadcasting and Publishing Ltd. Canada 1937; Partner Thomson Cooke Newspapers 1937–52; Pres. Radio Station CKEY, Toronto Canada 1944–61; Liberty of Canada Ltd. 1947–61; Toronto Maple Leaf Baseball Club Ltd., 1951–64; Consolidated Frybrook Industries Ltd. 1952–61; Micro Plastics Ltd. Alton, Canada 1955–60; Precision Die Casting Ltd. Toronto 1955–60; Robinson Industrial Crafts Ltd. London, Ont. 1957–63; First Vice Pres. Pro. Football Inc. Washington D.C. 1960—; Pres. Aubyn Investment Ltd. 1961–68; Jack Kent Cooke Inc. 1964–68; Continental Cablevision Inc. 1965–68; Chmn. Bd. and Pres. Calif. Sports Inc. 1965—; Chmn. Bd. Transamerican Microwave Inc. 1965–69; Pres. The Forum of Inglewood Inc. 1966—; Dir. Chmn. Exec. Cttee., H & B American Corp. 1969–70; Dir. Tele Prompter Corp. 1970—; Pres. Forum Boxing Inc. since 1972. Trustee, Little League Foundation; City of Hope; Gov. Arthritis Found; Dir. Nat. Athletic Health Institute. *Address: office* The Forum, Manchester and Prairie Avenue, Inglewood, Calif. 90307, U.S.A.

**COOKE, James Negley, Jr.** American director and marketing consultant. *B.* 1908. *Educ.* Salisbury (Conn.) Sch., and Princeton University. *M.* (1) 1932. Frances Ann Bonfoey; (2) 1941, Nancy Reynolds. *S.* James Negley III, Peter Reynolds, Christopher Creighton. *Dau.* Mrs. Peter A. Coombs. *Career:* Mgr., Monroe Chem. Co. Ltd., London, England, 1932 (Sales Manager of the Company in N.Y. 1933–34); Gen. Mgr., Wells & Richardson Co. Inc., Burlington 1935–40; The Cummer Products Co., and The Molle Co., Bedford, Ohio 1940–43; Subsidiaries, Sterling Drug Inc. Div; Vice-Pres., Sterling Drug Inc., Brattleboro, Vt. 1943–50; Dir. Mad River Corp. Burlington Vt. 1946–72; Mount Mansfield Co. Stowe, V.T. 1948—; Dir. of Marketing Sterling Drug Inc. N.Y.C. 1950–56. Pres. Glenbrook Laboratories (Div. of Sterling Drug Inc.) 1958–72; Sterling Drug Inc. N.Y.C. Sen. Vice-Pres. 1972–74; Advisory Dir. since 1974; Director, Brand Names Foundation, N.Y.C. 1962—; Vice-Pres. and Dir. 1960—; Chairman of The Board 1969–71. Trustee, Holderness School, Plymouth N.H., and Brattleboro Mem. Hospital, Brattleboro, V.T. Chairman, U.S. Ski Team Fund; Hon. Trustee U.S. Ski Educational Foundation Inc.; Hon. Dir. U.S. Ski-Team Inc. since 1975; Republican. Past Pres. & Dir., Proprietary Assn., Washington, D.C. 1969—; Board of Governors Human Resources, Albertson, N.Y. *Clubs:* Bedford Golf, Tennis (Bedford); Princeton, Pinnacle (N.Y.C.); Cap & Gown (Princeton, N.J.); Explorers (N.Y.C.). *Address: office* Sterling Drug. Inc., 90 Park Avenue New York City 10016, U.S.A.

**COOKSON, Roland Antony,** CBE, DCL. British industrialist. *B.* 12 Dec. 1908. *Educ.* Harrow School; Magdalen College, Oxford. *M.* (1) 1931, Rosamond Gwladys Barwick, dec'd. *Dau.* Cynthia Anne (Hoare). (2) Dr. Elizabeth Anne Milburn Aitchison. *Career:* In business since leaving the University. Past Pres., Tyneside Chamber of Commerce; Chmn. Consett Iron Co. 1966–67 (Dir. 1955, Acting Chmn. 1964), Vice-Chmn., North Regional Board for Industry 1949–65. Chmn. of Appointments Bd. of Universities of Newcastle and Durham 1962–73; Director, Lloyds Bank Ltd.; Dir. Lead Industries Group Ltd.; Man. Dir. 1952–62, Chmn. 1962–73. *Member:* Northern Economic Planning Council 1965–68; Northern Regional Council C.B.I. (Chmn. 1971–73); Member, Court and Council Univ. of Newcastle upon Tyne. *Address:* Howden Dene, Corbridge, Northumberland.

**COOLEY, Sir Alan Sydenham,** Kt cr. 1976, CBE 1972 Australian. *B.* 1920. *Educ.* Geelong Grammar School and Melbourne Univ. (BEngSc.). *M.* 1949, Nancie C. Young. *Daus.* Margaret Ann, Janet Chisholm, Helen Nancie and Katherine Joan. *Career:* Cadet Eng., Dept. of Supply 1940–43; Eng. Representative, Lond. 1951–52; Manager, Echuca Ball Bearing Factory 1953–55; Supply Representative, Washington 1956–57; Manager, Small Arms Factory, Lithgow 1958–60; First Asst. Secretary (Management Services and Planning), Dept. of Supply 1961–62; Controller-General of Munitions Supply, Department of Supply, 1962–66; Sec., Dept. of Supply, Commonwealth of Australia 1966–71; Chmn. C'wealth Public Service Board, Canberra since 1971. MIE, Australia. *Clubs:* Commonwealth (Canberra); Melbourne Cricket: *Address:* 27 Garsia Street, Campbell, A.C.T.; and *office* Public Service Board, Canberra, A.C.T. 2600.

**COOLIDGE, William Appleton.** American company director. *B.* 1901. *Educ.* Harvard Coll. (AB *cum laude* 1924), Balliol Coll., Oxford (MA 1927; Hon. Fellow 1963), and Harvard Law School (LLB *cum laude* 1936). *Career:* Previously with

Paine, Webber, Jackson & Curtis 1927–33, and Ropes, Gray, Boyden & Perkins, Boston 1936–41. With U.S. Navy Dept. (Chief, Financial Section, Material Div., Office of Under-Secretary of the Navy) 1941–46. Pres., New Enterprises Inc., Boston 1946–54; Chmn. of Board, National Research Corp., Cambridge 1954–63; Dir., The Coca-Cola Co.; Invest Inc. Pres. Bd. Trustees, Episcopal Theological School; Trustee, Boston Theological Inst.; Bishop Rhinelander Foundation; Chmn., Visiting Comm., Harvard Divinity School; Harvard Museum of Comparative Zoology; Massachusetts Half-Way House Inc.; Dir. The Episcopal Church Foundation. *Awards:* Hon. Fellow, Balliol Coll. (Oxford); Certificate of Merit, U.S. Government. *Clubs:* A.D; The Brook; Metropolitan; Myopia Hunt; Racquet & Tennis; River; Somerset; Tennis & Racquet. *Address: office* 70 Memorial Drive, Cambridge 02142, Mass., U.S.A.

**COOLS-LARTIGUE, Sir Louis,** OBE. *B.* 1905. *Educ.* Convents, St. Lucia and Dominica; Dominica Grammar School. *M.* 1932, Eugene Royer. *S.* 2. *Daus.* 4. *Career:* Entered Dominica Civil Service 1924; Chief Clerk to Administrator & Clerk of Cncls. 1932; Colonial Treas., Dominica 1940, St. Vincent 1945; Asst. Administrator, St. Lucia 1949; Chief Secy., Windward Is. 1951–60; Speaker, Legislative Cncl., House of Assembly, Dominica 1961–67. British. Governor, Dominica, West Indies, Nov. 1967—. *Address:* Government House, Roseau, Dominica, West Indies.

**COOMBS, Charles A.** American *B.* 1918. *Educ.* Harvard (AB 1940; PhD 1951). *M.* 1945, Ilona C. Karman. *Dau.* Claire. *Career:* Director of various companies and Financial Consultant; Senior Vice-President, Foreign Department, Federal Reserve Bank of New York 1959–75. Special Manager, Federal Open Market Account. Financial Adviser, Amer. Mission for Aid to Greece 1947; member, Presidential Task Force on Promoting Foreign Investment in U.S.A. 1962. *Publishing:* Treasury and Federal Reserve Foreign Exchange Operations, (1962), and subsequently: Conversations on International Finance, (Aug. 1963); The Arena of International Finance (1976). *Address:* Box 38, Green Village, N.J., U.S.A.

**COOMBS, Derek Michael.** Political journalist. *B.* 1931. *Educ.* Rydal Prep. School & Bromsgrove School. *M.* 1959, Patricia O'Toole. *S.* 1. *Dau.* 1. *Career:* Director, S & U Stores Ltd. 1960, Jt. Man. Dir. 1970–76, Chmn. 1976; Director Metalrax Holdings Ltd. 1975; & various companies; Member of Parliament for Yardley, Birmingham (Cons.) 1970–74; successfully introduced unsupported Private Member's Bill for Relaxation of Earnings Rule, 1972, establishing parliamentary record for a measure of its kind. Pioneered New Conservative Rate Scheme for Oct. 1974 Gen. Election. *Publications:* numerous articles on home, economic and foreign affairs. *Address:* 14 Chester Street, London, S.W.1; and Shottery Grange, Shottery, Stratford-on-Avon, Warks.

**COOMBS, Herbert Cole,** Australian. *B.* 1906. *Educ.* University of Western Australia (MA); London School of Economics (PhD); Fellow, Australian Academy of Science; Fellow, Austr. Acad. of Social Sciences; Fellow, Austr. Acad. of the Humanities. Hon. Fellow, London Sch. of Economics; Hon. LLD, Melbourne; Hon. LLD Sydney; Hon. LLD Aust. National Univ. (Canberra); Hon. DLitt (W. Aust.). *Career:* Asst. Econ., Commonwealth Bank of Australia 1935; Econ. to Commonwealth, Treasury 1939; member of Commonwealth Bank Board 1942; Director of Rationing 1942; Director-General of Post-War Reconstruction 1943; Governor, Commonwealth Bank of Australia 1949–60. Chmn., Commonwealth Bank Board 1951–60; Governor, Reserve Bank of Australia 1960–68; Chmn., Reserve Bank Board 1960–68. Chancellor, Australian National University: Chmn., Council for the Arts 1967–74; Council for Aboriginal Affairs 1967–76; Chmn. Royal Comm. on Australian Govt. Admin. 1974–76; Visiting Fellow, Centre for Resource & Environmental Studies, Australian National Univ. 1976—. *Publication:* Other People's Money (1971). *Address:* 119 Milson Road, Cremorne, N.S.W., Australia.

**COOPER, Arthur George Stening,** CBE, MB, ChM. British consulting radiotherapist. *B.* 1899. *Educ.* Sydney Grammar School, Sydney University (MB, ChM), and Univ. of London (DMR), FFR, FCRA. *M.* 1924, Marguerite Henry. *S.* Dr. David H. Cooper. *Daus.* Mrs. R. I. Meyers and Dr. Lorna M. Ruffle. *Career:* Graduated in Medicine 1923, Univ. of Sydney. House Physician and House Surgeon, Royal Hants County Hospital, England 1923–24. General Practitioner, Denman, N.S.W. 1925–37. Obtained Diploma in Med. Radiology, Univ. of London Oct. 1938. Radiologist, New Plymouth, N.Z. 1939–40; Radiological Supervisor, Brisbane Hosp. 1940–44; Radiotherapist-in-Charge, Q'land. Radium Inst. 1944–46 (Director 1946–65). Director, Queensland Radium Institute 1946–65, Consulting Radiotherapist 1965. *Publications:* articles on radiotherapeutic subjects in various medical journals. Foundation Fellow, College of Radiologists of Australia; Emeritus Fellow, International Club of Radiotherapists; Fellow, Faculty of Radiologists. *Member:* Australian Medical Association; Hon. member Japan Radiological Society. *Clubs:* The Queensland; Clayfield Bowling. *Address:* 19 Apex Street, Clayfield, Qld., Australia.

**COOPER, Donald Bashford.** Financial consultant. Director: Viking Investments Inc., Connecticut Venture Capital Corp., and Capital Reserve Corp. *B.* 1901. *Educ.* Ohio Wesleyan Univ. (BA) and Harvard Univ. (MBA 1925). *M.* 1954, Primrose Fardel. *S.* Cole and Peter. *Dau.* Suzanne. *Career:* Commercial banking, Boston 1925–30; Investment Counsel, Boston 1931–36; Federal Government Service, Washington, D.C. (Securities and Exchange Commission, and Lend-Lease Administration) 1936–43; Research, Transportation Economics, N.Y.C. 1944–45. Republican. *Club:* Harvard (N.Y.C.). *Address:* 25 Norwalk Avenue, Westport, Conn. 06882, U.S.A.

**COOPER, Herston M.** Consulting criminologist. *B.* 1901. *Educ.* Birmingham-Southern College, AB, MA. Member of the Bar, State of Alabama. *M.* 1931, Claire Virginia Averyt. *S.* William A. *Daus.* Beverly C. Stapleton and Valerie C. Geiger. *Career:* Criminologist 1933. Formerly Chancellor, National Law Enforcement Academy, Secretary, National Commission on Law Enforcement Standards; Exec. Vice-Pres. International Academy of Criminology. *Member:* Amer. Society of Criminology, Retired Officers' Assn. Amer., Association of Criminology. *Publications:* numerous articles and several Books. *Address:* 9216 Dickens Avenue, Surfside Miami Beach, Fla. 33154, U.S.A.

**COOPER, James Gollan.** Australian. *B.* 1913. *Educ.* Devonport High School; Fellow: Australian Society of Accountants (FASA), Chartered Institute of Secretaries (FCIS) and Australian Institute of Management (FAIM). *M.* 1939, Enid Joy Andrews. *S.* Ian Gollan, Graeme McNeill. *Career:* Accountant, Associated Pulp & Paper Mills Ltd., and Paper Makers Pty. Ltd. 1941–47; Asst. Manager and Secretary, Davies Bros. Lrd. 1948–52; Secy., Davies Bros. Ltd. group of companies, and Business Manager, The Mercury Newspaper Pty. Ltd. 1952–55; Director and General Manager, Mercury Press Pty. Ltd. 1955–70. Director, Company Dir.: The Mercury Newspaper Pty. Ltd., Platypus Publications Pty. Ltd., Mercury Press Pty. Ltd., The Critic Pty. Ltd., Packaging Investments Pty. Ltd.; Managing Director Mercury-Walch Pty. Ltd., Hobart, Tasmania, 1970—; Chief Exec. Davies Brothers Ltd. since 1972. Federal Vice-Pres. Australian Society of Accountants 1955–56 (Federal Councillor 1952–62; Tasmanian President 1958–59); Jaycees International 1953 (Life Member 1953); Member, Faculty of Commerce, University of Tasmania 1949–68; Federal President, Printing and Allied Trades Employers Federation of Australia 1964–65, (Elected an honorary member 1974); Tasmanian Councillor, Inst. of Directors since 1971; Trustee, Cttee. for Economic Development of Australia since 1972; Tasmanian State Cttee., C'wealth Scientific and Indust. Res. Org. since 1974. *Clubs:* Athenaeum; Royal Hobart Bowls; Royal Autocar. *Address:* Box 1206 M, G.P.O., Hobart, Tasmania; and *office* 93 Macquarie Street, Hobart, Tasmania.

**COOPER, John Neve,** OBE. British. Oil Company Director. *B.* 1916. *M.* 1942, Mary Linda Barrett. *S.* Ian Neve. *Career:* With the Shell Group since 1933; Chmn.: Steaua Romana (British) Ltd., and Director of the following Shell Company subsidiaries: ES Enterprises, Lithuania, Latvia, and Bulgaria. Director: Grozny-Sundja Oilfields Ltd., New Schibaieff Petroleum Co. Ltd., North Caucasian Oilfields Ltd., Guest Industrials Ltd., and Ural Caspian Oil Corp. Ltd. Dep. Chairman: Anglo-Yugoslav Trade Council; Deputy Chairman, East European Trade Council, Vice-Pres. & Chmn. of Overseas & USSR and Yugoslav Sections; London Chamber of Commerce and Industry, Chmn. Overseas Trade Liaison Cttee., Assoc. British Chambers of Commerce; Hon. Treas., Great Britain/East Europe Centre Governing Body. *Member* Brit. O'seas Trade Advisory Council; British-Soviet Chamber of Commerce Exec. Council; Royal Institute of International Affairs. *Clubs:* Trugeniks; Muscovite; Nazdrowian. *Address:* 45 Lee Road, Blackheath, London, SE3 9RT; and *office* Shell Centre, London, SE1 7NA.

**COOPER, Leon N.** U.S.A. Physicist. *B.* 1930. *Education.* Columbia Univ. AB (1951), AM (1953), Ph.D. (1954); Dr. of

Sciences Columbia (1973), Sussex Univ. (1973), Univ. Illinois (1974), Brown Univ. (1974), Gustavus Adolphus (1975), Ohio State Univ. (1976). *M.* 1969, Kay Anne. *Daus.* 2. *Career:* Res. Assoc. Univ. of Illinois 1955–57; Assist. Professor, Ohio State Univ. 1957–58; Associate Prof. Brown Univ. 1958–62; Prof. Brown Univ. 1962–66; Henry Ledyard Goddard Prof. Brown Univ. 1966–74; Thomas J. Watson Professor of Science, Brown Univ. since 1974. *Fellow:* American Physical Soc.; Am. Acad. of Arts and Sciences. *Member:* American Philosophical Soc.; National Acad. of Sciences. *Awards:* Comstock Prize (with J.R. Schrieffer) National Acad. of Sciences (1968); Nobel Prize (with J. Bardeen and J. R. Schrieffer) 1972. *Publications:* An Introduction to the Meaning and Structure of Physics; about 50 technical publications. *Club:* University (Providence, RI). *Address:* 31 Summit Avenue, Providence, RI 02906, U.S.A.; and *office*: Dept. of Physics, Brown Univ., Providence, RI 02912, U.S.A.

**COOPER, Roland Henry.** Liberian diplomat *B.* 9 Oct. 1916. *Educ.* Liberia, Sierra Leone, and U.S.A. *M.* 1943, Elizabeth Barclay. *S.* 1. *Daus.* 2. *Career:* Clerk, Dept. of State 1938; Passport Officer 1940; Vice-Counsul Savannah, U.S.A. 1943, and N.Y. 1944; Counsul, N.Y. 1947; Actg. Counsul-Gen. N.Y. 1949; Liberian Director, Liberia Port Management Co., New York; Proxy Director, Libera Company, New York 1950; Delegate to U.N. 1949–50–51–53–54–57–61; Commercial Attaché, Embassy of Liberia; Washington, D.C. 1948; Delegate to Conference on Import-Export Controls, Department of Commerce, Washington, D.C. 1948; member, Liberian Trade Mission to Europe 1951; Special Envoy to Havana 1948 and to Philippines 1946; Counsul-General, Hamburg, Sept. 1952; En. Ex. and Min. Plen. to Bonn 1953–55; Ambassador Apr. 1955, and En. Ex. & Min. Plen. to Sweden 1959–60; Ambassador, June 1960; Former Ambassador to Italy and to Yugoslavia. Ambassador to Japan and concurrently to the Republic of China and S. Korea since 1969. *Address:* Ministry of Foreign Affairs, Monrovia, Liberia.

**COOPER, Lt.-Col. William Kenneth.** British *B.* 1911. *Educ.* University Coll., Nottingham. *M.* 1937, Kathleen Nutton. *S.* William John. *Dau.* Philippa. *Career:* Served in World War II, 1939–45. Managing Director, Fisons Chemicals (S.A.) (Pty.) Ltd. 1949—; Fisons Pest Control (S.A.) Pty. Ltd. *Address:* 45, 1st Avenue, Illovo, Johannesburg, South Africa.

**COOPER, William O'Brien.** Bronze Star Medal (U.S.A.), Medal of Liberation (France); American. *B.* 1909. *M.* Vera Lucille Bozeman 1935. *S.* Don Cooper. Director U.S. Economic Assistance to Sudan 1961–67; Secretary General, World Veterans Federation, France 1967—. National Cmdr., Disabled American Veterans 1960–61. *Address: office* 16 rue Hamelin, Paris 16.

**COOREY, Clarence Oswald,** MBE. Ceylonese, Ambassador of Ceylon. *B.* 1910. *Educ.* BA (Cantab.); Bsc (Lond.). *M.* 1934. Isobel Margaret. Indian Civil Service 1933–48; Dir. and Secy., Ceylon Tea Board 1949–66. High Commissioner for Ceylon in Australia, 1966–69; Ambassador in the United Arab Republic 1969. *Club:* Taharir Cairo. *Address:* c/o Ministry of Foreign Affairs, Colombo, Sri Lanka.

**COOTE, Captain Sir Colin Reith,** DSO. *Educ.* Chilverton Elms, Dover; Rugby; Balliol College, Oxford; BA. 1914. *Career:* served in World War I (wounded and gassed) 1914–18; MP (CL), Isle of Ely Div. 1917–22. Managing Editor, the Daily Telegraph and Morning Post 1950–64 (deputy editor 1945–50); Legion of Honour 1954. Knight Bachelor 1961. *Publications:* Italian Town and Country Life (1925); In and About Rome (1926); Maxims and Reflections of The Rt. Hon. Winston Churchill (1948); (with R. H. Mottram) Through Five Generations: The History of the Butterley Company (1950); (with P. D. Bunyan) Sir Winston Churchill: A Self-Portrait (1954). Editorial (Autobiography 1965); A Companion of Honour (Biography of Walter Elliot 1965); The Government We Deserve (1968); A History of the Other Club (1971); (part-author) The History Makers (1973). *Address:* 16 Bigwood Road, London, N.W.11.

**COPE, John Ambrose,** FCA, MP. British chartered accountant and politician. *B.* 1937. *M.* 1969, Djemila Lovell Payne. *Daus.* 2. *Career:* Personal Asst. to Rt. Hon. Anthony Barber MP (now Lord Barber) 1967–70; Special Asst. to Secy. of State for Trade & Industry 1972–74; Conservative Member of Parliament for South Gloucesteshire since 1974. Sec., Parliamentary Group for Concorde; Sec., Conservative Smaller Business Cttee; Sec., Conservative Parliamentary Finance Cttee. *Address:* House of Commons, London SW1.

**COPELAND, Lammot du Pont.** American. *B.* 1905. *Educ.* Harvard Univ. (BS in Industrial Chemistry) 1928; LLD Univ. of Del., Univ. of Penna.; American Univ. ScD, Jefferson Medical Coll., Dr. of Humanities, Washington Coll., D. of Science in Commerce, Drexel Inst.; D. of Engineering, PMC College. *M.* 1930, Pamela Cunningham. *S.* Lammont du Pont, Jr. and Gerret van S. *Dau.* Louisa d'Andelot du Pont (Biddle). Chairman of the Board 1967–71, and Director, E. I du Pont de Nemours & Co., Wilmington, Del. (Sec. 1947–54, Vice-President 1954–62, President 1962–67); Director, Vice-President, Christiana Securities Co., Wilmington; Director, Du Pont of Canada, 1949–63; Director, member of Trust and Audit Committee, Wilmington Trust Co. 1943; Director, member Exec. and Fin. Cttees., Pennsylvania Railroad Co., Philadelphia 1953–59. *Awards:* Officer, Legion of Honour (France), Order of Leopold (Belgium); Commander, Order of the Couronne de Chene (Luxembourg). Gold Medal, Netherlands Socy. of Phila. 1968. Trustee-Treas. Eleutherian Mills-Hagley Foundation, Wilmington; Trustee, Pres., Longwood Foundation, Wilmington; Vice-Chmn. of the Bd., Delaware Safety Council; Dir., Family Service of Northern Delaware 1938–59; Dir., General Motors Corp. 1949–59 and United States Rubber Co. 1942–46. Trustee, Univ. of Pennsylvania, Phila.; Hon. Dir., Wilmington Socy. of Fine Arts; member, Bd. of Mgrs., Wilmington Inst. (Free Library); Trustee. Pres., Henry Francis du Pont Winterthur Museum; Member Bd. Overseers Harvard Coll. 1965–71. *Clubs:* Greenville C.C., Wilmington, Great Oak Yacht, Capitol Hill and City Tavern. *Address:* Du Pont Building, Wilmington, Del. 19898, U.S.A.

**COPHAM, Francis Michael Gerrard,** TD. British. *B.* 1911. *Educ.* Ealing Priory School, London. Served in World War II (Major, Queen's Own Yorkshire Dragoons; Palestine, Western Desert and Italy) 1939–45; Territorial Army 1935–56. Director and Chief Executive Green's Economiser Group Ltd.; Vice-Chmn., E. Green & Son Ltd.; Dir., J. W. Harrison Ltd., Spurr, Inman & Co. Ltd., Archibald Johnstone (Engrs.) Ltd.; Green and Tancred Ltd. *Club:* Cavalry (London). *Address:* Mar House, Arkendale, Knaresborough, Yorkshire.

**COPPÉE, Baron Evence.** Belgian. *B.* 1929. *Educ.* Collège St. Michel à Bruxelles (Greek and Latin Humanities); Université Catholique de Louvain (Civil Engineer-Mining); MIT (Grad. course in Economics). *M.* 1969, Bonne Béatrice Greindl. *S.* 9. *Daus.* 2. *Career:* Chmn. Compagnie Coppée de Développement Industriel S.A. Coppée-Rust, and SIAS; Admin. S. Generale de Banque; Administrator of other Belgian and foreign companies. *Awards:* Officier de l'Ordre de Léopold. *Address:* 33 avenue Franklin Roosevelt, Brussels 5; and *office* 103 boulevard de Waterloo, Brussels 1, Belgium.

**COPPIETERS, Emmanuel** (Coppieters de ter Zaele, Chevalier Emmanuel), Professor International Economic Organization. *B.* 1925. *Educ.* Univ. of Louvain (DEcon, DJuris); London University (MScEcon) *S.* 3. *Daus.* 1. *Career:* Professor International Economic Organization, National Faculty of Economics, University of Antwerp since 1954; Royal Military Academy Brussels 1963–66; Dir. Gen. Institut Royal des Relations Internationales, Brussels since 1954; Editor Studia Diplomatica formerly Chronique de Politique Etrangère since 1954; Co-editor Internationale Spectator Tijdschrift voor Internationale Politiek since 1961; Minister Chargé d'Affaires a.i. of Honduras to the European Communities 1973–77, and Consul-General of Honduras in Belgium since 1961; Public Auditor of banks since 1962; Barrister 1947–58; Reserve Lieutenant-Colonel. *Member:* Belgian Royal Academy of Overseas Sciences since 1963; Academia Mexicana de Derecho Internacional since 1975; Belgian Council of Statistics 1959—, Belgian Nat. Commission UNESCO 1955—; Governor Assoc. pour l'Etude des problèmes de l'Europe, Paris 1959—; Secretary General of the Belgian Cttee, for the European Cultural Foundation and of the Cultural Fund of the Council of Europe 1960—; Governor European Foundation for Culture since 1973; Mem., Mexican Academy of Int'l. Law. *Awards:* Commdr., Ordre de la Couronne; Officer Order of Leopold; Resistance and War Volunteer Medals; Commdr. Order of Orange Nassau (Netherlands), Luxembourg, Senegal, Holy Sepulchre; Orders of Rwanda, Polonia Restituta, the Leopard (Zaire); Knight, Order of Malta. *Publications:* English Bank Note Circulation 1694–1954; L'accord monétaire Européenet les Progès des Monnaies; La intergracion monetria y fiscal Europae culminacion de la integrecion politica; International Organisaties en Belgische economie. Les conséquences economiques pour la Belgique d'un éventuel désarmement. *Address:* 88 Avenue de la Couronne 1050 Brussels and Vijverskasteel 8021 Loppem by Brugge, Belgium.

**COQUELIN, Pierre-Edouard.** French. *B.* 1907. *Educ.* Polytechnic School. *M.* 1933, Jacqueline Polaillon. *S.* Gérard. *Daus.* Christiane and Brigitte. *Career:* Former Insp. of Finances; President-Director-General: Cie. pour le Financement d'Investissements Immobiliers 'Cofidim'; Société pour Favoriser l'Accession à la Propriété Sofapi. *Address:* 15 bis, Av. Theophile Gautier Paris 16 éme, France.

**CORBETT, James Davidson.** *B.* 1910. *Educ.* Dartmouth Coll. and New York Univ. (BS) *M.* 1935, Amy Seinknecht. *Daus.* Suzanne (Cooper), Martha (Leith), Jane (Floyd). *Career:* With Moody's Investment Service 1934–41; Hanover Bank 1941–43; with Merrill Lynch, Pierce, Fenner & Smith Inc. 1943–71, Partner 1952–59, Senior Vice Pres, and Dir. (ret.) 1971; Rebublican. *Clubs:* Union League; Wheatley Hills Golf; Hempstead Harbour; Dartmouth. *Address:* Box 32 Huletts Landing, N.Y. 12481, U.S.A.

**CORBIN, Clive Wilson,** CEng, FIEE, FIE Aust. British company director; Managing Director, Adelaide & Wallaroo Mt. Lyell Fertilizers Ltd., Chmn., Nairne Pyrites Pty. Ltd.; Director: Sulphuric Acid Pty. Ltd., Fertilizer Sales Pty. Ltd., Wallaroo Mount Lyell Fertilizers Ltd. *B.* 1910. *Educ.* St. Peters College, Adelaide; Univ. of Adelaide (B.E.); Professional qualifications FIEE, FIE Aust. *M.* 1947, Josephine Frances Hope (née Moulden). *S.* 1. *Career:* Engineer, Metro. Vickers Elec. Co. Manchester 1931–34; Engr. Australian General Electric Ltd., Melbourne 1934–40; served in World War II (Lieut.-Col. A.I.F.; Royal Australian Engineers; Middle East, New Guinea, Australia) 1940–46. *Address:* 12 Fuller Street, Walkerville, S.A., Australia.

**CORBIT, Ross.** American distillery executive. *B.* 1899. *Educ.* Schools of Toronto. *M.* 1928, Agnes May Miller (*Dec.* Jan. 1954). *Dau.* 1. *Career:* In steel industry prior to 1935; affiliated with Hiram Walker-Gooderham & Worts Ltd. and/or its subsidiaries from 1935. Vice-President & Director, Hiram Walker-Gooderham & Worts Ltd., Walkerville, Ont. Director: Hiram Walker & Sons Inc., Detroit, Mich. 1955—; Hiram Walker Inc., Detroit 1948—; Hiram Walker Importers Inc., Detroit 1952—; Hiram Walker Distributors Inc., New York City 1948—; Hiram Walker Distributing Co., Chicago, Ill. 1948—; Jas. Barclay & Co. Ltd., Detroit 1961—; Gooderham & Worts Ltd., Detroit 1961—; Associated Distillers Inc., Peoria, Ill. 1961—, and Associated Importers Inc., Detroit since 1961. *Clubs:* Detroit Athletic; Detroit Yacht; Marco Polo (N.Y.C.). *Address: office* 2072 Riverside Drive East, Walkerville, Ont., Canada.

**CORCORAN, David Merle.** American. *B.* 1903. *Educ.* Princeton University (AB); Harvard Graduate School of Business Administration MBA). *M.* 1942, Joan Woltman. *S.* 3. *Daus.* 2. *Career:* Tokyo Manager, General Motors Corporation, 1930–33. President: Sterling Products International Inc. 1939–73; The Sydney Ross Co. 1940–73; Winthrop Products Inc. 1948–73; Dorothy Gray Inc. 1967; Valmont Inc. 1967–73 (all New York); Vice-Pres. and Dir., Sterling Drug Inc., New York 1966–76. *Address:* Waterville Valley, N.H.03223, U.S.A.

**CORCORAN, Hon. James Desmond.** Australian. *B.* 1928. *M.* 1957, Carmel Mary Campbell. *S.* 4. *Daus.* 4. *Career:* Member for Millicent, House of Assembly in the South Australian Parliament, March 1962–July 1975; Member for Coles July 1975—; Minister of Lands, Minister of Repatriation and Minister of Irrigation, Nov. 1965–May 1967; Minister of Lands, Min. of Repatriation, Min. of Irrigation & Min. of Immigration June 1967–March 1968; Deputy Premier, Minister of Lands, Minister of Repatriation, Min. of Irrigation, Min. of Immigration and Tourism, Mar. 1968–April 1968; Deputy Leader of Opposition April 1968–June 1970; Dep. Premier, Minister of Works & Marine, since 1970. Member Australian Labour Party. *Address:* Aringa Court, Rostrevor, SA; and *office* Parliament House, North Terrace, Adelaide 5000, S.A.

**CORDER, Clive Sinclair.** South African chartered accountant and company director. *B.* 25 Nov. 1904. *Educ.* Rondebosch High School and University of Cape Town (BCom), FSAA; Hons LLD. *M.* 1929, May Noel Koster. *S.* Peter Derek. *Daus.* Margot Ilse (Gawith), Tessa Noel (de la Harpe) and Judy Vera (Smuts). *Career:* Hon. President, Syfret and South African Trust Co. Ltd.; Southern Sea Fishing Enterprises (Pty.) Ltd. *Address:* 'Mintaka', Monterey Drive, Constantia 7800, (PO Box 206) C.P., South Africa.

**CORDLE, John Howard.** British. *B.* 11 Oct. 1912. *Educ.* City of London School. *S.* 4. *Daus.* 3. *Career:* Served R.A.F. (commissioned) 1940–45; Managing Dir. & Chmn. E. W. Cordle & Son Ltd., 1946–68, Chmn. since 1968; Member of Parliament for Bournemouth East 1959–77; Member, Archbishops of Canterbury & York Commission on Evangelism 1945–46; Church Assembly 1946–53; Oxford Trust of Churches Patronage Bd. 1947; Lloyd's 1952; Founders Livery Co. and Freeman of City of London 1956; Chmn. West Africa Affairs Cttee. Conservative Commonwealth Council; Anglo-Libyan Parly. Group; Member, UK Delegations to Council of Europe (Strasbourg) & to Western European Union (Paris); Chmn., Church & Parliament Parly. Group; Life Governor, St. Mary's & St. Paul's Coll. Cheltenham; Epsom College. *Awards:* African Star, Liberia 1965. *Member:* Royal Commonwealth Society. *Clubs:* Carlton; English Speaking Union. *Address:* Malmesbury House, The Close, Salisbury, Wilts.

**CORETH, (Count) Johannes,** LLD. Austrian. diplomat. *B.* 1912. *Educ.* Universities of Vienna and Innsbruck (LLD); Consular Academy Diploma Vienna. *M.* 1941, Christiane von Karabacek. *S.* Clemens and Christian. *Career:* Austrian Civil Service 1936–38; re-entered Austrian Diplomatic Service 1945; Secy., Legation Wash. 1946–48; Counsellor, Embassy London 1951–54; various appointments in Austrian Foreign Office (Political Section); Austrian Ambassador to Switzerland 1956–61; to the Holy See 1961–66. Min. Plen. in Austrian Foreign Office 1967–68; Ambassador to the Netherlands since 1969. Order of Merit in Gold (Austria) and various foreign decorations. *Address:* 90 Zeestraat, The Hague, The Netherlands.

**CORFIELD, Rt. Hon. Sir Frederick Vernon.** PC, QC. British, *B.* 1915. *Educ.* Cheltenham College (Scholar) and Royal Military Acad. *M.* 1945, Elizabeth Mary Tuth Taylor. *Career:* Commissioned Royal Artillery 1935, retd. 1946; Member of Parliament Conservative for S. Glos. 1955–74; Parly. Secy. Min of Housing and Local Govt. 1962–64; Opposition Front Bench Spokesman on Land 1964–65 and on Power and Trade 1966–67; Opposition Front Bench Spokesman on Aviation 1967–70. Barrister-at-Law (Middle Temple). Minister of State, Board of Trade, June–Oct. 1970; Minister of Aviation Supply 1970–71; Minister for Aerospace 1971–72; Queen's Counsel since 1972. Privy Council. 1970. Knighted 1972; Mem. Brit. Waterways Board since 1974. *Publications:* Corfield on Compensation, (1959); Guide to the Community Land Act (1976). *Clubs:* Army & Navy. *Address:* 9. Randolph Mews, London, W.9; *office* 2 Paper Buildings, Temple, London EC4; and Guildhall chambers, 23 Broad Street, Bristol BS1 2HG.

**CORMACK, Patrick,** BA, MP. British politician. *B.* 1939. *Educ.* Havelock School Grimsby; Univ. of Hull (BA Hons) English & History. *M.* 1967, Mary MacDonald. *S.* 2. *Career:* Second Master, St. James School, Grimsby, 1961–66; Education Training Officer, Ross Group Ltd. 1966–67; Asst. Housemaster Wrekin Coll. Shropshire 1967–69; Senior History Master, Brewood Grammar School, Staffs. 1969–70; Member of Parliament Conservative for Cannock 1970–74, & SW Staffs. since 1974; Parly. Private Secy. Dept. of Health, Social Security 1970–73; Chmn. All Party Parly. Cttee. for Soviet Jewry 1971–74; Chmn. All Party Group for Widows & Single Parent Families 1974; Secy. All Party Heritage Cttee.; Vice-Chmn., Heritage in Danger. *Publication:* Heritage in Danger (1976). *Clubs:* Constitutional. *Address:* Somerford Grange, Brewood, Stafford; and 1a Heathview Gardens, London SW15; and *office* House of Commons, London, S.W.1.

**CORMIE, Donald Mercer,** QC. Canadian. *B.* 1922. *Educ.* Univ. of Alberta (BA 1944; LLB 1945) and Harvard Univ. (LLM 1946). *M.* 1946, Eivor Elisabeth Ekstrom. *S.* John Mills, Donald Robert, James Mercer, Neil Brian, Bruce George and Robert Ekstrom. *Daus.* Allison Barbara and Eivor Emilie. *Career:* Partner, Smith, Clement, Parlee & Whitaker, Barristers and Solicitors, Edmonton, Alta. 1947–53; Sessional Instructor in the Faculty of Law 1949–53 and Faculty of Business 1971–72. Senior Partner, Cormie, Kennedy, Fitch, Patrick, Cook & Campbell, Barristers and Solicitors. President & Director: Principal Group Ltd., Collective Securities Ltd., Principal Savings & Trust Co., The Principal Life Insurance Co., Principal Investors Corp. (U.S.A.), Principal Certificate Series Inc. (U.S.A.), Principal Venture Fund Ltd., and

Collective Mutual Fund Ltd. Secy. and Dir., Geo. M. Cormie Enterprises Ltd. *Publications:* The Power of the Courts to Review Administrative Decisions (1945); Treaty Making by Canada (1946); The Nature and Necessity of Administrative Law 1960; Administrative Problems of Government—Alberta (1964); The Administrative Agency in 1965 (1965). *Member:* Alberta Law Socy., Canadian Bar Assn.; (Memb. of Council 1961–70; Chmn. Administrative Law Section 1963–65; Vice-Pres., for Alberta 1968–69; Young Presidents' Organization Inc., Alberta Chmn. 1966–67; Dir. North Pacific Area, Vice-Pres. 1969–70; Dir.: Banff School of Advanced Management 1968–71; Citadel Theatre 1968–70. *Clubs:* Edmonton, Royal Glenora, Edmonton Petroleum, Derrick Golf & Country, Hillcrest Country. *Address:* 12436 Grandview Drive, Edmonton; and *office* 1600 Cambridge Building, Edmonton Alta., Canada.

**CORNELIUS, Dr. Karl.** German. *B.* 1912. *Educ.* jur. und betriebswirtschaftliches Studium (studied law and commerce). Director: Dortmunder Brückenbau C. H. Jouch, Dortmund (bridge building); J. Gollnow & Sohn, Stahlbau-Eisenhandel (iron and steel), Karlsruhe; Jucho Export GmbH, Dortmund; Baugesellschaft Ost GmbH, Dortmund (building society); Adviser, Dr. Schumacher & Co., Dortmund; Joint Proprietor, Elu-Elektro Union GmbH, Dortmund, Gosheim, Iobenbüren. *Address:* Landhaus am Vöckenberg, 581 Witten-Annen; and *office* Jüchostr. 100, 46 Dortmund, Germany.

**CORNELL, Drew.** American. *B.* 1914. *Educ.* Specialist Student, Texas A. & M. College in geology and petroleum engineering 1931–38. *M.* 1938, Delta Bergean. *S.* Robert John, *Daus.* Ann and Nell. *Career:* With Amerada Petroleum Corp. 1933–35; Continental Oil Co. 1935–43; Bates & Cornell 1943–54; Drew Cornell 1954—; Circle Drilling Co. 1945—. President, Drew Cornell Inc. Vice-President, Circle Drilling Co. *Member:* AIME, (SPE), AAPG, SIPES. *Clubs:* Petroleum (Lafayette); Engineers (Dallas). *Addresss: office* P.O. Box 1267, Lafayette, La., U.S.A.

**CORNELL, Ward Maclaurin.** Canadian. *B.* 1924. *Educ.* Pickering College; Univ. of Western Ontario (Canada). *M.* Georgina Saxon. *S.* 3. *Daus.* 2. *Career:* Free Lance Broadcaster 1946–72; Lecturer English & History, Pickering Coll. Ont. 1949—54; Gen. Mgr. Broadcast Div. (Radio) Free Press Printing Co. 1954–67; Pres. Ward Cornell Ltd. Creative Projects in Communications 1967–72; Visiting Lecturer Conestoga Coll. 1968–72; Agent General, for the Province of Ontario in the United Kingdom since 1972. *Clubs:* London; Lambs; London Hunt & Country; Celebrity, (Canadian); Pilgrims; Canada; Royal Overseas League; Royal Commonwealth Society (U.K.). *Address:* Ontario House, Charles II Street, London, S.W.1.

**CORNELSEN, Franz.** German publisher. *B.* 1908. *Educ.* Grammar School, University and Tech. High Schools in Berlin, Munich and Hanover. Civil Engineer. *M.* 1938, Hildegard Friedrichs. *S.* 1. *Career:* Engaged in industry (Head of foreign trade dept. at Siemens & Halske 1933–45); Manager & Partner, Franz Cornelsen Verlag KG 1946; Owner of Velhagen & Klasing (founded 1835) since 1954; Chmn. of Franz Cornelsen Stiftung who owns Cornelsen-Velhagen & Klasing Verlag für Lehrmedien (Educational Publishing house specialising in English Language teaching, science & social studies for schools & adult education). *Address: office* Lützowstr. 105–106, Berlin 30, Germany.

**CORNER, Frank Henry.** New Zealand diplomat. *B* 1920. *Educ.* Victoria University (Wellington), MA. *M.* 1943, Lynette Robinson. *Daus* 2. *Career:* Joined N.Z. Department of External Affairs 1943; First Secretary, Washington 1948–51; Senior Counsellor, N.Z. High Commission, London 1952–58; Deputy Secretary of External Affairs, Wellington 1958–62; Permanent Representative of New Zealand to the United Nations 1962–67: Ambassador to the U.S.A. 1967–72; Permanent Head of the Prime Minister's Dept. N. Zealand 1973–75; Secretary of Foreign Affairs 1973—. Represented N.Z. at many international conferences, including Peace Conference of Paris 1946, meetings of Commonwealth Prime Ministers 1944–58, 1973–77; and U.N. General Assembly 1949–52, 1955, 1960–68, 73, 75. N.Z. Rep. U.N. Trusteeship Council 1962–66, (Pres. 1964–65). Chmn., U.N. Visiting Mission, Micronesia, 1964. N.Z. Rep. to U.N. Security Council, 1966. *Address:* Ministry of Foreign Affairs, Wellington, New Zealand.

**CORRADO, Benjamin William.** American marketing research consultant. *B.* 1911. *Educ.* N.Y. School of Commerce (N.Y. Univ.); Economics Major. *M.* 1939, Virginia Margaret McCormick. *Career:* Statistician, Investment Counsellor, Standard Statistics Co. 1933–38; Metal Specialist, Poor's Publishing Co. 1939–41; Cleveland Editor, Iron Age 1941–42; Junior Economist U.S. W.P.B. (Munitions) 1942–43; News Editor and Washington Editor, Amer. Machinist 1944–46; Asst. P.R. Dir. Amer. Iron & Steel Inst. 1946–48; Special Asst. to Pres. and Co-ordinator of Advertising and Market Research Industries 1948–50; own Business, Marketing Consultant 1950–55; Vice Pres. Market Research 1955–64, Vice Pres. Industry Relations, National Distillers Products Corp, since 1964. *Publications:* Liquor Revenue (1941); Survey of Metalworking Equipment (1945); Liquor Consumption by States (1945–55); U.S. Beer Report (1951, 1952); Corrado's Liquor Handbook (1954–55); contributions to various publications. Industrial Marketing Award for Outstanding Research 1945. *Member:* Bourbon Inst. (Vice-Pres., Dir.); Kentucky Distillers Assn. (Vice-Pres., Dir.); Maryland Distillers Assn. (Vice-Pres.); Amer. Marketing Assn.; Amer. Management Assn.; Natl. Assn. of Business Economists. *Clubs:* National Press; Rear Guards, *Address:* The National Press Club, Washington 4 DC, U.S.A.

**CORREA da COSTA, Sergio.** Brazilian diplomat. *B.* 1919. *Educ.* National Faculty of Law, University of Brazil (LLD 1942); post-graduate work at University of California, Los Angeles 1949–50, and War College of Brazil 1951. *M.* 1943, Zazi Aranha. *S.* Oswald-Sergio. *Daus.* Zazi-Thereza and Maria Ignez. *Career:* diplomat since 1939. Secretary, Buenos Aires and Washington 1944–47; Acting Delegate, Council of O.A.S., Washington 1947–48; Delegate to IA-ECOSOC, Washington 1947–48; Consul, Los Angeles 1949–50; Deputy Director, Economic Dept., Ministry of External Affairs 1958–59; Acting President, Natl. Technical Assistance Committee 1954–58; Head of Brazilian Migration Service in Europe, Rome 1959–60; Minister-Counsellor Rome 1959–62. Resident Representative to FAO, Rome 1961–62. Brazilian Ambassador to Canada, July 1962–66. Under Secretary of State, March 1966–67; Secy. Gen. of the Min. of External Relations 1967–68; Ambassador to London 1968–75; Perm. Rep. to the UN since 1975. *Awards:* Grand Crosses (GCVO (G.B.); Das Grosse Verdienstkreuz (Germany); Aguila Azteca (Mexico); S. Gregorii Magni (Holy See); Infante Dom Henrique (Portugal); Den Kongelige Norske St. Orden (Norway); Pro Merito Melitensi and Magistral Grace (Malta); Isabel la Catolica (Spain); Grand Collar of the Bright Star (China); Order of Rio Branco (Brazil); Order of Sacred Treasury (Japan); Libertador (Argentina); Merit of the Republic of Korea (Korea); Grand Officer Aeronautical Merit & Naval Merit (Brazil); Al Merito della Republica Italiana (Italy). *Member:* Brazilian and American Societies of International Law; Brazilian Historical and Geographical Institute Brazilian Socy. of Geography. *Publications:* Every Inch a King (biography of Pedro I, Emperior of Brazil) (1950, 1965 and 1972); As Quatro Coroas de Pedro I (1941); Pedro I and Metternich (1942); A Diplomacia do Marechal (1944); A Diplomacia Brasileira na Questao de Leticia (1943). *Clubs:* Rio de Janeiro Yacht; Circolo della Caccia (Rome); Country, Rideau (both in Ottawa); White's Travellers (London). *Address:* Brazilian Mission to UN, 747 Third Ave, New York, NY 10617, U.S.A.

**CORREA, Henry Alvarez,** BS. American. *B.* 1917. *Educ.* St. Louis Univ. (BS (Bus. Admin.)). *M.* 1944, Elizabeth Winchester. *Career:* Vice Pres. Foreign Operations ACF 1958–59, Marketing 1959–63, Exec. Dept. 1964, Exec. Vice Pres. 1965–66; Pres. Dir. ACF Industries Inc.; ACF (Canada); Dir. ACF (Great Britain): Nat. Starch & Chemical Corp.; Polymer Corp.; Dir. Railroad Progress Inst.; Transportation Assoc. of America; MAPI Council Technological Advancement; Metropolitan Opera Guild Inc.; Metropolitan Opera Association. *Clubs:* Sky; Union; Yacht; Opera; Economic; New York; Chicago. *Address: office* 750 3rd Ave., New York, N.Y. 10017.

**CORSCADDEN. Henry Sadleir.** British banker. *B.* 1907. *Educ.* Portora Royal School, and Trinity College, Dublin (BA, LLB 1928, LLD 1931); and Incorporated Law Society of Northern Ireland (Silver Medallist 1931). *M.* 1934. Joyce Aimée Kathleen Wolf. *S.* Alastair Pentland. *Dau.* Jennifer Ann (Pulham). *Career:* Legal Assistant, Ministry of Finance, Northern Ireland 1931; Asst. Solicitor 1934, Solicitor 1940, Director 1953, Ulster Bank Ltd.; Senior Managing Director, Ulster Bank Ltd. 1964–69, Deputy Chmn. since 1969. *Publications:* of articles in Northern Ireland Legal Quarterly, Irish Law Times. *Member:* Institute of Directors; English-Speaking Union; Belfast Rotary Club; Northern Ireland Chamber of Commerce & Industry. *Clubs:* Ulster Reform;

Malone Golf. *Address:* Ulster Bank Ltd., Waring Street, Belfast 1, Northern Ireland.

**CORT, Stewart Shaw.** American business executive. *B.* 1911; *Educ.* Yale Univ. (BA), Harvard Univ. (MBA). *M.* 1961, Elizabeth Fiske Bumiller. *Career:* With Bethlehem Steel Corporation, Vice-Pres. in charge of sales for Pacific Coast 1954–60; Asst. Gen. Mgr. of sales 1960–61; Vice-Pres. (Pacific Coast) 1961–63. Director, Bethlehem Steel Corporation 1963—; Dir. Continental Illinois National Bank & Trust Co. 1965—; Dir. Conill Corporations 1969—; Dir. Met-Mex Pinoles S.A.; Pres. Bethlehem Steel Corp. 1963–70, Chmn., Chief Exec. Officer 1970–74. *Awards:* Decorated, Insignia of Grand Commander of the Order of African Redemption (Liberal); hon vice-pres. American Iron & Steel Institute; *Member:* The Pennsylvania Society; Hon LLD, Moravian College, Lehigh Univ.; LLD Christian College of Oklahoma; The Newcomen Society, Yale Development Board. *Clubs:* Saucon Valley Country; Links; Augusta National Golf; Cypress Point; Pacific-Union; San Francisco Golf. *Address:* 437 Main St., Suite 310, Bethlehem, Pa. 18018, U.S.A.

**CORWIN, Walling.** American chemist and author. *B.* 1895. *Educ.* Ohio State University (BSc 1919; MSc 1921); *M.* Alethea Ray. *Dau.* Mrs. Barbara Adams. *Career:* High School Teacher 1923–42; Chemist, Dupont Remington Arms 1942–44; Research Chemist: Armco Steel (1944–46), National Cash Register Co. (1946–48), Pollock Paper Co. 1949–54; Broker, Green & Ladd (members of the New York Stock Exchange) 1954–56. Chemist, Los Angeles County Smog Control 1956–63. Chemist, Air Pollution Control, Los Angeles County, Calif. 1956–64. *Publications:* Trails ToDay; Junior High School Science; Science of Human Living; Science of Plant and Animal Life; Science of Discovery and Invention; Living Things (a high school biology). Mason; Eastern Star; White Shrine; United States Chess Federation. *Address:* Box 58, Yucaipa, Calif., U.S.A.

**COSGRAVE, Liam.** Irish politician. *B.* 1920 (eldest son of William T. Cosgrave, Pres. of Exec. Council of the Irish Free State 1922–32). *Educ.* Christian Brothers' School Dublin; and Castleknock College, Co. Dublin. *M.* 1952, Vera Osborne. *S.* Liam and Ciaran. *Dau.* Mary. *Career:* Called to the Bar 1943; served in the National Army, first as a private and later in commissioned rank. Member of Dail 1943; Parliamentary Secretary to the Taoiseach (Head of Government) and to the Minister for Industry and Commerce 1948–51; Minister for External Affairs 1954–57; Chairman and Leader of the first Irish Delegation to the General Assembly of U.N. 1956; Senior Counsel 1958; Prime Minister 1973–77, & Minister for Defence 1976. *Awards:* Knight Grand Cross of Pius IX (Ordine Piano), March 1956. Hon. LLD; Duquesne Univ. (Pittsburgh, U.S.A.). St. John's Univ. (Brooklyn, N.Y.), De Paul Univ. (Chicago), National Univ. of Ireland (1974) and Dublin Univ. (1974). *Address:* Beechpark, Templeogue, Co. Dublin.

**COSTA, Rubens Vaz da.** Brazilian banker. *B.* 1927. *Educ.* George Washington University, U.S.A. (Degree in Economics and MA). *Career:* Chief Economist, BNB (1956–59); Economist Pan-America Union (1960); various appointments Inter-American Development Bank, including Deputy Programme Adviser and Deputy Director, Loan Division, South America, participated in important missions, visited Europe in the capacity of adviser. Superintendent of the Superintendency of the Development of the Northeast (Sudene) 1966–67; Pres. Bank North East Brazil 1967–71; Pres. National Housing Bank since 1971–74; Vice-Pres. Quatro-Rodas Hotels de Nordeste SA since 1974. *Address:* and *office* Av. Octaviano Alves de Lima 800, Sao Paulo, Brazil.

**COSTE-FLORET, Paul.** French politician. *B.* 9 April 1911. *Educ.* College Saint-François Régis de Montpellier; Faculté de Droit, Montpellier (D en D). *Career:* Assistant Professor, Faculté de Droit, Paris 1935–37, Professor, Faculté de Droit, Algiers Jan. 1938, Montpellier 1947; Pres., Univ. of Montpellier since 1977; joined Resistance Movement 1940, member of Association of Liberation; Assistant Director, Office of the Keeper of the Seals, Ministry of Justice 1944–45; Counsellor of State 1945–46; Deputy (M.R.P.) for Hérault, Constituent Assembly Oct. 1945, re-elected to Natl. Assembly 1946–51–56–58–62–67; Min. of War Jan.–Oct. 1947; Member, Financial Commission, National Assembly 1949; Minister of Overseas Territories Nov. 1947–Oct. 1949 and July 1951; Minister of Information, Faure Cabinet Jan.–March 1952; Minister of State, Mayer Cabinet Jan.–June 1953; Minister of Public Health in Laniel Cabinet 1953–54; Mayor of Larnalou les bains 1953–59, and since 1971; Counsellor, Herault since 1967. Member of Constitutional Council since 1971. *Awards:* Officier de la Légion d'Honneur; Croix de Guerre avec palme; Médaille de la Résistance, Grand Cross, Sovereign Order of Malta. *Address:* 16 rue du Cardinal-de-Cabrières, 34 Montpellier, France.

**COT, Jean Alexandra.** French commercial consultant (foreign trade) and manufacturer. *B.* 1912. *Educ.* secondary. *M.* 1954, Françoise Ragot. *S.* Stephane. *Dau.* Nathalie. *Career:* Consultant (economic) in private practice 1956—; Adviser to the Higher Committee on Customs and Tariffs; Expert in French Customs affairs. Exclusive importer to France (1960–66). UNOX (Unilever). *Member:* Franco-British Chamber of Commerce; French Exhibition Committee; Republican Committee for Commerce, Belgian/Luxembourg Chamber of Commerce; Industry and Agriculture; National Committee of Advisers in Foreign Trade; General Agent: Philippe & Canaud, Nantes 1937–57; Bel, La Vache qui Rit 1950; Droste, Haarlem; Importer since 1970, Conalvia & Santi-pasta. *Publications:* of several official publications on the opportunities for the exportation of French goods. *Member:* Aero Club de France; Cercle Carpeaux; Golf de la Boulie; Racing Club de France; Chevalier de Tastevin; Membre de l'Ordre Militaire Hospitalier St. Lazare de Nazareth, Malta. *Address: office* 62 rue des Lombards, Paris, France.

**COTTLE, Ronald Edward Waverley.** British. *B.* 1915. *Educ.* Downside Sch. *M.* 1940, Phyllis Mary Gossage. *S.* 1. *Dau.* 2. *Career:* Dir. John Rose & Son. Ltd.; Chmn. Bowring, Camper & Nicholsons Ltd.; *Clubs:* Royal Thames Yacht; Royal Ocean Racing. *Address:* 1 Fordie House, 82 Sloane Street, London, SW1X 9PA; Battery Hill, Castle Point, Salcombe, Devon.

**COTTON, Dr. Robert Henry.** *B.* 1914. *Educ.* Bowdoin College (BS); MIT (MS), and Pennsylvania State Univ. (PhD). *M,* 1948, Mildred W. Smith. *S.* Leonard W. and Thomas C. *Dau.* Dorothy (Kirkwood) (by previous marriage). *Career:* Asst. Pro., Pennsylvania State Univ. 1943–45; Director, Plymouth Florida Div. of National Research Corp. 1945–47; Prof., Univ. of Florida 1947–48; Director of Research: Holly Sugar Corp. 1948–53, Huron Milling Corp. 1954–58, I.T.T. and Continental Baking Co. 1958—. Vice-President 1965—, Continental Baking Co. & Chief Scientist, ITT Food Products. Research director and food chemist. Chairman, U.S. Department of Agriculture-American Bakers' Assn. Technical Liaison Cttee.; the Amer. Inst. of Baking Scientific Advisory Cttee.; Ctte. on Cereal & general products, A.B.M.P.S., NRC, National Academy of Science; Member, Panel V3 White House Conference on Food, Nutrition & Health 1969; Advisor, National Academy of Science N.R.C. Cttee. on Nutritional Guide Lines for Foods 1970; Dir.-Gen., Fundacion Chile, Santiago 1975–77, & Mem. Bd. of Dirs. 1977. *Publications:* of about 60 patents and scientific publications in nutrition chemistry and food technology. Award as Pioneer in Food Technology by Food Industries magazine (for development of frozen orange juice concentrate). President, Rotary Club (Harbor Beach, Michigan) 1959. *Member:* Amer. Chemical Society; Amer. Assn. for Advancement of Science; Inst. of Food Technology; Amer. Assn. of Cereal Chemists (Pres. 1964); Assn. of Research Directors. *Clubs:* Chemists (N.Y.C.); Manursing Island (Rye, N.Y.). *Address: office* ITT, 1351 Washington Blvd., Stamford, CT 06902, U.S.A.

**COTTRELL, Sir Alan (Howard),** Kt 1971. DSC, MA, PhD, FRS. British. *B.* 1919. *Educ.* Moseley Grammar School; Univ. of Birmingham. BSc. (1939), PhD. (1942); Univ. of Cambridge ScD (1976). *M.* 1944, Jean Elizabeth Harber. *S.* 1. *Career:* Lecturer in Metallurgy 1943–45, Professor, Physical Metallurgy, Univ. of Birmingham 1949–55; Deputy Head, Met. Div. Atomic Energy Research Est., Harwell 1955–58; Goldsmiths' Professor, Cambridge Univ. 1958–65; Deputy Chief Scientific Adv. (Studies), Min. of Defence 1965–67; Chief Adviser 1967; Deputy Chief Scient. Adviser to HM Govt. 1968–71; Chief Scientific Adviser 1971–74; Master of Jesus Coll, Cambridge since 1974; Part-time Mem. UKAEA 1962–65; Member Adv. Council on Scientific Policy 1963–64, Central Adv. Council for Science and Technology 1967—; A Vice-President, Royal Society 1964, 1976, 1977; Fellow Royal Swedish Academy of Sciences; Hon. Fellow, Christ's College, Cambridge, 1970; (Fellow, 1958–70). Foreign Hon. Mem., American Academy of Arts and Sciences 1960; Foreign Associate, Nat. Acad. of Sciences, U.S.A. 1972; Hon. Member, American Society for Metals 1972; Fellow, 1974; Foreign Associate, Nat. Acad. of Engineering, U.S.A. 1976; Hon. Member, The Metals Society 1977. *Awards:* Hon. D.Sc. Columbia Univ. 1965; Newcastle Univ. 1967; Liverpool Univ. 1969; Manchester Univ. 1970; Warwick Univ.

1971; Sussex Univ. 1972; Bath Univ. 1973; Strathclyde Univ., Cranfield Institute of Technology, Univ. of Aston in Birminham, 1975; Rosenhain Medallist of the Inst. of Metals; Hughes Medallist, Royal Society, 1971; Inst. of Metal (Platinum) Medal, 1965; Reamur Medal, Société Francaise de Metallurgie, 1964; James Alfred Ewing Medal, I.C.E., 1967; Holweck Medal, Société Francaise de Physique 1969; Albert Sauveur Achievement Award, American Society for Metals, 1969; James Douglas Gold Medal, American Institute of Mining, Metallurgy & Petroleum Engineers, 1974; The Rumford Medal of the Royal Society, 1974; Harvey Prize (Technion, Israel), 1974; Acta Metallurgica Gold Medal, 1976; Guthrie Medal & Prize, Inst. of Physics, 1977. *Publications:* Theoretical Structural Metallurgy (1948, 2nd Ed. 1955); Dislocations and Plastic Flow in Crystal (1953); The Mechanical Properties of Matter (1964); Theory of Chrystal Dislocations (1964); An Introduction to Metallurgy (1967); Portrait of Nature (1975); scientific papers to numerous Journals. *Club:* Athenaeum. *Address:* The Master's Lodge, Jesus College, Cambridge.

**COTTRELL, Anthony Ian.** CBE. New Zealand. Barrister and Solicitor and Notary Public; Dir. of various companies. *B.* 1907. *Educ.* Christs College, Christchurch Univ. *M.* (1) 1934, Florence Catherine Webb (*dec'd*). *S.* Anthony Richard, Hugh Paul and Hugh Crispe. *Daus.* Anna Catherine and Caroline Maude. (2) 1972, Claudia Lilliam Shand (*dec'd*). *Career:* With N.Z. Rugby Football teams 1929–30–31–32. District Governor of Rotary 1959–60; Rotary Information Counsellor 1960–61; N.Z. and Canterbury President, Royal Overseas League 1949–58. President: Canterbury Law Socy. 1947; Christchurch Football Club 1954–74; Christs Coll. Old Boys Assn. 1960–61; Christchurch Rotary 1947. Captain, 20th Bn., N.Z. Division 1940–45 (Prisoner-of-War 1942–44). Chmn., Commonwealth Games Promotion Cttee.; Chmn., N.Z. Medical Research Council; Chmn. C. H. Upham VC & Bar Scholarship Fund since 1946; Vice-Pres. Commonwealth Games Organization Committee. *Clubs:* Canterbury; Canterbury Officers. *Address:* 9 Farnham Place, Christchurch, N.Z.; and *office* 141 Cambridge Terrace, Christchurch, New Zealand.

**COUGHRAN, Tom B.** Banker. *B.* 1906. *Educ.* Stanford University (AB 1927). *M.* 1930, Florence Montgomery. *Dau.* Jane. *Career:* Joined Bank of America N.T. & S.A. 1927; served in various capacities until 1942, which was followed by four years of military duty, including service with the Supreme HQ Allied Expeditionary Forces Europe, and culminated in grade of Lieutenant-Colonel in General Staff. Returned to Bank of America N.T. & S.A. in 1946 as Vice-President and served in capacity of Vice-Pres. & Manager International Banking Dept. until 1957. Accepted appointment from President Eisenhower as Asst. Secretary of U.S. Treasury in 1957. While serving in that capacity also occupied other U.S. Governmental positions, viz., U.S. Director, International Bank for Reconstruction and Development and International Finance Corporation 1957–58; Director, U.S. Development Loan Fund 1958. Executive Vice-President, Bank of America International 1959–69. Also member: U.S. Delegation to NATO 1957; Colombo Conference 1958; Presidential Fact-Finding Commission to Central America 1958, U.S. Management Advisory Committee to the O.E.C.D 1962–67, Chmn. 1967–69; Director, Bank of America International; Capitol Industries; EMI; Vice-Chmn. Bank of America International 1969–71; Chmn. Wobaco Holding Co. and World Banking Corporation 1971–75. Republican. *Clubs:* Links India House, Council on Foreign Relations (N.Y.C.); F Street, International; Metropolitan (Washington); Pacific Union, Bohemian (San Francisco). *Address:* 923 5th Avenue, New York City 10021; and *office* 41 Broad Street, New York City 15, U.S.A.

**COULSON, Sir John Eltringham,** KCMG. British diplomat. *B.* 13 Sept. 1909. *Educ.* Rugby School and Corpus Christi College, Cambridge (1st Cl. Hons. in Classics and Modern Languages). *M.* 1944, Mavis Beazley. *S.* 2. *Career:* entered diplomatic service 1932; served at Bucharest, Foreign Office, Ministry of Economic Warfare and War Cabinet 1934–46; Counsellor, Embassy, Paris 1946; Deputy to Permanent U.K. Representative at U.N. 1950; Assistant Under-Secretary of State, Foreign Office 1952; Minister, Embassy, Washington Oct. 1955–57; Asst. to the Paymaster-General for European Free Trade questions 1957–60; Ambassador to Sweden, May 1960–63; Deputy Under-Secretary of State, Foreign Office 1963–65; Secretary General of European Free Trade Association 1965–72. *Address:* The Old Mill, Selborne, Hants.

**COULTER, Borden McKee.** American. *B.* 1917. *Educ.* Univ. of Calif. at Los Angeles (BS Mech Eng; BS Industrial Eng; MBA Business Administration). *M.* 1950, Emily Sawtelle. *S.* Borden, Leigh and Richard. *Dau.* Terry Lynn. *Career:* Research Analyst, Australian National Railway 1939–40; Senr. Industrial Engr., Lockheed Aircraft Corp. 1940–47; Div. Industrial Engr., U.S. Steel Corp. 1947–48; Manager Production Control, Bakwell Products 1948–49; Supervisor Organization and Procedure, Norris Industries 1950–53; Gen. Mgr. Road Engineering Associates 1940–53; Principal, The Emerson Consultants Inc. 1953—. Vice-President and Director, Emerson Consultants Inc., N.Y.C. 1965—. *Publications:* Scientific Office Management; Guaranteed Annual Wage Review. *Member:* Blue Key; Kappa Psi; Alpha Kappa Psi; Tau Kappa Alpha; Phi Gamma Delta. Amer. Inst. Industrial Engrs. (Past Pres.); System & Procedure Assn.; Amer. Management Assn. (Speaker and Chmn.); Amer. Inst. of Plant Engr.; Natl. Assn. of Accountants; United States Naval Inst.; Navy League of the United States; International Maintenance Inst.; International Platform Assn.; Inst. of Management Consultants; Int. Maintenance Institute; Nat. Register, Prominent Americans; The Newcomen Society. *Clubs:* Houston; Houston International; Petroleum Club of Houston. *Address:* 2112 Amberly Court, Houston, Tex. 77042; and *office* 30 Rockefeller Plaza, New York 20, N.Y., U.S.A.

**COULTER, Warren Raymond.** Canadian mechanical engineer. *B.* 1911. *Educ.* University of Toronto (BASc Mech); Professional Engineer, Ontario. *M.* 1937, Helen Patricia Aldington. *S.* Michael Arthur and Terence Douglas. *Career:* With Coulter Cooper & Brass Ltd., Trainee 1933; Supervisor, Metalsmithing Div. 1934; Chief Engineer 1941; Director 1944; Vice-Pres. 1956; President: Coulter Copper & Brass Ltd., Toronto, Booth-Coulter Coppersmithing Ltd. 1958; Bd. Chmn., Coulter Copper & Brass Ltd. 1976. Montreal, and Aluminium Swimming Pools Canada Ltd., Toronto. *Member:* Professional Engineers of Ontario; C.S.M.E. *Club:* Rotary (Islington, Ont.). *Address:* 97 Valecrest Drive, Islington, Ont. M9A 4P5; and *office* 140 The East Mall, Toronto, Ont. M8Z 2M2.

**COULTRAP, James W.** American. *B.* 1910. *Educ.* Ohio Wesleyan University (BA; and Hon LLD) and University of Michigan (JD). *M.* (1) 1937, Virginia Lees (*Div.* 1973). *S.* James Jr. *Daus.* Ginna Kline and Barbara Zachar. (2) Cornelia Doty. *Career:* President: Village of Hinsdale, Ill. 1961–65. Chairman, Miehle-Goss-Dexter Inc. 1968–70. *Member:* Amer. and Chicago Bar Associations; Chicago Assn. of Commerce and Industry; Machinery and Allied Products Inst.; National Printing Equipment Assn.; Phi Beta Kappa. *Clubs:* Chicago, Economic (Pres. 1964–66); Hinsdale Golf (Pres. 1969). *Address:* 840 South Elm St., Hinsdale, Ill. 60521, U.S.A.

**COURAU, Albert Marie Rene.** French engineer. *B.* 22 Feb. 1905. *Educ.* Ecole Polytechnique (BSc). *M.* 1929, Anne de Penfentenyo de Kervereguin (*Dec.*). *S.* 7. *Daus.* 3. *Career:* Worked on construction of submarines 1927–40; Professor École de Navigation Sous-Marine 1929–31; Secretary-General of the Merchant Marine 1948–53. President: Cie de Transports Océaniques 1954–60; Cie de Navigation Sud-Atlantique 1961–65; Cie Fabre-SGTM 1965–71; Nouvelle Cie de Paquebots, 1969–71; Cie de Navigation Paquet 1968–70; International Cargo Handling Association 1954–62. *Member:* Académie de Marine 1959; Administrateur du Port autonome de Marseille 1966—75. *Awards:* Commandeur de la Légion d'Honneur; Grand officier ordre National du Merite; Commandeur du Mérite Maritime; Commandeur du Ouissam Alaouite (Morocco); Commander, Orange Nassau (Netherlands); Commandeur Mérite Senegalais. *Address:* 19 Rue Michel-Ange, 75016 Paris, France.

**COURBIER, Jean** (Frédéric Victor Marie). French. *B.* 1904. *Educ.* Polytechnic (Lic en D 1924). *M.* 1934, Geneviève Delarue Caron de Beaumarchais. *Daus.* Anne (Vollant) and Christine (Piaton). President and Director-General, Sté. Gerland, June 1960—. *Awards:* Officer Legion of Honour; Officer Order of the Crown (Belgium); Chevailer, St. Gregory the Great. *Member:* Society of Political and Social Economy, Lyons (Hon. Pres.); Lyons Chamber of Commerce and Industry (Hon. Pres.); Directors of Industry for Social and Economic Progress (Hon. Pres.). *Clubs:* Rotary (Lyons); *Address:* 87 rue Pierre Brunier, 69 Caluire et Cuire, France; and *office* 49 rue de la République, 69 Lyon 2 ème, France.

**COURT, Hon. Sir Charles Walter Michael,** OBE (Mil), MLA. Australian. *B.* 1911. *Educ.* Fellow: Institute of Chartered

Accountants in Australia, of the Chartered Institute of Secretaries of the Australian Socy. of Accountants and Inst. of Sales and Marketing Executives. *M.* 1936, Rita Maud Steffanoni. *S.* 5. *Career:* Practising Chartered Accountant since 1933 (Partner in the firm of Hendry, Rae & Court, Chartered Accountants, 1938–70). War Service, AIF (from Private to Lt.-Col. 1940–46). Member of the Legislative Assembly for the electorate of Nedlands in the Parliament of Western Australia since 1953. Deputy Leader of the Opposition 1956–59. Minister for Industrial Development. and the North-West in the Govt. of Western Australia 1959–71, Min. for Rlys 1959–67; Deputy Leader of the Opposition 1971–72; Leader of the Opposition 1972–74; Premier of Western Australia since 1974. *Member* and patron of a number of sporting and cultural bodies; Pres. West. Austr. Band Assn. 1955–59; Political affiliations: Liberal Party. *Award:* Hon. Doctor of Laws Univ. of Western Australia 1969; Hon. Col. West. Aust. Univ. Regt. Aust. Military Forces 1969–75, and Hon. Col. Special Air Services Regt., Aust. Military Forces 1976; Senator Junior Chamber International 1971; Knight Bachelor 1972. *Publications:* Author of several papers on technical matters within the Accountancy profession and on matters of State and National development. *Clubs:* Commercial Travellers (Perth); Rotary; Lions (Nedlands). *Address:* 46 Waratah Avenue, Nedlands, W.A.; and *office* Parliament House, Harvest Terrace, Perth, W.A., Australia.

**COURTOIS de VICOSE, Gilbert.** French. *B.* 1908. *Educ.* LLD and Diploma of School of Political Science, Paris. *M.* 1936. Jenny Aron de Mengersen. *S.* Axel, François and Jean-Louis. *Dau.* Anne. *Career:* Chief of Section at the Secretariat-General of the International Chamber of Commerce, Paris 1937–39; Secretary-General, Courtois Bank 1940–47. President and Director-General, Courtois Bank 1942—. Consul-General of Belgium in Toulouse since 1947. *Awards:* Officier Legion of Honour (France), Order of Leopold I, and Order of the Crown (Belgium). *Club:* Toulouse Golf (Hon. President). *Address:* 3 rue Mage, Toulouse; and *office* Banque Courtois, 33 rue de Rémusat, Toulouse.

**COURVOISIER, Jean.** French; Chevalier Legion of Honour; Croix de Guerre. *B.* 1904. *Educ.* Alsatian School and National High School of Mines, Paris (Mining Civil Engineer). *M.* 1930, Denise Moutou. *S.* Pierre, Daniel and Robert. *Daus.* Muriel (Mme. Herrenschmidt) and Maryse. *Career:* President: the Evangelical Missionary Society of Paris; the Protestant Federation of France. President, Banque Odier Bungener-Courvoisier, Paris. *Address:* 44 rue Cardinet, Paris 17e; and *office* 57 avenue d'Iena, Paris, 16e.

**COUSINS, Rt. Hon. Frank,** PC. *B.* 1904. *Educ.* King Edward School, Doncaster. *M.* 1930, Annie Elizabeth Judd. *S.* 2. *Daus.* 2. *Career:* Organiser Road Transport Section T.G.W.U. 1938; National Officer (Road Transport Section) 1944; National Secretary (Road Transport Section) 1948; Assistant General Secretary T.G.W.U. 1955. *Member:* British Transport Joint Consultative Council 1955–63; General Secretary, Transport and General Workers Union 1956–69; Min. of Labour Natl. Jt. Adv. Council 1956–64, 1966—; Exec. Council Internatl. Transport Workers Fed. 1956 (Pres. 1958–60, 1962–64); Colonial Labour Adv. Cttee. 1957–62; London Travel Cttee. 1958–60; Political Economy Club 1967; Governor, Natl. Inst. for Economic and Social Research 1958; Member, Council for Scientific and Industrial Research 1960–64; (Seconded as Minister of Technology, Oct. 1964–July 1966). Export Credit Guarantee Dept. Advisory Cncl. 1962. Member of General Council of the Trades Union Congress, the National Economic Development Council 1962—, and Institute of Transport. Privy Councillor, Oct. 1964. Hon LLD Univ. of Strathclyde 1965. Chmn., Community Relations Commission. 1968–70. Member Labour Party. *Address:* 93 Park Drive, Sprotborough, Doncaster, S. Yorkshire.

**COUTTS, Sir Walter Fleming,** GCMG 1962, Kt Bach 1961, MBE. British civil servant (colonial administration). *B.* 1912. *Educ.* St. Andrew's Univ. (MA 1934). *M.* 1942, Janet Elizabeth Jamieson. *S.* David Fleming. *Dau.* Jacqueline Cameron. *Career:* Dist. Officer, Kenya 1936; Dist. Comm. 1947; Administrator, St. Vincent 1949; Minister for Education, Labour and Lands, Kenya 1956; Governor of Uganda 1961, Governor-General 1962; Chief Sec., Kenya 1958—. Assam African Investments Ltd. Secretary, Dulverton Trust 1966. Assistant Vice-Chancellor (Administration) Univ. of Warwick, 1969; Chmn. Pergamon Press 1972–74; Dir. Farmington Trust since 1972. *Publications:* Three papers on African elections: Kenya 1955, Zanzibar 1956, Kenya 1960 (with E. N. Griffiths-Jones, KBE, CMG, QC). *Clubs:* Royal Overseas League; Nairobi (Kenya). *Address:* 6 Stanmore Gardens, Mortimer, Berkshire.

**COUVE DE MURVILLE, Maurice.** *B.* 1907. *Educ.* École des Sciences Politiques L es L, D en D. *M.* 1932, Jacqueline Schweisguth. *Daus.* Juliette (Vieljeux), Dorothée (Matter), Beatrice (Hervey). *Career:* Inspector of Finance 1930; Dep. Director, Mouvement Général des Fonds 1938; Secretary-General to the Commandement en Chef, Algier 1943; member of the National Liberation Committee and Commissioner of Finance 1943; Amb. Ex. and Plen. to Italy 1944–45; Director-General of Political Affairs, Ministry of Foreign Affairs 1945–50; Amb. Ex. and Plen. to Egypt 1950–54; to U.S. 1955; to Bonn 1956–58; Minister for Foreign Affairs 1958–68; Prime Minister of France 1968–69; Deputé in Paris 1973; Commandeur de la Légion d'Honneur. *Address:* 3 rue Jean Goujon, Paris 8.

**COVERT, Frank Manning,** QC, DFC, OBE. Canadian barrister and solicitor. *B.* 1908. *Educ.* Dalhousie University (BA, LLB). *M.* 1934, Mary Covert. *S.* 2. *Daus.* 2. *Career:* Partner, Stewart, McKeen & Covert, barristers and solicitors, Halifax, N.S.; admitted to Bar of Nova Scotia 1930; Received K.C. 1944; Assistant General Counsel, Department of Munitions and Supply, Ottawa 1940–42; served in World War II (Navigator, R.C.A.F.) 1942–45; Director, The Royal Bank of Canada, Sun Life Assurance Coy. of Canada. Minas Basin Pulp and Power Co. Ltd., National Sea Products Ltd., Bowater Mersey Paper Co. Ltd., Maritime Steel and Foundries Ltd., Petrofina Canada Ltd., and Phoenix Assurance Co. Ltd., Canadian Keyes Fibre Co. Ltd. President, Maritime Paper Products Ltd.; Dir. Molson Cos. Ltd.; Dir. Standard Brands Ltd. *Member:* Board of Governors, Dalhousie University. *Address:* Spring Garden Terrace Apt., Halifax, N.S., Canada.

**COWAN, Irving.** American diplomat. *B.* 1927. *Educ.* Univ. of Miami (Florida) *M.* 1956. Mariorie Friedland. *S.* 1. *Daus.* 2. *Career:* Honorary Consul of the Republic of Korea since 1970. *Member:* Consular Corps of Miami; Consular Corps College and International Consular Academy. *Address:* 1615 Diplomat Parkway, Hollywood, Florida U.S.A.; and *office* 3515 South Ocean Drive, Hollywood, Florida, U.S.A.

**COWDEN, Dudley J.** *B.* 1899. *Educ.* Grinnell Coll., Univ. of Chicago (AM 1922) and Columbia Univ. (PhD 1931). *M.* 1926, Mercedes Siedler. *Career:* Instructor in Economics: Lafayette College 1926–29, St. John's University (Brooklyn) 1931–34 and William College 1934–35; Assoc. Prof. of Economics, University of North Carolina 1935-40; Professor of Economics Statistics 1940–71; Professor Emeritus since 1971. *Publications:* Applied General Statistics (with F. E. Croxton 1939, 1955); Practical Business Statistics (with F. E. Croxton 1938–48–60); Statistical Methods in Quality Control (1957). Phi Beta Kappa; Beta Gamma Sigma. *Member:* Amer. Statistical Assn. (Fellow). *Fellow:* Amer. Assn. for the Advancement of Science. *Address:* 304 Country Club Road, Chapel Hill, N.C.; and *office* 300 D Hanes Hall, University of North Carolina Chapel Hill, N.C., U.S.A.

**COWDRAY, Viscount,** of Cowdray (Weetman John Churchill Pearson, TD). British landowner & Company Chairman. *B.* 27 Feb. 1910. *Educ.* Eton; Ch Ch, Oxford. *M.* (1) 1939, Lady Anne Pamela Bridgeman (marriage dissolved 1950). *S.* 1. *Daus.* 2. (2) 1953, Elizabeth Georgiana Mather Jackson. *S.* 1. *Daus.* 2. Director, Lazard Brothers & Co. Ltd.; Chmn., S. Pearson & Son, Ltd. *Address:* Cowdray Park, Midhurst, Sussex; Dunecht, Skene, Aberdeenshire, and Millbank Tower (17th Floor), Millbank, London, SWIP 4QZ.

**COWEN, Prof. Sir Zelman,** Kt, GCMG, QC. Australian. *B.* 1919. *Educ.* Scotch Coll., Melbourne; Univ. of Melbourne—BA, LLM; Oxford Univ.—MA, DCL. *M.* 1945, Anna Wittner. *S.* 3. *Dau.* 1. *Career:* Fellow of Oriel Coll., Oxford 1947–50; Prof. of Public Law & Dean of the Faculty of Law, Univ. of Melbourne 1951–66; Vice-Chancellor, Univ. of New England 1967–70; Vice-Chancellor, Univ. of Queensland 1970–77; Governor-General of Australia since 1977. *Member:* Fellow, Acad. of Social Sciences of Australia 1972; Fellow, Aust. Coll. of Education 1972; Foreign Hon. Mem., American Acad. of Arts & Sciences, 1965; Academic Governor of the Bd. of Govs., Hebrew Univ. of Jerusalem 1969—; Bd. of Dirs., Australian Opera 1969–77; Bd. of International Assn. for Cultural Freedom 1970–75; Fellow, Royal Soc. of Arts, 1971; Pres., Aust. Inst. of Urban studies 1973–77; Club of Rome 1974—; Chmn., Bd. of Govs., Utah Foundation 1975–77; Law Reform Commissioner, Commonwealth of Australia

1976–77; Chmn., Aust. Vice-Chancellors' Cttee. 1977. Mem. of Gray's Inn, Barrister-at-Law, mem. of Victorian & Queensland Bars. *Decorations:* Companion, Order of St. Michael & St. George, 1968; Queen's Counsel, 1971; Knight Bachelor, 1976. *Publications:* Specialist Editor, Dicey: Conflict of Laws (1949); Australia & the United States: Some Legal Comparisons (1954); (with P. B. Carter) Essays on the Law of Evidence (1956); American–Australian Private International Law (1957); Federal Jurisdiction in Australia (1959); (with D. Mendes da Costa) Matrimonial Causes Jurisdiction (1961); The British Commonwealth of Nations in a Changing World (1964); Sir John Latham & Other Papers (1965); Sir Isaac Isaacs (1967); Introduction to 2nd edn., Evatt: The King & His Dominion Governors (1967); The Private Man (A.B.C. Boyer Lectures, 1969); Individual Liberty & the Law (Tagore Law Lectures, 1975); chapters in books, articles & essays in journals in Australia, U.K., U.S.A., Canada & Europe on legal, political, social & university matters. *Club:* Queensland (Brisbane). *Address:* 55 Walcott Street, St. Lucia, Queensland 4067, Australia.

**COWLES, Gardner.** American publisher and editor. *B.* 1903. *Educ.* Phillips Exeter Academy and Harvard University (AB 1925); Hon LLD, Drake University, 1942; Coe College, 1948; Long Island University, 1955; Hon LHD, Bard College, 1950, Cornell College, 1951; Hon LittD, Iowa Wesleyan College, 1955 Hon SScD, Simpson College, 1955; LHD Mundelein College (Hon), LLD Hobart and William Smith Colleges (Hon), Phi Beta Kappa College (Hon). *M.* (1) 1933, Louis Thornburg (*Div.* 1946). *S.* Gardner III *Daus.* 2. 1956, Jan Streate. *Dau.* 1. *Career:* President, Des Moines Register 1943–71, Chmn. 1971–73; Founder *Look* Magazine 1936; Hon. Chairman of Board, Cowles Communications Inc.; Director Emeritus, United Air Lines; Member, Board of Trustees, Univ. of Miami, Teachers College, Columbia Univ.; Domestic Director, Office of War Information, Washington, D.C. 1942–43; resigned; accompanied Wendell Wilkie on round-the-world flight 1942. Republican. *Address:* Suite 1612, 630 Fifth Avenue, New York, N.Y. 10020, U.S.A.

**COWLES, John.** American newspaper publisher and editor. *B.* 1898. *Educ.* Harvard (AB 1921); Hon Degrees: LLD Boston Univ. 1941; Grinnell Coll. 1955; Harvard 1956; Macalester (Minn.) College 1958; Rochester Univ. 1959; Carleton Coll. 1961; Allegheny Coll., 1963; LittD Jamestown Coll. 1946; Centennial Award, Northwestern Univ. 1951; LHD Coe Coll. 1956; Minnesota Award for Distinguished Service in Journalism, Univ. of Minnesota 1956; LHD; Simpson Coll. 1957; Drake (Iowa) Univ. 1958. *M.* 1923, Elizabeth Morley Bates. *S.* John, Jr. and Russell II. *Daus.* Elizabeth Morley (Ballantine) and Sarah Richardson (von Eggers Doering). In newspaper work since 1920. Chairman, Minneapolis Star and Tribune Co. (and previously president, predecessor corporations) 1935–73; Chairman of Board, Des Moines (Iowa) Register and Tribune Co. 1945–70; Dir., First Natl. Bank of Minneapolis 1940–68; member, Business Council 1952–69, Hon. member 1969—. Presidential Cert. of Merit for War Service. *Member:* Hoover Commission on Nat. Defence Estab. 1948, Cttee. White House Conference on Education 1954–55, National Citizens Commission for Public Schools 1950–56. Consultant to Natl. Security Council 1953. *Publications:* author of chapter of Journalism in America Now (1938); also newspaper series Britain Under Fire (1941); Report on Asia (1956). Trustee: Ford Foundation 1950–68; Gardner Cowles Foundation; Minneapolis Society of Fine Arts; American Assembly. Member, General Advisory Committee to U.S. Arms Control & Disarmament Agency 1962–69. Associated Press (2nd Vice-President 1929; 1st Vice-President 1930; member, Board of Directors 1934–43); Audit Bureau of Circulations (Dir. 1929–33); Overseers Harvard (member of Bd. 1944–50) 1960–66; Harvard Alumni Assn. (Pres. 1953–54); Trustee, Carnegie Endowment for International Peace 1960–69, Hon. Trustee 1969—, and Phillips Exeter Academy 1936–54. Hon. National President, Sigma Delta Chi 1954; Hon. member, Alpha Kappa Psi; Sons of American Revolution; American Legion. Mason. *Clubs:* Minneapolis; Woodhill; Des Moines (Iowa); Mill Reef (Antigua, W.I.). *Address:* Minneapolis Star and Tribune, Minneapolis, Minn. 55415, U.S.A.

**COWPER, Edward William Harington.** Australian. *B.* 1917. *Educ.* Crist Coll., New Zealand. *M.* 1940, Jean Maxwell. *S.* 1. *Daus.* 2. *Career:* Hobart (Tasmania) Mgr., Liverpool & London & Globe Insurance Co. 1946–48. Captain, Royal Australian Artillery, Australian Imperial Force 1940–45; Commercial Relations Director Alfred Dunhill (Australia) Pty. Ltd. *Clubs:* Australian (Sydney); Elanora Country (N.S.W.). *Address:* 4/116 Milson Road, Cremorne, N.S.W.; and *office* 23–25 O'Connell Street, Sydney, N.S.W. 2000, Australia.

**COWPER, Sir Norman Lethbridge,** CBE, Australian solicitor and company director. *B.* 1896. *Educ.* University of Sydney (BA, LLB). *M.* 1925, Dorothea Huntly McCrae. *Daus.* 3. Chairman of Directors of several public companies; *Publications:* numerous articles in Australian Quarterly, Australian Outlook and other periodicals. *Clubs:* Australian, (Sydney). *Address:* 9 Millewa Avenue, Wahroonga, Sydney; and *office* 2 Castlereagh Street, Sydney, N.S.W., Australia.

**COX, Sir (Ernest) Gordon,** KBE, TD. British. *B.* 1906. *Educ.* Univ. of Bristol (DSc). *M.* (1) Lucie G. Baker (*D.* 1962). *S.* Keith Gordon. *Dau.* Patricia Ann. (2) 1968, Mary R. Truter, DSc. *Career:* Res. Asst., Davy-Faraday Lab., Royal Instn. 1927; Chemistry Dept., University of Birmingham 1929–40; Vice-Pres., Inst. of Physics 1950–53. Special scientific duties, War Office and 21 Army Group 1942–45. Appointed to Chair in Leeds Univ. 1945. Secy., Agricultural Research Council, 1960–71; Treas. Royal Institution of Gt. Britain 1971–76. Mem. Agricultural Res. Council 1957–60. *Publications:* of numerous scientific papers in journals of various learned societies, chiefly on the crystal structures of chemical compounds. *Awards:* Hon DSc (Newcastle and Birmingham), Hon LLD (Bristol). FRS, 1954. *Fellow:* Royal Institute of Chemistry, and of Institute of Physics; Hon. Associate Royal Coll. Veterinary Surgeons; Hon. DSc Bath and East Anglia 1973. *Clubs:* Athenaeum; English-Speaking Union, Lansdowne. *Address:* 117 Hampstead Way, London, N.W.11.

**COX, Sir Geoffrey Sandford,** MA, BA, CBE. British television executive. *B.* 1910. *Educ.* Southland High School; Otago Univ. New Zealand; Oxford Univ. England. *M.* 1935, Cecily Barbara Talbot Turner. *S.* 2. *Daus.* 2. *Career:* Editorial Staff London News Chronicle and Daily Express 1935–40; New Zealand Army, Captain, service in Middle East 1940–42; First Secy. N. Zealand Legation Washington 1942–43; New Zealand Army, Major, service Italy 1944–45; News Chronicle, Political Correspondent Asst. Editor 1945–56; Editor Independent Television News London 1956–68; Deputy Chmn. Yorkshire Television Ltd. 1968–72; Chmn. Tyne Tees Television 1972–74, Dir. Trident Television since 1970; Chmn., LBC & IRN since 1977. *Fellow:* Royal Television Socy.; British Kinematographical Society. *Publications:* Defence of Madrid (1937); Red Army Moves (1941); Road to Trieste (1946). *Clubs:* Garrick (London). *Address:* Trident Television, 16 Brooks Mews, London, W1Y 1LF.

**COX, Harry Bernard,** CBE. British. *B.* 1906. *Educ.* BA (Oxon). *M.* 1955, Joan Alma Munn. *S.* Edward Henry. *Dau.* Janet Mary. *Career:* With H.M. Overseas Service 1930–57, and John Holt & Co. (Liverpool) Ltd. 1958–66; Deputy Chairman, Thos. Wyatt & Son (West Africa) Ltd. Consultant, Knight, Frank & Rutley. *Club:* Oriental (London). *Address:* c/o Barclays Bank, 4 Vere Street, London W.1.

**COX, Ray Basil.** Australian. *B.* 1909. *Educ.* Matriculation. *M.* 1934, Edna Margaret Hyatt. *S.* 1. *Daus.* 3. *Career:* Production Media & Account Exec. Richardson Cox Pty. Ltd. 1948–52; Dir. Noel Paton (Vic.) Pty. Ltd. 1953–54; Dep. Man. Dir. O'Brien Publicity (Vic.) Pty. Ltd. 1954–64; Man. Dir. John Higgins Advertising Assoc. Pty. Ltd. 1964–72; Thomson White & Partners (Vic.) Pty. Ltd. 1972–75; Public Relations Consultant 1976. Councillor Malvern City Council. Hon. Life Fellow, Advertising Inst. of Australia; A. Mus. A.; L.L.C.M.; L.C.M.; Fellow Market Research Socy.; Inst. Sales & Marketing Exec.; Business Administration. *Member:* S.P.E.A.; Chmn. Vic. Div. Aust. Assn. of Advertising Agencies 1960–63; Chmn. Education Bd, 1960–63; Councillor Royal Automobile Club, Vic. 1972—. *Clubs:* Kiwanis, Royal Automobile (Victoria); Riversdale. *Address:* 23 Durward Road, Chadstone, 3148, Vic. Australia.

**COYLE, Donald Walton.** American. *B.* 1922. *Educ.* Amherst (Mass.) Coll. (BA). *M.* 1946, Patricia Robinson. *S.* D. Lorne. *Daus.* Deborah A. and Sharon R. *Career:* Industrial Analyst, Commercial National Bank & Trust, N.Y. 1947–50; from 1950 with Amer. Broadcasting Co.; Mgr., radio and TV Network research; Dir., TV network and radio research; Dir., TV sales development and research; Vice-Pres. of ABC Internatl. Television Inc. 1959; President, ABC International Television Inc. 1960–70; Founder & President, Intercontinental Communications Inc., New York; Member Bd. of Dirs., Intercontinental Comm. Inc.; Exec. Vice-Pres. & Dir., CTV Television Network Ltd., Toronto, Ont.,

Canada. *Publications:* Recommended Standards for Radio and Television; Program Audience Size Measurements, 1954. *Address:* 86 Plymbridge Road, Willowdale, Ontario, Canada.

**COYNE, James E.** Former Governor of the Bank of Canada. *B.* 1910. *Educ.* Univs. of Manitoba (BA) and Oxford (BCL). Admitted to Bar of Manitoba 1934; practised as solicitor and barrister 1934–38. Financial Attaché, Canadian Embassy, Washington 1941; Member (Dep. Chmn.), Wartime Prices and Trade Board, Ottawa 1942; Assistant to Governors of Bank of Canada 1944–49; Dep.-Governor 1950–54; Governor 1955–61. *Address:* 29 Ruskin Row, Winnipeg 9, Manitoba, Canada.

**CRAFT, Robert Homan.** *B.* 1906. *Educ.* University of Pennsylvania (BS 1929). *M.* 1938, Janet M. Sullivan. *S.* Robert Homan and George Sullivan. *Dau.* Carol Ann (Schaefer). *Career:* Asst. Treas., Guaranty Trust Co. of N.Y. 1937–40; 2nd Vice-Pres. Vice-Pres. and Treas. 1943–52. Exec. Vice-Pres. and Dir., Amer. Securities Corp. N.Y. 1953–56; Pres., Vice-Chmn., Chase Int. Investment Corp. 1956–60; Pres., Chmn., Exec. Cttee., Paribas Corp. 1960–64, & since 1965 Dir. Mississippie River Corp., Chmn Board 1971–73, Financial Vice-Pres. 1965–70, Chmn. Finance Cttee. 1971–74; Dir. Chmn. Finance Cttee. since 1956 & Mem. Exec. Cttee. since 1962 of following companies: Missouri Pacific Railroad Co., Missouri Illinois Railroad Co., Missouri Improvement Co., American Refrigerator Transit Co., Chicago & E. Illinois Railroad Co., and Texas & Pacific Railway Co.; Dir. Chmn. Finance Cttee. River Corporation; Dir. & Mem. Exec. Comm., New York Bank for Savings; Chmn. Investment Policy Cttee., Massachusetts Mutual Life Ins. Co.; Mass. Mutual Corporate Investors; Mass Mutual Income Investors; Mercantile Trust Co., St. Louis Chemical Bank N.Y. Trust Co.; Lower Manhattan Adv. Board; U.S. Life Mutual-Fund; Dir. & Chmn. Finance Comm., Combined Communications Corporation. *Clubs:* Augusta Natnl. Golf, Wall St. (Gov.), Bond University, Fox Meadow Tennis, Scarsdale Golf; Colony (Springfield, Mass.); Blind Brook, Shenorock Shore, Rockfeller Center Luncheon, Desert Forest Golf (Carefree, Ariz.). *Address:* 2 Rectory Lane, Scarsdale, N.Y. 10583; and *office* 600 Third Ave. New York, NY 10016, U.S.A.

**CRAGIN, Stuart Wilson.** American. *B.* 1906. *Educ.* Phillips Acad., Andover (Grad. 1924) and Yale Univ. (PhB 1928). *M.* 1932, Mary Elizabeth Washburn. *S.* Stuart Wilson, Jr. *Daus.* Alison Washburn (Herzig) and Mary Elizabeth (Waters III). Capt., U.S. Marine Corps in World War II (Bronze Star; Pacific Theatre I Star). *Career:* Vice-Pres., J. P. Morgan & Co. 1940–55; Senior Vice-Pres. 1955–59; Senior Vice-Pres., Morgan Guaranty Trust Co. 1959–64; Chmn., Credit Policy Cttee., Morgan Guaranty Trust Company 1964–71. *Member:* Markle Foundation Greenwich Hospital Assn. (Trustee); Sons of the American Revolution. *Clubs:* Hollenbeck; Round Hill. *Address:* Pheasant Lane, Greenwich, Conn.; U.S.A.

**CRAIG, (Albert) James (Macqueen),** CMG. British Diplomat. *B.* 1924. *Educ.* Liverpool Inst. High Sch.; Queen's & Magdalen Colleges, Oxford—MA. *M.* 1952, Margaret Hutchinson. *S.* 3. *Dau.* 1. *Career:* Lecturer in Arabic, Durham Univ. 1948–55; Principal Instructor, Middle East Centre for Arab Studies 1955–58; Foreign Office 1958–61; H.M. Political Agent, Trucial States 1961–64; 1st Sec., British Embassy, Beirut 1964–67; Counsellor, British Embassy, Jedda 1967–70; Fellow of St. Antony's Coll., Oxford 1970–71; Head of Near East & North Africa Dept., Foreign & Commonwealth Office 1971–75; British Dep. High Commissioner, Kuala Lumpur 1975–76; British Ambassador, Damascus since 1976. *Decorations:* Companion of St. Michael & St. George, 1975. *Clubs:* Travellers' (London). *Address:* c/o Foreign & Commonwealth Office, London SW1.

**CRAIG, Hon. James Frederick.** MLA (Toodyay 1959—). Australian. *B.* 1911. *Educ.* Scotch College, Perth (W.A.). *M.* 1936, Marie Haynes. *S.* Ian. *Daus.* Joan and Judith. Minister for Transport and Police, Apr. 1962. Chief Secretary and Minister for Police and Traffic in the Government of Western Australia, since 1965. Member Australian Country Party. *Clubs:* W. A. Turf; Commercial Travellers Assn.; W.A. National Football League Members; City Beach Bowling. *Address: office* S.G.I.O. Buildings, 184 St. George's Terrace, Perth, W.A., Australia.

**CRAIG, John W.** *B.* 1907. *Educ.* University of Dayton (BSME). *M.* 1928, Thelma G. Stevens. *Dau.* Judith Irene (Wilhoit). *Career:* Refrigerating Engineer, Frigidaire Division, General Motors Corp. 1927–37; Chief Refrigerating Engineer, Crosley Division, Avco Manufacturing Corp. 1937–40) Works Mgr. 1945–48; Vice-Pres. and Gen. Mgr. 1948–53). Pres., Aluminium Industries Inc. 1953–54; Vice-Pres., Radio Corp of America 1954–55; Vice- Pres., Gen. Mgr., Major Appliance Div., Westinghouse Electric Corp. 1955–63; Vice-Pres., Director, Hupp Corp. 1963–65; Vice-Pres., Operations Appliance Div., Admiral Corp. 1965–68; Sen. Vice-Pres. 1968–69. Exec. Vice-Pres. Admiral Corp. since 1969. Recipient, Navy Bureau of Ordnance Development Award, U.S. Navy. *Member:* American Society of Heating, Refrigerating & Air Conditioning Engineers; Historical and Philosophical Socy. of Ohio; Newcomen Socy. in N. America. Republican. *Clubs:* Queen City, Recess (Cincinnati). *Address: office* 3800 W. Cortland Street, Chicago 47, Ill., U.S.A.

**CRAIG, William Sutherland.** Canadian industrial executive. *B.* 1912. *Educ.* BSc in Engineering. *M.* 1936, Charlotte Mary Colwill. *S.* Michael Robert. *Daus.* Patricia Eleanor, Judith Mary and Elizabeth Kathleen. *Career:* Metallurgist, International Harvester Co. of Canada 1935–39; Sales Engineer, International Nickel Co. of Canada 1939–40; Chief Engineer. Small Arms Ltd. 1940–46; Pres. and Mgr. Dir., Stamped and Enamelled Ware Ltd., Hespeler, Ont. 1946–63. Management Consultant 1964–65. General Manager, Canadian Operations, The General Fire-proofing Co., Georgetown 1966–68; Pres., Pica Data Services Ltd. 1968–74, Galt; Vice-President, Programmed Learning of London 1968–74; Industrial Development Consultant, Ontario Govt., 1974–77. *Member:* Assn. of Professional Engineers (Prov. of Ontario); Amer. Socy. for Metals; Canadian Manufacturers Assn.; Canadian Ceramic Socy.; Boy Scouts Assn.; Industrial Accident Prevention Assn. *Clubs:* Kiwanis; Waterloo Golf and Country: Galt Curling. *Address:* Grand Ridge Drive, Cambridge, Ontario, Canada.

**CRAIGMYLE, Ronald Muirhead.** Investment banker. *B.* 1896. *Educ.* Columbia Univ. (AB 1920; BS 1921). *M.* 1923, Louise de Rochemont. *S.* Ronald M., Jr., and Robert de Rochemont. *Dau.* Mary Louise (Magee). *Career:* Limited Partner, Fahnestock & Co., members of N.Y. Stock Exchange. Chmn, and Dir., Giant Portland Cement Co. Former Trustee, Columbia University. Republican. *Clubs:* Piping Rock, Beaver Dam; Bond, Columbia University, Metropolitan, University, Bankers, Recess, Creek, Seawanhaka Corinthian Yacht (N.Y.), Everglades, Bath & Tennis, Seminole Golf, Palm Beach; California (Los Angeles). *Address:* Piping Rock Road, Locust Valley, N.Y.; and *office* 110 Wall Street, New York City, U.S.A.

**CRAIK, Duncan Robert Steele,** OBE, BEcon, FASA, FAIM. Australian. Auditor-General for Australia. *B.* 1916. *Educ.* Fort Street (Sydney) High School; Univ. of Sydney, Grad. Bach. Economics. *M.* 1943, Audrey Ion. *Daus.* 4. *Career:* with Commonwealth Bank 1933–40; Commonwealth Treasury Taxation Branch 1940–60; Asst. Secy. Gen. Financial and Economic Policy Branch 1960–66; First Asst. Secy. Social Services Branch 1966–69; Deputy Secy. Supply & General 1969–73; Auditor-Gen. for Australia since 1973. *Member:* Economic Socy. of Australia & New Zealand; Royal Inst. Public Admin. (A.C.T. Branch); Aust. Admin. Staff Coll. Association. *Award:* Fellow Aust. Socy. of Accountants; Fellow, Aust. Inst. of Management. *Club:* Commonwealth (Canberra). *Address:* 15 Meehan Gardens, Griffith, Canberra, 2603 and *office* Canberra House, Marcus Clarke Street, Canberra City, 2601 A.C.T., Australia.

**CRAIN, Lacy E.** American. *B.* 1910. *Educ.* Southern State Coll. and Somerville Law School. *M.* 1934, Margie Lynn Cowan. *Career:* Past Pres. National Sanitary Supply Assn., Chicago 1955, and Conaid Inc., Dallas 1962. President: Crain Chemical Co. Inc., Dallas 1945—, Petro Manufacturing Corp., Dallas 1955—, Pipe Line Chemical Co. Inc., Dallas 1960—. Chairman of the Board: Quimico Crain de Mexico, Mexico City, and Crain Chemical Industrial Products Corp. (also Pres.), Dallas. Board of Directors: City Bank & Trust Co., Dallas, and Exchange Club of Dallas; International Trade Assn.; Dir. Preston State Bank of Dallas. *Member:* Amer. Inst. of Chemical Engineers; Chemical Specialties Manufacturers Assn.; National Sanitary Supply Association. *Clubs:* Exchange; Lancers. *Address:* 7348 Elmridge, Dallas, Tex.; and *office* 2630 Andfon Dr., Dallas, Tex., U.S.A.

**CRAINZ, Vittorio.** Italian. *B.* 1918. *Educ.* Univ. of Rome (Law Degree 1940). *M.* (1) 1945, Laura Bachetoni Rossi Vaccari (Div.). (2) 1972, Pauline Anne Douglass. *Daus.* Paola and Lucilla. *Career:* Military service (Lieut. mountain troops; awarded Cross of War) 1937–38 and 1941–42; on editorial staff of Giornale d'Italia 1942–43; Editor, then Chief Editor, of Domenica 1944–46; Chief Editor, Junior 1947–48, and Elefante 1949–50; Joint Director SIPR 1957–66; Managing Director EPI (Edizioni Periodiche Industriali a r.l. 1961–66). Managing Director, SEPA (Società Editrice Pubblicazioni Aziendali a r.l.) 1951—, and SIPR (Studio Italiano Public Relations) 1966—. Director, PR International Inc., New York 1963—. *Member:* IPRA (International Public Relations Assn.); FERPI (Federazione Relazioni Pubbliche Italiana); Fiprega (Federation Internationale Presse Gastronomique et Vinicole); and CIST Centro Internazionale Stampa Turistica). *Club:* Navy. *Address:* 7 Largo Messico, 00198 Rome; and *office* 5 Via Tomassetti, 00161 Rome, Italy.

**CRAMER, Hon. Sir John Oscar,** KtB, FREI, REIV, QRV. *B.* 1897. *Educ.* State public schools and business coll. *M.* 1921, Mary Earls. *S.* 2. *Daus.* 2. *Career:* M.H.R. for Bennelong, N.S.W. 1949–74; Minister for the Army, Commonwealth of Australia 1956–63; sen. partner, Cramer Bros., real estate auctioneers; Mng. Dir., Higgins (Buildings) Ltd.; member, Exec. of Building Industry Congress of N.S.W. *Member:* Statutory Cttee. on Public Works 1949–56 (Chmn. 1955–56); Chmn., Sydney C.C. 1946–49; Mayor, N. Sydney 1940–41; a founder and member of executive of Liberal Party of Australia (N.S.W. Div.); Member, Joint Cttee., Foreign Affairs, House of Representatives, Aust. *Address:* Commonwealth Parliament Offices, Martin Place, Sydney, N.S.W. 2000, Australia.

**CRAMER, Morgan Joseph, Jr.** American business executive. *B.* 1906. *Educ.* Lehigh University. *M.* 1933, Miriam Jeanette Fuchs. *Dau.* Cynthia Jeanette. *Career:* Pres. and Chief Exec. Officer, P. Lorillard Company 1962–65. President and Chief Executive Officer, Royal Crown Cola International Ltd. 1966–70. President, Morgan J. Cramer Associates Inc., 1970—. Trustee, N.Y. Polyclinic Hospital; Dir., Greater N.Y. Fund. *Member:* National Foreign Trade Council; The Advertising Council; International Center in New York Inc. (Dir. and Member Exec. Cttee.); Defense Supply Assn. *Clubs:* Sky, Lehigh University, Sales Executive (all in N.Y.C.); Pelham (N.Y.) Country; The Stanwich (Greenwich, Conn.). *Address:* 530 East 72nd Street, New York, 15021, U.S.A.

**CRAMP, George Chatfield,** MBE. British. *B.* 1904. *Educ.* Hobart High School. *M.* 1933, Beatrice A. Garrett. *S.* Peter. *Daus.* Jennifer and Mary. *Career:* Managing Director, Wm. Crosby & Co. (Tas.), Horbart, Tasmania; and Concrete Products Co. Director: Crisp & Gunn Co-operative; Tasmanian Stevedoring Co.; F. Hammond Pty. Local Board, Commercial Insurance Co. Trustee, Tasmanian Museum & Art Gallery; Past Cr. and Treasurer, Hobart Chamber of Commerce; Past Chmn., Salmon & Fresh Water Fisheries; Past Master, Warden, Hobart Marine Board. *Member:* Royal Society; President, Miniature Camera Club (Tasmania). *Clubs:* Athenaeum, Royal Yacht, Royal Autocar. *Address: office* 119 Collins Street, Hobart, Tasmania.

**CRANDALL, Kenneth Hartley.** American geologist; *B.* 1904. *Educ.* Stanford Univ. (AB 1924). *M.* 1929, Claire Wofford. *S.* Kenneth Hartley, Jr. and William Wofford. *Career:* Geologist with The California Co. (1925), and Standard Oil Co. of Texas (1931); successively Superintendent of Exploration (April 1941), Vice-Pres., Exploration (Feb. 1942), Pres. (Sept. 1945), Vice-Chmn. of Board (Oct. 1947), The California Co.; Dir., Standard Oil Co. of Texas, May 1948; Vice-Chmn. of Board, The California Standard Co., March 1949; successively Exec. Asst. (March 1949), Dir. (June 1962), Vice-Pres., Exploration (May 1950) Standard Oil Co. of California; Director of various subsidiary companies; Consulting Professor, Stanford Univ. since 1969. Member, Phi Beta Kappa. Sigma Xi; Fellow, Geological Soc. of America; Pres. Amer. Assn. Petroluem Geologists. *Clubs:* (both of San Francisco. Pacific-Union; Stock Exchange. *Address:* 209 Crocke) Avenue, Piedmont, CA94610, U.S.A.

**CRANDALL, Lloyd Milton.** Canadian industrialist. Began as Production Manager, Pembroke Shook Mills Ltd. 1930; Chairman of Board 1933–60. Vice-President, Planning and Development, Canadian Canners Ltd., Hamilton. Ont. 1950–52. Joined present Co. as Mng. Dir. 1952, Pres. and Chmn. of Bd. 1953–63. Chairman of the Board: Eddy Match Co. Ltd. 1963—, and Canadian Splint & Lumber Corp. Ltd. Vice-Pres. and Dir., Ottawa Valley Television Co. Ltd. Director: Kootenay Forest Products Ltd., Canadian Canners Ltd. and Pembroke Electric Light Co. Ltd. *Member:* Adv. Cttee., Forest Products Lab., Dept. of N. Affairs and National Resources. Freemason (32°; Shriner). Protestant. *Clubs:* Engineers' (Montreal); Albany (Toronto). *Address: office* 7 King Street East, Toronto 1, Ont., Canada.

**CRANDON, Albert Seabury.** *B.* 1893. *Educ.* Worcester (Mass.) Polytechnic Institute (BSc Civil Eng). *M.* (1) Grace Monro Scully, (2) 1957, Margaret Banker. (3) 1971 Matilda Foster. *S.* Albert Seabury, Jr. *Dau.* Mary Crandon Baker. *Career:* Captain, U.S. Corps of Engineers and G2, 79th Div. 1916–18; Field Engineer, American Bridge Co. (1918–23) and American Window Glass Co. (1923–37); Furnace Engineer, Hartford Empire Co. 1937–42; Exec. Vice-Pres. (1942–45) and President (1945–55) and Chmn. of Board (1955–58). American Window Glass Co. and Blue Ridge Glass Co. merged in May 1958, into American-St. Gobain Corporation, now A.S.G. Industries, Inc. 1970. Consultant and Director Emeritus A.S.G. Industries, Incorporated, since 1958. *Publications:* assisted in preparation of Surveying Manual-Ives (1914), and Field Engineering-Searles & Ives (1915). *Member:* Tau Beta Pi, and Sigma Xi. *Clubs:* Duquesne; Pittsburgh Athletic Association. Republican. *Address:* Little Compton, West Main Road, RI 02837, U.S.A.

**CRANE, Douglas P.,** BA, MBA. American. *B.* 1928. *Educ.* Rochester Business Inst. (ABA); Goddard Coll. (BA); Univ. of Chicago Graduate Sch. of Business (MBA). *M.* 1950, Lois W. Barton. *S.* 1. *Daus.* 3. *Career:* Vice-Pres. Perkin-Elmer Corp.; Pres. & Gen. Man. Coleman Instruments; Pres. & Man. Dir. Perkin-Elmer de Mexico S.A.; Senior Vice-Pres. The Wickes Corporation; Dir. affiliated Companies; Vice Pres. Group Exec. AMF Inc; Chmn. Bd. AMF Tuboscope Inc; Dir. AMF Canada Ltd.; Pres. Bendix Automotive, Dir. affiliated cos. *Member:* Bd. Fellows Saginaw Valley College. *Address:* 4525 Dow Ridge Rd., Orchard Lane, Michigan, U.S.A

**CRANE, Thomas Grenville.** British. *B.* 1912. *Educ.* Highgate School and Royal College of Science, London (BSc; ARCS). *M.* 1940, Dorothy A. A. Exner. *S.* Peter and Harvey. *Dau.* Carol. *Career:* Chemist, Monsanto Chemicals Ltd., London 1932–50. Managing Director, Monsanto Chemicals (Australia) Ltd. 1951–65, Chairman, 1965–68; Dir. Aust. Paper Manufacturers Ltd. 1957—; Colonial Gas Holdings Ltd. 1968–74; Dir. Gas and Fuel Corp. of Victoria 1975. Chairman, Australian Petro-Chemicals Ltd. 1960–68; Dir. 1968—; Chmn. N.K.S. Holdings Ltd. since 1970. Member, R.A.C.I. *Clubs:* Australian, Sciences, R.A.C.V. (Melbourne); Frankston Golf; Eccentric (London). *Address:* 4 Mernda Road, Kooyong, Vic. 3144, Australia.

**CRAWFORD, Douglas,** MP. Scottish Politician and Company Director. *B.* 1939. *Educ.* Glasgow Academy; Cambridge Univ. (MA). *M* . 1964, Joan Burnie. *S.* 1. *Dau.* 1. *Career:* Features Editor, "Business" Magazine 1960–62; Industrial Correspondent, Glasgow Herald 1962–67; Editor, "Scotland" 1967–70; Dir., Polecon since 1970; Dir., MCS/Robertson & Scott since 1975; MP (SNP) for Perth & East Perthshire since 1974. *Clubs:* Edinburgh Press; Scottish Arts; Savile; Oxford & Cambridge. *Address:* 43 Coates Gardens, Edinburgh EH2 2EF; and *office* House of Commons, London SW1.

**CRAWFORD, Sir Douglas Inglis,** CB, DSO, TD, LLD. British. *B.* 1904. *Educ.* Uppingham; Magdalene College, Cambridge (BA). *Career:* Previously: Chairman, William Crawford & Sons Ltd.; Vice-Chairman, United Biscuits Ltd.; Chairman, D. S. Crawford Ltd.; Dep. Chmn. Martins Bank; Director: Royal Insurance Ltd. Chmn., West Lancs. T.A. Assn. 1951–66; High Sheriff, County Palatine of Lancaster, 1969, First Lord Lieut. Metropolitan County of Merseyside, LLD Liverpool Univ. *Clubs:* Boodles; Whites; Royal & Ancient; The Hon. Company of Edinburgh Golfers. *Address:* Fernlea, North Mossley Hill Road, Liverpool, 18.

**CRAWFORD, Sir Frederick,** GCMG, OBE. Former British colonial administrator. *B.* 9 March 1906. *Educ.* Hymers College; Oxford University (BA). *M.* (1) 1936, Maimie Alice Green (*D.* 1960). *S.* Francis Macnab, Robin Macnab. *M.* (2) 1962, Clio Georgiades. *Career:* Cadet, Tanganyika 1929; Assistant District Officer 1931; District Officer 1941; seconded East African Governors' Conference 1942–43, 1945–46; Economic Secretary, Northern Rhodesia 1947–48; Director of Development, Northern Rhodesia 1948–51; Governor and C.-in-C., the Seychelles 1951–53; Deputy Governor, Kenya 1953–57; Governor, Uganda, Jan. 1957–61. Retired Director Resident, Rhodesia, Anglo-American Corporation. *Address:* Charter House, P.O. Box 1108, Salisbury, Rhodesia.

**CRAWFORD, Frederick Coolidge.** American industrialist: *B.* 19 March 1891. *Educ.* Harvard University (AB); Harvard

Graduate School of Applied Sciences (MCE). *M.* (1) 1932, Audrey C. Bowles (*Dec.*); (2) 1975, Kathleen M. Saxon. Trustee, Musical Arts Association (operating the Cleveland Orch.) from 1946-72; Director, National Assn. of Manufacturers, Hon. Vice-Pres. 1949—; Director, Armstrong Cork Company 1947-71; Hon. Dr. Eng., Case Western Reserve Univ.; Hon ScD, Clarkson College of Technology; Hon. LLD Case Western Reserve Univ., and Temple University. Trustee and President, American School of Classical Studies at Athens 1957-71. Chmn. 1971—; Pres. (1933-53). Chairman of Board (1953-58) of Thompson Products Inc., now known as TRW Inc., Honorary Chairman of the Board since 1963. Hon. Chmn. of Board, Case Western Reserve Univ. 1967—. Bd. of Overseers, Harvard College 1952-58; Chairman, Board Trustees, Cleveland Zoological Society; Pres., Western Reserve Hist. Socy.; member, Board of Overseers, Hoover Inst. on War, Revolution & Peace; Hon. Fellow, National Air Museum, Smithsonian Inst. Hon. degree, Dr. of Space Science, Fla. Inst. of Technology. *Clubs:* Union (Cleveland); Explorers; Bohemian, San Francisco; Cat Cay Club, Ltd., Bahamas. *Address:* P.O. Box 17036, Cleveland 44117, Ohio, U.S.A.

**CRAWFORD, Hector William,** OBE, FIAL. Australian radio and TV production exec. and orchestral conductor. *B.* 1913. *Educ.* St. Paul's Cathedral, Melbourne and Melbourne Conservatorium of Music. *M.* 1950, Glenda Raymond (coloratura soprano). *Career:* Member Sidney Myer Music Bowl Trust Executive Committee; Member Council Melba Memorial Conservatorium of Music; Member Victorian Selection Committee. Churchill Memorial Trust Advisory Cttee.; Conductor and Director of Music for the People; Managing Dir., Broadcasting Exchange of Australia Pty. Ltd., 1941-45. Managing Director, Crawford Productions Pty. Ltd.; T.V. Programmes, Film and Radio Feature Producers, Melbourne. Mem. Bd. of Dirs. Australian National Memorial Theatre Ltd.; Mem. Council of Austr. Film and T.V. school; Mem. Interim Bd. to Austr. Film Commission. *Clubs:* Athenaeum; West Brighton; Lorne Aquatic; Company Directors Assn. of Australia. *Address:* 1 Southampton Crescent, Abbotsford, 3067, Australia.

**CRAWFORD, Sir Robert Stewart,** GCMG, CVO. British *B.* 1913. *Educ.* Oxford University 1932-35 (Degree in Philosophy, Politics and Economics). *M.* 1938, Mary Katharine Corbett. *S.* 3. *Dau.* 1. *Career:* Counsellor of Embassy, Oslo 1954-56; Counsellor and later Minister, Baghdad 1957-59; Minister, U.K. Delegation to O.E.E.C., Paris, 1959-60; Assistant Under-Secretary of State, Foreign Office 1961-65; Political Resident Persian Gulf 1966-70. Deputy Under-Secretary of State, Foreign and Commonwealth Office, 1970-73. *Member:* Royal Society for Asian Affairs; Royal Geographical. *Club:* United Oxford and Cambridge University (London). *Address:* 5A Manchester Street, London, W.1.

**CRAWFORD, William Fowle.** American. Corporate Executive, Consultant. *B.* 1911. *Educ.* Northwestern Mil. & Naval Acad. 1925-29, and Univ. of Chicago 1929-31. *M.* 1935, Ruth M. Fellinger. *S.* 1. *Daus.* 3. *Career:* Secy. of Edward Valves Inc. (formerly The Edward Valve & Manufacturing Co. Inc.), East Chicago 1931-37 (Vice-Pres. 1937-41, Pres., Dir., 1941-63); Pres., Dir., Republic Flow Meters Co., Chicago 1957-61; Pres., Dir., Valve Products Inc., Knox, Ind. 1950-63; Pres., Dir., W. E. Bowler Co., Philadelphia, Pa. 1954-63. Vice-President and Director, Rockwell Manufacturing Co., Pittsburgh, Pa. 1945-73 (Chmn. Finance Ctee. 1963-73), Advisory Dir., Rockwell International, Pittsburgh, 1973—; Vice-Pres., Dir., Chicago Fittings Corp., Chicago; Dir., Washington Steel Corp. (Pa.), First National Bank of East Chicago, Ind., U.S. Flexible Metallic Tubing Co., San Francisco, Atlantic India Rubber Works Inc., Flex-Weld Inc., Keflex Inc., Tec-Line Products Inc., all of Chicago, Mogul Rubber Corp., Goshen, Ltd., Rubbernek Fittings Ltd., Birmingham, England; Chmn. W. F. Crawford & Assocs., Chicago. Trustee, Illinois Inst. of Technology, IIT Research Inst., The Crawford Foundation, Chicago; Pres., The Valve Manufacturers Assn., 1959-61, 1964-65; *Member:* Valve Industry Advisory Cttee. War Production Bd. 1941-45, 1950-52, Amer. Soc. Mechanical Engineers, Newcomen Soc. of North America, Art Inst., Chicago, Field Museum of Natural History, Chicago, Delta Upsilon. Republican. Congregationalist. *Clubs:* Union League, Tavern, Adventurers, Economic, all of Chicago; Duquesne, Pittsburg. *Address:* 4950 Chicago Beach Drive, Chicago, Ill. 60615; and *office* 185 North Wabash Avenue, Chicago, Ill. 60601, U.S.A.

**CRAWFORD and BALCARRES, The Rt. Hon. The Earl of, (Robert Alexander Linday),** PC. *B.* 1927. *Educ.* Eton; Trinity Coll., Cambridge. *M.* 1949, Ruth Beatrice Meyer-Bechtler. *S.* 2. *Daus* 2. *Career:* Member of Parliament (Con.) Hertford Div. of Hertfordshire 1955-74, and for Welwyn & Hatfield Div. Feb.-Nov. 1974; PPS to Financial Secy. of the Treasury 1955-57; to Minister of Housing & Local Government 1957-60; Minister of State for Defence 1970-72, for Foreign & Commonwealth Affairs 1972-74. Pres., Rural District Councils Assn. 1959-65; Chmn. Nat. Assn. for Mental Health 1963-70; Created Privy Councillor 1972 and Life Peer 1975; Director; National Westminster Bank, Sun Alliance & London Insurance Group; Chairman Lombard North Central; Dannatt Sheppard Architects Consortium; Historic Buildings Council for Scotland. *Address:* House of Lords, London SW1.

**CRAWLEY, Desmond John Chetwode,** CMG, CVO. *B.* 1917. *Educ.* Oxford University (Hons Degree in Modern History). *M.* 1945, Daphne Lesley Mockett. *S.* 2. *Dau.* 1. *Career:* Served in the Indian Civil Service and Indian Political Service in Madras and Baluchistan 1939-46; in British High Commission in India (in Madras and Calcutta) 1947-50; in Commonwealth Relations Office, London 1950-53, 1955-58 and 1963; British Embassy, Washington 1953-55; British Deputy High Commissioner in Pakistan (Lahore) 1958-61; Student, Imperial Defence College, London 1962; British. High Commissioner, Sierra Leone 1963-66; British Ambassador in Bulgaria 1966-70; British Minister to the Holy See 1970-75. *Clubs:* United Oxford & Cambridge University; various other clubs in India, Pakistan and Sierra Leone. *Address:* 35 Chartfield Avenue, London, S.W.15; and c/o Foreign and Commonwealth Office, London, S.W.1.

**CRAWSHAW, Sir Edward Daniel Weston,** QC (Aden). British. Commissioner with the Foreign Compensation Commission, London 1965-75 (Ret'd). *B.* 1903. *Educ.* St. Bees School; BA (Cantab.), Selwyn Coll., Cambridge; Solicitor, Supreme Ct. of Judicature, England 1929; Barrister-at-Law (Gray's Inn) 1946. *M.* 1942, Rosemary Treffry. *S.* 1. *Daus.* 2. *Career:* Solicitor, Northern Rhodesia 1930. Entered Colonial Legal Service, Tanganyika 1933-37; Administrator General, Zanzibar 1939; Attorney General, Aden 1947; Puisne Judge, Tanganyika 1952. Justice of Appeal, Court of Appeal for Eastern Africa 1960. Commissioner with the Foreign Compensation Commission, London 1965-75. Brilliant Star of Zanzibar; Coronation Medal. *Clubs:* Royal Overseas League (London); County Club, Guildford. *Address:* 1 Fort Road, Guildford, Surrey.

**CRAYS, Dwight L.** American banker. *B.* 1898. *Educ.* Northwestern University (BS); Law School, Iowa University. *M.* 1928, Irma Gibson. *Dau.* Patricia Crays Dixon. *Career:* Vice-Pres. Rockville National Bank 1926-32; Examiner, Reconstruction Finance Corp., Washington, D.C. 1932-33; Examiner, Board of Governors, Federal Reserve System Washington 1933-44; President and Director, Rockville National Bank (Rockville, Ind.) 1946-70; Dir. Chmn. Bd. since 1970. Director: Parke County (Ind.) Development Committee (1957); member, Hospitalization Committee, Indiana Bankers Association (1957). Chmn. 1958-59. Secretary-Treasurer, Region 6, Indiana Bankers Association 1952-53 (member Legal Affairs Cttee. 1960-61); Pres. & Dir., Consolidated Schools Building Corp., Rockville 1960-61; Past-Pres., Wabash Valley Conference of National Association of Bank Auditors and Comptrollers; formerly a speaker on banking subjects, and subjects of current interest. Past Trustee, First Methodist Church (Rockville). *Publication:* Two Poems (1940). Member Phi Beta Kappa (Northwestern Univ.); received Award of Merit in the field of Human Relations in Business and Industry, 1957. Republican. *Address:* 702 West Ohio Street, Rockville, Ind., U.S.A.

**CREAN, Frank,** MHR. Australian. *B.* 1916. *Educ.* Melbourne University (BA Hons); BCom; DPA; qualified Accountant (FASA). *M.* 1946, Mary Findlay. *S.* Stephen, Simon and David. *Career:* Income Tax Assessor, 1936-45; MLA Victoria 1945-51; Chairman, Council for Adult Education 1946-74; President, Victoria Fabian Society 1947-63; Member, House of Representatives (Lab. Melbourne Ports) 1951—. Member of Parliamentary Executive, Australian Party 1956-72 (specializing in public finance and economic policy). Previously Member of Legislative Assembly (MLA) of Victoria; Federal Treasurer 1972-74; Minister for Overseas Trade since 1974; Dep. Prime Min. 1975. Trustee, State Library of Victoria 1946-63. *Address:* *office* Australian Parliament Offices, Melbourne, Victoria, Australia.

**CREAN, John Gale.** Canadian. *B.* 1910. *Educ.* B. Commerce, University of Toronto, 1932. *M.* 1939, Margaret Dobbie. *S.*

John F. M. *Daus.* Jennie S., Susan M., Patricia L. *Career:* President: Robert Crean & Company Limited 1947—. Director, Scythes & Co. Ltd., Toronto. Director: Kelsey-Hayes Canada Ltd.; Chairman of the Board, The Centennial Centre of Science and Technology 1964–69. Canadian Centenary Council 1964–67; Chmn. of Canadian Business and Advisory Cttee. to the Organization for Economic Co-operation and Development 1972–74; Chmn. of the Cncl., Bishop Strachan Sch. 1953–63; former Pres., Board of Governors, Hillcrest Hospital now Director emeritus; Canadian Chamber of Commerce: Chairman, Ontario Regional Committee 1952–53; Vice-Chairman of Executive Council 1952–53; Chairman of Canada-U.S. Committee 1961–62 and member 1950–53, 1961–66; Immigration Committee 1949; national President 1955–56. Pres., Canadian Council, International Chamber of Commerce 1970–72 and 1974–75; Vice-Pres. International Chamber of Commerce, 1970–72, 1974–75, & Pres. 1975–76; Chmn., Canadian Business Group for Multinational Trade Negotiations 1973—; Chmn., Canadian Cttee. on the Multinational Enterprise 1974—; Canadian Employer Delegate to Int. Labour Organization (Geneva, 1974); Member, Bd. Adv. Int. Mangt. and Development Inst. Washington; Exec. Cttee. Canadian Inst. of International Affairs. Grand Master. Delta Epsilon Chapter, Kappa Sigma Fraternity 1931–32. *Member:* Exec. Cttee. Trinity Coll., Univ of Toronto 1968–74; Champlain Society; Canadian Institute of International Affairs; Canadian Historical Association; Hudson Bay Record Society; Canadian Political Science Association. Liberal. *Clubs:* Royal Canadian Yacht; Badminton & Racquet; St. James's Montreal; University. *Address:* 161 Forest Hill Road, Toronto, Ont. M5P 2N3, Canada.

**CREEDON, Gerrard Anthony.** Irish. *B.* 1921. *M.* Patricia Mary Reynolds. *S.* Brian Gerrard, Shane Peter, Mark Anthony and Michael Cornelius. *Daus.* Eileen Patricia, Anna Maria and Micah Geraldine. *Career:* Managing Director, Gypsum Industries Ltd. Director: M. Creedon Ltd.; Creedon Acoustics Ltd.; Emalux (Ireland) Ltd. and Portobello Investments Ltd., Dublin; First National Building Society, Dublin. *Address:* Goleen, Cross Ave., Blackrock, Co. Dublin; and *office* Clonskeagh Road, Dublin 14.

**CRESSMAN, Harry Gordon.** American. *B.* 1927. *M.* 1948, Barbara Brodine. *S.* 2. *Dau.* 1. Chairman BSG International Ltd., Dir. 60 BSG subsidiary companies; Dir. Charterhouse Group (Midlands) Ltd.; Dir. W. Ribbons Holdings Ltd.; Dir. Aston Villa Football Club; Dir. American Chamber of Commerce in U.K. *Club:* American (London). *Address:* Eastcote Paddocks, Hampton-in-Arden, Warwicks; and *office* BSG International Ltd., 1270, Coventry Road, Birmingham B25 8BB.

**CRICHTON-BROWN, Sir Robert,** CBE, TD. Australian. *B.* 1919. *Educ.* Sydney Grammar School. *M.* 1941, Norah Isabell Turnbull. *S.* Robert Anthony. *Dau.* Bernice Lesley. *Career.* Served War, 1939–45, BEF; Major Royal Artillery and Gen. Staff, France, Iceland, India, Burma (despatches twice). Exec. Chmn. and Man. Dir. Edward Lumley Ltd. 1952—; The Security & General Insurance Co. Ltd. 1952—; Chmn. Security Life Assurances Ltd., 1961—, John Thompson (Australia) P/L, Clark Chapman (Australia) P/L; Dir. Rothmans of Pall Mall (Aust.) Ltd., Commercial Banking Co. of Sydney Ltd., Westminster Dredging Australia Pty. Ltd., Ham-Dredging (Aust.) Pty. Ltd., H.C. Sleigh Ltd.; Fed. Pres. Institute of Directors in Australia (Chmn., N.S.W. Branch); Director, Royal Prince Alfred Hospital; Pres. Postgraduate Medical Research Foundation; Member Finance Committee, Royal Australasian College of Physicians. Area Pres. E. Metropolitan Area, Scout Association of Australia (N.S.W. Branch). Member Advisory Board—Salvation Army. Underwriting Member of Lloyds, 1946. *Clubs:* Royal Yacht Squadron; Cruising Yacht Club of Australia; Royal Sydney Yacht Squadron; Royal Prince Alfred Yacht; Australian. *Address:* 11 Castlereagh Street, Sydney, N.S.W. 2000, Australia.

**CRISP, Leslie Finlay.** Australian university professor. *B.* 19 Jan. 1917. *Educ.* Universities of Adelaide and Oxford (MA). *M.* 1940, Helen Craven Wighton. *S.* 1. *Dau.* 2. *Career:* With Australian Commonwealth Public Service 1940–50; Director-General, Department of Post-War Reconstruction 1949–50; Professor of Political Science, Australian National University, Canberra; Dir. since 1974, Chmn. since 1975, C'wealth Banking Corp; Dir, Univ. Co-op. Bookshops Ltd. since 1973. *Publications:* The Parliamentary Government of the Commonwealth of Australia; The Australian Federal Labour Party 1901–51; Ben Chifley; Australian National Government. *Address:* 47 Stonehaven Crescent, Deakin, Canberra, Australia.

**CRISP, Hon. Sir (Malcolm) Peter,** Kt 1969. *B.* 1912. *Educ.* St. Ignatius College (Riverview, N.S.W.) and University of Tasmania (LLB). *M.* 1935, Edna Eunice Taylor. *Daus.* Felicity Anne and Penelope Katherine Peta. *Career:* Admitted to Bar 1933; Crown Prosecutor 1938; Crown Solicitor 1946; Solicitor General and Queen's Counsel 1951; Royal Commission, Fluoridation of Public Water Supplies 1967–68; Lecturer in the Law of Property, Univ. of Tasmania 1947–52; A Justice of the Supreme Court of Tasmania 1952–71; Chairman, State Library Board of Tasmania 1956–77; member: Council of National Library of Australia 1960–71, Chmn. 1971; Chmn., Aust. Advisory Council on Bibliographical Services 1973—. Enlisted (with rank of Capt.) Australian Imperial Force 1940; served in Australia, U.K., Netherlands East Indies and Borneo with the Artillery; Liaison and Formation Staffs; rank of discharge (1946) T/Colonel. *Address:* 10 Anglesea Street, Hobart, Tasmania.

**CRISP, Raymond Floyd.** American corporation executive. *B.* 1919. *Educ.* University of Idaho (BS in EE). *M.* 1945, Barbara Fraser Foote. *S.* Steven Fraser. *Dau.* Linda Rae. *Career:* Vice-Chairman, Board of Directors, Associated Missile Products Corp. (President 1955–58); Project Engineer, Sperry Gyroscope Co. 1942–47, General Communications Co. 1947–51; Chief Electronics Engineer (1951–59) and Manager, Technical services (1953–55) Hycon Manufacturing Co.; President, Associated Missile Products Corp. 1955–58; Vice-President, Daniel Mann Johnson & Menderstall Inc. 1958–59; President, American Corporate Services 1959–61; Manager, Marketing Raytheon Co. 1962–67. Corporate Director, Division Development, Sanders Associates Inc. since 1963. Holder of Radio Amateur World's Record (5,250 megacycles) 1945–57. Senior Member, Institute of Electrical & Electronic Engineers. *Member:* Institute of Aeronautical Sciences; American Ordnance Association; American Management Association; American Marketing Association; Navy League; Adv. Cncl. on Nava Affairs; Armed Forces Communications & Electronics Assn.; Kappa Sigma. *Address:* *office* Sanders Associates, 24 Simon Street, Nashua, N.H. 03060 U.S.A.

**CRITCHFIELD, Robert.** American lawyer and industrialist; *B.* 1903. *Educ.* Western Reserve University (AB) and George Washington Univ. (LLB). *M.* 1951, Margaret Parsons. *Dau.* Cynthia. *Career:* President: Medal Brick & Tile Co. Director: Rubbermaid Inc., Diebold Inc., Premier Industrial Corp., Chmn. Bd. First Federal Savings & Loan Assn; The Wooster Brush Company Trustee, College of Wooster. *Address:* Gay Acres Farm, 2306 Sylvan Road, Wooster, Ohio, U.S.A.

**CRITCHLEY, Julian,** MP. British politician, writer & journalist. *B.* 1930. *Educ.* Shrewsbury; The Sorbonne; Pembroke Coll., Oxford (MA). *M.* 1965, Heather Goodrick. *S.* 1. *Daus.* 3. *Career:* Conservative MP for Rochester 1959–64; Editor, Town Magazine 1966–67; Critic and Columnist for The Times since 1967; Conservative MP for Aldershot since 1970; Public Affairs Consultant, SSCB/Lintas Ltd. since 1976; Chmn., Conservative Party's Media Cttee. *Publication;* (with Prof. O. Pick) Collective Security (1974). *Address:* The Brewer's House, 18 Bridge Square, Farnham, Surrey.

**CRITCHLEY, Thomas Kingston,** AO, CBE. Australian diplomat. *B.* 1916. *Educ.* North Sydney Boys' High School and Sydney University (Bachelor of Economics). Research Officer, Premier's Dept., Sydney 1938–41; R.A.A.F. 1941; Assistant Economic Adviser, Department of War Organization of Industry 1943–44; Head, Research Section, Far Eastern Bureau, New Delhi, British Ministry of Information 1944–46; Head, Economic Relations Section, Dept. of External Affairs, Canberra 1946–47; Australian Rep. U.N. Good Offices Cttee. on Indonesian Question 1948–49, and U.N. Commission for Indonesia 1949–50; Actg. Australian Commisioner for Malaya 1951–52; Aust. Rep. on U.N. Commission for Unification and Rehabilitation of Korea 1952–54; Head, Pacific and Americas Branch, Dept. of External Affairs 1954–55; Aust. Commissioner in the Fed. of Malaya 1955–57; High Commissioner in Malaysia 1957–65. Senior External Affairs, Representative London 1966–69. Ambassador to Thailand 1969–74; High Commissioner of Papua New Guinea 1974–Sept. 1975; Australian High Commissioner in Papua New Guinea since Sept. 1975. *Publications:* Australia Foots the Bill (joint author 1941); Australia and New Zealand, 1947. *Address:* c/o Department of Foreign Affairs, Canberra, A.C.T., Australia.

**CRITTALL, John Francis,** DL, JP (Essex) 1946. British. *B.* 16 Oct. 1911. *Educ.* Felsted Sch.; Cambridge University (MA). *M.* 1936, Ariel Margaret Mercer. *S.* Francis William Ariel, Charles John. *Daus.* Harriet Elizabeth Ariel, Laura Margaret. *Career:* Joined Crittall Manufacturing Co. Ltd. 1934, retired 1976; served in World War II with Royal Engineers 1942–45. Director, Equity & Law Life Assurance Society Ltd.; Lloyds Bank Eastern Counties Regional Board; Crittall & Winterton Ltd.; Pro-Chancellor, Essex Univ.; Treasurer, Royal Coll. of Art; Chmn. Governors of Felsted School. *Address:* Park Hall, Great Bardfield, Essex.

**CRIVELLI, Roger Leo.** Australian. *B.* 1907. *Educ.* Melbourne Grammar School and Melbourne Univ. (BA; BCom). *M.* 1938, Gwendolyn Boyd. *S.* Michael Urban. *Dau.* Marguerite Hélène. *Career:* Leader writer and financial editor, Sydney Morning Herald 1939–55; Commercial Manager, Australian Atomic Energy Commission 1955. International Atomic Energy Agency, Vienna 1963–66. Director of Information Services, Australian Atomic Energy Commission 1960—. Contributor to reviews—The Economist, Round Table, etc. *Clubs:* Melbourne Union (Sydney). *Address* and *office* 45 Beach Street, Coogee, N.S.W., Australia.

**CROCKER, Howard Graham.** Canadian. *B.* 1912. *Educ.* Harkins Academy; Harkins High School; Mount Allison Academy; Mount Allison Univ. *M.* 1936, Muriel Cross. *S.* Donald Graham. *Dau.* Muriel Anne. *Career:* T. W. Crocker Co. Accountant 1933; Secy.-Treas. 1934. President No. 10 Branch, Canadian Legion 1949–53; District Commissioner, Northumberland-Kent District, Canadian Legion 1952; Minister of Lands and Mines, Legislative Assembly of New Brunswick 1960—. Member of the Legislative Assembly of New Brunswick. 1960—. Chairman, Army Benevolent Fund, New Brunswick Board, 1957; New Brunswick Electric Power Commission, 1965–70. President & Gen. Mgr., T. W. Crocker & Co. *Member:* Bd. of Governors, Canadian Corps of Commissionaires (N.B. & P.E.I. Division). *Clubs:* Northumberland Lodge A.F. & A.M. (Past Master); Scottish Rite Luxor Temple. *Address:* 503 King George Highway, Newcastle, NB., Canada.

**CROCOMBE. Frederick Francis,** FRAeS. British. *B.* 1901. *Educ.* Imperial Coll. of Science & Technology, London (BSc, ACGI, DIC). *M.* 1933, Olive Ethelberta Chilton. *Career:* Aerodynamic Research, Imperial Coll. 1924–26; Technical Asst., Fairey Aviation Co. 1926–29; Technical Engr., Monospar Co. 1929–31; with General Aircraft Ltd.: Asst. Designer 1931–33, Chief Designer 1933–45, and Technical Dir. 1945–49; Principal Designer, Blackburn & General Aircraft Ltd. 1949–50. Technical Director, Boulton Paul Aircraft Ltd. 1951–66. *Address:* 7 Heathside, Hanger Hill, Weybridge.

**CROMER, Earl of,** KG, GCMG, MBE, PC (George Rowland Stanley Baring). Deputy Lieutenant County of Kent. *B.* 1918 *Educ.* Eton and Cambridge University. *M.* 1942, Hon. Esmé Harmsworth *S.* 2. *Dau.* 1. *Career:* Page of Honour to H.M. The King 1931–35; Lieut-Col. Grenadier Guards; Private Secretary to Marquess of Willingdon on official visits to South America (1938), and Australia and New Zealand (1940). Served in World War II (despatches; MBE); member, Inter-Parliamentary Mission to Brazil 1954; Managing Dir., Baring Bros. & Co. Ltd. 1947–61. On leave 1959–61 when he was Head of Treasury Delegation and British Economic Minister in Washington and U.K. Exec. Dir. of the International Monetary Fund, International Bank for Reconstruction and Development, and International Finance Corp.; Governor of the Bank of England, July 1961–June 30, 1966; Managing Dir. Baring Bros. & Co. Ltd. 1967–70; H.M. Ambassador to U.S.A. 1971–74; Adviser to Baring Brothers & Co. Ltd. since 1974; Chmn. IBM (UK Ltd.); Chmn. London Multinational Bank Ltd., *Director:* Compagnie Financiere de Suez; Shell Transport and Trading Co. Ltd.; Peninsular and Oriental Steam Navigation Co. Ltd, Imperial Group Ltd.; Daily Mail and General Trust Ltd. *Award:* Hon LLD, New York Univ. 1966. *Clubs:* White's, Brooks's, Beefsteak, Brook (N.Y.), Metropolitan (Washington). *Address:* 88 Leadenhall Street, London, EC3A 3DT.

**CROMER, D'Arcy Ananda Neil.** Australian. *B.* 1910. *Educ.* Univ. of Queensland (DScFor), Univ. of Adelaide (MSc) and Australian Forestry School, Canberra (DipFor). *M.* 1935, Edna May Featherstone. *S.* Robin Neil. *Dau.* Wendy Elizabeth. *Career:* Professional Forester, Forestry Commission of N.S.W. 1934–41; Sqdn. Leader, R.A.A.F. 1942–45; Officer-in-Charge, Research Divisions, Commonwealth of Australia Forestry & Timber Bureau 1946–63; Director, Forest Research Institute, Canberra, June 1963–70; Director-General, Forestry & Timber Bureau, Canberra, 1970–75 Secy., British Commonwealth Forestry Conf. 1957; Deleg., 10th Pacific Science Congress, Hawaii 1961; 11th Congress, Tokyo 1966. Chmn., Standing Cttee. on Forestry, Pacific Science Association 1967–75. Leader, Australian delegation to the 14th Congress International Union of Forestry Research Organizations, Munich 1967—. Senior Rapporteur F.A.O. Man-Made Forests Symposium, Australia 1967. Chmn. National Sirex Fund Cttee., 1970–75. Member, Permanent Committee of I.U.F.R.O. 1967–76; 15th Congress Florida 1971; Advisory Cttee. on Forestry Education, Aust. Nat. Univ.; Exect., Timber Industry Standards Cttee., Standard Assoc. of Aust. *Awards:* ISO 1976; Ernest Ayers Scholarship (Univ. Adelaide 1933); Bronze Medallion and Award of Merit, Royal Life Saving Socy.; Bronze Medal, Surf Life Saving Socy. *Fellow:* Inst. of Foresters of Australia 1969 (Pres. 1949–53; Past. Chmn. N.S.W. and A.C.T. Divisions; awarded N.W. Jolly Memorial Medal 1964); Governing Council, C'wealth Forestry Assn. *Publications:* New Approaches in Forest Mensuration (1961); and Bulletins of Forestry & Timber Bureau; numerous papers in scientific journals. *Clubs:* Canberra Alpine (Life Member). *Address:* 11 Guilfoyle Street, Yarralumla, Canberra, A.C.T., Australia.

**CROMIE, Peter Esmond.** Canadian. *B.* 1920. *Educ.* Univ. of British Columbia (BCom). *M.* 1948, Inez Patricia Knight. *S.* Ronald, Dana and Edward. *Daus.* Lin and Jane. *Career:* Secretary, Sun Publishing Co. Ltd. 1947–55; Mgr., Sun-printing (Div. of Sun Publishing Co. Ltd.) 1951–56; Pres. & Mgr., Plato Industries Ltd. 1957—. Formerly: President Graphic Arts Assn. of British Columbia; Dir. Printing Industry of Amer.; President: Plato Industries Ltd. 1957—, Thunderbird Ridge Properties Ltd. 1959—, Dolly Varden Mines Ltd. 1965–75, Copper Cliff Mines Ltd. 1964–75, Kitsault Silver Mines Ltd. 1964–75. D.C. Projects Ltd. Tunstall Estates Ltd. Dir. American Humanist Assn. Member, Vancouver Board of Trade. *Clubs:* The Vancouver; Vancouver Lawn Tennis & Badminton. *Address:* Suite 900 1685 West 14th Avenue, Vancouver, B.C. V6J 2J3, Canada.

**CROMWELL, James Henry Roberts.** American. *B.* 1898. *Educ.* Fay Sch.; Lawrenceville Sch.; Wharton Sch. of Finance & Commerce; Univ. of Pennsylvania. *M.* (1) 1920, Delphine Dodge (Div.); (2) 1935, Doris Duke (Div.); (3) 1948, Maxine MacFetridge (*D.* 1968); (4) 1971, Germaine Benjamin. *Career:* Lt. U.S.N. 1917–18; Capt. U.S.M.C.R. 1918–24; began with Drexel & Co.; Pres. Cromwell Dodge Corp. 1921–25; American British Improvement Corp. 1925–30; Vice-Pres. Peerless Motor Car Co. 1930–34; Pres. Cromwell & Co. 1934–40; U.S. Envoy to Canada 1940; Democratic Candidate U.S. Senate Amer. Ad. to Pres. Syngman Rhee of Korea 1941–45; Pres. Cromwell & Co. 1945–55; Bonnyville Oil & Refining Co. 1955–57; Kardar Canadian Oils 1957–69; Chmn. Realty & Petroleum Corp. 1961–64; Dir. Westates Petroleum Co. of Calif. since 1972. *Clubs:* Metropolitan N.Y. Bathing Corp. SN. N.Y.; St. Nicholas Society. *Member:* American Legion; Military Order of Foreign Wars. *Publications:* Voice of Young America (1932); in Defense of Capitalism (1957); Pax Americana (1940). *Address:* 4E 66th Street, N.Y. 10021 and Gin Lane, SN, N.Y. 11968.

**CROOK, Lord** (created 1947), JP. Reginald Douglas Crook; British administrator. *B.* 2 March 1901. *M.* 1922, Ida Gertrude. *S.* Douglas Edwin. *Career:* Organising Secretary, Poor Law Officers' Union 1920–24; Editor, Poor Law Gazette 1922–24; General Secretary, Ministry of Labour Staff Association 1925–51. Chairman, London Electricity Consultative Council 1967–72; Member, London Electricity Board 1967–72; General Practice Finance Corp. 1966–75; member, National Whitley Council 1925–51; Editor, Civil Service Argus 1927–51; Vice-Chairman and Chairman, North Islington Labour Party 1926–30; Secretary, Federation of Ministry of Labour Staff 1943–51; U.K. Delegate, General Assembly, United Nations 1950; Vice-President, Administrative Tribunal of United Nations 1951–71; Royal Society for the Prevention of Accidents; Chairman, National Dock Labour Board 1951–65; Pres., British Association of Industrial Editors 1954–56 K. St. J. Member of Chapter General of the Order; Pres. Pre-Retirement Assn.; Pres. Cystic Fibrosis Foundation; a Freeman of the City of London; master (1963–65) of the Company of Spectacle Makers; Past-Master & Life member, Court of Assistants of Guild of Freemen of City of London. An Apothecary. *Address:* Breedene, 25 Princes Avenue, Carshalton, Surrey.

**CROOK, Kenneth Roy.** British diplomat. *B.* 1920. *Educ.* Prescot Grammar School; Skerry's Coll. Liverpool. *M.* 1943,

Freda Joan Vidler. *Dau.* 1. *Career:* with Board of Trade, London 1937–39; On Loan, Ministry War Transport 1939–41; Served Royal Navy 1941–46; Board of Trade 1946–49; Asst. Principal. S. Asian Dept. Commonwealth Relations Office 1949–51; Canberra 1951–54; Principal in Defence Dept. Comm. Relations Office 1954–56; Madras 1956–59; Information, Cultural Relations Dept. C. R. Office 1959; Deputy High Commissioner Peshawar 1962, Dacca 1964–67; Asst. Head Information Dept. Foreign & Comm. Office 1967; Head of Dept. 1969; Governor of the Cayman Islands 1971–74; Ambassador to Afghanistan since 1975. *Address:* British Embassy, Kabul, Afghanistan.

**CROOK, Roy Dallas.** Australian oil executive; *B.* 1916. *Educ.* Adelaide Univ. (BSc). *M.* 1944, Loulie Mary. *S.* 2. *Daus.* 3. *Career:* Chemist Shell, Adelaide 1938–40; Shell Refinery Curacao, N.W.I. 1941; various positions 1942–49, finally Asst. Refinery Manager, Suez; Manager, Cracking Dept., Stanlow, England 1950–53; Manager, Refinery, Geelong 1953–62. Managing Director, Shell Refining (Australia) Pty. Ltd. 1962—. *Address:* 45 Bruce Street, Toorak, S.E.2, Vic., Australia.

**CROOKSTON, James Ian.** Canadian investment banker. *B.* 1910. *Educ.* Stowe (England). *M.* 1937, Cynthia D. Copping (*D.* 1975). *S.* James George. *Daus.* Andrea D. and C. Dana. *Career:* With Nesbitt, Thomson & Co. Ltd. since Jan. 1935. Chmn. and Director: Nesbitt, Thomson & Co. Ltd., Toronto; Director: Preston Mines Ltd. (Toronto); Newconex Holdings Ltd., Toronto; Norcen Energy Resources Ltd.; Rio Algon Mines Ltd., Fidelity Mortgage & Savings corp.; Trustee Heitman Realty Investors. *Clubs:* The Link's New York; Toronto Hunt; Toronto: York all (Toronto). *Address:* 70 Ardwold Gate, Toronto M5R 2W2, and *office* P.O. Box 35, Toronto Dominion Centre, Toronto M5K 1C4, Ont., Canada.

**CROSBIE, Hon. John Carnell,** MHA. Canadian. *B.* 1931. *Educ.* Queen's Univ., Kingston, Ont. (Hons BA Pol Sc and Economics) and Dalhousie Law School, Dalhousie Univ., Halifax N.S. (Hons LLB); Univ. of London (post-grad. Law). *M.* 1952, Jane Ellen Audrey Furneaux. *S.* Chesley Furneaux and Michael John. *Dau.* Beth. *Career:* Practised as Barrister and Solicitor in St. John's 1957–66 (partner in firm of Lewis, Aylward & Crosbie). Elected to City Council of St. John's Nov. 1965; appointed Deputy Mayor of St. John's Jan. 1966—; resigned 19 July 1965 when appointed Minister of Municipal Affairs and Housing. Minister in the Government of Newfoundland and Labrador, July 1966—. Member of House of Assembly for the District of St. John's West Sept. 1966–67; Minister of Health 1967–68; Re-elected St. John's 1971 (Progressive Conservative); Minister of Finance, Pres. Treasury Board, Minister of Economic Development since Jan 1972; Reappointed Min. of Finance & Pres. of Treasury Board April 1972. *Publications:* Local Government in Newfoundland (1954) 1972. *Awards:* University Medal: in Political Science (Queen's Univ.) 1953, and in Law (Dalhousie Univ) 1953, and in Law (Dalhousie Univ.) 1956; awarded Viscount Bennett Fellowship of the Canadian Bar Association 1956–57. *Member:* Law Socy. of Newfoundland; Canadian Bar Assn.; Canadian Tax Foundation. Liberal. *Clubs:* Rally Haly Golf and Country: Laurier; City. *Address: office* Department of Municipal Affairs and Housing, Confederation Building, St. John's, Newfoundland, Canada.

**CROSBY, Lucius Osmond, Jr.** *B.* 1907. *Educ.* Jefferson Military Coll.; Univ. of Mississippi (BS in Comm 1931). *Career:* Employee relief administrator and farm manager, Goodyear Yellow Pine Co. 1931–33; personnel and farm manager 1934–35; Vice-Pres. i/c sales and manufacturing, Crosby Lumber & Mfg. Co. 1936–41; President & Director, Crosby Forest Products Co. since 1941; President & Director, Pearl River Valley Railroad Co. since 1950; Pres., Pine Burr Area Council, Boy Scouts of America 1955–57; Past Dir., State and local YMCA; past Dir., Southern States Industrial Council; Dir., National Assn. of Manufacturers 1951–54. Mayor, City of Picayune 1957–61; Chairman, Region V., Boy Scouts 1958–62; Chairman National Explorer Committee Boy Scouts of America 1968. Member, Mississippi Dept. of Archives and History; Director of Mississippi Forestry Assoc. Recipient: Picayune Citizen of the Year Award for 1948; Man of the Year in the Tung Industry Award for 1960; Silver Beaver, Silver Antelope and Silver Buffalo (1963); Boy Scouts. *Clubs:* Capital City (Jackson, Miss.); Hattiesburg (Miss.) Country; International House (New Orleans); Millbrook Golf & Country (Picayune); Plimsoll. New Orleans; Bienville; New Orleans Country. *Address:* 1630 Third Avenue, Picayune, Miss.; and *office* 200 South Crosby Street, Picayune, Miss., U.S.A.

**CROSS, Francis Stewart,** JP. Australian. *B.* 1910. *Educ.* State Schools. *M.* 1942, Norma Kathleen Rutherford. *S.* Douglas. *Daus.* Vivienne and Dale. *Career:* With Western Australian Employers' Federation: Industrial Officer and Advocate 1926–46, Asst. Secretary and Chief Advocate 1946–53, and Secretary 1953–59. Director, Western Australian Employers' Federation Inc. 1959–74; Exec. Dir. Confed. of Western Australian Industry since 1975. *Member:* Economic Socy. of Australia and New Zealand; Australian & N.Z. Assn. for the Advancement of Science; Australian Inst. of Management; Inst. of Personnel Management (Australia); Indust. Relations Socy. of W. Australia; Justices' Assn. of Western Australia; Rotary Club of Perth. *Clubs:* The Perth; Hannans; Commercial Travellers. *Address:* 13 Dunkeld Street, Floreat Park, W.A.; and *office* 188 Adelaide Terrace, Perth, W.A., Australia.

**CROSS, William Redmond, Jr.** American. *B.* 1917. *Educ.* Yale Univ. (BA 1941). *M.* 1958, Sally Curtiss Smith. *S.* William Redmond III and Frederic Newbold. *Dau.* Pauline Curtiss. *Career:* With the Hanover Bank 1941–43; The New York Trust Co. 1946–59 (Asst. Treas., Asst. Vice-Pres. 1948–51, Vice-Pres. 1951–59); Morgan Guaranty Trust Co. of N.Y. 1959–64 (Vice-Pres. Head Fifth Avenue Office 1961–62, and Head, Midtown Offices 1962–65): Senior Vice-President, Morgan Guaranty Trust Company of New York, 1964–73, Exec. Vice-Pres. 1973—; Senior Credit Officer, General Banking Division 1971–72; Head, Metropolitan Group, 1965–71; Dir. Crompton Co. since 1970; Dir. The New York Times since 1973; Dir. Axax Inc. since 1974. Director, Valeria Home Inc. 1955—; Trustee, The Children's Aid Society 1962–75, Chapin School 1969–75, Rippowam-Cisque School, Bedford N.Y. 1973–77. *Clubs:* Yale, Racquet & Tennis, Sky (N.Y.C.); Bedford (N.Y.) Golf & Tennis. *Address:* R.D. 2, Box 299 So. Bedford Road, Mt. Kisco, N.Y. 10549; and *office* 23 Wall Street, New York, N.Y. 10015, U.S.A.

**CROSTHWAIT, Timothy Leland,** CMG, MBE. *B.* 1915. *Educ.* Wellington College and Peterhouse, Cambridge (MA). *M.* 1959, Anne Marjorie Penney. *Career:* Joined Indian Civil Service 1938; Assistant Private Secretary to the Viceroy 1942–44; Air Ministry 1948–55; Deputy High Commissioner Colombo 1957–61 and Malta 1965–66. High Commissioner Zanzibar 1963–64, Guyana 1966–67; Ambassador Madagascar 1970–75. *Club:* United University (London). *Address:* 39 Eaton Terrace, London SW1.

**CROWDER, Edmund.** British. *B.* 1918. *Educ.* Univ. of Alberta (BSc Chem Eng). *M.* 1943, Josephine M. Irving. *S.* Joseph Roger and Harry Edmund. *Career:* With Consolidated Mining & Smelting Co., Trail, B.C. 1942–55; Best Fertilizers, Lathrop, Calif. 1956–57; Northwest Nitro Chemicals, Medicine Hat, Alta. 1957–63. General Manager, Border Fertilizer Ltd., Winnipeg 1964–67; General Manager, Vice-Pres. & Dir., Simplot Chemical Co. Ltd. Brandon. *Member:* Assn. of Professional Engineers (Manitoba Branch). *Address:* 2517 Rosser Ave, Brandon, Manitoba R7B OE8; and *office* Box 940, Brandon, Man., Canada.

**CROWE, Sir Colin Tradescant,** GCMG. *B.* 1913. *Educ.* Stowe Schoo land Oriel College Oxford (MA). *M.* 1938, Bettina Lum. *Career:* Chargé d'Affaires, United Arab Republic 1959–61; Ambassador to Saudi Arabia 1963–64; Chief of Administration of H.M. Diplomatic Service 1965–68. British High Commissioner to Canada 1968–70. Deputy Permanent Representative in the U.K. Mission to the United Nations 1961–63. Permanent Representative, U.K. Mission to the United Nations, 1970–73. *Club:* Travellers' (London). *Address:* Pigeon House, Bibury, Glos.

**CROWN, Henry.** American business executive. *B.* Chicago, 1896. *Educ.* Public Schools, Chicago. *M.* (1). 1920, Rebecca Kranz (*D.* 1943). *S.* Robert, (*Dec.*). Lester, John Jacob. *M.* (2), 1946. Gladys Kay, *Career:* Clerk, Chicago Fire Brick Co. 1910–12; Traffic Manager, Union Drop Forge Co. 1912–16; Partner, S.R. Crown & Co. 1916–19; Treasurer, Material Service Corp., bldg. materials 1919–21, Pres. 1921–41, Chmn. Bd. 1941–59; Dir. and Chmn. Exec. Cttee. General Dynamics Corp. 1959–66; Dir. and Chmn. Exec. Cttee of Corp. since 1970; Chmn. Bd. Henry Crown & Co. since 1967; Dir. Waldorf Astoria Corporation; Vice-Pres. and Dir. 208 S. La Salle St. Building Corp. Member Chicago Civil Defense Corps. Bd. Dirs. Chicago Boys Clubs. Trustee, DePaul Univ., Univ. of Chicago Cancer Research Foundation. Member, Loyola Univ. Citizens Bd., Univ. of Ill. Citizens Cttee., Northwestern University Associates; Associate and Fellow, Brandeis Univ.; Fellow, St. Joseph's College, Rensselaer, Ind.; Mem. Nat. Council Boy Scouts Am. Served as Col., Corps of Engrs.,

A.U.S., World War II. Member, Mil. Order World Wars, Mason (Shriner 33°). *Awards:* Legion of Merit, Corps of Engineers 1942–45; Chevalier De La Legion D'Honneur France; The Gold Cross, Royal Order of the Phoenix Greece; Order, Ruben Dario, Republic of Nicaragua; Horatio Alger Award, Amer. Schools & Coll. Assn.; Damen Award Loyola Univ. Chicago Ill; Julius Rosenwald Memorial, Jewish Fed & Welfare Fund; Humanitarian Service Award for Industry, Eleanor Roosevelt Cancer Res. Foundation. *Clubs:* Mid-Day, Standard, Executives, Tavern (Chgo.), St. Louis (Mo.). *Address:* 900 Edgemere Ct., Evanston, Ill.; and *office* 300 W. Washington St., Chicago.

**CROWSON, Benjamin F. Jr.** American biographer and publisher, Crowson International Publications. *B.* 1918. *Educ.* William & Mary Coll. (AB); special work at Univ. of Mexico. *Career:* Topical Spanish instructor, U.S. Army and Navy officers 1942–44; English Instructor to diplomats, Washington, D.C. 1949–50, and to the army officers, Mexico City Defense Dept. 1954–55, to police officers. Victoria, Mexico 1962, and Zacatecas, Mexico 1965 and 1966. Editor, Inter-Nations Biographical Record (18 volumes already published); International Researcher and Biographer of World Personalities 1946—. Editor: Our Southern Neighbors in Review; Inter-Nations Highlight Series (75 countries); Topical Spanish Research Series; 1001 Highlights on Mexico (1967–68); Highlights of Latin American Commerce; Practical Spanish Handbook; Revised topical, Key Word, English Method 1968; Survey Chart on Arab Nations 1969; Modern Language Word Chart 1969; Survey charts on Scandinavian and African countries; Biographical Reports, Latin American Presidents 1973–74. *Awards:* Cross of Eloy Alfaro Foundation, Rep. of Panama. *Member:* Sigma Nu fraternity. *Address:* Charlotte Hall, Md., U.S.A.

**CROWTHER-HUNT of Eccleshill, Baron** (Norman Crowther-Hunt). British Political Scientist and Politician. *B.* 1920. *Educ.* Cambridge University, History Tripos (1st Class Honours) (1946, 1947); Ph.D. Cantab. (1951). *M.* 1944, Joyce Stackhouse. *Daus.* 3. *Career:* Research Fellow, Sydney Sussex Coll.; Cambridge 1948–51; C'wealth Fund Fellow, Princeton Univ., U.S.A., 1951–52; Fellow and Lecturer in Politics, Exeter College since 1952; Visiting Professor, Michigan State Univ. 1961; Constitutional Adviser to the Government 1974; Min. of State, Dept. of Education and Science 1974–76; Min. of State, Privy Council Office, 1976. *Member:* Political Studies Association; Study of Parliament Group; Cttee. on the Civil Service, 1966–68; Commission on the Constitution, 1969–73 and Principal Author of the Minority Report. *Award:* Created Life Peer 1973. *Publications:* Two Early Political Associations (1961); (Editor) Whitehall and Beyond (1964); (Editor) Personality and Power (1970). *Address:* 14 Apsley Road, Oxford; and *office* Exeter College, Oxford.

**CRUGER, Frank Marion.** Industrial engineer. *B.* 1905. *Educ.* Indiana Univ. *M.* 1931, Sara Elizabeth Hutto. *S.* Sterling R. and Kenneth J. President: National Small Business Association, Washington, D.C., and of National Industrial Distributors Association, Philadelphia. Board Chairman, American Assn. of Small Business, New Orleans. *Member:* National Advisory Council (Chairman, Management Assistance Div.); Chairman, Small Business Administration, and of World Trade Advisory Committee, U.S. Department of Commerce; Director, National Export Expansion Council, Washington, D.C.; Chmn. Small bus. Cttee. U.S. Dept. Commerce; Director, Indianapolis Chamber of Commerce (Chairman, National Legislative Committee); Director, National Schools Committee for Economic Education, New York; Director, F. H. Langsenkamp Co.; National Federation of Independent Business, San Mateo, Cal.; Vice-Pres. Chmn. Finance Cttee, Nat. Fed. Independent Business; Director, International Executive Service Corps., N.Y. President and, Trustee, American Good Government Socy. Chmn. Electoral College Reform Committee (both of Washington, D.C.). Pres., Indiana Mfrs. Supply Co., Indianapolis. Vice-Pres. and Director, C & CC Car Care Systems Inc. Vice-Pres., Machine Products Corp., Dayton, Ohio. Owner and operator of cattle and hog farm in Hancock County, Ind. Vice-Pres., Sons of the American Revolution, and the Indiana Society. *Publications:* Small Business Moves Ahead; The Fifth Estate; A Five-Cent Nickel; Progress Sharing; How Industrial Distributors Help Small Manufacturers; The Persistent Nature of Small Business; SBA Management Aid, Pointers on Preparing an Employee Handbook; Trade Mission to East Africa; Command versus Demand. *Member:* U.S. Trade Mission to Africa 1960; U.S. Trade and Investment Mission to South Vietnam 1965; Navy League; Amer. Ordnance Assn.; U.S. Trade Missions to Fed. of Malaysia, Hongkong, Greece 1963. Leader of Small Scale Enterprise Mission to the Soviet Union, Oct. 1962; member Newcomen Society; Bd, member Int. Mangt. and Dev. Inst. Washington. D.C. *Clubs:* Mt. Kenya Safari; Athletic, Columbia, Athenaeum Turner. (Director), all of Indianapolis; Southern (Past Pres.); 32 Deg. Mason; Shriner; English-Speaking Union; Kiwanis. *Address:* *office* 2260 Profit Drive, Park Fletcher, Indianopolis 6, Ind., U.S.A.

**CRUICKSHANK, William Patrick.** British. banker. *B.* 1906. Educ. George Watson's College (Edinburgh). *M.* 1951, Kathleen M. Brebner. *S.* 1. *Career:* Held various executive appointments in India and Ceylon with James Finlay & Co. Ltd. (Merchant bankers and East India merchants) 1925–38; Eastern Gen. Manager, Venesta Ltd. 1938 (Overseas Dir. of the Board 1946); Chairman: Venesta Tea Chest Co. Ltd., Acme Tea Chest Co. Ltd., Dir., Chest Components Ltd. Member London Committee, Bank of India 1958–70. Group Chairman, Venesta Ltd. 1964–68. Fellow, Inst, of Directors, *Club:* Oriental (London); New (Edinburgh). *Address:* Westerlea, Abbotsford Road, North Berwick, East Lothian.

**CUBER, John F.** American. Professor and author *B.* 1911. *Educ.* Western Michigan Univ. (AB) and Univ. of Michigan (PhD). *M.* (1) 1949, Armine Gulesserian. *M.* (2) 1964, Peggy B. Harroff. *Dau.* Armine Anne. *Career:* Chairman, Sociology and Economics, Sioux Falls College 1935–36; Asst. Prof., Sociology and Economics, Marietta College 1936–37; Asst. Prof. to Professor, Kent State University 1937–44; Professor, Sociology Ohio State Univ. 1944—. *Publications:* Sociology—a synopsis of Principles (1947–51–55–59–63–68); Problems of American Society (1948–52–56); Social Stratification in the U.S. (1955); Readings in Sociology: Sources and Comment (1962); The Significant Americans (1965). Fellow, Amer. Sociological Assn. *Member:* Amer. Assn. of University Professors. RI Mt. Gilead, Ohio; and *office* Ohio State University, Columbus, 43210 Ohio, U.S.A.

**CUDLIPP, Reginald.** British. *B.* 1910. Educ. Cardiff Technical College. *M.* 1945, Rachel Joyce Braham. *Career:* With News of the World: Special Correspondent in America 1946–47, Features Editor 1948–50, Deputy-Editor 1950–53, Editor 1953–59; Director, News of the World Ltd. 1955–60. Director, Anglo-Japanese Economic Institute, London, since 1961. *Publications:* numerous contributions to newspapers and periodicals on Japanese affairs; Editor, Japan (quarterly review); lectures on Japan's economic and industrial progress. *Member:* Japan Society of London; Royal Central Asian Society; Royal Inst. of International Affairs. *Address* 342/6 Grand Buildings, Trafalgar Square, London, W.C.2.

**CULLEN, Barbara Jocelyn.** OBE. Australian; *B.* 1908. *Educ.* Secondary School (Ascham Sydney). *M.* 1930, William Hartland Cullen (dec'd). *Daus:* Rosemary and Jennifer. *Career:* State Pres., County Women's Assn. of N.S.W. 1953–56; Vice Pres. Council, Social Service N.S.W. 1955–73; National Pres., Country Women's Assn. of Australia 1956 and 1957; Member, Immigration Advisory Council 1957–71; Vice-Pres., Associated Country Women of the World 1959–62; and of Good Neighbour Council of N.S.W. 1957–61 (Vice-Pres. 1963—77); Chmn., Council of Social Service of N.S.W. 1957–59; Vice-Chairman, Old Peoples Welfare Council of N.S.W. 1960–69; Exec. Member, Aust. Outward Bound Memorial Foundation 1961–68; Vice-Pres. Rachel Forster Hospital since 1963. Nat. Exec. Mem. Freedom from Hunger Campaign 1962–73; Mem. Convocation Macquarie Univ. since 1970. Cttee. Member, Home Help Service of N.S.W. 1964—; Deputy Pres., Associated Country Women of the World 1962–68; Consumer Goods & Service Industries Advisory Cttee. to the Metric Conversion Board since 1970. *Clubs:* Queen's and Imperial Service (Sydney). *Address:* Bimbimbie, Gilligans Road, Dural, N.S.W., Australia.

**CULLEN, George Jocelyn,** MBE, ED. Australian company director. *B.* 1902. *Educ.* Repton School (Derbyshire, U.K.). *M.* (1) 1929, Eleanore Fordyce Wheeler; (2) 1942, Loraine Hamilton McLachlan. *S.* Samuel Sydney Cullen. *Career:* Enlisted and served in Australian Imperial Force (Western Desert, Syria, Palestine, Owen Stanleys (Papua) and Bougainville (Solomon Is.)—in short, Middle East and S.W. Pacific Area) 1939–45; Dir. Aldershot Ltd. 1952—. *Clubs:* Australian; Imperial Services; Royal Sydney Yacht Squadron. *Address:* 5 Hillside, 412 Edgecliff Road, Woollahra, N.S.W.; and *office* 36 AMP Centre, Bridge Street, Sydney, N.S.W., Australia.

**CULLEN, Paul Alfred,** CBE, DSO & Bar, ED, FCA. Australian chartered accountant. *B.* 1909. *Educ.* Cranbrook School,

Sydney; FCA. *M.* (1) 1932, Phyllis Marjorie Sampson. *S.* Christopher Samuel. *Dau.* Dinah Helen (Harvey). *M.* (2) 1962, Jean Cecily née Drake-Brockman. Brigadier, Australian Military Forces 1954, Maj.-General 1961. Senior Vice-Pres., Royal Blind Society 1950. *Member:* Inst. of Chartered Accountants. *Clubs:* Australian, University Imperial Service (Sydney); Elanora Country. *Address:* 'Cranston', Aston Gardens, Bellevue Hill, Sydney, N.S.W., Australia.

**CULLIMORE, William Rae.** British solicitor and company director. *B.* 1918. *Educ.* Shrewsbury School and Caius College, Cambridge (MA). *M.* Stella Mabel Florence Russell. *S.* John Douglas Charles. *Dau.* Vivienne Stella. *Career:* Partner in the firm of Birch, Cullimore & Co., Solicitors, Friars, White Friars, Chester. Associate, Royal Institute of Chartered Surveyors. *Club:* Farmers (London). *Address:* Faulkners Lodge, Christleton, Chester.

**CULLITON, Hon. Chief Justice Edward Milton.** Chief Justice of Saskatchewan Province of Canada. *B.* 1906. *Educ.* University of Saskatchewan (BA; LLB Hon DCL). *M.* 1939, Katherine M. Hector. *Address:* 1303–1830 College Avenue, Regina, Saskatchewan S4P 1C2; and *office* Court House, Regina, Sask. S4P 3E4, Canada.

**CULLMAN 3rd, Joseph F.,** AB. American. *B.* 1912. *Educ.* Hotchkiss Sch.; Yale Univ. (AB). *Dau.* 1. *Career:* Vice-Pres. Benson & Hedges 1946–53, Exec. Vice-Pres. 1953–55, Pres. 1955–61; Vice-Pres. Philip Morris Inc. 1954, Exec. Vice-Pres. 1955–57, Pres. Chief Exec. Officer 1957–66; Chmn. Bd. Chief Exec. Officer since 1967; Dir. IBM World Trade Europe/M. East/Africa Corp., Bankers Trust Co., Ford Motor Co.; Levi Strauss & Co.; Whitney M. Young Jun. Memorial Foundation (& Pres.); Mission Viejo Company; World Wildlife Fund—U.S. Appeal. *Member:* Yale Development Bd.; Exec. Cttee. Tobacco Inst. Wash. D.C.; Trustee New York State Nature & Historical Preserve Trust; Amer. Museum Natural History; Trustee Colonial Williamsburg Foundation; Member, Port Authority of New York & New Jersey; Member National Board of the Smithsonian Associates; President International Atlantic Salmon Foundation. *Decorations:* Ordre du Mérite Commercial et Industriel, France 1966; Commander, Order of Merit of the Republic of Italy. In Tobacco Industry's Hall of Fame. *Clubs:* Yale; Century Country; Union League of N.Y. *Address:* (*office*) 100 Park Ave., New York, N.Y. 10017, U.S.A.

**CULLWICK, Prof. Ernest Geoffrey,** OBE; Captain (L), RCN (R), retd. Canadian; Emeritus Professor of Electrical Engineering, Univ. of Dundee; Hon. Prof., Univ. of Kent, Canterbury. *B.* 1903. *Educ.* Downing College, Cambridge University (Mech Sci Tripos 1925, BA; MA Cantab. 1929; DSc St. Andrews 1953). *M.* 1929, Mamie Ruttan Boucher (of Peterborough, Ont., Canada). *S.* Ernest Robert Alan (Lieut. Cdr. C.A.F.). *Dau.* Evelyn Catherine May. *Career:* With British Thomson-Houston Co., Rugby, and Canadian G.E. Co., Canada 1925–28; Assistant Professor of Electrical Engineering, University of British Columbia 1928–34; Lect. in Elect. Eng., Military College of Science, Woolwich 1934–35; Assoc. Prof. of Elect. Eng. Univ. of British Columbia 1935–37; Prof. and Head, Dept. of Elect. Eng., Univ. of Alberta 1937–46; Director of Electrical Engineering, Royal Canadian Navy, Ottawa 1942–47; with Defence Research Board, Ottawa 1947–49; Professor Univ. of St. Andrews, 1949–67, and Univ. of Dundee 1967–73; Dean of the Faculty of Applied Science, same Universities, 1955–60 and 1966–71. *Publications:* The Fundamentals of Electro-magnetism (Cambridge University Press, 1939); Electromagnetism and Relatively (Longmans Green, 1957); various papers in scientific and technical journals. Fellow, Institution of Electrical Engineers (Chmn., North Scotland Sub-Centre 1957–58, Chairman, Scottish Centre 1961–63); Fellow, Royal Society of Edinburgh (Member of Council 1958–61). *Address:* 20 Riverdale, River, Dover, Kent.

**CULMANN, Dr. Herbert (Ernst).** Dr. jur; German. *B.* 1921. *Educ.* Neustadt/Weinstrasse Gymnasium, and University of Heidelberg. *M.* 1949, Angelika Küstner. *S.* 2. *Dau.* 1. *Career:* With German Navy and Air Force 1939–45; Legal studies and practice 1945–53; Deutsche Lufthansa since 1953 (Member, Exec. Board since 1964). Chairman, Executive Board of Deutsche Lufthansa AG. Chairman, Bd. of Directors: Condor Flugdienst GmbH; Member, Hanse-Merkur Krankenvers. VVaG; Member, Adv. Board Colonia National AG. *Publications:* Völkerrechtliche Stellung der Handelsschiffe, (1951); various other publications. *Member:* Anwaltskammer, Cologne; International Law Assn.; International Air and Space Law Committee; *Club:* Rotary. *Address:* Neuer Trassweg 30, 5060 Bensberg-Refrath; and *office* Von Gablenz-Strasse 2–6, 1, 5000, Colgne, 21, Germany.

**CUMBERLAND, Julian O.,** MBA. American. *B.* 1921. *Educ.* Princeton Univ.; Univ. of Michigan (MBA); London Sch. of Economics (Graduate Study). *M.* 1943, Ruth Woodward. *S.* 2. *Daus.* 2. *Career:* Financial Vice-Pres. Newmont Mining Corp.; Asst. Treas. Aramco Overseas Co. & Financial Co-ordinator, Arabian American Oil Co. 1948–59; Vice-Pres. & Treas. American Independent Oil C. 1959–62; Financial Vice-Pres. American International Oil Co., 1962–68; Exec. Vice-Pres. Commonwealth Oil Refining Co. Inc. since 1972; Mem. American Petroleum Inst.; Mining Club Inc.; Middle East Inst.; American Foreign Policy Assoc.; Cerebral Palsy League. *Clubs:* Ridgewood Country; Princeton (N.Y.). *Address: office* 200 Park Ave., New York, N.Y. 10017, U.S.A.

**CUMES, Dr. James William Crawford.** Australian diplomat. *B.* 1922. *Educ.* BA (Queensland); PhD (London). *Career:* 3rd & 2nd Sec., Dept. of Foreign Affairs, Canberra 1944–49; served in Paris, London, Bonn (Chargé d'Affaires 1955–56), Berlin (resident Head of Australian Military Mission 1956–58) 1949–58; Asst. Sec., Economic Relations, Dept. of Foreign Affairs 1958–61; Chargé d'Affaires, Australian Embassy, Brussels 1961–65; Australian High Commissioner to Nigeria 1965–67; 1st Asst. Sec., Dept. of Foreign Affairs 1968–74; Australian Ambassador to Belgium, Luxembourg & the European Communities 1975–77; Australian Ambassador to Austria & Hungary, Resident Rep. to IAEA & UNIDO since 1977. *Publications:* The Indigenot Rich (1971); Inflation: A Study in Stability (1974); Their Chastity was Not Too Rigid (1978). *Clubs:* Royal Oree, Chateau St. Anne (Brussels). *Address:* 35 Peter Jordan Strasse, 1190 Vienna; & *office* 2–4 Mattielli Strasse, A-1040 Vienna, Austria.

**CUMMING, William Richard,** CVO. *B.* 1911. *Educ.* Univ. of Queensland (BA), Univ. of Sydney (LLB; Diploma in Public Administration); Barrister-at-Law, New South Wales. *M.* 1939, Evelyn Joyce Paul. *S.* 1. *Dau.* 1. *Career:* With Australian Army 1939–45; Adviser, Federal Taxation Dept. 1947–51; Senior Exec. Officer, Prime Minister's Dept., Canberra 1951–55 (Asst. Secy. 1955–60); Dir., Royal Visit, A.C.T. 1953–54 and 1957–58, Director-General, Royal Visit 1959; Secretary, Commonwealth Literary Fund (Australia) 1955–60, and 1967–70; of Commonwealth Art Advisory Board 1955–60, and 1966–70; and of Commonwealth Composers Bd. 1967–70; Dep. High Commissoner (Acting), London 1965–66; 1972–73; Official Secretary, Australian High Commission London 1960–66; 1970–73; Extra Gentleman Usher to the Queen 1962–66, 1971–74; Australian Delegate, International Tin Council 1961–66. Assistant Secretary, Prime Minister's Dept., Canberra, 1966–70; Counsellor, Cultural Affairs Aust. High Commission, London 1973–74; Consultant, Australia Council 1974–76; Chmn., Public Lending Right Cttee., Australia Council since Oct. 1976. *Member:* Inst. of Management; Inst. of Public Administration; Cncl. of National Library of Australia 1968–70; Cncl. Inst. of Aboriginal Studies 1968–70. *Clubs:* Univ. (Sydney); Oriental (London). *Address:* Australia Council, Northside Gardens, Walker Street, North Sydney, Australia.

**CUMMINS, Maurice William B.** British. *B.* 1908. *Educ.* Univ. of Sydney Sch. of Pharmacy. *M.* 1933, Kathleen Mary Glass. *S.* 1. *Dau.* 1. *Career:* Man. Dir. Quaker Chemicals (A'asia) Pty. Ltd.; Dir. Ripolin Paints (Aust.) Pty. Ltd.; Man. Dir. Chronol Industrial Chemicals Pty. Ltd. & Decol Detergents Pty. Ltd. 1950–59; Gen. Man. Chemical Materials Ltd. 1960–63; Exec. Chmn. Beith Chemical Materials Ltd. *Clubs:* Tattersalls, Sydney; Australian Golf, Sydney. *Address: office* 27/45 Federal Rd., Glebe, N.S.W., Australia.

**CUMMINGS, Nathan.** Industrialist. *B.* 1896. *Educ.* Public School and Economist Training School, New York City. *M.* (1) 1919, Ruth Lillian Kellert (*Dec.* 1952). *S.* Herbert K. and Alan H. *Dau.* Beatrice (Mayer). *Career:* Founder, Hon. Chmn. Consolidated Foods Corp., Chicago; Dir.-Gen. Dynamics Corp. St. Louis; Chmn., Magnatex Ltd.; Dir., Maxwell Inc.; Governing Life Member of Art Institute of Chicago; Honorary Trustee, Metropolitan Museum of Art; Patron, Montreal Museum of Fine Arts; Patron and Governing Member, Minneapolis Socy. of Fine Arts. *Member:* Citizens Bd., Univ. of Chicago; Northwestern Univ. Associates; Whitney Museum of American Art; Life Governor, Jewish General Hospital of Montreal; Patron, Lincoln Centre for the Performing Arts. *Awards:* Officier de la Légion d'Honneur (France); Commendatore dell Ordine Al Merito della Repubblica Italiana; Comendador Orden Al Merito por Servicios

Distinguidos República Peruana; LLD Citadel Military Coll. and Univ. of New Brunswick. DHum. Florida Southern College. Dr. of Humane Letters, Kenyon Coll., Gambier, Ohio; Catholic Univ., Wash., D.C. *Clubs:* Mid-America; Canadian; The Chicago. *Address:* 100 E. 50th Street, N.Y.C. N.Y. 10022; and *office* 375 Park Avenue, New York, N.Y. 10022, U.S.A.

**CUMMINS, John Edward,** OBE. Governor. Ian Clunies Ross Memorial Foundation, Australia. *B.* 1902. *Educ.* BSc (WA); MSc (Wis.). *M.* 1927, Elizabeth Margaret Lamborne. *Dau.* Helen Carol (Noble). *Career:* With C.S.I.R. Australia 1927–48 (successively Officer-in-Charge, Wood Preservation Research; Information Service; Director, Scientific Liaison Bureau; Officer-in-Charge, Information Service); Scientific Adviser and Chief Scientific Liaison Officer, London 1948–54; Scientific Counsellor and Chief Scientific Liaison Officer, Australian Embassy, Washington 1954–57; Director, International Atomic Energy Agency, Vienna 1958–60; Senior Principal Research Officer, C.S.I.R.O. Australia 1961–62. Author: contributor to various scientific journals. *Fellow:* Royal Institute of Chemistry (England) and of Royal Australian Chemical Inst. *Club:* Kelvin, The Sciences (Melbourne), Farmers' Club (London). *Address:* 10 Mortimer Street, Kew, E.4, Vic.; and *office* 191 Royal Parade, Parkville, Vic., 3152, Australia.

**CUNNINGHAM, Sir Charles Craik.** GCB, KBE, CVO . *B.* 1906. *Educ.* Harris Academy, Dundee; University of St. Andrews (MA; BLitt; LLD). *M.* 1934, Edith Louisa Webster. *Daus.* 2. *Career:* Entered Scottish Office 1929; Private Secretary to Secretary of State 1935–39; Secretary, Scottish Home Department 1948–57. Permanent Under Secretary of State, Home Office 1957–66. British. Deputy Chairman, United Kingdom Atomic Energy Authority 1966–71; Chmn. The Radiochemical Centre Ltd., 1971–74; Chmn. Uganda Resettlement Board 1972–74. *Address:* Bankside, Peaslake, Surrey, GU5 9RL.

**CUNNINGHAM, Sir Graham,** KBE, FSGT. *B.* 1892. *Educ.* Bancroft's School, Woodford, Essex; London University (LLB). *M.* (1) 1924, Marjorie Minshaw Harris. *S.* 2. *Dau.* 1. (2) 1934, Olive St. John Williams. (3) 1958, Edith Ellen Smith. *Career:* Served in World War I, Royal Fusiliers 1915–19; Deputy Director-General, Children's Overseas Reception Board 1940; Director of Claims, War Damage Commission 1941; Chief Executive & Controller General, Munitions Production, Ministry of Supply 1941–46; Chairman, Dollar Exports Board 1949; Chairman and Managing Director, Triplex Safety Glass Co. Ltd. 1929–61; Chmn., Shipbuilding Advisory Cttee. 1946–60; member, Economic Planning Board 1947–61; Crown Governor 1944–68; Hon. Fellow, Imperial College of Science & Technology; U.S. Medal of Freedom with Silver Bar, Past Pres. Socy. of Glass Technology; Past Pres., Socy. of British Gas Industries; Past Master Curriers Company and Glaziers Company. *Address:* Woolmers, Mannings Heath, Horsham, Sussex.

**CUNNINGHAM, Ira James,** CBE. New Zealand. *B.* 1905. *Educ.* New Zealand Univ. (MSc 1928, DSc 1959), Aberdeen Univ. (PhD 1931), and Sydney Univ. (BVSc 1938), Hon. DVSc Melbourne Univ. 1967. *M.* 1933, Marion Margaret MacOwan. *S.* Alastair James and Roderick Bayne. *Dau.* Margaret Christine. *Career:* Superintendent, Wallaceville Animal Research Station, Department of Agriculture, New Zealand 1945–58; Assistant Director-General, Dept. of Agriculture 1958–62. Dean, Faculty of Veterinary Science, Massey University of Manawatu, Palmerston North, N.Z. 1962–71 (retd.). *Award:* Medallist Royal Socy. of New Zealand. *Publications:* numerous scientific papers on nutrition and disease in animals. Fellow, Royal Society of N.Z. (F.R.S.N.Z.). *Member:* R.S.N.Z.; N.Z. Veterinary Assn. (Pres. 1945); N.Z. Socy. of Animal Production (Pres. 1946; life memb. 1969); Vice-Pres. Aust. Coll. of Veterinary Scientists 1971. *Address:* 562 Featherston Street, Palmerston North, New Zealand.

**CUNNINGHAM, Dr. John Anderson,** MP. British Politician *B.* 1939. *Educ.* BSc, PhD. *M.* 1964, Maureen. *S.* 1. *Daus.* 2. *Career:* Research Fellow in Chemistry, Durham Univ. 1966–68; Regional Organiser, General & Municipal Workers Union 1969–70; MP (Lab.) for Whitehaven, Cumbria since 1970; Parly. Under-Sec. of State for Energy since 1976. *Address:* House of Commons, London SW1A 0AA.

**CUNNINGHAM, Kenneth Stewart.** Australian educationist. *B.* 1890. *Educ.* Melbourne University (MA Dip. Ed.); Columbia University (PhD). *M.* 1920, Ella Mrytle Tuck. *S.* Kenneth Graeme. *Daus.* Marjory Lesley Ella. Winchester, *Career:* Lecturer at Teachers College and at Univ. of Melbourne 1920–30; Director, Australian Council for Educational Research 1930–54; U.N.E.S.C.O. consultant in teacher training and educational research, Indonesia 1955–57. Holds following honorary positions: Hon. Fellow, Australian Psychological Society; Hon. Member, Australian Library Assn.; Hon. Fellow, Inst. of Industrial Management; Hon. Fellow, Social Sciences in Aust. Monash University, Vic., in 1966 established K. S. Cunningham Chair of Education. *Publications:* The Measurement of Early Levels of Intelligence; Primary Education by Correspondence; Educational Observations and Reflections; Children Need Teachers (co-author); Review of Education in Australia (co-author) 1937 and 1938; Inspection and Supervision of Primary Schools (co-author); Education in Indonesia; Training the Administrator (co-author); An Australian School at Work 1967; History of S.S.R.C. 1966; chapters on Australian Education in various publications, especially the Year Book of Education. *Address:* 11 Wedge Court, Glen Waverley, Vic. 3150, Australia.

**CUPLER, John A., II.** American. *B.* 1912. *Educ.* West Virginia Univ. *M.* 1942, Margaret R. Durst. *S.* 1. *Dau.* 1. *Career:* Pres. Nat. Jet Corp., Nat. Jet drill Corp., Nat. Jet Sales Corp. Mem. American Assoc. of Tool Engineers; Dir. Sacred Heart Hospital. *Clubs:* 32nd Degree Mason; Shrine. *Address: office* 10 Cupler Drive, La Vale, Md., U.S.A.

**CURLE, Sir John Noel Ormiston,** KCVO, CMG. Director of Protocol, Hong Kong. *B.* 1915. *Educ.* Marlborough; New Coll. Oxford; Laming Travelling Fellow of Queen's Coll. Oxford; MA (Oxon.). *M.* (1) Diana Deane, and (2) 1948, Pauline Roberts (née Welford). *S.* 2. *Daus.* 3. *Career:* With Irish Guards 1939; Captain 1941; War Cabinet Secretariat 1941–44; Counsellor Stockholm 1956, and Athens 1959; Consul-Gen., Boston (U.S.A.) 1962; Ambassador to Liberia 1967–70, to Guinea 1968–70 and Philippines 1970–72; Vice-Marshal of the Diplomatic Corps 1972–75. *Club:* Beefsteak; Guards (London). *Address:* Appletree House, nr. Aston Le Walls, Daventry, Northamptonshire; and c/o Government Secretariat, Hong Kong.

**CURLETT, John Newton.** Business executive. *B.* 1905. *Educ.* Graduate of Ohio Wesleyan Univ. (AB 1928). *M.* 1932, Sarah Neilson. *S.* John N., Jr. and Charles Neilson. *Daus.* Sarah Louise (MacLeod) and Mary Carolyn (Cooper). *Career:* Management Trainee. McCormick & Co., Oct. 1930; member, original Jnr. Bd. of Executives (a part of Mutiple Management) 1932. Mgr., Flavouring Extract and Insecticide Depts. 1934; elected to Snr. Bd., McCormick & Co. Inc. 1935; Vice-Pres. 1936, Exec. Vice-President 1950. President 1955–70; (Ret. active participation), Chmn. Bd. 1969, Chmn. Emeritus 1977; Advisory Dir., Noxell Corp., Maryland National Bank, Former positions: Chmn. Governor's Exec. Reorganization Cttee; Dir. Maryland Properties Inc. Hunt Valley; Provident Savings Bank of Baltimore; United States Fidelity and Guaranty Co.; Baltimore Ice Sports Inc.; The Industrial Corp. Baltimore; Trustee, The Greater Baltimore Center. *Member:* Adv. Cttee. Church Home and Hospital; Trustee, the Greater Baltimore Medical Center; Phi Gamma Delta Fraternity; Omicron Delta Kappa; Mason (32 Degree K.T. Shriner). *Awards:* Ohio Wesleyan Univ. Distinguished Citizenship Award, and Hon. LLD Bd. of Govnrs., Acad. of Food Marketing St. Joseph's Coll., Philadelphia; Former Chmn., Commission for Modernization of the Exec. Branch of the Maryland Government (appointed by the Governor of the State); Former Chairman Commission for the Expansion of Public Higher Education in Maryland. *Clubs:* The Baltimore Country, The Maryland, Hunt Valley Golf; The Elkridge, (all of Baltimore), Seaview Country (Absecon, N.J.). *Address: office* McCormick & Co. Inc., 11350, McCormick Road, Hunt Valley, Md. 21031, U.S.A.

**CURLEY, Walter Joseph Patrick, Jr.** American. *B.* 1922. *Educ.* Yale Univ. (BA) and Harvard Univ. (MBA). *M.* 1948, Mary Taylor Walton. *S.* W.J.P. III, John Walton and James Mellon. *Dau.* Margaret Cowan. *Career:* With U.S. Marine Corps Reserve 1942–62; Active duty Pacific Theater (Captain) 1943–45, California Texas Oil Co. 1948–57; Caltex: India 1948–52. Italy 1952–55, and New York 1955–57; San Jacinto Petroleum Co. 1958–60; Dir. Curley Land Co. 1958—; Partner J. H. Whitney & Co. N.Y.C. 1961–75; Dir. Lenox Hill Neighbourhood Assn. 1967; Commissioner of Public Events and Chief of Protocol for New York City 1973–74; U.S. Ambassador to Ireland, 1975–77. Trustee Barnard Coll. (N.Y.); Buckley School (N.Y.). *Awards:* Breast Order of Cloud and Banner (Chinese Repub.); Bronze Star (U.S. Army); Letter of Commendation (U.S. Marine Corps.); Presidential Unit Citation; Hon. LLD, Trinity College, Dublin 1976. *Publications:* Monarchs in Waiting; Letters from the Pacific. Republican. *Clubs:* The Links, Union, Yale (all in N.Y.C.); Rolling Rock (Pittsburgh); Pittsburgh Golf; Bedford Golf; Kildare Street, St. Stephen's Green (Dublin). *Address:* 791 Park Avenue, N.Y.C.; Bedford Village, New York; Rossyvera, Newport, Mayo, Ireland; and *office* 630 Fifth Av., N.Y.C., U.S.A.

**CURRAN, Rt. Hon. Sir Lancelot Ernest.** Lord Justice of Appeal Supreme Court of Judicature, Northern Ireland 1956–75. *B.* 1899. *Educ.* Royal Belfast Academical Institution, and Queens Univ. Belfast (BA, LLB); Barrister N. Ireland 1923. *M.* 1924. Doris Lee. *S.* 2. *Dau.* 1 (*Dec.*) QC, 1943. *Career:* Served in World War I (R.F.C. and R.A.F. 1917–18); and in World War II (army, Major); M.P. Carrick Division, Co. Antrim 1945–49; Parly. Sec., Ministry of Finance and Chief Whip 1945; Attorney General 1947–49; Judge of the High Court 1949–56; Lord Justice of Appeal Supreme Court 1956–75. *Address:* Wentworth, Deramore Park, Belfast 9, Northern Ireland.

**CURRIE, William Masterton,** Canadian. *B.* 1910. *Educ.* Public and High Schools, Medicine Hat, Alta. *M.* 1956, Audrey Margaret Echlin. *S.* 1. *Daus.* 2. *Career:* Entered the service of the Canadian Bank of Commerce (est. 1867) 1927; served at branches in Alberta and the West Indies. Naval service Apr. 1943–July 1946; returned to duty with the Bank and posted to London (England) branch. Appointed: Assistant Manager, Kingston, Jamaica 1950; Manager, MortgageDept., Head Office 1954; Chief Inspector 1955;, Regional Superintendent, Winnipeg 1956; Asst. General Manager, Winnipeg 1957, and Ontario 1959; Dep. General Manager Head Office 1959; appointed Dep. General Manager at amalgamation with Imperial Bank of Canada 1961; Chief General Manager 1963 Elected Director May 1964, Vice-Chmn. of Board 1968–73; Retired 1973. Director: General Accident Assurance Co. of Canada; Scottish Canadian Assurance Corp.; Canadian Pioneer Insc. Co.; Crown Trust Co.; President, Canadian Bankers' Association June 1963–Dec. 1964. *Clubs:* Toronto, York (Toronto), Vancouver Club. *Address:* 1864 West 19th Ave., Vancouver BC, V6J 2N9, Canada.

**CURRY, George Austen.** South African. *B.* 1911. *Educ.* Clifton College, and Imperial College of Science & Technology. *M.* 1937, Olive Annie Frances Mather. *Daus.* Kahnia and Hilary. *Clubs:* Rand; Johannesburg Country; Royal Johannesburg Golf. *Address:* 5 Fifth Ave., Lower Houghton, Johannesburg, South Africa.

**CURTIS, Colin Hinton Thomson,** CVO, ISO. Australian. *B.* 1920. *Educ.* Junior Univ. *M.* 1943, Anne Catherline Drevesen. *S.* 1. *Career:* Secretary to the Premier 1949–63; Asst. Under-Secy., Premier's Dept. 1961–64; Associate Dir. and Director of Industrial Development 1964–66; Under-Secy. Premier's Dept. and Clerk of the Exect. Council 1966–70; Agent General for Queensland. London 1970–71; Chmn. Metropolitan Public Abattoir Bd. Brisbane. *Club:* RQYC. *Address:* Metropolitan Public Abattoir Board, Brisbane, Queensland, Australia.

**CURTIS, Dunstan Michael Carr,** CBE, DSC (and bar). Croix de Guerre. *B.* 1910. *Educ.* Eton and Trinity College, Oxford (Hons. in philosophy, politics and economics); after leaving the University studied law and qualified as a solicitor. *M.* Patricia Elton Mayo. *S.* 1. *Dau.* 1. *Career:* Commander, R.N.V.R. Practised as a solicitor in the City of London 1936–39; served in World War II (Commander, Royal Navy; D.S.C. and bar; Croix de Guerre) 1939–45; Liberal Candidate in General Election 1945; Second Secretary, British Embassy, Paris 1946–47; Deputy Secretary-General, the European Movement 1948–49; Counsellor (in charge of Assembly Committees), Secretariat-General of the Council of Europe 1950–54, Deputy Secretary-General 1955–62 (Registrar of the Assembly *pro tem.* 1955–56, and Secretary-General *pro tem.* 1956–57). Secy.-General European Conservative Group, Europ. Parliament since 1973. *Address:* European Parlt., CP 1601, Luxembourg.

**CURTIS, Frank Robert.** British. *B.* 1913. *M.* 1951, Evelyn Jane Watson Ferrier. *Daus.* 2. *Career:* Man. Dir. 1936–75, Chmn. 1954–75, Ranleigh Ware Pty. Ltd.; Dir. Horwood Bagshaw Ltd. since 1972. Fellow: Australian Inst. of Management (Pres. Adelaide Div. 1959–61), Inst. of Directors and of Australian Marketing Inst. (Hon.). *Member:* S. A. Chamber of Manufacturers Inc. (Press 1965–67); Assoc. Chambers of Manufacturers Aust. (Pres. 1965–67) Metal Industries Assn. of S.A. (Pres. 1963–65); Australian Association of National Advertisers, S.A. Branch (Chairman 1960–61); Australian Association of National Advertisers (Vice-Pres. 1960–61). *Clubs:* World Trade (San Francisco, U.S.A.); C.T.A. Commonwealth (S.A.); No. 10 (London, Eng.). *Address: office* 135 Shepherds Hill Road, Eden Hills, South Australia.

**CURTIS, Michael Howard.** British. *B.* 1920. *Educ.* MA Cantab (Economics, Law). *M.* 1962, Marian Joan Williams. *S.* 2. *Daus.* 2. *Career:* Editor, News Chronicle (London) 1953–57. Chairman, Nation Newspapers Ltd., Kenya, and Kenya Litho Ltd.; Executive Aide to H.H. The Aga Khan. Member, International Press Institute. *Clubs:* Garrick (London); Muthaiga (Kenya). *Address:* La Vieille Maison, Villemétrie, 60300 Senlis, France.

**CURTIS, Ronald Bryant,** MBE. Australian public accountant & business consultant. *B.* 1908. *Educ.* Wesley College, Melbourne. *M.* 1935, Gwendoline Laurel Guinea (*Dec.*). *Career:* Secretary: H. V. McKay Charitable Trust 1933–38, H. V. McKay Massey Harris (Qld.) Ltd. 1938, and Glaxo Laboratories (Aust.) Pty Ltd. 1938–47. General Secretary and Manager, The Australian Dried Fruits Association, June 1947–73; Editor, Australian Dried Fruit Journal. Secretary, Murray Industries Development Assn. Ltd., Jan. 1948–73; The Dried Fruits Stabilization Committee Ltd., May 1965–73; Director, Crowe and Newcombe Ltd., McLaren Vale Fruit Packers Ltd., Jack Horner Products Ltd., all of Adelaide. Fellow, Australian Socy. of Accountants; Associate, Chartered Inst. of Secretaries. *Clubs:* Naval & Military, (Adelaide); Melbourne Cricket; Royal Melbourne Tennis; Royal Automobile of Victoria. *Address:* 32 Kenmare Street, Mont Albert, Australia.

**CUTLER, Sir Arthur Roden,** VC, KCMG, KCVO, CBE, KStJ. Governor of New South Wales. *B.* 1916. *Educ.* Sydney Univ. (BEcon.) LLD (Hon.); Univ. of New South Wales DSc (Hon.); Univ. of Newcastle DSc (Hon.). *M.* 1946, Helen Gray Annetta Morris. *S.* 4. *Career:* Justice Dept., New South Wales, Public Trust Office 1935–42; War Service 2/5th Field Regt. A.I.F. Middle East 1940–42; State Secretary Returned Serviceman's League, N.S.W. 1942–43; Member, Aliens Classification and Advisory Committee to Advise Commonwealth Government 1942–43; Assistant Deputy Director, Security Service, N.S.W. 1943; Commonwealth Assistant Commissioner of Repatriation 1943–46; High Commissioner to New Zealand 1946–52; High Commissioner to Ceylon 1952–55; En. Ex. and Min. Plen. to Egypt July 1955–Nov. 1956; Sec.-General, Third S.E.A.T.O. Council and Military Advisers' Meeting, Canberra, March 1957; Chief of Protocol, Canberra 1957–58; Pres. Ret. Servicemen's League, Aust. Cap. Territory 1958; Australian High Commissioner to Pakistan 1959–61; Aust. Representative to Independence of Somali Republic 1960; Consul-General, New York, July 1961–65; United Nations General Assembly Delegate 1962–63–64 and Aust. Rep. to Fifth Cttee. 1962–63–64; Ambassador to the Netherlands 1965–66. Hon. Air Commodore 22 Sqn. R.A.A.F.; Hon. Col. Royal N.S.W. Reg. and of Sydney Univ. Reg. *Address:* Government House, Sydney, N.S.W., Australia.

**CUTTS, Trevett Wakeham.** Australian. *B.* 1914. *Educ.* University of Melbourne (LLB); Barrister and Solicitor of the Supreme Court of Victoria. *M.* 1945, Maidie Phyllis Stuhmcke. *S.* James, Alexander. *Career:* Joined Australian Department of External Affairs in 1946 after five years of active service in Australian Navy; apart from periods of service with that Department in Canberra, has held the following positions abroad: Attached to Australian diplomatic missions in Singapore and Indonesia 1946–50; Official Secretary, Australian High Commission, Ottawa 1952–54; Counsellor, Australian Mission to U.N., New York 1954–57; Chargé d'Affaires, Embassy, Moscow 1959–60; Consul General, San Francisco 1960–62; Ambassador to the Philippines 1963–66. High Commissioner in Pakistan, Feb. 1966–68. Ambassador to South Africa 1968–72; High Commissioner to Malta G.C. 1972–75. *Clubs:* Royal Canberra Golf. *Address:* c/o Ministry of Foreign Affairs, Canberra, ACT, Australia.

**CYRANKIEWICZ, Jozef.** *B.* 1911. *Educ.* Jagellon Univ. (Cracow). Secretary, Cracow organization of the Polish Socialist Party 1935; interned in Oswiecim (Auschwitz) concentration camp (was one of the leaders of the resistance movement there) 1941–45; General Secretary, Polish Socialist Party 1945–48. Prime Minister of Poland 1947–52 and 1954–70; Chmn. Council of State 1970–72; Member, Political Bureau of Polish United Workers Party 1948–71; Central Ctteo. Polish United Workers Party 1971; Presidium of Werld Peace Council since 1973. *Address:* Ogolnopolski Komitet Pokoju, ul. Rajcow 10, Warsaw, Poland.

# D

**DADDAH, Moktar Ould.** President of the Islamic Republic of Mauritania, Minister of Foreign Affairs, and of Defence, and Secretary-General of the People's Party—Hisb Al-Chaab. *B.* 1924. *Educ.* Medersa of Boutilimit (primary); and School of Interpreters in St. Louis, Senegal (secondary). *Career:* An interpreter 1942–49, a student in France 1949–54, when he received his baccalaureat at Nice and his licence in law in Paris; finally he graduated from the School of Oriental Languages in 1955. Returning home, he became a registered lawyer at the Dakar Bar. In 1957, politics attracted him as a means to national autonomy. Elected Territorial Councillor of the Adar in March of that year, he became Vice-President of the Governing Council and Minister of Youth, Sports and Education. In the following July he decided to transfer the capital of Mauritania from St. Louis to Nouakchott, and thus elaborated his plans for the new capital. Served successively as Vice-Pres. and Pres. of the Council, and Minister of Information and Inter-Territorial Affairs Jan.–Nov. 1958. Became Secretary-General of the Provisional Executive Committees of the Mauritanian Regroupment Party (P.R.M.), June 1958; Pres. Min. of Nat. Defence and Min. of Foreign Affairs since 1961. Pres. Org. Commune Africaine et Malgache 1965; Leader, Parti du Peuple. *Address:* The Presidential Residence, Nouakchott, Mauritania.

**DAENZER, Bernard John,** LLB, CPCU. *B.* 1916. *Educ.* Fordham Univ. (AB *cum laude* 1937) and Fordham Law School (LLB 1942). *M.* 1941, Valerie Antoinette Lee. *S.* Peter, John and Richard. *Dau.* Jean. *Career:* Exec. Vice-Pres. and Director, Security-Connecticut Companies 1943–57. American. President and Director, Wohlreich & Anderson Ltd.; Pres. and Dir., Drake Insurance Co. of N.Y.; Director, Alex Howden Group Ltd., 3 Billiter Street, London, E.C.3, England 1957—; RLI Corp; Cranford Insurance Co. *Publications:* Insurance Marketing in the United States 1963. Excess & Surplus Lines Manual 1970; Fact Finding Techniques in Risk Analysis 1970. *Member:* Trustee and Vice-Chmn., College of Insurance; Chartered Property and Casualty Underwriting; Member Lloyd's of London; American and New York Bar Associations; American Management Association. *Clubs:* Orange Lawn Tennis (South Orange, N.J.); Union League (N.Y.C.); Echo Lake Country (Westfield); Ocean Reef; Key Largo. *Address:* (summer) 19 Coleman Lane, Lavallette, N.J. 08735; and (winter) 29 Anglefish Cay Drive, Key Largo, Fla. 33037; and *office* 6 Commerce Drive, Cranford, N.J. 07016, U.S.A.

**DAHL, George Leighton.** American councilman and architect. City Councilman, Highland Park, Dallas, also Member, City Planning Committee. *B.* 1894. *Educ.* University of Minnesota (Bach. Arch.); Harvard University (MArch); Harvard Fellowship, American Academy, Rome. *M.* 1922, Lille Olsen (*Dec.*). *Dau.* Gloria Lille Dahl Akin. *Career:* Dahl, Braden Jones & Chapman (partner). *Publications:* Doors and Portals of France; monographs. Hon. Fellow Amer. Inst. of Architects. *Member:* American Institute of Architects; Military Engineers; Texas Society of Architects; City Planning Committee. *Clubs:* Harvard; Dallas Country; Book Hollow Golf; City; Dallas; Lancers; Petroleum. *Address:* 3601 Turtle Creek Boulevard, Dallas, Texas; and *office* Suite 310 Turtle Creek Village, #2, Dallas, Texas, U.S.A.

**DAHLGAARD, Tyge.** Danish Diplomat. Ambassador to Japan and Korea 1972–76, to the Netherlands since 1976. *Address:* Royal Danish Embassy, Koninginnegracht 30, The Hague, Netherlands.

**DAHLMAN, Sven Werner.** Swedish diplomat. *B.* 1905. *Educ.* Upsala University (BA). *M.* 1936, Brita Westberg. *Career:* Journalist (Upsala Nya Tidning) 1933–36; Press Attaché, Helsingfors 1936–39; First Secretary and Counsellor of Legation, Washington, D.C. 1940–46; Chief of Press Section, Foreign office 1946–48; Dir. of Political Affairs, Foreign Office 1948–52; En. Ex. and Min. Plen. to the Netherlands 1952–56; Ambassador 1956–61; Ambassador to United Arab Republic 1961–62. Adviser on International Relations, Federation of Swedish Industries 1962–70; Lord in Waiting to The King of Sweden 1969–1973. *Address:* c/o Ministry of Foreign Affairs, Stockholm, Sweden.

**DAHRENDORF, Prof. Ralf.** German Professor and Director of London School of Economics. *B.* 1929. *Educ.* Univ. of Hamburg, Dr. phil; London School of Economics PhD.; Fellow Imp. Coll. Sc. & Tech. (London) *M.* 1954, Vera D. Banister. *Daus.* 3. *Career:* Assistant (since 1954) and Privatdozent (since 1957) of Sociology at Univ. of the Saar (Saarbrücken); Fellow, Centre for Advanced Study in Behavioral Sciences, Palo Alto 1957–58; Prof. of Sociology at Hamburg 1958; Tubingen 1960, Constance 1964–66; Chmn. Commission on Compr. Univ. Planning 1967–68; mem. German Council on Education 1966–68; Adviser on educ. questions of the Land Govt. of Baden-Wurttemburg 1964–68; Vice-chmn. of founding cttee. of University of Constance 1964–66; chmn. of commission on comprehensive University Planning (Hochschulgesamtplan) 1967–68; mem. of German Council on Education 1966–68; Mem. of Free Democratic Party 1967, mem. of Fed. Exec. of FDP 1968–74; mem. of Land Diet of Baden-Württemberg and Vice-chmn. of FDP parly. party 1968–69; mem. of Fed. parlt. (Bundestag) and Parly. Secy. of State in For. Office 1969–70; mem. of Commission of Euopean Communities since 1970, responsible for external relations and for. trade 1970–73, research in science and education 1973–74; Dir. of London School of Economics since Oct. 1974. *Honours:* hon degrees at Reading (D. Litt.), Manch. (Ll.D), New Univ. of Ulster (D.Sc), Open Univ. (D.Univ.), Kalamazoo Coll. (DHL), hon fellow of LSE; hon. mem. Royal Irish Academy, Trinity Coll., Dublin (Litt. D) 1975; Université Catholique de Louvain (Hon. Dr.) 1977; Wagner Coll., N.Y. (LLD) 1977; Univ. of Bath (DSc) 1977; Foreign Hon. Mem., American Acad. of Arts & Sciences since 1975; Senator of Max-Planck-Gesellschaft since 1975; Trustee of the Ford Foundation since 1976; Fellow, Royal Acad. of Arts 1977; Foreign Assoc., Nat. Acad. of Sciences, Washington, D.C. 1977; Foreign Mem., American Philosophical Soc., Philadelphia 1977; Fellow, British Academy 1977; Chmn., Social Science Council of the European Science Foundation since 1976; Mem. on Royal Commission on Legal Services, 1976; Mem. of the Cttee. to Review the Functioning of Financial Institutions 1977. *Awards:* Journal Fund Award for Learned Publications, 1966; Reith Lecturer 1974; Grosses Bundesverdienstkreuz mit Stern und Schulterband, 1974 (FRG); Grosses goldenes Ehrenzeichen am Bande fur Verdienste um die R. Ost. (Republic of Austria); Grand Croix de l'Ordre du Mérite du Sénegal 1971; Grand Croix de l'Ordre du Mérite du Luxembourg 1974; Grand Croix de l'Ordre de Léopold II 1975 (Belgium). *Publications:* many including: Marx in Perspective (1953); Industrie—und Betriebssoziologie (1956, trans into 4 langs); Playdoyer fur die Europaische Union (1973); The New Liberty (1975). *Address:* London School of Economics and Political Sc., Houghton St., London WC2A 2AE.

**d'AILLIERES, Fernand Comte.** Chief of Protocol to H.S.H. the Prince of Monaco. Minister of Monaco in Belgium 1960–65. *B.* 1916. *Educ.* Univs. of Paris, Brussels, London and Geneva. *M.* (1) 1940, Jurien de la Gravière; and (2) 1951, Countess Eve Mörner of Morlanda. *Dau.* Catherine. *Career:* in the service of the Prince since 1945; Minister of Monaco in Belgium 1960–65; in Switzerland 1965; Luxembourg 1970; Federal Republic of Germany 1970. *Awards:* Médaille Militaire; Croix de Guerre 1939–45; Grand Cross Order of the Crown (Belgium), Order of Leopold II, Order of Merit (Luxembourg); Comdr., Order of St. Charles (Monaco), Order of Grimaldi (Monaco); Chevalier Merit (Italy); Ouissam Alaouita; Comdr. de l'Etoile Noire du Benin; Chevalier de Polonia Restituta. *Clubs:* Jockey; St. Cloud Country; Racquet & Tennis (New York). *Address:* Palace of Monaco, Principality of Monaco.

**DAKIN, Allin Winston,** *B.* 1905. *Educ.* State Univ. of Iowa (BA 1926, MA 1927) and Harvard Univ. Business School (MBA 1931); unmarried. *Career:* Instructor in Commerce, State Univ. of Iowa 1926–29; with J. & W. Seligman & Co., international banker, N.Y.C. 1931–34; Bursar and Instructor, Robert College, Istanbul (Turkey) 1934–39; Comptroller, Associated Colleges (Pomona, Scripps, Claremont), California 1940–44. Administrative Dean, State University of Iowa, Iowa City 1944–73; Dean Emeritus since 1973. Rotary International: Vice-Pres. 1956–57, Governor 1953–54, Chairman: Fellowships Committee 1955–57; Miami International Convention 1960; Finance Committee 1962–64; (Program Planning Committee 1964–66; Youth Activities Cttee., 1968–69; Public Relations Cttee. 1966—; Iowa Community Service 1970–71. Director, Iowa City Chamber of Commerce 1957–60; Partners for the Alliance for Progress; Chmn., Airport Commission. *Awards:* Hon. LLD Westmar Coll. 1961; Service to Mankind Award from Sertoma International 1976; Citation of Merit, Iowa City Rotary Club 1976; Hancher-Finkbine Medallion from Univ. of Iowa for Leadership, Learning, Loyalty; Scroll of Honor, UN Assn., Iowa.. Pres. U.N., Iowa Div. (1962–70). Contributor of articles to various magazines. Republican. *Member:* Amer. Geographical Socy. (Fellow); Archaeological Inst. of Amer. (Fellow). *Member:* Foreign Policy Assn., Natl. Geographic Socy., Natl. Education Assn., Sigma Nu, Delta Sigma Rho, Omicron Delta Kappa, Alpha Phi Omega; Boy Scouts; Nat. Council; Regional & local Eagle Silver Beaver and Antelope Awards. *Clubs:* Triangle. Athletic (Iowa City); Harvard (N.Y.C.); Elks. Shrine. Masons. *Address:* 329 Ellis Avenue, Iowa City, Ia. 522240; U.S.A.

**DALE, Claude O.** American professional engineer. *B.* 1916. *Educ.* Univ. of Montana School of Mines (BS Min. Eng.). *M.* 1948, Valora Fairbanks. *S.* Gregory J. *Daus.* Gayla and Sandra. *Career:* Previously: Asst. Gen. Mgr., Mining and Milling Operations, Illinois-Wisconsin, The Eagle-Picher Co. 1950–57; Asst. Gen. Mgr., Mining and Smelting Div. same company. Manager, Mining, and Vice-President, Eagle-Picher Industries Inc. to 1975; Pres., Sam-Bear Gold Co. since 1975. *Member:* Amer. Zinc. Inst.; A.I.M.E.; Amer. Mining Congress; Professional Engineers; National Defense Executive Reserve; Miami Chamber of Commerce (Dir.); Mason; Jesters; Elks. *Clubs:* Miami Country; Lions. *Address:* Box 302, Twin Bridges, Mont. 59754, U.S.A.

**DALE, John Denny.** American economist. *B.* 1916. *Educ.* Hamilton Coll. (AB 1936); Graduate School of Business, New York University (MBA 1954, PhD 1962). *M.* 1938, Louise Boyd Lichtenstein (*Div.* 1960). *S.* John Denny, Jr. *Dau.* Anne Boyd. *M.* (2) 1961, Madeline Houston McWhinney. *S.* Thomas Denny. *Career:* Divisional Mngr., Amer. Steel Export Co. 1936–40; successively Asst. to President 1940, Vice-President and Director 1941–45 and President-Chairman 1945–55, Charles Hardy Inc.; Active duty World War II and Korean War; commissioned 1943 2nd Lt. AUS; Man. Dir., Dale Chemurgy Co. 1946–50; Chmn., Manufacturers Marketing Co. 1949–50. Retd. Col., U.S. Army Reserve (1974) also Adviser: War Production Board 1941 and Chief Ordnance, U.S. Army 1952–55. Past-Pres. & Dir., Alumni Assn.; Dir., N.Y. University Alumni Fed.; Chmn. and Pres., Dale Elliott & Co. Inc. 1956–65; Former Chairman, Charles Hardy Inc; Director, Airport Industries Inc.; Technical Director: Charles Hardy Ltd., London; Steep Rock Iron Mines Ltd.; Premium Ores Ltd.; Leaseway Ltd.; Sea-Pool Fisheries Ltd.; Chmn., Dale, Elliott & Co. Inc.; Economist with Dept. of Labor & Industry, State of New Jersey. *Member:* National Planning Council; Trustee, Monmouth Medical Center, and Advisory Bd., Root Art Center; Pres., Amer. Defense Preparedness Assn, and Hudson River Conservation Socy. *Awards:* Legion of Merit; Meritorious Service Medal, Army Comm. Medal (with pendant). *Clubs:* University Glee; Racquet & Tennis; Knights of Malta; New York Athletic; Explorers; Bohemians (N.Y.C.); Rumson Country; Navesink Country. *Address:* P.O. Box 458, Red Bank, N.J. 07701, U.S.A.

**DALE, Ralph David.** British company director. *B.* 1914. *Educ.* Eton. *M.* 1937, Elizabeth Grace Marriage. *S.* Peter David Sandwith. *Dau.* Helen Elizabeth (Hornett). *Career:* Articled Clerk to Deloitte, Plender, Griffiths & Co. (qualified 1937) 1931–37; Mgr., J. H. L. Manisty, Stockbrokers, Johannesburg 1937–39; Military Service with Union of South Africa Defence Forces (Transvaal Scottish; final rank Major) 1939–46; Information Officer, The Diamond Corp. London 1946–48; Assistant to Directors in London, Anglo American Corp. of South Africa Ltd. 1948–49; Sales Executive, Rhokana Corp., London 1949–50; Dir., Brandhurst Co. Ltd.. Metal Brokers, London 1951–61; Man. Dir., Fergusson, Wild & Co. Ltd. 1961–62 & Chmn. 1962–72 & 1973–76; Chmn., Fergusson, Wild (Metals) Ltd., 1962–72 & 1973–76; Joint Man. Dir., E. A. Gibson Fergusson Wild (Shipbrokers) Ltd. 1962–69 & Joint Chmn. 1969–73; Chmn., Burton Rowe & Viner Ltd. 1965–68; Burton Rowe & Viner (Overseas) Ltd. 1965–68; Burton Rowe & Viner (Life & Pension) Assurances Ltd. 1965–68; Dir., William Baird Mining Ltd. 1966–69 & Man. Dir. 1969–76; Dir. Gibson Transportation Ltd. 1966–73; Joint Chmn. Gibson, Fergusson Wild, Clark Ltd. 1967–72; Dir., Gibson Shipbrokers Ltd. 1968–73; Swire, McGregor. Gibson Pty Ltd. 1969–71; Uni/Logistics Consultants Ltd 1969–73; Canada Marine Chartering Ltd. 1969–73; Chmn., William Baird Services Ltd. 1969–72 & 1973–76; Pres., Aumas, Fergusson Wild Ltd. 1969–72 & Dir. 1973–76; Dir., William Baird Services (Prospecting) Ltd. 1969–76; Chmn., Baird Travel Ltd. 1969–72 & Dir. 1973–76; Dir., Baird Mining (Australia) Pty Ltd. 1969–76; Chmn. W. & M. Gale Ltd. 1970–72; Chmn. Worldwide Hotel Property Services Pty. Ltd. 1971–72; Chmn., Worldwide Mining Services Pty. Ltd. 1971–76; Chmn., Worldwide Purchasing & Management Services Pty. Ltd. 1971–76; Dir. William Baird Finance & Services Ltd. 1972–73 and Deputy Chmn. 1973; Pres., Overseas Mining Assn. 1975; Dir., William Baird & Co. Ltd. 1969–72 & Dep. Chmn. since 1972; Sierra Leone Development Co. Ltd. since 1969; Dir. Mining & General Services Ltd. since 1969; Governor & Dir. The Old Malthouse School Trust Ltd. 1957–74 & Chmn. since 1974. Fellow Institute of Chartered Accountants in England and Wales. *Clubs:* Junior Carlton, 20–Ghost, Rolls-Royce Enthusiasts' (all London); Rand, Country (both Johannesburg), Rolls-Royce Owners (U.S.A.). *Address:* Lord's Hill Cottage, Shamley Green, Surrey GU5 0UZ; and *office* William Baird & Co. Ltd., City Wall House, 84/90 Chiswell Street, London EC1Y 4TP.

**DALEY, Air Vice-Marshal Edward Alfred,** CBE KStJ. Hon. Physician to H.M. The Queen 1953–61 and formerly to H.M. King George VI. *B.* 1901. *Educ.* Caulfield Grammar School, Melbourne, and University of Melbourne (MB, BS); Diploma Tropical Medicine, Liverpool University; Fellow, Royal Australian College of Physicians (FRACP). *M.* 1927, Katharine. *G. Dau.* of J. S. Wrightsmith. *Career:* Joined resident hospital staffs in Victoria until 1928; Hon. Surgical Clinical Asst., Royal Melbourne Hosp. 1927–36; Flt.-Lieut., R.A.A.F. Medical Service 1928; graduated as pilot 1930; promoted Squadron-Leader 1933; exchange duty with R.A.F. 1936–38; Wing-Commander and Dpty. D.M.S. 1938; Group-Captain 1940; served with R.A.A.F. in Middle East with air ambulance unit 1941; served in England, Europe and Pacific areas 1944; Air Commodore and Dpty. Director-General (later Dir.-Gen.) of Medical Services 1945; duty in England with R.A.F. 1950; and in Japan and Korea 1951 and 1953; Air Vice-Marshall 1952; Director-General, Medical Services, R.A.A. 1945–61. Former Chairman, St. John Ambulance Association, Melbourne (now Australian Priory, Director of Ambulance); Initial Chairman, Aviation Medicine Section (British Medical Association), Australia; Vice-Pres., Aero Medical Assn. Washington 1954–55; former member, Council of Australian Red Cross Society; President Royal Flying Doctor Service, 1965–68. *Publications:* Reaction Time and Flying Ability (1932); Modern Trends in Aviation Medicine (Med. Jnl. of Australia 1952); Casualty Air Evacuation (Aircraft Jnl. 1951); Aviation Medicine Progress in Australia over Twenty-Five years. *Address:* 24 Nott Street, East Malvern, Victoria, Australia.

**DALLEY, Christopher Mervyn,** CMG, MIMechE, FInstPet. British. *B.* 1913. *Educ.* Epsom Coll.; Queens' Coll., Cambridge (MA Hons). *M.* 1947, Elizabeth Alice Gammell. *S.* 1. *Daus.* 3. *Career:* Formerly Chmn. Iraq Petroleum Co. Ltd., Basrah Petroleum Co. Ltd., Abu Dhabi Petroleum Co. Ltd., Qatar Petroleum Co. Ltd. and associated cos.; formerly Dir. Iranian Oil Producing Co.; Chmn. Oil Exploration Holdings Ltd.; Chmn. Viking Jersey Equip. Ltd.; Dir. Viking Resources Trust Ltd. *Address:* 6 Godfrey St., London S.W.3; Mead Hse., Woodham Walter, Nr. Maldon, Essex.

**DALTON, Harry L.** *B.* 1908. *Educ.* Duke University (BA, Hon. LHD), New York Univ. (post-graduate work), and Call. of Technology, Manchester (Eng.). *M.* 1928, Mary Keesler, *S.* David McRae. *Dau.* Mary Elizabeth. *Career:* Member of Board, AVC Corp. Chmn. of Board, Shaw Manufacturing Co. (Charlotte, N.C.), and Falco Corp. Press., Kartox Oil Co. Chairman: Wachovia Bank & Trust Co. (Charlotte), and Adv. Cttee. of Chase National Bank. Director: Minerals Research & Development Corp., Ree Viking Corp., Carlton Yarn Corp., and Microtron Corp. Chmn. Exec. Cttee., American Credit Corp. Member Exec. Cttee. and Dir.: Pyramide Life Insurance Co., and Carolina Capital Corp. Member, Advisory Board, National Securities Corp; Delta Associates; Bruce Johnson Trucking; Investment

Life & Trust. Chmn. Patrons' Cttee. Queen's Coll., and of Friends Library, Duke Univ. Advisory Bd. of Visitors: Davidson, Queen's Furman and Wingate Colleges; Pres. Melodaire Friends UNC; Bd. N.C. Museum of Art Mint Museum; N.C. Arts Council; Bd. Charlotte, Country Day Alexanders Children Home. *Address:* 1212 Wachovia Bank & Trust Co., Charlotte. N.C., U.S.A.

**DALY, Francis P.** Irish. *B.* 1922. *Educ.* Ampleforth College. *M.* 1947, Margaret Daly. *S.* 3. *Daus.* 3. *Career:* Joint Managing Director, James Daly & Sons Ltd., Cork. Director, James Daly & Sons (Overseas) Ltd., Nomed Ltd.; British Fondants Cake Decorations Ltd.; Guardian Foods Ltd.; James Daly & Sons (Machinery) Ltd. *Address:* Coole, Tivoli, Cork; and *office* 30 Shandon Street, Cork, Ireland.

**DALY, Patrick Joseph.** Irish. *B.* 1925. *Educ.* Ampleforth Coll. (York) and Cambridge Univ. (BA in Law); FCA. *M.* 1956, Ann Newman (Toronto, Canada). *S.* Patrick and Julian. *Daus.* Sarah and Martina. *Career:* Man. Dir. James Daly & Sons Ltd. since 1954. Dir. Nomed Ltd. since 1960; Dir. Ulster Bank Ltd. 1969; Dir. Brit. Fondants Cake Decorations Ltd. 1969. *Member:* Inst. of Chartered Accountants in Ireland; Inst. of Marketing. *Clubs:* Lions International. *Address: office* James Daly & Sons Ltd., Shandon Castle, Cork, Ireland.

**DALYELL, Tam,** MA, MP. British politician. *B.* 1932. *Educ.* Cambridge Univ. History & Economics. *M.* 1963. Kathleen Wheatley. *S.* Gordon. *Dau.* Moira. *Career:* Teacher Bo'ness Academy 1957–60; Director of Studies on Shipschool Dunera 1960–62; Member of Parliament for West Lothian since 1962; Member Public Accounts Cttee. 1963–66; Parly. Private Secy. Rt Hon. Richard Crossman 1964–70; Science & Technology Select. Cttee. 1966—68; Scottish Trade Delegation China 1971. Chmn. Parly. Labour Party. Foreign Affairs Group 1974–75; Parly. Labour Party Liaison Cttee. Vice-Chmn. since 1974; Vice-Chmn., Parly. Labour Party 1974–75; Member of European Parlt. and Budget Cttee, and Socialist Bureau of Europ. Parlt. since 1975. *Publications:* The Case for Ships-Schools (1959); Ships-School Dumera (1962); Devolution: The End of Britain? (1977); Columnist New Scientist since 1968, Daily Record 1967–70. *Clubs:* Queens Tennis. *Address:* Binns, Linlithgow; and *office* House of Commons, London, S.W.1.

**d'AMELIO, Count Carlo.** Italian lawyer and publicist. *B*. 1902. *Educ.* Univ. of Rome. *M.* Anna Rocca de Sangro. *S.* 1. *Daus.* 6. *Career:* Title of nobleman; Vatican and Maltese decorations. Pres.: Consigliere Superiore, and Pres. Cons of Regenst della Banca d'Italia. *Publications:* Books and articles on juridical subjects. *Clubs:* Circolo degli Scacchi; Governor Rotary, Rome. *Address:* Piazza Paquale Paoli 3, Rome, Italy.

**DAMON, Roger Conant.** American banker. *B.* 1906. *Educ.* Hotchkiss Sch., Yale College (BA, and Stonier Graduate School of Banking. *M.* 1931, Ruth T. Hawley. *Dau.* Martha H. (Ward, Jr.). *Career:* Joined staff of The First National Bank of Boston 1929; Vice-Pres. 1943; Senior Vice-Pres. 1952; President 1959. Chairman of the Board and Chief Exec. Officer, The First National Bank of Boston 1966–71; First National Boston Corp. 1970–71 (Director 1956–75; Hon. Dir. since 1975). Director: New England Mutual Life Insurance Co.; Raytheon Co.; Howard Johnson Co.; Hon. Dir., Liberty Mutual Insurance Co. & Liberty Mutual Fire Insurance Co.; Trustee Mitre Corp.; Trustee: The Children's Hosp. Medical Center; LLD Northeastern Univ. 1971. Member of Corp., Museum of Science; North Eastern University. *Address:* 100 Federal Street, Rm. 7121, Boston, Mass., 02110, U.S.A.

**DANAHER, Eugene Ives.** American. Director of Material Control and Traffic, *B.* 1923. *Educ.* Univ of Calif. (BS 1943), and Stanford Univ. Graduate School of Business (MBA 1945; PhD 1946). *M.* 1946, Betty LaVerne Kefauver. *S.* Eugene Albert, Brian Grayson and Scott Ives. *Career:* Plant Manager: Fisher Body St. Louis Plant 1962–65, and Fisher Body Framingham Plant 1960–62; Plant Superintendent, Fisher Body Baltimore Plant 1958–60; Production Manager, Fisher Body Pontiac Plant 1956–60; Dir. of Material Control and Traffic, Fisher Body Div. Gen. Motor Corp. 1960–70; Group Dir. of Material Handling and Traffic since 1970. *Publications:* Apprenticeship Practice in the United States (1945); The Federal Training Within Industry Program (1946). *Member:* Beta Gamma Sigma; Phi Beta Kappa; Society of Automotive Engineers; Engineering Society of Detroit (Mich.). *Address: office* 30001 Van Dyke Boulevard, Warren, Mich. 48090, U.S.A.

**DĂNĂLACHE, Florian.** Romanian politician. *B.* 1915. *S.* I. *Dau.* I. *Career:* with Grivita Railway Workshops 1929–45; Minister of Railways 1966–69; Chmn. Central Council, General Fed. Romania's Trade Unions 1969–71; Minister Transport & Telecommunications 1971–72; Chmn., Central Union of Handicraft Co-operatives since 1972. *Member:* Romanian Communist Party 1944—; Secy. Prahova Regional Cttee. R.C.P. 1952–54; First Secy. Bucharest Town Cttee. R.C.P. 1954–66; Member Central Cttee. R.C.P. 1955—; Exec. Cttee. CC. of R.C.P. 1967—; Nat. Council, Exec. Bureau of the Front of Socialist Unity since 1970; Hero of Socialist Labour 1971. *Address:* UCECOM, Calea Plenne; 46, Bucharest, Romania.

**DANDISON, Basil Gray.** *B.* 1900. *Educ.* Univ. of Michigan (AB). *M.* 1930, Minnie Joy Remick. *S.* Basil Gray, Jr. *Daus.* Mrs. John A. Paton and Mrs. Edmund F. Nolan. *Career:* In U.S. Marine Corps 1918–23; Dir. McGraw-Hill Publishing Co. Ltd. Maidenhead (Eng.) 1958—; McGraw-Hill Co. of Canada Ltd. Toronto 1959—; Senior Vice Pres. McGraw-Hill Book Co. N.Y.C. 1961—; Air Dispatch Inc. since 1967. *Trustee:* U.S. Council, International Chamber of Commerce 1959—; Bureau of University Travel 1947—, and H. H. Powers Fellowship Fund 1957—. *Publications:* Color Media (Jnl. of Applied Psychology). Recipient, as Director of International Div. of McGraw-Hill Book Co. of 'E' for Export Award from President of U.S. 1962. Chmn., Foreign Trade Committee, American Textbook Publishers Inst. *Member:* Japan Society; Chmn., Committee on Piracy, American Book Publishers Council. Consultant in Brazil for Agency for International Development on book distribution in Higher Education. Consultant in Lebanon for International Exec. Service Corp. on book publishing, and in Indonesia for Agency for Int. Development on book distribution. Republican. *Club:* Univ. of Michigan (N.Y.C.). *Address: office* 330 West 42nd Street, New York City, U.S.A.

**DANFORTH, Douglas Dewitt.** *B.* 1922. *Educ.* Syracuse Univ. (BS Mech. Eng. 1947). *M.* 1943, Janet M. Piron. *S.* Douglas Dewitt, Jr. *Daus.* Barbara L., Susan J. and Debra L. *Career:* Vice-Pres., Industrial Group, Westinghouse 1963–64 (Vice-Pres., Industrial Control 1961–63); Exec. Vice-Pres., Industria Electrica de Mexico (Westinghouse affiliate) 1955–60. Plant Mgr., Locke Insulator, General Electric 1953–55; Vice-Pres.-Gen. Mgr., General Electric of Mexico 1948–53; Supt. of Planning, Easy Washer Machine Corp. 1946–48; Exec. Vice-Pres. Components & Materials Westinghouse Electric Co. since 1964; Pres. Westinghouse Electric Corp. since 1974. *Award:* Westinghouse Silver 'W'—Order of Merit. *Member:* N.E.M.A. and G.A.M.A. *Clubs:* Longvue (Pittsburgh); Chartiers Country (Pittsburgh). *Address: office* Westinghouse Bldg. Gateway Centre, Pittsburgh, Pa., U.S.A.

**DANIEL (Elbert) Clifton, Jr.** Newspaperman. *B.* 1912. *Educ.* Univ. of North Carolina (AB 1933), LLD DLitt 1970. *M.* 1956, Margaret Truman. *S.* Clifton Truman, William Wallace, Harrison Gates and Thomas Washington. *Career:* Associate Editor, Daily Bulletin, Dunn N.C. 1933–34; reporter News & Observer, Raleigh, N.C. 1933–37; with Associated Press in New York City, Washington, Berne, and London 1937–43. With N.Y. Times 1944—, stationed in London, with SHAEF HQ. in Paris, in Middle East, in Germany, U.S.S.R. 1954–55; New York City 1955—; Assistant Managing Editor 1959–64, Managing Editor 1964–69. Associate Editor, The New York Times since 1969; Washington bureau chief 1973–76. *Awards:* Overseas Press Club for best reporting abroad, 1955. *Club:* Century Association. *Address:* 229 West 43rd Street, New York City 10036, U.S.A.

**DANIEL (Mrs.) Eleanor S.** Economist. *B.* 1917. *Educ.* Mount Holyoke College (BA 1936), and Columbia University (MA 1937). *M.* 1952, John Carl Daniel. *S.* Charles Timothy. *Dau.* Victoria Ann. *Career:* Research Economist, U.S. Steel Corp. 1938; Lecturer in Economics, Brooklyn Coll. 1939–40; with Mutual Life Insurance Co. of N.Y. since 1940; has served on various technical advisory committees of National Bureau of Economic Research; Director of Economic Research, The Mutual Life Insurance Co. of New York 1955–72; Chief Economist, Vice-Pres. since 1972.; Insurance Director, American Finance Assn. 1957–59; member, Life Ins. Investment Research Committee 1957–61; testified before Joint Economic Committee of U.S. Congress 1955; Consultant to Board of Governors of Federal Reserve System 1955. Chairman, Downtown Economists. (N.Y.C.) 1964–66; Business Research Advisory Com., B.L.S. (U.S. Dept. Labor); Grants Review Panel, U.S. Dept. Health, Ed., Welfare; Economic Advisory Board (U.S. Dept. Commerce) 1971; Pres. Women's Bond Club 1972—. *Publications:* Our National Debt and Our

Savings (Committee on Public Debt. Policy); contributor to professional publications. Williston Senior Prize Scholar; Spalding Latin Scholar, and Bardwell Fellow, Mt. Holyoke; Perkins Fellow. Columbia University; Phi Beta Kappa. *Clubs:* Vice-Pres. Bond Club, New York; Sect.-Treas. Forecasters, N.Y. *Address: office* 1740 Broadway, New York City 19, U.S.A.

**DANIELS, Jonathan Worth.** American editor and author. *B.* 1902. *Educ.* Univ. of North Carolina (AB 1921; MA 1922); Columbia Univ. (studied law and passed N.C. Bar exam. but never practised law). *M.* (1) 1923, Elizabeth Bridgers (*Dec.* Dec. 1929). (2) Lucy Cathcart Daniels. *Daus.* Elizabeth (Squire) (by first marriage), Adelaide (Key), Lucy (Inman) and Cleves (Weber). *Career:* Staff writer, Fortune magazine 1930; Associate Editor, The News & Observer 1932; Assistant Director of Civilian Defence, Washington, D.C. 1942; Administrative Assistant and Press Secretary to President Roosevelt 1942–45; Executive Editor, The News & Observer 1947; Editor 1948–70; Editor Emeritus since 1970. *Publications:* Clash of Angels (which gained Guggenheim Fellowship 1930) (1930); A Southerner Discovers the South (1938); A Southerner Discovers New England (1940); Tar Heels—A Portrait of North Carolina (1941); Frontier on the Potomac (1946); The Man of Independence (1950); The End of Innocence (1954); Prince of Carpetbaggers (1958); Mosby, Gray Ghost of the Confederacy (1959); Stonewall Jackson (1959); Robert E. Lee (1960); The Devil's Backbone—The Story of the Natchez Trace (1962); They Will be Heard (1965); The Time Between the Wars (1966); Washington Quadville (1968); Ordeal or Ambition (1970); The Randolphs of Virginia (1972); The Gentlemany Serpent (1974); White House Witness (1975). Democrat. *Address:* Hilton Head Island, S.C., U.S.A.

**DANIELS, Troy Cook.** American professor of pharmacy, pharmaceutical chemistry and allied subjects. *B.* 1899. *Educ.* University of Michigan (BS); Indiana University (PhD). *M.* 1929, Elizabeth C. Holland. *S.* Troy Edward. *Dau.* Margaret Jean. *Career:* Instructor (1923–24), Assistant Professor (1924–27), Washington State College; Assistant in Organic Chemistry, Indiana University (1928–29); Assistant Professor of Pharmacy (1929–33), Professor of Pharmaceutical Chemistry 1933–67; Assistant Dean, College of Pharmacy (1937–43), and Dean, School of Pharmacy, University of California 1944–67; member, American Chemical Society (Chmn. Calif. Section 1944–45). President, Amer. Assn. of Colleges of Pharmacy 1952–53; Revision Committee of U.S. Pharmacopoeia 1950–60; Fellow, N.Y. Acad. of Sciences; Hon. member, Japanese Pharmaceutical Association, and Pharmaceutical Socy. of Japan; Chairman, House of Delegates, American Pharmaceutical Assn. 1956–57 (member of the Council—3-year term from May 1958; re-elected for a further term Nov. 1960); LLD (Hon.). Univ. of Calif., DSc Hon. Univ. of Mich. Hon. President American Pharmaceutical Association 1967–68; Dean Emeritus and Prof. Emeritus. Charter member, Western Pharmacology Society; Life member, American Pharmaceutical Association; Hon. member, Council of Deans, National Association on Standard Medical Vocabulary; Member, Editorial Advisory Board, Journal of Pharmaceutical Sciences 1961–66. *Publications:* More than 80 (scientific and educational). *Address:* School of Pharmacy, University of California, San Francisco 94143, California, U.S.A.

**DANIYALOV, Abdurakham Danilalovich.** Party leader, statesman. *B.* 1908; graduated from the Water Economy Engineering Institute 1935, and the Correspondence Branch of the Higher Party School at the C.P.S.U. Central Committee 1948. *Career:* Has held leading government and Party posts since 1937. Chmn. Council of Ministers, Daghestan Autonomous Soviet Socialist Republic 1940–48; First Secretary, Daghestan Regional Cttee. of the Communist Party, 1948–68; Alternate Member, C.P.S.U. Central Cttee. (Member 1956—); Deputy to the Daghestan Autonomous S.S.R. 1958—; Chairman, Presidium of the Supreme Soviet of the Daghestan Autonomous Soviet Socialist Republic 1968—; Member, Presidium of the Supreme Soviet of the Union of Soviet Socialist Republic's (USSR) 1950–62 and 1966—. Member of the Central Committee of the Communist Party; Deputy to the Supreme Soviet of the U.S.S.R. Recipient of Orders and Medals of the U.S.S.R. *Address:* Presidium of the Daghestan A.S.S.R. Supreme Soviet, Makhachkala, Daghestan A.S.S.R., U.S.S.R.

**DANJCZEK, William Emil.** American executive. *B.* 1913. *Educ.* Columbia University (N.Y.C.) and Charles University, Prague (Dr. juris 1935). *M.* 1935, Erna Lob. *S.* Thomas Arthur, Michael Harvey and David William. *Daus.* Mrs. Wm. Downes, Mrs. Mark A. Jorgensen. *Career:* Market Research, L. & C. Hardtmuth (Great Britain) Ltd., Croydon, England 1938–39; President: Koh-i-Noor Rapidograph Inc., Bloomsbury, N.J. 1947–75, Chmn. of the Bd. 1975–77, Lifetime Hon. Chmn. of the Bd.; Pres., Moser Jewel Co. Inc., Perth Amboy, N.J. *Member:* American Office Supply Exporters Association (Past President); Pencil Makers Association (Past Pres.); Phillipsburg (N.J.) Chamber of Commerce (Past Pres.); Phillipsburgh Rotary (Past Pres.). *Awards:* Named Knight of St. Gregory by Pope Paul VI (1975); Citizen of 1976 by Phillipsburg Chamber of Commerce. *Clubs:* Rancho Bernardo. *Address:* Verano Drive, San Diego, Ca. 92128, U.S.A.

**DANSEREAU, Bernard.** Canadian. *B.* 1914. *Educ.* Querbes Academy, Outremont; Jean-de-Brebeuf College (BA 1934); University of Montreal Faculty of Law (LLB 1937). *M.* 1940, Viola Prevost. *Career:* Practised law originally with Hon. John Hall Kelly, QC, MLC, New Carlisle, Quebec 1938–40. Royal Canadian Navy 1940–45 (Canadian Volunteer Service Medal with clasp, 1939–45 Star). Director, Law Dept., Imasco Ltd., Apr. 1964— (Solicitor 1946, General Solicitor 1953, General Counsel, Feb. 1963), Vice-President 1969–72. *Member:* Bars of Montreal and Province of Quebec; Canadian Bar Assn.; Assn. of Canadian General Counsel. *Address: office* 4 Wesmount Square, Montreal, 216 P.Q., Canada.

**DANSON, Hon. Barnett (Barney) Jerome.** Canadian politician. *B.* 1921. *Educ.* Toronto schools. *M.* 1943, Isobel Bull. *S.* 4. Served overseas with Queen's Own Rifles of Canada, 1939–45, retired with rank of Lieutenant; mem. Canadian House of Commons since 1968; Mem., Standing Cttee. on Finance, Trade & Economic Affairs; Vice-Chmn., Standing Cttee. on External Affairs & Nat. Defence; Parly. Sec. to Prime Minister Pierre Trudeau 1970–72; Min. of State for Urban Affairs 1974–76; Min. of Nat. Defence since 1976. *Member:* Canadian co-chmn., Canada/United States Inter-Parliamentary Group. *Address:* House of Commons, Ottawa, Ontario K1A 0A6, Canada.

**DANZIN, André Marcel.** French. Elec. Engr. *B.* 1919. *Educ.* École Polytechnique; École Supérieure d'Electricité. *M.* 1943, Nicole de la Poix de Freminville. *S.* Charles, Dominque, Alain. *Career:* Research Engr. Baccarat Crystal Mfg. Co. 1940–43. Research Engr. C.S.F. (Gen. Co. TSF) 1943–52; Mgr. Physico-Chim. Research Center CSF 1952–64; Chmn. Ducati-Elettrotecnica (Bologne) 1961–72; Member Bd. Sait Electronics (Bruxelles) 1962–72; Gen. Mgr. CSF Vice-Pres. Gen. Mgr. Thomson-CSF 1964–72; Vice-Pres. Comité Consultatif de la Recherche Scientifique et Technique 1964–68; Prés. Gen. Mgr. Cie Financière pour l'Information (Fininfor) 1969–72; Member Scientific Cttee. Nuclear Energy 1971–75; Dir. French Research Governmental Inst. Computer Sciences & Automatism Institut de Recherche d'Information et d'Automatique (IRIA) since 1972; Chmn. CEPIA; Member Bd. Govs. Atlantic Inst. Int. Affairs; Chmn., Eiropean Cttee. for Research and Development, 1975. *Member:* Scientific Societies. *Awards:* Officer Legion of Honour; Officer Palmes Acad.; Officer Nat. Order of Merit. *Address:* 41 Avenue Kleber 75016 Paris; and *office* IRIA-Domaine de Voluceau 78150 Le Chesnay, France.

**DAOUD KHAN, Sardar Mohammad.** Afghan army officer and politician. *B.* 1909. *Career:* Major General 1932; General of various provinces 1934–39; Commander, Kabul Army Corps. 1939–46; Minister of Defence 1946; Minister in Paris 1948; Prime Minister 1953–63, concurrently Minister of Defence & of the Interior; led coup deposing King Mohammad Zahir Shah, July 1973; Pres., Prime Minister, Minister of Foreign Affairs & Nat. Defence of the Republic of Afghanistan since 1973. *Address:* The Presidential Residence, Kabul, Afghanistan.

**DAOUDY, Adib.** Order of Merit (UAR), Ambassador of Syria. *B.* 1923. *Educ.* Damascus University (Baccalaureat, Lic.-en.-D.; and Paris University LLD). *M.* 1955, Amal Khartabil. *Daus.* 4. *Career:* Entered Ministry of Foreign Affairs, Damascus 1942; Secretary to Foreign Minister during negotiations to establish the Arab League, Cairo 1943–44; at Paris Legation 1945–49; Director of Palestine Refugees in Damascus 1952–55 (Representative at Adv. Committee to U.N. Relief and Works Agency for the refugees 1953–54); Counsellor-Chargé d'Affaires, London 1955; First Counsellor, New Delhi 1957, and at Embassy of U.A.R., Karachi 1958; promoted Minister, Prague Embassy 1961; attended Bandung Conference of Afro-Asian countries; Ambassador to India, 1962–64; Asst. Secretary General, Political Affairs,

Ministry of Foreign Affairs, 1964–69; attended over 12 sessions of the U.N. General Assembly & represented Syria at Security Council Debate on Arab-Israeli Conflict in 1967; Leader of Syrian Delegation to The International Conference on Human Rights, Teheran 1968; Arab League Conference, Beirut 1968. Ambassador of Syria to Belgium, The Netherlands and Luxembourg 1969–74; Political Advisor to President of Syria since 1974; accompanied the President on many state visits to Bulgaria, France, Jordan, Iran, North Korea, Romania, Saudi Arabia & Yugoslavia & the non-aligned Fifth Summit Conference in Colombo, Aug. 1976. *Decorations:* From Belgium, France, Iran, Jordan, Saudi Arabia, Senegal, UAR. Elected Member of Comm. on Human Rights and Prevention of Racial Discrimination, 1969 and 1970. *Address:* c/o Ministry of Foreign Affairs, Damascus, Syria.

**DARBY, John Herbert.** American. *B.* 1903. *M.* 1934, Jean MacPhail (*Dec.*) 1967. Pres. Ellicott Clinic and Hospital. President and Treasurer: Niagra Transformer Corp. 1959—; Erie Electric Co. Inc. 1930—; Erie Machinery Corp. 1964—; and Erie Fan & Blower Co. Inc. 1955—. Republican. *Clubs:* Buffalo; Buffalo Athletic; Park Country· Elma Gun & Field (Secretary 1955—); Rotary (Vice-Pres. 1955: Treasurer 1954). *Address:* 161 Brantwood Road, Snyder 26, N.Y., U.S.A.

**DARDEN, Eugeen C. P.** Belgian accountant. *B.* 1908. *Educ:* Athenée Royale, Antwerp (various diplomas including accountancy). *M.* 1949, Marie Elizabeth Van Nieulande. *Career:* Manager, Ascenseurs Daelemans 1934–38; in practice as accountant since 1938; expert of the Court of Justice. Member of Honour of the Belgian National Assoc. of Accountants; Member, Inst. of Company Surveyors. Dir. of Accountants company, Swaelen, Darden & Co. *Awards:* Officer, Order of the Crown; Knight, Order of Leopold; Golden Mark of Honour Accountancy, Delivered by State of Belgium. *Address:* 25 Rubenslei, 2000-Antwerp; and *office* Italielei 241, 2000-Antwerp, Belgium.

**DARGUSCH, Carlton Spencer.** Brig.-General U.S.A.R. Attorney-at-Law specializing in public finance and taxation. *B.* 1900. *Educ.* Indiana Univ., and The Ohio State Univ. (LLB 1925). *M.* 1923, Genevieve Johnston. *S.* Carlton Spencer, Jr. *Dau.* Evelyn B. (Lanphere). DSM (U.S. Army) 1946, and Commendation Ribbon (2) 1946; U.S. Army Exceptional Civilian Service Award 1950; Distinguished Service Award (Ohio State Univ.) 1960. *Career:* Attorney 1925–32, Chief Counsel 1932–33, Tax Commission of Ohio; Tax Commissioner, State of Ohio 1933–37; Counsel to Governor of Ohio 1937–38, and to Senate Tax Committee, Ohio General Assembly 1939; Trustee, Ohio State Univ. 1938–59 and 1963—; Dep. Dir., Selective Service System, U.S. Govt. 1941–47; Asst. Dir., Office of Defense Mobilization, U.S. Govt. 1955–57; Partner in law firm of Dargusch & Dargusch, Columbus, Ohio, Counsel Engineers Joint Council & Engineering Manpower Commission, American Institute of Industrial Engineers, New York; National Selective Service Scientific Advisory Group; National Defense Executive Reserve. Chairman of Board, Henrite Products Corp.; Director, The Clark Grave Vault Co.; Vice-Pres. and Gen. Counsel, the Ohio Tuberculosis and Health Association; Trustee, Mount Carmel Hospital. Member, 1953 Committee on Manpower Resources of ODM (Appley Cttee.), of 1956 U.S. Delegation, Vienna (Austria) Conf., Organization of Applied Research in Europe, of 1958 U.S. Delegation to India to study operation of ICA programme in higher institutions of learning, and of 1960 Delegation from Engineers Joint Council (sponsored by Natl. Science Foundation) to U.S.S.R. *Member:* Amer., Federal, Ohio and Columbus Bar Associations; Sphinx Honorary (Ohio State Univ.); Omicron Kappa Upsilon (Hon. Dental Fraternity); Kappa Sigma; Phi Delta Phi; Military Order of the World Wars. Mason. *Publications:* Estate & Inheritance Taxation (with John R. Cassidy 1930); The Operation of Selective Service in World War II (1956); numerous articles on public education, public finance, and manpower resources problems. Republican. *Clubs:* Chevy Chase (Md.); Army & Navy (Washington); Columbus Country, Columbus University (all of Columbus, Ohio); Engineers, Players (N.Y.C.); Union (Cleveland); Fort Henry Wheeling, Queen City (Cincinnati). *Address: office* 218 East State Street, Columbus, Ohio, 43215, U.S.A.

**DARLING of Hillsborough, Rt. Hon. Lord** (George Darling), PC *B.* 1905. *Educ.* Cambridge (MA). *M.* 1938, Dorothy Hodge. *S.* 1. *Dau.* 1. *Career:* Member of the Labour Party. Minister of State, Board of Trade, Oct. 1964–68; Member of Parliament (Labour) Co-op, Hillsborough 1950–74; Delegate to Council of Europe and Western Union Assemblies since 1970. *Address:* 17 Amersham Road, Beaconsfield, Bucks.

**DARLING, Sir James Ralph.** CMG, OBE, MA, DCL, LLD. Australian. *B.*. 1899 *Educ.* Repton School and Oriel College, Oxford; MA (Oxon.); MA (Hon.) (Melb.); DCL (Hon.) (Oxon.). *M.* 1935, Margaret Dunlop Campbell. *S.* 1. *Daus.* 3. *Career:* Headmaster, Geelong Grammar School 1930–61. 2nd Lieut., R.F.A. 1918–19 (France and Germany). Asst. Master: Merchant Taylors' School (Crosby, Liverpool) 1921–24, and Charterhouse School (Godalming) 1924–29. In charge of Public Schools Empire Tour to N.Z. 1929. Hon. Secy., Headmasters Conf. of Australia 1931–45 (Chmn. 1946–48). *Member:* Commonwealth Universities Commission 1942–51; Australian Broadcasting Control Board 1955–61 Chairman: Australian Broadcasting Commission 1961–67, Australian Frontier Commission 1961–71; and Australian Road Safety Council 1961–71; Hon. Fellow and past Pres., Australian Coll. of Educ. Member: Melbourne Univ. Council 1933–71 and Chairman, Immigration Publicity Council 1962–70; President, Australian Elizabethan Theatre. *Publications:* The Education of a Civilised Man (1962); Timbertop (with E. H. Montgomery) (1967). *Clubs:* Melbourne (Melbourne); Australian (Sydney). *Address:* 3 Myamyn Street, Armadale, Vic. 3143, Australia.

**DARLING, Philip Eustis.** Consulting engineer. *B.* 1905. *Educ.* Masschusetts Inst. of Tech. (BS Chem. Eng. 1927). *M.* 1928, Isidora Casas de Ponce. *Daus.* Gertrude Ponce (Lewis), and Wendy Moira (Perry). *Career:* Chemist and Chief Plant Chemist, American Smelting & Refining Co. 1927–30; various positions 1931–33; with American Oil Co., Texas City, Texas: Engineer, Chief Engineer 1934–54; Asst. Manager, Engineering 1955–58; Director, Professional Recruiting 1958–59; Head Engineer, Co-ordination, General Engineering Dept., American Oil Co. (Retired), Whiting, Ind. (1960–63); Pres. Doran Co. Consultants since 1969; Lecturer Physics, Univ. St. Thomas since 1973. *Publications:* Internal Insulation for High Temperature (A.S.M.E. Paper). Honorary Service Award, and Section Chairman Honorary Award, A.S.M.E. *Member:* A.S.M.E.; N.S.P.E.; *Address:* 3600 Link Valley Dr., Houston, Texas, 77025, U.S.A.

**DARLING, Stanley.** OBE, DSC (2 bars), VRD. Australian. *B.* 1907. *Educ.* Hutchins School, Hobart (Tasmania) and Univ. of Tasmania (B Eng.); unmarried. *Career:* War Service; in command of anti-submarine vessels, Atlantic Ocean 1939–46; Senior Officer, Royal Australian Naval Reserve until 1961; promoted Captain, Dec. 1952. *Clubs:* University Imperial Service (Sydney). *Address:* 29–205 Birrell Street, Waverley, N.S.W., Australia.

**DARROW, Richard W.** Public relations counsel. *B.* 1915. *Educ.* Ohio Wesleyan University (BA 1936). *M.* 1938, Nelda V. Darling. *S.* William R. and John H. *Career:* Reporter and Assistant City Editor, Columbus (Ohio) Citizen 1936–41; Assistant Director of Public Relations and Advertising, Curtiss Wright Corporation 1941–45; Asst. to the President, The American Meat Institute 1945–46; Director of Public Relations & Advertising, The Glenn L. Martin Co. 1946–52; joined Hill & Knowlton 1952. Chmn. Bd. Chief Exec. Officer. Hill & Knowlton Inc.; Chairman, Civilian Public Relations Advisory Committee, U.S. Military Academy (Committee member since 1955). Trustee, Ohio Wesleyan University 1957—; Chmn. 1968–72. Member: Public Relations Socy. of America (Natl. Exec. Cttee.; Pres. N.Y. Chapter 1957–58, Vice-Chmn., Counselors Section 1962–63); Bd. Dirs. Exec. Cttee. Regional Plan Assn.; Aviation/Space Writers Assn.; Assn. of Petroleum Writers; Nat. Exec. Board & Nat. Chmn. Public Relations, Boy Scouts of America 1962—; Chmn. Int. Relationships Cttee. 1972—; Mem. World Scout PR Adv. Cttee., Scarsdale Town Club 1963, Pres. 1964–65; Chmn. Scarsdale Youth Relations Cttee. Mem. Scarsdale (N.Y.) Board of Trustees and Police Commissioner 1967–71; Mayor 1971–73; *Awards:* Named Outstanding Young Man of the Year, Baltimore, Md. 1950; Silver Beaver 1963; Silver Buffalo 1966; Distinguished Eagle 1969; Public Relations News PR Professional of the Year 1971; U.S. Army Outstanding Civilian Service 1972. *Publications:* co-author, Dartnell Public Relations Handbook (1967). Author of articles on aviation, public relations and youth activities. *Clubs:* The Cloud; Overseas Press; National Press; Scarsdale Golf: Union League: The Blind Brook: Burning Tree. *Address:* 50 Barry Road, Scarsdale, N.Y., U.S.A.

**DART, Jack Calhoon.** American chemical engineer. *B.* 1912. *Educ.* Albion (Mich.) Coll. (AB 1934), Univ. of Michigan;

BSE (CE) 1935; MSE (ChE) 1937. *M.* 1940, Rachel Cecilia Henderson. *S.* James Laurance. *Daus.* Dianne Cecilia, Linda Lenore and Janis Jennette. *Career:* Chemical Engineer, American Oil Co. 1937–43, Magnolia Petroleum Co. 1943–44, Esso Research & Engineering Co. 1944–47; successively for Houdry Process Corporation, Director of Development 1947–52; Gen. Mgr., Research and Development 1952–55; Vice-Pres. and Gen. Mgr., Chemicals Div. 1955–58; Vice-Pres., Sales and Service Division 1958–62; Partner, Weinrich & Dart 1962–63; Owner, J. C. Dart & Associates 1963—; Dir., Houdry Process Corp. 1955–62; Houdry-Brazilian Co. 1955–62; Houdry-Belgium Co. 1955–62; Member, Bd. of Supervisors, Katalysatorenwerke Houdry-Huels, G.m.b.H.; Bd. of Directors, Montecassino, S.p.A. *Publications:* numerous technical papers and patents involving petroleum processing, particularly in the fields of alkylation, hydrocarbon synthesis, catalytic cracking, and catalytic reforming. *Member:* Amer. Chemical Socy. (Div. of Petroleum Chemistry); Amer. Inst. of Chemical Engineers; Amer. Inst. of Chemists; Kappa Mu Epsilon; Iota Alpha; Tau Kappa Epsilon. *Clubs:* Congressional Country (Washington). *Address:* 10101 Gary Road, Potomac, Md.; and *office* 1518 K Street, N.W., Washington D.C., 20005, U.S.A.

**DART, Justin Whitlock.** American company executive. *B.* 1907. *Educ.* Northwestern Univ. (BA 1929). *M.* (1) 1929, Ruth Walgreen (*Div.* 1939), and (2) 1940, Jane O'Brien. *S.* Justin W., Jr., Peter W., Guy Michael and Stephen Murray. *Dau.* Jane. *Career:* With Walgreen Drug Stores Co., Chicago 1929–41; General Manager (1939–41), Director (1934–41); Chmn. Bd. Dart Industries Inc., Los Angeles; Director and Vice-President, Rexall Drug Co. (now Dart Industries) 1941; Chmn. Bd. Dart Industries Inc. Los Angeles; Dir. Member Exec. Cttee., United Air Lines; Dir. Cowles Communications Inc. Chmn. Bd. Trustee Univ. Southern Calif. 1967–71; Vice Chmn. 1972; Trustee L.A. County Museum of Art; Hospital of Good Samaritan, Los Angeles; Dir. Eisenhower Medical Center, Palm Desert California. Republican. *Clubs:* Los Angeles; Country (Calif.); Bohemian (San Francisco); Cypress Point (Pebble Beach); El Dorado Country (Palm Desert). *Address:* P.O. Box 3157, Terminal Annex, Los Angeles, Calif. 90051, U.S.A.

**DARVALL, Sir Roger,** CBE, Kt. 1971. Australian company director. *B.* 1906. *Educ.* FASA (Fellow, Australian Society of Accountants). *M.* 1931, Dorothea May Vautier. *Daus.* 2. *Career:* Gen. Mgr., Australia and New Zealand Bank Ltd., 1961–67; Asst. London Mgr. 1949; London Office Mgr., Australia & New Zealand Bank 1951; Mgr., 351 Collins Street, Melbourne, A.N.Z. Bank 1952 (Deputy Gen. Mgr., 1954). Chmn., L. M. Ericsson Pty. Ltd., Electrolux Pty. Ltd., Grosvenor International (Aust.) Holdings P/L, Penguin Books Australia Ltd.; Dir.: Australia New Guinea Corp. Ltd., Longmans of Australia Pty. Ltd., H. C. Sleigh Ltd.; Australian Eagle Insurance Co. Ltd. *Clubs:* Melbourne, Australian, Athenaeum (Melbourne). *Address:* 2 Martin Court, Toorak, Melbourne, 3142; and *office* 460 Bourke St., Melbourne 3000, Vic., Australia.

**DARVILL, Frank Ongley,** CBE. *B.* 1906. *Educ.* Dover Coll., University of Reading (BA), University of London (BA and PhD), Columbia University (AM). *M.* 1931, Dorothy Edmonds. *S.* John Anthony (*D.*). *Career:* Pres., Natl. Union of Students 1927–29; Commonwealth Fund Fellow 1929–31; Assoc. Sec., Dept. of Internat. Studies, Internat. Students Service 1931–32; Dir., Students Internat. Union, Geneva 1933; Lecturer, Econ. and Hist., Queen's College, London 1933–36. Dir. of Research & Discussion and Public Relations Officer, The English-Speaking Union 1936–39; Deputy Dir., American Div. Min. of Inform., London 1939–45. British Consul, Denver, 1945–46. First Sec., Embassy, Washington 1946–49. Member, Council of Liberal Party 1938–39 and 1939–40. Editor 'The University' 1928–29, and 'The English-Speaking World' 1951–53; Extension Lecturer, Cambridge and London Universities 1933–39. British Director-Gen., English-Speaking Union of the Commonwealth 1949–57; Chairman of Bd. Congress of European-American Assns. 1954–57; European Editor, World Review 1958–59; Hon. Director, U.K. Committee Atlantic Congress 1959; attached to office of U.K. High Commission in Cyprus 1960–62. Director, British Information Services, Eastern Caribbean (1962–66). H.M. Consul, Boston 1966–68. H.M. Diplomatic Service Retd. Foreign and Commonwealth Office, London 1968–70; Lect. in Politics & International Affairs, Alvescot Coll. 1970–72 (Dean of Academics 1970–71, Vice-Pres. 1971–72). *Publications:* Popular Disturbances and Public Order in Regency England (1934); The Price of European Peace (1937); The American Political Scene (1939), and articles in British and American newspapers. *Clubs:* Travellers, Anglo-Belgian. *Address:* c/o Lloyds Bank Ltd., 46 Victoria Street, London, S.W.1.

**DASHEFSKY, Edward Leo.** American. *B.* 1914. *Educ.* Mass. Institute of Technology (BS). *M.* 1938, Rose Zelermyer. *S.* Barry. *Dau.* Gloria. *Career:* Aerodynamics and structural design engineer at Sikorsky Aircraft Co. 1937; Curtiss-Wright Airplane Co. 1938–45; Chief of structures and project engineer on Lark missile at guided missile division of Fairchild Engine & Airplane Co. 1946–51; Manager, Sparrow III missile production plant at Raytheon Co. 1951–60; Bd. of Dirs., Machlett Laboratories Inc., Springdale, Conn.: New Japan Radio Co. Ltd., Tokyo, Japan; Switchcraft Inc., Chicago, Ill.; Manager, Microwave and Power Tube Div. Raytheon Co. 1961, Vice-Pres. 1962; Senior Vice-Pres. since 1969. *Member:* American Institute of Aeronautics & Astronautics; Association of the U.S. Army; The Air Force Historical Foundation; Armed Forces Communications and Electronics Assn.; American Logistics Assn. *Address:* 15 Great Meadow Road, Newton Centre, Mass. 02159; and *office* Raytheon Co., Willow St., Waltham, Mass. 02154, U.S.A.

**da SILVEIRA, Antonio F. Azerada,** *B.* 1918. *Career:* joined diplomatic service 1943; Consul-general in Paris 1961–63; Head of Brazilian delegation to UNO in Geneva 1966–68; Ambassador in Buenos Aires 1969–74; International delegate including Il UNCTAD 1966–68 and Panama meeting of special cttees of Organisation of American States, 1966; Chmn. of a group of 77, head of various Brazilian delegations to UNCTAD, GATT and other meetings. *Address:* Ministry of External Relations, Brasilia, Brazil.

**DATTELS, David Roland.** Investment dealer *B.* 9 Dec. 1909. *Educ.* Toronto Schools. *M.* 1943. *S.* 4. *Daus.* 2. *Career:* Naval Service Lieut. 1940, Royal Canadian Navy 1940–45; Retired Commdr. Lieut. 1945; Pres. Dattels & Co. Ltd. Kitchener, Ontario; Pres. Caledon Mountain Recreational Properties Ltd. Toronto; Vice-Pres. and Secy. Cluthe Sales (Waterloo) Ltd. Waterloo Ont. *Member:* Dir., Ontario Socy. for Crippled Children; Rotary Club of Kitchener Ontario. *Clubs:* Toronto Financial Analysts; National (Toronto); Caledon Mountain Trout; Riding & Hunt (Caledon); Westmount Golf & Country *Address:* Meadowlands, R.R., 2, Caledon, Ontario and *office* Suite 402, 305 King Street West, Kitchener NG2 1B9, Ontario, Canada.

**DAUB, Erwin,** Dr. jur. German, adviser and business executive. *B.* 1893. *Educ.* Lausanne, Munich, and Marburg-Lahn Univ. (law and political science); 2nd state exam. 1922; Dr. jur, since 1920. *M.* 1924, Margarete Zinn. *S.* Peter C. and Dr. Johann Heinrich. *Career:* Legal Adviser, Deutsch-Luxemburgische Bergwerks & Hütten AG (mining and steel corp.), Dortmund 1922; Power-of-Attorney, Vereinigte Stahlwerke AG (mining and steel), Administration Office, Berlin 1926; Manager, Stahlverein GmbH für Bergbau und Industriewerte (holding company), Berlin 1934; Director-General and President of Management Board, Gebr. Böhler & Co. AG, Vienna 1938; Adviser, Vereinigte Stahlwerke AG, Düsseldorf 1948. Chairman, Board of Directors, Edelstahlwerk Witten AG (specialty steel plants), Witten 1952, Chmn. of Honour since 1970 and of Seereederei Frigga AG (ore and coal shipping corporation), Hamburg 1960—. *Member:* Max Planck Society for Advancement of Science, Munich; Verein Deutscher Eisenhüttenleute, Düsseldorf. *Club:* Industrial (Düsseldorf). *Address:* Kaiser Friedrich Ring 78, Düsseldorf-Oberkassel, Post fach 262, Germany.

**DAULER, Lee Van Voorhis.** American. *B.* 1912. *Educ.* Yale University (BS). *M.* 1938, Margaret B. Hodge. *S.* Lee V., Jr. *Dau.* Margaret (Wilson). *Career:* Dir., and Pres., Neville Chemical Co., Pittsburgh, Pa. Jan. 1954—. Director, Neville Cindu Chemie N.V., Uithoorn, Netherlands, Nov. 1959—; Manufacturing Chemists' Assoc.; Dir and Pres. Neville-Synthese Organics, Inc. 1970—. *Member:* American Chemical Society; Manufacturing Chemists' Association; National Association of Manufacturers; Tristate Industrial Association; National Paint, Varnish & Lacquer Association. *Clubs:* Duquesne, Yale, Fox Chapel Golf; Yale, Pinnacle (N.Y.C.); Rolling Rock, Laurel Valley Golf (Ligonier, Pa.). *Address:* 708 Squaw Run Road, Pittsburgh, Penna. 15238; and *office* Neville Chemical Co., Pittsburgh, Pa. 15225. U.S.A.

**DAULTANA, Mumtaz Mohammad Khan.** Pakistani Diplomat. *B.* 1916. *Educ.* St. Anthony's Sch., Lahore; Government Coll., Lahore—BA (Hons.); Corpus Christi Coll., Oxford—MA; Called to the Bar, Middle Temple, 1940. *M.* 1943, Almas

Jehan. *S.* 1. *Dau.* 1. *Career:* Gen. Sec., Punjab Muslim League 1944; Sec., All India Muslim League Central Cttee. of Action 1945; elected member of Punjab Assembly 1946; Constituent Assembly of India 1947; Constituent Assembly of Pakistan 1947; Finance Minister, Punjab 1947–48; Pres., Punjab Muslim League 1948–50; Chief Minister of Punjab 1951–53; Finance Minister, West Pakistan 1955–56; Defence Minister, Pakistan 1957; Pres., Pakistan Muslim League 1967–72; Ambassador to the Court of St. James's since 1972. *Publications:* Agrarian Report of Pakistan Muslim League (1950); Thoughts on Pakistan's Foreign Policy (1956); Kashmir in present day context (1965). *Clubs:* United Oxford & Cambridge University; Travellers; Gymkhana (Lahore). *Address* 8 Durand Road, Lahore, Pakistan; and 56 Avenue Road, London NW8; and *office* Pakistan Embassy, 35 Lowndes Square, London SW1.

**DAVENPORT, Robert Charles.** American. *B.* 1907. *Educ.* American Univ. (BS 1949) and Univ. of Maryland (PhD 1960); MIT (Certificates). *M.* 1943, Catherine Hamby. *S.* William. *Dau.* Deborah. *Career:* With U.S. Army (Private to Captain) 1942–46. Senior Field Representative, Urban Renewal Administration, U.S. Govt. 1952–57; Housing Manager, National Capital Housing Authority, U.S. Govt. 1949–52; Special Asst. to Administrator, War Assets Administration, U.S. Govt. 1946–47; Lecturer, Dept. of Economics, Univ. of Maryland 1959–63. President, Robert Davenport Associates Inc., Consulting Economists since 1957. *Publications:* Economic Study of Milwaukee, Wisc. (1973); The Economics of Urban Renewal—An Evaluation of the Federal Program, (1960). U.S. Army Commendation Ribbon 1946. *Member:* Amer. Economic Assn.; National Association of Business Economists; International Fed. for Housing and Planning; Regional Science Assn.; Urban Land Inst.; Amer. Socy. of Planning Officials. *Clubs:* Kenwood Golf and Country; National Economists. *Address:* 8746 Preston Place, Chevy Chase, Maryland 20015, U.S.A.

**DAVEY, Geoffrey.** American. *B.* 1913. *Educ.* London (BSc); Southern Methodist University, Dallas, Tex. MS; University of Michigan (JD), and New York Univ. (LLM). *M.* 1970, Muriel Rowan. *Career:* Vice-President and Secretary, The Continental Corporation, New York. Director, American Title Insurance Co., Miami, Florida; National-Ben Franklin Ins. Co., Illinois, Chicago; National-Ben Franklin Ins. Co. of Michigan, Detroit; National-Ben Franklin Life Ins. Corp., Milwaukee, Wisconsin; Appleton & Cox Inc., New York; INSCO Systems Corp., Neptune, N.Y. *Member:* Amer. and New York State Bar Associations; and N.Y. County Lawyers Association. *Clubs:* University (N.Y.C.); Stanwich (Greenwich, Conn.). *Address:* Cooper Road, Navesink, N.J. 07752; and *office* 80 Maiden Lane, New York, N.Y., U.S.A.

**DAVID, Michel.** French consulting engineer. *B.* 1920. *Educ.* Docteur en Droit. *M.* 1942, Henriette Bégué. *S.* François, Dominique and Pascal. *Career:* Member, Académie des Sciences Commerciales. Director of Organisation and Studies, Centre d'Etudes du Commerce 1946–64; of Studies Institut Français du Libre Service; and Magazine Libre Servicee Actualités 1968. Conseiller Technique, Chambre de Commerce et d'Industrie de Paris; Admin. Assn. Internationale Urbanisme et Commerce. Pres., Assoc. Internationale du Libre Service 1974–77; Professor in various institutions for higher education; Specialist on Tzigane (Hungarian Gypsy) music and record reviewer for the Review "Etudes Tziganes." *Publications:* Le marché noir (1945); Le Commerce intérieur en Russie Soviétique (1946); L'Evolution des formes d'exploitation commerciale (in Histoire du Commerce), (1950); Commerce et productivité aux Etats-Unis (in collaboration) (1951); Les Magasins Collectifs d'independants, (1968); Profils de Postes et Emplois Nouveaux Dans La Distribution Moderne (1970); Le Vol Dans Les Supermarchés (1970); Organisation du Commerce intérieur et extérieur (1956). Tableau de Bord de la Distribution Francaise (1974), Numerous articles, studies and reports on the subject of commerce and distribution, especially self-service, supermarkets, commercial town-planning, prices, etc. *Awards:* Chevalier Ordre National du Mérite; Officier du Mérite Commercial et Industriel; Chevalier de l'Economie Nationale. *Address:* 2 rue Barrault, Paris 13; and 46 rue de Clichy, Paris 9, France.

**DAVID, Paul Theodore.** American political scientist. *B.* 1906. *Educ.* Antioch Coll. (BA 1928) and Brown Univ. (MA 1930; PhDEcon. 1933). *M.* 1935, Opal Mary Davis. *Career:* Asst. Economist, Interstate and Foreign Commerce Cttee., U.S. House of Representatives 1932–33; Economist, Tennessee Valley Authority 1933–36; Staff member, President's Cttee. on Administrative Management 1936; Secy., U.S. Advisory Cttee. on Education 1936–39; Assoc. Dir. American Youth Commission of the American Council on Education 1939–42; Chief Fiscal Analyst, U.S. Bureau of the Budget 1942–46; Alternate Representative of U.S., International Civil Aviation Organization 1946–50; Chairman, U.S. Deleg. Conf. on Joint Financing of Air Navigation Facilities, London 1949; Senior staff member, Brookings Inst. 1950–60; Chairman 1964–66 (Prof. 1960–77, Prof. Emeritus 1977–), Woodrow Wilson Dept. of Govt. and Foreign Affairs, University of Virginia. Fellow, Center for Advanced Study in Behavioral Sciences 1959–60; Faculty member, Salsburg Seminar in American Studies, 1963; Vis. Professor, Univ. of Kent at Canterbury, 1974. Democrat. *Member:* Amer. Political Science Assn.; Amer. Socy. for Public Admin.; Amer. Economic Assn.; Nat. Planning Assn. *Publications:* The Economics of Air Mail Transportation (1934); The Administration of Foreign Affairs and Overseas Operations (with others) (1951); Presidential Nominating Politics in 1952 (with others), 5 vols., (1954); Executives for Government (with Pollock), (1958); The Politics of National Party Conventions (with Goldman and Bain, 1960); The Presidential Election and Transition (1960–61); Party Strength in the United States 1872–1970. *Clubs:* Cosmos, National Capital Democratic (of Washington, D.C.); Colonnade (Charlottesville). *Address:* Route 5 Box 335-B, Charlottesville, Va. 22901, U.S.A.

**DAVID, Václav.** Czechoslovak diplomat. *B.* 1910. *Educ.* Commercial Academy. Worked in CKD factory 1929–32; while there participated in the foundation of a Komsomol branch in the factory, and acted as its representative in the district and regional branches; joined the Czechoslovak Communist Party 1935. Worked also as Secretary of the Bohemia branch of the Union of Friends of the Soviet Union. During the occupation, was a member of the 4th underground Central Committee of the C.P. of Czechoslovakia, and participated actively in the Prague uprising. After liberation he became Deputy of the National Assembly. Is a member of the Central Committee of the C.P. of Czechoslovakia, of which he became Secretary in 1951; Minister of Foreign Affairs of the Czechoslovak Socialist Republic 1953–68; Ambassador, Sofia 1969–71; Vice-Chmn. of the Federal Assembly of CSR & Chmn. of its House of the People 1971—; Chmn. of the Central Cttees. of the Union of Czech-Soviet Friendship. *Address:* Ministry of Foreign Affairs, Prague, Czechoslovakia.

**DAVID, Walter.** Dr. juris. German. General Counsel of Carl-Zeiss-Foundation; Firm of Carl Zeiss, Heidenheim. *B.* 1913. *Educ.* Referendar und Assessor, Dr. juris. Counsel in the firm of Carl Zeiss, September 1943. *Publication:* Die Carl-Zeiss-Stiftung—ihre Vergangenheit und ihre gegenwärtige rechtliche Lage, (1954); contributor to various technical journals. *Address:* Otto-Kocher-Strasse 8, 792 Heidenheim, Germany; and 7082 Oberkochen, Germany.

**DAVID, Wilmot Alphonsus.** Ambassador of Liberia. *B.* 1911. *Educ.* St. John's Academic & Industrial School, Cape Mount; Liberia College (now Univ. of Liberia) BA. *M.* 1941, Irene Cooper. *S.* 1. *Daus.* 3. *Career:* Various appts. in Dept. of State 1934–44; Private Secy. to Secy. of State on Spl. Mission, Sierra Leone, 1944; Consul-General, U.K. 1945–48; First Secy. Legation, & Consul-General, London 1948–52; Counsellor, Liberian Embassy, Washington, 1952-56; Envoy Extraordinary and Min. Plen. Italy, 1956–57; Ambassador: Haiti 1957–58, Ghana 1958–60; Under Secretary of State 1960–64. Special services incl.: Chairmanship, Delegations to Paris 1945, London 1947, Brussels 1950, Washington 1953; Delegate: U.N. London 1946, Paris 1949, UNESCO, Paris 1949, F.A.O. Rome 1955; UNESCO, Paris 1964. Accompanied Pres. William V. S. Tubman on several State Visits 1960–64 .Ambassador to France 1964–68 and to Italy 1968. *Awards:* Gold Medal for Public Service; Kt. Cdr. Humane Ord. of African Redemption; Grand Ord. Star of Africa, Ord. Most Ven. Order of Knighthood of Pioneers of Republic of Liberia, K.B.E., and many others. *Address:* Viale Bruno Buozzi 64, Rome, Italy.

**DAVIDSON, Brian.** CBE. British. solicitor. *B.* 1909. *Educ.* Winchester Coll.; New Coll., Oxford (BA). *M.* 1935, Priscilla Margaret Chilver. *S.* Rollo (*Dec.*) and Nicholas Ranking. *Dau.* Christian Priscilla. *Career:* Barrister-at-Law 1933–36; Solicitor 1939; with Air Ministry and Ministry of Aircraft Production 1940–43; Director, Bristol Aeroplane Co. 1950–68; Solicitor with Gas Council 1969–75; Member, Concorde Committee of Directors (Engines) 1962–68; Chairman, Contracts Cttee., Society of British Aerospace Companies, 1964–68; Management Committee, I.E.C. Wine Society,

1966—. *Member:* Gloucestershire C.C. 1953–60; Monopolies Commn. 1954–68. *Address:* Sands Court, Dodington, Avon, BS17 6SE.

**DAVIDSON, Hon. Sir Charles William,** KBE, OBE (Mil.), Australian. *B.* 1897. *Educ.* Townsville (Qld.) Grammar School. *M.* 1929, Mary Gertrude Godschall Johnson. *S.* John Alexander. *Daus.* Joan Mary and Margery Elizabeth. *Career:* began sugar farming 1925; Served in World Wars I and II (Lieut., Australian Imperial Force. France, 1916–18, and Lieut.-Col. A.I.F., New Guinea, 1939–45); Member (Country Party) House of Representatives for Capricornia 1946–49; Dawson (Qld.) 1949–63; Deputy Government Whip, 1950–56; Chairman, Commonwealth Air Beef Panel, 1955. Postmaster-General, Jan. 1956–63 and Minister for the Navy, Oct. 1956; Consultant Plessey Telecommunications Pty. Ltd.; Dir. Magellan Petroleum Australia Ltd.; Pres. Asthma Foundation of Queensland 1964–73. *Clubs:* United Services (Brisbane), Mackay. *Address:* 439 Brisbane Corso, Yeronga, Brisbane, Qld. 4104, Australia.

**DAVIDSON, Francis Joseph.** Australian press director. *B.* 1904. *Educ.* Aquinas College, Perth, W.A. *M.* 1928, Mavis Alice Robinson. *S.* Ronald, Lawrence. *Career:* Director: Western Press, Ltd., Art Photo Engravers Pty. Ltd., Country Newspapers Pty. Ltd., Suntimes Broadcasters Ltd. *Address:* 34 Stirling Street, Perth 6001, Western Australia.

**DAVIDSON, George Forrester.** Canadian public servant. *B.* 1909. *Educ.* University of British Columbia (BA); Harvard Univ. (MA, PhD). *M.* (1) 1935, Elizabeth Ruth Henderson. *S.* Roger Reynolds, Craig Sullivan. *Dau.* Barbara Louise. (2) 1975, Anneke Irene Henderson. *Career:* Executive Dir., Canadian Welfare Council 1942; member, Canadian Delegation to E.C.O.S.O.C. 1946–57; Canadian Representative to U.N. Social Commission 1947–50; President, Canadian Conference on Social Work 1952–54; Deputy Minister of National Welfare 1944–60; member, Canadian Delegation 8th Gen. Assembly, U.N. 1953, and Chmn., Social, Cultural and Humanitarian Cttee. of the Assembly: Pres., Int. Conference on Social Work, 1956–60; Deputy Minister, Dept. of Citizenship and Immigration, 1960–63; Director, Bureau of Government Organization 1963–64; Secretary to Treasury Board, Govt. of Canada 1964–68. Pres., Canadian Broadcasting Corporation, 1968–72; U.N. Under-Secy. Gen. for Admin. and Mgmt. since 1972; Pres., U.N. Economic and Social Council 1958. *Address:* 400 East 54 St., Apt 24c, New York City, NY 10022; and *office* United Nations, New York 10017, U.S.A.

**DAVIDSON, James Alfred,** OBE. British Diplomat, *B.* 1922. *Educ.* Christ's Hospital; Royal Naval Coll., Dartmouth; Barrister-at-Law, Middle Temple; holds Master Mariner's Certificate of Service. *M.* 1955, Daphne. *S.* (Stepsons) 2. *Daus.* 2. *Career:* Royal Navy 1939–60 (war service Atlantic, Mediterranean & Far East); commanded HM Ships Calder & Welfare; Commander 1955; retired 1960; Called to the Bar 1960; joined Commonwealth Office (later incorporated into Diplomatic Service) 1960; served Port of Spain, Phnom Penh (periods as Chargé d'Affaires 1970 & 1971), Dacca (Chargé d'Affaires, later Dep. High Commissioner 1972–73); Visiting Scholar, Univ. of Kent 1973–74; High Commissioner in Brunei since 1974. *Decorations:* Officer, Order of the British Empire 1971. *Clubs:* Army & Navy. *Address:* High Commissioner's House, Brunei, S.E. Asia.

**DAVIDSON, Sir (Leybourne) Stanley (Patrick),** MD. British professor of medicine. *B.* 1894. *Educ.* Cheltenham College, Trinity College, Cambridge and Edinburgh University; BA (Cantab.), MB, ChB (Edinburgh Univ.); 1st Class Hons. MD, Gold Medal, MD Oslo, FRCP Edinburgh, FRCP London, LLD. Edin. and Aberdeen. *M.* 1927, Isabel Margaret Anderson. *Career:* Regius Professor of Medicine, Univ. of Aberdeen; Senior Physician, Royal Infirmary, Aberdeen 1932–38; Hon. Physician to King George VI in Scotland 1947–52; Physician to H.M. The Queen in Scotland 1952–61; Extra Physician to H.M. The Queen 1961; Professor of Medicine and Clinical Medicine, Univ. of Edinburgh 1938–59; Physician-in-Charge, Royal Infirmary, Edinburgh 1938–59. *Publications:* Pernicious Anaemia (monograph) with Professor G. L. Gulland (1930); A. Textbook of Medical Treatment (with D. M. Dunlop and J. W. McNee) (1939); A Textbook of Dietetics (with I. A. Anderson) (1940); The Principles and Practice of Medicine (with Staff of Edinburgh Univ. Dept. of Medicine) (1952); Human Nutrition and Dietetics (with A. P. Meikeljohn and R. Passmore) (1959); articles in medical journals. *Address:* 28 Barnton Gardens, Davidsons Mains, Edinburgh 4.

**DAVIES, Barrie Nicholas.** British statistician *B.* 1914. *Educ.* Univ. Coll. of Wales (BA Hons.) and Univ. of Manchester. *M.* 1940, Edith Joanna Howells. *Dau.* Joanna Catharine. *Career:* Statistician, Central Statistical Office, London 1940–48; Senior Statistician, U.N. Statistical Office, New York, U.S.A. 1948–53; Dir. Statistics Div. United Nations Economic Commission for Europe, Geneva, since 1953. Fellow Royal Statistical Socy. *Member:* International Statistical Inst. and International Assn. for Research in Income and Wealth. *Address:* 29 Malagnou, 1208 Geneva; and *office* Palais de Nations, Geneva, Switzerland.

**DAVIES, Bryan,** MP. British politician. *B.* 1939. *Educ.* University Coll., London (BA), London School of Economics (BSc). *M.* 1963, Monica R. M. Shearing. *S.* 2. *Dau.* 1. *Career:* Labour Member of Parliament for Enfield North since 1974; Parliamentary Private Secy. to Rt. Hon. Fred Mulley at Dept. Education & Science 1975, to Rt. Hon. Edward Short, Lord Privy Seal 1976, & to Rt. Hon. Joel Barnett, Chief Secy. to the Treasury 1977. *Clubs:* Enfield Highway Working Men's & Broxbourne Sports Club. *Address:* 28 Churchfields, Broxbourne, Herts.

**DAVIES, David Arthur.** British meteorologist. *B.* 1913. *Educ.* University of Wales (MSc). *M.* 1938, Mary Shapland. *S.* 1. *Daus.* 2. *Career:* Secretary-General, World Meteorological Organization since Aug. 1955; Technical Officer, Meteorological Office, London 1936–39: War service R.A.F. as Meteorological Officer 1939–47 (despatches 1943); Principal Scientific Officer, Meteorological Office, London, 1947–49; Director, East African Meteorological Department, Nairobi, Kenya 1949–55; elected Fellow Institute of Physics, London 1943; Member, Royal Inst. Public Administration, London 1950; Honorary Mem. American Meteorological Society 1970; Hon. Mem. Hungarian Meteorological Society 1975. Dr. h.c. Physics, Univ. of Bucharest 1970; Eötvös Lorand Univ., Budapest 1976. *Publications:* Various meteorological papers and articles dealing mainly with the applications of Meteorology through international collaboration. *Address:* Secretariat, World Meteorological Organisation, Avenue Guiseppe Motta, Geneva, Switzerland.

**DAVIES, Hon. Edward David Grant.** British investment manager. *B.* 1925. *Educ.* Gordonstoun; Upper Canada College (Toronto); King's College, Cambridge. *M.* 1949, Patricia Elizabeth Musto. *S.* 1. *Daus* 3. *Career:* Chairman, National Carbonising Co.; Director, Cambrian and General Securities Co., C.S.C. Investment Co., London Trust Ltd., Dinam Investment Co., Cambrian Land Co., Temple Bar Investment Trust Ltd., General Finance & Investment Co. (Wales) Ltd., and others. *Address:* 30 Southacre, Hyde Park Crescent, London W2.

**DAVIES, Ernest Albert John.** British author and journalist. *B.* 1902. *Educ.* Wycliffe College; London University (Diploma in Journalism). *M.* (1) 1927, Natalie Rossin. (2) 1944, Peggy Yeo. *S.* 2. *Daus.* 2. *Career:* Editor, Clarion 1929–32; Associate Editor, New Clarion 1932; with British Broadcasting Corporation 1940–45; Editor, Traffic Engineering & Control, 1959—, and Antique Finder 1962–72. MP (Lab.), Enfield Division of Middlesex 1945–50. Enfield East 1950–59; Parliamentary Private Secretary to Minister of State 1946–50; Parliamentary Under-Secretary of State for Foreign Affairs 1950–Oct. 1951; Chmn., Parly. Labour Party Transport Group 1945–50 and 1951–59, British-Yugoslavia Socy. 1958— Vice-Pres., European-Atlantic Group, 1966—; Hon. Secy. British Parking Assn. since 1970. *Address:* 6F Observatory Gardens, London W8 7HY.

**DAVIES, The Rt. Hon. John Emerson Harding,** PC, MBE. MP. British. *B.* 1916. *Educ.* St. Edward's School, Oxford. *M.* 1943, Vera Georgina Bates. *S.* 1. *Dau.* 1. *Career:* trained as an Accountant; Enlisted R.A.S.C. 1939; Commissioned 2nd Lt. 1940. G2 (Tech.) Combined Ops. Experimental Establishment (C.O.X.E.) 1945–46. Joined Anglo-Iranian Oil Co. 1946; served in Stockholm, London and Paris 1946–55; Gen. Mgr. Markets 1956–60. Dir., BP Trading 1960; Vice-Chmn. and Mng. Dir., Shell-Mex and B.P. 1961–65; Dir. Gen. Confederation, British Industry 1965–69; Director of the Hill Samuel Group Ltd., 1969–70 and 1974; Member of Parliament, Knutsford Division of Cheshire, 1970—; Secy. of State for Trade & Industry, Pres. Bd. of Trade 1970–72; Minister of Technology 1970; Chancellor of the Duchy of Lancaster and Minister for Europe 1972–74; Shadow Foreign & Commonwealth Secretary 1976—. *Member:* N.E.D.C. 1964–69; Transport Adv. Cncl. 1965; Nat. Joint Council Advisory to Minister of Labour 1965–69, British Productivity Council 1966–69; British Nat. Exports Council 1966–69; Council of

Industrial Design 1966–70; Gov. St. Edwards School Oxford; Windlesham House School Trust; ACA 1939; FCA 1960. Hon. Col. R.C.T. 1961; F.R.S.A. 1964. J. Dip. MA 1965. Doctor (Hon.) University of Essex; Hon. D.Sc. Univ. of Loughborough. *Club:* Oriental. *Address:* House of Commons, London, S.W.1.

**DAVIES, Richard Lloyd.** American Executive. *B.* 1910. *Educ.* Yale Coll. *M.* 1935, Mary Margaret McKee. *S.* John David McKee and Richard Bonar. *Career:* Delegate of Presbyterian Church in U.S.A. to World Council of Churches 1954—; Chairman, Foreign Policy Association of Philadelphia, 1945–49; President, Presbyterian Hospital, Philadelphia, 1948–55; President, Pennsalt International Corporation, 1949–57; Pres., Klein & Saks Inc., Davies & Associates Inc., International Management Consultants, Washington, D.C.; Exec. Dir. The Silver Inst. Inc. International Assn. since 1971; Man. Dir., The Gold Institute/L'Institut de l'Or since 1976. *Publications:* The Christian Role of Management in the Free Nations of the World (Trend Magazine); Cleaning Steel—Chemically (Chem. & Metall. Engng.); Establishing Operations in Latin-America (Univ. of Penna. Press); Women in African Economics (Johns Hopkins SAIS Review); Incentive Compensation for Executives (National Stationer). Process for Dissolving Cellulose and Reclaiming Rubber (U.S. Patent); Process for Making Alkali Subsilicates (U.S., Canadian, British, French, Argentine, Brazilian, Japanese and Swiss Patents); Process for Purifying Electrolytic Cell Liquor (U.S. Patent); Process for Making Sodium Aluminate U.S. Canadian and British Patents); Electrolytic Process, 1970 (U.S., Canadian, French & Swiss Patents). King Christian X Medal of Liberation (Denmark). *Clubs:* Cosmos, International (Washington); Yale, Chemists (N.Y.C.). *Address:* 3206 P Street, N.W., Washington 7, D.C.; and *office* Connecticut Avenue, Washington 20036, D.C., U.S.A.

**DAVIES, Richard Townsend.** American diplomat. *B.* 1920. *Educ.* Columbia Univ., AB; Middlebury College (Vermont) and Columbia Univ. (Russian Lang. and Area Studies). *M.* 1949, Jean Stevens. *S.* 4. *Career:* 3rd Secy. American Embassy, Warsaw (Poland) 1947–49; 2nd Secy. American Embassy, Moscow (USSR) 1951–53; Political Officer, International Staff, NATO, Paris 1953–55; 2nd Secy. American Embassy, Kabul (Afghanistan) 1955–58; Public Affairs Adviser, Office of Eastern European Affairs, Dept. of State, Washington DC 1958–59; Public Affairs Adviser, Office of USSR affairs, Dept. of State, Wash. DC 1959–61; 1st Secy. American Embassy, Moscow (USSR) 1961–62, Political Counsellor, 1962–63; Fellow 6th Seminar in For. Policy, For. Service Inst. Washington DC 1963–64; Deputy Exec. Secy. Dept. of State, Wash. DC 1964; Assist.-Dir. (Soviet Union and E. Europe) US Information Agency, Washington DC 1965–68; American Consul-Gen. Calcutta, India 1968–69; Member, Planning and Co-ordination Staff, Dept. of State, Wash. DC 1969–70; Deputy Assist. Secy. of State for European Affairs, Dept of State Washington DC. 1970–72; USA. Ambassador to Poland since 1972. *Member:* American Foreign Service Assn. (Wash. DC). *Award:* Superior Honor Award, US Inf. Agency, 1968. *Publications:* The Fate of Polish Socialism (in A Foreign Affairs Reader: The Soviet Union, 1922–62) 1963; article in International Control of Propaganda. *Address:* Warsaw Dept. of State, Washington DC, 20520; and American Embassy, Warsaw, Poland.

**DAVIES, Robert Henry.** American. Lieut. (jg) U.S.N.R. *B.* 1912. *Educ.* U.S. Naval Academy, Annapolis, Md. 1930–34 (BSc). *M.* 1941, Nettie Mary Bloom. *S.* Robert H., Jr.; Geoffrey L.; Daniel R.; and Christopher D. A. *Daus.* Mary K. and Cynthia L. *Career:* With Parker-Hannifin Corp. since 1939; Engineering Mgr. 1946–54. Scientific Consultant, U.S. Army SHAEF, Technical Industrial Intelligence Committee 1945; Corporate Vice-President, Parker-Hannifin Corporation 1955—; President of the International Division of the Corporation 1961—. Chairman of Board: Parker-Hannifin (U.K.) Ltd. 1963—, and Parker Hannifin N.M.F. GmbH 1962—. Member Aurora Board of Public Affairs 1950–57; Pres. Board of Education, Aurora Local School District 1958 and 1964. *Publications:* Design of German Aircraft, Hydraulic Systems and their Components; co-author of SHAEF Report on Developments in the German Aircraft Accessory Industry. Owner of 17 patents. Certificate of Achievement (U.S. Navy); Army Ordnance Distinguished Service Award; Dept of the Army Certificate of Appreciation. Registered Professional Engineer, States of Ohio and California. *Member:* Socy. Automotive Engineers; Amer. Socy. Mechanical Engineers; Cleveland Engineering Socy.; Amer. Management Assn. *Clubs:* Reform (London); Aurora Country; Clevelander. *Address:* 156 Shawnee Trail, Aurora, Ohio 44202; and *office* Parker-Hannifin Corporation, 17325 Euclid Avenue, Cleveland, Ohio 44112, U.S.A.

**DAVIES, Robert Wright,** QC. Partner in firm of Harris, Keachie, Garrow, Davies & Hunter, Barristers and Solicitors, Toronto. *B.* 1918. *Educ.* University of Toronto (BA 1940), and Osgoode Hall Law School 1946. *M.* (1) 1942, Audrey Rena (*D.* 1958); (2) 1972, M. Audrey M. *S.* Gordon Gray. *Dau.* Lynn Victoria. *Career:* Served with Canadian Army 1942–45 (Lieut., Toronto Scottish Regt. and Roya Regt. of Canada; P.o.W. Germany 1944–45). *Member:* Past President, Borough of York Assoc. for the Mentally Retarded, National Officer, Sigma Chi Fraternity; Canadian Bar Assn.; York County Law Assn.; Law Socy. of Upper Canada. Progressive Conservative Service. *Club:* Canadian Progress; Past Pres., Toronto Central-Branch, National Man-of-the-Year 1970. *Address: office* Suite 330, 165 University Avenue, Toronto 1, Ont., Canada.

**DAVIES, William Leslie Carrington,** Australian. *B.* 1919. *Educ.* Pulteney Grammar Sch., Adelaide; R.A.N. Coll., Flinders Naval Depot, Victoria. *M. Dau.* 1. *Career:* Man. Dir. Southern Television Corp. Nov. 1958–74. Director, News Ltd.; Group General Manager, Radio & Television News Ltd.; Full Time Member Australian Broadcasting Control Bd. 1974–75; Dir.-Gen. for Trade & Development, Premier's Dept., S.A., Nov. 1975; Bd. mem., South Australian Film Corp. April 1976; Bd. mem., Pipeline Authority of South Australia. *Address:* 12 Delamere Avenue, Netherby, S.A., Australia.

**DAVILA, Oscar M.** Bolivian. Mining and metallurgical engineer. Co-owner of tin mines in Bolivia, and Consultant Engineer. *B.* 1920. *Educ.* Escuela de Minas de Orure (Mining Eng.), Colorado School of Mines (Metall. Eng.), and Missouri School of Mines (MSc Met. Eng.). *M.* 1948, Graciela Poblete. *S.* Gonzalo. *Dau.* Sonia. *Career:* Metallurgical Engineer, Patiño Mines 1947–49; Mill Superintendent: Castro Virreyna Metal Mines (Lima, Peru) 1952, and Empresa Minera de Catavi (largest tin concentration in the world) 1952–57; General Mill Supt., Corporación Minera de Bolivia 1958–63 (Asst. Research Manager 1963–65); Professor of Mineral Dressing 1959—(working mines on private basis and doing consulting work). Professor of Ore Dressing, Escuela de Minas de Oruro. *Publications:* Methods to Improve the Metallurgy of Tin (1958); How Empresa Minera de Catvi Concentrates Tin Ores, E. and M.J. (1957). *Award:* Straight A Student of Colorado School of Mines. *Member:* Amer. Inst. of Mining & Metallurgical Engineers; Bolivian Socy. of Engineers (Pres. Oruro Section); Colorado School of Mines Alumni Assn. *Clubs:* Oruro Social; Oruro Rotary. *Address:* Escuela de Minas de Oruro, Oruro, Bolivia.

**DAVIS, Bernard George.** American publisher. *B.* 1906. *Educ.* Univ. of Pennsylvania, Columbia Univ., Univ. of Pittsburgh (BS 1927). *M.* 1930, Sylvia Friedman. *S.* Joel. *Dau.* Carol. *Career:* Editor of Pitt Panther, Univ. of Pittsburgh 1926; Secretary-Treasurer, Association of College Comics of the East 1926–27; Vice-Pres. and Dir., Ziff-Davis Publishing Co. 1936–46; President 1946–57; Director (1955–68), Treasurer (1959–67); Magazine Publishers Assn.; Pres. 1957–68, Chmn. 1968; Davis Publications, Inc.; U.S. Delegate Civil Air Patrol, International Cadet Exchange Programme Conference, Lisbon (1955) and Lima (1956). *Member:* National Panel of Arbitrators, American Arbitration Assoc., 1956–67; American Council on Education for Journalism, 1959–67; Dir., International Programs Univ., Palm Beach, since 1969; Dir. 1971, Ibis Isle Central Condominium Assn. Inc. Pres. 1972. Pi Beta; Sigma Delta Chi. *Club:* Ocean Beach. *Address: office* 229 Park Avenue, New York, N.Y., U.S.A.

**DAVIS, Charles J.** American resort and land developer. *B.* 1914. *M.* 1940, Isla B. Small. *S.* 2. *Career:* Pres. Davis Mfg. Inc.; Pres. & Gen. Man. Mid-Western Industries, Inc., 1950–57; Gen. Man. Massey Ferguson Industrial Div. 1957–59; Pres. New Davis Mfg. Inc. 1960–68, merged with Tenneco Inc., 1968; Davis Mfg. Co. Div. J.I. Case Subsidiary, Tenneco 1968–71; Owner Shangri La & Shangri La Estates Afton Oklahoma since 1969; Mem. Local, State & Nat. Chamber of Commerce; Nat. Assoc. of Mfrs. *Address:* Rt 3, Afton, Oklahoma 74331, U.S.A. and *office* c/o Shangri-la, Rt. 3, Afton, Oklahoma, 74331, U.S.A.

**DAVIS, C. Malcolm.** American. *B.* 1918. *Educ.* School of Commerce, N.Y. Univ. (BS) and Harvard Graduate School of Business Administration. *M.* (1) (*divorced*). *S.* Craig M., Bruce G. and Grant H. *Dau.* Susan K. (2) 1974, Mildred

Wright Oschwald. *Career:* Chairman, Fidelity Union Trust Co.; Director: Bamberger's, N.J.; Prudential Insurance Co. of America; Public Service Electric & Gas Co.; Pennwalt Corp., Allied Bank International; Chmn. Bd. Fidelity Union Bancorporation, & Allied Bank International. Vice-President, Newark Museum; Member, Newark Fiscal Advisory Board, Republican. *Clubs:* Somerset Hills Country; Baltusrol Golf; Essex; Down Town; Links Club. *Address:* 199 Lake Rd., Morristown, N.J. 07960, U.S.A.; and *office* 765 Broad Street, Newark, New Jersey 07101, U.S.A.

**DAVIS, Geoffrey George John.** Cement manufacturer. *B.* 1908. *Educ.* Durham University. *M.* 1946, Mary Winteringham. *S.* (adopted) Michael. *Career:* Managing Director: The Associated Portland Cement Manufacturers Ltd. 1953— (Director 1948—), and The British Portland Cement Manufacturers Ltd. 1953— (Director 1948); Chairman: Anchor China Clay Ltd. 1948—, Nottingham Gypsum Products Ltd. 1951—, and Riddlesdown Lime Co. Ltd. 1952—; Aberthaw and Bristol Channel Portland Cement Co. Ltd.; Atlas Stone Co. Ltd.; Standard Portland Cement Co. Ltd., de Mixcoac S.A. (Mexico), Commonwealth Portland Cement Co. Ltd. (Sydney), Commonwealth Portland Cement Nominees Pty. Ltd. (Sydney), Golden Bay Cement Co. Ltd. (Wellington, N.Z.), La Tolteca, Compania de Cemento Portland S.A. (Mexico), Metropolitan Portland Cement Co. Ltd. (Sydney), Victoria Portland Cement Co. Pty. Ltd. (Sydney), West African Portland Cement Co. Ltd. (Lagos), and White South African Portland Cement Co. Ltd. (Johannesburg), Associated Portland Cement Mfrs. (Australia) Pty. Ltd., Associated International Cement (Australia) Pty. Ltd., Bamburi Portland Cement Co. Ltd. Freeman of the City of London; Member, Worshipful Company of Fanmakers. *Clubs:* East India & Sports; Devonshire; Institute of Directors. *Address: office* Portland House, Stag Place, London, S.W.1.

**DAVIS, Sir John Henry.** British companv director *B.* 1906. *Educ.* City of London School. *Career:* President of The Rank Organisation Ltd.; Joint President Rank Xerox Ltd.; Director, Eagle Star Insurance Co. Ltd.; Chmn. of Children's Film Foundation Ltd. *Address:* 38 South Street, London, W1A 4QU.

**DAVIS, John Herbert.** Economist and administrator. *B.* 1904. *Educ.* Iowa State Univ. of Science and Technology (BS) and Univ. of Minnesota (MA and PhD). *M.* 1928, Edna Frazier. *S.* James F. and H. Lowell. *Career:* Vocational agricultural teacher and Superintendent of Schools, Douda, Iowa 1928–35; Economist, U.S. Dept. of Agriculture 1935–36; Superintendent of Schools, Story City, Iowa 1937–39; graduate work and research, Univ. of Minnesota 1939–41; Economist, U.S. Dept. of Agriculture 1941–42; Chief, Wheat Section, Commodity Credit Corp. 1942–44; Exec. Vice-Pres., National Council of Farmer Co-operatives 1944–52; General Manager, National Wool Marketing Corp. 1952–53; Asst. Secretary of Agriculture, President of Commodity Credit Corp., and Pres., Federal Crop Insurance Corp. 1953–54; Director, Program in Agriculture and Business, Graduate School of Business Administration, Harvard Univ. 1954–59; Commissioner-General, United Nations Relief and Works Agency, Beirut, Lebanon 1959–64. Exec. Vice-Chmn. Bd. of Trustees, American University of Beirut, 1964–67, Pres., American Middle East Refuge Aid, Inc. 1968–76. Vice-Chairman of the Board of Trustees and Director of New York Office, American University of Beirut 1964–67; Pres., Musa Alami Foundation 1967—. *Awards:* Citation, outstanding public service (N.J. Alumni, Notre Dame Univ.); Plakett citation, distinguished public service (Norske Flyktningerad, Norway); Grand Officer, Order of Cedars (Lebanon), of Order of the Star (Jordan) and Order of Merit (Syria); Citation, U.S. Cttee. for Refugees; Alumni Merit Award (Iowa State Univ. of Science and Technology); Knight, Order of the Hospital of St. John of Jerusalem (U.K.). *Publications:* An Economic Analysis of the Tax Status of Farm Co-operatives; A Concept of Agribusiness, and Farmer in a Business Suit, The Evasive Peace. *Clubs:* Cosmos (Washington); Harvard (N.Y.C.); Farmers (London). *Address:* 2500 Massachusetts Ave., N.W., Washington, D.C. 20008; and *office* ANERA, 733 15th St. N.W., Washington D.C. 20005, U.S.A.

**DAVIS, Malcolm Chris.** British. *B.* 1917. *Educ.* Christ's Coll. N.Z.; Clifton Coll. England. *M.* 1948, Rosalie Markham Carter. *S.* 2. *Career:* Man. Dir. Davis Consolidated Industries Ltd., Dir. subsidiaries; Chmn. Mercantile Mutual Insurance Co. Ltd., Australian General Insurance Co. Ltd.; Mercantile Mutual Life Insurance Co. Ltd; Mercantile Investment Co. Ltd; Mercantile Pacific Finance Co. Ltd.; Dir. The Australian Gas Light Co., Amalgamated Batteries Ltd. & Acmil Ltd. *Clubs:* Australian; Australasian Pioneers'; Kuring-gai Motor Yacht; Fellow Australian Inst. of Management; Life Governor N.S.W. Police-Citizen's Boys' Clubs. *Address:* 12 Cherry Place, Castle Cove, N.S.W., Australia 2069; and *office* Spring St., Botany, N.S.W.

**DAVIS, Martin S.,** Sr. American company executive. *B.* 1927. *Educ.* New York University; City College of N.Y. *M. S.* Martin jr., Philip. *Career:* Executive Vice President and member of executive committee of Gulf and Western Industries Inc. since 1969. Dir.: Gulf and Western Industries Inc.; Institute of Collective Bargaining and Group Relations. City College of New York Campaign Steering Committee; Dir., National Multiple Sclerosis Society. *Address:* 1 Gulf Western Plaza. New York, N.Y. 10023, U.S.A.

**DAVIS, Morgan Jones.** American petroleum consultant. *B.* 1898. *Educ.* Texas Christian Univ.; Univ. of Texas (BA in Geology) 1925; Harvard Graduate School of Business Administration (Advanced Management 1947; DEng (Hon.), Colorado Schl. of Mines, 1964). *M.* 1926, Veta Clare Moore. *S.* Morgan J., Jr., and James Harrison. *Career:* Ranchhand on Texas cattle ranch 1915–16; Engineer, later Asst. Supt., Tulsa Spavinaw Water Project 1921–24; Geologist: Humble Oil & Refining Co. 1925, Nederlandsche Koloniale Petroleum Mij. Sumatra, 1929–34. District Geologist (1934), Humble Div. Geologist 1936, Chief Geologist (1941), Manager of exploration (1946), Director i/c of exploration (1948), Vice-Pres. (1951), Exec. Vice-Pres. (1956), Pres. Apr. 1957–61, Chmn. of Bd. & Chief Executive Officer 1961–63, Humble Oil & Refining Co. Member of Bd. of Dirs., First City Nat. Bank, Houston; Dep. Chairman, Board of Dirs., Fed Reserve Bank of Dallas 1961–63. Mem., Amer. Assn. of Petroleum Geologists (Pres. 1952–53); Member of Board, Amer. Petroleum Inst.; Mem., Amer. Inst. of Professional Geologists; Amer. Inst. of Mining, Metallurgical and Petroleum Engineers; Geological Socy. of America (Pres. 1969); Mid Continent Oil & Gas Assn. (Recipient Distinguished Service Award, Texas 1960; Trustee. AAPG Fdn.; Advisory Council to the Geological Fdn., Univ. of Texas (Past Chmn.); Adv. Council-Geology, Rice Univ.; Houston Geological Society (Life Member); American Geographical Society; American Geophysical Union; Texas Academy of Science; Amer. Geological Inst. Member of Bd. of Trustees, Kinkaid School, Houston, Texasi *Member:* Philosophical Soc. of Texas; Past. Pres., Houston Museum of Natural Science; Trustee. Space Hall of Fame (For. Pres.) Sigma Gamma Epsilon, Sigma Iota Epsilon, Delta Kappa Epsilon, Mason. *Clubs:* Houston Country; River Oaks Country; Petroleum; Ramada; Bayou; (all of Houston); St. Charles Bay Hunting (Rockport, Tex.); Boston (New Orelans); Mill Reef (Antigua, W.I.); Twenty-Five Year; Petroleum Ind. (Pres. 1963). *Address:* 3207 Inwood Drive, Houston 77019, Tex., U.S.A., and Mill Reef Club, Antigua, W.I.; and *office* 1300 Main, Suite 709, Houston, Texas 77002.

**DAVIS, Nathanael Vining.** American. *B.* 1915. *Educ.* Harvard Coll. (AB 1938), London School of Economics. *M.* 1941, Lois Howard Thompson. *S.* James Howard Dow. *Dau.* Katharine Vining. *Career:* President and Director, Alcan Aluminium Ltd. 1947–72; (with the Company since 1939), Chmn. Bd. & Chief Exec. Officer since 1972; Dir. Aluminum Co. of Canada, Ltd. and other subsidiaries in Alcan group; The Canada Life Assurance Co.; Bank of Montreal; Governor, The Canadian Association for Latin America; Former member Bd. Oversees, alma mater, Harvard College. *Trustee:* The American School of Classical Studies (Athens, Greece). *Clubs:* The Mount Royal, Saint James's (Montreal); Somerset (Boston); The Country (Brookline, Mass.); The University, The Links (New York City). *Address:* 3050 Trafalgar Avenue, Montreal, P.Q. Canada, H3Y 1H4; and *office* P.O. Box 6090, Montreal Canada, H3C 3H2.

**DAVIS, Nathaniel.** American Diplomat. *B.* 1925. *Educ.* Phillips Exeter Acad.; Brown Univ.—MA; Fletcher Sch. of Law & Diplomacy—Dr. Phil; Hon. LLD, Brown Univ. 1970. *M.* 1956, Elizabeth Kirkbride Creese. *S.* 2. *Daus.* 2. *Career:* U.S. Naval Reserve 1943–46; entered Foreign Service 1947, served in Prague, Florence, Rome & Moscow; Desk Officer & Dep. Officer i/c Soviet Affairs, Dept. of State 1956–60; 1st Sec., Caracas 1960–62; Special Asst. to the Peace Corps Dir. 1962–63; Dep. Assoc. Dir. of the Peace Corps 1963–65; American Minister to Bulgaria 1965–66; Senior Staff, Nat. Security Council, White House 1966–68; American Ambassador to Guatemala 1968–71, to Chile 1971–73; Dir.-Gen. of the U.S. Foreign Service 1973–75; Asst. Sec. of State for African Affairs, Apr.–Dec. 1975; Ambassador to Switzerland 1975–77. *Member:* Chmn., Inner City Children's & Youth Program of the National Capital Area Council of Churches 1958–59; Bd. of Dirs., Northwest Settlement House in

Washington; Vice-Chmn. of Bd. of Dirs., American Foreign Service Assoc. *Decorations:* Hartshorn Premium, 1942; Caesar Misch Premium, 1942; Cinco Aguilas Blancas alpinism award, Venezuela 1962. *Address:* c/o Fife, 613 Hudson Street, Hoboken, N.J.; and *office* c/o Department of State, Washington, D.C. U.S.A.

**DAVIS, Norman.** Chartered Chemist. *B.* 1924. *Educ.* Sydney (N.S.W.) Technical College (Dipl. Chem.). *M.* 1947, Peggy A. Kerr. *S.* Christopher W. *Dau.* Jennifer R. *Career:* Senior Chemist, Michael Nairn (Aust.) Ltd., N.S.W. 1944–46; Chief Technical Officer, Ready Mixed Concrete (N.S.W.) Pty. Ltd. 1946–52, and Ready Mixed Concrete Ltd., U.K. 1952–54, Technical Director 1954–68. Deputy Managing Director, Ready Mixed Concrete Ltd. and subsidiary associated companies since 1962. Associate: Royal Australian Chemical Institute (A.R.A.C.I.), and Member: Royal Inst. of Chemistry (M.R.I.C.). *Address:* Windlegate, Sunningdale, Berks.; and *office* 53 High St., Feltham, Middlesex.

**DAVIS, Owen Lennox.** Australian diplomat. OBE. *B.* 1912. *Educ.* Sydney Univ., BA (Hons.); LLB (Hons.), *M.* 1940, Alison Mary Nicholas. *Career:* Barrister-at-Law, Sydney 1938; Australian Imperial Forces (Staff Capt., Malaya) 1940–45; joined Australian Dept. of External Affairs 1946; First Secretary, Embassy, Washington (1948–51) and High Commission, Karachi 1952–53; Acting High Commissioner, Wellington, N.Z. 1955–56; Senior External Affairs Representative, Australia House, London 1957–59; Ambassador to South Africa 1959–62; Ambassador to Brazil 1962–64; Chairman, Joint Intelligence Cttee., 1964–67; First Assistant Secretary, Dept. of External Affairs, Canberra 1967–69. Ambassador to Belgium and EEC 1969–72, Luxembourg 1970–72, and Mexico 1972–74; Perm. Mission to UN, Geneva 1974–77; Australian Rep. to UN Commission of Human Rights 1978. *Member:* Australian delegation to U.N. 1946, Delegate 1962 and 1968; and to Japanese Peace Conference 1951. *Club:* Royal Sydney Golf. *Address:* Apartado 140, Mijas, Malaga, Spain.

**DAVIS, Paul Herbert.** American college consultant. *B.* 1897. *Educ.* Stanford Univ. (BS 1922; EE 1923) and Chapman College LLD 1961; Pepperdine Univ. LLD 1972. *M.* 1928, Helen Meyer Brack. *S.* Herbert Paul; Brack (MD), and Forster Adams. *Career:* Aviation Section, U.S. Army 1917–20; Consultant, The Readers Digest 1956—. *Address:* P.O. Box 6087, Carmel Valley Manor, Carmel, California, 93921, U.S.A.

**DAVIS, Roy Wright.** American. *B.* 1914. *Educ.* John Marshall High School (Richmond) and Virginia Mechanics Inst. (Richmond); Certificate in business administration and accountancy; CPA Virginia 1936. *M.* 1945, Dorothy Mae Kenyon. *S.* Roy Wright II, and Christopher Kenyon. *Dau.* Linda Gaye. *Career:* C.P.A., Ernst & Ernst, Richmond 1936–42; Special Agent, Fed. Bureau of Investigation, U.S. Dept. of Justice, Washington, D.C. 1942–48; Reynolds Metals Co., Richmond, Va., Assistant to Treas. 1948–53, Asst. Treasurer 1953–61; Treasurer 1961–75; Financial Vice-Pres. 1975; Officer and director of various subsidiaries of Reynold Metals Co.; Director, Home Capital Funds Inc. (Austin, Tex.) Columbia Ventures, Inc. Washington D.C.; Southern Bank shares Inc. & Southern Bank and Trust Co., Richmond *Member:* Society of Former Special Agents of the F.B.I.; Amer. Inst. of C.P.A.s; Virginia Socy. of C.P.A.s; Newcomen Socy. of America; Virginia Assn. of Professions, Inc.; Finance Division Council of American Management Assns, *Club:* Hermitage Country (Richmond; Past Pres.). *Address:* 207 Wexleigh Drive, Richmond, Va. 23229; and *office* Reynolds Metals Company, P.O. Box 27003, Richmond, Va. 23261, U.S.A.

**DAVIS, Shelby Cullom.** American. diplomat. *B.* 1909. *Educ.* Princeton Univ., AB; Columbia Univ., AM Univ. of Geneva, Dr. Political Science. *M.* 1932, Kathryn Edith Waterman. *S.* Shelby Moor. *Dau.* Diana. *Career:* First Deputy Superintendent State of New York, 1944–47; Ambassador to Switzerland 1969–74; Trustees College of Insurance: Jackson Laboratory; Lieut. Gov. General Society of Colonial Wars; Former Pres., Financial Analysts Federation: Chmn., History Advisory Council, Princeton University. Republican. *Publications:* Reservoirs of Men (1934); The French War Machine (1937); Your Career in Defense (1942); America Faces the Forties (1940); LLD Bradley Univ. (1966). *Clubs:* Knickerbocker; Univ.; Princeton (N.Y.); Sleepy Hollow Country; Everglades( Palm Beach); etc. *Address:* c/o State Dept. Washington, D.C. 20520, U.S.A.

**DAVIS, Stanley Clinton,** LLB, MP. British politician and solicitor. *B.* 1928. *Educ.* Hackney Downs Sec. School; Mercers School; King's College London University. *M.* 1954, Frances Jane Lucas. *S.* Henry. *Daus.* Joanna Sara, Susanna, Melissa Gay. *Career:* Councillor, Metropolitan Borough of Hackney 1959–64; London Borough of Hackney 1964–71; Parly. Candidate for Portsmouth, Langstone 1955, Yarmouth 1959, Yarmouth 1964; Chmn. Welfare Cttee., London Borough, Hackney 1967–68; Mayor 1968–69; Member Parliament, Hackney Central 1970—; Joint Secy. All Party Parly. Solicitors Group 1970–74; Joint Secretary. Parly. Labour Party Anglo-Chilean Group 1972–74; Member Exec. Cttee. Socy. Labour Lawyers 1973–74; Parly. Under-Secy. of State Dept. of Trade with responsibilities for companies, aviation and shipping since 1974. *Member:* Law Socy.; London Criminal Courts Solicitors Assn.; Socy. Labour Lawyers; National Council, Civil Liberties. *Address:* Essex Lodge, 354 Finchley Road, Hampstead, London, NW3 7HA; and *office:* Clinton Davis & Co., 343a—345a Mare Street, Hackney, London, E.8.

**DAVIS, Thomas Potter,** BA, Legion of Merit. American banker. *B.* 1904. *Educ.* Yale Univ. (BA). *Career:* Officia. First Nat. City Bank 1926–63; Resident Vice Pres. First Natl City Bank in Japan 1960–64; Asahi Fiber Glass Co. Ltd.; Koyo-Lindberg Co. Ltd.; Terasaki-Nelson Ltd.; Travel Center of Japan; Senior Adviser, Seattle First National Bank. *Member:* Asiatic Socy. of Japan; Councellor, International Hse. of Japan; American-Japan Socy.; Auditor, Grew Foundation. *Clubs:* Tokyo; Foreign Correspondents, Tokyo; Metropolitan, New York; Rotary, Tokyo. *Address:* 15–14 Shimo-Meguro 6-chome, Meguro-ku, Tokyo, Japan.

**DAVIS, True.** *B.* 1919. *Educ.* Cornell University. *M.* 1948, Virginia Bruce Motter. *S.* William True III, Bruce Motter and Lance Barrow. *Career:* Served as Lieut. (s.g.) U.S.N.R. 1942–45 (chief test pilot, Naval Air Station, Pearl Harbor); Colonel on Staff of Governor of Missouri 1949–54, 1960–65, and Governor of Kentucky 1953–54. President and Chmn. of the Bd., Research Laboratories, Inc. 1952–60; Pets' Best Co. 1954–60; Peters Serum Co. 1956–60; Wilke Labs. Inc. of Tennessee 1956–60; West Plains 1956–60; Peerless Serum Co. 1956–60; Medical Industries Inc. 1956–63; Gothic Advertising 1956–60; Certified Labs. Inc. 1956–60; Carolina Veterinary Supply Inc. 1956–60; World Health Inst. Ltd. 1958–60; Anchor Serum Companies of New Jersey, Newark, N.J. and Indiana 1959–60; Anchor Serum Co., Minnesoto 1960–63; Chemico Labs. Inc., Miami 1960–63. Director, Preferred Fire Ins. Co., Topeka, Kan. 1957–65; St. Joseph Belt Railroad Co. 1959–63; St. Joseph Light & Power Co. 1963–69; Livestock Financial Corp., New York 1962–63; The National Bank of Washington 1968–73; Vice-Pres. and Dir. Philips Electronics and Pharmaceutical Industries Corporation 1959–63; Chairman of the Bd., Thomson Hayward Chemical Co., Kansas City 1961–63; The National Bank of Washington D.C. 1969–73; Exec. Dir. Inter-American Development Bank 1966–68; President, Anchor Serum Co., St. Joseph 1950–60; Philips Roxane Inc. 1959–63; The National Bank of Washington D.C. 1970–73; PEPI (Philips Electronics & Pharmaceutical Ind. Corp.) New York since 1972. Member, National Serum Control Agency 1947–58; Director, Little League 1958–60, and Natl. Assn. of Boys Clubs of America 1952–63. Police Comm., St. Joseph, Mo. 1949; Bd. of Governors, Amer. Royal, Kansas City 1960—; Dir., Mo. State Chamber of Commerce 1952–54; member, V.F.W. Americanism Chairman for State of Mo. 1960–63; Natl. V.F.W. Americanism Cttee. 1961–63; member: Exec. Cttee. United Fund 1960, N.A.M. Nuclear Energy Cttee. 1961–63, Cornell Univ. Council 1962–68. Trustee, Missouri Public Expenditure Survey 1962–63. Democrat (active National and Local). Asst. Secretary of the Treas. Wash. D.C. 1965–68, Chairman U.S. Port Security N.Y. Pier, and Public Adv. Cttee. on Customs Admin. 1966–68, Delegate to International Marine Coordinating Organization (United Nations), May 1966. Advisor to U.S. 'Dumping' Delegation, GATT, 1966. Advisor, U.S. Delegate, Annual Meeting, Bd. of Govns. of the Int. Bank for Reconstruction and Development and the Int. Monetary Fund, Washington, D.C., September 1966. Member, U.S. Del. Inter-American Development Bank Governors' Conference, Washington, D.C., April 1967, and U.S. Del., American Chiefs of State Summit Meeting, Punta del Este, Uruguay, April 1967. Alternate Treasury Member, Foreign Trade Zones Board 1966–68. Ambassador to U.S. to Switzerland 1963–65. *Awards:* V.F.W. Outstanding Citizen Award, St. Joseph, 1960, and St. Joseph Chamber of Commerce Boss of the Year Award 1960; Guest Lect. All Amer. Conference to Combat Communism 1967; U.S. Treas. Exceptional Service 1968, and many others. Life member New York Academy of Sciences. *Publications:* Americanism v. Communism (1962); The Partnership between the Federal Government and American Universities in Financing Scientific Enquiry (1967). *Clubs:* Benton (Pres. 1949–50); Keeneland; Thoroughbred of America (Lexington, Ky.); Brook (N.Y.C.); Metropolitan (Wash. D.C.); Minnesouri Angling, Alexandria, Minn. (Pres. 1961—); *Address:* 2860 Woodland Drive, N.W. Washington D.C., U.S.A.

**DAVIS, W(illard) Kenneth.** Engineering executive. *B.* 1918. *Educ.* College of Chemistry, Univ. of California, and Massachusetts Inst. of Technology (BS and MS, chemical engineering). *M.* 1941, Margaret Ellen Bean. *S.* Warren Kenneth. *Daus.* Kerry Suzanne and Gail Marie, *Career:* Asst. Director, M.I.T. School of Chemical Engineering Practice 1941–42; Sen. Research Eng. California Res. Corp. 1942–47; Senior Engineer, Ford, Bacon & Davis Inc. 1947–49; Prof. of Engineering Univ. of Calif. 1949–53, Assoc. Prof. 1949–52, Prof. 1953; Mgr. of Research, California Research & Development Co. 1951–54; Dir. of Reactor Development, U.S. Atomic Energy Commission 1955–58; Vice Pres. Bechtel Corp, 1958—; Bechtel Nuclear Corp, 1958—; Dir. 1960–68, Pres. 1964–66, Atomic Industrial Forum, Hon. Dir. since 1968. *Awards:* Arthur S. Fleming Award, 1956; Professional Progress Award, American Inst. of Chemical Engineers, 1958; Regents Lecturer, Univ. of California, 1961. Robert E. Wilson Award. AICe, 1969; National Academy of Engineering, 1970. *Member:* American Institute of Chemical Engineers (Chairman, Nuclear Engineering Division 1958); American Nuclear Society (Fellow); American Chemical Society; American Society of Mechanical Engineers; Amer. Socy. for Engineering Education; Sigma Xi; British Nuclear Energy Society. *Publications:* many articles and technical publications in fields of nuclear engineering, engineering education, and chemical engineering; also on mountaineering subjects. *Clubs:* Cosmos (Washington); Engineers', World Trade (San Francisco); Sierra. *Address:* 209 Fairhills Drive, San Rafael, Calif. 94901; and *office* 50 Beale St., P.O. Box 3965, San Francisco, Calif. 94119; 3280 Edgewater Drive, Tahoe City, Calif. 95730, U.S.A.

**DAVIS, William E., Jr.** American Attorney-at-Law, Corporate, Tax, Business and Estate Planning since 1956. *B.* 1909. *Educ.* Creighton University (Omaha, Neb.); PhB 1931 and LLB 1933. *M.* 1933, Margaret May Tomlinson. *Dau.* Mrs. Elizabeth Davis Meyers. *Career:* Prior to 1940 with Regional Agricultural Credit Corp., Omaha; Standard Oil Co. of Nebraska, and National Bank of Commerce, Houston, Texas; served in World War II (Lt.-Col. Ret., U.S. Army) 1940–47; Executive Director, Tax Research Association, Houston, 1947–52; successfully completed the Federal Income, Estate and Gift Tax course of the Practising Law Institute, New York City, 1948; Instructor in Municipal Government at the University of Houston, 1948–52; successfully completed the 4th annual Tulane Tax Institute, 1954; Associate Attorney, Vinson, Elkins & Weems & Searls, Houston, 1952–54; Head Treasury Dept. and Asst. Treasurer, Schlumberger Well Surveying Corp., Houston, 1955–56; Exec. Vice-Pres. and Treasurer, Gulf Coast Leaseholds, Inc., Houston, 1955–56. Admitted to practice in Texas, Nebraska, Fifth and Seventh Federal Circuit Courts of Appeal, U.S. Tax Court, Federal District Court of Texas, and before the Treasury Department. Was charter member, Southern Institute of Management. *Member:* Texas, Nebraska and Harris County Bar Associations and Delta Theta Phi Fraternity. Presbyterian. *Publications:* numerous works and articles on taxation, organization and finance. *Address:* 3036 Locke Lane, Houston 19, Tex.; and *office* 1416 Esperson Building. Houston Texas 77002. U.S.A.

**DAYAN, Moshe.** Israeli Politician. *B.* 1915. *Educ:* Univ. of Tel Aviv—LLB. *M.* 1973, Rachel. *S.* 2. *Dau.* 1. *Career:* Chief of Gen. Staff 1953–58; Minister of Agriculture 1959–64; mem. of Knesset since 1965; Minister of Defence 1967 & 1969–74; Minister of Foreign Affairs since 1977. *Publications:* Story of My Life (1976). *Address:* 11 Yoav Street, Zahala; and *office* Ministry of Foreign Affairs, Jerusalem, Israel.

**DEACON, Donald MacKay,** MC. Canadian stockbroker. *B.* 1920. *Educ.* Univ. of Toronto (BA 1940). *M.* 1947, Florence Campbell. *S.* Campbell, David, Douglas, Richard and Colin. *Dau.* Martha. *Career:* Served with Royal Canadian Artillery 1940–46; Chmn., F. H. Deacon, Hodgson, Inc. Liberal. *Clubs:* York Downs, Toronto. *Address:* Glenburn Farms, Unionville, Ont.; and *office* 105 Adelaide Street W., Toronto, Ont., Canada.

**DEAKINS, Eric Petro,** BA Hons. MP. British politician. *B.* 1932. *Educ.* Tottenham Grammar School; London School of Economics; London University. *Career:* Marketing Executive, F.M.C. (Meat) Ltd., 1956–69; Gen. Manager, Pigs Div. F.M.C. (Meat) Ltd., 1969–70; Member of Parliament, Walthamstow West 1970–74; Waltham Forest, Walthamstow since 1974; Parly. Under-Sec. of State for Trade 1974–76; Parly. Under-Sec. of State for Health & Social Security 1976—. *Publications:* A Faith to Fight For (1964). *Address:* House of Commons, London, S.W.1.

**DEAN, George Morley.** *B.* 1901. *Educ.* Univ. of Idaho (BA). *M.* 1929, Alice Jean Frazier. *Daus.* Charlotte (Bushue) and Susan (Harward). *Career:* Commissioned 2nd Lieut. U.S. Army Inf. (ORC) 1924; Capt. U.S. Army Field Artillery 1940; Major 1941; Lt.-Col. 1942; Colonel 1944; Vice Pres., Pacific Telephone & Telegraph Co., San Francisco 1957–67; (Engineer 1924; Vice Pres. & Gen. Mgr., Washington and Idaho Area 1953–56). Asst. Vice Pres. American Telephone & Telegraph Co., New York 1956–57; Bd. of Directors, Independent College of Northern California 1964–67; Citizens Comm. for Higher Edu, State of California 1964–67; San Francisco Bay Area Council (Trustee 1953–67); United Bay Area Crusade (Bd. of Govs. 1958–65, Vice Pres. 1962–63); Bd. of Governors San Francisco Symphony Assn. 1961–66; S.F. Chapter Assn. of US Army (Pres. 1965–66), and San Francisco Sixth Army Advisory Committee, since 1959; *Director:* Telecommunications Technology Inc., Sunnyvale, Ca.; Microform Data Systems, Inc., Mountain View, CA since 1971; Plantronics, Inc., Santa Cruz, CA since 1969; Computer Transmission Corp, El Segundo, CA since 1971; Coastal Parks Assn. since 1972; *Trustee,* San Mateo College Foundation since 1971; Endowment Fund, Congregational Church of San Mateo since 1975; California State Horsemen's Assn. Charitable Trust since 1969. *Chairman,* California Recreation Trails Committee 1968–76; *President:* Fort Point and Army Museum Assn. *Member:* Telephone Pioneers of America; San Mateo and California State Horsemen's Assns. Exec. Bd. San Mateo County Council; Boy Scouts of America 1958–74; Western Region Boy Scouts Exec. Bd. since 1959. *Awards:* Legion of Merit, Army Commendation Award; Hon Comdr. of British Empire (Mil.). *Clubs:* Alpha Kappa Psi; Sigma Chi; Presidio Officers' Club, San Francisco, CA. *Address:* 540 Laurent Road, Hillsborough Calif., U.S.A.

**DEAN, John Gunther.** American Diplomat. *B.* 1926. *Educ.* Harvard Univ.—BA, MA; Univ. of Paris—doctorate. *M.* 1952, Martine Duphenieux. *S.* 2. *Dau.* 1. *Career:* Consul, Togo 1959–60; Chargé d'Affaires, Mali 1960–61; Dept. of State 1961–63; mem., U.S. Delegation to 18th UN General Assembly 1963; Dept. of State 1963–65; American Embassy, Paris 1965–69; Fellow, Harvard Univ. 1969–70; Deputy to 24th Corps Commander, Vietnam 1970–72; Chargé d'Affaires, Laos 1972–74; American Ambassador to Cambodia 1974–75, and to Denmark since 1975. *Member:* American Foreign Service Assoc. *Decorations:* Commander of the National Order of Vietnam; Grand Officer of Sahametrei of the Khmer Republic; Superior Honor Award, Meritorious Honor Award, Dept. of State; etc. *Clubs:* Harvard Club of N.Y.C.; Kenwood Country Club of Washington, D.C. *Address:* Rydhave, Strandvej 259, 2920 Charlottenlund; and *office* American Embassy, Dag Hammarskjolds Allé 24, 2100 Copenhagen, Denmark.

**DEAN, Sir Maurice Joseph,** KCB, KCMG. British civil servant. *B.* 16 Sept. 1906. *Educ.* St. Olave's; Trinity Coll., Cambridge; Hon. LLD Strathclyde, 1970. *M.* 1943, Anne Gibson. *S.* 1. *Dau.* 1. *Career:* entered Civil Service 1929; Assist. Principal, Air Ministry 1929; Asst. Under-Sec. of State 1943; Dep. Sec. Control Office for Germany and Austria 1946; Deputy Under-Secretary of State, Foreign Office (German Section) 1947; Deputy Secretary Ministry of Defence 1948; 3rd Secretary, Treasury 1952; 2nd Secretary, Board of Trade 1952–55; Permanent Under-Secretary of State, Air Ministry 1955–63; Second Secretary, H.M. Treasury 1963–64; Joint Permanent Under-Secretary, Dept. of Education & Science 1964; Permanent Secretary, Ministry of Technology 1964–66. 1966–71, Director, British Printing Corporation. *Address:* 27 Bathgate Road, London, S.W.19.

**DEAN, Sir Patrick Henry,** GCMG. British. *B.* 1909. *Educ.* Rugby School and MA Cantab. Hon. LLD Lincoln Wesleyan Univ. 1961; Chattanooga Univ. 1962; Hofstra Univ. 1964; Columbia Univ. 1965, Univ. of S. Carolina 1967; and Coll. of William and Mary 1968. Hon. Fellow, Clare Coll., and Gonville and Caius College 1965. *M.* 1947, Patricia Wallace Jackson. *S.* 2. *Career:* Practised at the Bar 1934–39; Hon. Bencher Lincoln's Inn 1965. Assistant Legal Adviser, Foreign Office 1939–45; Head of German Political Department, Foreign Office 1946–50; Minister at Rome 1950–51; Senior Civilian

Instructor at Imperial Defence College 1952–53; Assistant Under-Secretary of State, Foreign Office 1953–56; Deputy-Secretary of State 1956–60; United Kingdom Permanent Representative at United Nations 1960–64; British Ambassador to U.S.A., April 1965–69; Chmn., Cambridge Petroleum Royalties Ltd.; Director, Taylor Woodrow Ltd.; Ingersoll Rand Holdings Ltd.; Amex Bank Ltd.; Jove Investment Trust; Chairman, English-Speaking Union, Gov. Body Rugby School. *Clubs:* Brook's; Beefsteak. *Address:* 5 Bentinck Mansions, Bentinck St., London, W.1.

**DEAN, Sidney Walter, Jr.** American. *B.* 1905. Educ. Yale (AB 1926). *M.* 1963, Eugenia Serios. *Career:* Vice-President, J. Walter Thompson Co. 1927–42; with Lend-Lease Administration (U.S.), and Office of Strategic Services (U.S.) 1942. Capt., Combat Intelligence, U.S. Air Force (Bronze Star Medal) 1943–45; Exec. Vice-Pres., Telecoin Corp. 1945–47; Vice-Pres. and Dir., McCann-Erickson (Interpublic) Inc. 1950–61. Director, Knickerbocker Federal Savings & Loan Association 1938—; Board of Directors, Americans for Democratic Action 1953—; Vice-Pres., City Club of N.Y., Vice-President, National Businessmen's Council 1958—; Director, Market Research Corporation of America 1961—; President, Ventures Development Corporation since 1961. *Publications:* Mass Communications in Modern Society (1948); Planning for Integrated Marketing (1949). *Member:* Sigma Xi; Natl. Planning Assn.; Amer. Marketing Assn.; Amer. Management Assn.; Amer. Economic Assn.; Audit Bureau of Circulations (Dir. 1957–61); Business Publications Audit (Treas. 1932–42); Metropolitan Educational TV Assn.; N.Y.C. (Trustee 1954–59). Democrat, Reform (N.Y.C.). *Clubs:* Yale, City (Trustee). *Address:* 27 Washington Square North, New York, N.Y. 10011, U.S.A.

**DE ANGELI, Dr. Carlo.** Cavaliere del Lavoro. *B.* 1906. *Educ.* DChem. degree in industrial pharmacy. *M.* 1931, Ernesta Gioia. *S.* Luigi and Floriano. Commendatore of the Italian Republic. Industrialist. Founder, President Istituto De Angeli s.p.a. (chemicals), Milan. *Publications:* Impiego dei Laureati in Farmacia e nell'Industria farmaceutica (1954); Lo stato attuale dell'Industria del Farmaco in Italia (1956); Caratteristiche e valore della produzione farmaceutica italiana (1957); Economia e fattori extra-economici nell' Industria farmaceutica (1960). *Member:* Board, Italian Pharmaceutical Sciences Co. *Clubs:* E.P.S. (Ente Produttori Selvaggina—private hunting reserves—President); Società del Giardino; Circolo del Clubino. *Address:* Via Serio 15, Milan, Italy.

**DEANS, Matthew Clifford.** Canadian. *B.* 1905. *Educ.* Queen's Univ., Kingston, Ontario (BCom.). *M.* 1930, Dorothy Ann Sutherland. *S.* Bruce and Roger. *Dau.* Judith (Damiani). *Career:* Employee 1927–45, Sales Manager 1945, Wood Gundy & Co., Toronto. Chairman, Bankers Securities of Canada Ltd., Investment Bankers, Toronto; Director: Northern and Central Gas Corp. Ltd., Toronto; Fittings Ltd.; Canadian Brass Ltd.; Canada Carbon & Ribbon Co. Ltd.; D. A. Stuart Oil Co. Ltd. (Toronto). *Member:* Toronto Board of Trade; Investment Dealers Assn. of Canada. Life Member, Queen's Univ. Alumini Assn. Conservative Party of Canada. *Clubs:* Royal Canadian Yacht; Toronto Board of Trade. *Address:* and *office* 112 King Street West, Toronto, Ont., Canada.

**de BARDIN, Claude.** French. President Director General, S.A. Applications Minérales et Chimiques. *B.* 1927. *Clubs:* Rallye Pique-Avant-Nivernais; Franco-Amerique; Automobile d'Isle de France; Sté. de Vénnerie. *Address: office* 9–11 Avenue Franklin Roosevelt, Paris 8e, France.

**de BARSY, Eugène Georges Isidore Léon.** Belgian. *B.* 1906. *Educ.* Commercial Engineer, Brussels Free Univ. *M.* 1928, Mariette Moerman. *S.* 4. *Career:* Professor, Brussels Free University 1929–75; Dir., Credit Agricole d'Afrique, March 1931–Apr. 1935; Attaché, Office of Minister of Finance, Apr. 1935–May 1936; Dir., Office de Liquidation des Interventions de Crise, May 1936. Manager (Feb. 1938); Pres. National Export Credit Guarantee Office 1941–75; Chmn. Banking Commission 1944–73. *Member:* Exec. Committee, and Deputy Governor (Aug. 1938), Société Nationale de Crédit à l'Industrie (National Industrial Credit Fund) until Nov. 1944; Pres., Office of Sequestration, Oct. 1944–March 1945. *Publications:* various books on legislation; numerous lectures. *Awards:* Grand Officier, Order of Leopold; Civil Cross 1st Cl.; Officer, Military Order of Christ (Portugal); Commander, Order of Oak Crown (Luxembourg); Officer Order of the Flag (Yugoslavia). *Clubs:* Assn. of Former Students of the Brussels Free University; Assn. of Commercial Engineers Graduates of the Brussels Free University (Hon. Chmn.); Member, Univ. Foundation. *Address:* 14 Avenue des Fleurs, Brussels 15; and *office* 99 Ave. Louise, 1050, Brussels, Belgium.

**de BECO, Georges.** French industrialist. *B.* 1920. *M.* 1942, Thérèse Cordonnier. *S.* Jean-Loup, Philippe and Benoit, *Daus.* Françoise (Madame J. C. Boulanger), Martine (Madame J. P. Cirier), and Pascal (Madame P. Beranger). *Career:* Pres. Director-General, Fenderies. Bouillot et Lebois Reunies, Louvroil 59; Manager: C. Bouillot fils et cie, S.A.R.L. Poincon & Matrice, Louvroil, and Sté Maubeugoise de Transports & Matériaux, Maubeuge: President, Syndicat des Fondeurs du Nord de la France; Vice-Pres., Syndicat General des Fondeurs de France. *Clubs:* Rotary (Maubeuge); Golf (Touquet). *Address:* 28 rue Jules Gallois, Louvroil (Nord), France.

**de BELFRAGE, Kurt-Allen.** Swedish. *B.* 27 Aug. 1907. *Educ.* Grenoble Univ. (L. ès L.); Stockholm Univ. (L. en D.). *M.* 1936, Renée Puaux. *S.* Patrick, Franck, Erik. *Career:* Attaché, Min. of Foreign Affairs 1930, Second Secretary 1935, Special Secy. 1936–38; First Secy., Bucharest and Sofia 1938–41, London 1943; Political Delegate to Algiers 1944; Counsellor of Embassy, Paris 1945–51; En. Ex. and Min. Plen. to Austria 1951; Deputy Chairman, Atlas Copco AB; Chairman, Swedish Export Council. *Awards:* Officer, Order of the North Star; Commandeur de la Légion d'Honneur. *Address:* Atlas Copco AB, Stockholm, Sweden.

**de BESCHE, Hubert Wathier August.** Swedish diplomat. *B.* 1911. *Educ.* Stockholm Univ.; Univ. of Grenoble; Univ. of Heidelberg. *M.* 1946, Eva Rhedin. *Daus.* Caroline, Gunilla. *Career:* Joined Swedish Foreign Ministry, 1936; London, 1937–40; Foreign Ministry, 1940–49; Charge Commission Trade and Commerce, 1947–49; Economic Counsellor, Embassy, Washington, 1949–53; Head, Trade Dept., Foreign Ministry, 1953–56; Dep. Secretary General, Foreign Ministry, 1956–64; Mem., Board of Trade, O.E.C.D., 1960–63; Chairman: Prep. Comm. European Free Trade Association, Stockholm, 1959; Swedish Trade Delegation to Finland, Spain, U.K., 1954–55; to G.A.T.T., 1955–60; Vice-Chairman; Free Trade Area Negotiations, Paris, 1956–58; European Free Trade Assoc., 1960–63; Ambassador to U.S.A. 1964–73, to Denmark since 1973. *Awards:* Grand Cross; North Star (Sweden); Order of Christ (Portugal); Homayoun, Iran; Sun Peru; Merit, Chile, Dannebrogen, Hon. K.B.E., and numerous other decorations. *Address:* Skr Annae Plads 15, 1250 Copenhagen K, Denmark.

**de BEUS, Dr. J. G.** Dutch diplomat. *B.* 18 Oct. 1909. *Educ.* California, The Hague and Amsterdam; Univ. of Leyden (LLD). *M.* 1960, Louise L. Broussard. *Dau.* Mariolijn. *Career:* attaché, Legation, Brussels 1936–38; Secy., Legation, Copenhagen 1938–39, Berlin 1939–40; Secy., Foreign Office and to Netherlands Prime Minister in London 1940–45; Counsellor, Embassy, Washington, D.C. 1945–47; Dutch Representative, United Nations Commission for Codification and Progressive Development of International Law 1947; Counsellor, Permanent Delegation to United Nations 1948; Alternate Delegate, Third General Assembly of United Nations and Head, Far Eastern Office of Foreign Office 1949; Deputy High Commissioner, Indonesia 1950; En. Ex. Min. Plen., Washington, D.C.; Ambassador to Pakistan 1954; to U.S.S.R. 1957; to Australia 1960–63, to Federal Republic of Germany 1967. Delegate to XVIII U.N. Assembly; Permanent Representative to U.N. Member of the Security Council; Asst. Sec.-Gen., U.N., & Exec. Dir., Fund for Drug Abuse Control 1975. *Awards:* Commander of Orange Nassau; Knight, Order of the Netherlands Lion; Grand Cross, German Order of Merit. *Publications:* The Jurisprudence of the General Claims Commission, U.S.A. and Mexico; De Wedergeboorte van het Koninkrijk; The Future of West (1953); In Rusland (1963); Morgen, by het aanbreken van de dag. *Address:* Palais des Nations, Geneva, Switzerland.

**DE BOECK, Jan Florent.** Belgian executive. *B.* 1913. *Educ.* Univ. of Louvain (Lic. Com. and Consular Sc.—grad. 1934). *M.* 1947, Noëlle-Eliane Van Luyten. *Daus.* Anne-Mary, Imelda, Margret, Godelieve. *Career:* Commenced as Secretary, Flemish Economic Union 1935; founded the Bank H. Vanden Broeck & Co. 1938; and was interested in several other financial firms, and in the meat trade; since 1954 has been connected with the dairy business; Chmn. and General Manager, Upeco, Grimbergen; member of the Boards of several other companies, member of a special group sent to the U.S.A. by O.E.C.E. to study the meat and dairy trade 1959. Awarded Order of Leopold II. *Clubs:* A.V.O.H.V.; V.E.V.; V.A.B. *Address:* 'Triboefikee', Keerbergen, B2850 Belgium; and *office* Gravenmolenstraat 10, 1850 B Grimbergen.

**de BOOS, Charles William Lane.** Australian banker. *B.* 1915. *Educ.* Fort Street Boys' High School, Sydney. *M.* 1941, Jean Morris. *S.* Brian. *Dau.* Elizabeth. *Career:* Entered Bank of N.S.W. 1932; Chief Manager for Tasmania 1961–63; Chief Manager for South Australia and Northern Terriroty, 1963–68; Manager Chief Office, Melbourne 1968–69. General Manager, Partnership Pacific Ltd., 1969–73; Asst. Gen. Mgr. Bank of N.S.W. 1973; Gen Man. Bank of N.S.W. 1975. *Fellow,* Australian Inst. of Management (F.A.I.M.); Inst. of Directors (F. Inst. D.). *Clubs:* Tasmanian; Adelaide; Australian (Melb.); Australian (Sydney); A/asian Pioneers; American National. *Address:* 4 Koowong Avenue, Beauty Point, N.S.W. 2088; and *office* Box 1, G.P.O. Sydney, N.S.W. 2001.

**de BOURBON-BUSSET, Comte Jacques Louis Robert Marie.** French writer. *B.* 27 April 1912. *Educ.* Ecole Normale Supérieure (L. es L.). *M.* Laurence Ballande. *Career:* Formerly Directeur du Cabinet, Ministry of Foreign Affairs 1948; Dir., Cultural Relations Dept., Min. of For. Affairs 1952; Minister Plenipotentiary 1954. Officier, Legion of Honour; Croix de Guerre 1939–45. *Publications:* Antoine mon Frère; Le Silence et la joie; Le remords est un luxe; Fugue à deux voix; Moi, César; Mémoires d'un lion; L'olympien; Les aveux infidèles; La Grande Conférence; Le Protecteur; La nature est un talisman, Les arbres et les jours; L'amour durable Comme le diamant Lejeude la Constance; Complices Laurence de Saintonge; Au Vent de la Mémoire; Editions Gallimard. *Address:* Campagne du Lion Salernes, Var, France.

**DEBRE, Michel,** D.-en-D. Former Prime Minister of France. *B.* 1912. *Educ.* Univ. of Paris. *Career:* Member, Conseil d'Etat 1934; before the 1939–45 war was attached to the office of the Minister of Finance. Cavalry officer 1939; taken prisoner but escaped to Morocco, where he became civil servant Secretariat-General of the Residence. Returned to France, joined Resistance; Commissioner of the Republic for the Region of Angers 1944; prepared the plans for administrative reform and for the statutes for the National School of Administration and Institutes of Political Studies 1945; Commissioner-General for German and Austrian Affairs 1946 (Secretary-General 1947); Senator for the Department of Indre-et-Loire (re-elected 1955). Member of the Council of Europe; Minister of Justice, De Gaulle Cabinet 1958; Premier of France 1959–62. Elected Deputy for Reunion, 1963. Minister of Economy and Finances 1966–68; Minister for Foreign Affairs 1968–69; Minister of State charge de la Defence National 1969–73. *Publications:* Demain la Paix (pseudonym: Jacquier in collaboration with Briére M. Emmanuel Monick); Refaire la France (Jacquier); La Mort de l'Etat Républicain; La République et son Pouvoir; La République et ses Problèmes; Ces Princes qui nous governent: Refaire une Démocratie, un Etat, un Pouvoir; Au Service de la Nation; Jeunesse, quelle France te faut-il ?; Une Certaine Idée de la France. *Awards:* Officer, Legion of Honour; Croix de Guerre (1939–45); Rosette of the Resistance; Free French Medal. *Address:* 18 Rue Spontini, Paris 16e, France.

**DE BRUYN, Joseph Henri Emelie.** Belgian Envoy Extraordinary & Minister Plenipotentiary. *B.* 1918. *Educ.* Lic. Commercial, Consular and Financial Sciences (1934–38). *M.* 1942, Reine M.P.M. Gilson. *S.* Peter D.J.M.V. *Career:* In government service since 1941; Dept. of Foreign Affairs 1946—; Vice-Consul, Milan 1947, Secretary of Legation, Pretoria 1948–51; in Central Administration 1952–54; Chargé d'Affaires en pied Bucarest 1954–57; Consul-General, Frankfurt/M. 1957–59; Consul-General, Düsseldorf 1959–66; Ambassador to Australia 1966–70; in Central Administration 1970–74; Consul-General, Milan since 1974. *Awards:* Grand Officer, Order of Leopold II; Commander, Order of Leopold (Belgium); Commander, Order of the Crown (Belgium); Commander, Order of Merit (W. Germany); Officer, Order of Orange-Nassau (Netherlands). *Clubs:* Lions (Klein Brabant). *Address:* c/o Ministry of Foreign Affairs, Brussels, Belgium.

**De CARVALHO E. Silva, Jorge.** Brazilian Diplomat. *B.* 1918. *Career:* Entered Brazilian Diplom. Service 1940; Vice-Consul in Portland 1944, and in Glasgow 1945; Consul in Glasgow (and chargé) 1945—47; Second Secy. in Washington Embassy 1947–50; Assist. to the Minister of Ext. Relations in Rio de Janeiro 1950–51; 2nd Secy. (1953) and 1st Secy. Paris 1953–55; 1st Secy. Rome (Embassy) 1955–58; Deputy-Head Polit. Sect. at Ministry of External Relations in Rio de Janeiro 1959 (also Head of Commercial Sect.), Counsellor 1959, Minister in 1961; Head of Section for Eastern Europe 1961–62; Min.-Counsellor at Embassy in Washington 1963–66; Brazil. Ambass. in Bogota 1966–69; Secy-Gen. Ministry Ext. Relations 1969–74: Brazil. Ambass. in Rome since 1974. *Address:* Brazilian Embassy, Piazza Navona 14, Rome, Italy.

**de CHEVIGNÉ, Comte Pierre Gabriel.** French politician and journalist. *B.* 16 June 1909. *Educ.* École Militaire de Saint Cyr. *M.* (1) 1931, Hélène Rodocanachi (*D.* 1939). *Daus.* 2. (2) 1945, Anne d'Ormesson. *Career:* Entered 1st Infantry Regiment 1929; left Army 1934; served in World War II, Captain, 127th Infantry Regiment 1939–40, joined Free French Forces in London, June 1940; commanded 1st Marine Infantry Battalion, Middle East 1940–41, Lieut.-Colonel; Directeur du Cabinet of General Catroux, High Commissioner to the Levant, Colonel 1941–42; Chief, Free French Military Mission to U.S.A. 1942–43; Chief of Staff to General Koenig, Commander of Free French Forces for the Normandy invasion 1944; Staff Major to General de Gaulle 1944–45; Deputy, Constituent Assembly 1945–46; High Commissioner to Madagascar and Dependencies 1948; Secretary of State for War 1951–54; Minister of National Defence, May 1958; Deputy (M.R.P.) Basses-Pyrénées, National Assembly 1945–58; President, General Council of Pyrénées-Atlantiques 1964–76. *Awards:* Commandeur de la Légion d'Honneur; Croix de Guerre; Compagnon de la Libération. *Address:* 11 rue Barbet de Jouy, 75007 Paris; and Liliteia, Biarritz, Pyrénées-Atlantiques, France.

**DECLERCQ, Guido Victor Alfons.** Belgian. *B.* 1928. *Educ.* Lic. Sc. Econ., Leuven 1950, and Bacc. Philosophie, Leuven 1953; C.R.B. Graduate Fellow, Columbia Univ. 1951–52. *M.* 1957, Josine Ghekiere. *S.* Dominik, Philip and Pieter. *Daus.* Magda, Beatrys and Marijke. *Career:* Manager, West Flanders Development Council, Bruges 1954–57; Managing Director, Bank van Roeselare en West-Vlaanderen, Roeselare 1957–63; Adviser to Minister of Economic Affairs 1958. General Administrator, Catholic University of Leuven 1967; Adviser, Banque Lambert, Brussels 1963–71; Director: Sté. d'Epargne, d'Hypothèques et de Crédit Atlanta S.A., Brussels 1964; Sté. Immobilière Bernheim Outremer Sibo S.A., Brussels 1967; Sté. de Location Financière de Biens d'Investissement Fininvest S.A., Brussels 1967–76; Chmn. N.V. Orda-B, Leuven 1971—. *Publications:* Structurele Werkloosheid in West Vlaanderen (with O. Vanneste) 1954; Kust en Hinterland (with O. Vanneste) 1955; Het arrondissement Ieper, 1958. *Address:* Patrijzenlaan 16, Kraainem, and *office* Catholic University of Leuven, Krakenstraat 3, Leuven/Louvain, Belgium.

**DE COSSÉ, DUC DE BRISSAC, (Simon Charles Timoléon) Pierre.** French. *B.* 1900. *Educ.* Ecole Polytechnique de Paris. *M.* 1924, Mary Schneider. *S.* François, Marquis de Brissac, and Gilles, Compte de Cossé Brissac. *Daus.* Marie-Pierre and Elvire. *Career:* Artillery Officer 1920–24. With Schneider & Co., Le Creusot 1924–65; Dir-Gen. S.W., Schneider Westinghouse 1939–48 (Chmn. 1948–64, Member Administrative Council 1964–65. *Publications:* La Duchesse d'Uzès; Histoire des Ducs de Brissac; Chasse; Longitudes; about 50 articles, prefaces, lectures, etc. *Awards:* Officier Légion d'Honneur; Comdr. Couronne de Chêne (Luxembourg); Officer, Etoile Noire (France); Ouissam Alaouite (Morocco). Chmn. Amis de Versailles; Amis des Châteaux de la Loire. Member, Académie des Sports. *Clubs:* Jockey (Pres.); St. Cloud Country; Automobile de France. *Address:* 36 Cours Albert Ier, Paris, France.

**DE COURSON DE LA VILLENEUVE, Tanguy.** French diplomat. *B.* 1911. *Educ.* Ecole des Sciences Politiques, Licence in Law, Diplomas Political Economy and Public Law. *M.* 1952, Francine Bérard. *Career:* French Consulate in London 1937–39; War service and POW 1939–42; French Embassy in Brussels 1944–49; French Military Govt. in Berlin 1949–51; French Foreign Office 1951–52; Counsellor in the Hague 1952–53; French Foreign Office 1953–56; Minister (Saarbrucken) 1956–59; Consul-general Dusseldorf 1960, Minister-counsellor in Bonn 1960–63; French Foreign Office 1963–68; Ambassador of France in Kinshasa (Zaire) 1968–70; Ambassador of France in Norway 1971–75 (ret'd). *President* (Hon.) French Chamber of Commerce in Saarebrucken. *Decoration:* Officer, Legion of honour, of Leopold and of crown of Belgium, and others. *Club:* Yeomanry. *Address:* Kalina, Place Maure, 06780 Saint Cezaire, France.

**de CROUY-CHANEL, Comte Etienne Marie René, L. ès L., L. en D.** French diplomat. *B.* 1905. *M.* 1942, Jacqueline Vallette-Viallard. *S.* Martial, Guillaume, *Daus.* Caroline, Véronique. *Career:* At League of Nations 1931–32; Private Sec. to Sec.-Gen. of Ministry of Foreign Affairs 1932–39; Liaison Officer to the Cabinet of General Commanding in Chief of the French Armies 1939–40. With French resistance forces 1944–45; Counsellor, Brazil 1945–48, Belgium 1948–50; Minister Plen. and Counsellor, London 1950–55; Director-General, Adj. of Political Affairs, Ministry of Foreign Affairs 1955–57; Permanent Representative to NATO Council 1957; Ambassador to Austria, Dec. 1958; to Netherlands,

Oct. 1961, to Belgium, Oct. 1965; Ministry of Foreign Affairs 1970–71. Commandeur Légion d'Honneur; Croix de Guerre 1944. *Address:* 4 Rue St. Florentin, Paris Ier, France.

**DEEB,** Michel. Canadian. *B.* 1930. *Educ.* M.Eng.; BSc Auto. Eng. Canada. *M.* 1960, Nicole Orfali. *S.* Derek. *Dau.* Carol. *Career:* Tech. Dir. of Workshops, Commercial Automobile Representation Co. (C.A.R. Co.; General Motors Agents), Mansourah, Aug. 1954–April 1964. Senior Engineer, Chief of Maintenance and Service Departments, National Spinning & Weaving Co., Alexandria (Egypt) April 1964–67. Plant Engineer, E. R. Squibb & Sons (Canada) Ltd. since 1968. (Special Studies); Air Pollution (1973); Engineering Management (1972); Design of Heat Transfer Equipment (1969); Machining Processes (1974); Design of Machining Equipment (1975). Member. Society of Engineers (Egypt); Order of Engineers of Quebec. Awarded the Degree of Safety Engineer 1965. *Address:* 314 Strasbourg Drive, Dollard-des-Ormeaux, Quebec H9G ISI, Canada.

**DEEDES, Rt. Hon. William Francis,** PC, MC, DL. *B.* 1913. *Educ.* Harrow School. *M.* 1942, Evelyn Hilary. *Career:* Member, Parliament (Con.) for Ashford 1950–74; Parly. Secy., Min. of Housing and Local Govt. Oct. 1954–Dec. 1955; Under-Secretary, Home Office 1955–57; Minister without Portfolio 1962–64; Editor, *The Daily Telegraph* since 1974. *Club:* Junior Carlton. *Address:* New Hayters, Aldington, Kent.

**de FARIA, Antonio Leite.** Portuguese diplomat. *B.* 1904. *Educ.* Law, Lisbon University. *M.* 1926, Herminia Cantilo. *S.* Jose Maria, Antonio Jose. *Career:* Attaché, Ministry of Foreign Affairs, Lisbon 1926; Secretary, Rio de Janeiro 1931; Paris 1933; Brussels 1934; London 1936; Counsellor, London 1939; Minister to Netherlands 1945; Director General Political Affairs, Acting Secretary General Foreign Affairs 1947; Ambassador: to Rio de Janeiro 1950; to NATO 1958; to Paris 1959; to the Holy See 1961, to the Court of St James's 1968–73. *Awards:* Grand Cross of Christ; Hon. GCVO. *Address:* Rua da Horta Seca, 11-2°. E, Lisbon 2, Portugal.

**de FERRANTI, Sir Vincent Ziani,** Kt 1948, LLD(hc), DEng (hc) FIEE. Chairman, Ferranti Ltd. 1930–63. *B.* 1893. *Educ.* Repton. *M.* 1919, Dorothy H. C. Wilson. *S.* 2. *Daus.* 3. *Career:* Served European War, 1914–19, Royal Engineers, Capt. (MC); 1939–45, Major Commanding Field Coy. RE, France, 1939–40, Lieut.-Col. Commanding 63rd County of Lancs Bn Home Guard, 1940–44; Hon. Col. 123 Field Engr. Regt. RE, TA, 1948–57. Chmn., International Exec. Council & British National Cttee., World Power Conf. 1950–62; Brit. Electrical & Allied Manufacturers Assoc.: Chmn. 1938–39, Vice-Pres. 1946–57, Pres. 1957–59; Pres. Inst. of Electrical Engineers, 1946–47; Pres. British Electrical Power Convention 1949–50; Pres. Television Soc. 1954–57. *Club:* Athenaeum. *Address:* Henbury Hall, Macclesfield, Cheshire.

**de FERRARIIS SALZANO, Carlo.** *B.* 1905. *Educ.* Dr. in International Law and in Political Sciences. *M.* 1933, Isabella Morra di San Massino. *Daus.* Beatrice and Fabrizia. *Career:* Great Cross, Order al Merito della Repubblica Italiana; several foreign decorations. Formerly Consul in Geneva and Cannes; Secretary, Embassy, Paris; Head of co-ordination office, Ministry of Foreign Affairs, Rome; First Secretary, Legation, Budapest; Head, Far East and American Division, Min. of For. Affs., Rome; Consul-General in Chicago and New York; Counsellor at Embassies in Maxico City and Brussels; Chief of Personnel and Secy.-Gen., Min. of For. Affs., Rome. Ambassador to Canada, July 1959, and to Switzerland, Oct. 1965. Permanent Representative of Italy to NATO Council 1967–70. *Address:* Via Bruno Buozzi 68, 00197 Rome, Italy.

**DE FRANCISCIS, Umberto.** Italian journalist and writer. *B.* 1912. *Educ.* DSCEcon. *M.* 1947, Marisa Margheritini. *S.* Carlo. *Career:* Editor of daily papers and contributor to periodicals since 1931. Formerly: Editor, Il Popolo di Roma, and Il Piccolo; contributor to Illustrazione Italiana, Omnibus, Oggi Storia di Ieri e di Oggi, Primato, Cinema, Documento (all before 1940, after the war: Chief Editor: Avanti, La Giustizia, Il Globo and Weekly Tempo. Head of the Correspondence Office in Rome of the monthly Successo, since 1964. Member of the Socialist Party 1944–48, but since then belongs to no party. *Member:* Parliamentary Press Association. Author of some comedies staged between 1936–40, and of historical essays on the Theatre, published by specialist journals. *Club:* Lions (Rome). *Address:* Via Ombrone 14, Rome; and *office* Via di Porta Pinciana 6, Rome, Italy.

**de FREITAS, The Rt. Hon. Sir Geoffrey Stanley,** KCMG, MP. British Parliamentarian. *B.* 1913. *Educ.* Haileybury, Clare College (Hon. Fellow) Cambridge (Pres. Cambridge Union 1934), and Yale Univ. (Mellon Fellow); Barrister-at-Law, Lincoln's Inn (Cholmeley Scholar). *M.* 1938, Helen Graham Bell (U.S.A.). *S.* 3. *Dau.* 1. *Career:* Served in World War II (R.A. and R.A.F.) 1939–45. Member of Parliament (Lab.), Central Nottingham 1945–50, Lincoln 1950–61, and Kettering 1964—. Member, Shoreditch Borough Council 1936–39; Bar Council 1939; Parliamentary Private Secy. to Prime Minister 1945–46; Under-Secy. of State for Air 1946–50, and at Home Office 1950–51; Chmn. House of Commons Select Cttee. on Overseas Development since 1964. Delegate to U.N. 1949 and 1965, Council of Europe 1951–54 and 1965–70 (Leader of U.K. Delegation), NATO Parliamentary Conference 1955–60 (Treasurer 1958–60), 1965–66. (Leader of U.K. Delegation) and since 1969 President, British Atlantic Cttee. 1965–68 and of Mouvement Gauch Européenne 1966–76. Chmn., Labour Party Housing Cttee. 1951–1954; Air Cttee. 1955–59; Agric. Cttee. 1960–61; Socy. of Labour Lawyers 1955–58; Atlantic Congress 1959; European-Atlantic Group 1968–75. Deputy-Chairman, British Council 1965–69; European Movement 1968—. Association of British Aero Clubs 1952–61; Nature Conservancy 1954–58. Member of Council, Royal Society of Arts, 1954–58 and 1964–67. Churches Social Responsibility Committee 1956–60; Agricultural Co-op. Association 1964–70; High Commissioner in Ghana 1961–63, in Kenya 1963–64. President of Consultative Assembly of Council of Europe 1966–69; Vice-Pres. Europ. Parlt. since 1975; Pres. of North Atlantic Assembly since 1976. *Clubs:* Reform, Garrick, Farmers, Guild of Air Pilots (London); Hawks (Cambridge) *Address:* House of Commons, London, S.W.1.

**de FRONDEVILLE, René.** French engineer Counsellor, *B.* 1908. *Educ.* Polytechnique, Ecole Nationale des Ponts et Chaussées. *M.* 1932, Sabine de Lanouvelle. *Daus.* 4. *Career:* Engineer, Dept. for Roads and Bridges 1931–36 and 1940–42; Maritime Engineer 1936–40; Asst. Dir., then Dir. for Industrial Equipment (preparation of the Monnet Plan; Resistance, 1st French Army) 1942–45; Asst. Dir., Ministry of Economic Affairs 1945–48; Engineer Counsellor, Banque de l'Union Parisienne 1948–69; Chairman: Sté: de Développement Régional de la Bretagne 1957–77, Hon. Pres. since 1977. *Awards:* Kt. Legion of Honour, Croix de Guerre (1939–45); Resistance Medal. Administrator of companies: Clin-Comar-Byla, Constr. Besson-St. Quentinoise C.B.S.; Ste de Developpement de la Region Mediterranéenne. *Address:* 79 Boulevard Raspail, Paris 75006, France.

**de GAIFFIER D'HESTROY, Baron Pierre Victor Felix.** Belgian diplomat. *B.* 27 Oct. 1909. *Educ.* University of Paris (D. en D.). *M.* Lucy Hsueh-Chien-Tou. *S.* Baron Edmond, Baron Paul. *Dau.* Diane. *Career:* Commissioned in Army 1934; entered Diplomatic Service 1936, Attaché, London 1937, Second Secretary, Teheran 1938, Chargé d'Affaires, a.i., Cairo 1942, First Secretary, Ottawa 1943, Washington, D.C. 1944; Delegate to the U.N. Conference, San Francisco 1945; First Secretary, London 1946; Delegate to I.T.O. Conference, Geneva and Cuba 1947; Counsellor of Embassy, Ottawa 1948; Chargé d'Affaires, Bangkok and Consul-General in Singapore, Malaya, North Borneo and Sarawak 1952–54; Min. Ex. and Plen. and Alternative Representative to U.N., New York 1957; Consul-General in Hong Kong and Macao, Sept. 1959; Ambassador to Argentina 1964–68; Belgian Foreign Office Head of Section of North, South America 1968–70; Del. U.N.O. 23rd Gen.-Assembly and 25th; Head Del. Geneva Red Cross Conference 1971; Ambassador to Mexico, Haiti and Jamaica, Consul General Cayman Islands 1972; Hon. Ambassador for Life since 1975. *Awards:* Chevalier, Ordre de Léopold, Commande, 1966; Officier, Ordre de Léopold II; Officier, Ordre de la Couronne 1952 (Commander 1957, Grand Officier 1972); Grand Croix, Ordre de San Martin; Médaille civique de Première Class; Médaille commémorative du Couronnement de Roi George VI et de la Reine Elisabeth (Angleterre). Grand Cross of the Liberator San Martin, 1965; Gran Cordon de la Orden de la clase del Aguila Azteca 1974; Croix civique de 1ére classe 1972. *Address:* 1026 16th Street, N.W., Washington D.C. 20036, U.S.A.; & 90 Eaton Place, London, S.W.1.

**de GARSIGNIES, Philippe.** French. *B.* 1909. *Educ.* BA (Law); Diploma, Ecole des Sciences Politiques. *M.* 1947, Odette de Saint Julien. *S.* 1. *Daus.* 2. *Career:* With La Nationale Incendie since May 1936. Inspector, Cie. d'Assurances contre l'Incendie La Nationale; General controler Cie Assurances Nationales. *Club:* Jockey. *Address:* *office* 44 rue de Chateaudun, Paris 9, France.

**de GUIRINGAUD, Louis.** French Diplomat. *B.* 1911. *Educ.* Diploma of Ecole Libre des Sciences Politiques, Faculty of Law, Univ. of Paris & Faculty of Letters, Sorbonne. *M.* 1955, Claude Mony. *S.* 1. *Career:* Staff mem., Min. of Foreign Affairs since 1936; Attaché, Ankara 1938–39; Special Asst. to Commissioner Foreign Affairs, Algiers 1943; First Sec., French Embassy, London 1946–49; Political Dir., French High Commn. in Germany 1949–52; Consul-Gen., San Francisco 1952–55; Dep. Perm. Rep. to UN 1955–57; Ambassador to Ghana 1957–60; Dir. Moroccan & Tunisian Affairs, Min. of Foreign Affairs, Paris 1960–62; Dep.High Commissioner, Algeria 1962–63; Inspector Gen., Diplomatic Posts 1963–66; Amb. to Japan 1966–72; Amb., Perm. Rep. of France to UN 1972–76; Pres. of Preparatory Meetings to Conf. on Int'l. Economic Cooperation, Paris, April & Oct. 1975; raised to rank of Ambassadeur de France, April 1975; appointed Minister of Foreign Affairs 1976. *Decorations:* Grand Officier de la Legion d'Honneur; Croix de Guerre 1939–45; Grand Cross, Rising Sun (Japan). *Clubs:* Jockey (Paris); Golf de Morfontaine. *Address:* 2 rue Cognacq-Jay, 75007 Paris, France; & Ministry of Foreign Affairs, Quai d'Orsay, Paris, France.

**DEHMEL, Richard Carl.** American. Engineering Executive. *B.* 1904. *Educ.* Univ. of California (BSc 1927), and Columbia Univ. (MSc 1930; DPh 1936). *M.* 1942, Madeleine Elizabeth Grim. *S.* Richard Charles. *Dau.* Marian Elizabeth. *Career:* Member Technical Staff, Bell Telephone Labs. 1927–43; Curtiss-Wright Corp. 1943–64; Chief Engineer, Development Div., 1943–45, Director of Engineering and Manufacturing, Electronics Div. 1945–60, Corporate Vice-Pres., Engineering and Research, General Office 1960–64; Consultant since 1964. Owner: 46 U.S. Patents on aircraft flight simulators, and 58 derived foreign patents. *Member:* Sigma Xi (N.Y. and Calif. Chapters); Tau Beta Pi; Epsilon Chi; Amer. Inst. of Aeronautics & Astronautics (Assoc. Fellow); Socy. Automotive Engineers; N.Y. Acad. of Sciences (Life Member). Licensed Professional Engineer, N.Y. State; Aircraft owner & Pilot (Commercial, Instrument, Multi-Engine). *Publications:* One Pair Loaded Emergency Cable (1933); The Potential Difference at Metal-Vapor, Vapor-Liquid and Liquid-Metal Interfaces of Partially Immersed Electrodes (1936); Aircraft Flight Simulation (1951); How Much Simulation? (1954); The Flight Simulator Modification (1955); New Simulation Techniques (1961). Numerous other articles on flight simulation. *Address:* 20 Barnsdale Road, Short Hills, N.J. 07078, U.S.A.

**DEHNE, Gerhard.** Dr. rer. pol. Director, Mannesmann AG Düsseldorf 1959—. *B.* 1900. *Educ.* Grammar School (with leaving certificate); Technical High School, Berlin (studies of machines and electric-technics); Commercial High School, Berlin (economics); Univ. of Berlin (law and economics). *M.* Waltraud Lammers. *Dau.* 1. *Career:* Engaged in professional work in industry 1924–29; Organizer, Second World Power Conference, Berlin 1929–30; Deputy Commercial Manager, Siemens 1931–33; Manager, Bakelite GmbH, Perutz Film GmbH, and Orenstein & Koppel AG 1933–41; Managing Director, Argus Motoren GmbH 1941–46; own enterprise 1947–49; Director, Rhein-Chemie GmbH 1949–50; Manager, German-American Trade Promotion Co. (dollar drive) 1950–53; member of the Board, Alweg AG and Manager, Alweg Forschungs GmbH, and member of the Board, Lohmann & Stolterfoht AG, and Manager, Fixatorenbau GmbH 1953–58. *Publications:* Books: Germany's Power Supply (1925, 1928); The Economics of German Electricity (1926); The Organizing of Meetings and Congresses (1934, 1962); articles in various newspapers and periodicals in Europe and America. *Address:* Lenggries/Obb., Am Schlosswald 10, Germany.

**DEHNKAMP, Willy.** German. Member Social Democratic Party 1920—; Blumenthal County Council 1929–33. Persecuted by the Nazis 1933–36; soldier 1942–45 (prisoner-of-war in Russia 1945–48). Official, Bremen-Blumenthal Community 1949–51; Senator for Education, Bremen 1951–65; Dep. Member, Bundesrat 1952–63; Pres., Standing Conf. of Ministers for Cultural Affairs, Fed. Repub. of Germany 1954–55 and 1962–63; Member, German Scientific Council 1957–65; Pres., Supreme Council of European Schools 1963–64; Burgermeister 1963–67; Pres. of the Senate of Bremen 1965—67; Member of Federal Council (Bundesrat) 1963–67; mem. of the Deutscher Bildungsrat 1968–72; Exect. Board of the German UNESCO Commission since 1968; Pres.. Gerhard-Marcks-Stiftung, Bremen since 1970; Mem., Admin, Bd., German Shipping Museum, Bremerhaven since 1971. *Address:* Bremen-Blumenthal, Ronnebecker Str. 87A, F.R.G.

**de JONQUIÈRES, Frederik Godfred de Dompierre.** Danish Ambassador. *B.* 1915. *Educ.* Bachelor of Law. *M.* 1945. Gladys Maria Zachariae. *S.* 3. Secy., Min of Foreign Affairs 1942; Second Secy. of Legation, Berne 1946; Secy. Min. of Foreign Affairs 1948; Head of Section Min. of Foreign Affairs 1949; First Secy. of Legation, Rome 1951; Head of Section, Min. of Foreign Affairs 1954; Counsellor of Legation, Chargé d'Affaires a.i., Baghdad 1957; Head of Dept. 1959; Ambassador to Djakarta 1961 (also accredited to Kuala Lumpur and Manila). Ambassador of Denmark to Teheran 1964—, also accredited to Karachi 1965— and Kabul 1966—; Ambassador, Consul-General of Denmark in Chicago 1972–74; Ambassador of Denmark to Peru, accredited to La Paz, Bolivia, 1974–76; Chief of Protocol, Ambassador, Ministry of Foreign Affairs, Copenhagen since 1976. *Awards:* Officer, Order of Dannebrog (Denmark) and various foreign decorations. *Address:* Østbanegade 15, 2100 Copenhagen Ø, Denmark.

**DE KEERSMAEKER, Paul Philip Marie Hubert.** Belgian politician. *B.* 1929. *Educ.* Greek-Latin Humaniora; Doctor in Law; Licence in Notariat. *M.* 1955, Nelly Limbourg. *S.* 1. *Daus.* 2. *Career:* Mayor of Asse 1959–77; Admin. of exec. board of the Intercommunal coop Haviland 1964; Mem. of chamber of deputies of Belgium 1968; Mem. of Exec. Bd. Brewery, NV de Keersmaeker since 1954; Member of Board of NV Seghers International since 1972; Mem. of European Parliament since 1974; Pres. of the Intercommunal Coop Havi-TV since 1975. *Club:* Rotary (Asse-Belgium). *Address:* Broekstraat 4, 1703 Kobbegem, Belgium; and *office* Brnsselstraat 1, 1703, Kobbegem, Belgium.

**De la BÈRE, Sir Rupert,** Bt, KCVO, KStJ. Company director. *Educ.* Tonbridge School. *M.* 1919, Marguerite Humphery. *S.* 2. *Daus.* 3. *Career:* Served in World War I (Capt. E. Surrey Regt. seconded to R.F.C. and R.A.F. graduated at Aboukir, Egypt) in Egypt, India, and Mesopotamia; Sheriff of City of London 1941–42. Lord Mayor 1952–53; a Member of Parliament since 1935; Alderman, Tower Ward; President of the Proprietors of Hay's Wharf Ltd., and other companies; Kt. Cmdr., Orders of Dannebrog (Denmark) and North Star (Sweden). *Address:* Crowborough Place, Crowborough, Sussex.

**de la COLINA, Rafael.** Mexican diplomat; Ambassador Representative of Mexico to the Organization of American States. *B.* 20 Sept. 1898. *M.* (1) 1920, Ruth Rosecrans (*D.* 1929). *S.* Rafael. *Dau.* Ruth (Silk). (2) 1944, Amanda Steinmeyer. *Career:* Held various posts in Consular Service 1918–34, Consul-General, San Antonio, Texas 1934–35, New York 1936–43; Minister Counsellor, Embassy, Washington 1943–44; En. Ex. and Min. Plen. to U.S.A. 1944–49; member of Delegation to many International conferences and United Nations Security Council 1946, General Assembly 1946–48; Amb. Ex. and Plen. to U.S.A. 1949–53; Perm. Rep. of Mexico to United Nations 1953–59; Ambassador to Canada 1959–62; Ambassador to Japan 1962–64; Ambassador-Representative of Mexico to Organization of American States, Washington 1965—. *Awards:* Orden al Mérito (Chile); Honneur et Mérite (Haiti); de Juan Pablo Duarte (Dominican Republic); de Vasco Nuñez de Balboa (Panama); Rising Sun (Japan); San Carlos Colombia; Libertador Venezuela; Order of the Sun (Peru). *Address:* 2440 Massachusetts Avenue, N.W., Washington, D.C. 20008, U.S.A.

**DELACOMBE, Maj.-Gen. Sir Rohan,** KCMG, KCVO, KBE, CB, DSO, LLD (Hon. Causa) Melbourne; LLD (Hon. Causa) Monash, KSt J. *B.* 1906. *Educ.* Harrow, R.M.C. Sandhurst, and Staff Coll., Camberley. *M.* 1941, Eleanor Joyce Foster (CStJ). *S.* Christopher Rohan (Major, The Royal Scots). *Dau.* Frances Anne. Commissioned 2nd Lieut., The Royal Scots, Feb. 1926; services in Egypt, Nth. China, India and Palestine. Active service Palestine 1937–39; (M.B.E. dispatches) France 1939–40, Norway 1940, Normandy DSO, 1944, Italy 1944–45, India and S.E. Asia 1945. C.O. 8th and 2nd Bn. The Royal Scots; Colonel, General Staff, H.Q. Rhine Army 1949; Commander 5th Infantry Brigade, Germany; (C.B.E.) Deputy Military Secretary, The War Office; General Officer Commanding 52 Lowland Div. and Lowland District; Col., The Royal Scots (The Royal Regt.) Jan. 1956–64; CB. British Commandant, Berlin 1959–62; Governor of Victoria 1963–74, Administrator of C'wealth Australia on 4 occasions. *Member:* Queen's Bodyguard of Scotland (Royal Company of Archers); Hon. Freeman of Melbourne; Hon. Air Commodore, R.A.A.F. Conducted a lecture tour in Canada (subject, The Berlin Problem). *Clubs:* The Royal Scots (Edinburgh); Army & Navy (London). *Address:* Shrewton Manor, nr. Salisbury, Wilts., England.

**DE LA CRUZ, Apolonio,** BSc (Bus. Admin.). Filipino. *B.* 1930. *M.* Nelia Ventura. *S.* 3. *Daus.* 3. *Career:* Treas. Theo H. Davies, Far East Ltd. & several associated Co's.; formerly Vice-Pres. & Gen. Man. T. J. Wolff & Co., Consolidated Electronics Industries, Inc.; Vice-Pres. DRB Marketing Corp.; Dir., Vice-Pres. & Gen. Man. Spectron Business Systems Corp.; *Member:* American Management Assoc.; Philippine Inst. of Certified Public Accountants; Junior Chamber of Commerce. *Clubs:* Rotary, Manila. *Address: office* P.O. Box 561, Makati Commercial Center, Makati, Rizal, Philippines.

**de La FORTELLE, Robert.** French. *B.* 1907. *Educ.* Diploma of Ecole des Hautes Etudes Commerciales. *M.* 1936, Hélène de Monplanet. *S.* 4. *Daus.* 5. *Career:* With the Crédit Lyonnais 1930–70; Hon. Chmn. Banque de la Réunion; Chmn. Société Anonyme de Pêche Maritime et de Ravitaillement. *Publications:* various articles on monetary problems. *Awards:* Officer Legion of Honour; Croix de Guerre (1939–45). Member, Société Française de Géographie Economique. *Club:* Union Interalliée (Paris). *Address:* 3 Avenue Rodin, Paris 16; and *office* SAPMER 32 rue la Boétie 75008 Paris, France.

**de LAJUGIE, François Jean-Marie.** French banker. *B.* 1924. *Educ.* Univ. of Bordeaux (Licence law). *M.* 1954, Artoni Simone. *Career:* Joined B.N.C.I. (now Banque Nationale de Paris) 1946; Inspector, B.N.C.I. (Afrique) 1948–52, Sub-Mgr., Bone, Algeria, 1953, Dep. Mgr. Constantine, Algeria, 1954, Manager, Baghdad, 1955–59, Nigeria Mgr. British & French Bank 1960, Gen. Mgr., United Bank for Africa Ltd. 1961–66; Pres. Dir. French American Banking Corp. N.Y. since 1967. *Awards:* Commd. Stella Della Solidarieta Italiana. *Clubs:* Overseas Bankers (London); France-America Socy.; Metropolitan; Automobile. *Address:* Les 3 Chênes, Tourrettes en Fayence, Var, France; *office* 120 Broadway, New York, N.Y. 10005.

**de la MARE, Sir Arthur James,** KCMG, KCVO. British diplomat. *B.* 1914. *Educ.* Victoria College, Jersey (C.I.) and Pembroke College, Cambridge (BA 1935). *M.* 1940, Katherine Elizabeth Sherwood. *Daus.* Kathleen, Marguerite and Elizabeth. *Career:* Joined Foreign Service 1936; served at Tokyo, Seoul and again Tokyo 1937–41; Washington 1942–44; London 1944–47; San Francisco (Consul) 1947–50; Tokyo (1st Secy.) 1950–53; London (Head of Security Dept.) 1953–56; Washington (Counsellor) 1956–60; London (Head of Far Eastern Dept.) 1960–63. H.B.M. Ambassador to Afghanistan 1963–65. Assistant Under-Secretary of State, Foreign Office, Dec. 1965. British High Commissioner, Singapore 1968–70; Ambassador Bangkok 1970–74; Business Consultant since 1975; Chmn., Anglo-Thai Society 1975—. *Clubs:* Oriental; Royal Commonwealth Society, London. *Address:* The Birches, Onslow Road, Burwood Park, Walton-on-Thames, Surrey.

**de la MOTTE-BOULOUMIE, Guy.** French. *B.* 1920. *Educ.* Inst. Sainte-Croix, Neuilly/Seine (Dipl. Sciences Politiques), *M.* 1955, Michèle Bertani. *S.* 1. *Daus.* 2. *Career:* Prés., Dir. Gén. Admin. Société Générale des Eaux Minérales de Vittel; various appointments with Soc. Gén. des Eaux Minérales de Vittel since 1949; Mayor, Vittel; Conseiller Gén. des Vosges; Pres. Dir. Gen. of the Societe Générale des Eaux Minerales de Vittel. Prés. Commn. Départementale des Vosges; Administrator: Soc. Nouvelle de Source Minérale à Contrexéville; Soc. Nancéienne de Crédit Industriel; SA Ricqles-Zan, Conseiller Regional de Lorraine. *Address:* 88 800 Vittel, Ave. Bouloumie, France.

**de la OSSA, Ernest George,** AB. American. *B.* 1915. *Educ.* Columbia Coll. (AB); Harvard Sch. of Business. *M.* 1950, Bonnie Slattery Walt. *S.* 2. *Daus.* 2. *Career:* Pres. Foremost International; Vice-Pres. & Dir. Foremost-McKesson Inc.; Dir. New Business Development, National Broadcasting Co., 1942–55; Vice-Pres. & Gen. Man. W. R. Grace & Co., 1955–61; Vice-Pres. Overseas Div. International Paper Co., 1961–62; Vice-Pres. Management Plan, Federated Department Stores Inc. 1962–64; Pres. Foremost International, SA, 1964–74; Vice-Pres. and Dir. Foremost McKesson Inc. since 1974. *Clubs:* Rotary, New York; Westchester Country; Pelham Country; Larchmont Yacht; Hyde Park Golf & Country. *Address:* 1435 Southdown Rd., Hillsborough, Cal. 94010, U.S.A.; and *office* Crocker Plaza, One Post Street, San Francisco, Cal., CA 94104, U.S.A.

**de la ROYÈRE, Bernard.** French. Manager of Sarl, Delaroière and Leclerco Group; Membre du Conseil de Surveillance, Origny-Desvroise S.A. *B.* 1907. *Educ.* Bachelor, Engineer I.T.R. *M.* 1932, Odette Fremaux. *S.* 1. *Dau.* 1. *Awards:* Officer, Legion of Honour (France); Commandeur de l'Ordre National du Mérite (France); Conseiller National de Commerce Exterier; Reservist Colonel. Member Comité de Direction du C.C.L. *Address:* 1 rue St. Fuscien, Amiens; and *office* 44 rue Riolan, Amiens, France.

**de las BARCENAS, Juan.** Spanish diplomat. *B.* 1905. *Educ.* Lic. en Derecho; BA (Oxon.). *M.* 1938, Baroness Elizabeth Charlotte von Franz. *S.* 2. *Daus.* 2. Grand Cross of Merit (Civil); Commander, Carlos III; Grand Officer, Crown of Italy, etc. *Career:* Entered Diplomatic Service 1929; League of Nations appointments at Geneva, Vienna and Beirut 1931–36; Chargé d'Affaires, Cairo 1939; Chief of Diplomatic Cabinet, Burgos-Madrid 1939–40; various appointments, Madrid, U.K. and Switzerland 1940–53; Dir.-General of Foreign Policy, Madrid 1953–57; Representative to 13th and 15th Sessions of Gen. Assembly U.N. 1958–60; Ambassador to Canada 1958–62; Consul General, Lisbon 1962; Ambassador in Norway 1970–74; in Switzerland 1974–75 (ret'd.). *Address:* Modesto Lafuente 32, Madrid 3, Spain.

**de la VALLÉE POUSSIN, Etienne,** D., L. ès D. en Sc. Econ. Belgian politician. *B.* 23 Nov. 1903; formerly member (P.S.C.) Senate; Delegate to Consultative Assembly, Council of Europe 1949–68; Vice-President, Administrative Council, Coll. of Europe. *Awards:* Grand Officier de l'Ordre de Léopold; Officier Ordre de la Couronne (Belgium); Chevalier de la Légion d'Honneur (France). *Address:* 64 Rue de la Limite, Brussels, Belgium.

**del BALZO di PRESENZANO, Giulio,** LLD, DEcon. Italian diplomat. *B.* 28 Nov. 1903. *M.* 1938, Marisa Cavalletti. *S.* Raimondo, Cristiano, Luca, Ludovico, Renato. *Career:* Entered Diplomatic Service 1927; Sec., London 1929–37; later, First Secretary, Budapest, Paris; Counsellor, Holy See 1946–48; En. Ex. and Min. Plen. to Australia 1948–51; Head of Political Dept., Ministry of Foreign Affairs, Rome 1952–54; Ambassador to Spain 1954–58; to Venezuela 1958–59; Head of Cultural Dept., Ministry of Foreign Affairs, Aug. 1959–64; Ambassador to the Holy See 1964–69; Chmn. Italian Center for International Conciliation. *Address:* via dei Barbieri, 6, Rome, Italy.

**DELBRÜCK, Adelbert.** German banker. Sleeping Partner: Delbrück & Co., Berlin, Cologne, Aachen, Hamburg and Frankfurt. *B.* 1898. *Educ.* Abitur 1915. *M.* 1923, Berta von Borcke. *Address:* St. Benedict-strasse 23a, Hamburg; and *office* Ballindamm 5, Hamburg 1, Germany.

**DE LEON, Fortunato.** Filipino lawyer, journalist and business man. *B.* 1904. *Educ.* Bataan High School; Coll. of Liberal Arts, Univ. of Phillipines, AA; Coll. of Law Univ. of Phillipines, LLB; UP Gold Meadal. *M.* 1942, Juana N. Gonzalez. *S.* 1. *Daus.* 2. *Career:* Staff member Manila Daily Bulletin 1924–29; Ed. in chief Philippine Collegian, 1929. Elected representative from Bataan to 9th Philippine Legation 1931–34; Presidental assistant 1955–56; Exec. Secy. to Pres. Ramon Magsaysay 1956–57; Exec. Secy. President Carlos P. Garcia 1957; Vice-Chmn. and Mem. Bd. of Directors, Philippine National Bank; Chmn. Bd. of Trustees, Multi-Million Peso Provident Fund; Mem. Bd. of Dirs., Philippine Exchange, Central Azucarero de Danao, and Ma-ao Sugar Central; PNB Delegate to Far-East-America Council of Commerce and Industry Conference (N.Y.C. 1958, 1960); Adviser Phil. delegation to World Bank and IMF Conf. (Washington D.C. 1960, 1966). *Member:* Bd. of Govs. Phil. Red Cross; (life) National Press Club; Philconsa Cttee. on Const. Amendments; Cttee. on Const. Enforcement; Bd. of Govs. Phil. Const. Assn.; Bd. of Trustees, World Peace Foundation 1970–71; Phil. Lawyers Assn. and Phil. Integr. Bar; Adviser, Bataan Bar Assn.; Dir. Malaban Lawyers' Assn. *Awards:* Phil. Nat. Red Cross; Phil. Nat. Bank. *Club:* Friday Breakfast. *Address:* 145 E. Abada St., cor. B Gonzales, Loyola Heights, Quezon City, Philippines; and *office* Suite 329 Madrigal Bldg., Escolta, Manila, Philippines.

**DELFIM NETTO, Mr. Antonio.** *B.* 1928. *Educ.* Univ. of St. Paolo (Degree in Economics). *Career:* Assist. Prof. Gen. Stats. and Economics 1952–54; Ind. Prof. Gen. Stats. and Economics 1954–59; Professor of Macroeconomic Analysis, National Accounting, Theory of Economic Dev., Brazilian Economy and Govt. planning since 1963; Dir. of the Insts. of Administration and Economic Research since 1963; Representative of Directorate of Faculty of Economics and Admin. on Univ. Council of Univ. of San Paolo; Adviser to S. Paolo Road Dept. and Commodities Market and member of several local and state councils; Secretary for Finance, state of

S. Paolo; Minister of Finance 1967–74; Brazilian Ambassador in Paris since 1975. *Publications:* Wheat in Brazil (part-author) (1960); The Sugar Market in Brazil (part-author) (1958); The Coffee problem in Brazil (1959); Aspects of Inflation in Brazil (1963); Agriculture and Development (1966); Twenty years of substitutes for Brazilian Coffee (1966); Economic Development Plan (1966) and numerous articles in technical journals. *Address:* Brazilian Embassy, Paris, France.

**DELISLE, Jean-Louis.** Canadian diplomat. *B.* 1912. *Educ.* Laval Univ. (BA, LLL (Law)) and Oxford University (BA Hon.; PPE, MA.). *M.* 1946, Constance Charette. *S.* 1. *Dau.* 1. *Career:* Advocate and Professor of Political Economy 1939–42; Secretary in the Cabinet of the Prime Minister of Canada 1942–46; 2nd Sec., Canadian Embassy, Rio de Janeiro 1946–49; Consul, Boston 1951–53; Chargé d'Affaires & Head of Post, Canadian Legation, Warsaw 1954–56; member U.N. Commission on Togoland under French Administration March–Sept. 1957, Head, Legal Div., Dept. of External Affairs, Sept. 1958–Aug. 1959; Counsellor, Press and Cultural Affairs, Canadian Embassy, Paris, Sept. 1959–61; Ambassador to Costa Rica, El Salvador, Honduras, Nicaragua, and Panama 1961–64; Ambassador to Turkey 1964–67; Ambassador Permanent Representative to the United Nations, Geneva 1967–70; Dir. Academic Relations Service, Department, External Affairs 1970–73; Consul-General Boston, U.S.A. 1973–76 (ret'd.); Lecturer, Laval Univ., Quebec since Sept. 1977. *Address:* 602–350 Chemin Ste-Foy, Quebec City, Quebec G1S 2J4, Canada.

**DE LISLE, Viscount,** (Sidney, William Philip) VC KG, PC,, GCMG, GCVO, FCA. British business executive. *B.* 1909. *Educ.* Eton and Magdalene College, Cambridge. *M.* (1) 1940, Hon. Jacqueline Corinne Yvonne Vereker (*D.* 1962). (2) 1966, Margaret Lady Glanusk, widow of 3rd Baron Glanusk. D.S.O. *Career:* Commn. Supplementary Reserve, Grenadier Guards 1929 and served World War II with regiment. MP (C) Chelsea, 1944–45; Parl. Secy., Min. of Pensions 1945; Secy. of State for Air 1951–55; Governor Gen. of Australia 1961–65; Trustee of the R.A.F. Museum; Chmn., Phoenix Assurance Co. Ltd., Dir., Phoenix Assurance Co. of New York; Yorkshire Bank Ltd.; The Diners' Club, Inc., N.Y.; Trustee Winston Churchill Memorial Trust. *Awards:* Hon. Fellow, Magdalene College, Cambridge, Hon. LLD Sydney University; KStJ, Hon. Fellow, Royal Institute of British Architects; Chancellor, Order of St. Michael & St. George 1968. *President:* British Heart Found. *Vice-President:* AA. *Address:* Penshurst Place, Tonbridge, Kent, and Glanusk Park, Crickhowell, Powys, S. Wales.

**DELL, Rt. Hon. Edmund,** PC, MP. *B.* 1921. *Educ.* Oxford University (MA 1st Cl. Hons.). *M.* 1963, Susanne Gottschalk. *Career:* Lecturer in Modern History, The Queen's Coll., Oxford, 1947–49; I.C.I. Executive 1949–63; Simon Research Fellow, Manchester Univ. 1963–64; Member Parliament Lab. for Birkenhead 1964—; Joint Parliamentary Secretary of State, Min. Tech. 1966–67, Joint Parliamentary Under-Secy. of State, Dept. of Economic Affairs 1967–68; Minister of State, Board of Trade, 1968–69; Dept. of Employment and Productivity, 1969–70; Chmn. Public Accounts Cttee 1972–74; Paymaster-General 1974–76; Sec. of State for Trade since 1976. *Publications:* The Good Old Cause (Editor with J. C. Hill) (1949); Brazil—The Dilemma of Reform (1964); Political Responsibility and Industry (1973). *Address:* 4 Reynolds Close, London, NW11 7EA.

**DELLMUTH, Carl Kugler.** Banker. *B.* 1908. *Educ.* Swarthmore College (AB). *M.* 1934, Margaret Ball. *S.* Carl Sturges. *Dau.* Nancy Gail. *Career:* Faculty and Administrative Officer of Swarthmore Coll. 1938–49; Exec. Secy., Penna. Bankers Assoc. 1949–52; Vice-Pres., Fidelity-Philadelphia Trust Co. 1953. Senior Vice-President and Director, The Fidelity Bank, Philadelphia 1957, Exec. Vice-Pres. 1964, Pres. 1966–72, Vice Chmn. Bd. since 1971. Member, Governor's Cabinet 1973; Secy. Banking for the Commonwealth of Pennsylvania. Board of Managers, The Franklin Institute. Present author of various articles on educational and banking subjects. Recipient, U.S. Navy Certificate of Merit 1944–45. *Member:* Pennsylvania Bankers Association Educational Federation (Chairman). *Clubs:* Midday; Swarthmore. *Address:* 323 Swarthmore Avenue, Swarthmore, Pa., U.S.A.

**DELP, George C.** American manufacturing executive. *B.* 1908. *Educ.* Manhaeim Township Schls. and Lancaster Business Coll. *M.* 1928, Grace M. Butz. *S.* Gervase. *Daus.* Georgia, Germaine, Gemma, Glenna, and Greta. *Career:* Asst. to Mgr., Farm Machinery Div., Dellinger Mfg. Co., Lancaster 1933–40. President, New Holland Div. of Sperry Rand Corp. 1947–69, Chmn. 1969—; Exec. Partner: State Equipment Co., Harrisburg, Pa. 1944—, and Lancaster Lincoln-Mercury Co., Lancaster, Pa. 1947—; Vice-Pres., Equipment Finance Inc., Lancaster 1945. Hon. DComSc, Franklin & Marshall Coll., 1953. Chmn., Lancaster Airport Authority; Dir., St. Joseph's Hospital (Lancaster). *Member:* Amer. Socy. of Agricultural Engrs. *Clubs:* Hamilton, Lancaster Country (Lancaster); Skytop (Skytop, Pa.); Canadian (N.Y.C.); Seaview Country (Atlantic City); Pine Valley (N.J.) Golf; Chicago. *Address: office* New Holland, Pa., U.S.A.

**DEL ROSARIO, Ramon V.** Filipino. *B.* 1919. *Educ.* BSc Com. 1938, Certified Public Accountant 1938. *M.* 1940, Milagros del Rosario. *S.* 6. *Dau.* 1. *Career:* Vice-Pres. and Gen. Mgr., IBM (Philippines) 1938–51. Exec. Vice-Pres. and Dir., Philippine American Life Insurance Co. 1951–57; Chmn. Home Savings Bank; First Continental Assurance Co. President: Trans-Asia Oil & Mineral Development Corp.; Bacnotan Cement Industries; Philippine Investment-Management Consultants, Inc.; United Pulp and Paper Co.; Kabankalan Sugar Co. Executive Vice-President, International Chamber of Commerce, Philippine Chapter; Vice-Pres., Chamber of Commerce of the Philippines; Trustee: De La Salle College; Asian Institute of Management. Director: Commonwealth Foods, Inc.; Far East Bank & Trust Co.; Elizalde Steel Rolling Mills; General Electric Appliance Co.; Member Harvard Business Alumni Assn.; Mem., Junior Chamber International (Past Injernational Pres., 1950). *Address: office* PHINMA Building, 166 Salcedo Street, Legaspi Village, Makati, Metro Manila, Philippines.

**DELRUELLE, Jules.** Belgian civil engineer. *B.* 1900. *Educ.* University of Liège (Civil Engineer). *M.* Marguerite Funck. *S.* Jacques, Gérard, Jean. *Career:* Secretary to the Board, S.A. Métallurgique de Prayon 1926; Dir. 1936; Man. Dir. 1941; Chmn.-Man. Dir. 1957—. Min. of Econ. Affairs 1944–45 Staff Officer, Special Force 1940–44; mem. of Belgian Government Consultative Committee, London 1942–44; member, Central Economic Council and Metal Industry Council since their formation 1949–62. Belgian National Committee of the I.C.C. *Awards:* Officer, Order of the British Empire (OBE); Commander, Order of Leopold; Officer, Order of the Crown: Croix de Guerre with Palm; Resistance Medal; Officer, Order of the Oak Crown; Grand Officer, Order of Leopold II; Hon. Chmn. Société de Prayon. *Address:* B-4940 Trooz, Belgium.

**DELSON, Robert.** American attorney specializing in international law and international economic development. *B.* 1905. *Educ.* Cornell Univ. (AB 1926); Columbia Univ. School of Law (LLB 1928); admitted to Bar 1929. *M.* 1941, Marjorie Feldman. *S.* Eric and James. *Career:* Associated with Wise & Seligsberg, attorney 1929–31; Assoc. General Counsel, Republic Pictures Corp. 1931–37. Associate and Partner, Delson & Gordon 1937—; Counsel for several foreign governments, International League for the Rights of Man, etc. *Publications:* The Status of the Republic of Indonesia in International Law; Trading with Insurgents; The Problems of the Foreign Merchant; Immunity from Taxation of Real Property Owned by Delegations to the United Nations; Nationalization of the Suez Canal—Issues of Public and Private International Law; Economic Development and International Law; Is a taking of an alien's property without compensation or in derogation of the terms of a contract in violation of public International Law? *Member:* N.Y. County Lawyers' Assn.; Amer. Bar Assn. and its Cttee. on Internatl. Law in the Courts of the U.S.; Amer. Branch, International Law Assn., American Society of International Law (and various committees); Patron, International Bar Assn.; Consular Law Socy.; Amer. Law Inst.; Amer. Foreign Law Assn.; Japan Socy.; U.S. Cttee., Inter-Amer. Assn. for Democracy & Freedom; Phi Beta Kappa; N.Y.S. Bar Assn.; Columbia and Cornell Alumni Assns. *Address:* 230 Park Ave., New York 17, N.Y., U.S.A.

**de MARGERIE, Bernard,** Amédée Marie. French banker. *B.* 1912. *Educ.* D.-en-D.; Diplomé de l'Ecole Libre des Sciences Politiques. *M.* 1939, Elisabeth de Salaberry. *S.* Gérard and Olivier. *Daus.* Anne and Marie-Hélène. *Career:* Inspector of Finances, 1938; Deputy of Finances in Alsace and the Moselle 1944; Director-Adjoint, Ministry of Finances 1947; Alternate Administrator, International Monetary Fund 1948; Secretary-General, Inter-ministerial Committee for International Economic Co-operation 1950. Directeur Général, adjoint Banque de Paris et des Pays-Bas. Président, de Paris Bas International; Prés. de la Société Nouvelle de la Banque de Syrie et du Liban; Prés. du Comité de Paris de la

Banque Ottomane; Prés. du Comité de Paris du Crédir Foncier Franco-Canadien; Vice-Prés. Banque de Madagascat & des Comores. *Award:* Officier de la Légion d'Honneur; Croix de Guerre 1939–45. *Address:* 7 avenue de La Bourdonnais, Paris 7, France.

**de MARTINO, Ciro.** Italian banker. Cav. di Gran Croce, Order of Merit of the Republic of Italy. *B.* 1903. *Educ.* Degree in economics and commerce. *M.* Renata Cametti. *Daus.* 2. *Career:* Entered Banca d'Italia, Cosenza Branch, 1927; Personal Secretary to the General Vice-Manager of the Bank, Aug. 1931; Assistant Inspector 1940. In 1944 he represented the Bank at the Interdepartmental Commission on the change of currency; in Feb. 1948 led the commission of Italian banking experts in re-establishing Italian bank branches in East Africa, and negotiating with the Occupation Authorities; in Jan. 1950 returned to Africa to assist in reopening Italian banks in Somali territory and to effect the withdrawal of British currency and the introduction of the Somali. Appointed Senior Inspector of the Banca d'Italia in charge of the General Inspectorate 1951, and Head of the Organisation Dept. 1953; appointed General Inspector and Head of the Banking Supervision Dept., Oct. 1960; resigned from the Bank, June 1964; Chairman Board of Directors, Banco di Sicilia, Palermo, Oct. 1965—. *Address:* Via Dei Colli Della Farnesina 118, Rome; and *office* Via Gen. Magliocco 1, Palermo, Sicily.

**DEMIREL, Suleiman.** Turkish Politician. *B.* 1924. *Educ.* Istanbul Tech. Univ. *Career:* Pres., Justice Party sine 1964; Dep. Prime Minister 1965; Prime Minister 1965–71, 1975–77, & since 1977. *Address:* Office of the Prime Minister, Ankara, Turkey.

**DEMPSEY, James Raymon.** Business Consultant-Independent Director. *B.* 1921. *Educ.* U.S. Military Academy (BSc 1943), and University of Michigan (MSc Aeronautical Engineering 1947). *M.* 1943, Dolores Barnes. *S.* David Barnes. *Daus.* Susan and Anne. *Career:* In United Air Force 1943–53 (Distinguished Flying Cross, Croix de Guerre, and Air Medal with oak cluster); Asst. to Vice-Pres. Planning, Convair Div., General Dynamics Corp. 1953–54; Program Director, Atlas Missile, Convair Div. 1954–57; Manager, Convair (Astronautics) Div. 1957–C1; Vice-Pres., Convair Div. 1958. President, General Dynamics/Astronautics, and Vice-President, General Dynamics Corp. 1961–65; Group Vice-President, Avco Corp. 1966–75. *Director:* Bunker Ramo Corp., Telcom Inc., Chase Convertible Fund of Boston Inc., Chase Special Fund of Boston Inc., Chase Frontier Capital Fund of Boston Inc., Income & Capital Shares Inc., Precious Metals Holdings Inc., Money Markets/Options Investments Inc. *Trustee:* The Chase Fund of Boston, Shareholder's Trust of Boston. Governor, National Rocket Club 1962–66. *Member:* Air Forc Assn.; American Rocket Socy.; American Astronautical Socy. (Fellow); American Inst. of Aeronautics & Astronautics (Fellow). *Clubs:* Burning Tree; Essex County. *Address:* 4081 Ridgeview Circle, N. Arlington, Va. 22207, U.S.A.

**DEMUYTER, Albert Ernest.** Belgian. Lord Mayor of Ixelles. *B.* 1925. *Educ.* Athénée Robert Catteau. *M.* Lydia Lisbeth Van den Berghe. *Career:* War service; political prisoner; agent of information and action; underground press activities; armed member of the Resistance; volunteer in Royal Navy. Man. Dir. in Africa of Ets. J. Valette at Bukavu 1947–49; Auditor, SABENA; Dir. S.A. Ballings 1947. Private Secy. to Minister for the Colonies 1954–58; Member of Parliament since 1965; Member National Standing Cttee. 1955, National Political Bureau 1962; Nat. Mgt. Cttee. P.L.P. Liberty & Progress Party 1962; Chmn. Brussels Branch P.L.P. Fed. 1966; (Chmn. Ixelles Branch); Senator since 1968. Member Bd. Liberal Party. *Awards:* Knight: Order of Leopold; Order of the Royal Lion; Resistance Medal; British War Medal. *Club:* Cercle Royal Africain. *Address:* 66 rue Paul Lauters, Brussels 5; and *office* Ixelles Town Hall, Brussels 5.

**de NAVASQUES, Count Emilio.** *B.* 1905. *Educ.* D. en D.; Lic. en Filos. *M.* 1935, Maria Elisa Bertrán. *S.* Joaquin. *Daus.* Pilar, Maria Elisa, Mercedes, Teresa and Maria Pia. *Career:* Third Secretary 1929; Secretary, Paris, Lisbon, Warsaw and Asuncion; Minister to The Hague 1948–50; Ambassador, Buenos Aires 1950–52; Dir.-Gen. of Dept. of External Commerce (1938–39) and Dept. of Political Economy 1944–46; Under-Secretary of Economy (1946–48) and of Ministry of External Affairs 1952–56; Ambassador to Italy Feb. 1956–May 1959; Ambassador of Spain. Director of Spanish Diplomatic Sch. 1959; Ambassador in Portugal 1972–74 Retired 1975. *Member:* Royal Acad. of Jurisprudence. *Awards:* Grand Cross of Orders of Isabel la Catolica Carlos III, Cristo de Portugal, Merito Argentino, Merito del Peru, etc. *Clubs:* Nuevo; Gran Peña, Puerto de Hierro (Madrid). *Address:* Avenida de Miraflores 31, Madrid 35, Spain.

**DENHOLM, Sir John (Carmichael),** CBE. British shipowner. *B.* 1893. *Educ.* Greenock Academy. *M.* 1926, Mary Laura Kerr. President, J. & J. Denholm, Ltd. Member of Council, Chamber of Shipping of United Kingdom. Pres. Chamber of Shipping of U.K. 1954; Regional Shipping Representative (West Scotland) Ministry of War Transport 1940–45. *Address:* 3 Octavia Terrace, Greenock, Scotland.

**DENHOLM, Col. Sir William Lang,** TD. British. *B.* 1901. *Educ.* Greenock Academy; Greenock Collegiate. *M.* 1925, Dorothy Jane Ferguson. *S.* 2. *Dau.* 1. *Career:* Chairman, Shipping Federation 1962–65; Joint Chmn.. National Maritime Board 1962–65. Deputy Lieutenant County of Renfrew. *Awards:* Chev. Ord. of St. Olav (Norway). *Clubs:* Western (Glasgow). *Address:* Glenmill. Kilmacolm, Renfrewshire; and *office* 120 St. Vincent Street, Glasgow, C.2.

**DE NICOLAY, Count Christian Marie Roger.** French Diplomat. *B.* 1910. *Educ.* Licence-ès-Lettres Latin and Greek, Licence in Law. *Career:* Attaché of Embassy, Washington 1941–43 Military Service, Lieut, in field, French Army 1943–45 Secy. French Embassy in Vienna 1946–48; Deputy-Dir. Press Service, Ministry For. Affairs 1948–50; U.N. Conciliation Commission for Palestine 1950–51; Sub-Dir. American Dept. Min. Foreign Affairs 1952–54; Counsellor of Embassy in Praque 1954–58; Counsellor of Embassy, Madrid 1959–62; First Counsellor of Embassy Vienna 1962–65; Ambassador in Asuncion Paraquay 1965–70; Ambassador in Wellington, N.Z. 1970–75 (also accredited as Ambass. in Fiji, Samoa and Tonga). *Decorations:* Officer of the Legion of Honour, Croix de Guerre (1940); Commander of the Order of Merit; Grand Cross of the Order of Merit, Paraquay; Doctor of the University of Paraquay. *Publications.* Sections diplomatie in Dictionnaire des Lettres Francaises; En Terre Sainte (editor). *Address:* 24 rue d'Artois, Paris, 8e, France.

**DENKTAS, Rauf.** Turkish Cypriot Politician. *B.* 1924. *Educ.* Barrister-at-Law, Lincoln's Inn, London. *M.* 1949, Aydin Munir. *S.* 2. *Daus.* 2. *Career:* Teacher 1942–43; Lawyer 1947–49; Legal Dept., Attorney-General's Office 1949–58; Lawyer & Chmn. of the Turkish Associations 1958–60; Lawyer & Pres. of the Turkish Communal Chamber, Cyprus 1960–73; Vice-Pres., Republic of Cyprus & Pres. of the Turkish Administration 1973–75; Pres. of the Turkish Federated State of Cyprus since Feb. 1975. *Publications:* Criminal Cases; Secrets of Happiness; Hell Without Fire; The Akritas Plan; The Cyprus Problem; Five to Twelve. *Address:* Selahattin Sonat Street, Lefkoşa, Mersin 10, Turkey.

**DENMAN, The Rt. Hon. Lord (Charles Spencer),** CBE, MC. British. *B.* 1916. *Educ.* Shrewsbury. *M.* 1943, Sheila Anne Stewart. *S.* Richard, James and John. *Dau.* Gillian (McCall). *Career:* Major, Duke of Cornwall's Light Infantry, 1939–45; Advisory Council, Export Credit Guarantee Dept., 1963–68; Cttee., Invisible Exports, 1966–67. Chairman, Tennant Guaranty Ltd.; Overseas Marketing Corp.; Tennant Budd Ltd.; Chmn., Marine & General Life Assurance Society; Director: Consolidated Goldfields; British Bank of Middle East; Challenge Corporation; Deputy-Chmn. C. Tennant Sons & Co. Ltd.; Chmn. Council for Middle East Trade 1971–75; Chmns. Cttee. of Cttee. on Invisible Exports. *Award:* Military Cross, 1942. Governor Windlesham House School. Member Lord Kitchener National Memorial Fund. *Club:* Brook's. *Address:* Highden House, Washington, Sussex; and *office* 82 Fenchurch Street, London, E.C.3.

**DENNERY, Etienne Roland.** French diplomat. *B.* 20 March March 1903. *Educ.* École Normale Supérieure; agrégé de l'Université. *M.* 1) 1949, Denise Fenard. (2) 1970, Marie Christine Angebault. *Career:* Secretary-General, Centre d'Etudes de Politique Etrangère 1935–39; Professor, École Libre des Sciences Politiques 1933–39; Free French Forces 1941–45; Director for America at the Ministry of Foreign Affairs, Paris 1945–50; Trustee, Ecole Nationale d'Administration; Ambassador to Poland; to Switzerland 1954; to Japan, Feb. 1961–64; Director General, Bibliothèque Nationale 1964—; Director French Libraries; Mem., UNESCO Exec. Council 1966—. *Address:* Bibliothèque Nationale, 58 rue de Richelieu Paris 2e, France; & 8 Rue des Petits Champs, 75002 Paris.

**DENNING, Rt. Hon. Lord** (Alfred Thompson Denning), PC. British judge. *B.* 23 Jan. 1899. *Educ.* Magdalen College

Oxford (MA). *M.* (1) 1932, Mary Harvey (*D.* 1941). *S.* 1. (2) 1945, Joan Stuart. *Career:* Served in World War I, Royal Engineers, in France 1917–19; called to Bar 1923; K.C. 1938; Judge of High Court 1944; Judge for Pensions Appeals 1945–48; Lord Justice of Appeal 1948; Chmn. of Cttee. on Procedure in Matrimonial Causes 1946–47; Lord of Appeal in Ordinary 1957; Master of the Rolls 1962—; conducted Profumo enquiry 1963. *Publications:* Freedom under the Law (Hamlyn Lectures); The Changing Law; The Road to Justice; The Denning Report. *Address:* 11 Old Square, Lincoln's Inn, London, W.C.2.

**DENNISON, Charles Stuart.** American international consultant. *B.* 1918. *Educ.* Columbia and New York Universities. *M.* 1951, Carol Frances Kruger. *Daus.* Laura Hardie and Deborah Irwin. *Career:* Export Sales Manager and acting Gen. Sales Mgr. Willy's Overland Motors Inc. 1946–51; Managing Director, Olin Mathieson Ltd. and E. R. Squibb Ltd., London (England) 1951–57; Vice-Pres. Chrysler Export Corp. 1957–58. Served to Capt., parachute inf., A.U.S. World War II. Vice-President, International Minerals & Chemical Corporation, Skokie, Illinois, U.S.A. to 1971; Director: International Minerals & Chemicals Ltd., London, Eng., (ANZ) Pty. Ltd., Australia, (Bahamas) Ltd., (Canada) Ltd., (Panama); Coromandel Fertilizers Ltd. Secunderabad, India, 1964–70; Compagnie Senegalaise des Phosphates de Taiba, Dakar, 1963–69; Azufrera Intercontinental S.A. de C.V., Mexico; Overseas Development Council; Senior Advisor International Industry, United Nations Environment Programme. *Director:* Bulletin of Atomic Scientists. *Member:* Cttee on Public Engineering Policy National Research Council; Environmental Panel National Commission on Materials Policy. *Awards:* Commander, Order of Merit (Senegal), Bronze Star (v) U.S. *Member:* President's Science Adv. Cttee. Panel on World Food Supply; Council on Foreign Relations; National Academy of Sciences, Board on Science & Technology for Development, Cttee. on International Development Inst.; Member U.S. Delegation to Conference, Science and Technology, Development of Latin Amer. Organization of American States; Exec. Cttee., FAO Industry Co-operative Cttee., Rome; Cncl. Socy. for International Development, Washington; Steering Cttee. Pacific Basin Economic Co-operation Cncl., Tokyo. Trustee of the Agricultural Developmental Council; Chmn National Academy Sciences Panel on Research Dev. & Engineering in Developing countries. *Clubs:* Metropolitan (N.Y.C.); International Club, Washington; English-Speaking Union. *Address:* 45 East 89th Street, New York, N.Y. 10028, U.S.A.

**DENNISON, Robert Lee.** Admiral U.S.N. (Retd.). *B.* 1901. *Educ.* U.S. Naval Acad. (BSc 1923); Post-graduate School, Annapolis; Penna. State Coll. (MSc 1930); Johns Hopkins Univ. (DEng 1935). *M.* 1937, Mildred Fenton Mooney Neely. *S.* Robert Lee, Jr. *Dau.* Lee. *Career:* Commissioned Ensign 1923; advanced through various grades to Admiral 1959. With Atlantic, Pacific and Asian Fleets; Cmd. U.S.S. Ortolan 1935–37 and Missouri 1947–48. Member, Joint War Plans Committee of the Joint Chiefs of Staff 1944–45; Asst. Chief of Naval Operations (political-military affairs) 1945–47; Naval Aide to President of U.S. 1948–53. Comdr. Cruiser Div. 4, U.S. Atlantic Fleet 1953–54; Dir. Strategic Plans Div., Asst. Chief Naval Operations (plans and policy). Office Chief Naval Operations 1954–56; member, Joint Strategic Plans Committee of Joint Chiefs of Staff; Comdr. First Fleet, U.S Pacific Fleet 1956–58; with DCNO (Plans and Policy), Navy Dept. 1958–59; Commander-in-Chief: U.S. Naval Forces, Eastern Atlantic and Mediterranean 1959–60, Atlantic Command, and U.S. Atlantic Fleet, and Supreme Allied Comdr. Atlantic 1960–63. D.S.M. Vice-Pres. 1963–74, and Dir. 1964–74, The Copley Press Inc., Washington, D.C. *Awards:* Distinguished Service Medal; Legion of Merit. Gold Star in lieu of 2nd Legion of Merit; Amer. Defense with Star; Asiatic-Pacific Area 2 stars, Philippine Defense with star; Navy Unit Commendation (U.S.S. Pennsylvania); Navy Occupation Service Medal (European Clasp); National Defense Servic Medal; Army Distinguished Unit Citation (Philippines) Amer. Area; World War II Victory (U.S.), Comdr. Order of Naval Merit (Brazil); Comdr. Order of Crown (Belgium); Officer Order of the British Empire; Comdr. Legion of Honour (France); Grand Cross Order of Orange-Nassau; Mil. Order of Aviz (Portugal). *Member:* Sigma Xi. *Clubs:* N.Y. Yacht; Metropolitan; Army-Navy (Washington); American (London); Ends of the Earth; Chevy Chase. *Address:* 5040 Westpath Terrace, Washington, D.C. 20016, U.S.A.

**DENNISTON, Alexander Churchill.** American banker. *B.* 1922. *Educ.* American Inst. of Banking; Instituto Mexicano de Administracion de Negocios (student and instructor). *M.* 1951, Barbara J. Carlson. *S.* 1. *Daus.* 2. *Career:* Joined American National Bank & Trust Co.. Mobile, Ala. 1938, Asst. Vice-Pres. 1948–67; Chmn., Arrendadora Serfin 1965—; Financiera Colon 1965–76; Vice-Chmn., Corporacion Inter-Americana Serfin 1967—. *Clubs:* University; De Vela la Pena Assn.; Pres., Amer. Benevolent Society 1972–75. *Address:* Cerrada de Corregidores 116, Mexico 10, D.F., Mexico.

**DENSON, John Boyd,** CMG, OBE. British Diplomat. *B.* 1926. *Educ.* Perse Sch.; St. John's Coll., Cambridge—MA. *M.* 1957, Joyce Myra Symondson. *Career:* Joined HM Diplomatic Service 1951; served in Hong Kong 1951–52, Tokyo 1952–53, Peking 1953–55, Foreign Office, London 1955–57, Finland 1957–59; 1st Sec., Washington 1960–62, Laos 1963–65; Asst. Head, Far Eastern Dept., FCO 1965–68; Chargé d'Affaires, Peking 1969–71; Royal Coll. of Defence Studies 1972; Counsellor & Consul-General, Athens, 1973–77; HM Ambassador, Kathmandu since 1977. *Decorations:* Officer of the Order of the British Empire, 1965; Companion of the Order of St. Michael & St. George, 1972. *Club* United Oxford & Cambridge University. *Address:* c/o Foreign & Commonwealth Office, London SW1.

**DENTON, Harold Morley.** New Zealand. *B.* 1913. *Educ.* Wesley Coll., Auckland, and Waitaki Boys High Schl., Oamaru. *M.* 1946, Ngaire E. Stewart. *S.* Paul J. *Dau.* Janet M. *Career:* Ten years in daily journalism (Ashburton Guardian and The Press, N.Z.) 1932–41. With 2 N.Z.E.F. in the Pacific in World War II (1941–45); R.N.Z.A.S.C. (Captain) 3 N.Z. Div. H.Q. Staff. Subsequently in commercial aviation with Air New Zealand (formerly TEAL), New Zealand's internl. airline, 1945–73, Operations Officer, Snr. Administrative Officer, Traffic Mgr., Sales and Traffic Mgr., Commercial Mgr.; Dir. Commercial Services; Assistant Gen. Mgr. 1969–73 (Ret.); Past Chmn. N.Z. Div. Ch. Inst. of Transport; Fellow (FCIT) and Fellow N.Z. Inst. of Travel (F.N.Z.I.T.); Life-mem. & former Pres. Pacific Area Travel Association. *Awards:* F.C.I.T.; F.N.Z.I.T. J.S.M. Malaysia 1972. *Address:* 7a Lingarth Street, Remuera, Auckland, 5, New Zealand.

**DEN UYL, Johannes Marten.** Netherlands Politician *B.* 1919. *Educ.* Protestant Lyceum Hilversum; Grad. Economics Municipal Univ. of Amsterdam. *M.* Children 7. *Career:* Ministry, Economics Affairs (Govt. Bd. Chemical Products) 1943–45; Social Affairs Editor Het Parool 1945; Vrij Nederland Nov. 1945–48; Dir. Wiardi Beckman Inst. (Labour Party Research Institute) 1949–62; Member, Second Chamber, States-General 1956–63; Alderman, Public Works Economic Affairs, Commercial and Port Affairs Amsterdam 1962–65; Minister, Economic Affairs, Cals Govt. 1965–66; Chmn. Parly. Party 1967; Head, List Candidates Election Campaigns 1967, 1971 and 1972; Prime Minister 1973–77. *Award:* Knight, Order of the Netherlands Lion. *Address:* The Ministry of General Affairs, Plein 1813 No. 4, The Hague, Netherlands.

**de PATOUL, Chevalier Jacques.** Belgian. *B.* 1907. *Educ.* Diplomas Civil Engineering (mining and electricity); Bachelor in Philosophy. *M.* 1937, Véronique Fallon. *S.* Dominique, Benoit and Philippe. *Dau.* Noëlle. *Career:* Formerly, Departmental Head, Compagnie des Métaux d'Overpelt-Lommel et de Corphalie, and Bureau d'Études Industrielles Fernand Courtoy. Administrator: Société NIFE Belge, and S.A. ESMALUX. Hon. Director, Compagnie d'Assurance Royale Belge. *Club:* Cercle Royal Gaulois (Brussels). *Address:* 72 Rue de la Faucille, Wezembeek, Belgium.

**De POUS, Jan Willem.** *B.* 1920. *Educ.* Economic Faculty, Municipal Univ. of Amsterdam (passed Doctoral Examination 1947). *M.* G. van Itterzon. *S.* 1. *Daus.* 2. Member of 'Trouw' resistance organization 1943–45; Secy. to Bd. of Directors of the daily newspaper Trouw until Jan. 1946; Member Bd., Christian National Press Association for the Netherlands. Dec. 1945—; Asst. to Prof. Dr. P. Hennipman, academic year 1945–46; Secy., Federation of Protestant Employers in the Netherlands Nov. 1949–Jan. 1953 (Economic Adviser 1953–59); Lecturer in Economic Theory, Free Univ. of Amsterdam Jan. 1953–June 1959; member, Privy Council Dec. 1958–May 1959; Minister of Economic Affairs of the Netherlands 1959–63. President, The Social Economic Council, 1964—; Chairman of Supervisory Board of K.L.M. Royal Dutch Airlines; Member of Supervisory Boards of: Philips' Gloeilampenfabrieken; Rijn-Schelde-Verolme Engineering Works & Shipyards; B.A.M. Batavian Contracting Co.; TCU, Information & Communication Co. *Awards:* Kt. of the Order of the Netherlands Lion; Commander of the Order Oranje-Nassau; Grand Cross of the Orders of Crown of Belgium; Merit (Peru); Merit (Argentina); Francisco Morazán (Honduras); White Elephant (Thailand); Oak Crown (Luxembourg); Grand Golden Mark of Merit (Austria). Member Christian Historian Union. *Address:* 65 Van Zaeckstraat, The Hague, Netherlands; and *office* 60 Bezuidenhoutseweg, The Hague.

**DEQUAE, André Joseph Paul Albert.** Belgian politician. *B.* 3 Nov. 1915. *Educ.* University of Louvain (Lic. Econ.). *M.* 1940, Agnes Vandemoortele. *S.* Henri, Paul, André. *Daus.* Maria, Anna, Christina. *Career:* Sec., Assn. Nationale des Tisseurs de Lin 1940; General-Secretary, Union Patronale Textile 1940; Regional Secretary, Association Nationale des Tisseurs de Tapis, Velours et Tissus d'Ameublement 1945; Minister of Reconstruction 1950; Minister for the Colonies 1950; Minister of Foreign Trade 1958; of Economic Co-ordination 1960; Minister of Finances 1961. First Vice-Pres. of Chamber of Representatives, 1965. Médaille de la Résistance; member, Chamber of Representatives (P.S.C.). since 1946; Assembly of Council of Europe, since 1966, Pres. of Agricultural Cttee; Pres. of Chamber of Representatives 1974, First Vice-Pres. since 1977. *Publication:* L'industrie linière belge. *Address:* Sint Elooidreef 36, Courtrai, Belgium.

**de QUAY, Jan Eduard.** *B.* 1901. *Educ.* St. Willibrordus Coll., Katwijk a/d Rijn; Univ. of Utrecht (DLitt., DPhil.); School for Reserve Officers. *M.* 1927. H. W. vander Lande. *S.* 5. *Daus.* *Career:* Lecturer in Psychotechnics, Catholic Economic High School, Tilburg 1928–33; Asst. at Psychological Laboratory, Rijksuniversiteit, Utrecht 1928–29; with Advisory Bureau for Business Organisations 1930; Psychotechnical Adviser to C. & A. Brenninckmeijer 1931–33; Prof. of Psychotechnics and Business Administration, Catholic Economic High School; Director of Technical Economic Institute and Editor-Secretary of periodical 'Economie' 1933–46; served in World War II, Army 1940; Chairman, Society for National Security until 1940; member, Netherlands Union 1940–41; prisoner at Haaren and St. Michaelsgestel 1942–43; Chairman, College van Algemene Commissarissen van Landbouw, Handel en Nivjerheid in the liberated southern provinces Oct. 1944–March 1945; Minister of War (Gerbrandy Cabinet) March–June 1945; Commissioner of the Queen, Province of North Brabant Nov. 1946–May 1959; Chairman of Board, K.L.M. Royal Dutch Airlines; 1964–73; Prime Minister and Minister for General Affairs of the Netherlands May 1959–Sept. 1963; Vice Prime Minister and Min. of Transport 1966–67; Pres., Carnegie Foundation 1964–73. *Awards:* Cmdr., Order of Orange Nassau, Order of Netherlands Lion. *Address:* Hiersenhof, Beers, bij Cuyk, Netherlands.

**DE RANITZ, Jonkheer Constant Johan Adriaan.** Dutch civic administrator. *B.* 3 April 1905. *Educ.* University of Leyden (LLD). *M.* 1945, Ariane Margaretha de Brauw. *Career:* Ministry of Education, Sciences and Arts 1931–36; Ministry of Social Affairs 1936–41; political prisoner 1941–42; staff of Dutch Red Cross 1944–45; Head, Section for University Education, Ministry of Education, Sciences and Arts 1945–48; President, Residentie Orkest 1946–48; Pres., Royal Dutch Alpine Club 1946–65, and Netherlands Bach Society 1947–74; Burgomaster of Utrecht 1948–70; Curator, State Univ. of Utrecht since 1954; Pres. 1972–73; Member Univ. Council 1973–76. *Awards:* Knighthood of Utrecht; Knight of Honour, Order of St. John of Jerusalem; Commander, Order of Orange-Nassau; Knight, Order of the Netherlands Lion; Cross of Honour, Family Order of Orange; Cross of Merit, Dutch Red Cross. Commander, Royal Victorian Order (U.K.); Commander, Order of George I (Greece); Commander, Order of the Lion (Finland); Officer, Order of the Crown of Belgium; Officer, Legion of Honour (France). *Publication:* Rechtspositie van de Rijksuniversiteit. *Address:* Loolaan 6–8, Driebergen, Netherlands; & Chalet 'Les Arcoraz,' 1885 Chesières, Switzerland.

**de RATULD, Jean.** French. *B.* 1909. *Educ.:* Breveté. National School of Overseas France; Lic. en Droit ès lettres, and Diploma from Natl. Sch. of Oriental Living Languages. *M.* 1943, Solange Demont. *S.* Yves, Michel and Alain. *Career:* Administrator in Overseas France 1932–35; Administrator of various companies. *Award:* Chevalier Legion of Honour; Officer of Commercial Merit; Officer of the National Economy; Chevalier Black Star. *Publications:* studies on the economics of petroleum in Bulletin de l'Association Française des Techniciens du Pétrole. *Address:* 3 Avenue Paul Doumer, Paris 16; and *office* 21 Rue Laffitte, Paris 9, France.

**DERBY, Stephen Arthur.** American retired banker. *B.* 1905. *Educ.* Yale (BS 1927). *M.* 1931, Dora Cooke. *S.* Philander Cooke and John Montague. *Daus.* Anna (Howe) and Martha (McDaniel). *Career:* New Business Investigator, Dillon, Read & Co., New York City 1927–30; Statistician. Hawaiian Pineapple Co. Ltd., Honolulu 1930–32; Senior Vice-Pres. Bank of Hawaii 1932–70; Director, Bank of Hawaii, 1948–75; Director, Molokai Ranch Ltd. 1957—; Kaluakoi Corporation 1969–76. *Award:* Silver Buffalo Award, Boy Scouts of America. *Member:* Yale Engineering Assn. Republican. *Clubs:* Pacific; Ironwood Hills Golf; Waialae Country. *Address:* 4340 Pahoa Ave. Apt. 18-D. Honolulu, Hawaii 96816.

**DEROY, Henri,** L. ès L., D. en D. French banker and company director. *B.* 12 June 1900. *M.* 1928, Marie Thérèse Toulouse. *S.* Hervé, Michel. *Daus.* Monique, Christiane. *Career:* Hon. Inspector-General of Finances; Hon. Director-General, Department of Deposits and Sinking Funds; Hon. Governor Crédit Foncier de France; Président honoraire de la Compagnie Financière de Paris et des Pays-Bas; (Hon.) Prés.: Cie Internationale des Wagons-Lits et du Tourisme; Vice-Chmn. Bank for International Settleements (Bâle); Administrator Banque Ottomane, Crédit foncier franco-canadien, Hachette, Paribas International. *Award:* Grand Officer, Légion d'Honneur. *Address:* 56 Avenue Foch Paris 16, France.

**DERRICK, Homer.** USA Banker and insurance executive. *B.* 1906. *Educ.* Univ. of S. Carolina; grad. Amer. Inst. of Banking. *M.* 1924, Mabel Ellison Beckham. *S.* Homer, Jr. *Daus.* Jeanne (Morris) and Betsy (Calvo). *Career:* Vice-Pres. South Carolina National Bank, Columbia and Greenville, S.C. 1926–50; President, Carolina National Bank, Easley and Pendleton, S.C. 1951–54. Founder and first President, Great Eastern Life Insurance Co., Greenville, S.C.; Atlantic & Gulf States Insurance Co., Easley; Eastern Fire & Casualty Insurance Co., Greenville. Former Director, Freedom Life Insurance Co., Greenville. Chairman of Board and President, First National Bank, Lexington, Va. 1955–73; Chmn. of the Bd., First Eastern Securities Corp.; and First Eastern Financial Corp.; Former Pres. and Director, Financial International Corp., Washington, D.C.; Director, Lexington Cadillac-Pontiac Inc., Lexington Va.; Appalachian Fruit Growers Cooperative Assoc., Raphine Va.; Partner, The Sherwood Co., Lexington. Democrat, Episcopalian. *Clubs:* Lexington Golf; Country: English-Speaking Union. *Address:* Windswept, Lexington, Va.; and *office* Drawer 1111, Lexington, Va., U.S.A.

**DERRICKSON, Vernon Blades.** Lieut. Col. Ret. *B.* 1900. *Educ.* Duke Univ. and Duke Univ. Law School. *M.* 1930, Jean Madeline Riveles. *S.* Vernon Blades, Jr. (Dec.). *Dau.* Joan (Slights). *Career:* Owner and operator of a chain of hotels. President: Derrickson Inc. (hotels and motels) 1940—, Derrickson Hotels Operating Co., Blades Corp. (hotels), V. & W. Hotel Corp., Derrickson Hotels Inc. Director: Farmers Bank of State of Delaware and Delaware Travel Council. Vice-Pres., Brandywine Raceway. Chmn. of Board, Ocean Highway; Chmn. Public Service Commission of State of Delaware. President, Great Lakes Conference on Public Utilities. Trustee: Wesley College, and People's Congregational Church now Moderator. *Member:* North Carolina State Bar; Amer. Cancer Socy.; Kappa Alpha fraternity; Gamma Eta Gamma legal fraternity; Cloverleaf-Standard Bred Owners' Assn. Inc.; Delaware Pony Breeders & Owners Inc.; Elks Lodge. Member Democrat State Committee 1949— (Chmn. Kent County Committee). *Club:* Maple Dale Country. *Address:* 128 Hazel Road, Dover, Del.; and *office* State House, Dover, Del., U.S.A.

**DESAI, Shri Moraji Ranchhodji,** BA. Prime Minister of India. *B.* 1896. *Educ.* Wilson Coll., Bombay. *M.* 1911, Shrimati Gajraben. *S.* 1. *Dau.* 1. *Career:* Entered Provincial Civil Service, Govt. of Bombay 1918; resigned to join the Civil Disobedience Campaign of Mahatma Gandhi 1930; convicted for taking part in the movement during 1930–34; Secy., Gujarat Pradesh Congress Cttee. 1931–37 and 1939–46; Minister for Revenue, Cooperation, Agriculture and Forests, Bombay 1937–39; convicted 1940–41; detained in prison 1942–45; Minister for Home and Revenue, Bombay 1946–52; Chief Minister of Bombay 1952–56; Minister for Commerce and Industry, Govt. of India 1956–58; Treasurer, All India Congress Cttee. 1950–58; Minister of Finance 1958–63. Resigned to do organizational work for Indian National Congress 1963; Chmn., Administrative Reforms Commission, Govt. of India 1966–67; Deputy Prime Minister and Minister of Finance, Mar. 1967–July '69; imprisoned June 1975 under the emergency declared by the Indira Gandhi Govt.;

released Jan. 1977; Chmn. of the Janata Party; Leader of the Janata Party. Party, March 1977; Prime Minister since March 1977. *Member:* All India Congress Cttee. 1931–69 (Treasurer 1950–58); Chancellor Gujarat Vidyapith; Pres. & Chmn. of many societies & trusts. Hon. Fellow, College of Physicians and Surgeons, Bombay 1956; Hon. LLD Karnatak Univ. 1957, Utkal Univ., Cuttack 1962. *Publications:* A View of the Gita; In My View; A Minister & his Responsibilities (Jawaharlal Nehru Memorial Lectures); The Story of my Life; Indian Unity: From Dream to Reality (Patel Memorial Lectures); Nature Cures. *Address:* Oceana, Marine Drive, Bombay, India.

**de SALIS, Rodo Théophile,** Dr. Jur. Swiss. *B.* 1910. *Educ.* Freie Protestantische Sch., Zürich; Kantonales Literar-Gymnasium, Zürich; Univs. of Zürich, Berlin, Berne. *M.* (1) 1939, Pierrette Dubied (Dec.), (2) 1955, Claude de Mulinen. *S.* 3. *Daus.* 2. *Career:* Chmn. Edouard Dubied & Cie S.A., Traversina S.A.; Vice-Chmn. Valves et Produits Industriels SA.; Chmn. Fonderie et Laminoirs Boillat S.A.; Fabrique d'aiguilles de machines a tricoter S.A. & affiliated cos. of Dubied Group; Dir., Metallica S.A.; Fosat S.A.; Metall-Serva A.G.; Swiss Federation of Machine Industries. *Clubs:* Grande Société, Berne; Cercle du Jardin, Neuchâtel. *Address:* 29 Chemin de Trois-Portes, Neuchâtel, Switzerland; and *office* 1 Rue du Musée, Neuchâtel.

**DESCHAMPS, Noel St. Clair.** Australian diplomat. *B.* 25 Dec. 1908. *Educ.* Pembroke Coll., Cambridge (MA). Rome, Brussels and Melbourne; *Career:* Australian Dept. of External Affairs 1937; Official Secy., High Commission in Canada 1940–43; Australian Official Representative, New Caledonia 1944–45: Chargé d'Affaires, Moscow 1946–47; Head, European American and Middle Eastern Division, Dept. of External Affairs 1948–49; Head, Australian Military Mission in Germany, Berlin 1949–52, with rank of Min. Plen.; Head, Australian Mission to Allied High Commission in Germany, Bonn 1950–52; Chargé d'Affaires, Bonn 1952; Head, Western Division, Dept. of External Affairs 1953; Counsellor, Paris 1953–58; Leader, Australian Delegation, First Antarctic Conf., Paris 1955; Liaison Press Officer, Suez Committee, London and Cairo, Sept. 1956; Australian Alternate, U.N. Committee for Hungary, Mar.–Apr. 1957; Chargé d'Affaires, Dublin, 1958–61; Acting H. Commissioner, S.A. 1960; Dept. of Ext. Affairs (Manila Treaty). 1961–2; Ambassador Cambodia 1962–9, Chile 1969–73; Pres. Aust. Soc. Latin Am. Studies since 1974. *Address:* 28 Kensington Rd., S. Yarra, Melbourne. Australia.

**DESCHATELETS, Hon. Jean Paul,** PC, QC (Lauzon). *B.* 1912. *Educ.* Valleyfield Seminary, St. Mary's Coll. (BA 1932), Univ. of Montreal, (LLB 1937). *M.* 1939, Fernande Duffresne. *S.* Bernard. *Daus.* Hélène and Andrée. *Career:* Barrister, Enforcement Counsel for the Prov. of Quebec, wartime Prices and Trade Board, 1942–51; Member House of Commons 1953—; Mem. of the Commonwealth Parliamentary Assn. to New Delhi, India, 1957. Delegate, NATO Conf. Paris, 1960, Delegate to Parl. Conf., Nigeria, 1962; Minister of Public Works 1963—; Asst. House Leader 1966: Senator 1966; Speaker of the Senate, 1968—; Delegate, Senatorial visit Czechoslovakia 1969; Council, Europe Conference Strasbourg 1969; Leader, Senate Del. Union Soviet Soc. Republic 1970; Leader Del. Expo 70, Japan, 1970. *Award:* Knight of Columbus 3rd degree. *Address:* The Senate, Ottawa, Canada.

**DE SCHRYVER, August Edmund,** D en D. Belgian lawyer and politician. *B.* 1898. *Educ.* St. Barbara College and State University Ghent; London School of Economics; Hon. Barrister, Court of Appeal, Ghent; member, Chamber of Representatives 1928–65. War volunteer 1916–18; Minister of Agriculture 1935; Minister of the Interior 1936; Minister of Justice 1939; Minister of Economic Affairs 1940; Minister of the Interior 1943; Deputy Prime Minister 1944; Minister for African Affairs 1959. Deputy Chairman, Belgian Delegation, U.N.C.I.O. 1945; Founder-President, Parti Social Chrétien 1945–49; member, Belgian Delegation U.N. 1950, 1964–65 and 1970; Chmn. Int. Union Christian Democrats 1949–59; Minister of State since 1948. *Address:* 52 Kwaadham, Ghent, Belgium.

**DESCLÉE de MAREDSOUS, Charles M. J.** Belgian director of business corporations. *B.* 1916. *Educ.* Doctor-in Law; Lic. Social and Political Economy. *M.* 1945, Bernadette Chaudoir. *S.* Philippe and Bruno. *Daus.* Isabelle, Pascale and Sibylle. *Career:* Economic Attaché, Belgian Embassy, London 1946–47; Economic Adviser, Ministry of Economic Affairs, Brussels 1947–49; Manager, H. Desclée et Cie. 1949–56; Dir. and Financial Adviser S.A. Electrobel 1956—; Dir. Sté Réunies Energie du Bassin de l'Escant E.B.E.S. 1956—; several other corporations; Man. Dir. Desclée Frères et Cie since 1958. Lieut. Col. of Reserve—Guides Regiment. *Award:* Commander, of LOrder eopold II; Officer, Order of the Crown. *Member:* Sté. Royale d'Economie Politique; Sté. Belge de Statistique; Econometric Society. *Club:* Officers of the Guides. *Address:* 16 avenue de Tervueren, Brussels 1040; and *office* 32 Ave. de Tervueren, Brussels 1040, Belgium.

**DESCLÉE de MAREDSOUS, Jules.** Belgian executive. Vice-Chairman, Member of the Executive Committee & Director, Banque Bruxelles Lambert. *B.* 1914. *Educ.* Univ. of Louvain (Doctor at Law). *M.* 1938, Marie Agnès, Baronne van der Straten Waillet. *S.* Benoit. *Daus.* Agnès, Marie-Cécile, Jacinte, Pauline, Anne-Marie. *Address:* 479 avenue Louise, Brussels; Le Chenoy, Maredsous; and *office* 2 rue de la Régence, Brussels, Belgium.

**DE SHARENGRAD, Erwin.** Swedish. *B.* 1905. *Educ.* Hogre Allmanna Laroverket, Malmo. *M.* 1933, Norah May Tillstone. *S.* 2. *Career:* Chief Eng., Skaninaviska Eternit AB, 1933–61; Man. Dir. A/B Gyproc 1955–71; AB Eternitror 1961–63; Pres. Nordisk Gipsskivef since 1971. *Clubs:* Kungl; Automobilklubben. *Address:* Anebergsg 15A, 21466 Malmo; and *office* Hans Michelsensg. 9, Malmo 1, Sweden.

**DESHLER, James II.** Corporation Official. *B.* 1909. *Educ.* William College, Williamstown, Mass. (AB 1931); New Jersey Law School (LLB 1934). *M.* (1) 1934, Carlyle L. Quackenboss. *Dau.* Elaine. (2) 1969, Elsa S. Palmer. *Career:* Admitted to N.J. bar, 1934, master-in-chancery, N.J. 1938. Associate Hicks, Kuhlthau & Thomson, 1934–38; Partner of same firm with name of Deshler added 1938–41; Assistant Secretary to General Counsel, Johnson & Johnson, New Brunswick 1941–45. Assistant Secretary: Industrial Tape Corporation; Ethicon Suture Corp.; Atlantic Diesel Corp. 1941–45; Ortho Pharmaceutical Corp. 1941–45 (Sec., Dir. 1945–47). Pres., Dir., Edgar Bros. Co. 1947–54; Chmn., Minerals & Chemicals Corp. of America, 1960–63; Dir., Engelhard Ind. Inc. Newark, N.J. 1963–67; Pres., Dir., Chmn., Exec. Cttee. Minerals & Chemicals Philipp Corp., Menlo Park, N.J. 1963–64, Vice-Chmn. of Bd., 1964–67. Pres., Dir., Chemstone Corp.; Cuyahoga Lime Co.; Porocel Corp. 1963–67 and Chmn. 1967–70. Chmn., Eastern Magnesia Talc Co. 1967–70; Minerals & Chemicals Div. of Engelhard Minerals & Chemical Corp., 1967–69; Dir. & Member Exec. Cttee., Engelhard Minerals & Chemicals Corp. 1967–70; Vamistor Corp., 1965–72; National Conference of Christians and Jews 1962—. Vice-Pres., Dir., New Brunswick Chpt. 1940–41; Community Chest. N.J. 1940–41; Trustee, Rutgers Prep. Sch., New Brunswick, N.J. 1959—. *Member:* New Jersey and Middlesex County Bar Assns.; Gargoyle Socy.; Zeta Psi; Upper Raritan Valley Watershed Assn. Episcopalian. *Clubs:* Country; Somerset Hills Country; The Little Club, Gulf Stream, Fla.; Country Club of Florida; Williams, Ocean (Florida); Delray Beach Yacht. *Address: office* Engelhard Minerals & Chemicals Corp., Menlo Park, Edison, New Jersey 08817, U.S.A.

**DESHMUKH, Hon. Shri. Chintaman Dwarkanath,** CIE. Indian administrator. *B.* 1896. *Educ.* Elphinstone High School and College, Bombay; Jesus College, Cambridge (BA). *M.* 1920 (1) Rosina Silcox (*D.* 1949), (2) 1953, Durgabai. *Dau.* Primrose. *Career:* Assistant Commissioner 1920–24, Deputy Commissioner and Settlement Officer, Raipur 1926–31; Under-Sec., Central Province Government 1924–25, Revenue Sec. 1932–33; Joint Secy., Second Round Table Conf. 1931; Financial Secy., Govt. of Central Province and Berar 1933–39; Joint Secy., Dept. of Education, Health and Lands, Govt. of India, later Officer on Special Duty, Finance Dept.; Custodian of Enemy Property 1939; Secy., Central Board, Reserve Bank of India, Bombay 1939–41, Deputy Governor 1941–43, Governor 1943–49; Delegate to World Monetary Conf. Bretton Woods 1944; Governor for India, Int. Monetary Fund and Int. Bank for Reconstruction and Development 1946–56, Chairman 1950; Financial Representative of Govt. of India in Europe and America 1949–50; Pres., Indian Statistical Inst. 1946–64; Pres. Council for Social Development 1964—; President, Indian Institute of Economic Growth, 1966–73; President, Population Council of India, since 1970. Member, Planning Commission 1950–59; Minister of Finance 1950–56; Chmn., University Grants Commission 1956–61; Chmn., National Book Trust, India 1957–60; Chmn., Admin. Staff Coll., Hyderabad 1960–73; Pres., Board of Trustees, India International Centre 1960—; Chairman, Indian Inst. of Public Administration 1964–65. Vice-Chancellor Univ. of Delhi 1962–67. Vice-

Chmn. U.N. Institute for Training and Research, 1966–70. *Awards:* Bar-at-Law Inner Temple London; Hon. Fellow Jesus Coll; Ramon Magsaysay Award; Doctorates (Hon. Cau.) Princeton, U.S.A.; Leicester U.K. many Indian Universities. *Address:* Indian International Centre, 40 Lodi Estate, New Delhi 3. India.

**DE SOUZA, Wilfred Raoul Eugène.** Benin diplomat. *B.* 1935. *Educ:* Quai D'Orsay, Diplomatic Studies, Licentiate (History), *M.* 1963, Francine Antonini, *Dau.* 1. *Career:* Assistant-Secy. at Ministry of Foreign Affairs 1961; Second Counsellor at the Dahomey Embassy in Bonn 1961–64; First Counsellor at the Dahomey Embassy in Paris 1964–68; Secy.-Gen. at the Ministry of Foreign Affairs with rank of Plenipotentiary 1968–70; Ambassadeur of Dahomey in Washington and Permanent Rep. of U.N. 1970–73; Ambassadeur of Dahomey in Paris (also responsible for London, Madrid, Algiers and (later) Malta) 1973–76. mem. oft he Dahomey delegation of the General Assembly of U.N. (notably for 21st, 23rd–27th sessions); Head of the Dahomey delegation, for the 12th, 13th and 14th sessions, of the council of Ministers of United African Organisation. *Decorations:* Knight of the National Order of Dahomey; Legion of Honour; Grand Cross of the Order of Merit of Malta; Cmmdr. of the Order of Merit (FGR). *Address:* c/o Ministère des Affaires Etrangères, Cotonou, Benin.

**DESRUISSEAUX, Senator Paul,** QC, LLD, Ph.D, KMT, CE, FAIM. Canadian barrister and editor. *B.* 1905. *Educ.* University of Montreal (BL); Babson Institute (post graduate) Harvard Univ. (post graduate); LLD Honoris Causa, University of Sherbrooke; Dr. Philosophy, Business Admin. Hamilton University. *M.* 1945, Céline Duchesne. *S. Louis (Dec.),* François and Pierre. *Dau.* Hélène. *Career:* Called to the Bar of Province of Quebec 1935; created K.C. 1948; was senior member of law firm of Desruisseaux, Fortin & Rouillard 1934–61. Served in World War I with Sherbrooke Fusiliers and Royal Canadian Artillery, until appointed Asst. Deputy Judge Advocate) 1940–45; Former Dir., Standard Brands Ltd. (Canada); Canadian Press and Daily Newspapers, Les quotidiens Canadian le Langue Francaise. Former Chairman, Melchers Distilleries Ltd. Pres., Desmont Research & Development Inc., Cablevision (Montreal) Inc.; Former Dir., PPG Industries; PPG Foundation; The Royal Bank of Canada, Canadian General Electric Co. Ltd., Westmount Life Assurance Co. Ltd., Mondev International Inc.; Governor, University of Sherbrooke, Sherbrooke Hospital; Chmn., Hon. Governors of Quebec Association of Retarded Children; Former Dir. The Canadian Council of Christians and Jews. Past President and one of the founders of the Federation of Junior Chambers of Commerce of the Eastern Townships; former Director: The Palestre Nationale; Sherbrooke Chamber of Commerce. Editor and Publisher 1955–67; La Tribune; The Telegram-Observer; contributed many articles and booklets. Fellow American Institute of Management. Member, Canadian, Province of Quebec and St. Francis Bar Associations. *Award:* Human Award of the Council of Christians and Jews. *Address:* 405 Victoria, Sherbrooke, Que.; and *office* The Senate, Ottawa, Ont. KIA OA6, Canada.

**de STRYCKER, Cecil.** Belgian. *B.* 1915. *Educ.* Univ. of Louvain (Dr. Com .Sc. 1939; Licenciate in Economics 1936). *M* 1948, Elisabeth Braffort. Governor, National Bank of Belgium. *Awards:* Grand Officer, Order of the Crown (Belgium); Officer, Order of Leopold (Belgium); Cmdr., Ordre du Chêne (Luxembourg); Officer Order of Merit of the Italian Republic; Officer, Order of the Lion (Finland). *Address:*14 Avenue Bois du Dimanche, Brussels 1150; and *office* National Bank of Belgium, Brussels.

**DESWARTE, Willem Pieter Alberic.** Belgian. *B.* 1906. *Educ.* Dr en Droit, Lic. en Sc. Pol., Lic. en Sc. Financ.; Diploma, Bureau of International Studies, Geneva; Dr. *Hon. Causa* (Academy of International Law, Mexico). *M.* 1940, Irène Tesch. *S.* 1. *Career:* Associate, Btonnier, Order of Belgian Advocates 1929; Secretary-General, later Director and Administrator and Director-General of the chain stores l'Innovation 1933; President, Belgian Maritime Tribunal in London 1945; Counsellor, Ministry of Finance 1946; Chief of Cabinet of the Prime Minister 1947, and of the Cabinet of the Minister of the Interior 1947; Director-General, Sabena 1949. Director-General, Sté. Anon. Belge d'Exploitation de la Navigation Aérienne (SABENA) 1949–71. *Publications:* La Limitation des Dividendes, (1942); L'impôt sur le capital appliqué aux Sociétés par actions 1946. *Awards:* Comdr. Order of Orange-Nassau; Officer Order of the Crown; Chevalier Legion of Honour; Commander Order of Leopold; Cross of the Voluntary Escapers in War; France-Germany Star; Brit. Defence of Britain Medal. *Member:* Institute of Air Transport (I.T.A.), Paris (Vice-Pres.); Committee of Institute of Organization and Management (University of Brussels). Member Belgian Socialist Party. *Address:* Chaussée de Charleroi 133, 1060 Brussels, Belgium.

**de TARDE, Jean Paul Marie Guillaume,** L ès L, L en D. French company director. *B.* 19 Nov. 1885. *M.* 1922, Marcelle Cléry. *Dau.* Françoise. *Career:* Auditor, Council of State 1910, Maître des Requêtes; Secretary-General, Protectorate of Morocco 1914–20; Manager, National Office of Foreign Trade 1922–27; Director, Compagnie des Chemins de Fer de l'Est 1927; Chairman, Compagnie des Chemins de Fer de l'Est since 1940; Vice-Chairman, Société Nationale des Chemins de Fer Français since 1940; Chairman, Société des Pétroles Serco since 1942; Chmn., Banque Nationale pour le Commerce et l'Industrie 1946–48 and 1957–60. Commandeur de la Légion d'Honneur. *Address:* 1 Avenue Camoens, Paris 16e, France.

**de TRAFFORD, Dermot Humphrey,** VRD, MA. British. *B.* 1925. *Educ.* Harrow School; Christ Church, Oxford (MA). *M.* (1) 1946, Patricia Mary Beeley. *S.* 3. *Daus.* 6. (2) Xandra Carandini Walter (née Lee). *Career:* Chmn., G.H.P. Group Ltd., Brentford Electric Ltd.; Calor Gas Holding Co. Ltd.; Dir., E. N. Bray Ltd., Hugh Smith (Glasgow) Ltd., Counting Instruments Ltd., Langley Alloys Ltd.; Grosvenor Hypower Ltd., London Hydraulic Power Co., Petrofina S.A., Monks Investment Trust Ltd.; Imperial Continental Gas Assoc., UNERG S.A. *Clubs:* White's; Royal Ocean Racing; Island Sailing. *Address:* 59 Onslow Square, London SW7; and *office* Battlebridge House, Tooley St., London, S.E.1.

**DETTWILER, Walter.** Swiss. *B.* 1925. *Educ.* in England, Switzerland and U.S.A. President Dettwiler Management Corporation. *Address:* 55 Moillebeau, 1209 Geneva, Switzerland.

**DEUTCH, Michael Joseph.** Consulting Engineer, and Economist, Washington D.C. 1946—. *B.* 1907. *Educ.* Univ. of Ghent (ME 1926, EE 1929, Dr Econ 1931). *M.* 1934, Dr. Rachel F. Fischer. *Children:* Nina, John Mark, Sara Anne. *Career:* Chief Engineer, Manager, electric development and research, Sofina Ltd., Brussels 1934–40; official delegate of Govt. of Belgium to World Power Conf., Washington 1936. Principal Consultant on the Engineering Staff of Warfare Analysis, Washington 1942; Chief, scheduling branch of W.P.B. and Special Asst. to Chmn. W.P.B. 1943–45, and to Dir. War Mobilization and Reconversion 1945–46; Consultant, Dept. of State 1966—, and on Logistics AC of S/G4, Army Gen. Staff. Member, U.S. Survey Mission to the Philippines, and U.S. Trade Mission to Mexico 1963, Poland and Roumania 1965, U.S. Embassy, Saigon 1966. U.S. Govt. official expert, Water for Peace Int. Conf. 1967; Head, Editorial Board Chemical Engineering International; Pres. Inst. of Global Dynamics Consultant Environmental Protection Agency Special Consultant on Energy, U.S. National Commission on Materials Policy 1972–73; Consultant & Snr. Staff Mem., Commission on Critical Choices for Americans 1974–75; Consultant on Energy, Materials & International Development & Financing 1976—; Mem., D.C. Board of Licensing of Professional Engineers 1977. Fellow, Am. Inst. of Chemical Engineers. *Member:* Am. Inst. Elect. Engineers, Am. Socy. Mech. Engrs., Socy. Mil. Engrs., Am. Petroleum Inst., Council on Foreign Relations, Co-op. Forum. Washington Inst. Foreign Affairs. *Publications:* Mémoire sur les Fraudes de Courant et les Dispositifs Techniques et Mesures Légales d'y prévenir, Brussels (1934) (trans. in Spanish, English, Italian, Rumanian and Czech); The Rationalization of Distribution of Electrical Energy, (1936); The Reorganization of Electrical Distribution in Great Britain, (1937); Methods of New Business Development in the Electric Light and Power Industry, (1938); Summary of Statutory Legislation on Electric Power Distribution in Different Countries, (1930); The Influence of Radio on the Demand for Electric Energy, Brussels and London, (1940); The U.S. Sulphur Industry, (1952); Industrial Development of the Philippines, (1953); Technological Developments of the U.S. Synthetic Rubber Industry, (1954); The Urea Technology, (1956); The Cost of Atomic Power for Small Reactors, (1959); Problems of Petrochemical Development, (1963); Management Methods in the Chemical Industry, (1963); Present Status of U.S. Petrochemical Development, (1963); Synthetic Fibres, (1964); Computer Application to Venture Analysis in the Chemical and Process Industries, (1969); Pollution Abatement Technology in the U.S. 1970 of Water Works, Liège

(Belgium); The U.S. Foreign Policy in the 1970s; The Cosmos Lecture, Washington, D.C. 1969. Air Pollution Technology and Investment Incentives; East West Trade (1976); ZEG and the Limits to Growth; Cybernetics of Environmental Protection (1972); Energy and Materials 1973; Nuclear Safety (1973); U.S. Energy Model 1973–1985; U.S. Energy Planning in an Independent World (1975); Energy & Environment (1976). *Clubs:* Cosmos, Lotos, Chemists', Petroleum (Houston) Presidents. *Address:* 2820 32nd Street, N.W., Washington, D.C. 20008, U.S.A.

**DEUTSCH, Charles Georges.** French. Officer Legion of Honour, Holder Gold Medal of Sports. *B.* 1911. *Educ.* Engineer Ecole Polytechnique, and Ecole Supérieure d'Electricité; Engineer-General of Bridges and Roads. *M.* 1947, Jacqueline Penin. *Daus.* Catherine and Françoise. *Career:* Engineer of Bridges and Roads, and in the Service of the Navigation of the Seine and Direction of the Hydrocarbures 1936–50; Adjoint Dir.-General Trapil 1951–60; Technical Counsellor to the Ministry of Industry 1956–57; Director-General Omnium Technique des Transports par pipe-line (OTP) 1957–67; Chairman du Groupement intersyndical pour l'équipment de l'industrie du Pétrole (GEP) 1964—. Delegate General, Scientific & Technical Questions Entrepose; Pres., G.E.P. Fisita. *Member:* I.C.F.; A.F.T.P.; S.I.A.; P.C.M. *Publications* numerous technical reviews. *Address:* 98 Avenue Suffren, Paris 75015; and *office* 75 Rue de Tocqueville, Paris 75017.

**de van der SCHUEREN, Johannes Baptista Geradus Maria.** Dutch administrator. *B.* 1899. *Educ.* Technical Univ., Delft. *M.* 1922, MA Th. Helmich. *S.* 4. *Daus.* 2. *Career:* General Manager, Neue Glansstoffwerke, Breslau 1927–30; Technical Manager, British Enka, Aintree 1930–44. Military Service Netherlands 1944–46. Governor, Province of Overijssel 1946–64. *Awards:* Grand Officer: Order of Orange Nassau, Order of Merit (Fed. Repub. of Germany), Order of Crown of Oak; Knight, Order of the Netherlands Lion; Commander, Order of the British Empire; Officer, Legion of Merit (U.S.A.); Bailiff, Sovereign and Military Order of Malta; Grand Cross pro Merits Melit. (S.M.O.M.); Grand Cross order St. Gregory. *Address:* Sophiaweg 117, Nijmegen (Gelderland), Netherlands.

**DE VASCONCELLOS, Dora Alencar.** Brazilian. *B.* 1920. *Educ.* Colegio Jacobina, Rio de Janeiro. *Career:* Secy. to the Brazilian Embassy in Montevideo 1947, Consul 1953; Asst. Consul, New York, 1952–58, Consul-General 1958–65. Alternate Deleg. on the Social, Humanitarian and Cultural Cttee. at the XIII Gen. Assembly in the U.N. 1958; Ambassador to Canada, 1966–69 to Trinidad and Tobago 1969–72. *Publications:* Palavra Sem Eco, (1952); Surdina do Contemplado, (1958); O Grande Caminho do Branco (1963). President, Society of Foreign Consuls in New York 1964–65; Member, Zonta International; Hon. Member, Women's Canadian Club of Ottawa. *Address:* c/o Ministry of Foreign Affairs, Brasilia, Brazil.

**De VIGIER, William A.,** Knight, Star of the North, Grand Cdr., Order of the Star of Africa. Swiss. *B.* 1912. *Educ.* La Chataigneraie, Coppet. *M.* 1939, Betty Kendall. *Daus.* 2. *Career:* Chmn., Acrow (Engineers) Ltd., Thos. Storey (Engineers) Ltd., Adamson & Hatchett Ltd., E. H. Bentall & Co. Ltd., Acrow Australia Ltd., Acrow Engineers (Pty.) Ltd. South Africa; Dir., Vigier Cement S.A., Switzerland, Acrow Argentina S.A., Acrow Peru S.A., Acrow India Ltd., Acrow Canada Ltd.; Inland Steel Pty. (Jo'burg); Steel Engineering Ltd.; Japan Steels Eng. Ltd. (Japan); Pres., Acrow Corp. of America; Chmn. Coles Cranes Ltd.; Priestman Bros. Ltd.; Coles France SA; Member British Airways Board. *Clubs:* Devonshire. *Address:* Tinkers Lodge, Marsh Lane, Mill Hill, London, N.W.7; and 'Sommerhaus,' 4500, Solothurn, Switzerland.

**DEVINE, Matthuw L.** American corporation executive. *B.* 1905. *Educ.* Northwestern Univ. (BS) and Georgetown Univ. (JD). *M.* 1928, Mary Ann Brailsford. *S.* Michael B. *Dau.* Beatrice Ann (Dellett). *Career:* Partner, Cresap, McCormick & Paget, Chicago 1947–60; management engineer, General Electric Co., Princeton, N.J. 1946–47; control officer, H.Q. Army Service Force and H.Q., U.S. Army Service of Supply, South West Pacific Area 1942–45; management engineer, Control Div. A.S.F., Washington 1942; Asst. Dir., Q.M. General's office, Const. Div., Washington 1940–42; Asst. and Dir., projects Div., Public Works Administration, Washington 1933–40; engineer, Graver Tank, Chicago 1929–33; Chmn., Amphenol Corp., Broadview, Ill. 1960–68. Director. Banker Ramo Corp.; Intercontinent Refining Corp. Ltd.; Parnter, Bowladrome Ltd. *Clubs:* Sunset Ridge (Winnetka, Ill.), Blue Lakes C.C. Twin Falls. *Address:* Pole Line Road, Rt. 3, Twin Falls, Idaho 83301, U.S.A.

**DEVLIN, Rt. Hon. Lord.** English judge; *B.* 1905. *Educ.* Stonyhurst; Christ's College, Cambridge. *M.* 1932, Madeleine Oppenheimer. *S.* Gilpatrick, Dominick, Timothy, Matthew. *Daus.* Clare, Virginia. *Career:* Called to the Bar Gray's Inn 1929; Prosecuting Counsel to the Mint 1931–39; KC 1945· Attorney-General, Duchy of Cornwall 1947–48; Master of the Bench, Gray's Inn since 1947; Justice of the High Court, Queen's Bench Division 1948–60; Chairman of Council, Bedford College, London, 1953–59, Wiltshire Quarter Sessions 1955—, Committee of Inquiry into the Dock Labour Scheme 1956; Nyasaland Commission of Inquiry 1959; Pres. of the Restrictive Practices Court 1956–60. Lord Justice of Appeal 1960–61; Lord of Appeal in Ordinary 1961–64; Chairman, Press Council 1964–69; a judge of the Administrative Tribunal of the ILO 1964—; High Steward of Cambridge Univ. 1966—. *Address:* West Wick House, Pewsey, Wilts.

**de WAAL, Dr. Anna.** Dutch scholar and politician. *B.* 25 Nov. 1906. *Career:* Teacher in Geography in Indonesia 1932–39; Assistant Professor in Human Geography, University of Utrecht 1947–52; member, Utrecht Town Council 1949–52; member of Parliament June 1952–Feb. 1953; State-Secretary of Education, Arts and Sciences 1953–57; member Provincial States of Utrecht 1958–62, Universities' Council 1961–62; President Neth. League of Women Voters 1959–66; Pres. Central Assn. for Public Libraries 1960–64; Teacher Library School Amsterdam 1964–70. *Address:* Prof. Winkleerlaan 365, Flat 05–10, Utrecht, Netherlands.

**DEWAR, H. H. (Hal).** American. *B.* 1902. *Educ.* Univ. of Texas (AB 1923). *M.* 1927, Hallie Ball. *S.* Robert L. B. *Daus.* Mrs. W. Keene L. Ferguson, and Mrs. J. Michael Bell. Partner, Hornblower & Weeks-Hemphill, Noyes (Securities Dealers, San Antonio, Tex.) 1967— (Partner, Dewar, Robertson & Pancoast 1932–67). *Member:* Exec. Cttee., Southwest Research Inst. 1954— (Vice-Chmn. 1962–67); United Fund of San Antonio (Pres. 1957); Texas Commission on Higher Education 1956–60 (Vice-Chmn.); Southern Regional Educational Board 1966—; National Assn. of Securities Dealers (Chmn. 1942); Investment Bankers Assn. of America (Pres. 1949); Board of Governors, New York Stock Exchange 1958–61. *Publications:* miscellaneous monographs and speeches on investment banking, higher education and united charities. *Clubs:* Racquet & Tennis, Bankers, Stock Exchange Luncheon (N.Y.C.); Bohemian (San Francisco); San Antonio Country, Argyle, St. Anthony (San Antonio, Tex.). *Address:* 10 Ironwood Road, San Antonio, Tex., U.S.A.

**DEWDNEY, Duncan Alexander Cox,** CBE. British. Legion of Merit (1945). *B.* 1911. *Educ.* Bromsgrove School; Univ. of Birmingham (BSc Hons.—Cadman Medallist). *M.* 1935, Ann Riley. *Daus.* Caroline and Christina. *Career:* Research Mgr., Esso Development Co. Ltd. 1945–51; Asst. Refinery Mgr., Esso Petroleum Co. Ltd. 1952–56; Dir., Esso Petroleum Co. Ltd. 1957; Chmn.: Irish Refining Co. Ltd. 1958–65, and Esso Chemical S.A. 1964–65. Chmn., Nat. Economic Development Cttee. for Mechanical Engineering 1964–68. *Member:* Inst. of Directors; Inst. of Petroleum; Inst. of Fuel; Managing Director, Esso Petroleum Co. Ltd. 1963–67, (Vice-Chmn., 1968). Member and Jt. Dep. Chmn. National Board for Prices & Incomes 1965–70; Exec. Dir., Riotintozinc Corp., 1969–72; Chmn., RT2 Britain 1969–72; Dep. Chmn. Manpower Services since 1974. *Club:* Travellers' (London). *Address:* 'Salters', Harestock, Winchester, Hants; and *office* 6 St. James's Square, London, S.W.1.

**DE WET, Dr. Carel.** South African Ambassador to the Court of St. James's, 1964–67 & 1972–76. *B.* 1924. *Educ.* Vrede High School, OFS; Pretoria Univ. (BSc); Univ. of Witwatersrand (MB, BCh). *M.* 1949, Rina Maas, BA. *S.* 1. *Daus.* 3. *Career:*Served at National Hospital, Bloemfontein; subseq. practised medicine at Boksburg, Transvaal, at Winberg, OFS, & from 1948 at Vanderbijlpark, Transvaal. Mayor of Vanderbijlpark 1950–52; MP for Vanderbijlpark 1953–64, when he was Mem. of various Parliamentary & Nat. Party Cttees.; Minister of Mines & Health, Govt. of South Africa 1967–72. *Clubs:* Wentworth, Les Ambassadeurs, Royal Automobile, Devonshire, Travellers, Eccentric, Here XVII (Cape Town), Constantia (Pretoria), Club RSA, Rand Park, Country Club, Eccentric Johannesburg, Maccauvlei Vereeniging, Emfuleni Vanderbijlpark. *Address:* P.O. Box 6424, Johannesburg 2000, South Africa.

**DEXTER, Robert R.** American aeronautical engineer and executive, Secretary and Administrator, Technical Information Programs. *B.* 1908. *Educ.* New York Univ. (BS 1930; AE 1932). *M.* 1935, Isabella McConnell. *S.* Robert R. and Reginald Thomas. *Dau.* Barbara Ann. *Career:* Sales Dept., Sun Oil Co., N.Y.C. 1932–34; Sales Engineer, Fred Buse Inc. N.Y. 1934–36; member of Staff, Inst. of Aeronautical Sciences, N.Y.C., as research worker 1936–39; Secretary, Inst. of Aerospace Sciences (now A.I.A.A.) since 1943; Member, U.S. Panel to NATO Advisory Group on Aeronautical Research and Development 1957–69; Exec. Secy., Inter. Coun. of the Aeronatical Sciences (ICAS) 1964—; Asst. Secy., Engineers' Council for Professional Development (ECPD) 1963–64. Dir., Paul Kollsman Library, and of technical information service 1939–43. Editor, ICAS Proceedings 1964 Paris, 1966, London and Haifa 1974, Ottawa 1976; Aeronautical Consultant & Exec. Sec., International Council of Aeronaut. Sciences 1974—. Associate Editor, Journal of Aerospace Sciences; Technical Advisor, Aerospace Engineering. Fellow: American Inst. of Aeronautics & Astronautics; Amer. Assn. for the Advancement of Science; Royal Aeronautical Socy.; Hon. Fellow, Canadian Aeronautical Inst.; member, Socy. of Automotive Engineers, and Aviation Writers Association. *Address:* 64 Underhill Road, Ossning, N.Y., U.S.A.

**d'HUART, Jean (Marie, Paul, Emile).** Luxembourger. *B.* 1903. *Educ.* Lic.-en-Sc. Com. *M.* 1934, Antoinette Funck. *S.* Paul, Jacques and Georges. Director, Banque Internationale à Luxembourg since 1957. President: Brasserie de Diekirch, Diekirch; Ancien President et Membre du Conseil, de la Fédération Bancaire Européene. Commandeur, Order of Adolphe of Nassau (with Crown); Officer, Order of the Oak Crown; Officer, Order of the Crown; Cmdr. Order of Merit (Luxembourg); Cmdr. L'Ordre de Merité (Ital). *Address:* 15 rue J P. Brasseur, Luxembourg; and *office* 2 Boulevard Royal, Luxembourg.

**DIAMOND, Rt. Hon. Lord (John Diamond),** PC. *B.* 1907. *Educ.* Leeds Grammar School. *Career:* (Lab. Blackley, Manchester 1945–51, and Gloucester 1957–70) Chief Secretary to the Treasury 1964–70. Member, General Nursing Council and Chairman of its Finance and General Purposes Committee 1947–53; Hon. Treasurer Fabian Socy. 1950–64; Dir. Sadler's Wells Trust 1957–64; Hon. Treasurer Labour Committee for Europe 1961–64; Member of Cabinet 1968–70; Baron cr. 1970 (Life Peer) of the City of Gloucester; Deputy-Chmn of Cttees H. of Lords 1974; Chmn. Royal Commission on Distribution of Income and Wealth since 1974; Chmn., Industry & Parliament Trust since 1977. *Publications:* Public Expenditure in Practice (1975); (part author) Socialism the British Way (1948). *Address:* House of Lords, London, S.W.1.

**DIAMOND, Walter Henry.** U.S.A. economist and editor. *B.* 1913. *Educ.* Syracuse Univ. (BA) and Syracuse Univ. Graduate School of Extension (AIB). *M.* 1947, Dorothy Blum. *Career:* Principal Hauser, O'Connor & Hylind, N.Y., 1966—; Exec. Editor and Dir. of Economics, United States Investor 1960–62; Editor, McGraw-Hill American Letter and Dir. of Economics, McGraw-Hill International Corp. 1952–60; Economist, Public National Bank 1946–52; Foreign Bond Analyst, Standard & Poor Corp. 1945–46; Foreign Analyst, Federal Reserve Bank of New York 1942–45; Asst. National Bank Examiner, U.S. Treasury 1941–42; Dir. of Research, Lincoln National Bank of Syracuse 1934–41; Director of Research, Foreign Credit Insurance Association; Editor and International Trade Consultant, Overseas Automotive Club, and of International Executives Association, Economic Consultant, Motor and Equipment Manufacturers Association. *Publications:* Foreign Tax & Trade Briefs (up-to-date service tax laws in 104 countries). Internat. Tax Treaty Guide; Tax Havens of the World; Internat. Tax Treaties of All Nations; Tax-Free Trade Zones of the World. Citation, Government of Honduras. Appointed to French Trade Mission. Investment adviser to twenty-one foreign governments. *Member:* Pi Delta Epsilon; International Executives Assn.; Motor & Equipment Manufacturers Assn.; Foreign Credit Interchange Bureau. *Clubs:* Overseas Press; Overseas Automotive; International Executives. *Address:* 9 Old Farm Lane, Hartsdale, N.Y.; and *office* Hauser, O'Connor & Hylind, 275 Madison Ave., New York, N.Y. 10016, U.S.A.

**DIBBA, Sherif Mustapha.** GCRE, MP. Gambian diplomat. *B.* 1937. *Educ.* Gambia. *M.* 1968, Oumie Barrie. *Daus.* 5. *Career:* Member, Gambian Parliament 1960—; Minister Local Government, Lands & Mines 1962–66; Minister, Works and Communications 1966–68; of Finance Comerce and Industry 1968–70; Vice-Pres. Minister of Finance 1970–72; Ambassador to Belgium and E.E.C. 1972–74; Minister of Economic Planning & Industrial Development since 1974. Pres. Gambia United Nations Association. *Award:* Grand Commander, Republic of Gambia. *Address:* Ministry of Economic Planning & Industrial Development, Marina Parade, Banjul, The Gambia.

**DICK, Alick Sydney.** British industrial consultant. *B.* 1916. *Educ.* Dean Close, Cheltenham; Chichester High School. *M.* 1940, Betty Melinda Eileen Hill. *S.* Michael John, Peter James, Nigel Alan. *Career:* Man. Director, Standard Triumph International Ltd., Coventry 1954–61; Purchasing Consultant, Volkswagenwerk AG, Wolfsburg; Audi NSU Union AG, Ingolstadt (both Germany) since 1968. *Address:* The Thatched Cottage, Hill Wootton, Warwickshire.

**DICKIE, Hon. Vance Oakley.** Australian MLC. *B.* 1918. *Educ.* Melbourne Church of England Grammar School. *M.* 1943, Dorothy Jean Malcolm. *S.* 2. *Dau.* 1. *Career:* MLC for Ballaarat since 1956; Minister of State Development 1964–65; Secretary to the Cabinet 1964; Minister of Health 1965–70. Minister of State Development; Minister for Environment Control, State of Victoria 1970–72; Minister, Housing; Minister Aboriginal Affairs, 1972–76; Chief Secretary 1976—. *Member:* Liberal Party of Victoria and Australia. *Clubs:* Melbourne Cricket, Victoria Racing: Moonee Valley Racing. Caulfield Racing. *Address:* 78 Lerderderg Street, Bacchus Marsh, Vic.; and *office* Old Treasury Building, Melbourne, Vic., Australia.

**DICKINSON, John Lawrence.** CBE, DL, FCA. British. *B.* 1913. *Educ.* Taunton. *M.* 1937, Bettine Mary Jenkins. *Daus.* 2. Holder Gold Medal Royal Patriotic Society of Sweden. *Career:* SKF (U.K.) Ltd. (M.D. Retired); Chairman SKF Tools (UK) Ltd.; SKF Steel Ltd.; Bofors (G.B.) Ltd.; Bofors Electronics Ltd.; British Rail Eastern Region Advisory Board; Weyroc Ltd.; Deputy Chairman Sheffield Twist Drill & Steel Co. Ltd.; Dir. SKF Tools Co. Sweden; Gen. Mgr., SKF Holding Co. Holland. Member, National Enterprise Bd., Chmn. of NEDO working Party. Closely associated with CBI, retired Sept. 1977. Dep. Chmn. of the Council, Cranfield Institute of Technology. High Sheriff of Bedfordshire 1972–73. Deputy Lieutenant of Bedfordshire 1977. *Address:* Arkle House, Upton End, Shillington, Herts. 2G5 3PG.

**DICKINSON, Ronald Arthur,** CMG. British. *B.* 1910. *M.* 1939, Helen Severs. *Career:* Under Secretary; Export Credits Guarantee Department 1965–70; Man. Dir., Exim Credit Management & Consultants since 1971. *Clubs:* Overseas Bankers. *Address:* 86 Regency Lodge, London, N.W.3.

**DICKINSON, Ronald Sigismund Shepherd,** CMG. British. *B.* 1906. *Educ.* Dulwich Coll. and London Univ. (London School of Economics). *M.* 1932, Vida Evelyn Hall. *Dau.* Eryll Francesca. *Career:* With National Provincial Bank 1925–41 (i/c Hayes Branch 1934–41); Finance Officer, Min. of Aircraft Production 1941–44; Civil Aviation Dept., Air Ministry 1944; Min. of Civil Aviation and its successors 1945–75; Asst. Secretary 1947. Head, International Relations Div. 1954–57; Civil Air Attaché to Washington and Mexico 1952–54; Civil Aviation Adviser to Fed. of West Indies Feb. 1961–July 1962; United Kingdom Representative on the Council of the International Civil Aviation Organization (ICAO), Montreal, 1962–69; Secy. Air Travel Reserve Fund Agency 1975—. *Member:* U.K. delegation to ICAO Assembly, Montreal 1955 Caracas (as Dep. Ldr.) 1956, Rome 1962, Montreal 1965, Buenos Aires 1968 as A/Chief Delegate, and the European Civil Aviation Conference, Strasbourg 1955. *Publications:* several articles on airport subjects, and of The Relationship of Civil Aircraft Design to Terminal Airport Development. Rees-Jeffreys Postgraduate Research Student, London School of Economics 1950–51. Associate Inst. of Bankers. *Club:* Royal Commonwealth, London. *Address:* 3 Sandrock Road, Tunbridge Wells, Kent.

**DICKSON, (Horatio Henry) Lovat,** MA. British. *B.* 1902. *Educ.* Univ. of Alberta (MA), LLD: DLitt, Univ. of Western Ontario 1976. *M.* 1934, Marguerite Isabella Brodie. *S.* Jonathan Lovat. *Career:* Editor: The Fortnightly Review 1929–32, and The Review of Reviews 1931–34. Man. Director, Lovat Dickson Ltd. (publishers) 1932–38. Director: Macmillan & Co. (publishers) 1941–64, The Reprint Society 1939–64, and Pan Books Ltd. 1946–64. Vice-Pres., St. Martin's Press, New York 1952–63. *Publications:* Half-Breed (biography of Grey Owl); Out of the West Land (novel); Richard Hillary (biography); The Ante-Room (autobiography); The House of Words (autobiography); H. G. Wells (biography); Wilderness Man (biography); Radclyffe Hall at the Well of Loneliness (biog.). *Club:* Garrick. *Address:* 21 Dale Avenue, Toronto, Canada.

**DICKSON, Raynes Waite Adrian**, LLB, ED. Australian solicitor and company director. *B.* 1904. *Educ.* Melbourne Church of England Grammar School, and Trinity Coll., Univ. of Melbourne (LLB). *M.* 1932, Eril M. (*Dec.* 1967), dau. of Sir Neville Howse, VC and Lady Howse. *Dau.* Tanis. *M.* Mary V. T. Urquhart. *Career:* Flying Officer, Citizen Air Force 1929–32; Wing-Comdr., R.A.A.F. 1939–45; Managing Trustee, Howey Estate Melbourne 1941–72; Chmn. Trustees RAAFWA Education Patriotic Fund 1947–74; Chmn. Dirs. Royal Insurance Co. Ltd; Chmn. Local Board 1951—; Chmn. Dirs. Castlemaine Brewery Co. (Melbourne) Ltd. 1952–73; Dir. Carlton & United Breweries Ltd. 1961—. *Clubs:* Melbourne, Naval & Military, Beefsteak, Royal Melbourne Golf, Royal South Yarra Tennis (all of Melbourne). *Address:* 17 Lansell Rd., Toorak, Vic.; and *office* Stock Exchange House, 351 Collins Street, Melbourne, Vic. 3000, Australia.

**DICKSON, Richard Arthur.** Australian. *B.* 1909. *Educ.* Sydney Church of England Grammar School. *M.* 1955, Anne Winsome Reid. *S.* 4. *Dau.* 1. *Career:* Chmn. & Man. Dir., Dickson Primer (Consolidated) Ltd.; Chmn. Brambles Industries Ltd.; Fiji Industries Ltd.; Dir., R.D.C. Holdings Ltd. Fellow, Australian Inst. of Management. *Clubs:* Royal Sydney Yacht Squadron; Australian Golf; Australian Club; Elanora Country; Imperial Service; Royal Prince Alfred Yacht; S.A.S.C.; Legacy; *Address:* Kelanoa, 35 Bangalla Street, Warrawee, Sydney, Australia; and *office* 60 Bathurst Street, Sydney, N.S.W.

**DIEDERICHS, Dr. Nicholaas**, DMS, State President of the Republic of South Africa. *B.* 1903. *Educ.* Boshof High School, Grey Univ. Coll. (now Univ. of O.F.S.) BA, MA; and Univ. of Munich, Cologne and Leiden, D.Litt. et Phil. (cl). *M.* 1932, Margaretha Jacoba Potgieter. *S.* 1. *Daus.* 2. *Career:* Lecturer, later Professor, Univ. of OFS; Entered politics 1948; Minister of Economic Affairs 1958–67; also Minister of Mines 1961–64; Minister of Finance, 1967–75; State President since 1975. Chancellor of Randse Afrikaanse Univ. Johannesburg. *Decorations:* Hon degrees: D.Com, Univ. of O.F.S. and of Randse Afrikaanse Univ., D.Com, Univ. of Stellenbosch and Univ. of Pretoria; Gold Medal (Paris); Order of Merit (Paraguay); Knight Grand Cross of Order of Merit (Italy); *Awards:* Business Statesman of the Year (SA) 1973; Businessman of the Year (SA *Sunday Times*). *Publications:* Numerous technical articles. *Clubs:* Various in South Africa *Address:* Private Bag X80, Pretoria, South Africa 0001.

**DIEFENBAKER, Rt. Hon. John George**, CH, PC, QC, MP. Chancellor of Univ. of Saskatchewan. *B.* 1895. *Educ.* Saskatchewan University (BA 1915; MA 1916; LLB 1919); recipient of honorary degrees from 35 universities, including DSL Victoria Coll., Toronto, and LLD Memorial Coll., St. John's, Nfd. *M.* (1) 1929, Edna Brower (*Dec.*); (2) 1953, Olive Freeman Palmer, BA, LLD, DCL (*Dec.* 1976). *Career:* Served in World War I (Lieut., Canadian Army) 1916–17; called to Bar of Saskatchewan 1919, Bar of British Columbia 1951 and Bar of Alberta 1953; Bar of Ontario 1959; Honorary Master of Grays Inn; appointed King's Counsel 1929, Unsuccessful candidate in the General Elections of 1925 and 1926; elected for Lake Centre, 1940–45–49, and Prince Albert 1953–57–58–62–63–65–68–72–74; Leader of the Progressive Conservative Party of Canada at Ottawa Convention Dec. 1956; Prime Minister of Canada, 1957–63, Leader of the Opposition, Apr. 1963–67, 1972 and 1974; Chairman of the First Conference of British Parliamentary Association (the first at which representatives of the Congress of the United States met with British Commonwealth and Empire representatives), Ottawa, 1943; adviser to the Progressive Conservative Delegation to U.N. Conference, San Francisco, Apr. 1945; member of Canadian Delegation to U.N., 1952; member, Canadian Delegation of the Empire Parliamentary Conference, Bermuda, 1946; member, Canadian Delegation to the Commonwealth Parliamentary Conference in New Zealand and Australia, Nov. 1950; member, Canadian Parliamentary Delegation to N.A.T.O., 1955; Vice-President, Canadian Bar Association, 1939–42. Freedom of the City of London, 1963; Chancellor of the Univ. of Saskatchewan; Companion of Honour 1975. *Clubs:* A.F. & A.M. (33rd Scottish Rite); Tunis Temple (Shrine); Kiwanis. *Address:* Prince Albert, Sask.; and *office* House of Commons, Ottawa, Ont., Canada.

**DIERGARTEN, Hans H. W.**, Dr-Ing. German civil engineer. Director in Ruhestand der SKF. Schweinfurt. *B.* 1901. *Educ.* Tech. Univ., Aachen (Dr Ing); Dr Ing habil, Tech. Univ., Munich. *M.* 1932, Ann-Margret Wendt. *Daus.* 3. Honorary Professor of Metallurgy and Ehrenbürger, Univ.. of Würzburg. Dr. Ing. E. h. Techn, Univ. of Berlin 1966 *Publications:* many, concerning gases in metal, assembly instructions, mechanization of heat treatment of metal lubrication, roller bearing technique, etc. Pres., German Association for Material Testing 1959–62; member of Board, Industrial Association for Tempering Techniques 1954–62, Pres. 1964—; and of the German Engineering Association. *Clubs:* Tennis; Hunting. *Address:* Elsa Brändstrom Str. 48, 872 Schweinfurt, Germany.

**DIESEL, Jurgen.** German Diplomat. *B.* 1926. *Educ.* Law, Univs. of Erlangen and Munich, Dr. Jur. *M.* 1954, Eleonore Freiin von Dungern. *S.* 1. *Daus.* 2. *Career:* German Embassy, Santiago 1954–56; German Embassy, Caracas 1956–60; Auswartiges Amt Bonn 1961–64; Mem. of German Delegation to UN (Geneva) 1964–68; Auswartiges Amt Bonn (Head of Eastern Affairs Div.) 1968–73; German Ambassador to Switzerland 1973–77, to Czechoslovakia since 1977. *Awards:* Chil. Orden al merito Bernado O'Higgins; Ven. orden al merito Simon Bdivar; Romanian order, Tudo Vladimirescu; Royal Swedish order of Northern Star. *Publications:* contributions on disarmament and arms control. *Address:* Lobkowicz Palais, Vlašska Ul. 19, Praha 1-Mala Strana, Czechoslovakia.

**DIETZ, David (Henry).** American editor and author. *B.* 6 Oct. 1897. *Educ.* Western Reserve University (AB); LittD; LLD Bowling Green State Univ. *M.* 1918, Dorothy B. Cohen. *S.* David Henry, Jr. *Daus.* Doris Jean, Patricia Ann. *Career:* Science Editor of the Scripps-Howard Newspapers since 1921; member, editorial staff, The Cleveland Press since 1915; lecturer in general science, Western Reserve University, since 1927; winner, Pulitzer Prize in Journalism, 1936; U.S. War Department Certificate of Appreciation 1945; Lasker Award for Medical Journalism 1954; James T. Grady Award, 1961. *Publications:* The Story of Science (1931); Medical Magic (1937); Atomic Energy in the Coming Era (trans. into 13 languages) (1945); Atomic Science, Bombs and Power (1954); All About Satellites and Space Ships (1958); All About Great Medical Discoveries (1960); All About the Universe (1965); Stars and the Universe (1969); The New Outline of Science (1972); article on 'Atomic Bomb' in the Encyclopaedia Britannica. *Address:* The Cleveland Press Building, Cleveland, Ohio 44114, U.S.A.

**DIGNAM, Hon William John.** Australian lawyer. *B.* 12 Sept. 1901. *Educ.* Christian Brothers School; University of Sydney (LLB). *M.* 1928, Mary Cerini Clark. *S.* Michael, Mark. *Daus.* Mary, Monica. *Career:* Called to Bar, New South Wales 1926; King's Counsel 1946; High Commissioner to Ireland 1946–50; Leader of Delegation, Copyright Convention, Brussels 1948; member of Delegation, United Nations General Assembly, Paris 1948; member, Workers' Compensation Commission, New South Wales 1950–71. *Address:* Kilmacduagh, 45 Coogee Bay Road, Randwick, N.S.W., Australia.

**DILHORNE, Rt. Hon. Viscount**, PC, DL (Reginald Edward Manningham-Buller). *B.* 1905. *Educ.* Eton: Magdalen College, Oxford (BA). *M.* 1930, Lady Mary Lilian Lindsay. *S.* 1. *Daus.* 3. *Career:* Called to the Bar, Inner Temple 1927; MP (Cons.) for Daventry 1943–50, Northamptonshire South 1950–62; Parliamentary Secretary to Ministry of Works May–Aug. 1945; member, Parliamentary Delegation to U.S.S.R. 1945, Anglo-American Committee on Palestine 1946; Solicitor-General 1951–54; Attorney-General 1954–62. Appointed Lord of Appeal in Ordinary May 1969. Lord Chancellor of the United Kingdom 1962–64. *Address:* 6 Kings Bench Walk, Temple, London, E.C.4, and Horninghold Manor, Market Harborough, Leicestershire.

**DILLE, Robert Crabtree.** *Educ.* Univ. of Chicago (BA); graduate work at Univ. of Chicago and Northwestern Univ. (Evanston, Ill.). *M.* 1945, Virginia L. Nichols. *S.* R. N. Flint. *Dau.* Lorraine Virginia. *Career:* Advertising copywriter, Homer J. Buckley and Associates 1944–45; membership Dir., National Safety Council 1945–46; Dir., Sales Markets, Methods, Encyclopedia Britannica 1946–48; Pres., Robert C. Dille and Associates Inc. 1948–52; various positions, National Newspaper Syndicate 1952—. President and member of the Board, National Newspaper Syndicate, Chicago 1957—; Pres. and Chmn. of the Board, John F. Dille Co., Chicago 1958—; President, Buck Rogers Co., Chicago 1959—; Vice-Pres. and member of the Board, Matrix Contrast Corp. (N.Y.) 1961–66. Director, Truth Publishing Co. and Communicana Group-operators of Elkhart Truth and Mishawaka Times, and WTRC Radio, WKJG-TV (Fort Wayne, Ind.) and WSJV-TV (South Bend Ind.)—1965—; *Publications:* articles in U.S. daily newspapers; Author-Editor collected works, Buck Rogers in the 25th Century (1969). *Member:* National Newspaper Promotion Assn. Republican. *Clubs:* Economic, Tower (Chicago). *Address: office* National Newspaper Syndicate, 20 N. Wacker Drive, Chicago 6. Ill., U.S.A.

**DILLON, Brendan.** Irish diplomat. *B.* 1924. *Educ.* O'Connell School Dublin, Blackrock College, Dublin; Univ. College Dublin, BA, MA. *M.* 1949, Alice O'Keeffe. *S.* 4. *Dau.* 1. *Career:* Chief of Protocol, EEC Headquarters 1968–70; Ambassador Extra. and Plenip. to Denmark and concurrently to Norway and Iceland 1970–72; Asst. Secy.-Gen. Headquarters 1972–73; Ambassador, Permanent Rep. of Ireland to European Communities since 1973. *Club:* Cercle Royal Gaulois. *Address:* Avenue Galilée 5, 1030 Brussels, Belgium.

**DILLON, Clarence Douglas.** American Investment Banker. *B.* 21 Aug. 1909. *Educ.* Groton School; Harvard Univ. (AB); Hon. degrees, Harvard, Princeton, Rutgers, Columbia, N. York and the Univ. of Pennsylvania; also Lafayette, Williams, Hartford and Middlebury Colls. *M.* 1931, Phyllis Ellsworth, *Daus.* Phyllis, Joan. *Career:* Member of the New York Stock Exchange 1931–36; Vice-Pres., Dillon, Read & Co. Inc. 1937, Chmn. of the Board 1946–53; Dir. of the U.S. and Foreign Securities Corporation and the United States and International Securities Corp. 1938; served in World War II, in United States Navy 1941–45; President of the United States and Foreign Securities Corporation and the United States and International Securities Corp. 1946, 1967 and 1968. Amb. Ex. and Plen. to France 1953; Under-Sec. of State for Economic Affairs 1958; Under-Sec. of State, June 1959; Secretary of the Treasury of U.S.A., 1961–65; Pres. Metropolitan Museum of Art, N.Y.C. since 1970; Chmn., United States and Foreign Securities Corp since 1969; Man. Dir. Dillon Read and Co. Inc. since 1971. *Awards:* Legion of Merit; Air Medal; Navy Commendation Ribbon. *Address:* Far Hills, N.J., U.S.A. and *office* Room 4302, 767 Fifth Ave., New York, NY 10022.

**DIMECHKIE, Nadim.** Lebanese. Ambassador to the Court of St. James's. *B.* 1919. *Educ.* American Univ. of Beirut (MA). *M.* 1946, Margaret Alma Sherlock. *S.* Riad, Ramez. *Career:* Director General, Minister of National Economy, 1943–44; Counsellor, Lebanese Embassy, London, 1944–49; Consul-General, Ottawa, 1950; Dir., Economic & Social Dept., Ministry of Foreign Affairs, 1951–52 & 1962–66; Chargé d'Affaires, Cairo, 1952; Minister, Cairo, 1953–55; Minister to Switzerland, 1955–57; Ambassador to U.S.A., 1958–62; Dir. Economic Affairs, Min. of Foreign Affairs 1962–66; Ambassador to the Court of St. James's since 1966. *Award:* Order of Cedars (Lebanon); Order of Ismail & Order of Merit U.A.R.); Order of Merit (Syria & Tunisia); Order of Phoenix (Greece). *Clubs:* Travellers; Hurlingham; R.A.C. (London); Metropolitan; Chevy Chase (U.S.A.); Cercle de Beirut; Aero (Beirut). *Address:* Lebanese Embassy, 21 Kensington Palace Gardens, London, W.8.

**DIMITRIOU, Nicos G.** Cypriot (Greek). *B.* 1920. *Educ.* Graduate of Pancyprian Lyceum (Larnaca) and Greek Gymnasium (Athens) and Maiden Erlegh School (Reading, Eng.). *M.* 1947, Nadina Poulia. *Daus.* 3. *Career:* Chmn. Cyprus Chamber of Commerce 1958–63. Member: Ethnarchy Council 1948–59, and Board of Directors, Bank of Cyprus Ltd. 1958–61; Royal Danish Consul-General, Cyprus 1961—; Man. Dir.: N. J. Dimitriou Ltd. (Merchant Bankers) 1962—, and Larnaca Oil Works Ltd. 1962—; Chmn. United Cyprus Oil Industries 1965–68; Cyprus Development Corp. Ltd. 1966–68; Chmn. Electricity Authority of Cyprus 1970–73; National & Grindlays Bank Ltd. Cyprus Regional Advisory Board 1970–73; Member, Bd. of Dirs. of several other commercial and industrial companies; Ambassador of Cyprus in the U.S.A. since 1974. *Member:* of Council Cyprus Chamber of Commerce and Industry 1963–68. Chmn. Larnaca Chamber, Commerce and Industry 1963–68; Pres. Cyprus Branch Chartered Inst. Secretaries. *Awards:* Comdr. Order of the Cedar (Lebanon); Cmdr., Order of Dannebrog (Denmark). Fellow Chartered Inst. of Secretaries. *Publications:* articles on political and economic subjects in newspapers and magazines in Cyprus and abroad. *Clubs:* Pezoporicos, Larnaca (Pres., 1940–68); Minister of Commerce and Industry 1968–70. Zeno Athletic (Secy., 1948–69); Rotary, Larnaca (District Governor of Rotary International 1962–63). International (Wash. DC); Cosmos (Wash. DC). *Address:* Artemis Avenue, Larnaca, Cyprus; and *office* 30 D.N. Dimitriou Street, Larnaca, Cyprus.

**DINSDALE, Hon. Walter Gilbert,** PC, DFC, LLD, M.P. Member of Canadian Parliament. *B.* 1916. *Educ.* McMaster Univ., Hamilton, Ont. (BA 1937); Univ. of Toronto (MA); pre-doctoral work in sociology at the Univ. of Chicago; LLD Brandon Univ., 1977. *M.* 1947, Lenore Gusdal. *S.* Gunnar, Gregory, Eric and Rolf. *Dau.* Elizabeth. *Career:* With Canadian Pacific Express Co., Brandon, Man. 1937; Social Worker, Salvation Army, Toronto and Montreal 1939; R.C.A.F. 1941; University 1945; Director and Adult Education and Asst. Professor, Social Science Dept., Brandon College 1946; won Federal by-election for Brandon-Souris 1951 (re-elected 1953–57–58–62–63–65–68–72–74; Parly. Asst. to Minister of Veteran Affairs 1957; Minister of Northern Affairs and National Resources, 1960–63. Progressive Conservative. Board of Directors, Western Region, Canadian Council of Christians and Jews; Delegate to U.N. General Assembly 1955, 1968 & 1974; General Chmn., Political Cttee. of the Atlantic Congress, London 1959; Chmn., Resources for Tomorrow Conference 1961; Delegate Commonwealth Parly. Seminar London 1971; World Federalists Conference Bressels 1972. *Member:* Canadian Legion; Canadian Rehabilitation Council, for Disabled. *Clubs:* Kiwani; Brandon Flying. *Address:* 1882 Norwood Avenue Ottawa; 461-11th Street, Brandon, Man.; and House of Commons, Ottawa, Ont., Canada.

**DIOUF, Abdou.** The Prime Minister of Senegal since 1970. *Address:* The Office of the Prime Minister, Dakar, Senegal.

**DIVELY, George Samuel.** American. Communications and information-handling equipment manufacturing executive. *B.* 1902. *Educ.* Univ. of Pittsburgh (BS in EE 1925) and Harvard (MBA 1929); Hon. DEng, Case Inst. of Technology 1961; Hon. DSc Eng, Univ. of Pittsburg 1962; Hon Dsc Florida Inst. of Technology 1972. *M.* 1933, Harriett F. Seeds (*Dec.* 1968). *S.* Michael. *M.* (2) Juliette Gaudin 1969. *Career:* With Harris Corp. 1937— (successively Asst. to Secy.-Treas., Asst. Treas., Secy.-Treas., Director, Vice-Pres., Gen. Mgr., Pres. 1947–54), Chief Exec. Officer 1952–68, Chmn. of Board and Pres. 1954–61; Chmn. of the Bd. Harris-Intertype Corp. 1954–72, Chmn. Exec. and Finance Cttee. 1972–75; Hon. Chmn. of the Bd. & Chmn. Financial Policy Cttee. since 1975. Hon Dir., Central National Bank of Cleveland; Dir. Council for Financial Aid to Education; Co-founder the Corporate One Per Cent Program for Higher Education. Fellow & Life Mem., Amer. Management Assn.; Hon. Trustee of Case Western Reserve Univ. *Member:* Visiting Cttee. Harvard Grad. School of Business Admin.; Mason. *Publications:* The Power of Professional Management. *Clubs:* Country; Peper Pike, Royal Palm Yacht & Country (Florida), Union, Harvard (Cleveland), Harvard (N.Y.C.). *Address:* 20776 Brantley Road, Shaker Heights, Ohio 44122; and *office* 55 Public Square, Cleveland, Ohio 44113, U.S.A.

**DIVERS, William Keeveny.** American lawyer. *B.* 12 Apr. 1905. *Educ.* University of Cincinnati (LLM, JD). *M.* 1935, Minna Rosenbaum. *Daus.* Lois, Diane. *Career:* admitted to Ohio Bar 1928; practised law Divers & Warm, Cincinnati 1928–33; legal staff, Federal Emergency Public Works Administration 1933–37; Regional Director for Mid-western Area, U.S. Housing Authority 1938–41; Regional Representative for Mid-western Area, National Housing Agency 1942–44; Assistant Administrator, National Housing Agency 1945; Special Assistant to National Housing Expediter 1946; Assistant Administrator, Housing and Home Finance Agency 1947; admitted to Supreme Court Bar 1935; former Chairman, Home Loan Bank Board, Board of Trustees, Federal Savings and Loan Insurance Corporation and Home Owners' Loan Corporation; now Chairman Exec. Cttee., The Savings and Loan Foundation Inc. (Pres. 1955–67). *Address:* 10654 Montrose Avenue, Bethesda, Maryland 20014, U.S.A.

**DIXON, Bernard.** British. *B.* 1906. *Educ.* Campbell Coll. Belfast; British Sch. of Malting & Brewing; Birmingham Univ. *M.* 1930, Olive Marie Watts. *Dau.* 4. *Career:* Chmn. Dixon International Ltd. & Subsidiaries, Dixon Malt Co. Ltd.; Chmn. & Man. Dir. Flowers Brewery Ltd., 1947–58. *Clubs:* Bath; R.A.C.; Kildare Street, Dublin; Mem. Inst. of Brewing. *Address:* Pampisford Place, Pampisford, Cambridge, CB2 4EW.

**DIXON, Philip Harold.** British. *B.* 1921. *Educ.* Charterhouse and Trinity Coll., Cambridge (MA). *M.* 1943, Barbara Elizabeth Vivian. *S.* Vivian Richard, Jonathan Murray and Nicholas Anthony. *Daus.* Susan Jennifer and Philippa Jane. *Career:* President, Employers Federation of Paper & Board Makers, 1968–74; Man. Dir. Peter Dixon & Son (Holdings) Ltd. 1971–74; Chmn. Graphic Systems International Ltd. since 1975. Chairman, Association of Yorkshire Chambers of Commerce 1965. Governor, Swinton Conservative College 1962–70. Member, Yorkshire Humberside Region Economic

Planning Council 1965–67. Pres., Sheffield Chamber of Commerce 1964–65. High Sheriff of Hallamshire 1969–70. *Member:* Decimal Currency Bd. 1967–71; Assn. of British Chambers of Comm. (Hon. Treas. 1965–71), Vice-Pres. 1971—; British Limbless Ex-Service Men's Assn. (on Exec. Council). Conservative Member of The Club (Sheffield); Chmn. BLESMA since 1975. *Address:* 19 Broadwalk House, Hyde Park Gate, S.W.7; and *office* GSI Ltd., 6 Dormer Road, Thame, Oxon.

**DJAMSON, Dr. Eric Christopher Kwaku.** Ghanaian Teacher, Lawyer, Banker & Diplomat. *B.* 1926. *Educ.* Wesley Coll., Kumasi, Ghana; Fircroft Coll., Birmingham; King's Coll., Univ. of London; Univ. of Nijmegen, Netherlands; LLB (Hons.), LLM, PhD, & Barrister-at-Law, Lincoln's Inn. *M.* 1960, Gladys Ofosua Nyamekye. *S.* 2. *Daus.* 2. *Career:* Teacher, Peki-Avetile Methodist Sch., 1948; Tutor, Wesley College, Kumasi 1949–52 & Prempeh Coll., Kumasi 1953–55; Legal Adviser, Ghana Commercial Bank, Accra 1962–63, then Secretary 1963–67, Chief Legal Adviser 1967–70 & Exec. Dir. 1968–70; Legal Practitioner 1970–72; Ambassador Ex. & Plen. to the Kingdom of the Netherlands since 1972, with concurrent accreditation to Belgium 1973–75 & Luxembourg 1973–75; Perm. Rep. to the EEC 1973–75. *Member:* Ghana Bar Assoc. *Publications:* The Dynamics of Euro-African Co-operation (an analysis & exposition of institutional, legal & socio-economic aspects of association/co-operation with the EEC). *Clubs:* The Hague Country & Golf Club, Wassenaar, Netherlands. *Address:* P.O. Box 7475, Accra, Ghana; and Groen van Prinstererlaan 12, Wassenaar, The Netherlands; and *office* Embassy of Ghana, Paleisstraat 6, The Hague, The Netherlands.

**DOBBINS, Cris.** Executive. *B.* 1904. *Educ.* Univ. of Denver (Bachelor Degree in Business Administration; and Hon. LLD). *M.* 1930, Elvira M. Bjork. *S.* Christopher and Michael Anthony. *Dau.* Felicity Anne. *Career:* Joined Ideal Cement Co. Oct. 1919; successively: Denver office and Portland Colorado plant 1921–30; Asst. Sales Manager 1930–41, and Sales Manager 1941–42, Colorado Cement Co.; Asst. to Pres., 1943–44; Vice-President and General Manager 1944–48, Exec. Vice-Pres. and Gen. Mgr. 1948–52, Pres. 1952–68; on 31 Dec. 1967 this Company and Potash Co. of America merged to become Ideal Basic Industries, Inc. Chairman and Director, Ideal Basic Industries Inc., Denver, Colo. Other companies (all of Denver unless stated otherwise): Dir. United Banks of Colorado Inc.; United Bank of Denver N.A.; Ideal Corp. Colorado & Southern Railway Co., Chmn. & Dir. Brown Palace Hotel Company; 1966–71; Chmn. and Trustee, Boettcher Foundation. Trustee: Tax Foundation Inc., Denver Museum of Natural History, Dir. Amer. Mining Congress (Pres. 1968–71); Director, The Air Force Academy Foundation Inc., National Industrial Conference Board, Central City Opera House Assoc. Pres., Treas. and Dir., the Dobbins Foundation; Alpha Kappa Phi. Beta Gamma Sigma (Hon. Scholastic Fraternity in Business). *Member:* American Society of the Most Venerable Order of the Hospital of St. John of Jerusalem. *Clubs:* Denver; Denver Country; Denver Athletic; Wigwam; Mile High; Tower; Pacific-Union; Burlingame Country; Garden of the Gods; Chicago (Chicago); Balboa (Mazatlan, Mexico); *Address:* 770 High Street, Denver, Colo. 80218; and *office* 950 Seventeenth Street, Denver, Colo. 80202, U.S.A.

**DOBROSIELSKI, Marian.** Phil. Dr. Polish. *B.* 1923. *Educ.* University of Zurich (Phil Dr); University of Warsaw. *M.* 1950, Ella. *Dau.* Ewa. *Career:* Served in Polish Army in France, WW11; with Ministry of Foreign Affairs since 1948; Polish Legation in Berne 1948–50; Head of Section at the Ministry of Foreign Affairs 1950–54; Asst. Professor, Warsaw Univ. and Polish Academy of Sciences 1954–57; First Secy. and later Counsellor of the Polish Embassy in Washington 1958–64; Counsellor to the Minister of Foreign Affairs 1964–69; Acting Dir. of Research Bureau, Min. of Foreign Affairs 1968–69; Associate Professor, Warsaw Univ. 1966; Vice-Dean, Faculty of Philosophy, Warsaw Univ. 1966–68; Chmn., Scientific Cncl., Institute of Philosophy of Warsaw Univ., 1969; Chmn., Editorial Board of Studia Filozoficzne, 1968–69; Secy., Polish Philosophical Socy., 1955–57 and 1965–69; Ambassador of the Polish People's Republic to the Court of St. James 1969–71; Dir. Polish Inst. International Affairs 1971—; Inst. of Philosophy Univ. Warsaw 1971–73; Vice Chmn. Cttee. European Security and Cooperation 1971, Chmn. since 1973; Assoc. Prof. Warsaw University, Ambassador and personam since 1973. *Publications:* A Basic Epistemological Principle of Logical Positivism, (1947); The Philosophical Pragmatism of C. S. Peirce, (1967); articles on philosophy and international problems in professional journals. Member, Polish Delegation to the United Nations G.A. 1952–53–58–66–72–76; Chmn. Polish Delegation Phase II on security & co-operation in Europe 1973–75. *Awards:* Banner of Labour; Knight's Cross of the Order of Polonia Restituta. *Address:* Polish Institute of International Affairs, 00-950 Warsaw.

**DOBROWOLSKI, Stanislaw Wincenty.** Polish jurist, economist and diplomat; *B.* 1915. *Educ.* Lic. en droit; Diploma, Jagiellone University, Cracow. *M.* 1947, Madame Irena Opechowska. *S.* Jacek and Marek. *Career:* At International Labour Office, Geneva 1938; active member of the resistance during the occupation; Secy.-Gen. and in the suite of the Vice-Pres., Society of University Workers 1945–48; Founder and editor-in-Chief, Swiat i Polska, Secy. of Central Council, and chief of the Foreign Section of the Socialist Party 1946–47; Director-in-chief, Central Maritime Council of Commerce 1948–51; Vice-Dir., Administration-General of Theatres, Ministry of Culture and Fine Arts 1951–56; Deputy of the Diet (National General Council 1947) 1946–52; Pres., Commission on Foreign Affairs 1947–50; at Ministry of Foreign Affairs 1957; Ambassador to Denmark 1957–63; At Polish Ministry of Foreign Affairs since 1963; Delegate to 16th Session, U.N. Gen. Assembly 1961; Chief of Polish Delegate, International Comm. for Supervision and Control in Vietnam 1968–69; Took part in negotiations Treaty, Polish Peoples Republic and Federal Republic, Germany 1970; Polish People's Republic Ambassador to Greece 1972–74; Polish Ministry of For. Affairs, Warsaw since 1975; LLD Jagiellonian Univ., Cracow. *Address:* Ministry of Foreign Affairs, 00–580 Warsaw, Poland.

**DOBSON, Donald Lorraine,** TD. British. *B.* 1915. *Educ.* Blundells School, Tiverton. *M.* 1938, Elizabeth Mary Evans. *S.* Ian, Jeremy and Guy. *Daus.* Sandra and Virginia. *Career:* Commissioned 2nd Lieut., Royal Devon Yeomanry (T.A.) 1936. War Service in Middle East, N. Africa, Sicily, Italy, India, and U.K. (Appointed I.G. (R.A.) 1941; attended Camberley Staff College 1943; appointed G.S.O. II. Territorial Decoration; now Hon. Major, Past Chairman, Coal Industry Socy. Gen. Commissioner, Inland Revenue 1961–70; Justice of the Peace, Torquay Borough (Devon) 1961–70. Chmn., Morter Investments. *Clubs:* RTYC; RCIYC; R.A.C. *Address:* Essex Castle, Alderney, Channel Islands.

**DOBSON, Ruth Lissant.** Australian Diplomat. *B.* 1918. *Educ.* Frensham, Mittagong (Aust); Sydney Univ. BA. *Career:* Dept. of Foreign Affairs, served in Canberra, Geneva, Wellington; represented Australia at many International Conferences, particularly U.N. and specialised agencies, including UNGA 1959, 60, 69; Seconded to Staff of Governor General as Personal Asst. to the Lady Casey 1965–66; First Secy, Manila 1967–68; Counsellor and Chargé d'Affaires Athens 1971–74; Ambassador in Copenhagen since 1974. *Club:* Commonwealth. *Address:* Australian Embassy, Kristianiagade 21, 2100, Copenhagen, Denmark.

**DOCKRELL, Maurice Edward,** LLD. Irish. *B.* 1908. *Educ.* St. Andrews Coll., Dublin (BCom; TCD; LLD *de jura dignitatis*). *M.* 1938, Isobel Myrick Pound (of Vancouver). *S.* Henry Morgan. *Daus.* Dianne, Lucinda and Caroline. *Career:* Director of Dockrells since 1930. Attended International Student Conferences in Rome 1927 and Bucharest 1931. Member of Dun Laoire Borough Council 1934. Member, Dublin Corp. 1940; Dail Eireann 1943–77; Chmn. Thos. Dockrell Sons & Co. Ltd. 1955—. Director: Irish Civil Service Building Society (Chmn.); Berger (Ireland) Ltd.; Fitzwilton Ltd.; Member, Council of State for Ireland since 1959. Governor, Adelaide Hospital 1940, and St. Patrick's Hospital 1944. Lord Mayor of Dublin 1960–61; Governor, Roy. Irish Academy of Music 1959; paid State Visit to Mansion House, London (the first during this century). Received Papal Legate as Lord Mayor during Patrician Year 1961. Formerly amateur swimmer and golfer. Member, Royal Dublin Socy. *Clubs:* University, Stephens Green (all in Dublin). *Address:* Kyelbeg, Mt. Anville Road, Dublin 14; and *office* 38–39 South Great Georges Street, Dublin 2, Ireland.

**DODDS-PARKER, Sir Arthur Douglas,** MA. British politician. *B.* 5 July 1909. *Educ.* Winchester College and Magdalen College, Oxford (MA). *M.* 1946, Aileen Beckett Coster. *S.* 1. *Career:* In Sudan Political Service 1930–39; served in World War II Grenadier Guards (2nd Lieut. 1939, Col. 1944), Middle East (despatches), North Africa, Italy and France, 1939–45; MP (Con.) Banbury Division of Oxfordshire 1945–59; Cheltenham 1964–74. Under-Secy. of State for Foreign Affairs 1953–54 and 1955–57; Under-Secy. of State for Commonwealth Relations 1954–55. Delegate, Council of Europe 1954, 1965–69 and 1970–72; Delegate Western Europe Union Assembly 1956—69 and 1970–72; Delegate North Atlantic Assembly 1968–73; Delegate European Parliament 1973–75. Legion of Honour and Croix de Guerre (France). *Address:* 9 North Court, Great Peter Street, London S.W.1.

**DODGE, Arthur Byron, Jr.** Corporation executive. *B.* 1923. *Educ.* Williams College, and Franklin & Marshall College (BS Econ). *M.* 1954, Margaretha Gerbert. *S.* Arthur B. III and Andrew Nikolaus. *Career:* With Dodge Cork Co. since 1946 (Production Mgr. 1947–50, Factory Mgr. 1952–57, Mgr., Foreign Division 1958–61); Dir., Frederick F. Wilkins & Co. Ltd., Lisbon, Portugal 1954—. Vice-President and Secretary, Dodge Cork Co. Inc., Lancaster, Pa. 1961—. Secretary, Dodge Cork Canada Ltd. 1976—. Director, Dodge Cork (Portugal) Lda. 1968—. *Publications:* Champagne Corks—their unique story and contribution to the Winemaker's Art, (1959). Trustee, Episcopal Church School Foundation 1958—. *Member:* Pennsylvania Society, Pennsylvania Committee for Employment of the Physically Handicapped; American Socy. for Testing Materials; Newcomen Socy.; Delta Upsilon. *Clubs:* Lancaster Country, Hamilton (Lancaster). *Address:* 1142 Marietta Avenue, Lancaster, Pa. 17603; and *office* 11 Laurel Street, Lancaster, Pa., U.S.A. 17604.

**DODGE, Cleveland E.** American company director and executive. *B.* 5 Feb. 1888. *Educ.* Princeton Univ. (AB); Hon. LHD, Springfield Coll., LLD New York Univ., LLD Columbia Univ., LittD, Univ. of Arizona; DPhil, Princeton Univ. *M.* 1919, Pauline Morgan. *S.* Cleveland Jr. *Daus.* Mrs. Bolling W. Haxall and Mrs. Frederic Rueckert, Jr. *Career:* With Phelps Dodge Corp. 1910–67 (mining, refining and manufacturing of copper and copper products); served as officer in World War I 1917–19; President; Y.M.C.A., New York City 1925–35, Mining and Metallurgical Society of America 1937 and Woodrow Wilson Foundation 1949–50; Alumni Trustee, Princeton University 1941–45; Director Emeritus, International House, New York City; now holds following appointments and offices: Mem. Exec. Cttee., International Committee Y.M.C.A.; Director, Y.M.C.A. of Greater New York; Board of Trustees, Teachers College, Columbia University; Director, Near East Foundation; Member, Council of Churches of the City of New York; Honorary Trustee, American Museum of Natural History; Trustee, Grant Foundation, Inc., and Atlantic Mutual Insurance Co.; Honorary Director, Phelps Dodge Corp. *Awards:* Grand Commander, Order of George I of Greece; Order of Homayoun (Iran). *Address:* Riverdale, New York City 71; and *office* 641 Lexington Avenue, New York, N.Y. 10022.

**DODGE, John V.** *B.* 1909. *Educ.* Northwestern University, Evanston, Ill. (BS); University of Bordeaux, France (Diplome d'Etudes). *M.* 1935, Jean Elizabeth Plate. *S.* John M. and Gerald C. *Daus.* Ann (Prochnow) and Kathleen E. (Nieman). *Career:* Editor of official publications of Northwestern University 1932–37; Exec. Secy., Northwestern Univ. Alumni Assn. 1937–38; Asst. Editor, Encyclopaedia Britannica and Associate Editor of Britannica Book of the Year 1938–43; Associate Editor, Ten Eventful Years (4-vol. historical summary of World War II period) (1947); Military Service (Anti-aircraft; 1st Lieutenant, Military Intelligence Service) (1944–46); Asst. Editor, Encyclopaedia Britannica 1946–50; Managing Editor 1950–60; Editor Britannica World Language Dictionary 1954; Exec. Editor Encyclopaedia Britannica 1960–64, Senior Vice-Pres., Editorial 1964–65, Senior Editorial Consultant 1965–70; Editorial Consultant, Encyclopaedia Universalis Paris since 1968; Britannica Intern. Encycl. (Tokyo) since 1969; Vice-Pres. International Editorial Encyclopaedia Britannica 1970–72; Encyl. Barsa (Mexico City) since 1974; Encycl. Mirador (RdeJ) since 1974; Chmn., Board of Editors, Encyclopaedia Britannica Publications since 1977. *Address:* 3851 Mission Hills Road, Northbrook, Ill. 60062, U.S.A.

**DODSON, Sir Derek Sherborne Lindsell,** KCMG, MC. British diplomat. *B.* 1920. *Educ.* Stowe School; Royal Military Coll. Sandhurst. *M.* 1952, Julie Maynard Barnes. *S.* John Gerald. *Dau.* Caroline. *Career:* served as a Commissioned officer, Royal Scots Fusiliers 1939–47; Military Asst. British Commissioner A.C.C. for Bulgaria 1945–46; Second Secy. Foreign Office Jan.–Sept. 1948; Vice Consul Salonika 1948–50; Second (later First) Secy. Madrid 1951–53; First Secy. Foreign Office 1953–58; First Secy. and Head of Chancery Prague 1958–62; H.M. Consul, Elisabethville 1962–63; Head, Central Dept. Foreign Office 1963–66; Counsellor British Embassy Athens 1966–69; British Ambassador to Hungary 1970–73; to Brazil 1973–77; to Turkey since 1977. *Awards:* Knight Commander, Most Distinguished Order, St. Michael and St. Georee; Military Cross; Grand Cross of Cruzeiro do Sul. *Clubs:* Boodle's; Travellers. *Address:* The Gabled House, Leadenham, Lincoln.

**DODSON, Leigh Frederick.** Australian. *B.* 1920. *Educ.* MB, BS, DCP (Sydney) and DPhil (Oxon). *M.* 1949, Mary Margaret McPhillips. *S.* Timothy, Peter, Simon and Mark. *Daus.* Caroline and Virginia. *Career:* R.M.O. St. Vincent's Hospital, Sydney 1943–44 (Pathology Registrar 1944–45; Asst. Pathologist 1945–50); Aust. Natl. Univ.: Travelling Scholar (Oxford) 1950–54; Senior Research Fellow, A.N.U. 1954–57. Director, National Standards Laboratory, Dept. of Health, Canberra 1958—. *Publications:* in the fields of Experimental Hypertension and Chemotherapy. *Member:* Aust. Physiological Socy.; Aust. Pharmaceutical Science Assn.; Canberra Medical Socy. *Clubs:* Canberra Yacht. *Address:* 25 Vasey Crescent, Campbell, Canberra, A.C.T.; and National Biological Standards Laboratory, Box 462 City, Canberra, A.C.T., Australia.

**DOESBURG, John Henry, Jr.** American Attorney-at-Law; *B.* 1908. *Educ.* Northwestern College of Law (JD) and Northwestern University (BS). *M.* 1941, Nell Rose. *S.* John Edward. *Career:* served in World War II (Lieut.-Commander, U.S.N.R.; Service Medal); Instructor Northwestern Univ. 1929–33; Attorney Chapman & Cutler 1933–35; General Counsel 1935–46; Secy.-Gen. Counsel Printing Industry of America 1949; Partner, Doesburg, Goddess & Bowes 1949—; Secy. Gen. Counsel R.R. Donnelley-Crawfordsville Co. Inc. 1946–49, R.R. Donnelley & Sons. Co. 1946–49; Johnsons-Coppock Co. 1949, Suburban Downs Inc. 1956; Dir. Michigan Lithographing Co. 1956; Secy. Dir. Pifer Printing Co. 1959—; Printway Inc. 1960—; Chmn. Bd. Canterbury Press Inc. since 1970. *Publications:* Contributions of the Open Shop to the Printing Industry; Elements of a Personnel Policy. Republican. *Address:* 116 W, Canterbury Lane, Phoenix, Arizona, U.S.A.

**DOGGETT, Leonard Wallace.** OBE. Australian. *B.* 1917. *Educ.* Brisbane Grammar School. *M.* 1948, Marjorie Doris Hill. *Daus.* 3. *Career:* Partner, Spry Walker & Co., Chartered Accountants, Brisbane. Director: Tableland Tin Dredging; Oilmin, Transoil; Uranium Consolidated; Peko Wallsend Ltd.; National Heart Foundation of Australia (Qld. Div.). Fellow, Institute of Chartered Accountants in Australia; State Chairman 1960–63. Member, General Council 1961–67; Queensland Chamber of Mines; Aust. Tin Producers Association. *Clubs:* Queensland, Tattersals (Brisbane). *Address:* 25 The Promenade, Isle of Capri, Qld. 4217; and *office* 27 Turbot Street, Brisbane, Qld., Australia.

**DOHA, Aminur Rahman S.** Bangladeshi Soldier, Journalist, Politician, Diplomat. *B.* 1929. *Educ.* BSc (Hons.), BA, & various military degrees. *M.* 1950, Shahnaz Begum. *S.* 2. *Career:* Asst. Mgr., Imperial Tobacco Co. Ltd. 1948–50; Commissioned Pakistan Artillery as 2nd Lieut. (Sword of Honour OTS, Kohat) 1952; Regimental Officer in Artillery Regiments 1952–61; Command & General Staff Coll., Quetta 1962; General Staff Infantry Brigade HQ 1963; Royal Military Coll. of Science & Technology, Shrivenham, Berks. 1964–65; School of Artillery & Guided Missiles, Oklahoma U.S.A. 1957–58; Senior Instructor, Gunnery 1965; General Staff, GHQ 1965–66; retired from Army 1966; Editor & Publisher, "Interwing," Rawalpindi 1968–71; Gen. Sec., Awami League, Rawalpindi 1969–71 & mem. of Working Cttee.; Bangladesh Ambassador to Yugoslavia & Roumania 1972–74, & to Iran & Turkey since 1974. Associate mem., Inst. of Strategic Studies, London. *Decorations:* Commander-in-Chief's Commendation 1964; several military awards & decorations; Yugoslav Order of the Lance & Flag, class 1. *Publications:* Arab-Israeli War, 1967; Aryans on the Indus. *Clubs:* Dacca Club; Chittagong Club; Diplomatic Club, Belgrade; Imperial Club, Tehran; Iran Club, Tehran. *Address:* 'Farm View,' Indra Road, Tejgaon, Dacca 15, Bangladesh & *office* Embassy of Bangladesh, 352 Kakh Avenue, P.O. Box 1189, Tehran, Iran.

**DOHERTY, Richard P.** American management consultant, television executive and economist. *B.* 1905. *Educ.* Clark Univ. (AB 1925) and Brown Univ. (AM 1926). *M.* 1933, Dorothy M. Sullivan. *Dau.* Judith Dale. *Career:* Professor of Economics, and Chairman, Economics Dept., Boston Univ.

1927–45; President, Television-Radio Management Corp.; Chairman, International Management Services, Inc. Vice-Pres., National Association of Broadcasters, U.S.A. 1946–54; Employer Member, U.S.A. National Wage Stabilization Board 1951–53; U.S.A. Employer Representative to International Labor Organization, Geneva 1948–63; Executive Director, Industrial Relations Council 1939–45; Member Joint (U.S.A.) International Labor Organization Committee 1952–60; Emergency Fuel & Food Administrator, Commonwealth of Massachusetts 1942–44; Int. Social Security Cttee. 1962—. *Publications:* Economic Organization of Society; Structure of American Business; Interpretation of Business and Financial Conditions; Business Cycles and Broadcasting; Prerequisites of Collecting Bargaining; numerous articles for magazines on business economics, employer-employee relations, and radio-TV broadcasting subjects. *Member:* Amer. Economics Society; Phi Beta Kappa. *Clubs:* Circumnavigators; Broadcasters; Assoc. Business Economists. *Address:* 10 Ezra Lane, Dennis, Mass., U.S.A.

**DOLD, Curt Hans.** Dr. Sc. techn., dipl. Chemical Engineer; Swiss. *B.* 1910. *Educ.* Higher Modern School studies. Department ETH of Swiss Institute of Technology. *M.* 1944. Dora Elsa Tschudy. *S.* Kurt Christian and Richard Johannes, *Dau.* Germaine Elisabeth. *Career:* Apprentice in his father's firm; co-partner since 1947; Owner and Manager Dold AG., Wallisellen, since 1947. *Publications:* Dissertation: Untersuchungen über Alkylphenolharzlacke unter besonderer Berücksichtigung ihrer materialtechnischen Eigenschaften. *Member:* Swiss Assn. of Manufacturers of Paint and Varnish (Pres. 1945–60); European Committee of Paint and Printing Inc. Manufacturers Assn. (Pres. 1955–57). *Club:* Rotary International (Past Governor District 200). *Address:* Rietstrasse 31, 8703 Erlenbach; and *office* Dold AG Hertistrasse 4, 8304 Wallisellen, Switzerland.

**DOLE, Robert.** American Politician. *B.* 1923. *Educ.* Univ. of Kansas; Washbourn Municipal Univ. *Career:* Senator from Kansas since 1968; Republican nominee for Vice-Presidency 1976. *Address:* New Senate Office Building, Washington D.C. 20510, U.S.A.

**DOLLEY, James Clay.** Educator and banker. *B.* 1900. *Educ.* McKendree College, Lebanon, Ill. (AB), Univ. of Illinois (AM) and Univ. of California (PhD). *M.* 1922, Lois Dee. *Dau.* Norma Lee (Kennedy, Jr.). *Career:* High School Teacher and coach of athletic teams (1919–26); Teaching Fellow (Economics), Univ. of California (Berkeley) 1926–28; at Univ. of Texas at Austin: Asst. Prof., Assoc. Prof. and Prof. of Finance 1928—; Vice-Pres. (in charge of Main Univ.) 1945–53; Acting Pres. 1952–53; Vice-Chancellor (Fiscal Affairs) Univ. System 1955—; Director of Research, Federal Reserve Bank of Dallas 1943–45; Director 1945—, President 1953–55, Austin National Bank. Vice-Chancellor (Fiscal Affairs), University of Texas System, and Professor of Finance & Director, Austin (Texas) National Bank. Vice-Pres., Natnl. Collegiate Athletic Assn. 1937–41; Pres., Southwest Athletic Conference 1943–44; Vice-Pres., Amer. Finance Assn. 1940–41. *Publications:* Principles of Investment (Harper & Bros., N.Y.) 1940; contributor to national, economic and financial periodicals. *Member:* Amer. Econ. Assn.; Amer. Finance Assn.; Fellow, Royal Economic Socy. (England); Economists National Committee on Monetary Policy. Honorary Societies: Beta Gamma Sigma; Artus. *Address: office* University of Texas, Austin 12, Tex., U.S.A.

**DOMAR, Evsey D.** American economist. *B.* 1914. *Educ.* Universities of California, Los Angeles (BA 1939) and Michigan (MA 1941), and Harvard Univ. (MA 1943); PhD 1947. *M.* 1946, Carola Rosenthal. *Daus.* Erica C. and Alice D. *Career:* Economist, Bd. of Governors, Federal Reserve System 1943–46; Asst. Prof. of Economics, Carnegie Inst. of Tech. 1946–47; Asst. Prof., Univ. of Chicago 1947–48; Assoc. Prof., The Johns Hopkins Univ. 1948–55 (Prof. 1955–58); Visiting Fulbright Prof., Oxford Univ. 1952–53; Dir. of Russian Studies, The Johns Hopkins Univ. 1949–51; Consultant, RAND Corp. 1951—, Ford Found. 1954–58, and Inter-University Cttee. on Travel Grants 1958–59; Brookings Inst. 1956–59; Professor of Economics, Massachusetts Institute of Technology 1958–72; Ford Professor of Economics since 1972; Visiting Professor, Harvard University 1962; Visiting Professor Stockholm School of Economics 1972; Visiting Prof., La Trobe Univ. Melbourne, 1974; Visiting Prof., Harvard Univ. 1976; Consultant, Batelle Mem. Inst. 1959–60; Natl. Science Fdn. 1958, 1967–69; Chmn., Committee on Slavic Grants, Am. Council of Learned Societies 1960–62; Consultant, OECD 1961–62, Institute for Defense Analysis 1961–62; Fellow, Econometric Socy. 1968—, Amer. Academy of Arts and Sciences 1962—, and Center for Advanced Study in the Behavioral Sciences 1962–63. *Member:* Executive Cttee., ASTE 1961–62; Board of Editors, American Economic Review 1957–59, Amer. Economist 1963—, & Journal of Comparative Economics 1976—; Exec. Cttee., Amer. Economic Assn. 1962–65; Pres. Comparative Economic Systems Assn. 1970; Vice-Pres. American Economic Association 1970; American Economic Assn.; Econometric Society; Royal Economic Society; Phi Beta Kappa; Pi Gamma Mu; Omicron Delta Epsilon the Honor Society in Economics. Recipient, John R. Commons Award, Dec. 1965. Member Exec. Cttee., Conference on Research in Income and Wealth 1965–69. *Publications:* Essays in the Theory of Economic Growth, Oxford Univ. Press 1957; contributor to professional periodicals. Democrat. *Club:* Faculty (M.I.T.). *Address:* 264 Heath's Bridge Road, Concord, Mass. 01742; and *office* Department of Economics E52-371, Massachusetts Institute of Technology, Cambridge 02139, Mass., U.S.A.

**DONALDSON, Sir John Francis** (The Hon. Mr Justice Donaldson). British High Court Judge. *B.* 1920. *Educ.* Charterhouse School; Trinity Coll. Cambridge. *M.* 1945, Dorothy Mary Warwick. *S.* 1. *Daus.* 2. *Career:* Barrister (QC 1961–66) 1946–66; Judge of High Court since 1966. Pres. Industrial Relations Court 1971–74. *Address:* Royal Courts of Justice, Strand, London, W.C.2.

**DONALDSON, John Geoffrey.** Australian. *B.* 1913. *Educ.* Scotch Coll., Melbourne. *M.* 1939, Alison A. Pollard. *S.* 3. *Career:* Dir. Nat. Bag Co. of Australia Ltd. 1951–64; Ramsay Surgical Ltd. 1953–77; Woodside Petroleum Ltd.; Woodside Oil Co. Ltd.; Mid Eastern Oil Ltd.; Mid-East Minerals N.L.; Vamgas Ltd.; Dir. R.V.B. Ltd.; Besser Vibrapac Masonry (W.A.) Ltd. 1962–72; Business & General Finance Corp. Ltd.; John Sackville & Sons, Ltd.; Santos Ltd. since 1972. *Member:* Stock Exchange, Melbourne, 1943–73. *Clubs:* Naval & Military; Athenaeum; R.A.C. of Victoria; Yarra Yarra Golf; Royal Melbourne Golf. *Address:* 42 West Toorak Rd., South Yarra, Vic., Australia; and *office* 351 Collins St., Melbourne 3000.

**DONALDSON, Rodgers.** American aircraft executive. *B.* 1908. *Educ.* Phillips Exeter Academy; Harvard College (BS 1930); Boston University (LLB *cum laude* 1933). *M.* 1940, Leslie Robinson Fisher. *S.* Rodgers, Jr. *Career:* Associated with Law firm of Choate, Hall & Stewart, Boston, Mass. 1933–39; Partner, Cunningham & Donaldson (general practice of law), Pittsfield, Mass. 1939–42; Counsel, Lockheed Aircraft Corp., Dayton, Ohio 1942; Asst. Manager Eastern District, Dayton and Washington 1942–45; Manager, New York Office 1946–48; General Counsel & Secretary, American Optical Co., Southbridge, Mass. 1949–54; Asst. Chief Counsel, Lockheed Aircraft Corp., Burbank 1954–61; Vice-President and General Counsel, Lockheed Aircraft Corp., 1961–71, Snr. Counselor since 1971; Director, Hollywood Presbyterian Hosp. Director, Los Angeles Metropolitan Y.M.C.A. *Member:* American and California Bar Associations. Republican. *Clubs:* Harvard (Southern California); Los Angeles Country; Rotary of Los Angeles. *Address:* 1950 South Beverley Glen Boulevard, Los Angeles 25, Calif.; and *office* Lockheed Aircraft Corp., P.O. Box 551, Burbank, Calif., U.S.A.

**DONELAN, Stephen Sydney,** OBE. Australian pastoralist and investor. Federal President, The Australian Primary Producers Union 1952–62; Councillor, Shepparton Agricultural Society 1948—; Executive Member of various Federal committees dealing with finances, wool, meat, wheat, fruit and dairying products. *B.* 1900. *Educ.* Xavier College, Melbourne. *M.* 1929, Ann Ryan. Recipient of Coronation Medal. Federal Life Member of A.P.P.U. Merino stud sheep breeder 1921–48; shorthorn beef cattle breeder; commercial fat stock grazier (fat lambs and vealers). *Publications:* Annual Federal Report of A.P.P.U. Member Federal Country Party; Graziers' Association; Royal Agricultural Societies. *Clubs:* Riverina Picnic Race Club; various social and racing clubs. *Address:* 33 Bruce Street, Toorak, Melbourne, 3142, Vic., Australia.

**DONNE, David Lucas,** MA. British. *B.* 1925. *Educ.* Stowe Sch.; Christ Church, Oxford (MA (Nat. Sci.)); Middle Temple. *M.* 1957, Jennifer Margaret Duncan (*Dec.* 1975). *S.* 2. *Dau.* 1. *Career:* Chmn. Williams Lea Group Ltd.; Crest Nicholson Ltd.; Fluidrive Engineering Co. Ltd.; Dep. Chmn. Dalgety Ltd.; Dir.: The Steetly Company Ltd.; The Royal Trust Co. of Canada and many other companies. *Clubs:* Vincent's, Oxford; Royal Thames Yacht. *Address:* 99 Abbotsbury Rd., London W14 8EP. and *office* 44 Baker Street, London, W1M 1DH.

**DONNELL, James C., II.** American Dir.: First National Bank (Findlay, O.) 1931—, National City Bank (Cleveland) 1949—, Armco Steel Corp. 1960—, Phelps-Dodge Corp. 1966—, New York Life Insce. Co. 1967—; Libbey-Owens-Ford Co. 1970—. *B.* 1910. *Educ.* Princeton Univ. (AB 1932). *M.* 1932, Dolly Louise Devine. *Dau.* Susan (Konkel). *Career:* With Marathon Oil Co.; Manager Crude Sales 1932–48, Director 1936, Vice-Pres. 1937–48, Pres. 1948–72, Chmn. 1972–75. Retired 1975. Recipient Grand Cross for Civil Merit (Spain). Hon. DSc Springfield Coll.; LLD Bowling Green State Univ.; George Williams Coll., Univ. of Wyoming; LHD Rose Polytechnic Inst., and Defiance Coll.; DH Findlay Coll.; Phi Beta Kappa. *Member:* Amer. Petroleum Inst., World Council and the National Council of the United States, Y.M.C.A.; The Conference Board. (Dir); National Petroleum Council; (Dir.); American Association of Petroleum Geologists. *Clubs:* Princeton, Links (N.Y.C.); Inverness (Toledo); Findlay Country, Bohemian (San Francisco). *Address:* 839 South Main Street, Findlay, Ohio; and *office* 539 South Main Street, Findlay, Ohio, U.S.A.

**DONNER, Frederic G.** American Foundation executive. Chairman, Alfred P. Sloan Foundatioo; Director, General Motor Corp. 1942–74. *B.* 1902. *Educ.* Univ. of Michigan (BA 1923). *M.* 1929. Eileen Isaacson. *S.* 1. *Dau.* 1. *Career:* Joined General Motors Corp. 1926; Assistant Treasurer 1934; Gen. Asst. Treasurer 1937; Vice-Pres. in Charge of Financial Staff and member of Administration Cttee. 1941; member, Board of Directors 1942; member, Financial Policy and Operations Policy Cttee. 1946; Exec. Vice-Pres. 1956; Chmn., Financial Policy Cttee. (now Finance Cttee.) 1956; Chmn. Bd of Dirs. 1958–67. Dir., Communication Satellite Corp.; Hon. LLD Michigan Univ. 1961, and Long Island Univ. 1966. Hon. Doctorate, Business Administration, Western Michigan University 1965. *Awards:* Comdr., Order of Leopold (Belgium); High Official. *Clubs:* The Links, University (N.Y.C.;) Creek Country; North Hempstead Country (Long Island, N.Y.). *Address: office* Room 2550, 630 Fifth Avenue, New York, N.Y. 10020, U.S.A.

**DONOVAN, Hedley.** American journalist. Editor-in-Chief, Time Inc., New York City, Apr. 1964—. *B.* 1914. *Educ.* Univ. of Minnesota (BA *magna cum laude* 1934) and Hertford College, Oxford Univ., Eng. (BA 1936). *M.* 1941, Dorothy Hannon. *S.* Peter Williams and Mark Vicars. *Dau.* Helen Welles. *Career:* Reporter, Washington Post 1937–42; Writer-Editor 1945–53, Managing Editor 1953–59, Fortune; Editorial Director, Time Inc. 1959–64. Lieut.-Comdr. U.S.N.R. (Retd.). Trustee, N.Y. Univ.; Ford Foundation; Carnegie End. for International Peace; Dir. Council on Foreign Relations. *Member:* Phi Beta Kappa; Delta Upsilon; *Clubs:* University (N.Y.C.); F. Street (Washington, D.C.); Manhasset Bay Yacht; Sands Point Golf (Port Washington N.Y.); Century (N.Y.). *Address: office* Time Inc., Time & Life Building, Rockefeller Center, New York City 10020, U.S.A.

**DONS, Erik.** Norwegian diplomat. *B.* 1915. *Educ.* Oslo Univ. (Law degree 1939). *M.* 1951, Cecilie Margrethe Jensen. *S.* Carl Erik and Paul Gustav. *Daus.* Helen Sirikit and Signe Margrethe. *Career:* Secretary 1940, Chief of Section Ministry of Foreign Affairs 1949; Counsellor and Deputy Permanent Representative to U.N. 1952; Minister to Thailand, Indonesia and the Philippines 1956. Member: Norwegian Deleg. to General Assembly U.N. (including Preparatory Commission) 1945–55, and 1967; Norwegian Deleg. to ECOSOC 1954–56, U.N. Conference on the Law of Treaties 1968; Ambassador to China 1959–63; Ambassador to Portugal 1963–67. Special Adviser to Ministry of Foreign Affairs 1967–76; Norwegian Deleg. negotiating for Membership European Communities 1970–71; Norwegian Delegate on Security and Co-operation in Europe 1973–74; Ambassador to the German Democratic Republic since 1976. *Publications:* (in Norwegian) Norwegian Nationality Law; The United Nations at Work. *Awards:* Chevalier, Order of St. Olav (Norway); Grand Cross Order of the Crown (Thailand); Grand Cross Order of Infante Dom Henrique (Portugal). *Address:* Ivar Aasensvei 30, Oslo, Norway.

**DOOLITTLE, Arthur K.** American chemical engineer and scientist; Professor of Chemistry, Drexel Inst. Philadelphia 1961–64 Senior Scientist, Research, Union Carbide Chemicals Co. 1955–61; Partner, Dorr Consultants 1959–61; President, Arcadia Institute for Scientific Research 1959–75. *B.* 1896. *Educ.* Columbia Coll. (AB 1919; BS 1920), and Columbia Univ. School of Engineering (ChE 1923). *M.* 1923, Dortha B. Bailey. S. Robert Frederick II. *Dau.* Elizabeth Doolittle Peckham. *Career:* Research Engineer, Dorr Co., 1923–25; Plant Engineer (1925–29) Chief, Lacquer Div., Sherwin Williams Co. 929–31; Development Engineer, Bowen Research Corp. 1931; Director, Lacquer Research, Bradley & Vrooman 1931–32; Technical Head Coatings Research (1932–44), Asst. Director of Research (1944–45), Carbide & Carbon Chemical Co. *Member:* A.C.S.; A.I.Ch.E.; A.I.C.; A.A.A.S., etc. *Awards:* Exceptional Contribution, Profession Chemical Engineering. Charlaston Section Aiche; Croce di Cavaliero of Merit, Italy; Fellow Aiche. *Clubs:* Columbia University. Chemists (N.Y.C.); Cosmos; Army & Navy; Quiet Birdmen (Washington), Daedalians (Harrisbury, Pa.). *Publications:* The Technology of Solvents and Plasticizers (John Wiley, N.Y. 1954); articles in scientific journals; chapters in books and encyclopedias; patents. *Address:* 406 Osborne Lane, Wllingford, Pa. 19086, U.S.A.

**DOOLITTLE, Gen. James Harold.** American aviation executive and aviator. Director, Mutual of Omaha 1961—, United Benefit Life Insurance Co. of Omaha 1964—, Tele-Trip Company Incorporated 1966—; Companion Life Ins. Co. 1968—; Mutual of Omaho Growth & Income Funds, 1968—. *B* 14 Dec. 1896. *Educ.* University of California (AB); Massachusetts Inst. of Tech. (DSc). *M.* 1917 Josephine E. Daniels. *S.* James H., John P. *Career:* served U.S. Army Air Corps 1917–30; Manager, Aviation Dept. Shell Petroleum Corp and Major, Reserve Corps., U.S. Army Air Corps 1930–40; member, Army Air Corps Investigating Cttee. 1934; Major Army Air Corps 1940, Brigadier-General 1942, Major-General 1942, Lieut.-General 1944; Commanding-General 8th Air Force in England and Okinawa; Chairman, Secy. of War's Board of Officer-Enlisted Men Relationship 1946; Led first air raid on Tokyo 1942; winner Schneider Cup Race 1925; established world's speed record for land planes 1932; first to fly outside loop; first to fly across U.S. in less than 24 hours 1922; first to take off, fly a set course, and land without seeing the ground, thus pioneering blind flying 1929; Vice-Pres. and Director, Shell Oil Co., N.Y. 1946–58: Dir. 1946–67; Chmn. of Board, Space Technology Laboratories, Jan. 1959–Jan. 1962; Director, TRW Inc., 1961–69; Vice-Chmn. Bd. of Trustees & Chmn. Exec. Cttee., Aerospace Corp. 1965–69. *Awards:* Congressional Medal of Honour; DSM with Oak Leaf Cluster; Silver Star; Bronze Star; Distinguished Flying Cross with two Oak Leaf Clusters; Air Medal with three Oak Leaf Clusters; Oficial, Orden del Condor de los Andes (Bolivia); Grand Officier de la Légion d'Honneur; Croix de Guerre avec palme (France); Knight Commander, Order of the Bath; Grand Officier, Ordre de le Couronne avec palme and Croix de Guerre avec palma (Belgium). *Address:* 5225 Wilshire Blvd., Room 702, Los Angeles, Calif. 90036, U.S.A.

**DORAND, Pierre René Léon Bernard.** French aeronautica constructor. Technical Director, Société Giravions Dorand 1950—; Director, Dorand Research Group. *B.* 1898. *Educ.* Baccalauréats, Latin Sciences, Philosophy and Mathematics; Engineer of Arts and Science; Dipl., Higher School of Electricity. *M.* 1951, Anne Marie Raimond. *S.* Jean-François and Pascal. *Dau.* Marie-Claire. *Career:* Served in World War I 1914–18. Engineer, Fabrications de l'Aéronautique 1922, and Société d'Aviation Louis Bréguet 1925; Technical Director, Gyroplane Research Syndicate 1931. Initiator of the Bréguet-Dorand gyroplane. In 1935, this was the first helicopter to realize flight in actual practice and to beat international records in speed, altitude, duration of flight and distance in a closed circuit. Served in World War II, 1939–45. Chief Engineer, Société Nationale de Constructions Aéronautiques du Centre 1945. *Awards:* Officer, Legion of Honour; Aeronautical Medal; Louis Bréguet Memorial Trophy. *Publications:* since 1923, various papers on aeronautics to Société Française de Navigation Aérienne; Association Française des Techniciens de l'Aéronautique; Association Technique Maritime et Aéronautique. In 1959 papers to Wissenschaftlicher Gesellschaft für Luftfahrt E.V. (W.G.I.), European Congress, Paris; Forum of American Helicopter Society; Royal Aeronautical Society. Member, American Helicopter Society Inc. Fellow of the Brit. Interplanetary Socy. *Clubs:* Aeroclub de France; Helicopter Club de France (President of Honour). *Address:* 3 rue du Général Lambert, Paris VII, France; and *office* Société Giravions Dorand, 5 Rue Jean Macé, 92, Suresnes.

**DORION, Hon. Frédéric.** Canadian. Chief Justice of the Superior Court for the Province of Quebec 1957–73. *B.* 1898. *Educ,* Laval University (Bach-ès-arts; lic. en droit). *M.* 1921, Emilienne Delisle. *S.* Guy, Judge. *Daus.* Michèle (Mme. Jean Bellavance) and Thérèse (Mme. Guy Thibondeau). *Career:* Called to Bar of Quebec 1920; KC 1940; served in World War I (with R.A.F.; in Canada Apr. to Sept. 1918; Comnd. Lieut. Nov. 1918 and proceeded overseas) 1918–19. Pres..

French Canadian Catholic Youth 1930. Elected to House of Commons for Charlevoix-Saguenay as independent in a by-election 1942, re-elected in the General Election of 1945. Bâtonnier of the Quebec Bar 1951–52. Headed judicial enquiry into charges of attempted bribery and coercion involving aid to two Federal Cabinet Ministers 1964; Chief Justice of the Superior Court for the Province of Quebec 1957–73. *Clubs:* Quebec Garrison; Cercle Universitaire Laval. *Address:* 2831 Sasseville Street, Ste Foy; and *office* 912 Chemin St.-Louis, Quebec 4, P.Q., Canada.

**DORIOT, Georges Frederic.** American businessman and educator. *B.* 1899. *Educ.* University of Paris (BS 1915). *M.* 1930, Edna Allen. *Career:* Asst. Dean 1926–31, and Associate Professor 1926–29; Professor, 1929–66. Harvard Business School. Directors: American Research & Development Corporation; The National Shawmut Bank of Boston; Advisory Dir. Technical Studies Inc. (channel tunnel study group), European Enterprises Development Co., EED, SA., Canadian Enterprise Development Corp.; The Boston Co. Inc.; Ionics. Inc.; and other companies. Brig.-Gen., U.S. Army 1941–47; Director of military planning division of Office of the Quartermaster General; Dep. Dir. for Research and Development, War Dept. Gen. Staff; Dep. Administrator of War Assets Administration; Office of the Asst. Chief of Staff G-4, 1946–59; Chmn. Dir. Exec. Cttee. American Research & Development Corp. Boston 1946; Professor Emeritus Harvard Univ. Graduate School of Business Administration since 1966; Dir. Digital Equipment Corp; Doll Research Inc; Textron Atlantic Inc; Sun Life Assurance Co. of Canada (U.S.). *Awards:* Distinguished Service Medal (U.S.A.); Outstanding Civilian Medal (U.S. Army); Commander, Order of the British Empire; Grand Officer, Ordre du Mérite Recherche et Invention (France); Commander, Legion of Honour (France); Hon. MA Harvard Univ. 1942; Hon. LHD, Union College 1938; Hon. MS Lowell Inst. 1952; Hon. LLD, Emerson College 1955; Hon. LLD, Ohio Univ. 1962. Trustee, Franklin Foundation; Geo-Transport Foundation, New England; The Institute for the Future. *Clubs:* The Brook, Harvard (N.Y.C.); Somerset (Boston). *Address:* 12 Lime Street, Boston 0218, Mass.; and *office* 200 Berkeley Street, Boston 16, Mass., U.S.A.

**DORLAND, Gilbert Meding.** American. Civil Engineer. Legion of Merit (U.S.A.); Order of the British Empire. *B.* 1912. *Educ.* U.S. Military Academy (BS 1936) and Univ. of California at Berkeley (MS in CE 1940). *M.* 1937, Lillian Okkerse. *S.* Gilbert N., John H., Peter G., and Richard L. *Dau.* Diane L. (Rixse). *Career:* Regular Army Officer, Corps of Engineers, U.S. Army 1936–56 (retired in grade of Colonel). Exec. Vice-Pres., Nashville Bridge Co. 1957–61; President, 1962–69; Dir. American Institute of Steel Construction 1959—, Vice-President 1968–71, President 1971–72; Vice-President, Nashville Area Chamber of Commerce 1960; Director, First American National Bank, Nashville 1961–69; Wachovia Bank and Trust Co. since 1971; North Carolina Citizens Assn. since 1971; Greater Greensboro Housing Foundation since 1971; President, Carolina Steel Corporation since 1971. Vice-Pres., Torres Mexicanas, S.A., 1962–68; Pres., National Waterways Conf. 1963–65; Pres., Cumberland Valley Assn. 1957–69; Registered Professional Engineer, Tennessee 1955. *Member:* National Council and Past Pres. Middle Tennessee Council, Boy Scouts of Amer.; Amer. Socy. of Civil Engineers (Fellow); National Socy. of Professional Engineers; Socy. of Amer. Military Engineers; Army & Navy Wash. D.C. *Clubs:* Kiwanis; Greensboro Country. *Address:* 1916 Granville Road, Greensboro, N.C. 27408, U.S.A.

**DORMAN, Sir Maurice (Henry),** GCMG, GCVO. K St J. *B.* 1912. *Educ.* Sedbergh School and Magdalene College, Cambridge (MA). *M.* 1937, Florence Monica Churchward D. St. J. *S.* John Douglas. *Daus:* Joanna Bridget Yeo, Elisabeth Bostock and Sibella. *Career:* Successively Administrative Officer 1935, District Officer 1937 and Clerk of Councils 1940–45, Tanganyika Territory; Assistant to the Lieut.-Governor, Malta 1945; Principal Assistant Secretary, Palestine 1947; seconded to Colonial Office as Asst. Secy. in charge of Social Services Department 1948; Director of Social Welfare and Community Development, Gold Coast 1950; Chief Secretary, Trinidad and Tobago 1952; Acting Governor for periods 1954–55; Governor, C.-in-C. and Vice Admiral Sierra Leone 1956–61; after Independence, Governor General, Sierra Leone 1961–62; Governor of Malta 1962–64; after Independence Governor-General, Malta 1964–71; Deputy Chmn. Pearce Commission Rhodesia 1971–72; Dir. MLH Consultants Ltd.; Ramsbury Building Society; Chmn. Wiltshire Area Health Authority since 1974; Trustee Imperial War Museum. Chief Commander St John Ambulance since 1975; Pres. Staffordshire Soc. 1974–77. *Awards:* Hon. DCL (Durham); Hon. LLD (Malta). *Address:* 42 Lennox Gardens, London S.W.1 and The Old Manor, Overton, Marlborough, Wilts.

**DORN, Richard Werner.** German publisher and book dealer. Partner, Otto Harrassowitz, Publisher and International Book Dealer, Wiesbaden 1947—. *B.* 1906. *Educ.* various schools in Sweden, Germany and Switzerland (Maturity Certificate from a Swiss Cantonal School). *M.* 1935, Marianne Dorn. *S.* Knut and Detlef. *Dau.* Gudula. *Career:* Apprenticed and later employed as a book dealer with various firms in St. Gall and Basle (Switzerland) and Munich (Germany) 1926–36; leading position with Otto Harrassowitz, Leipzig 1936–40; military service 1940–45; re-establishment of the firm in Wiesbaden and appointed director of same 1947, Partner 1964—. *Member:* Max Planck-Gesellschaft zur Förderung der Wissenschaften, Börsenverein für den deutschen Buchhandel; Goethe-Gesellschaft; English, Australian and Vienna Goethe Societies; Schiller-Gesellschaft; Freies Deutsches Hochstift; Gesellschaft der Bibliophilen a.o. *Award:* Bundesverdienstkreuz am Bande. *Address:* Beethovenstr. 6a, Wiesbaden; and *office* Taunusstr. 5, Wiesbaden, Germany.

**DORRANCE, John Thompson, Jr.** *B.* 1919. *Educ.* St. George's School (Grad. 1937) and Princeton Univ. (AB 1941). *S.* John T. III and Bennett. *Dau.* Mary Alice and Keith (step-daughter) Bassett and Langdon Mannion. *Career:* With U.S. Army July 1941–Dec. 1945. With Cambell Soup Co. since Apr. 1946. Chairman of the Board, Campbell Soup Co., Camden, N.J., U.S.A. Mar. 1962—. Director: Morgan Guaranty Trust Co. of N.Y.; John Wanamaker, Philadelphia; Trustee. Penn Mutual Life Insurance Co. *Member:* English Speaking Union; The Pilgrims of the U.S.A. Republican. *Clubs:* Racquet; New York Yacht; Corinthian Yacht (Phila.); Links; Union; Pinnacle; Oakland; Colonial (Princeton Univ.). *Address: office* Campbell Place, Camden 08101, N.J., U.S.A.

**DORTICOS TORRADO, Osvaldo.** Cuban Statesman. *B.* 1919. *Educ.* Univ. of Havana; admitted to Bar and practised law. Leader of Castro movement, Cienfuegos 1957–58; imprisoned 1958 but escaped and went to Mexico; returned on success of Castro's revolution. Minister of Revolutionary Law 1959; President of Cuba 1959–76; Minister of Economy & President of Central Planning Board 1965–76; Mem. Council of State & Political Bureau since 1976. *Address:* Consejo de Estado, Havana, Cuba.

**dos SANTOS, Sir Errol Lionel,** CBE. British company director. *B.* 1 Sept. 1890. *Educ.* St. Mary's College, Trinidad. *M.* (1) 1915, Lilian Evelyn Coleston. *S.* 1. *Dau.* 1. (2) 1939, Enid Hilda Jenkin. *Daus.* 2. Financial Secretary, Trinidad 1941–46, Colonial Secretary 1947–48; Dir., Alstons Ltd. 1948, Chmn. 1953–61; Caribbean Development Co. Ltd. 1953; Carib Glassworks Ltd. 1955. *Address:* Knaggs Hill, St. Ann's, Trinidad, West Indies.

**DOTY, Paul (Mead).** Professor. *B.* 1920. *Educ.* Pennsylvania State University (BS 1941); and Columbia University (PhD 1944). *M.* 1954, Helga Boedtker. *S.* Gordon Sutherland (by 1st marriage). *Daus.* Marcia, Rebecca and Katherine. Professor of Chemistry, Harvard University 1956—. Member, President's Science Advisory Committee 1961–65; Consultant to the U.S. Disarmament Agency, Department of State and National Security Council; Chmn. American Academy Committee on International Studies in Arms Control; Rockefeller Fellow, Cambridge, England 1946–47; Assistant Professor Harvard 1948–50 (Associate Prof. 1950–56; Professor 1956–68; Mallinckroft Professor of Biochemistry 1968—; Dir. Program for Science and International Affairs since 1973. *Award:* American Chemical Society Award in Pure Chemistry, 1956. *Member:* National Acad. of Science (Fellow); Amer. Socy. of Biological Chemists; Amer. Acad. Arts and Sciences (Fellow); Philosophical Socy. (Fellow). Democrat. *Address:* 4 Kirkland Place, Cambridge, Mass., U.S.A.

**DOUBLEDAY, George Chester.** *B.* 1904. *Educ.* Princeton Univ. (BA). *M.* 1933, Mary P. Kelley. *Daus.* Mrs. Henry C. Irons, Jr., Mrs. C. Austin Buck, and Mrs. Paul Massey *Career:* Vice-President 1952–68; and Director 1953–76, Ingersoll-Rand Co., Woodcliff Lake, New Jersey; Secy. Treasurer Beaverkill Farm, Incorporated. *Member:* Society of Naval Architects and Marine Engineers; Amer. Inst. of Mining, Metallurgical & Petroleum Engineers; Sons of the Revolution; Socy. of California Pioneers. *Clubs:* Racquet & Tennis; Downtown Association; Piping Rock. *Address:* Beaverkill Farm, Millboro, Virginia, U.S.A.

**DOUCET, Gerald Joseph,** QC. Canadian barrister-at-law. *B.* 1937. *Educ.* St. Francis Xavier Univ. (BA) and Dalhousie Univ. (LLB). Divorced. *S.* Gerald and Paul. *Daus.* Michelle, Dana and Denise. *Career:* Shareholder, Officer and Director: Canso Realties Ltd.; Shando Holdings Ltd.; Island Properties Ltd.; Canso Straight Development Ltd. Gulf Sands Retreat Ltd.; Chairman Central & Nova Scotia Trust Co. Advisory Board (Port Hawkesbury Br.); President Eastern Broadcasters Ltd.; Vice-Pres. Pharmacie Acadienne Ltd. *Member:* Nova Scotia Barristers' Socy.; St. Francis Xavier Univ. Atlantic Fund Raising Cttee; Governor & N.S. Vice-Pres. of Atlantic Provinces Economic Council; mem. of Nova Scotia Law Reform Commission. *Address:* P.O. Box 69, Church Street, Port Hawkesbury, Nova Scotia BOE 2VO, Canada.

**DOUGLAS, Donald Wills, Jr.** American. *B.* 1917. *Educ.* Stanford Univ. and Curtiss-Wright Technical Inst. *M.* (1) 1939, Molly McIntosh (*Dec.*); (2) 1950, Jean Cooper. *Daus.* (by first marriage) Victoria and Holly. *Career:* Engineer, Douglas Aircraft Co. 1939; Dir., Douglas testing division 1943–48; Dir. Contract Admin. 1948–49; Dir. Research Labs. 1949–51. Corporate Vice-Pres. 1951–57; President, 1957–68. Director, Stanford Research Inst. 1955—. Member, National Industrial Conference Board 1958—; Senior Corporate Vice-President (Administration) McDonnell Douglas Corporation 1971–72; Pres. Chief Exec. Officer Douglas Development Co. since 1972. *Award:* Chevalier, Legion of Honour (France 1961); Officer, Order of Merit of the Republic (Italy). *Member:* Pres. Eisenhower's Cttee. on Youth Fitness; Natl. Defense Transportation Assn.; Aerospace Industries Ass. (Chmn. 1964); Natl. Air Cncl.; Amer. Ordnance Assn. *Clubs:* Conquistadores del Cielo; Burning Tree C.C. (Washington D.C.); California Yacht; Transpacific Yacht; Los Angeles Country; Los Angeles Press; Confrerie de la Chaine des Rotisseures; Confrerie des Chevaliers du Tastevin; National Aviation; St. Francis Yacht (San Francisco); St. Louis, Bellerive Country (St. Louis). *Address:* and *office* P.O. Box 516, St. Louis, 63166, U.S.A.

**DOUGLAS, (John) Harold.** Irish. *B.* 1912. *Educ.* St. Stephen's Green School and Dublin Univ. (B.A., BCom). *M.* 1941, Hazel Malcolm. *S.*1. *Daus.* 2. *Career:* Peace Commissioner. Managing Director: John Douglas & Sons Ltd., and Irish Stylewear Co. Ltd. Director: Friends' Provident & Century Life Office; Commissioner of Irish Lights. *Member:* Dublin Corporation 1945–54, and Irish Senate 1954–57. Council Member, Dublin Chamber of Commerce (Pres. 1958). *Clubs:* University, Royal Irish Automobile. *Address:* Wenden, Delgany, Co. Wicklow; and *office* 18 Wexford Street, Dublin, 2, Ireland.

**DOUGLAS, Keith Humphrey,** AMI Mech E., MSAE. British. *B.* 1923. *Educ.* Claremont; Leamington Tech.; Leicester Govt. Eng. Training Centre. *M.* 1944, Joan L. Sheasby. *S.* 2. *Career:* with R.A.F. 1943–48; Marketing Dir., G.K.N. Transmissions Ltd.; Dir. Keith Douglas (Motor Sport) Ltd.; various previous appointments with GKN. *Clubs:* R.A.C.; Steering Wheel; British Automobile Racing; British Racing Drivers; *Member:* British Motor Racing Marshals (Vice-Pres.); Chmn. SMMT Motor Sports Cttee.; U.K. Rep. B.P.I.C.A., Paris; Member R.A.C. Motor Sports Council; Midland Road Develop. Group. *Address:* 281 Four Ashes Rd., Dorridge, Solihull, Warwicks; and *office* P.O. Box 405, Chester Road, Birmingham B24 0RB.

**DOUGLAS, Lloyd V.** American Business Educator. *B.* 1902. *Educ.* State Univ. of Iowa (BSCom, MA, and PhD) and Blackstone Inst. of Law, Chicago (LLB). *M.* (1) 1925, Grace A. Waddell (dec'd). (2) 1973, Virginia V. Marston. *Career:* High School business teacher 1923–25; Superintendent of Schools 1925–30; Junior College Instructor 1930–34; Head, Dept. of Commerce, New Mexico Highland Univ. 1934–37; Professor and Head, Department of Business Education, University of Northern Iowa (formerly Iowa State Teachers College) 1937–70. Visiting Prof. and Lecturer, State Univ. of Iowa, Univ. of Wisconsin, Univ. of Iowa, Univ. of Colorado, Northwestern Univ., and Oklahoma State Univ. Distinguished Professor, Michigan State Univ.; War Service leave 1942–44 (Head of Recruiting Section, 8th U.S. Civil Service District; Supervisor of Naval Disbursing, Naval Training School, Indiana Univ.); Visiting Professor Northern Illinois Univ. 1970–71; Professor Emeritus since 1970. *Publications:* Teaching Business Subjects, (1958); The Business Education Program in the Expanding Secondary School (Editor and co-author), (1956); Modern Business; An Introduction to Problems & Principles (1948); Business Education, (1963); contributor to numerous professional magazines. *Awards:* John Robert Gregg Award, 1960; Cedar Falls Representative Citizen, 1966; Hon. member, Delta Pi Epsilon (Beta); Pi Omega Pi (Past Natl. Pres.); elected to Phi Delta Kappa. *Clubs:* Cedar Falls Den of Lions International (Past Pres.); Cedar Falls Chamber of Commerce (Past Pres.). *Address:* 1114 West 19th Street, Cedar Falls, Ia., U.S.A.

**DOUGLAS-HAMILTON, Lord James Alexander,** MA, LLB, MP. British. *B.* 1942. *Educ.* Balliol Coll., Oxford (MA, Modern History); Edinburgh Univ. (LLB). *M.* 1974, Hon. P. Susan Buchan. *Career:* Pres., Oxford Union Society; Scots Advocate 1968; Edinburgh Town Councillor 1972; Conservative Member of Parliament for Edinburgh West since 1974. *Publications:* Motive for a Mission; The Story Behind Hess's Flight to Britain (1971). *Clubs:* New Club (Edinburgh); Hon. Company of Edinburgh Golfers; Puffins. *Address:* 3 Blackie House, Lady Stair's Close, Edinburgh EH1 2NY; & House of Commons, London, S.W.1.

**DOWD, Bernard John.** Australian. Chairman and Managing Director, Dowd Associates Pty. Ltd., Burwood, Melbourne. *B.* 1913. *Educ.* Wesley Coll., Melbourne. *M.* Roma Wenlock Moore. *S.* 4. *Daus.* 3. Life Member, The Australian-American Association. *Clubs:* Institute of Directors (London); Victoria Racing, Royal Victorian Motor Yacht, Public Schools, Victoria Golf (Melbourne); Germania (U.S.A.). *Address:* 'Whernside', Albany Road, Toorak, Vic.; and *office* Dowd Associates Pty. Ltd., Burwood, Melbourne, Vic., Australia.

**DOWN, Alastair Frederick,** OBE, MC, TD; Kt Cdr Order of Orange Nassau with Swords (Netherlands). British oil executive. *B.* 1914. *Educ.* Edinburgh Academy (Scotland) Marlborough College (England). *M.* 1947, Maysie, Hilda Mellon. *S.* Richard Charles Alastair and Nigel Stuart Vernon. *Daus.* Diana Caroline and Melinda Jane. *Career:* After qualification as a Chartered Accountant, joined British Petroleum Co. Ltd. in London (England), serving in Palestine (now Israel) 1938–40, Iran 1945–47, London 1947–53, Canada 1953–62. Served in World War II, W. Desert-Egypt 1940–44; Capt., Maj., Lt.-Col.; Italy 1944–45; Lt.-Col. H.Q., 8th Army; North-west Europe 1945; full Col. and Col. 'Q', H.Q. First Canadian Army. Man. Dir. British Petroleum Co., Mar. 1962–74, Dep. Chmn. 1969–74; Chmn. of Burmah Oil Co. since 1975. *Member:* Review Body on Remuneration of Doctors and Dentists; Television Adv. Cttee.; Fellow of the Royal Society of Arts. *Member:* Socy. of Chartered Accountants. *Award:* Kt. Cdr. Order of Orange Nassau with Swords (Netherlands). *Clubs:* Bath (London); Ranchmen's (Calgary); Toronto (Toronto); Mount Royal (Montreal). *Address:* Burmah House; Pipers Way, Swindon, Wiltshire SN3 1RE.

**DOWNER, Hon. Sir Alexander Russell,** KBE. *B.* 1910. *Educ.* Geelong Grammar School and Brasenose Coll., Oxford (MA Dip. of Economics and Pol. Science); Called to Bar (Inner Temple) 1934; admitted to South Australian Bar 1935. *M.* 1947, Mary I. Gosse. *S.* 1. *Daus.* 3. *Career:* Served 8th Div. A.I.F. 1940–45 (P.o.W. Changi Camp, Singapore for 3½ years). Member of Bd., Electricity Trust of South Australia 1946–49; MP (L.) Angas, Australia 1949–64; Minister for Immigration 1958–63; High Commissioner for Australia in the United Kingdom, Oct. 1964–72. *Member:* Australian Parliamentary Foreign Affairs Committee 1952–58; Australian Constitution Review Cttee. 1956–59; Commonwealth Parly. Deleg. to Coronation 1953; Board of National Gallery, S. Aust. 1946–63. Pres., Royal Over-Seas League (S. Aust. Branch) 1946–62; Governor, English Speaking Union, 1973. *Awards:* Freeman, City of London 1965. Fellow Roy. Socy. of Arts 1968; Hon. Doctor of Laws (LLD) Birmingham 1973. *Publications:* various lectures. *Clubs:* Brooks's, Junior Carlton, (Hon.) Cavalry (Lond.); Adelaide (Adelaide); Union (Sydney). *Address:* Martinsell, Williamstown, South Australia; and 26/27 Queens Gate Gardens, London SW7.

**DOWNER, Samuel Forsythe.** American. *B.* 1918. *Educ.* Ohio Univ. (BSc Com *cum laude*); Harvard Business School (Advanced Management (Programme), I.B.M. Corp. (Executive Computer Concepts Courses I and II), and American Inst. of Banking (Lecturer on economics and business administration). *M.* 1940, Jessie Stuart Cooper. *S.* Philip Stuart. *Dau.* Benita (Rountree). *Career:* Trustee & Receiver, Bankruptcy Cases; Gen. Partner, A Properties Ltd.; Managing Agent, Creditors Trust of Hill Properties Ltd.; Vice-Pres., Finance, Treasurer & Dir., LTV Aerospace Corp.; Dir., Kentron Hawaii Ltd., Service Technology Corp., Park Towers Inc.; Asst. to Exec. Vice-Pres., Finance and Administration, Corporate Secy. and Asst. Treasurer, Continental Can Co. Inc. 1960–65; Vice-Pres., Exchange National Bank, Colorado Springs 1957–60; Sales Representative, Burroughs Corp., Colorado Springs 1948–57; Asst. to Pres., Asst.

General Sales Mgr., Jessop Steel Co., Washington, Pa. 1942–48; Sales Representative, Burroughs Corp., Wheeling, West Va. 1940–42. *Awards:* Exceptional Service Award, U.S.A.F. (highest civilian decoration); Recognition Affiliation. Colorado Socy. of Certified Public Accountants; Life Membership, Burroughs Corp. All Star Sales Club. *Member:* Amer. Socy. of Corporate Secretaries Inc.; Association of U.S. Army (Vice-Pres.); Bd. of Governors, American National Red Cross. *Clubs:* Nanhook Yacht; Lancers. *Address:* 3310 Fairmount, Dallas, Tex. 75201; and *office* 3310 Fairmount, Dallas, Tx. 75201, U.S.A.

**DOWNES, Ronald Geoffrey.** Australian. *B.* 1916. *Educ.* BAgrSc (Melb.) 1937, MAgrSc (Melb.) 1939, DAgrSc (Melb.) 1971. *M.* 1940, Gwenyth Edith Dodds. *S.* Michael, Stephen, and Nicholas. *Career:* With C.S.I.R.O. (Division of Soils) 1939–50. Member, Soil Conservation Authority 1950 Depty. Chmn. 1952, Chmn. 1961–73; U.N.F.A.O. Consultant in Land Use and Hydrology Conservation of Natural Resources in Israel 1960 and 1965 and Iran 1967, Near East Land & Water Use Commission 1967; Dryland Farming Conference U.S. 1969, Algeria 1972; Deputy Chmn. Land Conservation Council 1971–73; Chmn. Environment Protection Council 1971–73; Fed. Pres. Aust. Inst. of Agric. Science 1971–72; Dir. Permanent Head Ministry for Conservation since 1973. *Member:* State Coordination Council 1976—; Chmn. Pesticides Review Cttee. 1966–76; Pres. Austr. Society of Soil Science 1961–63; Vice-Pres. Aust. Conservation Foundation 1965–73. *Publications:* articles in various scientific journals, and separate publications on land use, origin and distribution of soils, soil physics, soil mechanics, ecology, hydrology and soil conservation. *Fellow:* Australian Inst. of Agricultural Science (F.A.I.A.S.), Soil Conservation Socy. of America, Aust. Acad. of Technological Sciences, and Commonwealth Fund of New York. *Member:* Royal Socy. of Victoria; Soil Science Socy. of Aust.; International Soil Socy.; International Union for Conservation of Natural Resources. *Address:* 95 Marshall Street, Ivanhoe, Vic.; and *office* Ministry for Conservation, 240 Victoria Parade, East Melbourne, 3002, Victoria, Australia.

**DOWNING, Edward Frank,** QC. Australian lawyer. *B.* 1908. *Educ.* Hale School, Western Australia. *M.* 1935, Phyllis Grace Thiel. *Daus.* 3. *Career:* Chairman of Directors, Amalgamated Collieries of Western Australia, BP Refinery (Kwinana) Ltd., and Nicholsons Broadcasting Service Ltd. Director: Bunning Timber Holdings Ltd., Swan Portland Cement Ltd. Chmn., Wigmores Ltd. *Club:* Weld (Perth). *Address: office* 21 Howard Street, Perth, W.A., Australia.

**DOWNING, Hon. Robert Reginald.** Australian politician. *B.* 1904. *Educ.* CBC, Goulburn, N.S.W.; Univ. of Sydney (LLB). *M.* 1932, Rose M. Ashcroft. *S.* 2. *Dau.* 1. *Career:* Minister of Justice and Vice-Pres., Exec. Cncl., N.S.W. 1941–56; Attorney-General, Minister of Justice and Vice-President of the Executive Council, New South Wales 1956–60; Attorney-General, and Vice-Pres. of Executive Council of N.S.W., 1960–65; Leader of the Opposition in N.S.W. Legislative Council, 1965–72; Trustee Taronga Zoological Park 1942–74; Member, Senate Sydney Univ. 1949–68; N.S.W. Cancer Council 1954—; Pres. Aust. Cancer Council 1967–70; Hon. Doctor of Laws Sydney Univ. 1972. *Address:* 117 Henley Marine Drive, Drummoyne, N.S.W., Australia.

**DOWNS, Leslie Hall,** CBE. British company director. *B.* 1900. *Educ.* Abbotsholme School; Christ's College, Cambridge (MA, FIMechE). *M.* 1930, Kathleen Mary Lewis. *Daus.* 3. *Career:* Chairman: Barnsley Canister Co. Ltd. Blundell-Permoglaze Ltd.; formerly: Chmn. & M.D., Rose, Downs & Thompson Ltd., Hull; Vice-Chmn., Power-Gas Corp. Ltd., Stockton-on-Tees; Vice-Chmn., Davy-Ashmore Ltd., Sheffied; Dir., Blundell-Permoglaze (Holdings) Ltd., London; Trustee, Hull Trustee Savings Bank; Treasurer, Univ. of Hull, Hon. Dr. of Science, Hull Univ. *Address:* King's Mill, Driffield, E. Yorks.

**DOWNSBROUGH, George Atha.** Physicist, Vice-Pres., The Singer Co., New York City Feb. 1965—. *B.* 1910. *Educ.* Rutgers Univ. (BS 1931, MS 1933, PhD 1936). *M.* 1948, Margaret E. McDougall. *S.* George A., Jr. and Bruce O. *Career:* Senior Physicist, Johns Manville Co., Manville, N.J. 1936–40; Bureau of Ordnance, Navy Dept., Washington, D.C. and Norfolk, Va. 1940–42. Successively Vice-Pres. & General Manager 1942–44, Pres. and Gen. Mgr. 1944–50, and Pres., Treasurer and Gen. Mgr. 1950–56, Boonton Radio Corp.; President and Dir., Boonton Radio Corp. 1956–63; Assistant to the President, American Radiator & Standard Sanitary Corporation, New York City, N.Y. 1963–65. *Member:* Inst. of Radio Engineers; Amer. Physical Socy.; American Assn. for Advancement of Science; Instrument Socy. of America; Scientific Apparatus Makers Assn. *Clubs:* Union League, Smoke Rise. *Address:* c/o The Singer Co., New York City, NY., U.S.A.

**DRAESEKE, Gordon Cecil Ladner.** Canadian. *B.* 1913. *Educ.* Univ. of B.C. (BA 1936); Law, Dalhousie 1939. *M.* 1957, Dorothy Roy. *S.* Douglas; stepsons Bruce and John Allan. *Daus.* Kathleen and Janice. *Career:* Admitted to B.C. Bar 1939. Engaged in practice of law 1939–40. Served in Royal Canadian Navy (retd. Lieut.-Comdr.) 1941–45; Secy. Alaska Pine Co. 1945–58; Dir. Secy. Western Forest Ind. 1946–48, Vice-Pres., Dir., Rayonier Canada Ltd., 1958–68; Vice-Pres. and Dir. Seaboard Shipping Co. and Seaboard Lumber Sales Co., 1964–68. President and Chief Executive Officer, Council of the Forest Industries of British Columbia since 1968. *Fellow:* Chartered Institute of Secretaries; Dir. Canadian Ass; Chmn. Bd. Trustees Vancouver Gen. Hospital. *Member:* Canadian Bar Assn.; Newcomen Society of North America; Port of Vancouver Authority (Fed. Gov.); Metric Commission (Fed. Gov.); Law Socy. of British Columbia. Freeman The District of Port Alice; Past-Pres., Medical Services Assn. 1963–64; Adv. Council Medical Service Assn.; Dir. Canadian Forestry Assn; President Canada-Japan Socy. of Vancouver; Newcomen Socy. North America. *Clubs:* Vancouver (Vancouver B.C.); Union of British Columbia (Vic. B.C.). *Address:* 1599 Angus Drive, Vancouver 9; and *office* 1500 Guiness Tower, 1055 West Hastings, Vancouver BC, Canada.

**DRAGAN, Constantin.** Romanian politician. *B.* 1922. *Educ.* Acad. of Economic Studies, Bucharest. *M.* Marioara Dragan. *S.* 2. *Career:* member Communist Party 1945—; Youth organizations 1947–54; Secy. Arges Region Cttee. 1954–59, Deputy to grand Nat. Assembly 1957—; Member State Council 1965—; Member Central Cttee. R.C.P. 1965—; Exec. Cttee. 1965—; Chmn. Gen. Union, Romanian Trade Unions 1965–67; First Vice Chmn. 1967–71; First Secy. Communist Party Cttee. Brasov County since 1971. Order of Labour 1962. *Address:* Central Committee of the Romanian Communist Party, Bucharest, Romania.

**DRAKE, Sir Eric,** CBE. British. *B.* 1910. *Educ.* Shrewsbury School and Pembroke College, Cambridge. *M.* (1) 1935, Rosemary Moore, and (2) 1950, Margaret Elizabeth Wilson. *S.* 2. *Daus.* 2. *Career:* With the British Petroleum Co. Ltd. 1935—; General Manager, Iran and Iraq 1950–51; Chairman, 1969–75, Deputy Chairman (1962–69) and Managing Dir. (1958–75), The British Petroleum Co. President, Chamber of Shipping of the United Kingdom 1964 (Vice-Pres. 1963; Member of Council 1958—); Dep. Chmn., The Peninsular & Oriental Steam Navigation Co., *Director:* Kleinwort Benson Lonsdale Ltd., Toronto-Dominion Bank (Canada), Hudson's Bay Co., BP Canada Ltd., Société Francaise des Petroles BP. *Member:* General Committee of Lloyd's Register of Shipping 1960—, and Court of Governors of The London School of Economics and Political Science 1963—. Representative in U.S. 1952–54. Governor of Pangbourne Nautical College 1958–69 and Shrewsbury School, since 1969; Hon. Mem., Gen. Council of British Shipping 1975—; Cttee. of Management RNLI 1975—. Hon. Fellow, Pembroke Coll., Cambridge; Fellow. Institute of Chartered Accountants.*Awards:* Commander, Order of the Crown (Belgium) 1969; Knight Bachelor 1970; Knight Grand Cross Order of Merit (Italy) 1970; Officer, Legion d'Honneur France 1972; Hon. DSc Cranfield 1972; Hon. Fellowship Univ. Manch. I.S.T. since 1974; Hon. Petroleum Advisor to Army; Hon. member. Hon. Company Master Mariners; Freeman City of London. 1974; Hon. Elder Brother of Trinity House, 1976; one of H.M. Lieutenants, City of London. *Clubs:* Royal Yacht Sqn.; Royal Cruising; Leander (Henley-on-Thames). *Address:* The Old Rectory, Cheriton, Alresford, Hants.; and *office* Britannic House, Moor Lane, London, E.C.2.

**DRAKE, Robert T.** Lawyer. Member of law firm of Foss, Schuman & Drake, Chicago. Board of Directors, of Independent Voters of Illinois. *B.* 1907. *Educ.* Dartmouth College (AB) and Columbia Univ. (LLB). *M.* 1929, Martha Bishop Swan. *Daus.* Janet (Morris) and Helen (Sanford). Arbitrator by appointment: Federal Mediation and Conciliation Service; and American Arbitration Service. Attorney, National Labor Relations Board 1942–47; Associate Professor, College of Law, University of Idaho 1947–49; Member Bd. Dirs. Illinois Division, American Civil Liberties Union 1949–69; United Nations Assn. of Chicago 1972. Referee, National Railroad Adjustment Board 1953; Dir. Bank of North Shore

1976—; Member Bd. Dirs. Sierra Club Legal Defense Fund. *Member:* Chicago, Illinois, and American Bar Associations; American Arbitration Association. Democrat. *Clubs:* University, City (Chicago); Skokie Country; Cliff Dwellers. *Address: office* 11 South LaSalle Street, Chicago 3, Ill., U.S.A.

**DRALANS, Arthur Ernest August.** Belgian banker and professor. *B.* 1908. *Educ.* Master, Economic and Consular Sciences; Reserve Lieut.-Colonel; FIBA. *M.* 1940, Augusta-Francine Rossien. *S.* Emmanuël, Erik, Fërederik and Patrick. *Daus.* Beatrix, Denise, Daniëlla, Patricia and Eveline. *Career:* Head of Market Research, Union Chimique Belge 1945–52; Professor at Institut Supërieur de Commerce de l'Etat, Antwerp 1947–55; Manager of Congo Branch, Banque de Paris et des Pays-Bas, Léopoldville 1955–60. Managing Director, Banque de Paris et des Pays-Bas (Zaire) 1960; First Dir., Banque de Paris et des Pays-Bas, Antwerp 1961; Professor, Antwerp State Univ. 1969; Chmn. Société de Développement Hôtelier et de Gestion 1970; Consul of Guatemala 1971; Vice-Pres., French Chamber of Commerce & Industry, Antwerp 1972; Vice-Pres., Belgian Section, Society for International Development; Member of the Board of Belgian & Zairese companies. *Awards:* Commander, Order of Leopold II; Officer, Order of Leopold; Order of the Crown; Order of the White Rose of Finland; Knight, Ordre Française du Mérite. *Publications:* Étude des marchés d'exportation; Commodity Price Forecasting; La Banque en Chine; Le Financement de la Construction d'Habitations Sociales; Economic & Financial Planning in Developing Countries; China Vandaag. *Clubs:* Mars & Mercury (Past Pres.); American-Belgian Assn. (Past Pres. & Gov.); Antwerp; Cercle Royal de Kinshasa; Cercle Royal 'La Concorde'; Orde van de Prince. *Address:* Banque de Paris et des Pays-Bas (Belgique), B-2000 Antwerp, Belgium.

**DRAYSON, George Burnaby,** TD, MP. British politician. *B.* 1913. *Educ.* Preparatory and Secondary. *M.* (1) 1939, Winifred Heath. *Dau.* 1. 2) 1962, Barbara Maria Teresa Radonska Chrzanowska. *Dau.* Celia Dingle. *Career:* London Stock Exchange; Officer, Territorial Army 1931, Captain 1938; Member London Stock Exchange 1935–54; War Service 1939–45, P.O.W. 1942–43; Member of Parliament for Skipton, Yorkshire since 1945. *Club:* Royal Automobile. *Address:* Linton House, Linton-in-Craven, Skipton, North Yorkshire.

**DREES, Willem.** Dutch Minister of State. *B.* 1886. *Educ.* High School of Commerce, Amsterdam (Dr Oec hc, Rotterdam; Dr of Laws hc, Univ. of Maryland). *M.* 1910, Catharina Hent (dec'd). *S.* Johannes Michiel, Willem. *Dau.* Anna Sophia. *Career:* Chmn. The Hague Section, Dutch Socialist Labour Party 1911–31; member, Municipal Council 1913–41; Alderman 1919–33; member, Provincial Council, Southern Holland 1919–41; member and later Vice-Pres. National Exec. Committee, Labour Party 1927–45; Vice-Pres., The Hague Tramway Co., 1927–42; member Second Chamber, States-General 1933–40; Chmn. Socialist Group in Parliament 1939–40; during the occupation imprisoned in Buchenwald Oct. 1940 till Oct. 1941, and as a hostage in St. Michiels-Gestel 1942; Chmn. of an illegal committee of the political parties and of the Central Cttee. of the Resistance Movement; member of Secret Cttee. representing the Netherlands Government in London; Minister of Social Affairs 1945–48; introduced Old Age Pension Act 1947; Prime Minister of Netherlands 1948–58; Minister of State 1958. *Awards:* Grand Cross of Adolf van Nassau (Luxembourg) Dannebrog (Denmark), Crown of Oak (Luxembourg), George I (Greece), Holy Trinity (Ethiopia), Leopold (Belgium), Legion of Honour (France), Star of Africa (Liberia), St. Olav (Norway), Vasa (Sweden), White Elephant (Thailand); St. Michael & St. George (U.K.); Netherlands Lion. *Address:* Beeklaan 502, The Hague, Netherlands.

**DRESCHFIELD, Ralph Leonard Emmanuel,** CMG, QC. British Barrister-at-Law. Attorney General, Uganda 1951–62; Chairman of Trustees, Uganda National Park; 1952–62; Secretary, Community Council of Essex 1963–76; Parliamentary Counsel Law Reform Bermuda 1976—. *B.* 1911. *Educ.* Trinity Hall, Cambridge (BA Hons.). *Club:* Royal Ocean Racing. *Address:* c/o Attorney General's Chambers, Hamilton, Bermuda.

**DRIMMEL, Heinrich,** Dr jur. Austrian statesman. *B.* 1912. *Educ.* University of Vienna, Phil. and Jur. Faculty (Dr jur 1935). *M.* Theresia Hehra. *Dau.* Marialiese. *Career:* Official at the Ministry of Education, Vienna 1933–71 (Minister, 1954–64) with a break from 1938 to 1945; Federal 1964–69; Consultant at the Catholic Academy of Vienna. *Member:* numerous Austrian student and academy associations; Austrian People's Party (Christian Democratic). *Awards:* Gold Medal of the Austrian Academy of Sciences; Grand Gold Medal on Ribbon (Austria); Grand Cross of Alfonso the Wise (Spain); Grand Cross of the Service Order (Germany); Grand Cross of the Gregorius Order (Holy Site); Hon. LLD Georgetown Univ. and Catholic Univ. of America; Hon. Senator Univ. of Vienna and Univ. of Salzburg. *Publications:* in the fields of Education; Political Science; Sport. *Address:* Landstrasser Gürtel 3/16, A-1030 Vienna III, Austria.

**DRINKALL, John Kenneth.** CMG. British diplomat. *B.* 1922. *Educ.* Haileybury Coll; Brasenose Coll. Oxford University. *M.* 1961. Patricia Ellis. *S.* 2. *Daus.* 2. *Career:* entered H.M. Diplomatic Service 1947; Third Secy. British Embassy, Nanking China 1948; Vice Consul, Acting Consul, British Consulate Tamsui Formosa 1949–51; Second Secy. Far East Dept. Foreign Office 1951–53; First Secy. Cairo Egypt 1953–56; Western Dept. Foreign Office 1957–60, British Embassy, Brasilia, Brazil 1960–62; First Secy. Later Counsellor (1964) Information Research Dept. Foreign & Commonwealth Office 1962–65; Counsellor, British High Commission, Nicosia Cyprus, 1965–67; British Embassy Brussels 1967–70; Head, Western European Dept. Foreign & Commonwealth Office 1970–71; Canadian National Defence Coll. Kingston Ont. Canada 1971–72; Ambassador to Afghanistan 1972–76; High Commissioner in Jamaica & Ambassador (non-resident) to Haiti since 1976. *Award:* Companion, Order of St. Michae and St. George. *Clubs:* All England Lawn Tennis; Royal Automobile. *Address:* Bolham House, Tiverton, Devon and *office* c/o Foreign & Commonwealth Office, London, S.W.1.

**DRINKWATER, Terrell Croft.** American airline executive. *B.* 1908. *Educ.* University of Colorado (AB, LLB, LLM). *M.* 1933, Helen Louise Kiddoo. *S.* Terrell Thomas. *Dau.* Dorsey Ann. Executive Vice-President, Director, General Manager, Continental Air Lines, Inc. 1942–44; Vice-President, American Airlines, Inc. 1944–47; President, Director, Western Air Lines, Inc. since 1947. *Address:* 6060 Avion Drive, Los Angeles 9, California, U.S.A.

**DRISCOLL, Hugh McPherson.** President and Director, First National Bank of Blue Island; Director, Vice Chmn. Union National Bank of Chicago, Former Visiting Lecturer, School of Banking, Univ. of Southern Illinois. *B.* 1898. *Educ.* Princeton Univ. (BA). *M.* 1936, Margaret Burton. *S.* Hugh M., Jr. and David Burton. *Career:* Sub-accountant, National City Bank of N.Y. 1921–23; Assistant Cashier, Old National Bank of Grand Rapids, Michigan Jan.–Sept 1924; Assistant Cashier and Assistant Vice-Pres., Boulevard Bridge Bank of Chicago 1924–33; Asst. Vice-Pres., Vice-Pres., Exec. Vice-Pres. and Vice-Chmn. of Board, National Boulevard Bank of Chicago 1933–65; Vice-Pres., Exec. Vice-Pres. and Vice-Chmn. and Dir., Civic Center Bank & Trust Co., 1966–70. Author of various articles in financial publications. Former Pres. and Dir., Robert Morris Associates; Pres. and Director, Harris School of Chicago; Trustee and Vice-Pres., Chicago Wesley Memorial Hosp.; Trustee, Chicago Methodist Episcopal Church Aid Socy.; Treas. and Trustee, Northwestern Univ. McGaw Medical Center; Chmn. Board of Trustees, Chicago Temple; Chicago Community Fund (former Chmn., Group Work Reviewing Committee; former Co-Chmn., Federation Reviewing Committee). Dir. and Pres., Off-the-Street Club (Chicago). *Member:* Amer. Bankers Assn., Economic Club, and Newcomen Socy. Republican. *Clubs:* University, Yacht, Arts (Former Treas. and Dir.), Bankers (Chicago). *Address: office* First National Bank of Blue Island, 13057 Western Avenue, Blue Island, Illinois 60406, U.S.A.

**DRUCKER, Daniel Charles.** U.S.A. Professor of Engineering. *B.* 1918. *Educ.* Columbia University (BS 1937; CE 1938; PhD 1940). *M.* 1939, Ann Bodin. *S.* David. *Dau.* Mady. *Career:* Chmn. Div. of Engineering, Brown Univ. 1953–59; Technical Editor, Journal of Applied Mechanics 1956–68; Chairman, Physical Sciences Council, Brown Univ. 1961–63. Dean of the College of Engineering, University of Illinois, Urbana, Illinois 1968; Member U.S. National Committee for Theoretical and Applied Mechanics, Delegate to Gen. Assembly; Treas. Int. Union of Theoretical & Applied Mechanics; Member, Editorial Board, Quarterly of Applied Mathematics. *Member:* Amer. Socy. of Civil Engineers Fellow Past Pres. New England Council; Pres. 1973–74 Amer. Socy. Mech. Engineers; Society for Experimental Stress Analysis (member Exec. Cttee. 1957—; President 1960–61, Hon. Member); Amer. Inst. of Aero and Astro (Assoc. Fellow); Amer. Socy. for Engineering Education (First Vice-Pres., Chmn. Eng.

Col. Council); Nat. Socy. for Professional Engineers; Nat. Academy of Engineering; Socy. for Rheology; Amer. Assn. for Advancement of Science: Tau Beta Pi; Pi Tau Sigma; Sigma Xi; Phi Kappa Pi; Sigma Tau; Registered Professional Engineer. *Awards:* Fellow, Amer. Acad. of Arts and Sciences; American Academy of Mechanics; Guggenheim Fellow 1960–61; Illig Medal, Columbia Univ. Marburg Lecturer A.S.T.M. 1966; Karman Medal A.S.C.E. 1966; Lamme Award A.S.E.E. 1967; Murray Lecture S.E.S.A.; SESA.MM Frocht Award 1971; NATO Senior Science Fellow & Fullbright Travel Grantee, 1968. *Publications:* over 130 works. *Club:* Cosmos (Washington D.C.). *Address:* 106 Engineering Hall, Univ. of Illinois, Urbana, Ill., U.S.A.

**DRUMALBYN, Rt. Hon. Lord** (Niall Malcolm Stewart Macpherson), PC, KBE. *B.* 1908. *Educ.* Fettes and Trinity College, Oxford (MA). *M.* 1937, Margaret Phyllis Runge. *Daus.* 3 (1 *Dec.*). *Career:* With Reckitt & Colman Ltd. 1931–39; Served in Army 1939–45 (Major). MP 1945–63. Joint Under-Secy. of State, Scottish Office, 1955–60; Parliamentary Secy., Board of Trade 1960–62; Minister of Pensions and National Insurance 1962–63; Minister of State, Board of Trade 1963–64; Chmn. Advertising Standards Authority 1965–70 and 1974–77; Minister Without Portfolio 1970–74. *Address:* House of Lords, London, S.W.1.

**DRURY, Hon. Charles Mills**, PC, CBE, DSO, QC, MP. *B.* 1912. *Educ.* Bishop's Coll. (Lennoxville, Que.), Royal Military Coll. (Kingston, Ont.), McGill Univ. and Univ. of Paris. *M.* Jane Ferrier Counsell. *Children* 4. *Career:* Brig.-Gen., World War II; Chief of UNRRA Mission to Warsaw 1945–47; Economic Div., Ministry to External Affairs 1947–49; Dep. Minister, Dept. of National Defence 1949–55; Dir., Avis Transport of Canada, Western International, Thermal Powers Ltd.; Member, House of Commons 1962—. Minister of Defence Production, Canada, Apr. 1963–68, and Minister of Industry, July 1963–68; Pres. of the Treasury Board 1968–74; Minister of Public Works & Minister of Science & Technology 1974–76. Formerly: President: U.N. Association in Canada; Canadian Centenary Council. Chairman: Montreal. Branch, Canadian Inst. of International Affairs, Pres. Montreal Board of Trade 1961–62. Member, Northwest Territories Council. *Address:* House of Commons, Ottawa, Ont., Canada.

**DRURY, Edward Nigel**, CBE. Australian. *B.* 1911. *Educ.* Brisbane Grammar School; FASA; ACIS. *M.* 1949, Valerie B. K. Thomas. *S.* 2. *Career:* Joined Staff of Queensland Trustees Ltd., 1927, and resigned from a senior position on entering politics, 1949. Enlisted as Gunner 1940; served with Australian Army in New Guinea and elsewhere in S.W. Pacific Area; discharged with rank of Major 1946. Member, Liberal Party of Australia (Chmn. of Toowong Branch, 1948–49). Member, Ryan Division, House of Representatives, Canberra, A.C.T., 1949–75 (Deputy Chairman of Committees, 1962–75); Member Printing Cttee. 1954–58; Member, Committee of Privileges since 1958; Chairman 1959–72; and Member Standing Orders Committee, 1959–72 & since 1974; Exec. member Inter-Parly. Union Aust. Branch 1959–70; Hon. Auditor 1959–75; Member Joint Select Committee of the New and Permanent Parliament House, 1965–70; Member Library Committee 1968–69; Chairman, Commonwealth Immigration Planning Council, 1962–67; Member, Joint House Cttee. 1969–72; Joint Statutory Cttee. on Broadcasting of Parliamentary Proceedings 1969–72; Exec. Member, Commonwealth Parliamentary Assoc. Aust. Branch 1970–75. *Clubs:* Queensland. *Address:* 49 Quinn Street, Toowong, Brisbane, Qld., Australia.

**DRUTO, Jan.** Polish Diplomat, *B.* 1909. *Educ.* Higher Education (Engineer). *M.* 1939, Gertrude Sawicka. *S.* 1. *Dau.* 1. *Career:* Commander, Order of Polonia Restituta. Previously research worker; Vice-Pres., Central Planning Office, Warsaw; Director, Economic Department, Ministry of Agriculture, Warsaw; Ambassador to Turkey 1948–51, to Italy 1951–59; Head of Dept., Min. of Foreign Affairs 1959–61; Amb. to France 1961–69; Head of Dept. for Cultural & Scientific Cooperation, Min. of Foreign Affairs 1969–72; Adviser to Minister of Foreign Affairs 1973—. *Member:* Polish United Workers Party. *Address:* Ministry of Foreign Affairs, Warsaw, Poland.

**DRYNAN, William Innes.** Canadian. Dir. (1943—) Canadian Canners Ltd. (fruits and vegetables), Hamilton, Ont. Dir., Aged Women's Home, Hamilton. *B.* 1900. *Educ.* Grad. Royal Military College of Canada, Kingston, Ont., and Osgoode Hall, Toronto. *M.* 1928, Mary Katharine Kirk. *S.* William Innes Kirk and George Sydney. *Dau.* Alice Mary. *Career:* Canadian Army attached to the British Imperial Army, India—5th (Royal Irish) Lancers and 18th (Queen Mary's Own) Hussars 1920–22; Royal Hamilton Light Infantry (War Reserve) Wentworth Regiment, Canadian Militia 1940–52 (Lieut-Col. last two years). Member, Hamilton and District Officers Inst. Vice-Chmn. 1965–68, Canadian Canners Ltd. (fruits & vegetables); member of Hamilton Advisory Board of the Royal Trust Co.; Hamilton Chamber of Commerce. *Clubs:* Hamilton; Albany (Toronto); Hamilton Golf and Country (Ancaster, Ont.); Tamahaac (Ancaster). *Address:* P.O. Box 214, 171 Lover's Lane, Ancaster, Ont., Canada.

**DRYON, Jacques Max.** Belgian. *B.* 1923. *Educ.* State Univ., Liége (Faculty of Applied Science). *M.* 1948, Genevieve R. Parein. *S.* 3. *Dau.* 1. *Career:* Dir. & Gen. Mgr. Heuze Malevez Simon; Dir. Soc. Financiere Industrielle et Coloniale, Fidelitas Insurance, Production Mgr., Sodemeca; Local Adviser Societe Generale de Banque; Chmn. S.A. Abrastone; Dir. Graphing. Antwerpse Bottle My; Devibel S.A., SA Fidacor. 1960–64. *Clubs:* Rotary, Auvelais-Bassesambre; Golf, D'Ardennes; Mem. Inst. Belge des Mecaniciens; Inst. Belge de la Soudure. *Address:* Rue Charles Heuze 51, Auvelais, Belgium; and *office* Auvelais, Belgium; & Quai des Vennes 1, 4020 Liége, Belgium.

**DU BOIS, J. Harry.** American plastics consultant. *B.* 1903. *Educ.* Univ. of Minnesota (BS). *M.* 1933, Kathryn E. Peterson. *S.* John Harry. *Dau.* Helen E. *Career:* Plastics Engineer, General Electric Co. 1928–36; Tool Engineer, The Gorham Co. 1937; Commercial Engineer, G.E.C. 1938–44; Executive Engineer, Shaw Insulator Co. 1944–50 (Vice-Pres. 1949–50); Manager, New Product Development & Sales Manager, Plax Corp. 1950–51; Vice-Pres., Engineering, Mycalex Corp. of American 1952–58. President: J. Harry Du Bois Co. 1958—, and Mykroy Ceramics Corp.; Director, Egan Machinery Co.; Delia Assoc.; Pavia Farny Co.; Arlington Ind. Inc. *Publications:* Plastics (five editions; Reinhold Pub. Co. (N.Y.); Plastics History U.S.A.; Co-author, Plastics Mold Engineering (2nd edn. Reinhold Publishing Co.); contributing author (with H. M. Richardson and V. W. Wilson), Fundamentals of Plastics (McGraw Hill Book Co., N.Y.); author-editor, motion picture film, Origin and Syntheses of Plastics Materials (U.S. Government of Education); author, Transfer Molding, Glass Bonded Mica (Modern Plastics Encyclopaedia); on editorial advisory board: A Manual of Plastics and Resins (Chemical Publishing Co. Inc., Brooklyn, N.Y.); The Expanding Polymer Horizon (S.A.E., June 1959); New Materials Survey (Modern Plastics, Dec. 1958). *Member:* Society of Plastics Engineers (Distinguished Member; National Pres. 1947); Society of the Plastic Industry; Plastic Pioneers; Plastics Institute (Great Britain); Eta Kappa Nu (Hon. Elect. Eng.). Recipient 1966 S.P.E. International Award in Plastics Science and Engineering; Charter Election to Plastics Hall of Fame 1973. *Address:* P.O. Box 346, Morris Plains, N.J. 07950, U.S.A.

**du BREIL, C. Alain V.**, BA, PhD. French. *B.* 1919. *Educ.* Univ. of Paris (BA); Law Univ. of Paris (PhD). *M.* 1950, Genevive Cambon. *S.* 2. *Dau.* 1. *Career:* Dir. Gen., Squibb Europe; Dir. E. R. Squibb & Sons Ltd., Squibb SpA, Squibb S.A., E. R. Squibb & Sons Ilaçlar A.S., Chem. Fabrik von Heyden AG. Laboratories Squibb, Squibb-Sogefar; formerly Vice-Pres. American Saint Gobain; Pres. Mondial United Corpn., 1953–61. *Clubs:* Nouveau Cercle, Paris. *Address:* *office* 17 Ave. Matignon, Paris 8, France.

**DUBS, LeRoy Cletus.** U.S.A. Company Chairman and Consultant. *Educ.* Ohio State Univ. (BS Industrial Management, 1931). *M.* 1936, Evelyn M. Richard, *S.* Robert Theodore and Richard. *Daus.* Elinor, Marie and Anne. *Career:* President: Stoker Manufacturers Association 1953–58, and Catholic Community League 1952–57; Director, Catholic Youth Council 1957–61; Chairman, Board of Advisers, Notre Dame Educational Center 1960–61; Service Director, Canton, Ohio 1964—; Pres. Canton Stoker Corp. and the Canton Pattern and Foundry Co; Director: Junior Achievement of Stork County Policy Cttee.; Muskingham Valley Water Quality Conference; Chmn. Solid Waste Disposal Cttee., Water and Sanitation Group; Canton Chamber of Commerce. Consult. to Structures Engineering. *Publications:* Technical Manual for Stokers, sponsored by Stoker Manufacturers Association and Air Pollution Control Association (co-author); Sewer Use Code (co-author) for City of Canton; Solid Waste Management Study (co-author) for Greater Canton area; Article on City Service Centers, American City Magazine, 1970; various articles in heating and power publications. *Member:* Air Polution Control Assn.; Stoker Manufacturers' Assn.; Chamber of Commerce; National Labor-

Managment Assn.; Incinerator Cttee., A.S.M.E.; Beta Gamma Sigma; Phi Kappa Theta; American Public Works Assn.; Board of Control, City of Canton; City Planning Commn., Canton, Ohio; Ohio Municipal League; Advisory Bd. American Security Council. Independent. *Clubs:* Canton, Rotary, Knights of Columbus, Catholic Men's Luncheon (Pres. 1947), Sales Executives (National). *Award:* Outstanding Merit from Junior achievement of Stork County. *Address:* 4623 Woodside Ave., N.W. Canton, Ohio 44709; and *office* City Hall, Canton, Ohio 44702, U.S.A.

**DU CANN, Col. Rt. Hon. Edward Dillon Lott,** MP, British Politician. *B.* 1924. *Educ.* Colet Court, Woodbridge School and St. John's College, Oxford (MA Law). *M.* 1962, Sallie Innes Murchie. *S.* 1. *Daus.* 2, *Career:* Chairman Association of Unit Trust Managers 1961; Joint Hon. Secretary U.N. Parliamentary Group 1961–62; Conservative Party. Finance Group 1961–62; Member, Select Cttee. on House of Lords Reform 1962; Economic Secy. to the Treasury 1962–63; Min. of State, Bd. of Trade 1963–64; Privy Councillor 1964; Chmn. Conservative Party Organization 1965–67; Chmn. Cannon Assurance Ltd. since 1972. Hon. Colonel 155 Regt. RCT. Wessex Volunteers. Member Lord Chancellor's Advisory Cttee. on Public Records 1960–62; Commodore, House of Commons Yacht Club 1962, Admiral since 1974; B.B.C. Advisory Council 1968. Chmn. Burke Club 1968—; Deputy-Chmn. Wider Share Ownership Cttee. 1970—; Family Planning International Campaign 1971—; First Chmn. Select Cttee. Public Expenditure 1971–73, mem. Public Acts. Cttee and Chmn. since 1974; Chmn. 1922 Cttee. since 1972. Founder of the Unicorn Group of Unit Trusts & creator of Equity-Limited life assurance contracts. *Publications:* Investing Simplified, (1959); articles on financial and international affairs, incl. The Control of Public Expenditure (1977). Director, Bow Group Publications Ltd. Elected first Freeman of Taunton Deane, 1977. *Clubs:* Pratt's (London); Carlton (London); Somerset County (Taunton); Royal Thames Yacht. *Address:* Cothay Barton, Greenham, Wellington, Somerset.

**DUCCI, Roberto.** Italian Diplomat. *B.* 1914. *Educ.* Rome Univ.—LLD. *M.* 1951, Wanda Alexandrovna Matyjewicz. *S.* 2. *Career:* Entered Italian Foreign Services 1937; Consul in Canada & U.S.A. 1938–41; Mem., Italian Delegation to Peace Conference 1946; First Sec., Warsaw, Rio 1947–50; Counsellor, Italian Delegation to NATO & OEEC 1950–55; Mem., Italian Delegation to Common Market Conference 1955–57; Chmn. Drafting Cttee., Rome Treaties 1956–57; Ambassador to Finland 1958–61; Chmn., Italian Delegation to EEC–UK Conference 1962–63; Dep. Dir.-Gen. for Political Affairs 1963–64; Amb. to Yugoslavia 1964–67; Amb. to Austria 1967–70; Dir.-Gen. for Political Affairs 1970–75; Amb. to the Court of St. James's since 1975; mem., Bd. European Investment Bank 1958–68. *Decorations:* Knight Grand Cross, Italian Order of Merit; Knight Grand Cross of the Orders of Finland, Yugoslavia, Austria, Ethiopia, Oman, etc.; Officer of the Légion d'Honneur, etc. *Publications:* Prima Età di Napoleone (1933); Questa Italia (1948); L'Europa Incompiuta (1971); D'Annunzio Vivente (1973); I Contemporanei (1976). *Clubs:* Circolo della Caccia (Rome); Reform, Garrick (London). *Address:* 4 Grosvenor Square, London W.1; and *office* 14 Three Kings' Yard, London W.1.

**DUCHEMIN, Jacques-Louis.** French company director. Special adviser on copyright. General Secretary, Société de la Propriété Artistique, des Dessins et Modèles (SPADEM); Arbitrator at the Tribunal de Commerce. Member (since 1925) of all committees, national and international congresses and diplomatic conferences concerned with copyright; member, Commission on Intellectual Copyright, Ministry of Education, and of the Higher Council of Industrial Rights, Ministry of Industry; member UNESCO Commission. *B.* 1895. *Educ.* School of Political Sciences (Lic. en Droit). *M.* 1922, Melle S. Huré, and (2) 1939, Mme N. Koucheleff. *S.* 1. *Daus.* 3. *Awards:* Chevalier, Legion of Honour (France); Croix de Guerre (1914–18); Chevalier, Crown of Belgium; various civil and military distinctions. *Address:* 12 rue Henner, Paris 9, France.

**DUCKMANTON, Talbot Sydney,** CBE. Australian broadcasting executive. *B.* 1921. *Career:* joined A.B.C. 1939; Aust-Imperial Force and RAAF 1939–45; Manager A.B.C. Tasmania 1953; Co-ordinator T.V. A.B.C. 1956; Controller, Admin. 1958, Asst. Gen. Mgr. (Admin.) 1959; Dep. Gen. Mgr. 1964, Gen. Manager 1965; Pres. Asian Broadcasting Union; Pres. Commonwealth Broadcasting Assn.; Trustee VISNEWS; Trustee, International Broadcast Inst.; Trustee Cttee. Economic Development, Mem. Council of Newington Coll. (Sydney) 1964—; Pres. Sydney Legacy 1964–65; Member Bd. of Austr. Film Develop. Corp. 1971–75. *Member:* Council Aust. Admin. Staff College. *Awards:* Commander, Order of the British Empire; Fellow Aust. Inst. Management. *Clubs:* Australian, Tattersall's. *Address:* Australian Broadcasting Commission, 145 Elizabeth Street, Sydney, N.S.W., Australia, 2000.

**DUCOMMUN, Charles Emil.** American. *B.* 1913. *Educ.* Harvard School, Los Angeles (Diploma), Stanford University (AB Econ 1935), and Harvard University (MBA *cum laude*, Business Administration 1942). *M.* 1949, Palmer Gross. *S.* Robert Constant. *Dau.* Electra Bradford. *Career:* With U.S. Navy: Lieutenant, USNR Aide to Chief to Staff, U.S. Fleet 1944–46; previously Ensign and Lieutenant (j.g.) 1942–44. Director 1938— and President 1950–73, Chmn. since 1973, Ducommun Inc.; Director 1938–69; and Vice-President 1947—, Ducommun Realty Co.; Pres. Ducommun Metals & Supply Co. 1950–65, Chmn. 1965–67; Dir. The Pacific Telephone and Telegraph Co. 1957—, and Security First National Bank since 1958; Security Pacific Corporation since 1973; Pacific Finance Corp. 1958–62; Security Pacific National Bank 1959; Investment Co. of America 1961—; Lockheed Aircraft Corp. 1961–71; Adv. Dir. Investment Co. of America 1961—; Dir. Kierulff Electronics Inc. 1961–70; Dillingham Corp. 1971–74; Trustee: Stanford Univ. 1961–71; Claremont Men's Coll. 1948—; and Cttee. for Economic Development 1958–76. *Member:* Los Angeles Area Chamber of Commerce: Director 1952–61; previously President 1957, Vice-President 1955, 1956, Treasurer 1958, Delegate to Japan-California Association since 1965; Dir. California Chamber of Commerce; Chairman Federal Affairs Cttee. 1952–56; Delegate Republican National Convention 1960 and 1968. *Member:* Central City Cttee. (Los Angeles); Los Angeles County Art Museum Associates, Trustee, Treas. and Vice-Pres. Visiting Cttee. Harvard Univ. Graduate School of Business Admin. 1962–68 & 1969–75; Fund Council 1956–57; Los Angeles Civic Light Opera Assn. (Pres. 1957–60). Republican. *Clubs:* California (Dir. and Treas. 1952–54); Los Angeles Country; Bohemian. *Address:* 237 Strada Corta, Los Angeles, Calif. 90024; and *office* 612 South Flower Street, Suite 460, Los Angeles, Calif. 90017 U.S.A.

**DUDDING, Sir John (Scarbrough).** British company director. *B.* 1915. *Educ.* Cheltenham College and Jesus College, Cambridge (BA Hons.). *M.* 1945, Enid Grace Gardner. *S.* Richard Scarbrough. *Dau.* Anne Rosamund. *Career:* Entered Administrative Service, Nigeria 1938. War service with Nigeria Regt. of R.W.A.F.F. 1940–45 (served Nigeria, India and Burma); Deputy Commissioner of Cameroons 1956–59; Permanent Secretary of Nigerian Federal Ministries of Works and Survey, Transport and Aviation, and Communications 1959–63; retired from the Service 1964. Chmn. Humberside Area Health Authority. *Fellow:* Royal Commonwealth Socy.; Royal Society of Arts. Deputy Lieutenant. *Address:* Scarbrough House, Winteringham, Scunthorpe, Lincs.

**DUDLEY, John Henry.** Business Executive. *B.* 1912. *Educ.* Michigan State Univ. (BA). *M.* 1940, Elizabeth Baird Dean. *S.* John Henry, Jr., and Thomas Dean. *Career:* With John Henry Co. since 1937; Chmn. Michigan United Fund; Vice-Pres. and Mem. Exec. Cttee., Past Pres. & Campaign, United Community Chest; Chmn. Project-HOPE; Past Area Chmn., United Negro Coll. Fdn.; Rehabilitation Centre; Past Chmn. Y.M.C.A. & Y.W.C.A.; Chmn. Special Study & Adv. Cttee. Y.M.C.A (Advisory Bd.).Amer. Cancer Socy., Ingham County Unit. Mem. State Bd., Michigan Cancer Socy.; Past Pres., Socy. of Amer. Florists; Past Chmn.: Natl. Advertising Cncl., Natl. Education Cttee.; Founder & Co-Chmn., All Florist Industry Congress; Past Bd. Mem., Florists Transworld Delivery Assn.; Past Pres., Michigan State Florist Assn.; Dir., Treasurer, Wholesale Florists and Florist Supplies of Amer.; Trustee, Secy. and Treas., Socy. of Amer. Florists Endowment; Member: United States, Michigan and Lansing Chambers of Commerce, Rotary International. Member Michigan Governors Special Cttee. on Traffic Safety. Served USNR 1942–45, Lieutenant to Lt. Commander. *Awards:* Navy Marine Medal, Navy Bronze Star, two battle stars, Unit citations; Colonel, Hon. Order Kentucky Colonels. Award; Florist Transworld Delivery Assn. Natl. Award: Michigan State Florist Assn. Natl. Award and State Award. *Clubs:* Lansing Country (Past Pres.); City of Lansing (Past Pres.); Lansing Automobile; Chicago Athletic; Detroit, Detroit Athletic; Detroit Economic; Marco Polo, N.Y.; Los Angeles Country, Los Angeles. *Address: office* P.O. Box 1410, Lansing, Mich., 48904, U.S.A.

**DUDLEY, Lindsay Robert.** Australian. *B.* 1921. *Educ.* Creswick School of Forestry (Dipl. Forestry), and Melbourne Univ. (BCom; LLB). *M.* 1956, Valda Adam. Forester: Victorian Forests Commission (1941–46) and Australian Newsprint Mills Ltd. 1947–49; Exec., Secretariat Pty. Ltd. 1950–56. Executive Dir., Master Builders' Federation 1957–68. Barrister-Solicitor, Supreme Court of Victoria. Member, Australian Tariff Board 1969–74; Consultant, Dept. of Administrative Services since 1974. *Clubs:* Athenaeum (Melbourne); Royal Canberra Golf; Commonwealth (Canberra). *Address:* 26 Quiros St., Red Hill, A.C.T. 2603; and *office* Dept. of Administrative Services, East Block, Canberra, A.C.T. 2600, Australia.

**DUFF, Sir (Arthur) Antony,** KCMG, CVO, DSO, DSC. British diplomat. *B.* 1920. *Educ.* R.N.C. Dartmouth. *M.* 1944, Pauline Marion Bevan. *Career:* Royal Navy 1937–46; Foreign later Diplomatic Service since 1946; Deputy High Comm. Kuala Lumpur 1969–72; High Commissioner, Nairobi 1972–75; Deputy Under-Secy. FCO since 1975. *Address:* Foreign & Commonwealth Office, London, S.W.1.

**DUFF, Donald James,** FRSA. Canadian. *B.* 1926. *Educ.* Univ. of Alberta (BEd 1949) and Columbia Univ. (MSc 1950). *M.* 1948, Beth Elinor Edwards. *S.* James Connor and Donald Jonathan. *Dau.* Julie Anita. *Career:* On editorial Staff, Southam Newspapers of Canada 1945–50; Director of Public Relations, British Columbia Health Centre 1951–54; Vice-Pres., G. A. Brakeley & Co. Ltd. 1954–61. President: Duff, Abbott & Associates Ltd., and Oceanways Ltd. *Member:* Canadian Public Relations Society. *Clubs:* Halifax; Halifax Golf & Country; Royal Nova Scotia Yacht Sqdn. 1 Montreal A.A.A.; Hudson Yacht; Whitlock Golf & Country; Arts and Letters, Toronto. *Address: office* 1400 Toronto-Dominion Centre, Toronto, Canada.

**DUFFUS, Sir Herbert George Holwell.** *B.* 1908. *Educ.* Cornwall College, Jamaica (Solicitor 1930; Barrister-at-Law, Lincolns Inn, 1956). *M.* 1939, Elsie Mary Hollinsed. *Career:* Posts in Jamaica: Resident Magistrate 1946; Puisne Judge 1958; Judge of Appeal 1962. President, Court of Appeal for Jamaica 1964; Chairman, Police Service Commission for Jamaica, Mar. 1958–Aug. 1968. Editor, Jamaica Law Reports, 1958–60; Joint Editor, West Indian Law Reports, 1959–61. British and Jamaican. Chief Justice of Jamaica, 1968–73; Acting Gov. General of Jamaica 1973. Knighted 1966. *Address:* Braywick Road, P.O. Box 243, Kingston, 6, Jamaica.

**DUFLOS, Jean-François Louis.** Ambassador of France (ret'd). *B.* 1908. *Educ.* Inst. of Sacred-Heart (Moulins), Law Faculty (Paris), Harvard Univ. Graduate: School of Political Science, and Higher Studies of Public Law and Political Economics. *M.* 1952, Janine Kleindienst. *S.* 3. *Dau.* 1. *Career:* Asst. Gen. Secy., Economic Commission for the Danube, 1937; Asst. Dir., Dept. of North America, French Ministry of Foreign Affairs, 1946; Counsellor of Embassy, Stockholm 1948; Consul-General, Düsseldorf, 1955–59; Head, Diplomatic Section, National Defence Inst. of Higher Studies, 1962–66; Ambassador of France to New Zealand 1966–70; Central Administration, Ministry of Foreign Affairs, Paris, since 1970. *Awards:* Officer Legion of Honour; Croix de Guerre (1939–45), and Médaille des Evadés. *Address:* 14 rue Greuze, Paris 16e, France.

**DUFOURNIER, Bernard.** French diplomat. *B.* 1911. *Educ.* Sorbonne and School of Political Sciences (Dipl.). Ambassador to Pakistan 1957–60; to Chile 1960–63, to Libya 1963–66 to Finland 1966–69 to Lebanon 1969–72 to Switzerland 1972–75. *Address:* Ministère des Affaires Etrangéres, 37 Quai d'Orsay, Paris, France.

**DUGGAN, Patrick Aloysius.** Irish. Partner, Patrick A. Duggan & Co., Chartered Accountants, Dublin. Director: National Bank of Ireland Ltd., Hibernian Insurance Co. Ltd., Odeon (Ireland) Ltd., Bank of Ireland Irish Cinemas Ltd., and Hospitals' Trust (1940) Ltd. *B.* 1909. *M.* 1936, Carmel Conolly. *S.* 1. *Daus.* 2. *Fellow:* Inst. of Chartered Accountants in Ireland. *Clubs:* St. Stephen's Green (Dublin); Royal Irish Yacht. *Address:* Walford, 24 Shrewsbury Road, Dublin; and *office* 28–30 Exchequer Street, Dublin, Ireland.

**DUHAMEL, Jean.** French diplomat. *Educ.* Univ. of Paris (Lic.-ès-Lettres; Lic.-en-D.). *M.* 1946, Esmeralda Lupesco. *Career:* Member of Paris and English (Gray's Inn) Bars. Private Sec., to French High Commissioner in London 1918–19. One of Counsel to the French Embassy in London 1928–34. Minister Plen. of the Principality of Monaco to France and Belgium 1956–60. *Publications:* (among others) Louis-Philippe et la Première Entente Cordiale (Couronné par l'Académie Française; pub. Sirey, Paris); De quelques Piliers des Institutions Britanniques (Sirey; translated into English (Pitman)); La Captivité de François 1er et des Dauphins; Un amour de Lady Hester Stanhope (Hachette); Les Cinquante Jours (Plon); many articles in periodicals and the press. *Awards:* Commander, Legion of Honour; Croix de Guerre (1914–18); Military Cross; Medal of American Legion; Grand Cross, Leopold II. *Club:* Union Interalliée. *Address:* 8 bis rue Margueritte, Paris 17, France.

**DUHAMEL, Roger.** Canadian diplomat. *B.* 1916. *Educ.* BA (1935), LL.L (1938), Dr. (Letters, 1960). *M.* 1941, Elaine Belanger. *S.* 2. *Daus.* 2. *Career:* Private Secy. to Mayor of Montreal 1938–40; Asst. Editor-in-Chief (dailies) Le Canada, 1938–40, Le Devoir, 1942–44, La Patrie, 1944–47; Editor-in-Chief (dailies) Montreal-Matin, 1947–52, La Patrie, 1952–58; Vice-Chmn. Bureau Broadcast Governors 1958–60; Queen's Printer 1960–69; Diplomat (Ottawa, New York etc.) 1969–72; Canadian Ambassador in Portugal 1972–77. *Member:* Royal Society of Canada; French Canadian Academy, Canadian Inst. of Inter. Affairs; *Governor:* Ottawa University 1965–72. *President* (former): of Canadian Writers' Assoc. *Award:* Duvernay Prize for Lietrary Achievements. *Decoration:* Comm. de l'ordre Academique de la lique Universelle de Bien Public. *Publications:* Les Cinqs Grands; Les Moralistes Francais; Litterature; Bilan Provisoire; Lettres A Une Provinciale; Aux Sources du Romantisme Francais; Lecture de Montaigne; Le Roman des Bonaparte. *Clubs:* Rideau Club (Ottawa); Gremio Literario (Lisbon); British Club (Lisbon); Univ. Club (Ottawa). *Address:* c/o Ministry of External Affairs, Ottawa, Ont., Canada.

**DUKE, Sir Charles Beresford,** KCMG, CIE, OBE. British diplomat. *B.* 1905. *Educ.* Charterhouse and Oxford Univ. (BA). *M.* 1938, Morag Craigie Grant. *Daus.* Elizabeth Ann Millicent, Sarah Chichele Assheton. *Career:* with Indian Civil Service, 1929–47, and British Foreign Service 1947–61. Amb. Ex. and Plen. to Jordan 1954–56; to Morocco 1957–61. Director-General, Middle East Assn., London, Nov. 1964–70. *Address:* 15 Westgate Terrace, London, S.W.10; & Cadenham Grange, Cadnam, nr. Southampton, Hants.; and *office* 71 Oxford Street, London, W.1.

**DUMONT, Camille.** Luxembourg diplomat. *B.* 1918. *Educ:* Doctor at Law. *Career:* Ministry of Economic Affairs 1947–49; For. Ministry 1949–51; Secy. to the Luxembourg Legation in London 1951; Mem. of Delegation to Gen. Assembly of UN 1952–53; Counsellor to Luxembourg Embassy in London 1956–58; European Economic Community 1958–60; Ambassador in the USSR 1960–63; Ambassador in Belgium 1963–68; Secy.-Gen. of Foreign Ministry 1968–71; Luxembourg Ambassador in France since 1971. *Address:* 8 Avenue Deschanel, Paris 75007; and *office* 33 Avenue Rapp, Paris 75007, France.

**du MONT, John Sanderson.** American. *B.* 1919. *Educ.* Deerfield Acad. and The Salisbury School. *M.* 1941, Mary Esther Robinson. *Daus.* Susanne Waller (Alexander), Mary Taliaferro (Nelson), and Ann Washburn. *Career:* Asst. Production Mgr., Millers Falls Co. 1939–43; served in 81st Infantry Div., Army of the U.S. 1943–46 (Bronze Star Medal). Vice-President and Director, The du Mont Corp., Greenfield, Mass. 1947–76 (Ret'd.). Presidents' (U.S.) E. Award 1966 (for excellence in exporting). Presidents E Star Award, 1969. Expansion Council by U.S. Sect. of Commerce, 1969. Kt. Comdr. O.St.J. Fellow, Company of Military Historians, 1957. *Member:* Order of Founders & Patriots; Socy. of Colonial Wars; Sons of Amer. Revolution; Mayflower Socy.; Pres. New York Socy. of the Cincinnati, Asst. Sec.-Gen. & mem. of The Standing Committee, 1971. Sons of Confederate Veterans, Pres. Greenfield Library Assn. 1953–74; Member, Exec. Cttee. Custer Battlefield National Monument Assoc.; Socy. of War of 1812; Trustee, P.V.M. Assn.; Vice-Chmn. Mass Ruffed Grouse Society; Order of the Stars and Bars; Trustee Wildlife Conservation Trust; Republican. *Publications:* Firearms in the Custer Battle, (1953); du Mont de Soumagne and Allied Families, (1961); Samuel Colt Presents, (1961); The Custer Battle Guns (1973). Contributor to various encyclopaedias, and magazines. *Address:* Brimstone Corner Road, Hancock, N.H. 03449, U.S.A.

**DUNCAN, John Spenser Ritchie.** CMG, MBE, British diplomat. *B.* 1921. *Educ.* George Watson's Boys Coll; Glasgow Acad; Dundee High School; Edinburgh University. *M.* 1950, Sheila Conacher. *Career:* entered Sudan Political Service

1941; Served in H.M. Forces 1941–43; Head, Personnel Dept. Diplomatic Service 1966–68; Minister, Canberra 1969–71; High Commissioner to Zambia 1971–74; Ambass. to Morocco since 1975. *Publications:* The Sudan: A Record of Achievement (1952); The Sudan's Path to Independence (1957). *Address:* British Embassy, Rabat, Morocco.

**DUNCAN-SANDYS, Rt. Hon. Lord Duncan Edwin.** Life Peer (cr. 1974) PC CH. British politician. *B.* 24 Jan. 1908. *Educ.* Eton; Magdalen College, Oxford (MA). *M.* (1) 1935, Diana (marriage dissolved 1960, *Dec.* 1963). *S.* 1. *Daus.* 2. *M.* (2) 1962, Marie-Claire, formerly Viscountess Hudson. *Dau.* 1. *Career:* Entered Diplomatic Service 1930, served at Foreign Office and British Embassy, Berlin; MP (Conservative) for Norwood (Lambeth) 1935–45, and Streatham 1950–74; Political Columist Sunday Chronicle 1937–39; Member Nat. Exec. Cons. Party 1938–39; served World War II with Expeditionary Force in Norway 1940–41 (disabled on active service 1941); Financial Secy., War Office 1941–43; Parliamentary Secretary to Ministry of Supply 1943–44; Chairman War Cabinet Committee for Defence against German 'V' weapons 1943–45; Minister of Works 1944–45; founded European Movement 1947 and was Chairman of International Executive until 1950; Member, General Advisory Council of B.B.C. 1947–51; Minister of Supply 1951–54; of Housing and Local Govt. 1954–57; of Defence 1957–59; Min. of Aviation 1959–60; Secy. of State Commonwealth Relations 1960–64; for the Colonies 1962–64; Member: Parliamentary Assembly, of Council of Europe & of Western European Union 1950–51 & since 1965 (Leader of British Delegation to both 1970–72); Pres. Civic Trust which he founded 1956; Chmn. Parly Council of European Movement 1950–51 and 1968–70; Pres. Europa Nostra since 1969; Chairman of Lonrho Ltd. since 1972; Jt. Chmn., Franco-British Council since 1972; Chairman of International Organising Cttee. for European Architectural Heritage Year 1975; Hon. Mem. Royal Town Planning Institute since 1956; Hon. Fellow RIBA since 1968; Grand Cross, Order of Merit, Italy 1960; Order of Sultanate of Brunei 1973; Medal of City of Paris 1974; Gold Cup of European Movement 1975; Goethe Gold Medal of FVS Foundation 1975; Grand Cross of Order of Crown of Belgium 1975. *Address:* 86 Vincent Square, London SW1P 2PG.

**DUNDAS SMITH, John Robert.** Australian executive, A Justice of the Peace. *B.* 1905. *Educ.* Sydney Grammar School. *M.* Frances Ethel Morgan. *S.* Robert John. *Daus.* Pamela Margaret and Jennifer Rosemary. *Career:* N.S.W. Honorary Consul for Chile in Sydney. Chairman of Directors: Dundas Smith & Son Pty. Ltd. and Associated Companies; Dundas Smith & Son (Textiles) Pty. Ltd.; A Hartrodt Pty. Ltd.; Chilean Nitrate Sales Corp. Pty. Ltd. Hon. Life member Aust. Red Cross. *Clubs:* Australian; Royal Orchid Society of N.S.W. (Foundation Member); Commander of the Order Merit (Chile). *Address:* 24 North Arm Road, Middle Cove, N.S.W. 2068; and *office* 7–9 York St., Sydney, N.S.W. 2000, Australia.

**DUNKELBERGER, Tobias Henry.** *B.* 1909. *Educ.* Dickinson Coll. (ScB 1930) and Univ. of Pittsburgh (PhD 1937). *M.* 1941, Esther Simons. *Daus.* 2. *Career:* Assistant Professor of Chemistry: N. Texas Agricultural Coll. 1936–37, Univ. of Idaho 1937–38, Duquesne Univ. 1938–41, and N.Y. State Coll. of Ceramics 1941–44; Prof. of Chemistry and Head, Chemical Dept., Duquesne Univ. 1944–52. Professor of Chemistry (1952—) and Administrative Officer (1952–63) of the Chemistry Department, Univ. of Pittsburgh; Univ. of Pittsburgh Faculties in Ecuador 1963–67; Asst. Section Editor, Chemical Abstracts 1962–63; Chief of Party Guatemala Project 1967–68. Associate Dean, Coll. of Arts and Sciences 1969–76 (ret'd., Prof. Emeritus). *Awards:* Pittsburgh section, Amer. Chemical Society 1970. *Publications:* (with C. J. Engelder and W. J. Schiller): Semi-Micro Qualitative Analysis (John Wiley & Sons), 1936, 1940; various papers on scientific subjects. *Member:* Phi Beta Kappa; Sigma Xi; Phi Lambda Upsilon; Keramos; Phi Eta Sigma; Alpha Epsilon Delta; Amer. Chemical Socy.; Amer. Assn. for Advancement of Science; Amer. Assn. of University Professors; Pennsylvania Acad. of Sciences; International Development Socy. *Club:* Pittsburgh Chemists. *Address:* 5132 Beller Street, Pittsburgh 15217, U.S.A.

**DUNKELMAN, Benjamin,** DSO. President, Carnel Investments Ltd. (operating Dunkelman Gallery). President and Director, Cloverdale Shopping Centre Ltd. *B.* 1913. *M.* 1948, Yael Lifshitz. *S.* David, Jonathan. *Daus.* Rose, Lorna, Deenah, Daphna. Served in World War II (DSO). *Member:* Canadian Military Inst.; Toronto Bd. of Trade. *Clubs:* Canadian; Alexandra Yacht. *Address:* 43 Prince Arthur Avenue, Toronto, Ont., Canada.

**DUNLOP, Robert Galbraith.** American company director. *B.* 1909. *Educ.* Elementary and High School; Collingswood, N.J.; Wharton School of Finance and Commerce; University of Pennsylvania. *M.* 1937, Emma L. Brownback. *S.* Richard G. *Dau.* Barbara E. Accountant, Barrow, Wade, Guthrie & Co. July 1931–33; Accountant, Sun Oil Company 1933–41, Assistant Comptroller 1941–44, Comptroller 1944–47. President 1947–69. Chairman Board, Sun Oil Co., 1970–74; Mem. Bd., Sun Co. Inc., & National Railroad Passenger Corp., Washington, D.C. *Address:* Sun Co. Inc., 100 Matsonford Road, Radnor, Pa. 19087, U.S.A.

**DUNLOP, Robert William Barr.** British company director. *B.* 1889. *Educ.* Merchiston Castle School, Edinburgh. *M.* 1931, Jean Mary Lorimer. *S.* 1. *Dau.* 1. *Career:* Joined Walter Duncan & Co., Glasgow 1908; assistant, Duncan Brothers & Co. Ltd., Calcutta 1912–28, Director 1928–39; Chairman, Indian Tea Association, Calcutta 1938, and London 1947, President 1953–54. Senior Partner, Walter Duncan & Co. 1949–51; Chairman, Walter Duncan & Goodricke Ltd. 1951–56. *Member:* Mercantile Bank Ltd. London Advisory Cttees.; Governor, Bd. Governors Sevenoaks School, Kent. *Clubs:* Oriental (London). Hon. Company, Edinburgh Golfers. *Address:* Toll Acre, Seal, near Sevenoaks, Kent.

**DUNN, Harry L.** American lawyer; Counsel, law firm of O'Melveny & Myers: Trustee, Claremont University Center. *B.* 1894. *Educ.* University of Calif. (AB), Columbia Law School, and Harvard Law School. *M.* (1) 1925, Louise Dodge Reding (*D.* 1952) and (2) 1955, Katharine Tilt McCay. *S.* (Dr.) Peter Reding. *Dau.* Priscilla Flynn. *Career:* Associate lawyer (with firm of Cravath, Henderson, Leffingwell & de Gersdorff, N.Y. City) 1921–24; Partner O'Melveny & Myers 1927–68; served with Commission for Relief in Belgium 1916–17; with American Field Service, France 1917; 1st Lt. 6th F.A., 1st div. A.E.F. 1917–19; with American Relief Administration in Poland 1919. *Member:* Low Angeles, Californian, and American Bar Associations; American Bar Foundation; Los Angeles World Affairs Council; Los Angeles Chamber of Commerce; Phil Delta Theta. *Clubs:* California; Annandale Golf; Valley Hunt; Twilight. *Address:* 1360 Hillcrest Avenue, Pasadena, Calif.; and *office* 611 West Sixth Street, Los Angeles, Calif. 90017, U.S.A., and 4 Place de la Concorde, Paris 8e, France; & 1800 M Street N.W., Washington, D.C. 20036, U.S.A.

**DUNN, Hugh Alexander.** Australian diplomat. *B.* 1923. *Educ:* Queensland Univ. BA; Oxford BA. *M.* 1968, Margaret Joan Anderson. *Dau.* 1. *Career:* Leader-writer Courier-Mail, Brisbane 1952–54; Lecturer in Chinese, Toronto Univ. Canada 1953–54; Dept. of For. Affairs (formerly external affairs) since 1954; Third Secy. Tokyo 1955–57; Australian Rep. on UNCURK (Korea) 1957–59; First Secy. Washington 1963–64; Indian National Defence College, New Delhi 1966; Counsellor Saigon 1967–68; Ambassador, Taipei 1969–72; Ambassador in Argentina and Uruguay since 1973, in Paraguay since 1974; in Peru 1973–74. *Member:* Australian Institute of International Affairs. *Publication:* Ts'ao Chih, The Life of a Royal Chinese Poet (1970). *Club:* Commonwealth (Canberra). *Address:* and *office* c/o Dept. of Foreign Affairs, Canberra, Australia; and (temporary) Australian Embassy, Buenos Aires, Argentina.

**DUNN, James Anthony,** KSG, MP, British statesman. *B.* 1926. *M.* 1954, Dorothy Larkey. *S.* 2. *Daus.* 2. *Career:* Member of Parliament for Kirkdale; Parly. Under-Sec. of State, Northern Ireland 1976. *Member:* Bd., British Inst. for the Achievement of Human Potential, Bridgwater, Somerset; World Org. of Insts. for the Achievement of Human Potential, Philadelphia, U.S.A.; International Playgrounds Association; Catholic Union, Gt. Britain; Pres. Merseyside Assn. for Brain-damaged children; Hon. LLD, Plano Univ., Texas 1976. *Address:* 45 Lisburn Lane, Tuebrook, Kirkdale, Liverpool L13 9AF; and *office* House of Commons, London SW1A 0AA.

**DUNNETT, Alastair MacTavish.** British. *B.* 1908. *Educ.* Hillhead High School, Glasgow. *M.* 1946, Dorothy Halliday. *S.* 2. *Career:* Commercial Bank of Scotland Ltd. 1925; Co-founder and Editor, The Claymore 1933; Acting Editor, Glasgow Weekly Herald, 1935; Art Editor, Daily Record, 1937; Chief Press Officer, Secretary of State for Scotland 1940; Editor, Daily Record 1946; Editor, The Scotsman Edinburgh 1956–72; Managing Dir. Scotsman Publications Ltd. 1962–70.

Chmn. Scotsman Publications Ltd., 1970–74; Mem. Exec. Board, Thomson Organization Ltd. 1974. Chmn. Thomson Scottish Petroleum Ltd. since 1972. Smith-Mundt Scholarship U.S.A. 1951. Council member Commonwealth Press Union; Gov. Pitlochry Theatre; member, Scottish Tourist Bd., 1956–69; Dir., Scottish Television Ltd. 1976. *Publications:* Quest by Canoe; Treasure at Sonnach; Heard Tell; Highlands and Islands of Scotland. *Plays:* The Original John MacKay (Glasgow Citizens' Theatre 1956), Fit to Print (Duke of York's, London, 1962). *Address:* 87 Colinton Road, Edinburgh.

**DUNNETT, Denzil Inglis,** OBE, CMG. British diplomat. *B.* 1917. *Educ.* Edinburgh Academy; Corpus Christi (Oxford). *M.* 1946, Ruth Rawcliffe (dec'd 1974). *S.* 2. *Dau.* 1. *Career:* Royal Artillery 1939–46; Editorial Staff, The Scotsman 1946–47; Foreign Office 1947–48; 1st Secy. HM Legation, Sofia 1948–50; Foreign Office (U.N. Dept.) 1950–53; UK Delegation to OEEC, Paris 1953–56; Commercial Secy. Buenos Aires 1956–60; H.M. Consul Elizabethville (now in Zaire); Commercial Counsellor, Madrid 1963–67; Seconded to Board of Trade 1967–70; Counsellor, Mexico City 1970–72; H.M. Ambassador Senegal, Mauritania, Mali, Guinea 1973–75; Diplomatic Service Chmn. of Selection Bd. at Civil Service Selection Bd. 1976—. *Decorations:* Order of the British Empire, Comdr. of St. Michael and St George. *Club:* Oxford and Cambridge University. *Address:* 11 Victoria Grove, London W8 5RW.

**DUNNETT, Sir George Sangster,** KBE, CB. British. *B.* 1907. *Educ.* Edinburgh Academy and Corpus Christi College, Oxford (MA). *M.* 1938, Margaret Rosalind Davies. *S.* 1. *Daus.* 3. Asst. Secy., Treasury 1942–46; Under-Secy., Ministry of Civil Aviation 1946–47; Deputy Secretary, Ministry of Agriculture 1947–56. Chairman of the Sugar Board Oct. 1956–70. *Club:* Athenaeum. *Address:* Basing's Cottage, Cowden, Kent.

**DUNNETT, Sir Ludovic James,** GCB, CMG. *B.* 1914. *Educ.* Edinburgh Academy and University College, Oxford (BA). *M.* 1943, Olga Adair. Entered Air Ministry 1936; Principal 1941; transferred to Ministry of Civil Aviation 1944; Asst. Secretary 1946, Under-Secretary 1949; transferred to Ministry of Supply 1951; Deputy Secretary 1953, Permanent Secy., Transport and Civil Aviation 1959–62; Min. of Labour 1962–66; Ministry of Defence, 1966–74. *Club:* Reform (London). *Address:* 2 Warwick Square, London, S.W.1.

**DUNNIGAN, (Mrs.) Alice Allison.** American newspaper woman. *B.* 1906. *Educ.* West Kentucky College (Diploma); Kentucky State College Teacher Training Division (Diploma); studied at Tennessee A. & I. State; Louisville Municipal College, and Howard University (Washington, D.C.). *M.* 1932, Charles Dunnigan. *S.* Robert William. Chief Washington Bureau, Associated Negro Press 1947–61; Vice-Chairman, Courtesy Committee, Women's National Press Club 1958—; member: Executive Committee, Capital Press Club 1959—, White House Correspondents Association 1947–61; State Department Correspondents Association 1948–61; Senate and House of Representatives Press Galleries 1947–61; appointed Educational Consultant to the President's Cttee. on Equal Employment Opportunity by Vice-Pres. Lyndon B. Johnson 1961; Asst. to Director of Information, President's Council on Youth Opportunity 1967–70. *Awards:* the Haitian Diploma and insignia of the Order of Honor and Merit. The title of Chevalier was awarded by President Duvalier of Haiti; Hon. PhD. Colorado State Christian Coll. 1973. Previously Federal employee 1942–46; School Teacher 1924–42. *Member:* Sigma Gamma Rho Sorority; National Council of Negro Women. *Publications:* reported national news for Associated Negro Press (serving 112 newspapers throughout America); columnist to West African Pilot (Lagos); contributing editor for Service and Sepia magazines; contributions to Foreign Service Journal, Opportunity, Valor, National Republic, Front Rank and the Employment Security Review; (autobiography) A Black Woman's Experience from Schoolhouse to White House. Democrat. *Clubs:* Women's National Press; Capital Press. *Address:* 1462 Ogden Street N.W., Washington, D.C. 20010, U.S.A.

**DUNPHIE, Maj.-Gen. Sir Charles Anderson Lane,** CB, CBE, DSO. *B.* 1902. *Educ.* Royal Naval Colleges of Osborne and Dartmouth and Royal Military Academy, Woolwich. *M.* 1931, Eileen Campbell. *S.* Christopher. *Dau.* Jane Lane. *Career:* Brigadier 1947; Acting Maj.-General 1944; Temporary Maj.-Gen. 1945; ret. 1948; H.M. Hon. Corps. of Gentleman at Arms 1952–62; Man. Dir. Vickers Ltd. 1957–62, Chmn. 1962–67. *Address:* Elliscombe House, Wincanton, Somerset.

**DUNSTAN, Donald Allan,** QC, MP. Australian. *B.* 1926. *Educ.* Suva Grammar School; St. Peter's College, Adelaide; Univ. of Adelaide (St. Mark's College), LLB. *M.* 1949, Gretel Ellis. *S.* 2. *Dau.* 1. *Career:* MP for Norwood, House of Assembly, 1953; Attorney-General, Minister of Social Welfare, Minister of Aboriginal Affairs, S.A., 1965–67; Premier, Treasurer, Attorney-General and Minister of Housing, S.A., 1967–68; Leader of the Opposition, S.A. Parliament, 1968–70; Premier & Treas., S.A. 1970—; Minister of Development & Mines 1970–73. *Member:* Australian Labour Party. *Clubs:* Democratic; Norwood; Redlegs. *Address:* 15 Clara Street, Norwood, South Australia, 5067; and *office* State Administration Centre, Victoria Square, Adelaide, South Australia, 5000.

**DUNTON, Arnold Davidson.** President, Carleton University, Ottawa 1958—. *B.* 1912. *Educ.* Grenoble, McGill, and Cambridge Universities, and University of Munich. *M.* 1944, Kathleen Bingay. *Daus.* Darcy and Deborah. *Career:* Reporter Montreal Star 1934 (Associate Editor 1957); Editor, Montreal Standard 1938; Wartime Information Board, Ottawa 1941 (General Manager 1944); Chairman, Canadian Broadcasting Corp. 1945. Hon. degrees: DSc., Laval; LLD, Univ. of Saskatchewan, Queen's University, University of British Columbia and McGill University. University of Toronto. *Clubs:* Rideau (Ottawa); Montreal Racket. *Address:* 410 Maple Lane, Rockcliffe, Ottawa 2, Ont., Canada.

**DUPERREX, Emile (Jacques).** Swiss. *B.* 1905. *Educ.* Doctor of Laws. *M.* 1931, Lina Grass. *Dau.* 1. *Career:* Previously at Dreyfus & Co., Frankfurt-on-Main, and at the Banque de Dépôts et Crédits, Geneva; active in Banque Populaire 1931–70. Former Director on Board of Management of Banque Populaire, Suisse, Geneva. Former Member & V.P., Federal Commission of Swiss Banks, 1967–75; Lecturer, Law Faculty, Geneva University until 1971. *Publications:* numerous articles in economic and financial journals; Financial Editor, Journal de Genève (1939–56); La Lettre de Gage (1931); Placements Suisse à l'étranger (1950); Evolution économique de la Suisse durant les 100 denieres années (1969); Loi fédérale les banques. (1973). Commander, Confrérie des Chevaliers de Tastevin; Hon. Pres. Fondation de Secours Mutuels aux Orphelins. *Member:* Association of Swiss Bankers Sté. Genevoise de Droit de Législation President 1967–69. *Club:* Swiss Alpine. *Address:* 17 rue de Saint-Jean, Geneva, Switzerland.

**du PLESSIS, Wentzel Christoffel.** South African. Director, several companies. *B.* 1906. *Educ.* Transvaal Univ. College (BA), D.Litt et Phil (h.c.). *M.* 1934, Marie Düring. *Dau.*1 *Career:* appointed to Dept. of External Affairs 1927; Administrative Secretary of the South African Delegation to the Imperial Conference 1930; Private Secry. to Prime Minister 1931; Legation; Secy., The Hague 1934; Chief, Diplomatic and Consular Division, Head Office 1938; Secy., Union Government's P.O.W. Cttee. 1941–45; Commerce and Industry 1945–48; MP (National Party) Standerton (Transvaal) 1948–54; High Commissioner to Canada (1954–56) and concurrently Permanent Representative to U.N. (June 1954–Aug. 1956); Ambassador of the Union of South Africa at Washington, D.C. 1956–60; Dir., Africa Institute, Pretoria 1960–61; Secretary of Dept. of Information, Pretoria, 1961–63. Administrator of South West Africa 1963–68. *Address:* 880 Pretorius Street, Arcadia, Pretoria, South Africa.

**duPONT, Edmond.** American investment banker. *B.* 1906. *Educ.* Andover Academy; Princeton Univ.; Oxford Univ. *M.* 1932, Averell Adelaide Ross. *S.* Anthony Averell and Edmond Rhett. *Career:* With Panhandle Eastern Pipeline 1930–32; Partner F. I. duPont, Glore Forgan & Co. 1933–68, Treas. Delaware Chemical Engineering Co. 1939–62; Financial & Foundation Exec. Dir. Winterthur Corp. 1950—; Episcopal Church Foundation 1950—; United International Fund Ltd. 1960–64; Chmn. Bd. 1968–70, Partner F. I. du Pont, Glore Forgan & Co. 1970–71. Director, Delaware Fund 1938–49, Pres. 1942–45. Trustee, Univ. of Delaware, 1950; Archives of American Art, 1967. Diocese of Delaware, 1957—. Chmn. Exec. Cttee Episcopal Church Foundation; HF Du Pont Winterthur Museum since 1950. *Clubs:* Wilmington (Wilmington, Del.); Wilmington Country; Greenville (Del.) Country; Chesapeake Bay Yacht (Easton, Md.). *Address:* P.O. Box 137, Montchanin, Del. 19710. and *office* P.O. Box 507, Wilmington, Del., 19899, U.S.A.

**DUPONT, Pierre.** Swiss diplomat. *B.* 1912. *Educ.* Lic. en D.; Advocate. *M.* 1939, Georgette Grillet. *S.* 1. *Dau.* 1. *Career:* Lawyer, Geneva Switzerland 1937; mem. Fed. Polit. Dept. Bern, 1939; at Legation, Paris 1939; Attaché, Vichy 1942; 2nd Sec., Brussels 1944 (1st Sec. 1947); with Swiss delegation to O.E.C.E., Paris 1948; Counsellor, Paris 1953; Consellor of Legation in Fed. Political Dept., Berne 1953; Minister to Venezuela and Panama since 1957. Ambassador to Poland 1961; the Netherlands 1965; France 1967. *Address:* Swiss Embassy, 142 rue de Grenelle, 75007 Paris, France.

**DUPRAZ, Joannès.** French journalist and government official. *B.* 3 July 1907. *Career:* Editor of numerous French and foreign newspapers and revues until 1939; worked with the League of Nations 1928–31; went on Official Mission to Latin America; Secretary-General of Information in Government of General de Gaulle 1944; Deputy for Indre-et-Loire 1945–58; formerly Secretary of State for Armaments and the Navy; Pres. French delegation at Economic Commission for Europe of U.N. 1955–73, of French Delegation at Economic Commission for Africa, and at Economic and Social Council of U.N. 1961–64. Secretary of State, Presidence du Conseil 1953; Delegate, General Assembly, U.N. 1957–63. *Address:* 4 rue Charles Dickens, Paris XVI, France.

**DUPUIS, Hon. Yvon,** PC. *B.* 11 Oct. 1926. *Educ.* Varennes and Longueuil Colleges, Montreal Jacques-Cartier Normal School and Edward Murphy Institute. *M.* 1954, Roberte Langevin. *S.* Yves and Langevin. *Daus.* Annie and Nathalie. *Career:* Has been in business as importer and distributor of educational books and records in Montreal and St.-Jean, P.C., 1954—. Member of the Quebec Legislative Assembly 1952–56; Member of the House of Commons (for St.-Jean-Iberville-Napierville, 1958–65. Member of the Federal Cabinet of Canada. Parly. Secy. to the Secretary of State, April 1963–64; Minister without Portfolio Feb. 1964; resigned Jan. 1965; remains a member of the Privy Council Publivox Inc. Radio Commentator CKVL, Montreal 1968–71 and CKAC 1971–72; Leader of the Creditiste Party of Quebec 1973; Leader Presidential Party since 1974; Pres. of Photo-Commerce Ltd., Montreal. *Clubs:* St. Johns R.C.A.F. Officers Mess, Pinegrove Country; Nautique de St.-Jean. *Address:* 620 Rang du Côteau, St. Jacques-le-Mineur, Quebec, Canada.

**DUQUE VILLARREAL, Alejandro A.** Panamanian. *B.* 1919. *Educ.* La Salle Military Academy; Univ. of Vermont. *M.* 1963, Vilma Maldonado. *S.* 5. *Career:* Asst. Gen. Man. Cerveceria Nacional S.A.; Dir. Cia Unida de Duque; Pres. Sociedad Agricola Marixenia S.A.; Council mem., Star & Herald Co. *Clubs:* Union; Golf; Sala de Armas John de Pool; Past Pres., Consejo Nacional de la Empresa Privada; Past Pres., Camara de Comercio Industria Agricultura de Panama. *Address: office* P.O. Box 495, Panama City, Panama.

**DUQUET, John Edward Lewis,** QC. Canadian. *B.* 1904. *Educ.* St. Charles Seminary (Commercial Diploma and BA *magna cum laude* issued by Univ. of Montreal) and Univ. of Montreal (Licentiate in Law *magna cum laude*). *M.* 1936, Aileen Caron. *Daus.* Dawn and Joan. *Career:* Read law with Laflamme, Mitchell, Calaghan & Kearney 1926–29. Senior Partner in law firm of Duquet, MacKay, Weldon and Bronstetter, Director, Vice-Pres. and General Counsel: Canadair Ltd., Dir. and Vice-Pres.: Canada West Indies Molasses Co. Ltd. Director: Royal Bank of Canada; Gillette of Canada Ltd.; Timmins Investments Ltd., Chromasco Ltd.; Liquid Carbonic Canada Ltd.; Wabasso Ltd. *Awards:* Hon LL D Univ of Sherbrooke 1960; Comdr. Order of St. Gregory the Great by His Holiness Pope John XXIII, 1959. *Clubs:* Mount Royal; St. James's Engineers'; Laurentian Golf; Laval-sur-le-Lac Golf; Mount Bruno Golf; Canadian. Member Montreal Board of Trade. *Address:* 99 Gordon Crescent, Westmount, P.G.; and *offices* Suite 3411, The Royal Bank of Canada Building, Place Ville Marie, Montreal, Quebec H3B 3J5, Canada.

**DURACK, Hon. Peter Drew,** LLB, BCL(Oxon). Australian barrister & politician. *B.* 1926. *Educ.* Aquinas Coll., W.A. Univ.; Lincoln Coll., Oxford (W. A. Rhodes Scholar 1949). *M.* 1953, Isabel Arnott Milne. *S.* 1. *Dau.* 1. *Career:* Tutor in law, Oxford 1952–53; Barrister, Grays Inn 1953; Practising law in Perth since 1954; M.L.A. (Lib.) for Perth, W.A. 1965–68; Pres., W.A. Liberal Party 1968–71; Senator (Lib.) for W.A. since 1971; appointed Attorney-General 1977. *Address:* 34 Melvista Avenue, Claremont, W.A. 6010, Australia.

**DURAND, Bernard Raymond Amédée.** French Diplomat. *B.* 1911. *M.* 1947, Anne Chatin. *S.* 1. *Dau.* 1. *Career:* Embassy, Madrid 1938–41; Rabat (Morocco) 1942–44; Foreign Ministry, Paris 1945–47; First Secy., French Embassy Cairo 1947–51; Counsellor, French Embassy 1951–55; Private Secy. to M. Pinay, Foreign Minister, Paris 1955–56; Counsellor, French Embassy, Athens 1956–61; Chief of Cabinet to M. Couve de Murville, Foreign Minister 1961–64; Chief of Protocol, 1964–69; Ambassador in Athens 1969–73; Ambassador in Lisbon 1973–76. *Decorations:* Commandeur de la Légion d'Honneur; Commandeur de l'Ordre National du Mérite. *Address:* 5 Rue de Lota, Paris XVI, France; and *office* Ministère des Affaires Etrangéres, 37 Quai d'Orsay, Paris, France.

**DURAND-RÉVILLE, Luc.** French. Company director. *B.* 1904. *Educ.* Diplomé HEC (Hautes Etudes Commerciales); Licencié en droit. Diplomé of the British Chamber of Commerce of Paris. *M.* 1926, Françoise Alice Warnod. *S.* Eric and Blaise. *Dau.* Eveline (Mme. Pierre Lobry, MD). *Career:* General Secretary, Society for the Economic Development of Oriental Countries 1925–31; with National City Bank of New York (France) 1931–35; Director, later Managing Director and Pres., Société du Haut-Ogooué 1936; Pres., Ets. R. Gonfreville et Cie 1942; Hon. Pres., Anciens Ets. Ch. Peyrissac et Cie 1956; Vice-Pres. Cie OPTORG; Dir COFINCAU. CFSO. Voltex. Former Senator 1946–59. *Member:* (Honorary) Economic and Social Council; Hon. Pres., Acad. of Overseas Sciences; Hon. Pres. Academy of Commercial Sciences; Vice-Pres., French Cttee., Internat. Chamber of Commerce; Hon. President Political Economy Society, and Anglo-French Parliamentary Friendship Group; Président, Amicale du Sénat; Président, Amicale du Conseil Économique et Social; President, French Association Albert Schweitzer; Member Correspondent de l'Institut 1972; (Academie des Sciences Morales and Politiques). *Publications:* numerous articles in the press and magazines, concerning the economics of the underdeveloped countries. *Award:* Officier de la Légion d'Honneur; Commander Ordre national du Mérite; Grande médalle d'argent de la République Autrichienne; Officer, Ordre Lion de Belgique; Knight Commander, Order of the British Empire. *Clubs:* Cercle France-Outer-Mer (Hon. Pres.); Dir. Cercle republican. *Address:* Chateau de Varenville, Bacqueville en Caux (Seine maritime); and 5 rue Bellini Puteaux (92), France.

**DUREPAIRE, Michel Aurele Jules Lucien.** French. *B* 1907. *Educ.* Ecole Supérieure d'Electricité (BSc; Qualified Engineer). *M.S.* 1. *Daus.* 3. *Career:* Engineer and then Director of Sté Industrielle des Procédés Loth 1931–38. Chairman and Director-General, Sté. Industrielle de Télécommande et de Télémécanique 1938—. Governor, Compagnie d'Electronique Industrielle Lepaute 1941—. *Publications:* Communications with the Académie des Sciences; articles in the Revue Générale de l'Electricité, and Bulletin de la Société française des Electriciens. Awarded Galitzine Prize 1958; Officer, Legion of Honour (France). *Member:* Syndicat National de la Mesure Electrique et Electronique (Hon. Chmn.); Centre National de l'Automatisation (Chmn.); Comité Intersyndical 'Mesure Régulation Automatisme' Hon. (Vice-Chmn.); Administrative Council of the Syndicat Géneral de la Construction Electrique. *Address: office* 26 rue Vauthier, Boulogne-sur-Seine (Seine), France.

**DURHAM, Joseph William.** American. *B.* 1922. *Educ.* Univs. of Tours, Oklahoma and Phillips; Colorado State Coll., PhD (1972). *Career:* Joined Guaranty Bank 1939, Cashier 1948. Brig. Gen. Confederate States Air Force. Vice-President, Guaranty Bank 1964—. Photographer and reporter: Enid Morning News, Watonga Republican, Cross Country News and other newspapers and periodicals. *Member:* Aviator Space Writers', Blaine County Historical (Fdr. and Dir.), Nat. Flying Farmers', Experimental Aircraft, Nat. Aeronautics, Internatl. Platform; Vice-Chmn. local housing Authority; Pres. Anti-Thief Assn. *Award:* Aviation Promotion. *Address:* Box 222 Okeene, Okla. 73763, U.S.A.

**d'URSEL, Comte Jean.** Belgian diplomat. *B.* 1917. *Educ.* École Abbatiale de Maredsous; University of Louvain (D en D). *M.* (1) 1942, Mlle Jeanne Lejeune de Schiervel (*D.* 1945). (2) 1947, Comtesse Arlette d'Oultremont. *S.* Lancelot, Aurian, Cédric, Gaël, Wauthier. *Career:* Ministry of Foreign Affairs 1946; Second Secretary, Teheran 1949–52; First Secretary, Ministry of Foreign Affairs 1952–54; First Sec., Madrid 1954, Counsellor 1955–59; Ministry of Foreign Affairs 1959–61; Ambassador to Khartoum 1961–62; Minister, Washington D.C. 1963–65. Min. Plen. at Ministry of Foreign Affairs 1965–71; Ambassador to Luxemburg 1972–73. *Address:* 1 Drève de Bonne Odeur, 1170 Brussels, Belgium.

**DU TOIT, Stephan Francois.** *Educ.* Universities of Stellenbosch and Cape Town. *Married,* 4 children. *Career:* admitted as Advocate of Supreme Court; entered Parliamentary Service 1920, Secy. of the Senate 1941–46. Successively S.A. Minister to Sweden, Chile, Argentine, Spain; Ambassador to Portugal, Italy, France. Leader S.A. Delegation to 8th session, Commission for Tech. Co-operation in Africa South of Sahra; Deputy-Leader S.A. Delegation to U.N. Assembly 1953. Pres., Huguenot Socy. of S. Africa, Board of Control Huguenot Museum; Bd. of Trustees, Huguenot Monument. *Member:* Council and Exec. Cttee., Univ. of Cape Town. *Publication:* Home and Abroad. *Address:* City & Civil Service Club, Box 50, Cape Town 8000, South Africa.

**DUTT, Bata Kristo.** Indian. *B.* 1910. *Educ.* BCom, Calcutta Univ. *M.* 1930, Uma Rani. *S.* 1. *Daus.* 4. *Career:* With New Standard Bank Calcutta 1930–45; Dep. Man, Dir., Comilla Banking Corp. 1945–50; United Bank of India 1950–73; Formerly: Chairman, Board of Industries, Govt. of West Bengal; Commissioner, Commissioners for the Port of Calcutta; Dir. Industrial Reconstruction Corp. of India 1971—; Chmn. West Bengal Ind. Development Corp. Ltd. 1972—; Chmn. Man. Dir. United Bank of India; Chmn. United India Credit and Devel. Co. Ltd. *Member:* West Bengal State Planning Bd; Bd. Govs. Indian Inst. of Social Welfare & Business Management; Council Indian Inst. of Bankers; Cttee. Fed. Indian Chamber, Commerce; Rotary Club of Calcutta. *Publications:* Monetary Discipline & Indian Banking (1960); Rural Banking Plan (1951); Banking-Plan—an Outline (1956); Hard Accounts; Unemployment amongst Engineers; Fundamentals of Banking; Employment Opportunities. frequent contributor to financial and economic press. *Address:* 35 Ballygunge Park, Calcutta-19; and *office* Benoy Bhawan, 27-B Camac Street, Calcutta-16.

**DUVALIER, Jean-Claude.** Head of State of Haiti. *B.* 1951. *Educ.* Univ. of Haiti Faculty of Law. *Career:* Following the death of his father installed as President for Life of the Republic of Haiti, 1971. *Address:* Palais National, Port-au-Prince, Haiti.

**DVORKOVITZ, Vladimir.** American. *B.* 1917. *Educ.* King's College, University of London (BSc Hons 1936; Chemistry Major; and PhD 1939 (Organic Chemistry). *M.* Betty McIntosh. *Dau.* Judith Ann. *Career:* Pres. and Gen. Mgr. Jensen-Salsbery Laboratories (subsidiary of Richardson-Merrell Inc.), Kansas City 1959–61 (Vice-Pres. 1955–59); Director of Research Diversey Corp., Chicago, 1945–55. Research Associate, Northwestern Univ., Evanston, Ill. 1940–42. Owner, Dr. Dvorkovitz & Associates, Ormond Beach, Fla since 1961. *Publications:* numerous scientific articles; owner of about 50 U.S. and foreign patents. *Member:* Amer. Inst. of Chemists (Fellow); Amer. Chemical Socy.; New York Acad. of Science; Licensing Executives Socy.; American Chamber of Commerce in U.K. *Address: office* 216S. Atlantic Boulevard, Ormond Beach, Fla., U.S.A.

**DWEK, Maurice.** British. *M.* 1963, Naomi. *S.* 2. *Dau.* 1. *Career:* Man. Dir. Cahn & Bendit Ltd., Vanderbilt (Fittings) Ltd., S. & M. Dwek (Developments) Ltd., S. Dwek & Sons (Holdings) Ltd., Tyrone Metalcraft Ltd., Dwek Investments Ltd.; Dir. M. & N. Dwek & Co. Ltd.; Man. Dir. Lancashire Metalcraft Ltd.; Westware Plastics Ltd.; Chmn. Dwek Group Ltd.; Atlas Plastics Ltd. *Address:* 1 Fairholme Close, Finchley, London, N.3 and *office* Dwek Works, Blackwall Lane, Greenwich, London SE10 0BG.

**DYAS, Richard Campbell.** American. *B.* 1905. *Educ.* Univ. of Illinois (AB) and George Washington Univ. (LLB). *M.* 1934, Mildred R. Wainwright. *S.* Richard Wainwright. *Career:* Counsel, Office of Comptroller of the Currency, U.S. Treasury Dept. 1933–38; General Counsel, RFC Mortgage Co. (subsidiary of Reconstruction Finance Corp.) 1938–44; Exec. Asst. to Bd. of Directors, Reconstruction Finance Corp. 1944–51, including following service with subsidiaries: Member of Board; RFC Mortgage Co., Defense Homes Corp. (also Pres.) and Federal National Mortgage Association (also Vice-Pres.). Director of Loans, Small Detense Plants Administration 1951–53. Vice-President and Treasurer, U.S. Steel Homes Credit Corp. and U.S. Steel Finance Corp., 1953–70; Exec. Vice-Pres. Government National Mortgage Assoc., 1970—. *Member:* Sigma Chi. Mason. *Club:* National Press. *Address:* 835 Herbert Springs Road, Alexandria, Va, 22308; and *office* 451 Seventh Street, S.W. Washington, D.C., U.S.A.

**DYKES, Hugh John,** MP. British Politician. *B.* 1939. *Educ.* Weston-super-Mare Grammar Sch.; Pembroke Coll., Cambridge. *M.* 1965, Susan Margaret Smith. *S.* 3. *Career:* Research Sec. of the Bow Group 1965; Conservative candidate in Tottenham for General Election 1966; Partner in Simon & Coates, Stockbrokers, since 1968; Chmn. of the Coningsby Club 1969; MP (Cons.) for Harrow East since 1970; Sec. of Cons. Parly. Finance Cttee.; PPS to three Service Ministers (Ministry of Defence); PPS to Parly. Under-Sec. of State, Cabinet Office & Civil Service Dept. 1973; Sponsor of the Heavy Commercial Vehicles Act 1973; mem. of the European Parliament 1974–77; Sec. of the Cons. Parly. European Affairs Cttee. 1975; Chmn., Parly. Cttee. for the Release of Soviet Jewry 1975–76; Vice-Chmn., Cons. Group for Europe 1977; Council mem., Wider Share Ownership Council; mem. Bd. of Govs., Royal National Orthopaedic Hospital. *Member:* London Stock Exchange; Farriers Livery Company; Freeman of the City of London. *Publications:* Author of numerous pamphlets & articles on political & financial subjects & two books on investment. *Club:* Beefsteak. *Address:* House of Commons, London SW1A 0AA.

**DYKSTRA, William Dwight.** American. President, William Dykstra Group. *B.* 1927. *Educ.* Hope College (AB 1949) and Indiana University (MBA 1950). *M.* 1957, Ann McGuiness. *S.* William Hugh. *Dau.* Mary Irene. *Member:* Amer. Economic Assn.; Amer. Inst. of Graphic Arts; Amer. Marketing Assn.; Acad. of Political Science; Phi Kappa Psi; Pi Kappa Delta; Reformed Church in America (Elder). Republican. *Publications:* Management and the Fourth Estate; New Profit Sources. *Awards:* Recipient of award for outstanding furniture, 1955; AIGA Package Design Award, 1965 and 1966; American Advertising Federation Award 1972, '74, '76. *Clubs:* La Coquille (Palm Beach); Otsego Ski; Great Lakes Cruising; Charlevoix Yacht; Rotary. *Address:* Tallmadge Grange 0–1845 West Leonard Road, Grand Rapids, Mich. 49504, U.S.A. and 1145 Edison N.W., Grand Rapids, Mich. 49504.

**DYSON, Arthur Albert,** OBE, CEng, FIEE, FIERE, SMIEEE. British. *B.* 1908. *Educ.* Wisbech Grammar School, Leamington Coll., and Coventry Tech. Coll. (Ordinary and Higher Certificates in Electrical Eng.). *M.* 1932, Edna Mary Poole. *S.* Arthur Frank and Edward John. *Career:* British Thomson-Houston Co. Ltd. and Ediswan, 1930–31; Tech. and Works Engr., Radio Recordion, Newcastle-on-Tyne 1931–32; Works Mgr. and Engr., Erie Resistor Ltd., 1932–36; Joint Mng. Dir. 1936–37, Chief Engr. and Mng. Dir. 1937–58. Chairman and Managing Director: Erie Electronics Ltd. (formerly Erie Resistor Ltd.) 1958–72; Erie Technological Products Ltd., Great Yarmouth, 1968–72. *Member:* Economic Planning Council (East A. Region) Industry & Communications Cttee.; National Electronics Council. Pres. I.E.R.E. 1972–73. CEngFIEE, CEngFIERE, SMIEEE. *Clubs:* R.A.C. (London). *Address:* 15 Marine Crescent, Great Yarmouth, Norfolk.

**DYUKAREV, Semyon Petrovich.** USSR Diplomat. *B.* 1914. *Educ.* Moscow State Univ. *M.* 1945, Lyudmila Bezverkhniaya *S.* 2. *Dau.* 1. *Career:* Secondary School teacher 1937–39; mem. of USSR Embassy, Japan 1939–41; Diplomatic Agent, Vladivostok 1943–45; Consul-General, Milan 1946–49; Counsellor, USSR Embassy, Burma 1951–55, & Thailand 1958–61; Ambassador, Somalia 1964–69, & Argentina since 1972. *Member:* Astronomic Soc. of the USSR. *Decorations:* Order of the Red Banner of Labour (twice); Order of the Peoples' Friendship; Order of the Sign of Honour; Grand Star of the Somalia Republic, and 5 medals. *Address:* USSR Embassy, Rodriguez Peña 1741, Buenos Aires, Argentina.

# E

**EADES, John Jesper.** British. *B.* 1920. *Educ.* Bootham Sch.; Emmanuel Coll., Cambridge. *M.* 1947, Beatrice Honor Butler. *S.* 3. *Career:* with Rea Bros. Ltd. Bankers 1946–50; Exec. Dir. Automatic Telephone and Electric Co. Ltd. 1950–71; Dir. Indian Telephone Ind. Ltd. 1952–63; Mitchell & Butlers Ltd. 1955–67; Plessey Overseas Ltd. 1962–65; Man. Dir. Plessey International Group of Companies 1965–71; Dir. The Plessey Co. Ltd. (Exec. Bd.) 1965–71; Chmn. EPI Holdings Ltd.; EPI-Ashdale Engineering Services Ltd.; Roderland Ltd.; Ashdale Consultancy Services Ltd.; Jesson Financial Services Ltd. *Member:* British National Export Council, Canadian Cttee. 1966–69, Dept. Chmn. 1969–71. Council Member Canada U.K. Chamber Commerce. *Club:* Carlton. *Address:* 151 Rice Lane, Liverpool L9 1AF.

**EAGLE, Roy Frank.** British. *B.* 1916. *Educ.* Sydney Church of England Grammar Sch. *M.* 1942, Vera Curtis. *S.* 1. *Dau.* 1. *Career:* Chmn. & Man. Dir. Kyabram Preserving Co. Ltd.; Dir. K-Y Sales Ltd. (London); Dir. & Gen. Man. P. Methven & Sons 1947–63. *Member:* Fruit Industry Sugar Concession Cmte. *Clubs:* R.A.C.V. Melbourne; R.A.C.A. Sydney. *Address* and *office* P.O. Box 111, Kyabram, Vic., Australia.

**EANES, General Antònio dos Santos Ramalho.** President of the Portuguese Republic. *B.* 1935. *Educ.* Castelo Branco High School; Higher Inst. of Applied Psychology; Lisbon Faculty of Law. *M.* 1970, Maria Manuela Duarte Neto Portugal. *S.* 1. *Career:* Enlisted in the Army School 1953; 2nd Lieut. 1957; service commission to Goa 1958–60; Lieut. 1959, Capt. 1961; service commission to Macau & Mozambique 1962–64, to Mozambique 1966–68; Physical Education Instructor at the Military Academy 1968; service commission to Guinea 1969, to Bissau (temporarily promoted to Major) 1970; Dir. of the Dept. of Cultural & Recreational Affairs at the Military Academy 1973 and promoted to Major; service commission to Angola 1973–74; after the Portuguese revolution of April 1974, recalled to Lisbon & named to the first ad-hoc cttee. for the mass media, then named Dir. of Programmes of Portuguese T.V. where he remained until March 1975, rising to become Chmn. of the Board of Dirs. of the T.V. Company; Lieut-Col. 1975, on the General Staff of the Armed Forces; temporarily promoted to four-star General & appointed Army Chief of Staff, Dec. 1975; Colonel 1976; elected 14th President of the Portuguese Republic, June 1976 & swore in the first Constitutional Government in July; Chmn. of the Council of the Revolution; Commander-in-Chief & Chief of the General Staff of the Armed Forces. *Decorations:* War Cross, 2nd Class; Silver Medal for Distinguished Services with Palm Leaf; Silver Medal for Exemplary Behaviour; Commemorative Medal of the Portuguese Armed Forces; Knight of the Military Order of Avis. *Address:* Office of the President, Lisbon, Portugal.

**EARNSHAW, John Frederick.** *B.* 1911. *M.* 1940, Joyce C. Scarfe. *Dau.* 1. *Career:* Mgr., Cambridge 1953; subsequently occupied executive positions in other New Zealand branches, Fiji, London and Head Office; Assistant General Manager, 1963. General Manager, Bank of New Zealand 1967–73; Dir. BNZ Finance Co. Ltd.; Chmn. First New Zealand International Ltd. *Address:* c/o Bank of New Zealand, Head Office, P.O. Box 2392, Wellington, New Zealand.

**EASON, Henry,** CBE, JP. British. *B.* 1910. *Educ.* Kings College, Durham University BCom); Barrister-at-Law (Gray's Inn); Hon. Fellow, Institute of Bankers. *M.* 1939, F. I. Stevenson. *S.* 1. *Daus.* 2. *Career:* Engaged in banking until 1939. Served in World War II (W/Cdr. R.A.F.; Despatches twice) 1939–46; Asst. Secy. 1946–56 and Dep. Secretary 1956–59, Secretary-General 1959–71. Inst. of Bankers. Vice President, The Institute of Bankers 1969–75. *Clubs:* Gresham, Overseas Bankers (London). *Address:* 12 Redgate Drive, Hayes Common, Bromley, Kent.

**EAST, Kenneth Arthur,** CMG. British diplomat. *B.* 1921. *Educ.* Taunton's School; Southampton University. *M.* 1946, Katherine Blackley. *S.* 2. *Daus.* 3. *Career:* served with H.M. Forces 1942–46; India Office, Commonwealth Relations Office 1946–50; Asst. Private Secy. to Secy. of State First Secretary Ottawa 1950–53; Colombo 1956–60; Head, East and General Africa Dept. CRO 1961–63; Head of Personnel Dept. CRO 1963–64; Counsellor, Diplomatic Service Administration 1965; Counsellor, Head of Chancery, Oslo 1965–70; Minister, British High Commission Lagos 1970–74; HM Ambassador Reykjavik since 1975. *Award:* Companion, Order of St. Michael and St. George. *Address:* c/o Foreign & Commonwealth Office, London, S.W.1 and *office:* British Embassy, PO Box 230 Reykjavik.

**EASTMAN, Allan James,** CBE. Australian diplomat. *B.* 1912. *Educ.* Sydney University (BA; LLB); University Medal for Law; several scholarships; Graduate of Imperial Defence College, London. *M.* 1941, Marie Adele O'Reilly. *S.* 1. *Daus.* 3. *Career:* Barrister-at-Law 1935–39; served in World War II (Australian Army; retired as Colonel) 1940–45; Consul-General, Bangkok, 1946–49; Dept. of External Affairs, Canberra, 1950; First Secretary and later Counsellor, London, 1951–53; Dept. of External Affairs 1954; Deputy Commissioner, Singapore 1955; High Commissioner in Ceylon 1956–58; Asst. Secy. 1959–60, and First Asst. Secy. 1961–62, Dept, of External Affairs. Senior External Affairs Representative, London, 1962–65; High Commissioner in Malaysia 1965–69; First Asst. Secy. Dept. Foreign Affairs 1969–71; Ambassador to Belgium, Luxembourg and the European Communities 1972–74; Ambassador to Mexico, Guatamala, Costa Rica, and Panama since 1975. *Address:* Australian Embassy, Paseo de la Reforma, 195, 5º Piso, Mexico, 5 DF Mexico.

**EASTON, Ernest Wright,** ISO. Australian business consultant. *B.* 1911. *Educ.* Brisbane Grammar School and Queensland University (MA; BCom); FASA. *M.* (1), Nell Stockree. (2) Elizabeth Donovan. *Daus.* 4. *Career:* Queensland: Economist, Bureau of Industry Commonwealth: Principal Research Officer, Australian Post Office (APO) 1948; Director, Finance and Public Relations, APO, 1954–59; Senior Assistant Director-General, Australian Post Office 1964–70; Assistant Director-General, APT 1959–64; Vice-Chairman, Overseas Telecommunications Commission (Aust.) 1961–64. Pres. Second Division Officers' Assn. 1965–69; Consultant, Victorian Railways since 1971; Member Prices Justification Tribunal. *Publications:* Wilderness to Wealth (1949); Social Services in Australia (part, 1939). *Clubs:* Athenaeum & Yarra Valley Country Club (both of Melbourne). *Address:* 78 Studley Road, Ivanhoe, Vic., Australia.

**EASTWICK, Joseph Lees.** American business executive. *B.* 1896. *Educ.* Tome School, Maryland; Cornell Univ. (BA). *M.* 1943, Suzanne Wister Fuguet. *S.* Stephen Fuguet. *Daus.* Suzanne Hancock and Stephanie Arndt. *Career:* Associated with James Lees & Sons Co. (which was established by his great grandfather, James Lees) since graduation from College in 1919. Served in World War I as 1st Lieut. in the Field Artillery. Former Chairman of the Board, James Lees & Sons Co. (carpet mfg.); member of Board, Burlington Industries Inc. (textiles), Central-Penn National Bank, The Budd Company, Pennsylvania General Insurance Co., Potomac Insurance Co., General Accident Insurance Co.; Chmn. Bd. Thomas Jefferson Univ. Medical Coll. & Medical Center, Republican. *Member:* Philadelphia Society for Promoting Agriculture. *Clubs:* River (N.Y.), Union League, Racquet, Rittenhouse (Philadelphia); Gulph Mills Golf; Pickering Hunt. *Address:* Springhead Farm Paoli, Pa. 19301, U.S.A.

**EASTWOOD, Sir John Bealby,** Civil Engineer and Farmer. *B.* 1909. *Educ:* Q. Elizabeth's Gr. School, Mansfield, Notts. *M.* 1929, Constance Mary. *D.* 2. *Career:* Man. Dir. JB Eastwood-Ltd. Group of Companies since 1969, Chmn. since 1963. *Decoration:* Knight Bachelor 1975. *Clubs:* Farmer's; Carlton. *Address:* Oxton Manor, Oxton, Newark, Notts; and *office:* Burns Lane, Warsop, Mansfield, Notts.

**EATON, William Mellon.** American lawyer, Founder of Eaton Van Winkle, Greenspoon & Grutman, 1968. Dir. of various corporations. *B.* 1924. *Educ.* Duke (BS); Harvard (JD). *M.* 1956, Elizabeth Waring Witsell. *S.* Alexander Mellon. *Daus.* Carolyn W., Sarah E. and Lisa. *Career:* Admitted to N.Y. Bar 1949, U.S. Supreme Court Bar 1961;

Associate, White & Case, N.Y. 1949–60; Partner, Hardy, Peal Rawlings, Warner & Maxwell, N.Y. 1960–65, own firm 1965–68; Pres. B.T. Capital Corp.; Trustee, Skowhegan School of Painting & Sculpture. *Member:* American (Cttee. Invest. Securities, chmn. 1969–73); Intl.; NYS (Chmn. Invest. Cttee.); & NYC Bar Assns.; St. Nicholas Socy.; Society Colonial Wars; The Pilgrims. *Clubs:* Union, Pinnacle; Profile; French Alpine; Appalachian Mountain. *Address:* 39th Floor, 600 Third Avenue, New York, New York 10016, U.S.A.

**EBAN, Abba Solomon.** Israeli statesman. *B.* 1915. *Educ.* MA Cambridge University; Hon DLitt and LLD, Boston, Maryland, New York, Cincinnatti, Lehigh, Brandeis, Temple, Yeshiva, Jewish Theological Seminary N.Y. and other Universities. *M.* 1945, Susan Ambache. *S.* Eli. *Dau.* Gila. *Career:* Lecturer in Oriental Languages, Cambridge Univ. 1938; Liaison officer between Allied H.Q. and the Jewish Agency for Palestine 1941–42; Vice-Principal, Middle East Arab Centre, Jerusalem 1943–48; Jewish Agency for Palestine 1946; Liaison officer, U.N. Cttee. to Palestine 1947; Israeli Representative at U.N. 1948; Ambassador to U.S.A. 1950–59. President, Weizmann Inst. of Science 1958–66. Member of Parliament 1959; Minister without Portfolio 1959; Min. of Education and Culture 1960–63; Dep. Prime Minister 1963–66. Minister for Foreign Affairs 1966–74. Foreign Member, American Academy of Arts and Sciences 1960. *Fellow:* World Academy of Art and Science 1964. *Publications:* Voice of Israel (1957); Tide of Nationalism (1959); My People (1968); My Country (1972). *Address:* The Knesset, Jerusalem, Israel.

**EBBESEN, Sven.** Danish Diplomat. *B.* 1911. *Educ.* Master of Theology (Copenhagen) 1935. *M.* 1937, Anna Elisabeth Olesen. *S.* 1. *Daus.* 3. *Career:* Asst. London Correspondent for Berlingske Tidende, Copenhagen 1939–40, 1945–47; Asst. Editor of Frit Denmark, London 1941–45; Asst. Press Attaché, Danish Embassy, London 1947–52; Dep. Dir. of Press Dept., Ministry for Foreign Affairs, Copenhagen 1952–55; Press Attaché, Danish Embassy, Oslo 1955–66; Dep. Dir.-Gen. of Press & Cultural Div., Ministry for Foreign Affairs, Copenhagen 1967–69 & Dir.-Gen. 1969–73; Ambassador to Israel since 1973. *Awards:* Commdr. of Dannebrog; Fortjenstmedaljen i sølv; Officer, Netherlands Order of Orange-Nassau; Commdr. Order of St. Olav (Norway); Store Fortjenstkors med Stjerne af Tyske Forbundsrepubliks Fortjenstorden. *Address:* Royal Danish Embassy, 23 Rehov Bnei Moshe, P.O.B. 21080, Tel Aviv 61210, Israel.

**EBREMARE, Gustave Gaspard Ghislain,** FCIS, AMBIM, FSCA. British. *B.* 1912. *Educ.* Athénée of Schaerbeek, Brussels; Inst. Supérieur des Sciences Financières. *Career:* Co. Secy. Leeds & Northrup Ltd.; Acct. Netherland Shipping & Trading Cttee. 1940–44; Chief Acct. Integra Co. Ltd.; Co. Secy. Integra Leeds & Northrup Ltd. 1953–61; Chmn. Birmingham & District Council 1972–73; Mem. of Council Inst. Chartered Secretaries & Administrators 1974 and 75; Chmn. Solihull & District Engineering Training Group 1977 (Vice-Chmn. 1971–76). *Member:* Council of Birmingham Chamber of Industry & Commerce 1974; Commerce-Industrial & Administrative Cttee of Solihull Coll. of Technology since 1975. *Award:* Chevalier de l'Orde de Léopold II Defense Medal. *Address:* The Beeches, 15 Widney Manor Road, Solihull West Midlands B91 3JG; and *office* Wharfdale Road, Tyseley, Birmingham B11 2DJ.

**ECCLES, Rt. Hon. Viscount,** PC, KCVO (David McAdam Eccles). British politician. *B.* 18 Sept. 1904. *Educ.* Winchester; New Coll., Oxford. *M.* 1928, Hon. Sybil Dawson. *S.* 2. *Dau.* 1. *Career:* Min. of Econ. Warfare 1939; Econ. Adviser to British Ambassadors, Madrid and Lisbon 1940–42; Min. of Production 1942–43; M.P. (Cons.) for Chippenham 1943–62. Minister of Works 1951–54; Minister of Education Oct. 1954; President of the Board of Trade 1957–59; Minister of Education Oct. 1959–62; Paymaster General with responsibility for the Arts 1970–73; Chmn. British Library since 1973. *Address:* Dean Farm, Chute, near Andover, Hants; and 6 Barton Street, London S.W.1.

**ECCLES, George Stoddard.** American executive. *B.* 1900. *Educ.* Utah State Agricultural Coll.; Univ. of Calfornia; Columbia School of Business, New York (BS); Hon LLD, Univ. of Utah 1963 and Utah State Univ. 1970. *M.* 1925: Dolores Doré. *Career:* Entered field of banking upon graduation and has been associated with the First Security System of banks, or predecessors, since the time. In order to study economic, financial and political conditions overseas visited South America 1953, Japan, Hongkong, Thailand, Singapore, and Australia 1955, and New Delhi and Far East, International Monetary Fund Conferences 1958, Int. Monetary Fund Hon. Life Member (has attended all subsequent meetings); also Vienna (and made a visit to Africa) 1961. Chmn. & Director: First Security Corp., Chmn. & Dir. First Security Bank of Utah, National Association, and Past Pres. Assn. of Registered Bank Holding Companies. Chairman of Executive Committee & Director, First Security Bank of Idaho, National Association; Hon. Director: American Bankers Life Assurance Co. of Florida, American Bankers Insurance Co. of Florida, Husky Oil Canada, Ltd. Mem. Exec. Cttee., Amal. Sugar Co.; Texasgulf; Husky Oil Co. (Dir. and mem. of Exec. Cttee); Cody, Wyo., Farmers Insurance Group, Los Angeles; Utah International, San Francisco; Union Pacific Railway Co. *Member:* Exec. Cttee., Aubrey G. Lanston & Col Inc., New York City. Chmn., International Monetary Conf. 1964. Member: Amer. Bankers Assn. Past Pres. Reserve City Bankers Assn. (former Chmn. of various Cttees.; Vice-Pres. and Pres.); National Industrial Conference Board, N.Y.C. (member, Bd. of Dirs.); member-at-large, National Council, Boy Scouts of America 1954, Discharged from the Army, 23rd Dec. 1918. Fraternities: Sigma Chi; Alpha Kappa Psi (Past Pres., Columbia Univ. Chapter); Salt Lake City Chamber of Commerce. Trustee, Los Angeles Foundation of Otology; Dir., Salt Lake Symphoney Orchestra. Hon LLD Univ. of Utah State University. *Clubs:* Alta, Fort Douglas Golf (Salt Lake City); Salt Lake Country; Ogden Golf & Country (Ogden); El Dorado Golf (Palm Desert, Calif.). *Address:* 1525 Penrose Drive, Salt Lake City; and *office* 79 South Main Street, Salt Lake City, Utah, U.S.A.

**ECCLES, Sir John Carew,** FAA, FRS. Australian scientist. *B.* 1903. *Educ.* Melbourne Univ. (MB; BS); Oxford Univ. (MA; DPhil); Hon ScD (Cantab); Hon DSc (Tas; UBC); Hon LLD (Melb.). *M.* (1) 1928, Irene Frances Miller (diss.). *S.* 4. *Daus.* 5. *M.* (2) 1968, Helena Táboříková. *Career:* Director: Kanematsu Memorial Institute of Pathology, Sydney 1937–44; Prof. of Physiology. University of Otago, Dunedin, N.Z. 1944–51; Professor of Physiology, Australian National University 1951–66; President, Australian Academy of Science 1957–61. Member, Inst. for Biomedical Research, Chicago, 1966–68. Waynflete Lecturer, Magdalen College 1952; Herter Lecturer, Johns Hopkins Univ. 1955; Ferrier Lecturer, Royal Society 1960; Sherrington Lect. Univ. Liverpool 1966; Distinguished Professor, State University of New York, Buffalo since 1968. Patten Lecturer Univ. Indiana 1972. *Awards:* Royal Medal, 1962; Nobel Prize 1963. Fellow: Exeter Coll., and Magdalen Coll., Oxford 1927–37. *Publications:* many papers in Proceedings of Royal Society, Journal of Physiology, and Journal of Neurophysiology; Reflex Acitivty of Spinal Cord (part-author) (1932); Neurophysiological Basis of Mind (1953); Physiology of Nerve Cells (1957); The Physiology of Synapses (1964); The Cerebellum as a Neuronal Machine (Part-author) (1967). The Inhibitory Pathways of The Central Nervous System (1968); Facing Reality (1970); The Understanding of the Brain (1973); (part author) The Self & Its Brain (1977). *Member:* F.R.A.C.P.; F.R.S.N.Z.; F.A.A.; F.R.S.; Pontifical Academy of Science; Foreign Member, Amer. Acad. Arts & Sciences, and Amer. Philosophical Socy.; Deutsche Akad. der Naturforscher Leopoldina (and recipient of Cothenius Medal); World Acad. of Art & Science (Fellow); Accad. Nazionale del Lincei (Foreign Hon. Member); Foreign Hon. Associate, Natl. Acad. of Sciences. *Address:* Cá a la Grá, CH6611 Contra (Ticino), Switzerland.

**ECCLES, Marriner Stoddard.** American financier and business executive. *B.* 9 Sept. 1890. *Educ.* Brigham Young College; Hon LLD, Univ. of Utah, LLD (Hon), Utah State Univ. *M.* (1) 1913, May Campbell Young. *S.* Marriner Campbell (*Dec.*), John David. *Dau.* Eleanore May (Steele); (2) 1951, Sara Madison Glassie. *Career:* Organized Eccles Investment Co., a holding company for interests in family estate 1916, Vice-President and General Manager until 1929 Pres. since 1929. President, First National Bank of Ogden and Ogden Savings Bank and successor banks; Organized First Security Corporation Bank Holding Co.; Pres. 1928–34, Chmn. 1951–75, Hon. Chmn. since 1975; Dir. 1916, Chairman, Amalgamated Sugar Co. 1941–76, Hon. Chmn. since 1976; First Security Bank of Utah, N.A.; Marcona Corp.; Elector, Hall of Fame for Great Americans, 1940—; Chmn., Utah Construction & Mining Co., 1941–71; Hon. Chmn. Utah International Inc. since 1971. Chairman, First Security Bank of Utah, N.A. 1955–70; Hon. Dir. Planned Parenthood-World Population, 1960; Sponsor, The Atlantic Council, 1962. Asst. to the Secy. of the Treasury of the United States 1934; Govnr. of the Federal Reserves Bd. 1934–36; Chmn. of the Bd. of Governors of the Federal Reserve System 1936–48. *Member:* Board of

Economic Stabilization 1942–46; National Advisory Council on International Monetary and Financial Problems 1945–48; Advisory Board, Export-Import Bank 1945–48; Board of Governors of the Federal Reserve System 1934–51; President Utah Bankers Assn. 1924–25; U.S. Delegate, Conference creating World Bank & International Monetary Fund 1944. Trustee, The American Assembly, Columbia Univ. 1959. *Address:* Hotel Utah, Salt Lake City, Utah, and 290 Lombard Street, San Francisco, and *offices* Desert Building, Salt Lake City, Utah; and 550 California Street, San Francisco, Calif., U.S.A.

**ECHEVERRIA-VILLAFRANCA, Eduardo.** Costa Rican diplomat and businessman. *B.* 1926. *Educ:* Escuela Juan Rudín; Escuela Comercio Castro Carazo; Liceo de Costa Rica; Centro Cultural Costarricense; Collegio Seminario; Universidad de Costa Rica; Escuela Normal; Alianza Francesa en Lisboa. *M.* 1953, Dona Flora Calzada Maduro. *S.* 2. *Daus.* 3. *Career:* Delegate to the Agricultural Marketing Conference, Amsterdam, 1952; Delegate to FEDECAME Conference, Haiti, 1954; Head of Protocol for Ambassadors Credentials, 1953; General Inspector of Consulates, 1954–62; Delegate of the Ministry of Foreign Affairs in Special Mission to U.S.A., England and Mexico, 1963; Assistant Manager A. Esquivel & Sons, Coffee Exporters; Vice-President of the National Association of Coffee Exporters; Manager of Autofores Ltda., Ford Motors Representative in Costa-Rica; Member of the Board of Directors of the National Factory of Cement; President of the Board of Directors of Club Unión, San José; Member of the Board of Directors of LACSA Airlines; Delegate of the Supreme Electoral Tribunal; Costa Rican Ambassador to Portugal; Special Delegate of the Costa Rican Government to act as Equerry to His Royal Highness Prince Philip during his visit to Costa Rica in 1975; Delegate of Costa Rican Govt. for the establishment of Diplomatic Relations with the Republic of Iran, 1975; Mem. of Delegation that accompanied President Lic. Don Daniel Oduber on his Official visit to Spain, 1976; Ambassador and Plenipotentiary of Costa Rica to the Court of St. James, and the European Economic Community 1974–77; Ambassador of Costa Rica at Large 1977. *President:* Lotificaciones Echeverria SA (R. Estate Dev.); Lotificaciones El Jardin, SA; Bd. of Dirs. Comp. Financiera de Inversiones y Financiones, SA; *Manager:* Sociedad Inversora de la Cía. *Chairman:* Board of Directors, Fraccio-namientos del Oeste SA; Urbanizaciones Especiales, SA; *Vice-Chmn.* Bd. of Dirs. of Urbanizacion Paseo Colon; Grupo y Desarrollo, SA; *Mem.* Bd. of Dirs. Tele-Com. SA of Nicaragua. *Representative:* GEC of Gr. B. in Costa Rica, Direlli-Gen. of Gt. B. in Costa Rica; Lamps and Lighting Co. of Gt. B. *Publication:* Biografia del Licenciado Don Manuel Echeverria- Aguilar. *Address:* P.O. Box, 1014, San José, Costa Rica.

**ECKARDT, Rt. Rev. Dr. Benjamin Clifford.** Canadian. *B.* 1906. *Educ.* Christian Seminary (LTheo), American School of Law, Chicago (LLB); Trinity Southern Seminary (DD); Ohio College of Podiatry (DEd); on University Circle. *M.* 1948, June Marie Fortner. President of Philathea College, London. Ont. 1946—. Chmn. of Frank Lloyd Wright Foundation Florida Southern College. Pastor of The First Church of Christ Disciples since 1928. Senator, University of Western Ontario 1947–55. Made a Bishop of the Free Protestant Episcopal Church 1958; Past Pres. The London Council of Churches. Appeared as Pres. of the 'Friends of the Forest' on behalf of Canada before the Congressional Judiciary Cttee. (U.S.A.) and is quoted in its records. *Awards:* Knight of Grace and Maltese Cross of Merit, Sovereign Order of St. John of Jerusalem; Eloy Alfaro Grand Cross (Panama); Justice Brandeis Gold Medal (U.S.A.). *Fellow:* International Academy; Hon LLD Florida Southern College (Lakeland) and of Nat. Police Academy; Chaplain General, Nat. Police Assoc. of America (Venice, Florida) and Trustee of their Nat. Police Coll. Member, Doctorate Assoc., N.Y. Educators, 1967. Member, The Royal Socy. of Arts, London 1970. *Publications:* Our Forest Future; Ontario's Forests; Our Forests Your Prosperity and Life. *Address:* 1033 Adelaide Street, London, Ont., Canada; and *office* Philathea Theological Seminary, Administration Building, 430 Elizabeth Street, London, 31 Ont., Canada.

**ECKHOFF, Ernst Fredrik.** Norwegian judge. *B.* 28 Apr. 1905. *Educ.* University of Oslo. *M.* 1937, Randi Eckhoff. *S.* 1. *Dau.* 1. Barrister 1937–45; Judge of the Supreme Court 1946–75; member, Board of Scandinavian Airlines System 1949–62; S.A.S. Assembly of Representatives 1962–68; Chmn. & mem. several official commns. since 1945. *Address:* Trosterudveien 5, Oslo 3, Norway.

**ECONOMIDES, Chris.** Cypriot business economist. *B.* 1908. *Educ.* BSc (Econ.) (London); Associate Institute of Bankers; Fellow of the Association of Certified and Corporate Accountants. *M.* 1942, Maria Economides. *S.* Phaedros. *Daus.* Ersi, Leda. *Career:* Chief Accountant, Agricultural Bank of Cyprus 1941–50; Pres. Cyprus Economic Society 1963–73; Council member International Economic Association. *Publications:* The Problem Confronting Cyprus—Solution compatible with the U.N. Charter, 1964; Should the Rich Countries Help the Poor and how they could do so, in The Gap Between Rich and Poor Nations (1972); Earned International Reserve Units—The Catalyst for Two Complementary World Problems: The Monetary and Development (1972). *Address:* 6 Dositheos Street, Nicosia, Cyprus (P.O. Box 1632).

**EDBERG, Rolf.** Governor of Värmland 1967. *B.* 1912. *M.* 1937, Astrid Persson. *S.* Jörgen. *Daus.* Ranveig and Birgitta. *Career:* Chief Editor: Oskarshamms Nyheter (1934–37), Oestgoeten, Linkoeping (1938–44), *Ny Tid*, Goeteborg (1945–56). Ambassador of Sweden to Norway 1956–67. Member of Parliament (Oestergoetland) 1940–44, and (Goeteborg) 1948–56; Pres., Swedish Press Club (Publicistklubben) 1951–53; Delegate to: Council of Europe (1949–52), United Nations (1952–55, 57, 60 and 61), Northern Council (1953–56), and Disarmament Conference 1961–65. *Publications:* On the Shred of a Cloud (1967); At the Foot of the Tree (1972); Letters to Columbus (1974); On Earth's Terms (1974); A House in the Cosmos (1974); The Spirit of the Valley (1976); Shadows Across the Savannah (1977) and several works on political subjects. *Award:* Dr. (h.c.) 1974; Good Medal, R. Swedish Acad of Science–Pro Mundo Habitabili (1974). *Address:* The Residence, Karlstad, Sweden.

**EDDY, G. Russell.** American. Registered Professional Engineer. *B.* 1912. *Educ.* Manlius School; Mass. Inst. of Tech. (BS, EE); Graduate School University of Nevada. *M.* 1964, Sara Lepper. *Career:* Founder Partner, The Eddy Group, Management Consultants 1948—; Pres., Dir. and Chief Exec. Officer: Hobam Inc. 1964–66; Screen Equipment Co. 1964–66; John E. Smith's Sons 1964–66; A.B. Stridh Maskiner 1964–66; Caribbean Crafts Inc. 1948–56; Marco Industries Inc. 1955–59; Dir., Chief Exec. Officer, Ludlow Valve Co. Inc. 1959–61; Pres. Dir. Chief Exec. Officer Conestoga Hardwoods 1961—; First Tower Corp. 1962—; Gen. Mgr.: Philadelphia Carpet Co. 1961–62, Doerr Carpet Co. 1961–62 and Jewelers Products Corp. 1948–50; Financial Consultant, Remington Corp. 1953–56; Exec. Vice-Pres., General Mgr., Medical Electronics Corp. 1965–66; Advisor to Minister for Finance, Republic of Singapore, 1968–69. Manufacturing Executive, Jingyih Enterprise Co. Ltd., Taipai Taiwan 1968—; Lecturer Syracuse Univ. Business Admin. Continuing Education. Patentee in electrical field. *Member:* Industry Adv. Cttee., War Production Board 1940–53; Nat. Cttee. man on Government Affairs; Wisdom Hall of Fame 1970 (Hon.) Community Leaders of America 1969 (Hon.); Nat. Assn. of Manufacturers; President's Cncl. Amer. Inst. Management; Internatl. Executive Service Corps. 1968–70; Internatl. Platform Assn. etc. *Clubs:* University (Syracus); Wyomissing (Reading, Pa.); Cruzana (St. Croix, V.I.); Cavalry (N.Y.). *Address:* Windrush, Manlius N.Y. 13104, U.S.A.

**EDDY, W. Paul.** Industrial Management and Engineering Consultant. *B.* 1899. *Educ.* Syracuse University (BSCh Eng) *M.* 1922, Gail Cushing. *S* .William P. III. *Daus.* Jean (Pullan) and Barbara (Brown). *Career:* Chief Engineering Operations, Pratt & Whitney Aircraft 1946–65; Chief, Materials Engineering, Pratt & Whitney Aircraft 1944–45; Chief Metallurgist, GMC Truck and Coach Division, General Motors Corporation 1930–43; Assistant Chief Metallurgist, Brown-Lipe-Chapin Division, General Motors Corporation 1928–30; Chief Metallurgist, The Geometric Tool Co. 1924–28; Chemist, Crucible Steel Co. of America 1922–24. Dir., S.E. Connecticut Economic Development Corp. (Pres. 1967–72); Dir., S.E. Connecticut Water Authority, (Chmn. 1968–71); Hon. Member, Society Automotive Engineers (Pres. 1957); Hon. Life Member, American Society for Metals. *Member:* Newcomen Socy., Noank Historical Socy.; Lyman Allen Museum; Conn. Aeronautical Historical Association; International Oceanographic Foundation; U.S. Power Squadrons; Secy. & Dir. E. Conn. Development Council; U.S. Naval Inst.; Chamber of Commerce S.E. Conn.; (Pres. 1971); E. Conn. Council Navy League of U.S. (Pres. 1973); Dir., New London YMCA; Service Corps Retired Exec. Conn. (Chmn. 1973); Mystic Seaport; A. F. & A. Masons; B.P.O.E.; Nat'l Sojourners; Dir., Lawrence & Memorial Benefactors Society; Fr. Mitchell College; Beta Theta Pi. *Publications:* 40 technical papers on metallurgical and engineering subjects in technical journals. *Clubs:* Hartford Engineers (Pres. 1964–65); Ram Island Yacht; Thames; Rotary (Pres. 1971–72); Syracuse Alumni Rowing Assn.; Conn. Council Automotive Organization Team (Pres. 1974). *Address:* 41 Neptune Drive, Groton Conn. 06340; and *office* Groton Professional Building, Groton, Conn., U.S.A.

**EDELING, Curt, Dr.-Ing.** German executive. *B.* 1913. *Educ.* Inst. of Technology, Karlsruhe (Engineering Diploma 1938; Dr.-Ing. 1944). *M.* 1944, Irmgard Schleiermacher. *S.* Wolfgang and Martin. *Dau.* Friederike. *Career:* Experimental Engineer, Industriewerke, Karlsruhe 1938–43; Superintendent, Hagenuk, Kiel 1943–45; Chief Engineer. Th Goldschmidt AG, Mannheim 1945–50, Works Director at Essen plant 1950–55. Vice-President, Th. Goldschmidt AG, Essen 1955–68; President since 1968. *Publications:* article on pulverizing drying; Research in Pulverizing 1947. *Club:* Rotary. *Address:* Waldsaum 37, Essen; and *office* Goldschmidtstr 100, 4300 Essen 1, Germany.

**EDEN, Rt. Hon. Sir John Benedict.** Bt. MP. British politician. *B.* 1925. *Educ.* Eton; St. Pauls School, U.S.A. *M.* (1) 1958, Belinda Jane Pascoe (divorced 1973). *S.* 2. *Daus.* 2. (2) 1977, Margaret Ann Drummond, Viscountess Strathallan. *Career:* Minister of State, Minister of Technology June–Oct. 1970; Min. for Industry, Dept. of Trade and Industry 1970–72; Minister of Posts and Telecommunications 1972–74; Mem. House of Commons Expenditure Cttee. 1974–76; Chmn., House of Commons Select Cttee. on European Legislation etc. 1976—; Pres., Wessex Area Conservatives 1974–77. Company Director. *Clubs:* Boodles; Pratts. *Address:* 29 Eldon Road, London W8 5PT.

**EDES, (John) Michael,** BA, MA. British diplomat. *B.* 1930. *Educ.* Blundells School; Clare Coll. Cambridge Univ.; Yale University. *Career:* H.M. Forces 1948–49; Third Secy. F.O. 1954; Middle East Centre for Arabic Studies 1955; Second Secy. Asst. Political Agent Dubai 1956–57; F.O. 1957–59; Private Secy. H.M. Ambassador, Rome 1959–61; F.O. 1961–62; First Secy. U.K. Delegation, 18 Nation Disarmament Conference Geneva 1962–65; F.O. 1965–68; Cabinet Office 1968–69; Asst. Head Arabian Dept., F.C.O. 1969–71; Ambassador Sana'a Yemen Arab Republic 1971–73; U.K. Del. Conference on Security and Cooperation in Europe, Geneva 1973–74; Head Permanent Under-Secy's Dept., F.C.O. 1974–76; on Sabbatical at Royal Inst. of International Affairs from 1977. *Awards:* Bachelor Arts (Cantab.); Master Arts, Yale University; Cavaliere del ordine de merito della Republica Italiana. *Clubs:* Athenaeum & Hawks (Cambridge). *Address:* 23 Newton Road, London, W.2. and *office* F.C.O., London, S.W.1.

**EDGAR, Grahame,** OBE, DVSc ARCVS, FACVSc. Australian. *B.* 1901. *Educ.* Sydney Grammar School; BVSc 1924, DVSc 1962 (Sydney). *M.* 1928, Mary Barnes Elliott. *S.* 1. *Dau.* 1. *Career:* Captain, Australian Army Veterinary Corps. (C.M.F.) 1924–40; Veterinary Research Officer and Senior Veterinary Research Officer, Glenfield Veterinary Research Station 1927–47; Director of Veterinary Research 1947–59; Assistant Under-Secretary, N.S.W. Department of Agriculture 1959–61. Director-General of Agriculture N.S.W. Dept. of Agriculture and Chairman, Roy. Botanic Gardens and Domain Trust (Syd.) 1961–66. Director, Wellcom (Australasia) Pty. Ltd. 1966–75 (ret'd.); Dir. 1959, Chairman, McGarvie Smith Institute since 1967. *Publications:* 72 papers in various scientific journals. Hon. Associate, Royal College of Veterinary Surgeons (A.R.C.V.S.) 1963. *Fellow:* of Senate, Univ. of Sydney 1966; Faculty of Veterinary Science 1960. *Member:* Australian Veterinary Assn. (President, 1948–49, N.S.W. Div. 1938; Australian Society of Animal Production (Pres. N.S.W. Branch 1962–63); Council World Poultry Science Association; Royal Agricultural Society of New South Wales; Australia and N.Z. Assn. for Advancement of Science; Council, N.S.W. Sheepbreeders' Assn.; Aust. Nat. Cttee. for UNESCO 1948–68. N.S.W. Cttee. for C.S.I.R.O. 1964. Awarded Farrer Medal (1966) for contributions to Australian agriculture, A.V.A. Gilruth Prize 1967. *Clubs:* Univ. (Sydney); Sydney Cricket Ground; Concord Golf. *Address:* 7 Wallis Avenue, Strathfield, N.S.W.; and *office* c/o Cooper (Aust.) Pty. Ltd., Phillip Street, Concord, N.S.W., Australia.

**EDGAR, Thomas Geoffrey,** CBE. British. *B.* 1908. Managing Director: A. G. Healing Ltd., and A. E. Goodwin Ltd. Group 1947–69. *Clubs:* American, Tattersall's; Killara Golf; Manly Golf; R.A.C.A. *Address:* 7/51 Wolseley Road, Point Piper, N.S.W., Australia.

**EDGE, Charles Geoffrey.** Canadian. *B.* 1920. *Educ.* BSc (Econ) Hons London; Registered Industrial and Cost Accountant (R.I.A.). *M.* 1940, Madeline Rita Tarrant. *Daus.* Christine Dorothy and Jennifer Wendy. *Career:* With Chemcell (1963) Ltd., Asst. to the Chairman: 1962–64, and Asst. Treasurer 1959–62. Asst. to the Chmn., Columbia Cellulose Co. Ltd. 1962–64. Dir., Management Services, Chemcell (1963) Ltd. 1964–68; Vice-Pres. Corporate Development 1969–70; Member National Energy Board since 1971 & Associate Vice-Chmn. since 1975. *Publications:* The Appraisal of Capital Expenditure. *Fellow:* Royal Statistical Socy.; Inst. of Statistics. *Member:* Financial Executives Inst. *Address:* 333 Chapel St., Apt 806, Ottawa Ont. and *office* National Energy Board, 473 Albert Street, Ottawa, Ont. Canada.

**EDGE-PARTINGTON, James Patrick Seymour.** British company director. *B.* 1926. *Educ.* Marlborough 1939–44; Scholarship Royal Coll. of Music 1944; Institute of Chartered Accountants 1951. *M.* 1951, Monica Madge Smith. *S.* Julian and Simon. *Dau.* Jane. *Career:* With Coldstream Guards 1944–48. Partner, Gordon Heynes & Co., Chartered Accountants 1954–59, then amalgamated with Allen, Baldry, Holman & Best, Chartered Accountants 1959–64 (retired 1964), Director 1961—. Chairman 1963—, Crown House Ltd.; Dir. 1975, Chmn. 1976 Tilbury Contracting Group Ltd. *Address:* Basing, Furnace Lane, Cowden, Kent; and *office* 2 Lygon Place, London SW1W 0JT.

**EDMENSON, Sir Walter Alexander,** CBE, DL. British shipowner. *B.* 1892. *M.* 1918, Doris Davidson. *S.* Walter Alexander (killed in action 1940). *Dau.* Elizabeth Ann (Maclaran). *Career:* Served World War I, North Irish Horse, Royal Field Artillery (despatches) 1914–19. Northern Ireland Rep., Ministry of War Transport 1939–45. President, G. Heyn & Sons. Ltd.; President, Ulster Steamship Co. Ltd. and other companies, Irish Lights Commissioner; member, Council of Chamber of Shipping 1943–73; Belfast Harbour Commissioner 1940–61; Lloyd's Register of Shipping 1949–74. *Award:* Medal of Freedom with Palms (U.S.A.). *Address:* 101 Bryansford Road, Newcastle, Co. Down BT33 0LF, Northern Ireland.

**EDMISTON, James Richard.** American. *B.* 1912. *Educ.* Westminster College, (AB degree). *M.* 1935, Ruth Hunter. *S.* James Hunter. *Career:* Sales Manager, Pillsbury Co. 1950; Merchandizing Manager, Lever Bros. 1955; Vice-Pres., Cudahy Packing Co. 1960. Governor, Swimming Pool Assn.; Dir., Amer. Meat Inst. Chairman of the Board: Swimrite Inc., Swimrite Manufacturing Co., and Swimming Pool Manufacturers. *Member:* Management Assn.; Vice-Pres., Chamber of Commerce 1949. Republican. *Clubs:* Larchmont New York Yacht; Chicago Athletic; Omaha Country, Interlochen Country. *Address:* 5038 Hazeltine Avenue, APT 301, Sherman Oaks, Calif. 91403; and *office* 15330 Oxnard Street, Van Nuys Calif. 91408, U.S.A.

**EDMONDS, Robert Humphrey Gordon.** CMG, MBE. British diplomat. *B.* 1920. *Educ.* Ampleforth; Brasenose Coll. Oxford. *M.* (1) 1951, Gorgina Combe (*Diss.* 1975). *S.* 4. (2) 1976, Enid Flora, widow of Dr. Michael Balint. *Career:* served Army 1940–46; Intelligence Officer, Western Desert, N. African and Italian Campaigns; Entered Foreign Service 1946, served Cairo, Rome, Warsaw and Caracas, 1947–65; Head, Amer. Dept. F.O. 1966–67; Head Medit. Dept. C'wealth Office 1967–68; Head, Southern European Dept. FCO 1968–69; Minister Moscow 1969–71; British High Commissioner Nicosia 1971–72; Visiting Research Fellow, Dept. Politics, Glasgow Univ. 1973; Asst. Under-Secy. of State, Foreign & C'wealth Office 1974–77; Visiting Fellow, Woodrow Wilson International Center for Scholars, Washington, D.C. since 1977. *Publications:* Soviet Foreign Policy 1962–73 (1975). *Address:* The Apple House, Cardross Stokes, Port of Monteith, Stirling FK8 3JY.

**EDMONDS, Victor Thomas.** British chartered accountant. Partner, Wrigley Cregan Todd & Co. (Chartered Accountants, Guildford, Surrey). *B.* 1916. *Educ.* Hove High School and Streatham Grammar School. *M.* 1946, Hazel Roy Linden. *S.* 1. *Daus.* 2. *Career:* Articled to Wrigley Cregan Todd & Co. until 1938–45 war; partner afterwards. Served with R.A.P.C. in U.K. and Middle East (Captain). Fellow, Inst. of Chartered Accountants in England and Wales (F.C.A.); Fellow, Institute of Chartered Secretaries and Administrators. *Address:* 6 Foxenden Road, Guildford, Surrey GU1 4DL and *office* 276 High Street, Guildford, Surrey, GU1 3JU.

**EDSALL, John Tileston.** American professor of Biochemistry. *B.* 1902. *Educ.* Harvard Univ. (AB 1923, MD 1928); studied at Cambridge Univ. 1924–26. *M.* 1929, Margaret Dunham. *S.* Lawrence Dunham, David Tileston, and Nicholas Cranford. *Career:* Instructor to Prof., Harvard 1928–51; Fellow, John Simon Guggenheim Fdn., California Institute of Technology 1940–41; Professor of Biological Chemistry, Harvard Univ. 1951–73; Fulbright Visiting Lecturer, Cambridge Univ. 1952; Visiting Professor, Collège de France, Paris 1955–56; Univ. of California, Berkeley, Summer 1960; Fulbright Lecturer, Univ. of Tokyo, 1964; Pres. Sixth International Congress of Biochemistry N.Y. 1964; Visiting Lecturer Australian National Univ. Canberra 1970. Editor, Journal of Biological Chemistry 1958–67: Professor of Biochemistry Emeritus since 1973; Chmn., Survey of Sources for the History of Biochemistry & Molecular Biology 1975—. *Publications:* Proteins, Amino Acids and Peptides (with E. J. Cohn), (1943); Biophysical Chemistry (with J. Wyman), vol. I, (1958). *Member:* Amer. Socy. of Biological Chemists (Pres. 1957–58); Amer. Chemical Socy. (Chmn. Div. of Biological Chemistry 1948–49, 1950–51); National Acad. of Sciences of U.S.A., Amer. Philosophical Socy.; Amer. Acad. of Arts & Sciences. Member, Royal Danish Academy of Sciences. Member, Deutsche Akademie der Natur Forscher Leopoldina (Halle); Chmn. Editorial Bd. Proceedings of National Academy of Sciences 1968–72; Foreign Member, Royal Swedish Academy of Sciences. *Awards:* Passano Fdn. Award 1966. DSc (Hon) Univ. Chicago and Western Reserve Univ. 1967. Hon DSc, Univ. of Michigan, 1968; Willard Gibbs Medal (Chicago Section, Amer. Chemical Socy. 1972; D. Phil (Hon.) Univ. of Göteborg. Sweden 1972. *Address:* 985 Memorial Drive, Cambridge, Mass., 02138 and Biological Laboratories, 16 Divinity Avenue, Harvard Univ., Cambridge 02138, Mass., U.S.A.

**EDSBERG, Mogens.** Danish Diplomat. *Address:* Danish Embassy, Apard. 61.169, Caracas 106, Venezuela.

**EDWARDS, Campbell William,** OBE, JP (Dorset). *B.* 1907. *Educ.* Trinity Coll., Cambridge (BA Hist and Pol Sc 1927; MA 1960). *M.* 1948, Pauline Joan Southwell. *S.* M. A. J. Southwell (stepson). *Dau.* Amanda Campbell. *Career:* Chmn. and Joint Mng. Dir., W. Edwards & Son (Bridport) Ltd. 1933. Flight Lieut. R.A.F.V.R. 1941–45. Chairman. Bridport-Gundry Ltd. since 1952. Deputy Chmn. 1971–72; Conservative. *Club:* Junior Carlton (London). *Address:* The Gables, Bridport, Dorset; and *office* Bridport-Gundry Ltd., Bridport, Dorset.

**EDWARDS, E. Augustin E.** Chilean publisher and industrialist. President: Empresa *El Mercurio* S.A.P.; Banco de A. Edwards y Cia; Seguros La Chilena Consolidada; and Technical University Federico Santa Maía. *B.* 1927. *Educ.* Heatherdown (England) Grange School; and School of Law, Univ. of Chile (Santiago). *M.* Maria Luisa del Rio. *Address:* c/o *El Mercurio,* Casilla No. 13-D, Santiago, Chile.

**EDWARDS, Edwin W.** American statesman. *B.* 1927. *Educ.* Marksville public schools; Louisiana State Univ. LL B (1949), LL D (1968). *M.* 1949, Elaine Schwartzenburg. *S.* 2. *Daus.* 2. *Career:* Practised law in Crowley, Sen. Partner Edwards, Edwards and Broadhurst since 1949; Elected to Crowley City Council 1954 and 1958; Louisiana State Senate (35th Dis.) 1964; U.S. Congress 1965 and 1966; Re-elected U.S. Congress 1968 and 1970; Lou-Miss Delegations' Whip 1967 and 1969; Governor of Louisiana since 1972. Chmn. Interstate Oil Compact Commission since 1974; Chmn. Ozarks Reg. Comm. (comprehensive planning for 5 states) since 1974; Mem. Natural Resources and Environ. Mgmt. Cttee for Southern Governors' Conference; Nat. Governors' Conference, New Orleans in 1975. *Member:* Crowley Lions Club (and former Pres.); International Rice Festival (and former Pres.); Greater Crowley Chamber of Commerce; America Legion, Acadia Post 15 (past adjutant), Major Civil Air Control. *Address:* State Buildings, Baton Rouge, Louisiana 70804, U.S.A.

**EDWARDS, Sir George Robert,** OM, CBE, FRS, BSc (Eng), Hon DSc, CEng, Hon FRAeS, Hon FAIAA. British. *B.* 1909. *Educ.* Univ. of London (BSc). *M.* 1935, Marjorie Annie Thurgood. *Dau.* 1. *Career:* Joined design staff of Vickers Aviation, Weybridge 1935; Experimental Manager 1940, and Chief Designer 1945. Chmn. British Aircraft Corp. Ltd. until 1975. *Publications:* various papers and lectures in the Journal of the Royal Aeronautical Society, American Institute of Aeronautical Sciences, and the Amer. Society of Automotive Engineers. *Member:* Royal Aeronautical Society (President 1958); Amer. Inst. of Aeronautics and Astronautics. *Awards:* Guggenheim Medal, 1959; R.S.A. Albert Medal 1972; Royal Institute Fellow Institute, Directors; Pro-Chancellor, Univ. of Surrey; Hons. DSc London, Manchester, Southampton and Cranfield. *Clubs:* Athenaeum. *Address:* Albury Heights, White Lane, Guildford, Surrey.

**EDWARDS, Keith William,** CBE. Australian. *B.* 1908. *M.* 1936, Lilian Catherine Thomson. *S.* 2. *Dau.* 1. *Career:* Manager, J. A. Hemphill & Sons Pty. Ltd., Perth, W.A. 1934–39; seconded to Australian Wheat Board (Accountant and at times Actg. Secy.) 1939–45; Manager, Westralian Farmers Transport Ltd., London 1945–50, Asst. Gen. Manager, Westralian Farmers Co-op. Ltd., Perth 1950–57, Gen. Mgr. 1958–73; Dir.: CSBP, Farmers Ltd. 1964; BP Refinery (Kwinana) Ltd. 1958–72; Australian Mutual Provident Society, Perth Branch, 1968—; The Australian Wool Marketing Corp. Pty. Ltd., 1970–72; British Petroleum Co. of Australia since 1972; Dir. Westralian Farmers Co-op. Ltd. since 1974. *Member:* Export Development Council 1960–67, and of Australian Coastal Shipping Commission (1956–60); Transport Industries Advisory Council 1971–74. Associate: Aust. Socy. of Accountants, and of Inst. of Chartered Shipbrokers. *Club:* Weld (Perth). *Address:* 191 Wellington Street, Mosman Park, W.A., Australia.

**EDWARDS, Kenneth Joseph.** American. Prince of Outer Baldonia. *B.* 1914. *Educ.* N.Y. Univ. Coll. of Engineering, Guggenheim School of Aeronautics (BSME-Aero). *M.* 1942, Edith Joan Young. *S.* Kenneth Joseph, Jr. *Dau.* Valerie Anne. Chmn. of the Bd. and Pres., Godfrey Products Co. 1948–50. Chairman of the Board and President, Alken-Lux Corp. 1963–69; Pres. and Chmn. of the Board (1963—) and Director (1937—), Alken-Murray Corp. Vice-Pres. 1961—, and Dir. 1957—, L. A. Lux Co. *Member:* A.S.L.E., A.M.A., V.T.A. *Clubs:* N.Y. University; Fauquier; Fauquier Springs. Hon. PhD., Hamilton State Univ. 1973. *Address:* Fenton Farm, Warrenton, Va.; and *office* 111 Fifth Avenue, New York, N.Y. 10003, U.S.A.

**EDWARDS, R. Nicholas,** MA, MP. British insurance Broker. *B.* 25 Feb. 1934. *Educ.* Westminster School; Trinity Coll. Cambridge. *M.* 1963, Ankaret Healing. *S.* 1. *Daus.* 2. *Career:* With Royal Welch Fusiliers 2nd Lieut., 1952–59; Trinity Coll. Camb. 1954–57; Employed at Lloyds by Brandt's Group 1957–76; Dir. Brandt's Ltd. 1974–76; Dir. of Globtik Tankers Ltd., Globtik Management Ltd., A. L. Sturge (Holdings) Ltd. 1971–76, Brandt's Underwriting Agencies Ltd. 1965–76, PA International & Sturge Underwriting Agency Ltd. Member of Parliament for Pembroke since 1970; Member of Shadow Cabinet and Conservative Front Bench Spokesman for Welsh Affairs. *Clubs:* City University, Cardiff County. *Address:* Pontesgob Mill, Fforest, nr. Abergavenny; & 20 Chester Row, London SW1; & Peach House, Rhos, nr. Haverfordwest; & *office* Moor House, 119 London Wall, London EC2.

**EDWARDS, Richard Cecil Churchill.** British (Australian) newspaperman. *B.* 1903. *M.* 1925, Lillian Edith Hamilton. Political Correspondent, Melbourne Sun 1925; Chief sub-editor: Star, Melbourne 1933, and The Herald 1936 (Asst. Editor 1948–56). Editor, The Herald, Melbourne 1956–64. *Publications:* Why Parties? (1943); What is Liberty? (1944); Bureaucracy, (1944); You and the Bomb, (1945); Bruce of Melbourne—Man of Two Worlds, (1966); Brown Power, (1970); John Monash (1971); The Editor Regrets (1972); Labor Pains (1974). *Address:* 2a Hopetoun Grove, Ivanhoe, Vic., Australia.

**EDWARDS, Robert,** MP. British. *B.* 1906. *Educ.* Council Schools and Technical College. *M.* 1933, May Edith Sandham (*Dec.* 1970). *S.* 1. *Career:* M.P. (Lab.-Co-op.) for Bilston since 1955 (contested Chorley, 1935; Stetford, 1939; Newport, 1945); MP, S.E. Wolverhampton; National Chairman, L.L.P., 1943–48; member Labour Party since 1949; 30 years' membership of the Co-operative Party. Journalist; engineer; chemical traveller; Captain in the Spanish Republican Army; Lancashire organiser of the Chemical Workers' Union, 1939–43; Assistant General Secretary, 1945–47. General Secretary of the Chemical Workers' Union 1947–71; Chmn. Section of Internat. Fed. of Chemical & General Workers Unions (ICF); National Officer, Transport & Gen. Workers Union 1971–76. Leader, British Deleg. to North Atlantic Assembly, 1967–69; Deputy Leader, British Deleg. to Assembly of Counc. of Europe, 1967–70; Vice-Pres. to Assembly 1969–70, also Assembly of Western Union; Chmn., Western European Union Defence and Armaments Cttee., 1965–70; Vice-Chmn., Local Authorities Cttee. of the Council of Europe; Member of European Parliament since 1977. *Publications:* United Socialist States of Europe; Chemicals, Servant or Master?;

War on the People; Freedom or Servitude; and many pamphlets. *Address:* House of Commons, London, S.W.1.

**EDWARDS, Willard Eldridge,** LittD; Lieut.-Comdr. U.S.N. (Ret.); Originator of The Perpetual Calendar. *B.* 1903. *Educ.* Massachusetts Institute of Technology; Univ. of Oklahoma (BS 1929); Univ. of S. California; Jackson Coll., Hawaii (MS 1960, MA 1961). *M.* 1942, Dorothy Shiell. *S.* Willard Eldridge and Arthur Lindley. *Daus.* Annabelle Hyder (*D.*) and Geraldine Ann. *Career:* Research Engineer, Radio Corp. of American. N.Y.C. 1926–28; Electrical Engineer, Alexander Aircraft Co.. Colorado Springs 1929; Telephone and Radio Engineer, Amer. Tel & Tel. Co. 1929–33; Radio Engineer at KFI 1933–40; Electrical Engineer, Lockheed Aircraft Co. 1940–41, 9th Region Civil Aero. Admin., Honolulu 1946–49, and 14th Naval District, U.S. Navy, Pearl Harbor, Hawaii 1949–65; Retired Lieut.-Comdr. (Electronics Engineer) 1942–46. Lecturer and writer on The Perpetual Calendar since 1922, in 350 cities in 104 countries on nine world tours; Originator of Presidents Day and proposals of Mon-holidays in U.S.A. *Publications:* The Perpetual Calendar (1943); American Samoa (1949); Origin of Christian Time (1955); Underground Corrosion and Cathodic Protection (1956); Time and the Calendar (1961); Marine Corrosion—Its cause and cure (1963); New-Year Days are Anniversaries (1973); The subject of The Perpetual Calendar is now before the U.S. Congress for study for possible international adoption. Republican. *Member:* Inst. of Radio Engineers; Socy. of Amer. Military Engineers; Amer. Inst. of Electrical Engineers; Nat. Assn. of Corrosion Engineers; A.A.A.S.; Hawaiian Astronomical Socy. Sigma Chi; Tau Omega; Alpha Sigma Delta; Alpha Eta Rho. Mason 32°; Int. Platform Assn. *Clubs:* Pearl Harbour Officers; Aero-Kokua; Toastmasters International; 100,000 Mile; Wollaston (Mass.) Yacht; Los Serranos (Calif.) Country. *Address:* 1434 Punahou St. Honolulu, Hawaii 96822, U.S.A.

**EDWARDS, William Bennett.** U.S.A. Technology Consultant. *B.* 1927. *Educ.* Univ. of Chicago. *M.* 1954. Virginia Jane Davis. Vice-President: MARS Equipment Corp. 1958–62 (also Technical Dir.), and Centennial Arms Corp., Chicago 1960–62. Founder and Technical Editor of Guns, Chicago 1954–61. Technical Editor: Shooting Goods Retailer 1956–61 and Guns Quarterly 1960–61. Arms Editor: Publisher's Development Corp., Chicago 1953–61, and Reynard Publishing Co., Chicago 1956–57. Asst. Editor, The Gun Digest 1952–55. Prior to 1948 was variously employed by Colt's, Hi-Standard (Gun) Mfg. Co. and by U.S. Government at Watertown (Mass.) Arsenal Laboratory. Research and Development Consultant to U.S. Dept. of the Army, and to private industry firms, such as Colt's, Remington Arms Co., Winchester Repeating Arms Co., Fabriques d'Armes Unies de Liège SA, Antonio Zoli Arms Factory (Italy), MARS Equipment Corp. (Chicago), Navy Arms Co. (Ridgefield, N.J.) and others. Owner of Benet Arms Co. Export-Import (estab. 1947) and Gold Rush Gun Shops, San Francisco, 1964. *Publications:* Guns of the Great War 1914–18 (1964); Civil War Guns (1962); This Is The West (contrib. anthology), (1958); Guns at Independence Hall, (1958); Let's Set the Record Straight, (1958); The Story of Colt's Revolver (1953); United States Steal (1975); Contributer, Encyclopedia Britannica; Straight Shooting Magazine (1970); numerous articles on arms and historical subjects. *Awards:* Best Western Non-Fiction (Western Writers of America) 1958; Tenth annual 1963 award in Criminal Investigation (Amer. Assn. of Criminology, of which he is Hon. Life Member); Advisor to White House on Armageddon Plan (1974); *Member:* California Atny.-Gen. Vol. Advisory Cttee.; Amer. Ordnance Assn.; National Rifle Assn.; Northern California Arms Collectors Assn.; Amer. Automatic Weapons Assn. Inc.; Consultant Staff of Amer. Assn. of Criminology Inc. Republican. *Address:* Ultramonte Manse, Afton, Va. 22920; and Benet Arms Proving Ground, Lowesville, Va., U.S.A.

**EDWARDS, William Henry.** American lawyer. *B.* 1898. *Educ.* Brown Univ. (AB 1919; Hon LLD 1965); Hon DHS Providence College and Hon LLD Univ. of R.I., 1967; Harvard Law School (LLB 1921). *M.* 1921, (1) Mabel Potter (*Dec.* 1969). *S.* Knight. *Dau.* Louise Edwards Saul; (2) 1969, Mary Rita McGinn. Service on various State Commissions; served U.S. Army, World War I, and in U.S. Navy in World War II. *Publications:* book reviews in various publications. *Clubs:* New York: Century, Harvard; Providence; University; Agawam; Art; Hope; Turks Head. *Address:* 154 Arlington Avenue, Providence 02906, R.I., U.S.A.

**EDWARDS, William Philip Neville,** CBE. *B.* 1904. *Educ.* Rugby Sch.; Corpus Christi Coll., Cambridge; Princeton Univ. (Davison Scholar). *M.* (1) 1931, Hon. Sheila Cary (*Dau.* of 13th Viscount Falkland) (*Dec.* 1976). (2) Joan Mullins (née Barker), widow of Norman Mullins. *S.* 2. *Career:* Joined Underground Electric group of companies 1927; later became Secy. to Lord Ashfield, Chmn., London Passenger Transport Bd.; Secy. of Standing Jt. Cttee. of Main Line Railway Companies and of L.P.T.B. 1933; Officer of Board as Personal Asst. to Gen. Mgr. of Railways 1937; Outdoor Supt. of Railways 1938; Public Relations Officer to Board 1939; Asst. to Chmn. of Supply Concl., Ministry of Supply 1941–42; Head, Industrial Inform. Div., Min. of Production and Alternate Dir. of Informn., British Supply Cncl. in N. America 1943–45; Dir. of Overseas Infmn. Div. Board of Trade 1945–46; Head, British Infmn. Services U.S.A. 1946–49; Dir., Confed. British Industry 1949–66; Mng. Dir. British Overseas Fairs Ltd. 1959–66 and Chairman 1966–68. *Address:* Dawes Mead, Leigh, Reigate, Surrey.

**EELLS, Richard S. F.** American. *B.* 1917. *Educ.* Whitman Co. (BA); Princeton Univ. (MA). Chief, Div. of Aeronautics, Library of Congress, 1944–49; Field Dir., Near East College Assn., 1949–50; Manager, Public Policy Research, General Electric Co., 1950–59. At Columbia Univ. 1959–present: Executive Editor and Director, Program for Studies of the Modern Corporation, and Adjunct Professor of Business, Graduate School of Business, Columbia University; Member, The National Development Board of the President of the University, Columbia University. Visiting Fellow, Center for the Study of Democratic Institutions, Santa Barbara, California, 1971. Trustee and Vice President, The Weatherhead Foundation, N.Y.; Trustee and Executive Vice President, Arkville Erpf Fund, N.Y.; Trustee and Executive Director, Midgard Foundation, N.Y.; Trustee, the New England Conservatory of Music, Boston; Member, Board of Overseers, Whitman College, Walla Walla, Washington; Trustee and Member of the Executive Committee, New York Council on Alcoholism. Former trustee of: the Municipal Art Socy. of N.Y., National Citizens' Cttee. for Broadcasting, and the American Shakespeare Theatre. Advisor, Committee for Economic Development, N.Y.C. *Publications:* Corporation Giving in a Free Society (1956); The Meaning of Modern Business (1960); Conceptual Foundations of Business (with Clarence Walton), (1961) (revised edition, 1969) (third edition, 1974); The Government of Corporations (1962); The Business System; Ideas and Concepts, 3 vols. (edited with Clarence Walton), (1957); The Corporation and the Arts (1967); Education and the Business Dollar (with Kenneth G. Patrick), (1968); Man in the City of the Future (edited with Clarence Walton), (1968); Global Corporations (1972), (revised edition 1976); Bribery & Extortion in World Business (with Neil Jacoby & Peter Nehemkis) (1977). *Awards:* Phi Beta Kappa; Guggenheim Chair of Aeronautics, Library of Congress, 1949; Alfred P. Sloan Foundation grant, 1959; Academy of Management and McKinsey Foundation Book Award, 1962; Rockefeller Foundation Grant, 1963. *Clubs:* Pilgrims of the U.S.; Socy. of Colonial Wars; Metropolitan (N.Y.); The Church (N.Y.); Cosmos (Washington, D.C.). *Address:* 251 East 51st Street, New York, N.Y. 10022; and *office*, Uris Hall, Columbia University, New York, N.Y. 10027, U.S.A.

**EFRAIMOGLOU, Minas,** BCom, MA. Greek. *B.* 1925. *Educ.* Greek-American Coll., Athens; Highest Sch. of Economic & Commercial Studies, Athens; London Sch. of Economics (MA (Bus. Admin.)). *M.* 1961, Agapie Thomas Lanaras. *S.* 1. *Daus.* 5. *Career:* Dir. & Gen. Man. Styloglou-Efraimoglou & Co.; Dir. & Financial Man. Efraimoglou Bros.; Dir. Efraimoglou-Aslanoglou & Co.; Member of Board, Profin Ltd.; Vice-Chmn. of Board, XYLEBORIA Ltd.; Gen. Sec. Federation of Greek Wool Industrialists; Mem. of Board Greek-American Educational Inst.; Vice-Chmn. of Board Karenta Ltd. *Clubs:* Royal Hellenic Yachting; Kifissia Lawn Tennis. *Address:* 6 Pavlou Mela Str., Filothei, Athens, Greece; and *office* 10 Kalamiotou St., Athens.

**EFRON, Samuel,** BA, LLB. American. Specialist Attorney. *B.* 1915. *Educ.* Lehigh Univ. (BA); Harvard Law Sch. (LLB). *M.* 1941, Hope Newman. *S.* 2. *Career:* Partner. Arent, Fox, Kintner, Plotkin & Kahn; Surrey, Karasik, Gould & Efron, 1954–61; Exec. Vice-Pres. Parsons & Whittemore Inc. 1961–69. *Member:* Bar Assoc. American, Federal, District of Columbia; Inter-American; Assn. of the Bar of the State of New York; American Soc. of International Law; Phi Beta Kappa. *Clubs:* Army-Navy; Capitol Hill; Cosmos; International; Federal Bar; Nat. Press (all Washington D.C.); Harvard; Lehigh; Lotos (all New York). *Award:* Knight of 1st Class Order of Lion of Finland, 1975. *Address:* 3537 Ordway St., N.W., Washington, D.C. 20016, U.S.A.; and *office* Federal Bar Bldg., 1815 H. Street, N.W., Washington, D.C. 20006.

**EGAN, William Constantine.** American. *B.* 1912. *Educ.* Harvard Univ., BS Degree 1936. *M.* 1939, Jane Calkins. *S.* Raymond C., William C., III. *Dau.* Nancy C. *Career:* Pres., Carrier-Houston Corporation, 1958; Vice-Pres., Special Products Group, Carrier Air Conditioning Co., 1962; Pres., Carrier-Transicold Co., 1970; Vice-Pres., Carrier Corp.; Pres., Day & Night Payne Company (Div. of Carrier Corp.) (1972) 1975–; Vice-Pres. & Exec. Asst. to the Chmn. of the Board of Carrier Corp. *Clubs:* Onondaga Golf & Country Club, Fayetteville, N.Y.; (Syracuse, New York); Harvard (N.Y.C.). *Address:* Duguid Road, Manlius, New York 13104; and *office* P.O. Box 4800, Carrier Tower, Syracuse, New York 13221, U.S.A.

**EGELAND, Leif.** South-African advocate and director of companies. *B.* 19 Jan. 1903. *Educ.* Univ. of S. Africa (MA, 1st Class); Oxford Univ. (MA, BCL); Hon. LLD (Cantab.); Official Fellow in Classics and Law, Brasenose Coll., Oxford (1927–30); Rhodes Scholar (Natal, 1924); elected Hon. Bencher, Middle Temple (1948). *M.* 1942, Marguerite de Zwaan. *Dau.* Margrethe Christine. *Career:* Member, Teaching Staff, Michaelhouse, Belgowan, Natal 1923–24; Vice-Consul of Norway in Natal 1931–43; S. African Min. Plen. and Env. Ex. to Sweden 1944–46, and to Belgium and Holland 1946–47; High Commissioner in London 1948–50. Member of Union House of Assembly (United Party) for Durban (Berea) 1933–38, and for Zululand 1940–43; Asst. Judge Advocate General in Union Defence Forces (with rank of Major) 1943; served with 6th S. African Armoured Div. in the Middle East 1943; S.A. delegate to San Francisco Conf. 1945, and to 6th Assembly, U.N. 1946; Leader of S.A. delegation to Final General Assembly, League of Nations 1946; S.A. delegate and President of the Italian Commission at Paris Peace Conf. 1946; delegate to 3rd Gen. Assembly of U.N. 1948; Chmn. Standard General Insurance (Co.) Ltd.; Pres. SA Guide-dog Assoc. for Blind; Chmn. Smuts Memorial Trust; Nat. Chmn. SA Inst. of International Affairs. Vice-Pres. South Africa Foundation. *Address:* 11 Fricker Road, Illovo, Johannesburg, South Africa.

**EGERAN, Enver Necdet.** Turkish petroleum geologist. *B.* 1907. *Educ.* Min. E., Geol. E., DSc. *M.* 1933, Sabi Olcmen. *S.* Birol and Erol. *Career:* Managing Director, Geological Department of MTA (Turkish Geological Survey) 1938–51 and Petroleum Department 1951–52; Chief Petroleum Adviser 1952–54; Vice-Pres., Petroleum Administration of Turkey 1954–56; Assistant to General Manager & Director, Mobil Exploration Mediterranean Inc. 1956–68. President, General Manager, E. N. Egeran Consulting Engineering Firm. *Publications:* Applied Geology (in Turkish) (1944); Tectonique de la Turquie (1947); Geology of Turkey (in Turkish) (1948); several technical papers on the geology of various mineral and oil deposits in Turkey. Past President: Turkish Association of Petroleum Geologists, Geological Society of Turkey, Union of Turkish Geologists, Association Franco-Turque d'Ingénieurs, and Turkish-American Association; General Secretary, Turkish National Committee for World Petroleum Congresses. *Clubs:* Rotary, Golf (Ankara). *Address:* Gunes Sokak 23/10, Kavaklidere, Ankara, Turkey.

**EGERTON, Sir Seymour (John Louis),** GCVO. British banker. *B.* 24 Sept. 1915. *Educ.* Eton. Served in World War II with Grenadier Guards 1939–45. Chairman, Coutts & Co., 1951–76, Regional Director, National Westminster Bank Ltd., and Dep. Chmn., Phoenix Assurance Co. Ltd. Dir., Romney Trust Ltd. Treas., Boy Scouts Assn. 1952–64. Sheriff of Greater London, 1968–69. *Address:* 440 Strand, London, W.C.2.

**EGGER, Rowland Andrews.** Professor of Politics and Public Affairs. *B.* 1908. *Educ.* Southwestern Univ. (AB *cum laude* 1926); Southern Methodist Univ. (AM 1927); Univ. of Michigan (PhD 1933); Southwestern Univ. (LLD 1959). *M.* 1932, Gretchen Lee Savin (MacIlwaine (*D.* 1952); stepson William Andrew MacIlwaine, MD Officer Order of Leopold (Belgium); Knight Commander, Order of the Condor (Bolivia); Commander, Order of the Cedars (Lebanon). *Career:* Instructor, Southern Methodist Univ. 1926–28; Univ. Fellow, Univ. of Michigan 1928–29; Instructor, Princeton Univ. 1929–31; Technical Consultant, State of New Jersey 1930–31; Associate Prof. of Pol. Science 1931–36, Prof. 1936–64, Univ. of Virginia; Director, Bureau of Public Administration, Univ. of Virginia 1931–56; Sec.-General, Joint Committee on Public Administration, Brussels 1935–36; Director of the Budget, Commonwealth of Virginia 1939–42; Administrative and Financial Adviser to the President of Bolivia 1942; Gen. Manager and Member of Board of Directors, Bolivian Development Corp. 1942–47; Visiting Prof. of International Organization and Administration, Columbia Univ. 1947–48; Vice-Pres., U.N. Administrative Tribuna 1949–51; Associate Director, Public Administration Clearing House 1950–53; Administrative Adviser, Prime Minister of Pakistan 1953; Near-East Representative, The Ford Foundation 1954–56; S.S.R.C. Senior Fellow 1958–59; sometime consultant to the U.N., U.N.E.S.C.O., White House, Dept. of State, Dept. of Commerce, Dept. of Agriculture, First Hoover Commission, Brookings Institution, Ford Foundation and various Congressional committees of inquiry. Visiting Professor of Government, Harvard University 1961. Special Representative of the President of the U.S. to Bolivia 1961–62. Member Pres. Johnson's Task Force on Government Organization 1964; Professor of Politics and Public Affairs 1964–72, Professor. Emeritus of Politics and Public Affairs Princeton Univ. since 1972; John Goodwin Tower Professor, Political Science Southwestern Univ. 1972–73; Eugene McElvaney Prof. Political Science, Southern Methodist Univ. 1973–77; Visiting Prof., Univ. of Virginia 1977–78. *Member:* Int. Inst. of Administrative Sciences (Exec. Cttee.); Royal Inst. of Public Administration (Haldane Prize 1960); Nat. Acad. of Public Administration; American Political Science Assn. American Society for Public Administration; American Academy of Political Science; Inter-University Case Program (Vice-Chmn., Trustee, Exec. Cttee.). Phi Beta Kappa. *Publications:* Retirement of Public Employees (1933); International Organizations in the Field of Public Administration (1936) Municipal Ownership of Electrical Undertakings (1937); Organization of Peace at the Administrative Level (1945); Research, Education and Regionalism (1949); The Improvement of Public Administration in Pakistan (1953); The Economic and Social Development of Boliva (1962); The President and Congress (1963). The President of the United States, (1971); Le Métier de Président (1970); O Presidente dos Estados Unidos (1974); Editor International Review of Administrative Sciences. Frequent contributor of articles to symposia, learned journals, etc. *Clubs:* Farmington Country (Charlottesville); Cosmos (Washington); Nassau (Princeton); Princeton (N.Y.C.); English-Speaking Union; Pi Kappa Alpha: Raven Society. *Address:* Institute of Government, Minor Hall, University of Virginia, Charlottesville, Virginia 22903, U.S.A.

**EGGLETON, Anthony,** CVO. Australian. *B.* 1932. *Educ.* King Alfred's College, Wantage (U.K.). *M.* 1953, Mary Stuart Walker. *S.* 2. *Dau.* 1. Director of Public Relations, Royal Australian Navy 1960–65; News Director, Australian Broadcasting Commission, Melbourne, 1956–60. Press Secretary to the Prime Minister of the Commonwealth of Australia 1965–71; Dir. of Information, Commonwealth Secretariat 1971–74; Special Adviser to Australian Leader of Opposition 1974; Federal Director, Liberal Party of Australia since 1975. Mem. Australian Journalists' Assoc. Received Public Relations Institute's first Award of Honour 1968. *Clubs:* National Press of Canberra (Fdn. President). *Address:* Parliament House, Canberra, Australia.

**EHRENBERG, Dr. Herbert.** German Politician. *B.* 1926. *Educ.* Wilhelmshaven-Rüstersiel Coll. of Labour, Politics & Economics; Göttingen Univ. *M.* 1963, Ilse Borreck. *Daus.* 2. *Career:* Lecturer in Sociology; Economic Research Dept. to the Governing Bd. of the Industriegewerkschaft Bau-Steine-Erden; entered ÖTV trade union 1949; Federal Service, latterly as Sec. of State, Federal Ministry of Labour & Social Affairs 1968–72; mem., Social Democratic Party (SPD) since 1955; mem., German Federal Diet since 1972; mem., SPD Executive, & Exec. Chmn. of the Economics & Finance Policy Commission to the Party Exec. of the SPD since 1975; Minister of Labour & Social Affairs since 1976. *Publications:* Lohnpolitik heute (1963); Die Erhard-Saga (1965); Durchbruch zum sozialen Rechtsstaat (1969); Vermögenspolitik für die siebziger Jahre (1971); Zwischen Marx und Markt (1973); Blick zurück nach vorn (1975). *Address:* 53 Bonn-Duisdorf, Rochusstrasse 1, Federal Republic of Germany.

**EHRNROOTH, Goran Robert.** Finnish banker. *B.* 1 Apr. 1905. *M.* 1930. Louise von Julin. *S.* Casimir, Clas Göran, Robert. *Dau:* Elsa. *Career:* Chmn. Bd. Finnish Steamship Co; Oy Tampella Ab; Oy Lohja Ab. *Address:* Södra Kajen 6, Helsinki, Finland.

**EIGENHEER, Charles Emile.** Swiss. *B.* 1914. *M.* 1947, Trudi Callus. *S.* 1. *Dau.* 1. *Career:* Man. Dir. Hasler Holding Ltd.; Hasler Ltd.; FAVAG SA; Hasler Cashregister Ltd.; Chmn., Hasler Signal Ltd.; Autelca Ltd.; Indim Ltd.; Neederlandse

Hasler Mij. *Member:* SIA (Schweiz Ingenieur & Architektenverein). *Address:* Schneiderstrasse 53, 3084 Wabern, Switzerland; and *office* Belpstrasse 23, CH-3000 Berne 14.

**EIMICKE, Victor W(illiam).** American industrial psychologist. President: V. W. Eimicke Associates Inc. *B.* 1925. *Educ.* New York University (AB 1945; MA 1946; PhD 1951). *M.* 1955, Maxine Howard Thome. *Daus.* Laura Suzanne and Alicia Karen. *Career:* Vice-Pres., Institute for Human Research in Industry 1947–48; various educational posts; New York University, Brooklyn Coll., City Coll. School of Business and Pace Coll. 1945–56; Pres., V. W. Eimicke Assos. Inc., N.Y.C. 1951—; Chmn., Eimicke Assoc. Ltd., London 1956–59; Pres., Action Aids, N.Y.C. 1969—, Laurel Office Aids Inc., 1969—; Dir., New England Grocer Supply Co., Worcester, Mass. 1964–68; Bd. Dir., Japan International Christian University Foundn., Nathan's Famous Inc., Wetson's Inc., American Trauma Soc., Laymen's National Bible Cttee. *Publications:* PhD Dissertation: 'The Effect of Intensive Sales Training Experience upon the basic Pattern of Abilities and Personality Characteristics of Salesmen Candidates'; contributor to various professional journals, magazines, etc., such as Journal of Marketing, Food Marketing, Institutions, Business Screen. *Member:* Phi Beta Kappa; Kappa Delta Pi; Phi Delta Kappa; N.Y. State Psychological Assn.; Westchester Psychological Assn.; Amer. Psychological Assn.; Eastern Psychological Assn. *Clubs:* Metropolitan Opera; Union League; Siwanoy Country; Field (Bronxville); University and Metropolitan (N.Y.C.); American Yacht. *Address:* 20 Hereford Road, Bronxville, N.Y.; and *office* Bronxville, N.Y., U.S.A.

**EISEMAN, Myron Joseph.** American. Chairman of the Board, United International, Division of United Merchants and Manufacturers Inc. April 1954 (Vice-Pres. 1958). Director: Panameritex de Panama, S.A. (Panama); Compagnie Generale du Vetement (France); United Merchants and Manufacturers (U.K.) Ltd. (England); The British Silk Dyeing Co. Ltd. (Scotland); Spun Glass Ltd. (England); Marglass Ltd. (Sherbrooke, England); Perifa Ltd. (France); Polimeros Colombianos S.A. (Colombia). *B.* 1919. *Educ.* New York Univ. (BBE) and Columbia Univ. (BE). *M.* (1) 1953, Marjorie Koenig (*Dec.*). *Daus.* Patricia Ann, Nancy Elizabeth. *M.* (2) 1967, Adrienne Kaster. *S.* Richard M. Heller. *Dau.* Robin Heller. *Career:* Started business career with the Cohn-Hall Marx Co., Division of United Merchants and Manufacturers in 1937, and has been with the Company, in various operations up to the present time. *Member:* Central American Chamber of Commerce (Charter Member); Internatl. Chamber of Commerce; Pan. Amer. Socy.; Ecuadorian Chamber of Commerce; Mexican-American Chamber of Commerce; Export Textile Advisory Cttee. of Washington; Amer. Arbitration Assn., General Arbitration Council. Served as member of various governmental agencies on international trade; Special Mission for International Monetary Fund. *Clubs:* Textile Exporters Assn.; Intercom; Beach Point Country (Mamaroneck .N.Y.). *Address:* Sunny Ridge Road, Harrison, N.Y.; and *office* 1407 Broadway, New York, N.Y. 10018, U.S.A.

**EISENHARDT, Karl John.** American corporation official, diplomat and engineer. *B.* 1897. *Educ.* Baltimore Polytechnic Institute. *M.* 1940, Virginia Ramona Cadotte-Millan. *S.* Eugene. *Career:* served as 2nd Lieut. Corps. of Engineers, U.S. Army 1917–19. Previously Engineering and Business Consultant, 1919–27; General Partner, Eisenhardt-Rutter & Co., Investment Bankers 1927–29; Pres. National Heating & Engineering Co. 1930–33; Chmn. Dist. I, Petroleum Transport Advisory Committee, Office of Defense Transportation; Chmn. Petroleum Transporters Conference, Atlantic Seaboard Committee (for Petroleum Administrator for War) 1941–43. Special Assistant for Economic Affairs to the Ambassador, Embassy of U.S., Caracas and Bogota; also Special Representative of Foreign Economic Administration and U.S. Commercial Corporation to Venezuela, Colombia, British Guiana, Surinam, French Guiana, West Indies, Trinidad, Tobago 1943–45. Chairman of Board: Coastal Tank Lines, Inc., 1940—; Atlas Steel Container Corp. 1957—. President and Director, Pennsylvania Petroleum Co. 1934—; Pan-American Transport Co. 1946—; Petroleum Transport Co. 1934—; Kroy Corp. 1949—; Petrolines, Inc. 1936—; Coastal Tank Lines, Inc. of Virginia, 1952—. Director, Farmile Company 1956—; Thermodynamics and Chemical Corp. 1964—. Republican. *Clubs:* Metropolitan (N.Y.); Cat Key (Bahamas); York Country (Penna.); Belleview-Biltmore Country Club. *Address:* Belleview Biltmore Villas, 100 Oakmont Lane, Belleair, Florida 33516, U.S.A.

**EISENTRAUT, Herbert.** German bookseller. Director, Einkaufszentrale für Öffentliche Büchereien GmbH (buying centre for public libraries), Bismarckstrasse 3, Reutlingen, Wurtt 1947—. *B.* 1909. *Educ.* Higher School Certificate 1930; study of philosophy at Universities of Leipzig and Graz; training for publisher. *M.* 1947, Aldona Petrilaitė. *S.* Jörg-Jurgis. Apprenticed to publisher 1933–34; founded own publishing firm, Goten-Verlag, Leipzig 1934; Head of Lithuanian State Publishers in Kaunas 1941–44. *Member:* Baltic Society; Exchange Association of the German Bookselling Trade. *Club:* Lions (Reutlingen). *Address:* Bergäckerweg 36, 7411 Reutlingen-Betzingen, Germany.

**EITELJORG, Harrison.** American. *B.* 1904. *Educ.* Indiana University Law School. *M.* 1958, Sonja Tarsey. *S.* Jack M. Harrison 11, Roger, James. *Dau.* Vivian. Chairman of Board, 2850 Corporation; Indianapolis, 1950—; Reliable Coal & Mining Co. Chicago, 1950—; Florida Commercial Development Corporation; Miami, 1961—; TSI Thermal Systems, Inc., St. Louis, 1967—; Senior Partner, Morgan Coal Co., Indianapolis, 1945—; President, Contractors & Strippers Supply Co., Indianapolis, 1940—; Sample Rock Co., Miami, 1958—; Energy Coal Co., Routt County, Colo., 1961—; Western Utility Coal Co., Chicago, 1963—. Director, Boys Club Association, Indianapolis, 1956—; Gulfstream Park Association, Hallandale, Fla., 1956—; Chmn. Board of Governors, Indianapolis Museum of Art, 1960; Morgan-Eiteljorg Foundation Indianapolis, 1948—. Gallery of Western Art and Museum Steamboat Springs Colo., 1968; Trustee National Academy of Western Art. *Member:* Delta Kappa; National Coal Assn. America Mining Congress; United States Chamber Comm. Newcomen Society. *Clubs:* Woodstock; Meridian Hills Country; Indianapolis Athletic; Traders Point Hunt; University; Hundred (all Indianapolis); Missouri Athletic (St. Louis); Surf, Indian Creek Country; Palm Bay; Committee of One Hundred (all Miami). *Address:* *office* 4567 Cold Spring Raod, Indianapolis, Indiana 46208.

**EKBLAD, Nils-Eric Gustaf,** LLM, MPhil. Swedish diplomat. *B.* 12 Nov. 1904. *M.* 1931, Märta Maria Gränström. *Daus.* Marie Louise (Stenström), Ulla Mae (von Gottberg). Attached Ministry of Foreign Affairs 1928, served Chicago, Tallinn, Riga, Kaunas, Berne, Omaha, Copenhagen; Ministry for Foreign Affairs 1940–43; Chargé d'Affaires, Caracas 1943–48; Chargé d'Affaires, Addis Ababa 1948–50; Ministry of Foreign Affairs 1950–52; Consul, Hamburg 1952–54; Consul-General, Hamburg 1954–60; Envoy Extraordinary and Minister plenipotentiary, Canberra 1960–63; Ambassador Extraordinary and Plenipotentiary at Dublin 1963–67. Ambassador to Teheran and Kabul 1967–70. *Address:* Apartado 140, Portimão, Portugal.

**EKLUND, Laurence Conrad.** American newspaperman. *B.* 1905. *Educ.* Univ. of Wisconsin (BA in Journalism). *M.* 1931, Ethel Chipman. *S.* John Conrad. *Career:* Reporter on Capital Times of Madison, Wis., 1927; staff of Milwaukee Journal 1927–70; Washington Correspondent of Milwaukee Journal 1947–70. Has reported local and state news, covered Wisconsin political campaigns and national party conventions. Covered economic and political stories in Scandinavia (1949 & 1959) appraising results of Marshall Plan and extent of economic recovery. Swedish-American Homecoming in Sweden (1965). Covered operation Deep Freeze 61 in Antarctica in autumn of 1960; wrote series of 28 articles Antarctica and its growing importance in scientific research on and as the result of signing of the Antarctic Treaty. *Member:* Antarctican Socy.; Amer. Polar Socy.; Swedish Pioneer Historical Socy.; Sigma Delta Chi; Theta Chi. *Awards:* Knight, Royal Order of the North Star 1975 (Sweden); Sigma Delta Chi; Wisconsin Newsman of the Year on retirement. *Clubs:* National Press, Gridiron (Washington) Milwauke (Pres.). *Address:* 5602 York Lane, Bethesda, Md., U.S.A.

**ELAHI CHAUDHRI, Fazal.** *B.* 1904. *Educ.* B.Sc (Agri.), MA, LL.B (Alig.). *M.* (1) 1920, Noor Begum (dec'd 1965), (2) 1939, Ghulam Fatima (dec'd 1969) *S.* 1. *Career:* Called to Gujrat Bar 1929; mem. Gujrat District Board 1932–53; District & City Pres., Gujrat Muslim League 1944; elected to Punjab Legislative Assembly 1945; Minister for Education and Health Punjab, 1948; returned to legal practice 1949; re-elected to Punjab Assembly 1951; Gen. Sec., Pakistan Muslim League 1954; Speaker West Pakistan 1956–58; Mem. Nat. Assembly (Indep.) 1962; Sen. Deputy Speaker Nat. Assembly 1964; MNA Pakistan People's Party 1970; Speaker Nat. Assembly 1971–73; President of Pakistan since 1973. *Award:* H.Q.A. (Hilal e Quaid-e-Azam). *Address:* Presidency, Rawalpindi, Pakistan.

**ELATH, Eliahu**, BA, PhD. Israeli. President Emeritus of the Hebrew University of Jerusalem. *B.* 30 July 1903. *M.* 1931, Zehava Zalel. *Career:* Reuter's Correspondent in Syria and Lebanon 1931–34; Amb. Ex. and Plen. to U.S.A. April 1949–July 1950–Oct. 1952; Amb. Ex. and Plen. to the Court of St. James's 1952–59. *Publications:* Bedouins, their life and manners; Transjordan; Israel and her Neighbours; San Francisco Diary; British Routes to India; Zionism and the Arabs; Zionism at the UN. *Address:* 17 Bialik St., Beth Hakerem, Jerusalem, Israel.

**EL-AYOUTY, Khairy Ahmed Ragheb.** Egyptian Diplomat. *B.* 1916. *Educ.* Faculty of Law, Cairo University, LLB, Master of Laws. *M.* Horeyya M. Hussein, Served in Ministry of Finance 1944–54; Consul Gen., Istanbul, 1957–59; Counsellor, Bonn, 1959; Consul-Gen., Hamburg, 1959–61; Counsellor in U.A.R. Ministry of Foreign Affairs, 1961; Deputy Director, Economic Dept.; Member, I.A.R. Delegation, Fourth Session Economic, Committee for Africa, Addis Ababa, 1962; Chargé D'Affaires, a.i. at U.A.R. Embassy Sierra Leone; Counsellor, U.A.R. Embassy Dar El-Salaam, 1963–67; (Appointed Minister Plenipotentiary, 1966) Dep. Dir., of Dept. of African Affairs, U.A.R. Ministry of Foreign Affairs, 1968–69; Ambassador of United Arab Republic in Australia 1969–74. *Awards:* Order of the Republic, 2nd Class; Order of Merit 1st Class. *Address:* Ministry of Foreign Affairs, Cairo, Egypt.

**EL-AZEM, Abdel Rahman.** *B.* 1922. *Educ.* American University, Beirut, and the Faculty of Law, Beirut. *M.* 1943, Souad El-Azem. *S.* 1. *Daus.* 2. *Awards:* Grand Cordon du Nil, Grand Cordon de la Republique (Egypt); Order of Omayyad, and Cordon of Merit (Syria); Gran Cruz de Isabel la Catolica (Spain). Member of Parliament 1947; member, Syrian Constituent Assembly 1949; Minister of Finance 1950–51–54; Ambassador of Syria to Egypt and the Sudan, and Permanent Representative of Syria in the Arab League 1956–58; Ambassador of the United Arab Republic to Spain and to Japan 1958–61. Ambassador of the Syrian Arab Republic to the Court of St. James's, Feb. 1962–63. *Address:* Ministry of Foreign Affairs, Damascus, Syria.

**ELDIN, Gérard.** International Civil Servant. *B.* 1927. *Educ.* Licencié ès Lettres, Licencié en Droit. Université d'Aix-en-Provence; Diplômé de l'Ecole Nationale d'Adminstration. *M.* 1960, Marie-Cêcile Bergerot. *S.* 2. *Daus.* 2. *Career:* Inspector of Finances 1954–58; Treasury Dept. 1958–63; Adviser, Private Office of M. Valéry Giscard d'Estaing, Min. of Finance & Economic Affairs 1963–66; Deputy Director, Ministry of Economy & Finances 1965–70; Deputy Sec.-Gen., OECD since 1970. *Decorations:* Chevalier de l'Ordre National du Mérite. *Address:* 63 bis rue de Varenne, 75007 Paris, France; & *office* 2 rue André Pascal, 75016 Paris, France.

**ELDJARN, Dr. Kristjan.** President of Iceland. *B.* 1916. *Educ.* Univ. of Copenhagen; Univ. of Iceland (MA. PhD.). *M.* 1947, Halldora Ingolfsdottir. *S.* 2. *Daus.* 2. *Career:* Assistant Curator National Museum of Iceland 1945–47; Director and State Antiquary 1947–68; President of Iceland since 1968. *Awards:* Grand Cross with Chain, Icelandic Order of the Falcon; Knight, Danish Order of the Elephant; Grand Cross with Chain, Norwegian Order of St. Olav; Grand Cross, Swedish Order, Northern Star; Grand Cross with chain. Finnish Order, White Rose. *Address:* Bessastadir, Iceland and *office* Reykjavik, Iceland.

**ELDRIDGE, Eric William**, CB, OBE. British. *B.* 1906. *Educ.* Millfields Central School and City of London College; Solicitor (Honours). *M.* 1936, Doris Margaret Kerr. *S.* David. *Dau.* Alison Mary Pritchard. Chief Administrative Officer, Public Trustee Office 1955–60; Assistant Public Trustee 1960–63. The Public Trustee 1963–71. Member of The Law Society. *Address:* 'Old Stocks', Gorelands Lane, Chalfont St. Giles, Bucks.

**ELEY, Sir Geoffrey Cecil Ryves**, CBE. British. *B.* 1904. *Educ.* Eton, Cambridge University (MA), and Harvard University (Davison Scholar). *M.* 1937, Penelope Hughes Wake-Walker. *S.* 2. *Daus.* 2. *Career:* Director, Bank of England 1949–66. Chairman: BDH Group Ltd. 1948–64; Richard Crittall Holdings Ltd. 1948–68; Dir., Thomas Tilling Ltd. 1950—76 (Chmn. 1964–76); Chmn., Richard Thomas & Baldwins Ltd. 1959–64; Dir., British Oxygen Co. Ltd. 1959–76 (Vice-Chmn. 1964–76); Chmn., Heinemann Group of Publishers Ltd. 1965–76; Dir., AIRCO Inc. U.S.A. 1974–76; Dir., British Bank of the Middle East 1949–77 (Dep. Chmn. 1952–77). High Sheriff of County of London 1954–55. High Sheriff of Greater London 1966–67. Director, Equity & Law Life Assurance Co. *Member:* Middle East Assn. (Vice-Pres.); and Committee of Royal U.K. Benevolent Assn. *Address:* 27 Wynnstay Gardens, Allen Street, London W8 6UR; and The Change House, Great Yeldham, Essex.

**EL HADARI, Dr. Osman.** Sudanese diplomat. *B.* 1920. *Educ.* Gordon College, Khartoum (Cambridge School Certificate) Khartoum School of Science (Preparatory Natural Sciences). and Faculty of Medicine, Univ. of Alexandria MB BCh. *M.* 1950, Fahima. Private medical practice 1950–56. Ambassador to Pakistan 1956–59; to U.S.A. 1959–64, to Egypt 1964. *Address:* Ministry of Foreign Affairs, Khartoum, Sudan.

**EL-HIBRI, Said T.** *B.* 1916. *Educ.* French University, Beirut (Dipl. Diplomatic and Admin. Sciences) and University of Freiburg, Switzerland (Lic Pol and Econ Sc); married: three children. Secy. Presidence of the Republic, Beirut 1944; Attaché Buenos Aires 1946; Chief, Latin-American Section, Ministry of External Affairs 1951; Secretary of Embassy, Rome 1953; Consul in Milan 1956; Consul-General, Alexandria 1957, and Milan 1958; Acting Chief of Protocol, Ministry of External Affairs 1959; Chargé d'Affaires New Delhi 1959; Chief, International Div., Ministry of External Affairs 1960, and of the Consular Div. 1961; Consul-General Sydney (with jurisdiction over Australia and New Zealand) 1962. Ambassador of Lebanon in Ghana 1966, and concurrently in Togo, Chad, and the Central African Republic 1967. *Awards:* Officer, Order of the Cedar (Lebanon); Chevalier, Order of Merit (Italian Republic). *Address:* Embassy of the Republic of the Lebanon, Box 562, Accra, Ghana.

**ELIJAH, Leo M.** American. Consulting Engineer on metallurgy, foundry and management problems. Registered Professional Engineer of Pennsylvania and Ontario. *B.* 1928. *Educ.* Univ of Wisconsin (MSc Metallurgical Engineering); University of Bombay (BSc Hons in Chemistry); National Foundry College, England (Post-graduate Diploma). *M.* 1961, Leah Raissa. *Daus.* Danielle-Simha and Daphne-Esther. Metallurgical Dir., George Sall Metals Co. Inc. 1958–62 (Chief Metallurgist 1962–66). *Publications:* Maximizing Soundness in Aluminium, (1961); Engineering Properties Vs. Composition in Binary Alloys, (1957); Aggressive Product Development for Leadership, (1958); How to Make Castings with Correct Composition, (1960); Cutting Metal Costs of Nonferrous Castings, (1961); How to Overcome Die-soldering in Aluminium Alloys, (1962); and numerous other titles; contributor to Metals Handbook. Contrived 50 inventions. *Member:* Amer. Socy. for Metals; Foundry Technical Group, etc. *Address:* 265 Sumac Street, Philadelphia, Pennsylvania, 19128, U.S.A.

**ELIOPOULOS, Elias-Georges.** Greek industrialist. *B.* 17 Mar. 1903. *Educ.* London University (BSc); General Agent for Greece, World Auxiliary Insurance Co. Ltd., London since 1928; Managing Director: Aspioti Elka Chrome Mines Co. Ltd. (amalgamated Co.); Hellenic Manganese Mines Co. Inc.; Paragon Hellas Co. Ltd., Kekrops Land Co. *Address:* Vouliagmenis 352, Athens 463, Greece.

**EL JISR, Hussein.** Lebanese diplomat. *B.* 1911. *Educ.* Faculty of Law, Beirut (Lic.-en-D. 1931). *M.* 1956, Nadima Akil. *S.* Ibrahim. Advocate 1931–39; entered the Lebanese Administration 1940; at Ministry for Foreign Affairs 1950; Ambassador to Saudi Arabia 1955, to Belgium 1959, to the Court of St. James's 1960 & to Spain. *Awards:* Grand Officer: Order of the Cedar (Lebanon); Order of Southern Cross (Brazil); Order of Merit (Italy). *Address:* General Sanjurjo 47, Madrid, Spain.

**ELKINS, Sir Anthony (Joseph)**, CBE. *B.* 1904. *Educ.* Haileybury. *M.* (1) 1930, Mabel Brenda Barker (*Dec.*). *S.* 3. *Dau.* 1; (2) 1944, Mrs. Ines Erna Miller (*nee* Neele). *M.* diss.; (3) Nora Christianne Elliot (*nee* Rowe). *Career:* With Gillanders Arbuthnot & Co. Ltd. in India 1924–54 (Chmn. 1945–54); Vice-Pres. Imperial Bank of India (Calcutta Local Board) 1949; President, Institute of Export 1967–70; President, Bengal Chamber of Commerce 1949, and Associated Chambers of Commerce of India 1949; Controller of Supplies (Bengal Circle) 1941–45; Chmn., Darjeeling Himalayan Railway, 1945–48; Former Chairman British Match Corporation Ltd.; Gestetner Holdings Ltd.; Vice-Chairman, Army & Navy Stores Ltd.; Pres. U.K. Citizens' Assn. of India 1953. Chmn. Bryant & May Ltd. 1955–64; Chmn. London Regional Industrial Cttee., National Savings Movement; Regular Forces Resettlement Service (D.E.P.), London & South-Eastern Region Cttee. 1961–69, Chmn. 1968–69. *Clubs:*

Oriental; Bengal; Royal Calcutta Turf. *Address:* Malindia, 23 Clontarf Street, Sorrento, Western Australia, 6020.

**ELKINS, Howard Frederic**, BA. American. *B.* 1934. *Educ.* St. Lawrence Univ. (BA). *M.* 1960, Helen G. Ferguson. *S.* 1. *Career:* Pres. Lloyd's Industries (U.S.A.) Ltd.; Chmn. Overseas Trade & Development Corp., Delaware; Dir. Kilvert-Hormel Import Agency, The Inter-Nation Holding Co., Delaware, The Intercorplan Group, Lloyds Trading Corp.; Deputy Sec. Gen. Metra International; Exec. Vice-Pres. Travel-Wide Syndicate 1957–60; Pres. R.E.T. International 1960–62. Dir. LI Holdings Ltd. Sydney, Hormel-Cerebos Pty. Ltd. Melbourne; First Enterprise Corp. Okinawa; Schneider-Hormel Corp. Canada; Lloyds-Tarber Switzerland; Tarber Trading Corp. Sweden; Okinawa Premier Corp., Naha, Japan, Vista Packaging Corp., Wisconsin, U.S.A.; Pres., Hormel International Corp., Delaware, U.S.A. Hon. Member: British Schools & Univ. Club of N.Y.; Mem. British American Chamber of Commerce, N.Y.; American Management Assoc.; Omicron Delta Kappa. *Clubs:* Royal Aero.; St. Lawrence; Columbia. *Address:* 75 Ivy Way, Port Washington, N.Y., U.S.A.; and *office* 680 5th Ave., New York, N.Y. 10019.

**ELLERN. Herman.** Israeli banker. *B.* 1892. *M.* (2) Eva Nussbaum. *S.* Heinz, Felix and Joshua. *Daus.* Esther Many, Margot Gross. *Career:* Hon. Consul of Republic of El Salvador. Chairman: Ellern's Investment Co. Ltd.; Elgar Investments Ltd.; Director: General Mortgage Bank Ltd.; Israel Can Co. Ltd.; Magam Rubber Works Ltd.; Sugat Sugar Ltd. *Publications:* (with Bessi Ellern) Facsimile of Documents of Herzl, Hechler, The Grand Duke of Baden & The German Emperor. *Address:* P.O. B. 7778, Jerusalem; and *office* Shalom Tower, 16th Floor, P.O. B. 29166, Tel. Aviv, Israel.

**ELLINGWORTH, Richard Henry**, MA. British diplomat. *B.* 1926. *Educ.* Uppingham School; Oxford Univ. Magdalen College. (M.A. 1st Lit. Hum.). *M.* 1952, Joan Mary Waterfield. *S.* 1. *Daus.* 3. *Career:* with British Army, Royal Art. and Intelligence Corps. 1943–47; British Embassy, Tokyo 1950–55; Foreign Office 1955–59; British Embassy Belgrade 1959–63; Tokyo 1963–68; Foreign and Commonwealth Office, Head of Oil Dept. 1968–72; Counsellor British Embassy Tehran 1972–75; Seconded to Dept. of Energy, London since 1975. *Member:* Assoc. Int. Inst. for Strategic Studies. *Publications:* An Anthology of Oratory (with A. N. Gilkes 1948); Japanese Economic Policy and Security (1972). *Clubs:* Travellers. *Address:* The Mount, Sparepenny Lane, Farningham, Kent; and *office* Energy, Policy and Conservation Div., Dept. of Energy; Thames House S., London S.W.1.

**ELLIOT, Alfred Johnston.** Canadian ophthalmologist. *B.* Aug, 1911. *Educ.* University of British Columbia (BA); University of Toronto (MD); Columbia University (Doctor of Medical Science); Diploma in Ophthalmic Medicine and Surgery. Royal Colleges of Physicians and Surgeons, London. *M.* 1942, Jean Kerr MacNaughton. *S.* George Kerr. *Daus.* Mary Elizabeth; Heather Jean; Barbara Lynn. *Career:* Undergraduate rotating internship, Toronto Western Hospital 1936–37; Graduate 1937–38; Basic Sciences in Ophthalmology, Institute of Ophthalmology, New York 1938–39; Residency in Ophthalmology, New York Eye and Ear Infirmary 1939–41; Certification in Ophthalmology; American Board of Ophthalmology 1941 and Royal College of Physicians and Surgeons of Canada 1946; Professor of Ophthalmology, University of Toronto 1946–61; Consultant, Department of Veterans Affairs, Toronto, July 1949–61; Professor of Ophthalmology, Univ. of British Columbia, and Ophthalmologist-in-Chief, Shaughnessy Hospital 1961–76. Adviser in Ophthalmology to Director-General, Treatment Services, Dept. of Veteran Affairs; Chmn. Professional Adv. Cttee. B.C. Medical Centre 1973–75; Hon. Consultant, Dept. of Ophthalmology, Toronto General Hospital. *Member:* B.C. Div. and Canadian Medical Associations, Canadian and American Ophthalmic Societies, American Academy of Ophthalmology; National Council, Can. Nat. Inst. for the Blind. *Publications:* author and co-author of numerous works on ophthalmic diseases. *Address:* Suite 1108 Fairmont Medical Building, 750 West Broadway Avenue, Vancouver, V5Z 1J1, B.C. Canada.

**ELLIOT, Sir John.** British. High Sheriff of Greater London, 1970–71. *B.* 1898. *Educ.* Marlborough; Sandhurst. *M.* 1924, Elizabeth Marjorie Cobbledick. *S.* David Arthur. *Dau.* Mary (Ivens). *Career:* 3rd Hussars, France & Germany 1917–20; Joined former Southern Railway 1925, in charge of public relations (first in U.K.) and advertising: Deputy General Manager 1937, Gen. Manager 1947; Chief Reg. Officer, Southern Region, British Railways, 1948–49; London, Midland Reg., Euston, 1950–51; Chairman, Rly. Exec. 1951–53; London Transport 1953–59; Pullman Car Co. 1959–63; Thos. Cook & Son Ltd., 1959–67; Willing & Co. Ltd., 1959–67. Director, Commonwealth Development Corp. 1959–66; Thos. Tilling Ltd. 1959–69. Chairman: London & Provincial Poster Group Ltd. 1966–71; Director: Cie Internationale des Wagons-Lits 1961–71. British Airports Authority, 1965–69. Railway Air Services Ltd. 1933–48; Channel Island Airways Ltd. Vice-President, International Union of Railways (U.I.C.) 1947 and 1951–53, F.B.I.M.; F.Inst.T. (President 1953–54); Vice-Pres. Essex Co. Cricket Club; Member, Société de l'histoire de Paris; Officer Leg. d'Honneur; Amer. Medal of Freedom. *Publications:* The Way of the Tumbrils (Paris during the Revolution); Where our Fathers Died 1914–18; Speaking of That; book reviews (military history) *Daily Telegraph*; many papers on transport. *Clubs:* Cavalry & Guards; M.C.C. *Address:* Stonyfield, Great Easton, Dunmow, Essex.

**ELLIOT, Robert Sherrard, Jr.** American financial consultant. *B.* 1901. *Educ.* Philips Exeter Academy 1919; Princeton Univ. (AB 1923). *M.* 1929, Jean P. Robertson. *Career:* With American Exchange National Bank, N.Y.C. 1923–26; The Equity Corp. (and predecessor companies) 1926–58 (Asst. Treas. 1927, Secy. 1931, Vice-Pres. 1936, Exec. Vice-President 1953–58). Executive Vice-Pres. Financial General Corp. 1953–66 and International Bank 1958–66. Chairman Finance Committee and Director, International Bank. Director: Alexandria National Bank, Clarendon Trust Co., Bankers Security Life Insurance Socy., Bankers Financial Life Co.; International General Industries Inc., Foster Wheeler Corp., Kliklok Corp., Woodman Co. Inc., Natl. Mortgage Corp., H. G. Smithy Co. Inc. *Clubs:* Union League (N.Y.C.); Washington Golf and County (Arlington, Va.); Belle Haven Country (Alexandria, Va.); Metropolitan (Washington, D.C.). *Address: office* 1701 Pennsylvania Ave. N.W., Washington, D.C., U.S.A.

**ELLIOTT, Byron K.** American lawyer and business executive; President (1957–65), Director (1945–69), Chairman Finance Cttee. (1961–69), Chairman of the Board (1963–69), John Hancock Mutual Life Insurance Co. (Boston). *B.* 1899. *Educ.* Indiana Uinversity (AB); Harvard Law School (LLB); North-Eastern Univ. LHD LLD (Hon) Indiana University; ScD (Hon) Lowell Technological Institute. *M.* 1938, Helen Alice Heissler. *S.* Byron Kent and David Randall. *Dau.* Barbara Helen (Niles). Director: Boston Opera Assn. Inc., Indiana University Foundation, Inst. of Life Insurance (Chmn. of Bd. 1965–66), Northeastern Region National Conference of Christians and Jews, United Fund of Greater Boston, Chmn. 1960 Campaign, World Wildlife Fund 1960–71, American Research & Development Corp. (1950–75), World Affairs Cncl. of Boston. Trustee: Wellesley College (1950–69), Boston Society of Natural History 1955–72, North-eastern Univ. (also Chmn. of Corp.); Independent College Funds of America 1959–73; the Provident Institution for Savings (1950–74), Tax Foundation; The Tufts Civic Education Center; Hospital Research and Educ. Trust (Amer. Hosp. Assn.) 1955–70; Natl. Trustee, Federal City Cncl. (Washington, D.C.). Fellow, Amer. Acad. of Arts and Sciences; Overseer, Boston Symphony Orchestra 1970–75. *Member:* Amer. Law Inst.; Amer. Judicature Socy.; Council on Foreign Relations; etc. Member, Elliott & Elliott 1923–25; Asst. Attorney-General of Indiana, 1925; Judge Superior Court, Indianapolis 1926–29; Pres., Curtiss-Wright Flying Service of Indiana 1927–29; Mgr. and General Counsel, Amer. Life Convention 1929–34; President, American Service Bureau, 1929–33 (Chairman of Board 1933–34); General Solicitor, Law Dept., John Hancock Mutual Life Ins. Co. 1934–35 (Gen. Counsel) 1936; Vice-Pres. and Gen. Counsel and Dir. 1937–47; Exec. Vice-Pres. and Dir. 1947–57. *Publications:* numerous booklets and articles on insurance law. *Clubs:* Chicago, Commercial (Pres. 1950–52), Algonquin, Dedham Country and Polo, St. Botolph, Brookline Country, Harvard (Boston); Tavern; Casino; The Sky (N.Y.C.). *Address:* 200 Berkeley Street, Boston 17, Mass., U.S.A.

**ELLIOTT, Charles Rainforth.** Canadian Chartered Accountant. *B.* 1905. *M.* 1935, Wilhelmina Wells (*Dec.*). *M.* (2) Isabelle Naylor. *S.* Charles Rainforth II, James Naylor, and Richard Linfield. *Daus.* Margaret (Hatcher) and Isabelle (Cureton). *Career:* With Clarkson, Gordon & Dilworth 1928–36; joined F. M. Connell Organization 1936; Chmn. of Board and Director, Conwest Exploration Co. Ltd.; Vice-Pres., Sec. and Director, Cassiar Asbestos Corp. Ltd.; Exec. Vice-Pres. & Director, Basin Oil Exploration Co. Ltd.; Director, Central Patricia Gold Mines Ltd. *Address:* 10th Floor, 85 Richmond Street W., Toronto 1, Ont., Canada.

**ELLIOTT, George Alexander.** Canadian economist. *B.* 1901. *Educ.* Univ. of Manitoba (MA). *M.* 1929, Mary Stewart Paul. *S.* David Francis. *Dau.* Joan Mary. *Career:* Asst. at Univ. of Manitoba 1924–25; Lecturer, Univ. of Man. 1925–26 and 1928 (six months); Asst. Professor, Univ. of Chicago 1928–29; Prof. and Chmn. of Dept., Univ. of Alberta 1929–46; Prof. Univ. of Toronto 1946–57; and Royal Commission on Co-operatives 1944–45. Managing Editor, Canadian Journal of Economics and Political Science 1948–57; Dir., National Bureau of Economic Research 1948–57; member, Canadian Social Science Research Council 1944–48 and 1957–61; Member, Tariff Bd. of Canada 1957–71; Mem. at large, Universities National Bureau Cttee. for Economic Research, 1962–71. Guggenheim Fellow 1953–54; LLD Queen's Univ. *Publications:* Tariff Procedures and Trade Barriers. *Member:* Canadian Political Science Assn. (Pres. 1957–58); American Economic Assn., Royal Economic Assn. Fellow, Royal Society of Canada. *Address:* 303 Clemow Avenue, Ottawa 1, Ont., Canada.

**ELLIOTT, Ronald Stuart.** Australian. *B.* 1918. *M.* 1944, Isabella Mansbridge Boyd. *S.* Stuart William. *Dau.* Vivien Joan. *Career:* Secretary, Commonwealth Banking Corp. 1960; Chief Manager, International Division, Commonwealth Trading Bank of Australia 1963; Chief Manager, Queensland, Commonwealth Banking Corp. 1964. General Manager, Commonwealth Development Bank of Australia 1965; Dep. Man. Dir., Commonwealth Banking Corp. 1975; Man. Dir., Commonwealth Banking Corp. 1976; Chmn., Australian European Finance Corp. Ltd. 1976, Associate, Bankers' Institute; Fellow, Australian Inst. of Management (F.A.I.M.). *Clubs:* Australian Golf; Rotary; Australian; Union (both Sydney). *Address:* 56 Milray Avenue, Wollstonecraft, N.S.W.; and *office* Pitt Street & Martin Place, Sydney, N.S.W., Australia.

**ELLIOTT, Russell Caldwell.** South African attorney and company director. *B.* 10 Feb. 1899. *Educ.* St. Andrew's College, Grahamstown (S.A.). *M.* 1925, Enid Muriel Cox. *S.* 1. *Dau.* 1. *Career:* Chairman, Northern Cape Technical Coll. since 1943; and R. C. Elliott Technical College; Hon. Life Pres., Northern Cape Regional Development Association and Northern Cape Agricultural Society; Freedom of City 1965; Past Pres. Rotary Club of Kimberley; previously member, Natural Resources Development Council; Director, S. African Iron and Steel Industrial Corp. Ltd.; Vanderbyl Engineering Corp. Ltd.; President, Technical College Association of S.A. 1951–52, 1959–60; Mayor of Kimberley 1942–44. President, Child Welfare Society, Kimberley 1940, British Empire Service League 1933 and of Northern Cape Agricultural Society 1967. *Publications:* S.A. Notary; Elliott's Legal Forms. *Address:* P.O. Box 578, Kimberley, South Africa.

**ELLIS, Sir Charles Drummond,** FRS. British scientist. *B.* 11 Aug. 1895. *Educ.* Harrow, Royal Military Academy and Trinity College, Cambridge (BA, PhD). *M.* 1925, Paula Warzcyewska. Fellow and Lecturer, Trinity College, Cambridge 1923–36; Wheatstone Professor of Physics, King's College, London University 1936–46; Scientific Adviser to the Army Council 1942–46; member National Coal Board 1946–55: Director, Finance Corporation for Industry; Scientific Adviser to the Gas Council, the British-American Tobacco Group, The Tobacco Research Cncl. and to Battelle Memorial Inst. *Address:* Seawards, Cookham Dean, Berks.

**ELLIS, George Hathaway.** *B.* 1920. *Educ.* Univ. of Maine (BA Econ 1941; and Harvard Univ. MA Econ 1948, PhD 1950). *M.* 1946, Sylvia Poor. *S.* George Milton and Randall Poor. *Daus.* Rebecca Anne and Deborah Josephine. *Career:* Graduate Assistant in Economics, Univ. of Maine 1945–46; Teaching Fellow in Economics, Harvard Univ. 1948–49; Asst. Prof. of Economics and Business Administration, Univ. of Maine 1949–51. With Federal Reserve Bank of Boston: Industrial Economist 1951–53, Dir. of Research 1953–57; Vice-Pres. and Dir. of Research 1957–61; Pres. 1961–68. President, Keystone Custodian Funds Inc. 1968–74; Pres. Home Savings Bank since 1975; Pres. Massachusetts Congreg. Funds; Dir., Central Maine Power Co., Savings Management Computer Corp.; Trustee, United Church of Christ, Pension Boards. *Publications:* many Federal Reserve Bank of Boston, including: Why New Manufacturers Locate in New England, (1949); The New England Chemical Industry, (1952); New England's Economic Progress, (1955); The Redevelopment of Industrial New England, (1956). Co-editor: The Economic State of New England, (1954); Economic Development in the United States, (1960). *Member:* Phi Beta Kappa, Phi Kappa Phi (Univ. of Maine); Hon LLD; Nasson Coll., Bates Coll., Univ. of Maine, Univ. of Mass.; Hon DCS Western New England Coll.; Gamma Chapter, Beta Gamma Sigma Socy. (Hon.) Univ. of Massachusetts, Trustees Advisory Council, Amer. Economic Assn.; Amer. Acad. Arts & Sciences; *Clubs:* Commercial Merchants, Wellesley, Economic (Boston). *Address:* 177 Benvenue Street, Wellesley, Mass.; and *office* Home Savings Bank, 69 Tremont Street, Boston, Mass., U.S.A.

**ELLIS, Ray C.** American. Consultant, Raytheon Co., Lexington, Mass., since 1945. *B.* 1898. *Educ.* BSc and MA. *M.* 1921, Aline. *S.* Ray, Jr., and Herbert. *Dau.* Ruth. Official, General Motors 1922–42; served in U.S. War Production Board 1942–45. *Address:* Dark Harbor, Maine 04848, U.S.A.

**ELLIS, Robert Thomas,** MP. British Politician. *B.* 1924. *Educ.* Univ. of Wales, BSc.; Univ. of Nottingham, BSc. (Min.). *M.* Nona Ellis. *S.* 3. *Dau.* 1. *Career:* Coal Miner 1947–52; Mining Engineer 1952–70; Labour Member of Parliament for Wrexham since 1970. *Member:* Fellow of the Inst. of Mining Engineers. *Publications:* Mines & Men. *Address:* Whitehurst House, Whitehurst, Chirk, Clwyd.

**ELLIS, Ulrich Ruegg.** Australian. *B.* 1904. *Educ.* Brisbane Grammar School. *M.* 1930, Ray Arnot Maxwell. *S.* Timothy Ruegg and George Maxwell. *Career:* Dir., Office of Rural Research, Canberra 1947–60; Executive member, New England New State Movement since 1948; Chief Liaison Officer, Department of Information 1946–47; P.R.O., Dept. of Post-War Reconstruction 1944–46; Asst. Controller, Materials Supply, Ministry of Munitions 1940–44; Commercial Intelligence and Exhibitions Officer, Dept. of Commerce 1936–40; Political Secy. to Sir Earle Page (Commonwealth Treas. and Leader of Country Party) 1928–36; Member, A.C.T. Adv. Council 1947–51; Chairman, Canberra Tourist Bd. 1935–40 (member 1940–43); Dir., Cncl., New State Referendum 1967; Campaign Director, New England New State Movement, May 1960–69; General Secretary, 1969–71; also Secretary, National Executive of New State Movements, Nov. 1964–69. Editorial writer, Northern Daily Leader, Tamworth, 1968–72; Patron, New State movement, Northern N.S.W. since 1972. Hon Life Member, New England New State Movement, 1970. *Publications:* New Australian States, (1933); The Country Party—a Social and Political History of the Party in N.S.W., (1958); A History of the Australian Country Party, (1963); Why New States are Vital to Australia, (1964); Self Government in the 70s (1971). contributions to Australian Encyclopedia, etc. *Address:* 8 Neridah Avenue, Tamworth, N.S.W., Australia.

**ELLNER, Charles H.** American. Counsellor-at-Law. *B.* 1901. *Educ.* Columbia Coll. AB cum; Columbia Univ. Law Sch. LLB, superseded by Jur. D. *M.* 1965, Libby Feingold. *S.* David C. *Dau.* Caryl P. (Rubenfeld). *Career:* Admitted to Bar N.Y. State 1926; U.S. District Courts 1927; Court of Appeals 1942; Tax Court 1944; Supreme Court 1947; Treasury Dept. 1944; Govt. Appeal Agent (Draft Bd.) 1941; Democr. County Comm; Elect. Distr. Capt. 1942–52; Del. N.Y. Jud. Conv. 1951; N.Y. Elect. Fr. Bur. Spec. Dep. Atty. Gen. 1944; Arbitrator, Amer .Arb. Assn. *Member:* N.Y. County Lawyers Assn.; Queens County Bar Assn.; Int. Inst. of Arts & Letters; Former Member Amer. Bar Assn.; Judicature Socy.; N.Y. State Bar Assn.; N.Y. State Trial Lawyers Assn.; Int. Academy, Law & Science; Int. Coll. of Angiolog (hon.). *Awards:* Phi Beta Kappa; Columbia Law Review Bd. of Editors; Hubbard Math. medal; Pulitzer & other scholarships; Selective Service medal. *Address:* 4712 N.W. 58 St., Ft. Lauderdale, Fla., U.S.A.

**ELMANDJRA, Mahdi.** Moroccan civil servant. *B.* 1933. *Educ.* Cornell Univ., BA; London School of Economics Ph.D (Econ). *M.* 1956, Amina Elmrini. *Daus.* 2. *Career:* Asst. Professor, Law Faculty, Rabat 1957–58; First Counsellor, Moroccan Mission to U.N. 1958–59; Dir.-Gen. Moroccan Broadcasting and TV 1959–60; Chief, Africa section, UNESCO 1961–63; Dir. Exec. Off. 1963–66; Asst. Dir.-Gen. for Social Sciences and Culture UNESCO 1966–70, Programming, Unesco 1971–74; Special Director to Director-General UNESCO 1975–76; Pres. of the Univ. Mohammèd V, Rabat since 1976; Pres. of the World Future Studies Federation (WFSF). *Award:* Chevalier Ordre Arts et Lettres (France). *Publications:* The league of Arab States (PHD 1957); The United Nations System, An Analysis (1973); several articles on economic, cultural and internation matters in various books and journals. *Address:* B.P. 53, Rabat, R.P., Morocco; & 12 Rue Dufrenoy, Paris 16, France.

**ELSEY, George McKee,** MBE. President, American National Red Cross. *B.* 1918. *Educ.* Princeton Univ. (AB *summa cum* *laude* 1939) and Harvard Univ. (MA 1940). *M.* 1951, Sally Phelps Bradley. *S.* Howard McKee II. *Dau.* Anne Bradley. *Career:* Comdr., U.S. Naval Reserve 1941–47; Administrative Assistant to the President, The White House Staff 1947–53; Vice-Pres., American National Red Cross 1953–61; Asst. to President and Chmn. Pullman Inc., 1961–70; Pres., ANRC 1970—. *Director:* American Security Corp.; American Security Bank; Peoples Life Insurance Co.; Security Storage Company; Perpetual Federal Savings & Loan Assn. *Trustee:* National Geographic Soc.; Brookings Institution; George C. Marshall Research Foundation; Harry S. Truman Library Inst.; Trustee Emeritus, National Trust for Historic Preservation. *Member:* National Archives Advisory Council; Columbia Historical Socy.; American Assn. for the Advancement of Science; English-Speaking Union; Newcomen Society in North America; National Presbyterian Church (Ruling Elder). *Awards:* Phi Beta Kappa; Legion of Merit; Order of the British Empire; Medals of the Finnish and Greek Red Cross Societies; Distinguished Public Service Medal Dept. of Defence; Grand Order of Tai Keuk (Republic of Korea). *Clubs:* Metropolitan, City Tavern Assn.; Princeton (N.Y.C.). *Address:* 2201 King Place, N.W., Washington, D.C. 20007; and *office* 17th & D Streets, N.W., Washington, D.C. 20006, U.S.A.

**ELSTUB, Sir St. John,** CBE. British. *B.* 1915. *Educ.* Rugby and Manchester University (BSc Hons Mech Engineering). *M.* 1939, Patricia Arnold. *Daus.* 2. *Career:* With ICI (Metals Division): Deputy Chief Engineer 1947–50, Production Director 1950–57, Joint Managing Director 1957–61. Chairman 1961–62. Managing Director, Imperial Metal Industries Ltd. 1963–72; Chmn. Man. Dir. 1972–74; Royal Insurance Co. Ltd. 1966–76; Guardian, Birmingham Assay Office since 1971; Dir. Rolls-Royce (1971) Ltd; Tube Investments Ltd. since 1974; Avery Ltd. since 1974; Samuel Hill (Group) Ltd. since 1974; Local Director (West Midland and Wales); National Westminster Bank Ltd. *Member:* Council of the University of Aston in Birmingham 1966–72; Court of Governors of Administrative College 1962–74, and Engineering Industry Training Board 1964–72; British Engine Insurance Co., 1970—; Past Pres. Institution of Mechanical Engineers; Review Board for Government Contracts—1975; Part-Time, Midlands Electricity Board 1966–76. *Awards:* Hon. Doctor of Science Univ. Aston, Birmingham 1971. *Address:* Perry House, Hartlebury, Worcestershire.

**ELTON, The Lord,** TD, MA. British publisher. *B.* 1930. *Educ.* Eton College; New College Oxford. *M.* 1958, Anne Frances Tilney. *S.* 1. *Daus.* 3. *Career:* Dir. Wakeley Farm Ltd. 1957–74; Asst. Master Loughborough Grammar School 1962–67; Fairham Comprehensive School Notts. 1967–69; Lect. Bishop Landale Coll. of Education Derby 1969–72; Founder Yendor Book, Educational Publishing House 1972; Opposition Whip 1974 & Spokesman since 1975; Dir., Overseas Exhibition Services Ltd. & Building Trades Exhibition Ltd. 1976. Succeeded Father, Godfrey 1st Baron Elton of Headington 1973. *Awards:* Territorial Decoration; Master of Arts (Oxon.). *Clubs:* Athenaeum; Cavalry; Beefsteak. *Address:* House of Lords, London, S.W.1.

**ELVINGER, Paul,** D. en D. Advocate of the Court of Appeal of Luxembourg. Minister of Justice, of Economic Affairs, and of the Middle Classes 1959–64. *B.* 1907. *Educ.* Docteur en Droit. *M.* Mme. Christiane Brasseur. *Career:* Barrister in the Luxembourg Court of Appeal 1932; President, Order of Barristers-at-Law 1956–58; Municipal Magistrate 1958; elected to Parliament Feb. 1959 and Dec. 1968; member of Luxembourg Government Mar. 1959–July 1964. Re-elected M.P. 1964 and 1969; M.P., Pres. of Foreign Affairs Cttee. *Publications:* Le contrat de travail des employés, (1952); Introduction à la profession d'advocat, (1957); L'Affaire Dreyfus, (1958). *Awards:* Commander, Order of the Oak Crown (Luxembourg); Grosses Verdienstkreuz (Fed. Germany); Grand Cross, Orders of The Crown (Belgium), Orange (Netherlands), Nassau (Luxembourg), Grosses Verdienstkreuz (Austria). Member of the Liberal Party; of the North Atlantic Assembly. *Address:* 84 Grand'rue, Luxembourg.

**ELWYN-JONES, Rt. Hon. The Lord,** CH. MA. (Frederick Elwyn Elwyn-Jones). British. *B.* 1909. *Educ.* Aberystwyth and Cambridge Univ. *M.* 1937, Pearl Binder. *S.* 1. *Daus.* 2. Recorder of Merthyr Tydfil 1949–53, of Swansea 1953–60, of Cardiff 1960–64, of Kingston-on-Thames 1968–74; Elected M.P. 1945, QC 1953; Attorney-General of England and Wales, 1964–70; Lord Chancellor since 1974. *Publications:* Hitler's Drive to the East; The Battle for Peace; The Attack from Within. Hon. LLD Univ. of Wales. Fellow of King's Coll. London; Pres. University Coll., Cardiff. *Address:* House of Lords, London S.W.1.

**ELY, Claire Gerald.** Vice-President, Marketing, The Maytag Co., Newton, Iowa 1957—; Member Board of Directors of the Company 1962—, and of subsidiary companies: Maytag Co. Ltd., Canada 1958; and Board of Directors, American Home Laundry Manufacturers' Assn. 1958–66. *B.* 1905. *Educ.* Univ. of Minnesota, 1923. *M.* 1926, Dorothy H. Moeller. *S.* Jon Moeller. *Dau.* Mary Alice (Slocum). *Career:* With Maytag: Salesman, Minneapolis 1929–45; Asst. Branch Manager and Branch Manager, Kansas City 1945–52; Manager Market and Product Planning, Newton 1952–54; General Sales Manager 1954–57. *Member:* National Assn. of Manufacturers. Republican. *Clubs:* Newton Country; Maytag Management; Chamber of Commerce; Desmoines. *Address:* *office* The Maytag Co., 403 West Fourth Street North, Newton, Iowa, U.S.A.

**ELYUTIN, Vyacheslav P.** Minister of Higher and Secondary Specialized Education of the U.S.S.R. *Address:* Ministry of Higher Education, Zhdanov Street 11, Moscow, U.S.S.R.

**EL-ZAYYAT, Mohamed Hassan.** Egyptian Diplomat. *B.* 1915. *Educ.* Cairo Univ.—BA, MA, Diploma of Oriental Studies; Oxford Univ.—DPhil. *M.* 1948, Amina Taha-Hussein. *S.* 1. *Daus.* 2. *Career:* Lecturer, Asst. Prof., Alexandria Univ. 1942–50; Cultural Attaché, Washington D.C. 1950–55; Charge d'Affaires, Teheran 1955–57; Mem. of UN Advisory Council for Somaliland 1957–60; Ambassador to India 1964–65; Government Spokesman 1967–69; Minister of Foreign Affairs 1972–73; Advisor to President of Egypt 1973–75; Visiting Prof., Univ. of Alexandria 1976. *Decorations:* Republic, 1st Grade (Egypt); Nile, Grand Cordon (Egypt); & Decorations from Iran, Somalia, Senegal, Mauritania, Poland & Italy. *Clubs:* Maadi (Cairo); Guezirah (Cairo). *Address:* One Midan Al Nasr, Maadi, Cairo, Egypt.

**EMERY, (John) Josiah.** American. *B.* 1898. *Educ.* Harvard University (BA) and Oxford University, England. *M* (1) 1926, Irene Langhorne Gibson (Deceased). *S.* Ethan. *Daus.* Irene (Goodale), Lela (Steele) and Melissa (Lanier). (2) 1975, Adéle H. Olyphant. *Career:* President; Thomas Emery's Sons, Inc.; Director and Member Executive Cttee., Emery's Industries, Inc.; Director, member Exec. Cttee. Emery Realty; former Dir. Cincinnati Equitable Fire Insurance Co. Hon. Dr. of Music, College-Conservatory of Music 1949; Hon. Dr. of Humane Letters, University of Cincinnati 1956. Trustee and Chairman of Board, Cincinnati Art Museum; Trustee Inst. of Fine Arts. Hon. Life Trustee, Cincinnati Children's Home; Trustee Emeritus of Board, Cincinnati Symphony Orchestra; Former, Director and Member of Executive Committee. Citizens. Development Committee. Previously member, Public Recreation Commission (1927–35). Republican. *Address:* *office* Carew Tower, Cincinnati, I.O., and Hopewell Road, Montgomery, O., U.S.A.

**EMERY, Peter Frank Hannibal,** BA, MA, MP. British. banker and industrial director. *B.* 27 Feb. 1926. *Educ.* Scotch Plains, New Jersey, U.S.A.; Oriel College, Oxford. *M.* Elizabeth Monnington. *S.* 3. *Daus.* 2. *Career:* Member Hornsey Borough Council, 1951–59; Chmn. Housing Cttee. 1953–57; Member of Parliament, Reading 1959–66 and for Honiton since 1967; Director, Phillips Petroleum (U.K.) Ltd. 1964–72; Institute of Purchasing and Supply 1961–72; and Property Growth Assurance Co. Ltd. 1969–72; Secy. Gen. European Federation of Purchasing 1962–72; Parly. Secy. Industry 1972; Parly. Secy. Industry & Consumer Affairs 1973; Parly. Secy. Energy 1974; Chmn. & Dir., Financial & Industrial Companies since 1974. *Member:* Council of Europe; Western European Union 1962–66 and 1970–72. *Clubs:* Carlton. *Address:* Tytherleigh Manor, Axminster, Devon; and *office* Shenley Trust Services Ltd., 29 Sackville Street, London W.1.

**EMERY, Raymond Victor Georges.** French. *B.* 1897. *Educ.* D en D (DES Droit Public D. E. S. Economie Politique). *M.* 1920, Eugenie Nelly Chevalier. *Career:* Controller, Banque Charles Weisweiller (now Sté. de Banque et de Crédit) 1923 (Chief Controller 1931–40; Chairman 1940–50). Managing Director, Caisse Générale de l'Industrie et du Batiment 1951–56. President, Director General, Metrostore SA, 1969–72; Hon. Vice-President: Société d'Economie Politique; Président d'Honneur de l'Association Générale des Officiers de Liaison et Interprètes de Réserve (Liaison Officers Reserve Association). *Publications:* 'Escompte en Compte-Courant et ses garanties (Discount in Current Account and its Sureties), (1933); Artillerie et F.T.A.-Dictionnaire militaire français-allemand et allemand-français, (1956) (Franco-German military dictionary). *Awards:* Officer Legion of Honour; Croix de Guerre; Comdr. Military Merit; Chevalier of the National Economy and of Social Merit. Hon. Chairman: Sté. de Banque et de Crédit; Caisse Générale de l'Industrie et du Batiment. *Address:* La Terrasse, Crécy-Couvé, Eure et Loir, 28500, Vernouillet, France.

**EMMINGER, Otmar.** Governor, Central Bank. *B.* 1911. *Educ.* Universities of Berlin, Munich, Edinburgh and London (law and economics); Dr. oec. publ., Munich; Law Assessor. *M.* 1939. *S.* 2. *Career:* in German Institute of Business Research, Berlin 1935–45; Bavarian Ministry of Economics 1947–49; with German delegation to O.E.E.C. 1949–50; with Bank deutscher Laender (Central Bank) since 1950 (member, Board of Managers, since March 1953); Member, Board of Directors and Board of Managers, Deutsche Bundesbank (Central Bank) since 1957; Chairman, Deputies of Group of Ten, 1964–67; Exec. Dir., International Monetary Fund, Washington 1953–59; Vice-Pres., Monetary Cttee. of EEC (Common Market) 1958–76; Chmn. Working Party Three of OECD, Paris since 1969. Deputy Governor Deutsche Bundesbank, 1970, Governor since 1977. *Publications:* Die englischen Währungs-experimente der Nachkriegzeit (1934); Die Bayerische Industrie (1947); Die Stellung Deutschlands in der Weltwirtschaft (1953); Währungspolitik im Wandel der Zeit (1966); numerous scientific articles. *Address:* Hasselhorstweg 36, Frankfurt/Main, Germany.

**EMMONS, Glenn Leonidas.** American Banker. *B.* 1897. *Educ.* Univ. of New Mexico. *M.* 1924, Dorothy Frances Hockaday, U.S. Commissioner of Indian Affairs 1953–61; Chairman & President, First State Bank, Gallup, New Mexico 1935–64. Pres., New Mexico Bankers Assn. 1949; Treasurer, American Bankers Assn. 1949–50; Board of Regents, Univ. of New Mexico 1930–33. Recipient, Distinguished Service Award of U.S. Dept. of the Interior; Certificate of Merit, N.M. Chapter, Daughters of the American Revolution; Hon. Dr. of Laws, Univ. of New Mexico 1977. *Member:* Amer. Bankers Assn. Republican. *Clubs:* Gallup Country; Albuquerque Country; Kiwanis. *Address:* 1512 Los Alamos Ave. S.W., Albuquerque, N.M. 87104, U.S.A.

**ENAHORO, His Excellency Edward O.** Diplomat. *B.* 9 Feb. 1925. *Educ.* Nigeria and United Kingdom. *M.* Children Three. *Career:* Joined Civil Service Nigeria 1943; Nigerian Foreign Service 1958; Period with British Embassy in Oslo 1959–60; External Affairs Ministry, serving Nigerian Missions in London, Bonn, and Rome. Former Deputy Permanent Secy. Ministry External Affairs; High Commissioner of Nigeria to Canada 1970–73; Ambassador to Zaire 1973–77; Ambassador to Yugoslavia since July 1977. *Address:* Nigerian Embassy, P.O. Box 1021, Belgrade, Yugoslavia.

**ENDEMANN, T. Johannes (John).** South African Diplomat. *B.* 1914. *Educ.* Univ. of S. Africa (BA). *M.* 1941, Elsa (Peggy) Mallander. *S.* 3. Chargé d'Affaires, Rome 1956; Consul-General, New York 1957–60; Chief of Protocol, Dept. Foreign Affairs 1961–64. Leader S. African delegation to U.N. Conf. on Consular Relations, Vienna 1963. Ambassador to Canada 1964–67, to the Netherlands 1967–74, to Sweden since Dec. 1974. *Address:* Bragevägen 8, Stockholm, Sweden.

**ENDERL, Kurt.** Austrian Diplomat. *B.* 1913. *Educ.* Vienna Univ., Doctor of Law. *M.* 1967, Adele Leigh. *Career:* War Work, London 1939–46; Austrian Political Representation, London 1946–47; Vice-Consul, New York 1947–48; Ministry for Foreign Affairs 1948–50; Chargé d'Affaires e.p., New Delhi 1950–53; Ministry for Foreign Affairs 1953–55; Minister, Tel Aviv 1955–58; Head of Multilateral Economic Dept., Min. for Foreign Affairs 1958–61; Ambassador, Warsaw 1962–67; Ambassador, Budapest 1967–72; Chef de Protocol, Min. for Foreign Affairs, Vienna 1972–74; Ambassador, London since 1975. *Awards:* many decorations from Austria & other Countries. *Clubs:* Queens; Hurlingham. *Address:* 18 Belgrave Square, London SW1.

**ENDSOR, Alan Victor, MA.** *B.* 1925. *Educ.* Royal Grammar Sch., High Wycombe, Bucks., and Jesus College, Oxford (MA). *M.* 1956, Sylvia Joy Rose. *S.* Aidan Robert, Alan. *Daus.* 2. *Career:* Successively Chief Accountant 1954, Secretary 1958, Finance Director 1962, Ready Mixed Concrete Ltd., Deputy Managing Director, Ready Mixed Concrete Ltd. since 1968; Man. Dir. Property & Leisure Dev. Division of RMC since 1972. Fellow (G.C.A.) of the Institute of Chartered Accountants in England and Wales (A.C.A.). *Address:* *office* RMC House, High Street, Feltham, Middx.

**ENG, Brynolf.** Swedish diplomat. *B.* 4 July 1910. *M.* 1945, Annelise Pedersen. *S.* Ulf Peter. *Daus.* Camilla, Monica. *Career:* entered Diplomatic Service 1933; served Berlin and Moscow 1934–39; First Secretary, Ministry of Foreign Affairs 1940, Helsinki 1942; Delegate to Provisional Polish Government 1945; Counsellor and Head of Consulate, Berlin 1947, Consul-General 1948; Acting Head, Mission to Allied High Commission for Germany 1949–50; Envoy Ex. and Minister Plen. to Colombia, Panama and Ecuador 1950, to Egypt, Lebanon and Syria 1955; Ambassador to Egypt and Saudi Arabia 1957, to the United Arab Republic 1958, to the Netherlands 1961 to Italy 1966; to the Soviet Union 1973. *Awards:* Knight of Dannebrog (Denmark), St. Olav, 1st Cl. (Norway). White Rose (Finland); Kt.-Cmdr., Order of Crown (Italy); Gold Cross of Merit (Poland); Grand Cross, El Merito (Ecuador), San Carlos (Columbia), Vasco Nunez de Balboa (Panama), Cedar (Lebanon), Order of the Republic (U.A.R.), Orange Nassau (Netherlands), Order of the Republic (Italy); San Silvestro (Vatican); Grand Officer: North Star (Sweden); Al Merito Industrial (Colombia), of Merit (Syria). *Address:* Ministry of Foreign Affairs, Stockholm, Sweden.

**ENGELHARDT, Nickolaus Louis.** Educational consultant. President and Chairman of the Board, Engelhardt & Engelhardt Inc., (planning of school buildings and direction of many community surveys analysing school needs). *B.* 1907. *Educ.* Sheffield Scientific Sch., Yale Univ. (BS 1929); Columbia Univ. (MA, PhD 1939). *M.* 1933, Florida B. Kramer. *S.* David. *Career:* Research Associate, Division of Field Studies, Teachers College, Columbia Univ. 1936–40; Director Research, Public School System, Newark, N.J. 1940–43; Educational Consultant, Civil Aeronautics Administration 1942; Director, Air Education, American Airlines 1943–47; Professor, Univ. of Florida 1939–40; Lecturer, Univ. of Wisconsin 1941; Professor, New York Univ. (summer) 1949. Recipient Frank B. Brewer Trophy for Outstanding Contribution to Aviation Education (by National Aeronautics Assn. 1947). *Publications:* School Building Costs; Planning Community Schools; Social Trends & The Schools; Standards for College Buildings; Section on Health, Recreation and Athletics; Education for the Air Age; New Frontiers of Our Global World; Elementary Schools; High Schools; Planning Secondary School Buildings; Planning Elementary School Buildings; School Planning Handbook; Complete Guide for Planning New Schools. *Address:* Harvest Hill, Purdy Station, Westchester County, N.Y. 10578, U.S.A.

**ENGELLAU, Gunnar.** Swedish academic engineer. *B.* 1907. *Educ.* Royal Technical University, Stockholm, 1931. *M.* 1933, Margit Höckert. *S.* John-Jacob. *Daus.* Christina, Birgitta, Margita, Caroline, and Susanne. *Career:* Head, workshops of the Swedish State Railways, Gothenburg, Orebro and Stockholm 1932–34; Head of Planning and Time-Study Departments of AB Motala Verkstad, Motala 1935–37; Purchase and Sales Manager in the same company 1937–39; Head, Technical Sales Department at Electrolux, Stockholm, and Motala 1939–43; Managing Director, Svenska Flygmotor AB, Trollhättan 1943–56; Man. Dir. AB Volvo, Gothenburg, Head Volvo Corp. 1956–71; Chmn. Bd. AB Volvo since 1971; AB Volvo Flygmotor, Trollhattan; The Gothenburg Bd. Skandinaviska Enskilda Banken; Safveåns AB, Gothenburg. Member Bd. SKF; AB Electrolux; Rederi AB Transatlantic; Park Hotel AB; Sukab AB; Volvo BM AB, Hevea; Sveriges Allmana Export förening. *Member:* Swedish Academy of Engineering Sciences. *Address:* Dicksonsgatan 6. 412 56 Gothenburg; and *office* AB Volvo, 405 08 Gothenburg, Sweden.

**ENGELLAU, John Gustaf,** Knight Commander of Wasa. Swedish. *B.* 1911. *M.* 1936, Irma Alexandra Stuart. *Daus.* 3. *Career:* Man. Dir. AB Bolinder-Munktell; Section Eng. Finspongs Metallverk 1935–36; Planning Eng. Eskilstuna Stalpressnings AB 1936–39; Dir. Purchase & Sales Dept. AB Motala Verkstad 1939–49; Vice-Man. Dir. AB Bolinder-Munktell 1950–64. *Address:* and *office* AB Bolinder-Munktell, Eskilstuna, Sweden.

**ENGI, Dr. iur. Jürg (Gadient).** Swiss. *B.* 1910. *Educ.* Univs. of Basle, Geneva, Berlin and Oxford (Doctor's degree of law, Basle 1934). *M.* 1942, Magrit Meyerhans. *S.* 1. *Daus.* 3. Mgr. of CIBA AG, Basle 1935–64. Chairman: Lonza AG and its subsidiaries, Basle 1964—; Dr. ès. sc. h.c.; Director of a number of other Swiss and foreign concerns. Hon. Mem. and Mem. of Exec. Cttee., International Assn. for Protection of Industrial Property (IAPIP). Hon. Consul General of Austria. *Club:* Lions (Basle). *Address:* Rebgasse 3, 4144 Arlesheim,

Switzerland; and *office* Lonza AG, Münchensteinerstrasse 38, Basle, Switzerland.

**ENGLAND, Robert,** MC, LLD. Canadian economist and author. *B.* 15 Sept. 1894. *Educ.* Queen's Kingston, Ont., (MA); High School Professional Certificate, Normal School, Saskatoon; Collège Libre des Sciences Sociales (Paris) and Sorbonne. *M.* 1919 (1) Amy Marion Hale (*Dec.* 1966), (2) 1969, Thelma Thomson. *Career:* Continental Superintendent in London of Canadian National Railways 1924–29; Western Manager, Colonization and Agriculture, Canadian National Railways 1930–36; Director of Extension and Assoc. Prof. of Economics, University of British Columbia 1936–37; Economic Adviser, Winnipeg Electric 1937–39; First Director Educational Services, Canadian Legion with Canadian Forces 1940; Exec. Sec. Rehabilitation Committee, Ottawa 1940–43; Assistant to Deputy Minister, National War Services and Veterans' Affairs 1944–46; Chairman, University Requirements Committee, Ottawa 1946; Consultant Advisory Board, Encyclopaedia Americana. *Publications:* The Central European Immigrant in Canada 1929; The Colonization of Western Canada 1936; The Threat to Disinterested Education 1937; Discharged 1942; Contemporary Canada 1948; Twenty Million World War Veterans 1951. Served in World War I (Military Cross); Hon LLD, Manitoba University; Fellow, Guggenheim Foundation. *Address:* 3916 Tudor Road, Victoria, B.C., Canada.

**ENGLISH, James Fairfield, Jr.** American. *B.* 1927. *Educ.* Graduated Loomis in 1944, Yale 1949; from 1949–51 held a Mellon Exchange Scholarship from Yale to Cambridge University (from which has a MA degree); received LLB degree from Univ. of Connecticut School of Law 1956. *M.* 1955, Isabelle S. C. Cox. *S.* James and William. *Daus.* Alice and Margaret. *Career:* Chairman and Director, The Connecticut Bank & Trust Co. 1966—. Director: Connecticut Gen. Insurance Corp. 1962—, Emhart Corp. 1964—, American Thread Co. Conn. Natural Gas Co. Chmn. Loomis Institute 1964—, Wadsworth Atheneum 1967—, Dir. Heublin Inc. and Connecticut Coll. 1967—. Director, Hartford Hospital 1965—. *Club:* Hartford. *Address:* 33 Fernwood Road, West Hartford, Conn. 06119; and *office* One Constitution Plaza, Hartford, Conn. 06115, U.S.A.

**ENGLISH, Michael,** MP. British Politician. *B.* 1930. *Educ* Liverpool Univ., LLB. *Career:* Councillor, Rochdale Counci 1953–65; Labour MP for Nottingham West since 1964· *Address:* House of Commons, London SW1.

**ENNALS, Rt. Hon. David Hedley.** British, M.P. *B.* 1922. *Educ.* Loomis Institute, Windsor, Conn. U.S.A. *M.* 1950, Eleanor Caddick. *S.* Richard, Paul and Simon. *Dau.* Susan. *Career:* Captain, R.A.C., 1941–46; Secretary: Cncl. for Education in World Citizenship, 1947–52; United Nations Assn., 1952–57. Overseas Secy., Labour Party, 1957–64; Member of Parliament for Dover 1964–70; Parliamentary Private Secy.: Minister of Overseas Development, 1964–66; Minister of Transport, 1966; Parliamentary Under Secy.: Army, 1966–67, Home Office, 1967–68. Minister of State, Dept. of Health and Social Security, 1968–70; Campaign Dir. National Assn. for Mental Health 1970; Chmn. Ockenden Venture; Minister of State for Foreign & Commonwealth Affairs 1974–76; Sec. of State for Social Services since 1976; Member of Parliament for Norwich North since 1974. *Publications:* Strengthening the United Nations (1957); Middle East Issues (1968); United Nations Peace Force (1960); United Nations on Trial (1962); Out of Mind (1974). *Address:* 8 St. Anne's Close, London N6.

**ENNOR, Sir Arnold Hughes,** CBE (known as Sir Hugh). Australian. *B.* 1912. *Educ.* Melbourne Univ. (DSc). *M.* 1939 Violet Argall. *S.* Philip. *Dau.* Janice. *Career:* Professor of Biochemistry, Aust. National Univ. 1948–67; Dean of John Curtin School of Medical Research, Aust. National Univ. 1953–67; Deputy Vice-Chancellor, Aust. National Univ. 1964–67. Secretary, Department of Education and Science, Commonwealth of Australia 1967–73; Secretary, Dept. of Science 1973–75; Secy. Dept of Science and Consumer Affairs 1975; Secy., Dept. of Science since 1976. Emeritus Professor, Aust. National Univ. Fellow: Aust. Acad. of Sciences, and of Royal Aust. Chemical Socy. Member, C.I.B.A. Foundation Advisory Panel. *Publications:* numerous articles in the field of Biochemistry. *Club:* Commonwealth (Canberra); Athenaeum (Melbourne). *Address:* 3A Vancouver Street, Red Hill, Canberra. A.C.T.; and *office* Department of Science, Scarborough House, Woden Offices, Phillip, A.C.T. 2606, Australia.

**EPANGUE, Michel Koss.** Cameroonian Diplomat. *B.* 1939. *Educ.* Baccalaureat (Serie Philos.); Licence en Droit (Paris, 1964); Diploma of Political Science; Ancien Auditeur de l'Acad de Droit Intern. de la Haye. *M.* 1974 Cecile-Yvonne Nseke. *S.* 1. *Career:* U.N. Div. Ministry of Foreign Affairs 1955–65; Dep. Dir. Intern. Orgs. 1965–68; Counsellor, Cameroon Embassy Washington DC 1968–73; Dir. Intern. Orgs., Ministry of For. Affairs 1973–74; Ambassador in Gt. Britain since 1974. *Address:* 2 Chalgrove Gardens, Finchley, London N3; and *office* 84 Holland Park, London W11 3SB.

**EPLEY, Marion Jay, Jr.** American. *B.* 1907. *Educ.* Tulane Univ. (LLB 1930). *M.* 1934, Dorris Glenn Ervin. *S.* Marion Jay III. *Dau.* Sara (Davis). Admitted to Louisiana Bar 1930; practised law at New Orleans 1930–47; General Attorney, Texaco Inc. 1948–58; Vice-Pres. and Asst. to Chmn. of Board 1958–61; Exec. Vice-Pres. 1961–64; Pres. 1965–70; Chmn. Bd. 1970–71, e.ected Director 1964; President, Mardor Financial Corporation since 1972; Lieut, U.S. Naval Reserve 1942–45. *Member:* American and Louisiana Bar Associations. Board of Visitors, Tulane University since 1962, *Clubs:* Boston (New Orleans); Everglades, Bath & Tennis, Sailfish, Seminole Golf, Palm Beach (Fla.). *Address:* The Everglades Club, Palm Beach, Florida 33480, U.S.A.

**EPPERT, Ray R.** American executive, Director: Burroughs Corp., Michigan Bell Telephone Co., Michigan Consolidated Gas Co., Cunningham Drug Stores Inc. *B.* 1902. *M.* 1923, Helen Marie Chaffee. Hon. D. Humanities, Hillsdale Coll. 1956; Hon LLD, Western Michigan Univ. 1961, and Michigan State Univ. 1962; Hon DSc in Business Admin., Detroit Inst. of Technology 1961. Joined Burroughs Corp. 1921; rose from ranks to Gen. Sales Manager 1941, Vice-Pres. in charge of Marketing 1946, Director 1948, Exec. Vice-Pres. 1951, Pres. 1958–66, Chairman and Chief Executive Officer, 1966–67. Member Adv. Cttee. on International Business, U.S. Dept. of State; Member Adv. Cttee. on Marketing, Harvard Graduate School of Business; Director and member Exec. Cttee., United Foundation of Metropolitan Detroit; Chmn. Board of Trustees, Harper Hospital; Pres., Detroit Medical Center Development Corp. Trustee, Hillsdale Coll.; Dir., Economic Club of Detroit; Dir., Trustee or Member: Detroit Area Council, Boy Scouts of America; Boys' Clubs of Detroit; International Cttee. Chamber of Commerce of U.S.; Inst. for Economic Education Inc.; Junior Achievement of Southeastern Michigan; Metropolitan Detroit Building Fund; Michigan United Fund; National Industrial Conference Board; Power Reactor Development Co.; U.S. Council, International Chamber of Commerce; Vice-Chmn., International Executive Service Corps. *Awards:* Cross of Chevalier, Legion of Honor 1962; Commander of the British Empire 1967; Hon. Dr. of Science, Univ. of Detroit 1967. *Clubs:* Detroit Athletic; The Detroit; Bloomfield Hills Country; Pine Lake Country Club. *Address:* 295 Lone Pine Court, Bloomfield Hills, Mich. 48013 and *office* Burroughs Corporation, Second Avenue and Burroughs, Detroit, Michigan 48232, U.S.A.

**EPPLER, Dr. Erhard.** German politician. *B.* 1926. *Educ.* Studied German and Philology and history, graduated 1946, Doctor's degree 1951. *M.* 1928, Irene. *S.* 1. *Daus.* 3. *Career:* Gesamdeutsche Volkspartei of Gustav Heinemann 1952; Member of S.P.D. 1956; SPD-County Chmn. of Rottweil 1958; Elected into City Council of Schwenningen and District Council of Rottweil 1959; Member of German Bundestag 1961–76; mem. of cttee of Foreign Affairs since 1965; Federal Minister for Economic Co-operation 1968–74; Leader of SPD Baden-Württemberg since 1975; Leader of Opposition in Landtag Baden-Württemberg 1976. *Member:* Chamber for Public Responsibility, EkD; Synod of EKD. *Publications:* Spannungsfelder, (1968); Wenig Zeit fur die Dritte Welt (1971); Ende oder Wende-Von der Machbarkeit des Notwendigen (1975). *Address:* Konrad-Adenauer-Str. 3, Haus des Landtags, D-7000 Stuttgart 1, FRG.

**ERDAL, Leif Crometie Bruun.** General Secretary, Norwegian Youth Hostel Association; member, Council of Norwegian Travel Association since 1952. *B.* 1918. *Educ.* Univ. of Oslo (MA). *M.* 1941, Edel Nilsen. *S.* 2. Widerøes Air Co. (tourist flights) 1937; Cruise Director on coastal steamer to North Cape 1938; Purser M.Y. 'Stella Polaris' on world cruise 1939; at headquarters of civil air raid defence Bergen 1940–44; finished studies at Oslo Univ. 1942 (Cand. mag.); Man. Dir. School of Languages, Bergen, 1940–47; Sec. Tourist Traffic Cttee. of Western Norway 1946–52. *Member:* Exec. Cttee. International Youth Hostel Fed. 1953–55; Vice-Pres. since 1956; Pres., Oslo Round Table 1954; Lecturer at American

Summer School, Univ. of Oslo since 1955; representative or delegate to several international conferences. *Address:* Carl Grøndals vei 10, Oslo, Norway.

**ERICHSEN, Eivind.** Norwegian government official. *B.* 1917. *Educ.* Oslo Univ. (Cand. oecon 1943); Rockefeller Fellow 1945. *M.* 1944, Ingrid Holmboe. Counsellor, Ministry of Commerce 1948; Director, Ministry of Finance 1952; Director, O.E.E.C. 1956; Permanent First Secretary of the Ministry of Finance 1958. Harvard University Project Director in Pakistan 1967–68, with leave from position in Norway, *Awards:* Commander, Order of St. Olav 1975; Government Cooperation Prize 1974. *Address:* c/o Ministry of Finance. Oslo Dept., Oslo 1, Norway.

**ERICKSON, Joseph Austin.** American banker. *B.* 8 Jan. 1896. *Educ.* Harvard University (AB); Graduate School of Business Administration; DBA (Hon) Tufts Univ. 1960. *M.* 1923, Esther R. Stevens. *S.* Joseph Austin. *Daus.* Nancy (Murphy), Carolyn (Sutcliffe). *Career:* Served World War I with 55th Artillery, C.A.C. (1st Lieut.). *Member:* Reparations Div. of the American Peace Commission following Armistice; joined National Shawmut Bank of Boston 1920, Vice-President 1928, Executive Vice-President 1942–48; President: Federal Reserve Bank of Boston, Dec. 1948–Mar. 1961; President, New England Council 1961–63, Chmn. 1963–65. Director: Sprague Electric Company, Boston Metro Chapter Amer. Red Cross, Greater Boston Chamber of Commerce, Foreign Bondholders Protective Council Inc. Trustee, New England Economic Research Foundation. *Address:* 1032 Statler Office Building, Boston, Massachusetts, U.S.A.

**ERICSSON, John August.** Swedish Member of Parliament and Managing Director of AB Vin- & Spritcentralen. *B.* 6 April 1907. *M.* 1928, Anna Karlström. *Daus.* 2. *Career:* MP (Soc. Dem.) since 1937; Head of Division, Vice-Chmn., State Labour Market Commission 1943; Minister without Portfolio 1945–48; Minister of Commerce 1948–55; Minister of Social Affairs, Labour and Housing 1955–Mar. 1957; President of the standing committee of ways and means 1959–70; Chmn. Bd. Dirs. Sveriges Riksbank 1970–74. *Address:* Reimersholmsgatan 5, Stockholm, Sweden.

**ERIKSON, Arval L.** *B.* 1909. *Educ.* Univ. of Idaho (BSAgric Econ 1937), and Iowa State Univ. (MS Econ 1938; and advanced work in Economics 1938–40). *M.* 1937, Lygia Parkinson. *S.* Stephen and Roger. *Daus.* Joan, Elizabeth and Eileen. Director of Foods, Office of Price Stabilization, U.S. Govt. 1951–52; Chief of Livestock and Livestock Products, Food & Agricultural Organization of the U.N. 1947–50; Price Executive, O.P.S. 1942–47; Professor, Univ. of New Hampshire 1940–42. Delegate to International Federation of Agricultural Producers, Stockholm 1950; and to American Assembly, Columbia Univ. 1955; Vice-Pres., Economic Advisor; Vice-Pres., Planning & Acquisitions; Oscar Mayer & Co., Madison, Wis., 1958—. *Member:* Amer. Farm Economic Assn.; National Planning Assn. (Trustee); Amer. Meat Institute. *Clubs:* Rotary, Professional Men's. *Address:* 5 Waushara Circle, Madison, Wis.; and *office* Oscar Mayer & Co., 910 Mayer Avenue, Madison, Wis. 53701, U.S.A.

**ERIKSON, Stig-Erik.** Swedish. *B.* 1924. *Educ.* Bergsing (Met Eng; MSc); KTH Stockholm 1950. *M.* 1950, Sargit Maria. *S.* 1. *Daus.* 3. *Career:* Research engineer, Sandviken Jernverks A.B. 1950; Assistant metallurgist ESAB, Göteborg 1951; Sales metallurgist ESAB, Göteborg 1956; Chief Editor, ESAB's journal Svetsaren 1963; Sales Manager for Sweden, ESAB 1965. Product Manager, Welding, AGA AB, Oct. 1966, AGA (UK) Welding Div., Man. Dir. 1972, AGA AB, Vice-Pres. Welding Div. 1976. *Member:* Amer. Socy. for Metals; Amer. Welding Socy.; F. Weld. I; International Inst. of Welding (Delegate); Svetskommissionen. *Publications:* about 30 papers on welding metallurgy in Swedish and European publications; and handbooks: Arc Welding, Electric Welding. *Address:* AGA AB, WV, Fack, S-181 81 Lidingo, Sweden.

**ERKIN, Feridun Cemal.** Turkish diplomat. *Educ.* Galatasaray Lyceum, Istanbul. *Career:* Faculty of Law, University of Paris; First Secretary, London 1928–29; Counsellor and Chargé d'Affaires, Berlin 1934–35; Consul-General, Beirut 1935–37; Director-General, Economic Dept., Ministry of Foreign Affairs 1937, Political Dept. 1939–42; Assist. Secretary-General, Ministry of Foreign Affairs 1942–45, Delegate, U.N. Conference, San Francisco 1945; Secretary-General 1945–47; Chairman, Turkish Delegation, final Session, League of Nations, Geneva 1946; Member, International Diplomatic Academy, Paris since 1949. Amb. Ex. and Plen. to Italy 1947–48; to U.S.A. 1948–55; to Spain 1955–57; to France 1957; to Gt. Britain 1960–62; Minister of Foreign Affairs 1962–65; Honorary chairman of the NATO Ministerial Council 1963: Senator 1970–72. *Awards:* Grand Cross of the Phoenix (Greece) and of Legion of Honour (France); Grand Officer, Order of the Crown of Yugoslavia, Order of Cedar (Lebanon); Grand Cross of Isabelle la Catolica (Spain); Grand Cross of Duarte Sanchez and Mella (Dominican Repub.); Grand Cross of Legion of Honour; Order of 'Grand Collier' of Pius IX; Grand Cross from Germany, France, China, Italy and of the British Empire. *Address:* Ayaztaşa Sarayarkasi, Sokak 24, Instanbul, Turkey.

**ERLANDER, Tage Fritiof.** Swedish politician. *B.* 13 June 1901. *Educ.* University of Lund. Phil. Dr. H.C., Lund. *M.* 1930, Aina Andersson. *S.* 2. *Career:* Member, Second Chamber, Riksdag 1933–44, First Chamber 1944–48; Under-Secretary of State for Social Affairs 1938–44; Chairman, Population Committee 1941–46, School Committee 1946; Assistant Minister of Social Affairs 1944–45; Minister of Education and Culture 1945–46; Prime Minister 1946–69; Chairman, Swedish Labour Party 1946–69; member. Second Chamber, Riksdag 1949–70. *Address:* Fyrverkarbacken 21,11260 Stockholm, Sweden.

**ERNST, Albert Edward.** American business consultant (oil). *B.* 1901. *Educ.* BSc; Beta Gamma Sigma. *M.* 1933, Anita Dolle. *S.* John DeBolt, Edward Selton, Frederick Vincent. *Career:* Engaged in international oil business in various countries of Asia, Africa, South America and Europe 1925–39; during World War II held following U.S. Government posts at Washington, D.C.: Chief, Petroleum Div., Lease-Lend Administration and Foreign Economic Administration 1943–46. Member Foreign Petroleum Committee 1943–45; alternate member, Petroleum Committee 1943–45; alternate member, Petroleum Board 1944–45; member, Enemy Oil Committee, Joint Chiefs of Staff 1944–45; Assistant to Chairman Board of Directors, California Texas Oil Co., Ltd. 1946–56, Vice-Pres. 1954–59. Vice-President, Continental Oil Co. (30 Rockefeller Plaza, New York City) 1959–66. Independent in politics. *Clubs:* Metropolitan (N.Y.); Graduate (New Haven); Council on Foreign Relations (N.Y.). *Address:* 369 Florida Hill Road, Ridgefield, Conn., U.S.A.

**ERROLL OF HALE, Rt. Hon. Lord** (Frederick James Erroll), MA, CEng, FIEE, FIMechE. *B.* 27 May 1914. *Educ.* Oundle and Trinity College, Cambridge (MA). *M.* 1950, Elizabeth Barrow. *Career:* Served in World War II (retd. as Colonel) 1939–45; M.P. (C.) for Altrincham and Sale 1945–64. Chmn. or Dir. of several companies. Parly. Secy. to Ministry of Supply April 1955–Nov. 1956; to Bd. of Trade, Nov. 1956–Oct. 1958; Economic Secy. to the Treasury, Oct. 1958–59; Minister of State, Bd. of Trade, 1959–61; Pres., Bd. of Trade 1961–63; Minister of Power 1963–64. Pres., London Chamber of Commerce 1966–69; Pres., Canning House, 1969–73; Dep. Chmn., Decimal Currency Bd. 1966–71; Chmn. Liquor Licensing Cttee. 1971–72. *Member:* National Economic Development Council 1961–63; Chmn. Inst. of Directors 1973–76, Pres. 1976; Chmn. Automobile Assn. since 1974. *Clubs:* Carlton. *Address:* 21 Ilchester Place, London, W.14.

**ERSKINE, Donald Seymour.** Chartered land agent. *B.* 1925. *Educ.* Wellington College. *M.* 1953, Catherine Annandale McLelland. *S.* 1. *Daus.* 4. *Career:* Served in World War II (R.A. Airborne; retired with rank of Capt.) 1943–47: student land agent Buccleuch Estates 1948–50; Assistant Northern Land Agent, The Country Gentlemen's Association, Edinburgh 1950–53; Northern Land Agent for the Association 1953–55; Factor to Mr. A. L. P. F. Wallace, Candacraig, Strathdon, Aberdeenshire 1955–61. Factor, Deputy Dir. to the National Trust for Scotland. Deputy Lieutenant, County of Kinross. *Member:* Queen's Bodyguard for Scotland, Royal Company of Archers. *Address:* Cleish House, Cleish, Kinross-shire.

**ERSKINE, Sir (Robert) George,** CBE. British company director. *B.* 5 Nov. 1896. *Educ.* Kirkcudbright Acad. Edinburgh Univ. (B.L.). *Career:* served in World War I; with National Bank of Scotland, 1913–29; then joined Morgan Grenfell & Co. Ltd., Dir. 1945–67, now mem. of Directors Advisory Cttee.; Director: London & Provincial Trust Ltd., and Alan Paine Ltd.; Pres. Institute of Bankers 1954–56; Dep. Chmn., N.A.A.F.I. 1941–52; Master of the Glaziers Co. 1960–61; High Sheriff of Surrey 1963–64. *Member:* Jenkins Cttee, on Company Law, 1960–62; Cncl. the R.A.F. Benevolent Fund; London Advisory Cttee., Scottish Council (Development and Industry). *Address:* Busbridge Wood, Godalming, Surrey.

**ERSMAN, Sven N.** Swedish. *B.* 1918. *Educ.* Univ. of Uppsala (LLB). *M.* (1) 1939, Britta Malmstroem. (*Dec.* 1967). *S.* 1. *Daus.* 2. *M.* (2) 1969, Elisabet af. Klint. *Daus.* 2. *Career:* At Stockholm Court of Appeal 1945–50; Vice-Pres., Administration, The Graengesberg Co. 1951, in charge of the management of the Lamco Joint Venture (Liberia) 1959–63; Exec. Vice-Pres., The Graengesberg Co., Stockholm 1963–71; Vice Chmn. Exec. Cttee. since 1971. *Member:* A.M.A. (U.S.) and I.P.M. (U.K.). *Address:* Strandvägen 39, Stockholm, 1; and *office* Gust Adolfs torg 18, Stockhom 16, Sweden.

**ERVIN, Samuel James.** American Lawyer & Politician. *B.* 1896. *Educ.* AB. Univ. N. Carolina; LLD; LLB Harvard; LLD, Western Carolina College; Dr. Public Admin. Suffolk Univ. Boston. *M.* 1924, Margaret Bruce Bell. *S.* 1. *Daus.* 2. *Career:* admitted to Bar 1919; General Practice Morganton 1922; Judge Burke County Criminal Court 1935–37; Assoc. Justice N.C. Supreme Court 1948–54; U.S. Senator N.C. 1954–74; Chmn., Senate Watergate Cttee. 1973. *Awards:* Wake Forest Univ., LLD, 1971; George Washington Univ., LLD, 1972; Davidson Coll., LLD, 1972; St. Andrews Presbyterian Coll., LHD, 1973; UNC-Charlottee, LLD, 1974; Catawba Coll., LittD, 1974; Drexel U., LLD 1974; Colgate U., LLD, 1974; Univ. of Cincinnati, LLD, 1974; Appalachian Univ., DConL, 1937. *Address:* Morganton, NC 28655, U.S.A.

**ERWIN, William James.** Textile manufacturing executive. Chairman of Board, Dan River Mills Inc., Danville, Va. 1966 Chairman of Board and Director: Dan River International Corporation, Wunda Weve Leasing Co., Schoolfield Finishers Inc. Director: Carolina & Northwestern Railroad, American National Bank & Trust Co., Woodside Mills, Iselin-Jefferson Co. Inc., Iselin-Jefferson Financial Co. President and Dir. Dan River Mills Foundation. Dir. and Chmn. of Board, Wunda Weve Leasing Co. Dir.: Webco Mills Inc., Webco Dyers Inc., Webco Realty Co. Inc., Dan River Cotton Co., John Preston Whse. Co., Crystal Springs Textiles, Inc. *B.* 1900. *Educ.* Clemson (S.C.) University (BS in Textile Engineering 1921); Hon Dr Tex Eng (Clemson 1960); Hon Dr of Textiles (Philadelphia College of Textiles & Science, 1966); Annual Textile Award, N.Y. Bd. of Trade Textile Section, 1966; Distinguished Alumnus Award (Clemson University, 1966); Omicron Delta Kappa (Virginia Poly. Institute Circle, 1966). *M.* 1930, Elizabeth Suttle. *S.* William James, Jr. *Career:* Textile Engineer, Consolidated Textile Corp., Lynchburg, Va. 1921; Manager, Ella Mills, Shelby, N.C. 1927; Assistant to President, Republic Cotton Mills, Great Falls, S.C. 1929, Vice-Pres. and Director 1939; Vice-Pres., J. P. Stevens & Co. Inc. 1946; Vice-Pres. and Director, Riegel Textile Corp. 1949. Trustee or Director: Danville Memorial Hospital; Union Theological Seminary; Stratford College; Hampden-Sydney College; Sirrine Foundation; North Carolina Textile Foundation; Danville Chamber of Commerce (Director); *Member:* Development Council, Virginia Polytechnic Institute. Vice-Pres. & Dir. Va. Industrial Corp.; Sponsor Trustee, Univ. of Virginia Graduate Business Sch.; Virginia Industrial Development Corp.; Advisory Council on the Virginia Economy (member); Virginia Foundation for Independent Colleges. *Member:* Newcomen Society in North America, N.Y. Southern Socy., National Cotton Council (Research Cttee.), Advisor to President, Nat. Assn. of Manufacturers (Research Committee). Director, American Textile Manufacturers Institute. Trustee: Clemson Univ. Foundation, and Randolph-Macon Woman's Coll. Member-at-large, Nat. Cncl. Boy Scouts of Amer. (Silver Antelope Award). *Clubs:* Danville Golf; Rotary (Danville); The Weavers, University (N.Y.C.). *Address:* *office* Dan River Mills Inc., Danville, Va., U.S.A.

**ESCALER, Ernesto.** Philippines. *B.* 1917. *Educ.* Ateneo Univ., Manila (BA; LLB). *M.* 1939, Maria Luisa de Leon. *S.* 5. *Dau.* 1. *Career:* Professor of Law, Ateneo University 1947–60: Director, Philippines Sugar Institute 1954–60. Chmn. of the Board: Bacnotan Consolidated Industries Inc., Aurea Ceramics Industries, Kabankalan Sugar Estate, Filagro Development Corp., Panel Lock Homes, Inc.; Pamplona Dev. Corp.; Luzon Commodities Corp., Resource & Finance Corp. Pres.: Aurea Inc., Executive Training Institute of the Philippines, Emel Inc. and Provident Insurance Co.: Exec. Vice-Chmn. National Life Insurance Co., and Philippine Sugar Assn. Chmn. Dir Pampanga Sugar Development Co., Inc. Member of Bd.: Bancom Development Co., Filoil Consolidated Industries, Philippine Investment & Management Consultants; Chmn. of the Board ESS Marine Products, Inc.; Alta Mar. Int'l Shipping Agencies; Member of the Board: Trans Asia Oil and Mineral Dev. Corp.; United Pulp and Paper Corp.; Wayfair Tours, Inc. (Alitalia Airlines); Design Center of the Phil.; Population Center of the Phil.; Population Center Foundation; Phil. International Trading Corp. *Member:* Philippine Society for International Law; Junior Chamber of Commerce International Senator; Philippines Sugar Assn.; Philippine Exec. Movement for Social Action (UNIAPAC); Catholic Action of the Philippines; Philippine Assn. of Papal Knights. *Address:* 726-E Quirino Avenue, Paranaque, Rizal, Philippines; and *office* 330 Regina Building, Escolta Street, Manila, Philippines.

**ESCHER, Alfred M.** Swiss diplomat. *B.* 1906. *M.* 1949, Mary Greenhalgh. *S.* 3. *Educ.* Universities of Zürich (D en D), Kiel and Berlin. Entered Political Dept. 1931; served in London and Bangkok; Consular Attaché 1933; Warsaw 1935; Secretary of Legation, 2nd Class 1936; Sec. of Legation, Berlin 1939; Ankara 1941; Consul, Baghdad 1942, Athens 1944; Counsellor of Legation 1945; Asst. to Minister, London 1945; appointed Commissioner for Aid to Refugees in Palestine by Int. Red Cross Committee 1948; En. Ex. and Min. Plen. to Persia since June 1951 and to Afghanistan 1953–54. *Member:* Neutral Nations Supervisory Cmmn. for the Armistice in Korea 1954; En. Ex. and Min. Plen. to Italy 1955; Ambassador 1957; Ambassador to Fed. Republic of Germany May 1959–64; to Austria 1964–72; Representative, Secy. Gen. United Nations for Namibia 1972. *Address:* Alte Landstrasse 34, 8702 Zollikon, Switzerland.

**ESENBEL, Melih.** Turkish diplomat. *B.* 1915. *Educ.* Lycée of Galatasaray, Istanbul; Faculty of Law, Univ. of Istanbul. *M.* 1937, Emine Dengiz. *Dau.* 1. *Career:* Joined Min. of Foreign Affairs and became 3rd Secy. in Secy.-Gen.'s cabinet 1936–44; 2nd Secy. Turkish Embassy Paris and 1st Secy. Min. of For. Affairs 1944–45; 1st Secy. and Counselor at Turkish Embassy Washington DC 1945–52; Dir.-Gen. Dept of International Economic Affairs 1952; Turkish Delegate to U.N. Gen. Assembly 1952 and 1953; Represented Secy. Gen. at negotiations for Bagdad Pact (1955); Asst.-Secy.-Gen. for Economic Affairs and Secy.-Gen. of Internat. Co-op. Admin. 1954–56; Secy.-Gen. of Min. of Foreign Affairs 1957–59 (Zurich-Lond. Conf. on creation of Indep. Cyprus 1959); Turkish Ambassador in U.S.A. 1960; Sen. Advisor to Min. of Foreign Affairs 1960; Turkish Ambassador in Japan 1963–66; Ambassador (2nd Time) of Turkey in U.S.A. 1967–74; Min. of Foreign Affairs of Republic of Turkey 1974–75 (6 months); Ambassador of Turkey in U.S.A. since 1975. *Decorations:* Legion d'Honneur Chavalier, France (1941); Isabel Catolica Cross, Spain (1956); Gran. Cruz del Mérito Civil, Spain (1959); Cavalière di Gran Croce, Italy (1957); First Class Order of the Sacred Treasure, Japan (1958); Grand Cordon of the Order of Brilliant Star, China (1958); Knight Grand Cross of the Royal Order of the Phoenix, Greece (1959); Sardar Ali, Afghanistan (1958); Grand Cross, Germany (1954). *Address:* Turkish Embassy, 1606 23rd St. NW, Washington DC 20008, U.S.A.

**ESFANDIARY, Mahmoud.** *B.* 1916. *Educ.* Lic. en Sc. Pol., Louvain and Liège (Belgium). *M.* 1951, Parvine Gharagozlou. *S.* Massoude. Commander, Order of North Star (Sweden); Order of Homayoun 3rd Cl. (Iran). Successively Chief of Personnel Division, Ministry of Finance Teheran; 1941–43; Ministry, Foreign Affairs 1943; Second Secy. Iranian Embassy Stockholm 1945–47; Second Secy. Berne 1948; Counseller Berne 1952; Stockholm 1953; Dir. of Staff 1955; Actg. Consul-General in Geneva and Permanent Delegate in U.N. office in Europe; Counsellor of Embassy Switzerland, and afterwards Stockholm; Chief of Personnel Div. and Budget, Ministry of External Affairs; raised to rank of Minister Plenipotentiary 1957. En. Ex. and Min. Plen. of Iran to Canada Aug. 1958, Amb. Plen. Jan. 1961–62; Permanent Under-Secy. for External Affairs 1962; Responsibility for Press Information 1969–70; Ambassador in Berne 1971–76. *Clubs:* Cercle des Amis de la Culture Francaise à Téhéran; Club Impérial; Grande Société á Berne. *Address:* Ministry of Foreign Affairs, Teheran, Iran.

**ESHRAGHI, H. E. Hossein.** Iranian Diplomat. *B.* 1921. *Educ.* London BA; Tehran. *M.* 1961, Fairdeh Behzadi. *S.* 1. *Daus.* 2. *Career:* Pte Secy. Min. of Foreign Affairs 1953; Vice-Consul San Francisco 1956–59, Consul 1959–61; 2nd Secy., Press and Information, Washington 1958, Head of Foreign Minister's Seretariat 1961–63; Delegate General Assembly CENTO 1963; Acting-Dir. Dept. International Co-operation 1963–64; Counsellor, Paris 1964–66; Consul-General San Francisco 1966–69; Dept. American Affairs Tehran 1970; Consul-Gen. New York 1971; Dir. (American Affairs Div.) 1972; Ambassador of Iran in Australia 1973–76, and Accredited Ambassador of Iran in New Zealand 1974–76. *Decorations:* Order of Homayoun (Iran) 1967. *Address:* Ministry of Foreign Affairs, Teheran, Iran.

**ESKELL, Maj. Gen. Hon. Stanley Louis Mowbray,** ED, MLC (N.S.W.). Australian company director. Member of Legislative Council of N.S.W. 1958—; Managing Director, Sangara (Holdings) Ltd.; Director, Wheelock Marden and Co. (Australia) Ltd.; Time-Life International (Aust.) Pty. Ltd.; Astor Consolidated Mills Ltd.; mem., Nuclear Research Foundation and Board, Water Research Foundation of Australia. *B.* 1918. *Educ.* Royal Military Coll., Duntroon (Graduate Staff Coll.); Graduate of U.S. Command and Staff School, Fort Leavenworth, Kansas. *M.* 1946, Denise Rachel Yaffa (*Div.* 1962). *S.* 2. *Dau.* 1. *M.* 1964, Joan Taubman Malmgren. A.I.F. Bde. Maj., 17 Aust. Inf. Bde., 6 Div., M.I.D., C.M.F. since 1948. *Member:* Liberal Party of Australia. *Clubs:* Imperial Service; Elanora Country; Royal Sydney Yacht Squadron; Royal Sydney Golf; R.A.C.A., American National. *Address: office* Box 127, Post Office Brickfield Hill, Sydney, 2000, N.S.W., Australia.

**ESMARK, Lars Hille.** Norwegian executive director. *B.* 1908. *Educ.* University of Oslo (Cand. jur.). *M.* 1938 Alexandra Magnusson. *S.* Lars. *Dau.* Lillen Kirsti. *Career:* Worked at Thomas Cook and Bennett's Travelbureau; Hotel Inspector for the Government 1936–46; Director of Tourist Traffic, Ministry of Communications since 1946; with U.N. Tech. Assistance Admin. as expert in organization and development of the tourist trade in Yugoslavia 1954; and Indonesia 1956; U.N. Technical expert in Cyprus 1960; returned to his permanent post in the Norwegian Government 1961; Technical Expert in Turkey as O.E.C.D. (Paris) consultant; President, Norwegian Tourist Assn.; Exec. Director, Bennetts Travel Bureau Ltd. 1964—. *Awards:* Orders of Dannebrog (Denmark); St. Olav (Norway); North Star (Sweden). *Address:* Midtasen 59, Ljan, Norway.

**ESSAAFI, M'Hamed.** Comdr. Order of the Tunisian Republic. *B.* 1930. *Educ.* Collège Sadiki, Tunis, and University of France (Sorbonne). *M.* 1956, Hedwige Klat. *S.* 1. *Dau.* 1. *Career:* With Secretariat of State for Foreign Affairs, Tunis; Secretary, Embassy, London 1956; First Secretary, Washington 1957; American Department, at Secretariat (Director with rank of Counsellor) 1960, and American and International Conference Department (Minister Plenipotentiary) 1962. Tunisian Ambassador to the United Kingdom 1964–69. Secretary General, Ministry for Foreign Affairs, 1969–70; Ambassador to the U.S.S.R. 1970–74; Ambassador to the Fed. Republic of Germany since 1974. *Member:* Parti Socialiste Destourien, Tunis. *Address:* Tunisian Embassy, Bonn-Bad Godesberg, Kolner-Str. 103, Federal Republic of Germany.

**ESSELENS, Maurits.** Belgian financial executive. *B.* 1916. *Married. Children:* 3. *Career:* Ministry of Finance, Belgium, culminating in appointment as Dir.-Gen. of the Treasury, July 1975. In this capacity has held the posts of Government Commissioner to the Banque Nationale de Belgique & Institut de Réescompte et de Garantie, Chmn. of the Comité du Fonds des Rentes, Dir. of the Caisse Autonome des Dommages de Guerre & of the Institut Belgo-Luxembourgeois du Change, & mem. of the Conseil Supérieur des Finances & of the Conseil des Institutions de Crédit Public. Vice-Chmn., European Investment Bank since 1976. *Address:* European Investment Bank, 2 Place de Metz, Luxembourg.

**ESSER, Werner,** Dipl. Kfm.; Dr. rer.pol.; German executive. Member, Board of Management, Stahlwerk Mannhein AG-Mannheim-Rheinau 1933—; Managing-Partner, West, deutsches Stahlkontor Esser & Co., Mannheim Rheinau 1951—. *B.* 1905. *Educ.* Mannheim Superior Business College, and University of Innsbruck. *M.* 1933, Elisbeth Wirtz. *S.* Carl-Heinrich and Werner-Michael. Entered service of Stahlwerke Mannheim AG 1930. *Member:* Industrial Committee of Mannheim Chamber of Industry and Commerce; Board of Management, Verband Württemberg-Badischer Mettalindustrieller, Mannheim. *Address: office* Stahlwerke Mannheim AG, Mannheim-Rheinau, Germany.

**ESTABROOK, Robert Harley.** *B.* 1918. *Educ.* Northwestern University (BA—Hons—*summa cum laude,* 1939), and Coe College (Cedar Rapids, Iowa)—extension work; Hon. L.H.D. (Doctor, Humane Letters) Colby Coll. 1972. *M.* 1942, Mary Lou Stewart. *S.* John, James and David. *Dau.* Margaret. City Editor, Emmet County Graphic, Harbor Springs, Mich. 1936; Editor, Daily Northwestern, Northwestern Univ. 1938–39; Reporter, Cedar Rapids (Iowa) Gazette 1939–40 (Editorial Writer 1940–42); Editorial Writer, Washington Post 1946–53, Editor, Editorial Page 1953–62. Chief Foreign Correspondent based in London 1961–65. United Nations Correspondent Washington Post 1966–71; Editor and Publisher, Lakeville (Conn.) Journal since 1971. *Awards:* Sigma Delta Chi Award for best editorial in an American newspaper, 1954; Sigma Delta Chi (professional journalism society) and Deadline Club Award, Distinguished U.N. Reporting, 1969; International Golden Quill Award for best Editorial, 1973; National Conference of Editorial Writers (a founder 1947; Chairman 1951); Council on Foreign Relations; *Member:* Phi Beta Kappa; Sigma Delta Chi. *Publications:* editorials and numerous articles in the Washington Post; articles in various magazines; chapter in 75 Prose Pieces (Rathburn-Steinman, Scribner's 1961); A Manual for Correspondents (1966). Delta Tau Delta fraternity. *Address:* Box 73, Lakeville Conn. 06039; and *office* The Lakeville Journal, Pocket Knife Square, Lakeville, Conn. 06039.

**ETEMADI, Nour Ahmad.** *B.* 1921. *Educ.* Esteklal College, Kabul. Joined Ministry of Foreign Affairs as Career Diplomat, 1946; successively Asst. Chief of Protocol; Dir. for Economic Relations Division; Dir. Gen. for Political Affairs; Secy. Gen. of Foreign Ministry; Ambassador to Pakistan, 1965–66; Min. for Foreign Affairs, First Deputy Prime Minister, 1966–67; Prime Minister, 1967–71; Ambassador to Italy 1972–73, to U.S.S.R. since 1973. Participated in the 5th and 13th sessions of the U.N., and in the Emergency Session of 1967. Former Prime Minister of Afghanistan. *Member:* Advisory Cttee. which drafted the new Constitution of Afghanistan; 'Loya Jirgo' (Great Council), 1964. *Address:* Embassy of Afghanistan, Ul. Vorovskogo 42, Moscow, U.S.S.R.

**ETHERINGTON-SMITH, Raymond Gordon Antony,** CMG, retired Diplomat. *B.* 1914. *Educ.* Downside and Magdalen College, Oxford (Doncaster Scholar, Hons. Modern Langs.). *M.* 1950, Mary Elizabeth Besly. *S.* Peter. *Daus.* Serena, Henrietta and Venetia. *Career:* Entered Foreign Office 1936; Berlin Embassy 1939, Coppenhagen 1939–40, Washington 1940—42, Chungking 1943–45, Kashgar 1945–46 Moscow 1947, Foreign Office 1947–52, Rome (Vatican) 1952–54; Counsellor Saigon 1954–57, The Hague 1958–61, and Office of the U.K. Commissioner-General for S.E. Asia, Singapore, Mar. 1961–Aug. 1963; Ambassador to Vietnam. Aug. 1963–66; Minister and Deputy-Commandant of British Sector of Berlin 1966–70. British Ambassador, Democratic Republic of the Sudan, 1970–73. *Member:* Contemporary Art Socy. The Cheshire Foundation Homes for the Sick. *Clubs:* Buck's; Oriental. *Address:* The Old Rectory, Melbury Abbas, Shaftesbury, Dorset SP7 0DZ.

**ETTELSON, Leonard B.** American lawyer. *B.* 1905. *Educ.* University of Michigan (AB 1924); University of Chicago (JD 1947); Hon LLD Illinois Wesleyan University 1955; LLH Barat College 1971. *M.* 1934, Luela Bone. *Dau.* Leanne. *Career:* Director: Lytton's, Henry C. Lytton & Co., Allied Structural Steel Co., Drovers National Bank; Chairman of Bd., First Drivers Corp.; Daybilt Corp., Emme Corp., National Council, Boy Scouts of America. Chmn. Bd. of Trustees: Barat College; Trustee, Henrotin Hospital. *Member:* American Illinois and Chicago Bar Associations; Michigan Alumni Association. Republican. *Clubs:* Tower, Mid-America Tavern (Chicago); Michigan Union (Ann Arbor); Bankers, Lawyers (N.Y.C.); Racquet (Palm Springs); La Quinta Country (Calif.). *Address: office* 208 South La Salle Street, Chicago, Ill. 60604, U.S.A.

**EUSTACE, Terence Henry.** South African. *B.* 1899. *Educ.* Transvaal University College (BA). *M.* 1935, Irene de Courcy Blakeney. *S.* Peter Blakeney and Michael de Courcy. *Dau.* Ann Maureen. *Career:* With Standard Bank of S.A. 1918–21; S. African Civil Service 1921–34; S. African Diplomatic Corps 1934–59 (served in Rome 1934–35, Stockholm 1935–39, Nairobi 1939–46; Counsellor of Embassy, Washington 1946–50; High Commissioner in Salisbury, Rhodesia 1950–56; Minister Plenipotentiary, Rio de Janeiro 1956–59). Dir.: Anglo-American Rhodesian Development Corp.; Rhodesian Acceptances Ltd.; Rhodesian Wattle Co. Ltd.; Gestetner (Rhodesia) Ltd.; Iron Duke Mine Ltd. *Address:* 4 Penray Drive, Highlands, Salisbury, Rhodesia) Ltd.; Iron Duke Mine Ltd. *Address:* 4 Penray Drive, Highlands, Salisbury, Rhodesia.

**EVANG, Karl.** Norwegian government official. *B.* 19 Oct. 1902. *Educ.* Oslo (MD) Univ. Oslo. England, France and Germany. *Career:* Began private practice, Medicine Oslo 1929; member staff of Oslo Municipal Hospital 1932–34; Medical Officer, State Factory Inspection Office 1937–38; Director-General of Public Health 1939–72 (Ret.); Professor of Social Medicine, Tromsoe, 1973; Chairman, Norwegian

Nutrition Council and FAO Committee 1946–53; Chairman, Norwegian State Council for Welfare on Seafarers since 1946, Joint I.L.O.-WHO Commission on Hygiene of Seafarers since 1949. *Member:* WHO Panel on Public Health Administration; Norwegian Society of Hygiene. Hon. Fellow, Royal Sanitary Inst. London, Norwegian Medical Society; Hon. FRSM London, Hon. Fellow, American Public Health Association; Chmn., Norwegian Delgn. 1st to 27th (inclusive) Assemblies of WHO, Geneva; Vice-Chmn., WHO-U.S.C. Medical Missions to Israel 1951 and 1959, India 1953; Chmn. WHO Exec. Board 1965 and many Ctts. and Boards in Norway. *Awards:* Leon Bernard Foundation Prize; Bronfman Prize (Amer. Public Health Assn.); Royal Order, St. Olav, Cmdr. with Star Chevalier Legion d'Honneur. *Publications:* Sex Education; Race Policy and Reaction; Silicosis in Norway; Health Services in Norway; Rebuilding the People's Health; Public Health Organization of Norway; Heath Clark Lectures; Use and Abuse of Drugs (1966); Current Narcotic Problems (1967); Drug Dependence, Health & Society (1974) and many articles, Medical, Health problems. *Address:* Maaltrostvn, 11B, Oslo 3, Norway.

**EVANS, Alfred Thomas,** BA Hons, Dip Ed, MP. British. *B.* 1914. *Educ.* University of Wales. *M.* Mary Katherine O'Marah. *S.* Andrew James. *Daus.* Mary Katherine and Elizabeth Siân. *Career:* Head of Dept. Bargoed Grammar School, 1937–49; Headmaster Bedlinog Secondary School, 1949–66; Headmaster Lewis Boys Grammar School, 1966–68; Member of Parliament, Caerphilly since 1968. Treas. Brit. German Democratic Republic Parly. Group. Member, Parly. Labour Panels for Education, Social Services, Disabled People, Fuel, Power and Steel. *Member:* Headmasters Assn. Clerical & Admin. Workers Union. *Clubs:* Labour Rargoed; Aneaurin Caerphilly Glam. *Address:* House of Commons, London, S.W.1.

**EVANS, Sir Bernard,** DSO, ED, CAV. Australian. *B.* 1905. *Educ.* Private school and Royal Melbourne Technical Coll. *M.* 1929, Dorothy May Ellis. *S.* 1. *Daus.* 2. *Career:* Architect; Raised 2/23rd Battalion, A.I.F. in World War II (served at Tobruk, El Alamein, Lae and Finschaven; DSO, ED; 3 times M.I.D.; Brigadier); Pres. Melbourne City Councillor (Gipps Ward) 1949; Commissioner Melbourne & Metropolitan Bd. of Works 1955–72; Pres. Princess Hill Village since 1958; Royal Melbourne Inst. of Technology 1958–60; Victorian Branch, Royal Commonwealth Socy. 1960—; Lord Mayor of Melbourne 1959–61; Consultant, Bernard Evans, Murphy, Berg & Hocking Pty. Ltd. *Fellow:* Royal Australian Inst. of Architects. *Member:* Inst. of Directors, London. *Clubs:* Athenaeum, Naval & Military, Victoria Racing, Victoria Amateur Turf, Royal Automobile (Vic.), Kelvin, West Brighton. *Address:* 735 Orrong Road, Toorak, 3142, Vic.; and *office* 2A Horne St., Elsternwick, Melbourne, Vic. Australia.

**EVANS, David Wyke.** Australian diplomat. *B.* 1934. *Educ.* Prince Alfred College, Adelaide; Univ. of Adelaide B(Econ); Univ. Oxford, MA. *M.* 1959, Pamela Rubina Stratmann. *S.* 2. *Dau.* 1. *Career:* Joined Australian Public Service 1959; Third and later Second Secy. Austr. Embassy Jakarta 1962–65; First Secy. Aust. Mission to U.N., New York 1968–70; Counsellor, Aust. Embassy Belgrade 1970–72; Dir. of Organisation, Staffing and Training, Dept. Foreign Affairs 1972–74; Austr. High Commissioner to Ghana, and Australian Ambassador to Senegal since 1974; Ambassador to Ivory Coast since 1975. *Decorations:* South Australian Rhodes Scholar (1957). *Clubs:* Commonwealth (Canberra); Royal Canberra Golf. *Address:* Dept. of Foreign Affairs, Canberra, ACT 2600.

**EVANS, Edward Gurney Vaux,** OBE, BA. *B.* 1907. *Educ.* Ridley College and Univ. of Manitoba (BA 1928). *M.* 1947, Lillian Jean Minnis. *S.* Douglas William. *Dau.* Sylvia Jane. *Career:* Joined Sanford Evans & Co. 1928. Elected to Manitoba Legislature (Progressive Conservative) for Winnipeg South 1953; re-elected for Fort Rouge 1958, 1959, 1962 and 1966; Minister of Mines and Natural Resources 1958–59 and 1966–67, also Minister of Finance 1966–69; Minister of Industry and Commerce 1959–66; Provincial Secy. 1959–1963; Partner, Woods Gordon & Co., 1969–72; Secy. Treas. Rock Ore Exploration & Development Ltd. since 1973. Served with Royal Canadian Ordnance Corp., Asst. Dir., Ordnance Services 1942–46; retired with rank of Lieut.-Col. Exec. Dir., Shaw-Carswell Commission, and of Red River Valley Board (Flood of 1950). *Member:* Chamber of Commerce; St. Luke's Church (Past Warden); Board of Governors, Ridley College; Civil Service Commission of Manitoba (Past Chairman); Board of Manitoba Hospital Service Assn.; Board of Governors, Univ. of Manitoba; Board of Canadian Corps of Commissionaires (Winnipeg); Winnipeg Welfare Council (Past Vice-Chmn.); English-Speaking Union, Winnipeg (Past Pres.). Chmn. Winnipeg Schools Orchestras. *Clubs:* Winnipeg Winter; Canadian (Winnipeg; Past-Pres.). *Address:* 309 Kelvin Blvd., Winnipeg, Man. R3P 0J1, Canada.

**EVANS, Edward Steptoe, Jr.** American corporation executive. *B.* 1906. *Educ.* Virginia Episcopal Schl., Univ. of Michigan, and Univ. of Lausanne (Switzerland); Hon. Doc. of Humanities, Hillsdale (Mich.) Coll. *M.* 1934, Florence Allington. *S.* Edward Steptoe III and John Derby. *Dau.* Virginia Beverley. *Career:* Vice-Pres., Evans Appliance Co. 1929–42; Exec. Vice-Pres., Evans Products Co. 1935–45; Director, Evans Products Co. 1935—. Chairman of the Board 1962–64, President 1945–62, Pres. & Director. Evans Products Co. Ltd., Vancouver, B.C. 1945–62. Chmn., Evarie Corp. 1964–74. Pres., Evans Communication Systems, Inc. 1968–70, Chmn. 1970–73; Dir. Modern Materials Corp. 1964–67; English-speaking Union since 1968; Bloomfield Inc. 1968–72; Capital Trinity Fund 1969–73; The Bethleham Corp. since 1973. Chmn. and Dir., Lockhart Mfg. Corp. 1964–70. Member: National Defense Transportation Assn.; Michigan Manufacturers Assn. (Dir. 1962–67); Greater Detroit Bd. of Commerce (Dir. 1960–67, Chmn. 1965–66); Industry Founders Cttee. of Applied Management and Technology Center of Wayne State Univ; Aviation Commission, City of Detroit 1962–67 (Pres. 1963–67). Newcomen Socy. in North Amer.; Advisory Council, Graduate School, Business Admin. Univ. of Virginia 1968–72. *Clubs:* Farmington Country, Greencroft (Charlottesville, Va.); Yondotega (Detroit); Mill Reef, Antigua, W.I.; Club Limited (since 1974). *Address:* Ragged Mountain Farm, Route 3, Charlottesville, Virginia 22901; and *office* Evarie Corp., 32840 West Eight Mile Road, Farmington, Mich. 48024, U.S.A.

**EVANS, Sir Francis Edward,** GBE, KCMG, DL. British diplomat. *B.* 4 Apr. 1897. *Educ.* The Royal Academy, Belfast; London School of Economics; LLD (Hon.) Queen's Univ. (Belfast); DCL (Hon.) Ripon Coll., Wisconsin, U.S.A.; DLitt New Univ. of Ulster. *M.* 1920, Mary Dick. *Career:* served in Consular Service 1920–45, and in Foreign Service 1945–57; Vice-Consul at New York, Boston, Colon; Consul at Los Angeles; Foreign Office 1939–43; Consul, New York 1943; Consul-General, New York 1944–50; Under-Secretary of State, Foreign Office 1951; En. Ex. and Min. Plen. to Israel Nov. 1951, Amb. Ex. and Plen. 1952–54; to Argentina 1954–57; Dep. Chmn., N. Ireland Development Council 1957; Agent of the Govt. of N. Ireland in Gt. Britain 1962–66. *Address:* Ardleevan, Dunmurry, Belfast, N. Ireland.

**EVANS, Dr. Gwynfor Richard,** MP. Welsh Politician. *B.* 1912. *Educ.* Barr; Primary & Grammar Schools; University College of Wales, Aberystwyth; Oxford Univ., MA, LLB. *M.* 1941, Rhiannon Gwyfor *née* Thomas. *S.* 4. *Daus.* 3. *Career:* Market Gardener 1939–74; MP for Carmarthen 1966–70, 1974—. *Member:* Pres. of Plaid Cymru; Mem. of the Court of the Univ. of Wales; Past Treasurer, Union of Welsh Congregationalists; Sec., Undeb Heddychwyr Cymru (Union of the Pacifists of Wales). *Awards:* Hon. Doctorate in Law, Univ. of Wales. *Publications:* Aros Mae; Land of My Fathers; Wales Can Win; History of Wales; A National Future for Wales. *Address:* Talar Wen, Llangadog, Dyfed, Cymru; & 8 Water Street, Caerfyrddin.

**EVANS, Sir Harold,** Bt, CMG, OBE. *B.* 1911. *Educ.* King Edward School, Stourbridge. *M.* 1945, Elizabeth Jaffray. *S.* 1 (*Dec.*) *Dau.* 1. *Career:* Journalist 1932–39; British Volunteers in Finland 1940; British Legation, Helsinki 1940–41; Ministry of Information Representative in West Africa (Staff of Resident Minister) 1942–45; Colonial Office 1946–57 (Head of Information Services 1953); Adviser on Public Relations to the Prime Minister 1957–64; Head of Information and Research, Independent Television Authority 1964–66; Adviser on Public Relations to the Vickers Board 1966–76. Chmn. Health Education Council 1973–76. *Publications:* Men in the Tropics (anthology). Address: 3 Challoners Close, Rottingdean, Sussex.

**EVANS, Henry James,** OBE. New Zealand. Geologist. *B.* 1912. *Educ.* Reefton School of Mines (Diploma in Mining and Geology). *M.* 1937, Helen McLean Watson. *S.* Peter William. *Dau.* Margaret Lea. *Career:* Mining Engineer, Dredging Corp., N.Z. 1933–36, and in N.Z. Dept. of Mines 1937–38; Geologist, Senior Geologist, N.Z. Petroleum Co. Oil Exploration 1938–45; Chief Geologist, Frome Broken Hill Co. 1946–49; Exploration Manager, Fissions Ltd. Potash Exploration in England 1949–51; Manager, Enterprise Exploration 1951–52, and Oil Exploration A.A.O. Uranium Exploration, Northern Territories. Aust. 1952–53; Chief Geologist, Frome Broken Hill Pty. Ltd. 1954–55; Field Superintendent, Comalco Industries 1955–58. Chief Geologist, Comalco Industries Pty. Ltd. 1958–74 (retired). C.R.A. Exploration Pty. Ltd. *Member:* Aust. Inst. of Mining & Metallurgy; Geological Socy, of Australia. Liberal. *Publications:* various papers and articles on geology and exploration. *Address:* 46 Warleigh Grove, North Brighton, Vic; and *office* 95 Collins Street, Melbourne Vic., Australia.

**EVANS, Leonard Arthur Ranson,** EM. Australian. *B.* 1907. *Educ.* Collegiate School of St. Peter; Chartered Accountant. *M.* 1937, Sydney May de la Poer Beresford. *S.* 1. *Dau.* 1. *Career:* Served 8th Div. A.I.F. 1941–46, P.O.W. 1942–45; Director, Australian Mutual Provident Society (South Aust. Board), Secretary 1945–76; Collegiate School of St. Peter, Walford Church of England Girls Grammar School. 1956–72; Wilderness School for Girls 1957–72; Warden of St. Peter's Cathedral, Adelaide, 1960–75, Synodsman 1950–77, Financial Board 1951–76, Diocese of Adelaide, and Australian Gen. Synod 1952–77. Member, Council of St. Barnabas Theological College, Adelaide. *Clubs:* The Adelaide (S. Aust.;) Royal Adelaide Golf. *Address:* 45 Church Terrace, Walkerville, Adelaide, S.A., Australia.

**EVANS, Leonard Battley,** CBE. Australian. *B.* 1906. *Educ.* St. Arnaud High School; Fellow of the Australian Society of Accountants. *M.* 1936, Elsie Bennetts Gellard. *S.* 2. *Daus.* 2. *Career:* With English, Scottish and Australian Bank Ltd. 1921–40; Secretary, Makower, McBeath & Co. Pty. Ltd. 1940–48. Managing Director, Makower McBeath & Co. Pty. Ltd. (Australia and New Zealand) 1948; Chairman: Beacon Investment Ltd. 1964—, Bryant & May Pty. Ltd. 1964—, Palladium Investment Ltd. 1964. Business Adviser, Dept. of the Navy, and Chairman Defence Business Board, Defence Dept. 1971; Chmn., Victorian Division of the Aus. Red Cross Society, 1970, Hon. Life Member, Australian Red Cross Society. 1962. *Address:* 8 Charles Street, Kew, 3101 Vic., Australia.

**EVANS, Richard Mark,** BA. British diplomat *B.* 1928 *Educ.* Repton School; Magdalen Coll. Oxford. *M.* 1973 Grania Birkett. *Career:* Third Secretary, London 1952–53; Peking 1958–57; Second Secy. London 1957–62; First Secy. Peking 1962–64; (Commercial) Berne 1964–68; First Secy. London 1968–70; Head, Near Eastern Dept. Foreign and Commonwealth Office London 1970–72; Head, Far Eastern Dept. Foreign and Commonwealth Office 1972–74; Fellow of Center for Intern. Affairs, Harvard Univ. 1974–75; Counsellor (commercial) Stockholm 1975–77; Minister (economic) Paris since 1977. *Clubs:* United Oxford and Cambridge (London). *Address:* 16 Trigon Road, London, S.W.8

**EVANS, Robert Eugene,** AB. American. *B.* 1925. *Educ.* Harvard Univ. (AB); Harvard Graduate Sch. of Bus. Admin. *Career:* Pres. & Chmn. Tedman Importing Co. Inc.; formerly with Markt & Hammacher; Dodge & Seymour Ltd.; Chmn. Evans International Inc. 1954–59; Pres. King Housewares Inc. Peck and Mack Co. *Clubs:* Hasty Pudding Inst. of 1770; Harvard Club. N.Y.C. *Address:* 11 Gramercy Park, S. New York, N.Y. 10003, U.S.A.; and *office* 668 Sixth Avenue, N.Y., N.Y. 10011, U.S.A.

**EVANS, Russell Wilmot,** MC, LLB. British. *B.* 1922. *Educ.* King Edward's Sch., Birmingham; Univ. of Birmingham (LLB). *M.* 1956, Pamela M. Hayward. *S.* 2. *Dau.* 1. *Career:* Man. Dir., Rank Organisation Ltd.; formerly Dir. Wood Pritchett (Holdings) Ltd., Wood Pritchett & Partners Ltd., Mechquip Ltd.; Sec. Massey-Ferguson Holdings Ltd., & subsidiary comp. in U.K. *Member:* Law Socy.; Inst. of Directors. *Clubs:* English Speaking Union; Roehampton. *Address:* Walnut Tree, Roehampton Gate, London SW15 5JR; and *office* 38 South St., London W1A 4QU.

**EVANS, Sir (William) Vincent (John),** GCMG, MBE, QC. British Barrister-at-Law and Diplomat. *B.* 1915. *Educ.* Merchant Taylors' School, Northwood; Wadham Coll. Oxford, BCL MA. *M.* 1947, Joan Mary Symons, *S.* 1. *Daus.* 2. *Career:* served in H.M. Forces 1939–46; Called to The Bar Lincoln's Inn 1939; Legal Adviser, British Military Administration, Cyrenaica 1945–46; Asst. Legal Adviser, Foreign Office 1947–54; Legal Counsellor, U.K. Perm. Mission to United Nations New York 1954–59; Deputy Legal Adviser, Foreign Office 1960–68; Legal Adviser, Foreign and Commonwealth Office 1968–75; U.K. Rep. on Council of Europe Steering Cttee. on Human Rights 1976—; Member of Human Rights Cttee. set up under International Covenant on Civil & Political Rights 1977—; Dir. (Chmn.) of Bryant Symons & Co. Ltd., London. *Member:* Int. Law Assn.; British Inst. Int. Comparative Law; Amer. Socy. of International Law. *Awards:* Knight Grand Cross, Most Distinguished Order, St. Michael and St. George; Order of the British Empire (Mil. Division); Queens Counsel; Bachelor Civil Law (Oxon), Master of Arts (Oxon). *Club:* Athenaeum. *Address:* 4 Bedford Road, Moor Park, Northwood, Middlesex; and *office* 2 Hare Court, Temple, London, EC4Y 7BH.

**EVANS OF HUNGERSHALL,** (Ifor Evans) Baron (Life Peer) 1967. Kt 1955. *B.* 1899. *Educ.* University College, London (MA; DLit); Hon. D.ès.L. Paris, Manchester University. *M.* 1923, Marjorie Ruth Measures. *Dau.* 1. *Career:* Prof. of Eng. Language and Literature, University College, Southampton 1925–26; Sheffield University 1926–33; University of London (Queen Mary College) 1933–44; Educational Director, British Council 1940–44; Principal of Queen Mary College, London 1944–51; Provost of University College, London 1951–66. Chairman of Observer Trustee 1957–66; Chmn. Educational Advisory Cttee. of Thames Television; The Linguaphone Institution; Chmn., Royal Society of Literature. *Awards:* Officer of the Legion of Honour (France); Chevalier. Order of the Crown (Belgium). Commander, Orders of Orange Nassau and Danebrog. *Publications:* Ed. Romeo and Juliet (1921) and Richard III (1922); William Morris and His Poetry (1924); Encounters (1926); Keats and the Chapman Sonnet (1930); English Poetry in the Later Nineteenth Century (1933); The Limits of Literary Criticism (1933); Keats, a biographical and critical study (1934); editions, with W. W. Greg, of The Commody of Susana and Jack Juggler (1937); Tradition and Romanticism (1940); A Short History of English Literature (1940); English Literature (for British Council) (1944); In Search of Stephen Vane (1946); The Shop on the King's Road (1947); Literature Between the Wars (1948); A Short History of the English Drama (1948); The Church in the Markets (1948); (with Mary Glasgow) The Arts in England (1948); The Use of English (1949); (with Marjorie R. Evans) A Victorian Anthology (1949); The Language of Shakespeare's Plays (1951); Science and Literature (1954); English Literature: Values and Traditions (1962). *Address:* 1317 Minister House, St. James' Court, Buckingham Gate, London, S.W.1.

**EVATT, Hon. Clive Raleigh,** QC, LLB. Australian barrister and former parliamentarian. *B.* 1900. *Educ.* Fort Street High School; R.M.C. Duntroon; Sydney University. *M.* 1928, Marjorie Hannah Andreas. *S.* Clive Andreas. *Daus.* Elizabeth, Penelope. *Career:* Formerly Minister for Education, Minister for Tourist Activities and Immigration, Minister for Housing and Assistant Treasurer of New South Wales; Chief Secretary, Minister for Co-operative Societies and Assistant Treasurer, New South Wales 1950; Minister for Housing and for Co-operative Societies 1952–54; resumed practice at the Bar. *Address:* 174 Phillip Street, Sydney, N.S.W., Australia.

**EVERSON, Sir Frederick,** KCMG, British economic consultant; Director, BPB Industries, Ltd. *B.* 1910. *Educ.* Tottenham County Sch.; BSc (Econ) London. *M.* 1937, Linda Mary Clark. *S.* 3. *Dau.* 1. Entered Civil Service 1928; Foreign Service 1934; Ambassador to El Salvador 1957–60; Commercial Counsellor, Stockholm, 1960–63. Economic Min., British Embassy, Paris, 1963–68. *Address:* 8 Gainsborough Court, College Road, Dulwich, London, SE21 7LT.

**EVRON, Ephraim.** Israeli Diplomat. *B.* 1920. *Educ.* Reali Secondary Sch., Haifa; Hebrew Univ., Jerusalem. *M.* 1943, Rivka Passman. *S.* 1. *Dau.* 1. *Career:* Joined Israel Foreign Service 1949; Political Sec. to Foreign Minister 1949–51, to Prime Minister 1951–52; Exec. Asst. to Defence Minister 1954–55; Minister, Embassy of Israel, London 1961–65, & Washington D.C. 1965–68; Ambassador, Stockholm 1968–69, & Ottawa 1969–71; Asst. Dir.-Gen. Foreign Ministry, Jerusalem 1972–73, & Dep. Dir.-Gen., 1973–76. *Address:* Ministry of Foreign Affairs, Jerusalem, Israel.

**EWAGNIGNON, Nicolas Amoussou.** Ambassador of Dahomey to the Federal Republic of Germany, Austria, Switzerland, Denmark, Sweden and Norway, 1964–73 (retired). *B.* 1915. *Educ.* Doctor of Medicine; Graduate, Faculty of Medicine of Paris and Catholic Univ. of Montreal. *M.* 1934, Honorine Faboumy. *S.* 2. *Daus.* 4. *Career:* In private practice on the Ivory Coast and in Dahomey 1953–57; Minister of Public Health in Dahomey 1957–59; Inspector-General of Medical Training Service 1959–62. Ambassador of Dahomey to Haiti Republic 1962–64. Great Officer, National Order of Dahomey. Commander National Order of Niger. Member National Union of Doctors in Dahomey. *Address:* P.O. Box 487, Cotonou, Benin.

**EWENS, John Qualtrough,** CMG, CBE. Australian barrister. *B.* 1907. *Educ.* Univ. of Adelaide (LLB). *M.* 1935, Gwendoline Wilson. *S.* 2. Admitted as Barrister and Solicitor, Supreme Court of South Australia 1929. Legal Officer, Commonwealth Attorney-General's Dept. 1933, Senior Legal Officer 1939; Asst. Parliamentary Draftsman 1944, PrincipalAssistant 1948. Parliamentary Draftsman 1949–70. First Parliamentary Counsel, Commonwealth of Australia 1970–72;. Member Council of Australian National University 1960–75. *Address:* 57 Franklin Street, Forrest, A.C.T. 2603, Australia.

**EWING, James Dennis.** Newspaper publisher. *B.* 1917. *Educ.* Princeton Univ. (AB). *M.* 1943, Ruth R. Dewing. *S.* 1. *Daus.* 2. *Career:* U.S. Naval Reserve 1943–46; Publisher, Bangor (Maine) Evening and Sunday Commercial 1946–54; Vice-Pres. The MacDowell Colony Inc.; Publisher, Keene (N.H.) Sentinel President, Valley Publishing Co., Lebanon, N.H.; Vice-Pres. and Treasurer, Newport (N.H.) Publishing Corp., and of Cheshire Engravers Inc., Keene; Director: Edward Durant Investment Co., Boston. *Member:* American Society of Newspaper Editors. *Award:* LHD, Univ. of New Hampshire 1973. *Club:* Rotary. *Address:* East Surry Road, Keene, N.H.; and *office* Keene Sentinel, Keene, N.H., U.S.A.

**EXETER, Marquess of** (David George Brownlow Cecil), KCMG, DL. British company director. *B.* 1905. *Educ.* Eton; Magdalene College, Cambridge. *M.* (1) 1929, Lady Mary Theresa Scott. *Daus.* 3; (2) Diana Mary, widow of Col. David Forbes. *Dau.* 1. Won Olympic 400 metre hurdles 1928. 2nd, 4th and 5th places in Los Angeles. MP (Conservative) Peterborough Division, Northants 1931–43; Parliamentary Private Secretary to Parliamentary Secretary, Ministry of Supply 1939–41 as Chmn. of Materials Cttee. & i/c Raw Materials for Tanks Dept.; served in Ministry of Supply 1941–42, on the Council of Ministry of Aircraft Production 1942–43 as Controller of Repairs & Overseas Supplies of Aircraft; Governor and C.-in.C. Bermuda 1943–45; Chairman, Organizing and Executive Committee, Olympic Games, London 1948; Leader, U.K. Industrial Mission to Pakistan 1950 and Burma 1954; Chairman, Birmid-Qualcast 1950–75; Director, National Westminster Bank 1935–75 and other companies; President, Radio Industry Council 1952–55, and of Federation of Chambers of Commerce of the British Empire 1952–54; Pres.: International Amateur Athletic Federation 1946–76; Amateur Athletic Association 1936–76; President, British Olympic Association; Vice-President International Olympic Cttee. 1954–66, now Doyen; Pres. Junior Carlton Club. Pres. B.T.A. 1966–69; Rector, St. Andrews University 1950–52; Mayor of Stamford 1961. Hon. LLD, St. Andrews; Hon. FRCS; Knight of Order of St. John of Jerusalem. *Address:* Burghley House, Stamford, Lincs.

**EXON, John James.** American statesman. *B.* 1921. *Educ.* Univ. of Omaha. *M.* 1943, Patricia Ann Pros. *S.* 1. *Daus.* 2. *Career:* Branch Man. Universal Finance Corp 1946–54; President Exon's Inc. 1954–70; Governor State of Nebraska since 1971. *Member:* Lincoln Chamber of Commerce; National Stationers and Office Equipment Assoc.; 32cd Degree Mason; Shrine; Elks; Lincoln Optomists Club (past pres.); American Legion. *Award:* Phillipines Campaign ribbons; Omaha World Herald, Man of the Year 1974. *Address:* Governor's Mansion, 1425 H Street, Lincoln, Nebraska 68508; and *office* State Capitol Building, Nebraska 68509, U.S.A.

**EXTER, John.** American consultant. Senior Vice-President, First National City Bank, 1960—; Vice-President, International Banking Corp., 1959—; Director: ASA Ltd. 1965—, and American Bureau for Medical Aid to China, 1964—. *B.* 1916. *Educ.* College of Wooster (BA); Fletcher School of Law and Diplomacy (MA); Harvard University. *M.* 1937, Marion Fitch. *S.* John K. and George F. *Daus.* Janet E. Butler and Nancy E. Downs. Governor, Central Bank of Ceylon 1950–53; Vice- Pres., Federal Reserve Bank of New York 1954–59. *Publications:* Report on the Establishment of a Central Bank for Ceylon (1949); Easy Money and the Balance of Payments (Investment Dealers' Digest, 1965); Financing Freedom's Future—Can we Moderate the Boom! (publ. Detroit Economic Club 1966); Real Gold or Paper Gold? (S. African Journal of Economics, Mar. 1967). Central Banking Adviser to the Philippine and Ceylon Govts. *Member:* Asia Socy.; Cncl. on Foreign Relations. *Club:* University. *Address:* 290 Boulevard, Mountain Lakes, New Jersey 07046, U.S.A.

**EXTON, William, Jr.** Management consultant, executive, author, speaker, educator, agriculturist; originator of EFAR (Error Factor Analysis & Reduction), & SAIS (Semantic Analysis of Information Systems) etc. *B.* 1907. *Educ.* Harvard (BA 1926); Columbia (MA 1951). *M.* 1966, Katherine Malandraki (of Athens). *S.* William III. *Career:* Lecturer N.Y. University also India, Greece, Prague, Karachi; Conducted Seminars, Univ. of Denver, Univ. of Chicago, London, Paris and elsewhere; State Univ. of New Mexico, etc.; Associate Director, Columbia Univ, Public Utility Management Workshop, and Research and Development Conference 1963. Banking 1926–29; journalism 1929–32; Mining 1932–37; N.Y. World's Fair 1935–6–7; radio work 1937–39; U.S. Navy 1941–47; Captain U.S.N.R. Ret. Sen. Consultant, William Exton Jr. and Associates 1947—; Associate in Univ. Seminars, Columbia University 1950—; Chmn. Columbia Univ. Seminar on Organization & Management; Lecturer, Graduate Faculty, N.Y. University 1948–52, and Faculty, New School of Social Science 1964; President: Growth of Democracy Inc. 1940—, Institute of Human Communication 1955—, and Pay-plus Inc. 1956—; Director, Council for International Progress in Management (U.S.A. Component of the Conseil Internationale pour l'Organization Scientifique); Vice-Pres., Institute of General Semantics. Consultant to U.S. Embassy in Paris 1950–51. Founder, first National City Planning Exhibition 1935–37; U.S. Junior Chamber of Commerce (principal sponsor). Incorporator, charter member, vice-president and director since 1958 of Society of Professional Management Consultants (Pres. 1974 & 5), elected Hon. Fellow 1977; Mem., Planning Cttee., North Am. Conf. of Mgt. Cons., 1974—; Co-founder, 1969, Institute of Management Consultants; Secy. 1975–76; made first presentation of Award for Excellence in Mgt. Consulting, 1976; Founder & First Chmn., Council of Mgt. Consulting Organisations 1975–76. Democrat. *Publications:* He's with the Destroyers Now, (1943); Audio-visual Aids to Instruction, (1947); Employee Benefits; Assets or Liability?, (1960); Enlargement of Managerial Capacity, (1959); Communication: Direct or Non-Direct, (1958); Communication: Non-verbal and Supraverbal, (1954); Communication: An Overview, (1960); Management Dynamics, (1962); Upgrading of Asian Crews on Tankers, (1966); The Information Systems Staff, (1969); The Age of Systems; Minimisation of Error, (1970); Error Factor Analysis & Reduction; Semantic Analysis of Information Systems: Motivational Leverage; A New Approach to Managing People, (1975); What Price Accuracy? (1976); & many articles & papers. *Clubs:* Harvard, Explorers, Columbia Faculty (N.Y.C.); Army-Navy Country (Washington); Millbrook Rod & Gun; Sandanona Beagles; Mensa, Chestnut Ridge Rod & Gun; Athens Golf. *Address:* Exton Plantations, R.D., Dover Plains, N.Y.; and 40 Central Park South, New York City 10019, U.S.A.; and 2, Amalias Ave., Athens, Greece.

**EYADEMA, Etienne Gnassingbe.** Togolaise. President of Togo. *B.* 1935. *Career:* Served French Army 1953–61; Indo-China, Dahomey, Niger and Algeria, commissioned 1963; Army Chief-of-Staff (Togo) 1965; President of Togo and Minister of Defence since 1967. *Awards:* Grand Officier de l'Orde National du Mono; A titre militaire francais, décoré de la Croix de la valeur militaire et Chevalier de la Légion d'Honneur. *Address:* Office of the President, Lomé, Togo.

**EYERS, Ernest Stanley,** OBE. Australian. *B.* 1910. *Educ.* Scotch College (Melbourne, Vic.). *M.* 1943, Margot Patricia Gallagher. *S.* 3. *Career:* With International Monetary Fund 1949–50; with Commonwealth Bank of Australia: Secretary 1951–54, Manager for South Australia 1954–57, Manager, London 1957–60; Reserve Bank of Australia: Manager for Victoria 1960–63, Adviser to the Governor 1963–65. Chairman and Managing Director, Housing Loans Insurance Corporation, 1965–71; Adviser to the Governor Reserve Bank of Aust. 1971–75 (ret'd.). A member of Australian delegations to ECAFE, IMF, and Commonwealth Finance Ministers' Conference. *Publications:* Debt Management Policy (SEANZA Lectures 1964); (Jointly) Housing for Australia-Philosophy & Policies (1975). Associate Banker's Inst. of Australasia; Fellow, Australian Inst. of Management. *Clubs:* Union, Killara Golf (both of Sydney) Melbourne. *Address:* 11 Silex Road, Clifton Gardens, N.S.W., Australia.

**EYRE, Dean Jack.** New Zealand Politician & Diplomatist. *B.* 1914. *Educ.* Hamilton High School and Auckland Univ. *M.* 1937, Naomi Patricia Arnoldson. *S.* 2. *Dau.* 1. *Career:* Initiated the importing business of D. J. Eyre & Co., owing to import restrictions took up business in Hawaii 1938; served in World War II (Lieut. R.N.V.R. in escort vessels North Sea and West Africa); re-opened business in New Zealand 1946; D. J. Eyre & Co. Ltd., now Airco (N.Z.) Ltd. Latterly, N.Z. and Australian assemblers & Distributors, Vespa Scooters. Elected MP (National Party) for North Shore 1949; Min. of Industries and Commerce and Customs 1954; Minister of Social Security and Minister for Tourist and Health Resorts from Mar. 1956; Minister of Police from

Dec. 1956; relinquished Social Security and appointed Minister of Housing and State Advances Feb. 1957; Minister of Defence 1957. In opposition from Dec. 1957 until Nov. 1960. On re-election of National Party in Dec. 1960 became Minister of Defence and Minister of Police, and from 1961 Minister of Tourist and Health Resorts; Minister of Defence, and Tourism and Publicity in Govt.; re-elected 1963, retained Ministerial Portfolios of Defence, Tourist and Publicity, retired 1966; High Commissioner in Canada 1968–73, re-appointed 1976 & concurrently accredited to Jamaica, Trinidad & Tobago, Barbados & Guyana. *Clubs:* Royal N.Z. Yacht Squadron; Northern Wellington; Officer's; Commercial Travellers'. *Address:* c/o Ministry of Foreign Affairs, Wellington, New Zealand.

**EYSKENS, Viscount Gaston.** Belgian. Former Prime Minister. *B.* 1. Apr. 1905. *Educ.* Columbia Univ; Université de Louvain, Master of Sciences; Docteur en Sciences politiques et sociales 1931; Docteur en Sc Com. at Financiércs 1930; Licencié en Sciences économiques 1929; Dr. h.c. Univ. Cologne; rhc. Columbia Univ. Dr hc Helvaïc Univ. Jerusalem. *M.* 1931, Gilberte de Petter. *S.* Marc. Eric. *Career:* Prof. at the Université de Louvain 1931—; Chef du Cabinet to Minister of Labour and Social Insurance 1934–35; mem. of the Conseil Supérieur des Finances 1936; Economic Councillor to the Minister of Economic Affairs 1939; member of the Chamber of Representatives (Social Christian Party) 1939–65, Member of Senate 1965–73; Minister of Finance Feb.–Aug. 1945; Minister of Finance Mar. 1947–Aug. 1949; Governor, Internat. Bank for Reconstruction and Development (Washington) 1947–49; Prime Minister Aug. 1949–June 1950; Minister of Economic Affairs and the Middle Classes June–Aug. 1950; Vice-Pres., Economic and Social Council U.N.O. 1951; Prime Minister June 1958–May 1961; Minister of Finance July 1965–Mar. 1966; Prime Minister 1968–72. *Member:* Royal Academy of Sciences. *Publications:* Le Port de New York dans son Rôle économique; De Arbeiders en de Bedrijfsleiding in Amerika; Les Indices de la Conjoncture économique du Congo Belge depuis les guerres; Vlaamse Volkskracht van heden; Les finances publiques depuis la guerre, etc. *Address* 60 rue de Namur, Louvain, Belgium.

**EYTAN, Walter.** Israeli statesman. *B.* 1910. *Educ.* St. Paul's School London; Queen's College Oxford, MA. *M.* Beatrice Levison. *S.* 2. *Dau.* 1. *Career:* Lecturer in German, Oxford Univ. 1934–46; Prin. Public Service College, Jerusalem 1946–48; Dir.-Gen. Ministry for Foreign Affairs of Israel 1948–59; Ambassador of Israel in France 1960–70; Political Adviser to Minister for Foreign Affairs 1970–72; Chmn Israel Broadcasting Authority since 1972. *Publications:* The First Ten Years: a Diplomatic History of Israel (1958). *Awards:* Commandeur de la Légion d'Honneur (1976). *Address:* 18 Rehov Balfour, 92 102 Jerusalem, Israel; and *office* POB 7139, 91 070 Jerusalem, Israel.

**EZPELETA, Mariano.** Ambassador of the Philippines. *B.* 1905. *Educ:* Philippine Law School, Manila (B). *M.* Gloria Ledesma. *S.* Mariano, Jr. *Daus.* Eugenia and Lourdes. Member: Philippine Constitutional Convention (and signed the Constitution) 1935; Congressional Secretary and Political Adviser (with rank of Under-Secretary) to the President 1946–47; Consul-General: Shanghai 1947–49, San Francisco 1949, and London (also Counsellor of Embassy) 1950–53; En. Ex. and Min. Plen to Mexico 1953–55; and to Vietnam, Cambodia and Laos 1956–57; Ambassador to Thailand and Fed. of Malaya 1957–59; Ambassador to Australia & Chief of Mission to New Zealand 1960–71. *Publication:* The Rules of Court (annotated). *Address:* Ministry of Foreign Affairs, Manila, Philippines.

# F

**FADER, Henry Isaac.** British. Companion, Most Exalted Order of the White Elephant of Thailand; Commander, Most Noble Order of the Crown of Thailand. *B.* 1902. *Educ.* St. John's College, Sydney, N.S.W. *M.* 1929, Florence Ella Rossiter. *S.* Julian Richard and Geoffrey Clement. *Career:* Formerly Chairman and Managing Director, Potter & Moore (Aust.) Pty. Ltd.; Director, W. J. Bush & Co. (Aust.) Pty. Ltd., J. H. Breck & Co. (Aust.) Pty. Ltd. and Hazel Bishop (Aust.) Pty. Ltd.; company director and Consul of Thailand at Melbourne 1956–62, Consul-General 1962—. Dir. of Marketing, O'Brien Publicity (Vic.) Pty. Ltd. 1959–66; Past Pres. Aust. Inst. of Advertising; Victorian Inst. of Advertising; Advertising Club of Vic.; Past Chairman, Cosmetic & Perfumery Industry of Victoria, formerly member of the Council, Victorian Chamber of Manufacturers; Victorian Chamber of Commerce, Drug & Allied Trade Council of Australia 1943–48; Council, Australian Association of National Advertisers. Manager, Frazer & Best Ltd. 1925–30; Manager, Perfumery Div., W. J. Bush & Co. Ltd. 1930–48. *Fellow:* Australian Institute of Management, Institute of Sales Management, Advertising, Institute of Australia, Australian Institute of Export, Royal Commonwealth Society; Inst. of Directors, London; member, National Sales Executive of U.S.A. *Address:* 15 Balaclava Road, East St. Kilda, Melbourne, Australia.

**FAGAN, Hon. Roy Frederick.** Australian. *B.* 1905. *Educ.* St. Virgil's College, Univ. of Tasmania (BA; LLB). *M.* 1947, Mavis I. Smith. *S.* 3. Attorney-General 1946–58; Ministry for Prices 1950–54; Deputy Leader, Tasmanian Parliamentary Labor Party 1948–59; Pres., Univ. Union of Tasmania 1931–33; Barrister, Hobart 1934–46; Lecturer in Law, Univ. of Tasmania 1943–46; Deputy Premier and Attorney-General of Tasmania 1959–69; Minister for Industrial Development 1959–69. Deputy Leader of the Opposition 1969–72; Minister, Industrial Development, Power and Forests 1972–74 (ret'd). *Club:* Tasmanian. *Address:* 732 Sandy Bay Road, Hobart, Tasmania.

**FAHMY, Lt. Gen. Mohamed Ali.** Chief of Staff of the Armed Forces of the Arab Republic of Egypt. *B.* 1920. *Educ.* Engineering Faculty, Cairo Univ.; Military Academy. *Married. S.* 2. *Dau.* 1. *Career:* Lieutenant, First Lieutenant, Captain & then Major in the Egyptian Army, 1939–50; Instructor in the Senior Officer's Studies Inst., 1952; Army Operations Dept., 1953; Lt. Colonel 1954, Colonel 1957; Cmdr. of the 2nd Light A/A Regiment 1958; Cmdr. of the 14th A/A Regiment 1958; Cmdr. of the 64th A/A Regiment 1959; Cmdr. of the 6th Art. Group 1961; Brigadier, 1962; Chief of Staff of the 5th Art. Division 1963; Major General 1965; Cmdr. of the 5th Art. Division 1966; Air Defence Chief of Staff 1968; Cmdr. in Chief of Air Defence Forces 1969; Lieutenant General 1973; Chief of Staff of the Armed Forces since 1975. *Decorations:* Many, incl. Order of Liberation, 1952; Medal of Merit 1949; Military Star Order, 1971; Merit Golden Medal from Army of German Democratic Republic, 1972; & others from Saudi Arabia, Syria, Yugoslavia etc. *Address:* c/o Ministry of War, Cairo, Egypt.

**FAHY, Charles.** American Circuit Judge. *B.* 1892. *Educ.* University of Notre Dame, Georgetown Univ. (LLB 1914), (LLD 1942). *M.* 1929, Mary Agnes Lane. *S.* Dom Thomas, OSB. *Daus.* Anne (Sheehan), Sarah (Sister Sarah Fahy, SND), and Agnes (Johnson). *Career:* Admitted to District of Columbia Bar 1914; war service 1917–19; practised in Washington until 1924 and from 1947–49; and in Santa Fe 1924–33; Chairman, Petroleum Administrative Board 1933–35; General Counsel, National Labor Relations Board 1935–40; Asst. Solicitor General of the U.S. 1940–41; member, President's Naval and Air Base Commission in London 1941; Solicitor General of U.S. 1941–45; adviser to U.S. Delegation to San Francisco Conference, U.N. 1945; the Legal Adviser, Military Governor, Germany 1945–46; the Legal Adviser, Dept. of State 1946–47; Adviser, U.S. Deleg. to Gen. Assembly, U.N. 1946; Alternate Representative 1947 and 1949; Chairman, Personnel Security Review Board, Atomic Energy Commission 1949; Chairman, President's Committee on Equality of Treatment and Opportunity in the Armed Forces 1948–50. President, Catholic Association for International Peace 1950–51. Nominated by Pres. Truman as Judge of the U.S. Court of Appeals for the District of Columbia, and assumed office 15 Dec. 1949. *Awards:* Robert S. Abbot

Memorial Award, 1951; John Carroll Award, 1952; Russwurm Award 1953, Awarded Navy Cross by Pres. Wilson, and the Medal for Merit by Pres. Truman. *Address:* U.S. Court of Appeals, Washington, D.C., U.S.A.

**FAINA, Carlo.** Cavaliere del Lavoro; Légion d'Honneur; Count of Civitella dei Conti; Italian industrialist. *B.* 1894. *Educ.* Dr. jur. and Rer, Econ. *M.* 1930, Myriam Balduino. *S.* Eugenio, Sebastiano and Alessandro. *Daus.* Maria Caterina and Angelica. Secretary, Vicenza Chamber of Commerce 1921; Branch Dir., National Bank of Agriculture 1922–26; Secy. of Pres. of Montecatini Co. 1926 (Dir.-General 1941; Managing Dir. 1946, Vice-Pres. and Managing Dir. 1952; Pres. and Managing Dir. 1956). Hon. President Montedison Co. 1966—. Author of many publications and studies on financial and economic subjects. *Clubs:* Rotary Clubino, Hunting (Rome). *Address:* Via S. Simpliciano, 6, Milan, Italy.

**FAIRBAIRN, Sir David Eric,** KBE, DFC, MA(Cantab.). Australian politician. *B.* 1917. *Educ.* Geelong Grammar School and Jesus College, Cambridge; MA (Cantab.). *M.* 1945, Ruth Antill Robertson. *Daus.* 3. *Career:* Farmer & grazier 1939–71; Served with R.A.A.F. in England and New Guinea 1940–45 (awarded DFC). Federal Member for Farrer 1949–75. Liberal. Minister of State for Air, Aug. 1962–June 1964 Minister of State for National Development of the Commonwealth of Australia and Leader of the House (1966), June 1964–69; Minister for Education & Science March–Aug. 1971; Minister for Defence 1971–72; Shadow Minister for National Development 1973–74; appointed Australian Ambassador to the Hague 1976. *Clubs:* Melbourne; Albury (N.S.W.); Commonwealth (Canberra). *Address:* 2/3 Tasmania Circle, Forrest, A.C.T., Australia.

**FAIRBAIRN of Fordell, Nicholas Hardwick,** QC, MP. Baron of Fordell. *B.* 1933. *Educ.* Loretto & Edinburgh Univ.—MA, LLB. *M.* 1962, Hon. Elizabeth Mackay. *Daus.* 3. *Career:* MP (Cons.) for Kinross & Perthshire West since 1974. *Clubs:* Beefsteak; New. *Address:* Fordell Castle, by Dunfermline, Fife; and *office* House of Commons, London SW1A 0AA.

**FAIRBAIRN, Sir Robert.** British. *B.* 1910. *Educ.* Perth Acad.; Beckett & Whitehead. Prizeman, Institute of Bankers, 1934. *M.* 1939, Sylvia Lucinda Coulter. *S.* Robert Coulter and Geoffrey Gibbon. *Dau.* Susan Elizabeth. *Career:* Joined service of Clydesdale Bank at Perth 1927; Midland Bank Ltd. 1934, Lt.-Cmdr. (S) R.N.V.R. 1939–46. Assistant General Manager, Clydesdale & North of Scotland Bank Ltd. 1951, General Manager 1958 (the name of that Bank was shortened to Clydesdale Bank, June 1963); Dir. and Gen. Mgr. Clydesdale Bank Ltd., Glasgow 1967–71, Vice Chmn. 1971, Chmn. 1975; Director: Forward Trust Ltd. 1958–67 and Forward Trust (Finance) Ltd. 1964–67; Vice-Chmn., Inst. of Fiscal Studies (Scotland) 1976. Director: Scottish Amicable Life Assurance Society since 1960 (Chmn. 1970 Dep chmn. 1975, Chmn. 1976); Midland Bank Finance Corp. Ltd. 1967–74, Clydesdale Bank Finance Corp. Ltd. since 1967, Commercial Union Assurance Group (Local Board; Clydesdale Bank Insurance Services Ltd.; Second Great Northern Investment Trust; Scottish Computer Services Ltd. (Chmn.); Scottish Western Investment Co.; Newarthill Ltd.; Dir., British Nat. Oil Corp. 1976; Chmn. Cttee. Scottish Bank General Managers 1963–66; Vice-Pres., Glasgow Chamber of Commerce 1970; Scottish Council (Development and Industry) Vice-Pres. 1967–68; Scottish Council of C.B.I.; Vice-Pres., Scottish Economic Society, Pres. 1966–69; Pres., Inst. of Bankers in Scotland 1961–63; Vice-Pres. British Bankers Assn. 1966–68; Chmn. Industrial Development Advisory Bd. Scottish. *Member:* Justice of the Peace for the City of Glasgow. *Fellow:* Royal Society of Arts. British Inst. of Management; Inst. Bankers; Inst. Bankers in Scotland; Hon. Fellow, Society of Industrial Artists & Designers. *Clubs:* Caldedonian; M.C.C.; Western (Glasgow); Royal and Ancient; Corinthian Casuals. *Address:* The Grange, Hazelwood Road, Bridge of Weir, Renfrewshire; and *office* 30 St. Vincent Place, Glasgow, G1 2HL.

**FAIRBANKS, Douglas Elton Jr.,** KBE, DSC. Actor, producer and corporation director. *B.* 1909. *Educ.* private schools and by tutors in N.Y., Los Angeles, London and Paris. MA (Oxon); visiting Fellow St. Cross Coll. Oxford Univ.; DFA (hon) 1966; Senior Churchill Fellow Westminster Coll. Fulton; LLD (hon) Univ. of Denver Coll. 1974. *M.* 1939, Mary Lee Epling. *Daus.* Daphne, Victoria and Melissa. *Career:* Began acting in films in Los Angeles 1923, became a 'star' and given production authority 1931; organized own production company in Great Britain 1934 and U.S. 1946; has appeared in over 75 films. Began stage career in Los Angeles 1927, appearing in approximately 15 stage productions in U.S. and U.K. First T.V. appearance 1950; began TV producing in Los Angeles and London 1952 (has since produced over 160 and acted in over 40 TV films). In 1927, began writing for national magazines, films and newspapers. Studied art in Paris; exhibited paintings, drawings and sculpture, illustrated own articles and contributed caricatures to national magazines. Public service: in 1939 helped organize and became Natl. Vice-Pres. of Wm. Allen White Cttee. to Defend America by Aiding the Allies; Franco-British War Relief (later British War Relief) 1939; and, later Fight for Freedom Cttee. Appointed by Pres. Roosevelt as Presidential Envoy on Special Mission to certain Latin American countries 1940–41. After World War II received numerous assignments by U.S. Department of State, U.S. Navy, E.C.A., Office of the Presidency, etc.; Post-war activities include: National Chairman (appointed by U.S. State Department) American Relief for Korea 1951–55; National Chairman, C.A.R.E. Cttee. and the Share Through C.A.R.E. Committee 1946–50; Vice-Pres., Amer. Assn. for the U.N. 1946–63; Member: Bd. of Directors, Refuge Defense Cttee. 1946–52 and English-Speaking Union of the U.S. 1950–63; Gov., Ditchley Foundation (U.K.). Trustee: Edwina Mountbatten Trust (U.K.); Wellington Charitable Trust; Council for Foreign Relations (U.S.); Board of Governors, Exec. Cttee. member Royal Shakespeare Theatre, Stratford-upon-Avon 1952—; American Museum in Britain since 1965; Denver Center of Performing Arts since 1973; Commissioned Lieut. (j.g.) U.S.N.R. Apr. 1941; and promoted through grades to Captain U.S.N.R. After North Atlantic Convoy and Arctic Patrol, Russian and Malta Convoy duty assigned to serve Admiral Lord Mountbatten, first on Planning and Research Staffs, and later as only U.S. officer in command of flotilla of raiding craft for Combined Operations (Commandos). From 1943 on staff of Commander Amphibious Forces, U.S. Atlantic Fleet, and of Commander U.S. Naval Forces, N.W. Africa Waters; also Operational Planner and Chief Staff Officer Operations for Special Operations Task Group, Mediterranean. After invasion of France assigned Strategic Plans Division of C.-in-C. U.S. Fleet H.Q., and as liaison between Chiefs of Staff and State Department in Postwar Plans Division, until end of active duty in 1946; Pres. Dougfair Corp.; Boltons Trading Corp.; owner The Fairbanks Co.; Fairbanks Int. Business Developments Inc.; Norlantic Development Inc.; Douglas Fairbanks Ltd.; Cavalcade Films Ltd.; Dir., Norlantic Record Co. Ltd.; Rambagh Palace Hotel (Jaipur, India); and Dir. or Consult. to several other U.S. and European Cos. *Awards:* U.S. Silver Star; Legion of Merit (valor) U.S.; K.J.St.J.(U.K.); Legion of Honour, Croix de Guerre with Palm; Order of Merit, Star of Italian Solidarity and War Cross for Military Valour; Order from Belgium, Italy, Netherland, Greece, Chile, Brazil, Korea; Orders and decorations. *Clubs:* The Brook; Century, Knickerbocker (N.Y.C.); Myopia Hunt (Hamilt.); Metropolitan (Washington); Racquet (Chicago); White's, Buck's; Garrick; Naval & Military (London); Puffin's (Edinburgh); Travellers' (Paris). *Address:* 575 Park Avenue, New York, N.Y. 10021; The Vicarage, 448 North Lake Way, Palm Beach, Florida, 33480, U.S.A.; *office* 10 Park Place, St. James's, London, S.W.1.

**FAIRCHILD, Clare E.** American business executive. *B.* 1911. *Educ.* University of Washington. *M.* 1947, Eleanor M. Donoghue. *S.* Mark Douglas. *Daus.* Brenda Sue and Linda Jean. Deputy-Sheriff, Worcester County. Member, Massachusetts Dept. Sheriff's Assn., and Mass. Restaurant Assn.; Developer, Highland Park, Brentwood, Estates; Designer-Builder, Fairbrook Hotel. Newspaper work, advertising, photography, New York City 1935–39; Construction Engineer and Technical Representative with U.S. Army and Navy in Los Angeles, Hawaii, New Guinea, North Africa, Italy 1939–44; Inspector, Bahrein Island, Persian Gulf 1944–45; Treas., Fairchild Bros. Inc. 1945–57; Pres.-Treas., Brentwood Corp. 1947—; Pres., Capital Investors of Florida. Rufus Putman Lodge A.F. & A.M.; Worcester Foundation for Experimental Biology; National Geographic Society; Worcester Art Museum; American Museum of Natural History; Pan American Union. Republican. *Clubs:* Fairbrook Country (Treas.); Palm Beach Athletic. *Address:* 242 8th Street, West Palm Beach, Fla. 33401, U.S.A.

**FAIRCLOUGH, Hon. Ellen Louks,** PC, FCA, LLD. *B.* 1905. *Educ.* Hamilton (Ont.) Public and Secndy. Schools. *M.* 1931, David Henry Gordon Fairclough. *S.* Howard. Chartered Accountant, public practice 1935–57; Alderman Hamilton City Council 1946–49; Controller 1950; elected to House of Commons as Progressive Conservative member for Hamilton West 1950 (re-elected at general elections 1953–57–58–62);

appointed Secretary of State for Canada 1957; Minister of Citizenship and Immigration 1958–62; Postmaster-General 1962–63. Defeated General Election Apr. 1963. Secy., Vice-Pres., Dir., Hamilton Trust and Savings Corp., Ont. 1963—. *Fellow:* Inst. Chartered Accountants of Ontario. *Member:* Zonta club of Hamilton; International Treas. Zonta International 1972; United Empire Loyalists Association, and Imperial Order Daughters of the Empire; Patron, Huguenot Society of Canada, Hon. LLD, McMaster Univ., 1975. *Address:* 25 Stanley Avenue, P.O. Box 887, Hamilton, Ont., L8N 3P8 Canada.

**FAIRFAX, James Oswald.** Australian. *B.* 1933. *Educ.* Geelong Grammar School (Australia) and Balliol College, Oxford (MA). *Career:* Chairman, John Fairfax Ltd., Sydney, N.S.W. (Publishers of Sydney Morning Herald, The Sun, The Sun-Herald, and other publications) 1977, Director 1957; Associated Newspapers Ltd. (Australia) 1958—, (Chmn. 1975). *Member:* Council International House Sydney Univ. 1967; Int. Council Museum of Modern Art, New York, 1971. Mem. Bd. Management, Royal Alexandria Hosp. for Children, 1968. *Clubs:* Garrick; Carlton (London); Union, Australia (Sydney); Melbourne (Melbourne). *Address:* 5 Lindsay Avenue, Darling Point, Sydney, N.S.W.; and *office* John Fairfax Ltd., Broadway, Sydney, N.S.W., Australia.

**FAIRFAX, Sir Vincent Charles, Kt Crt 1971, CMG.** Australian newspaper, bank and assurance director, and grazier. *B.* 1909. *Educ.* Geelong Grammar School, Victoria, and Brasenose College, Oxford; BA Oxon. *M.* 1939, Nancy Heald. *S.* 2. *Daus.* 2. *Career:* staff John Fairfax & Sons Pty. Ltd. 1933; Advtg. Mgr. 1937–38; Dir. 1946–53; Grazier in S. Queensland; Director, Bank of New South Wales 1953; Australian Mutual Provident Society 1956 (Chairman 1966); Chmn., Australian Section, Commonwealth Press Union 1950–73; Chmn. Stanbroke Pastoral Co. Pty. Ltd. 1964. *Member:* Council Royal Agricultural Socy., N.S.W. 1950, Treas. 1959. Dep. Pres., Royal Agricultural Socy. of the Commonwealth 1966 and 1969, Pres. 1970; Chief Commissioner of Boy Scots Assn. (N.S.W. Branch) 1958–69; Chief Commissioner, Australia, of Boy Scouts Assn. 1969–73; Chairman Boys Brigade, 1950, Pres. 1973; Member, Church of England Property Trust 1950–71; Scout Assn. of Australia; Trustee of Walter & Eliza Hall Trust 1953; Vice-Pres., Art Gallery Society 1954–69; Major A.I.F. *Clubs:* Union Univ.; Imperial Service; Melbourne Club (Vic.); Roy. Sydney Golf; Bath, Leander (London). *Address:* 550 New South Head Road, Double Bay, N.S.W., Australia.

**FAIRFAX-ROSS, Basil Edward,** CBE (Civil). Australian. *B.* 1910. *Educ.* The King's School, Parramatta. *M.* 1946, Jessie Agnes Dalton. *Daus.* Jennifer Robyn, Gillian. *Career:* Plantation Manager, Inspector for Burns Philp & Co. Ltd. 1932–39; War service (Middle East 1940–42, New Guinea 1942–45; Major; Mentioned in Dispatches twice; Medal of Freedom of U.S.A.); Medal of Freedom, Hon. Colonel 35 Cadet Batt. Aust. Cadet Corps; Gen. Mgr. British New Guinea Development Co. Ltd. 1951–71; Dir., Kanosia Estates Pty. Ltd.; South Pacific Post Pty. Ltd.; Bougainville Copper Ltd.; Burns Philp (New Guinea) Ltd. Pres. Planters Assn. of Papua 1949–71, MLC PNG 1951–63; PNG Copra Marketing Board 1951–73, Chmn. 1970–73; Copra Industry Stabilization Board (Chmn.) 1956–74; Administrative Council 1961–63; Member, Council Univ. of PNG 1968–71. *Clubs:* Union; Imperial Service; Australian Jockey (all Sydney); Papua (Port Moresby). *Address:* 8 Superba Parade, Mosman, N.S.W. 2088, Australia.

**FAIRHALL, Hon. Sir Allen,** KBE. *B.* 1909. Founded and controlled Commercial Broadcasting Station 2KO 1931–47; Supervising Engineer, Radio and Signals Supplies Div., Ministry of Munitions 1942–45; elected to Federal Parliament for the Div. of Paterson 1949; member. Liberal Party of Australia. Member, Australian delegation 10th Sessions U.N. Gen. Assembly 1955; Minister for the Interior and Works 1956–58; Chmn. Parliamentary Committee on Public Works, 1959–61. Member of Federal Parliament of Australia 1949–69. Minister for Defence 1966–69; for Supply 1961–66. *Fellow:* RSA. *Award:* DSc Hon Newcastle. *Address:* 7 Parkway Avenue, Newcastle, N.S.W. 2300, Australia.

**FAIRHURST, William Albert, CBE, LLD, FICE, FI Struct E, M Inst HE, FNZIE.** British. Consultant. *B.* 1903. *Educ.* Cavendish Road School, W. Didsbury; Manchester College of Technology. *M.* 1937, Elizabeth Robertson Jardine. *S.* Michael Jardine. *Dau.* Elizabeth May. *Career:* Senor Designer British Reinforced Concrete Co. Ltd., Stafford, 1928–31; Chief Engineer, F. A. Macdonald & Partners, Glasgow, 1931–38; W. A. Fairhurst & Partners, Senior Partner 1940–70. Technical Director, Cement & Concrete Association 1948–50 (part time appt.); Chmn. Bridge Design Consultant's Pty Ltd. Sydney. Member, Royal Fine Art Commission for Scotland 1963–72; (Designer of the New Tay Road Bridge, Dundee, and of the Kingston Bridge, Glasgow). Hon. LLD, St. Andrews, 1968. *Member:* Institute of Highway Engineers, Association Consulting Engineers, Soc. des Ingen eurs Civils France. *Awards:* Fellow. Inst. Civil Engineers, Inst. Structural Engineers; Int. Chess Master British Chess Champion 1937; Commonwealth Champion 1951. *Publications:* Arch Design Simplified; Design and Construction of Reinforced Concrete Bridges (jointly); numerous papers on bridges and structural engineering to engineering institutions. *Club:* R.A.C. *Address:* 59 Luton Avenue, Pakuranga, Auckland, New Zealand; and *office* Bridge Design Consultants Pty Ltd., 3 West Street, North Sydney, Australia.

**FAIRMAN, Milton.** American public relations executive; *B.* 1904. *Educ.* Loyola University, Chicago and Chicago University. *M.* 1929, Kathryn M. McSweeney. *S.* Roger Milton. *Career:* Writer and Editor: City News Bureau, Chicago American, Chicago Post, and Chicago Herald & Examiner 1925—34; Assistant Publicity Director, XXVIII Eucharistic Congress 1926; Asst. Dir. of Information, U.S. Dept. of Interior and U.S. Pub. Wks. Admin. 1935–36; Dir. of Pub. Relations: Borden's Dairy & Ice Cream Co., Columbus, Ohio 1937–43; and The Borden Co., N.Y.C. 1943–63, Vice-Pres. 1963–67. Editor, Public Relations Journal 1954–55, 2nd 1968–71. Editor Public Relations Journal 1954–55, 1968–71. *Publications:* Managing the External Function (Top Management Handbook) (1960); Consultant, Standard Dictionary, Internatl. Ed. (1958); contributor, World Book Encyclopedia (1959); various articles on public relations in trade and professional journals. *Member:* Public Relations Socy. of America (Pres. 1951); mem. Accreditation Bd. 1963–66; Public Relations Socy., N.Y.. (Past Chmn.); International Public Relations Assn. Trustee, Foundation for Public Relations Research and Education, 1961— (Pres. 1961–65). *Clubs:* Overseas Press, (N.Y.C.). *Address:* 80 East Hunting Ridge, Stamford, Conn. 06903, U.S.A.

**FALCK, Ragnvald.** Partner in the shipbroking firm of Ragnv. Falck A/S, Oslo 1955—. *B.* 1924. *Educ.* Matriculation and School of Commerce. *M.* 1951, Edel Ohlsson. *S.* Stian and Fridtjof. Chartering Clerk. Oslo 1945–46; Nortraship, London 1945–46; Chartering Clerk, N.W. Spratt & Co. Ltd., London 1946, and Jones, Lane & Co. Ltd., London 1947; Chmn., Oslo Shipbrokers Assn. 1967–69. *Address:* Holmendammen Terrasse 14, Smestad, Oslo, Norway.

**FALETAU, Inoke Fotu.** Tongan diplomat. *B.* 1937. *Educ.* St. Peter's School, Cambridge N.Z.; Tonga High School. Auckland Grammar School N.Z.; Univ. of Wales, Manchester Univ. United Kingdom. *M.* Evelini Maata Hurrell. *S.* 3; *Daus.* 3. *Career:* civil servant Exec. Tonga Civil Service 1958–65; Asst. Secy. Prime Ministers Office 1965–69; Secy. to Government 1969–71; Resources & External Relations Officer. Univ. of the South Pacific Fiji 1971–72; Tonga High Commissioner to United Kingdom & Ambassador to France since 1972, Ambassador to German Federal Republic 1976, to Netherlands, Belgium, Luxembourg & EEC 1977. *Clubs:* Royal Commonwealth Socy; Travellers (Hon.); Nuku'alofa Yacht, Tonga. *Address: office* Tonga High Commission N.Z. House, Haymarket, London, S.W.1.

**FALK, Sir Roger Salis,** OBE. British. *B.* 1910. *Educ.* Haileybury and Geneva University (Wife *D.* 1958). *S.* 1. *Daus.* 2. *Career:* Chmn.: Furniture Development Council, Central Council for Agricultural and Horticultural Co-operation; P.E. International Ltd.; Member, Monopolies Commission. Formerly with D. J. Keymer & Co. Ltd.; Director-General, British Export Trade Research Organization; British European Assoc. Publishers Ltd.; Former Member, Council of Industrial Design; Television Advisory Cttee. *Publications:* The Business of Management (Pelican). Fellow, and Mem. of Council, Royal Society of Arts. *Clubs:* Garrick. *Address:* 603 Beatty House, Dolphin Square, London, S.W.1. and *office* 14–20 Headfort Place, London, S.W.1.

**FALKINGHAM, Robert Percy.** Australian executive. General Manager, John Fairfax Ltd. 1970—. Dir.: Associated Newspapers Ltd. and several related companies 1959—; Amalgamated TV. Services Pty. Ltd. 1959—; Australian Newsprint Mills Holdings Ltd. 1963—; Tasman Pulp & Paper Co. Ltd. 1963—. *B.* 1915. *Educ.* Perth Modern School and Univs. of Western Australia and Queensland (BA; BCom; Diploma in Commerce); Fellow, Australian Socy. of Accountants; Fellow, Bankers Inst. of Australasia; Associate, Commonwealth

Inst. of Valuers. *M.* 1939, Elsie Beryl Clayton. With Bank of New South Wales 1933–57 (Sub-Chief Accountant 1954–57). Lieut., Australian Military Forces 1942–47. Treasurer, John Fairfax Ltd., 1957–69. *Member:* Australian Institute of Management (Associate Fellow); Constitutional Association of Australia; Economic Society of Australia & New Zealand; Royal Economic Society; Australian Institute of Political Science; Sydney University Union. *Club:* The Sydney. *Address:* 7 Byora Crescent, Northbridge, N.S.W.; and *office* 235–243 Jones Street, Broadway, Sydney, N.S.W. Australia.

**FALLE, Sir Samuel,** KCVO, CMG, DSC. British diplomat. *B.* 1919. *M.* 1945, Merete Rosen. *S.* 1. *Daus.* 3. *Career:* British Consul-General, Gothenburg, 1961–63; Head, United Nations Political Dept., Foreign Office, London, 1963–67; Adviser to Lord Shackleton in Aden, 1967; Deputy High Commissioner, Kuala Lumpur, 1967–69; Ambassador to Kuwait 1969–70; High Commissioner, Singapore 1970–74; Ambassador to Sweden 1974–76; High Commissioner, Nigeria since 1976. *Address:* British High Commission, Lagos, Nigeria.

**FALZ-FEIN, Baron Eduard Alexander von.** Liechtenstein. *B.* Sept. 1912. *M.* 1951, Virginia Curtis-Bennett (London). *Dau.* Ludmila. *Address:* Villa Askania Nova, Schloss Strasse, Vaduz; and Quick Tourist Office, Vaduz, Principality of Liechtenstein.

**FANFANI, Amintore,** D Econ. *B.* 6 Feb. 1908. *M.* 1975, Mariapia Tavazzani. *S.* 2. *Daus.* 5. Min. of Labour June 1947–Jan. 1950, Min. of Agriculture, 1951–53; Min. Int, 1953–54; Pres. Minister's Cncl. July 1958–Feb. 1959, July 1960–June 1963; Foreign Office Min., Mar. 1965–June 1968; Pres. of Senate 1968–73. Secretary, Democratia Cristiana Party 1954–59 and 1973–74. Formerly Prime Minister and Foreign Minister of Italy; Professor of Economic History, University of Rome. *Publications:* Storia Economica; Storia dottrine economiche; Capitalismo e partecipazione, etc. *Address:* Senate Della Repubblica, Rome.

**FANSHIER, Chester.** American (of French descent), business executive, professional engineer. *B.* 1897. *M.* 1918, Ina Muriel Goens. *Dau.* Norma Elaine (Rice). *Career:* Commissioner from Tulsa Presbytery to 156th General Assembly of the Presbyterian Church in the U.S.A.; General Manager, Bart Products Co. 1932–39; President, Sunday Evening Federation of Churches 1937–38; Registered Professional Engineer in the State of Oklahoma. President and Gen. Manager, Metal Goods Manufacturing Co. since 1939. Vice-President, Rotary Club of Bartlesville 1955–56; President 1956–57. *Member:* Professional Photographers of America Inc.; Oklahoma Society of Professional Engineers (Charter member, Bartlesville Chapter), National Society of Professional Engineers, Engineers Club of Bartlesville (Charter member and Director 1948–49 and 1954–55). American Society of Mechanical Engineers (Hon. Life Member;) American Society for Testing and Materials, Bartlesville Chamber of Commerce, National Rifle Association (Life Member), American Defense Preparedness Association (Life Member). *Award:* Wisdom Award of Honor 1970. Republican. *Address:* c/o Metal Goods Mftg Co., 309 West Hensley Boulevard, Bartlesville, Oklahoma 74003, U.S.A.

**FARBOWSKY, Kurt.** Austrian Ambassador to Belgium, formerly Federal Ministry of Foreign Affairs, Vienna. *B.* 1911. *Educ.* Univ. of Vienna (LLD). *M.* 1947, Martha Vida. *Dau.* Pia. Formerly Ambassador to the Lebanon, Greece and Cyprus, and Austrian Minister to Iraq, Jordan, Syria and Saudi-Arabia. *Awards:* Commander, Order of Merit (Austria); Officer, Order of Leopold (Belgium); Grand Cordon, Order of the Cedars (Lebanon); Grand Officer, Order of Merit (Syria); Grand Cross, Royal Order of George I (Greece) Cmdr., Order of Merit (Austria); Grand Cross, Order of the Crown (Belgium); Grand Cordon, Royal Jordan Order of Independence. *Address:* Ambassade d'Autriche, Bruxelles.

**FARMER, Edward Hinde.** American. Management, Engineering and Investment Consultant 1961—. *B.* 1906. *Educ.* Case Inst. of Technology (BS and ME) and Harvard Graduate School of Business (MBA). *M.* 1929, Robina Smith. *S.* Robert Hollingsworth. *Dau.* Patricia Jane. Division Mfg. Mgr., E. W. Bliss Co. 1954–59; Vice-Pres., Pacific Airmotive Corp. 1953; Works Mgr., Lockheed Aircraft Corp. 1941–52, Mgr. U.S. Chemical Milling Corp. 1960–61. *Member:* American Socy. of Mechanical Engineers; Amer. Society. for Metals; Amer. Inst. of Aeronautics and Astronautics; Socy; of Automotive Engineers; Amer. Ordnance Assn. and Socy; of Financial Analysts. *Clubs:* Jonathan; Bel Air Country; Eldorado Country. *Address:* 1228 Chantilly Road, Los Angeles, Calif. 90024, U.S.A.

**FARMER, Sir (Lovedin) George (Thomas),** LLD, MA, FCA, JDip, MA. British industrialist. *B.* 1908. *Educ.* Oxford High Sch.; Fellow Inst. of Chartered Accountants. *M.* 1938, Edith Mary Fisher. *Career:* Chairman, Rover Co. Ltd. 1963–73; Deputy-Chmn. British Leyland Motor Corp. Ltd. 1971–73; Second Vice-Chmn. and member of Advisory Cttee., Metalurgica de Santa Ana, S.A., Madrid 1960–74; Dir. Empress Nacional de Autocamiones, S.A., Madrid 1970–73; Chmn. The Zenith Carburretter Co. Ltd. since 1974; Past President: Birmingham Chamber of Commerce, and Society of Motor Manufacturers and Traders and Chmn. Executive Committee 1968–72; Past member of Advisory Council of Export Credits Guarantee Department. Member U.K. Committee of Commonwealth and British Chambers of Commerce; Pror Chancellor, Univ. of Birmingham 1966–75; Govn. Chmn. of Exec. Council and of Finance Cttee, Royal Shakespeare Theatre 1955–75. Pres., Loft Theatre. Member Court of Worshipful Company of Coach & Coach Harness Makers. *Club* Fly Fishers; Bath (London); Royal and Ancient. *Address:* Fairfold, 8 Hill Park, Ballakillowey, Colby, Isle of Man.

**FARNIER, Charles Joseph.** French banker. Director: Crédit National, Banque de l'Indochine, Union pour le Crédit à l'Industrie Nationale (U.C.I.N.A.), Compagnie Financière France-Afrique, Compagnie Française Thomson-Houston, Denain-Nord Est, Usinor. *B.* 1894. *M.* Sabine Imbert-Bail (*D.* 1962). Commander, Legion of Honour (France). Inspector of Finance 1919; Chief of Cabinet, Minister of Finance 1926; Directeur de Mouvement des Fonds 1929; Assistant Governor, Banque de France 1930 (Hon. 1934); Chairman, Comptoir National d'Escompte de Paris 1959 (Hon. 1964). *Address: office* 14 rue Bergère, Paris 9, France.

**FAROLAN, Modesto.** Filipino. Ambassador of the Philippines to Indonesia and Papua New Guinea, concurrently Secretary General of ASEAN (Association of Southeast Asian Nations). *B.* 1900. *Educ.* Philippine Schools. *M.* 1939, Manuela Tolentino. *S.* 4. *Daus.*2. Pre-War D-M-H-M Newspaper exec.; Press Secy. to President of the Philippines 1946; Consul General Hawaii 1946–49; Editor and Publisher, Philippines Herald (one of DMHM 1949–56; Commissioner of Tourism 1956–63; Pres. Pacific Area Travel Association (PATA) 1952–53, and of International Union of Official Travel Organizations (IUOTO—now WTO) 1960–61; Ambassador to Vietnam, Laos and Cambodia 1963–65; Ambassador to Switzerland and Austria 1965–68. Special Envoy of Pres. of the Philippines to Malasia, 1964, and to Indonesia and Malaysia, 1966. *Awards:* Commander, Order of Knights of Rizal (Philippines); Grand Officer, National Order of Vietnam; Grand Officer, Royal Order du Sahametrei (Cambodia); Hon. Doctorate in Education, Bagulo Colleges Foundation, Philippines; Life Mem., IUOTO–WTO Court of Honour & of PATA. *Member:* National Press Club (Philippines); Manila Overseas Press Club; Perhumas, Indonesian P.R. Society; Jakarta Press Club, International Cultural & Academic Relations: Bayanihan Folk Arts Assn. (Philippines); Jajasan Mitra Budaya (Indonesian Cultural Assn.); Int. Acad. of Tourism (Monaco); Inst. of Int. Relations (Indonesia); Centre for Strategic & Int. Studies (Indonesia). *Clubs:* Jakarta (formerly Manila) Rotary & Skal Clubs; Philippine Columbian Assn.; Club Filipino; Phillippine Ambassadors' Club. *Address:* Philippine Embassy, 6–8 Jalan Imam Bonjol, Jakarta, Indonesia.

**FARQUHARSON, Robert Alexander.** CMG. British diplomat. *B.* 1925. *Educ.* Harrow School; Kings Coll., Cambridge. *M.* 1955, Joan Elizabeth Mallet. *S.* 3. *Dau.* 1. *Career:* with Royal Navy 1943–46; British Embassy Moscow 1950–52; Foreign Office 1952–55; British Embassy, Bonn 1955–58, Panama 1958–60, Paris 1960–66; Foreign Office 1966–67; Dir. British Trade Development S. Africa 1967–70; Minister Madrid 1970–73; British Consul-General, San Francisco, U.S.A. 1973–77; British Ambassador, Belgrade since 1977. *Clubs:* Naval and Military, Flyfishers (London); Bohemian (San Francisco). *Address:* Tollard Royal, Wiltshire.

**FARRAR, Irwin E(lmer).** American executive. *B.* 1893. *Educ.* Univ. of Southern California, Leland Stanford Univ., Alexander Hamilton Inst. Admitted to Practice of Law by Supreme Court of the State of California 1916. *M.* 1917, Lois Barbara Peebles. *S.* Robert Irwin (AB Stanford 1948). *Dau.* Mary Elizabeth (AB 1940, MA 1948 Stanford). *Career:* Private practice of law 1916–17; Secy., Corona Chamber of

Commerce 1916–17; Dir., California Secretaries Assn. 1916–17; Pres. and Dir., La Sierra Alfalfa Co. 1919–46; Pres., Hemet Valley C. of C. 1919–21; Pres. and Dir., Riverside Alfalfa Growers Assn. Inc. 1930–46; President and Director, Farrar-Loomis Seed Co. Inc. 1934–64; Vice-Pres. and Dir., Hemet Growers Inc. 1943–71; Dir., Inland Division Board and Member of Exec. Cttee., Security-Pacific National Bank 1952—; Director, Metropolitan Water District of Southern California 1951— (Member, Executive Committee; Vice-Chairman, Water Problems Committee; Member, Legal Committee); Member of Council, Water Resources Center, University of California 1959–65; Director, Eastern Agricultural Association Inc. 1961–69. Chmn., Riverside County Committee (which formed the Riverside County Flood Control District 1945–46, of which he was Commissioner 1946–51); Pres. and Dir.: San Jacinto River Conservation District 1946–55, and of Eastern Municipal Water District 1950–58. Member War Labor Board, Riverside County 1942–45; Dir., Southwest Conf. of Congregational Churches 1956–59; Dir., Calif. Hay & Grain Dealers 1938–40; Pres., Riverside County C. of C. 1937–41; Representative for Riverside Co. on Flood Control and Water Problems in Washington, D.C. 1947–48. *Publications:* Riverside County Water Pioneer (1974); articles in Proceedings of Amer. Socy. of Sugar Beet Technologists, and in California Citrograph. Active member, 7th Annual Global Strategy Discussions, U.S. Naval War Coll., Newport, R.I.; Dir. President Riverside County Chamber Commerce 1938–42. *Member:* State Bar of Calif.; Sons of Amer. Revolution; Navy League of U.S.; Amer. Socy. of Sugar Beet Technologists (Charter Member); Calif. State C. of C.; Citizens Cttee., Univ. of Calif. at Riverside. Republican. Phi Alpha Delta; Kiwanis International (Past Pres.; Past Disgrict Officer). *Address:* 25661 Cornell Street, Hemet, Calif., U.S.A.

**FARRELL, James A., Jr.** American. Comdr. U.S.N.R. (Rtd.). Chairman of the Board, Farrell Lines Inc. 1964—. Director: Argonaut Lines. *B.* 1901. *Educ.* Yale University, BS; Hon. BSc Duquesne Univ. *M.* 1934, Emilie Hill (of Evanston, Ill.). Co-founder of Farrell Lines Inc., with brother, John J. Farrell (*Dec.*). *Awards:* Comdr. Star of Africa; Grand Cross Humane Orders of Africa Redeemed. Naval Order of the U.S. Fellow, Royal Society of Arts. Trustee: Emigrant Industrial Savings Bank; American Bureau of Shipping (Exec. Cttee.); Marine Historical Socy. Director: Amer. Merchant Marine Inst.; National Foreign Trade Council; Maritime Assn. of Port of N.Y.; Socy. of Naval Architects & Marine Engineers; Amer. Socy. of Mechanical Engineers; Delta Phi; St. Elmo Socy.; Pilgrims Socy.; Newcomen Socy. *Clubs:* India House; N.Y. Yacht; Edgartown Yacht; Westminster Kennel; Norwalk Yacht; Royal Thames Yacht. *Address: office* One Whitehall Street, New York, N.Y. 10004, U.S.A.

**FARRIS, Clyde Augustus.** American. *B.* 1922. *Educ.* Lenoir-Rhyne College, Hickory, N. Carolina, BA. 1944; Medical College of Virginia Postgraduate work, 1944. *M.* 1945, Marion Elizabeth Edwards. *S.* Clyde Alexander and Thomas Frederick. *Dau.* Elizabeth Faith. President. Water Services Inc. Knoxville Tennessee; Water Services Caribbean, Inc. Carolina P.R. and Farris Chemical Co. Inc. *Award:* Dictionary of International Biography for Water Treatment Research, 1969. *Member:* North Carolina Socy. of Engineers; American Chemical Socy.; Association of Textile Chemists & Colorists; Socy. of Heating, Refrigeration & Air Conditioning Engineers; Water Works Association, Knoxville Technical Society. *Clubs:* Deane Hill Country; Ski Chalet Village Owners. *Address:* 203 North Weisgarber Road, Knoxville, Tennessee 37919; and *office* P.O. Box 10126, Lovell Road, Knoxville, Tennessee 37919, U.S.A.

**FARRUKH, Dr. Phil. Omar A.** Lebanese educationist and author. *B.* 8 May 1906. *Educ.* American University of Beirut (BA), University of Erlangen, Germany (PhD). *M.* 1940, Amneh A. Hilmi. *S.* Usama, Marwan, Mazin. *Daus.* Linah, Lamis. *Career:* Member, Arab Academy, Damascus, Islamic Research Association, Bombay, Arab Academy, Cairo, and Lebanese National Committee; Prof. of Islamic Philosophy and Arabic literature at Maqâsid College, Beirut; Visiting Professor at the Syrian University in Damascus on History of Muslim Spain; 1951–60; Teacher of History and Geography, Najah School, Nablus, Palestine 1928–29; Professor of Muslim History, High Training School, Baghdad (1940–41). Member of Council, Professor of History of Arab Science and Islamic Studies, Arab University of Beirut. *Awards:* First Order of Education (Lebanon) 1948; Star of Pakistan, Order of Qaid Azam, 1968; National Merit of the Cedars, Knight's Order Lebanon 1971. *Publications:* Islam, a Social System (in English): Das Bild des Frühislam in der arabischen Dichtung von der Higra bis zum Tode Umars (a thesis in German); in Arabic: Islam at the Crossroads (trans); The Incubation of Western Culture in the Middle East (trans.); Missionaries and Imperialism (trans. into Russian, Persian, Turkish and Urdu); Arab Genius in Science and Philosophy (a translation into English: Washington 1954); Influence of Muslim Philosophy on European Thought; Mysticism in Islam; Greek Philosophy and the story of its translation into Arabic; The Family in Muslim Jurisprudence; Islam and the Arabs in the Eastern Mediterranean; Islam and the Arabs in the Western Mediterranean; A History of Arab Thought; A History of Arab Literature I, II; III, History of Arab Science; Trans. into Arabic of H.E. Muhammad Khan's Friends not Masters; and many other volumes on similar subjects. *Address:* P.O. Box 941, Beirut, Lebanon.

**FARUGK, Dr. Gholam.** Afghan politician. *B.* 15 May 1909. *Educ.* Berlin. Resident Physician, Women's Hospital 1940–42; Chief Medical Officer, Central Jail 1942–45; Dean, Faculty of Medicine 1945–47; Under-Secretary of State, Health Ministry 1947–50; Acting Minister, Ministry of Health 1950–51; Minister of Health 1951–55; Minister to Bonn 1955; Ambassador Oct. 1958; Minister to Berne July 1958; Ambassador of Afghanistan in Bonn and concurrently Ambassador in Stockholm. *Address:* Embassy of Republic of Afghanistan, 53 Bonn-Rottgen 2, Liebfrauenweg Ia, Germany.

**FASCIONE, Pietro,** Dott. Ing. Italian. *B.* 1921. *M.* 1948. Antonia Scaramuzzi. *Dau.* 1. *Career:* formerly Chief Engineer, Italian Affiliate of Svenska Tandstiks Aktiebolaget, 1949–53; Mfg. Man. Metalmeccanica, 1953–58; Production Man. Forni e Impianti Industriali Ingg. De Bartolomeis S.p.A., 1958–64; Man. Dir. Chmn. Cia. Italiana Westinghouse and Cia; Italiana Westinghouse Meridionale; Ideal Standard S.p.A. 1964–69; Man. Dir. Gen. Mgr. Reggiane O.M.I. S.p.A.; Man. Dir. Breda Meccanica Bresciana S.p.A.; Breda Standard S.p.A. 1969–73; Man. Dir. Costruzioni Aeronautiche Giovanni Agusta S.p.A.; Meccanica Verghera S.p.A.; Elicotteri Meridionali S.p.A.; Vice Pres. Siai-Marchetti S.p.A. Pres. O.T.B. Officine Termotecniche Breda S.p.A. di Bari; F.O.M.B. Fonderie e Officine Meccaniche di Benevento S.p.A.; Industria Aeronautica Meridionale S.p.A. di Brindisi. *Address:* Via del Ghisallo 20, 20151 Milan, Italy.

**FAST, Morris.** Canadian. *B.* 1917. *Educ.* Univ. of Saskatchewan (BSc Mech Eng 1942). *M.* 1945, Simone Marie Frigon. *Dau.* Louise. Engineer: Northern Electric Co. Ltd. 1937–39; Ottawa Car & Aircraft Co. Ltd. 1939–40; Aluminium Co. of Canada Ltd. 1940–48. President: Locweld & Forge Products Ltd. since 1948, Scaffold-Fast Ltd. since 1950, Locweld Industries Ltd. since 1955, and Cabot Holdings Ltd. since 1960. *Member:* Corp. of Professional Engineers of Quebec; Engineering Inst. of Canada. *Address: office* 50 Iberville Ave., Candiac, P.Q., Canada.

**FATAYI-WILLIAMS, The Hon. Mr. Justice Atanda.** Nigerian. Justice of the Supreme Court of Nigeria. *B.* 1918. *Educ.* Trinity Hall, Cambridge Univ. (MA, LLB). *Career:* Barrister-at-Law (Middle Temple). Crown Counsel 1950–55; Deputy Commissioner for Law Revision 1955–58; Editor, Western Nigeria Law Reports 1955–58; Chief Registrar, High Court of Western Nigeria 1958–60; Judge of the High Court of Western Nigeria, 1960–67; Justice of Appeal, Court of Appeal Western State in Nigeria, 1967–69; Justice of the Supreme Court of Nigeria 1969; Assignments; Chairman, Arbitration Board (Ports) 1969; All Nigeria Law Reports Committee; Chmn. Bd. of Trustees, Van Leer Nigerian Education Trnst since 1973; Mem., Legal Practitioners' Privileges Cttee. since 1975. *Member:* Body of Benchers, Council of Legal Education, Nigeria; Nigerian Museum Socy; Nigerian Inst. International Affairs. *Address:* Supreme Court, Lagos, Nigeria.

**FAUL, Albert Harold.** Australian company director and engineer. *B.* 1906. *Educ.* Melbourne Univ. (BA; BMechE; BEE). *M.* 1935, Ellis Nicholson. *Dau.* Barbara. *Career:* Lecturer, Engineering Design, Melbourne Univ. 1930–35; Engineer, Factory Manager, Deputy Chmn. British Tobacco Co. (Australia) Ltd. 1936–65; Dir. Automatic Totalisators Ltd.; AMF (Aust.) Ltd.; Worthington (Aust.) Ltd.; Delta Minerals N.L.; Omega Oil N.L *Clubs:* Australian, Elanora Golf (Sydney); Athenaeum (Melbourne). *Address: office* Box 145, G.P.O., Sydney, N.S.W., Australia.

**FAULDS, Andrew Matthew William,** MP. British. *B.* 1923. *Educ.* George Watsons, Edinburgh; King Edward VI Grammar School, Louth; Daniel Stewart's. Edinburgh;

High School, Stirling; Glasgow University. *M.* 1945, Bunty Whitfield. *Dau.* Susanna. *Career:* Many TV and radio performances, over 30 films; Member Parliament, Labour, Smethwick 1966–74; Warley East since 1974; Parly. Private Sec. to Minister of Aviation, 1967–68; to Postmaster-Gen. 1968–69; Opposition Spokesman for the Arts, House of Commons 1970–73. *Member:* British Actors Equity. *Address:* 14 Albemarle Street, London, W.1; and *office* House of Commons, London, S.W.1.

**FAULKNER, Sir Eric (Odin),** MBE. British banker. *B.* 21 Apr. 1914. *Educ.* Bradfield College; Corpus Christi College, Cambridge (Hon. Fellow). *M.* 1939, Joan Mary Webster. *S.* 1. *Dau.* 1. Served in World War II, Leicestershire Yeomanry and Royal Artillery (dispatches) 1939–45; Director, Lloyds Bank Ltd., Vickers Ltd.; Dep. Chmn., Finance for Industry Ltd.; created knight 1974. *Address:* 71 Lombard Street, London, E.C.3.

**FAULKNER, Rt. Hon. J. Hugh,** PC. Canadian Politician. *B.* 1933. *M.* 1973, Jane Meintjies. *Career:* MP for Peterborough since 1965; Chmn., Standing Cttee. on Labour & Employment 1966; Dep. Speaker of Parliament 1968; Parly. Sec. to Sec. of State 1970; Sec. of State 1972–76: Minister of State for Science & Technology 1976, for Indian & Northern Affairs since 1977. *Address:* House of Commons, Ottawa, Ont., Canada.

**FAURE, Edgar,** D en D. French statesman. *B.* 18 Aug. 1908. Barrister-at-law, Paris Court of Appeal; Director of Legislative Services, Committee of French National Liberation 1943–44; Deputy Chief Prosecutor in trial of war criminals at Nuremberg; Deputy (Rad. Soc.) for Jura Nov. 1946; Financial Secretary of State 1949; Minister of the Treasury and the Budget, Pleven Cabinet July 1950–Mar. 1951 and in Queuille Cabinet Mar.–Aug. 1951; Minister of Justice, Pleven Cabinet Aug. 1951; Prime Minister Jan.–Mar. 1952, and Feb. 1955–Feb. 1956; Ministre de Finance et des Affaires Economiques (May 1958); Sénator de Jura (May 1959); Professeur à la Faculté de Droit et des Sciences Economiques de Dijon; Ministre de l'Agriculture 1966; Elected Pompidou Cabinet 1967, 1968, 1969; Ministre de l'Education 1969; Professor à la Faculté de Droit et des Sciences economiques de Besancon 1970; Pres. de la Commission Internationale sur le developpement de l'Education de l'UNESCO 1971–72; Minister d'Etat Charge des Affaires Sociales; President de l'Assemblée Nationale. *Address:* 128 rue de l'Université, Paris 75007, France.

**FAURE (Guillaume) Jean (Marie).** French. *B.* 1892. *Educ.* Docteur en Droit. *Career:* At the Bank of France 1910–52 (successively clerk, Inspector, Director of Discount, Inspector General, Director-General of Titles, Director-General of Discount, and Director-Général Honoraire since 1952); Pres. bank de financement Immobilier; Union Mobilère d'investissement. Administrator, Credit Electrique et Gazier; Cavia; Compagnie Cherifienne des Textiles; Union of Credit et de Financement. *Awards:* Officer Legion of Honour; Military Medal; Croix de Guerre; Officer of Agricultural Merit. *Address:* 6 rue du Vieux Colombier, Paris 6è; and *office* 19/21 rue de la Bienfaisance, Paris 8ème, France.

**FAURE, Hubert Rene Joseph.** Chevalier, Legion of Honour. French. *B.* 1919. *Educ.* Ecole Libre des Sciences Politiques. *Career:* Pres. Otis Elevator Co., New York; Vice-Pres. Ascinter Otis, Paris; Dir. Stigler Otis, Milan; Dir. Otis Elevator Co. Ltd., London; Grands Magasins Jones Paris; Imetal Paris; Pres. Otis Europe SA, Paris: formerly Sales Man. Ateliers Metallurgiques de St-Urbain; Dir. United Technologies Corp.; Dir. Saxby, Paris; Otis Elevator International Inc.; Pres. and Chief Executive Officer; Dir. Nippon Otis Elevator Co. Tokyo. *Clubs:* Nouveau Cercle; Racquet & Tennis. *Address:* 960 5th Ave., New York City, NY; and 245 Park Ave., New York, NY 10017, U.S.A.

**FAVEREAU, André Joseph Emile.** French diplomat. Officer Legion of Honour; Companion of the Liberation; Croix de Guerre; Medal of the Resistance, etc. *B.* 1907. *Educ.* Lic. en Droit. *M.* 1953, Françoise Gallot. *S.* Jean-Marie. *Dau.* Sylvie. *Career:* Deputy Administrator of Establishments, Vendeuvre 1930–42; Head of Cabinet of the Commissioner of Foreign Affairs, Algeria 1944; Director of Cabinet of the Ministry for Prisoners, Deportees and Refugees, Paris 1945; Governor of the Palatinat, later Rheinish-Palatinat 1946–53; in post in London, Beirut and Jerusalem; Technical Counsellor to the Governor-General of Algeria 1955–56; Associate to Commandant of the College of Defence, N.A.T.O. 1961–63; in charge of mission on the Direction of Personnel of the Ministry of Foreign Affairs 1965–67; Ambassador in Australia 1967–71. *Club:* Commonwealth (Canberra). *Address:* 15 rue de Bourgogne, Paris 7, France.

**FAVRETTI, Luciano.** Ambassador of Italy. *B.* 1911. *Educ.* Torino University (Dr. juris and Political Science, 1932 and 1933). *M.* 1938, Liana Lambert. *S.* Umberto. *Career:* Entered Diplomatic Service 1936; at Central Administration 1936; Consular Attaché 1937; joined the Minister's Cabinet 1937; Vice-Consul Sangallo 1938; Third Secretary Madrid 1941; at Central Administration 1943. Head of Italian Delegation at Italo-Soviet Commission 1951; Head of Department, Ministry of Foreign Affairs, Rome 1952; Pres., Italian Delegation Italo-Greek Economic Commission 1952; Vice-Pres. Italian Cttee. of COCOM 1953. Member of various Italian delegations at conferences on the European Community, Rome 1953; European Council, Strasbourg 1953 and 1954, Tenth Session of C.E.C.A., Luxembourg 1953. Chief of Cabinet of the President of the Assembly of C.E.C.A. 1954. Counsellor in 1955 and joined the Cabinet of the Minister of Foreign Affairs 1957. Member of various delegations to CEE and Euratom, Paris, Brussels and Strasbourg 1958; Minister-Counsellor, Ankara 1958; Min. Ex. and Plen. 1962; Ambassador to Lebanon 1964–68, to Tunisia 1968. *Club:* Circolo degli Scacchi (Rome). *Address:* Ministry of Foreign Affairs, Rome, Italy.

**FAZEKAS, Janos.** Romanian politician. *B.* 1926. *M.* Elisabeta *S.* 2. *Career:* member Communist Party 1945—; Central Cttee. Communist Youth 1950–54; Secy. Central Cttee. 1950; Member, Central Cttee. R.C.P. 1954—; Deputy Grand Nat. Assembly 1954; Minister, Food Industry 1961–65; Vice Chmn. Council of Ministers 1965; Member Exec. Cttee. Central Cttee. 1967—; Nat. Cttee. Socialist Unity Front 1968; Academy Social & Political Sciences 1970. Hero of Socialist Labour 1971. *Address:* Central Committee of the Romanian Communist Party, Bucharest, Romania.

**FECHTER, Rudolf.** German diplomat. *B.* 1912. *Educ.* Gymnasium Karlsruhe; Univs. Innsbruck, Frankfurt/M, Vienna and Heidelberg; Dr. phil. (History). *M.* 1941, Maria Claeys. *Daus.* 2. *Career:* Editor (Foreign Affairs) of a German weekly 1949–52; Cultural and Press Attaché at German Embassy Mexico 1953–54; Counsellor, Foreign Office Bonn 1955–60; Consul General (1960–62) and Ambassador Damascus 1960–64; First Counsellor, German Embassy Paris 1964–69; Ambassador, German Embassy, Addis Ababa 1969–73; German Ambassador in Dublin 1973–77. *Decorations:* Bundesverdienstkreuz I. KI (German); Commdr. of the Order of Merit, France; Grand Cordon Order of Merit of Syria; Grand Cordon Star of Honour of Ethiopia. *Address:* Ahornweg 3, D7825 Lenzkirch, Federal Republic of Germany.

**FEDELE, Carlo Riccardo,** LLD. Swiss International Civil Servant. Chief, External Relations, World Health Organization June 1961—. *B.* 1918. *Educ.* Degree in Commercial Sciences, Bellinzone (Tessin), and Univ. of Berne (LLD). *M.* 1944, Janine Herren. *S.* Marco Giovanni. *Dau.* Cristina Manuela. Jurist, Dept. of Public Economy, Secretariat General, Swiss Confederation 1942; Federal Political Dept. 1943–53; Attaché, Press and Information Service, Berne 1943–46; Secretary of Legation, Bogotá 1946–49; Chargé d'Affaires, Caracas 1949–50; Division of International Organizations, Berne 1950–53. Special Mission to Brazil 1952. With Inter-governmental Committee for European Migration (ICEM) 1953–61: Deputy Chief, ICEM Mission in Rio de Janeiro 1953–56; Chief of Section of Latin-America, Geneva (Hq.) 1956–61. On Missions to Uruguay 1953 and 1954, and to other Latin-American countries 1960. *Publications:* La Dichiarazione di Scomparsa nel Diritto svizzero (Thesis of doctorate, Univ. of Berne 1942); various articles in Swiss and foreign newspapers and weeklies. Member of numerous other literary and social circles in Switzerland and abroad. Pres. Lions Club 1966–67. *Address:* La Marmottíere, 1248 Hermance, Geneva; and *office* WHO, 1211, Geneva 27, Switzerland.

**FEDERA, Henry Appleton.** American. *B.* 1913. *Educ.* Univ. of Louisville (BA 1935; LLB *magna cum laude* 1937). *M.* 1948, Mary D. Stafiniak. *Daus.* Pamela, Danielle and Judith. *Career:* Asst. Attorney-General of Kentucky 1939–42. U.S. Army (Capt. J.A.G.D.) 1943–45. Attorney, U.S. Steel Corp. 1946–50; Secy., General Counsel and Dir., Orinoco Mining Co. 1950–52; President, Greater Council of Manhasset Civic Association 1967–68. Senior Vice-President, Secretary and General Counsel, Raymond International Inc. 1952—(Director 1964—). *Publications:* several legal papers. *Member:* American-Texas Bar;; Kentucky Bar Assns. Amer. Soc.

Corporate Secretaries; Delta Upsilon (Pres. and Chmn. 1959–65). *Address:* 11502 Habersham Houston, Texas 77024; and *office* 2801 South Post Oak Road, Houston, Texas 77027.

**FEGAN, David A.** American. Attorney-at-Law *B.* 1918. *Educ.* George Washington University, Harvard College and National University Law School (LLB). J.D. *M.* 1943, M. Lorraine Coyle. *S.* David and Stephen. Partner, Morris, Pearce Gardner & Pratt 1943–60; Attorney-at-Law 1943—; General Counsel, Cruise-Along Boats 1949–57; Legal Counsel, British Embassy Washington 1957—; Vice Pres. Dir. MarBer Development Co. 1960—; Cavalier Finance Co. 1962–69; Old Line Brick & Tile Co. Inc. 1963—; Calvert Bank & Trust Co. 1963—; General Counsel, Amer. Inst. Biological Science 1963—; Vice Pres. Chmn. Bd. Dirs. Capital Clay Products Inc. *Publications:* Abstracts of the Law of the District of Colombia (The Lawyers' Directory); Abstracts of the Federal Income Tax Laws (The Lawyers' Directory). *Member:* Apex Honor Socy.; Sigma Nu Phi. Member: Bars of the Supreme Court of the United States, United States Court of Appeals for the District of Columbia, of the States of Maryland, South Carolina, and District of Columbia; American Bar Assn. *Clubs:* Army-Navy; Kenweel Country; Calvert Country; Reciprocity (Natl. Treas. 1968). *Address:* 8709 Seven Locks Road, Bethesda, Md.; and *office* Suite 711 Wire Building, Washington. D.C., U.S.A.

**FEHLE, Armin G.** Austrian. Managing Partner Dorland Advertising, Vienna. *B.* 1932. *Educ.* Vienna School of Economics and Business Administration (Dipl. Int. Com). *M.* 1956, Marianne Fessler. *Daus.* Aglaja Maria Christina, Constanze Marie-Therese and Isabelle Katia Maria. *Career:* Graduated, College of the Humanities; six months study tour in Spain, and six months in Great Britain. Director, Franz Baumgartner, A.G., Linz; Man. Director: Interpublic K.G., Vienna 1959–61; and Ogilvy & Mather, Vienna 1961–68; International Advertising Association former Secy. now Vice-Pres. *Decorations:* Commander of the Order of the Temple (Tempelherren); Grand Officer of the Order of the Holy Cross (Constantinople). *Publication:* Die syndikalistische Wirtschaftsverfassung im neuen Spanien (1956). *Member:* Schlaraffia (Linz/Donau); Lions (Wien/Papageno). Pres.; Austrian-South African Club, Vice-Pres. *Address:* Blaasstrasse 13. Vienna XIX (34-71-78); and Vienna I., Kärntnerstraße 25, Austria.

**FEHMERS, Frank Wilhelmus Tilman.** Dutch. *B.* 1942. *Educ.* Mendel Coll., Haarlem. *M.* 1964, Cynthia Franchette Bennett. *Career:* Dir. & Owner Frank Fehmers Productions; formerly with Herder Verlag; Paul Brand Pub.; Coebergh Booksellers; Paulist Press, N.Y. *Clubs:* Royal Rowing Club 'De Hoop'. *Address:* Herengracht 487, Amsterdam, Holland.

**FEICHTINGER, Arne F.** Swedish executive. *B.* 1906 (Orby, Sweden). *Educ.* MS in Engineering. *M.* 1934, Ruth Inez Krutmeijer. *Career:* With Svenska Siemens AB, Stockholm since 1929, successively Engineer, Sales Manager, Man. Dir. 1954–70, Chmn. 1970–72. Member Bd. Dirs. Dansk Siemens AS, Copenhagen 1953–60; Swedish Electric Mfg. Assn. Stockholm 1956–72; Employers Assn. Swedish Elec. Stockholm 1961–70; Telub AB, Växjö, Sweden 1967–69; Elema-Schönander AB, Stockholm 1970–72; Siemens Corp. New York 1970–76. *Member:* Assn. Engineers and Architects; Royal Swedish Acad. of Engineering Science (Ind. Council); Swedish Assn. Inventors; Swedish Physicists; Swedish Radio Engineers Socy.; Swedish Nat. Cttee. International Chamber of Commerce; Stockholm Chamber of Commerce (all of Stockholm); Inst. Electrical and Electronic Engineers, New York; Royal Socy. of Arts London. *Awards:* Knight (First Class); Order of Vasa. *Clubs:* Royal Swedish Automobile; International; Swedish American Society. *Address:* Villavägen 27, S-182 75 Stocksund, Stockholm, Sweden.

**FEILDEN, Geoffrey Bertram Robert,** CBE, MA (Cantab), FIMechE, FEng, Hon. FIStructE, FRS. British. *B.* 1917. *Educ.* Bedford School (Scholar) and King's Coll., Cambridge (Scholar); DSc (Hon); DTech (Hon). *M.* (1) Elizabeth Gorton. *S.* Richard. *Daus.* Jane and Fiona. (2) Diana Angier *née* Lloyd. *Career:* Technical Trainee with Unilever Ltd. 1939–40; Engineer with Power-Jets Ltd. 1940–46; with Ruston & Hornby Ltd.; Engineer i/c Gas Turbine Div. 1946, Chief Engineer 1949, and Engineering Director 1954; Managing Dir. Hawker Siddeley Brush Turbines Ltd. 1959–61; Group Technical Director, Davy-Ashmore Ltd., London. Director of principal operating companies of Davy-Ashmore Group 1961–68; Deputy Director-General, British Standards Institution 1968–70; Dir. General since 1970; Non-exec. Dir., Averys Ltd. 1974—; Dep. Chmn., Design Council 1976—. *Publications:* A Standard Gas Turbine to Burn a Variety of Fuels (1956); First Bulleid Memorial Lecture, Nottingham Univ. 1959; Engineering Design (Report published by D.S.I.R., London) (Chairman of Cttee.). CBE 1966. Fellow of Royal Society 1959, Vice-Pres., 1967–69. *Club:* The Athenaeum (London). *Address:* 'Greys End', Rotherfield Greys, Henley-on-Thames; and *office* 2 Park St., London, W1A 2BS.

**FEIN, A. Edwin.** American marketing-management-research consultant. *B.* 1898. *Educ.* Columbia and New York Universities. *Career:* Formerly: Chairman, Cttee. on Markets and -arkating Research, National Federation of Sales Exec., Vice-Pres. and Chmn., Research National Federation of Sales Exec., Vice-Pres. and Chmn., Research Cttee. Society for Advancement of Management (appointed Fellow, May 1958); lecturer to various sales executives clubs, American Marketing Assn., Edison Electric Institute, Socy for Advancement of Management, and other organizations; Marketing-Technical Consultant to Walter Kiddie & Co., and Curtis Furniture Co.; Manager, Colonial Div., William H. Knox & Co. 1919–23; Pres., National Radium Products Corp. 1924–25; Pres., Sparklets Corp. 1925–35; Dir. Sales, Doughnut Corp. of America 1936–38. Chmn. Research Company of America, 654 Madison Ave., New York, N.Y. Feb. 1939—; Vice-Pres. and Secy. United Industrial Corporation, New York, N.Y. since 1959; Secy. Affiliated Hospital Products Inc. since 1971. *Member:* Four Freedoms Foundation; Int. Platform Assn.; Assn. for Corporate Growth; American Socy. of Corporate Secretaries; Fellow, Socy. for Advancement of Mgmt; Chmn. Industry Group, N.Y. Zoological Society. *Publications:* Survey of Brewing Industry in United States, Canada and Mexico (27 annual editions); A Basic Marketing Chart of United States (10 annual editions); An Outline of Radium and its Emanations; Psychological Merchandising; Management Research; This is My Life; Research with a Practical Accent; How Consumers Spend their Income; (co-author) 8-M Plan for Industrial Communities. *Address:* 660 Madison Ave., New York, N.Y. 10021, U.S.A.

**FEITH, Dr. Hans.** *B.* 1910. *Career:* Member of Supervisory Board of the Deutsche Bank AG; Chmn. of Supervisory Bd.; Deputy-chmn. and member of several Supervisory Boards. *Address:* Gr. Gallusstr. 10–14, Frankfurt-am-Main, Germany.

**FELBER, John Edward.** American. *B.* 1926. *Educ.* Columbia Univ. and Rutgers Univ. Unmarried. *Career:* Vice-Pres. Printing Consultants (publishers) 1945—; Editor Chief Analyst, International Import Index 1949—; City Printer, City of Newark, N.J. 1950–55; Ed. U.S. Export Extract 1956—; Ed. Founder, Int. Intertrade Index 1959—; Ed.-Compiler, Traders Marketing Maps 1960—; Trade Promotion Adviser, Finance Dept. Govt. of Kuwait 1960–63; Editor-Compiler Traders Marketing Maps 1960—; Ed. Japanese Export-Import Studies 1960–65; Tourism Editor, Hammond Map Co. 1962–65; Analyst, Canadian Marketing Service 1963–66; Foreign Trade Editor, Printing Impressions Magazine 1964—; Ed. American Tourist Manuals 1964–66; Foreign Trade Editor, Printing Impressions Magazine since 1964; Tour Dir. Exec. Patent-License Trade Mission, London–Moscow, Tokyo 1972; Accredited Editor, Canton Trade Fair, Min. of Information, People's Republic of China, 1978. *Publications:* Imports to Expand Business (1959); Kuwait Welcomes Commerce; Manual for Soviet-American Trading (1967); Hammon Map Tourist Guides (1962); Executives International Travel Guide (1956); American Tourist Manual for USSR, 1977; Guide for People's Republic of China, 1977; New Products China Newsletter 1977. *Member:* Guild U.S. World Trade Fair Assn.; Amer. Authors League; Amer. Radio Relay League; N.J. State Guard Assn. *Clubs:* Antique Collectors; Overseas Buyers. *Address:* 636 Buchanan Street, Hillside, N.J. 07205; and *office* 744 Broad Street, Newark, N.J. 07101, U.S.A.

**FELGATE, James Gordon.** Australian. *B.* 1908. *Educ.* Brisbane Grammar School; Associate Australian Society of Accountants. *M.* 1936, Beryl Telford. *S.* 2. *Dau.* 1. *Career:* With the Adelaide Steamship Co. Ltd.; manager, Cairns, Qld 1946 and Brisbane 1950; Company Secretary 1956. Chairman, The Adelaide Steamship Co. Ltd. 1973–76 (Ret'd); Director: Port Adelaide Haulage Co. Ltd.; Lensworth Finance Ltd.; Seatainer Terminals Ltd.; J. & A. Brown & Abermain Seaham Collieries Ltd.; Hexham Engineering Co. Pty. Ltd.; Boral Resources (Sth. Aust.) Pty. Ltd.; Bulkships Ltd.; Alt. Dir., Tasman Union Ltd.; Union Steamship Co. of New Zealand Ltd. *Clubs:* Adelaide; Queensland; Grange Golf. *Address:* 2 Moore Street, Toorak Gardens, S.A., Australia.

**FELICETTA, Cesare.** Italian financial and administrative director. *B.* 1930. *Educ.* Rome Univ.; Revisore Ufficiale dei Conti. *M.* 1956, Raffaella Agostinelli. *S.* Fabio. *Career:* Auditor, Rome office of Price Waterhouse & Co. 1949–54; Chief Accountant, Squibb S.p.A. 1954–58; Controller of L.A.I. Italian Airlines during top-management change-over 1957; Manager, Admin. Services Dept., Milan office of Arthur Andersen & Co., Chicago 1958–60; Controller, Bowater Europea S.p.A., Rome 1960–64. Man. Dir. and General Manager, COBEVA S.p.a., Rome 1964–67; Director of Finance and Administration, Warner-Lambert Co., Morris Plains, N.J. (U.S.A.) 1967–71. Vister S.p.A., Angiolini S.p.A. 1967–70, Milan, Eastern Hemisphere, Slough U.K. 1970–71; Director of Finance and Administration Merck Sharp & Dohme (Italia) SpA, Rome 1971–73; Dir. of Finance and Admin. Romana Calcestruzzi SpA, Rome since 1974; Professor of Personnel Administration at Post Graduate Law School, University of Camerino Italy 1967–70. *Awards:* Gentleman to H.H. the Pope; Sovereign Military Order of Malta; Order of Merit (Italian Republic); Order of St. Gregory the Great; St. Sepulchre of Jerusalem; St. Agata (San Marino); Southern Cross (Brazil); Teutonic Order; Pontifical Lateran Cross (1st Cl.); Constantinian Order of St. George. *Clubs:* Scacchi, Golf Acquasanta, Vela Anzio, Rotary, Parioli Tennis (all of Rome); Clubino, Dadi (Milan); Bath (London). *Address:* 21 Via Siracusa, Rome 00161; and *office* Via Di Tor Fiorenza 35, Rome 00199, Italy.

**FELL, Anthony,** MP. British Politician. *B.* 1914. *Educ.* State Education in New Zealand. *M.* 1938, Dorothy Jane Ada Warwick. *S.* 1. *Dau.* 1. Conservative MP for Yarmouth 1951–66, 1970—. *Address:* 11 Denny Street, London, S.E.1.

**FELLINGHAM, Warren L.** American. *B.* 1902. *Educ.* Dartmouth College (BS *magna cum laude*). *M.* 1928, Dorothy Park. *S.* John H., Warren L., Jr., David A. *Career:* Vice-Pres. and Chmn., Trust Investment Committee, Harris Trust and Savings Bank 1949–66; Vice-Pres. and Treasurer, Pioneer Investment Co. 1950–66; Treasurer and Trustee, Shedd Aquarium Society 1942–66; member Adv. Committee Visiting Nurse Assn. of Chicago 1933–66; Dartmouth Alumni Council 1956–58; Pres., Dartmouth Alumni Assn. of Chicago 1954–55; Board of Education, School District, Cook County 25 1944–51; Treasurer, Inverness Assn. 1957–59; Board of Stewards, Barrington Methodist Church 1962–68. *Publications:* various articles in professional publications. *Member:* Phi Beta Kappa; Acad. of Political Science; Federation of Fly Fishermen. Republican. *Clubs:* University (Chicago); Dartmouth Alumni Assn.; Kappa Sigma Fraternity. *Address:* 852 North Sterling Road, Inverness Countryside, Palatine, Ill. 60067, U.S.A.

**FELLNER, William John.** American economist. *B.* 1905. *Educ.* Univ. of Budapest; Federal Institute of Technology, Zürich (BS 1927); Univ. of Berlin (PhD 1929). *M.* 1936, Valerie Korek. *Dau.* Anna Valerie (Thomas). *Career:* Partner in a manufacturing enterprise, Budapest 1929–38; member, Dept. of Economics, Univ. of California 1939–52 (Prof. of Economics 1947–52); Prof. of Economics, Yale Univ. 1952—, Chairman, Dept. of Economics 1962–64. Alfred Marshall Lecturer, University of Cambridge 1957; Consultant U.S. Treasury 1945 and 1969. Sterling Professor of Economics, Yale University 1959–73; Emeritus since 1973; Member of President's Council of Economic Advisers 1973–75; Resident Scholar American Enterprise Institute, Washington DC since 1975. Member of International Committee of Independent Experts of O.E.E.C. and co-author of Cttee. report on the Problem of Rising Prices 1959–61. *Publications:* Monetary Policies and Full Employment (Univ. of Calif. Press 1946); Competition Among the Few (Alfred A. Knopf 1949); Trends and Cycles in Economic Activity (Henry Holt 1955); Emergence and Content of Modern Economic Analysis (McGraw-Hill 1960): Probability and Profit (Richard D. Irwin); Towards a Reconstruction of Macroeconomics (American Enterprise Inst. 1976); also contributes to periodicals and symposia. *Member:* Amer. Acad. of Arts & Sciences; Amer. Economic Assn.; Royal Economic Socy.; Phi Beta Kappa (Hon.) President, American Economic Association, 1969. *Clubs:* Graduates (New Haven); Yale (New York); Cosmos (Washington). *Address:* American Enterprise Inst., 1150 17th str. NW, Washington, DC 20036, U.S.A.

**FENECH ADAMI, Eduard.** Maltese Politician & Lawyer. *B.* 1934. *Educ.* LLD; BA (Econ., Philosophy & English). *M.* 1965, Mary Sciberras. *S.* 4. *Dau.* 1. *Career:* Joined Nationalist Party 1961; co-opted to Parliament 1969; elected to Parliament 1971, re-elected 1976; Asst. Gen. Sec., Nationalist Party 1963–75; Editor, *Il-Poplu* party paper 1963–70; Shadow Minister of Labour, Social Security & Emigration 1971–76; elected Party Leader & Leader of the Opposition 1977. *Member:* Chamber of Advocates, Valletta. *Club:* Casino Maltese (Valletta). *Address:* 176 Main Street, Birkirkara; and *office* 171 Old Bakery Street, Valletta, Malta.

**FENTON, David Ewan.** Canadian. *B.* 1925. *Educ.* Junior matriculation; Chartered Accountant. *M.* 1951, Ruth Lenore Pike. *S.* Richard Barry and Paul Anthony. *Dau.* Leslie Anne. *Career:* Director and Vice Pres. Finance, Commonwealth Construction Co. Ltd., and Comco Distributers Ltd. *Member:* Inst. of Chartered Accountants; Chmn. Official Bd. Financial Executives Inst. *Clubs:* Hollyburn Country (Past Pres.); Rotary. *Address: office* 700 Taylor Street, Vancouver, 3, B.C. Canada.

**FENTON, Roy Pentelow,** CMG. British. *B.* 1918. *Educ.* Salford Grammar School. *M.* 1941, Daphne Cheason. *S.* Timothy. Previously: Governor, Central Bank of Nigeria, 1958–63. *Career:* Chief of Overseas Department, Bank of England, 1965–75; Chief Exec., Keyser Ullmann (Holdings) Ltd. Vice-Chairman, Managing Board of European Monetary Agreement, 1968–72. *Clubs:* East India and Sports; Overseas Bankers. *Address:* Flat k, 23 Warwick Sq., London SW1V 2AB; and *office* Keyser Ullmann Ltd., 25 Milk Street, London, EC2V 8JE.

**FENTON, Roy Stanley,** AAII. Australian executive. *B.* 1901. *Educ.* Sydney Tech. High School. *M.* 1926, Marjorie Graburn McLean. *S.* 1. *Dau.* 1. President, Constitutional Association of Australia, Jan. 1958–61. Director, Transcity Discount Ltd., City Mutual General Insurance Ltd., Permanent Building Society of Australia Ltd. Gen. Manager (Retd.), Queensland Insurance Co. Ltd. *Clubs:* Warrawee Bowling. *Address:* 32–650 Pacific Highway, Killara, N.S.W., Australia.

**FERBER, Robert.** Economist and statistician. *B.* 1922. *Educ.* City College of New York (BS 1942); University of Chicago (MA 1945; PhD 1951). *M.* 1946, Marianne Abeles. *S.* Don Richard. *Dau.* Ellen J. Citation: Outstanding Contribution of Field of Marketing (Amer. Marketing Assn.) 1950; Parlin Award 1972. Statistician, Industrial Surveys Co. 1943–45; Economist & Statistician, I Devegh Co., N.Y. 1946–47; Research Asst. Prof. Univ. of Illinois 1948–51 (Research Assoc. Prof. 1951–55); Pres., American Marketing Association 1969–70. Research Professor of Economics, Professor of Marketing, Director Survey Research Laboratory, Univ. of Illinois; Coordinating Editor and Editor, Applications Section, Journal of the American Statistical Association 1969–76; Editor, Journal of Consumer Research 1977—. *Publications:* Statistical Techniques in Market Research (1949); Factors Influencing Durable Goods Purchases (1951); The Railroad Shippers Forecasts (1953); Cases and Problems in Marketing Research (co-author) (1955); A Study of Aggregate Consumption Functions (1950); Employers' Forecasts of Manpower Requirements (1959); A Basic Bibliography of Marketing Research (co-author 1956, revised 1963 and 1974; Collecting Financial Data by Consumer Panel Techniques 1960; Research Methods in Economics & Business (co-author) (1962); Motivation & Market Behavior, (1959); Marketing Research (1963); The Reliability of Consumer Reports of Financial Assets and Debts (1966); Estudios Fundamentales de Mercado technia (1970); Handbook of Marketing Research (1974). *Address:* 606 S. Western Av., Champaign, Ill. and *office* 414 David Kinley Hall, Univ. of Illinois, Urbana, Ill. 68101, U.S.A.

**FERDERBER, Joseph.** American. *B.* 1919. *Educ.* Case Inst. of Technology (BS in EE 1942). *M.* 1942, Georgia Lucille Pesek (Div. 1970). *S.* Lawrence Joseph and Michael James. *Dau.* Julie Ann. Manager, El Segundo Div. 1956 (Vice-Pres. 1962); Vice-Pres. Manufacturing 1966. Vice-President, Hughes Aircraft Co. 1962—. *Member:* Eta Kappa Nu; Tau Beta Pi; Sigma Xi. *Address:* 27553 Sunnyridge Road, Palos Verdes Peninsula, Calif. 90274; and *office* Hughes Aircraft Co., Florence & Teale, Culver City, Calif. 90230, U.S.A.

**FERGUSSON, Ian Victor Lyon.** British. *B.* 1901. *Educ.* Berkhamsted School. *M.* 1927, Hannah Grace Gourlay. *S.* John Norris, Kenneth Mackenzie Neil and Malcolm Lyon. *Dau.* Anne Everett. *Career:* Joined Evans Medical Ltd. (then Evans Sons Lescher & Webb) 1919; Director 1927, Man. Dir. 1941, Chmn. & Man. Director 1943–62. Director, Glaxo Group Ltd. 1961–62. President, Chemists Friends Association 1940–41; Chairman, Association of British Pharmaceutical Industry 1946–48; Member of Council, Association of British Chemical Manufacturers 1948–61; Elected Member of Grand

Council of Federation of British Industries 1949–56; Chairman, Pharmaceutical Industry's Negotiating Committee 1952–60; Member, Liverpool Regional Hospital Board 1958–61. *Address:* Orchard Lodge, Avon Dassett, Warwickshire.

**FERNANDEZ ESCALANTE, Dr. Fernando.** Argentine Diplomat. *B.* 1920. *Educ.* Degrees in Law, Econ., & Business Admin. *Career:* Ministry of Foreign Affairs, Buenos Aires 1937–45; Sec. of Embassy, Uruguay, Belgium & Spain 1946–50; Counsellor of Embassy, Chargé d'Affaires, Brazil & Colombia 1951–54; Counsellor, UN Mission 1955–56; practice as lawyer & journalist 1956–62; Mgr. & Gen. Mgr., Ford Motor Argentina 1963–68; Vice-Pres., Industrial Bank & National Development Bank, Argentina 1968–73; Ambassador, Dir. in Ministry of Foreign Affairs 1974–75; Ambassador to India 1976–77. Prof. & Dir., Argentine Universities & Catholic Univ. of Argentina (Business & Law) 1963–76. *Member:* Indian Inst. of Internat. Law; Argentine Public Relations Assoc.; Assoc. for Study & Research on Information (AIERI); Argentine Lawyers Assoc.; Argentine Diplomatic Circle; European Management Assoc. *Decorations:* Commander, Southern Cross of Brazil; Commander, Order of Isabel la Catolica (Spain). *Publications:* Public Relations (1968, 1972); Direction & Organization of Public & Private Enterprises (1974); & many articles in newspapers & magazines on international law & management. *Clubs:* Jockey Club (Argentina); Gymkana Club (New Delhi); Kennel Club (India). *Address:* Charcas 3074, Buenos Aires, Argentina; and 3/11 Shantiniketan, New Delhi 21, India.

**FERNANDO, Joseph Leslie Michael.** Ceylonese lawyer and company director. *B.* 1909. *Educ.* St. Catherine's, Oxford (BA); MA (Oxon. 1953). Barrister-at-Law; Gray's Inn (Hons. Jurisp.). *M.* 1939, Edith Dias. *S.* Lalin and Lalith. *Daus.* Kamalika and Sharmila. Advocate of the Supreme Court of Ceylon 1932–50; Lecturer to Council of Legal Education in Constitutional Law, Legal History and Legal Systems; Chmn., Bd. of Examiners for Advocates and Proctors 1938–49; First Chmn., Air Ceylon Corp. 1951, Managing Director 1956–60. Chairman: Pegasus Hotels of Ceylon Ltd.; Lanka Salu Sala Ltd.; Leahmi Estates Co. Ltd. (Hatton and Poolbank Estates). Director: Millers Ltd., Usha Industries Ltd., Warner Hudnut (Lanka) Ltd., Orient Club Co. Ltd. President: Ceylon National Chamber of Commerce, and of Income Tax Payers' Assn. of Ceylon. *Clubs:* Orient, Turf, Rotary, Fishing. *Address:* 185 Turret Road, Colombo, 7, Sri Lanka.

**FERNANDO, Thusew Samuel, CBE, QC.** *B.* 1906. *Educ.* Royal College (Colombo); Univ. College, London (LLB); called to the Bar (Lincoln's Inn). *M.* 1943, Malini Wickramasuriya. *S.* Harendra. *Career:* Appointed Crown Counsel, Ceylon 1938; Solicitor-General 1952–54; Acting Attorney-General 1954–56; Justice of the Supreme Court of Ceylon 1956–68; Pres. Court of Appeal Ceylon 1971–73; President, International Commission of Jurists, Geneva, 1966—; member, International Committee of the Institute of Man and Science, New York; High Commissioner for Sri Lanka in Austr. and N.Z. since 1974. *Address:* 3 Cosmos Avenue, Barnes Place, Colombo 7, Sri Lanka.

**FERREIRA, Otavio Salgado.** Brazilian. Economist and business consultant. *B.* 1922. *Educ.* Univ. of Brazil (BSc Econ 1950) and Univ. of Philadelphia (post-graduate studies 1955–56). *M.* 1948, Maria Adelaide C. Salgado Ferreira. *S.* Sergio. *Daus.* Eliane, Lilian Heloise and Luciana. *Career:* Manager, Marketing Services Dept., Shell Brazil S.A. 1961–63; Controller, Cia. Brasileira de Gás 1963–66; Financial and Cost Analyst, Philco Radio e Televisao S.A. 1967. Sao Paulo's Master Plan: Project Director of Administration and Control 1968—. ASPLAN S.A.—Assessoria em Planejamento; Senior Economic & Financial Analyst Banco Nacional do Desenvolvimento Econômico; Economist, Emp. Brasileira de Infraestrutura Aeroportuaria; Civil Aviation Dept. Planning Group. *Member:* Sociedad Brasileira de Estaticíca; Amer. Economic Assn.; Amer. Finance Assn. *Club:* de Regatas Flamengo. *Address:* Rua Prudente de Morais, 101 apto. 802, Ipanema (ZC-95), 20000 Rio de Janeiro, RJ, Brazil.; *office* Santos Dumont Airport, DAC (SPL), Rio de Janeiro, RJ, Brazil.

**FERRERS, The Rt. Hon. The Earl, Robert Washington** (Viscount Tamworth, Sir Robert Shirley). British. *B.* 1929. *Educ.* Winchester Coll.; Magdalene Coll. Cambridge (MA degree in Agriculture). *M.* 1951, Annabel Mary Carr. *S.* 2. *Daus.* 3. *Career:* served in Army, Coldstream Guards, Malaya 1948–50; Undergraduate Cambridge University 1950–53; Farms in South Norfolk 1954; Delegation of both Houses to Singapore 1965; CPA delegations to Nigeria 1965; Member of IPU Delegation to Italy 1957; Lord-in-Waiting to H.M. Queen, Government Whip, House of Lords 1962–64; Special Ambassador to Liberia to Represent H.M. the Queen 1964; Opposition Whip, House of Lords 1964–67 CPA delegation to Gambia 1967; Mem., Inter-Parliamentary Union Delegation to Japan and Indonesia 1969; Lord-in-Waiting to H.M. Queen; Govt. Whip, House of Lords 1971–74; CPA Delegation to Canada 1974; IPU Delegation to Switzerland 1974; Parly. Secy. Ministry Agriculture, Fisheries and Food 1974; Dir. of Norwich Union Life Ins. Socy., Scottish Union and Nat. Ins. Co.; and Maritime Ins. Co. Ltd. since 1975; represented Commonwealth Parliamentary Assn. on the occasion of the Independence of the Seychelles 1976; Joint Dep. Leader of Opposition in the Lords since 1976; Mem., Armitage Cttee. on the Political Activities of Civil Servants 1976. *Member:* Council Hirstpierpoint Coll. Sussex 1959–68; Trustee, East Anglian Trustee Savings Bank; later Vice-Chairman; Chmn., Trustee Savings Bank of Eastern England 1977—. *Club:* The Beefsteak. *Address:* Hedenham Gall, Bungay, Suffolk.

**FERRIER, Dr. Johan Henri Eliza.** President of Surinam. *B.* 1910. *Educ.* Elementary School; Teacher Training Coll., Univ. of Amsterdam. *M.* 1951, Edmé C. Vas. *S.* 4. *Daus.* 2 (by previous marriage). *Career:* Teacher 1927–50; Dir., Teacher Training Coll. 1950–51; Dir., Dept. of Education 1951–55; Prime Minister, Minister of General Affairs, Minister of Internal Affairs 1955–58; Counsellor, Ministry of Education, Arts & Sciences (Netherlands) 1958–65; Dir., Billiton Bauxite Co., Surinam 1966–67; Governor of Surinam 1967–75; President of the Republic of Surinam since 1975. *Awards:* Dr. of Letters & Philosophy, Univ. of Amsterdam; Commander, Order of Orange; Knight, Order of the Netherlands Lion; Commander, Order of the Netherlands Lion. *Address:* Presidential Palace, Paramaribo, Surinam.

**FERRIERE, Jean André Marie.** Honorary French shipbroker. *B.* 1897. *Educ.* Bachelier Enseignement Secondaire. *M.* 1923, Simone Dubos. *Daus.* Danielle (Mme Cazenave), Claude (Mme Blanchy) and Maylis (Mme Pitteloud). Union, Hon. Vice-Pres., Chamber of Comm. of Bordeaux. Hon. Pres.: Maritime Federation of Bordeaux; Hon. President of Sworn Shipbrokers of France. *Awards:* Officier Legion of Honour; Croix de Guerre (1914–18); Chevalier Mérite Maritime; Officer Mérite; Officer Orange Nassau. *Address:* 8 cours Xavier Arnozan, Bordeaux, France.

**FERRIS, George F.** American. Chairman of Board and Director, Raymond International Inc. Dir. and Member Exec. Cttee., Jones & Laughlin Steel Co. Director: Firemen's Fund Insurance; Celanese Corp. of America. *B.* 1902. *Educ.* Univ. of Florida (BSCE 1924). *M.* 1942, Barbara Evans. *Dau.* Carole Denham. *Career:* Engaged in miscellaneous engineering work, State of Florida 1924–29; from Supt. to Vice-Pres. and Dir., Turner Construction Co., New York City 1929–45. With Raymond International Inc. (formerly Raymond Concrete Pile Co.) 1946—, from Vice-Pres. and Gen. Mgr. to Pres., and then to Chmn. of the Board. Chmn., Operating Cttee., Pacific Naval Air Base Construction for U.S. Navy 1940–44. Hon. DEng (Lafayette Univ. 1960); Distinguished Public Service Medal, 1947. *Member:* Amer. Socy. of Civil Engineers; The Moles. *Clubs:* The Links, Recess (N.Y.C.); Clove Valley Rod & Gun (N.Y.); Bohemian (San Francisco); Woodbury Golf (Stamford, Conn.). *Address:* and *office* 140 Cedar Street, New York City, U.S.A.

**FESTA, Giuseppe.** Italian Doctor in International Law and Professor of Political and Financial Economy. Head of Service for Studies, Commercial Commission, Ministry of Foreign Commerce; concurrently Vice-Director, Ufficio Italiano del Cambi (exchange). *B.* 1906. *Educ.* Dipl. in Accountancy and Degree in Economics and Commerce. *M.* 1947, Maria Vespasiani. *Daus.* Rosalba, Carla and Laura. *Career:* Engaged in organizational work with financial and banking concerns 1926–45. From 1945 onwards: Head of Missione dell' Istcambi (verification of currencies); joined Ministry of Labour as technical consultant to the Commission of Enquiry into the organization of the administrative services; collaborated in the co-ordination of prices, cost of living, land and sea transport, agriculture, etc., and (Nov.) with the Economic and Technical Secretary of the Ministry of Industry & Commerce in editing of the Piano di Massim for industrial imports and exports; later, at the request of the Ministry of Foreign Affairs, assumed the direction of the official enquiry into economic management (Mar. 1946); Interested Field of the valutary compared Legislation, several countries respectively of franc, sterling and U.S.A. dollar. *Publications:* several works, including Beveridge e la Realtà

Italiana (1957); La Crisi e la Prospettive Sociali del Mercato Commune Europeo (1958); Riforme Monetarie Europee e Riflessi in Africa (1959); Politica Valutaria e Dinamica dell'a Integrazione (1960); The balance of Italian Municipalities and one hundred other studies in economics and finance (1967); numerous articles, concerned with political and financial economy in the Italian and foreign scientific journals, newspapers and magazines; compiler of Enciclopedia Zuffi (economic-judicial); Per l'avvio dell Unione Monetaria European; del sistema bancario communitario (1970); La Banca ed il Regime Valutario Italiano (1974). *Member:* Intern. Press. Association for the Study of Overseas Problems. *Address:* Via S. Tommaso d'Aquino 98/108, Rome.

**FETHERSTON, Donald Ivan.** British. *B.* 1919. *Educ.* Campbell Coll. *M.* 1949, Beatrice Anne Medlock. On leaving school (1937) engaged for two years in accountancy. Served in World War II 1940–46 (Royal Artillery and Sherwood Foresters 7th Bn.—The Robin Hoods—as Captain). *Clubs:* Ulster; Royal Belfast Golf; *Address:* 'Highfields', Clandeboye, Bangor, Co. Down, N. Ireland.

**FETRIDGE, William Harrison.** Corporation executive. *Educ.* Northwestern Univ. (BS 1929) and Central Michigan Univ. (LLD). *M.* 1941, Bonnie Jean Clark. *S.* Clark Worthington. *Dau.* Bonnie Blakley (Bundy). *Career:* Lieut. Cmdr., U.S. Navy 1942–45; Exec. Vice-Pres., Diamond T Motor Track Co., Chicago, Ill. 1961–65 (Vice-Pres. 1959–61). Exec. Vice Pres. Popular Mechanics 1953–59); Pres., The Dartnell Corp., Chicago, Ill. 1965—; Dir. Bank of Ravenswood National Vice-Pres., Boy Scouts of America 1958–76; Hon. Pres. United Republican Fund of Illinois; Trustee, American Humanics Foundation; Lake Forest Coll. 1969–77; Past Pres., Board of Trustees, The Latin School of Chicago; Pres. United States Foundation for International Scouting. Chmn. Midwest Volunteers for Nixon-Lodge 1960; Campaign Manager, Merriam for Mayor of Chicago 1955. Past Regional President, Navy League of the U.S. Editor: The Navy Reader, 1943; The Second Navy Reader, 1944; American Political Almanac, 1950. Author: With Warm Regards, 1976. Alternate Delegate-at-Large, Republican Natl. Convn., 1956, and Delegate-at-Large 1968; Support Cttee of Scouts World Cttee. *Awards:* Silver Buffalo, Silver Beaver and Silver Antelope, Boy Scouts of America; Bronze Wolf, World Conference of Scouting; Chevalier, Knights of St. John, Jerusalem. Republican. *Member:* Republican National Finance Cttee. *Clubs:* The Chicago; The Union League; The Saddle & Cycle; The Casino; Chikaming C.C.; Stevensville Yacht (Vice Commodore). *Address:* 2430 North Lakeview Avenue, Chicago 60614; and *office* 4660 Ravenswood Avenue, Chicago 60640, Ill., U.S.A.

**FETZER, John Earl.** American business and radio-television executive. *B.* 1901. *Educ.* Purdue Univ.; National Radio Inst.; Andrews Univ. (AB 1927); Univ. of Michigan; Hon. LLD Western Mich. Univ., 1958 and Kalamazoo Coll. 1972. Hon. LittD Elizabethtown Coll. Pennsylvania 1972. *M.* 1926, Rhea Maude Yeager. *Career:* Chmn. owner, Fetzer Broadcasting Co. (Kalamazoo-Grand Rapids) 1930—; Cornhusker Television Corp. (Lincoln, Neb.) since 1953; Amalgamated Properties Inc. Kalamazoo-Grand Rapids) 1955–68; Fetzer Television Inc. 1958–70; Fetzer Music Corp. 1958–70; Chairman, Parkway Development Inc., Kalamazoo, 1957–64; Major League Television Cttee. 1963–71; Wolverine Cablevision Inc. since 1967; Owner and Pres. John E. Fetzer, Inc. 1968—; Medallion Broadcasters, Inc. 1969—; owner and Pres., Detroit Tiger American League Baseball Club 1956—; Owner, Chmn. Fetzer Television Corp. since 1970. *Member:* Board of Directors, American National Bank & Trust Co. (Kalamazoo) 1947—73; Board of Trustees, Kalamazoo College 1954—; Radio Research 1919–24; Asst. Dir., U.S. censorship in charge of radio, supervising 900 domestic radio stations and all shortwave broadcasts beamed at Germany and Japan 1944–46; reporting to General Eisenhower, engaged in ETO radio studies to rehabilitate German people, as well as postwar communication problems involving international radio between U.S., England, France, Russia, Germany Italy and other countries 1945; Foreign Correspondent, radio-television-newspaper mission to Europe and Middle East, interviewing heads of state 1952; Mission, Radio Free Europe, Munich and Austro-Hungarian border 1956; broadcasters' mission to Latin America, under auspices of State Dept. 1962; Associated Press tour of Europe, 1966. *Awards:* Golden Ear Award, 1962; Broadcast Pioneers' Award, 1968; National Association of Broadcasters' Distinguished Service Award, 1969; Michigan Frontiersman Award, 1969; Citation for Contribution to the development of Nebraska Educational Television System, 1968. *Publications:* One Man's Family (1964); The Men from Wengen and America's Agony (1971). *Address:* 2714 Clovelly Road, Kalamazoo, Mich., and *office* Kalamazoo, Mich., U.S.A.

**FEUCHTWANGER, Walter.** Israeli and German. Banker. *B.* 1916. *Educ.* Primary School, followed by Humanistisches Gymnasium (interrupted before matriculation in 1933, due to Hitler's rise to power); full education and subsequent activity as Banker in Germany and several other countries. *M.* 1958. Christina-Alisa Campbell. *Daus.* 2. Member Advisory Board, Allgemeine Deutsche Credit-Anstalt, amalgamated with W. Feuchtwanger Bank K.G., Munich; 1970. President, Feuchtwanger Corp. of N.Y.; Former Director: Feuchtwanger (London) Ltd. until 1972; Dir., City of San Paulo Improvement & Freehold Land Co. Ltd., Panama-São Paulo, and various other companies. Patron of the Munich International School; Representative of the Scottish Council Development and Industry, Edinburgh; Member of German-Israel Chamber and several others. Nominated Handelsrichter (Judge in Commercial Court, Landgericht, München I). *Club:* Founder-member Anglo-Bavarian, Munich. *Address:* 8131 Aufkirchen Kirchweg 15; and *office* Financial Counsellors, 8 München 22, Widenmayerstr. 11, Germany.

**FEY, E. Georg.** Swiss. President: Georg Fey Co. Inc. (paint manufacturers, founded by George Fey Snr.), St. Margrethen since 1942, and of Lackfabrik Fey Ltd., Feldkirch, Austria since 1955. *B.* 1912. *Educ.* Univs. of Zürich and Leipzig (chemistry) and Munich Polytechnic (Dipl lic oec). Active in the firm since 1938, and in visits to many countries outside Switzerland. Member of several boards of industrial organizations; Pres. EFTA Paint and Printing Ink Makers' Group 1965–68, and of European Cttee. of Paint, Printing Ink and Artists' Colours Mfrs. Assoc. 1968–70. *Club:* Rotary. *Address:* Birkengut, CH-9430 St. Margrethen; and *office* George Fey Co. Inc., Lackfabrik, CH-9430, St. Margrethen, Switzerland.

**FICKLEN, Joseph Burwell III.** American consulting chemical engineer. *B.* 1902. *Educ.* Univ. of Virginia; California Institute of Technology (BS Chem Eng 1928); Yale Univ. *M.* 1938, Irene Louise Poole. *S.* Joseph B. IV. Supt., Rappahannock Electric Light & Power Co. 1920–23; Engineer, Travelers Insurance Co., 1928–41; Consultant, City of Los Angeles Health Dept. 1941–42; Special Health Officer, County of Los Angeles, 1941–42; Asst. Mgr., U.S. Rubber Co. (Charlotte), 1942–44; Engineer (Major) U.S. Public Health Service 1944–46; Special Health Officer, County of Los Angeles 1946—; Research Engineer, North American Aviation, Inc. 1946–56; Owner, Joseph B. Ficklen III (manufacturer of air sampling instruments) 1953—; Consultant, American Machine & Foundry Co., 1955–56; Consultant, North American Aviation, Inc. 1956—; Adviser, Bur. of Occ. Health, New Zealand since 1964; Christ Church-Lyttelton Tunnel Authority N.2. since 1964 and Bur. Occ. Health Dept. New S. Wales Aust. since 1964. *Publications:* Manual of Industrial Health Hazards 1940; Some Methods for the Detection and Estimation of Poisonous Gases and Vapours in Air (translation; A. S. Zhitkova—Russian) about 20 scientific papers dealing principally with detection and estimation of small amounts of materials in air. *Fellow:* Southern California Academy of Sciences; American Institute of Chemists. Republican. *Clubs:* Chemists' (N.Y.C.); Unive sity (Hartford, Conn.). *Address:* 1848 East Mountain Street, Pasadena 7, Calif., U.S.A.

**FIDGE, Sir (Harold) Roy.** Australian. *B.* 1904. *Educ.* Geelong and Ormond Colleges and Univ. of Melbourne (LLB). *M.* (1) 1934, Mavis Melba Jane Burke (*D.* 1948). *S.* James Edward. *Dau.* Helen Roberta. *M.* (2) 1949, Nance Davidson. Hon. Secy.-Treas.: Assn. of Apex Clubs of Aust. 1934–40, 1945–47; and Geelong Law Assn. 1933–40, 1945–54, Pres. 1959–60. Lt.-Comdr. Royal Aust. Navy 1940–45. Pres. Geelong East Technical School Council 1961–65 and of East Geelong Branch, Aust. Red Cross Socy. 1961–67. Formerly Senior Partner, Price Higgins & Fidge, Solicitors, Geelong (now retired). Councillor, City of Geelong (1939–40) and since 1946; Mayor, 1954–56 and 1964–68; Commissioner. Geelong Harbor Trust Jan. 1956—, Chairman 1963—. Member Exec. Cttee. Municipal Assn. of Victoria 1964—; Council, Aust. Port Authorities Assn. since 1968. Hon. Member Geelong Rotary 1966; Awarded Community Service Award for State of Victoria by Develop Victoria Council for 1966. *Member:* R.S.S.A.A. Imperial League of Aust.; Ex-Navalmen's Assn.; Victoria League. *Clubs:* Geelong; Geelong Legacy; Royal Geelong Yacht. *Address:* 23 Meakin Street, Geelong, Vic 3219, Australia.

**FIDLER, Michael M., JP.** British business consultant and textile specialist; Founder & National Director, Conservative Friends of Israel, since 1974. *B.* 10 Feb. 1916. *Educ.* Salford Grammar School, Salford Royal Technical College. *M.* 1939, Maidie Davis. *S.* 1. *Dau.* 1. *Career:* Managing Dir. H. & L. Fidler Ltd. 1941–70, Michael Lewis Ltd. 1942–70; Joint Chmn. Clothing Advisory Cttee. British Board of Trade, 1942–49; Vice-Chmn. British Rainwear Manfcts. Fed. 1948–63; Friends of the Hebrew Univ. Manchester 1948–58; Councillor, Borough, Prestwich 1951–63, Alderman 1963–74, Mayor 1957–58, Deputy Mayor 1958–59; Dep. Chmn. Prestwich Local Govt. Re-organization Cttee. 1958–67 and Central Area Re-development Cttee. 1963–68; Pres. Council of Manchester & Salford Jews, 1966–68 and Holy Law Congregation, 1967–70; Dep. Chmn. Manchester Victoria Memorial Jewish Hospital, 1967–69; Member World Jewish Congress Gov. Board since 1975; Vice-Chmn. World Conference, Jewish Organizations 1967–73; Chmn. WJC Org. Commission since 1975; Chmn. Trustees, Chaim Weizmann Yough Centre, Manchester since 1967; Governor, Inst. of Cont. Jewry, Hebrew Univ. of Jerusalem since 1967; Life Vice-Pres. Jewish Bd. of Guardians and Jewish Social Services since 1967; Pres. Bd. Deputies of British Jews 1967–73; Pres., General Zionist Organisation of Great Britain since 1973; Vice-Pres. Children & Youth Aliyah Cttee. for Gt. Britain & Mizrachi Hapoel Hamizrachi Fed. of Gt. Britain & Ireland since 1968; Member Parliament, Bury & Radcliffe Div. 1970–74. Pres. Prestwich Horticultural Socy. since 1956 and Heys Amateur Football Club since 1964. *Fellow:* Royal Geographical Socy.; Royal Asiatic Socy.; Royal Economic Socy.; Inst. of Industrial & Commercial Accounts; Patron, The All Party Cttee. The Release of Soviet Jewry 1971–74; USSR Regional Group Chmn., Foreign and C'wealth Cttee., Conservative Party. Party 1974; Chmn. Foreign Affairs Cttee. and Chmn. Soviet Jewry Cttee., both of Board of Deputies of British Jews since 1973; Treas. Parliamentary Migraine Group 1971–74. *Publications:* One Hundred Years of the Holy Law Congregation (1964); La Puiss Economique De La Grande Bretagne (1966). *Address:* 1 Woodcliffe Lodge, Sedgley Park Road, Prestwich, Manachester, M25 8JX.

**FIELD, Henry.** American anthropologist. *B.* 1902. *Educ.*Eton Coll. (1916–21); New Coll., Oxford (1921–26); BA 1925; Diploma in Anthropology 1926; MA 1929; DSc 1937. *M.* 1953, Julia Rand Allen. *Daus.* Mariana (by previous marriage) and Juliana. *Career:* Curator of Physical Anthropology, Field Museum of Natural History 1926–41; Government Research on Near East 1941–45. Hon. Associate in Physical Anthropology, Peabody Museum, Harvard University 1950—; Adjunct Professor of Anthropology, University of Miami 1959—; *Member:* Royal Geographical Socy.; Royal Central Asian Socy.; Zoological Socy.; Royal Asiatic Socy.; Royal Anthropological Institute; American Assn. of Physical Anthropologists, etc. *Publications:* The Anthropology of Iraq; Contributions to the Anthropology of Iran; Anthropology of the Caucasus; An Anthropological Reconnaissance in West Pakistan (1955); North Arabian Desert Archaeological Survey 1925–50 (1960), The Track of Man (1953); Ancient and Modern Man in S.W. Asia (I, 1956, II,1961); Bibliography on S.W. Asia; I–VII (1953–63). *Club:* Explorers (New York). *Address:* 3551 Main Highway, Coconut Grove, Miami, Fla. 33133; and *office* Peabody Museum Cambridge, Mass. 02138, U.S.A.

**FIELD, Stanley Alfred.** British. *B.* 1913. *M.* 1950, Doreen Plunkett. *S.* 1. *Daus.* 2. *Career:* Chmn. William Baird & Co. Ltd., Winterbottom Trust Ltd.; Dir. Harvey Butterfield Ltd., Dawson International Ltd., Automobile Association Ltd., Merchants Trust Ltd., Expanded Metal Co. Ltd.; Cook International Ltd.; Lloyd's Underwriter; formerly senior Partner, W. N. Middleton & Co. 1946–53; Man. Dir. Prestige Group Ltd. 1953–58; Dir. Venesta Ltd. 1956; Chmn. 1958–64. *Clubs:* Carlton; City Livery; Liveryman, Glass Sellers Company; Alderman, City of London. *Address: office* City Wall Hse., 84–90 Chiswell St., London, E.C.1.

**FIELDING, Elizabeth M.** American. *B.* 1917. *Educ.* American Univ. Sch. of Public Affairs, MA 1944; Grad. with Honours, in political and social science, Connecticut College for Women. B.A. 1938. *Career:* Administrative Aide, GOP Platform Cttees., Republican National Conventions, 1944, 1948, 1952 and 1956; former public relations director, National Federation of Republican Women, & Editor, The Republican Clubwoman 1961–68; Assoc. Dir., Research Div., Republican National Cttee., 1944–56; Legislative Analyst and Editor, Nat. Assn. of Electric Companies, 1957–60; Legislative Aide to Senator Alexander Wiley (R. Wis.), 1953–54; Dir., special activities for the women's div. of United Citizens for Nixon-Agnew campaign 1968; Finance co-ordinator, 1969 Inaugural Cttee. Special Assistant to the Assistant Postmaster-General 1969–71; Public Affairs Director, President's Council on Youth Opportunity 1970–71; Asst. Administrator for Public Affairs, National Credit Union Administration 1971–73; Public Information Officer 1973–75; Editor NCUA Bulletin, NCUA Quarterly, NCUA Report 1971–75; Pres. Professional Enterprises since 1975; Legislative Asst., U.S. House of Representatives 1976—. *Member:* Phi Beta Kappa; Methodist Church; Public Relations Socy. of America; Columbia Historical Socy.; Amer. Political Science Assn.; Amer. Assn. for the Advancement of Science; Amer. Socy. for Public Administration; Amer. Academy of Political and Social Science; International Platform Assoc.; South Potomac Environmental Council; Connecticut State Socy.; National Assn. of Government Communicators; National Assn. of Women Business Owners; National Trust, Historic Preservation; National Parks Conservative Assoc.; Treasure Cove Citizens' Assoc. (Pres.). *Awards:* NFRW Dist. Service; NFRW Outstanding Service; Connecticut Coll. Medal of Achievement 1971. *Clubs:* Capitol Hill; National Press; Washington Press; American Newspaper Women's Antique Automobile Club of America; Packards International; U.S. Senate Staff Club. *Address:* 1312 Thornton Parkway, Oxon Hill, Md. 20022; and *office* 1018 Longworth House Office Building, Washington, D.C. 20515, U.S.A.

**FIFE, Hon. Wallace Clyde,** MP. Australian. *B.* 1929. *Educ.* Secondary School. *M.* 1952, Marcia Hargreaves Stanley. *S.* David Robert and Allan Anthony. *Daus.* Carolyn Elizabeth and Susan Gay Mary. *Career:* M.L.A. for Wagga Wagga, Parliament of New South Wales, 1957–75; Asst. Minister for Education 1965–67; Minister for Mines, 1967–75; Minister for Conservation 1971–72; Minister for Power and Assistant Treasurer 1972–75: Min. for Transport and Highways 1975; M.H.R. for Farrer, Commonwealth Parliament 1975—; Minister for Business & Consumer Affairs 1977. *Member:* Liberal Party of Australia. *Address:* R.M.B. 636 Tarcutta Road, Wagga Wagga, N.S.W. 2650; and *office* 512 Swift Street, Albury, N.S.W. 2640, Australia.

**FIGAROLO di GROPELLO, Adalberto.** Italian diplomat. *B.* 1910. *Educ.* Doctor in Law. Vice-Consul: Nice (France). Aug. 1937, Tangier July 1939. Consul Casablanca (Morocco), May 1942. First Secretary Damascus 1942; Representative of Govt. of Italy in Eritrea Nov. 1949; Counsellor Moscow Aug. 1951; Consul-General Hong Kong Oct. 1956; Ambassador to Pakistan, 1962–64; to Norway, 1964–67; Ambassador of Italy to Algeria, 1967–71; and to Switzerland since 1971. *Address:* Italian Embassy, Berne, Switzerland.

**FIGUERES, José.** *B.* 1906. *Educ.* High School, Costa Rica; Elect. Engin. course; studied English & hydraulics; Hon. PhD. *M.* (1) José Marti y Muni; (2) 1954, Karen Olsen, *Daus.* 3. *Career:* Lived in rural area of U.S.A. 1922–26; Was exiled and lived in Mexico, Guatamala and El Salvador (1942); Leader of War of National Liberation against Comm. Party since 1948; Provisional President 1948–49; const. President of Republic of Costa Rica 1953–58. Visiting Professor on Latin America Affairs, Harvard Univ. 1963–64, State Univ. of New York 1967; Constitutional President of Costa Rica 1970–74; Head of National Liberation party (during periods when not President). *Awards:* From 18 European and Latin-American countries. *Publications:* Several books and papers on political science. *Address:* Apartado No. 4820, San José, Costa Rica.

**FINGLAND, Stanley James Gunn,** CMG. Diplomat *B.* 1919, *Educ.* Royal High School of Edinburgh. *M.* 1946, Nellie Lister. *S.* Peter David Gunn. *Dau.* Patricia Mary. *Career.* War Service 1939–46 (Major, Royal Signals, in N. Africa, Sicily, Italy and Egypt). Service in British High Commissions in: India, 1948–51, Australia 1953–56, and Nigeria 1960. Advisor on Commonwealth and External Affairs: to Governors-General of Nigeria 1958–60, West Indies Federation 1960–61, and to Trinidad and Tobago 1962. British Deputy High Commissioner in Trinidad 1962–63, and in S. Rhodesia 1964–66; British High Commissioner in Sierra Leone, Aug. 1966–69. Assistant Under-Secretary of State Foreign and Commonwealth Office, 1969–72; H.M. Ambassador in Havana, Cuba 1972–75; British High Commissioner in Kenya since 1975. *Club:* Royal Overseas League. *Address:* Foreign and Commonwealth Office, King Charles Street, S.W.1.

**FINK, Donald Glen.** Electrical engineer. *B.* 1911. *Educ.* Mass. Inst. of Technology (BSc Elec Eng 1933) and Columbia Univ. (MSc Elec Eng 1942). *M.* 1948, Alice M. Berry. *S.* Stephen Donald. *Daus.* Kathleen Marion and Susan Carol.

*Career:* Editor: Electronics 1946–52 (Editorial staff 1934–46), and Proceedings of the Institute of Radio Engineers 1956–57; Expert Consultant, Office of the Secretary of War 1943–45; Consultant: Bikini Atom Bomb Tests, U.S. Navy Dept. 1946, and to the Belgian Govt. (Television Systems) 1952; Director of Research, Philco Corp. 1952–61; Exec. Dir. and General Manager, Institute of Electrical and Electronics Engineers, 1963–74, Exec Consult. since 1975; Vice-Pres., Research, Philco Corp. 1961–62. Staff member, M.I.T. Radiation Laboratory 1941–43. *Publications:* Books: Engineering Electronics (1938); Principles of Television Engineering (1940) Radar Engineering (1947); Microwave Radar (1942); Television Engineering (1952); Television Engineering Handbook (1957); Physics of Television (1960); Computers and the Human Mind (1966); Television Standards and Practice (1942) (Editor); Colour Television Standards (1954) (Editor); Standard Handbook for Electrical Engineers, (1968) (Editor); Electronics Engineers Handbook (1975) (Editor): many papers and articles in scientific and technical periodicals *Awards:* Medal of Freedom; American Technologist Award, 1958; SMPTE Journal Award, 1955; Presidential Certificate of Merit, 1948; Eta Kappa Nu Recognition of Outstanding Young Electrical Engineers, 1941; Outstanding Civilian Service Medal, U.S. Army 1969. Eminent Member, Eta Kappa Nu. 1965. Member, National Academy of Engineering. Fellow Inst. of Radio Engineers (President 1958); American Institute of Electrical Engrs.; Socy of Motion Picture and Television Engineers; Inst. of Electrical and Electronics Engineers, 1963. *Member:* Eta Kappa Nu; Sigma Xi; Tau Beta Pi. Republican. *Clubs:* Cosmos (Washington); Heritage Hills N.Y.) Country. *Address:* 103-B Heritage Hills, Somers, N.Y. 10589; and *office* 345E. 47th Street, New York, N.Y. 10017, U.S.A.

**FINN, Francis M.** American banker. *B.* 1905. *Educ.* England and Continent of Europe. *M.* 1935, Janet Catherine Smith. *Dau.* Nancy Ruth. *Career:* With Banca Commerciale Italiana 1923–38, and Swiss Bank Corporation 1939–46; Vice-President, Marine Midland Grace Trust Co. of New York 1947–68. Representative for North America, Wm. Brandt's Sons & Co. Ltd., Merchant Bankers, London 1968–70; International banking consultant. *Clubs:* (New York) Economic; City Midday; British Luncheon; St. George's Society (Director); Richard Whittington Society; Old Londinians; Canadian. *Address:* 59 Elston Road, Upper Montclair, N.J., U.S.A.

**FINNE-GRÖNN, Jorgen Magnus.** Norwegian diplomat. *B.* 1905. *Educ.* Oslo Univ. (Law). *M.* Margareta Christiansen. *Dau.* Lilli Margarethe, Entered Foreign Service 1931; served Min. of Foreign Affairs, Oslo, 1931–33; France 1933–34; Turkey 1934–35; Oslo 1936–37; New York 1937–41; First Secretary, Embassy, London, 1941–46; Brussels 1946–48; Counsellor, Min. of Foreign Affairs, Oslo, 1948–50; Chief of Protocol 1950–52; Minister to Czechoslovakia 1952–58, concurrently accredited to Hungary; Norwegian Defence College 1959–60; Ambassador to Chile 1960–66, concurrently accredited to Peru and Bolivia; Ambassador to Portugal 1966–72. *Awards:* Commander Order of St. Olav (Norway); Grand Cross Al Merito (Chile); Kt.-Commdr. North Star (Sweden); Officer Belgian Crown. *Clubs:* Norske Selskab; Oslo Golf; Estoril Golf. *Address:* Ministry of Foreign Affairs, Oslo, Norway.

**FINNISTON. Sir Harold Montague**, FRS, BSc, PhD, DSc (Hon.), D Univ. (Surrey), DCL (Hon.), ARCT. Dir. Sears Holdings Ltd. & Chmn. Sears Engineering Ltd. 1976—. *B.* 1912. *Educ:* Glasgow Univ. and Royal Colleges of Sciences and Technology. *M.* 1936, Miriam Singer. *S.* 1. *Dau.* 1. *Career:* Chief Research Officer at Scottish Coke 1937–40; Metallurgist in Royal Naval Scientific Service 1940–47; Chief Metallurgist, UKAEA Harwell 1948–58; Technical Director of C. A. Parsons & Co. Ltd., and Managing Director of International Research & Development Co. Ltd. (both at Newcastle/Tyne) 1959–67. Deputy-Chmn. and Chief Exec. British Steel Corporation 1967–73, Chmn. 1973–76; Dir. GKN 1976—; Chmn. International Combustion (Holdings) 1977—; Pro-Chancellor, Univ. of Surrey 1977; Chmn. Council of Scottish Business School 1976—; Dir. Cluff Oil 1976—. Member National Research Development Corporation 1963–73; Chairman of International Research & Development Co. Ltd. (Newcastle upon Tyne), since 1968; Chmn. of Political and Economic Planning 1975; Editor of: the Rarer Metals Series (Butterworth Publications) and Progress in Nuclear Energy (Pergamon Press). *Fellow:* Inst. of Metallurgists, FInst P; Royal Socy. of Arts; Univ. Manchester Inst. Science & Technology. *President:* Inst. of Metals 1967; Metals Society 1974–75; Institution of Metallurgists 1975–76; *Member:* Ministry of Technology Advisory Council Research and Development 1966–73; Exec. Cttee. Political and Economic Planning 1966–73; Academic Advisory Cttee. Cranfield Institute of Technology; Vice-Pres. Iron & Steel Inst.; The Royal Society 1971–72; Vice-Chmn. British Non-Ferrous Metals Research Assoc. 1969–72; Gen. Secretary, British Assoc. the Advancement of Science 1970–73. *Member:* BBC Science Consultative Group 1971–74; Vice-Pres. ASLIB 1974, Pres. 1976—; Hon, Mem. American Iron and Steel Inst. 1974; Hon. Mem. Indian Inst. of Metals 1977; (Hon.) Iron and Steel Inst. Japan 1975. *Award:* Bessemer medalist, 1974; Tawara Gold Medalist. *Publications:* numerous publications on scientific matters. *Club:* Athenaeum (London). *Address:* 40 Duke Street, London W1M 6AN; & Flat No. 72, 33 Prince Albert Road, St. John's Wood, London, N.W.8.

**FINSBERG, Geoffrey, MBE, JP, MP.** British politician. *B.* 1926. *Educ.* City of London School. *M.* 1969, Pamela Benbow Hill. *Career:* Member, Hampstead Borough Council 1949–65; Camden Borough Council 1964–74; Chmn. Post Office Cttee. Confederation of British Industry since 1969; Chief Personnel Officer, The Great Universal Stores Ltd. since 1968; Member of Parliament, Conservative for Hampstead since 1970; Member; Post Office Users National Council since 1970; Vice-Chmn. of Conservative Party; House of Commons Select Cttee. on Expenditure. *Fellow:* Institute of Personnel Management. *Address:* 80 Westbere Road, London, N.W.2; and *office* Universal House 251–256 Tottenham Court Road, London, W1P 0AE.

**FIRESTONE, Roger Stanley.** Director, The Firestone Tire & Rubber Co.; President, Firestone Plastics Co. *B.* 1912. *Educ.* Princeton Univ. (AB). *M.* 1946, Anne Joers. *S.* Peter Stanley and John Davis. *Daus.* Gay (Wray), Cinda Joers and Susan Clark. *Career:* President, The Firestone Rubber & Latex Products Co. 1938; Lieutenant-Commander, U.S. Navy 1942; President, Firestone Aircraft Co. 1945; Director, The Firestone Tire & Rubber Co. 1945; President, Firestone Plastics Co. 1947; and Firestone Synthetic Fibers Co. 1959–68. Hon. LHD, Central College, Pella, Iowa; Pres., United Cerebral Palsy Research and Educational Foundn. *Clubs:* Union League (Philadelphia); Brook, River (New York); Augusta (Ga.) Golf; Metropolitan (Washington, D.C.); Crown Colony (Bahamas); Key Largo Anglers (Florida). *Address: office* P.O. Box 699, Pottsdown, Pa., U.S.A.

**FIRTH, Jolyon Rex.** New Zealand. *B.* 1932. *Educ.* Victoria and Auckland Universities. *M.* 1961, Julia Naughton. *Career:* Chartered Accountant in Public Practice, Chartered Secy; Foundation Board Member, Onehunga Jaycees 1957; National Party Candidate, Waitemata electorate 1960; Electorate Chmn., Auckland Central Electorate, N.Z. National Party 1962; National Party Candidate, Grey Lynn Electorate 1963. Principal Jolyon Firth & Co., Chartered Accountants, Auckland. President: Auckland Junior Chamber of Commerce 1963. First President and Founder, Auckland Toastmasters Club 1963; Auckland Public Relations Bd. 1963—, Cncl of Management Auckland Festival Socy. 1964—; Pres. New Zealand Toastmasters Council 1967; Elected to Auckland City Council 1968—; Auckland Metropolitan Fire Bd. 1971–76; Foundation Trustee N.Z. Retirement Life Care Residence Trust since 1972; Winner, N.Z Jaycee 'Stotter' oratory contest 1960. *Member:* N.Z. Socy of Accountants, Chartered Inst. of Secretaries and N.Z. Inst. of Management. *Clubs:* Remuera Squash; Auckland Kiwanis (Pres. 1968). *Address:* 26 Lochiel Road, Remuera, Auckland; and *office* 11 Lorne St., Auckland, New Zealand.

**FISCHER, David Anthony Valdemar.** South African diplomat. *B.* 1920. *Educ.* Univ. of Cape Town (BA 1940); post-graduate studies in law, diplomatic practice and history. *M.* 1946, Patricia Emily Hingle. *S.* Michael David and Patrick John. *Daus.* Diana Valerie and Adrienne Margaret. Military Service in Africa, Middle East and Italy 1941–45; South African Department of External Affairs (Athens, Pretoria, Washington 1945–57; served on several delegations to international meetings, including three sessions of the General Assembly of U.N.; appointed First Secy. of Embassy 1957) Director of External Liaison & Protocol, International Atomic Energy Agency, Vienna 1957; Asst. Dir.-Gen., International Atomic Energy Agency, Vienna 1976. *Member:* Economic Society of South Africa. *Club:* Kelvin Grove (Cape Town). *Address: office* International Atomic Energy Agency, Vienna I, Austria.

**FISCHER, Ernst Otto.** German professor of chemistry. *B.* 1918. *Educ.* Theresiengymnasium (Munich); Munich Tech. Univ., Dip Chemistry (1949). *Career:* Military Service 1938–

45, P. of W. 1945; Scientific Asst. at Inorganic Chemistry Inst. Munich 1949–52; Worked in field of research of complex chemical and chelate problems and other work at Munich Tech. Univ. 1952–54, Appointed lecturer 1954, U.S. Study tour 1956, Appointed Sen. Lectr. 1957, Professor of Inorganic chemistry (Munich Univ.) 1959; Appointed to Chair of Inorganic chemistry Munich Technical Coll. 1964; Lecture tours in U.S.A., Australia, Venezuela, Brazil, Israel, Lebanon and numerous European Countries and USSR; Firestone Lecturer at Univ. of Wisconsin, (U.S.A.) 1969, and first Inorganic chem. Pacific West Coast Lectr., Lecturer at Mass. Inst. of Technology Cambridge (U.S.A.) 1973; Visiting Distinguished Lecturer at Univ. Rochester N.Y.; FMC Lecturer at Princeton Univ. NJ 1975; and Venable Lecturer at Univ. of N. Carolina, NC (U.S.A.). *Member:* Mathematical and Sc. Div. of Bavarian Academy of Sciences 1964; German Academy of Scientists. Leopoldina 1969; Austrian Acad. of Sciences 1976; Accademia Nazionale dei Lincei 1976. *Awards:* Hon. Degree Dr. of Nat. Sciences, Munich, 1972; Nobel Prize for Chemistry (with Prof. G. Wilkinson, Imp. Coll. London) 1973; Hon. Degree of Dr. of Science, Strathclyde Univ. 1975; Hon. Degree Dr. of Nat. Sciences, Univ. Erlangen-Nürnberg 1977; Amer. Chemical Society Centennial Foreign Fellow 1976; Foreign Hon. Fellow, Amer. Acad. of Arts & Sciences 1977. *Address:* IC Laboratory, Tech. Univ. of Munich, 8 Munchen 2, Arcisstrasse 21, Postfach Nr 20 24 20, Germany.

**FISCHER, John.** *B.* 1910. *Educ.* Univ. of Oklahoma (BA); Rhodes Scholar, Oxford. *M.* 1935, Elizabeth Wilson. *Daus.* Nicolas and Sara. Vice-Pres., Harper & Row, Publishers, Inc. 1947–65; Editor and writer 1944–47; Officer of Board of Economic Warfare and other agencies of U.S. Govt., and economic intelligence officer on staff of General Joseph W. Stilwell, Comdr., China-Burma-India theatre 1940–44. Economist, U.S. Dept of Agriculture 1937–40 Washington Correspondent, Associated Press 1935–37; Editor-in-chief Harpers Magazine 1953–58, Assoc. Editor since 1968. Hon. Doctorates from Univ. of Massachusetts, Bucknell Univ., and Kenyon Coll. *Member:* Amer. Political Science Assn.; Amer. Acad. of Political and Social Sciences Trustee Brookings Institution and Educational Broadcasting Corporation. *Publications:* Why They Behave Like Russians (1947); Master Plan: U.S.A. (1951); The Stupidity Problem (1964); Six in the Easy Chairs (1971); Vital Signs (1975); many articles in magazines and professional journals. *Clubs:* The Century Association. *Address:* 21 Shell Beach Road, Guilford, Conn. 06437, U.S.A.

**FISCHER, Dr. Karl Ingmar Roman,** ao u. bev. Botschafter. Austrian Diplomat. *B.* 1922. *Educ.* Volkschule, Realgymnasium, Universität (Doktor der Rechte). *Career:* Federal Ministry of Foreign Affairs 1949–53; Austrian Legation, Lisbon (2nd Secretary) 1953–55; Embassy, Washington (1st Secretary) 1955–59; Counsellor, Min. of Foreign Affairs 1954–63; Embassy, Paris 1963–70; Min. of Foreign Affairs, in charge of Bilateral Economic Relations 1970–74; Ambassador Stockholm since 1974. *Address:* Kommendörsgatan 35/V, S-114 58 Stockholm, Sweden; and Wehlistrasse 366/V, A-1020 Vienna, Austria.

**FISCHER, Paul Rudolf.** Swiss. *B.* 1913. *Educ.* Commercial Coll.; 46th AMP Harvard Univ. *M.* 1940, Annie Simmen. *S.* 1. *Dau.* 1. *Career:* Senior Vice Pres. CPC/E; Chmn., Knorr Nährmittel A.G., Thayngen; Dir., Knorr Zürich A.G., Monda Alimenta A.G., Indamid A.G., Knorr G.m.b.H., Cosmonda Voedingsmiddelen N.V., S.A. Monda, Knorr Portuguesa S.A.R.L., Knorr Anglo Swiss Ltd., OKA A.G.; Chmn., Société des Produits du Mais, Clamart/France; formerly Senior Accountant & Financial Expert, Schweizerische Revisionsgesellschaft A.G. *Member:* AMA; Chaine des Rôtisseurs. *Club:* Savoy. *Address:* Freudenbergstrasse 75, 8044 Zürich, Switzerland; and *office* c/o CPC/E, Tour Louise, 149 Avenue Louise, 1050 Brussels.

**FISCHER, Walker Hans.** Swiss. *B.* 1912. *Educ.* Cantonal College of Zürich and London School of Economics. *M.* 1935, Jane Proudfoot Elliott. *S.* George Walter. *Dau.* Agnes Nancy. General Manager, Zürich Bolting Cloth Co. Ltd. 1941–61, Man. Dir. since 1961. *Member:* Chamber of Commerce, Zürich; Zürich Silk Manufacturers Assn.; SFUSA, Zürich; Swiss Friends of U.S.A., Zürich. *Clubs:* Zürich Rowing; Montana Ski (both of Zürich). *Address:* Kurfirstenstr. 66, 8002 Zürich; and Moostr 2, 8803 Ruschlikon, Switzerland.

**FISHER, Arthur John Malcolm,** TD. Legion of Merit (U.S.A.); Canadian electrical engineer. *B.* 1913. *Educ.* City & Guilds of London Institute (Elect. Eng.). *M.* 1937, Dorothy Edith Hipkin. *S.* Peter John and Hugh Anthony. *Daus.* Gillian and Valerie. With Callenders Cable & Construction Co. 1932; Johnson & Phillips Ltd. 1936; Lieut.-Colonel, Royal Artillery 1939–45; Atomic Energy Research Establishment, Harwell 1945; Fiberglas (Canada) Ltd. 1948—. President and Director, Fiberglass (Canada) Ltd. 1956—, Chmn. of the Bd. & Pres. 1976. Director: Dominion Explorers Ltd. 1958—, Vermiculite Insulation Ltd., Great West Steel Industries Ltd. 1976—. Hon. Vice-Pres., Canadian Arthritis & Rheumatism Society. *Member:* Institution of Electrical Engineers. Professional Engineer, Ontario. Honoris Causa, Doctor of Engineering. *Clubs:* Granite (Toronto); Rosedale Golf; Badminton & Racquet (Toronto). *Address:* 8 Maytree Road, Willowdale, Ont.; and *office* 48 St. Clair Avenue W. Toronto, Ont., Canada.

**FISHER, (Edwin) Shelton.** American publisher. *B.* 1911. *Educ.* Columbia Univ. and U.S. Naval Acad. (BS 1934). *M.* 1936, Louise Tait. *S.* Shelton Tait, Anthony Kent and Christopher Alan. *Dau.* Anne Louise (Colby). *Career:* With Curtis Publishing Co. 1935–38; McCann Erickson Adv. 1938–40; successively Promotion Mgr., Business Week 1940–42; Asst. Publisher, Science Illustrated 1946–49, and Publisher: Power 1949–57, Fleet Owner 1954–59 and Electrical Merchandising 1957–59; Senior Vice-Pres., Publications Division, McGraw-Hill Publishing Co., 1958–63, Pres. 1963–66; President 1966–74, Chief Executive Officer 1968, Chmn. of Board since 1974, McGraw Hill Inc. *Member:* Delta Kappa Epsilon. *Clubs:* Wee Burn C.C.; University (N.Y.C.). *Address:* 1221 Ave. of Americas, New York 10020, N.Y., U.S.A.

**FISHER, Gordon Henderson.** American. *B.* 1918. *Educ.* University of Texas (BS 1938; MS 1941). *M.* Elinor P. Armstrong. *S.* 1. *Daus.* 2. *Career:* Petroleum Engineer, Phillips Petroleum Co., Bartlesville, Okla. 1939–41; Geology Technician, Geologist, Chief Petroleum Engineer; Executive Assistant to Vice-Pres., Mgr. Supply and Services, Mgr. Production, Gulf Oil Corp., Fort Worth, Tex. 1941–55; Vice-Pres., Plymouth Oil Co. Sinton Tex. (also Dir.) 1955–62; Pres., General Minerals Co., Houston, Tex. 1962–63. Vice-President-Asst. to the President, Kennecott Copper Corp. 1976—. (Asst. to Pres. 1963–68; Vice-Pres.-Planning 1968–76). Director: Quebec Columbium Ltd. 1966—, and Peabody Coal Co. 1968–77; Chmn. Bd. of Peabody Coal Co. 1971–72 Dir. Engineers Joint Council 1972–74. *Member:* Tau Beta Pi; Sigma Gamma Epsilon; Amer. Inst. of Mining Engrs.; Amer. Assn. of Petroleum Geologists; Amer. Petroleum Inst. *Clubs:* Fort Worth (Fort Worth); Wee Burn Country (Darien); Pinnacle (N.Y.C.); Landmark (Stamford, Conn.). *Address:* Ridge Acres Road, Darien, Conn. 06820; and *office* 161 East 42nd Street, New York, N.Y. 10017, U.S.A.

**FISHER, Harold Wallace.** American Chemical Engineer. *B.* 1904. *Educ.* Massachusetts Inst. of Technology (BSc). *M.* 1930, Hope Elisabeth Case. *S.* Dean W., II. *Career:* Joined Standard Oil Co. (N.J.) 1927; Dir. Esso Standard Oil Co. and Pres. Enjay Co. Inc. 1945; Refining Co-ordination, S.O. Co. (N.J.) 1950; Resided in London 1954–59; U.K. Representative for Standard Oil (N.J.) and Chairman of its Co-ordination Committee for Europe 1954–57; Joint Managing Director, Iraq Petroleum Co. Ltd. and Associated Companies 1957–59; Director 1959–69 and Vice-President 1962–69, Standard Oil Co., N.J., now Exxon Corporation; Hon. DSc Clarkson College of Technology; Chmn., Bd. Of Trustees, Sloan-Kettering Inst. for Cancer Research 1970–74; Nat. Acad. Eng. 1969; Vice-Chmn. and Chmn. Exec. Cttee. Community Blood Council Gr. N.Y., 1969–71. *Member:* Amer. Chemical Socy.; Socy. of Chemical Industry; Amer. Inst. of Chemical Engineers. *Clubs:* Pilgrims, American (London); University (N.Y.C.). *Address:* P.O. Box 1792 Duxbury Massachusetts 02332; and *office* One, Rockefeller Plaza, New York, N.Y. 10020, U.S.A.

**FISHER, Sir Nigel Thomas Loveridge,** MC, MP. *B.* 1913. *Educ.* Eton and Trinity Coll. Cambridge (Hons. Degree Law; MA). *M.* (1) 1935, Lady Gloria Vaughan. *S.* 1. *Dau.* 1. (2) 1956, Patricia Smiles. Member of Parliament (Con.) for Hitchin Div. of Hertfordshire 1950–55, Surbiton since 1955; Parliamentary Private Secretary: to Minister of Food 1950–55, to Secy. of State for the Home Dept. 1955–57. Parliamentary Under-Secretary of State: for the Colonies July 1962–Oct. 1963, for Commonwealth Relations and for the Colonies 1963–64. Official Opposition spokesman for Commonwealth and Colonial Affairs 1964–66; Treasurer. Commonwealth Parliamentary Assoc., 1966–68 & of the UK Branch of the C.P.A. since 1977; Mem. of the Exec. of the 1922 Cttee. 1959–62 & since 1969; Mem. of the National Exec. of the Conservative Party 1945–47 & since 1971; Pres., British-Caribbean

Assoc.; Vice-Pres., Building Societies Assoc.; Vice-Chmn., U.K. Branch of the C.P.A. 1975–76. War service: volunteered 1939; Commissioned Welsh Guards; served overseas; wounded; mentioned in dispatches; awarded Military Cross in the Field 1944 (Capt. 1940; Major 1944); Received knighthood 1974. *Publications:* Iain MacLeod (1973); The Tory Leaders (1977). *Address:* 16 North Court, Great Peter Street, London, S.W.1; Portavo Point Donaghadee Co. Down, N. Ireland; St. George's Court, St. George's Bay, Malta, G.C.; and House of Commons, London, S.W.1.

**FISHER, Norman Henry,** AO. Australian. *B.* 1909. *Educ.* University of Queensland (BSc 1931; MSc 1933; DSc 1941). *M.* 1937, Ellice Marguerite Summers. *S.* William Norman. *Career:* Geologist, Mt. Isa Mines 1932–34; Government Geologist, Territory of New Guinea 1934–46; Chief Geologist, Mineral Resources Survey, Australia 1942–46; Chief Geologist, Bureau of Mineral Resources, Geology and Geophysics, Commonwealth of Australia 1946–69. Director 1969–74; United Nations Advisor on Mineral Development—to Bolivia 1954–55 (one year) and to Israel 1963–64 (three months); Chmn. of Organizing Cttee & Pres. 25th Intern. Geological Congress. *Member:* Geological Socy. of Australia; Socy. of Economic Geologists; Socy. for Geology Applied to Mineral Deposits (Editorial Adviser); Australasian Inst. of Mining and Metallurgy; Australian and New Zealand Assn. for Advancement of Science. *Awards:* Officer of the Order of Australia 1976; Spendiarov Prize 1976. *Publications:* Geological Bulletins 1 to 3 (Territory of New Guinea); The Fineness of Gold (Economic Geology, 1945); Catalogue of Active Volcanoes of the World (Part V, Melanesia); numerous scientific papers. *Club:* Commonwealth (Canberra). *Address:* 68 National Circuit, Deakin, Canberra, A.C.T., Australia.

**FISHER, Philip Sydney,** OC, CBE, DSO, DSC. Canadian executive. *B.* 1896. *Educ.* McGill Univ. (BA and LLD *h.c.*); DCL (*honoris causa*), Bishop's Univ. and Waterloo Lutheran Univ. *M.* 1920, Margaret L. Southam. *S.* Guy Southam, John Philip, Gordon Neil. *Daus.* Sydney Mary (Duder), Margaret Claire (Kerrigan), Martha June (Hallward). *Career:* Served in World War I (R.N.A.S., Flight-Cmdr.; retired Captain, R.A.F.); joined Southam Co., Jan. 1924. Chairman, Southam Press Ltd. (newspapers, magazines and printing 1961–71. *Clubs:* (Montreal) St. James's; Royal, St. Lawrence Yacht. *Address:* 3130 Cedar Avenue, Montreal 6, P.Q., Canada H3Y 121.

**FISHER, Ruth Kinyon Whiteside (Mrs. Robert Fisher),** (*nee* **Kinyon**). American. *B.* 1914. *Educ.* Univ. of Missouri (BSc. Bach. Journalism). *M.* (1) Prof. Horace E. Whiteside; (2) 1959, Robert Fisher. *Career:* Man. Dir. Overseas Features Ltd.; Jt. Man. Dir. Robert Fisher (Packing & Shipping) Ltd.; Man. Dir. Robert Fisher (Holdings) Ltd; Research & Public Relations, Charles W. Hoyt Advertising Co. Inc., 1941–51; Board of Directors, Advertising Fed. of America, 1944–46; Treas. Int. Assoc. Woman in Radio & Television; Mem. American Women in Radio & Television; Advertising Women of New York Inc.; Nat'l. Pres. Gamma Alpha Chi; Advertising fraternity 1944–46; Assoc. member Junior Carlton Club, London. *Clubs:* Women's Press; American Women's Club of London. *Address:* 22 St. James's Close, Prince Albert Road, London, N.W.8; and *office* 32 Lexington St., London, W.1; and Gulf View Beach Club, 2171 Gulf Shore Boulevard North, Naples, Florida 33940, U.S.A.

**FISHER, Sterling Wesley.** *B.* 1899. *Educ.* Univ. of Texas (BA) and Univ. of California (MA). *M.* 1923, Jean Alice Callahan. *S.* Sterling and William Murray. *Career:* Professor of English, Kwansei Univ., Kobe, Japan 1924–29; Sub-editor, Associated Press, N.Y.C. 1929–30; Far Eastern Editor, New York Times 1930–37; Dir. of Education, Columbia Broadcasting System 1937–42; Mgr. of Public Affairs, National Broadcasting Co. 1942–50; Mgr. for Far East, Reader's Digest 1950–56; Executive Director, Reader's Digest Foundation 1956–70. *Publications:* many magazine articles, including New York Times Magazine. Adviser on Broadcasting, Dept. of State, Washington 1942–49. Mayor of Tarrytown, N.Y. 1947–49; Pres., Amer. Chamber of Commerce in Japan 1951–52; Vice-Pres., America-Japan Soc., Tokyo 1952–56; Chairman, Board of Directors, World Press Inst., St. Paul, Minn. 1963–70. *Award:* Columbia Univ. School of Journalism 50th Anniversary Award (1963). *Club:* Overseas Press (N.Y.C.). *Address: office* Reader's Digest, Pleasantville, N.Y., U.S.A.

**FISK, James B(rown).** American executive. *B.* 1910. *Educ.* Massachusetts Institute of Technology (BS; PhD); Trinity College, Cambridge, England (Redfield Proctor Travelling Fellow); Hon. Degrees: MA, Harvard 1947; ScD, Carnegie Inst. of Tech. 1956, Williams College 1958, Newark College of Engineering 1959, Columbia Univ. 1960, Colby College 1962, New York Univ. 1963, Dr. of Eng. Univ. of Michigan 1963. Univ. of Akron 1963; ScD, Rutgers State Univ. 1967. Hon. Degrees: LLD, Lehigh Univ. 1967 and Illinois Institute of Technology 1968; DSc, Drew Univ. 1968 and Harvard 1969; DLitt. Newark State College 1969; LLD Fairleigh-Dickinson Univ. 1973. *M.* 1938, Cynthia Hoar. *S.* Samuel Hoar, Zachary and Charles Brown. *Career:* Society of Fellows, Harvard University 1936–38; Associate Professor of Physics, University of North Carolina 1938–39; Gordon McKay Professor, Harvard University 1948–49. Director of Research, U.S. Atomic Energy Commission 1947–48; Bell Telephone Laboratories 1938–47 and 1949–74 (Director of Research, Physical Sciences 1952–54; Vice-President, Research 1954–55; Executive Vice-President 1955–58). Member, President's Science Adv. Cttee 1957–60; Pres. Bell Telephone Laboratories, Murray Hill N.J. 1959–73; Consultant 1960—; Chmn. Bd. Bell Telephone Laboratories 1973–74. *Member:* National Academy of Sciences; Amer. Physical Socy.; Amer. Academy of Arts and Sciences; Inst. of Electrical & Electronics Engineers; Amer. Philosophical Society; National Academy of Engineering. *Publications:* contributed articles to professional periodicals. *Clubs:* Harvard (N.Y.C.); Ausable (Adirondack Mt.); Somerset Hills Country (New Jersey). *Address:* c/o Bell Telephone Laboratories, Murray Hill, N.J. 07974, U.S.A.

**FISKE, Robert B.** Exec., Retd. V-Pres. & Dir., American Cyanamid Co.; Dir.: The Pillsbury Co., Rhodia Inc., Howe Folding Furniture Co. Inc., Foreign Policy Association; Nat. Advisory Council, Hampshire Coll.; Trustee, Dry Dock Savings Bank; Governor, International Planned Parenthood Federation. *B.* 1900. *Educ.* Yale College (BA 1924) and Yale Law School (LLB *magna cum laude*) 1926. *M.* 1929, Lenore Seymour. *S.* Robert B., Jr., McNeil S. and John A. With law firm of Root, Clark, Buckner, Howland & Ballantine 1926–34; Reconstruction Finance Corp. 1931–32; Dir., American Cyanamid Co. 1947–59 (Vice-Pres. 1948–62); Asst. General Secretary of NATO for Production and Logistics (onleave of absence from Cyanamid) 1959–60. Order of the Coif 1926; Editor-in-Chief, Yale Law Journal 1926. Phi Delta Theta. Republican. *Clubs:* University, Anglers (N.Y.C.(; Phelps Association, Graduates (New Haven); Old Lyme C.C.; Balsam Lake. *Address:* Cove Road, Lyme, Conn., U.S.A.

**FISSER, Carl (Heinrich Ernst).** Dr. jur. German ship owner, and coal importer and wholesaler. Partner, Fisser KG. *B.* 1896. *Educ.* Grammar School (with leaving certificate); studied law (Dr. jur.). *M.* Bertha Ellersdorfer. *S.* Dr. Frank M. Fisser. *Club:* Overseas (Hamburg). *Address:* Böttgerstrasse 9, Hamburg 13, Germany.

**FITCH, Ernest Alan,** JP, MP. British Politician. *B.* 1915. *Educ.* Kingswood Sch., Bath. *M.* 1950, Nancy Maude. *S.* 1. *Dau.* 1. *Career:* MP (Lab) for Wigan since 1958; Asst. Whip 1964–66; Lord Commissioner of the Treasury 1966–69; Vice-Chamberlain of the Royal Household 1969–70; Chmn. of the North West Regional Council of the Labour Party since 1967; mem. of Assembly of Council of Europe 1966–69; mem. of Mr. Speaker's Panel of Chairmen since 1971. *Member:* Rotary Club, Wigan. Justice of the Peace, 1958. *Club:* Royal Automobile. *Address:* 117 The Avenue, Leigh, Lancs.; and *office* 20 King Street, Wigan, Lancs.

**FITE, Dean Pickering.** American. *B.* 1912. *Educ.* University of Cincinnati (degree in Comml. Engng. 1935). *M.* 1936, Norma Conard. *S.* David C. *Dau.* Nancy L. (Stockmann). *Career:* Joined Buckeye Cotton Oil Co. (subsid. of Procter & Gamble) 1937. Entered U.S. Army 1942, and left as a Major in 1945, and returned to Cost Dept. of P & G 1945; subsequently Mgr., Budgets and Proced. Dept. 1951; Mgr., Cost Dept. 1952; Chief Accountant 1955; Associate Comptroller 1957; Comptroller 1958; Vice Pres. and Comptroller 1961, Vice-President, Corporate Affairs and Member Board of Directors, The Procter-Gamble Co. 1961–75 (retired); Vice Pres. Group Exec. 1972–75; Director, Cincinnati Milacron; The Tool Steel Gear & Pinion Co.; Gradison Cash Reserves Inc. *Member:* Board of Trustees, Hamilton County Regional Airport Authority; Financial Executives Institute; Chmn. Bd. Trustee's, Cincinnati Museum of Natural History. *Clubs:* Queen City, Commercial (Cincinnati). *Address:* 6915 Winding Way, Cincinnati, Ohio 45236, U.S.A.

**FITZMAURICE, Sir Gerald Gray,** GCMG, QC. International Law Consultant. *B.* 1901. *Educ.* Malvern; Caius College,

Cambridge (BA, LLB 1924); Hon. Fellow 1961; Hon. LLD, Edinburgh 1970, Cambridge 1972. *M.* 1933, Alice Evelina Alexandra Sandberg. *S.* 2. *Career:* Called to the Bar (Gray's Inn) 1925; practised 1925–29; Q.C. 1957; Bencher of Gray's Inn 1961; 3rd Legal Adviser to Foreign Office 1929; Legal Adviser to Ministry of Economic Warfare 1939–43, and to U.K. Delegations at Paris Peace Conference 1946, U.N. Assembly 1946 and 1948–59. Japanese Peace Conference, San Francisco 1951, and Berlin and Manila Confs. 1954; Counsel for U.K. in several cases before the International Court of Justice; 2nd Legal Adviser to Foreign Office 1945–53; Legal Adviser, with rank of Deputy Under-Secy. 1953–60; Judge of European Court of Human Rights, Strasbourg 1974–; Judge of the International Court of Justice at The Hague, 1960–73. *Member:* Permanent Court of Arbitration 1961—; Internatl. Law Comm. of U.N. 1955–60 (Pres; 1959); Inst. of Iternational Law (Pres. 1967–69); Grotius Socy. (President 1956–60). Hon. Doctorates of Law University of Cambridge, Edinburgh & Utrecht. *Publications:* articles in British Year Book of International Law; American Journal of International Law and other legal journals; three sets of Lectures in Hague Recueil: five Reports on the Law Treaties in the Yearbook of the International Law Commission. *Clubs:* Athenaeum, United Oxford & Cambridge University (London). *Address:* 2 Hare Court, Temple, London, E.C.4; and 3 Gray's Inn Square, London, W.C.1.

**FLAHERTY, Eugene Dewey.** American. Captain, U.S.N.R. (Ret.). Ocean Shipping Consultant. *B.* 1898. *Educ.* Los Angeles College of Law. *M.* 1923, Georgiana Boenau. *S.* Robert and William Patrick. *Dau.* Mary Eileen (Galloway). *Career:* U.S. Railroad administration 1917–20; Sec. and Dir., Seaboard Development Co. 1922–38; Director, Marblehead Land Co. 1936–38; Assistant to Chairman, American President Lines 1938–41; Commanding Officer, U.S. Naval Armed Guard Center Pacific (received U.S. Navy Commendation for Services) 1942–46; Secretary, American President Lines 1946–48; Vice-Pres., Operations 1949–50; Vice-Pres., Southwestern Division 1950–63; Pres. and General Manager, Marine Exchange of Los Angeles-Long Beach Harbor Inc. 1963–68. *Member:* The Maritimers; Propeller Club of U.S.A., Amer. Socy. of Traffic and Transportation, Life Member, National Defense Transportation Association, and Association Internationale des Skål Clubs. Delta Phi Epsilon (foreign trade and service fraternity), Japan-American Society of S. Calif. Hon. Life member Los Angeles Steamship Association. *Publications:* articles and addresses on shipping matters and American Merchant Marine. Democrat. *Address:* 1232 Leisure Lane 8, Rossmoor, Walnut Creek, CA 94595., U.S.A.

**FLAMM, Donald.** Director and owner of radio stations, including WMMM (AM) and WDJF (F.M.) which serve the Connecticut, New York and Long Island areas; co-producer of stage plays in New York and London; officer and director of various business and real estate corporations in various parts of the United States; member, Bd. of Directors, Oscar Lewenstein Plays Ltd., London; served as Chairman, Civil War Centennial Commission, State of New Jersey (appointed by the Governor of the State); President, Flamm Realty Corporation (N.Y.C.); Officer and member, Board of Directors, Hebrew Free Loan Socy. of N.Y. and The Manfred Sakel Inst. *B.* 1899. *Educ.* Public Schls. of N.Y., including extension courses at New York University. Magazine and book publisher 1921–30; owner, operator, radio stations WMCA (New York, N.Y.) 1925–41, WPCH (New York, N.Y.) 1927–32; co-owner WPAT (Paterson, N.J.) 1942–48; Pres. & Man. Dir. Intercity Network (Regional American Network along Eastern Seaboard) 1927–41; served as special liaison officer, U.S. Office of War Information, World War II. In that capacity (devising plans for psychological warfare) he formulated the original plan for ABSIE (American Broadcasting Station In England) so that American propaganda could be easily picked up in all occupied countries. As head of the Inter-City Network (with stations from Boston to Washington, D.C.) he openly fought the Nazis. Soon after Hitler came to power his radio station WMCA was recognized as the official mouthpiece of the Anti-Nazi League of America; and when America was neutral, he was obliged, as owner of the station, to ensure that no foreign spokesman was afforded the use of his facilities for propaganda purposes; nevertheless, he worked in the Allied cause, and fought a long and bitter war against pro-Nazi elements in America. He sponsored the 'Bundles for Britain' movement and the British-American Ambulance Corps; and it was his own idea that resulted in hundreds of refugee British children speaking to their parents and relatives at home from his New York studios and then by way of short-wave station WRUL in Boston; this was a regular WMCA feature for many months. He was also energetic in his support of the John Logie Baird System of television in America as far back as 1932, when he appeared before the Federal Radio Commission, in Washington, D.C., to urge the American use of the English system over his New York radio outlet. *Clubs:* Friars, Rockfeller Luncheon (N.Y.C.); Alpine Country; Catholic Actors Guild; El Morocco; Le Club; Annabel's; The Atriam; United Hunts; White Elephant. *Address:* Closter, N.J.; and *office* 25 Central Park West, New York City 23, U.S.A.

**FLECK, G. Peter.** Officer, of Orange Nassau. *B.* 1909. *Educ.* Amsterdam Lyceum (Grad. 1927), Hochschule für Welthandel Vienna 1928. *M.* 1939, Ruth Alice Irene Melchior. *Daus.* Miriam Ann (Henderson), Andrea Emily (Clardy) and Marjorie Elizabeth (Withers). *Career:* with Erlangers Ltd., London 1928–29; Banque des Pays de l'Europe Centrale, Paris 1929–30; Bank für auswärtigen Handel, Berlin 1930–31; Continental Handelsbank, Amsterdam 1931–40 (becoming Vice-President 1936); emigrated to United States 1941, became United States citizen 1945. Organized and became President of Amsterdam Overseas Corporation 1947; Chmn. New Court Securities Corp. N.Y.C. successor Co. Amsterdam Overseas Corporation; Dir. N. M. Rothschild & Sons Ltd. London, Banque Rothschild, S.A. Paris; Pierson Heldring and Pierson, Amsterdam; N.Y.C.; Magnum Fund, Amsterdam; Compagnie Lambert, Brussels; Pres. Dir. Five Arrows Securities Co. Curaco, N.A. Director, Netherland-America Foundation; Chairman: Meadville Theological School, Chicago; Hon. D.H.L. Starr King School, Ministry Berkeley Calif.; Hon. D.L. Meadville, Lombard Theological School Chicago. *Member:* Council of Foreign Relations. *Clubs:* Wall Street; Netherlands (of N.Y.C.); St. James' London. *Address:* Quanset Road, South Orleans, Mass. 02662, U.S.A.; and *office* One, Rockefeller Plaza, New York City 10020, U.S.A.

**FLEISCHER, Julius Christian August.** *B.* 1907. *Educ.* Passed Diplomatic Exam. 1939. *M.* 1941, Magnhild Othilie Sundby. *S.* Christian August. *Daus.* Anne-Carine, Vibeke Cecilie and Marit Benedicte Sophie. *Career:* Secretary, Foreign Ministry, Attaché Legation, Warsaw 1937; Secretary Legation, Stockholm 1940 (First Secretary 1943); Counsellor in Foreign Ministry 1947; Chargé d'Affaires, Athens, 1949; Consul General, Cape Town 1951. Ambassador to Argentina 1958–62, and Minister to Uruguay and Paraguay 1959–62. Consul-General of Norway in New York 1962–70; Ambassador of Norway in Berne, Switzerland 1970–73. *Awards:* Commander, Order of St. Olav; Commander, Order of Vasa (Sweden); Queen Elizabeth Coronation Medal in Silver; Grand Cross Order de Mayo (Argentina). *Address:* c/o Ministry of Foreign Affairs, Oslo, Norway.

**FLEISCHER, Michael.** American geochemist. *B.* 1908. *Educ.* Yale (BS 1930; PhD 1933). *M.* 1934, Helen Anna Isenberg. *S.* Walter H. and David A. Asst. Physical Chemist, Carnegie Inst. of Washington 1936–39. Geochemist, U.S. Geological Survey 1939—; Assistant Editor, Chemical Abstracts 1941—; Professorial lecturer, George Washington University 1957–65. *Member:* Mineralogical Socy. of America (Vice-Pres. 1951; Pres. 1952); Amer. Chemical Socy.; Mineralogical Socy. of Great Britain; and the Mineralogical Societies of Italy, Switzerland, France, Canada; Socy. of Economic Geologists; Geochemical Socy. (Vice-Pres. 1963, Pres. 1964); Geochemistry Commission, Int. Union of Pure & Applied Chemistry (Pres. 1953–57); Commission on new minerals, Int. Mineralogical Assn. (Pres. 1959–74). *Award:* Roebling Medal Mineralog. Socy. Award (1975); Friedrich Becke Medal, Mineral Soc. Austria (1976). *Publications:* about 100 scientific papers. *Address:* 3104 Chestnut Street, N.W., Washington, D.C. 20015; and *office* U.S. Geological survey, Reston, Va. 22092, U.S.A.

**FLEMING, Allan Percy,** OBE. Australian. *B.* 1912. *Educ.* Melbourne University (BA). *M.* 1940, Margaret Patterson. *Dau.* 1. *Career:* Journalist (Argus, Melbourne; Courier Mail, Brisbane; Sun, Melbourne, Leader writer) 1932–39 and 1946–47; Served with 2nd A.I.F. (Middle East, Greece, New Guinea, Philippines (Lt.-Col., O.B.E.; twice M.I.D.)) 1939–46. Trade Commissioner, Paris, and (for nine months) Acting Special Commercial Adviser, Australian High Commission, London 1959–62; at Department of Defence (Director, Joint Intelligence Bureau; Asst. Secretary; Controller, Joint Service Organisations) 1947–59; variously First Asst. Secy. (Int. Trade Relations Policy), (Int. Trade Organisations) Dept. of Trade 1962–66. Special Commercial Adviser, High Commission, London, 1967. Commonwealth

Parliamentary Librarian 1968–70; National Librarian 1970–73 (Ret'd.); Co-ordinator, V.I.P. Security 1976–77. *Publications:* various articles and short stories. *Club:* Naval & Military (Melbourne). *Address:* 60 Gellibrand Street, Campbell, Canberra, A.C.T.

**FLEMING, Hon. Donald Methuen,** PC, QC, BA, LLB, DCL, LLD. Managing Director: Bank of Nova Scotia Trust Co. (Bahamas) Ltd. and subsidiaries. General Counsel to Bank of Nova Scotia. *B.* 1905. *Educ.* Univ. of Toronto (BA 1925); LLB 1930); Osgoode Hall Law School 1928. *M.* 1933, Alice Mildred Watson. *S.* David and Donald. *Dau.* Mary. *Career:* Barrister and Solicitor; called to the Bar 1928; Toronto Board of Education 1938; Toronto City Council 1939–44; elected M.P. for Toronto-Eglinton 1945–49–53–57–58–62. Minister of Finance and Receiver General of Canada 1957–62; member of H.M. Privy Council for Canada (June 1957); Governor of International Bank for Reconstruction and Development; International Monetary Fund; Director: International Finance Corp. (1957–63); International Development Assn. 1957–63; Chmn., Organization for Economic Co-operation and Development, 1961–62; Minister of Justice and Attorney-General of Canada 1962–63. *Awards:* Greek Red Cross Medal 1953; Created KC 1944. Progressive Conservative. *Member:* Canadian Political Science Assn.; Canadian Bar Assn.; Ionic Lodge A.F. and A.M.; Scottish Rite; Shrine, Independent Order of Foresters; Chevalier de la Société du Bon Parler Français (Montreal); Royal Order of Scotland. *Publications:* contributed to legal periodicals, including Canadian Encyclopedic Digest, Canadian Bar Review, Canadian Abridgement, etc. *Clubs:* Canadian; Empire; National; Granite; Rosedale Golf; Toronto Cricket; Queens (all of Toronto); Rideau; Country (Ottawa); Lyford Cay; East Hill (Nassau). *Address:* Bayview, P.O. Box N3016, Nassau, Bahamas; and *office* The Bernard Sunley Bldg., P.O. Box N3016, Nassau, Bahamas.

**FLEMING, John G.** U.S. citizen. Professor of Law. University of California 1960—. *B.* 1919. *Educ.* Oxford University (MA; DPhil; DCL). *M.* 1946, Valerie Joyce. *S.* 3. *Dau.* 1. Previously Dean and Robert Garran Professor of Law, Australian National University; Editor-in-Chief, American Journal of Comparative Law; Cecil Shannon Turner Professor of Law, Univ. of Cal. since 1960. *Publications:* Law of Torts (5th edn. 1977); Introduction to Law of Torts (1966). *Member:* Lincoln's Inn. London (Barrister-at-Law); American Law Institute; International Acad. of Comparative Law; Vice-Pres., International Assoc. Legal Science. *Address:* 836 Spruce Street, Berkeley Calif., 94707, U.S.A.; and *office* Law School, University of California, Berkeley, Calif., U.S.A.

**FLEMING, Robert Ingersoll,** BA. American. *B.* 1918. *Educ.* Yale Univ. (BA); Oxford Univ.; London Sch. of Economics· *M.* 1942, B. Slayton. *S.* 2. *Career:* Consultant on International Development, Checchi & Co.; Vice-Pres. & Res. Dir. (W. Africa) Mid-America International Development Assoc. Inc., Glore Forgan, Wm. R. Staats & Co., Wm. Blair & Co. Asst. & Public Relations Adviser to Gen. Mans. of Mobil Oil affiliates, Nigeria, Ghana, Sierra Leone & Liberia (1954–58); Dir. W. Africa Program, Rockefeller Bros. Fund (1958–63); Man. Dir. Life Flour Mill Ltd.; Dir. U.S.-Nigeria Foundation; Dir. & First Vice-Pres. African-American Chamber of Commerce; Operation Crossroads—Africa. *Member:* Nigerian-American Chmbr. of Comm.; Nat. Urban League. *Clubs:* Yale of N.Y. *Address:* 45 Livingston St., New Haven, Conn., U.S.A.

**FLEMING, Samuel Milton.** American banker. *B.*1908. *Educ*·, Vanderbilt Univ. (BA 1928). *M.* 1930, Josephi ne Cliffe. *S* Daniel Milton. *Dau.* Joanne Cliffe. Lieut.-Commander. U.S.N.R. 1942–45. *Career:* Director, Third National Bank, Nashville, Tennessee 1950–70; Chmn. 1970–72, Dir. Chmn. 1972–73, Chmn. Trust Board 1973–74; Pres., American Bankers Association 1961–62; Vice-Pres., 1960—; Director, Williamson County Bank, Franklin, Tenn.; Murray Ohio Mfg. Co.; Span-Deck; Seaboard Coast Line Industries; National Life & Accident Insurance Co.; Dir. NLT Corporation; Dir. Ralston Purina Co.; Dir. Nasturtle and Decatin RR; President, Board of Trust, Vanderbilt Univ 1975; Federal Advisory Council 1965–67; Treasurer, Tennessee Hist. Socy. *Trustee:* Battle Ground Academy, Franklin, Nashville. *Clubs:* Belle Meade Country; Richland Country; Cumberland (Nashville); Augusta (Ga.) National Golf; University, Links; Gulfstream Golf. *Address:* 810 Jackson Boulevard, Nashville, Tenn.; and *office* Third National Bank, 170 Fourth Avenue North, Nashville, Tenn., U.S.A.

**FLEMMING, Hon. Hugh John,** PC, LLD, DCL. Canadian. *B.* 1899. *Educ.* Grade and High Sschools. *M.* 1946. Aida Boyer McAnn. *S.* Hugh John and Frederick Gerard. *Career:* Municipal Councillor, Carleton County 1921–35; elected (Progressive Conservative) New Brunswick Legislature 1944; re-elected 1948–52–56–60; sworn in as Premier Oct. 1952. His Government unsuccessful in Provincial election of June 27th, 1960; resigned office July 12th. Resigned seat in New Brunswick Legislature, October 8th 1960, and elected Member of the House of Commons, October 31st 1960. Sworn in as Member of the Privy Council and Minister of Forestry 1960; Re-elected Member of the House of Commons 1962, 1963 and 1965 for the constituency of Victoria-Carleton, New Brunswick; 1968 for newly created constituency Carleton-Charlotte. Minister of Forestry, Government of Canada, 1960–63; Minister of National Revenue 1962–63; Premier of New Brunswick, Canada 1952–60; Minister of Public Works, Province of New Brunswick 1952–58; Minister of Municipal Affairs, Province of New Brunswick 1958–60. Retired from Political Activity 1972. Since 1972: Pres. & Dir. of Flem ming Industries Ltd., North Carleton Land Co. Ltd., Sussex Lumber & Pulpwood Ltd., Carleton Development Co. Ltd., Evandale Lumber & Pulp Ltd., Caldwell Transport Ltd. *Member:* Knights of Pythias and Masonic Lodge. *Address:* Juniper, New Brunswick; 252 Waterloo Row, Fredericton, New Brunswick E3B 1Z3, Canada.

**FLETCHER, Hon. Sir Alan Roy.** Australian. *B.* 1907. *Educ.* State School and Scots College, Warwick. *M.* 1934, Enid Thompson. *S.* Mostyn and Murray. *Daus.* Lyndsey and Jillian. *Career:* Member for Cunningham in the Queensland Legislative Assembly 1953—. Speaker, Qld. Legislative Assembly 1957–60; Minister for Lands, State of Qld. 1960–68; Member Exec. Council 1960—; Minister for Education and Cultural Activities State of Queensland 1968–74 (Retired).; Member, Pittsworth Shire Council (10 years), Chmn. 9 years. Director, Qld. Co-operative Milling Assn. Chmn., Presbyterian Schools Council, Warwick. Pres., Old Boys' Assn., Scots Coll. Member, Australian Country Party (Qld.); Birthday Honours Knighted 1972. *Address:* 'Te Mata', Mount Tyson, via Oakey, Qld. 4356, Australia.

**FLETCHER, Andrew.** American Engineer (executive). *B.* 1895. *Educ.* Yale University (PhBMech. Eng. 1916); Hon. DEng. University of Missouri 1949 and Montana School of Mines 1964; Hon. LLD, St. Francis Xavier University 1953, and Seton Hall University 1957. *M.* 1918, E. Dorothea Camp. *S.* Andrew, Jr. *Daus.* Mrs. Victor G. Balboni and Mrs. Patrick W. Robinson. Shipyard mechanic, Harlan & Hollingsworth, Wilmington, Del. 1916–17; Foreman, Baltimore (Md.) Dry Dock Co. 1917–18; Secretary, W. & A. Fletcher Co., Hoboken, N.J. 1918–24; in charge Fletcher Shipyard 1924–29. Director, Industrial Hygiene Foundation of America; Past President, American Institute of Mining, Metallurgical and Petroleum Engineers; Past President and Trustee, United Engineering Trustees Inc.; Trustee, Engineering Foundation Board; Dir., Amer. Bureau of Metal Statistics: Hon. Member and Director, Amer. Mining Congress (Washington, D.C.); Past Pres. and Dir., Lead Industries Assn.; Dir., Amer. Zinc Inst. Honorary-Chairman, St. Joe Minerals Corp.; Past President & Director, Mine La Motte Corp., Meramec Mining Co. *Member:* Socy. of Naval Architects and Marine Engineers (life member); Yale Engineering Assn.; Holland Lodge No. 8, F. & A.M.; Mining & Metallurgical Socy.; Institute of Metals (London); Australasian Inst. of Mining and Metallurgy. Mayor, Borough of Mendham, N.J.; Pres. & Trustee, Mendham Public Library. *Clubs:* Roxicutus Country; Mining; Yale; University. *Address:* 'Three Fields', Cherry Lane, Mendham, N.J., U.S.A.

**FLETCHER, Cyril Scott.** American management and communications consultant. *B.* 1904. *Educ.* Newington College, Sydney (Australia) and Sydney University (Dipl. Econ. and Com.); Hon. LHD, Southwestern College, Memphis, Tennessee; LittD, University of Akron, Ohio. *M.* 1929, Olga Noreen Brigg. *S.* Douglas. *Daus.* Barbara and Wendy. *Career:* With Studebaker Corporation of Australasia, Sydney, N.S.W. 1926–29; Studebaker Corp., South Bend, Ind. 1929–33 (successively as Special Representative in West Indies, China, Japan, Korea, Philippines; Regional Supervisor, Australasia and S. Africa); General Sales Manager, Studebaker Corp. of Canada, Windsor, Ontario 1934–36, and Studebaker Corporation, South Bend 1937–42. Director, Field Development Committee, Committee for Economic Development, Washington 1942–44 (Exec. Dir., N.Y.C. 1944–46); Trustee, Committee for Economic Development 1946–52; Pres., Encyclopaedia Britannica Films, 1946–51;

member, Board of Editors, Encyclopaedia Britannica, Chicago 1948–51. President, The Fund for Adult Education (established by the Ford Foundation 1951), White Plains, N.Y. 1951–61; financed first 30 Education TV stations in U.S.A.; Director, Fund for Advancement of Education (established by the Ford Foundation) New York City 1951–60; Consultant to the President, Univ. of Miami. Coral Gables, Florida 1961–63; Snr. Consultant, National Association of Educational Broadcasters, Washington D.C. 1964–71. *Member:* Adv. Committee on Commercial Activities of the Foreign Service of the U.S. Depts. of State and Commerce 1944; Dir., Great Books Foundation 1947–49; Natl. Assn. Educational Broadcasters 1965–69; First Actg. Pres., National Educational Television & Radio Center est. and financed by AE fund. 1952 (Dir. 1952–57); Consultant for The Int. Co-operation Admin., Washington in collaboration with the European Productivity Agency, Paris 1954 and 1955; member, Advisory Committee on New Educational Media—Title VII of the National Defence Education Act of 1958–64, Dept. of Health, Education & Welfare, Washington 1958–61; Chmn., Advisory Council on Adult Education of the Board of Regents of the Univ. of the State of New York 1958–61; Chief Exec. Officer, National Educational TV Stations, Wash, D.C. 1964–71; Pres. & chmn. Exec. Cttee., Channel 2, WPBT-TV, Community Television Fdn. of South Florida, Inc. 1969–70, Dir. & Snr. Cnslt. 1970–73; Omicron Delta Kappa; Campaign Dir. Exec. vice-chmn. Martin Co. Citizens, Save Our Beaches Cttee., since 1972. *Publications:* Education for Public Responsibility; Education, The Challenge Ahead. *Clubs:* Izaak Walton League; Stuart; Sailfish; Anglers; The National Audubon Society (all Martin Co., Fla.). *Address:* 25 Sewalls Point Road, Jensen Beach, Florida 33457, U.S.A.

**FLETCHER, Edward Joseph,** MP. British. *B.* 1911. *Educ.* St. Mary's School and Fircroft Coll., Birmingham. *M.* 1946, Constance Lee. *Daus.* 2. *Career:* Trade Union Official, Clerical and Administrative Workers Union 1948–64; Member of Parliament for Darlington since 1964. *Address:* House of Commons, London, S.W.1.

**FLETCHER, James Muir Cameron.** New Zealand. *B.* 1914. *Educ.* Waitaki Boys' High School; Auckland Grammar School; A.C.A. *M.* 1942, Margery Vaughan Gunthorp. *S.* James Roderic, Hugh Alasdair and Angus Gregor. *Career:* Chmn. Man. Dir. Fletcher Holdings Ltd.; Chmn. of Dirs. B.P. New Zealand Ltd.; Marac Finance Ltd.; Pacific Steel Ltd.; Tasman Pulp & Paper Co. Ltd.; Lusteroid Holdings (N.Z.) Ltd.; Dep. Chmn. The South British Insurance Co. Ltd. Dir. Alcan New Zealand Ltd.; Australian Newsprint Mills Holdings Ltd.; Dalgety New Zealand Ltd.; New Zealand United Corp. Ltd. *Member:* Lloyds Register of Shipping, New Zealand Committee; *Clubs:* Northern; Auckland; Auckland Racing; Pakuranga Hunt. *Address:* Apartment 3, 2 Crescent Road, Auckland (Private Bag, Auckland); and *office* Fletcher Holdings Ltd., Private Bag, Auckland.

**FLETCHER, John Callachor,** CBE. Australian. *B.* 1906. *M.* 1930, Eugenie Fahy. *S.* Francis and Gerald. *Dau.* Therese. *Career:* In N.S.W. Public Service since 1922. Joined Rural Bank 1935; Secretary, Rural Reconstruction Board 1948–50; Commissioner, Rural Bank 1960–61. President, Rural Bank of New South Wales 1961–71; Chmn. Totalizator Agency Bd. N.S.W., and Racecourse Devel. Cttee. since 1973. Fellow, Australian Inst. of Management (F.A.I.M.). Dep. Chmn., Prince Henry and Prince of Wales Hospitals (Chmn. 1961–62). *Member:* Past President and Life mem. Bankers' Institute of Australasia; Exec. Bd. mem., Nat. Parks & Wild life Foundation of N.S.W.; Coun. Austr. Opera Auditions council and Tech. Ed. Advisory Council. *Clubs:* Australian Jockey; Bowlers; Coogee Bowling; Randwick Rugby. *Address: office* Totalizator Agency Board, 495 Harris St., Ultimo, Sydney, N.S.W., Australia.

**FLETCHER, John Clarkson.** British engineer. *B.* 11 May 1908. *Educ.* Stonyhurst College (England). *M.* 1934, Maureen Mulock Bentley. *S.* 1. *Dau.* 1. *Career:* Joined Staff of Johnson & Fletcher Ltd., Bulawayo as junior mechanical engineer 1932. Director, Johnson & Fletcher, Ltd.; Dir., Rhodesian Engineering & Steel Construction Co., Ltd.; Pres., Rhodesian Federated Chambers of Commerce 1953–54; Company director, Sims & Hill (Pt.) Ltd.; U.D.C. Rhodesia Ltd.; Keystone Joinery. *Address:* P.O. Box 588, Salisbury, Rhodesia.

**FLETCHER, Leopold Raymond,** MP. Politician, journalist. *B.* 3 Dec. 1921. *M.* 1947, Johanna Klara Elisabeth Ising (*D.* 1973). *Career:* Served (first) Indian Army, (second) British, terminating service BAOR 1941–50; Free Lance Journalist, Lecturer National Council Labour Colleges 1950–58; Worked on Tribune 1958–64; Columnist on The Times, contributor Encounter & New Statesman; Member of Parliament for Ilkeston, Derbyshire since 1964; Chmn. All Party Parly. Airships Group; Secy. Anglo-German Parly. Group *Member:* Inst. Strategic Studies. Council member Airship Association; Former Leader of Brit. Delegations to West European Union and the Council of Europe; Former Vice-Pres. of Parly. Assembly of Council of Europe; Mem., North Atlantic Assembly. *Publications:* £60 a Second on Defence (1963); & various scripts. *Address:* 304 Frobisher House, Dolphin Sq. London S.W.1 and *office* House of Commons, London, S.W.1.

**FLETCHER, Robert Irving.** American. Financial Consultant. Financial Vice-Pres. (1965) & Dir. (1966), Newport News Shipbuilding & Dry Dock Co., Newport News, Va. 1953—. *B.* 1899. *Educ.* Univ. of Pennsylvania (BS Econ. 1921); Certified Public Accountant, N.Y. State 1928. *M.* 1928, Gladys Caroline Ruhberg. *Dau.* Marjorie Ann. Vice-Pres. & Comptroller, Newport News Shipbuilding & Dry Dock Co. 1939–53; Managing Accountant, R. G. Rankin & Co., New York City 1937–38; Comptroller: Long Island Lighting Co., N.Y.C. 1934–36, and Central Hudson Gas & Electric Corp., Poughkeepsie, N.Y. 1929–33; Staff Accountant, Price Waterhouse & Co., New York City 1924–28; Director, Virginia and Peninsula Heart Assns. *Member:* Amer. Inst. Certified Accountants; N.Y. and Virginia Societies of Certified Public Accountants; Financial Executives Institute. *Clubs:* Univ. of Pennsylvania, Engineers (N.Y.C.); James River Country (Newport News). *Address: office* c/o Newport News Shipbuilding & Dry Dock Co., Newport News, Va., U.S.A.

**FLIGHT, Lionel Bruce.** Australian. Sales promotion, public relations and advertising. *B.* 1906. *Educ.* St. Kilda Park School, Melbourne. *M.* 1938, Nancy Golda Davies. *Daus.* Joan Golda and Helen Nancy. *Career:* Sales Director, A'Beckett Auto Sales Pty. Ltd., Melbourne 1930–35; Manager, Delandro Ltd., North Sydney 1935–40; R.A.A.F. Finance Office, Southern Area 1940–46; Asst. Sales Manager 1946–52 and Advertising Manager Rootes (Australia) Ltd. 1952–66. Sales Manager, The Victoria Hotel, Melbourne, Vic., 1967–70; Gen. Mgr. Park Associates Pty. Ltd.; Paget Associates Pty. Ltd. Melbourne 1970–74. *Member:* Australian Assn. of National Advertisers 1954–70; Victorian Chmn. 1958–59. *Clubs:* Journalists; Victoria Amateur Turf; R.A.C.V. *Address:* 840 Toorak Road, Hawthorn, Vic., Australia.

**FLINT, Einar Philip.** American chemist. *B.* 1908. *Educ.* University of Washington (BS); George Washington University (MA), and University of Maryland (PhD). *M.* 1937, Adele Cavanagh. *S.* Robert Bryan and James Federick. Chemist, National Bureau of Standards, Washington, D.C. 1930–44; Manager, Ceramics & Minerals Dept., Armour Research Foundation, Chicago 1944–54; Director of Inorganic Research, Mallinckrodt Chemical Works, St. Louis 1954–55; with Arthur D. Little Inc. 1955–62; Asst. to Pres., Ipsen Industries Inc., Rockford, Ill. 1962–65. Manager, Materials Dept., American Machine & Foundry Co., Alexandria, Va. 1965–66; Staff Metallurgist, U.S. Bureau of Mines, Interior Building, Washington, D.C. 1966–73; Consultant & Freelance Writer since 1973. *Publications:* articles in technical journals on chemistry of portland cement, ceramics, etc. *Member:* American Ceramic Society, American Chemical Society, American Institute of Mining, Metallurgical & Petroleum Engineers, American Soc. for Metals. *Club:* Cosmos. *Address:* 6229 Radcliff Road, Alexandria, Va., U.S.A.

**FLOE, Carl Frederick.** American. Professor of Metallurgy and Consulting Metallurgist; *B.* 1908. *Educ.* Washington State University (BS 1930; MS 1932); Mass. Inst. of Technology (ScD 1935). *M.* 1954, Beverly Brooks. *S.* Charles Pennell and Jonathan Tyndall. *Daus.* Carol Sherry and Joan Proctor. Asst. Prof., University of Notre Dame 1936–39, and at M.I.T. 1939–44; Assoc. Prof. 1944–50; Prof. M.I.T. 1950— (Asst. Provost 1952–56; Asst. Chancellor 1956–57); Administrative Vice-Chancellor 1957–59; Vice-Pres., Research Administration, Massachusetts Institute of Technology, Cambridge, Mass., 1957–72. Fellow, American Academy of Arts and Sciences. *Publications:* contributions to technical societies and journals in field of surface hardening of steel, and heat treatment of steel. *Clubs:* Algonquin (Boston); University (New York); St. Botolph (Boston). *Address:* 40 Howells Road, Belmont 02178, Mass.; and *office* Massachusetts Inst. of Technology, Cambridge 02139, Mass., U.S.A.

**FLOREZ, Genaro Alwin.** American management consultant. *B.* 1907. *Educ.* University of Chicago and Wisconsin (BA). *M.* 1930, Catharine Elizabeth Wood. *S.* Gerard W. and John W. *Dau.* Jean Louise. *Career:* With F. W. Pearson Inc. 1929–31; Jam Handy Organization 1931–33; Plymouth Division, Chrysler Corporation 1933–34; Associated Sales 1934–38; Pres., Visual Training Corp. 1938–42; Pres. and Chmn. of the Bd., Florez Incorporated 1942–71; Florez, Phillips & Clark 1944–48; Founder and Chmn. Florez Consultants since 1971. *Publications:* numerous magazine articles and special texts for company clients. *Address:* 15418 Bowling Green Drive, Sun City, Arizona 85351, U.S.A.

**FLORIAN, Ludwig.** German economist and banker. *B.* 18 Jan. 1900. *Educ.* University of Münster (Dr. rer. pol.). *M.* 1926, Margarethe Faupel. *Dau.* Rosemarie. Served in World War I 1918; General Secretary of various economic and political organizations 1925–35; economic adviser in an industrial undertaking 1935–41, Departmental Director 1941–45; business manager of a chamber of commerce and a departmental director in the Economic Ministry of Land Hesse 1946–47; Administrator and Trustee, Mitteldeutsche Creditbank 1947–52; Vice-Pres. of Police, Frankfurt 1953–65. *Address:* Gartenstrasse 72, Frankfurt-am-Main, Germany.

**FLÖTTMANN, Wilhelm,** Dr Sc (Hon.), PhC, FCS, FIL. German. *B.* 1921. *Educ.* Chemical School in Wiesbaden; State Examination; extra-mural studies, Cologne, Danzig, London and Paris Universities. *M.* 1943, Inge Tinzmann. *S.* Geribert, Holger, Hendrik, Till, Torsten. *Daus.* Berit, Mareile. *Career:* Assistant at Bayer Leverkusen; translator (English, French, Italian, Russian and Spanish) to important drug manufacturers; Court of Honour German Interpreters' Association; Specialist translator (into English & into Italian) in the fields of biochemistry, pharmacology & related subjects; ghost writer for various university professors, consultants & free-lance scientists. Sworn Translator, Chamber of Industry and Commerce, Oct. 1947—. *Publications:* articles on medico-linguistic problems in professional journals (Die Fremdprache, Lebende Sprachen, etc.); translations of medical papers and philosophical essays and books; Saper, Amare, Estetica, Essays on Faith and Morals, Invitation to Pilgramage, Recovery of Faith, Why Smash Atoms ?, Chemotherapy of Malignant Tumours, etc. *Member:* Socy. of German Scientists and Physicians; Assn. of German Translators; Chemical Socy. (London); Inst. of Linguists (London); Socs. de chimie biol. (Paris), Dantesca (Florence), and Alighieri (Rome), Am. Chem. Society (Washington); corresponding mem., World Federation of Scientific Workers. *Address:* 11 Schlüterstrasse, Gütersloh, Germany.

**FLOWER, Desmond John Newman,** MC. Officier, Legion of Honour (France). *B.* 1907. *Educ.* Lancing College and King's College, Cambridge (MA). *M.* (1) 1931, Margaret Cameron Coss (Diss. 1952), and (2) 1952, Anne Elizabeth Smith (Diss. 1972). *S.* Nicholas and David Newman. *Daus.* Susan Elizabeth Cayetana and Caroline Louise. *Career:* Entered Cassell & Co. 1930 (Director 1931, Literary Director 1938, Dep. Chairman 1952, Chairman 1958–71); Pres., Cassell Australia Ltd. 1965–69; Dir., Michael Joseph Ltd. 1962–70; Dir., Folio Society 1948–71; President des Comités d'Alliance Française en Grande Bretagne 1963–72; Editorial consultant, Sheldon Press since 1974. *Publications:* Founder and Editor (with A. J. A. Symons) Book Collectors' Quarterly (1930–34); Complete Poetical Works of Ernest Christopher Dowson (1934); The Pursuit of Poetry (1939); Voltaire's England (1950); History of 5th Bn. Argyll & Sutherland Highlanders (1950); Editor (with James Reeves) The War 1939–45 (1960); Letters of Ernest Dowson (with Henry Maas) 1967; numerous translations from French, Hon D.Litt. University of Caen. *Clubs:* Brooks'; Royal and Ancient (St. Andrews). *Address:* 187 Clarence Gate Gardens, London, N.W.1.

**FLOWER, John Humphrey Kyle.** Australian journalist, *B.* 1921. *Educ.* North Sydney Boys' High School. *M.* 1944. Audrey Ethel Wilson. *S.* 1. *Daus.* 2. *Career:* Associate Nieman Fellow, Harvard Univ. 1952–53; Chief, Reporting Staff, The Sydney Morning Herald 1953–55; London Representative, John Fairfax & Sons Ltd. 1956–59; Advertising Manager, The Sydney Morning Herald 1959–61; Gen. Mgr. Newcastle Morning Herald & Miner's Advocate Pty. Ltd. 1961–65, Circulation Mgr. 1965–70; Chief Circulation Mgr. John Fairfax & Sons Pty. Ltd. since 1970. *Clubs:* Press (London) *Address: office* 235–243 Jones Street, Broadway, Sydney. N.S.W., Australia.

**FLOYD, George C.** American. Vice-President and Assistant to the President, Sharon Steel Corp., Sharon, Pa. *B.* 1904. *Educ.* Univ. of Montana (ABChem. 1927) and Cornell Univ. (PhDChem. 1933). *M.* 1935, Marie Gebel. *S.* James and David. *Dau.* Linda. *Member:* A.I.S.A.; A.S.M.; A.I.M.E. *Clubs:* Duquesne (Pittsburgh); Trumbull Country (Warren, Ohio). *Address:* 2107 Arms Drive, Logan Arms, Girard, Ohio 44420; and *office* Sharon Steel Corporation, Sharon, Pa., U.S.A.

**FOCKE, Arthur E.** Metallurgical engineer. *B.* 1904. *Educ.* The Ohio State University (BMetE; MS; PhD). *M.* (1) 1929, Mona Gale (*D.* 1966). (2) 1968, Janis Lyons. *Career:* Research Metallurgist and Chief Metallurgist, Diamond Chain Co. Inc., Indianapolis, Ind. 1930–51; Manager, Materials Development, Aircraft Nuclear Propulsion Department. General Electric Co., Cincinnati 1951–62. President, A. E. Focke Corp. Prof Emeritus of Metallurgical Engineering. University of Cincinnati. Consultant, Clyde Williams & Co. *Member:* Sigma Xi; Tau Beta Pi; Amer. Socy. for Metals (Pres. 1950); A.I.M.E.; A.S.T.M.; Amer. Nuclear Socy.; The Metals Socy (U.K.); Republican; *Publications:* over 20 technical & professional articles. *Address:* 7799 E. Galbraith Road, Cincinnati, Ohio 45243; and *office* 206 Whitehall, 8041 Hosbrook, Cincinnati, Ohio 45236, U.S.A.

**FOLEY, Milton Joseph,** AB. Canadian. Vice-President and Director, Anglo-Canadian Pulp and Paper Mills Ltd. Director: Brooks-Scanlon Inc. (Bend, Oregon), Suwannee Lumber Manufacturing Co. (Shamrock, Florida). *Clubs:* Royal Quebec Golf, Garrison (Quebec); Vancouver (Vancouver). *Address:* 10–16 Boulevard des Capucins, Quebec 2, P.Q., Canada.

**FOLEY, Thomas John Noel,** CBE. Australian company director. *B.* 1914 *Educ.* Univ. of Queensland (BA, BCom.). *Career:* Chmn. of Dir.: Allied Manufacturing & Trading Industries Ltd. (AMATIL); Director: Bank of N.S.W.; CSR Ltd.; Chmn. of Dir., Courage Breweries Ltd.; Australian United Corp. Ltd. *Address:* 71–79 Macquarie Street, Sydney, N.S.W., Australia.

**FOLGER, John Clifford.** American. *B.* 1896. *Educ.* State College of Washington (BS 1917; MS 1918). *M.* 1929, Mary Kathrine Dulin. *Career:* Chmn. of Board: Folger Nolan Fleming Douglas Inc. (Investment Bankers) 1931—, and Cumberland Trust Co. 1941—. Chmn. of Board: Universal Ball Co., Bingham & Taylor, Piedmont Mortgage Co.; Dir.: International Business Machines, Hilton Hotels Corp., International World Banking Corp. Ltd. (Nassau), Virginia Industries Inc. Ambassador to Belgium 1957–59. *Member* of Board. Washington Cathedral. Bd. of Governors, New York Stock Exchange 1946–49; Chmn., National Republican Finance Cttee. 1955–57 and 1960–61; General Chairman, Washington Community Chest 1940; Chairman, D.C. Chapter American Red Cross 1942 (now Hon. Chmn.); Pres., American Investment Bankers Association of America 1943–45. Member, National Inst. of Social Science, *Clubs:* The Alfalfa, The Brook (N.Y.); Chevy Chase; Metropolitan (Washington, D.C.); 1925 F Street Club (Washington, D.C.); Down Town Association (N.Y.); Pilgrims; Lyford Cay (Nassau); Everglades, Bath & Tennis (Palm Beach). *Address: office* 725 Fifteenth Street, N.W., Washington 5, D.C.

**FOLKERS, Karl A(ugust).** American scientist. *B.* 1906. *Educ.* Universities of Illinois (BS 1928) and Wisconsin (PhD 1931). *M.* 1932, Selma Johnson. *S.* 1. *Career:* Pres., Stanford Research Inst. 1963—; Prof. of Chemistry (by courtesy) Stanford Univ., and lecturer in Vitamin Chemistry, University of California, Berkeley 1963—; Ashbel Smith Professor of Chemistry, Director, Institute for Biomedical Research, University of Texas, 1968—. *Member:* Natl. Acad. Sciences; Amer. Chem. Society; American Socy. of Biological Chemistry; Amer. Assn. Advancement of Science; Chemical Socy. of London, and several others. Alpha Chi Sigma; Phi Lambda Upsilon; Sigma Xi. Member, Cttee of Revision of U.S. Pharmacopeia. *Awards:* American Chemical Socy., Mead Johnson; Harrison-Howe (and Lecturer); Merck Scientific; Julius Stumer Lecture; Spencer; and Perkin Medal, and Presidential Certificate of Merit. Chmn Adv. Council, Dept. of Chemistry, Princeton 1957–64; President, American Chemical Socy. 1962; Hon. DSc. Phila. Coll. of Pharmacy and Science 1962. Post-doctorate Research Fellow in Organic Chemistry, Sterling Lab. at Yale 1931–34; associated with Merck & Co. 1934–63 (various posts in organic, biological and fundamental research; Vice-Pres. for Exploratory Research 1962–63). Honourary member, Societa Italiana di Scienze Farmaceutiche; Int. Robert A. Welch Medal, research on Life Processes 1972. *Publications:* over 400, including Inhibition of Influenza Virus Multiplication by Alkyl Derivatives of Benzimidazole III—Relationship between Inhibitory Activity and Chemical Structure (1953); Determination of Structure of beta, delta-Dihydroxy-beta-methyl-valeric Acid (Mevalonic Acid) (1957); Structure Studies on the Coenzyme Q Group (1958); Biological Studies with Coenzyme Q on Sperm Motility, Animal Nutrition 1961–66; Exploration of Coenzyme Q in Human Medicine 1963–66. Co-recipient Van Meter Prize of the American Thyroid Association for 1969. *Address:* 6406 Mesa Drive, Austin, Texas; and *office* Institute for Biomedical Research, The University of Texas, Austin, Texas 78712, U.S.A.

**FOLLETT, Sir David Henry.** British. *B.* 1907. *Educ.* Rutlish School, Brasenose College, Oxford (MA) and Birkbeck College, London (PhD). *M.* 1932, Helen Alison Wilson. *Career:* Keeper of Department of Electrical Engineering and Communications, Science Museum, London 1957–60; Dir. and Secy. Science Museum, London 1960–73; Governor, Imperial Coll. of Science & Technology 1960–73; Trustee, Imperial War Museum 1960–73; Vice-Pres., Institute of Physics and Physical Socy. 1965–69; Member, Ancient Monuments Board for England 1966–77. *Member:* Inst. of Physics; Royal Inst.; Newcomen Socy. *Publications:* papers in journals of learned societies. *Club:* Athenaeum. *Address:* 3 Elm Bank Gardens, Barnes, London, S.W.13.

**FOLLIS, Ralph Gwin.** *B.* 1902. *Educ.* Princeton Univ. (BSc). *M.* 1929, Opal Ann Young. *S.* James Gwin. *Dau.* Mary Bell. *Career:* With Standard Oil of California: Engineer helper 1924–25; crude still operator 1925–26; specialist research department 1926–27; refinery supt. 1928–32; cracking plant manager 1933–36; manufacturing dept. manager 1937–42; Director 1942–68; Vice-Pres. 1942–45; Pres. 1945–47; Vice-Chmn. 1948–49; Chmn. 1950–68; Former Chairman of the Board, Standard Oil Co. of California. Director: (Emeritus) Crocker National Bank, San Francisco; San Francisco Palace of Fine Arts League. *Trustee:* National Industrial Conference Board; M.H. de Young Memorial Museum; Grace Cathedral; Princeton University (Charter Trustee). Member San Francisco Council of Churches. *Member:* Amer. Petroleum Inst. (Dir.); 25-Year Club Petroleum Industry (Pres. 1955). *Clubs:* Pacific-Union. Bohemian (San Francisco). *Address:* 555 Market Street, San Francisco, Calif. 94105, U.S.A.

**FONER, Philip S.** American professor of History. *B.* 1910. *Educ.* City College of New York (BA 1932) and Columbia Univ. (MA 1933; PhD 1940). *M.* 1939, Roslyn Held. *Daus.* Elizabeth and Laura. *Career:* Instructor of History, Coll. of City of N.Y. 1933–41; Publisher, The Citadel Press 1945–66. Professor of History, Lincoln University, Pennsylvania since 1967. *Member:* Amer. Historical Assn; Socy. of American Historians; Editorial Bd. Journal of Negro Life and History; Phi Beta Kappa: *Award:* Fellow Columbia University. *Publications:* 25 works, including: History of the Labor Movement in the United States; The Complete Writings of Thomas Paine; The Life and Writings of Frederick Douglass; Jack London: American Rebel; Helen Keller; Thomas Jefferson; Abraham Lincoln; Franklin D. Roosevelt; The Bolshevik Revolution; The Jews in American History; The Black Panthers Speak; W.E.B. DuBois Speaks; The Voice of Black America; When Karl Marx Died; American Labor Songs of the 19th Century; Organized Labor & The Black Worker; Labor & The American Revolution; Comments in 1883. *Address:* Lincoln University, Pennsylvania 19352, U.S.A.

**FOOKES, Janet Evelyn,** BA, MP. British. *B.* 1936. *Educ.* Hastings & St. Leonards Ladies Coll. Hastings High School for Girls and Royal Holloway Coll. Univ. of London. Bachelor of Arts (Hon.) Medieval & Modern History Univ. of London. *Career:* Teacher, various Independent Schools 1958–70; Councillor, County Borough of Hastings 1960–61 and 1963–70; Chmn. Hastings Education Cttee. 1967–70; Member of Parliament for Merton and Morden 1970–74; MP for Plymouth, Drake since 1974; Mem. of Select Cttee. on Expend., and chmn. of its Educ. Arts and Home Affairs sub-cttee; Mem. of the Speaker's Panel of Chairmen; Member of Council of RSPCA & National Canine Defence League. *Address:* 11 Branksome Road, St. Leonards-on-Sea, Sussex and *office* House of Commons, London, SW1A 0AA.

**FOOT, Rt. Hon. Sir Dingle Mackintosh,** PC, QC, British barrister-at-law and politician. *B.* 24 Aug. 1905. *Educ.* Bembridge School and Balliol College, Oxford (MA). *M.* 1933, Dorothy Mary Elliston. Called to the English (1930), Ghana (1948), Ceylon (1951), Nigerian (1955), Northern Rhodesian (1956), Sierra Leone (1959), Indian (1960) and Bahrain (1962); Malayan, Southern Rhodesian (1964); Northern Ireland (1969); Bars. MP (Lib.), Dundee 1931–45; (Lab.) Ipswich 1957–70; Parliamentary Secretary, Ministry of Economic Warfare 1940–45; member of British Delegation of United Nations Conference, San Francisco 1945; Chairman of Observer Trust 1953–57. Solicitor-General, Oct. 1964–67. *Address:* 2 Paper Buildings, Temple, London, EC4Y 7ET.

**FOOTS, Sir James (William),** BME. Australian mining engineer. *B.* 1916. *Educ.* Melbourne University (Bachelor of Mining Engineering). *M.* 1939, Thora Hope Thomas. *S.* 1. *Daus.* 2. Chairman; M.I.M. Holdings Ltd. and Mount Isa Mines Ltd., Queensland 1970; Dir. Bank of New South Wales 1971. *President:* Austr. Inst. of Mining and Metallurgy 1974; Austr. Mining Industry CI, 1974 and 1975. *Member:* Senate Univ. of Queensland 1970. *Address:* G.P.O. Box 1433, Brisbane, Australia, 4001.

**FORACE, Joseph Leonard.** Maltese Diplomat. *B.* 1925. *M.* 1948, Frances Troisi. *Daus.* 2. *Career:* Ambassador of the Republic of Malta to People's Republic of China, Democratic People's Republic of Korea, High Commissioner to Australia & Dean of the Diplomatic Corps in Australia. *Decorations:* Knight Grand Cross, Order of St. John of Jerusalem; Knight Grand Cross of Merit, Order of St. Agatha. *Address:* 261 La Perouse Street, Red Hill, Canberra 2603, Australia.

**FORBES, Alexander James,** MC, BA (Hons.), DPhil. (Oxon.). Australian. *B.* 1923. *Educ.* Adelaide Univ. (BA) Hons. and Oxford Univ. (DPhil.). *M.* 1952, Margaret A. Blackburn. *S.* 2. *Daus.* 3. *Career:* Lecturer Univ. of Adelaide 1954–56; Minister of State for the Navy, 1963–64. Minister of State for the Army, 1963–66; Minister of State for Health, Jan. 1966–71, Minister for Immigration 1971–72; Opposition Spokesman on Defence 1973–75. Member Liberal Party. *Club:* Adelaide. *Address:* 77 Church Terrace, Walkerville, S.A. 5081; and *office* A.M.P. Building, 2 King William Street, Adelaide, S.A., 5000, Australia.

**FORBES, Sir Archibald Finlayson,** GBE. British chartered accountant and business executive. *B.* 6 Mar. 1903. *Educ.* Glasgow Univ. *M.* 1943, Angela Ely (*Dec.* 1969). *S.* Alasdair Charles. *Daus.* Angela Clare, Cynthia Rose. Formerly member of firm of Thomson McLintock & Co.; member of various committees and commissions appointed by Min. of Agriculture 1932–39; Dir. of Capital Finance, Air Ministry 1940; Dep. Secy. Ministry of Aircraft Production 1940–43; Controller of Repair, Equipment and Overseas Supplies 1943–45; member, Aircraft Supply Cncl. 1943–45; Chmn., First Iron and Steel Board 1946–49; Pres., F.B.I. 1951–53; Chmn.: Iron and Steel Board 1953–59, The Midland Bank 1964–75 (now Pres.); Pres., Spillers Ltd.; Chmn. Debenture Corp. Ltd. *Address:* 40 Orchard Court, Portman Square, London, W.1.

**FORD, Benjamin Thomas,** MP. *B.* 1925. *Educ.* Elementary & Central School. *M.* 1950, Vera Ada Fawcett. *S.* Anthony and Ivan. *Dau.* Paula. *Career:* Member, Clacton Urban District Council 1959–62; Alderman, Essex County Council 1959–65; Justice of the Peace Essex 1963–67; Member of Parliament for Bradford North since 1964; Vice-Chmn. U.K. Branch, I.P.U.; Chmn. Br.-L-A Joint Parly. Group. Chmn. Anglo-Malaysian, Anglo-Portuguese A. Brazilian, Parly. Group; V-Chmn. Anglo-Argentinian, Venezuelan Parly. Groups; Chmn., Joint Cttee. on Sound Broadcasting. *Clubs:* Royal Automobile. *Address:* House of Commons, London, S.W.1.

**FORD, Frank R.** American journalist. *B.* 1898. *Educ.* Marietta (Ohio) College; Hon. LittD. *M.* 1923, Bernice Perry Brown. *Dau.* Caroline. Editor: Warren (Pa.) Tribune, 1927–28; Evansville (Ind.) Press 1935–51; San Francisco (Cal.) News 1951–56; Editor, Scripps-Howard Newspaper Alliance 1956–59. Chief Editorial Writer, Scripps-Howard Newspapers 1959–66. *Address:* 440 Hesmer Road, Evansville, Ind.; and *office* 777 Fourteenth St., N.W. Washington D.C., U.S.A.

**FORD, Gerald Rudolph.** President of the United States 1974–76. *B.* 1913. *Educ.* Grand Rapids High School; Univ. Michigan, BA (Polit. Science and Economics) 1935; Yale Univ. Law School. *M.* 1948, Elizabeth Bloomer. *S.* 3. *Dau.* 1. *Career:* War Service; Elected to U.S. Congress 1948; member

Appropriations Cttee. 1951; member Select Cttee. on Astronautics and Space Exploration 1957–59; Chmn. Republican Conference 1963; Elected Party Leader (Republican) 1965; Nominated Vice-President United States 1973–74; President of United States 1974–76. *Awards:* Honorary Doctorates from: Univ. of Pennsylvania, Notre Dame Univ., Ohio State Univ., Western Michigan Univ., Grand Valley State Colleges, Univ. of Notre Dame duLac, Univerditatis Dominae Nostrae Laru, North Carolina Central Univ., Chicago State Univ., Univ. of Nebraska, Yale Univ. & many others. *Address:* Post Office Box 927, Rancho Mirage, Ca., U.S.A.

**FORD, Henry II.** American. Chmn. of Board and Chief Exec. Ford Motor Co. *B.* 4 Sept. 1917. *Educ.* Detroit University School; Hotchkiss School, Lakeville, Conn.; Yale University. *M.* (1) 1940, Anne McDonnell (*Div.*). *S.* Edsel Bryant II. *Daus.* Charlotte (Forstmann), Anne (Uzielli). (2) 1965, Maria Cristina Vettore Austin. *Career:* Director, Ford Motor Company since 1938, with Company since 1940; Executive Vice-President 1944, Pres. 1945, Chairman since 1960; co-Chmn. Detroit Renaissance. Member: Business Council. *Address:* Grosse Pointe Farms, Mich., U.S.A.; and *office* The American Road, Dearborn, Michigan, U.S.A.

**FORD, Sir John Archibald,** KCMG, MC, MA. British diplomat. *B.* 1922. *Educ.* St. Michael's Coll. Tenbury; Sedburgh School, Yorks; Oxford University. *M.* 1956, Emaline Burnette. *Daus.* 2. *Career:* Officer, Royal Artillery (Major) 1942–46; Third Secy. British Legation, Budapest 1947–49; Second Secy. Foreign Office 1949–52; Private Secy. to Permanent Under-Secy. Foreign Office 1952–54; H.M. Consul San Francisco 1954–56; Seconded to Treasury 1956–59; Attended Admin. Staff Coll. Henley 1959; Head, Chancery Political Residency Bahrain 1959–61; Asst. Personnel Dept. For. Office 1961–63; Head, Establishment Dept. For. Office 1963–66; Counsellor (Commercial) British Embassy Rome 1966–70; Asst. Under-Secy. Foreign Office 1970–71; H.M. Consul-General, New York, Dir.-General British Trade Development in the U.S.A. 1971–75; British Ambassador in Jakarta since 1975. *Awards:* Knight Companion Order of St. Michael and St. George; Military Cross; MA Oxford University. *Clubs:* Travellers; Farmers. *Address:* Jalan Imam Bonjol 1, Jakarta Indonesia, and *office* Jalan MH, Thamrin 75, Jakarta, Indonesia.

**FORD, John Peter,** CBE. British executive. *B.* 1912. *Educ.* Caius Coll., Cambridge; BA (Hons.) 1934, MA (Cantab.) 1937. *M.* 1939, Phoebe Seys Wood. *S.* Nigel Peter. *Daus.* Penelope Susan (Grenside) and Sandra Claire (McLeod). *Career:* Air Ministry 1939–40; Asst. to Chmn., Coventry Gauge & Tool Co. Ltd. 1941–45; Gen. Mgr., British Engineers Small Tools & Equipment Co. Ltd., and Gen. Mgr., Scientific Exports (Great Britain) Ltd. 1945–49; Managing Director, Brush Export Ltd., Associated British Oil Engines (Export) Ltd., National Oil Engines Export Ltd. and director of other associated companies of the Brush Group 1949–55. Director Associated British Engineering Ltd. and subsidiaries 1957–58; Managing Dir. Coventry Climax International Ltd. 1958–63. Dir. Plessey Overseas Ltd. 1963–70; Dir. Bryant & May (Latin America) Ltd. 1970–73; Chmn. and Man. Dir. International Joint Ventures Ltd. since 1974. *Member:* Council, Inst. of Export 1946–70 (Chmn. 1954–56 and 1965–67); Member of Cncl. London Chamber of Commerce 1951–72; Vice-Pres. since 1972; Pres. Socy. of Commercial Accountants 1970–75; Member B.N.E.C. Cttee. for Exports to Latin America 1964–70; Chmn. 1968–70; Member, London Court of Arbitration, 1970–73; Chmn. British Shippers Council 1972–75, Member, NEDO Cttee, Movement of Exports 1972–75; Member British O'Seas Trade Advisory Council since 1975. *Decorations:* Commander, Order of the British Empire 1969; Order of Rio Branco (Brazil) 1977. Contributor to technical press; Broadcaster on International Trade subjects. CEng, Comp IMechE, CompIMar E, MIEE, FIProd E. *Clubs:* Oxford and Cambridge; City Livery; M.C.C.; Royal Wimbledon: Hawks (Cambridge); London Athletic (Pres. 1964–65). *Address:* 40 Fairacres, Roehampton Lane, London, S.W.15.

**FORD, Richard R.** British. *B.* 1910. *Educ.* Cambridge University (MA). At Conservative Central Office, London, 1933; Odeon Theatres Ltd., 1937; British Information Services, New York, and British Embassy, Washington, D.C., 1939–43; U.N.R.R.A. 1945–47; International Trade, Havana Conference, 1947–48; Head, Information Service General Agreement on Tariffs and Trade (GATT) 1948–70. *Publications:* Children in the Cinema 1938; various articles on international trade. *Address:* c/o Palais des Nations, Geneva, Switzerland.

**FORD, Robert Arthur Douglas.** Canadian Ambassador to the Soviet Union. *B.* 1915. *Educ.* Univ. of Western Ontario (BA; DLitt 1965) and Cornell Univ. (MA). *M.* 1946, Maria Thereza Gomes. *Career:* Entered Canadian Department of External Affairs 1940; 3rd Secy., Legation, Rio 1941; promoted to 2nd Secy. 1944; with United Nations in London 1946; transferred to Moscow 1946–47; to London as 1st Secy. 1948; Ottawa 1949; Chargé d'Affaires, Moscow 1951–54; Head, European Div., Ottawa 1954–57; U.N. Assembly 1956–57; Ambassador to Colombia, March 1957; to Yugoslavia, Jan. 1959; to United Arab Republic May 1961; to Soviet Union since 1964. *Awards:* Hon. DLitt University of Western Ont., 1965; Gold Medal, Professional Institute of Canada; Companion of Order of Canada. *Publications:* A Window on the North (winner of Governor-General's Award for Poetry) 1956; The Solitary City (1969). *Address:* Canadian Embassy, 23, Starokonyushenny Pereulok, Moscow, U.S.S.R.

**FORDE, Rt. Hon. Francis Michael,** PC. Australian politician and diplomat. *B.* 18 July 1890. *Educ.* State School; Christian Brothers College, Toowoomba; School Teacher; Electrical Engineer. *M.* 1925, Veronica C. O'Reilly. *S.* Francis Gerard. *Daus.* Mary Thérèse, Mercia Philomena, Monica Clare; MLA (Lab.), Rockhampton, Queensland 1917–22; MHR (Lab.), Capricornia, Queensland 1922–46; member, Royal Commission on Motion Picture Industry 1927–28; Minister for Trade and Customs 1930–31 and 1932; Acting Minister for Markets and Transport 1930–31; Deputy Leader, Federal Labour Party and of Opposition 1932–41; Deputy Prime Minister, Deputy Leader of Federal Labour Party, and Minister for the Army 1941–46; attended Commonwealth Ministers Conference, London as Deputy Prime Minister March–April 1945; Prime Minister 6–12 July 1945; Acting Prime Minister for periods during 1944–45–46; Leader, Australian Delegation, United Nations Security Conference, San Francisco 1945; High Commissioner to Canada 1946–53; elected to Queensland Parliament as Member for Flinders, March 1955; and 1956–57. Official Representative at furneral of General MacArthur, Norfolk, Va. 11 Apr. 1964. Hon. LLD Ottawa, Laval and Montreal Univs.; Hon. LLD Queensland Univ. 1972. *Address:* 44 Highland Terrace, St. Lucia, Brisbane, Qld. 4067, Australia.

**FORDER, Howard Poulsom.** British industrialist. *B.* 1911. *Educ.* Tonbridge School. *M.* 1938, Cecily Mary Rust. *S.* 1. *Dau.* 1. *Career:* Chmn. Arthur Lee & Sons Ltd.; Gen Manager, Samuel Fox & Co. 1956–64; Joint Man. Dir. United Steel Co. 1965–67; Man. Dir. Special Steel Div. British Steel Corporation 1970–72. *Address:* Gorse Hill, Curbar, Sheffield; and *office* Trubrite Works, Meadowhall, Sheffield.

**FOREMAN, Philip Frank,** CBE, CEng, Hon DSc, FIMechE, FRAeS, FI, ProdE, FBIM, DL. British. Managing Director, Short Brothers Ltd. *B.* 1923. *Educ.* Loughborough College (1st class Hons. Mech. Engineering). *M.* 1971, Margaret Cooke. *Publications:* Papers to Royal Aeronautical Society & Institution of Mechanical Engineers. *Address:* 7 Rushfield, Helens Bay, Co. Down, Northern Ireland; and *office* Queens Island, Belfast, Northern Ireland.

**FORMAN, Howard I,** PhD. American. *B.* 1917. *Educ.* St. Joseph's Coll., Phila. (BSChem. 1937), Temple Univ. (LLB 1944), Univ. of Pennsylvania (MA 1949; PhD 1955). *M.* 1938, Ada Pressman. *S.* Kenneth J. and Harvey R. *Career:* Successively Research Chemist, Patent Attorney, and Chief of Patents Branch, Frankford Arsenal, Philadelphia 1940–56; Lecturer (evenings), Political Science, Temple Univ. 1956–63; Consultant to Chmn., Government Patent Board 1950–55, Patent and Trademark Attorney, Rohm and Haas Co., Philadelphia 1956–76; Dep. Asst. Sec. of Commerce & Dir., Office of Product Standards 1976—. Member of Bar of District of Columbia, Pennsylvania, Court of Customs & Patent Appeals, U.S. Court of Claims and U.S. Supreme Court. Advisor to Asst. Secy. of State for Economic Affairs relative to International Intellectual Property Matters 1968–71; Dir., Patent Law Courses, Engineers' Club of Phila. 1960–64; Chmn., National Council of Patent Law Assoc. 1967–68. Dir. & Sec.: Rohm & Haas Asia Inc. 1973–76, Far East Chemical Services Inc. 1973–76, Rohm & Haas GmbH (Switzerland) 1973–76; Dir., Brilliant International Inc. since 1972, U.S. Pharmaceutical Corp. since 1975, Dir., American National Standards Inst. since 1977. *Publications:* Patents—Their Ownership and Administration by U.S. Government (1957); Inventions, Patents and Related Matters (1958); Patents, Research and Management (Editor) (1961); Law of Chemical, Metallurgical and Pharmaceutical Patents (1967); Chapters on Patent Law in 8 books and more than 40 articles on patent law and related subjects in legal journals. *Member:* Philadephia Patent Law Association (President 1964–65 and 1965–66); American Patent Law Association; Bd. of Managers 1970–72, American Association for Advancement of Science; Amer. Chemical Socy.; Research Socy. of Amer.; American, Federal and Philadephia Bar Assns.; National Lawyers Club; Fellow, Amer. Institute Chemists. Dir., School Board, Lower Moreland Township, Montgomery County 1969–75, & School Board, Eastern Montgomery County Vocational-Technical School 1969–75. *Club:* Somerton (Penna.) Country. *Address:* 1033 Corn Crib Drive (Corner, Windmill Circle) Huntingdon Valley, 19006, Pa.; and *office* U.S. Dept. of Commerce, 14th Street & Constitutional Avenue, Washington, D.C. 20230, U.S.A.

**FORNANDER, Sven Gunde Edvin.** Swedish. Companion, Order of Vasa (Sweden). Technical Director and Genera. Manager, Surahammars Bruks AB 1958–77 (ret'd.); Consultant. *B.* 1913. *Educ.* Royal Institute of Technology (Bergsingeniör); FilDr(hon. causa) Göteborg 1974. *M.* 1939, Marianne von Friedrichs. *Daus.* 3. *Career:* Assistant, Inst. of Metals Research 1939–41; Production Engineer, later Research Engineer, Surahammars Bruks AB 1941–51; Technical Director, Jornkontoret (Swedish Ironmasters' Assn.) 1952–57; Tech. Dir. and Gen. Man. Surahammars Bruks AB since 1958. *Publications:* of articles in Swedish, English and American journals. Fellow, Swedish Acad. of Engineering Sciences 1959; Life Member, Amer. Inst. of Mining & Metallurgical Engineers 1955; Hon. Life Member, Amer. Society of Metals 1955. *Member:* Science Advisory Council of the Government 1962–68; and Jernkontoret's Technical Council 1967—. Member of Board, Swedish National Testing Laboratory 1954–70; Member, Swedish Research Council for Natural Science 1971–77; Iron and Steel Inst.; Verein deutscher Eisenhüttenleute. *Address:* Åsgatan 8, 71060 Grythyttan; and *office* Surahammars Bruks AB, Surahammar, Sweden.

**FORNARI, Giovanni.** Italian diplomat. *B.* 21 May 1903. *M.* 1934, Maretta Arnaldi. *S.* Ranieri, Luca. *Dau.* Maria Cristina (Marquise Litta Modignani); 2nd Lieut., 2nd Regt. of Dragoons 1924; Doctor Juris, Rome Univ. 1925; joined Diplomatic Service 1925; served in France 1926–30, at the Central Admin. 1930–34; Sec. of the Italian Delegation to the League of Nations 1932; First Secretary, Madrid 1934–36, Morocco 1936–38, Athens 1938–40, Foreign Affairs 1941–42; on mission to Turkey 1933; to Yugoslavia 1940; in charge of Italian interests in the Netherlands 1943; Head of Department of the Secretary-General of the Ministry of Foreign Affairs, Rome 1944–45; Chargé d'Affaires, Buenos Aires 1947–48; Amb. Ex. and Plen. to Chile 1948–49; Administrator of Somalia 1950–53; Italian Delegate to the United Nations 1950; Special Representative of Somalia to the Trusteeship Council of the United Nations 1951; Italian Delegate to the Nairobi Conference 1951; Amb. Ex. and Plen. to Brazil 1953–55; to United Arab Republic 1955–61; General Director of Political Affairs, Foreign Office, Rome, May 1961–64; Amb. to France 1964–69; President of Electroconsult (ELC) since 1969; President of Italia Francia Assn. since 1970; *Address:* 1951 via Cassia (Olgiata), Rome, Italy.

**FORREST, Sir James (Alexander).** Australian. *B.* 1905. *Educ.* Caulfield Grammar School and Melbourne University. *M.* 1939, Mary Christina Armit. *S.* Alexander James, William John, and Hugh David. *Career:* Served in R.A.A.F. and Department of Aircraft Production 1942–45. Chairman 1959—, and Director 1950—, The National Bank of Australasia Ltd.; Director, Australian Mutual Provident Society 1961–77 (and Chairman 1957–77, Victorian Branch Bd.); Partner, Hedderwick Fooks & Alston 1933–70; Consultant, 1970–73; Chmn. Chase-N.B.A. Group Ltd., 1969—; Chairman, Alcoa of Australian Ltd. 1970—; Dir., Western Mining Corp. Ltd., 1970—; Chmn. 1953–77, & Dir. 1950, Australian Consolidated Industries Ltd.; member Ctte Royal Children's Hospital Research Foundation; Victoria Law Foundation 1969–75; Member of Council of Monash Univ. 1961–71. Fellow (by special election), Australian Academy of Science 1977. *Clubs:* Melbourne, Australian, Naval & Military (Melbourne), Union (Sydney). *Address:* 11 Russell Street, Toorak, Melbourne; and *office* 19th Floor, A.M.P. Tower, 535 Bourke Street, Melbourne, Vic. 3000.

**FORSTER, Walter Leslie, CBE.** British engineering consultant. *B.* 1903. *Educ.* Leeds University (BSc). *M.* 1936, Lorna Bonstow. *S.* 1. Awarded Legion of Merit (U.S.A.). *Career:* Employed by Royal Dutch-Shell group in Mexico, Venezuela, Rumania, and other countries in various capacities 1925–40; Served in World War II in military and civilian service, mainly in connection with petroleum in the Middle East countries, the Soviet Union, Burma, U.S.A. and elsewhere 1940–46; Colonel in charge of Economic Section, British Mission in Rumania 1944–46; General Manager, Royal Dutch-Shell companies in Colombia 1946–47, and in Venezuela 1947–50. Director: Candiac Development Corp.; Petrofina Canada Ltd.; Gen. Star Ltd. and other companies. *Clubs:* (all of Montreal): University; St. James's; Mount Royal; Montreal. *Address:* 61 Summit Crescent, Westmount, P.Q., Canada.

**FORSYTH, Charles Morris,** BS. American. *B.* 1923. *Educ.* Princeton Univ. (BS (Aeronautical Eng.)). *M.* 1947, Rebecca Lee Ramsey. *S.* 1. *Dau.* 1. *Career:* Exec. Vice Pres. Douglas Aircraft Co.; Assoc. Fellow American Inst. of Aeronautics & Astronautics; Princeton Advisory Council, Dept. of Aerospace & Mechanical Sciences; Princeton Engineering Assoc. *Clubs:* Bel Air Country; Los Angeles. *Address* and *office* Lakewood Blvd., Long Beach, Calif. 90846, U.S.A.

**FORSYTHE, Carl S.** American lawyer. *B.* 1910. *Educ.* Princeton Prep. School; Univ. of Michigan (AB 1932; LLD 1935). *M.* 1936, Virginia Cluff. *S.* Carl S. III. *Awards:* Certificate of Merit, Bronze Star (U.S.); Golden Medal of Vasa (Sweden). *Career:* Associated with O'Connor & Farber, N.Y.C. 1935–37; partner, Townley, Updike & Carter, N.Y.C. 1937–51; Forsythe, McGovern, Pearson & Nash, N.Y. 1951—. Director: Crompton & Knowles Corp., McCorquodale Process Inc., Chemical Enterprises Inc. (Chmn., Vice-Pres. and member Exec. Cttee.), Joseph Steel International Corp., John M. Maris Inc., Peters, Griffin, Woodward Inc. Republican. *Member:* Judge Advocate Generals' Assn.; New York State Bar Assn.; Bar Assn. City of New York; American Bar Assn.; American Legion; Theta Delta Chi; Sigma Delta Chi. *Clubs:* Union League (N.Y.C.); Greenwich Country, Indian Harbor Yacht (both of Greenwich, Conn.). *Address:* Dingletown Road, Greenwich, Conn., U.S.A.

**FORT, Rufus Elijah, Jr.** American insurance executive. and business consultant. *B.* 1910. *Educ.* Virginia Military Inst. (BS 1931); taught mathematics at V.M.I. for one year, 1932. *M.* 1933, Agnes M. Stokes. *Daus.* Mrs. Livingfield More, Mrs. John J. Hooker Jr., Mrs. Terrence Fails, and Louise (Merritt, Jr.). Commenced with Natl. Life & Accident Insurance C9. 1932; successively Leader, next 6 years; Asst. Manager, Orinary Dept. 1938; developed training school and manpower development programme 1947; Asst. Vice-Pres. and Supt. of Agencies, Texas and Pacific Coast 1950; Vice-Pres., Field Research Planning and Development Dept. 1953; Senior Vice-Pres., Selling and Servicing, 1962; Senior Vice-Pres., Special Assignments 1964–66. Member, Bd. of Trustees, Life Underwriters Training Council 1962—. Member Executive Cttee., National Life 1959— (Member, Bd. of Dirs. 1940—); Member of Bd., Tennessee State Retirement System 1949—. Member, A. & S. Cttee., Combination Cos. of LIAMA 1955; Chairman, Combined Cttee. and member of Bd. of LIAMA and Chmn. of Comb. Co. Cttee., American Life Convention. Fourth Service Command Recruiting Officer, Atlanta, Ga. 1940–44. Adjutant-General, State of Tennessee 1945. *Clubs:* Belle Meade Country; The Exchange; Capitol; The Cumberland (all of Nashville, Tenn.); International (Chicago); Capital City (Atlanta, Ga.); Farmington C.; University (N.Y.C.). *Address: office* P.O. Box 2641, Nashville, Tenn. 37219, U.S.A.

**FORTESCUE, Trevor Victor Norman,** BA, MA. British. *B.* 1916. *Educ.* Uppingham School and Kings Coll. Cambridge. *M.* (1) 1939, Margery Stratford. *S.* 2. *Dau.* 1. (2) 1975, Anthea Maureen. *Career:* Colonial Admin. Service Hong Kong 1939–47; Food and Agricultural Organization U.N. Washington D.C. 1947–49; Colonial Admin .Service Kenya 1949–51; Food & Agric. Organization U.N. Rome 1951–54; Chief Mkt. Officer Milk Mkt. Board England & Wales 1954–59; Mgr. Nestle Group of Companies Switzerland 1959–63 & London 1963–66; Member of Parliament for Liverpool Garston 1966–74; Asst. Govt. Whip 1970–71; Lord Commissioner of the Treasury 1971–73; Sec. General, Food and Drink Industries Council since 1973. *Address:* 34 Stanford Row, London W.8.; and *office* 1/2 Castle Lane, London, S.W.1.

**FORTIER, D'Iberville.** Canadian Diplomat. *B.* 1926. *Educ.* Coll. Jean de Brebeuf; Coll. Stanislas—BA; Univ. of Montreal—LSP, LLB; PhD, Paris. *M.* Marie Thérèse Allegret. *S.* 1. *Dau:* 1. *Career:* Called to Quebec Bar 1948; various Govt. positions 1952–58; Dep. Canadian Commander to Int. Comm; for Supervision & Control in Cambodia 1959; Seconded to NATO Secretariat 1961; Head of Press Office, Dept. of External Affairs, Ottawa 1964–68; Chmn., Working

Group, Privy Council Office on Govt. Information 1968–69; Ambassador to Tunisia & Libya 1969; Asst. Under-Sec. of State for External Affairs 1972; Ambassador to Italy since 1976. *Address:* Via della Camillucia 641, 00135 Rome; and *office* Canadian Embassy, Via G.B. de Rossi 27, 00161 Rome, Italy.

**FORTIER, Robert.** Canadian. *B.* 1914. *Educ.* Universities of Ottawa (BA) and Montreal (LLB); QC 1953. *M.* 1954, Monique Salvas. *S.* Claude. *Dau.* Anne-Marie. *Career:* Practised law, 1937–42; private secretary to Minister of Public Works, 1942–53; Private Secy. to Chmn. Canadian Delegation, Economic & Social Council U.N. Geneva 1950; Dept. Secretary, Dept. of Public Works, 1953–66; Director, Administrative Services, Dept. of Public Works, 1966–68; Clerk of the Senate and Clerk of Parliaments, 1968—; Vice-Pres., Assn. of Clerks-at-the-Table, Canada, 1969–70. *Member:* Bar of Quebec; Hull Bar; Quebec Rural Bar Association. *Address:* 9 Hadley Blvd., Hull, Quebec; and *office* The Senate, Parliament Buildings, Ottawa, K1A 0A4, Ontario, Canada.

**FOSTER, Sir Robert (Sidney),** GCMG 1970, KCVO, 1970, KCMG (1964; CMG 1961). KStJ 1968. Officer of the Legion of Honour 1966. *B.* 1913. *Educ.* Eastbourne College and Peterhouse, Cambridge; BA (Hons.) Mechanical Sciences. *M.* 1947, Margaret Walker. *Career:* Cadet, Colonial Service, Nthn. Rhodesia 1936 (District Officer 1938). Released for War Service 1940–43 (2nd N. Rhodesian Regt.; Major). Provincial Commissioner 1957, Secretary, Ministry of Native Affairs 1960, Northern Rhodesia; Chief Secretary, Nyasaland 1961, Deputy Governor 1963; High Commissioner Western Pacific, 1964–68; Governor and Commander in Chief Fiji, 1968–70. Governor General and Commander in Chief Fiji 1970–73. *Clubs:* Leander (Henley-on-Thames). *Address:* Kenwood, 16 Ardnave Crescent, Bassett, Southampton SO1 7FJ.

**FOSTER, Walter Horton.** American. *B.* 1914. *Educ.* Heffley Business School, Brooklyn; American Institute of Banking, N.Y.C.; American Savings & Loan Institute; Alexander Hamilton Institute; Public Relations Course, Syracuse University. *M.* 1936, Ann J. Chianese. *S.* Walter H. Jr. and Arthur L. *Dau.* Claire A. *Career:* Pres., Glen Ridge, N.J. Savings & Loan Assn.; Past Pres., Essex County Savings & Loan League. *Member:* American S/L Institute, United States S/L League, New Jersey S/L League, Essex County S/L League; Past-Pres., Glen Ridge Republican Club. Past-President of Glen Ridge Rotary Club; Past Director, Glen Ridge Taxpayers Association, Glen Ridge Rotary; Senior member, Residential Appraisors; member: Glen Ridge Volunteer Fire Department; Glen Ridge First Aid Squad; Glen Ridge Battalion Forum; Board of Realtors of Glen Ridge, Nutley and Bloomfield. *Publications:* articles in savings and loan periodicals. *Address:* 9 Winsor Place, Glen Ridge, N.J., U.S.A. and 156 Eagle Rock Ave., Roseland, New Jersey 07068, U.S.A.

**FOSTER, William Chapman,** Ret. U.S. Government Official. *B.* 27 April 1897. *Educ.* Massachusetts Institute of Technology. *M.* 1925, Beulah Robinson. *S.* Seymour Robinson. *Career:* With Pressed and Welded Steel Products Co. Inc. 1922–46; resigned as President to become Under-Secretary of Commerce 1946–48; deputy U.S. representative to E.C.A. in Europe 1948–49; Deputy Administrator, E.C.A. 1949–50; Administrator, 1950–51; Deputy Secretary of Defence 1951–53; served in World Wars I Lieut. (Res. Mil. Aviator) and II (Dir., Purchases Div., Army Services Forces and special representative under-secretary on procurement for A.A.F.); Chairman of Board, Porter International Co. (resigned, Sept. 1961). President, Manufacturing Chemists' Association, Inc. 1953–55; Executive Vice-Pres. and Dir., Olin. Mathieson Chemical Corp.; Chmn. Bd. of Dirs., Reaction Motors, Inc., 1955–58; Pres., United Nuclear Corp. 1961. Dir., Detroit Edison Co., National Savings & Trust Co. Pres., Federal City Council, Washington, D.C.; Dir., Atlantic Institute (resigned from latter five posts Sept. 1961). Vice-Pres., Sen. Adviser, Olin Mathieson 1958–61. Director, U.S. Arms Control and Disarmament Agency 1961–69; Chmn. Arms Control Association since 1966. *Awards:* Hon. LLD Syracuse Univ. 1957; DHL (Hon.) Kenyon College 1968: and LLD Hon. at Rutgers Univ. 1968, Bowdoin Univ. 1968 and Yale Univ. 1969. Hon.Dir. of Public Service, George Washington Univ. 1963. *Address:* 3304 R Street, Washington 7, D.C., U.S.A.

**FOSTER, William Frederick John.** Australian. *B.* 1906. *M.* 1931, Mona Daphne Masters. *S.* Peter John. *Dau.* Janice Mary. *Career:* Melbourne Mgr., McIlwraith McEacharn Ltd. 1949–55, Gen. Man. 1955–59; Man. Dir. 1960–70. Director, McIlwraith McEacharn Ltd., Melbourne; Dep. Chmn., The Bellambi Coal Co. Ltd., Sydney. Past Commissioner, Melbourne Harbor Trust; Former mem. of INL Shipping Federation; Joint Maritime Comm., INL Labour Organisation. *Address:* 22 Wanderah Avenue, Avalon, N.S.W. 2170, Australia.

**FOUCHE, Hon. Jacobus Johannes,** DMS. South African. *B.* 1898. *Educ.* Grey College, Bloemfontein; Boys' High School, Paarl; Victoria College, Stellenbosch (now Stellenbosch Univ.) *M.* 1920, Letta Rhoda McDonald. *S.* 1. *Career:* Member of Parliament: for Smithfield, 1941–50; for Bloemfontein West, 1960–68; Administrator, Orange Free State, 1951–59; Minister of Defence, 1959–66; Minister of Agricultural Technical Services and of Water Affairs, 1966–68; State President of the Republic of South Africa 1968–75. *Awards:* Hon. DPhil., Univ. of Stellenbosch, 1966; Hon. Colonel, Regiment President Steyn, Bloemfontein; Decoration Meritorious Service (RSA); Nat. Order of Merit (Paraguay). *Address:* 9 De Jongh Street, Strand, South Africa.

**FOURIE, Bernardus Gerhardus.** South African Diplomat. *B.* 1916. *Educ.* B.Com. (Pretoria); MA (New York). *M.* 1962, Daphne Madeleine Doyle. *S.* 1. *Dau.* 1. *Career:* Dept. of Foreign Affairs; S.A. Legation, Berlin, Stockholm, Brussels, 1938–39, South Africa House, London 1940–47; Mem., South African Perm. Mission to U.N., New York 1947–52; Head Office, Dept. of Foreign Affairs 1952–58; S.A. Perm. Rep. & Amb. to U.N. 1958–62; Sec. for Information 1963–66; Sec. for Foreign Affairs since 1966. *Club:* Pretoria Country Club. *Address:* Department of Foreign Affairs, Union Buildings, Private Bag X141, Pretoria, South Africa.

**FOURNIER, Fernando.** Costa Rican lawyer. *B.* 13 Sept. 1916. *Educ.* Univ. of Costa Rica (Master of Laws) and Harvard Univ. (Master of Laws). *M.* 1945, Virginia Facio. *S.* Fernando, Gaston, Arturo, Marco Vinicio. *Daus.* Virginia and Ivette. *Career:* Civil Attaché, Embassy, Washington 1941–42; member, Drafting Ctte., for new Constitution of Costa Rica 1948; member, Constituent Assembly of Costa Rica 1949; Delegate, 5th Assembly U.N. 1950; Prof. of Legal History, Univ. of Costa Rica since 1947: member, law firm of Facio, Fournier & Cañas, now reorganised as Fournier, Gutierrez & Asociados since 1942; Member, Exec. Cttee. Inter-American Bar Assn.; member Bar of Repub. of Colombia; Vice-Minister of Foreign Relations of Costa Rica 1953–55; Amb. Ex. and Plen. to U.S.A. 1955–56; Pres., Costa Rican Bar Assn. 1960–61; member, Internat. Commission of Jurists 1961—; Pres. Inter. Amer. Bar Assn. 1965–67; member, National Liberation Party. *Address:* P.O. Box 1571, San José, Costa Rica.

**FOWLE, Ernest Percy,** KStJ. South African advocate and notary public. *B.* 29 July 1898. *Educ.* Durban High School and Natal University College (Matriculated, Cape); Advocates' Examination. *M.* 1925, Harriet Mary Wood. *Daus.* 3. Member, Provincial Council, Natal since 1943; Chief Scout, Union of South Africa; Knight of the Order of St. John. Served in S.A. Field Artillery 1916–18; Captain, Senior Cadet Detachment (Durban) 1939–45; Liaison Officer, Civilian Protection Services 1939–45; Member, St. John Ambulance Assocn; United Party (S.A.). *Address:* 209 Main City Building, Longmarket Street, Pietermaritzburg, South Africa.

**FOWLER, Gerald Teasdale.** British Academic & Politician. *B.* 1935. *Educ.* Northampton Grammar Sch.; Lincoln Coll., Oxford (MA); Univ. of Frankfurt-am-Main. *M.* 1968, Julie Marguerite Brining. Lecturer, Hertford & Lincoln Colleges, Oxford 1959–65; Lecturer, Univ. of Lancaster, 1965–66; MP for the Wrekin 1966–70; Parliamentary Sec., Min. of Technology 1967–69; Min. of State, Dept. of Education & Science (D.E.S.) 1969–70; Visiting Prof., Univ. of Strathclyde 1970–74; Asst. Dir., Huddersfield Poly. 1970–72; Prof. of Educational Admin., the Open Univ., 1972–74; M.P. for the Wrekin since 1974; Min. of State, D.E.S., 1974; Min. of State, Privy Council Office 1974–76; Min. of State, D.E.S 1976; Professor Associate, Brunel Univ., 1977. *Member:* Society for the Promotion of Roman Studies; British Educational Admin. Society; Assn. for the Teaching of Social Sciences (Pres.); Assn. for Recurrent Education (Pres.); Assn. for Liberal Education (Pres.); Chmn., Youth Aid Trust. *Publications:* Education in Great Britain & Ireland (with Bell & Little), 1973; Decision-making in British Education (with Morris & Ozga), 1973; & numerous articles, chapters etc. *Address:* 18/36 Buckingham Gate, London, SW1E 6PB.

**FOWLER, Henry Hamill.** Investment Banker. *B.* 1908. *Educ.* Roanoke Coll. (AB 1929) and Yale (LLB 1932; JSD 1933);

LLD Roanoke Coll. 1962; William and Mary Univ. 1966; Wesleyan Univ. 1966. *M.* 1938, Trudye Pamela Hathcote. *Daus.* 2. *Career:* Admitted to Bars of Virginia 1933 and the District of Columbia 1946; Counsel, Tennessee Valley Authority 1933–38; Asst. General Counsel 1939; Special Asst. to Attorney-General and Chief Counsel to Sub-committee of U.S. Senate Committee on Education & Labor 1939–40; Special Counsel to Federal Power Commission 1941; Assistant General Counsel of Office of Production Management 1941, and War Production Board 1942–44; Economic Adviser to U.S. Mission for Economic Affairs, London, England 1944; Special Asst. to Foreign Economic Administrator 1945; Dep. Administrator and Administrator, National Production Authority 1951–52; Administrator, Defense Production Administration 1952–53; Dir. Office of Defense Mobilization, and member of National Security Council 1952–53; Senior member, Fowler, Leva, Hawes & Symington, Washington, D.C. 1946–51, 1953–61, 1964–65. Under-Secretary of the Treasury 1961–64; Secretary of the Treasury, 1965–68; General Partner, Goldman Sachs & Co. (N.Y.C.) since 1969; Dir. Corning Glass Works, U.S. Industries Inc; U.S. & Foreign Securities Corporation; Norfolk & Western Rly. *Member:* Council, Foreign Relations; Pi Kappa Phi; Phi Delta Phi; Trustee Roanoke Coll.; Alfred P. Sloan Foundation; Carnegie Endowment for Peace; Chmn. Institute of International Education; Chmn. Atlantic Council, United States; Councillor, Conference Bd. Democrat. *Awards:* Distinguished Alumni, Tau Kappa Alpha and Roanoke College. *Clubs:* Links, Recess, Pinnacle (N.Y.C.), Metropolitan (Washington), *Address:* 209 South Fairfax Street, Alexandria, Va.; 200 East 66th St., New York, N.Y., and *office* c/o Goldman, Sachs & Co., 55 Broad St., New York, N.Y., U.S.A.

**FOWLER, John Murray.** Australian. *B.* 1928. *Educ.* St. Peter's College, Adelaide. *M.* 1951, Mary Suzanne Marriott. *S.* Nicholas John. *Daus.* Sally Ann and Alexandra Mary. *Career:* Entered radio 1947; Despatch Clerk, Programme Officer, Continuity Manager; Asst. Advertising Manager 1958–60; Manager, The Advertiser Broadcasting Network (5AD-PI-MU-SE) 1960–66. General Manager, Television Broadcasters Ltd. (ADS7) 1966–76 (Dir., 1971–76); Gen. Mgr., Reg Grundy Productions Pty. Ltd. 1976—. Chairman, Organizing Committee, *Carols by Candlelight* 1961–66. *Member:* Management Council, Crippled Children's Assn. of South Australia 1961–66; Chmn. Management Cttee., Somerton Crippled Children's Home 1965–66. *Club:* Commercial Travellers; Royal SA Yacht Squadron. *Address:* 21/3 Mosman Street, Mosmans Bay, N.S.W.; and *office* 448 Pacific Highway, Artarmon, N.S.W., Australia.

**FOWLER, (Peter) Norman.** MP. British Politician. *B.* 1938. *Educ.* Cambridge, MA. *Career:* Staff of The Times 1961–70; Elected Conservative MP Nottingham South 1970–74 (constituency disappeared due to redistr.); PPS Northern Ireland Office 1972–74; MP Sutton Coldfield since 1974. Opposition Spokesman Home Affairs 1974–75; Chief Opposition Spokesman Social Services 1975–76; Chief Opposition Spokesman Transport 1976—. *Member:* National Union of Journalists. *Publications:* political pamphlets including: Cost of Crime (1973) and press articles. *Address:* Grounds Cottage, Ox Leys Road, Wishaw, Sutton Coldfield; and *office* House of Commons, Westminster, London S.W.1.

**FOWLER, Sir Robert William Doughty,** KCMG. *B.* 1914. *Educ.* Queen Elizabeth's Grammar School, Mansfield: and Emmanuel College, Cambridge (BA). *M.* 1939, Margaret MacFarquhar MacLeod. *S.* 1. *Dau.* 1. *Career:* In Burma Civil Service 1937–48; Burma Army 1944–46. Home Civil Service from 1948 and appointed to Commonwealth Relations Office; United Kingdom Mission to United Nations, New York 1950–53; British Deputy High Commissioner in Pakistan 1957–58, Canada 1960–62, Nigeria 1962–64; Imperial Defence College 1959. British High Commissioner to the United Republic of Tanzania Aug. 1964 to break in diplomatic relations Dec. 1965; Diplomatic Service from 1965; Ambassador to Sudan 1966, to break in diplomatic relations June 1967; Gibraltar Referendum Administrator Sept 1967. British Ambassador to Sudan, 1968–70; Panel of Chmn. Civil Service Selection Board 1972. *Club:* Royal Commonwealth Society (London). *Address:* 7 Leicester Close, Henley-on-Thames, Oxon.

**FOX, Abijah Upson.** American investment banker and broker. *B.* 1905. *Educ.* Rutgers Univ. (LittB *cum laude*). *M.* 1935, Isabel Place Sullivan. *S.* Abijah Shawhan and Jarvis Powell. *Dau.* Suzanne Angevine. *Career:* Accountant, Natl. City Bank of N.Y., Tokyo 1926–34: Partner, Swan, Culbertson and Fritz, Shanghai 1934–41; Deputy Director, Foreign Funds Control, U.S. Treasury Department, Washington, D.C. 1941–46; Director, Surplus Property Division, Deputy Director Finance Division, Military Government OMGUS, Frankfurt, Germany 1945–46; Chairman, Mathieson Alkali Works, N.Y. 1946–48; Vice-President, Secretary-Treasurer, Director, American Thread Co., N.Y. 1948–59. Vice-President, Director Hayden, Stone Incorporated New York 1959–72; Connecticut State Legislature Representative, 1968—; Senior Investment Exec. Riter, Pyne Kendall & Hallister 1972; Harris Lipham and Co. since 1973. *Member:* Governor's Advisory Council on Aging 1971–76; Juvenile Justice Comm. 1976—; Comm. to Revise & Recodify the Fiscal Statutes of the State 1977—. *Clubs:* Indian Harbor Yacht. *Address:* 200 North Street, Greenwich, Conn., U.S.A.

**FOX, Benjamin,** BS. Russian. *B.* 1907. *Educ.* Inst. Normale Electrotechnique, Brussels (BS (Elect. Eng.)); Temple Univ. (Plastics Eng.) *Career:* Chmn. Elco Corpn.; Dir. Brant Jewellers, Dir. International Elco (Denmark) Dir. Deutsche Elco, Dir. Interelco of France; Dir Elco Belge; Varelco Ltd.; Board Mem. National Pop Warner Program; Dir. American Technion Socy. *Member:* Advisory Board of Mayor's Science and Technology Council; Socy. of Plastic Engineers; Jewish National Fund of Philadelphia; Mem. American Management Assoc.; American Ordnance Assoc.; Sen. Mem. Inst. of Electrical & Electronics Engineers; Le High Consistory (Mas.); American Defense Preparedness Assn. *Address:* 1475 Hampton Rd., Rydal, Pa. 19046, U.S.A.; & Willow Grove, Pa. 19090, U.S.A.

**FOX, Herbert W.,** Dipl. Ing. German. *B.* 1903. *Educ.* Humanist Grammar School (matriculation); Universities of Halle and Erlangen; Technical University of Berlin (Dipl. Ing.); official training as Inspector of Mines, Bergassessor. *Publications:* Handbook of German Brown Coal (lignite) Mining; The Prussian State Mining Over the Years; various articles in technical journals (Gluckauf, VDI-Zeitschrift, Kali und Steinsalz). *Member:* German Socy. for Mineral Oil Science and Coal Chemistry; Boring Technologists' Assn.; Retired Member of the Board; Wintershall AG, and Burbach-Kaliwerke AG, and of various subsidiary companies of Wintershall AG. Possessor of Grosses Bundesverdienstkreuz. *Clubs:* Lions (Lugano); Reifensteiner Verband E.V.; Christliches Jugenddorfwerk Deutschlands E.V. *Address:* CH 6918 Figino/TI, La Torretta, Switzerland.

**FOX, John Holloway,** OBE. Canadian. Consulting professional engineer. *B.* 1903. *Educ.* Univ. of Toronto (BA Sc Eng. 1927). *M.* 1936, Elizabeth Hunter Walker, *Dau.* Marion. *Career:* Asst. Engineer: C. A. Dunham Co. Ltd. 1927–35, and Minneapolis-Honeywell 1935–39. In Canadian Army: Britain and N.W. Europe (Lt.-Col., Royal Cdn. Elect. & Mech. Engrs.) 1939–46. Honeywell Controls Ltd. 1946–48, former Vice President. Elected Fellow, Amer. Socy. of Heating, Refrigerating and Air Conditioning Engineers 1964. *Member:* Assn. of Professional Engineers of Ontario (Past Pres.); Engineering Inst. of Canada; Inst. of Mechanical Engineers. *Clubs:* Engineers, Royal Canadian Military Inst. (Toronto). *Address: office* Leaside, Toronto 17, Ont., Canada.

**FOX, Kenneth Russell.** American. *B.* 1916. *Educ.* Lowell Textile Inst. (BTE 1938) and MIT (SM Tex. Tech. 1940); Hon. MSc (1951) and Hon. DSc (1954), Lowell Technological Inst.; Scholastic Medal, National Assn. of Cotton Mfrs. 1938; Certificate of Appreciation, Dept. of the Army 1951. *M.* 1941, Eleanor Inez Pihl Fox. *S.* Stephen Russell. *Daus.* Karen Elisabeth (Evans), Linda Pearson (Kugel) and Janet Wilson (Fleming). *Career:* Asst. Prof. in Textile Technology, M.I.T. 1940–45; Pres., Lowell Technological Inst. 1945–50; Vice-Pres. and Assoc. Dir., Fabric Research Laboratories 1942–50; Vice-Pres. and Technical Dir., Burlington Mills Corp. 1950–53. Vice Chmn., Fabric Research Laboratories Inc., Dedham, Mass. 1953–70, Chmn., 1970–73; Vice-Pres., Albany Intern. Corp., Albany N.Y. since 1973; Director, Troy (N.H.) Blanket Mills; Industry Aids to Education Inc. *Member:* Pres. Bd. Member, Lowell Technological Inst. Library Assn. since 1958. Committee on Organic Materials, Materials Advisory Board, National Academy of Sciences, National Research Council 1959–62, and Board of Directors, Lowell Technological InstituteAlumni Association 1953–76; Member and Chmn., Bd. of Trustees, Mass. State Colleges 1966–70; Member, 1966. *Publications:* Application of Rank Correlation to the Development of Testing Methods (with E. R. Schwarz); Effect of Relative Humidity on Load-Elongation Properties of Certain Fibers (with H. Hindman); New Method for Quantitative Determination of Moth Damage to Textile Fibers (with W. J. Hamburger); Study of The Tongue-Tear Test (with C. M.

Krook); The Place of Research in Textile Colleges; Technical Problems of the Textile Industry; Relationship Between Structure of Dyes and Their Dyeing Characteristics in Hydrophobic Fibers; Engineering Aspects of Textile Structures; A New Process of Compacting Textile Materials (with W. J. Hamburger); Survey & Trends in Fabrics and Fabric Processing Machinery. Difficulties with Data (with R. D. Wells); The Development of Stretch Fabrics by Use of the FRL Compactor (with L. N. Backer); Jute—New Visions for an Old Fiber (with F. K. Burr & J. S. Panto); The Role of Research and Development in Modern Management of the Textile Industry; Mechanical Finishing with the F.R.L. Compactor (with T.T. Constantine). *Address:* 107 Marmion Way, Rockport, Mass., U.S.A. and *office* F.R.L., 1000 Providence Highway, Dedham, Mass., U.S.A.

**FOY, Frank James.** Australian. *B.* 1911. *Educ.* North Sydney High School; Fellow, Australian Socy. of Accountants (FASA); Associate, Chartered Inst. of Secretaries (ACIS). *M.* 1936. *Career:* With B.H.P. Co. Ltd., Sydney 1927–45; Executive, Angus & Coote Pty. Ltd., Sydney 1945–49; Victorian Manager, Irish Linen, Spinning & Weaving Co. Pty. Ltd., Melbourne 1949–54. General Secretary, Real Estate & Stock Institute of Victoria 1954–71; Australian Secretary, Real Estate & Stock Institute of Australia 1959–73; and of Australian Chapters International Real Estate Fed. 1964–73; Asia Pacific Real Estate Federation 1971–73; Organisation and Methods Man. Holmes and Stephenson since 1973; Adv. Cttee. for Commonwealth Hostels Limited, 1967–73. *Publications:* Homebuyers. Guide; many property articles. *Member:* Socy. of Assn. Secretaries of Victoria (Pres. 1958–59). Alderman and Public Relations Officer, Mosman Municipal Council, N.S.W. 1946–49 (Deputy Mayor 1948–49). *Club:* Royal Automobile (Victoria). *Address:* 23 Wharton St., Surrey Hills, Vic. 3127; and *office* 505 Lt. Collins St., Melbourne, Vic. 3000, Australia.

**FOY, Frederick Calvert,** American. *B.* 1905. *Educ.* University of California (AB Econ.). *M.* 1929, Elizabeth Hamilton. *S.* Frederick Calvert, Jr. *Daus.* Ann Elizabeth (Gunn) and Sara Virginia (Dixon). *Career:* Asst. Public Relations Manager San Joaquin Light & Power Corp., Fresno, Calif., 1928–30; with J. Walter Thompson Co., San Francisco, 1930–31; Asst. General Manager, Seattle Gas Co. 1931–32; Manager, Los Angeles Office, J. Walter Thompson Co. 1932–33; Advertising Manager, Shell Oil Co. 1933–38; Vice-Pres., Wilding Pictures, 1938–39; Young & Rubicam 1939–42; Vice-Pres., J. Walter Thompson Co., Detroit, 1945–48; Vice-Pres. and Sales Mgr., Koppers Co. Inc. 1948, Chmn. and Pres. 1958–60, Chmn. and Chief Exec. Officer 1960–67; Chmn. 1968–70. *Award:* Legion of Merit (U.S.A.). Republican. *Address:* Star Route, Rector, Pennsylvania 15677, U.S.A.

**FOY, Lewis Wilson.** American. Chmn. and Dir., Bethlehem Steel Corporation. *B.* 1915. *Educ.* Duke, George Washington and Lehigh Universities. *M.* Marjorie Werry. *Daus.* Susan (Heller) and Jane (Karaman). *Career:* Dir., American Iron and Steel Institute, International Iron & Steel Inst., Brinco Ltd., J. P. Morgan & Co. Inc., Morgan Guaranty Trust Co. of N.Y., Fluoruros S.A., Bituminous Coal Operators Association, United Negro College Fund. *Member:* The Business Council; The Newcomen Socy. in North America; The Business Roundtable; The Board of Governors, United Way of America; The Pennsylvania Society. Trustee, Moravian College; Council of the Americas. *Awards:* Moravian Coll. Hon. Dr. Laws 1971; Univ. of Liberia Dr. Civil Laws, 1973; Lenigh Univ. Hon. Dr. Laws 1975. *Clubs:* Saucon Valley Country; Bethlehem; Union League; Sky; The Economic (New York); Laurel Valley Golf; Everglades; Blind Brook; The Links; Rolling Rock; The Presidents; Augusta National Golf. *Address:* The Elms, Saucon Valley Road R.D. 4, Bethlehem, P.A. 18015; and *office* Martin Tower, Bethlehem, Pa. 18016, U.S.A.

**FRAGA-IRIBARNE, Manuel.** Spanish diplomat, Professor and politician. *B.* 1922. *Educ.* Institute of Coruña, Villalba and Lugo; Santiago de Compostela and Madrid Universities. *M.* 1948, Maria del Carmen Estévez. *S.* 2. *Daus.* 3. *Career:* Entered Diplomatic Service, Legal Adviser to the Cortes since 1945 Professor, Political Law at University of Valencia since 1948; Political Science and Constitutional Law, Univ. of Madrid 1953; Secretary-General, Instituto de Cultura Hispánica 1951–55; Prof. of Polit. Science and Constit. Law, Univ. of Madrid since 1953; Secy.-Gen. Ministry Education 1955–61; Director Inst. Political Studies 1961; Minister, Information and Tourism 1961–69; Spanish Ambassador to Court of St James 1973–76; Minister of the Interior 1976 (Resigned); Co-founder Popular Alliance Party, 1976. *Member:* Royal Academy Moral, Political Sciences and Corresponding member, Academies and Societies in Europe and America. *Awards:* Grand Crosses of Isabel la Católica, Mérito Civil, Cisneros, San Raimundo de Panafort, Mérito Militar, Naval, Aeronáutico, El Sol Peru; Holy Sepulchre of Jerusalem (Holy See), Grimaldi (Monaco), many others. *Publications:* various books on Law, Political Science, History, Sociology and one on the British Parliament. *Clubs:* The Athenaeum; Travellers; St. James'. *Address:* Joaqíun Maria López 72, Madrid 15, Spain.

**FRAIN, Frank Lord.** American. Aircraft Corp. advisor, business consultant. *B.* 1912. *Educ.* American Institute of Banking; Harvard Univ. Advanced Management Program. *M.* 1938, Phyllis Thomas. *S.* Lee. *Daus.* Pamela and Marilyn. *Career:* Senior Vice Pres. Dir. Lockheed Aircraft Corp.; Treasurer 1956, Senior Advisor since 1971; Dir. and mem. Investment Cttee. Allendale Mutual Insurance Co., Rhode Island; Dir. and Chmn. Audit Cttee AMCAP Fund Inc. L.A.; Director and Consultant, R & D Associates Ca. *Member:* Financial Executives Inst., Los Angeles, Calif. *Clubs:* Catalina Island Yacht. *Addrss:* 10 Rue Valbonne, Newport Beach, Ca. 92660; and *office* R & D Associates, P.O. Box 9695, Marina del Rey, Ca. 90291, U.S.A.

**FRANCE, Sir Arnold William,** GCB. British. *B.* 1911. *Educ.* Bishop's Stortford College. *M.* 1940, Frances Margaret Linton (née Palmer). *Daus.* 4. *Career:* Third Secretary, H.M. Treasury 1960–63; Deputy Secy., Ministry of Health 1963–64; Permanent Secy. 1964–68; Chmn. Bd. Inland Revenue 1968–73; Chmn. Central Board of Finance, Church of England, since 1973; Chmn., Cttee. of Mgmt. Lingfield Hospital School since 1974; Dir., Pilkington Bros., Rank Organisation, Tube Investments. *Club:* Reform (London). *Address:* Thornton Cottage, Lingfield, Surrey.

**FRANCFORT, Pierre.** French diplomat. *B.* 1908. *M.* 1946, Nadine Labey. *S.* 2. *Dau.* 1. Entered diplomatic service 1934; Secretary Peking 1935–38 and Madrid 1938–39; Counsellor London 1942–48, Moscow 1948–50, Washington 1951–53; Minister to Rumania 1954–57; Private Secretary to the Minister of Foreign Affairs 1957–58; Charge de Mission 1959–61; Ambassador to Hungary 1962–65; to Yugoslavia, 1965–70; Ambassador to Sweden 1970–73; Ministry of Foreign Affairs since 1973. *Address:* 31 Rue de Bellechasse, Paris 7; and Faverolles 28, France.

**FRANCIS, Wilfrid Edwin Robert,** CBE. Australian. *B.* 1899. *Educ.* Grafton High School, Sydney Grammar School, and Univ. of Sydney (BA; LLB). *M.* 1925, Eileen Sylvester McCauley. *S.* Ian Wilfrid and Alan Brian. *Dau.* Valerie Eileen (Perriman). Hon. Secretary, Council of Wesley College, University of Sydney 1932–69; Hon. Solicitor, Sydney Hospital 1948—; Vice-Pres., Hon. Treas. and Pres. (1960–61) Law Council of Australia; Vice-Chairman, Trustees of Sydney Grammar School 1960—. Pres., Incorporated Law Inst. of New South Wales 1954. *Publications:* Summary of New South Wales Companies Act (1961). *Clubs:* Australian, Schools (Sydney). *Address: office* 167 Kent Street, Sydney, N.S.W., Australia.

**FRANCIS, Sir Frank Chalton,** KCB, MA, FSA, FLA, FMA. British Librarian. *B.* 1901. *Educ.* Liverpool Inst., Liverpool and Cambridge Univs. *M.* 1927, Katrina McClennon. *S.* 2. *Dau.* 1. *Career:* Asst. Master, Holyhead Co. School 1925–26; Entered British Museum Library 1926; Secretary 1946–47; Keeper, Dept. of Printed Books 1948–59; Dir. and Principal Librarian, British Museum 1959–68; *President:* Library Assoc. 1965 (Council 1948–59, Chmn. Exec. Cttee. 1954–57); ASLIB 1957–58; Int. Fed. of Library Assocs. 1963–69; Vice-Pres. UNESCO Int. Adv. Cttee. on Bibliography 1954–60. *Chairman:* Circle of State Librarians 1947–50; Int. Cttee. of Library Experts, UN 1948; Council, British Nat. Bibliography 1949–59; Anglo-Swedish Socy. 1964–68; Trustee, Imperial War Museum; Governor, Birkbeck Coll.; Master, Company of Clockmakers 1974. *Member:* Bibliographical Socy. of America; Corresp. Mem., Massachusetts Historical Socy.; Foreign Hon. Mem., American Acad. of Arts and Sciences; Hon. Mem., Kungl. Gustav Adolfs Akademien. Editor, The Library 1936–53; Jt. Ed. Journal of Documentation 1947–68; Adv. Ed. Library Quarterly; Assoc. Ed. Libri. *Awards:* Hon. FLA; Hon. DLit—Trinity College, Dublin, Liverpool, British Columbia, Leeds, Exeter, Oxford, New Brunswick, Wales. *Clubs:* Athenaeum; Royal C'wealth Socy.; Grolier (N.Y.). *Address:* The Vine, Nether Winchendon, Aylesbury, Bucks.

**FRANK, Dr. Paul.** German Diplomat. *B.* 1918. *Educ.* Study of econ. at Zurich (Switzerland); Freiburg (Br.) and Fribourg (Switzerland), Dr. rer. pol. *M.* 1950, Irma Sutter. *S.* 2. *Career*- Joined Federal Foreign Office 1950; Head of Political Dept. 1968; State Secy. 1970; State Secy., Chief of the Office of the President of Federal Republic of Germany since 1974. *Address:* Bundespräsidialant, 53 Bonn, Kaisar-Friedrich-Str 16, F.R.G.

**FRANK, Morton.** American. *B.* 1912. *Educ.* University of Michigan (BA 1933). *M.* (1) 1944, Agnes Dodds (div. 1957); (2) 1963, Elizabeth Welt Pope. *S.* Allan Dodds and Michael Robert. *Dau.* Marilyn Morton. *Career:* Advertising Manager, Braddock Daily News Herald 1933–34; Editor, Asst. Mgr. Braddock (Pa.) Free Press 1934–35; Rotogravure Mgr. The Pittsburgh (Pa.) Press 1936–42; Ensign to Lieutenant, U.S. Naval Reserve 1942–45; Vice-Pres. Business Manager Arizona Times Inc. (Ariz.) 1946; Publisher Canton Economist 1946–58; Stark County Times Canton 1950–58. Lorain (Ohio) Sunday News 1948–49; Strasburg (Ohio) Gazette 1949–50; Salem (Ohio) Farm & Dairy 1951; Pres. and Manager, Tri-Cities Telecasting Inc., Canton, Ohio 1953–61. President and Publisher, Family Weekly magazine since 1966. President, Property Development Co., Canton, 1956–58, and Printype Inc., Canton 1956–58. *Member:* INAE, INPA, ANPA, IPI, NAB, ICMA, SNPA, TDNA, CNPA. Trustee, Alfred University; Chmn., Comm. Corresp. Indep. & Priv. Coll. & Univ. New York State. *Clubs:* Deadline (Pres.); Sigma Delta Chi; Overseas Press; The Players. *Address:* 115 East 67th Street, New York, 10021, N.Y., U.S.A.

**FRANKEL, Sir Otto Herzberg.** Australian. *B.* 1900. *Educ.* DSc (N.Z.); DAg (Berlin). *M.* 1939, Margaret Anderson. *Career:* Geneticist, later Chief Executive Officer, Wheat Research Institute, D.S.I.R., New Zealand 1928–49; Director, Crop Research Div., D.S.I.R., N.Z. 1949–51; Chief, Div. of Plant Industry, C.S.I.R.O., Australia 1951–62; Member of Executive, C.S.I.R.O., Aust. 1962–66; Consultant on Plant Exploration, FAO, Rome 1966. Senior Research Fellow, Division of Plant industry, C.S.I.R.O., July 1966—*Publications:* over 80 scientific papers on genetics, plant breeding, etc. in British, N.Z. and Australian journals. Honours: F.R.S.; F.A.A.; F.R.S.N.Z.; F.W.A.; F.A.I.A.S. *Member:* Australian and N.Z. Genetical Societies, etc.. *Address:* 4 Cobby Street, Canberra, A.C.T. 2601; and *office* Division of Plant Industry, C.S.I.R.O., P.O. Box 1600, Canberra City, A.C.T. 2601, Australia.

**FRANKENHOFF, William Pollner.** American management consultant. *B.* 1925. *Educ.* Phillips Exeter Academy; and Yale College, Yale Univ. (BAEcon. 1945), and Yale Engineering Schl., Yale Univ. (BEMech. Eng. 1945). *M.* 1961, Jill T. Hyland. *Career:* Naval Service 1942–46 (Civil Engineering Corps—service in Philippines; O.C. naval construction battalion). With Stone & Webster Securities Corporation 1946–47; Turck, Hill & Co. (consulting engineers) 1947–50; Vice-President, Davis Filtration Equipment Co. 1950–53. Chmn. William E. Hill & Co. Inc. (Management Consultants, New York, London and Brussels) 1953—. Dir.: Molson Industries Ltd., William E. Hill & Co. Inc., Dexter Corp., and Weil-McLain Co., Roanwell Corp.; Trustee St. Vincent's Hospital. *Member:* American Management Association; Speaker before various business and professional associations, and contributor of articles to technical and trade journals. *Address: office* 640 Fifth Avenue, New York City 10019, U.S.A.

**FRÄNKL, Dr. jur. Otto.** Swiss. *B.* 1897. *Educ.* Univ. of Vienna. *M.* 1936, Nora Lundborg. *S.* 2. *Dau.* 1. President of Weleda Ltd. 1958–70. *Publications:* Fifteen books. *Member:* General Anthroposophical Society; PEN Club. *Address:* CH 4143, Dornach, Larchenweg 3, Switzerland.

**FRANKLIN, Henry,** OBE. *B.* 1906. *Educ.* Exeter College, Oxford (BA Oxon.) and Lincoln's Inn (London); Barrister-at-Law. *M.* 1928, Hilda Margaret Hadfield. *S.* Henry Clive. *Dau.* Tonia Margaret. *Career:* Colonial Service 1928–51 (Inspector of Education, District Officer, District Commissioner, Resident Magistrate. Asst. Secy. Native Affairs, Director of Information and Broadcasting Services); War Correspondent 1943–45; Radio Development Adviser to British Ever-Ready (Berec) 1951–54. Minister of Education and Social Services 1954–59, and of Transport & Works, Northern Rhodesian Government Mar. 1961–62. Later journalist, playwright, and farmer. *Publications:* Ignorance is No Defence; 'Crash': Don't Go To Centa; Unholy Wedlock; The Flag Wagger. *Address:* Warren House, Warren Lane, Froxfield, Petersfield, Hants.

**FRANKS, Lord** (Oliver Shewell Franks), PC, GCMG, FBA, KCB, OM, CBE (baron 1962, U.K. life peer). *B.* 16 Feb. 1905. *Educ.* Queen's College, Oxford (MA). *M.* 1931, Barbara M. Tanner. *Daus.* 2. *Career:* Fellow and Lecturer, Queen's College, Oxford 1927–37, Provost 1946–48, Hon. Fellow 1948; Professor of Moral Philosophy, Glasgow Univ. 1937–45; entered Ministry of Supply 1939, Permanent Secy. 1945–46; Amb. Ex. and Plen. to U.S.A. 1948–52; Chairman, Lloyds Bank Ltd., London 1954–62; Chmn., Friends' Provident & Century Life Office 1955–62; Provost of Worcester College, Oxford 1962–76. Member, Nat. Economic Development Council 1962–64; Trustee, Rockefeller Foundation 1961–70; Chmn. Cttee. Official Secrets Act, Section 2 1971–72. *Address:* Blackhall Farm, Charlbury Road, Oxford OX2 6UU.

**FRASER, Sir Douglas Were,** ISO. Adviser on Civil Defence Activities, Queensland. *B.* 1899. *Educ.* State High School, Gympie, Qld.; *M.* 1927, Violet Pryke. *S.* 3. *Career:* Secy. to Qld. State Public Service Commr. 1939; Snr. Public Service Inspector 1947; Deputy Public Service Commr. 1952, Commissioner 1956–65. War-time Asst. Dir. of Civil Defence and Secy. to Public Safety Adv. President, Queensland Ambulance Transport Brigade 1967—; Chmn. Council Queensland Conservatorium 1971—; Dir. Civil Defence since 1973. *Member:* Qld. Univ. Senate since 1967; Associate in Accountancy, Univ. of Qld. (AAUQ). *Fellow:* Aust. Socy. of Accountants (FASA), Royal Inst. of Public Administration (FRIPA), Aust. Inst. of Management (FAIM) and Inst. of Civil Defence (FICD). *Address:* 76 Prince Edward Parade, Redcliffe, Qld., Australia, 4020.

**FRASER, Hon. Hugh Charles Patrick Joseph,** MBE, PC, MP *B.* 1918. *Educ.* Ampleforth; Balliol Coll., Oxford; Sorbonne. *M.* 1956, Lady Antonia Pakenham; *Career:* Served in World War II (Lovat Scouts, Phantom and Special Air Service). Ex-President Oxford Union; Member, Parliament (Con.) Stone Division 1945, Stafford & Stone Division 1950—; Parliamentary Private Secretary to Secretary of State for the Colonies 1951–54; Under Secy. of State & Financial Secy. War Office 1958; Parly. Under Secy. State for Colonies 1960; Secy. of State for Air 1962–64; Member of Privy Council, 1962. *Awards:* Order of Orange Nassau, Order of Leopold with palm, Croix de Guerre (Belgium)l *Clubs:* White's. *Address:* 52 Campden Hill Square, London, W.8; and Eilean Aigas, Beauly, Inverness-shire.

**FRASER, John Denis,** MP. British solicitor. *B.* 1934. *Educ.* London Univ. (Matriculation); Coll. of Law, Solicitor (Hons.). *M.* 1960, Ann. *S.* Mark and Andrew. *Dau.* Sarah Ann. *Career:* Councillor Borough of Lambeth 1962–68; Member of Parliament for Norwood since 1966; Parly. Private Secy. Dept. of Employment and Productivity 1968–70; PPS to Rt. Hon. Barbara Castle 1970–71; Opposition spokesman on Home Affairs 1972–74; Under-Secy. State, Dept. of Employment 1974–76; Minister of State, Dept. of Prices & Consumer Protection 1976—. *Member:* Law Society. *Address:* 44 Pymers Mead, London, S.E.21.

**FRASER, Rt. Hon. John Malcolm,** CH, MP. Australian Prime Minister. *B.* 1930. *Educ.* Melbourne Grammar School and Oxford (MA Oxon.). *M.* 1956, Tamara Margaret Beggs. *S.* John Mark and Hugh Neville. *Daus.* Angela and Phoebe. *Career:* Member of Parliament for Wannon (Victoria) since 1955. Member: Joint Parliamentary Cttee. on Foreign Affairs Mar. 1962–Jan. 1966; and Council of Australian National Univ. Mar. 1964–Jan. 1966; Minister of State for the Army 1966–68; Minister for Education & Science 1968–69; Minister of State for Defence, 1969–71; Minister of State for Education and Science 1971–72; Opposition spokesman, Primary Industry Jan–Aug. 73; Labour & Immigration 1973–75; Leader of Opposition then Prime Minister since 1975. *Member:* Australian Inst. of Agriculture Science; and Australian Inst. of Political Science. Member Liberal Party of Australia. *Club:* Melbourne. *Address:* Nareen, Vic.; and Parliament House, Canberra, A.C.T., Australia.

**FRASER, Sir Robert Brown,** OBE. British television administrator. *B.* 26 Sept. 1904. *Educ.* St. Peter's School, Adelaide; Trinity College, University of Melbourne (BA); London University (BScEcon). *M.* 1931, Betty Harris. *Dau.* 1. *Career:* Leader Writer, Daily Herald 1930–39; entered Empire Division, Ministry of Information 1939, Director of Publications Division 1941, Controller of Production 1945–46; Director-General, Central Office of Information 1946–54;

Director-General, Independent Television Authority 1954–70; Chmn. Independent Television News 1971–74. Hon. Fellow London School of Econ. 1965. *Club:* Athenaeum. *Address:* Flat 5M, Portman Mansions, Chiltern Street, London, W.1.

**FRAZIER, John Earl.** American professional mechanical and ceramic engineer. *B.* 1902. *Educ.* Washington and Jefferson College (BSc), (Life member of Bd. of Trustees of the College); Massachusetts Institute of Technology (SM) and University of Brazil (ScD). *M.* Frances Sprague Lang 1936. *S.* John Earl II and Thomas Gibson. *Career:* Chief Chemist and Engr., Owens-Illinois Glass Co., 1924–26; Fuel Engr., Simplex Engineering Co., 1926–28; Asst. Secy. and Asst. Treas. 1928–30, Secy. and Treas., 1930–38; Vice-Pres. and Treas., Frazier-Simplex Inc. 1938–45; Pres. and Treas., Frazier-Simplex, Inc. (Washington, Pa.) 1945—; Vice-Pres., Asst. Secy. of Bd. of Trustees, Washington & Jefferson Coll.; Past Member Adv. Bd. Dept. Ceramic Engineering, Univ. of Illinois; Pres. and Dir., Washington Union Trust Co.; 1960–62. Member Advisory Bd., Pittsburgh Natl. Bank. Secy. and mem., Washington City Planning Commn. 1950–61. Pres.; Washington City Chamber of Commerce 1950; Washington Lions Club 1932–33; Fortnightly Literary Club 1961–64 (Estab. 1884); Pennsylvania Ceramics Assn. (now Dir.); Life-Member N.Y. Academy of Sciences, Charter Member Pa. Inst. of Chemists; Washington County Motor Club 1958–62 (now Dir.); Executive Club 1950. Trustee and Secy., Washington City Hospital 1937—. Pres. & Trustee, Penn. Western State School and Hospital 1963–73. Dir., United Fund (Washington Community Chest) 1962. Mem. Adv. Bd. Culver Fathers Assn.; Culver Military Acad. (Culver, Indiana) 1959–61. (Chmn., Orton Memorial Cttee. A.Cer.S. 1968. *Fellow:* Royal Socy. of Arts (Hon. Benjamin Franklin); Amer. Assn. for Advancement of Science; Socy. of Glass Technology of England; Amer. Ceramic Socy. (Vice-Pres. 1967–68, Treasurer 1968–69, Pres. Elect 1969–70), Pres. 1970–71. *Member:* Amer. Socy. of Test Materials; Nat. Inst. of Ceramic Engrs.; N.I.C.E. Judge of P.A.C.E. Award for 1962; Past Chmn. Glass Industry Board; Phi Beta Kappa; Phi Chi Mu; Sigma Xi; Keramos Library at Pennsylvania State Univ. (Col. of Mineral Industries), Dept. of Ceramic Science (named Frazier-Keramos Library as honour); Druids; Masons; Shrine; Jesters; Amer. Legion; Newcomen Socy. of N. America; Pennsylvania & New York Acad. of Science. *Awards:* Kappa Sigma Fraternity Man of the Year 1964 (Distinguished Alumni Award 1962); Distinguished Citizen Award by Washington and Pennsylvania City Cncl. 1960; Achievement Citation (Engineering), Washington and Jefferson College 1953; elected to Greaves-Walker Roll of Honour, Keramos Fraternity 1967; Washington, Pa. Lion of the Year 1970; Wisdom Award of Honour Wisdom Socy. 1970; Knight of Saint Patrick Alfred 1971; Phoenix Award Com. 1974–77; A.V. Bleininger Award 1969; John Jeppson Award 1976. *Publications:* contributions to Colliers National Encyclopaedia; Glass Sand and A Glass Industry (co-author) in Puerto Rico; contributions to Venezuelan Government, Amer. Ceramic Socy., Amer. Mining and Metallurgical Engineers and Alfred (N.Y.) Univ. publications. Republican. *Clubs:* Bassett (Wash., Pa.); Chemists (N.Y.C.); M.I.T. (N.Y.C.); Century. *Address:* President, Frazier-Simplex Inc., P.O. Box 493, Washington, Pa., 15301, U.S.A.

**FREDE, Karl, Dr.** utr. jur. German. *B.* 1903. *Educ.* Univ. of Freiburg (Dr. utr. jut. 1927). *M.* 1938, Mathilde Goebel. *Dau.* Eva. *Career:* Officer of the Reichsbank 1924— (Dir. polit. econ. Dept., Berlin 1943); Member, Management Board, Landeszentralbank für Württemberg und Hohenzollern, Reutlingen 1948–53, and Landeszentral bank von Baden-Würtemberg, Stuttgart 1953–57 (Vice-Pres. 1958—). Member Management Board, Stuttgart Exchange 1956—. *Address:* and *office* Marstallstrasse 3, Stuttgart, Germany.

**FREDGA, Prof. Arne.** Swedish professor of organic chemistry. *B.* 18 July 1902. *Educ.* BSc 1924; DSc 1935. *M* .1931, Märta Brita Öhlin. *S.* Sven, Karl, *Daus.* Kerstin, Märta. Assistant at the Chemical Institute, Uppsala University 1930–35; Assistant Professor 1935–39; Professor 1939–69; Member, Nobel Committee of Chemistry 1944–75; Pres. 1972–75; National Science Research Council 1952–54; President, Swedish History of Science Society, 1968—; Trustees, Nobel Foundation 1972–75; K.N.O. *Publications:* about 180 papers in organic chemistry and the history of chemistry. *Address:* Börjegatan 3A Uppsala, Sweden.

**FREEDMAN, Hon. Chief Justice Samuel.** Judge of the Court of Appeal, Mar. 1960—. *B.* 1908. *Educ.* BA (Hon) 1929, University of Manitoba, Manitoba Law School LLB; Hon. LLD Univ. of Windsor (Ont.), Hebrew Univ. of Jerusalem, N. Dakota State Univ., Univ. of Toronto, Univ. of Manitoba, McGill Univ., Brock Univ. and Queen's Univ.; Hon DCnL St. John's Coll., Winnipeg. *M.* 1934, Claris Brownie Udow. *S.* Martin Herbert. *Daus.* Susan Ruth and Phyllis Claire. *Career:* Called to Bar of Manitoba 1933; member of law firm of Steinkopf, Lawrence & Freedman 1935–45, and of Freedman & Golden 1946–52; appointed K.C. Dec. 1944; Lecturer at Manitoba Law School 1941–58; Chancellor of Univ. of Manitoba 1959–68; President, Manitoba Bar Assn. 1952; Judge of the Court of Queen's Bench for Manitoba 1952–60. Bencher of the Law Socy. of Manitoba 1949–52; Chmn., Winnipeg Branch of the Canadian Institute of International Affairs, 1947–48; Hon. President, University of Manitoba Student's Union, 1949–50; member, Board of Governors, The Hebrew University, Jerusalem, since 1955; Co-chairman, Central Division, Canadian Council of Christians and Jews 1955–59; Chairman, The Manitoba Heart Foundation, 1957–58. Served as one-man Industrial Inquiry Commission on Canadian National Railways run-through problem 1965. *Awards:* Hon LLD Dalhousie Univ. York Univ. 1971; Hon. LLD Trent Univ. 1972; Univ. of Western Ontario 1973; William Mitchell Coll. of Law 1973; Appointed Chief Justice of Manitoba 1971. *Publications:* occasional contributions to Canadian Bar Review and Manitoba Bar News (editor of the latter 1942–46). *Address:* 425 Cordova Street, Winnipeg; and *office* Judges Chambers Court House, Winnipeg, Man., Canada.

**FREEMAN, Sir Bernard,** CBE. Australian executive. *B.* 1896. *M.* 1926, Marjorie Arabel Bloom. *S.* Geoffrey John. *Dau.* Pamela Evelyn. *Career:* Established Metro-Goldwyn-Mayer in Australia, New Zealand and South Pacific in 1925; Managing Director 1925–66; Chairman, 1967—. Member, Lord Mayor's Comforts Fund 1939–45; and Administrator of the British Centre 1945; Chairman: Anzac House Appeal 1944–45, and Anzac House Trust 1946—; N.S.W. Chairman, the Miss Australia Quest 1948–49; Nat. Chairman, UNICEF 1952; Chairman, World Refugee Year Appeal of N.S.W. 1960; President, Rotary Club of Sydney 1960–61; Chmn., Universities Internat. Houses Appeal 1962, and of N.S.W. and Canberra Anzac Memorial and Forest in Israel. World War I, A.I.F. and Australian Flying Corps. Member, Exec. Cttee., Sydney Opera House Trust, Bds. of Mgment., Int. Houses Univ. of Sydney and N.S.W. Life member, N.S.W. State Branch, Returned Services League of Australia. Life Govr.: Royal N.S.W. Inst. for Deaf and Blind Children; Vic. Ear and Eye Hosp.; Vic. School for Deaf Children. *Clubs:* Aust. Flying Corps. Assn.; Rotary (Sydney); American National; City Bowling; *Address:* The Penthouse, 'Santina', 85 Yarranabbe Road, Darling Point, N.S.W., Australia.

**FREEMAN, Douglas Haig,** CBE. Australian. *B.* 1917. *Educ.* Sydney Univ. (BSc Hons 1 1938), and Univ. of New Zealand (MSc 1941). *M.* 1940, Joyce Gwenyth Hosking. *S.* Murray Douglas. *Daus.* Marilyn Joy, Diana Louise, and Kathryn Alexandra. *Career:* Managing Director, Union Carbide Australia Ltd., since 1961 Regional Director, Union Carbide Eastern Inc. since 1966; Managing Dir., Union Carbide Australia and New Zealand Ltd. since 1969. Chairman, Export Development Council; Chemical Industry Advisory Council; since 1969; Dir. Australian Industry Development Corp. since 1971; Past. Pres., Australian Chemical Industry Council. *Clubs:* Royal Sydney Yacht Sqdn.; Amer. National; Avondale Golf, Commonwealth. *Address: office* Union Carbide Australia and New Zealand Ltd., 167–187 Kent Street, Sydney, N.S.W. 2001, Australia.

**FREEMAN, Rt. Hon. John,** PC, MBE. British. *B.* 1915. *Educ.* Westminster School and Brasenose College, Oxford (MA). *M.* 1961. *S.* Matthew John Aylmer and Thomas Alexander. *Daus.* Lucy Catherine and Elizabeth Margaret Melville (adopted). *Career:* Financial Secy. War Office 1946–47, and Parly. Under-Secy. of State 1947–48; Parly. Sec. Ministry of Supply 1948–51; Asst. Editor, New Statesman 1951–55, Deputy Editor 1955–61, Editor 1961–65; British High Commissioner in India 1965–68. Ambassador to the U.S.A. 1969–71; Chmn. London Weekend Television Ltd. since 1971; Chmn., Independent Television News since 1976. Member H.M. Privy Council, and of the Order of the British Empire (Mil. Div.); Croix de Guerre, Member National Union of Journalists. *Address:* c/o Barclays Bank, 58 Southampton Row, London, W.C.1.

**FREEMAN, Capt. Spencer,** CBE. British consulting business engineer. *B.* 1892. *Educ.* Johannesburg College (Scholarship) and Technical Inst., York. Pa., U.S.A. *M.* 1924, Hilda Kathleen Toler. *S.* Brian Sidney. *Career:* In automotive industry, U.S.A.; Pullman Motor Car Co., York, Pa. and Chalmers Motor Corp., Detroit 1910–14; in British Army (held every non-commissioned rank, finally promoted to Capt.); responsible for salvage and repair work of all automotive parts and components used by British Army in France 1914–19; Principal Director, Regional and Emergency Services Organization, Ministry of Aircraft Production (responsible for restoration of production following enemy action or other causes, such as fire, etc., in all factories engaged in manufacturing munitions 1940–45); Business mem. Industrial & Export Council 1944–45; mem. Radio Board (a cttee. of British War Cabinet); mem. Radio Planning & Production Cttee., Radio Production Executive; seconded to Board of Trade to assist reconversion of industry to peacetime production 1945–46; Executive Director, Hospitals Trust Ltd. Dublin. *Awards:* Commander, Order of the British Empire 1942; Mons Star; Mentioned in Dispatches (W. War I). *Member:* Socy. of Automotive Engineers (U.S.A.); Liveryman of the Company of Newspaper Makers and Stationers (London, England). *Publications:* Production Under Fire (Fallon, Dublin); Take Your Measure; You Can Get to The Top. *Clubs:* Naval & Military (London); Kildare St. & University (Dublin). *Address:* Knocklyon House, Templeogue, Dublin 14; and *office:* Hospitals Buildings, Ballsbridge, Dublin, Ireland.

**FREEMAN, William Miser,** BA, AMP. American. *B.* 1919. *Educ.* Dartmouth Coll. (BA); Harvard Business Sch. (AMP). *M.* 1941, Winifred C. Stevens. *S.* 1. *Daus.* 2. *Career:* Dir. Standard of America Financial Co., Gary-Wheaton Bank (Chmn. of the Board), Horton Steel Works; Dist. Man. N.Y. Contracting Office, Chicago Bridge Iron Co. 1960–64; Vice-Pres. International 1964–67, Vice-Pres. Sales 1967–70, Chicago Bridge Iron Co. Sen. Vice-Pres. Finance and Treasurer since 1970; Dir. Uarco, Inc. *Member:* Chicago Commonwealth Club. *Club:* Hinscale Golf. *Address:* 219 E. 7th St., Hinsdale, Ill. 60521, U.S.A.; and *office* 800 Jorie Blvd., Oak Brook, Ill. 60521.

**FREESE, Carl Gates.** American savings banker. *B.* 1892. *Educ.* Harvard Coll. (AB 1915). *M.* 1924, Dorothy Helen Clapp. *S.* Carl Gates, Jr., MD. *Dau.* Mrs. Boardman Brown. *Career:* Represented Southern Railway in Argentina 1914; American Ambulance with French Army (Croix de Guerre) 1917–18; American Commission to Negotiate Peace, Paris 1919; Investment Banker, R. L. Day & Co. (Partner 1928–43) 1920–43; Vice-Pres., Connecticut Savings Bank 1944–48, Pres. 1948–63; Senior Trustee since 1963; Chairman, Committee on Government Securities & Public Debt 1957–63; Director: First New Haven National Bank 1944–66; Southern New England Telephone Co. 1957–65; Security Insurance Co. 1950–69; Articles in banking magazines, and on urban redevelopment. *Member:* Newcomen Society of England; Society of Colonial Wars. *Clubs:* Harvard (N.Y.C.); New Haven Lawn; Kiwanis; Graduates. *Address: office* 47 Church Street, New Haven, Conn., U.S.A.

**FREETH, Hon. Gordon,** LLB. Australian diplomat. *B.* 1914. *Educ.* Church of England Grammar School (Sydney), Guildford Grammar School, University of W.A. *M.* 1939, Joan C. Baker. *S.* 1. *Daus.* 2. *Career:* Barrister and Solicitor, W.A. 1938. Rowed for Australia in British Empire Games, Sydney 1938. Served in World War II (Pilot R.A.A.F.) 1942–45. M.H.R. for Forrest, W.A. 1949–69; Minister for Interior and Works, Commonwealth of Australia 1958–63; Minister for Shipping and Transport 1963–68; Minister Assisting the Attorney-Gen. 1962–64; Minister for Air, Min. Assisting the Treasurer 1968; Min. External Affairs 1969; Australian Ambassador to Japan 1970–73; practiced law in Perth, W.A. 1973–77; High Commissioner for Australia in London since April 1977. *Address:* Australian High Commission, Australia House, Strand, London WC2.

**FREI MONTALVA, Eduardo.** *B.* Jan. 1911. *Educ.* Catholic University of Chile and became a lawyer. *Career:* Was for a few years Professor at this University and at Elvira Matte de Cruchaga College. Elected Senator for Atacama and Coquimbo 1949, and for Santiago 1957. Has occupied the posts of Minister of Public Works, and of Transport and Communications; was also Senate Representative to the Council of Social Services and National Insurance. Was sent to Europe as Secretary-General of the Ibero-American Congress in Rome 1933–34. Former member Exec. Committee of Conservative Youth; one time Pres. of the organization and of the National Falange. President of Chile, Sept. 1964–70. *Publications:* Unknown Chile; Politics and Spirit; History of the Political Parties of Chile; Truth Will Prevail (for which he received the Chilean Literature Prize in 1956). *Address:* c/o Partido Demócrata Cristiano, Santiago, Chile.

**FREIBERGER, Heinrich,** Dr-Ing., Dipl.-Ing. Member, Bayrischer Senat; Ehrensenator der Technischen Universität Fridericiana Karlsruhe. *B.* 1900. *Career:* Chairman: Board of Directors Münchner Messe- und Austellungs GmbH. Munich; Advisory Committee, Allianz-Versicherungs A.G., Munich. Member, Administrative Committee, Deutsches Museum. President: Verein der Bayer. Met. Ind., Munich; Vereinigung der Arbeitgeberverbände in Bayern. Vice-President Gesamtverband de Metallindustriellen Arbeitgeberverbände, Köln. Co-editor 'die atomwirtschaft'. Member of the Board of Management, Grobes Verdienstkreuz mit Stern Federal Republic of Germany; Gossen & Co. GmbH. *Awards:* Gold ring in honour of the Deutsches Museum; Bayer. Verdienstorden. *Address:* 3 Faistenbergerstrasse, 8 Munich 90, Germany.

**FREIHA, Bassam,** BA. Lebanese. *B.* 1939. *Educ.* Political Science, American Univ. Beirut. *Career:* Man. Dir. Dar Assayad S.A.L. publishers, Al-Anwar (daily), Achabaka (wkly. mag.), Assayad (wkly.), Attayar (daily), Samar (wkly.): Weekly Observer (in Eng.), Al-Idary (monthly), Arab Defence Journal (monthly), Reports & Backgrounds (weekly, in Arabic). *Member:* International Adv. Assn. Press Syndicate, Beirut. *Awards:* Medal, Republic of Egypt; Star of the Imperial Order, Morocco; Sudan Nile Decoration. *Address: office* Dar Assayad S.A.L., P.O.B. 1038 Beirut, Lebanon.

**FREIHA, Said.** *B.* 1903. *M.* Mrs. Hassiba Koukhi. *S.* Issam, Bassam. *Dau.* Ilham. *Career:* Pres. Bd. Dirs. Dar Assayad S.A.L., Publishing & Printing House; Founder Al Anwar daily newspaper; Assayad weekly and Achabaka weekly magazine. Attayar daily newspaper; Samar weekly magazine; Weekly Observer (in Eng.); Al-Idary (monthly); Arab Defence Journal (monthly); Reports & Backgrounds (weekly, in Arabic). *Member:* Press Syndicate. *Awards:* Egypt's Medal; Jordanian; French; Cyprus; Spanish; Lebanese Orthodox Patriach medals; Order of the Cedars. *Address: office* P.O. Box 1038, Beirut, Lebanon.

**FRENCH, Henry John Sawyer,** OBE. British company director. *B.* 7 Jan. 1913; son of late Herbert Stanley French, M.D., C.M.G., etc., late Physician-in-Ordinary to the Royal Household and Senior Physician, Guy's Hospital, London. *Educ.* Rugby School and Christ Church, Oxford (MA, BCL); Barrister-at-Law (Grays Inn). *M.* (1) 1935, Susan Davies-Colley. *S.* 2. *Dau.* 1. *M.* (2) 1962, Philippa Piehler. *Career:* Served in World War II (Lt.-Col.; Officer, U.S. Legion of Merit); City Editor, The Sunday Times 1938; Director, London and Yorkshire Trust, Ltd. 1947–69; Chairman, Issuing Houses Assn. 1959–61; Chairman, Melbourne Brewery (Leeds) Ltd. 1954–60; Russels & Wrangham Ltd. 1958–60; Site Improvements Ltd. since 1960; Chmn. Test and Itchen Fishing Assoc. *Address:* Itchen Gate, Itchen Abbas, Hants.

**FRENCH, Neville Arthur Irwin,** CMG, MVO. British Diplomat. *B.* 1920. *Educ.* London Sch. of Economics & Political Science, Univ. of London—BSc (Econ.). *M.* 1945, Joyce Ethel Greene. *S.* 1. *Daus.* 2. *Career:* Colonial Admin. Service & H.M. Overseas Civil Service, Tanganyika (later Tanzania), District Commissioner 1948–60; Principal Asst. Sec., Prime Minister's Office, Dar es Salaam 1961–62; First Sec., Central African Office, London 1963–64; First Sec. (Political), British, High Commission, Rhodesia 1964–66; Head of Chancery, British Embassy, Rio de Janeiro 1966–69; Asst. Head, Western Organisations Dept., FCO London 1970–72; Counsellor & Charge d'Affaires, British Embassy, Havana 1972–74; Governor & C-in-C, Falkland Islands, & High Commissioner, British Antarctic Territory 1975–77; British Dep. High Commissioner in Southern India (Madras), July 1977. *Member:* Diplomatic Service Association, London; Mem. of Convocation, Univ. of London. *Decorations:* Companion of the Most Distinguished Order of St. Michael & St. George; Member of The Royal Victorian Order (4th Class); Commander of the Order of Rio Branco (Brazil). *Clubs:* Royal Commonwealth Soc., London. *Address:* c/o Foreign & Commonwealth Office, London, S.W.1.

**FRENSLEY, Herbert J.** American. *B.* 1906. *Educ.* Southern Methodist Univ. of Texas; Univ. of Texas. *M.* 1935, Evelyn Sundberg. *Dau.* 1. *Career:* Former Pres., Chief Exec. Officer & Dir. Brown & Root, Inc.; Texas Eastern Transmission Corp., Texas; Medical Center Inc., First City National Bank, Gordon Jewelry Corp.; Vice-Chmn., Baylor College of Medicine

*Member:* American Inst. of Accountants; Texas Soc. of C.P.A.'s; Trustee, Brown Foundation Inc. *Clubs:* River Oaks Country; Sky, N.Y.; Ramada. *Address: office* Suite 2910, 2 Houston Center, Houston, Texas 77002, U.S.A.

**FRENZEL, Otto N.** American banker. *B.* 1899.*Educ.* Cornell University. *M.* 1925, Eleanor Dickson. *S.* Otto N. III. *Dau.* Eleanor (Bookwalter). *Career:* United States Navy WWI; Chairman, Merchants National Bank & Trust Company of Indianapolis, & Merchants National Corp.; Director: America States Insurance Co., American States Fire Insurance Co., American States Life Insurance Co., Indianapolis Chamber of Commerce; Riley Hosp. Assn. Crown Hill Cemetery Assn.; United Fund (now United Way) of Greater Indianapolis; Trustee, Butler Univ.; Director and Life Member, Indiana State Chamber of Commerce, Indianapolis Chamber of Commerce, Y.M.C.A. *Address:* 1 Merchants Plaza, Indianapolis 46204, Ind., U.S.A.

**FRETHEY, Albert Roy.** British. *B.* 1902. *Educ.* Eltham Public School; Stratford District High (both New Zealand); Diploma in Banking; A.C.A.N.Z. *M.* 1964, Marie Agnes Joan Mallard. *Career:* Bank of New Zealand: Assistant Manager, Wellington 1944–45; Manager, Sydney, 1950–54, Manager, London 1954–62. Director: Bank of New Zealand (London Board) 1962–76; Foley Bros. (London) Ltd., London; Weber Cook & Garnham Ltd., London; Union Steamship Co. of N.Z. Ltd.; Union Steamship Co. (Union U.K.) Ltd.; Pacific & World Travel Ltd. *Address:* Green Ridges, Pelhams Walk, Esher, Surrey.

**FREUD, Clement Raphael.** MP. Writer, broadcaster and politician. *B.* 1924. *M.* 1950, Jill Flewett. *S.* 3. *Daus.* 2. *Career:* apprenticed Dorchester Hotel London; War Service, Royal Ulster Rifles, Liaison Officer Nuremberg 1946; Sports Writer, Cookery Editor, Sports & Columnist for many newspapers and magazines since 1956; Liberal Party Spokesman on Education and Science; Rector of Dundee Univ. Dir. Genevieve Restaurants London; Dir. Trustee Playboy Club of London Ltd.; Berkeley Hotel Southampton; Consultant New Mauritius Hotels Ltd. Curepipe; Member Parliament (Lib.) Isle of Ely since 1973. *Club:* Saville. *Address:* 7 Boundary Road, London, N.W.8.

**FREY, Emil.** German. Hon. Teaching Professor Economics *B.* 1904. *Educ.* Humanist Grammar School, Kiel; Studied Jurisprudence at Kiel and Munich; Court Assessor 1933. *M.* 1929, Margaret Flichtenhoefer. *S.* Dr. Peter. *Daus:* Elisabeth (Wildhagen), Irene and Anette (Rinne). *Career:* Trainee and scientific asst. Schleswig-Holstein State Fire Insurance Office, Kiel 1929–32 (Legal Representative 1932–37, Manager 1938–45). Officer of the Reserve 1939–45; Independent business consultant 1946–49. Member of Board Mannheim Insurance Co. 1949 (Chairman 1950); Professor Economics High School Univ. of Mannheim 1954—; Chairman, Mannheim Life Insurance Co. 1965. *Publications:* books: Forms of Organisation of Insurance Undertakings, (1962); The Principle of Co-operation in the Management of Businesses, (1960); Transport Insurance, (1959); the Law of Property Insurance, (1936); and numerous articles in German and French journals. *Awards:* War honours; Federal Cross of Merit; Silver Badge of Honour (Federal Traffic Guard). Board of Trustees, Max-Planck Inst. for Foreign and International Private Law (Chmn.); Board of Trustees, Seebull Ada and Emil Nolde Foundation, and of Friedrich Naumann Foundation; Bd. Trustees, The Heinrich Lanz Krankenhaus Foundation (Chmn.). *Clubs:* Rotary; Montag; Kreis Mars & Merkur. *Address:* Schwarzwaldstr. 39, Mannheim; and *office* Augusta-Anlage 65, 6800 Mannheim, 1, Germany.

**FRIEDMAN, Sidney.** American. *B.* 1907. *Educ.* Yale Law School (LLB 1931), Brown University (PhB 1928, MA 1931). *M.* 1930, Blanche Banner. *S.* Stuart. *Daus.* Nancy and Susan Dimitris. *Career:* Member, Board of Ethics of Nassau County, N.Y. later Chmn; Director: Citizens Development Corp. Chairman of the Board, National Bank of North America 1964–73; Director: CIT Financial Corp. 1966–73; Chmn. of the Bd., Pres. & Chief Exec. Officer, Farmers Bank of State of Delaware 1976—. *Awards:* Metropolitan Award of Yeshiva Univ. 1966; Tree of Life Award; Boys Town Jerusalem. Citizen of the Year Award; Adelphi Coll. 1968; National Conf. Christians and Jews 1969; Fellow, Phi Beta Kappa Assoc.; Hon. Finance, Post Coll. L.I.U. 1972. *Member:* Assn. of the Bar of the City of New York and Nassau County and American Bar Assns.; Trustee, Hofstra Univ.; Assoc. Trustee North Shore Hospital. *Address:* 15 Wensley Drive, Great Neck, N.Y.; and *office* 1345 Avenue of the Americas, New York City, U.S.A.

**FRIEDRICH, Rudolf,** Dr. Eng. Prof. Universität Karlsruhe (Thermische Strömungsmachinen). *B.* 1909. *Educ.* Technical High Schools at Breslau and Hanover (Engineer's Diploma; Doctor of Engineering). *M.* 1936, Ruth Proell. *S.* 3. Constructor and projection engineer, Junkers Aircraft Works, Dessau 1933–36; Engineer for turbine power, Junkers Motor Works, Magdeburg 1936–39, and at Heinkel, Rostock 1939–41; development of air compressors and gas turbines, Bruckner-Kanis, Dresden 1941–47. Head of thermo-energy instruction and development of gas turbines, Siemens-Schuckertwerke AG, Mülheim/Ruhr 1948–64. *Publication:* a book on gas turbines with equal pressure combustion. *Member:* Association of German Engineers; Scientific Society for Aviation. *Address:* Elbingestr. 24b, Karlsruhe-Waldstadt; and *office* Universität Karlsruhe, Kaiserstrasse 12, Germany.

**FRIEND, Albert Wiley.** Consulting Engineer and Physicist. *B.* 1910. *Educ.* Harvard University DSc in Communication Engineering (1948); West Virginia University (MSc in Physics; BSEE in Elec. Eng.). *M.* 1931, Evelyn Augusta Hall. *S.* Albert W., Jr. and John Robert. *Dau.* Evelyn Joyce (Everett). *Career:* Monongahela W. Penn. Public Service Co. 1929–30; Transmission and Distribution Engineer, Ohio Power Co. 1933–34; Engineering Consultant 1931–39; Instructor in Physics 1934–37 and Associate Professor of Physics 1937–44, W. Virginia Univ.; on leave 1939–44; Research Fellow and Instructor in Physics and Communications Engineering, Cruft Lab., Harvard Univ. 1939–41; Research Fellow, Blue Hill Met. Obser. 1939–43; Research Associate and Staff Member, Massachusetts Inst. of Technology (Radiation Lab. M.I.T. Radar School, and Heat Research Lab.) 1941–44; Resident Staff, Electronic Research Lab., Harvard Univ. 1946–47 Development & Research Staff Engineer, Radio Corp. of America, Camden, N.J. 1944–47, and Princeton, N.J. 1947–51; Director of Engineering, Inst. Div., Daystrom Inc. 1951; Director of Engineering and Development, Magnetic Metals Co. 1951–53; practising Consulting Engineer and Physicist 1953—; President, Acoustex Inc. 1961—. Lecturer in Architectural Acoustics, Univ. of Penn., 1965. Holder of 40 U.S. patents on electronics and television. *Awards:* R.C.A. Laboratories Award (for outstanding work in research, for ingenuity in developing and designing magnetic circuits for tri-colour kinescopes), 1950; Inst. of Radio Engineers Fellowship Award (contributions to tropospheric echo research and to the development of magnetic materials and circuits) 1954; National Electronics Conference Award (for his paper, 'The Use of Powdered Iron in Television Deflecting Circuits'—a contribution of major importance to the advancement of the electronic art). *Publications:* numerous articles for technical journals, including many delivered papers since 1931, on electro-magnetic wave propagation and pulse sounding of the ionosphere and troposphere by radio or radar signals, vibration of plates and membranes, cathode ray indicator presentations, television deflection and high voltage systems and components, colour television picture tubes and systems, magneto-optic devices, magnetic recording and reproducing systems, ferro-magnetic materials and devices, vacuum tubes; telemetering acoustics, noise abatement and reliability. Engineering of large communications, command and control systems, satellite communications systems and space vehicle communications, command, control and telemetering systems and acoustical facilities, electromagnetic/acoustic shielding enclosures and industrial vibration reduction design. Consultant and Expert witness in patent and other litigation. *Fellow:* Amer. Assn. for Advancement of Science (Life Member), American Physical Society, and Institute of Electrical and Electronic Engineers. *Member:* Acoustical Society of America, American Geophysical Union, American Inst. of Physics, Amer. Meteorological Socy., Air Force Assn., Amer. Ordnance Assn. (Life member). Audio Engineering Socy., Franklin Inst. of State of Pennsylvania; The Pennsylvania Society; Sigma Pi Sigma (Physics), Sigma Xi (Science), Tau Beta Pi (Engineering). *Clubs:* Cosmos (Washington, D.C.); Engineers (Philadelphia); Harvard (Philadelphia); Harvard Engineers and Scientists (N.Y.C.). *Address:* P.O. Box 34420, West Bethesda, Md. Branch, Washington, D.C. 20034, U.S.A.

**FRIESEN, Albert P.** Canadian Chartered Accountant; *B.* 1915; Chartered Accountant (C.A.); Fellow, Chartered Institute of Secretaries (F.C.I.S.). *M.* 1946. *S.* Robert. *Daus.* Patricia and Carol. *Career:* With Department of National Revenue, Ottawa, 1947–52; with Dept. of Munitions and Supply, Ottawa 1943–45; Clarkson Gordon & Co. Chartered Accountants, Toronto 1945–47; The White Pass & Yukon Corp. Ltd. 1953–74 (Ret'd. as President). *Address:* P.O. Box 2141, Vancouver, B.C., Canada.

**FRIMANNSSON, Svanbjoern.** *B.* 1903. *M.* 1938, Holmfridur Andrésdóttir. *S.* Andrés and Agnar. *Dau.* Sigridur. Chief Cashier, Landsbanki Islands 1937–42; Chairman, The Icelandic Importboard 1942–45; Asst. Manager Landsbanki Islands 1945–57, General Manager 1957—; Governor Central Bank of Iceland since 1971. *Address: office* Central Bank of Iceland (Sedlabanki Islands), Reykjavik, Iceland.

**FROCK, Edmond Burnell.** American industrialist. *B.* 1910. *Educ.* Catawba College (AB). *M.* 1936, Rebecca Black. *S.* Edmond B., Jr.; J. Daniel James W. *Dau.* Judy. *Career:* Merchandise Manager, Atlantic & Pacific Tea Co., Hanover, Pa. 1933. President, Hanover Wire Cloth, 1945—. Vice-President, Continental Copper & Steel Industries Inc. 1948—. President and Director, Bank of Hanover & Trust Co.; Continental Copper and Steel Industries, Inc., Continental Rubber Works; Exec. Vice-Pres. Continental Copper & Steel Ind. Inc. since 1974; Pres. Wire Weavers' Assn.; Dir. & Vice-Pres. Hanover Gen. Hospital. President, Hanover Public Library 1955; Bd. of Trustees Catawba College. *Address:* 7 Oak Street, Hanover, Pa.; and *office* E. Middle St., Hanover, Pa., U.S.A.

**FRODSHAM, Anthony Freer.** British. *B.* 1919. *Educ.* Ecole Lacordaire (Paris), Mayfield College (Sussex) and Faraday House (London). *M.* 1953, Patricia Myfanwy Wynne-Edwards. *S.* Simon Hugh and David George. *Career:* Engineer Officer, Royal Navy 1940–46; Management Consultant. P-E Consulting Group Ltd. 1947–72, Manager Midlands Area 1954, Director 1956 Man. Dir. and Group Chief Exec. 1963–72; Dir. Gen. Engineering Employers' Fed. since 1975; Chmn. Machine Tools EDC since 1973; Group Specialist Adv. United Dominions Trust Ltd 1973–74; Dir. Arthur Young Management Services since 1973. *Member:* Council Management Consultants Assn. 1960–72, Chmn. 1968–70; Council Fédération Européenne des Assns. de Conseils en Organization 1960–72; BNEC Canada Cttee. 1970–71 (Chmn. Machinery Group); Council, Inst. Management Consultants 1962—74 (Pres. 1967–68); Engineering Industries Training Board (Board Member); CBI (Council Member); Gen. Comm. of Tax; *Publication:* Ed. Bd. Handbook for Managers 1971–75. *Fellow:* Institution of Mechanical Engineers; British Inst. of Management. Institute of Directors. *Clubs:* Carlton; The Naval. *Address:* 1 The Grange, Wimbledon Common; and *office* Broadway House, Tothill St., London SW1H 9NQ.

**FROHNE, Hugo.** German businessman (with diploma). *B.* 1904. *Educ.* Grammar and Commercial High Schls. *M.* 1944, Liselotte Gunning. *S.* 1. *Daus.* 2. *Career:* With Osnabrück Bank AG 1922–27; Preussenkasse, Berlin, and Landesgenossenschaftskasse, Stettin 1931–33; Secretary and Member of Board, Pommersche Bank AG, Stettin 1933–38; Director, Vereinsbank, Hamburg 1938–54; General Manager 1955. Member of the Bd. of Dirs. Vereinsbank, Hamburg 1955—. Handelsbank in Lübeck; Handel Privatbank Köln; Chmn. of Administrative Cncl.; 'Aurum' Beteiligungs. und Verwaltungs-Gesellschaft mbH. & Co., Hamburg; Member of Administrative Council; Otto-Versand KG., Hamburg; Trustee: Pommersche Bank AG., Stettin, für das Bundesgebeit. Vice-Pres., Hanseatische Wertpapierbörse, Hamburg. *Club:* Lions (Hamburg). *Address:* Westend 8, Hamburg-Othmarschen, Germany.

**FROMENT-MEURICE, Gérard.** French banker. President, Crédit Privé, Paris. *B.* 1896. *Educ.* Faculty of Letters, Paris. *M.* Elisabeth Lefèvre-Pontalis. *S.* Henri. *Dau.* Geneviève (Baronne C. Evain). Officer, Legion of Honour; Croix de Guerre (1914–18); Croix du Combattant Volontaire, and Officer Mérite National. With the Banque Nationale pour le Commerce et l'Industrie 1923–53 and with De Rothschild 1953–63. Président d'honneur du Crédit Privé. *Club:* Cercle Interallié (Paris). *Address:* 321 boulevard Saint-Denis, Courbevoie (Seine); and *office* 5 Rue Louis le Grand, Paris 2.

**FROMER, Leo.** Swiss lawyer. *B.* 1911. *Educ.* University of Basle (Dr. jur. 1935; lawyer's brevet 1938). *M.* 1960, Jacqueline Sarasin. *S.* Martin Andreas. *Daus.* Christine Doris, Liliane. *Career:* As well as being a lawyer, is adviser to economic associations and member of boards of different corporations in industrial practice 1929–30; studied law at Basle and Paris, 1930–33; practised at the Courts and Law Office 1936–38; Partner, Meyer Fromer 1939–43; specializes in corporation and fiscal law. Partner, Fromer, Schultheiss, Altwegg & Speiser since 1944; Fromer, Schultheiss, Böcht, 1968—. *Publications:* Die Abtretung künftiger Forderungen; Die Treuepflicht des Aktionärs; Die Kollision von Bundessteuerrecht mit kantonalem Steuerrecht; numerous articles on juridical and fiscal questions. Schutz der Aktiengesellschaft vor fremden Einfluss. *Address:* Im Klosteracker 15, Binningen; and *office* St. James-St. 7, Basle, Switzerland.

**FROSST, John, B.** *B.* 1900. *Educ.* PhG. *M.* 1929, Alice Snow. *S.* Martin S. *Daus.* 2. Followed all his business career with Charles E. Frosst & Co., and affiliated companies. *Address:* 3223 Trafalgar Avenue, Montreal P.Q. H3Y 1H8 Canada.

**FROST, Alan Charles Hamlyn.** Australian Electrical Engineer. *B.* 1914. *Educ.* Univ. of London, BSc(Eng) 1st Class Hons. *M.* 1938, Edith Thomas. *S.* 3. *Career:* Merz & McLellan Consulting Engineers, London 1936–43; Royal Engineers, U.K. & India 1943–46 (Major); Merz & McLellan, Newcastle on Tyne 1947–51; Snowy Mountains Authority, Australia 1951; Chief Engineer, Electrical & Mechanical, Snowy Mountains Authority 1967–74; Chief Engineer, Snowy Mountains Engineering Corp. 1974–75; Asst. Dir., Snowy Mountains Engineering Corp. since 1975. Fellow, Inst. of Electrical Engineers; Fellow, Inst. of Engineers, Australia. *Club:* Rotary (Past Pres., Paul Harris Fellow). *Address:* 19 Nimby Place, Cooma North, N.S.W. 2630; & *office* Box 356 Post Office, Cooma North, N.S.W. 2630, Australia.

**FROST, Jack.** American geologist. Chairman of Board, Toreador Royalty Corp. Director: Alco Oil & Gas Corp., and Leon Land & Cattle Co. President, Treasurer & Director, Frost Oil Co. *Educ.* Hardin-Simmons Univ. (Abilene, Tex.) and Southern Methodist Univ. (Dallas, Tex.). *M.* 1948, Adele Patterson. Geologist, various companies 1918–30; Independent Oil Producer 1930–69. *Member:* Amer. Assn. of Petroleum Geologists; American Petroleum Inst.; Socy. of Independent Professional Earth Scientists; Permian Basin Petroleum Pioneers; South and West Texas Geological Societies. *Clubs:* Brook Hollow Country, Terpsichorean (Dallas, Tex.); Menger Patio, Argyle, San Antonio, Fiesta San Antonio Commission (San Antonio, Tex.). *Address: office* 1802 National Bank of Commerce, San Antonio, Tex. U.S.A.

**FRY, Maurice Alec.** British *B.* 1915, *Educ.* Bancroft School (Woodford Green, Essex). *M.* 1947, Betty May Slaughter. *S.* Christopher Maurice. *Daus.* Shirley Ann and Julia Marion. *Career:* Chmn. Electronic Rentals: Visionhire Ltd.; Colorent GmbH (Germany); City Link Ltd.; Orbit Cargo Services Ltd.; Director: Fry & Cowell (Pindisports) Ltd.; Telerenta S.A.; Colour TV Rentals Ltd. Hong Kong. *Member:* Inst. of Directors. *Clubs:* Army & Navy, St. George's Hill Golf, St. George's Hill Tennis. *Address: office* Electronic House, Churchfield Road, Weybridge, Surrey.

**FRY, Peter Derek,** MP. British Politician. *B.* 1931. *Educ:* Royal Grammar Sch., High Wycombe; Worcester Coll., Oxford—MA(Hons). *M.* 1956, Edna Roberts. *S.* 1. *Dau.* 1. *Career:* MP (Cons.) for Wellingborough since 1969. *Club:* Royal Automobile. *Address:* 27 Poplars Farm Road, Barton Seagrave, Kettering, Northants.; and *office* House of Commons, London SW1A 0AA.

**FRYDENLUND, Knut Olav.** Norwegian politician. *B.* 1927. *Educ.* Graduated 1946; law degree 1950. *M.* Grethe Nilsen. *S.* 3. *Career:* In Ministry of For. Affairs 1952–53; Secy at Embassy, Bonn 1953–55; Secy. later Counsellor at For. Min. 1956–62 (personal secy. to former For. Min. for several years); Press Counsellor Brussells 1962–63; Perm. Rep. at Council of Europe 1963–65; Head of Division of For. Min. 1966–69; Consultant with Research Office of Labour Movement 1967–69; Member of Parl. for Oslo 1969–73; Min. of For. Affairs since 1973. *Address:* 12 Borgenveien, Oslo 2, Norway; and *office* Min. of For. Affairs, 7 Juni-plassen 1, Oslo Dep., Norway.

**FRYER, Dr. Geoffrey,** DSc, PhD, FRS. British biologist. *B.* 1927. *Educ.* Huddersfield College. *M.* 1953, Vivien Griffiths Hodgson. *S.* 1. *Dau.* 1. *Career:* Colonial Research student 1952–53; H.M. Colonial (later Overseas) Research Service (Malawi, Zambia, Uganda) 1953–60; with Freshwater Biological Association since 1960. *Member:* Linnean Socy. of London; Socy. Study of Evolution; Int. Socy. Theoretical and applied Limnology; British Ecological Society. *Publications:* (with T. D. Iles) The Cichlid Fishes of the Great Lakes of Africa: their Biology and Evolution. *Awards:* Doctor of Science, Doctor of Philosophy, London University; Fellow of the Royal Society. *Address:* Elleray Cottage, Windermere, Cumbria; & Laboratory, The Ferry House, Far Sawrey, Ambleside, Cumbria.

**FULBRIGHT, James William.** United States Politician. *B.* 9 Apr. 1905. *Educ.* University of Arkansas (AB); Pembroke

College, Oxford (MA); George Washington University (LLB). *M.* 1932, Elizabeth K. Williams. *Daus.* Elizabeth, Roberta; Attorney, Department of Justice 1934–35; Law Instructor, George Washington and University of Arkansas 1935–39; President, University of Arkansas 1939–41; Member, U.S. House of Representatives (Democrat) 1942–45; U.S. Senator from Arkansas 1945–74; Chmn. Senate Cttee. on Foreign Relations 1959–74. Democrat. *Address:* 1000 Shrewsbury, Fayetteville, Arkansas, U.S.A.

**FULD, Stanley Howells.** American attorney-at-law. *B.* 23 Aug. 1903. *Educ.* College of City of New York (AB); Columbia University (LLB). *M.* 1930, Florence Geringer (Dec'd). *Daus.* Hermine (Nessen), Judith (Miller). *Career:* Admitted to New York Bar 1926; private practice, New York City 1926–35, 1944–46; Assistant District-Attorney New York County, in charge of Indictment Bureau and Appeals Bureau 1935–44; Special Assistant Attorney-General New York State, Liaison Counsel various State investigations May 1944–Dec. 1945; Associate Judge of Court of Appeals of the State of New York 1946–66. Elected and served as Chief Judge of Court and of State of New York 1967–73; On retirement (from bench) Special Counsel to Kay, Scholer, Fierman, Hays and Handler since 1974; Hon, LLD, Columbia Univ., Hamilton College, Union Coll., Yeshiva Univ., New York Law School, New York Univ., Syracuse Univ., Jewish Theological Seminary of America; St. John's Univ.; City Univ. of New York; Republican. *Address: office* 425 Park Ave, New York, NY 10022, U.S.A.

**FULLER, Curtis G.** American *B.* 1912. *Educ.* Univ. of Wisconsin (BA) and Northwestern Univ. (MS). *M.* 1938, Mary Margaret Stiehm. *S.* Michael Curtis. *Dau.* Nancy Abigail. *Career:* Newspaper reporter 1933–37; Assistant, Journalism, Northwestern Univ. 1936–37; Assoc. Editor, National Almanac and Year Book 1937–38; Information Director, State of Wisconsin 1938–39; Associate Editor, Better Roads magazine 1939–43; Managing Editor, Flying magazine 1943–48, Editor 1948–51; Editorial Director, Publishers Development Corp. 1951–53; Pres. Clark Publishing Co. 1952—; Editor, Advertising Publications Inc. 1953–55; Managing Director, Modern Castings magazine 1955–56; Vice-Pres., Greenleaf Publishing Co. 1956–57; Pres., Oak Ridge Atom Industries Sales Corp. 1960–62; Woodall Publishing Co. 1965; Publisher, Fate Magazine 1952—; Trailer Travel Magazine 1965—; Woodall's Mobile Home Park Directory 1965—; Woodall's Trailering Parks & Campgrounds Directory since 1967. *Member:* Sigma Delta Chi, Illinois Socy for Psychic Research; Spiritual Frontiers Fellowship. *Publications:* Fate Magazine (1952); Trailer Travel Magazine (1965); Woodall's Trailering Parks & Campgrounds Dir. (1967). *Address:* 500 Hyacinth Place, Highland Park, Ill., 60035, U.S.A.

**FULLER, Fred Ellsworth.** American. Lawyer (Ret'd.). General Counsel, Glass Container Manufacturers Institute & Owens-Illinois Inc. *B.* 1901. *Educ.* Ohio Wesleyan Univ. (AB 1923) *cum laude,* and Ohio State Univ. (JD 1926) *summa cum laude. M.* 1923, Mary Isabelle Beetham. *S.* Fred Ellsworth Jr. *Daus.* Anne Crete (Boyd), Bess Isabelle (Brownell) and Margaret Renna (Sandberg). *Career:* Admitted to Ohio Bar 1926, and Supreme Court 1936. Officer, Medical Admin. Corps. 1928–34. Partner in firm of Fuller, Seney, Henry & Hodge (formerly Tracy, Chapman & Welles) 1926—; Dir., Toledo Edison Co., 1968–73. Trustee: Ohio Wesleyan Univ. 1932–70; Gen. Counsel Owen-Illinois Inc. 1945–67; Ohio Wesley Associates (First Chmn.), Ohio Historical Socy. Trustee 1966–75. (Sites, Investments and Ex. Coms.) and Toledo Area Chamber of Commerce Trustee 1967–69. *Member:* American Bar Assn. (former Chmn. of Anti-trust Section; presented with bronze plaque for Distinguished Services 1958, 1972; member of Section of Admin. Law; former member, Standing Cttee. on Federal Judiciary), Ohio State, New York State, Toledo, Inter-American (member, Special Sub-section for the U.S. on the Food, Drug and Cosmetic Law Section), and International Bar Associations, and Association of the Bar of the City of New York, Life Fellow Amer. Bar Foundation: Fellow, American College of Trial Lawyers. Life Fellow, Ohio State Bar Foundation. Member, U.S. Attorney General's National Committee to Study the Anti-trust laws; American Judicature Society; International Association of Insurance Counsel; American Law Institute; Newcomen Society of North America; Ohio Society in New York; Order of the Coif; Chi Phi; Phi Delta Phi; Delta Sigma Rho. Methodist. Mason. Republican. *Clubs:* Inverness, Rotary, Skytop (Skytop, Pa.); Toledo. *Address:* 3905 (East) Hillandale Road, Toledo 43606, Ohio; and *office* 1200 Edison Plaza, Toledo 43604, Ohio, U.S.A.

**FULLER, Hon. Sir John Bryan Munro,** MLC. Australian politician. *B.* 1917. *Educ.* Knox Gammar School, Wahroonga. *M.* 1940, Eileen Webb. *S.* Bryan Antony. *Dau.* Sally Llewellyn. *Career:* Grazier; MLC since 1961; Leader of Opposition in Legislative Council since May 1976; Vice-pres. Exec. Council and Leader of Govt. in Legislative Council 1968–76; Min. for Decentralization and Develop. 1965–73; Min. for Planning and Environment 1973–76; knighted 1974. Chairman Australian Country Party, N.S.W. 1959–64; Vice-President, Graziers' Association of N.S.W. 1965; Vice-Chmn., Australian Country Party (Federal) 1962–68. *Clubs:* Australian (Sydney); Associated Schools; American. *Address:* 'Kallateenee', Coolah, N.S.W.; and *office* Parliament House, Sydney, N.S.W., Australia.

**FULLER, Robert Garfield.** Business Executive. *B.* 1904. *M.* Gwendolen Sherwood Ferrey, 1927. *S.* Robert Ferrey. *Dau.* Daphne Sherwood Ferrey (*Dec.* 1940). *Career:* With 1st Natl. Bank NYC 1925–55, Asst. Cashier, 1928, Asst. Vice-Pres., 1942, Vice-Pres., 1945–55; Vice-Pres., First National City Bank, N.Y.C. 1955–58, Senior Vice-Pres., 1958–66; Chmn. Exec. Commn., Erie Lackawanna RR Co., 1965–67, Chmn. of Bd. 1967–68 Chairman, Voting Trustees, Railway Express Agency, Inc. 1968–69; Director & Member Executive Cttee. Amstar Corp. Dir. & Mem. Exec. Cttee., Seaboard Surety Co.; Director Discount Corp.; Chmn. Ad. Cttee. Pension Investment, Penn Central Trans. Co. Member, Cttee. of Separate Accounts A.C. & D., Equitable Life Assurance Socy. Council on Foreign Relations. Phi Beta Kappa. Psi Upsilon, Republican. Baptist. *Clubs:* Harvard (N.Y.C.); Sky Club (N.Y.C.); Scarsdale Golf (Scarsdale, N.Y.); Everglades (Palm Beach); Blind Brook (Port Chester, N.Y.); Lost Tree (North Palm Beach Fla.). *Address:* 6 Olmsted Road, Scarsdale, New York 10583, U.S.A.

**FUNK, Wilfred (John).** American writer, editor and publisher; President of several publishing companies. *Educ.* Princeton University LittB; Oglethorpe University LittD. *M.* 1915, Eleanor MacNeal Hawkins. *S.* Wilfred John (*k. in action* 1943), Peter Van Keuran. *Daus.* Eleanor Joan and Sally McNeal. With Funk & Wagnalls Co., publishers, since 1909; Secretary 1912; Vice-Pres. 1914–25; Pres. 1925–40; resigned to start Wilfred Funk Inc., N.Y. City; Editor-in-Chief, Literary Digest 1936–37; Pres. and Dir. The Kingsway Press, Inc.; Editor-in-Chief, Publications, Inc.; Your Health Publications, Inc.; Owner and Editorial Director (magazines): Your Life; Your Health 1928–51; Trustee, Montclair (New Jersey) Public Library; Organizer and First Pres., Montclair Community Chest; Dir., Knickerbocker Growth Fund; *Member:* Linguistic Society of America. *Clubs:* Players; The Lambs; Dutch Treat; Montclair Golf; National Golf, Southampton, Meadow, Southampton Yacht, Southampton Beach (Southampton, L.I.); Society of Illustrators; Artists and Writers. *Publications:* Manhattans, Bronxes and Queens (verse) (1931); Light Lines and Dears (verse) (1933); So You Think It's New (prose) (1937); It Might Be Verse (verse) (1938); When the Merry-Go-Round Breaks Down (prose) (1938); If You Drink (prose) (1940); 30 Days to a More Powerful Vocabulary (1942); Love, Life and Laughter (verse) (1942); Vocabulary Power and Culture (prose) (1946); Word Origins and Their Romantic Stories (prose) (1950); 6 Weeks to Words of Power (prose) (1953); 25 Magic Steps to Word Power (1960); Dr. Wilfred Funk's Book Shelf (1961); Selected Verse of Wilfred Funk (1963); author of Reader's Digest feature, 'It Pays to Increase Your Word Power'; Editorial Advisor of new edition of the New Practical Standard Dictionary; also fact and fiction in magazines. Independent Democrat. *Addiess:* 16 Erwin Park Road, Montclair, N.J.; and *office* Room 1520, 342 Madison Avenue, New York City 17, U.S.A.

**FURLONGER, Robert William.** Australian Civil Servant. *B.* 1921. *Educ:* Sydney High Sch.; Univ. of Sydney—BA. *M.* 1944, Verna Lewis. *S.* 3. *Dau.* 1. *Career:* Australian Army 1941–45; Dept. of Foreign Affairs: London 1947–48; The Hague 1948–51; Jakarta 1952–54; Singapore 1954–55; Karachi 1958–59; Imperial Defence Coll. 1960; High Commissioner, Lagos 1961; Perm. Rep. to European Office of UN 1961–64; Minister, Washington 1965–69; Dept. of Defence: Dir., Joint Intelligence Org. 1969–72; Ambassador, Jakarta 1971–74, Vienna (also accredited to Budapest & Prague) 1974–77; Dir.-Gen., Office of National Assessments, Canberra since 1977. *Club:* Commonwealth (Canberra). *Address:* 12 Norman Street, Deakin, A.C.T. 2600; and *office* Office of National Assessments, West Block, Canberra, A.C.T. 2600, Australia.

**FURNESS, Rt. Hon. The Viscount** (William Anthony Furness). Knight of Justice (Grand Officer of Merit), Sovereign

Military Order of Malta; Knight of Justice Order of St. John; Knight Commander with Star, Order of St. Gregory the Great; Grand Officer, Order of Merit (Italy); Knight Grand Cross of the Constantinian Order of St. George. *B.* 1929. *Educ.* Downside and in the U.S.A. Special Assistant to Vice-Pres. and Gen. Mgr. American Express Co., London 1948–50; Member of the House of Lords 1950—; Served in Welsh Guards 1946–47; extra A.D.C. to Gov. and Cmdr.-in-Chief Bahamas 1953; Delegate, Inter-Parliamentary Union Conferences, Washington 1953, Vienna 1954, Helsinki 1955, Warsaw 1959, Brussels 1961, Belgrade 1963; Chairman, United & General Trust Ltd. 1955—, Managing Director 1963—. Member, Sovereign Cncl. of Sovereign Military Order of Malta 1960–62. Secy., British Assn., Sovereign Military Order of Malta 1956–65, Secretary General 1965. *Member:* Inter-Parliamentary Union; University of London Catholic Chapliancy Association; American Academy of Political Science; Founder-Chmn., Anglo Monogolian Society 1963; Pres. Aged Poor Society, etc. Conservative. *Clubs:* Carlton, Boodles (London); Travellers (Paris). *Address:* 60 St. James's Street, London, S.W.1.

**FURSTENBERG, Hans (Jean)**, Chev. Légion D'Honneur, France, Great Cross of Merit with Star, Fed. Rep. of Germany Commander, Ordre du Chêne, Luxembourg. French. *B.* 1890. *Educ.* Univ. of Munich & Berlin. *M.* 1930, Eugénie. *Career:* Hon. Chmn. Berliner Handels-Gesellschaft; Frankfurter Bank, Rheinische Bank; Partner, Berliner Handelsgesellschaft 1919–35; Dir. 1935–37; Dir. in Frankfurt 1948–52; Vice-Chmn. A.E.G., 1928–35; Vice-Pres. Assoc. Internationale de Bibliophilie, Paris; Pres. Fondation Furstenberg-Beaumesnil. *Clubs:* Grolier, N.Y. *Address:* 16 Rue de Beaumont, Geneva, Switzerland; Château de Beaumesnil, Beaumesnil, Eure, France; and *office* 10 Bockenheimer Landstrasse, Frankfurt-Main, W. Germany.

**FURUKAKI, Tetsuro.** *B.* 1900. *Educ.* Univ. of Lyons (D.-en-D.). *M.* Masuko Kikuta. Grand Officer, Al Merito (Italy); Commander, Order of the British Empire; Grand Cross, Legion of Honour (France). Previously: official of the League of Nations; Director of *Asahi* (newspaper); Senator; President, Japanese Radio and Television (N.H.K.); Ambassador to France 1956–61; Adviser to Ministry of Foreign Affairs, Japan, Oct. 1961–67; Pres. Japan Association UNICEF; Hon. Adviser, N.H.K. *Publications:* League of Nations and World Peace; International Mandate System of the League of Nations; International Arbitration; Melancholy of London; Geneva Express; Pink Handkerchief; Vol de Nuit; Paris qui Vit, etc. *Address:* c/o NHK, Tokyo.

# G

**GAAR, Ernst.** Austrian civil engineer and businessman. *B.* 1904. *Educ.* Bundes School for machine engineering and electro-technique, Technical High School, Graz. *M.* 1930, Lia Ackerl. *S.* 1. *Daus.* 2. *Career:* Technical official 1923–29; owner of Ing. Gaar 1930. Partner, Ing. Gaar & Co., Graz 1958— (electric, gas, water, central heating and ventilation installations). *Address:* Burgasse 6, Graz; and *office* Conrad von Hötzendorf Strasse 66a, Graz, Austria.

**GAGE, John Edward.** BCom. Canadian executive. *B.* 1910. *Educ.* Philips Academy, Andover, Mass.; McGill Univ. (BCom). *M.* 1935, Ruth Powers. *S.* John Charles and Gordon Russell. *Daus.* Julie Elizabeth and Kelley Ann. *Career:* Dir. and General Manager, Pacific Elevators Ltd., Vancouver, B.C. Dir.: Federal Grain Ltd., The Alberta Pacific Grain Co. (1943) Ltd., Burrard Terminals Ltd., Buckerfields Ltd., and Green Valley Chemical & Fertilizer Co. Ltd.; Vice-Pres.: Federal Grain Ltd.; Alberta Pacific Grain Co. (1943) Ltd. *Clubs:* The Vancouver; Capilano Golf & Country; Shaughnessy Golf & Country. *Address:* 2688 Marine Crescent, Vancouver 14, and *office* 531 Marine Building, Vancouver 1, B.C., Canada.

**GAGGERO, Sir George**, OBE, JP. British. *B.* 1897. *Educ.* Gibraltar, Germany and England. *M.* 1925, Mabel Andrews-Speed. *S.* 2. *Dau.* 2. *Career:* Chairman M. H. Bland & Co., Ltd. (1914–70) and Bland Group of Companies, including Rock Hotel Ltd., Bland Cable Cars Ltd., Bland Line, Thomas Mosley & Co. Ltd., and M. H. Bland & Co. (U.K.) Ltd. President, Gibraltar Airways Ltd. (Chairman 1947–66). Dir. Rock Fire Assurance Co. Ltd. 1927–52; Gibraltars Transporter Ltd. 1930–66; Mackintosh & Co. (Gibraltar) Ltd. 1943–67; Chmn. Gibraltar Stevedoring Co. Ltd. 1948–59, Stevedoring & Cargo Handling Co. Ltd. 1959–65; Hon. Pres. M. H. Bland & Co. Ltd. since 1970; Hon. Pres. Bland Ltd. since 1977. City Councillor 1921–24. Unofficial Member of Exec. Council 1924–30 and 1936–43. Chmn. Bench of Justices 1949–59. Chief A.R.P. Warden Gibraltar 1938–40. Chmn. Bd. of District Commissioners 1940–43. Mem. Public Service Commn. 1956–58. Chmn. Gibraltar Shipping Assn. 1956–60; Chmn. Merchant Navy Welfare Cttee. 1943–47. Mem. Merchant Navy Club Cttee. Served on many local Cttees. appointed by the Governor in connection with public matters. Swedish Consul 1939, Swedish Consul-General 1954–66. F.R.S.A. Coronation Medals 1937 and 1953. Chevalier (1st class) Royal Swedish Order of Vasa. *Clubs:* Royal Thames Yacht, Royal Gibraltar Yacht. *Address:* 75 Prince Edward's Road, Gibraltar.

**GAGLARDI, Hon. Philip Arthur.** *B.* 1913. *Educ.* Northwest Bible College, Seattle, Washington State (ordained Minister of Religion—Pentecostal). *M.* 1938, Jennie Marguerette Sandin. *S.* Robert and William. *Career:* prominent in British Columbia politics since 1952; elected for Constituency of Kamloops 1952; Former Minister, Public Works; Minister of Highways and Minister without Portfolio; Chmn. Provincia. Alliance of Businessmen; Minister of Rehabilitation & Social Improvement, Govt. of the Province of British Columbial Plastor of Calvary Temple (Pentecostal Church), Kamloops, B.C.; won national fame for his Sunday school and youth work (the Sunday school with 1125 members is the largest in British Columbia; the youth work takes the form of an organized hobby shop where boys of all faiths are taught woodwork, metalwork, steel and wood lathe work and welding); first to introduce transport of children of all faiths to Sunday school by means of omnibuses owned by Calvary Temple. Member of Social Credit Party in British Columbia. Has travelled extensively in Europe, Asia, Africa, South America, North American and Australia. *Clubs:* Hon. member: Rotary, Kiwanis, Gyro and Lions. *Address:* Parliament Buildings, Victoria, B.C., Canada.

**GAIENNIE, L. René.** American psychologist and business executive. *B.* 1912. *Educ.* AB; MS; MBA; PhD. *M.* 1941, Beatrice Clark. *S.* Clark Réne and William Grant (*Dec.*). *Career:* Vice-President: Fairbanks, Morse & Co. 1948—; Industrial & Public Relations, A.C.F. Industries 1958. Senr. Vice-Pres. and Dir., Canadian Fairbanks. Morse Co. Ltd., Montreal 1959—. President & General Manager, Howe Richardson Corp., Clifton, N.J., U.S.A. 1962; Dir. Corporate Analysis, The Singer Co. N.Y. U.S.A. Order of the British Empire; Phi Beta Kappa; Sigma Xi. Asst. Vice-Pres., The Richardson Co. 1945–48; Lieut.-Cmdr., U.S. Navy 1942–45. *Publications:* numerous articles in psychological and business journals. Republican. *Clubs:* Union League (Chicago); Executive; Economic; University (N.Y.C.); Montclair Golf, and Pennington. *Address:* 10 Belleclaire Place, Montclair, New Jersey, U.S.A.

**GAINEY, Daniel C.** Jewelry manufacturer. *B.* 1897. *Educ.* Hamline University, St. Paul, Minnesota (BA). *M.* 1924, Harriette Swearingen; and 1962, Elaine L. Frock. *S.* Daniel J. *Career:* Pres., Jostens 1933–59, Chmn. 1933–68; Instructor and Athletic Coach 1921–22; Natl. Treas., Republican Party 1958–60. Chairman Emeritus of Board, and Director Jostens Inc. 1968—. Arabian Horse Registry of America Inc., Governing member 1942–73; Dir. 1948–73; Pres. 1958–72; Univ. of Minnesota 1939–73; Trustee Emeritus, American Graduate School of International Mgmt. since 1956; Trustee, Hamline University, St. Paul, 1966—. *Awards:* Hon. Doctor of Business Administration, Hamline Univ.; Hon. Dr. Letters Coll. of St. Thomas, St. Paul, Minn. *Member:* Natl. Assn. of Manufacturers (Past Dir.); Educational Jewelry Mfrs. Assn. (Past Pres.); Jewelers Vigilance Committee Inc.

(Past Dir.); Minnesota State Employers Assn. (Past Dir.); Officer, The Gainey Foundation (philanthropic). Republican. *Clubs:* Minneapolis (Minneapols); Minikahda (Minneapolis); Paradise Valley Country (Phoenix, Ariz.). *Address:* Route 2, Box 1, Owatonna, Minn.; and *office* 138 East Broadway, Owatonna, Minn. 55060, U.S.A.

**GAIRDNER, John Smith.** Canadian investment dealer. *B.* 1925. *Educ.* Univ. of Toronto. *M.* 1946, Ivy Jane Brothwell. *S.* John Lewis and Robert Donald. *Dau.* Brenda Leigh. *Career:* With R.C.A.F. 1943–45. Chairman of Board and Director, Gairdner & Co. Ltd. 1965–73; Pres. and Director, Gairdner International Ltd. Chmn. and Pres. Security Trading Ltd. since 1973; Vice-President and Director: Trafalgar Investments Ltd., all Toronto. Mem. Bd. of Governors, Appleby Coll., Oakville. Vice-Chmn. The Gairdner Foundation. *Clubs:* National (Toronto); Toronto Golf (Mississauga); St. James's (Montreal); Hamilton; Oakville; Oakville Golf (Oakville); Caughnawana Hunting & Fishing; La Jolla Country (Calif., U.S.A.). *Address:* Suite 4706 Manulife Centre, 44 Charles Street West, Toronto, Ont., Canada M4Y 1R8.

**GAIRY, Rt. Hon. Sir Eric Matthew,** PC, Kt. Grenadian Politician & Trade Union Leader. *B.* 1922. *Educ.* St. Andrew's R.C. School. *M.* 1949, Cynthia Bernadette Clyne. *Daus.* 2. *Career:* Elected Member of the Legislative Council 1951–54, re-elected 1954–57; Premier & Minister of Finance 1961–62, re-elected Premier 1967–72, 1972–76; first Prime Minister of Grenada & Minister of Foreign Affairs since 1974, re-elected P.M. 1976; Pres., Grenada Manual, Maritime & Intellectual Workers' Union since 1950; Founder Pres. & Political Leader, Grenada United Labour Party since 1951. *Member:* Fellow of the Royal Society of Art. *Decorations:* Order of the Liberator (Venezuela); Knight Grand Cross of Jerusalem; Hon. Dir. of Political Science; Medal of the Americas; Hon. LLD; Grand Gwanghwa Medal—Order of Diplomatic Service Merit (Republic of Korea); Knight Grand Cross of St. Denis of Zante; Knight of Malta; Privy Councillor; Knight Bachelor (1977). *Address:* Mount Royal, St. George's, Grenada; and *office* Botanical Gardens, St. George's, Grenada.

**GALBALLY, Hon. John William,** MLC, QC. Victoria; Australian politician and lawyer. *B.* 2 Aug. 1910. *Educ.* Univ. of Melbourne (LLB). *M.* 1937, Sheila M. Kenny. *S.* 2. *Daus.* 3. Minister-in-Charge, Electrical Undertakings 1952–55; Minister of Labour 1954–55; member, Australian Labor Party. *Address:* 410 Glenferrie Road, Kooyong, Victoria, Australia.

**GALBRAITH, Prof. J. Kenneth.** American economist. *B.* 1908. *Educ.* Univ. of Toronto (BS 1931), Univ. of California (PhD 1934), and Cambridge Univ. (England). *M.* 1937, Catherine Atwater. *S.* 3. *Career:* Research Fellow, Univ. of California 1931–34; Instructor and Tutor, Harvard 1934–39; Asst. Prof. of Economics, Princeton Univ. 1939–42; Economic Adviser, National Defence Advisory Commission 1940–41; Asst. Administrator i/c Price Div., Office of Public Administration 1941–42 (Deputy Administrator 1942–43); Director, U.S. Strategic Bombing Survey 1945; Dir., Office of Economic Security Policy, State Dept. 1946; Member Bd. of Editors, Fortune 1943–48; Lecturer, Harvard 1948–49; Paul M. Warburg Professor of Economics, Harvard Univ. 1949–75, now Emeritus Prof.; Ambassador of the U.S.A. to India, Apr. 1961–63; Fellow, Social Science Research Council 1937–38; Fellow, Amer. Acad. of Arts and Sciences; member: Amer. Economic Association, Amer. Farm Economics Association and National Institute of Art and Letters. Awarded Medal of Freedom 1946. *Publications:* several books, including American Capitalism (1951); A Theory of Price Control (1952); The Great Crash (1955); The Affluent Society (1958); The Liberal Hour (1960); Made to Last (1964); The New Industrial State (1967); The Triumph (1968); Indian Painting (with M. S. Randhawa 1968); The Affluent Society, Rev. ed. 1969; How to Control the Military, (1969); Ambassador's Journal (1969); Economic Peace & Laughter (1971); A China Passage (1973); Economics & Public Purpose (1974); Money: whence it came, where it went (1975); The Age of Uncertainty (1976); articles in scientific journals. *Clubs:* Century Association; Federal City. *Address:* 30 Francis Avenue, Cambridge, Mass. 02138, U.S.A.

**GALBRAITH, Rt. Hon. Thomas Galloway Dunlop,** MA, LLB, MP. British. *B.* 1917. *Educ.* Aytoun House, Glasgow; Wellington Coll. Christ Church, Oxford; Glasgow University. *M.* 1956, Simone du Roy de Blicquy. *S.* Thomas and Charles. *Dau.* Ghislaine. *Career:* Member of Parliament for Hillhead Div. of Glasgow since 1948; Scottish Unionist Whip, 1950–57; Lord Commns. of the Treasury, 1951–54; Comptroller, Her Majesty's Household, 1954–55; Treasurer, 1955–57; Civil Lord of the Admiralty, 1957–59; Parly. Under Sec. of State for Scotland, 1959–62; Parly. Sec. Minister of Transport, 1962–64. Pres., Scottish Georgian Soc. 1970. *Clubs:* Carlton; Conservative (Glasgow); New (Edinburgh). *Address:* Old Barskimming, Mauchline, Ayrshire, Scotland; and *office* 2 Cowley Street, London, S.W.1.

**GALLAGHER, John Edward Patrick.** Canadian. *B.* 1916. *Educ.* Univ. of Manitoba (BSc Geol). *M.* 1949, Kathleen Marjorie Stewart. *S.* James Stewart, Thomas Patrick and Frederic Michael. *Career:* Geologist: Canadian Geological Survey 1936–37; Shell Oil Co., California 1938; Standard Oil (New Jersey) 1939–49 (in Egypt and in Central and South America); Asst. Production Mgr., Imperial Oil Ltd. (Western Canadian Division) 1949–50; Exec. Vice-Pres., Dome Petroleum Ltd. 1950–52, President 1953–74, Chmn. of the Board & Chief Exec. Officer since 1974; and Provo Gas Producers Ltd. 1956—; Dir. Canada Development Corp.; Panarctic Oils Ltd.; Research Council of Alberta. *Address:* 4315 Britannia Drive, Calgary, Alta, Canada; and *office* 706 7th Avenue S.W., Calgary, Alta., Canada.

**GALLAGHER, Patrick Joseph,** DFC. British. *B.* 1921. *Educ.* Prior Park Coll., Bath. *M.* 1950, Veronica F. Bateman. *S.* 1. *Career:* Dir. Ogilvy & Mather Ltd., 1961–66; Consultant, Urwick, Orr & Partners Ltd., 1958–60; Dir. Finlay Engineering Co. Ltd., 1959–64; Adviser, Raisman Commn., Nigeria, 1957–58; Man. Dir. London Broadcasting Co. Ltd. and Independ. Radio News Ltd. since 1975. Chmn. Radio Sales and Marketing Ltd, since 1975; Pres. Glendinning Cos. Inc. 1971–74. *Address:* (Office) Communications House, Gough Square, London, E.C.4.; (Home) 5/30 Hans Road, London SW3.

**GALLESE, Guido.** Italian executive. *B.* 1903. *Educ.* Doctor in Pure Chemistry; Fellow, Textile Technologies; appointment in silk technology, Finishing Course in Textile Industries, Milan Polytechnic; Professor Titular with filature technologies in Textile Institute, Como, Italy. *M.* 1931, Mafalda De Filippi. *S.* Giuseppe and Enrico. *Dau.* Giovanna. Managing Director, Development office for textile applications, SNIA Viscosa, Milan; Manager, Messrs. Giuseppe Gallese, Milan; Director, at the Silk Experimental Station, Milan; Manager, Societa Industriale Serica (S.I.S.) (Industrial Silk Co.), Milan; Manager, Filande Tessiture Costa, Genoa. *Publications:* Technology of Silk; Crop and drying of cocoons (vol. 1); Silk filature (vol. 2); Twisting of silk (vol. 3); Torsion vivacity in yarns (Textile Review 1960); Artificial and Synthetic Fibres and their Applications; International Convention for artificial and synthetic fibres and for enemistry, Busto Arsizio Sept. 1960, L'impiego delle fibre sintetiche nelle camicie per uomo—Convegno Internazionale per le fibre tessili artificiali e stintetiche e della chimica—Settembre 1961—Busto Arsizio; Le fibre 'man-made' caratteristiche ed impieghi-Rivista Tessile N. 3 Marzo 1963. *Address:* Via Castelfidardo 11, Milan, Italy.

**GALLI, Luigi Michele.** Italian Politician. *B.* 1924. *Educ.* Doctorate in Economics. *M.* 1951, Attilia Briata. *S.* 3. *Dau.* 2. *Career:* Member of Italian Parliament since 1953, of European Parliament since 1968. *Address:* Cajello di Gallarate (Varese), Italy; & Camera dei Deputati, Rome, Italy.

**GALLIENNE, Georges Joseph Mathieu.** French business executive (formerly in the automobile industry). Président de la Prévention Routière Internationale; Founder Pres., International Road Federation; Président d'Honneur de la Prévention Routière Française et de l'Union Routière de France; Vice-Prés. de la Société Concessionnaire Française pour la Construction et l'Exploitation du Tunnel Routièr sous le Mont-Blanc; Prés. du Groupe d'Etude des Problèmes Routiers du Marché Commun; Administrateur de l'Office National de Securité Routière. *Member:* Commission de Gestion du Fonds Routier; Conseil Supérieur des Transports. *Educ.* Ecole Alsacienne, Paris. *M.* 1945, Yvonne Delporte. Grand Officier Légion d'Honneur; Croix de Guerre (1914–18). *Address:* La Maison Blanche, Chemin des Alluets, Chambourcy 78240; and *office* Prévention Routière Internationale, Linas, 91310 Montlhéry, France.

**GALLUP, George Horace.** Public opinion statistician. *B.* 1901. *Educ.* University of Iowa (BA 1923, MA 1925, PhD 1928); Northwestern University (MA, PhD; Hon LLD); Hon DSc Tufts Coll.; Hon LLD, Rutgers College, Univ. of Iowa, Drake Univ. Boston Univ., Chattanooga Univ., Hon Dr.

Humanities, Colgate Univ. & Hon. Degrees at Rider Coll., Pepperdine, Okla, Christian Coll., Georgian Court Coll. & Beaver Coll. *M.* 1925, Ophelia Smith Miller. *S.* Alec Miller and George Horace, Jr. *Dau.* Julia. *Career:* Head, Dept. of Journalism, Drake Univ. 1929–31; Prof. of journalism and advertising, Northwestern Univ. 1931–32; Dir. of Research, Young & Rubicam Advertising Agency 1932–47; Pres., Market Research Council 1934–35. Prof., Pulitzer School of Journalism, Columbia Univ. 1935–37. Chairman, American Institute of Public Opinion; Chairman Emeritus, Gallup & Robinson Inc. President, Public Opinion Surveys Inc., Chairman of Board, The Gallup Organization Inc., Pres., Gallup Int'l. Research Institutes Inc. *Publications:* The Pulse of Democracy; A New Technique for Measuring Reader Interest; Guide to Public Opinion Polls; The Miracle Ahead (1964); The Sophisticated Poll Watcher's Guide (1976), numerous articles on public opinion; Editor, Gallup Political Almanac, Award for distinguished achievement, Syracuse Univ. and others. *Member:* Quill & Scroll (Founder); National Municipal League; Amer. Assn. of Public Opinion Research (Pres. 1954–55); World Assn. for Public Opinion Research; Sigma Delta Chi; Sigma Alpha Epsilon. *Address:* The Great Road, Princeton, N.J.; and *office* 53, Bank St., Princeton, N.J., U.S.A.

**GALSWORTHY, Sir Arthur Norman,** KCMG. *B.* 1916. *Educ.* Emanuel School and Corpus Christi College, Cambridge (BA 1937). *M.* (1) 1940, Margaret Agnes Hiscocks (dec'd 1973). *S.* 2. (2) 1976, Aylmer Jean Martin. *Career:* On active service 1939–45. Head, International Relations Department, Colonial Office, London 1947–51; Chief Secretary, West African Inter-Territorial Secretariat, Accra 1951–54; Head of Finance Dept., Colonial Office 1954–56; Assistant Under-Secy. of State, Colonial Office 1956–65; Deputy Under-Secy. of State; Colonial Office 1965–66; Commonwealth Office, 1966–68; Foreign and Commonwealth Office, 1968–69. British High Commissioner, New Zealand, Oct. 1969–73. Tonga (non-Resident) 1970–73. W. Samoa (non resident) 1970–73; Governor of Pitcairn 1970; Amb. to Republic of Ireland 1973–76. *Club:* Oxford & Cambridge University. *Address:* c/o FCO, London SW1.

**GALSWORTHY, Sir John Edgar,** KCVO, CMG. British diplomat. *B.* 1919. *Educ.* Emanuel School, Corpus Christi Coll. Cambridge. *M.* 1942, Jennifer Ruth Johnstone. *S.* 1. *Daus.* 3. *Career:* with H.M. Forces 1939–41; Foreign Office 1941–46; Third Secretary, Madrid 1946; Second Secy. Vienna 1949; First Secy. Athens 1951; Foreign Office 1954; Bangkok 1958; Counsellor, Brussels U.K. Delegation to EEC 1962; Counsellor (Economic) Bonn 1964–67, Paris 1967–70; Minister, European Economic Affairs Paris 1970; Ambassador to Mexico 1972–77. *Award:* Knight Commander of the Royal Victorian Order; Companion, Order of St. Michael & St. George. *Club:* United Oxford and Cambridge University. *Address:* c/o Foreign and Commonwealth Office, London, S.W.1.

**GALVIN, John Michael.** Chairman of the Executive Committee and Chief Executive Officer, The Marine Midland Trust Co. of Western New York, Buffalo, N.Y., May 1962—. *B.* 1905. *Educ.* Millard Fillmore Coll. of the Univ. of Buffalo, and the American Inst. of Banking. *M.* 1936, Grace Kleinbauer. *S.* John Michael and Richard James. *Dau.* Grace Ann. With the Marine Trust: Asst. Treas. 1933; successively Asst. Vice-Pres., Vice-Pres., Vice-Pres. and Dir. of Public Relations, Senior Vice-Pres., Exec. Vice-Pres 1961. *Awards:* 'Man of the Year' 1963 Award (Greater Buffalo Advertising Club); Magistral Knight, Sovereign Military Order of Malta in U.S. 1962; Hon LLD Canisius Coll. 1959; 'One of ten outstanding citizens of Buffalo for 1961' (Buffalo Evening News); 1964 National Brotherhood Citation (Natl. Conf. Christians and Jews). *Member:* Amer. Bankers Assn.; N.Y. State Bankers Association; Association of Reserve City Bankers. *Clubs:* Automobile; Buffalo Athletic; Buffalo; Capitol Hill; Country (Buffalo); Frontier Press; Mid-Day. *Address:* 241 Main Street, Buffalo, N.Y. 14203, U.S.A.

**GAMASY, General Mohamed El-.** Egyptian Soldier & Statesman. *B.* 1921. *Educ.* Military Academy (Bachelor of Military Sciences); Staff College; Nasser Higher Military Academy. *Married. S.* 1. *Daus.* 2. *Career:* Rose to rank of Lietuenant Colonel by 1954; Asst. Dir., Mobilization Dept. 1954–55; Commander of the 5th Recce Regiment 1955–57; Promoted Colonel, 1957; Staff Officer, Armours Corps 1957; Cmdr., 2nd Armoured Brigade 1959; Cmdr., Armour School 1961; Brigadier, 1962; Major General, 1965; Chief of Army Operational Branch 1966; Chief of Staff, Eastern Mil. Zone 1967; Dep. Dir., Recce & Intelligence Dept. 1968; Cmdr. Operational Group of Syrian Front 1970; Chief of Armed Forces Training Dept., 1971; Chief of Operations Dept. & Dept. Chief of Staff of Armed Forces 1972; Lieutenant Gen., 1973; Chief of Staff of Armed Forces 1973; General 1974; Minister of War & Cmdr. in Chief of the Armed Forces 1974; Deputy Prime Minister. Min. of War & Cmdr. in Chief of the Armed Forces since 1975. *Decorations:* Many, incl. Liberation Order, 1952; Memorial Order of the U.A.R. Establishment, 1958; Medal of the 10th Aniversary of the Revolution, 1962; Medal of the 6th of October, 1974; & others from Army of the G.D.R., Iran, Libya, Saudi Arabia, Sudan, Syria, etc. *Address:* c/o Ministry of War, Cairo, Egypt.

**GAMBERINI, François.** French banker. *B.* 1899. *Educ.* ESCP. *M.* 1937, Suzanne Semaille. *Dau.* Rosine. *Career:* Manager and Partner, Seligman & Co. 1926–55; General Manager, Union Financière de Paris 1950–56; Administrator; Compagnie Franco-Hellénique de Chemins de Fer 1943–55, Société de Transports et Manutentions Industriels (STEMI) 1943–55; Pres. Fonderies Modernes de l'Automobile 1956–60; Vice-Pres., Cie Européene de Réassurances 1943–65. Westinghouse Electric Europe (Paris) 1960–65; Gen. Manager C.O.F.P.A. 1956–68 President, Société Alsacienne-Lorraine de Recherches et de Participation (SALREP) 1956–75; Administrator, S.A. Ruberoid 1966–74; Société d'Electricité MORS 1960–75, and Omnium d'Assainissement 1963–72; Fiat France 1968–75; Assistant General Manager Banque Rothschild Paris 1968–72. *Clubs:* Golf de La Boulie; Automobile Club de France. *Address:* 2 Avenue Emile Bergerat, Paris 16; and Vera Cruz, 15 Boulevard des Nations, Juan les Pins (A.M.) France; and *office* 20 rue d'Athens Paris 9.

**GAMBLE, Bertin Clyde.** American. *B.* 1898. *Educ.* Grade and High School; Hon LLD Univ. of North Dakota, June 1965. *M.* 1927, Gladys Pearson. *S.* Jerry David (*Dec.*). *Dau.* Karen (Gamble Hubbard). *Career:* Chairman of the Board, Gamble-Skogmo Inc. (also Director) 1963—. Director: Gambles Canada Ltd., Aldens Inc., Red Owl Stores Inc. and Retailers Growth Fund Inc.; Abbott Northwestern Hospital Corp. Minneapolis. Patron Minneapolis Socy. of Fine Arts. Trustee: Ripon Coll. (Ripon, Wis.), College of the Desert, Palm Desert, Calif.; and Nat. Bd. of Boys Clubs of America; *Member:* National Citizens Bd. Eisenhower Medical Center, Calif. *Award:* Theodore Roosevelt Roughrider. *Clubs:* Minneapolis; Minneapolis Athletic; Minkahda (Minneapolis); Eldorado Country (Palm Desert, Calif.); Woodhill Country (Wayzata, Minn.). *Address:* 5100 Gamble Drive, Minneapolis; Minn. 55416, U.S.A.

**GAMBLE, Sir (Frederick) Herbert,** KBE, CMG. British diplomat. *B.* 21 May 1907. *Educ.* Portora Royal School, Enniskillen and Trinity Coll., Dublin (BA). *M.* 1942, Janine Corbisier de Cobreville. *Daus.* 2. Entered Levant Consular Service 1930; Consul, Suez 1945–46; Commercial Counsellor, Baghdad 1948–52 and Athens 1952–55; Amb. Ex. and Plen. to Ecuador 1955–59; Consul-General, Los Angeles 1959–64; Amb. to Bolivia, June 1964–67. *Address:* Santana, Delgany, co. Wicklow, Ireland.

**GAMBRELL, E(noch) Smythe.** American lawyer. *B.* 1896. *Educ.* Univ. of South Carolina (AB 1915) and Harvard Univ. (LLB 1922). *M.* 1927, Alice Kathleen Hagood (*Dec.*). *S.* Robert H. (*Dec.*) and David H. *Career:* Principal, Public Schools, Bannockburn, S.C. 1915–16; Supt. of Schools, Pelzer, S.C. 1916–18; active front line duty, machine-gun unit, A.E.F., France 1918; Instructor in English, A.E.F. Univ., Beaune, Côte d'Or, France 1919; Prof. of Law, Emory Univ. 1922–40. General practice in Atlanta, Ga. 1922—. Senior partner in law firm of Gambrell, Russell, Killorin, Forbes; Director and General Counsel, Eastern Air-Lines Inc. 1940—. Pres., Georgia State Chamber of Commerce 1952–54; Trustee, Shorter Coll. 1957–60; Hon. LLD, Univ. of S.C. 1953, Southern Methodist Univ. 1956, Univ. of Montreal 1956, Emory Univ. 1964; awarded Amer. Bar Assn. Medal for conspicuous service to cause of Amer. Jurisprudence 1958. *Member:* Visiting Cttee. Harvard Law School; Amer. Bar Assn. (Pres. 1955–56); Amer. Bar Foundation (Pres. 1955–56; Chmn. of Fellows 1956–58); Lawyers Club of Atlanta (Pres. 1948–49); Atlanta Legal Aid Socy. (Founder and Pres. 1924–40); Phi Beta Kappa; Order of the Coif; Amer. Judicature Socy.; Acad. of Political Science; Amer. Coll. of Trial Lawyers; Assn. of the Bar of New York City. *Clubs:* Piedmont Driving; Capital City; Commerce; Harvard. *Address:* 4000 First National Bank Tower, Atlanta, Ga., U.S.A.

**GAMBRILL, Howard, Jr.** American business executive; *B.* 1907. *Educ.* Yale University (BS). *M.* 1939, Mary Greenwood Butler. *S.* James Howard. *Daus.* Betsy Greenwood

(Clark), Mary Howard (Aydelott). *Career:* Vice-Pres., Gillette Safety Razor Co. 1947–52; Vice-Pres. & Dir., The Gillette Co. (1952–60); Corporator, Boston Five-Cents Savings Bank (1952—); Incorporator, Trustee, South Boston Savings Bank (1959–73). Dir. Rivett Lathe & Grinder Inc. (1960–65); Chmn. Affiliated Hospitals Center, Boston (1963–66); Trustee, R. B. Brigham Hospital (1950; Pres. 1960–66); Concord (Mas.) Academy (1959–69; Treas. 1960–66); Dir. Cliff Realty Corp. (1953—); Pres., Yale Club of Boston (1956–58); Vestryman, St. Peter's Church, Weston (1948–61); Trustee, Socy. for Relief of Widows & Orphans of Clergymen of the Protestant Episcopal Church; Simon's Rock School, 1965–72; Exec. Ctte., Simon's Rock, Inc. (1965–76), Golden Ball Tavern Trust (1965—); Treas. Margaret Kendrick Blodgett Foundation 1964–76; Council Socy. for Preservation New England Antiquities 1968–71, 72–75; Pres., Union Club of Boston 1970–72; Mem. Bd. of Trvstees, Weston Visiting Nurse Assn.; Trustee, Historic Deerfield 1976—. *Address:* 39 Crescent Street, Weston, Mass.; and *office* 79 Milk Street, Boston, Mass. 02109, U.S.A.

**GANCAYO, Hon. Emilio A.**, KSGG. Filipino jurist and associate Justice, Court of Appeals. *B.* 1921. *Educ.* Jose Rizal Institute, AA, LLB, Univ. of the Philippines. *M.* 1947, Herminia Mejia. *S.* 4. *Dau.* 1. *Career:* World War II 1942–44, Legal Asst., Phil. Army; Private Law Practice since 1949; Spec. Prosecutor, Dept. of Justice 1955–60, chief Prosecuting Attorney 1962, Chief State Prosecutor 1963–71; Assoc. Justice, Court of Appeals 1972; Professor of Law, Univ. of the Phils. & Univ. of the East; Chmn. Conf. Cttee on Law Reform, UP Law Centre 1965, Spec. Lect. on Law & Procedure 1968; Vice-Pres. & mem. Bd. of Dirs. YMCA of the Phils.; Bd. of Dirs. Quezon City YMCA; Nat. Commander Govt. Employees World War Veterans League 1967–69, & 1969–70; Vice-Pres. Family Life Workshop of Philippines; Pres. Bataan Bar Assn.; Nat. Pres. Catholic Action of the Philippines; Pres. San Fernando Dioc. Council. *Member:* Bd. Consumers' Union of Phils.; Nat. Bd. Exec. Cttee. YMCA World Alliance; Upsilon Sigma Phi; Phil. Society International Law; Philippine Constitution Assn. *Awards:* Special Prosecutor of the Year (1960); Leadership and Achievement (1964); Most Outstanding Professional; Papal Knighthood of St. Gregory the Great. *Address: office* Court of Appeals, Manila, Philippines.

**GANDHI, Mrs. Indira Priyadarshini.** Former Prime Minister of India. *B.* 19 Nov. 1917. *Educ.* India, Switzerland & Somerville Coll., Oxford. *M.* 1942, Feroze Gandhi (*D.* 1960). *S.* 2. *Career:* Founded Vanar Sena Congress Childrens' Organization 1929; Joined Indian National Congress 1938; Member Working Cttee. 1955; Pres. Congress Party 1959–60; Chmn. Citizens Central Council 1962; Minister, Information and Broadcasting 1964–66; Leader, Congress Party 1966–77; Prime Minister of India 1966–77; Concurrently Minister for Atomic Energy; Chmn. Planning Commission; Min. of External Affairs 1967–69; Min. of Finance 1969–70; Min, of Home Affairs 1970–73; Min. of Information & Broadcasting 1971–74; Min. of Defence 1975–77. *Awards:* Received Honorary Degrees from many Universities, incl. Oxford, Baghdad, Moscow State, Andra, Bangladore, etc. *Address:* 12 Willingdon Crescent, New Delhi, India.

**GANDY, Christopher Thomas.** British. Retired diplomat. *B.* 1917. *Educ.* Marlborough College and King's College, Cambridge (MA 1938). Served with Army and R.A.F. 1939–45, Entered Foreign Office Nov. 1945; served at Teheran 1948–51, Cairo 1951–52, Foreign Office 1952–54, Lisbon 1954–56, Libya 1956–59, NATO Defence College 1959–60, Foreign Office 1960–62. Appointed British Minister to Yemen, Aug. 1962; Counsellor, British Embassy, Kuwait, 1963; Minister (Commercial) Rio de Janeiro, April 1966. *Member:* Iran Society; C.A.A.B.U.; Royal Central Asian Society. *Club:* Travellers' (London). *Address:* 60 Ambleside Drive, Headington, Oxford OX3 OAH.

**GARBA, J. M.** Diplomat and Economist. Ambassador of Nigeria. *B.* 1918. *Educ.* C.M.S. Grammar School, Lagos; Igbobi Coll. Yaba; Dept. Economics and Political Science, London School of Economics. *M.* Amina Adamu. *S.* 4. *Daus.* 2. *Career:* joined Foreign Service 1957; Asst. Secy. Office, Nigerian Commissioner London 1957; Second Secy. Office United Kingdom High Commissioner Ottawa Canada 1958; First Secy. Office Nigerian Comm. London 1958; Nigerian Pilgrim Office Khartoum Sudan 1959; Counsellor, Charge d'Affairs, Minister Embassy of Nigeria Washington D.C. 1960; Asst. Perm. Secy. Federal Min. of Finance Lagos 1962–63; Exec. Dir. International Bank for Reconstruction and Development; Int. Dev. Assn. and Int. Finance Corp. for 23 African and one Caribbean States, 1963, 1964–66; Nigerian Ambassador to the Republic of Italy 1966, Concurrently accredited to the Republics of Greece, Cyprus and Spain 1970; Ambassador to the United States of America 1972–75. *Address:* c/o Ministry for External Affairs, Lagos, Nigeria.

**GARBISCH, Edgar William.** American. *B.* 1899. *Educ.* Washington and Jefferson Coll. (BA 1921), Hon. Doctor Fine Arts 1972. U.S. Military Acad. (BS 1925). *M.* 1930, Bernice Chrysler. *S.* Edgar William, Jr. *Dau.* Mrs. David E. Severance. *Career:* sales dept., Postum Cereal Co. 1926–27; Institutional Sales Manager, same company 1927–28; Mgr. of Sales, Post Products Co., N.Y.C. 1928–29; Vice-Pres. 1929; Manager of Sales, General Foods Sales Co., N.Y.C. 1929–30; Winthrop Mitchell & Co., N.Y.C. 1930–31; Pres. & Dir., Cellulose Products Corp., also successor company, Tish, Inc. (later Kernap, Inc.), 1931–42; Vice-Pres. and Dir., J. Sterling Getchell, Inc., advertising agency, N.Y.C. 1933–37; Vice-Pres. and Dir., Ruthrauff & Ryan, Inc. (advertising agency), N.Y.C. 1937–42. Major Corps of Engineers, A.U.S. Mar. 1942; Lt.-Col. Dec. 1942; District Engineer, Providence, R.I., Dist. (1943–44) and New York District; Colonel May 1944; honorably discharged Dec. 1945. Legion of Merit 1946. Dir., Hudhattan Corp., N.Y.C. 1937–54; Dir., Island Creek Coal Co., Huntington, W. Va. 1941–43; Dir., W. P. Chrysler Building Corp. 1948–53; Dir. Grocery Store Products Co. 1937; Chmn., Finance Cttee. 1937–45; Pres. 1945–47; Chmn. Bd. 1947–71, Hon. Chmn. Bd. since 1971. Trustee, Maryland Historical Society; Metropolitan Museum of Art (Fellow in Perpetuity); Patron, National Trust for Historic Preservation; Life member, American Federation of Arts. Hon. Trustee, Assn. of Graduates, U.S. Military Acad.; (Dir. 1953; Treas. 1955–59. Vice-Pres. 1959–70; Vice-Chmn. of the Board, 1970—. Exect. Cttee. 1955–70). National Football Foundation (elected to Hall of Fame 1954); Helms Athletic Foundation's College Football Hall of Fame, Aug. 1959; Trustee, Phi Gamma Delta Educational Foundation; member. Board of Managers, St. Barnabas Hospital, N.Y.C. 1956–61. *Clubs:* University, Metropolitan Opera, Sky, Touchdown, Phi Gamma Delta (all of N.Y.C.); Everglades; West Beach Fishing; Bath and Tennis; (Palm Beach, Fla.); Cambridge Yacht and Cambridge Country (both Cambridge, Md.); Touchdown Club of America. *Address:* Route 3 Box 44, Cambridge, Maryland 21613, U.S.A.

**GARCIA HERNANDEZ, Sr. Don. Jose.** Spanish Politician. *B.* 1915. *Educ.* Madrid Univ. (Faculty of Law) Law Degree. *M.* 1946, Esmeralda Alexiades. *Career:* Pres. Guadalajara Co. Council 1941–47, Governor Province of Lugo 1947–48; Governor Province of Las Palmas (Canary Is.) 1948–51; Gen.-Dir. Dept. Local Govt. 1951–57; Mem. Spanish Cortes since 1952; Min. of Int. Span. Govt. 1974–75; First Vice-Pres. of Spanish Govt. 1974–75; Vice-Pres. & Man. Dir. of the Banco Exterior de España since 1975. *Member:* Guild of Lawyers; Spanish Assoc. of Financial Law; Genova Finance Club. *Decorations:* Grand Cross Civil Merit; Commander of Order of Cisneros; Grand Cross, Yoke and Arrows; Grand Cross Carlos III. *Club:* Madrid Country. *Address:* Paseo Castellana 10 Madrid-1, Spain; and *office* Carrera San Jerónimo 36, Madrid 14, Spain.

**GARDINER, Cyril**, FCIS. Ceylonese. *B.* 1922. *Educ.* St. Joseph's College, Colombo. *M.* 1959, Mavis Henry. *S.* 1. *Career:* International Dir., Pacific Area Travel Assn. (PATA); Dir., Development Finance Corp. of Ceylon; Hotels: Chmn. & Man. Dir. The Galle Face Hotel Co. Ltd.; Deputy Chmn. Hotel Services; Ceylon Inter. Continental; Dir. Nuwara Eliya Hotels; Chmn., Ceylon Tourist Hotels Assn.; Automobiles: Founder Chmn. The Autodrome Ltd.; Gardiner Motors Ltd., Union Co. Ltd. representing General Motors; Cadillac, Buick (U.S.), Pontiac (Canada), Vauxhall Cars & Bedford Trucks (Britain) and Opel Cars (Germany); *Deputy Chmn.* Ceylon Theatres Ltd.; Dir. Global Films Ltd., Ceylon Bulbs & Electricals Ltd.; Chief Executive Union Secretaries; Founder Managing Editor, The Financial Times; Trustee Sir Chittampalam A. Gardiner Trust; Cyril Gardiner & The Aloysius' Charitable Fund; Committee Member Children's Trust; Ceylon, Australia, New Zealand Assn.; Fellow Institute of Chartered Secretaries: *Member:* Corporation of Certified Secretaries; Faculty of Corporate Secretaries; London Institute of Directors. *Clubs:* Nuwara Eliya Golf: Royal Colombo Golf: Sinhalese Sports; Tamil Union. *Address:* Box 330, 323 Union Place, Colombo-2. Sri Lanka.

**GARDINER, Frederick Keith**, FJI, JP. British. *M.* 1929, Ruth Dixon. *S.* Douglas K. and J. Duncan *B.* Held various positions with newspaper companies in the South of England,

Darlington, York, Oxford and Sheffield. Editor and Director, Sheffield Telegraph & Star Ltd. 1937–55; Past Chairman, Sheffield Magistrates' Courts Committee; Past Chmn. Neepsend Ltd.; Pres. Hallamshire Golf Club. *Clubs:* The Sheffield; Hallamshire Golf. *Address:* 5 Chorley Road, Fulwood, Sheffield 10.

**GARDINER, Lord Gerald Austin,** PC, CH, Baron of Kittisford; British. *B.* 1900. *Educ.* Harrow School; Magdalen College, Oxford; called to the Bar of the Inner Temple, 1925. *M.* (1) 1925, Lesly Trounson (*Dec.* 1966). *Dau.* Carol Susan. (2) 1970, Muriel Box. *Career:* Chairman, General Council of the Bar, 1958 and 1959. Lord High Chancellor of Great Britain, 1964–70. LLD (Universities of Southampton and London); Dr. University of York; Chancellor of the Open University; Master of the Bench of the Inner Temple; Hon. Pres. Socy. of Labour Lawyers. *Address:* 1 Harcourt Buildings, Temple, London, EC4Y 9DA.

**GARDINER, Robert David Lion.** American. *B.* 1911. *Educ.* Columbia University (BA). *M.* Eunice Bailey Oaks. Hon. Doctor's Degree, Humane Letters, Southampton Coll., 1970. *Career:* Lieut.-Comdr. U.S.N.R. Candidate for the New York State Senate 1960. Suffolk County Planning Commissioner, at present on Suffolk County Board of Boy Scouts of America; Candidate, Congressman United States 1st District New York 1972. Conservative. Trustee, Bard Coll.; Long Island Univ.; Director Hala Enterprises. *Awards:* Grand Officer, Knights of the Holy Sepulchre (Holy See), and of St. Denis of Zante (Greek Orthodox). *Member:* Society of the Cincinnati. *Clubs:* New York Yacht; Turf & Field; Racquet & Tennis; Downtown Assn.; University (Washington); Everglades (Palm Beach). *Address:* Gardiner's Island, N.Y. 11937; and *office* 230 Park Avenue, New York, N.Y. 10017, U.S.A.

**GARDNER, Charles Joseph Thomas,** OBE, AFRAeS. British. *B.* 1912. *Educ.* King Edward VI School, Nuneaton; R.A.F. College, Cranwell. *M.* 1935, Eve Fletcher. *S.* 2. *Dau.* 1. Air Correspondent 1937–39, War Correspondent 1939–40, B.B.C. Serving Officer R.A.F. 1940–45; Air Correspondent B.B.C. 1946–53; Assistant to Managing Director, Vickers-Armstrongs (Aircraft) Ltd. 1953–54; Information and P.R. Manager, same company 1952–60. Publicity Manager, British Aircraft Corp. 1960—. *Publications:* A.A.S.F.; Gen. Book; Modern British Aircraft; Come Flying with Me; History of Brooklands (Editor); Astro-Navigation; The Great Trog Conspiracy; Trogs Afloat. *Member:* Guild of Air Pilots. *Clubs:* M.C.C.; R.A.F.; R.A.F.Y.C. *Address: office* B.A.C. Weybridge, Surrey.

**GARDNER, Edward Lucas,** QC, MP. British *B.* 1912. *Educ.* Hutton Grammar Sch. *M.* Joan Elizabeth Belcher. *S.* 2. *Daus.* 2. *Career:* After War Service, called to the Bar, Gray's Inn, 1947; Master of the Bench of Gray's Inn, 1968; Dep. Chmn. of Quarter Sessions, East Kent 1961–71; Country of Kent 1962–71; Essex 1968–71; Conservative M.P., Billericay Div. of Essex 1959–66; PPS to Attorney-General 1962–63; Chmn. Justice Working Party on Bail & Remands in Custody, 1966; Bar Council Ctte on Parliamentary Privilege, 1967; Exec. Ctte. Justice, 1958; Conservative M.P. for South Fylde since 1970; a Recorder of the Crown Court since 1972. *Member:* Departmental Ctte on Jury Service, 1963; Ctte on Appeals in Criminal Cases, 1964; Commonwealth War Graves Comm. 1971. Governor of Thomas Coram Foundation for Children since 1962 & Queenswood Sch. since 1975. *Publications:* (Part author) A Case for Trial. *Clubs:* Garrick; United & Cecil (Chmn. 1970). *Address:* 4 Raymond Buildings, Gray's Inn, London WC1; & Outlane Head Cottage, Chipping, Lancs.

**GARDNER, George P., Jr.** Investment banker. *B.* 1917. *Educ.* St. Mark's School (Southboro, Massachusetts) and Harvard Coll. (AB 1939). *M.* 1947, Tatiana Stepanoff. *S.* George Peabody 3rd. *Daus.* Alexandra and Tatiana S. *Career:* Mem. of expedition to Peru on behalf of Museum of Comparative Zoology 1939–40. Served from Ensign to Lieutenant-Commander, U.S.N.R. 1940–46. Advertising Department, Boston Herald Traveler 1947–48; Account Executive, Batton, Barton, Durstine & Oxborn (advt.) 1948–51; Snr. Vice-Pres. and Dir. Paine, Webber, Jackson & Curtis Incorporated Boston 1955— (with this firm since 1952). Dir. Barry Wright Corp.; W. R. Grace & Co.; Instron Corp., Stanley Home Products. Life member, Corporation of Massachusetts Institute of Technology. Fellow American Academy of Arts and Sciences. Trustee: John F. Kennedy Library, Children's Hospital Medical Center, Boston Museum of Science, Escuela Agricola Panamericana (Honduras). Institute for Defense Analyses; Pan American Society of New England. *Clubs:* A.D. (Cambridge, Massachusetts); Tavern (Boston), Links (N.Y.C.). *Address: office* 100 Federal Street, Boston, Mass., U.S.A.

**GARNER, Baron** cr. 1969 (Life Peer) of Chiddingly; **(Joseph John) Garner,** GCMG. *B.* 1908. *Educ.* Highgate School; Jesus Coll., Cambridge; BA (Hons). *M.* 1938, Margaret Beckman (of Indiana, U.S.A.). *S.* 2. *Daus.* 1. *Career:* appointed to Dominions Office; Private Secretary to successive Secretaries of State 1940–43; Senior Secretary, Office of the High Commissioner for the U.K., Ottawa 1943–46; Deputy High Commissioner, Ottawa 1946–48; Asst. Under-Secretary of State, Commonwealth Relations Office 1948–51; Deputy U.K. High Commissioner in India 1951–53; Depty Under-Secretary of State, Commonwealth Relations Office 1952–56; British High Commissioner in Canada 1965–61; Permanent Under-Secretary of State, Commonwealth Relations Office 1962–65, Commonwealth Office 1965–68; Head of the Diplomatic Service 1965–67; Chmn. Commonwealth Scholarship Commission in the U.K. since 1968; Bd. of Management, Royal Postgrad. Medical Sch. since 1971; London Board, Bank of Adelaide since 1971. *Publications:* The Books of the Emperor Wu Ti (transl. from the German 1930). LLD, Univ. of Brit. Columbia 1958; LLD, Univ. of Toronto 1959; Governor of Highgate School 1962; Registrar Order of St. Michael and St. George 1962–66 and Secretary of Order 1966–68; Chmn. Bd. of Governors, Commonwealth Inst. 1968–74. *Address:* 1 Courtenay Square, London SE11 5PG.

**GARNER, Paul.** Dean & Professor of Accounting. Emeritus. *B.* 1910. *Educ.* Duke University (AB 1932; AM 1934); Columbia University; University of Texas (PhD 1940); CPA Texas 1938, Alabama 1942; LLD (Hon.) Alabama; Dr Econ (Hon) Korea. *M.* 1934, Ruth Bailey. *S.* Thad Barclay and Walter Samuel, *Dau.* Sarah Jane. *Career:* Instructor: Duke University 1934–35, Mississippi State University 1935–37 and University of Texas 1937–39; Assoc. Professor of Accounting, Univ. of Alabama 1939–43 (Head Dept. of Accounting 1949–55). State Accountant for O.P.A. 1942; Comer lecturer, Univ. of Georgia 1957 & Distinguished Visiting Prof. at 14 different Universities; Professor of Accounting 1943–71, and Dean, School of Business Administration 1954–71, University of Alabama. Member of firm of Knight & Garner, Certified Public Accountants 1942–49. Consultant on Education to Comptroller General of U.S. 1955–61; Consultant on Graduate Education U.S. Office of Education 1965–69; and on Management Education, U.S. Department of Defense, 1965–68. *Member:* Committee on International Accounting 1964—; Committee on Program and Activities 1965—; and many other bodies. U.S. delegate to Int. Congress on Management Paris 1957, Sydney and Melbourne 1960, Int. Congress on Accounting, Amsterdam 1957, and Pacific-Asian Accounting Convention, Melbourne 1960 & 16 other International Conferences; educational assignments for U.S. State Dept., 1958–68. *Publications:* Elementary Cost Accounting (with G. H. Newlove), 1941, 1949, Spanish Edn. 1952; Advanced Accounting; Advanced Accounting Problems; Handbook of Modern Accounting Theory (1955); Education for the Professions (1955); Readings in Cost Accounting, Budgeting & Control (1955); Evolution of Cost Accounting to 1925, 1954 (Japanese edn. 1956); Readings in Accounting Theory (1965); numerous contributions to professional journals. *Address:* 1016 Indian Hills Drive, Tuscaloosa, Ala.; and *office* The University, Alabama, U.S.A.

**GARRAN, Sir (Isham) Peter,** KCMG. *B.* 15 Jan. 1910. *Educ.* Melbourne Grammar School and Trinity College, Melbourne University (BA 1st Cl Hons). *M.* 1935, Mary Elisabeth Stawell. *S.* 2. *Dau.* 1. *Career:* Joined Foreign Office 1934. Served at Belgrade 1937–41; Lisbon 1941–44; Berlin (seconded to Control Commission) 1947–50; The Hague 1950–52; Inspector of Foreign Service Establishments 1952–54; Minister (Commercial), Washington 1955–60; Ambassador to Mexico 1961–64; Ambassador to the Netherlands 1964–70. Director, Lend Lease Corp., Sydney, Australia; London Board, Australian Mutual Provident Society; Property Holdings International (Bermuda); Chmn. Securicor Nederland BV. *Address:* Roanoke, Bosham Hoe, Sussex.

**GARRATT, Arthur John,** MBE, BSc, FInstP, FRSA. British. *B.* 1916. *Educ.* Salesian Coll., Farnborough; Univ. Coll., London (BSc (Hons. Physics)). *M.* 1948, Eileen Mena Mary Pearson. *S.* 2. *Career:* Man. Dir. Value Engineering Ltd., Phillips & Garratt (Opticians) Ltd., Cougar Films Ltd., Management Advisory Group Ltd.; formerly Dir. International Scientific Research Exhibitions Ltd., 1958–60. *Member:* Soc. of Film & Television Arts; Royal Institution;

British Science Writers; Mem. International Science Writer: Assoc.; Sen. Warden of Worshipful Co. of Scientific Instrument Makers. *Clubs:* Nat. Liberal. *Address: office* Value Engineering Ltd., John Cunningham House, Lower Sloane Street, London, S.W.1.

**GARRETT, Arthur.** American lawyer. *B.* 1904. *Educ.* Yale (BA 1926) and University of Washington JD (1939). *M.* 1926, Marguerite Wuest. *Daus.* Nancy Ann (Brown), Eleanor (Smith) and Barbara (Griffith). *Career:* Successively Analyst, Chief, Organization & Methods Division, Secy. to Chief Executive Cities Service Co. (60 Wall Street, N.Y.C.) 1926–37 Business Mgr., Parsons College, Fairfield (Iowa) 1940; Special Agent, Farm Security Administration, U.S. Dept. of Agriculture 1940–45; Prosecuting Attorney, Jefferson County 1945–46. Chairman of the Board, Alaska Power & Telephone Co. National Utilities Inc.; Pacific Water Co. Inc.; Alectric Inc. President Garrett Industries Inc. *Address:* 702 Water Street, Port Townsend, Washington 98368. U.S.A.

**GARRETT, Sylvester.** American attorney and arbitrator. *B.* 1911. *Educ.* Swarthmore Coll. (AB 1933); Univ. of Pennsylvania (LLB 1936). *M.* 1938, Molly Yard. *S.* James and John. *Dau.* Joan. Professor of Law, Stanford Univ. 1949–51; Co-ordinator of Labor Relations, Libbey-Owens-Ford Glass Co. and Pittsburgh Plate Glass Co. 1946–49; Vice-Chmn., National Wage Stabilization Board 1945–46; Chmn., Third Region, National War Labor Board 1942–45; Chief Counsel, Textile Leather and Apparel Div., Office of Price Administration 1941–42. Author: Management Problems Implicit in Multi-Employer Bargaining (with Dr. L. Reed Tripp). Chmn. Cttee. on Ethics and Grievances since 1965; Chmn. Board of Arbitration, U.S. Steel Corporation and United Steelworkers of America; Impartial Chmn. U.S. Postal Service and Postal Worker Unions. *Member:* National Acad. of Arbitrators, Pres. 1963–64; Amer. Bar Assn.; Amer. Arbitration Assn.; Industrial Relations Research Assn. *Address: office* 2412 Grant Building, Pittsburgh 15219, Pa., U.S.A.

**GARRETT, William Edward,** MP. British Engineer. *B.* 1920. *Educ.* Elementary Sch.; London Sch. of Economics; Evening Classes. *M.* 1946, Beatrice Kelly. *S.* 1. *Career:* Engineer, Imperial Chemical Industries 1945–64; 18 years in Local Government 1946–64; Labour M.P. for Wallsend since 1964. *Member:* Labour Party since 1938; Amalgamated Engineering Union. *Clubs:* Numerous working-mens Clubs. *Address:* 84 Broomhill Road, Prudhoe, Northumberland; & House of Commons, London SW1A 0AA.

**GARRIGUE, Pierre Louis.** French mining engineer; Officer Legion of Honour (France). General Manager in Peru of Compagnie des Mines de Huaron, Nov. 1947—. Also member of the Board of Directors of: Sociedad de Mineria y Petroleo; Cámara de Comercio Franceca; Banco Wiese Ltdo.; Cia. Minera San Juan de Lucanas; Hornos Eléctricos Peruanos; Panisndustria; Cia. Internacional de Segures del Perú; Compañia Peruana de Créditos; Amial Peruana; Colegio Franco-Peruano; Alliance Française; Cia. Minera San Jorge; Clínica Internacional. *B.* 1910. *Educ.* Ecole des Mines, Paris. *M.* 1936, Isabelle Miranda. *S.* Pierre. *Dau.* Evelyne. Mining engineer in Spain (Société Minière et Métallurgique de Peñarroya) 1934–36, and in Peru (Compagnie des Mines de Huarón 1937–41), Chief Engineer of latter company 1941–47. Officer, Legion of Honour, and Croix de Guerre (both of France). *Member:* Patronato de la Universidad Nacional de Ingeniería del Peru; Instituto de Ingenieros des Minas del Peru; American Inst. of Mining, Metallurgical and Petroleum Engineering. *Clubs:* De la Banca; Lima Golf. *Address:* Los Laureles 337, San Isidro, Lima, Peru.

**GARSON, Hon. Stuart Sinclair,** QC, PC (Can). Canadian barrister-at-law. *B.* 1 Dec. 1898. *Educ.* University of Manitoba (LLB). *M.* 1933, Emily Joyce Topper. *Daus.* Marjorie Joyce (Beam), Eleanor Frances (Swainson). *Member:* Manitoba Legislature for Fairford 1927–48. Provincial Treasurer of Manitoba 1936–48; Minister in charge of Manitoba Telephone System and Manitoba Power Commission 1941–48; Premier of Manitoba and Minister of Dominion-Provincial Relations 1943–48; Minister of Justice and Attorney-General of Canada 1948–57; M.P. (Lib.) for the Manitoba constituency and Marquette 1948–57; Chairman of Continuing Committee of Attorneys-General set up by the Constitutional Conference of Federal and Provincial Governments 1950; Chairman, Canadian Delegation, Sixth General Assembly, United Nations, Paris 1952; Hon LLD. *Address:* 139, Ash Street, Winnipeg, Manitoba, Canada.

**GARTSIDE, Edmund Travis.** British. *B.* 1933. *Educ.* Winchester College and Trinity College, Cambridge (MA 1957). *M.* 1959, Margaret Claire Nicholls. *S.* Michael Travis. *Dau.* Vanessa Perry Anne. *Career:* Major, The Lancashire Fusiliers T.A. Service 1954–69; With Shiloh Spinners Ltd.; Management trainee 1957; successively Manager Park Mill; Personal Assistant to Mng. Dir.; General Mgr. Roy Mill; Mng. Dir. 1965—. Director: Royton Textile Corp. 1960–65. Chairman, 1966— (Deputy Chairman 1963–66), Managing Director 1965—, Director 1960—, Shiloh Spinners Ltd.; Chmn. Parklite Insulation Ltd. 1965—. *Award:* (T.D. 1968). *Address: office* Shiloh Spinners Ltd., Holden Fold, Royton, nr. Oldham, Lancs.

**GARVEY, Sir Ronald Herbert,** KCMG, KCVO, MBE, KStJ. British administrator. *B.* 4 July 1903. *Educ.* Trent College; Emmanuel College, Cambridge (MA). *M.* 1934, Patricia Dorothy Edge McGusty. *S.* 1. *Daus.* 3. *Career:* entered Colonial Service and attached to Western Pacific High Commission, Suva, Fiji 1926; District Officer, British Solomon Islands 1927–32; Assistant Secretary, Western Pacific High Commission 1932–40; Assistant to Resident Commissioner, New Hebrides Condominium 1940–41; District Officer, Nyasaland Protectorate 1942–44; Administrator, Saint Vincent, Windward Islands, B.W.I. 1944–48; Acting-Governor of Windward Islands 1946, 1948; Governor and C-in-C., British Honduras 1948–52; Gov. and C.-in-C., Fiji, and Governor of Pitcairn Island; Consul-Gen. for Western Pacific; Senr. Commissioner for U.K. in S. Pacific Commission 1952–58; Lieut.-Governor, Isle of Man 1959–66. Dir. Garveys (London) S.A.; Member, East Anglian Tourist Board; Sec., Soil Assn. 1967–71. *Address:* The Priory, Wrentham, Beccles, Suffolk.

**GARVEY, Sir Terence Willcocks,** KCMG. British. *B.* 1915. *Educ.* Univ. Coll., Oxford (BA 1938). *M.* 1957, Rosemary Margaret O'Neill. *S.* 2. *Dau.* 1 (all by previous marriage). *Career:* Foreign Office 1951–54; British Embassy Cairo 1954–56; Belgrade 1958–62; Chargé d'Affaires Peking 1962–65; Asst. Under-Secy. of State Foreign Office 1965–68; Ambassador to Yugoslavia 1968–71; High Commissioner in India 1971–73; Ambassador to U.S.S.R. 1973–75. *Club:* Travellers' (London). *Address:* 11a Stonefield Street, London N1.

**GARWARE, Bhalchandra Digamber,** JP. Indian. *B.* 1903. *Educ.* Public High School. *M.* 1929, Vimlabai. *S.* 4. *Career:* Founded Garware Group of Industries, comprising of Garware Nylons Ltd; Garware Plastics Private Ltd.; Garware Synthetics Private Ltd.; Garware Filament Corp. Private Ltd.; Garware Motors and Engineers Private Ltd. and Garware Finance Corp. Private Ltd.; Held Presidentship of Maharashtra Chamber of Commerce and the All India Plastics Manufacturers' Org.: Chmn. 1956–64 and Pres. 1965 of the Maharashtra Economic Devel. Council, and is connected with State, Central and International Orgs; Chmn. of Maharashtra State Financial Corp; Past Vice-Chmn. of State Bank of India; Past Dir.: Central Board of State Bank of India; Past Dir. of Sutlej Cotton Mills Ltd. Bajaj Electricals Ltd., Svadeshi Mills Co. Ltd.; Past President of Assn. of Synthetic Fibre Industry; Trustee: Building Cttee of Maharashtra Chamber of Commerce; Founder of several Charity Trusts *Address:* Kapur Mahal, Netaji Subhash Road, Bombay 400 020, India.

**GASCON, Charles-Auguste.** Financier. *B.* 1885. *Educ.* Bilingual Commercial course. *M.* 1913, Rose Dubuc. *S.* 7. *Daus.* 4. In wholesale dry goods 1901–13, and in food business 1913–40; President: Christin Ltd.; former President, Retail Merchant Association of Canada. Chevalier de l'Ordre Equestre du Saint-Sépulcre de Jérusalem. *Address:* 6377 Avenue de Vimy, Montreal H35 2R5, Canada.

**GASE, Walther.** German statesman. *B.* 20 June 1901. *Educ.* Universities of Freiburg, Breslau, Göttingen, and Marburg (Dr. jur.). *Career:* Judge, District Court, Berlin 1927; at Finance Ministry 1928, and 1932–39; Ministry of Labour 1929–32; Financial Adviser and Director of companies 1939–45; Chief Finance Departments, Kassel, 1945; Depty., Finance Minister of Hessen, Wiesbaden, 1947–50; State Secretary in Marshall Plan Ministry 1950–53; Chief, Dept. of Finance, Intergovernmental Committee for European Migration, Geneva 1953–55. *Member:* Bd. of Dirs., Deutsche Centralbodenkredit Actiengesellschaft, Köln and Berlin. *Publication:* Gisberts-Gase, 'Handbuch des deutschen Siedlungwesens'. *Address:* Drachenfelsstr. 21, Bonn-Bad Godesberg, Germany.

**GASON, Anthony Wyndham.** British. Lt.-Col. (Retd. 1962). Property owner and real estate operator. *B.* 1917. *Educ.* Cheltenham Coll., R.M.C. Sandhurst, and Staff Coll. Camberley (p.s.c.). *M.* (1) 1942, Mary Patricia Russell; and (2) 1958, Dorothy deMercado. *Daus.* 3. *Career:* Served with Duke of Cornwall's Light Infantry 1938–62. Served in World War II 1939–45 (Dunkirk, Holland and Roer; twice wounded); Instructor at various schools, including the Royal Military College and Greek School of Infantry and Greek Senior Officers' School; fought with Greek Army on Military Mission to Greece 1947–50; DAAG Southern Command 1951–53; Staff Officer to British Commandant, Berlin 1956–58; G.S.O. 1 Military Training. HQ BAOR 1958–60: GSO 1 Military Training HQ Allied Land Forces, SE Europe 1960–62. Owner, Jamaica All-Island Yacht Agency 1962—; Dir. Jamaica Assn. of Villas and Apartments; Chmn. Man. Dir. Resort Rentals & Real Estates Ltd. Recipient NATO Certificate of Merit 1962; Tumlaren 20 sq. meter Champion 1947; British Berlin Star Class Champion 1956. *Member:* Jamaica Family Planning Assn. *Clubs:* Royal Southern Yacht; Royal Cornwall Yacht; Royal Jamaica Yacht; Royal Thames Yacht; Royal Ocean Racing; Island Sailing Club; Royal Yachting Assn.; Landsdowne; Liguanea; Jamaica etc. *Address:* Turtle Cove, Box 89, Port Antonio, Jamaica; & Triangle Towers, Cordell Ave., Bethseda, Maryland 20014; & Box 4543, Pasadena, Calif. 91106, U.S.A.

**GASS, Sir Michael David Irving,** KCMG. British Diplomat (Ret'd.). *B.* 1916. *Educ.* King's Sch., Bruton; Christ Church, Oxford (MA); Queens' Coll., Cambridge (BA). *M.* 1975, Elizabeth Periam Acland-Hood. *Career:* Colonial Admin. Service, Gold Coast (Ghana) 1939–58; War Service 1939–45; Gold Coast Regiment, RWAFF (East Africa & Burma; Major; Twice mentioned in despatches); Chief Sec., Western Pacific High Commission, 1958–65; Colonial Sec., Hong Kong 1965–69; High Commissioner for the Western Pacific & British High Commissioner, New Hebrides 1969–73 (Ret'd.); Member, Somerset County Council 1977. *Decorations:* Knight Commander of the Most Distinguished Order of Saint Michael & Saint George. *Address:* Broadway, Butleigh Wootton, Glastonbury, Somerset.

**GASSMANN, Walter Otto.** Member of the German Bundestag. *B.* 1903. *Educ.* High School. *M.* 1937, Maria Elisabeth Meyer. *S.* Günter and Dieter. *Dau.* Michaela. Vice-Chmn., International Social Security Assn.; Chmn., German Pensions Insurance Institutes 1955; Mem. Exec. Cttee., Federal Institute for Work Procurement and Unemployment Insurance 1957; member German Bundestag 1957. Previously Mgr. of public savings bank 1925; public auditing official; entered service of Daimler-Benz 1938; Dep. Member, Board of Directors, Daimler-Benz AG. *Publications:* numerous articles and lectures on social problems. Hon. Member, Senate of Univ. of Tübingen; Commander, Order of the Holy Sepulchre. Member Christian Democratic Party. *Member:* Württemberg Automobile Assn. *Address: office* c/o Daimler-Benz AG, Stuttgart-Untertürkheim, Germany.

**GASSNER, Richard.** Austrian commercial Kommerzialrat; *B.* 1912. *Educ.* Coll. of the Humanities, Feldkirch, and High School of International Commerce (Diplomé). *M.* 1939, Gerda Schallgruber. *S.* Andreas. *Daus.* Monika and Gabriele. Entered Getzner, Mutter & Cie. 1936; granted power of attorney 1938; General Manager-Partner 1948; Pres., Board of Managers 1954. Managing Director, Textilwerke Getzner, Mutter & Cie., Bludenz; Hon. Pres. Association of Austrian Industrialists. Land Group, Vorarlberg 1972; Hon. member Association of Austrian Industrialists, Vienna 1972. *Publications:* Lectures; article in various Austrian journals. *Club:* Rotary (Vorarlberg). *Address:* Werdenbergerstrasse 44, Bludenz; and *office* Bleichestrasse 1, Bludenz, Austria.

**GATES, Thomas S.** Chairman of the Board, Morgan Guaranty Trust Co. *B.* 1906. *Educ.* University of Pennsylvania (AB 1928). *M.* 1928, Millicent Anne Brengle. *S.* Thomas S. (*D*). *Daus.* Millicent Anne, Patricia S. and Katherine Curtin. With Drexel & Co., Philadelphia 1928–53. Partner 1940. Under-Secretary of the Navy 1953–57; Secretary of the Navy 1957–59; Secretary of Defence of United States 1960–61. Served overseas (Commander U.S.N.R.) in World War II, 1942–45. *Awards:* Bronze Star and Gold Star in lieu of 2nd Bronze Star. Hon LLD, Univ. of Pennsylvania, and Columbia and Yale Univs. Republican. *Clubs:* The Links (N.Y.C.); Metropolitan, Chevy Chase (Washington); Philadelphia, Racquet (Philadelphia); Pine Valley Golf (Clementon, N.J.); Gulph Mills (Pa.) Golf. *Address:* Mill Race Farm, Devon, Pa. 19333, U.S.A.

**GAUDIAN, Martin Ferdinand.** *B.* 1902. *Educ.* Trinity College, Hartford, Conn. (BS 1923); Ohio State Univ. (MA 1926). *M.* 1937, Evelyn Gettings. *Daus.* Barbara Lee, Evelyn Augusta (Parks) and Edythe Mae (Kleinpeter III). *Career:* Professor: Univ. of Cincinnati, Butler Univ. and Univ. of Colorado 1927–33; U.S. Savings & Loan League 1933–37; North Carolina Building & Loan League 1937–41; Producers' Council 1944–45. Executive Vice-President, National Association of Cemeteries 1944—. As the Executive Officer of the National Association of Cemeteries, he has taken a leading part in the growth of this new type of cemetery which has proved so popular in the U.S. and developed so fast; many of the new ideas and much of this new cemetery development originated in his office. *Member:* Amer. Socy. of Association Executives; English-Speaking Union; Sigma Nu. *Publications:* Cemetery Yearbook (Editor); Cemetery Selling; Cemetery Counselor Handbook; The Operation of a Cemetery; Sales Contests Manual. *Clubs:* Arts (Washington); Fairfax Hunt; International. *Address:* 3425 S. Ocean Boulevard, Delray Beach, Florida 33444, U.S.A.

**GAUTREY, Peter,** CMG, CVO, DK (Brunei). British diplomat. *B.* 1918. *Educ.* Abbotsholme School Derbyshire. *M.* 1947, Marguerite Etta Uncles. *S.* 1. *Dau.* 1. *Career:* Home Office 1936–39; Royal Artillery 1939–45; Home Office 1946–48; Asst. Principal Commonwealth Relations Office 1948–50; First Secy. British Embassy Dublin 1950–53; British High Commission, New Delhi 1955–57; Counsellor 1960–63; Deputy-High Commissioner, Bombay 1963–65; Corps of Diplomatic Service Inspectors 1965–68; High Commissioner, Swaziland 1968–72; High Commissioner, Brunei 1972–75; High Commissioner, Guyana since 1975 & Concurrently Ambassador (non-res.) to Surinam. *Member:* Royal Society of Arts; Royal Commonwealth Society. *Awards:* Companion, St. Michael and St. George; Commander, Royal Victoria Order; DK (Brunei). *Club:* Royal Automobile. *Address:* 24 Fort Rd., Guildford, Surrey; c/o FCO, King Charles Street, London SW1A 2AH and British High Commission, 44 Main Street, Georgetown, Guyana.

**GAUVIN, Michel,** OC, CVO, DSO. Canadian. *B.* 1919. *Educ:* BL; BA. Divorced 1972. *S.* Jean and Marc. *Career:* Served with Canadian Army during World War II; French-speaking Secretary to the Prime Minister of Canada 1946–50. Exec. Assis. to Under-Secy. of State for External Affairs 1950–51; served at Ankara 1951–53, Lisbon 1953–55, Saigon 1955–56, Carcas 1958–59, Buenos Aires 1959–60, Leopoldville 1961–63; National Defence College, Kingston, Ont. 1963–64; Special Mission to Kenya, Ethiopia and Congo during Stanleyville crisis Nov. 1964, and to Dominican Republic, May–June 1965; Canadian Ambassador to Ethiopia 1966–69; to Portugal, 1969–70; to Greece 1970–75; Temporary duty Vietnam, as Head, Canadian Del. to the ICCS Jan-July 1973; Canadian Consul-Gen., Strasbourg since 1975. *Member:* Professional Inst. of Public Service of Canada; Assn. des Anciens du Collège des Jésuites de Québec; l'Amicable du Régiment de la Chaudière; Carleton University Alumni Association. *Award:* Made Officer of Order of Canada 1973. *Publications:* Le Geste du Régiment de la Chaudière. *Clubs:* Royal Ottawa Golf; Cercle Universitaire d'Ottawa. *Address:* c/o Department of External Affairs, Ottawa, Ont., Canada; and 1 Rue Joseph Massol, 67000 Strasbourg, France.

**GAY, Geoffrey Charles Lytton.** English real estate consultant (international). FRICS. *B.* 1914. *Educ.* St. Paul's School. *M.* 1947, Dorothy Ann. *S.* 1. *Daus.* 2. *Career:* served War 1939–45, Durham Light Infantry B.E.F. 1940; Staff Coll. Camberley and India; Lt-Col. Chief of Staff, Sind District 1943; Gen. Commissioner for Inland Revenue 1953; Member, Westminster City Council 1962–71; Vice-Pres., City of Westminster Chamber of Commerce; World President, International Real Estate Federation 1973–75; Senior Partner Knight Frank & Rutley. Liveryman of the City of London; Worshipful Company of Broderers; St. John Council for London; Governor, Benenden School. *Awards:* Chevalier de l'Ordre de l'Economie Nationale; Officer of the Order of St. John of Jerusalem. *Clubs:* Carlton; Oriental; M.C.C. *Address:* C2 Albany, Piccadilly, London W1V 9RF.

**GAY, Georges-Henry.** French banker. *B.* 1898. *Educ.* Licencié en Droit. *M.* 1949, Irene Chaurand. Officieur, Legion of Honour. *Career:* Barrister at the Paris Courts 1919–22; Member of the Cabinet of the Under-Secretary of State to the Leader of the Cabinet, and to the Minister of Finance 1925; then turned to banking. Partner of Lazard Frères & Cie Bank, Paris; President, Credit Mobilier Industriel Sovac, Sovaclux Vice-Pres., Central Branch of Reescompte and of Credit

Electrique. Director, Compagnie pour le Crédit à moyen terme, Banque Française Immobilière Sovac; Compagnie de Location de Véhicules; Locatel; France Bail; Sovabail; Sofi-Sovac. *Member:* Conseil National du Crédit; Conseil de l'Assn. Professionnelle des Banques. *Address:* 10 rue du Conseiller Collignon, Paris 16; and *office* 5 rue Pillet Will, Paris 9, France.

**GEDDES, Sir (Anthony) Reay (Mackay),** KBE (1968), OBE (1943), Hon DSc (Aston 1967), Hon LLD (Leicester 1969), Hon DTech (Loughborough 1970). *B.* 1912. *Educ.* Rugby and Cambridge. *M.* 1938, Imogen. *S.* 2. *Daus.* 3. *Career:* Chmn., Dunlop Holdings Ltd., 1968; Director, Midland Bank Ltd., 1967, The 'Shell' Transport and Trading Co. Ltd., 1968; The Rank Organisation 1975; Adela Investment Co. S.A. 1976; Pres. Socy. of Motor Manufacturers & Traders 1958–59; Part-time member, U.K. Atomic Energy Authority 1960–65: Member, Nat. Econ. Development Council 1962–65; Chmn., Shipbuilding Inquiry Cttee. 1965–66. *Club:* Caledonian. *Address:* 13 Wilton Crescent, London, S.W.1, and *office* Dunlop House, Ryder Street, St. James's, London, S.W.1.

**GEDDES, Ford Irvine,** MBE. British. *B.* 1913. *Educ.* Loretto School and Gonville and Caius College, Cambridge (BA). *M.* 1945, Barbara Parry-Okeden. *S.* David. *Daus.* Jennian, Merryn, Fiona and Ailie. *Career:* Director: Bank of New South Wales (London Advisory Board). Chmn., British United Turkeys Ltd.; Chmn, British Shipping Federation Ltd., 1965–68; Pres., International Shipping Federation, 1967–69; Chmn., Peninsular & Oriental Steam Navigation Co. 1971–72; Dir., The Equitable Life Assurance Society (Pres. 1963–71) 1955–76. *Clubs:* City of London; Union (Sydney). *Address:* The Manor, Berwick St. John, Shaftesbury, Dorset SP7 0EX.

**GEIER, Frederick V.** American machine tool and Industrial Products manufacturer and business executive. *B.* 1893. *Educ.* Williams College (BA 1916); Hon LLD, Univ. of Cincinnati 1956 Williams Coll. 1963. *M.* 1918, Amey Massey Develin *S.* Frederick V., Jr., and James Aylward. *Daus.* Mary Alice (Turner), Amey Acheson (Garber). *Career:* Ordnance Sergeant U.S. Army 1917–19. Entered The Cincinnati Milling Machine Co. (now Cincinnati Milacron Inc.) 1916; President 1934–58, Chmn. Bd. 1958–63, Chmn. Executive Cttee. 1963—. Director: Cincinnati Milacron Inc., McCurdy & Co., and Little Miami R. R. Co. Trustee: The Herman Schneider Found. (Pres. 1942–47), University of Cincinnati Endowment Fund Assn. (Treas. 1940–48), Williams College 1953–63. The Children's Home, Cincinnati Museum of Natural History (Chmn. 1957–63; Hon. Member (Vice-Chmn. 1948–49), Business Cncl., Dept. of Commerce (served on Reciprocal Trade and Labor Policy Cttees.); Dir., Cincinnati Post of Amer. Ordnance Assn. (Pres. 1944 and 1945) 1930–63; Citizens Development Committee (Vice-Pres. 1949, Pres. 1950 and 1951, Chmn. Exec. Cttee. 1952–53) 1943–60. Community Chest of Cincinnati and Hamilton County (Co-Chmn. 1953–54); member Exec. Cttee., Ohio Valley Civil Defense Authority 1955–62; Chmn., Nat. Sponsoring Cttee., Univ. of Cincinnati 50th Anniversary of Co-operative Education; member, Nat. Affairs Cttee. Cincinnati Chamb. of Commerce 1951–52. Dir., Ohio Mechanics Inst. 1934–49; Asst. Chief, Cincinnati Ordnance District 1938–40; National Dir., Army Ordnance Assn. 1938; Pres., National Machine Tool Builders' Assn. 1941 (Vice-Pres. 1940, Treas. 1930); Member, Exec. Cttee., Machinery & Allied Products Inst. 1936–39, National Assn. of Manufacturers National Defense and Mobilization Cttee. 1939–40; Economic Co-operation Administration Industrial Adv. Cttee. 1948; Chmn., Cincinnati Cttee. for Economic Development 1943–46; Trustee, The Cttee. for Economic Development 1946–48; member, Foreign Economic Administration Cttee. to Survey Axis Machine Tool Industries 1945; Dir., Cincinnati Branch, Federal Reserve Bank of Cleveland 1943–46; member, Machine Tool Industry Adv. Task Cttee., Army and Navy Munitions Board 1947–50; Dir.: Cincinnati Community Development Co. 1948–54; Union Central Life Insurance Co., 1933–69; Central Trust Co., 1934–69. *Member:* Comm. Club of Cincinnati, Amer. Socy. Mech. Engineers, Newcomen Socy. N. Amer., Cincinnatus Assn., Cincinnati Chamber of Commerce, Engineering Socy. of Cincinnati; Phi Beta Kappa; Zeta Psi Fraternity; Omicron Delta Kappa. *Awards:* Harrison Medal, Distinguished Ordnance Service; Boy Scouts of Amer. Silver Beaver; Amer. Ordnance Assn. Fiftieth Anniversary Gold Medal; Great Living Cincinnatian Award. *Clubs:* Camargo, Queen City, Cincinnati Country. *Address:* 8880 Old Indian Hill Road, Indian Hill, Cincinnati 45243; and *office* 4701 Marburg Avenue, Cincinnati 45209, Ohio, U.S.A.

**GEIGER, Marion B.** Doctor (PhD) of Chemistry. *B.* 1903. *Educ.* Georgetown (Ky.) College (BS *cum laude*, mathematics and physics); Massachusetts Inst. of Technology; Engineering Administration, Univ. of Michigan (MS; PhD—Chemistry, Physics). *M.* 1928, Bonnie Castle Hart. *Daus.* Bonnie B. and Phyllis H. *Career:* Instructor (Chemistry) Georgetown Coll. 1924 (Physics 1924–25; Chemistry 1927–29); Head, Science Dept., Paintsville High School 1926–27; Teaching Assistant, Chemistry Dept., Univ. of Michigan 1929–31. With Oldbury Electrochemical Co.; Chemist 1932–35, Asst. Works Manager 1935–47; Works Manager 1947–53; Exec. Vice-Pres. 1953 until merger with Hooker end of 1956. Director, International Development, Hooker Chemical Corp., New York City; Associate, Chemical Projects Associates Inc., 30 Rockefeller Plaza, N. York 20, N.Y. 1961—. *Member:* Amer. Chem. Socy.; Amer. Inst. of Chemical Engineers; Amer. Inst. of Chemists (Fellow). *Clubs:* Niagara Falls Country; Rotary of N.Y.C.; Niagara; Navy League of America; University, N.Y. City. *Address:* 465 Mountain View Drive, Lewiston, N.Y. 14092; and *office* Chemical Projects Associates, Inc., 30 Rockefeller Plaza, New York City 20, U.S.A.

**GEIGER, Raymond Aloysius,** AB. American. *B.* 1910. *Educ.* University of Notre Dame (AB *magna cum laude*). *M.* 1948 Anna Marie Hueber. *S.* Eugene Gregory, Peter Edward, Kenneth Christopher and Michael Terence. *Dau.* Barbara Elaine. Editor, Farmers' Almanac since 1934; American Farm and Home Almanac. President: Geiger Bros.; Almanac Publishing Co., Lewiston; Martin Meyers Co. Philadelphia, Pa.; Adtech Industries, Strayer Beitzel, of York, Pa.; Bandrich-Geiger International, Puerto Rico; Geiger Bros.—New York, Syracuse, N.Y. Past President Associated Industries of Maine. *Member:* Board of Overseers of St. Joseph Coll., North Windham, Maine; National Academy, Television Arts and Sciences. Advisory Bd. Airline Passenger Assn. National Press Club. Past Governor Inter. Platform Assn.; Past Pres., Advertising Speciality National Assn.; Past Director of the New England Council; Past-Pres., Lewiston-Auburn Chamber of Commerce. *Address:* 650 Main Street, Lewiston, Maine; and *office* Mount Hope Avenue, Lewiston, Maine, U.S.A.

**GEIJER, Dr. Lennart.** Swedish lawyer, politician. *B.* 1909. *Educ.* Doctor of Law, Univ. of Lund and Stockholm. *M* 1944, Signe Löfgren. *S.* Bengt Johan and Christoffer. *Daus.* Ann Charlotte and Agneta. *Career:* Secretary and Legal Adviser, Swedish Union Clerical & Technical Employees in Industry 1939–57; The Central Organization of Salaried Employees in Sweden 1957–66. *Member:* The Riksdag (Social Democrat) 1962–76; Consultative Assembly Council of Europe 1964–76; Minister without Portfolio 1966–69; Minister of Justice 1969–76. *Publications:* Employer and Employees as Judges in the Labour Court (1958). *Address:* Armfeltsgatan 18, 115 34 Stockholm, Sweden.

**GEILE, Willhelm,** Dr rer pol. German. *B.* 1902. *Educ.* Dipl. Kaufm. Dr rer pol. *M.* 1932, Helma Küch. *S.* 1. *Dau.* 1. *Career:* Chmn. Ausfsichtsrat der Demerag Donau-Main-Rhein-Schiffahrts-A.G. Regensburg; Pres., Central Committee for German Inland Shipping. *Address: office* Zentral-Verein für deutsche Binnenschiffahrt, Beethovenstr. 43, Bonn-Beuel, Germany.

**GEISE, Harry Fremont.** American meteorologist. *B.* 1920 *Educ.* University of Chicago; Meteorology Service School (Marine Corps). Lakehurst, New Jersey. *M.* 1974, Juanita Calmer. *S.* 3. *Daus.* 2 by previous marriages. *Career:* Pioneered private weather services, starting in Chicago in 1937, first private meteorologist on Radio WLS Chicago 1941–42–46, issuing first week in advance forecasts to the public; Chief Meteorologist, Kingsbury Ordnance 1943; instituted thunderstorm warning system, using radio static (at ordnance plant) which became model for many U.S. ordnance plants; Meteorologist, U.S. Marine Corps 1944–45; published forecast of drought in plains states, based on solar output and weather relationships 1946; Meteorology Instructor Santa Rosa Junior College 1964–66 and Soroma State College 1967–68; discovered a relationship between a particular weather type and rash type tornado outbreaks in the midwestern part of the U.S. 1965; originated transatlantic weather radio programmes from Geneva and London to California, Dec. 1965; Revealed micrometeorological approach to tornado forecasting 1966. Associate, Dr. Irving P. Krick, Meteorological Consultant 1947–49; developed new temperature forecasting technique in research for Air Force, at California Institute of Technology, and American Institute of Aerological Research; conducted radio and T.V. shows in various markets including Chicago and San Franscico Bay during early fifties prior to rejoining Krick Associates as Media Director 1955–59; recognized relationship between specified solar emissions and major changes in earth weather patterns 1956; conducted weather programmes on KNXT, CBS, Hollywood 1957–58; on Panorama Pacific, Columbia Pacific Television Network 1957; Columbia Pacific Radio Network 1956–58; produced over 70 radio programmes per day across U.S. in 1959; WCBS TV N.Y. Weather Director and Chief Meteorologist 1966–67. Demonstrated long range forecasts up to two years in advance (at WCBS TV). Forecasts for Industry & Agriculture. Has been guest on all major T.V. and Radio networks in U.S. Resumed private weather business 1962, broadcasting on a dozen Radio & TV stations & providing long range forecasts a year or more in advance to industry, agriculture & Government, including State of Calif. Corps of Engineers, Bureau of Reclamation. Member, National Defense Executive Reserve 1968–75. *Publications:* contributions to various journals, newspaper, radio and TV networks and several TV films. Professional member, Amer. Meteorological Socy. Life Foreign Member Royal Meteorological Society. *Address:* 1770 Avenida del Mundo # 1404 Coronado, Cal. 92118, U.S.A.

**GEISEL, Gen. Ernesto.** Head of State of Brazil. *B.* 1907. *Educ.* Military Colleges. *Career:* Joined the Army on graduation in 1928; Head of the General-Secretariat of the National Security Council, 1946; Military Attaché in Montevideo, 1947–50; Dep. Chief of the Military Household of Pres. Café Filho, 1955; Head of the 11th Military Region, Brasilia 1960–61; Head of the Military Household of Pres. Castello Branco, 1964–67; Mem. of the Supreme Military Court, 1967–69. Civil Duties: Sec.-Gen. & Head of Dept. of Public Security, State of Rio Grande do Norte, 1931; State Sec. for Finance, Agriculture & Public Works, State of Paraíba, 1934–35; Superintendent of the Cubatão Oil Refinery, 1955–56; Mem. of the Nat. Petroleum Council, 1957–60; Pres. of the State Oil Corp. (PETROBRÁS), 1969–73. Elected President of the Republic of Brazil, 1974. *Address:* Office of the President, Brasília, Brazil.

**GEISER, Auguste.** Swiss diplomat. *B.* 6 May 1916. *Educ*' Paris (lic en d). *M.* 1944, Lilli Weber. *S.* 1. Following commercial and banking activities, entered Federal Dept. of Public Economy 1941; Political Dept. (Foreign Affairs), Berne 1945; Secretary, Swiss Embassy, Ottawa 1952; Delegate to 8th Session I.C.A.O., Montreal 1954; First Secretary, Legation, Prague 1958 (Chargé d'Affaires a.i. Apr. 1960–Mar. 1961); Deputy Chief, Finance & Econ. Section, Political Dept., Berne, June 1961; Chief, Swiss Delegation, Neutral Nations Supervisory Commission, Korea, May–Nov. 1964; Chief of Section, Div. of Commerce, Dept. of Public Economy 1966; Economic Counselor, Swiss Embassy, Washington 1968; Ambassador to Colombia and Ecuador since 1975. *Address:* Swiss Embassy, Bogota, Colombia.

**GELISSEN, Prof. Henri Caspar Joseph Hubert.** Dutch engineer. *B.* 15 May 1895. *Educ.* Technical University, Delft; Technische Hochschule, Berlin. *M.* 1920, W. B. M. Roos. *S.* 1. *Dau.* 2. *Career:* Former Professor of Technology; Minister of Economic Affairs and Min. Plen.; former Dir., Limburg Electricity Co.; Hon. President, Netherlands Chamber of Commerce for Germany; Dr. tech. sc. TH Delft; Dr. h.c. TH Aachen; Senator h.c. University of Cologne; Dr. h.c., University of Louvain; Senator h.c., Commercial Univ., Mannheim, Dr. h.c., Univ. of Gent; Dr. h.c. University Grenoble; hon. citizen, Province of Limburg and town of Venlo, town of Maastricht. Pres. of Honour, Europ. Electroheat Union; Hon. Pres., Assn. of Directors of Netherlands Electricity Undertakings. Hon. Member of Unipede; Hon. member Union of Polish Engineers; *Awards:* Grand Officer, House Order of Orange; and of Order of Orange Nassau; Knight, Order of Netherlands Lion; Grand Cross de l'Ordre de la Couronne (Belgium); Grand Cross, Order of North Star (Sweden), Order of White Rose of Finland, Order of Rumanian Star, Order of St. Olav (Norway); Grand Cross of Merit (Austria); Grand Cross Aztec Eagle (Mexico); Grand Cross, Order of Polonia Restituta; Grã Oficial, Ordem do Cruzeiro do Sul (Brazil); Grand Officer, Order de la Couronne de Chêne (Luxembourg); Grand Cross, Order of Merit (Germany); Cmdeur., Légion d'Honneur (France); Cmdeur., Order of Commercial and Industrial Merit (France); Grand Cross, Order of the Crown (Thailand); Cmdeur., St. Gregorius the Grand; Grand Cross Order of Merit Luxembourg. Member of Board of several companies. *Publications:* more than 250 articles and books. *Address:* Stoephout, flat 27, Stoeplaan 11, Wassenaar, Netherlands.

**GELZER, Carl Otto Michael.** Swiss Diplomat. *B.* 1916. *Educ.* High Sch. & Univ. of Basel—Dr. iur. *M.* 1964, Marie Christiane Sarasin. *S.* 2 *Career:* Dep. Attorney-Gen. of Canton Basle-City 1943–45. Federal Political Dept., Berne 1946–51; 2nd Sec., Swiss Legation, Bucharest 1951–55; 1st Sec., Swiss Delegation in Berlin, Dep. Chief of Mission 1955–57; Chief of Section, Federal Political Dept., Berne 1957–61; Counsellor of Embassy & later Dep. Chief of Mission, Washington, D.C. 1961–66; Dep. Chief of Division for Political Affairs, Dep. Dir., Chief Division for Political Affairs, Fed. Political Dept., Berne 1966–73; Ambassador to the Federal Republic of Germany since 1973. *Address:* Goethestrasse 66, D-5000 Köln 51; and *office* Gotenstrasse 156, D-5300 Bonn-Bad Godesberg, Federal Republic of Germany.

**GENEEN, Harold S.** *B.* 1910. *Educ.* Suffield Prep. School; Bachelor Science Accounting & Finance New York University. *M.* June Elizabeth Hjelm. *Career:* with New York Stock Exchange 1926; Chief Accountant Amer. Can Co. 1942; Vice Pres. and controller Jones & Laughlin Steel Corporation; Exec. Vice-Pres. and Dir. Raytheon Co. 1956–59; Pres. Chief Exec. Officer International Telephone & Telegraph Corp. 1959–64; Chmn. of the Bd. since 1964, also Pres. and Chief Operating Exec. since 1973, also chmn. of Exec. Cttee since 1974; Chmn. U.S. Industrial Payroll Savings Cttee.; Communications Cttee; National Citizen's Commission, 1965 Int. Cooperation Year; Pres. Int. Mngt. Education Foundation; Dir. International Rescue Cttee.; U.S. Council Intern. Chamber of Commerce. *Awards:* Commander Belgian Order of the Crown; Order of Merit (Peru); Grand Cross of Isabel the Catholic (Spain). *Address:* 320 Park Avenue, New York City, N.Y. 10022, U.S.A.

**GENEST, Jacques,** CC, BA, MD, FRCP(Can.), FACP, FRSC. Canadian. *B.* 1919. *Educ.* BA; MD. *M.* 1953, Estelle Deschamps. *S.* Paul; Jacques, Jr. *Daus.* Suzanne, Marie, and Hélène. *Career:* Formerly Research Physician Rockefeller Institute. Chmn., Department of Medicine, University of Montreal 1964–69. Chief Nephrology Hypertension Service, Hotel-Dieu Hospital, Montreal 1963–76. Director, Clinical Research Institute, Montreal since 1964. *Awards:* Hon. LLD, Queen's Univ. (Kingston Ont., Canda) 1966; Hon. LLD Univ. Toronto, 1970; Hon. DSc Laval Univ. 1973; Hon. DSc Sherbrooke Univ. 1974; Companion Order of Canada; recipient Gairdner Award Toronto 1963, Flavelle Award of Royal Society 1968, Archambauld Medal, ACFAS Canada 1965; Stouffer Award, 1969; Sims Commonwealth Travelling Professor, 1970. *Member:* Royal Society of Canada; Royal College of Physicians of Canada; Endocrine Society; Peripatetic Club (U.S.A.); Assn. of American Physicians; Amer. Clinical & Climatological Association. *Publications:* some 400 articles on hypertension and renal physiopathology, aldosterone and clinical research. *Address:* 1171 Boulevard Mont-Royal, Outremont, Montreal; and *office* Hotel-Dieu Hospital, and Clinical Research Institute of Montreal, Montreal H2W 1R7, P.Q., Canada.

**GENOCK, Edouard Paul.** American. Advertising (television) executive. *B.* 1907. *Educ.* London University (BSc-1st Cl Hon) and Columbia University (MA). *M.* 1936, Eva Sofia Beckman. *S.* Robert Paul. *Dau.* Ann Patricia. *Career:* Recording Engineer, Brunswick Balke Col., 1927–29; Chief Recording Engineer, Decca Record Co., London, 1929–30; Sound Engineer, Paramount News, 1930–32; Cinematographer, N.Y.C., 1930–36; March of Time, 1936–37; Production Manager, Paramount News, London, 1936–39; British War Correspondent (Paramount News, London, and freelance for News Chronicle and Associated Press) in Egypt, Greece, Iraq, Iran, Ethiopia, Eritrea, Singapore 1939–42; in Indonesia and Borneo for Paramount, 1942–49; News Editor, Telenews Television Service 1949–52; Editor-in-Chief 1952–54; Dir. Media Development, Mercer County Community Coll. N. Jersey; Dir. TV Programming, Eastman Kodak Co. 1954–72; Dir. Media Product. Mercer Coll., Trenton, (NJ), 1972–74. *Fellow:* Society of Motion Picture and Television Engineers. *Publications:* War Correspondent; I Shot the War; American Mercury (1942); Mechanics Illustrated (1942). *Address:* 80 Flagg Road, West Hartford, Conn., U.S.A.

**GENSCHER, Hans-Dietrich.** German politician. *B.* 1927. *Educ.* Leipzig and Hamburg Univs. *M.* Barbara Schmidt. *Dau.* 1. Vice-Chancellor and Minister of Foreign Affairs since 1974. Chmn., Free Democrats (FDP). *Address:* 53 Bonn-Bad-Godesberg, Eschenweg 3, F. R. Germany.

**GENTNER, Professor Wolfgang.** German. Director, Max-Planck-Institut für Kernphysik, Heidelberg. Professor of Physics, University of Heidelberg. *B.* 1906. *Educ.* Universities of Erlangen and Frankfurt (PhD). *M.* 1931, Alice

Pfaehler. *S.* Ralph. *Dau.* Doris. *Career:* Scientific Assistant, Univ. of Frankfurt, 1931–32; Fellowship at Institut du Radium de la Sorbonne, Curie Laboratory, Paris, 1933–35; Scientific Asst. at Institute of Physics of Kaiser-Wilhelm Institute for Medical Research, Heidelberg, 1936–46; Lecturer in Physics, University of Frankfurt, 1937–41; Fellowship at Radiation Laboratory, University of California, 1938–39; Lecturer in Physics, University of Heidelberg, 1941–45; Professor of Physics & Dir., Institute of Physics, University of Freiburg 1946–58; Prorektor, University of Freiburg, 1947–49; Dir. Synchro-Cyclotron, CERN, 1955–59. Corresponding Scientific Member, Max-Planck Society, 1950—; Scientific Member, Max-Planck Society, 1958—. *Member:* Heidelberger Akademie der Wissenschaften; Bayerische Akademie der Wissenschaften; Akademie Leopoldina, Halle. Officer, Legion of Honour; Hon. Fellow, Weizmann Institute of Science. *Address: office* Max-Planck Institut für Kernphysik, Postfach 1248, Heidelberg, West Germany.

**GEOFFREY-LLOYD, Baron, of Broomfield, Kent, Geoffrey William**, PC. British politician. *B.* 17 Jan. 1902. *Educ.* Harrow;Trinity College, Cambridge (MA). *Career:* Contested (Cons.) S.E. Southwark 1924, Ladywood 1929; Private Secretary to Rt. Hon. Sir Samuel Hoare 1926–29, and to Rt. Hon. Stanley Baldwin 1929–31; Parliamentary Private Secretary to Rt. Hon. Stanley Baldwin (Lord President of the Council) 1931–35, (Prime Minister) 1935; M.P. (Unionist) for Ladywood, Birmingham 1931–45; Parliamentary Under-Secretary, Home Office 1935–39; Secretary for Mines 1939–40, for Petroleum 1940–42; Chairman, Oil Control Board 1939–45; Minister in Charge of Petroleum Warfare Department 1940–45; Parliamentary Secretary (Petroleum), Ministry of Fuel and Power 1942–45; Minister of Information 1945; Governor of B.B.C. 1946–49; M.P. (Con.) for King's Norton, Birmingham 1950–55; Minister of Fuel and Power 1951–55; M.P. (Con.) for Sutton Coldfield 1955–74; Minister of Education, 1957–59; Pres. Birmingham Conservative and Unionist Assn. 1946–76. Created Life Peer 1974. *Clubs:* Carlton; Pratts, Cons. (B'ham). *Address:* 77 Chester Square, London, SW1W 9DY.

**GEORGE, Bruce Thomas**, MP. British Politician. *B.* 1942. *Educ.* Mountain Ash Grammar; Univ. of Wales—BA; Warwick Univ.—MA. *Career:* Asst. Lecturer in Government, Glamorgan Poly. 1964–66; Lecturer in Government, Manchester Poly. 1968–70; Senior Lecturer in British Politics, Birmingham Poly. 1970–74; MP (Lab.) for Walsall South since 1974. *Address:* 42 Wood End Road, Walsall, West Midlands; and *office* House of Commons, London SW1A 0AA.

**GEORGE, William Brooks**, BS. American. *B.* 1911. *Educ.* Coll. of William & Mary (BS). *M.* 1934, Elizabeth Harman Simmerman. *S.* 2. *Career:* Dir. The Bank of Virginia, Larus & Brother Co. Inc., Lawyers Title; Chmn. Bd. House of Edgeworth Larus & Brother Co. Inc.; Vice Pres. Central Virginia Educational Television; Dir. Tobacco Merchants Assoc.; Tobacco Inst.; Assoc. Tobacco Mfrs.; Pipe & Tobacco Council; Tobacco Tax Council; Grocery Mfrs. of America; Pres. National Tobacco Festival; Richmond Chamber of Commerce; United Givers Fund; Mem. Nat. Tobacco Advisory Cttee.; Bd. Visitors Coll. of William and Mary School of Business Admin. Inc.; Vice-Pres. Dir. Richmond Eye Hospital; Dir. Richmond Symphony.*Member:* Newcomen Socy. of America; Kappa Sigma; Phi Beta Kappa; *Clubs:* Country; Commonwealth. *Address:* 106 Berkshire Rd., Richmond, Va. 23221, U.S.A.; and *office* 5643 South Laburnum Avenue, Richmond, VA. 23231, U.S.A.

**GEORGE-BROWN, The Rt. Hon. Lord (George Alfred)**, PC. British politician. *B.* 2 Sept. 1914. *Educ.* Elementary and Secondary Schools. *M.* 1937, Sophie Levene. *Daus.* Frieda, Patricia. *Career:* District Official, Transport & General Workers Union from 1936; MP (Lab.) for Belper Division of Derbyshire 1945–70. Parliamentary Private Secretary to Minister of Labour and National Service 1945–47, to Chancellor of the Exchequer Mar.–Oct. 1947; Joint Parliamentary Sec., Min. of Agriculture and Fisheries 1947–51; Min. of Works Apr.–Oct. 1951; Deputy Leader of the Labour Party 1960–70. First Secretary of State, and Secretary of State for Economic Affairs. Oct. 1964–66; for Foreign Affairs 1966–68; Productivity Counsellor, Courtaulds Ltd. 1968–73; Dir. First Fortune Holdings Ltd. since 1973; Chmn. Stewart Title U.K. Ltd. since 1974. *Address:* House of Lords, London S.W.1.

**GEORGES-PICOT, Jacques Marie Charles.** French. Hon. Chmn. La Compagnie Financière de Suez. *B.* 1900. *Educ.* BA (Law), BA; Dipl Pol Sc. *M.* 1925, Angéline Pellé. *S.* 5. *Career:* Finance Inspector 1925; Assistant Director, then Director, Ministry of Finance 1931–37; General Secretary 1949, Director-General 1953, Compagnie Universelle du Canal de Suez; Chairman and Director-General, Cie. Financière de Suez 1957–70; Vice-Pres., Compagnie de Pont-à-Mousson 1966–70. *Awards:* Commander, Legion of Honour; Knight Commander, Order of the British Empire. Administrator: Fondation de Sciences Politiques; Institut Catholique de Paris. *Clubs:* Cercle Interallié (Paris). *Address:* 2 Square Mignot, Paris 16; and *office* 1 rue Astorg, Paris, 8.

**GERALD, J(ames) Edward.** Professor of Journalism. *B.* 1906. *Educ.* West Texas State Teachers Coll. (BA); Univ. of Missouri (BJ; MA) and Univ. of Minnesota (PhD). *M.* 1930, Opal Dutton. *S.* James Edward III. *Dau.* Patricia Ellen (Bourne). *Career:* Staff correspondent, United Press Associations 1928; Editor and Mgr., Canyon (Tex.) News 1929; Instructor, Univ. of Missouri 1929 (Asst. Prof 1930; Assoc. Prof. 1935–46; part-time service 1936–41, while serving respectively as a copy reader, St. Louis Star-Times 1936–37, and Mgr., Missouri Press Assn. Inc. 1937–41); Actg. Dean 1941–42; on leave 1943–45; Prof. Univ. of Minnesota 1946–74 (retired); Stewart Riley Prof. of Journalism, Indiana Univ., Bloomington, 1974–75. *Publications:* The Press & The Constitution, 1931–47, Univ. of Minn. Press. (1948); British Press Under Government Economic Controls, U.M.P. (1956); Social Responsibility of the Press. U.M.P. (1963); research papers in Journalism Quarterly, and other journals dealing with Law and the press as social institution. *Member:* Assn. for Education in Journalism; Amer. Political Science Assn.; Inst. of Newspaper Controllers & Finance Officers (Associate); Secy. Grievance Cttee. Minnesota Press Council; Sigma Delta Chi; Kappa Tau Alpha; charter member Minnesota Press Council 1971–74; secy. 1973–74. *Club:* Campus (Univ. of Minn.). *Address:* 2530 N.E. Ulysses Street, Minneapolis 55418, U.S.A.

**GERARD, Ronald.** British. Joint Managing Director, London & Provincial Shop Centres (Holdings) Ltd. *B.* 1925. *M.* 1952, Patricia Krieger. *S.* Michael. *Dau.* Celia. *Fellow:* Institute of Directors; Royal Society of Health; Incorporated Society of Valuers; Member of Lloyd's. *Club:* Marylebone Cricket. *Address:* 28 South Street, Park Lane, London, W.1.

**GERARD, William Geoffrey**, CMG. *B.* 1907. *Educ.* Adelaide Technical High School. *M.* 1932, Elsie Lesetta Lowe. *S.* 1. *Dau.* 1. *Career:* Man. Dir. Gerard Industries Pty. Ltd. S. Australia 1930–76; Chmn. of Dirs., Gerard Industries Pty. Ltd. S. Australia 1950—; President: S.A. Chamber of Manufactures 1953–54; Assoc. Chambers of Manufactures of Australia 1955; S.A. Metal Industries Assn. 1952, 1957; Australian M.I.A. 1962–64; Liberal & Country League (S.A. Div. of Liberal Party of Australia) 1961–64; Australian-American Assn. in S.A. Inc. 1961–63. Past Pres.: Electrical Development Assn. of S.A., and Electrical Manufacturers' Assn. of S.A. Chmn., National Employers' Assn. 1964–66; Vice-Chmn. Standards Assn. of Australia 1956—; *Member:* Commonwealth Immigration Planning Council 1956–74; Commonwealth Manufacturing Industries Adv. Council 1958–62. *Clubs:* Adelaide; Commonwealth; Captain, Kooyonga Golf S. Aust. 1953–55. *Address:* 9 Robe Terrace, Medindie, S.A., Australia.

**GERLI, Paolino.** American business executive. *B.* 1890. *Educ.* Dr. Schmidt's School (St. Gaul, Switzerland) and Leo XIII College (Milan, Italy). *M.* 1910, Peal Kingston Egan (*Dec.*). *S.* Francis M. *Dau.* Pauline (Sullivan). During World War II served in O.S.S. and as Consultant to the Govt. Agency. Previously: President: Silk Assn. of America (later Natl. Federation of Textiles), and of Natl. Raw Silk Exchange; Vice-Pres.-Dir., Commodity Exchange; Chmn.-Dir.: Julius Kayser & Co., and Belding Heminway Co.; Dir.: Interstate Dept. Stores, and British & Foreign Insurance Co. Chairman of the Board: Gerli & Co. Inc., and Cheney Brothers Inc. President: International Silk Assn. (Hon. Chmn.). Trustee: St. Patrick's Cathedral, Manhattan College, St. Vincent's Hospital. Former Trustee Emigrant Ind. Savings Bank. Hon. Mem. Board Manufacturers Hanover Bank. Honours: LLD Manhattan College. *Awards:* Emanuel d'Alzon Medal; Knight Commander, Orders of the Holy Sepulchre, the Sacred Treasure of Japan, the Italian Crown; Knight of Malta; Dr. of Textile Industries, Clemson Coll. *Clubs:* Greenwich Country; Manhattan; Metropolitan. *Address: office* 155 East Forty-Fourth Street, New York, N.Y. 10017, U.S.A.

**GERNAERT, Manuel Paul Louis Raymond**, Knight, D-en-D. General Secretary Société Générale de Banque S.A. Belgian.

*B.* 1911. *Educ.* Docteur en Droit; LLD Lic Fiscal and Financial Sc; Graduated Advanced Management Program—School of Business Administration Harvard University. *M.* 1940, Marianne Thys. *S.* Baudouin, Charles-Hubert. *Daus.* Christine, Wivine and Isabel. *Awards:* Officer Order of Leopold; Officer Order of the Crown; Croix du Mérite de la République Fédérale d'Allemagne, Médaille de la Résistance, Médaille Commémorative de la guerre 1940/1944. *Address:* 'Les Chênes', Humbeek, Belgium.

**GERRITY, Edward Joseph,** Jr. American. *B.* 1924. *Educ.* University of Scranton (BS, Hon. LLD; Columbia University, MS. *M.* 1956, Katharine Casey. *S.* Edward, Joseph III. *Dau.* Katharine. *Career:* With AUS 1942–45. Senior Vice-President, director, Corporate Relations and Advertising. Director: American Cable and Radio Corporation; ITT World Communications Inc.; ITT World Directories Inc.; Sen. Vice-Pres. Corporate relations & advertising ITT since 1964; Chmn. PR Cttee., Cardinal's Cttee. of the Laity, Archdiocese of N.Y.; Bd. member Adv. Council; Int. Economic Policy Ass.; Catholic Big Brothers; Advisory Bd. mem. St. Vincent's Hospital & Medical Center, Westchester Branch. *Member:* Association of Knights of Malta, the Sovereign Military Order of Malta; Public Relations Society of America; International Public Relations Assoc. (Dir.); Sigma Delta Chi. *Award:* Silver Star, Bronze Star with Cluster; P.R. Professional of the Year 1971. *Clubs:* Overseas Press (N.Y.C.); National Press (Washington); Westchester Country; Metropolitan (Washington). *Address:* Plymouth Road, Rye, N.Y. 10580; and *office* ITT, 320 Park Avenue, New York, N.Y. 10022, U.S.A.

**GERSON, Frederick T.,** BASc, PEng, AIM. Canadian. *B.* 1921. *Educ.* Lindisfarne Coll.; Univ. of Toronto (BASc); Christ's Coll., Cambridge. *M.* 1954, Margo Simon. *S.* 1. *Dau.* 1. *Career:* Pres. F. T. Gerson Ltd.; Vice-Pres. & Dir. Freeze-Dry Products Ltd; Dir. Kuypers, Adamson, Norton Ltd.; Dir. Corvend Ltd.; Dir. Varsity Fund; Man. Research & Development, John Dale Ltd. 1949–52; Gen. Man. & Dir. John Dale (Canada) Ltd. 1952–60; Vice-Pres. Modern Containers Ltd. 1959–60; Pres. Engineering Alumni Assn. Univ. Toronto 1970–72. *Member:* Board of Trade, Toronto; Assoc. of Professional Engineers, Ontario; Inst. of Metallurgists, London. *Club:* University. *Address:* 138 Oakes Drive, Port Credit, Ont., Canada; and *office* 67 Yonge St., Toronto. Ont. M5E 1J8.

**GERSTLEY, James Mack.** Vice-Chairman of the Board and Director, United States Borax & Chemical Corp. *B.* 1907. *Educ.* in England—St. Aubyns (Prep.) School, Rottingdean; Cheltenham College; Peterhouse, Cambridge. *M.* 1934, Elizabeth Lilienthal (of San Francisco). *S.* James Gordon. *Dau.* Ann Lilienthal. *Career:* Sales and General Office Work, Great Western Electro Chemical Co., San Francisco 1930–33; With Pacific Coast Borax Co., Division of Borax Consolidated Ltd. of London (successively Asst. to General Manager, Vice-Pres. and Asst. General Manager, Vice-Pres. and General Manager, President) 1933–56; President, United States Borax & Chemical Corp. (formed by merger of Pacific Coast Borax Co. and United States Potash Co.) 1956–61; Vice-Chmn. Asian Art Commission; Vice-Chmn, and Treas., Asian Art Foundation of San Francisco: Trustee Pomona College. *Member:* Friends of Colleges at Claremont; Friends of Huntington Library; Los Angeles Art Museum; Los Angeles County Museum; Brandeis University. *Clubs:* Sharon Heights & C. C. Menlo Park, Calif., Fifth Avenue (N.Y.C.). *Address: office* 3075 Wilshire Boulevard, Los Angeles 5, Calif., U.S.A.

**GESTRIN, (Lars Olof) Kristian.** Finnish Politician. *B.* 1929. *Educ.* Univ. of Helsinki—Bachelor of Law, LLM. *M.* 1962, Monica Eddina Furuhjelm. *S.* 1. *Daus.* 2. *Career:* Mem. of Town Council in Helsinki 1961–64; Mem. of Parliament since 1962; Minister of Defence 1970–71, 1972–74; Minister of Trade & Industry 1974–75, of Justice 1975–77, of Education since 1977; Chmn., Swedish People's Party 1973–74. *Decoration:* Commander, Order of the Finnish Lion. *Address:* Tammitie 10, 00330 Helsinki 33; and *office* Ministry of Education, 00170 Helsinki 17, Finland.

**GETTING, Ivan Alexander.** American. *B.* 1912. *Educ.* Massachusetts Inst. of Technology (SB); and Oxford Univ., England (DPhil). *M.* 1937, Dorothea L. Gracy. *S.* Ivan C. and Peter A. *Dau.* Nancy Louise (Resch). *Career:* Staff Member, M.I.T. Radiation Laboratory 1940–45; Professor, M.I.T. 1945–50; Asst. for Development Planning U.S.A.F. 1950–51; Vice-Pres. Raytheon Co. 1951–60; Pres. Aerospace Corp. since 1960 .*Awards:* Junior Fellow, Harvard 1935–40. Hon. DSc Northeastern Univ. Medal for Merit (U.S.A.); Exceptional Service Award (U.S.A.F.); Ordnance Award (U.S.N.). Fellow, American Physical Socy., I.E.E.E., Amer. Acad. of Arts & Sciences, A.I.A.A. Member National Academy of Engineering. *Publications:* various contributions to professional and technical journals. *Clubs:* Cosmos; California Yacht. *Address:* 312 Chadbourne, Avenue, Los Angeles, 90049, Calif.; and *office* Aerospace Corporation. El Segundo Boulevard, El Segundo, Calif., U.S.A.

**GIACOMUZZI, Luciano.** Italian company director. *B.* 11 Dec. 1899. *Educ.* Milan Polytechnic (DEng). *M.* 1933, Bianca Moore. *S.* Lorenzo, Enrico, Lionello, Gianni. General Manager, Lincolnshire and Central Electric Supply Co. Ltd., London 1931–38; Managing Director, Mid-Lincolnshire Electric Supply Co. Ltd., Grantham 1931–38, Campbeltown and Mid-Argyll Electric Supply Co. Ltd. 1935–38, Thurso and District Electric Supply Co. Ltd. 1935–38; Managing Director, Società Elettrica Coloniale Italiana, Rome 1939, Società Industrie Elettriche di Rodi (EGEO) 1939; Director, Società Elettrica della Venezia Giulia, Trieste; Man. Dir., Società Elettrica Carnica, Udine; Director, Banca Cattolica Del Veneto; Managing Director, Società Friulana Di Elettricita, Udine; Mgr., Regional District Enel, Triste; Past President, Rotary Club of Udine; Commander, Order of St. Gregory the Great (Holy See); Chamberlain of Honour of Sword and Cape (Holy See). *Publication:* Energia Elettrica. *Address:* Via Marinoni 11, Udine, Italy.

**GIBBON, General Sir John Houghton,** GCB, OBE. British Army General. *B.* 1917. *Educ.* Eton; Trinity Coll. Cambridge. *M.* 1951, Brigid Rosamund Bannerman. *S.* 1. *Career:* Commissioned, Royal Artillery (2 R.H.A.), regim. duty and on staff France, Belgium, Greece, Western Desert and Sicily 1939–44; Part, Normandy Invasion forces 1944–45; Brigade Major (R.A.)1945–47; Inst. and Chief Instructor R.M.A. Sandhurst 1947–51; Battery Commander 2 R.H.A. 1953–54; A.Q.M.G., War Office 1955–58; Commanding Officer R.A. in BAOR 1959–60; Cdr. 3 Inf. Brig. Group and Dhekelia Area, Cyprus Mar.–Oct. 1962; Brigadier D Plans, War Office 1962–64; Dir. Defence Plans Ministry of Defence 1964–65; Secy. Chiefs of Staff Cttee. Min. of Defence and Dir. Defence Operations Staff 1966–68; Dir., Army Staff Duties, Min. of Defence 1969–71; Vice-Chief, Defence Staff 1972–74; Master-General of the Ordnance, Ministry of Defence 1974–77. *Club:* Naval & Military. *Address:* Moth House, Brown Candover, Nr. Alresford, Hants.

**GIBBONS, James.** Irish Politician & Farmer. *B.* 1924. *Educ.* Presentation Convent, Kilkenny; Christian Brothers' Sch., Kilkenny; St. Kieran's Coll., Kilkenny; University Coll., Dublin. *M.* 1950, Margaret O'Neill. *S.* 5. *Daus.* 6. *Career:* Mem. of Kilkenny County Council 1954–57; elected to Dail Eireann (Irish Parliament) 1957; Parly. Sec. to Minister for Finance 1965–69; Minister for Defence 1969–70; Minister for Agriculture & Fisheries 1970–73; mem. of European Parliament 1973–77; Minister for Agriculture since 1977. *Address:* Dunmore, Ballyfoyle, Co. Kilkenny; and *office* Agriculture House, Kildare Street, Dublin 2, Eire.

**GIBBS, Allan George,** AO. Australian. *B.* 1911. *Educ.* Adelaide University (Dipl. Applied Science; BEng). *M.* 1937, Beryl Marjorie Bowley. *S.* Peter William and Roger Harry. *Career:* Superintendent, Tooling 1936–45; Personnel Manager 1946–59; Mechanical Manufacturing Manager 1960–63. Dir. 1963–73; Manufacturing Manager, General Motors-Holden's Pty. Ltd., Melbourne and Managing Dir. 1970–73; Chmn. Victorian Railways Board since 1973; Chmn., interim board, Australian Telecommun. Authority 1974–75; Chmn. O'seas Telecommunications Commission 1974–75; Chmn., Australian Railways Research & Development Organisation since June 1977. Fellow Inst. of Engineers Aust. *Member:* Melbourne Underground Rail Loop Authority; Faculty of Engineering, Melbourne Univ.; Victorian Aust. American Association. *Decorations:* Order of Australia, 1975. *Address:* Victorian Railways, Spencer Street, Melbourne, Vic.; and 4 Chelmsford Street, North Balwyn, Vic., Australia.

**GIBBS, Rt. Hon. Sir Harry Talbot,** K.B.E. Australian. Justice of High Court of Australia. *B.* 1917. *Educ.* Univ. of Queensland (BA, LLM). *M.* 1944, Muriel Dunn. *S.* 1. *Daus.* 3. *Career:* Judge of Supreme Court of Queensland 1961–67; Judge Federal Court of Bankruptcy and Aust. Capital Territory 1967–70; Justice of High Court of Australia since 1970. *Awards:* Knight Commander of British Empire; Member, Most Honourable Privy Council. *Clubs:* Australian (Sydney);

Queensland (Brisbane). *Address:* High Court of Australia, Sydney, Australia.

**GIBBS, The Rt. Hon. Sir Humphrey,** PC, GCVO, KCMG, KSTJ, OBE. Governor of Rhodesia, Jan. 1960–69. *B.* 1902. *Educ.* Eton and Trinity Coll., Cambridge. *M.* 1934, Dame Molly Peel Nelson. *S.* 5. Went to Rhodesia in 1927. Farmer and director of companies. *Clubs:* Athenaeum; Salisbury; Bulawayo. *Address:* Private Bag 5583 W., Bulawayo, Rhodesia.

**GIBBS, Oswald Moxley,** CMG. Grenadian Diplomat. *B.* 1927 *Educ.* St. George's Sch. Grenada; Sec. Sch. and City of London Coll. BSc (Econ); *M.* 1955, Dearest Agatha Mitchell. *S.* 2. *Daus.* 2. *Career:* Law Clerk 1949–51; Operator at Petroleum Refinery 1951–55; Civil Servant, Grenada 1955–57; London Transport 1957–59; Clerical Officer at West Indies Commission, London 1961–62; Welfare and Migrants Office, Eastern Caribbean Comm. London 1965–67, Trade Secy. 1968–72, Deputy Commissioner 1972–74, Acting Comm. 1973–75; High Commissioner in London for Grenada since 1974. *Member:* Brit. Inst. of International and Comparative Law. *Decorations:* Companion, Order of St. Michael & St. George, 1976. *Club:* Travellers. *Address: office* Grenada High Commission, Kings House, 10 Haymarket, London SW1Y 4DA.

**GIBBS, General Sir Roland (Christopher),** GCB, CBE, DSO, MC, ADC Gen. British Army Officer. *B.* 1921. *Educ.* Eton; Royal Military Acad., Sandhurst. *M.* 1955, Davina Merry. *S.* 2. *Dau.* 1. *Career:* Commissioned into King's Royal Rifle Corps, 1940; Commanding Officer, 3rd Parachute Bn 1960–62; British Army Staff, Washington 1962–64; Commander, 16 Parachute Brigade Group 1964–66; Chief of Staff, HQ Middle East Land Forces 1966–68; Commander, British, Forces, Gulf 1969–72; General Officer Commanding 1st (British) Corps 1972–74; C-in-C, UK Land Forces 1974–76; Chief of the General Staff since 1976. *Member:* British Inst. of Management. *Decorations:* Knight Grand Cross, Order of the Bath, 1976; Commander of the Order of the British Empire, 1968; Distinguished Service Order, 1945; Military Cross, 1943; Aide de Camp General to Her Majesty the Queen, 1976. *Club:* Turf. *Address:* Shalden Lodge, Shalden, Alton, Hants.; and *office* Ministry of Defence, Whitehall, London SW1.

**GIBBS, Stephen.** British. *B.* 1920. *Educ.* Oldbury Grammar Sch. *M.* 1941, L. G. Pattison. *S.* 1. *Career:* Dep. Chmn., Turner & Newall Ltd.; Fellow, Rubber & Plastics Inst. (FPRI). *Address:* Nicholas Green, Pumphouse Lane, Hanbury, Nr. Droitwich, Worcs. WR9 7EB.

**GIBSON, Charles (Arnold).** American textile manufacturer. (Ret.). *B.* 1906, *Educ.* Dartmouth College (BA 1927). *M.* (1) 1932, Mary Alice Burns, (*Dec'd*). *S.* 1. *Daus.* 2. (2) 1974 (Mrs.) June Collinson. *Career:* President B.I. Cotton Mills; Director: South Carolina National Bank; Trustee, South Carolina Association of Independent Colleges, Textile Hall Corp., Sirrine Textile Foundation; St. Francis Hospital; Trustee Greenville County Library, Presbyterian College. *Member:* Donaldson Center Management Cttee.; South Carolina Chamber of Commerce; South Carolina Textile Manufacturers' Association (Vice-Pres., Pres., 1952–53). American Textile Manufacturers' Institute (Past Director). Past Trustee, Greenville Hospital; St. Francis Hospital; Pres. Greenville County Chamber Commerce 1972. Presbyterian. *Address:* 305 Riverside Drive, Greenville, S.C. 29605, U.S.A.

**GIBSON, Sir Donald,** CBE, DCL, PPRIBA, Dis TP (Distinction in Town Planning), MTPI. British. Consultant. Formerly Controller General, Ministry of Public Building and Works, London, S.E.1. *B.* 1908. *Educ.* Manchester Grammar School and Manchester University (BA (Hons.) Architecture; MA). *M.* 1936, Winifred Mary McGowan. *S.* 3. *Dau.* 1. Entered Civil Service, Building Res. 1935; Deputy County Architect, Isle of Ely 1937; City Architect and Town Planning Officer, City of Coventry 1939; County Architect, Nottinghamshire 1955; Dir. Gen. of Works, War Office 1958–62. Dir. Gen. of Research and Development, M.P.B.W. to Dec. 1967; Controller-Gen. 1967–69; Member, Central Housing Cttee. 1951–53–54. Pres. R.I.B.A. 1964–65. *Publications:* articles on architecture, planning and housing in various professional journals. *Address:* Bryn Castell, Llanddona, Anglesey.

**GIBSON, Hon. Phil. Sheridan.** *B.* Grant City, Mo. *Educ.* Univ. of Missouri (AB; LLB); post-graduate student, Inns of Court. London (Eng.); LLD; Univs. of California. Missouri, Southern California, Pacific, Southwestern Univ. and McGeorge College of Law. *M.* Victoria Glennon. *S.* Blaine Alan. *Career:* served as Prosecuting Attorney 1915–17; Served in World War I (1st Lieut. U.S. Army). Served State of California as Director of Finance; Chmn. Board of Control and Lands Commission; Member of Emergency Council, Water Project Authority, and Governor's Council. Pres. Board of Directors, Hastings Coll. of Law; Chmn. Judicial Council, and Commission on Judicial Appointments. Assoc. Justice of Supreme Court of California 1939–40, Chief Justice 1940–64. Chief Justice, Retired, Supreme Court of California 1940–64. Appointed by Pres. Eisenhower in 1958 as Member of Commission on International Rules of Judicial Procedure, and by Pres. Johnson in 1964 as Chmn., National Commission on Food Marketing. *Address:* 4130 Segundo Drive, Carmel, California 93921, U.S.A.

**GIBSON, Lord (Richard Patrick Tallentyre).** British company director. *B.* 1916. *Educ.* Eton College and Magdalen College, Oxford (MA Oxon.). *M.* 1945, Elisabeth Dione Pearson. *S.* 4. *Career:* London Stock Exchange 1937–39; served European War (mentioned in dispatches; prisoner-of-war .Italy 1941–43) 1939–45. Chairman, Pearson Longman Ltd.; Chmn. Financial Times; Deputy Chairman, S. Pearson & Son Ltd.; Director Westminster Press Ltd., Economist Newspaper Ltd.; Mem. Council Cttee. (Chmn. elect) The National Trust; Exec. Cttee. National Art Collections Fund. *Clubs:* Brooks's; Garrick. *Address:* Penn's Rocks, Groombridge, Sussex and *office* 17th Floor, Millbank Tower, Millbank, London SW1.

**GIBSON-WATT, Rt. Hon. James David,** PC, BA, MC, DL, JP, FRAgS. British. *B.* 11 Sept. 1918. *Educ.* Cambridge (BA History). *M.* 1942, Diana Hambro. *S.* 3 (1 *dec'd*). *Daus.* 2. *Career:* Major, Welsh Guards 1939–46; Forester and Farmer; Chmn., Livestock Export Council, 1962–64; In Charge, Livestock Section, British Agric-Exhibition, Moscow, 1964; Member of Parliament for Hereford 1956–74; Minister of State Welsh Office 1970–74; Chmn. of Council of Royal Welsh Agric. Soc.; Forestry Commissioner 1976—. *Clubs:* Boodles. *Address:* Doldowlod, Llandrindod Wells, Powys.

**GIDDENS, Willard A.** Corporation executive. *B.* 1910. *Educ.* University of Texas (Bachelor of Business Admin.). *M.* 1932, Elizabeth Ann McDonnel. *S.* Warren W. (MD) and Paul J. (student). *Dau.* Jean A. Cass. Special Agent, Federal Bureau of Investigation, U.S. Dept. of Justice 1934–42; Asst. Comptroller, Oil Well Supply Co. (Division of U.S. Steel Corp.) 1942–47. Certified Public Accountant (CPA) Texas and Ohio; guest lecturer on accounting. Vice-President and Treasurer, Director, and Chmn. Finance Cttee., Hupp Corp.; Vice-Pres., Hupp Canada Ltd., Vice-Pres. and Treas. Hupp Caribbean Corp.; Vice-Pres. and Dir. Hupp Americana S.A., Inc. Treasurer, French American Neutronic Corp. Dir., Cleveland Trenchen Co. *Member:* Financial Executives Inst.; Amer. Inst. of Accountants; Texas and Ohio Certified Public Accountants Societies. Dir., Marymount Hospital, Cleveland. *Clubs:* Cleveland Athletic; Canterbury Golf. *Address* and *office* 1135 Ivanhoe Road, Cleveland 10, Ohio, U.S.A.

**GIDEONSE, Harry David.** American College President. *B.* 17 May 1901. *Educ.* Columbia Univ. (BS, MA); Diplome des Hautes Etudes Internationales. Univ. of Geneva; LLD, St. Lawrence Univ., Western Reserve Univ.; LHD Hebrew Union College; LLD Columbia Univ.; Lake Forest Univ. *M.* 1926, Edmee Koch. *S.* Hendrik David and Martin Cornelius. *Career:* with Eastman Kodak Co. (Chemical Research) 1919–21; Lecturer (Econ.), Barnard and Columbia Colleges (Columbia Univ.) 1924–26; Director, International Students' Work, Geneva 1926–28; Asst. Prof. (Econ.) Rutgers Univ. 1928–30; Assoc. Prof. (Econ.), Univ. of Chicago 1930–38, Prof. of Economics, Columbia Univ., and Chmn., Dept. of Economics and Sociology, Barnard College 1938–39; Pres., Brooklyn College of the City Univ. of New York from 1939 to 1966; Chancellor, The New School for Social Research since 1966. Chmn., Board of Directors, Freedom House; Past Pres., Woodrow Wilson Foundation (various positions held in Freedom House since 1942 and in Woodrow Wilson Foundation since 1941). *Publications:* Transfert des Reparations et Plans Dawes (1928); The International Bank (1930); The Commodity Dollar (1936); The Higher Learning in a Democracy (1937); Organized Scarcity and Public Policy (1939); Against the Running Tide (1966); American editor, Revue Economique Internationale (Brussels) 1928–41; editor, Public Policy Pamphlets (Univ. of Chicago) 1932–42; Joint author, United States Foreign Policy—Its Organization and Control (1952). *Awards:* Kt.-Commander, Order of Orange,

Nassau (Netherlands); King Christian X Order of Liberation (Denmark); Chevalier of the Legion of Honour (France). *Address:* 15 Mills Lane, East Setauket, N.Y. 11733, U.S.A.

**GIFFORD, Alfred Silva Harril,** OBE, KStJ, DCM, LLB. Australian solicitor and company director. *B.* 1897. *Educ.* Prince Alfred College, South Australia, and Univ. of Adelaide (LLB 1922); Admitted South Australian Bar 1919, and Victoria 1920. *M.* 1922, Gwen Leaver. *S.* 1. *Dau.* 1. *Career:* Chairman of Directors, Andrews Bros., Pty., Ltd., Melbourne (branches in all Australian States and London); Chairman of Directors. The Union Assurance Society of Australia Ltd. 1960–73; Served in World War I (Australian Imperial Forces; Signals Officer; DCM) 1916–19. Vice-Pres. Australian Red Cross Socy., 1968—, Senior Vice-Chmn., 1949–60; member, National Council since 1939; Chmn., Stores Cttee. 1939–44; Chief Commissioner, Field Force 1941–43; Hon. Treas. 1945–47; Pres., Federated Taxpayers' Association of Australia 1939–46; Chairman, Victorian Government Prices Advisory Committee 1948–54; Vice-Pres. and Executive Member, Tweddle Baby Hospital 1946–72; Trustee, The Scots Church, Melbourne 1951–60. *Award:* Knight of Grace, Order of St. John of Jerusalem 1947; Officer, Order of the British Empire 1972. *Clubs:* Melbourne Cricket; Rotary; Royal Automobile of Victoria (all of Melbourne). *Address:* 52–58 Chetwynd Street, Melbourne West 3003, Vic., Australia.

**GILBERT, Carl Joyce.** Lawyer. *B.* 1906. *Educ.* Univ. of Virginia (AB 1928) and Harvard Law School (LLB) 1931; Hon. LLD Boston College 1958, Hon. LHD Northwestern Univ. 1976. *M.* 1936, Helen Amory Homans. *S.* Thomas Tibbals. *Awards:* Silver Star and Bronze Star Medals. *Career:* Admitted to Massachusetts Bar 1931; practised in Boston as associate of the law firm of Ropes, Gray, Boyden & Perkins 1931–38, member of the firm 1938–48; Treasurer, Vice-Pres., The Gillette Co. (formerly Gillette Safety Razor Co.), Boston 1948–56, Pres. 1956–58, Chairman 1958–68; Special Rep. Trade Negotiations, rank of Ambassador, exec. office, the President, Washington 1969–71. Trustee Carnegie Inst. of Washington; Tax Foundation Inc.; and member Exec. Cttee. Tufts University; Trustee Cttee. Economic Development. *Member:* Boston Bar Association. *Clubs:* Somerset, Dedham Country & Polo (Boston); Links (N.Y.C.). *Address:* Strawberry Hill Street, Dover, Mass., U.S.A.

**GILBERT, Ernest Bert.,** AM. Australian. *B.* 1918. *Educ.* Melbourne Grammar Schools & Melbourne Univ. (BA Hons. Economics). *M.* 1942, Gwendoline Charlotte Steel. *S.* Robert Kent and Barry Steele. *Dau.* Lynette Kaye. Victorian Division Manager, Kraft Foods Ltd. 1952–55; Australian Govt. Trade Commissioner to U.K. 1955–58; General Manager, Overseas Div., Dewey & Almy Pty., Ltd., and Director, Dewey & Almy (New Zealand) Ltd. 1958–62. General Manager, Australian Dairy Produce Board 1962–75; Dir., Melbourne Grammar Foundation 1976—. *Member:* Australian National Dairy Cttee. 1963–70; Vice-Chmn. XVIII International Dairy Congress; Previously Australian Government Trade Commissioner in the United Kingdom (1955–58); Created member of Order of Australia, 1975. *Publications:* various publications and contributions. At one time Assistant Secretary, Economic Society of Australia and New Zealand (Victorian Div.). *Clubs:* Royal Automobile (Victoria); Melbourne Cricket; Lonsdale Golf; Kew Golf. *Address:* 3 Ellerslie Place, Toorak, 3142 Australia.

**GILBERTSON, Arthur Geoffrey,** JP (Co. Glamorgan). British. *B.* 1913. *Educ.* Shrewsbury School. *M.* 1937, Hilarie Williams-Thomas. *Daus.* Elizabeth Phebe, Annette Ruth, and Diana Ellen. *Career:* Trainee with W. Gilbertson & Co. Ltd., Steelworks 1932–35, and Youngstown Sheet & Tube Co. (Ohio, U.S.A.) 1935–37; Richard Thomas & Baldwins Ltd., Ebbw Vale, 1937–49; Brown Lenox & Co. Ltd. 1949–71; Dir. Stevens & Williams Ltd. (Royal Brierley Glass Works, Staffs.); Consultant Dir. B.W.G. (Duisburg). Pres. South Glamorgan Branch BRCS. *Club:* M.C.C. *Address:* Castle Cottage, Llanblethian, Cowbridge, South Glamorgan.

**GILBRIDE, John Thomas.** American. *B.* 1916. *Educ.* Univ. of Pennsylvania (BA); Brooklyn Polytechnical Institute and Pratt Institute. *M.* 1940, Rosemary Shelare. *S.* Francis Joseph, John Thomas and Gary George. *Career:* General Mgr., Los Angeles Division 1946–58, Asst. Gen. Mgr. of the Division 1946; General Superintendent, Brooklyn Division 1945–46; Supt. in charge of Naval Repairs, Brooklyn Div. 1942–45. President 1958–75, Chmn. 1975—, And Director 1951—, Todd Shipyards Corp. *Member:* Lloyd's Register, Shipping, American Cttee. Director Chmn. Exec. Cttee. Shipbuilding Cttee. Shipbuilders Council of America; Hon. Vice-Pres. (for life), Society Naval Architects and Marine Engineers. Member, American Society Naval Engineers; Board of Managers, American Bureau of Shipping; Board of Governors, National Maritime Council; Trustee, Atlantic Mutual Insurance Co.; Dir., Centennial Insurance Co.; Advisory Board, U.S. Merchant Marine Academy; Mem. of Board, The Oceanic Education Foundation; U.S. Naval Inst.; Maritime Assn., Port New York; Amer. Welding Society; National Defense Transportation Assn.; Navy League U.S.; North East Coast Inst. Engineers Shipbuilders (England); Newcomen Society of N. America; Marine Historical Socy.; Chase Manhattan Bank Advisory Board; American Shipping Society; Propeller Club of the U.S. Bd. of Trustee United Seaman's Service Council. *Clubs:* Phi Sigma Kappa; Whitehall Luncheon (Vice-Pres. and Bd. Govs.); India House (Bd. of Governors); Chiselers; N.Y. Yacht; Oslo Golf. *Address:* Apt. 4B, 447 East 57th Street, New York, N.Y. 10022; and *office* One State Street Plaza, New York, N.Y. 10004, U.S.A.

**GILCHRIST, Hugh.** Australian Diplomat. *B.* 1916. *Educ.* Cranbrook Sch., Sydney; Univ. of Sydney—BA, LLB. *M.* 1950, Elizabeth Dalton Richardson. *S.* 1. *Daus.* 2. *Career:* Entered Australian Dept. of External Affairs 1945; 2nd Sec., London 1947; 2nd Sec., Paris 1949; 1st Sec., Jakarta 1951; 1st Sec.,Pretoria & Cape Town 1955–59; Aust. High Commissioner in Tanzania 1962–66; Asst. Sec., Information & Cultural Relations, Dept. of Foreign Affairs, Canberra 1966–68; Ambassador to Greece 1968–72; 1st Asst. Sec., Legal & Treaties Div., Dept. of Foreign Affairs, Canberra 1972–76; Ambassador to Spain since 1976. *Publications:* Australia's First Greeks (*Canberra Historical Journal*, March 1977). *Clubs:* Commonwealth Club, Canberra; Real Club de Puerta de Hierro, Madrid. *Address:* Australian Embassy, Avda. del Generalisimo 61, Edificio Cuzco 1, Madrid, Spain.

**GILCHRIST, James.** Director of companies. *B.* 12 Sept. 1901. *Educ.* Scotland and Southern Rhodesia; widower with 1 *Dau.* *Career:* settled in Rhodesia in 1912, and has since been connected with the cattle industry (rancher, dealer and auctioneer); has interests in various companies operating in Rhodesia. Hon. French Consul, Chevalier de l'Etoile Noire. *Address:* Fortunes Gate (P.O. Box 551), Bulawayo, Rhodesia.

**GILES, Sir Henry Norman,** OBE. *B.* 1905. *Educ.* Christ Church Grammar School (West Aust.). *M.* 1929, Eleanor Barker. *S.* 1. *Dau.* 1. *Career:* Served in World War II (R.A.A.F.; CF/Lt.; Australia and New Guinea) 1941–44; joined Elder, Smith & Co. Ltd. 1922; W. Aust. Manager 1947–48 (Asst. General Manager for Australia 1948–52; General Manager 1952–55); Managing Dir. 1955–62 (until amalgamation, when name changed to Elder, Smith, Goldsbrough Mort Ltd.); General Manager 1962–67, Chmn. 1967–76, Director: Commonwealth Banking Corporation 1959–77 (Deputy-Chairman 1959–62; 1967–75); Babcock Australian Holdings Ltd. 1959–76; P. & O. Australia Ltd. 1959–75, Chairman 1969–75; Elder Smith Goldsbrough Mort Group Companies 1962–76; Gove Alumina Ltd. 1969–72; Reyrolle Pty. Ltd. Group 1973–76; Reyrolle Parsons of Australia Ltd. (Group) 1971–76. *Member:* Commonwealth Export Development Council, 1965–70, Executive 1966–70; Deputy Chairman 1966–70; South Australia Industrial Advisory Council 1967–70. Academy of Science Industry Forum 1967–72; Cncl, of Australian Admin. Staff College 1956–75. Fellow of Cncl. for C. of E. Schs. (W.A.) 1933–53; Australia Institute, Rotterdam 1965–76; Australia-Japan Business Cooperation Committee, 1966–75; C.S.I.R.O.-S.A. State Committee 1962–71; Pacific Basin Economic Council 1968–75; Australian Wool Industry Advisory Cttee., 1970–71; Vice-President and on Executive Committee, West Australian Chamber of Commerce 1947–50; member: General Executive Committee, National Council Wool-selling Brokers of Australia 1947–62; W. Australia 1947–52; S. Australia 1956–62; Council of H.R.H. The Duke of Edinburgh's Third Commonwealth Study Conference, 1966. *Address:* 31 "Strathearn", 16 King's Park Avenue, Crawley, WA 6009, Australia.

**GILKEY, Professor Herbert James.** American; professor and engineering consultant; Professor (theoretical and applied mechanics), Iowa State University. *B.* 1890. *Educ.* Oregon State Univ. (BS Civ. Eng. 1911), Massachusetts Institute of Technology (SB 1916), Harvard University (BS 1916), Univ. of Illinois (MS 1923); ScD, Hon. Buena Vista College, 1939. *M.* 1923, Mildred Virginia Talbot. *S.* Herbert Talbot and Arthur Karr (*D.* 1953 on K-2 Exped.). Civil Engineering (Government, State and private practice), Oregon and California, 1911–14; Asst. Engineer on construction, Pennsylvania R.R., Chicago, 1916–17; 1st Lieut. and Captain of Engineers in U.S. and France, 1917–18; American Relief Administration at Paris HQ of Herbert Hoover, 1919; Structural Engineer with Arthur R. Lord, Chicago, 1920; research and teaching under A. N. Talbot Univ. of Illinois, 1921–23; Professor, Civil Engineering, Univ. of Colorado, 1923–31; organized Department of Theoretical and Applied Mechanics, Iowa State Univ. (serving as Professor and Head of Dept.) 1931–55. Concurrent supplementary assignments: member, Third U.S. Joint Committee on Concrete (Report publ. 1940); member, American Society of Engineering Education Special Committee on Aims and Scope of Engineering Education in U.S. (Report 1940); Consultant, Hoover Dam Concrete Research Board, 1931–33; National Vice-Pres., American Society for Engineering Education, 1943–44; National Pres., American Concrete Institute, 1950; Wason Medal 1939; Henry C. Turner Gold Medal, Amer. Concr. Inst., 1958; Hon. Member, American Society for Testing Materials 1956, and American Concr. Inst. 1959. Iowa Engineering Socy. Distinguished Service Plaque 1959. *Publications:* about 150 papers, discussions, bulletins and books dealing largely with research in engineering materials and engineering education; contributed the concrete sections of Urquhart's Civil Engineering Handbook, and the Kirk-Othmer Encyclopedia of Chemical Technology; also joint author of Engineering Foundation Arch Dam Report vol. 2 (1934). *Address: office* Room 102 Lab. of Mechanics, Iowa State University, U.S.A.

**GILL, Ernest Clark,** BA, LLD, FSA, FCIA. *B.* 1903. *Educ.* Queen's University (BA with Gold Medal 1923); Fellow, Society of Actuaries 1926; Fellow Can. Inst. of Actuaries; Hon. LLD Queen's University 1957. *M.* 1929, Mercedes Rae. *Dau.* 1. *Career:* Joined Canada Life Assurance Co. 1923; Asst. Actuary 1927; Asst. Treasurer 1930; Treasurer 1938; Asst. General Manager and Treasurer 1939; General Manager 1946; member, Board of Directors 1946; Vice-Pres. and General Manager 1947; President, 1951. Bd. Dirs. The Canada Life Assurance Co. 1964–74. *Clubs:* Granite; Eastbourne Golf; York. *Address:* 77 Hillholm Road, Toronto, Ont. M5P IM4, Canada.

**GILL, Merwyn C.** American reinforced plastics manufacturer and chemical engineer. *B.* 1910. *Educ.* BS Chemical Engineering; AB Chemistry. *M.* 1939, Ellen Wildy. *S.* Stephen Edward and Phillip Carl. *Dau.* Debaney Dianne. *Career:* Asst. Product Control foreman, U.S. Rubber Co. 1937–42; Research and Development Chemical Engr., A. O. Smith Corp. 1942–45; New Products Development Chemical Engineer, Swedlow Aeroplastics 1945–46; President, Peerlees Plastic Products 1946–47; Head of Corrosion Laboratory, Aerojet Engineering Corp. 1948–51. President, M. C. Gill Corporation since 1951. *Publications:* Treatise on Reinforced Plastics (1951); Paper on post-forming polyester laminates (1946); author of several patents and manufacturing processes. *Address:* 1385 El Mirador Drive, Pasadena, Calif. 91103; and *office* M. C. Gill Corporation, 4056 Easy Street, El Monte, Calif. 91731, U.S.A.

**GILL, His Hon. Judge Stanley Sanderson,** MA. British. Circuit Judge. *B.* 1923. *Educ.* Queen Elizabeth Grammar School Wakefield; Magdalene Coll. Cambridge. *M.* 1954, Margaret Mary Patricia Grady. *S.* 1. *Daus.* 2. *Career:* Royal Air Force 1942–46; Barrister-at-Law 1950–71; Asst. Recorder Bradford 1966–69; Chmn. Yorks Rent Assessment Cttee. 1967–71; Deputy-Chmn. West Riding Quarter Sessions 1968–71; County Court Judge 1971; Circuit Judge since 1972. *Member:* Middle Temple. *Award:* Master of Arts (Cambridge). *Address:* Downe, Baldersby, Thirsk.

**GILLEN, Stanley James.** American. *B.* 1911. *Educ.* St. Frederick's High School (Pontiac, Mich.) and University of Detroit (BSc). *M.* 1935, Mary Elizabeth Marks. *Daus.* 3. *Career:* With Fisher Body Div., General Motors Corp. 1933–47; with Ford Motor Co. U.S.A.: Contract Administrator, Defence Products 1947–48; Controller, Steel Div. 1948–55, and Tractor and Implement Div. 1955–56; Asst. Gen. Mgr., Steel Div. 1956–60, General Mgr. 1960–61; Gen. Mgr., General Parts Div. 1961–65; Mng. Dir. and Chief Exec. Officer, Ford of Britain 1965–67; Director, Ford Credit Co. Ltd. 1965–67; Chmn. Autolite Motor Products Ltd. 1962–65; Dir., Henry Ford & Son Ltd., Cork, 1965–67; Vice-Pres., Manufacturing, Ford of Europe Inc. 1967–69; Chmn. & Chief Exec Officer, Ford of Europe Inc. 1969–71; Vice-Pres., Ford Motor Co. U.S.A. 1967–71; Dir. Ford of Europe Inc., Ford of Britain, 1965–71, Sangamo Weston Ltd. 1972—; Sangamo Electric Co. U.S.A. 1973–75; Ford Werke Germany 1969–71; Brown Brothers Corp. Ltd, England 1976—; Ambac Industries Inc., U.S.A. 1976—; Ambac B.V., Holland 1976—; FABRICA Espanola Magnetos S.A., Spain 1976—. *Member:* British Manufacturers' Executive Committee, Society of Motor Manufacturers & Traders Ltd. 1965–67; and Natl. Adv. Council for Motor Manufacturing Industry (NACMMI) 1966–67; Dir. Amer. Chamber of Commerce 1967—. *Award:* Lord Wakefield Gold Medal 1971. *Address:* 58 Campden Hill Ct., Campden Hill Road, London W8.

**GILLES, Dennis Cyril,** BSc, DIC, PhD. British. University Professor. *B.* 1925. *Educ.* Sidcup Grammar School; Imperial Coll. Univ. of London. *M.* 1955, Valerie Mary Gardiner. *S.* 2. *Daus.* 2. *Career:* Assistant Lecturer, Imperial Coll. London 1947–49; Univ. of Liverpool 1947–49; Mathematician, Scientific Computing Service Ltd. London 1949–55; Research Fellow, Univ. of Manchester 1955–57; Dir. Computing Laboratory 1957–66, Professor of Computing Science University of Glasgow since 1966. *Fellow,* Royal Socy. of Edinburgh; Inst. Mathematics and its Applications; British Computer Socy.; Royal Socy. of Arts. *Publications:* edited and revised The Computer and Business (1972); Papers in iournals. *Address:* 7 The University, Glasgow G12 8QG; and *Office:* Computing Science Department, University of Glasgow, Glasgow G12 8QQ.

**GILLETT, Charles.** American. U.S. Army Bronze Star; Army Commendation Medal. Executive Vice-President, New York Convention & Visitors Bureau 1965. Chairman, Inter Continental Committee, International Association of Convention Bureaus 1967—. Director, Discover America Travel Organizations, 1969—. *B.* 1915. *Educ.* Univ. of Cincinnati (BAEcon). *M.* 1949, Virginia Littman. *S.* David, Brian P. and Peter G. *Dau.* Valerie. Promotion Director, N.Y. Convention & Visitors Bureau 1946–55 (Vice-Pres. 1955–65); Chairman of Board, National Association of Travel Organizations 1966–68. Vice-Pres. International Festivals Assn. 1967–69. *Publication:* The Bridge. Awarded Midwest Travel Writers Assn. 'Most Original Travel Idea in 1964'. Award of Merit by Natl. Assn. of Travel Organizations, 1966. *Member:* Amer. Socy. of Association Executives; International Assn. of Convention Bureaus; Public Relations Socy. of America; Socy. of Amer. Travel Writers; Amer. Socy. of Travel Agents; Hotel Sales Managers Assn. *Club:* Overseas Press. *Address: office* 90 East 42nd Street, New York, N.Y. 10017, U.S.A.

**GILLIES, Mary Davis** (Mrs. Joseph E. Johnston). *B.* 1900. *Educ.* Univ. of Washington (BS; MA). *M.* Joseph E. Johnston. Instructor, Univ. of Oregon 1926–27; Textile Division, U.S. Bureau of Home Economics 1927–28; Account Executive, Gardner Advertising 1928–29. Interiors and architectural editor, McCall's Magazine 1929–67. Interior Design Consultant 1968—. *Publications:* Books: Popular Home Decorating; All About Modern Decorating; How to Keep House; McCall's Book of Modern Houses McCall's Fabulous Decorating Book. *Member:* Amer. Home Economics Assn.; Architectural League; Fashion Group, National Home Fashions League (Pres. 1954–55); Amer. Inst. of Design; N.S.I.D.; Design Writers International. Dorothy Dawes Furniture Industry Award 1954, 1961; Gold Medal; Valley Forge Freedom Foundations Award 1949. *Address:* 444 S. State Street, Apt 209, Bellingham, WA 98225. U.S.A.

**GILLIN, John (Philip).** American anthropologist. *B.* 1907. *Educ.* Univ. of Wisconsin (BA; MA); Harvard Univ. (AM; PhD); attended London School of Economics 1928. *M.* 1934, Helen Norgord. *S.* John Christian. *Career:* Research Professor of Anthropology, Univ. of N. Carolina 1946–59; Associate Prof. of Anthropology, Duke Univ. 1941–46; Asst. Prof. of Anthropology, Ohio State Univ. 1937–41; Asst. Prof. of Anthropology and Curator, Univ. of Utah 1935–37; Peabody Museum of Harvard 1934–35. Dean of Social Sciences and Prof. of Anthropology, Univ. of Pittsburgh 1959–62, Research Professor 1962–72. *Member:* Amer. Anthropological Assn. (Pres. 1965–66); Socy. for Applied Anthropology (Pres. 1959–60); Amer. Ethnological Assn.; Amer. Sociological Assn.; Amer. Assn. of Physical Anthropologists. *Publications:* The Barama River Caribs of British Guiana (1936); The Quichua-Speaking Indians of Ecuador (1941); Archaeological Investigations in Nine Mile Canyon, (1938); Archaeological Investigations in Central Utah (1942); An Introduction to Sociology (1942); Moche, a Peruvian Coastal Community (1947); Cultural Sociology (1948); The Ways of Men (1948); The Culture of Security in San Carlos (1951); For a Science of Social Man (1954); San Luis Jilotepeque (1959); (with others) Social Change in

Latin America Today (1960); Human Ways (1969). *Address:* 1115 Sourwood Drive, Chapel Hill, N.C. U.S.A.

**GILLIS, Marvin B.** American. *B.* 1920. *Educ.* University of Georgia (BSA Agric 1940) and Cornell Univ. PhD Biochemistry, Org. Chem. Physiology 1947). *M.* 1946, Helen Reed. *S.* 2. *Dau.* 1. *Career:* Student Asst. Univ. of Georgia 1940; Research Asst. Cornell Univ. 1942. Military Service, U.S.A.A.F., U.S. and Saipan 1942–45 (DFC with Oak Leaf Clusters, Air Medal with 3 Oak Leaf Clusters). Research Associate, Cornell Univ. 1945–47; Res. Chem.-Sup. Nutr. Res. IMC, Skokie, Ill. 1947–51: Supervisor, Biol. Research IMC 1951–54; Manager of Research, Organic and Biological Sciences, IMC, 1954–56; Asst. Director of Research, IMC, 1956–57; Director of Research and Development (Corporate) IMC, 1957–64; Project Dir., Animal Health and Nutrition Products, 1964–66; Division Vice-Pres. Europe, Dir. Continental Ore Corp., Lavino South Africa, Eufaula Bauxite Mining Co. (Subsidiaries of IMC). Corporate Vice-President Business Development 1970–71; Sen. Vice-Pres. Industrial Products Group, International Minerals & Chemical Corp. 1971–73; Soc. Vice-Pres. Agric. Operations since 1972; Dir. International Minerals & Chem. Corp. (Canada) Ltd. since 1972; Dir. IMC Chemicals Corp., Dir. I.M.C. Development Corp. since 1973. *Publications:* Contributor to Journal of Nutrition, Journal of Biological Chemistry, Official Report 8th World's Poultry Congress (Copenhagen), and 9th Congress (Paris); Poultry Science, and many other journals. *Member:* Agricultural Research Institute (Past-Pres.); A.C.S.; Dir. I.M.C. Foundation. *Address: office* IMC, Plaza, Libertyville, Illinois, U.S.A.

**GILMOUR, Rt. Hon. Ian (Hedworth John Little)**, PC, MP. *B.* 1926. *Educ.* Eton; Balliol Coll. Oxford. *M.* 1951, Lady Caroline Margaret Montague-Douglas-Scott. *S.* 4. *Dau.* 1. *Career:* served with Grenadier Guards 1944–47; 2nd Lieut 1945; Called to the Bar Inner Temple 1952; Member, Parliament (Con.) Central Norfolk 1962–74, for Chesham & Amersham since 1974; Minister of State for Defence Procurement, Ministry of Defence 1971–72, for Defence 1972–74; Sec. of State for Defence 1974. *Publications:* The Body Politic (1969). *Address:* The Ferry House, Old Isleworth, Middx.

**GILMOUR, Colonel Sir John E.** Bt, DSO, TD. British Member of Parliament. *B.* 1912. *Educ.* Eton; Trinity Hall, Cambridge; Dundee Sch. of Economics. *Married. S.* 2. *Career:* Fife County Council ,1955–61; Conservative M.P. for East Fife since 1961; Vice-Chmn., Conservative Party Scotland 1963–65 & Chmn. 1965–67. *Decorations:* Distinguished Service Order; Territorial Decoration. *Clubs:* Cavalry; Royal & Ancient Golf Club St. Andrews. *Address:* Montrave, Leven, Fife; & House of Commons, London SW1A 0AA.

**GINSBURG, David**, MA, MP. British. *B.* 1921. *Educ.* Ballio Coll. Oxford University. *M.* 1954, Louise Cassy. *Career:* War Service specially employed Captain, Intelligence, 1942–45; Senior Research Officer Govt. Social Survey, 1946–52; Sec. Research Dept. Policy Cttee. Labour Party, 1952–59; Market Research Consultant since 1957; Member, Parliament, Labour for Dewsbury since 1959; Chmn. Parly. Scientific Cttee. 1968–71, Deputy-Chmn. 1971—; Member, Select Cttee. Science and Technology; Broadcaster, Can I Help You! French Service BBC, since 1965; Dir. various Research Companies since 1966. *Address:* 3 Bell Moor, East Heath Road, London N.W.3.

**GINSBURG, Marcel.** Diamond merchant. *B.* 1 Apr. 1891. Hon. President, Beurs voor Diamanthandel, Commander, Ordre de la Couronne; Officier, Ordre de Léopold. *Address:* 88 Rue du Pélican, Antwerp, Belgium.

**GINZBERG, Eli.** Hepburn Professor of Economics. *B.* 1911. *Educ.* Columbia University (AB 1931; AM 1932; PhD 1934); Heidelberg University 1928–29; Grenoble University 1929; LLD (Hon.) 1969; DLitt (Hon.) 1966. *M.* 1946, Ruth Szold. *S.* Jeremy. *Daus.* Abigail and Rachel. Recipient Exceptional Civilian Service Medal (War Dept. 1947); Gold Medal of Int. University of Social Studies, Rome. *Career:* Prof. Economics, Columbia Univ. N.Y. 1935—; Dir. of Research, United Jewish Appeal 1939; Consultant, Executive Office of President 1941–42; Special Assistant, Chief Statistician, War Dept. 1942–43; Dir., Resources Analysis Div., Surgeon-General's Office 1944–46; Dir., N.Y. State Hospital Study 1948–49; U.S. Representative. five-power Conf. on Reparations, Paris 1946. Director, Conservation of Human Resources Project, Columbia University 1950—; Director of Staff Studies, National Manpower Council, Columbia University 1951–61. Consultant: U.S. Department of Army 1945—; Department of Labor 1954—; Department of State 1953–56, 1966—; Defence 1965— and Commerce 1965. Chmn., Committee on Studies, White House Conf. for Children and Youth 1960; Chmn. National Manpower Advisory Cttee. 1962–74; Chmn. Nat. Commission for Manpower Policy since 1974; Consultant to the President 1964–68. Member, Scientific Advisory Board U.S. Air Force, 1969–73; Inst. of Medicine, Nat. Academy of Sciences. *Publications:* House of Adam Smith; Illusion of Economic Stability; Grass on Slag Heaps—The Story of the Welsh Miners; The Unemployed; The Labor Leader; Agenda for American Jews; Occupational Choice; The Uneducated; What Makes an Executive?; The Negro Potential; Effecting Change in Large Organizations; Human Resources; The Ineffective Soldier (3 vols.); The Nation's Children (ed. 3 vols.); Planning for Better Hospital Care; The Optimistic Tradition and American Youth; The American Worker in the Twentieth Century; Democratic Values and the Right of Management; Technology and Social Change; The Troublesome Presence; Talent and Performance; The Negro Challenge to the Business Community; The Pluralistic Economy; Life Styles of Educated Women; Keeper of the Law—Louis Ginzberg; Educated American Women; The Development of Human Resources; Manpower Strategy for Developing Nations; The Middle Class Negro in the White Man's World; Manpower Agenda for America; Manpower Strategy for the Metropolis; Business Leadership and the Negro Crisis; Men, Money and Medicine; Urban Health Services, Career Guidance; Manpower for Development; New York is very Much Alive; Corporate Lib.; Women's Challenge to Management; The Manpower Connection: Education and Work; and others. Fellow, American Assn. for Advancement of Science; Hon. member: Medical Consultants, World War II; Governor, Hebrew Univ., Jerusalem 1956–59. *Member:* American Econ. Association; Academy of Political Science. *Club:* Columbia Univ. *Address:* 845 West End Avenue, New York City 25; and *office* Columbia Univ., New York City, U.S.A.

**GIOLITTI, Antonio**, Dott in Leg. Italian. *B.* 1915. Under-Secretary for Foreign Affairs, June–Oct. 1946; Minister of the Budget Dec. 1963–July 1964; Pres. of Industry Commission in the Camera dei Deputati, Nov. 1964–70: Chmn. Parly. group. Italian Socialist Party. Minister of the Budget 1970–72, 1973–74; EEC Commissioner 1976. *Publications:* Reforms & Revolution (1957); Communism in Europe (1960); Socialism is possible (1967). Member of Italian Socialist Party. *Address:* Camera dei Deputati, Rome, Italy.

**GIRARD, S. A.** American. *B.* 1913. *Educ.* Univ. of Washington. *M.* Laurina Banks. *S.* Stephen. *Daus.* Julie Ann (Miller), Caron Jeanne (Cox), and Stephanie (Le Boutillier). President and Chief Executive Officer, Kaiser Jeep Corp. 1959–70; (joined the Kaiser organization as Superintendent of Grand Coulee Dam project 1938). Dir. & Vice-Pres. Kaiser Industries Corp. Pres. and Dir.: Kaiser Jeep Intnl. Corp., and Jeep Sales Corp.; Pres. Bd. of Directors, Kaiser Jeep Overseas S.A. (Italy); Chmn. Bd. of Dirs., Willys Motors Australia Pty. Ltd. Director: Kaiser Jeep of Canada Ltd., Industrias Kaiser Argentina S.A., Mahindra & Mahindra Ltd. (India), E. Ilin Industries Ltd. (Israel), Kaiser Jeep Afrika (Pty.) Ltd. (S. Africa), and Turk-Willys Overland Fabrikalari A.O. (Turkey). Pres. Kaiser Resources Ltd., Vancouver BC, Canada 1972–73; Senior Vice-Pres. Kaiser Ind. Corp. 1973–74; President Group Operations, Kaiser Industries Corp. since 1974. *Member:* Sigma Nu; Automobile Mfg. Assn.; Socy Automotive Engineers; President's Council, Amer. Inst. of Management; Automotive Safety Foundation (member Bd. Trustees). *Award:* Order of Vasco Nunez de Balboa (Panama). *Clubs:* Toledo, San Francisco Golf; Rolling Rock. *Address:* Kaiser Center, 300 Lakeside Drive, Oakland, Calif. 94666, U.S.A.

**GIRAUD, Pierre René.** French Senator. *B.* 1913. *Educ.* Univ. *M.* 1936, Ann Pinçon. *S.* 1. *Dau.* 1. *Career:* University Teacher and Professor 1936–1968; Counsellor (Seine) 1953–68, (Paris) 1953–71; Senator 1958 and 1968–75. Member of North Atlantic Assembly & of European Parliament. *Decoration:* Chevalier de la Legion d'honneur. *Publications:* Articles in la Revue Socialité and le Droit de Vivre. *Address:* 14 rue de Vouille, 75015 Paris, France; and *office* Palais du Luxembourg, Paris.

**GIRDWOOD, Charles P.** Canadian mining engineer. *B.* 1910. *Educ.* McGill Univ. (Bachelor of Engineering). *M.* 1936, Edna MacKay. *S.* Allan. *Dau.* Margaret. *Career:* Plant Operator, Consolidated Mining & Smelting Co., Trial, B.C. 1929–31; Prospector, engineer, assayer, mine superintendent various prospects in Ontario and Quebec 1933–39; Asst. to Gen.

Mgr., M. J. O'Brien Ltd. 1936–39; Chief Engineer 1939–47, Gen. Superintendent Dome Mines Ltd. 1947–53, Gen. Mgr. 1953–72; Vice-Pres. Director, Dome Mines, South Porcupine, Ont. 1953–76, Consultant 1976—; Director, Sigma Mines (Quebec) Ltd. Clinton Copper Mines Ltd.; Gamma Mines Ltd; Hon. Pres., Porcupine General Hospital; former Dir. and Vice-Pres., Ontario Hospital Assn.; Former Commissioner, Ontario Northland Rly.; Dir., Star Transfer Ltd. Hon. Pres. Porcupine Div., Canadian Cancer Socy.; Porcupine Div. St. John's Ambulance Socy.; Past President and Director Ontario Mining Association; Past President, Mines Accident Prevention Association of Ontario. *Member:* Professional Engineers of Province of Ontario. *Life Member:* Canadian Institute of Mining and Metallurgy. (Former Vice-Pres.), American Institute of Mining and Metallurgical Engineers. *Award:* Distinguished Service 1972; CIMM. *Publications:* various technical articles for mining and metallurgical journals. *Clubs:* Prescott Golf. *Address:* Dome Mines Ltd., South Porcupine, Ont., PON 1HO, and R.R.I. River Road, W., Prescott, Ont. KOE 1TO, Canada.

**GIRI, Varahagiri Venkata.** Indian. *B.* 10 Aug. 1894. *Educ.* Kallicote Coll. Berhampur; National University Ireland. Barrister-at-Law. *M.* 1917, Smt. Sarasvathi Bai Giri. *S.* 4. *Daus.* 7. *Career:* Advocate, Madras High Court; Member, Indian National Congress & Home Rule League; Trade Union Leader, Gen. Secy. and President, All India Railwaymen's Federation; Pres. Trade Union Congress 1926 & 1942, Indian Workers Del. to Int. Lab. Conf. Geneva 1927; Workers Rep. Second Round Table Conf. London 1931; Member, Central Legislative Assembly 1934–37; Minister, Labour, Industries, Co-operation & Commerce Madras 1937–39 and 1946–47; High Commissioner India, in Ceylon 1947–51; Minister for Labour, Govt. India 1952–54; Pres. Indian Socy. Labour Economics since 1957 and Indian Conference, Social Work since 1958; Governor, Uttar Pradesh 1957–60, Kerala 1960–65, Mysore 1965–67; Vice-Pres. India 1967–69; President, India 1969–74. *Awards:* DLitt (hc) Banaras Hindu Univ. and Andhra Univ.; LLD (hc) Agra University; Dr. of Literature (hc) Lucknow Univ. (1972); Dr. of Law (hc) Bratislava Univ. (1973); Dr. of Law (hc) Moscow Univ. (1970); Univ. of Sofia (1970). *Publications:* Industrial Relations, Labour Problems in Indian Industry; Jobs For Our Millions. *Address:* 4 Giri Road, T'Nagar, Madras; and No 1, III Block, Jayanagar, Bangalore II, India.

**GISCARD d'ESTAING, (Jean) Edmond (Lucien);** *B.* 29 March 1894; *educ.* Licencié ès-lettres; Docteur en droit; *m.* 1923, Melle. May Bardoux; *s.* Valery (President of Republic of France), Oliver; *daus.* Sylvie (Comtesse de Las Cases), Isabelle (Comtesse de Lasteyrie du Saillant), Marie-Laure (Comtesse de Froissard de Brossia). *Career:* Financial Dir., French High Commission in the Rhineland 1921–26; on financial missions to Czechoslovakia, Germany and A.O.F.; administrator of various industrial organizations; Hon. President, Société Financière pour la France et les Pays-d'Outremer, and Hon. Pres., International Chamber of Commerce; member of l'Institut; former Inspector of Finances. *Awards:* Croix de Guerre (1914–18); Grand Officer of the Legion of Honour and Order of Isabelle la Catholique; Commander, Crown of Belgium; Cmdeur., Order of St. Gregory the Great, Dannebrog; Chevalier of Malta. *Publications:* Misère et Splendeur des Finances allemandes (1924); Capitalisme (1930); La Maladie du Monde (1933); Le Chemin de la Pauvreté (1947); La France et l'Unification Economique de l'Europe (1953); Les Finances, Terre inconnue; numerous reviews. *Address:* 101 Avenue Henri Martin, Paris 16; Château de Varvasse, Chanonat par St.-Amant-Tallende (P.d.D.); and *office* 23 rue de l'Admiral d'Estaing, Paris 16.

**GISCARD d'ESTAING, Valery.** President of Republic of France. *B.* 1926. *Educ.* Ecole Polytechnique; Ecole Nationale d'Administration. *M.* Anne Aymone de Brantes. *S.* 2. *Daus.* 2. *Career:* Armed forces 1944 to 1945; Inspector of Finance 1954; Principal Private Secretary to Pres. of Council 1954; Deputy Puy-de-Dome 1956; Re-elected Clermont-North and South-West (1958, 1962, 1967, 1968–73); Sec. of State for Finance 1959; Minister of Finance 1962 (Jan.–April); Minister of Finance and Economic Affairs 1962–66, 1969–72 and 1972–74; Elected Pres. of Republic of France 1974. *Chmn.* OLCD 1970. *Address:* Palais de L'Elysée, 55 rue du Saubourg, Saint Honore, 75008 Paris, France.

**GISEL, William George.** American. *B.* 1916. *Educ.* Miami Univ. (BS 1937). *M.* 1944, Katherine Lee. *S.* William George, Jr. *Daus.* Sarah Lee (Green) and Barbara Koehl. *Career:* With Goodyear Tire & Rubber Co.; (Jamestown, N.Y.) 1937–39; Bank of Jamestown 1939–40; Joined Bell Aircraft Corp. 1940; Chief Accounting Officer, 1952. Secy. 1954, Treas. 1956, Vice-Pres. 1957, Secy. 1954, Comptroller 1952–56, Actg. Gen. Mgr. 1959, Gen. Mgr. 1960; President, Bell Aerosystems Co. 1960–70. President, Bell Aerospace Co., Div. of Textron Inc. since 1970, name changed to Bell Aerospace Textron, Div. of Textron Inc. from 1976. Director: Associated Industries of New York State Inc.; Dunlop Tire & Rubber Corp.; Marine Midland-Western (Board Mem.); Buffalo Fine Arts Academy; Vice-Pres. and Dir. James H. Cummings Foundation Inc.; Niagara Share Corp. *Member:* Aero Club of Buffalo, Aerospace Ind. Assn. of America Inc.; Air Force Assn.; AFA Lawrence D. Bell Chapter; Assn. of U.S. Army; Assoc. of Old Crows; Buffalo Area Chamber of Commerce; Aviation Hall of Fame; Natl. Defense Transportation Assn.; Natl. Security Industrial Assn.; Natl. Space Club; Niagara Falls Chamber of Commerce; U.S. Naval Inst.; Navy League United States; Dean's Associate of School of Business Admin.; of Miami Univ.; National Aviation Club; Trustee Western N.Y. Savings Bank; The Children's Hospital Advisory Cttee; Vice-Chmn. Niagara Frontier Transportation Authority. *Clubs:* Buffalo; Cherry Hill; Country Club of Buffalo. *Address:* 58 Rumsey Road, Buffalo, New York 14209; and *office* P.O. Box One, Buffalo, New York 14240, U.S.A.

**GISLASON, Gylfi.** Icelandic. *B.* 1917. *Educ.* Frankfurt am Main and Vienna Universities, Dr rer pol., Dr. Econ. h.c. Univ. of Iceland. *M.* 1939, Gudrun Vilmundardottir. *S.* Thorsteinn, Vilmundur and Thorvaldur. *Career:* Lecturer of Economics, University of Iceland 1941–46; Professor 1946-56; Member of Parliament 1946—; Minister of Education and Industries 1956–58; Education and Commerce 1959–71; Governor for Iceland, International Monetary Fund 1956–65; Governor for Iceland, International Bank for Reconstruction and Development 1965–71; Chmn., State Research Council 1965–71; Chmn. Social Democratic Party 1968–73; Chmn., Parly. Group Social Democratic Party since 1968; Prof. of Economics Univ. of Iceland since 1971; President of Icelandic Parliament 1974. *Member:* Icelandic Science Society. Nordic Council since 1971; Chmn. of its Cttee for Cultural Affairs since 1971; Chmn. of Finance Cttee since 1975; *Publications:* General Business Theory (1941); Bookkeeping (1942); Finance of Private Business Enterprises (1945); Management of Industrial Enterprises (1953); Accountancy (1955); The Marshall Plan (1948); Socialism (1949); Capitalism, Socialism and the Co-operative Movement (1950); The Foreign Policy of Iceland (1953); Enterprise and Society (1974); Essays in Business Administration (1975); Fisheries Economics (1975); The Problems of being an Icelander (1973); past, Present and Future. *Address:* Argata 11, Reykjavik, Iceland; and *office* Althingi, Reykjavik, Iceland.

**GITTLEMAN, Morris.** American. Consulting metallurgist; professional engineer, chemical and metallurgical engineering. Inventor of MG coupling; Consultant. *B.* 1912. *Educ.* Brooklyn Coll. (BS *cum laude* 1934), Polytechnic Inst., of Brooklyn (grad. studies 1947–48) and Pratt Inst., Manhattan College School of Engineering. *M.* 1937, Clara Konefsky. *S.* Michael Jay and Arthur Paul. *Career:* Metallurgical Engr. N.Y. Naval Shipyard 1942–47; Metallurgist; Technical and Production Mgr. Pacific Cast Iron Pipe & Fitting Co., South Gate 1948–58; Instructor of Physics, Los Angeles Harbor Coll. 1958–59; Instructor of Chemistry, Western States Coll. of Engineering 1961–68. Consultant: Valley Brass Co., El Monte, Calif. 1958–61; Anaheim Foundry Co. Calif. 1958–63; Vulcan Foundry, Haifa, Israel 1958–65; Hollywood Alloy Casting Co., Calif. 1960–70; Spartan Casting Corp., Buena Park, Calif. 1961–62; Familian Pipe & Supply Co., Van Nuys, Calif. 1962–72; Overton Foundry Co., South Gate, Calif. 1962–71, Gen. Mgr. 1970–71; Commercial Enameling Co., Los Angeles 1963–75; Universal Cast Iron Manufacturing Co., South Gate 1965–71; Pres. MG Coupling Co. Div. of Familian Corp. since 1972. *Member:* Amer. Assn. for Advancement of Science; Amer. Socy. for Metals; Amer. Foundrymen's Society. Contributor to technical and professional journals. *Address:* 8232 Blackburn Avenue, Los Angeles, Calif. 90048, U.S.A.; and *office* 12353 Wilshire Boulevard, Los Angeles, Calif. 90025, U.S.A.

**GIUSTI DEL GIARDINO, Justo.** Italian diplomat. *B.* 19 Mar 1908. *Educ.* Padua Univ. (LLD). *M.* 1938, Matilde Chieri. *S.* Giovanni, Vettor. *Daus.* Sandra, Marina, *Career:* Entered Italian Foreign Service July 1933; Vice-Consul, Calcutta and Djibuti; Second Secretary, Peking and Athens; Consul, San Sebastian; Consul-General, Paris; General Director for Emigration; Chief of many delegations to I.L.O., O.E.C.E.,

I.C.E.M., Council of Europe; President, pro tem, of I.C.E.M.; Ambassador Extraordinary and Plenipotentiary to Venezuela 1954–58; to India 1958; and concurrently to Nepal, 1960; Ambassador to Japan, 1968; President of Italian Delegation of 10th Assembly of I.C.A.O.; Chief of the Special Italian Embassy in the Dominican Republic, Aug. 1957; Italian Observer at 17th ECAFE Conference, Italian Permanent Representative at the International Agencies in Geneva, Dec. 1964; Chief of Italian delegations at 20th and 22nd Session of the Economical Commission for European Aid. Italian Observer at 41st session of E.C.O.S.O.C.; Deputy Chairman, Council of C.E.R.N. *Awards:* Knight of Great Cross Merito Republica Italiano; Commander, Legion of Honour and of Isabel la Catolica; Officer, S.S. Maurizio e Lazzaro; Chevalier, Crown of Italy and of the Colonial Star; holder of Italian Cross of War for Gallantry. *Publications:* Articles in various reviews on labour and migration problems. *Address:* 2 via Giardino Giusti, Verona, Italy.

**GIUSTINA, Pietro (Luigi).** Italian business executive. *B.* 1922. *Educ.* DMechEng, Politecnico, Turin 1946. *M.* 1947, Bruna Valle. *S.* Marcello. *Dau.* Manuela. *Career:* With the Giustina Co. since 1946. President and Chairman, Giustina Co., Sp. Az., Turin (grooving lathes, grinding machine manufacturers, made by Giustina Engineering or under Farrel Co. and Bendix Besly Welles and Sheffield (U.S.A.) licences). *Publications:* various technical publications on some particular aspects of grinding operations and surface finish; contributions to technical journals. *Clubs:* Rotary (for machine tools, Subalpino Turin); UCID (Turin); IDE (Rome); N.S.A. (N.Y.C.). *Address:* Strada Valsanmartino Superiore 7, Torino 10131, Italy; and *office* P.O. Box 510-Strada Statale 11, Settimo Torinese, Italy; and 450 West 44th Street, New York City, N.Y. 10036, U.S.A.

**GLADWYN, Lord** (Hubert Miles Gladwyn Jebb), GCMG, GCVO, CB; Grand Cross, Legion of Honour. British diplomat, writer and Parliamentarian. *B.* 25 Apr. 1900. *Educ.* Eton; Magdalen College, Oxford. *M.* 1929, Cynthia Noble. *S.* 1. *Daus.* 2. *Career:* Entered Diplomatic Service 1924; Private Secy. to Parly. Under-Secy. of State 1929–31; to Permanent Under-Secretary of State 1937–40; Asst. Under-Secretary, Ministry of Economic Warfare 1940; Acting Counsellor, Foreign Office 1941, Head of Reconstruction Department 1942–45; Acting Secretary-General, United Nations Feb. 1946; Deputy to Secretary of State on Council of Foreign Ministers Mar. 1946; Asst. Under-Secretary of State, Foreign Office, May 1946–49. Deputy Under-Secretary of State 1949–50; United Kingdom Representative to the United Nations 1950–54; Amb. Ex. and Plen. to France Apr. 1954–Sept. 1960. Retired 1960; Created Peer Apr. 1959. Deputy Leader of Liberal Party in House of Lords 1967—; Member Parliamentary Delegation, Council of Europe and Western Union 1966–73; Member European Parliament 1973–76. Ex-Pres., Atlantic Treaty Assn.; Vice-Chmn., European Movement; Chmn. 'Campaign for a European Political Community'; Governor, Atlantic Inst. Hon. DCL. Oxford, Essex, and Syracuse, Hon. Fellow Magdalen Coll. Oxon. *Publications:* several works on international tension and Cold War problems; also of The European Idea (1966); Half-Way to 1984 (1967); de Gaulle's Europe, or Why the General Says No (1969); Europe After De Gaulle (1970); The Memoirs of Lord Gladwyn (1972). *Address:* Bramfield Hall, Halesworth, Suffolk; and 62 Whitehall Court, London, S.W.1.

**GLASS, Sir Leslie Charles,** KCMG. *B.* 1911. *Educ.* Bradfield College; Trinity Coll., Oxford (MA); School of Oriental Studies, London University. *M.* (1) 1942, Pamela Gage (*dissolved* 1956). *S.* Nicholas and Luke. *Dau.* Julia. *M.* (2) 1957, Betty Hoyer-Millar. *Step-daughters* Lindsay and Nicola Hoyer-Millar. *Career:* Entered Indian Civil Service 1934; Burma 1934–42; Far Eastern Bureau, British Ministry of Information, New Delhi 1943; Lieut.-Col., Head of Burma Section, Psychological Warfare Division of S.E.A.C. 1944; Head of Information Division British Military Administration, Burma 1945; Foreign Office 1947; Oriental Secretary, British Embassy, Rangoon 1948; Foreign Office 1949; Head of Chancery, Legation, Budapest 1950; Head of Information Division, British Middle-East Office, Beirut 1953; Director-General of Information, Government of Cyprus 1955; Consul-General, Washington 1957; Director-General of British Information Services in U.S.A. 1959–61; Minister in the Foreign Office, Sept. 1961–62; Asst. Under Secretary of State 1963–65; Ambassador to Romania 1965–67; Ambassador and Deputy Permanent Representative to the U.N. 1967–69. High Commissioner, Nigeria, 1969–71; Chmn. Anglo-Romanian Bank; Chmn. Civil Service Selection Bd.; Trustee Thomson Foundation; Governor Bradfield College. *Club:* East India Sports & Public Schools (London). *Address:* Stone House, Ivington, Leominster, Herefordshire.

**GLASSER, Georges Charles,** Commandeur, Legion of Honour, Grand Officer Order of Orange-Nassau, commander, Order of Lion, Finland. French. *B.* 1907. *Educ.* Ecole Polytech.; Ecole Nationale des Ponts et Chaussees. *M.* 1934, Hugette Farjon. *Daus.* 3. *Career:* Pres. d'Honneur, Soc. Alsthom, Pres. & Man. Dir., Stein Industrie et CGEE Alsthom. *Clubs:* Tennis-Club de Paris; Automobile-Club de France; Aero-Club de France. *Address:* 3 rue Dangeau, 75016 Paris, France; and *office* 38, Ave. Kleber, Paris 16e.

**GLASSPOLE, Florizel A.** The Governor General of Jamaica. *B.* 1909. *Educ.* Ruskin Coll., Oxford. *M.* 1934, Ina Josephine Kinlocke. *Career:* Mem., House of Representatives 1944; Vice-Pres., People's National Party; Minister of Labour 1955–57; Leader of the House 1955–62; Min. of Educ. 1957–62; Mem., House of Reps. Cttee. which prepared Jamaica's Independence Constitution; Mem. of Delegation to British Govt. completing constitution Document, 1962; Gov. Gen. of Jamaica since 1974. *Address:* The Residence of the Governor General, Kingston, Jamaica.

**GLENCONNER, Lord** (Sir Christopher Grey Tennant, Bt). British peer and company director. *B.* 14 June 1899. *M.* (1) 1925, Pamela Winefred Paget, and (2) 1935, Elizabeth Powell. *S.* (by 1st marriage) 2, (by 2nd marriage), *S.* 1. *Daus.* 2. Director, Silvermines Lead & Zinc Co. Ltd.; Dir. Tennant's Estates Ltd. *Adress:* Rovinia, Liapades, Corfu, Greece.

**GLENIE, Jack Patrick.** New Zealand. *B.* 1909. *Educ.* Auckland Univ. (Barristers Professional Examination). *M.* 1937, Gwen Gibson Gardner. *S.* John Andrew and Richard James. *Daus.* Margaret Jill, Alison Jean and Robin Leslie. *Career:* Born in England; emigrated to N.Z. 1912; practised law 1928–35. Governing Dir.: A. W. Gardner & Co. Ltd., H. A. Bell Ltd., Gardner Fashions Ltd., Empire Frocks Ltd., and Gardners (Taumarunui) Ltd. (all of Auckland) Past Pres. Auckland Chamber of Commerce; Former Pres. Associated Chamber of Commerce N.Z.; Bureau of Importers (Auckland). *Club:* Auckland. *Address: office* P.O. Box 1569, Auckland, New Zealand.

**GLENKINGLAS, Rt. Hon. Lord (Michael Antony Cristobal),** PC, *B.* 1913. *Educ.* Eton and Magdalen Coll., Oxford. *M.* 1940, Anne Pearson. *Daus.* 4. *Career:* Served in R.A.F.V.R. 1941–45. Memb. Parliament for Argyllshire (Cons.) 1958–74; Parly. Secy. to Secy. of State for Scotland 1959; Asst. Government Whip 1960; a Lord Commissioner of the Treasury 1961–62. Secretary of State for Scotland 1962; Chmn. Unionist Party in Scotland 1962–63; Chmn. Associated Fisheries Ltd. 1966–70; Pres. Board of Trade 1970–72; Minister for Trade 1970–72. Chmn. Brit. Agricultural Export Board 1973–77; Dir., John Brown Engineering since 1973, Monteith Holdings since 1974; Mem. of Council of Royal Zoological Soc. of London 1975—. *Clubs:* Boodle's (London); New (Edinburgh); Royal Scottish Automobile (Scotland). *Address:* Strone, Cairndow, Argyll.

**GLENN, Sir (Joseph Robert) Archibald,** OBE, BCE, MIChemE, FIE (Aust.). *B.* 1911. *Educ.* Scotch College, and Melbourne Univ.; Harvard Univ. (AMP) 1957; Fellow, Australian Institute of Management. *M.* 1939, Elizabeth Balderstone. *S.* 1. *Daus.* 3. *Career:* Design and Construction Engineer, ICIANZ 1935–46; Explosives Dept., I.C.I., England 1945–46; Construction Controller, ICIANZ 1947–48; Controller, Nobel Group ICIANZ 1948–50, Gen. Manager 1950–53; Managing Dir. ICIANZ 1953–63. Chairman and Managing Director Imperial Chemical Industries of Australia and New Zealand Ltd. (ICIANZ) (ICI Australia since 1973) 1963–73; Director, Bank of New South Wales 1967—; ICI Ltd. London 1970–75; Alcoa of Australia Ltd. 1973—; Tioxide Aust. Ltd. 1973— (Chmn. 1977—); Newmont Pty. Ltd. 1977—; Chmn. IMI Aust. Ltd. since 1973; Chmn. Collins Wales Pty. Ltd. since 1974; I.C. Insurance Australia Ltd. 1973—. *Member:* Manufacturing Industry Advisory Council 1963–77; Governor, Atlantic Institute International Affairs since 1973; Industrial Design Council of Australia; Chancellor, La Trobe Univ. 1964–72; Chairman Scotch College Council, Ormond College Council 1976—. *Clubs:* Australian; Melbourne; Royal Melbourne Golf; Victoria Racing; Frankston Golf; Melbourne University Boat. *Address:* 3 Heyington Place, Toorak, 3142, Vic., Australia.

**GLENTORAN, Rt. Hon. Lord,** (Daniel Stewart Thomas Bingham Dixon), PC, KBE. *B.* 1912. *Educ.* Eton and R.M.C.

Sandhurst. *M.* 1933, Lady Diana Mary Wellesley. *S.* 2. *Dau.* 1 *Career:* with Grenadier Guards; served in World War II, 1939–45 (dispatches), retired with rank of Hon. Lieut.-Col. H.M. Lieutenant, City of Belfast since 1950, Lord Lieutenant since 1975. MP (U) Bloomfield Div. of Belfast, N. Ireland Parliament 1950–61; Parliamentary Secy., Ministry of Commerce 1952–53; Minister of Commerce 1953–61. Hon. Col. 6th Bn. Royal Ulster Rifles 1956–61 Minister in and Leader of the Senate of Northern Ireland 1961—. Speaker of the Senate 1964–73. *Clubs:* Ulster (Belfast). *Address:* Drumadarragh House, Ballyclare, Co. Antrim, Northern Ireland.

**GLIGOROV, Kiro.** Yugoslavian Politician & Economist. *B.* 1917. *Educ.* Belgrade Faculty of Law. *M.* 1943, Nada Misev. *S.* 1. *Daus.* 2. *Career:* Mem. Anti-Fascist Council of National Liberation 1943–44; Mem., Presidium, Provisional National Assembly 1944–45; Assist.-Min. of Finance 1947–52; Professor, Faculty of Economics, Univ. of Belgrade 1952–55; Secy. Gen. Economic Affairs 1955–62; Secy. of Finance & Mem. of Cabinet 1962–67; Vice Prime-Minister, Yugoslavia 1967–69; Mem., Exec. Bureau, Presidium, League of Communists 1969–74; President, Assembly of SFR of Yugoslavia since 1974; Mem. Presidium, Central Cttee. League of Communists since 1974. *Member:* Yugoslav. Assoc. of Economists. *Decorations:* several national and foreign. *Address:* Bulevar Oktobarske Revolucije 14, Belgrade, Yugoslavia; and *office* Bulevar Lenjina 6, Belgrade.

**GLOVER, Alan (Marsh).** *B.* 1909. *Educ.* Univ. of Rochester (BA, MA, PhD). *M.* 1949, Janet Mary Briggs. *S.* Keith Terrot and John Carroll. *Dau.* Beth Marsh. Fellow, Univ. of Rochester, N.Y. 1935; Physicist, Lawrence College (Wis.) 1935–36; Radio Corp. of America 1936—; Technical Adviser Radio Corp. of America since 1971. *Publications:* Photo-electricity, Proc. IRE 1938. Phi Beta Kappa; Sigma Xi. Fellow, Inst. of Electrical & Electronic Engineers. *Address:* *office* Radio Corp. of America, Harrison, N.J. U.S.A.

**GLUBB, Lieut.-General Sir John Bagot,** KCB, CMG, DSO, OBE, MC. British army officer. *B.* 16 Apr. 1897. *Educ.* Cheltenham College; R.M.A., Woolwich. *M.* 1938, Muriel Rosemary Forbes. *S.* 2. *Daus.* 2. *Career:* Served in World War I in France (wounded 3 times); served in Iraq as Lieutenant, R.E. 1920; resigned commission in 1926 and became Administrative Inspector to the Iraq Government; transferred to Trans-Jordan 1930; Officer Commanding Desert Area 1932; Chief of General Staff, Arab Legion 1939–56. *Publications:* Story of the Arab Legion (1948); A Soldier with the Arabs (1957); Britain and the Arabs (1959); War in The Desert (1960); The Great Arab Conquests (1963); The Empire of the Arabs (1963); The Course of Empire (1965); The Lost Centuries (1967); The Middle East Crisis (1967); Syria, Lebanon, Jordan (1967); A Short History of the Arab Peoples (1969); The Life and Times of Muhammad (1970); Peace in The Holy Land (1971); Soldiers of Fortune (1973); The Way of Love (1974); Haroon Al Rasheed & The Great Abbasids (1976); Into Battle: A Soldier's Diary of the Great War (1978). *Address:* c/o Lloyds Bank, 6 Pall Mall, London, S.W.1.

**GLUCK, Samuel Emanuel.** American philosopher and mining geologist. *B.* 1925. *Educ.* Ohio State Univ. (BA 1947); Columbia Univ. (MA Philos, 1954, PhD Philos 1960); Certif., Industrial College of the Armed Forces, U.S.A. 1952. *M.* 1956, Phyllis R. Gold. *S.* Josiah Nicholas, Theodore Eugene, Sebastian Matthew. *Career:* Director of Research and Development, Bonded Scale and Machine Co., 1948–63; Instr., School of Politics, Dept. of Sociology and Anthropology, New School for Social Research 1958–60; Adjunct Instructor, Dept. of Philosophy, Rutgers Univ. 1958–60; Departmental Representative, Department of Philosophy, Bernard M. Baruch School of Business and Public Administration, City Univ. of New York 1960–63; Associate Professor of Management, Marketing, and Business Statistics, Hofstra University 1963–71; Professor, Industrial Management, Graduate School of Business Hofstra Univ. since 1971. Active as consultant on management education, as well as on mineral beneficiation, chemical processing and coal preparation, and the socio-economic problems of the basic extractive industries. Recipient, Shell Research Grants 1964, 1966, Hofstra Research Grant, 1968, 1971. N.Y. Acad. Sc. representative 1967, to ACHEMA Congress, Frankfurt and International Mining Congress Moscow, Korcula. Jugoslavia Summer School, Philosophy 1971, Pneumotransport Conference Cambridge 1971. *Publications:* Manufacturing Management: An Overview (1969); Screens in The Chemical Processing Industries (1966); numerous articles. monographs and reviews in philosophy, the social sciences and engineering. Numerous articles in Encyclopedia International.Ed itor, Education for Management in the Technical Trade Press (1969). Fellow Amer. Assn. for the Advancement of Science. *Member:* International Congress of Philosophy (Vienna) 1968; Royal Institute of Philosophy, England (Life member); American Philosophical Assn.; American Institute of Mining, Metallurgical and Petroleum Engineers (and member of its Cncl. of Education); Canadian Inst. of Mining and Metallurgy. The Royal Canadian Institute; Renaissance Society of America (Charter member); Operations Research Soc. of Amer.; Franklin Institute; N.Y. Academy of Sciences; Ohio Academy of Science; American Society for Engineering Education (mem., Ethics Cttee.); Pi Sigma Epsilon; Mu Gamma Tau; Mem. of Columbia Univ., Seminar on Management in a Dynamic Society. *Address:* 305 Riverside Drive, New York 25, N.Y., U.S.A.

**GLYN, Dr. Alan,** ERD, MP. British politician. *B.* 1918. *Educ.* Westminster; Caius Coll., Cambridge (BA Hons); St. Bartholomew's Hosp. & St. George's Hosp. *M.* 1962, Lady Rosula Caroline Windsor Clive. *Daus.* 2. *Career:* Served in war of 1939–45; Far East 1942–46; psc 1945; Bde Major 1946; Capt. (hon. Major) Royal Horse Guards (E.R.); Medical Practitioner Qualified 1948; Barrister at Law Middle Temple 1955; Co-opted member L.C.C. Educ. Cttee. 1956–58; Member No. 1 L.C.C. Divisional Health Cttee. 1959–61; Member Inner London Local Medical Cttee. since 1967; Member Chelsea Borough Council 1959–62; Governing Body British Post Grad. Medical Fed. (London Univ.); Greater London central valuation panel; Member of Parliament Conservative for Wandsworth (Clapham) 1959–64: Elec. member Inner London Medical Cttee. 1967; Member of Parliament for Windsor Div. Berkshire 1970–74; MP for Windsor and Maidenhead since 1974. *Publications:* Witness to Viet Nam: The Containment of Communism in South East Asia (1968). Freeman, Worshipful Society of the Art & Mystery of Apothecaries of City of London, 1961. Pro-Hungarian Medal of Sovereign Military Order of Malta. *Clubs:* Carlton. *Address:* 17 Cadogan Place, London, S.W.1; and *office* House of Commons, S.W.1.

**GLYN, John Patrick Riversdale,** C.B.E. British banker. *B.* 1913. *Educ.* Eton and Oxford University; BA. *M.* 1937, Audrey Stubbs. *S.* 2. *Daus.* 2. *Career:* Managing Director, Glyn Mills & Co., 1950–70. Chairman, Agricultural Mortgage Corp., Ltd. Alexanders Discount Co. Ltd., Yorkshire Bank Ltd.; Deputy-Chmn. Exchange Telegraph Co., Ltd.; Chmn. First National Finance Corporation; Dir. Stockholders' Investment Trust Co. Ltd. *Address:* The Dower House, Chute Standen, Andover, Hants.

**GNÄGI, Rudolf.** Swiss Lawyer & Politician. *B.* 1917. *Educ.* Secondary, Bienne; Law studies Berne Univ; Qualified an Advocate, Berne 1943. *Career:* Lawyer since 1943; Secy. Peasants' Fed. of Berne 1946; Secy. Farmers' Tradesmen's and Burghers Party of Berne 1946, of Switzerland 1947; Govt. Councillor for Canton of Berne 1952, National Council 1953–65; Swiss Federation Council member, head of Min. of Transport Communications and Power 1965–67; head of Federal Military Dept. since 1968; Vice-Pres. of Federal Council 1970, 1975 & Pres. 1971, 1976. *Address:* Steingrubenweg 8, Spiegel-Bern, Switzerland.

**GOBURDHUN, Ram Chundur.** Barrister-at-law; Indian diplomat. *B.* 19 Sept. 1911. *Educ.* Royal College, Mauritius; l'Institut Français du R.U.; University of Lille, France; Middle Temple, London. *M.* 1949, Kamala Sinha, PhD, MA, LLB. *Career:* Practised law at the Supreme Court of Mauritius 1939–44; Magistrate of the Industrial Court of Mauritius 1945–46; First Secretary, Embassy of India, Prague, 1948–50; Chargé d'Affaires, Prague 1950–52; Deputy-Secretary, Ministry of External Affairs, Jan–Feb. 1953; Counsellor, Embassy of India in Peking 1953–55; Counsellor of Embassy, Paris, 1955–58; Director of External Publicity, Ministry of External Affairs Mar.–Dec. 1958; Ambassador to Morocco and Tunisia 1958–62; Chmn., International Commission for Supervision and Control, Saigon, Vietnam 1962–64; Amb. to Algeria, 1964–66, to Turkey 1967–69; Presently Legal Consultant, Supreme Court of India. *Address:* 30 Lawyers Chambers, Supreme Court of India, New Delhi, India.

**GODBER, Rt. Hon. Joseph Bradshaw,** PC, MP. *B.* 1914. *Educ.* Bedford School. *M.* 1936, Miriam Sanders. *S.* 2. *Career:* MP (Con.), Grantham Division of Lincolnshire 1951—. Assistant Govt. Whip 1955–57; Joint Parly. Secy., Ministry of Agriculture, Fisheries & Food 1957–60; Parly. Under-Secy. of State. Foreign Office 1960–61; Minister of State for Foreign Affairs 1961–63; Secy. of State for War June–Oct. 1963; Minister of Labour Oct. 1963–64. Minister of State for Foreign Affairs, 1970–72; Minister of Agriculture, Fisheries and Food 1972–74; Chmn. Tricentrol Ltd. 1976; Chmn. SC Banks Ltd. 1974; Dir. Booker McConnell Ltd., 1974; Dir. British Home Stores 1977; Consultant Beecham Foods 49, 1974; Chmn. Retail Consortium 1976. *Club:* Carlton (London). *Address:* Willington Manor, nr. Bedford.

**GODCHOT, Jacques Emmanuel.** French Economist. *B.* 1910. *Educ.* Sorbonne (LLD, Ma, Science) and Brevet Centre Hautes Etudes Administratives. Paris. *M.* 1942, Geneviève Schieffer, *S.* Jean-Pierre. *Dau.* Elisabeth. Chevalier de la Légion d'Honneur. *Career:* Free French Forces 1939–44; Lecturer, Paris Univ. 1944; Deputy-Director, Ministry of Reconstruction and Town Planning, Paris 1947, Specialist, Social Science Programme, UNESCO 1948–51; Middle East Representative, Dept. of Social Sciences, UNESCO 1961–57; Expert, French National Commission for UNESCO 1958; French Delegate, OECD; Resident Representative for Technical Assistance in Turkey. *Publications:* Theses in the Social Sciences (UNESCO); Les Constitutions du Proche et du Moyen-Orient (Sirey); Les Sociétés d'Economie Mixte et l'Aménagement du Territoire (Berger-Levrault). *Club:* Kiwanis International. *Address:* 92 Boulevard Péreire, Paris 75017.

**GODFREY, Alan Wilfred,** JP, AASA, AAII. *B.* 1914. *M.* 1938, Jean Beer. *S.* John Alan. *Career:* Commenced with United Insur. Co. Ltd. 1930; Statistical Officer 1947; Asst. Secy. 1952; Secty. 1953; Inspector of Branches 1959; Manager for Australia, Skandia Insurance Co. Ltd. 1961–66; General Manager, Mortgage Guaranty Insurance Corp. of Australia Ltd. Sydney, N.S.W., 1966—. Associate, Australian Society of Accountants (AASA) and Australian Incorporated Insurance Institute (AAII). *Address:* 27 Benelong Crescent, Bellevue Hill, N.S.W., Australia.

**GODFREY, Hon. John Morrow,** QC. Canadian Senator, Barrister and Solicitor. *B.* 1912. *Educ.* Osgoode Hall Law School. *M.* 1940, Mary Burwell Ferguson. *S.* John Ferguson and Stephen Burwell. *Daus.* Sally Mary Helen and Anne Isobel. *Career:* With Royal Canadian Air Force (Wing-Commander) 1940–45. Partner: Campbell, Godfrey & Lewtas; Appointed to Senate of Canada 1973. Director: Dover Industries Ltd.; Montreal Trust Co.; Governor Canadian Council, Social Development. Liberal. *Clubs:* Toronto; Toronto Golf; Osler Bluffs Ski. *Address:* 99 Elm Avenue, Toronto, Ont., Canada.

**GODINE, Morton Robert.** Business executive. *B.* 1917. *Educ.* McGill University (BA 1938, MA 1939) and Harvard Univ. (PhD 1948). *M.* 1941, Bernice Beckwith. *S.* David. *Daus.* Amy and Louise. *Career:* Sometimes Tutor and Teaching Fellow, Dept. of Government, Harvard Univ. 1943, 1946–49, Served in U.S. Navy in World War II. Vice-Pres., Market Forge Co., Everett Mass.; Division, Beatrice Foods Inc.; Board of Selectmen, Brookline, Mass.; Dean, Massachusetts College of Art. *Member:* Mass. Cttee. Children & Youth; Mass. Advisory Council on Education. *Publications:* The Labor Problem in the Public Service (Harvard Univ. Press 1950); town reports, etc. *Clubs:* Rotary, Everett, Mass. (former Pres.); University (Boston); Kernwood Country (Salem, Mass.). Newcomen Socy. *Address:* 9 Cary Road, Chestnut Hills 67, Mass., U.S.A.

**GODRON, Jacques.** French. Chairman, Sté, du canal des Mines de Fer de la Moselle. *B.* 1901. *Educ.* Ecole Polytechnique (Civil Mining Engineer; BA Law). *M.* 1925, Marcelle Langlois. *S.* 3. *Daus.* 2. From Asst. Engineer to Head of the Technical Dept., Comité Central des Houillères de France 1925–27; Secy. to the Board, U.C.P.M.I., Forges et Aciéries d'Hagondange 1927–33 (Attaché to Board of Directors 1933–44, General Secy. 1944–57, Asst. Director to the Chairman and Director-General 1957–63); Asst. Dir.-Gen., Sté. Mosellane de Sidérurgie 1963—. *Member:* Sté. des Ingénieurs Civils de France. *Address:* 2 rue de Narbonne, Paris 7.

**GOEDECKE, Otto.** American cotton merchant. *B.* Bremen (Germany) 1906. *Educ.* N. Carolina State College and Houston (Texas) Law School (LLD 1933); admitted to Texas State Bar 1933. *M.* 1929, Margaret Neumann. *S.* Otto Ernst and Curtis Harold. *Daus.* Waltraut (Duckworth) and Ursula (Aston). *Career:* Went to U.S. under sponsorship of Cotton Co-operatives Organization, and spent first five years in gaining experience with this organization in N. Carolina, and with Oklahoma Cotton Growers Association in their sales office at Houston; founder and President, Otto Goedecke Inc., and subsidiary companies. The first started as a proprietorship in 1932 and was incorporated in Texas 1946, when it inaugurated modern merchandising of cotton by scientific methods, and has continued as a pioneer in this work. *Member:* New York Cotton Exchange, Houston Cotton Exchange and Board of Trade; Texas Academy of Science, Hon. LLD, Texas Lutheran Coll., Seguin, Texas 1962. *Address:* P.O. Box 387, Hallettsville, Texas, U.S.A.

**GOEMAERE, Valère Nathalis Achilles Marie.** Belgian industrialist. *B.* 1912. *Educ.* Univ. of Louvain (Ing. Mechanics and Electricity). *S.* 1. *Dau.* 1. *Career:* Asst., University of Louvain 1935–36; Cockerill-Ougrée Shipyard until 1960. Member Bd. of Dirs., Stefens Electrical Works, Antwerp. Knight, Order of the Crown (Belgium). *Member:* Inst. of Marine Engineers; S. R. Belge Ingénieurs et Industriels; Union des Ingénieurs de l'Université de Louvein; Mars et Mercure; Union Belge des Ingénieurs Navals. *Club:* Rotary. *Address:* 23, Leo Baekelandstraat, 2520 Edegem, Belgium.

**GOETZE, Roger.** French banker. Finance Inspector. Governor, Crédit Foncier de France, 1967 (Asst. Gov., 1957–67). *B.* 1912. *Educ.* BSc, BA, and BA (Law). *M.* 1935, Marcelle Charpentier. *S.* Joan-René. Finance Inspector since 1937; General Director, Les Finances d'Algérie Nov. 1942–July 1949; Financial Director of the Budget in Paris July 1949–Dec. 1956. Chairman and Chief Director, Sté. Nationale de Recherche et d'Exploration du Pétrole en Algérie (SN. REPAL) 1946–66. *Award:* Grand Officier, Légion d'Honneur, Croix de Guerre 1939–45. *Address: office* C.F.F., 19 rue des Capucines, Paris, France.

**GOGSTAD, Odd.** Norwegian shipowner. *B.* 1909. *Educ.* Matriculation and Commercial College. *M.* 1933, Edle Prydz. *S.* 1. *Daus.* 2. Previously: Thb. Engø. Oslo. 1929–30 and 1931–33; Watts, Watts & Co., Newcastle-on-Tyne, 1930–31; Leif Høegh & Co. A/S 1933–40; Manager, Norwegian Shipping & Trade Mission (Tanker Division), New York, 1940–46. Director, Leif Høegh & Co. A/S since 1933; Shipping editor. Norwegian weekly Farmand since 1935; Chairman of Board, Mutual Insurance Club SKULD; Mem. of Bd. Nordisk Skibsrederforening and Norwegian Veritas. Member, Oslo Høyre (Conservatives). *Address:* Drammensveien 82 D, Oslo, Norway.

**GOHEEN, Robert Francis.** U.S. Diplomat & educator. *B.* 1919. *Educ.* Princeton Univ.—BA 1940, PhD 1948; Phi Beta Kappa; Hon. Degrees: LLD LHD, & LCD from 26 institutions. *M.* 1941, Margaret M. Skelly. *S.* 2. *Daus.* 4. *Career:* Instructor & Asst. Prof., Princeton Univ. 1948–57; Dir., Woodrow Wilson Fellowships, Assn. of American Univs. 1953–56; President, Princeton Univ. 1957–72; Chmn., New York City Council on Foundations 1972–76; Pres., Edna McConnell Clark Foundation 1977; Pres. Emeritus, Princeton Univ. since 1977; Dir., Equitable Life Assurance Soc. U.S. 1968–77; U.S. Ambassador, India since 1977. *Member:* American Acad. of Arts & Sciences; American Philology Assn. *Awards:* Bronze Star with two clusters; Combat Infantry Badge with four arrowheads; Legion of Merit medal. *Publications:* The Imagery of Sophocles' Antigone (1951); The Human Nature of a University (1970). *Clubs:* Cosmos, Nassau, Eastward Ho! (Chatham, Mass.), Pretty Brook (Springdale), Princeton, Century Assn., University. *Address:* American Embassy, New Delhi, Department of State, Washington, D.C. 20520, U.S.A.

**GOLDBERG, Hon. Arthur J.** *B.* 1908. *Educ.* City College of Chicago; and Northwestern University (BSL 1929 and summa cum laude, JD 1930). *M.* 1931, Dorothy Kurgans. *S.* Robert M. *Dau.* Barbara L. (Cramer). *Career:* Admitted to Illinois Bar 1929; practised law, Chicago and Washington, D.C. 1930–61; General Counsel, Congress of Industrial Organizations (CIO) 1948–55, and United Steelworkers of America 1948–61; Special Counsel AFL-CIO 1955–61. Secretary of Labor 1961–62; appointed by President Kennedy Associate Justice of the Supreme Court, Aug. 1962; confirmed by Senate Sept. 1962; Asso. Justice of the U.S. Supreme Court 1962–65; Ambassador of U.S. to United Nations 1965–68. Senior Partner, Paul, Weiss, Goldberg, Rifkind, Wharton & Garrison, 1968–71; Charles Evans Hughes Prof. Princeton Univ. 1968–69; Distinguished Prof. Columbia Univ. 1969–70; Practice of Law Wash. D.C. since 1971; Univ. Professor of Law & Diplomacy Amer. Univ. Wash. D.C. 1971–73; Formerly, Chairman: President's Committee on Migratory Labor, President's Missile Sites Labor Commission, President's Committee on Youth Employment, President's Temporary Committee on the Implementation of the Federal Employee-Management Relations Program, Workers' Advisory Committee on U.S. *Member:*

International Labor Organization, Employer's Advisory Cttee. on U.S., and Inter. Labor Organ. Chmn.: President's Advisory Cttee. on Labor-Management Policy; President's Committee on Equal Employment Opportunity; member: President's Committee on Psychological Warfare, President's Committee on Juvenile Delinquency and Youth Crime, President's Council on Ageing, Trade Policy Committee, President's Council on Youth Fitness, Advisory Council on Employment of the Handicapped Federal Radiation Council, President's Commission on the Status of Women, President's Cabinet Textile Advisory Committee, Advisory Commission on Intergovernmental Relations, Distinguished Federal Civilian Service Awards Board, Cabinet Committee on Federal Office Space, Advisory Committee to the Secretary of Defense; ex-officio member, Ad Hoc Participant, National Security Council; legal adviser to several unions. Major, U.S.A. (O.S.S.) in World War II; member, American, Illinois and Chicago Bar Associations. *Publications:* AFL-CIO; Labor United (1956); Defenses of Freedom (1967); Equal Justice, The Warren Era of the Supreme Court (1972); contributions to various legal journals and magazines of public opinion. *Address:* 1101 17 Street NW, Washington DC 20036, U.S.A.

**GOLDEN, William T.** American corporate director and Trustee. *B.* 1909. *Educ.* University of Pennsylvania (AB); Harvard Graduate School of Business Administration; Columbia Univ. 1961—; DSc (Hon.), Polytechnic Inst. of New York, 1975. *M.* 1938, Sibyl Levy. *Daus.* Sibyl Rebecca and Pamela Prudence. Assistant to Pres., Cornell, Linder & Co. (industrial and financial management) 1931–34; with Carl M. Loeb & Co. and Carl M. Loeb, Rhoades & Co. (investment brokers and bankers) 1934–41. Lieut. to Lieut.-Cmdr., U.S.N.R., active duty 1941–45; Assistant to Commissioner, U.S. Atomic Energy Commission, 1946–50, consultant 1950–58; Special consultant to President Harry S. Truman (to review organization of government's military-scientific activities incident to Korean War) 1950–51; Consultant to U.S. Director of Budget 1950–51; member, military procurement task force of Commission on Organization of the Exec. Branch of Government (Hoover Commission) 1954–55; Member, Advisory Committee on Private Enterprise in Foreign Aid, U.S. Department of State 1964–65; mem., National Science Foundation's special advisory cttee. on Sacramento Peak Observatory 1976–77; mem., National Acad. of Public Administration's panel advising National Aeronautics & Space Administration on space transportation operations 1976–77. System Development Corporation (Trustee 1957–66, Chairman 1961–66); Chairman of the Board Nat. U.S. Radiator Corp., and successor companies, 1954–74. Director: General American Investors Co. Inc., Block Drug Co., Verde Explorations Ltd. Chmn., Bd. of Trustees City Univ. Construction Fund, 1967–71; Member and Trustee, Marine Biological Laboratory (Wools Hole, Mass.); Trustee: Amer. Museum of Natural History (Vice-Pres.); trustee (Vice-Chmn.) Barnard College, Haskins Laboratories, Columbia Univ. Press 1974–77; John Simon Guggenheim Memorial Foundation, Bennington College 1971–76; Carnegie Institution of Washington (Secy.); Mitre Corp., 1958–72, 1976—; Mount Sinai Hospital, Mount Sinai School of Medicine, Riverside Research Institute 1967–76, New York City—Rand Institute 1969–75; Center for Advanced Study in The Behavioural Sciences 1970–76, Hebrew Free Loan Society, New York Foundation; University Corporation for Atmosphere Research 1965–74; Director; Associated Hospital Service of New York (Blue Cross) 1959–74; Public Member, Hudson Institute; Vice-Chairman of Governing Council, Courant Institute of Mathematical Sciences (N.Y. Univ.). *Member:* Visiting Cttees. at Harvard (Medical School, 1971–77; Engineering and Applied Physics 1971–77; Astronomy); Columbia (School of General Studies); Princeton (Astronomy); Univ. of Pennsylvania (Faculty of Arts & Sciences); Assoc. of Univs. for Research in Astronomy 1973–76; Dir. and Treasurer, Amer. Assn. for Advancement of Science, Member, New York City Commission on Delivery of Personal Health Services (Piel Commission) 1966–67; Mayor Lindsay's Advisory Task Force on CATV and Telecommunications. 1967–68. Recipient, letter of commendation from Secretary of Navy (with commendation ribbon) and from Chief of Bureau of Ordnance for invention of a naval gunfire device used in World War II. Fellow, New York Acad. of Sciences; Benjamin Franklin Fellow, Royal Society of Arts, London. *Member:* Council on Foreign Relations; American Psychosomatic Society; Society of Protozoologists. *Clubs:* Army & Navy, Cosmos (Washington); City Midday, Century Association (N.Y.C.). *Address:* 730 Park Avenue, New York City 10021; and *office* 40 Wall Street, New York City, 10005, U.S.A.

**GOLDING, John,** BA, MP. British politician. *B.* 1931. *Educ.* London School of Economics; Univ. College of N. Staffs (BA II Hons.) History, Econ. Politics. *M.* 1955, Thelma. *S.* Thomas Richard and Simon James. *Career:* Officer Post Office Engineering Union (Research, Education, Politics) since 1960; Member Select Cttee. Nationalized Industries; Lord Commissioner of the Treasury; former Labour Whip (and PPS to Eric Varley); Member of Parliament for Newcastle under Lyme since 1969; Parly. Under Sec. of State, Dept. of Employment 1976. *Publications:* Productivity Bargaining; Trade Unions—on to 1960. *Clubs:* King St. WMC; Parksite Miners Welfare Institute. *Address:* 8 Ashbourne Drive, Silverdale, Newcastle, Staff.; and *office* House of Commons, London, S.W.1.

**GOLDS, Anthony Arthur.** CMG. MVO. British diplomat. *B.* 1919. *Educ.* King's School Macclesfield, New Coll. Oxford (Scholar). *M.* 1944, Suzanne Macdonald Young. *S.* 1. *Daus.* 1. *Career:* with H.M. Forces (War Service) 1939–46; Commonwealth Relations Office 1948–51; B.H.C. Calcutta and Delhi, First Secretary, Head of Chancery, British Embassy Ankara; British High Commission Karachi, Pakistan 1951–61; Counsellor C.R.O. and Foreign Office 1962–65; British Embassy Rome 1965–70; H.M. Ambassador Yaounde 1970–72; British High Commissioner, Bangladesh (Dacca) 1972–74; Snr. Civilian Instructor, R. Coll. of Defence Studies, London 1974–76; Dir., British National Cttee., International Chamber of Commerce since 1977. *Awards:* Companion, St. Michael and St. George; Member, Royal Victorian Order; Master of Arts, Oxford. *Address:* 6/14 Dean Farrar Street, London, S.W.1.

**GOLDSCHMIDT, Bertrand Léopold.** French atomic scientist. *B.* 1912. *Educ.* School of Physics & Chemistry, Paris (Engineer; D. ès Sciences). *M.* 1947. Naomi de Rothschild. *S.* Paul. *Dau.* Emma. Comdr. of the Legion of Honour (France). *Career:* Assistant at the Faculty of Sciences, Paris 1938–40; Section Leader (1942–45) and Head of Chemistry Division (1946), Anglo-Canadian Atomic Energy Project; Director of Chemistry, French Atomic Energy Commission 1946–59; Exec. Vice-Pres., European Atomic Energy Society 1955–59. Governor for France at the International Atomic Energy Agency 1957—. Dir. of Planning and External Relations, French Atomic Energy Commission (Commissiariat à l'Energie Atomique) 1959–70, and Dir. of International Relations since 1970. *Address:* 11 Blvd. Flandrin, Paris 16; and *office* 29 Rue de la Fédération, 75752 Paris, France.

**GOLDSCHMIDT, Carel.** American. *B.* 1904. *Educ.* Openbare Handel-school (Amsterdam) and Lyceum Alpinum (Zuoz, Switzerland). *M.* 1925, Helena Woodruffe Jelliffe. *S.* Dolf Leeming and Smith Ely. *Career:* Partner, Gebing & Lieftinck (brokers Indonesian tobacco), Amsterdam 1922–48, and Goldschmidt & Jiskoot (importers Sumatra and Java leaf tobacco), New York City, 1922–43. Pres. and Dir.: Imperial Commodities Corp. (Hartford, Conn.) 1942–68, American Sumatra Tobacco Corp. (N.Y.C.) 1956–68; Dir.: Anglo-American Corp. (Singapore) 1945–68. President & Director: Imperial Production Corp. (San Antonio, Tex.) 1947—, The Goldschmidt Foundation; Corrie MacCall & Sons Ltd. (London) 1952–68, Corrie MacCall Trading Corp. (London) 1952–68, Commonwealth Tobacco Co. (Richmond, Va.) 1962–68; Chmn. Jelliffe Corp. (N.Y.C.) 1968—, Jelliffe Associates, Inc. N.Y.C. since 1970. Trustee: Smith Ely Jelliffe Trust; Member, Man. Bd. & of Exec. Cttee., N.V. Deli-Maatschappij (Amsterdam, Neth.) 1956–68. Member: N.Y.C. Cancer Cttee.; Socy. of the New York Hospital. *Clubs:* Wall Street, Recess, Netherlands (all in N.Y.C.); Lake George (Warren County, N.Y.). *Address:* 110 East 57th Street, New York City; and 205 South Bedford Road, Mt. Kisco, N.Y.; and *office* 641 Lexington Avenue, New York, N.Y. 10022, U.S.A.

**GOLDSMITH, Bertram M.** Bronze Star, Croix de Guerre (2), Corono d'Italia, Medaglio Argento Croce Rosa. American. *B.* 1907. *Educ.* Princeton Univ. BA) 1926. *M.* 1934, Fannie Newman. *S.* 2. *Career:* Manager Bond Dept., Ira Haupt & Co. 1933–41; Partner 1940–62; Exec. Officer Allied Mil. Gov. Florence, Italy 1944–45; Man. Partner 1958–62; Salomon Bros. & Hutzler, 1963; Dir. Servo Corpn. of America, 1954–59; Cott Beverages 1955–59; Partner, L. F. Rothchild & Co.; 1964–69; Originator Municipal Bond Investment Trust. Founding *Member:* Municipal Bond Forum; American Horticultural Soc.; American Orchid Soc.; N.Y. Philharmonic Society. *Clubs:* Princeton N.Y.; Nassau; Tower. *Address:* Watercress Farm, Annandale, N.J. 08801, U.S.A., and Boco-Hi Apt, Del Ray Beach, Fla.

**GOLDSMITH, Clifford Henry.** *B.* 1919. *Educ.* Graduate, Bradford Inst. of Technology (Bradford, Yorks., England). *Daus.* Corinne Elizabeth; Audrey Jane and Alexandra Eve. *Career:* With Glenside Mills Corp., Skaneateles, N.Y. 1940–41; Falls Yarn Mills, Woonsocket, R.I. 1941–42; Aldon Spinning Mills, Talcottville Conn. 1942–43; U.S. Army 1943–45; Benson & Hedges, New York 1945–54; Philip Morris Inc. since 1954, now Exec. Vice-Pres. & Dir.; Pres., Phillip Morris U.S.A.; Dir., Central Nat. Bank, Central Nat. Corp., Richmond, Va. *Member:* Associate Textile Institute (Manchester, Eng.). *Club:* Chemists' (N.Y.C.); C'wealth Club, Richmond; Downtown (Richmond). *Address:* 875 Park Avenue, New York City; and *office* 100 Park Avenue, New York City, U.S.A.

**GOLDSON, Philip Stanley Wilberforce.** Belizean Lawyer, Legislator & journalist; Managing Director, The Billboard Press Ltd. British Honduran Leader of the Opposition, Mar. 1965–74, and of the National Independence Party Mar. 1961–Oct. 1974; Secretary, National Independence Party July 1958. *B.* 1923. *Educ.* Cambridge Overseas School Certificate. *M.* 1954, Hadie Ellen Jones. *S.* Philip Stanley Paul, Dale David, and Adrian Joseph. *Daus.* Karen Ann Marie and Ann-Margaret Stephanie. Editor, Belize Billboard 1950; Asst. Secy., People's United Party 1950; Gen. Secy., General Workers' Union 1951; Acting Mayor, Belize City 1951. Served eight-month term in Belize prison for political agitation 1951–52; Asst. Gen. Secy., General Workers' Union 1952; elected member of British Honduras Legislative Assembly and of the Exec. Cncl. 1954; member for Social Services 1955; Foundation member, Dep. Leader and Secy., Honduras Independence Party 1956 (this Party merged with the National Party of Honduras under the name of National Independence Party, July 1958). *Publication:* Social Views (1956). *Address:* P.O. Box 79, Belize City, Belize.

**GOLDSWORTHY, George Walter, Jr.** Executive. Representative U.S. Banknote Corp. (International) 1965—. *B.* 1905. *Educ.* Shadyside Academy (Pittsburgh, Pa.) and Bowdoin College (Brunswick, Me.), BS. *M.* 1930, Sarah M. Feltyberger. *S.* George Walter III. Successively Estimating, Sales Depts. 1927–30, Assistant to President 1930–33, Vice-Pres., Director 1933–42, Republic Banknote Co. Exec. Vice-Pres., Director 1942–52, President, Director 1953–57, Security Banknote Co. Director, Security Columbian Banknote Co. 1958–63. President, Lanston Monotype Machine Co. 1955–56; Director, Lanston Industries 1955–63. Vice-Pres., Security Columbian Banknote Co. 1958–67. *Member:* Beta Theta Pi. *Address:* P.O. Box 506, Bryn Mawr, Pa.; and *office* 55th and Sansom Streets, Philadelphia 39, Pa., U.S.A.

**GOLDWATER, Senator Barry M.** Republican of Phoenix, Arizona. *B.* 1909. *Educ.* Staunton Military Academy and Univ. of Arizona. *M.* 1934, Margaret Johnson. *S.* Barry and Michael. *Daus.* Joanne Butler and Margaret Holt. With U.S. Air Force 1941–45; Brig.Gen. USAFR. Elected to city council of Phoenix 1949; re-elected 1951. Elected to U.S. Senate Nov. 1952, Senator from Arizona 1952–64, 1969—; Republican Presidential nominee 1964. Episcopalian. Mason. *Member:* Sigma Chi; American Legion. *Address:* United States Senate, Washington, D.C. 20510, U.S.A.

**GOLE, Victor Leslie.** Australian chartered secretary. *B.* 1903. *Educ.* State School scholarship; Brisbane Grammar School; Brisbane Technical College. *M.* 1929, Eve Bartle Gillard. *S.* Barton Victor. *Dau.* Wilma Lee. *Career:* Was secretary of Allied Bruce Small Ltd. and subsidiary companies for 26 years until 1953, when he set up his own consulting business on accounting, taxation, finance, and other professional services. Hon. Auditor: Y.M.C.A. Melbourne, Defence Forces Committee, and Y.M.C.A. Youth Clubs 1942—. Fellow, Inst. of Directors. *Member:* Australian Society of Accountants (Councillor since 1953); Chartered Institute of Secretaries (President Victoria Branch, April 1961); Australian Institute of Management. *Publications:* Accounting for Businessmen; Australian Proprietary Companies—Management Finance and Taxation; Fundamentals of Financial Management in Australia; 4th Ed. Fitzgeralds, Analysis and Interpretation of Financial Statements. *Club:* R.A.C.V. *Address:* 72 Canberra Grove, Vic.; and *office* 1 Palmerston Crescent, South Melbourne, Vic., Australia.

**GOMULKA, Wladyslaw.** Former First Secretary, Central Committee of the Polish United Workers' Party. Member. State Council of Polish People's Republic 1957–71 (Ret'd.). *B.* 1905. At age of 16 he set up the workers' youth organization, *Strength*; at 21 he became secretary of his trade union; on the eve of the *coup d'etat* of May 1926 he was arrested, but under pressure by the workers (during the general strike of the Krosno Basin) he was released from prison; he was then one of the active leaders of the left-wing trades union and secretary of the Chemical Industry Workers Union; Secretary of the organizing committee of the left-wing trades unions, and worked among miners in the Dabrowa Basin and Silesia, the metal workers in Silesia and the textile workers in Lodz; in 1932 he was sentenced to four years' imprisonment, but on account of his ill-health was released before the completion of the term; arrested again on eve of May Day 1936 and remained in prison until the declaration of war; took part in the workers' battalions in the defence of Warsaw; after the establishment of the Polish Workers' Party he began work in its ranks; in 1942 became Secretary of the Warsaw organization and, in the same year, a member of the Central Committee of the Party; he became General Secretary in 1943; he was responsible for the formation of the People's Guards and was one of the initiators of the National Council; after the Liberation became Deputy Prime Minister of the Provisional Government, Minister of the Regained Territories and Deputy of the Legislative Seym; was also Deputy Prime Minister in the National Unity Government; after unification of the workers' parties, became a member of the Central Committee of P.U.W.P.; removed from the Committee by the Third Plenum of the Central Committee and arrested in Nov. 1951; was cleared of all charges by the Seventh Plenum in July 1956; at the Eighth Plenum again became a member of the Committee and was elected First Secretary of the Central Committee 1956–70; Member of Parliament (the Seym) 1957–72. *Address:* Central Committee of the Polish United Workers' Party, Warsaw, Poland.

**GONTARD, Dr. Heinrich.** Austrian executive. *B.* 1906. *Educ.* Theresianum, Vienna, and Univ. of Vienna Faculty of Law; Dr. jur. March 1930. *Career:* Employee, Erzhütte AG, Vienna 1926–28; entered Gebr. Böhler & Co. 1928; Procurist 1945—, Director 1953—. Member, Austrian People's Party. *Clubs:* Cottage Tennis (Vienna); Austria Automobile and Touring (Vienna), First Vienna Football, Vereinigung ehemaliger Theresianisten (Vienna). *Address:* A 1180 Wien, Colloredogasse 6, Austria.

**GONZALES, Ramon A.** Filipino lawyer and constitutionalist. *B.* 1925. *Educ.* Iloilo public schools; Univ. San Agustin B.Comm., LLB. *M.* 1953, Lilia Yusay. *S.* 1. *Daus.* 8. *Career:* Admitted to Phil. Supreme Court 1956; Munic. Councilo of Lambunao (Iloilo) 1959, Elected Delegate to 1971 Con vention. *Member:* Phils. Const. Assn., Phils. Chamber o Commerce; Phils. Bar Assn.; Phils. Integrated Bar. *Awards:* Most Outstanding Lawyer of the Year 1965–69; Lawyer of the Year 1970; Cert. of merit & other distinctions. *Clubs:* Manila Breakfast; Tuesday. *Address:* 23 Sunrise Hill, New Manila, Quezon City, Philippines; and *office* Mariwasa Bldg., Aurora Blvd., Quezon City, Philippines.

**GONZALEZ-CAMINO, Fernando.** Spanish. Secretary of the Embassy of Spain in Paris, April 1968. *B.* 1936. *Educ.* Licentiate in Law. *M.* 1965, Maria Ruiz de Bucesta. *Dau.* Almudena. Officer of the Order of Civil Merit. With Ministry of Foreign Affairs, Madrid, June 1965—; Secretary of the Embassy of Spain in Yaoundé 1965–68. *Address:* 13, Ave. Georges V, Paris 8, France.

**GOOD, Robert Crocker.** American. *B.* 1924. *Educ.* Haverford College. BA Philosophy 1945; Yale Divinity School. BD Social Ethics 1951; Yale University PhD International Relations 1956. *M.* 1946, Nancy Louise Cunningham. *S.* Stephen Laurence. *Daus.* Karen Louise and Kathleen Jennifer. Research, School of Advanced International Studies, Johns Hopkins Univ. and Washington Center of Foreign Policy Research; Co-ordinator of President John Kennedy's Task Force on Africa; Director, Office of Research and Analysis for Africa, Dept. of State 1961–65; U.S. Ambassador to Zambia 1965–68; Dean, Graduate School of International Studies 1965–69; Dir., Social Science Foundation, Univ. of Denver 1965–69; Pres. of Denison Univ., Granville, Ohio, since 1976. *Publications:* (Co-author or Co-editor) Alliance Policy in the Cold War (1959); Reinhold Niebuhr on Politics (1960); Neutralism and Non-Alignment (1962); Foreign Policy in the Sixties (1965); (author) UDI The International Politics of the Rhodesian Rebellion (1973). *Award:* Superior Honour Award, Dept. of State 1964; Haverford Award 1976. *Member:* International Studies Assn.; Amer. Political Science Assn.; Society on Religion in Higher Education; Governing Bd., National Univ. of Lesotho; Council on Religion in International Affairs; Patterson School of Intern. Diplomacy & Commerce. Democrat. *Address:* Office of the President, Denison University, P.O. Box B, Granville, Ohio 43023, U.S.A.

**GOODALL, His Honour Judge Anthony Charles,** MC, MA. British Circuit Judge. *B.* 1916. *Educ.* Eton; King's Coll. Cambridge. *M.* 1947, Anne Valerie Chichester. *S.* 1. *Daus.* 2. *Career:* Called to Bar (Certificate of Honour) 1939; served 1st Royal Dragoons 1939–46; Practised as Barrister 1946–67; County Court Judge (Circuit No. 40, Bow) 1968–72; Circuit Judge in Devonshire since 1972. *Member:* Inner Temple. *Address:* Mardon, Moretonhampstead, Devon.

**GOODE, Sir William (Allmond Codrington).** GCMG. *B.* 1907. *Educ.* Oakham School; Worcester College, Oxford (Classical exhibitioner); Barrister-at-Law (Gray's Inn), 1936. *M.* (1) 1938, Mary Armstrong Harding (*D.* 1947), and (2) 1950, Ena Mary McLaren. *Dau.* 1. Joined Malayan Civil Service 1931; Deputy Economic Secretary, Fed. of Malaya 1948; Chief Secretary, Aden 1949–53; Acting Governor, Aden 1950–51; Col. Secretary (later Chief Secy.), Singapore, 1953; Gov., Singapore 1957–59; first Yang di Pertuan Negara, and U.K. Comm., Singapore 1959; Gov., North Borneo 1960–63. Chairman Water Resources Board 1964–74. *Address:* East Streatley House, Streatley, Berks., England.

**GOODENOUGH, Howard Linus.** American mining company executive. *B.* 1904. *Educ.* New York Univ. (BSc Com. *cum laude,* 1927). *M.* 1930, Hildegarde E. Gerson. *S.* Howard Linus, Jr., and Edwin Day. *Dau.* Phyllis Luverne (Collins). Assistant to Production Manager, Standard Underground Cable Co. 1922–26; Accountant Auditor, Scovell, Wellington & Co., N.Y.C. 1927–28 and 1934–37; General Auditor, General Bronze Corp., Long Island City 1928–34; Asst. Comptroller, American Smelting & Refining Co. 1937–52; Comptroller, American Smelting & Refining Co., 120 Broadway, N.Y.C. 1952–69. *Member:* Beta Gamma Sigma; Financial Executives Inst.; National Assn. of Accountants. Overseer, Old Sturbridge Village Inc.; Trustee of East Jersey Olde Towne, Inc.; Chmn., Metuchen Senior Citizens Housing Corp. Republican. *Clubs:* Bankers (of America). *Address:* 21 Cliffwood Place, Metuchen, N.J., U.S.A.

**GOODHART, Philip Carter,** MP. *B.* 1925. *Educ.* Hotchkiss School (U.S.A.) and Trinity Coll., Cambridge (BAHist.; MA). *M.* 1950, Valerie Forbes Winant. *S.* Arthur Winant, David Forbes and Daniel Lehman. *Daus.* Sarah Cecilia, Catherine Rachel, Harriet Mary and Helen Rebecca. *Career:* With K.R.R.C. and Parachute Regt. 1943–47. Editorial Staff: Daily Telegraph 1950–55, and Sunday Times 1955–57. Contested (Cons.) Consett, Co. Durham, General Election 1950. Member L.C.C. Education Cttee. 1956–57; Member Parliament (Cons.) for Kent, Beckenham 1957–74, for Bromley, Beckenham since 1974; P.P.S. to Julian Amery at War and Colonial Offices 1958–60; Member, Council of Consumers' Association 1959–68 and since 1970; Joint Hon. Secy. 1922. Committee 1960—; Member of British Delegations: Council of Europe and W.E.U. 1961–63; and U.N. 1963; Chmn. Cons. Parly. Defence Cttee. 1972–74, Vice-Chmn. since 1974. *Publications:* The Hunt for Kimathi with (Ian Henderson, G.M.), 1958; In the Shadow of the Sword (1964); Fifty Ships that Saved the World (1965); War Without Weapons (with Christopher Chataway) (1968); The 1922 Referendum (1971); History of the 1922 Committee (with Ursula Branston, 1973), various pamphlets. Conservative. *Clubs:* Athenaeum, Beefsteak, Carlton, Garrick, Saville (all of London). *Address:* 27 Phillimore Gdns., London W.8; and Whitebarn, Boars Hill, Oxford.

**GOODMAN, Cyril William,** CBE. Australian. *B.* 1893. *Educ.* Univ. of Adelaide (BEng.). *M.* 1917, Ruth, dau. of late Sir Richard Butler. *S.* 1. *Dau.* 1. *Career:* Consultant to G.E.C. English Electric Pty. Ltd., Australia. *Member:* Australian British Trade Assn. (Past Pres.). *Fellow:* Institution of Electrical Engrs.; Inst. E. Aust. *Clubs:* Australian (Sydney). *Address:* P.O. Box 109 Terrigal, N.S.W. 2260, Australia.

**GOODRICH, L. Keith.** American publishing executive. *B.* 1906. *Educ.* Univ. of Michigan (AB) and Advanced Management Program, Harvard Univ. *M.* 1934, Margaret Gillan. *S.* John Keith. Accountant and Travelling Auditor, General Electric Co. 1928–35; Asst. Treasurer, General Electric X-Ray Corp. 1935–41; Plant Accountant, General Electric Co. 1941–45. With McGraw-Hill Publishing Co.: Asst. Treasurer 1945–49; Asst. Treasurer and Asst. Vice-Pres. 1949–54; Asst. Treasurer and Vice-Pres. 1954–57; Vice-Pres. and Treasurer 1957–61; Exec. Vice-Pres. and Treasurer 1961–63. Executive Vice-President and Chairman of Finance Committee, McGraw-Hill Inc. 1961—. Director: McGraw-Hill Inc. 1961—, Newton Falls Paper Mill Inc. 1961—, McGraw-Hill Publishing Co. Ltd., London, and McGraw-Hill of Canada, Toronto. Standard & Poor's Inc. 1966—; Milo Electronics Corp. 1966—. *Member:* Financial Executives Institute (National Pres. 1936–64; National Chmn. of Board 1964–65); Dir. at Large 1965—, and Financial Executives 59). *Address:* 16 Foxhall Place, Scarsdale, N.Y., U.S.A.

**GOODWILLIE, John Morley.** American advertising executive. *B.* 1910. *Educ.* Williams College (Williamstown, Mass.); BA. *M.* (1) 1939, Mary Louise Rhodes (divorced 1961). *Dau.* Susan Rhodes. *M.* (2) 1961, Lee Marko. *Dau.* Kate. *M.* (3) 1976, Muriel Stiefel Rafalsky. Assistant to Director, The Limited Editions Club 1933–35; Advertising Mgr., R. H. Macy & Co., New York 1935–42; U.S. Army Air Force (European Theatre of Operations in Combat Intelligence, Eighth Air Force; discharged 1945, rank of Major) 1942–45; Creative Supervisor, Benton & Bowles Inc., N.Y. 1945–48; Vice-President for Advertising and Public Relations. Alexander Smith Inc., White Plains, N.Y. 1948–52; Account Executive, Young & Rubicam Inc., N.Y. 1952–55; Exec. Vice-Pres., C. J. LaRoche Inc. 1955–65; Senior Vice-President, Norman, Craig & Kummel Inc., New York 1965–68; Pres., John Goodwillie Inc. N.Y. since 1968. Bd. Dirs., Irvington House 1950. Zeta Psi Fraternity. *Address:* 1185 Park Avenue, New York, N.Y. 10028, U.S.A.

**GOODWIN, George.** *B.* 1917. *Educ.* Washington and Lee Univ. (AB degree with certificate in Journalism 1939). *M.* 1940, Lois Milstead. *S.* Clark and Allen. *Career:* Reporter on Atlanta Georgian 1939; later reporter and special writer on News and Courier, Charleston, S.C.; Times Herald, Washington, D.C.; Miami Daily News, Florida; Intelligence Officer, PT Boats, U.S. Naval Reserve 1942–45; reporter Atlanta Journal 1946–52; Exec. Dir., Central Atlanta Improvement Association, July 1952–September 1954; Exec. Vice-Pres. Bell & Stanton Inc. since 1965. *Awards:* Winner of Pulitzer Prize for local reporting 1948; Sigma Delta Chi National Reporting Award 1948; Pall Mall Big Story Award 1949. *Trustee:* Oglethorpe University, Atlanta Arts Alliance; Bell & Stanton Inc. *Member:* Delta Tau Delta, Sigma Delta Chi, Omicron Delta Kappa, Public Relations Society of America. *Address:* 3302 Ivanhoe Drive, N.W., Atlanta, Ga. 30327; and *office* 229 Peachtree Street N.E. Atlanta, Ga. 30303, U.S.A.

**GOODWIN, Jonathan.** American banker. *B.* 1917. *Educ.* Deefield Academy 1936; Brown University 1940. *M.* 1950, Betsy Bent. *S.* Charles Brockett. *Career:* With Phoenix State Bank & Trust Co. 1940; served in World War II (1st Lieutenant A.C.; mainly in SouthWest Pacific Area) 1943–46; returned to Phoenix Bank 1946; Asst. Trust Officer 1949; Trust Officer 1953. In 1954 Phoenix State Bank & Trust Co. and Hartford Connecticut Trust Co. merged to form Connecticut Bank & Trust Co. Director, (& mem. of Exec. Cttee.) Hartford Fire Insurance Co. and its subsidiary, Accident & Indemnity Co. 1953— (also member of the Finance Cttee. & Chmn. of Audit Cttee.); Assistant V.P., Connecticut Bank & Trust Co. 1954–76 (Ret'd.); Dir., Amer. Schl. for the Deaf; Trustee, Hartford College. *Clubs:* Old Lyme Beach. *Address:* Mill Pond Lane, Old Lyme, Ct. 06371, U.S.A.

**GOODWIN, Michael Felix James.** *B.* 1916. *Educ.* Privately. *M.* 1944, Pamela Alison Trower. *S.* Toby Michael Giles. *Dau.* Caroline Mary. Drama Dir., B.B.C., 1938–39; War service, R.A.; Editor: The Twentieth Century (formerly The Nineteenth Century and after) 1947–52; Bellman Books 1952–55; Director: Contact Publications Ltd. 1955–60; Newman Neame Ltd. 1960–65; Mng. Dir., Information Bulletin Ltd. and C.S.F. Publications Ltd. 1966–67. Administrative Director, Institute for the Study of Conflict; Sec. & Treas., International Assn. for Cultural Freedom 1967–71; Director, International Projects Assessment Ltd. 1971—. *Publications:* Nineteenth Century Opinion (Penguin Books, 1949); Artist and Colourman (1966); Concise Dictionary of Antiques Collectors' Terms (1967). *Club:* Traveller's. *Address:* 16 Cope Place, W.8.

**GOODWIN, Sir Reginald Eustace,** CBE, DL. British. *B.* 1908. *Educ.* London County Council Grammar School. *M.* 1943, Penelope Mary Thornton. *S.* 2. *Dau.* 1. *Career:* Asst. Gen. Secy. National Assn. Boy's Club 1936–45, General Secy. 1945–73; H.M. Forces 1939–45; Member Bermondsey Borough Council 1937–64, Leader of Council 1946–64; Member, London County Council, Chmn. various Cmttee's including Housing and Finance 1946–64; Greater London Council 1964—; Leader of Opposition 1967–73, 1977—; Leader of Council 1973–77; Member Inner London Education

Authority 1964—; The Court of University of London 1964—; Bd. Basildon New Town Corp. 1966—, Vice-Chmn. since 1968. *Awards:* Commander of the most excellent Order of the British Empire; Deputy-Lieut. of Greater London. *Address:* The County Hall, London, SE1 7PB.

**GOODYEAR, George Forman.** American lawyer. *B.* 1906. *Educ.* Yale University (PhB 1927); Harvard Law School (LLB 1931); Harvard Graduate School (Chemistry, 1932); Allen University Columbia SC, LHD 1974. *M.* 1932, Sarah Norton. *Daus.* Anne (Appel), Mary Forman (Gurney, Jr.), Sarah Coakley (Wadsworth). *Career:* With DuPont Rayon Co., Buffalo 1932–37; Bean, Brooks, Buckley & Bean, Buffalo 1937–42; Lake Ontario Ordnance Works, Niagara Falls 1942–43; Airplane Division, Curtiss-Wright Corporation 1943–45; Hewitt Rubber Corp., Buffalo 1945–52; WGR Corp., Buffalo Pres. and Chmn. Bd. until merger into Transcontinental Television Corp. in 1957; Dir.: Marine Trust Co. of Western New York, Niagara Share Corp., Ontario Marine Inc., Director: Buffalo Philharmonic Orchestra Society (Pres. 1968–69); Buffalo and Erie Historical Society (Vice-Pres.); Buffalo Society of Natural Sciences (Pres. 1948–65); Buffalo Urban League (Pres. 1960–61, 1964–67); Chmn. Review and Planning Council of Western N.Y. Hospital 1961–65; Member Board of Education, City of Buffalo, 1965— (Pres. 1967–68); Secretary, Council of the University of Buffalo (1953–62). *Member:* New York State, Federal, Erie County, and American Bar Associations; Amer. Chemical Society; Amer. Patent Law Assn.; Amer. Assn. of Museums; Buffalo Fine Arts Academy. *Clubs:* Saturn (Dean 1963); Buffalo Country (Pres. 1960–61); Pack (Pres. 1955–56); Buffalo Tennis & Squash (Pres. 1949–50). *Address:* 82 Middlesex Road, Buffalo, N.Y. 14216, U.S.A.

**GOOLD-ADAMS, Richard John Moreton,** CBE, MA. British. *B.* 1916. *Educ.* Winchester College; New College, Oxford. *M.* 1939, Deenagh Blennerhassett. *Career:* Dir. in Guthrie group of companies 1953–69; Assistant Editor, The Economist 1954–55; Chairman, British Atlantic Committee 1959–62; International Institute for Strategic Studies 1963–73; S.S. Great Britain Project since 1968; Vice-President, British Atlantic Committee; Academic Councillor, Wilton Park, 1963—; Governor, Atlantic Institute in Paris (1963–71). Councillor; Royal Institute of International Affairs since 1957, and National Institute of Industrial Psychology 1956–70. *Publications:* South Africa To-day and Tomorrow (1936); Middle East Journey (1947); The Time of Power—a Reappraisal of John Foster Dulles (1962); The Return of the Great Britain (1976); numerous articles in the press, and many radio and TV contributions. *Club:* Travellers'. *Address:* Highfield House, Binley, Andover, Hants.

**GOONERATNE, Tilak E.** Civil Servant & Lawyer of Sri Lanka. *B.* 1919. *Educ.:* London Univ. BA; Attorney at Law. *M.* 1947, Pamela Jean Rodrigo. *Daus.* 2. *Career:* Sri Lanka Civil Service 1943–65; Dep.-Secy. to Treasury 1963–65; President, Colombo Plan 1964–65; Dep.-Secy.-General, Communications Secretariat 1965–70; High Commissioner for Sri Lanka in UK 1970–75; Chmn. Bd. of Representatives C'wealth Fund for Tech. Co-operation since 1974; Ambassador to EEC and concurrently to Belgium since 1975. *Address:* 21–22 Avenue des Arts, 1040 Brussels, Belgium.

**GOONEWARDENA, Hylton Samuel Fonseka,** BA. Sinhalese development Banker. *B.* 1924. *Educ.* Royal College, Colombo and University of Ceylon. *M.* 1948, Chandra. *S.* Michael. *Dau.* Sandra. Staff Asst., Dept. of Food Supplies, 1946–48; Secy., Agricultural & Industrial Credit Corp., 1948–51. General Manager, Agricultural & Industrial Credit Corp. of Ceylon, 1952—. *Member:* Ceylon Assn. for the Advancement of Science; Productivity Assn. of Ceylon; Wild Life Protection Socy. of Ceylon; Fellow, Economic Development Inst., Washington D.C.; Fellow, Asian Development Inst., Bangkok. *Address:* 192 Newala Road, Rajagirya, Ceylon; and *office* 292 Galle Road, Colombo 3, Ceylon.

**GOOSSE, Marcel,** Dr. pol. econ. soc. Sc. Belgian diplomat. *B.* 21 Aug. 1897. *M.* 1921. Served in World War I; entered Foreign Service 1921; served in Berlin, Ottawa, Montreal, Belgrade, Alexandria and Calcutta; Consul-General, Bombay 1940–46; Economic Adviser to Belgian Military Mission in Berlin, rank of Colonel. Chargé d'Affaires, Belgian Embassy, Pakistan, and Legation, Afghanistan (rank of Minister) 1948–52; En. Ex. and Min. Plen.; Min. of For. Affairs and Foreign Trade 1952–55; Amb. Ex. and Plen. to Pakistan 1955; Ambassador and Chief of Treaties Dept., Min. of Foreign Affairs 1957; Ambas. to Yugoslavia 1960; His Belgian Majesty's Ambassador 1962—. *Address:* 56 Quai Bonaparte, 4020 Liège, Belgium.

**GOPALLAWA, William,** President Republic of Sri Lanka. *B.* 1897. *Educ.* Dharmaraja College, Kandy, St. Anthony's College, Kandy and Law Coll., Colombo. *M.* 1928, Seila Rambukwella (*D.* 1977). *S.* Asoka and Moithra. *Daus.* Iranganie and Chintha. *Career:* Teacher; Supreme Court of Ceylon 1924; practised in Matale, his home town, 1924–39; entered local politics and elected member of Matale Urban Council 1927–39 (Chmn. for nearly six years); Commissioner, Kandy Municipal Cncl. 1939; Municipal Commissioner of Colombo 1952; retired 1957. Ambassador to People's Republic of China 1958; to Washington (and concurrently to Cuba and Mexico) 1961; Gov. General of Ceylon 1962–72; DLitt Vidyodaya Univ. 1962; Pres. of the Republic since 1972; as President is Chancellor of Univ. of Sri Lanka. *Address:* President's House, Colombo, Sri Lanka.

**GORDON, Donald McDonald,** CMG. British diplomat *B.*1921. *Educ.* Robert Gordons Coll. Aberdeen; Aberdeen University, *M.* 1948, Molly Denise Norman. *S.* 3. *Career:* with H.M. Forces (R.A., Mentioned in despatches) 1941–47; joined H.M. Diplomatic Service, served in Lima, Vienna, London. Rangoon 1947–63; Counsellor, British Embassy South Africa 1963–65; Attended Imp. Def. Coll. London 1966; Counsellor, Consul-General Saigon 1967–69; Head, S.E. Asian Dept. Foreign and Commonwealth Office 1969–72; Deputy-British High Commissioner, Kuala Lumpur 1972–75; High Commissioner to Cyprus. 1975. *Address:* British High Commission, Nicosia, Cyprus. and *office* c/o Foreign and Commonwealth Office, King Charles Street, London, S.W.1.

**GORDON, George Blair.** Canadian company director. *B.* 1900. *Educ.* Lower Canada College; McGill Univ. (BSc). *M.* (1) Dorothy Mann (*Dec.*). *S.* James Blair (*Dec.*). (2) Mary A. McCulloch. *S.* Christopher Brooks. *Dau.* Linda Blair. President, Blair & Co. *Address:* and *office* Suite 1440, 1245 Sherbrooke Street West, Montreal, Quebec, Canada.

**GORDON, James Franklin.** American electronic equipment design and development engineer. *B.* 1912. *Educ.* Montana Public Primary Schools; intensive private study and experimentation. *M.* 1932, Helen Elizabeth Wells (*Dec.* 1967). *S.* James Wells. *Dau.* Helen Elizabeth Wells. *Career:* Civilian Engineer, U.S. Army Signal Corps. 1941–43; Junior Engineer, Bendix Radio Div. of Bendix Aviation Corps. 1941–43; and successively Asst. Project Engineer 1944–45; Project Engineer 1945–47; Research Engineer 1947–50; Principal Research Engineer 1950–52; Chief Engineer, Berkeley Div. of Beckman Instruments Inc. 1952–55; Chief Development Engineer, Helipot Div. of Beckman Instruments Inc. 1955–58; Engineering Mgr., Pacific Scientific Co. 1958–63; Design Consultant since 1963. *Publications:* regular contributor to U.S. technical journals. Numerous patents issued (U.S. and other countries); other patents pending. *Address:* 14320 Sunnyvale-Saratoga Road, Saratoga, Calif., U.S.A. 95070.

**GORDON, James Roycroft.** Canadian corporation executive. *B.* 1898. *Educ.* Queen's Univ., Kingston, Ont. BSc (Chem.) 1920, LLD (Hon.) 1955. *M.* 1922, Margaret Belle Arthur (*Dec.*). *M.* 1955, Joan Ehretia Windus. *S.* James Arthur Leonard, David Holmes and Brian (stepson). *Daus.* Mrs. Ralph Harrison and Mrs. F. C. Parrott. *Awards:* Platinum Medal, Canadian Institute of Mining & Metallurgy 1948; James Douglas Gold Medal, American Institute of Mining, Metallurgical and Petroleum Engineers 1958. Research Metallurgist, M. J. O'Brien Ltd. 1920–29; Asst. Director of Research, Ontario Research Foundation 1929–36. Joined The International Nickel Co. of Canada Ltd., 1936; successively: at Copper Cliff, Ont.: Dir. of Research 1936; Asst. to Vice-Pres. 1941; Asst. Vice-Pres. 1947; Asst. Gen. Mgr. 1952; Vice-Pres. and Gen. Mgr. 1953; at New York: Vice-Pres. 1 Jan. 1955; Exec. Vice-Pres. Jan. 1957; Pres. April 1960; Advisory Member of Cttee., The International Nickel Co. of Canada Ltd. *Clubs:* University (New York); Toronto (Toronto). *Address:* One New York, Plaza, New York, N.Y. 10004, U.S.A.

**GORDON, Hon. Walter Lockhart,** PC, FCA, LLD. Canadian. *B.* 1906. *Educ.* Upper Canada Coll., Toronto; and Royal Military Coll., Kingston Ont. *M.* Elizabeth M. L. Counsell. *Children,* 3. *Career:* Chartered Accountant and Mgmt. Consultant. Chairman: Royal Com. on Administrative Clarifications in the Public Service 1946; Royal Com. on Canada's Economic Prospects 1955; Cttee. on the Organizations of Govt. in Ontario 1958. Min. of Fin. and Receiver-General, Canada 1963—65 (until resignation in Nov.); Re-appointed to Cabinet as Minister without Portfolio Jan. 1967–Apr

1967; President of Privy Council Apr. 1967-68. Member House of Commons 1962–68; Chmn. Canadian Corporate Mgmt. Co. Ltd., Toronto; Dir. Toronto Star Ltd.; Chancellor, York University; Snr. Fellow, Massey Coll. in Univ. of Toronto. *Address:* 22 Chestnut Park Road, Toronto, Canada M4W 1W6.

**GORDON, Wilfred,** QC. Master of Hebrew Letters. Canadian. *B.* 1909. *Educ.* Univ. of Chicago (PhB 1931), McMaster Univ. (BA 1931); Hebrew Theological College, Chicago (Master of Hebrew Letters); Barrister and Solicitor, Osgoode Hall 1935. *M.* Balfoura Feldman. *S.* Jared and Daniel. *Dau.* Phyllis. *Career:* President: Brown's Line Investments Ltd., Twenty-Seven Wellington West Ltd., Cloverdale Park Ltd., Terry Investments Ltd., Keygor Investments Ltd., Halgor Investments Ltd., Islington Park Ltd.; Silver Dawn Estates Ltd., Abgor Investments Ltd., Cloverdale Shopping Centre Ltd., Mountain Theatres Ltd., Yarn Realty Ltd., Bellgor Management Ltd. Secretary-Treasurer: Yorkleigh Investments Ltd., Yorkville Financiers Ltd. Gen. Manager: One Hundred Simcoe Street Ltd., Queen City Leaseholds Ltd. Director: Tower-Chisholm Ferguson Ltd., Charitable Foundations: J. Wolinsky, J. B. Goldhar and H. Abramsky. Past President, Camp Massad of Ontario 1954; Pres., Hebrew Day High School of Toronto. Past Pres., Associated Hebrew Schls. of Toronto 1962. National Vice-President, Canadian Friends of Bar-Ilan Univ. 1961. Chmn.: Negev Dinner 1962, and Ner Israel Yeshiva College of Toronto. Dir., Central Fund for Traditional Institutions 1961–62; United Jewish Welfare of Toronto, and Keren Hatarbut of Canada. Member of Synagogues: Forest Hill Anshei Lide Congregation; Member Exec. Mizrachi Organ. of Canada, 1970; Regional Vice-Pres. Nat. Comm. on Torah Educ. 1970 and Shaarei Shomayim Congregation. Dr. of Rabbinical Studies, Ner Israel Rabbinical Coll., Baltimore 1972. *Address:* 200 Dunvegan Road, Toronto 7, Ont.; and *office* Suite 1919, 390 Bay Street, Toronto, Ont., Canada M5H 2Y2.

**GORDON-SMITH, David Gerard,** CMG, BA. British diplomat. *B.* 1925. *Educ.* Rugby School; Trinity Coll. Oxford University. *M.* 1952, Angela Eugenie Kirkpatrick Pile. *S.* 1. *Dau.* 1. *Career:* Legal Assistant, Colonial Office 1950–53, Senior Legal Assistant 1954–63; Senior Legal Assistant Commonwealth Relations Office 1963–65; Asst. Legal Adviser Colonial Office 1965–66; Legal Counsellor, Commonwealth Office 1966–68, Foreign and Commonwealth Office, 1968–72; Deputy-Legal Adviser Foreign and Commonwealth Office 1973–76; Legal Service, Secretariat of Council of Ministers, European Community, Brussels since 1976. *Member:* Inner Temple, London. *Awards:* Companion, Order St. Michael and St. George; Bachelor Arts (Jurisprudence: Oxford). *Address:* Kingscote, Westcott, Surrey; and 14 Avenue Ptolémée, 1180 Brussels, Belgium.

**GORDON WALKER of Leyton, Rt. Hon. Lord Patrick Chrestien,** PC. British politician. *B.* 7 April 1907. *Educ.* Wellington College and Christ Church, Oxford (MA, BLitt). *M.* 1934, Audrey Rudolf. *S.* 2. *Daus.* 3. History Tutor, Oxford 1931; MP (Lab.), Smethwick 1945–64; Parliamentary Under-Secretary of State for Commonwealth Relations 1947–50; Secretary of State for Commonwealth Relations 1950–Oct. 1951. Foreign Secretary 1964; M.P. for Leyton 1966–74; Secy. of State, Education and Science 1967–68; Minister with Portfolio 1967; Member European Parly. since 1975. *Publications:* Europe in the Sixteenth and Seventeenth Centuries; Outline of Man's History; The Lid Lifts; Restatement of Liberty; The Commonwealth; The Cabinet. *Address:* 105 Frobisher House, Dolphin Square, London S.W.1.

**GORE-BOOTH, Lord Paul Henry,** GCMG, KCVO. *B.* 1909. *Educ.* Eton and Balliol Coll., Oxford. *M.* 1940, Patricia Mary Ellerton. *S.* David Alwyn, Christopher Hugh. *Daus.* Celia Mary, Joanna Rosamond Georgina. *Career:* Entered Foreign Office 1933; transferred to Vienna 1936 and Tokyo 1937; seconded to Shanghai Oct.–Nov. 1941; transferred to Washington 1942. Member: U.K. Delegation to Inter. Food Conf., Hot Springs, and U.N.R.R.A. Conf., Atlantic City 1943, Dumbarton Oaks Conversations, Washington and Civil Aviation Conf., Chicago 1944; San Francisco Conf. 1945. Returned to Foreign Office 1945; Secretary to U.K. Delegation to the first meeting of U.N. General Assembly, London, Jan. 1946; Head of Refugee and U.N. Economic and Social Departments 1947; Head of European Recovery Department 1948; C.M.G., Jan. 1949; Director-General, British Information Services in U.S.A. 1949; Ambassador Ex. and Plen., Burma 1953–56; Dep. Under-Sec. for Economic Affairs. Foreign Office 1956–60; British High Commissioner in India 1960–65; Permanent Under-Secretary of State, Foreign Office 1965–68; Head of the Diplomatic Service, 1968–69; Permanent Head of Foreign Office & Commonwealth Office, 1968–69; Director National & Grindlays Bank, 1969–; United Kingdom Provident Institution 1969—. Created Baron, June 1969; Chmn. Gov. Body, School of Oriental and African Studies since 1975. *Publications:* With Great Truth and Respect (autobiog., 1974); various articles on public relations; Sherlock Holmes; Speaking Among Friends. President of the Sherlock Holmes Society of London, 1966. Chmn., Save the Children Fund, 1970–76; Chmn., Windsor Music Festival 1971–73; Chmn., Disasters Emergency Cttee. 1974—. *Address:* 70 Ashley Gardens, London, SW1P 1QG.

**GORNICK, Alan Lewis.** American lawyer and consultant. *Educ.* Columbia Coll. (BA) and Columbia Univ. School of Law (BA). *M.* 1940, Ruth L. Wilcockson (*Dec.* 1958). *S.* Alan, Jr. and Keith Hardin. *Dau.* Diana (Richard). *Career:* Law practice with Millbank, Tweed, Hope & Hadley, N.Y. 1941–47; Associate Counsel in charge of Tax Matters, Ford Motor Co., Dearborn Mich. 1947–49; Tax Counsel, and Dir., Office of Tax Affairs 1949–63. Consultant 1964—. Director: Castleton Industries Inc. 1967—, Brooks and Perkins, Inc. 1968—, Caprex International Inc. 1961—, Boulevard Center Corp. 1963—, Seagate Hotel and Beach Club, Delray, Fla. 1962—. *Publications:* Taxation of Partnerships, Estates & Trusts (1952); Divorce, Separation & Estate Taxes, Estate Tax Handbooks (1952, 1959); Arrangements for Separation & Divorce, Handbook of Tax Techniques (1952, 1960); Big Taxes: A Challenge and Opportunity for Management (1954); Tax Incentives and Our National Foreign Policy (1954). *Awards:* Medal for Distinguished Alumni Accomplishment 1947; Award, Most Outstanding Student 1935, Field Prize Award 1935 (all from Columbia Univ.); Governor's Special Award, State of Colorado 1952. *Member:* N.Y., Michigan and Federal Bars; Amer. Bar Assn.; City of Detroit & State of Michigan Bar Assns.; International Law Assn.; Ntnl. Foreign Trade Council Tax Committee; U.S. Council, International Fiscal Assn. (National Reporter: Brussels Congress 1952, and Basle Congress 1960); Council for Foreign Relations. Mem. Bd. Trustees: Council on World Affairs. *Clubs:* Detroit Athletic; Detroit; Bloomfield Hills Country; Bloomfield Open Hunt; University (Washington); Church (N.Y.C.). *Address: office* Bloomfield Center Offices, Bloomfield Hills, Mich., U.S.A.

**GORST, John Michael,** MA. British politician. *B.* 1928. *Educ.* Ardingly Coll. Sussex: Corpus Christi Coll. Cambridge. *M.* 1954, Noel Harington Walker. *S.* Julian, Sebastian, Tarquin, Tamburlaine and Jasper. *Career:* Advertising & Public Relations Mgr. of Pye Ltd., 1953–63; Public Relations Consultant, John Gorst & Assocs. Ltd. since 1964; Sec. Local Radio Assn. 1964–71; Member of Parliament, Hendon North 1970–74, Barnet, Hendon North since 1974. *Club:* Garrick. *Address:* House of Commons, London, S.W.1.

**GORTON, Rt. Hon. Sir John Grey,** CH (1971), MA, (PC 1968). *B.* 1911. *Educ.* Geelong Grammar School, Brasenose Coll., University of Oxford (MA). *M.* 1935, Bettina, daughter of G. Brown, Bangor, Me., U.S.A. *S.* 2. *Dau.* 1. *Career:* Senator for State of Victoria, Parliament of Commonwealth of Australia 1949–68; Govt. Leader in the Senate 1967–68; Minister for the Navy 1958–63; Minister Assisting the Minister for External Affairs 1960–63 (and Acting Minister during periods of absence overseas of the Minister); Minister in Charge of C.S.I.R.O. 1962–68; Minister for Works, and under the Prime Minister, Minister in Charge of Commonwealth Activities in Educ. and Research 1963–66; Minister for the Interior 1964; Minister for Works 1966–67; Minister for Educ. and Science 1966–68; Prime Minister of Australia 1968–71; Elected to House of Representatives February 1968; Minister for Defence & Deputy Leader, Liberal Party March–Aug. 1971. Member, Parly. Liberal Party Exec. & Spokesman on Environment and Conservation, Urban & Regional Development 1973–75; Deputy Chmn. Parly. Joint Cttee. on Prices 1973; Independent member 1975, retired from politics Dec. 1975. Previous profession, Orchardist Councillor Kerang Shire 1947–52 and Pres. of Shire; Member Lodden Valley Regional Cttee. Enlisted Royal Australian Air Force Nov. 1940; served in U.K., Singapore, Darwin, Milne Bay. Severely wounded in air operations, discharged with rank of Flight Lieutenant 1944. *Address:* 12th Floor, National Mutual Centre, Darwin Place, Canberra City, ACT 2601, Australia.

**GOSPER, James Murray,** OBE. Australian. *B.* 1905. *Educ.* Sydney Grammar School and Univ. of Sydney (St. Andrew's Coll.), (BE). *M.* 1936, Evelyn Mary Mitchell. *S.* James Murray Marsden. *Career:* Chartered Engineer, Australia. Exec. Director, Australian Inst. of Building 1956—; Council of

University of N.S.W. 1962—; Technical Education Advisory Council of N.S.W. 1954—; Council of N.S.W. Institute of Technology 1967—. Board of Directors: Prince Henry Hospital (Sydney) 1966—; Prince of Wales Hospital (Sydney) 1966—; Eastern Suburbs Hospital (Sydney) 1968—; Matured Pine Trees Ltd. Pres., Standing Cttee. of Convocation (Univ. of Sydney) 1968–69; International House (Univ. of N.S.W.) 1964— (Chmn. 1968—); Council of Medical Benefits Fund of Australia 1950—; Building Regulations Adv. Cttee., Ministry of Works & Local Govt., N.S.W. 1940–45; Technical Bodies Adv. Cttee., Ministry of Post War Reconstruction 1944; Building Industry Adv. Cttee., same Ministry 1945–46; Timber Adv. Cttee., Ministry of Supply 1940–41. Dir. Australian Fed. of Civil Engineering Contractors 1959–63. Hon. Organizer of Australia's First Construction Industry Fair and Convention 1952. Hon. Abstracter (Engineering Section), Australian Science Abstract 1935–39. Member: Institution of Engineers Australia. *Member:* Council 1962–67 and 1969—); Australian Inst. of Building (Fellow; Member of Council 1951–56); Building Industry Congress of N.S.W. (Hon. Member). *Clubs:* University (Sydney); Newcastle (Newcastle); Royal Sydney Yacht; Australian Jockey. *Address: office* 110 Alfred Street, Milson's Point, N.S.W., Australia.

**GOTAAS, Harold B.** American environmental engineer and educator. *B.* 1906. *Educ.* Univ. of South Dakota (BS 1928); Iowa State College (MS 1930); Harvard Univ. (SM 1937; ScD 1942). *M.* 1931, Alice McLaughlin. *S.* Richard. *Career:* Assistant Prof. of Civil Engineering, Univ. of S. Dakota 1932–36; Asst. Prof. to Prof., Graduate School of Public Health, Univ. of N. Carolina 1937–42; served as Exec. Vice-Pres. and Pres. of the Institute, 1944–46); Chief Engr. and Dir., Div. of Health and Sanitation, Inst. of Inter-American Affairs 1942–44; U.S. Army, Capt. to Col. Prof. of Sanitary Engineering, Univ. of California 1946 (Chmn., Civil Engineering Div. 1948–53; Dir., Engineering Laboratories 1949–57), Dean 1957–70; W. P. Murphy Professor of Technological Institute, Northwestern Univ. 1957–75; Consultant to WHO 1954—; member, National Advisory Health Council of U.S. Depart. of Health, Education and Welfare 1956–60. Director: Engineering College Research Council 1958–61; Eng. Coll. Admin. Council ASEE 1964–67; Engineering Science Panel, National Sciences Foundation; Chmn. Water Resources Cttee. and Solid Waste Mgt. Cttee; N.E. Illinois Metro. Area Planning Commission 1962–77; Chairman, Closed Ecological Systems Panel, National Res. Council 1958–60; Washington Award Commission, Great Lakes Commission 1961–72; Board of Visitors, U.S. Army Transportation School 1961–64. Member, Rockefeller Mission to Latin America (for President Nixon) 1969; Chmn. Nat. Research Council, Adv. Cttee. Military Environmental Research Council, Adv. Cttee. Military Environmental Research; Walter P. Murphy Professor and Dean Emeritus since 1970. *Awards:* Legion of Merit (United States); Orders of the Condor of the Andes (Bolivia), of Merit (Chile) of Honor and Merit (Haiti); Cross of Boyaca (Columbia); Kenneth Allen Award; Harrison P. Eddy, James R. Cross, Rudolph Hering and Gordon M. Fair Marston Medals; Engineer of Year Award 1962 (Illinois Society of Professionl Engineers); Civil Engineer of the Year 1974 (Ill. section ASCE). Hon. DSc University of S. Dakota; Hon. Dr. Eng. Rose Polytechnic Institute 1969; National Academy of Engineers; Honorary member Amer. Society, Civil Engineers. *Member:* American Public Health Association; American Society of Civil Engineers (Chmn. Sanitary Engineering Division 1953, and Research Committee); American Waterworks Association; American Society for Engineering Education; Inter-American Assn. of Sanitary Engineering; Natl. Socy. of Professional Engineers; Water Pollution Control Fed.; Hon. Member 1972. Western Socy. of Engrs.; American Academy of Sanitary Engineers (Trustee and Vice-Pres.); Phi Kappa Phi; Tau Beta Pi; Sigma Xi; Delta Omega; Chi Epsilon. *Publications:* over 100, dealing with chemical, biological and engineering studies in the public health, environmental control, water and waste treatment areas, education and economic development, including Composting of Irganic Wastes for Sanitary Disposal and Reclamation (1956). *Address:* 618 Colfax Street, Evanston, Ill.; and *office* Technological Institute, Northwestern University, Evanston, Ill., U.S.A.

**GOTHARD, Sir Clifford (Frederic),** OBE, JP. British. chartered accountant. *B.* 1893. *Educ.* Burton-on-Trent Grammar School and Birmingham Univ. (BSc Eng. 1915). *M.* 1961, Margaret Vera Hall. *Career:* Served in World War I (Capt. R.A.) 1914–18. Associate 1924, Fellow 1929, Institute of Chartered Accountants. in practice, Coxon Bannister & Gothard, Burton-on-Trent 1925—; Dir., Marston, Thompson & Evershed Ltd.; Chmn., Burton Daily Mail Ltd.; Portland Motor Group Ltd. and subsidiaries and other companies. His interests include religious, educational and agricultural institutions, and supervision of Air Training Corps 1939–45. Formerly Member of various committees of Assn. of British Chambers of Commerce; Pres. Burton Div., Conservative and Unionist Assn. 1945. J.P., County Borough of Burton-on-Trent 1940—. *Club:* Abbey (Burton-on-Trent). *Address:* Bearwood House, Burton-on-Trent.

**GOTT, Edwin Hays.** American. *B.* 1908. *Educ.* Lehigh University, Bethlehem, Pa. (BS 1929). *M.* 1934, Mary Louise Carr. *S.* Edwin H., Jr. *Daus.* Elizabeth (Byerly, Jr.) and Barbara (Martha). *Career:* Spent seven years with Koppers-Philadelphia Coke Co. Joined U.S. Steel Corporation as industrial engineer at Ohio works 1937; transferred to Clairton works in 1939 and to Gary works in 1941. At Gary began as plant industrial engineer and then became assistant division superintendent—rolling, assistant div. supt.—maintenance, and later assistant general superintendent—services. Appointed assistant general superintendent at South works, Chicago 1949, and 1951, general superintendent of Youngstown District operations, and, two years later, Gen. Mgr., operations—steel; Vice-Pres., operations—steel, July 1956, and in 1958 Vice-Pres. production—steel, producing divisions; named Administrative Vice-Pres., central operations (steel and coal), May 1959; Exec. Vice-Pres. Production, Nov. 1959; Pres. July 1967. Chairman and Chief Exec. Officer, United States Steel Corp., 1969–73, currently Director; Dir. International Husky Inc.; Dir. Pittsburgh Baseball Club; Dir. International Wilderness Leadership Foundation; Director, Allegheny Trails Council, B.S.A.; Chmn., National Flag Foundation. *Member:* Exec. Cttee. U.S. Steel; Assn. of Iron & Steel Engineers; Business Council Engrs' Socy of Western Pennsylvania; Trustee, Children's Hospital of Pittsburgh, Carnegi-Mellon University; Lehigh Univ.; Member American Iron & Steel Institute; *Clubs:* Duquesne, Longue Vue. Fox Chapel Golf (all of Pittsburgh); Rolling Rock (Ligonier, Pa.); Pine Valley (N.J.) Golf. *Address:* c/o United States Steel Corporation, 600 Grant Street, Pittsburgh, Pa. 15230, U.S.A.

**GOTT, Rodney Cleveland.** American business executive *B.* 1911. *Educ.* U.S. Military Academy (BS 1933). *M.* 1933, Lydia G. McAdam. *S.* Peter H., Rodney C., Jr., and Alan V. *Career:* Officer, U.S. Army 1933–35; Assistant to Sales Manager, American Radiator & Standard Sanitary Corporation, N.Y. 1935–41; Colonel w/Brig. General Command, U.S. Army Field Artillery 1941–46; American Machine & Foundry Co. 1946; successively Asst. to President, Manager Commercial Research & Development Department, Vice-President, Dir. & Exec. Vice-President until assuming present post. Chairman, Chief Executive officer AMF Inc. since 1962, President 1962–75; Director of all subsidiaries and divisions. Director, The Black & Decker Manufacturing Co., Townson, Md.; Bulova Watch Co.; Associated Dry Goods Corp. (N.Y.C.). Trustee: Franklin Savings Bank, N.Y. City; American Museum of Natural History, N.Y. City. *Awards:* Silver Star; Legion of Merit; Bronze Star with Oak Leaf Cluster; Purple Heart; Croix de Guerre avec Palme (France). *Clubs:* Union League, The Links (N.Y.C.); Shenorock Shore (Rye, N.Y.); Bedford Golf & Tennis (Bedford, N.Y.). *Address:* Sarles Street, Mount Kisco, N.Y. 10549, U.S.A.

**GOULD (Mrs.) Beatrice Blackmar.** American. *Educ.* State University of Iowa (BA); Columbia University School of Journalism (MS). *M.* 1923, Charles Bruce Gould. *Dau.* Sesaly (Krafft). Newspaper reporter, writer and woman's editor, New York Sunday World 1926–29; writer for magazines 1929–35. Editor, Ladies' Home Journal 1935–62. *Publications:* author (with Bruce Gould) of the plays, Man's Estate (1929); The Terrible Turk (1931); Autobiography—American Story 1968. *Clubs:* Cosmopolitan (N.Y.); Oxford and Cambridge University (London, Eng.). *Address:* Hopewell, N.J., U.S.A.

**GOULD, Charles Bruce.** American. *B.* 1898. *Educ.* Grinnell (Iowa) College; State University of Iowa (AB); Columbia University (grad. study). *M.* 1923, Beatrice Blackmar. *Dau.* Mrs. Frederic B. Krafft. Reporter, Des Moines (Ia.) Tribune 1922, New York Sun 1923–24, and New York Evening Post 1924–27; Literary Editor (1927–28) and Aviation Editor (1928–31) New York Evening Post; Dramatic Critic, Wall Street News 1927–30; Associate Editor, Saturday Evening Post 1934–35. Editor, Ladies' Home Journal 1935–62. *Publications:* Sky Larking (1929); Flying Dutchman (1931); Conversations on the Edge of Eternity (1965); American Story (1968); Plays (written with wife) Man's Estate (1929). The

Terrible Turk (1931), and Reunion (film play) (1936). *Clubs:* The Players; Dutch Treat; Nassau (Princeton, N.J.); Century; University. *Address:* Hopewell, N.J., U.S.A.

**GOULD, Sir Ronald.** British union official. *B.* 9 Oct. 1904. *Educ.* Shepton Mallet Grammar School and Westminster College, London. *M.* 1928, Nellie Denning Fish. *S.* 2. *Career:* Chairman, Norton Radstock U.D.C. 1937–47; President, World Confederation of Organizations of the Teaching Profession 1952–70; General Secretary, National Union of Teachers 1947–70; Vice Chmn. Independent Television Authority 1967–72. Hon. Fellow Educational Inst. of Scotland 1955. Hon. LLD British Columbia 1962; McGill 1964; St. Francis Xavier 1969, Leeds 1971, York, 1972. *Award:* Officier de l'ordre des palmes académiques 1970. *Address:* "Little Croft", 12 St. John's Avenue, Goring-by-Sea, Worthing, Sussex BN12 4HU.

**GOULDEN, Mark.** British publisher. *B.* Bristol. *Educ.* Clifton, Bristol. *M.* 1935, Jane Moore. *S.* 2. *Dau.* 1. *Career:* Managing Dir. and Editor, Eastern Morning News and Evening News, Hull 1923–30. Managing Ed.: Evening News, Leeds 1930–32, and Sunday Referee, London 1932–36; Editor-in-Chief, Argus Press, London 1936–39. Director, Illustrated Publications and various magazines 1939–41. Chairman, W. H. Allen & Co. Ltd., London 1939–76; Dir., Howard & Wyndham Ltd. 1971–76. *Publications:* Lectured and written extensively on Press, publishing and advertising. *Clubs:* Savage, Press, Paternosters; Players (N.Y.C.). *Address:* Mayfair House, 14 Carlos Place, London, W.1; 37 East 64th St., New York 22; and *offices* 44 Hill Street, London, W.1; and 200 East 42nd St., New York 10017, U.S.A.

**GOULDING, Edgar Dunlop.** Canadian investment dealer. *B.* 1902. *Educ.* Univ. of Toronto Schools and Univ. of Toronto. *M.* 1926, Vera Grace Woolnough. *Dau.* Virginia Clare. Vice-Pres., Goulding, Rose & Turner Ltd. 1949—; *Clubs:* National, Granite, Royal Canadian Yacht. *Address:* 96 Cheltenham Avenue, Toronto; and *office* 11. King St. W. Toronto, Canada.

**GOULDING, Sir (Ernest) Irvine,** MA. British. Judge at High Court of Justice. *B* .1910. *Educ.* Merchant Taylors' School London; St. Catharine's Coll. Cambridge. *M.* 1935, Gladys Sennett. *S.* 1. *Dau.* 1. *Career:* Instructor Lieutenant, Royal Navy 1931–36; (Called to the Bar Inner Temple 1936) Practised at the Bar 1936–39; Served, Royal Navy (promoted Inst. Lieut-Comdr.) 1939–45; Practised at the Bar 1946–71 (Queen's Counsel, 1961; Bencher of Lincoln's Inn 1966); Judge of the High Court of Justice, Chancery Division since 1971. *Member:* International Law Assn. (Pres. British Branch since 1972). *Awards:* Hon. Fellow, St. Catharine's Coll. Cambridge; Master of Arts, Univ. of Cambridge. *Club:* Travellers'. *Address:* 9 Constitution Hill, Woking, Surrey, GU22 7RZ; and *office:* Royal Courts of Justice, London, W.C.2.

**GOURD, Jean-Joffre,** QC. Canadian. *B.* 1916. *Educ.* Collège Jean de Brébeuf (BA 1938); University of Montreal (law studies 1939–41). Admitted to Montreal and Quebec Bars 1941; Queen's Counsel 1961. *M.* 1943, Germaine Monette. *Career:* Law practice with firm Monette, Filion, Meighen & Gourd 1943–51; Partner, Gourd & Monette 1951. President: St. Lawrence Columbium & Metals Corp., Chairman of the Board: Northern Radio – Radio Nord Inc., Radio LaSarre Inc. Vice-President: Anaconda Iron Ore (Ontario) Ltd Director: Canada Permanent Trust Co., Quebec Columbium Ltd. and several other companies. Expertise Cttee. Quebec Council of Universities. Ntnl. Dir., Canadian Council of Christians & Jews; Life Member, Montreal Museum of Fine Arts; Governor, Ntnl. Theatre School of Canada. Gov. Notre-Dame Hospital. *Member:* Quebec Bar Assn.; Canadian Inst of Mining & Metallurgy; The Montreal Board of Trade; American Institute, Mining Metallurgy and Petroleum Engineers. *Clubs:* Canadian (Montreal and N.Y.C.); Saint-Denis; Mount Stephen (Montreal); Marco Polo (N.Y.C.); Newcomen Socy. *Address:* 1010 St. Catherine Street W. (Suite 1011), Montreal, H3B 3R8, P.Q. Canada.

**GOWON, General Yakubu,** jssc, psc. Nigerian. Army Officer and Politician. *B.* 1934. *Educ.* Saint Bartholomew's School, Wusasa, Zaria; Government (Barewa) College, Zaria (full High School education); Eaton Hall OCS and Royal Military Academy, Sandhurst (England). Staff College, Camberley and Joint Services Staff College, Latimer (England). *M.* 1969, Victoria Hansatu Zakari, *S.* Ibrahim. *Dau.* Saratu. *Career:* First Nigerian Officer to become Adjutant in the Nigerian Army, March 1960; as Captain and Adjutant in the 4th Bn. Nigerian Army saw service with U.N. peace-keeping forces in the Congo (Nov. 1960–June 1961) and again as Major and Brigade Major from Jan. 1963 to June 1963; Adjutant-Gen. Nigerian Army 1963–65; Chief of Staff 1966; Commander-in-Chief of the Armed Forces of the Federal Republic of Nigeria, Aug. 1, 1966–July 29, 1975 (Major-General June 1967; General 1971); Undergraduate at Univ. of Warwick, Coventry Oct. 1975. *Address:* c/o Dept. of Politics, University of Warwick, Coventry CV4 7AL.

**GOYDER, George Armin,** CBE. British. *B.* 1908. *Educ.* Mill Hill School and London School of Economics. *M.* 1937, Rosemary Bosanquet. *S.* 5. *Daus.* 3. *Career:* General Manager, Newsprint Supply Co. 1940–47 (responsible for supply, control and rationing of newsprint to British Press during World War II). Director, Geographical Magazine 1935–58 (Chairman 1956–58). Chairman and Managing Director, British International Paper Ltd. 1935–75. Chmn. Liberal Party Standing Committee on Industrial Partnership 1966. Hon. Sec. British North American Cttee. Governor, Chmn. International Briefing Centre, Farnham; Founder-Trustee, William Blake Trust. *Publications:* The Future of Private Enterprise (Blackwell, 1951, 1954); El Porvenir de la Empresa Privada (Madrid, 1957); L'Avvenire Dell' Impressa Privata (Milan, 1955); The Responsible Company (Blackwell, 1961); Japanese editions (1959–64); The People's Church (1966); The Responsible Worker (1975). *Club:* Reform. *Address:* Pindars, Rotherfield Greys, Henley-on-Thames.

**GOYER, Hon. Jean-Pierre,** PC, QC, MP, BA, LLB. Minister of Supply & Services & Receiver General for Canada. Lawyer. *B.* 1932. *Educ.* Schools & Collegiate Insts. in Montreal; studied law at Univ. of Montreal, graduated in 1957. *M.* 1960, Michelle Gascon. *Daus.* 3. *Career:* Called to the Bar of Quebec, practised law in Montreal, created QC in 1976; first elected to House of Commons in Montreal-Dollard in 1965, re-elected 1968, '72, '74; appointed Parly. Sec. to Sec. of State for External Affairs 1968; called to the Cabinet & appointed Solicitor General of Canada 1970; appointed Minister of Supply & Services & Receiver General for Canada 1972. *Address:* 300 Driveway, Townhouse #6, Ottawa, Ontario K1S 3M6; and *office* Parliament Buildings, Room 215-S, Ottawa, Ontario K1A 0A6, Canada.

**GRAAFF, Sir de Villiers,** Bt, MBE. *B.* 1913. *Educ.* Cape Univ. (BA) and Oxford Univ. (MA, BCL); (LLD) Rhodes University. Barrister-at-Law (Inner Temple). *M.* 1939, Helena Le Roux. *S.* 2. *Dau.* 1. MP for Rondebosch 1958–77 (for Hottentots Holland 1948–58). Served in World War II (prisoner). Advocate of the Supreme Court of South Africa; Leader of the United Party of S.A. 1956–77; Leader of Official Opposition 1956–77. *Club:* Civil Service (Cape Town). *Address:* De Grendel, Tijgerberg, Cape, South Africa.

**GRABOWSKI, Franz.** German. Member Board of Dirs.: Commerzbank AG, Frankfurt. *B.* 1897. *Member:* Board of Directors, AG Ferrum, Kattowitz 1932–45. With Buderus'-schen Eisenwerke: Director 1946, Chairman 1953–67. Hon. Senator: Justus-Liebeg-Universität, Giessen, Techn. Hochschule, Darmstadt; Hon. Dr. Ing., Techn. Hochschule, Aachen. Grosses Bundesverdienstkreuz mit Stern. *Address:* Vogelsang 40, 633 Wetzlar, Federal Republic of Germany.

**GRACE, J. Peter.** American business executive. *B.* 25 May 1913. *Educ.* St. Paul's School, Concord; Yale University. *M.* 1941, Margaret Fennelly. Pres. and Chief Exec. Officer of W. R. Grace & Co. since 1945. *Address:* Grace Plaza, 1114 Avenue of the Americas, New York, N.Y. 10036, U.S.A.

**GRADL, Johann Baptist.** Dr. rer. pol. *B.* 1904. University of Berlin (Diplomvolkswirt) and University of Halle (Dr. rer. pol.). *M.* 1908, Marianne Brecour. *S.* Michael and Winfrid. *Daus.* Roswitha and Bergita. *Career:* Bank clerk and official 1922–24; Editor 1926–30; Executive Member, Sparkassen and Girobanks, Berlin 1931–38; Executive Member, Reichsgruppe Banken, Berlin 1938–45; Economist 1945–47; newspaper publisher 1948–65. Member of the Bundestag 1957—; Bundesminister für Vertriebene, Flüchtlinge und Kriegsgeschädigte 1965–66. Member of Executive Committee Christian Democrat Party 1953–71; Executive Member, Association of Exiles 1948—. *Publications:* Geschichte der deutschen Reparationssachleistungen, Berlin (1933); Zinsvereinbarungen und Wettbewerbsbestimmungen im Kreditwesen, Berlin (1936); numerous political articles since 1945. *Member:* German Central Party 1926–33; German Christian Democratic Union since 1945. *Address:* Zerbster Str. 28, 1 Berlin, 45 Lichterfelde; and *office* Bundeshaus, 53 Bonn, Germany.

**GRAF, Dr. Ulrich.** German. *B.* 1912. *Educ.* Matriculation 1931, Junior Barristers' Examination 1935, and University of Erlangen (took Degree 1936). *M.* Helga Oetjen. *Dau.* 1. *Career:* Export Salesman with Allgemeine Elektricitäts Gesellschaft 1936; Manager, Bremen Chamber of Trade 1945; Senator for Justice and Constitution and for Ecclesiastical Affairs, 1959–71. *Publications:* Der Ausschluss von Gestaltungsrechten durch die Rechskraft (technical book on German Law). Vorsitzender des Kuratoriums der Stiftung Worpswede. Mem. Cncl., Norddeutsche Finanzierungs sclien Paster. *Club:* Carl Schurz (Pres.). *Address:* No. 2862 Worpswede, auf der Heidwende 11, Germany.

**GRAHAM, Eric Richard.** Canadian chartered accountant. *B.* 1912. *Educ.* McGill University. *S.* David. *Daus.* Sandra, Lynn and Susan. *Career:* Vice-President (I/C Finance) and Dir., Pilkington Bros. (Canada) Ltd.; Director and Controller, Pilkington Glass Manufacturing Co. Ltd.; Franklin Paint & Glass Co., Pilkington Paint Ltd.; Director: Pilkington Glass Ltd., Duplate Canada Ltd. *Clubs:* University (Toronto); Toronto Rotary; Toronto Board of Trade. *Address:* 44 Charles Street W, Toronto, Ont., Canada M4Y 1R8.

**GRAHAM, Ford Mulford.** *B.* 1911. *Educ.* Alma (Mich.) Coll. (AB); and Univ. of Michigan (Law Degree). *M.* 1933, Maxine Ingold. *S.* John Joseph. *Dau.* Shirley (Wiginton). *Career:* Area Land Manager (Louisiana-Mississippi), Humble Oil & Refining Co. 1946; Louisiana Manager, Minerals Division, Gaylord Container Corporation 1946–54; Chairman of the Board, Citizens National Bank 1954–57; Vice-Pres., Monterey Oil Co. 1957–60, and The Louisiana Land & Exploration Co. 1960–61, Pres. 1961—, Chairman of Board, Dir. 1967—; Chief Exec. Officer 1967–72; Dir. Halliburton Inc. Member, National Petroleum Council of U.S.A. 1963; Trustee, Gulf South Research Institute 1964—. *Clubs:* Houston, Racquet (N.Y.C.); New Orleans Country; Boston, N.O., La. *Address:* 225 Baronne Street, Hammond, La. (P.O. Box 939, Hammond), U.S.A.

**GRAHAM, James Alexander, Jr.** American mechanical engineer. *B.* 1907. *Educ.* University of Arizona. *M.* 1939, Alice Neal-Burnett Holderby. *Career:* Draftsman-designer, Shell Oil Co. (Refinery Div.) 1926–31; Engineer, Nolder Dehydrating Co. 1933–36, and Southern California Water Co. 1936–40. Asst. Chief Engineer (1940–44), Chief Engineer (1944–48), and Executive, Contract Admin., Century Metalcraft Corp. 1948–56; Sales Executive, Harvill Corp. 1956–61. President, Air Borne Foundries, Inc. 1961—; A.F.A. Corp. since 1962; Bd. member KPA Nuclear, Inc. since 1969; Sales & Eng. Dir., Los Angeles Aluminium Casting Corp. 1970–72; Bd. Member, Omega Corp. since 1971; Pres. James A. Graham Co. since 1972. *Publications:* many papers, articles and texts on light metals fabrication. *Member:* Californian Professional Engineers; Phi Delta Theta. *Address:* 3198 West Seventh Street, Los Angeles 90005, Calif., U.S.A.

**GRAHAM, Hon. Sir (John) Patrick,** QC (1953). British Judge. High Court of Justice. *B.* 1906. *Educ.* Shrewsbury School and Gonville & Caius Coll., Cambridge (BA). *M.* 1931, Annie Elizabeth Newport Willson. *S.* Anthony, Robert, William, and Dan Washington. Group Captain R.A.F. (V.R.) 1939–45; Judge of the High Court of Justice, Chancery Div. since 1969; knighted 1969. *Publications:* Awards to Inventors. *Address:* Tall Elms, Radlett, Herts.; and *office* Royal Courts of Justice, Strand, London, W.1.

**GRAHAM, Pierre Robert.** U.S.A. Diplomat. *B.* 1922. *Educ.* University of Chicago, MA (1949). *M.* 1968, Dr. Helgard Planken. *Daus.* 3. *Career:* 3rd Secy. American Legation, Tangier, 1951–54; 2cd Secy. American Embassy, Beirut, 1954–57, Paris 1957–68; 1st Secy. American Embassy Dakar 1958–61; Personnel Officer, Dept. of State, Washington 1962–64; Counselor, American Embassy, Conakry, 1964–66; Dep. Dir. 10/PES, Dept. of State 1967–69; U.S. Perm. Rep. UNESCO Paris, 1969–73; Counselor, American Embassy, Amman, 1973–74; Chief of Mission, American Embassy, Ouagadougou, Upper Volta, since 1974. *Address:* Ouagadougou, Dept. of State, Washington D.C., 20520, U.S.A.

**GRAHAM, Robert Klark.** American. *B.* 1906. *Educ.* Michigan State Univ. (AB 1933); Ohio State University (BSc 1937). *M.* 1960, Marta Ve Everton, MD. *S.* 5. *Daus.* 3. *Career:* Associate, Bausch & Lomb 1937–40; Western Mgr., Univis Lens Co. 1940–44; Asst. Sales Mgr. 1945; Sales Mgr. 1945–46; Vice-Pres., Dir., Research Plastic Optics Co. 1946–48. President, Armorlite Inc. 1948—; Special Lecturer, Loma Linda Univ. Inventor, variable focus lens; Director of development of hard resin lens. Friederik William Herschel Medal (Germany). Mensa. *Publications:* A Variable Focus Lens (1940); Reduction of Reflections (1946); A New Light Weight and Unbreakable Plastic Lens (1947); The Corneal Lens (1949); A Hard Plastic Spectacle Lens; Control of Ultra-violet Problems (1957); The Evolution of Corneal Lenses (1959); The Future of Man (1970). *Address:* 3024 Sycamore Lane, Escondido, CA 92025 U.S.A.

**GRAINGER, Isaac B.** American banker. *B.* 15 Jan. 1895. *Educ.* Woodberry Forest School, Orange, Va., and Princeton University. *M.* Catherine Garrett. *S.* Isaac B., Jr., William G., J. Victor, III. *Career:* With Murchison National Bank, Wilmington, N.C., until 1929. Vice-Pres., North Carolina Bank & Trust Co. 1929–34; Pres., Montclair Trust Co., New Jersey 1934–43; Vice-Pres., Chemical Bank New York Trust Co. 1943–50; Pres. 1956–60; Adviser Director of Union Electric Co.; Director: Fort Myers Southern R.R. Co., Hartford Fire Insurance Co., Hartford Accident & Indemnity Co., American Manufacturing Co., Shearson Capital Fund Inc.; Dir. Shearson Appreciation Fund. Service in World War I (Captain, Infantry). Institute for the Crippled and Disabled. *Member:* St. James' Episcopal Church in N.Y. City; N.Y. Chamber of Commerce; Southern Society; N. Carolina Socy.; Society of Colonial Wars in the State of New York; Newcomen Society of England; Pilgrims of the U.S. *Clubs:* Links; Princeton (all of N.Y.); Tiger Inn, Princeton, New Jersey; Bond Club of N.Y.; Links Golf Club, Roslyn, N.Y.; Pine Valley Golf Club, New Jersey; Royal and Ancient, St. Andrews, Scotland, Augusta National Golf; Cape Fear Country, Wilmington (N.C.). *Address:* 200 East 66th Street, New York City; and *office* 11 West 51st Street, New York City, U.S.A.

**GRAINGER, John Frederick.** Canadian. Vice-President, Southam Press Ltd. Publisher, The North Bay Nugget. *B.* 1915. *M.* 1938, Anne M. Sadick. *S.* William, *Dau.* Barbara Hogan. *Club:* Rameses Shrine. *Address:* 1049 Premier Road, North Bay, Ont.; and *office* 259 Worthing Street West, North Bay, Ont. P1B 8J6, Canada.

**GRANADO, Donald Casimar.** Trinidadian. *B.* 1915. *M.* 1959, Anne-Marie Faustin Lombard. *S.* 1. *Daus.* 2. *Career:* Minister of Labour & Social Services 1956; Minister of Health & Housing 1961; Deputy Leader. House of Representatives 1961; Secretary, People's National Movement 1956; Secretary-Treasurer Fed. of Trade Unions 1952–54; Secretary, Union of Commercial & Industrial Workers 1952–54; Leader, Deleg. to I.L.O. 1957 and 1958; Ambassador to Venezuela 1963–64. High Commissioner to Canada 1964–69; Ambassador to Brazil and to Argentina 1965–69; High Comm. U.K. 1969–71; Ambassador to E.E.C. France, Germany, Holland, Belgium, Italy, Luxembourg, Switzerland 1969–71; *Member:* People's National Movement. *Decorations:* Trinity Cross. *Publications:* poems; plays; Autobiography. *Clubs:* various. *Address:* 20 Grove Road, Valsayn Park North, Curepe, Trinidad.

**GRANDE, George Kinnear.** Canadian diplomat. *B.* 1919. *Educ.* McGill Univ. (BA 1940) and Osgoode Hall Law School. *M.* 1947. *S.* Robert Malcolm, John Kinnear and Donald Masson. *Dau.* Susan Elizabeth. *M.* 1975. Diane Dekens. *Career:* Joined R.C.A.F. 1941; served in United Kingdom, India and Ceylon; discharged 1945 (F/Lieut.). With War Assets Corp., Montreal 1945–46. Joined External Affairs Dept. as F.S.O.I., Dec. 1946; Secy., Deleg. to AEC Sept. 1947; Advisor, C.P.D.U.N., New York, Jan. 1948; Ottawa, Aug. 1950; First Secy., Athens, Dec. 1952; Ottawa, Nov. 1954; First Secy., Berlin, July 1957; Counsellor, Berlin, July 1958; Ottawa, July 1960; High Commissioner in Ceylon 1964–66; Foreign Service Mem. of the Directing Staff, National Defence College, Kingston Ont. 1966–68; Ambassador to Norway and Iceland 1968–72; Dir. Defence Relations Div. Ottawa 1972–73; Ambassador, Head Canadian Del. The Mutual and Balanced Force Reduction Talks Vienna, Austria 1973–76; Amb. to South Africa & High Commissioner to Lesotho, Botswana & Swaziland since 1976. Member, Graduate Society of McGill University. *Address:* The Canadian Embassy, Pretoria, South Africa.

**GRANDIN, John Livingston, Jr.** American. *B.* 1910. *Educ.* Harvard (SB 1932) and Harvard Graduate School of Business (MBA 1934). *M.* 1940, Susanne Preston Wilson. *S.* John L. III, Edward W. and Preston B. *Career:* Secretary, The Gillette Co., Boston, Mass. 1948–72; Dir., Boston Safe, Deposit & Trust Co., 1942–72; Constitution Exchange Fund Inc. *Trustee:* Northfield Mount Hermon School 1938—.

*Member:* Corporation of University Hospital, and Northeastern University; Corporation, Museum of Science, Boston. Trustee, Office of J. L. Grandin 1934–41; Lt.-Comdr., U.S. Naval Reserve 1942–46. *Clubs:* Commercial, Merchants (Boston); The Country (Brookline, Mass.). *Address:* 169 Chestnut Hill Road, Chestnut Hill, Mass. 02167; and *office* One Boston Place, Boston, Mass. 02106, U.S.A.

**GRANJON, Jacques.** French. *B.* 1909. *M.* 1932, Jeanne Main. *S.* 2. *Daus.* 3. *Career:* Ingenieur Chimiste EPCI; Président Dir. Général de Nobel Bozel; Pres. Dir. Général Bozel Electrometallurgie. *Address:* 53 Rue Pergolese, Paris 16, France; and *office* Tour Roussel Nobel. 3 Avenue du Général de Gaulle, 92800 Puteaux.

**GRANO, Thomas Anthony.** Australian. *B.* 1916. *Educ.* Melbourne Univ. (LLB) and Queensland Univ. (Dipl. Com.). *M.* 1942, Marie Aconley. *Daus.* Julie Maria and Suzanne. *Career:* Commonwealth Government Service (Legal Officer for War Organization of Industry; Commonwealth Rent Controller; Secy., Snowy Mountains Hydro-Electric Investigational Committee; Secy. Commonwealth Fire Board) 1942–49; Director, Queensland Press Ltd. (controlling body of leading Queensland newspapers, broadcasting stations with television associates), Sept. 1956—. *Member:* Queensland Law Socy. Inc.; The Law Socy. of N.S.W.; *Fellow,* Inst. of Directors. *Clubs:* The Brisbane; Royal Queensland Golf; Queensland Turf. *Address:* 32 Austral Street, St. Lucia, Brisbane, Australia.

**GRANT, Alexander Ludovic,** TD, DL JP. British. *B.* 1901. *Educ.* Winchester College and New College, Oxford; MA (Oxon) History Honours. *M.* 1946, Elizabeth Langley-Buxton. *Daus.* 2. Joined Barclays Bank 1925; Local Director, Liverpool 1930, and Manchester 1940; Main Board 1945–73; Chmn. of Manchester Local Board 1946–73; Director, Barclays Bank D.C.O. 1948–72. *Clubs:* Pratt's and M.C.C. *Address:* Marbury Hall, Whitchurch, Salop.

**GRANT, Bruce Alexander.** Australian Author & Diplomat. *B.* 1925. *Educ.* Melbourne Univ. BA; Harvard, Nieman Fellow. *M.* 1962, Joan Constance Pennell. *S.* 2. *Career:* Film and Theatre Critic of 'The Age' Melbourne 1950–54; For. Correspondent in Europe (1954–57); Asia (1959–63) and U.S.A. (1964–65); Fellow in Political Science, Univ. of Melbourne 1965–68; Public Affairs Columnist for 'The Age' 1968–73; Councillor of Monash Univ. Melbourne 1970–73; Australian High Commissioner in India and Ambassador to Nepal 1973–76; George Scott Visiting Fellow, Ormond Coll., Univ. of Melbourne 1976; Associate, International Inst. for Strategic Studies, London 1976–77. *Member:* Austr. Inst. of International Affairs; Australian Soc. of Authors; Australian Journalists Assoc. *Publications:* Indonesia; The Crisis of Loyalty; Foreign Affairs and the Austr. Press; Arthur and Eric. *Address:* 83 Grey Street, E. Melbourne, Vic. 3002, Australia.

**GRANT, Charles Henry.** British engineer and executive. *B.* 1906. *Educ.* at Melbourne C. of E. Grammar School 1; Trinity Coll., Melbourne Univ. 1925–30 (BEE). *M.* Dorothy Gwendoline Smith. *S.* 3. *Career:* With Tasmanian Hydro-Electric Commission 1930–31; Metropolitan-Vickers Co., Ltd. 1931–33; Manager, Australian Magnesium Co., Ltd. 1934–40; Engineer, Munitions Factory, Hobart 1941–44; Chairman and Managing Director, Market Place Pty. Ltd. 1944; Chmn. of Directors, Hobart Gas Co. since 1951. Director: Cascade Brewery Co., Ltd. 1944 (Chmn. 1965—); Perpetual Trustees and National Executors of Tasmania Ltd. 1945—; Chmn. 1968—; Dir., Traders Pty. Ltd. 1944 (Chmn., 1965—); Perpetual Insurance & Securities Ltd. 1948–77); Richardsons Meat Industries Ltd. 1952–76; Tasmanian Breweries Pty. Ltd. 1951—; (Chmn., 1965—); Burgess Bros. Ltd. 1965—; Eastlands Pty. Ltd. 1967–76. *Member:* Inst. of Engrs. (Australia); Inst. of Directors in Australia; Chmn. Trustees, Property of C. of E. in Tasmania. *Address:* High Peak, Neika, Tasmania.

**GRANT, John Douglas,** MP. British politician. *B.* 1932. *M.* 1955, Patricia Julia Ann. *S.* Miles Christopher and David Stephen. *Dau.* Susan Patricia. *Career:* Journalist, Daily Express since 1955; Chief Industrial Correspondent 1967–70; Member of Parliament for Islington East 1970–74; Opposition spokesman, Policy Broadcasting and The Press 1973–74; MP for Islington Central since 1974; Parly. Secy. to Civil Service Dept. 1974; Under Secy. of State for O'seas Dev. 1974–75; Under Secy. of State for Employment 1976—. *Address:* House of Commons, London, S.W.1.

**GRANT, Keith Henry.** Australian. *B.* 1927. *Educ.* Wesley College (Melbourne) and Melbourne University (BCom.); FCIS, ACA. *M.* 1963, Denise Audrey Kidd. *S.* Alistair Beith. *Career:* Public Accountant 1951–60. Senior Partner, Grant & Falk, Public Accountants 1960–75; Senior Partner, Grant Falk Thomas & Co., Chartered Accountants 1976—. Director: Australian Development Ltd. 1957—; Chmn. Barrier Exploration N.L. 1968–; Chmn. Jimberlana Minerals N.L. 1970—. *Clubs:* Royal Automobile (Victoria); Lonsdale Golf; Latrobe Golf. *Address:* 1 Blythswood Court, Kew, Melbourne, Vic.; and *office* 356 Collins Street, Melbourne, Vic., Australia.

**GRANT, Walter Randolph.** Business executive. *B.* 1910. *Educ.* Univ. of Pennsylvania (BSc 1934). *M.* 1949, Joyce A. Gafford. *Daus.* Kathleen S., Sally E., Nancy M. and Laurie J. *Career:* Travelling Auditor, General Electric Co. 1934–45; Secy.-Treas.: Locke Insulator Co. 1945–47, and Hotpoint Inc. 1947–52 (Vice-Pres. 1950–52); Vice-Pres.: Packard Motor Co. (and Treas.) 1952–54, and Studebaker-Packard Corp. (of Finance) 1954–55; Vice-Pres.-Finance, New York Central Railroad Co., 1955–68; Exec. Vice-Pres. Penn. Central 1968. Executive Vice-President, Consolidated Edison Co. of N.Y. 1968—. *Clubs:* Indian Harbor Yacht; The Milbrook (both of Greenwich, Conn.). *Address: office* 4 Irving Place, New York City 3, U.S.A.

**GRANVILLE, Sir Keith,** CBE. British. *B.* 1910. *Educ.* Tonbridge School. *M.* (1) 1933, Patricia Capstick. *S.* 1. *Dau.* 1. *M.* (2) 1946, Truda Bellis. *S.* 1. *Daus.* 4. *Career:* Joined Imperial Airways as trainee 1929; Manager African and Middle East Division BOAC 1947; Commercial Director 1954; Deputy Managing Director BOAC 1958–60; Chairman BOAC Associated Companies 1960–64. Managing Director BOAC 1969–70 Deputy Chairman 1964–70; Chmn. Chief Exec. 1971–72; Deputy Chmn. British Airways Board 1972–74; Member of the Board 1959–72, BOAC. Inst. of Transport (Pres. 1963–64); Pres. IATA 1972–73; Maplin Development Bd. 1973–74. *Clubs:* Naval & Military. *Address:* Speedbird, Chateau D'Oex, Switzerland.

**GRASSBY, Albert Jaime.** Australian politician. *B.* 1926. *Educ.* Australia and overseas; studied Arts Univ. SW England; special studies Agric. Extension, Univ. of Calif (Berkeley). *Career:* Entered journalism, U.K., member Commonwealth Parliamentary Press Gallery, Canberra; Tasmanian Parliamentary Press Gallery; Joined CSIRO as Specialist Officer in Information; transferred M.I.A. Agricultural Extension Service, N.S.W. Department of Agriculture; Executive Officer Irrigation Research and Extension Organisation; War Service: Enlisted British Army 1945, served infantry and Intelligence Corps; As member of Australian Labor Party held offices at local, state and federal electorate level, state level and at Federal Executive Committee level; Independent trade missions go Asia, Europe and South America 1959–60 Attached U.S. Dept of Agriculture., Washington, D.C., special studies extension 1962. Special study mission with Food and Agriculture Org of U.N. in Italy 1956; Elected Member for Murrumbidgee, N.S.W. Parliament 1965; Secretary N.S.W. Parly. Party Rural and Resources Cttee. 1965–68; Shadow Minister for Agriculture and Conservation, 1968–69; Elected Member for Riverina, 1969; Member Joint Cttee on Broadcasting; Secretary Rural and Resources Cttee Parly. Labor Party; member Immigration Cttee, Parly. Labor Party; Re-elected member for Riverina 1972; Minister for Immigration; Special Consultant to Australian Government on Community Relations, 1974–75; Appointed Australia's First Commissioner for Community Relations 1975. *Decorations:* Knight Commander of Order of Solidarity of Italian Republic, 1970 by President Saragat. Knight of Military Order of St. Agata of Paterno 1969; Grand Cross of Military Order, 1974; Citation of University of Santo Tomas, Republic of Philippines; Freedom of Sinopoli and Plati (Italy), Platynos & Akrata (Greece). *Publications:* Contr. to many journals and ref. publs. *Address:* P.O. Box E280, Canberra, ACT, Australia; and *office* Administration Building, Canberra ACT, Australia.

**GRASSO, Ella Tambussi.** American Politician. *B.* 1919. *Educ.* Mount Holyoke College, BA 1940, MA 1942. *M.* 1942, Dr. Thomas A. Grasso. *S.* 1. *Dau.* 1. *Career:* Connecticut House of Representatives 1953–55; Sec. of State, Connecticut, 1958–70; Congressional District, Connecticut 1970–74; Member, U.S. House of Representatives; Governor, State of Connecticut since 1975. *Address:* Woodland Hollow 2, Windsor Locks, Connecticut, U.S.A.; & *office* Executive Chambers, State Capitol, Hartford, Conn., U.S.A.

**GRAUPNER, Ernest Arnold.** AB. PhD. American. *B.* 1908. *Educ.* Duke Univ. (AB); Harvard Univ; Graduate School of Bus. Admin; Univ. of Wisconsin; Webster Univ. (PhD). *M.* 1947, Gabriella Le Dorf. *Career:* manager Int. Div. American Potash & Chemical Corp. 1945–58; Pres. & Dir. Sulphur Export Corporation. *Member:* Sigma Chi. *Clubs:* Harvard Business School N.Y.; Duke Univ; Export Managers, N.Y. *Address:* 20 East 74 Street, New York, N.Y. 10021, U.S.A. and Pond Brook Farm, Newtown, Conn., U.S.A.

**GRAY, Allan Verdun.** Australian. *B.* 1916. *Educ.* Mordialloc High School. *M.* (1) 1939. *S.* 2. (2) 1969, Marjorie Jean McDonald. *Career:* Sales Representative, Eliza Tinsley Pty. Ltd. 1942–43; Supply Manager, Rheem Australia 1943–48; Supply Manager and Assistant to Managing Director, Ansett Transport Industries 1948–51; General Manager, Regent Motors (Holdings) 1952–55. Executive, Managing Director, Volkswagen Australasia Ltd. 1955–66; Regional Dir., Wormald International (Aust.) Pty. Ltd. since 1967. Fellow, Australian Inst. of Management. *Clubs:* Barwon Heads Golf Club; Australian; M.C.C.; Melbourne Rotary. *Address:* 12–18 Clowes St., South Yarra, Vic. Australia. and *office* 447–459 Williamstown Road, Port Melbourne, Australia.

**GRAY, Arthur, Sr.** American banker. President, Arthur Gray Corporation since 1939. *B.* 1891. *Educ.* Public Schools. *M.* 1920, Beatriz Lerner. *S.* Arthur, Jr. Member, New York Stock Exchange. *Dau.* Joan (Untermyer II; *Dec.* 1962). Chairman: Lerner Marine Laboratory, Bimini. Bahamas, B.W.I.; American Museum of Natural History; Governor, International Game Fish Association; American Museum of National History; Director: National Hospital for Speech Disorders, and of American Arbitration Association (Founder 1922). Republican. *Address:* 2 East 61st Street, New York City; and *office* 730 Fifth Avenue, New York City 19, U.S.A.

**GRAY, Arthur, Jr.** Investment Counselor. *B.* 1922. *Educ.* The Lawrenceville School and Massachusetts Inst. of Technology. *M.* (1) 1944, Adele Hall. (2) 1964, Betty Jean Johnson. *S.* Michael H. and John M. *Daus.* Kathleen W., Wendy L., Lydia B., Elizabeth C. *Career:* Served as 1st Lieut., Navigator, U.S.A.F. 1942–45; Distinguished Flying Cross, Air Medal—4 Oak Leaf Clusters, European Campaign—4 Battle Stars and Presidential Unit Citation. Association with Kuhn ,Loeb & Co. 1945–53; Pres., Michael Myerberg Productions 1953–56; Exec. Vice-Pres. and Dir., A. M. Kidder & Co. Inc. 1957–59; Senior Partner, Gray & Co., member of New York Stock Exchange 1959–74; First Vice-Pres. Mitchell Hutchins Inc. (member NYSE) since 74; Chmn., Tallasi Management Co. since 1975; Dir., Prudential Lines Inc. 1977—; Chmn. Exec. Cttee. Boys' Athletic League 1960—; Dir. Amer. Arbitration Assn.; Trustee, Amer. Museum of Natural History; Vice-Pres. and Dir., Lerner-Gray Foundation Inc.; member, Advisory Cttee., U.S. Committee for U.N.; Chmn., Special Events, Citizens for Eisenhower-Nixon 1952; Dir., ICD Rehabilitation & Research Center. Sigma Alpha Epsilon. *Clubs:* The Wall Street; The Lambs. *Address:* Bliss Tavern, Haverhill, New Hampshire 03765; and *office* One Battery Park Plaza, New York, N.Y. 10004, U.S.A.

**GRAY, Gordon.** American. *B.* 1909. *Educ.* Univ. of North Carolina (BA) and Yale Law School (LLB). *M.* 1956, Nancy Maguire Beebe. *S.* Gordon, Jr., Burton Craige, C. Boyden and Bernard. *Stepdaughters,* Cameron, Alexandria and Schuyler Beebe. *Career:* Practised law in New York and North Carolina 1933–37. N. Carolina State Senate 1939–42. Served in Army 1942–45; Asst. Secy. of Army 1947, Secretary 1949. President, Univ. of North Carolina 1950–55; Asst. Secy. of Defense 1955; Director, Office of Defence Mobilization 1957; Special Assistant to the President for National Security Affairs 1958–61. Chairman of the Board, Summit Communications Inc.; Winston-Salem, N.C.; Director of the Board, R. J. Reynolds Industries, Inc. and American Security & Trust Co. Chmn. Media General,; Chmn. Emeritus, The National Trust for Historic Preservation; Brookings Institution 1971–75; Trustee Fed. City Council; Member, President's Foreign Intelligence Advisory Board 1961–77. *Member:* Phi Beta Kappa. Democrat. *Clubs:* Metropolitan; Brook; Burning Tree. *Address:* 1224–30th Street, N.W., Washington, D.C. 20007, U.S.A.

**GRAY, Harold James,** CMG. British. *B.* 1907. *Educ.* London Univ. (BSc; MSc; LLB), Gray's Inn, Harvard (MPA); MInstP; FRSA; Cmnwlth. Fund Fellow. *M.* 1928, Katherine Starling, *Dau.* Ann Betty. *Career:* Customs and Excise Dept. 1927; Asst. Examiner Patent Office, 1930, Examiner 1935; Board of Trade 1938; Ministry of Supply 1939, Asst. Secretary 1942; Board of Trade 1946; Under-Secy. 1954. U.K. Senior Trade Commissioner and Economic and Commercial Adviser to High Commissioner: in Australia 1954–58, and in Union of South Africa 1958–60. Director National Association of British Manufacturers 1961–65; Dir. Legal Affairs Confederation, British Industry 1965–72; Numas Management Service Ltd. 1961—; Chmn since 1970. *Publications:* Economic Survey of Australia; Electricity in the Service of Man: Dictionary of Physics; New Dictionary of Physics (Gray & Isaacs). *Clubs:* Devonshire; East India; Sports & Public Schools. *Address:* Oaken Wood, Red Hill, Wateringbury, Kent.

**GRAY, J. H. N. (Hamish),** MP. British company director. *Educ.* InvernessRoyal Academy. *M.* 1953, Judith W. Brydon. *S.* 2. *Dau.* 1. *Career:* Served, Queens Own Cameron Highlanders, 1945–48; Director, Family & other Companies, 1948–70; Member, Council Highland Chamber of Commerce, 1960–65 and Inverness Town Council 1965–70; Member of Parliament, Conservative for Ross and Cromarty since 1970; Government Whip 1971–73; Lord Commissioner to the Treasury 1973–74; Opposition Whip 1974–75; Opposition Spokesman on Energy since 1975. *Clubs:* Highland (Inverness) St. Stevens (London). *Address:* The Cedars, Drummond Road, Inverness, Scotland; and *office* House of Commons, London, S.W.1.

**GRAY, Milton H.** American lawyer. *B.* 1910. *Educ.* Northwestern Univ. (BA, JD). *M.* 1937, Florence A. Subin. *S.* James. S. *Dau.* Roberta (Katz). *Career:* Chmn., Corporation and Securities Law Section Illinois Bar 1947–48; Corporation Law Cttee. Chicago Bar 1948–50; Securities Law Cttee. Chicago Bar 1951–1953; Lecturer, American Institute of Banking 1943–45; University of Illinois Law School 1953; Northwestern University Law School, 1956; Harvard University, 1967; American Bar Association Committees on State Regulation of Securities 1961—, and Federal Regulation of Securities 1961—, and Corporate Law & Accounting since 1971; Partner in law firm of Altheimer and Gray; Vice-Pres. & Dir., Blackstone Manufacturing Co.; Secretary and Director; Noma-World Wide, Inc., Alloy Manufacturing Co. Member, Board of Managers, Chicgo Bar 1966–68; Pres. Chicago Bar 1971–72; Special Master U.S. District Court since 1973. *Member:* Chicago, Illinois, American Bar Associations, International Bar Association; World Association of Lawyers; American Judicature Society. Order of the Coif, Past Pres. (1957–59) Northeast Illinois Council; Chairman (1968–70) Executive Bd., Region VII, Boy Scouts of America (Silver Beaver, 1959; Silver Antelope, 1963); Mem. Natl. Exec. Bd. 1968–70. Boy Scouts of America; National Adv. Council 1970—. *Awards:* Distinguished Eagle Scout Citizen, Northwestern Univ. Alumni Award of Merit. *Publications:* Illinois Not for Profit Act; Illinois Securities Law (codrafter). Editorial Board, Illinois Business Corporation Act Annotated; contributor to legal publications. *Clubs:* Standard; Tavern; Northmoor Country. *Address:* 420 Lakeside Place, Highland Park, Chicago; and *office* One IBM Plaza, Chicago, Ill., U.S.A.

**GRAY, W. Latimer.** Consultant. *B.* 1894. *Educ.* Harvard (BS 1917). *M.* 1931, Margaret Morton Platt. *S.* William Latimer and Samuel Packwood Morton. Successively Clerk, Vice-Pres., and Senr. Vice-Pres., & Dir. First National Bank of Boston 1917–59. Director Platt & Co. Inc., Helmerich & Payne Inc. *Clubs:* Country (Brookline); Harvard, Somerset (Boston); Beverley Yacht; Kittansett (Marion); Bourne's Cove Yacht (Wareham). *Address:* "Saffron Walden", Wareham, Mass. 02571, U.S.A.

**GREATHOUSE, Glenn A(rthur).** American nuclear chemist and physicist. *B.* 1903. *Educ.* PhD. *M.* 1925, Edith Bennett. *Daus.* Rosemary and Glenna Lu. *Career:* Graduate Assistant, Univ. of Illinois 1927–30; Duke Fellow, Duke Univ. 1930–31; Assistant Professor, Biochemistry and Biophysics, Univ. of Maryland 1931–36; Project Leader, U.S. Dept. of Agriculture 1936–40; Consultant to Defense Dept. 1940–42; Office of Scientific Research & Development 1942–45; Project Director, National Academy of Sciences 1945–55; Professor and Head, Nuclear Engineering Dept., Univ. of Florida 1956–60; Head Nuclear Consultant, Commonwealth of Mass. 1960–64. President, Nuclear Research Chemicals Inc. 1954–67. Special Consultant to Mallingkrodt Chemical Works 1967–72. *Publications:* seventy or more technical papers. *Member,* U.S.-British Scientific Mission, England, Europe, Africa and Panama; U.S. Delegate, World Conference, Atoms for Peace. National Defense Research Committee. *Awards:* Bureau of Ordnance Development Award, U.S. Navy; King's

Medal (United Kingdon); The Two Thousand Man of Achievement, 1971; Wisdom Hall of Fame and others. *Member:* American Chemical Socy.; American Nuclear Socy.; American Physical Socy., and others. *Club:* Cosmos. *Address:* P.O. Box 6, Winter Park, Fla. 32789, U.S.A.

**GREDLER-OXENBAUER, Dr. Willfried Andreas Kolomann.** Austrian diplomat. *B.* 1916. *Educ.* Univ. of Vienna, Dr. in Law and Economics 1939; Foreign Trade Inst, in Vienna 1944; other univs. incld. Berlin 1942–44; Harvard 1954. *M.* 1954, Elfriede Jirgl. *Daus.* 3. *Career:* Asst. at Court of Justice in Vienna 1939–40; Exec. Dir. of Austrian Banking Corp. Vienna 1945–63; Member of Austrian Parly. 1953–63; Opposition leader (F.P.O.-Austr. Nat. Liberal Party) in Austrian Parly. 1956–63; Ambassador Extraord. and Plenipotent, and Permanent Delegate for Austria at Europ. Council in Strasbourg 1963–70; Ambass.-Extraord. and Plenipot. to the Federal Republic of Germany since 1970. Former Vice-Chmn. F.P.O., Austrian Nat. Lib. Party, & Chmn. of Austrian Section of Liberal International; Secy.-Gen. European League of Economic Co-operation (Europ. Movement). *Decorations:* Grand Cross FRG; Grand Silver Cross Republic of Austria; Officer's cross of Order of Malte; Officer's cross of Order of Constantin. *Publications:* Various on economic questions, European integration, human rights and minority rights. *Club:* Rotary. *Address:* D-5300 Bonn, Friedrich-Wilhelmstrasse 14, Federal Republic of Germany.

**GREEN, Alan,** CBE. British. *B.* 1911. *Educ.* Brighton College. *M.* Hilda Wolstenholme. *Daus.* 3. *Career:* Schoolmaster 1931–35; Scapa Dyers Ltd. Blackburn 1935–61; served in World War II (Royal Artillery) 1940–46. Vice-Chairman: Scapa Dyers and Subsidiaries 1953–61, Wolstenholme Bronze Powders Ltd. 1953–61. Director, Walmsley (Bury) Ltd. and Subsidiaries 1951–61; Chairman, Walmsleys Ltd. and Subsidiaries 1955–61. Member of Parliament (Con.), Preston South 1955–64. Parliamentary Secretary to Ministry of Labour June 1961; Minister of State, Board of Trade, July 1962–63: Financial Secretary to the Treasury 1963–64. Director: Walmsley (Bury) Group 1964—; Chairman 1970—; Wolstenholme Bronze Powders Ltd.; Barclays Bank, Manchester; Scapa Group Ltd. 1965—; Member of Parliament Preston South 1970–74; Member Nationalised Industries Cttee. 1970–74; Select Cttee. on European Legislation since 1973; Speakers Conference 1973–74. *Member:* Estimates Cttee. House of Commons 1958–61. *Clubs:* Reform, R.A.C. (London). *Address:* The Stables, Sabden, nr. Blackburn, Lancs.

**GREEN, E. Ellsworth, Jr.** American Insurance Executive. *B.* 1911. *Educ.* Univ. of Kansas City; Southwestern Institute for C. of C. Executives; Univ. of North Carolina; Indus. Coll. of Armed Forces (Lincoln, Nebraska); Natl. War Coll. (Wash.); Chillicothe Business Coll., *M.* 1932, Ada Frick. *Daus.* Ellie L. and Martha A. Accountant. Missouri Power & Light Co., Mexico, Mo. 1929–36; Manager 1936–37, Operator 1937–38, Auto Agency, Mexico; Manager, Poplar Bluff (Mo.) C. of C. 1938, Sedalia (Mo.) C. of C. 1938–47, and Freeport (Ill.) C. of C. 1947–49; Exec. Mgr., Kansas City (Kan.) C. of C. 1949–62; Exec. Vice-Pres., Dayton (Ohio) Area C. of C. 1962–63 & El Paso, Texas C. of C. 1963–65; Economic Development Consultant (Ellsworth Green, Jr. & Associates). Broadcaster (radio and TV); public speaker; Chmn., Kansas Citizens Commn. on Ageing; U.S. Dept. of Labor delegate to San Juan, P.R. (to study economic condition of industries) 1943; member six-man USAF team to observe W. European Air Bases Community Relations Program 1956; Alternate member, U.S.A.R. Forces Policy Committee 1961; member, National Vale Advisory Board, American Security Council; National Agricultural Hall of Fame; Speakers Bureau. 2nd Lieut. to Major, U.S.A.A.F., World War II (Lt.-Col. Reserve); Bronze Star Medal. Mem.: Kansas (Past Pres.) and American (Chmn. Better Business Bureau Liaison Cttee.) C. of C. Executives; U.S. (Pres., mem. labor relations council) and Kansas (Chmn. Adv. Cncl. and Dir.) Chambers of Commerce. *Member:* American Industrial Development Council; Disabled Amer. Veterans (Natl. Chief of Staff and local and State Commander 1959–60); Air Force Association (Director); National Association of Executives; American Legion; Military Order of World Wars; 40 and 8; C.B.I. Veterans Ass. (past Natl. Comdr.; Past Speaker Bureau Labor Relations Council, President, National Dir. U.S. Junior Chamber Comm., Bureau Labor Relations and Chamber of Comm., U.S.); Author of magazine articles. *Address:* 2811 N. 45th Terrace, Kansas City, Kan., U.S.A.

**GREEN, George Grafton.** British. *B.* 1907. *M.* Brigid Maxwell the novelist). London Editor. Manchester Evening News 1933–39; during World War II built up and directed for the Ministry of Information the world's largest features agency; London Editor, Daily Dispatch 1947–48; Asst. Editor, Daily Graphic 1948; Editor, Empire News & Sunday Chronicle. London 1949–57. Executive Producer, The Rank Organization Special Features Division 1957–70; Controller, The Rank Organization Information Services 1971–72; Dir. European League for Economic Co-operation. Films include: the Look at Life series, Honeymoon Island, Wedding in Springtime (the wedding of Princess Margaret), White Rose Wedding (Duke of Kent), Wedding of the Year (Princess Alexandra), Churchill—A Nation's Homage, The Open Door, Palaces of a Queen, Return to the Island, The Post Office Tower of London. The Saints Went Marching Out, A Man Who Shook the World, and the television series, Sea War. *Award:* C. P. Robertson Memorial Trophy for Services to R.A.F. 1966. *Address:* 16 Regency Street, London, S.W.1.

**GREEN, Henry William Jerome,** KCGM, OSJ, JP. Australian executive. *B.* 1908. *M.* 1939, Jean Colbey. *S.* 1. *Dau.* 1. Previously High School teacher and artist. Principal, Adelaide College of Music 1941–76; Director, Adelaide Conservatorium of Music 1953–75; Perth College of Music 1961–74; Public Relations International 1963—; Executive Director: Stradivarius Co. of Australia Ltd., Associated Music Colleges of Australia Ltd., Harry J. Green & Co. Ltd., and other companies 1950–74; Director: The London & Lancashire Insurance Co. Ltd. 1956–75, Prudential Finance Ltd. 1957–64, and Queensland College of Music 1950–74; Chmn. of Directorate: Australian-American Association 1956–61, Senior Vice-President, 1962–63, 1971–72; President 1963–65. President: Australian-Italian Association 1958–63, Catholic Blind Association 1958—, and Gilbert and Sullivan Society 1949–67; Federal President: Music Teachers Federation of Australia 1956—, and National Accordian Organisation of Australia 1958—; Exec. Australian-Asian Association 1958–64, Vice-Pres. 1961–64; Pres. City of Adelaide Lions International 1971–72. Member, Regional Committee, U.S.A. Education Foundation 1958–76. Chairman, Music League of S.A. Inc. 1941—. *Awards:* Fellow, Institute of Directors (London) 1962. Life Governor, Adelaide Children's Hospital. Created Knight Commander of Grace, Knights of Malta, Sovereign Order of St. John of Jerusalem 1967. *Clubs:* Bacchus, Lions. *Address:* 50 Sunnyside Road, Glen Osmond, S.A., Australia.

**GREEN, Johannes.** Danish. *B.* 1904. *Educ.* Univ. of Copenhagen (LLB). *M.* 1931, Vibeke Marie Neergadar. *S.* Per. *Dau.* Birgitte (Hassel). *Career:* JP since 1939; Asst. Gen. Mgr. 1940, Privatbanken, Copenhagen, Deputy Gen. Mgr. 1950, Gen. Mgr. 1953–67; Federation of Danish Banks 1955–69 (Chmn. 1955–58 and 1964–67). Member: Danish National Committee of the International Chamber of Commerce 1964–69 and Board of the Frontier Foundation; Irma Fabrikerne A/S 1970; Kredit-Finansierings-Kompagniet. A/S 1970; Member, Board of Dir. Nordisk Factoring A/S 1970; and Karl Pedersens og Hustrus Industrifond 1970. Admitted to Quorum of Justice 1974. *Publications:* The Stock Exchange Manual, Greens Danske Fonds go Aktier; various articles and papers on economic subjects. Commander of the Dannebrog; Grand Knight of the Icelandic Falcon. *Member:* Institute International d'Études Bancaires 1956–70; Academy of Technical Sciences 1963–70; Chmn. of the Academy's Financial Cttee. 1966–70; Chmn. Danish E.D.P. Council, 1968–70. *Address:* 429 Strandvej, Klampenborg; and (summer) Davrup Hovedgaard, Jyderup, Denmark.

**GREEN, John Michael,** CB, MA. British civil servant. *B.* 1924 *Educ.* Merchant Taylors' School Rickmansworth; Jesus Coll. Oxford, MA. *M.* 1951, Sylvia Crabb. *S.* 1. *Dau.* 1. *Career:* Assistant Principal Inland Revenue 1948–52, Principal 1952–55, 1957–62; Principal H.M. Treasury 1956–57; Asst. Secy. Inland Revenue 1962–71; Under-Secretary, Commissioner Board of Inland Revenue 1971–73; Deputy-Chmn. since 1973. *Club:* Reform. *Address:* 5 Bylands, White Rose Lane, Woking Surrey; and *office* Board Room, Inland Revenue, Somerset House, London, W.C.2.

**GREEN, Raymond Newman.** American. *B.* 1909. *Educ.* Ohio Wesleyan University. *M.* 1937, Emmy Lou Cable. *S.* 1. *Daus.* 2. *Career:* Dir. Eng. Fostoria Pressed Steel Corp. 1939–45; Vice-Pres. & Treas, Wagner-Green Co. 1946–61; Vice Pres. Sales Fostoria Corp. 1961–65; Vice Pres. Secy. & Gen. Mgr. 1965–68; Pres; Fostoria Industries Inc. Fostoria; Exec. Vice Pres. TP1 Corporation, Johnson's Tenn.; Ret'd. Jan. 1976; currently Management Consultant to Seneca Wire Manufacturing Corp., Fostoria, Ohio. Trustee Kaubisch Memorial Public Library. *Member:* Reserve Officers Assoc.;

Illuminating Eng. Socy.; Ind. Heating Equipment Association. *Clubs:* Cleveland Athletic. *Address:* 508 Mt. Vernon Drive, Fostoria, Ohio 44830, U.S.A.

**GREENAWAY, Sir Derek,** Bt., CBE, TD, JP, DL. President, Daniel Greenaway & Sons Ltd. *B.* 1910. *Educ.* Marlborough College. *M.* 1937, Sheila Beatrice Lockett. *S.* John Michael Burdick. *Dau.* Anne Jennifer Hewson. *Career:* Served in World War II (attained rank of Major). Joint Master, Old Surrey and Burstow Foxhounds 1958–66. Chmn., Sevenoaks Cons. & Unionist Assn. 1960–63 (Pres. 1963–66). Asst. Area Treas., S.E. Area Nat. Union of Cons. Assn. 1966; Treas. 1969, Chmn. 1975; Hon. Col., 44 (H.C.) Signal Regt. (Cinque Ports) T.A. 1966; and 36th (Eastern) Signal Regt. (V) 1967–74; High Sheriff of Kent 1971; Master of Worshipful Co. of Stationers and Newspaper-makers 1974. *Clubs:* Carlton, City of London, M.C.C. (all of London). *Address:* Dunmore, Four Elms, Edenbridge, Kent; and *office* Greenaway House, 132 Commercial Street, London, E.1.

**GREENBOROUGH, Hedley Bernard,** CBE. British oil company executive. *B.* 1922. *Educ.* Wandsworth School, London. *M.* 1951, Gerta Ebel. *S.* 1 (stepson). *Career:* Commercial Dir. Exec. Vice-Pres. Shell Argentina Ltd. 1960–66; Vice-Chmn. British Chamber of Commerce in Argentina 1962–66; Area Co-ordinator (Far East) Shell International Petroleum Co. 1967–69; Man. Dir. (Marketing) Shell Mex & B.P. Ltd. 1969–71; Chief Exec. Man. Dir. Shell Mex and B.P. Ltd. 1971–75; Man. Dir. and Dep. Chmn. Shell UK Ltd. since 1976; Governor Ashridge Mgmt. College since 1971, Chmn. of Govs. 1977; Pres. Nat. Socy. Clean Air 1973–75. Fellow, Brit. Inst. of Management, Chmn. Bd. of Fellows 1976; Pres., Inst. of Petroleum since 1976; Chmn., U.K. Petroleum Industry Advisory Cttee. since 1971; Member, CBI Council; Economic Policy & Finance Cttees.; Dep. Pres. CBI 1977; Pres., Incorporated Society of British Advertisers since 1976; Mem., National Economic Development Council 1977. *Clubs:* Junior Carlton; M.C.C.; Royal Wimbledon Golf; Royal & Ancient Golf. *Address:* 30 Burghley House, Somerset Road, Wimbledon Common, London, S.W.19; and *office:* Shell-Mex House, Strand, London, W.C.2.

**GREENE, Sir Hugh (Carleton),** KCMG, OBE. British. *B.* 1910. *Educ.* Berkhamsted School and Merton College, Oxford (BA 1935; MA 1958). *M.* 1970, Tatjana Sais. *M.* 1951, Elaine Shaplen (*Diss.* 1969) (previous marriage to Helga Guinness. *M.* 1934, dissolved 1948). *S.* 4. *Career:* Daily Telegraph, Berlin staff 1934; Chief Correspondent 1938; expelled from Germany as reprisal, May 1939; Warsaw correspondent 1939; after the outbreak of war reported events in Poland, Rumania, Bulgaria, Turkey, Holland, Belgium and France. Joined BBC as head of German Service 1940 (after service in R.A.F.); Controller of Broadcasting in British Zone of Germany 1946–48; Head of BBC East Europ. Service 1949–50; Head of Emergency Information Services, Fed. of Malaya 1950–51; Asst. Controller, BBC Overseas Services 1952–55, Controller 1955–56; Chmn., Federal Commission of Inquiry into Organization of Broadcasting in Fed. of Rhodesia and Nyasaland 1955. Dir. of Administration, BBC 1956–58; Dir. of News and Current Affairs BBC 1958–59; Dir.-Gen. of the British Broadcasting Corp. (BBC) 1960–69. Chmn, The Bodley Head 1969—; Governor of the BBC 1969–71; Report for Israeli Govt. Operations of Israeli Broadcasting Authority 1973; Report for Greek Government on constitution of Greek Broadcasting 1975. *Address:* Earls Hall, Cockfield, nr. Bury St. Edmunds.

**GREENE, Hon. John James (Joe).** Canadian. *B.* 1920. *Educ.* Univ. of Toronto (BA 1948) and Osgoode Hall (Law Degree 1950). *M.* Corinne Bedore (of Arnprior, Ont.). *S.* 2. *Daus.* 3. *Career:* Established law practice in Arnprior, and was on Arnprior municipal council 1951–56, and Renfrew County Council 1956–59; elected Member of Parliament 1963. Delegate to 54th Inter-Parliamentary Union Conf., Dublin, March 1965. Minister of Agriculture for Canada, Dec. 1965–68; Minister of Energy, Mines & Resources 1968–72. Served in World War II (Flt.-Lieut. RCAF; awarded D.F.C.; mentioned in dispatches). *Member:* Canadian Bar Assn.; Law Society of Upper Canada. Liberal. *Clubs:* University (Toronto); Rideau (Ottawa); Royal Ottawa Golf; Niagara Falls (Canada). *Address:* 323 John Street, Arnprior, Ont.; and The Senate, Ottawa, Ont. K1A 0A4, Canada.

**GREENEBAUM, Richard Walter.** American editor and executive. Editor, The Gallatin Service, Copley International Corp.; Consultant on Latin America, Committee for Economic Development; Director, University of the Andes Foundation. *B.* 1920. *Educ.* Harvard (AB 1942; LLB 1949). *M.* 1944, Carmen de Zulueta. *S.* John and Edward. *Dau.* Mary. Executive, International Basic Economy Corp., New York and São Paulo 1949–63; Director of Brazilian subsidiaries of I.B.E.C. and representative of Hon. Nelson A. Rockefeller in Brazil 1953–57. From Private to Captain, Military Intelligence, U.S. Army 1942–46; Interpreter and Instructor, Command and General Staff School, Ft. Leavenworth, Kansas 1944–46 (Army Commendation Ribbon). *Publications:* The Mobilization of Local Capital in Latin America Through Open-end Investment Companies, 1963; Editor, The Gallatin Letter and The Gallatin Annual of International Business. *Address:* 437 East 84th Street, New York City 28, U.S.A.

**GREENEWALT, Crawford Hallock.** American industrialist. *B.* 16 Aug. 1902. *Educ.* William Penn Charter School; Massachusetts Institute of Technology (BS). *M.* 1926, Margaretta Lammont du Pont. *S.* David, Crawford Hallock. *Dau.* Nancy (Frederick). *Career:* With E. I. du Pont de Nemours & Co., Inc., since 1922; Asst. Dir. Experimental Station, Chemical Dept. 1939, Director, Chemical Division, Grasselli Chemicals Dept. 1942, Technical Director, Explosives Dept. 1943, Assistant Director, Development Dept. 1945, Asst. Gen. Mgr., Pigments Dept. 1945–46, Vice-Pres. 1946, Vice-Pres. and Vice-Chairman of Exec. Cttee., 1947, Pres. 1948, Chairman of the Board 1962. Director, E. I. du Pont de Nemours & Co., Inc. since 1942, (Chairman of the Finance Cttee. 1967–74, Member since 1974); Christiana Securities Co. since 1944; Boeing Co. 1964–74; Morgan Guaranty Trust Co. of New York 1963–72. *Awards:* Hon. DSc, University of Delaware and Northeastern Univ. and Philadelphia Coll. of Pharmacy and Science; LLD (Hon.) Williams Coll., Columbia Univ., Temple Univ., Kansas State Univ., Kenyon Coll.; Hon. LLD, Boston Univ. Hon. DSc(Comm.) New York Univ., and Drexel Inst. of Technology; Dr. Eng, Poly. Inst. of Brooklyn; Dr. Eng (ED), Rensselaer Poly. Inst.; DHL (Hons.), Jefferson Medical Coll.; Hon. LLD, Univ. of Pennsylvania, Swarthmore Coll., Bowdoin Coll., and Univ. of Notre Dame; Hon. DSc Yale Univ. 1969; Hon. DSc Hamilton Coll. 1970. *Address:* Du Pont Building, Wilmington, Delaware 19898, U.S.A.

**GREENFIELD, Bruce Harold.** Col. U.S. Army Reserve. *B.* 1917. *Educ.* Duke University (BA) and Yale Law School (LLB). *M.* 1955, Adele Gersh. *S.* Gregory Richard. *Daus.* Elizabeth Susan and Margaret Alison. *Career:* Office of Tax Legislative Counsel, U.S. Treasury Dept. 1941–48; absent on military service with U.S. Air Force 1942–46; Partner, Folz, Bard, Kamsler, Goodis & Greenfield (Attorneys) 1949–53; Vice-Pres. Bankers Securities 1953–59; Exec. Vice-Pres. 1959–70. Dir. Bankers Bond and Mortgage Guaranty Co. of America 1956—; Treas. & Dir. Bellevue Stratford Co. 1957—; Dir. City Stores Co. and Continental Bank 1959—; Pres. & Dir. Bankers Securities Corp. since 1970. Contributor of articles on Federal Taxation to Practising Law Institute; Prentice-Hall Tax Ideas Service; Taxes Magazine. Lecturer at New York Univ. Tax Inst., Tulane Univ. Tax Inst., and Amer. Univ. Tax Inst., the proceedings of which were all published. Graduated Duke Univ. *summa cum laude*; Phi Beta Kappa. *Member:* Tax Executives Inst. (Pres. Phila. Chapter 1964–65); American, Pennsylvania, Philadelphia and Federal Bar Assns.; Adv. Group to U.S. Commissioner of Internal Review, since1965; Democrat. *Clubs:* Yale, Locust, Variety. *Address:* 210 Barker Road, Wyncote, Pa.; and *office* 1401 Walnut Street, Philadelphia, Pa. 19102, U.S.A.

**GREENFIELD, Sir Harry,** KBE, CSI, CIE. British. *B.* 1898. Served European War in Berkshire Yeomanry and Tank Corps 1916–19. In Civil Service in India 1919–47, retiring as Chairman, Central Board of Revenue Government of India. Delegate of India to Narcotics Commission of U.N. 1946. Director of The Chartered Bank 1953–73 and of various companies: President, 1953–68. Permanent Central Board elected to U.N. under Inter. Convention of 1925 relating to Dangerous Drugs (Vice-Pres. 1948–52); Chmn. Institute for the Study of Drug Dependence 1968–75; Pres., International Narcotics Control Board, 1968–75; Governor, The Polytechnic of Central London. Vice-Chmn., Westminster Chamber of Commerce 1963–65 and of Commission on Formalities in International Trade, International Chamber of Commerce 1962–74. *Member:* Committee to review Customs and Excise Organization 1951–53; and of Adv. Cttee. Chelsea School of Art 1958–64. Chairman: Council of the Leprosy Mission, 1962–74; Royal Society for India, Pakistan and Ceylon 1963–75. *Clubs:* Oriental (London). *Address:* Ruthven Holmewood Ridge, Langton Green, Tunbridge Wells, Kent.

**GREENHILL of Harrow, Baron (Denis Arthur),** GCMG, OBE. British. *B.* 1913. *Educ.* Bishops Stortford College and Christ Church, Oxford (MA). *M.* 1942, Angela Doris McCulloch. *S.* Nigel and Robin. *Career:* With Royal Engineers 1939–45. Foreign Office 1945–47; First Secretary: Legation, Sofia 1947–49, and Embassy, Washington 1949–52; Foreign Office 1952–53; Imperial Defence Coll. 1954; Counsellor: U.K. Delegation, NATO, Paris 1954–56, Singapore Commissioner-General's Office 1956–58, and Washington 1959–62 (Minister 1962–64); Asst. Under-Secy., Foreign Office 1964–66. Under-Secretary, Foreign Office, London 1966–69. Permanent Under-Secretary, Foreign & Commonwealth Office; Head of Diplomatic Service, 1969–73; Govt. Dir. British Petroleum Ltd; Governor BBC; Dir.; Clerical Medical and General Life Assurance Socy.; Dir. British Leyland Ltd.; Dir. S. G. Warburg & Co. Ltd.; Dir. Wellcome Foundation Ltd. since 1974; BAT Industries Ltd.; Hawker Siddeley Group; Trustee of Rayne Foundation; Gov. Wellington Coll.; Created Baron (Life Peer) 1974; Hon. Student, Christ Church. *Club:* Travellers (London). *Address:* Hamilton House, Vicarage Gate, London, W.8; and *office* S. G. Warburg & Co. Ltd., 30 Gresham Street, London EC2P 2EB.

**GREENWAY, Chester Alan.** Australian. *B.* 1927. *M.* 1960, Jeanette Anne Blake. *Dau.* 2. *Career:* Chmn. & Man. Dir. Travelodge Australia Ltd.; Dir. Travelodge International, Inc. San. Diego, Calif.; Chmn. Aust. Tourist Commission; Dir. Trust Houses Forte Ltd. London.; Southern Pacific Properties Ltd . London Fellow Inst. of Directors. *Clubs:* Royal Automobile, Australian Golf; Royal Motor Yacht. *Address:* Travelodge Australia Ltd., Box 2 PO, Edgecliff, N.S.W. 2027 Australia. 754 New South Head Road, Rose Bay, N.S.W. 2029, Australia and *office* 110 Bayswater Road, Rushcutters Bay, N.S.W. 2011.

**GREENWOOD, of Rossendale. The Rt. Hon. the Lord (Arthur William James Anthony Greenwood.)** PC, DL, JP, Company Director and Planning Adviser. *B.* 1911. *Educ.* Merchant Taylors' School and Balliol Coll. Oxford (MA). *M.* 1940, Gillian Crawshay Williams. *Daus.* Susanna and Dinah. *Career:* Member of Parliament 1946–70; J.P. 1950; Vice-Chmn. Parly. Labour Party 1950 and 1951; Member National Exec. Labour Party 1954–70; Chmn. Labour Party 1963–64; Secy. of State for the Colonies 1964–65. Minister of Overseas Development Dec. 1965–66. British Minister of Housing and Local Government 1966–70; Chmn. Britannia Bldg. Socy. 1975–76; Dir. C'wealth Development Corp. since 1970. *Member:* Bureau Socialist International 1960–70; Pres., River Thames Society since 1970; Chmn. Local Government Staff Commission since 1972; Pro-Chancellor, Univ. Lancaster since 1972; Pres., British Trust for Conservation Volunteers since 1974; Pres., Housing Centre; Chmn., U.K. Housing Assn. 1972—; Pro-Chancellor, Univ. of Lancaster since 1972; Pres., British Trust for Conservation Volunteers since 1974; Chmn. Local Govt. Training Board since 1975; Deputy-chmn. Housing Corp. since 1974. Chmn. Isle of Man Parly. Group 1975; Conciliator, Internat. Centre for Settlement of Investment Disputes 1975; Pres. Nehru Memorial Trust, 1975; Chmn., Integrated Professional Development Services since 1975; Mem., Advisory Bd. on Redundant Churches since 1975. *Address:* 38 Downshire Hill, Hampstead, London, N.W.3. Tel. 01-435 3276.

**GREENWOOD, Lawrence George.** Canadian. *B.* 1921. *Educ.* Regina (Sask.) Central Collegiate. *M.* 1947, Margaret Purser. *Career:* With Canadian Imperial Bank of Commerce: Manager: Seattle, Wash., U.S.A. 1956, and Toronto Branch 1958; Asst. Gen. Mgr., Head Office 1962; Regional Gen. Mgr. 1963; Dep. Chief General Manager, Head Office 1964; Chief General Manager 1964, Pres. 1968, Vice-Chmn since 1971. Dir. Canadian Imperial Bank of Commerce, Toronto. Imperial Life Assurance Co. of Canada; Dir. Canadian Export Assn. Canadian Executive Service Overseas. Member Bd. Trustees Queen's Univ.; Bd. Dirs. Cdn. Council International Chamber of Commerce; Canadian Advisory Board, Liberty Mutual Insurance Co. *Member:* Board of Trade of Metropolitan Toronto; National Trust for Scotland; Prospectors & Developers Assn.; Amer. Management Assn.; Canadian Inst. of Mining & Metallurgy; Canada-Netherlands Council Canadian Chamber of Commerce; Can. Economic Policy Cttee.; C. D. Howe Research Inst. *Clubs:* St. James's; The Mount Royal; Mount Bruno Country; Mount Royal Tennis; Canadian; Toronto; York; Empire (of Canada); The Forest and Stream; Granite. *Address:* c/o Canadian Bank of Imperial Commerce, Commerce Court, Toronto, Ontario M5L 1A2, Canada.

**GREGG, Guion, Jr.,** GRI, CRB. *B.* 1917. *Educ.* Texas Technological College (BS Textile Engineering). *M.* 1945, Helen Ladner. *S.* John D. Appleby, Guion III and William III. *Career:* Served in World War II (Midshipman to Lieutenant); participated in 5 battles in Pacific theatre; wounded in action; recipient Purple Heart; honourable discharge May 1946. Engaged since 1939, appraising and selling Dallas residential real estate; Owner-manager, Guion Gregg, Realtors since 1952; Licensed Real Estate Broker; Insurance Broker; Notary; Fee Appraiser, Texas Highway Dept. *Member:* Dallas Real Estate Board (Past President); Texas Real Estate Assn. (Dir.); Representative, National Inst. of Real Estate Brokers; Texas Technological College Ex-Students Assn. (Past-Pres.); Circle Ten Council Boy Scouts; National Association of Real Estate Boards; National Inst. of Real Estate Brokers; Dallas Multiple Listing Service; Dallas and North Dallas Chambers of Commerce; Socy. of Residential Appraisers (Assoc. member): Park Cities Lions Club (Past Pres.); District 2x1, Lions International (Past Zone Chmn.); Dallas Chapter, Texas Technological Ex-Students Assn. (Past Pres.), Cotton Bowl Athletic Assn. (Dir.); Pres. Park Cities Chapter Amer. Cancer Society (Past Pres.); National Homes for Living Network. *Awards:* Dallas Board of Realtors, Easterwood Cup 1973; Realtor of the Year Award 1973–74. *Clubs:* Dallas Knife & Fork (Past Pres.); Saturday Morning Quarterback (Dir., Past Pres.). *Address:* 7618 Bryn Mawr, Dallas, Tex.; and *office* 6906 Snider Plaza, Dallas 5, Texas, U.S.A.

**GREGOIRE, Pierre.** Luxembourgeois. *B.* 1907. *Educ.* Cours Supérieurs (Dipl. by Exam.). *M.* 1932, Octavie Schmit. *S.* Jean-Pierre. *Career:* Administrative career 1929–33; Editor, Luxembourger Wort 1933–59. Member of the Government; Minister 1959–69; Minister of Foreign Affairs, Jan. 1967; Pres. of Chamber of Deputies until 1974. *Publications:* many and varied works on the theatre, history, romance, philosophy, literary criticism. *Award:* Grand Cordon, Crown of Belgium; Grand Cross, Order of Orange-Nassau (Netherlands); and many other decorations and honours. Member Christian Social Party. *Member:* Association of Journalists of Luxembourg (Hon. Pres.); Association of Catholic Writers (Hon. Pres.). *Address:* 177a route d'Arlon, Strassen, Grand Duchy of Luxembourg.

**GREGORY, Jack Norman,** FRACI. Australian scientist. *B.* 1920. *Educ.* Wesley Coll., Melbourne and Melbourne Univ. (BSc; MSc; DSc). *M.* 1945, Sheila Muriel Ewan. *S.* Ian Raymond. *Dau.* Susan Margaret. *Career:* Research Officer, Division of Tribophysics, C.S.I.R.O., Melbourne 1942–48; Senior Research Officer and Principal Research Officer in C.S.I.R.O. (later Australian Atomic Energy Commission); seconded for duty to U.K. Atomic Energy Research Establishment at Harwell 1948–56; returned to Australia, Chief of Isotope Division, 1956, Australian Atomic Energy Commission 1955–74; Program. Man. Nuclear Science and Applications Program, Australian Atomic Energy Commission since 1974. *Member:* Radiological Advisory Council of N.S.W. 1957–64. Mem. Cttee., N.S.W. Branch of Royal Australian Chemical Institute 1968. Hon. Associate, Dept. of Medicine Sydney Univ. 1969—; Member Adv. Cttee. Nuclear Medicine, Health Commission, N.S.W. since 1970. *Publications:* The World of Radioisotopes (1966); numerous scientific papers in various journals. Fellow of the Royal Australian Chemical Institute (F.R.A.C.I.). *Address:* 13 Nellella Street, Blakehurst, N.S.W. 2221; and *office* Australian Atomic Energy Commission Research Establishment, Private Bag, Sutherland, N.S.W. 2232, Australia.

**GREGORY, Reginald Edward.** MBE. Australian director, The Myer Emporium Ltd., Melbourne. *B.* 1911. *M.* 1937, Laura Read. *Member:* Australian Socy. of Accountants (Life Member); Chartered Inst. of Secretaries (Fellow). *Club:* The Athenaeum. *Address:* 21 Albany Road, Toorak, 3142, Vic.; and *office* Myer House, 250 Elizabeth Street, Melbourne, 3000, Vic., Australia.

**GREGORY, Wilfrid Palmer,** QC. Canadian lawyer. *B.* 1912. *Educ.* University of Toronto (BA) and Osgoode Hall Law School; Barrister-at-Law. *M.* 1940, Ann Patricia Stevenson. *S.* John Davidson. *Daus.* Catherine Jane and Elizabeth Ann. (McMillan). *Career:* Practised law on his own account 1936–42 and 1946. With Canadian Army 1943–45. Practised law with Gregory, Anderson, Ehgoetz & Bell 1947–56; Bencher, Law Society of Upper Canada 1951–68; Queen's Counsel 1952. Man. Dir. British Mortgage & Trust Co. 1957–65; Senior Partner Gregory, McDonald and Linley; Dir. of several Corporations. *Member:* Canadian Bar Assn., Member of Council 1946–65; Canada Council for Arts, Humanities and Social

Sciences 1965–58; Vice-Pres. Nat. Liberal Fed. 1954–57; Pres. Ontario Liberal Assn. 1955–56; Chairman, Stratford Parks, 1969; Stratford City Alderman, Mayor, 1955–56; Chmn. Conf. Governing Bodies, Legal Profession in Canada 1959; Pres. Stratford Shakespearean Festival Foundation of Canada 1959–61; Former Dir., Stratford Art Assn. Liberal. *Clubs:* Stratford (Ont.) Country. *Address:* 41 Delamere Ave., Stratford, Ont.; and *office* 168 Ontario Street, Stratford, Ont., Canada.

**GRENFELL, Lord (Hon. Julian Pascoe Francis St. Leger)**, 3rd Baron (1976). British International Civil Servant. *B.* 1935. *Educ.* Eton & King's Coll., Cambridge—BA (Hons.). *M.* (1) 1961, Loretta Maria Reali (*Diss.* 1970). *Dau.* 1. (2) 1970, Gabrielle Katharina Raab. *Daus.* 2. *Career:* TV Journalist, London 1960–65; Joined World Bank, 1965; Information & Public Affairs Dept., Washington D.C. 1965–69; Chief of Information & Public Affairs in Europe, Paris 1969–72; Dep. Dir., European Office, Paris 1972–74; Special Rep. to UN Organizations, New York since 1974. *Clubs:* Travellers; Royal Green Jackets. *Address:* 55 East 72nd Street, New York City, N.Y. 10021, U.S.A. and *office* Room 2435, United Nations, New York City, N.Y. 10017, U.S.A.

**GREY, of Naunton, Baron (Life Peer) Ralph Francis Alnwick**, GCMG, GCVO, OBE. *B.* 1910. *Educ.* Wellington (N.Z.) College, Auckland University College and Pembroke College, Cambridge; LLB (N.Z.); Hon. LLD Queen's Univ. Belfast. *M.* 1944, Esmé Kirkcaldie C. St. J. *S.* 2. *Dau.* 1. *Career:* Barrister and Solicitor, Supreme Court of N.Z. 1932; Associate to Hon. Mr. Justice Smith 1932–36; Probationer, Colonial Administrative Service 1936; Cadet, Admin. Service, Nigeria 1937; Asst. Fin. Secy. 1949; Admin. Officer (Cl. I) 1951; Development Secy. 1952; Secy. to Gov.-General and Cncl. of Ministers 1954; Chief Secy. of the Federation 1955–57; Dep. Gov.-Gen., Fed. of Nigeria 1957-59; Governor and Commander-in-Chief British Guiana, Nov. 1959–64; Governor and Commander-in-Chief Bahamas 1964–68, and of Turks and Caicos 1965–68; Governor, N. Ireland 1968–73; Deputy-Chmn. Commonwealth Development Corp. since 1973; Chmn., Royal Overseas League since 1976. *Awards:* GCStJ; Hon. Bencher, Inn of Ct. Northern Ireland; Hon. Freeman City of Belfast; Borough of Lisburn; Bailiff of Egle, Order of St. John 1975. *Clubs:* Travellers; Ulster (Belfast). *Address:* Overbrook, Naunton, Glos.

**GRIBKOV, Colonel-General Anatoly.** Chief of Staff of the Warsaw Pact. *B.* 1919. *Career:* First Dep. Commander, Leningrad Military District 1969; Commander 1973; Elected Candidate Member, Soviet Communist Party's Central Cttee. 1975; Commanded "Sever-76" Military Manoeuvres in Leningrad area June 1976; Appointed Chief of Staff, Warsaw Pact, Oct. 1976. *Address:* Ministry of Defence, Naberezhnaya M. Thoreza 34, Moscow, U.S.S.R.

**GRIEVE, Alan Thomas.** British. *B.* 1928. *Educ.* Cambridge University (MA (Hons.) LLB). *M.* (1) 1957, Anne Dulake. *S.* *S.* 2. *Dau.* 1. (2) 1971, Karen Louise Dunn. *S.* 1. *D.* 1. *Career:* Solicitor to The Prestige Group Ltd. 1953–56. Partner in Taylor & Humbert, Solicitor. Chairman, Colibri Lighters Ltd.; Irvine Sellars Ltd.; Reliance Nursing & Social Care Services Ltd.; Director Baggeridge Brick Co. Ltd.; Jones Sewing Machine Co. Ltd.; Stenham Ltd.; Vigers, Stevens & Adams and other companies. *Publications:* Purchase Tax. *Member:* Law Society. *Address:* Brimpton House, Brimpton, Berks.; and *office* 2 Raymond Buildings, Gray's Inn, London, WC1R 5BN.

**GRIEVE, William Percival, QC, MA, MP.** British barrister and politician. *B.* 1915. *Educ.* Privately & Trinity Hall Cambridge. *M.* 1949. Evelyn Raymonde Louise. Mijouain. *S.* Dominic Charles Roberts. *Dau.* Oriane Georgina Aletta. *Career:* Barrister-at-Law, Middle Temple since 1938; Served Middlesex Regt. & Gen. Staff Hon. Major 1939–46; Asst. Recorder Leicester, 1956–65; Deputy Chmn. Quarter Sessions 1962–71; Queen's Counsel since 1962; Member of Parliament Conservative for Solihull since 1964; Recorder of Northampton 1965–71; Recorder since 1972. Master of Bench Middle Temple since 1969; Member of House of Commons Select Cttee. on Race Relations & Immigration, 1968–70; British Delegation to Council of Europe & W.E.U. since 1969. (Chmn. Rules of Procedure Cttee.), Hon. Vice-Pres. Franco British Parly. Relations Cttee. Chmn. 1970–75; Vice Chmn. Parly. Anglo-Benelux Group 1974; Chmn., Luxembourg Society 1975. *Member:* International Law Association; *Awards:* Chevalier de la Legion d'Honneur (France); Commandeur de l'Ordre de Merite (Luxembourg); Officer with Crown, Order of Adolphe of Nassau; Chevalier, Order of Couronne De Chêne; Croix de Guerre with Palms (Luxembourg); Bronze Star (U.S.A.). *Clubs:* Royal Automobile; Hurlingham. *Address:* 32 Gunterstone Road, London, W.14; and *office* 1 King's Bench Walk, Temple, London, E.C.4.

**GRIFFIN, Sir David**, CBE. Australian. *B.* 1915. *Educ.* LLB Sydney. *M.* 1941, Jean Falconer Whyte. *S.* Edward and Alastair. *Career:* Dep. Chmn. Oil Search Ltd. 1954—; Chmn. Australasian Petroleum Co. Pty. Ltd. 1958—; Island Exploration Co. Pty. Ltd. 1958—; Nabalco Pty. Ltd. 1964—; Dep. Chmn. Swiss Aluminium Australia Ltd. 1964—; Dir. Zellweger (Aust) Pty. Ltd. 1965—; Gove Joint Venture 1968—; Robert Bosch (Aust.) Pty. Ltd. 1972—; Vanguard Insurance Co. Ltd. 1972; Aetna Life of Australia & New Zealand Ltd. 1972—; Man. Dir. Swiss Aluminium Mining Australia Pty. Ltd.; Barclays Austr. Ltd.; Lord Mayor of Sydney 1972–73. *Publications:* The Happiness Box. *Clubs:* Union (Sydney); Elanora Country; Royal Sydney; Pine Valley (U.S.A.). *Address:* 7 Mildura Street, Killara, N.S.W. 2071; and *office* 1 Alfred Street, Sydney, N.S.W., Australia.

**GRIFFIN, William Thomas.** American Attorney and Counsellor-at-Law. *B.* 1905. *Educ.* Holy Cross College (AB *summa cum laude*) and Fordham (LLB *cum laude*). *M.* 1934, Joan Mannix. *S.* William and Peter. *Daus.* Christine and Gabrielle. Admitted to New York Bar 1931; law practice in New York since. Former Vice-Pres., Law, New York, New Haven and Hartford R.R. Co.; Corp. member, American Bar Association, Federal Bar Association, New York County Lawyers Association Interstate Commerce Commission Practitioners, New York Law Institute; Amer. Judicature Socy.; Internatl. Socy. of Barristers, New York Assn. of Trial Lawyers. *Clubs:* Lawyers (N.Y.C.); National Lawyers (Washington, D.C.); Richmond County Country (S.I., N.Y.); Princess Anne Country (Virginia Beach, Va.); New York Athletic; Drug and Chemical; Manhattan (N.Y.S.); Quinipiaque (New Haven, Conn.). *Address:* 37 Howard Avenue, Grymes Hill, S.I., N.Y.; and *office* 161 William Street, New York, N.Y. 10038., U.S.A.

**GRIFFITH, Hon. Sir Arthur Frederick.** Australian. *B.* 1913. *Educ.* Public Schools. *M.* 1940, Gweneth L. Macaulay Evans. *Dau.* 1. M.L.A. for Canning, W.A. 1950–53; M.L.C. for Suburban 1953–65; Leader of Opposition, Legislative Council, 1958–59; Minister for Mines, Housing and Justice 1959–71; M.L.C. for North Metropolitan Province; Leader of Opposition 1971–74; Pres. Legis. Council 1974–76. Member Liberal Party. Knight Bachelor 1977. *Address:* 16 St. James' Park Road, Crawley, W.A., Australia; and *office* Parliament House, Perth, W.A., Australia.

**GRIFFITH, Wilbur L.** Business executive and consultant. *B.* 1902. *Educ.* Oklahoma Univ. *M.* 1955, Betty Boucher. *S.* Wilbur Linn, Jr. *Daus.* Sally Elizabeth and Julie Anne. *Career:* With Gulf Oil Corp. 1926–45; independent oil operator 1945–59. President: Power Farms Ltd., Plateau Land Development Co. Ltd.; H. C. Bauer Welding Associates Ltd.; British Columbia Lightweight Aggregates Ltd; Pres. Del Rio Ranch Ltd.; Dir., Orbit Oil & Gas Inc.: Pinebrook Golf & Country Club. *Clubs:* Petroleum, Ranchmen's; Calgary, Golf & Country (Calgary); Glencoe. *Address:* R.R. 2, Calgary, Alta., Canada.

**GRIFFITH-JONES, Sir Eric (Newton)**, KBE, CMG, QC. Barrister-at-Law (Gray's Inn 1934). *B.* 1913. *Educ.* Cheltenham Coll. and Gray's Inn, Barrister-at-Law 1934. *M.* 1946. Mary Patricia Rowland, née Heagerty. *S.* 2. (1 *Dec.*). *Daus.* 2. *Career:* Advocate and Solicitor, Straits Settlements & Johore 1935 (Crown Counsel 1939); Capt. Straits-Settlements Vol. Force (P.O.W. Far East 1942–45) 1942–46; Efficiency Medal; Crown Counsel, Malayan Un. 1946; Senior Federal Counsel, Federation of Malaya 1948; Legal Adviser, Selangor 1948 and Perak 1949–51; Acting Solicitor-General and Acting Attorney-General, Fed. of Malaya 1951; Solicitor-General, Kenya 1952–55; member of Legislative Council 1952–61; Council of Ministers, 1955–63; Deputy Speaker and Chairman of Committees, Kenya Legislative Council 1954–55; Attorney-General and Minister for Legal Affairs 1955–61; (occasions) Acting Chief Secretary and Governor's Deputy 1956–61; Acting Governor, Kenya, 1959–63 (occasions); Deputy Governor 1961–63. Chairman and Director: The Guthrie Corp. Ltd. and associated companies; The Commonwealth Development Corp., Property Holdings (Pennine) Ltd., Sutcliffe Mitchell (Insurances) Ltd., Dir.: Provident Mutual Life Assurance Association: Vice-Pres. Liverpool School of Tropical Medicine; Fellow BIM. *Clubs:* Royal & Ancient Golf, St. Andrews; Karen Country & Nairobi

(Kenya); Port Dickson (Malaysia). *Address:* The Combe, Rogate, nr. Petersfield, Hants.; and *office* 52–54 Gracechurch Street, London, E.C.3 and 33 Hill Street, London, W.1.

**GRIFFITHS, Paul Coghlan,** MD. New Zealand barrister & solicitor. *B.* 1905. *Educ.* University of New Zealand (Law) *M.* 1938, Dorothy Nannette Hazard. *Dau.* Gaye Nannette, Barrister and Solicitor (Griffiths, Gill, Hooker, Auckland, N.Z.). Consul for Republic of Panama. Dean, Auckland Consular Corps. Member N.Z. Law Socy. *Clubs:* Racing; Golf; Trotting; Officers (all Auckland); Avondale Jockey. *Address: office* N.I.M.U. Building, Auckland, New Zealand.

**GRIFFITHS, William Balcombe,** OBE, MC, ED. British architect. *B.* 1907. *Educ.* Geelong Grammar School; Trinity College, Melbourne University (B Arch); FRIBA; (Life Fellow) RAIA. *M.* 1942, Rachel Cockburn Salmon. *S.* Allan Balcombe. *Dau.* Deirdre Balcombe. *Career:* Commissioned Australian Army 1929; Lieut-Col., War Service 1939–45 (2/5 Aust. Inf. Bn. 17th Bde., A.I.F.). Foundation Partner, Yuncken Freeman, Architects 1933, Non-Exec. Chmn. 1977; Chairman, Ozapaper Ltd. *Fellow:* Royal Inst. of British Arch. (RIBA); Life Fellow, Royal Australian Institute of Architects (RAIA); Past Pres. Royal Victorian Institute of Architects 1953–54 and Building Industry Cong. of Victoria 1956–57. *Clubs:* Melbourne; Naval & Military (Melbourne); Royal Melbourne; Golf; Barwon Heads, Golf. *Address:* 7 Ethel Street, Malvern, Melbourne; and *office* 411 King Street, Melbourne, Victoria, Australia.

**GRIMOND, Rt. Hon. Joseph,** PC, TD, LLD, DCL, MP. Director, Manchester Guardian & Evening News Ltd. *B.* 1913. *Educ.* Eton and Balliol Coll., Oxford; 1st Class Hons. (Politics, Philosophy and Economics). *M.* 1938, Laura Bonham-Carter. *S.* 3. *Dau.* 1. MP (Lib.) Orkney and Shetland since 1950; called to Bar 1937; served World War II (Fife & Forfar Yeomanry) 1939–45; Director of Personnel, European Office, U.N.R.R.A. 1945–57; Secretary, National Trust for Scotland 1947–49. Leader Parliamentary Liberal Party Nov. 1956 to Jan. 1967. Elected Rector of University of Edinburgh 1960–63; Rector Aberdeen Univ., 1969–72; Chancellor Univ. of Kent, 1970. *Address:* Old Manse of Firth, Kirkwall, Orkney.

**GRIST, Ian,** MP. British. *B.* 1938. *Educ.* Repton School; Jesus Coll., Oxford (Open Scholar), Hons. Philosophy, Politics, Economics. *M.* 1966, Wendy Anne White. *S.* 2. *Career:* Plebiscite Officer, Southern Cameroons Plebiscite 1960–61; Stores Manager, United Africa, Company, Nigeria 1961–63; Conservative & Unionist Central Office, Wales 1963–74; Conservative Research Dept., 1970–74; Conservative MP for Cardiff North since 1974; Sec., Welsh Conservative Parliamentary Members since 1974; Sec., Conservative Parliamentary Group for the Deaf since 1975. *Address:* 18 Tydfil Place, Roath Park, Cardiff; & House of Commons, London, SW1A 0AA.

**GRISWOLD, Benjamin Howell, III.** American investment banker. Director: Mercantile-Safe Deposit & Trust Co.; Fidelity & Deposit Co. of Maryland 1949—, Black and Decker Mfg. Co. 1964—, Ellicott Machine Corp. 1953—, The Rouse Co. Partner of Alex. Brown & Sons, Baltimore 1935—. *B.* 1911. *Educ.* Princeton University (AB 1933). *M.* 1936, Arabella Leith Symington. *S.* Benjamin H., IV and Jack Symington. *Daus.* Lelia Leith and Nancy Montague. Served in World War II (Lieutenant U.S. Navy) 1942–45. *Award:* Legion of Merit (U.S.A.); Gold Star in lieu of 2nd Legion of Merit (U.S.A.); Dis. Service Cross (G.B.); Croix de Guerre. Member: Board of Governors, New York State Stock Exchange 1953–56, and Board of Governors, Association of Stock Exchange Firms 1946–51 (President 1949–50). *Clubs:* Maryland (Baltimore); Elkridge-Harford Hunt; Metropolitan (Washington); Bucks (London); Pilgrims of the United States, and The Links (both of N.Y.C.). *Address: office* 135 East Baltimore Street, Baltimore 2, Md., U.S.A.

**GRISWOLD, John Carroll.** American business consultant. *B.* 1901. *Educ.* Millikin Univ.; Hon. LLD (Decatur, Ill.). *M.* 1922, Louise Bessire. *S.* David Ross. *Dau.* Jacqueline Louise (Moore). *Career:* General Partner, Eastman Dillon, Union Securities & Co. 1964–72; W. R. Grace & Co. (Vice-Pres. 1949, Dir. 1950–72; Exec. Vice-Pres. 1955–64). Pres. & Dir., Griswold & Co. Inc. 1945–62, J. C. Griswold & Co. Inc. 1945–62, Griswold & Co. Inc. of California 1947–62; Metromedia Inc., Safety First Shoes Inc. *Trustee:* Millikin University; Postgraduate Inst. of Osteopathic Medicine and Surgery (also Treasurer); Athens College in Greece; New York Inst. of Technology. *Member:* Sigma Alpha Epsilon; Phi Delta Phi; Bd. of Govs., New York Coll. of Osteopathic Medicine. *Clubs:* U.S. Seniors Golf Association, The Links, The Brook, The Wall Street, The River (N.Y.C.); Chicago; Pacific Union (San Francisco); The Pilgrims of America, The Bohemian (San Francisco). *Address:* 375 Park Avenue, New York City, N.Y. 10022, U.S.A.

**GROENING, William Andrew, Jr.** American lawyer. *B.* 1912. *Educ.* University of Michigan (BA, JD). *M.* 1940, Virginia J. Gann. *S.* 2. *Daus.* 3. *Career:* With Legal Department of the Dow Chemical Co. since 1937, Assistant General Counsel 1951–67, General Counsel 1968–77, Assistant Secretary 1955–71, Vice-Pres. since 1971; Finance Cttee. mem. 1972–77; The Dow Chemical Company; Secretary and Director; Dow Corning Corp. Dir. Special Counsel 1977, Dow Chemical International; Director and Secretary, Kartridge Pak. Co. Republican. *Clubs:* Midland Country; Saginaw Valley Torch; Rotary Midland Country; Knights of Columbus. *Address:* 4204 Arbor Drive, Midland, Mich., 48640, U.S.A.

**GROMBACH, John V.** American; general business and public relations consultant, executive and director of various corporations since 1946. *B.* 1902. *Educ.* U.S. Military Academy (West Point): BS; CE. *M.* Olga Lohinecz 1959. Licensed professional engineer, New York. Cadet, West Point 1919–23; Officer, U.S. Regular Army, U.S. and overseas (resigned) 1923–28; Engineer, N.Y. Subway System and later for sound studio 1928–29; President Grombach Productions, Inc., and other companies, production radio and television programmes for national advertisers, recording for broadcasting sales, promotion and advertising counsel 1929–41; Colonel, War Dept. Gen. Staff 1941–46; Chief of Liaison Branch 1942–46; Legion of Merit; Commendation Medal; N.Y. State Distinguished Service Cross. Brig.-Gen. N.Y.N.G. Res. 1956—. President, Universal Service Corporation of Delaware; Industrial Reports Inc.; U.S. consultant to leading European and U.S. commercial and industrial organizations. *Publications:* The Saga of Sock, How to Box; Touch Football; The Olympics; The Olympic Cavalcade of Sports; Wine, Women and Duels; Army Athletic Manuals; 1964–68 Olympic Guide. *Member:* U.S. Olympic Games Cttee. 1956–68; U.S. Inter-collegiate Heavyweight Boxing Champion, 1922–23; U.S. Olympic Boxing Term, 1924, and of many international fencing teams, 1926–52; Runner-up, U.S. National Epée Open, 1929; winner U.S. National Epée Open, 1950; international competitor, rifle and pistol; Adv. coach, U.S. Olympic Modern Pentathlon Team 1928–64; Secretary General, International Fencing Federation 1960–64. *Address:* 40 Park Avenue, Newton, New Jersey, 07860 and *office* 111 West 57 Street, New York, N.Y. 10019. U.S.A.

**GROMYKO, Andrei Andreevich,** DScEcon. Soviet diplomat; *B.* 1909. *Educ.* Minsk Institute of Agriculture; Moscow Institute of Economics. *Career:* worked as senior research scientist of the Institute of Economics of the Academy of Sciences 1936–39; Editorial Secretary of Problems of Economics; entered Diplomatic Service 1939; directed American Department of the Commissariat of Foreign Affairs; Counselor, U.S.S.R. Embassy, Washington 1939–43; Amb. Ex. and Plen. to United States and En. Ex. and Min. Plen. to Cuba 1943–46; U.S.S.R. Representative on Security Council of U.N.O. 1946–48; participated in the Yalta and Berlin Conferences of the Great Powers; member, U.S.S.R. Delegations to U.N.O. Conference, San Francisco and First Session of General Assembly in London and New York; supervised U.S.S.R. Delegation's work at Dumbarton Oaks; Deputy to Supreme Soviet of the U.S.S.R. since 1946; Deputy Minister for Foreign Affairs 1947–52; Amb. Ex. and Plen. to Court of St. James's 1952–53; 1st Deputy Minister of Foreign Affairs 1953–57, Minister, Foreign Affairs since 1957. *Address:* Ministry of Foreign Affairs, 32–34 Smolenskaya-Sennaya Ploshchad, Moscow, U.S.S.R.

**GRÖNER, Hans Christian Brodtkorb.** Norwegian. *Educ.* Univ. of Oslo. *M.* 1950, Kari. *S.* 2 *Daus.* 2. *Career:* with Norske Shell 1947–60; Exec. Vice Pres. Borregaard A/S; Member of Aufsichtsrat in Borregaard Österreich Aktiengesellschaft; Chmn. of Bd., Rasch & Co. A/S; Chmn. of Cttee. of Shareholders' Reps. in Rena Kartonfabrik A/S; Member of the Board: A/S Denofa og Lilleborg Fabriker, Folldal Verk A/S, Borregaard Industries Ltd. (Norway), A/S And. H. Kiaer & Co. Ltd., Stabburet A/S, & A/S Securus. *Address:* Sarpsborg, Norway.

**GROOM, John Murray Stanley,** JP, FCA, FASA. Australian chartered accountant. *B.* 1905. *Educ.* Perth Modern Schl.; FCA, FASA. *M.* 1939, Mary Louise Wright (marriage diss.

1955). *S.* Peter John Flaxman. *Dau.* Penelope Jane Flaxman. Pres.: Federated Taxpayer's Associations of Australia 1954–55; Taxpayers' Association of Western Australia 1952–57; Australian Society of Accountants (W.A. Div.) 1957–59; Justices' Assn. of W. Australia 1957–58. President, Australian Society of Accountants 1962–64; Hon. Trustee and Councillor, The Justices Association of Western Australia 1952. Member: Royal Perth Hospital Board of Management 1967–75; Companies' Auditors Bd.; Parliamentary Salaries Tribunal (W. Australia). *Publications:* What Income Tax shall I Pay? (various editions to 1943); Modernizing Australian Tax Legislation (1959); Tax and Estate Planning (1961); various articles in technical journals. Member, Liberal Party of Australia. *Fellow:* The Inst. of Chartered Accountants in Australia, and The Australian Socy. of Accountants (Foundation General Councillor), created life member 1968. *Clubs:* Weld, Perth, C.T.A. (all of Perth). *Address:* Lawson Flats, 6 Esplanade, GPO Box A29 Perth W.A. 6001; and *office* 191 St. George's Terr., Perth, W. Australia.

**GROOM, Sir (Thomas) Reginald.** Australian chartered accountant and company director. *B.* 1906. *Educ.* Brisbane Grammar School, and Univ. of Queensland; BA, BCom. *M.* 1932, Jessie Mary Grace Butcher, OBE, BA. *S.* Edward Graeme and Peter Roy. *Dau.* Elaine. *Career:* Lord Mayor of Brisbane 1955–61. Chairman Greater Brisbane Town Planning Committee 1958–61; Dir. M. I. M. Holdings Ltd.; Consolidated Rutile Ltd.; P. & O. Australia Ltd.; Chmn. Woodland Ltd.; Elder Smith Goldsbrough Mort Ltd.; Chmn. Queensland Adv. Bd.; Governor Australian Elizabethan Theatre Trust. *Member:* Australian Nat. Airlines Commn. 1961–75; C'wealth Banking Corp. 1962–73. *Clubs:* Queensland, Johnsonian (Brisbane); Athenaeum (Melbourne), Union (Sydney). *Address:* 31 Jerdanefield Tower, Jerdanefield Rd., St. Lucic, Brisbane; and *office* Watkins Place, 288 Edward Street, Brisbane, Qld., Australia.

**GROOT, Per. S.** Danish Diplomat. *B.* 1924. *Educ.* Graduated in Law, Copenhagen Univ., 1949. *M.* 1974, Inger Sorensen. *S.* 1. *Dau.* 1. *Career:* Sec., Min. of Foreign Affairs 1949–54; First Sec., NATO Secretariat, Paris 1954–57; First Sec., Min. of Foreign Affairs 1957–61; Dep. Perm. Rep., NATO, Paris 1962–64; Head of Dept., Min. of Foreign Affairs 1964–67; Asst. Under-Secy. of State, Min. of Foreign Affairs 1967–73; Amb. to the GDR 1973–76; Amb. to Tokyo & Seoul 1976. Pres., Danish Lawyers' Assoc. 1970–73. *Decorations:* Officer, Order of Dannebrog (Denmark); Officer, Order of Tadj (Iran); Commander, Order of Merit (Italy). *Address:* c/o Ministry of Foreign Affairs, DK-1218 Copenhagen, Denmark.

**GROS, Andre.** French. Judge at the International Court of Justice, The Hague. *B.* 19 May 1908. *M.* 1940, Dulce Simoes Correa. *S.* François, Marcel. Professor of Public Law, Universities of Nancy (1934), Toulouse (1937), Rio de Janeiro (1939), Poitiers (1945); Legal Adviser to French National Committee, London 1943; Delegate, U.N. War Crimes Commission 1943–48; to the European Advisory Commission 1944–45; Legal Counsellor, French Embassy, London 1946–47; Legal Adviser, French Delegation to Peace Conference, Paris 1946; to Council of Foreign Ministers 1946–50; member, Permanent Conciliation and Arbitration Commission between Denmark and Greece (1949) and Chairman of Commission between Denmark and Turkey (1953); Legal Adviser to The Ministry of Foreign Affairs (1947), First Delegate to Central Rhine Commission 1950; Agent of French Government to International Court of Justice 1950; member, Permanent Court of Arbitration 1950; Counsellor of State 1954. Member, Institute of International Law 1965; member, International Law Commission 1961; Judge 1964; Member, Court of Arbitration Argentine-Chile 1976 & France-United Kingdom 1976. *Publications:* Survivance de la raison d'Etat (1932); Le statut international actuel de l'Egypte (1937); Les problemes politiques de l'Europe (1942) (translated into Spanish 1943); La condition juridique de l'Allemagne (1947); Les recours contre les decisions d'organismes internationaux (1950), La conciliation internationale (1956); La négociation diplomatique (1958); La conservation des ressources de la haute mer (1959); Traites et Documents diplomatiques (1960). L'enquête du Tavignano (1968). Commander of the Legion of Honour, Croix de Guerre (1939–45). *Address:* 12 Rue Beaujon, Paris 8, France.

**GROSE, Frederick Trerice.** Australian insurance executive and company director. *B.* 1911. *Educ.* St. Peter's Coll., Adelaide, S.A. *M.* 1938, Laura Lillian Fanning. *S.* Peter F. and Douglas J. *Career:* With Commercial Union Assurance Co., Adelaide 1927. A.I.F. 1942–45 (7th Div. Engineers). Asst. Manager for Queensland, Manufacturers' Mutual Insurance Ltd. 1952. Queensland Mgr. 1953, N.S.W. Mgr. 1957, Asst. Gen. Mgr. 1961, General Manager, The Western Australian Insurance Co. (Canberra) Ltd. 1961; Gen. Mgr. Manufacturers' Mutual Insurance Ltd. Sydney 1962; Man. Dir. The Western Ins. Co. (Canberra) Ltd. 1962; Dir. A.I.A. Insurance Ltd; The Australian Aviation Underwriting Pool Pty. Ltd; Famua (N.S.W.) Ltd; Federation Manufacturers Life Assurance Co. of Australasia Ltd.; Fed. Retirement Ltd.; Victory Reinsurance Co. of Aust. Ltd.; The Worker's Compensation Pool of N.S.W. Ltd. *Member:* Royal Commonwealth Socy.; Executives' Assn. of Australia; Royal Australian Historical Society. *Clubs:* The Australian; Royal Sydney Yacht Squadron; New Zealand Services; Elanora Country; Palm Beach Golf. *Address:* 30 Bilga Avenue, Bilgola Plateau, N.S.W.; and *office* Manufacturers Mutual Insurance Ltd., Head Office, 60 York St. Sydney, N.S.W., Australia.

**GROSSE, Aristid Victor.** Research chemist *B.* 1905. *Educ.* Dr. Engin., Technische Hochschule, Berlin-Charlottenburg, Germany. *M.* 1932, Irene Lieven. *S.* Aristid Victor, Jr. *Career:* Research Chemist, Kaiser Wilhelm Inst. for Chem., Germany 1927–28; Isolated Pa (element 91) 1927; Med. Analysis Laboratories, Shanghai 1928–39; Research Associate, Technische Hochschule 1929–32; Visiting Asst. Prof., Dept. of Chemistry, Univ. of Chicago 1931–40; Research Assoc., Universal Oil Products Co., Chicago 1930–35 (Assoc. Dir. of Research 1935–40); fission of Pa, 1939; John Simon Guggenheim Research Fellow, Dept. of Physics, Columbia Univ. 1940–41; associate with H. C. Urey in war research labs., Columbia Univ. (Manhattan Project) 1942–43; Consultant on synthetic rubber, Houdry Process Corp., Philadelphia since 1942; Chief Consultant on synthetic rubber, W. P. B., Washington 1942–43; Dir. of Research, Houdry Labs., Houdry Process Corp. 1943–48. Member of American Rubber Mission to Soviet Union 1942–43. President, Germantown Laboratories Affiliated with The Franklin Institute, formerly The Research Institute of Temple University, Philadelphia since 1948. *Member:* Amer. Chemical Socy.; Amer. Assn. for Advancement of Science; Amer. Physical Socy.; Amer. Inst. Aero & Astro.; Sigma Xi. *Award:* Special Recognition from U.S. Atomic Energy Commission, discovery of U235-fission and dev. Oak Ridge Diffusion Process for separating U235. *Publications:* (with E. Krause), Chemie der Metallorganischen Verbindungen, (1937); numerous scientific papers. Specialized in catalytic chemistry of hydrocarbons, radioactivity, high temperature research; flame studies; new oxidizers and fuels for rocket propulsion and detonation; ozone studies; containment of liquid metallic substances up to 5000°K and properties of liquid metals (density, viscosity, electrical and thermal conductivity, self-diffusion, vapor pressure) up to their ctitical temperature; noble gases, solidification. efflux time, natural life of soap bubbles, liquid pillars, desert agriculture. Republican. *Address:* 456 Glynwynne Road, Haverford, Pa. 19041; and *office* 4150 Henry Avenue, Philadelphia, Pa. 19144, U.S.A.

**GROSSENBACHER, Marcel (Alfred).** Swiss diplomat. *B.* 12 Aug. 1913. *Educ.* Lic en D. *M.* 1915, Hélène Steiner. *Dau.* 1. *Career:* Secretary in Swiss Fed. Military Administration 1939–46; Vice-Consul, Bregenz, 1946–47; Jurist, Fed. Political Dept. 1947–49; 2nd Sec., Legation Prague, 1949–53; 1st Sec., Teheran 1953–56; adjoint Federal Political Dept., Berne 1956–58; Counsellor of Embassy, Tokyo 1958–63; Moscow 1964–67; Ambassador in Manilla 1967–70, in Buenos Aires 1970–75 & in Canberra since 1976. *Address:* c/o Swiss Embassy, 7 Melbourne Avenue, Canberra/Forrest, ACT 2603, Australia.

**GROSSMAN, Allan.** Canadian Government Official. *B.* 1910. *Educ.* Jarvis & Harbord Collegiate Schs.; Grad. Univ. of Toronto Extension Course; Dr. Criminology (Hon.), Univ. of Ottawa 1971. *M.* 1936, Ethel Audrey Starkman. *S.* 1. *Daus.* 2. *Career:* Alderman, Toronto City Council 1952–55; Charter Mem., Met. Toronto Council 1953–55; Mem., Ont. Legislative Assembly 1955–75; Minister without Portfolio 1960–63 & Chief Comm. Liquor Control Bd. of Ontario; Minister Reform Instns. 1963–68; Minister Correctional Services 1968–71, Trade & Development, & Responsible for Housing 1971–72; Minister of Revenue & Responsible for Housing 1971–74, also Vice-Chmn. Mgmt. Bd. of Cabinet 1972–74; Provincial Sec. for Resources Devel. 1974–75, also Mem. Mgmt. Bd. Cabinet; Mem. Pol. & Priorities, Bd. of Cabinet; appointed Chmn. of Criminal Injuries Compensation Bd. 1976. Bd. Dirs. Jewish Nat. Fund: Past Nat. Pres. Jewish Immigrant Aid Services; Bd. Dirs., St. Alban's Boys Club,

Mt. Sinai Hosp., Canadian Found. Jewish Culture, Hon. Dir. Jewish Vocational Service, Baycrest Centre for Geriatric Care, Mem. Assn. C.L.U.'s., Mem. Progressive Conservative Party, Jewish Religion. Mem. B'Nai B'rith (Past Pres. Toronto Lodge). *Clubs:* Primrose; Canadian, R.A.M., Mount Sinai Lodge A.F. & A.M., Variety. *Address:* 325 Rosemary Road, Toronto, Ont. M5P OE4, Canada; & *office* 505 University Avenue, 3rd Floor, Toronto, Ont. M5G 1X4, Canada.

**GROSSMANN, Bernd.** American. *B.* 1928. *M.* 1952, Dora Maria. *S.* 2. *Career:* Gen. Mgr. Herder & Herder Inc. New York 1959–61; Vice Pres. Prentice-Hall International Inc; United Kingdom European Div. 1961–69; Man. Dir. Int. Book Distributors Ltd. 1961–69; Pub. Dir. Int. Holt Rinehart & Winston Inc. 1969–70; Exec. Vice-Pres. and Chief Exec. Officer (N.Y.) Springer-Verlag New York Inc. *Address:* Short Hill Road, Croton-on-Hudson, N.Y. 10520, U.S.A.; and *office* 175 Fifth Avenue, Suite 1900, New York, N.Y. 10010, U.S.A.

**GRØSTAD, Einar Johan.** Norwegian civil servant. *B.* 3 Aug. 1902. *Educ.* University of Oslo (Cand. jur.); NATO's Defence High School Paris. *M.* 1932, Liv Vinje. *S.* Paul Michael, Finn. *Career:* Judge 1928; Secretary in the Ministry of Finance 1930, Chief of Division 1935; Chairman, State War Risk Hull Insurance; member, U.N.E.S.C.O. Advisory Panel on Finance and Administration 1948; Dir. General Economy and Law, Ministry of Defence 1948–54; Director, Ministry of Finance 1954–72; Chmn. Norwegian Bd. Nordic Admin. Assn. 1963–71. *Awards:* Knight 1st Class, Order of St. Olav; Commander, Order of Danneborg, Commander, with Star Order of Yugoslav Flag. *Address:* Sigbjørn Obstfelders v. 12, Oslo 3, Norway.

**GROSVENOR, Melville Bell.** *B.* 1901. *Educ.* U.S. Naval Academy (BS 1923). *M.* (1) 1924, Helen North Rowland; and (2) 1950, Anne E. Revis. *S.* Alexander Graham Bell, Gilbert Melville, and Edwin Stuart. *Daus.* Helen Rowland (Lemmerman) and Sara Anne. *Career:* Emeritus Chairman of the Board and Editor, National Geographic Society, Washington, D.C. 1967— (current membership: worldwide 9,651,162; United Kingdom and Republic of Ireland 161,008; other Commonwealth nations 1,021,640). Dir.: Riggs National Bank; member: Board of Trustees, The George Washington Univ., Univ. of Miami. President and Editor, National Geographic Society, 1957–67. *Publications:* numerous articles in National Geographic Magazine (which grew from 2 million to 6 million in circulation under his editorship); Editor in Chief: Man's Best Friend, the Book of Dogs (revised edition); America's Wonderlands, The National Parks (enlarged edition 1966, 650,000 copies total); Wild Animal of North America; America's Historylands, Landmarks of Liberty; Men, Ships and the Sea; National Geographic Atlas of the World (rev. ed. 1970; 260,000 copies total); Great Adventures with National Geographic; Wondrous World of Fishes; Song and Garden Birds of North America; Water, Prey and Game Birds of North America; This England; Everyday Life in Bible Times; Greece and Rome; Builders of Our World; The Age of Chivalry; The Renaissance. Hon. ScD, Univ. of Miami 1954; LLD, George Washington Univ. 1959; LittD, Boston Univ. 1970. *Awards:* Hon. DSc. Univ. of New Brunswick; *Clubs:* Cruising Club of America; Cosmos, Metropolita, Chevy Chase Country, National Press. *Address:* 5510 Grosvenor Lane, Bethesda, Md.; and *office* National Geographic Society, Washington, D.C. 20036, U.S.A.

**GROVER, Sir Anthony.** British. *B.* 1907. *Educ.* Westminster Schl. *M.* 1931, Marguerite Beatrice Davies. *S.* Anthony Michael. *Dau.* Sheila Margaret Alison (Smyth). *Career:* Chmn. of Lloyd's 1959–60. Chairman: Lloyd's Register of Shipping, 1963–73; and Lifeguard Assurance Ltd. 1964–76. *Awards:* Cmdr.; Order of Leopold II (1967); Orange Nassau (1968); Commander Order of Dannebrog (1972). *Clubs:* White's; Pratt's; Guards; Golf; Royal St. George's Golf (Sandwich); Hon. Company of Edinburgh Golfers; Rye Golf, Swinley Forest Golf; Woking Golf. *Address:* Dial Cottage, Firbank Lane, St. John's, Woking, Surrey.

**GROVES, Wallace.** American financier. *B.* 1901. *Educ.* Georgetown University, Washington, D.C. (BSc, MA. LLB, LLM); Hon. LLD Ursinus College, Collegeville, Pa, *M.* 1940, Georgette Cusson. *S.* Gordon, Gary and Graham. *Daus.* Gene and Gayle. *Career:* Founder The Grand Bahama Port Authority Ltd., Freeport, Bahamas 1955. Practised law until 1931; engaged in reorganization and management of industrial and financial concerns from 1931 to World War II, during which time engaged in construction and government war projects. In 1955 founded Freeport, Bahamas, under special act of Govt. of Bahamas with broad concessions for 99 years under agreement to build a deep-water free port and to develop an industrial and financial area. The Grand Bahama Port Authority Ltd. is the corporation operating the concessions. *Address:* P.O. Box 5, Freeport, Bahamas and P.O. Box 340, 939 Coral Gables, Florida 33134.

**GRUBER, Karl.** Austrian statesman. *B.* 3 May 1909. *Educ.* Universities of Innsbruck and Vienna (Dr. jur.). *M.* 1939, Helga Ahlgrimm. With Post Administration 1934–38; dismissed by Nazis as a pronounced opponent 1938 and found employment in private industry, simultaneously studying Jurisprudence, joined resistance movement in which he assumed a leading part; under his leadership the Tyrol was practically cleared of Nazidom prior to the arrival of Allied troops; re-organized the administration of Tyrol and was Governor of Tyrol 1945; member (O.V.P.), Nationalrat and Minister of Foreign Affairs since 1945; Vice-President, O.E.E.C. 1949–54; Ambassador to U.S.A. Mar. 1954; Special Adviser to the Director-General, International Atomic Energy Agency, 1958; Ambassador to Spain 1961; to Fed. Republic of Germany 1966; to U.S.A. 1969; to Switzerland 1972; Secy. of State in the Fed. Chancellery (Ret'd.). *Publications:* Politik der Mitte; Voraussetzungen der Vollbeschäftigung; Zwischen Freiheit und Befreiung; Die Letzte Chance Der Freien (by Politicus); Ein Politisches Leben (Molden Ed. 1976). *Address:* Rennweg 6a, 1030 Vienna, Austria.

**GRUENTHER, General Alfred M.** American army officer (retd.). *B.* 1899. *Educ.* U.S. Mil. Acad. Instructor, West Point 1927–32; Asst. Professor and Instructor 1934–36 and 1937–38; Chief of Staff, Third Army 1941–42; Deputy Chief of Staff, Allied Force H.Q. 1942–43: Chief of Staff, Fifth Army 1943–44, 15th Army Group 1944–45; Deputy Commanding General, U.S. Forces in Austria 1945; Deputy Commandant, National War College 1945–47; Director, Joint Staff, Joint Chiefs of Staff 1947–49; Deputy Chief of Staff for Plans and Combat Operations, Army General Staff 1949–51; Chief of Staff, S.H.A.P.E., 1951–53; Supreme Allied Commander, Europe 1953–56; President American Red Cross, Jan. 1957–64. Director: Pan American World Airways 1960–72; New York Life Insurance Co. 1960–73; Dart Industries Inc. since 1964; Federated Department Stores since 1964; Chairman, English-Speaking Union of U.S. 1966–68. Hon. President World Bridge Federation. *Member:* Board of Trustees Institute for Defense Analyses since 1964; President's Committee on Arms Control and Disarmament 1966–69, also Cttee. on Foreign Assistance 1965–69; Business Council, Council on Foreign Relations; Executive Cttee., Atlantic Council; President's Commission on an All-Volunteer Armed Force 1969–70. Hon. degrees from 38 colleges and universities. *Address:* 4101 Cathedral Avenue, N.W. Washington, D.C. 20016, U.S.A.

**GRUNBERG, J. Julien.** American. *B.* 1902. *Educ.* Inst. Superieur de Commerce de l'Etat (Antwerp), University of Brussels (BCom and Consular Sc), and Oxford University extension (proficiency in English with honours). *M.* 1949, Lorraine M. Levine. *Dau.* Mrs. Ghity H. Penney. *Career:* Naval War Correspondent, United Press and British United Press 1942–46; War Correspondent, Palestine Post 1942–43. Manager, Oppenheimer & Co. (members New York Stock Exchange) 1954–59. Managing Director: Establissements Bamco (Egypt) 1934–50, and National Bottling Co. (Pepsi-Cola, Cairo, Egypt) 1948–51. Chairman of Board, Pennsylvania Securities Co. Division, Pennsylvania Life Co. (brokers and general insurance agents) 1960—. Director, Glenwood Securities Inc. Lecturer, Upsala Coll., East Orange, N.J. Instructor, West Orange Adult Schl. 1956—. *Member:* Philadelphia Baltimore Stock Exchange 1961–63 (Assoc. Mem., 1968—); Natl. Assn. of Securities Dealers 1959—; Assn. of N.J. Securities Dealers; Legislative Cttee., Livingston Arts Assn. (Chmn. Pres. 1966–69). *Publications:* Belgium Carries On (1943); Market Comments (weekly column) in Newark Star Ledger and Scranton (Pa.) Times; The War at Sea (Cairo Broadcasts 1942–45); numerous articles on naval and economic affairs. Democrat. *Address:* Llewelyn Gates, 24 Hutton Avenue, Apt. 44, West Orange, N.J. 07052, U.S.A. and *office* 44 Glenwood Avenue, East Orange, N.J., 07017, U.S.A.

**GUDMUNDSSON, Gudmundur I.** Ambassador of Iceland. *B.* 1909. *M.* 1942, Rosa Ingolfsdottir. *S.* 4. *Educ.* Reykjavik Gr. S.; Univ. of Iceland (Law Grad.). *Career:* Solicitor and Barrister 1934–39; Barrister to Supreme Court 1939; Member Central Cttee., Social Democrats 1940–65, Vice-Chmn.

1954–65; Sheriff and Magistrate 1945–56; Member of Parliament (Athling) 1942–65; Minister of Foreign Affairs 1956–65; Min. of Finance 1958–59; Chmn. Icelandic Del. to U.N. Conference on Law of the Sea (Geneva) 1958, 1960; Ambassador of Iceland to U.K. 1965–71, and concurrently to Netherlands, Spain and Portugal; Ambassador to U.S.A. 1971–73; Ambassador to Sweden since 1973, & concurrently to Finland & Austria. *Member:* Board of Directors, Fishery Bank in Reykjavik 1957–65. *Awards:* Comdr. with Star, Order of Falcon, 1957; Est. of Rep. Medal, 1944; Grand Cross Order of White Rose (Finland), North Star (Sweden), Orange-Nassau (Netherlands), Chene (Lux.), Southern Cross (Brazil), St. Olav (Norway), Phoenix (Greece); Hon. K.B.E. *Address:* Embassy of Iceland, Kommendorsgatan 35, 114 58 Stockholm, Sweden.

**GUERRA, Ruy de Camoes Teixeira.** Portuguese ambassador. *B.* 1902. *Educ.* University of Lisbon (graduated in Law) and School of Public Administration, Harvard University. *M.* 1925, Mariana de Calça e Pina. *S.* António. *Daus.* Maria da Graça and Helena. *Career:* Practised Law in Lisbon 1925–32. Entered Portuguese Foreign Service 1932; held diplomatic and consular posts in Canada, Germany, U.S.A., Great Britain and France. Portuguese representative in committee of European Economic Co-operation, Paris 1947; Head, Portuguese Delegation to O.E.E.C. until Jan. 1956; Chairman of Executive Committee of latter organization Feb. 1955–Jan. 1956, when he was appointed Director-General of Economic Affairs, Ministry of Foreign Affairs; held this post until July 1960. Ambassador to Switzerland, 1960–67; Head of Portuguese Delegations to E.F.T.A. 1960–67; and G.A.T.T. 1962–67. Led Portuguese delegations in numerous bilateral negotiations and attended several meetings of NATO and the Economic Commission for Europe; led Portuguese Delegation leading to establishment of E.F.T.A. and accession of Portugal to G.A.T.T.; Leave of absence 1967–70; recalled to active service 1970; Chmn. of the Interministerial Commission for External Economic Co-operation, led at Official level the Portuguese Delegation, negotiations between Portugal and the European Economic Communities. Signed in Brussels, July 22nd 1972, with the Portuguese Minister for Foreign Affairs the Treaty between Portugal and the Common Market. *Awards:* Portuguese and foreign include: Grand Cross of the following Orders, Christ of Portugal, North Star (Sweden), Order of Merit (Federal Republic of Germany), St. Olav (Norway), Southern Cross (Brazil), Order of the Crown (Thailand); Order of Merit (Spain), Grand Officer, Legion of Honour (France), Order of the Phoenix (Greece), Order of Leopold (Belgium), Officer, Orange-Nassau (Netherlands). *Address:* Rua de Angola, 2, Paco de Arcos, Portugal.

**GUIDOTTI, Gastone.** FRSA. Italian diplomat. *B.* 1901. Entered Diplomatic Service 1925. Vice-Consul: Zürich 1926, Dortmund 1928; Consul, Pernambuco 1930; Secretary, Prague 1932; Head of Dept., Ministry for Foreign Affairs, Rome 1935; First Sec.: Belgrade 1938, Stockholm 1942. Italian Rep. to the Allied Governments in London 1945. In charge of Legation: Prague 1945, Athens 1946. Head of Liaison Office of Ministry for Foreign Affairs with the Allied Government in Trieste 1947; Director General of Political Affairs, Ministry for Foreign Affairs, Rome; and member of various Italian Delegations to NATO Conferences 1948; Head of Italian Representation to UNO 1951. Ambassador: Belgrade 1955, Vienna 1958, Bonn 1961 and London 1964–68; Counsellor of State, Rome since 1968. *Clubs:* Unione (Florence), Circolo della Caccia (Rome). *Address:* Piazza Cap Di Ferro No. 13, Rome, Italy.

**GUILD, Henry Rice.** American lawyer (retired from partnership). *B.* 1896. *Educ.* Noble & Greenough, Harvard Coll. (AB 1917), and Harvard Law School (LLB 1922). *M.* 1927, Martha Pintard Bayard. *S.* Henry R., Bayard S. *Dau.* Sheila (Iselin). *Career:* Ensign and Lieut., (J.G.), Chief Quartermaster, U.S.N., World War I, Partner, Herrick, Smith, Donald, Farley & Ketchum (now Herrick & Smith) 1922, now Counsel; Gen. Chmn. Greater Boston Community Fund Campaign 1941; Chmn. Exec. Ctte. of Greater Boston Community Fund 1944–46; Chmn. of Advisory Council of Massachusetts Dept. of Public Welfare 1945–46; Formerly: Pres. and Dir. of Massachusetts Hospital Life Ins. Co.; Dir. and Member of Exec. Cttee.; Boston Edison Co. and Massachusetts Audubon Soc.; Dir. and Exec. Cttee. of Fiduciary Trust Company. *Director:* Massachusetts Investors Growth Fund, Tampa Electric Co., Massachusetts General Life Insurance Co., Boston Fund; *Trustee:* Boston Personal Property Trust, Century Shares. Public Reservations; Vice President, Trustee, Massachusetts General Hospital. *Clubs:* Longwood Cricket (Pres. 1932–35); Harvard (Boston—Pres. 1951–53) New England Lawn Tennis Assn. (Pres. 1936–37); Badminton & Tennis (Governor). *Address:* 1150 South Street, Needham, Mass 02192; and *office* 100 Federal Street, Boston, Mass. 02110, U.S.A.

**GUILD, Robert Park.** British company director. *B.* 1905. *Educ.* Glasgow Academy and Sedbergh School. *M.* 1930, Elizabeth Wainwright Hamilton. *S.* Robin Hamilton and David Park. Chairman, Vogue Ltd. *Address:* 4 Taverngate Hawksworth, Guiseley, Yorks.

**GUILLAUMAT, Pierre.** French civil servant. *B.* 1909. Formerly student of the Polytechnique School; and the Paris Mining School; Engineer of the Mining Corps. *Career:* Chief, Service of Mines in Indo-China, and later in Tunis 1934–43; Chief of the Petroleum Division and Chairman of the Petroleum Bureau 1945–58; President of the Atomic Energy Commission 1951–58. Minister of the Armed Forces 1958; Deputy to the Prime Minister 1960–62; Pres.: Union Générale des Pétroles 1962–65; Electricité de France 1964–66, Entreprise de Recherches et d'Activités Pétrolières 1966–77; Société Nationale Elf-Aquitaine 1966–77. *Award:* Grand Officer Legion of Honour; Croix de Guerre (1939–45). *Address:* 7 rue Nélaton, Paris 15, France.

**GULBRANSEN, Olav.** Norwegian. *B.* 1899. *Educ.* Commercial School and High School. *M.* 1929, Olga Danielsen. Has varied business and banking experience; studied banking laws, political economy, industrial management and foreign languages. Managing Director, Håndverkernes Sparebank, Oslo. *Awards:* Badge of Honour from Oslo Håndverks- og Industriforening; and The King's Gold Medal of Merit. *Address:* Sofies Gate 16, Oslo, Norway.

**GULDBERG, Ove.** Danish politician. *B.* 1918. *Educ.* MSc (Civil Eng.); Graduate in Law. *M.* 1921 Else Christiansen. *S.* 3. *Career:* With Vejle City Admin. 1942; with K. Hindhede, Civi. Eng. Contractor 1943; City Engineer's Office, Copenhagen 1944–46; Res. Lab. Min. of Fisheries 1946–47; mem. Central Cttee, Inst. of Danish Engineers 1946–48; Secy. 1948, Dir. 1952–65; Man. of the building, Inst. of Danish Engs. 1956; Liberal mem. Folketing Parlt. 1964–77; Min. for Transport and Communications 1968–71; Mem. European Parlt. 1973–74; Min. for Foreign Affairs 1973–75; Vice-Pres., European Parlt. 1975. *Member:* Sec. Conf. of Reps. from Eng. Socs. of W. Europe and U.S.A. (E.U.S.E.C.) 1955–58; Civil Defence Union (pres. 1962–65); Civil Defence Council 1962–68; Inst. of Danish Civil Engineering; American Socy. of Civil Engineering. *Decorations:* Commdr. Order of Dannebrog (1st Class); Grand Cross St. Michael and St. George; Grand Cross Tyske Forbundsrepublik Grand Cross St. Olav, Norge; Grand Cross Det Jugoslaviske Flag; Orden del Merito Civil. *Address:* Skovvangen 18, DK 2920 Charlottenlund, København, Denmark.

**GULICK, Merle Amerson.** American. Life insurance executive. *B.* 1906. *Educ.* Hobart Coll., Geneva, N.Y. (BS). *M.* 1962, Helen Hindmarsh. *S.* Peter Lee. *Career:* Vice-Pres., Public Corporate Affairs Equitable Life Assurance Society of the U.S. N.Y.C. Legion of Merit. Capt. U.S.S.G.R. Chairman: Board of Trustees, Hobart and William Smith Colleges, Geneva, N.Y. 1956–68; Exec. Committee. American Cancer Society Inc., N.Y. Div. 1964—; Insurance Cttee., 1966–68, Special Cttee, on Urban Affairs, N.Y. Chamber of Commerce. Pres., Natl. Cncl. on Alcoholism 1963–65. Chmn. Greater N.Y. Men's Cttee. United Negro Coll. Fund 1953, and of Greater N.Y. Cttee. Natl. Fund for Medical Educn. 1955. Member: Exec. Cttee. and Bd., Football Foundation and Hall of Fame 1959; Board of Directors, Natl. Assn. for Prevention of Blindness 1965—; Council of Executives on Company Contributions of Natl. Industrial Conf. Bd. 1965; Health Insurance Inst. Assn. Public Relations Cttee. 1965; Inst. Life Ins. Adv. Cttee. on Co. Public Relations 1961; Adv. Cttee. on Vocational Education of City of N.Y., N.Y. Chamber of Commerce 1966. LLD Hobart Coll.; Marts & Lundy Medal; Natl. Football Hall of Fame. *Member:* P.R. Socy. of America; Newcomen Socy.; Holland Socy. Sons of Amer. Revolution; Reserve Officers Assn.; Coast Guard League. *Clubs:* Overseas Press; Touchdown; Hobart (N.Y.); Madison Square Garden; River (N.Y.). *Address:* and *office* Equitable Life Assurance Society of the U.S., 1285 Avenue of the Americas, New York, N.Y. 10019, U.S.A.

**GÜMRÜKÇÜOĞLU, Rahmi Kamil.** Turkish Diplomat *B.* 1927. *Educ.* Haydar Pasha Lycee, Istanbul; Faculty of Political Sciences, Ankara Univ.; Masters Degree in Political

Economy & Government, Harvard Univ., U.S.A. *M.* 1956, Elcin Makbule Benice. *S.* 1. *Dau.* 1. *Career:* Turkish Embassy, London, 2nd Sec. 1952–58, 1st Sec. 1958; Head of Section dealing with International & Economic Affairs, Ministry of Foreign Affairs, Ankara 1958–60; Counsellor at Turkish Embassy, Cairo 1960–63; Dep. Dir.-Gen., Dept. of International & Economic Affairs, Min. of Foreign Affairs, Ankara 1963–65; Head of Special Bureau dealing with Co-operation between Turkey & the Soviet Union 1965–67; Dir.-Gen. of Dept. of International & Economic Affairs 1967–71; Turkish Ambassador to Council of Europe, Strasbourg 1971–75; Turkish Ambassador to Iran since 1975. *Publications:* Various Articles & Booklets on Foreign Investment, Questions of Economic Development, Soviet Economic Development, Economic Integration amongst developing countries. *Address:* Turkish Embassy, 314 Avenue Ferdowsi, Tehran, Iran.

**GUNA-KASEM, Pracha.** Thai Diplomat. *B.* 1934. *Educ.* Dhebsirindra Sch., Bangkok; Marlborough Coll.; Hartford Coll., Oxford—BA (Hons.) & MA in Jurisprudence; Yale Univ.—MA & PhD in International Relations. *M.* 1962, Sumanee Chongcharoen. *S.* 1. *Career:* Chief of Section, Political Div., Dept. of International Organization 1960–61; 2nd Sec., SEATO Div., Dept. of Int. Org., & Alternate Member for Thailand in the Permanent Working Group 1962–63; Royal Thai Embassy, Cairo 1964–65; Chief, Foreign News Analysis Div., Information Dept. 1965–69; Chief, Press Div., Information Dept. 1970–71; Thai Consul-General, Hongkong 1971–73; Dir.-Gen., Information Dept. 1973–75; Ambassador & Perm. Rep. of Thailand to the UN since 1975. *Member:* Siam Society; Council on World Affairs & International Law, Bangkok; Oxford & Cambridge Soc., Bangkok. *Decorations:* Knight Grand Cross, Order of the Crown of Thailand; Knight Commander, Order of the White Elephant. *Publications:* Domestic Jurisdiction in the League of Nations & the UN (1956); The Thai-Indo-Chinese Dispute 1939–41 (1957); Thailand & the UN 1945–57 (1959). *Clubs:* Royal Bangkok Sports; Navatanee Golf. *Address:* 19 Fanshaw Avenue, Yonkers, New York 10705; and *office* 20 East 82nd Street, New York, N.Y. 10028, U.S.A.

**GUNDERSON, Harvey.** American, corporation executive and lawyer. *B.* 1906. *Educ.* Univ. of Michigan, AB, JD. *M.* 1933, Alwayne Burkhart. Director: Glenn L. Martin Co., Baltimore 1947–50; Denver & Rio Grande R.R. Co. 1949–51; Eastern Representative, Transamerica Corp. 1950–53; Dir., Reconstruction Finance Corp. 1945–50. President and Director, Wylin Corporation. Director: Columbia Corp. Pres. Capitol Parking Inc. Republican. *Address:* 3335 Stuyvesant Place N.W., Washington, D.C. 20015, U.S.A.

**GUNDY, Charles Lake.** Canadian investment dealer. *B.* 1905. *Educ.* Appleby College, Oakville, Ont., and University of Toronto. *M.* 1939, Virginia Diana Antoinette Ritchie. Hon. LLD, Univ. of Toronto 1969. *Career:* Chairman and Director, Wood Gundy Ltd., Toronto; Director: Abitibi Paper Co. Ltd., Canada Cement Lafarge Ltd.; Massey-Ferguson Ltd.; Simpsons Ltd.; Simpsons-Sears Ltd.; United Corporations Ltd.; Hon. Chmn., Board of Trustees, Hospital for Sick Children, Toronto. *Member:* Toronto, Montreal and Canadian Stock Exchanges; Hon. member, Canadian Socy. for Clinical Investigation 1966; Hon. Pres. Investment Dealers' Assn. of Canada. Chmn., Senior Advisory Cttee., Investment Dealers' Assn., of Canada 1969. Zeta Psi Fraternity. *Clubs:* Toronto; Toronto Golf; York (Toronto); Mount Royal, St. James's (both of Montreal); Vancouver; Canada (London, England); Beaver Winter; Hunt Gun; Griffith Island; Glenmajor Angling. *Address:* 43 Russell Hill Road, Toronto, Ontario, Canada.

**GUNN, Nigel Hamilton.** Canadian. *B.* (Edinburgh, Scotland) 1910. *M.* 1938, Eleanor Jessie Secord. *S.* Neil H. *Dau.* Patricia H. *Career:* President, Investment Dealers' Association of Canada 1956–57; Chmn. Bd. and Dir. Bell Gouinlock & Co. Ltd.; Governor Toronto East General Hosp. *Clubs:* Rosedale Golf; National; Toronto Cricket, Skating & Curling. *Address:* 255 Glencairn Avenue, Toronto, Ont. M5N IT8 Canada.

**GUNN, Sir William Archer,** KBE, CMG. Australian grazier and company director. *B.* 1914. *Educ.* The King's School, Parramatta, N.S.W. *M.* 1939, Mary Phillipa Haydon. *S.* Bill Haydon. *Daus.* Helen Rosemary (Savill); Mary Isabel (Evans). *Career:* Chairman: Australian Wool Board 1963–72; International Wool Secretariat 1961–73; Queensland Advisory Board, Development Finance Corp., 1962–72; *Chairman:* Cattle Investments Ltd.; Livestock Mgmt. Pty. Ltd.; Gunn Devel. Pty. Ltd.; Eagle Corp. Ltd.; Moline Pastoral Co. Pty. Ltd.; Unibeef Aust. Pty. Ltd.; Roper Valley Pty. Ltd.; Coolibah Pty. Ltd.; Mataranka Pty. Ltd. Director: Rothmans of Pall Mall (Australia) Ltd.; Clausen Steamship Co. (Aust.) Pty. Ltd.; Walter Reid & Co. Ltd.; Grazcos Cooperative Ltd.; Gunn Rural Management Pty. Ltd. *Member:* The Commonwealth Bank Board 1952–59; Australian Meat Board 1953–66; Australian Wool Bureau 1951–63 (Chairman 1958–63); Australian Woolgrowers' Council 1947–60 (Chairman 1955–58); Grazier's Federal Council of Australia 1950–60 (Pres. 1951–54); Australian Woolgrower's and Graziers' Council 1960–65; Export Development Council 1962–65; Australian Wool Testing Authority, 1953–63); International Wool Secretariat 1958. (Chmn. 1961–73); Council of the Natl. Farmers' Union of Australia 1951–54; Reserve Bank Board 1959—; Executive Cncl., United Graziers Assn. of Qld. 1944–69. (Pres. 1951–59). (Vice-Pres. 1947–51); CSIRO State Cttee. 1951–68. Faculty of Veterinary Science, Queensland Univ. 1953—; Queensland Board, National Mutual Life Assn. of Australasia, 1955–67; Aust. Wool Corp. 1973. Chmn., The Wool Bureau Inc., New York, 1962–69. *Trustee:* Queensland Cancer Fund. Justice of the Peace. *Awards:* Coronation Medal 1953; CMG 1955; KBE (Civil) 1961; Golden Fleece Achievement Award 1962; Award of Golden Ram (NWGA of SA). *Clubs:* Queensland (Brisbane); Union (Sydney); Tattersalls (Brisbane). *Address:* 98 Windermere Road, Ascot, Brisbane, Qld., 4007 Australia; and *office* Wool Exchange, 69 Eagle Street, Brisbane, Qld., 4000 Australia.

**GUNNENG, Arne.** Norwegian diplomat. *B.* 1914. *Educ.* Oslo Univ.; LLB. *M.* 1939, Ingrid Fleischer. *Daus.* 3. *Career:* First Secretary, Embassy, Washington 1945–48; Chief of Division, Ministry of Foreign Affairs, Oslo 1948–50; Chargé d'Affaires, Warsaw 1950–51; Counsellor, Embassy, Stockholm 1951–52; Deputy permanent Representative to North Atlantic Council, Paris 1952–55; Ambassador to Canada 1955–59; Director Gen. of Political Affairs, Ministry of Foreign Affairs, Oslo 1959–62; Ambassador to Sweden 1962–66, to U.S.A. 1966–73; to Italy since 1973. *Address:* Via di Porta San Sebastiano 13/A, 1-00 179 Rome, Italy.

**GUNNING, J. Henry.** American aircraft engineer. *B.* 1905. California Institute of Technology and Massachusetts Institute of Technology (BS 1928). *M.* 1938, Violet R. Bartosh. Associate Fellow, Institute of Aeronautical Sciences. Sales Engineer, Steelform Contracting Co., Los Angeles 1928–29; Engineer, Douglas Aircraft Co. Inc., Santa Monica 1929–36; charge of Aircraft Weight and Balance Control 1936–41; charge of Engineering Standards and member of National Aircraft Standards Committee (representing Douglas Aircraft Co.) 1941–43; Asst. Exec. Engineer 1943–47; Research Engineer on Special Weapons Project 1947–49; Strength Engineer; 1949–57, Structures Engineer 1957–65; Senior Engineer/Scientist 1965–67; Consulting Engineer 1967—. Manufacturer of Caddie Chum Golf Carts 1949—. U.S. Army Air Corps Reserve Officer 1928–42; Registered Professional Engineer in Civil and Mechanical Engineering, State of California. *Member:* Beta Theta Pi, Scabbard & Blade, and Gnome Club. *Address:* 211 South Rockingham Avenue, Los Angeles, Calif. 90049, U.S.A.

**GUNTER, John Wadsworth.** American. *B.* 1914. *Educ.* Univ. of North Carolina (BS Com 1935; MA 1939; PhD 1942). *M.* (1) 1939, Lola Hatcher (*Div.* 1963), (2) 1970, Margaret Dozier Underwood. *Daus.* 2. *Career:* With U.S. Treasury Dept.; Economist 1941–47; served as Treasury Representative in Cairo 1943–44 and London 1946–47; Deputy Director, Office of International Finance 1947–48; Associate Professor of International Trade, Univ. of Texas 1948–49; U.S. Member of Greek Currency Committee, Athens 1949–51; Alternate U.S. Representative, Tripartite Commission on German Debts, London 1951–53; Asst. Dir., then Acting Dir., Middle Eastern Dept., I.M.F. 1953–77; Consultant on International Finance, the First Boston Corp. *Member:* Phi Beta Kappa; Beta Gamma Sigma; Amer. Economic Assn.; Southern Economic Assn. *Address:* 7024 Buxton Terrace, Bethseda, Maryland 20034, U.S.A.

**GURNHAM, Charles Frederick.** American. President, Gurnham and Associates Inc., Pollution Control Consultants. *B.* 1911. *Educ.* Yale Univ. (BS 1932) and New York Univ. (MChE 1940; DEngSc 1942). *M.* 1934, Vivian Wikander. *S.* Robert Henry and Roy Frederick. *Daus.* Sandra (Barman) and Diane (LaPorte). *Career:* 17 years in industry 1932–49. Chmn., Dept. of Chemical Engineering, Tufts Univ. 1949–52, and similar position at Michigan State Univ. 1952–61. Chmn., Dept. of Environmental Engineering, Illinois Institute of Technology, 1962–68; Dir., Peter F. Loftus Corp., Pittsburgh. Honour: Distinguished alumni citation, N.Y. Univ. 1955; Amer. Inst. Plant Engrs., Mr. Pollution Control 1970; *Member:* Alpha Chi Sigma; Phi Lambda Upsilon; Sigma Pi Sigma; Sigma Xi; Tau Beta Pi; Amer. Inst. Chem. Engrs.; Amer. Socy. Civil Engrs.; Amer. Chem. Socy.; Amer. Inst. Chemists; Amer. Acad. Environment Engrs.; Water Pollution Control Federation. *Publications:* (books) Industrial Wastewater Control (1965); Principles of Industrial Waste Treatment (1955); also numerous articles and chapters. *Address:* 505 N Lake Shore Drive, Chicago, 60611; and *office* 223 W. Jackson Boulevard, Chicago, Ill. 60606, U.S.A

**GUSHMAN, John Louis.** Lawyer and corporation executive. *B.* 1912. *Educ.* Ohio State Univ. (BA 1934; JD 1936) and Inst. of Management, Northwestern Univ. (Certificate of Completion). *M.* 1937, Helen Louise Little. *S.* John Louis, Jr. *Daus.* Sally (Gillespie) and Susan (Fetters). *Career:* Admitted to Ohio Bar 1936; practised law with Williams, Eversman & Morgan, Toledo, Ohio 1936–47; Owens- Illinois Inc. 1947–61; Pres., Owens-Illinois International 1953–61. Chmn. of the Bd. Chief Executive Officer and Director, Anchor Hocking Corp., Lancaster, Ohio; Director: Dana Corp.; Huntington Bancshares Inc.; Western Electric; Libby-Owens-Ford; F. W. Woolworth Co.; Keyes Fibre Co.; The Richman Bros. Co.; *Chairman and Director:* Anchor Hocking Interm. Corp.; Anchor Hocking Puerto Rico Ltd.; Anchor Cap & Closure Corp. of Canada Ltd.; Premier Plastics Ltd.; Ravenscroft Ltd.; *President and Director:* Standard Glass Mftg. Co., *Director:* Plastics Inc.; The Phoenix Glass Co.; Moldcraft Inc. *Member:* American Bar Assn.; Order of the Coif; Phi Beta Kappa; Phi Delta Theta; Lancaster Country Club; Trustee, Ohio State University. *Address:* 6 Timberlance Heights, Lancaster, Ohio 43130; and *office* Anchor Hocking Corp., Lancaster, Ohio 43130, U.S.A.

**GUT, Gottlieb,** Dr jur. Swiss diplomat. *B.* 31 July 1912. *Educ.* Berne, St. Gallen, London. *Career:* First Secretary of Legation at Belgrade; Chargé d'Affairs (en pied), Bucharest 1956; Counsellor of Embassy, Stockholm, 1957; Counsul General, Saigon 1961. First Chief of Section in the Federal Political Department, Berne 1964; Ambassador Guatemala, Honduras, El Salvador, Panama, Nicaragua, Costa Rica. *Publications:* Schicksal in Freiheit (1965). *Address:* Département Politique Fédéral, Berne, Switzerland.

**GUTIERREZ-OLIVOS, Sergio.** Chilean diplomat and international lawyer. Grand Cross of Libertador San Martin. *B.* 1920. *Educ.* Sacred Heart School, Santiago (Bachelor); Catholic Univ. of Chile (Lic. in Law and Lawyer); Inter-American Law Inst., N.Y.C. (post-grad. studies). *M.* 1945, Margot Yrarrázaval Larrain. *S.* Sergio, Rodrigo and Juan Francisco. *Career:* Law practice with Sergio Gutiérrez Olivos & Sons (Chile); Assoc. Prof. in Civil Law 1944 and Prof. of International Law, Catholic Univ. 1951 (Dir. of Univ. School of Law 1951–54). Delegate to Quadripartite negotiations on S. Pacific Maritime Zone 1955, U.S. Conf. on Law of the Sea (Geneva 1958), Consultative meeting, Minister of Foreign Affairs (Santiago 1959), and Punta del Este Economic Conf. 1961. Chmn. Chilian Management Assoc., 1958–59; Member, Business Advisory Cttees; O.A.S.: Interamerican Bank (BID); & Latin American Advisory Cttee. of International Business. Ambassador: to Argentina, 1959–62; to U.S.A. 1963–65. *Publications:* Compromise Agreements before Law and Judicial Decisions (1945); Territorial Sea and Modern Law (1955); Alberdi (1963); Chilean Development Banks (1965); The Brain Drain and the Chilean Case (1965). *Member:* Chilean Bar Assn.; Spanish Bar Assn.; Chilean Management Assn.; Amer. Socy. of International Law: Spanish-Portuguese-American Inst. of Law. *Address:* Bandera 341 of, 757 Santiago, Chile.

**GWINN, William Persons.** American. *B.* 1907. *Educ.* Gunnery Prep. School; Dr Eng (Hon.), Rensselaer Polytechnic Inst.; Dr Sc (Hon.), Trinity College. *M.* (3rd) 1970 Rachel Coleman Witman. *S.* William Clark and Michael Persons. *Dau.* Linda Clare. *Career:* General Manager, Pratt & Whitney Aircraft Div. UAC, 1944–56: with United Aircraft Corp.: Vice-Pres. 1946, Pres. and Dir. 1956–58; Former Chairman, Chief Executive Officer until 1972, Former Dir. United Aircraft Corp., East Hartford, Conn. until 1974. Director: Shell Oil Co.; Connecticut Mutual Life Insurance Co.; F. & M. Schaefer Corporation. Dir., Hartford Hospital. Trustee: Rennsselaer Polytechnic Institute of Connecticut, Inc.; Marine Historical Assn., Inc.; Mystic Seaport; Life Trustee, Trinity College, Hartford. Chmn., U.S. Industrial Payroll Savings Bonds Cttee., 1968. Member, Industry Advisory Council, Dept. of Defence; Trustee, Naval Aviation Museum Association. Republican. *Clubs:* Hartford Golf; New York Yacht; Essex Yacht; Conquistadores del Cielo; Fishers Island Country; Delray Beach Yacht; Everglades, Palm Beach; Country (Florida). La Coquille (Palm Beach); Key Largo (Anglers). *Address:* 3060 South Ocean Boulevard, Palm, Beach, Florida 33480, U.S.A.

**GWYNNE-EVANS, Sir Ian William,** Bt. British. *B.* 1909. *Educ.* Royal Naval College, Dartmouth. *M.* (1) 1935, Elspeth Collins; and (2) 1946, Monica Dalrymple. *Daus.* 2 (by first marriage). *Career:* In Royal Navy 1922–34, and again 1939–45. Chairman. Real Estate Corporation of South Africa Ltd. 1950–73; Joint Deputy Chmn. (merger with Guardian Assurance Group) since 1973. *Club:* Rand (Johannesburg). *Address:* 57 Eastwood Road, Dunkeld, Johannesburg; and *office* 201 Palace Buildings, 52 Pritchard Street, Johannesburg, South Africa.

**GYORY, Jean Charles Henri.** Belgian. *B.* 1923. *Educ.* Univ. of Louvain. *M.* 1952, Mona Morren. *S.* 1. *Dau.* 1. *Career:* Dir. Pres. & Pub. Relations Belgian National Tourist Office; Secy. Gen. Belgian Congress Association. *Award:* Commander of Merit, Italian Republic. *Address:* 72 Rue Armand Campenhout, Brussels, 5, Belgium and *office* 7 Blvd. de l'Imperatrice, Brussels.

# H

**HAAK, Jan Friedrich Wilhelm.** South African. *B.* 1917. *Educ.* BA, LLB. *M.* 1954, Maria Theron. *S.* 1. *Daus.* 2. *Career:* Attorney, Bellville, Cape Town 1945–46; Advocate, Cape Bar 1960; Mayor of Bellville 1949–52; MP 1953–70. Deputy Minister of Economic Affairs 1961–64; Department Minister of Mines 1962–64; and Deputy Minister of Planning 1962–64. Minister of Mines and Planning 1964–67. Minister of Economic Affairs 1967–70; Pres. Afrikaans Handelsinstitute 1976. *Member:* Chief Council of Nationalist Party 1951–71.; Nationalist Party. *Club:* Here Sewentien. *Address:* 8 Governor Street, Welgemoed, Bellville, Cape, South Africa.

**HAASTRUP, Prince Adedokun.** Nigerian. Legal Practitioner & Notary Public; Chmn. S.I.ME (Nigeria); Proprietor, Adehunmi Oruleola Trading Co. & A. Haastrup Enterprises, 1976—. *B.* 1921. *Educ.* LLB Hons. (London); Barrister at Law of the Middle Temple; Postgraduate Studies in International Law, Comparative, Constitutional Law, Administrative Law & Local Government. *M.* 1948, Olabisi Sadare. *S.* 3. *Daus.* 2. *Career:* A.D.O. & acting Asst. Local Inspector 1954–56; Private Sec. to the Premier Western Nigeria 1956; Acting Trade Officer, Western Nigeria Office, London 1957; various diplomatic positions in Washington, D.C. & New York 1957–60; Counsellor, Ministry of External Affairs 1961–64; High Commissioner to India 1964–66; Ambassador to Ethiopia 1964–68; Ambassador to Western Germany 1968–73; Ambassador to Italy, Spain & Greece & High Commissioner to Cyprus 1973–76; Perm. Rep. to F.A.O. 1975–76. *Member:* Mem. & Vice-Chmn., UN Cttee. on the Elimination of Racial Discrimination 1970–74, Chmn. 1974–76. *Publications:* Problems of International Law, Diplomatic Relations & Reciprocity—an address to the Indian Society of International Law & the Indian Academy of International Law & Diplomacy, 1965. *Clubs:* Metropolitan; Island; Saturday Circle; Four Hundred; All Lagos; Nigeria Society. *Address:* Prince Chambers, 10 Alhaji Ribadu Road, S.W. Ikoyi, Lagos, Nigeria.

**HABACH, George F.** American engineer. *B.* 1907. *Educ.* Stevens Inst. of Technology (ME 1929) and Polytechnic Institute of New York (MME 1936); Dir. Eng. (Hon.) 1977. *M.* 1939, Helen S. Wislicenus. *Dau.* Elizabeth M. *Career:* With Worthington Corporation; successively Development Engineer, Application Engineer, and Product Engineer, Centrifugal Pumps 1929–45; Chief Engineer, Cent. Pumps and Compressors 1945–51; Manager of Engineering, Harrison Div. 1951–55; Vice-Pres. Engineering 1955–59, Vice-Pres. Admin. 1959–67; Vice-Pres. Administration and Engineering, 1964–67, Pres. 1969–70; Worthington Corp. 1960–69; Vice-Pres. Administration Studebaker Worthington Inc. 1967–71; Vice-Pres. and Dir. management Div. Creative Logic Corp. Pres: Worthington Foundation; Consultant, Burns & Roe; with Polytechnic Inst. of Brooklyn: Instructor, Evening Undergraduate School 1937–44; Adjunct Professor 1944–52, Trustee 1971—; Citizenship Cttee., New Jersey Chamber of Commerce; Advisory Cttee., Dept. of Mechanical Engineering, Newark College of Engineering. 87th Pres., American Socy. of Mechanical Engineers (1968–69). President, Stevens Alumni Assns. 1969–70; American National Standards Inst., Dir. since 1971, Mem. Board of Standards Review since 1972, Chmn. since 1975; Stevens Inst. of Technology, Trustee since 1973; United Eng. Foundation, Trustee since 1972. *Fellow:* Amer. Socy. of Mechanical Engineers; Standards Engineers Socy.; Engineers Club (Life Member); Natl. Socy. of Professional Engineers; Tau Beta Pi; Pi Tau Sigma. *Publications:* Control of the Engineering Functions in a Decentralized Company; Management Opportunities and Problems in Standardization; Importance of Continuing Education of Engineers—A Company Case Study. *Club:* Engineers N.Y.C. *Address:* 20 Cambridge Road, Glen Ridge, N.J., 07028, U.S.A.

**HABICHT, Frank H.** American. *B.* 1920. *Educ.* Purdue Univ. (BSME). *M.* 1943, Jeanne Patrick. *S.* Frank H. H. *Daus.* Pamela and Patricia. *Career:* U.S. Naval Officer 1942–46. Previously with George Gorton Machine Co.; Clearing Machine Corp.; Kellog Switchboard & Supply Co.; Chmn. Pres. United Technical Corporation; Pres. & Dir. Marshall & Huschart Machinery Co.; M. & H. Engineering Co.; Dir. Paxall Corp; American Sip Corp. (Swiss); Security Industrial Co.; Consolidated American Life Insurance Co.; Sterling Precision Corp.; Manitou Systems, Inc.; Vice Chmn. Dir Cone-Blanchard Machine Col (U.S.); Dir. Cone-Blanchard Machine Co. Ltd. (U.K.). *Member:* Amer. Socy. of Mechanical Engineers; Amer. Machine Tool Distributors' Assn. (Pres., 1957–58); Aircraft Owners' and Pilots' Assn.; Dir. and mem. exec. cttee. Fabricating Manufacturers Assn.; Exec. Council, National Industrial Conference Board. *Publications:* Modern Machine Tools (Van Nostrand Co., N.Y., London, Toronto, 1963). *Address:* 2801 South 19th Avenue, Broadview, Illinois 60153, U.S.A.

**HABICHT, Max.** Swiss international lawyer. *B.* 6 Mar. 1899. *Educ.* Universities of Neuchatel, Berne, Berlin, Zurich and Harvard (Dr jur utri, Zurich, and Dr sc jur, Harvard). *S.* John-Peter. *Dau.* Margareta. *Member:* Geneva Bar; Legal Section, League of Nations Secretariat 1934–39. Assistant Diplomatic Adviser to U.N.R.R.A. 1944–45; Lecturer, Hague Academy of International Law 1934. *Publications:* Die Erbschaftsteilung im schweizerischen Recht; The Exception of Public Order and the Application of Soviet Laws (American Journal of International Law, vol. 21, 1927); Post-War Treaties for the Pacific Settlement of International Disputes (1931); Le pouvoir du juge international de statuer *ex aequo et bono* (1934); The Special Position of Switzerland in International Affairs (vol. 39, International Affairs, London) (1953); Proposals of World Federalists for United Nations Charter Revision (1954); Conflict Resolution by Peaceful Means (1966); Co-founder of World Movement for World Federal Government. *Address:* Rebwisstrasse, CH 8702 Zollikon, Switzerland.

**HACKER, Louis Morton.** American university professor, author and editor. *B.* 17 Mar. 1899. *Educ.* Columbia College and Columbia University (AB, AM, LHD) MA (Oxford), LLD (Hawaii). *M.* (1) 1921, Lillian Lewis (*D.* 1952), and (2) 1953, Beatrice Larson Brennan (*D.* 1977). *S.* Andrew. *Dau.* Betsy Dexheimer. *Career:* Asst. editor, New International Encyclopedia, 1923–25 and 1928–29; contributing editor, New International Yearbook, 1924–35; asst. editor, Encyclopedia of Social Sciences, 1932–34; contributor, Columbia Encyclopedia, 1934–35. Harmsworth Prof. of American History at Oxford 1948–49; Fellow of Queen's College; Prof. of Economics (since 1948) and Dean of the School of General Studies, Columbia University 1949–58; Chmn., Academic Freedom Cttee., Amer. Civil Liberties Union. Editor, American Century Series. *Publications:* United States since 1865 (1932); Farmer is Doomed (1933); Short History of the New Deal (1934); The United States: a Graphic History (1937); American Problems of To-day (1938); Triumph of American Capitalism (1940); Shaping of the American Tradition (1947); England and America: The Ties that Bind (1948); The New Industrial Relations (1948); Government Assistance to Universities in Great Britain (1952); The United States in the Twentieth Century (1952); Capitalism and the Historians (1954); Alexander Hamilton in the American Tradition (1957); American Capitalism (1957, trans. into several languages); Larger View of the University (1961); Major Documents in American Economic History (2 vols., 1961), The World of Andrew Carnegie, 1865–1901 (1968); The Course of American Economic Growth and Development (1970); Proskauer: His Life & Times (with M. D. Hirsch) (1977). *Address:* 430 West 116th Street, New York 10027, U.S.A.

**HACKERMAN, Norman.** American educator and research chemist. *B.* 1912. *Educ.* Johns Hopkins Univ. (AB 1932; PhD in chemistry 1935). *M.* 1940, Gene Allison Coulbourn. *S.* Stephen Miles. *Daus.* Patricia Gale, Sally Griffith and Katherine Elizabeth. *Career:* Assistant Prof. 1945, Assoc. Prof. 1946, Univ. of Texas; Research Eng., Manhattan Dist. Project at Kellex Corp., N.Y.C. 1944; Asst. Prof. Virginia Poly. Inst. Blacksburg, Va.; 1941–43; Chemist, U.S. Coast Guard Station, Staten Island, N.Y. 1939–41; Asst. Prof., Loyola Coll., Baltimore, Md. 1935–39; Research Chemist, Colloid Corp., Baltimore 1935–40. Professor of Chemistry 1950—; Technical Ed., Journal of the Electrochemical Society 1950—; Chairman Dept. Chemistry 1952–61, and Dean of Research and Sponsored Programmes 1960–61; Vice-President and Provost, Univ. of Texas 1961–63; Vice-Chancellor for Academic Affairs, Univ. of Texas, 1963–67. President, Univ. of Texas, at Austin, 1967–70. President Rice Univ. since 1970; Bd. Gordon Research Conf. 1970. National Science Board, National Science Foundation since 1968, Chmn. since 1974. *Member:* U.S. Nat. Acad. Scis. 1971; Board of Editors of Monograph Series of the American Chemical Socy. 1956–64; Amer. Chemical Socy; Amer. Philosophical 1972; Hon. member, Electrochemical Society 1973. *Awards:* 1965 Southwest Regional Award of the Socy.); Electrochemical Socy. Palladium Medallist, 1965; selected to give 16th Joseph L. Mattiello Memorial Lecture, 1964); Faraday Socy.; Amer. Assn. for Advancement of Science; National Assn. of Corrosion Eng. (winner of their Whitney Award); Phi Lambda Upsilon; Sigma Xi; Alpha Chi Sigma (all scientific societies); Phi Kappa Phi (honor society). *Clubs:* River Oaks Country; Houston (Houston). *Address:* President's House, Rice University; and Dept. of Chemistry, Rice University, P.O. Box 1892, Houston, Texas 77001, U.S.A.

**HADDOW, Sir (Thomas) Douglas,** KCB. British. *B.* 1913. *Educ.* George Watson's Coll., Edinburgh; Edinburgh Univ. (MA (Hons.)); Cambridge Univ. (BA Hons.). *M.* 1942, Margaret Ross Steven Rowat (*D.* 1969). *S.* David George and Christopher Sloan. *Career:* Secretary Dept. of Health for Scotland 1959–62, and Scottish Development Department 1962–64; Permanent Under-Secy. of State Scottish Office 1965–73; Chmn. North of Scotland Hydro-Electric Board since 1973. *Awards:* Hon. LLD Univ. of Strathclyde (1967), FRSE (1968); Hon. D. Litt Heriot-Watt Univ. (1971) *Clubs:* Royal Commonwealth Society (London). *Address:* The Coach House, Northumberland Street Lane S.W., Edinburgh, EH3 6JD; and *office* 16 Rothesay Terrace Edinburgh EH3 7SE.

**HADFIELD, Lloyd Dyson.** Australian. *B.* 1922. *Educ.* BSc, BE (Hons). *M.* 1956, Cherie Anne Rudder. *Daus.* 3. *Career:* With A.I.F. 1942–46. Research Engineer, E.M.I. Ltd. 1948–53; Senior Scientific Officer, Dept. of Supply (Aust.) 1953–55; Dir., Technical Services, Australian Broadcasting Commission 1955–60; Chief Engineer (Electronics) Clyde Industries Ltd., Sydney 1960; Gen. Mgr., Automatic Electric Telephones Pty. Ltd. 1961; Product Planning Executive, Plessey Pacific, Sydney 1965–66. General Divisional Manager, Plessey M. & T. Divisions, 1966–70; Managing Dir. Aust. and New Zealand Region, Plessey Pacific Ltd. (Aust.) since 1971. *Publications:* a number of articles (particularly television) and patents. *Member:* MIEE; FIE (Aust.), FAIM. *Clubs:* Pymble Golf. Australasian Pioneers; Sydney Rotary. *Address:* 5 Pibrac Avenue, Warrawee, New South Wales 2074, Australia; and *office* Plessey Pacific Pty. Ltd. Commonwealth Street, Sydney, Australia.

**HADOW, Sir Michael,** KCMG, *B.* 1915 *Educ.* Berkhamsted School and Cambridge Univ. (MA). *M.* 1976, the Hon. Mrs.

Michael Sieff. *Career:* With Indian Civil Service 1937–47; Private Secretary to Minister of State, Foreign Office 1949–52; Head of Levant Dept., Foreign Office 1958–59; Counsellor, Paris Embassy, 1959–62; Head, News Dept., Foreign Office 1962–65; H.M. Ambassador to Israel, 1965–69 and to Argentine 1969–72; Chmn. Anglo-Israel Association since 1976. *Club:* Travellers' (London). *Address:* Quorn House, Hingham, Norfolk.

**HÆKKERUP, Per Christen.** Danish statesman. *B.* 1915. *M.* Grete Hækkerup. *S.* Klaus, Hans and Niels. *Career:* Chairman, Social Democratic Youth of Denmark 1946–52; Member of the Folketing (Parliament) 1950 (elected to Social Democratic Party); General Secretary, International Union of Socialist Youth 1946–54; Member, City Council of Copenhagen 1946–50, and of Consultative Assembly, Council of Europe 1953–71; Appointed to Foreign Affairs Committee of the Folketing 1955. Member Nordic Council 1957–71; President, Danish Society 1960; Head of Danish Delegations to UN 1961; Foreign Minister, Sept. 1962–66; Minister, Economic and Budget Affairs 1971–73; Minister of Economic Affairs 1975 & concurrently Minister for Trade 1976–77. Member Folketing Parliament. *Publications:* Danish Foreign Policy, 1965; formerly an editor, has contributed articles on economic policy to Social-Demokraten (now Aktuelt). *Address:* Stubberup, 4880 Nysted, Denmark.

**HAEUSSERMANN, Dr.-Ing. Walter.** American. *B.* 1914. *Educ.* Institutes of Technology of Stuttgart (Vordiplom/BS 1935) and Darmstadt (Dipl. Ing/MS 1938, and Dr-Ing/PhD 1944). *M.* 1940, Ruth Knos. *Career:* Asst. Engineering Office, Science and Engineering Directorate, George C. Marshall Space Flight Centre, Nat. Aeronautics and Space Admin.; Member Auburn Univ. Graduate Faculty, Ala. since 1966; Chmn., Space Cttee. of International Federation of Automatic Control. *Awards:* Exceptional Civilian Service Award, Department of the Army 1959; National Aeronautics and Space Administration Medal for Outstanding Leadership 1963; ION Superior Achievement Award 1969; NASA Exceptional Service Medal 1968 and 1969. *Member:* (Fellow) Amer. Astronautical Socy.; Inst. of Navigation (ION); (Fellow) Amer. Institute of Aeronautics and Astronautics; Sigma Xi; Rocket City Astronomical Association. *Publications:* some 25 works on space vehicles, space carrier vehicles, Saturn launch vehicles, guidance and control, aeronautical research and development, etc. *Address:* 1607 Sandlin Avenue S.E., Huntsville, Ala. 35801; and *office* NASA, George C. Marshall Space Flight Center, Huntsville, Ala. 35812, U.S.A.

**HAFFNER, Charles C., Jr.** American manufacturer. *B.* 15 Mar. 1895. *Educ.* Yale (AB). *M.* 1925, Clarissa Donnelley. *S.* Charles C. *Daus.* Clarissa G., Frances Ann, Phoebe Louise. *Career:* Served World War II, Major-General, U.S. Army; Director and Chairman of Finance Committee, R. R. Donnelley & Sons Co., Chicago. *Awards:* Distinguished Service Medal (U.S.A.); Légion d'Honneur; Croix de Guerre avec Palme (France). Independent. *Address:* 2223 King Drive, Chicago, Ill. 60616, U.S.A.

**HAFSLUND, Bjørn Arnulf.** Norwegian public affairs manager. *B.* 1919. *Educ.* Master of Arts. *M.* 1944, Sonja R. Brekke. *Daus.* Marit Sonja and Astrid Bergliot. *Career:* Previously: Manager, Swedish Relief to Norway; Headmaster, Commercial High School, Drammen; Associate Professor, Oslo University; Asst. Director of Public Relations, Scandinavian Airlines System and Information Section, Norwegian Fed. of Industry, Oslo; Former Pres. Norwegian Public Relations Assn. Author of various textbooks on Economic Geography. *Address:* Konvallvn 28, Sandvika, Baerum, Norway; and *office* A/S Norske Esso, Oslo, Norway.

**HAFSTAD, Lawrence Randolph,** PhD. American Physicist. *B.* 1904. *Educ.* Univ. of Minnesota (BSc 1926) and Johns Hopkins Univ. (PhD (physics) 1933). *M.* 1949, Mary Cowan. *S.* William A. Engr. N. W. Bell Telephone Co. 1920–28; Assoc. Physicist, Carnegie Instn. 1928–33, Physicist 1933–45; Member National Defense Research Commission, Office of Scientific Research and Development 1941–46. From Research Physicist to Director, Applied Physics Laboratory, Johns Hopkins Univ. 1942–47; Exec. Secy. Research and Development Board, Dept. of Defense 1947–49. Director, Inst. of Co-operative Research Johns Hopkins Univ. 1947–49; Director, Nuclear Reactor Development Div., Atomic Energy Commission 1949–55; Atomic Energy Div., Chase Manhattan Bank 1955; Vice-Pres., General Motors Corp. Research Laboratories 1955–69; Chairman, General Advisory Committee, Atomic Energy Commission 1962— (Chmn. 1964). Ad Hoc Consultant, Executive Office of the President, Navy Department, and Department of Defense. Chairman, Board of Advisers, Naval Postgraduate School. Trustee: Johns Hopkins University and Carnegie Endowment for International Peace. Member, Board of Regents, Tulane University, Cranbrook Institute of Science, and General Motors Institute. Member-at-Large, National Research Council (National Academy of Sciences). Member, Nat. Academy of Engineering. *Publications:* more than 120 scientific. *Awards:* Medal of Merit, U.S.N. 1946; King's Medal for Defence of Freedom, British Govt. 1946; Distinguished Service Award, Atomic Energy Commn. 1954. Proctor Prize, Scientific Research Socy. of America 1956. Charles F. Kettering Award, Patent Inst., George Washington Univ., 1967; Sisquiantannial Award, Univ. of Mich. 1967; Atomic Energy Commission Citation, 1968; Nuclear Socy. Inst. of Electric & Electronic Engineers. *Member:* Amer. Assn. for Advancement of Science; Geophysical Union; Scientific Research Socy. of America. *Clubs:* Cosmos (Washington); Orchard Lake (Michigan) Country; Century Association (N.Y.C.); Economic (Detroit). *Address: office* National Acad. of Sciences, Washington, D.C., U.S.A.

**HAFSTEIN, Johann.** Icelandic. *B.* 1915. *Educ.* University of Iceland, Cand. jur. 1938; Further studies in International Law, University of London. *M.* 1938, Ragnheidur, born Thors. *S.* Haukur, Johann, Julius, Petur Kristjan. *Career:* General Secy. Independence Party, 1940–52; Member, City Council of Reykjavik, 1946–58; Member, Althing Parliament 1946—; Director, The Fisheries Bank of Iceland 1952–63; Representative of Iceland, UN Assembly, 1953 and 1959; Nato Parliamentarian Conference, 1955–64; Rep. and Head of Delegation to the Council of Europe, 1961–64; President, Board of Directors of the Development Bank of Iceland, 1955–56 and 1961–67, when the Development Fund of Iceland took over the functions of the Bank 1970–71; Minister of Justice, Ecclesiastic Affairs, Health & Industry 1961 and 1963–70; President of the Board of Directors of the Fund 1967–71; Minister of Industry & Prime Minister 1970–71; Vice Chmn. Independence Party 1965–70, Chmn. 1970–73. *Publications:* Numerous articles on Politics in newspapers and magazines. *Awards:* Grand Cross of the Icelandic Order of the Falcon; Grand Cross of the Norwegian Order of St. Olav; Grand Cross, Order of Couronne de Chenne; The Medal of the Church of Skalholt Icelandic. *Address:* Sjálfstaedisflokkurinn, Laufásvegi 46, Rekjavik, Iceland.

**HAGEMANN, H(enry) Frederick, Jr.** Bank executive. *B.* 1906. *Educ.* Washington Univ. (BSc). *M.* 1940, Leita Perkins Amory. *S.* Henry Frederick Hagemann III. *Daus.* Louise, Amory, Helen Ann and Leita. Municipal Bond Dept., Kauffmann-Smith & Co., St. Louis, 1926–29; Boatman's National Bank, St. Louis, 1929–46, Vice-Pres. 1938–46; Pres., National Rockland Bank of Boston 1948–61; Pres. combined institution, State Street Bank and Trust Co. Boston 1961–65, Chmn. and Pres. 1965–71 Chmn. Bd. 1970–71; Dir. and member Exec. Cttee. State Street Bank since 1971. Director and Member of Finance Committee, New England Mutual Life Insurance Co.; Southwestern Public Service Co., Dallas, Texas; Petrolite Co., St. Louis; Trustee and Member of Investment Committee, Provident Institution for Savings in Boston. Pres., 18th Street Building Co., St. Louis. Member: Northeastern Univ. Corp., Sigma Chi, Beta Gamma Sigma. *Clubs:* Country (Brookline); Somerset, Algonquin (Boston); Kittansett (Marion). *Address:* 548 Point Road, Marion, Mass.; and *office* 225 Franklin Street, Boston, U.S.A.

**HAGEN, Everett Einar.** *B.* 1906. *Educ.* St. Olaf Coll. (BA); Univ. of Wisconsin (MA; PhD). *M.* 1937, Ruth Alexander. Instructor in Economics, Michigan State Coll. 1937–42; Federal Government 1942–48 (including Director, Division of Planning, Office of War Mobilization & Reconstruction 1945–46, and Fiscal Economist, Bureau of the Budget 1946–48); Prof. of Economics, Univ. of Illinois 1948–51 (Chmn. of Dept. 1950–51); Economic Adviser, Government of the Union of Burma 1951–53; Visiting Professor of Economics, M.I.T. 1953–59, Professor 1959–72; Professor Emeritus since 1972; Dir. Center for International Studies 1970–72; Consultant to various foreign govts. since 1956. *Publications:* Handbook for Industry Studies (1958); On the Theory of Social Change: How Economic Growth Begins (1962); The Economics of Development (1968); numerous articles, including Population & Economic Growth (1959); An Economic Justification for Protection (1958). Editor, Planning Economic Development (1963). *Member:* American Economic Association; Royal Economic Society; Phi Beta Kappa; Amer. Acad. of Arts & Sciences. *Address:* 65 Pasture Road, Cataumet, Mass 02534; and *office* Massachusetts Institute of Technology (Center for International Studies), Cambridge, Mass. 02139, U.S.A.

**HÄGERSTRÖM, Sven (Haaken).** Finnish company director. *B.* 29 Mar. 1906. *Educ.* LLB. *M.* 1935, Ruth Elisabeth Mellin. *S.* 1. *Daus.* 2. *Career:* Assistant Manager, The Paper Exporters of Finland 1935–38 (Managing Director 1939–45); Director, Finnish Cellulose Union Finncell 1945–52; Man. Dir. 1952–71; Chmn. Suomen BP Oy (The British Petroleum). *Awards:* Finnish Cross of Liberty (Cl. 3 and Cl. 4); Commander Cl. 1; Order of Finnish Lion; Knight Commander, Order of British Empire; Commander Order of White Rose (Finland), Commander Order of Vasa (Sweden) and of St. Olav (Norway). *Address:* Rehbindervägen, 3, Helsinki, 15, Finland.

**HAGGERTY, Lawrence G.** American business executive. *B.* 1916. *Educ.* Marquette University College of Engineering (BMech Eng). *M.* 1942, Mary Ellen Sweeney. *S.* Michael, Patrick and Timothy. *Daus.* Catherine (Lenahan), Eileen (Mundy), Margaret, Sheila, Maureen and Monica. *Career:* R.C.A. Victor, Div. of RCA, various management positions leading to Man. of Manufacturing, Radio and Television Div., Indianapolis, Ind. 1940–48; with F. L. Jacobs.; Gen. Man., Home Appliance Div. and Gen. Mngr., Parts Manufacturing Div. 1948–50; with International Telephone & Telegraph Corp., Capehart Farnsworth Co. (successively Dir. of Manufacturing, Vice-Pres., Manufacturing, Vice-Pres. and Gen. Mgr., Tech. Products Div. and Pres. and Dir.); Pres., Farnsworth Electronics Co. 1950–58. President, Director and Chief Executive Officer, Warwick Electronics Inc. 1958–66. President & Director, Lawrence G. Haggerty & Associates, Inc. since 1967; Chmn., Lava-Simplex Internationale Inc. 1976; Dir. Wilton Corp.; Trustee Marquette Univ. *Member:* Tau Beta Pi, Alpha Sigma Nu, Pi Tau Sigma; Sigma Phi Delta. Roman Catholic. *Clubs:* Bob O'Link Golf; Highland Park (Ill): North Shore Country (Glenview, Ill.); Lyford Cay (Bahamas); Metropolitan N.Y. *Address:* 850 Alles Road, Winnetka, Ill. 60093, U.S.A.

**HAGGERTY, Patrick Eugene.** *B.* 1914. *Educ.* Marquette Univ., Milwaukee (BS EE); *M.* 1938, Beatrice E. Manne. *S.* Patrick E. Jr. and Michael Gamble. *Daus.* Sheila Margaret, Kathleen Mary, Teresa Ann. *Career:* Assistant General Manager, Badger Carton Co., Milwaukee 1936–42; Officer, U.S. Naval Reserve, Assigned to the Bureau of Aeronautics, Department of the Navy, Washington, D.C. 1942–45; Texas Instruments Incorporated and predecessor companies since 1945; Pres. 1958–66; Chmn. 1966–76; Dir. 1976—. Graduate Study, Southern Methodist Univ., Dallas; Director, Texas Instruments Ltd., Bedford, England; Fellow, Institute of Electronic Engineers (President, I.R.E., predecessor Society 1962). Member, Natl. Academy Engineering; Dir. A. H. Belo Corp.; International Advisory Cttee. Chase Manhattan Bank; Chmn. Bd. of Trustees, Rockefeller University, Univ. of Dallas. *Awards:* Hon. LLD St. Marys Univ. 1959. Hon. Dr. Eng. Poly. Inst of Brooklyn 1962, Rensselaer Poly. Ins. 1972; Hon. DSc. North Dakota State Univ. 1967, Hon. LLD Univ. of Dallas 1964, Catholic Univ. 1971; Distinguished Alumni, Marquette Univ. 1966. *Publications:* Management Philosophies and Practices of Texas Instruments Incorporated; The Productive Society; miscellaneous technical and management articles and papers. *Address:* 5455 Northbrook Drive, Dallas 75220; and *office* Texas Instruments Inc., 13500 North Central Expressway, Dallas, Texas 75222, U.S.A.

**HÄGGLÖF, Gunnar Richardsson.** Swedish diplomat. *B.* 15 Dec. 1904. *M.* Anna Folchi-Vici. *S.* 1. *Career:* Entered Diplomatic Service 1926; served in Paris, London, Moscow, Geneva; Minister without Portfolio 1939; led Swedish Delegations to Berlin, London, Washington 1939–45; En. Ex. and Min. Plen. to Belgian and Dutch Governments in London 1944, to U.S.S.R. 1946–47; Permanent Delegate to United Nations 1947–48; Amb. Ex. and Plen. to Court of St. James's 1948; Amb. to France 1967–71. *Address:* 9 Rue de Harigan, Paris 8me, France.

**HÄGGQVIST, Sven (Halvar).** Swedish. *B.* 1910. *M.* Muriel Wilson *S.* 2. *Daus.* 1. *Career:* Managing Director, (Ret.) Eriksbergs Mek, Verkstads AB, Göteborg. *Chairman:* Bd. Mo & Domsiö AB; Bd. AB Platmanufaktur; Bd. Gunnebo Bruks AB. *Dep.-Chairman* Fegersta AB; AB Gullfiber; AB Industrivärden. *Director*: Svenska Handelsbanken; *Address:* Johannebergsgatan 18. 412,55 Göteborg, Sweden: and *office* Eriksbergs Mek. Verstads AB, Fack 402,70 Göteborg 8, Sweden.

**HAGLUND, Tor Fjalar.** Finnish banker. *B.* 1908. *Educ.* Studies of Law, Univ. of Helsinki. *M.* 1934, Annagreta Sahlberg. *Daus.* 2. *Career:* Commenced banking career 1926; Asst. General Manager, Nordiska Föreningsbanken Pohjoismaiden Yhdyspankkl 1953–55; General Manager 1955–59; Dept. Chief General Manager 1959–73; Consultant Northern Europe for Bank of America, N.T. and S.A. 1973–75; Chmn. Finnish Chemicals OY. *Address:* Myntgatan 3B, Helsinki 16.

**HAGRUP, Knut.** Norwegian. *B.* 1913. *Educ.* Technische Hochschule, Darmstadt; Royal Air Force Coll. Oslo. Commercial Coll. Oslo. *M.* 1944, Ester Skaugen. *Daus.* 2. *Career:* Chief Eng. Norwegian CCA 1945; Dir. South America & Far East Air-Line 1946; various appointments with S.A.S since 1947; Pres. Scandinavian Airlines System (SAS) *Chairman:* Commission on Air Transport ICC (Paris); Scanair (Scand. Charter Consortium); Sweden. *Member:* IATA Exec. Committee; Chmn. Bd. SAS Catering; various boards. *Decorations:* Commander of the Northern Star (Sweden); Commander of the Order of St. Olav (Norway). *Address:* Slottsvagan 58, S 183 52 Täby, Sweden and *office* Stockholm-Bromma 10.

**HAGUENAUER, Léon.** French. *B.* 1893. *M.* 1922, Alice Weil. *Daus.* Yvette and Nicole. *Career:* Chairman and Chief Director, Fabrique Alsacienne de Levure et Alcools 1951—, Member; Board of Directors: Sucreries et Raffineries d' Erstein 1935—; Société pour la Fabrication de Antibiotigus (SIFA) 1949–70;, and Crédit Foncier d'Alsace et de Lorraine 1959—; Chief Manager, Société Industrielle de Levure Fala, 1968—; Member Bd. Dirs. Ets. Fould-Springer since 1972. *Address: office* 60 rue Pierre Charron, Paris 8, France.

**HAIG, General Alexander Meigs, Jr.** American army officer, government official. *B.* 1924. *Educ.* student Univ. Notre Dame; B.S. U.S. Military Acad.; MA. Georgetown Univ.; Grad. Naval War Coll.; Army War College. *M.* 1950, Patricia Antoinette Fox. *S.* 2. *Daus.* 1. *Career:* with U.S. Army Commander 1947; advanced to Brigadier 1969; Dept. Chief of Staff, Operations, Dept of Army 1962–64; Asst. to Secy. and Deputy Secy. of Defence 1964–65; Military Asst. to Asst. to the President, National Security Affairs 1969–70; Asst. to the President, National Security Affairs, Washington 1970–73; Vice-Chief of Staff 1973; Asst. to President 1973–74; Commander-in-Chief, United States European Command since 1974; Supreme Allied Commander since 1974. *Awards:* D.S.C. Silver Star with oak leaf clusters; Bronze Star; Air Medal; Nat. Order 5th Class Cross of Gallantry with gold palm (Vietnam); National Order of Vietnam, Degree of Grand Officer; UN Service Medal; Republic of Vietnam Campaign Medal; Medal of King Abd El-Aziz, Second Class (Saudi Arabia); Defense Distinguished Service Medal; Army Distinguished Service Medal; Legion of Merit with Two Oak Leaf Clusters; Distinguished Flying Cross with Two Oak Leaf Clusters; Army Commendation Medal; Purple Heart. *Address:* 32 Chausee De Binche, B. 7000 Mons, Belgium.

**HAIGHT, Gordon Sherman.** American professor and writer. *B.* 1901. *Educ.* Yale (BA 1923; PhD 1933). *M.* 1937, Mary Treat Nettleton. *Career:* Master in English, The Kent School 1924–25, and The Hotchkiss Sch. 1925–30; Yale Univ. 1933; Visiting Prof. of English, Columbia Univ. 1946–47, and the Univ. of Oregon 1949; Master of Pierson Coll. 1949–53. Guggenheim, 1946–53–60; Emily Sanford Professor of English Literature, Yale University 1966–; Emeritus, 1969. Fellow Royal Society of Literature, and Corr., British Academy; Fellow Pierpont Morgan Library. *Awards:* James Tait Black; Heinemann, Royal Society of Literature; Van Wyck Brooks, 1969; National Institute of Arts and Letters. *Publications:* Mrs. Sigourney (1930); George Eliot and John Chapman (1940); The George Eliot Letters (7 vols. 1954–55); George Eliot, A Biography (1968); contributions to Dictionary of American Biography (1935); Ency. Britannica (1962); Literary History of the United States (1948); From Jane Austen to Joseph Conrad (1959); George Eliot and Edith Simcox (1961); A Century of George Eliot Criticism (1965); Imagined Worlds (1968); Notable American Women (1971); editions of De Forest, Franklin, DeFoe, Emerson. FitzGerald, Bacon, Whitman, Thoreau, and George Eliot; and about 50 articles in learned journals. *Member:* Modern Language Assn.; Connecticut Acad. of Arts & Sciences. *Clubs:* Century, Yale (N.Y.C.); Elizabethan; Berzelius. *Address:* 145 Peck Hill Road, Woodbridge, Conn. 06525, U.S.A.

**HAILSHAM OF ST. MARYLEBONE, Baron. Rt. Hon. Quintin McGarel Hogg,** CH, FRS, DCL, LLD (formerly Viscount Hailsham, which title he relinquished Nov. 1963). *B.* 1907. *Educ.* Eton and Christ Church Oxford (Scholar); Fellow All Souls Coll. Oxford; President, Oxford Union Soc.

*M.* 1944, Mary Evelyn Martin. *S.* 2. *Daus.* 3. *Career:* Served World War II (Rifle Bde.; Middle East, Western Desert, Egypt, Palestine, Syria; wounded; Major 1942) 1939–45; MP (Con.) Oxford City 1938–50, and St. Marylebone 1963–70. Joint Parly. Under-Secy. of State for Air 1945; First Lord of the Admlty. 1956; Min. of Educ. Jan. 1957, Lord Pres. of the Cncl. 1957–59; Chmn. Conservative Party 1957; Lord Privy Seal 1959–60. Lord President of the Council 1960–64; Leader of the House of Lords 1960–63; Secy. of State for Education and Science 1964; Lord Chancellor 1970–74. *Awards:* Hon. Doctor of Laws, Westminster College, Fulton, Missouri 1960; Hon. LLD (Cambridge) 1963; Hon. DCL, Newcastle University 1964; Hon. Fellow Inst. Structural Engineers 1960, Civil Engineers 1963 and Electrical Engineers 1972. Hon. LLD Delhi Univ. 1972; Hon. DCL Oxford 1974; Companion of Honour 1974, Fellow Royal Society 1973. *Publications:* The Law of Arbitration (1935); One Year's Work (1944); The Law and Employers' Liability (1944); The Times we Live in (1944); Making Peace (1945); The Left was Never Right (1945); The Purpose of Parliament (1946); The Case for Conservatism (1947); The Law of Monopolies, Restrictive Practices and Resale Price Maintenance (1956); The Conservative Case (1959); John Findley Green Memorial Lecture 1960, Glasgow Rectorial Address, 1961; Science and Politics (1963); The Devil's Own Song & Other Verses (1968); The Door Wherein I went (1975); Elective Dictatorship (1976). *Clubs:* Carlton; Alpine; M.C.C.; R.A.C. *Address:* The House of Lords, London, S.W.1.

**HAINWORTH, Henry Charles,** CMG. British diplomat (retired) *B.* 1914. *Educ.* Cambridge University (BA). *M.* 1944, Mary Ady. *Daus.* 2. Diplomatic Service appointments in Tokyo, London, Bucharest, Nicosia, Brussels & Vienna. Ambassador to Indonesia, 1968–70; Permanent UK Delegate, Disarmament Conference, personal rank of Ambassador 1971–74. *Address:* c/o Barclays Bank Ltd., 50 Jewry St., Winchester, Hants.

**HAJEK, Jiri.** Czechoslovak diplomat and lecturer. Professor of the History Institute of the Czechoslovak Academy of Science. *B.* 1913. *Educ.* Charles University, Prague (Graduate of the Faculty of Law). *Career:* Deputy Minister of Foreign affairs active in resistance movement in World War II; held various posts in sphere of youth education 1945–47; Lecturer, College of Political and Social Sciences, Prague 1947–48; Professor at the Coll. 1948–52; Professor in the History of International Relations, Charles University 1952–55; Member of the National Assembly 1945–46 and 1948–54; Chairman of Foreign Affairs Committee 1952–54; took part in various international conferences; head of Czechoslovak delegation to General Conference of UNESCO 1954 and 1966. Ambassador to U.K. 1955–57; Head of Czechoslovak Delegation to 18 Nations Disarmament Cttee., Geneva, 1962; Permanent Czechoslovak Delegate to U.N., New York; Vice-Pres. Econ. & Social Cncl. 1963; Representative on Security Cncl. 1964. Minister of Education 1965. Minister of Foreign Affairs 1968; Dir., Inst. of Political Science, Czechoslovak Acad. of Sciences 1969. *Publications:* various books on recent Czechoslovak and world history; numerous pamphlets, essays and articles. *Address:* Academy of Sciences, Narodni Tr. 3, Prague 1, Czechoslovakia.

**HAKIM, George.** Lebanese diplomat and educator. *B.* 1913. *Educ.* American University of Beirut (BA 1932; MA 1934); University of St. Joseph, Beirut (Lic en D 1937). *M.* 1951, Laura Belle Zarbock. *S.* 1. *Dau.* 1. *Career:* Instr. Econ. (1934–43) and Adjunct Professor (1943–46), American Univ. of Beirut; Counsellor of Legation, Washington 1946–52; Alternate Delegate (1946–49) and Chief Delegate (1949) to ECOSOC: Alternate Governor (1947–48) and Governor (1949–51) of Lebanon to International Monetary Fund and International Bank; Chief Lebanese Delegate to U.N. Conference on Trade and Employment, Havana 1947–48; Delegate to Gen. Assembly U.N. 1946–65 and to several international conferences 1946–59; Chairman, groups of experts appointed by Sec.-General, U.N., to study problem of economic development of under-developed countries Feb.–May 1951; Chairman, U.N. Commission on Human Rights 1962; Rapporteur, U.N. Conf. on Trade and Development 1964; Minister of Finance and National Economy of Lebanon 1952–53; Minister of Foreign Affairs 1953, 1965, and 1966–68. Minister of National Economy Mar.–June 1956; Minister (1955–58) and Ambassador (Oct. 1958–Jan. 1959) to Fed. Repub. of Germany. Ambassador, Permanent Rep. of Lebanon to U.N. 1959–66. Vice-President, American University of Beirut, May 1968—. *Awards:* Grand Officer: Cedar (Lebanon), Rafidain (Iraq), Ismail 1st Class (Egypt); Chevalier, Grand Cross Order of Merit of Italian Republic; Grosskreuz des Verdienstordens der Bundesrepublic Deutschland Hon. LLD St. John's Univ., Jamaica N.Y. *Publications:* two chapters on industry and fiscal system in Economic Organization of Syria (ed. Said B. Himadeh 1936); one chapter on monetary and banking system in Economic Organisation of Palestine (ed. Said B. Himadeh 1939); chapters in other books and numerous articles on the general subject of economic development of under-developed countries. *Address:* American University of Beirut, Beirut, Lebanon.

**HAKSAR, Sundar Narain.** Indian diplomat. *B.* 4 Dec. 1909. *Educ.* MA, BSc (Hons.). *M.* 1936, Chunni Atal. *S.* 1. *Career:* joined Indian Civil Service 1933 and served in various posts in the Punjab; transferred to Foreign Service 1947; Counsellor, Embassy, Cairo 1948–49; Joint Secretary, Ministry of External Affairs 1950–53; Minister, Embassy, Washington 1953–54; Ambassador to Turkey 1954–56; to Afghanistan 1957–60; to Italy May 1960–64; to U.A.R. 1964–1966; to the Netherlands July 1966. *Address:* Ministry of External Affairs, New Delhi, India.

**HALBOUTY, Michel T.** Consulting geologist and petroleum engineer and independent producer and operator since Sept. 1945. *B.* 1909. *Educ.* BS and MS in Geology and Petroleum Engineering; Professional Degree in Geological Engineering; DEng (hc). *M.* 1945, Fay Renfro. *Dau.* 1. *Career:* Junior Geologist and Petr. Engr. 1931–33; Chief Geologist and Petr. Engr. 1933–35, for Yount-Lee Oil Co.; Chief Geologist and Petr. Engr., Vice-Pres. and Gen. Mgr. for Glenn H. McCarthy Interests, Houston, Aug. 1935–May 1937; Consulting Geologist and Petr. Engr. 1937–42, when called to active service as Chief (with rank of Lieut.-Col.) of Petroleum Production Section, Planning Division, Army-Navy Petroleum Board. Owner of present firm since Sept. 1945. *Publications:* Over 200 works, articles, theses and several books on the subject of geology in its relation to petroleum production, and exploration which appeared either as separate works, or in professional journals. *Address:* The Halbouty Center, 5100 Westheimer Road, Houston, Texas 77056, U.S.A.

**HALDANE-STEVENSON, Rev. James Patrick,** MA, TD. Scottish Broadcaster and writer. *B.* 1910. *Educ.* King Edward's School Birmingham and St. Cath. College Oxford. *M.* 1938, Leila Mary Flack (*Div.*). *S.* 2. *Dau.* 1. *Career:* Second Lieut. Royal Tank Corps (S.R.) 1931); Lieut. 1934; Territorial Chaplain 1937; Dunkirk 1940; Eighth Army 1944; Major 1945; Lieut.-Col. 1946; Commandant, Chaplains' Centre (Italy and Austria) 1946–48, N. Ireland 1948–51, Germany 1951–54; Larkhill 1954–55. Australian correspondent, Le Monde 1969–73. Gen. Synod Canon Law Commission. *Publications:* Religion and Leadership (1948); Poems (1948); Beyond the Bridge (1973). The Backward Look (1975); editor, In Our Tongues (S.P.C.K.) (1944); contributor, Soldiers also Asked (1943), Padre Presents (1944). Poems from Italy (1945); articles and reviews in press, literary and church journals. *Clubs:* Athenaeum (London); Melbourne, Naval & Military (Melbourne). *Address:* St. Silas' Vicarage, North Balwyn 3104, Australia.

**HALE, Arthur.** British company director. *B.* 1916. *Educ.* Caulfield Grammar School (Melbourne); Mount Albert Grammar Sch. (Auckland, N.Z.); Auckland Univ. Coll. and Melbourne University. *M.* 1942, Norrie Elaine Holyman. *Dau.* Mary. *Career:* With Alliance Assurance Co. Ltd., Auckland, N.Z. 1933–37; Shell Co. of Australia Ltd. Melbourne 1937; Norwich Union Fire Insurance Soc., Melbourne 1938; Asst. Manager, Royal Insurance Co. Ltd., Melbourne 1938–56. With A.I.F.; Captain; 3rd Australian Corps. R.A.A.; Officers Pre-selection Board, and Officers for India Pre-selection Board 1939–45; Dir. Australian & International Insurances Ltd. 1956–68; Gen. Mgr., The Nippon Fire & Marine Insurance Co. Ltd., Australia 1958–68; Man. Dir. Associated General Contractors Insurance Co. Ltd. 1960–72; Chmn. Consolidated Insurances of Australia Ltd. 1960–68; Dir. Underwriting & Insurance Ltd. 1962–72; A. & I. Discounters Ltd. 1962–67; Credits Pty. Ltd. 1964–67; Machinery Insurance Services Pty. Ltd. 1964–68; Hale-Holyman (Aust.) Pty. Ltd. and Artnor Pty. Ltd., Chmn. since 1972; Arton Holdings Pty. Ltd. Chmn. since 1972; Chmn., Essex Insurance Brokers Pty. Ltd. 1972–76, Essex Assurance Consultants Pty. Ltd. 1973–76. Member, Councils of Fire, Accident & Marine Underwriters of Australia 1956–72; Fellow, Inst. of Sales & Marketing Executives (FISM); Associate, The Corporation of Insurance Brokers of Australia (ACIBA). *Clubs:* Stock Exchange; Naval & Military; West End; Royal

Automobile. *Address:* 1 Dion Street, Burwood, Vic., Australia.

**HALE, Clayton G.** American; Independent Property Insurance Agent, Broker and Consultant (with licences in 12 States and Province of Ontario, Canada). *B.* 1902. *Educ.* University of Michigan (AB 1924); Fenn College (BBA 1932); Hon. LLD Fenn College 1956; LLD Baldwin-Wallace Coll., 1975; Fellow, Insurance Inst. of Amer.; Student in Economics, Univ. of Michigan. *M.* 1927, Laura Bartlett. *S.* 1. *Dau.* 1. *Career:* Chmn. The Hale & Hale Co. 1939—; Edtl. Consultant for interpetation of insurance statistics and trends (on staff of The Spectator (America) 1948–53); Asst. Chief. Insurance Div., Navy Dept. for control of insurance expenditure under re-arming contracts 1942–43; U.S. Navy Dept. in negotiations resulting in establishment of British Insurance Communications Office (BICO), N.Y. 1943; Professor of Insurance, School of Business Admin., University of Michigan 1948–56; Office of Secretary of Defence, to integrate insurance practice of Army, Navy and Air Force in Korean police action 1950; delegate, White House Committee on Highway Safety (1954–58); Insurance consultant to U.S. Dept. of Defence 1950–62; and to Ohio Turnpike Commission 1953–58; Chmn. Fenn Educational Foundation. *Publications:* 'An Approach to Fire Insurance'; approximately 70 technical articles for various journals, including an annual commentary on property insurance developments (1931–53). *Member:* Committee on General Insurance Terminology of Amer. Risk and Insurance Association 1960–70; Visiting Cttee., Graduate School of Business Administration, Univ. of Michigan. *Address:* 208 The Arcade, Cleveland, Ohio 44114, U.S.A.

**HALE, Hamilton Orin.** Lawyer. Counsellor for commercial airlines and related enterprises. *B.* 1906. *Educ.* University of Illinois (BS) and Northwestern University (JS). *M.* 1946, J. Elizabeth Hale. *S.* Hamilton O., Jr. *Daus.* Jean and Jamie. *Career:* With Pruitt & Grealis, Chicago 1931–40; Partner, Pruitt, Hale & MacIntyre, N.Y.C. 1940–48; founded Hale, Russell & Stenzel, 1948–70; Member Joslyn & Green 1970—; Dir. Emeritus and Asst. Secy. Allegheny Airlines 1972. Decorated Knight, Order of St. Olav (Norway). Order of the Coif. *Member:* Amer. and Illinois State Bar Assns., and Assn. of the Bar of the City of New York. *Club:* Turnberry, Woodstock Country. *Address: office* 145 Virginia Street, Crystal Lake, Ill., U.S.A.

**HALEFOGLU, Vahit Melih.** Turkish diplomat. *B.* 1919. *Educ.* Antakya College; Uniteraity of Ankara, MA (Polit. Science). *M.* 1951, Zehra. *S.* 1. *Dau.* 1. *Career:* Turkish Ministry of Foreign Affairs 1942–47; Vienna 1947–49; Moscow 1949–51; Turkish Ministry of Foreign Affairs 1951–53; London 1953–59; Dir.-Gen. 1st Polit. Dept. Ministry of Foreign Affairs, Ankara 1959–62; Ambassador of Turkey in Lebanon 1962–65, concurrently Kuwait 1964–65; Ambassador in USSR 1965–66; Ambassador in Netherlands 1966–70; Deputy Secy.-Gen. for Political Affairs, Ministry of Foreign Affairs, Ankara 1970–72; Ambassador of Turkey in F. Republic of Germany since 1972. *Decorations:* Knight Comdr. Victorian Order; decorations from Lebanon, Finland, Greece, Italy, Germany and Spain. *Address:* Turkish Embassy, D 53 Bonn-Bad Godesberg, Utestr. 47, Federal Republic of Germany.

**HALFORD-MacLEOD, Aubrey Seymour,** CMG, CVO. British. *B.* 1914. *Educ.* King Edward's School, Birmingham, and Magdalen Coll., Oxford (Doncaster Scholar); BA 1st Cl. Hons. 1936; Paget Toynbee Prize 1939; MA 1964. *M.* 1939, Giovanna Mary Durst. *S.* 3. *Dau.* 1. *Career:* Deputy Secy.-Gen. Council of Europe 1949–52; Counsellor, Embassy, Tokyo 1953–55; Chargé d'Affaires Seoul (S. Korea) 1954; Counsellor, Embassy, Benghazi 1955–57; Political Agent, Kuwait 1957–59; Consul-General, Munich 1959–65. H.M. Ambassador to Iceland, Feb. 1966; (Retd) Diplomatic Service; Adviser, Scottish Council (Development of Industry) since 1971; Dir. Scottish Opera Ltd.; Pres. Scottish Socy. for Northern Studies. *Publications:* The Kabuki Handbook (1956); regular contributions to Opera since 1964. *Address:* Mulag House, N. Harris, Inverness-shire; and 37 Buckingham Terrace, Edinburgh.

**HALCK, Henning.** Danish Ambassador in Nigeria. *Address:* Royal Danish Embassy, P.O. Box 2390, Victoria Island, Lagos, Nigeria.

**HALL, A. Douglass.** American. *B.* 1910. *Educ.* Princeton University (BA *summa cum laude*). *M.* 1938, Marie LeMoyne Noyes. *S.* Andrew Douglass, Jr. and Benjamin Thomas. *Daus.* Mrs. Emlen F. Guggenhime, Anne Drury, and Linda (MacKay). *Career:* With Bonbright & Co. 1932–36; Buying Dept., Morgan Stanley & Co. 1936–45; with Diamond Match Co. (which changed its corporate name to Diamond Gardner Corp. and currently is Diamond International Corporation): successively Asst. to Pres. 1946–48, Vice-Pres. and Asst. Treas. 1949–50, Financial Vice-Pres. 1950–58, and Director 1952–59; Partner, Morgan Stanley & Co. 1959–62; Vice-Pres. and Dir., Stauffer Chemical Co. 1962–68 President, Chairman, Waran Associates, Inc.; President, Homar International, Inc. Trustee, The Worcester Foundation for Experimental Biology, 1958—. *Member:* Phi Beta Kappa. *Clubs:* River, Recess, Princeton (all in N.Y.C.); Bedford Golf & Tennis (Bedford, N.Y.). *Address:* David's Hill Road, Bedford Hills, N.Y.; and *office* 16th Floor, 380 Madison Avenue, New York, N.Y. 10017, U.S.A.

**HALL, Albert Earl.** Canadian banker. *B.* 1913. *Educ.* Grey, Ontario. *M.* 1941, Mildred Lucille Echlin. *Daus.* 2. *Career:* Entered service of the Bank in Thornbury, Ont., 1930, and subsequently served in Hamilton, Galt, Meaford and Toronto. Manager of Queensway and Royal York Road branches, Toronto, Mar. 1947; Manager, Eglinton and Bathhurst, Toronto, Feb. 1949; Inspection Dept., Head Office, Feb. 1951; Manager, Sarnia, Ont. 1952; Supervisor, Western Div., Winnipeg, Oct. 1955; Superintendent, Alberta Div., 1956; General Manager, Dec. 1960; Vice Pres. and Dir. The Toronto-Dominion Bank 1962; Chmn. of the Bd. & Chmn. of the Exec. Cttee., The Bank of British Columbia; Chmn. & Trustee, BBC Realty Investors; Chmn. & Dir., BBC-RI Services Ltd.; Dir. BBC Realty Ltd.; Dir. Burrard-Yarrows Group; Dir. P. A. Woodward Found.; Hon, Treasurer Brentford Coll. Fund. *Clubs:* Shaughnessy Golf & Country; The Vancouver. *Address:* 5276 Connaught Drive. Vancouver, B.C. V6M 3G4; and *office* 1725 Two Bentall Centre, Vancouver, B.C. V7X 1K1, Canada.

**HALL, Sir Arnold (Alexander),** MA, Hon. FAIAA. Hon. FI MechE, Hon. FIEE, DEng. DSc. FRS, Hon. FRAeS,Hon. ACGI, C.Eng., D. Tech. British aeronautical engineer. *B.* 23 Apr. 1915. *Educ.* Clare College, Cambridge, *M.* 1946, Dione Sykes. *Daus.* Elizabeth Ann. Veronica Clare. *Career:* Principal Scientific Officer, Royal Aircraft Establishment 1938–45; Zaharoff Prof. of Aviation, Univ. of London, and Head of Dept. of Aeronautics, Imperial Coll. of Science and Tech. 1945–51; Dir. Royal Aircraft Establishment, Farnborough 1951–55; Director, Hawker Siddeley Group 1955–63; Man. Dir., Bristol Siddeley Engines Ltd. Nov. 1958–63; Vice-Chmn. & Man. Dir., Hawker-Siddeley Group, 1963–67. Chairman and Managing Director, Hawker Siddeley Group Ltd., 1967–; Director, Lloyds Bank Ltd.; Phoenix Assurance Co. Ltd. 1969–; Imperial Chemical Industries Ltd. since 1970; Onan Corp. since 1976. *Address:* Hawker Siddeley Group Ltd., 18 St. James's Sq., London, S.W.1.

**HALL. Joan V.,** British. *B.* 1935. *Educ.* Queen Margaret's School, Escrick, near York; Ashridge House of Citizenship, Berkhamstead. *Career:* As a Secretary worked in the United Kingdom, Denmark, Switzerland and France; Member of Parliament for Keighley 1970–74; Parly. Private Secy. to Rt. Hon. Anthony Stodart MP Min. State, Ministry of Agriculture 1972–74. *Address:* Highfield, High Hoyland, Barnsley, S. Yorkshire.

**HALL, Sir John,** OBE, MP. British industrialist and politician. *B.* 1911. *Educ.* Private. *M.* 1935, Nancy Doreen Hampton Blake. *S.* John Andrew Hampton. *Dau.* Felicity (De Burgh Codrington). *Career:* Served War, Staff Appointments, Rank Lt. Col. 1939–45; Member, Grimsby Borough Council, 1946–48; President of companies concerned with cellulose, Plastics and Brewing since 1948; Member of Parliament Conservative for Wycombe Div. of Bucks since 1952; P.P.S. to Minister, Fuel & Power, 1956–57, Supply 1957–59; Member Select Cttee. Public Accnts. 1958–64; Vice-Chmn. Parly. Trade & Industry Cttee. 1964–65; Vice-Chmn. Finance Cttee. 1965–69, 1970–72 and since 1974 (Chmn. 1973–74); Vice-Chmn. 1922 Cttee. since 1970; Chmn. British Group I.P.U. 1970–72, Deputy-Pres. Inter-Parly.: Union 1970–73; Chmn. Select Cttee. Nationalised Industries 1973–74. Member, Select Cttee. Expenditure; Chmn. Sub-Cttee. Environment 1970–72 *Awards:* Fellow Royal Society of Arts; Created Knight Batchelor 1973; Order of Diplomatic Merit (Rep. of Korea) 1975. *Clubs:* Naval & Military. *Address:* Marsh, Kimble, Aylesbury, Bucks; and *office* Vistec House, London Road, Croydon, Surrey.

**HALL, Sir John Hathorn,** GCMG, DSO, OBE, MC. British colonial administrator. *B.* 1894. *Educ.* St. Paul's School; Lincoln College, Oxford (BA). *M.* Torfrida Trevenen Mills.

*Daus.* 2. *Career:* Served World War I, France and Belgium 1914–18: member of staff, Minister of Finance, Egypt 1919–21; Colonial Office, London 1921–32, Foreign Office 1932–33; Chief Sec. to Govt. of Palestine 1933–37; British Resident, Zanzibar 1937–40; Gov. and Commander-in-Chief, Aden 1940–44; Gov. and Commander-in-Chief, Uganda 1944–51; dir. or chmn. of various companies 1952–73. *Address:* 128 Rivermead Court, London, S.W.6.

**HALL, Joseph Rex**, OBE, ED, AASA. Australian. Dir.: Farm & Pastoral Supplies Pty. Ltd. 1923—. *B.* 1894. *M.* 1922, Dr. Margaret H. Anderson (*Dec.*). *S.* Graham Anderson, BAgSc (Melb.). Served in both World Wars, Gallipoli and Palestine; Staff Capt. Imperial Camel Brigade and 5th Australian Light Horse Brigade 1914–18; in 1939–45 war Commanded 20th Light Horse Rgt. and later 23/21st Infantry Bn. Director of Rehabilitation, Australian Military Forces 1943–47; retired as Colonel 1949. *Publications:* The Desert Hath Pearls (1975); The World is Mine (1977); sundry press articles (subjects mainly military). *Clubs:* Legacy, Naval & Military (Melbourne); Peninsula Golf (Frankston, Vic.). *Address:* 1638 Malvern Road, Glen Iris, Vic. 3146, Australia.

**HALL, Per.** Canadian civil engineer. *B.* 1911. *Educ.* Royal Technical College, Copenhagen (MSc—Civil, 1936); Post-graduate studies, Univ. of Toronto 1940; awarded Larsen Foundation (1937) and Otto Monsted (1939) Scholarships. *M.* 1937 Nina Monsted. *S.* Peter William. *Daus.* Karen Agnete, and Ingrid Marianne. *Career:* Project Engineer, A/S Manniche & Hartmann 1935–37; Manager, A/B ASA Stockholm and Gothenburg, Sweden (a subsidiary of A/S Manniche & Hartmann) 1937–38; travels in S.E. Europe; Designing Engineer, Christiani & Nielsen 1939; Project Engineer, Aluminium Co. of Canada Ltd. 1940–46; Designing Engineer, The Foundation Co. of Canada Ltd. 1946–49; Assistant Chief Engineer, The Foundation Co. of Canada Ltd. 1949–53; Vice-Pres., Foundation of Canada Engineering Corp. Ltd. (FENCO) 1953–57, Exec. Vice-Pres. 1957–58; Pres. 1958–61. President, Per Hall Associates Ltd., Consulting Engineers. Chmn., General Engineering Co. Ltd. Dir. and President, Up-Hill Ltd. Trustee, Canadian-Scandinavian Fdn. *Publications:* Novel Concret; Headframes for Asbestos Mine, E.I.C. Journal, (1947); Deas Island Tunnel (co-author) Proceedings of Amer. Socy. of Civil Engineers Journal of the Structural Div., (1957); Deas Island Tunnel Four-Lane Rectangular Tunnel Placed by Trench Method (co-author), Civil Engineering (1958); Deas Island Tunnel (co-author), The Engineering Journal, (1959). *Clubs:* University (Montreal); Royal St. Lawrence Yacht; Royal Vancouver Yacht. *Address:* 46 Summit Circle, Westmount, Montreal 217, P.Q., Canada.

**HALL, Robert King.** American international consultant (Education and Industrial Development). *B.* 1912. *Educ.* Lake Forest Univ. (AB 1934), Harvard Univ. (AM Physics 1935), Univ. of Chicago (AM, Educ. Law and Administration 1936); Columbia Univ. (AM Pol Sc and Oriental Studies 1944); School of Asiatic Studies, N.Y. (AM Middle East Studies 1950); Univ. of Michigan (Phd Comparative Educ. 1941); Universidad de Buenos Aires research in Educ. Law 1935); Catedrático Honorario CH) Univ. of San Marcos, Lima; LLD, Lake Forest Univ.; Hon. Lecturer, Teachers Coll., Columbia Univ. *M.* 1938, Margaret Wheeler. *S.* Marshall King. *Daus.* Mrs. Louise Wheeler Chaffin and Margaret Jean. *Career:* Laboratory Assistant in Physics, Lake Forest Univ. 1929–32; Master in Maths. and Spanish, Cranbrook School 1936–40; Dir. of Research and Guidance, Milwaukee Country Day Schools (six months; resigned to go to Harvard); Asst. Dir., Commission on English Language Studies, Harvard Univ., 1941–43; Lieut.-Commander, U.S.N.R. (34 months; 11 months overseas); Associate Prof., Teachers Coll., Columbia Univ. 1947–50; Prof. of Education (same college) 1950–55; American Joint Editor, Yearbook of Education, London 1952–57; Asst. Dir. of Training, Arabian American Oil Co. June 1955–July 1957 (Director 1957–60). Senior Adviser Univ. of Petroleum and Minerals, Saudi Arabia since 1964; Vice-Pres. & Treas., CPM Foundation since 1977. *Publications:* 14 books and 7 monographs, including: A Basic English for South America; Education for a New Japan; Kokutai No Hongi (with J. O. Gauntlett); Shūshin; The Ethics of a Defeated Nation; Report on the Seven-Year Economic Development Plan for Iran; Educacíon en Crisis; El Dilema de la Universidad Estandounidense (in honour of 400th anniversary of San Marcos de Lima); A Strategy for the Inner City. *Address:* University of Petroleum and Minerals, Dhahran, Saudi Arabia.

**HALL, Ronald William.** BA, MA. British. *B.* 1929. *Educ.* Oxford Univ. (BA); Stanford Univ. (MA). *M.* 1957, Anne Hatton Delaforce. *S.* 1. *Career:* Dir. European Operations ConAgra Inc.; former senior appointments with W. R. Grace & Co.; Man. Dir. Saprogal (Spain); Nebiosa (Spain); ConAgra Europe Inc. (Spain); Española (Spain) Sapropor (Lisbon). *Clubs:* Real Madrid. *Address:* Charquia, 1 Somosaguas, Madrid-11, Spain.

**HALL, Theodore Parsons.** American aeronautical engineer, business executive and inventor; *B.* 1898. *Educ.* Syracuse Univ. (Elec. Eng. Deg.); Massachusetts Inst. of Technology (MSc Aeronautics). *M.* 1929, Marion E. Parsons. *Daus.* Marguerite P. (Stitt), Janet C. (Backer), Theodora P. (Burton). *Career:* Served in World War I (26th Div., U.S. Army; citation for bravery). Chief Development Engineer, Consolidated Vultee Aircraft Corp. 1935–48. President and Chief Engineer, T. P. Hall Engineering, San Diego, Calif., 1950—. Developed Hall Flying Automobile and many outstanding military airplanes. Holder of many patents. *Publications:* numerous articles in technical journals and magazines. *Member:* Socy. of Automotive Engineers; Inst. of Aeronautical Sciences; Ancient Free and Accepted Masons; Acacia Fraternity; Theta Tau. *Address:* 2006 Orizaba Avenue, San Diego, Calif. 92103, U.S.A.

**HALL, William O.** American. *B.* 1914. *Educ.* University of Oregon (AB); University of Minnesota. *M.* 1939. Jayne B. *S.* William J., Robert B. *Dau.* Dr. Sarah H. Sternglanz. *Career:* Research assistant, assistant director, city hall office League of Oregon Cities, 1936–38; acting exec. sec., Bureau of Municipal Research, 1939–40; Budget examiner & administrative analyst, U.S. Bureau of the Budget, 1940–44; supervisor, Bureau of Administrative Management and Budget, U.N., 1946; Dir.: Office of Budget and Planning, U.S. State Dept., 1947–50; Office of International Conferences and Administration, 1950–52; Deputy Rep., Interim Commission, General Assembly, U.N., 1952–56; Counsellor of Embassy, London, 1956–58; Deputy Assistant Secretary of State, 1958–59; Minister, Counsellor, Deputy Chief of Mission, Embassy, Karachi, Pakistan, 1959–63; Asst. Administrator. Agency for International Development, State Dept., 1963–67. Ambassador to Ethiopia, 1967–71; Dir. Gen. Department of State, the Foreign Service, 1971–73; Prof. Int'l Affairs, Lewis & Clark Coll., Portland, Oregon since 1974. *Member:* Phi Beta Kappa: American Foreign Service Assn.; American Public Administration Society; Int. Development Socy. *Clubs:* Cosmos, Washington; Rotary International; City (Portland). *Address:* Lewis & Clark College, Portland, Oregon 97201, U.S.A.

**HALL-JONES, Frederick George,** OBE. British (New Zealand). Barrister and Solicitor. *B.* 1891. *Educ.* BA, LLB. *M.* 1919, Marjorie Bush. *S.* 4. Served in World War I. *Publications:* Historical Southland; King of the Bluff; Kelly of Inverkelly; Invercargill Pioneers; Early Timaru; Rotary in New Zealand, 1955, 1971. Sir Wm. Hall-Jones; etc. *Member:* Rotary (District Governor); Founder, Southland Historical Committee, Centennial Association, Beautifying Society, Art Gallery Trust Board, Lennel Art Trust. *Club:* Invercargill. *Address:* 88 Albert Street, Invercargill, New Zealand.

**HALLE, (Kaarlo) Pentti.** Finnish. *B.* 1908. *Educ.* Graduate, Institute of Technology, Helsinki, 1933. *M.* 1936, Irja Peltoniemi. *S.* Arto. *Dau.* Enni-Liisa. *Career:* With Enso-Gutzeit Osakeyhtiö since 1934; Director 1950; Manager Kaukopää Mills 1948–62. President Enso-Gutzeit Osakeyhtiö (pulp and paper) 1962–72. *Awards:* Knight 1st Cl. Order of the Lion (Finland); Cross of Liberty 4th Cl. with oak leaves and swords, and Medal of Liberty 2nd Cl. Member: T.A.P.P.I.; *Address:* Koivuniemi, 55800, Imatra 80, Finland.

**HALLER-GRIFFITS, Alexander Edgar.** British professional engineer and educationist. *B.* 1909. *Educ.* Christ's Hospital; Imperial Coll. of Science & Technology (Diploma); Univ. of London (1st Cl. Hons.; BScEng); Assot., City & Guilds of London Inst.; Diploma, Pub. Admin., Univ. of Tasmania. *M.* 1941, Dorothy Lilian Achard. *S.* Peter Alexander. *Dau.* Merrilyn Dorothy (Evans). *Career:* Graduate-Apprentice, Associated Equipment Co. Ltd., London 1930; Engineer-Apprentice Supervisor, Leyland Motors Ltd. 1932; Scientific Officer, Admiralty Research Lab., Teddington 1934; Lecturer in Mech. Engng., Univ. of Tasmania 1948; Principal, Hobart Technical Coll., Tasmania, 1954; Consulting Engineer 1974. *Fellow:* Inst. of Mech. Engineers (Automobile Div.; Member, Inst. of Engineers, Australia; Fellow, Aust. Inst. of Management. *Member:* Aust. Coll. of Education; Royal Inst. of Public Administration. *Clubs:* Hobart Speakers; Royal

Automobile (Tasmania); Christ's Hospital. *Address:* **458** Elizabeth Street, North Hobart, Tasmania, 7000.

**HALLGRIMSSON, Hallgimur Frederick,** CBE Icelandic. *B.* 1905. *Educ.* grad. High School, Baldur, Manitoba, Canada. *M.* 1928, Margaret Thors. *Daus.* Margaret Thora and Elina Benta. Cmdr.: Order of the Falcon (Iceland); Order of St. Olavs (Norway). *Career:* Chmn. of the Bd. of Directors, Oliufelagid Skeljungur h.f. *Clubs:* The East India, Sports and Public Schools (London); Rotary (Reykjavik). *Address:* Suderlandsbraut 4, Reykjavik, Iceland.

**HALLOWELL, Charles Joseph.** British. *B.* 1909. *Educ.* Warrnambool High School. *M.* 1939, Valerie Hickman. *S.* John and Robert. *Dau.* Janine. *Career:* Joined commercial department of Warrnambool Standard Pty. Ltd. 1924 (Secy. 1936, Director 1942). Chairman of Directors 1963—and Managing Director 1942–74, Warrnambool Standard Pty. Ltd.; Dir. and Secy. Provincial Daily Press Association of Victoria Pty. Ltd. 1962—. Director: Victorian Board, Australian United Press Ltd. 1953—, and of Central Board, Regional Dailies of Australia Ltd. since 1963; Chmn., Regional Dailies of Australia Ltd. 1974–75. *Member:* Commonwealth Press Union; Warrnambool and District Base Hospital (Life Governor), *Club:* Warrnambool Rotary (Past-Pres.). *Address:* 327 Timor Street, Warrnambool, Vic., Australia.

**HALLOWELL, Henry Richardson.** American investment banker. *B.* 1898. *Educ.* William Penn Charter School (Philadelphia) and Yale Univ. (BA). *M.* 1919, Dorothy Saylor. *S.* Henry Richardson, Jr.; and J. Wallace III. *Daus.* Dorothy (Fetterolf) and Bertinia (Bailey). *Career:* Agent, George H. McFadden & Bros. New Bedford Mass. 1919–25; Proprieter Henry R. Hallowell & Son 1925–30; Registered Rep. Lee Higginson Corp. 1931–32; Bryan, Pennington & Colket 1933–37; Manager, Investment Dept., Eastman Dillon & Co. 1937–45; Partner Hallowell SulzBerger, Jenks & Co. 1945–73; Vice Pres. Hoppin, Watson Inc. New York since 1973. Director: Alleghany Airlines Inc., Member, Board of Governors, P.B.W. Stock Exchange; Amer. Stock Exchange; Assoc. Member, N.Y. Stock Exchange. Ex. Pres. & Director, Merion Civic Assoc., and Botanical Society of Lower Merion Township. *Clubs:* Union Leagure, Yale, Ex. Pres. Penn (Pres.); Philadelphia Country, Rotary; Rittenhouse (all of Philadelphia); *Address:* 'Berberrie' Greystone & Blancoyd Roads, Merion Station, Pa., U.S.A.

**HALLSTEIN, Walter.** President of European Movement. *B.* 1901. *Educ.* Law and Economics (Referendar, Doctor's Degree, Privatdozent); *Career:* Assistant, Faculty of Law, Berlin Univ. 1925; Referent (Research Fellow), Kaiser Wilhelm Inst. of Foreign and International Private Law 1927; Professor, Rostock Univ. 1930; Professor and Director, Institute of Comparative Law, Frankfurt University 1941, Rector Frankfurt Univ. 1946–48; Guest Professor, Georgetown University, Washington 1948–49; Chairman, U.N.E.S.C.O. German Committee 1949–50; led German delegation, Schuman Plan Conference, Paris, 1950; State Secretary, Federal Chancellery 1950; State Secretary, German Foreign Office 1951; elected Pres., Commission of European Economic Community 1958–67; Pres. European Movement 1968; Member, Bundestag 1969–72. *Awards:* Charlemagne Prize for services to the cause of Western unity, 1961; Robert Schuman Prize 1969. Dr. of Law, Univs. of Georgetown, Washington, D.C., Padua (Italy), Tufts (Medford, Mass.), Harvard, Cambridge (Mass.), and Colby Coll. (Waterville, Maine), Adelphi Univ. (Garden City, Maine), Wesleyan, Omaha, Nebraska, Columbia, New York, N.Y., Johns Hopkins Univ. (U.S.A.), and Univ. of Liège (Belgium), Jussex Nancy Louvain (Belgium), Hamburg, Tübingen; Bradford (Gt. Britain); Oviedo (Spain). Grand Cross of the following Orders: Merit (Germany), of Merit (Bavaria), St. Sylvester (Holy See), Merit (Italy), George I (Greece), Merit (Argentine), do Sul (Brazil), Falcon (Iceland), White Elephant (Thailand), Homayun 1st Cl. (Iran), Merit (Peru), Merit (Austria), Libertador (Venezuela), Aztec Eagle (Mexico), Polar Star (Sweden), Bernardo O' Higgins (Chile) the Crown (Belgium), African Redemption (Liberia), Condor of the Andes (Bolivia), Oak Crown (Luxembourg), Carlos Manuel de Céspedes (Cuba), National Order (Republic of Niger), Netherlands Lion, Holy Sepulchre; Grand Officer, National Order of the Republic (Upper Volta); Order of 'du Mono' (Togo); Commander, National Order of Value (Cameroun); Cross, Order of Merit (Central African Republic) Grand Cross, National Order (Chad). *Publications:* Der unvollendete Bundesstaat (1969); Comparative studies civil law, commercial and industrial law, especially company law; on cultural policy with particular reference to higher education; on foreign policy; co-editor Deutsche Juristenzeitung since 1946. *Address:* 5439 Rennerod (Oberwesterwaldkreis) Federal Republic of Germany.

**HALSTEAD, Hon. Eric Henry,** ED. New Zealand business consultant. *B.* 26 May 1912. *Educ.* Auckland Grammar School and Auckland Univ. College; MA (Hons.), BCom, FPANZ, FCIS; is a chartered Accountant and company director. *M.* 1940, Millicent Joan Stewart. *S.* 3. *Dau.* 1. *Career:* Staff, Seddon Memorial Technical College 1936–39; served in World War II (Middle East and Italy 2 N.Z.E.F.; rank, Major) m.i.d. 1940–45; Head of Commercial and Accountancy Department Seddon Memorial Technical College 1945–49; MP for Tamaki (National Party) 1949–57; entered N.Z. Cabinet 1954; Minister of Social Security and Minister in Charge of Tourist and Health Resorts 1954–56; Minister of Industries and Commerce and Minister of Customs 1956–57, 1958–69. In practice with Mabee, Halstead & Kiddle, Chartered Accountants, Auckland; Pres., Auckland Savings Bank; Dir. Air New Zealand; Auckland Univ. Councillor; Appointed N.Z. Ambassador to Thailand & Laos 1970–74; Council Rep. SEATO; Rep. N.Z. ECAFE Conference 1970, 1972; Deputy Chmn. Asian Inst. of Technology; Business Cnslt. & Co. Director since 1974; Appointed N.Z. Ambassador to Italy, Yugoslavia, Egypt, Iraq & Malta 1976. *Publications:* Six campaign booklets of 2 N.Z.E.F. (N.Z. Army Board); Text books and contributions on finance, economics and politics. *Address:* 5 Pere St., Remuera, Auckland, NZ.

**HALSTEAD, Ronald,** CBE. British co. dir. *B.* 1927. *Educ.* Lancaster Royal Grammar Sch.; Queen's Coll. Cambridge. *M.* 1968, Yvonne Cecile de Monchaux. *S.* 2. *Career:* Research Chemist H. P. Bulmer and Co. Ltd. 1948–53; Mftg. Man. Macleans Ltd. 1954–55; Factory Man. Beechams Products Inc. (U.S.A.) 1955–60; Asst. Man. Dir. Beecham Research Labs. Ltd., 1960–62; Pres. Beecham Research Labs. Inc. (U.S.A.) 1962–64 (now Beecham Pharms.); Vice-Pres. Marketing, Beecham Products Inc. (U.S.A.) 1962–64; Chmn. Food and Drink Div. Beecham Group Ltd. 1964–67; Chmn. Beecham Products since 1967, and Man. Dir. Beecham Group Ltd. (all consumer-products) since 1973. *Fellow:* Royal Soc. of Arts; B.I.M.; Inst. of Marketing. Council Mem. Food Manufacturers' Federation Inc. since 1966 (Pres. 1974–76); Council Mem., British Nutrition Foundation since 1967 (Chmn. 1970–73); Governor, Ashridge Mgmt. College since 1970. Hon. Vice-Pres., Proprietary Assn. of Gt. Britain since 1977 (Vice-Chmn., 1968–77); Vice-Chmn. Advertising Assn. since 1973. *Member:* (Council) C.B.I. since 1970; (council) B.I.M. since 1972; Board, Nation Coll. of Food Technology since 1977. *Awards:* Commander of the British Empire (1976); MA, BSc, FRIC. *Clubs:* Royal Thames Yacht; Hurlingham; Junior Carlton; Lansdowne. *Address:* 37 Edwardes Square, London W8 6HH; and *office* Beecham Products, Beecham House, Brentford, Middx. TW8 9BD.

**HAMAKER, Dr. John Charles, Jr.** *B.* 1924. *Educ.* Univ. of Michigan (BSE 1945, MSE 1947, PhD 1952, all in metallurgical engineering). *M.* 1947, Phyllis Bourbonnais. *S.* John C. III. *Dau.* Joanne C. *Career:* Lieut. (j.g.) U.S.N.R. (Fighter Direction Officer on aircraft carrier) 1945–46. Research Engineer International Nickel Co. Research Laboratory 1948; Consultant, Foundry Services Inc. 1950; Plant Metallurgist, General Iron Works 1951–53. With Vanadium-Alloys: Research Metallurgist 1953–54; Manager Research 1955–58; Director of Res. & Metallurgical Engineering 1959–61. President, Rodney Metals, 1968—. Vice-Pres. Technology & Director: Vanadium-Alloys Steel Co. U.S.A. 1961–68, Vanadium Alloys Steel Co. Canada Ltd. 1961—, and Vasco Metals Corp. U.S.A. 1965–68. Co-author: Tool Steels (Amer. Socy. for Metals 1962); Tool Steels (metals engineering textbook 1958). Author of technical papers published in Europe; contributor to professional journals and associations. Owner of several patents in high alloy steels and special heat treatments. Sigma Xi, Tau Beta Pi, Phi Lambda Upsilon, Phi Kappa Phi, Phi Eta Sigma. Delivered over 100 lectures in U.S. and Canada; member of several advisory board panels of Natl. Acad. of Sciences; Chmn. Standards Cttee. A.S.A. *Member:* Amer. Socy. for Metals (National Trustee) (Chmn. Natl. Tech. Council); Amer. Inst. Mining & Met. Engineers; Iron & Steel Inst. (London); American Iron & Steel Inst. (Chmn. High Strength Steel Cttee.); Socy. Automotive Engrs. American Vacuum Socy. *Clubs:* Rotary, Country (New Bedford); Aircraft Owners & Pilots Assn. *Address:* *office* Rodney Metals, 1257 E. Rodney French Blvd., New Bedford, Mass., U.S.A.

**HAMBURGER, Ferdinand, Jr.** Dr. of Engineering. *B.* 1904. *Educ.* BEng 1924; Dr Eng 1931. *M.* 1931, Opal Leavitt.

*Career:* Electrical testman, Consolidated Gas, Electric Light & Power Co., Baltimore 192 4–25;Research Asst., Johns Hopkins Univ. 1925–29; from 1931, successively Instructor, Associate, Associate Professor, and Professor in Electrical Engineering 1947. Instructor, night courses in technology 1929–42; Special Master, U.S. District Court 1936–37, 1939. Chief Test Engineer, Bendix Radio Division 1942–45; Consultant, National Defense Research Council 1944–45; and Research and Standards section, Bureau of Ships, Navy Department 1945–46; Research Contract Director, contracts between Dept. of Defense and Johns Hopkins 1945–70; Dir., Carlyle Barton Laboratory, Institute for Co-operative Research, The Johns Hopkins University 1958–70. Consultant to May Oil Burner Corp., Adler Safety Control Co., Maryland State Police, Radio Station W.C.A.O., Bendix Radio Div., Radio Corp. of America. Professor of Electrical Engineering. Chairman, Electrical Engineering Department, The Johns Hopkins University 1954–70; Prof. Emeritus, Electrical Engineering since 1970; Dir. of Centennial Planning 1970–76. *Publications:* numerous papers on electronics, radio, instrumentation, dielectrics in professional journals. *Member:* Inst. of Electrical & Electronics Engineers (Fellow; Director 1963–64); Sigma Xi; Tau Beta; Eta Kappa Nu. *Clubs:* Engineers (Baltimore); Johns Hopkins (Pres., 1969–71). *Address:* 3900 North Charles Baltimore, Street, Md. 21218, U.S.A.

**HAMDANI, Dr. Viqar Ahmed.** Ambassador of Pakistan. *B.* 1911. *Educ.* Deccan Coll., Poona; Jesus Coll., Oxford (BA; DPhil); Lincoln's Inn, London; Bombay Univ. (MA Hons. Gold Medallist); James Mew Arabic Scholar (Oxford Univer.). *M.* 1942, Nafisa Panchasi. *S.* 1. *Daus.* 4. *Career:* Formerly Tutor to Heir Apparent of Junagadh State; Prof. of Islamic Culture, Bahaudin Coll., Junagadh. Joined Pakistan Foreign Service June 1950; Chargé d'Affaires, Djakarta 1951–52; Alternate Representative of Pakistan to U.N. until 1955; Counsellor, Cairo 1955–56; Dep. Secretary, Ministry of Foreign Affairs, Karachi 1956–58; Consul General, Damascus (U.A.R.) 1959–61; Minister, Deputy Permanent Representative of Pakistan to U.N., New York, 1961–64; Ambassador to Sudan and Ethiopia 1964. *Address:* c/o Ministry of Foreign Affairs, Karachi, Pakistan.

**HAMER, Alan William.** Australian. *B.* 1917. *Educ.* Geelong Grammar School, Melbourne Univ. and Oxford Univ. (MA, BSc—1938 Victorian Rhodes Scholar). *M.* 1948, Margaret Elizabeth Angas. *S.* Angas William Fife, Michael David and Jonathan Mark. *Dau.* Victoria. *Career:* Joined I.C.I. of Aust. and N.Z. 1941; successively Works Manager, Yarraville 1950–52, Technical Manager, Chemicals 1953–55, Development Controller 1956–58; Operations Director, I.C.I. of Australia and New Zealand 1959. Chairman, I.C.I. Group of Companies in India, Apr. 1968–71; Joint Man. Dir. I.C.I. Australia Ltd. since 1971. *Member:* Royal Aust. Chemical Inst.; Inst. of Directors. *Clubs:* Melbourne, Royal Melbourne Golf, Barwon Heads Golf, Royal Melbourne Tennis, Royal & Ancient Golf, Oriental. *Address:* ICI Australia Ltd., ICI House, 1 Nicholson Street, Melbourne, Australia.

**HAMER, Ian Malcolm.** Canadian professional engineer and consultant. *B.* 1914. *Educ.* Univ. of Toronto (BASc 1937; Fellowship 1938). *M.* 1941, Gladys Johnston. *S.* David Ian Wallace. *Daus.* Kathryn Eryl, and Mary Margot. *Career:* Dir., Vice-Pres. and General Manager, Dowty Equipment of Canada Ltd. 1956–60; Dir. and Pres., Cametoid Ltd. 1956–60, and Dowty Mining Ltd. 1958–60; Technical Dir. 1952–56, Chief Engineer 1941–52, Dowty Equipment of Canada Ltd.; Consultant to Royal Commission on Government Organization 1960, Privy Council of Canada. *Fellow:* Royal Aeronautical Society, and Canadian Aeronautics and Space Institute (Founding Councillor); member, Engineering Institute of Canada. *Clubs:* University (Toronto). *Address:* 'Westlea', 701 King Street, Whitby, Ont., Canada.

**HAMILTON, Anthony Mordaunt.** South African Diplomat. *B.* 1909. *Educ.* University of Johannesburg (BA Hons.) and New College, Oxford, *M.* 1938, Emily Cardross Grant. *S.* Timothy Patrick. *Daus.* Vanesas and Catherine. *Career:* First Secy., London 1947–53; Counsellor, Washington 1954–57; High Commissioner in Australia 1957–61. Member, South African Delegation to U.N. 1947, 1948 and 1950. Special High Commissioner at Malayan Independence Celebrations 1957, and Ceylon's 10th Anniversary Celebrations 1958; Ambassador to Sweden and Finland 1961–65; Ambassador of the Republic of South Africa to Spain, Sept. 1965–68; Deputy Secretary, Foreign Affairs, Pretoria, 1969–70; Consul-Gen. of South Africa in Tokyo 1970. *Clubs:* Pretoria and Country (Pretoria). *Address:* Department of Foreign Affairs, Pretoria, South Africa.

**HAMILTON, Sir (Charles) Denis,** DSO. *B.* 1918. *Educ.* Middlesbrough High School. *M.* 1939, Olive Wanless. *S.* 4. *Career:* Staff of Evening Gazette (Middlesbrough) 1937–38; Evening Chronicle (Newcastle) 1938–39; Served in World War II (Officer T.A.) Durham Light Infantry; Lieut.-Col. Comdg. 11th Bn. D.L.I. and 7th Bn. The Duke of Wellington's Regt. in 21 Army Gp.) 1944–45, Personal and Editorial Assistant to Viscount Kemsley 1946–50; Editorial Dir. of the Kemsley (now Thomson) Newspapers 1950–67; Chmn. Natl. Council, Training of Journalists 1956–57; Editor, The Sunday Times 1961–67; Editor in Chief and Chief Executive, Times Newspapers Ltd. 1967–70; Chmn. and Editor in Chief since 1971; Dir. Reuters Ltd. *Member:* Council, Newspaper Publishers' Association Press Council; Chmn. British Museum Publications; Gov. Brit. Inst. Florence; Trustee, British Museum; Mem. Bd. of the British Library; British Overseas Trade Bd. *Decorations:* Knight Batchelor 1976. *Publications:* Kemsley Manual of Journalism (Jnt. Editor), 1950. *Address:* 25 Roebuck House, Palace St., London, S.W.1; and *office* PO Box 7, New Printing House Square, Gray's Inn Rd., London WC1X 8EZ.

**HAMILTON, Hon. (Francis) Alvin (George),** PC, MP, *B.* 1912. *Educ.* Saskatchewan Teachers College Saskatoon, and Univ. of Saskatchewan (BA 1937; BA with Hons. in History). *M.* 1936, Constance Beulah Florence Major. *S.* Robert Alexander and William Alvin. *Career:* Rural School Teacher 1931–34; Teacher, Nutana Collegiate, Saskatoon 1938–41; Navigator with R.C.A.F. with service in Canada, Gt. Britain, N. Africa, Northern India and Burma (discharged with rank of Flight-Lieut.) 1941–45; returned to teaching at Nutana Collegiate 1945–48; travel and study 1948; Provincial Leader and Provincial Organizer for Progressive Conservative Party in Saskatchewan 1949–57. Minister of Agriculture 1960; sworn to the Privy Council. Federal Government of Canada 1957 as Minister of Northern Affairs and National Resources; elected Member (Progressive Conservative Party) for Qu'Appelle 1957, re-elected Mar. 1958 and June 1962. Federal Candidate for the Party, Rosetown-Biggar 1945 and 1949, and Qu'Appelle 1953; Provincial Candidate for the Party, Rosetown 1948, Lumsden 1952 and Saskatoon 1956. *Member:* Royal Canadian Air Force Assn.; Canadian Legion; Canadian NATO Parliamentary Assn.; Commonwealth Parliamentary Assn. *Club:* Kiwanis. *Address:* c/o Parliament Buildings, Ottawa, Ont., Canada.

**HAMILTON, Hamish.** British publisher. *B.* 1900. *Educ.* Rugby School and Caius College, Cambridge (MA; LLB). *M.* 1940, Countess Yvonne Pallavicino. *S.* Alastair Andrew. *Career:* Medical Student 1919–20; Barrister-at-Law, Inner Temple 1926; Man. Dir. Hamish Hamilton Ltd. 1931–72, Chmn. since 1931. Chevalier de la Légion d'Honneur (1953); Grande Ufficiale, Order of Merit, Italy (1976). *Clubs:* Garrick; Leander; MCC. *Address:* 35 Cumberland Terrace, London NW1.

**HAMILTON, Michael Aubrey.** British Politician. *B.* 1918. *Educ.* Radley; Oxford. *M.* 1947, Lavinia Ponsonby. *S.* 1. *Daus.* 3. *Career:* Conservative M.P. for Wellingborough 1959–1964, and for Salisbury since 1965. *Address:* Lordington House, Chichester, Sussex.

**HAMILTON, Sir Patrick George, Bt.** *B.* 1908. *Educ.* Eton and Oxford Univ. (MA). *M.* 1941, Winifred Mary (Stone), OBE, MA. *Career:* Chairman: Expanded Metal Co. Ltd. Director: Lloyds Bank Ltd.. Renold Ltd.. Simon Engineering Ltd.; Possum Controls Ltd.; Dir., Propeller Production, Min. of Aircraft Production 1942–44; Chmn., Adv. Cttee. on Commercial Information Overseas 1957–59; Dep.-Chmn., Exports Publicity Cncl. 1959–62; Chmn., Transport User's Consultative Cttee., N.W. area 1957–64; Member, Central Transport Consultative Cttee. 1963–64; Chmn. Mgmt. Cttee. Central Middlesex Hospital, 1964–70; Member ITA, 1965–69; Member, Airline Users Cttee. *Club:* Carlton. *Address:* 23 Cheyne Walk, London, S.W.3.

**HAMILTON, Hon. William McLean,** PC. *B.* 1919. *Educ.* Bachelor of Science (Commerce), Sir George Williams Univ. 1943. *M.* 1954, Ruth I. Seeman. *Career:* City Councillor, City of Montreal 1950–57; Member Canadian Parliament 1953–62; Postmaster-General of Canada 1957–62: Dir. Wasteco Disposal Ltd.; Foursome Development Ltd.; Richmond Landfill Ltd.; Phoenix Assurance Co. of Canada; Chmn. of the Bd., Fidelity Life Assurance Co. and Century Insurance Co. of Canada, 1968—; Pres. Brink Hamilton Enterprises

Ltd.; Past Pres. Vancouver Board of Trade; Pres. and Chief Exec. Officer, Employers' Council of British Columbia since 1973. *Awards:* National Brotherhood; Businessman of the Year; Gold Medal Assn. of Canadian Advertisers; Toastmasters' International Communication and Leadership Award. Member, Progressive Conservative Party of Canada. *Address:* 1630–1055 West Hastings St., Vancouver, B.C., Canada V6E 2E9.

**HAMILTON, William Maxwell,** CBE. British (N.Z. citizen) *B.* 1909. *Educ.* Auckland Univ. (DSc) and Massey Agric. Coll., (MAgrScDip Hons); Hon. DSc. *M.* 1945, Alice Annie Morrison. *S.* David John. *Dau.* Margaret Lyn. Joined D.S.I.R. 1936 (Scientific Liaison Officer, London 1937–40. Asst. Secy. 1948). Director General, Department of Scientific and Industrial Research, Apr. 1953–71. *Publications:* The Dairy Industry in New Zealand (1944); White Island (1959); Little Barrier Island (1961); about 30 scientific papers. *Fellow:* Royal Socy. of N.Z.; N.Z. Inst. of Agricultural Science; *Member:* Hon. Life N.Z. Socy. of Animal Production; N.Z. Ecological Socy. *Address:* P.O. Box 180 Warkworth, New Zealand.

**HAMMAR, Birger.** Swedish. *B.* 1917. *Educ.* Lundsberg School; Stockholms Stad's Business School. *M.* 1945, Ylva Lagercrantz. *S.* 1. *Dau.* 1. *Career:* Man. Dir. Hammar & Co. AB; Chmn. Rank-Xerox AB; Hector & Co. all Stockholm. *Clubs:* Stora Sällskapet, Stockholm; Djursholms Golf, Djursholm. *Address:* Apelvägen 31, Stocksund, Sweden and *office* Nybrokajen 7, S111 48, Stockholm.

**HAMMARÉN, Eugen Arthur Lennart.** Finnish executive. *B.* 1923. *Educ.* Econ.cand; Authorized Auditor. *M.* 1953, Marita Hakola. *Career:* Office Manager with G. A. Serlachius oy Tako, Tampere 1955–59; Assistant Auditor with Wideonius, Sederholm & Someri 1952–55. Member of the Board, Nordiska Föreningsbanken, Nov. 1962. *Address:* c/o Aleksanterinkatu 30, Helsinki, Finland.

**HAMMARSKJOLD, Knut Olof Hjalmar Akesson.** Swedish. Minister Plenipotentiary, Swedish Foreign Service. *B.* 1922. *Educ.* Stockholm University. *Career:* Joined Swedish Foreign Service 1946, postings to Stockholm, Paris, Vienna, Moscow, Bucharest, Sofia, Kabul, Swedish delegate O.E.C.D. (Paris); Swedish Civil Aeronautics Bd., 1957–59. Dep. Secy. Gen., E.F.T.A. (Geneva) 1960–66. Director General, International Air Transport Association, since 1966. *Awards:* Cmdr. 1st Class Order of the North Star (Sweden); Cmdr. Order of Lion (Finland); Order of the Falcon (Iceland); Commander of Orange Nassau (Netherlands); Order of the Black Star (France); Grand Officer, Order of Al-Istiqlal (Jordan); Hon. Fellow, Canadian Aeronautics & Space Inst., Ottawa; Member, Institute Transport (London); Academician, Honoris Causa, Mexican Academy of International Law. *Publications:* articles on political economic and aviation topics. *Address:* 1000 Sherbrooke Street West, Montreal, P.Q. H3A 2R4, Canada; and 26 Chemin de Joinville, 1216 Cointrin, Geneva, Switzerland.

**HAMMERLE, Rudolf.** Australian industrialist (textiles). *B.* 1904. *Educ.* Technical High School (Dipl Eng). *M.* 1940, Anita Becher. *S.* Hanno. *Dau.* Monika. *Career:* Member of Parliament (Nationalrat) 1962–71; Bd. of Dirs. F. M. Hammerle, Dornbirn (Austria); Town Councillor of Dornbirn 1958–71. Consul for Sweden since 1958. *Publications:* of a genealogical and heraldic nature. Mem. of the People's Party. *Club:* Rotary Int. (Past Pres.). *Address:* Oberdorfstr. 2, Dornbirn, Austria.

**HAMMERSHAIMB, V. U.** Danish Diplomat. *B.* 1914. *Educ.* Copenhagen Univ., Law Degree; Harvard Law Sch., Master of Laws. *M.* 1947, Evelyn Adams Holt. *S.* 2. *Daus.* 2. *Career:* Sec., Min. of Foreign Affairs, Copenhagen 1939–45; Vice-Consul, Consulate-General, New York 1945–50; Dep. Head of Dept., Min. of Foreign Affairs 1950–54; Dep. Chief, Danish Military Mission, Berlin 1954–58; Head of Dept., Min. of Foreign Affairs 1958–61; Asst. Sec. for Political Affairs, Copenhagen 1961–62; Ambassador to Venezuela 1962–66; Under-Sec. for Administration, Copenhagen 1966–73; Ambassador to the U.S.S.R. since 1973. *Awards:* Commander of the Order of Dannebrog. *Address:* Royal Danish Embassy, 9 Pereulok Ostrovskovo, Moscow, U.S.S.R.

**HAMMOND, Caleb D., Jr.** American. *B.* 1915. *Educ.* Worcester (Mass.) Polytechnic Inst. (BSc in Mech. Eng.). *M.* 1940. Patricia Treacy Ehrgott. *S.* C. Dean III. *Daus.* Beth L. and Wendie H. *Career:* Sales Engineer, The Texas Co. 1937–39; Produc. Mgr., C. S. Hammond & Co. 1939–42 (Vice-Pres. 1945–48). Officer (various ranks), U.S. Coast Guard Reserve 1942–45. Chairman of the Board, Hammond Inc., Maplewood, N.J. 1968—. Director, Maplewood Bank & Trust Co. Trustee, Hospital Center at Orange (N.J.). *Member:* American and Royal Geographical Societies and American Assoc. of Publishers. *Club:* Maplewood Country. *Address: office* 515 Valley Street, Maplewood, N.J., U.S.A.

**HAMMOND, E. Cuyler,** ScD. American. *B.* 1912. *Educ.* Yale Univ. (Major in Zoology; William R. Belknap Award in Biology 1935) and Johns Hopkins Univ. Sch. of Hygiene and Public Health (Thesis: Experiment Population Problems in Lower Organisms); MA (hon.) Yale Univ. 1953. *M.* 1948, Marian E. Thomas. *S.* 3. *Career:* Consultant, Dept. of Biology, Brookhaven Natl. Laboratory 1961–64; Prof. of Biometry, Yale (Dir. of Graduate Studies in Statistics; Chmn. of Univ. Exec. Cttee. on Statistics) 1953–58; Natl. Lecturer for Socy. of the Sigma Xi 1957–58; Lecturer in Statistics, Dept. Public Health, Yale 1952–53; U.S.A.A.F. (1st Lt., Capt., Major), Chief Statistics Dept. 1942–46; Vice-President, Epidemiology & Statistics, Amer. Cancer Socy. Inc., Sept. 1946—. Clinical Professor in Community Medicine, Mt. Sinai Sch. of Medicine, N.Y. 1966—. Lecturer in Preventive and Environmental Medicine, Albert Einstein College of Medicine. Member, Scientific Advisory Panel, Research to prevent blindness Inc. Civilian in Requirements Branch, Office of the Quartermaster-General, U.S. Army (Research into equipment, etc.) 1942; Consultant, Medical Research Section, Bureau of Aeronautics, U.S. Navy (personal selection tests) 1941–42; Associate Statistician, Div. of Industrial Hygiene, National Institute of Health, U.S. Public Health Service (research on fatigue in truck drivers, toxic vapour, etc.) 1938–42; Special Consultant to the Surgeon-General of the U.S.A.F. 1966. *Address:* 164 East 72nd Street, New York, N.Y. 10021, U.S.A.

**HAMMOND, John Payne.** American petroleum consultant. *B.* 1913. *Educ.* Univ. of Tulsa (BSPetEng). *M.* 1937, Katharine R. Rees. *Daus.* Grace (Betzer, Jr.), Patricia Kay (Watt), and Sara Jo. *Career:* With Amerada Petroleum Corp. since 1941; Asst. General Production Supt. 1951–58; Exec. Asst. 1959; Vice-Pres. 1960–62; Senr. Vice-Pres. 1962—; Exec. Vice-Pres. 1967; Director 1963–69. Executive Vice-President, Director, Amerada Hess Corp. 1969–71; President, Amerada Division, Amerada Hess Corp., 1969–71; Senior Vice-President 1962—, and Board of Directors 1963—, Amerada Petroleum Corp. *Member:* AIME (past Vice-Pres. and Dir.); Socy. of Petroleum Engineers of AIME (past Pres.); API; Mid-Continent (Dir.), RMOGA Oil and Gas Assn.; First National Bank and Trust Co., Tulsa. *Clubs:* Petroleum (Tulsa); Southern Hills; Country; Summit. *Address: office* Box 2902, Tulsa, Okla., U.S.A.

**HAMNER, Homer Howell.** University professor and public finance consultant. Holder of Edward L. Blaine Chair in Economic History, University of Puget Sound, Tacoma, Washington 1963. *B.* 1915. *Educ.* Glendale (California) College (AA), and University of Southern California (AB; JD; MA; PhD). *M.* 1947, Marjorie Dittus, *Daus.* Jean Lee (Nicholson) and Elaine Annette. *Career:* With Army of U.S. 1941–44 (Master Gunner) A.A.; Instructor, Department of Economics, University of Southern Calif. 1945–49; Chmn., Dept. of Economics, Baylor University, Waco, Texas 1949–55; Chairman Department of Business Administration and Economics, University of Puget Sound 1955–59. Consultant, State of Washington Tax Advisory Council 1957–58, Expenditure Advisory Council 1960; Dir. American Triad Corp. since 1965. Graduate School Fellow, U.S.C. 1945–48; Fellow, Central Banking Seminar, Federal Reserve Bank of Dallas, 1952; Fellow, Foundation for Economic Education 1953; Fellow, Institute for Freedom and Competitive Enterprise 1955; Director, School of Business Administration and Economics, University of Puget Sound 1959–63. Awarded Certificate of Merit for Distinguished Service, London 1973. *Publications:* Population Change in Metropolitan Waco, (1950); Economic Trends & Human Freedom (1954); The Basic Textbook—It is Adequate? Abstract of PhD Dissertation, The Journal of Finance (1954); various book reviews. Seminar-Fellow, Pacific Northwest Bell Tel. Co., 1970. *Member:* Phi Beta Kappa, Phi Kappa Phi, Order of Artus, Delta Theta Phi, Phi Rho Pi, Amer. Assn. of University Professors; Amer. Economic Assn.; Amer. Finance Assn.; Natl. Tax Assn.; Mu Sigma Delta; Alpha Kappa Psi; Pi Gamma Mu. *Address:* 4404 North 44th Street, Tacoma 98407, Wash.; and University of Puget Sound, Tacoma 98407, Wash., U.S.A.

**HAMYLTON JONES, Keith.** British diplomat. *B.* 1924. *Educ.* St. Paul's School (London); Balliol (Oxford) MA (Greats). *M.* 1953, Eira Morgan. *Dau.* 1. *Career:* HM Welsh Guards (Ensign; Lieut. in Italy; Staff Captain in France) 1943–46; HM Diplomatic Service: 3rd Secy. Warsaw, 2nd Secy. Lisbon, 1st Secy. Manila, Head of Chancery and HM Consul Montevideo 1962; Head of Chancery, Rangoon 1967; Asst. Head of S.E. Asia Dept., FCO 1968; HM Consul-Gen. Lubumbashi 1970–72; Counsellor, FCO 1973–74; Ambassador to Costa Rica since 1974. *Publications:* The Ideal World (Peter Myllent); The Real World (in preparation). *Address:* 71 Peel Street, Campden Hill, London W8; and Cedar Cottage, Tinkers Lane, Nr. Blackboys, Sussex.

**HAN, Dr. Pyo-Wook.** Korean Diplomat. *B.* 1916. *Educ.* Yun Hui Coll., Yonsei Univ., Seoul—AB (English); Syracuse Univ., N.Y.—AB (Phil.); Harvard Univ., Mass.—MA (Government); Univ. of Michigan—PhD (Political Science). *M.* 1942, Chungnim Choi. *S.* 1. *Career:* 1st Sec. & Dep. Chief of Mission 1949–54, Counsellor & Dep. Chief of Mission 1951–54, Minister Plenipotentiary & Dep. Chief of Mission 1954–60, Korean Embassy, Washington, D.C.; Research Fellow, Harvard Univ., Cambridge, Mass. 1961–62; Professorial Lecturer in International Relations & Politics, Graduate Sch. of George Washington Univ., Washington, D.C. 1963–65; Ambassador & Chief of Mission of Republic of Korea to UN HQ, Geneva 1966–68; Ambassador to Thailand & concurrently to The Maldives 1968–71; Perm. Observer of Rep. of Korea to UN, New York & concurrently to The Maldives 1971–73; Ambassador to Austria & concurrently to The Maldives 1973–77; Ambassador to the Court of St. James's since 1977. *Member:* American Soc. of International Law; American Political Science Assn.; Council on Foreign Relations, USA; National Pres. Club, USA; International Inst. for Strategic Studies. *Decorations:* ARENTS Medal, Alumni Award, Syracuse Univ., N.Y. 1956; LLD, Willamett Univ., Salem, Oregon 1957; Order of the White Elephant, Thailand 1971; Order of Kwang Wha Jang (1st Class Service Medal), Rep. of Korea 1976; Grand Decoration of Honour, Austria 1977. *Clubs:* Sunningdale Golf; Coombe Hill Golf; Travellers'. *Address:* Embassy of the Republic of Korea, 4 Palace Gate, London W8 5NF.

**HANCOCK, Sir Patrick Francis,** GCMG. *B.* 1914. *Educ.* Winchester Coll. and Trinity Coll., Cambridge. Entered Foreign Office 1937; P.P.S. to Foreign Secy. 1955; Head, Western Dept., Foreign Office 1956; Ambassador to Israel 1959–63; to Norway 1963–65. Deputy Under-Secretary of State, Foreign Office; Ambassador to Rome 1969–75; Secretary of the Pilgrim Trust. *Address:* The Old Vicarage, Affpuddle, Dorset.

**HANCOCK, Ronald Philip.** British. *B.* 1921. *Educ.* Shrewsbury House Prep. School and Epsom College; FCIB, ACII. *M.* 1958, Stella Florence Mathias. *S.* William Philip, Richard Henry. *Dau.* Anne Marie. *Career:* Lieut. R.N.V.R. 1940–46, Alexander Howden & Co. Ltd. 1938–40; Dir. Bland, Welch & Co. Ltd. 1946–70; Deputy Chmn. 1955; Dir. River Thames Insurance Co. Ltd.; River Severn Insurance Co. Ltd.; Deputy Chmn. Group Man. Dir. L. Hammond & Co. Holdings Ltd. 1971; Dir. International Risk Management Ltd. 1972—; American Risk Management Inc. 1972—; Chmn. European Risk Management Ltd, 1972—; Chmn. A.R.M. International Ltd. since 1972; Common Bros. Insurance Services Ltd. since 1973; Medical Insurance Agency Ltd. since 1974; Member of Lloyds. Freeman of the City of London. *Member:* Associate Chartered Insurance Inst. (ACII); Fellow Corporation of Insurance Brokers; member Worshipful Company of Carmen. *Clubs:* Royal Thames Yacht; Royal Burnham Yacht; Lloyd's Yacht City Livery. *Address:* Hillside Farm, Shere Road, West Horsley, Surrey; and *office* Walnut Tree House, Woodbridge Park Industrial Estate, Guildford, Surrey, GO1 1EJ.

**HANCOCK, Sir (William) Keith,** KBE, FBA, FAHA. Cav. Ufficiale Ord. del Merito, Italy 1961. Australian professor of history. *B.* 1898. *Educ.* Melbourne Grammar School; Melbourne Univ. (MA); Rhodes Scholar, Oxford Univ. (MA); DLitt (Rhodes, Cape Town, Oxford A.N.U.); LittD: Cambridge, Birmingham, Melbourne, Adelaide, Western Australia. *M.* 1925, Theaden Brocklebank (*D.* May 1960). *M.* 1961, Marjorie Eyre. *Career:* Director, School of Social Sciences (1956–61) and Professor of History, Australian National University 1956–65, Emeritus Professor 1966—. Fellow All Souls Coll., Oxford 1924–30; Prof. of Modern History, Univ. of Adelaide 1924–33; Prof. of History, Birmingham Univ. 1934–44; Chichele Prof. of Economic History, Univ. of Oxford 1944–49; Dir., Inst. of Commonwealth Studies and Prof. of Commonwealth Affairs, Univ. of London 1949–56; appointed to War Cabinet Offices as Supervisor of Civil Histories; Hon. Member, Amer. Historical Assn. (1961); Amer. Academy of Arts and Sciences (1963); Hon. Fellow, Balliol College (1966). *Publications:* Ricasoli (1926); Australia (1930); Survey of British Commonwealth Affairs (1937, 1940–42); Argument of Empire (1943); Politics in Pitcairn (1947); (with M. M. Gowing) British War Economy (1950); Wealth of Colonies (1950); Country and Calling (1954); War and Peace in This Century (1961); Smuts: The Sanguine Years 1870–1919 (1962) (ed. with J. vander Peol) the Smuts Papers, Vols. I–IV (1966): Smuts: The Field of Force 1919–50 (1968); Discovering Monaro (1972); Professing History (1976). *Address:* The Australian National University, Canberra, A.C.T., Australia.

**HAND, Avery Chapman, Jr.** American Banker. *B.* 1918. *Educ,* Wharton School of Finance, University of Pennsylvania. Philadelphia (member Tau Chapter, Psi Upsilon Fraternity (National); Exchange Student, archaeological field work for Irish National Museum, Dublin, Eire). *M.* 1946, Mariann Stander. *Daus.* Jo Lynn, Jill Carla, Heidi Belinda, Holly Anne. *Career:* Served in World War II (Private to Major; overseas active service; Pre-Pearl Harbor Ribbon, E.T.O.; Ribbon with five stars, Victory Ribbon, etc.; Active Reserve Service 1946–48). With the Tracy & Avery Company (wholesale grocers), Marchand Markets (super-market chain) as executive, buyer, merchandiser, salesman 1939–41; President, Director, First National Bank of Mansfield, Ohio 1947—. Member, Board of Directors: The Euclid Coffee Co., Cleveland (Vice-Pres.); Industrial & Technical Sales & Service Inc., Mansfield; Lynn Realty & Construction Inc. (Treasurer), Mansfield; The Tracy & Avery Company (Vice-Pres.); Mansfield; former Chmn. Bd. Ohio Chamber of Commerce. Has visited 38 foreign countries. Congregationalist. *Clubs:* Westbrook Country (Bd. Trustees; Past Pres.), University, Fifty-One, The Our (Hon.), Bluecoats (all of Mansfield); Great Lakes Cruising; Huron (O) Yacht. *Address:* 145 South Linden Road, Mansfield, Ohio; and *office* The First National Bank of Mansfield, Ohio, U.S.A.

**HANDLER, Arieh Leon.** British *B.* 1915. *Educ.* Magdeburg (Matriculation); Rabbinic Seminary, Berlin (Teacher's Dipl.); London School of Economics (Post-graduate studies). *M.* 1940, Henny Prilutzky. *S.* Daniel and Gabriel. *Career:* Director: Religious Jewish Youth Organisation in Germany 1937–38, and the same organization for Great Britain, Ireland and Western Europe 1939–47, and World Movement of Religious Zionist Workers Organisation 1948–55 (also Treasurer of that organization in Israel 1948–55). Managing Director, Migdal Insurance Co. in U.K. 1956–61. Financial Consultant. Chairman, Bachad Fellowship. Member: Council of Jewish Colonial Trust and Actions Cttee World Zionist Movement; Mem. of World Exec. of Movement of Religious Zionists; Founder Member Jewish Agency Assembly; Mem. of Bd. of Deputies of British Jews. Founder and Editor of Chayenu Organ of Religious Youth 1937–47. *Publications:* on a number of educational and economic problems. *Member* Inst. of Directors; Inst. of Bankers; Insurance Inst. of London. *Clubs:* Reform. (London). *Address:* 24 Wellington Road, London, N.W.8.

**HANDS, H. William.** American *B.* 1913. *Educ.* Dartmouth Coll. (AB) and Amos Tuck School of Business Administration (MBA). *M.* 1937. Alice Carew Macdonald. *S.* Geoffrey W. *Dau.* Deirdre Macdonald. *Career:* Vice-Pres., Abbott Laboratories, Chicago 1961–64; and Vice-Pres. International, Amer. Hosp. Supply Co., Evanston, Ill. 1958–61; Gen. Sales Mgr. (Peru) Standard Oil Co. (N.J.) 1954–58; Gen, Mgr., Flowerfield Bulb Farm, N.Y. 1940–45; Buyer, B. Altman & Co., Fifth Ave., N.Y.C. 1936–40. Director International Marketing, H. K. Porter Co. Inc., New York City 1965—. Trustee, Barat College, Lake Forest. Ill. 1961–72. Dir., Intl. Executives Assn. 1976. *Publications:* The Used-Car Problem, (1936); Fall Bulbs (magazine article. 1944). *Clubs:* University (N.Y.C.); Old Lyme Country Club; Old Lyme Beach Club. *Address:* Lyme, Conn.; and *office* 405 Park Avenue, New York City, U.S.A.

**HANDSCHIN, Eric Charles.** Swiss manufacturer. *B.* 20 Sept. 1913. *Educ.* Liestal (Switzerland) and Bendigo (Australia) Schools, Textile Technical College, Reutlingen, Württemberg and studies in Paris and Milan. *M.* 1945, Trudi Kriesemer. *S.* 3. *Daus.* 1. *Career:* Chairman, Hanro Ltd., and subsidiary companies. Member of Board; Ed. Dubied & Cie. S.A., Neuchatel; Swissair, Zürich; Balair Ltd. Basle; and Bl. Hypothekenbank, Liestal. Member, Basle Chamber of Commerce. *Address:* Hanro Ltd., 4410 Liestal, Switzerland.

**HANES, John Wesley, Jr.** American. *B.* 1925. *Educ.* Deerfield (Mass.) Academy and Yale Univ. (BA 1950). *M.* 1949, Lucy Pomeroy Deans. *S.* John Wesley III. *Daus.* Lucy Pomeroy, Carol Mitchel and Lindsay Philips. *Career:* with Army of U.S. (from Private to Captain) 1943–46: Economic Specialist, Office of High Commissioner, Germany/Frankfurt/M, Berlin Munich) 1950–52; Special Asst. to Secy. of State 1953–57; Dep. Asst. Secy. of State for International Organization Affairs 1957–59; Asst. Secy. of state (Administrator of Security and Consular Affairs) 1959–61. General Partner, Wertheim & Co. Inc. New York City 1964–72; (Associate 1961–63); Senior Vice Pres. 1972–75; Limited Partner since 1975; Chmn. of the Board, Inverness Capital Corp. Inc. since 1975; President and Member, Board of Directors, the Hanes Foundation 1952—. Member, Board of Directors: Ohio Plate Glass Corp. Toledo; Olin Corp. 1963—; Squibb Corp., New York City 1967— (Member Executive Cttee.). Experience: U.S. Representative at Executive Committee of U.S. High Commissioner for Refugees, Geneva 1957–58; U.S. Delegate to World Health Organization, Minneapolis 1958; Vice-Chmn., U.S. Delegation and U.S. Delegate to UNESCO, Paris 1958; Member, Commission International Rules of Judicial Procedure 1959—61; U.S. Representative at Council of Inter-Governmental Committee for European Migration, Geneva 1959–60; Co-Commissioner and Chmn. of U.S. Section of the Caribbean Commission 1960–61. Republican. *Clubs:* Capitol Hill, Metropolitan, Nineteen Twenty-Five F. Street (Washington, D.C.); Boone & Crockett, Links, Explorers (all of N.Y.C.). *Address:* Gunnell's Run Farm, P.O. Box 64, Great Falls, Va. 22066; and *office* Wertheim & Co., 1 Chase Manhattan Plaza, New York, N.Y. 10005, U.S.A.

**HANGER, Hon. Sir Mostyn,** KBE. Australian Judge. *B.* 1908. *Educ.* Univ. of Queensland (BA; LLM)). *M.* 1936, Greta Lumley Robertson. *S.* John Mostyn, David Sydney and Richard Ian. *Dau.* Kathryn Gertrude. *Career:* Flight Lieut., Royal Australian Air Force, 1942–45; began practice at Bar, Feb. 1932; appointed KC 1950. Judge of the Supreme Court of Queensland since 1953, and Pres. of the Industrial Court, Nov. 1961–71; Senior Puisne Judge of Supreme Court, 1970—; Acting Chief Justice, 1970—; Chief Justice since 1971. *Club:* Queensland; United Services. *Address:* 73 Seventh Avenue, St. Lucia, Brisbane, Qld., Australia.

**HANKE, Lewis Ulysses.** American historian. *B.* 1905. *Educ.* Northwestern Univ. (BS) and Harvard Univ. (PhD). *M.* 1926, Kate Ogden Gilbert. *S.* Jonathan and Peter. *Daus.* Susan and Joanne. *Career:* Instructor, Univ. of Hawaii 1926–27; Adjunct Prof., American Univ. of Beirut 1927–30; Tutor, Harvard Univ. 1934–39; Director, Hispanic Foundation, Library of Congress 1939–51; Professor of Latin American History 1951–61, and Director, Institute of Latin American Studies 1951–58, Univ. of Texas; Professor of History, Columbia Univ. 1961–67; Univ. of California, Irvine, 1967–69. Professor of Latin American History, Univ. of Massachusetts, 1969—; member, Board of Trustees, Hispanic Society of America, Apr. 1961—. *Publications:* First Social Experiments in America, (1935); Spanish Struggle for Justice in the Conquest of America, (1949); Aristotle and the American Indians, (1959); Modern Latin America—Continent in Ferment (2 vols. 1966); History of Latin American Civilization (2 vols. 1967). Editor: Handbook of Latin American Studies, 1937–40; Hispanic American Historical Review, 1954–60, (with Manuel Giménez Fernández), Bartolomé de las Casas—Bibliografía Critica; Historia de la Villa Imperial de Potosí (3 vols.) (with Gunnar Mendoza 1965); Orden del Sol (Peru); Cruzeiro do Sul (Brazil); Condor de los Andes (Bolivia). Beveridge Prize, American Historical Association 1947; Doctor Honoris Causa, Universidade de Bahia 1959; Univ. Tomás Friás 1965, and Univ. de Sevilla 1966. Texas Institute of Letters Prize 1960. *Member:* American Historical Assocn, President 1974; Corresponding Member: historical academies of Argentina, Cuba, Spain, Guatemala, Venezuela. *Clubs:* Cosmos (Washington); Beta Theta Pi. *Address:* Dept. of History, Univ. of Massachusetts, Amherst, Mass. 01002, U.S.A.

**HANKEY, Lord** (Robert Maurice Alers Hankey), KCMG, KCVO. British diplomat. *B.* 1905. *Educ.* Rugby; New College, Oxford (BA). *M.* 1930, Frances Bevyl Stuart-Menteth (*D.* 1957). *S.* 2. *Daus.* 2. *M.* (2) 1962, Joanna Riddell, dau. of late Rev. James Wright and Mrs. Joanna Campbell Wright. *Career:* Entered Foreign Service 1927; appointed to British Embassy, Berlin 1927, Paris 1928; Private Secretary to Rt. Hon. Anthony Eden, Foreign Office 1933–36, Warsaw 1936–39, Bucharest 1939, Cairo 1941, Teheran 1942, Warsaw 1945, Head of Northern Department 1946–49; Chargé d'Affaires, British Embassy, Madrid 1949–51; En. Ex. and Min. Plen. to Hungary 1951–53; Amb. to Sweden 1954–60; U.K. Permanent Delegate and Official Chairman to O.E.E.C., Paris 1960–61; U.K. Delegate to O.C.E.D. 1961; Chairman Economic Policy Cttee. 1960–65. Grand Cross Order of North Star (Sweden 1956). Vice-Pres. European Inst. of Business Administration 1962—. Member, International Council of United World Coll. & Council International Baccalaureat; Director, Alliance Building Society; President Anglo Swedish Society, London 1970–75. *Address:* Hethe House, Cowden, Edenbridge, Kent.

**HANKEY, Hon. Henry Arthur Alers,** CMG, CVO. British diplomat. *B.* 1914. *Educ.* Rugby School and New College Oxford (Hons degree in Philosophy, Politics and Economics). *M.* 1941. Vronwy Mary Fisher. *S.* 3. *Dau.* 1. *Career:* First Secy. British Embassy, Madrid 1946, First Secy., British Embassy, Rome 1946–49. First Secy., Foreign Office 1949–50; Consul, San Francisco, California 1950–53. First Secy., British Embassy, Santiago 1953–56; Head of American Dept., Foreign Office 1956–62; Counsellor, Beirut 1962–66. Ambassador to Panama 1966–69. Under Secretary of State, Foreign & Commonwealth Office 1969–74; Dir. Lloyds Bank International Ltd., Antofagasta (Chili) and Bolivia Railway Co. Ltd. since 1975. *Club:* United University (London). *Address:* Hosey Croft, Hosey Hill, Westerham, Kent.

**HANKS, Stedman Shumway.** Col., U.S.A.F. (retd.); airport engineer and author. *B.* 1889. *Educ.* Groton School; Harvard (AB 1912); Columbia (AM 1946). *M.* 1952, Helen Chappell. *S.* Roger Stedman (by previous marriage). *Career:* Secy. to American Ambassador, London, 1912; U.S. Dept. of State, Washington 1915; Secy. to Pres., Amer. International Corp. 1915–20; Pres. Amer. Airports Corp. 1927–29; member, Mass. Cttee. for Aeronautics 1936–39; Major, Military Pilot, World War I; Colonel, World War II. President Stedman Hanks & Co. 1920—; Trustee, American Flight Strips Assn. 1936—; Associate Fellow, Inst. of Aerospace Sciences 1944—; Editor, Masterscope 1953—. *Publications:* International Airports (Ronald Press) (1929); Aviation Gets Down to Earth (1940); Frontiers Are Not Borders (Coward-McCann) (1955); Le Barzoi: Le Plus Noble des Lévriers (Perrin) (1960), with a German translation and an Annex (1962); Making an American (Vantage Press) (1976); many pamphlets and articles. Originated (1936) plan for combining local and federal funds for ground facilities for aircraft—called flight strips; and holds trade-mark registry for these auxiliary airfields. Republican. *Member:* Early Birds of Aviation; Society of Cincinnati; Socy. of Colonial War; Socy. of Mayflower Desc; Sons of Amer. Revolution (N.Y.). Socy. of War 1812; St. Nicholas Socy.; Order of Daedalians. *Clubs:* Piping Rock (Locust Valley, N.Y.); Union and Harvard (N.Y.). *Address:* 19 East 72nd Street, New York, N.Y. 10021, U.S.A.

**HANNAH, Air Marshal Sir Colin Thomas,** KCMG, KCVO, KBE, CB, KStJ. Australian. Governor of Queensland 1972–77. *B.* 1914. *Educ.* Hale School Perth; Royal Aust. Air Force Coll. Point Cook. *M.* 1939, Patricia Tracey Gordon. *Dau.* 1. *Career:* Commanding Officer No. 6 Squad; Officer Commanding No. 71 Wing New Guinea 1943–44; Royal Air Force Staff Coll. 1946–47; Senior Air Staff Officer R.A.A.F. Overseas H.Q. London 1947–49; Dir.-Gen. Personnel 1951–54; Imperial Defence Coll. 1955; Senior Air Staff Officer R.A.F. Far East Air Force 1956–59; Dir-Gen. Plans and Policy Dept. of Air 1959–61; Deputy-Chief, Air Staff 1961–65; Air Officer Commd. Operational Command R.A.A.F. 1965–68; Support Command 1968–70; Chief, Air Staff R.A.A.F. 1970–72; Governor of Queensland 1972–77. *Awards:* Knight Commander, Order of St. Michael and St. George; Knight Commander Royal Victorian Order; Knight Commander, Order of the British Empire; Companion Order of the Bath; Knight of the Order of St. John; Doctor of Griffith Univ. *Clubs:* Australian (Sydney). *Address:* c/o National Bank of Australasia Ltd., 308 Queen Street, Brisbane, Queensland 4000, Australia.

**HANNAH, Paul Francis.** American Lawyer. *B.* 1905. *Educ.* Dartmouth Coll. (BS) and George Washington Univ. (JD). *M.* 1933, Elizabeth Wingfield Jackson. *S.* Paul F., Jr. and Richard J. *Career:* Served in World War II (Bronze Star; Legion of Merit), Asst. Ed., Nature magazine, Washington, D.C. 1928–32, Associated with Morris, Kixmiller & Baar, Washington 1932–41; Junior Partner 1936–41, Raytheon Co., Gen. Counsel 1946–63; Vice-Pres. 1960–63; Partner Law Firm Gadsby & Hannah, Mass. since 1963. *Member:* American, House of Delegates 1966–75; Chmn. Public Contracts Section 1975–76; Massachusetts, Federal and Boston Bar Assns.;

Association of General Counsel; District Columbia Bar Assn.; Adv. Council, Amer. Arbitration Association. Fellow, American Bar Foundation; Republican. *Clubs:* Barristers; Union (Boston); Metropolitan (Washington); Chevy Chase (Md.); Brae Burn Country (Newton, Mass.). *Address:* 44 Hubbard Road, Weston 93, Mass. 02193; and *office* 140 Federal Street, Boston, Mass. 02110, U.S.A.

**HANNES, Jack Dieter**, BE, MIE (Aust.), FAIM. Australian. *B.* 1923. *Educ.* Buxton (Derbyshire U.K.) College, and Sydney University (BE). *M.* 1949, Morna Jean Houghton. *S.* Martin Roy and John Anthony. *Dau.* Vicki. *Career:* Graduated from Sydney Univ. with degree in Mechanical and Electrical Engineering 1943. Planning Engineer with Standard Telephones & Cables 1944; formed own company, Hanimex Pty. Ltd. as importers and distributors of photographic equipment 1947; built a first-class light engineering factory on seven acres at Brookvale, Sydney, and became first Australian company to specialize in complete design and manufacture of photographic equipment 1956; Company listed on all Australian stock-exchanges in 1957, and on London Stock Exchange 1964. Managing Dir. Hanimex Corp. Ltd. and subsidiary companies in Australia, New Zealand, U.K., U.S.A., Canada, Japan, Hongkong, France, Belgium, Switzerland, Ireland and Germany 1947—. *Member:* Institution of Engineers (Associate), Australia; Australian Inst. of Management (Fellow); Inst. of Directors; Royal Commonwealth Society. *Clubs:* Royal Prince Alfred Yacht; Comwlth. (Canberra); Royal Motor Yacht, Sydney. *Address:* 'Sonning', 1754 Pittwater Road, Bayview, N.S.W.; and *office* Hanimex Pty. Ltd., Old Pittwater Road, Brookvale, N.S.W., Australia.

**HANSEN, Prof. Kurt**, Dr-Ing, Dipl Kfm. German *B.* 1910. *Educ.* Technical High School, Munich (Dr-Ing; Dipl-Kfm). *M.* 1937, Irmi Strähuber. *S.* Gert. *Dau.* Karin. *Career:* With I.G. Farbenindustrie AG Bayer AG, Leverkusen, since 1936. Manager: Wuppertal-Elberfeld factory Apr. 1956; Member, Managing Board (responsible head of the production plants and research facilities for pharmaceuticals and crop protection products) July 1957; Chmn., Managing Bd., Farbenfabriken Bayer AG 1961–74; Chmn. Supervisory Board since 1974. Ehrensenator: Tierärzlischen Hochschule Hanover, Univ. of Bonn, and of Mainz; Hon. Prof. der Math. Naturwissenschaftl. Fakultät der Universität Köln; Vice-Pres. des Bundesverbandes der Deutschen Industries e.V.; Member of the Praesidium, Verband der Chemischen Industrie e.V.; Treasurer, Gesellschaft Deutscher Naturforscher und Arzt e.V. Foreign Correspondent in Germany of Conference Board, New York. Member, Supervisory Board, Hapag-Lloyd AG; Kaufhof AG; Veba AG. Allianz Versicherungs AG.; Siemens AG.; Otto Wolff AG. *Address:* Sürder Strasse 14, 509 Leverkusen-Schlebusch; and *office* 509 Leverkusen-Bayerwerk, Germany.

**HANSON, Bennie Teabeaut** (Mrs. Howell Ross Hanson). American. President, Atlanta Biltmore Hotel 1936—. Chmn. of Board, Edgewater Estates, Inc., Florida. *Educ.* Andrew College (AB 1908) and Randolph-Macon Women's College (AB 1912). *M.* (1) 1913, William Candler. *S.* William, Jr. *Dau.* Rena (Chambers). *M.* (2) 1938, Howell Ross Hanson. Named Woman of the Year in Business. Dir., American Cancer Society; Vice-Pres.: English Speaking Union, Crippled Children's Socy., and Uptown Assn. Sponsor, 'Women of the Year' Organization, 1960. Trustee, Randolph-Macon Women's College; Dir., Opera Guild; Hon. Steward, St. Mark's Methodist Church. *Member:* Advisory Board, Who's Who in Dining and Lodging on North American Continent (1958); Hostess for Gone With the Wind, 1960. *Clubs:* Capital City (Atlanta); Union League (Phila. and N.Y.); Surf (Miami Beach, Fla.). *Address: office* The Atlanta Biltmore Hotel, 817 West Peachtree Street, N.E., Atlanta, Ga., U.S.A.

**HANSON, Clarence Bloodworth, Jr.** American publisher, *B.* 1908. *Educ.* Univ. of Virginia (BS 1929); Hon. LittD. Univ. Alabama 1974. *M.* 1929, Elizabeth Fontaine Fletcher. *S.* Victor Henry II. *Career:* Maj. U.S. Army Air Force 1942–45. Previously: Advt. Dept., Indianapolis (Ind.) Star 1929–30, and The Birmingham News 1930–34; Natl. Advt. Mgr. (1934–36), and Vice-Pres. and Dir. (1936–45), The Birmingham News. Publisher The Birmingham News 1945—; Pres. and Dir. The Birmingham News Co. 1945—. Director and member Exec. Cttee.: The First National Bank of Birmingham; Ala. Bancorporation; Mercury Express Inc.; Dir. and Chmn. Exec. Cttee., Royal Crown Cola Co. *Member:* Associated Press (Vice-Pres. 1952–56), American Newspaper Publishers Association, Southern Newspaper Publishers Association (Pres. 1949–50), Alabama Press Association Pres. 1951–52); Trustee, Birmingham Mus. of Art, Eye Foundation Hosp., and Alabama Mus. of Natural History. Phi Gamma Delta. *Clubs:* Mountain Brook Country, Birmingham Country, Relay House, Birmingham; Hon. Co. of Edinburgh Golfers (Muirfield). *Address:* 4055 Old Leeds Road, Mountain Brook, Birmingham 35213, Ala.; and *office* 2200, 4th Avenue North, Birmingham 35202, Ala., U.S.A.

**HANSSON, Per M.** Norwegian. *B.* 1905. *Educ.* BA 1922; LLB Oslo University 1926. *M.* 1939, Astri Aubert. *S.* Christian, Per, Nils. *Daus.* Lucy, Ellen. *Career:* Chmn. Bd., Storebrand Insurance Co. Ltd., and of affiliated companies and Director of various manufacturing companies. *Awards:* Comdr., Order of St. Olav (Norway), and Kt. of Dannebrog (Denmark), Commander Order of El Merito (Chile); the Icelandic Falcon; Lejons Order (Finland). *Address:* Gregers Grams vei 3, Oslo 3. Norway.

**HARA, Sumio.** Japanese. Banker. *B.* 1911. *Educ.* Graduated Tokyo Imperial Univ. Dept. of Jurisprudence. *M.* 1939, Kazuko Mimura. *S.* 2. *Dau.* 1. *Career:* Joined Ministry of Finance Japanese Government 1934; Dep.-Dir. Budget Bureau, Min. Finance 1953–56; Dir.-Gen. Tax Bureau, Ministry of Finance 1956–60; Commn. Nat. Tax Admin. Agency 1960–62; Joined The Bank of Tokyo Ltd., elected Dep.-Pres. 1962–65; President 1965–73, Chmn. 1973–77, Exec. Adviser since 1977; Chmn. Bd. Dirs. Bank of Tokyo (Switzerland) Ltd.; Chmn. Exec. Cttee, Private Investment Co. for Asia (PICA) SA; Special Adviser to the Pres., Japan Chamber of Commerce and Industry; Dep. Pres., Tokyo Chamber of Commerce and Industry; Adviser Nat. Personnel Authority; Chmn. Examination Cttee. on Cert. Tax Acc (NTAA); Vice-Pres. Japan Tariff Assn.; The External Dev. Cooperation Council, (Prime Minister's Office); Tobacco Cultivation Council (Japan Monopoly Corp.); Economic Council (Prime Minister's Office); Japan–U.S. Economic Council; Trilateral Commission; Rockefeller Univ. Council; Internat. Advisory Board, Sperry Rand Corp. *Club:* Rotary. *Address:* 26–14 Tsutsujigaoka, Midori-Ku, Yokohama City, Kanagawa-Ken, Japan; and *office* 1–1, Muromachi 2-chome, Nihombashi, Chuo-ku, Tokyo, Japan.

**HARBEK, Odd.** MSc. Norwegian. *B.* 1922. *Educ.* Tech. Univ. of Denmark, Copenhagen (MSc.). *M.* 1958, Helen Wilhelmsen. *S.* 1. *Career:* Pres., A/S Oil Services. *Member:* Royal Institution Naval Architects; Norwegian Assoc. Chartered Engineers. *Address:* Glassverkvn, 25c-N 1322 Hoevik, Norway; and *office* Dronning Mauds gt. 3; P.O. Box 1714 Vika, Oslo 1, Norway.

**HARCOURT, Viscount (William Edward)**, KCMG, OBE, MA. *B.* 1908. *Educ.* Eton; Christ Church, Oxford. Widowed. *Daus.* 3. *Career:* Man. Dir., Morgan Grenfell & Co. Ltd. 1938–69, Chmn. 1969–73; Minister (Econ.) H.M. Embassy, Washington; Head British Treasury Deleg. in U.S.; Exec. Dir. Internat. Monetary Fund; also of International Bank for Reconstruction and Development (all 1954–57); Chairman: Legal and General Assurance Society Ltd. 1958–77. *Member:* Departmental (Radcliffe) Cttee. on Monetary and Credit Policy, 1957–59; and of Prime Minister's (Plowden) Cttee. on the Reorganization of the Representational Services Overseas, 1962–64. Hon. Fellow, St. Anthony's Coll., Oxford: Chmn. Governors of Museum of London; Rhodes Trust; Oxford Preservation Trust; Vice-Lieut, Oxfordshire. Conservative. *Clubs:* Whites; Pratts; *Address:* Stanton Harcourt, Oxford, and *office* 23 Great Winchester Street, London EC2P 2AX.

**HARDEEN, Theodore.** American. *B.* 1905. *Educ.* Univ. of Virginia (LLB 1930). *M.* 1952, Elizabeth Brett. *S.* Theodore Brett. *Career:* Administrative, Defence Air Transportation Administration 1952–63; U.S. Representative to NATO Civil Aviation Planning Cttee; Chmn. U.S. Delegation 1955–63. General Counsel, Virginia Stage Lines Inc., Mar. 1964—. *Award:* U.S.A.F. Commendation Medal, Air Medal. *Clubs:* University (Washington); Tavern (Chicago); Farmington Country, Boars Head, Farmington Hunt (all of Charlottesville, Va.); Everglades (Palm Beach, Fla.). *Address: office* 114 4th Street, S.E., Charlottesville, Va., U.S.A.

**HARDER, Hudson Orlan.** American oil executive. *B.* 1905. *Educ.* Univ. of Oklahoma (AB). *M.* 1929, Lucille Roby. *Dau.* Hope. *Career:* Petroleum Engr. and Supt. Prodn., Cities Service Oil Co. 1927–45; Gen. Supt. Prodn., Sunray Oil Corp. 1945–49; Vice-Pres. and Manager Prodn. 1949–52; Vice-Pres. and Mgr. Explor. 1952–55; Vice-Pres. and Mgr. Explor., Sunray Mid-Continent Oil Co. 1955–59. (Snr. Vice-Pres. & Dir. 1959–62). Executive Vice-Pres. and Director, Sunray DX Oil Co., 1962–66; Dir., Pacific Petroleums Ltd.;

Chmn. Univ. Oklahoma Foundation. *Member:* Amer. Petroleum Inst.; Amer. Inst. of Mining and Metallurgical Engineers; Ind. Petroleum Assn.; Landmen's Petrol. Assn. of Amer. Phi Kappa Sigma; Pi Tau Epsilon; Sigma Tau; Beta Gamma Sigma. Republican. Member, Reorganized Church of Jesus Christ of Latter Day Saints. Mason (Consistory K.T.). *Address:* 3914 South Delaware Place, Tulsa, Okla., U.S.A.

**HARDER, Lewis Bradley.** American mining executive. *B.* 1918. *Educ.* Harvard (BA 1941). *M.* 1941, Dorothy Butler. *Daus.* Deirdre and Diana. *Career:* Distinguished Service Cross (U.S. Naval Aviator). Partner, Harris Upham & Co., Investment Bankers 1946–54. Chairman, International Mining Corp. since 1956. Director: Pato Consolidated Gold Dredging Ltd. since 1956, Madison Fund Inc. 1956—, Molybdenum Corp. of America; Indian Head, Inc.; Crane Co.; Bancroft Convt. Fund; Brascan Ltd.; Kawecki-Berylco Industries; Roman Corp.; Pittsburg & West Virginia R.R. since 1961; Dir. Chicago Rock Island & Pacific Railroad Co.; Dir. First National Stores. *Clubs:* Brook; Bedford Golf and Tennis; National Golf; Seminole Golf. *Address: office* 280 Park Avenue, New York City, U.S.A.

**HARDER, William Hartman.** *B.* 1908. *Educ.* Cornell Univ. (AB 1930), and New York Univ. (Business Admin.) 1930–34. *M.* 1935, Jane Torrence. *S.* William H., Jr. and Torrence C. *Daus.* Luella and Sarah Jane. *Career:* Clerk: First National Bank of Boston 1930–32, and First Boston Corp. 1932–37 (Mgr. Buffalo office 1937–46); successively Mgr. Bond Dept. Buffalo Savings Bank 1947, Vice-Pres., 1948, Trustee, 1954, Exec. Vice-Pres., 1960, Pres. 1961, Chmn. Bd. Chief Exec. Officer 1972–73; Chmn. Buffalo Savings Bank 1961–73. Director: Institutional Investors Mutual Fund, National Fuel Gas Co., Savings Bank Trust Co.; Cornell Univ. Council; Manufacturers & Traders Trust Co. of Buffalo, and Buffalo Chamber Commerce. Pres., Children's Foundation of Erie County; Trustee, Buffalo Seminary; Treas. Millard Fellmore Hospital. *Member:* Newcomen Socy. of North America; International Platform Assn. *Clubs:* Buffalo; Midday; Country; Cornell (N.Y.C.). *Address:* 8000 Feddick Road, Hamburg, N.Y. 14075; and *office* Buffalo Savings Bank, 545 Main Street, Buffalo 3. N.Y., U.S.A.

**HARDIE, Sir Charles (Edgar Mathewes),** CBE. British. *B.* 1910. *Educ.* Aldenham School; qualified as chartered accountant. *M.* (1) 1937 Dorothy Jean Hobson (*Dec.* 1965), *S.* 1. *Daus.* 3. (2) 1966, Mrs. Angela Richli (*diss.* 1973). (3) 1975, Rosemary Margaret Harwood. *Career:* Chartered Accountant, Partner, Dixon Wilson and Co. since 1934; Director: British American & General Trust Ltd.; British Printing Corp. Ltd.; Wm. Cook & Sons (Sheffield) Ltd.; Mann Egerton & Co. Ltd.; Royal Bank of Canada; Trust Houses Forte Ltd.; Westminster Property Group Ltd. *Fellow:* Institute of Chartered Accountants in England and Wales; Legion of Merit, U.S.A. *Clubs:* Naval & Military; Canada. *Address:* The Old School House, Sturminster Newton, Dorset; 207 Cranmer Court, London SW3 3HG; *office:* Gillett House, 55 Basinghall Street, London EC2V 5EA.

**HARDING, Charles Malim,** OBE, BA. Canadian executive. *B.* 1911. *Educ.* Univ. of Toronto Schools; Univ. of Toronto (entered 1928 on Edward Blake Scholarship in Mathematics; graduated in Political Science 1931; Gold Medallist). *M.* 1947, Constance Hope. *S.* Charles Malim Victor. *Daus.* Stephanie Hope Magee and Debora Mary. *Career:* With Canada Packers Ltd. 1931–33, and Harding Carpets Ltd. 1933—; Served in World War II 1939–45 (overseas with 54th Battery 1st Field Regiment RCHA 1939, served in various capacities including GSO-1 Fourth Canadian Armoured Div. in England, and GSO-1 First Candian Div., and finished war with rank of Colonel as Chief Instructor, Royal Military College, Kingston, Ont.); Chairman of the Board, Harding Carpets Ltd., Union Gas Co. of Canada Ltd.; Director: Confederation Life Assn., Toronto-Dominion Bank; Director, Canadian Corporate Mgmt. Co. Ltd. *Awards:* OBE; Hon. LLD, Univ. of Toronto 1977. *Clubs:* Toronto, Toronto Golf, Queens, York (Toronto); Mount Royal (Montreal). *Address:* 48 Rosedale Road, Toronto, Ont.; and *office* 60 Yonge Street, Toronto, Ont. ME 1H5, Canada.

**HARDING, George William,** CMG, CVO. British Diplomat. *B.* 1927. *Educ.* Aldenham Sch., Hertfordshire; St. John's Coll., Cambridge—MA (Hons.). *M.* 1955, Sheila Margaret Ormond Riddel. *S.* 4. *Career:* Lieut., Royal Marines 1946–48; joined HM Diplomatic Service 1950; served in Singapore, Rangoon, Maymyo, Paris (twice), Santo Domingo, Mexico City; HM Ambassador, Lima since 1977. *Member:* Fellow of the Royal Geographical Society. *Decorations:* Companion of the Order of St. Michael & St. George, 1977; Commander of the Royal Victorian Order, 1972. *Clubs:* Garrick (London); Leander (Henley-on-Thames); Los Inkas Country Club (Lima). *Address:* Embajada Britanica, Apartado 854, Lima, Peru.

**HARDING, Hon. James McKay,** QC. Canadian. *B.* 1926. *Educ.* Acadia Univ. (BA) and Dalhousie Univ. (LLB). *M.* 1961, Mary Patricia Spitler. *S.* James, Donald, Rance and Trevor. *Career:* Minister of Public Welfare, Province of Nova Scotia, 1964–69, and Minister in charge of Nova Scotia Housing Commision 1964, Minister of Fisheries 1969–71. *Member:* Legislative Assembly for Shelburne 1956–60–63–67; Canadian Bar, and N.S. Bar Society. Progressive Conservative. *Club:* Royal Nova Scotia Yacht Squadron. *Address:* The Progressive Conservative Party, Halifax, N.S., Canada.

**HARDMAN, David Rennie,** MA, JP. British educational adviser and consultant. *B.* 18 Oct. 1901. *Educ.* Christ's College, Cambridge (MA, LLB). *M.* 1946, Barbara Lambert. *S.* 1. *Daus.* 2. *Career:* First Socialist Pres., Cambridge Union Society. *Member:* Cambs. C.C. 1937–46. Elected to Parliament 1945; Parly. Private Sec. to Lord Privy Seal 1945; Parly. Sec. Min. of Education 1945–51; service in World War II: A.B.C.A. lecturer to the three Services; Leader, UNESCO delegation of U.K., having served on London Preparatory Commission previously, Paris, Beirut, Mexico City, Paris and Florence 1946–52; Chmn., U.K. Education UNESCO Commission, and of UNESCO national committee for Wales; Justice of the Peace since 1940; President, Holiday Fellowship 1962; Professor of English Literature, Elmira Coll., N.Y. 1964–66; Barclay Acheson Prof. International Studies, Macalester Coll., Minn. 1967. Chmn., Inst. of Educational Television, London. Secretary, Cassel Educational Trust; Secretary, Stafford Cripps Memorial Trust. *Publications:* What About Shakespeare? (1939); Poems of Love and Affairs (1950); Telscombe—A Village in Sussex (1964); and other works and articles. *Club:* Savile. *Address:* Bankyfield, Hurstpierpoint, Sussex.

**HARDMAN, Sir Henry,** KCB. *B.* 1905. *Educ.* Manchester Central High Sch., and Univ. of Manchester. *M.* 1937, Helen Diana Bosanquet. *S.* 1. *Daus.* 2. *Career:* Lect., W.E.A. 1929–34; Tutor in Econ., Univ. of Leeds 1934–45. Joined Min. of Food 1940; Dep. Head, British Food Mission to North America 1946–48; Under-Secy., Min. of Food 1948–53; Minister, U.K. Permanent Delegation, Paris 1953–54; Dep. Secretary, Ministry of Agriculture, Fisheries and Food 1955–60; Dep. Secretary, Min. of Aviation 1960; Permanent Secy., Ministry of Aviation, 1961–63; Permanent Under-Secy. of State, Ministry of Defence 1963–66; Member & Deputy Chmn. Monopolies Commn. 1967–70. Chairman: Covent Garden Market Authority 1967–75; Home-Grown Cereals Authority 1968–77. Hon. LDD, Manchester 1965. *Clubs:* Reform. *Address:* 33 Durand Gardens, London SW9 0PS.

**HARDMAN, Lamartine G.,** *B.* 1908. *Educ.* Univ. of Georgia (BSc). *M.* 1934, Dorothy Shell. *S.* Lamartine G. III and John B. *Dau.* Dorothy Shell. *Career:* Pres. American Cotton Mfs. Inst. 1957–58, and Georgia Textile Mfs. Association Inc. 1950–51. JR. President-Treasurer, Harmony Grove Mills Inc., Commerce, Ga.; Chmn., First National Bank; Dir., Georgia Power Co. 1957—, Bibb. Mfg. Co. 1962—, and Citizens & Southern National Bank. Democrat. Phi Delta Theta Fraternity. *Clubs:* Piedmont Driving, Capital City (Atlanta, Ga.). *Address: office* Harmony Grove Mills, Commerce, Ga., U.S.A.

**HARDY, Peter,** MP. British. *B.* 1931. *Educ.* Wath Upon Dearne Grammar School; Westminster Coll. London; Sheffield Univ., Coll. of Preceptors. *M.* 1954, Margaret Ann Brookes. *S.* 2. *Career:* Royal Air Force, 1949–51; Schoolmaster South Yorkshire, 1953–60; Councillor Wath Upon Dearne U.D.C. 1960–70; Head of Dept. Mexborough C. Secondary School, 1961–70; Parly. Labour Candidate Scarborough & Whitby, 1964 and Sheffield Hallam, 1966; Member of Parliament for Rother Valley; PPS to Secretary of State for the Environment; PPS to Sec. of State for Foreign & Commonwealth Affairs since 1976; Member of UK Delegation to the Council of Europe. *Member:* National Union, Public Employees; Socialist Educational Association. *Clubs:* Rawmarsh Trades & Labour; Kennel. *Address:* 53 Sandygate, Wath upon Dearne, Rotherham, Yorks.; and *office* House of Commons, London, S.W.1.

**HARDY, Thomas Walter.** Australian business executive. *B.* 1924. *Educ.* Brighton Primary School, St. Peters Coll., and Univ. of Adelaide (BSc). *M.* 1948, Barbara R. Begg. *S.* 4. *Career:* President, Winemakers Assn. of South Australia 1957–60 Vice-Pres. 1956–57); Chairman, Allied Liquor

Industries Charities Committee 1959–60; Pres., Federal Wine & Brandy Producers Assn. of Aust. 1965–68. Royal S.A. Yacht Squadron Committee 1949–60; Vice-Commodore 1956–57; Rear-Commdr. 1957–60. Mng. Dir., Thomas Hardy & Sons Ltd. (winemakers; establ. 1853). Pres. St. Peters Old Collegians Assn. 1971–73; Council Member, Royal Automobile Assn. of S.A. Inc. 1966—; Aust. Wine Research Institute 1970–76. *Member:* The Australian Wine Board, 1970—, Chmn. 1973–76; *Clubs:* Adelaide; Kooyonga Golf; Royal S.A. Yacht Squadron; Public Schools; Thebarton Rotary. *Address:* 44 Maitland Terrace, Seacliff, S.A., and Tintara House, Mile End, S.A., Australia.

**HARE, Raymond Arthur.** American diplomat. *B.* 3 April 1901. *Educ.* Grinnell Coll. (AB). *M.* 1932, Julia Cygan. *S.* Raymond Arthur, Paul Julian. *Career:* Entered American Foreign Service April 1927; Chief, Div. of Middle Eastern and Indian Affairs, Aug. 1947; Chief, Div. of S. Asian Affairs, Sept. 1947; Dep. Dir., Office of Near Eastern & African Affairs, July 1948; Deputy Assistant Secretary of State for Near Eastern, S. Asian, and African Affairs, Oct. 1949; Amb. Ex. and Plen. to Saudi Arabia and Minister to Yemen 1950; Ambassador to Lebanon 1953–54; Dir.-Gen., U.S. Foreign Service 1954–56; Amb. to Egypt 1956; to United Arab Republic 1958, and Minister to Yemen 1959; Dep. Under-Secy. of State; Personal Representative of President with rank of Special Ambassador to head U.S. Delegation at inaugural ceremonies in Ghana; FSO, Class of Career Ambassador 1960; Ambassador to Turkey 1961. Asst. Secy. of State for Near Eastern and South Asian Affairs, Sept. 1965–Nov. 1966. President, Middle East Institute, Washington D.C. 1966–69. National Chairman, M.E.I. 1969—. *Address:* 3214-39th Street N.W., Washington, D.C. 20016, U.S.A.

**HARKINS, Maurice James.** JP. Australian. tourism counsellor *B.* 1905. *Educ.* Licensed Shorthand Writer (L.S.W.). Supreme Court of Victoria. *M.* 1939, Mary Elizabeth Booke. *Career:* Administrative Officer, Victorian Railways 1920–34; Victorian Government Tourist Officer 1934–58. Served in World War II (2nd A.I.F.; Major) 1940–46. Director of Accommodation, Olympic Civic Committee 1955–56; Acting Dir., Vic. Promotion Cttee. 1957. Director of Tourist Development, Govt. of Victoria, Australia 1958–70; Dir. Ministry of Tourism 1970–71; Accommodation Eucharistic Congress 1972–73. Life member, Travel League (Vic.); Mem., Pacific Area Travel Assn.; National Parks Assn.; National Trust of Australia (Vic.). *Clubs:* Victoria Racing; Naval & Military; Skal; Melbourne Walking; Royal Automobile (Vic.); Kew Golf; Melbourne Rotary. *Address:* 1 Howitt Street, Glen Iris, 3146, Vic. Australia.

**HARKNESS, Lt.-Col. Hon. Douglas Scott,** PC, GM, ED, *B.* 1903. *Educ.* University of Alberta (BA). *M.* 1932, Frances Elisabeth MacMillan. *S.* Kenneth Blair. *Career:* Previously High School Teacher, and engaged in farming and livestock; served in World War II (Maj. and Lt.-Col., R.C.A.; Sicily, Italy and North-west Europe) 1940–45; Reserve of Officers, Aug. 1945; C.O. 41st Anti-tank Regt. (S.P.), R.C.A. (Reserve Army) 1948–49. First elected to House of Commons 1945; re-elected 1949–53–57–58–62–63–65–68, Ret. 1973. appointed to Cabinet as Min. of North. Affairs and Natnl. Resources and Acting Minister of Agriculture (June 1957); Minister of Agriculture 1957–60. Minister of Defence, 1960–63. Director, Metropolitan Trust Co., Toronto; United Western Oil & Gas Co. Calgary. Is a Progressive Conservative. *Clubs:* Rachmen's, Petroleum (Calgary); Rideau (Ottawa); Canadian Legion (Calgary). *Address:* 716 Imperial Way, S.W. Calgary, Canada.

**HARKNESS, Philip Vaughan,** JP. New Zealand *B.* 1933. *Educ.* University of New Zealand (Dip. Journ.), University of Missouri (U.S.A.) BJ; Stanford Univ. (U.S.A.) MA. *M.* 1964, Leonie Diane, d. of late J. L. Phillips. *S.* 1. *Dau.* 3. *Career:* Mg. Dir. Newspapers of Fiji Ltd., publisher of Fiji Sun and Sunday Sun; Exec. Board Internat. Press Institute (Zurich) since 1970; Dir., New Zealand Press Association, 1963–65, Correspondent, Antarctica, 1962, U.S. Official Observer Vietnam, 1965, N.Z. Delegate to Commonwealth Press Union Conference, Bermuda, 1965; Scotland 1970; International Press Inst Conference, Hong Kong, 1970; Germany 1972; Turkey 1973; Japan 1974. Editor and Managing Director, The Times, N.Z. 1962–. Director: Independent Publishers Ltd. 1968—; Independent Broadcasting Ltd., 1968—; Chairman, Waikato Arts Cncl., 1967–68. *Publications:* Various articles U.S. newspapers and magazines, Pres.: Waikato Justices of the Peace Assn. 1970; Vice-Pres. Crippled Children's Society; Marriage Guidance Cncl. 1967; Hamilton Amateur Operatic Society. Trustee. Southwell School, Hamilton, 1964. Director, Hamilton Rotary Club, 1969—. Patron, Playbox Repertory Society, 1965; Kappa Tau Alpha, Honorary journalism soc. U.S.A. *Member:* Newspaper Proprietors Assn. (N.Z.); Commonwealth Press Union; New Zealand Press Assn.: International Press Institute; Sigma Delta Chi (U.S.A.). *Clubs:* Royal New Zealand Yacht Squadron; Wellington; Hamilton (N.Z.); Fiji. *Address:* 2 Central Terrace, Wellington, New Zealand; and Wadigi Island, Mamamuca Group, Fiji; and *office* P.O. Box 354, Suva, Fiji.

**HARLECH, Rt. Hon. Lord,** PC, KCMG, DL (William David Ormsby Gore). *B.* 1918. *Educ.* Eton; New College, Oxford. *M.* (1) 1940, Sylvia Lloyd Thomas (*D.* 1967). *S.* 2. *Daus.* 3. (2) 1969. Pamela T. Colin. *Dau.* 1. *Career:* MP (Con.) Oswestry Div. of Salop 1950–61; Parliamentary Private Secy. to Minister of State for Foreign Affairs 1951–55; Parliamentary Under-Sec. of State for Foreign Affairs 1956–57; Minister of State for Foreign Affairs 1957–61; Ambassador to Washington Oct. 1961–65; Deputy Leader of the Conservative Party in the House of Lords 1966–67. Chairman, Harlech Television; Pilgrim Trust; Kennedy Memorial Trust; Pres., British Board of Film Censors, K. St. J.; Trustee, Tate Gallery; Shelter. *Club:* Pratt's. *Address:* Glyn Talsarnau, Gwynedd, N. Wales; and 14A Ladbroke Road, London, W.11.

**HARLEM, Gudmund,** MD. Norwegian statesman. *B.* 1917. *Educ.* Oslo Univ. (MD; recipient Albert Laskar Award 1960). *M.* 1938, Inga Brynolf. *S.* Erik and Lars. *Daus.* Gro and Hanne. *Career:* Underground student leader during German occupation 1941–43; Research in Social Medicine 1946–48; Physician-in-Charge, State Rehabilitation Centre, Oslo 1946–55 and 1965–77 (full-time job from 1948; in charge of the Centre from 1953); Professor, Norwegian Univ. of Technology 1977—. Member, Norwegian Research Cncl. 1949–57; studied rehabilitation in Gt. Britain 1947–48 and 1950, and in U.S.A. 1949–50; Technical Expert, U.N. Rehabilitation Work in Egypt 1954, and in Greece and Italy 1955; Cabinet member 1955–65, Minister of Health and Social Affairs 1955–61; Minister of Defence Feb. 1961–65; Pres. Rehabilitation International 1966–69; Created Dr. Med. 1976; Chmn. Cttee. on Environment Pollution 1970–76; Chmn. Cttee. on Work Environment 1977—; Chmn., Norwegian Student Socy. 1945. *Member:* Oslo City Council 1946–47, Oslo Board of Schools (and Chmn. of Cttee. for Special Education) 1948–55; Central Committee, Labour Party 1949–57, and Board of International Union of Socialist Youth 1946–51. Vice-Chmn., Oslo Labour Party 1952–57. *Address:* Sigbforn Obstfelders Vei 2, Oslo 3; and *office* Sinsenveien 76, Oslo 5, Norway.

**HARLEY, Sir Stanley Jaffa.** DL, BSc, CEng, FIMechE, FIProdE. British. *B.* 1905. *Educ.* Birmingham Univ. *M.* 1931, Rhona Townsend. *S.* 2. *Dau.* 1. President, Coventry Gauge Ltd. *Clubs:* R.A.C. *Address:* Sunnycrest, Ashorne, Warwick.

**HARMAN, Avraham.** Ambassador of Israel. *B.* 1914. *Educ.* BA Oxford. *M.* 1940, Zena Stern. *S.* David. *Daus.* Naomi and Ilana. *Career:* Ambassador to the U.S.A. 1959–68; Executive, Jewish Agency for Israel 1956–59. Asst. Director-General, Israel Ministry for Foreign Affairs 1955–56; Consul-General, New York 1953–55; Director, Israel Office of Information 1950–53; Consul-General, Montreal 1949–50; Deputy Director, Press and Information Office, Govt. of Israel 1948–49; President, Hebrew Univ. Jerusalem since 1968. *Address:* Hebrew University of Jerusalem, Israel.

**HARMAR-NICHOLLS, Lord (of Peterborough) (Sir Harmar Nicholls) JP.** British politician and surveyor. *B.* 1912. *Educ.* Queen Mary's School, Walsall. *M.* 1940, Dorothy Edwards. *Daus.* 2. *Career:* contested Nelson and Colne General Election 1945 and Preston by-election 1946; Member, Parliament (Con.) for Peterborough 1950–74; Secy. to Asst. Postmaster-General 1951–55; Junior Minister of Food; Parliamentary Secy., Ministry of Agriculture and Fisheries Apr. 1955, and Min. of Works 1957; Under writer at Lloyds. Director: Radio Luxembourg (London) Ltd.; J. & H. Nicholls (Paints) Ltd.; Nicholls & Henessay (Hotels) Ltd. Chairman Malvern Theatre Trust; Cannon Assurance Ltd.; Public Co., Pleasurama Ltd. since 1970. *Address:* Abbeylands, Weston, Stafford.

**HARMER, Sir Frederic Evelyn,** Kt, CMG. *B.* 3 Nov. 1905. *Educ.* Eton; King's Coll. Cambridge. *M.* (1) 1931, Barbara Susan Hamilton (*dec'd*). *S.* 1. *Daus.* 3. (2) Daphne Shelton Agar. *Career:* Employed at Treasury 1939, temporary assistant secretary 1943–45: served in Washington, U.S.A. in 1944 and 1945. British company director. Dept. Chmn. and Mng.

Dir., Peninsular and Oriental Steam Navigation Co., retd. 1970. Former Director Natl. Westminster Bank Ltd., B.P. Tanker Co. Ltd.; and other companies. Chmn., International Chamber of Shipping 1968–71. *Address:* Tiggins Field, Kelsale, Saxmundham, Suffolk.

**HARNESS, J. King.** American patent lawyer. *B.* 1897. *Educ.* Detroit College of Law (LLB). *M.* 1920, Vera Gregory. *S.* Don Kenneth, Jerry King and Hugh Gregory. *Dau.* Joan Dianne. Patent Counsel, Ford Motor Co. 1919–21. Senior Partner, Harness, Dickey & Pierce 1921—; Chief Patent Counsel, Chrysler Corporation 1921–62; Patent Consultant since 1962. *Member:* Michigan Patent Law Assn. (Past Pres.); American and Detroit Bar Assns. *Clubs:* Athletic, Rotary, Golf (all of Detroit Past Pres. of all); Recess (Past Governor). *Address:* P.O. Box 6493, Litchfield Park, Arizona 85340; and *office* 1500 North Woodward, Birmingham, Michigan 48011, U.S.A.

**HARPER, David Augustine.** OBE. JP. British *B.* 1913. *Educ.* Liverpool University (BSc, PhD); FRIC, *M.* 1939, Nora Mary Bark. *S.* Christopher. *Daus.* 2. *Career:* Chmn. Storey Bros. & Co., Ltd., Lancaster, England. *Publications:* various contributions to scientific journals. *Club:* Lansdowne (London). *Address:* Applegarth, 8 Hest Bank Lane, Hest Bank, Lancaster LA2 6DG.

**HARPER, John Dickson.** American. Director & Chairman of the Exec. Cttee., Aluminium Company of America. Director: Metropolitan Life Insurance Co., Proctor & Gamble Co., COMSAT (Communication Satellite Corp.), Crutcher Resources Corp., Mellon Bank, Mellon National Corp. etc. *B.* 1910. *Educ.* University of Tennessee (Elec. Eng. degree). *M.* 1937, Samma Lucille McCrary. *S.* Rogers, McCrary, John Dickson, Jr., and Thomas William. *Career:* The Aluminium Association Hon. DEng: Lehigh Univ., Maryville College, Rensselaer Polytechnic; Hon. LLD Univ. of Evansville; Hon. Degree Science, Clarkson Univ.; Nathan W. Dougherty Award, Univ. of Tennessee. Fellow I.E.E.E.; Vice-Chmn., Business Council, National Alliance of Businessmen; Visiting Cttee., Stanford Graduate School of Business; The Business Roundtable (Chmn.); Communications Satellite Corporation—COMSAT (Dir.); Mellon National Corporation (Dir.); International Primary Aluminium Institute (Chmn.); President's Export Council (Member); U.S.-Korea Economic Council (Dir.); The Rockefeller Univ. Council (Founding member); Woodrow Wilson International Center for Scholars (Advisory Cttee). *Member:* American Institute of Electrical Engineers; American Society Mech. Engineers; Engineers Society of Western Pa.; Tau Beta Pi; Eta Kappa Nu; Beta Gamma Sigma. Trustee: Council for Latin Amer.; Cttee. for Economic Development; Carnegie Mellon University of Tennessee Development Board; American Society of Metals (Dist. Life Member); National Academy of Engineering; United States Council of the International Chamber of Commerce, Inc. (Member). *Awards:* Hon. Doctor of Commercial Science, Widener College, Chester, Pa.; Knight's Cross, Order of St. Olav (Norway); Gold Medal, Pennsylvania Society. *Clubs:* Burning Tree (Maryland); Duquesne, Fox Chapel, St. Clair Country (Pittsburgh); International (Wash. D.C.); Laurel Valley, Rolling Rock (Ligonier); The Links, Racquet & Tennis, Sky (N.Y.); University; Tres Vidas En la Playa, Acapulco, Mexico. *Address: office* 3040 Alcoa Building, Pittsburgh, Pa. 15219, U.S.A.

**HARPHAM, Sir William,** KBE CMG. British. *B.* 1906. *Educ.* Christ's College, Cambridge (BA 1928, MA 1931). *M.* 1943, Isabelle Marie Sophie Droz. *S.* 1. *Dau.* 1. *Career:* Counsellor (Commercial), Berne 1947–50; Head of General Department, Foreign Office 1950–53; Deputy to U.K. Delegate to O.E.E.C. 1953–56; Minister, Tokyo 1956–59; Economic Minister, Paris 1959–63; Ambassador to Bulgaria 1964–66. Director, Great Britain—East Europe Centre 1967—. *Publications:* various official. Bulgarian Order, Madara Horseman, 1969. *Clubs:* Travellers'; Royal Automobile. *Address:* 9 Kings Keep, Putney Hill, London SW15 6RA.

**HARRIMAN, E. Roland.** American company director and banker. *B.* 24 Dec. 1895. *Educ.* Yale University (BA); Hon. LLD, Columbia 1955, Yale 1960. *M.* 1917, Gladys C. C. Fries. *Daus.* Elizabeth (*Dec.*), Phyllis. Partner, Brown Brothers Harriman & Co.; Hon. Trustee, Amer. Museum of Natural History; Hon. Chairman of the Board, Union Pacific Corporation. *Address:* 59 Wall Street, New York, N.Y. 10005, U.S.A.

**HARRIMAN, Leslie Oriseweyinmi.** Nigerian diplomat. *B.* 1930. *Educ.* Govt. School Benin; Edo College Benin, Govt. College Ibaadan, Pembroke College Oxford. Imp. Defence Coll. London. *M.* Clara Edewor. *S.* 3. *Dau.* 1. *Career:* Manager UAC Lagos 1955–58; 2nd Secy. Brit. Embassy Spain 1958–59; Counsellor and Ag. High Commissioner for Nigeria in Ghana 1961–63; Dep. Perm. Secy., Ministry of External Affairs Lagos 1965–66; High Commissioner for Nigeria in Uganda 1966–69, in Kenya 1966–70; Ambassador of Nigeria in France and Tunisia 1970; Perm. Delegate of Nigeria to UNESCO, Paris 1970; Perm. Rep. of Nigeria to the UN since 1975. *Address:* Office of the Permanent Delegation of Nigeria to the UN, 757 Third Avenue, 20th Floor, New York, N.Y. 10017, U.S.A.

**HARRIMAN, William Averell.** American banker-diplomat-statesman. *B.* 15 Nov. 1891. *Educ.* Groton School and Yale Univ. (BA). *M.* (1) 1915, Kitty Lanier Lawrence, (2) 1930, Marie (Norton) Whitney, (3) 1971, Pamela Digby Churchill Hayward. *Daus.* (by 1st m.) Mary Averell (Fisk), Kathleen Lanier (Mortimer, Jr.). *Career:* Dir. 1913, Chmn. of Board 1932, Union Pacific R.R. Co. (resigned both posts 1946); Dir. 1915 and Chmn. Exec. Cttee. 1931, Illinois Cent. R.R. Co. 1931; resigned as Chmn. 1942, and as Dir. 1946; organized Merchant Shipbuilding Corp. (which built many ships for the U.S. Government during World War I) 1917; Chmn. 1917–25; in 1920 organized W. A. Harriman Co., Investment Bankers; consolidated with Brown Bros. into present private banking firm of Brown Bros. Harriman & Co. 1931; Chmn., New York State Cttee. of Nat. Recovery Admin. 1933; member, Business Advisory Cncl., Dept. of Commerce since its inception 1933; Chairman 1937–39; Chief, Materials Branch in Production Div., Office of Prod. Management 1941; Pres. Roosevelt's Special Rep. in Great Britain to facilitate material aid to British Empire from 1941 (headed what was then known as the Harriman Mission); Spec. Rep. and Chmn. of President's Special Mission to U.S.S.R. 1941 (in this capacity went to Moscow with Lord Beaverbrook heading a British Mission), and negotiated provision of Anglo-American supplies to Soviet Union; represented Pres. at meeting of Churchill and Stalin, Moscow Aug. 1942; Amb. to U.S.S.R. 1943–46; returned to U.S., there to receive Medal for Merit 'for exceptionally distinguished conduct in a position of great responsibility'; during the war attended all but one of the bi-lateral and both of the tri-lateral meetings of Pres. Roosevelt, including Atlantic Conf., Washington and Quebec Confcs., all of the Big Three Confcs. at Teheran, Yalta, and Potsdam, the Cairo preliminary to Teheran Conf., meeting of Churchill and Stalin (Oct. 1944), and several confcs. of For. Mins. at Moscow, London, and San Francisco; Amb. to Great Britain April–Oct. 1946; Sec. of Commerce 1946; Chmn. of President's Cttee. on Foreign Aid (June 1947), which laid groundwork for E.C.A.; Spec. Rep. in Europe for E.C.A.; Spec. Asst. to the President July 1950–Oct. 1951; to Teheran, to discuss Anglo-Iranian problems concerning oil July 1951; Chmn. in Paris of N.A.T.O. Sept. 1951; Dir. for Mutual Security 1951–53; Candidate, Democratic Party Nomination for President U.S.A. 1952. Governor of New York State, Jan. 1955–Nov. 1958; Ambassador-at-Large 1961; Asst. Secretary of State for Far East, 1962; Under-Secretary of State for Political Affairs, 1963; Ambassador-at-Large 1965–69; U.S. Representative to Paris Peace Talks on Vietnam, May 1968–Jan. 1969. *Address:* 3038 N St., N.W., Washington, D.C. 20007, U.S.A.

**HARRINGTON, Conrad Fetherstonhaugh,** CD, KStJ. *B.* 1912. *Educ.* Selwyn House School (Montreal), Trinity College School (Port Hope, Ont.), McGill Univ. (BA 1933, BCL 1936), Univ. of Besançon (France). *M.* 1940, Joan Roy Hastings. *S.* Conrad. *Daus.* Jill and Susan. *Career:* Practised Law in Montreal (called to Bar of Quebec 1937) 1937–39; served in World War II with Royal Canadian Artil. 1940–45; U.K., Italy, N.W. Europe with 5.2.17 Canadian Field Regts; twice mentioned in dispatches; Res. Army 1945–51; O.C. 37 Canadian Field Regt.; Hon. Lieut.-Col., 42nd Medium Regt. 1961–63 (RCA) Hon. Col. 2nd. Field Regt. (RCA) 1967. Joined Royal Trust Co. 1945; served at Toronto 1952–63 as Manager, Asst. Gen. Mgr. and Vice-Pres. and Supervisor of Ontario branches, Pres. 1965, Chmn. & Chief Exec. Officer 1970, Chmn. of the Bd. Exec. Cttee. 1973; Director: Royal Trust Co. and subsidiaries: Gerling Global Life Ins., General & Reinsurance Companies; R L Crain Ltd.; Consumers Glass Co. Ltd. MPG Investment Corp.; Stone and Webster Canada Ltd.; Chairman: Redpath Industries Ltd.; Glaxo Canada Ltd. *Governor:* Canadian Council on Social Development, Trinity Coll. School, Port Hope, Ontario; McGill Univ.; Montreal Childrens' Hosp.; Montreal Gen. Hosp.; Douglas Hosp.; Chancellor of McGill University since 1976. *Director:* (hon) Quebec Council, St. John Amb.; (hon) Anglican Foundation of Canada; VON, Montreal Branch; The London House Assn. of Canada. *Vice-President:* (hon)

Boy Scouts of Canada (Montreal); *Chairman:* McGill Fund Council; Montreal Advisory Bd.; Salvation Army. *Member:* Council of the Montreal Museum of Fine Arts; Zeta Psi. *Clubs:* York, The Toronto, Toronto Golf (Toronto), University; St. James's; Mount-Bruno Golf; Zeta Psi Fraternity; Mount Royal; Forest & Stream. *Address:* 556 Lansdowne Avenue, Montreal H3Y 2V6, Canada.

**HARRINGTON, Harry Francis.** American banker. *B.* 1900. *Educ.* Graduate of Stonier Graduate School of Banking, Rutgers Univ. 1941. *M.* 1940, Edwina G. Daly. *Career:* With The Boatmen's National Bank of St. Louis 1915–70. (Vice-Pres. 1937–54, Dir. 1947–73, Pres. 1954–61, Pres. and Chmn. of Board 1961–65; Chmn. 1965–70). Director: Federal Reserve Bank of St. Louis 1963–68, United Fund of Greater St. Louis: Director, Member of Exec. Cttee., Campaign Chmn. 1963–64, Pres., 1967–68, Treas. 1958–59, St. Louis Univ.; General Chmn. Leadership Program; Chmn., Foundation Cttee.; Exec. Cttee. for Priority Needs Campaign 1959–63. Panel Examiner, Stonier Graduate School of Banking 1946–59. Member, Assn. of Reserve City Bankers (Dir. 1963–66). Pres. 1966–67, and Dir.: Catholic Charities of St. Louis, and Downtown St. Louis Inc. Pres. St. Louis Clearing House Assn. 1960–61. Chmn., Amer. Bankers Assn. Federal Agency Relations Commn., 1963–67; Chamber of Commerce of Metropolitan St. Louis. Vice-Pres. 1961–67 and Dir. Civic Progress Inc., and St. Louis Bicentennial Corp., 1963–66. Director Civic Center Re-development Corp.; Municipal Theater Assn. of St. Louis (Treas. 1957–63); St. Louis Symphony Socy., St. Louis Crime Commission; Better Business Bureau of Greater St. Louis. Vice-Pres., Member Board of Trustees, Jefferson National Expansion Memorial Assn. *Member:* Board of Trustees, Governmental Research Inst.; President's Cncl., St. Louis Univ. (Chmn. of the Cncl. 1954–57); Financial Exec. Institute; St. Louis Ambassadors Inc.; State of Missouri Appellate Judicial Commission 1949–52; U.S. Joint Commn. on the Coinage. Recipient of Papal Decorations, Knights of Malta; Knight Equestrian, Order of the Holy Sepulchre; Brotherhood Citation, National Conf. of Christians and Jews: Silver Beaver Award, Boy Scouts of America. *Clubs:* Bellerive, Missouri Athletic, Saint Louis. *Address:* 57 Briarcliff, St. Louis, No. 63124, U.S.A.

**HARRINGTON, John Maurice.** Canadian diplomat. *B.* 1924. *Educ.* St. Illtyd's Coll. Cardiff (Wales) 1938–39; Central Collegiate London, Ontario 1938–42; Univ. of W. Ontario 1942–46, BA, 1946–47, MA; London Sch. of Economics 1947–49 (MSc. Econ.). *M.* 1950, Dorothy Pocock. *S.* 1. *Career:* Asst.-Professor St. Francis Xavier Univ. 1949–50; Dept of External Affairs since 1950: 3rd Secy. Belgrade 1952–55; 1st Secy. London (HC) 1958–62; Counsellor Tokyo 1965–68; Dir. Pacific Affairs, Dea, Ottawa 1968–72; High Commissioner Kingston, Jamaica 1972–76; University Visitor, Trinity Coll., Toronto 1976–77; appointed Dep. Commandant, National Defence Coll. of Canada 1977. *Member:* Georgian Socy.; Canadian Political Science Assn. *Address:* National Defence College, Fort Frontenac, Kingston, Ontario, Canada.

**HARRINGTON, R(ussell) Paul.** Professor and Head of Department of Aerospace Engineering, and Director, Institute for Space Sciences, University of Cincinnati 1960—. *B.* 1905. *Educ.* BSE 1930, MSE 1931, Michigan; Sheehan Scholar 1930–31; Univ. Fellow 1930–32; ScD 1936; *Fellow:* Guggenheim Airship Inst. 1932–34. *M.* (1) 1929, Emogene Dyson (*Dec.*). *Daus.* Marigene, Julia Ann and Cynthia Lynne. *M.* (2) 1966, Babette Marshall. Chevalier, Order of Leopold (Belgium). *Career:* Metallurgist, Whitman-Barnes Inc., Michigan 1926–28; Instructor, Mech. Engineering, and i/c of Aeronautics, Polytechnic Institute, Brooklyn 1934–36 (Asst. Prof. Aeronaut. Eng. 1936–39, Assoc. Prof. 1939–41; Prof. and Head, Department of Aeronautical Eng. & Applied Mechanics 1941–50); Rensselaer Polytechnic Inst. 1950–60 (Head of Dept. 1950–56); Director, Training Centre for Experimental Aero-dynamics, NATO, Brussels 1956–58; Scientific Adviser, U.S. Army Air Corps 1945; Consultant, AFOSR 1951–54, and to Dept. of Defense Research & Development 1956–57. *Publications:* about 20 reports on aerodynamics, fluid dynamics and mechanics. Associate Fellow: Inst. of Aeronautical Sciences (Member of Council 1942–46), Royal Aeronautical Socy., and Amer. Inst. for Aeronautics & Astronautics. *Member:* Amer. Rocket Socy., Amer. Socy. for Engineering Education (Chmn. Aerospace Div., 1967–68), Gesellschaft für Angewandt Math. and Mech., Engineering Socy. of Cincinnati; Sigma Xi, Tau Beta Pi, Phi Kappa Phi, Iota Alpha hon. societies. *Address:* Department of Aerospace Engineering, Univ. of Cincinnati, Cincinnati, Ohio, U.S.A.

**HARRIS of GREENWICH, LORD, (John Henry).** British Journalist/Politician. *B.* 1930. *Educ.* Pinner Gr. School M'sex. *M.* 1952, Patricia Margaret Alstrom. *S.* 1. *Dau.* 1. *Career:* Journalist on newspapers in Bournemouth, Leicester, Glasgow and London; Mem. Harlow Council (Essex) 1957–63, Chmn. 1960–61; Personal Assist. to Mr. Hugh Gaitskell 1960–62; Dir. of Publicity Labour Party 1962–64; Spec. Assist. to Foreign Secy. 1964–66; Spec. Assist. Home Secy. 1966–67; Spec. Assist. to Chancellor of Exchequer 1967–70; Minister of State, Home Office since 1974. *Club:* Reform. *Address:* House of Lords, London SW1; and Home Office, Queen Anne's Gate, London SW1.

**HARRIS, Albert.** American. Operator of Harris Hotels. *B.* 1897. *Educ.* University of Cincinnati. *M.* 1923, Sadie Linowitz. *S.* Irving. *Dau.* Bernice Friedman, *Career:* Commenced in mercantile business but turned to real estate and building; has built over a hundred buildings in the city of Cincinnati; holds World Wars I and II medals; Republican. *Address:* 4115 Paddock Road, Cincinnati, O.; and *office* 35 E Seventh Street, Cincinnati, U.S.A.

**HARRIS, Chauncy Dennison.** American. *B.* 1914. *Educ.* Brigham Young Univ. (AB); Oxford Univ. (BA, MA, D.Litt.) and Chicago Univ. (PhD). *M.* 1940, Edith Young. *Dau.* Margaret. *Career:* Professor of Geography 1947—; Dean, Graduate Division of the Social Sciences, Univ. of Chicago 1954–60; Chmn. Cttee. on Non-Western Area Programs and Other International Studies, same Univ. 1960–66; Director, Centre for International Studies, Univ. of Chicago since 1966; Samuel N. Harper Distinguished Service Professor 1969—; Vice-Pres. for Academic Resources, 1975—; U.S. Delegate 17th General Conference UNESCO, Paris 1972. *Member:* Assoc. American Geographers (Secy. 1946–48 Pres. 1957); Amer. Assn. for Advancement of Slavic Studies (Pres. 1962); Amer. Geographical Soc. (Vice-Pres. 1969–74); International Geographical Union (Vice-Pres. 1956–64), Secy.-Gen. & Treas., 1969–76; Inst. British Geographers; Assn. de Géographes Français. *Publications:* International List of Geographical Serials; Annotated World List, Selected Current Geographical Serials in English, French & German; Editor: Soviet Geography, Accomplishments and Tasks; Economic Geography of the USSR; Cities of the Soviet Union, Studies in Their Functions, Size, Density and Growth; Guide to Geographical Bibliographies and Reference Works in Russia or on the Soviet Union; Bibliography of Geography: Part 1. Introduction to General Aids. *Awards:* DEcon (*h.c.*), Catholic Univ. of Chile; Hon. Corresponding Member, Royal Geographical Soc.; Ehrenmitglied: Gesellschaft für Erdkunde zu Berlin and Frankfurter Geographische Gesellschaft; Membre d'Honneur, Société de Geographie de Paris; Socio Corrispondente, Società Geografica Italiana; Societa di Studi Geografici. Hon. Member, Polskie Towarzystwo Geograficzne; Alexander de Csoma Körösi, Medal, Hungarian Geographical Society; Honors Award, Assn. of American Geographers; Distinguished Service Award, Geographic Society of Chicago; Lauréat d'Honneur, International Geographical Union. *Club:* Quadrangle. *Address:* Center for International Studies, University of Chicago, 5828 University Avenue, Chicago, Ill. 60637, U.S.A.

**HARRIS, David J.** American. *B.* 1913. *Educ.* Univ. of Chicago (BA). *M.* 1936, Evelyn R. Carr. *S.* 2. *Dau.* 1. *Career:* Entered securities business Mar. 1935 for Sills, Minton & Co. (Exec. Vice-Pres. 1944 and Pres. 1945); continued as Pres. with its successor organizations, Sills Fairman & Harris Inc., and Fairman Harris & Co., until the latter merged with Bache & Co. in May 1956; Resident Partner, Bache & Co. Chicago 1956–64; Vice-Pres., Investment Bankers Assn. of America 1960–63, Pres. 1963–64. Chairman & Chief Executive Officer, The Chicago Corp. 1964—; Chmn. Midwest Stock Exchange 1964–66; Director: CIC Financial Co., Sentry Insurance, Chicago Board Options Exchange Inc.; Governor, Association of Stock Exchange Firms; Governor Western Golf Assn. since 1971. *Member:* Investment Bankers; Assn. of America; Allied Member, N.Y. Stock Exchange; Midwest Stock Exchange; American Stock Exchange. Republican. *Clubs:* The Chicago; University (Chicago); Exmoor Country; The Attic; Delta Kappa Epsilon. *Address: office:* 208 So. La Salle Street, Chicago 60604, Ill., U.S.A.

**HARRIS, Frank Meredith.** AAII. British. *B.* 1904. *Educ.* Hobart High School, Tasmania. *M.* 1940, Dorothy E. Sloane. *Career:* Gen. Mgr. Transport & General Insurance Co. Ltd.; Asst. Mgr. Melbourne Union Insurance Socy. of Canton Ltd., 1939–47; Exec. Dir. Shield Life Assurance Limited; Dir.,

Leigh Clark (Aust.) Pty. Ltd. Past Pres. Non-Tariff Insurance Assn. *Club:* Australian; Sydney. *Address:* 10–20 Almora Street, N.S.W. Australia and *office:* Wynyard House, Sydney, N.S.W. 2000.

**HARRIS, Irving Brooks.** American businessman. *B.* 1910. *Educ.* Yale Univ. (BA 1931). *M.* (1) 1932. *S.* William Wolpert. *Daus.* Roxanne Harris Meyer and Virginia Harris Polsky. (2) 1974, Joan Frank. *Career:* Executive Vice-President, The Toni Company 1946–53; Exec, in aircraft part business 1944–46; Exec. in finance business 1932–42; with U.S. Govt. Board of Economic Warfare, OPA 1942–44; President and Director, Standard Shares Inc.; Chmn., Pittway Corporation. Board of Trustees, Univ. of Chicago; Chmn. Chicago Educational Television Association. *Address:* 209 E Lake Shore Drive, Chicago, Ill. 60611, U.S.A. and *office* One First National Plaza, Chicago, Ill., U.S.A.

**HARRIS, Lloyd John.** Australian, Newspaper Publisher. *B.* 1921. *Educ.* BSc Univ. of Tasmania; Australian Administrative Staff Coll. *M.* 1952. Marigold June Elizabeth Harding. *S.* Nigel Andrew. *Daus.* Robyn Elizabeth and Donna Marion. *Career:* Senior Demonstrator, Chemistry School, Univ. of Tasmania, 1943–46; Dir. Harris & Co. Ltd. and Subsidiaries, 1952—; Dir. and Former Chmn., Regional Dailies of Australia Ltd.; Dir., Bass Permanent Building Society 1977—. Mgr., The Advocate Newspaper Pty. Ltd. 1963—. President Students' Representative Cncl., Univ. of Tasmania, 1943. Life Member, Assoc. of Apex Clubs (Burnie Club); Freeman, Burnie No. 4, Rostrum Clubs of Australia; Member of Council, Univ. of Tasmania; Chmn., North West Cttee. on Post Secondary Education 1975—; Member, State Cttee. of Enquiry into Education (TEND) 1976–77; Foundation Chmn. Assn. North Western Chambers of Commerce. *Clubs:* Rotary; Seabrook Golf; Burnie Gentlemen's; Burnie Tennis; Patron, Burnie Yacht Club. *Address:* 275 Bass Highway, Ocean Vista, Burnie, Tasmania; and *office* 56 Mount Street, Burnie, 7320 Tasmania, Australia.

**HARRIS, Milton.** American. *B.* 1906. *Educ.* Oregon State College (BSc); Yale Univ. (PhD); Univ. of Washington. *M.* 1934, Carolyn Wolf. *S.* Barney Dreyfuss (adopted) and John Andrew. *Career:* Research Associate, American Association of Textile Chemists & Colorists, National Bureau of Standards 1931–37; Director of Research for the Textile Foundation and Textile Research Institute 1938–44; Founder and Pres. Harris Res. Laboratories 1945–61; Member Bd. of Directors, Orbit Industries 1962–65 and 1966; also of Hazelton Laboratories 1967–68. Vice-President & Director of Research, The Gillette Co. and subsidiaries 1956–66. Pres., American Inst. of Chemists 1960–61. Chairman of the Board, American Chemical Society 1966–71; Head Exec. Cttee., and Member Bd. of Directors, Sealectr Corp. 1966; Member Bd. Dirs. Warner Lambert Corp. 1972–75; Acorn Fund; Science Service. *Member:* Editorial Bd., Science. 1968–70; Dept. of Agriculture's Utilization Res. and Development Advisory Cttee., 1966—; National Science Foundation's Advisory Cttee. for Planning 1968—; Nation Acad. of Engineering; American Socy. Biological Chemists, Amer. Assn. for Advancement of Science, American Chemical Socy., Society of Chemical Industry, Washington Academy of Sciences, American Panel, Textile Institute; Advisory Committee, National Bureau of Standards; Chmn., Experimental Technology Incentives Panel of U.S. Dept. of Commerce; mem., Science Advisory Bd. of Environmental Protection Agency; mem., various cttees. on energy, environment, and the distribution of scientific information of the National Research Council; Sub-Committee, F.A.O. (Director Textile Section); Yale Alumni Board; Chairman, Panel on Civilian Technology, President's Science Advisory Committee; Consultant in Executive Office of the President 1962–65; Member, Research & Development Division Planning Council of Amer. Management Assn. 1963–66; Yale Development Bd. 1964–67, Yale Univ. Cncl. 1964–69; visiting cttees. of chemistry depts. of Yale Univ., Univ. of California at San Diego, College of Human Ecology of Cornel Univ.; Directors of Industrial Research and Industrial Research Institutes. Cosmos Club (Washington), Chemists Club (N.Y.), Sigma Xi, Tau Beta Pi, Phi Lambda Upsilon, Phi Kappa Phi, Gamma Alpha. *Awards:* Olney Medal for Textile Research 1945; Award of Washington Academy of Sciences 1943; Hon. Degree of Textile Science, Philadelphia Textile Institute; Perkin Medal, American Section of the Socy. of the Chemical Industry, 1970; Wilbur Lucius Cross Medal, Yale Univ., 1974. *Fellow:* Textile Institute, and New York Academy of Sciences; Award of Honour, American Institute of Chemists; Distinguished Service Award, Oregon State Univ. 1967; Harold DeWitt Smith Memorial Medal, American Socy. for Testing and Materials 1966. *Publications:* Editor, Harris' Handbook of Textile Fibers (1954); Co-Editor, Chemistry in the Economy (1973); Editor, Natural & Synthetic Fibers; Assoc. Ed., Textile Research Journal, contributing ed. to numerous books, scientific journals, etc.; author of over 200 scientific papers. *Address:* 4101 Linnean Avenue, N.W., Washington, D.C., U.S.A.

**HARRIS, Richard William.** Canadian executive (retd.). *B.* 1899. *Educ.* Maritime Business College. *M.* 1922, Helen Margaret Outhit. *S.* 1. *Dau.* 1. *Career:* President, Allied Investments Ltd.; Amalgamated Investments Ltd., and Can-Amera Export Refining Co. Ltd. *Address:* (May–Oct.) Tantallon, Nova Scotia, Canada BOJ 3JO; and (Nov.–Apr.) 1922 South Ocean Lane, Fort Lauderdale, Florida, 33316, U.S.A.

**HARRIS, Roland Allen,** OBE. Canadian. *B.* 1906. *Educ.* Univ. of Toronto (BA) and Staff College, Camberly (p.s.c.). *M.* 1933, Dae Lyon. *S.* John R. *Dau.* Molly D. *Career:* President; Canada Cycle & Motor Co. Ltd. 1958–61, and Walker Stores Ltd. 1957–58. Vice-Pres. Gordon Mackay & Co. Ltd. 1953–58; Managing Director, C. H. Smith Co. Ltd. 1945–53; Vice-President, Marketing, B. F. Goodrich Co. Ltd. 1961–67; Director: David & Henderson Ltd. 1961—; Economical Mutual Insurance Co. 1966—; Canadian General Tower Ltd., 1968—; Perth Insurance Company since 1970; Whitman Golden Ltd. since 1971. *Clubs:* University, Racquet (all of Toronto); Westmount Golf. *Address:* 10 Westgate Walk, Kitchener, Ont., Canada.

**HARRIS, William Cranfield.** Canadian Investment Underwriter. *B.* 1900. *Educ.* University of Toronto (BCom). *M.* 1926, Ethel Mary Bowles. *S.* William B. *Career:* Hon. Chmn. Harris Dominion Securities; Director, Bank of Nova Scotia; Imperial Life Assurance Co. of Canada. *Address:* *office* Commerce Court South, Box 21, Toronto M5L 1A7, Canada.

**HARRIS, William Gibson.** American lawyer. *B.* 1916. *Educ.* Princeton Univ. (BA *summa cum laude* 1939); Univ. of Virginia Law School (LLB 1942); Univ. of Berlin (post-graduate studies 1945–46). *M.* 1942, Jane Hardy. *S.* William Gibson II. *Dau.* Loring Hancock. *Career:* Legal Adviser, U.S. Office of Military Government for Germany, Berlin 1945–46. Editor, Univ. of Virginia Law Review 1941–42. Partner, McGuire, Woods & Battle, Richmond, Va.; Chairman of the Board, Southern Industries Inc., Va. Capital Corporation, Richmond, Cologne Life Reinsurance Co. Inc.; and Solaronics Inc., Paris; Pres. Virginia Bar Association 1973–75; Pres. Church Schools in (Episcopal) Diocese of Va. *Member:* Democratic Party. Finance Chmn., Va. Democratic Campaign for U.S. Senate 1966. Phi Beta Kappa; Order of the Coif; O.D.K. *Clubs:* Country; Commonwealth, Downtown (all of Richmond); Farmington Country (Charlottesville, Va.); Princess Anne Country (Virginia Beach, Va.); Princeton (New York); Racquet & Tennis (N.Y.); Racing Club of France (Paris); Bucks, (London), Gulfstream & County (Delray, Florida); Mid-Ocean (Bermuda). *Address:* 122 Tempsford Lane, Richmond, Va.; and *office* Ross Building, Richmond, Va. 23219. U.S.A.

**HARRIS, William Melish.** Advertising. *B.* 1907. *Educ.* Mass. Inst. of Technology, and Boston Univ. College of Business Administration (BS in BA *cum laude* 1930). *M.* 1931, Elizabeth Woodman. *S.* William Melish, Jr., Robert Woodman, and Peter Bronwell. *Career:* Dir. Merchandizing, National Biscuit Co. 1947–48, and Advertising & Sales Promotion, National Dairy Products Corp. 1945–47; Business Manager, National Assn. of Manufacturers 1944–45; Director, Business Methods Dept., American Cyanamid Co. 1942–44; Director, Procurement Policy, Office Machinery & Equipment, War Production Board, Washington, D.C. 1941–42; Exec. Vice-Pres., First National Bank, Greenwich, Conn. 1935–42. President: Wm. Melish Harris Associates, New York City 1948—; National In-Store Advertising 1960—; Formfelt Inc. 1962—. *Publications:* numerous articles and speeches on technical subjects from advertising research to personnel management. Republican. *Clubs:* New York Yacht Greenwich (Conn.) Country; Indian Harbor Yacht. *Address:* *office* 518 Fifth Avenue, New York City 36, U.S.A.

**HARRIS, William Stewart.** British journalist and research fellow. *B.* 1922. *Educ.* Marlborough College and Clare College. Cambridge; Hons. in History; MA. *M.* 1955, Mary Orr Deas. *S.* Nicholas Grant and Alastair James. *Daus.* Karina and Iona Kate. Canberra (Australia) Correspondent of The Times,

London 1957–73; Snr. Research Fellow in Res. School of Pacific Studies at Austr. National Univ. Canberra 1973–77. *Address:* 93 Hawkesbury Crescent, Farrer, Canberra, A.C.T. 2607, Australia.

**HARRISON, Alastair Brian Clarke.** Australian. *B.* 1921. *Educ.* Geelong Grammar School (Australia) and Trinity College, Cambridge. *M.* 1952, Elizabeth Hood Hardie. *S.* Michael. *Dau.* Susanna Mary. *Career:* Previously: Captain, A.I.F. Member Parliament for Maldon 1955–74; Parliamentary Private Secretary to: Minister of State Colonial Office 1955–56; Secretary of State for War 1956–58; Minister of Agriculture 1958–60. Director: Commercial Bank of Australia Ltd. (London Board) Agricultural Investment Aust. Ltd. Member, Victoria Promotion Committee, London; former member One Nation Group which published The Responsible Society; One Europe. *Clubs:* Carlton; Pratts (London); Melbourne (Melbourne). *Address:* Copford Green Farm House, Colchester, Essex.

**HARRISON, Sir Cyril E.** British. *B.* 1901. *Educ.* Burnley Grammar School; MA (*h.c.*), Victoria Univ. of Manchester. *M.* Ethel Wood. *S.* 2. Fellow: Chartered Inst. of Secretaries, and British Institute of Management; Companion, Textile Institute. *Career:* Member: Court of Governors Univ. of Manchester; N.W. Elec. Bd.; S. Manchester Hosp. Management Committee 1957–74; Council Manchester Business School. Formerly President F.B.I. (Chairman N.W. Region Council 1957–59); President Shirley Institute; Deputy-Chairman, Williams and Glyn's Bank Ltd., 1967–73; Chamber of Commerce (Pres. 1958–60). Chmn. Board of Governors United Manchester Hosps. 1966–74; Member Natl. Economic Development Cncl. 1962–64; Past Chmn., English Sewing Cotton Co. Ltd. *Address:* 8 Harefield Drive, Holly Road South, Wilmslow, Cheshire.

**HARRISON, Sir Harwood, Bt, MA, TD, MP.** British politician. *B.* 1907. *Educ.* Northampton Grammar School and Trinity College, Oxford (Hons. deg. jurisprudence 1928; MA 1946). *M.* 1932, Peggy Alberta Mary Stenhouse. *S.* 1. *Dau.* 1, *Career:* Member of Parliament (Con.), Eye Div. of Suffolk 1951—. Served in World War II (Capt. 1939, Major 1940; captured at Singapore: on Burma railway); Lieut.-Col. 1947; Brevet-Col. 1951. Presented and sponsored Private Member's Bills, The Road Transport Lighting (Rear Lights) Act 1953 and The Road Traffic Act 1964; P.P.S. to Minister of Housing and Local Government 1953–54; Assistant Whip 1954–56; a Lord Commissioner of the Treasury 1956–59; Comptroller of H.M. Household 1959–61; President, National Conservative and Unionist Association Eastern Area, 1963–66 (Chairman 1956–59); Chmn. Unionist Club since 1966; Chmn. Sub-Cttee of Expenditure Cttee since 1971; Chmn. Inter-Parly. Union 1973–74. *Clubs:* Carlton, Pratts; Commodore, House of Commons, Yacht. *Address:* House of Commons, London, S.W.1; and 17 Tufton Court, London, S.W.1.

**HARRISON, Henry Stuart.** American. *B.* 1909. *Educ.* Yale University (AB 1932). *M.* 1943, Suzanne Brookhart. *S.* Henry Stuart, Jr. *Daus.* Mary Suzanne (Lansing) and Virginia Foster (Knight). *Career:* Director: The Cleveland Trust Co.; The Cleveland Cliffs Iron Co.; Medusa Portland Cement Co.; Midland Ross Corp.; Republic Steel Corp. Trustee & mem. of Finance Cttee., Cleveland Inst. of Art; Trustee, Vice-Chmn. & mem. of Exec. Cttee., University Hospitals of Cleveland; Trustee, Federation for Community Planning (Cleveland), United Torch, & Cleveland Council of World Affairs; Past mem. of Bd. & Exec. Cttee., American Iron and Steel Institute; American Mining Congress; Chmn., Distribution Cttee., Cleveland Foundation. Corrigan-McKinney Steel Co. 1932–33, Central Hanover Bank & Trust, N.Y.C. 1933–35, Lionel D. Eddie & Co., New York City 1936–37. Pres. Munising Wood Products 1942–46; Executive Vice-President 1958–60; joined the Cleveland-Cliffs Iron Co.: 1937, Asst. Treas. 1940, Vice-Pres.-Finance 1953, Exec. Vice-Pres. 1958, Pres. 1960, Chmn. and Chief Exec. Officer since 1974, Chmn. of the Bd. since 1976. *Awards:* Hon. LLD, Michigan Tech. Univ. 1964, & North Michigan Univ. 1967; Alumni Award, Univ. School (Cleveland) 1971; Business Statesmanship Award, Harvard Business School Club of Cleveland 1973. *Address:* 22089 Shaker Boulevard, Shaker Heights, Ohio 44122; and *office:* 1460 Union Commerce Building, Cleveland, Ohio 4415, U.S.A.

**HARRISON, Sydney Herbert.** *B.* 1913. *M.* 1943, Joan Morris. *Career:* Journalist with various newspapers, including Glasgow Herald, News of the World, Glasgow Weekly Herald, News Chronicle. Served in World War II: Lt.-Colonel. Dir., Paisley Building Society. Vice-Chairman, Managing Director, Paton & Cook Ltd., Proprietors, Paisley and Renfrewshire Gazette series of newspapers. Director, International Film Associates (Scotland) Ltd. Previously Editor of Scottish Field; Former Member: Scot. Cttee., Cncl. of Industrial Design, Scottish Council for Physical Recreation; Member, Scottish P.E.N.; Councillor, 4th District Council of Renfrewshire. *Address:* Aviemore, Stanley Drive, Brookfield, Renfrewshire.

**HARROD, Sir Roy Forbes,** FBA. British economist. *B.* 1900. *Educ.* Westminster School (Scholar); New College, Oxford (Scholar: 1st Class *Liberae Humaniores*; 1st Class Modern History); Hon. D Litt, Glasgow and Warwick; Hon. LLD Poitiers, Aberdeen, University of Pennsylvania & of Stockholm; Bernard Harms Prize (Kiel) 1966 Hon. Student of Christ Church since 1967; Hon. Fellow New Coll. since 1975. *M.* 1938, Wilhelmine Cresswell. *S.* Henry Mark and Dominick Roy. *Career:* Lecturer Christ Church Oxford until 1967. *Member:* Council of Royal Economic Society 1933—(President, 1962–64); Pres., Economic Section of British Association for the Advancement of Science 1938; member of Sir Winston Churchill's private statistical staff 1940–45 (after 1942, part-time only); member, U.N. Sub-Commission on Employment and Economic Stability 1947–49; and of Research Staff of International Monetary Fund 1952–53. Student (Mem. of Governing Body) of Christ Church, Oxford, 1924–67; Reader in International Economics, Oxford 1953–67; Member Overseas Migration Bd. Commonwealth Relations Office 1953–66. Joint Editor, Economic Journal 1945–61. *Publications:* International Economics (1933) (fully revised 1939, 1958 and 1973); Trade Cycle (1936); Are These Hardships Necessary? (1947); Towards a Dynamic Economics (1948); Life of John Maynard Keynes (1951); Economic Essays (1952); The Dollar (1953); Foundations of Inductive Logic (1956); Policy Against Inflation (1958); The Prof. (1959); Topical Comment (1961); The British Economy (1963); Reforming the World's Money (1965); Towards a New Economic Policy (1967); Money (1969); Ed. Translation, Nicod's Geometry and Induction (1970); Sociology, Morals and Mystery (1971). Liberal (contested Huddersfield Div. in Genl. Election 1945) until 1948; since then Conservative. *Clubs:* Anthenaeum; Beefsteak (London); Norfolk (Norwich). *Address:* 51 Campden Hill Square, London, W.8: and Old Rectory, Holt, Norfolk.

**HARRY, Ralph Lindsay.** Australian diplomat. *B.* 1917. *Educ.* Launceston Church of England Grammar School; LLB (Tasmania); BA (Oxon.); Rhodes Scholar for Tasmania (1937). *M.* 1944, Elsie Dorothy Sheppard. *S.* 1. *Daus.* 2. *Career:* Entered Australian Department of External Affairs 1940; served in High Commission, Ottawa 1943–45; Embassy, Washington and Australian Mission to the United Nations, New York 1945–49; Counsellor, Dept. of External Affairs, Canberra 1949–53; Consul-General, Geneva, and Permanent Delegate to European Office of U.N. 1953–56; Commissioner for Australia in Singapore, Brunei, Sarawak and North Borneo 1956–57; First Asst. Secretary, Department of External Affairs 1957–65; Ambassador to Belgium and the European Communities 1965–68. Ambassador to the Republic of Vietnam 1968–70; Federal Republic of Germany 1971–75; Ambassador, perm. rep. of Australia to UN, New York since 1975. *Address:* Department of Foreign Affairs, Canberra, A.C.T., Australia.

**HARSHAW, David H.** *B.* 1904. *Educ.* Wharton School, Univ. of Pennsylvania (BSEcon) and Stetson Univ. (DCom Sc). *M.* 1930, Frances D. Drewes, *S.* 1. *Dau* 1. (2) 1974, June W. French. *Career:* Vice-Chmn. and Director; John B. Stetson Company 1947—, (President 1947–66); Director: First Pennsylvania Banking & Trust Co., American Mutual Liability Ins. Co., John B. Stetson Company (Canada) Ltd.; Dir., Danbury Hat Co.; Greater Phila Movement; North City Corp.; Amer. Sunday School Union; First Penn. Corporation. Trustee, West Park Hospital; Stetson Univ., Dehand, Fla. *Clubs:* Philadelphia Country; Union League (Philadelphia). *Address:* 537 Brookfield Road, Drexel Hill, Pa, 19026; and *office* 5th Street and Montgomery Avenue, Philadelphia, Pa., U.S.A.

**HART, F. Donald.** American. *B.* 1915. *Educ.* Cornell Univ. (ME 1936; Master's Degree in Engineering 1937). *M.* 1942, Ann S. Wright. *Daus.* Anne, Charlotte and Jane Malvern. *Career:* Management Engineer, E. I. DuPont de Nemours Co. 1937–44; Exec. Vice-Pres., TEMCO Inc. 1944–47 (Pres. 1957–64); Pres. Lear Siegler International (Wiesbaden, Germany) 1964–66. Pres. American Gas Assn., Arlington, Va. 1967—, Member of Board: Indusmin Ltd.; Clarendon

Trust Co. Past Pres.: Nashville Cncl. of the Navy League; Volunteer Post of Amer. Ordnance Assn.; Inst. of Appliance Manufacturers, Nashville Chamber of Commerce; Gas Appliance Manuf. Assn. Locally has served on following boards: United Givers Fund; Amer. Red Cross Chapter; Travellers' Aid; Nashville Children's Museum and Nashville Better Business Bureau. Bd. Former Member: Amer. Ordnance Assn.; Southern Divl. Vice-Pres., Nat. Assn. of Manufacturers. *Clubs:* Belle Meade Country; Union League; Pinnacle N.Y.; Cornell (N.Y.C.); International Washington Golf. *Address: office* 1515 Wilson Blvd., Arlington, Virginia 22209, U.S.A.

**HART, George Arnold Reeve,** MBE, LLD, DCL, DCSc. *B.* 1913. *Educ.* Public and High Schools, Toronto. *M.* (1) 1939, Jean C. Gilbert (*Dec.*). *Dau.* Diane (Keeling). *M.* (2) 1961, Patricia I. Plant. *Career:* Entered Bank of Montreal at Toronto 1931; held various posts; Joined Canadian Army Oct. 1941; discharged with rank of Major and awarded MBE, Military Division, 1946. Returned Bank of Montreal Head Office, became Asst. Gen. Mgr. 1954, Dep. Gen. Mgr. 1956, Gen. Mgr. 1957, Chief Exec. Officer 1959–74: President 1959–67, Chmn. of the Board 1964–75; Chmn. of the Exec. Cttee. 1964–77; Dir. and member Exec. Cttee, Bank of Montreal; Consolidated—Bathurst Ltd.; Sun Life Assurance Co. of Canada; Inco Ltd.; Dir. Canadian Pacific Ltd.; Bathurst Paper Ltd.; Royal Insurance Co. of Canada; Roins Holding Ltd.; BM-RT Realty Investments; Chmn. Canadian Investment Fund Ltd.; Canadian Fund Inc.; Dir. Uniroyal Inc.; Pratt & Whitney Aircraft of Canada Ltd. *Member:* Canadian Economic Policy Cttee.; Advisory Board, Concordia Univ.; The Conference Board Inc.; Bd. Governors, Canadian Export Assn.; C. D. Howe Research Inst.; Royal Victoria Hospital; Corp./Fdn. Hon. Vice-Pres. Boy Scouts of Canada, Montreal Region; St. John Ambulance (Quebec Council). *Awards:* Hon. LLD Univs. of Saskatchewan 1961 and Montreal 1962; Hon. DCL Bishop's Univ. 1963; Acadia Univ. 1970; Hon. DSc Univ. of Sherbrooke 1965. *Clubs:* Saint James's Mount Royal, Forest & Stream, Mt. Bruno Country (St. Bruno); Ranchman's (Calgary). *Address:* 1700 McGregor Street, Montreal, P.Q. H3H 1B4; and *office* 129 St. James Street West, Montreal, P.Q. H2Y 1L6, Canada.

**HART, Mrs. Judith Constance Mary,** PC. British politician. *Educ.* Clitheroe Royal Grammar School; London School of Economics; London University (BA Hons.). *M.* 1946, Anthony Bernard Hart. *S.* Richard, Stephen. *Career:* Joint Parliamentary Under Secretary of State for Scotland, 1964–66; Minister of State, Commonwealth Office, 1966–67; Minister of Social Security, 1967–68; Paymaster General, 1968–69; Minister, Overseas Development, 1969–70, 1974–75 & since Feb. 1977. Member. National Exec. Cttee., Labour Party & Chmn. of its Industrial Policy & Finance & Economic Sub-committees. *Publications:* Aid and Liberation (1973). *Address:* House of Commons, London, S.W.1.

**HART, Lawrence Albert.** American. *B.* 1912. *Educ.* Yale Univ. (BA 1936); Harvard Business Schl. (MBA 1938). *M.* 1941, Sally Green. *Career:* Pres., Hart & Cosby 1947, Fox-Hart-George Pipe Line Co. 1955, and Hart & Burns Inc. 1948. Dir., National City Bank (Dallas) 1948; President and Director: Home Furniture Co. 1940—, Chairman, 1970—. Hart Investment Co. 1940—, Chicago Oil Co. 1941—, Hart Bowl 1959—, Hart Farm 1951—, Evergreen Building Co. 1962—. President, Kibbe Hart Mining Enterprises 1967—, Dallas Fire Insurance. Co. Vice-Pres.: Hart Furniture Co. 1934—, United Distributing of Texas Inc. 1964—. Chmn., L. A. Hart Distributors 1967—. Dir.: Texas Industries Inc. 1948—. Dallas Citizens Cncl. 1953—, Action Cttee. 1963—, Choate Schl. Alumni Fund 1963—; General Partner, Heyrer and Hart. Aust. Major, U.S. Marine Corps. 1942–45 (Presidential Unit Citation). Recipient: First Report Award, Harvard Business School, 1937; Choate Alumni Seal Prize, 1977. All-American Water Polo, Yale 1935. Alpha Sigma Phi Dir., Central Business Dist. Association. *Member:* Canyon Greek Shopping Center (Pres.); Yale Alumni Fund (chmn.), Board for Fundamental Education; Y.M.C.A. Board; Board of Boys' Club of Dallas; Greater Dallas Planning Council; Board of Caruth Memorial Rehabilitation Center (Pres. since 1966); Trustee, the Choate School. *Clubs:* Brook Hollow Golf; Terpsichorean; Dallas; Hesitation; The Beach; Pebble Beach, Calif.; Cypress Point Golf. *Address:* 5050 Ravine Drive, Dallas, Tex. 75220, U.S.A.; and *office* 3725 Blackburn, Dallas 1, Tex. 75219, U.S.A.

**HART, Parker Thompson.** American businessman. *B.* 1910. *Educ.* Dartmouth Coll. (BA 1933), Harvard Univ. (MA 1935); Graduate Institute of International Studies, Geneva (Dipl. 1936). *M.* 1949, Jane Constance Smiley. *Daus.* 2. *Career:* Rank in the U.S. Foreign Service is that of Career Minister. Joined the Service 1938; served successively in Vienna, Pará (Brazil), Dhahran, Saudi Arabia, Washington, Dhahran, Washington, Cairo, Damascus 1958; Deputy Assistant Secretary of State, Washington 1958–61. Appointed Ambassador to Jordan 1958, but could not present credentials due to federation of Jordan with Iraq; Minister to the Yemen, June 1961–Dec. 1962; Ambassador: to Kuwait 1962–63; to Saudi Arabia 1961–65; to Turkey 1965–68; Asst. Secy. of State for Near East & South Asian Affairs, 1968–69; Director, Foreign Service Institute 1969; President, The Middle East Institute (Washington D.C.) 1969–73; Independent Business Consultant. Trustee, Amer. Univ. of Beirut, American Univ. (Washington); Member Council Foreign Relations of (N.Y.C.). Bd. of Advisors, National Defense Univ.; Washington Inst. Foreign Affairs. Royal Socy. for Asian Affairs (London); Bd. of Govs. of The Middle East Institute; American Research Center in Egypt; Trustee, Center for Applied Linguistics; Co.-Pres., American Turkish Socy., Inc., for Commerce, Industry & Cultural Understanding; Mem., International Advisory Cttee., American Security Bank, Wash., D.C. *Publications:* Application of Hanbalite and Decree Law to Foreigners in Saudi Arabia (article in the George Washington Univ. Law Review, Dec. 1953); & numerous articles on Middle East Affairs. *Club:* Cosmos. *Address:* 4705 Berkeley Terrace, N.W. Washington, D.C., U.S.A. 20007.

**HARTCH, Fred Ernest.** American lawyer and financial consultant. *B.* 1908. *Educ.* AB, Cornell Univ.; MBA, New York Univ.; LLB, JSD, Brooklyn Law School. *M.* Florence Ruth Ferguson; 1933. *S.* Thomas Ferguson. *Career:* Treasurer and Trust Officer, Greenwich Trust Co. 1942–46; Deputy Chief and Chief Property Control & External Assets Officer, Mil. Govt. Berlin and Wiesbaden, Germany, 1946–49. President, General Equities Corp. 1953–72; Chairman, Fairfield Home Oil Co. 1953–72; President, The Vianda Playter Williams Foundation, 1969—. *Member:* Phi Delta Phi Legal Fraternity. *Clubs:* Metropolitan; Sky (both N.Y.); Greenwich Country; Indian Harbour Yacht (both Greenwich, Conn.). *Address:* Lake Avenue, Greenwich, Conn., U.S.A.

**HARTL, Karl Ernst.** Austrian diplomat. *B.* 30 June 1909. *Educ.* Commercial Academy. *M.* 1936, Franziska Gruenhut. *Dau.* 1. *Career:* Businessman and writer, Vienna 1932-38; Political Refugee in France 1938–45; Austrian Commissioner for Repatriation of War Prisoners from France 1945—47; First Secretary of Legation, Rome 1947–49; Consul-General in Israel 1950–55; Counsellor of Legation, Foreign Office, Vienna 1955–58; Ambassador to Turkey Apr. 1958–63; to Yugoslavia 1963–68. Director, Cultural Department, Federal Ministry for Foreign Affairs. *Publications:* How—When—Where; Why—What for; Life's Way. *Address:* Auswärtiges Amt, Vienna, Austria.

**HARTLAND-SWANN, Julian Dana Nimmo.** British Diplomat. *B.* 1936. *Educ.* Stowe; Lincoln Coll., Oxford. *M.* 1960, Ann Deirdre Green. *S.* 1. *Dau.* 1. *Career:* Joined Foreign Office 1960; 3rd Sec., Bangkok 1961–65; 2nd, later 1st Sec., Foreign Office 1965–68; 1st Sec., Berlin 1968–71; 1st Sec. & Head of Chancery, Vienna 1971–74; Foreign & Commonwealth Office 1975–77; HM Ambassador, Ulan Bator since 1977. *Address:* 5 Burgh Street, Islington, London N.1.; and *office* Foreign & Commonwealth Office, King Charles Street, London SW1A 2AH.

**HARTLEY, Eric Llewellyn,** MBE, O St J, ED, CD. Officer, Order of Orange-Nassau (Netherlands); Canadian civil engineer. *B.* 1912. *Educ.* Queen's Univ., Kingston, Ont. (BSc.) *M.* 1937, Audrey Grace Rolston. *S.* Sydney Frederick, Eric Robert and Timothy James. *Career:* President: Dominion Structural Steel Ltd. 1959–62, and Western Bridge Warehouses Ltd. 1957–62; Chmn. Frankel Structural Steel Ltd.; Chmn. Frankel Steel Construction Services Ltd. Pres. Kelsteel Ltd. 1964–75; Vice-Pres., Western Bridge & Steel Fabricators Ltd. 1957–62; Past Pres., Ontario Fed. of Construction Assocs; Past Chmn. and Pres. and Hon. Life member Canadian Construction Assoc. Hon. Col. Roy. Canadian Engineers, Toronto. Fellow Engineering Inst. of Canada; Fellow, Royal Socy. of Arts. *Member:* Prof. Engineers of British Columbia; Prof. Engnrs. of Ontario; Canadian Inst. of Steel Constn. (Past Pres. and Hon. Dir.); Ontario Council, St. John Ambulance. *Clubs:* Seigniory (Montebello, P.Q.); York; Granite; Royal Canadian Military Institute; Empire (Toronto); Terminal City (Vancouver). *Address:* Apt. 2406, 355 St. Clair Avenue, Toronto, Ont. M5P IN5, Canada.

**HARTLING, Poul.** Former Prime Minister of Denmark. *B.* 14 Aug. 1914. *Educ.* Matriculated in 1932, graduated in Divinity 1939. *M.* 1940, Elsebeth Kirkemann. *S.* Niels, Ole and Svend. *Dau.* Ida. *Career:* Secy. to Christian Academic Socy 1934–35; Denmark's Christian Movement, Senior Secondary Students 1939–43; Curate, Frederiksberg Church 1941–45; Chaplain, St. Luke Foundation 1945–50; Principal, Zahle's Teachers Training Coll. 1950–68; Member, Folketing (Parliament) 1957–60 and since 1964; Chmn. Liberal Party's Parly. Group 1965–68; Member, Nordic Council 1964–68, (Pres. 1966–68) and Parly. Foreign Affairs Cttee. Minister for Foreign Affairs, Baunsgaard Cabinet 1968–71; Prime Minister 1973–75. *Awards:* Comdr. Order of Dannebrog; Grand-Croix de l'Ordre de le Couronne, Belgique; Grand-Croix de l'Ordre de Mennlik II: Ethipie; Grosskreuz des Verdienstordens der Bundesrep Deutschl; Grand Croix de l'Ordre du Faucon Islandais. *Publications:* Sursum Corda, Growth of Church Idea in the Missionary Field (1945); The Danish Church (1964 and 1967); From 17 years in Danish Politics. *Address:* Emilievej 6 E. 2920 Charlottenlund; and *office* Christiansborg, Copenhagen K, Denmark.

**HARTLMAYR, Dr. Fritz.** Austrian ambassador. *B.* 1909. *Educ.* Univ. of Vienna (LLD). *M.* 1938, Helly Stempfl-Landegg. *Career:* Judicial practice 1933; Austrian Civil Service (financial administration) 1933–47; Austrian Foreign Service May 1947–Dec. 1974; Consul, French Zone of Occupation, in Germany 1948–50; Consul-General Zurich 1951–54; Chargé d'Affairs, Pakistan 1954; En. Ex. and Min. Plen. Feb. 1956–59. Ambassador to Pakistan 1959–60; Japan 1961–67; Nigeria 1967–69; to Brazil 1971–75. *Publications:* articles on Constitutional and International Law in various journals. Sec.-Gen., Austrian U.N. Association. *Address:* 1060 Wien, Köstlergasse 5/19a, Austria.

**HARTMAN, John W.** American. *B.* 1922. *Educ.* Colgate & Duke Universities. *M.* 1947, Esther Kelly Bill. *S.* 1. *Dau.* 1. *Career:* Chmn. Bd. Bill Communications; Magazine Publishers Association. Past Pres. & Dir. Young President's Organization; Adv. Research Foundation. *Clubs:* Wee Burn Country; Camp Fire Club of America; Old Lyme Country. *Address:* 364 Laurel Road, New Canaan, Conn., U.S.A.; and *office* 633 Third Avenue, New York, N.Y. 10017.

**HARTNETT, Sir Laurence John,** CBE, FRSA, FIE (Aust.). British Chartered Engineer. *B.* 1898. *Educ.* Epsom College, Surrey (England). *M.* 1925, Gladys Winifred Tyler. *Daus.* 3. *Career:* Lieut. R.N. Air Service and R.A.F. 1917–19; own engineering business, England 1919–23; Guthrie & Co, Ltd., Singapore 1923–26; General Motors Corp. (India. U.S.A., Sweden) 1926; Vauxhall Motors Ltd., England 1929; Managing Director, General Motors Holdens Ltd.; concurrently (1936–37) Regional Director for Australia and New Zealand; Vice-Pres., General Motors Export Co. (1936) 1934–47; Director: Commonwealth Aircraft Corp. Pty. Ltd. 1935–47, and Ordnance Production, Ministry of Munitions (Australia) 1940–45; Chairman, Inventions Directorate, Australia 1942–46; Chairman & Governing Director, Hartnett Holdings Pty. Ltd. 1949—; Chairman, John Hart Pty. Ltd. 1948—; Chmn., Ferro Corp. (Aust.) Pty. Ltd. 1947—. Trustee, Inst. of Applied Science, Victoria (Past-Chmn. & Treasurer) 1945—. Governor, Corps of Commissionaires (Victoria) Ltd. 1946—. Fellow, Royal Society of Arts (London); *Member:* Institution of Engineers, Australia; Institution of Automotive & Aeronautical Engineers (Past Pres.); Society of Automotive Engineers Inc. of New York; Fellow, Australian Institute of Management; member of Executive and Past Pres., Australian Industries Development Association; Co-opted Member, Standards Association of Australia. *Award:* BBM (Public Service Star) Republic of Singapore. *Clubs:* Athanaeum (Melbourne); Royal Aero (London). *Address:* 'Rubra' Watts Rd., Mount Eliza, 3930 Vic., Australia; Flat 4, 24 Hill Street, Toorak, 3142, Vic., Australia.

**HARTOG, Robbert.** Canadian manufacturer. *B.* 1919. *Educ.* Ecole Libre des Sciences Politiques, Paris (Diplomé 1940) and University of Toronto (MA 1942). *Career:* With Société Astra, Paris 1939–40; Massey Harris & Co. Ltd., Toronto 1942–43. Royal Netherlands Army 1943–46. President and Director, Waltec Enterprises Ltd.; Foreign Investment Trust Inc.; Kindred Industries Ltd., Dolmar N.V.; Dir.: Hugh Russel Ltd.; Dalex Co. Ltd. *Publications:* De l'Utilité du Contrôle de Change en Temps de Guerre (1941). *Member:* Canadian Economic Association; Royal Economic Society. *Club:* Granite. *Address:* RRI Perkinsfield, Ont.; and *office* P.O. Box 936, Cambridge, Ont. N1R 5X9, Canada.

**HARTOGH, Abraham Frans Karel.** Netherlands Diplomat. *B.* 1913. *Educ.* Univ. of Leyden—Master's Degree in Law. *M. S.* 2. *Career:* Practitioner in Law in U.S. & the Netherlands 1936–40; Ministry of Social Affairs, London 1941–43; Reserve Flying Officer 1943–48; Ministry of Economic Affairs 1948–52 onwards; Netherlands Delegation to OEEC, Paris 1952–59; on loan to Ministry of Economic Affairs 1960–62; Dir.-Gen. European Cooperation, Ministry of Foreign Affairs 1962–73; Perm. Rep. of Netherlands to North Atlantic Council since 1974. *Decorations:* Knight, Order of Netherlands Lion; Commander, Order of Orange Nassau. *Address:* Franklin Roosevelt-laan 77, 1050 Brussels, Belgium; and *office* Boulevard Leopold III, 1110-NATO-Brussels, Belgium.

**HARTZ, Raymond E.** American. Corporation executive. *B.* 1899. *Educ.* Univ. of Minnesota (BS 1922). *M.* 1932, Elizabeth Keiser. *S.* Raymond E. and John C. *Dau.* Elizabath. *Career:* Service in the Army 1919. Sales Dept. Brown & Bigelow, St. Paul, Minn. 1923–25; Special Agent Prudential Insurance Co., Minneapolis 1923–25; Special Agent Prudential Insurance Co., Minneapolis 1925–28; Vice-Pres. Estate Planning Corp., Mpls., Chicago and N.Y.C. 1928–48 (Pres. 1948–53, Chmn. of Bd. 1954–61); Exec. Vice-Pres. Management Planning Inc. 1941–48. Associated with Fiduciary Counsel Inc. 1931— (Dir. 1948—, Vice-Pres. 1949–54, Pres. 1954–62). Chairman of the Board 1962—and Director 1948, Chmn. Emeritus since 1971, Fiduciary Counsel Inc. Trustee, Four Oaks Foundation. *Publications:* Fiscal Counsel Plus, (1946); A New Concept for Conserving Estates, (1953); How to Protect Capital Against all Hazards, (1958). *Member:* Alpha Delta Phi, Beta Gamma Sigma. Episcopalian. *Clubs:* Somerset Hills Country; Grolier; Wall Street. *Address:* 20 Park Place, Morristown, N.J., U.S.A.

**HARVEY, Arthur.** American oil executive. *B.* 1895. *Educ.* Public Schools. *M.* 1929, Sylva Vogelsong. *S.* Arthur Herbert. *Daus.* Elizabeth Inez (Holcomb) (Dec.), Sylva Anne (Lynn Smith). *Career:* Discoverer several large oil fields in Texas and Illinois; crude oil producer; sole owner Tex-Harvey Oil Company since 1939; organizer Tex-Harvey Gasoline Plant, Midland (Texas); Organized Harvey Park Company (Denver) which converted Colorado cattle ranch into a portion of Harvey Park, the largest political sub-division of the City and County of Denver; Special Agent, Intelligence Unit. Bureau of Internal Revenue, Dept. of U.S. Treasury 1920–39; served as private to sergeant, U.S. Inf. Div., World War I, 1917–19; reserve officer, 2nd Lieut. to Major, 1926–55; Major AF-RET, 1955— served as Capt. to Major, 449th Bombardment Group, Heavy, in Italy 1942–45. *Address:* 334 Peerman Place, Corpus Christi, Texas, 78411, U.S.A.

**HARVEY of Prestbury, Baron** (cr. 1971 Life Peer) **Arthur Vere,** CBE, Kt. 1957. *B.* 1906. *Educ.* Framlingham College Suffolk. *M.* (1) 1940, Jaqueline Anne Dunnett (Dis). *S.* 2. (2) 1955, Mrs. Hilary Charmian Williams. *Career:* With Royal Air Force 1925–30, Air Commodore 1943 (twice mentioned in despatches); Conservative MP for Macclesfield 1945–71; Dir., Far East Aviation Co. Ltd. and Far East Flying School Ltd. (Hong Kong) 1930–35. Hon. rank of Major-General 1932–35; Tradewinds Airways Ltd.; Vice-Pres., British Air Line Pilot's Assn. Chmn. Film Corp. of America (U.K. Ltd.), Honorary Freedom, Borough Macclesfield, 1969; Congleton, 1970; Chairman 1922 Cttee. 1965–70. *Awards:* Commander, Order of Orange Nassau; Hon. Doctor Science Salford University, 1969. *Clubs:* Buck's, Royal Yacht Squadron, Royal Malta Yacht. *Address:* Villa Wardija, Malta.

**HARVEY, Ian Douglas,** TD. British Independent Consultant, Advertising and PR. *B.* 1914. *Educ.* Fettes Coll., Edinburgh, and Christ Church, Oxford (MA); Pres. Oxford Union 1926. *M.* Clare Mayhew (*sep*). *Daus.* Margaret Aylwin and Amanda Clare. *Career:* P.A. to Vice-Chmn., Mather & Crowther Ltd. 1937–39. Adjutant and Brigade-Major, GSOII (Ops.); Staff Coll., Camberley 1944; p.s.c.; Lt.-Col. Commanding R.A., T.A. Regiment 1947–50. Executive 1945–49; Director 1949–56, W. S. Crawford Ltd. Member of Parliament, Harrow East (Parly. Under-Secretary of State Foreign Office 1957–58; Parly. Secy., Ministry of Supply 1956–57). With Colman Prentis & Varley Ltd.; Independent Consultant, Advertising and P.R. 1959–60; Manager, International Div. 1960–62; Exec. Director 1961–62; Director 1962–63. Advertising Director, Yardley of London Ltd. and Yardley Internl. Ltd. 1964–66; Associate Douglas Stephens Associates Ltd. *Member* Royal Borough of Kensington 1946–51; London County Council 1949–53; Secy. Iain Macleod Trust since 1974; Vice-Pres. Campaign for Homosexual Equality; Chmn. Gaycon. Conservative. *Publications:* Talk of Propaganda: the Technique of Persuasion; Arms of Tomorrow; To Fall

Like Lucifer. *Club:* Royal Automobile. *Address:* 28a Star Street, London W2 1QV.

**HARVEY, John Edgar.** British. *B.* 1920. *Educ.* Xaverian Coll., Bruges; Lyme Regis Grammar School. *M.* 1945, Mary Joyce Lane. *S.* Richard John. *Career:* Member of Parliament, Walthamstow East, 1955–66. Director of various subsidiary companies of The Burmah Co. Ltd.; Deputy Chmn., Burmah Castrol Europe S.A. 1968—. *Publications:* Contributor, with others, to Conservative Party publications: Monopoly and the Public Interest and The Rising Tide, dealing with educational and young people's problems. *Member:* Inst. of Directors; Inst. of Export; Inst. of Petroleum. *Clubs:* Carlton; City of London. *Address:* 43 Traps Hill, Loughton, Essex; and *office* Burmah House, Pipers Way, Swindon, Wilts. SN3 1RE.

**HARVIE ANDERSON, Rt. Hon. (Margaret) Betty,** PC, OBE, TD, DL. British Member of Parlaiment. *Educ.* St. Leonard's School; St. Andrews. *M.* 1960, John Francis Penrose Skrimshire, MD, FRCP. *Career:* Conservative MP. for East Renfrewshire since 1959; Member, Exec. Cttee of 1922 Cttee, 1962–70, 1974—; Chairman's Panel, House of Commons, 1966–70; Dep. Chmn. of Ways & Means, House of Commons 1970–73. *Member:* Historic Buildings Council for Scotland, 1966; Royal Commission on Local Government in Scotland 1966–69; Mr. Speaker's Conf., 1966–68. *Address:* Quarter, by Denny, Stirlingshire, Scotland.

**HARVIE-WATT, Sir George Steven,** Bt., TD, DL, QC. British politician and company director. *B.* 1903. *Educ.* George Watson's College, Edinburgh; Univs. Glasgow and Edinburgh. *M.* 1932, Jane Elizabeth Taylor. *S.* 2. *Dau.* 1. Cons. Member of Parliament for Keighley Division of Yorks 1931–35, Richmond, Surrey, 1937–39; Parly. Private Secy. to late Rt. Hon. Euan Wallace 1937–38; Asst. Govt. Whip 1938–40; Parly. Private Secy. to Rt. Hon. Winston S. Churchill 1941–45; Member of Queen's Bodyguard for Scotland, Royal Co. of Archers; A.D.C. to H.M. the Queen 1952–58; D.L. (Greater London) 1966; President Consolidated Gold Fields Ltd.; former Chmn. The Monotype Corp.; Dir. Midland Bank Ltd.; Dir. Eagle Star Insurance Co.; Dir. The Clydesdale Bank Ltd. *Member:* Borough Council R.B. of Kensington 1934–45. *Address:* Earlsneuk, Elie, Fife, Scotland.

**HARWOOD, Edward Crosby.** American economist and retired Officer, Corps of Engineers, U.S. Army. *B.* 1900. *Educ.* U.S. Military Academy, West Point (BSc) and Rensselaer Polytechnic Institute (CE; MCE; MBA). *M.* (1) 1921, Harriet Haynes, and (2) 1938, Helen L. Fowle. *S.* Edward L., Richard F., William F., Frederick C. *Daus.* Marjorie H., Eve. C., and Katherine S. *Career:* Commissioned 2nd Lieut., U.S. Army 1920; advanced through the ranks to Colonel, 1943; retired 1937; returned to active duty 1940; executive engineers service, E.T.O., 1942–43 chief of mobilization division, War Department, 1943; Corps of Engineers, XI Corps, 1943–44; Chief of Staff, Army Service Command, S.W. Pacific Theatre, 1944; retired as Colonel 1946; Associate Professor of Military Science, Massachusetts Institute of Technology, 1930–34, 1940–42; executive, U.S. district engineer, Boston, in charge of Cape Cod Canal Improvement Programme, 1934–36; in charge of flood control surveys of New England, 1936; Director, American Institute for Economic Research (since 1934); Trustee, Henry George School of Social Science; Director, Economic Education League; Treasurer, Behavioral Research Cncl.; Trustee, Progress Foundation; Dir. Cttee. for Monetary Research and Education. *Publications:* Cause and Control of the Business Cycle; Useful Economics; The Counter Revolution—American Foreign and Domestic Policy and Economic Aspects of National Defence; Reconstruction of Economics; Twentieth Century Common Sense; The American Crisis of the 1960s; Useful Procedures of Inquiries; A Current Appraisal of the Behavioural Sciences; numerous articles in leading journals. *Address:* Great Barrington, Mass., U.S.A.

**HASEK, Joseph Karel,** Dr. American. *B.* 1911. *Educ.* Charles Univ. Prague, Ph.D. Law & Economics). *M.* 1938, Karla Policka, (Div.). *S.* 1. *Dau.* 1. *Career:* Pres. Hasek & Co. Bankers; Comm. Court of Justice 1935; Law Firm E. Schwartz 1936; N. M. Rothchild & Sons London 1937; Czechoslovak Export Inst. and Bank of Manhattan Co., New York 1938. Member, 1945 Czechoslovak Govt. Economic Mission to England; Dir. Czech-Am. Ch. of Commerce 1947; Marketing Project for US Govt 1948; Cslt. and lectr. on Intern. Trade & Fin.; Pres. Combined Agencies Corp. since 1948; Exec. International Bank of Washington 1951–53; U.S. citizen since 1954; Dir. Aeromaritime Inc.; Kenwood Development Corp. since 1957. Chmn. Export Cttee. Washington Bd. of Trade; Appt. to US Export Expansion Councils 1968–74. *Member:* Am. Assn. Intl. Execs.; Amer. Chamber of Commerce in London. *Clubs:* Kenwood Golf & Country; City Tavern; Chevaliers du Tastevin (all Washington D.C.). *Address:* 4207 45th Street, N.W. Washington, D.C. 20006, U.S.A.; and *office* 910 17 Street, N.W., Washington, D.C. 20006.

**HASELGROVE, Harry Ronald,** OBE. *B.* 1900. *Educ.* Roseworthy Agricultural College, South Australia (Dipl.). *M.* 1926, Elsie Janet Wigan. *S.* Richard Frederick and Ronald James Cleveland. *Daus.* Mrs. O G. Woodward, Mrs. A. Keeves and Mrs. P. Wilksch. Director, Mildara Wines Ltd., Merbein, Vic. Liberal. *Clubs:* Royal South Australian Yacht; Mildura. *Address:* 5 Wootoona Terrace, St. Georges, S.A.; and *office* Mildara Wines, Ltd., Merbein, Vic., Australia.

**HASELTON, William Raymond.** American. *B.* 1925. *Educ.* Rensselaer Polytechnic Institute (BS Chem. Eng.) and Lawrence Univ. (MS; PhD). *M.* 1948, Frances C. Crooks. *Daus.* Susan, Judith and June. *Career:* With Rhinelander Paper Co. 1953–61, Vice-Pres. and Gen. Mgr. 1957–61; Dir. R. W. Paper Co. Longview 1962–75; Pacific National Bank of Washington 1962–75; Dir. St. Regis Paper Co. New York, N.Y. since 1971; Dir. Southland Paper Mills Houston, Texas since 1973.; Vice-Pres. St. Regis 1964–69, Senior Vice-Pres. 1969–72, Exec. Vice-Pres. 1972–73; Pres. St Regis Paper Co., New York, since 1973. Recipient Westbrook Steel Award, Inst. of Paper Chemistry 1953. *Address:* 16 Shagbark Road, Darien, Connecticut 06820; and *office* 150 East 42nd Street, New York, New York 10017, U.S.A.

**HASKETT, Hon. Wesley Irwin.** Canadian. Patent Attorney in the City of Ottawa. Minister of Transport for Ontario. *B.* 1903. *Educ.* Lisgar Collegiate (Ottawa). *M.* 1936, Vera Moorhead. Minister of Reform Institutions for Ontario Nov. 1961–Aug. 1963. Past President: Ottawa Board of Trade, and Ontario Chamber of Commerce; President, Ottawa Association for the Blind; Hon. Treasurer, St. John's Ambulance Association. Member Progressive Conservative Party. *Clubs:* Metropolitan Board of Trade; Ottawa Ski (Life Member); Eagle Fish & Game (Past Pres.); Ottawa Hunt & Golf; Albany (Toronto). *Address:* 3 Frederick Place, Ottawa; and *offices* Parliament Buildings, Ferguson Tower, Toronto; and Patent Attorney Office, 53 Queen Street, Ottawa, Ont., Canada.

**HASKINS, Caryl Parker.** American scientist and educator. *B.* 1908. *Educ.* Yale (PhB 1930); Harvard Univ. (PhD 1935); Tufts College (DSc 1951); Union College (DSc 1955); Northeastern Univ. (DSc 1955); Yale (DSc 1958); Hamilton (DSc 1959); LLD Carnegie Inst. of Technology, Univ. of Cincinnati, and Boston Coll. (all in 1960) and Washington & Jefferson College (1961); Univ. of Delaware (1965); George Washington Univ. (DSc 1963); Pace Univ. (1974). *M.* 1940, Edna Ferrell. *Career:* Staff member, research laboratory, General Electric Co., Schenectady 1931–35; Research assoc., Massachusetts Inst. of Technology 1935–44; Pres. and Research Dir., Haskins Laboratories, Inc. 1935–55; Pres., National Photocolor Corp. of New York City 1939–55; Research Professor, Union Coll., Schenectady, 1937–55; Asst. Dir., Survey of Research in Industry, National Research Council 1940–41; Asst. Liaison Officer, Office of Scientific Research and Development 1941–42, Senior Liaison Officer 1942–43; Exec. Asst. to Chmn., National Defense Research Committee 1943–44 (Deputy Exec. Officer 1944–45); Scientific adviser, Policy Council, Joint Research and Development Board of the Army and Navy, 1947; Scientific adviser, Research and Development Board of the National Military Establishment, 1947–51; Consultant, Secretary of Defence, since 1948; Chairman, Special Advisory Committee to the Secretary of Defence, 1947–49; Consultant, Secretary of State since 1950; member, President's Science Advisory Committee 1955–58; Consultant, President's Advisory Committee 1959—. President, Carnegie Institution of Washington (1956–71). *Member:* Board of Directors, Haskins Laboratories, Inc. (1935), Chmn. of Board 1969—; Council on Foreign Relations Inc. 1961–75; Trustee and Member of the Corporation, Yale Univ. 1962–77; Trustee: Carnegie Corporation of New York (Chmn. Bd. 1975—.); Marlboro Coll.; Centre for Advanced Study in the Behavioral Sciences 1960–76; Carnegie Institution of Washington, Population Council. Member of the Corporation, Woods Hole Oceanographic Institution; Regent, Smithsonian Institution; Dir., E. I. du Pont de Nemours & Co.; Trustee, American Museum of Natural History. *Publications:* Of Ants and Men (1939);

The Amazon (1943); Of Societies and Men (1951); Scientific Revolution and World Politics (1964); The Search for Understanding (Editor) 1967; Chmn. Ed. Board, *American Scientist* 1970—; numerous articles and professional papers on scientific subjects. *Address:* 2100 M Street N.W., Washington D.C., 20037, U.S.A.

**HASKINS, Edna (Ferrell).** American. Writer, Scientist. Member, Board of Directors, Haskins Laboratories 1943–71. *B.* 1911. *Educ.* King's College, Durham University (England) BSc 1933; Radcliffe College and Harvard University, MA, 1937; PhD, King's College, Durham University, 1937. *M.* 1940, Caryl Parker Haskins, naturalized 1943. State Scholar, King's College, Durham Univ., 1930–34; Saville Shaw Memorial Medal of the Society of Chemical Industry, England, 1933; Johnston Memorial Chemical Prize, Durham Univ. 1934; Johnston Memorial Chemical Fellow, Durham Univ., 1934–35; Augustus Anson Whitney Fellow, Radcliffe College and Harvard Univ., 1935–36; Rose Sidgwick Memorial Fellow of the British and American Association of University Women, Radcliffe College and Harvard Univ., 1936–37. Senior Research and Administrative Staff, War Department, Royal Arsenal, Woolwich, England, 1937–38; H.M. District Inspector of Factories in the Ministry of Labour and National Service and in the Home Office, England, Nov. 1938–April 1939; Acting District Inspector of Factories, April 1939–July 1940; Staff member, Haskins Laboratories 1940–55; member, Board of Directors, National Photocolor Corporation, New York City 1943–56 (Secretary 1945–55). *Fellow:* New York Academy of Sciences, 1957; Member, Women's Council, N.Y. Public Library, Capital Public Speakers Club, Am. Assn. Advancement of Science, (Life Mem.) Am. Chem. Socy., Calif. Acad. of Sciences, N.Y. Zoological Socy., Am. Museum of Natural History, N.Y. Botanical Garden, Brooklyn Botanic Garden, Radcliffe Club (N.Y. & Washington), English-Speaking Union, Metropolitan Museum of Art, former Mem., Brit Assn. Adv. Science. *Publications:* contributor to American and British periodicals. *Address:* 2100 M. Street N.W., Washington, D.C. 20037 U.S.A.

**HASKINS, George Lee.** American lawyer, historian and educator. *B.* 1915. *Educ.* Harvard Univ. (AB; LLB); Oxford Univ. (special student). Fellow, Royal Historical Soc.; Consejero del Instituto Internacional para Unification del Derecho Publico (Madrid); Corresponding Member, Masschstts. Hist. Soc.; Hon. Fellow, American Socy. for Legal History (1975); several prize fellowships, and military decorations. Henry Fellow, Merton Coll., Oxford 1935–36; Socy. of Fellows, Harvard 1936–42; MA (honoris causa) Univ. of Pennsylvania 1971. *Career:* Lecturer in Sociology, Harvard 1938–39; Lowell Lectures, Boston 1939; Associate in law firm of Herrick & Smith, Boston 1942; U.S. Army General Staff 1942–46; U.S. Army Reserve Corps 1946–54; Assistant Professor of Law, University of Pennsylvania 1946–48; Associate Prof. 1948–49; Prof. 1949—. Councillor, Mediaeval Academy of America, 1958–60; A. S. Biddle Professor of Law since 1974. Corresponding Secretary for Pennsylvania of the Selden Society. Advisory Council for the Humanities. Station WHYY (Philadelphia) 1976—. President, American Society, Legal History 1970–74, Board of Dirs. 1977–80; Council, Association Internationale d'Histoire du Droit et des Institutions, 1970—. Member of panel of authors preparing official History of U.S. Supreme Court authorised by U.S. Congress. Member, Advisory Board of Editors of Speculum, 1948–68. Special Attorney, Consulting Counsel, Pennsylvania Railroad Co., Penn Central Railroad since 1951. Dir., Pennsylvania Mutual Fund 1961–68. Edit. Adv. Cttee. Papers of John Marshall; Justice Bradley Papers; Asst. Reporter, Supreme and Superior Courts, Pennsylvania, 1970–71. Seminar Research Associate, Columbia Univ., Société Internationale Pour l' Etude de Philosophie Médiévale, Member Titulaire 1971. *Member:* Genealogical Socys. of Amer. & Pennsylvania; Council and Editorial Board, Institute Early American History and Culture; Board of Editors, William & Mary Qtly., 1969–71; Panel of Arbitrators, American Arbitration Assoc.; American Judicature Soc.; Maine Bar Association, Massachusetts, Pennsylvania, Philadelphia and American Bar Associations; Bar Association, City of New York; Interstate Commerce Commission Practitioners Association; American Law Institute; American Historical Association; Maine Historical Socy.; Hancock County (Maine) Bar Assn.; Mediaeval Academy of America; International Law Socy.; Socy. of Comparative Legislation; Colonial Socy. of Massachusetts Swedish Colonial Socy.; Pennsylvania Colonial Soc. (Governor's Council, 1977); Virginia Historical Soc.; Socy. of Colonial Wars; Socy. of Mayflower Descendants; Socy. War of 1812; Socy. Sons of Amer. Revolution; Internatl. Commsn. for History of Representative and Parly. Institutions; Amer. Antiquarian Socy.; National Socy. of Literature and Arts; Societé Jean Bodin (Brussels), New England Land Title Assn.; Delegate American Council of Learned Socys. Conference on British Studies; Phi Beta Kappa; Order of the Coif; Philadelphia Art Alliance; various clubs in Boston, Philadelphia and Washington; Library Co. of Philadelphia, U.S. Court Tennis Assoc.; Boston Athenaueum, Royal Automobile (London). Official Mem. Town of Hancock (Maine) Bicentennial Cttee. (1975–76). *Publications:* The Statute of York and the Interest of the Commons (1935); The Growth of English Representative Governments (1948); The American Law of Property (with others) (1952); Pennsylvania Fiduciary Guide (1957 and 1962); Law and Authority in Early Massachusetts (1960 and 1968); Editor, Death of a Republic, by John Dickinson (1963); numerous articles on history, constitutional law, the law of property and of decedents' estates, and govt. regulation of business in U.S. and European periodicals. *Address:* Paoli Pa. 19301 and 3400 Chestnut Street, Philadelphia 19104, Pa., U.S.A.

**HASLUCK, Rt. Hon. Sir Paul Meernaa Caedwalla,** GCMG, GCVO, PC, KStJ. Australian. *B.* 1905. *Educ.* Univ. of Western Australia (MA). *M.* 1932, A. M. M. Darker. *S.* Rollo (*Dec'd*), Nicholas. *Career:* engaged in journalism 1922–38; Lecturer in History, University of Western Australia 1939–40; in Australian Diplomatic Service 1941–47; Acting Representative, United Nations Security Council and Atomic Energy Commission and Australian Representative, United Nations Headquarters 1946–47; Research Reader in History, University of Western Australia 1948; Political Historian for Australian Official War History; M.P. (Lib.) 1949–69; Commonwealth Minister for Territories 1951–Dec. 1963; Minister for Defence Jan.–May 1964; Minister for External Affairs May 1964–69. Privy Councillor 1966; Governor-General of Australia 1969–74. *Address:* 95 St. George's Terrace, Perth, Western Australia.

**HATCH, H. Clifford.** Canadian executive. *B.* 1916. *Educ.* St. Michael's College School, Toronto. *M.* 1940, Joan Ferriss. *S.* Henry Clifford and Richard Ferris. *Daus.* Gail Elizabeth (Todgham), Sheila Mary (McNamara). *Career:* with T.G. Bright & Co. Ltd., Niagara Falls, Ont. 1933–37; Hiram Walker-Gooderham & Worts Ltd., Walkerville, Ont. since 1937, Dir. 1946. Pres. since 1964; Dir. various subsidary companies; Toronto Dominion Bank, Toronto and T. G. Bright & Co. Ltd., Niagara Falls; Dir., Bell Canada; Dir., Curtis Co. Ltd. *Clubs:* Rosedale Golf (Toronto); Essex Golf, Windsor Curling (Windsor); Detroit Athletic. *Address:* 7130 Riverside Drive East, Windsor, N8S 1C3, Ont.; and *office* 2072, Riverside Drive East, Walkerville N8Y 4S5, Ont., Canada.

**HATCH, William Douglas.** Canadian. *B.* 1923. *Educ.* Univ. of Toronto 1946. *M.* 1946, Irene Frances McLaughlin. *S.* 2. *Career:* Served in World War II (R.C.N.V.R. 1942; active service; Sub-Lieut. 1943, Lieut. 1944, demobilized 1945) Joined present company as Laboratory Asst. 1947; Export Mgr. 1948; Asst. to Vice-President.—Sales and Advertising Mgr.—1949; Director 1952; Secy. 1952; Vice-President Sales 1959; Director and President, T. G. Bright & Co. Ltd. (estab. 1874) June 1963—. Director: Canada Malting Co. Ltd.; Canada Permanent Trust Co.; Associate Member, Canadian Wine Inst. (Past Pres.), Member Internatl. Oceanographic Fd., Miami; Naval Officers' Assn. (Toronto Branch); Knights of Malta; Advisory Cncl. Hotel Dieu Hospital, St. Catherines. *Clubs:* Granite, R.C.Y.C., Rosedale Golf, Ontario Jockey (all Toronto); St. Catharines Golf; St. Catharines; Cherry Hill (Ridgeway); Niagara Falls (Ont.). *Address:* 173 Highland Avenue, St. Catharines, Ont.; and *office* Dorchester Road, Niagara Falls, Ont., Canada.

**HATELY, Furness Hall.** American industrialist. *B.* 1905. *Educ.* Mass. Inst. of Technology (ME 1927). *M.* 1947, Alba Luz Bayonet. *S.* Furness Hall, Jr. *Dau.* Pamela Maria. *Career:* Lieut. to Major, U.S. Army 1943–45; Assistant General Manager, European Cyanamid Export Co. Ltd., London (Eng.) 1927–32; Development Sales Engr., Whitehead Metal Products Co., N.Y.C. 1932–35; Research Development Director, American Felt Co., Glenville, Conn. 1935–38; Assistant to President, Semet Solvay Corp., N.Y.C. 1938–41, and Interlake Iron Corp., Cleveland 1942–43; Management Consultant, Bigelow, Kent, Willard & Co., N.Y.C. 1945–47, and San Juan, P.R. 1947–49; Director 1954–62, Treasurer 1955–61, Secretary 1960–61, Farrington Manufacturing Co., Needham, Mass.; Dir. 1955–61, Exec. Vice-Pres. 1959–61, The Farrington Corp. Dir.: Electralab

Inc., Needham 1954–61, and Electralab Printed Electronics Corp. 1959–61; Dir. 1954–61, Secretary-Clerk 1960–61, Farrington Texol Corp., Walpole; Dir. 1954–61, Secretary 1960–61, Farrington Mfg. Co. Ltd., Toronto; Dir., Intelligent Machines Research Corp., Alexandria, Va. 1959–61; Dir., Secretary-Clerk 1960–61; Farrington Packaging Corp. (Needham), Casco Mfg. Co. Inc. (Westbrook, Maine), Farrington Electronics Inc. (Needham), and Farrington Business Machines Corp. (New Bedford, Mass.); Dir., Pickard & Burns Inc., Needham 1955–60; Exec. Vice-Pres., Treas., Dir., Cushman & Wakefield of Puerto Rico Inc., Hato Rey 1962–70; Pres., Dir., Hately Financial Corp., Hato Rey, Puerto Rico since 1962. *Member:* Controllers Inst. of America, Amer. Management Assn., A.I.M., Beta Theta Pi A.F. & A.M., A.A.O.N.M.S. Episcopalian. *Clubs:* University (Boston); Milton:Hoosie (Milton, Mass.); Tennis & Swimming, San Juan, P.R.; Berwind Country, Rio Grande, P.R. *Address:* 136 Barcelona, Santurce, Puerto Rico; and *office* Banco Popular Center (P.O. Box 326), Hato Rey, Puerto Rico.

**HATFIELD, Benjamin Frank.** Col. U.S. Army (Retd.). *B.* 1906. *Educ.* Univ. of Tennessee (BS Elec. Eng.; BS Mech. Eng.); U.S. Army Engineer School (No. 1 Graduate 1935); U.S. Army Signal Corps School. *M.* 1930, Ada Ella Hatcher. *S.* Benjamin Frank, Jr, (*dec'd*). *Dau.* Ada Joyce (Coleman). *Career:* Installer, Western Electric Co., Memphis Tenn. 1924–25; Switchman, Cumberland Tel. & Tel. Co., Memphis 1925–26; With Southern Bell Tel. & Tel. Co.; Engineer, Atlanta, Ga. 1930–32, 1936–41, Switchman, Louisville, Ky. 1932–36, Maintenance and Practices Engineer 1946–48, Chief Engineer, New Orleans 1949–53; Executive (telephone industry); Asst. Vice-President, Southern Bell Telephone & Telegraph Co., Atlanta, Ga. 1953–71; Public Utility Consultant, Steinhauer, Hatfield and Good Assoc.; Vice-Pres. A. L. Groce Assoc., Public Utility Consultants; With U.S. Army: Captain, Corps of Engineers, Camp Blanding, Fla. 1941; with Signal Corps: Major-Lieut.-Col., Ft. McPherson, Ga. 1942—44; Lieut.-Col., Col., India-Burma Theatre 1944–46 (Bronze Star Medal, Burma Campaign Battle Star, Commanding Officer Meritorious Service Unit). Junior Engineering Prize, Univ. of Tenn., and Krusi Prize in Electrical Engineering Univ. of Tenn. *Member:* Inst. of Electrical and Electronics Engineers; Georgia Arch. and Engin. Socy.; Armed Forces Comm. and Electronics Assn.; Internat. Inst. of Community Services. Military Order of the World Wars. Tau Beta Pi; Phi Kappa Phi. *Address:* 3916 Land O'Lakes Drive N.E., Atlanta Georgia 30342, U.S.A.

**HATFIELD, Edgar Wakeman.** American attorney and counsellor-at-law (N.Y.). *B.* 1908. *Educ.* Bard College—then St. Stephens College of Columbia University (LLD *honoris causa* 1956) and Harvard Law School (LLB 1934). *M.* (1) 1940, Muriel Campbell Hunter (D. 1970). *Daus.* Ellen Elizabeth (Feverhake), Barbara Campbell and Joan Carleton, (2) 1972, Nancy Elenore Walker. *Career:* Law clerk with Gifford, Woody, Carter & Hays (then Merrill, Rogers, Gifford & Woody), N.Y.C. 1932; Admitted N.Y. Bar Mar. 4, 1935; partner, Gifford, Woody, Carter & Hays 1942–48; entered single law practice 1948; formed Mason & Hatfield partnership 1950—. Former Dir.: The General Package Co., Liberty Lithographing Co. Inc.; Allied Lithographing Co. Inc.; Copy Reproductions Inc.; The Blakeslee Forging Co.; J. H. Dunning Corp.; Biddeford Box Co., The Green Co. Inc., Plastic Sheet Fabrication, Inc., The Four Five Eight Corp., Corrugated Metal Products. Partner, Hatfield & Brady (formed 1964), N.Y.C., Hatfield, Brady & Taft (formed 1968). Director & Secretary of Cross County Wines and Liquors, Inc.; John J. Langan, Inc.; Roger S. Smith Associates, Inc.; University Graphics, Inc.; W. A. McClelland Inc.; Debro Enterprises, Inc.; Lizanda Enterprises Inc.; Clover Lane Enterprises Inc. *Member:* Amer. and N.Y. State Bar Assns.; Harvard Law Schl. Assn.; New York Republican County Cttee.; Paramus Historical & Preservation Socy.; N.Y. Genealogical & Biographical Socy; National Geographic Socy.; Marine Historical Assn. of Mystic Conn.; Holland Socy. of N.Y.; New York Chapter, Empire State Society, Sons of the Amer. Revolution; The St. Nicholas Socy. of the City of New York; Military Order Loyal Legion United States; Sons of the Revolution; The Order of Lafayette; St. George's Socy. of New York; The New England Socy. in the City of New York; Ridgewood Art Assn.; Learned Hand & Ely Law Clubs, Harvard Law School. Trustee, and First Vice Chmn. Bd. Trustees Bard Coll.; Trustee, Gen. Legal Counsel; Asst. Secy. Asst. Treas. Hoosac School; Trustee, Secy. Treas. Wooley-Clifford Foundation; Trustee, Loyal Legion Foundation. *Award:* Fellow of the Amer. College of Probate Counsel. *Clubs:* Kappa Gamma Chi; Ridgewood Country Skytop; Franklin Lake Indian Trail; Englewood Yacht; Saddle River Power Squadron; Health Roof; New York Yacht, *Address:* Apt. 17-B, 180 East End Avenue, New York City, N.Y.; and *office* 277 Park Avenue, New York City, N.Y., U.S.A.

**HATFIELD, Richard B.**, Canadian politician. Premier of New Brunswick. *B.* 1931. *Educ.* Rothesay Collegiate School; Hartland High; Acadia Univ. (BA); Dalhousie Univ. (LLB). *Career:* with Law Firm Smith, Matthews and Grant 1956; Exec. Asst. Minister of Trade and Commerce Ottawa 1956–58; Sales Mgr. family firm Hatfield Industries Ltd., Hartland 1958–65; Leader of Opposition in the Legislature 1968; Leader of Progressive Conservative Party, N.B. 1969; Premier of New Brunswick since 1970. *Member:* Exec. N.B. Div. Canadian Red Cross Socy.; Prov. Council Boy Scouts, Canada; Governor, Beaverbrook Art Gallery; Past member Bd. Dirs., Maritime School, Social Work. *Awards:* LL.D. Univ of Moncton N.B.; LL.D Univ. of New Brunswick; LLD St. Thomas Univ.; Mount Allison Univ. 1975; Chief, Maliseet & Micmac tribes (Chief Rolling Thunder); Received the Canada-Israel Friendship Award. *Address:* P.O. Box 6000, Fredericton, New Brunswick E3B 5H1, Canada.

**HATTERSLEY, Roy Sydney George.** PC, MP. British politician. *B.* 1932. *Educ.* Sheffield City Grammar School; Univ. of Hull. *M.* 1956, Molly Loughran. *Career:* Under Secretary of State, Department of Employment and Productivity, 1967–69. Minister of Defence (Administration), 1969–70; Principal Opposition Spokesman on Defence Matters 1972; Principal Opposition Spokesman on Education 1972–74; Minister of State for Foreign and Commonwealth Affairs 1974–76; Sec. of State for Prices and Consumer Protection since 1976. Visiting Fellow, Institute of Politics, Univ. of Harvard 1971. Member, Privy Council (1975). Member, Labour Party. *Club:* Reform. *Address:* House of Commons, London, S.W.1.

**HAUGE, Armand.** Norwegian. *B.* 1914. *M.* 1939, Marwell Larsen. *S.* Sigurd-Armand. *Dau.* Eva. *Career:* Chmn. and Chief Exec. Collett-Marwell Hauge A.S. *Address:* Troster-Udveien 8, Slemdal, Oslo 3, Norway.

**HAUGE, Egil Hiis.** Director. *B.* 1908. *Educ.* Bergens Katedralskole (Matric. Degree 1927) and Univ. of Oslo (Grad. in Law 1931). *M.* 1937, Liv Hannaas. *S.* Eivind Hiis (Prof., Dr. techn. N.T.H.). *Daus.* Ingerid Hiis Helstrup and Astrid Hiis Reinton. *Career:* Deputy Judge 1932–33; Secretary, City Dept. 1934–36; Assessment Secretary 1936–44; Legal Adviser 1944–45. At Norwegian Finance Ministry in London 1945; Vice-President. Bergens Skillingsbank. Bergen 1945–49, President 1949–53. Managing Director, Bergens Privatbank, Oslo 1953–59, General Managing Director, Bergens Privatbank, Bergen 1959–64. Legal and Economic Adviser, Bergen 1964—(Malaysia 1966); Chmn. Industrial Research Development in Western Norway 1969—; Bergens Byfornyingsinstitutt A/S 1966—, Hotel Norge 1968—; Board mem., Holms Hotel (1970), Jinse Hotel (1971); Member, Cttee, Representative (Council), A/S Investa since 1971, Oil Cttee. of Bergen (1977). Member of Council, Norway-America Assn. 1963—; Norwegian Advocates Assn.; Bergen Trade Assn.; Bergen Industry Assn. *Publications:* Creditinstit (1970); Taxes (1971); Bank Taxes (1974); The Norwegian Bank and Credit System (1976); Moderne Kredittvesen (1977); plus legal and economic articles. *Address:* Natlandsveien 23, pc 5030 Landaas, Norway.

**HAUGHTON, Daniel J.** Chairman, Lockheed Aircraft Corp. 1967–76. *B.* 1911. *Educ.* Univ. of Alabama (BS). *M.* 1935, Martha Jean Oliver. *Career:* With Lockheed since 1939, Exec. Vice Pres.. 1956, Dir., 1958, Pres., 1961, Chmn. 1967–76. Dir. Southern Calif. Edison Co.; United Calif. Bank; Los Angeles World Affairs Council. *Member:* Aviation Hall of Fame, numerous Professional and Technical Assns.; Dir. Chmn. Nat. Multiple Sclerosis Society. *Awards:* National Defense Transportation Assn.; Sales & Marketing Executives; Int. Marketing Executive; Nat. Aviation Club Achievement Tony Jannus; Headliner of Year Los Angeles Press Club; Fellow, Amer. Inst. of Austronautics and Aeronautics. *Address:* 12956 Blairwood Drive, Studio City, Calif. 91604, U.S.A.

**HAUPT, Arthur Wing.** American botanist and biologist. Doctor of Philosophy. President, Haupt Botanical Laboratory, Inc. ,North Av .Chicago. *B.* 9 Aug. 1894. *Educ.* Univ. of Chicago (BSc, PhD). *M.* 1921, Hazel MacMillen. *S.* 1. *Daus.* 2. *Career:* Professor of Biology, Carthage College, Ill. 1919–20; Professor of Biology, St. Lawrence University, Canton N.Y.

1920–23; Professor of Botany, University of California 1924–60; Professor Emeritus 1961—. *Publications:* Fundamentals of Biology; An Introduction to Botany; Plant Morphology; also numerous articles based on original investigations in plant morphology and cytology. *Address:* 164 Lake Shore Drive, Barrington, Ill. 60010, U.S.A.

**HAUSNER, Henry H.** Consulting metallurgist. *B.* 1901. *Educ.* Technical University, Vienna (EE 1925; DEng. 1938). *M.* (1) 1927, Elizabeth Wallner (*Dec.*). *M.* (2) 1962, Hedda M. John (*Dec.*). *M.* (3) 1970, Ada Berger. *Career:* Laboratory Director, Elin A.G. 1938–40; Research Engineer, American Electro Metal Corporation 1940–41; Chief Research Engineer, General Ceramics Corporation 1942–46; Adjunct Professor, New York University 1946–48; Manager of Engineering. Sylania Electric 1948–56; Professor Polytechnic Inst. Brooklyn 1951; Chairman, Power Metallurgy Cttee., A.I.M.E. 1953–63; Director, American Nuclear Science Corp. 1957—; Instructor, Univ. of California, N.Y. Univ.; Research Scientist, Rensselaer Polytechnic Inst. 1959–64. *Publications:* Powder Metallurgy (1947); Materials for Nuclear Power Reactors (1955); Powder Metallurgy in Nuclear Reactor Construction (1961); Editor, Modern Materials; Nuclear Fuel Elements (1957); New Types of Metal Powders (1964); Fundamental Phenomena in the Material Sciences (1964); International Journal of Powder Metallurgy (ed.) (1965); Beryllium—Its Metallurgy: Modern Development in Powder Metallurgy, Vol. 1–11 (1966–77); Handbook of Powder Metallurgy (1973); 140 articles in technical and scientific journals *Member:* American Institute of Mining and Metallurgical Engineers; American Association for Advancement of Science; British Japanese and German Institutes of Metals; *Hon. Member:* International Inst. for the Science of Sintering; Powder Met. Assoc. of India. *Club:* Metal Science. *Address:* 67 Red Brook Road, Kings Point, N.Y. 11024, U.S.A.

**HAVARD, John Francis.** American. *B.* 1909. *Educ.* Montana School of Mines and Univ. of Wisconsin (PhB, PhM, BS, EM). *M.* 1943, Faith Hartley. *S.* 3. *Dau.* 1. *Career:* Successively mining engineer, mine supt. (1935–41), plant manager (1941–47), and Chief Engineer Mines (1947–52), U.S. Gypsum Co., Western U.S. and Chicago. Asst. Resident Mngr., Potash Co. of Amer., New Mexico. Vice-Pres. (Mfg.) Pabco Products Inc. 1953–57, and Fibreboard Corp. 1957–62; Vice-President, Minerals Division, Kaiser Engineers, Oakland, California 1963–74, Sen. Vice-Pres. since 1974. *Publications:* numerous articles in professional and trade journals. Registered Professional Engineer, Montana, Nevada, Wisconsin and California; Registered Geologist California. *Member:* Amer. Inst. of Mining, Metallurgical and Petroleum Engineers; Pres. Soc. Mining Engineers of A.I.M.E.;; Canadian Inst. of Mining and Metallurgy; Geological Society of America; Society of Economic Geologists. *Fellow:* American Association for the Advancement of Science. *Address:* Augustine Rd., Box 142A Nevada City, Calif. 95959, U.S.A.; and *office* 300 Lakeside Drive, Oakland, Calif, U.S.A.

**HAVERS, Sir Michael Robert Oldfield,** QC, MP. British. *B.* 1923. *Educ.* Westminster School; Corpus Christi Coll. Cambridge. *M.* 1949, Carol Elizabeth Lay. *S.* Philip, Nigel. *Career:* Barrister, Inner Temple 1948—; Queen's Counsel 1964—; Chancellor of Diocese, St. Edmundsbury and Ipswich 1965–73; of Ely 1969–73; Recorder of Dover 1962–68, of Norwich 1968–71; Deputy-Chmn. West Suffolk Q.S. 1961–65; Chmn. West Suffolk Q.S. 1965–71; Member Parliament (Cons.) Wimbledon 1970–74, for Merton, Wimbledon since 1974; Solicitor General 1972–74; Shadow Attorney-General since 1974; Member, Select Cttee. on Privileges 1977. Knighted 1972; Privy Councillor, Jubilee Honours List 1977. *Club:* Garrick. *Address:* 6B Woodhayes Rd., Wimbledon, London SW19; White Shutters, Ousden, Newmarket, Suffolk; and *office* Chambers, 6 King's Bench Walk, London, E.C.4.

**HAVILAND, Denis William Garstin Latimer,** CB. *B.* 1910. *Educ.* Rugby School; St. John's College, Cambridge, (MA Exam. of AM Inst. T). IDC, FBIM, FRSA. *Career:* With L.M.S. Railway, 1934–39; Army (Col. R.E.), 1940–46; Principal, Control Office for Germany & Austria, 1946; Asst. Secretary, 1947; transferred to Foreign Office (GS) 1947; seconded to I.d.c., 1950; transferred to Ministry of Supply, Asst. Sec., 1951–53; Under Sec., 1953–59; Deputy Sec.; 1959; Transferred to Ministry of Aviation, 1959–64; Chmn., Preparatory Commission, European Launcher Development Org. 1962–64; Jt. Man. Dir. & Dep. Chmn. Staveley Industries, 1964. Chairman & Managing Director, Staveley Industries Ltd., 1965–69. Director, Short Bros. & Harland, Belfast; Wheelabator Corporation Mishawaka, U.S.A. 1967–72; Organised Office Designs. Member of Court, Cranfield Institute of Technology, Consultant. *Club:* Bath. *Address:* 113 Hampstead Way, London, N.W.11; and *office* Portland House, Stag Place, London, S.W.1.

**HAWES, Roderick Travers,** TD. British. Chairman, Price Forbes (Holdings) Ltd. and subsidiary companies 1964–65. *B.* 1905. *Educ.* Eton Coll. and Trinity Coll. Oxford (BA Hons.). *M.* 1932, Julie Evan Spicer. Served in Royal Artillery 1939–45 (Lt.-Col.) and T.A. 1952–53 (Col.). *Awards:* Order of Orange-Nassau; Croix de Guerre (France); Member of Court of Haberdashers Coy. (Master 1968–69); Chmn., Royal Humane Society. *Clubs:* Oriental; Royal St. George's; Royal Cinque Ports; Chislehurst Golf. *Address:* 37/8 St. James's Place, London, S.W.1; and Pedlinge, Herschell Road East, Walmer, Kent.

**HAWKE, Robert James Lee.** Australian Trade Union Executive. *B.* 1929. *Educ.* Perth Modern Sch.; Univ. of Western Australia—LLB, BA (Econ.); Oxford Univ. (Rhodes Scholar)—BLitt. *M.* 1956, Hazel Masterson. *S.* 1. *Daus.* 2. *Career:* Research Scholar, Aust. National Univ. 1956–58; Research Officer & Advocate, Aust. Council of Trade Unions 1958–69; Pres., Aust. Council of Trade Unions since 1969; Senior Vice-Pres., Aust. Labor Party 1971, Pres. since 1973; member: Bd. of Reserve Bank of Australia since 1973; Aust. Population & Immigration Council since 1976; Aust. Council for Union Training since 1976; Aust. Manufacturing Council since 1977; Governing Body of International Labor Org. *Address:* Australian Council of Trade Unions, 254 La Trobe Street, Melbourne, Victoria 3000, Australia.

**HAWKER, Sir (Frank) Cyril.** British. *B.* 1900. *Educ.* City of London School. *M.* Marjorie Ann Pearce. *Daus.* Mrs. J. P. Smith, Mrs. B. Rissik, Mrs R. McKenzie. *Career:* Entered Bank of England 1920; Deputy Chief Cashier 1944; Chief Accountant 1948; Adviser to Governors 1953; Executive Director 1958. Chairman: The Standard Bank Ltd. 1962–74; Standard Chartered Banking Group Ltd. 1970–74; Chmn. Chartered Bank Ltd. 1973–74; Director: Head Wrightson & Co. Ltd. 1962–69; Deputy-Chmn. Midland and International Banks Ltd. 1964–74; Chmn. Union Zaroise De Banques 1971–74; Dep. Chmn. Agric. Mortgage Corp. 1962–73; Vice-Pres. National Playing Fields Assn.; President, M.C.C. 1970–71; Hon. Vice-Pres. Football Assn.; Pres. Amateur Football Alliance 1972–73. *Clubs:* Athenaeum M.C.C. *Address:* Pounsley Lodge, Blackboys, Nr. Uckfield, Sussex.

**HAWKER, Sir Richard George.** Australian. *B.* 1907. *Educ.* Geelong Grammar School (Victoria) and Trinity Hall, Cambridge (MA Cantab.). *M.* 1940, Frances C. Rymill. *S.* 2. *Daus.* 2. *Career:* Manager, Bungaree Merino Stud 1932—. Director: Adelaide Steamship Co., Ltd. since 1945 (Chmn. 1960–73); Coast Steamship Co. Ltd. 1963–74; and S.A. Tug Co. 1963–67; Director: Coal & Allied Industries since 1961; Associated Steamship Proprietary Ltd. 1963–71; and Waratah Tug & Salvage Co. 1963–69; Chairman of Advisory Council, Roseworthy Agricultural College 1964–73; President, Australian Assn. of Stud Merino Breeders 1968–70; Committee Member, South Australian Stud Merino Breeders Assn. *Clubs:* Bath, Oriental (London), Adelaide (South Australia), Australian (Sydney). *Address:* Bungaree, via Brinkworth, SA 5464, Australia.

**HAWKINS, Paul,** FRICS, TD, MP. British Chartered Surveyor and Member of Parliament. *B.* 1912. *Educ.* Cheltenham Coll. *M.* 1937, Joan Snow. *S.* 2. *Dau.* 1. *Career:* Royal Norfolk Regt. 1933–45 (Captain 1940; P. O. W. 1940–45); Partner in a firm of Chartered Surveyors started by his grandfather, since 1945; County Councillor for Downham Market, Norfolk 1949–70; Conservative MP for SW Norfolk since 1964; Member of Brit. Delegation to Council of Europe & Western European Union 1976. *Member:* Royal Inst. of Chartered Surveyors; Central Assoc. of Agricultural Valuers. *Decorations:* Territorial Decoration and Bar. *Club:* Carlton. *Address:* Stables, Downham Market, Norfolk; & House of Commons, London SW1A OAA.

**HAWLEY, Donald Frederick,** CMG, MBE, MA. British diplomat. *B.* 1921. *Educ.* Radley; New Coll. Oxford. *M.* 1964, Ruth Morwenna Graham Howes. *S.* 1. *Daus.* 3. *Career.* H.M. Forces 1941–44; Sudan Political Service 1944–47; Sudan Judiciary 1947–55; Foreign Office 1956–58; H.M. Political Agent Trucial States 1958–61; Head of Chancery, British Embassy Cairo 1962–64; Counsellor, Head of Chancery British High Commision Lagos 1965–67; Sabbatical Visiting Fellow, Durham Univ. 1967–68; Counsellor

(Commercial) British Embassy Baghdad 1968–71; H.M. Ambassador to Sultanate of Oman, Muscat 1971–75; Asst. Under Secy. of State, Foreign and C'wealth Office 1975–77; British High Commissioner in Malaysia 1977. *Awards:* Companion, Order St. Michael and St. George; Member, Order British Empire; Master of Art's Oxford. *Publications:* Courtesies in the Trucial States (1965); The Trucial States (1970); Oman & its Renaissance (1977); Courtesies in the Gulf Area (1977). *Club:* Athenaeum. *Address:* West Pulridge, Little Gaddesden, Herts; and *office* Foreign & Commonwealth Office, London SW1.

**HAWLEY, Edmund Blair.** American. Consultant to Federal and State Government and to industry. *B.* 1924. *Educ.* Yale University. (BA), Harvard Univ. (MBA) and Tufts Univ. Grad. School. *M.* 1949, Greta Aileen Crocker. *S.* 5. *Dau.* 1. *Career:* Formerly: Vice-Pres. and Dir. Clayton Securities Corp.; Dir.: Cambridge Hotels Inc., Jarrell Ash Co., Pickard & Burns Inc., Investment Research Corp., Flow Corp., Dunn Engineering Associates. Exec. Secy. Formula Fund of Boston 1950–54; Staff Lecturer, Boston Center for Adult Education 1950–53; National Panel of Consultants to Amer. Cncl. of Independent Savings & Loan Assns. 1960; Consultant to: Schirmer Atherton & Co. 1960–61, and Commissioner of Administration, C'wealth of Massachusetts 1966–67; Director Programme Planning and Research, Exec. Office for Administration and Finance, Commonwealth of Massachusetts 1967—. Deputy Commissioner for Central Services, 1967—. Governor's Adv. Council on Civil Defence 1966, and of Adv. Committee on State Planning 1967—; Member, Faculty Phillips Exeter Academy, 1970—and Faculty Thayer Academy 1971—; Chmn. Secondary School Panel, Youth Foundation Inc. since 1970. Vice-Pres. New England Lawn Tennis Assn., and Dir. N.E.T. Patrons 1954–58. Active office-holder in many civic, social and religious organizations. *Awards:* Citation for Outstanding Achievement (from Boston Junior Chamber of Commerce 1955). *Member:* Amer. Socy. of Public Admin.; Socy. Mayflower Descendants; Military Order of World Wars; Sons of the Revolution; Socy. of Colonial Wars; Founders & Patriots; St. Nicholas Socy.; Huguenot Socy. Served in World War II (Counter-Intelligence Service; S.W. Pacific; Presidential Citation). *Publications:* The Sword and the Spirit (study on philosophy of world affairs). *Clubs:* Harvard; Yale; State; Winchester Country; Coral Beach & Tennis (Bermuda), Pequosette Lodge; Longwood Cricket. *Address:* Hawcrest, Winchester, Mass.; and Holly Acres, Smith's Parish, Bermuda; *office* State Office Building, Room 909, 100 Cambridge Street, Boston, Mass. 02202, U.S.A.

**HAWORTH, Robert Downs.** British chemistry professor. *B.* 15 March 1898. *Educ.* Manchester University (BSc, MSc, PhD, DSc); Oxford University; FRIC, FRS. *M.* 1930, Dorothy Stocks. *Dau.* Elizabeth. *Career:* Lecturer in Chemistry, Armstrong College, Durham Univ. 1927–39; Firth Professor of Chemistry, Sheffield University 1939–55, and Head of Department of Chemistry 1955–63; Emeritus Prof. 1963; Hon. DSc Sheffield Univ., 1974; Tilden Lecturer 1942; Pedler Lecturer 1961; Davy Medallist of Royal Society 1956; Leverhulme-Royal Society Visiting Professor at Madras University 1963. *Address:* 67 Tom Lane, Sheffield S10 3PA, Yorks.

**HAWTHORNE, Professor Sir William Rede,** CBE, FRS. *B.* 1913. *Educ.* Trinity Coll., Cambridge; MA (Cantab.); Massachusetts Inst. of Technology (ScD). *M.* 1939, Barbara Runkle. *S.* 1. *Daus.* 2. *Career:* Development Engineer, Babcock & Wilcox Ltd. 1937–39; Scientific Officer, Royal British Aircraft Establishment 1940–44; British Air Commission, Washington 1944; Dep. Director Engine Research, Ministry of Supply 1945; Assoc. Prof. of Mechanical Engineering 1946–48; George Westinghouse Prof. of Mechanical Engineering, M.I.T. 1948–51; Jerome C. Hunsaker Prof. of Aeronautical Engineering, M.I.T. 1955–56; Visiting Institute Professor M.I.T. 1962–63; Fellow Trinity Coll. Cambridge 1951–68; Head, Eng. Dept., Camb. Univ. 1968–73, Professor of Applied Thermodynamics, Univ. of Cambridge (Hopkinson and I.C.I.) since 1951. Master of Churchill College since 1968; *Fellow:* Royal Socy.; Inst. of Mechanical Engrs.; Royal Aeronautical Socy.; Foreign Associate of U.S. Nat. Acad. of Engineering; Foreign Associate of U.S. Nat. Acad. of Sciences; Hon. FIAA; American Academy of Arts and Sciences. *Chairman:* Advisory Council on Energy. *Trustee:* Winston Churchill Foundation of U.S.A. *Member:* Electricity Supply Research Council. *Director:* Cummins Engine Co.; Dracone Developments Ltd.; *Awards:* Commander Order of British Empire (1959); Medal of Freedom, U.S.A. (1947); Knight Bachelor (1970); Hon. D.Eng., Sheffield Univ. 1976. *Publications:* (Ed) Aerodynamics of Compressors and Turbines Vol. X; (Co-Ed) Design and Performance of Gas Turbine Power Plants Vol XI; High Speed Aerodynamics and Jet Propulsion (Princeton); Papers on fluid mechanics, aero engines, flames and flexible barges in scientific and technical journals. *Club:* Athenaeum (London). *Address:* The Master's Lodge, Churchill Coll., Cambridge (England); and 19 Chauncy Street, Cambridge, Mass. 02138, U.S.A.

**HAY, Alexander Frederic.** Swiss banker. *B.* 1919. *Educ.* University of Geneva (L.-en-D.). *M.* 1945, Helene Morin Pons. *S.* 2. *Daus.* 2. *Career:* Practised Law 1942–45; served Federal Political Dept., Berne 1945–48; Swiss Legation, Paris 1948–53; Director, Vice-President, Swiss National Bank since April 1966. *Address:* Banque Nationale Suisse, Berne, Switzerland.

**HAY, Andrew Mackenzie,** CBE. American. *B.* 1928. *Educ.* St. John's Coll. Cambridge (MA). *Career:* Pres. Calvert, Vavasseur & Co. Inc.; Red V Coconut Co. Inc. Dir. British-Amer. Chamber Commerce (Pres. 1966–68); Pres. Philippine-Amer. Chamber of Commerce; Amer. Importers Association; Chmn. Board, Barretto Peat, Inc., N.Y.C.; Chef du Protocole d'Amerique Confrerie des Chevaliers du Tastevin. *Publication:* A Century of Coconuts. *Clubs:* Down Town Assn. N.Y.; Bath, London. *Address:* 162 East 64th Street, New York, N.Y. 10021, U.S.A.

**HAY, David Osborne,** CBE, DSO, BA. *B.* 1916. *Educ* Universities of Oxford and Melbourne (BA). *M.* 1944' Alison Adams. *S.* Andrew and David. *Career:* Joined Australian diplomatic service 1940; Served in Australian Infantry in World War II 1940–45; Imperial Defence College 1954; Ambassador to Thailand, and SEATO Council Representative 1955–57; Assistant Secretary, Department of External Affairs, Canberra 1957–61; High Commissioner to Canada 1961–64; Ambassador to U.N. 1963–65; First Assistant Secretary, Department of External Affairs, Canberra 1965–66; Administrator, Territory of Papua and New Guinea 1967–70. Secretary, Department of External Territories, Canberra, 1970–73; Defence Force Ombudsman 1973–76; Secretary Dept. of Aboriginal Affairs since 1976. *Clubs:* Melbourne; Australian; Naval & Military; Commonwealth. *Address:* 10 Hotham Crescent, Deakin, A.C.T., Australia.

**HAY, Hamish Grenfell.** New Zealand. *B.* 1927. *Educ.* St. Andrew's College and Canterbury Univ. (BCom); FCA; awarded New Zealand Socy. of Accountants Travelling Scholarship 1949. *M.* 1955, Judith Leicester Gill. *Daus.* Juliet Christina, Gillian Davina, Celia Margaret and Diana Felicity. *S.* James Malcolm Gill. *Career:* Secy. Hay's Ltd. 1955–62; Deputy Managing Dir., Haywrights Ltd. Department Store Group 1962–74; Dir. Challenge Finance Ltd.; Chmn., N.Z. Socy. of Accountants (Canterbury Branch) 1948; Councillor, Christchurch City Council 1959–74 and Mayor since 1974. Chmn. Town Hall Board since 1962; Trustee, Canterbury Savings Bank 1962—(Pres. 1973–75); Chmn. Christchurch Arts Festival 1965–74; Dir. Commercial Services Ltd.; Pres. Christchurch Civic Music Council; Pres. Canterbury Aged Peoples' Welfare Council; Univ. of Canterbury Council 1974—; Canterbury Museum Trust Board 1974—; Queen Elizabeth II Arts Council 1976—; Canterbury Orchestra Trust Bd. 1976—. *Address:* 70 Heaton Street, Christchurch, N.Z.; and *office* Mayor's Office, P.O. Box 237, Christchurch, New Zealand.

**HAY, John Albert,** British solicitor and company director. *B.* 1919. *Educ.* Brighton, Hove and Sussex Grammar School. *M.* (1) 1947, Beryl Joan Found (*dec'd*). *S.* 1. *Dau.* 1. (2) Janet Spruce. *Career:* Served in World War II (Sub-Lieut. and Lieut. R.N.V.R.; invalided 1944). Member, British Delegation to Congress of Europe 1948; MP (Con.) Henley Div. of Oxfordshire 1950–74; P.P.S. to President of Board of Trade 1951–55; member, U.K. Delegations to Council of Europe and Western European Union; Chmn. of Conservative Party Housing and Local Government Cttee. 1956–59. Parliamentary Secretary, Ministry of Transport 1959–63; Civil Lord of the Admiralty 1963–64; Parliamentary Under Secy. of State for Defence Royal Navy 1964; Chmn. Brit. Section Council of European Municipalities 1971–77, Pres. 1977; former Vice-Pres. Urban District Councils Association. *Address:* 62/66 Whitfield Street, London, W.1.

**HAYAKAWA, Dr. Samuel (Sam) Ichiye.** U.S. Senator & Academic. *B.* 1906. *Educ.* Calgary & Winnipeg public schools; Univ. of Manitoba—BA (English); McGill Univ.—MA (English); Univ. of Wisconsin—PhD (English & Amer.

Lit.). *M.* 1937, Margedant Peters. *S.* 2. *Dau.* 1. *Career:* Instructor in English, Univ. of Wisconsin (extension) 1936–39; Instructor to Assoc. Prof. of English, Illinois Inst. of Technology 1939–47; Lecturer, Univ. of Chicago 1950–55; Prof. of English, San Francisco State College 1955–68; Acting Pres. 1968; Pres. 1968–73; Pres. Emeritus 1973, San Francisco State Univ. (formerly College); Republican Senator from California since 1977. *Member:* Senate Cttees. on Agriculture, Nutrition & Forestry, The Budget, & Human Resources; U.S. Senate Republican Policy Cttee.; National Republican Senatorial Cttee. *Fellow:* American Psychological Assn.; American Assn. for the Advancement of Science; American Sociological Assn.; Royal Society of Arts. *Awards:* Hon. degrees: DFA, California Coll. of Arts & Crafts; DLitt, Grinnell Coll.; LHD, Pepperdine Univ.; LLD, The Citadel. *Publications:* Oliver Wendell Holmes: Selected Poetry & Prose, with Critical Introduction (1939); Language in Action (1941); Language in Thought & Action (1949, 4th edn. 1978); Language, Meaning & Maturity (1954); Our Language & Our World (1959); The Use & Misuse of Language (1962); Symbol, Status & Personality (1963); Editor, Funk & Wagnall's Modern Guide to Synonyms (1968); Editor, *ETC, A Review of General Semantics* (1943–70); columnist, *Chicago Defender* (1942–47); columnist, Register & Tribune Syndicate (1970–76). *Address:* 6217 Dirksen Senate Office Building, Washington, D.C. 20510, U.S.A.

**HAYCRAFT, Howard.** American publisher and author. *B*, 1905. *Educ.* University of Minnesota (AB 1928). *M.* 1942. Mary Randolf Costain. *Career:* On staff of University of Minnesota Press 1928; joined H. W. Wilson Co. 1929; successively Dir. 1934—, and Pres. 1953–67. Specialist War Department 1942; served as Capt. to Major, U.S. Army Service Forces 1942–46; accorded Outstanding Achievement Award. Univ. of Minnesota 1954; member President's Committee on Employment of the Handicapped, 1963—; Pres., Mystery Writers of America, 1963–64. Chairman, The H. W. Wilson Co. (publishers of indices and reference works), New York City 1967—. *Publications:* author, editor, or joint editor; Authors Today and Yesterday (1933); Junior Book of Authors (1934); Boys' Sherlock Holmes (1936); British Authors of the Nineteenth Century (1936); Boys' Book of Great Detective Stories (1938); American Authors—1600–1900 (1938); Boys' Second Book of Great Detective Stories (1940); Murder for Pleasure—The Life and Times of the Detective Story (1941); Crime Club Encore (1942); Twentieth Century Authors (1942); Art of the Mystery Story (1946); Fourteen Great Detective Stories (1949); British Authors Before 1800 (1952); Treasury of Great Mysteries (1957); Ten Great Mysteries (1959); Five Spy Novels (1962); Three Times Three Mystery Omnibus (1964); Books for the Blind 1968; contributions to literary publications. *Member:* Players (N.Y.); Kappa Sigma, Episcopalian. *Address: office* 950 University Avenue, New York 10452, N.Y., U.S.A.

**HAYDN, Hiram.** American. *B.* 1907. *Educ.* Amherst College (AB 1928); Western Reserve University (AM 1938); Columbia University (PhD 1942); LittD Western Reserve University 1963. *M.* (1) 1935, Rachel Hutchinson Norris, and (2) 1945, Mary Wescott Tuttle. *S.* Michael Wescott and Jonathan Olmstead. *Daus.* Mary Rachel and Miranda Merriman. *Career:* Instructor, Hawken School, Cleveland 1928–41; Lecturer, Cleveland College, Western Reserve Univ. 1939–41; Asst. Prof. (1942–43) and Associate Professor (1943–44), Woman's College, Univ. of N. Carolina; Exec. Secy., United Chapters of Phi Beta Kappa 1944–45; Editor, The American Scholar 1944—; Instructor, New School for Social Research 1947–60; Associate Editor, Crown Publishers, Inc. 1945 (Editor-in-Chief 1948–50); New York Editor, The Bobbs-Merrill Co. Inc. 1950–54; Senior Editor, Random House, Inc. 1955 (Editor-in-Chief 1956–59); Alternating Vice-President and President, Atheneum Publishers 1959–64; co-publisher, Harcourt, Brace Jovanovich Inc. 1964–73, Consulting Editor 1973—. Visiting Prof. of Communications, Annenberg School of Communications 1965–66, Prof. of Communications 1966–73; Dir., Amer. Book Publishers' Council 1958–59. *Publications:* The Counter Renaisance; By Nature Free; Manhattan Furlough; The Time is Noon; The Hands of Esau; Report from the Red Windmill; editor: The Twentieth Century Library series; The Portable Elizabethan Reader; co-editor: The Makers of the American Tradition series; The Papers of Christian Gauss; Explorations in Living; A World of Great Stories. A Renaissance Treasury; The American Scholar Reader. *Address:* R.F.D. Vineyard Haven, Mass. 02568, U.S.A.

**HAYDON, Walter Robert (Robin),** CMG. British Diplomat. *B.* 1920. *Educ.* Dover Grammar School. *M.* 1943, Joan Elizabeth Tewson. *S.* 1. *Daus.* 2 (1 Dec'd). *Career:* H.M. Forces 1939–46; 3rd Secy. Berne, 1946–47; Foreign Office 3rd Secy. 1947–48; Vice-consul Turin 1948–52; Vice-Consul and 3rd Secy. Sofia 1952–53; 2nd Secy. Bangkok 1953–56; 1st Secy. Foreign Office 1956–58; 1st Secy. and Head of Chancery, Khartoum 1958–61; 1st Secy. U.K. Mission to U.N. New York 1961–65; Washington Counsellor 1965–67; Head of News Dept. and Counsellor, Foreign Office 1967–71; High Commissioner Blantyre, Malawi 1971–73; Chief Press Secy. (10 Downing St.) 1973–74; High Commissioner (Valletta) Malta 1974–76; Ambassador to Rep. of Ireland since 1976. *Award:* Companion, Order of St. Michael & St. George (1970). *Clubs:* Travellers; Royal Commonwealth Society. *Address:* c/o Foreign & Commonwealth Office, London SW1.

**HAYES, Alfred.** *B.* 1910. *Educ.* Grad. Milton (Mass.) Acad.; Harvard; Yale (BA 1930); Harvard Graduate School of Business Administration; New College, Oxford, England (Rhodes Scholar; BLitt 1933); Hon. Fellow of New College since 1975. *M.* 1937, Vilma F. Chalmers. *S.* Thomas. *Dau.* Anita Robertson (Gratwick). *Career:* Investment Analyst, City Bank Farmers Trust Co., N.Y.C. Bond Dept., National City Bank of N.Y. 1940–42; Asst. Secy., investment division, N.Y. Trust Co. 1942–47; Asst. Vice-Pres., foreign division 1947–49 (Vice-Pres. 1949–56); Pres. Federal Reserve Bank of New York 1956–75; Vice-Chairman, Federal Open Market Committee 1956–75; Chmn., Morgan Stanley International Inc. 1975—; Advisory Dir., Morgan Stanley & Co. Inc. 1975—. *Clubs:* Century Association, River Club (N.Y.C.). *Address:* 401 Brushy Ridge Rd., New Canaan, Conn. 06840, U.S.A.

**HAYES, Nathaniel Perkinson.** American. *B.* 1901. *Educ.* University of North Carolina (BA 1921); BSc Civil Eng. 1922. *M.* 1927, Louise Hull. *S.* 1. *Career:* Engineer, McClintic-Marshall Co., Pittsburgh 1922–26; Carolina Steel Corporation, Greensboro 1926 (Sales Mgr. 1930; Director 1941; Vice-Pres. 1949–51 Pres. 1951—); Pres., Salem Steel Co., Winston-Salem, N.C. 1951—, Greenville (S.C.) Steel & Foundry Co. 1959—, Greensboro Industries, Inc. 1953—. Chairman, Carolina Steel Corporation, Carolina Steel Salem Steel Co., Greenville Steel Co.; Hickory Steel Co.; Burlington Engineering Sales Co.; Arnold Stone Co.; Director: North Carolina National Bank 1966—, Home Federal Savings & Loan Co. 1965—, and Greensboro TB Assoc. 1949—; The Pomona Corp. Greensboro N.C.; Vice Pres. Southern Div. National Assoc., Manufacturers 1972–76. Member, American Institute of Steel Construction, Inc. (Dir. 1946, Vice-Pres. 1952; 1st Vice-Pres. 1954; Pres. 1956–58), Amer. Socy. of Civ. Engrs.; Pres., Greensboro Chamber of Comm. 1951, Business Foundation of North Carolina Inc. 1958; Dir. N.C. Engineering Foundation 1958. Trustee, Moses H. Cone Memorial Hospital, Greensboro, N.C.; Bennett Coll., Greensboro, N.C. 1975—; Oak Ridge Acad., Oak Ridge, N.C. 1965—. *Address:* Carolina Steel Corporation, P.O. Box 20888, Greensboro, N.C., U.S.A.

**HAYHOE, Barney (Bernard) John,** CEng, MIMechE. British. politician. *B.* 1925. *Educ.* State Elementary & Technical Schools, Borough Polytechnic. *M.* 1962 Anne Gascoigne Thornton. *S.* Crispin and Dominic. *Dau.* Sarah. *Career:* Engineering Tool Room Apprentice 1941–44; Armament Design Establishment, Ministry of Supply 1944–54; Inspectorate of Armaments 1954–63; Dir. Ariel Foundation 1963–65; Conservative Research Department 1965–70; Member of Parliament for Heston & Isleworth 1970–74, for Brentford & Isleworth since 1974; Parly. Private Secy. to Lord President and Leader of the House of Commons 1972–74; Opposition Front Bench Spokesman on Employment since 1974; Governor of Birkbeck Coll., 1976—. *Club:* Carlton. *Address:* 20 Wool Road, London, S.W.20.

**HAYMAN, Helene Valerie,** MP. British Politician. *B.* 1949. *Educ.* Wolverhampton High Sch.; Newnham Coll., Cambridge—MA (Law). *M.* 1974, Martin Heathcote Hayman. *S.* 1. *Career:* Shelter, National Campaign for the Homeless 1969–71; London Borough of Camden, Social Services 1971–73; Dep. Dir., National Council for One Parent Families, March–Oct. 1974; MP (Lab.) for Welwyn & Hatfield since 1974. *Address:* House of Commons, London SW1A 0AA.

**HAYMAN, Sir Peter Telford,** KCMG, CVO, MBE. *B.* 1914. *Educ.* Stowe (Scholar) and Worcester College, Oxford (Exhibitioner); BA (Oxon) in history. *M.* 1942, Rosemary Blomefield. *S.* Christopher Wilmot Arden. *Dau.* Virginia Rosemary. *Career:* Asst. Principal, Home Office 1937; Asst. Principal in War Room, Ministry of Home Security 1939; Asst. Private Secy. to the Home Secretary (Mr. Herbert

Morrison). Served in World War II (Major, Rifle Brigade) 1942–45; Principal, Home Office 1946–49; Asst. Secy., Ministry of Defence 1949–52; Counsellor, U.K. Delegation to NATO 1952–54, and in Belgrade 1955–58; Adviser to Governor of Malta 1958–59; Counsellor in Baghdad 1959–61; Director General, British Information Services in New York 1961–64; British Minister and Deputy Commandant, Berlin 1964–66; Assistant Under Secy. of State, Foreign and Commonwealth Office, 1966–68. Deputy Under Secretary of State, Foreign Office and Commonwealth 1968–70; High Commissioner in Canada 1970–74; Chmn., Estates House Investment Trust 1975—; Dir., Delta Overseas 1974—; Consultant, Seatrade Publications 1974—; Governor, International Student Trust 1974—; Exec. Cttee., Grenfell Assn. 1974—. *Clubs:* Travellers'; Army and Navy; M.C.C. *Address:* Uxmore House, Checkendon, Oxon.

**HAYNES, Sir George Ernest,** CBE. British social administrator; knighted 1962. *B.* 24 Jan. 1902. *Educ.* Liverpool Univ. (BSc). *M.* 1930, Kathleen Norris Greenhalgh. *Daus.* Pamela, Judith. *Career:* Warden of University Settlement, Liverpool 1928–33; joined staff of Natl. Cncl. of Social Service 1933; Director, 1940–67; Chmn., Temporary International Council for Educational Reconstruction of U.N.E.S.C.O. 1947–50; Chmn. Prep. Cttee. World Assembly of Youth 1948–49; member of various government committees including Lord Chancellor's Committee on Legal Aid 1950–75; President, International Conference of Social Work 1948–56; Hon. Pres. 1956–70; Chmn. Social Services Cttee., N.A.M.H. 1955–58; René Sand International Award 1958; Vice-Chairman, British National Conference on Social Work 1948–68; President, British Association of Residential Settlements 1960–69; Chmn., Standing Conference of British Agencies for Aid to Refugees 1953–60; National Bureau for Co-operation in Child Care 1963–68; Invalid Children's Aid Assn. 1966–69; Rural Industries Bureau Advisory Council 1964–68; Crown Trustee City Parochial Foundation 1966–75; President, National Birthday Trust. Chairman, Rural Industries Loan Fund, 1949–68; U.K. delegate to U.N .Social Cttee. 1962–67. Chmn., Social Science Cttee. of Natl. Fund for Research into Crippling Diseases 1967–71; Chmn. Gen. Cttee. of Clinic of Psychotherapy 1971–73; Member Council of British Red Cross Society 1960–76; Pres., British Assn. for Counselling; Pres., Nat. Assn. of Citizen's Advice Bureau. *Address:* 103 Richmond Hill Court, Richmond, Surrey.

**HAYNES, Ulric St. Clair, Jr.** American Diplomat. *B.* 1931. *Educ.* Amherst Coll.—BA; Yale Law Sch.—LLB. *M.* 1969, Yolande Toussaint Haynes. *S.* 1. *Dau.* 1. *Career:* Exec. Asst., N.Y. State Dept. of Commerce 1956–59; Admin. Officer, UN European Office 1959–60; Asst. Rep., The Ford Foundation (Nigeria) 1960–62; Asst. Rep., The Ford Foundation (Tunisia) 1962–63; Foreign Service Officer, U.S. Dept. of State 1963–64; Staff, National Security Council 1964–66; Pres., Management Formation Inc. 1966–70; Senior Vice-Pres., Spencer Stuart & Assoc. 1970–71; Vice-Pres. Mgmt. Development, Cummins Engine Co. 1971–73; Vice-Pres. Mid East & Africa, Cummins Engine Co. 1973–77; American Ambassador to Algeria since 1977. *Member:* Council on Foreign Relations; Overseas Development Council. *Publications:* Equal Job Opportunity—The Credibility Gap (*Harvard Business Review,* May–June 1968); Preparation for the Overseas Assignment (Indiana Univ. *Business Horizons,* June 1977). *Clubs:* The Yale Club of NYC; The National Democratic Club. *Address:* American Embassy, B.P. 549, Alger Gare, Algiers, Algeria.

**HAYS, Howard H., Jr.** American. Editor and Co-publisher. *B.* 1917. *Educ.* Stanford Univ. (BA 1939) and Harvard University (LLB 1942). *M.* 1947, Helen Cunningham. *S.* William Ross and Thomas T. *Career:* Admitted to California Bar 1939; Special Agent, F.B.I. 1942–45; Reporter, San Bernardino (Calif.) Sun 1945–46; Asst. Editor, Riverside Press-Enterprise 1946—49; Editor and Co-publisher Riverside Press-Enterprise Calif. since 1949. Director, Palm Desert Publishing Co. *Awards:* Recipient of Distinguished Award by California Junior Chamber of Commerce 1951 (newspaper awarded Pulitzer prize for public service, 1968); Publisher of the Year, California Press Assn. 1968. *Member:* California Bar Association; Pres. American Society of Newspaper Editors 1974; Kappa Tau Alpha; Dir. Amer. Press Institute, Vice-Chmn. 1976—; Advisory Board on the Pulitzer Prizes 1976–80; Exec. Board, International Press Inst. 1977—; Stanford Alumini Association. *Address: office* 3512, 14th Street, Riverside, Calif., U.S.A.

**HAYWARD, Sir Edward Waterfield, KStJ.** Australian merchant and grazier. *B.* 1903. *Educ.* Collegiate Sch. of St. Peter, Adelaide. *M.* 1972, Jean Katherine Bridges. *Career:* Lieut.-Col. 2nd A.I.F.; Middle East., New Guinea and Borneo. Chmn. Dir., John Martin & Co. Ltd. Coca-Cola Bottlers (Adelaide) Ltd. Director: Finance Corporation of Australia, Bennett & Fisher Ltd.; Bank of Adelaide; Pres. of the Council of St. John in South Australia. Owner of Silverton Park Hereford Stud, Delamere, and Hill Billy' Poll Hereford Stud. S.A. (M.I.D. 1944; New Guinea; 1945 Borneo; American Bronze Star Medal 1945). *Clubs:* The Adelaide, The Naval, Military & Air Force, The Royal Adelaide Golf, Adelaide Polo; The Melbourne; The Australian, The Royal Sydney Golf (Sydney). *Address:* Carrick Hill, Springfield, S.A.; and *office* 100 Rundle Street, Adelaide, S.A., Australia.

**HAYWARD, Thomas Z.** American marketing consultant and Lecturer. *B.* 1901. *Educ.* Northwestern Univ. Coll. of Commerce; Diploma; Service Award 1950; Merit Award 1959. *M.* 1938, Wilhelmenia White. *S.* Thomas Z., Jr. and Peter White. *Dau.* Wilhelmenia. *Career:* Formerly Senior Vice-President, Marketing, Joseph T. Ryerson & Son Inc.; Chmn. of Bd., Protectoseal Co. Republican. *Member:* Steel Service Center Institute; National Aluminium Distributors Assn.; Farm Equipment Inst.; Newcomen Society in N. America; Animal Crackers of America; Rancheros Visitadores; Sons of American Revolution. Mason. *Clubs:* Economic, Barrington Hills Country. *Address:* Out of Bounds Hill, Route 2, Box 9, Barrington, Ill. 60010, U.S.A.

**HAZARD, John Newbold.** Professor of Public Law, Columbia University, New York 1946—, Emeritus 1977. *B.* 1909. *Educ.* Yale Univ. (AB 1930), Harvard Univ. (LLB 1934); Moscow Juridical Institute (Certificate 1937); Univ. of Chicago (JSD 1939); LLD Univ. of Freiburg 1969; Lehigh Univ. 1970; Univ. of Leyden 1975; Univ. of Paris I 1977. *M.* 1941. Susan Lawrence. *S.* John Gibson and William Lawrence. *Daus.* Nancy and Barbara Peace. Awarded President's Certificate of Merit 1947. *Career:* Managing Editor, American Slavic & East European Review 1951–60; Dep. Dir., U.S.S.R. Branch, Foreign Econ. Admin. and predecessor agencies, U.S. Govt. 1941–45; Adviser on State Trading, Dept. of State 1945–46, and on Soviet Law to U.S. Prosecutor (Nuremberg Indictment) 1945; Fellow, Institute of Current World Affairs (delegated to study Soviet Law), N.Y. 1934–39; member N.Y. Bar 1939–41; Member Bd. of Editors American Journal of Comparative Law 1950—; and International Law 1957–72; Hon. Ed. since 1973; Fulbright Prof. of Law, Univ. of Cambridge and London School of Economics 1952–53; Visiting Prof., Univ. of Tokyo, summer 1957; member, Int. Faculty of Comparative Law, Luxembourg 1958–60; member, International Faculty for Teaching Comparative Law. Strasburg 1961—; Visiting Prof., Graduate Int. of Internat. Studies, Geneva 1959–60; Visiting Prof. Teheran Law Faculty 1966; Senior Specialist, East-West Center, Univ. of Hawaii, 1967; Visiting Prof., Univ. of Sydney, Lent 1978; Pres., Internatn. Assoc. of Legal Science, 1968–70. *Member:* Amer. Philosophical Socy. 1972—; Amer. Socy. Int. Law; Vice-Pres. 1970–73, Hon. Vice-Pres. since 1973; The Socy. of Public Teachers of Law (U.K.); Int. Law Assn.; Pres. American Branch 1973—Société de Legislation Comparée (France); Intl. Academy of Comparative Law 1963—; Amer. Acad. of Arts & Sciences 1977—. Fellow Inst. for Advanced Study of the Behavioural Sciences, Stanford 1961–62; Corresponding member, The British Academy since 1973; American Foreign Law Assn. Pres. 1973–76. *Publications:* Soviet Housing Law (1939); Law and Social Change in the U.S.S.R. (1953); The Soviet System of Government (1957 rev. 1960, 1964, 1968); Settling Disputes in Soviet Society (1960); Communists and Their Law (1969), Editor, Soviet Legal Philosophy (1951); editor (with M. L. Weisberg) Cases and Reading on Soviet Law (1950); (with Isaac Shapiro) The Soviet Legal System (1962). *Clubs:* Century, Yale (N.Y.C.); University (Washington); Authors' (London, Eng.). *Address:* 20 East 94th Street, NY 10028; and *office* Columbia University, 435 West 116th Street, New York City 27, U.S.A.

**HAZELTINE, Sherman.** American. *B.* 1907. *Educ.* Leland Stanford Univ., Stanford, Calif. (BA, Econ.), LLD, Univ. of Northern Arizona. *M.* 1932, Mary Temple Favour. *Daus.* Mary Favour Hazeltine Slater and Cynthia C. *Career:* President, Bank of Arizona, Prescott, Arizona. Past Pres., Nat. Bank Division, Amer. Bankers' Assoc.; Past Pres. and Secy., Arizona Bankers Assoc. Chairman, First National Bank of Arizona, Phoenix. Director; Sperry Rand Corp., New York; Director, Inspiration, Consolidated Copper Co. N.Y.; American Graduate School, Int. Management, Phoenix; Heard Museum, Phoenix. *Clubs:* Phoenix Country; Paradise

Valley Country; Arizona; Valley of Sun Kiwanis; Metropolitan, N.Y.C. *Address:* 6021 East Sage Drive, Scottsdale, Arizona 85253; and *office* First National Bank of Arizona, P.O. Box 20551, Phoenix, Arizona 85036, U.S.A.

**HÁZI, Dr. Vencel.** Hungarian diplomat. *B.* 1925. *Educ.* Technical Univ. and Univ. of Economics, Budapest. *M.* Judith Zell. *Dau.* 1. *Career:* Press Att. Hungarian Legation, London 1951–53; Counsellor, Hungarian Legation, Stockholm 1957–58; Ambassador to Iraq and Afghanistan 1958–61; Ambassador to Greece and Cyprus 1962–64; Head of Western Dept. Min. of Foreign Affairs 1964–68; Dept. For. Minister 1968–70; Ambassador for Hungary to Court of St. James's 1970–76; Dept. of Foreign Affairs since 1976. *Awards:* Golden Grade of Merit for Labour; Medal of Merit of Hungarian People's Republic; Grand Cordon of Order of Omayoum, Iran. *Address:* Ministry of Foreign Affairs, 1395 Budapest, Hungary.

**HAZLITT, Henry.** American editor and author. *B.* 28 Nov. 1894. *Educ.* College, City of New York. *M.* 1936, Frances S. Kanes. *Career:* Member, staff of Wall Street Journal 1913–16; financial staff, New York Evening Post 1916–18; wrote monthly financial letter of Mechanics and Metals National Bank, New York 1919–20; Financial Editor, New York Evening Mail 1921–23; Editorial Writer, New York Herald 1923–24; The Sun 1924–25; Literary Editor 1925–29; Literary Editor, The Nation 1930–33; Editor, American Mercury 1933–34; on editorial staff, New York Times 1934–46; Associate, Newsweek (magazine), and writer of column, Business Tides 1946–66; syndicated columnist for Los Angeles Times Syndicate 1966–69; co-founder and co-editor with John Chamberlain of The Freeman 1950–52; Editor-in-Chief 1953. *Publications:* Thinking as a Science (1916) and 1969; Instead of Dictatorship (1933); The Anatomy of Criticism (1933); A New Constitution Now (1942 and1974); Economics in One Lesson (1946); Will Dollars Save the World? (1947); Time Will Run Back (1951 and 1966); What You Should Know About Inflation (1960 and 1965); The Free Man's Library (1956); The Failure of the "New Economics"; An Analysis of the Keynesian Fallacies (1959 and 1973); The Foundations of Morality (1964 and 1972); Man vs. The Welfare State (1969); The Conquest of Poverty (1973); edited, A Practical Programme for America (1932); The Critics of Keynesian Economics (1960). Hon. LittD, Grove City (Pa.) College, 1958; Hon. LLD, Bethany (W Va) College 1961; Hon. ScD., Universidad Francisco Marroquin (Guatemala) 1976. *Address:* 65 Drum Hill Road, Wilton, Conn. 06897, U.S.A.

**HEAD Rt. Hon. Viscount** (Antony Henry Head), PC, GCMG, CBE, MC. *B.* 1906. *Educ.* Eton; Royal Military College, Sandhurst. *M.* 1935, Lady Dorothea Ashley-Cooper. *S.* 2. *Daus.* 2 (1 deceased). *Career:* Adjutant, Life Guards 1934–37; Staff College 1939; Brigade Major, 20th Guards Brigade 1940; Asst. Secy., Committee on Imperial Defence 1940–41; G.S.O. 2, Guards Armoured Division 1941–42; MP (Cons.) for Carshalton 1945–60; Secretary of State for War 1951–56; Min. for Defence Oct. 1956–Jan. 1957; British High Commissioner to the Fed. of Nigeria 1960–63; British High Commissioner in the Fed. of Malaysia 1963–66; Trustee, The Thomson Foundation, 1967—; Chairman, Royal National Inst. for the Blind, 1968–75, Pres. since 1975. Colonel Commandant, SAS Regiment, 1968; Chmn. Wessex Regional Cttee. The National Trust since 1970. *Address:* Throope Manor, Bishopstone, Salisbury, Wilts.

**HEAD, James Wilson.** Doctor of Law. *B.* 1912. *Educ.* Piedmont College (AB; LLD); Oglethorpe Univ. (AB). *M.* 1935, Corinne Payne, and (2) 1959, Sarita Cibula. *S.* James Payne. *Dau.* Gloria Ann (Martin). *Career:* Superintendent, Oglethorpe Univ. Press 1935–37; Engineer, Public Service Electric & Gas Co. of New Jersey 1937–38; self-employed as Radio Engineer 1938–40; Engineer: American Television Laboratories, Chicago 1940–41, Continental Motors Corp., Detroit 1941–42, and Commercial Research Laboratories, Detroit 1942–43. President & Founder: Industrial Electronics Inc. 1943—, and Electronics Institute of Technology 1946—. *Publications:* Electronic Pressure Measuring System, 1944, Electronic Instruments for Industry, 1944, 1945; Electronic Training for Industry, 1956; Thickness Gage for Moving Sheets, 1948. LLD, Piedmont Coll. *Member:* Advisory Committee, Michigan Dept. of Economic Development; Detroit Television Council; Instrument Socy. of America; Photographic Socy. of America; Inst. of Radio Engineers. *Clubs:* Vortex; Plum Hollow Golf; Oakland County Sheriff's Posse; Economic (Detroit); Appaloosa Horse Assn. Inc.; Michigan Appaloosa Horse Assn. Inc. *Address:* and *office* 2473 Woodward Avenue, Detroit 1, Mich., U.S.A.

**HEALD, Darrel Verner.** Canadian. *B.* 1919. *Educ.* University of Saskatchewan (BA, LLB). *M.* Doris R. Hessey. *S.* Brian. *Dau.* Lynn. *Career:* Att.-Gen. Prov. Secretary of Saskatchewan, 1924; Judge of the Court of Appeal, Canada. *Member:* Regina Bar Assoc.; Law Society of Saskatchewan; Regina Curling, Wascona Golf, Wascona Winter. *Address:* and *office* Room 338 Legislative Building, Regina, Saskatchewan, Canada.

**HEALD, Rt. Hon. Sir Lionel Frederick,** PC, QC. British barrister-at-law and politician. *B.* 7 Aug. 1897. *Educ.* Charterhouse; Christ Church, Oxford (BA). *M.* (1) 1923, Flavia Forbes. *S.* 1. *Dau.* 1. (2) 1929, Daphne Constance Price. *S.* 2. *Dau.* 1. *Career:* Served in World War I, Royal Engineers 1915–19; called to the Bar, Middle Temple 1923, Bencher 1946; Junior Counsel to Board of Trade in technical matters 1931–37: served in World War II. R.A.F.V.R. 1939–45; Vice-Chmn., Bar Council 1957; MP (Cons.) for Chertsey 1950–70; Attorney-General 1951–54. *Address:* Chilworth Manor, Guildford, Surrey.

**HEALEY, Rt. Hon. Denis Winston,** PC, MBE, MP. *B.* 1917. *Educ.* Bradford Grammar School and Balliol Coll., Oxford (1st Cl. Mods., 1st Cl. Greats, MA 1945). *M.* 1945, Edná May Edmunds. *S.* Timothy. *Daus.* Jenifer and Cressida. *Career:* Member Parliament (Lab.) Leeds since 1952; British Secretary of State for Defence, Oct. 1964–70; Shadow Foreign Secretary 1970–72; Shadow Chancellor of the Exchequer 1972–74; Chancellor of the Exchequer since 1974. *Publications:* The Curtain Falls (1951); New Fabian Society (1952); Neutralism (1955); Fabian International Essays (1956); A Neutral Belt in Europe (1958); NATO and American Security 1959); The Race against The H-Bomb (1960); Labour Britain and the World (1963). *Address:* House of Commons, London, S.W.1.

**HEALY, George William, Jr.** American. *B.* 1905. *Educ.* Univ. of Mississippi (AB). *M.* 1927, Margaret Alford. *S.* George W. III. *Awards:* Order of Leopold II (Belgium); Star of Solidarity (Italy); Order of Christopher Columbus (Dominican Republic). *Career:* Correspondent, The Associated Press and ten daily newspapers 1922–26; Reporter, the Knoxville Sentinel 1926; successively Reporter (1926–30), City Edr. (1930–35), Mng. Edr. (1935–52), and Edr. The Time-Picayune, New Orleans 1952–72. Corresponding Edr., Collier's Magazine 1934–44. Editor, Vice-Pres. and Director, The Times-Picayune Publishing Corp. 1952—; President, American Socy. of Newspaper Editors 1958–59; Director, The Associated Press 1957–66. Democrat. *Publications:* A Life on Deadline (1976). *Clubs:* Boston; Louisiana; Recess; Southern Yacht (all New Orleans); National Press (Washington, D.C.); Mount Kenya Safari (E. Africa); Circumnavigators (New York). *Address:* 2110 State Street, New Orleans, La., U.S.A.

**HEARST, William Randolph, Jr.** *B.* 1908. *Educ.* University of California. *M.* 1948, Austine McDonnell. *S.* William Randolph III and John Agustine Chilton. *Career:* with New York American, N.Y.C. 1928; reporter, assistant to city editor, publisher 1936–37; Publisher, N.Y. Journal-American, N.Y.C. 1937–56; War Correspondent 1943–45. Chairman of the Board, The Hearst Corporation; Editor-in Chief of the Hearst Newspapers. *Awards:* Pulitzer and Overseas Press Club Awards; Order of the Southern Cross (Brazil); Grand Cross Order of Merit (Peru); Order of the Philippine Legion of Honour, and others. Member, American Society of Newspaper Editors. *Clubs:* Brook, Madison Square Garden, Sigma Delta Ch. (N.Y.C.); National Press, Metropolitan, Burning Tree, Fi Street, Sulgrave (Washington); Bohemian; W.P.I. & 70th C-Fox, (San Francisco). *Address:* 810 Fifth Avenue, New York, N.Y. 10021; and *office* 959 Eighth Avenue, New York, N.Y. 10019, U.S.A.

**HEASLIP, Lloyd Howard,** OBE, JP. Australian. *B.* 1911. *Educ.* Primary and High Schools and Prince Alfred College, S.A. *M.* 1936, Thelma Hawthorne. *Daus.* Heather, Annette and Judith. *Career:* Member, Wool Research Committee 1953–68. Vice-Pres., National Farmers' Union of Australia 1961–68. Exec. Member, Australian Wool Industry Conference 1963—; Chmn. United Farmers & Graziers Co-operative Socy. 1966–71; Lay member Aust. Trate Practices Tribunal 1968–73; Past Member International Wool Secretariat; Australian Wool Board; President: Aust. Wool & Meat Producers Federation and of Northern Fire Fighting Assn. Former Chmn.: South Australia (S.A.) Wheat & Wool-growers Assn. Inc.; S.A. Wheat & Wool-growers Co-operative Society and of S.A. Co-operative Bulkhandling Co.; mem. Austr. Wool Industry Policy cttee. since 1972; Controls pastoral interests at

Wirrabarra and Tintinara, S.A., Merino Stud at Wirrabarra and Avonmore Investment Co. *Member:* Prince Alfred Old Collegians Assn. *Club:* Unley Park Bowls. *Address:* 17 Cudmore Avenue, Toorak Gardens, S.A. 5065, Australia.

**HEATH, Benjamin Wild.** American executive and engineer. *B.* 1914. *Educ.* Marquette University (BMech. Eng.). *M.* 1942, Aloise Buckley. *S.* James, John, Buckley and Timothy. *Daus.* Pamela, Priscilla, Alison, Jennifer, Elizabeth and Janet. *Career:* Aviation Cadet, U.S. Air Corps 1941–42; graduated Dec. 1942; U.S. Air Forces (formerly Army Air Corps) 1941–46; rank of major; director of aircraft maintenance for Eastern Flying Training Command; U.S.A.F. representative on War Dept. Manpower Board. Joined Coastal Petroleum Co. as Secy. and Gen. Mgr. June 1946; Vice-Pres. 1950; Pres. 1952. President and Director: Coastal Petroleum Co., and Magellan Petroleum Corporation; Chairman, Magellan Petroleum Australia Ltd.; President and Director, Coastal Caribbean Oils and Minerals Ltd.; President, The Catawba Corp. (N.Y.C.); Director: Canada Southern Oils Ltd., and United Canso Oil & Gas Ltd. Member, Tau Beta Pi, National Honorary Engineering. *Clubs:* Union League (NYC); Hertford Golf; University (Hartford). *Address:* 29 Colony Road, West Hartford, Conn.; and *office* 37 Lewis Street, Suite 500, Hartford, Conn., U.S.A.

**HEATH, Rt. Hon. Edward Richard George,** PC, MBE, MP *B.* 1916. *Educ.* Chatham House School, Ramsgate; Balliol College, Oxford (Scholar Hon. Fellow 1969). *Career:* Pres. Oxford Univ. Cons. Assn. 1937; Chmn. Fed. Univ. Cons. Assn. 1938; Pres. Oxford Union 1939; Oxford Union debating tour, Amer. Universities 1939–40; Fed. of Univ. Conservative & Unionist Assn. 1959—; Served War of 1939–45 (despatches, MBE); in Army 1940–46; France, Belgium, Holland, Germany), Gunner in R.A. 1940; Lt.-Col. 1945. Admin. Civil Service (1946–47) resigning to become prospective candidate for Bexley; MP for Bexley since 1950; Asst. Con. Whip 1951; Lord Commissioner of Treasury 1951; Joint Deputy Govt. Chief Whip 1952; (Deputy Govt. Chief Whip 1953–55); Parly. Secy. to the Treasury and Govt. Chief Whip Dec. 1955–Oct. 1959; Minister of Labour, Oct. 1959–July 1960; Lord Privy Seal with Foreigh Office responsibilities 1960–63; Secretary of State for Industry, Trade and Regional Development and President of the Board of Trade 1963–64. Leader of the Opposition 1965–70; Prime Minister & First Lord of the Treasury 1970–74; Leader of Oppos. 1974–75. *Member:* Council, Royal Coll. Music 1961–70; Chmn. London Symphony Orchestra Trust 1963–70; Vice Pres. Bach Choir 1970—; Chmn. Commonwealth Parly. Assn. 1970–74. *Awards:* Smith-Mundt Fellowship, U.S.A.; Vis Fellow Nuffield Coll. Oxford; Hon. Fellow 1970; Cyril Foster Memorial Lecture, Oxford; Godkin Lecturer Harvard Univ.; Hon. DCL Oxon 1971; Hon. DTech Bradford; Hon. LLD Westminster Coll., Salt Lake City 1975; Dr. honoris causa Univ. of Paris-Sorbonne 1976; Freiherr Von Stein Foundation Prize; Estes J. Kefauver Prize; Stresseman Gold Medal; Charlemagne Prize; Winner, Sydney to Hobart Ocean Race 1969; Captain, Britain's Admiral's Cup Team 1971. *Publications:* One Nation—a Tory Approach to Social Problems (1950). Old World New Horizons (1970). Sailing—A Course of My Life (1975). Music—A Joy for Life (1976); Travels-People & Places in my Life (1977). Carols—The Joy of Christmas (1977). *Clubs:* Carlton; Buck's; Royal Yacht Squadron. *Address:* House of Commons, London, S.W.1.

**HEATH, Frederick Jack.** British. *B.* 1915. *Educ.* City of London School. *M.* 1941, Diana Barrett. *S.* 2. *Dau.* 1. *Career:* Works Manager, M.R.P. Ltd. Enfield Cable Works Ltd. 1942–45; District Sales Manager, Proctor & Gamble Ltd. 1945–55; Horticultural Manager, Fisons Ltd. Fertilizer Div. 1955–61. Chmn. and Managing Director, Fisons Horticulture Ltd. 1963–66; Director: Fisons Ltd. Apr. 1964—; Deputy Chairman and Managing Director Fertilizer Division. 1966–73; Chmn. Fertilizer Division 1973–76, Vice-Chmn. Fisons Ltd. 1973, Dep. Chmn. since 1976. Fellow Inst. of Marketing, F.R.H.S. *Address:* Barton Wood, Stone Lodge Lane, Ipswich, Suffolk; and *office* Harvest House, Felixstowe, Suffolk.

**HEATH, Sydney Francis.** Australian company director. *B.* 1905. *Educ.* Sydney Grammar School; Associate, Australian Society of Accountants. *M.* 1933, Elizabeth Joan Anderson. *S.* 2. *Daus.* 2. *Career:* Man. Dir. Woodheath Pty. Ltd., and T. W. Heath Agencies Pty. Ltd. 1950–73, Chmn. of Dirs. since 1973; Chairman, N.S.W. State Council of Australian Association of British Manufacturers 1954–57. *Address:* G.P.O. Box 1389, Sydney, N.S.W., Australia.

**HEATHCOTE-SMITH, Clifford Bertram Bruce,** CBE. British. *B.* 1912. *Educ.* Malvern College and Pembroke College Cambridge. *M.* 1940, Thelma Joyce Engström. *S.* 2. *Career:* Diplomatic Service 1936–72, at Peking and various posts in China 1937–42; Teheran 1942–43, Foreign Office 1944–47. Political Adviser, Hong Kong 1947–50; Commercial Counsellor, Ankara 1956–60. Copenhagen 1961–64, and Washington 1964–65; British Deputy High Commissioner, Madras, June 1965–68; Foreign and Commonwealth Office 1968–72; Snr. Clerk (Acting) in Dept. of Clerk of House of Commons. 1973–77. *Address:* Lampool Lodge, Maresfield, Sussex TN22 5DR.

**HEATON, Kenneth Louis.** Industrial psychologist. *B.* 1902. *Educ.* Indiana Univ. (AB) and Univ. of Chicago (PhD). *M.* 1926, E. Allison Bolitho. *Daus.* Elizabeth (Skinner) and Janet (Thomas). *Career:* Dir., Michigan Bureau of Research 1933–41; Chief Training Officer, U.S. Office of Civil Defence 1942–43; Chief. Program Development, Civilian Personnel and Training, Secretary of War 1944–46; Dean of Administration, Boston Univ. 1946–50; Vice-Pres., Richardson, Bellows, Henry & Co. 1950–55; Partner, Heaton, Floyd & Watson 1956—. Consultant to U.S., European and Latin American industries. Research Consultant, U.S. Strategic Bombing Survey 1945; Chmn., Secretary of War's Post-war Planning Cttee. for Civilian Personnel 1945–46; Director, confidential evaluation of U.S. foreign economic program for President 1952–54; Consultant to Office of President, Secretary of Defence, and U.S. Senate committees 1935—. *Publications:* Guide for Industrial Managers; Identifying Worker in Need of Training; A Curriculum Based on Functional Needs; Personnel Selection Manuals; Overseas Management and the Local Community; professional articles, and confidential reports for government and industries. *Member:* Phi Beta Kappa; Phi Delta Kappa; Amer. Assn. for Advancement of Science (Fellow); Amer. Educational Research Assn.; Industrial Relations Assn. *Clubs:* Cosmos (Washington); St. Botolph (Boston); Urban (Philadelphia); Yacht Club (St. Petersburg). *Address:* 830 North Shore Drive, St. Petersburg, Fla. 33701, U.S.A.

**HECHINGER, Fred. M.,** MBE. U.S.A. Editor & Foundation Executive. *B.* 1920. *Educ.* The City College of New York (BA). *M.* 1958, Grace Bernstein. *S.* Paul David and John Edward. *Career:* Correspondent, Educational Supplement, The Times, London 1946–48; edcn. columnist, The Washington Post 1946–49; Correspondent, Overseas News Agency 1946–49; Edcn. Editor, New York Herald Tribune 1950–56; Assoc. Publisher and Exec. Editor, Bridgeport (Conn.) Sunday Herald 1956–59; Education & Cultural Relations Div., U.S. Military Govt. in Germany (special consultant to the Director) 1948; Education Editor, The New York Times 1959–69; Member of the Editorial Board since 1969, Asst. Editor of Editorial Page since 1976; Pres., The New York Times Company Foundation since 1977; contributing Editor to the Saturday Review since 1976. *Publications:* Handbook of the German Police, British War Office and U.S. War Dept. (co-author); An Adventure in Education; Connecticut Points the Way; The Big Red Schoolhouse, Teen-Age Tyranny, Morrow (co-author with wife, Grace Hechinger); Pre-School Education Today; New York Times Guide to New York City Private Schools (co-author with Grace Hechinger); Growing Up in America (co-author with G.H.). *Awards:* U.S. Army Citation; Hon. LLD Kenyon College; Hon. LHD Bard Coll.; Washington College, Wilkes, Coll.; Rider Coll.; Paine Coll.; Trinity; St. Josephs; City Coll. of New York; Hon. LLD Bates College; Univ. of Notre Dame; Education Writers' Assn. Annual Prize (six times); George Polk Memorial Award (twice); Fairbanks Award; Townsend Harris Medal; Soc. of Silurians Editorial Writing Award (twice). *Member:* Education Writers Assn. (Past Pres.); Phi Beta Kappa; English-Speaking Union. Trustee: American-Scandinavian Foundation; Acad. for Educational Development. *Clubs:* Coffee House, Century Assn. *Address:* 40 East 88th Street, New York City 28; and *office* The New York Times, 229 West 43rd Street, New York City, 36, U.S.A.

**HECHT, George Anthony.** American publisher, bookseller. *B.* 1910. *M.* 1937, Dorothea Rallinhs Ackermann (div.). *Daus.* Karen and Dorothea. *M.* 1956, Elaine Ann Kelly (div. Oct. 1964). *S.* George Anthony, Jr.; remarried first wife Nov. 1964. *Career:* Clerk, Doubleday Page Book Shops, N.Y.C. 1925–29; Publishing representative, Doubleday Doran Book Shops 1930–37; Asst. Gen. Mgr., Doubleday Doran Book Shops 1937–40; Gen. Mgr. Doubleday Book Shops 1940–75, Pres. 1972. Director, Council on Books in Wartime 1941–46; Armed Services Editions 1941–46; Treasurer,

Overseas Editions 1944–46; member, American Book Travellers (Pres. 1937); American Booksellers Association (Pres. 1946–47; Chmn. of Board 1948); Vice Pres. Doubleday & Co. 1948–75; Pres. Old Corner Book Store 1950–75; Doubleday Book Shops 1972–75. *Publications:* Notes on a Modern Bookshop (1941). Democrat. *Address:* 176 Bay Avenue, Hampton Bays, N.Y. 11946, U.S.A.

**HECKSCHER, August.** Journalist, author, and public official. *B.* 1911. *Educ.* St Paul's School (Concord, N.H.), Yale Univ. (BA 1936) and Harvard (MA 1939). *M.* 1941, Calude Chevreaux. *S.* Stephen August, Philip Hofer and Charles Chevreux. Instructor in Government, Yale 1939–41; Editor, Auburn (N.Y.) Citizen-Advertiser 1946–48; New York Herald-Tribune (N.Y.C. Editorial writer 1948–56; Chief Editorial writer 1952–56); Military service, Civilian in Office of Strategic Services, serving in N. Africa 1942–45. Director, The Twentieth Century Fund, N.Y.C. 1956–67; Special Consultant on the Arts to President Kennedy, The White House, March 1962–63. Commissioner of Parks & Administration of Cultural Affairs, New York City, 1967–74. *Publications:* These are The Days (1936); A Pattern of Politics (1947); The Politics of Woodrow Wilson (1956); Diversity of Worlds (with Raymond Aron 1957); The Public Happiness (1962). Hon. LLD Fairleigh-Dickinson Univ. and Adelphi Univ.; Hon. LittD: Regents of Univ. of State of N.Y., and C. W. Post Coll.; Hon. DHL: Temple Univ. and Brandeis Univ. *Member:* Phi Beta Kappa; Jonathan Edwards Coll., Yale (Fellow). *Club:* Century (N.Y.C.). *Address:* 159 East 94th Street, New York, N.Y. 10021, U.S.A.

**HEDGES, Dennis Mitchell, CBE.** British company director. *B.* 1917. *Educ.* Felsted School; Lausanne University; St. Catharine's College, Cambridge (MA Hons.). *M.* 1951, Margaret Janet Belcham. *S.* 2. *Career:* Administrative Cadet (1940); Asst. District Commissioner (1944); District Commissioner (1949); Administrative Officer, Grade II (1957), Sierra Leone; Former Chief Secretary, British Guiana. Member, Royal Commonwealth Society. *Address:* Forshem, Elvetham Road, Fleet, Hants.

**HEDLUND, Charles John.** American. *B.* 1917. *Educ.* Univ. of Minnesota (Bach. Chem. Eng. and of Business Admin.). *M.* 1940, Helen Marie Thorstenson. *S.* Christopher. *Daus.* Susan, Patricia and Ann. *Career:* Mgr. Co-ordination and Petroleum Economics Dept. Standard Oil Co. (N.J.) New York, 1954–60; Pres., Dir., Esso Standard Italiania, Genoa 1960–62; Svenska Esso-Stockholm 1962–66; Vice-Pres., Esso Europe, London, 1967; Vice-President, Standard Oil Co. (N.J.), New York. Director, Arabian American Oil Co., Dhahran and New York. *Clubs:* Queens, Lansdowne (London); Beacon Hill, Summit (N.J., U.S.A.). *Address:* *office* 30 Rockefeller Plaza, New York, N.Y., U.S.A.

**HEERING, Peter.** Danish distiller. *B.* 1908. *Educ.* University of Copenhagen. *M.* 1933, Lissen Ipsen. *S.* Peter, William. *Dau.* Rosemarie (*Dec'd*). *Career:* Co-partner, Peter F. Heering 1934; Sole-partner, 1936–69; Co-partner with sons Peter Jr. and William since 1969; Chmn. Nye Danske Lloyd; The Danish Sugar Corp; Incentive AS Vilh. Christiansen, P. Weile & Son; and other companies and associations. *Address:* Overgaden N.V.11, Copenhagen K.; and Nordhusvej 33, 3220, Tisvildeleje, Denmark.

**HEES, Hon. George H., PC.** *B.* 1910. *Educ.* Trinity College School, The Royal Military College, University of Toronto, and Cambridge University, England; Hon. LLD, Waterloo Lutheran Univ. 1961. *M.* 1934, Mabel, dau. of Hon. E. A. Dunlop. *Daus.* Catherine, Martha and Roslyn. *Career:* Directed the manufacturing firm of George H. Hees Co. Ltd. (founded by his grandfather in Toronto), but severed his connection with the firm when he became President of the Conservative Party in 1954. Sworn of the Privy Council and appointed Minister of Transport June 21, 1957. President, Montreal Stock Exchange, Canadian Stock Exchange. Former Minister of Trade and Commerce in the Goverment of Canada. Member, Progressive Conservative Party. *Clubs:* Toronto Golf; Toronto Badminton & Racquet; University; Woodgreen Community Centre (Director); St. James's; St. Denis; Montreal; Royal Montreal Golf. *Address:* 7 Coltrin Place, Ottawa, Canada.

**HEFFELFINGER, Totton Peavey.** Commander, U.S. Naval Reserve (Retd.). *B.* 1899. *Educ.* Yale Univ. *M.* (1) 1922, Mildred Virginia Kidder (*D.* July 1931). *S.* Frank T., II, and Marcus W. K. *Dau.* Lila K. (Coleman). *M.* (2) 1933, Elsmore G. Anderson. *S.* John H. and Christopher B. Past-Commander, American Legion Department of Canada; Past-President, U.S. Golf Association 1952–53. *Address:* 3 Birdie Lane, Chaska, Minnesota 55318; and *office* 730 Second Avenue South, Minneapolis, Minnesota 55402, U.S.A.

**HEFLER, Richard James.** American. *B.* 1912. *Educ.* Dartmouth Coll. (AB *summa cum laude* 1936), Univ. of Southern California (MBA 1954) and Fordham Univ. Law School. *M.* 1946, Edith A. Timmins. *S.* Richard James. *Dau.* Olivia Catherine. *Career:* Financial Analyst, Hanover Bank, N.Y. 1936–41; Special Studies Analyst, E.I. Du Pont de Nemours Co., Wilmington, Del. 1941–42; Controller, Royal Heaters Inc., Alhambra, Calif. 1946–47; joined American Potash & Chemical Corp. 1948, Secretary 1953–57, Vice-Pres. 1958–67; Dir. 1959–70; Vice-Pres. Kerr-McGee Corp; Dir. Oklahoma Chamber of Commerce. Member, Dartmouth Coll. Alumni Council. Commander USNR. *Member:* Phi Beta Kappa. *Clubs:* Bohemian (San Francisco); Oklahoma City Golf & Country. *Address:* 2525 Pembroke Terrace, Oklahoma 73116, U.S.A.

**HEINEMANN, Edward Henry.** American aeronautical engineer. Aerospace Consultant; Vice-Pres., Engineering, General Dynamics Corp., New York. *B.* 1908. *Educ.* Public Schools in Saginaw (Mich.) and Los Angeles; through High School; private instruction in aircraft engineering. *M.* 1959, Zell Shewey. *Dau.* Mrs. Allan Lamont. *Career:* First employed as Aircraft Design Engineer by Douglas Aircraft Co. 1926; has been continuously with this firm until 1960 with the exception of four years with International Aircraft, Moreland Aircraft and Northrop Aircraft; Design and Project Engineer, Douglas Aircraft Co. (then Northrop Corp.) 1932; Chief Engineer, El Segundo Div. of Douglas Aircraft Co. Inc. 1936–58; Director of Combat Aircraft Systems, Engineering, General Offices, Santa Monica 1958–60; Vice-President, European Sales, Douglas Aircraft Co. Apr.–July 1960. As Chief Engineer has directed the design and development of Dauntless, Boston, Havoc, Invader, Destroyer, Skyraider, Skystreak, Skyrocket, Skynight, Skyshark, Skywarrior, Skyray, Skyhawk and Skylancer planes. Exec. Vice-President of Guidance Technology Inc. (formerly Summers) Santa Monica, Calif. 1960–62. *Awards:* Sylvanus Albert Reed Award 1952; Collier Trophy 1953; Southern Calif. Aviation Man of the Year Award 1954, Calif. Fashion Creators' Distinguished Achievement Award (Aviation) 1955, F.A.I. Paul Tissandier Diploma 1955. *Clubs:* Jonathan (Los Angeles); Lake Arrowhead Yacht (Past Commodore). *Address:* 1248 Casiano, Los Angeles, California, U.S.A.

**HEINTZELER, Wolfgang.** Dr. jur. German. *B.* 1908. *Educ.* studied law at Tübngen, Munich and Berlin 1926–30; junior period 1930–33; took degree 1931. *Career:* Assessor in Württemberg Judicial Service 1933–34; County Court official in State Ministry of Justice 1934–36; lawyer with BASF 1936, manager 1950, member of the Board 1952. Member of the Supervisory Board of BASF Aktiengesellschaft, Ludwigschaften 1974; Supervisory Board, Pfälzische Hypothekenbank, Ludwigshafen. *Member:* Working circle of Evangelical Employers; member Max-Planck-Inst. for foreign and international patent-original and competition-rights; Mem.: Bds. of Trustees of: Max-Planck Inst. for foreign statute and international law; Hon. Senator, High School for Administrative Science, Speyer 1957. *Address:* 6900 Heidelberg, Schloß-Wolfsbrunnen-Weg 78, Germany.

**HEINZ, Henry John II.** American industrialist. *B.* 1908. *Educ.* Yale University (BA): Trinity College, Cambridge. *S.* 1. President (1941–59), Chairman, H. J. Heinz Co. 1959—; Agribusiness Council; Yale Univ. Art Gallery, Governing Board; Member, Yale Univ. Economic Growth Center, Advisory Cttee.; Council of Management, British-Ditchley Business Cttee. for the Arts; Dir., Pittsburgh Symphony Soc.; The Smithsonian National Associates Board; World Affairs Council of Pittsburgh; Trustee, Carnegie Inst.; Carnegie-Mellon Univ.; Nutrition Foundation; Cttee. for Economic Development; U.S. Council of the International Chamber of Commerce. *Awards:* Commander of the Royal Order of the Phoenix (Greece); Chevalier de la Légion d'Honneur; Comdr. Order of Merit (Italian Repub.). *Address:* c/o H. J. Heinz Company, P.O. Box 57, Pittsburgh, Pennsylvania, 15230, U.S.A.

**HEIPERTZ, Otto Erich Sigismund.** German diplomat. *B.* 1913. *Educ.* Law and Economics, Dipl. Volkswirt (MEcon). *M.* 1940, Regina Frank. *S.* 1. *Career:* Air Min. Berlin (Test Field Rechlin Peenemünde) 1934–42; Prussian State Ministry, Gov. Couns. 1942–45; Econ. Admin. Berlin and Minden 1945–48; State Chancellery Hannover 1948–51; Min. For. Affairs Bonn 1952–56; Consul Cape Town 1957–62; Couns.

Emb. Damascus 1962–65; Min. For. Affairs African Aff. Pers. Div. 1965–67; Head of Trade Mission to USSR, Prague 1968–74; Ambassador Extraordinary and Plenipotentiary in Oslo, Norway since 1974. *Decorations:* Order of Merit (Madagascar); Order of Valour (Cameroun); Order of the Mono (Togo); Order of Merit First Class (F. Rep. of Germany). *Clubs:* YMCA, Christian Youth Village Organisation. *Address:* Embassy of the Federal Republic of Germany, Oscarsgt. 45, Oslo 2, Norway.

**HEISBOURG, Georges Louis Dominique.** *B.* 1918. *Educ.* Athenaeum (Luxembourg), and Universities of Grenoble, Innsbruck and Paris (Sorbonne); Lic.-ès-Let. *M.* 1945, Hélène Pinet. *S.* Pierre and François. *Dau.* Jeanne. *Career:* Director Information & Press Service, Prime Minister's Office, Luxembourg 1944–45; Attaché 1945–48 and Secy. of Legation, London 1948–51; Counsellor of Legation, Chief of Section of International Organizations, then Dir. of Political Division, Min. of Foreign Affairs 1952–58; Ambassador of Luxembourg to U.S.A. 1958–64, Canada and Mexico 1959–64; Permanent Representative of Luxembourg to U.N. 1958–61; Ambassador to the Netherlands 1964–67, to France, 1967–70; Permanent Representative to O.E.C.D. 1967–70: Secy. General of Western European Union 1971–74; Ambassador to USSR 1974–77; Ambassador-at-Large since 1977. *Awards:* Grosse Goldene Ehrenzeichen fur Verdienste um die Republik (Austria); Grand Officier de l'Ordre de Léopold II (Belgium); Grand Officier de l'Ordre du Mérite, Officier de la Legion d'Honneur (France); Grosses Verdienstkreuz des Verdienstordens der Bundesrepublik (Germany); Commandeur de l'Ordre Al Merito della Republica (Italy); Aguilla Azteca, Banda de Primera Clase (Mexico); Grand-Croix de l'Ordre d'Orange-Nassau, Grand-Croix de Ordre de la Maison d'Orange (Netherlands); Commandeur de l'Ordre de mérite civil et militaire d'Adolphe de Nassau. Chevalier de l'Ordre National de la Couronne de Chêne, Grand Officier de l'Ordre de Mérite (Luxembourg). *Address:* Ministry of Foreign Affairs, 5 rue Notre-Dame, Luxembourg.

**HEITLER, Walter Heinrich,** FRS. Irish physicist. *B.* 2 Jan. 1904. *Educ.* Universities of Berlin and Munich; PhD (Munich). *M.* 1942, Kathleen W. Nicholson. *S.* Eric. *Career:* Privat docent, Göttingen 1929–33; Research Fellow, University of Bristol 1933–41; Prof. of Theoretical Physics Dublin Inst. for Advanced Studies 1941–49 (Director 1946–49); Prof. for Theoretical Physics, Univ. of Zürich since 1949. *Member:* Akademie der Wissenschaften; der Literature, Mainz. Royal Irish Academy; Member, Royal Society of Sciences, Uppsala (Sweden); Academy Leopoldina, Halle; Kgl Norske Videnskabers Selskab. *Awards:* Fellow, Royal Society, London; Hon. DSc, National University of Ireland; Hon. Dr. rer, nat. University of Göttingen; Hon. Dr. phil Univ. of Uppsala, Max Planck Medal, 1968; Marcel Benoist Prize 1969. *Publications:* Theory of Chemical Bond (with F. London 1927); Quantentheorie und homöopolare Bindung (1934); Quantum Theory of Radiation, Oxford 1936 (3rd ed. 1954); Elementary Wave Mechanics, Oxford 1945 (2nd ed. 1956); Der Mensch und die naturwissenschaftliche Erkenntnis, Vieweg 1961 (4th ed. 1966); English trans., Man and Science, Oliver & Boyd (1963); Naturphilosophische Streifzüge,, Vieweg (1970) Naturwissenschaft ist Geisteswissenschaft, Waage (1972); Die Natur und das Göttliche, Klett u Balmer (1974, 3rd edn. 1976, Literaturpreis der Stiftung für abendlandische Besinnung); papers on theory of radiation, Meson Theory, cosmic rays, quantum electrodynamics, philosophical problems. *Address:* Am Guggenberg 5, Zürich 53, Switzerland.

**HEKMAN, Edward J.** *B.* 1914. *Educ.* Southwest Christian Schools; Grand Rapids Christian High School, and Calvin College (all of Grand Rapids, Mich.). *M.* 1937, Florence Stuart. *S.* John. *Daus.* Marilyn (Clark), Judy (Thompson) and Susan. *Career:* With Keebler Co. of America, Hekman-Supreme Baker, Grand Rapids: Sales Dept. 1935–43, Vice-Pres. and Asst. Gen. Mgr. 1946–51, Pres. and Gen. Mgr. 1951–60. With Keebler Co. of America, Melrose Park, Ill. Director, 1950—, Vice-Pres. 1954–59, Exec. Vice-Pres. 1959–60, President 1960—; Vice Chmn. Bd. Dirs. since 1960. Director, Old Kent Bank & Trust Co., Grand Rapids 1958—. Enlisted in U.S. Navy Reserve, Dec. 1943 (Ensign); discharged Feb. 1946 (Lieut. j.g.). Past-President, Kent County (Mich.) Community Chest; Past Campaign Chairman, Kent County United Fund Campaign; Past member of Board, Grand Rapids YMCA; Past Vice-Pres. and Director, Grand Rapids Chamber of Commerce; State Chmn. 1958, Advisory Board 1958–61, Michigan Week; member: Commission on Michigan's Economic Future (COMEF), and Calvin College Campus Committee 1959—. *Trustee:* The National Jewish Hospital. Denver. Member, Grace Evangelical Lutheran Church of River Forest, Ill. *Clubs:* Newcomen Society; Union League, Executives Economic (Chicago); River Forest Tennis. *Address:* and *office* Keebler Co., 677 Larch Avenue, Elmhurst, Ill. 60126, U.S.A.

**HELENIUS, Veli Arthur.** Finnish diplomat. *B.* 1910. *Educ.* Bachelor of Law, Helsinki. *M.* 1941, Leila Selma Anita Ignatius. *S.* Kari Gustav Woldemar. *Career:* Attaché, Tokyo 1941–43; Second Secy., Tokyo 1943–45; Secretary of Bureau, Ministry for Foreign Affairs 1945–47; Second Secretary, The Hague 1947–49; First Secretary, Ankara 1949–54; Chief of Bureau, Ministry 1954–56; Deputy Director of Commercial Affairs, Ministry 1956–58; Consul-General & Trade Representative, Cologne 1958–61; Ambassador at New Delhi (and concurrently Ambassador in Bangkok and Rangoon and Minister in Colombo and Djakarta) 1961–64. Director of Admin. Affairs, Ministry for Foreign Affairs 1964–67. Ambassador at Peking 1967–74; Ambassador at Copenhagen since 1974. *Awards:* Liberty Cross 4th class with swords (Finland); Cmdr. 1st Class, Order of White Rose of Finland; Cmdr., 1st Class Lion of Finland; Grand Cross, Order of St. Gregory the Great (Holy See); Grand Cross Merit with star of the Federal Republic of Germany; Cmdr., Order of Polonia Restituta (Poland); Officer, Orange-Nassau (Netherlands). *Address:* Embassy of Finland, Copenhagen, Denmark.

**HELGASON, Sigurdur.** Icelandic. *B.* 1921. *Educ.* Columbia Univ., New York. *M.* 1952, Unnur Einarsdottir. *S.* Helgi and Sigurd. *Daus.* Olof and Edda. *Career:* Man. Dir., Flugleidir H.F., Reykjavik, Iceland (Holding Company of Iceland's two Airlines—Loftleidir/Icelandic, and Flugfelag/Icelandair), 1974; Vice-Chmn., Loftleidir/Icelandic Airlines H.F.,Reykjavik, Iceland 1953; Gen. Mgr. and Chief. Exec. Officer, International Air Bahama, 1969. *Member:* Pres., Icelandic/American Socy., Reykjavik; Hon. Citizen, City of Winnipeg, Manitoba. Trustee, International House, New York. *Clubs:* Wings (N.Y.); Rotary (Reykjavik). *Address:* Skildinganes 52, Reykjavik, Iceland; and *office* Reykjavik Airport, Reykjavik, Iceland; and 630 Fifth Avenue, New York, N.Y. 10020

**HELGELAND, Hans Andreas.** Norwegian managing director. *B.* 1911. *Educ.* Univ. of Trade, and studies in England and U.S.A. *M.* 1937, Gunvor Haehre. *S.* Axel Emil. *Career:* Member of Board, Norges Handelsstands Forbund 1960–64 and 1970–72 (Vice-Pres., 1969, Pres. 1970–72): Norges Grossistforbund, Chmn. Bd. 1972–74. Member Bd. Norges Jernvarehandleres Forbund, og Bygningsartikkelgrossistenes Landsforbund; Park Hotel (A/S; Lier Jernvareforretning A/S. Th. Marheim A/S, and Bragerhagen 35–37 A/S; Man. Dir. Axel Helgeland A/S. Drammen. Member, Cncl. for Industrial and Trade Research in Norway, 1968–72. *Awards:* War decorations and others of distinction in different trades. *Address:* 3425 Reistad, Norway.

**HELLER, Paul.** Mechanical engineer (ret.). *B.* 14 Dec. 1911. *Educ.* Cambridge Univ. (BA 1933; MA 1940) and Pitman's Intensive Business Course. *M.* 1936, Edwina Patron. *Daus.* 2. *Career:* Manager and Director, Horace Heller Co., Ltd., Warsaw, Poland 1934–39; Director, Central Lumber Export Company Ltd., Warsaw 1938–39; Engineer at Stewart Warner Alemite Co., Belville, Ontario 1941; Pres., Granite Bay Timber Co. Ltd.; Vice-Pres. and Dir., Triangle Pacific Forest Products Ltd., formerly Pacific Pine Co. Ltd. until 1970; Past Pres., Glulam Products Ltd., New Westminster; Past Chmn., Forestry and Logging Division, Council of Forest Industries, B.C.; Past Pres. Independent Timber Convertors Assn.; Chmn., Rental Housing Council of British Columbia, Vancouver, B.C. 1976. *Address:* 4815 Belmont Avenue, Vancouver, B.C. V6T 1A8, Canada.

**HELLESTAM, Sigvard.** Swedish. *B.* 1919. *Educ.* Teknologilicentiat (DSc). *M.* 1945, Ragnhild Franzen. *S.* Anders, Ak, and Sven. *Dau.* Eva. *Career:* Technical Director of Reymersholm 1954; Vice-Pres. Förenade Superfosfat 1957. Gen. Mgr., Reymersholm Gamla Industri Aktiebolag 1961–66. Chmn., NPK-Engrais, Sfax, Tunisia 1964–68. Vice-Pres. ISMA, London 1962–64. Vice-President, Boliden AB., 1966—. *Member:* Royal Acad. of Engineering (IVA); Vice-Pres. Swedish Assn. of Engineers (STF). *Club:* Rotary. *Address:* Drottinggatan 153, Helsingborg, Sweden; and *office* Boliden, Helsingborg, Sweden.

**HELLMUTH, Edward John William,** CBE. British banker. *B.* 1907. *Educ.* Wilson's Grammar School. *M.* 1937, Erica Schollar. *Dau.* 1. *Career:* Dir. The Chartered Bank; Scottish and Continental Invest. Co. Ltd.; The Standard Bank Ltd.; Standard & Chartered Banking Group; European Arab

Bank. *Member:* CBI Europe Cttee.; CBI Overseas Cttee.; European Trade Cttee. of BOT Board; Chmn. Sub-Cttee. Europe, Invisible Exports. *Awards:* Croix de Guerre, Order of Orange Nassau; Companion, Order of the British Empire 1976. *Club:* Overseas Bankers. *Address:* 43 Somerset House, Oakfield, Somerset Road, Wimbledon, London, S.W.19; and *office* 29 Gresham Street, London EC2V 7EX.

**HELLWEGE, Heinrich.** German politician and merchant. *B.* 18 Aug. 1908. *M.* 1934, Lieschen Ahlers. *S.* Johann. *Daus.* Gisela, Erika. *Career:* Merchant until 1939; served in World War II, Air Force 1939–45; Landrat in Stade 1946; member, Land Synod of the Evangelical Land Church, Hanover; member of Committee Stade Chamber of Industry and Commerce; member, Zonal Council of British Zone: Landtag of Lower Saxony 1947–49; Chairman, Deutsche Partei 1946—; member (D.P.), Bundestag 1949–55; Minister for Affairs of the Bundesrat 1949–55; Minister-President, Land Niedersachsen 1955–59. Gro Bkreuz VO. BRD 1955; u. Kgl. Griech. St. Georgs-Orden 1956 Ehrensenator TH Hannover, Inaber der nieders. Landesmedaille. *Address:* 2152 Neuenkirchen Nr. 52, Germany.

**HELLYER, Hon. Paul Theodore,** PC. Canadian politician. *B.* 1923. *Educ.* High School (Waterford Ont.), Curtiss-Wright Technical Institute of Aeronautics (Glendale, Calif.) and Univ. of Toronto (BA). *M.* Ellen Jean Ralph. *S.* 2. *Dau.* 1. *Career:* Served in World War II with R.C.A.F. and Royal Canadian Artillery. Member House of Common- 1949–57 and 1958–74. Parliamentary Asst. to Minister of Natl. Defence, 1956–57, Minister 1963–67, (Associate Minister Apr.–June 1957). Sworn of Privy Council 1957; Minister of Transport, Minister responsible for Central Mortgage & Housing Corp., 1968–69; Chmn., Task Force on Housing and Urban Development, 1968. Resigned from Government on matter of principle, 30 April 1969; Distinguished Visitor, York Univ. Graduate Faculty of Environmental Studies 1969–70; Foundling Chmn. of Action Canada 1971; Joined Progressive Conservative Party 1972, Candidate for Leadership 1976; Joined Canadian Parly Press Gallery 1974 (columnist); Fellow, the Royal Socy for encouragement of the Arts. *Publications:* Agenda A plan for Action (1971). *Address:* 1982 Rideau River Drive, Ottawa, Ont., Canada.

**HELM, Harold Holmes.** American. Comdr. Order of St. Olav (Norway). *B.* 1900. *Educ.* Princeton Univ. (AB 1920); Hon. LLD Hampden-Sydney Coll., Center Coll., and Bloomfield Coll.; Hon. D.C.S. New York Univ.; Hon. D.L.C. Univ. of the South. *M.* Mary G. Rodes. *S.* John R. *Dau.* Eleanor B. (Ketcham). *Career:* Employed Chemical National Bank 1920; junior officer 1926, Vice-Pres. 1929, Dir. 1941, First Vice-Pres. 1946, Pres. 1947, Chmn. Bd. Dirs. 1956); Chmn. Exec. Cttee. 1966; Chmn. Dirs. Adv. Cttee. since 1973. Director: Chemical Bank, Hon. Dir. Member Trust Cttee.; Garden Services Inc., Readers Digest Association. *Member:* Advisory Bd. Hoover Institution (Palo Alto Calif.), Central Presbyterian Church, Montclair; Fed. Hall Memorial Associates; Montclair Historical Socy.; National Inst. of Social Sciences. *Clubs:* Bond (N.Y. Hon, Mem.); Campus (Princeton); Economic Filson Inc. (Louisville, Ky.); Kentuckians (N.Y.C.); Links; Monclair Golf (N.J.); Sons of the Revolution (State, N.Y.); Ristgouche Salmon Quebec (Treas.); University (N.Y.C.; Past Pres.); U.S. Seniors' Golf Association. *Address:* 49 Glenwood Road Upper Montclair, N.J.; and *office* Chemical Bank New York Trust Co., 277 Park Avenue, New York, N.Y. 10017, U.S.A.

**HELMS, Hermann Christian.** German. *B.* 1928. *Educ.* Bremen, Rosenheim, Neubeuren and Traunstein. *M.* 1958, Bettina, Elisabeth Melchers. *S.* Christian Hermann and Niclas Carl Sebastian. *Career:* Basic Shipping training, Carl Scholle, Bremen, 1944–47; Lykes Bros. Steamship Co. Inc. Bremen & New Orleans, 1947–51; Shipping work in India, France and Gt. Britain, 1951–52; with D.D.G. Hansa Bremen, 1952. Member, Bd. of Directors, Deutsche Dampfschiffahrts-Gesellschaft, Hansa Bremen; Member of Supervisory Bd. Hansa B.V. Rotterdam; Offshore Supply Assocn. Ltd. London; Albingia Versicherungs AG, Hamburg; Klöckner Werke AG, Duisburg; Atlantica S.p.A. Genoa. *Address:* 28 Bremen-Oberneuland Hoogenkamp Oberneulander Landstr. 35- *office* 28 Bremen, Schlachte 6, Fed. Rep. of Germany.

**HENCKEN, Hugh O'Neill.** American archaeologist. *B.* 8 Jan. 1902. *Educ.* Princeton Univ. (AB); Cambridge Univ. IBA, PhD, MA, ScD); National University of Ireland (Hon. DLitt.). *M.* 1935, Thalassa Cruso. *Daus.* Ala, Thalassa, Sophia. *Career:* Archaeological excavation in England 1928, 1930, 1931; Ireland 1932–36: Morocco 1947; Algeria 1949; special University Lecturer, London and Oxford Universities 1947; Monro Lecturer, Edinburgh University 1959; Curator of European Archaeology, Peabody Museum of Harvard Univ. 1932–72; Director, American School of Prehistoric Research 1945–72, Chmn, 1960–72. *Award:* Honorary Fellow St. Johns College, Cambridge 1969. *Publications:* Archaeology of Cornwall (1932); Tarquinia Villanovans and Early Etruscans, 1968; Tarquinia and Etruscan Origins, 1968; numerous archaeological reports. *Address:* Peabody Museum, Harvard University, Cambridge, Mass 02138, U.S.A.

**HENDERSON, Rt. Hon. Lord** (created baron 1945), William Watson Henderson, PC. British politician and journalist. *B.* 8 Aug. 1891. *Educ.* Queen Elizabeth Grammar School, Darlington. *Career:* Private Secretary to Leader of Labour Party, 1911; Editorial Secretary, Daily Citizen 1913–14; served World War I 1914–18; Private Secy. to Minister of Labour 1917; London Correspondent, European News Agency 1919–21; Parliamentary Correspondent to Labour Press Dept. 1919–21; Secretary to Labour Party Press and Publicity Dept. 1921–45; M.P. (Lab.) for Enfield (Middx.) 1923–24 and 1929–31; Parly. Private Secy. to Secretary of State for India 1929–31; Personal Assistant to Rt. Hon. Arthur Greenwood, M.P. (Minister without Portfolio) 1940–42; A Lord-in-Waiting to the King 1945–48; Additional member of the Air Council 1945–47; Parliamentary Under-Secretary of State, Foreign Office 1948–51; A British Rep. at Assembly of Council of Europe 1954 and 1955; Labour Peers Rep. on Parly. Cttee. of Parly. Labour Party 1952–55. Dir. Alliance Building Soc. 1955–75 (Chmn. 1966–72). *Address:* 707 Collingwood House, Dolphin Square, London, S.W.1.

**HENDERSON,** (Andrew) Maxwell, OBE. *B.* 1908. *Educ.* Institute of Chartered Accountants of Ontario (Fellow). *M.* 1935, Beatrice J. Maltby. *S.* David J. *Career:* Formerly: Comptroller, Canadian Broadcasting Corp.; Secretary-Treasurer, Distillers Corp. Ltd. and subsidiaries of Distillers Corp. Seagrams Ltd. in Canada. Auditor-General of Canada 1960–73. *Member:* Inst. of Chartered Accountants of Ontario and of Quebec. *Clubs:* Rideau (Ottawa). *Address:* 17 Coulson Ave., Toronto, Canada.

**HENDERSON, Edward Firth,** CMG, Retired British diplomat. *B.* 1917. *Educ.* Clifton Coll.; BNC Oxford. *M.* 1960, Jocelyn Nenk. *Daus.* Anna Maria, Lucy Emma Firth. *Career:* with the Army 1939–48; Petroleum Concessions Ltd. 1948–56; Seconded to Foreign Service 1956–59; Foreign (later Diplomatic) Service, Served in Middle East and Foreign and Commonwealth Office 1959, Political Agent Doha, Qater 1969; H.M. Ambassador Doha, Qatar 1971–74; Director M and G Securities Ltd. *Award:* Commander St. Michael and St. George. *Club:* Travellers. *Address:* c/o Barclays Bank, Pall Mall, London, S.W.1.

**HENDERSON, Horace Edward.** American executive, diplomat and politician. *B.* 1917. *Educ.* College of William & Mary, and Yale University. *M.* Vera S. Schubert. *Daus.* Terri (Kelley) and Elizabeth (Cosgrove). *Career:* Chmn., Congressional Speaker Reform Cttee., Washington 1976; Exec. Vice-Pres., American Lawmakers Assn.; Chairman of the Board and Pres.: Community Methods Inc. 1969–76; Asst. Dir. Scranton for President Campaign 1964; Deputy Assistant Secretary of State 1959–60; Director, Special Liaison Staff, Dept. of State 1958; Dir., Exile Political Organizations, Free Europe Cttee. 1961–62; Chairman, Americans for Asia Security and Freedom, 1961; President, Horace E. Henderson Agency, Real Estate & Insurance, McLean, Virginia 1964; Chairman Republican Party of Virginia 1964, Candidate U.S. Senator 1972; Candidate for Congress 1956. Cand., Lieut-Governor of Virginia 1957; Pres., Powhatan Hist. Assn. 1956–57; Pres., U.S. Jr. Chamber of Commerce 1952–53; Vice-Pres., Junior Chamber International 1951–52. Outstanding Jaycee of the World 1954; U.S. Delegate, WHO, ILO, UNESCO, FAO, ECOSOC and United Nations 1959–60; Director-General World Peace Through Law Center 1964–69; Exec. Dir., World Assocn. of Judges 1968–69; Assocn. Co-ordinator, National Automobile Dealers Association, 1954–56. Republican Nat. Committee, 1962–64; U.S. Committee for the U.N.; (Dir.) 1954; Chamber of Commerce of the U.S. (Director) Chmn. Convention for the Peaceful Settlement of International Disputes 1972; President International Domestic Devel. Corps 1974; *Publications:* articles on international affairs and proposed legislation. *Clubs:* Iktinos, Yale; Sigma Alpha Epsilon. *Address:* 1136 York Lane, Virginia Beach, Va. 23451; and *office* Suite 700, 1522 K Street, N.W., Washington, D.C. 20005, U.S.A.

**HENDERSON, Ian Thomson,** TD. Director of various companies. *B.* 1908. *Educ.* Uppingham and Magdalen College, Oxford (MA; 2nd Cl. Hons. History); Qualified Solicitor 1932. *M.* (1) 1932, Monica Wingfield Verner (*Dec.* 1962). *S.* Andrew David Thomson. *Daus.* Venetia Mary and Nicola Susan Thomson; (2) 1963, Imelda Davey. *S.* Anthony Patrick Thomson. *Career:* Mem. of Stock Exchange 1935–51; Vice-Chmn., Mental Health Foundation. Served in World War II (mentioned in despatches). *Publications:* Pictorial Souvenirs of Britain (David & Charles); Consulting Editor of Pictorial Souvenirs and Commemoratives of North America (Dutton). *Clubs:* Bath, City University, M.C.C. (all of London). *Address:* Pond House, Crawley, nr. Winchester, Hants; and *office* Cayzer House, 2 and 4 St. Mary Axe, London, E.C.3.

**HENDERSON, James McInnes.** Attorney. Private practice; former General Counsel, Federal Trade Commission of the United States. *B.* 1911. *Educ.* Univ. of Texas, and George Washington Univ. (JD 1938). *M.* 1954, Marie B. York. *S.* John McInnes, James Craig and William Morgan. *Dau.* Mary Gainer. *Career:* Special Asst. to the Attorney-General 1938–46; Legal Adviser to General McArthur, Supreme Commander for Allied Powers, Tokyo, Jan.–Dec. 1946; Philippine Alien Property Administrator 1947–51; General Counsel, Economic Stabilization Agency 1951; Director, Rent Stabilization for U.S. 1951–52; private practice of law 1952–58; General Counsel, Government Activities Cttee., House of Representatives 1958–61; General Counsel, Federal Trade Comm. 1961–69. *Publications:* Contributions to various law journals. *Member:* American and Federal Bar Associations; American Judicature Society; Delta Theta Phi; Hon. Legal Fraternity, Democrat. *Club:* National Lawyers. *Address:* Upper Horse Valley Farms, Upper Strasborg, Pa., U.S.A.

**HENDERSON, Joseph Harrison, Jr.** American. *B.* 1909. *Educ.* Louisiana State Univ. (LLB). *M.* 1945, Constance Randolph Wilbur. *S.* Joseph Harrison III. *Daus.* Constance Randolph and Ann Clothilde. *Career:* Pres. Henderson Oil Co., Bosko Oil Co., La Cable T.V. Inc., National Cable Co. and St. Landry Cable T.V. Inc. Pres.: LSU Alumni Assn., and LSU Foundation. *Member:* Rapides Parish, Louisiana, and Amer. Bar Assn., and Amer. Judicature Socy.; Phi Delta Phi (Hon. Legal Socy.), Sigma Alpha Epsilon; Knights of Justice; Louisiana Land Marks Socy.; New Eng. Histl. and Genealogical Socy.; Louisiana Historical Socy.; Amer. Numismatic Socy.; Mid-Continent Oil & Gas Assn. Democrat. *Clubs:* Petroleum, New Orleans Country, Lake Wood Golf and Country (all New Orleans); Alexandria (La.) Golf & Country; So Big Hunting Lodge; The Coastal; Duck (Cameron Parish, La.); Louisiana Sports Assn.; Elks. *Address:* 2612 Marye Street, Alexandria, La.; and *office* P.O. Box 1907, Alexandria, La., U.S.A.

**HENDERSON, Sir Nicholas,** GCMG. British ambassador. *B.* 1919. *Educ.* Stowe School; Hertford Coll. Oxford. Hon. Fellow 1974. *M.* 1951, Mary Barber Cawadias. *Dau.* 1. *Career:* served Minister of State's Office, Cairo 1942–43; Asst. Private Secy. to the Foreign Secy. 1944–47; H.M. Embassy Washington 1947–49; Athens 1949–50; Permanent Under-Secy. Dept. Foreign Office 1950–53; Embassy Vienna 1953–56, Santiago 1956–59; Northern Dept. Foreign Office 1959–62; Perm. Under-Secy's Dept. 1962–63; Head Northern Dept. 1963; Private Secy. to the Secy. of State, Foreign Affairs 1963–65; Minister in Madrid 1965–69; H.M. Ambassador to Poland 1969–72 to Federal Republic of Germany 1972–75, and to France since 1975. *Publications:* Prince Eugen of Savoy (biography), various stories and articles. *Clubs:* Brooks's. *Address:* British Embassy, 35 Rue du Faubourg, St. Honore, Paris 8, France; School House, Combe, nr. Newbury, Berks.

**HENKEL, Erich.** Dr.-Ing. German. *B.* 1922. *Educ.* studied chemistry at the Technical Univ., Berlin-Charlottenburg; took degree 1952. *Career:* Joined BASF 1952. Dir. 1964, Deputy Member, Board of Exec. Directors, 1966. Member of the Board since 1968. Member, Board of Exec. Directors, BASF Aktiengesellschaft, Ludwigshafen am Rhein. *Address:* c/o BASF Aktiengesellschaft, Ludwigshafen am Rhein, Germany.

**HENLE, Günter,** Dr. jur., Dr. phil. h.c. German businessman. *B.* 1899. *Educ.* Dr. jur. Universities of Würzburg and Marburg. *M.* 1933, Anne-liese Küpper. *S.* 2. *Dau.* 1. *Career:* In German diplomatic service (Auswärtiges Amt, Berlin; Holland, Argentine, Brazil, United Kingdom) 1921–35; Partner & General Manager, Klöckner & Co., Duisburg 1937–76, Partner with limited liability. 1977—. Hon Chairman: Klöckner-Werke AG, Duisberg; Klöckner-Humboldt-Deutz AG, Köln; ALLIANZ Versicherungs AG, München. Founder and owner of G. Henle Musik Verlag, München 1947. *Member:* Frankfurter, Wirtschaftsrat (Frankfort Economic Council) 1947–49, Bundestag (Bonn) 1949–53 (Christian Democratic Union), and Common Assembly, European Coal & Steel Community, Strasbourg 1952–53. President, German Society for Foreign Politics, Bonn, 1955, Hon. Pres. since 1973. Author of his biography ('Weggenosse des Jahrhunderts') and its Amer. Trans. (Three Spheres) Regnery, Chicago and various publications. *Club:* Niederrheinischer Golf, Duisberg (Hon. Pres.). *Address:* Klöcknerhaus, Duisburg, Germany.

**HENLEY, Dr. William Ballentine.** American educationalist and member of the Bar, Religious leader and rancher. *B.* 19 Sept. 1905. *Educ.* University of Southern California (AB, AM, MSPA, JD) Willamette University (LLD Hon.), Kansas City College of Osteopathy and Surgery (ScDHon.); Los Angeles College of Optometry (LHD Hon.); Pepperdine College (ScD Hon.). *M.* 1942, Helen McTaggart. *Career:* Director of Coordination, University of Southern California, 1936–40; Acting Dean, School of Government, University of Southern California; 1936–38; Associate Professor, Public Administration, Univ. of S. California (and Dir. of In-Service Governmental Training, Civic Centre Division) 1938–40; Pres., Los Angeles Rotary Club 1955–56 (Vice-Pres. 1954–55); Guest Observer, U.N. Conf., San Francisco 1945; Pres., California College of Medicine, Los Angeles, Calif. 1940–65; Provost, Univ. of Calif., Irvine Calif. Coll. of Medicine 1965—. Member, Board of Water and Power Commissioners, City of Los Angeles 1944–62; of many learned societies and the California, American and Los Angeles Bar Associations. Past Pres., Amer. Assn. of Osteopathic Colls.; member, International Platform Assn.; Pres. Western Dvsn. 1950–51; Chairman, Rotary Conf., Dist. 160-A; Gov., District 528, Rotary Int. 1959–60; member, Legislative Council, Rotary International 1959–61 (and Community Service Consultative Group 1960–61); Chairman Host, Club Executive Committee, Rotary International, 1962 Convention; R.I. President's Representative in India, Israel and England 1964. *Member:* Rotary Internatl. World Community Cttee. 1966–67; Amer. Assn. for the Advancement of Science; Amer. Management Assn.; Amer. Assn. for History of Medicine; Amer. Acad. of Political and Social Science; Defense Orientation Conference Assn.; American Inst. of Management; Board of Governors, Welfare Federation of Los Angeles area, operating the Community Chest; of the Board of Glendale Community Hospital; Vice Pres. Los Angeles Safety Council 1971—. Member, Board of Directors, Southern California Cancer Center; Calif. member, Western Inter-State Commission on Higher Education 1961–70; member, General Motors Corporation Speakers' Bureau. President, United Church of Religious Science, 1969—. *Publication:* History of the University of South California; Man's Great Awakening (Beautiful Mud) 1974. *Address:* 3251-West 6th Street, Los Angeles, Calif. 90020; and (Owner Operator) Creston Circle Ranch, Paso Robles, Calif., U.S.A.

**HENNESSY, Sir Patrick.** *B.* 18 April 1898. *Educ.* Christ Church School, Cork, Eire. *M.* 1923, Dorothy Margaret Davis (*D.* 1949). *S.* 2. *Dau.* 1. *Career:* Chmn. Henry Ford & Son, Ltd., Cork 1955—; (successively assembler, road representative, service manager and production manager 1920–31) with Ford Motor Co. Ltd., Dagenham (successively Purchase Manager, General Manager and Director) 1931–48; Managing Director 1948–57; Deputy Chairman 1950–56; Chairman 1956–68; formerly member, Advisory Cncl., Min of Aircraft Production. Chairman, Henry Ford & Son Ltd., Cork, 1955—; Director, Montego Freeport Ltd. Jamaica. President, Society of Motor Manufacturers & Traders Ltd. 1965 and 1966; Deputy President 1967 and 1968. *Address:* 'Larkmead', TheydonBo is, Essex.

**HENNIKER-MAJOR, Hon. Sir John (Patrick Edward Chandos)** KCMG, CVO, MC. *B.* 1916. *Educ.* Stowe School and Trinity College, Cambridge (BA). *M.* (1) 1946, Margaret Osla Benning (dec'd.). *S.* 2. *Dau.* 1. (2) 1976, Julia Marshall Poland. *Career:* Entered H.M. Foreign Office and Diplomatic Service (3rd Secretary) 1938; served in World War II (Rifle Brigade; Western Desert; wounded 1942; and Military Mission to Yugoslavia). Army major, The Rifle Brigade 1940–45; H.M. Embassy, Belgrade 1945–46; Assistant Private Secretary, Secretary of State for Foreign Affairs 1946–48; Foreign Office 1948–50; 1st Secy. (Head of Chancery) Buenos Aires 1950–52; Assistant (1952), and Head of Personnel, Foreign Office 1953–60; Ambassador to Jordan 1960–62; to Denmark, 1962–66; Civil Service Commission, 1966–67; Asst. Under-Secy. of State F.O. 1967–68. Director-General of British Council, 1968–72; Dir. Wates Foundation since 1972. *Club:* Special Forces Club (London). *Address:* The Red House, Thornham Magna, Eye, Suffolk.

**HENNING, John Francis.** American diplomat. *B.* 1915. *Educ.* St Mary's College, California (BA). *M.* 1939, Marguerite M. Morand. *S.* John F., Jr., Brian H., Patrick W., Daniel M., and Thomas R. *Daus.* Nancy R. and Mary T. *Career:* Director, California State Dept. of Industrial Relations 1959–62; U.S. Under-Secretary of Labor 1962–67; Ambassador to New Zealand 1967–74. Hon. LLD, St. Anselm's Coll. (Manchester, N.H.) 1965; DScCom., St. Bonaventure (N.Y.) Univ. 1966. *Awards:* St. Mary's Coll. Alumni Assn. Alumnus of the Year Award 1959; Univ. of San Francisco 1961; St. John Francis Regis Award for distinguished service in field of labor-management relations, and 1966 Berlin Award from Inst. of Industrial Relations for similar outstanding services; Los Angeles Catholic Labor Inst. Distinguished Public Service Award, 1962; The John F. Henning Perpetual Histadrut Scholarship Fund for Under-privileged Children of Israel, February 1963, under joint auspices of Los Angeles Fed. of Labor, AFL-CIO and American Trade Union Council for Israel; Most Distinguished Citizen Award, Mexican-American Political Assn. of California, 1966. Democrat. *Address:* c/o Department of State, Washington, D.C. 20520, U.S.A.

**HENNINGS, John Dunn,** CMG, MA. British diplomat. *B,* 1922. *Educ.* Ipswich School; University Coll. Oxford. *M.* 1953, Joanna Anita Reed. *S.* 2. *Career:* Royal Air Force. Flt. Lieut. 1942–45; Joined British Civil Service 1947; Foreign Office and Berlin (Special Asst. to the Financial Adviser) 1947–49; Asst. Principal Colonial Office 1949–51; Principal 1951–53; West African Inter-Territorial Secretariat Accra 1953–55; Principal, Colonial Office 1956–60; Colonial Attaché, British Embassy Washington 1960–63; Counsellor H.M. Diplomatic Service, London 1963–66; Head British Residual Office, Salisbury, S. Rhodesia 1966–68; Head, Chancery British High Commission New Delhi India 1968–72; Acting High Commissioner, Kampala Uganda 1972—; British High Commissioner, Jamaica and H.M. Ambassador (Non-Resident) in Haiti 1973–76; Asst. Under-Sec. of State, FCO 1976; High Commissioner, Singapore since 1977. *Awards:* Companion, Most Distinguished Order of St. Michael and St. George; Master of Arts, Oxford University. *Clubs:* Travellers. *Address:* c/o FCO, Downing Street, London, S.W.1.

**HENRIKSEN, Finn Benjamin.** Norwegain. banker. *B.* 1918. *Educ.* Graduated in Law 1945. *M.* 1948, Anna-Margrete Lyssand. *Daus.* 3. *Career:* Joined Bergens Privatbank 1937; practised as Deputy Judge 1946–47; Legal Consultant Bergens Privatbank 1949–59; Chief General Manager, Bergens Sparebank 1959–64; General Manager, Bergens Privatbank 1964, Man. Dir. since 1968. from 1975 in Bergen Bank. Member Bd., Norwegian Bankers' Association, Chmn. 1969–72; A/S Eksportfinans, Oslo, Chmn. since 1974; Scandinavian Bank Ltd. London; Scandinavian Far East Ltd., Hong Kong; Banque Scandinave en Suisse, Geneva; Bergen Bank International S.A., Luxembourg, Chmn. since 1976. *Award:* Knight 1st Class St. Olav's Order. *Address:* Fjellveien 133, N-5000 Bergen; and *office:* Torgalmenning 2, Bergen, Norway.

**HENRIKSEN, Hans Chr.** Managing Director, Norwegian-America Line, Oslo (and affiliated companies). *B.* 1909. *Educ.* Matric. 1927; Univ. of Neuchatel (Lic.-es-sc. econ. et com.) 1931; London 1931–32. *M.* 1934, Agnes Cecilie Egeberg. *S.* Hans Gustav. *Career:* Chmn. Bd. of Governors, Oslo Stock Exchange, and Norsk Marconi Co.; Member of Board A/S Meraker Smelteverk; Electric Furnace Products Co. Ltd.; A/S Saudefaldene; Assuranceforeningen Skuld; Det. Norske Livsforsikringesselskap Fram A/S; Polaris Assuranceselskap A/S; Akers Mek. Verksted; Nylands Verksted; Christania Bank og Kreditkasse; Den Norske Krigsforsikring for Skib; joined Norwegian-American Line in Oslo 1933; Asst. Manager, N.A.L., Inc., New York 1934–39; Asst. Manager, Oslo 1939; Director 1947; Managing Director 1948. *Awards:* Knight, Orders of St. Olav and Vasa; Officer, Order of Orange-Nassau; Officer, Legion of Honour; Commander Mérite Nationale (France). *Address:* Ths. Heftyes gate 38; and *office* Den norske Amerikalinje A/S Jernbanetorvet 2, Oslo.

**HENRIKSEN, Rein.** Norwegian. *B.* 1915. *M.* Cecilie Eger. *S.* 2. *Dau.* 1. *Career:* Pres. & Chief Exec. Officer, Dir. Aktieselskapet Borregaard, Dir. of Subsidiaries. *Awards:* Knight, Order of St. Olav, Norway; Grand Cross, Order for Services to Austrian Republic; Commander, Homayon Order, Iran. *Address:* Borregaard Hovedgard, Sarpsborg, Norway.

**HENRY, Hugh Fort.** Physicist. B.,1916. *Educ.* Emory & Henry Coll. (BA, BS 1936); Univ. of Virginia (PhD-Physics 1940). *M.* 1942, Emmaline Rust. *S.* Hugh Littell, Howell George and Harold William. *Dau.* Margaret Fort. *Career:* Head, Safety Fire and Radiation Control Dept., Oak Ridge Gaseous Diffusion Plant, Union Carbide Nuclear Co. 1949–61; Assoc. Prof. of Physics, Univ. of Georgia 1941–49; Head, Dept. of Physics and Mathematics, College of the Ozarks 1940–41. U.S. Delegate to TC-85, International Standards Organization 1958, 1960 and 1965. Chairman, Dept. of Physics, DePauw University Sept. 1961—; Pres. Indiana Section, Amer, Assn. of Physics Teachers; Pres. Bd. Dirs. Central States Universities Inc., 1967; Vice Chmn. Amer. Standards Assn. Committee No. 7, 'Radiation Protection' (Chairman, Sub-committee No. 7-3; member, Sub-committees N-7.2 and N-6.8); Consultant, Union Carbide Corp.; Goodyear Atomic Corp.; U.S. Atomic Energy Commission. *Member·* Amer. Physical Socy.; Amer. Assn. of Physics Teachers; Amer. Nuclear Socy.; Health Physics Socy.; Amer. Assn. for Advancement of Science; Sigma Xi. Pres., Board of Directors, Central States Universities. *Publications:* TID-7019, Guide to Shipment of U-235 Enriched Materials; K-1380, Studies in Nuclear Safety, K-1019, Criticality Data and Nuclear Safety Guide Applicable to ORGDP; articles in several scientific and technical journals, including Chap. 3-2 in Progress in Nuclear Safety, Series IV, Vol. 3; Fundamentals of Radiation Protection (1969). *Clubs:* Rotary (Pres.); Elks. *Address:* 404 Linwood Drive, Greencastle; and Department of Physics, DePauw University, Greencastle, Ind., U.S.A.

**HENRY, Rene Paul.** American. Financial Consultant, Tulsa Okla. *B.* 1917. *Educ.* Baylor University (BA 1937), University of Texas (LLB 1940), and Harvard University Graduate Schl. of Business Administration (IA 1943). *M.* 1939, Ernestine Ryan. *S.* Rene Paul, Jr. *Daus.* Mary Louise and Grace Christine. *Career:* Attorney, Office of Chief Counsel, Bureau of Internal Revenue, Washington, D.C. 1946–49; Treasurer, Tax Counsel, Mid-Continent Petroleum Corp., Tulsa 1949–55; Vice-Pres., Financial and Dir., D-X Sunray Oil Co., Tulsa 1955–58; Vice-Pres. Financial, Treasurer and Dir., Sunray Mid-Continent Oil Co., Tulsa 1958–62. Senior Vice-Pres., Treasurer, and Director, Sunray DX Oil Co., Tulsa, 1962–64, Senior Vice-Pres. of Finance & Planning and Dir., 1964–68; Director & Vice President Sun Co., Philadelphia, 1969–71. *Member:* Amer. Petroleum Inst.; American, Oklahoma, Texas Bar Assn.; Southwestern Legal Foundation; Amer. Bar Assn.; Independent Petroleum Assn. of America. *Address:* 2113 E.60 Street, Tulsa, Okla., U.S.A. and *office:* 710 Philtower Bldg., Tulsa, Okla,. U.S.A.

**HENRY, Rodney Wilton,** CBE. British. *B.* 1915. *Educ.* Ormond College, Univ. of Melbourne (BSc). *M.* 1941, Margaret Rouvray Kirton. *S.* Roger John Wilton and Peter James. *Daus.* Denita Jayne and Sabrina Rouvray. *Career:* Engaged at Technical Development Dept., I.C.I. (Australia) 1938–45; General Manager Australian Newsprint Mills Ltd. Tasmania 1947–62, Managing Dir. since 1962. *Publications:* contributions to trade and technical journals. *Member:* Australian and N.Z. Pulp and Paper Assn. (Pres. 1958–59); pulp and paper advisory committee, FAO, Rome 1960—: Tasmanian University Council 1962—, Dep. Chancellor since 1972; T.A.P.P.I.; Nat. Pres. National Safety Council Australia since 1973; Aust.-Britain Socy. Dep. Pres. since 1973; Mem. Economic Advisory Group, Federal Govt. 1976. *Clubs:* Australian (Melbourne); Tasmanian, Athenaeum (Hobart); M.C.C. *Address:* Derwent Terrace, New Norfolk, Tasmania; and *office* A.N.M. Ltd., Boyer, Tasmania.

**HENTY, The Hon. Sir Norman Henry Denham.** *B.* 1903. *Educ.* Launceston (Tasmania) Church of England Grammar School. *M.* 1930, Faith Gordon Spotswood. *S.* 2. *Dau.* 1. *Career:* Managing Dir. T. Norman Henty Pty. Ltd. 1937–50; Alderman Launceston City Council 1943–49; Mayor 1948–49; Senator Commonwealth Parliament 1950–68; Chairman, Commonwealth Public Works Cttee. 1956; J.P. (Tasmania) 1957; Minister for Customs and Excise 1956–64; for Civil Aviation 1964–66; for Supply 1966–68; Leader of the Government in the Senate 1966–67; Commission Overseas Telecommunications Commission since 1968. *Member:* Liberal Party. *Clubs:* Tasmanian (Hobart), Launceston, Northern (Launceston). *Address:* 11 Beaulah Gardens, Launceston, 7250 Tasmania Australia.

**HEPPEL, Richard Purdon,** CMG. Retired. British diplomat. *B.* 2 Oct. 1913. *Educ.* Rugby School, Balliol College, Oxford

(1st Cl. Classical Mods, 2nd Cl. *Litt. Hum., prox. acc.* Craven and de Paravicini Scholarships and Gaisford Greek Verse Prize) and Queen's College, Oxford (Laming Travelling Fellow). *M.* 1949, Ruth Theodora Matthews. *S.* 2. *Dau.* 1. *Career:* Entered Diplomatic Service 1936; Third Secretary, Rome 1939–40; Foreign Office 1940–42; Second Secretary, Teheran 1942–44; First Secretary, Athens 1945–46; Secretary, U.K. Delegation to U.N. Assembly 1947; First Secretary, Karachi 1948; Madrid 1951; Counsellor, Saigon 1953; Ambassador at Phnom Penh, 1954; Minister at Vienna 1956; Head of South East Asia Dept., Foreign Office 1959; Imperial Defence College 1960; Head of Consular Department 1961–63; Consul-General at Stuttgart 1963–69; Admin. Officer, Grad. Business Centre, The City Univ. 1969–70: Appeals Secy. Cancer Research Campaign since 1970. *Address:* Barn Piece, Nether Winchenden, Aylesbury, Bucks; and Lacona 43, Isola d'Elba, Italy.

**HEPWORTH, William Roy.** Australian. *B.* 1921. *M.* Noelle Wynifred Turnbull. *S.* Ian William and David Andrew. *Career:* Managing Director, The United Distillers Pty. Ltd., Port Melbourne, Vic. Director: The Distillers Corp. Pty. Ltd. Founder, Victorian Field and Game Association. *Clubs:* Athenaeum, Naval & Military, Toorak Services, Melbourne Cricket, Huntingdale Golf, Barwon Heads Golf, Victoria Racing, Victoria Amateur Turf, Moonee Valley Racing, Melbourne Racing; Royal Melbourne Tennis. *Address:* 124 Kooyong Road, Caulfield, Vic., Australia; and *office* United Distillers Pty Ltd., P.O. 132, Port Melbourne 3207.

**HERBERT, Hon. John Desmond,** MLA. Australian. Minister Queensland State Government, *B.* 1925. *M.* 1948, Yvonne May Cranston. *S.* 5. *Career:* Appointed to Cabinet 1965; Min. for Community Welfare Services and Min. for Sport; Past Pres. National Trust of Queensland; Liberal Party of Australia (Queensland Div.). *Address:* 22 Randolph Street Graceville, Brisbane, Qld.; and *office* Second Floor, Legacy House, Mary Street, Brisbane, Qld., Australia.

**HERBISON, (Miss) Margaret McCrorie.** British. MA, Hon. LLD. Lord High Commissioner to General Assembly, Church of Scotland, 1970–71, Lay Observer since 1976. *B.* 1907. *Educ.* Bellshill Acad. and Glasgow University (MA). *Career:* Under-Secretary of State for Scotland February 1950–October 1951. Minister of Pensions and National Insurance, Oct. 1963–67. Minister of Social Security 1966–67; Mem. of Royal Commission on Standards of Conduct in Public Life 1974–76. *Member:* Glasgow Graduates Assoc. *Address:* 61 Shottskirk Road, Shotts, Lanarkshire.

**HERBOSCH, Antoine Pierre Elise.** Belgian Administrator of Companies. *B.* 1902. *Educ.* Classical studies and degree in Commercial and Consular Science. *M.* 1929, Jenny Ceurremans. *Career:* Consul General of Monaco; Commissioner-General of Monaco at Brussels International Exhibition 1958; Secretary-Treasurer Consular Corps of Antwerp; Hon. Censor National Bank of Belgium; Hon. Judge Trade Tribunal; Administrator Royal Society for Encouragement of Fine Arts; Pres. Peter Benoit Fund; Pres. Music Commission of the Royal Society for Zoology of Antwerp; Vice-Pres. Cttee for the Patrimony of the Royal Conservatory for Music of Antwerp. *Awards:* Commander Orders of Leopold II; of St. Charles; of Grimaldi; of the National Merit (Italy); of St. Sylvester and the Sovereign Order of Malta. Grand Officer Order of St. Sava. Officer of the Crown (Belgium); of the National Merit (France). Chevalier Order of Leopold. Hon. Dean of Works Inland Navigation. *Clubs:* Royal Society Concorde and Philotaxe. *Address:* Jan Van Rijswijcklaan 26, B-2000 Antwerp, Belgium.

**HERD, John Victor.** American company director. *B.* 1902. *Educ.* Public Schools in Milwaukee, Kansas City and St. Louis. *M.* 1937, Pauline Hoffman. *Daus.* Pauline and Victoria. *Career:* Exec. duties America Fore Insurance Group 1927–30, Secy., Vice-Pres. 1942, Exec. Vice-Pres. & Dir. since 1956; Vice-Pres. & Dir., Fire Assn. of Philadelphia 1930–42. Chairman, The Continental Corpn. and The Continental Insurance Companies (formerly known as America Fore Loyalty Group) 1957–71. Director: The Security Reinsurance Corp. Ltd. (Bermuda) Ltd.; London Guarantee & Reinsurance Co. Ltd.; Tishman Realty & Construction Co. Inc. *Member:* N.Y. Advisory Board, The Salvation Army. *Clubs:* Downtown Association, The Links, The Union League (all of N.Y.C.); Arcola Country (N.J.). *Address: office* 80 Maiden Lane, New York City 10038, U.S.A.

**HEREIL, Georges Jules Bernard Victor.** French. *B.* 1909. *Educ.* Doctor in Law. *M.* 1939, Fernande Gilot. *Career:* Hon. Judicial Liquidator on Commercial Tribunal of the Seine. Hon. President: Sud-Aviation, Union of Aeronatic Industries, Moroccan Aviation, La Chapelle Paper Works, Lehman Brothers International. Founder Pres. of A.E.C.M.A.S. Presiding Director-General, Chrysler France, 1963–71; Former Vice-Pres.: Chrysler International; Hon. Pres. since 1971. Member of the Board, Chrysler España, Dec. Vice-President du Conseil de Surveillance Hewlett Packard France. Président du Conseil de Surveillance de la Société Agache-Willot. *Awards:* Cmndr.; Legion of Honour, Order of National Economy, of Touristic Merit, and of French Courtesy; Gold Medal of Advancement of Progress, Research and Invention Medal; Comdr.: Order of Merit (Italy), Vasa (Sweden), White Rose (Finland), Orange-Nassau (Netherlands), Merit (German Fed. Repub.) and of Crown (Belgium). *Publications:* Revue Générale du Droit des Faillites et des Etudes Pratiques de Droit Commercial. *Clubs:* Des Cent; Automobile (France). *Address:* 9B Plateau de Frontenex, Geneva, Switzerland.

**HERFORD, Harold Neale,** ED, JP. Australian executive. *B.* 1904. *Educ.* Cleveland Street Inter. High School and Technical High School, Sydney; P.S.C. (Duntroon 1944). *M.* 1928, Laurel Bancroft. *S.* Harold Graham. *Dau.* Margaret Laurel (Harris). *Career:* Army Service: part-time 1924–40, full-time 1940–45; R. of O. 1945–54; Colonel 1942; Director, Herfords Pty. Ltd. 1932–74 (Herfords Holdings Pty Ltd. since 1947; President: Leathergoods and Allied Trades Assn. of N.S.W. 1934–38, 1947–49; Federal Council of Leathergoods Manufacturers of Australia 1946–56; Rotary Club (Ashfield, N.S.W.) 1957–58; Vice-Pres., State Industrial Leather Advisory Committee 1949–55. *Member:* Commonwealth Reconstruction Training Scheme 1946–50; Federal Council of Leathergoods Manufacturers of Australia (Pres. 1946–56); State Apprenticeship Council (Leather) 1946–61; Pres., Chamber of Manufacturers of N.S.W. 1961–63; Dir., Manufacturers Mutual Insurance Ltd. since 1963. Hon. Treasurer, Associated Chambers of Manufactures of Australia 1962–70, Pres. 1970–71. *Clubs:* Imperial Service; Killara Golf. *Address:* 564 Pacific Highway, Killara, N.S.W., Australia.

**HERINGTON, Gordon Ross.** Canadian. *B.* 1914. *Educ.* Victoria Coll. Univ. of Toronto (BA; CA). *M.* 1949, Marjory Lindsay Torrance. *S.* Gordon Ross. *Dau.* Heather Louise Watt. *Career:* Vice-Pres.: Rootes Motors (Canada) Ltd. and Rootes Motors Inc. U.S.A. 1948–50, and A.R. Williams Machinery Co. Ltd. 1950–54. Secy-Treas. and subsequently Vice-Pres. and President, 1954–69, Corby Distilleries Ltd. With Price Waterhouse & Co. (Chartered Accountants), 1936–41, 1945–46, and Paris (France) 1946–48. President, Association of Canadian Distillers, 1970–74; Pres. and Chief Exec. Officer, Melchers Distilleries Ltd. 1975–76, Dep. Chmn. 1976—. *Member:* Canadian Inst. of Chartered Accountants; Inst. of Chartered Accountants of Ontario; Royal Commonwealth Society; Newcomen Society. Life Governor, Montreal General Hospital. Dir., Zellar Foundation; Dir. United Church Homes for Elderly People, Montreal 1970—(Pres. 1974–75). *Clubs:* Mount Stephen; Royal Montreal Golf. *Address:* 250 Laird Boulevard, Montreal, Quebec H3R 1Y2; and *office* 56 Fundy, Place Bonaventure, Montreal H5A 1R1.

**HERLIN, Heikki Hugo.** Finnish company director. *B.* 7 Feb. 1901. *Educ.* Technological University of Helsinki (grad. Mech. Engineer; Councillor of Mining). *M.* 1930, Anna Maria Oittinen. *S.* 1. *Daus.* 3. *Career:* Employed by various American companies 1927–28; Dep.-Production Manager, Kone ja Siltarakennus Oy 1928–32; Manager, Emali Osakeyhtiö 1932–43; Chairman, Kone Osakeyhtiö, Helsinki. *Awards:* Commander of the Order of Finnish Lion; Cross of the Order of the Cross of Liberty, 3rd and 4th Class; Knight of the Order of White Rose of Finland, 1st Class; Medal of the Order of the Cross of Liberty, 2nd Class (all Finnish Orders). Grand Cross Order of Yugoslav. Flag and Cross (2nd Class); Grand Officer, Ordre de la Republique Tunisienne; Hon. Doctorate, Rostock Univ. 1969. *Address:* Munkkiniemen Kartano, Helsinki 33, Finland.

**HERMON, Richard,** BSc, FICE. British. *B.* 1912. *Educ.* The Edinburgh Academy; Univ. of Edinburgh (BSc Hons Civil Eng.). *S.* 1. *Daus.* 3. *Career:* Resident Partner Sir Alexander Gibb & Partners (Africa) 1950–57; Jt. Man. Dir. Butterley Co. Ltd. 1957–63; Man. Dir. 1963–66; Dir. Nat. Council of Building Material Producers, Building Materials Export Group. *Member:* French Socy. Civil Engineers. *Fellow:* American Socy. of Civil Engineers. *Address:* Langar House, Langar, Notts. and *office* 26 Store St., London WC1E 7BT.

**HERNBERG, Gunnar (Robert Alarik).** General Manager, Finnish Sugar Corporation. *B.* 1904. *Educ.* MA 1928; MSc (Eng) 1932; Major 1941. *M.* 1932, Helmi Charpentier. *S.* 1. *Dau.* 1. *Career:* Chemist, Töölö works of the Finnish Sugar Corp. 1926 (Local Director 1946); Member of Board of Managers, Finnish Sugar Corporation 1947; Managing Director 1948; Director-General 1949—, and Chairman of the Board of Mgrs. 1953–70. Pres., Federation of Finnish Industries 1955–60; Pres., Foodstuff Industries Assn. 1954; Vice-Pres., Fnd. for the Promotion of Technology 1949; Vice-Pres., Board of Directors, Finnish Employers' General Group 1954; Pres., Rationalization Bureau 'Oy Rastor Ab' 1950–60; Pres., Foundation for Productivity Research 1953; Pres., Board of Managers, Naantali Raw Sugar Works (Juurikassokeri Oy) 1951, and of the Kotka Raw Sugar Works (Itä-Suomen Raakasokeritehdas Oy) 1951; Vice-Pres., Board of Managers, Turenki Sugar Works (Turengin Sokeritehdas Oy) 1948, and of the Salo Raw Sugar Works (Salon Sokeritehdas Oy) 1954; Vice-Pres. Cttee. European des Fabr de Suere 1969–70. *Publications:* numerous lectures on technical, industrial and economic subjects. *Awards:* Cross of Liberty (3rd and 4th Cl.); Commander, Order of the Lion of Finland; Cross of the St. Olav Order of Norway. Commander, Order of Vasa. *Address:* Saunalahdentie, Helsinki 33, Finland.

**HERRERA, Felipe.** Chilean. *B.* 1922. *Educ.* University of Chile (Degree in Law and Social Sciences); London School of Economics. *M.* 1961, Ines Olmo de Herrera. *S.* 1. *Career:* Legal Department, Central Bank of Chile 1943–47; Attorney for Bank and Law Practice 1947–52; Under-Secretary of Economy and Commerce of Chile 1952; Minister of Finance, 1953; General Manager, Central Bank of Chile, 1953–58; Executive Dir., Internat. Monetary Fund, 1958–60; Exec. Dir. International Monetary Fund Rep. Argentina, Bolivia, Chile, Equador, Paraguay and Uruguay 1958–60; Pres. Inter-American Development Bank 1960–71; Consultant to UNESCO and member of its International Educational Commission; Vice-Chairman UNITAR'S Board of Trustees; Member of Organizational Cttee U.N. University; International Council Educational Development and International Inst. for Environmental Affairs; General Coordinator ECIEL Program (Joint Studies on Latin American Economic Integration). *Publications:* Central Bank of Chile; Economic Policy; Fundamentals of Fiscal Policy; Elements of Monetary Management; Latin America Integrated; Latin American Development and its Financing; Latin American Nationalism. *Awards:* Hon. degrees: Univ. of San Marcos, Lima; Nat. University of Asuncion; Amer. Univ. of Washington, D.C.; University of America, Bogota; Pittsburgh; Columbia; California; Los Angeles; Federal Univ. of Bahia, Brazil, San José (Costa Rica), Miami (Fla.), Clinton (NY), Chile. *Decorations:* Camilo Torres Gold Medal, Colombia; Great Cross for Dist. Service, Fed. Repub., Germany; Cavalier, Grand Cross, Italian Republic, Peru, Dominica, Nicaragua, Colombia, Brasil, Panama, Ecuador, Paraguay and Mexico. *Address:* Calle del Cerro 1991, Pedro de Valdivia, Norte Santiago, Chile.

**HERRIDGE, Geoffrey Howard,** CMG. British. *B.* 1904. *Educ.* The Crypt School, Gloucester, and St. John's College, Cambridge, MA (Cantab.). *M.* 1935, Dorothy Elvira Tod. *S.* Leslie Charles and Michael Geoffrey. *Daus.* Mary Christina and Elizabeth. Joined Turkish Petroleum Co. Ltd. (later Iraq Petroleum Co. Ltd.), Iraq 1926; served in Iraq, Jordan, Palestine 1926–47; General Manager in the Middle East, Iraq Petroleum Co. and Associated Companies 1947–51; Executive Director, London 1953–57, Managing Director 1957–63. Dep. Chmn. 1963–65. Director Ottoman Bank (London Committee), Mar. 1964—. Chmn. Petroleum Industry Training Board 1967–70; Chairman, Iraq Petroleum Co. and Associated Companies, Jan. 1965–70. *Fellow:* Royal Geographical Socy. *Club:* Oriental. *Address:* Flint, Sidlesham Common, Chichester, Sussex.

**HERRING, Lieut.-General Hon. Sir Edmund Francis,** KCMG, KBE, DSO, MC, ED, QC, KStJ. Australian administrator. *B.* 2 Sept. 1892. *Educ.* Melbourne Church of England Grammar School; 1912 Rhodes Scholar Victoria; Trinity College, University of Melbourne and New College, Oxford (MA, BCL) (Hon. DCL Oxford 1953. *M* .1922, Mary Ranken Lyle (MB, BS; DBE). *Daus.* 3. *Career:* Served in World War I, King Edward's Horse, R.F.A., B.E.F., in France and Macedonia 1914–19; called to Bar, Inner Temple 1920, Victoria 1921; Commander, Royal Artillery, 6th Australian Division A.I.F. 1939–41; Commanded 6th Australian Division A.I.F. 1941–42; G.O.C., Northern Territory Force 1942, New Guinea Force 1942–43, 1st Australian Corps 1942–44; Chancellor, Diocese of Melbourne 1941—: Chief Justice of the Supreme Court of Victoria 1944–64; Lieutenant-Governor of Victoria 1945–72; Leader of Australian Contingent to the Coronation 1953. Hon. Fellow, New College, Oxford; Military Cross (Greece) D.S.C. (U.S.A.). Chmn., Board of Management, Australian War Memorial, Canberra 1959–74; Hon. Bencher, Inner Temple 1963; Pres. Australian Boy Scouts Assn. 1959—; Hon. Doctor of Law Monash University 1973. *Address:* 226 Walsh Street, South Yarra, Victoria 3141, Australia.

**HERRMANN, Curt Rudolf,** Dr. Ing. German. *B.* 1917. *Educ* Deutsche Technische Hochschule, Brünn (Dipl. Ing.; Dr. Ing.). *M.* 1940, Emmi Baier. *Dau.* 1. *Career:* Vice-Pres. Demag AG; Member Bd. American DEMAG Corp., U.S.A.; Member Bd. (non-representative) Nichidoku Jukogyo Yugen Kaisha Japan; Chmn. Bd. Sidernaval Equipos Siderurgicos S.A., Spain; Member, Bd. Maschinenfabrik Briem-Hengler & Cronemeyer KG, Krefeld, Germany. *Member:* VDEH; British Iron & Steel Institute. *Address:* Kiefernweg 8, Duisburg, W. Germany.

**HERRON, Robert Henry Cowell,** T.D. British. *B.* 1909. *Educ.* Wrekin Coll. and Univ. of Newcastle (Armstrong Coll. in the Univ. of Durham); Solicitor of the Supreme Court (Hons. 1933). *M.* 1939, Lilian Mary Blench. *S.* 2. *Dau.* 1. *Career:* Asst. Solicitor with Watson Burton Booth & Robinson from 1935 until entering partnership in 1938; Senior Partner, Watson Burton, Solicitors and Notaries of Newcastle-upon-Tyne 1961, Consultant 1975. Chmn., Grainger Building Socy. Served in Territorial Army 1928–39, and then War Service until 1945 (Royal Artillery; rank Lt.-Col.). *Member:* The Law Society. *Clubs:* Constitutional (Newcastle-upon-Tyne); Royal Northumberland Yacht. *Address:* 27 Reid Park Road, Newcastle-upon-Tyne NE2 2ER; and *office* 20 Collingwood Street, Newcastle-upon-Tyne NE1 1LB.

**HERTZLER, John Rowe.** American management consultant. *B.* 1905. *Educ.* Lehigh University (Mech. Eng.); MA. 1962, University of Connecticut. *M.* 1944, Priscilla Bennett. *S.* Bennett, Timothy, Samuel and Daniel. *Career:* Deputy Secretary of Commerce of Pennsylvania 1955; Vice-Pres. and General Sales Mgr., York Corp., York, Pa. (manufacturers and contractors of air-conditioning and refrigeration plant) 1945–54; Member of Board of Directors of the Corp. 1951–54; Lieut.-Commander, U.S.N., assigned to the War Production Board (General Industrial Equipment Div.), Washington 1942–45. President, Hertzler Enterprises Inc., York, Pa. since 1954. *Publications:* School and Society—a Layman's Slant on Merit Rating in public education (1958); technical articles in Journal of American Society of Heating, Refrigerating and Air-Conditioning Engineers; numerous articles in trade magazines, electrical power journals, etc. Republican (candidate for Representative in Congress, Pennsylvania 19th Congressional District, May 1956). *Member:* Amer. Socy. Heating, Refrigerating and Air-Conditioning Engineers. *Clubs:* Rotary of Willimantic, Conn. (Pres.. 1963–64). *Address:* R.D. No. 1, Mansfield Centre, Conn. 06250, U.S.A.

**HERTZOG, Dr. Albert.** South African advocate. *B.* 4 July 1899. *Educ.* Stellenbosch University (BA); Oxford University (BCL); Leyden University (LLD). *M.* 1933, Katharine Marjorie Whiteley. *Career:* Member, Cncl. of Univ. of S. Africa 1936–39; member, Pretoria City Council 1944–51; MP (Nationalist), Ermelo 1948–70; Minister of Posts and Telegraphs, and of Health 1958–69; Leader Herstigte Nationale Party; Dir. Afrikanse Boubeleggings; Koopkrag Bank; Strydpers. *Publications:* Saaklike Reg en Eiendom. *Address:* 10 Edward Street, Waterkloof, Pretoria, South Africa.

**HERWARTH VON BITTENFELD, Hans Heinrich.** German diplomat. *B.* 1904. *Educ.* Universities of Berlin, Breslau and Munich (Law and Nat. Econ.). *M.* 1935, Elisabeth, Baroness von Redwitz. *Dau.* 1. *Career:* Entered Foreign Office 1927; Attaché Paris 1930; Second Secretary and Personal Secretary to Ambassador (Count von der Schulenburg). Moscow 1931–39; military service 1938–45; Government Counsellor, Director, Bavarian State Chancellery 1945–49; Ministerialdirigent and Chief of Protocol, Federal German Government 1950; appointed Minister Plenipotentiary 1952; Ambassador Ex. and Plen. to Court of St. James's, May 1955–Sept. 1961; State Secretary, Chief of the Office of the Federal President, Sept. 1961–March 1965. Ambassador to Republic of Italy, 1965–69. President, Commission for the Reform of the German Diplomatic Service, 1969–71; Pres. Goethe-Institute, Munich 1971–76. *Awards:*

Grand Cross 2nd Class, Order of Merit (Fed. Repub. Germany); Grand Cross Royal Victorian Order (U.K.) and other decorations. *Address:* 8000 München, 80 Menzelstr. 7, West Germany.

**HERZBERG, Gerhard.** Canadian physicist. *B.* 1904. *M.* 1929, Luise Oettinger (dec'd). *S.* 1. *Dau.* 1. (2) 1972 Monika Tenthoff. *Career:* Lectr. in Physics, Darmstadt Inst. of Tech. 1930–35; Res. Prof. of Physics, Univ. of Saskat. 1935–45; Prof. of Spectroscopy, Yerkesobservatory (Univ. of Chicago) 1945–48; Princ. Research Officer, Div. of Physics, Nat. Research Council of Canada 1948–49; Dir. Div. of Physics, NRC 1949–55; Dir. Div. of Pure Physics, NRC, 1955–69; Distinguished Research Scientist, Div. of Physics, NRC 1969–75; Dist. Research Scientist, Herzberg Inst. of Astrophysics, NRC, since 1975. *Fellow:* Royal Socy. of Canada, 1939 (Pres. 1966–67); Royal Socy. of London, 1951 Chemical Socy. of London (Hon.) 1968. *Member:* Pontifical Academy of Sciences 1965; (For. Associate) National Academy of Sciences Washington, 1968 and Royal Academy of Belgium 1974; Hon. mem., Japan Academy 1976. *Decorations:* Companion of the Order of Canada; Chancellor of Carleton Univ. Ottawa (since 1973). *Awards:* Henry Marshall Tory Medal, RSCan. (1953); Joy Kissen Mookerjee Gold Medal, IACS (1954); Gold Medal Can. Assn. of Physicists 1957; Medals of Univs of Liège and Brussels (1960); Frederick Ives Medal, Optical Socy. of Am. 1964; Willard Gibbs Medal, Am. Chemical Socy. 1969; Faraday Medal, Chem. Socy. of London, 1970; Royal Medal, Royal Socy. of London 1971; Linus Pauling Medal, Am. Chem. Socy. 1971; Nobel Prize in Chemistry 1971; Chem. Inst. of Canada Medal 1972; Many Hon. Degrees incl. DSc (Oxon) and ScD (Cantab.). *Publications:* Atomic Spectra and Atomic Structure (1937, 1944, also Russ. Ital. and Jap. trans.); Molecular Spectra and Molecular Structure; (1) Spectra of Diatomic Molecules (1939, 1950, also Russ. and Hung. trans.); (2) Infrared and Raman Spectra of Polyatomic Molecules (1945, also Russ. & Hung. trans.); (3) Electronic spectra and Electronic Structure of Polyatomic Molecules, (1966 and transl. Russ.); The Spectra and Structures of Simple Free Radicals: An Introduction to Molecular Spectroscopy (1971, also Germ. Russ. and Jap. trans.). *Address:* 190 Lakeway Drive, Ottawa, Ontario K1L 5B3, Canada; and *office* National Research Council of Canada, Ottawa, Ont. K1A OR6, Canada.

**HERZOG, Major General Chaim.** Israeli Lawyer & Diplomat. *B.* 1918. *Educ.* LLB, London Univ.; Barrister at Law, Lincoln's Inn; Advocate, Israel. *M.* 1947, Aura Ambache. *S.* 3. *Dau.* 1. *Career:* British Army, W.W. II, 1940–46; Israel Defence Forces (Dir. of Military Intelligence, Governor of the West Bank, various Field Commands) 1948–62; Managing Dir., Industrial Investment Group 1962–72; Senior Partner, Herzog Fox & Neeman, Advocates, Tel-Aviv 1962–75; Dir. of various Corporations, Banks, etc., and Commentator, Broadcaster and Writer in Israel and the UK, 1962–75; Perm. Rep. of Israel to the UN since 1975. *Member:* Honourable Society of Lincoln's Inn; International Ambassador, Variety International; Vice Chmn., World ORT Union, Geneva. *Decorations:* Hon. Knight Commander of the British Empire (KBE); Hon. Doctor of Literature, Yeshiva Univ., New York; S.Y. Agnon Medal, Hebrew Univ., Jerusalem; Hon. Doctor Hebrew Letters, Jewish Theological Seminary, New York; Hon. Doctor Laws, Bar Ilan Univ., Israel. *Publications:* Israel's Finest Hour (1967); Days of Awe (1973); The War of Atonement (1975); (Editor) Judaism, Law and Ethics (1974). *Clubs:* Harmonie, New York. *Address:* 800 2nd Avenue, New York, N.Y. 10017, U.S.A.

**HESELTINE, Michael Ray Didbin,** MP. *B.* 1933. *Educ.* Shrewsbury School; Pembroke Coll., Oxford, BA Second Class in Politics, Philosophy and Economics. *M.* 1962, Anne Harding Williams. *S.* 1. *Daus.* 2. *Career:* National Service (comm.) Welsh Guards 1959; Dir. Bow Publications 1961–65; Member, Parliament (Con.) Tavistock 1966–74; Henley-on-Thames since 1974; Opposition Spokesman, Transport 1969; Parly. Secy. Min. of Transport June–Oct. 1970; Parly. Under-Secy. of State 1970–72; Dept. of Environment 1970–72; Minister, Aerospace and Shipping 1972–74; Opposition Spokesman for Industry 1974–76. for the Environment since 1976. *Address:* Thenford House, nr. Banbury, Oxon.

**HESS, Walther.** Dr. jur. German diplomat. *B.* 12 Mar. 1900. *Educ.* High School, Frankfort-on-Main; Universities of Giessen, Tübingen, Munich and Göttingen. *M.* 1942, Johanna Schuhmann. *S.* Andreas, Helmut. *Daus.* Ingeborg, Anna-Elizabeth, Irene. *Career:* Attaché, Foreign Office 1925; Vice-Consul, Thorn 1927–28: Secretary of Legation, Kowno 1927–28; Vice-Consul. Jerusalem 1929–32; Secretary of Legation, Belgrade 1822–38; left Diplomatic Service 1938; Representative of the firm H. F. & Ph. F. Reemtsma (Hamburg) for Greece and Turkey 1938–45; re-entered Foreign Service 1950; Amb. Ex. and Plen. of the Federal Republic of Germany to Australia 1952–58; to Mexico 1958–60; Deputy Chief, Economic Division of the German Foreign Office 1960–62; Ambassador to Morocco 1962–65. *Address:* 8 München 60, Marsop-Str. 4, Germany.

**HESSELBACH, Walter,** (Dr. h. C.). German banker. *B.* 1915. *Educ.* Matriculation, 1 year Bank Acad., Berlin; apprenticeship in Banking. *M.* 1953, Hedwig Huth. *Daus.* 3. *Career:* In the period 1933–58, successively with Dreyfus & Co., Frankfurt; Deutsche Uberseeische Bank, Berlin; E. Merck, Chem. Fabrik, Darmstadt; Georg von Opel, Frankfurt, Army and P.O.W. 1940–47; Landeszentralbank von Hessen, Frankfurt (Member, Bd. of Managers 1952–58); Bank Deutscher Länder; President. (Vorsitzender des Vorstands), Bank für Gemeinwirtschaft Aktiengesellschaft, Frankfurt/M 1961–77; Town Councillor, City of Frankfurt, 1952–77; Pres. (Vorsitzender des Vorstandes) Beteiligungsgesellschaft fur Gemeinwirtschaft AG, Frankfurt/M; Chmn. Board of Directors, Allgemeine Hypotheken Bank, Deutsche Lufthansa AG, Köln, Bau und Handelsbank AG, Frankfurt & Israel-Continental Bank Ltd., Tel Aviv; Boswau & Knauer AG, Düsseldorf, Deputy-Chmn., Bank für Sparanlagen und Vermögensbildung AG, Frankfurt, RWE Rheinisch-Westfäl Elektrizitätswerke AG, Essen and Investitions-und Handlesbank, Frankfurt; Braunschweig-Hannoversche Hypothenbank, Hannover; Pres., Friedrich-Ebert-Foundation, Bonn and Deutsch-Israelische Wirtschaftsvereininigung eV. President of Board and Board of Administrators, International Co-operative Bank Ltd., Basel. *Member:* Board of Directors, Bank für Gemeinwirtschaft AG, August Thyssen-Hütte AG, Duisburg-Hamborn, Krupp GmbH, Essen; Volkswagen AG; Wolfsburg Salzgitter Hüttenwerk AG; Isrop Israel/European Comp. S.A.; and other Corporations. Chmn., Banking Cttee. of the International Cooperative Alliance, Chmn. Administrative Council P.T.T.F.R. of Germany. *Address:* Ginnheimer Stadtweg 148, 6-Frankfurt/Main; and *office* Mainzer Landstrasse 16–24, Frankfurt/Main, Germany.

**HETHERINGTON, Charles Ray.** Canadian oil company executive. *B.* 1919. *Educ.* University of Oklahoma (BS 1940; MS 1941); Massachusetts Institute of Technology (ScD 1943). *M.* (1) 1943, Jane Helen Childs. *S.* William Leslie II and Childs Pratt. *Daus.* Helen Jane and Gail Ann. (2) 1967, Rose Scurlock. *Career:* Research Engineer with Research and Development Dept. of Standard Oil Co. of California, and subsequently California Research Corp., Richmond, Calif., 1942; Engineer with Ford, Bacon & Davis Inc. Engineers, N.Y.C., engaged in professional consulting engineering with particular emphasis on petroleum and natural gas technology; Man. Dir. Pacific Petroleums Ltd. 1957; Pres. Cancrude Oil & Gas Co. Ltd. 1959—; President & Chief Exec-Officer, Panarctic Oils Ltd., formerly Vice-President, West-Coast Transmission Co. Ltd., 1967—; Charles R. Hetheringl ton & Co. Ltd., Consulting Engineers to the Oil and Gas Pipeline and Production Industry. President and/or Director of various subsidiary companies of Pacific Petroleums Ltd. *Publications:* numerous articles on the oil and gas industry. *Clubs:* Calgary Petroleum; Calgary Golf & Country, E' Dorado Country. *Address:* 2205 Amherst Street S.W., Calgary, Alberta; and *office* 703 6th Av. S.W., Calgary, Canada.

**HETTINGER, Albert J., Jr.** Investment banker. *B.* 1891. *Educ.* Stanford Univ. (BA; MA) and Harvard Univ. (PhD). *M.* 1929, Catherine Zirpoli. *S.* Albert John III. *Career:* Prof. Harvard Graduate School of Business Administration 1920–1926; Pres. Investment Research Corp. 1926–35; Vice-Pres. General American investors Corp. 1935–43; General Partner, Lazard Frères & Co. 1943—. Director: General Reinsurance Corporation and General Reinsurance Life Corp. (Fin. and Exec. Cttee.), Harcourt Brace Jovanovich Inc.; Dir. General Reassurance Corp; Herbert Clough Inc.; North Star Reinsurance Corp.; Lincoln National Life Insurance Co., Honorary (Inv. Cttee.); Lincoln National Corp., Honorary; National Fire Insurance Co.; Transcontinental Ins. Co. (Inv. Cttee.); Olivetti Corp. of America (Exec. Cttee.); Emeritus Owens-Illinois, Inc.; Piedmont Adv. Corporation; Chmn. Providentia Ltd.; Chmn., Instoria Inc.; Independent Counsellor, U.S. Steel and Carnegie Corp. Pension Fund. Trustee: Salzburg Seminar in American Studies, Honorary; National Bureau of Economic Research. *Clubs:* Cosmos (Washington); Rockefeller Center Luncheon (NYC). *Address:* 40 Fifth Avenue, New York City; and *office* One Rockefeller Plaza, New York City, U.S.A.

**HEWARD, (Arthur) Brian (Augustus).** Canadian stockbroker. *B.* 1900. *Educ.* Lower Canada College and St. John's College, Cambridge, England (MA). *M.* 1925, Anna Barbara Lauderdale Logie. *S.* Chilion. *Daus.* Barbara, Efa (Greenwood), and Faith (Berghuis). *Career:* With P. S. Ross & Sons, Chartered Accountant 1921; Oswald & Drinkwater, Stockbrokers 1922; Partner Jones Heward & Co. Ltd., Stockbrokers 1925–45, Senior Partner 1945–64, Chairman since 1964. Chairman of Board, Consumers Glass Co. Ltd., Montreal. *Clubs:* Montreal, Mount Royal, University (Montreal); Mount Bruno Country (St. Bruno, Que.); Brockville (Ont.) Country; Leander (Henley-on-Thames, Eng.); Royal & Ancient Golf (St. Andrews, Scotland). *Address:* 249 St. James Street, Montreal H2Y 1M8, Canada.

**HEWES, Leslie.** Professor Emeritus of Geography. *B.* 1906. *Educ.* Universities of Oklahoma (BA 1928) and California (PhD 1940). *M.* 1933, Elma Graham Beary. *S.* Robert Willis. *Dau.* Carolyn Louise (Toft). *Career:* Instructor, Asst. Prof., Assoc. Prof. of Geography, Univ. of Oklahoma 1932–45; Professor of Geography, University of Nebraska 1945–74 (Chairman of Department 1946–68). Guest Prof. (Fulbright Lecturer), Univ. of Vienna 1958–59. *Publications:* Huepac, Village of Sonora (1935); Oklahoma Ozarks, Land of Cherokees (1942); Indian Land in Cherokee Country (1942); Features of Early Woodland and Prairie Settlement, Iowa (1950); Northern Wet Prairie of U.S. (1951); Occupying the Wet Prairie, Central Iowa (with Philip E. Frandson) (1952); Lincoln Nebraska Area (1952); Tontitown, Ozark Vineyard Center (1953); Die Entwässerung der nordlichen nassen Prärien der Vereinigten Staaten (1953); Risk in Central Great Plains: Wheat Failure in Nebraska (1931–52) (with Arthur C. Schmieding 1956); Wheat Failure, Western Nebraska 1931–54 (1958); Causes of Wheat Failure in Central Great Plains (1965); Conservation Reserve as Measure of Maladjustments in Agriculture in Great Plains (1967); The Suitcase Farming Frontier (1973). *Member:* Phi Beta Kappa (Pres. Okla. 1944–45; Nebraska 1959–60); Sigma Xi (Pres. Neb. 1952–53); Assn. of American Geographers, Council 1954–57; National Advisory Committee in Geography, Fulbright Programme 1955–58; Amer. Geographical Socy. *Club:* Lincoln Tennis. *Address:* 3022 South 27th Street, Lincoln, Neb. 68502; and *office* Department of Geography, University of Nebraska, Lincoln 68508, Neb., U.S.A.

**HEWITT, William Alexander.** American. *B.* 1914. *Educ.* University of California (AB Econ.). *M.* 1948, Patricia Wiman. *S.* 1. *Dau.* 2. *Career:* Dir., Deere & Company 1951—, Exec. Vice-Pres. 1954, President and Chief Executive Officer 1955; Chmn. and Chief Exec. Officer since 1964; Dir. American Telephone & Telegraph Co. 1962—, Continental Illinois National Bank and Trust Company of Chicago 1955—, Continental Oil Co. 1965—; Continental Illinois Corp. since 1968; United Nations Assn. 1970–73; Hon. LLD: Augustana College, Rock Island (Ill.); St. Ambrose Coll., Davenport (Iowa); Knox College, Galesburg (Ill.). *Member:* Harvard University Grad. School of Design and Visual Arts Visiting Cttee 1967–73; the Business Council; Farm and Industrial Equipment Inst.; Stanford Research Institute Council; Chase Manhattan Bank, Int. Adv. Cttee.; The Conference Board; Harvard University Grad. School Business Administration Visiting Cttee. 1962–67; American Inst. Architects; Atlantic Inst. Int. Affairs; Chmn. National Council, U.S.A.–China Trade; Business Cttee. for the Arts, Inc.; Socy. Automotive Engineers; Ill. Council, Economic Education; The Trilateral Commission. Trustee, United States Cncl., Internl. Chamber of Commerce; California Inst. of Technology; Carnegie Endowment, International Peace 1971–75; National Safety Council; Council of the Americas; Hon. Trustee, Cttee. for Economic Development. Business Roundtable; U.S.A.-U.S.S.R. Trade and Economic Council (Director); National Endowment for the Humanities 1975—; Harvard Univ. visiting cttee. on East Asian Studies 1977—. *Clubs:* Bohemian, Burlingame Country, Pacific-Union (San Francisco); Chicago; Pilgrims of U.S. *Address:* 3800 Blackhawk Road, Rock Island, Ill. 61201; and *office* Deere & Company, John Deere Road, Moline, Ill. 61265, U.S.A.

**HEWLETT, Lord (Sir Thomas Clyde),** CBE, MA, FBIM, FPRI MIEx. British. *B.* 1923. *Educ.* Clifton Coll., and Magdalen Coll., Cambridge (BA 1948; 2nd Cl. Hons. Economics and Politics Tripos). *M.* 1949, Millicent Taylor. *S.* 2. *Career:* joined Anchor Chemical Company Ltd. 1949, Export Dir. 1950, Joint Man. Dir. 1961, Man. Dir. since 1965, Deputy-Chmn. 1968, Chmn. since 1971, Chmn., Anchor Italiana S.P.A.; Anchor Chemical Co. (Pty.) Australia Ltd.; Anchor Chemical South Africa (Pty.) Ltd., Borg-Warner Chemicals UK Ltd.; Burco-Dean Ltd.; Vice-Chmn. Young Conservatives 1953; Pres. Cam. Union and Chmn. Univ. Conservative Assn. 1948; Member Manchester City Council, 1949–56; Chmn. North West Area Conservative Assn. 1961–66, and North West Branch Inst. of Export 1961–66. Chairman, Executive Committee National Union of Conservative and Unionist Associations 1965–71; Chmn., North West Industrialists' Council since 1971; Pres., Conservative Political Centre since 1974; Pres., Nat. Union of Conservative Party since 1976; Fellow of the British Institute of Management, 1970. *Member:* Court of Governors University of Manchester; Plastics and Rubber Inst. (Fellow); Corporate Member, Institute of Export; Manchester & Salford Street Children's (Wood Street) Mission Management Cttee. 1950—; Govn. Clifton College (1972); Vice-Pres., City of Manchester County Scout Council 1972; Council of Clifton Coll. 1973; Pres., Northern Lawn Tennis Club 1973; Council, Nat. Rifle Assn. 1973; Trustee, Royal Exchange Theatre & Jt. Chmn. of the Trust Appeal Cttee. 1974; Vice-Chmn., Manchester Naval Officers 1974; Pres., Plastics & Rubber Inst. 1975 (Pres. IRI 1972–74); Court of Victoria Univ. of Manchester 1976; Pres., North West Branch Economic League 1976. *Clubs:* Carlton, Cambridge Union. *Address:* Dane Edge, Swettenham, Congeleton, Cheshire, CW12 2LQ; and *office* Anchor Chemical Co., Ltd., Clayton Lane, Clayton, Manchester M11 4SR.

**HEWLETT, William R.** American business executive. *B.* 1913. *Educ.* Stanford University, BA (1934); EE (1939); MIT.—MS 1936; UC Berkeley—LLD (1966). *M.* Flora Hewlett. *S.* 3. *Daus.* 2. *Career:* Co-founder and Partner Hewlett-Packard Co. 1939–46; Exec. Vice-Pres. and Dir. 1947–64; Pres. and Dir. 1964–69; President-Chief Exec. Officer and Dir. since 1969. *Director:* Chase Manhattan Bank NYC since 1969, Chrysler Corp., Detroit, Mich. since 1966; Kaiser Foundation Hosp. and Health Plan Board, Oakland, Ca. since 1972; Utah International, San Francisco since 1974, Overseas Develop. Council, Washington DC since 1969; Bd. of Science and Technology (NASc.) Washington DC, since 1974; *Trustee:* California Acad, of Sciences (Hon) since 1969; San Francisco Bay Area Council since 1969; Carnegie Inst. of Washington since 1971. *Fellow:* Am. Acad. of Arts and Sciences since May 1970; Inst. of Electrical and Electronic Engineers (pres. 1954). *Member:* Emergency Cttee. for American Trade since 1969; National Acad. of Engineering since 1965; Instrument Socy. of America (Hon. lifetime) since 1963; also past member and trustee of numerous cttees, councils and organisations. *Awards:* Calif. Manuf. of Year (1969); Business Statesman of the Year (1970); Medal of Achiev. (WEMA) 1971; IEEE Founders Medal (1973); Other awards. *Publications:* Co-author technical articles. *Clubs:* Bohemian; Pacific Union (both San Franc.); Menlo Country (Woodside, Cal.). *Address:* 1501 Page Mill Road, Palo Alto, California, U.S.A.

**HEYER, John Whitefoord.** Australian. Film producer director. *B.* 1916. *Educ.* Scotch College, Melbourne. *M.* 1942, Dorothy Greenhalgh; (*Dec.* 1969). *S.* Frederick. *Daus.* Elizabeth and Catherine. *Career:* Sound Engineer, Efftee Production, Melbourne 1934–36; Cameraman, Zane Grey Corporation, Los Angeles 1936–37; Director, Australian Documentary Films 1938–39; Producer, Allied Works Council; Film Adviser, Prime Minister's Committee; member, Film Committee; Services Education Council 1940–45; Producer, Australian National Film Board 1945–48, Shell Film Unit 1948–56 and Shell International Petroleum London 1956–67; Governor and Executive Member, Australian Film Institute 1958–74; Film Consultant, Rank Organization 1967–73; Consultant, Producer Aust. Broadcasting Commission 1967–74; Aust. Conservation Foundation 1970–75; Man. Dir. John Heyer Film Co. Pty. Ltd. London & Sydney. *Awards:* First British film director to win Venice Grande Prise Assoluto; First Australian Film Director to be honoured by the Queen, OBE, 1970. Productions: Documentary films: The Back of Beyond (Venice Grand Prix 1954, Gran Premio, Montevideo 1956); Playing with Water (Grand Prix, Cortina); The Forerunner (1st Prize, Melbourne 1957, Special Award, Venice 1958, 1st Prize, Padua 1958, An Outstanding Film of the Year, London 1958); The Paying Bay (2nd Prize, Turin 1961); Tumut Pond (An Outstanding Film of the Year, London 1962); Publicity Films; Man's Head (1st Prize, Venice 1958); Dream Sound (Honourable Mention); The Professor (Hon. Mention, Cannes 1959); The Duel (1st Prize, Venice 1960); Jack (Diploma, Venice 1960); The Chameleon (Dipl., Venice 1960); Hands (2nd Prize, Trieste 1961); Like New (Diploma, Cannes 1963); The Sleeper (Diploma, Cannes 1967). President, Fed. of Film Societies, Sydney 1944–56; Vice-Pres., Scientific Film Assn., Sydney

1950–56; Pres., Sydney Film Socy. 1944–54. *Member:* N.S.W. Govt. Film Council 1947–56: British Film Institute 1944—; Australian Council for the Arts, 1970–75. *Address:* 3 Ulva Road, London, S.W.15.

**HEYES, Sir Tasman Hudson Eastwood**, CBE. *B.* 1896. *Educ.* Melbourne. *M.* 1921, Ethel Brettel Causer. *S.* 1. *Dau.* 1. *Career:* Served in World War I (A.I.F.; France and Flanders) 1916–19. Attached to Committee of Imperial Defence, London, and War Departments in Ottawa, Washington and Wellington 1924–28; Director, Australian War Memorial, Canberra 1939–42; Dept. of Defence, Melbourne 1942–46; Secretary, Dept. of Immigration, Commonwealth of Australia 1946–62. Awarded Nansen Medal 1962. *Club:* Melbourne. *Address:* 3/5 36 Toorak Road, Toorak, Melbourne, Australia.

**HEYNES, William Munger**, CBE. British. *B.* 1903. *Educ.* Warwick School; Apprentice Humber Ltd. *M.* 1932, Evelyn Blunt. *S.* Simon William, Jonathan. *Career:* With Humber Ltd. (Rootes): Student Apprentice 1922; Design Technician 1926; Chief Technical Officer 1930. With Jaguar: Chief Engineer 1935; Technical Director 1946. Vice-Chmn. and Technical Director, Jaguar Cars 1961–69. Member of Council and Management, Motor Industry Research Association. *Publications:* The Jaguar Engine; Design of a Sports Car; Milestones in the Life of an Automobile Engineer. Honours: Starley Premium; Clayton Award (Engineering). *Award:* CBE (1969) for services to export. *Member:* M.I. Mech.E.; N. Soc. Automotive Eng. (U.S.A.); M. Inst. Director; Hon. Member, Motor Research Assn. *Clubs:* Royal Automobile; Royal Smithfield; Automobile D'ouest (France); Hon. member, Racing Mechanics. *Address:* Wolverton Grange, Stratford-on-Avon, Warwicks.

**HIBBERD, Sir Donald James**, Kt. 1977, OBE. Australian. *B.* 1916. *Educ.* Sydney University (BEc). *M.* 1942, Florence A. Macandie. *S.* Adrian. *Dau.* Christine. *Career:* With Commonwealth Department of Trade & Customs 1939–46; Executive Assistant, Commonwealth Treasury 1946–53; Director, Commonwealth Oil Refinery Ltd. 1949–51; Member, Australian Aluminium Production Commission 1953–57; First Asst. Secy., Banking, Trade & Industry Branch, Commonwealth Treasury 1953–57; Exec. Director, Commonwealth Aluminium Corp. Pty. Ltd. 1957–61; Managing Director, Comalco Industries Pty. Ltd. 1961–69: Director, Conzinc Riotinto of Australia Ltd. (previously Consolidated Zinc Pty. Ltd.), Melbourne 1962–71; Member, Board of Reserve Bank of Australia since 1966; Chairman, Comalco Ltd., 1969—; Chmn., Munich Reinsurance Australia Ltd. 1970—. *Member:* Melbourne University Council, 1968—; Cttee. of Management, Royal Victorian Eye & Ear Hospital 1958—. *Clubs:* Athenaeum; Commonwealth; Royal Melbourne Golf; Frankston Golf and Royal Canberra Golf. *Address:* Apt. 13-2, 193 Domain Road, South Yarra, 3141; and *office* 95 Collins Street, Melbourne, Vic., Australia.

**HIBBERT, Donald Raymond.** American. *B.* 1926. *Educ.* BA Michigan State Univ., East Lansing, Mich., 1950 Michigan C.P.A., 1953. *M.* 1951, Marilyn Joyce Vickers. *S.* 1. *Dau.* 1. *Career:* Supervisor, Touche, Ross & Co., Detroit, 1950–58; Vice-Pres., Dir., Treasurer, Wyandottte Chemicals Corp., and of principal subsidiaries 1958–69; Treasurer Bendix Corp. (Mich.) 1969–70; Exec. Vice-Pres. Kimberley-Clark Co. (Wis.) since 1970; Dir. mem. Exec. Cttee., Spruce Falls Power & Paper Co.; 1st Nat. Bank of Neenah Wis.; Assoc. Bank Services Inc. *Member:* Amer. Institute of Certified Public Accountants, Financial Executives Institute, Beta Alpha Psi; Beta Theta Pi. *Clubs:* Union League Club, New York City, Detroit Athletic Club. *Address:* 3 Westfield Ridge, Neenah, W1 54956; and *office* N. Lake St., Neenah, W1 54956, U.S.A.

**HICKERSON, John Melancton.** Marketing executive. *B.* 1897. *Educ.* State Univ. of Iowa (BA). *M.* 1929, Annette Adrean. *Daus.* Ann and Martha. *Career:* With General Electric Co. 1920–29; Lord & Thomas Advertising Agency 1929–39; established J. M. Hickerson Inc. 1939–50; President, Albert Frank-Guenther Law Inc. 1950–52; re-established J. M. Hickerson Inc. 1952. Regional Vice-Pres., United Student Aid Funds, N.Y. 1962—. *Publications:* Ladd Plumley of State Mutual (1972); Ernie Breech: The Story of his remarkable career at General Motors, Ford & TWA (1968); How to Get What You Want Out of Life (1961); How I made the Sale that Did the Most for Me (Prentice-Hall 1951); Entering the Advertising Field (1949). *Member:* Sigma Delta Chi; Omicron Delta Kappa; Acacia. Republican. *Clubs:* Sales Executives, University (N.Y.C.); Scarsdale Golf. *Address:* 187 Garth Road, Scarsdale, N.Y.; and *office* 200 E. 42nd Street, New York City 17, U.S.A.

**HICKINBOTHAM, Sir Tom**, KCMG, KCVO, CIE, OBE; former colonial administrator. *B.* 27 April 1903. *Educ.* R.M.C. Sandhurst. *Career:* Entered Indian Army 1923, served with 5th Btn. Baluch. Regt. 1924; transferred to Indian Political Service 1930; served in Aden 1931–32, 1933–35 and 1938–39; Political Agent, Muscat 1939–41, Kuwait 1941–43, Bahrein 1943–45, Kalat, Baluchistan 1945–47; Chairman, Aden Port Trust 1948–51; Governor, Aden Colony and Protectorate 1951–56; Trustee of the London Clinic. *Address:* Travellers Club, 106 Pall Mall, London, S.W.1.

**HICKING, Clive Richard Hinson.** Australian public accountant and company director. *B.* 1902. *Educ.* FASA, FCIS. *M.* 1942, Adeline Ethel Bennett. *Career:* In New South Wales Public Service 1918–22; Accountant, Matthews Thompson & Co. Ltd. 1923; Director of the Company and of its 40 subsidiaries 1945–61. Sydney Junior Chamber of Commerce (Chmn. 1936–38); Sydney Chamber of Commerce (Councillor 1944–48); Australian Exporters' Federation (Vice-Pres. 1949–53). *Member:* Chartered Institute of Secretaries (Australian Pres. 1951–53); Australian Society of Accountants (Foundation Pres. 1953–1955). Sydney Club. *Address:* 54 Beaconsfield Parade, Lindfield 2070, N.S.W., Australia.

**HICKMAN, Edgar Laurie.** British merchant. *B.* 1907. *Educ.* Lakefield Prep. School, Ontario, and Tonbridge School, England. *M.* 1940, Ethel Beatrice Fudge. *S.* 2. *Dau.* 1. *Career:* Chmn. & Dir. A. E. Hickman Co. Ltd.; Hickman Motors Ltd.; Hickman Leasing Ltd.; Vice-Pres., Purity Factors Ltd.; St. John's Operating Co. Ltd Director: Canadian Imperial Bank of Commerce; Canamark Ltd.; Dir. Dougall Paintings (1965) Ltd.; Wilson Equipment Ltd.; Verdon Sales Ltd.; Ranrod Ltd.; Pres., Atlantic Insurance Co. Ltd.; Dir. and Pres. Hickman Insurance Services Ltd. Chmn. Hickman Equipment Ltd. these companies are estabished in Newfoundland. Chmn. Nfld. Adv. Board of Canada Permanent Trust Co. Former chmn. Newfoundland Bd. of Trade. *Address:* P.O. Box 790, St. John's, Nfld., Canada.

**HICKMAN, John Kyrle**, CMG, BA. British diplomat. *B.* 1927. *Educ.* Tonbridge School; Cambridge University. *M.* 1956, Jennifer Love. *S.* 2. *Dau.* 1. *Career:* War Office 1950–58; Commonwealth Relations Office 1958–59; First Secy. British High Commission Wellington (N.Z.) 1959–62; Commonwealth Relations Office 1962–64; Foreign Office 1964–66; First Secy. British Embassy Madrid 1966–67; Counsellor and Consul-General Bilbao 1967–69; Deputy-High Commissioner Singapore 1969–71; Head, South West Pacific Dept. Foreign and Commonwealth Office 1971–74; Counsellor Brit. Embassy Dublin 1974–77; Ambassador to Ecuador since 1977. *Awards:* First Class Hons. Historical Tripos. pts. 1–11, Cambridge University; Companion, Order of St. Michael & St. George, 1977. *Club:* Oxford and Cambridge University. *Address:* 3 Weltje Road, London W.6; and *office* F.C.O., Downing Street, London, S.W.1.

**HICKMAN, Richard Allan.** American; Consultant on State Govt. Relations. *B.* 1908. *Educ.* Park Coll. and Univ. of Missouri (BS 1930); Grad. Sales Analysis Inst. *M.* 1934, Martha Lucile Sehnert. *S.* David Coleman, *Dau.* Alana de Nise. *Career:* With production, market research, and technical sales departments, E.I. du Pont de Nemours & Co. 1929–45. Asst. Chief, Packaging Branch, Office of Chief of Ordnance, U.S. Army, Washington, D.C. 1945. Manager, Plastic Glazing, Dobeckmun Co., Cleveland, Ohio 1946–47; Sales Manager, Northern Central California 1947–51; Director Market Research 1951–53; Sales Manager, Industrial Products 1953–56; Field Sales Manager 1956–58; Manager for Market Planning 1958–62; Sales Administration, Personnel, The Dow Chemical Co. 1962–63; Manager, U.S. Government Sales 1963–71; Manager, State Government Relations 1971–73 (retired); Associate Professor, Goldengate College 1947–51; Guest Lecturer, Santa Clara Univ., Univ. of San Francisco and Univ. of California 1947–51. *Member:* American Marketing Assn. (Vice-Pres. Northern Calif.); Sigma Phi Epsilon. Presbyterian (Elder); active in Nat. Security Industrial Assn, 1963–73, last serving as Chmn. Planning Group Dist. Adv. Cttee. 1972; Awarded Hon. Membership 1974. *Publications:* Articles on packaging to trade magazines & to Encyclopedia Britannica; Author: Desirable Types of Cellophane and Combinations of Cellophane with other Materials and New or Expanded Applications (American Chemical Society's 125th Annual Meeting, Kansas City 1965). A Businessman's Look at Proposals for New Laws on Lobbying, Public Financing of Campaign and Financial Disclosure (The Citizens Conference on State Legislatures Meeting on Legislative Openness, Williamsburg, Va. 1974). *Clubs:* Midland, Michigan Country; Bella Vista, Arkansas Country; Northwest Arkansas Gun; Life Mem., Amateur Trapshooting Assn.; Life Mem., Michigan Trapshooting Assn.; Pres., Benton County Republican Men's Club 1974–75–76; Active Mem., Republican Party in Arkansas, Pres., Chapter 620 AARP 1976–77. *Address:* Route # 4, Yocum Road, Rogers, Arkansas 72756, U.S.A.

**HICKS, Hon. Henry Davies,** CC, QC. Candian. Politican and educator. *B.* 5 Mar. 1915. *Educ.* Mount Allison Univ. (BA); Dalhousie Univ. (BSc); Exeter Coll., Oxford (MA, BCL); Hon DEd, College of Ste. Anne 1952, DCL, Univ. of King's Coll. 1954 and Univ. of New Brunswick 1963; LLD. Mount Allison Univ. 1956. *M.* 1945, Paulene Agnes Banks (D. 1964). *S.* Henry Randolph Harlow, John George Herbert. *Daus.* Catherine Kinney, Paulene Jane Francess. *M.* 1965, Margaret Gene MacGregor Morison. *Career:* Called to Bar 1941; served World War II, Royal Canadian Artillery 1941–45. *Member:* Nova Scotia Legislative Assembly (Lib.) 1945–60; Minister of Education 1949–55; Provincial Secretary 1954–56; Premier of Nova Scotia 1954–56; Deane of Arts & Science, Dalhousie Univ. 1960; Vice-Pres., Dalhousie Univ. 1961; President & Vice-Chancellor, Dalhousie Univ. 1963; Appointed Canadian Senate 1972. *Address:* 6446 Coburg Road, Halifax, Nova Scotia, Canada.

**HICKS, Robert,** BSc Hons, MP. British. *B.* 1938. *Educ.* Queen Elizabeth's Grammar School, Devon; Univ. of London; Univ. of Exeter, Cert. Education. *M.* 1962, Maria E. A. Gwyther. *Daus.* Alison and Katrina. *Career:* Assistant Master St. Austell Grammar School, 1961–64; Lecturer, Regional Geography, Weston-Super-Mare, Tech. College, 1964–1970. Member of Parliament, Bodmin, Cornwall, since 1970; Asst. Govt. Whip 1973–74; Member Select Cttee. European Secondary Legislation since 1973. Vice Chmn. Cons. Parly. Cttee. for Agriculture 1972–73, and since 1974; Chmn. Horticultural Sub committee 1971–73. *Fellow:* Royal Geographical Society. *Member:* Economic Research Council. *Clubs:* Carlton; M.C.C. *Address:* Parkwood, St. Keyne, Liskeard, Cornwall; and *office* House of Commons, London, S.W.1.

**HIDAJAT, Raden.** Ambassador of Indonesia. *B.* 1916. *Educ.* High School, Royal Military Academy Netherlands); studied for inspector of railways and transports. *M.* 1940, Ratu Aminah. *Career:* Deputy Chief of Staff. Indonesian Armed Forces (rank of Colonel) 1948; Quarter-Master General (rank of Colonel) 1949; Secretary-General, Ministry of Defense 1953, Vice-Minister (rank of Brig. General) 1959; Deputy Minister of National Defense (rank of Maj.-General) 1960; Minister Seconded to the Deputy First Minister for Defense and Security (rank of Lieut.-General) 1962; Minister for Land Communication, Posts, Telegraphs and Tourism 1963–66; Ambassador to Canada 1966. *Awards:* National and foreign decorations. President: National Automobile Association; and National Yacht Association. *Address:* c/o Ministry of Foreign Affairs, Jakarta, Indonesia.

**HIDAKA, Teru,** LLB. Japanese. *B.* 1905. *Educ.* Tokyo Imperial Univ. (LLB). *M.* 1931, Tsune Ogura. *S.* 1. *Dau.* 2. *Career:* Dir. Industrial Bank of Japan Ltd., 1950, Man. Dir. 1951; Vice-Pres. Nissan Chemical Industries Ltd. 1960, Pres. 1962–64. Pres. Yamaichi Securities Co. Ltd. 1964–72, Chmn. since 1972; Dir. Tokyo Shoken Building Inc., Tokyu Hotel Chain Corp; *Member:* Man. Dir. Fed. of Economic Orgs; Man. Dir. Japan Federation of Employer's Assns; Councillor, Japanese Commission BIAC. Governor Tokyo Stock Exchange; Dir. Members' Assn. T.S.E. *Address:* 22–3 Oyama-cho, Shibuya-ku, Tokyo, Japan; and *office* 1-1, Yaesu 5-chome, Chuo-ku, Tokyo 104, Japan.

**HIDAYATULLAH, Hon. Mr. Justice Mohammad,** OBE. Indian judge. *B.* 1905. *Educ.* Nagpur University (BA) and Trinity College, Cambridge (MA); called to Bar (Lincoln's Inn) 1930. *M.* 1948, Pushpa Shah. *S.* Arshad. *Dau.* Avni (*D.* 1960). *Career:* Lecturer in Jurisprudence, University College of Law, Nagpur 1934–43; Government Pleader 1942; Advocate General 1943–46; Dean, Faculty of Law, Nagpur Univ. 1948–53. Former member of Senate: Faculty of Law Nagpur, Sagar, Vikram and Aligarh Univs. Judge, High Court of Judicature, Nagpur 1946–54, Chief Justice 1954–58; Judge, Supreme Court of India 1958–68; Chief Justice of India 1968–70; Acting Pres. of India 1969; Ex-Council World Assembly of Judges; Former Chief Commissioner (MP) and Vice-President National Council Bharat Scouts and Guides (awarded Silver Elephant) 1950–53. *Awards:* Bencher Lincoln's Inn. Hon. LL.D., University of the Philippines, Hon. LL.D., Ravishankar; Hon. LLD., Rajasthan; Order, Yugoslav Flag with Sash. Medallion and Plaque of Merit of Philconsa; Knight of Mark Twain (1974); Bronze Medal (Life-Saving) 1969. *Publications:* Democracy in India & the Judicial Process, Mullas Mohammedan Law, Editor 18th Edition. The South West Africa Case; A Judge's Miscellany; U.S.A. and India (in press). *Address:* A-10 Rockside, 112 Walkeshwar Road, Bombay, 400006, India.

**HIDY, Ralph Willard.** Business historian. *B.* 1905. *Educ.* Miami Univ. (BA 1926); Clark Univ. (MA 1928); Harvard Univ. (Ph.D 1935). *M.* 1928, Muriel Emmie Wagenhauser. *Dau.* Ann Helen. *Career:* Instructor in History, Norwich Univ., Northfield, Vt. 1928–30; from Instructor to Professor, Wheaton College, Norton, Mass. 1932–47. Lieut., Lieut.-Cmdr., Cmdr., U.S. Navy 1941–46; Senior Associate in Research, Business History Fdn. 1947–50; Prof. of History and Editor of Business History Series of N.Y. Univ. Press 1950–57. Isidor Straus Professor of Business History Emeritus, Graduate School of Business Administration, Harvard Univ. Editor Harvard Studies in Business History. Editor-in-Chief, Business History Review 1962–65. *Member:* Phi Beta Kappa; American Historical Association (Beveridge Award Committee 1952–56; Chairman 1956); Organization of America Historians; Economic History Association (Secy. 1950–62), Pres. 1970–71; Economic History Society (England); Minnesota Historical Society; Lincoln Educational Foundation Inc.; Business History Foundation Inc. (President 1960—). *Publications:* The House of Baring in American Trade and Finance—English Merchant Bankers at Work 1763–1861 (1949); with Muriel E. Hidy; Pioneering in Big Business 1882–1911—History of Standard Oil Co. (New Jersey 1955); The World of Business (co-author) (1962); Timber and Men; The Weyerhaeuser Story (1963). *Address:* 108 Radcliffe Road, Belmont, Mass.; and *office* Aldrich 135, Harvard Graduate School of Business Administration, Boston, 02163 Mass., U.S.A.

**HIEBERT, John Mark,** MD; business executive. *B.* 1904. *Educ.* Tabor College (AB 1929) and Boston University School of Medicine (MD 1932). *M.* 1933, Dorothy Prior, MD. *S.* John Mark, Jr. *Career:* Medical House Officer, Massachusetts General Hospital 1933–1934; joined Sterling Drug. 1934; Exec. Vice-Pres., Winthrop Laboratories (a division of Sterling Drug) 1941–44; Vice-Pres. and Gen. Mgr., Frederick Stearns & Co. (a division of Sterling Drug) 1944–47; elected Vice-Pres., Sterling Drug 1945, Director 1949; Exec. Vice-Pres. 1950, Chmn. of Board 1960–73 (Pres. 1955–63), Hon. B.Sc. in Pharmacy, New England Coll. of Pharmacy June 1952; Dir. New York Chamber, Commerce & Industry; Trustee Boston University; Bd. of Trustee, The Proprietary Association of America; Founding Chmn. Council for Family Health; Trustee, Tabor College; Dir. W. R. Grace & Co.; Irving Trust Co. *Member:* Amer. Medical Assn.; N.Y. Acad. of Sciences; N.Y. Acad. of Medicine; Medical Socy. of State of N.Y.; Medical Socy. of County of N.Y.; Amer. Assn. for Advancement of Science; Newcomen Socy. in N. Amer. Author of numerous scientific papers relating to medical research published in professional journals. *Clubs:* Union League; Ocean; Delray Beach Golf; Schuyler Meadows. *Address:* 83 Island Drive So., Harbour Island, Delray Beach, Fla. 33444; and *office* 90 Park Avenue, New York City 10016, U.S.A.

**HIGDON, John Cline.** American. *B.* 1897. *Educ.* University of Texas (AB 1917) LLD, Park Coll. 1971. *M.* 1918. Aimée Vanneman. *S.* William E., Robert V., J. Kenneth and Donand T. *Dau.* Ruth (Knudtson). *Career:* Hon. Chmn., Business Men's Assurance Company 1968—. Past Chmn., United Funds. Past President: Health Insurance Assn. of America; American Life Convention, Past Chmn. and Honorary Director, Kansas City Crime Commission, Honorary Trustee, Rockhurst Coll. and Park College, Bd. of Governors Amer. Royal Assocn.; Adv. Board and Former Vice-Pres., Kansas City Area Cncl. Boy Scounts of America; recipient Silver Beaver Award, Alumnus of the Year 1967, Manual High Sch. of Indianapolis. Honorary Dir. and Past Chmn. Kansas City and Jackson County Chapter of American Red Cross; Past Dir., Past Pres., Kansas City Chamber of Commerce; Member, Natl. Planning Council of Natl. Planning Assn.; Member, Kansas City Art Inst. & Schl. of Design. Became associated with Business Men's Assurance Co., December 1923; served as Asst. Secy., Actuary and Secretary; Vice-President 1931; Director 1934; Executive Vice-President 1944; President in 1945 and Chairman in 1960. Served in World War I (U.S..A.A.C.—2nd Lieut.) with Near East Relief 1919; Vice-Consul, Tabriz (Iran) 1919. Moved to Kansas City 1921, and served as Consulting Actuary until 1923. Republican. Presbyterian. Phi Beta Kappa. Delta, Kappa Epsilon. *Clubs*: Man of the Month; Mercury; River; Kansas City; Mission Hills Country; Saddle and Sirloin; Advertising & Sales Executives. *Address:* 3610 Wyncote Lane, Shawnee Mission, Kansas 66205, U.S.A.

**HIGGIN, Spencer Perceval,** OBE. British. *B.* 1904. *Educ.* N.S.W. Australia. Married. *S.* 1. *Dau.* 1. *Career:* Practising Chartered Accountant, Australia 1929–39; War Service, Royal Australian Air Force 1940–45 (Wing Commander); Man. Dir., Australian Sisalkraft Ltd. 1953–57; Pres., American Sisalkraft Corp. 1957–60; Chmn., St. Regis International Ltd. 1961–76; Dir., St. Regis Paper Co. 1972–76; Chmn. J.H. Sankey & Son Ltd.; Dir. A.P.V. Holdings Ltd.; Zellstoff-Und Papierfabrik Frantschach A.K. (Austria); La Rochette-Cenpa (France). *Clubs:* Junior Carlton, Royal Thames Yacht, American. *Address:* Redford, Midhurst, Sussex.

**HIGGINS, Terence Langley,** MP. British. *B.* 1928. *Educ.* Alleyn's School, Dulwich; Gonville and Caius Coll. Cambridge; President, Cambridge Union Society 1958. *M.*1961, Rosalyn Cohen. *S.* 1. *Dau.* 1. *Career:* Lecturer in Economic Principles, Dept. Economics Yale Univ. 1958–59; Economist Unilever 1959–64; Member, Parliament (Con.) Worthing since 1964; Opposition Spokesman, Treasury and Economic Affairs 1966–70; Minister, State Treasury 1970–72; Financial Secy. to the Treasury 1972–74; Opposition Spokesman on Trade 1974–76. *Address:* 18 Hallgate, Blackheath Park, London, S.E.3.

**HIGHLAND, Harold Joseph.** Professor. *B.* 1917. *Educ.* College of the City of New York (BS 1938, MS 1939) and New York University (PhD 1942). *M.* 1940, Esther Harris. *S.* Joseph Harris. *Career:* Teacher, School of Education, College of City of N.Y., and part-time teacher with N.Y. Council for Adult Education 1938–41; Managing Editor, Education Abstracts 1940–43; Dir. Research Int. Statistical Bureau Inc. N.Y.C. 1942–50; Editor (part-time) Modern Distribution, N.Y.C. 1948–50; Editor, Publisher Plastics Merchandising 1950–52; Vice Pres., Research, Robert Shook Associates N.Y.C. 1950–54; Editor, The Family Handyman, Education Editor Tom Thumb with Universal Publishing Co. 1952–54; Dir. Home Auto Mechanic, book & encyclopedia publishing 1952–58; Editorial Dir. How-To Associations, N.Y.C. and Modern Hardwaring; contributing editor to Parade, Sunday Edition, The New York Times 1952–58; Pres. Highland-Bass Inc. (advertising, public relations advisors to industry and schools) 1956–58; Dir. Graphic Communications Center, audiovisual communications and industrial education, Long Island City 1958–60; Director of Computer Center and Chairman of Data Processing Department, Agricultural and Tech. Coll. State Univ. at Farmingdale 1967—; Fulbright Professor, Computer Science, Helsinki Univ. of Technology (Otaniemi Finland) 1970–71; Lecturer, The City Univ. London (England) 1971; Editor, ACMSIGSIM since 1971. *Publications:* Books on the subject of Modeling and simulation, Statistical probability, general science, etc. Fellowship in Education, Coll. of City of N.Y. 1938; Ford Foundation Fellowship in Computer Science 1964–65; Economics in Action Fellowship, Case Inst. of Technology 1966. *Address:* State University Technical College, Farmingdale, N.Y., U.S.A.

**HILALY, Agha.** Pakistani diplomat. *B.* 1911. *Educ.* BA (Hons) Cantab; MA Madras. *M.* 1938, Malek Taj Begum. *S.* 3. *Career:* Entered I.C.S. 1936; Magistrate (Bengal) 1938; Under-Sec., Ministry of Finance, Govt. of Bengal 1939; Under-Sec., Ministries of Agriculture, Food, Commerce and Education, Govt. of India 1941; Deputy Sec., Ministry of Finance, Govt. of Bengal 1943; Deputy Sec., Ministry of Commerce, Govt. of India 1947; Joint Secretary, Ministry of Foreign Affairs and Commonwealth Relations, Govt. of Pakistan 1947; Acting Secretary same Ministry 1954; Imperial Defence College, London 1955; Ambassador to Sweden, Norway, Denmark and Finland 1956–59. *Member:* Pakistan Delegation to 13th Session of U.N. Gen. Assembly, N.Y. 1958. Ambassador to U.S.S.R. and Czechoslovakia 1959–61; High Commissioner to India and Ambassador to Nepal 1961–63; High Commissioner to U.K. and Ambassador to Ireland 1963–66; Ambassador to U.S.A., Mexico, Jamaica and Venezuela 1966–71; Mem., Bd. of Dirs., State Bank of Pakistan 1972—; Chmn., Bd. of Govs., Pakistan Inst. of Stategic Studies 1973—. *Address:* 25-C Block-6, P.E.C.H. Society, Karachi 29, Pakistan.

**HILDEBRAND, Joel Henry.** American professor of chemistry. *B.* 16 Nov. 1881. *Educ.* University of Pennsylvania (BS, PhD. ScD. Hons.; LLD Hon, Univ. of California; Berlin University (post doctoral). *M.* 1908, Emily Alexander. *S.* Alexander. Milton, Roger Henry. *Dau.* Louise Hildebrand Klein. *Career:* Posts held in University of California; Asst. Professor 1913, Associate Professor 1917, Professor 1918–52. Professor Emeritus 1952, Dean, College of Letters and Science 1939–43, Dean, College of Chemistry 1949–51; Military Service: World War I—Lieut.-Col. Commandant, Experimental Field and A.E.F. Gas Officers' School, Chemical Warfare Service; Distinguished Service Medal; World War II—Scientific Liaison Officer, American Embassy, London 1943–44; member, National Academy of Sciences, American Philosophical Society; Hon. Life Member, Faraday Society; Hon. Fellow, Royal Society, Edinburgh. *Fellow:* American Phys. Soc. *Member:* Amer. Chemical Soc. (Pres. 1955). *Awards:* Nichols Medal, Gibbs Medal, King's Medal for Service in the Cause of Freedom, Priestley Medal, James Flack Norris Award, 1961; William Proctor Prize 1963; Joseph Priestley Award 1965. Madison Marshall Award 1967. Oct. 1966 Univ. of Calif. dedicated new $4,500,000 Chemical lab. as Hildebrand Hall. *Lectures:* Walker Memorial, Romanes (Edinburgh); Spiers Memorial (Faraday Society); Guthrie, Phys. Soc. (London); Bampton (Columbia Univ.); Westman Memorial (Chem. Inst., Canada). *Publications:* Principles of Chemistry (with R. E. Powell) 7th Ed. 1964; Solubility of Nonelectrolytes (with R. L. Scott 3rd Ed. 1950); Science in the Making (containing the Bampton Lectures 1956); Regular Solutions (with R. L. Scott 1962); Introduction to Molecular Kinetic Theory (1963); Is Intelligence Important? (1963; with J. M. Prausnitz & R. L. Scott) Regular and Related Solutions (1970); Lind Lectures (Tennessee) 1974; Viscosity & Diffusivity: A Predictive Treatment (1977); 270 scientific papers. *Address:* 500 Coventry Road, Berkeley 7, Calif. 94707, U.S.A.

**HILEY, Joseph.** British. *B.* 1902. *Educ.* West Leeds High School; Leeds University. *M.* 1932, Mary M. Boyd. *Daus.* 3. *Career:* Junior Partner with Hiley Bros., Armley, Leeds, 1920–24; Managing Dir. J. B. Battye & Co. Ltd. 1946–68; Lord Mayor Leeds 1957–58; Pres.: Leeds Chamber of Commerce 1962–63; J. B. Battye Co. Ltd., 1924–73; Dir., Readicut International Ltd. 1946–72; former Member of Parliament for Pudsey, Honorary Alderman, Leeds City Council; Deputy-Lieut. of West Yorkshire. *Member:* Lloyds. *Clubs:* Leeds; Conservative, Pudsey. *Address:* Elmaran, Layton Road, Horsforth, Leeds LS18 5ET; and *office* Kirk Lane Mills, Yeadon, Nr. Leeds LS19 7LX.

**HILL, Sir Austin Bradford,** CBE; FRS; (1954); British professor. *B.* 8 July 1897. *Educ.* Chigwell School; London Univ. (DSc, PhD); Hon. DSc, Oxford; Hon. MD Edinburgh. *M.* 1923, Florence Maud Salmon. *S.* 2. *Dau.* 1. *Career:* Member of Staff of Medical Research Council 1923–33; London University Reader in Epidemology and Vital Statistics 1933–45; Professor of Medical Statistics at London School of Hygiene and Tropical Medicine 1945–61 (Dean 1955–57); Hon. Director, Statistical Research Unit of Medical Research Council 1945–61; member, Medical Research Council 1954–58; Past-Pres. and Gold Medallist, Royal Statistical Society; Galen Medallist, Society of Apothecaries, London; Harben Gold Medallist, Royal, Institute of Public Health & Hygiene 1961, Heberden Society Medallist 1965. Past President, Sections of Epidemiology and Occupational Medicine and Hon. Fellow and Jenner Medallist of Royal Society of Medicine; Hon. Fellow, Royal College of Physicians; The Faculty of Community Medicine; Fellow of University College (London); Hon. Fellow American Public Health Association; Hon. Fellow, London School of Hygiene & Tropical Medicine; Hon. member, Institute of Actuaries; Socy. of Occupational Medicine; Socy. of Social Medicine; Faculty of Medicine, University of Chile; Socy. of Community Medicine; International Epidemiological Association. *Publications:* Principles of Medical Statistics; Statistical Methods in Clinical & Preventive Medicine. *Address:* Green Acres, Little Kingshill, Great Missenden, Bucks.

**HILL OF LUTON, Rt. Hon. Lord** (Charles Hill), PC, MA, MD, DPH, Hon LLD, Created Life Peer 1963. *B.* 15 Jan. 1904. *Educ.* St Olave's Sch. & Trinity Coll., Cambridge. *M.* 1931, Marion Spencer Wallace. *S.* 2. *Daus.* 3. *Career:* MP (Nat. Lib-U.) for Luton 1950–63 Parliamentary Secy., Min of Food 1951–55; Postmaster-General 1955–57; Chancellor of the Duchy of Lancaster 1957–61; Minister of Housing & Local Government 1961–62; Chairman, Laporte Industries Ltd. 1962–70; Chmn. Abbey National Building Society; Chairman, National Joint Council for Local Authorities' Administrative, Professional, Technical & Clerical Services. Previously House Physician and Receiving Room Officer, London Hospital; Extension Lecturer in Biology, London University; Deputy Medical Officer of Health, City of Oxford; President World Medical Association; Hon. Secy. Commonwealth Medical Conference; President (formerly Chairman) Central Council for Health Education; Secretary, British Medical Association, Chmn. Independent Television Authority 1963–67; Chmn. British Broadcasting Corp. 1967–72. *Publications:* What is Osteopathy? (1937); Reprinted Broadcasts 1941–50; Both sides of the Hill (1964); Behind the Screen (1974). *Address:* House of Lords, London, S.W.1.

**HILL, Fred Greenhalgh.** British. Airline Executive. *B.* 1917. *Educ.* Whangarei Boys' High School. *M.* 1947, Bobbie Rose Winstone. *Daus.* 2. *Career:* State Advances Corp. 1938; War Service: N.Z. Artillery (Capt.) and Royal N.Z. Air Force (F/O), qualified pilot. Served in New Zealand, Canada and Pacific 1939–46; joined (renamed Air New Zealand) TEAL Operations Div., 1947; appointed first Station Supt., Wellington 1950, and Station Mgr., Christchurch 1951; District Manager: Christchurch 1958, Auckland 1962, Regional Mgr., New Zealand 1966. Manager Commercial Policies Head Office 1969; Mgr., Administration Services 1976. Founder and Past Pres., Canterbury Travel League, Past President Travel League N.Z.; Auckland City Councillor; Former member Canterbury Chamber of Commerce Council. *Member:* N.Z. International Trade Fair Cttee.; N.Z. Inst. of Travel. *Clubs:* Auckland Commercial Travellers. *Address:* 5 Stoneyroyd Gardens, Remuera, Auckland; and c/o Air New Zealand Ltd., Air New Zealand House, 1 Queen Street, Auckland, New Zealand.

**HILL, Sir James William Francis,** CBE. *B.* 1899. *Educ.* Trinity College, Cambridge; MA, LL.M, Litt.D. *Career:* Service in King's Royal Rifle Corps 1918; and Solicitor 1926. Chairman, Association of Municipal Corporations 1957–1966; President, European Conference of Local Authorities, 1966–68; Alderman, City of Lincoln 1946–74; Pres. of Council 1948–67, and Pro-Chancellor 1959–72 Chancellor since 1972 of University of Nottingham; President International Union of Local Authorities 1967–71; Company Director. *Awards:* Hon. LLD Nottingham and Birmingham; Hon.D Litt Leicester; Hon. Freeman, City of Lincoln; Hon. Vice-Pres., Royal Historical Society. *Publications:* Medieval Lincoln; Tudor & Stuart Lincoln; Georgian Lincoln; Victorian Lincoln; Banks Family Papers. Conservative. *Club:* United Oxford & Cambridge. *Address:* The Priory, Lincoln.

**HILL, William Edwin.** American management consultant; *B.* 1910. *Educ.* Sheffield Scientific School, Yale Univ. (BS 1932). *M.* 1938, Jane E. Herrmann. *Daus.* 2. *Career:* Engineer with industrial companies in Cuba, and Instructor, Ruston Acad., Havanna 1932–36; Manager, Commercial Department, American Radiator and Standard Sanitary Corporation, New York City 1936–38; co-founder and partner, Turck, Hill & Co., Inc., Consulting Engrs., N.Y.C. 1938–53; founder, William E. Hill & Co. Inc., Management Consultants. New York City 1953–71; Chmn. Mgmt. Consulting Division, Dun and Bradstreet Cos. Inc., Pres. Management Consulting Division; Pres. Willian E. Hill International; Inc. Dir. William E. Hill & Co. Inc.; The Fantus Co. Inc.; William E. Hill Int. Inc.; Bangor Punta Corp.; Dead River Company; Eltra Corp.; Swiss Re Holding (N.A.) Inc.; Iroquois Brands Ltd.; North American Reinsurance Corp.; North American Reinsurance Co.; Swiss Reinsurance Co. (N.A.) Inc. Trustee, Emigrant Saving Bank; member, N.Y. City Youth Board 1954–58; Director (and former Pres.), Catholic Youth Organization; Director (and member, Executive Committee), Boys Clubs of America; Trustee, Children's Aid Society. Trustee (and Vice-Pres.) National Institute of Social Sciences. *Publications:* Fundamentals of Distribution (Funk & Wagnalls 1948); contributor of articles of technical and professional journals. *Address:* 640 Fifth Avenue, New York, N.Y. 10019, U.S.A.; and *offices* 43 quai de Grenelle, 75015-Paris, France; and 13 Truderinger Strasse, 8000 Munich 80, Federal Republic of Germany.

**HILL-NORTON, Admiral of the Fleet Sir Peter (John),** GCB. British. *B.* 1915. *Educ.* Royal Navy College, Dartmouth; Royal Naval College, Greenwich. *M.* 1936, Margaret Eileen Linstow. *S.* 1. *Dau.* 1. *Career:* Went to Sea 1932, Commissioned 1936; War Service in Arctic Convoys & NW Approaches 1939–45; Naval Attaché, Argentina, Uruguay, Paraguay 1953–55; Flag Officer Second in Command, Far East Fleet 1964–66; Deputy Chief of the Defence Staff (Personnel & Logs) 1966; Second Sea Lord & Chief of Naval Personnel 1967; Vice Chief of Naval Staff 1967–68; Commander-in-Chief, Far East 1969–70; Chief of the Naval Staff & First Sea Lord 1970–71; Chief of the Defence Staff 1971–73; Chmn., NATO Military Cttee. 1974–77. *Member:* Royal Naval Officers; The Navy League (Life Fellow); Royal United Services Inst. (Vice-Pres.); Pres., Sea Cadet Assn. *Decorations:* Commander of the Honourable Order of the Bath (1964), Knight (1967), Knight Grand Cross (1970). *Clubs:* Royal Thames Yacht; Royal Navy Club of 1765; Naval & Military. *Address:* King's Mill House, Kings Mill, South Nutfield, Redhill RH1 5NG.

**HILLENBRAND, Martin Joseph.** American diplomat. *B.* 1915. *Educ.* Univ. of Dayton, BA (1937); Columbia Univ. (N.Y.) MA (1938); Harvard Univ. (Mass.) PhD (1948), post-grad. (1949–50). *M.* 1941, Faith Stewart. *S.* 2. *Dau.* 1. *Career:* Vice-Consul Zurich 1939–40, Rangoon, Burma 1940–42, Calcutta, India 1942–44, Laurenco-Marques 1944–45; Consul Bremen 1945–50; Dept. of State, Bureau of German Affairs 1950–52; Consul Paris 1952–56; Political Adviser Berlin 1956–58; Director, German Affairs, Dept. of State 1958–62; Minister, U.S. Embassy Bonn 1963–67; Ambassador of America in Hungary 1967–69; Asst.-Secy. for Europ. Affairs, Dept. of State 1969–72; American Ambassador in Fed. Republic of Germany 1972–76; Dir.-Gen., Atlantic Inst. for International Affairs. *Member:* Council on Foreign Relations N.Y.; Am. Polit. Science Assn.; Am. Foreign Service Assn. *Awards:* Litt. D. (hon causa) Univ. of Dayton (1963); LLD Univ. of Maryland (1973). *Publications:* Power and Morals (1949); (co-auth.) Zwischen Politik und Ethik (1968). *Address:* 3313 O Street, N.W., Washington D.C. 20037, U.S.A.

**HILLERY, Dr. Patrick John.** Irish Statesman. *B.* 1923. *Educ.* Miltown-Malbay National School. Rockwell College, Cashel; and University College, Dublin (B.Sc 1943; MB, B.Ch, BAO 1947; DPH 1952). *M.* 1955, Mary Beatrice Finnegan. *S.* 1. *Dau.* 1. *Career:* Member of Health Council 1955–57; Medical Officer, Miltown-Malbay Dispensary District 1957–59; Coroner for West Clare 1958–59. Minister for Education in the Government of Ireland 1959–65; Minister for Industry & Commerce, 1965–66; Minister for Labour, 1966–69; Foreign Affairs 1969–72; Vice-Pres. Commission, European Communities, Commissioner for Social Affairs 1973–76; President of Ireland since 1976. MRIA. T.D. Clare 1951; LLD Hon. Causa 1962. *Address:* Spanish Point, Co. Clare, Ireland.

**HILLIER-FRY, William Norman.** BA, British diplomat. *B.* 1923. *Educ.* Colfe's Grammar School; St. Edmund Hall, Oxford (Bachelor of Arts). *M.* 1948, Elizabeth Adéle Misbah. *S.* 2. *Daus.* 2. *Career:* with Army 1942–45; Foreign Office 1946–47; Vice-Consul Isfahan and Meshed 1947–48; Oriental Secretary Tehran 1949–52; Foreign Office 1952–55; Vice-Consul Strasbourg 1955–56; Commercial Secy. Istanbul and Ankara 1956–59; Foreign Office 1959–61; Consul and Commercial Secy. Prague 1961–63; Foreign Office 1963–68; Counsellor, U.K. Del Geneva 1968–71; Head, Middle East Dept. Overseas Development Administration 1971–74; Consul-General Hamburg since 1974. *Address:* Foreign and Commonwealth Office, London, SW1A 2AH.

**HILTON, Conrad Nicholson.** American hotel executive. *B.* 1887. *Educ.* N.M. Military Inst., St. Michael's Coll. (Santa Fe) and N.M. School of Mines. *M.* (1) 1925, Mary Barron, (2) Sari Gabor. *S.* 3. *Career:* Partner with father in mercantile business; organiser, cashier and Pres. (1915), N.M. State Bank (San Antonio, Tex.) 1915; Representative in first State Legislature of N.M. 1912–13. Built Hilton Hotel, Dallas (Tex.) 1925, and Hilton Hotels in Waco, Longview, Plainview, Lubbock, El Paso and Marlin (all in Tex.) 1926–1931. Chairman of Board, Hilton Hotels Corp. (which owns, operates or has under management or franchise contract 114 hotels in various cities in the U.S.A.), and Chmn., Hilton International Co. (which operates or has under management contract 63 hotels in Europe, Middle and Far East, North, Central and S. America, the Caribbean and Pacific areas, and in the Far East). With 1st R.O.T.C., Presidio, Cal., 1917; served with A.E.F. as Lt. Q.M. Corps. *Awards:* Brotherhood Award, Natl. Conf. Christians and Jews; 1951 Freedoms Foundation Award; LLD Barret and Adelphi Colls. and Sophia Univ.; DLitt De Paul Univ. 1953. *Publication:* Be My Guest (autobiography 1957). *Address:* 10644 Bellagio Road, Bel Air, Los Angeles 90024, Calif.; and *office* 9990 Santa Monica Boulevard, Beverly Hills, Calif. U.S.A. 90212.

**HILTON, John David,** FCA. British. *B.* 1926. *Educ.* Rydal School. *M.* 1949, Dorothy Gwendoline Eastham. *S.* 1. *Daus.*

2. *Career:* Accountant, Kirkless Ltd. 1951–56; Group Acct. Hall Engineering Holdings Ltd. 1956–61; Chmn. Kennedy Industrials Ltd.; Kennedy Securities Ltd.; Kennedy Wagstaff Ltd.; Dir. Kennedy Smale Ltd.; Dorman Machinery Sales Ltd.; Dorman Properties Ltd.; Hilmax Engineering Ltd.; Spenhouse Development Ltd.; Harrott & Co. Ltd. *Address:* Wyndsway, Woodside Hill, Chalfont St. Peter, Gerrards Cross, Bucks.; and *office* 153 Parker Drive, Leicester.

**HINKLE, Samuel Forry.** American. *B.* 1900. *Educ.* Pennsylvania State Univ. (BS Chem Eng); Hon. DSc, Elizabethtown (Pa.). *Career:* Chemist, Norton Co., Chippawa, Ontario, Canada 1922–23; Chief Chemist: National Abrasive Co., Niagara Falls, Ontario, Canda 1923–24; Chief Chemist and Director of Research, Hershey Chocolate Corporation 1924–1947 (Plant Manager 1947–56); Dir. & Vice-Pres, Penn. Manufactrs. Assoc.; Dir. Penn. Manufactrs. Assoc. Insurance Co., Mem. and former Pres. Historical Foundation of Penn.; Chairman of the Board 1963–65, President 1956–65, and Director 1948–65, Hershey Foods Corp., Hershey, Pa. Pres., Hershey Chocolate of Canada Ltd. 1961–65; Bd. of Dirs.; Americans for the Competitive Enterprise System (Central Penn. Ch.). *Award:* Distinguished Alumnus Award Penna. State Univ. for 1957; Hon. Alumnus, Milton Hershey School 1971; DSc. (Hon.) Elizabeth Town Coll; Honorary Alumnus, Eliz. Town Coll. *Member:* Board of Managers, Emeritus Harrisburg (Pa.) Hospital, and Board of Governors; Trustee Penna. State Univ.; Amer. Assn. of Candy Technologists; Amer. Chemical Socy.; Chmn. Med. Affairs Comm. of Milton S. Hershey Medical Center, Penna. State Univ.; Charter Member Institute of Food Technologists; American Legion (World War I); The Newcomen Socy. in North America; Sons of American Revolution. Mason 33°. Republican. Board of Associates, Gettysburg College; Lancaster County (Pa.) Historical Socy.; Board of Governors, and Vice-Pres. Penn. Manufacturers Assoc.; Penn. German Socy.; Penn. Socy., Phi Kappa Phi; Phi Lambda Upsilon; Alpha Chi Sigma; Alpha Kappa Psi. *Award:* The Stroud Jordan Medal. *Clubs:* Hershey Country; Rotary of Hershey. *Address:* 112 Para Avenue, Hershey, Pa.

**HINRICHS, Albert Ford.** Economist. Professor Emeritus Business Administration. *B.* 1899. *Educ.* Columbia Univ. (BA 1921; MA 1922; PhD 1923). *M.* 1922, Edith F. Pendreigh. *Daus.* Elisabeth, Barbara and Carolyn. *Career:* Chief of a party of statistical advisers to Govt. of Repub. of China 1965–67. Prof. of Business Admin. and Dir. of Grad. Studies, Coll. of Business Admin., Syracuse Univ. 1957–64, Professor emeritus since 1964; Principal Statistical Adviser to Govt. of Pakistan 1959–61; With Inst. of Public and Business Admin., Univ. of Karachi 1955–57; Assistant Divisional Chief, Division of Finance & Fiscal Policy, E.C.A. (U.S. Government) 1948–53; Acting Commissioner of Labor Statistics 1940–46, and Chief Economist, U.S. Bureau of Labor Statistics 1934–40, U.S. Dept. of Labor; Assoc. Prof. of Economics, Brown Univ. 1927–34; Dir. of Research, N.Y. State Bureau of Housing & Regional Planning 1924–27. *Publications:* United Mine Workers of America and Non-Union Coal Fields; Printing Industry in New York; National Economic and Social Planning; Wages in the Cotton Textile Industry; miscellaneous articles in numerous technical and professional journals. *Member:* American Statistical Assn. (Fellow); American Economic Assn. University Fellow in Economics, Columbia Univ. *Address:* 4200 Cathedral Ave., N.W. Washington, 20016, D.C., U.S.A.

**HINTON OF BANKSIDE, Lord** (Christopher Hinton), OM, KBE, FRS; British engineer. *B.* 1901. *Educ.* Chippenham Grammar School; Trinity Coll., Cambridge (MA 1926); Hon. Fellow, Trinity Coll. (1957); Hon. DEng, Liverpool (1955); Hon. DSc(Eng.), London (1956), Hon. DSc. Oxford (1957); Hon. LLD, Edinburgh (1958); Hon. ScD, Cambridge (1960); Hon. DSc, Southampton (1962); Hon. DSc Durham 1966; Hon. DSc. Bath 1966. Hon. Associate, Manchester Coll. of Science and Techn. *M.* 1931, Lillian Boyer (*dec'd*). *Dau.* Susan Mary. *Career:* Engineering apprenticeship, Gt. Western Railway Co. 1917–23; Brunner Mond & Co. (later part of Imperial Chemical Industries Ltd.); Chief Engineer, I.C.I. (Alkali) Ltd. 1930–40; Ministry of Supply (Dep.-Director-General, Royal Filling Factories; Deputy Controller, Production Division, Atomic Energy Organization) 1940–54; member of Board and Managing Director, Industrial Group, U.K. Atomic Energy Authority 1954–57; Chairman, Central Electricity Generating Board 1957–64; Chairman, International Exec. Cncl., World Power Conference, 1962–68. Special Adviser to the World Bank 1965–70; Depty Chmn. Electricity Supply Research Cncl. 1965—; Chancellor of Bath Univ. 1966; Pres. of the Council of Engineering Institutions 1976, & Pres. of the Fellowship of Engineering *Awards:* Fellow of: The Royal Society; The Royal Society of Arts; Institution of Chemical Engineers; (Hon) Institution of Civil Engineers; Institution of Mechanical Engineers (Pres. 66/67); Institution of Electrical Engineers; Institution of Gas Engineers; Institute of Welding & the Welding Society; The Metals Society (Hon) Member of American Socy. of Mech. Engineers; Foreign Associate, National Acad. of Engineering in America; Imperial Order of the Rising Sun, 2nd Class (Japan). *Publications:* Engineers and Engineering; various technical papers. *Address:* Tiverton Lodge, Dulwich Common, London SE21 7EW.

**HIRACHAND, Lalchand,** BA. Indian Industrialist. *B.* 1904. *Educ.* Bombay Univ. (BA). *M.* Lalitabai. *S.* 3. *Dau.* 1. *Career:* Chairman: Premier Automobiles Ltd., Indian Hume Pipe Co. Ltd., Walchandnager Ind. Ltd., Premier Construction Co. Ltd., Copper Engineering Ltd., Tiwac Industries Ltd.; Chmn. & Man. Dir., Hindustan Construction Co. Ltd.; Dir., The Scindia Steam Navigation Co. Ltd., The Kesar Sugar Works Ltd. President: Indian Merchants' Chamber 1959; Maharashtra Chamber of Commerce 1960–64; Automotive Manufacturers' Assn. of India 1954–59; Assn. of Indian Automobile Manufacturers 1960–61; Member, Bombay Leg. Council 1939; Rajya Sabha 1952–58; former Mem., Import Adv. Council of the Govt. of India; Pres. Swatantra Party, Bombay Region, 1968–71. *Address:* Neela House, M. Deshmukh Marg, Bombay-400 026; and *office* Construction House, Walchand Marg, Ballard Estate, Bombay 400 038, India.

**HIRSCHSPRUNG, Asger M.** Danish. *B.* 1909. *Educ.* High School in Rungsted Statsskole; trained in cigar industry in Copenhagen, Amsterdam and Mannheim, with later study in London (Eng.). *M.* 1962, Grethe Elisabeth Henningsen. *Daus.* (by former marriage) Sonja and Ruth. *Career:* Joined A. M. Hirschsprung & Sønner Ltd. 1926, Confidential Clerk 1938, Man. Dir. 1945–73. Member Board of Directors, Association of Danish Cigar and Tobacco Manufacturers 1939–72, and the Association's Executive Committee 1945–72. Member of the Board of Directors of Danske Salgslederes Faellesråd (Assn. of Danish Sales and Marketing Executives) 1958–70. (Pres. 1958–63). *Award:* Knight of the Icelandic Order of the Falcon (1975). *Clubs:* Rotary; various within the world of music and tennis. *Address:* Ordrupvej 2, DK-2920 Charlottenlund, Denmark.

**HITCHCOCK, John Oliver.** British. *B.* 1909. *Educ.* London Univ. (BSc). *M.* Majorie Tolley. *S.* 1. *Daus.* 2. *Career:* Joined International Nickel Ltd. 1927, Vice-President of International Nickel Co. of Canada Ltd. 1967–72; Chmn., Engelhard Industries Ltd. since 1972. *Member:* Institution of Metallurgists; Institution of Mining and Metallurgy. Fellow, The Royal Aeronautical Socy, Vice-pres., The Metals Socy. *Publications:* various contributions to technical journals. *Club:* Naval and Military (London). *Address:* High House, Underriver, nr. Sevenoaks, Kent; and *office* Engelhard Industries Ltd., St. Nicholas House, Sutton, Surrey.

**HJORTH-NIELSEN, Henning.** Danish Diplomat. *B.* 1913. *Educ.* Master of Law. *M.* 1947, Ernestine Hjorth-Nielsen. *Career:* Sec., Ministry of Justice, Copenhagen 1938; Sec. to Governor of the Faroe Islands 1939; Joined British Forces 1944; Danish Liaison Officer to Germany 1945; Entered Danish Foreign Service 1946; Served on Danish Delegation to North Atlantic Council 1951–52; at International Secretariat of NATO 1952–54; Head of Danish Delegation to OEEC in Paris 1954–57; Consul General in London 1959–63; Ambassador to the Netherlands 1963; Ambassador & Perm. Rep. of Denmark to the North Atlantic Council in Brussels 1966–73 (and since 1967 also Ambassador to Belgium & Luxembourg); Ambassador to Canada 1973–75; Ambassador & Perm. Rep. of Denmark to the UN, New York 1975–77; Ambassador to Sweden since 1977. *Address:* Embassy of Denmark, Gustaf Adolfs Torg 14, Stockholm 11186, Sweden.

**HLADIK, Dr. Theodor.** Austrian industrialist (textiles). *B.* 1923. *Educ.* Doktor der Wirtschaftswissenschaften, Diplomkaufmann. *M.* 1953, Ingeborg Brioschi. *S.* Markus and George. *Dau.* Astrid. *Career:* Member of the Bd. of Directors, F. M. Hämmerle Textilwerke A. G. Dornbirn. Procurist: Hämmerle & Böhler; Iris-Taschentuchfabrik Dornbirn, F. M. Hämmerle & Co., Meersburg; Dreihammer AG, St. Gall. Vorarlberg Petroleum Co.; Anglo-Elementar Assurance, Vienna. *Address:* c/o Textilwerke F. M. Hämmerle, Steinebach 9, Dornibirn, Vorarlberg, Austria.

**HOADLEY, Walter Evans.** American financial executive and economist. *B.* 1916. *Educ.* Univ. of California (AB 1938, MA 1940, PhD. 1946) and Franklin & Marshall Coll. (Hon, DComSc 1963); LLD Golden Gate Univ. 1968. *M.* 1939, Virginia Alm. *S.* Richard. *Dau.* Jean Elizabeth (Price). *Career:* Collaborator U.S. Bur. Agricultural Economics 1938–39; Research Economist and Teaching Fellow, Univ. of Calif. 1938–41; Supervisor, Industrial Management, War Training Office 1941–42; Senior Economist, Federal Reserve Bank of Chicago 1942–49; Economic Adviser, University of Chicago Civil Affairs Training School 1945; Economist Treas., Vice-Pres., Armstrong Cork Co. 1949–66; Chairman, Federal Reserve Bank of Philadelphia 1962–66; Dir., Armstrong Cork Co., Lancaster, Pa. 1962—; Executive Vice-Pres. and Chief Economist and member Managing Cttee., Chmn. Baimco (subs.), Bank of America NT & SA 1966—. *Member* of Faculty, Graduate School of Banking, Univ. of Wisconsin 1958–66. Adviser to various U.S. Govt. agencies. Member: White House. Rev. Committee for Balance of Payments Statistics 1963–65; President Nixon's Task Force on Economic Growth. Fellow American Statistical Assn. (Vice-Pres., Dir. 1952–54, Pres. 1958). Member Amer. Finance Assn. (Dir. 1955–56, Pres. 1969); Conf. Business Economists (Chmn.) 1962; C. of C. of the U.S.; Amer. Mktg. Assn.; Amer. Econ. Assn.; Western Economic Assn.; Financial Analysts of S.F. Fellow, Nat. Assen. Business Economists; The Conf. Bd. (economic forum): Business Cncl. Tech. Cons. (Chmn. 1963–66); Amer. Bankers Assn. Cttee. Urban and Community Affairs, Chmn. 1972–73; National Commission, Study of Nursing & Nursing Education, Advisory Cttee.; Presidential Task Force, Land Use and Urban Growth 1972–73; Board of Trustees, U.S. Council, International Chamber of Commerce 1976—; Economic Adv. Com., Amer. Bankers Assn. 1976—; Panel of Economic Adv., U.S. Congressional Budget Office 1976—; U.S.–Japan Shimoda Conference 1977; Trustee Conservation Foundation. International Conference, Commercial Bank Economists and others. Phi Beta Kappa. Methodist. *Awards:* Hon. D.Com.Sc. 1963; Hon. Dip. El Inst. Tecnol. Autonomo de Mexico 1974. *Clubs:* Commonwealth; Pacific Union, Silverado Country; St. Francis Yacht; Bankers of S.F. *Address:* 999 Green St., San Francisco; and *office* Bank of America NT & SA, San Francisco, Calif., U.S.A.

**HOBART, Donald Marcene.** American business consultant, Hilton Head Island, S.C. *B.* 1897. *Educ.* Wooster College (Ohio); Univ. of Pennsylvania (BS.Econ. 1920); Hon. DBA, Bowling Green State Univ., Ohio 1957. *M.* 1931, Elizabeth Ostrom Cross. *Daus.* Elizabeth Joan (Valle), and Rachel Laramy (Thornton). *Career:* Elected to Hall of Fame in Distribution, Oct. 1953; Parlin Memorial Lecturer 1954; Pres., Amer. Marketing Assn. 1945; Instructor in Merchandising, Wharton School, Univ. of Pennsylvania, Philadelphia; Speaker and Writer on marketing, marketing research, advertising, selling and selling subjects; Consultant, Foreign Agriculture Service, Dept. of Agriculture and Sea Pines Plantation Co. *Publications:* Marketing Research Practice (1950); Praxis Der Markt-Forschung (1952); Selling Forces (1953); Verkaufs-Dynamik (1955). *Address:* 3 Cedar Waxwing Road, Hilton Head Island, S.C. 29928, U.S.A.

**HOBART, George Maxwell.** Canadian Chemical engineer; *B.* 1894. *Educ.* McGill Univ. (Chem. Eng.). *M.* 1924, Marguerite Tuckey. *S.* George M. Jr., R. R. and D. G. *Dau.* Mary Elizabeth (Fuller). Past Chairman of Board, Consolidated Bathurst Ltd. Director: Belgium Standard, Ltd. *Member:* Professional Socy. of Engrs. of Ont. LLD, Sir J. W. Williams University. *Clubs:* St. James, University. *Address:* 3940 Côte des Neiges (Apt. B92), Montreal; and *office* 800 Dorchester Blvd., Montreal, P.Q., Canada.

**HOBBS, Marvin.** American. Member, Board of Directors, A.R.F. Products, Inc. *B.* 1912. *Educ.* Tri-State College (BS Elec. Eng.); Univ. of Chicago. *M.* 1936, Bernadine Weeks. *Career:* Consultant, Radio Corp. of America 1946–49; Dir., Electronics Div. Supply and Logistics Office, Secy. of Defense, Washington 1950–62; Member, Electronics Production Bd., Office of Defense Mobilization, U.S.A. 1951–52; U.S. Dept. of Defense representative at NATO Cttee. meetings in London and Rome, 1951–52; Vice-Pres., Harvey-Wells Electronics Inc., Southbridge 1953–54; Asst. to the Exec., Vice-Pres., General Instrument Corp. 1958–62; General Mgr., Design Service Co., Inc., Division of Dictaphone Corp., 1963–68; Dir., New Programmes, American Bosch Arma Corp.; Director of Marketing, American Machine & Foundry Co., Boston, 1955–56; Gladding Corp., 1968—. *Publications:* Modern Communications Switching Systems (1974) and numerous articles on frequency modulation, radar, magnetrons and audio; and books on missiles, rocketry and spacecraft. *Address:* 655 W. Irving Park Road, Chicago, Ill. 60613, U.S.A.

**HOBBS, Ranald Purcell.** American publisher. *B.* 1907. *Educ.* Dartmouth College. *M.* 1936, Vera Ingeborg Andren. *S.* Ranald Dearborn. *Dau.* Linda Andren. *Career:* with The Macmillan Co., New York 1935–43; Rinehart & Co. Inc. 1943–60; member: Board of Education, Darien, Conn. 1948–55 (Chairman 1950–52); Representative Town Meeting, Darien 1957–59; Director, American Textbook Publishers Institute 1956–59. President: Hobbs International Inc. 1962–64; Hobbs Context Corp. 1964–77; Editorial Hobbs-Sundamericana S.A., Buenos Aires; Executive Vice-President, Rinehart & Co. Inc. 1955–60; The Bobbs-Merrill Co. Inc. 1960–61; Vice-Pres. and Secy. BCMA 1971–77, Vice-Pres. & Treas. 1977—; Reg. vice-pres. United Students' Aid Funds 1973–77. *Clubs:* Dutch Treat; Dartmouth (NYC). *Address:* Shagbark Road, Wilson Point, S. Norwalk, Conn., U.S.A.

**HOBDEN, Reginald Herbert.** British Diplomat. *B.* 1919. *Educ.* Sir William Borlase's Grammar School. *M.* 1945, Gwendoline Ilma Vowles. *S.* 2. *Dau.* 1. *Career:* Colonial Office 1936–64; War Service with RAF (Squadron Leader) 1940–46; Seconded to Dept. of Technical Cooperation 1961–62; UK Commission, Malta 1962–64; H.M. Diplomatic Service since 1964; Counsellor, Dar Es Salaam 1968–69; Counsellor (Economic & Commercial), Islamabad 1970–75; High Commissioner to Lesotho, since 1976. *Decorations:* Distinguished Flying Cross (1944); Mentioned in Despatches (1942). *Clubs:* Royal Commonwealth Society, London. *Address:* 14 Belmont Close, Uxbridge, Middx.; & c/o Foreign & Commonwealth Office, London SW1.

**HOBEL, Adolf Heinrich,** LLD. *B.* 1910. *Educ.* Univ. of Vienna (LLD). *M.* 1959, Edith Leitner (Comm. Dipl.). *Career:* Entered Civil Service (Finance) 1933; Ministry of Social Administration 1937 (Secy. 1945); diplomatic service in Vienna 1948; Pol. Representation of Austrian Govt. in Moscow 1949–52; Counsellor 1951; in Fed. Chancellery, Foreign Affairs 1952–54; Chargé d'Affaires, Sofia 1954–58; Head of Dept. Fed. Min. Foreign Affairs 1958–60; En. Ex. and Min. Plen. 1959; Minister to Finland 1960; Ambassador to Finland 1961–64. Ambassador of Austria to South Africa 1964–68; Ambassador, special mission, Independence ceremonies of Botswana 1966, and Lesotho 1966; Head, Consular Dept., Federal Ministry of Foreign Affairs, 1968–72; Ambassador to Chile since 1972. *Awards:* Grand Cross Order of Finnish Lion; member Osterreichische Gesellschaft f. Aussenpolitik und, Internationale Beziehungen. *Publications:* Osterreichische Apothekengesetzgebung, 1948. *Address:* Vienna 1, Ballhaus Platz 2, Austria.

**HOBERECHT, Earnest Trevar,** BA American businessman insurance executive. *B.* 1918. *Educ.* Univ. of Oklahoma (BA). *Career:* Chief Correspondent and Manager for Japan, United Press 1948; Gen. Mgr., Asia 1951; Vice President, United Press International 1953; War Correspondent World War II, Korean War, Vietnam War; Owner & Pres., Blaine County Abstract Co. Inc.; The Watonga Abstract Co. Inc.; Owner, Ernest Hoberecht Insurance; Pres., Oklahoma Land Trust; Pres., American Suppliers Inc.; Pres., American Southeast Asia Corporation, Saigon. *Member:* (Life) Sigma Delta Chi; Foreign Correspondents Club of Japan; Oklahoma Journalism Hall of Fame; Assn. Insurance Agents; National Assn.; Oklahoma Land Title Assn. (Pres. 1977). Amer. Land Title Association. *Publications:* Tokyo Romance (English & Japanese); Tokyo Diary; Democratic Etiquette; Fifty Famous Americans; Shears of Destiny (Japanese); Asia Is My Beat. *Awards:* Oklahoma Hall of Fame, 1977. *Address:* Oklahoma Land Trust, Box 368, Watonga 73772, U.S.A. 1317 North Noble, Watonga, Okla., U.S.A. and *office* 100 W. Main, Watonga, Okla.

**HOBSON, John Waller,** CBE. British company director. *B.* 23 Sept. 1909. *Educ.* Rugby and King's College, Cambridge (MA); Fellow (Pres. 1965–67), Institute of Practitioners in Advertising (FIPA); FRSA. *M.* 1935, Barbara Jane Davenport. *S.* 3. *Dau.* 1. *Career:* Hon. Pres. Ted Bates Ltd. and Hon. Chmn. Bates International, Europe; with London Press Exchange, Ltd. 1930–40: Ministry of Lab. 1940–43, Ministry of works 1943–45. Dir., Colman, Prentis & Varley Ltd. 1945–55; Chairman, John Hobson & Partners Ltd. 1955–59; Chmn. & Man. Dir., Hobson Bates & Partners Ltd. 1959–72; Dir., Ted Bates N.Y. 1959–72; Chairman, Advertising Assocn., 1971–75; Pres. European Assn. of Advertising Agencies 1971–75. *Publications:* Hulton Readership Survey (1947–53); The Selection of Advertising Media (1955); The Influence and Techniques of Modern Advertising (Cantor Lectures, R.S.A.). *Address:* Thunderdell, Ringshall, nr. Berkhamsted, Herts.

**HOCHOY, Sir Solomon,** TC, GCMG, GCVO, OBE; *B.* 1905. *Educ.* St. Mary's Coll., Port-of-Spain. *M.* 1935, Thelma Edna Huggins. *Dau.* 1. *Career:* Served in Trinidad Government: Clerk 1928; Labour Officer 1944, Dep. Industrial Adviser 1946; Commissioner of Labour 1949; Dep. Colonial Secretary 1955; Colonial Secretary 1956; Governor 1960–62; Governor Gen. Comm.-in-Chief 1962–72. Chmn. Nat. Scout Council; Hon. Patron, World Scouting. *Awards:* Queen's Coronation Medal; Knight Grand Cross, Order of St. Michael and St. George; Knight Grand Cross, Royal Victorian Order; Officer of the Order of the British Empire; Knight, Venerable Order, St. John of Jerusalem. *Clubs:* Royal Commonwealth Society. Corona. *Address:* Blanchisseuse, Trinidad and Tobago.

**HOCHWALT, Carroll Alonzo.** *B.* 1899. *Educ.* Univ. of Dayton (BChE; DSc); Hon. DSc. Washington and St. Louis Univs. *M.* 1922, Pauline Rosemaire Burkhardt. *S.* 2, *Dau.* 1. *Career:* Research Chemist, Gen. Motors Corp. 1920–24; Prod. Mngr., Ethyl Gasoline Corp. 1924–25; Vice-Pres., Thomas & Hochwalt Labs. 1926–36; Assoct. Dir., Central Research Dep. Monsanto Chemical Co. 1936–45; Co-ordinator of Research, Development and Patents 1948; Vice-Pres. May 1947; elected to Board of Directors March 1949; appointed member, Executive Committee Nov. 1950; in charge of Research, Development and Engineering, 1954–64. Member, Research Cttee. Witco Chemical Corp., Policy Cttee., Mallinckrodt Chemical Works. President and Director, St. Louis Research Council 1964–67, Dir. 1964—. Director, The Boatmen's National Bank of St. Louis since 1949, The Chemstrand Corp. 1949–50 (Pres. April 1949–Nov. 1950), Carboline Co. of St. Louis, Petrolite Corp. of St. Louis. Trustee, Univ. Dayton Catholic Univ. of America, Washington D.C. and Kettering Foundation. *Awards:* Midwest, Amer. Chemical Socy.; Distinguished Alumnus, Univ. of Dayton; Brotherhood Citation, Nat. Conf. Christians & Jews; Cardinal Gibbons, The Catholic Univ. of America; Socy. Chemical Industry, Amer. Section; Knight of Malta, Pope Paul VI. *Publications:* Diplumbic Hexaethide: A New Organic Compound (1924); Ferrous Selenide as a Contact Catalyst for Cracking (1924); Effect of Alkali-metal Compounds on Combustion (1928); Effect of Dehydration of Nitrocellulose on Orange Peel of Sprayed Lacquer Films (1933); Hydrogenation of Freshly Distilled Spirits (1936); Alkyl Esters of Phosphoric Acid (1942). *Address:* 7 Upper Ladue Road, St. Louis, Missouri.

**HOCKADAY, Arthur Patrick,** CB, CMG, MA. British. Government service. *B.* 1926. *Educ.* Merchant Taylors' School Northwood; St. John's Coll. Oxford (1st class, Literae Humaniores). *M.* 1955, Peggy Prince. *Career:* with Admiralty London and Bath 1949–62; Private Secy. to Secy. of State Ministry of Defence London 1962–65; NATO International Staff 1965–69; Asst. Secy. Gen. for Defence Planning and Policy 1967–69; Asst. Under Secy. of State Min. of Defence London 1969–72; Under Secy. Cabinet Office 1972–73; Deputy-Under Secy. of State, Ministry of Defence 1973–76; Second Perm. Under-Secy., Min. of Defence since 1976. *Awards:* Companion, Most Honorable Order of the Bath and Most Distinguished Order, St. Michael and St. George; Master of Arts (Oxford University). *Address:* 2 Toll-Gate Drive, Dulwich, London, SE21 7LS; and *office* Ministry of Defence, Whitehall, London, SW1A 2HB.

**HOCKING, Sidney Jack Fenn,** CMG. Australian newspaper editor (Ret.). *B.* 1901. *M.* 1927, Iris Grace Kyle. *S.* 2. *Daus.* 3. *Career* devoted mainly to working journalism. Chairman of Directors, Hocking & Co. Pty. Ltd., publishers of Kalgoorlie Miner (daily), and director (ret'd chmn.) of West Australian Newspapers Ltd., Perth, publishers of the West Australian (morning daily) and the Daily News (afternoon daily. *Member:* Commonwealth Press Union; Regional Daily Press Association. *Award:* Order of Companion St. Michael & St. George. *Clubs:* Hannans (Kalgoorlie); Perth (Perth). *Address:* 60 Egan Street, Kalgoorlie, W.A.; and *office* West Australian Newspapers, 125 St. George's Terrace Perth, W.A., Australia.

**HODGES, Parke Abernethy.** American. Consulting mining engineer. *B.* 1902. *Educ.* Harvard College (B.Sc. 1925) and Massachusetts Institute of Technology (M.Sc. Mining Engineering 1927). *M.* 1937, Margaret Ann Lennihan, *Career:* Engineer and Foreman, Braden Copper Co., Rancagua, Chile 1927–30; Evaluation Engineer, Compania Transvias Luz y Fuerza de Puebla S.A. 1930–32; Consulting Engineer, Mexico City 1932–34; Mine Superintendent, Compania Kildun y Anexas S.A., Matauala S.L.P., Mexico 1935–37; Consulting Engineer, Northern Mexico 1937; Mining and Chief Field Engr., Climax Molybdenum Co. 1938–48; Consulting Engr. and Geologist, Vanadium Corp. of America in Southern Rhodesia 1948–49; Consulting Engineer, Behre Dolbear & Co. Inc. 1949— (Secy. 1950–55, Vice-Pres. and Director 1950–66 Pres. and Dir. 1967–73. Engaged in examination, evaluations and economic studies of mineral deposits in U.S., Canada, Mexico, Central America, South America, Africa, Australia, Philippines, and Turkey. Mineral Adviser, Republic of Haiti 1956; Consultant to International African-American Corp. on iron deposits in Liberia 1957–58; to Min. of Mines & Hydrocarbons, Venezuela 1958–61; to Salt Cttee., Danish Academy of Technical Sciences 1958–59; Benquet Consolidated Philippine Islands 1967–70; Member, operating committee, and Director Compagnie des Potasses du Congo 1964–66. *Member:* Amer. Inst. of Mining & Metallurgical Engineers; Canadian Inst. of Mining & Metallurgy; Socy of. Economic Geologists; Mining & Metallurgical Socy. of America (Secy. 1955–56). Republican. *Publications:* articles in the technical press. *Clubs:* Mining (N.Y.C.); Harvard; M.I.T.; Military Order of the Loyal Legion; Explorers; Cambridge (Md.) Yacht; Greenville Country (Del.). *Address:* 1401 N. Broom Street, Wilmington, Del.; Hunyani Landing, P.O. Box 431, Cambridge, Md.; and *office* 299 Park Avenue, N.Y.C. 10017, U.S.A.

**HODGSON, James Day.** American. Chmn. of the Board Lucky Mc Uranium Co. *B.* 1915. *Educ.* Univ. of Minnesota (AB), Graduate Works, Univ. and UCLA. *M.* 1943, Maria M. Denend. *S.* Frederic. *Dau.* 1. *Career:* Jr. Exec. Trainee, Dayton Co. Minn. 1938–40; Supervisor, Youth Employment State of Minn. 1940–41; Numerous Industrial Relations positions including: Director of Industrial Relations 1941–68; Corporate Vice-Pres., Lockheed Aircraft Corp., Calif., 1968–69; Under Secy. of Labour, Washington D.C. 1969–70; Secretary of Labour 1970–73; Senior Vice-Pres., Lockheed Aircraft Corp. 1973–74; Ambassador to Japan 1974–77; Regents Lecturer, UCLA 1977–78; Adjunct Scholar, American Enterprise Inst. 1977–78. *Member:* Aerospace Industries Assn.; National Industrial Conference Board; Amer. Mangt. Assn.; Dir., Bullock Fund; Ticor Corp.; ARA Industry; Japan-Amer. Soc., N.Y.: Hewlett Packard. *Awards:* Univ. of Minnesota's Distinguished Achievement 1970; Doctor of Laws, Temple Univ. 1971; Doctor of Laws Univ. Cincinnatti 1972. *Publications:* Employing the Unemployables; Automation; Federal Regulation of Unions; Management Thinking; Japan's Production Machine. *Clubs:* Burning Tree Country, Bethesda, Washington D.C.; Los Angeles Country. *Address:* 10132 Hillgrove Drive, Beverly Hills, Calif. 90210, U.S.A.

**HODGSON, John Brailsford.** Company director. *B.* 1926. *Educ.* Hilton Coll., Natal; Witwatersrand University. *M.* 1949, Ruth Reid Robson. *S.* 1. *Daus.* 2. *Career:* Joined S.A. Army 1943; service, Italy with Royal Natal Carbineers, after demob. studied Civil Engineering, Wits Univ.; Joined Darling & Hodgson 1947, Appt. to Bd. 1952, Chmn. & Chief Exec., Darling & Hodgson Ltd.; Chmn., Darling & Hodgson Industrial Holdings Ltd.; Chmn. following companies and operating subsidiaries: Ready Mixed Concrete (S.A.) (Pty.) Ltd.; Tanker Services (Pty.) Ltd.; Embecon S.A. (Pty.) Ltd.; Project Engineering Co. (Pty.) Ltd.; Paul's Industrial Investments (Pty.) Ltd. RF Materials (Pty.) Ltd. and subsids.: Waste-tech. Holdings (Pty.) Ltd. *Dir.:* Savage & Lovemore Holdings (Pty.) Ltd. *Clubs:* The River, Bryanston Country; Durban Country. *Address:* Sunbury, Witkoppen Road, Bryanston, Sandton, 2021 Tvl.; and *office* P.O. Box 41104, Craighall, Tvl. 2024, South Africa.

**HODGSON, Percy.** American (naturalized). *B.* (Yorks.) 1901. *Educ.* Bradford Durfee Technical Inst. (MSc); DScO, Curry College (Milton, Mass.), LLD, Pepperdine College and Univ. of Rhode Island; D. Hum., Silliman Univ.; *M.* 1924, Edith Mary Parkin. *Career:* Vice-Pres., Park & Shop Inc., Pawtucket, R.I.; Director: Blackstone Valley Gas & Electric Co. Eastern Utilities Associates, Old Colony Co-operative Bank, Eastern Edison Electric Co. President and Treasurer, Parkin Yarn Mill. Inc., Pawtucket, R.I.; Pres., Pawtucket Business Chamber Realty Corp. DSc Business Administration, Bryant College, Providence R.I. St. Andrew's School, New England Council, Y.M.C.A., Salvation Army; President, British Empire Club, Providence, R.I.; Pres. Emeritus, Visiting Nurse Association; formerly Pres., Rotary International (1949–50); Pres., Pawtucket Business Chamber; Pres. Blackstone Valley Electric Co., Bradford Durfee Coll.

of Technology; Trustee, Rhode Island Textile Assn., Old Slater Mill Museum, Barrington College; Pres., R.I. Fed. of Craftsmen's Clubs; Pres. (for State of R.I.), Natnl. League of Masonic Clubs; Vice-Chmn., R.I. Development Assn.; past officer, U.S. Chamb. of Comm.; former Dir. Valley Gas Co., Past Pres. of British Empire Club. Sen. Warden Emeritus, Christ Church (Episcopal). Also served as Chairman of the Mayor's Advisory Cttee. for the City of Pawtucket: acclaimed by Meadowbrook Club of Pawtucket as 'the outstanding citizen of the year'; received National Award of National Conference of Christians and Jews; fourteen trips around the world; as Pres. of Rotary International (1949 and 1950) travelled more than 200,000 miles in 79 countries, to visit and address Rotary Clubs; Member of Rhode Island Commodores; Hon. Citizen of many cities and states of U.S.A. *Awards:* include the following Orders; Condor of the Andes (Bolivia), Cruzeiro do Sul (Brazil), Al Merito (Chile), Juan Pablo Duarte (Dom. Repub.), Al Merito (Ecuador), Cedars (Lebanon), E. Sol. del Peru (Peru), San Carlos ((Columbia S.A.), and Legion of Honour (France). *Publication:* Service is my Business. *Address:* "Alta Vista", 65 Grand View Avenue, Lincoln, R.I. and *office* Parkin Yarn Mill, Inc., 21 Commerce Street, Pawtucket, R.I., U.S.A.

**HODKINSON, James.** British. *B.* 1910. *Educ.* Manchester Coll. of Technology. *M.* 1938, Marjorie M. Harris. *Career:* Dir. Wickman Ltd.; Dir., Wickman Machine Tools (Overseas) Ltd.; Dir., Wickman (Australia) Pty. Ltd.; Drury Wickman Ltd.; Johannesburg, Machine Tools (India) Ltd.; Billington & Co. Ltd (New Delhi). *Clubs:* Directors; Leamington and County Golf; Royal Calcutta Golf. *Address:* 9 Northumberland Road, Leamington Spa, Warwicks and *office* Banner Lane, Tile Hill, Coventry.

**HODSON, Rt. Hon. Lord,** MC (Life Peer). British. *B.* 17 Sept. 1895. *Educ.* Cheltenham College; Wadham College, Oxford (MA) Hon. Fellow. *M.* 1918, Susan Blake. *S.* 1. *Dau.* 1. *Career:* Served World War I with Gloucs. Regt. (Capt.) 1914–17; called to the Bar, Inner Temple 1921, Bencher 1938; Junior Counsel to Treasury (Probate Division) 1935; President, International Law Association 1956; Judge of the High Court of Justice (Probate, Divorce and Admiralty Division) 1937–51; Lord Justice of Appeal 1951–60; Lord of Appeal in Ordinary 1960–71. Order of the Crown of Italy. *Address:* Rotherfield Greys, Oxfordshire.

**HØEGH, Ove D.** Norwegian. *B.* 1936. *Educ.* Royal Norwegian Naval Academy; Harvard Graduate School of Business Administration (MBA). *M.* 1960, Nora Meyer. *S.* Leif Ovesøn, Thomas Christian. *Dau.* Anette. *Career:* Chairman and Manager, Leif Høegh & Co., Oslo; member of the Board, Norsk Elektrisk & Brown Boveri (NEBB), Oslo, *Address:* Hoffsjef Løvenskiold's vei 26, Oslo 3, Norway; and *office* Parkveien 55, Oslo 2, Norway.

**HOFF, Trygve J. B.** Norwegian publisher and editor. *B.* 12 Nov. 1895. *Educ.* Universities of Harvard and Oslo (PhD). *Career:* President, Hoffs Faelleskontor since 1922; Editor, Farmand since 1935, Owner and Publisher since 1938; Director, various Banks, Insurance & shipping companies. *Publications:* Economic Calculation in Socialist Societies; Peace and the Future—The Way of Liberocracy. *Address-* Roald Amundsengate 1, Oslo, Norway.

**HOFFMANN, Ralf Ludwig.** Canadian executive. *B.* 1910. *M.* 1945, Ingeborg Seepacher. *S.* Christopher. *Career:* Chmn. Canadian Hoechst. Ltd. 1957—. Member of Board: Trans-American Chemicals Ltd., Hoechst Industries Ltd., S.K.W. Electro Metallurgy Canada Ltd. *Member:* Canadian Inst. of International Affairs; The Chemical Inst. of Canada; Society of Chemical Industry. Dir., Canadian Chemical Producers Association. *Clubs:* St. James (Montreal); Canadian. *Address:* 2095 Hanover Road, Town of Mount Royal, Montreal; and *office* 4045 Côte Vertu Blvd, Montreal, 383, P.Q., Canada.

**HOFFMEYER, Professor Erik,** DSc. Danish economist and banker. *B.* 1924. *M.* 1949, Eva Kemp. *Career:* With the Danmarks Nationalbank 1951–59; studied in U.S.A. on Rockefeller Fellowship 1954–55; lecturer on economics, Univ. of Copenhagen 1956 (Prof. at the Univ. 1959–64); DSc (Econ) 1958; Economic Counsellor, Danmarks Nationalbank 1959–62; Governor Bikuben Savings Bank 1962–64 (Chairman of Board 1964). Pres., Assn. of Political Economy 1951–53; member, Bd. of Management, Nationaløkonomisk Forening (Economic Socy.) 1960–66, of the presidency of the Economic Council 1962–65, and of the Academy of Technical Sciences 1963. Economic Council 1965, Governor and Chairman of the Board of Governors of the Danmarks Nationalbank 1965—; Governor for Denmark to the International Monetary Fund 1965—; Danish Science Advisory Council 1965, C. L. David Collection, 1967; The Housing Mortgage Fund, 1969–72; Member Bd. of Dirs., European investment Bank 1973–77; Chmn. of the Cttee. of Governors of the Central Banks of the EEC Countries 1975–76. *Publications:* Dollar Shortage and the Structure of U.S. Foreign Trade (thesis 1958); Stabile priser og fuld beskæftigelse (1960); Strukturændringer på penge—og kapitalmarkedet (1960); Velfærdsteori og velfærdsstat (1962); Industriel vækst (1963); Monetary History of Denmark (1968), contributions to Nationaløkonomisk Tidsskrift and international economic journals. *Address:* Hegelsvej 22, 2920 Charlottenlund, Denmark; and *office* Danmarks National-Bank, Havnegade 5, DK-1093 Copenhagen K, Denmark.

**HÖGBERG, Petrus Emanuel.** Swedish shipowner. *B.* 23 March 1891. *Educ.* Commercial Schools. *M.* (1) Annie Malberg. *S.* Curt, Ake, Rolf. (2) 1945, Elsa Maria Malmgren. *Career:* Managing Director, Rederi AB Fredrika 1923–33, and of Stockholms Rederi AB Svea 1934, Chairman 1960–71; President, Baltic and International Maritime Conference 1949–51; Chairman of various companies. *Awards:* Commander, Grand Cross, Order of the North Star; Commander 1st Class, Order of Vasa; Commander 1st Class, Order of Lion (Finland); Commander, Order of White Rose of Finland; Cross of Eagle 2nd Class (Estonia); Officer Ordre de la Couronne (Belgium); Officer, Order of Orange Nassau (Netherlands); Cmdr. 1st. Cl. Order of Dannebrog (Denmark); Cmdr. with Star, Order of St. Olav (Norway). *Address:* Karlavägen 11, Stockholm and Skeppsbron 30, Stockholm.

**HOGG, Sir John Nicholson.** British banker. *B.* 4 Oct. 1912. *Educ.* Eton; Balliol Coll., Oxford (MA); Fellow of Eton College 1951–70. *M.* 1948, Barbara Mary Elisabeth. *S.* Malcolm, *Dau.* Susan. *Career:* Joined Glyn Mills & Co. 1934; served World War II with King's Royal Rifle Corps in Greece, Crete, Western Desert, Tunisia and N.W. Europe; rejoined Glyn Mills & Co. 1945; Dep. Chmn. Gallaher Ltd.; Dir., Prudential Assurance Co. Ltd.; Dir., National & Commercial Banking Group Ltd.: Dep. Chmn. Williams & Glyns Bank Ltd.; Dir. Honeywell Ltd.; Chmn., Brown Harriman & International Banks Ltd.; Chmn., Export Credit Guarantee Dept. Advisory Council 1962–67; Chmn., Abu Dhabi Investment Board 1968–75. *Address:* 67 Lombard Street, London EC3P 3DL.

**HOGGART, Richard,** BA, MA. English Educator & Author. *B.* 1918. *Educ.* Leeds LEA Schools; Leeds University. *M.* 1942, Mary Holt France. *S.* 2. *Dau.* 1. *Career:* Staff Tutor, Univ. of Hull 1946–56; Visiting Professor Univ. of Rochester, N.Y., U.S.A., 1956–57; Staff Tutor Univ. of Hull 1957–59; Sen. Lecturer Univ. of Leicester 1959–62; Professor, English Univ. of Birmingham 1962–73, Dir. Centre for Contemporary Cultural Studies 1964–73; Asst. Dir.-Gen. for the Social Sciences, Humanites and Culture at UNESCO 1973–75; Leverhulme Fellow, Univ. of Sussex 1975; Warden, Goldsmiths' Coll., Univ. of London since 1976. *Member:* Albemarle Cttee. Youth Services; Pilkington Cttee. Broadcaster; Edit. Bd. Universities Quarterly; Reith Lecturer; Gov., Royal Shakespeare Theatre; Arts Council; Chmn., Arts Council Drama Panel; New Statesman Board. *Awards:* BA 1st class Hons. English, Leeds Univ.; MA Leeds Univ.; Hon. D.Litt., Open Univ.; Docteur Honoris Causa de l'Univ. de Bordeaux. *Publications:* Auden (1951); The Uses of Literary (1957); W. H. Auden (1957); W. H. Auden—A Selection (1961); Teaching Literature (1963); Speaking to Each Other Vol. I, About Society (1967) and Speaking to Each Other Vol. II, About Literature (1970); Only Connect (Reith Lectures, 1972). *Address:* Norton's Field, Beavers Hill, Farnham, Surrey; Goldsmith's College, New Cross; London SE14 6NW.

**HOGLUND, Erik Anders Rune,** MA, PhD. Swedish. *B.* 1920. *Educ.* Stockholm School of Economics (PhD). *M.* 1947, Anne Marie. *S.* 2. *Career:* Department Store executive, Professor Stockholm School of Economics 1953; Consultant Svenska Handelsbanken 1954–55, member Mangt. Staff 1955, Exec. Vice-Pres. 1960–66. Pres. 1966–70; Chief Gen. Mgr., President, NK-Åhléns AB since 1970; Chmn. AGA AB, Almedahl-Dalsjöfors AB, Handelns Arbetsgivare-organisation; Försäkrings AB Trygg-Hansa, Sandrews, Svenska Arbetsgivareföreningen. *Awards:* Commander Order Vasa; Al Merito della Repubblica Italiana. *Address:* Sturegatan 38, Stockholm, Sweden and *office* Regeringsgatan 25, Stockholm.

**HOGUET, Robert Louis.** Inv. bkr. and broker. *B.* 1908. Harvard, A.B., 1931, M.B.A. 1933. *M.* Constance M. Roberts. *S.* Robert Louis III, George Roberts. *Dau.* Constance Middleton. *Career:* Office of Sec. U.S. Treasury Dept.,

Washington, 1933–35, with First Nat. City Bank N.Y. 1936–70; Exec. V.P. 1962–70; Vice Chmn. trust bd. 1968–70; Partner Tucker, Anthony & R. L. Day, N.Y.C. 1970–75; Chmn., Tucker, Anthony & R. L. Day, Inc. since 1975; Dir. Internat. Banking Corp. N.Y.C. 1954–70; N.Y. London Trustee Co. Ltd. 1964–70; Consumers Power Co. 1955–65, Anaconda Co. 1964–70; Bd. Dirs. Lincoln Center Performing Arts Inc. 1961–70; Pres. Repertory Theater of Lincoln Center 1961–70; Bd. overseers Harvard Coll. 1965–71; Chmn. of exec. cttee. 1969–70; Served from Lt. to Comdr. USNR 1942–45; Presently serving as Dir. London Guarantee & Accident Co. N.Y., Phoenix Assurance Co. N.Y.; Meb. Bd. Mgrs. Hosp. for Spl. Surgery, N.Y.C.; Trustee, Vice Chmn. Bd. Barnard Coll.; Bd. Dirs. French Inst., Fedn. French Alliances, Mem. Soc. Friendly Sons St. Patrick, Council Fgn. Relations. *Clubs:* Links, Century, River, Down Town Assn. (N.Y.C.) Maidstone, Piping Rock. *Address:* 1 E. 66th St., New York City 10021, U.S.A. and *office:* 120 Broadway, New York City 10005, U.S.A.

**HOHLER, Henry Arthur Frederick**, CMG. *B.* 1911. *Educ.* Eton College and Royal Military College, Sandhurst. *M.* 1945, Eveline Susan Hood. *S.* 2 (by previous marriage). *Daus.* 2. *Career:* Second Lieut., Grenadier Guards 1931. Entered Foreign Office 1934; served in Budapest, Berne, Helsinki, Moscow, Rome, Saigon and Paris. Head of Northern Dept., Foreign Office, 1951–56. Ambassador to Switzerland 1967–70. *Member.* Liveryman of the Grocers' Company. *Club:* Boodle's. *Address:* 16 Egerton Terrace, London SW3 2BT.

**HOHNEN, John Harold**, JP, ChEng, ACSM, FIMM, MAustM & M, FGS. Australian Mining Engineer. *B.* 1911. *Educ.* Camborne School of Mining, Cornwall. *M.* 1943, Frances Margaret Merrifield. *S.* Giles, David, Mark and John. *Dau.* Berta Jane. *Career:* Former Man. Dir., New Guinea Goldfields Ltd. and Rio Tinto Mining Co. of Aust.; Dir. of Operations, Conzinc Rio Tinto of Aust. in West Australia 1969. Since 1936 engaged in professional assignments India, West Africa, Australasia, incl. N.G. 12 years (New Guinea Goldfields). Former Official Member N.G. Legislative Council and Chmn. Native Apprenticeship Bd. Wartime service included Min. of Econ. Warfare (Enemy Resources Intelligence) and Min. of Supply, London. *Clubs:* Melbourne; Weld (Perth). *Address:* Flat 101, "Lawson", The Esplanade, Perth 6000, Western Australia.

**HOHOL, Dr. Albert Edward**, PhD. Canadian. *B.* 1922. *Educ.* Alberta Normal School; Univ. of Alberta; Univ. of Oregon in Eugene PhD. *M.* Katherine. *S.* 1. *Dau.* 1. *Career:* Teacher and Principal, Clover Bar School Division 1947–55; School Principal, Two Hills 1955–57; Asst. Principal 1957–59; Supt., Junior High Schools Special Services 1959–60; Admin. Assistant, West Jasper Place School Division 1963–64; Asst. Supt., Pupil Personnel Services Edmonton Public School Bd. 1964–68; Assoc. Supt., Educ. Administration 1969–71; Minister Manpower and Labour Province of Alberta 1971–75; Minister of Advanced Education and Manpower since 1975. *Member:* Canadian Mental Health Assn.; Bd. Governors; Prov. Adv. Cttee., Juvenile Delinquency; H.R.D.A. Cttee., Misuse of Drugs & Narcotics. *Address:* Department of Advanced Education and Manpower, Office of The Minister, Legislative Building, Edmonton, Alta., Canada T5K 2B6.

**HOLBROOK, David Stearns.** Canadian industrialist. *B.* 1912. *Educ.* Univ. of Pittsburgh (BS Mech.Eng.). *M.* 1931, Marguerite Somers. *S.* David Stearns, Jr., and Richard Lyman. *Dau.* Diane S. *Career:* Held various engineering and operating positions, U.S. Steel Corp. 1933–40; Asst. Chief Engineer, Homestead Works (in charge of Defense Plant Corporation Project), U.S. Steel Corporation 1940–44; Asst. Gen. Manager, Algoma Steel Corp., Sault Ste. Marie, Ont. 1944–45 (Exec. Asst. to Pres. 1945; Vice-Pres. 1946; Exec. Vice-Pres. 1949; Pres. 1956). Chairman of Board, Algoma Steel Corp. Ltd. Director: Royal Bank of Canada; and of Du Pont of Canada Ltd. *Member:* Iron & Steel Inst.; Association of Iron & Steel Engineers. Professional Engineer of Ontario and Pennsylvania. *Award:* LLD, Laurentian University; American Iron & Steel Institute Medal; International Nickel Co. Medal; Benjamin F. Fairless Award of Amer. Inst. of Mining, Metallurgical & Petroleum Engineers, Inc. (AIME). *Clubs:* Mount Royal (Montreal); York (Toronto); Sault Ste. Marie Golf and Country. *Address:* 44 Charles Street W, Box 4108, Toronto, Ont.; and *office* 503 Queen Street East, Sault Ste. Marie, Ont., Canada.

**HOLBROOK, Elmer Allen**, BS. American. *B.* 1919. *Educ.* Univ. of Pittsburgh (BS Industrial Eng.). *M.* 1941, Nancy Robling. *Career:* Gen. Mgr., Production Planning K.A.C.C. 1956–57; Marketing Mgr., Kaiser Aluminium & Chemical Corp. 1957–59; Vice-Pres., Gen. Mgr., Kaiser Aluminio S.A., Buenos Aires 1959–64; Gen. Mgr. and Dir., Comalco Industries Pty. Ltd. 1964–69; Exec. Vice-Pres., Kaiser Trading Co.; 1969–71, President since 1971; Corporate Vice-Pres., Kaiser Aluminum & Chemical Corp. 1975; Vice-Pres., Purchasing & Distribution. *Address:* 300 Lakeside Drive, Oakland, Calif., U.S.A.

**HOLBROOKE, Richard**, American Diplomat. *B.* 1941. *Educ.* Brown Univ.—BA. *M.* 1977, Blythe Babyak. *S.* 2. *Career:* Foreign Service Officer 1962–72; Pearce Corps Dir., Morocco 1970–72; Editor, Foreign Policy Magazine 1972–77; Dir. of Publications, Carnegie Endowment 1973–77; Asst. Sec. of State for East Asia & Pacific Affairs since 1977. *Member:* Inst. of Strategic Studies; Council on Foreign Relations. *Publications:* Various articles in *New York Times, Washington Post, The Atlantic*, etc. *Address:* 2101 Connecticut Avenue, N.W., Washington, D.C. 20008; and *office* Department of State, Washington, D.C. 20520, U.S.A.

**HOLDSWORTH, David Lindesay Bethune.** British. Business executive. *B.* 1922. *Educ.* Royal Naval Coll., Dartmouth; Royal Naval Staff Coll., Greenwich. *M.* 1948, Lorraine Graham Bacon. *S.* David Crispian Alsted Bethune. *Daus.* Lorraine Lindesay Graham and Mary Caroline Stuart. *Career:* Commissioned Midshipman R.N. 1939, advanced through grades to Commander 1957. Exec. Asst. to Head of the U.K. Deleg., Military Staff Cttee. to U.N., and Advisor to U.N. Security Cncl. 1947–48; re-organization duties with Royal N.Z. Navy 1949–51; Staff Officer (Operations) to Admiral Sir Walter Couchman, British Aircraft Carrier Squadron 1951–53; Staff Officer (Tactic) to Director, Tactical and Staff Duties, Admiralty, London 1954–56; Staff Officer (Plans) to the Admiral, British Naval Staff, Washington, D.C. 1957–59; Asst. U.K. National Liaison Officer to Supreme Allied Commander Atlantic 1957–1959; Deleg., Planning Bd. for Ocean Shipping 1958–59; Asst. Vice-Pres., Islands Investment Corp. 1961–62; Vice-Pres. 1962–65; Exec. Vice-Pres., Federal Union Inc., Washington D.C. 1976—; Dir., Sprat Bay Corp., U.S. Virgin Islands 1964—; Dir. Treas., Belmont Estates Ltd. 1965—; Partner and Secy., Chelsea Co. Inc. 1965–70; Partner, Brunswick Associates. Pres., Georgetown Pike Assn.; Vice-Pres., The Navy League; Dir., McLean Citizens Assn.; Trustee, Nat. Cybernetics Found. *Member:* Internat. Oceanographic Found., Washington Bd. of Trade and Nat. Assoc. of Real Estate Bds. *Clubs:* Naval and Military (London); Union (Malta); Metropolitan (Washington, D.C.); Royal Naval Officers (N.Y.C.); La Confrerie des Chevaliers du Tastevin. *Address:* Langley Ordinary, 1101 Chain Bridge Road, McLean, Va. 22101, and (summer) State Road, Chilmark, Mass.

**HOLE, George Vincer**, CBE. Former Chief Exec., British Airports Authority. *B.* 1910. *Educ.* Wilson's Grammar Sch., London Sch. of Economics, BSc (Econ.) 1933. *M.* 1938, Gertraud Johanna Anna Koppe (Baroness von Broesigke). *S.* 2. *Career:* Asst. Auditor, Exchequer and Audit Dept. 1929; passed First Div. Exam. 1935; Under-Secy. 1958; Min. of Aviation 1959–66; Chief Exec., British Airports Authority 1966–72; Consultancy & Academic work principally for the International Civil Aviation Organisation (ICAO), Montreal since 1972. Chmn. First Div. Assoc. 1949–50; Chmn. OEEC Prod. Group on Traffic Engineering and Control, U.S.A. 1954; Chmn. W. European Airports Assoc. 1970. *Member:* Council, Int. Bd. of Airport Operators 1970; Bd. Int. Civil Airports Assoc. (Chmn.); Bd. Airports Assocs. Co-ordinating Council (First Chmn.); FCIT; Hon. Treas. Caravan Club 1960–66. *Awards:* Officer, Order of Orange Nassau, Netherlands 1946; Officer, Order of Crown, Belgium 1946. *Clubs:* Reform; United Service; Royal Aero. *Address:* 6 St. Germans Place, Blackheath, London, S.E.3.

**HOLLADAY, Howard K.** Insurance, general agent. *B.* 1928. *Educ.* University of Georgia (BBA 1953). *M.* 1961, Jonnet Jean Kerns. *Career:* General Agent, Boston Agency, National Life Insurance Co. of Vermont, Boston, Mass. Recipient, National Quality Award 1957–59. Life member, Million Dollar Round Table 1957; Leaders Club 1954; Charter member, President's Club 1958; Leaders Round Table of Georgia 1957; Dir., Citizen's Commn. for Good Government; member, Junior Chamber of Commerce; Dir., Chamber of Commerce; Inter-Fraternity Council (Past Pres.); Pres. Holladay Associates of Boston. *Member:* Sigma Chi; Blue Key; Omicron Delta Kappa; Young Republicans. Episcopalian. *Clubs:* Sphinx; Bachelors'; University, Union (Boston); University (Augusta, Ga.); Augusta Country;

Gridiron. *Address:* 11 Chestnut Street, Boston 02108; and *office* P.O. Box 270, Boston 02117, Mass., U.S.A.

**HOLLAI, Imre.** Hungarian Diplomat. *B.* 1925. *Educ.* Political Sciences. *M.* 1949, Margit Fejes. *S.* 1. *Career:* Entered Foreign Service 1949; Counsellor, Dep. Perm. Rep. of the Hungarian People's Republic to the UN 1956–60; Head of International Dept. of the Central Cttee. of the Hungarian Socialist Worker's Party 1960–63; Ambassador to Greece, concurrently accredited to Cyprus 1964–70; Dep. Foreign Minister 1970–74; Perm. Rep. of the Hungarian People's Republic to the UN since 1974. *Decorations:* Order of the Hungarian People's Republic 1951; Order of Liberty, 1957; Order of Labour, Golden Degree, 1955, 1975; Royal Order of King George of Greece, 1964. *Address:* 425 East 58th Street, New York, N.Y.; and *office* 10 East 75th Street, New York, N.Y. 10021, U.S.A.

**HOLLAND, Sir (John) Clifton Vaughan,** Kt. cr. 1974, BCE, FIE (Aust.), FAIM, FAIB. Australian. *B.* 1914. *Educ.* Queen's Coll., Univ. of Melbourne (BCE). *M.* 1952, Emily Joan Atkinson. *S.* 3. *Dau.* 1. *Career:* Lieut.-Col. Royal Australian Engineers 1939–65 (War service: Middle East 1940–42; S.W. Pacific 1942–45). Managing Director: John Holland Construction Group 1949–72; John Holland Holdings Ltd. 1963–72; Chmn., Victoria Div. of Australian Outward Bound 1963—; National Chmn., Aust. Outward Bound 1973–74; Foundation Pres., Fed. Civil Eng. Contractors 1958–63; Councillor, Australian Civil Engineering Contractors 1962–67; Dir., T. & G. Mutual Life Society since 1972; Dir., Australia & New Zealand Group Holdings Ltd.; Mem., Economic Consultative Advisory Group to the Treasurer. *Member:* Committee of Management, Royal Melbourne Hospital 1963—. Churchill Fellowship Selection Cttee.; Rhodes Scholarship Selection Cttee. 1970–72; Export Dev. Council 1972–75; Consultative Cttee., Snowy Mts. Eng. Corp. 1971—; Inst. Public Affairs Council 1970—; Dir., Winston Churchill Memorial Trust; Chmn., Matthew Flinders Bi-Centenary Celebrations 1973; Foundation Fellow Acad. of Technological Sciences; Chmn., History Advisory Council of Victoria; Fellow, Inst. of Engineers Australia (FIE). Liberal. *Awards:* Peter Nicoll Russell Memorial Medal, 1974. *Clubs:* Naval & Military, Australian (Melbourne); Royal Melbourne Golf; Frankston Golf. *Address:* 14 North Road, Brighton, Vic.; and *office* 492 St. Kilda Road, Melbourne, 3004, Vic., Australia.

**HOLLAND, Sir Jim Sothern,** Bt., TD. *B.* 1911. *Educ.* Durnford, Marlborough, and Trinity College, Oxford (MA). *M.* 1937, Elisabeth Hilda Margaret Prickard. *Daus.* 2. *Career:* Served in World War II (City of London Yeomanry) 1939–45. A.D.C. to Lord Gort when Governor and Commander-in-Chief Malta. Director, Price & Pierce Ltd. 1959–67; Alternate Director, Charter Consolidated Ltd., Dir., Central Mining & Investment Corp. Ltd., Dir. Central Mining & Investment Corp. Ltd., Central Mining Finance Ltd., Rhodesia Railways Trust Ltd. Chairman, Wall Trust Ltd .1964–69. *Club:* Bath (London). *Address:* Dderw, Rhayader, Powys; and Pond Cottage, Westwell, Burford, Oxon.

**HOLLAND, Philip Welsby,** MP. *B.* 1917. *Educ.* Sir John Dean's School Northwich, Cheshire. *M.* 1943, Josephine Hudson. *S.* Peter Welsby. *Career:* Parliamentary Private Secy. to Minister of Pensions & National Insurance, 1961–62; to Chief Secretary to Treasury, 1962–64; Joint Secy. of the Conservative Parliamentary Cttee. on Employment & Productivity, 1967–70. Member, of Estimates Cttee. 1966–67 and Public Accounts Cttee., 1967–70. Member for Carlton Notts; P.P.S. to Ministry of Aviation Supply, for Aero space 1970–72; Vice-Chairman, Conservative Parliamentary Cttee. on Employment & Productivity, June–Oct. 1971; Personnel Management Adviser to Standard Telephones & Cables Ltd. 1969—; PPS to Minister for Trade 1972. Conservative. *Address:* 2 Holland Park Mansions, Holland Park Gardens, London, W.14.

**HOLLAND-MARTIN, Edward.** British banker. *B.* 8 March 1900. *Educ.* Eton and Christ Church, Oxford. *M. Dau.* 1. *Career:* Martins Bank Ltd. 1923–33; Director, Bank of England 1933–48; Dep. Chmn., Bank of London & South America Ltd., 1949–70; Vice-Pres. Council for Protection of Rural England (Hon. Treas. 1928–71); Hon. Treas. National Trust 1945–68. Director: Racecourse Holdings Trust Ltd. *Address:* 28 St. James's Place, London, S.W.1. and Overbury Court, Tewkesbury, Glos.

**HOLLANDER, Stuart David,** MA, CEng, MIMechE, MIProdE, FCI. British. *B.* 1932. *Educ.* Oundle School: Kings Coll., Cambridge (MA Mech Sci Tripos Part 1). AMI Mech E, MI Prod. E, C Eng. *M.* 1956, Gillian Sachs. *S.* 1. *Daus.* 2. *Career:* Hawker Aircraft Ltd. 1955–56; P.E. Consulting Group Ltd. 1956–59; E.M.S. Electrical Products Ltd. 1959–65, Director Kurt Salmon Associates Ltd.; Man. Dir. European Div. and Sen. Vice-Pres., Kurt Salmon Assoc. Inc. (Atlanta, Ga.). *Member:* Inst. of Directors; Fellow, Clothing Inst. *Address:* 19 Sandy Lodge Road, Moor Park, Rickmansworth, Herts.; and *office* 119/120 High St, Eton, Berks.

**HOLLEBONE, Derek Graeme,** British Shipping Conferences Chairman. MBE, MC, TD. *B.* 1916. *Educ.* Brighton Coll. *M.* 1946, Phoebe Rollo Howitt. *S.* 2. *Career:* Director, Port Line Ltd. 1963—. Director: Blue Star Port Lines (Management) Ltd., 1968—. Crusader Shipping Co. Ltd.; Associated Container Transportation Australia Ltd. *Address:* Moor Hill, Hindhead, Surrey.

**HOLLITSCHER von HOLLENWARTH, Karl,** RPD. Austrian reinsurance broker. Co-owner of Heckscher & Gottlieb, Cologne (founded Vienna 1874), Hollitscher & Gottlieb, Vienna, and Hollitscher & Co., Basle (Swtzerland). *B.* 1905. *Educ.* High School and University (Dipl. Pol. Econ. and D.Pol.Sc. *M.* 1948. Margarete Paltinger. *S.* Carl. *Publication:* International Reinsurance, Berlin (1931). *Address:* Nonnenweg 4, CH-4055 Basel, Switzerland.

**HOLLOM, Sir Jasper (Quintus),** KBE. British banker. *B.* 1917. *Educ.* King's School, Bruton. *M.* 1954, Patricia Elizabeth Mary Ellis. *Career:* Deputy Chief Cashier, Bank of England 1956–62; Chief Cashier, 1962–66; Director, Bank of England 1966–70, Deputy Governor since 1970. *Address:* Highwood, Selborne, nr. Alton, Hants.; and *office* Bank of England, London, EC2R 8AH.

**HOLLOMON, John Herbert.** Educator; Licensed professional engineer in New York State. *B.* 1919. *Educ.* Augusta Military Acad. (Fort Defiance, Va.) and Massachusetts Inst. of Technology (BS 1940; Ph.D. 1946); Hon. Ph.D.Eng.; Worcester Poly. Inst. Michigan Tech. Univ. and Rensselaer Polytechnic Institute; Carnegie-Mellon, Northwestern and Akron Univs. *M.* (1) 1941, Margaret Knox Wheeler (*Dec.*); (2) Nancy Elizabeth Gade. *S.* Jonathan Bradford, James Martin and Duncan Twiford. *Dau.* Elizabeth Wheeler Vrugtman. *Career:* Instructor, Harvard Univ. Graduate School of Engineering 1941–42; U.S. Army 1942–46; successively Research Associate, Research Laboratory 1946–49; Asst. to Manager, Metallurgy Research Dept. 1949–51; Manager, Metallurgy & Ceramics Research Dept. Research Laboratory 1952—60; General Manager, General Engineering Laboratory, General Electric Co. 1960–62. Asst. Secy. of Commerce, for Science & Technology 1962–67, also Acting Under-Secy. 1967–68; President, Univ. of Oklahoma 1968–70; Consultant to President and Provost 1970–72; Dir., Center for Policy Alternatives; Prof. of Engineering, Mass. Inst. of Technology since 1972. *Awards:* Legion of Merit (U.S.); Rossiter W. Raymond Award of American Inst. of Engineers 1946; Alfred Nobel Award of Combined Engineering Societies 1947; Rosenhain Medal, Inst. of Metals (England) 1958. *Publications:* some 300 papers and a textbook on Ferrous Metallurgical Design; Advisory Editor for a series of science books, Science & Technology of Materials. *Member:* Metallurgical Socy. of Amer. Inst. of Mining, Metallurgical and Petroleum Engineers; Amer. Socy. for Metals; Amer. Physical Socy. (Fellow); Natl. Acad. of Engineering (founding member); Amer. Acad. of Arts and Sciences (Fellow); Amer. Assn. for the Advancement of Science (Fellow, 1977); Socy. for Hist. of Technology; Elected Foreign Member, Royal Swedish Acad. of Engin. Sciences (1974); Sigma Xi, Kappa Sigma. *Clubs:* Harvard (Boston); Cosmos (Washington). *Address:* 121 Carlton Street, Brookline, Mass. 02146, Mass., U.S.A.

**HOLM, John Ferdinand,** DSC. New Zealand. *B.* 1912. *Educ.* Wellington College, Rongotai College (Univ. Entrance). Foreign-Going Master Mariner's Certificate (with sailing-ship endorsement). *M.* 1944, Marion Ogilvie Bell. *S.* 2. *Daus.* 2. *Career:* Served in Merchant Navy (sailor, officer, Master) 1930–40, and in the Royal Navy (Lieut.-Comdr.) in World War II. Managing Director, Holm & Co. Ltd., Wellington; Burgess Holm & Co. Ltd., Southern Traders Ltd., Huddart-Parker Building Ltd.; Fellow Inst. Chartered Shipbrokers; Fellow Chartered Inst. of Transport. *Member:* N.Z. Company of Master Mariners (Master); Inst. of Chartered Shipbrokers (London); Inst. of Transport; (Past) President N.Z. Shipowners Federation; Wellington Chamber of Commerce; Rongotai OB Assn. (Hon. Life Member) Bd of Govs. combined Wellington Colls; Wellington Harbour Board. *Clubs:* United Services Officers (Wellington); Royal Naval Reserve

Officers (London); Royal Port Nicholson Yacht; Lions. *Address:* 21 Newport Terrace, Seatoun Heights, Wellington 3, New Zealand; and *office* Holm & Co. Ltd., P.O. Box 1391, Wellington, New Zealand.

**HOLM, Tryggve O. A.**, Swedish Co. Chmn. *B.* 1905. *Educ.* Mining and Metallurgical Engineer, Royal Institute of Technology, Stockholm 1929. *M.* 1929. Gunvor Bruu. *Daus.* Inger-Marie (Zetterqvist) and Margareta (Berg). *Career:* Engineer, AB Bofors, Bofors, Sweden, 1929–30; Hess Bright Mfg. Co., Philadelphia 1930–31; Engineer, steel works AB Bofors, 1932–36 (Chief Engineer and Manager 1936–39); President, AB Svenska Järnvägsverkstäderna, Linköping, 1940–50, Saab Aktiebolag, Linköping, 1950–67; Chairman Swedish Employers' Confederation 1967–76 (Vice-Chmn. 1957–67. Member Board of the Federation of Swedish Industires 1967—. Chairman Board of Gusums Bruk AB 1964–76, Hexagon AB 1965–76, Skandinaviska Traimport AB 1967— (mem. Bd. 1940—), Vegete Insurance Co. 1968–75; Chmn. Bd. of AB Bofors since 1974 (mem. since 1968); Alfa-Laval AB 1970—. Member of Board: AB Svenska Järnvägsverkstäderna 1940–74, Saab Aktiebolag 1947—, Holmens AB 1955—, Allmana Pensionsfonden (National Pension Insurance Fund) 1959—, Skandinaviska Enskilda Banken 1969–75; SILA 1950—, ABA 1957—, Assembly of Representatives Scandinavian Airlines System 1962— (mem. Bd. 1957–62). Consul for Denmark 1949—. Chmn. Swedish Metal Trades Employers Assn. 1955–67. *Decorations:* Cdr. Order of Vasa (Sweden, 1st class); Grand Commander, Order of Nordstjernan; Cdr. 1st Class, Order of Dannebrog. *Address:* Vasavägen 13, Linköping, Sweden; and *office* Nygatan 54, Linköping, Sweden.

**HOLM, Wilton Robert.** American physicist. *B.* 1914. *Educ.* St. Ambrose Coll. (BS); Univ. of Iowa (grad. work). *M.* 1942, Helen L. Richtman. *Dau. Career:* As physicist is at present concerned with product planning, research and development of photographic (optical and magnetic) systems; Physics Instr., Univ. of Iowa 1941–42; Research Physicist, Naval Research Laboratory 1945; Officer, U.S.N.R. 1943–46; Colour Consultant, Cincecolor Corp., 1946–47; Asst. Dir. of Research & Development 1948; Dir., Photographic Services & Chief Colour Consultant 1949–52; Motion Picture Specialist and Technical Administrator E.I. Dupont de Nemours & Co., 1952–68; Vice-President, Association, Motion Pictures & T.V. Producer; Executive Director, Motion Picture and Television Research Centre 1968–77. Former President, Society of Motion Picture & T.V. Engineers. *Member:* Academy of Motion Picture Arts & Sciences; Society of Photographic Scientists & Engineers; American Society of Cinematographers; Optical Society of America; American Physical Society Fellow, Society of Motion Picture and Television Engineers (SMPTE). *Award:* outstanding service to U.S. Navy as a naval officer in World War II. *Publications:* various articles and works dealing with physical optics, photography and electronics. *Address:* 3149 34th Street, Rock Island, Ill. 61201, U.S.A.

**HOLMER, Paul Cecil Henry**, CMG. British diplomat. *B.* 1923. *Educ.* King's School Canterbury; Balliol Coll. Oxford. *M.* 1946, Irene Nora Beater. *S.* 2. *Daus.* 2. *Career:* Lieut., Royal Artillery 1942–46; Asst. Principal, Colonial Office 1947–49; Third Secy., Foreign Office 1949–51; Office, Commissioner General for the UK, SE Asia, Singapore 1951–55; First Secy., Foreign Office 1955–58, British Embassy, Moscow 1958–59, British Military Govt., Berlin 1960–64, Foreign Office 1964–66; Deputy High Commissioner, Singapore 1966–69; Counsellor, Foreign & Commonwealth Office 1969–72; Ambassador to the Ivory Coast, Upper Volta and Niger 1972–75; British Dep. Perm. Rep. at NATO, Brussels, since 1976. *Awards:* Master of Arts; Companion, Most Distinguished Order, St. Michael & St. George. *Club:* Travellers (London). *Address:* Stoke Park Farm Cottage, Guildford, Surrey and *office* c/o Foreign and Commonwealth Office, King Charles Street, London, S.W.1.

**HOLSCHUH, Carl G.** *B.* 1909. *Educ.* Rutgers University (BS 1931). *M.* 1935, Mary A. Hobbs. *S.* Frederick C. and John C. *Dau.* Anne E. *Career:* Employed by Sperry Gyroscope Co. since 1933 in various research and manufacturing positions, becoming President and General Manager of Sperry Gyroscope Div. of Sperry Rand Corp. from 1957–58 and Exec. Vice-President of Sperry Rand Corp. from 1958–65. Group Vice-President, Marine Systems General Dynamics Corporation, New York, 1965—. Hon. Dr. Eng., Rutgers Univ., 1950. *Member:* Aerospace Industries Assn. *Clubs:* Burning Tree; Deepdale Golf; Huntington Crescent: University. *Address:* 56 Cove Road, Huntington, N.Y.; and *office* One Rockefeller Plaza, New York City 10020, U.S.A.

**HOLTA, Halvor B.** Norwegian. Director-General, Tinfos Papirfabrik, Tinfos Jernverk A/S, and Notodden Calcium-Carbidfabrik A/S, all of Notodden. *B.* 1896. *Educ.* Civil Engineer, Norwegian Technical High School. *Awards:* Commander, Order of St. Olav (Norway); Commander, Order of the White Rose (Finland). *Address:* Notodden, Norway.

**HOLTEN-EGGERT, Christian D.** Danish diplomat. *B.* 18 Apr. 1912. *Educ.* Metropolitanskolen (Bachalaureat 1930) and University of Copenhagen (LLM 1936). *M.* 1942, Stéphanie Antoine-Feill. (*Dec'd* 1966). *Career:* Entered Danish Foreign Service 1937; Chief of Section, Foreign Office 1946 Deputy Permanent Rep of Denmark to U.N., New York 1949; Chief of Dept., Foreign Office 1953; Ambassador to Egypt 1956–61; Concurrently Ambass. to Ethiopia and Lebanon, Iraq, Jordan, Sudan & Syria. Ambassador to the Soviet Union 1961–66. Ambassador to Spain 1966–71, to Poland 1971–74; Ambass. to Austria 1974–77; Concurrently Ambassador to Hungary and Resident Rep. of Denmark in Vienna to IAEA; and to UNIDO; Head of Danish Delegation to MBFR in Vienna; Legal Advisor on International Affairs since 1977. Chairman, Danish Government delegations for negotiating trade and payment agreements 1946–49 and 1953–56; Ambassador on Special Mission to Argentine 1954, to Iraq 1959 and to Somalia 1960. *Publications:* Articles on Intern. and Danish Private Law. *Award:* Grand Cross, Orders of Merit (Austria), Independence (Jordan), Cedar (Lebanon), of the Republic (UAR) and of Isabella (Spain); Grand Officer, Order of Dannesbrog (Denmark) & of Merit (Syria); Commander, Order of Legion of Honour (France) and Order of Merit (Italy); Officer: St. Olav (Norway), and of Christ (Portugal). *Address:* Altenhof Castle, A-4142 Hofkirchen i.M., Austria.

**HOLTROP, Marius Wilhelm.** Dutch banker. *B.* 2 Nov. 1902. *Educ.* University of Amsterdam (Dr. Sc. Oecon.); Dr. h.c. Netherlands School of Economics; Univ. of Basle. *M* (1) 1926, Josina Juchter (*Dec.*). *S.* Ernst Jan. Wouter Herman. *Dau.* Marijke Elizabet. *M.* (2) 1965, Cathrin M. Peltenburg. *Career:* With Royal Dutch Blast Furnaces and Steel Works, IJmuiden 1929; Vice-Pres., Shell Chemical Company, San Francisco 1936; Mng. Dir., Royal Dutch Blast Furnaces and Steel Works IJmuiden 1939; Pres., De Nederlandsche Bank 1946–67; member of Board, Bank for International Settlements 1946–67, Chmn. of Board and Pres. 1958–67; Alternate Governor, International Monetary Fund, Washington 1947–52; Governor 1952–67. *Awards:* Knight, Order of Netherlands Lion; Grand Cross, Order of Orange Nassau (Netherlands); Grand Cross Order of the Crown (Belgium). *Address:* c/o De Nederlandsche Bank, Westeinde 1, Amsterdam; and Zomerzorgerlaan 2, Bloemendaal, Netherlands.

**HOLYMAN, Keith Cameron.** Australian company director. *B.* 7 Sept. 1911. *M.* 1933. Jean McRae. *S.* Peter Ross, Robin T. J. *Daus.* Mary Cameron, Elizabeth J. S. *Career:* Chmn. Wm. Holyman & Sons Pty. Ltd.; Chairman Associated Stevedores Pty. Ltd.; Electrical & Engineering Supplies Pty. Ltd.; Dep. Chmn., Kilndried Timber Industries Ltd. Director, E. R. Charman & Co. Ltd., Holyman Bros. Pty. *Address:* Mount Pleasant, South Launceston, Tasmania; and *office* Holyman House, Brisbane Street, Launceston, Tasmania, Australia.

**HOLYOAKE, Rt. Hon. Sir Keith (Jacka)**, GCMG, CH, PC, Governor-General of New Zealand. *B.* 11 Feb. 1904. *Educ:* Tauranga, Hastings and Motueka, Hon. LLD., Victoria University N.Z. 1966; Hon. LLD (Agric.) Seoul National University Korea, 1968. *M.* 1935, Norma Janet Ingram. *S.* Roger Henry Jacka, Peter Garden. *Daus.* Diane Flora, Lynley Norman, Keitha Jennifer, Mary. *Career:* Former Provincial Pres., Nelson Farmers' Union, later Dominion Vice-Pres.; Chmn. N.Z. Hop Marketing Cttee. 1938–41; Member, Executive, N.Z. Tobacco Growers' Federation and Fruit Exporters' Association. MP (National) for Motueka 1932–38; MP National Party Pahiatu Electorate 1943; New Zealand Delegate to World Conference of Farmers, London 1946; Deputy Prime Minister and Minister of Agriculture 1949; Prime Minister & Minister for Maori Affairs 1957; Leader of H.M. Opposition 1958–60; Prime Minister 1960–72; Minister of Foreign Affairs 1960–72; Member of H.M. Opposition 1972–75; Minister of State 1975–77; Gov.-Gen. of New Zealand since 1977. Pres., U.N. Food & Agric. Organisation Conference, Rome 1955. Chmn. of Anzus cncl. meetings in Wellington in 1963 and of Anzus Seato, and The Vietnam

Allies in Wellington 1968; Conference on Cambodia in Djakarta, 1970; Commonwealth Heads, Govt. Conference Singapore 1971; Five-Power Conference, Defence and Annual Ministerial Meeting SEATO, London 1971; South Pacific Forum, Canberra 1972. Freeman, City of London. *Clubs:* Ruahine (Dannevirke); Pahiatua; National (Wellington); Wellington (Wellington). *Address:* Government House, Wellington, New Zealand.

**HOMBERGER, Heinrich,** Dr. rer. cam.; Swiss commercial and industrial executive. *B.* 1896. *Educ.* St. Gall Commercial Univ. of Lausanne (Dr. hc); studied social economy and law, Univs. of Zürich and Paris (Dr. rer. cam.). *M.* 1922; Anny Liechti. *S.* 1. *Dau.* 1. *Career:* Del. Swiss Union of Comm. & Industry since 1950 (Secy. 1922; Dir. since 1939); President Swiss Life Insurance and Pension Co. Zurich. *Publications:* Aussenhandelspolitik (1939); Schweizerischer Handels- und Industrie-Verein (1939); Die Schweiz in der internationalen Wirtschaft (1949); Die schweizerische Aussenhandelspolitik und die Krise der Zahlungsbilanzen im Zeichen der internationalen Zusammenarbeit (1953); 2 Vorträge zur schweizerischen Zolltarifrevision (1957); Die Schweiz und die europäische Wirtschaftsintegration (1958); Die Entwicklung der europäischen Integration zum wirtschaftlichen Konflikt, und die Lage der Schweiz (1961), L'intégration Européene et la Suisse (1962); Schweizerische Handelspolitik in Wandel der Zeiten, 1965; Schweizerische Handelspolitik im Zweiten Weltkrieg, 1970. *Address:* Krähbühlstr 78, 8044 Zürich Switzerland.

**HOME, Baron,** of The Hirsel of Coldstream (Alexander Frederick). PC. *B.* 1903. *Educ.* Eton and Oxford Univ. *M.* 1936, Elizabeth Alington. *S.* 1. *Daus.* 3. *Career:* MP (Cons.), South Lanark 1931–45; Parliamentary Private Secretary to the Chancellor of the Exchequer 1936, to the Prime Minister 1937–40; Joint Under-Secretary of State for Foreign Affairs 1945; MP (Conservative) Lanark Division, Feb. 1950–51; Minister of State, Scottish Office 1951–55; Secretary of State for Commonwealth Relations 1955–60. Leader of the House of Lords 1957–60. Lord President of the Council 1957. Foreign Secretary 1960–63; MP for Kinross & West Perth 1963–74; Prime Minister and First Lord of the Treasury, Oct. 1963–64; (Formerly 14th Earl of Home; renounced peerage on becoming Prime Minister 1963); Leader of Opposition 1964–65. For. Secy. 1970–74. *Address:* The Hirsel, Coldstream, Berwickshire; and Castlemains, Douglas, Lanarkshire.

**HOMER, Sidney.** Investment banker. *B.* 1902. *Educ.* Harvard College (AB 1923). *M.* 1924, Marion Symmes. *Daus.* 3. *Career:* With Gilbert Eliott & Co. 1925–32; Homer & Co. Inc. (President) 1932–43; Foreign Economic Administration, Washington 1943–45; Scudder, Stevens & Clark (Manager, Bond Dep.) 1945–61; Partner, Salomon Brothers 1961–71; *Publications:* A History of Interest Rate 200 BC to the Present (1963); Inside the Yield Book (1973). *Address:* 36 Gramercy Park, New York City 3; and *office* 60 Wall Street, New York City, U.S.A.

**HOMMEL, Nicolas.** Luxembourg Diplomat. *B.* 1915. *Educ.* Louvain and Paris (Docteur en Droit). *M.* 1959, Denise Ruffié. *Career:* Barrister-at-Law in Luxembourg 1939–41; Counsellor-at-Law 1944–46; Member, Council of the Order of Barristers; Entered diplomatic service 1946; member, Luxembourg Military Mission in Berlin and delegate to Inter-Allied Reparations Agency in Brussels 1946–48; Permanent Rep. to OEEC 1949–59; Permanent Rep. to NATO 1949–59; Ambassador to Belgium 1959–62, and to France, 1963–67; Secy. Gen., Ministry of Foreign Affairs, 1967–68. Ambassador to the Federal Republic of Germany, 1968–73; Secy. General, Council of the European Communities since 1973. Has represented Luxembourg in several international negotiations. *Awards:* Grand Officer de la Légion d'Honneur; Grand Croix de l'Ordre de Léopold; Grand Croix de l'Ordre de la Couronne; Commandeur de l'Ordre d'Orange-Nassau; Commandeur de l'Ordre d'Adolphe de Nassau; Officier de l'Ordre du Mérite du Grand-Duché de Luxembourg; Chevalier de la Couronne de Chêne. *Address:* 170 Rue de la Loi, Brussels, Belgium.

**HONE, Sir (Herbert) Ralph,** KCMG, KBE, MC, GCSt.J., TD, QC, LLB. Colonial administrator and lawyer. *B.* 1896. *Educ.* Varndean Grammar School, Brighton; London Univ. *M.* (1) 1918, Elizabeth Daisy Matthews (marriage dissolved). *S.* 1. *Dau.* 1; (2) 1945, Mrs. Sybil Mary Simond. *S.* 1. *Career:* Served World War I with B.E.F. 1915–19; Assistant Treasurer, Uganda 1920; called to the Bar, Middle Temple 1924; Registrar of High Court, Zanzibar 1925–28; Resident Magistrate 1928–30; Crown Counsel, Tanganyika 1930; Attorney-General, Gibraltar 1933, Uganda 1937; Commandant, Uganda Defence Force 1940–42; Chief Civil Affairs Officer, Middle East 1942–43 (Major General), Malaya 1945–46; Secretary General to Governor-General, Malaya 1946–48; Deputy Commissioner-General (colonial affairs) S.E. Asia 1948–49, Governor and C.-in-C., North Borneo 1949–54; Head of Legal Division, Commonwealth Relations Office 1954–61; resumed practice at the Bar 1961; Constitutional Adviser, Kenya, Dec. 1961–Mar. 1962; Constitutional Adviser to Secretary of State for African Affairs July to Oct. 1962 and to South Arabian Govt. Oct. 1965 to Feb. 1966 and to Bermuda Govt. July to Nov. 1967; Standing Counsel, Grand Bahama Port Authority 1962–74. *Address:* 1 Paper Buildings, Temple, London, E.C.4; and 56 Kenilworth Court, Lower Richmond Road, London, S.W.15.

**HOOD, Harvey Perley.** Dairy industry executive. *B.* 1897. *Educ.* Phillips Andover Academy, Andover, Mass.; Dartmouth College (BS, Hon. LLD); Harvard Graduate School of Business Administration, Boston. *M.* 1928, Barbara Churchill. *S.* Charles Harvey II. *Daus.* Helen Olivia, Barbara Ellen Churchill, and Olivia Churchill. *Career:* Director: New England Telephone & Telegraph Co., Boston 1950–70, International Paper Company, New York 1952–69, and United Shoe Machinery Company, 1958–1969. President 1936–62, Chairman of the Board 1962–69, and Director since 1922, H. P. Hood Inc. Director, State Street Bank & Trust Co. Life Trustee, Dartmouth Coll., Hanover, N.H. 1941–67. *Address:* Masconoma Street, Manchester, Mass.; and *office* 500 Rutherford Avenue, Boston, Mass. 02129, U.S.A.

**HOOKER, DeWest.** American. *B.* 1918. *Educ.* Cornell University (BA). *M.* 1942, Mary Barbey (div. 1962). *S.* Grant Barbey, John Ensley, Kellogg Griggs and Thomas Beecher. *Dau.* Mary Katherine. *M.* 1963, Elena Brunelli. *Dau.* Jacqueline Anne. *Career:* Packager of television shows (all networks) in U.S.A. 1948–54; featured in film, Miracle of the Living, 1946; Actor and State Manager of Broadway play, Command Decision 1946–47; Pres., Film Network Inc. 1953–57. President and Managing Director, Seven-up Italia, Milan, Italy 1958–75. *Member:* Actor's Equity Association; Screen Actors' Guild; Academy of Political Science. *Clubs:* Ambrosiano Tennis, British-American (Milan); Fredericksburg Country (Virginia U.S.A.). *Address:* Via Pordenone 19, Milan, 20132 Italy.

**HOOLE, William Stanley.** American. *B.* 1903. *Educ.* Wofford Coll. (AB 1924; AM 1931; LittD 1954); Duke Univ. (PhD 1934); North Texas Univ. (AMLJ 1943); Univ of Alabama, LLD (1975). *M.* (1) 1931, Martha Sanders (*Dec.* May 1960); (2) 1970, Addie Shirley Coleman. *Daus.* Martha DuBose and Elizabeth Stanley. *Career:* Teacher, Spartanburg (SC) High School 1924–25, and Darlington (SC) High School 1927–31; Fellow, Duke Univ. 1931–34; Asst. Prof. of English, Birmingham (Ala.) Southern Coll. 1934–35 (Librarian 1935–37); Librarian: Baylor Univ. 1937–39, North Texas Univ. 1939–44. Dean of Libraries, University of Alabama 1944–71; Editor, Alabama Review 1947–67. Editor, Confederate Centennial Studies 1956–65. Research Consultant, U.S. House of Representatives Committee on Special Education 1957–58; Research Consultant, U.S. Office of Education 1959–60; Research Consultant, U.S. House of Representatives Select Cttee. on Government Research 1963–64; Professor, Library Service Univ. of Alabama 1970–73. *Awards:* Alabama Library Assn. Literary Award 1958; Fulbright Scholar to Great Britain 1956–57. *Publications:* numerous books; and articles in professional and popular journals. *Member:* Phi Beta Kappa; Phi Alpha Theta; Pi Tau Chi; Kappa Phi Kappa; Newcomen Society. *Club:* University (University of Ala.). *Address:* 39 University Circle, Tuscaloosa, Ala.; and P.O. Box 1712, University, Ala. U.S.A.

**HOOPER, Sir Leonard James,** KCMG, CBE, jdc. *B.* 1914. *Educ.* Alleyn's School, Dulwich and Worcester College, Oxford. *M.* 1951, Ena Mary Osborn. *Career:* Assistant Director G.C.H.Q. 1952–60, Dep.-Director 1960–64; Director 1965–73; Deputy-Sec. Cabinet Office since 1973. *Clubs:* Royal Automobile (London); New (Cheltenham). *Address:* 3c Carlisle Place, London, S.W.1.

**HOOPER, Sir Robin William John,** KCMG, DSO, DFC. *B.* 1914. *Educ.* Charterhouse and The Queen's Coll. Oxford. *M.*. 1941. Constance Mildred Ayshford Sanford. *S.* 3. *Career:* Third Secy., Foreign Office 1938–40. Served in World War II (Wing-Comdr. R.A.F.) 1940–44. Secy., Embassy Paris 1944–46; First Secy. Lisbon 1947–49; Counsellor, F.O. 1950; Head, Personnel Dept. 1950–53: Counsellor. Embassy

Baghdad 1953–56; Head, Perm. Under-Secy's. Dept. 1956–60; Asst. Secy.General (Political) N.A.T.O. 1960–66; Ambassador to Tunisia 1966–67; to People's Republic of Southern Yemen, 1968. Deputy Secretary, Cabinet Office, 1968–71; H.M. Ambassador to Greece 1971–74; Chmn., Anglo-Hellenic League 1975—; Mem., NATO Appeals Board 1976—; Dir., Benguela Railway Co. 1976—. *Award:* Chevalier Legion of Honour; Croix de Guerre (2 palms). *Club:* Travellers. *Address:* F. 3, Albany, Piccadilly, London, W.1., Brook House, Egerton, Ashford, Kent.

**HOOSE, York Erwin.** German banker. *B.* 27 March 1911. *Educ.* Gymnasium. *M.* 1946, Hilde Eisenbarth. *S.* 1. *Daus.* 2. *Career:* Commenced banking with Eichborn & Co., Breslau; with Deutschen Reichsbank, Berlin 1937–48; member, Board of Managers of Landeszentral-bank der Freien und Hansestadt Hamburg, Hamburg 1948–52; President, Landeszentralbank von Niedersachsen, Hanover since 1952; member, Zentralbankrat (Bd. of Dirs.) der Bank deutscher Länder since 1952; Pres., Landeszentralbank in Niedersachsen and member, Zentralbankrat (Bd. of Dires.) der Deutschen Bundesbank Aug. 1957–June 1962; Member, Bd. Managers, Westbank AG, Hamburgh-Altona since 1962. *Address:* Gudrunstrasse 76 (68), Hamburg-Rissen, Federal Republic of Germany.

**HOOSON, Tom (Thomas Ellis).** British. Director of Communications, Conservative Party, since 1977. *B.* 1933. *Educ.* Rhyl Grammar Sch.; University College, Oxford—MA; Gray's Inn. *Career:* With Benton & Bowles Inc. 1961–76—Senior Vice-Pres. & Dir. of European Operations; contested Caernarvon as Conservative Parly. Candidate, 1959; Chmn. of Bow Group 1960–61. *Member:* Inst. of Practitioners in Advertising (qualified with distinction 1959). *Publications:* (Co-author) Work for Wales (1959); (contributor) Lessons from America (1974). *Club:* Carlton. *Address: office* 32 Smith Square, London S.W.1.

**HOOVER, Herbert William, Jr.** *B.* 1918. *Educ.* Choate School, and Rollins Coll. (AB 1941); Hon. LLD Mount Union Coll. 1959. *M.* 1941, Carl Good. *S.* Herbert William III. *Dau.* Elizabeth Lacey. *Career:* Served in U.S. Army as 2nd Lieut. 1943–45. Former Offices held The Hoover Co., North Canton, Ohio; Exec. (Exec., Sales) 1941; Dir. (Dir., Public Relations) 1945; Asst. Vice-Pres. 1948; Vice-Pres., Field Sales 1952; Exec. Vice-Pres. 1953; Pres. 1954. Dir (1952), Pres. (1954), The Hoover Co. Ltd., Canada; Director (1954), Chairman (1956), Hoover Ltd., England; Director and President: Hoover Inc., Panama 1955; Hoover (America Latina) S.A., Panama 1955; Hoover Mexicana, S.A. de C. V., Mexico 1955; Director, The Hoover Co. (Pres. and Chmn. 1959–66). Hoover Industrial y Comercial S.A., Colombia 1960, Pres. & Dir., Hoover Worldwide Corp., N.Y., 1960, Dir., S. A. Hoover, France, 1965. Dir., Harter Bank & Trust Co., Canton. O; Dir., Miami Heart Institute. Past Regional Vice-Chmn., U.S. Committee for U.N. July 1965. *Awards:* Dr. of Laws Mt. Union College 1959; Chevalier of the French Legion of Honour, July 1965; Chevalier du Tastevin. Member N.Y. Sales Executives Club; Y.M.C.A.; Council on Foreign Relations. *Member:* Amer. Socy. of the French Legion of Honour. *Clubs:* Bath (Miami); Canton; Key Largo Anglers (Fla.); New York Yacht; Rolling Rock (Ligonier, Pa.); Surf (Miami, Fla.); Union (Cleveland, O.); Travelers of Paris; Indian Creek Country (Florida); Trustee, Univ. of Miami; Key Biscayne Yacht Club, Miami, Fla. *Address:* 70 Park Drive, Bal Harbour, Fla., 33154, U.S.A.

**HOPE, Sir Archibald Philip,** Bt, OBE, DFC, AE. British. *B.* 1912. *Educ.* Balliol Coll., Oxford (BA 1934). *M.* 1938, Ruth Davis. *S.* John Carol Alexander and Charles Archibald. *Career:* With Royal Auxiliary Air Force 1939–45; Airwork Ltd. 1945–56; D. Napier & Son Ltd. 1956–60; Napier Aero Engines Ltd. 1960–68; Director and Chief Executive, Napier Aero Engines Ltd. 1962–68; Management Executive The English Electric Company Ltd. 1963—. Chmn., The Air League 1965–68. Group Treasurer, G.E.C., 1970, Dep. Chmn. Airline Users Cttee of Civl Aviation Authority. Fellow, Inst. of Chrtd. Accountants (FCA); Fellow, Royal Aeronautical Society. *Clubs:* Bath; R.A.F. (London): New (Edinburgh); Nairobi (Nairobi). *Address:* Upton Grey Lodge, nr Basingstoke, Hants; and *office* 1 Stanhope Gate, London, W.1.

**HOPE, Sir Peter,** KCMG, TD. British diplomat. *B.* 1912. *Educ.* Oratory School, London; London and Cambridge Universities, BSc(Hons.), ACGI. *M.* 1936, Hazel Mary Turner. *S.* 3. *Career:* Royal Artillery 1938–46; First Secretary, Paris 1946–59; Foreign Office 1950–53; Counsellor. Bonn 1953–56: Head of News Dept., F.O. 1956–59; H.M. Minister, Madrid 1959–62; H.M. Consul-General, Houston 1962–64; Alternative British Delegate to the U.N. 1965–68; Ambassador, Mexico City, 1968–72; Mem. of Acad. of Intern. Law and Intern. Cons. in London since 1972. *Clubs:* Whites (London). *Address:* North End House, Heyshott, Midhurst, Sussex.

**HOPE-JONES, Sir Arthur,** KBE, CMG. British company director and adviser. *B.* 1911. *Educ.* Kirkby Lonsdale; Christ's Coll. Cambridge; Columbia University. *M.* 1938, Lucile Owen, New York. *S.* 1. *Dau.* 1. *Career:* Fellow Christ's Coll. Cambridge, Lecturer in University 1937–46; War Service 1939–45; Economic Adviser, Kenya Government 1946–48; Minister for Commerce and Industry 1948–60; Director of Companies and Adviser to several Public Companies since 1960. *Awards:* Knight Commander, Order of the British Empire; Companion Order of St. Michael and St. George. *Publication:* Income Tax in the Napoleonic Wars (1938). *Clubs:* East India; Mutharga; Nairobi (Kenya). *Address:* 1 Buckland Court, Buckland, Betchworth, Surrey.

**HORD, Stephen Young.** American banker. *B.* 7 Nov. 1897. *Educ.* Yale University (BA). *M.* 1926, Catharine Norcross (Dec.). *S.* Stephen Y., Frederic N. *Dau.* Catharine Brent (Malarkey). *Career:* Served World War I in 5th Regt. U.S. Marine Corps, with A.E.F. 1918; with Northern Trust Co., Chicago 1921–27; Associated with Lee, Higginson & Co., Chicago 1927–32; with Brown Brothers Harriman & Co. since 1932; General Partner since 1945; Dir. Illinois Central Railroad Co. 1945–72; Amer. Auto. Ins. Co. 1947–69; Rotary Elec. Steel Co. Detroit 1952–57; American Ins. Co. 1956–69; Assoc. Indemnity Corp. 1957–69; Calvert Drilling, Inc. 1957–61; Syminton Wayne Corp. 1957–68; Illinois Central Industries Inc. 1962–72; National Surety Corp. 1964–69: Abex Corporation 1968–72; Northwestern Memorial Hospital, Chicago; Trustee, Cowles Commission for Research in Economics, Trustee Emeritus, Phillips Academy, Andover, Mass. Member, Chicago Panel of Arbitrators, N.Y. Stock Exchange. *Address:* 135 South La Salle Street, Chicago, Ill., 60603, U.S.A.

**HÖRJEL, Nils Johan.** Swedish. Governor of Province o Malmöhus län. *B.* 1917. *Educ.* Lund Univ. LLB (jur.kand). *M.* 1945, Elly Holst. *S.* 2. *Dau.* 1. *Career:* With Ministry of Eucation and Culture: Principal Assistant Secretary 1952–53, Budget Secretary 1953–55, and Chief of Division 1955–58; Under-Secretary of State, Ministry of Communications 1958–64; Director-General of Posts 1965–73; Governor of Malmöhus län since 1973; Chairman of the Board: Swedish National Devel. Co., AB Linjeflyg, AB Umeforsen; investigation Committee on TV Commercials; invest. cttee on regional traffic in Sweden; investigation on videogram; Member of the Board: AB Aerotransport; Scandinavian Airlines System, Government Employee Negotiation Bd. Natl. Cncl., Personnel Questions; Mediator between Employer and Employee Organisations appointed by the Govt. Chmn. of Bd. of the "Skansen". *Publications* various articles in reviews and professional journals. *Address:* Stortorget 1. S211 22 Malmö; and *office:* Governor of the province of Malmöhus län, S-205 15 Malmö, Sweden.

**HORN, John Chisholm.** American management consultant. *B.* 1915. *Educ.* Cornell Univ. (AB and Grad. Eng.). *M.* 1938, Solveig Elizabeth Wald. *S.* John C. Jr., Stephen L., Eric L., Robert G., Thomas W. and James M. *Daus.* Phyllis D. and Dorothy T. *Career:* Chmn., Huntingdon County Airport Cttee. 1965–67; Pres.; Juniata Mountains Devel. Assn. 1956–60, Huntingdon County United Fund 1959–61; Juniata Valley Cncl., B.S.A. 1948–50, 1957; Dir.: Huntingdon Business and Industry 1958–62, Central Penn. Synod, Lutheran Church 1962–67; Pres., Bd. of Trustees, Susquehanna Univ. 1962; Chmn.; Wald Foundation 1960, Highway Traffic Products Group, Inst. of Traffic Engineers 1966; Dir., Materials and Services Div., Amer. Road Buildings' Assn. 1967; Member, Industrial and Advisory Cncl., Coll. of Engineering, Penn. State Univ. 1967; Lutheran Church in America—Bd. Publication 1967—. Consultative group organizational change, LCA. Pres.: Wald Industries Inc. 1951–69; Prismo Safety Corp. 1962–69. President, Prismo Universal Corp., 1969–70; Director, Long Siding Development Corp. 1955, Prismo-France, S.A. 1966–70; Exec. Dir. Church Management Service since 1970; Pres. John C. Horn Associates since 1970. *Publications:* Traffic Paint Systems (Ascho, 1964); Tonedown Treatment of Runaways (1967); New Technology in Traffic Markings (1967); Traffic Operations in Japan (Co-author, 1964). Hon. LLD Susquehanna Univ. 1965; Recipient of Silver Beaver and other awards. *Member:* Amer. Management Assn., Nat. Assn. Manufacturers, Amer. Road Builders

Assn., Army Ordnance Assn.; Affil. Inst. of Traffic Engrs; Internat. Road Fed. *Clubs:* Huntingdon Country; Indian; Juniata College; Alexandria Garden. *Address:* Kilmarnock Hall, Alexandria, Pa. 16611; and *office* 301 Penn Street, Huntingdon, Pa, 16652, U.S.A.

**HORNBLOWER, Henry II.** American investment banker, *B.* 1917. *Educ.* Harvard College (BS 1941). *M.* (1) 1942, Dorothy M. Shapard (divorced). *S.* Henry III. *Daus.* Harriet, Augusta, Eleanor. (2) 1974, Mrs. Malabar S. Brodeur. *Career:* Vice-Pres., Hornblower, Weeks, Noyes & Trask, Inc. Director and President, The Cape Cod Co.; President, Plimoth Plantation Inc., and H. & W. Agency Inc. *Member:* Massachusetts Historical Society; Club of Odd Volumes. *Clubs:* Somerset; Union. *Address:* 160 Franklin Street, Boston, Mass. 02110, U.S.A.

**HORNE, Charles Frederick, Jr.** Rear Admiral U.S.N. (Ret.) and Consultant. *B.* 1906. *Educ.* U.S. Naval Academy, Annapolis (BS 1926); U.S.N.A. Post-Graduate School 1933–34; Harvard University (Communications and Electronics, NS 1935). *M.* 1930, Evelyn Tuttle. *S.* Charles F. III. *Dau.* Anne (Trevithick). *Career:* Commissioned Ensign 1926; Commanding Officer, U.S.S. Long 1940–41; Staff Commander, Battleships 1941; Communications Officer, South Pacific Area 1942–43; Communications, Radar Officer, Amphibious Forces, Pacific 1944–45; Deputy Chief Naval Communications 1946–48; Dir., Federal Airways 1949–50; retired as Rear Admiral 1951. Administrator of the U.S. Civil Aeronautics Administration 1951–53; Manager, Convair (Pomona), a Division of General Dynamics Corporation 1953–57; Vice-Pres. 1957, Convair (Pomona), a Division of General Dynamics Corp.; Pres., General Dynamics, Pomona Div. & V.P. Gen. Dynamics Corp. 1961–71, Consultant since 1971. *Awards:* Twice decorated Combat Legion of Merit; 9 battle stars; recipient, National Region Medal CAA; E.I.A. Medal of Honor. Management Man of the Year, N.M.A. Gold Knight Award. Second Annual Governor's Award (CAGVE). Fellow Institute of Electrical & Electronics Engineers 1958. Electronic Industries Assn. (Past Pres.); Bd. of Dirs.: Los Angeles State Chambers of Commerce; Industry- Education Council of California; Fellow Inst of Adv. of Engineering; American Defense Preparedness; American Assn. for Advancement of Science; Nat. Advisory Council on Nat. Guard and Reserve Employer Support; American Inst. of Aeron and Astronaut. Associate Fellow; Chmn. Los Angeles County Overall Economic Devel. Program. Pres. Industry Education Councils of America Education Cttee.; Chmn. Los Angeles Area Chamber of Commerce; Chmn., Technology Use Task Force; Armed Forces Communications & Electronics Assn.; American Radio Relay League; National Aeronautics Assn. Aircraft Owners and Pilots Assn.; Navy League, Naval Order of U.S. (Life Member). Claremont Colls.; Member, Assoc. of U.S. Army. *Publications:* Reliability and National Security, Signal (1962); Guided Missiles: Past-Present-Future, Navigation (1957); Engineering Recruitment, Electronic Industries (1957); Electronics in New Weapon Systems, Signal (1957); The Importance of Engineering to National Defense. U.S.C. Engineer, (1957). *Address:* P.O. Box 2507, Pomona, California, U.S.A.

**HORNE, Donald Richmond.** Australian writer. *B.* 1921. *Educ.* Sydney Univ. and Canberra Univ. College. *M.* 1960, Myfanwy Gollan. *S.* Nicholas. *Dau.* Julia. *Career:* Served A.I.F. 1941–44. Diplomatic Cadet 1944–45; Australian Consolidated Press 1946–49, and 1953–63; Editor; Weekend 1954–61, The Observer 1958–61; Quadrant 1964–67; The Bulletin 1961–62, 1967–72. Research Fellow, Univ. N.S.W. since 1973; Contributing Editor, Newsweek 1973–77. *Publications:* The Lucky Country; The Permit; Southern Exposure; The Education of Young Donald; God is an Englishman; The Next Australia; But What If There are No Pelicans?; The Australian People; Death of the Lucky Country; Money Made Us; His Excellency's Pleasure. *Address:* 53 Grosvenor St., Woollahra, N.S.W. Australia.

**HORNE, McDonald Kelso, Jr.** Economic consultant. *B.* 1909. *Educ.* University of Mississippi (AB); University of North Carolina (AM; PhD). *M.* 1942, Mary Elizabeth Cobb. *S.* McDonald Kelso and Robert Chapman. *Career:* Director of Economic Research 1939–41, Dir. of Utilization Research 1945–47, National Cotton Council of America; Staff, Committee on Agriculture, United States House of Representatives 1945; U.S. Naval Reserve, Commissioned Officer on active duty 1942–45; Staff, Board of Economic Warfare 1942. University of Mississippi: Prof. & Dir., Bureau of Business Research 1941–42; Chmn., Dept. of Economics 1947–49; Dean, School of Commerce & Business Administration 1949–50; Chief Economist, National Cotton Council of America 1950–69. Member, Advisory Committee to the Secretary of Agriculture on Economics Research 1958–63. *Publications:* various articles on the economics of cotton; Price and the Future of U.S. Cotton (with Frank McCord and George Townsend) (1955). *Address:* 372 Grandview, Memphis, Tenn.; and *office* P.O. Box 12,285, Memphis, Tenn., 38111, U.S.A.

**HOROWITZ, David.** Israeli Statesman. B. 15 Feb. 1899. *Educ.* Vienna and Lwow. *Career:* Economic Adviser and Secretary, American Economic Committee for Palestine 1932–35; Director, Economic Department, Jewish Agency for Palestine; member, various Govt. Cttees. under Mandatory Regime, and director various enterprises 1935–48; former Lecturer at High School for Law and Economics, Tel-Aviv; Liaison Officer to U.N. Special Cttee. on Palestine 1946; member Jewish Del. to Lake Success 1947; Head of Israel Del. Financial Talks on Sterling Releases between Israel and Great Britain London and in negotiations between Israel and Great Britain on economic and financial affairs in connection with the termination of the Mandate 1948. Head of Israeli Del. to Economic Survey Comm. of U.N. 1948; former Director-Gen., Ministry of Finance (resigned 1952); Governor, Bank of Israel (Central State Bank) 1954–71; Chmn. Advisory Cttee. and Council since 1971; Head, Israel deleg. to U.N. Conf. on Trade and Development, Geneva 1964; and New Delhi, 1968; Chmn., Bd. of Dirs. Elizer Kaplan School of Economics and Social Sciences, The Hebrew Univ. Member: Exec. Council, Weizmann Institute of Science; Member, Bd. Trustees, Truman Research Centre. Chmn. Israel Assn. for Friendship with Sweden; Hon Pres. Instituto per le Relazioni Internazionali Rome. *Awards:* Dr. Honoris Causa Hebrew Univ. and Tel-Aviv University; Israel Prize for Social Sciences. *Publications:* Aspects of Economic Policy in Palestine (1936); Jewish Colonisation in Palestine (1937); Economic Survey of Palestine (1938); Palestine Jewry's Economic War Effort (1942); Post-War Reconstruction (1942); Prediction and Reality in Palestine (1945); State in the Making (1963); Hakimum Ubaayotav Beolam Ubaaretz Israel (1946); Hakalkal Haerezisraelit Behitpatchuta (1948); Kalkalat Israel (1954); Halacha Kalkalit Umediniyut Kalkalil Beistrael (1956); Zel Ha-Etmol ve-ergar ha-machar (1962); Anatomie Unserer, Zeit (1964), Hemispheres North and South (1966); The Economics of Israel (1967); The Abolition of Poverty (1969): Ha-etmol Sheli; My Yesterday (1970); The Enigma of Economic Growth (1972); Chaim. Bamoked (1975); Mavo Lebeayot Zmanenu (1976). *Address:* 4 Halamed-Hé Street, Katamon, Jerusalem, Israel.

**HORSLEY, Caperton Braxton.** American. Executive Vice-President and Chief Engineer, Braxton Corporation (Medfield, Mass.), Dec. 1963—. *B.* 1903. *Educ.* Virginia Military Institute, Univ. of Virginia, and Univ. of Cincinnati (Elec. Eng.). *M.* 1937, Margaret Weymouth Alderson. *S.* Allen Caperton. *Daus.* Lucile Mouat (Blanchard), Eliza Braxton (Miller), Emily Caperton and Rose Shelton (de Cruz). *Career:* Consulting Engineer, Union Carbide Corporation and others 1960–63; President and Chief Engineer, Sonic Research Corp., Boston, Mass. 1948–60; Vice-Pres. i/c Engineering, Ultrasonic Corp., Cambridge, Mass. 1945–48; Consulting Engineer, Machlett Laboratories Inc., the Technical Industrial Intelligence Committee of the U.S. Govt., and others 1943–45; Pres. and Gen. Mgr., Sutton-Horsley Co. Ltd., Toronto, Canada 1938–43: Chief Engineer, Picker X-Ray Corp., Waite Mfg. Div. Inc., Cleveland, Ohio 1931–38; Engineer, Bell Telephone Laboratories Inc., N.Y.C. 1929–31; Engineer i/c Engineering Dept., Engeln Electric Co. 1924–29. Patents: Forty issued U.S. Patents, as sole of joint inventor. *Address:* 32 Linden Street, Wellesley, Mass., 02181 and *office* Braxton Corporation, Janes Avenue, Medfield, Mass., U.S.A.

**HORTON, Alexander Romeo.** *B.* 1923. *Educ.* Morehouse College, Atlanta, BA Economics; Univ. of Pennsylvania, Wharton School of Finance & Commerce, MBA. *M.* 1956, Mary Eliza Cooper. *S.* 1. *Dau.* 1. *Career:* Assistant Economic Adviser to the President of Liberia 1955–63; President, Bank of Liberia 1955—; Bankers Association of Liberia; Secy. of Commerce and Industry, Republic of Liberia, 1964–68; First Chmn., Economic Commission for Africa, Cttee. of nine, on the Establishment of the Development Bank for Africa, 1962–63; Chmn., Steering Cttee. of African Businessmen's Conference, 1960–61; Chmn., Bd. of Directors, Liberian National Airlines, 1964–68. Member Bd. of Directors, Agricultural Credit Corporation; Liberia Produce Marketing Corporation. *Publications:* Free Enterprise in West Africa; How to Improve the Climate for Private Foreign Investment; The Development of Industrial Institutions in West Africa through International Co-operation; Supply, Demand and Value of the Dollar in Liberia. *Awards:* Morehouse Coll. Atlanta, Hon. LLD; Knight Cmdr., Order of African Redemption, Liberia, 1959; Officer of the National Order of the Ivory Coast, 1962, and many more. *Address:* Office of the President, Bank of Liberia, Monrovia, Liberia.

**HORWOOD, Owen Pieter Faure.** South African. *B.* 1916. *Educ.* Bach. of Commerce (Cape Town); Postgraduate Diploma in Actuarial Science. *M.* 1946, Helen Mary Watt. *S.* Peter. *Dau.* Diana. *Career:* Professor of Economics, Univ. of Rhodesia and Nyasaland 1956–57; William Hudson Professor of Economics, Univ. of Natal 1957–65; Principal and Vice-Chancellor, University of Natal 1966–70; Director: Natal Regional Survey 1958–70; Financial Adviser to the Government of Lesotho 1966–72; Lesotho National Development Corp. 1967–72; Member S.A. Senate since 1970; Minister of Indian Affairs and Tourism 1972–74; Minister of Economic Affairs 1974; Min. of Finance since 1975. Chancellor, Univ. of Durban-Westville Natal since 1973; Life member, Royal Economic Socy.; Vice-Pres. Economic Socy. of S. Africa. *Publications:* numerous journal articles; Economic Systems of the Commonwealth (C.U.P.); Gen. Editor: Natal Regional Survey publications. *Clubs:* Durban; Western Province Cricket; Cape Town Cricket. *Address:* 2 Amos Street, Colbyn, Pretoria 0002, S.A.; and *office* Private Bag X115 Pretoria, 0001, South Africa.

**HOSKIN, Thomas Leslie Borrowman.** Canadian educationalist (administration and student personnel services). *B.* 1914. *Educ.* Univ. of W. Ontario (BA); Univ. of Toronto (Dipl. Pedagogy); Northwestern Univ. (MA). *M.* 1938, Vera E. MacMartin. *Dau.* Elizabeth Ann. *Career:* Teacher, London Central Collegiate 1936–41; Leave 1941–45; Canadian Army overseas (member of Officer Selection and Appraisal Centre Staff) 1941–45; Dean of Men, Coordinator of Student Services, University of Western Ontario 1945; Pres., Canadian Mental Health Assn. (Ontario), 1970—. General Cttee., Leonard Foundation. Award of Merit 1966, Canadian Student Affairs Assn. Chairman, Ontario Cttee. on Student Awards 1967. Univ. Air Liaison Officer, U.W.O., London 1947–55. Canadian Univ. Counselling and Placement Assn. (Pres. 1956–58). Delegate: Intnatl. Colloquium Student-Aid in Madrid 1957; to UNESCO Conf., Paris 1956; I.A.A.S.U.P. Conference on Education in Developing Countries, Paris 1962; Deputy-Chmn. English-Speaking Union. *Publications:* The Ivy is Green (1958); On Getting a Head (1961); Careers in Higher Education (Canada) (1962). *Clubs:* London (Ont.) Hunt & Country. *Address:* 707 Plaza Tower, 190 Cherryhill Circle, London, Canada N6H 2M3.

**HOTCHKIS, Preston.** American lawyer. *B.* 1893. *Educ.* University of California; Hon. LLD, Whittier College (1957) and Pepperdine College (1955). *M.* 1923, Katharine Bixby *S.* 2. *Daus* 2. *Career:* Seaman to Ensign U.S. Navy World War I, 1918–19; co-founder Dir. Vice-Pres. Pacific Finance Corp. 1920; Dir. Exec. Vice-Pres. Pacific Indemnity Co. 1926; Dir. Exec. Cttee. Consolidated Western Steel Corp. 1929; Dir. Pres. Central Business Properties Inc. 1929; Dir. Pres. Vice-Chmn. Founders' Insurance Co. 1946; Chmn. Bd. Bixby Ranch Co. Los Angeles. *Member:* Pres. Calif. Alumni Assn. 1934–36; Regent Univ. of California 1934–36; Chmn. Navy Relief Socy. Campaign, Southern Calif. 1942–43; Citation by Secy. Navy; Pres. Calif. State Chamber, Commerce 1942–44, Dir. 1934–62; War Manpower Board for S. Cal. 1942–45 U.S. Rep. Econ & Social Council 1954–55; Past Member Hoover Commission Task Force Fed. Lending Agencies; Official Host, City of Los Angeles; Chmn. Greater Los Angeles Area War Chest Campaign; Present, Trustee Mills Coll. Oakland; Harvey Mudd Coll. Claremont; Southwest Museum, Good Hope Medical Foundation (Vice-Pres.); Co-Founder Hon. Dir. Past Pres. Los Angeles World Affairs Council; Japanese Philharmonic Socy. Los Angeles; Member Mayor's Adv. Cttee.; Girl Scouts of U.S. Nat. Ad. Council; Chmn. Local Agency Formation Comm. Los Angeles County; Southland Water Cttee.; Pres. Bd. Pepperdine Coll.; Adv. Council Univ. of Redlands; Adv. Council Calif. State Parks Foundation; Dir. Property Owners Tax Assn. of Calif. Inc.; Trustee, Calif. Alumni, Foundation, Univ. of Calif. *Publications:* History of Lost Angels Camp. *Clubs:* (Los Angeles) California; University; (Pasadena) Valley Hunt; (San Francisco) Pacific Union; Bohemian; Twilight. *Address:* 1415 Circle Drive, San Marino, Calif. 91108 and *office* 523 West Sixth Street, Los Angeles 90014, Calif., U.S.A.

**HOTTINGUER, Rodolphe.** Baron. French banker. *B.* 1902. *Educ.* Grade Universitaire—Diplomé H.E.C. *M.* 1934, Odette Basset. *S.* Henri and Paul. *Daus.* Caroline and Véronique. *Career:* Partner in firm of Hottinguer et Cie, former Vice-Pres. Paris Chamber of Commerce, Censor, Credit Foncier de France. Administrator, Kleber Colombes, Châtillon Commentry, Trefimetaux Schneider, and Vieille Montagne; Grindlays Bank Ltd. President of the International Chamber of Commerce. Commander of the Legion of Honour; Croix de Guerre (1939–45). *Clubs:* Jockey; Interallie; Union Saint Cloud. *Address:* 4 rue de la Baume, Paris 8; and *office* 38 rue de Provence, Paris 9, France.

**HOUCK, George C.** American company Vice-Pres. *B.* 1913. *Educ.* Ohio Wesleyan Univ. (BA 1935). *M.* 1935, June Waldorf. *S.* John C. *Dau.* Ann Louise. *Career:* With Harris-Seybold Co., a Div. of Harris-Intertype Corp., Controller Dayton (Ohio) plant, Asst. Treasurer, Asst. to General Manager, Asst. to President, Director of Planning, Vice-Pres. for Operations, Vice-President and General Manager, Group Vice-Pres. Printing Equipment Group, Sen. Vice-Pres. Printing Equipment; National Printing Equipment Assn. (Dir. and Pres.); National Scholarship Trust Fund, Graphic Arts Technical Foundation. *Clubs:* Cleveland Yachting; Union. *Address:* 2208 N. Carriage Lane, Port Clinton, Ohio 43452, U.S.A.; and *office* 55 Public Square, Cleveland, Ohio 44113, U.S.A.

**HOUGHTON, Amory.** *B.* 1899. *Educ.* St. Paul's School (Concord, NH); Harvard (AB 1921); Hon. LLD Hobart and William Smith Colleges 1947, Alfred University 1948, New York and Colgate Universities 1969; Hon. DEng, Rensselaer University 1949. *M.* 1921, Laura DeKay Richardson. *S.* Amory, Jr., Alanson Bigelow and James Richarson. *Daus.* Elizabeth (Weinberg) and Laura De Kay (Beer). *Career:* Asst. to President 1926–28, Exec. Vice-Pres. 1928–30, Pres. 1930–41; Chairman 1941–61, Chairman of Exec. Cttee. 1961–64, Hon. Chairman of the Bd. 1964–71, Chmn. Emeritus 1971; Corning Glass Works, Corning, N.Y. War-time government service: Asst. Dep. Director, Materials Division, O.P.M. 1941–42; Dep. Chief, Bureau of Industry Branches W.P.B. 1942; Dir. General of Operations 1942; Dep. Chief Mission for Economic Affairs 1943–44; Ambassador of the United States to France 1957–61; Cmn., U.S. Cncl. Interntl. Chamber of Commerce 1962–64; Vice-Chmn., Int. Chamber of Commerce, 1962–64. Trustee and Member, Exec. Cttee., U.S. Council Int. Chamber of Commerce 1965. *Awards:* Order of Merit Bernardo O'Higgins 1952. Grand Cross of the Legion of Honour, France 1961. Republican. *Clubs:* University, Harvard, Links (N.Y.); Elmira County, Corning County, Chevy Chase (Md.); National Golf; Royal and Ancient (St Andrew's); Golf de Saint Cloud; Golf de Monfontaine; Metropolitan (Washington, D.C.). *Address:* 12 South Road, Corning, N.Y. 14820. U.S.A.

**HOUGHTON, Arthur Amory, Jr.** *B.* 1906. *Educ.* St. Paul's School and Harvard Univ.; LHD Lehigh Univ.; Univ. of Maryland; LittD, Washington Coll.; Trinity Coll.; Hofstra Coll.; St. John's Univ. (Minn.); LitD Beaver Coll.; LLD Univ. of Rochester; Wesleyan Univ.; Alfred Univ., Salisbury Coll.; DSc Hobart and William Smith Colls., Bucknell Univ. and DFA Washington, Jefferson College and MacMurray College. Senior Fellow, Royal Coll. of Art; Fellow, Royal Society of Arts. *M.* 1973, Nina Rodale. *S.* Arthur Amory III. *Daus.* Jane Olmsted (Mrs. Robert G. Hankey), Sylvia Bigelow (Garrett), Hollister Douglas (Haggard III). *Career:* Dir.; Corning Glass Works; Former Dir. United States Steel Corp.; New York Life Insurance Co.; President, Steuben Glass, New York 1933–73. Chmn. since 1973; Former Trustee, Rockefeller Foundation; Hon. Trustee U.S. Trust Company; Trustee Emeritus and Past Chmn. Copper Union; Past Chairman; Inst. of International Education; Hon. Trustee and Past Chmn. Parsons School of Design; Hon. Trustee, The New York Public Library; Trustee Emeritus, former Pres. and Chmn. Metropolitan Museum of Art; Trustee Emeritus and Past Vice-Pres., Piermont Morgan Library; Past Chmn., Philharmonic-Symphony Society of N.Y.; Director-at-Large, Nat. Bd. and Past Pres., English-speaking Union; Past Pres., Keats Shelley Assn. of America; Chmn. and Pres. Wye Inst. (Md); Dir., France-American Society; officer and member of numerous other educational and cultural institutions; Curator of Rare Books, The Library of Congress 1940–42; World War II; Army Air Force; Lt.-Col. Association. *Awards:* Commander, OSJ, Officer French Legion of Honour; Commandeur de l'Ordre des Arts et des Lettres. *Address:* Wye Plantation, Queenstown, Maryland 21658; and *office* 715 Fifth Avenue, New York, N.Y. 10022, U.S.A.

**HOUGHTON, Rt. Hon. Lord (Douglas), PC, CH.** British Member of Parliament. *B.* 1898. *Educ.* Long Eaton (Derbyshire)

Secondary Schl. *M.* 1939, Vera Travis. *Career:* Civil Servant 1915–22; broadcaster in BBC Home and Overseas Programmes 1941–49; elected Member of Parliament (Lab.) 1949; Secy., Inland Revenue Staff Federation 1922–60; Alderman, London County Council 1947–49; member, Gen. Cncl., British Trades Union Congress 1952–60; Chmn.: Staff Side, National Whitley Council 1956–58; Public Accounts Cttee., House of Commons, 1963; Chancellor of Duchy of Lancaster, Oct. 1964–66; Minister Without Portfolio 1966–67; Chairman, Parliamentary Labour Party 1967–74; Member, Royal Commission on the Constitution 1968–73; Chmn. Teachers' Pay Inquiry 1974; Chmn. Cttee. on Aid to Political Parties 1975–76; and of Commonwealth Scholarships Commission 1967–68; created Life Peer 1974. *Address:* 110 Marsham Court, London, S.W.1.

**HOUPHOUET-BOIGNY, Felix.** President of the Republic of the Ivory Coast. *B.* of a family of tribal chiefs 1905. *Educ.* Dakar School of Medicine (grad. with Hons. 1925); practised as a physician until 1940; founded African Agricultural Syndicate of the Ivory Coast 1944, and the R.D.A. 1945: Territorial Councillor, then deputy 1946–60; Mayor of Abidjan 1956–60; Gen. Councillor. Elected to the First Constituent Assembly of the Government of France, 1945; Ivory Coast deputy to Fr. Republic Nat. Assembly 1946–48; Acting Pres. of Council 1956–57; Min. of State 1955; Min. of Public Health 1957–58; Min. of State 1958–59; French Govt. Min-advising the Fr. Govt. on For. Affairs 1959–60; Pres. of Conseil d'Entente (with Upper Volta, Dahomey and Niger) 1959; Prime Minister of Ivory Coast 1959–60; Pres. Republic of Ivory Coast since 1960, concurrently Minister of Foreign Affairs 1961, of Interior, Education & Agriculture 1963, of Defence 1963–74; Pres., Parti Démocratique de la Côte d'Ivoire. *Address:* The Presidency (B.P. 1354), Abidjan, Ivory Coast.

**HOUPT, Wilmer Kenneth.** American executive. *B.* 1917. *Educ.* Atlantic City (N.J.) High School; Syracuse Univ. (BSc, ME). *M.* 1941, Emily Louise Herrick. *S.* Paul Kenneth. *Dau.* Linda Louise. *Career:* Successively Experimental Engine Tester 1939–40, Development Engineer 1940–41, Technical Manager, Washington office 1941–42, Wright Aeronautical Corp., Paterson, N.J.; Asst. Manager, Washington office 1942–44, Manager, Military Co-ordination Section, Wright Aero. Div. 1944–45, Asst. Sales Manager, Wright Aero. Div. 1945–48 (Sales Manager 1948–50), Vice-Pres., Sales 1954–58, Curtiss Wright Corp., Wood-Ridge, N.J. President: Major Cleaners and Launderers, Major Cleaners Corp., Major Services, and Correct Cleaners & Launderers 1958—. Member: Inst. of Aero Sciences; Aircraft Owners & Pilots Assn.; Pres. West Hudson, South Bergen (Counties) Chamber of Commerce. *Clubs:* Packanack Lake Country (Past Governor); Comet Class Yacht Racing Association (Past Fleet Captain); Packanack Lake Yacht (Past Commodore); U.S. Power Squadrons; Boat Owners Council of America; American Ordnance Association. *Address:* 100 Lake Drive West, Wayne, N.J. 07470; and *office* 787 Kearny Avenue, Kearny, N.J., U.S.A.

**HOWARD, Harry Nicholas.** American University Professor. *B.* 19 Feb. 1902. *Educ.* William Jewell College (AB); University of Missouri (MA); University of California at Berkeley (PhD; *M.* 1932, Virginia Faye Brubaker. *S.* Robert, Norman. *Career:* Assistant Professor of Modern History, University of Oklahoma 1929–30; Asst., Assoc. Prof. and Prof. of History, Miami University, Oxford, Ohio 1930–42; Lecturer, University of Cincinnati 1937–42; Visiting Professor of History (at various periods) Universities of Missouri, Indiana, Colorado, Columbia and California; in Dept. of State, Washington 1942–56; Head, E. European Unit, Div. of Territorial Studies 1942–45; member, Div. of International Organisation Affairs 1945–46; Technical Expert, U.S. Deleg. U.N. Confce. on Internatl. Organization 1945; member, U.S. Special Interrogation Mission to Germany 1945; Chief, Near East Branch, Div. of Research for Near East and Africa 1946–47; Adviser, Office of Greek, Turkish and Iranian Affairs 1947–49; Adviser, U.S. Delegation, U.N. Gen. Assembly 1947–50; Security Council Commission of Investigation in Greece 1947; U.N. Special Committee on the Balkans 1947–50; U.N. Adviser, Bureau of Near Eastern, South Asian, and African Affairs 1949–56; U.S. Rep., Advisory Commission, U.N.R.W.A., Beirut 1956–61; former Foreign Service Officer, Dept. of State, Washington; member, American Historical Assn., Middle East Inst.; Special Asst., U.N.R.W.A., Commissioner-General, 1962–63; Professor of Middle Eastern Studies. American Univ. 1963–68, Adjunct. Prof. since 1968; Associate Editor, Middle East Journal, 1963—; Chmn., Program in Near East & N. African Country Studies, Foreign Sc. Inst., Dept. of State, summer 1966, 1971–73; Faculty Adv., Fr. Serv. Inst. Dept. of State 1966—; Reserve Cons. Department of State 1966—; Chief Consultant, Middle East Cincinnati Council on World Affairs 1967–69. Lecturer, Middle East U.S. Army War Coll. 1971–72; Book Review Editor, Middle East Journal; Board of Directors, American Near East Refugee Aid; Bd. of Governors, Middle East Institute. *Publications:* The Partition of Turkey (1931); (with R. J. Kerner) The Balkan Conferences and the Balkan Entente (1936); The Problem of the Turkish Straits (1947); Greece and the United Nations (1947); The King-Crane Commission (1963); Turkey, the Straits and United States Policy (1974); contrb. to various journals; Book Review Editor of Middle East Journal. *Address:* 6508 Greentree Road, Bethesda, Maryland 20034.

**HOWARD de WALDEN, Lord,** TD (John Osmael Scott-Ellis, also Lord Seaford). British peer. *B.* 27 Nov. 1912. *Educ.* Eton; Magdalene College, Cambridge (MA). *M.* 1934, Countess Irne Harrach (dec'd). *Daus.* Hazel, Susan, Jessica, Camilla. Director, Howard de Walden Estates Ltd. and other companies. *Address:* Avington Manor, Hungerford, Berks.

**HOWE, Sir (Richard Edward) Geoffrey,** MA, LLB, QC, MP. British. *B.* 1926. *Educ.* Winchester Coll. Exhibitioner; Trinity Hall, Cambridge. *M.* 1953, Elspeth Rosamund Morton Shand. *S.* 1 *Daus.* 2 *Career:* Lieut. Royal Signals 1945–48; Chmn. Camb. Univ. Cons. Assn. 1951; Called to the Bar, 1952; Chmn. Bow Group 1955; Contested (C) Aberavon, 1955 & 1959; Managing Dir. Crossbow, 1957–60; Mem. Gen. Council of the Bar, 1957–61; Editor Crossbow, 1960–62; Mem. Council of Justice, 1963; Secy. Con. Parly. Health & Social Security Cttee, 1964–65; MP for Bebington, 1964–66; Opposition Front Bench Spokesman, Labour & Social Sec. 1965–66; Interdept. Cttee on Age of Majority, 1965–67; QC 1965; Dep. Chmn. Glamorgan Quarter Sessions, 1966–70; Bencher, Middle Temple since 1969; Mem. Council of Management, Private Patients Plan, 1969–70; Chmn. Ely Hospital Cardiff Inquiry 1969; Kt. 1970; Solicitor General, 1970–72; Member of Parliament for Reigate 1970–74, for East Surrey since 1974; Minister of Trade and Consumer Affairs 1972–74; Opposition Front Bench Spokesman on Social Services 1974–75; on Treasury and Economic Affairs since 1975. Director: Sun Alliance & London Insurance Co. Ltd. 1974—; AGB Research Ltd. 1974—; EMI Ltd. 1976—. *Address:* c/o Barlcays Bank, 4 Vere Street, London, W.1.

**HOWE, William Frederick.** British. *B.* 1916. *Educ.* Humphrey Perkins School; Loughborough College. *M.* 1947, Brenda Lilian Hibberd. *Career:* Gen. Mgr. & Dir. David Brown Industries Machine Tool & Tool Div. 1959–63; David Brown-E.M.I. (Electronics) Ltd. 1962–63; Man. Dir. Millspaugh Ltd. 1963–64; Man. Dir. Mono Pumps Ltd., J. & E. Arnfield; Man. Dir. Mono Pumps (Eng.) Ltd.; Dir., Saunders Valve Co. Ltd.; Chmn. Metering Pumps Ltd.; Chmn. F. A. Hughes & Co. Ltd.; Chmn. Stainless Steel Pumps Ltd., Chmn. E. T. Oakes Ltd. 1964–76; Industrial Consultant. *Member:* Inst. Production Engineers. *Address:* Longridge, West Lees Road, Bamford, Derbyshire; and *office* Mono House, Clerkenwell Green, London, E.C.1.

**HOWELL, David Arthur Russell,** MA, MP. British politician and Journalist. *B.* 1936. *Educ.* Eton Coll., King's Coll. Cambridge 1st Class Hons. Econ. *M.* 1967, Davina Wallace. *S.* 1. *Daus.* 2 *Career:* Economic Section, H.M. Treasury, 1959–60; Leader Writer, special Correspondent Daily Telegraph, 1960–64; Chmn. Bow Group, 1961–62; Editor, Crossbow, 1962–64; Dir. Conservative Political Centre, 1964–66; Member of Parliament for Guildford, Surrey since 1966; Hon. Sec. British Council European Movement, 1968–70; Parly. Sec. Civil Service Dept. Lord Commissioner, H. M. Treasury 1970–72; Parly.-Under-Sec. Dept. of Employment 1971–72; Parly. Under Secy. of State Northern Ireland Office 1972; Minister of State, Northern Ireland Office 1972–74; Min. of State, Dept. of Energy 1974. *Publications:* The Conservative Opportunity; New Directions in World Trade; A New Style of Government (1970). *Club:* Bucks. *Address:* and *office* House of Commons, London, S.W.1.

**HOWES, Alfred S.** *B.* 1917. *Educ.* Brown and Syracuse Universities and University of Alabama. *M.* 1942, Elizabeth Hoffner. *Daus.* Wendy, Mary and Constance. *Career:* Pres. New York State Association of Life Underwriters June 1962—. President: Employee Incentive Plans of America Inc.; Bering Trading Corp.; Century Planning Corp.; Killip Laundering Co.; Chairman, Utica Duxbak Corp. Dir.: Nursing Homes, Inc., APMEW, Inc.; Winchester Knitting Mills, Inc., Placid's Parkas, Inc., American Pulp & Paper

Co., Utica Bulk Terminal, Inc., Hurd Shoe Company, American Paper Machinery, Inc., Killip Laundering & Dry Cleaning Co. Inc.; Mechanical Technology Inc.; Past Pres. New York State Assn. of Life Underwriters; Dir. and Pres. Hyden Inc., Wood Realty Inc., Wood and Hyde; Publisher and Dir. of the Gray Letter; Dir. Insulating Shapes Inc., Emerson Plastronics Inc. Life member, Million Dollar Round Table (Chairman Public Relations Committee, 1960–62); Secretary, Estate Planning Council, City of New York 1959–61; Chairman, New York State Association of Life Underwriters Committee on cooperation with the Temporary New York State Commission on the Revision of Laws pertaining to Estates. *Clubs:* Collectors; Fort Schuyler (Utica, N.Y.), University (Albany); Brown (N.Y.C.). *Address: office* 551 Fifth Avenue, New York, N.Y. 10017, U.S.A.

**HOWLAND, William Goldwin Carrington,** QC. Canadian. *B.* 1915. *Educ.* University of Toronto (BA; LLB; LLD); Barrister-at-Law, Osgoode Hall. *M.* Margaret Patricia Greene. *Career:* Partner in law firm of McMillan, Binch; Dir. Monarch Investments Ltd., Monarch Construction Ltd., Taylor Woodrow of Canada Ltd., Kent Cambridge Ltd., Zenith Radio Corp. of Canada Ltd., Eve Ltd., A. I. & P. Canada Properties Ltd., Kerr Bros. Ltd., Franklin Electric of Canada Ltd., St. Hilda's Investments Ltd.; Gruen Industries Inc.; Gruen Watch Co. of Canada Ltd.; B. D. Wait Co. Ltd.; Credit Heights Ltd.; Pypotenax of Canada Ltd.; P. A. Monaghan Holdings Ltd.; Cliffrich Ltd.; The Toronto Symphony. Hon. Lecturer, Osgoode Hall Law School 1956–67. Natl. Pres., U.N. Association in Canada 1959–60; Pres. Univ. Coll. Alumni Assoc. 1958; Churchwarden, Grace Church On-the-Hill, Toronto 1959–61; Capt., Canadian Army 1942–45; Cncl., Canadian Bar Assoc. 1959–62. Author: Special Lectures, Law Socy. of Upper Canada 1951, 1960. Life Bencher and Past Treasurer (Head) Law Society of Upper Canada. *Publications:* Practice in Mortgage Actions in Ontario (2nd edn.); engaged on Falconbridge & Howland, Law of Mortgages (4th Edn.). Member: Bd. of Governors of Upper Canada College, 1968–70; Senate of York Univ. 1968–69. Council of Governing Bodies of the Legal Profession, 1968–70, Vice Pres. 1971; Canadian Bar Association; U.N. Association in Canada; Canadian Inst. for International Affairs. *Clubs:* Toronto, Toronto Hunt, Granite, Canadian, Empire, Lawyers'. *Address: office* 20 King Street West, Toronto, Ont., Canada.

**HOWSON, Hon. Peter.** Australian. *B.* 1919. *Educ.* Stowe School (England) and Cambridge University (MA). *M.* 1956, Christina Synnot. *S.* 1. *Career:* Mentioned in Dispatches (World War II) 1942; Dir. Foy & Gibson Ltd. 1951–56; Chief Government Whip 1963–64; Minister of State for Air, June 1964–68, and Minister Assisting the Treasurer, Jan. 1966–68. Chairman, Commonwealth Parliamentary Association Executive Committee 1968–70; Minister of State for the Environment, Aborigines & the Arts since 1971. Pres. Royal Victorian Eye and Ear Hospital 1956–64; Gen. Councillor, Commonwealth Parly. Assn. 1962 and 1965; Chmn. Foreign Affairs Cttee. 1964. Min. of State for the Environment, Aborigines and Arts 1971–72. Chmn. Australian Deafness Council since 1974. Member, Advisory Council for Inter-Government Relations 1977—. Fellow Australian Inst. of Management. Member, Liberal Party. *Clubs:* Melbourne; Naval & Military; Royal Melbourne Golf. *Address:* 40 Kensington Road, South Yarra 3141, Melbourne, Vic., Australian.

**HOXHA, Enver.** Albanian political leader and statesman. *B.* 16 Oct. 1908. *Educ.* Korca and France. *Career:* Founder of the Communist Party of Albania (the Party of Labour), Sec.-Gen. 1943–48, 1948–54, First Sec. of Central Cttee. since 1954; Organized and led the Albanian people in the Anti-fascist Nat. Liberation War; Leader Socialist Construction; Prime Minister and Supreme Commander, Armed Forces 1944–54; Minister of Foreign Affairs 1946–53; Chmn., General Council of Democratic Front; Mem., Presidium People's Assembly of Albania. *Awards:* Hero of the People (twice); Hero of Socialist Labour; Order of Suvorov, First Class. *Address:* The Party of Labour, Tirana, Albania.

**HOXTER, Curtis Joseph.** American. *B.* 1922. *Educ.* New York Univ. (BA, MA). *M.* 1945, Grace Lewis. *S.* Ronald Alan. *Daus.* Victoria Ann and Audrey Theresa. *Career:* Staff Contributor, AUFBAU Reconstruction 1939–40; Editor, writer, Office of War Information 1943–45; Feature writer, reporter, Long Island Daily Press, 1940–42; Public Information Officer, Dept. of State, 1945–47; Freelance magazine writer 1947–48; Dir. of Public Relations, U.S. Cncl. Internatl. Chamber of Commerce 1948–53; Adviser to U.S. Deleg. to London Disarmament Conf. 1954; Exec. Vice-Pres., George Peabody & Associates 1953–56; Department of State, Psychological Warfare Branch; Economic Co-operation Administration (Marshall Plan); White House (Information Adviser on Trade Matters); President, Curtis J. Hoxter Inc. since 1956—. *Publications:* weekly column The Economic Scene (Scripps-Howard Newspapers); magazine articles, Europe, Latin America, U.S.; specialist in international, Economic and financial matters. *Member:* Public Relations Society of America. *Clubs:* Overseas Press; National Press; Royal Auto; National Aviation; International (Wash.); Bankers' (San Juan); Friars; Atrium. *Address:* 34 Broadfield Road, New Rochelle, New York; and *office* 745 Fifth Avenue, New York, N.Y. 10022, U.S.A.

**HOYLE, Eric Douglas Harvey,** JP, MP. British. *B.* 1930. *Educ.* HNC in Mechanical Engineering. *M.* 1952, Pauline Spencer. *S.* 1. *Career:* British Rail 1946–51; AEI Ltd., Manchester 1951–53; C. Weston Ltd., Salford 1953–74; Labour MP for Nelson & Colne since 1974. *Member:* Vice-Pres., Association of Scientific, Technical & Managerial Staffs. *Clubs:* Pres., Adlington Cricket Club. *Address:* House of Commons, London SW1A OAA.

**HSIA, Ching-Lin.** Chinese. Professor. United Nations official. *B.* 17 Jan. 1896. *Educ.* Glasgow (BSc) and Edinburgh (MA, PhD) Universities. *M.* Wai-tsung New. *S.* David Yi-Yung, MD. *Career:* Prof. International Law and Political Science at various universities in Shanghai 1922–31; Delegate, Institute of Pacific Relations Conferences 1929, 1931, 1942; First Sec., Chinese Embassy, London 1931–32; Washington 1932–33; member, Chinese Delegation, World Disarmament Confce., Geneva 1932; member, Legislative Yuan (National Senate) 1934–43; Principal Rep., Chinese Ministry of Information, England 1938–40; U.S. 1940–46; Dir., Chinese News Service U.S. 1940–46; member, Chinese Delegation, Dumbarton Oaks 1944; San Francisco Confce. 1945; Dep. Chinese Rep., Security Cncl., U.N. 1946–52; Alternate Delegate, U.N. Gen. Assembly 1946–51; delegate, U.N. Gen. Assembly 1952–55; member, Advisory Cttee. on Administrative and Budgetary Questions 1947–51; member, Headquarters Advisory Cttee. 1947–52; member, Human Rights Commission 1946; Rep. of China on Economic and Social Cncl. (with rank of Ambassador) 1952–55; Chief Delegate, U.N. Opium Confce. 1953; Adviser to Chinese Ministry of Foreign Affairs 1956—. *Publications:* Studies in Chinese Diplomatic History; Status of Shanghai; translator of Chinese Civil Code and of Chinese Criminal Code; My Five Incursions into Diplomacy (memoir). *Address:* 8 Nassau Drive, Great Neck, New York, 11021 U.S.A.

**HSIUNG, Shih-I,** DPh. Chinese author. *B.* 14 Oct. 1902. *Educ.* Teachers' College; National University, Peking, *M.* 1923, Dymia Tasi. *S.* 3. *Daus.* 3. *Career:* Chinese Delegate, Internatl. Pen Congress, 1934–47; Delegate to First Congress of the Intl. Theatre Inst. 1948; Dean, College of Arts, Nanyang Univ., Singapore 1954–55; Member of Universities China Committee since 1935; Hon. Sec., China Society, London, since 1936; Pres. Tsing Hua College, Hong Kong 1963—. Visiting Prof. Univ. of Hawaii, Honolulu 1965–66. Author of Lady Precious Stream, The Western Chamber, The Professor from Pekin, The Bridge of Heaven, The life of Chiang Kai-Shek; The Story of Lady Precious Stream; The Gate of Peace; The Money-God; Mencius Was a Bad Boy; A Treasury of Chinese Proverbs; Lady on the Roof. *Address:* 41 Buckland Crescent, London, N.W.3, England and Tsing Hua College, Kowloon, Hong Kong.

**HSU, Shuhsi.** Chinese diplomat. *B.* 3 April 1892. *Educ.* Hong Kong University (BA), Colombia University (MA, PhD). *M.* 1921, Grace Wenchuang Liu. *S.* Yuanyo, Fucheng, Chichang. *Career:* Professor of Political Science 1923–37, Dean of College of Public Affairs, Yenching University 1929–32; Adviser to the Chinese Delegation to the League of Nations 1932–33; member, Commission on National Defence Planning 1933–35, Commission on National Resources, National Government, 1935–38; Adviser to the Ministry of Foreign Affairs 1936–38 and 1940–49; technical member 1945–47, Minister Plenipotentiary 1947–52; Ambassador, Chinese Delegation to the United Nations 1952–56; Ambassador to Peru and Bolivia 1956–63; Canada 1963–67; member, United Nations International Law Commission 1948–61; Representative at U.N. Gen. Assembly 1958, 60, 62. *Publications:* The Manchurian Question; The North China Problem; Chinese Foreign Relations; The Chinese Situation; China in Five Eras; etc. *Address:* 26 Mohawk Trail, Westfield, N.J. 07090 U.S.A.

**HUBBELL, John William.** *B.* 1899. *Educ.* Dartmouth College (BA). *M.* 1934, Ruth Seanor. *S.* John W., Jr. *Daus.* Jean, Susan Leland and Patricia Ruth. *Career:* Vice-President & Dir. Simmons Co., New York. Vice-President, Union League Club of New York, and Board of Governors of United States Seniors' Golf Assn.; Bd. of Trustees: United Hospital; Dir., Nat. Assn. of Bedding Manufacturers; Board of Directors: Sales Executives Club of New York, and of Brand Names Foundation; Dir. Marketing Policy Inst. *Member:* National Executive Reserve of U.S. Government. National Co-ordinator for Polio Campaign. *Awards:* Wentworth Bowl for distinguished service to Dartmouth; Exceptional Service, Nat. Assn. of Bedding Manfts.; Man of the Year, Furniture World; Distinguished Service (Markt. Policy Inst., Nat. Home Furn. Assoc., Southern Furn. Assoc.). *Clubs:* Apawamis; Union League (Vice-Pres.); Ekwanok Country; The Pilgrims. *Address:* Windcrest Road, Rye, N.Y.; and *office* Simmons Company, 280 Park Avenue, N.Y. City 10017, U.S.A.

**HUDDLE, Thornton Cosby,** CPA. American independent oil operator. *B.* 1908. *Educ.* Oklahoma Univ. (BS 1929). *M.* Frances Worley. *Dau.* Denise Diana. *Career:* Accountant and Auditor, Continental Oil Co. 1929–36; Treas. and Chief Accounting Officer, Fleetburn Oil Corp. 1936–38; Chief Accounting Officer, W. B. Osborn Enterprises 1938–43; Partner, Eaton & Huddle, C.P.A. firm, San Antonio, Tex. 1943–58; Exec. Vice-Pres., Imperial Production Corp. 1953–61; Pres., Viking Drilling Co. 1956–61, and Shoreline Petroleum Corp. 1945–61. President: River Rock Materials Co. Inc. 1963–74; and of Tectonic Oil Inc. 1961—. *Member:* Texas Independent Producers & Royalty Owners Assn.; Mid-Continent Oil & Gas Assn.; Amer. Institute of C.P.A.s; Texas Society of C.P.A.s; Pi Kappa Phi; Alpha Kappa; Psi; Presbyterian Church. *Address:* 103 Roleto, San Antonio, Tex. 78213 and *office* 900 N.E. Loop Expressway, San Antonio, Tex. 78209, U.S.A.

**HUET, Pierre Marie Jean.** French. Conseiller D'Etat. *B* 1920. *Educ.* Lauréat of the Faculty of Law, Paris, and of the School of Political Science; Diploma of Higher Studies in Law. *M.* Catherine Vienot. *S.* 1. *Daus.* 2. *Career:* Member Council of State 1946; Legal Adviser and later General Counsel of the Organization for European Economic Co-operation (OEEC) 1948; Director and later Director-Gen., European Nuclear Energy Agency 1956. Chairman, Association Technique pour l'Energie Nucléaire (ATEN), Paris 1965; Chmn. Centre d'Informatique (CEDIJ) 1971; Vice-Chmn. European Atomic Forum (FORATOM) 1973; Chmn. Bureau pour de Développement de la Production Agricole (BDPA) 1977. *Awards:* Officer, Legion of Honour; Officier Ordre du Mérite; Comdr. Order of Leopold (Belgium) and of Order of Merit of the Austrian Republic. *Address:* 128 Boulevard Malesherbes, 75017 Paris, France.

**HUGHES, Rt. Hon. Cledwyn,** PC, CH, MP. British. *B.* 1916. *Educ.* Holyhead Grammar School and Univ. of Wales (LLB); Solicitor. *M.* 1949, Jean Beatrice Hughes. *S.* Harri Cledwyn. *Dau.* Ann Cledwyn. *Career:* Member of Parliament (Lab.) for Anglesey; Chairman, Welsh Parliamentary Labour Party 1953–54; Minister of State for Commonwealth Affairs 1964–66; Secretary of State for Wales 1966–68; Min. of Agriculture, Fisheries and Food 1968–70; Opposition Spokesman on Agric., Fisheries and Food 1970–72. Pres. Univ. Coll. of Wales, Aberystwyth. *Member:* Law Society, Hon. LLD, Univ. of Wales 1970. *Publications:* Conditions in St. Helena (1957). *Address:* House of Commons, London SW1A OAA; and Swynol Le, Trearddur, Holyhead, Anglesey.

**HUGHES, Hon. Sir Davis,** Kt 1975. Agent General, New South Wales. *B.* 1910. *Educ.* Launceston High School. *M.* 1940, Joan Philip Johnson. *S.* 1. *Daus.* 2. *Career:* with Tasmania Educ. Dept. 1927–35; Squadron Leader R.A.A.F. 1939–45; Deputy Headmaster, The Armidale School 1947–50; Mayor Armidale 1954–56; M.L.A. for Armidale, N.S.W. 1950–73; Leader, Country Party N.S.W. 1958–59 (Res.); Minister, Public Works, N.S.W. 1965–73; Agent General, in London since 1973. *Clubs:* East India and Sports; Australasion Pioneers; Air Force Officers (Sydney). *Address:* 15 Chester Street, Belgravia, London SW1.

**HUGHES, John Robertson.** *B.* 1898. *M.* 1925, Lexy Whittall. *Daus.* Barbara Elizabeth (Warner) and Catherine Janet (Gill). Entire business career with Royal Securities Corp. Ltd., Montreal. Former Chairman and Director, Royal Securities Corp. Ltd. Director: Canadian International Power Co. Ltd., Hunting Associates Ltd., Maritime Electric Co. Ltd., Monterey Railway Light & Power Co. Past President, Investment Dealers Assn. of Canada. *Member:* Atlantic Salmon Assn. *Clubs:* Forest & Stream, Montreal. *Address:* Three Westmount Square, Apt. 916, Montreal 216, Quebec, Canada.

**HUGHES, Roy,** MP. British Politician. *B.* 1925. *Educ.* Ruskin Coll., Oxford—Diploma Economics & Political Science. *M* 1957, Marion Appleyard. *Daus.* 3. *Career:* MP (Lab) for Newport since 1966; Chmn. All Party Sports Cttee. since 1974; Chmn., Parly Labour Party Environment Group since 1976; Vice-Chmn., Labour Middle East Council since 1973. *Clubs:* St. Pierre (Chepstow); United Service Men's (Cardiff); Workingmen's Clubs (Pontllanfraith). *Address:* 34 St. Kingsmark Avenue, Chepstow, Gwent NP6 5LY; and *office* House of Commons, London SW1A 0AA.

**HUGHES, Walter Laurence.** British. *B.* 1917. *Educ.* Sydney University (BE; BSc) and Oxford University (DPhil). *M.* 1950, Elizabeth Muriel Baird. *S.* Christopher Laurence. *Dau.* Jacqueline Kay. *Career:* Officer-in-Charge Ship Construction, Whyalla Shipyard, South Australia 1951–54; Director and General Manager, Walkers Ltd., Maryborough, Queensland. 1954–75, Man. Dir. 1975—; Member, Australian Universities Commission, 1965–77, Member Universities Council June 1977—; Consultative Council Export Payments Insurance Corp. 1967–73; Chmn., Export Finance & Insurance Corp. 1977—; Chmn., Aust. Shipbuilders Assn. 1972–73; Dir. Hyne & Son Pty., Ltd. since 1973; Dir. M.I.M. Holdings since 1973; Queensland Council Metal Trades Employers Association since 1954. Is a New South Wales Rhodes Scholar. *Member:* Institution of Mechanical Engineers; Australian Inst. of Management; Inst. of Marine Engineers: North-East Coast Inst. of Engineers & Shipbuilders; American Bureau of Shipping; Manufacturing Industries Council. *Clubs:* Queensland; Brisbane; Maryborough & Wide Bay Club. *Address: office* Walkers Ltd., Maryborough, Qld. 4650, Australia.

**HULME, Hon. Sir Alan Shallcross,** KBE, FCA. *B.* 1907. *Educ.* North Sydney Boys' High School. *M.* 1938, Jean Archibald. *S.* 2. *Dau.* 1. *Career:* Hon. Treas. King's Univ. College 1944–49; Pres. Qld. Div. Liberal Party of Australia 1946–49 & 1962–64; M.H.R. for Petrie, Qld., 1949–61 and 1963–72. *Member:* Commonwealth Parly. Public Accounts Cttee. 1953–58. Chmn., Special Cttee. investigating depreciation under income tax acts 1955; Chmn., Commonwealth Immigration Planning Council 1955–58. Former Vice-Consul for Portugal; Minister for Supply 1958–61; Postmaster General 1963–72; Acting Minister for Defence 1965–66; Vice-Pres. of the Exec. Council Commonwealth of Australia 1966–72. *Club:* Brisbane. *Address:* Alcheringa Drought-master Stud, Eudlo, Qld. 4554, Australia.

**HULTON, Sir Edward George Warris.** British magazine publisher and author. *B.* 29 Nov. 1906. *Educ.* Harrow; (scholarship) Brasenose College, Oxford. *M.* 1942, Princess Nika Yourievitch. *S.* 2. *Dau.* 1. *Career:* Conservative Parliamentary Candidate, Leek Division of Staffordshire 1929, and Harwich Division of Essex, stood down in National interest 1931; called to Bar, Inner Temple 1936; practised on South-Eastern Circuit; Chairman and Managing Director, Hulton Publications Ltd.; Member, National Cttee., British Council of the European Movement; Pres., European-Atlantic Group, 1968–70; Vice-President. European League for Economic Co-operation. Freeman of City of London since 1945; Nato Peace Medal 1969; F.R.S.A. 1971. *Publications:* The New Age; When I Was a Child; Conflicts (1966). *Address:* Flat 9, 24 Carlton House Terrace, London SW1; Haycroft House, Sherbourne, Cheltenham, Glos.; and *office* 237 Cromwell Mansions, Cromwell Road, London SW5 OSD.

**HUMMEL, Arthur W., Jr.** American. *B.* 1920. *Educ.* University of Chicago (MA). *M.* 1951, Betty Lou Firstenberger. *S.* Timothy, William. *Career:* U.S. Foreign Service: Hong Kong 1952–55; Tokyo 1955–57; Rangoon, 1957–60; Taiwan, 1965–68; Dep. Chief of Mission, U.S. Embassy Taiwan 1958–68; Deputy Director, Voice of America, 1961–63; Deputy Assistant Secretary of State for Cultural Affairs, 1963–65; Ambassador to Burma 1968–71; Dep. Asst. Secy of State, East Asia Bureau 1972–75; Ambassador to Ethiopia 1975–76; Asst. Secy. of State, East Asia Bureau 1976–77; Ambassador to Pakistan since 1977. *Member:* Association for Asian Studies; Phi Beta Kappa. *Address:* c/o East Asia Bureau, Department of State, Washington, D.C., U.S.A.

**HUMPHREY, Senator Hubert H.** Democrat-Farmer-Labor of Waverly Minn. *B.* 1911. *Educ.* South Dakota schools; Denver College of Pharmacy (grad. with degree), Univ. of

Minnesota (AB), (Phi Beta Kappa); Louisiana State Univ.—MA degree; Hon. Doctorate degrees from 40 Colleges and Universities. *M.* Muriel Buck. Four children. *Career:* State Director War Production Training 1942; Asst. Dir. War Manpower Commission 1943; Professor in Political Science, Macalester Coll. 1943 and 1944; Mayor of Minneapolis 1945 and 1947; member, First Congregational Church of Minnesota; Elected to U.S. Senate Nov. 1948, for the term commencing Jan. 1949; re-eelcted 1954 and 1960 for term ending Jan. 1967; U.S. Delegate to United Nations 1956–57; Senate Majority Whip 1961–64; Vice-Pres. 1965–69; Democratic nominee for Pres. United States 1968; Prof. political science and Int. Affairs Macalester Coll. 1969–70; Prof. social science program, Univ. of Minnesota 1969–70; Chmn. Board of Consultants, Member Bd. Dirs. Encyclopaedia Britannica Educational Corp.; and Mem. Bd. Dirs. Encyclopaedia Britannica Inc. 1969–70; Chmn. Bd. Trustees Woodrow Wilson International Center for Scholars 1969–72; Elected to United States Senate 1970 for 6 year term commencing Jan. 1971; Chmn., Congressional Joint Econ. Cttee. 1975; Re-elected to Senate for 6 year term commencing Jan. 1977. *Address:* 550 N. Street, S.W., Washington, D.C., U.S.A.

**HUMPHREYS, David Colin.** British Civil Servant. *Educ.* Eton (King's Scholar); Kings College Cambridge, MA. *M.* 1952, Jill Allison Cranmer. *S.* 2. *Dau* 1. *Career:* Air Ministry since 1949, Private Secy. to Secy of State for Air 1959–60; Counsellor, UK Delegation to NATO 1960–63; Air Force Dept 1963–69; Student Imperial Defence College 1970; Civilian-Dir. Defence Policy Staff 1971–72; Assist. Secy. Gen. for Defence Planning and Policy, NATO 1972–76; Asst. Under Secy. (Naval Staff), Ministry of Defence, London since 1977. *Address:* Rivendell, Northdrive, Virginia Water, Surrey.

**HUMPHREYS, Sir Kenneth Owens.** Australian Chartered Accountant. *B.* 1918. *Educ.* Fellow Institute of Chartered Accountants; FCA.; Fellow Aust. Inst. of Management. *Career:* Accounting Profession, then R.A.A.F. until 1945; Gen. Mgr. and Dir. Clyde Industries Ltd. 1951–55. Chmn.: The Commonwealth Industrial Gases Ltd.; International Pacific Corp. Ltd.; United Telecasters Sydney Ltd.; Director: Australian Reinsurance Co. Ltd.; The Commercial Bank of Australia Ltd.; Qantas Airways Ltd.; Councillor, New England Univ.; Member, Australian/Japan Foundation. *Address:* 26th Floor, Royal Exchange Bldg., 56 Pitt Street, Sydney 2000, Australia.

**HUND, Prof. Friedrich (Hermann).** German physicist. *B.* 4 Feb. 1896. *Educ.* Göttingen University (Dr phil). *M.* Dr. Ingeborg Seynsche. 5 children. *Career:* Reader in Theoretical Physics, Göttingen 1925; Associate Professor 1927, and Professor, Rostock University 1928; Guest Reader, Harvard University 1929; Professor at the Universities of Leipzig 1929, Jena 1946, Frankfurt 1951 and Göttingen 1956; Professor of Theoretic Physics, University of Göttingen 1956–64. *Publications:* works on the Theory of Atoms & Solids, Molecules, since 1967 on History of Physics. *Address:* Charlottenburgerstr. 19, Gottingen, Federal Republic of Germany.

**HUNDELSHAUSEN, Von Freiherr Wilhelm Heinrich Karl Rolf,** first class Cross of Merit Fed. Republic of West Germany; *B.* 1905; *Educ.* German Wilhelmsgymnasium; Hamburg Univ.; *M.* 1939. Olga Haydee Mendoza-Pohl. *S.*1. *Career:* Man. Dir. CAISA; Consultant of Exec. Board Banco Salvadoreño; Mem. Assoc. Azucarera of El Salvador; Mem. Exec. Board Central Reserve Bank, El Salvador, 1934–36; Gen. Man. Banco Hipotecario, 1935–40; *Clubs:* Ubersee, Hamburg; Club Salvadoreno. *Address:* Blvd. Hipodromo 662, Col. San Benito, San Salvador; and *office:* San Salvador, 2a Ave. Norte 120, El Salvador.

**HUNDERTMARK, Dr. jur. Hans.** German banker. *B.* 1909. *Educ.* studied Law and Political Science Univs. of Jena, Kiel and Greifswald. Legal Advsr. 1930–33; Law Assessor 1934; Doctor-at-Law, Jena 1931. *M.* 1946, Ina Hein. *S.* Frank. *Career:* From 1934, Solicitor and Rural Borough Counsel, Anklam; from 1945, Co-partner and General Manager, Deutsche Sauna-Gesellschaft Wagner & Company, Hamburg; from 1948 Solicitor, Hanseatischen Oberland Court, Hamburg; from 1951, Legal Adviser to Lastenausgleichsbank, Bank for Refugees and Injured Persons, and from 1962 Ordinary Member of the Board of the Bank; Managing Dir. 1970–74. *Member:* Arminia Association (former students of Jena); Burgkeller (Mainz); Internat. Club. *Address:* Rolandstr. 36, D-5300 Bonn-Bad Godesberg, Federal Republic of Germany.

**HUNT, Sir David Wathen Stather,** KCMG, OBE; Bronze Star (U.S.). British. *B.* 1913. *Educ.* Oxford University (MA First Class Hons; Diploma in Classical Archaeology). *M.* (1) 1948, Pamela Medawar (diss.). *S.* John and Richard. (2) Iro Myrianthousi. *Fellow:* Magdalen Coll. Oxford 1937. *Career:* Served in 1st Bn. Welch Regt. and Gen. Staff in Middle East, Balkans, N. Africa, Sicily, Italy (desp. 3 times; O.B.E.; Bronze Star) 1940–46. Attached to staff of Gov. General of Canada 1946–47. Entered Diplomatic Service 1947; First Secy., Pretoria 1948–49; Private Secretary to Prime Minister (Mr. Attlee and Mr. Churchill) 1950–52; Deputy High Commissioner Lahore 1954–56; Asst. Under-Secy. of State 1959; Deputy High Commissioner Lagos 1960–62; High Commissioner: Uganda 1962–65; Cyprus 1965–66; Nigeria 1967–69. Ambassador in Rio de Janeiro, Brazil 1969–73; Chmn. C'wealth Inst. since 1974. *Publications:* articles in Annual of British School of Archaeology in Athens, and in the Journal of Hellenic Studies; A Don at War (1966) On the Spot (1975). Is an Hon. Colonel. *Member:* Press Council; Central Council, Royal Overseas League; Council, Hellenic Society; British Legion; Brazilian Academy of Arts. *Clubs:* Athenaeum (London), PEN (Brasil). *Address:* Old Place, Lindfield, Sussex RH16 2HU.

**HUNT, Sir Joseph Anthony,** MBE. British. *B.* 1905. *Educ.* St. Gregory's School, Farnworth; Royal Technical College, Salford; Manchester College of Technology. *M.* 1960, Esme Jeanne Langston. *S.* 2. *Dau.* 1. *Step-dau.* 1. *Career:* Director and General Manager, The Hymatic Engineering Co. Ltd. 1938–65. Director: The Chloride Electrical Storage Co. Ltd. 1965–73; Industrial Training Service Ltd.; Chairman (1968) The Hymatic Engineering Co. Ltd., The Hydrovane Compressor Co. Ltd. 1969—; Porvair Ltd.; Chmn. Fairey Co. Ltd. 1970–75; Dir. Inmont Corp. New York 1973–77. Pro-Chancellor, University of Aston in Birmingham 1966–70; Chmn. Huntleigh Investments Ltd. since 1974; Hunt Cttee. on Intermediate Area 1967–69; Nat. Adv. Council on Education for Industry and Commerce 1967–74; Chmn. Hymatic Industrial Controls since 1974; Chmn. Kellogg-American Inc. 1975—; Dir., FlowtronAire Ltd. 1975—; Dir., Aston Technical Services 1975—; Dir., Nicholas Mendes and Associates 1975—; Dir. MIT since 1975. Pres. B.A.C.I.E., Vice-Pres. City & Guilds of London Institute. *Member:* Central Trng. Cncl., Hon DSc (Aston), LLD (Birmingham). *Fellow:* British Inst. of Management. *Address:* 16a Ampton Rd., Ampton Green, Edgbaston, Birmingham 15. and *office* Claybrook Drive, Redditch, Worcs.

**HUNT, Roland Charles Colin,** CMG. British. *B.* 1916. *Educ.* Rugby School and Queen's College Oxford. *M.* 1939, Pauline Garnett. *S.* 3. *Daus.* 2. *Career:* British Deputy-High Commissioner; Malaysia 1957–59, and Pakistan 1962–65. High Commissioner in Uganda 1965–67. Under-Secretary of State, Foreign and Commonwealth Office 1967–70. High Commissioner in Trinidad and Tobago, 1970–73; Dir Brit. National Cttee. International Chamber of Commerce 1973–76. *Address:* Charlton Lodge, Charlton, Banbury, Oxon.

**HUNT, Sydney A.** Vice-President, Meldrum & Fewsmith, Cleveland, Ohio. *B.* 1909. *Educ.* Haverford College (BA). *M.* 1948, Frances E. Conover. *S.* Nicholas B. *Daus.* Patricia A. and Margaret S. *Career:* Teaching Fellowship of International Goodwill from American Friends' Service Committee 1932–33; Editor, Arab Federation newspaper in Jerusalem, Palestine 1933–34; copywriter, N.W. Ayer 1935–41, and Lee Anderson 1942; catalogue editor, Firestone Tire & Rubber Co. 1942–43 Account Executive, Fuller, Smith & Ross 1944–53; joined Meldrum & Fewsmith 1953; Vice-Pres. (Creative Director 1953–60; Group Supervisor, Consultant on Corporate Reputation Communications 1960–67; Board of Directors, 1963–67); Vice-Pres. and Bd. Dirs., Opinion Builders (P.R.) 1964–67. *Publications:* numerous articles on travel, advertising and commerical communications, Near East politics, investments, etc. Past Clerk: Detroit Society of Friends, and Cleveland Society of Friends. *Member:* Ohio Republican Information Committee; Ohio Cancer Society P.R. Committee; Children Crusade (Chmn. 1946); Society for Prevention of Infantile Paralysis (Vice-Pres. Cleveland Chapter). *Clubs:* Novel, Athletic, City, Advertising, Ski (Cleveland); Soc. Am. Travel Writers. *Address:* Virgin Gorda, Box 52, British Virgin Islands.

**HUNT, Wallis Glynn Gunthorpe.** British. *B.* 1922. *Educ.* Wellington College. *M.* 1943, Susan Noel Wentworth Davis. *S.* 4. *Daus.* 2. *Career:* War Service 1941–47. Managing Director, Balfour, Williamson & Co. Ltd. 1961–65; Dalgety 1965–69; Sir Frederick Snow and Partners 1970–72; Gen. Manager Hedderwick, Stirling, Grumbar & Co. since 1972. *Member:*

Court of Common Council of City of London 1962—; Chmn. of Police Cttee. 1966–69; Chmn. Music Cttee. 1971–74; Chmn. City Lands and Bridge House Estates Cttee. (chief Commoner) 1975. Gvnr. of Cripplegate Foundation 1961— (Chmn. 1965–66); Member Court of Gold and Silver Wyre Drawers; Dir. City Arts Trust 1971—; Chmn. Assn. British Orchestras since 1973; Governor, Sadlers Wells 1977. *Publications:* Heirs of Great Adventure (History of Balfour, Williamson & Company). *Address:* Moorlands, The Drive, Belmont, Surrey.

**HUNTER, Sir (Ernest) John,** CBE, DSc, DL. *B.* 1912. *Educ.* Oundle School, Cambridge University; Durham University; BSc. *M.* 1949, Sybil Gordon. *S.* 2. *Career:* Started Apprenticeship at Swan, Hunter & Wigham Richardson Ltd., Wallsend Shipyard in 1930 on the Sandwich System; graduated in the Degree of BSc in 1935; after leaving Univ., spent two years in the Drawing and Design Office of Wallsend Shipyard, following which joined staff of Barclay Curle & Co. Ltd., first in North British Engine Works and subsequently at Elderslie Dry Docks (1937–39). Returned to Dry Dock Department of Swan, Hunter & Wigham Richardson as an Assistant Manager (July 1939), Assistant General Manager of the Dept. 1941, General Manager 1943, and a Director of Swan, Hunter & Wigham Richardson 1945. Held position of Director and General Mgr. until May 1957, when appointed Chmn; Exec. Chairman Swan Hunter Group Ltd., Chmn. N.E. Broadcasting Co. Ltd.; Dir.: Newcastle and Gateshead Water Co., Common Brothers Ltd., Midland Bank Ltd.; Dorman Long Swan Hunter (Pty.); Swan Hunter Africa (Proprietary) Ltd.; Swan Hunter International Ltd.; Past Chmn.: North East Coast Shiprepairers Assn. 1957–58, Tyne Shipbuilders' Assn. 1955–57, Dry Dock Owners & Repairers Central Cncl. 1961–62, Central Training Cncl. 1964–68; Past Pres.: North-East Coast Institution of Engineers and Shipbuilders 1958–60, Shipbuilding Employers' Federation 1956–67; British Emlpoyers' Confederation; Institute of Marine Engineers 1965–66; Shipbuilding and Repairers National Asscn. 1968–70. *Member:* Royal Institution of Naval Architects, Institution of Marine Engineers, Inst. of Shipbuilders & Engineers in Scotland, Council of Lloyd's General Committee and Executive Board. Council of Confederation of British Industry Exec. Board of SRNA. Liveryman of Worshipful Company of Shipwrights. Freeman, City of London (by Redemption) and of the Borough of Wallsend. *Club:* Northern Counties. *Address:* The Dene, Stocksfield, Northumberland; and *office* Sunley House, Regent Centre, Gosforth, Newcastle upon Tyne NE3 3QA.

**HUNTER, Brigadier Ian Murray,** CVO, MBE. Australian soldier, company director. *B.* 1917. *Educ.* Cranbrook School Sydney; Royal Military Coll. Duntroon; Staff Coll. Middle East, Australia and U.S.A. *M.* 1947, Rosemary Jane Batchelor. *S.* 2. *Daus. Career:* Staff Captain Infantry Brigade Brigade 1940–41; D.A.Q.M.G. 1–6 Division 1941–42; A.Q.M.G. N.T. Force 1942–43; G.S. 3 Corps and Advanced L.H.Q. 1943–44; A.Q.M.G. and Col. Q.B.C.O.F. 1946–47; A.A. and Q.M.C. 3 Div. 1948–50; Prime Minister Dept. Exec. Officer, Commonwealth Jubilee Celebrations, Royal Visits 1952 and 1954, 1959; C.O. 4 R.A.R. 1953; Commandant Aust. Staff Coll. 1963–65; Papua New Guinea Command 1966–69; D.Q.M.G. A.H.Q. 1969; Chmn. Allied Rubber Products since 1970. *Awards:* Commander, Royal Victoria Order; Member, Most Excellent Order, British Empire; Fellow Aust. Inst. Management; Aust. Inst. Directors. *Clubs:* Australian; Queensland; United Service and Royal Sydney Golf. *Address:* Garthland, 42 Charlton Street, Ascot, 4007, Qld., Australia; and *office* 10 Wolverhampton Street, Stafford, 4053, Qld.

**HUNTING, Lindsay Clive.** Chairman, Hunting Group of Companies. *B.* 1925. *Educ.* Loretto, and Trinity Hall, Cambridge (MA Cantab). *M.* 1952, Shelagh Mary Pamela Hill-Lowe. *S.* Peter Eric Lindsay. *Dau.* Deborah Ruth. *Career:* Joined Hunting Group 1950, Dir., 1952, Vice-Chmn. 1962, Chmn. 1975. Group comprises companies engaged in Shipowning, Ship and Oil Broking, Aviation Support, Engineering, Boat-Building, Industrial Painting and Survey and Consultancy, in Britain, France, Canada, Australia and Southern Africa. Other appointments; Chmn., Donkin & Co. Ltd. 1952—; Pres., British Independent Air Transport Assoc. (1960–62), Pres., Fedn. Internationale de Transporte Aerien Privée (1961–63), Chmn., Air League (1968–71); Pres., Air Education & Recreation Org. 1970—. *Clubs:* City Livery (London); Royal London Yacht (Cowes). *Address:* Fugelmere Grange, Fulmer, Bucks. SL3 6HN; and *office* Avenfield House, 118–127 Park Lane, London W1Y 4HN.

**HURD, The Hon. Douglas Richard,** MP. British. *B.* 1930. *Educ.* Eton & Trinity Coll., Cambridge (First Class Hons. in History). *M.* 1960, Tatiana Eyre. *S.* 3. *Career:* H.M. Diplomatic Service 1952–66; Conservative Research Dept., 1966–70; Political Sec. to the PM 1970–74; Conservative MP for Mid Oxfordshire since 1974 and Cons. Spokesman on European Affairs since 1976. *Decorations:* Commander of the British Empire (1974). *Publications:* The Arrow War; Send Him Victorious; Smile on the Face of the Tiger; Scotch on the Rocks; Truth Game; Vote to Kill. *Clubs:* Travellers. *Address:* 2 Mitford Cottages, Westwell, Burford, Oxon.; and House of Commons, London SW1A 0AA.

**HURD, Leslie Vernon,** JP. South African. *B.* 27 Aug. 1900. *Educ.* Jeppe High School (matric.). Life Associate of the Chartered Insurance Institute, London. *M.* 1929, Violet May Bashforth. *S.* 1. *Dau.* 1. *Career:* Served with R.A.F. in World War I, and part-time (Capt.) in World War II (trans. to Reserve of Officers with rank of Capt.); served with the following firms; New Zealand Insurance Co. Ltd. (1919–20), Ocean Accident & Guarantee Corpn. Ltd. (1920–21), African Guarantee & Indemnity Co. Ltd. (1921–22), Ocean Accident & Guarantee Corpn. Ltd. (1922–28), General Motors (S.A.) Ltd. (1928–31); operated own business 1931–58; W. H. Davis Ltd.; The African City Properties Trust (1952) Ltd.; Property Renting Corp. Ltd.; S.A. Mutual Fire & General Insurance Co. Ltd.; now with the Metal Industries Group Medical Aid Fund; Pres., The Inst. of Estate Agents and Auctioneers of South Africa 1944–45; Vice-Chmn. of the Southern Transvaal Branch of the same Institute 1939–40 and 1948–49 (Chmn. 1940–45, 1949–53, elected Life Member 1954); Vice-Chmn., Transvaal Branch, South African Institute of Valuers 1948–50 and elected Life Member 1971; elected to City Council of Johannesburg 1947 (Chmn. or Vice-Chmn. of several committees, including Non-European Affairs Cttee, of which he was Chmn. 1951–54); Chmn. Health and Social Affairs Committee 1956–57; Dep. Mayor 1954–55; Mayor 1955–56; Chmn., Special Licensing Committee 1957–58 (Vice-Chmn. 1961–67; five successive unopposed returns); Pres., Rotary Club of Johannesburg 1951–52; Chairman (Hon. Pres. 1955–61) of Johannesburg Youth Weeks (1949–52), Johannesburg Youth Council (1952–63), Hon. Life Pres., Johannesburg Council for the Care of the Aged 1958—, and Johannesburg Publicity Association 1953–59. *Address:* 'Lamorbey', Cor. Eildon and Rambler Roads, Kensington, Johannesburg; and *office* Metal Industries House, 3rd Floor, Corner, Marshall & Simmonds Streets, Johannesburg, South Africa.

**HURLEY, Donald Joseph.** American lawyer. *B.* 1907. *Educ.* Harvard Coll. (AB *magna cum laude* 1928); Harvard Law School (LLB 1931). *M.* 1937, Miriam Greene. *S.* Donald, Jr. and Stephen Nash. *Daus.* Cornelia Greene and Rosamond Page. *Career.* Admitted to Massachusetts Bar 1931; with Goodwin, Practer & Hoard, Boston 1931—, Counsel, Mass. Pardon and Parole Commn. 1938–40; Partner, Goodwin, Practor & Hoar 1939—. Chmn. Dir., Northkraft Industries Inc. Chmn., Dir., Merrimac Paper Co. Inc. Pres. & Dir., Massachusetts Business Development Corp.; Trustee and member board of investment Charlestown Savings Bank; Dir. and Mem. Exec. Cttee., Boston Co. and Boston Safe Deposit & Trust Co.; Secy', Federal Street Capital Corp.; Dir. & Mem. Exec. Cttee, Boston Old Colony Insurance Co.; Dir. Lilly Chemical Products, Inc.; Dir., Carling Brewing Co., Inc.; Dir., Carling O'Keefe, Ltd.; Trustee, George Putnam Fund of Boston, Putnam Growth Fund; Dir., Putnam Convertible Fund, Inc., Putnam Duofund, Putnam Equities, Inc., Putnam Income Fund, Putnam Investors Fund, Putnam Mariner Fund, Putnam Vista Fund, Putnam Voyager Fund; Dir., J. L. Hammett Co.; International Center of New England; Honorary Trustee, Concord Academy; Trustee, New England Aquarium; Chmn. & Dir., Aquamac Corp; Trustee, Boston Urban Foundation; Pres. & Dir. Committee of the Permanent Charity Fund, Inc., of Boston; and Dir. of 9 other corporations or insurance coys. Special Counsel to Governor of Mass. in preparation of charter of Mass. Business Development Corp. 1953; Chmn., Boston Mid-Century Jubilee 1950; General Chmn., 25th reunion Harvard Class of 1928, 1953; Trustee, Lowell Technological Inst., 1955–58. Member: Harvard Univ. Overseers Committee to Visit the Dept. of Economics; Greater Boston C. of C. (Pres. 1954–56, Chmn. Exec. Cttee. 1957, Dir. 1949—); Civic Foundation for Boston (Trustee); Mayor's Cttee. for Civic Progress in Boston (Chmn.); Boys' Clubs of Boston (Overseer); Mass. General Hospital (Member of Corp.); Plimoth Plantation (Trustee); Museum of Science (Mem. of Corp.). *Member:* American Law Institute; American and Boston Bar Associations. *Clubs:* Edgartown Reading

Room (Martha's Vineyard, Mass). Union (Boston); Harvard (N.Y.C.); Weston (Mass.); Golf. *Address:* 41 Aberdeen Road, Weston 93, Mass.; and *office* 28 State Street, Boston 9, Mass., U.S.A.

**HURLEY, Sir John Garling,** Kt 1967, CBE 1959, FAIM, JP. Australian. *B.* 1906. *Educ.* Sydney Tech. High School. *M.* (1) 1929, Alice E. Saunders (*D.* 1975). *Daus.* 3. (2) 1976, Desolie M. Richardson. *Career:* With Berlei group of companies since 1922, including Berlei (UK) Ltd., London 1931–36; Man. Dir. Berlei Ltd. 1948–69; Chmn. William Adams Ltd. 1963–74, Dep. Chmn. 1974–76. *Director:* Development Finance Corp. Ltd. 1967—; Australian Fixed Trusts Ltd. 1970—; Manufacturers' Mutual Insurance Ltd. 1954; Royal North Shore Hospital of Sydney 1969–76. *Member:* Manufacturing Industries Advisory Council 1958–71; Pres., Associated Chambers of Manufactures of Australia 1955–56 & of N.S.W. Chamber of Manufactures 1955–57; Leader of Aust. Trade Mission to India & Ceylon 1957; Chmn. Standing Cttee. on Productivity, Commonwealth Ministry of Labour Advisory Council 1957; Mem. Technical & Further Education Advisory Council N.S.W. 1958–76; Mem. Industrial Design Council of Australia 1958–76 (Dep. Chmn. since 1970); Mem. Council of Abbotsleigh School 1960–66; Mem. Aust. Advertising Standards Advisory Authority 1974—; Chmn. & Trustee, Museum of Applied Arts & Sciences N.S.W. 1958–76; Councillor, Nat. Heart Foundation of Aust. (N.S.W. Div.) 1969—; Mem., Royal Agricultural Soc., Sydney Cricket Ground, Aust.-Amer. Soc., Aust.-Britain Soc., Nat. Trust of Aust. *Clubs:* Australian (Sydney); Australasian Pioneers (N.S.W.); Royal Sydney Yacht Squadron; Warrawee Bowling. *Address:* 1 Arnold Street, Killara, N.S.W. 2071, Australia.

**HUSAK, Dr. Gustav.** Czechoslovakian Statesman. *Career:* General Secretary, Central Committee of the Communist Party of Czechoslovakia. President of Czechoslovakia since 1975. *Address:* Prague, Czechoslovakia.

**HUSSEIN, Amin Ahmed,** GCVO, OBE. Ambassador of the Republic of the Sudan to the Court of St. James's 1961–66. *B.* 1913. *Educ.* Gordon Memorial College. *Career:* Joined Ministry of the Interior as Sub Mamur (Police), promoted to the post of Commissioner of Police in Dec. 1954. Deputy Under-Secretary for Security in the Ministry of the Interior 1957; transferred to the Ministry of Foreign Affairs as Deputy Permanent Under-Secretary with the personal rank of Ambassador Sept. 1957. *Address:* c/o Ministry of Foreign Affairs, Khartoum, Sudan.

**HUTCHENS, Hon. Cyril Douglas,** CBE. Australian. *B.* 1904. *Educ.* Black Rock Primary School. *M.* 1927, Edith Myrtle Lewis. *S.* 1. *Dau.* 1. *Career:* President 1950–52–54–59, and Secy. 1955–57, Hindmarsh, A.L.P. District Committee. M.H.A. for Hindmarsh, S.A. 1950–70. Member, Central Executive of Australian Labor Party (A.L.P.), S.A. Branch 1950–70. Pres. S.A. Branch 1955–56; Bd. Member Electricity Trust, South Australia since 1970. Deputy Leader, Parliamentary Labor Party 1960–67; Awarded, CBE 1970. Member, Adelaide Univ. Cncl. 1953–56. Min. of Works and Min. of Marine, S. Australia 1965–68. *Member:* Hindmarsh Cncl., Croydon Ward 1947–51; Hindmarsh Branch, Royal Dist. & Bush Nursing Socy. 1946—; Pres., Hindmarsh Historical Socy. 1968. *Clubs:* Democratic. *Address:* 57 La Perouse Ave., Flinders Park, S.A., Australia.

**HUTCHINSON, Hon. Sir Ross,** DFC (RAAF). Australian. *B.* 1914. *Educ.* Wesley College, Perth (W.A.). *M.* 1939, Amy Strang. *S.* 1. *Dau.* 1. *Career:* member, Cottesloe 1950—; Chief Secy. Minister for Health and Fisheries in State Govt. of Western Australia 1959–65; Minister for Works and Water Supplies in the State Government of Western Australia. 1965–71; Speaker 1974–77. *Member:* Liberal Party of Western Australia. *Club:* Royal King's Park Tennis. *Address:* *office* Parliament House, Perth 6000, Australia.

**HUTCHISON, Michael Clark,** MA, MP. British. Barrister-at-Law. *B.* 1914. *Educ.* Eton Coll., Trinity Coll., Cambridge. *M.* 1937, Anne C. R. Taylor. *S.* George Alexander Clark. *Dau.* Virginia Helen (Hon. Mrs. William Beckett). *Career:* Called to Bar Gray's Inn 1937; Australian Army, Campaigned Middle East, Ceylon and Pacific Theatre. Passed Staff Coll. discharged rank of Major 1939–46; Officer, Colonial Admin. Service, Palestine and Aden 1946–54; Member of Parliament Conservative, for Edinburgh South, since 1957. *Awards:* Mentioned in dispatches (Military). *Club:* New Club (Edinburgh). *Address:* 16 Maunsel Street, London, S.W.1; and *office* House of Commons, London, S.W.1.

**HUTCHISON, Col. Paul Phelps,** ED, QC. Canadian barrister and Solicitor. *B.* 1895. *Educ.* McGill University (BA 1916; BCL 1921); LLD Southern Methodist Univ. (1956); DCL McGill (1956). *M.* 1930, Mary Meredith Thorburn. *Dau.* Mary Jane. *Career:* Counsel to McMaster, Minnion, Patch, Hyndman, Legge, Camp & Paterson (this law firm was founded in 1823); Pres., Canadian Bar Association 1955–56; Vice-Pres., Int. Bar Association 1956–57; served with The Black Watch (R.H.R.) of Canada 1915–46; commanded Regt. 1939–46. *Member:* Council, The Canadian Bar Association since 1940 (Hon. Treasurer 1947–50; Vice-Pres. for Quebec 1951–52; Dominion Vice-Pres. 1954–55). Hon. Life Member American Bar Assn., and Law Socy of England and Wales. *Publications:* Five Strenuous Years; The 73rd Bn. Royal Highlanders of Canada; Canada's Black Watch; various military, legal and historical articles. *Address:* 129 St. James Street West, Montreal, P.Q., Canada.

**HUTCHISON, William Bruce,** Canadian author and journalist. *B.* 1901. *Educ.* Public Schools. *M.* 1925, Dorothy Kidd McDiarmid. *S.* Robert Bruce. *Dau.* Joan Edith. *Career:* Newspaper reporter, free-lance magazine writer and author; has worked on the Winnipeg Free Press and Victoria Daily Times. Editorial Director, Vancouver Sun, Vancouver, B.C. Editor, Victoria Daily Times, Victoria, B.C., Dec. 1950–63. *Publications:* The Unknown Country (1943); The Hollow Men (1944); The Fraser (1950); The Incredible Canadian (1952); The Struggle for the Border (1955); Canada—Tomorrow's Giant (1957); Mr. Prime Minister. Has written numerous articles published in The Saturday Evening Post, Cosmopolitan, The Reader's Digest, American, Maclean's, Harper's. Hon LLD, Univ. of British Columbia; Governor-General's Award for three of his books; three times winner for entires in the annual National Newspaper Awards; won 'Commonwealth & International Affairs classification in Bowater awards for Canadian journalism,' 1960; first winner of award for distinguished journalism in the Commonwealth awarded by Royal Society of Arts, London, 1961; Service Medal of The Order of Canada, 1967. *Address:* 810 Rogers Avenue, Victoria, B.C., Canada.

**HUTTON, (David) Graham,** OBE. British independent economic consultant. *B.* 1904. *Educ.* Christ's Hospital, and BSc (Econ) (Lond); Barrister-at-Law. *M.* 1958, Marjorie Bremner (U.S.A.) PhD. *Daus.* 3 (by former marriage). *Career:* in business in City of London 1922–25; Student, Fellow and Tutor, London School of Economics 1925–33 and Hon. Fellow 1971; Assistant Editor, The Economist 1933–38; Foreign Office and Ministry of Information in U.K. and U.S.A. 1939–45. *Publications:* Nations and the Economic Crisis (1932); The Burden of Plenty (1935); Is it Peace? (1936); Danubian Destiny (1939); Midwest at Noon (1946); English Parish Churches (1952); We Too Can Prosper (1953); All Capitalists Now (1960); Inflation and Society (1960); Mexican Images (1963); Politics & Economic Growth (1968); English Parish Churches (Joint Author) (1976). *Clubs:* Reform, English-Speaking Union (London). *Address:* 38 Connaught Square, London, W2 2HL.

**HUTTON, Pierre Norman.** Australian diplomat. *B.* 1928. *Educ.* St. Virgil's College Hobart, Univ. of Tasmania, B. Com.; Univ. Coll. Canberra, Diplomatic Studies. *M.* 1964, Judith Mary Carnegie. *S.* 1. *Daus.* 4. *Career:* Joined Austraian Diplomatic Service 1949; 3rd Secy. Bangkok 1952–54; 2cd Secy. Ottawa 1955–58; Acting Consul Noumea 1958; Private Secy. to Minister for External Affairs 1959–60; 1st Secy. Jakarta 1960–62; Dept. of External Affairs 1962–64; Counsellor, Perm. Mission to UN (Geneva) 1964–67; Public Inf. Officer 1967–70; High Commissioner to Nigeria 1970–73, Ambassador of Australia to Lebanon 1973–75, Ambassador to Iraq 1974–75; Ambassador to Jordan 1975 and Ambassador to Syria 1975 (concurrent appointments); Dept. of Foreign Affairs 1975—. *Address:* c/o Dept. of Foreign Affairs, Canberra ACT 2600, Australia.

**HUUN, Christian Einar.** Norwegian; Managing Director, Hop, Norway. *B.* 1905. *Educ.* Engineer. *M.* 1930, Else Hausvik. *S.* Einar and Christian Petter. *Dau.* Ingrid. Knight Order of St. Olav. *Address:* Hop pr., Bergen, Norway.

**HUVELIN, Paul.** French company president. *B.* 1902. *Educ.* l'Ecole Polytechnique. *M.* 1928, Madeline Giros. *S.* Henry, François, Bernard, Michel, Xavier, Gérard. *Daus.* Dominique, Brigitte. *Career:* Ingénieur, Societé Metallurgique de Normandie, 1924–27; Director, then Administrator, l'Eléctrique de Lille-Roubaix-Tourcoing, 1928–40; P.D.G., l'Enérgie Eléctrique du Nord de la France, 1940–46; Vice-President, Administrateur Délégué de Kleber-Colombes,

1947–59. President & Dir. Gen.: Kléber-Colombes, 1959–70. President d'Honneur Kléber-Colombes. Administrator, Thomson-Brandt; Cie Péchiney; Cie Suez. Cie Française Thomson CSF; CGE Societe Generale d'Entreprises; Sogelerg; Sté. Générale des Ets. Bergougnan. President, Conseil National du Patronat Français, 1966–72; President d'Honneur since 1972; Pres. de l'unice 1971–75, Vice-Pres. since 1975. *Clubs:* Automobile; Cercle Interallié. *Address:* 37 rue de Sèvres Paris 6°, and *office* 21 rue du Pont Halles, 94536 Rungis, France.

**HUXLEY, Sir Leonard (George Holden),** KBE. British. *B.* 1902. *Educ.* Rhodes Scholar (Tasmania) 1923; New College, Oxford; MA, DPhil (Oxon); Jessie T. Rowden Scholar 1927; Scott Scholar, University of Oxford 1929. *M.* 1928, Ella Mary Child Copeland. *S.* George Leonard. *Dau.* Margaret Ella. *Career:* Staff member, C.S.I.R. Sydney 1929–30; Lecturer, University College, Nottingham 1930; Head, Dept. of Physics, University College of Leicester 1931–39; Principal Scientific Officer, T.R.E., Ministry of Aircraft Production 1940–46; Reader, University of Birmingham 1946–49; Elder Prof. of Physics, University of Adelaide 1949–60; Chairman, National Standards Commission 1953–65. Member: National Library Council 1960—. Member of Executive, C.S.I.R.O. 1960; Vice-Chancellor, The Australian National University, 1960–67 (retired); Bd. of U.S. Educational Fndn. in Australia 1960–68; First Pres. Australian Institute of Physics 1963–65; Chairman, Board, Britannica-Australia 1964–74; Chmn. of Bd. Aust. US. Educational Foundation 1965–68. Member, Council, Canberra College of Advanced Education 1968—. *Publications:* Wave Guides (Cambridge Univ. Press 1949); numerous papers on gaseous electronics, the Ionosphere, The Diffusion and Drift of Electrons in Gases (with R. W. Crompton-Wiley, 1974); electro-magnetism and related subjects. Hon DSc (Tasmania); Professor Emeritus (University of Adelaide). *Fellow:* Australian Acad. of Science (Foundation Fellow); First President of Australian Inst. of Physics (Fellow); Inst. of Physics and Physical Socy. (U.K.). *Club:* The Commonwealth (Canberra). *Address:* 19 Glasgow Place, Hughes, Canberra, A.C.T. 2605, Australia.

**HYDE, Louis Kepler, Jr.** American corporation and government executive. *B.* 1901. *Educ.* Groton School; Yale College (BA); Corpus Christi College, Cambridge (post-graduate studies). *M.* 1924, Penelope Overton. *S.* Louis Kepler III and Richard Witherington. *Career:* Vice-Pres. Union County Investment Co., Plainfield (N.J.) 1926–39; Riverside Coal and Timber Co., N.J. and Kentucky 1926–41; Wasserman, Nelson, Barringer & Hyde Inc., Philadelphia 1935–41; Partner, Barringer, Nelson & Hyde 1941–48; Pres., Simplex Universal Joint Inc.. Plainfield and Flemington (N.J.) 1929–32; Delaware Fund Distributors Inc., Philadelphia 1938–48; mem., Bd. of Man., Plainfield Savings Bank 1940–41; Dir., Muskogee (Okla.) Elec. Trac. Co. 1936–51; Vice-Pres., Sec. and Treas., Delaware Fund Inc., Philadelphia 1938–48; Dir. 1938–51; Deputy Dir., Planning and Development Staff and Special Asst. to Deputy Administrator, Lend-Lease Administration 1942–43; Deputy Trade Relations Adviser, Foreign Economic Administration (in charge of trade relations staff), Washington 1943–44; Asst. to Sec. of State, in charge of policy review and analysis 1945; Asst. to Chmn., U.S. Deleg. to U.N. Conf. on International Organization, San Francisco 1945; Advisor to U.S. Delegation, 1st to 4th Sessions, U.N. General Assembly (London 1946, New York 1947, 1949; Paris 1948); 1st to 10th sessions of U.N. Economic & Social Council; member, Permanent U.S. Mission to U.N. and Adviser to U.S. representative in U.N. Economic & Social Council 1946–50; alternate U.S. Representative, U.N. International Children's Emergency Fund 1948–50; Vice Pres, E. W. Axe & Co., Inc. 1950–64; Sr, Vice Pres. 1964–67; Chmn. of Board 1967–73; Pres., Axe-Houghton Fund A, Inc. 1967–72, 1975–76; Vice Pres. Axe Scientific Corporation 1967–74; Vice Pres. and Dir., Axe Science Management Co., Inc. 1967–74; Dir., Planning Counsellors, Inc. 1969–74; Chmn of Investment Committee, E. W. Axe & Co., Inc Vice Pres., Axe-Houghton Fund A, Inc., Axe-Houghton Fund B, Inc., Axe-Houghton Stock Fund. Inc.; Dir., E. W. Axe & Co., Inc., Axe Securities Corporation, Axe-Houghton Fund A, Inc., Axe-Houghton Stock Fund, Inc., The Henry W. T. Mali & Co., Inc., Hardigg Industries, Inc., Church Society for College Work; Dir., Exec. Committee, & Treas., American Fund for Czechoslovak Refugees; Trustee, Bedford Free Library, N.Y. *Publications:* The United States and the United Nations: Promoting the Public Welfare (pub. by Carnegie Endowment for International Peace, 1960). Contributor and staff writer, Fortune Magazine 1933–34; articles on trade and international organization in U.S. Government journals and bulletins, and in trade publications. *Address:* Airlie Farm, Bedford, N.Y. 10506; and *office* c/o E. W. Axe & Co., Inc., Tarrytown, New York, 10591, U.S.A.

**HYDER, Sajjad,** SPk, SQA, PFS. Pakistani diplomat. *B.* 1920. *M. Career:* saw active service in South East Asia, Commissioned Officer; Indian Foreign Service Third Secy., New Delhi 1947; Second Secy., Washington 1948; Rep. Pakistan Int. Emergency Food Council, Washington; Secy. Del. Tripartite Conference, Cape Town 1950; Trade Mission, Japan 1951; Second Secy., First Secy. and Counsellor, London 1952; Dir. Pakistan Foreign Office, Karachi 1955; Deputy High Commissioner, New Delhi 1957; Deputy High Comm., London 1959; Ambassador to Baghdad 1961–65; to U.A.R. 1965–68; High Commissioner in India 1968–71; Ambassador of Pakistan to Federal Republic of Germany 1972–75, to the Soviet Union since 1975. *Address:* Embassy of Pakistan, 17 Sadora Kudrinskaya, Moscow, U.S.S.R.

**HYLE, Les J.** Australian Radio Manager. *B.* 1935. *Educ.* Brighton Gr.S. Victoria. *Career:* Anncr./Copywriter (3SR) 1951–57 & (3BA) 1956–58; Anncr., News-Reader, Supervisor & Asst. Mgr. (3UZ) 1958–65; Gen. Mgr. (3KZ) since 1965; Rep. of FARB on Advertising Club of Vic. Board of Mgt. for 5 years; President of Advertising Club of Vic. 1963–65; Member of the Melbourne Kiwanis Club since 1968 (Service org), Vice-President 1971–72, President 1972–73; Member State Executive of FARB, Cttee. Mem. Australian Radio Advertising Bureau (FARB Research & Promotional Division) from 1967–73; Cttee. Mem. FARB Joint Industry Research Committee, Chairman 1976–77; Federal Councillor of FARB since 1971, Snr. Vice-Pres. FARB 1972–73, Pres. FARB 1973–74. *Clubs:* RACV (Melb.), Kelvin (Melb.), Savage (Melb.). *Address:* c/o 3KZ Broadcasting Company Pty. Ltd., Bryson Centre, 186 Exhibition Street, Melbourne, Vic 3000, Australia.

**HYNES, Sir Lincoln Carruthers,** O.B.E. Former Australian executive (radio network). *B.* 1912. *Educ.* Sydney High School and Sydney Univ. *M.* 1939, Enid May Brunskill. *Daus.* Cynthia, Michelle and Stephanie. *Career:* Former sports executive, Macquarie Broadcasting Service, successively Sales Manager 1949, Gen. Manager 4BC 1951; Gen. Manager, Queensland Network (4BC, 4GR, 4RO, 4MB) 1952; Gen. Mgr. 2UW and Queensland Network 1956; Senr. Vice-Pres., Federation of Australian Commercial Broadcasters 1969–71, Pres. 1958–59, 1971–72; Chmn., C.B.N. Sales Pty. Ltd. 1970–74; Chief Gen. Mgr. of Radio Station 2UW and Commonwealth Broadcasting Network (2UW, 4BC, 4GR, 4MB and 4RO) 1956–74; Dir. Fidelity Radio 1956–74, Australian Television Facilities Co. Pty. Ltd. 1960–75, and Darling Downs TV Ltd. 1960—, Chairman since 1969; Chmn., Thos. Cook Pty. Ltd. since 1973; Pres. 1969–71; Dir. City Mutual Life Assurance Society Ltd. 1976—. Vice-Pres. Aust. Hospital Assn. 1971—; Senior Vice-Pres. Aust. Hospital Assn. 1972–74. President 1974; Member o Council Federation of Australian Commercial Broadcasters 1952—, Chmn. 2UW Blind Appeal 1956–74; Chmn. 1968, Royal North Shore Hospital, Dir. 1960–68; Hon. Vice-Pres. Paraplegic Quadriplegic Assn. of N.S.W. 1971—; Dir. Community Systems Foundation 1972–74, Chmn. 1974–75. *Clubs:* Rotary of Sydney; Contact Amer. Natl.; Bowral Bowling; Killara Bowling; Cricketers of N.S.W.; Northbridge Bowling. *Address:* 35 Powell St., Killara, N.S.W., 2071, Australia.

# I

**IBARRA-FORT, Alejandro Antonio.** Dominican banker and physician. *B.* 1914. *Educ.* Univ. of Santo Domingo (MD); Santa Ana Academy, Santo Domingo (Commercial Expert); Superior Normal School (B Physical and Natural Sciences) Master of Spanish. English, French and Russian. *M.* 1943, Margarita Gómez Báez. *S.* Alexis Antonio; Francis Guillermo; Juan Alejandro. *Dau.* Honna Amelia. *Career:* Practised as a physician (Gynaecologist) 1943–45; as an Accountant 1943—. Pres. and Mgr., Banco de Credito y Ahorros (Bank of Credit & Savings), Nov. 1949—. Manager of several real estate and loan companies (Nueva Caja de Prestamos; Solares y Huertos; Negocios en General; Compañia Anonima La Fe; Juan Alej. Ibarra Sucs. C. por A.) 1945—; Rank of Ambassador in Dominican Foreign Affairs Office. Hon. Consul of Paraguay in Santo Domingo. *Publications:* La Taquicardia Atropínica en la Sexualidad Gravídica (medicine); Retiro Médico en la Republica Dominicana (medicine); La Capitalización de Ahorros (finance). *Address:* Avenida Independencia 333, Santo Domingo, Dominican Republic.

**IBSEN, Henri Georg.** American; Vice-Chairman, Constitution Reinsurance Corporation. *B.* 1908. *Educ.* various diplomas from schools and colleges in Denmark, England and France. *M.* 1940, Nell Priscott. *S.* Max Emil. *Career:* Joined Baltica Insurance Co., Ltd., Copenhagen 1929; studied insurance and economics in England, France and Germany, 1935–38; in charge of Baltica's London office, 1939–47; Pres., Constitution Reinsurance Corporation 1947–69. *Member.* Insurance Society of New York. *Clubs:* (New York): Drug & Chemical. *Address:* 315 Forest Drive, Short Hills, N.J.; and *office* 110 William Street, New York, 10038, U.S.A.

**IDE, Chandler.** American. *B.* 1909. *Educ.* Pomona Coll., California (BA). *M.* 1934, Helen Evans. *Daus.* Susan (Junta) and Deborah (Palmer). *Career:* Exec. Asst. to Deputy Petroleum Administrator for War 1941–46; Assoc. Dir. Oil & Gas Div., Dept. of the Interior 1947; Vice-Pres., Secy. & Treas., American Independent Oil Co. 1954–58 (Secy. and Treas. 1948–58); Director, Secy. and Treas., American Independent Oil Co. of Iran 1955–58; President, Natomas Co. 1966–74, Chmn. of the Bd. since 1974 (Vice-Pres., Secy. and Treas. 1956–66). Director: West Indies Oil Co. Ltd. 1962–75, Chairman 1969–75. Bank of California; Dir., Chmn., of Bd., American President Lines, Ltd.; Director and Pres., Secy. and Treas., Natomas Co. of Peru; Chmn. Bd. Natomas International Corp.; Chmn. of Bd. of Natomas Arabian Oil Co., Natomas of Canada Ltd. and Independent Indonesian American Petroleum Co. *Publications:* History of Petroleum Administration for War (Government Printing Office). *Clubs:* Berkeley Tennis; Commonwealth. *Address:* St. Helena, Calif.; and *office* 601 California Street, San Francisco, Calif., U.S.A.

**IDENBURG, Philippus Jacobus.** Netherlands educational and statistical expert. *B.* 1901. *Educ.* Univ. of Leyden (LLD). *M.* 1952, C. S. Kohnstamm. *S.* Jacobus, Philip, Petrus. *Daus.* Johanna and Margaretha. *Career:* Deputy Secy., Netherlands Schoolboard for Schools with the Bible 1924–26; Secy., Economy Committee dealing with general efficiency of State-apparatus of the Netherlands 1927–28; Chief of division for cultural statistics of Central Bureau of Statistics 1929–38; Dir., Central Bureau of Statistics 1939–45; Dir. General of Education 1946; Director-General of Statistics 1947–66; and Professor of Education, Univ. of Amsterdam 1956–72. *Awards:* Hon. Degree, Univ. of Durban. Comm. Order of Orange Nassau, Order of Netherlands Lion, Order of Leopold II of Belgium, and Order of the Oak Crown of Luxembourg. *Address:* Rue d'Eglise 129, 6925 Fays-Famenne, par Wellin, Belgium.

**IGNATIEFF, George.** Canadian. Provost of Trinity College, Toronto, diplomat. *B.* 1913. *Educ.* BA Toronto; MA Oxon. *M.* 1945, Alison Grant. *S.* Michael and Andrew. *Career:* Rhodes Scholar (Ontario) 1936; New College, Oxford 1936–38; joined Department of External Affairs 1940; 3rd and 2nd Secretary, London 1940–44; Ottawa 1944–46; Adviser, Canadian Permanent Delegation to U.N. 1947–48; Counsellor of Embassy, Washington 1949–54; Imperial Defence College 1954–55; Department, Ottawa 1955–56; Ambassador of Canada to Yugoslavia 1956–59; Deputy High Commissioner for Canada in United Kingdom 1959–60; Asst. Under Secy. of State for External Affairs Ottawa 1960–62; Ambassador and Permanent Representative of Canada to North Atlantic Council Paris 1962–66, to the United Nations New York 1966–69; Ambassador, Permanent Representative of Canada, European Office, United Nations, Geneva 1970–72; Provost, Trinity Coll. since 1972. *Awards:* LLD (Hon.) Brock Univ. 1969; LLD (Hon.) Univ. of Toronto 1969; LLD (Hon.) Univ. of Guelph 1970; LLD (Hon.) Univ. Saskatchewan 1973; DCL (Hon.) Bishop's Univ. 1973; DLitt (Hon.) Victoria Univ., Toronto 1977; Companion, Order of Canada 1974; Chmn. of Board of Trustees, Nat. Museum of Canada. *Address:* Trinity College, Toronto, Ont., Canada.

**IHLEN, Alf.** Norwegian. *B.* 1900. *Educ.* University of Wisconsin (BSc Mech Eng 1921) and Massachusetts Institute of Technology (MSc metallurgy and business admin. 1923). *Career:* Pres., A/S Strømmens Verksted 1923. Pres. and General Manager, A/S Strømmens Verksted. Chairman of the Board, Den Norske Creditbank, Oslo and Det Norske Zinkkompani. Chmn. of the Board of Representatives, Norsk Hydro A/S, Oslo; and A/S Borregaard, Sarpsborg. Chairman, Norwegian Chapter of the International EFTA Action Committee (estab. Jan. 1961). *Award:* Commander, Order of St. Olav (Norway); Hon. Member, Polytechnic Society, Norway. *Address:* Holmenveien 4, Oslo 3; and *office* Strømmen, near Oslo, Norway.

**ILIESCU, Ion.** Romanian politician. *B.* 1930. *Educ.* Bucharest Polytechnic Institute. *M.* Elena. *Career:* member Union Communist Youth 1944; Gen. Cttee. 1949; Communist Party 1953; National Assembly 1957—; Member Cen. Cttee. R.C.P. 1968—; First Secy. Cen. Cttee. U.C.Y. Minister Youth Problems 1967–71; Alt. member Exec. Cttee. Cen. Cttee R.C.P. 1969—; Pres. Union Student Assns. 1957–60; Member Acad. Social & Political Sciences since 1970; First Secy. Regional Cttee. & Pres. of Regional Peoples' Council of Lassy 1974. *Address:* Central Committee of the Romanian Communist Party, Bucharest, Romania.

**ILLIES, Kurt,** Dr Ing (marine engineering). Professor: Technical University. *B.* 1906. *Educ.* Technical High Schools of Munich (Dipl Eng), and Braunschweig (Dr Eng). *M.* 1934, Irmgard Kissel. *S.* 1. *Daus.* 2. *Career:* Practical experience on board ship 1930–35; Constructional Engineer, Blohm & Voss, Hamburg (ship machinery and boiler making) 1935 (Chief Constructional Engineer 1941) Hon. Professor, University of Hamburg 1952. *Publications:* Ships' Boilers (vols. 1, 2, 3); numerous publications on Marine eng. President, Association of Shipbuilders (STG). *Member:* Verein Deutscher Ingenieure (Society of German Engineers); Bonnsery Scientific Soc. Silver and Gold Medal, STG. *Address:* Babendiekstr. 20, Hamburg-Blankenese; and Technical University, Hanover, Germany.

**INAYATULLAH.** *B.* 1924. Pakistani Statesman. *Educ.* Univ. of Punjab MA (Hist); Harvard Univ, Master's Degree (Public Administration). *M.* 1955, Attiya. *S.* 2. *Dau.* 1. *Career:* Civil Service in Pakistan 1947–73, this included various positions: Assistant commissioner, Dep. Commissions and District Registrate, Secy to Govt. of W Pakistan in numerous depts., Addit. Est. Secy & Cabinet Secy., set up first Federal Ministry of Tourism and Minority affairs, Chmn. Lahore Improvement Trust; Chmn W. Pakistan Municipal Re-org. Cttee: Mem. Nat. Pay Commission; Chmn. Azed Kashmir Admin. Reorg. Cttee. Chmn. Northern Areas Re-org, cttee; chmn. Pakistan Tourism Devel. Corp; Pakistan Ambassador in Nepal. *Member:* SID; EROPA; DAGA; Am Soc. Public Admin. and Comp. Admin Group; Chmn. Pakistan Mgmt. Group, and its chmn. for study of local govt. *Publications:*—contr. to Development of Administration in Asia; Editor, Public Administration Review; edited many books and contributed articles on Admin. *Clubs:* Lahore

Gymkhana, Rawalpindi Club, Royal Nepal Golf. *Address:* Ambassador's Residence, Ambassador of Pakistan to Nepal, Kathmandu, P.O. Box 202, Nepal.

**INCHBALD, Geoffrey Herbert Elliot.** British. *B.* 1896. *Educ.* Winchester Coll. and Oriel Coll. Oxford; BA (Law) Oxon. *M.* (1) 1919, Rosemary Evelyn Ilbert (*Dec.*), and (2) 1958, Mary Sylvia Woods. *S.* Michael John Chantrey and Anthony Ilbert (killed in Italy 1943). *Dau.* Presiley June. *Career:* Commissioned, Army (Berkshire Yeomanry) on leaving Winchester College in 1915; served in Egypt, Sinai, Palestine and Jordan with regiment and Imperial Camel Corps; wounded 1918; Oxford Univ. 1920–22. Ptnr. in firm of Bischoff & Co., Solicitors 1929–67 (Snr. Ptnr. 1951–67). Commissioned, Army (Royal Berkshire Regt.) 1940; Staff 1941–45 (Major). Dir., Royal Trust Company of Canada, 1956–69. *Member:* Law Society. *Publications:* Camels and Others (1968); Imperial Camel Corps. (1970). *Address:* Flat 28, 2 Porchester Gardens, London, W.2.

**INCHCAPE, Earl of (Kenneth, James William Mackay).** British company director. *B.* 27 Dec. 1917. *Educ.* Eton; Trinity College, Cambridge (MA). *M.* (1) 1941, Aline Thorn Hannay (divorced, 1954). *S.* 2. *Dau.* 1; (2) 1965, Caroline Cholmeley Harrison. *S.* 3. *Career:* Served World War II, Major Royal Armour Corps, 12th and 27th Lancers, France, Middle East and Italy 1940–45; Chmn. Inchcape & Co. Ltd.; P. & O. Steam Navigation Co.; Director: Guardian Royal Exchange Assurance; British Petroleum Co. Ltd., Standard & Chartered Banking Group and other companies; Pres. Gen. Council of British Shipping 1976–77; Prime Warden, Fishmongers Company 1977–78. *Address:* Quendon Park, Saffron Walden, Essex; Glenapp Castle, Ballantrae, Ayrshire and 40 St. Mary Axe, London, E.C.3.

**INCLEDON-WEBBER, Lieut.-Col. Godfrey Sturdy,** TD, DL, MA. British. *B.* 1904. *Educ.* (Radley Coll. 1st Classical Scholar 1918); Eton Coll. 1918–23; Magdalen Coll. Oxford 1923–26 (BA 1926, MA 1947). *M.* 1931, Angela Lacy. *Daus.* Diana Mary (Bury), Elizabeth Angela (Dodge) and Priscilla Mary (Smith-Bingham). *Career:* Partner, Cutler & Lacy Stockbrokers, Birmingham 1932–52. Joined Royal Devon Yeomanry Artillery 1925; served in World War II (Lt.-Col. commanding 136 Lt. A.A. Regiment R.A. 1942–45). T.D. 1943. Man. Dir., British Trusts Assn. Ltd. 1953–73. Director: United Dominions Trust Ltd. 1959–73, English Insurance Company Ltd. Chairman: Osborn and Wallis Ltd. 1954–73, M. Hyam Ltd. 1956–73, and Incledon Estate Co. Ltd. Represented Eton at rackets, football and cricket 1922–23; Oxford University at tennis and squash rackets 1925–26. *Member:* British Squash Racket team in U.S. and Canada 1927. Alderman and Justice of the Peace for City of London 1963–71; one of H.M. Lieutenants for City of London 1963. Sheriff City of London, 1968–69. *Awards:* O.St.J.; Commander of National Order of the Niger 1969; Cmdr. of the Order of Merit., the Italian Republic 1969, and Order of the Lion of Finland 1969. Elected Master Worshipful Company of Clothworkers 1975—, excused service; Past-Master, Worshipful Company of Saddlers; Hereditary Freeman of Barnstaple, Lord of the Manor of Croyde and Putsborough, Devon; Deputy Lieutenant County of Devon 1969. High Sheriff of Devon 1970–71; F.R.S.A. *Clubs:* White's, Carlton, City of London, City Livery. *Address:* 1a Ennismore Gardens, London, S.W.7; and *office* 39 King Street, London, E.C.2.; Buckland Manor, Braunton, North Devon.

**INGERSOLL, Ralph McAllister.** American editor and publisher. *B.* 1900. *Educ.* Hotchkiss School (Lakeville, Conn.); Yale (BS 1921); Columbia Univ. *M.* (1) 1925, Mary Elizabeth Carden (*Div.* 1935) (*D.* 1965). *M.* (2) Elaine Brown Keiffer (*Dec.* April 1948). *S.* Ralph McAllister II, Ian Macrae. *M.* (3) 1948, Mary Hill Doolittle (*Div.* 1962). *M.* (4) Thelma Bradford. *Career:* Mining Engineer, Reporter, New Yorker 1925, Mgng. Ed. 1925–30; Assoc. Ed., Fortune 1930, Mgng. Ed. 1930–35; Vice-Pres. & Gen. Mgr., TIME, Inc. (publishing Time, Life, Fortune, and the Architectural Forum, and sponsoring radio and cinema productions of 'The March of Time') 1935–38; Publisher also of Time 1937–39; resigned, April 1939 to organize and finance company subsequently to publish PM (N.Y.) daily evening newspaper; Pres., The R. J. Company Inc. (investments, principally newspapers, including Middletown (N.Y.) Times Herald and Port Jervis Union Gazette) 1948–59; Pres. Dir. New England Newspapers Inc. (publishing The Pawtucket (R.I.) Times); Pres. Dir., Mid Atlantic Newspapers Inc., publishing The Daily Journal, N.J.; Dir., Capitol City Publishing Co., publishing The Trentonian, Trenton, N.J.; Pres. Dir., Auburn Newspapers Inc. (Citizen-Advertiser & Camillus Advocate) since 1973; Pres. Dir., Community Service Publishing Inc. (Coatesville (Pa.) Record) since 1973; Pres. Dir., Erie-Niagara Publishing Inc. (Tonawanda (N.Y.) News & Kenmore Record Advertiser) since 1973; Pres. Dir., Eagle Publications Inc. (Daily Eagle & Vermont Times-Reporter) since 1974; Pres. and Dir., Central States Publishing Co., publishing The Delaware County Daily Times, Chester, Pa. 1961—, and Shenandoah Valley Publ. Corp. publ. Shenandoah (Pa.) daily Evening Herald; Pres. Dir., Riverdale Publishing Company Inc., publ. Riverdale (N.J.) bi-weekly Trends; Pres. Dir., Milford Publishing Co. Inc., publ. Milford (Conn.) Milford Citizen; Pres. Dir., Mid-Hudson Publications Inc., publ. Pottstown (Pa.) Mercury; Pres. Dir., Northeast Publishing Inc., publ. Fall River (Mass.) Herald News; Pres. Dir., Acme Newspapers Inc., publ. Ardmore (Pa.) Main Line Times, Upper Darby (Pa.) News of Delaware County, Germantown (Pa.) Record American; Pres., General Publications, Inc. (newspaper management) 1959—; Director, Public Welfare Foundation, Washington, D.C. 1970–74; Recording for the Blind 1972–74. Enlisted as private, Engr. Amphibian Comm., U.S. Army 1942; advanced Lt.-Col., Gen. Staff Corp.; served overseas in Africa, England, Italy, France, Belgium and Germany on staffs of Gen. Jacob Devers, F.M. Montgomery and Gen. Omar Bradley; Legion of Merit; Bronze Arrowhead (assault landing in Normandy); 7 campaign stars; Officer, Order of the Crown (Belgium). Episcopalian. *Publications:* Report on England (1940); Action on All Fronts (1941); The Battle is the Payoff (1944); Top Secret (1946); The Great Ones (1948); Wine of Violence (1951); Point of Departure (1961). *Clubs:* Racquet & Tennis; Brook (N.Y.C.). *Address:* Cornwall Bridge, Conn., U.S.A.; and *office* c/o Newspaper Management Inc., 641 Lexington Avenue, New York, N.Y. 10022.

**INGLES, Dr. José D.** Under-Secretary for Foreign Affairs, Philippines. *B.* 1910. *Educ.* Univ. of the Philippines; Univ. of Sto. Tomas (Manila); Columbia Univ. PhB, LLB, LLM, DCL. *M.* 1942, Josefina M. Feliciano. *S.* 2. *Daus.* 2. *Career:* Practising Attorney, Manila 1932–36; Private Secy. to Justice Jose P. Laurel, of Supreme Court of the Philippines 1936; Legal Asst. to the Pres. of the Philippines 1936; Secy. and Tech. Asst., Code Cttee. 1941; Chief, Law & Research Div. (with rank of Sol.-Gen.), Dept. of Justice 1942; Judge-at-large 1942; Capt. of Resistance Movement 1942–45; Asst. Exec. Secy., Office of the President 1943–44; Legislative Counsel in the Senate 1945–47; Prof. of Constitutional Law, Philippine Law School 1946–47; Law Officer, Office of Permanent Rep. of the Philippines at U.N. 1947; Foreign Affairs Officer, Class I, with rank of Minister 1954; Chargé d'Affaires a.i., Philippine Mission to U.N. 1949–50–55; Deputy Permanent Representative at U.N. 1955; Minister to Fed. Germany 1956, Ambassador 1958–62; Ambassador to Thailand 1962–65; Council Representative SEATO 1962–66, and Assn. of S.E. Asian States (ASA) 1963–66; Under-Secy. Foreign Affairs since 1966. Rep. or Alternate Representative (at various periods 1946–74) to General Assembly, Security Council, Economic and Social Council, Trusteeship Council, Commission on Human Rights; Representative: Special Session of UNESCO, Paris, Sept. 1948; UNESCO General Conference Paris 1970; Oral Argument before the International Court of Justice, May 1950; Philippine Delegation (Chmn.) to Economic and Social Council (Santiago, Chile 1951; New York 1951 and 1952; Geneva 1951 and 1953); Vice-Chmn., 4th Cttee., 6th session, General Assembly, Paris 1951–52; Vice-Chmn. Special Pol. Cttee., 18th and 20th Sessions General Assembly 1963–65; chmn. credentials cttee 29th session, 1974; Vice-Chmn. Philippine Delegations to General Assemblies 1955–63–67; acting Pres. UN General Assembly 29th session, 1974; Chmn. Philippine Del. Fifth Ministerial Meeting, Assn. South east Asian Nations (ASEAN) Singapore 1972; member, Sub-Commission on Prevention of Discrimination and Protection of Minorities 1954–74; Rapporteur 1954–58; Vice-Chmn. 1959; Chmn. 1960–62; Member, Cttee., Elimination of Racial Discrimination 1970–77; Acting Secy. of foreign affairs at various times 1966–77; has attended many other intl. conferences, too numerous to mention here. *Lectures:* Democracy—its Appeal and Prospects in South East Asia (Mt. Holyoke Coll., Mass.) 1956; A Philippine View of the World-Wide Struggle for Freedom (Earlham College, Richmond, Va.) 1956); Wirtschaftliche-Partnerschaft, von Asien ausgesehen (Univ. of Aachen) 1961. *Member:* National Research Council, Philippines; Phil. Socy. of Internatl. Law; World Peace Congress. *Publications:* Neutralization of the Philippines (1936); The Philippines and its Economic Structure (1959); The Philippines and Madagascar: A Comparative Study of Malagasy and Tagalog (1960); Freedom and Non-Discrimination in the

Right of Emigration & Travel (a U.N. study, N.Y., 1962). *Address:* 1 Vinzons St., Heroes Hill, Quezon City, Philippines.

**INGLESON, Philip,** CMG, MBE, MC. British. Freelance Export Consultant. *B.* 1892. *Educ.* Rossall School and Queen's College, Cambridge (BA Senior Classical Scholar). *M.* 1921, Gwendoline Fulton. *Dau.* Joan. *Career:* Served in World War I (France, Royal Fusiliers and Staff Captain 198th Inf. Brigade 66 Div. MC. Despatches) 1914–19. Joined Sudan Political Service 1919. Governor: Halfa Province 1931, Berber Province 1932, Bahr-el-Ghazal Province 1934, Darfur Province 1935–44. Ministry of Production 1944; Board of Trade 1945; U.K. Trade Commissioner in Queensland 1949–53, and in Western Australia 1954–56; Former Pres., Revel Industrial Products Ltd. (now Grampian Furniture Ltd.), Chair Centre Ltd. 1958–72. *Award:* Order of the Nile. *Clubs:* Bath (London). *Address:* 36 Campden Hill Court, London, W.8.

**INGRAM, George, Jr.** American. Business Executive; Pres. Chief Exec. Officer & Dir., Reed-Ingram Corp., N.Y.C. *B.* 1920. *Educ.* Yale Univ. (BS) and Stevens Inst. of Technology (MS). *M.* 1947, Olive May Holtz. *S.* George III and John. *Daus.* Patricia (Bone) and Sata. *Career:* various engineering positions, Radio Corp. of America 1942–45. Senior Consultant, Stevenson, Jordan & Harrison Inc. 1945–51; Riegel Paper Corp. Asst. Controller 1951–53. Controller 1953–57; With Raytheon Co. Controller 1957–61, Vice-Pres. 1960–61; Vice-Pres. Finance 1961–63, Senior Vice-Pres. and Dir. 1963–68; U.S. Plywood Champion Papers Inc. Senior Vice-Pres. and Dir. 1968–69; Exec. Vice-Pres. 1969–72, Dir. 1968–72; Pres. Chief Exec. Off. Reed-Ingram Corp. NYC, from 1972; Dir. chmn. Bd. Dir. Deerfield Splty Papers Inc. 1973; Oneida Packaging Products Inc.; Canadian Glassine Co. Ltd. since 1973; Dir. Microwave Assn. Inc. Burlington, Mass. *Member:* Financial Executives Inst.; American Socy. of Mechanical Engineers. American Management Assn. Foundation; Coll. of Wooster (Wooster O). Trustee, Financial Executive Research. *Clubs:* Wall Street (N.Y.C.); Canadian; Nantucket Yacht; (N.Y.C.). *Address:* 502 East 87th Street, New York, N.Y. 10028, U.S.A.

**INKABI, Dr. James Edward.** American. *B.* 1943. *Educ.* Cape Coast Methodist Boy's Sch., Adisadel Coll., Agric. Sch., Kumasi, Ghana; DSc (Oxon). *Career:* Teacher, Anglican Sch., Nsawam Sept.–Dec. 1962 & May–Sept. 1966; Writer on English Language 1968–77; Patron, Foundation for Law, Defence & Education Inc. (Ink Fund Inc. Newsweek Issue) since 1970; with Office of Commissioner for Oaths July–Sept. 1977. *Member:* U.S. Civil Rights Movement; National Assn. for the Advancement of Coloured People. *Address:* G55/2 Tantri Road, Cape Coast, Ghana.

**INOUYE, Kaoru.** Japanese banker. *B.* 1906. *Educ.* Graduated from Tokyo Imp. Univ. *M.* 1933, Mitsuko Shibuya. *S.* 2. *Dau.* 1. *Career:* Joined Dai-Ichi Kangyo Bank (formerly Dai-Ichi Bank) 1929, Dir. 1954–58, Sr. Man. Dir. 1958–62; Pres. 1962–66, 69–71, Chmn. 1966–69, and since 1971; Dir. Asahi Mutual Life Ins. Co.; Taisei Fire and Marine Ins. Co. Ltd.; K. Hattori and Co. Ltd.; Auditor Furukawa Electric Co. Ltd.; Adviser Kawasaki Heavy Industries Ltd.; exec. dir. Fedn. Econ. Org.; exec. councillor Tokyo C. of C. and Industry. *Address:* 3-16-14 Nishi-Shinagawa Shinagawa-ku, Tokyo, Japan; and *office* 6-2 Marunouchi I-chome chiyoda-ku, Tokyo, Japan.

**IRELAND, Relph Leonard.** American professor of pedodontics. *B.* 1901. *Educ.* Univ. of Nebraska (Dr. of Dental Surg. 1927; BSc 1929; MSc 1944). *M.* 1935, Marian Becker. *S.* Robert M. Private pract. dentistry, Lincoln, Neb. 1929–36; joined Fac. of Coll. of Dentistry, Univ. of Nebraska as Instructor 1936; Asst. Prof. of Operative Dentistry 1938; Prof. of Pedodontics and Chmn. of the Dept. of Pedodontics 1940–58. Dean Emeritus and Professor of Pedodontics, Coll. of Dentistry, Univ. of Nebraska, Feb. 1968—. *Publications:* Secondary Dentine Formation in the Deciduous Teeth; Introducing Dentistry to the Child; The Effects of Sodium Fluoride Application on the Dental Caries Experience in Adults; Recent Advances in Operative Dentistry for Children; Photo-elastic stress Analysis of Buccolingual Sections of Class II Cavity Restorations; Measurements of the Primary Teeth, *et al. Clubs:* University, Country (Lincoln). *Address:* 3280 South 31st Street, Lincoln, Neb.; and *office* College of Dentistry, University of Nebraska, East Campus, Lincoln, Neb. 68503, U.S.A.

**IREMONGER, Valentin.** Irish diplomat. *B.* 1918. *M.* 1948, Sheila Manning. *S.* 1. *Daus.* 4. *Career:* Entered Irish Foreign Office as Third Secy. 1946; Second Secy. and Private Secy. to Foreign Minister 1948–50; First Secy. Dept For. Affairs Dublin 1950–55; First Secy. Embassy London 1956–59; Counsellor, Embassy London 1959–64; Ambassador of Ireland to Sweden, Norway and Finland, April 1964–68. Ambassador of Ireland to India 1968–73; and to Luxembourg since 1973. *Publications:* On the Barricades (poems) (1944); Reservations (poems) (1950); Contemporary Irish Poetry (anthology) (1949); Beatha Muire (translation into Irish of Rilke's Das Marienleben) (1955); Irish Short Stories (anthology) (1960); The Hard Road to Klondyke (trans. 1961); The Irish Navvy (trans.) (1963); Horans Field and other Reservations (1972); literary and critical articles and poems in Irish, English and American magazines. *Address:* Embassy of Ireland, 28 Route d'Arlon, Luxembourg.

**IRIBARREN BORGES, Dr. Don Ignacio.** Ambassador *B.* 1912. *Educ.* Don Bosco College (Valencia, State of Carabobo); Central Univ., Caracas (Dr Pol and Soc Scs). *M.* 1938, Carolina Terrero Aguerrevere. *S.* Ignacio Leopoldo and Gonzalo. *Dau.* Maria Carolina. *Career:* Appointed District Attorney, Valencia 1936; Judge of the Primary Court of Claims (Civil and Mercantile), City of Valencia 1936–39; Prof. of Roman Law, Miguel Jose Sanz School of Law, Valencia 1938–39; Assist. Prof. of Civil Law, Central Univ. (also took over Chair of Civil Law from time to time) 1940–44; Councillor, Univ, City Inst. 1945–47; Ambassador of Venezuela to Court of St. James's 1959–64; Minister for Foreign Affairs 1964–69. *Member:* Examination Bd. in Civil Law for many years; University Council representing post-graduate students 1946–47. Subsequent appointments included Presidency of The National Corporation of Hotels (Conahotu Co. Ltd.), and Secretary of the Venezulean Government Junta, presided over by Dr. Edgard Sanabria, until the transfer of power to the Constitutional President of the Republic. *Awards:* Grand Cordon of the Order of the Liberator; Grand Cross. Papal Order of San Sylvestre. *Club:* Travellers' (London). *Address:* Cerro Quintero, Urbanizacion Las Mercedes 3, Quinta Pandora, Caracas, Venezuela.

**IRISH, Sir Ronald Arthur,** Kt, OBE, FCA (Aust). Australian. *B.* 1913. *Educ.* FCA (Aust). *M.* 1960, Noella Jean Fraser. *S.* 3. *Career:* Chmn.: Rothmans of Pall Mall (Aust.) Ltd.; International Cellars Australia Ltd.; Director, Wood Hall Ltd.; Partner, Irish Young and Outhwaite, Chartered Accountants. Chairman, Manufacturing Industries Advisory Council 1966–72; President, Tenth International Congress of Accountants 1972. *Publications:* Auditing. *Life Member:* Institute of Chartered Accountants in Australia (Pres. 1956–58); Australian Socy. of Accountants. *Member:* Inst. of Directors. *Clubs:* Union; Australian; Killara Golf. *Address:* Cootharinga, Castle Hill, N.S.W.; and *office* 127 Kent Street, Sydney, N.S.W., Australia.

**IRVINE, Rt. Hon. Sir Arthur James,** QC, MP. *B.* 1909. *Educ.* Universities of Edinburgh (MA) and Oxford (MA). *M.* 1937, Eleanor. *S.* 4. *Career:* Pres., Oxford Union, 1932; Secretary to the Lord Chief Justice of England, 1935–40; MP, 1947—; Recorder of Colchester, 1965–67. Solicitor-General, 1967–70. Member of the Labour Party. *Address:* 20 Wellington Square, Chelsea, London, S.W.3.

**IRVINE, Bryant Godman,** MA, MP. Canadian. farmer, Barrister at Law. *B.* 1909. *Educ.* Upper Canada Coll.; St. Paul's School; Magdalen Coll., Oxford, Master of Arts, Inner Temple; Companion Inst. Civil Engineers 1934–73. *M.* 1945, Valborg. Cecilie Carslund. *Daus.* 2. *Career:* to the Bar 1932; Served with R.N.V.R. Lieut. Commdr. 1939–45; Chmn. Young Conservative Union 1946–47; Member Exec. Cttee. East Sussex N.F.U. & former Branch Chmn. since 1947; Chmn. Agricultural Land Tribunal, S.E. Province 1954–56; Member of Parliament for Rye since 1955; P.P.S. to Minister of Education to Parly. Secy. Min. of Ed. 1957–59; Joint Secy. Vice-Chmn. Cons. Commonwealth Affairs Cttee. or Foreign & Commonwealth Affairs Cttee. 1957–76; P.P.S. Financial Secy. to the Treasury 1959–60; Chmn. Cons. Horticulture Sub-Cttee. 1960–62; Pres. British Resorts Assn. since 1962; Vice-Chmn. Cons. Agriculture Cttee. 1964–70; Member Exec. Cttee. U.K. Branch Commonwealth Parly. Assn. 1964–76; Chmn. All Party Tourist & Resort Cttee. 1964–66; Speaker's Panel of Chairmen of the House of Commons and Standing Cttee. 1965–76; a Dep. Chmn. of Ways & Means & a Dep. Speaker since 1976; Joint Secy. 1922 Cttee. 1956–68 (Exec. Cttee.) Hon. Treasurer 1974–76; Member House of Commons Select Cttee. on Agriculture 1966–69; General Councillor, Commonwealth Parly. Assn. 1969–73; Treas. Commonwealth Parly. Assn. 1970–73. *Clubs:*

Carlton; Pratt's; Naval; Dormy House Rye. *Address:* Great Ote Hall, Burgess Hill, Sussex.

**IRVING, Harold Rupert.** Australian chartere d accountant. Chairman of Directors of several companies. *B.* 1899. *Educ.* Melbourne High School. *M.* 1927, Valda Marie Satchell (*Dec.*). *S.* John Satchell. *Career:* Private Secy. to Minister for Trade & Customs 1927–28; Research Officer, Royal Commission on Coal Ind. 1930; Inspector, Taxation Office, Dept. of the Treasury 1930–33. Part-time lecturer and Member Accountancy Advisory Panel, Univ. of N.S.W. 1958–70; Editor, Taxation in Australia 1965–74; Part time Lecturer Univ. of Sydney since 1974; Dir. R.C.A. Ltd; Australian delegate 9th International Congress of Accountants, Paris 1967; 5th Conference of Asia & Pacific Accountants, New Zealand, 1968; 6th Conference, Asian & Pacific Accountants, Singapore and Kuala Lumpur 1970; International Tax Conference, Kingston, Jamaica 1972, and Singapore 1974. Member, Public Accountants Registration Bd., and Companies Auditors Bd. for New South Wales 1968–74; Fellow: Institute of Chartered Accountants; Inst. of Chartered Secretaries and Administrators Australian Society of Accountants Member N.S.W. State Cncl. 1953–76; N.S.W. Pres. 1960–62; Member General Council 1961–71; Federal Exec. 1962–69; Aust. Vice-Pres. 1962–66 and Aust. Pres. 1966–68. Honorary Life Member 1971. Taxation Inst. of Australia Founder 1943 (Member Gen. Council 1943–77, Hon. Life Mem. 1974, Gen. Secy. 1943, Exec. Dir. 1971–72); Editor, Taxation in Australia 1963–74; Inst. of Directors (Member N.S.W. Council 1963–67). *Member:* Federal Institute of Accountants (N.S.W. President 1943–44). *Publications:* Taxation Amendments since 1936; Pay Roll Tax in Australia; Commonwealth Sales Tax Law and Practice. *Clubs:* Masonic; Mosman Bowling. *Address:* 19 Queen Street, Mosman, Sydney; and *office* 13–15 O'Connell Street, Sydney, N.S.W., Australia.

**IRVING, Rt. Hon. Sydney,** PC, MP, British politician. *B.* 1918. *Educ.* London School of Economics (BSc Econ; Dip Ed). *M.* 1942, Mildred Weedy. *S.* Julian (Dec.), Stephen John. *Dau.* Susan Anne. *Career:* Member of Parliament, Dartford, 1955–70, and since 1974; Treasurer of H.M. Household & Deputy Chief Government Whip, 1964–66. Chmn. of Ways and Means; Deputy Speaker, House of Commons 1968–70. A Deputy Pro-Chancellor, University of Kent at Canterbury 1968–71; Chmn. Dartford and Darenth Hospital Mangt. Cttee. 1972–74; Dartford District Council since 1973 and Chmn. 1973–74; Director of the Foundation Fund, Univ. Kent, Canterbury 1971–74. Member: Labour Party. *Address:* 10 Tynedale Close, Dartford, Kent; and House of Commons, London SW1A 0AA.

**IRWIN, Basil William Seymour,** MC, TD, DL. British banker. *B.* 1919. *Educ.* Tonbridge School. *M.* 1949, Eleanor Ruth Burgess. *Career:* Served in World War II (London Irish Rifles and Special Forces) 1939–46; ADC 1968–73; Vice Chmn. Ionian Bank Ltd. Director: Leda Investment Trust Ltd.; Dir. Archimedes Investment Trust. *Club:* Special Forces. *Address:* The Thatch, Stansted, Essex; and *office* c/o Ionian Bank Ltd., 64 Coleman Street, London, E.C.2.

**IRWIN, Charles Wright.** American. *B.* 1917. *Educ.* Peabody Institute; Western Maryland College. *M.* 1950, Jacqueline Grace Kelly. *S.* Kelly and Kevin. *Dau.* Becky. *Career:* With Chesapeake Broadcasting Corp.: Sales Manager 1950, Member of Board of Directors 1960; Director, First Harford Federal Savings & Loan 1958; Secretary, First Harford Federal Savings & Loan 1963, Vice-Pres. 1976; Dir. Chesapeake Broadcasting Corporation 1960, Vice-Pres. and Treas. 1972—. Partner Mayfield Development Co. 1959—. Director, Aberdeen National Bank 1965—. Vice-President, Multiview Cable Co. Ltd. 1966—. Dir., Maryland Development Credit Corp. 1976—. District of Columbia Delaware Broadcasters 1970–71; Appt. Harford State Central Cttee. by Gov. Mandel 1971. *Member:* Bd. of Directors Harford Memorial Hosp.; Harford Cecil Adv. Board Salvation Army; Harford County Board of Directors American Cancer Society; Maryland, Del., D.C. Broadcasting Assn.; American Legion—Veteran of Foreign Wars. *Club:* Rotary (Bel Air), Pres., 1969–70. *Address:* 201 Finney Avenue, Churchville, Maryland 21028 U.S.A.; and *office* Box 97 Havre de Grace, Maryland, U.S.A.

**IRWIN, Emmett MacDonald.** Engineer and business executive. *B.* 1902. *Educ.* California Institute of Technology (BSHons 1924). *M.* 1927, Laura A. Wolcott. *S.* William W. *Dau.* Charlotte G. Huntley. With General Electrical Co. 1924–29; Ford W. Harris, patent attorney 1929; Staff Electrical Engineer on 200″ telescope, California Inst. of Technology 1938; Electrical Engineer, Diesel plant, City of Vernon 1932; Asst. Consulting Engineer, power development, Imperial Irrigation District 1934; Private consulting practice 1931–39; Chief Engineer, Magnetest Corp. 1940–42; Manager, West Coast Branch, Waugh Laboratories 1946; President, Induflux Inc. and Irwin Laboratories 1946—. *Member:* Tau Beta Pi; I.E.E.E.; Registered Professional Engineer, E.E. & M.E. Republican. *Address:* 4621 Surrey Drive, Corona del Mar, California; and *office* 1238 South Gerhart Avenue, Los Angeles 90022, California, U.S.A.

**IRWIN, Sir James (Campbell).** OBE (Mil.), ED, psc. Australian Architect. *B.* 1906. *Educ.* St. Peter's College and St. Mark's College, University of Adelaide. *M.* 1933, Kathleen Agnes Orr. *S.* 1. *Dau.* 1. *Career:* Partner, Woods, Bagot, Laybourne-Smith & Irwin (Architects) 1930–74; With Australian Imperial Force (Lt. Col. Royal Australian Artillery) 1940–46; Alderman Adelaide City Council 1953–72; Lord Mayor of Adelaide 1963–66; Pres. Royal Australian Inst. of Architects 1962–63; Pres. Adelaide Festival of Arts 1964–66, Chairman 1969–73. *Member:* National Capital Planning Committee 1964–70. President, Home for Incurables 1966—. Colonel Commandant, Royal Australian Artillery (Central Command) 1966–71. *Fellow:* Royal Institute of British Architects, Royal Australian Institute of Architects, Hon. Fellow St. Marks Coll. (1973). *Awards:* psc. Haifa 1942; OBE (Mil.); Created Knight 1971; Australian Efficiency Decoration. *Clubs:* Adelaide; Naval Military & Air Force (South Australian). *Address:* 35 Barnard Street, North Adelaide, S.A., 5006, Australia.

**IRWIN, John Arnold.** Canadian Diplomat. *B.* 1917. *Educ.* (BA Hons. in History). *S.* 2. *Career:* with R.C.A.F. 1941–45. Joined Dept. of External Affairs 1945. Third Secy. Dublin 1946, Second Secy. Prague 1948, Dept. External Affairs 1950, First Secy. Djakarta 1953; Canadian Rep. to International Civil Aviation Organization 1954, Dep. Head, U.N. Div., Dept. of External Affairs 1957, Counsellor, Cairo 1959, Imperial Defence College 1962, Ambassador, Warsaw 1963–65. Head, Administration Services Div., Dept. of External Affairs, 1965–67; High Commissioner to Tanzania concurrently Zambia and Mauritius 1967. Member, Central Staff, Dept. External Affairs, Ottawa 1971–73; Dir. Inspection Services Div. 1973–75; Ambassador to the Philippines since 1975. *Club:* Cercle Universitaire, Ottawa. *Address:* c/o Mail Room, Dept. of External Affairs, Ottawa, Canada.

**IRWIN, William Arthur,** Canadian journalist and diplomat. *B.* 1898. *Educ.* Univs. of Manitoba and Toronto (BA Pol Science). *M.* (1) 1921, Jean Olive Smith (*D.* 1948), and (2) 1950, Patricia K. Page (a Canadian poet and winner of the Oscar Blumenthal Prize, and author of As Ten as Twenty; won the Governor-General's Award for Poetry with her book The Metal and the Flower). *S.* Neil A. *Daus.* Sheila A. Irving and Patrica J. Morley. *Career:* High Commissioner for Canada in Australia 1953–56; Government Film Commissioner and Chairman National Film Board 1950–53; sometime Rodman, Canadian Northern Railway; later Reporter, Toronto Mail and Empire; subsequently Reporter, Correspondent (Parl. Press Gallery, Ottawa) and Editorial Writer, Toronto Globe; Associate Editor, Maclean's Magazine 1925–42; Managing Editor 1943–45; Editor 1945–50; served in World War I with Canadian Expeditionary Force in France; former President, Toronto Writers Club; former Chairman, Toronto Branch, Canadian Institute of International Affairs; former member, National Executive and Research Committee, Can. Inst. of Int. Affairs; delegate to British Commonwealth Conference, London 1945; Canadian delegate to U.N. Conf. on Freedom of Information, Geneva 1948; Ambassador to Brazil 1957–59; Alternate Delegate to 14th Assembly, U.N. 1959, and 15th 1960; Ambassador to Mexico 1960–64. Publisher Victoria Daily Times & Vice-Pres., Victoria Press Ltd., Victoria, B.C. 1964–71. *Awards:* Officer, Order of Canada; LLD, Univ. of Victoria. *Publications:* Co-editor, Canadian Writers' Market Survey (1931); The Wheat Pool, Motor Vehicle Transportation Briefs—Royal Commission on Railways and Transportation (1932); ditto, Royal Commission on Transportation in Ontario (1937); The Machine (an ice-ballet) (1938). *Address:* 3260 Exeter Road, Victoria, B.C., Canada.

**ISAAC, Charles Martin,** MBE. American business executive. *B.* 1896. *Educ.* The George Washington University, Washington, D.C. (AB). *M.* 1920, Gula Louise Welsh. *Dau.* Marijean. *Career:* Served as member of staff of Inspector General, S.O.S., Am.E.F., France in World War I (decorated with Purple Heart and Certificate of Merit); engaged in retail business 1922–34; President and Executive Manager Canton (O.), Retail Merchants Bd. 1934–42; executive assistant to president, Am. Retail Federation, Washington D.C. 1942–44; manager, Domestic Distribution Department, Chamber of Commerce of the United States, Washington, D.C. 1944–51; member, National Distribution Council 1944–52; Lecturer on distribution, National Institute, Northwestern University Aug. 1943, Yale University Aug. 1946, University of Penn., Nov. 1946, New York University, Jan. 1958; Vice-President, Retail Jewelers of America Inc. 1951–60; Pres. Behr Enterprises Inc. 1960–69; Real Estate Assoc. Fort Lauderdale, Fla. since 1969. *Address:* 3201 N.E. 19 Avenue, Suite D, Fort Lauderdale, Florida 33306, U.S.A.

**ISAACS, David Victor**, MBE. Australian consulting engineer. *B.* 1904. *Educ.* Melbourne Univ. (B Civil Eng. 1925; M Civil Eng 1928). *M.* 1928, Rebecca Winstein. *S.* Phillip Daryl. *Dau.* Audrey Miriam (Bersten). *Career:* Stawell Research Scholar and on staff, Univ. of Melbourne 1926; Stuctural Engr. in Victorian Govt. 1927–33; private practice as Consulting Engineer (Consultant to Tasmanian Govt. for design of Bridgewater Bridge—welded steel rail and road bridge—and Hobart Bridge, 3,178 ft. floating Concrete Bridge. Designed equipment for salvaging £2,379,000 in gold bullion from 438 ft. below sea level, sunk in S.S. Niagara in World War II) 1934–42; Civil Engineer, war projects, Aust. Commonwealth Govt. 1942–44. Dir., Commonwealth Experimental Building Station (government building research) 1944–69; Consulting engineer, private practice since 1969. *Publications:* Metallic Arc Welding (1938). *Member:* FICE, FIE Aust. *Address:* 27 Cultowa Road, Pymble, N.S.W., 2073, Australia (private and office).

**ISAACS, Harry Columbus.** AB. American. *B.* 1910. *Educ.* Boston Latin School; Harvard Univ. (AB). *M.* 1935, Natalie Strauss. *S.* 2. *Dau.* 1. *Career:* Dir. Merchandise Development, Butler Bros. 1945–53; Pres. McCrory Int. Inc; Corporate Vice Pres. Int. Affairs & Dir. B.V.D. Co. Inc. Vice Pres. Intercontinental Industries Inc. since 1973. *Clubs:* Harvard (N.Y.C.); Harvard (Westchester). *Address:* 516 Forest Avenue, Rye, N.Y. U.S.A. and *office* 95 Madison Avenue, RM 709–10 New York, N.Y. 10016.

**ISAACS, Kenneth L.** American trustee and banker. *B.* 1904. *Educ.* Lehigh University (ME 1925); Harvard University (MBA 1927). *M.* 1949, Helen Coolidge Adams. *S.* Kenneth Coolidge Adams. *Dau.* Anne Carpenter Richards. *Career:* Director: Southern Pacific Company 1943, Phelps Dodge Corporation 1949; General Public Utilities Corp. 1962. Trustee: Children's Hospital, Boston 1957; Suffolk Franklin Savings Bank 1939. Lehigh University 1959. Massachusetts Investors Trust 1936; made Trustee 1937. National City Co. (Buying Dept.) 1927–30; private investment work 1930–32; Assistant Comptroller specializing on Endowment Fund Investments, Cornell Univ. 1932–36. Formerly Chmn., Trustee, Massachusetts Investors Trust; Chmn. and Dir., Massachusetts Investors Growth Stock Fund. *Clubs:* Somerset (Boston); Brook, Knickerbocker, Harvard (New York). *Address:* 68 Beacon Street, Boston, Mass.; and *office* 200 Berkeley Street, Boston 16, Mass., U.S.A.

**ISARABHAKDI, Vadhana.** Thai diplomat. *B.* 1913. *Educ.* Faculty of Law and Political Science, Chulalongkorn University; Bachelor of Laws, Barrister-at-Law, Middle Temple, London; London School of Economics. *M.* 1947, Vijni Umananda. *Career:* Appointed one of H.M. Judges 1939; joined Thai Foreign Service 1946; Second Secy., Royal Thai Legation, Delhi 1949 (later promoted First Secy. of Embassy); Chief, Commerce Division, Ministry of Foreign Affairs 1954–55; Chief, South and South-East Asia Division 1955; Director, SEATO Affairs 1956; Executive Secretary, SEATO 1956–57; Legal Adviser, Ministry of Foreign Affairs 1958; Ambassador of Thailand to Australia 1959–66, and to New Zealand 1959–64. Member of Constituent Assembly of Thailand 1959; Dean of Diplomatic Corps in Australia 1963. Member, Siam Society. *Clubs:* Old England Students Association; Royal Bangkok Sports; Royal Turf (Thailand). *Address:* Ministry of Foreign Affairs, Bangkok, Thailand.

**ISHII, Mitsujiro.** Japanese politician. *B.* 18 Aug. 1889. *Educ.* Hitotsubashi University. *M.* 1918, Hisako Kuhara. *S.* Koichiro, Daijiro. *Daus.* Kyoko (Asabuki), Yoshiko. *Career:* Man. Dir., The Asahi Press May 1940–Nov. 1945; joined the Japanese Liberal Party Feb. 1946; Minister of Commerce and Industry Jan.–May 1947; Minister of Transport 1952–54; Gen. Sec. Liberal Party 1955; Chmn. Exec. Bd. Liberal Democratic Party 1956 and 1957; Dep. Prime Minister in the Kishi Cabinet 1957–58; Chmn., Exec. Board, Liberal Democratic Party July 1959–60; Minister of International Trade and Industry July 1960; Minister of Justice 1965–66. Speaker of the House of Representatives 1967–76. *Address:* 10-63, 4-Chome, Takanawa, Minato Ku, Tokyo, Japan.

**ISHKANIAN, George Abraham.** Egyptian. *B.* 1908. *Educ.* American Univ., Cairo (Diploma 1926). American School of Aviation Chicago (Diploma 1929); Holder of British and Egyptian Ground Engineers Licence; Egyptian Commercial Pilot's Licence. *Career:* Storekeeper, Recholampe Commercial Assn. 1926–29; Apprentice Rigger, Imperial Airways Ltd. 1929–31; Ground Engineer 1931–34; MISR Airwork Ltd. 1934–44, Works Man. 1940–44; Chief Engineer, National Air Services 1945–49; Technical Manager, S.A.I.D.E. (Egypt Internatl. Airlines) 1949–53; Technical Director and co-owner of a collapsible tube factory 1953–64; factory nationalized and taken over by the Supreme Organization for Drugs, Mar. 1964; Technical Adviser Cairo Mantle Company. *Member:* Exp. Aircraft Assn. (Milwaukee USA). *Club:* Heliopolis Sporting. *Address:* 43 Ramses Street, Heliopolis, Egypt, A.R.E.

**ISMAIL bin Mohamed Ali**, PMN. National of Malaysia, Governor Central Bank of Malaysia. *B.* 1918. *Educ.* Victoria Institution, Kuala Lumpur, Malaysia; Cambridge University, Middle Temple, England. *M.* 1949, Maimunah binti Abdul Latiff. *Career:* Joined Malayan Civil Service 1946; Asst. State Sec., Selangor State Secretariat 1948–50; Asst. Sec., Economic Division of the Treasury 1950–53; Economic Officer, Penang 1954–55; Controller, Trade Division, Ministry of Commerce and Industry 1955–57; Minister 1957–58, Economic Minister 1958–60, at Federation of Malaya Embassy, Washington 1957–60; Executive Director, International Bank for Reconstruction and Development, and its affiliates International Finance Corp. and International Development Assn., Washington 1958–60; Deputy Governor, Central Bank of Malaysia 1960–62. Governor, Central Bank of Malaysia 1962—. Member, National Development Planning Cttee. 1962—; Director, Malaysian Industrial Development Finance Ltd. since 1963, Chmn. since 1969; Chairman, Capital Issues Cttee. 1968—; Advisor, National Corporation (PERNAS) 1971—; Member, Foreign Investment Cttee. 1974—; Fellow, Malaysian Inst. of Management (Pres. 1966–68); Member Bd. of Governors, Asian Inst. of Mgmt., Manila since 1971. *Awards:* Order of Panglima Mangku Negara (Malaysia) 1964; Order of Panglima Negara Bintang Sarawak (Sarawak) 1976; Hon. Dr. Laws (Univ. of Malaya) 1973. *Clubs:* Royal Selangor Golf (Pres. 1964). *Address:* 23 Jalan Natesa, Kuala Lumpur; and *office* Central Bank of Malaysia, P.O.B. 922, Kuala Lumpur, Malaysia.

**ISMAN MAS, Major-General.** Indonesian. *B.* 1924. *Educ.* Faculty of Law of Indonesia. *M.* 1953, Elsje Wowor. *S.* 4. *Daus.* 2. *Career:* Commander, Student Regiment 1945–50 (prominent guerrilla leader); Army Headquarters, Djakarta 1950–55; Personal Assistant to the Army Chief of Staff and attached to the office of the Prime Minister 1956–57; member, Indonesian Delegation to United Nations 1958; Minister, Chargé d'Affaires *ad interim*, Indonesian Embassy, Rangoon 1959–60; Ambassador to Thailand 1961–64; Ambassador to the United Arab Republic 1964–66. *Awards:* Medals of Honour: fighting with the first and second Dutch aggression; for the members of the Indonesian Armed Forces continuously active in the Military Services 1945–53; Loyalty Service for eight years; Medals: of the first Dutch Military Action Affairs; the second Dutch Military Action Affairs; and Madiun Affairs in the year of 1948. *Clubs:* Royal Bangkok Sport (Bangkok); Djakarta Golf. *Address:* 34 Djalan Tjik Ditiro, Djakarta, Indonesia.

**ISPAHANI, Mirza Abol Hassan.** Pakistan. *B.* 1902. *S.* of late Mirza Mohamed Ispahani and late Sakina Sultan. *M.* (1) 1930, Ameneh Sultan Shushtary. *S.* 2. *Dau.* 1; (2) 1954, Ghamar Azimi. *Educ.* St. John's College, Cambridge. *Career:* joined family business of M. M. Ispahani 1925; was Director of M. M. Ispahani Ltd., and other business undertakings; Pres. Muslim Chamber of Commerce, Calcutta; Leader, Indian Trade Deleg. to Middle East, 1947; elected to Calcutta Corp. 1933; resigned to work for introduction of separate electorates in Calcutta Corp. 1935; re-elected 1940; Dep. Mayor 1941–42; member Bengal Legislative Assembly 1937–47; member All India Muslim League Working Cttee. until end of 1947; Pakistan Constituent Assembly; represented Muslim League at New York Herald Tribune Forum 1946; toured U.S. as Personal Representative of Quaid-i-Azam, M.A. Jinnah; Ambassador of Pakistan to U.S.A. 1947–52; Dep. Leader Pakistan Deleg. to U.N. 1947: Leader Pakistan Deleg. to

Havana Conf. on Trade and Employment 1947; member Pakistan Deleg. to U.N. (Jammu and Kashmir); High Comr. for Pakistan in the U.K. 1952–54; Minister of Industries and Commerce 1954–55; Ambassador of Pakistan to Afghanistan 1973–74. *Publications:* 27 Days in China, Leningrad to Samarkand, and Qaid-e-Azam Jinnah As I knew Him (1966), second revised and enlarged edition (1968); Qaid-e-Azam Jinnah-Ispahani Correspondence (1974). *Address:* 2 Reay Road, Karachi, Pakistan.

**ITANI, Khalil.** Lebanese ambassador. *B.* 1923. *Educ.* MA (with distinction) in History and Political Science. *M.* 1949, Atcha Itani. *Career:* First Counsellor, Paris 1960–64; Head Arabic Dept. U.N. Secretariat 1955–60; Pres Secy. Washington 1952–54; Member Lenanese Deleg. to U.N. Gen. Assembly 1953–54; Head U.N. Div. and Press Service, Lebanese Min. of Foreign Affairs 1949–52; Head Press Service 1946–49; Professor and journalist until Jan. 1946. Ambassador to Ghana 1965–67, and concurrently to Togo, Central African Republic and Chad to Saudi Arabia 1967–69; to Libya (L.A.R.) 1969–71; Ambassador to Algeria since 1971. *Publications:* Histoire Diplomatic du Liban—1840–1864 (thesis for MA degree); Mouhammed Ali Pacha—Ses avocats & ses adversaires (thesis for BA degree); History and Political Science; various articles in newspapers and magazines. Commandeur: Order of National Merit (France) and Order of National Merit (Syria). *Address:* Embassy of Lebanon, 9 rue Caïd Ahmed, El Biar, Algiers, Algeria.

**ITOH, Kyoichi.** Japanese. *B.* 1914. *Educ.* Kobe University. *M.* Chikako. *S.* 1. *Daus.* 2. *Career:* Man. Dir. Kureha Spinning Co. Ltd. 1956–63, Pres. 1963–66; Vice-Pres. Toyobo Co. Ltd. 1966–73, Chmn. 1973–74, General Adviser since 1974; Chmn. Nippei Industrial Co. Ltd. since 1968; Chmn. Toyo Pulp Co. Ltd. since 1975; Hon Consul-General of El Salvador, Osaka. *Club:* Osaka Rotary. *Address:* 11–17, Sumiyoshi-Yamate 4 chome, Higashinada-ku, Kobe, 658 Japan; and *office* 8 Dojima Hamadori 2-chome, Kita-Ku, Osaka.

**IVES, Walter,** CBE. Australian. *B.* 1917. *Educ.* Master of Economics. *M.* 1945, Betty Elnor Henderson. *S.* 1. *Dau.* 1. *Career:* Associate Member of Executive, C.S.I.R.O. 1962; Member of Executive, Commonwealth Scientific and Industrial Research Organization, Australia 1965–68; Secy. Australian Dept. of Agriculture since 1969. *Address:* 79 Parkhill Street, Pearce, A.C.T. 2607; and *office* Australian Dept. of Primary Industry, Barton A.C.T. 2600, Australia.

**IVEY, Peter John.** Canadian executive. *B.* 1919. *Educ.* Univ. of Western Ontario and Harvard Business School (AMP). *M.* Barbara Campbell Smith. *S.* John Campbell. *Daus.* Barbara, Alexandra. *Career:* With Canadian Army Overseas (Captain R.C.A.S.C.) 1941–45. Director, Emco Ltd.; Pres., Cambarex Investments Ltd.; Pres., Benmiller Estates Corp.; Mem. Bd. of Govs., Junior Achievement of Canada. *Clubs:* London; London Hunt & Country. *Address:* 1132 Richmond Street, London, Ont. N6A 3K8; and *office* 784 Richmond Street, London, Ont., Canada N6A 3H5.

# J

**JABLONSKI, Henryk.** Chairman of Council of State of Polish People's Republic. *B.* 1909. *Educ.* Warsaw Univ., degrees M. Philosophy & Dr. of History. *Career:* Army Hist. Office 1932–33; Teacher People's Univ. Warsaw 1933–39; Conscripted into Polish Army 1939; War Service, part with Allied Corps and including Polish resistance 1939–44; Secy. Central Exec. Cttee of Polish Socialist Party, and Chmn. Warsaw PSP Cttee 1945; Lecturer, modern history, Acad. of Polit. Science, Warsaw 1946–48; Asst. Prof. recent history, Warsaw Univ. 1948–50, Prof. since 1950; Under-Secy. of State, Min. of Education 1947–53; Dep. Chmn. PSP Exec. Cttee 1948; Elected corresp. mem. Polish Academy of Sciences 1952, mem. since 1956; Scientif. Secy. to Polish Acad. of Sciences 1955–65; Min. of Higher Education 1965–66; Min. of Education & Higher Learning 1966–72; Mem. Political Bureau since 1970; Chmn. of Council of State of Polish People's Republic since 1972. *Awards:* Member of Soviet Acad. of Sciences, Czechoslovak Acad. of Sciences, Acad. of the Romanian Socialist Republic, Acad. of the Mongolian Socialist Republic; Hon. doctorates Univ. Moscow, Budapest & Wroclaw; Order of Builders of People's Poland; Grand Cross Order of Polonia Restituta; also state decorations *Publications:* Aleksander Warszkowski (Warsaw 1937); Opinion, Parliament and the Press (Warsaw 1947); Polish National Autonomy in the Ukraine: 1917–1918 (Warsaw 1918); The Policies of the Polish Socialist Party during the war of 1914–18 (Warsaw 1958); The Birth of the Second Republic 1918–19 (Warsaw 1962); School, Teacher, Education (1972). *Address:* The Belvedere, Warsaw, Poland.

**JABRE, François.** Lebanese. *B.* 1922. *Educ.* Bachelor of Laws. *M.* 1950, Souad Noujaim. *Daus.* 3. Honorary Consul Gen. of Iceland. Chairman, Board of Directors, Brasserie et Malterie Almaza, S.A.L. 1959—; Managing Director, Jute National Industries, S.A.L. since 1969. *Member:* Assn. of Industrialists of Lebanon. *Address:* P.O. Box 110608, Beirut, Lebanon.

**JACKEL, Simon S.** Chemist. *B.* 1917. *Educ.* Coll. of the City of New York (BS 1938) and Columbia Univ. (AM 1947; PhD 1950). *M.* 1954, Betty Carlson. *S.* Glenn Edward. *Dau.* Phyliss Marcia. *Career:* Instructor, Army Air Force Engineering Officers' School, Yale Univ. 1941–44; Research Chemist, The Fleischmann Labs. 1944–47; Research Assistant, Chem. Dept., Columbia Univ. 1947–49; Head, Fermentation and Yeast Division, Fleischmann Labs. 1949–59; Pres. Plymouth Technical Services 1950—; Vice-President and Director of Research, Vico Products Co. 1959–61. Director of Laboratory, Research and Development, Quality Bakers of America New York 1961—, Vice-Pres. 1976—; Dir. of Research & Development, Bakers Research Development Service, New York 1969—; Pres., Plymouth Technical Services, N.Y. 1951—; Dir., Hearing Aid Audiology, Jewish Home & Hospital for the Aged, N.Y. 1951–76; Technical Editor, Bakery Production & Marketing 1969—; Chmn. Engineers Information Service, Amer. Socy. of Bakery Engineers since 1970; Chmn., Technical Liason Cttee. with U.S.D.A., American Bakers Assn. since 1974; Chmn., Milling & Baking Div. (1973–74), N.Y. Section (1973–74), American Assn. of Cereal Chemists. *Publications:* 74 publications in Journal of Biological Chemistry, Archives of Biochemistry & Biophysics, Science, Cereal Chemistry, Bakers Digest, Bakery Production and Marketing, Cereal Science Today, Instruments, Encyclopedia of Chemistry. Holder of 9 patents in areas of Food & Bakery products and processing. Phi Lambda Upsilon; Sigma Xi (Hon. Fraternities); Wisdom Hall of Fame. *Fellow:* American Institute of Chemists; American Association for Advancement of Science. *Member:* American Chemical Society; New York Academy of Science; IllinoisAcademy of Science; Amer. Association of Cereal Chemists; Inst. of Food Technologists; Chemists' Club; American Society of Bakery Engineers; American Managernent Assn.; American Society for Testing Materials; Association for Environment Protection; Nutrition Cttee. Amer. Bakers Assn.; Technical Liaison Cttee. U.S. Dept. Agriculture ABA; Scientific Adv. Cttee. Amer. Inst. of Baking; Industry Adv. Cttee. North Dakota State University. *Address:* 46 Kings Highway North, Westport, Conn. 06880; and *office* 1515 Broadway, New York 10036, N.Y., U.S.A.

**JACKLING, Sir Roger William,** GCMG. HM Diplomatic Service (Ret'd.). *B.* 1913. *Educ.* Felsted and Law Society's School of Law. *M.* 1938, Joan Tustin. *S.* Michael Brook and Roger Tustin. *Career:* Solicitor, Supreme Court 1935; Vice-Consul, New York 1940; Commercial Secy., Quito 1942; First Secy., Washington 1943–47; Asst. Secy. Cabinet Office 1950–51; Commercial Counsellor, The Hague 1951–53; Economic Adviser, British High Commission, Bonn 1953–55 (and Minister (Economic) there 1955–57); Counsellor, Washington 1957–59; Asst. Under-Secy. of State, Foreign Office 1959–63; Deputy U.K. Permanent Representative to U.N., New York 1963–67 (appointed Ambassador there 1965); Deputy Under-Secy. of State, Foreign Office, London 1967–68; H.M. Ambassador, Bonn 1968–72; Leader U.K. Delegation, U.N. Conference, Sea Bed and the Law of the Sea; Chmn., Anglo-German Foundation for the Study of Industrial Society.

*Club:* Travellers' (London). *Address:* 37 Boundary Road, London, N.W.8.

**JACKMAN, Henry Rutherford,** OC, K St J, QC. Canadian. *B.* 1900. *Educ.* Univ. of Toronto (LLB 1924), Osgoode Law School, and Graduate School of Business Administration, Harvard Univ. *M.* 1930, Mary Coyne Rowell. *S.* 3. *Dau.* 1. MP for Toronto-Rosedale 1940–49. *Career:* Pres.: Dominion and Anglo Investment Corp. Ltd.; Electra Investments (Canada) Ltd. Hon. Chmn.: Empire Life Insurance Co.; Canadian & Foreign Securities Co. Ltd.; Hon. Director: Bank of Nova Scotia; Dominion of Canada General Insurance Co.; Canadian Internatl. Investment Trust Ltd.; Vice-Chmn., Canadian Cttee. for the Atlantic Congress, London 1959; Secy. Exec. Cttee., Empire Parliamentary Conference, Ottawa 1943. Queen's Counsel; Officer of the Order of Canada; Knight of the Venerable Order of St John; Grand Cross of the Order of St. Lazarus of Jerusalem. Former Chairman Canadian Red Cross Pension Fund; Member Canadian Institute of International Affairs. *Life Member:* Commonwealth Parliamentary Assn.; and A.F. & A.M. Harvard and Ionic Lodges; The Royal Socy. of Arts; Pres. Art Gallery of Ont. 1959–61. *Clubs:* York, Toronto, National, Albany, Badminton & Racquet, Toronto Hunt, Eglinton Hunt. *Address:* 10 Cluny Drive, Toronto, Ont. M4W 2P7; and *office* 10th Floor, 165 University Ave., Toronto, Ont. M5H 3B8, Canada.

**JACKSON, Prof. Clarence Evert.** American. *B.* 1906. *Educ.* Carleton Coll. (BA Hons. in Phyics 1927) and Graduate work, George Washington Univ. 1932. *M.* 1936, Anne Scott. *S.* 1. *Daus.* 2. *Career:* Engaged in research and development: Union Carbide Corp. 1946–64, and U.S. Govt. 1930–46; Professor of Welding Engineering, Ohio State University, Columbus, Ohio 1964—; Consultant on welding and metallurgy since 1964. *Member:* Amer. Welding Socy. (Natl. Pres. 1963–64; Miller Gold Medal, Adams Lecture, Science of Arc Welding 1959; Life Member); Amer. Socy. for Metals (Life Member); Amer. Inst. Metallurgical Engineers; Australian Inst. of Welding (Hon. Member); Hon. Fellow British Inst. of Welding; Member, French Socy. of Welding Engrs. *Publications:* numerous technical papers on welding and metallurgy; Editor, Arc welding book. *Address:* 866 Mission Hills Lane, Worthington, Ohio 43085; and *office* Ohio State University, Columbus Ohio, U.S.A.

**JACKSON, Elmer Martin, Jr.** Comdr. U.S.N.R. (Rtd.). *B.* 1906. *Educ.* St. John's College, Annapolis (BA 1927). *M.* (1) 1929, Mary Waters Conard (*Div.* 1972). *S.* Elmer III and Allen C. *Dau.* Pamela Conard White. (2) 1972, Doris Grace Blummer. *Career:* Reporter Associated Press 1927–29; successively Sports Editor, City Editor, Man. Editor, Editor, and Gen. Mgr., The Evening Capital, Maryland Gazette and The County News 1947–69; Publisher and Editor, Anne Arundel Times 1969—; President Jackson Printing Inc. 1975—. Prior to 1941, Correspondent, Associated Press, Washington Star, Philadelphia Evening Bulletin, N.Y. Times, N.Y. Herald-Tribune, and Boston Globe. Newspaper editor and publisher. Editor, The Evening Capital and Maryland Gazette, Annapolis. Publisher: Carroll, County Times, Westminster, and Worcester Democrat, Pocomoke City, Md.; Annapolis Times and Glen Burnie Times. Former member, Maryland Legislature, Annapolis City Council, and Maryland Representative on Federal Council of State Governments, Chicago. President: Library Association, Annapolis Chamber of Commerce 1959–64, and Chesapeake District, Assoc. Press 1934–42, and again 1960—; Md. Press Association 1948–52. *Publications:* Annapolis: Three Centuries of Glamour; The Baltimore Oriole; Maryland Symbols. *Member:* Sigma Delta Chi; Amer. Socy. of Newspaper Editors; Maryland Press Assn.; Amer. Newspaper Publishers Assn.; Newcomen Socy.; Commission on Higher Education (Middle States Div.); Maryland Historical Socy.; Naval Acad. Alumni Assn. (Hon.); Civitan International (Past Pres. and Past District Governor). Good Neighbour Award (U.S. Naval Acad.); King William Award for Achievement (St. John's Coll.) 1926; Honored by State of Maryland, 1965, as Patron of the Arts. *Clubs:* Naval Acad. Officers'; Naval Acad. Golf; Army-Navy (Washington); University, Annapolis Yacht, Nat. Press Club, Washington, Annapolitan. *Address:* 219 Claude Street, Annapolis, Md. 21401, U.S.A.

**JACKSON, Sir Geoffrey (Holt Seymour),** KCMG. British diplomat (ret.), author and broadcaster. *B.* 1915. *Educ.* Cambridge Univ. (MA). *M.* 1939, Patricia Mary Evelyn Delany. *S.* 1. *Career:* Vice-Consul, Beirut and Cairo and Acting Consul-General, Basra 1937–46; First Secy., Bogota 1946; appointed to Foreign Office, served at U.N. 1950; First Secretary, Berne 1954; Minister at Tegucigalpa 1956; Ambassador 1957–60; Consul-General, Seattle 1960–64; Senior British Trade Commissioner in Ontario 1964. Ambassador to Uruguay 1969–72; Deputy Secy. of State 1973. *Publications:* The Oven-Bird (1972); People's Prison (1973); Surviving the Long Night (1974). *Address:* 63B Cadogan Square, London, S.W.1.

**JACKSON, Gordon Noel,** CMG, MBE. British ambassador. *B.* 1913. *Educ.* King's School, Worcester and abroad. *M.* 1959, Mary April Nettlefold. *S.* Nigel David Frederick. *Daus.* Gillian Mary and Amanda Jane. *Career:* With Indian Political Service until 1947, then joined the British Foreign Service. Political Officer, Sharjah 1947; Political Agent, Kuwait 1949; Consul at St. Louis (U.S.A.) 1953; Consul-General, Basra 1955–57, Lourenço Marques 1957–60, and Benghazi 1960–63; Ambassador to Kuwait 1963–67 to Equador 1967–70. *Publications:* Effective Horsemanship (for dressage, three-day event, jumping and polo); (Co-Editor with William Steinkraus) The Encyclopedia of The Horse. *Member:* Royal Central Asian Society. *Address:* Lowbarrow House, Leafield, Oxon. OX8 5NH.

**JACKSON, Henry Martin.** American senator. *B.* 31 May 1912. *Educ.* University of Washington Law School (LLB). *Career:* Law Associate in firm of Black & Rucker, Everett, Wash. 1935–38; Prosecuting Attorney, Snohomish County, Washington 1938–40; Member of the House of Representatives 1940–52. U.S. Senator from Washington State Jan. 1953—; Chmn. Interior and Insular Affairs Cttee.; Member Armed Services, Joint Atomic Energy, and Government Operations Committees. Democrat. Chairman, Democratic National Committee 1960–61. *Awards:* Bernard M. Branch Prize (with Charles A. Lindbergh) 1968; Hon. LLD (Alaska). *Address:* 1703 Grand Avenue, Everett, Washington 98201 U.S.A.

**JACKSON, John Tillson.** American. *B.* 1921. *Educ.* Cornel. Univ. (BS in AE-ME 1942). *M.* 1953, Suzanne H. Bartley. *S.* John T., Jr. *Daus.* Suzanne B. and Jennifer T. *Career:* Major, Ordnance Corps U.S. Army 1942–46; with International Telephone & Telegraph Corp. 1953–60 (Vice-Pres. 1959–60); George S. Armstrong & Co. 1946–53 (Vice-Pres. 1949–53); Vice-Pres. Remington Office Equipment Division, Sperry Rand Corp., 1960–66. President, Sperry Rand International Corp. 1962–66; Senior Vice Pres. International Utilities Corp (now I.U. International Corporation) 1969–73, Exec. Vice-Pres. & Dir. 1973, Chmn. Exec. Cttee. and Dir. since 1973; Chmn. & Dir., C. Brewer & Co. Ltd. since 1975. *Member:* A.S.M.E. *Clubs:* Union League; University (both of N.Y.C.); Racquet; Merion Golf (both Philadephia). *Address:* 155 Rose Lane, Haverford, Pa. 19041; and *office* 1500 Walnut Street, Philadelphia, Pa., 19102, U.S.A.

**JACKSON, Commander Sir Robert Gillman Allen,** KCVO, CMG, OBE. *B.* 1911. *M.* 1950. *S.* 1. *Career:* With Royal Australian Navy 1929–37; transf. to Royal Navy, staff of Vice-Adm., Malta 1938; Chief Staff Officer to Govnr. and C.-in-C., Malta 1940; Staff of British Min. of State in Middle East, and Dir.-Gen., Middle East Supply Centre 1942–45; Senior Dep. Dir.-Gen. U.N.R.R.A. and in charge of U.N.R.R.A. operations in Europe (1945), 1945–47; Assistant Sec.-General, U.N. 1948; at H.M. Treasury 1949; Permanent Secretary, Ministry of National Development, Australia 1950–52; Adviser on Development to Government of India 1952–57 and 1962–63, and Pakistan 1952; Chairman Volta River Multi-Purpose Project 1953–56. Member and Consultant to Volta River Auth. 1962—, and Chmn. Ghana Development Commission 1957–62; organization of Royal Tours in Ghana 1959 and 1961; Senior Consultant to Administrator, U.N. Development Programme 1963–71; Chmn. of Expert Group on Zambia's Economic Security 1966; Personal Adviser to Pres. of Liberia 1962–75; Advisory Cttee., Mekong Project, Mekong S.A. Asia 1962–76; United Nations Commissioner i/c of Survey of U.N. development system 1968–71; United Nations Under Secy. Gen. in charge Relief of Bangladesh 1972–74; Co-ordinator for UN Asst. to Zambia since 1973; to Cape Verde since 1974; to Indo-China since 1975; to Sao Tome & Principe since 1977. Services recognized by various governments in Europe and Asia. *Address:* Palais Des Nations, Geneva, Switzerland.

**JACOB, Hon. Lieut.-General Sir (Edward) Ian (Claud),** GBE, CB, DL. British army officer (retired). *B.* 1899. *Educ.* Wellington College; Royal Military Academy, Woolwich; King's College, Cambridge (BA). *M.* 1924, Cecil Bisset Treherne. *S.* John Claud, Willian Le Grand. *Career:* 2nd Lieutenant, Royal Engineers June 1918; Staff College, Camberley

1931–32; G.S.O.3, War Office 1934–36; Brigade Major, Canal Brigade, Egypt 1936–38; Military Assistant Secretary, Committee of Imperial Defence 1938; Military Assistant Secretary, War Cabinet 1939–46; Controller, European Services. B.B.C. 1946–48; Director, Overseas Services, B.B.C. 1948–52; Chairman, Covent Garden Market Authority 1961–66; Director-General of the B.B.C. 1952–60. Director, Electrical & Musical Industries Ltd. 1960–73 and Fisons Ltd. 1960–70; Chmn., Matthews Holdings 1970–76; President' European Broadcasting Union 1950–52, and 1954–60. County Councillor, East Suffolk 1960–70: Alderman, 1970–73. C. Councillor, Suffolk 1973–77. Commander, Legion of Merit. *Address:* The Red House, Woodbridge, Suffolk.

**JACOBS, Dr. Maurice.** Publisher (retd.). *B.* 1896. *Educ.* Univ. of Maine (BA, LLD) and Hebrew Union Coll. (DHL 1948. *M.* 1926, Elsa Wohlfeld. *Daus.* Elizabeth (Klatzkin) and Ruth Steele). *Career:* Director, National Jewish Welfare Board 1940–62; Hon. Dir., Jewish Chautauqua Socy. 1944—; Governor, American Association for Jewish Education 1940–62; Dir., Yivo Institute for Jewish Research 1940–62; co-founder and Dir. 1940–62, and Vice-Pres. 1958–66, Jewish Book Council of America; Chmn. Maurice Jacobs Inc. 1969–70. Hon. Dir., National Federation of Temple Brotherhoods 1944—; member, Exec. Council, American Jewish Historical Society 1947–69;, Hon. 1969— Treas. 1947–53, Chmn. 1972–75, Pres. since 1975. Member, B'nai B'rith National Vocational Service Commission 1950–62, (Chairman 1955–62); member editorial board, The Jewish Digest 1955—; Trustee, Union of American Hebrew Congregations 1957—; Pres., Pennsylvania Council of the Union of American Hebrew Congregations 1960–64; Dir., Jewish Occupational Council 1958–62; Hon. Overseer, Gratz College 1966—; Hon. Trustee, Reform Congregation Keneseth Israel 1953—; Hon. Dir., Advisory Board for Jewish Students (Hillel) 1959—; Trustee, Federation of Jewish Agencies 1956–62; National U.N. Day Cttee. *Publications:* Universal Jewish Encyclopedia, National Jewish Monthly, Jewish Book Annual, and Jewish Digest. Citations: Boston Jewish Advocate (1940), Jewish Book Council 1948, National Inter-Fraternity Conference Silver Medal 1952 (the same Conference awarded him a gold medal for distinguished service to American Youth 1954), University Lodge B'nai B'rith 1955, World Union for Progressive Judaism 1955, American Jewish Historical Society 1956, Phi Epsilon Pi 1956, National Federation of Temple Brotherhoods 1957, Gratz College 1958, Keneseth Israel 1961, B'nai B'rith 1961, Phi Epsilon Pi Founder's Medal 1961. Served as Chief Petty Officer, U.S.N. in World War I. *Member:* Socy. of Biblical Literature; Amer. Jewish Historical Socy. (Gold Medal, 1966). *Address:* 520 Rittenhouse Claridge, Philadelphia 3, Pa., U.S.A.

**JACOBS, Nathan Elias.** American public relations and advertising exec. *B.* 1901. *Educ.* Univ. of Missouri (Bachelor of Journalism 1924). *M.* 1966, Gladys Frost Brandeis. *S.* Anthany Smith. *Dau.* Linda (Mraz). Worked on three Omaha newspapers after graduation from the School of Journalism of Univ. of Missouri; Commercial editor, Omaha Daily News 1924. Correspondent for trade publications in fourteen industrial and commercial fields 1924–25. Senior Consultant, Bozell & Jacobs Inc.; Director of Public Relations: International Trade Fair, Chicago 1950, and for the Illinois Committee for Constitutional Revision in 1950–52–54–58–60 Campaigns; member, Glencoe Civil Defense Committee 1941–55; War Bond Campaigns for U.S. Treasury 1943–44; Director of Public Relations for Illinois Citizens Committee for Eisenhower-Nixon in 1956. Member, Board of Governors of United Republican Fund of Illinois. Appointed to Joint Civilian Defense Orientation Conference by Secretary of Defense Wilson. Guest of Honour, Paris International Fair 1951. *Awards:* first 'Anvil Award' in 1946 for achievement of public relations, presented by American Public Relations Assn.; Recipient, Charles Award National Hairdressers and Cosmatologists Assoc., 1970. Colonel on staff of Governor of Kentucky; Admiral in the Great Navy of the State of Nebraska; Hon. Texan; Hon. Citizen of New Orleans. *Member:* Public Relations Socy. of Amer.; Art Inst. of Chicago; Adler Planetarium; Chicago Historical Society; Chicago Natural History Museum; Board of Directors, Jewish Welfare Fund, and of Jewish Telegraphic Agency; Chairman, Chicago Chapter, American Jewish Committee 1960–61; National Exec. Board, American Jewish Committee. Member, Nebraska Historical Land Mark Council, 1969—; U.S. National Commission for U.N.E.S.C.O. 1970—. U.S. Public Representative, First Special of Organization of American States, 1970. Republican. *Clubs:* Kiwanis, The City, Executives, Press, Publicity, International (all of Chicago); Plaza (Omaha); Capitol Hill, National Press (Washington). *Address:* 9755 Lafayette Plaza, Omaha, Nebraska 68114; and *office* 10250 Regency Circle, Omaha, Neb. 68114, U.S.A.

**JACOBS, Samuel.** American civil engineer and designer, *B.* 1911. *Educ.* Tri-State Col. (BS in Civ Eng 1935). *M.* 1937' Mildred Kirschner. *S.* Lester Martin and Lawrence Edward. Served in World War II, Lt.-Cdr., U.S.N. 1942–45; Capt., U.S.N.R. *Career:* President and Chairman of Board, Adirondack Construction Co. R.P. (which he founded in 1937) 1950—; Pres., Inter-Development Systems Inc., and Queensbury Development Corp.; Director, Glens Falls Investors; Community Chest; Opera Festival Assoc. Dir. and Trustee, Crandall Library; member: Exec. Cttee., General Building Contractors (GBC); Bd. of Dirs., Glens Falls Savings & Loan Assn; General Building Contractors of New York City; Naval Inst.; Public Works Officer, U.S.N.R.T.F., Glens Falls; World Center for handicapped; Capt. USNR (Ret.). Member, Naval Reserve Assn.; Naval Inst. Vice-Pres., Glens Falls Investors. *Awards:* holder of Commendation Medal and other U.S.N. decorations, and N.Y. State Conspicuous Service Cross. Foreman of construction N.Y. State exhibit, World's Fair, Chicago 1933; Civil Engr., Duplex Construction Co. 1935–47; Pres., United Fund, Advisory Board Albany Savings Bank. *Publications:* Construction, Methods, Design Procedures. *Member:* Glens Falls (N.Y.) Forum; Geriatrics Foundation; Glens Falls Contractors; Y.M.C.A.; Schl. Bd.; Conference on Safety (Pres. 1958–62); Exec. Cttee., Building Industry Employees, N.Y. State; Amer. Socy. of Civil Engineers; Amer. Socy. of Military Engineers; Tri-County Socy. of Professional Engrs.; Navy League; American Legion. Mason. Elk. *Clubs:* Glens Falls Country; Kiwanis. *Address:* 34 Garrison Road, Glens Falls N.Y.; and c/o East Lake, George, N.Y. U.S.A.

**JACOBS, Sir Wilfred (Ebenezer),** OBE, QC. British. Governor of Antigua, West Indies. *B.* 1919. *Educ.* Grenada Boys' Secondary School and Gray's Inn. London; Barrister-at-Law. *M.* 1947, Carmen Sylva Knight. *S.* Walter William. *Daus.* Flora Diana and Jennifer Margaret. *Career:* Registrar, St. Vincent 1946; Magistrate, Dominica 1947, and St. Kitts 1949; Crown Attorney, St. Kitts 1952; Attorney-General: Leeward Islands 1957–59, and Antigua 1960. Acting Administrator: Dominica, St. Kitts, Antigua, various periods 1947–60. Legal Draftsman and Acting Solicitor-General, Trinidad and Tobago 1960; Solicitor-General and Acting Attorney-General, Barbados 1961–63; Member Privy Council and Legislative Council of Barbados 1962–63; Director of Public Prosecutions 1964, and Judge of the Supreme Court of Judicature, Barbados 1967; Governor, Antigua since 1967. *Member:* Gray's Inn, London; Imperial Socy. of Knights Bachelor; West India Committee; Royal Commonwealth Socy.; British Red Cross Socy. (Antigua Branch). K St J, 1968. *Clubs:* Oxford and Cambridge Univ.; West Indian (London). *Address:* Governor's Residence, Antigua, West Indies.

**JACOBS, William Ketchum, Jr.** Private Financial Consultant. Director: and Chmn. Audit Cttee. Govt. Employees Insurance Co., Criterion Insurance Co., Govt. Employees Life Insurance Co., Govt. Employees Financial Corp.. Advisory Dir.: Worldwide Special Fund N.V. (Curacao, N.W.1.), World wide Securities Ltd. (Bermuda). Executor and/or Trustee of numerous estates and trust funds. Pres. and Dir., The Tebil Foundation Inc., N.Y.C. *Member:* The N.Y. Socy. of Security Analysts Inc., and The Tax Inst., Princeton, N.J. *Address:* 895 Park Avenue, New York, N.Y. 10021; and *office* 660 Madison Avenue, New York, N.Y. 10021, U.S.A.

**JACOBSEN, Frithjof.** Norwegian diplomat. *B.* 1914. *Educ.* Faculty of Law, Oslo University (cand. jur.). *M.* 1941. *S.* 1. *Daus.* 2. *Career:* Entered diplomatic service 1938; Served in embassies in Paris, Moscow, London; Director of Political Affairs, Ministry of Foreign Affairs, Oslo 1955–59; Ambassador to Canada 1959–61; Ambassador of Norway to U.S.S.R. 1961–66. Under Secretary of State, Oslo, 1966–70; Ambassador to U.S.S.R. 1970–75; Ambassador to Court of St. James (London), and Dublin since 1975. *Address:* Royal Norwegian Embassy, 25 Belgrave Square, London S.W.1.; and Foreign Ministry, Oslo, Norway.

**JACOBSON, Alfred Thurl.** American. *B.* 1919. *Educ.* Univ. of Utah (AB Geol. 1940, MA Geol. 1941). *M.* 1942, Virginia Lorrain LaCom. *S.* Alfred Thurl, Jr. *Daus.* Wendy Jean and Deborah Ann. *Career:* With Amerada Petrol Corp.; Mgr. Foreign Ops. 1960–61, Vice-Pres. 1961–62, Senr. Vice-Pres. 1962–63. Exec. Vice-Pres. 1963–67. Pres. and Chief Exec.

Officer Amerada Petroleum Corp. 1968–69. President, Amerada Hess Corporation, 1969–72; Petroleum Consultant since 1972. Served with FA, Aus. 1941–46 ETO; decorated Croix de Guerre (France). *Member:* Phi Beta Kappa; Phi Kappa Phi; Amer. Petroleum Inst.; Amer. Assn. Petroleum Geologists; Amer. Inst. of Mining, Metallurgical and Petroleum Engineers. *Address:* 358 Oxford Drive, Short Hills, New Jersey 07078, U.S.A.

**JACOBUS, Gilbert Chester.** American attorney-at-law and management consultant. *B.* 1907. *Educ.* Georgetown University (JD); New York University (MBA); Rutgers Univ. (BSc Civil Eng.). *M.* 1930, Ruth Mary Jane Keisler. *S.* Gilbert Randall. *Dau.* Nancy Elizabeth. *Career:* Assistant Engineer, New Jersey Bell Telephone Co. 1929–40; U.S. Army Colonel 1940–48; Division Dir. and Special Assistant to Chairman, National Security Resources Board, Executive Office of the President 1948–52; Asst. Dir. Public Affairs Office, Federal Civil Defence Administration 1952–54; Dir. Instruction, The Army Command Management School 1954–56; Consultant Exec. Development & Education, various Federal Govt. Departments 1957–65; Dir. Army Logistics Research 1957–65; Special Consultant and Visiting Professor, Graduate School of Public and International Affairs, Univ. of Pittsburgh 1959–67; Dir. Management Research Group, School of Government, Business & International Affairs 1961–65; Professor of Public Administration, George Washington Univ. 1956–65; member, Bd. of Dirs., Research Found., Federal Bar Assn. 1960–69. Admitted to practice District of Columbia and U.S. Supreme Court, Director, Research Activities, D.C. Chapter, Society for Advancement of Management 1961–62; Exec. Dir. Federal Bar Foundation 1962–69; Digital Computer Systems Administrator, Office ot Chief of Staff U.S. Army 1965–67; Special Assistant to Director, Coast and Geodetic Survey 1967–69; Lecturer, George Washington Univ. 1949–60, 1966–69, 1972—; Professor, Public Administration Graduate School of Public & International Affairs, Univ. Pittsburgh; Visiting Prof. Faculty of Economics and Administration, Univ. of Malaya 1969–71. Consultant to National Ocean Survey 1972–74; Adviser to Bd. of Directors Foundation of Federal Bar Assn. since 1972. *Awards:* U.S. Legion of Merit; Officer, Order of the British Empire; Cross of Liberation (Norway); Officer, Order of Leopold (Belgium); Croix de Guerre avec Palme (awarded by both France and Belgium). *Publications:* articles on management, management development and operations research (The Petroleum Engineer, Advanced Management, Armed Forces Management, Personnel) and Journal, Malaysian Inst. Management *Member:* American and Federal Bar Associations; Washington Operations Research Council; Engineering Society of Rutgers University; Bd. Trustees, Fairfax Hospital, Virginia 1962–69; Management Consultant, Univ. of Malaya Hospital 1969–71. *Clubs:* National Lawyers; Army-Navy Country. *Address:* 1528 Hardwood Lane, Chesterbrook Woods, McLean, Va. 22101, U.S.A.

**JACOBY, George Alonzo.** American. *B.* 1904. *Educ.* Georgetown (Ky.) Coll. (AB 1924) and Columbia Univ. Schl. of Business (MS 1927). *M.* 1928, Ruth B. Burtner. *S.* Dr. George A.; John B. *Career:* Joined Irving Trust Co., N.Y. 1925 (Asst. Secy. 1929; Asst. Vice-Pres. 1937); Asst. Personnel Dir., Buick Div., Gen. Motors Corp., Flint, Mich. 1941–45; Labor Relations Staff, General Motors Corp. 1945–46; Dir. of Personnel Services 1946–56; Dir. of Personnel Relations 1956–69; Exec. Dir., Cttee. for Educational Grants & Scholarships 1955–69; Member, Board of Regents, General Motors Inst., Feb. 1957–69; Member, Board of Trustees, Alma College 1956–70, and Bd. of Directors, Cranbrook Schl. 1956–71. *Awards:* Hon. LLD, Georgetown Coll. 1958, Alumni Achievement Award 1953; Medal for Distinguished Alumni Service, Columbia Alumni Fedn., 1943. *Member:* Natl. Safety Cncl. (Dir. 1947–66); Industrial Hygiene Federation (Trustee 1957–62); Member Exec. Cttee., Inst. for Economic Education, Detroit 1959–69; Member, Board of Governors, Inst. of Industrial Health, Univ. of Michigan 1959–69; Member, Federal Advisory Council of Employment Security (1952–54); Unemployment Benefit Advisors (Vice-Pres. 1948–60). Republican. *Clubs:* Orchard Lake Country (Orchard Lake, Mich.); The Recess (Detroit). *Address:* 245 Puritan Road, Birmingham, Mich. 48009; U.S.A.

**JACOME, Alexander German.** American. *B.* 1904. *Educ.* Univ. of Arizona (BS Com). *M.* 1934, Estela Valles. *S.* Alex Fred and Philip Carlos. *Dau.* Margarita Emilia. *Career:* Chmn. of the Board since 1972, Jacome's Department Stores, Tucson, Ariz., (Clerk 1928; Vice-President 1928–32; Pres. 1932–72). Pima County Hospital Advisory Committee. Member, Board, United States Selective Service. Representative of State of Arizona to Pan-American Highway Congress, Mexico City 1940; Pres., Tucson Merchants Association 1941; Hon. Vice Consul of Mexico 1949; member, Policy Holders Examining Committee, Northwestern Mutual Life Insurance Co., Milwaukee, Wis.; Chmn., U.S. Delegation to Inter-American Indian Congress, La Paz 1954; Official representative of U.S. to Governing Board, Inter-American Indian Institute 1955; Chmn., Exec. Cttee., Mexico City 1956; Pres., Board of Regents Univ. of Arizona and State College 1959—. Member, U.S. Trade Mission to Spain 1959; Adv. Bd. Arizona Sonora Desert Museum 1960; Hon. member Blue Key Society. *Awards:* Citation, Alpha Kappa Psi, Outstanding Businessman of 1962; U. of A. Alumni Distinguished Citizen Award 1966; Meritorious Service Award, U.S. Selective Service System 1971; Hon. Dr. of Laws Univ. of Arizona 1974. *Member:* Elks, Rotary (Pres. 1945–46); Old Pueblo; Tucson Country; Skyline Country. Arizona Cttee., Newcomen Soc. of North America. *Address:* 60 Calle Primrosa, El Encanto Estates, Tucson, Arizona 85716, U.S.A.; and *office* 77 N. Stone Avenue, Tucson, Ariz., U.S.A.

**JACOMET, Andre A.** French. *B.* 1917. *Educ.* Lycee Carnot, Paris; Univ. of Paris, diplome d'Etudes superieures de Droit public et d'Economie Politique, Licencie es Lettres, diplome de l'Ecole Nationale des Sciences Politiques. *M.* 1942, Helene Cathala. *Career:* Registered with the Paris Court of Appeal as Lawyer, 1938; Junior member Conseil d'Etat, 1946–52, Maitre des Requêtes 1952; Legal Counsellor to French High Commissioner in Germany, 1949–52; Advisor to Secy. of State for Air Force, 1956–58, and to Minister of Construction, 1958; Secretary in charge of Administrative Affairs in Algeria, 1958–60; Employed by Compagnie Pechiney 1961; Head of Australian operations, 1963, Australian and American operations, 1964–67; Vice-President of Pechiney, 1966; In charge of operations in North and South America, Pacific and Spain, 1967–69; President and Director, Howmet Corp. Connecticut 1970–71; Senior Vice Pres. Pechiney Ugine Kuhlmann (France), in charge of copper and North America operations 1972–75; Chmn. & Pres., Trefimetaux 1973–75; Exec. Vice-Pres. for International Affairs, Pechiney Ugine Kuhlmann 1975–77; Président du Groupe Français de la Fondation Européenne pour l'Economie since 1974. *Award:* Knight of the Legion of Honour (France). *Address:* 45 rue Scheffer, 75016 Paris; and *office* 14 rue de la Baume, 75008 Paris, France.

**JACQUES, Lord John Henry,** JP, BA (Com). British. Retired chief executive. *B.* 1905. *Educ.* Elementary School; Co-operative Coll. Stanford Hall, Loughborough; Victoria Univ. Manchester. *M.* 1929, Constance White. *S.* 2. *Dau.* 1. *Career:* Man. Secy. Co-operative Socy. Moorsley Co. Durham 1926–29; Lecturer Co-operative Coll. Loughborough 1929–42; Accountant Co-operative Socy. Plymouth Devon 1942–45; Chief Exec. Co-op Socy. Portsmouth 1945–65; Chmn. Co-operative Union Manchester 1964–70. Pres. Distributive Trades and Training Council 1971–75; Lord-in-Waiting 1974–76. *Publications:* Accounting for Co-operative Societies; Management Accounting for Co-operative Societies; Management Manual for Co-operative Societies. *Club:* Co-operative Portsmouth. *Address:* 23 Hilltop Crescent, Cosham, Portsmouth, PO6 1BB and House of Lords, Westminster, London S.W.1.

**JAEGER, Rudolph Hans Carl.** West German. *B.* 1908. *Educ.* Gustav, Bertram Junior School, Hamburg; and German Gymnasium Hamburg (Abitur 1927). *M.* 1942, Nora Elisabeth Booth. *S.* 3. *Daus.* 2. *Career:* Apprentice Arndt & Cohn, Hamburg (iron and steel exporters and fish oil importers) 1927–30; Trainee, William Hollins & Co. Ltd., London (manufacturers) 1930–31; Junior Executive, H. A. & Gustav Küchler, Hamburg (Brokers for vegetable oils and naval stores) 1931–34; Senr. Executive, Gebrüder Noggerath, Hamburg (similar type of firm), Head of Foreign Dept. 1934–45. Owner, firm of Rudolph C. Jaeger (import and export of chemicals, naval stores, oils and fats), Oct. 1945—. *Member:* Hamburg Chamber of Commerce; 'Grofor', Hamburg (Assn. of Oils, Fats and Oilseeds); 'Harzverein', Hamburg (Naval Stores Assn.). *Clubs:* Hamburger Polo; Anglo-German; Overseas; Club on the Alster; Amerika Gesellschaft. *Address:* Rainweg, 7, Hamburg 20, West Germany; and *office* Oderfelder Str. 42, Hamburg 13, West Germany.

**JAFFAR, Khalid Mohammed.** Ambassador of the State of Kuwait. *B.* 1922. *Educ.* Mubarakia School. *M.* 1942, Miriam Abdulaah Lal-Askar. *S.* 4. *Daus.* 3. Teacher 1940; Chief Cashier, Municipality 1943; with Kuwait Oil Co. 1945; Chief of Goodwill Mission to Latin America 1961; Lord Chamberlain to H.H. the Amir 1961; Head of Cultural and Press Department, Ministry of Foreign Affairs 1962; Ambassador to the Court of St. James's 1963–65, to Lebanon 1965–70, concurrently to France 1965–67, to Turkey 1968–73, concurrently to Bulgaria & Greece 1971–73, to U.S.A. since 1975. Member of Delegation to United Nations 1962. *Awards:* Knight Grand Cross, Order of St. Gregory the Great. *Clubs:* Travellers', Hurlingham (London); Habara (Kuwait). *Address:* Embassy of the State of Kuwait, 2940 Tilden Street, N.W., Washington, D.C. 20008, U.S.A.

**JAFFÉ, Bernard Frederick Victor.** British director of companies. *B.* 1890. *Educ.* Doctor of Law, Rostock. *M.* 1931, Countess Armgard Platen-Hallermund. *S.* Bernard W. (MA Cantab). Regular and reserve service, Royal Saxon Army 1908–18; member, German Peace Delegation, Versailles 1919. Engaged in business 1924—; with International Telephone and Telegraph Corporation 1928; Vice-Pres. & Dir., subsidiary International Standard Electric Corp. 1928–63; Chairman (later Hon. Chmn.) Standard Elektrik Lorenz AG, Stuttgart, Hanseatish, Industrie Bet. GmbH. *Address:* 13 Flurweg, Bottmingen (Basel Land), Switzerland; Standard Elektrik Lorenz AG, Hellmuth- Hirth-Str. 42, Stuttgart-Zuffenhausen, Germany; and Hanseatische Industrie Bet. GmbH., Hünefeldstr., Bremen-Flughafen, Germany.

**JAKOBSEN, Arnt-Jakob.** Norwegian diplomat. *B.* 1913. *Educ.* Laywer (Admitted to Bar of Oslo 1946). *M.* 1950, Laila Jespersen. *Career:* Secretary, Ministry of Foreign Affairs, Oslo 1945; Vice-Consul New York City 1947; Secy. of Legation Belgrade 1950; Head, Section Ministry Foreign Affairs 1951; Consul 1956, Consul-General Genoa 1964, Sydney 1965; Ambassador to Australia, Canberra 1969 to New Zealand 1970; Chief of Protocol, Min. of For. Affairs, Oslo 1973. *Awards:* Grand Cross (Dannebrog); Comdr with Star (Swedish). Commander Order of St. Olav; Commander. Icelandic Falcon Order. *Address:* Ministry of Foreign Affairs, Oslo, Norway.

**JAKOBSON, Max.** Finnish diplomat. *B.* 1923. *M.* 1957. Marilyn Medney. *S.* Ralph and David. *Dau.* Linda. *Career:* Reporter, Finnish News Agency 1941–42; United Press Helsinki 1944–45; B.B.C. London 1946–48; London Correspondent, Helsinki newspaper UUSI Suomi 1948–53; Press Attache Finnish Embassy, Wash. D.C. 1953–58; Head, Press Bureau Min. Foreign Affairs Helsinki 1958–61; Dir. Political Affairs 1961–65; Permanent Rep. Finland to U.N. 1965—; Ambassador to Sweden 1972–74; Man. Dir. of Council of Economic Orgs. in Finland since 1975. *Awards:* Commemorative War Medal 1941–44; 1st Class Order Lion (Finland), 1st Class Order North Star (Sweden); 1st Class Dannebrog (Denmark); 1st Class Order Olaf (Norway), 1st Class Polonia Restituta (Poland), Hon. Doctor, Helsinki Univ.; Hon. Doctor Brandies University. *Publications:* Diplomacy of the Winter War (1960); Finnish Neutrality (1968). *Address:* Rahapajankatu 3B, Helsinki 16, Finland.

**JAMES, Edgar P. H.** American marketing and advertising executive. *B.* 1904. *Educ.* Coopers Company's School, London, Eng. *M.* 1943, Laura Wyatt-Brown. *S.* Wyatt E. F. and Christopher C. *Dau.* Phyllis V. *Career:* Advertising & Sales-Promotion Mgr., Natl. Broadcasting Co. 1927–41; U.S. Army Air Forces 1942–45; Vice-Pres., Mutual Broadcasting System 1945–49; Pub. Relations Dir., Corning Glass Center (1949–51) and Television Station KVOA (Tucson, Ariz.) 1952–54. Vice-Pres., A. C. Nielsen Co. 1954–69. Former Director: United Broadcast Audience Research Ltd., Television Audience Measurement Ltd., Television Press Agency Ltd., Eurobar N.V. (Netherlands). *Publications:* The Technique of Market Research (McGraw-Hill); contributor to U.S. and British trade journals in advertising and marketing fields. *Member:* Royal Television Socy. (U.K.); Broadcast Pioneers (U.S.). *Address:* 7 Byfield Gardens, Barnes, London SW13 9HP.

**JAMES, Murray Willoughby.** Australian. *B.* 1913. *Educ.* Alma Public School and Broken Hill High School. *M.* 1937, Ethel M. Taylor. *Daus.* 2. *Career:* Reporter, Barrier Miner, Broken Hill 1930; The News, Adelaide 1935; Air Crew R.A.A.F. 1942–44; Melbourne Herald Cable Service, London 1946–48; Chief of Staff and Associate Editor, The News, Adelaide 1948–60. Managing Director, Western Press Ltd., Perth, W.A. 1960—. Director: Country Newspapers Pty. Ltd., Art Photo Engravers Pty. Ltd. 1960—. Suntimes Broadcasters Ltd. since 1968. *Clubs:* Weld; Perth, Perth Rotary, Royal Perth Golf. *Address:* 71 Mount Street, Perth, W.A.; and *office* 34–36 Stirling Street, Perth, W.A., Australia.

**JAMIESON, Hon. Donald C.** Canadian politician. *B.* 1921. *Educ.* Schools in St. John's, Newfoundland. *M.* 1946, Barbara Oakley. *S.* 1. *Daus.* 3. *Career:* Former broadcasting exec.; mem., Federal Govt. Cttee. on Canadian broadcasting, 1963; Pres., Canadian Assoc. of Broadcasters 1962–65; former adviser to Board of Broadcast Governors & mem. of Consultative Cttee. on Private Broadcasting; mem. Canadian House of Commons since 1966; mem., Cttee. for Broadcasting, Films & Assistance to the Arts; mem., Parly. Standing Cttees. for fisheries & for transport & communications; Minister of Defence Production 1968–69, of Transport 1969–72, of Regional Economic Expansion 1972–75, of Industry, Trade & Commerce 1975–76; Sec. of State for External Affairs since 1976. *Publications:* The Troubled Air (1966)—an analysis of Canadian broadcasting. *Address:* House of Commons, Ottawa, Ontario K1A 0A6, Canada.

**JANAS, Sigmund.** American financier. *B.* 23 Nov. 1899. *Educ.* Sacramento Institute 1912–15; University of California (money and banking); St. Ignatius University (AB). *M.* Kennan Hamilton (*D.*). *S.* 2. (2) Laura V. Cook. *Career:* Served from Pte. to 1st Lt. World War I. Comml. Editor, Asst. Financial Editor, San Francisco Chronicle 1919–20; Chief Dept. Supt. Banks of Cal. 1923–25; Asst. Pres., Richfield Oil Co. of Cal. 1925–28; Pres., Silver Peak Mining Co. 1928; Asst. Pres. Am. Airlines 1933–38; Western Air Express 1930–33; Chmn. Board, Central Airlines Inc. 1936–37; Pres., Dir., Colonial Airlines Inc. 1938–52; Pres., Janas Investment Company; Pres. Dir. Scientific Oil Processers. *Address:* 16 Fairlane Harbour, Vero Beach, Fla. 32960 U.S.A.

**JANES, John Douglas Webster,** CB. British. Government official. *B.* 1918. *Educ.* Trinity Academy, Edinburgh; Southgate County School, Middx.; City & Guilds Coll. Univ. of London, BSc (Eng), ACGI; DIC. *M.* 1943, Margaret Isabel Smith. *S.* 1. *Daus.* 2. *Career:* Asst. Engineer, Post Office Eng. Dept. 1939–47; Military Service (Major REME) 1939–45; Principal MHLG 1947–56, Fuel and Power 1956–58; MHLG 1958–59; Asst. Secy. Min. HLG 1959–60; H.M. Treasury 1960–63; MHLG 1963–64; Min. Land & Natural Resources 1964–67; MHLG 1967–68; Under Secy. (Principal Finance Officer) MHLG Dept. of the Environment 1968–73; Deputy Secy. Dept. of the Environment Mar.–Nov. 1973; Chief Exec. Maplin Development Authority 1973–74; Dep. Secy. N Ireland Office since 1974. *Awards:* Companion of the Bath; Bachelor of Science (Eng); Assoc. City and Guilds Inst.; Diploma Imperial College. *Address:* 136 Waterfall Road, Southgate, London N14 7JN.

**JANITSCHEK, Hans Walter.** Austrian. *B.* 1934. *Educ.* Vienna and Haverford College. *M.* 1959, Elfriede Ruisinger. *S.* Stefan. *Dau.* Angela. *Career:* Staff corres. U.P.I. Vienna 1955–57. Foreign editor Kurier, Vienna 1957–65. Austrian Foreign Service 1964–67. Gen. Sec. Socialist Internat. London 1967–76; Special Asst. for Public Relations, UN, New York since 1977. Mem. Austrian Socialist Party, British Labour Party, Portuguese Socialist Party & New Democratic Party of Canada. Bd. Dirs. Aneurin Bevan Foundation, Inst. Social History. *Club:* Pilgrims (London). *Address:* 84 Addison Way, London, NW11; and *office* United Nations, New York, U.S.A.

**JANNER, Antonino,** Dr jur. Swiss diplomat. *B.* 1917. *Educ.* Basle Gymnasium and Universities of Basle (Dr jur) and Perugia. *M.* Adriana Janner, *S.* Marco, *Daus.* Francesca Sabina, Faustina. *Career:* Federal Political Dept. 1942; Attaché 1944; Second Secretary, Rome 1946; Fed. Political Dept. 1950; Second Head of Section, Berne 1952; First Secy., Bonn-Cologne, 1952; Counsellor, Bonn-Cologne 1957; First Head of Section, Berne 1961; Dep. Chief, Div. of Political Affairs, Berne 1963. Ambassador to Argentina and Paraguay 1968—; Ambassador, Chief Div. of Administrative Affairs, Berne 1970—. *Publications:* Wandlungen der Bereicherungslehre im Schweizerischen Recht (1943) La Puissance protectrice en Droit international (1948). *Address:* Frohbergweg 11, Berne, Switzerland.

**JANNER. Hon. Greville Ewan,** QC, MP. British politician, lawyer, writer. *B.* 1928. *Educ.* Trinity Hall, Cambridge, Master of Arts; Harvard Law School, U.S.A. *M.* 1955, Myra Sheink. *S.* Daniel Joseph Mitchell. *Daus.* Marion Juliette, Laura Naomi. *Career:* Barrister at law since 1954; Member of Parliament for Leicester N.W. (now Leicester W.) since 1970; Queen's Counsel 1971; Founder All Party Parly. Group for Homeless People; Vice-Chmn. Parly. Group for Release of Soviet Jewry; Chmn., All Party Industrial Safety Group; Hon. Sec., All Party Retirement Group. *Member:* Academy, Forensic Sciences; Howard League for Penal

Reform; Socy. of Labour Lawyers; Senior Vice-Pres. Bd. Deputies British Jews; Vice-Pres. Association, Jewish Ex-Servicemen; Assn. for Jewish Youth. Founder Member Internat. Coun. on Human Rights. *Publications:* 25 Books, Legal and Professional subjects. *Address:* 2 Linnell Drive, London, N.W.11; and *office* 1 Garden Court Temple, London, E.C.4 and House of Commons, S.W.1.

**JANSSEN, Baron Charles-Emmanuel.** Belgian company director. *B.* 1907. *M.* 1930. Marie Anne Boel. *S.* 3. *Career:* Vice Chairman, Cia. Española para la Fabricacion Mecanica del Vidrio 'Celo' S.A. 1951; Director: Credit Industriel et Commercial 1960—; Hon. Chairman UCB, Glaverbel-Mecaniver; Dir. La Royale Belge 1964—; Vice Chmn. Société Genérale de Banque 1965—. *Awards:* Commander de l'Ordre de la Couronne; Commander de l'Ordre de Leopold; Officer de la Legion d'Honneur. *Address:* 'Claire Colline', La Hulpe, Belgium.

**JANSSEN, Paul-Emmanuel,** D-enD. Belgian. *B.* 1931. *Educ.* Doctor in Law. *M.* 1961, Baronne Nadine van der Straten Waillet. *S.* Emmanuel. *Daus.* Valérie and Stéphanie. *Career:* Managing Director, Société Générale de Banque, Brussels. Chairman, Belgian Banks Association, Brussels. Chairman, Antwerpse Diamantbank N.V. Antwerpen. Chairman, Caisse Interprofessionnelle de Virements et de Dépôts de Titres CIK, Brussels. Vice-Chairman, Banque Européenne de Crédit à Moyen Terme, Brussels. Director, European-American Banking Corp. New York. Director, European-American and Trust Cy New York. Director, S.A. Solvay & Cie, Brussels. Director, Compagnie Belge d'Assurance-Crédit, Brussels. Director, European Banking Cy Ltd, London. Director, H. de Bary, Amsterdam. *Address:* "Le Bonnier", La Hulpe, Belgium.

**JAPHET, Ernest I.** Banker. *B.* 1921. *M.* Ella Gilead. *S.* 2. *Daus.* 3. *Career:* Chmn & Chief Exec. Bank Leumi le-Israel B.M.; Chmn. Bank Leumi Trust Company of New York; Bank Leumi (U.K.) Ltd.; Bank Leumi le-Israel (France) S.A.; Bank Leumi le-Israel (Switzerland); Union Bank of Israel Ltd.; Bank Leumi Investment Co. Ltd.; Otzar Letaasia; Mimonim Ltd.; Dir. Otzar Hityashvuth Hayehudim B.M.; Jewish Colonial Trust; Dagon Batey Mamguroth le-Israel Ltd.; Dir. Member Exec. Cttee. Paz Ltd.; Paz Investment Ltd.; Member: Adv. Council & Adv. Cttee. Bank of Israel; Pres. Association of Banks in Israel & Chmn. Exec. Cttee.; Dep. Chmn., Bd of Govs. Hebrew Univ. of Jerusalem; Mem. Bd. of Govs. and Chmn. Funds Cttee. Tel Aviv Univ.; Chmn. Financial Cttee. and Mem. Bd. of Govs. Technion Haifa; Mem. Bd. of Govs. Haifa Univ.; Dep. Bd. of Govs., Chmn. Exec. Cttee., Weizmann Inst. of Science; Chmn. Bd. of Trustees, Maurice Falk Inst. for Econ. Research. *Address:* Bank Leumi le-Israel B.M., 24–32 Yehuda Halevi Street, Tel Aviv, Israel.

**JARDINE PATERSON, Sir John Valentine.** British company director. *B.* 1920. *Educ.* Eton College and Jesus College, Cambridge. *M.* 1953, Priscilla Mignon Nicolson. *S.* Jonathan. *Daus.* Tessa, Sarah and Anna Serena. *Career:* Managing Director, Jardine Henderson Ltd., Calcutta 1952–67, Chairman 1963–67. Director, McLeod Russel & Co. Ltd. since 1967. Chairman Indian Jute Mills Assn. 1963–64. President: Bengal Chamber of Commerce & Industry 1966–67, and Associated Chambers of Commerce of India 1966–67. *Clubs:* Bengal; Royal Calcutta Turf (both Calcutta); Oriental (London). *Address:* Norton Bavant Manor, Warminster, Wiltshire; and *office* Vintry House, Queen Street Place, London, E.C.2.

**JARMAIN, Edwin R.** Canadian professional engineer. *B.* 1907. *Educ.* University of Toronto (BASc) and University of Western Ontario (MA Business Admin). *M.* 1936, Ruth Winifred Secord. *S.* William Edwin Charles, Walter Kelly, Eric Robert. *Daus.* Ann Lowell, Julia Helen. *Career:* General Manager, Jarmain's Cleaners. London, Ont. 1932–34, Proprietor 1934–61; Dollar-a-Year Man, Federal Government, Dept. of Munitions & Supply 1942–44; Asst. Dir., War Industries Dept. of Labour 1944–45. Founded Jarmain's (Stratford) Ltd. 1947, Pres., Dir. 1947–52; Founder and Manager, Jarmain Cablevision 1952–59; Dir. 1940–46, Kelco Engineering Ltd. Chmn. Bd. 1946–70, Vice Pres. 1970–73; Exec. Vice Pres. London Cable TV 1959–70, Pres. since 1971; Pres. Canadian Cable Television Assn. (Ottawa) 1965–66; Pres. & Dir. Jarmain Cable TV (Brantford; Newmarket) 1965–74; Pres. & Dir., Cablesystems Engineering (formerly Jarmain Teleservices Ltd.) (London 1966–71; Chmn. & Dir. 1971—; Vice Pres. Pine Ridge Cable TV (Oshawa) 1967—; Dir. Chatham Cable TV Ltd. (Chatham) 1967—; Chmn. & Dir. Jarmain Cablesystems Ltd. (London) 1969–73; Dir. Canadian Cablesystems Ltd. (Toronto) since 1971. *Member:* Adv. Bd. Parkwood Hospital, London, Ont.; and McCormick Home, London; Ontario Engineering Adv. Council; Inst. of Electrical & Electronic Engineers; Professional Engineers of the Province of Ontario. *Address:* 97 Commissioners' Road East,London, Ont.; and *office* 800 York Street, London, N5W 2T1, Ont., Canada.

**JARMAN, Walton Maxey.** American business executive. *B.* 1904. *Educ.* Massachusetts Institute of Technology; Hon. LLD, Stetson Univ. and Georgetown Univ. *M.* 1928, Sarah Anderson. *S.* Franklin Maxey. *Daus.* Anne (Taylor) and Eugenia (Elliott). *Career:* Secy.-Treasurer, Jarman Shoe Co. 1925–32; Pres. (1932–47) and Chmn. (1947–69). Nashville City Bank. Trustee: Mutual Life Insurance Co., New York; Financial Federation; Dir., Nashville City Bank. Republican. Trustee: Moody Bible Institute; Christianity Today; Vice-Pres. American Bible Socy. *Member:* Theta Delta Chi; Theta Tau; Eta Mu Pi; Pi Delta Epsilon. *Clubs:* Everglades, Palm Beach; Bath & Tennis; Bell Meade (Nashville). *Address:* 4410 Gerald Place, Nashville, Tenn., U.S.A.

**JÄRNSTEDT, Bo Gunnar.** Swedish Diplomat. *B.* 1911. *Educ.* Degrees in Law, Business Admin. & Public Admin. *M.* 1939, Margareta (Gunvor) Lundgren. *S.* 1. *Dau.* 1. *Career:* Asst. Military Attaché, Berlin Jan.–Sept. 1940; joined Swedish Foreign Service Oct. 1940; served Stockholm, Finland, Canada 1940–52; Chargé d'Affaires, Wellington 1953–57; Counsellor of Embassy, New Delhi 1957–59; Consul-Gen., Chicago 1959–62 & 1964–73; Ambassador to Liberia, Ghana, Ivory Coast, Sierra Leone & Guinea 1962–64; Ambassador to Ireland since 1973. *Decorations:* Grand Officer, Order of the North Star (Sweden); Grand Cross, Order of Redemption (Liberia); Officer, Order of Dannebrog (Denmark); Chevalier, Orders of White Rose (Finland), Phoenix (Greece), & Orange Nassau (Netherlands). *Address:* Embassy of Sweden, Dublin 4, Eire.

**JARRATT, Alexander Anthony.** British company director. *B.* 1924. *Educ.* Royal Liberty Grammar School; Birmingham Univ. B.Comm. *M.* 1946, Mary Philomena Keogh. *S.* 1. *Daus.* 2. *Career:* Civil Service, Min. of Power, Treasury, Cabinet Office, Nat. Board for Prices and Incomes, Dept. of Employment and Productivity, all 1949–70; Man. Dir. IPC 1970–73; Chmn. and Chief Exec. IPC and Chmn. IPC Newspapers 1973–74; Chairman Reed International Ltd. since 1974. *Director:* Goodyear Tyre and Rubber Co.; ATV; ICI. *Governor:* Henley Admin. Staff College; London Grad. School of Business Studies; National Inst. of Economic and Social Research. *Fellow:* British Inst. of Mgmt. *Member:* Supervisory Board Thyssen Bornemisza; Court of Cranfield Inst. of Tech.; Chmn. of the Industrial Society; CBI Economic Policy Committee; National Economic Development Council. *Award:* Companion of the Bath. *Club:* Saville. *Address:* Reed International Ltd., 82 Piccadilly, London, W1A 1EJ.

**JARRIN AMPUDIA, Gustavo.** Ecuadorian Naval Attache. *B.* 1928. *Educ.* Ecuadorian Naval Academy; Argent. Naval Academy; US Naval Post-Grad. School; US Deslant Eng. School; US Bupers Mgmt. Course; Ecuad. Naval War College, Brazilian Naval War and Staff College. *M.* 1956, Gladys Maria Tamajo Ocampo. *S.* 3. *Career:* CO of BAE 'Velasco' 1964–65; Assist. Naval Attaché in Washington DC 1967–68; Operations Officer, Eucadorian Naval Staff 1968–69; CO of BAE '25 de Julio' (Ensign Ship) 1969–70; Chief of Staff, Ecuadorian Navy 1972; Min. of Natural Resources and Energy (Ecuador) 1972–74; Alternate Governor of Interamerican Dep. Bank for Ecuador 1972–74; Pres. of the XL & XLI Conferences of OPEC 1974; President of the Ecuadorian Delegation to UN (6th session) 1974; President of 2nd Conference of Latin-American Ministers on Energy 1973; Naval Attaché to Ecuadorian Embassy in London 1974. *Awards:* Fuerzas Armadas (3a, 2a, 1a); Abdon Calderon (2a); Academia de Guerra (1a Class); Comandante Moran Valverde Grados Comendador y Gran Cruz (all Equad.); Bernardo O'Higgins, Grado Comendador, Estrelle al Merito Militar (both Chile) Ordo Nacional al Merito, Grado de Gran Cruz (Peru); Orden de 'El Libertador', Grado Gran Cordon (Venezuelan); Cruz Del Merito Naval (la Distint. Blanco) (Spain); Orden Tudor Vladimiriscu (1a) (Romania). *Address:* Comandancia General de Marina, PO 2095, Quito, Ecuador.

**JARRING, Gunnar Valfrid.** Swedish diplomat. *B.* 1907. *Educ.* Lund Univ. (PhD). *M.* 1932, Agnes Charlier. *Dau.* Eva. *Career:* Attaché, Ankara 1940–41; Chief. Section B, Teheran

1941; Chargé d'Affaires a.i., Teheran and Baghdad 1945, Addis Ababa 1946–48; En. Ex. and Min. Plen. to India 1948–51, also to Ceylon 1950–51; En. Ex. and Min. Plen. to Persia, Iraq and Pakistan 1951–52; Director, Political Div., Min. of Foreign Affairs, Stockholm, 1953–56; Ambassador and Permanent Representative to U.N. 1956–58; Ambassador to U.S.A. 1958–64; to U.S.S.R. 1964–73; also to Mongolia 1965–73; Representative of Sweden in the Security Council 1957–58; Special Representative of the Secretary-General of the U.N. for the Middle East 1967—. *Awards:* Grand Cross, Order of North Star. *Publications:* Studien zu einer osttürkischen Lautlehre; The Contest of the Fruits—an Eastern Turki Allegory; The Uzbek Dialect of Qilich, Russian Turkestan; Uzbek Texts from Afghan Turkestan; On the Distribution of Turk Tribes in Afghanistan; Materials to the Knowledge of Eastern Turki (Vols. 1–4); An Eastern Turki-English Dialect Dictionary. *Address:* Karlavaegen 85, S11459, Stockholm, Sweden.

**JARVIE, Basil Johnstone.** South African diplomat. *B.* 1907. *Educ.* CIS; BEcon (South Africa). *M.* 1936, Marie-Jose Beumont. *Career:* Under-Secy., Department of Foreign Affairs, Pretoria 1960; Attaché, The Hague 1934, Brussels 1935–38; Vice-Consul, Hamburg 1938–39; Legation Secretary, Paris 1939–40; Dept. of Foreign Affairs, Pretoria 1940–41; Consul in Charge, Cairo 1941–46; Chargé d'Affaires to Greek Govt. in exile 1945–46; Chargé d'Affaires, Brussels 1946–47; South African Delegate to Inter-allied Reparation Agency, Brussels 1946–47; Dept. of Foreign Affairs 1948–50; Delegate on South African Delegation to U.N. Session 1950; Counsellor, Washington, 1951–53; Consul-General, New York 1954–55; Minister to Sweden and Finland 1955–58; to Brazil 1959–60. *Address:* 320 Marais Street, Pretoria, South Africa.

**JAWARA, Sir Dawda (Kairaba)** Kt., GMAG, GCMG. President of the Republic of The Gambia. *B.* 1924. *Educ.* Archimota Coll. Univ. of Ghana, and Glasgow Univ. *Career:* Veterinary Officer, Kombo St. Mary 1954–60. Principal Veterinary Officer, Gambia Govt. 1954–59; Diploma in Trop. Vet. Med., Edinburgh, 1957. Min. of Education 1960–61; Premier 1962. Prime Minister of The Gambia 1963–70. President since 1970. Leader, People's Progressive Party 1960. *Address:* State House, Banjul, The Gambia.

**JAY, Rt. Hon. Douglas (Patrick Thomas)**, PC, MP. British journalist and economist. *B.* 23 Mar. 1907. *Educ.* Winchester Coll., New Coll., Oxford. *M.* (1) 1933, Margaret Christian Garnett (Div.). *S.* Peter, Martin. *Daus.* Helen, Catherine. (2) 1972, Mary Lavinia Thomas. *Career:* On the staff of The Times 1929–33; Fellow of All Souls Coll., Oxford; 1930–37 and since 1968; on the staff of The Economist 1933–37; City Editor of the Daily Herald 1937–40; Assistant Secretary, Ministry of Supply 1940–43; Principal Assistant Secretary, Board of Trade 1943–45; Personal Assistant to Prime Minister 1945–46; Member of Parliament (Lab.) for Battersea North since 1946; Parliamentary Private Secretary to the Rt. Hon. Hugh Dalton, Chancellor of the Exchequer 1946–47; Economic Secretary to the Treasury 1947–Feb. 1950; Financial Secretary to the Treasury Mar. 1950. President Board of Trade, Oct. 1964–67; Director, Courtaulds Ltd. 1967–70; Fellow, All Souls; Dir., Trades Union Unit Trust; Chairman, Common Market Safeguards Campaign 1970–76; London Motorway Action Group. *Address:* 6 Hampstead Grove, London, N.W.3; and Monument Cottage, Britwell Saiome, Watlington, Oxford.

**JAY, Peter.** British. *B.* 1937. *Educ.* Winchester Coll.; Christ Church, Oxford—MA (1st class hons.). *M.* 1961, Margaret Ann Callaghan. *S.* 1. *Daus.* 2. *Career:* Midshipman & Sub-Lieut., RNVR 1956–57; Asst. Principal 1961–64, Private Sec. to Joint Perm. Sec. 1964, Principal 1964–67, HM Treasury; Economics Editor, The Times 1967–77; Assoc. Editor, Times Business News 1969–77; Presenter, Weekend World, ITV 1972–77, The Jay Interview, ITV 1975–77; HM Ambassador, Washington, D.C. since 1977. *Awards:* Political Broadcaster of the Year, 1973; Harold Wincott Financial & Economic Journalist of the Year, 1973; Royal TV Soc's Male Personality of the Year (Pye Award), 1974; Shell Int. TV Award, 1974. Wincott Memorial Lecturer 1975. *Address:* British Embassy, 3100 Massachusetts Avenue, N.W., Washington, D.C. 20008, U.S.A.

**JAY, R. Harry.** Canadian Diplomat. *B.* 1919. *Educ.* McGill Univ. (BA 1941; BCL 1948). *M.* 1945, Dorothy V. Andrews. *S.* 3. Deputy Permanent Representative, Canadian Delegation to NATO 1963–65; High Commission for Canada in Jamaica 1965–68: Ext. Affairs Rep. on Directing Staff Nat. Defence Coll. Kingston, Ont. 1968; Dir.-Gen. Bureau of UN Affairs, Dept. of Ext. Affairs Ottawa 1971–73; Ambassador of Canada in Sweden 1973–76; Canadian Amb. and Perm. Rep. to the UN at Geneva, and to the Conference of the Cttee. on Disarmament, Aug. 1976—. *Member:* Bar Assn., Province of Quebec, Sigma, Chi. *Club:* Jamaica. *Address:* 10A Avenue de Budé, 1202 Geneva, Switzerland.

**JAYEWARDENE, Junius Richard.** Ceylonese politician. *B.* 17 Sept. 1906. *Educ.* Royal College, Colombo; Ceylon University and Law Colleges. *M.* 1935, Elina B. Rupesinghe. *S.* Ravindra. *Career:* Hon. General Secy., Ceylon National Congress 1940–47; Treas., United National Party 1947; Vice-Pres., United National Party 1958. Leader: Ceylon Delegation to Sterling Talks, London 1948–52; Co-Author of the Colombo Plan for aid to underdeveloped Asiatic countries 1950; Ceylon Delegation to Commonwealth Talks in Sydney, to International Monetary Fund and World Bank Meeting in Paris, Commonwealth Talks, London; Ceylon Deleg. Japanese Peace Treaty Conf., San Francisco 1951; Member, Municipal Council, Colombo 1940–43; Member (United Nat.) for Kelaniya 1943–56; MP (United Nat.) 1947–56; Governor, World Bank and International Monetary Fund, 1947–52; Min. of Agric. and Food, and Ldr., House of Representatives 1953–56; Minister of Finance: 1947–52, 1952–Oct. 1953, Mar.–July 1960 and Leader of the House 1960; MP for Colombo South 1960–65; 65–70; since 1970, and Chief Opposition Whip, July 1960–65. Minister of State, Parliamentary Secretary to the Prime Minister and Minister of Defence and External Affairs, and Chief Government Whip in the House of Representatives. 1965–70: Leader of the Opposition 1970–77; Sec., United Nat. Party 1972, Leader 1973; Prime Minister since 1977. Ex-Pres., Ceylon Cricket Assn.; Advocate, Supreme Court, Ceylon. *Publications:* Buddhist Essays; Stome Sermons of the Buddha; In Council; Buddhism and Marxism. *Address:* 66 Ward Place, Colombo 7, Sri Lanka.

**JEAN, Hon. Bernard,** QC. Canadian Judge *B.* 1925. *Educ.* St. Joseph's University, N.B. (BA 1946; MA Econ 1949). *M.* 1955, Corinne Lanteigne. *S.* Rodrigue and Maurice. *Daus.* Suzanne, Monique, Françoise and Isabelle. *Career:* Barrister, admitted to NB Bar 1951; Elected as Liberal Member to NB Legislature 1960–63–67–70; Speaker of the House of Assembly 1963–66; Mem. Senate of Univ. of New Brunswick 1965–70; Minister of Justice and Attorney-General, Province of NB, Canada 1966–70; Judge of the County Court of New Brunswick, 1972. *Address:* Caraquet, New Brunswick; and *office* Fredericton, N.B., Canada.

**JEANNENEY, Jean-Marcel.** D-en-D; Officier, Legion of Honour. French professor. *B.* 1910. *Educ.* Lic-es-L; Diploma of the School of Political Sciences; D-en-D; Agrégé, Economic Science. *M.* 1936, Marie-Laure Monod. *S.* 2. *Daus.* 5. *Career:* Assistant Professor, Faculty of Law, Grenoble 1937; Director of Cabinet of the Minister of State in the Provisional Government 1944–45; Dean of the Faculty of Law, Grenoble 1947–51; Professor of Political Economy, Faculty of Law and Economic Sciences of Paris 1952—; Director of studies of economic activity, National Foundation of Political Science; member of the Committee of Experts (responsible for reform of economy and finance) 1958; Minister of Industry Jan. 1959–Apr. 1962; Ambassador to Algeria 1962–Jan. 1963; Member, Economic and Social Council 1964–65; Conseillor general de la Haute-Saône 1965–76; Minister of Social Affairs 1966–68; Maire de Rioz (Haute-Saône) 1967; Deputé de L'Isère 1968, Ministre d'Etat 1968–69; Professor Universite' Pantheon Sorbonne 1969. *Publications:* Le mouvement des prix en France depuis la stabilisation du franc 1927–35; Economie et Droit de l'Electricité, L'Economie alpine, Les Commerces détail en Europe Occidentale, Forces et faiblesses de l'Economique française, 1945–59; Textes de droit Economique et Social français, 1789–1857; Comptabilité interégionale française pour 1954; A mes Amis Gaullistes; Elements d'Economie Politique. *Address:* 102 rue d'Assas, Paris 6e, France.

**JEANNERET, Marsh.** Canadian. *B.* 1917. *Educ.* Univ. of Toronto (BA Hon—Law), LLD McGill Univ. *M.* 1938, Ethel Beatrice Mellon. *S.* 2. *Career:* Director, Copp, Clark Co. 1952; Director, University of Toronto Press 1953—. Chmn., Canadian Copyright Institute 1965–67; Board of Governors, Council of Printing Industries 1963–66; President, Association of American University Presses, 1970–71. Pres., Canadian Book Publishers' Cncl. 1968–69; Ontario Royal Commission, Book Publishing 1971–73. *Publications:* Story of Canada: Notre Histoire; Canada in North America;

History's Mystery; From Cartier to Champlain. *Clubs:* University, Arts and Letters (Toronto). *Address:* R.R.1, King City, Ont., Canada; and *office* University of Toronto Press, Front Campus, University of Toronto, Toronto M5S 1A6, Ont., Canada.

**JEBSEN-MARDWEDEL, Hans.** German. Professor Dr. phil. habil. Gold Gehloff-Ring. Otto Schott Múnze; Ehrenmitglied, Deutsche Glastechnische Gesellschaft e.V. *B.* 1899. *Educ.* Studied Natural Sciences at the Universities of Heidelberg and Cologne and at the Technical High School of Aachen. *M.* Margot Stang. *S.* Roland Ing. (*Dec.*). *Daus.* Karin (Frau Luhn) and Frauke. *Career:* Formerly: Mgr., Siegwart Glassworks; Head of Laboratory, Prokurist, Technical Director and Member of the Board of the Deutschen Libbey-Owens Gesellschaft for machine-made glass; Training Officer for Glass Technology at the Institute of Metallurgy of the Technical High School of Aachen, Hon. Prof. *Publications:* Glastechnische Fabrikationsfehler (manufacturing defects in glass) (Springer-Verlag); also numerous publications on glass technology. *Member:* Deutsche Glastechnischen Gesellschaft; Fraunhofer-Gesellschaft; Fellow, Society of Glass Technology. *Address:* Unterzeismering 14, 8132 Tutzing/Obb, Germany.

**JEFFERY, Alexander Haley,** QC, BA. Canadian Barrister and Solicitor of Jeffery & Jeffery (estab. 1890), 174 King Street (P.O. Box 2095), London, Ontario. *B.* 1909. *Educ.* Victoria Public School; London South Collegiate Institute; University of Western Ontario; Osgoode Hall, Toronto: BA (Honour Economics and Political Science); *Career;* Read Law with Jeffery & Jeffery, called to Bar of Ontario, June 1934; with Jeffery & Jeffery since 1934. *M.* 1934, Eulalie E. Murray. *S.* 1. *Dau.* 1. *Career:* President, London Life Insurance Company; President and Director: Forest City Investments Limited; Director of the following companies: Thames Valley Investments Ltd.; London Realty Management and Rentals Ltd.; London Winery Ltd.; Two Hundred Queens Avenue Ltd.; Canada Trust; Huron & Erie. *Member:* Canadian Bar Association; Member: American Association of Life Insurance Counsel; elected to constituency of City of London, June 1949–53 .*Clubs:* London Hunt & Country (London, Ont.); Royal Canadian Yacht, University (Toronto); Kanagio Yacht (Port Stanley, Ont.); Windsor Yacht (Windsor, Ont.); Sarnia Yacht (Sarnia, Ont.); Trans-Erie Sail (Pt. Stanley). Societies: The Tuscan Lodge, No. 195; A.F. & A.M., G.R.C.; Life Member in London Sovereign Chapter of Rose Croix A. & A.S.R.; Life member, Moore Sovereign Consistory, S.P.R.S. 32nd Degree, A. & A.S.R. Liberal. *Address:* 104 Commissioners Road East, London N6C 2T1, Ont.; and *office* P.O. Box 2095, London N6A 4E1, Ontario, Canada.

**JEFFERYS, Gordon Greaves Hunt.** British. *B.* 1922. *Educ.* St. John's Preparatory School, Essex, and Harlow College. *M.* 1944, Nancy Yvonne Edgeworth-Nichols. *Career:* Served in World War II (R.A.F. Pilot; rank Flight Lieutenant) 1940–46; with Blue Star Line Ltd., London 1946–47; with Blue Star Line Agents (Parry, Leon & Hayhoe Ltd.) in South Africa 1947–52; rejoined Blue Star Line when previously mentioned subsidiary was opened up as Head Office in Republic of S. Africa 1952. Director and Gen. Manager, Blue Star Line (South Africa) (Pty.) Ltd. since Apr. 1952; Director, Compass Line (Pty) Ltd.; ACT (S.A. Pty) Ltd.; Terminal Properties (SA) Pty Ltd.; Containerbases (Pty) Ltd. Fellow, Institute of South Africa Shipbrokers. *Clubs:* Kelvin Grove & City (Cape Town). *Address:* 'Amalfi', Hillside Road, Fish Hoek, C.P., South Africa; P.O. Box 4446, Cape Town.

**JEFFRIES, Robert Joseph.** Engineer. educator. business executive. Trustee, Univ. of Bridgepott (Conn.). *B.* 1923. *Educ.* BSEE *cum laude*, Univ. of Connecticut, MSE 1946, and Eng-Dr, Johns Hopkins University. *M.* 1945, Anna Darling Cumming. *S.* Bruce Cumming. *Dau.* Christine Darling. *Career:* Electrical Engineer, National Advisory Commission for Aeronautics 1944–46; Electronic Design Engineer, Johns Hopkins Univ. 1946–48; Assoc. Prof. Eng., Michigan State Univ. 1948–54; Dir., Tec-Search Inc. 1953—; Technical Planning Adviser, Schlumberger Instrument Co. 1954–56; Asst. to Pres. Daystrom Inc. 1956–57; Pres., Data-Control Systems Inc. 1957–66; Dir. Foundation for Instrumentation Education and Research 1958–69; General Science Corp. 1968–70; Van Dyck Corp.; Life Energies Research Inc. Metraplex Corp.: Evergreen Fund Inc.*Publications:* papers and articles. *Member:* National Academy of Sciences (Nat. Res. Council 1959); Vice-Chmn. Conn. Comm. for Higher Education, 1965–77; Instrument Society of America (Past Pres.); American Inst. of Electrical Engineers; Amer. Socy. of Mechanical Engineers. Universalist-Unitarian Assn. *Club:* University (N.Y.C.); Cedar Point Yacht (Conn.). *Address:* Owenoke Park, Westport, Conn.; and *office* Room 332, North Hall, Univ. of Bridgeport, Bridgeport, Conn., U.S.A.

**JEJEEBHOY, Sir Jamsetjee,** Bt. Landlord, Managing Director Beaulieu Investment Private Ltd. *B.* 19th April 1913. *Educ.* St. Xavier's College (BA) Bombay University. *M.* 1943, Shirin Jehangir H. Cama. *S.* Rustom. *Dau.* Ayesha. *Career:* Chmn. Sir Jamsetjee Jejeebhoy Charity Funds, Sir J. J. Parsee Benevolent Institution, Bombay Panjrapole, Seth Rustomjee Jamsetjee Jejeebhoy Gujrat Schools' Fund, Wadia Atash-behram, Parsi Charity Organisation Society, Iran League etc.; Trustee Sir J. J. School of Arts, Byramjee Jeeheebhoy Parsi Charitable Institution, Eranee Charity Funds & Dharamshala, Zoroastrian Building Fund, The K. R. Cama Oriental Institution; Exec. Committee B. D. Petit Parsee General Hospital. *Clubs:* Willingdon Sports Club, W.I.A.A. Club, Western India Turf Club, Bombay. *Address:* Beaulieu, 95 Worli Seaface, Bombay 25; and *office* Maneckji Wadia Bldg, Mahatma Gandhi Road, Fort, Bombay 1.

**JENKIN, The Rt. Hon. Charles Patrick Fleeming,** PC. MP. *B.* 1926. *Educ.* Jesus Coll. Cambridge (MA). *M.* 1952, Monica Graham. *S.* 2. *Daus.* 2. *Career:* Adviser, The Distillers Co. Ltd. 1957–70; Non-Exec. Dir. Tilbury Contracting Group Ltd. since 1974; Royal Worcester Ltd., and Continental and Industrial Trust Ltd. since 1975; Barrister-at-Law (Middle Temple). Member of Parliament (Cons.) for Wanstead and Woodford since 1964; Governor, Westfield Coll. London Univ. 1964–70; Opposition Front Bench Spokesman on Treasury, Trade and Economic Affairs 1965–66, 1967–70. Vice-Chmn. Conservative Party Trade and Power Cttee. 1966–67; Financial Secy. to the Treasury 1970–72; Chief Secy. 1972–74; Minister for Energy Jan.–March 1974; Shadow Minister for Energy 1974–76; Shadow Sec. of State for the Social Services 1976; member Shadow Cabinet since 1974. Privy Councillor, 1973. *Club:* West Essex Conservative. *Address:* 9 Hurst Avenue, Highgate, London, N.6, and House of Commons, London, S.W.1.

**JENKINS, Sir Evan Meredith,** GCIE, KCSI. *B.* 2 Feb. 1896. *Educ.* Rugby School; Balliol College, Oxford. *Career:* served in World War I; entered Indian Civil Service 1920; Deputy and Joint Secretary, Department of Industries and Labour, New Delhi 1933–36; Chief Commissioner, Delhi 1937–40; Secretary, Supply Department 1940–43; Private Secretary to Viceroy and Personal Secretary to Governor-General 1943–45; Governor, Punjab 1946–47. *Address:* 24 Ashley Gardens, Westminster, London, S.W.1.

**JENKINS, Hugh Gater,** MP. British Politician. *B.* 1908. *M.* 1936, Marie. *Career:* Insurance Official, 1930–39; R.A.F. Officer, 1940–45; Dir. English programmes, Rangoon Radio, 1945–46; Research & Publicity Officer NUBE. Editor, The Bank Officer, 1946–50; Asst. Gen. Sec. British Equity, 1950–64; Member of Parliament for Putney since 1964. Former Chairman, Theatres Advisory Council; Standing Adv. Cttee. Local Authorities & Theatre; Minister of Arts 1974–76; Dep. Chmn., Theatres Trust; Chmn., Parly. Labour Party Arts sub-cttee. *Address: office* House of Commons, London, S.W.1.

**JENKINS, Leslie Augustus Westover,** CBE. British. *B.* 1910. *Educ.* Lancing College. *M.* 1936, Ann Barker Bruce. *Career:* Man. Dir., John Wright & Sons (Veneers) Ltd. 1945, Chmn 1956–59; Man. Dir., I. & R. Morley Ltd. 1959–62. A Deputy Chmn., British Natl. Export Council 1966–73; Director: Restall Brown & Clennel Ltd. 1963–77; National Industrial Fuel Efficiency Service 1953–72, Chmn. 1968–73; Haden Carrier Ltd. 1967—; Dir. Airscrew-Weyroc 1971–73; Consultant 1973–77. *Member:* Industrial Coal Consumers' Council 1947–73, Deputy-Chmn. 1971. Pres., National Assn. of British Manufacturers 1962–65, Chairman, Forestry Commission, U.K. 1965–70. Vice-Pres., C.B.I. 1965–68. Member of Council, 1968; European Coal & Steel Consultative Cttee. since 1973. Hons.: M. Inst. Fuel; Bd. of Fellows, B.I.M. 1968; FRSA 1972. *Club:* Royal Ocean Racing. *Address:* Lyneham Lodge, Hook Park, Warsash, Hants.

**JENKINS, Rt. Hon. Roy,** PC. President of the Commission of the European Communities since 1977. *B.* 1920. *Educ.* Abersychan Grammar Schl. and Balliol Col., Oxford, First Class Hons. Sch. of Philosophy, Politics & Economics. *M.* 1945, Jennifer Morris. *S.* 2. *Dau.* 1. *Career:* Served War of 1939–45 in RA 1942–46, Captain 1944–46; Contested (Lab.) Solihull at

Gen. Election 1945; Elected for Central Southwark 1948, for Stechford div. of Birmingham 1950–77; on Staff, Industrial & Commercial Finance Corp. Ltd. 1946–48. Parly. Private Secy. to Secy. of State, Commonwealth Relations 1949–50; Member, Exec. Cttee. of Fabian Socy. 1949–61, Chmn. 1957–58; Cttee. Management, Socy. of Authors 1956–60; Dir. of Financial Operations, John Lewis Partnership 1962–64; Minister of Aviation 1964–65; Home Secy. 1965–67; Chancellor of the Exchequer 1967–70; Deputy-Leader, The Labour Party 1970–72; Home Secy. 1974–76; Pres. of Britain in Europe for the referendum campaign 1974; Past Vice-Pres. Britain in Europe; Dept. Chmn. Common Market Campaign: Chmn. Labour European Cttee. Pres. United Kingdom Coun. of the European Movement; Hon. Fellow Balliol Coll. Oxford & Berkeley Coll., Yale; Hon. D Litt, Glasgow & City Univ., London; Hon. LLD, Leeds, Harvard, Pennsylvania, Dundee, Loughborough, Keele & Aston (Birmingham). *Publications:* Purpose and Policy, A Volume of the Prime Minister's Speeches (1947); Mr. Attlee, An Interim Biography (1948); Contributor of New Fabian Essays (1952); Pursuit of Progress (1953); Mr. Balfour's Poodle (1954); Sir Charles Dilke, a Victorian Tragedy (1958); The Labour Case (1959); Contributor to Hugh Gaitskell, A Memoir (1964); Asquith (1964); Essays and Speeches (1967); What Matters Now (1972); Afternoon on the Potomac (1972); Nine Men of Power (1974). *Clubs:* Brooks's (London). *Address:* St. Amand's House, East Hendred, Wantage, Oxon.; and 10 Rue de Praetere, Brussels 1050, Belgium.

**JENKS, James Lawrence, Jr.** Chairman of the Board, Sanborn Co. 1961–63 (Pres. 1942–61). *B.* 1896. *Educ.* Moses Brown Prep. School, Providence, R.I.; and Brown University (AB 1920). *M.* 1921, Evelyn S. A. Makant. *Career:* Engineer in research laboratory, American Radio & Research Corp. 1920–25; American Appliance Co. (now Raytheon Co.) 1925; Sanborn Co. 1925–63; Director, Hewlett-Packard Co., 1962–67. Publisher of bimonthly magazine, Praying Hands. With Dr. Francis Benedict, took pioneer electrocardiogram on an elephant 1936; participated in a scientific expedition to Alaska with Drs. Paul Dudley White, Robert L. King and recorded pioneer electrocardiogram on a whale 1952. Hon. Trustee and member, Corporation of New England Baptist Hospital; and Boston Museum of Science. *Clubs:* Institute of Directors (London); Algonquin (Boston); Brown (Boston); Winchester Country; Beta Theta Pi. *Address:* 12 Myopia Hill Road, Winchester, Mass.; and *office* 28 Church Street, Winchester, Mass. 01890, U.S.A.

**JENNINGS, Sir Albert Victor,** Kt. Australian. *B.* 1896. *M.* 1922, Ethel Sarah Johnson. *S.* 2. *Career:* Founder A. V. Jennings Industries (Australia) Ltd. 1932—. Ret. 1972. Fellow, Australian Inst. of Building (Past Pres.). Member: Council of Master Builders Association. Manufacturing Industries Adv. Council; Victorian Decentralisation & Development Adv. Cttee. 1965–68; Commonwealth Building Research & Development Adv. Cttee. 1949–71; Fellow, Australian Inst. of Management (FAIM). Australian Institute of Building Medal, 1970; Fellow, Institute of Building (UK). Member, Metric Conversion Board, 1970–72. *Awards:* Sir Charles McGrath Award, 1976. *Address:* Ranelagh House, Rosserdale Crescent, Mt. Eliza, Victoria 3930, Australia.

**JENNINGS, (Richard Edward) Christopher,** MBE (Mil.), DL. Editor, The Motor (London) 1946–60; High Sheriff Carmarthenshire, 1957–58. *B.* 1911. *Educ.* Repton School. *M.* 1937, Margaret Allan. *S.* 1. *Career:* Apprentice, Riley (Coventry) Ltd.; with same firm 1930–37; Midland Editor, The Motor 1937–39; Served in World War II (Western Desert, Greece Crete, Syria and Europe; MBE) 1939–44. Director, Trust Houses Ltd., Buckley's Brewery Ltd., and British Automatic Co. Ltd. *Publication:* a military work dealing with the fall of Greece and Crete. *Address:* Gelli-deg, Kidwelly, Dyfed.

**JENSEN, Hans Waldemar.** Finnish company director. *B.* 7 Aug. 1913. *Educ.* BS in Bus. Adm. Textile engineer. *M.* 1938, Märta Marita von Wendt. *S.* 3. *Dau.* 1. Managing-Director, Suomen Trikoo Oy.-Ab 1953–70, Chmn. since 1970. Vice-Consul for Belgium at Tampere 1951–71. *Address:* Box 65, 33101 Tampere 10, Finland.

**JENSEN, Ray Victor.** American. President and Owner, Radio Station KIRT, Mission, Texas. *B.* 1899. *Educ.* Fremont (Nebraska) Normal School; Midland College, Fremont. *M.* 1934, Edith Sutcliffe Bunker. *Daus.* Geraldine (Starmer), Joan (Callahan). *Career:* Previously: Sales Mgr.: Radio Station KTRI, Sioux City, Iowa; Radio Station KOAM, Pittsburgh, Kansas; Regional Supervisor, Sioux City, Wincharger Corp.; Mgr., Radio Station KSAL Salina 1944–59; Pres., Salina Y.M.C.A. 1949 and U.S.O. Bd., 1948–49; Mem., Governor's World Affairs Cttee., 1952–53; Chmn.: Communications Div., Civil Defence; C.R.O.P. (overseas programme) 1952–53; Mem., Kansas Governor's Refugee Relief Cttee.; Pres., Service Men's Centre; Mem.: Kansas State College Advisory Council Radio and Television Dept.; Kansas Assn. of Radio Broadcasters (Sec.-Treas. 1951–52; Pres. 1952–53); First Vice-Pres., Chamber of Commerce; Pres., Rotary Club of Salina 1949; Mem., Mission Chamber of Commerce Trade Development Cttee. *Member:* Kansas State Radio and TV Council, National Radio and TV Executive Society; Kansas Refugee Relief Committee; Governor's World Affairs Committee; Military Affairs Committee of Chamber of Commerce. President U.S.O. of Salina. Sentinel Harmony Chapter, Order of Eastern Star. Mason 32°; Shriner; Lutheran. *Publications:* Sponsor; Broadcasting. *Clubs:* Salina Country (Dir.); Northview Country; Shary Country; Rotary (Mission, Tex.); Rio Grande Valley Advertising (Chartered member); Wichita Sales Executives (Kansas); Radio; Television Exec. Socy.; Nomad Shrine. *Address:* 802 Country Club Drive, Mission, Texas 78572; and *office* Shary Building, Mission, Tex., U.S.A.

**JEPHCOTT, Sir Harry,** Bt, DSc, FRIC, FPS. Formerly Chmn., Glaxo Group Ltd. *B.* 1891. *M.* 1919, Doris Gregory, FPS. *S.* 2. *Educ.* King Edward's School, Birmingham. Called to Bar (Middle Temple) 1925; *Career:* Chmn., Council Department Scientific and Ind. Research 1956–61; President, Royal Institute of Chemistry 1953–55; Chairman, Association of British Chemical Manufacturers 1947–52; President 1952–55; member, Advisory Council Scientific Policy 1953–56; Chairman, Committee Detergents 1953–55; Chairman, School of Pharmacy, University of London 1948–69; Governor, London School of Economics 1952–68; Governor, North London Collegiate School 1957—. Hon. Fellow, Royal Society of Medicine 1961. *Club:* Athenaeum. *Address:* Weetwood, 1, Cheney St., Pinner, Middlesex.

**JEPSON, Norman.** British. *B.* 1906. *Educ.* Queen Elizabeth's Grammar School, Blackburn, and Univ. of London. *Career:* Chmn. and Mng. Dir., The Walpamur Co. Ltd., and Dir., The Wall Paper Manufacturers Ltd. until retirement in 1963. Managing Dir., Crabtree Engineering Group (Colne) Ltd., since 1964. Freeman City of London. *Member:* Livery of the Worshipful Company of Painter-Stainers; Chmn., N.W. Postal Region Users Cttee.; Chmn. of General Commissioners of Taxes for Blackburn & District. *Clubs:* Brooks', East India, Sports and Public Schools (both of London); District & Union (Blackburn). *Address:* 17 Park Lee Road, Blackburn; and *office* Crabtree Engineering Group, Green Works, Colne, Lancs.

**JERRETT, Robert Jr.** American. *B.* 1913. *Educ.* Brown Univ. (BA). *M.* 1941, Hope Janet Harkness. *S.* Robert III, David Harkness and Steven MacNiven. *Career:* City Sales, Mgr., Asst. Gen. Sales Mgr. 1935–39; Dir. of Economic Planning, American Airlines Inc. 1939–46; Asst. to Pres., Wiggins Airways 1946–47; Research Fellow, Harvard Univ., Graduate School of Business Admin., 1947–49; Senior Associate, McKinsey & Co. 1949–57; Vice-Pres. and Gen. Mgr. and Dir., American Tackle & Equipment Corp. 1957–59; Asst. Vice-Pres., Controller, Daystrom Inc. 1963–68; Cambridge Systems Inc. 1967–69. Pres., Treasurers and Dir., Venture Resources Inc., 1968–71; Financial Consultant and Assist. to President, Emerson College since 1971; Director: S.M.C.S. Inc. 1966—, Parker River Marine Inc. 1966—, James E. Graves Inc. 1968—, Trustee, Salem Five Cents Savings Bank, 1969—, Treasurer, Ortec Inc. 1967. *Publications:* Airline Competition (Harvard University Press, 1949); The Financial Manager's Job (American Management Assn. 1957); Financial Executive's Handbook (Dow-Jones-Irwin Inc. 1968); Contr. to Life. *Member:* American Management Assn.; Financial Executives' Inst.;. *Clubs:* New York Yacht; Corinthian Yacht (Marblehead, Mass.); Yacht-Racing Union of Mass. Bay; Brown Univ. (Boston). *Address: office* 150 Beacon Street, Boston, Mass. 02116, U.S.A.

**JESPERSEN, Iver.** Danish publisher. *B.* 21 Oct. 1904. Educ. cand. phil. *M.* 1928, Kirstine Korsgaard. *S.* Hans, Ole Søren. *Dau.* Birte. *Career: Examen artium* 1922; trained as a bookseller and publisher in Copenhagen, Geneva, Boston, New York, and Stockholm; joined Jespersen og Pio, Copenhagen 1927; owner since Jan. 1952; member, Board of Danish Publishers' Association 1941; Vice-President 1947; President 1953–59; Pres., Danish Booksellers' Schl., 1961–69. *Address:* Sølystvej 11, 2930 Klampenborg, Denmark, and Les Charmettes, 10 rue Paul Morillot, 06500 Menton, France.

**JESSEL, Toby F. H.**, MP. British. *B.* 1934. *Educ.* Royal Naval Coll., Dartmouth; Balliol Coll., Oxford (MA). *Career:* Conservative Member of Parliament for Twickenham since 1970; Mem., Parly. Assemblies of Council of Europe & Western European Union. *Clubs:* Garrick, Hurlingham. *Address:* Old Court House, Hampton Court, East Molesey, Surrey.

**JESSUP, Philip C.** American. Lawyer, educationist, diplomat and international judge. *B* 5. Jan. 1897. *Educ.* Hamilton College (AB); Columbia University (MA, PhD); Yale University (LLB). *M.* 1921, Lois Walcott Kellogg. *S.* Philip C. *Career:* Served World War I, U.S. Army Expeditionary Forces; Asst. to the Pres. and Asst. Cashier, First National Bank of Utica N.Y. 1919–21; admitted to D.C. Bar 1925, New York Bar 1927; member, Parker and Duryea, New York Law firm 1927–43; taught International Law, Columbia 1925–61; Hamilton Fish Professor of International Law and Diplomacy 1946–61; Associate, Rockefeller Foundation 1960–61. Visiting Professor, Harvard Law School, 1938–39; Assistant Solicitor, Dept. of State 1924–25; Assistant to Elihu Root, Conference of Jurists on the Permanent Court of International Justice, Geneva 1929; Legal Adviser to American Ambassador to Cuba 1930; Chief of Division, Office of Foreign Relief. Dept. of State 1943; Assistant Secretary General, First Council Session of U.N.R.R.A. 1943, and of Bretton Woods Conference 1944; Adviser, U.S. Delegation at U.N. Conference, San Francisco, 1945; Associate Director, Naval School of Military Government and Administration 1942–44; U.S. Representative at various Sessions of the Security Council and General Assembly of the Un. Nations 1948–53; Ambassador at Large, Mar. 1949–Jan. 1953; Chmn., Chile–Norway Permanent Conciliation Commission 1958—; Chmn., Perm. Austro–Swedish Commission for Reconciliation and Arbitration 1976—; Storrs Lecturer, Yale Univ. Law School 1956; Cooley Lecturer, Michigan University Law School 1958; Blaustein Lect. Columbia Univ. 1970; Sibley Lect. Univ. of Georgia Law School 1970. Member, Curatorium of the Hague Academy of International Law 1957–68; Trustee of Hamilton College 1958–61; Trustee Woodrow Wilson Foundation 1948–57, Pres. 1957–58; Carnegie Endowment for International Peace, 1937–60; Vice-Pres. Institute de Droit Internat. 1959–61 and 1973–75; Hon. Member, Inter-American Institute of International Legal Studies 1964—; Hon. Mem., Academia Mexicana de Derecho Internacional, 1965—; Hon. Pres., American Socy. of International Law, 1969–73, 1976—; Hon. Pres. American Branch International Law Association, Senior Fellow, Council Foreign Relations, 1970–71. Judge, International Court of Justice 1961–70. Hon. member, Governing Council, Inst. for Unification of Private Law (UNIDROIT). *Awards:* Hungarian Cross of Merit, Class II; Oficial Ordem Nacional do Cruziero do Su (Brazil); Grand Officer, Order of the Cedars (Lebanon); Distinguished Service, Connecticut Bar Assn.; Hon. LLD Western Reserve, Brown, Seoul National, Rutgers, Michigan, Pennsylvania, Columbia, St. Lawrence and Yale Universities, Middlebury, Hamilton and Colby Colleges; Johns Hopkins Univ. Brandeis Univ. JD Oslo University; Doc hc University of Paris; LittD of Hanoi; LCD Colgate University and Union College; Manley O. Hudson Gold Medal; Wolfgang G. Friedmann Memorial Award; Columbia Univ. School of Law Alumni Assn. Medal for Excellence, 1977; Graduate Faculties Alumni of Columbia Univ. Award for Excellence, 1977. *Publications:* The Law of Territorial Waters and Maritime Jurisdiction; American Neutrality and International Police; The United States and the World Court; International Security; Neutrality, Its History, Economics and Law —Vol. I, The Origins (with Francis Deak), Vol. IV, Today and Tomorrow; Elihu Root; International Problem of Governing Mankind; A Modern Law of Nations; Transnational Law; The Use of International Law; Controls for Outer Space and the Antarctic Analogy (with Howard Taubenfeld); The Price of International Justice (1971); The Birth of Nations (1974). *Address:* off Windrow Road, Norfolk, Conn. 06058, U.S.A.

**JEWETT, Frank B., Jr.** *B.* 1917. *Educ.* California Inst. of Technology (BS Mec Eng), and Harvard University Graduate School of Business Administration (MBA); Registered Professional Engineer, Minnesota. *M.* 1942, Edar von L. Fleming. *S.* Frank B. III and Robert F. *Daus.* Rebecca L. and Edar F. *Career:* Graduate Research Asst., Harvard Graduate School of Business Admin. 1940–41; with National Research Corp. (final position, Vice-Pres. and Manager, Vacuum Equipment Div.) 1941–47; General Mills Inc. (final position, Vice-Pres. and Dir. Engineering Research and Development, Mechanical Div.) 1947–55. President, Vitro Corporation of America N.Y.C. (Director 1956–69; Pres., Chief Exec. 1960–69); Chairman, Vitro Minerals Corp. 1961–69; Dir., Vitro Italiana, 1961–65; Vitroselenia 1963–65; Chmn. and Pres., Technical Audit Associates Inc. since 1970; Trustee; Tabor Academy 1952—, and Rockford College 1949—. Member of Corporation, Woods Hole Oceanographic Institution 1960—. *Award:* Certificate of Merit, Crusade for Freedom. *Member:* Amer. Socy. Mechanical Engineers; Amer. Ordnance Assn.; New York Academy, Sciences. *Clubs:* Vineyard Haven (Mass.) Yacht (Governor); Union League, New York Yacht (N.Y.C.). *Address:* 589 Oenoke Ridge, New Canaan, Conn.; and *office* 420 Lexington Ave., New York City. N.Y. 10017, U.S.A.

**JEWETT, Robert H.** American *B.* 1910. *Educ.* Univ. of Minnesota (Bach., Aeronautical Engineering). *M.* 1940, Marjorie J. Fjerstad. *S.* John Robert, Donald Scot and Charles William. *Career:* Chief Engineer, The Boeing Co. 1954; Vice Pres. Gen. Mgr. Missile and Information Systems Div. since 1960. Asst. Gen. Manager, Aero Space Group, 1963. Received Outstanding Achievement Award, University of Minnesota. *Fellow:* Amer. Inst. of Aeronautics and Astronautics. *Address:* 3645 Hunts Point Road, Bellvue, Washington 98004; and *office* The Boeing Co., Seattle, Washington, U.S.A.

**JEWKES, Prof. John**, CBE, MA (Oxon), MCom (Manchester). *B.* 29 June 1902. *Educ.* Barrow Grammar School; University of Manchester; Hon. DSc. (Econ.) Hull. *M.* 1929, Frances Sylvia Butterworth. *Dau.* Anne Gillian. *Career:* Lecturer in Economics, University of Manchester 1926–29; Rockefeller Foundation Fellow 1929–30; Professor of Social Economics, University of Manchester, 1936–46; Stanley Jevons Professor of Political Economy, University of Manchester 1946–48; Professor of Economic Organization, University of Oxford 1948–69; Emeritus Fellow of Merton College 1948. Visiting Professor in the University of Chicago 1953–54; Visiting Professor, Princeton Univ. 1961; Dir. of the Industrial Policy Group 1969–74; Economic Adviser, Arthur Guinness Son & Co. Ltd. *Publications:* Wages and Labour in the Cotton Spinning Industry (with E. M. Gray); the Juvenile Labour Market (with Sylvia Jewkes); Ordeal by Planning; The Sources of Invention (with D. Sawers and Richard Stillerman); The Genesis of the British National Health Service (with Sylvia Jewkes); Value for Money in Medicine (with Sylvia Jewkes); Public and Private Enterprise; The New Ordeal by Planning. *Address:* Entwood, Boars Hill, Oxford.

**JHA, Lakshimi Kant.** Indian. Governor Jamma and Kashmir State. *B.* 1913. *Educ.* Benares Hindu University (BA); Cambridge University (BA Hons). *M.* Mekhala. *S.* 1. *Daus.* 2. *Career:* Deputy Secretary, Government of India Supply Dept., 1942–46; Chief Controller, Imports & Exports, 1947–50; Chmn.: Contracting Parties, G.A.T.T., 1957–58; U.N. Interim Cttee. for Co-ordination of International Commodity Arrangements, 1959–61; Jt. Secy., Ministry of Commerce & Industry, 1950–56; Secy.: Ministry of Heavy Industries, 1957–60; Ministry of Finance, Dept. of Economic Affairs, 1960–64; to Prime Minister, 1964–67; Gov. Reserve Bank of India 1967–70; Ambassador to U.S. 1970–73; Chmn. U.N. Group, Multinational Corp. 1973–74; Gov. Jamma and Kashmir State since 1973; Chmn., Indirect Taxes Enquiry Cttee. 1976—; Chmn., Commonwealth Group of Industrial Specialists 1976—. *Publications:* Shortages & High Prices: The Way Out. *Address:* Raj Bhawan, Stringer, Kashmir, India.

**JOERGES, Harald**, Dr jur. German. Gen. Dir., Deutsche Bundesbank; Head of the Department of International Organizations and Agreements (Ret'd. 1975). *B.* 1909. *Educ.* Student of Law in Lausanne, Berlin and Göttingen. *Career:* Legal Adviser 1931; Dr. iur (Göttingen) 1933; Legal Assessor in Berlin 1934; *M.* Dr. Ing. Maria J. Heyden 1939. *S.* Christian. *Dau.* Franziska. Official of the former Reichs Ministry of Economics, Berlin 1934–45. *Publications:* Foreign Trade and Inter-Zonal Traffic (loose-leaf collection since 1954), German Economic Service, Cologne (with Kühne); International Monetary Fund, World Bank IFC and IDA (with Schleiminger) 1965 (Knapp/Verlag, Frankfurt/Main); numerous articles and book reviews. *Member:* Deutsch.-franzosische Gessellschaft, Frankfurt/Main. *Address:* Anton-Radl-Pfad 12, Frankfurt/Main; and *office* Deutsche Bundesbank, Wilhelm-Epstein, Str. 14, Frankfurt/Main, Germany.

**JOHN, Robert Michael.** British diplomat. *B.* 1924. *Educ.* Merchant Taylors' School, Sandy Lodge. *M.* 1952, Anne Phebe Clifford Smith. *Daus.* 2. *Career:* Indian Army (9th Jat Regt.) 1942–47; Foreign Office 1950–52; Second Secy. Commissioner-General's Office Singapore 1952–56; First Secy. British Embassy, Rio de Janeiro 1956–60: Foreign

Office 1960–64; First Secy., later Counsellor (Commercial) British Embassy Warsaw 1964–67; British Consul-General, Osaka, Japan 1967–71; Minister (Commercial) Rio de Janeiro 1971–72; British Consul-General, Rio de Janeiro 1972–74; British Ambassador, Panama since 1974. *Club:* Travellers. *Address:* British Embassy, Panama; and c/o Foreign and Commonwealth Office, London, S.W.1.

**JOHNS, Alan Tutton**, CBE, PhD (Cantab). New Zealand scientist. *B.* 1917. *Educ.* MSc (N.Z.); PhD (Cantab); FRSNZ. *M.* 1943. Marion Carvile Jacobs. *S.* Brian, Ian, Tony, David and Douglas. *Career:* With Second N.Z. Expeditionary Force (Army) 1941–45; at Clare College, Cambridge 1945–48; on Staff of Plant Chemistry Div. 1949–56, Director 1956–65. Director, Plant Chemistry Division, D.S.I.R., Palmerston North 1956–65. Pro-Chancellor, Massey University 1963–68; Mem., National Research Adv. Council 1966–77; Dir.-Gen., Ministry of Agriculture & Fisheries 1968–77; Mem., F.A.O. Council, Rome 1969–72, 1975–76; Chmn., F.A.O./W.H.O. Codex Alimentarius Cttee. on Meat Hygiene 1971—; Mem., N.Z. Wool Board 1974–77; Chmn., University Grants Cttee, 1977—. Author of 47 scientific papers. Commonwealth Fund Fellow 1954–55, Univ. of California. *Member:* Royal Inst. of Chemistry; N.Z. Inst. of Chemistry; Member Royal Socy. of N.Z.; Animal Production Socy.; N.Z. Grasslands Assn. *Awards:* Commander, Order of the British Empire, 1977; DSc (h.c.), Cant. *Address:* University Grants Committee, P.O. Box 12–348, Wellington, New Zealand.

**JOHNS, Frederic Peter.** Australian company director; *B.* 1905. *Educ.* Wesley Coll. Melbourne. *M.* 1930, Ena Margaret Clarke. *S.*1. *Daus.* 2. *Career:* Chmn. Johns and Waygood Perry Engineering Ltd. and subsidiary companies. Dir.: Mount Lyell Mining & Rly. Co. Ltd., Renison Ltd., National Mutual Life Association of Australasia Ltd., The Commercial Banking Company of Sydney Ltd., Australian Equity Corp. Ltd. *Member:* Cttee. of Management, Royal Children's Hospital. *Address:* 162 Mont Albert Road, Canterbury, Vic., Australia.

**JOHNSON, Arno Hallock.** American. *B.* 1901. *Educ.* Michigan State Univ. (BS Mech Eng) and Harvard Graduate School of Business Administration, Harvard Univ. (MBA 1924). *M.* 1925, Marian Lettenberger. *S.* Elliott Hallock and Dean Marshall. *Career:* Research Supervisor, Bureau of Business Research, Harvard, 1924–26; Market Analyst, J. Walter Thompson Co. 1926–29 (Dir. Research 1932–56; Vice-Pres. 1946); Dir. Research, J. Walter Thompson Co. Ltd., Montreal 1930–31, and London, England, 1931–32. Vice-President and Senior Economist. J. Walter Thompson Co., New York City 1956—. Member, Market Research Council of N.Y. (Past Sec.-Treas., Vice-Pres. and Pres. 1940–41); Chmn. Bd. of Directors, Advertising Research Foundation; member American Statistical Assn., American Marketing Assn., (Vice-Pres. 1954–55), Tau Beta Pi, Alpha Delta Sigma, Pi Alpha Mu, Scabbard and Blade, Acacia; Mason; Republican; member, Editorial Board, Harvard Business Review. *Publications:* several books on economics, including Market Potentials (1948); Consumer Purchasing Power (1949); Marketing Opportunities (1950); Hidden Pressure for Expansion (1953); The Challenge to America (1955); Advertising: a Dynamic Force in Economic Growth (1961); Explosive Growth of World Markets Ahead (1961); Are we Shackling Economic Growth by Overlooking the Consumer? (1962); The Decade of Opportunity. World-Wide 1966 to 1975 (1965); The American Market of The Future (1966). Delivered speech '57 Million Jobs—A Post-War Goal and Opportunity', before Governor's Conference, Mackinac Island (July 1945) and to clubs; initial winner of annual American Marketing Association award for Leadership in Marketing; Hall of Fame in Distribution, Boston Conference on Distribution, 1953. *Club:* Harvard (N.Y.C.). *Address:* 701 East Camino Real, Boca Raton, Fla., U.S.A.; and *office* c/o J. Walter Thompson Co., 420 Lexington Avenue, New York City, U.S.A.

**JOHNSON, David Gale.** American professor of economics. *B.* 1916. *Educ.* Iowa State Coll. (BS 1938, PhD 1945), Univ. of Wisconsin (MS 1939), and Univ. of Chicago. *M.* 1938. Helen Wallace. *S.* 1. *Dau.* 1. *Career:* Prof. of Agricultural Economy, Iowa State Coll. 1941–44; Univ. of Chicago (Research Assoc., Asst. Prof., Assoc. Prof., Prof. of Economics) 1944—, Assoc. Dean of Div., of Social Sciences 1957–60. Dean, Division of the Social Sciences 1960–70. Acting Director, Univ. of Chicago Library 1971–72; Chmn. Dept. of Economics, Univ. Chicago 1971–75; Vice-President and Dean of Faculties since 1975. *Member:* President's National Advisory Commission on Food and Fibre, 1965–67; Division of Behavioral Sciences, National Academy of Sciences, Amer. Economic Assn.; Commission on Population Growth and the American Future, 1970–72; Pres. Amer. Farm Economic Assn.; 1964–65, Fellow 1967; Pres. National Opinion Research Center 1962–75. Research Council 1968–75; Phi Kappa Phi; Alpha Zeta. *Publications:* Forward Prices for Agriculture (1947); Trade and Agriculture (1950); Grain Yields and the American Food Supply (with R. Gustafson, 1962); World Agriculture in Disarray (1973). *Address:* Univ. of Chicago, 1126 East 59th Street, Chicago, Ill. 60637, U.S.A.

**JOHNSON, Derek Harry.** British, *B.* 1921. *Educ.* Harrow. *M.* (1) 1952, Diana Clare Fitzgibbon. *S.* 1. *Dau.* 1. (2) 1973, Joan Elizabeth Clinch. *Career:* Chmn. H. & R. Johnson-Richards Tiles Ltd.; Johnson Tiles (Pty.) Ltd.; H. & R. Johnson (India) Ltd.; H. & R. Johnson (Aust.) Pty. Ltd.; H. & R. Johnson (Canada); H. & R. Johnson Inc.; H. & R. Johnson (N.Z.) Ltd.; Richards Ceramic (Pty.) Ltd.; Richard Tiles (Aust.) Pty. Ltd.; Ceramic Aust. Pty. Ltd.; Philkeram-Johnson S.A.; Malkin Tiles Ltd.; H. R. Johnson Ltd. (Hereford); H. & R. Johnson (Trent); Thos. Peake Engineers Ltd.; Drayton Kiln Co. Ltd.; Building Adhesives Ltd.; Stoke Central Offices Ltd.; British Ceramic Tile Council and Johnson Quarry Tiles. *Clubs:* Country, Johannesburg. *Address:* Boden Hall, Scholar Green, Ches., and *office* Highgate Tile Works, Tunstall, Stoke on Trent, Staffs.

**JOHNSON, Ernest Clayton, Jr.** American consulting engineer. *B.* 1903. *Educ.* University of Illinois (BSc); Yale-Sheffield Scientific School (MSc). *M.* (1) 1934, Jean S. Hill (*D.*1954). *S.* 2. *Daus.* 2. *M.* (2) 1957, Mrs. Neill P. Overman. *Career:* Engineer, hydrometallurgy, Inspiration (Ariz.) Copper Co. 1926–29; Development Engineer, non-ferrous metals, Western Electric Co., Kearney, N.J. 1929–32; Research Engineer, electro-metallurgy, U.S. Metals Refining Co., Carteret, N.J. 1933–34; with Gibbs & Hill Inc., Consulting Engineers, Designers and Constructors, N.Y. City 1934–53; successively Asst. Engineer (1934–39), Engineer (1936–46), Vice-Pres.-Sec. (1939–45), Dir. (1941), Exec. Vice-Pres. (1945–48), Chmn.-Pres. (1948–53). *Member:* Port of New York Authority Engineering Board 1948–56. Mason. *Address:* 7236 Pine Needle Road, Sarasota, Fla., 33581, U.S.A.

**JOHNSON, Hon. George.** Canadian (Icelandic origin). *B.* 1920. *Educ.* University of Manitoba (BSc; MD 1950; LMCC 1950). *M.* 1943, Doris Marjorie Blondal. *S.* 2. *Daus.* 4. *Career:* M.L.A. for Grimli constituency 1958—. Minister of Health and Welfare 1958; Minister of Health 1961. Minister of Education, Province of Manitoba, Canada 1963–68; Minister of Health and Social Services, 1968–69. *Member:* Canadian and Manitoba Medical Associations; General Practitioners Association. Conservative. *Clubs:* Kinsmen; Masonic Lodge. *Address:* c/o Legislative Assembly, Winnipeg, Man., Canada.

**JOHNSON, Henry Clay.** American insurance executive and lawyer. *B.* 1910. *Educ.* Univ. of Notre Dame (AB 1932; JD 1934) and Catholic University of America (LLM 1935). *M.* 1945, Rosemary Fitzpatrick. *S.* Michael Clay and Peter H. *Daus.* Catherine S. and Anne Marie. *Career:* Counsel for Reconstruction Finance Corp. 1935–41; Special Asst. to President of N.Y. Stock Exchange 1941; returned to Reconstruction Finance Corp. to resume work in connection with the Government rubber procurement programme during World War II, serving as Vice-President and General Counsel of Rubber Development Corporation; also active in formation of Government war damage insurance programme, serving as Vice-Pres. of War Damage Corp. 1941–45; joined Royal-Globe Insurance group as General Counsel 1945, subsequently becoming Pres., Chmn. of the Board, and Dir., of all companies in the group; currently Counsel to firm of McCarthy, Fingar, Donovan & Alatthaar, White Plains, N.Y.; former Chmn. Underwriters Laboratories; Member Bd. Dirs. Lincoln First Banks, Inc. of Rochester N.Y.; Dir. Nat. Bank of Westchester. Law Adv. Council Univ. of Notre Dame; former Pres. United Hospital Port Chester 1967–75; Mayor, City of Rye, N.Y., 1962–65. *Member:* Amer. Bar. Assn.; New York State Bar Assn.; Insurance Socy. of New York; The Pilgrims of the United States. *Award:* Knight of Malta; Knight of Holy Sepulchre. *Clubs:* Manursing Island; University (New York). *Address:* 164 Grandview Avenue, Rye, N.Y. 10580, U.S.A.

**JOHNSON, Herbert Fisk.** American. *B.* 1899. *Educ.* Cornell Univ. (AB); LLD, Northland College 1958, Univ. of Wisconsin 1963; Dr. Hum. Law, Carthage Coll. 1963—. *M.* (1) 1941, Irene Purcell. *S.* Samuel Curtis. *Dau.* Karen (Keland) (2)

1974, Georgea W. Cushman. *Career:* Chairman Emeritus, S. C. Johnson & Son, Inc., Racine, Wis., U.S.A.; National Industrial Conference Board (N.Y.C.). *Member:* Hon. Trustee, Council of Profit Sharing Industries. Trustee: Profit Sharing Research Foundation; member-at-large, National Council, Boy Scouts of America; Trustee Emeritus Cornell Univ., Northland College (Ashland, Wis.) and Ashville (N.C.) School. Dir., Univ. of Wisconsin Foundation, Madison, Wis.; Hon. Chmn. The Johnson Foundation Inc.; Trustee: The James S. Kempter Foundation; U.S. Cttee. of the Dag Hammarskjold Foundation, and People-to-People Program. Chevalier, National Order of Southern Cross Brazil 1957. *Clubs:* American (London); Racine Country; University (Milwaukee); University (Chicago); Metropolitan (New York); Bohemian (San Francisco). *Address:* 4400 Lighthouse Drive, Racine, Wis.; and *office* S. C. Johnson & Son, Inc., Racine, Wis. 53403, U.S.A.

**JOHNSON, Howard Cooper, Jr.** American. *B.* 1909. *Educ.* Swarthmore College (AB 1930); Harvard (MBA 1932); Centre de Préparation aux Affaires, Chambre de Commerce, Paris (Grad.). *M.* 1945, Betty Doan Young. *S.* Richard. *Daus.* Pamela and Christina. *Career:* Investment Banking 1933–41; Stroud & Co., Philadelphia 1933–34; Lazard Frères & Co., N.Y. 1934–36; Morgan Stanley & Co., N.Y. 1936–41; U.S.N. Material Inspection Administration, Washington 1941–43; Assistant to Secretary, Joint Chiefs of Staff, U.S. Navy, Washington 1943–45; U.N. Conference on International Regulations, San Francisco, 1945; with Office of U.N. Affairs, Department of State 1945–52; Asst. Chief, Division of International Security Affairs 1947 (Chief 1947–49); Adviser on Planning, U.N. Planning Staff 1949–51; National War College 1951–52; Special Asst. to Dir. of Psychological Strategy Board, 1952; Ford Foundation 1952–55; Asst. to Chmn. of Board, U.S. Steel Corp. 1956–60; Dir., Stockholder Relations, 1960–63; Dir., New York Office, International Bank for Reconstruction & Development, and International Finance Corp., 1963–67; Pres. World Banking Corp. Nassau 1968–72; Vice-Pres. Aspen Inst. for Humanistic Studies 1972; Pres. The Plasmine Corp. 1972–73. *Member:* Socy. of Friends. *Address:* South Freeport Road, Box 81, South Freeport, Maine 04078, U.S.A.

**JOHNSON, James, MP.** British Politician. *B.* 1908. *Educ.* Leeds Univ.—BA; London Univ.—DPA. *M.* 1937, Evelyn Green. *Dau.* 1. *Career:* Schoolmaster, Queen Elizabeth Grammar Sch., Atherstone 1931–34; Scarborough High Sch. 1934–43; Bablake Sch., Coventry 1943–48; Coventry Tech. Coll. 1948–50; MP (Lab.) for Rugby 1950–59; Trade Union Organiser, Kenya 1960–61; Education Adviser, Republic of Liberia 1961–64; MP (Lab.) for Hull West since 1964. Fellow, Royal Geographical Soc. *Decorations:* Knight Commander, Star of Africa (1st class). *Address:* 70 Home Park Road, London, SW19; and *office* House of Commons, London, SW1A 0AA.

**JOHNSON, James Kimball.** *B.* 1901. *Educ.* Case Inst. of Technology BSc; MSc). *M.* 1960, Virginia Knapp. *S.* James Kimball, Jr. *Career:* Civil and Sanitary Engineer 1924–32; Public Welfare Administrator 1933–41; Regional Executive, War Manpower Commission, and U.S. Employment Service, 1942–48; Regional Director, U.S. Department of Health, Education and Welfare 1948–54. Director, The Cleveland Foundation 1954. *Publications:* articles on public welfare and philanthropy, published in various magazines. Phi Kappa Psi and Tau Beta Pi fraternities; Distinguished Service Award, from United Appeal of Greater Cleveland 1959. Board member of various health and welfare organizations in Cleveland; Officer, National Council on Community Foundations; Board member, Shaker Heights Library, Ohio Citizens Council for Health & Welfare. *Member:* Amer. Socy. for Public Administration; formerly Trustee, Foundation Library Centre, New York City. *Club:* Mid-day (Cleveland). *Address: office* 700 National City Bank Bldg., Cleveland, Ohio 44114, U.S.A.

**JOHNSON, Olafur O.** Icelandic company director. *B.* 1931. *Educ.* Valley Forge Military Acad., Nichols Coll. (ABA) and Adelphi Coll. U.S.A. *M.* 1954 Gudrun Gunnlaugsdottir. *S.* Fridthjofur, Gunnlaugur and Olafur. *Dau.* Helga Gudrun. *Career:* Dir.: O. Johnson & Kaaber hf.; Arvakur hf.; Drangar hf.; Heimilistacki sf.; Chmn. Iceland Food Centre Ltd., London; Pres., Jnr. Chamber, Iceland 1964; Representative in Iceland for Confederation of British Industries. Dir. Icelandair Loftleidir Icelandic Airlines, Geysir hf.; Member of Board, Chamber of Commerce of Iceland 1956–58, 1962–63, and 1965–72. *Address:* Neshagi 8, Reykjavik, Iceland.

**JOHNSON, Richard Lester.** American certified public accountant. *B.* 1909. *Educ.* University of Illinois (BS with Hons.); Graduate School of Business Administration, Harvard University (MBA with Distinction). *M.* 1940, Ruth Twenhoefel. *Career:* Vice-Pres. Finance, Martin Aircraft Co., Baltimore, Jan. 1950–May 1952; Controller, Economic Co-operation Administration in Greece, Germany, U.S. Department of State, Jan.–Dec. 1949; Asst. to Vice-Pres.-Controller, Douglas Aircraft Co., Santa Monica, Jan. 1942–Dec. 1948; Asst. Manager: Investment Research, The Northern Trust Co., Chicago 1934–41; Manager, Special Financial Projects; Assistant Treasurer, Ford Motor Co. 1952–60; Dir.: Ford Motor Credit Co., American Road Insurance Co. Treasurer, Ford Motor Company, Dearborn, Mich., U.S.A., Jan. 1961–May 1966. Financial Consultant since June 1966. *Publications:* Co-author, Supplemental Unemployment Benefit Plans; several articles on economic financial, industrial relations and related subjects in various financial and business journals. American Institute of Certified Public Accountants; Phi Beta Kappa; Swiss American Society (Bern). *Club:* Rotary (Interlaken). *Address:* Jungfraustrasse 69, 3800 Interlaken, Switzerland.

**JOHNSON, Robert White.** Company director. *B.* 1912. *Educ.* Rossall School. *M.* 1950, Jill Margaret Preston. *S.* Robert Charles, Timothy Stewart. *Dau.* Susan Monica. *Career:* with Messrs. Robert Bradford & Co. Ltd., London (Insurance Brokers) 1931–35; served in World War II, Officer in Dept. of the Provost Marshal, R.A.F. 1939–46; Director: Patent Shaft and Axletree Co. Ltd., Wednesbury, Staffs, 1946–51; Cammell Laird & Co. Ltd. 1946–70; Metropolitan-Cammell Carriage and Wagon Co. Ltd., Birmingham 1946–64; North Western Line Mersey Ltd. 1964–70; La Mont Steam Generator Ltd., London 1951–54; Bradley Shipping Ltd., Scottish Aviation Ltd.; Director of Coast Lines Ltd., 1968–71. *Address:* The Oaks, Well Lane, Heswall, Wirral, Merseyside, L60 8NE.

**JOHNSON, Samuel Curtis.** American business executive. *B.* 1928. *Educ.* Cornell University (BA and Harvard Business School (MBA). *M.* 1954, Imogene Powers. *S.* Samuel Curtis III and Herbert Fisk III. *Daus.* Helen Powers and Winifred Conrad. *Career:* With S. C. Johnson & Son Inc.: Asst. to Pres. Racine 1954–55; New Products Director 1955–58; Service Products Division Vice-Pres. 1958–60; Vice-Pres. & Regional Director, Johnson's Wax International (London) 1960–62; International Vice-Pres. 1962–63; Exec. Vice-Pres. 1963–66; Pres. 1966–67. Chairman & President, S. C. Johnson & Son Inc., Racine, Wis. 1967—. Director, Deere & Co., Heritage Bank; Inland Financial Corp.; Chmn. Johnson Foundation Inc.; Chairman, The Prairie School. Trustee: Eisenhower Exchange Fellowships; Cttee. for Economic Development. *Publications:* How to Organize for New Products (Harvard Business Review); How Common is the Common Market? (Business Horizons Magazine of Indiana University). *Member:* Public Trustee, Mayo Fdn.; Trustee and mem. Exec. Cttee. Board Cornell University, U.S. Council International Chamber of Commerce; Chi Psi Fraternity; Visiting Committee, Harvard Business School; Business Cttee. for the Arts; U.S. Dept. of Commerce International U.S. Chamber of Commerce; Chmn. Racine Environment Cttee., New Advisory Council for Minority Enterprises; Steering Cttee., National Urban Coalition: Trustee American Crafts Council, selected as "International Advertising Man of the Year" by International Advertising Assn., in London 1967. *Clubs:* Cornell (N.Y. and Milwaukee), Harvard Business School Club (Milwaukee); Bluffs (Canada); Crane Lake Game Preserve (Bath, Ill.); Racine Country; Somerset; University (Milwaukee); American (London). *Address:* 4815 Lighthouse Drive, Racine, Wis., U.S.A.; and *office* 1525 Howe Street, Racine, Wis., U.S.A.

**JOHNSON, U. Alexis.** American diplomat. *B.* 1908. *Educ.* Occidental College, AB (1931); Georgetown Univ. School of Foreign Service. *M.* 1932, Patricia Ann Tillman. *S.* 2. *Daus.* 2. *Career:* Joined USA State Dept., language officer Tokyo 1935–37; Seoul, Korea—Tientsin, China 1937–39; Mukden, Manchuria 1940–42; 2nd. Secy. American Embassy, Rio de Janeiro 1942–44; American Consul, Manila; detailed headquarters SCAP Tokyo 1945; Consul-General, Yokohama 1947–50; Deputy Dir. Office NE Asian Affairs 1950, Director 1951; Depity Asst. Secy. Bureau FE Affairs 1951–53; Ambassador to Czechoslovakia 1953–58 (detailed co-ord. Geneva Conf 1954–55); U.S, Rep to Geneva Amb. Negotiations with Communist China for release US–Chinese citizens 1955–58; Ambassador to Thailand–SEATO Council 1958–61; Deputy Under-Secy. State for Political Affairs 1961–64; Deputy Ambassador to Vietnam 1964–65; Deputy Under-Secy. of State for Political Affairs 1965–66; Ambassador in Japan 1966–69; Under Secy. State for Political Affairs

1969–73; Ambassador-at-Large, Chief of US Delegation to Strategic Arms Limitation Talks with USSR since 1973. *Member:* American Foreign Service Assn. (Pres. 1963–64, 1965–66). *Decoration:* Medal of Freedom 1946. *Awards:* Hon LLD (1957); Career Service Award, Nat. Civil Service League (1964); Rockefeller Public Service (1965); President's Dist. Civilian Service (1971). *Club:* Chevy Chase. *Address:* 3133 Connecticut Ave, N.W., Washington DC 20008; and *office* Dept. of State (S/AJ), Washington DC 20520.

**JOHNSON SMITH, Geoffrey.** BA, MP. British politician. *B.* 16 April 1924. *Educ.* Charterhouse School; Lincoln Coll., Oxford Univ. Bachelor of Arts. *M.* 1951, Jeanne Pomeroy, MD. *S.* 2. *Dau.* 1. *Career:* Royal Artillery Captain 1942–47; Lincoln Coll. Oxford Univ. 1947–49; Information Officer, British Consulate Gen. San Francisco 1950–52; BBC. TV. Current Affairs, Interviewer and Reporter 1953–59; MP. Holborn and St. Pancras South 1959–64; Private Parly. Secy. to Parly. Secy. Board of Trade 1960–62 and Minister of Pensions 1962–64; Member of Parliament for East Grinstead Sussex since 1965; Opposition Whip 1965; Vice Chmn. Conservative Party Organization 1965–71; Under Secy. of State for Defence (Army) 1971–72; Parly. Secy. Civil Service Department 1972–74. *Clubs:* Travellers. *Address:* House of Commons, London, S.W.1.

**JOHNSTON, Hon. Lord.** A Senator of the College of Justice in Scotland. *B.* 1 Feb. 1907. *Educ.* Aberdeen Grammar School; St. John's College, Oxford (MA); University of Edinburgh. *M.* 1936, Doris Isobel Kidd. *S.* 2. *Daus.* 2. *Career:* Served World War II, Lt.-Col. R.A. K.C. 1947. Solicitor-General for Scotland 1947–Oct. 1951; M.P. (Lab.) for Paisley 1948–Jan. 1961. Hon. Fellow R.I.A.S. 1970. *Address:* Dunosdale, 22 Cammo Crescent, Barnton, Edinburgh, Scotland.

**JOHNSTON, Alton Vincent.** Canadian. *B.* 1909. *Educ.* Queen's University Kingston, Ontario (BScEng). *M.* 1940, Grace Irene Gray. *S.* 2. *Career:* With Canadian National Railways: various positions in operating and maintenance departments 1927–40; Asst. Div. Engr. 1940–42, Div. Engr. 1942–46; Office Engr. and Asst. Chief Engr., Central Region 1946–50, and System 1950–55; Chief Engr., System, Canadian National Railways, June 1955–68. General Manager, International Consulting Division, Canadian National Railways, 1968–71; Pres. Canac Consultants Ltd. (subsidiary of CN) 1971–74; Exec. Consultant 1974–75. *Member:* Amer. Railway Engineering Assn. (Pres. 1965); Engineering Inst. of Canada; Corpn. of Engineers of Quebec; Assn. of Professional Engineers of Province of Ontario. *Address:* 18 Woodland Road, St. Thomas, Ontario, N5P 1P4.

**JOHNSTON, Edgar Charles,** DFC. Australian aviation expert. *B.* 30 April 1896. *Educ.* Guilford Grammar School, Western Australia; University of Western Australia. *M.* 1921, M. A. Gibb Maitland. *S.* 1. *Dau.* 1. *Career:* Served in World War I; Superintendent of Aerodromes, Civil Aviation Department 1921; Deputy Controller of Civil Aviation 1929; Representative on Air Accidents Investigation Committee; Acting Controller 1931; Chairman, Inter-Departmental Committee on Air Communications; Controller of Civil Aviation 1933–36; Controller-General of Civil Aviation and Chairman, Civil Aviation Board 1936–39; Australian representative, Tasman Air Commission 1940–47; Assistant Director-General of Civil Aviation 1939–55; member, Australian National Airlines Commission 1946–52; International Adviser to Qantas Empire Airways 1955–67. *Address:* 12 Southey Street, Sandringham, Victoria, Australia.

**JOHNSTON, Ian Strachan,** CBE, DSO and Bar, QC. Canadian barrister and solicitor. *B.* 1908. *Educ.* Upper Canada College Preparatory; Bishop Ridley College; Royal Military College (Kingston, Ont.); Osgoode Hall. *M.* 1947, Debora E. Armstrong (née Coulson). *S.* Strachan Leys. *Daus.* Alice Leys and Victoria. *Career:* Called to Bar 1933; associated with firm of Tilley, Johnston, Thomson & Parmenter; Partner, Johnston, Tory & Johnston 1936; Commissioned 48th Highlanders of Canada, C.A.S.F. 1939; Commanded 48th Highlanders 1943; Commanded 11th Canadian Infantry Brigade 1944; Commanded 5th Canadian Armoured Division 1945; Partner, Johnston, Heighington & Johnston 1946. Partner, Lash, Johnston, Sheard & Pringle, Toronto 1964–71. *Awards:* CD, ED, LLD, Chevalier, Legion of Honour; Croix de Guerre avec Palme. *Address:* 24 Chestnut Park Road, Toronto 5, Ont., Canada.

**JOHNSTON, James Campbell,** CBE, ACA, Dip.Com. *B.* 1912. *Educ.* Melbourne Univ. (Dipl. Com.); Associate, Inst. of Chartered Accountants in Australia. *M.* 1938, Agnes Thomas. *S.* Richard Edwin and Thomas Campbell. *Dau.* Rosemary Anne. *Career:* Member of the Stock Exchange of Melbourne 1947—. (Chairman 1972—; Member of the Committee 1954—). Senior Partner, J. B. Were & Son, Share Brokers Melbourne 1967—. Chairman: Capel Court Corp. Ltd., and Australian Foundation Investment Co. *Clubs:* Melbourne; Australian; Athenaeum; Royal Melb.; V.R.C. *Address:* 13 Monaro Road, Kooyong, Vic.; and *office* 379 Collins Street, Melbourne, Vic., Australia.

**JOHNSTON, Sir John Baines,** GCMG, KCVO.HM Diplomatic Service (ret'd.). *B.* 1918. *Educ.* Banbury Grammar School, and Queen's Coll., Oxford (MA; Eglesfield Scholar). *M.* 1969, Elizabeth Mary Crace. *S.* 1. *Career:* War Service 1940–46 (Adjt. 1st Battalion Gordon Highlanders 1944; D.A.Q.M.G. 30 Corps. District 1945); Assistant Principal, Colonial Office 1947. Principal 1948; Asst. Secretary, West African Council, Accra 1950–51; Principal Private Secy. to Secy. of State for the Colonies 1953; Assistant Secretary 1956; Head of Far Eastern Dept., Colonial Office 1956; transferred to Commonwealth Relations Office 1957; Deputy High Commissioner for U.K. in South Africa 1959–61; High Commissioner in Sierra Leone 1961–63; in Federation of Rhodesia and Nyasaland 1963–64 in Rhodesia 1964–65. Asst. later Deputy Under-Secretary of State, Foreign & Commonwealth Office 1965–71: British High Commissioner in Malaysia 1971–74, in Canada 1974–78 (Ret'd.). *Clubs:* United Oxford & Cambridge (London), Rideau (Ottawa). *Address:* Earnscliffe, Sussex Drive, Ottawa, Canada.

**JOHNSTON, Hon. Raymond T.** Canadian. *B.* 1914. *Educ.* Ottawa University, St. Patrick's College. *M.* 1941, Grace Bowie. *Daus.* Gail, Ann (Beriau), Carol (Kavanagh), Kim, Mary (Lafleur, Jr.). *Career:* Elected Member of the National Union Party of the Province of Quebec, 1948; re-elected 1952–56–60–62–66; Party Whip from 1953–58. Apptd. Parliamentary Assistant to Minister of Tourism, Fish and Game for P.Q. 1958–60 and party whip 1960–66. Minister of Revenue, Province of Quebec, June 1966–70. *Awards:* Queen's Medal (World War II); Order of Knights of Gregory the Great. *Member:* Pontiac Lions Club (Hon.); Bishop Smith 4th Degree Knights of Columbus; Royal Canadian Legion; Deputy District Governor, Vice Commander. *Address:* Otter Lake, Pontiac County, P.Q., Canada.

**JOHNSTON, Robert E.** *Educ.* Allegheny High School Cumberland; Univ. Pittsburgh (Bachelor, Science Chemical Engineering). *Career:* Joined Bethlehem Steels, management trainees Group 1942; Supt. Industrial Engineering Dept., Steelton 1951; Plant Industrial Engineer 1956; Asst. Gen. Mgr., Sparrows Point 1960; Vice-Pres., Mfg. Products, Steel Operations, Bethlehem Steel Corporation 1972–74, Vice-Pres. Production, since 1974. *Member:* Assn. Iron & Steel Engineers; Amer. Iron & Steel Institutes. *Address:* Bethlehem Steel Corporation, Bethlehem, Pennsylvania.

**JOHNSTON, Russell,** MP. British Politician. *B.* 1932. *Educ.* Carbost Public School, Portree High School, Isle of Skye; Edinburgh Univ., MA (Hons) History; Moray House Coll. of Education. *M.* 1967, Joan Graham Menzies. *S.* 2. *Career:* Teacher, Liberton Secondary Sch., 1961–63; Research Asst., Scottish Liberal Party 1963–64; Liberal MP for Inverness since 1964; Member, European Parliament 1973–75, 1976—; Member, Royal Commission on Local Government in Scotland 1966–69; Leader, Scottish Liberal Party since 1974. *Publications:* Highland Development (1964); To be a Liberal (1972). *Clubs:* Scottish Liberal (Edinburgh). *Address:* Glendruidh, by Inverness IV1 2AA; and House of Commons, London, SW1A 0AA.

**JOHNSTONE, William Harcourt.** American. Director, April 1957–67, and Chairman, Finance Committee, Bethlehem Steel Corporation, July 1965–67 (retired). *B.* 1899. *Educ.* Univ. of Michigan (AB) and Harvard Univ. (LLB); Hon. LLD Lehigh Univ. *M.* 1935, Mildred Thomas. *Stepson* 1. Trustee, American Academy in Rome. *Clubs:* University, The Leash, Sky (N.Y.C.); Saucon Valley Country (Bethlehem). *Address:* 870 United Nations Plaza, New York, N.Y. 10017, U.S.A.

**JONATHAN, Rt. Hon. Chief Leabua.** The Prime Minister of Lesotho. *Address:* The Residence of the Prime Minister, Maseru, Lesotho.

**JONES, Rt. Hon. Aubrey,** PC. British economist and industrialist. *B.* 1911. *Educ.* London School of Economics (BScEcon.; 1st Cl. Hons., Gladstone Memorial Prizewinner, and Gerstenberg Post-graduate Scholar). *M.* 1948, Joan Godfrey-Isaacs. *S.* 2. *Career:* On foreign and editorial staffs of The

Times 1937–39 and 1947–48; served in World War II (Army Intelligence Staff, War Office, and Mediterranean); MP (U.) Birmingham, Hall Green, 1950–65; joined British Iron & Steel Federation 1949; General Director 1955; formerly Parly. Private Sec. to Minister of Materials; Minister of Fuel and Power Dec. 1955; Minister of Supply Jan. 1957–Oct. 1959. Formerly Director: Guest, Keen Iron & Steel. Co. Ltd. (renamed Guest, Keen & Nettlefolds Steel Co., Ltd., Jan. 1961), March 1960–65; Courtaulds Ltd., 1960–63; Staveley Industries Ltd., May 1962 (Chmn. 1964–65.) Chairman, National Board for Prices and Incomes 1965–70; Chmn., Laporte Industries (Holdings) Ltd. 1970–72; Dir., Thomas Tilling Ltd. 1970—; Chmn., Cornhill Insurance Co. Ltd. 1971–74; Dir. since 1971; Dir., Black & Decker Ltd. 1977—; Member, Plowden Cttee. of Enquiry into Aircraft Industry; Adviser to Nigerian Public Service Review Commission 1973–74; Economic Adviser to Iranian Govt. 1974; Panel Member, International Centre for Settlement of Investment Disputes 1974—. *Awards:* Hon. Fellow L.S.E. 1959; Member Court of Governors, 1964; Hon. Fellow Commoner, Churchill Coll. Cambridge, 1972–73; Pres., Oxford Energy Policy Club 1976—. *Publications:* The Pendulum of Politics (1946); Industrial Order (1950); The New Inflation—the Politics of Prices and Incomes (1973). *Address:* 4 Plane Tree House, Duchess of Bedford's Walk, London, W8 7QT.

**JONES, Bernard Thomas McColl.** Australian. *B.* 1918. *Educ.* Xavier Coll., Melbourne. *M.* 1942, Kathleen Mary Ryan. *S.* 4. *Dau.* 1. *Career:* Governing Dir., Bernard Jones (Aust.) Pty. Ltd. 1954–59; Chmn., Reckitt & Colman (Aust.) Pty. Ltd. *Member:* Royal Agricultural Society. *Clubs:* Pennant Hills Golf; Sydney Turf; American National. *Address: office* 239 Pacific Highway, Artarmon, N.S.W., Australia.

**JONES, Charles Beynon Lloyd,** Australian. Consul General of Finland. Officer, Order of Merit (Italy). *B.* 1932. *Educ.* Cranbrook School and University of Sydney. *Career:* Dir., David Jones Ltd., Sydney 1957—, Chairman of Directors 1963—. Pres., Retail Traders Association of N.S.W.; French Chamber of Commerce, Sydney (also Vice-Pres.); Vice-Chmn., Finnish Chamber of Commerce. Trustee: Sir Wm Dobell Art Foundation; Vice-Pres., Art Gallery of N.S.W.; Councillor, Australian Retailers Assn. *Club:* Royal Sydney Golf. *Address:* "Rosemont", 14 Rosemont Ave., Wollahra, Sydney, N.S.W.; and *office* David Jones Ltd., Sydney, N.S.W., Australia.

**JONES, Hon. Eric S.,** MHA. (District of Forgo, Sept. 1966—); *B.* 1914. *M.* 1940, Nina F. Smith. *S.* Eric R. *Daus.* Maxine (White), Doreen (Parrot) and Sharon. *Career:* Magistrate, Harbour Breton and Grand Banks 1944–56. Member South Coast Commission 1955–56, Minister of Highways, Government of Newfoundland and Labrador, Dec. 1964. Member Liberal Association. *Clubs:* Laurier; Masonic; Lions. *Address: office* Confederation Building, St. Johns, Nfld., Canada.

**JONES, Edmund Angus,** CMG. Australian. *B.* 1903. *Educ.* Christchurch Boy's High Schl., N.Z.; Harvard Univ., U.S.A. *M.* 1926, Elsie May Townley. *S.* Bryan Campbell and David Campbell. *Dau.* Rena. *Career:* Vacuum Oil Co. Pty. Ltd., New Zealand 1928–43, Gen. Mgr. 1939–43, Dir. Melbourne 1944–48; Director; Mobil Oil Australia Ltd., 1944–70. Standard Vacuum Oil Co., New York 1948–51; Dir., Vacuum Oil Co. Pty. Ltd., Melbourne 1951–54; Man. Dir., Mobil Oil, Australia Ltd. 1954–65; Chmn. 1962–67; Dir. Gilbert Lodge Holdings Ltd. 1965—; Equity Trustees Ltd. 1966—; Luke Ltd. 1966—; Liquid Air Aust. Ltd. since 1966. Fellow, Australian Inst. of Management; Fellow, Institute of Directors. *Publications:* various articles on management. *Clubs:* Athenaeum (Melbourne); Royal Melbourne Golf; Melbourne Rotary; Victoria Racing. *Address:* 61-546 Toorak Road, Toorak, Vic., Australia.

**JONES, Rt. Hon. Sir Edward Warburton.** British. Lord Justice of Appeal. *B.* 1912. *Educ.* Portora Royal School, Enniskillen N. Ireland; Trinity Coll. Dublin. *M.* (1) 1941, Margaret Anne Crosland Smellie (dec'd 1953). *S.* 3. (2) 1953, Ruth Buchan Smellie. *S.* 1. *Career:* Barrister-at-Law Bar of N. Ireland 1936; Private Soldier in Army 1939–40; Regimental Duties 1940–43; Asst. Adjutant-Gen. Allied Land Forces, South East Asia 1944–45; Queen's Counsel 1948—; Attorney-General, N. Ireland 1964–68; Call to Bar by Middle Temple London 1965; Judge, High Court N. Ireland 1968–72; Lord Justice of Appeal N. Ireland since 1972, Knighted 1973. *Clubs:* Army and Navy; Pall Mall, London. *Address:* The Lodge, Spa, Ballynahinch, Co. Down, Northern Ireland; and Craig-y-Mor, Trearddur Bay, Anglesey, N. Wales.

**JONES, Sir Glyn Smallwood,** GCMG, MBE. British. *B.* 1908. *Educ.* King's School, Chester, and St. Catherine's Society, Oxford Univ. (MA). *M.* 1942, Nancy Madoc Featherstone. *S.* 1 (decd.). *Dau.* 1. *Career:* Joined Colonial Service, later Overseas Civil Service in Northern Rhodesia; Cadet 1931; District Officer 1933; Commissioner for Native Development 1950; Acting Development Secy. 1956; Provincial Commissioner 1956; Resident Commissioner, Barotseland 1956; Secy. for Native Affairs 1958; Minister for Native Affairs and Chief Commissioner 1959, Chief Secretary, Nyasaland 1960–61, Governor 1961–64. Governor-General, Malawi 1964–66. *Clubs:* Athenaeum; Royal Commonwealth Society; Chester City. *Address:* Little Brandfold, Goudhurst, Kent, TN17 1JJ.

**JONES, Gwilym Wyn,** CBE. British Governor. *B.* 1926. *Educ.* Llanrwst Grammar Sch.; UCNW, Bangor—BA (Hons.). *M.* 1951, Ruth Thomas. *S.* 1. *Dau.* 1. *Career:* Admin. Officer, Gilbert & Ellice Is. Colony 1950–61; Admin. Officer 1961–67, Snr. Admin. Officer 1967–74, Dep. Chief Sec. 1974, & Sec. to Chief Minister & to Council of Ministers, Solomon Islands 1974–76; Governor, Montserrat since 1977. *Decorations:* Commander of the British Empire. *Address:* Government House, Montserrat.

**JONES, Sir Harry Ernest.** CBE. British diplomat. *B.* 1911. *Educ.* Stamford School; St. John's School, Cambridge. *M.* 1935, Phyllis Eva Dixon. *S.* 1. *Dau.* 1. *Career:* entered Northern Ireland Civil Service 1934; Asst. Secretary Ministry of Commerce 1942; Permanent Secretary 1955; Industrial Development Adviser in Great Britain for N.I. Ministry of Commerce 1969; Agent in Great Britain for Northern Ireland 1970–76. *Awards:* Knight Bachelor 1971; BA (Cantab). *Address:* 51 Station Road, Nassington, Peterborough.

**JONES, Sir Henry Frank Harding,** GBE, British. *B.* 1906. *Educ.* Harrow School and Cambridge Univ. (MA). *M.* 1934, Elizabeth Angela Langton. *S.* 3. *Dau.* 1. *Career:* Chmn. East Midlands Gas Board 1949–52; Dep. Chairman The Gas Council 1952–59. Chairman, The Gas Council, Jan. 1960–71. Chairman, British National Committee, World Energy Conference, May 1968–71, (Vice-Chmn. 1962–68); Vice-Chmn. International Executive Council 1970–73, Hon. Vice-Chmn. since 1973. *Publications:* articles, addresses and lectures in scientific and technical journals. *Members:* Institution of Civil Engineers; Institution of Gas Engineers (Hon. Member). Institution of Chemical Engineers. Hon. LLD Leeds University 1967; Hon. DSc Leicester University 1970; Hon. DSc. Salford 1971. *Clubs:* Athenaeum; Bath; M.C.C. *Address:* Pathacres, Weston Turville, Aylesbury, Bucks.

**JONES, Hervey West.** South African. *B.* 1892. *Educ.* Dalhousie University (Halifax, N.S., Canada); BA with Distinction. *M.* 1917, Gertrude Marion Murphy. *Dau.* Mrs. Hildred Edith Senger. *Career:* Managing Editor, The Halifax (N.S.) Chronicle 1925–32; Manager, New Consolidated Gold Fields Ltd., Johannesburg 1942–51; Director: Woodside Holdings Ltd. Life member, Royal Nova Scotia Yacht Squadron (Halifax). *Clubs:* Rand, Country (of Johannesburg). *Address:* Suikerbossie House, Bryanston, Johannesburg, South Africa.

**JONES, Jack (James Larkin),** CH, MBE, FCIT, FRSA. British Trade Union Official. *B.* 1913. *Educ.* Elementary School, Liverpool. *M.* 1938, Evelyn Mary Taylor. *S.* 2. *Career:* District Secretary Confederation, Engineering and Shipbuilding Unions 1939–55; Justice of the Peace 1950–63; National Exec. Cttee. Labour Party 1964–67; Deputy-Chmn. National Ports Council 1967—; Dir. Tribune 1968—; Gen. Council T.U.C. 1968—; General Secretary, Transport & General Workers Union since 1969; Vice-Pres. Internat. Transport Workers' Federation. *Member:* Exec. Bd. ICFTU and ETC; Chartered Inst. Transport; Royal Inst. Int. Affairs; Royal Socy. Arts, Manufacturers and Commerce. *Publications:* The Incompatibles (1968); Industry's Democratic Revolution (1974), Contributions. *Address:* 74 Ruskin Park House, Champion Hill, London S.E.; and *office* Transport House, Smith Square, London, S.W.1.

**JONES, John Hugh Mowbray.** Canadian industrialist (Ret.). *B.* 1905. *Educ.* Public Schools; Upper Canada College; University of Toronto (Graduated 1927, Mechanical Engineering—Hons.); Hon. DEng., Nova Scotia Technical College 1959. *M.* 1934, Phyllis Lucille Hodges. *S.* Daryl Douglas and Dereck Mowbray (twins). *Daus.* Jenepher (Cupitt), Sandra Kennedy (Caines) and Stephanie Cartwright (Evans). *Career:* With Engineering Department, Spanish River Pulp & Paper Company Ltd., 1927–28; Engineer, Abitibi Pulp & Paper Co. Ltd., 1928; With Mersey Paper Company

Ltd. (successively Resident Engineer, Chief Engineer, Mill Manager, Vice-President & Director, Pres. & Gen. Mgr.) 1928–58; Pres., Bowater's Newfoundland Pulp & Paper Mills Ltd. 1958. Mersey Paper Co. Ltd. became Bowater's Mersey Paper Co. Ltd. 1959; President, Bowaters Corp. of N. American 1962; Bowaters Case Corp., 1966; Ben's Holdings Ltd., Halifax; Director and Pres., White Point Beach Lodge Ltd., White Point (N.S.); Director and President, Chateau Bonne Entente Inc., Ste. Foy (P.Q.), and Glencannon Corp., Ste. Foy Dir., Halifax Development Ltd.; Hermes Electronic Ltd.; Dartmouth N.S. Dir., Halifax International Containers Ltd., Halifax; Chmn. Dir. Maritime Coastal Containers Ltd. Halifax; White Point Estates Ltd.; Lt.-Govt. Maritime Div., Kiwanis International 1937; Serving Brother, Order of St. John of Jerusalem; Chmn. of Board, Queens General Hospital Assn. (Liverpool) (N.S.); member: Assn. of Professional Engineers of Nova Scotia (Pres. 1944). Served in Reserve Army 1943–45 as Major and O.C. 20th (R) Field Co., R.C.E. Delta Kappa Epsilon. Conservative. Anglican. *Address:* Apt 5, 5885 Spring Garden Road, Halifax, Nova Scotia, Canada.

**JONES, Sir Philip Frederick,** Kt. 1971, ACA, AASA. British. *B.* 1912. *Educ.* Barker College, Sydney; ACA; AASA. *M.* 1942, Josephine Nancy Kirschlager. *Career:* With Department of the Treasury until 1951. General Manager, Herald and Weekly Times Ltd. 1953–63; Dir. since 1957, Vice-Chmn. 1966–70; Chmn. of Directors since 1970; Dir. since 1957; Chmn., West Australian Newspapers since 1971; Dir., Queensland Press Ltd. since 1970, Advertiser Newspapers, Adelaide, since 1974. *Clubs:* Melbourne; Athenaeum, V.R.C.; V.A.T.C.; Moonee Valley Racing Club; Metropolitan Golf. *Address:* 25 Griffith Street, New Farm, Brisbane, Queensland, Australia.

**JONES, Ronald Francis.** Australian banker. *B.* 1916. *Educ.* Sydney Boys' High School and Univ. of Sydney (BEc.). *M.* 1942, Eleanor Catherine Bulmer. *S.* 1. *Daus.* 2. *Career:* Senior Economist, I.M.F., Washington 1951–55; Superintendent Banking Operations, Reserve Bank of Australia 1960–63. Manager for Tasmania, Reserve Bank of Australia 1963—. *Member:* Economic Society of Australia and New Zealand; Australian Institute of Management (Fellow of); Counc. Royal Agric. Soc. of Tasmania. *Clubs:* The Tasmanian; Athenaeum; Kingston Beach Golf. *Address:* 66 Waimea Avenue, Sandy Bay, Tasmania; and *office* 111 Macquarie Street, Hobart, Tasmania.

**JONES, Sir Samuel (Owen),** Kt. 1966, FIREE (Aust.), FIE (Aust.), Chmn., Standard Telephones & Cables Pty. Ltd. 1968–76 (Man. Dir. 1961–69); Chmn.: Concrete Industries (Monier) Ltd. 1969–76, Austral Standard Cables Pty. Ltd. 1967–69 & 1972–75, & Export Finance & Insurance Corp. 1975–77; Dir., Overseas Corp. (Aus.) Ltd. 1969–75. *B.* 1905. *Educ.* Warracknabeal High Sch.; Univ. of Melbourne. *M.* 1932, Jean Sinclair. *Daus.* 2. *Career:* Engineering Branch, PMG's Dept. 1927–39; Lt. Col. commanding Div. Signal Unit, AIF abroad 1939–41; CSO Aust. Home Forces 1941–42; Dir. Radio & Signal Supplies, Min. of Munitions 1942–45; Technical Mgr., Philips Electrical Industries Pty. Ltd. 1945–50, Technical Dir. 1950–61; Chmn.: Telecommunications Co. of Australia 1956–61, Aust. Telecommunications Development Assn. 1967–70 (Mem. 1963–75), Consultative Council Exports Payments Insurance Corp. 1970–75; Dir., Television Equipment Pty. Ltd. 1960–61; Cannon Electric Aus. Pty. Ltd. 1964–68; National Pres., Australian Inst. of Management 1968–70; Councillor Chamber of Manufactures of NSW 1968–72; Mem., Govt.'s Industry Adv. Cttee. on Telecommunications 1955–72; Export Dev. Council 1969–74; Council, Macquarie Univ. 1969–74; Council, National Library of Australia 1971–74; Australian Universities Comm. 1972–75. *Publications:* several technical articles. *Clubs:* Union, Royal Automobile of Aus., Royal Sydney Yacht Squadron (all in Sydney); Naval & Military (Melbourne). *Address:* Apartment 11, 321 Edgecliff Road, Woollahra, NSW 2025; & "Mummuga Lodge", Dalmeny, NSW 2546, Australia.

**JONES, Walter Selby Kennedy,** QC, DCL, LLB. BA. *B.* 1919. *Educ.* King's Coll. and Dalhousie Univ. (BA 1940; LLB 1942) and King's Coll. (DCL 1958). *Career:* Read law with J. MacG. Stewart, QC, Halifax; called to Bar of Nova Scotia 1942; created QC 1957; practised law with Stewart, Smith, MacKeen & Rogers, in Halifax, N.S. 1946–49; entered private practice in Liverpool, N.S. 1949; Town Solicitor of Liverpool 1955–60. Served in World War II with Canadian Army 1942–45 (West N.S. Regt. and 3rd Bdge. HQ in Italy; retired to reserve with rank of Capt.). Elected to N.S. Legislature 1953; Speaker of Leg. Assembly 1957–60; Minister: Public Welfare & Provincial Secretary 1960–64, in Charge of Civil Defence 1962–64, and Under the Water Act 1962–65. Min. of Trade and Industry 1964–68; Commissioner of Atlantic Provinces at Expo. Montreal 1967; Minister of Finance and Economics 1968–69. Minister of Municipal Affairs 1969–70: Business Consultant 1971–74; Corporate Consultant Atlantic Region, Canadian National Railways 1971–74; Agent, Atlantic Canada of Mitsui and Co. Canada Ltd. 1972–74; Returned to practice of Law in Liverpool (N.S.) since 1974. Former member, Board of Governors: Univ. of Kings College, and King's College School, Windsor, N.S. Member, Nova Scotia and Canadian Bar Assns. *Address:* 212 Main Street (PO Box 1420), Liverpool, Nova Scotia, Canada.

**JONES, William James Kenyon.** MBE. British. *B.* 1911. *Educ.* Monmouth School; Jesus Coll., Oxford (BA). *M.* 1948, Barbara Esme Barton. *Dau.* 1. *Career:* with various Unilever Cos. 1933–45; Man. Dir., Birds Eye Holdings Ltd. 1945–50; Chmn. & Man. Dir., Ronson Products Ltd. (retd. 1975) Dir. Trade Promotion Services Ltd. *Award:* Bronze Star (U.S.) *Club:* Oxford & Cambridge University. *Address:* Knowle House, Froxfield, Marlborough, Wilts.

**JONSSON, Agnar Klemens.** Icelandic diplomat. *B.* 13 Oct. 1909. *Educ.* University of Iceland (Cand. jur.). *M.* 1944, Ólöf Bjarnadóttir. *Daus.* 2. *S.* 1. *Career:* Entered Foreign Service 1934; Acting Consul-General, New York 1941–42; Chief of Section, Ministry of Foreign Affairs 1942–44; Permanent Under-Secretary, Ministry of Foreign Affairs 1944–51; En. Ex. and Min. Plen. to Court of St. James's March 1951; En. Ex. and Min. Plen. to the Netherlands April 1951; Amb. Ex. and Plen. 1956; Ambassador to France, July 1956, and concurrently En. Ex. and Min. Plen. to Spain, Portugal, Belgium and Italy 1957, and also Amb. to Greece. March 1960; Secretary-General, Ministry of Foreign Affairs, Ambassador to Norway, 1969, and to Denmark 1976. Asst. to Turkey, Israel and Italy. *Awards:* Grand Cross, Orange Nassau; Grand Knight, Order of Falcon; Grand Cross, Order of Dannebrog (Denmark); Grand Cross, Order of St. Olav (Norway); King's Medal for Service in Cause of Freedom (Great Britain). *Publication:* Biographies of Icelandic Lawyers 1736–1964; The Central Administration of Iceland 1904–67. *Address:* Icelandic Embassy, Copenhagen, Denmark.

**JONSSON, Eysteinn.** Icelandic politician. *B.* 13 Nov. 1906. *Educ.* Co-operative Business College. *M.* 1932, Solveig Eyjolfsdóttir. *S.* Eyjólfur, Jon, Thorbergur, Finnur. *Daus.* Sigrídur, Olöf Steinunn. *Career:* Head of Tax Bureau, Reykjavik 1930–34; Minister of Finance 1934–39; Minister of Commerce 1939–42; Dir., Printworks Edda 1943–47; Minister of Education 1947–49; member (Progressive), Althing 1933–74; Leader of Parliamentary Party 1943–69; Leader of Party 1962–68; Vice-Pres., Co-operative Union of Iceland 1946–75, and Pres. since 1975; Minister of Finance 1950–58; Speaker of the United Althing 1971–74. Chmn. of Icelandic Nature Conservation (Board) Council since 1972. *Address:* Asvallkagata 67, Reykjavik, Iceland.

**JONSSON, John Erik.** *B.* 1901. *Educ.* Rensselaer Polytechnic Institute (ME 1922; Hon. Dr. Engineering 1959). *M.* 1923, Margaret Elizabeth Fonde. *S.* Philip R. and Kenneth A. *Dau.* Margaret (Charlton). *Career:* With Aluminium Co. of America 1922–23; Aluminium Index Co. (Alcoa subsidiary) 1923–27; Dumont Motor Car Co. Inc. 1927–29; Aluminium Co. of America 1929–30; Texas Instruments Inc. and predecessor company 1930—, President 1951–58; (Chairman of Board 1958–66; Honorary Chairman of the Board Texas Instruments Inc., Dallas, Tex. 1966–77, Hon. Dir. 1977—; Director Republic of Texas Corp. 1955—; Assoc. Dir., Citizens Bank, Richardson, Tx.; Assoc. Dir., Republic National Bank, Dallas, Tx.; President, Excellence in Education Foundation; Honorary Trustee, The Hockaday School, (Chmn. 1954–64); member, Bd. of Trustees, University of Dallas; Skidmore Coll., Saratoga Springs, N.Y.; Rensselaer Polytechnic Inst., Troy, N.Y.; Chmn., Bd. Lamplighter School, Dallas; Dallas/Ft. Worth Regional Airport 1968–77; Chmn., Educational Facilities Laboratories; Hon. Member, American Inst. Architects; Academy of Texas; Member, former Chmn., Bd. of Visitors, Tulance Univ.; Former Dir., Amer. Management Assn.; Member Bd. Dirs., Foundation for Callier Center and Communication Disorders; Mayor of Dallas 1964–71. *Awards:* Hon. DSc.; Hobart William Smith, and Austin Colleges; Hon. Degree, Univ. of Dallas Doctor of Civil Laws 1968. Hon. LLD Southern Methodist Univ.; Skidmore College; Carnegie-Mellon; Hon. Dr. Engineering, Rensselaer Polytechnic Inst., Troy 1959; Dr. of Humane Letters, Oklahoma Christian College; Amer. Socy. of Metals Advancement Research Award 1964; Society of Industrial Realtors

Industrialist of the Year Award 1965; Gantt Medal, 1968. Hoover Medal, 1970, National Academy Engineering Founders Medal 1974; Fortune Mag. (Bus. Hall of Fame) 1975 and many others. *Member:* Society of Exploration Geophysicists, Newcomen Society of North America. *Clubs:* Dallas Country; Dallas Petroleum; Brook Hollow Golf; Chaparral. *Address:* 3300 Republic Bank Tower, Dallas, Texas 75201.

**JOPLING, Thomas Michael,** MP. British Politician. *B.* 1930. *Educ.* Cheltenham Coll.; King's Coll., Newcastle upon Tyne—BSc Agric. *M.* 1958, Gail Dickinson. *S.* 2. *Career:* Mem., Thirsk Rural District Council 1958–64; mem., Nat. Council, Nat. Farmers' Union 1962–64; MP (Cons.) for Westmorland since 1964; Joint Sec., Cons. Parly. Agric. Cttee. 1966–70; PPS to Minister of Agric. 1970–71; an Asst. Gov. Whip 1971–73; a Lord Commissioner, HM Treasury 1973–74; an Opposition Whip, March–June 1974; an opposition spokesman on agriculture 1974–75; & 1976—; Shadow Minister of Agric. 1975–76. *Member:* UK Exec., Commonwealth Parly. Assoc. since 1974. *Club:* Beefsteak. *Address:* Ainderby Hall, Thirsk, North Yorks; & Pine Rigg, Windermere, Westmorland.

**JORDAN, Donald Lewis.** Business executive. *B.* 1896. *Educ.* Cluster Springs Academy, and American Institute of Banking (Grad.). *M.* 1924, Mary Preston Hughson (*D.* 1971). *S.* Donald Lewis, Jr. and Charles Frederick (*D.* 1976). *Career:* With First National Bank, Roanoke, Va. 1913–24; First National Exchange Bank, Roanoke 1925–27. With Johnson-Carper Furniture Co., Accountant 1927, Asst. Secy.-Treas. 1928, Secy.-Treas. 1932, Vice-Pres. 1937, Pres. and Gen. Mgr. 1937–64, Chmn. of Bd. 1964–70; Chmn., Singer Home Furnishings Div. 1945–72; Member, Exec. Committee, Colonial-American National Bank, Roanoke 1953, director 1945—; Virgina Advisory Board, Liberty Mutual Insurance Co., Richmond 1951—; Dir· Community Hospital, Roanoke Valley. *Awards:* Honours: Hon.D Comm.Sc (Roanoke Coll.); Man-of-the-Year in Furniture Industry 1950 and 1966 (by American Furniture Mart Building Board of Governors, Chicago); George Washington Hons. Medal (Freedoms Foundation); Hon. member, Beta Gamma Sigma, Washington & Lee Univ. 1956; Silver Beaver Award, Boy Scouts of America 1959; Silver Antelope Award, Boy Scouts of America, 1966. Roanoke 1965 Father of the Year for Youth Leadership. Roanoke Jaycees 1966 Boss of the Year. *Member:* Ntl. Assn. of Manufacturers; (Chmn. Exec. Cttee. 1967); Southern Furniture Manufacturers Assn. (Pres. 1942–44); Chmn., Finance Cttee., 1968–69; (National Assn. of Manufacturers) Virginia Manufacturers Assn. (Pres. 1956); Roanoke Area Manufacturers Assn.; Roanoke Valley Industries (Pres. 1964–65); President, Furniture Factories Marketing Association of the South 1967–69; Member of Board of Governors, American Furniture Mart, Chicago; Southern Furniture Exposition Building, Dallas Center; Member: Board of Trustees, Virginia Foundation for Independent Colleges, World Trade Committee, 1967—, National Emergency Committee, on National Council on Crime Delinquency, 1967–69. Mason (Scottish Rite Shriner). *Clubs:* Rotary, Country (Roanoke); Shenandoah; Farmington Country. *Address:* Patrick Henry Hotel, P.O. Box 2241, Roanoke, Va., U.S.A.

**JORGENSEN, Anker,** Danish Politician. *B.* 1922. *M.* 1948, Ingrid. *S.* 2. *Daus.* 2. *Career:* Vice-Chmn. and Chmn. Trade Union 1950–62; Member City Council Copenhagen 1961–64; Member of Parliament since 1964; Chmn. DASF 1968–72; Prime Minister of Denmark 1972–73, and 1975—; Chmn. Social Democratic Party since 1973. *Address: office* Statsministeriet, Christiansberg, 1218 Copenhagen K, Denmark.

**JORGENSEN, Hemming Kristian.** MSc, FIMechE. Danish. *B.* 1919. *Educ.* Royal Tech. Univ., Copenhagen (MSc.). *M.* 1944, Ilona Frank. *S.* 3. *Dau.* 1. *Career:* Man. Dir., Impact Extrusions Ltd., Middx; Abmaco A/S Copenhagen; Asst. Dir., Andersen & Bruuns Fabriker A/S Copenhagen; Man. Dir., Disa, Dansk Industri Syndikat A/S; Chmn. Bd., Disamatic Inc.; Chicago, Disa Elektronik G.m.b.H.; Disa Electronique S.A.R.L. Paris; Disa Elettronica S.r.1, Milan; Industrihaer deriet A(S; Boy Transportmateriel A/S; Motorfabriken Bukh A/S; P. Rasmussen & Co. A/S Member Bd., Fabrikantforeningen (Assn. of Manfrs.) Copenhagen; Pharma-Plast A/S; Maersk Kemi A/S; Dansk Boresel skab A/S; Sophus Berendsen A/S; Academy of Technical Science; Vice-Chmn. Bd., Fed. Danish Industries. *Address:* Schimmelmanns Have 9, 2930 Klampenborg, Denmark; and *office* Herlev Hovedgade 17, 2730, Herlev, Denmark.

**JOSEPH, Henry Oscar,** OBE. British. *B.* 1901. *Educ.* Westminster School, London. *Career:* Former Man. Dir., Leopold Joseph & Sons Ltd., Bankers; Director, Bank Leumi (U.K.) Ltd.. Past President, International Council on Jewish and Welfare Services; Joint Pres. (Past Chmn.); Central British Fund for Jewish Relief and Rehabilitation; Chmn. Jewish Trust Corporation for Germany Ltd.; Chmn. Jewish Youth Fund Advisory Committee. *Address:* 16 Park Lodge, St. John's Wood Park, London NW8 6QT.

**JOSEPH, Rt. Hon. Sir Keith Sinjohn,** Bt, PC, MP. *B.* 1918. *Educ.* Harrow and Magdalen Coll., Oxford. *M.* 1951, Hellen Louise Guggenheimer (of New York). *S.* 1. *Daus.* 3. *Career:* Served in World War II (Capt. R.A.; Italy; wounded; despatches) 1939–46. Fellow, All Souls Coll.; Oxford 1946–60, 1972—; Barrister (Middle Temple) 1946; Councillor City of London 1946 (Alderman 1946–49); Liveryman (Vintners' Company); Member of Parliament Con. for Leeds N.E. since 1956. P.P.S. to Parly. Under-Secretary of State, Commonwealth Relations Office 1957–59; Parly. Secy. Ministry of Housing and Local Govt. 1959–61; Minister of State, Board of Trade, 1961–62; Minister of Housing and Local Government and Minister for Welsh Affairs, 1962–64; Dep. Chmn. Bovis Holdings Ltd. 1964–70. Founder and First Chmn. Mulberry Housing Trust 1965–69; Secretary of State for Social Services 1970–74; Fellow, Inst. of Builders. Co-Founder, Foundation of Management Education; Founder and Chmn of Mgmt. Cttee of Centre for Policy Studies Ltd since 1974. *Club:* Carlton. *Address:* 23 Mulberry Walk, London, SW3 6DZ.

**JOSEPH, Sir Leslie.** British engineer and company director. *B.* 1908. *Educ:* The Kings School, Canterbury. *M.* 1934, Emily Irene Mruphy. *Daus.* Mary Lesley and Christine. *Career:* Major RE 1940–46; Chairman: Housing Production Board for Wales 1952–53, Association of Amusement Park Proprietors of Great Britain, 1949–51, Amusement Caterers' Association 1953–54, Circus Proprietors Association 1959–61, National Amusements Council 1950–51; Vice-Chairman, Trust Houses Forte Ltd., Chairman Entam Ltd., Director: of other companies; High Sheriff Mid-Glamorgan 1975–76. *Fellow:* Royal Society of Arts; Royal Horticultural Society; Zoological Society. *Address:* Coedargraig, Newton, Porthcawl, Glam., and *office* Forte House, Piccadilly Circus, London, W.1.

**JOSEPHS, Ray.** Public relations consultant, author, lecturer. *B.* 1912. *Educ.* University of Pennsylvania. *M.* 1941, Juanita W. Wegner. *Career:* Chairman of Board, Ray Josephs-David E. Levy, Inc. (representing U.S. companies); Chmn., International Public Relations Co. Ltd. (N.Y.C.); contributor of articles to leading magazines and newspapers in U.S., Canada, Great Britain, Latin America and the Far East. Lecturer at American Management Assn., leading business organizations, universities, etc., on business subjects; previously on Latin America. General correspondent for Philadelphia Evening Bulletin 1929–40; Columnist, Buenos Aires Herald 1940–44; Correspondent at various times for Washington Post, Christian Science Monitor, Pittsburg Post-Gazette, Newark Star Leger, Chicago Sun, Time magazine, Variety, National Monthly, and others. Later, special consultant on Latin American affairs for British Ministry of Information, R.K.O. Pictures, R.C.A. and National Broadcasting Corp. *Publications:* Argentine Diary (1944); Spies & Saboteurs in Argentina (1943); Those Perplexing Argentines (with former Ambassador James Bruce (1952); How to Make Money from Your Ideas (1954); How to Gain an Extra Hour Every Day (1955); Our Housing Jungle and Your Pocketbook (Oscar Steiner 1960); Streamlining Your Executive Workload (1960); The Magic Power of Putting Yourself Over with People (Stanley Arnold 1962); and many other titles. *Member:* Writers Guild of America; Founders Committee, Tobé Lecture Series; Harvard Grad. School of Business Administration. *Clubs:* American (Buenos Aires); Overseas Press (N.Y.C.); Society of Magazine Writers. *Address:* 860 United Nations Plaza, New York City 10017; and *office* 230 Park Avenue, New York City 10017, U.S.A.

**JOUBIN, Francis Renault.** Canadian mining geologist. *B.* 1911. *Educ.* Univ. of British Columbia; BA & Sc and MA & DSc (Chem., Geol.); Leonard Gold Medal of Engineering Institute of Canada; Selwyn Blaylock Gold Medal of Canadian Institute of Mining and Metallurgy. *M.* 1939, Mary Torvinen. *Dau.* Marion Frances. Technical Adviser, U.N. Bureau of Technical Assistance. *Publications:* Structure of Canadian Ore Deposits; Modern Methods of Mineral Exploration in Canada; Geology of the Algoma Uranium Field; Geology of the Pioneer and Bralorne Mines, etc. *Address:* 170 Bloor Street West, Toronto, Ont., M5S IT9, Canada.

**JOUVE, Géraud Henri.** French diplomat. *B.* 1901. *Educ.* University Fellow. *M.* 1933, Elizabeth Krausz. *S.* 1. *Career:* Dir., Havas Agency at Budapest, Warsaw, Berlin, Amsterdam and Bucharest 1931–40; Alger-Paris 1944–45; Deputy, National Assembly 1946–51; Permanent French Delegate to the Council of Europe 1951–55; Ambassador to Finland 1955–60. French Delegate to U.N. High Commission for Refugees, April 1960–66. *Award:* Officier, Legion of Honour. *Publications:* De Munich à Brazzaville (Paris 1945); Voici l'Age atomique (Paris 1946). *Address:* 104 Boulevard Azago, Paris, France.

**JOVA, Joseph John.** American diplomat. *B.* 1916. *Educ.* Dartmouth College (AB); Mt. St. Mary Coll. (LHD); Dowling Coll. (JD). *M.* 1949, Pamela Johnson. *S.* Henry, Thomas. *Dau.* Margaret. *Career:* Counsellor of Embassy Santiago, Chile, 1961–65; Ambassador to Honduras, 1965–69. Ambassador to the Organization of American States. 1969–74; Ambassador to Mexico 1974–77; Pres., Meridian House International. *Member:* Board of Trustees, Mount Saint Mary College; American Society for Public Administration; Amer. Foreign Service Association; Member, Inter-Amer. Cttee. for Peaceful Settlement; Head, U.S. Delegation to 14th Session, U.N. Economic Commission for Latin America; Member, Mexican Academy of History; Mexican Academy of International Law; Inst. of Hispanic Culture (Spain); Trustee, Arizona Sonora Desert Museum. *Awards:* Knight of Malta (Amer. Chapter); Order of Morazan (Honduras); Order of Aztec Eagle (Mexico); Constantinian Order of St. George. Rotarian. *Address:* 1630 Crescent Place N.W., Washington, D.C., U.S.A.

**JOVANOVICH, William.** AB. DLitt. American. *B.* 1920 *Educ.* Univ. of Colorado (AB). Harvard & Columbia Univs. (Grad. Study). *M.* 1943, Martha Davis. *S.* 2. *Dau.* 1. *Career:* Pres., Harcourt Brace & Co. 1954–60; Harcourt, Brace & World 1960–69; Chmn. & Chief Exec., Harcourt Brace Jovanovich Inc. since 1970. *Member:* Phi Beta Kappa. *Awards:* D.Litt. Univ. of Colorado, Colorado Coll.; Ohio State Univ.; Adelphi Univ.; Middlebury Coll., Univ. of Alaska. Regent of the State of New York since 1974. *Address:* 757 Third Avenue, New York, N.Y. 10017, U.S.A.

**JOWSEY, Frederick H.** Canadian mining executive. *B.* 1914. *Educ.* Public and High Schools, Toronto. *M.* 1940, Florence Barber. *Career:* Began in March 1933 as Assistant at God's Lake Mines (assaying, surveying, diamond drilling, etc.); prospecting in Northern Canada 1946–50; associated with Teck Exploration Co. 1950–53; Manager, Bobjo Mines Ltd. 1953–55; President: Aggressive Mining Ltd., Canuc Mines Ltd.; Dir. Globex Mining Enterprises Inc.; Denison Mines Ltd.; Stanford Mines Ltd.; Rock-Ore Mines Ltd. Member, C.I.M.M. (Toronto Branch). *Clubs:* Engineers', Canadian, Yorkdowns Country (Toronto); Manitoba (Winnipeg). *Address:* 9 Glengowan Road, Toronto; M4N 1E9, Ont., Canada.

**JOYCE, James Herbert.** Canadian. *B.* 1913. *Educ.* Univ. of Toronto (BComm 1934). *Unmarried. Career:* Investment Analyst, Confederation Life Association 1934–44; Investment Editor, Financial Post 1944–52; Treasurer, Crown Trust Co. 1952–54. Executive Vice-Pres., Crown Trust Co. 1965–71, (Assistant Gen. Mgr. and Treas., Toronto 1954–63; Assistant General Manager 1963–64), Vice-Pres. Special Assignments 1972–73; Chmn. of the Board, Ontario Development Corp. since 1974 & Chief Exec. Officer since 1975; President, Dominion Mortgage and Investment Assn. 1964–65. *Member:* Bd. Trade of Metropolitan Toronto; English-Speaking Union; St. George's Society; Moore Park Ratepayers' Assn. (Dir. and Treas. 1954–71). Member, Senate, Univ. of Toronto 1962–68; Governing Council Univ. of Toronto since 1972; Member Adv. Bd., Grenfell Labrador Medical Mission Inc., Toronto; Trustee and Vice-Chmn. of Council, Wycliffe College; Chmn. of Advisory Bd. Bloorview Children's Hospital since 1965, Chmn. of Adv. Bd. 1966–69, 1972–75. *Clubs:* Granite (Dir. 1952–69; Hon. Dir. 1970—; Chmn. Management Committee 1960–61; Vice-President 1962–63, Pres. 1964–65; Chmn. of Bd. 1966–67; Hon. Pres. 1968–69); Royal Canadian Yacht; National; Canadian; Empire Club of Canada; Rosedale Golf. *Address:* 306 Rose Park Drive, Toronto, Ont., M4T 1R7 Canada.

**JUDD, Frank Ashcroft, BSc, MP. British. *B.* 28 March, 1935. *Educ.* City of London School, London School of Economics.** *M.* 1961, Christine Elizabeth Louise Willington. *Daus.* Elizabeth and Philippa. *Career:* Short Service Commisn. R.A.F., 1957–59; Sec. Gen. International Voluntary Service, 1960–66; Chmn. Parliamentary Labour Party Overseas Aid and Development Group, 1966–70; Member, Public Accounts Cttee. 1966–69, Select Cttees. Overseas Aid, 1969–74; Member Parliament Portsmouth W.. 1966–74 and Portsmouth N. since 1974; Parly. Private Secy. to Leader of Opposition 1970–72; Member, British Delegation to WEU and to Council of Europe 1970–73; Mem., Opposition Front Bench Defence Team 1972–74; Parly. Under-Secy. State for Defence 1974–76; Parly. Sec. for Overseas Development and Minister of State 1976–77; Minister of State, Foreign & Commonwealth Office 1977—; Chmn. Fabian Society 1974. *Publications:* Radical Future; Fabian International Essays (1970); Purpose in Socialism; Various papers and articles on current affairs. *Address:* 84 Kingston Crescent, North End, Portsmouth, Hants.; and House of Commons, London SW1A 0AA.

**JUDGE, Edward Thomas.** British Engineer. *B.* 1908. *Educ.* Royal Grammar School, Worcester, and St. John's College, Cambridge Univ. (MA, Mech. Sciences Tripos). *Director:* Dorman Long Vanderbijl Corp. Ltd., Cleveland Scientific Institution, BPB Industries Ltd., Pilkington Brothers Ltd., ETJ Consultancy Services, Fibreglass Ltd., The Zenith Electric Co. Ltd. *Career:* Joined Dorman Long 1930 and held various appointments, becoming Chmn. and Gen. Man. Dir. 1961–67; Chmn. Reyrolle Parsons Ltd. 1969–74; Mem. of North-Eastern Electricity Board 1952–62; Hon. Vice-Pres. of The Iron and Steel Institute 1958; Pres. British Iron and Steel Federation 1965–67; Iron and Steel Institute Bessemer Gold Medalist 1967; Pres. of The British Electrical and Allied Manufacturers' Association 1970–71. *Address:* Wood Place, Woodside, Aspley Guise, Milton Keyes, MK17 8EP.

**JUDGE, Thomas L.** American State Governor. B. 1934. *Educ.* Univs. of Notre Dame & Louisville. *M.* 1966, Carol Anderson. *S.* 2. *Career:* Second Lieut. U.S. Army 1958; Advertising Exec., Louisville Courier Journal 1959–60; Pres., Judge Advertising 1960–73; State Rep., Lewis & Clark County 1960–66, State Senator 1967–68; Lieut.-Gov. of Montana 1968–72, Governor 1973–76 and since 1977. Democrat. *Address:* Office of the Governor, State Capitol, Helena, Montana, U.S.A.

**JUKES, Thomas Hughes.** Biological chemist, Space Sciences Laboratory, Univ. of Berkeley, Calif. *B.* 1906. *Educ.* Univ. of Toronto (BSA 1930; PhD 1933); DSc h.c. Univ. of Guelph 1972. *M.* 1942, Marguerite Esposito. *S.* Kenneth Hughes. *Daus.* Caroline Elizabeth (Knueppel), Dorothy Mavis. *Career:* National Research Council Fellow in Medical Sciences 1933–34, Instructor 1934–39. Assistant Professor 1939–42, University of California; Director of Nutrition & Physiology Research, Lederle Laboratories Div., American Cyanamid Co. 1942–59, Agricultural Division 1959–63; Professor in Residence, Div. of Medical Physics, Associate Director, Space Sciences Laboratory, Univ. of California 1963—. *Awards:* Borden Award of the Poultry Science Association, 1947. *Member:* Amer. Socy. Biological Chemists; Amer. Inst. of Nutrition, Fellow 1973; Socy. Experimental Biology & Medicine; Amer. Chemical Socy.; Amer. Socy. for Animal Science (Fellow 1961); Biophysical Society. *Publications:* B-Vitamins for Blood Formation; Antibiotics in Nutrition; Molecules and Evolution (books); about 250 articles in scientific journals dealing with vitamins, antibiotics, cancer chemotherapy, molecular evolution and other biochemical subjects. *Address:* 170 Arlington Avenue, Berkeley, Calif.; and *office* Space Sciences Laboratory, Univ. of California, Berkeley, Calif. 94720, U.S.A.

**JULIN, Jacob Albert Carl Gustaf von.** Finnish industrialist. *B.* 23 July 1906. *Educ.* Universities of Helsinki and Cambridge. *M.* 1939, Brita Enqvist. *Daus.* Albertina, Mariana, Sophie. *Career:* Assistant Dir., Finnish Cellulose Union 1938–42; Managing Director, Oy Kaukas Ab. 1942-67; Chmn. since 1951; Chairman: O/Y Fiskars AB since 1947, Finnish Cellulose Union 1962–73; Vice-Chairman, Union Bank of Finland 1961–73, Chairman 1973–74. *Address:* Unionsgatan 4, Helsinki, Finland.

**JUNG, Charles Chester.** American business executive. *B.* 1903. *Educ.* Univ. of Michigan (AB). *M.* 1927, Gwen Drew, and (2) 1951, Elizabeth Norse. *S.* Charles Chester, Jr. *Daus.* Nancy Ellen and Constance Drew. *Career:* With Halsey-Stewart & Co., Chicago 1926–28; A. G. Becker & Co., Chicago 1928–34; Exec. Vice-Pres., Gen. Mgr., Dir., Sheridan, Farwell & Morrison Inc. 1940–49; Pres., Dir., Scudder, Stevens & Clark Inc., Chicago 1949–53 (Dir. 1953–60); Vice-Pres.,

Calumet & Hecla 1953–62. Chairman of Board: California Cold Storage & Distributing Co. 1955—; and Hayward Marum Inc. 1958—; General Finance Corp., State National Bank, Evanston; Universal Oil Products Co. Chmn. of Bd.; Calumet & Hecla Inc. 1962–68. *Clubs:* University, Swedish (Chicago); Skokie Country (Glencoe, Ill.); Lauderdale Yacht; Tower Club, Fort Lauderdale. *Address:* 1508 Hinman Avenue, Apt. 6C, Evanston, Illinois 60201 and 3333 N.E. 34th Street, Apt. 1208 Fort Lauderdale, Fla., U.S.A.

**JUNOR, John.** Editor and Chairman, Sunday Express, London. *Educ.* Glasgow Univ.; MA (Hons. English). *M.* 1942, Pamela Welsh. *S.* Roderick. *Dau.* Penelope Jane. Assistant Editor, Daily Express 1951–53; Deputy Editor, Evening Standard 1953–54. *Address:* Wellpools Farm, Charlwood, Surrey.

**JURAN, Joseph M.** American author, lecturer and consultant in management. *B.* 1904. *Educ.* Univ. of Minnesota (BS in EE 1924), and Loyola University (JD 1935). *M.* 1926, Sadie Shapiro. *S.* Robert, Charles and Donald. *Dau.* Sylvia. With Western Electric Co. 1924–41; Lend Lease Administration 1941–43; Foreign Economic Administration 1943–45; New York University 1945–50; freelance author, lecturer and consultant 1950—. *Fellow:* Amer. Socy. of Mechanical Engineers; Amer. Management Assn.; Socy. for Advancement of Management; International Academy of Management; Am. Assoc. for Advancement of Science, Am. Inst. of Industrial Engineers; Hon. member Quality Control societies in USA, Europe, Japan, Australia, Argentina, Britain and Philippines. *Awards:* Various medals and scrolls from institutions in U.S.A., Japan, Czechoslovakia, Hungary, Australia, Philippines and Spain. *Publications:* Bureaucracy (1944); Management of Inspection and Quality Control (1945); Quality Control Handbook (1951; 3rd edn. 1974); Case Studies in Industrial Management 1944); Lectures in General Management (in Japanese 1955); Managerial Breakthrough (McGraw-Hill 1964); The Corporate Director (with J. Keith Louden). American Management Association (1966); Quality Planning and Analysis (with F. M. Gryna, Jr. 1970). *Address:* 860 United Nations Plaza, New York, N.Y. 10017, U.S.A.

**JUROW, Irving H.** American lawyer. *B.* 1905. *Educ.* New York Univ. (BS 1926) and Harvard Law School (JD 1929). *M.* 1929, Mae Wechsler. Vice-President and General Counsel, Schering Corp. 1959–70. *Member:* American, N.Y. State and Dist. of Col. Bar Associations. *Clubs:* National Lawyers (Washington); Harvard (N.Y.C.). *Address:* 4701 Willard Avenue, Chevy Chase, Md. 20015; and *office* 1019 19th Street, N.W. Washington, D.C. 20036, U.S.A.

**JURY, Peter Charles Cotton.** British. *B.* 1919. *Educ.* Rugby School and King's Coll., Cambridge. *M.* 1953, Ursula Joan Abraham. *Daus.* Sophie and Polly. *Career:* Captain 13/18 Royal Hussars 1939–46. Managing Director, Shelbourne Hotel, Dublin 1947; Director, Cairnes Brewery, Drogheda 1952–60; Chairman, Preston Bros. Ltd., Drogheda 1960–63. Managing Director, Trust Houses (Ireland) Ltd. 1960–72. Director: S.A. de l'Hotel Moderne. Chmn., International Airport Hotel, Dublin; Chmn., Trust Houses Forte Ireland Ltd. *Member:* Irish Hotels Fed. (Pres. 1957–59); International Hotel Assn. (member Exec. Cttee. 1962; Vice-Pres. 1970, Deputy chmn. 1975–76, Pres. since 1977). *Clubs:* Cavalry (London); Kildare Street (Dublin). *Address:* Struan Hill, Delgany, Co. Wicklow; and *office* 27 St. Stephens' Green, Dublin.

# K

**KADOORIE, Sir Lawrence,** CBE, LLD, KStJ(A), JP. Officier de la Legion d'Honneur; Officer of the Order of Leopold. British industrial financier and philanthropist. *B.* 1899. *Educ.* Cathedral Schl. (Shanghai), Ascham St. Vincents (Eastbourne, Eng.), Clifton College (Bristol), and Lincoln's Inn (London). *M.* 1938, Muriel Gubbay. *S.* Michael David. *Dau.* Rita Laura. *Career:* Partner, Sir Elly Kadoorie & Sons; Chairman Sir Elly Kadoorie Successors Ltd.; China Light & Power Co. Ltd.; Franki Piling & Engineering (H.K.) Ltd.; Nanyang Cotton Mills Ltd.; Hong Kong Carpet Manufacturers Ltd.; and other companies. Director: Sir Elly Kadoorie Continuation Ltd.; Cross-Harbour Tunnel Co. Ltd.; Peninsula Electric Power Co. Ltd.; Hong Kong Fire Insurance Co. Ltd.; Lombard Insurance Co. Ltd. Hon LLD Univ. of Hong Kong 1962; Ramon Magsaysay Award Mamila, 1962; Solomon Schechter Award, New York, 1959. *Member:* Inst. of Dirs. (London); Hong Kong General Chamber of Commerce; Employers' Federation of H.K.; Council and Court, Univ. of H.K.; St. John Ambulance Assn. and Brigade; Kadoorie Agricultural Aid Assn.; Photographic Socy. of H.K. *Clubs:* Motor Sports, Hong Kong, Jewish Recreation, Country (all of Hong Kong); Royal Automobile, Number Ten (London). *Address:* 24 Kadoorie Avenue, Kowloon, Hong Kong; and *office* Sir Elly Kadoorie & Sons, St. George's Building 24 fl., 2 Ice House Street, Hong Kong.

**KAHN, Alfred Jr,** MD. American. *B.* 1916. *Educ.* Washington & Lee Univ. (BA) and Harvard Medical School (MD). *M.* 1941, Redith Aline White. *S.* Alfred III. *Daus.* Susan J. and Marion White. *Career:* With U.S. Army Medical Corps 1942–45; Vice-pres. and Medical Director, National Equity Life Ins. Co. 1951–60; Chief of Staff, St. Vincent's Infirmary 1966–67, and Chief of Medicine Arkansas Baptist Hospital 1954–55. President, Kahn Medical Corp. 1955—; Editor, Journal of Arkansas Medical Society 1955—; Medical Director, Union Life Insurance Co. 1964–74; Associate Clinical Professor, Internal Medicine, University of Arkansas School of Medicine; Chief of Medicine, St. Vincent's Infirmary; Vice-Pres., Donaghey Foundation. *Member:* Arkansas Atomic Energy Commission; Pulaski County Red Cross (Dir.); Pulaski County Medical Socy. (Vice-Pres. and Secy. 1952–57); Little Rock Acad. of Internal Medicine; American Medical Assn.; American Board of Internal Medicine (Diplomate); American College of Physicians (Fellow); Little Rock Boys Club (Dir. and past Pres.). Member, Board of Trustees, George W. (Dir. and past Pres.). George W. Donaghey Foundation (President). *Publications:* more than 50 articles on Medicine. *Clubs:* Top of the Rock; Rotary; Pres., Little Rock Rotary (Past Pres.); Little Rock Yacht (Dir.); Little Rock Country. *Address:* 10 East Palisades, Little Rock, Ark.; and *office* 1300 West 6th Street, Little Rock, Ark., U.S.A.

**KAHN, Prof. Alfred Edward.** American, *B.* 1917. *Educ.* New York Univ (BA 1936, MA 1937) and Yale Univ. (PhD). *M.* 1943, Mary Simmons. *S.* 1. *Daus.* 2. *Career:* Prof. of Economics, Cornell Univ. 1947— (also Member, Bd. of Trustees 1964–69; Dean, College of Arts and Sciences, 1969–74); Chmn., Civil Aeronautics Bd. 1977. Senior Staff, U.S. Council Economic Advisers to the President 1955–57; Chmn., Dept. of Economics, Cornell Univ. 1958–63; Economic Adv. Council, Amer. Tel. & Tel. Co. 1968–74; Chmn. New York Public Service Commission 1974–77; Special Consultant, National Economic Research Assoc. Inc. N.Y.C. 1961–74; Board of Editors American Economic Review 1961–64; Special Consultant: (a) U.S. Dept. of Justice, 1964, (b) U.S. Dept. of Agriculture 1960–63, (c) U.S. Federal Trade Commission 1965; Member, Economic Advisory Cttee. Chamber of Commerce of the U.S. 1965–67; member, U.S. Attorney-General's National Cttee. to study the Anti-Trust Laws 1953–55; Director, Tomkins County Economic Corp. 1968–69; Member, Exec. Comm., Nat. Assn. of Regulatory Utility Commissioners. *Publications:* (books) Great Britain in the World Economy (1946); Fair Competition, the Law of Economics of Antitrust Policy (with J. B. Dirlam, 1954); Integration and Competition in the Petroleum Industry (with M. G. de Chazeau 1959); The Economics of Regulation (1970, 1971). *Member:* Phi Beta Kappa: Amer. Economic Assn. *Address:* 910 Independence Avenue S.E., Washington, D.C. 20003; and *office* Civil Aeronautics Board, 1825 Connecticut Avenue N.W., Washington, D.C. 20428, U.S.A.

**KAHN, Claude D. H.,** Dr. oec. publ. Swiss. *B.* 1929. *Educ.* Doctor of Economics. *M.* (1) 1955, Yvonne Carasso; (2) 1969, Ruth Wyss. *S.* Patrick C. and Francis M. *Dau.* Dominique V. Personal Partner of Hugo Kahn & Co., Bankers, Zürich 1961— (Executive member of the Company 1955—).

Director of various companies. *Publications:* Die Besteuerung des Kapitalgewinns (Taxation of Capital Gains); contributor to various newspapers. *Address: office* Stockersti, 38 (Bleicherhof), 8002 Zürich, Switzerland.

**KAHN, Ellison.** South African advocate. *B.* 1921. *Educ.* BCom, LLB, LLM, LLD; Barrister-at-Law (Middle Temple); Advocate of the Supreme Court at South Africa. *M.* 1945, Adèle Sonnenberg. *S.* 2. *Daus.* 1. *Career:* Member Johannesburg Bar 1945–48; Senior Lecturer in Law, University of the Witwatersrand 1948–54. Deputy Vice-Chancellor and Honorary Professor of Law, University of the Witwatersrand, Johannesburg. *Publications:* South Africa: The Development of its Laws and Constitution (co-author); the South African Legal System and its Background (co-author); Contract and Mercantile Law Through the Cases; The South African Law of Domicile; some 200 articles and papers in various books and learned journals; Editor, South African Law Journal; Member Editorial Bd., Annual Survey of South African Law. Member, International Advisory Bd., Comparative and International Law Journal of Southern Africa; Editorial Cttee. Businessmans Law. *Address:* University of the Witwatersrand, Johannesburg, South Africa.

**KAHN, Hans Jacob.** MSc. British. *B.* 1922. *Educ.* Dulwich Coll.; London Univ. (MSc.). *M.* 1946, Barbara Clare McKellan. *S.* 1. *Daus.* 2. *Career:* former Chmn., International Div. Fisons Ltd.; Chmn., Agrochemical Div. Fisons Ltd.; Dir., Vice-Chmn., Fisons Ltd. *Address:* 39 Gilmerton Court, Long Road, Trumpington, Cambridge and *office* Harston, Cambridge.

**KAHN, Robert.** Certified management consultant. *B.* 1918. *Educ.* Stanford Univ. (BA Hons) and Harvard Graduate School of Business (MBA; elected Baker Scholar 1939). *M.* 1945, Patricia E. Glenn. *S.* Christopher Glenn. *Dau.* Roberta Ann. *Career:* With R. H. Macy & Co., N.Y.C. 1940–41; U.S.A.A.F. (2nd Lieut. to Major; Iran, Philippines, Japan) 1941–46; Controller, Smiths, Oakland 1946–50; U.S. Air Force (Major to Lieut.-Col.; French Morocco) 1951–52; Vice-Pres. and Treas. Sherwood Swan & Co., Oakland 1952–56; Dir. Staco Inc.; Simon Stores Inc.; Walnut Creek; Piedmont Grocery Co. Oakland; Vice-Pres. and Dir. Marc Paul Inc. (and subsidiaries) Oakland; Coast Medical Corp, Alarm Systems Inc. both Walnut Creek; Pres., Kahn & Harris Inc. 1974—; Vice-Pres., Hambrecht & Quist 1977—. Phi Beta Kappa 1938. Trustee, Kahn Foundation. *Member:* United Bay Area Crusade (Board of Governors; Executive Cttee. 1955–66, Treas 1961–66); Alameda County United Fund (Bd. of Governors; Exec. Cttee. 1953–63, Vice-Pres. 1961–63); American Red Cross (Dir. Oakland Chapter 1956–64); Controllers Congress; Natonal Retail Merchants Assn.; Dir. San Francisco Bay Girl Scout Council 1969—; (Vice-Pres., 1976—); Founding member Inst. of Management Consultants 1969—; Member 1965—; Trustee 1968—; Assn. of Management Consultants, Vice-Pres. since 1970 (Pres. 1977–78). *Publications:* approximately 40 articles in various periodicals, chiefly in the retail field. Editorial Columnist, The Sun Newspapers, Lafayette, California. *Awards:* Hon. LLD, Franklin Pierce College, 1977. *Address:* 3684 Happy Valley Road, Lafayette, Calif.; and *office* P.O. Box 343, Lafayette, Calif., U.S.A.

**KAI, Fumihiko.** Japanese diplomat and businessman. *B.* 1912. *Educ.* Univ. of Tokyo, Faculty of Law. *M.* 1946, Ayako Kimura. *S.* 1. *Daus.* 2. *Career:* Chief of Second Section, Research Bureau, Ministry of Foreign Affairs 1945; Consul-General, Jakarta, 1952; Counsellor, Embassy of Japan, Holland 1953; Consul-General, Berlin 1955, and Hamburg 1957; Dir., Economic Co-operation Bureau, Min. of Foreign Affairs 1962; Ambassador to Malaysia 1964–67; Ambassador of Japan to Australia 1967–69; to Fed. Republic of Germany 1970–73 (Ret'd.); Man. Dir.. Nissin Sugar Mfg. Co. 1973—. *Clubs:* Tokyo (Japan); Hodogaya Golf Country (Japan); Royal Selangor Golf (Malaysia); Royal Canberra Golf and Commonwealth (Canberra). *Address:* 10–14 2-Chrome, Hatanodai, Shinagawa-ku, Tokyo, Japan.

**KAISER, Edgar Fosburgh.** American industrialist. *B.* 1908. *Educ:* Univ. of California. *M.* (1) 1932, Sue Mead (dec'd). *S.* Edgar F., Jr., Henry Mead, Kim John. *Daus.* Mrs. Franklin Stark, Mrs. Martin Drobac, Mrs. Wallace Gudgell. *M.* (2) 1975 Nina McCormick. *Career:* Started as supt. of a pipeline project in the Midwest; shovel foreman and later supt. of canyon excavation, Hoover Dam; admin. mgr., main spillway, Bonneville Dam; project mgr., Grand Coulee Dam; former mgr. of three shipyards in Portland, Oregon; former gen. mgr., Kaiser-Frazer Corp.; pres., Kaiser Industries Corp., 1956–67. Now *Chmn. of Board:* Kaiser Industries Corp.; Kaiser Aluminium & Chemical Corp.; Kaiser Steel Corp.; Kaiser Resources Ltd.; Kaiser Cement & Gypsum Corp.; Kaiser Foundation Health Plan, Inc.; Kaiser Foundation Hospitals; Stanford Research Institute; and Oakland Symphony Orchestra Assoc. Trustee: Henry J. Kaiser Family Foundation; Council of the Americas. Dir.: Bank-America Corp.; Hindustan Aluminium Corp.; Mysore Cements Ltd.; Volta Aluminium Co. Ltd.; U.S.–U.S.S.R. Trade and Economic Council. Member: National Advisory Council, Opportunities Ind. Centers of America; San Francisco Opera Assoc.; The Business Council; East-West Center; Former Member, President's (U.S.A.) Advisory Cttee. on Refugees; Advisory Board, Oakland Museum Assoc.; International Industrial Conference; Pan American Soc.; Nat. Cttee. on U.S.–China Relations. Vice Chmn.: U.S. Section, Bulgarian–U.S. Economic Council. Trustee and former chmn., (San Francisco) Bay Area Council. *Awards:* Hon. LHD Univ. of Calif. 1969; Alumnus of the Year, Univ. of Calif. 1969; Hon. LLD Univ. of Portland, Pepperdine Coll., Mills Coll., Golden Gate Univ. and Univ. of the Pacific; New Oakland Cttee. Award for National Achievement 1976; Int. Achievement Award, World Trade Club, 1975; Golden Beaver Award for Mgmt., 1975; Grand Officer Republic Ivory Coast, 1972; Fell. American Acad. Arts and Sciences 1970; First Annual International Key Award Opportunities Indus. Centers of America, 1970; Presidential (U.S.A.) Medal of Freedom, 1969; Hoover Medal, 1969; Engineering News-Record's Const. Man of Year, 1968; Calif. Mus. of Science & Industry's Industrialist of Year, 1966; Cdr., Brazil's National Order of Southern Cross, 1966; National Chmn., U.N. Day 1966. *Address:* Kaiser Center, 300 Lakeside Drive, Oakland California 94666, U.S.A.

**KAISER, Khwaja Mohammed,** Bangladesh Diplomat. *B.* 1918. *Educ.* Dacca Univ. (BA Hons (History) 1939). *M.* 1936, Sayeeda Alimullah. *S.* Junaid and Javed. *Daus.* Laila and Shama. *Career:* Joined India Police Service 1941 (Asstt. Inspector-General 1950); appointed 2nd Secy. Office of Deputy High Commissioner for Pakistan in Calcutta 1950; Officer on Special Duty (with rank of Deputy Secy.) Ministry of External Affairs, Dacca; transferred to Karachi as Deputy Secy. 1951; posted to Embassy of Pakistan at Peking 1955; appointed Consul-General, New York 1957; High Commissioner for Pakistan in Australia and New Zealand, 1962–65; Minister of Embassy, Washington 1960; Director-General, Ministry of Foreign Affairs, Govt. of Pakistan. 1965–66; Ambassador to Sweden, Denmark and Norway; Ambassador of Pakistan to the People's Republic of China 1969–72; Declared allegiance to join the Government of the People's Republic of Bangladesh; Appointed Bangladesh's Ambassador to Burma, Thailand, North Vietnam, P.R.G. of South Vietnam and Democratic Republic of Korea and High Commissioner of Singapore 1972–75; Leader of Bangladesh Delegation to the 1st & 2nd Law of the Sea Conferences at New York; currently Permanent Representative of Bangladesh to the United Nations. *Clubs:* Dacca; Dacca Club Gymkhana Races; Melbourne (Hon.). *Address:* Permanent Mission of Bangladesh to the U.N., 130 East 40th Street, 5th Floor, New York, N.Y. 10016, U.S.A.

**KAISER, Philip M.** U.S. Diplomat. *B.* 1913. Univ. of Wisconsin—AB; Balliol Coll., Oxford (Rhodes Scholar)—BA, MA. *M.* 1939, Hannah Greeley. *S.* 3. *Career:* Economist, mem. Bd. of Govs., Federal Reserve System 1939–42; Chief, Project Operations Staff, Chief Planning Staff, Enemy Branch, Bd. of Economic Warfare 1942–46; Expert on Internat. Org. Affairs, Dept. of State 1946; Exec. Asst. to Sec. of Labor in charge of Internat. Labor Affairs, Dept. of Labor 1947–49; Asst. Sec. of Labor for Internat. Labor Affairs 1949–53; Labor Adviser to Cttee. for Free Europe 1954; Special Asst. to Gov. of New York 1955–58; Prof. of Internat. Labor Relations, Sch. of Internat. Service, American Univ. 1958–61; U.S. Ambassador to Republic of Senegal, Islamic Republic of Mauritania 1961–64; Minister, American Embassy, London 1964–69; Chmn., Encyclopedia Britannica International Ltd., London 1969; Dir., Guinness Mahon Holdings Ltd. 1975–77; U.S. Ambassador to People's Republic of Hungary since 1977. *Member:* American Assoc. of Rhodes Scholars; Council on Foreign Relations; American Political Science Assoc.; Phi Beta Kappa. *Publications: Woodrow Wilson* in The History Makers, ed. Sir John Wheeler-Bennett (1973); (Co-author) *Old Problems & New in International Relations* in Great Ideas Today (1976). *Clubs:* Brooks, Queens (London); National Democratic (Washington). *Address:* American Embassy, Budapest, Hungary; and c/o Department of State, Washington, D.C. 20520, U.S.A.

**KAKITSUBO, Masayoshi,** BA. Japanese diplomat. *B.* 1907. *Educ.* Cambridge University. *M.* 1947, Noriko Kanakura. *Daus.* Masako and Yoko. *Career:* Dir., Information and Culture, Japanese Foreign Ministry 1952; Counsellor of Embassy, Australia, 1953–56; Deputy Perm. Representative to U.N., New York, 1957–62; Ambassador to Pakistan 1962–65, and to U.A.R. 1965–67. Ambassador of Japan to Switzerland 1967–69; Dir., U.N. Asian Inst. for Economic Development and Planning, Bangkok 1970–74. *Address:* c/o Ministry of Foreign Affairs, Tokyo, Japan.

**KALBACH, Harrison LeVan.** Chemical engineering executive. *B.* 1918. *Educ* .Virginia Polytechnic Inst. (MS Chem Engr); University of Florida (BS Chem Engr); Drexel Inst. of Technology; Wharton School of University of Pennsylvania; American Management Assn. *M.* 1947, Ann Elizabeth Shively. *S.* Harrison LeVan, Jr., and Stephen Hopkins. *Dau.* Suzanne Audrey. *Career:* Chemist, Southern Kraft Corp., Panama City, Fla. 1938; Chemical Engineer, Jos. E. Seagram Sons, Louisville, Ky. 1939; Chemical Engineer 1940–45; Technical Adviser 1945–47; Purchasing Manager, Atlantic Richfield Co. Philadelphia Pa. 1948–71; Chief Exec. Officer and Treas. King of Prussia Technical Co. Inc. Bryn. Mawr. Pa. 1971–72; Chmn. Chief Exec. Officer, WasteNot Inc. since 1972; Consulting Engineer & Economist, London since 1974; Dir., Monckton Equities Ltd., London since 1976. Committee Member, U.S. Govt. Petroleum Administration for War 1942. Registered Professional Engineer. *Member:* Amer. Inst. of Chemical Engineers; Amer. Chemical Socy.; Republican. *Publications:* Ortho Phosphoric Acid as an EKA-catalyst in the alkylation of Pipe Still Vapors. Several patents pending. *Clubs:* Philadelphia Country; Engineers of Philadelphia (Treasurer); Sigma Nu. *Address:* Box 544, Bryn Mawr. Pa.; and *office* Box 544, Bryn Mawr, Pa., U.S.A.

**KALES, Robert Gray.** American. *B.* 1904. *Educ.* Phillips Exeter Academy (Diploma); Massachusetts Institute of Technology (BSc, CE); Harvard Graduate School of Business Administration (MBA). *M.* (1) 1932, Jane Webster (*Div.* 1944). *S.* 2. *Daus.* 2. (2) 1945, Miriam Wallin (*Div.* 1949). *S.* 1; (3) 1951, Herma Lou Boyd (*Div.* 1961); (4) 1961, Shirley L. McBride. *S.* 1. *Dau.* 1. *Career:* With Whitehead & Kales Co. 1928–31; Secy. Treasurer, Investment Counsel, Inc., Detroit; Founded Kales Kramer Investment Co., Detroit, with Charles B. Kramer in 1933 and has been President of the Co. since its incorporation in 1935; Chmn. Bd., Jefferson Terminal Warehouse 1934—; Pres. Dir., Kales Realty Co. 1935—; Pres. Dir., Midwest Underwriters Inc. 1938—; Modern Construction Inc. 1938–60; Vice-Pres., Dir., Basin Oil Co. 1947—; Industrial Resources Inc. 1950–70; Chmn. Bd., General Discount Corp. 1951–62; Dir., Liberty Life & Accident Insurance Co. 1952–66; Independent Liberty Life Insurance Co. 1966—; Chmn. Bd., Automotive Bin Service Co. Inc. 1967— (Ohio & New York); Michigan 1968–71; Chmn., Sea Cadet Cttee., U.S. Naval Sea Cadets 1965—; Instructor, Detroit Power Squadron 1966—. *Member:* Academy of Political and Social Sciences; Amer. Inst. of Management; Amer. Legion; Assn. des Croix de Guerre; Masonic Order (Kt. Templar, York Rite Coll.); Military Order of the Wars (Past Natl. Cdr. in Chief); Navy League of the U.S. Past Pres., Southeastern (Michigan Cncl.); Order of Lafayette; Sigma Chi Fraternity; Sons of the Amer. Revolution. *Clubs:* Bayview Yacht; Country (Detroit); Detroit Athletic; Grosse Pointe Yacht. *Address:* 87 Cloverly Road, Grosse Pointe Farms, Michigan 48236, U.S.A.; and *office* 1900 E. Jefferson, Detroit, Michigan 48207, U.S.A.

**KALMANSON, Anthony,** MA Oxon. British. *B.* 1929. *Educ.* Balliol Coll., Oxford. *M.* 1962, Mette Marene Nielsen. *S.* John Stephen. *Daus.* Susan Eva and Monica Ann. *Career:* Man. Dir. and alternating Chmn.. Amalgamated Packaging Inds. Ltd. 1957–65. President, Canadian Overseas Packaging Inds. Ltd., Quebec, and Dir. of that Company's subsidiaries in Jamaica, Trinidad, Kenya and U.K. Director, Hesperus Holdings Ltd.; Iran Carton Ltd. *Clubs:* Bath & Landsdowne (London). *Address:* Butts Hill, Chobham, Surrey.

**KALODNER, Harry E.** American judge. *B.* 28 Mar. 1896. *Educ.* Univ. of Pennsylvania (LLB); LHD Yeshiva Univ. *M.* 1925, Tillie Poliner. *S.* Philip P., Howard I.; admitted to Pennsylvania Bar 1917; Sec. of Revenue, Commonwealth of Penn. 1935; Judge, Court of Common Pleas, No. 2 Philadelphia County 1936–37; Judge, U.S. District Court, Eastern District of Pa. 1938–46; Judge, U.S. Court of Appeals, 3rd Circuit since 1946; member, Bd. of Dir. Phila. Psychiatric Center; Federation of Jewish Agencies; member, Bd. of Trustees Yeshiva Univ.; National Conference of Christians and Jews; Chmn. Bd. of Governors, Cancer Inst.; Hahnemann Medical Coll. and Hosp. Philadelphia, (Penn). *Address:* U.S. Court House, Philadelphia, Pa., U.S.A.

**KAMITZ, Reinhard,** Dr. rer. com. *B.* 1907. *Educ.* Realgymnasium and Hochschule für Welthandel, Vienna (Diploma 1929, Doctor's Degree 1934). *M.* 1938, Margarete Schaudy. *S.* Reinhard, Jr. (Dr.). *Dau.* Roswitha. *Career:* After work on a foreign paper (Czechoslovakia) and in iron and steel industry (France) joined research staff of the Austrian Institute for Cyclical Research 1934–38; Asst. Professor, Hochschule für Welthandel, Vienna 1939 (Senior Lecturer on political economy in same school 1944–46); leading functions, Austrian Chamber of Commerce 1939–52; Federal Minister of Finance 1952–60; Governor of World Bank for Austria 1952–60. President, Austrian National Bank 1960–68. Governor, International Monetary Fund for Austria, Honorary Professor of Political Economy and Finance, Vienna University. Author of various publications on monetary, financial and economic subjects. Honours: GrGE/B; GrKr ddVO; GrKdbelg KrO; bayr VO; Gr Kdspan ZVO; Hon. Prof. Vienna University; Hon. Doctor. Univ. of Los Angeles. President: Austrian Committee of the Friends of the European Forum of Alpbach, Austrian Road Federation, Inst. for Advanced Studies, and Internat. Freedom Academy. *Member:* Board of the Austrian Institute for Economic Research, Institut d'Etudes politiques, Vaduz; and many other associations. *Address: office* 1013 Vienna, Renngasse 10, Austria.

**KAMM, Jacob Oswald.** American economist, writer, lecturer and business executive. *B.* 1918. *Educ.* Baldwin-Wallace College (AB 1940, LLD 1963); Brown Univ. (AMEcon. 1942); Ohio State Univ. (PhD Econ); Erskine Coll. LLD 1971. *Career:* Asst. in Economics Brown Univ. 1940–41; Instructor of Economics, Ohio State Univ. 1945–46; Associate Prof. and Chmn. Dept. of Economics Baldwin-Wallace College 1946–48; Dir., School of Commerce, Baldwin-Wallace College 1949–53 (also Prof. of Economics); Elected Vice-Pres. Cleveland Quarries Co. 1953, Exec. Vice-Pres. 1953; President 1955–67; Chmn. of the Bd. of Directors and Chief Exec. Officer since 1967; Exec. Vice-Pres. and Treas. The American Ship Building Co. Later Pres. 1967–69, Pres. 1973–74. Chmn., Lorain County Republican Finance Cttee. 1968–70; M.B.R. Ohio Republican Finance Cttee. 1970–71. Dir., Baldwin Corp.; United Screw & Bolt Corp.; Cleveland Quarries Co.; Fairmont Foods Co.; Nordson Corp.; MTD Products Inc.; Gowe Printing Co.; Oatey Co.; Bibb Co.; Cardinal Federal Savings & Loan Assn. and Vice-Chmn. (Cleveland); "Investment Policy Cttee," of Portfolio Advisory Company (a Division of the National City Bank of Cleveland); Trustee and Chmn., Ohio Manufacturers Association. *Member:* Ohio Society of New York; Ohio Board of Regents 1969–72; Bd. of Trustees and Chmn. Investment Cttee; Baldwin-Wallace College, Fellow for Life, Cleveland Zoological Scoy.; Presidents' Club of Ohio State University; St. Luke's Hosp.; Lake Ridge Academy 1963–64; Counsellors of Erskine College; John Baldwin Society; Newcomen Society; Association, Ohio Commodores; Royal Economic Socy.; American Economics Association; American Finance Association; American Association of University Professors. Member: Delta Phi Alpha; Delta Mu Delta; Beta Gamma Sigma; Phi Beta Kappa; Phi Alpha Kappa. *Publications:* (Books): Economics of Investment, (1951); Making Profits in the Stock Market, 1952, 1961, 1966, and 1971; Investors' Handbook, (1954). Articles in Journal of Finance, Journal of Marketing, Review of Economics & Statistics, etc. Contributing Editor, Webster's New World Dictionary. Columnist on Economics for Cleveland Plain Dealer; Decentralization of Securities Exchanges, 1942. *Clubs:* Brown Univ. of New York; Union (Cleveland); Duquesne (Pittsburgh); Clifton (Lakewood); Lake Placid. *Address:* Route 1, Huron, O, 44839, Amherst, Ohio 44001, U.S.A.

**KAMMERMEYER, Karl.** Professor and Head, Department of Chemical Engineering, University of Iowa 1949–73. Emeritus 1974. *B.* 1904. *Educ.* BSE, MSE, DSc in Chemical Engineering; BSE in Mathematics. *M.* 1930, Cordelia G. Meyers. *S.* John Karl. *Career:* Development Engineer, Standard Oil Co. of Indiana 1933–36; Refinery Chief, Chemist and Chemical Engineer, Pure Oil Co. 1936-39; Asst. Prof. of Chemical Engineering, Drexel Inst. of Technology 1939–42; Dir. of Research Publicker Industries Inc. 1942–47; Manager, Research and Development, Chemicals Div., The Glenn L. Martin Co. 1947–49 Consultant: U.S. Veterans Hospital, Iowa City, Iowa; Monsanto Research Corp., Dayton, Ohio. Author of 70 publications and 4 books. *Member:* A.A.A.S.;

Amer. Chemical Socy.; A.S.E.E.; Sigma Xi; Tau Beta Pi; Fellow I.Ch.E. *Club:* Triangle. *Address:* 116 Ferson Avenue, Iowa City, Ia.; and *office* 121 Chemistry Building, University of Iowa City, Ia., U.S.A.

**KANAKARATNE, Neville.** Diplomat of Sri Lanka. *B.* 1923. *Educ.* Univ. of Ceylon—BA (Hons.) in History; Univ. of Cambridge—MA, LLB; Middle Temple—Barrister-at-Law. *Career:* Crown Counsel, Attorney General's Dept., Ceylon 1951–57; First Sec. and Legal Adviser, Perm. Mission of Ceylon to the UN and Member of Ceylon's Delegations to UN General Assembly 1957–61; Legal Adviser to UN Sec.-General's Special Rep. in the Congo 1961–62; Political and Legal Adviser to Commander of UN Peace-Keeping Force, Middle East 1962–64; Legal Adviser to Sec.-General's Mediator and to Commander of UN Force, Cyprus 1964–65; Senior Fellow, School of International Studies, New York Univ. 1965–66; Minister, Ceylon High Commission, London 1967–70; Ambassador to U.S.A. and Mexico since 1970. *Address:* 2503 30th Street N.W., Washington D.C. 20008, U.S.A.; and *office* Embassy of Sri Lanka, 2148 Wyoming Avenue N.W., Washington D.C. 20008.

**KANE, David S.,** LLB. American senior Partner in law firm of Kane, Dalsimer, Kane, Sullivan & Kurucz, New York City. *B.* 1907. *Educ.* Far Rockaway High School, Washington Square College, New York Univ., and New York Univ. School of Law (LLB). *M.* 1931, Mildred Thompson. *S.* 1. *Daus.* 2. *Career:* Director, Becton, Dickinson & Co., and C. F. Mueller Co. Partner, Duell & Kane 1934–52; Senior Partner, Kane, Dalsimer & Kane 1952–65. Senior Partner, Kane, Dalsimer, Kane, Sullivan & Kurucz, and predecessor firms 1952—; Mayor of Incorporated Village of Sands Point. Trustee, New York University Law Center Foundation, C. F. Mueller Scholarship Foundation. *Member:* New York State and American Bar Assns.; Assn. of Bar of City of New York; New York County Lawyers Association; American Judicature Society; Phi Delta Phi. Mason. *Clubs:* Union League, Pinnacle, New York University (N.Y.C.); Naples (Florida) Yacht; Royal Poinciana Golf Club. *Address:* Millertown Road, Bedford, N.Y. 10506; and 140 Second Avenue North, Naples, Florida; and *office* 420 Lexington Avenue, New York, N.Y. 10017, U.S.A.

**KANELLOPOULOS, Panayotis.** Greek politician. *B.* 13 Dec. 1902. *Educ.* studied law and political science at the Universities of Athens, Heidelberg and Munich (apptd. LLD at Heidelberg). *M.* 1935. Nitsa Poulikakou. *Career:* Sec.-Gen., Ministry of National Economy 1926–27; Prof. of Sociology, Univ. of Athens 1929–35; organized and became leader of National Unionist Party 1935; volunteer, Albanian Campaign, Greek-Italian War 1940–41; escaped to Middle East on account of his national activities during German occupation 1942; Deputy Prime Minister and Minister of Defence of exiled Greek Govt. 1942–43; Minister of Finance and Reconstruction 1944; Prime Minister, Nov. 1945; elected Member of Parliament (Athens, Salonica and Patras), Mar. 1946; Minister without Portfolio 4–17 Apr. 1946; Ministry of Navy, Jan.–Apr. 1947; Minister of Air, Feb.–Aug. 1947; Minister of War 1949–50; re-elected MP (Athens and Patras) Mar. 1950; organized (with M. Stephanopoulos) Popular-Unionist Party, which he disbanded to co-operate with the Greek Rally under Marshal Papagos, Jan. 1951; again elected MP (Athens and Patras), Sept. 1951, and Nov. 1952 (Patras); Min. without Portfolio 1952; Min. of Nat. Defence 1952–54; Prime Min. and Min. of Nat. Defence 1954–55; Dep. Prime Min. 1959–61; Prime Minister 1967, later called for gen. election and arrested by army junta. *Awards:* Grand Cross, Order of Phoenix (Greece); Grand Cross, Italy, Germany, Yugoslavia and Ethiopia; Greek War Cross, Albanian Campaign Medal, Middle East Campaign Medal. *Publications:* The League of Nations (1926); Social Progress and Social Policy (1927); The Sociology of the Imperialistic Phenomena (1927); Karl Marx (1931); The Society of our days (1932); Progress of Technique and Economy (1933); The Man and the Social Conflicts (1934); Philosophical and Sociological Problems of History (1936); Simple Sounds (verse) 1939); The History of the European Spirit (1941–47); I Shall Tell you The Truth (1945); The Cycle of Sonnets (verse) (1946); The Twentieth Century (1950); Christianity and our Era (1952); Prolegomena to Metaphysics (1955); Athenian Dialogues (1956); The End of Zarathustra (1956); I war Born in 1402 (1957); Poetry and Truth in Modern Greek Life (1959); From Marathon to Pydna (3 Vols 1963); Mistra: The Akropolis to Christian Greece (Ger. and Engl., 1963); The Years of the Great War (1964); Athens (Engl., French and Ger. 1964); Ascent to Faith (Am. 1964); History of the European Spirit (3 vols); *Address:* Akadima Athinon, Odos Panepistimiou, Athens, Greece.

**KANIAK, Gustav.** Austrian judge. *B.* 30 July 1907. *Educ.* University of Vienna (Dr jur); Judge 1936–47; Official in Austrian Federal Chancellor's Office, Constitution Service 1947–50; Judge, Verwaltungsgerichtshof since Sept. 1950; Verfassungsgerichtshof since 1955. *Publications:* Österreichische Strafprozessordnung; Österreichisches Strafgesetz; Kommentar zum Amtshaftungsgesetz; Das vollkommene Gesetz-Prolegomena zu einer Thesmologie. *Address:* Schloss Schönbrunn Nr. 24, Vienna XIII, Austria.

**KANIDINC, Salahattin.** Turkish. *B.* 1927. *Educ.* First High School Istanbul; Defenbaugh School of Lettering, Minnesota; Zanerian Coll. of Penmanship Ohio; State Univ. of Iowa; Univ. of Minnesota; Univ. of California. *M.* 1957, Seniha Ustun. *S.* Sanver, Somer. *Career:* Chief Calligrapher, Naval Printing House, Istanbul 1950–61; Lettering Specialist, Buzza-Cardoza, Anaheim, Calif. 1962–63; Asst. Art Dir., Rustcraft Publishers, Dedham Mass. 1964; Lettering Specialist Tiffany & Co. 1964–72; Owner-Creative Dir., Kanidine International since 1972; World Program Dir. for Calligraphic Arts, Who's Who Biographies. *Member:* The Int. Center, Typographic Arts; Int. Assn. Master Penmen, Teachers of Handwriting; Queens Council of the Arts; Nat. Socy. of Literature and the Arts; International Panel of Designers, United Nations Philatelic Programme; Nat. Advisory Board, American Security Council. *Awards:* High Moral, by Turkish Government; Community Leader of America; Summo Cum Honore, Honors Register U.S.A.; Distinguished Service, Art of Calligraphy; Diploma, Two Thousand Men of Achievement; National Register Prominent Americans. *Address: office* 55 Liberty Street, New York, N.Y. 10005, U.S.A.

**KANJANA-VANIT, Rachan.** Thai. Thailand District Superintendent for: Tongkah Harbour Tin Dredging Bd. 1964—, Aokan Tin Bd. 1967—, Southern Kinta Consolidated Ltd. 1964—. Kamunting Tin dredging Ltd. 1964—. *B.* 1921. *Educ.* Stanford University, California (AB and AM). *M.* 1951, Yonglarp Vasuvat. *Daus.* Jaruloch and Kesary. *Career:* Language Technician, U.S. Office of War Information 1943–45; Mining Engnr., Dept. of Mines, Bangkok, 1947–51; Valuation Engnr., British-Thai War Commn. 1948–51; Mining Engnr., Tongkah Harbour Tin Dredging Ltd., Southern Kinta Consolidated Ltd. and Kamunting Tin Dredging Ltd. 1951–64; Phuket Municipal Councillor 1953–62; Chmn., Siam International Mining Assn. 1975. *Member:* Thai Inst. Engrs.; Phi Eta Sigma. *Award:* Order of White Elephant 4th Class. *Clubs:* Lions; Royal Banckok Sports; Phuket Yacht; Phuket Golf; Royal Turf; Royal Dusit Golf. *Address:* 35/1 Damrong Road, Phuket (Bhuket), Thailand; and *office* 10 Soi Span Hin, Phuket (Bhuket), Thailand.

**KANSARA, Tribhuvan Damodar,** BSc, MA. Indian. *B.* 1906. *Educ.* Bombay Univ.; Cambridge Univ. *M.* (1) Anjuben Purshottam Gadhwala; (2) 1943, Shardaben Liladhar Amratlal Mehta. *S.* 2. *Dau.* 1. *Career:* With Bank of India: Asst. Gen. Mgr. 1954, Dep. Gen. Mgr. 1960, Gen. Mgr. 1960–68; Chmn., Foreign Exchange Dealers' Assn. of India for 1967; Vice-Chmn. Indian Banks' Assn. 1962–65; Dir., Refinance Corp. for Industry Ltd. 1963–64. Chairman, whole-time Director and Chief Executive Officer, Bank of India 1968–70; Director: Agricultural Finance Corp. Ltd. (India) 1968–70; and Bank of India (U.K.) Nominees Ltd. 1960–70. *Member:* Man. Cttee., Indian Banks' Assn. 1960–70; Custodian, Bank of India 1969–70. Financial consultant to several Companies; Chmn., Board of Trustees, Hindu Education Fund, Bombay, 1959—. *Clubs:* Willingdon Sports Bombay; Royal Western India Turf (Bombay & Poona). *Address:* 11A Mayfair Gardens, Little Gibbs Road, Bombay, 6; and *office* c/o Bank of India, 70/80 M.G. Road, P.O. Box No. 238, Bombay 1, India.

**KANU, Dr. Sheka Hassan.** Sierra Leonean University Lecturer & Diplomat. *B.* 1932. *Educ.* Fourah Bay Coll.—Teacher's Advanced Cert. & BA (Hons); Univ. of Alberta (Canada)—MA, PhD. *M.* 1965, Fatmatta Rawdatu Bangurah. *S.* 2. *Daus.* 4. *Career:* Asst. Master, West African Methodist Collegiate Sch., Freetown 1956–61; Service Asst. 1966–67, Teaching Asst. 1967–69, & Lecturer 1970–71, Univ. of Alberta, Edmonton, Canada; Lecturer, Njala Univ. Coll., Sierra Leone 1971–72; Dep. High Commissioner for Sierra Leone in London 1972–73; Ambassador Ex. & Plen. to West Germany, Holland, Belgium, Luxembourg & the EEC since 1973. *Decorations:* Mem. of the Order of the

Republic of Sierra Leone. *Publications:* A World of Everlasting Conflict: Joyce Cary's View of Man & Society (1974). *Address:* 5300 Bonn, Johanniterstr. 30, West Germany; and *office* Embassy of the Republic of Sierra Leone, Ubierstr. 88, 5300 Bonn-Bad Godesberg, West Germany.

**KAPITONOV, Ivan V.** Party Leader, member of the Central Committee of the Communist Party of the Soviet Union, and Deputy to the Supreme Soviet of the U.S.S.R. *B.* 1915; graduated at Moscow Institute of Municipal Construction Engineers 1938. *Career:* Engaged in economic, Party and government work since 1938. First Secretary of the Moscow (1954–59) and Ivanovo (1959–64) Regional Committees of the C.P.S.U. Member of Central Committee since 1952, of the Secretariat since 1965; Member of the Presidium of the Supreme Soviet 1954–62. Recipient of Orders and Medals of the Soviet Union. *Address:* Central Committee of the C.P.S.U., Staraya ploshchad 4. Moscow, U.S.S.R.

**KAPITZA, Prof. Peter Leonidovitch.** Russian scientist, physicist and academician. *B.* 1894. *Educ.* Petrograd Polytechnical Institute (Faculty of Electrical Engineering); PhD (Cantab.); D. Physical Sciences (Academy of Sciences of U.S.S.R.). *M.* 1927, Anna Alekseevna Krylova. *S.* Sergei and Andrei. *Career:* Lecturer, Petrograd Polytechnical Institute 1919–21; Clerk Maxwell Student, Cambridge Univ. 1923–26; Asst. Dir. of Magnetic Research, Cavendish Laboratory, Cambridge 1924–32; Royal Society Messel Research Professor 1930–34; Director, Royal Society Mond Laboratory, Cambridge 1930–34; Director, The Institute for Physical Problems of the Acad. of Sciences of U.S.S.R., Moscow 1934–46; Prof. of the Moscow Univ. 1944–46; Head of Chair of Physics of the Moscow Physico-Technical Institute 1947–50; Senior Scientific Worker of the Institute of Crystallography of the Acad. of Science of U.S.S.R. 1950–55. Director, Institute for Physical Problems of the Academy of Sciences of U.S.S.R. 1955—; Editor, Journal of Experimental and Theoretical Physics. *Member:* Cambridge Philosophical Society; Hon. Member, Trinity College, Cambridge; Royal Society of London; Physical Society of England; Fellow, Inst. of Physics, England. Hon. Member, Moscow Society of Naturalists. Member: Acad. of Sciences of U.S.S.R.; International Academy of Astronauts, 1964. Hon. Member: Institute of Metals, England; Franklin Inst. (U.S.A.); Academy of Science, Denmark; Foreign Associate, National Acad. of Sciences (U.S.A.); Hon. Member: New York Academy of Science; Royal Irish Acad.; National Academy of Sciences, India; International Acad. History of Sciences 1971; Foreign mem., Royal Netherlands Academy of Sciences 1969; Swedish Academy of Science; National Institute of Science, India; Hon. Member, German Academy of Naturalists 'Leopoldina'; Polish Acad. of Sciences. Foreign Hon. Member, American Academy of Arts & Sciences, 1968; Serbian Academy of Sciences & Arts 1971. For. Mem. Finnish Acad. of Sciences and Arts 1974. *Awards:* Academician: Twice Hero of Socialist Labour; Order of Lenin; Order of the Red Banner of Labour. Order: Yugoslav Banner with Ribbon 1967. *Publications:* Collected Papers, 3 vol. 1964–67; various publications on physics, mainly on magnetism, cryogenics and high temperature plasma in scientific journals. *Address:* B–334, Vorobjevskoe Shosse 2, Moscow, U.S.S.R.

**KAPLAN, Sheldon Zachary.** American international lawyer; specialist in Latin American affairs. *B.* 1911. *Educ.* Yale Coll (AB 1933); Oxford University School of Jurisprudence (BA Hons 1937; MA 1945); also attended Harvard Law School and the Faculté de Droit, Univ. of Paris; Doctor (Hon. Causa), Inca Garcilaso de la Vega Univ. Peru, 1970. *M.* 1947, Megan Vondersmith. *S.* Eldon Miles, Daniel Barclay and Philip Jeremy. *Daus.* Deborah, Rebecca and Abigail. Awarded Bronze Star Medal (U.S.); Medaille de la Reconnaissance Française and Orden del Quetzal (Guatemala); Order al Merito (Peru). *Career:* U.S. Army, from private to captain 1942–46. Associated with law firm of Elder, Whitman & Weyburn, Boston 1937–40; private practice, Boston 1940–42; Asst. to Legal Adviser, U.S. Dept. of State 1946–49; Staff Consultant, House Foreign Affairs Committee, U.S. Congress 1949–57; partner, law firm of Dodd & Kaplan, Washington, D.C. 1957–58. Counsel, law firm of Wilkinson, Cragun & Barker, Washington, D.C. 1962; U.S.A. Counsel SAHSA (Honduras) Airlines, 1963—; Counsel: Central Bank of Honduras 1962–65; Partner, Law firm, Bechhoefer, Sharlitt & Lyman, Washington D.C. 1975—. Candidate (Republican) for U.S. Congress, Md. 1974. Member of U.S. Special Missions: Costa Rica 1949, El Salvador 1950, Uruguay 1955; Congressional Adviser, U.S. Deleg. to U.N. 1955. Delegate, Govt. of Nicaragua, 18th and 19th Sessions, Internatl. Sugar Council (London 1964 and 1965). Member of Board, Glaydin School (Leesburg, Va.) June 1965—. Legal Adviser in U.S., Government of Guatemala 1960–62; General Counsel, Latin American Sugar Cncl., 1963–65 & 1977; Mem., U.S. Advisory Board, Campion Hall, Oxford 1974—. *Publications:* Crime Without Punishment, (1947); Toward a Law-Governed World, (1948); The Eightieth Congress & the United Nations, (1948); Background Information on Korea, (1950); Increasing the Flow of Private Capital into Underdeveloped Areas, (1952). Contributor, 'Panama Canal Issues and Treaty Talks, (Mar. 1967 Center for Strategic Studies, Georgetown Univ.). *Member:* Amer. Socy. Composers, Authors & Publishers; Inter-Amer. Bar Assn.; Brasenose Socy.; Amer. Socy. International Law; Washington Foreign Law Socy.; Amer. Bar Assn.; Boston Bar Assn.; District of Columbia Bar Assn. *Clubs:* Yale; Army & Navy; Cosmos (all of Washington, D.C.); Yale; Sugar; British Schools & Universities; National Steeplechase & Hunt Assn. (all of N.Y.C.). *Address:* 7810 Moorland Lane, Bethesda, Md. 20014; and *office* 1747 Pennsylvania Avenue, N.W., Washington, D.C. 20006, U.S.A.

**KARAMANLIS, Constantine G.** Prime Minister of the Republic of Greece. *B.* 1907. *Educ.* Univ. of Athens. *Career:* Began practising law in Serres in 1932; elected mem. of Parliament for Serres 1935, 1936, & again 1946, 1950; Minister of Public Works, Nov. 1946–Jan. 1947, & Jan.–Feb. 1947; Minister of Transport May–Nov. 1948; Minister of Social Welfare, Nov. 1948–June 1949, & June 1949–Jan. 1950; Minister of National Defence Sept.–Nov. 1950; re-elected mem. of Parliament for Serres 1951, 1952; Minister of Public Works, later Min. of Communications & Public Works, Dec. 1954–Oct. 1955; Prime Minister 1955–56; founded the National Radical Union (ERE); Prime Minister 1956–58, 1958–61, 1961–63; resigned from leadership of ERE & left for Paris, Dec. 1963; recalled in July 1974 to head National Emergency Government; founded New Democracy Party which won the elections of Nov. 1974; Prime Minister since 1974. *Decorations:* numerous, incl. Grand Cross of George I, Commander's Cross of the Order of the Redeemer, of the Legion of Honour, of Merit (Austria), of the Belgian Crown, of Orange-Nassau (Netherlands), etc. *Address:* 2, Herod Atticus Street, Athens, Greece.

**KARAMEH, Rashid.** *B.* 1921. *Educ.* Fuad-al-Awal Univ., Cairo. Minister of Economy and Social Affairs 1954–55; Prime Minister 1955–56 (also Minister of the Interior) and 1958–60 (also Minister of Economy and Information 1958–59, and Minister of Finance and Defence 1958–60). Prime Minister and Minister of Finance, Lebanon 1961–71; Prime Minister 1975–76. *Address:* Rue Karm Elle, Beirut, Lebanon.

**KARAN SINGH, Dr.** *B.* 9 Mar. 1931. *Educ.* Doon School; Jammu and Kashmir University (BA); Delhi University (MA Pol; PhD). *M.* 1950, Princess Yasho Rajya Lakshmi of Nepal. Regent of Jammu and Kashmir State June 1949; elected as first Head of State Nov. 1952; re-elected Sadar-i-Riyasat 1957, 1962, Governor, J. & K. 1962–67; joined Union Cabinet 1967; represents Udhampur constituency of J. & K. in Lok Sabha. Minister of Tourism and Civil Aviation 1967–73; Minister of Health and Family Planning Govt. of India 1973–77. Sec., Jawaharlal Nehru Mem. Fund; Chmn., Indian Board for Wildlife and Project Tiger; Convenor, National Cttee, Sri Aurobindo Centenary. *Address:* 3 Nyaya Marg. Chanakyapuri, New Delhi, India.

**KARAYAZICI, Fuat Ilhan.** Turkish consulting and mining engineer. *B.* 1920. *Educ.* University of Pittsburg (BS Mining Engineer) and Columbia Univ. (MS Mining Eng); London School of Economics (Grad., research in economics of ind.). *M.* Birgen. *S.* Oral, Eral. *Career:* With Eregli Coal Mining Co.; Colliery Eng. 1944–45; Chief Plan. Eng. 1950–51; District Manager 1953–54; Asst. Gen. Mgr. 1954–56; Adviser, Etibank, Ankara 1956–57; Director, Plan. Dept. T.K.I. Ankara 1957–62. Gen. Dir., Wire Rope and Wire Industry Ltd., Istanbul 1962–67. Assistant Director General for mining, Etibank Ankara, 1967–71; Vice-Chairman, Black Sea Copper Works Corp. 1968–71; Consultant to Zinc and Lead Corporation; Executive Board Member Industrial Minerals Ltd.; Partner Dir. TE-TA Engineers and Consultants Ltd. since 1972. *Publications:* articles on the nationalized industries, economics of fuel, power, mining and research in Turkey. *Member:* Turkish Mining Engineers Association, Chamber of Turkish Engineers and Architects. *Address:* 1 Bestekâr Sokak, Ankara, Turkey.

**KARDELJ, Edvard.** Yugoslav statesman. *B.* 27 Jan. 1910. *Educ.* Teacher's College, Ljubljana; Hon. mem. Slovene Acad. of Sciences and Art: Bosnian & Herzegovinian;

Macedonian mem. Serbian Acad. Sciences & Art; Dr. h.c. Ljubljana. *M. S.* 1. *Dau.* 1. *Career:* Member, of The Presidium of League of Communists of Yugoslavia 1969—; Executive Bureau of the Presidium of the League of Communists of Yugoslavia, 1969–72, and of Cncl. of the Fed. 1963–74; mem. of Presidency of SFR of Yugoslavia since 1974; After graduation (1929) was arrested on account of his political activities and sentenced to two years' hard labour, but continued his activities in the movement against the regime of the 'Sixth of January' dictatorship; completed short course at the Lenin School, Moscow, 1934–37; on return to Yugoslavia and until World War II was engaged as a publicist; under the pseudonym 'Sperans'. One of the founders of the Liberation Front in Slovenia and Vice-President of its Exec. Cttee. 1941; became member of the Supreme H.Q. of the National Liberation Army and Partisan Detachment of Yugoslavia; elected Vice-Pres. of Natl. Cttee. of the Liberation of Yugoslavia; Vice-Pres. of the Federal Govt. since Mar. 1945 and Minister of Foreign Affairs 1948–53; since the constitutional reform in 1953, has been Vice-Pres. of the Fed. Exec. Cncl.; Pres. Federal Assembly of Yugoslavia 1963–67; Chief of Yugoslav delegation to Peace Conference, Paris (1946) and to U.N. 1947; participated in Conference of Council of Ministers of Foreign Affairs, Moscow, 1947; Chief of delegation to 3rd Session of U.N. 1948, 4th Session 1949, and 5th Session 1950; Secy., Cent. Cttee. League of Communists of Yugoslavia 1948–66, also of Cent. Cttee. of Communist League of Slovenia, visited Belgium and Norway at the invitation of the Labour Parties of those countries. Visited Denmark, Sweden, Norway, Greece, the U.A.R., India, Indonesia, Iraq, Sudan, Tanzania, Zambia, Uganda, Kenya, Chile, Peru, Mexico at the invitation of the governments of those countries. Head of Yugoslav parly. delegations to Czechoslovakia, German Democratic Republic, Belgium, the U.A.R., Poland, U.S.S.R., Mali and Guinea; Member, Del. to Algiers Conf. of non-aligned countries 1973; visited Poland, UAR, USSR, 1974; Hungary, Czechoslovakia and Romania 1975; Member of Yugoslav Delegation at the Conference on Co-operation and Security in Europe at Helsinki; Chmn. of the Constitutional commission, played active role in drafting the new Constitution of Yugoslavia. *Awards:* National Hero; Partisan Star; National Liberation; Brotherhood and Unity; Order of Merit for the People; Order of Valour; Order of Hero of Socialist Work; Order of the Great Yugoslavia Star. *Publications:* The Development of the Slovenian National Question (1939); The Road of New Yugoslavia; The Foundations of the Social and Political Orders; Problem of our Social Development; Problems of Socialist Policy in the Countryside; Socialism and War; The Problems of Socialist Development (9 vols.); The New Constitution of Socialist Yugoslavia; Notes on our Social Criticism, The Bureaucracy, the Working-class; Crossroads in the Development of our Socialist Society; Contradictions of Social Property in Contemporary Socialist Practice; Basic Causes and Directions of Constitutional changes; The Historical Roots of Non-Alignment; a large number of brochures, essays and articles on foreign and internal policy. *Address:* Presidency of SFR of Yugoslavia, Belgrade, Yugoslavia.

**KARHILO, Aarno Eino.** Finnish Diplomat. *B.* 1927. *Educ.* Helsinki Univ., Master of Laws. *M.* Liisa Karttunen. *Daus.* 2. *Career:* Posts at the Ministry of Foreign Affairs, Helsinki, & in Washington, D.C. & Rio de Janeiro 1952–61; Embassy of Finland. Rome 1961–63; Counsellor and Dep. Perm. Repr., Mission of Finland to the UN, New York 1963–65; Chief of Bureau, UN Affairs, Min. of Foreign Affairs, Helsinki 1965–66; Counsellor & Dep. Head of the Embassy of Finland, Moscow 1966–68; Dep. Dir. for Political Affairs, in charge of Security Council Affairs & International Organizations, Min. of Foreign Affairs, Helsinki 1969–71; Ambassador to Japan 1971–72; Perm. Rep. of Finland to the UN, New York 1972–77; Ambassador to France since 1977 & Perm. Rep. of Finland to UNESCO 1977—. *Decorations:* Order of the Lion, Finland; Order of the Southern Cross, Brazil; Order of Merit; Italy; Order of the Tunisian Republic. *Publications:* articles on Foreign Policy. *Address:* 58 Avenue Foch, Paris; and *office* 2 rue Fabert, Paris, France.

**KARJALAINEN, Ahti Kalle Samuli.** *B.* 1923. *Educ.* Univ. of Helsinki (Dr. of Political Science). *M.* 1947, Päivi Helinä Koskinen; 4 children. *Career:* Secy. to the Prime Minister 1950–56; Member of Board, Post Office Savings Bank 1956—; Minister of Finance 1957–58; Member Board of Directors, Bank of Finland 1958—; Minister of Trade and Industry 1959–61; Minister of Foreign Affairs 1961-62: Prime Minister 1962–63; Minister of Foreign Affairs of Finland, 1964–70; Member of Parliament 1966—; Prime Minister 1970–71; Minister of Foreign Affairs of Finland 1972–75; Special Economics Minister & Vice Premier 1976–77. *Address:* Perustie 13, Helsinki, Finland.

**KARSH, Yousuf.** Canadian portrait photographer. *B.* 1908. *M.* (1) 1939, Solange Gauthier (*Dec.* 1961). *M.* (2) 1962, Estrellita Nachbar. *Career:* Studied photography in Boston with John H. Garo 1928–32; opened Ottawa studio 1932. Since 1941 has photographed most of the world's significant figures in politics, industry, business, religion, the arts and sciences, including H.M. Queen Elizabeth, King George VI, George Bernard Shaw, Winston Churchill, Albert Schweitzer, Albert Einstein, Ernest Hemingway, Picasso, Presidents Eisenhower, Kennedy, and Lyndon Johnson, and Popes Pius XII, John XXIII and Paul VI. Numerous one-man exhibitions. *Awards:* Hon. LLD: Carleton University, Ottawa 1960, and Queen's Univ., Kingston, Ont. 1960; Hon DHL, Dartmouth College, Hanover, N.H. 1961, Athens (Ohio) Univ. 1965, Hon LLD, Mount Allison Univ. 1968, New Brunswick. Hon DCL, Bishops Univ., Quebec, 1969; Hon Deg DHL, Emerson Coll., Boston, Brooks Inst. 1969. Canada Council Medal, 1965; Order of Canada (Service Medal), 1968. Photographic Adviser, Expo 70, Osaka, Japan. Visiting Prof. of Fine Arts, Ohio Univ. 1970; Fine Arts Emerson Coll. Boston 1972–73. Trustee, Phot. Arts & Sciences Foundation; Fellowship Rochester Science Center Rochester N.Y.; Hon. Fellow, Royal Photographic Socy. of Great Britain; Fellow, Royal Canadian Acad. of Arts 1975. *Publications:* Faces of Destiny (1946); This is the Mass (1958); Portraits of Greatness (1959); This is Rome (1960); This is the Holy Land (1961); In Search of Greatness (autobiography) (1962); These are the Sacraments (1962); The Warren Court (with John Frank) (1965); Karsh Portfolio (1967); Faces of our Time (1971); Karsh Portraits (1976). *Address:* Little Wings, Box 1931, Prescott Highway, Ottawa; and *office* Chateau Laurier Hotel, Ottawa, Canada.

**KARSTEN, Christian Friedrich,** DSc (Econ). *B.* 1917. *Educ.* DSc (Econ). *Married. S.* 3. *Dau.* 1. *Career:* Successively Economist 1945, Secretary to the Managing Directors 1948, Asst. Gen. Mgr. 1948–52, Rotterdamsche Bank N.V. Managing Director: Rotterdamsche Bank N.V., Rotterdam 1955–65; Amsterdam-Rotterdam Bank N.V. (merger Rotterdamsche Bank N.V. and Amsterdamsche Bank. N.V.) 1966—; Professor, Erasmus Univ. of Rotterdam since 1972, Dir. of several companies, a.o. Kon. Ned. Hoogovens Holland-Amerika Lijn Nationale-Nederlanden N.V. Van Doorne's Autombielfabrieken N.V. *Publications:* Het Amerikaanse Bankwezen; Banking without Cheques; Competition between Commercial Banks and other financing institutions; The Role of Banks in Industrial Financing; EWG-Perspektiven des Bankwesens; Transfer Systems: Should Europe restrict U.S. Investments? Banking in the Netherlands 1955; Ueberfremdung oder Intergrierung der Europäischen Industrie, (1970); Enkele recente ontwikkelingen in het Amerikaanse Bankwezen; Analysis of a Crisis (1973); Some recent changes in the Dutch commercial banking system International Economics and Banking (1974). *Address:* 15 Rijksweg Oost. Laren (NH); and *office* 595 Herengracht, Amsterdam, The Netherlands.

**KASDI, Sudarsono,** Indonesian diplomat. *B.* 1945. *Educ.* Sec. and High Schools; Indonesian Naval Academy (Commando Corps) 1964–68. *Career:* Joined Indonesian Navy as Marine Cadet Officer (Indon. Naval Acad. in Surabaya) 1964–68; served as Sub-Liet. KKO, attached to Marine Platoon Commandant in Jakarta 1970–73; ADC to Chief of Staff of Indonesian Navy 1973–74; served with rank of Captain (KKO), attached to Indonesian Embassy as Private Secy. to U.K. Ambassador since 1974. *Decoration:* Satya Lencana Wira Dharma (Indon.). *Address:* Nusantara, Bishop's Grove, The Bishop's Ave., London N.2; and *office* Indonesian Embassy, 38 Grosvenor Square, London W.1.

**KASTEEL, Petrus Albertus.** Dutch diplomat and essayist. *B.* 4 Nov. 1901. *Educ.* Dr Pol & Soc Sc. *M.* 1927, M. J. A. Baltussen. *S.* 3. *Daus.* 2. *Career:* Netherlands Ministry of Justice, London 1940–41; Governor of Curaçao 1942–48; En. Ex. and Min. Plen. to Chile 1948–55; Ambassador Oct. 1955; En. Ex. and Min. Plen to Ireland 1955, Ambassador, 1958–64; to Israel Oct. 1964–67 (Retd.). *Awards:* Knight, Order of Netherlands Lion; Cross of Merit, Netherlands Red Cross; Grand Croix, Ordre d'Honneur et Mérite (Haiti); Gran Cruz, Orden al Mérito (Chile) and Grande Oficial, Orden de Simon Bolivar (Venezuela), Orden del Mérito Juan Pablo Duarte (Dominican Republic), Orden del Sol del Peru, Ordem do Cruzeiro do Sul (Brazil), Order of St. Gregory the Great (Holy See); Medal of Freedom with Silver Palms (U.S.A.);

Commandeur de la Légion d'Honneur. Knight Holy Sepulchre. *Publication:* Abraham Kuyper. *Club:* Circolo di Roma. *Address:* Palazzo Rusticucci, Via della Conciliazione 44, 00193 Rome, Italy.

**KATER, Sir Gregory Blaxland.** Australian. *B.* 1912. *Educ.* Cambridge University (MA). *M.* 1937, Catherine Ferris-Scott. *S.* 2. *Dau.* 1. *Career:* With A.I.F. 1939–45—four years overseas service—Major. Chairman: Commercial Banking Co. of Sydney, Ltd., Colonial Sugar Refining Co. Ltd., Electrical Equipment of Australia Ltd., Mercantile and General Reinsurance Co. of Australia Ltd., Metal Manufacturers. Ltd., Oil Search Ltd., Permanent Trustee Co. of N.S.W. Ltd. Director: H. E. Kater & Son Pty. Ltd., Vickers Australia Ltd.; and W. R. Carpenter Holdings Ltd.; Vice-President, N.S.W. Society for Crippled Children. *Award:* Created Knight Bachelor 1974. *Member:* F.I.E.E.; F.I.E. (Aust.). *Clubs:* Australian, Junior Carlton, Royal Sydney Golf, Union. Liveryman of the Worshipful Company of Borderers. *Address:* 106 Victoria Road, Bellevue Hill, N.S.W.; *and office* 56 Pitt Street, Sydney, N.S.W., Australia.

**KATZ, Israel.** American engineer. *B.* 1917. *Educ.* North-eastern Univ. (BSME) Massachusetts Inst. of Technology (Naval Architecture); Cornell Univ. (MME). *M.* 1942, Betty Steigman. *Daus.* Susan Joanne, Judith Melanie, Ruth Ellen. *Career:* Test engineer, General Electric Co. 1938–42; Engineer-in-Charge, Submarine Propulsion Machinery, U.S. Naval Diesel Engineering Laboratory, Cornell Univ. (Civilian Capacity) 1942–46; Assistant Professor, Graduate School of Aeronautical Engineering, Cornell University 1946–48; Associate Professor of Mechanical Engineering and Professor-in-Charge of the Aircraft Powerplants Laboratory, Cornell University 1948–57; Manager-Liaison and Consulting Engineering, General Electric Advanced Electronics Center at Cornell Univ. 1957–63; Director, Benwill Pub. Corp. 1964; Editor in Chief, Technology Transfer Times 1976—; Dean of the Center for Continuing Education, North-eastern Univ. 1967–74; Prof. & Dir. of Advanced Engineering Programs 1974—; Member, Panel on Yield of Electronic materials & Devices, National Materials Advisory Bd. 1970; Chmn. Subcttee. for Research and Education; Cttee. on Materials Science Application and Coordination, National Research Council 1972–73; Consultant, Engineering, National Academy of Sciences since 1971; Chmn. C.E.S. Division, American Soc. for Engineering Education 1975–76; Developments and Programme Participation: Endodontic Pressure Syringe (with Greenberg); Semi-automatic High-Speed Dynamometer, High-Speed Marine Propeller Test Tunnel, Ribbonwire Tensile Test Machine, Low-pressure Injection Oil Engine Turbo-compound Radial Engine, Early-Warning Airship, AN/TPQ-10 Close Support Bombardment System, Submarine-Launched Missile System Study, Atlas Missile Radio Guidance System, WS-125A Nuclear-Propelled Strategic Penetrator, MSQ Bomber-Fleet Automatic Traffic Control, CAMAL Strategic Alert System, Global Surveillance Satellite System. *Member:* Temple Beth El, Ithaca, N.Y. (Chairman, Board of Trustees 1958–62; President of the Congregation 1956–58); Fidelity Lodge No. 51 F. and A.M.; Kalurah Temple; Institute, Electrical and Electronics Engineers; Research Society of America; Tau Beta Pi; Senate Socy., Cornell Socy. of Engineers; Amer. Socy. for Engineering Education; President, Daniel Rothschild Lodge (Bnai Brith) 1962–63; Amer. Assn. for the Advancement of Science *Publications:* Some aspects in Fuel Injection in Aircraft Engines (1947); Principles of Aircraft Propulsion Machinery (1949); Ballistics of Continuously Propelled, Radar Directed Missiles (1953); Optimum Flow Dilution in Ducted Fan Engines (1955); Electro-magnetic Propagation Relating to ICBM (with Matt and Einbinder) (1957); Hazardous Environmental Factors Relating to Supersonic Bomber Defense (1958); Technological and Sociological Factors Affecting the Military Use of Space Vehicles (1959); Scientific Education in the Space Age (1961); Functional and Operational Requirements for the Military Uses of Man in Space (1962); Guidelines for Continuing Engineering Studies in Urban Centers (1966); Structures of Terrestrial and Extra-terrestrial Atmospheres (1966); The Boston Stone for UNICEF fable book. 'Friends' (1968); Design of Continuing Engineering Studies for the Aerospace Field (1969); Higher Continuing Education, Handbook of College and University Administration (1970); An Emerging Role for Universities (1970); The Critical Reaction in Mankind (1971); The Theory and Practice of Higher Continuing Education (MIT 100th Anniversary of Women Graduates) 1973. A Case Study of Post-Experience Higher Education that Supplements and Stimulates Learning on the Job (UNESCO IIEP Seminar on Educational Planning, 1974); Motivation of Engineers Electro-76). *Clubs:* Shrine. *Address:* 40 Auburn Street, Brookline, Mass., U.S.A.

**KATZ, Milton.** American lawyer and diplomat. *B.* 29 Nov. 1907. *Educ.* Harvard Univ. AB, JD. *M.* 1933, Vivian Greenberg. *S.* John, Robert, Peter. *Career:* Anthropological expedition across Central Africa for Peabody Musuem, Harvard 1927–28; Member of Bar since 1932; various official posts U.S. Government 1932–39; Professor of Law, Harvard University 1940–50; served World War II with War Production Board and as U.S. Executive Officer, Combined Production and Resources Board 1941–43, thereafter Lt.-Comdr., U.S.N.R. until end of war; Deputy U.S. Special Representative in Europe with rank of Ambassador, 1949–June 1950; U.S. Special Representative in Europe with rank of Ambassador, July 1950–Aug. 1951; U.S. Representative on the North Atlantic Defence, Finance and Economic Committee, July 1950–Aug. 1951; U.S. Representative, Economic Commission for Europe July 1950–Aug. 1951; Associate Director, Ford Foundation Aug. 1951–June 1954 (thereafter Programme Counsellor); Dir., Internat. Legal Studies and Henry L. Stimson Prof. of Law, Harvard Law School since July 1954, and Dir., International Programme in Taxation, 1961–63; Trustee: Chmn. Bd. of Trustees, Carnegie Endowment for Internation Peace; (Exec. Cttee.), World Peace Foundation; Pres. Citizens Research Foundation; Inter-American Univ. Foundation; Brandeis Univ.; Chmn. Bd. of Trustees, International Lega Center; Case Western Reserve University. Fellow & Cnclr., American Academy of Arts and Sciences; Member, Corp. Boston Museum of Science. Member Cttee. on Foreign Affairs Personnel 1961–63; Exec. Cttee., Cttee. on Compaign Contributions and Expenditures; Chmn. Cttee. on Life Sciences and Social Policy, National Academy of Science, National Research Council 1968–75. Member, Panel on Technology Assessment, National Academy of Sciences 1968–69; Visiting Committee for the Humanities, MIT, 1970–73; Mem. Adv. Bd. Energy Lab., MIT, since 1974; Sherman Fairchild Distinguished Scholar Calif. Inst. of Technology 1974; Chmn. Energy Advisory Cttee. & Consultant U.S. Office, Technology Assessment. *Award:* Legion of Merit; Commendation Ribbon; LLD hon causa (Brandeis). *Publications:* Cases and Materials on Administrative Law; Government Under Law and the Individual (Co-author and editor); The Law of International Transaction and Relations; Cases and Materials (with Kingman Brewster, Jr.); The Things that are Caesar's; The Relevance of International Adjudication; The Modern Foundation: Its Dual Nature, Public and Private; Man's Impact on the Global Environment (contributor with others); Assessing Biomedical Technologies (with others); *Address:* c/o Harvard Law School, Cambridge, Mass. 02138, U.S.A.

**KATZIR, Ephraim.** Biophysicist, President of Israel. *B.* 1916. *Educ.* Hebrew Univ. of Jerusalem, MSc, PhD. *M.* 1938, Nina Gotlieb. *S.* 1. *Dau.* 1. *Career:* Asst., Dept of Theoretical Chemistry, Hebrew Univ. 1941–45; Research Fellow, Polytechnic Inst., Brooklyn 1946–48; Acting Head & Head, Dept. of Biophysics, Weizmann Inst., Israel 1949–73; Visiting Prof. of Biophysics, Hebrew Univ. Jerusalem 1953–61; Guest Scientist at Harvard Univ. 1957–59; Chief Scientist, Israel Defense Ministry 1966–68; Elected Fourth President of Israel, 1973. *Member:* Royal Society, London, Foreign Member; National Academy of Sciences, U.S.A.; American Chemical Society, Centennial Foreign Fellow; Leopoldina Academy of Science, Germany; World Academy of Art & Science; CIBA Foundation, Scientific Advisory Panel. *Awards:* Israel Prize in Natural Science, 1959; Linderstrom Lang Gold Medal, 1969; Hans Krebs Medal, 1972. *Publications:* Numerous Scientific Papers in Professional Journals. *Address:* President's Residence, 3 Ha-Nassi Street, Jerusalem, Israel.

**KAUFFMANN, Kurt.** Financial consultant and travel writer. *B.* 1900. *Educ.* Heidelberg (PhD econ). *M.* 1934, Nelly Baade. *Career:* Consultant to families and business firms in Germany, Switzerland, Liechtenstein, U.S.A. 1937–51 in New York (Wall Street). Became citizen of U.S.A. Travels in 73 countries of 4 continents. Since 1961 in Switzerland. Owns important collection of old maps. Fellow, Royal Geographical Society. *Address:* Lindenfeldsteig 9, Lucerne, Switzerland.

**KAUFMAN, Gerald Bernard,** MA, MP. British politician. *B.* 1930. *Educ.* State Schools, Oxford University. *Career:* Asst. Gen. Sec. Fabian Society 1954–55; Political Staff, Daily Mirror, 1955–64; Political Correspondent, New Statesman, 1964–65; Parly. Press Liaison Officer, Labour Party, 1965–70; Under-Sec. of State, Dept. of the Environment, 1974–75;

Under-Secy. of State, Dept. of Industry, 1975; Minister of State, Dept. of Industry, since 1975; Member of Parliament for Ardwick. *Member:* National Union of Journalists. *Publications:* How to Live Under Labour; The Left; To Build The Promised Land. *Clubs:* Bellevue British Legion. *Address:* 87 Charlbert Court, Eamont Street, London, NW8 7DA and *office* House of Commons, London, S.W.1.

**KAUFMANN, Arthur Coblens.** American. *B.* 1901. *Educ.* Peabody High School, Pittsburgh. *M.* 1936, Dorothy Blatt. *Daus.* Susan and Jane. *Career:* Exec. Head, McCreery & Co., Pittsburgh 1928–34; Vice-Pres. & Dir., Gimbel Brothers Inc., N.Y.C.; Executive Head of Gimbel Stores in Philadelphia 1934–58; Civilian Aide to the Secretary of the U.S. Army 1956–64. Re-appointed for the First Army Area, 1969—. President, Arthur C. Kaufmann & Assoc. Inc. Trustee; Lankenau Hospital, The Pennsylvania Acad. of Fine Arts, Devon Horse Show. *Awards:* Star of Italian Solidarity (bestowed twice); Chevalier, Order of Merit (Rep. of Italy); Order of Commercial Merit, and Chevalier, Order of National Economy (France); Cross, Order of the Crown (Belgium); Order of Orange-Nassau (Netherlands). Hon. DHL Temple Univ. 1956, Thomas Jefferson Univ. 1976; 4 Awards, U.S. Dept. of the Army 1949–53–62–64; American Congress Award for Civic, Social and Industrial Achievement 1948; Man-of-the-Year Award (Men's Wear Industry) 1948; Pioneers of Industry Award (Murrell Dobbins Vocational School, Phila.) 1951. Member, Pennsylvania Socy. *Clubs:* Peale; The Urban, City Business of Phila.; Union League of Philadelphia. *Address:* 214 Cheswold Lane, Haverford, Pa., U.S.A.; and *office* 1617 John F. Kennedy Boulevard, Philadelphia Pa. 19103, U.S.A.

**KAUNDA, Kenneth David.** President of Zambia, (formerly Prime Minister N. Rhodesia). *B.* 1924. *Educ.* Lubwa Training School (also Teacher and Headmaster there) and Munali Secondary School. *M.* 1946, Betty Banda. *S.* 7. *Daus.* 2. *Career:* Offices in African National Congress: District Secy. 1950–52; Provincial Organizing Secy. 1952–53; Secy.-Gen. 1953–58; Natl. Pres.: Zambian African Natl. Congress 1958–59; and United Natl. Independence Party 1960; Chmn. Pan-African Freedom Movement for East, Central and South Africa 1962. Minister of Local Govt. and Social Welfare, N. Rhodesia 1962–63; Prime Minister of Northern Rhodesia Jan. 1964–Oct. 1964; Pres. of Zambia since 1964. Hon LLD Universities of Fordham (U.S.A.), Sussex, Dublin, York, Windsor (Canada) and Chile. Chancellor. Univ. of Zambia, 1966—. *Publications:* Black Government (1961); Zambia Shall Be Free (1962); Humanism in Zambia and a Guide to its Implementation (1967). *Address:* State House, P.O. Box 135, Lusaka, Zambia.

**KAWAKITA, Nagamasa.** Japanese. *B.* 1903. *Educ.* Nat. Univ. of Peking. *M.* 1928, Kashiko Takeuchi. *Dau.* 1. *Career:* Vice Pres. China Film Corp. 1939–45; Dir. Nat. Film Corp. 1942–45; Chmn., Toho-Towa Corp.; Man. Dir. Unijapanfilm; Dir. Toho Co. Ltd.; Pres. Motion Picture Co. *Member:* Industrial Rationalization Cttee.; Ministry of International Trade; Dir. Fed. of Motion Picture Industries; Pres. Foreign Film Importers Distributors Association. *Awards:* Commander of Republic, Italy; Officer, Arts & Letters; Chev. Legion of Honour (France); Medal of Merit, Blue Ribbon, Order of Sacred Treasure, 2nd class (Japan). *Clubs:* Tokyo; Maison Franco-Japonaise. *Address:* 2-2 Yukinoshata, Kamakura-shi, Kanagawa-Ken, Japan and *office* 2-2 Ginza, Chuo-Ku, Tokyo.

**KAWAWA, Rashidi Mfaume.** Tanzanian Politician. *B.* 1929. *Educ.* Secondary School, Tabora. *Career:* Pres., Tanganyika Fed. of Labour; Vice-Pres., Tanganyika African National Union (TANU); Member Central and National Executive Cttees. Minister of Local Government and Housing 1960–61: Minister Without Portfolio 1961–62; Prime Minister Jan.–Dec. 1962; Vice-Pres. 1962–64; 2nd Vice-Pres. 1964–72; Prime Minister and 2nd Vice-Pres. 1972–77; Minister of Defence & National Service 1977—. *Address:* Ministry of Defence, Dar-es-Salaam, Tanzania.

**KAYLA, Ziya.** Turkish economist. *B.* 1912. *Educ.* School of Political Sciences, Istanbul. *M.* 1967, Sevinc Cenk. *Career:* Ministry of Finance 1934–63; Asst. Inspector, Inspector and Chief Inspector, 1934–60; Deputy Min. of Finance, 1960–63; Chmn., Bd. of Directors and Dir. General, Central Bank of Turkey 1963–66. Member, Board of Controllers of the Prime Ministry 1966–70; Chmn. of Bd. Türkiye Vakiflar Bank 1971–76. *Publications:* Emission Movements in Turkey (1967); Treasury and Central Banks Relations (1970). *Address:* Mesnevi sokak 8/8, Ankara, Turkey.

**KAYRA, Ömer Cahit.** Turkish politician. *B.* 1917. *Educ.* Univ. (Econ.). *M.* 1950, Gönül. *S.* 2. *Career:* Insp. of Finance, Min. of Finance 1939–50; Consult to the Revenue Dept., Min. of Finance 1950–55; Economic Financial Consultant 1955–59; Head of Foreign Trade Dept. Min. of Trade 1959–60; Head of Turkish Delegation to the GATT, Geneva 1960–63; Asst. Secy. Min. of Finance, 1963–64; Head of Turkish Delegation to OECD-Paris 1964–67, Head of Research Dept., Min. of Finance 1968–72; Member of Parliament since 1973, Min. of Energy and Natural Resources 1974. *Publications:* Balance of Payments of Turkey (1972); Free Trade of Gold in Turkey (1971); Foreign Aid (1970); A Rational Customs Policy (1969); Foreign Trade Policy of Turkey (1964); A Guide to the Turkish System of Taxation (1959—in English). *Address:* Kavaklidere, Güvenevleri, Ic Ŝokak, no 3/4, Ankara, Turkey; and *office* Turkish Parliament, Ankara, Turkey.

**KEARNS, Amos Ragan.** *B.* 1905. *Educ.* Staunton Military Acad., and Duke Univ. (AB 1927). *M.* 1933, Louise Copeland. *S.* Amos R., Jr. *Dau.* Jane Edgerton (Marlowe). *Career:* Member of City Council, City of High Point, N.C. 1938–51; Mayor 1951–53; Dir., N.C. Bd. of Conservation & Development, and Chmn., State Parks Cttee. 1953–61. Chmn. of the Board & Treasurer, Crown Hosiery Mills Inc., High Point, North Carolina; Vice-President & Secretary, G.A.C. Corp. (real estate); Vice-Chmn. and Director, Tom Haggai and Associates. Trustee: Duke University (and member Executive Committee, and Chairman Board of Visitors, Medical Center); and Wesley Memorial Methodist Church; and Angier B. Duke Memorial, Inc. *Member:* Board of Trustees, Duke Endowment; Advisory Council to Maryfield Nursing Home Inc.; Advisory Board to Westchester Academy. Director: Research Triangle Foundation of North Carolina United Community Services, North Carolina Citizens Assoc. Inc.; member, Bd. of Dir., High Point Bank & Trust Co.; Hon. Trustee, Emeritus for Life, High Point Memorial Hospital. *Clubs:* Rotary; Emerywood Country; Union League (N.Y.C.); String and Splinter (Past Pres.). *Address:* 600 Emerywood Drive, High Point, N.C.; and *office* 449 South Wrenn Street, High Point, N.C., U.S.A.

**KEARNS, Frederick Ronald.** *B.* 1924. *Educ.* McGill Univ. School of Commerce. *M.* 1948, Elizabeth Black. *S.* 3. *Daus.* 2. *Career:* Canadian Dept. of National Defence, Ottawa 1940–42; Fighter Pilot R.C.A.F., 1942–45; (McGill Univ.); joined Canadair, 1949; Chief cost accountant, 1951–53; Assist. Comptroller 1953–57; Vice-Pres. and Comptroller, 1957–60; Exec. Vice-Pres., Sales and Finance, 1960; Board of Directors, 1961; Exec. Vice-Pres., 1963; President & Chief Exec. Officer of Canadair Ltd., 1965—. Chmn. of Board, Air Industries Assoc. of Canada 1974–75; Dir., Asbestos Corp. Ltd.; Dir., Quebec Industrial Relations Inst., Canadian German Chamber of Commerce; Board of Governors, Canadian Assoc. of Latin America. Mem: Financial Executives Inst. (Dir. 1957–60), Montreal Board of Trade, Canadian Chamber of Commerce (Exec. Council) and Canadian Aeronautics and Space Inst. *Clubs:* Royal Montreal Golf, Royal Ottawa Golf, Mount Royal. *Address: office* P.O. Box 6087, Montreal 101, P.Q., Canada.

**KEATE, James Stuart.** Canadian. publisher. *B.* 1913. *Educ.* Prince of Wales HS, Vancouver; Univ. of British Columbia (BA 1935). *M.* 1939, Letha Katherine Meilicke. *S.* Richard Stuart. *Dau.* Kathryn Jane. *Career:* Vancouver Daily Province 1935–37; Toronto Daily Star 1937–38; Vancouver Daily Province 1938–42; Royal Canadian Navy Volunteer Reserve 1942–45; Time, Inc., New York and Montreal 1945–50; Publisher, Victoria Daily Times 1950–64; Publisher Vancouver Sun since 1964. *Member:* The Int. Press Institute, Dir. Can. Cttee.; former Pres., Canadian Daily Newspaper Assn.; former Pres., The Canadian Press, Hon. life member. The Canada Council 1966–69, former Dir. and Pres. of several orgs. *Awards:* National Press Club Award, 1966; Centen. Medal 1967; Mem. Canadian Hall of Fame 1974. *Publications:* contributions to Maclean's Saturday Night, Reader's Digest, New York Times Book Review, London Times, 'Canada' supplement. Press and Public: Canadian Club Lecture, Univ. of B.C. 1955 Lecturer (Can. Club); Report on CBC programme for Can. Govt. (This Hour has 7 days). Liberal. *Clubs:* Vancouver Union (Victoria); Capilano Golf & Country (West Vancouver), Shaughnessy Golf & Country (Vancouver); Victoria Golf (Victoria). *Address:* 3455 Marpole Avenue, Vancouver 9, Canada.

**KEELING, Sir John (Henry).** British company director. *B.* 18 Aug. 1895. *Educ.* Eton. *M.* Dorothy Finucane. *S.* 3. *Dau.*

1. *Career:* Served in World War I, Queen's Royal West Surrey Regiment and Coldstream Guards 1914–18. Ministry of Aircraft Production 1940–45; Director-General of Aircraft Distribution 1943–45; Vice-Chairman, Bowater Paper Corp., Ltd. (1945–67); Dep.-Chmn., British European Airways Corporation 1948–65; Director of London & Yorkshire Trust Holdings Ltd. 1923–70 (Chmn. 1923–65), West Riding Worsted and Woollen Mills Ltd. 1944–68 (Chmn. 1944–62); Safeguard Industrial Investments Ltd. 1953–69, (Chmn. 1953–66). *Address:* Hurst House, Sedlescombe, Sussex, and Flat 148, Grosvenor House, London, W.1.

**KEENER, Jefferson Ward.** *B.* 1908. *Educ.* Birmingham Southern College (AB 1928); Univ. of Chicago (MA 1930); Graduate work at Ohio State Univ., Hon LLD Birmingham Southern College 1955, and Ohio Wesleyan Univ. 1959; Hon. Dr. Com Sci Millikin Univ. 1959; Hon Dr. of Law Univ. of Akron. *M.* 1931, Marian Feudner (Dec.). *S.* 3. *Career:* Service with Office of Price Administration and War Production Board (U.S.A.) in World War II; Mutual Security Programme evaluation study of Germany 1953; Industry member, Wage Stabilization Board 1950–51; Adviser, U.S. Dept. of State at rubber study group meetings (Paris 1947, Brussels 1950, Monrovia 1955, Hamburg 1958, Kuala Lumpur 1960, Washington 1962, Tokyo 1964; Chief Exec. Officer 1958–72; Dir. 1957—; The B. F. Goodrich Co., Akron, Ohio, Dir. of following: Campbell Soup Co., Ohio Bell Telephone Co., Federal Reserve Bank of Cleveland. Member, Advisory Committee on Civilian Personnel in U.S. Army 1954–56. Member, President's Adv. Cttee. on Labour-Management Policy, and of U.S. Dept. of Commerce Foreign Direct Investments Adv. Committee. Decorated U.S. Army Medal for Exceptional Civilian Achievement 1956. Instructor, Assistant Professor of Economics, Ohio Wesleyan University 1929–37 and 1938–39. Director of business research, B. F. Goodrich 1939–44; Asst. to Financial Vice-Pres., Asst. to Pres. 1944–46; Vice-Pres. 1946–56; Exec. Vice-Pres. 1956; Pres., Chief Exec. Officer; Dir. 1957; Chmn. Chief Exec. Officer 1967–72; Chmn. Exec. Cttee 1972–73. *Publications:* Cutting the Cost of Bank Loans (1939); various speeches and magazine articles. *Address: office* 500 S. Main Street, Akron 11, Ohio, U.S.A.

**KEENLEYSIDE, Hubert Brock,** CBE (Mil). British-Canadian. *B.* 1900. *Educ.* University of Toronto BASc Mech Eng. *M.* (1) 1926, Margaret Anne McIntosh (*D.* 1945), and (2) 1951, Mary Olive Wall (*D.* 1968). *S.* (Dr.) Hubert Brock, Jr., (Dr.) John Gordon and David Anthony, P.Eng. *Career:* Industrial Engineer, Toronto Industrial Commission 1929, Gen. Mgr. 1931; Asst. Gen. Mgr., Robert Simpson Eastern Ltd., Toronto 1936; Gen. Mgr., Robert Simpson Western Ltd., Regina, Sask. 1939; Colonel, Director of Ordnance Services, Canadian Army Overseas 1942; served in the U.K., Italy & N.W. Europe; Brigadier, ADQMG (AE) 1943, and Deputy Quartermaster-General 1945; Operating Manager, Mail Order Division, Robert Simpson Eastern Ltd. and Robert Simpson Western Ltd. 1945; Pres. & Dir. Photo Engravers & Electrotypers Ltd. 1946–66 (Retired from active business, Ap . 1966). *Address:* 561 Avenue Road, Apt. 1406, Toronto Ont., Canada M4V 2J8.

**KEENLEYSIDE, Hugh Llewellyn.** *B.* 7 July 1898. *Educ.* University of British Columbia (BA); Clark University (MA, PhD). *M.* 1924, Katherine Hall Pillsbury. *S.* Miles. *Daus.* Mary, Anne, Lynn. *Career:* served World War I, Canadian Field Artillery and 2nd Canadian Tank Bn. 1918; member, Canada-U.S. Permanent Joint Board on Defence 1940–45, and Joint Economic Committee of Canada and U.S. 1940–44; Asst. Under-Sec. of State for External Affairs 1941; Amb. Ex. and Plen. to Mexico 1944; member, Canadian Deleg., 1st Gen. Assembly, U.N. 1946; Canadian Delegation to 25th Gen. Assembly U.N. 1970; Dep. Min. of Mines and Resources 1947–50; Commissioner of Northwest Territories 1947–50; Head, Canadian Deleg. to U.N. Scientific Conf. on Conservation and Utilization of Resources 1949; Deputy Minister of Resources and Development Jan. 1950; Director-General, U.N. Technical Assistance Administration 1950–58; U.N. Under-Secy General for Public Administration 1959; Chmn. British Columbia Hydro and Power Authority, Vancouver, B.C. 1959–69; Chancellor Notre Dame Univ. of Nelson since 1969. *Awards:* Hon. Degrees from various Univs.; Haldane Medal, Vanier medal, Inst. of Public Administration of Canada; Companion of Canada, 1969. *Publications:* Canada and the United States; History of Japanese Education (with A. F. Thomas) International Aid. *Address:* 3470 Mayfair Drive, Victoria, B.C., Canada.

**KEITH, Sir Kenneth (Alexander).** British merchant banker and company director. *Educ.* Rugby School. *M.* (1) Lady Ariel Baird. *S.* 1. *Dau.* 1 (dissolved 1958) and (2) Mrs. Nancy Hayward (dissolved 1972); (3) Mrs. Marie Hanbury. *Career:* Served in World War II; Welsh Guards; 2nd Lieut. 1939, Lieut.-Col. 1945; in N. Africa, Italy, France and Germany (despatches, Croix de Guerre with Silver Star); Assistant to Dir. Gen. Political Intelligence Dept., Foreign Office 1945–46. Trained as Chartered Accountant. London 1934–39; Chmn. Phillip Hill Investment Trust, Chmn. Hill Samuel Group Ltd.; Chmn. Rolls-Royce Ltd., since 1972; Vice-Chmn. Beecham Group Ltd., since 1974, Dir. 1949; Vice-Chmn. B.E.A. 1964–71; Dir. The Times Newspapers Ltd. and other companies. *Member:* NEDC 1964–71, 1974; Defence Industries Council, National Defence Industries Council, S.B.A.C.; Vice-Pres. Engineering Employers' Federation; Chmn. Economic Planning Council for East Anglia 1965–70; Gov. Nat. Inst. of Economic and Social Research; Council Mem. Manchester Business Sch.; Fellow, British Institute of Management. *Clubs:* White's; Pratt's; City of London; The Brook, Racquet & Tennis (N.Y.C.). *Address:* 80 Eaton Square, London, SW1 9AP; and The Wicken House, Castleacre, Norfolk.

**KEKKONEN, Hon. Urho Kaleva.** President of the Republic of Finland. *B.* 3 Sept. 1900. *Educ.* University of Helsinki (LLD). *M.* 1926, Sylvi Uino. *S.* Matti, Taneli. *Career:* Jurist, Federation of Rural Communities 1927–32; Administrative Secretary, Ministry of Agriculture 1933–44; Minister of Justice 1936–37, 1944–46; Minister of Interior 1937–39; Dir., Central Bureau for Evacuated People 1940–43, Office of Rationalisation 1943–45, Speaker of the Diet 1948–50; MP (Agrarian) 1936–56; member, Board of Managers, Bank of Finland 1946–56; Prime Minister and Minister of Interior, Mar. 1950–Jan. 1951; Prime Minister 1951–53; Minister for Foreign Affairs 1952–53 and 1954; Prime Minister, Oct. 1954; elected President of the Republic of Finland, Feb. 1956; re-elected 1962 and 1968. *Awards:* Finland: Grand Cross, White Rose (with Chain), Cross of Liberty, Lion and Holy Lamb; Olympic Cross (1st Cl.) of Merit; Gold Cross Merit of Finnish Sports. Numerous foreign decorations. Dr. hc, Univs. of Moscow, Aix-en-Provence, Waterloo, Warsaw, Delhi, Budapest and Prague. *Address:* Presidential Palace, Helsinki, Finland.

**KEKWICK, Bruce Huntley.** Company director. *B.* 1910. *Educ.* State School; Adelaide Technical High School. *M.* 1971, Rhonda Mary Wildman. *Career:* Founder and Inaugural Secy., Launceston Philharmonic Socy. 1947. M.H.R. for Bass (Tasmania) 1949–54; Chmn., L'ton Shipping Advisory Committee, 1950–54; Chmn., Govt. Industrial Relations Cttee. (Canberra) 1951–54; Pres., L'ton Branch Navy League 1953–56; served in World War II (Lieut. R.A.N.R.); Music Dir. and Conductor, Launceston Philharmonic Socy. since 1963; Proprietor of Bruce Kekwick Promotions; Partner, Bruce Kekwick & Associates; Chmn., John Batman Historical Activities Cttee. Member, State Advisory Cttee., Australian Broadcasting Commission; Inaugural President, Aust. Centre Party, founded in Launceston. Good Neighbour Council (Tas.). *Address:* 35 Riverside Drive, Launceston, Tasmania.

**KELFA-CAULKER, Dr. Richard Edmund.** Sierra Leonean Diplomat. *B.* 1909. *Educ.* Albert Academy, Sierra Leone; Otterbein College, Westerville, U.S.A. (BA 1935); Oberlin (Ohio) College (MA 1937); Teachers' College, Columbia University (Dip Ed 1947). *M.* 1940, Olivette Hannah Stuart. *S.* Richard Edmund, Jr. *Daus.* Imodale Olivette, Lucilde Yamita, Joyce Elaine, Velma Geneve and Sheila Yankete. *Career:* Printing Instructor, Albert Academy, Freetown 1929; College student, U.S.A. 1931–37; Senior Tutor, Albert Acad. 1938; Principal of the Academy 1939; Commissioner for Sierra Leone and Gambia in London 1959–61; Ambassador to U.S.A. 1961–64; High Commissioner to the U.K. 1964–66; Ambassador to Liberia 1969–73. *Publications:* articles on various aspects of education in Sierra Leone in various local magazines. Hon DHL, Otterbein Coll., Westerville, Ohio, U.S.A. 1947. *Club:* Junior Dinner (Freetown). *Address:* c/o Ministry of Foreign Affairs, Freetown, Sierra Leone.

**KELLAS, Arthur Roy Handasyde,** CMG. British. *B.* 1915. *Educ.* Aberdeen Grammar School, Aberdeen University (MA), and Balliol College, Oxford University (BA). *M.* 1952, Katharine Bridget Le Rougetel. *S.* Ian and Roger. *Dau.* Miranda. *Career:* First Secretary, Legation Helsinki 1949–51, Cairo 1952–53, and Baghdad 1954–58; Counsellor, Teheran 1958–62; Counsellor-Consul-General Tel Aviv 1964–65. Ambassador to Nepal, Feb. 1966–70. Ambassador to Aden,

1970–72; High Commissioner to Tanzania 1973–75. Pres., Britain-Nepal Socy.; Fellow, Royal Geographical Socy. *Club:* United Oxford and Cambridge University. *Address:* Laurel Villa, Culworth, Banbury, Oxon.

**KELLEHER, John Arnold.** N.Z. journalist. *B.* 1925. *Educ.* St. Patrick's Coll., Wellington. *M.* 1953, Ursula Jean Sheehan. *S.* Jeremy John, Christopher Joseph and Kevin Sheehan. *Daus.* Erin Mary and Lisa Marié. *Career:* Pres.: N.Z. Journalists' Assn. 1959–60, 60–61, 61–62; and of Wellington Journalists' Union 1958–59; on reporting staff of Hutchinson (Kansas) News 1960 (on Foreign Specialist Grant awarded by U.S. State Dept.). Employed on a number of newspapers in N.Z. and Australia, and as news compiler, N.Z. Broadcasting Service before joining Wellington Publishing Co. Chief Reporter, The Dominion 1962–65 (Columnist 1956–62). Editor, Dominion Sunday Times 1966–68; Editor, The Dominion (morning daily), Wellington, since 1968. Exec. member, N.Z. Branch, Commonwealth Press Union. Cowan Memorial Prize for Journalism 1954, Teal Aviation Literary Prize 1957, and Baird Journalism Award 1964. *Address:* 34 Chartwell Drive, Wellington, 4, New Zealand.

**KELLER, Rene Jacques.** Swiss. *B.* 1914. *Educ.* Trinity Coll., Cambridge; Univ. of Geneva (Law and Doctor's degrees). *M.* 1942, Marion Werder. *S.* Pierre. *Daus.* Jocelyne and Florence (Barbey). *Career:* Head of News Department, Ministry of Foreign Affairs, Berne, 1954–56; First Counsellor of Embassay, Paris, 1957–60; Ambassador to Ghana, Guinea, Liberia, Mali and Togo, with res. in Accra, 1960–62, and Turkey 1962–65; Head of Perm. Mission to U.N. Office and Specialized Agencies in Geneva 1966–68. Ambassador to the Court of St. James's, 1968; Head of Direction International Organizations Ministry of Foreign Affairs 1971; Ambassador to Austria since 1976. *Publications:* Thesis: L'Accreditif documentaire. *Club:* Travellers'. *Address:* Swiss Embassy, Prinz Eugenstr. 7 & 9, A-1030 Vienna, Austria.

**KELLETT-BOWMAN, (Mary) Elaine,** M.P. British Politician. *B.* 1924. *Educ.* Queen Mary Sch., Lytham; The Mount, York; St. Anne's Coll., Oxford—post graduate distinction in welfare diploma. *M.* (1) 1945, Charles Norman Kellett (Dec'd). (2) 1971, Edward Thomas Kellett-Bowman. *S.* 3. *Dau.* 1. *Career:* Contested Nelson & Colne 1955, South West Norfolk, March & Oct. 1959, Buckingham 1964, 1966; Camden Borough Council: Alderman 1968–74, Vice-Chmn. Housing Cttee. 1968, Chmn. Welfare Cttee. 1969; Called to Bar, Middle Temple 1964; Lay Member, Press Council 1964–68; Gov., Culford Sch. 1963; mem., Union European Women 1956; Delegate to Luxembourg 1958; MP (Cons.) for Lancaster since 1970; mem., European Parliament since 1975. *Awards:* No. 1 Country Housewife, 1960; Christal MacMillan Law Prize, 1963. *Club:* English Speaking Union. *Address:* 42 Schoolhouse Lane, Halton on Lune, Lancaster; and *office* House of Commons, London SW1A 0AA.

**KELLEY, Clarence M.** American. *B.* 1911. *Educ.* Univ. of Kansas, BA; Univ. Kansas City (Mo.), LLB (1940); Admitted to Missouri Bar 1940. *M.* (1) Ruby (*Dec'd.*). (2) 1976, Shirley Ann Dyckes. *S.* 1. *Dau.* 1. *Career:* Special Agent Federal Bureau Investigation 1940; U.S. Navy 1944–46; F.B.I. Headquarters Washington D.C. 1951; Field supervisor F.B.I. Kansas City 1951; Asst. Special Agent in charge F.B.I. Houston Office 1953–55, Seattle Office 1955–56, San Francisco Office 1956–57; Special Agent in charge Birmingham and Memphis 1957–61; Chief of Police, Kansas City 1961–73; Director of F.B.I. since 1973. *Member:* Numerous Cttees. and Missouri organisations while Chief of Police, and past Pres., of Missouri Peace Officers Association. *Awards:* J. Edgar Hoover Gold Medal (1970); Outstanding Officer of the Year Award (1972); Alumnus of Year Kansas City School of Law (Univ. Mo.); 17th Annual Award from the Society of Professional Investigators Hon. LLD, Baker Univ. (Ks.), Culver-Stockton Coll. (Mo.); Hon. Dr. of Political Science, Westminster College (Mo.). *Address:* United States Dept. of Justice, F.B.I., Washington D.C. 20535, U.S.A.

**KELLIHER, Sir Henry (Joseph).** *B.* 1896. *Educ.* Clyde School. *M.* 1917, Evelyn Sproule. *S.* 1. *Daus.* 4. *Career:* Chmn. and Man. Dir. (Founder) Dominion Breweries Ltd. 1929—; Dir., Bank of New Zealand 1936–42. Purchased Puketutu Island 1938; developed and established Ayrshire Studs 1940, Aberdeen Angus 1942. Thoroughbred & Standard bred horses 1950. Kt 1963 KStJ 1960. *Publications:* New Zealand at the Cross Roads (1936); Why your £1 buys less and less (1954). *Address:* Puketutu Island, Manukau Harbour, Auckland, New Zealand.

**KELLOGG, Lester S.** Economist and statistician. *B.* 1903. *Educ.* Northwestern University (AB, 1927, AM 1928); Univ. of Chicago (graduate work 1929–31). *M.* 1928, Mildred Baker. *Dau.* Milles Ann. Instructor in Statistics, Univ. of Buffalo 1931–35; (Asst. Dean., School of Business Administration, same Univ.) 1932–35; Asst. Prof. Statistical Research, Bureau of Business Research, Coll. of Commerce, Ohio State Univ. 1935–46 (on leave 1940–46); Asst. Chief, Munitions Branch, and Editor of War Progress, Div. of Statistics, War Production Board 1940–42; Chief, Prices and Cost-of-Living Div., U.S. Dept. of Labor 1942–47. Consulting Economist 1966–67; Director of Economics Research, Deere & Co. 1948–66; U.S. Bureau of Labor Statistics, Business Research Adv. Council Chairman 1963–64; member, Board of Directors, Iowa-Illinois Gas & Electric Co. 1955–72. *Publications:* Business and Economic Statistics (with Wm. A. Spurr and John H. Smith), 1961; Chapter on 'Prices', Government Statistics for Business Use (1956); Chapter on 'Agriculture' in Determining the Business Outlook (1954). *Member:* Natl. Council on Religion in Higher Education (Fellow); Amer. Assn. (Fellow); Amer. Economic Assn.; Conf. of Business Economists; National Assn. Business Economists. *Address:* RTE 4, Fairlane-south, Columbus, N. Car. 28722, U.S.A.

**KELLOU, Mohamed Messaoud.** Lawyer and diplomat. *B.* 1931. *Educ.* Studied law at Montpelier (LLB 1954; Diploma of advanced studies 1955). Before the revolution in Algeria he was active as a militant nationalist and later directed the General Union of Algerian Moslem Students; was also member of the Algerian National Liberation Front. Represented F.N.L. in Great Britain 1957–61; later represented the provisional government of the Algerian Republic as head of the diplomatic mission to Pakistan until July 1962. In charge of African, Asian and Latin-American affairs 1962; Ambassador to Great Britain 1963–64; Ambassador Czechoslovakia 1964–70; Ambassador to Argentina, Chile, Peru. Uruguay and Bolivia 1970–75; to People's Republic of China 1975; elected to Algerian Parliament, Feb. 1977, & now Chmn., Foreign Affairs Cttee. of the People's National Assembly. *Address:* Assemblée Nationale Populaire, 40 Boulevard des Martyrs, Alger, Algeria.

**KELLY, Arthur Francis.** American aviation official. *B.* 1913. *Educ.* University of Utah (BA). *M.* 1942, Sally Payne. *S.* James J., Arthur F. *Career:* Worked in Department of Airports, Salt Lake City, Utah 1933–35, United Air Lines 1935–37, Western Air Lines, Los Angeles since 1937; Spec. civilian consultant to US Mil. Dir. of Civil Aviation 1941–42; Deputy Chief of Staff of Europ. Div. of Air Transport Command, USAF, World War II (Colonel); Returned to Western Airlines and became Vice-Pres. 1949, Senior Vice-Pres. 1965, Elected to Bd. of Directors 1968. Exec. Vice-Pres. 1972, Pres. and chief exec. officer 1973, Chmn. and chief exec. officer 1976. *Director:* National Space Assn. *Member:* Bd, of Governors of Arthritis Foundation (S. Calif. chapter); Bd. of Directors for over 15 councils and organisations; Bd. of Fellows, Univ. Santa Clara; Advisory Cttee of RIF (Reading is Fundamental). *Award:* Several decorations for advance air base planning in Eastern Europe. *Address:* 6060 Avion Drive, Los Angeles 90045, U.S.A.; and *office* P.O. Box 92005, World Way Post Center, Los Angeles 90009.

**KELLY, Crosby Moyer.** American. *B.* 1918. *Educ.* University of Arizona BA; University of Mexico, Graduate Study. *M.* 1951, Willah Mary Smith. *Career:* Ford Motor Co. 1941–48; Dean, Merchandising School, 1947). Dir., Advertising & Pub. Rel., Rapid Standard Co. Inc. 1949. Exec. Dir., Chicago World's Fair 1950. Sales Representative, Central Services Inc. 1951. Owner-Manager, Importing-Distributing Co. 1952–55. Litton Industries Inc., 1955–65, Vice-Pres. 1960–65, Snr. Vice-Pres. 1963–75; Chairman, Performance Measurements Co., 1965–70. President, Advertising Measurementt, Inc., 1965–70. President, Crosby M. Kelly Associates, Ltd., 1965–73; Vice-Pres., Rockwell International 1976—. Owner, AMPR Associates, Inc., 1968. Member, Steering Committee, Pacific Basin Economic Cooperation Committee, 1968–70; Director, Western World Insurance Co.; 1973—; Senior Vice-Pres. Litton Industries Inc. Head, American Delegation International Congress Air Force Assns. 1964. Guest Lecturer European Inst. Business Administration 1966. Deleg. U.N. Industrial Development Organization 1st World Symposium 1967; Advisor, International Economics Affairs Cttee. National Assn. of Manufacturers 1967–69; Member, Southeast Asia Business Conf. 1968; Dir. Albertus Magnus Coll. 1971–73. *Member:* Stanford Research Institute International; Public Relations Soc. of America; Public Affairs Council, Machinery & Allied Products Inst.;

Public Affairs Council, Aerospace Industries Assn. *Awards:* Decoration-Commendatore, Ordine de Mérito, Republican. Italiana, 1969. *Clubs:* Los Angeles Country, University (N.Y.). Banker's (N.Y.), Allegheny (Pittsburgh). *Address:* Park Mansions, 5023 Frew Avenue, Pittsburgh, Pa 15213; and *office* Rockwell International, 600 Grant Street, Pittsburgh Pa 15219, U.S.A.

**KELLY, Sir Theo,** Kt. cr. 1966, OBE, FRSA, FAIM. *B.* 1907. *M.* 1944, Nancy Margaret Williams. *S.* 2. *Daus.* 2. *Career:* Wing Commander R.A.A.F. 1942–44; Dir., R.A.A.F. Canteen Services Board 1944–59; Chairman: Woolworths Ltd. & subsidiary companies since 1963 (Man. Dir. 1945–70); Woolworths (New Zealand) Ltd. (Dir. & Gen. Mgr. 1934–71); Woolworths Properties Ltd.; Computer Sciences of Australia Ltd.; mem., Board of the Reserve Bank of Australia 1961–75; Dep. Chmn., Australian Mutual Provident Soc. since 1967; Fellow. Univ. of Sydney Senate 1968–75; mem., Board of the Royal North Shore Hospital 1969–77; Trustee, National Parks & Wildlife Foundation since 1969; Fellow, Royal Soc. of Arts (London) since 1971 & Australian Inst. of Management since 1967; Life Governor of the Royal Life Saving Society. Justice of the Peace 1946. *Clubs:* Sydney Rotary; Royal Motor Yacht; American National; Australian Golf. *Address:* 73 Yarranabbe Road, Darling Point, N.S.W. 2027; and *office* Woolworths Ltd., 540 George Street, Sydney 2000, Australia.

**KELSICK, Osmund Randolph,** DFC. British. *B.* 1922. *Educ.* Private Prep. School; Montserrat School; Oxford Univ. *M.* 1950, Doreen Avis Hodge. *S.* 1. *Daus.* 2. *Career:* War Service, Fighter Pilot, Squadron Leader, 1940–47. A.D.C. to Governor, Leeward Islands, 1946–47; Commissioner, Carriacou, 1947–51; Asst. Chief Secretary, Windward Islands, 1951–52; Asst. Administrator, St. Vincent, 1952–55; Administrator, 1955–56; Asst. Trade Commissioner for W. Indies in London, 1956–57; Exec. Secy., Reg. Economic Cttee., Barbados, 1957; Chief Secy. and Governor's Deputy, Leeward Is., 1957–60. President and Managing Director, Antigua Holdings Ltd. 1962—. Chairman: Bottlers (Antigua) Ltd., 1967— and Yigie Beach Hotel Ltd. St. Lucia. Man. Dir.: Carib Enterprises Ltd., operating Blue Waters Beach Hotel, Antigua; Antigua Land Development Co. Ltd.; Investment Consultants Ltd. Dir.: Caribbean Consultants Ltd.; Anguilla Beaches Ltd.; Thos. H. Kelsick Ltd., Montserrat; Liat (1974) Ltd.; Past President, Caribbean Hotel Assn., Puerto Rico, Vice-Pres.: Caribbean Travel Assn., New York. *Member:* West India Cttee., Royal Victoria League. *Award:* F.R.S.A. 1973. *Clubs:* West India (London); Celebrity (Toronto); New (Antigua). *Address:* Blue Waters Beach Hotel, Antigua; and *office* P.O. Box 256, St. John's, Antigua.

**KEMBALL-COOK, Denis Basil.** American executive. *B.* 1910. *Educ.* Shrewsbury School and Balliol College, Oxford. *M.* 1935, Mary Virginia Ricks. *S.* Richard and Stephen. *Dau.* Virginia. *Career:* Joined Shell Oil Co. 1932; Dir., Compania Shell de Venezuela 1953; Vice-Pres. and Dir., Asiatic Petroleum Corp. and Shell Caribbean Petroleum Co., New York 1957. Exec. Vice-Pres. and Dir. 1958–71; Mem. of Exec. Cttee. 1961–71; Chief Operating Officer 1968–69; Pres. Chief Exec. Officer, 1970–71; Shell Oil Company. Director, American Petroleum Institute; Vice-Chmn., Bd. of Trustees, Skidmore Coll., Saratoga Springs, N.Y.; Fellow, Royal Society of Arts. *Clubs:* New York Yacht; Noroton (Conn.) Yacht. *Address:* 58 Andrews Drive, Darien, Conn., U.S.A.

**KEMP, Sir Leslie Charles,** KBE, CE, FICE, MIEE, ACGI. Comdr., Royal Order of George I of Greece 1951. British civil engineer. *B.* 1890. *Educ.* Forest Hill House School and London Univ. (BSc Eng—1st Class Hons). *M.* (1) 1918, Millicent Constance Matland (*Dec.* 1958). *S.* 2. *M.* (2) 1961, Melina Enriquez. Engineer with Fraser & Chalmers, Erith 1910–14; Capt. R.G.A., France 1914–19; Contract Eng., English Electric Co. 1919–23; Tech. Advisor, Power & Traction Finance Co. 1923–25; Midlands Branch Manager, English Electric Co. 1924–26; Managing Director, Athens-Piraeus Electricity Co. 1926–41; Manager, Asmara War (land-plane repairs) Base, Eritrea 1942–43; Deputy Regional Director, Middle East, B.O.A.C., Cairo 1943–44; Vice-Chairman & Managing Director: Athens-Piraeus Electricity Co., and Société Générale Héllenique 1944–56. Vice-Chaiman, General Development Corp. Athens. *Clubs:* Junior Carlton, Royal Thames (London); Royal Yacht Squadron (Cowes); Royal Corinthian Yacht (Burnham-on-Crouch): Royal Hellenique Yacht (Athens). *Address:* 12 Queen Amalia Avenue, Athens, Greece.

**KEMP, Oliver,** CMG, OBE. *B.* 1916. *Educ.* Wakefield Grammar School and Queen's College, Oxford (MA Lit Hum). *M.* 1940, Henrietta Taylor. *S.* Peter M. and John R. *Career:* Served in World War II 1939–45; appointed to H.M. Foreign Service 1945; served in Moscow, Egypt, Indonesia, Yemen, Laos, West Africa and Mongolia. Deputy Head of the U.K. Delegation to the European Communities, Luxembourg, 1965–67. H.M. Ambassador to Togoland 1962–65. H.M. Ambassador. Ulan Bator, 1967–68; F.C.O. European Economic Community Affairs 1970–73; Dir. British Steel Corp. Office Brussels since 1973. *Address:* 10 Manor Gardens, Hunmanby, N. Yorks; and 7 rue de la Fontaine, Genval, Belgium.

**KEMPNER, Robert Maximilian Wasili.** Min. Dir. a.D; Dr. jur. utr. International lawyer and political scientist; expert in war crimes prosecutions and post-war indemnification. *B.* 1899. *Educ.* Univs. of Berlin, Breslau, Freiburg and Pennsylvania. *M.* Ruth Hahn (pen name Benedicta Maria K.). *S.* Lucian W. F., André Basil Franklin. *Dau.* Bettina. *Career:* Asst. to State Prosecutor, Berlin 1926–28; Chief Legal Counsellor to the 76,000-man Prussian Police Administration, Prussian Ministry of Interior, and Judge, Disciplinary Court, Berlin 1928–33; Pres. and Professor, Fiorenza College, Florence (Italy) and Nice (France) 1937–39; Research Associate, Government Institute, Univ. of Pennsylvania 1939–41; Expert Consultant on Foreign governmental and police systems to the Dept. of Justice, of War and Office of Strategic Service, Washington 1941–45; U.S. Staff Prosecutor, Internatl. Military Tribunal, Chief Prosecutor, Wilhelmstrasse Trial, Nuremberg 1945–49; Expert Consultant to American, German and Israeli courts and prosecutors, *e.g.* in foreign agent trials in the U.S. and in the Adolf Eichmann trial in Jerusalem 1941–61. Co-plaintiff in murder trials of Anne Frank and Edith Stein 1967 and the murder of Berlin Jews, and other cases. *Awards:* Member of the German Bar. Many honours and decorations; Honorary fellow, Univ. of Jerusalem. *Member:* Amer. Socy. of International Law; Amer. Political Science Assn.; and West German Bar. *Publications:* Co-author or annotator, Prussian Code of Police Administration (1930); Security Police (1932); The Nazi Underground (1945); The Cicero Spy Case (1950) The Judgement of the Wilhelmstrasse Case (1951); Eichmann and Accomplices (1961 and 1963); SS Elite Guards under Cross-Examination (1964); Edith Stein and Anne Frank. Two of hundred thousand (1968). The Third Reich under Cross-examination (1969); The Murder of 35,000 Berlin Jews (1971); edited German edition of Warren Report on President Kennedy's assassination; many scientific articles. Holds various degrees and awards. *Address:* 112 Lansdowne Court, Lansdowne, Pa. 19050, U.S.A.

**KEMSLEY. The Rt. Hon. The Viscount (Geoffrey Lionel Berry),** DL, K. St. J. *B.* 1909. *Educ.* Marlborough; Magdalen College, Oxford. *M.* 1933, Lady Helen Hay, O. St. J. *Daus.* Mary Anne, Pamela Jane Margaret, Caroline Helen, Catherine Frances Lillian. MP (Cons. for Buckinghamshire) 1943–45; Master, Spectacle Makers Co. 1949–51 and 1959–61; C.C. (Northants) 1964–70, Deputy Chairman. Kemsley Newspapers Ltd. 1938–59. High Sheriff of Leic. 1967; DL (Leics) 1972; Member of the Chapter General of the Order of St. John; Chmn., St. Andrew's Hospital, Northampton; Pres., Assn. of Independent Hospitals. *Address:* Thorpe Lubenham, Market Harborough, Leics.

**KENDALL, William Denis.** British. *B.* 1903. *Educ.* Trinity Coll.; Halifax Technical Coll.: FIMechE; FRSA; MIAE; Chartered Engineer. PhD. *M.* 1952, Margaret Burden. *Career:* Asst. to Chief Inspector, Budd Mfg. Co. (Philadelphia) 1923; Dir. Manf. Citroen Motor Car Co. Paris 1929–38; Man. Dir. British Manufacture & Research, Grantham (England) 1938–45; Consultant, Pentagon Washington on high velocity small arms 1938–45; Cadet in Royal Fleet Auxiliary; Member Churchill's War Cabinet Gun Board 1941–45; Member of Parliament (Ind. Grantham) 1942–50. President and Chairman of the Board, Dynapower Systems Corp., Santa Monica, Calif.; Exec. Vice-Pres. Brunswick Ordnance Corp. (New Brunswick, N.J.) 1952–55; Vice-Pres. Ops. Mack Truck Corp. 1952–55; Pres., Chmn. Bd. Amer. M.A.R.C. 1955–61; Pres. Kendall Medical International Inc., Los Angeles. *Member:* President's Council, Amer. Management Assn. 1957. Governor, King's School, Grantham 1942–50. Mason (32°; Member of the Shrine); Al Malaikah Temple; Worshipful Co. of Clockmakers; Religious Society of Friends (Quakers). *Awards:* Freeman, City of London 1943; Chevalier, l'Ordre du Oissam Alouite Cherifien. *Clubs:* International Sportsmen's: Riviera Country; Pacific Palisades (Calif.); National Liberal (London); Royal Norfolk

& Suffolk Yacht (Lowestoft); Cave des Rois (Los Angeles). *Address:* 1319 North Doheny Drive, Los Angeles, Calif. 90069, U.S.A.

**KENDREW, Maj.-Gen. Sir Douglas Anthony,** KCMG, CB, CBE, DSO, KStJ. British. *B.* 1910. *Educ.* Uppingham School. *M.* 1936, Nora Elizabeth Harvey. *S.* 1. *Dau.* 1. *Career:* Bde. Comd. 1944–45; World War II and Korea 1952–53; G.O.C. Cyprus and Dir. of Operations 1956–58; Dir. of Infantry, War Office 1959–61; Head of British Defence Mission, Australia 1961–63; Governor of Western Australia 1963–73. Pres., Hon. Society of Knights of the Round Table 1975—; Commissioner, Royal Hospital, Chelsea 1974—. Imperial Defence College 1954. Colonel, Royal Leicestershire Regt. 1963–65; Hon. Col. S.A.S. Regt., Australia 1966–74, and Hon. Col. R.W.A.R. 1966–74. Hon. LLD, W.A. Univ. *Club:* Army & Navy (London). *Address:* The Manor House, Islip, Northants.

**KENISON, Frank Rowe.** American judge. *B.* 1 Nov. 1907. *Educ.* Dartmouth College, Hanover, N.H. (AB); Boston University Law School (LLB). *M.* 1939, Loretta Mary Landry. *S.* Thomas Rowe, Frank Edson. *Dau.* Mary Ann. *Career:* Carroll County Solicitor 1935–37; Assistant Attorney-General 1937–40; Attorney-General 1940–42 and 1945–46; served in World War II with U.S.N.R. 1942–45; Associate Justice, Supreme Court 1946–52; Chief Justice, Supreme Court (N.H.) since April 1952. LLD Dartmouth Coll. (1954); Boston Univ. (1955); Univ. New Hampshire (1966); Franklin Pierce Coll. (1966). D Jur Sc, Suffolk Univ. (1959). *Address:* Supreme Court Bldg., Concord, N.H. 03301, U.S.A.

**KENNAN, George F.** American. Prof Emeritus. *B.* 1904. *Educ.* St. John's Military Academy (Delafield, Wis.) and Princeton Univ. (AB 1925); Diploma, Berlin Seminary for Oriental Languages 1930; Hon. LLD; Yale (1950), Dartmouth Coll. (1950), Colgate (1951), Notre Dame (1953), Kenyon Coll. (1954), The New School for Social Research (1955), Princeton (1956), Michigan (1957), Northwestern (1957), Brandeis Univ. (1958), Wisconsin, Harvard (1963), Denison (1966), Rutgers (1966); JCDLC, Oxford (1969); Hon. Dr. Jur. Marquette Univ. 1972. *M.* 1931, Annelise Sorenson. *S.* Christopher James. *Daus.* Grace, Joan Elisabeth, Wendy Antonia. *Career:* Apptd. U.S. Foreign Service Officer, Sept. 1926; Vice-Consul, Geneva 1927, Hamburg 1927, Berlin 1928, Tallinn 1928; Third Secy., Riga (Kovno & Tallinn) 1929; Language Offr., Berlin 1929; Third Secy., Riga 1931; accompd. Ambassador Bullitt to Moscow (to re-open American Embassy) 1933; Consul, Vienna 1935; Second Secy., Moscow 1935; Dept. of State, Washington 1937; Second Secy., Prague 1938 (Consul 1939); Second Secy., Berlin 1939 (First Secy. 1940); interned at Bad Nauheim 1941; repatriated in June 1942; Dept. of State, Washington 1942; Counsellor, Lisbon 1942; Counsellor, American Delegation to European Advisory Commission, London 1943; Minister-Counsellor, Moscow 1944; Deputy for Foreign Affairs, National War College, Washington 1946; Director, Policy Planning Staff, Dept. of State, Washington 1947; Counsellor, Dept. of State 1949; Leave-of-absence (at Inst. for Advanced Study, Princeton) 1950; Charles B. Walgreen Fdn. Lecturer at Univ. of Chicago 1951; Ambassador to U.S.S.R. 1952; retired from the Foreign Service, July 1953. Member, Inst. for Advanced Study, Princeton 1953; Stafford Little Lecturer, Princeton Univ. 1954; Leave-of-absence, George Eastman Visiting Prof., Balliol Coll., Oxford Univ. 1957–58; Prof., Sch. of Historical Studies, Institute for Advanced Study, Princeton, Jan. 1956–61; Ambassador to Yugoslavia, Feb. 1961–63; Member National Inst. of Arts and Letters, 1965–67; American Academy of Arts & Letters, 1968. Benjamin Franklin Fellow, Royal Society of Arts, London, 1968.; Fellow Woodrow Wilson Intern. Center, Smithsonian Inst. Wash. DC (1974–75), Pres. Am Academy of Arts and Letters 1967–71. *Publications:* American Diplomacy, 1900–1950 (Freedom House award 1951), 1951; Realities of American Foreign Policy (1954); Das Amerikanisch Russische Verhältnis (1954); Russia Leaves the War, Vol. 1, Soviet-American Relations 1917–20 (National Book Award; Pulitzer Prize) 1956; Russia, The Atom and The West (1958); The Decision to Intervene, Vol. II, Soviet-American Relations 1917–1920 (1958); Russia and the West under Lenin and Stalin (1961); On Dealing with The Communist World (1964); Memoirs 1925–50 (National Book Award, Pulitzer Prize) 1967; From Prague After Munich (1968); Democracy and; The Left (1968) the Student Marquis de Custine and His Russia in 1839 (1971); Memoirs 1950–63 (1972). *Address:* 146 Hodge Rd., Princeton, N.J.

**KENNEALLY, Joseph Thomas.** American. *B.* 1926. *Educ.* Univ. of Minnesota (BA Econ 1949; MA International Law and International Economics 1950). *M.* 1955, Patricia Steele. *S.* 5. *Dau.* 1. *Career:* With Houston Oil Field Material Co. Inc.; Exec. Vice-Pres. 1959–60, Pres. 1960–61, Chmn. of Bd. 1964—; Chairman of Board; International Systems & Controls Corp., Houston, Tex.; and of Black, Sivalls & Bryson Inc., Kansas City, Mo.; Gen. Partner, Kenro & Co., N.Y.C. Vice-Chmn., Nat. Council for U.S.–China Trade; & Iran–U.S. Business Council; Director: Romanian–U.S. Economic Council; Brazil–U.S. Business Council; Governor, ADELA S.A.; Director: Univ. of St. Thomas, Houston; Houston Chamber of Commerce. *Member:* Phi Beta Kappa. *Clubs:* Petroleum (Houston); Kansas City (Kansas City); River Oaks Country. *Address: office* Suite 2280, 2727 Allen Parkway, Houston, Tex. 77019, U.S.A.

**KENNEDY, David Matthew.** American diplomat. *B.* 1905. *Educ.* Weber Coll., Ogden, Utah (MA), and George Washington Univ. (AB; LLB); Graduate, The Stonier Graduate School of Banking, Rutgers Univ. *M.* 1925, Lenora Bingham. *Daus.* 4. *Career:* Technical Asst., Div. of Bank Operations, Economist in Div. of Research and Statistics, and Asst. to Chairman of the Board 1930–46, Board of Governors of Federal Reserve System; Vice-Pres., Continental Illinois National Bank & Trust Co. of Chicago 1946–53 (Vice-President in charge of Bond Department 1954–56; elected a Director and President, Nov. 1956); Asst. to Secy of U.S. Treasury 1953–54; Chairman, Board of Directors, Continental Illinois National Bank & Trust Co. of Chicago 1959–69; Secretary, United States Treasury, 1969–71; Ambassador-at-Large 1971–73; Ambassador to Nato 1972–73; Spec. Rep. of First Presidency of Church of Jesus Christ Latter-Day Saints, 1974. Director: Abbot Laboratories, International Harvester Co., Commonwealth Edison Co., Pullman Co., Swift & Co., and United States Gypsum Co., Communications Satellite Corp., Adela Investment Co., Radio New York World Wide. Trustee: Equitable of Iowa, and Savings and Profit Sharing Pension Fund of Sears, Roebuck & Co. Chairman Executive Board, Committe for Economic and Cultural Development of Chicago; Chmn., Chicago Clearing House Assn. Trustee, Committee for Economic Development (CED). Director: Chicago Central Area Committee; Trustee; Univ. of Chicago, Presbyterian-St. Luke's Hospital, Brookings Institution, and George Washington Univ. *Member:* Assn. of Reserve City Bankers, Associates of the Graduate School of Banking of Univ. of Chicago. *Address:* 3793 Parkview Drive, Salt Lake City, Utah, U.S.A.

**KENNEDY, Douglas Strother.** American. *B.* 1919. *Educ.* Brown Univ. (BA). *M.* 1966, Gertrude E. Bohner. *Career:* Associate Editor, Time magazine 1950–54; Reporter, N.Y. Herald-Tribune 1945–50; Vice-Pres. Adventures Unlimited 1956—. Presidential Unit Citation; Purple Heart, Editor-in-Chief, True, The Man's Magazine. *Member:* Lambs; Artists & Writers; Amer. Socy. of Magazine Editors. *Clubs:* Overseas Press; Sakonnet Golf. *Address:* Little Compton, R.I., Stuart, Fla., U.S.A.

**KENNEDY, Dr. Eamonn.** Irish. *B.* 1921. *Educ.* Univ. Coll. Dublin (MA, BComm); Nat. Univ. of Ireland (PhD). *M.* Barbara Jane Black. *Children:* 2. *Career:* Dept. Foreign Affairs, Dublin, 1943; Consul, New York, 1947; Second Secy., Irish Embassy, Ottawa 1947–49; First Secy., Irish Embassy, Washington, 1949–50; First Secy., Irish Embassy, Paris 1950–54; First Secy. and Acting Chief of Protocol Dept. of Foreign Affairs, Dublin, 1954–56; Counsellor, Permanent Mission of Ireland to United Nations 1956–61; Delegate of Ireland to General Assembly of United Nations, New York, 1956–60; Rapporteur of UN South West Africa Cttee. in New York 1959, and of 4th Cttee. (Trusteeship) of UN General Assembly New York 1960; Ambassador Extraordinary and Plenipotentiary of Ireland to Fed. Rep. of Nigeria 1961–64, to Fed. Rep. of Germany 1964–70, and to France 1970–74; Permanent Representative of Ireland to United Nations, with rank of Ambassador Extraordinary and Plenipotentiary since 1974. *Decorations:* Grand Cross of Merit of F.R. of Germany with star 1970; Grand Cross of Merit of French Republic with plaque 1974. *Address:* Perm. Mission of Ireland to UN., 885 Second Ave., New York, NY 10017, U.S.A.

**KENNEDY, Edward Moore.** U.S. Senator. *B.* 1932. *Educ.* Harvard (AB); Univ. Virginia (LLB); Amer. Int. Coll. (Hon. Degree). *M.* 1958, Virginia Joan Bennett. *S.* 2. *Dau.* 1. *Career:* served with AUS 1951–53; Admitted to Mass. Bar 1959; Asst. District Attorney, Suffolk County 1961–62; U.S. seantor from Mass. since 1963; Asst. Majority Leader, U.S. Senate 1969–71. *Member:* Corp. Northeastern U. Mass. General Hospital; Trustee John F. Kennedy Library; Boston

Symphony; John F. Kennedy Memorial Foundation; Adv. Bd. Emmanuel College. *Awards:* Order of Merit Italy; Grand Commander, Order of the Phoenix (Greece); Named one of 10 outstanding young men of 1967. U.S. *Address: office* Senate Office Building, Washington DC. 20510, U.S.A.

**KENNET, Lord, (Wayland Hilton Young).** British author and politician. *B.* 1923. *Educ.* Stowe; Trinity Coll. Cambridge; Perugia; Harvard Univ. U.S.A.; *Career:* R.N. 1942–45; Foreign Office 1946-7, 1949–51; Rapporteur, Defence Cttee. Parly. Assembly W.E.U. 1962–65, Parly. Secy. Min. of Housing and Local Govt. 1966–70; Opposition Spokesman on For. Affairs and Science Policy 1970–74; *Chairman:* Adv. Cttee. for Oil Pollution of Sea 1970–74. CPRE 1971–72; Internat. Parly. Conferences on Environment since 1971; Dir. Europe Plus Thirty Project. *Award:* Hon FRIBA (1970). *Publications:* Editor, Disarmament and Arms Control 1962–65; (as Wayland Young): The Italian Left (1949); The Deadweight (1952); Now or Never (1953); (with E. Young) Old London Churches (1956); The Montesi Scandal (1957); Still Alive Tomorrow (1958); Strategy for Survival (1959); (with E. Young) The Socialist Imagination (1960); (with E. Young) Disarmament: Finnegan's Choice (1961); The Profumo Affair (1963); Eros Denied (1965); Thirty-Four Articles (1965); (as Wayland Kennet) Preservation (1972); (ed.) Existing Mechanisms of Arms Control (1965). *Address:* 100 Bayswater Road, London, W.2.

**KENNEY, F. Donald.** American. investment Banker. *B.* 1918. *Educ.* Harvard Univ. (MA); Oxford Univ.; Harvard Graduate School of Business Administration (MBA). *Career:* U.S. Naval Reserve—Ensign. to Lt. Comdr. 1942–46; Teaching Fellow, Harvard Univ. 1947–51; with Harriman Ripley & Co. Inc. subsequently Drexel Harriman Ripley 1951–70, Asst. Vice-Pres. 1958–61; Vice-Pres. and Dir. 1961–, 70; Pres. and Dir. Harriman Ripley (Canada) Ltd. 1960–70; Gerant General, Harriman Ripley International 1964–70; Chairman, Merril Lynch, Pierce, Fenner & Smith Securities Underwriter Ltd. since 1974 (Vice-Chmn. 1970–74); Dir., Finnish Amer. Chamber of Commerce since 1967. Dir. Merrill Lynch-Brown Shipley Bank Ltd. *Member:* Council on Foreign Relations; International Finance Committee of Securities Industry Assn.; Pilgrims. *Awards:* Order of the Lion, Finland; Commander, Order of Merit, Luxembourg. *Clubs:* Knickerbocker, Harvard, Down Town Assn. (N.Y.C.); Harvard (Boston). *Address:* 785 Park Avenue, New York, N.Y. 10021; and *office* One Liberty Plaza, 165 Broadway, New York, N.Y. 10006, U.S.A.

**KENNEY, William John.** American lawyer. *B.* 16 June 1904. *Educ.* Stanford University (AB); Harvard Law School (LLB). *M.* 1931, Elinor Craig. *S.* John Franklin, David Torrence. *Daus.* Elinor (Brown), Priscilla (Streator). *Career:* Associated with the law firm of Orrick, Palmer & Dahlquist, San Francisco 1929–36; Chief of the Oil and Gas Unit of the Securities and Exchange Commission 1936–38; practised law in Los Angeles, California 1938–41; Special Assistant to the Hon. James Forrestal, Under-Secretary of the Navy, Jan. 1941; Assistant Chief, Procurement Legal Division Office of the Under-Secretary of the Navy 1941–June 1944; Chairman of the Price Adjustment Board, Department of the Navy, June 1944–Feb. 1945; The General Counsel, Department of the Navy, Feb. 1945–April 1945; Vice-Chief of Procurement and Material, Department of the Navy, April 1945–Dec. 1945; Deputy to the Assistant Secretary of the Navy in addition to position as Vice-Chief of Procurement and Material, Department of the Navy, Aug. 1945–Dec. 1945; Assistant Secretary of the Navy, Mar. 1946–Sept. 1947; Under-Secretary of the Navy, Sept. 1947–May 1949; Chief of the Economic Cooperation Administration Mission to the United Kingdom, July 1949–Nov. 1950; Deputy Director for Mutual Security 1952; Partner in law firm of Sullivan, Shea & Kenney 1950–71; Director: Merchants Transfer & Storage Co. (Washington, D.C.); Riggs National Bank Porter International Co. (Washington, D.C.); Partner in Law Firm, Cox Langford and Brown since 1971. Medal for Merit. Democrat. *Address:* 78 Kalorama Circle, Washington 8; and *office* 21 Dupont Circle, Washington 36, D.C., U.S.A.

**KENT, Sir Harold Simcox,** GCB. British barrister-at-law. *B.* 1903. *Educ.* Rugby School (Scholarship) and Merton College, Oxford (classical Postmastership); MA (Oxon). *M.* 1930, Zillah Lloyd. *S.* James Michael. *Career:* Called to the Bar (Inner Temple) June 1928. Parliamentary Counsel to the Treasury 1940–53; Treasury Solicitor and Queen's Proctor 1953–63. Standing Counsel to the Church Assembly (now General Synod) 1964–73; Vicar-General of Province of Canterbury 1971–76; Dean. Arches Court of Canterbury; Auditor, Chancery Court of York 1972–76; Queens Counsel since 1973. *Clubs:* United Oxford & Cambridge University. *Address:* 36 Whitehall, London, S.W.1; and Oak Meadow, Broad Campden, Glos.

**KENYATTA, Jomo.** President of Kenya. *B.* (approx.) 1899. *Educ.* Church of Scotland Mission (Kenya) and London School of Econs. *M. S.* 4. *Daus.* 2. *Career:* Gen. Secy., Kikuyu Central Assn.; founded first African-owned journal, Mwigwithania 1928; sent by Kenya Africans to Britain to press case for independence. Travelled extensively in Europe; rep. Ethiopia at the Lge. of Nat. briefly in its early stages. Pres., first Pan-African Cong., Manchester, England, 1945; Pres., Kenya African Union 1947–52; imprisoned 1952–61; elected Pres. *in absentia* of Kenya African National Union whilst in restricted residence at Lodwar 1960. Member. Legislative Council 1962. Minister of State for Constitutional Affairs and Economic Planning 1962. Prime Minister, Minister for Internal Security and Defence, and Foreign Affairs, June 1963–64; Pres. since 1964. *Publications:* Facing Mount Kenya; Kenya, The Land of Conflict; My People of Kikuyu; Harambee; Suffering Without Bitterness. *Address:* P.O. Box 30510, Nairobi, Kenya (Tel. Nairobi 27411). Permanent address: Ichaweri, Gatundu, Kenya.

**KÉRÉKOU, Lt. Col. Mathieu.** Benin Army Officer and Politician. *B.* 1933. *Educ.* St.-Raphael Military Coll., France. *Career:* Chmn., Military Revolutionary Council 1967–68; Deputy Chief of Staff 1970–72; President, Prime Minister and Min. of National Defence since 1972. *Address:* The Presidency, Cotonou, Benin.

**KERNAGHAN, Kenneth Watt,** QC. Canadian. *B.* 1916. *Educ.* Trinity Coll., Univ. of Toronto (BA 1937) and Osgoode Hall Law School, Toronto; called to the Bar of Ontario 1940; QC 1958. *M.* 1941, Edna Mortley Button. *Career:* Trust Offr. in Toronto for The London & Western Trust Co. Ltd. 1940–41, and at London, Ont. 1942–44 (Manager of Toronto office 1944–45). Joined The Robert Simpson Co. Ltd. June 1945, as Solicitor (Asst. Secy. 1953, Secy. 1958, Vice-Pres. and Secy. 1968). Vice-President and Secretary: Simpsons Ltd. 1958—; Director and Secretary, Simpsons Acceptance Co. Ltd.; The Robert Simpson Co. Ltd. (and all subsidiaries); Greenridge Investment Ltd.: Limestone Hall Farms Ltd.; Secy. Pinerocks Ltd.; Director: Woodbine-Sheppard Shopping Centre Ltd., Lakeshore Shopping Plaza Ltd.; Les Galeries d'Anjou Ltée; Micmac Shopping Centre Ltd.; Secy. Simpsons Profit Sharing Retirement Fund; Burton Charitable Foundation. *Member:* Canadian Bar Association; County of York Law Assn.; Assn of Canadian General Counsel; The Chartered Inst. of Secretaries (Affiliate); Board of Trade of Metropolitan Toronto; Canadian Manufacturers Assn.; Phi Delta Phi Fraternity. Conservative. *Clubs:* Canadian; Granite; Lawyers'; Empire. *Address: office* The Simpson Tower, 401 Bay Street, Toronto, M5H 3K2 Ont., Canada.

**KERR, James W.** Canadian executive. *B.* 1914. *Educ.* BSc in applied science and engineering. *M.* 1940, Ruth Eleanor Marrs. *S.* David. *Dau.* Barbara. *Career:* Joined Canadian Westinghouse Ltd. 1937, holding various positions, Vice-President and Gen. Manager, Apparatus Products Group, 1956; Pres. and Chief Exect. Officer TransCanada PipeLines, 1958; Chmn. of the Bd. and President 1961, Chmn. Chief Exec. Officer since 1968; Chmn. Chief Exec. Officer and Dir. Trans Canada Pipelines, Toronto; Director, Manufacturers Life Insurance Co., Great Lakes Gas Transmission Co.; Canadian Imperial Bank of Commerce; Bell Canada; Lehndorff Corp.; International Minerals & Chemical Corp. (Canada) Ltd.; McMaster Univ. Medical Centre Foundation. Vice-Pres., Board of Governors and trustee, Queen Elizabeth Hospital, Toronto; Pres. International Gas Union; Member Nat. Adv. Cttee. on Petroleum, Member, Bd. Governors, Ontario Research Foundation. Past President, Canadian Gas Association, Toronto Board of Trade. *Member:* Engineering Inst. of Canada; Assn. of Professional Engineers for the Province of Ontario. *Address:* P.O. Box 54, Commerce Court West, Toronto, M5L 1C2, and 3 Highland Avenue, Toronto, Ontario M4W 2A2, Canada.

**KERRIDGE, Sir Robert James,** CStJ. *B.* 1901. *M.* 1923, Phyllis Elizabeth Roland. *S.* Robert, Roland and John. *Daus.* Vanessa and Gail. *Career:* Founder of Kerridge Odeon Corp.—the largest theatre organization in the Southern Hemisphere, and of diversified group of companies in fields of Entertainment, Tourism, Hotels, Advertising, Catering, Publishing, Recordings, Merchandising, Property and Finance. Managing Director, Kerridge Odeon Corp. Ltd. Auckland, N.Z.

*Awards:* International Order of the Lion. Chevalier, Order of Merit (Italian Repub.). *Address:* 1 Judge Street, Parnell, Auckland; and *office* 246 Queen Street, Auckland, New Zealand.

**KERSHAW, (John) Anthony,** MC, MP. British Politician. *B.* 1915. *Educ.* Eton; Balliol Coll., Oxford. *M.* 1939, Barbara Crookenden. *S.* 2. *Daus.* 2. *Career:* Mem., London County Council 1946–49, & Westminster City Council 1948–51; MP (Cons.) for Stroud since 1955; Parly. Sec., Ministry of Building & Works 1970; Under-Sec. of State, FCO 1970–73, & Defence (RAF) 1973–74; Vice-Chmn., British Council since 1975. Barrister-at-Law. *Decorations:* Military Cross. *Club:* White's. *Address:* The Tithe Barn, Didmarton, Badminton, Glos.; and *office* House of Commons, London SW1A 0AA.

**KESERÜ, Etelka.** Hungarian politician. *B.* 1925. *Educ.* Graduated from the University of Economy. *M.* 1948, *S.* János. *Dau.* Etelka. *Career:* Active in state and social organizations, in responsible posts 1949–67; Deputy Minister, Domestic Trade 1971; Minister of Light Industry since 1971. *Award:* Golden Grade of Order of Labour. *Address:* Könnyüipari Minisztérium, 11. Fö. U. 68, Budapest, Hungary.

**KESSEL, Lawrence R.** American business executive. *B.* 1903. *Educ.* Harvard Coll. (BS *magna cum laude*) special work at the Univs. of Goettingen, Sorbonne, Munich, Berlin; Columbia and Harvard Business Schools. *M.* 1933, Marie Adler. *Dau.* Laura. *Career:* Business Consultant; Operated mining, farming and retail store enterprises as entrepreneur and consultant, HQ., Kansas City, Mo. 1925–48. Partner, Lawrence Kessel & Associates; President & Chairman of the Board, Adam Hat Stores Inc.; Director: Utica Knitting Co., Straus-Duparquet, United Cities Realty, Greater New York Development Co., Sidney Blumenthal & Co. Inc., American Type Founders Co., Rutland Railway Corp., The Thew Co., The Curtis Publishing Co.; Saturday Evening Post Co.; United American Life Insurance Co. Vice-Pres. & Dir., Landis Machine Co., Arrow Machinery Co.; Dir. and member Exec. Cttee., Dean Phipps Stores Inc.; Norwich & Worcester RR. Co.; Brantford Coach & Body Ltd.; Vice-Pres., Chmn. of Exec. Cttee. & Dir., Cockshutt Farm Equipment Ltd.; Dir. and member of Exec. Cttee., Ogdensburg Terminal Corp.; Dir., C.K.P. Developments Ltd., A.S. Beck Shoe Corp., Delaware & Hudson Railroad Corp., and United Service for New Americans; Director and Member Finance Cttee., Champlain Nat. Securities; Inc.; Manager, Champlain National Corp.; Manager and Member, Finance Cttee., The Delaware and Hudson R. R. Co.; Dir., Pibly Fund Inc. Trustee, Missouri Society of N.Y. *Member:* Amer. Finance Assn.; N.Y. Socy. of Security Analysts; Harvard-Yale-Princeton '25 Assn. (Secretary). *Clubs:* Harvard (N.Y.C.); Harvard (Kansas City); Executives International (Switzerland). *Address:* 4 East 78th Street, New York City, 10021, U.S.A.; and Rue de la Paix 11, Montreux, Switzerland.

**KESSELL, Stephen Lackey,** MBE. Australian Director, Australian Newsprint Mills Ltd. *B.* 1897. *Educ.* MSc (Adelaide); Diploma of Forestry (Oxon.). *M.* 1924, Barbara Morton Sawell. *Dau.* Julia Lesley Cleland. Conservator of Forests, W.A. 1923–40; Commonwealth Timber Controller 1940–46. *Publications:* numerous technical papers on forestry subjects, including reports on forestry administration in N.S.W. (1934) and in Tasmania. *Clubs:* Australian (Melbourne); Tasmanian (Hobart). *Address:* 3 Monomeath Ave., Toorak, S.E.2, Vic.; and *office* Australian Newsprint Mills Ltd., 461 Bourke Street, Melbourne, Vic., Australia.

**KESWICK, Sir William Johnston.** British. *B.* 1903. *Educ.* Winchester Coll. and Trinity Coll. Cambridge (MA). *M.* 1937, Mary, dau. late Rt. Hon. Sir Francis Lindley. *S.* 3. *Dau.* 1. *Career:* Previously Director, Jardine, Matheson & Co. Ltd., Chmn., Shanghai Municipal Council of the Internl. Settlement; member British Shipping Mission at Washington in World War II; Brigadier Staff Duties 21 Army Group; member Royal Commission on Taxation of Profits and Income; Chmn. Matheson & Co. Ltd. 1946–66; Governor Hudson's Bay Co. 1952–65. Former Director, Matheson & Co. Ltd., British Petroleum Ltd., Bank of England, British Petroleum Ltd. and Hudson's Bay Co. *Clubs:* White's. *Address:* Theydon Priory, Theydon Bois, Essex; and *office* 3 Lombard Street, London, E.C.3.

**KETCHUM, Alton Harrington.** American advertising executive. *B.* 1904. *Educ.* Western Reserve Univ. (BA). *M.* 1940, Robyna Neilson. *Dau.* Deborah (Lambert). *Career:* Foreign Corr. for United Press in 20 countries around the world 1926–27; associated with smaller advertising agencies, and a year with New York World-Telegram 1933–34; joined McCann-Erickson 1934; in London office 1937–38; Special Assistant to Petroleum Administrator for War 1943–44; wrote many war effort campaigns, including Red Cross, war bonds, salvage; active in World Government organizations; Vice-Pres. and Creative Director, International Div. McCann-Erickson Inc. 1948–63; Consultant to U.S. Information Agency 1956—and to United Nations Postal Administration, 1966—; Advisory Council American Review, Rome 1961–65; Advertising Committee, Civil War Centennial Commission, 1961–65; Editor, The Inst. of Marketing Communications Bulletin; Vice Pres. Infoplan (world wide public relations) 1963–64; Corporate Staff Executive Interpublic 1964–69; Man. Dir. Harrington's Historical Resources since 1970. member, Exec. Council of Federal World Government 1947–51; member, Bd. of Dirs., World Government News 1949–52. *Awards:* Medal for Outstanding Service to Advertising, by Advertising Federation of America 1961; Freedoms Foundation Award, 1949; Award of Merit, U.S. Information Agency, 1956 (also member Exec. Reserve); Governor's Award for Achievement, State of Ohio, 1965. Worked on over 200 advertising accounts in many fields. *Publications:* wrote Advertising Cncl. campaign to explain Amer. Econ. System (1948–41) and key booklet, The Miracle of America (3 million printed, and 5 million reprinted); wrote story of man's world-wide impulse for freedom for U.S. Information Agency Greek campaign (1951); The March of Freedom, at request of State Dept.; Let Freedom Ring (the place of the American citizen in world affairs); Our Hopes March Side by Side (for USIA 1954, translated into 10 Indian languages); Follow the Sun (on world travel, 1930); Uncle Sam, the Man and the Legend (first book about Samuel Wilson, the original of Uncle Sam, 1959); Editor, Principles and Practices of Marketing Communications (1967); article on advertising for Doubleday, Encyclopedia of Careers; numerous magazine and newspaper articles. Designed People's Capitalism exhibit for U.S. Information Agency, opened by President Eisenhower 1956; planned show, The Golden Key (for U.S. Dept. of Commerce; offering facilities to business), 1956; organized Westchester-Fairfield Cttee. of American Assn. for United Nations (to promote site there for U.N.), 1946; gave original designs for Baton and Badge for Marshals of France (formerly owned by Marshal Berthier, Napoleon's Chief of Staff) to the French people. *Member:* Assn. of American Geographers; Amer. Acad. of Political & Social Science; Greenwich Historical Socy.; Amer. Historical Socy.; Historical Assn. of Great Britain; National Planning Assn.; India-America League (Pres. 1960–64). *Address:* 333 Cognewaug Road, Cos Cob, Conn. 06807, U.S.A.

**KEVILLE, Sir (William) Errington,** CBE. British shipping director. *B.* 1901. *Educ.* Merchant Taylors' School. *M.* 1928, Ailsa Sherwood McMillan. *S.* 3. *Daus.* 2. *Career:* Member, Council of Chamber of Shipping of the United Kingdom 1940 (Pres. 1961); Chmn., General Council of British Shipping 1961. Director: National Bank of New Zealand Ltd. 1946–75; Chmn. Furness Withy Group, 1962–68; International Chamber of Shipping 1963–68; Air Holdings Ltd., 1968–69. Cttee. of European Shipowners 1963–65. *Address:* Stroud Close, Grayswood, Haslemere, Surrey GU27 2DJ.

**KEYSERLING, Leon H.** American economist and lawyer. President, Conference on Economic Progress. *B.* 22 Jan. 1908. *Educ.* Columbia University (AB 1928); Harvard (LLB 1931) (Hon. Dr Bus Sc Bryant 1965); Hon. Member Faculty, Industrial College Armed Forces 1966—. *M.* 1940, Mary Dublin. *Career:* Asst., Dept. of Econ., Columbia 1932–33; Legisl. Asst. to Senator R. F. Wagner, 1933–37; Deputy Administrator and General Counsel, U.S. Housing Authority, 1937–41, Acting Commissioner, 1941–42; General Counsel National Housing Agency, 1942–46; Consultant to various Committees and Members of U.S. Senate and House of Reps., 1938—; Vice-Chairman, President's Council Economic Advisers, 1946-49 (Chairman, 1949-53). Now Economist devoted full-time to voluntary public service. Dir.: Park Electro-Chemical Corp.; North River Securities Co. *Awards:* The Ten Thousand Dollar; Prize in the 1944 Pabst Post-War Employment Awards for essay. 'The American Economic Goal; A Practical Start Toward Post-war Full Employment.' Main Draftsman of major national legislation on employment, labour relations, housing, public works and fiscal policy, 1933—. *Member:* Phi Beta Kappa. *Publications:* Redirecting Education (co-author) 1934; Inflation—Cause and Cure (1959); The Federal Budget and the General Welfare (1959); Jobs and Growth (1961); Key Policies for Full Employment (1962); Taxes and the Public Interest (1963); Two Top Priorities to Reduce Unemployment (1963); The Toll of Rising Interest Rates (1964); Progress or Poverty

(1964); Agriculture and the Public Interest (1965); The Role of Wages in a great Society (1966); Goals for Teachers' Salaries in Our Public Schools (1967); Achieving Nationwide Educational Excellence (1968); Israels Economic Progress (1968); Taxation of Whom and For What (1969); Growth with Less Inflation or More Inflation without Growth (1970); Wages, Prices and Profits (1971); The Coming Crisis in Housing (1972); The Scarcity School of economics (1973); Full Employment without Inflation (1975); Toward Full Employment Within Three Years (1976). *Address:* 2610 Upton Street N.W., Washington, D.C. 20008, U.S.A.

**KEYSERLINGK, Robert Wendelin Henry.** Canadian. *B.* 1905. *Educ.* Univ. of British Columbia (BA); LLD Univ. of Ottawa. *M.* 1930, Sigrid, Baronesse von der Recke. *S.* Robert, Edward, Alexander, Henry and John. *Dau.* Cecile. *Career:* With United Press 1930–61; Managing Director, British United Press 1930–61; Managing Director, British United Press 1936. President; Palm Publishers Ltd., and International Publishers (Canada). Director, Ivag Investments Ltd. Chairman of the Board, Globe, Modern Curriculum Press. *Award:* Count, Grand Cross Bailiff of Obedience Order of Malta; Comdr. Order of Merit (Chile). *Publications:* Unfinished History (Robert Hale, London, 1948); Fathers of Europe (1972). *Clubs:* University (Montreal and Toronto); Vancouver; Cercle Universitaire (Ottawa). *Address:* 450 Racine, Dorval, Que.; and *office* P.O. Box 2267, Dorval, P.Q., Canada.

**KHALAF, Kadhim, M.** *B.* 1922. *Educ.* American University of Beirut (BA); Institute of Advanced Studies, Paris. *Career:* Joined Foreign Service, 1944. Director, Western and Economic Sections, Political and Economic Departments, Foreign Office, 1945. Manager, Rafidain Bank, Southgate Branch, Baghdad, 1951–55. Deputy and Acting Representative for Iraq to the U.N., and Member, U.N. Advisory Committee on Administrative and Budgetary matters, 1955–58. Chargé d'Affairs, Bonn, 1959–60. Director General, Department of the U.N. and International Conference, Foreign Office, 1961–63. Iraqi Representative: the General Conference of the International Labour Organization and the World Health Organization; the Foreign Ministers' Preparatory Meeting for the 2nd Afro-Asian Conference in Jakarta and Algiers, and the Foreign Ministers' Preparatory Meeting for the 2nd Non-Aligned Conference in Colombo, 1964; the Security Council, the Economic and Social Council, the General Assembly, of the U.N., and its different Committees. Member, Iraqi delegation to the 2nd Non-Aligned Conference in Cairo, 1964. Permanent Under-Secretary for Foreign Affairs, 1965–66, and 1967–68. Ambassador, Permanent Representative of Iraq to the U.N., 1966–67. Head of the Iraqi delegation to the International Conference on Human Rights in Tehran, 1968. Ambassador to the Court of St. James's, 1968–72. *Address:* Ministry of Foreign Affairs, Baghdad, Iraq.

**KHALATBARY, Dr. Abbas Ali.** Iranian diplomat. *B.* 1912. *Educ.* Univ. of Paris (PhD, Law and Political Science). *Career:* Joined Ministry of Foreign Affairs; Dept. of Protocol and Third Political Division 1942; Second Secretary, Berne 1945; Member Delegation to the U.N. Gen. Assembly; First Secretary, Warsaw 1947; Acting Head, Dept. of International Organizations 1950 (Director 1951); Alternative member Delegate U.N. Gen. Assembly 1951; Counsellor of Embassy, Paris 1953; Dir.: Third Political Div. 1957; Protocol Dept. Dir. 1958; Ambassador at Warsaw and Minister at Bucharest 1959; Member Del. 13th Session Gen. Assembly; Delegate, Gen. Council U.N. Relief, Rehabilitation Administration (UNRRA) 1960; Sec.-General, Central Treaty Organization (CENTO) 1962–68. Deputy Minister of Foreign Affairs, Imperial Iranian Government; Under-Secy. for Political Affairs at the Imperial Ministry of Foreign Affairs since 1968; Vice Minister, Imperial Iranian Ministry of Foreign Affairs since 1970; Minister for Foreign Affairs since 1971; Chief of Iranian Delegation to the U.N. Gen. Assembly in 1971; Head of Iranian Delegation to the summit Islamic conference, Lahor 1974; Head of Iranian Delegation to Iran-Iraq Treaty 1975. *Address:* Farmanieh, Shemiran, 26 Benafsheh Street, Tehran, Iran; Imperial Iranian Ministry of Foreign Affairs, Teheran, Iran.

**KHALID, Dr. Mansour,** Sudanese. diplomat. *B.* 1931. *Educ.* Univ. of Khartoum (LLB); Univ; of Pennsylvania (LLM); Univ. of Paris (LLD). International Law. *Career:* Attorney, Khartoum 1957–59; Legal Officer, United Nations New York 1962–63; Dept. UN Resident Representative Algeria 1964–65; UNESCO Paris 1965–69; Visiting Prof. of International Law, Univ. of Colorado 1968; Minister Youth and Social Affairs 1969–71; Chmn. Sudan Del. XXV Session, U.N. 1970; Special Consultant, Personal Rep. UNESCO, Dir. Gen. UNRWA fund raising mission 1970; Permanent Rep. to the UN April to July 1971; Minister, Foreign Affairs 1971–75; Chmn. Sudan Delegation XXVI Session of the UN 1971; President Security Council 1972; Chmn. OAU Minst. Cttee. on impact of Petrol price increase in Africa 1973–75; Min. of Educ. 1975–77, of Foreign Affairs since 1977. *Address:* Ministry of Foreign Affairs, Khartoum, Sudan.

**KHALIFA ABBAS, El-Obeid Sayed.** Sudanese diplomatic advisor. *B.* 1915. *Educ.* Old Gordon Memorial Coll.; School of Arts Khartoum. *M.* 1945, Sayida Safiya Hamid. *S.* Tewfik, El-Fateh. *Daus.* Igbal, Huda, Eman. *Career:* Sudanese Railways Asst. Commercial Supt. & District Traffic Manager 1933–54; Dep. Under-Secy. Special Functions External Affairs 1955–56; Dep. Permanent Under-Secy. Min. Foreign Affairs, Sudan 1956–57; Ambassador of the Sudan to Ethiopia 1957–59, to Iraq, Lebanon, Jordan & Turkey 1959–64; to United States of America 1965–66; Perm. Under Secy. Min. Foreign Affairs Khartoum 1966–68; Chmn. Bd. of Dirs. National Bank (Nationalised National & Grindleys) Khartoum, 1969–70; Diplomatic Foreign Service Expert Qatar Foreign Service & Advisor to the Embassy, State of Qatar in London 1972. *Awards:* Grand Cordon, Star of Ethiopia; Independence of the Kingdom of Jordan; The Cedar of Lebanon. *Address:* c/o Ministry of Foreign Affairs, Khartoum, Democratic Republic of the Sudan.

**KHAMA, H. E. Sir Seretse.** KBE. MP. President of Botswana. *B.* 1921. *Educ.* University Coll. Forte Hare (BA); Balliol Coll. Oxford; Inner Temple. *M.* 1948, Ruth Williams. *S.* 3. *Dau.* 1. *Career:* Member, Exec. Council 1961–65; Legislative Assembly 1965–66; Prime Minister, Bechuanaland 1965–66; President of Botswana since 1966. *Awards:* Knight Commander, British Empire; Bachelor of Arts; Hon. PhD; Hon. LLD; Hon. Fellow Balliol Coll. Oxford. *Address:* State House, Gaborone, Botswana and *office* Private Bag 001, Gaborone, Botswana.

**KHAN, Sultan Muhammad.** B.Z. Pakistani diplomat. *B.* 1919. *Educ.* Ewing Christian Coll; Allahabad Univ. B.A. *Career:* Commissioned Indian Army 1942; Indian Political Service 1946; Pakistan Diplomatic Service 1947; Pakistan High Commission New Delhi 1947, Cairo and Rome 1948–50; Embassy, Peking and Ankara 1953–57; Deputy High Comm. London 1957–59; Ministry External Affairs Karachi 1959–61; High Commissioner, Canada 1961–66, concurrently accredited High Commissioner Jamaica 1963–66, Trinidad and Tobago 1963–66; Ambassador to Cuba 1964–66; Ambassador to People's Republic of China 1966–68; Additional Foreign Secy., Foreign Affairs 1969–70; Foreign Secy., Foreign Affairs 1970–72; Ambassador to U.S.A. 1972–73; Concurrently accredited as Ambassador to Jamaica 1972–73; Venezuela 1972–73; Mexico 1972–73; Ambassador to Japan 1974–76. *Address:* c/o Ministry of Foreign Affairs, Islamabad, Pakistan.

**KHARAS, Jamshed Gustadji.** Pakistani diplomat. *B.* 1919. *Educ.* BSc (Eng). *M.* 1949, Miss K. M. Dinshaw. *S.* Homi. *Dau.* Purveen. *Career:* Joined Indian civil service 1942; held executive appointments under the former Government of Sind; opted for service in Pakistan and was appointed Deputy Secretary to the Govt. of Pakistan 1951; attended Imperial Defence College, London 1958; Joint Secretary, Ministry of Foreign Affairs, Karachi 1959. Represented Pakistan on various delegations, and attended the meeting of the SEATO Council of Ministers in Wellington, N.Z. 1959, Paris 1963; High Commissioner for Pakistan in Australia and New Zealand 1960–61; Director-General, Ministry of Foreign Affairs, Government of Pakistan 1962–63. Ambassador to Spain, July 1963–Mar. 1967 with concurrent accreditation to the Holy See 1966–67; to Yugosolavia Mar. 1967 with concurrent accreditation to Greece from Dec. 1967—; Ambassador of Pakistan to the Federal Republic of Germany 1970–72; Ambassador to the Netherlands with concurrent accreditation to Denmark 1972–75; Ambassador to the Republic of Italy with concurrent accreditation to the People's Socialist Republic of Albania since July 1975. *Address:* Embassy of Pakistan, Lungotevere delle Armi 22, 00195 Rome, Italy.

**KHATRI, Major General Padma B.** Nepalese Diplomat. *B.* 1915. *Educ.* Calcutta. *M.* Hari Kumari. *S.* 3. *Dau.* 1. *Career:* Military Attaché to Nepalese Embassy in London 1947–49; Nepalese Liaison Officer to British Brigade of Gurkhas, Malaya, 1950; Represented Nepal at First Asian-African Conf., Indonesia, 1955; Chmn., Nepal-China Boundary Committee 1959–61; Defence Secy., HMG, 1961–63; Foreign Secy. 1963–64; Ambassador in U.S.A., Canada, Chile, Argentina, 1964–69; Perm. Rep. to U.N. 1964–72; Foreign Secy. 1972–75; Ambassador to the U.S.A. since 1976. *Awards:* Order of Nepal Tara (Cl. 1); Trishakti Patta (Cl. 1); KCVO, Gr. Cross Fed. Republic of Germany, Officer de Legion D'Honneur (France); Hon. ADC to HM King of Nepal. *Address:* Royal Nepalese Embassy, 2131 Leroy Place N.W., Washington, D.C. 20008, U.S.A.

**KHILNANI, Khemchand Rewachand Fatchchand.** Barrister-at-Law, Counsel Supreme Court of India and High Court of Punjab. *B.* 1913. *Educ.* Bombay Univ. (BA Hons.) and Cambridge Univ. (BA Hons.; MA Hons.); Called to the Bar (Lincoln's Inn, London 1937). *M.* 1941. *S.* 1. *Daus.* 5. *Career:* Assistant Commissioner-General (Economic Adviser), Paris 1949; First Secretary (Com.) Prague, and Trade Commissioner to Poland, Hungary, Albania, Rumania, and Bulgaria 1949–51. First Secy. (Com.), Indian High Commission, Colombo, and Indian Embassy, Rome 1955–57; Counsellor (Com.) Cairo 1957–59; Joint Secy. Ministry of Commerce and Industry 1959–61; Commissioner in British East Africa, Nairobi 1961–63 (concurrently accredited to Fed. of Rhodesia and Nyasaland, and (as Consul-General) to Raunda Burundi); Ambassador to Rumania and concurrently to Bulgaria until Mar. 1967; Ambassador to Senegal (and concurrently to Ivory Coast, Upper Volta, Mauretania, and (as High Commissioner) to Gambia, July 1967–68. Dir.: State Trading Corporation and Shipping Corporation of India 1959–61; President 3rd Committee on Trade (ECAFE); Leader, Indian Trade Delegations to East European and West Asian countries; Member Cttee. Bhartiya Vidya Bhavan, Delhi; Fellow Royal Economic Society; Industrial Consultant. *Club:* Gymkhana (New Delhi). *Address:* 18, Eastern Avenne, Maharani Bagh, New Delhi-14, India.

**KHIN, U.** Burmese. *B.* 1917. *Educ.* Univ. of Rangoon (BA 1938) and Univ. of Minnesota, U.S.A. (MA Journalism 1950); (MA History Univ. of London 1970). *M.* 1952, Gladys Hirjee. *S.* 2. *Daus.* 2. *Career:* In Burma Civil Service 1940; Sub-Lieut., Burma R.N.V.R. 1941; Information Assistant. U.S.I.S., Rangoon, 1947; Burma State Scholar 1948–50; Announcer and Commentator, Voice of America 1951–53; Information Officer, Ministry of Information, Rangoon 1953–57; Deputy Director of Information; Burma (Rangoon) 1957–66; On Deputation to B.B.C. London 1966–71; Former Editor, Forward magazine; Dir. of Information. Information and Broadcasting Department since 1972. *Member:* Sigma Delta Chi; Freemasons. *Publications:* Public Opinion and Role of Newspapers in pre-Independent Burma; Japanese Psychological Warfare in S.E. Asia during World War II; The Peasant's Revolt of Burma 1930. *Address: office* BBS Building, Prome Road, Rangoon, Burma.

**KHOMAN, Dr. Thanat.** *B.* 1914. *Educ.* School of Political Sciences, Paris; University of Paris (LLD). *Career:* Joined Ministry of Foreign Affairs, Bangkok 1940; served at the Embassies in Japan, U.S.A. and India; Director-General, Economic Affairs Dept. and concurrently Acting Director, General of U.N. Affairs Dept. 1949–52; Dep. Permanent Representative, Permanent Mission to Thailand to U.N., New York 1952–57; Ambassador to U.S.A. 1957–58; Minister of Foreign Affairs of Thailand Feb. 1959–71; Mem., Admin. Council, Administrative Reform Cttee. 1976. Member, International Law Commission 1957; Chairman of Committee on South-west Africa of U.N. 1952–57; Chmn., U.N, Trusteeship Committee 1957. *Address:* 123 Petchburi Road, Bangkok, Thailand.

**KHURANA, Madan Mohan,** BSc, LLB. Indian. *B.* 18 Jan. 1919. *Educ.* Govt. Coll. Lahore; Delhi University. *Career:* Commissioned, Indian Army 1941; served under Netaji Subbas Chandra Bose in Malaya; Joined I.F.S. Oct. 1948; Second Secy. Indian Commission, Trinidad then Singapore, 1948–53; First Secy. Singapore 1953. Member, Afro-Asian Conf. Secretariat, Bandung, 1955; Asst. Commissioner for India, Salisbury, Rhodesia, 1959–60; Chargé d'Affaires, Helsinki, 1960–63; Commercial Counsellor, Indian Embassy, Bonn, 1963–67. High Commissioner for India in Malawi, 1967–71; Ambassador of India to Argentina, Uruguay and Paraguay 1971–74; High Commissioner for India in Mauritius since 1974. *Clubs:* Gymkhana; Golf (New Delhi); Jockey (Buenos Aires). *Address:* c/o Ministry of External Affairs, New Delhi, India.

**KIA, F. Nouredin.** Iranian diplomat. *B.* 1918. *Educ.* Univ. of Tehran (BA) and Sciences School, New York (BA). *M.* 1954, Afsar. *S.* Bahman. *Dau.* Afsoun. *Career:* Joined Ministry of Foreign Affairs 1939. Vice-Consul, Palestine and Jordan (Jerusalem) 1942–47; Asst., U.N. Department, Ministry of Foreign Affairs 1947–49; Adviser and Counsellor, Permanent Delegation of Iran to U.N. 1949–54; Member, Iranian Delegation to Economic & Social Council 1950–53; Representative in 5th Committee of General Assembly; elected Alternate Member, U.N. Staff Pension Committee 1953–55, and 1956–59. Head, 4th Political Department (North and South American Affairs), Minister of Foreign Affairs 1954–56; Minister and Consul-General Istanbul 1956–60; Member and Vice-Chmn., Committee on Contributions of U.N. 1959–70; Director-General, Iranian Foreign Ministry 1960. Member, Iranian Delg. to 18th Session of U.N. Gen. Assembly. Elected Commissioner-General of Iran for the Montreal International Exposition of 1967, 1965. Ambassador of Iran to Canada, Nov. 1962–67, to Japan, Philippines, Republic of China, South Korea 1968–72; Head, Iranian Friendship Mission to N. Korea 1973; Inspector-General, Ministry of Foreign Affairs since 1972. *Awards:* Order of Homayoun of First Class; Order of Rising Sun, First Class; Order, Diplomatic Merit of First Class; Medal of City of Istanbul. *Address:* Ministry of Foreign Affairs, Tehran, Iran.

**KIDDE, John Frederick.** Industrialist. *B.* 1905. *Educ.* Princeton Univ. (AB 1926), Stevens Inst. of Technology (ME 1928); Hon. LLD, Upsala Coll. 1957. *M.* 1929, Katharine Lyon (*Div.*), and 1942, Mary Taylor MacKenzie. *S.* John Lyon. *Dau.* Katharine. *Career:* Dir., Clara Maass Memorial Hospital, Belleville, N.J. Trustee; Stevens Inst. of Technology, Hoboken. N.J.; With Cities Services Co., N.Y.C. 1928–29; J. R. Williston & Co., N.Y.C. 1929–34; Dir. 1931—; Advertising Manager, Walter Kidde & Co. Inc. 1934–37, Vice Chmn. Bd. 1961—; Treasurer: Walter Kidde & Co., and Walter Kidde Constructors Inc. 1937–43; Pres., Walter Kidde & Co. Inc. 1943–61. Chmn. of Exec. Cttee., Walter Kidde & Co. Inc. 1967–69; Dir. Midatlantic National Bank (formerly National Newark & Essex Bank). *Member:* National Assn. of Manufacturers; Republican. *Clubs:* Montclair (N.J.) Golf; National Golf Links of America (Southampton, N.Y.); Westhampton Beach (N.Y.) Country; Links (N.Y.C.); Stevens Metropolitan (N.Y.C.); C.C. of Florida; Delray Beach Yacht; Ocean of Florida. *Address:* 12 South Mountain Avenue, Montclair, N.J.,; and *office* 9 Brighton Road, Clifton, N.J., U.S.A.

**KIDRON, Abraham.** Israeli Diplomat. *B.*1919. *Educ.* Graduate of Hebrew Univ. of Jerusalem. *M.* Shoshana Kidron. *Daus.* 2. *Career:* Captain, Israel Defence Forces 1948; various posts at Ministry of Foreign Affairs, Jerusalem 1949–50; Attaché, Embassy of Israel, Rome 1950–52; Ministry of Foreign Affairs, Jerusalem 1953–54; Consul, Cyprus 1954–56; First Sec. (Press), Embassy of Israel, London 1957–59; Head of Research Dept. & Spokesman for Ministry of Foreign Affairs, Jerusalem 1959–63; Minister, Israel Legation, Yugoslavia 1963–65; Ambassador of Israel to the Philippines 1965–67; Asst. Dir.-Gen. 1969–71, Dep. Dir.-Gen. 1972–73, Dir.-Gen, 1973–76, Ministry of Foreign Affairs, Jerusalem; Amb. of Israel to the Netherlands 1976–77; Amb. of Israel to the Court of St. James's since 1977. *Address:* Embassy of Israel, 2 Palace Green, London W.8.

**KIENZL, Dr. Heinz,** Dkfm. Austrian Banker. *B.* 1922. *Educ.* Humanistisches Gymnasium; Hochschule für Welthandel. *M.* 1951, Erna. *Career:* Head of Economics Dept., Austrian Trades Union Congress 1950–69; Generalrat (Councillor) Austrian National Bank 1961–69, Deputy-Man. Dir. 1969–73, Man. Dir. since 1973. *Publications:* Wirtschaftstheorie und Wirtschaftspolitik; contributions to technical magazines and economic and social science publications. *Address:* 1130 Wien, Turgenjewgasse 7, Austria; and *office* 1090 Wien, Otto Wagner-Platz 3, Austria.

**KIESINGER, Dr. h.c. Kurt Georg.** *B.* 1904. *Educ.* studied law, history and philosophy. *Married*, two children. *Career:* Practised law in Berlin 1935–40; drafted for work in the German Foreign Ministry as a scientific assistant 1940. After the war he opened a legal practice in Tübingen and entered politics; mem. Bundestag from 1949 until he became Prime Minister of the State of Baden-Württemberg (1958–66) and from 1969 on when he represented a constituency of the Christian-Democratic Union (Chmn. 1967–71) in the Bundestag (the federal parliament), Hon Chmn since 1971; became Chmn. of the Bundestag Foreign Affairs Cttee. 1954. Federal Chancellor of the Federal Republic of Germany from 1966–69. When, during the political crisis in Bonn he was asked to stand as a candidate for the Chancellorship, he persuaded the Social Democrats to enter his government, and was able to assemble his Cabinet with a speed unheard of in Bonn's political history. He pursued a policy of reconciliation with Germany's eastern neighbours; established diplomatic relations with Rumania and Yugoslavia. *Address:* 53 Bonn Bundeshaus, Federal Republic of Germany.

**KILFEDDER, James Alexander.** BL, BA, MP. British (Ulster Unionist) politician. *B.* 1928. *Educ.* Dublin University. Barrister-at-Law. *Career:* Member of Parliament for Belfast West 1964–66 and for North Down since 1970; Elected Member, Northern Ireland Assembly 1973; Elected Member of Northern Ireland Convention 1975; Member, Trustee Savings Banks Parly. Cttee. since 1970. *Address:* Eastonville, Millisle, Co. Down, Northern Ireland; 7 Grays Inn Square, London, W.C.1; and House of Commons, London, S.W.1.

**KILGOUR, Bayard Livingston, Jr.** American executive. *B.* 1904. *Educ.* Harvard Univ. (BS 1927). *M.* 1931, Kate E. Gray. *S.* David Gray and Bayard L. III. *Career:* Engaged in commercial and statistical work with American Telephone & Telegraph Co., New York City 1927–30; plant dept. Asst. to Pres., Cincinnati & Sub. Bell Telephone Co. 1930–31, Dir. 1930, Vice-Pres. 1931, Chmn. 1965, retd. 1969, Dir.-Emeritus; Dir. Emeritus Central Trust Co.; Dir. Union Central Life Insurance Co., and Central Bancorporation, Inc. Trustee, Cincinnati Museum Association; member, American Institute of Electrical Engineers, Caledonian Socy., Cincinnati Historical Socy., and Cincinnati Nature Center; Cttee. to visit Dept. of Slavic Languages and Literatures, Harvard, Library Overseers' Cttee. to visit Harvard Library (Hon. Curator of Slavic Collections in the Harvard Coll. Library), Harvard Engineering Society, and Newcomen Society. *Clubs:* Harvard, The Brook (N.Y.C.); Bohemian (San Francisco); Queen City, Harvard, Commonwealth, Commercial, Cincinnati Country; (all of Cincinnati); Fly (Cambridge, Mass.); Balboa Club; Mazatlan; Mexico. *Address:* 4500 Drake Road, Cincinnati, Ohio 45243; and *office* 225 E. 4th Street, Room 200, Cincinatti, Ohio 45202, U.S.A.

**KILLEFER, Tom.** American lawyer and financier. *B.* 1917 *Educ.* Stanford Univ. (AB Econ); Harvard Univ. (JD); Rhodes Scholar at Oxford Univ. 1947, Bach. Civil Law degree. *M.* 1948, Carolyn Clothier. *S.* Wade. *Daus.* Caroline, Gail and Anne. *Career:* Admitted to California Bar 1946 and U.S. Supreme Court Bar 1953; Partner in law firm in San Francisco 1956–59; Executive Dir. American Steamship Lines 1959–60; First Vice-President, Vice-Chairman and Director, Export-Import Bank, Washington, 1960–62; Executive Director, Inter-American Development Bank, and Spl. Asst. to Secy. of Treasury, 1962–66; with Chrysler Corp.: Executive Assistant to Vice-President Legal Affairs 1966, Vice-President in same year, Vice-President Finance 1967. Vice-President, Finance and General Counsel, Chrysler Corp., 1968–76; Chmn., Pres. & Chief Exec. Officer, United Trust Co. of New York since 1976. *Member:* Amer. Assn. of Rhodes Scholars, etc. *Clubs:* Detroit; Country Club of Detroit; Yondotega; Metropolitan, Chevy Chase, Alibi, Alfalfa (all Washington); Pacific-Union, (San Francisco); The Links (New York); The River Club (N.Y.). *Address:* 30 East 65th Street, New York, N.Y. 10021; and *office* 45 Wall Street, New York, N.Y. 10005, U.S.A.

**KILLEN, Bryce Geoffrey Lyle.** Australian. *B.* 1923. *Educ.* Edgecliff Prep School and Sydney Grammar School. *M.* (1) 1942, Medea Hinsby. *S.* 1. *M.* (2) 1950, Rosanne Rofe. *S.* 2. *Dau.* 1. *Career:* Chmn. Airfast Services Group; Helicopter Utilities Pty. Ltd.; Westernair Navigation Pty. Ltd.; Northern Meat Exporters P/L. Dir.: Country Life Newspapers; Queensland Country Life Newspaper. Vice-President, Northern Territory Pastoral Lessees Assn. General Manager, Moonagee Merino and Poll, Shorthorn Studs. *Member:* N.S.W. University Wool Technology Advisory Panel; and Water Development Association of Eastern Australia. Lieut 2/8, Commando Squadron (served in the Islands). Member, Australian Woolgrowers & Graziers Council 1962–66; Vice-Pres., Grazier's Assn. of N.S.W. 1962–65. Pres. Federal Inland Development Organization since 1964. Member, Australian Wool Industry Conference since 1962. *Clubs:* Australian (Sydney); Queensland (Brisbane); Royal Sydney Golf. *Address: office* Suite 2710, Australia Square Tower, Sydney, N.S.W. 2001, Australia.

**KILLIAN, James R., Jr.** College administrator (Ret'd.). *B.* 1904. *Educ.* M.I.T. (SB 1926). *M.* 1929, Elizabeth Parks. *S.* Rhyne Meredith. *Dau.* Carolyn (Mrs. Paul R. Staley). *Career:* Asst. Managing Editor, The Technology Review 1926–27 (Managing Editor 1927–30; Editor 1930–39); Exec. Asst. to the President, M.I.T. 1939–43 (Exec. Vice-Pres. 1943–45; Vice-Pres. 1945–48; Pres. 1948–59); on leave 1957–59 to assume post of Special Asst. to President of U.S. for Science & Technology. Chairman of the Corporation, Massachusetts Institute of Technology (M.I.T.) 1959–71; Hon. Chmn. since 1971. *Awards:* President's Certificate of Merit 1948; Certificate of Appreciation 1953, and Decoration for Exceptional Civilian Service, Dept. of the Army 1957; Public Welfare Medal, National Acad. of Sciences 1957; Officer, Legion of Honour (France) 1957; Hoover Medal, 1963; George Foster Peabody Awards 1968 and 1975. Honorary Degrees: LLD: Colleges: Union, Bowdoin, Williams, Amherst, William & Mary, Providence, Meadville Theological School; Universities: Northeastern, Duke, Boston, Harvard, Lehigh, Pennsylvania, Chattanooga, Tufts, California, Brandeis, New York and Johns Hopkins, Temple, South Carolina; ScD: Colleges: Middlebury, Bates, Lowell Technological Institute, Wooster, Oberlin, Worcester Polytechnic Institute; Universities: Havana (Cuba), Notre Dame, Columbia, Maine, Akron. DEng: Drexel Institute of Technology, University of Illinois, University of Massachusetts; DAppl Science, University of Montreal; EdD Rhode Island College; HHD, Rollins College; DPS Detroit Inst. of Technology. *Member:* Amer. Acad. of Arts & Sciences, Nat. Acad. of Engineering; Hon. Mem., Amer. Socy. for Engineering Education. *Clubs:* St. Botolph (Boston); Century Association, University (N.Y.C.). *Address:* 100 Memorial Drive, Cambridge, Mass. 02142; and *office* 77 Massachusetts Avenue, Cambridge, Mass. 02139, U.S.A.

**KILLICK, Sir John Edward,** KCMG. British diplomat. *B.* 18 Nov. 1919. *Educ.* Latymer Upper School London; Univ. Coll. London; Bonn University. *M.* 1949, Lucy Lynette Du Preez Leach. *Career:* Foreign Office London 1946–48; Control Commission for Germany, Berlin, Frankfurt and Bonn 1948–51; Private Secy. to Parly. Under Secy. F.O. 1951–53; British Embassy, Addis Ababa 1953–57; Canadian National Defence Coll. 1957–58; Asst. Head, Western Dept. F.O. 1958–61; Imperial Defence Coll. London 1962; Head of Chancery, British Embassy Washington 1963–68; Asst. Under Secy. of State F.O. 1968–71; British Ambassador at Moscow 1971–73; Deputy Under Secy. of State F.C.O. 1973–75; UK Perm. Rep. to NATO since 1975. *Award:* Knight Commander of the Order of St. Michael & St. George. *Clubs:* Brooks's; East India Sports and Public Schools; Royal Commonwealth Socy. Royal African Society. *Address:* Pennycross, Park Road, Limpsfield, Oxted, Surrey; and *office* Foreign & Commonwealth Office, Downing Street, London, S.W.1.

**KILLICK, Paul Victor St John,** OBE. British diplomat. *B.* 1916. *Educ.* St. Paul's School, London. *M.* 1947, Sylva Leva. *S.* 1. *Daus.* 2. *Career:* with H.M. Forces 1939–46; H.M. Diplomatic Service, Singapore 1946–47; Tokyo 1947–50; Katmandu 1950–53. Foreign Office 1953–55; Oslo 1955–58; San Francisco 1958–60; Djakarta 1961; Rome 1962–66; Pretoria 1966–71; Tangier 1971–72; H.M. Ambassador, Santo Domingo 1972–76 (Ret'd.). *Award:* Order of the British Empire. *Address:* c/o Foreign and Commonwealth Office, London, SW1A 2AH.

**KILLOUGH, Walter William,** OBE (Hon.). American industrialist. *B.* 1904. *Educ.* Oklahoma State Univ. *M.* 1927, Allie Nell Watson. *S.* Walter William, Jr. *Dau.* Mickey June (Emerson Lynn, Jr.). *Career:* Arrived in Australia 1944. Previously: Pres., International Harvester Co. of Canada Ltd., Hamilton, Ont. 1961–62; Chmn. and Mng. Dir. International Harvester Co. of Australia Pty. Ltd., Melbourne 1950–61. A director of the U.S. Educational Foundation in Australia Administration 1954–61; Military Vehicles Industry Advisory Cttee. 1954–61; Export Development Council 1959–61; Productivity Council 1959–61; Council of Inst. of Public Affairs, Victoria 1956–66; Council Monash Univ. 1958–61; Pres. Australian Inst. of Management (Melbourne Div.) 1955–57 (Federal Pres. 1958, 1960; Hon. Life Member). Dir., Construction Industry Manufacturers Assn. 1966–68; Vice-Pres., International Harvester Co. (Construction Equipment Div.), Chicago, Ill. Nov. 1963–68; Chamber of Commerce (Arlington), Construction Industry Manufacturers Association 1966–68. *Member:* Melbourne Rotary Club 1951–61. *Clubs:* Athenaeum, Australian (Melbourne); Tattersall's (Sydney); Association of the U.S. Army (Chicago); Chicago Assn. of Commerce & Industry; Fort Worth (Fort Worth Texas.). *Address:* 1215 Canterbury Court, Arlington, Texas 76013, U.S.A.

**KILPATRICK, Sir William John,** KBE. British. *B.* 1906. *Educ.* Wolongong N.S.W. *M.* 1932, Alice Margaret Strachan.

*S.* William John. *Daus.* Margaret Ruth (Randall), Roslyn Ann (King), Susan Elizabeth (Griffin). *Career:* Chmn. Mulford Holdings and Associated Companies 1945—; Dir. Kilpatric Investments Pty. Ltd. 1946—; Guardian Assurance Group 1958; Dep. Pres. Nat. Heart Foundation of Australia, 1960–64; Pres. Aust. Cancer Socy. 1961–64; World Chmn. Finance Cttee. International Union Against Cancer 1961—; National Chmn. Winston Churchill Memorial Trust 1965—; Drug Education Sub-Cttee. Commonwealth Government 1970; Plastic & Reconstructive Surgery Foundation 1970. Pres. Australia Cancer Socy. (1974); ESU (Vic. Branch); Chmn. of Trustees, Alcoholism, and Drug dependence Foundation; National undergrads working visit to Australia scheme (UNVAS) 1969–74. *Member:* Melbourne City Council, 1958–64. *Clubs:* Naval & Military; Victoria Golf. *Address:* 8 Hopetoun Road, Toorak, Vic. 3142; and *office* Mainline Building, 434 St. Kilda Road, Melbourne, Australia.

**KILROY-SILK, Robert,** MP. British. *B.* 1942. *Educ.* Secondary Modern Sch., Grammar Sch., London Sch. of Economics—BSc (Econ.). *M.* 1963, Jan Beech. *S.* 1. *Dau.* 1. *Career:* Lecturer, Univ. of Liverpool 1966–74; Labour MP for Ormskirk since 1974; Select Cttee. on Public Accounts since 1975; Vice-Chmn., Parly. Labour Party Home Affairs Group 1977—. *Publications:* Socialism Since Marx (1972); (co-author) Role of Royal Commissioners in Policy Making (1973); and articles in Political Studies, Political Quarterly, Parliamentary Affairs, etc. *Address:* Trees, Lock Mead, Maidenhead, Berks.

**KIMBALL, Charles Newton.** American. Chairman scientific research organization. *B.* 1911. *Educ.* Northeastern Univ. (BEE 1931); Harvard Univ. (SM 1932; ScD 1934); Hon. EngD, Northeastern Univ. 1955; Hon. ScD Park Coll. 1958; *M.* 1951, Mary Louise Theis Kimball. *S.* John Theis. *Dau.* Susanne Louise. *Career:* Director: Hallmark Cards Inc.; Trans-World Airlines Inc.; Trustee, Cttee. for Economic Development; Fellow, Institute of Electrical and Electronics Engineers; Board of Trustees, Menninger Foundation; Trustee, Hallmark Foundation; Research Engineer, Radio Corporation of America 1935–41; Vice-Pres., mbr. of the Bd., Aircraft Accessories Corporation 1941–46; Vice-President, member of the Board. C. J. Patterson Co. 1946–48; Tech. Dir., Research Lab., Div., Bendix Aviation Corp. 1948–50; Pres. Midwest Research Inst. 1950–75; Chmn. of not for profit scientific research organisation, 1975—. *Publications:* Technology in a Changing World (1966); Interface, Technology-Society (1972); and many other works, articles and papers. *Address:* Midwest Research Institute, 425 Volker Boulevard, Kansas City, Mo. 64110 U.S.A.

**KIMBLE, George H. T.** British Geographer. *B.* 1908. *Educ.* BA and MA (London) and PhD (Montreal). *M.* 1935, Dorothy Stevens Berry. *S.* Stephen. *Dau.* Gillian. *Career:* Rushton Foundation Lecturer 1952, Borah Foundation Lecturer, Univ. of Idaho 1956, and Haynes Foundation Lecturer, Univ. of Redlands 1966. Asst. Lecturer in Geography: Univ. of Hull (1931–36) and Univ. of Reading (1936–39); Lieut. (later Lieut.-Comdr.), Royal Naval Meteorological Service 1939–44; First Professor & Chairman, Dept. of Geography. McGill Univ. 1945–50; Director: American Geographical Society (1950–53) and Tropical African Survey (Twentieth Century Fund) 1953–60; Secy.-Treas., International Geographical Union 1949–56; Visiting Professor, Univ. of California (Berkeley) 1948–49, Stanford Univ. 1961, Stockholm School of Economics 1961. Director, U.S. Geography Project (20th Century Fund) 1962–68. Professor, Department Geography, Indiana Univ., Sept. 1957–66; Chairman, Department of Geography, Indiana University 1957–62; Chmn., Commission on the Humid Tropics, Intl. Geographical Union, Aug. 1956–61. *Publications:* Geography in the Middle Ages (1938); The World's Open Spaces (1939); The Weather (1943); The Way of the World (1953); Our American Weather (1955); Tropical Africa (2 vols., 1960); Tropical Africa Today (with Ronald Steel, (1966); Man and His World (1972); From The Four Winds (1973). *Member:* Royal Geographical Socy.; Royal Meteorological Socy. *Address:* Summerclose, Stoodleigh, Tiverton, Devon.

**KIMCHI, Aaron D.,** MM. Israeli banker. *B.* 1924. *Educ.* Hebrew Univ., Jerusalem (MAEcon). *M.* Aliza Schneerson. *Daus.* 2. *Career:* On Government service as Deputy Director of State Revenue and Deputy Controller of Foreign Exchange 1951–59. General Managing Director, The Israel Industrial Bank Ltd. *Address:* 13 Montefiore Street, Tel-Aviv, Israel (P.O. Box 29179, Tel.-Aviv).

**KINAHAN, Sir Robert George Caldwell,** ERD, JP, DL, LLD. *B.* 1916. *Educ.* Stowe School (Buckingham). *M.* 1950, Coralie Isabel deBurgh. *S.* 2. *Daus.* 3. *Career:* Councillor and Alderman, Belfast Corporation 1949–64; Member of Parliament, Northern Ireland 1958–59; Lord Mayor of Belfast 1959–60, 1960–61. High Sheriff of Belfast 1955, and County Antrim, 1969. Chairman: Bass Ireland Ltd. 1958; Inglis & Co. Ltd. 1962—, E. T. Green Ltd. 1964—; Ulster Bank Ltd., Deputy-Chmn., 1964, Chmn. 1970; Dir. Nat. Westminster Bank Ltd. since 1973; Director, Eagle Star Insurance Co. (Local); Gallaher Ltd. Interests (holds office on): Board of St. Anne's Cathedral, Belfast, and 'Samaritans'. *Club:* Ulster (Belfast). *Address:* Castle Upton, Templepatrick, Co. Antrim, Northern Ireland; and *office* Ulster Bank Ltd., 35–47 Donegall Place, Belfast BY1 5AU.

**KINDLEBERGER, Charles P.** American professor. Bronze Star, Legion of Merit. *B.* 1910. *Educ.* Univ. of Pennsylvania (AB 1932) and Columbia Univ. (MA 1934, PhD 1937). *M.* 1937, Sarah Bache Miles. *S.* Charles P. III and Richard S. *Daus.* Sarah, Elizabeth (Randall). *Career:* Adviser on European Recovery (German reparations), Dept. of State 1945–48. G-2 Section, 12th Army Group, U.S. Army 1944–45. Office of Strategic Services 1942–44. Professor of Economics, Massachusetts Institute of Technology (M.I.T.). *Publications:* ten books, of which the latest are: Europe's Postwar Growth (1967); American Business Abroad (1969); Power and Money (1970); The world in Depression 1929–39 (1973); Dhc Univ. of Paris 1966. *Member:* Amer. Economic Assn.; Royal Economic Socy.; Academy of Arts and Sciences; Phi Beta Kappa. *Address: office* 52–380 Massachusetts Institute of Technology, Cambridge, Mass. 02139, U.S.A.

**KING, Cecil Harmsworth.** *B.* 1901. *Educ.* Winchester Coll.; Christ Church, Oxford (MA); Hon D Litt Boston Univ. 1974. *M.* (1) 1923, Agnes Margaret Cooke. *S.* Michael, Francis, Colin (*D.* 1977). *Dau.* Priscilla; (2) 1962, Ruth Railton. *Career:* Worked with Glasgow Daily Record 1922, London Daily Mail 1923–26, Daily Mirror since 1926, Director 1929, Chairman 1951–63, Sunday Pictorial, Dir. 1935, Deputy-Chmn. 1942, Chmn. 1951–68; Chmn.: Fleetway Publications 1959–61. Chmn. International Publishing Corporation 1963–68, Newspaper Proprietors Assn. 1961–68. Dir., Bank of England 1965–68. Chmn., Reed Paper Group 1963–68. *Member:* Countryside Commission 1966–69 and (part-time) National Coal Board 1966–69. *Publications:* Strictly Personal (1969); With Malice Towards None (1970); Without Fear or Favour (1971); Cecil King's Diary 1964–70 (1972); Cecil King on Ireland (1973); Cecil King's Diary 1970–74 (1975). *Address:* 23 Greenfield Park, Dublin 4, Ireland.

**KING, Evelyn Mansfield,** MA, MP. British. *B.* 30 May 1907. *Educ.* Kings Coll., Cambridge. *M.* 1935, Hermione Edith Crutchley. *S.* 1. *Daus.* 2. *Career:* Headmaster Clayesmore School, Dorset, 1935–40; Army Lieut.-Colonel, Gloucestershire Regiment, 1940; MP Penryn & Falmouth 1945–50; Parly. Sec. Ministry, Town & Country Planning 1947–50; Farming & Writing, 1950–64; Member of Parliament for South Dorset since 1964. *Publications:* Biography of Luke Hansard. *Clubs:* Carlton; Royal South Dorset Yacht. *Address:* Embley Manor, Romsey, Hants; and 11 Barton Street, London, S.W.1.

**KING, Hilary William,** CBE. Former British diplomat. *B.* 1919. *Educ.* Sherborne School (Dorset) and Corpus Christi College, Cambridge (BA Classics, Modern Languages). *M.* 1947, Dr. Margaret Helen Grierson (née Borrowman). *S.* 1. *Daus.* 3. *Career:* Served in World War II (Royal Signals 1939–45); Vice-Consul Sarajevo and Ljubljana 1947–48; Acting Consul Skopje 1948; Foreign Office 1949–51; British Embassy, Vienna 1951–53, and Washington 1953–58; Foreign Office 1958–59; British Embassy, Moscow 1959–62; Ambassador to Republic of Guinea, Nov. 1962–65. St. Anthony's Coll., Oxford 1965–66; Counsellor, British Embassy, Warsaw 1966–67; Foreign and Commonwealth Office (U.N. Economic and Social Department) 1968–71; Consul General Hamburg 1971–74. *Clubs:* Clyde Cruising. *Address:* Fuaim an Sruth, South Cuan, Oban, Argyll, PA34 4TU.

**KING, Thomas Jeremy (Tom),** MA, MP. British. *B.* 13 June 1933. *Educ.* Rugby & Emmanuel Coll., Cambridge, Master of Arts, (Hons.). *M.* 1960, Jane Tilney. *S.* Rupert. *Dau.* Elisa. *Career:* Trainee, various positions to Div. Gen. Manager, E. & A Robinson Ltd. 1956–69; Dir. Sale Tilney & Co. Ltd. 1965–71, Chmn. since 1971. Member of Parliament for Bridgwater since 1970; Parly. Private Secy. to Ministry of Posts & Telecommunications 1970–74; P.P.S. to Minister, Industrial Development 1972–74; Vice-Chmn. Conservative Industry

Cttee. 1974; Conservative Front Bench Spokesman for Industry 1975–76, for Energy since 1976. *Address:* House of Commons, London, S.W.1.

**KINGSBURY, Frederick Hutchinson, Jr.** American banker. *B.* 1907. *Educ.* The Hill Sch., Pottstown, Pa. 1923–25, and Princeton Univ. (AB 1929). *M.* (2) 1962, Eleanor Bried O'Donnell. *S.* 1. *Dau.* 1. *Career:* Partner, Brown Brothers Harriman & Co., N.Y.C. 1949—. Chmn. of the Board; Prudential Insurance Co. of Gt. Britain, N.Y.C. 1957–73, and Hudson Insurance Co. 1957—. Director: Netherlands Chamber of Commerce in U.S.A., N.Y. 1955–72; Chmn. U.S. Exec. Cttee., Skandia Insurance Co., Stockholm 1957–74; Chmn. Skandia America Reinsurance Corporation, New York, since 1974; Director: Interpace Corp.; Parsippany, N.J. 1952—; Bangor Punta Corp.; Greenwich Connecticut 1956—; Deputy-Chmn. Brown Harriman & International Banks Ltd. 1972–77. *Member:* International Advisory Committee of American Bankers Association, 1962–65. *Award:* Officer, Order of Oranje Nassau (Netherlands). *Clubs:* Blooming Grove Hunting and Fishing (Hawley, Penn.); India House, The Links, The University (all of N.Y.C.); Pine Valley Golf (Clementon, N.J.); University Cottage (Princeton, N.J.). *Address:* 655 Park Avenue, New York, N.Y. 10021; and *office* Brown Brothers Harriman & Co., 59 Wall Street, New York, N.Y. 10005.

**KINGS NORTON, Lord** (Sir Harold Roxbee Cox). British engineer. *B.* 1902. *Educ.* Kings Norton Grammar School and Imperial College of Science & Technology (DIC, PhD). *M.* 1927, Doris Marjorie Withers. *S.* Christopher Witners Roxbee, Jeremy William Roxbee. *Career:* With Austin Motor Co. 1918–22; University 1922–24; held various government posts concerned with airships, and aircraft 1924–31; Royal Aircraft Establishment 1931–37; Chief Engineer, Air Registration Board 1938–39; Supt., Scientific Research Royal Aircraft Estab. 1939–40; Deputy Dir. Min. of Aircraft Production 1940–42; Dir., Special Projects M.A.P. 1942–44; Chmn. and Man. Dir., Power Jets (Research and Development) Ltd. 1944–46; Director, National Gas Turbine Establishment, 1946–48; Chief Scientist, Ministry of Fuel & Power 1948–54; Chairman: Council for National Academic Awards 1964–71; Air Registration Board 1966–72; The Metal Box Co. Ltd. 1961–67, Coll. of Aeronautics 1962–70. Berger, Jenson & Nicholson Ltd. 1967–75, Sidney-Barton Ltd., 1968–73; Director: Dowty Rotol Ltd., 1958–75. Ricardo & Co., Engineers (1927) Ltd., 1965–77; President, Royal Institution, 1969–70; Chancellor Cranfield Inst. of Techn., 1969—. Chairman, Civil Aircraft Research Committee 1953–59; Pres., Royal Aeronautical Socy. 1947–49; Chmn.: Council for Scientific and Industrial Research 1961–65; and Naval Education Advisory Cttee. 1957–60. *Awards:* Fellow of Imperial College of Science & Technology 1960; Fellow, Thames Polytechnic; Fellow, City & Guilds Institute (FCGI) 1976. Hon. DSc (Birmingham); Hon. DTech (Brunel); Hon. LLD (CNAA); Hon. DSc (Cranfield. *Address:* Westcote House, Chipping Campden, Glos.

**KINLOCH, Donald Ian.** British insurer. *B.* 1917. *Educ.* Associate, Chartered Insurance Institute. *M.* 1948, Nadine Dickler-Doukelsky. *Daus.* 2. *Career:* Pres. and General Manager, Compagnie Nouvelle d'Assurances, Paris; Legal Representative in France, Insurance Co. of North America and INA Reinsurance Co. *Clubs:* Rand (Johannesburg); Interallée (Paris). *Address:* 7 rue de la Paix, Paris 2e, France.

**KINNEY, Abbott Ford.** American radio executive, writer, historian. *B.* 1909. *Educ.* Dermott High School and Arkansas College, Batesville 1925–27 (education interrupted by illness; while recuperating assisted in development of X-ray technique at Saranac Lake, N.Y., and conducted state-wide drive for expansion of library at Arkansas State Tuberculosis Sanatorium, Booneville; also taught high school courses for patients unable to finish school because of illness). *M.* 1943, Dorothy Jeffers. *Daus.* Colleen, Joyce and Rosemary. *Career:* Columnist and free-lance writer 1934—; Editor, Dermott (Ark.) News 1934–39; Partner, Delta Drug Co. 1940–49; during World War II was member of District Office of Price Administration Board; Pres., Post-War Planning Council; member, United Service Organizations. Conducted research in early aeronautics for Inst. of Aero. Sciences, N.Y. 1941; conducted research in castor bean production 1941–42; Pres. Gen. Mgr. Southeast Arkansas Broadcasters Inc. since 1951. Honoured by observance of Abbott Kinney Day by civic organizations and schools of Southeast Arkansas 1955; Donor of annual Kinney Athletic Award (dating from 1915). *Member:* Arkansas Geological and Conservation Commission 1959–66: Mississippi River Parkway Commission 1961–70; Arkansas Planning Commn., 1963–80; Exec. Bd. member and Past Pres., De Sota Area Council, Boy Scouts of America; Charter member, Ark. Econ. Assn. and Ark. Historical Assn.; member: Amer. Inst. of Management, International Broadcasters Society (Mem., International Adv. Editorial Bd.); National Assn. of Radio and Television Broadcasters, Arkansas Broadcasters Association, Hospital Adv. Board, Southeast Arkansas C.-of-C., Country Board of American Red Cross, Bd. of County Tuberculosis Assn., County Library Commission, and Park Commission (Secy.). Methodist. *Awards:* Silver Beaver (Boy Scouts of America); Outstanding Leader in Arkansas (1969); State Conservation Award (1974). *Publications:* newspaper editorials (some were instrumental in adoption of Arkansas automobile drivers' licence law); articles of local history used in local school courses; radio editorials. *Clubs:* Delta Country; Rotary (Past Pres. and Secy.). *Address:* 202 Trotter Street, Dermott, Ark. 71638, U.S.A.

**KINNEY, Samuel Marks Jr.** American. *B.* 1925. *Educ.* Lawrenceville School; Allegheny Coll., Pennsylvania State Coll. (BA); Rutger's Univ. JD. *M.* 1946, Kathryn Clouser. *S.* Samuel Marks III and Brian Scott. *Dau.* Kathryn Lee. *Career:* With Daystrom Inc.; Counsel, Manager Army Contracts, 1951–54, Asst. Secy. & Counsel 1954–57, Secy. and Counsel 1957–59, Asst. Vice-Pres. 1959–61, Vice-Pres. and Gen. Counsel 1961–62. Vice-President and Secretary, Union Camp Corp. 1962–69, Sen. Vice-Pres. 1969–70, Exec Vice-Pres. 1970–72, Dir. since 1967, Pres. Mem, Exec. Cttee since 1972; New Jersey Life Insurance Co. 1964—, Cartonajes Union S.A. (Spain) 1965—. Lafarge Emballage S.A. (France) 1967—. *Director:* Philibert Delastre (France) since 1974; C.F. Mueller Co. since 1972; First Nat. State Bancorporation since 1973; First National State Bank of NJ. since 1973. *Trustee:* N.J. State Safety Council since 1975. *Publications:* various speeches and papers in the field of corporate mergers and acquisitions and commercial development. *Member:* New Jersey Bar, U.S. Supreme Court Bar, Amer. Bar Assn. *Clubs:* Echo Lake Country (Westfield, N.J.); Phi Delta Fraternity; Union League (N.Y.). *Address: office* 1600 Valley Road, Wayne, N.J. 07470, U.S.A.

**KINNOCK, Neil Gordon,** MP. British. *B.* 1942. *Educ.* BA (Wales) Industrial Relations; BA (Wales) History; Diploma of Education (Wales). *M.* 1967, Glenys Elizabeth Parry. *S.* 1. *Dau.* 1. *Career:* Labour MP for Bedwellty since 1970; Commons Select Cttee. on Public Expenditure 1971–73, and on Nationalised Industries since 1974; PPS to Sec. of State for Employment 1974–75 (resigned). Member, General Advisory Council, BBC 1976—. *Publications:* (Pamphlet) Wales and the Common Market (1972); As Nye Said (1977); and many newspaper and magazine articles. *Address:* House of Commons, London, SW1A 0AA.

**KINTNER, Earl W.** Mbr. of the Washington (D.C.) law firm of Arent, Fox, Kintner, Plotkin & Kahn, Mar. 1961—. *B.* 1912. *Educ.* DePauw Univ. (AB 1936), LLD 1970 and Indiana University School of Law (JD 1938). *M.* 1948, Valerie Patricia Wildy. *S.* Christopher. *Career:* In general law practice, Princeton, Ind. 1938–44; City Attorney, Princeton 1939–42; Prosecuting Attorney, 66th Indiana Judicial Circuit 1943–44; re-elected 1944 and 1946 but resigned due to military service. U.S. Navy: Ensign to Lieutenant 1944–46 (Amphibious Forces 1944–45). Period 1946–48: Deputy U.S. Commissioner, U.N. War Crimes Commission, serving as Co-Chairman of Committee reviewing Allied war crimes matters; Chmn., Legal Publications; Cttee and Editor of law reports; edited official volume on Development of Laws of War, and privately edited volume, The Hadamar Trial. Federal Trade Commission 1948, trial attorney on anti-monopoly; 1951, legal adviser; 1953–54, Delegate to President's Conference on Administrative Procedure, Chairman, Committee on Hearing Officers; planned and edited Commission's Manual for Attorneys; 1953–59, General Counsel; sworn in 9 June 1959 as member of Federal Trade Commission for unexpired term ending Sept. 1960; designated Chairman by President Eisenhower 11 June 1959; served as Commissioner and Chairman until expiration of Government service on 21 Mar. 1961; Special Consultant to U.S. Patent Office, in charge of Management Survey of Office 1961–62. *Member:* Federal Bar Assn. (Pres. 1956–57, 1958–59); Foundation of F.B.A. (Pres. 1957—); Federal Bar Building Corp. (Pres. 1958—); National Lawyers Club (Pres. 1959—); Amer. Legion; DAV (Life Member); Phi Delta Phi (Pres. Province II 1962–65); Pi Sigma Alpha; Delta Sigma Rho; Sigma Delta Chi, Washington Professional Chapter; American Bar Association; American Judicature Socy. and other legal organizations. Mason (Shriner and Past Master). Member, Episcopal Church, Washington, D.C. Chairman, Section of Administrative Law, A.B.A. 1959–60; House of Delegates, A.B.A. 1957–58, and 1959–60; member, Council, Section of Anti-Trust Law, A.B.A. 1958–61; Board of Directors, American Judicature Society 1960–64; member, Exec. Cttee., N.Y. State Anti-Trust Law Section 1957–60. Adjunct Professor, N.Y. University School of Law 1958; admitted to practice, Indiana and District of Columbia, U.S. Supreme Court and other bars. Distinguished Alumni Service Award, Indiana Univ. 1960, and DePauw Univ. 1965. *Publications:* An Antitrust Primer: A Guide to Antitrust and Trade Regulation Laws for Businessmen (1964); A. Robinson Potman Primer (1970); A Deceptive Business Primer (1970); A Primer on the Law of Mergers (1973); An International Anti-Trust Primer (Co-author) (1975); An Intellectual Property Primer (Co-author) (1975); A Legislative History of the Anti-Trust Laws of the United States, 11 vols. (1977); Kintner on the Anti-Trust Laws of the United States, Vol. 1 (1977). *Clubs:* Cosmos, Capitol Hill, National Lawyers, National Press (all of Washington, D.C.), Union League, N.Y.; Coral Beach & Tennis (Bermuda). *Address:* 3542 Newark Street, N.W., Washington, D.C.; and *office* 1100 Federal Bar Building, 1815 H Street, N.W., Washington, D.C. 20006, U.S.A.

**KIPPING, Sir Norman Victor,** GCMG, KBE, JP. British Administrator. *B.* 1901. *Educ.* University College School; DSc Loughborough Univ.; (FIEE, FIPE); Hon. Fellow, Brit. Inst. Management. *M.* 1928, Eileen Rose. *S.* John Philip Brenchley, Michael Norman Brenchley. *Dau.* Pamela Mary. *Career:* Junior engineer in Research Dept., G.P.O. 1920–21; Transmission Engineer, International Western Electric Co. 1921–26; Standard Telephones and Cables Ltd. successively as Engineer of Manufacture, Technical Superintendent and Works Manager 1927–42; Head of Regional Division, Ministry of Production 1942–45; Under-Secretary, Board of Trade 1945; Director-General, Federation of British Industries 1946–65; Chairman, British Overseas Fairs Ltd. 1958–66. Director, Pilkington Brothers Ltd. 1966–73, Joseph Lucas Industries 1966–73; Chairman, Governing Council, Univ. Coll. School 1960–71; Vice-Chmn., Fulton Cttee. on the Civil Service 1966–68. *Awards:* Commander: 2nd Class, Order of Dannebrog (Denmark); 1st Class, Order of the Lion (Finland); Order of Merit of Italian Republic; 1st Class, Order of Vasa (Sweden). *Address:* 36 Barrydene, Oakleigh Road North, Whetstone, N20 9HG.

**KIRBY, Sir Arthur Frank,** GBE, CMG, OStJ. British. *B.* 1899. *Educ.* London University; F.C. Transport. *M.* 1935, Winifred Kate Bradley. *Dau.* 1. *Career:* Trained with Great Western Railway, England, 1920–28; Assistant Secretary, Takoradi Harbour, Gold Coast, June 1928; Traffic Manager, Gold Coast Railway, 1937; Asst. Supt. of the line, Kenya and Uganda Railways, 1938; General Manager, Palestine Railways, 1942; Supt. of the line, East African Railways and Harbours, 1948; Asst. Commissioner for Transport, East Africa, 1951; General Manager, East African Railways and Harbours, 1953; Commissioner for East Africa, London, 1958–62. Chairman, British Transport Docks Board 1963–67; Chairman, National Ports Council 1967–71. Pres. Shipping and Forwarding Agents Inst., 1966. Dep. Chmn. Gt. Ormond St. Hospital 1963–69; Royal Commonwealth Society, 1965–68; Council Socy. of Art 1966–71; Governor, National Hospital, Nervous Diseases, 1966–69: Chmn. Palestine Assn.: Vice-Pres. British Inst. in Eastern Africa. *Address:* 6 Baltimore Court, The Drive, Hove BN3 3PR, Sussex.

**KIRBY, Hon. Sir Richard Clarence.** Australian judge. *B.* 22 Sept. 1904. *Educ.* University of Sydney (LLB). *M.* 1937, Hilda Marie Ryan. *Daus.* Kathrin and Susan. *Career:* Called to the Bar 1933; Judge, District Court of N.S.W. 1944–47; member, Australian War Crimes Commission 1945–46; Australian Representative on War Crimes to S.E. Asia Command H.Q. 1945; Australian Representative, U.N. Committee of Good Offices on Indonesian Question (Security Council) 1947–48 (conducting negotiations for settlement of dispute between Netherlands Government and Indonesian Republic, leading to recognition of the United States of Indonesia); Royal Commissioner conducting special enquiries on different occasions for Australian and N.S.W. Governments 1947, and Tasmanian Government 1946; Chairman, Australian Stevedoring Industry Commission 1947–49; Judge of the Commonwealth Court of Conciliation and Arbitration Aug. 1947–56; Chief Judge 1956–73; President, Commonwealth Conciliation and Arbitration Commission Aug. 1956–73; Chmn., Australian Advertising Standards Authority since 1973. *Publications:* various papers on industrial relations. *Clubs:* Atheneum (Melbourne); Victoria Racing; Vic. Amateur Turf; Mooney Valley Racing. *Address:* 85 Park Tower, 201 Spring Street, Melbourne 3000, Australia.

**KIRCHEIS, John Reinhardt.** United States Citizen. Vice-Pres., Mobil South Inc. *B.* 1916. *Educ.* Buena Vista College; Drake University; Univ. of Iowa; Cornell Univ.; Univ. of Chicago; Harvard University. *M.* 1940, Jean Ohme. *Daus.* 2. *Career:* Teacher and Principal, Bode Public Schools, 1937–40; Account Analyst, General Motors Corporation 1940–42; Lt.-Cdr. U.S.N.R. 1942—46; Assignments Mobil Oil Corp. 1946–66; Vice-Pres., Area Manager Mobil Europe Inc. 1966–68; Man. Dir. Mobil Oil Co. Ltd. 1968–69; Chmn. Chief Exec. Mobil Oil Co. Ltd. 1969–75; Vice-Pres., Mobil South Inc. since 1976. *Member:* Royal Inst. International Affairs; Inst. of Directors; British Inst. Management; Inst. Petroleum; Amer. Chamber of Commerce. *Clubs:* Directors: Royal Automobile; Highgate; Marco Polo; Burning Tree Country Club. *Address:* 3 South 155 Field Point Road, Greenwich, Conn. 06830; and *office* 150 East 42nd Street, New York, N.Y. 10017, U.S.A.

**KIRCHSCHLAGER, Rudolf,** LLD. Federal President of Austria. *B.* 1915. *Educ.* University of Vienna. *M.* 1940, Herma Sorger. *S.* Walter. *Dau.* Christa. *Career:* Judge until 1954; Deputy Legal Adviser, Foreign Affairs Dept. of Fed Chanc. 1956–63; Chef de Cabinet, Minister Foreign Affairs 1963–67; Envoy Extraordinary and Minister Plenipotentiary in Prague 1967–70; Federal Minister, Foreign Affairs 1970–74; Federal President of Republic of Austria since 1974; taken part in various international negotiations including Austrian state Treaty and Constitutional Neutrality Act. *Awards:* Grand Star Order of Merit, Austria, and other decorations. *Publications:* Wörterbuch des Volkerrechts 1960–63). *Address:* 1014 Wien, H ofburg, Austria.

**KIRK, Grayson.** American university professor and administrator. *B.* 12 Oct. 1903. *Educ.* Miami University (BA); Clark University (MA); University of Wisconsin (PhD); Hon. LLD Miami, Waynesburg, Brown, Union, Columbia, Puerto Rico, Clark, New York Univ., Princeton, U. of Wisconsin, Jewish Theological Sem., Syracuse, Williams, U. of Penna., Harvard, Central Univ. (Caracas), Univ. of the Andes (Merida), Zulia, Delhi, Thamasset (Thailand), Johns Hopkins, Washington Univ. (St. Louis), Amherst, Dartmouth, Northwestern, Tennessee, St. Lawrence, Denver, Notre Dame, Bates College, Univ. of Michigan, and Univ. of Sussex (Eng.). Hon. DCL, University King's College (Halifax, N.S.); LHD North Dakota; Hon. PhD Bologna. *M.* 1925, Marion Louise Sands. *S.* John Grayson. *Career:* Prof. of History, Lamar Coll., Texas, 1925–27. Instructor of Political Science, University of Wisconsin 1929–30; Assistant Professor 1930–36; Associate Professor 1936–38, Professor of Political Science 1938–40; Associate Professor of Government, Columbia 1940–43 (Prof. 1943–47); Professor of International Relations, Columbia University 1947–49; Head, Security Section, Division of Political Studies, U.S. Department of State 1942–43; on U.S. Delegation Staff, Dumbarton Oaks Conference 1944; Executive Officer, Third Commission (Security Council), U.N. Conference on International Organization, San Francisco 1945; Research Associate, Yale University, Institute of International Studies 1943–44; Vice-President and Provost, Columbia University 1950–53, Bryce Professor Emeritus of History of International Relations 1972; President and Trustee 1953–68; President and Trustee Emeritus 1968—; International Business Machines Corp. (Dir.); member, American Philosophical Soc.; Acad. of Pol. Science, (Dir.) Asia Foundation (Trustee); Council on Foreign Relations; France-America Society (Dir.); Institute of Internat. Education (Trustee); Pilgrims of the U.S. (Vice-Pres.); Director: Belgian-American Education Foundation, Dividend Shares Inc., Nation-Wide Securities; Trustee, Greenwich Savings Bank; President, American Socy. of French Legion of Honour; American Academy of Arts and Sciences. Trustee, The Tinker Foundation, Lycée Français of New York. *Awards:* Hon. Knight Comdr., Order of the British Empire; Commander of Orange-Nassau (Netherlands), Grand Officer, Legion of Honour (France); Grand Officer, Order of Merit (Italy); KStJ (Great Britain), Order of Taj (Iran). *Publications:* Philippine Independence; Contemporary International Politics (with Walter Sharp); The Study of International Relations in American Colleges and Universities; War and National Policy, Syllabus (with R. P. Stebbins). *Address:* 125 Maiden Lane, Columbia University, New York, N.Y. 10038 U.S.A.

**KIRK, Rt. Hon. Herbert Victor,** PC. *B.* 1912. *Educ.* Queen's Univ., Belfast. *M.* 1944, Gladys Dunn. *S.* 3. *Career:* Chartered Accountant. MP (U), Windsor Div. of Belfast, N.

Ireland Parliament 1956—; Minister of Labour and National Insurance, N. Ireland 1962–64; Minister of Education 1964–65; Minister of Finance 1965–72, and Jan.–May 1974 (resigned); Unionist mem. for South Belfast, Northern Ireland Assembly 1973–75. *Address:* 38 Massey Avenue, Belfast BT4 2JT, Northern Ireland.

**KIRK, Kenneth Burson.** American investment banker and engineer. *B.* 1901. *Educ.* Pennsylvania State University (BSc Eng). *M.* Helen Grace White. *Daus.* Cynthia Grace and Helen Cecilia Victoria. *Career:* Director, Radelin Kirk Ltd.; Chairman of Board, Coachella Savings & Loan Association; President, Kirk Dial of Texas, Kirk Dial Corp., Helken Engineering Corp., and director of several other corporations. Pres., Desert Hospital District 1951–67 and 1969–71. Governor Rotary International 1956–57; Pres., California Association of Hospitals Districts (1952–53). Member, California Health Review and Program Cncl.; Los Angeles Rotary Club (1951–52); Chmn.: Business Advisory Cttee. Beverly Hills, Community Chest 1947, Desert Circus, Palm Springs 1951; Treasurer: Desert Hospital District, Desert Hospital Authority; Vice-Mayor, Palm Springs. *Clubs:* Royal Canadian Yacht (Toronto), Chapparrel (Dallas), Bel Air Bay (Pacific Palisades, Calif.), O'Donnell Country, Palm Springs Tennis, Racquet (Palm Springs, Calif.), Committee of Twenty-Five Club, Phi Gamma Delta Fraternity; Mount Kenya Safari Club. *Address:* 702 North Bedford Drive, Beverly Hills, Calif. and *office* 144 South Beverly Drive, Beverly Hills, Calif.; (winter) 155 South Belardo Road, Palm Springs, Calif., U.S.A.

**KIRKENDALL, Ernest O.** American. Trade Assoc. executive. *B.* 1914. *Educ.* BSc 1934; MSc in Engineering 1935; DSc 1938. *M.* 1938, Maxine Marrs. (*d.* 1969). *S.* Howard E. *Daus.* Carol J. (Leunk) and Barbara J. (Davis). *Career:* Instructor (1937–41) and Asst. Professor (1941–46) Wayne University; Asst. Secy. Amer. Inst. of Mining, Metallurgical & Petroleum Engineers 1946–55 (Gen. Secy. 1955–63); Secy. and Gen. Mgr., United Engineering Trustees 1963–65. Vice-President, American Iron & Steel Institute 1968— (Metallurgical Engineer, 1965–66; Asst. Vice-Pres. 1966–68). *Member:* Sigma Xi; Tau Beta Pi; Phi Lambda Upsilon; The Metals Society (London); Verein Deutscher Eisenhüttenleute (Düsseldorf); Assn. des Ingénieurs sortis de l'Ecole de Liège (Belgium). *Publications:* Rates of Diffusion of Copper & Zinc in Alpha Brass (with Thomassen and Upthegrove), Trans. AIME, (1939); Diffusion of Zinc in Alpha Brass, Trans. AIME, (1942); Zinc Diffusion in Alpha Brass (with Smigelskas), Trans. AIME, (1947). *Address:* Apt. 114, 1330 New Hampshire Avenue, N.W., Washington, D.C. 20036; and *office* 1000 16th Street, N.W. Washington, D.C. 20036, U.S.A.

**KIRKPATRICK, Dr. Forrest Hunter.** American business executive. *B.* 1905. *Educ.* Bethany College (AB); Columbia Univ. (AM, Prof. Dipl.); Univ. of London; Univ. of Pittsburgh; LLD, Bethany College, College of Stuebenville and Drury College. *Career:* Dean and Professor, Bethany College (West Va.) 1927–41; Gen. Mgr. of Personnel & Labor Relations, Radio Corp. of America, N.Y.C. 1941–46; Consultant to U.S. State Dept. 1944, to U.S. Post Office Dept. 1953, to U.S. Labor Dept. 1965–68. Visiting Professor at Columbia Univ., and Univ. of Pittsburgh 1946–52; also management consultant 1946–52; Wheeling-Pittsburgh Steel Corp., Wheeling, W. Va. 1952–70, Vice-Pres., 1964–70; Visiting Professor, West Virginia University since 1970; State Water Resources Board since 1974. *Clubs:* University (Pittsburgh, Pa.), Fort Henry (Wheeling), Duquesne (Pittsburgh), University (N.Y.C.). *Address:* Tally-Ho Apartments, Wheeling, W. Va., U.S.A.

**KIRKWOOD, Sir Robert Lucien Morrison,** Kt Bach (1959); KCMG 1972, OJ 1974. British. *B.* 1904. *Educ.* Wixenford, Harrow; Le Rosey, Switzerland. *M.* 1925, Sybil Attenborough. *S.* Francis Lyle. *Daus.* Lady Peek, Mrs. Cyrus Merrell. *Career:* Joined Tate & Lyle 1922; Mgr. Director, The United Sugar Co. 1929–36; Director, Yorkshire Sugar Co., 1928–36 and Central Sugar Co. (Peterborough) 1929–36; Joined Board, Tate & Lyle 1935; Mgr. Director, West Indies Sugar Co. Jamaica, 1937; Dir. Caroni Ltd. Trinidad, 1937; M.L.C. Jamaica, 1942–62; Chmn. Citrus Growers Assn. 1946–61; Chairman, The Sugar Manufacturers Assn. (of Jamaica) Ltd., 1945–74, Pres. since 1974; West Indies Sugar Association, 1961–74. Rep. West Indies at Commonwealth and International Sugar Conferences; Chmn. International Sugar Council, 1966; President, Sugar Club of New York 1965–66. *Publications:* A Farm Production Policy for Jamaica. *Clubs:* Whites; Queens; Royal St. George's (Sandwich); The Brook (New York). *Address:* Haven House, Sandwich, Kent.

**KISSINGER, Dr. Henry Alfred.** AB. MA. PhD. American Secretary of State 1973–77. *B.* 1923. *Educ.* Harvard. *M.* (1) 1949, Ann Fleischer. (Div. 1964). *S.* 1. *Dau.* 1. (2) 1974, Nancy S. Maginnes. *Career:* Exec. Dir. Harvard Int. Seminar 1951–69; Lect. Dept. Govt. 1957–59; Dir. Defence Studies Program 1958–69; Asst. to Pres. of U.S.A. for Nat. Security Affairs 1969–77; Chief Negotiator America and Vietnam Peace Treaty 1973; and Middle East Ceasefire 1973, 1974; Secretary of State 1973–77; Visiting Prof. of Diplomacy, Univ. of Georgetown Sch. of Foreign Service, Washington 1977–78. *Award:* The Nobel Peace Prize for 1973, awarded jointly with Mr. Le Duc Tho. *Address:* Suite 520, 1800 K Street, N.W., Washington, D.C., U.S.A.

**KITCHEN, Geoffrey Fort.** British. *B.* 1916. *Educ.* Princeville School's Bradford Tech. College. *M.* 1941, Joan Gunilda Birtles. *S.* 1. *Dau.* 1. *Career:* Man. Dir. Woolcombers Ltd. (Lanolin Div.); Pres. Westbrook Lanolin Co., Belge S.A.; Westbrook Lanolin Co. Inc., U.S.A.; Dir. Woolcombers (Holdings) Ltd.; Pura-Lanolin Ltd.; Laisterdyke Investments Ltd. Member of the Yorkshire Water Authority (Ministerial Appointment). *Member:* Sté Royale d'Harmonie, Verviers. *Address:* Far Hills House, Wibsey, Bradford, Yorks; and *office* Argonaut Works, Laisterdyke, Bradford.

**KITTIKACHORN, Field Marshal Thanom.** Former Prime Minister. *B.* 1911. *Educ.* Graduated from the Royal Military Academy, Bangkok 1931; Army School of Survey 1934, School of Infantry 1939, and National Defence College 1956. *Career:* Made tours to Europe, U.S.A., Japan and Korea 1951; toured Philippines 1952, Taiwan 1957, Singapore 1959 and U.S.A. and Okinawa 1959. Previously, Deputy Prime Minister, Dep. Supreme Commander of Thai Armed Forces, Commandant National Defence College, Lecturer in Royal Military Academy, and Rector of Thammasat University. Prime Minister of Thailand, and Minister of Defence 1963–73; Exiled 1973; returned to Thailand as Ordained Buddhist Monk. *Address:* c/o Ministry of the Interior, Bangkok, Thailand.

**KITTO, Rt. Hon. Sir Frank Walters,** PC (1963), KBE. Formerly Australian judge. *B.* 1903. *Educ.* Sydney Univ. (BA, LLB). *M.* 1928, Eleanor May Howard. *Daus.* Kathleen, (*Dec.*) Margaret, Lindsay, Elizabeth. Practised at New South Wales Bar 1927–50; KC 1942; Justice of the High Court of Australia 1950–70. Deputy Chancellor, Univ. of New England, 1968–70; Chancellor, Univ. of New England since 1970; Chmn., Australian Press Council 1976—. *Address:* Jindalee, Armidale, N.S.W., Australia.

**KIVEKÄS, Lauri Jaakko.** Finnish Councillor of Mining. Director-General, and lawyer. *B.* 7 July 1903. *Educ.* Univ. of Helsink. (grad. in law) and School of Law, Paris. *M.* 1926, Elsa Aaltonen. *S.* 1. *Daus.* 3. *Career:* Chmn. Bd. of Dirs (since 1949), Aaltosen Tehtaat Oy; Chmn. Bd. of Dirs. Oy Nokia Ab, Oy Finlayson Ab; mem. of Bd. and Vice-chmn., Emil Aaltonen Foundation. Chmn., Bank of Kanslalis-Osake-Pankki (1965–72); Honorary Chmn., Central Union of Shoe Factories and Finnish Plastics Assn. Chmn. Finnish Plastics Association (1941–49); member of Town Council of Tampere 1940–47, and the Town Govt. 1940–46; Minister of Commerce and Industry 1957 and 1958. *Address:* Tampere, Finland.

**KJÖRNAS, Jon Didrik.** Norwegian. *B.* 1924. *Educ.* High School; Univ. in Oslo. *M.* 1952, Gerd Alhaug. *S.* Arne Didrik. *Dau.* Kari. *Career:* advocate 1950–71; Man. Dir. Ringerikes Sparebank, Hönefoss since 1971. *Address:* Ringerikes Sparebank, Hönefoss, Norway.

**KLAGSBRUNN, Hans A(lexander).** American lawyer. *B.* 1909. *Educ.* Vienna Gymnasium; Yale Univ. (BA 1929; LLB 1932); Harvard Law School. *M.* 1932, Elizabeth Mapelsden Ramsey. *Career:* Admitted to D.C. Bar and to Bar of U.S. Supreme Court 1935; associated with Reconstruction Finance Corp. and affiliates 1933–45; Exec. Vice-Pres., Gen. Counsel, Dir. and member Exec. Cttee., Defense Plant Corp.; Dir., surplus property and Asst. Gen. Counsel, Reconstruction Finance Corp.; R.F.C. member, Hancock Contract Settlement Board and Clayton Surplus Property Board in office of War Mobilization; Dep. Dir., Office of War Mobilization and Reconversion, The White House 1945–46; senior member, law firm of Klagsbrunn & Hanes 1946–68; Counsel to successor firm since 1969. Member, Army Chemical Corps Reorganization Committee 1955–56;

member, Health and Welfare Council (Budget steering cttee. member 1956–61; Chmn., Budget Cttee. 1958–61; member, Board of Directors 1958—; Vice-Pres. 1960–61; Pres. 1961–63); Past Pres. and Member Bd. of Dirs., Friendship House; Dir., Columbia Hospital for Women; Mem., D.C. Commissioners Juvenile Delinquency Working Cttee.; HWC Community Service Awards, 1961 and 1963. Mem. Piedmont (Va.) Environmental Council, since 1975. Mem., Judicial Conf. of the D.C. Circuit 1964–65–66 (Chmn. Cttee. on Criminal Indigents); Mem. U.S. Court of Appeal Cttee. on Admissions and Grievances 1967–74; Chmn. 1972–74; Bar Assn. of D.C. Chmn., U.S. Ct. of Appeal Cttee. 1966–68, (council member, Admin. Law Section 1952–55); American Bar Assn. (chmn. special committee Impact Atomic Attack 1956–59; Chmn., Cttee. on Congressional Cttee. 1958–59; council member, Administrative Law Section 1955–58); Federal Bar Assn.; Amer. Bar Foundation; Natl. Planning Assn.; Amer. Arbitration Assn. (mem., Natl. Panel); Amer. Inst. of Management; Amer. Judicature Socy.; Newcomen Socy.; Phi Beta Kappa; Order of Coif; Phi Beta Kappa Associates; National Symphony Orchestra Assn. *Clubs:* Metropolitan, Yale, National Press, City Tavern. *Address:* 3420 Q Street, N.W., Washington, D.C. 20007; Salem Farm, R.D.1, Purcellville, Va., 22132; and *office* Ring Building Washington,, D.C. 20036, U.S.A.

**KLAUS, Josef**, Dr jur. Lawyer. *B.* 1910. *Educ.* University of Vienna (Dr jur). *M.* 1936, Erna Seywald. *S.* Michael, Norbert and Bernhard. *Dau.* Uta. *Career:* Governor of Salzburg 1949–61; Federal Minister of Finance 1961–62; Leader of Austrian People's Party 1963–70; Fed. Chancellor 1964–70. *Awards:* Silver Order with Sash (1st Class) and Gold Order with Star (1st Class) for services rendered to the Austrian Republic; Cross of St. Sylvester (Holy See); Cross of Merit with Star and Sash of the Order of Merit of the Federal Republic of Germany; Grand Cross, Order of Leopold (Belgium); Bavarian Order of Merit; Cross of the Iranian Order of Homayoun. *Address:* A-1130 Vienna, Sauraugasse 11, Austria.

**KLAVENESS, A. Fredrik.** Norwegian shipowner. *B.* 8 Nov. 1903. *Educ.* commercial education in Norway and abroad. *M.* 1938, Brita Zahle. *S.* Anton F., Erik. *Daus.* Nini Therese, Helene. *Career:* Chairman, A. F. Klaveness & Co. A/S and affiliated Board of Directors, Vega Insurance Co.; board of Representatives, Thoresen Car Ferries. *Address:* Lagaasen, Fjellveien 5, Lysaker-Oslo, Norway.

**KLAVENESS, Dag.** Norwegian shipowner, landowner and company director. *B.* 1913. *Educ.* Matric. 1931. *M.* 1939, Wanda Young Fearnley. *S.* Nils Olav. *Daus.* Turi, Wanda, Therese. *Career:* Military Academy 1932; Ecole Sup. de Commerce, Neuchâtel 1933; Lic. ès sciences commerciales et économiques, Univ. of Neuchâtel 1935; studied commercial and industrial organization, economics and law at Univs. of Berlin, Berne and Neuchâtel; connected with shipping and industrial firms in Norway and abroad 1936–38; Director, A. F. Klaveness & Co. A/S and associated shipping companies since 1939 (Chmn. 1974); Chairman, Skipsassuranseforeningen Unitas 1955; Dir: A/S Kvaerner Industrier, Den Norske Krigsforsikring for Skib, Norsk Sjøfortmuseum, Norske Fina A/S; Chmn., A/S Meraker Brug 1972; Cttee. mbr. Det Norske Veritas; Pres. of the Norwegian Shipowners' Assn. and the Norwegian Shipping Employers' Assoc. 1971–73; Chmn. Oslo Shipowners' Ass. 1962–64, A/S Selco 1956–65, A/L Robergmyrene 1956–73. *Clubs:* Norske Selskab; Oslo Shipping. *Address:* Nedre Ringi gård, 1300 Sandvika, Norway.

**KLEFFEL, Dr. Andreas.** Member of the Board of Managing Directors of the Deutsche Bank AG; member of several Supervisory Boards. *B.* 1916. *Address:* Königsallee 45–47, D-4000 Düsseldorf, Germany.

**KLEINIG, Cyril.** Australian. *B.* 1912. *Educ.* Scotch Coll. (S. Aust.); Adelaide School of Mines; Perth Technical Coll. *M.* 1939, Rona Thiele. *S.* John. *Dau.* Barbara. *Career:* With Mac. Robertson Miller Airlines, Adelaide: Engineer, Chief Pilot, Chief Engineer, Adelaide 1934–39, Asst. Managing Dir. 1947–55. Director 1955—, Managing Director 1955–69, Gen. Manager: Mac. Robertson Miller Airline Services, Perth since 1969; Chmn. Austr. National Travel Assn. W.A. 1973–75; Hon. Fellow, Inst. of Sales and Marketing Executives. Fellow and Past Pres., Australian Inst. of Management. Member: Inst. of Transport; Inst. of Automotive & Aeronautical Engineers (Past Chmn.); W.A. Transport and Advisory Council; Vice-Pres. Royal C'wealth Socy. *Clubs:* Western Australia; Perth Rotary (Past Pres.); Weld. *Address:* 82 Victoria Avenue, Dalkeith, W. A.; and *office* International House, 26 St. George's Terrace, Perth, W.A., Australia.

**KLEINWORT, Sir Cyril Hugh**, Kt., DLL. British. *B.* 1905. *Educ.* private. *M.* 1933. Elisabeth Kathleen Forde. *Daus.* Elizabeth, Charlotte and Susanna. *Career:* Partner 1927–47 and Dir. 1947–66, Kleinwort Sons & Co. (this Company became Kleinwort, Benson Ltd. in 1961); Dir. 1935–57, Chmn. 1957–68 of former North British & Mercantile Insurance Co. Vice-Chairman, Commercial Union Assurance Co. Ltd. 1959–75; Kleinwort Benson (Europe) SA, 1964–71; Chairman: Kleinwort, Benson Ltd. 1966–71; Kleinwort, Benson, Lonsdale Ltd. 1968—, Kleinwort, Benson (Geneva) S.A. 1968–71; Cttee on Invisible Exports 1968–75; Chmn. British National Export Cncl. 1968–72; Director and Chairman, Board of Transatlantic Fund Inc. New York. Member, British Overseas Trade Board. 1972; Inst. of Directors (London); Advisory Cttee., Queen's Award to Industry 1976. *Club:* Royal Yacht Squadron. *Address:* Eyford House, Upper Slaughter, Cheltenham, Glos. GL54 2JN; and *office* 20 Fenchurch Street, London, E.C.3.

**KLEIS, John D.** American. Physicist & Metallurgist. *B.* 1912. *Educ.* Univ. of Buffalo (BA Physics 1932, MA Physics 1933); Yale Univ. (PhD Physics 1936). *M.* 1951, Marie E. Dahl. *S.* John D., II. *Daus.* Lynne and Cheryl. *Career:* Engineering Physicist 1936–43; Chief Physicist 1943–51; Mgr. Engineering and Research 1951–55; Vice-Pres. Electrical Div. 1955–62; Vice-Pres. Research Fansteel Inc. 1955–62; Vice Pres. and Dir Electronics Div. 1957–69; Vice-Pres. C.S. Brainin Corp. 1969—; Pres. J. Cooper & Sons since 1971. *Publications:* Ferromagnetic Anistropy of Ni-Fe Crystals at Various Temperatures; Various Articles on Electrical Contacts. *Member:* Amer. Physical Socy.; Amer. Socy. for Testing Materials; Socy. of Automotive Engineers. Republican. *Clubs:* Lake Forest; Yale (N.Y.C.); Harvard (N.Y.C.). *Address:* 320 Washington Street, Mount Vernon, N. York 10553.

**KLEPSCH, Dr. Egon Alfred.** German Politician. *B.* 1930. *Educ.* Secondary Sch., Abitur; Univ. of Rostock and Marsburg an der lahn—Dr. Phil. *M.* 1952, Anita Wegehaupt. *S.* 3. *Daus.* 3. *Career:* Consultant in the Bonner Berichte office, 1955–59; Lecturer on International Politics on the Scientific Research and Teaching Staff of the Federal German Army 1959–65; Planning Consultant in the Federal Chancellor's Office 1965; Member of the Bundestag 1965—, re-elected 1969, 1972, nominated again 1976; Member of European Parliament 1973; Spokesman for CDU/CSU in European Parliament 1975; Chmn. of Federal Security Policy Cttee of CDU 1972; Rep. of the CDU on the International Steering Bodies at Party Level 1973. *Decorations:* Commendatore della Repubblica Italiana. *Publications:* Deutsche Russlandpolitik unter Streseman (Thesis, 1954); Der Kommunismus (Handbook No. 1 of Political Acad., Eichholz); numerous essays and publications. *Address:* D-5400 Koblenz-Pfaffendorf, Lüderitzstrasse 41, Federal Republic of Germany; and *office* D-5300 Bonn-Bundeshaus, Fed. Republic of Germany.

**KLINE, Sidney Delong.** American. *B.* 1902. *Educ.* West Reading and Reading High Schools; Dickinson Coll.; Dickinson School of Law; Albright Coll. *M.* Leona Clarice Barkalow. *S.* Sidney D. Jr. and Robert Cornelius. *Daus.* Joan Clarice (Gingrich) and E. Susan (Hart). *Career:* Trust Officer, Colonial Trust Co. of Reading 1929–33; Vice-Pres. and Trust Officer, Berks County Trust Co. 1933–44, Pres. 1944–60; Pres. and Chmn. of Bd. 1960–64; Pres. and Chmn. of Bd., Amer. Bank & Trust Co. (formerly Berks County Trust Co.) 1964–68. Chairman of the Board and Chief Executive Officer, American Bank & Trust Co. of Pa. 1968–72; Chmn. of the Board, American Bank and Trust Co. of Pa. since 1972; Chairman of the Board and Director, Berks Title Insurance Co.; Director: Frankhouser Associates Inc., Colonial-Berks Real Estate Co. Pres. & Dir., Greater Berks Development Fund; Dir. & Treas., Berks County Advisory Cncl.; Trustee: Albright Coll., Bethany Children's Home. Womelsdorf; Dickinson College. Member, Board of Incorporation, Dickinson School of Law. *Member:* Amer., Penna. and Berks County Bar Assn., also Penna. Bankers' Assn. (Past Pres.) etc. *Clubs:* Wyomissing; Berkshire Country. *Address:* 62 Grand-View Boulevard, Wyomissing Hills, Reading, Penna. 19609, U.S.A.

**KLINGELE, Werner F.**, Dr.rer.pol. Royal Swedish Consul General for Baden-Württemberg. *B.* 1915. *Educ.* Universities of Basle, Geneva and Heidelberg (Dipl. Volkswirt 1937, and Dr.rer.pol 1938). *M.* 1960, Dr. Brigitte Ogrinz. *S.* Jan Haiko. *Dau.* Fiona Christina. *Career:* German manufacturer, Managing Director, Klingele Papierwerke, and Klingele GmbH.

Chairman, Association of Corrugated Cardboard Manufacturers 1948–64, Hon. Chairman 1964—. President, Federated Association of Paper and Plastic Board Converters 1948–68, Hon. Pres. since 1968; Pres. Fédération Européenne des Fabricants de Carton Ondulé 1961–64, Vice-Pres. 1952–61, 1964–72; Pres. International Corrugated Case Assoc. 1963–64, Mem. of Board since 1964; Mem. Exec. Board Federal Assoc. German Industry 1955–56, 1958–60, 1964–66; Chmn. Assoc. Baden-Württemberg Industries 1962–72, Vice-Chmn. 1960–62, and since 1972. *Club:* Rotary. *Address:* 7 Stuttgart, Gustav Siegle-Strasse 50; and *office* Klingele Papierwerke, 7064 Remshalden, Germany.

**KLINGLUND, Carl Ake.** Swedish (KVO). *B.* 1912. *Educ.* Sweden, England, and U.S.A. *M.* 1938, Christina Ahlin. *Dau.* 1. *Career:* With International Match Corp. 1932–36; International Business Machines Corp. 1937–44 (activities both in Sweden and U.S. in respect of these two concerns); with Electrolux in Sweden, Denmark, Australia, Canada, South Africa, Japan and The Far East 1944–71; Dir. Herald International Ltd. Hong Kong; Consul for Sweden in Johannesburg 1949–64. *Address:* 35 Bisney Road, Pokfulam, Hong Kong.

**KLOMPE, Margaretha Albertina Maria.** Doctor in Mathematics and Physics. *B.* 1912. *Educ.* studied mathematics and physics at the State University of Utrecht (graduated 1941). *Career:* Teacher, Nijmegen Lyceum, *Mater Dei* 1932–49; Vice-President, Women's Voluntary Service 1943–53; one of the founders of the R.C. Debating Society for Women 1945; Member of Second Chamber of the States-General, for the Catholic People's Party 1948–56 and 1963–66; member, Consultative Assembly of the Council of Europe 1949–56, and of the Common Assembly of the European Coal & Steel Community 1952–56. Minister of Social Welfare, Government of the Netherlands Oct. 1956–63. Minister of Culture, Recreation and Social Welfare 1966–71. Has several times attended the General Assembly of U.N. as a member of Netherlands Delegations. International President of FERES (Fédération internationale des instituts de recherches sociales et socio-religieuses) 1965–70; Minister of State since 1971; Pres., National UNESCO Commission 1972—; Pres., National Commission Justice and Peace 1972—. *Address:* Smidswater 5, The Hague, Netherlands.

**KNAPP, J(oseph) Burke.** American. *B.* 1913. *Educ.* Stanford Univ. (AB 1933) and Oxford Univ. (BA; BLitt; MA 1933–36). *M.* 1939, F. A. Hilary Eaves. *S.* 2. *Daus.* 2. *Career:* With Federal Reserve Board, Washington, D.C. 1940–47, and Department of State, Washington 1948–52. Rhodes Scholar, Oxford Univ. 1933–36; Senior Vice Pres. International Bank for Reconstruction and Development since 1972. *Clubs:* Metropolitan, International (both of Washington). *Address:* 3701 Curtis Court, Chevy Chase, Md.; and *office* 1818 H Street N.W., Washington, D.C. 20433, U.S.A.

**KNAPP, Joseph Grant.** American. Retired as Administrator of Farmer Co-operative Service, now engaged as an independent author and consultant. Is preparing A History of Co-operative Enterprise in the United States. *B.* 1900. *Educ.* Univ. of Nebraska (BS 1922; MA 1923) and Stanford Univ. (PhD 1929). *M.* 1929, Carol M. West. *S.* John Laurence. *Dau.* Sheila Margaret (Woodward). *Career:* Member of Staff, Brookings Instn. 1926–29; Assoc. Prof., North Carolina State Univ. 1929–34; Senior Agricultural Economist, Principal Agricultural Economist, Assoc. Chief, Co-operative Research and Service Div., Farm Credit Admin. 1934–53; Administrator, Farmer Co-operative Service, U.S. Dept. of Agriculture 1953–66. *Awards:* Hon. DSc. Univ. of Nebraska and N. Carolina State Univ.; Pioneer Award, Amer. Inst. of Co-operation. *Member:* Amer. Economic Assn. Amer. Farm Economics Assn. Amer. Marketing Association. *Publications:* (books) The Co-operative Marketing of Livestock (with Edwin G. Nourse 1931): The Hard Winter Wheat Pools (1933); Stokdyk-Architect of Co-operation (1953); Seeds that Grew—A History of the Co-operative Grange League Federation Exchange (1960); Farmers in Business (1963); An Appraisement of Agricultural Co-operation in Ireland (1964); An Analysis of Agricultural Co-operation in England (1965). Editor: Great American Co-operators (1967); The Glen Haven Story (1967); The Rise of American Co-operative Enterprise (1969); The Advance of American Co-operative Enterprise (1973). *Club:* Cosmos (Washington). *Address:* 7119 Fairfax Road, Bethesda, Md. 20014, U.S.A.

**KNIGHT, Derek Walter,** JP. British. *B.* 1926. *Educ.* Ashville Coll. and New Coll., Giggleswick (School Certificate of Oxford and Cambridge). *M.* 1950, Mary Kathleen Bussey. *S.* 3. *Daus.* 2. *Career:* Chmn. London Wool Terminal Market Assn. 1963–64 and 1969–70. Dir., Sir James Hill & Sons Ltd. (1960) and subsidiary companies: Robinson & Peel Ltd., Colonial Combing Co., LANA Ltd., Y.S.F. Converters Ltd. and Commissareon of S.T.I. NV Zundert, nr. Breda, Holland; Dir. Woolcombers Mutual Assn. Ltd.; Booth Hill (Pty.) Aust. Ltd.; Chmn. Taber Travel Ltd.; Intasun-North Ltd. *Publications:* Working of the London Wool Futures Market (special number published by Forward Markets Commission, Govt. of India) 1963. Councillor, Bailon Urban District, 1969–74; Chmn. Shipley Constituency Conservative Assn. 1970–74. *Clubs:* No. 10 (London); Ilkley Golf; Union (Bradford). *Address:* Baildon House, Baildon, Yorks.; and *office* c/o Sir James Hill & Sons Ltd. Dalton Lane, Keighley, West Yorkshire.

**KNIGHT, Frederick Falkiner,** CBE, Retired. Australian company director. *B.* 1895. *Educ.* Melbourne Church of England Grammar School; Trinity College, Univ. of Melbourne, LLB. *M.* 1925, Jean Agnes Nicholas (*Dec.*). *Career:* Served in 1st A.I.F. 1915–19; R.A.A.F. 1926–47; admitted to Victorian Bar 1922; non-practising since 1939. Dir.: F. S. Falkiner & Sons Pty. Ltd. 1952–63, Falkiner Holdings Ltd. 1954–74. Pres., Taxpayers' Association of Victoria 1947–72; Pres., Federated Taxpayers' Assn. 1952–54. *Address:* 3 Woorigoleen Road, Toorak, Vic.; and *office* 99 William Street, Melbourne, Vic., Australia.

**KNIGHT, Harold Murray,** DSC. Australian banker. *B.* 1919. *Educ.* Scotch College, Hawthorn, Victoria; Univ. of Melbourne (MComm). *M.* 1951, Gwenyth Catherine Pennington. *S.* 4. *Dau.* 1. *Career:* Commonwealth Bank of Australia 1936–40, 1946–55; Served with Australian Imperial Forces and Royal Australian Navy 1940–46; awarded Distinguished Service Cross; in Statistics Division, Research and Statistics Department of I.M.F. 1955–59, (Assistant Chief 1957–59); Research Economist, Reserve Bank of Australia 1960, Assistant Manager, Investment Department 1962–64, Manager, Investment Department 1964–68; Deputy Governor Reserve Bank of Australia, Deputy Chmn. of the Bank's Board 1968–75; Governor and Chmn. of Bd. since 1975. *Address: office* Reserve Bank of Australia, 65 Martin Place, Box 3947, Sydney, N.S.W. 2000, Australia.

**KNIGHT, William W., Jr.** Legion of Merit (U.S.A.). Royal Order of VASA (Sweden). *B.* 1905. *Educ.* Yale Univ. (AB) and Harvard School of Business Administration (MBA). *M.* 1931, Elsie Stranahan. *S.* John Lord. *Dau.* Diana (Foster). *Career:* Assistant General Manager and Director, Wyandotte Chemical Corporation 1929–40; Pres. and Dir., Ford Building Co. 1935–42; Adm. Asst. to W. E. Knudsen, Deputy Chief, Tank and Combat Vehicle Section 1940–42; Major, U.S. Army Ordnance Dept. 1942–43; Commanding Officer, Milan Arsenal 1943–44; Lieut.-Col. Chief., Powder & Explosives Section of Field Directors Office 1944–45; Asst. to Exec. Vice-Pres., Libbey-Owens-Ford Glass Co. 1945–47; Pres. and Gen. Mgr., Plaskon Division, LOF Glass Co. 1947–53; Pres. Knight Land Co. Inc. 1963—, Chmn. of the Board, Knight Land Co. 1976; President, Nicholas Corp. 1956–67. Chairman of Board, Toledo-Lucas County Port Authority 1956–73; Dir. and Vice-Chmn. since 1974; Pres. and Dir. Bimini's Blue Water Ltd. since 1963; Dir. Dana Corp. 1960–75; Mem. Dana Finance Cttee 1960–75; Dir. International Oceanographic Foundation since 1972; Dir. Toledo Hosp. Endowment Fund since 1958 (chmn. since 1967); Mem. St. Lawrence Seaway Devel. Corp. Adv. Board since 1969; Nicholas Corporation 1967–70; Dir. member Exec. Committee. *Member:* Amer. Legion; National Defense Transportation Assn.; Amer. Ordnance Assn.; Univ. of Toledo Research Foundation; (Vice-Pres.) Amer. Red Cross (Toledo Chapter) (Dir.); Cancer Cytology Research Fund of Toledo (Dir.): and Institute of Medical Research, Toledo Hospital. *Clubs:* Belmont Country, Ohio; Florida Country; Toledo Yacht; Ocean (Florida); Delray Beach (Fla.). *Address:* 9753 Carnoustie Road, Perrysburg, Ohio 43551; and *office* 1026 National Bank Building, Toledo, Ohio 43604, U.S.A.

**KNOPPERS, Antoine Theodoor,** MD. American. *B.* 1915. *Educ.* Amsterdam (Netherlands) Gymnasium (Sciences): Univ. of Amsterdam (MD 1939); Univ. of Leyden (D Pharmacology 1941). *M.* 1939, Maria Johanna Willemsen. *S.* Bastiaan A. *Daus.* Maria H., Anneke C., Elisabeth E. *Career:* Director of Pharmacology, Amsterdamsche Chininefabrik 1943–49; member, Managing Board, Comb Amsterdamsche Bandoengsche en Nederlandsche Kininefabrieken 1950–52; Manager, Medical Services, Merck Inc. 1952. With Merck Sharp & Dohme International: Dir., Med. Services 1953, Dir., Scientific Activities 1955: Vice-Pres. and General Mgr.

1955. Pres., Merck Sharp & Dohme International 1957–67. Senior Vice-Pres., Merck & Co., Inc. 1967–71; Pres., 1971–73; Vice-Chmn. 1974–75. *Publications:* approximately 60 scientific papers in field of pharmacology, endocrinology, etc.; co-author: Malaria (1950); Chemotherapy (1950). *Club:* Netherlands (N.Y.C.). *Address:* 38 Lenox Road, Summit, N.J. 07901; and *office* Merck & Co., Inc., Rahway, New Jersey 07065, U.S.A.

**KNOWLES, James Wiley.** Consulting economist. *B.* 1913. *Educ.* City College of the College of the City of New York (BSS 1936) and Columbia University (MA 1939). *M.* 1936, Viola Helene MacIntyre. *Career:* Instructor, Dept. of Economics, College of the City of New York 1938–44; Senior Statistician, Research project on post-war economic problems, State of New York 1944; Senior Economist, Econometric Institute Inc. 1944–50; Senior Economist, Joint Econ. Cttee., U.S. Congress, 1950–62; Exec. Dir., 1963–67. Director of Research, Joint Economic Committee, U.S. Congress 1967–72. *Publications:* A Guide to the Use of Statistics (1948); Potential Economic Growth of the United States during the Next Decade (1954); Productivity, Prices and Incomes (1957); Potential Economic Growth in the United States (1960); numerous research articles in economics. Honors in Economics, College of the City of New York 1936. Fellow, American Statistical Assn. 1966. *Member:* Amer. Economic Assn.; Amer. Statistical Assn.; Econometric Society; Nat. Assn. of Business Economists. *Address:* 6005 Berkshire Drive, Bethesda 14, Md., D.C., U.S.A.

**KNOWLES, Hon. Sir Leonard Joseph,** Kt 1974, CBE 1963. Chief Justice of the Bahamas since 1973. *B.* 1916. *Educ.* Queen's Coll., Nassau; Faculty of Laws, King's Coll., Univ. of London—LLB; first Bahamian student to take and pass Higher School Certificate in Bahamas, 1934; LLB Hons 1937, Cert. of Hon. in Bar examinations. *M.* 1939, Harriet Hansen. *S.* 2. *Career:* Called to Bar, Gray's Inn, London, 1939; Lord Justice Holker Scholar, Gray's Inn 1940; practised law in Liverpool for some years; served War of 1939–45 in Royal Air Force (radar); returned to Nassau 1948 & was called to local Bar; Attorney-at-Law & Acting Attorney-General of the Bahamas 1949; Registrar-General 1949–50; past Stipendiary & Circuit Magistrate; Chmn., Labour Board, Bahamas 1953–63; MLC (upper House of Legislature) 1960–63; President, Senate 1964; re-elected 1967, 1968 & continued to hold that office until 1972. Has always been an active lay preacher. Chmn., Fund-raising Cttee. of Persis Rodgers Home for the Aged, Bahamas. *Club:* Royal Commonwealth Soc., London. *Address:* P.O. Box N-862, Nassau, Bahamas; and *office* Supreme Court, Nassau, Bahamas.

**KNOX, David Laidlaw,** BSc, MP. British. *B.* 1933. *Educ.* Lockerbie Academy; Dumfries Academy; London Univ. (Econ. Hon.). *Career:* Management Trainee, G. Waterson & Son 1953–56; Printing Executive, E. Bayliss & Son 1956–62; O & M Consultant J. Lucas Ltd. 1962–70; Member of Parliament for Leek since 1970; Secy. Conservative Finance Cttee. 1972–73; Parly. Private Secy. to Secy. of State for Defence 1973–74; Vice-Chmn. Conservative Party 1974–75; Secy., Conservative Employment Cttee. since 1976. *Address:* House of Commons, Westminster, London, S.W.1.

**KNUDTZON, Harald.** Knight, Order of Dannebrog (1st Class). *B.* 1897. *Educ.* Matriculation Degree 1915; Bachelor of Arts. *M.* 1937, Thyra Aletta Ingeborg Castenskiold. *S.* Henrik. *Dau.* Michala Benedicte. *Career:* Commercial and banking education in Denmark 1916–21; training in banks in Paris, London and Hamburg 1921–25. Employed Den Danske Landmandsbank 1925; Asst. General Manager 1934, Deputy General Manager 1950, General Manager 1954–66, Member Bd. 1966–73; Board member: Grenaa Steam Weaving-Mill Ltd. 1949–60, Danish Textile Equipment Ltd. 1949–60, and Reckitt & Colman, Ltd. 1942–54. Director, Den Danske Landmandsbank, Copenhagen. Chairman, BP Olie-Kompagniet Copenhagen (a subsidiary Co. of the British Petroleum Co. Ltd., London) 1956–72. *Address:* Maltevangen 13, Gentofte, Denmark.

**KNUTH, Count Eggert Adam.** Ambassador of Denmark. *B.* 1901. *Educ.* cand jur. *M.* 1934, Countess Lily Rantzau. Ambassador: to Reykjavik, 1956–59; Brussels and Luxembourg 1961–67, Rome, 1967–68, Oslo 1968–71. *Address:* Krengerup, 5620 Glamsbjerg, Fyn. Denmark.

**KNUTH-WINTERFELDT, Count Kield Gustav.** Danish diplomat. *B.* 17 Feb. 1908. *Educ.* University of Copenhangen (Cand jur). *M.* 1938, Gertrud Lina Baumann. *S.* Aksel-Ivar, Ditlev Helge. *Dau.* Isabel Suzanne. *Career:* Student, Cathedral School, Roskilde 1926; law degree, Univ. of Copenhagen 1931; entered Foreign Ministry Feb. 1931; Vice-Consul, Hamburg 1935; Secretary of Legation, Tokyo 1938; Secretary, Foreign Ministry 1939; Deputy Chief of Section 1945; Chief of Section 1950; En. Ex. and Min. Plen. to Argentina, Bolivia, Chile, Paraguay and Uruguay 1950–54; Chief, Trade Information Dept., Min. of Foreign Affairs 1954; Deputy Director, Economic Division, Ministry of Foreign Affairs 1956. Represented Denmark in Ghana as Ambassador on the occasion of Ghana's Independence celebrations 1957; Leader of the Danish Trade Mission to India and Ceylon, Jan.–Feb. 1957, to Peiping, Nov.–Dec. 1957, and to Moscow, July–Aug. 1958; Ambassador to the United States 1958; to France 1965; to Fed. Repub. of Germany 1966–72 Lord Chamberlain of Her Majesty Queen Margrethe II of Denmark and His Royal Highness Prince Henrik of Denmark 1972–76. *Address:* Rosendal by Fakse, Denmark.

**KOBAYASHI, Koji.** D.Eng. Japanese. *B.* 1907. *Educ:* Tokyo Imperial Univ. (D.Eng.). *M.* 1935, Noda Kazuko. *Daus.* 3. *Career:* Dir. Nippon Electric Co. 1949, Senior Vice-Pres. 1956, Exec. Vice-Pres. 1961, Senior Exec. Vice-Pres. 1962, Pres. 1964, Chmn. of the Board and Chief Exec. Officer 1976; Chmn. Nippon Aviotronics Co. Ltd.; Nippon Electric Yamagata Ltd.; Nippon Electric Tohokur Ltd.; Member, International Advisory Council of the Canadian Imperial Bank of Commerce; Member, Club of Rome; Foreign Assoc., National Acad. of Engineering. *Clubs:* Rotary, Tokyo, South. *Address:* 15–10 Denenchofu 5-Chome, Ohta-Ku, Tokyo 145, Japan; and *office* 33-1 Shiba Gochome, Minato-Ku, Tokyo, 108, Japan.

**KOCH, Colonel Erwin T.,** DHum, PhD, DLitt, DFA, OSJ, OSH, FAS, OCM, GCAB, LLB, LLM. *Educ.* City Coll.; Univ. of Mo.; St. Louis Univ. *Publications:* Subject of articles by Dr. Marcus Bach in Good Business & Adventures in Faith. *Awards:* from 30 States, 101 Counties & 1475 cities in the U.S.A.; & from 41 cities outside the U.S.A.; numerous other American & International Awards. Life Member of numerous American & International Organizations. *Address:* 4501 Lindell Blvd., St. Louis 63108, Mo., U.S.A.

**KOCH, Hans Henrik.** Danish civil servant. *B.* 17 Apr. 1905. *M.* 1932. *S.* Jørgen, Christian, Niels. *Career:* Asst. Principal Officer, Ministry of Social Affairs 1930, Principal Officer 1937 and in Ministry of Labour and Social Affairs 1940; Chief of Employment Department, Ministry of Social Affairs 1941; Permanent Secretary, Ministry of Social Affairs 1942–57; Chmn. Exec. Board, Danish Atomic Energy Commission 1956–75; member, Steering Committee, European Nuclear Energy Agency; Government Delegate to International Atomic Energy Agency General Conference. Government Delegate to International Labour Conference 1946–56; Chairman, Greenland Commission 1949–50, and Greenland Council 1964. Member, Danish F.O. Disarmament Cttee. (Chmn., 1968). *Awards:* Grand Cross Order of Dannebrog and Silver Cross. *Address:* Gronningen 17, Dk-1270-Copenhagen K, Denmark.

**KOCH, Roderic Malcolm.** *B.* 1904. *Educ.* Evansville College and Univ. of Wisconsin (AB Bus Admin.) *M.* 1925, Loretta M. Kaltenbacher. *Dau.* Constance Kathleen. *Career:* President, Standard Industrial Products Inc. 1932—; Executive Vice-President, George Koch Sons Inc. 1956—. Dir.: Evansville Museum of Arts & Sciences 1945—, Evansville Numismatic Society 1958—, Evansville Coll. Alumni Assn. 1963—, and Evansville Manufacturers Association 1956–60; Treasurer, Evansville Public School 1941–45. *Member:* American Pharmaceutical Association; American Astronomy League; American Association for Advancement of Science (Life Member); American Museum Association (Life Member); Amer. Numismatic Assn. (Life Member). *Clubs:* Petroleum; B.P.O.E.; Kennel. *Address:* 2200 Lincoln Avenue, Evansville, Ind., U.S.A.

**KOCH, Walter Karl.** *B.* 1901. *Educ.* Univ. of Colorado (AB 1923); Univ. of Denver (JD, 1925). *M.* 1945, Ruth Brooks Reid. *Daus.* Wanda Elizabeth (Wilson), Ellen Janet (Buchholz). *Career:* Student, The Mountain States Telephone & Telegraph Co. 1923 (Traffic Chief, Denver 1928; Gen. Sales Manager, Denver 1930; Utah Commercial Supervisor, Salt Lake City 1933; Colorado Commercial Supervisor, Denver 1935; General Commercial Supervisor, Denver 1939; General Commercial Manager, Denver 1945; Vice-Pres. and Dir. 1949, Pres. 1952–66); Attorney Holme Roberts & Owen law firm, 1700 Broadway,Denver, Colorado 80202. *Director:* Capitol Life Insurance Co., (former Dir.)

Denver Dry Goods Co., Associates Corporation of N. America; Children's Hospital; Past Dir., Silver States Savings and Loan Association; Trustee, Boettscher Foundation; Past Dir., Denver Real Estate Investment Association, Univ. of Denver; Denver Museum of Natural History; Denver Symphony; Past Pres., Mile High United Fund. Dir.: Air Force Acad. Found.; Colorado Assn. of Commerce & Ind.; Lutheran Hosp. & Medical Center; Hon. Director, Mountain States Telephone & Telegraph Co.; Civilian Aide to Secy. of the Army for Colorado. *Awards:* Univ. of Colorado, Disting. Service Award 1953, Beta Gamma Sigma, Delta Sigma Rho, Phi Alpha Delta; Alpha Kappa Psi. 1965 Marquis Award for outstanding citizenship (Amer. Inst. of Management); Certificate of Achievement (Assn. U.S. Army) 1965; Evans Award as outstanding alumnus (University of Denver), 1966. Brotherhood Award, National Conference of Christians & Jews, Colorado Region, 1963; U.S. Savings Bond Patriots Medal, 1965. Distinguished Alumni Award, Delta Sigma Rho-Tau Kappa Alpha Forensic Socy., 1966; Liberty Bell Award, Lutheran Brotherhood, 1966; Distinguished Service to Safety Award, Natl. Safety Cncl., 1966; Hon. Eng.D. Colorado School of Mines 1958; Hon. LLD Colorado Coll. 1962. *Clubs:* Athletic, Denver, Country (Denver); Cherry Hills Country; Amer., Colorado and Denver Bar Assns.; Colorado and U.S. Senr. Golfers Assns.; Rotary (Pres. 1966–67). *Address:* 33 Sunset Drive, Englewood, Colo. 80110, U.S.A.

**KOECHLIN, Raymond.** Swiss civil engineer. *B.* 23 Apr. 1903. *Educ.* Zurich (graduated with civil engineering diploma ETH). *M.* 1934, Colette de Merveilleux. *S.* 1. *Daus.* 2. *Career:* Engaged in dam construction in Italy 1926–27; Engineer, then Chief Engineer, of Société Energie Electrique du Rhin, Mulhouse, in construction of dam and hydro-electric plant at Kembs (Rhine), and the hydro-electric project of Lac Blanc and Lac Noir (Vosges) for pumping storage 1928–40; Managing Director, Conrad Zschokke Ltd., Geneva 1941–73, Vice-Chmn. since 1974 (this firm is engaged in civil engineering building and steel construction—dams, hydro-electric power plants, roads, airports, housing schemes, bridges, steel dam-gates, turn-key contracts, etc.). *Publications:* contributions to several journals concerned with civil engineering and steel construction. *Address:* 1246 Corsier-Port, Geneva; and *office* 42 Rue du 31-Décembre, 1211, Geneva 6, Switzerland.

**KOENIG, Frederick Gilman, Jr.** American coal mining and coke manufacturing executive. *B.* 1915. *Educ.* Birmingham-Southern Coll. (AB 1935); Harvard Univ. (LLB 1938). *M.* 1946 ,Mary Anne Geisking. *S.* Donald Clayton. Bronze Star (World War II). *Career:* Private law practice Birmingham, Ala., 1938–41; Tennesse Valley Authority 1941–42, 1946–47; served from private to Captain, Army of the U.S. 1942–46 (European Theatre of Operations, 1944–45, including service with 44th Infantry Div. 1944–45); Major, U.S.A.R., Retd.; Attorney, Alabama By-Products Corp. 1947–53 (Asst. Secy. 1948–54; Vice-Pres. 1953–54). Pres., Dir. and Member Executive Committee, Alabama By-Products Corp. 1968; President and Director, Ketona Chemical Corp. 1968—; *Member:* Socy. of Mayflower Descendants; Socy. of Colonial Wars; Sons of the Revolution; Sons of the Amer. Revolution; Omicron Delta Kappa; Tau Kappa Alpha; Sigma Alpha Epsilon; Birmingham, Alabama and American Bar Associations. *Clubs:* Birmingham Country, The Mountain Brook. *Address:* 3401 East Briarcliff Road; Birmingham 35223, Ala.; and *office* P.O. Box 354, Birmingham 3520–2, Ala., U.S.A.

**KOENIG, Robert P.,** OBE. *B.* 1904. *Educ.* Harvard (AB 1924; graduated with highest honours in geology); Hon. DEng, School of Mines, Montana University 1958. *M.* Angela Pow. *S.* Robert Julian, Harold Otto, and John Lauriston. *Daus.* Margarette Whittemore and Rosalie Angela. *Career:* Assistant Geologist, Cerro de Pasco Copper Corp. 1925–27; Engineer, New Verde Mines Co. 1927–30, International Mining Corp. 1930–33; Vice-Pres. & General Manager, Montezuma Corp. 1933–35; Engineer to Lehman Bros. 1935–36; Vice-Pres., Pres. & Dir., Electric Shovel Coal Corp. 1936–39, Pres. and Dir., Ayrshire Collieries Corp. 1939–50; Chmn. of the Bd. of Dirs., Cerro Corporation, New York City. Director: Southern Peru Copper Corp. 1955–72; Atlantic Cement Co. Inc. 1960–72; Trustee, Mutual Life Insurance Co. of New York 1954; Director, Compañia Minera Andina S.A. 1960–70; Arabian Shield; Golden Cycle Corp.; since 1970. Dir., Bancroft Fund; Cheapside Dollar Fund; Foote Mineral Co.: St. Joe Minerals. On leave of absence with Corps of Engineers, U.S. Army 1942–45; overseas July 1942–Aug. 1945, in Central and North Africa, Mediterranean and European Theatres of Operations. Promoted Colonel May 1944. Final assignment, Chief of Solid Fuels Section, SHAEF (Gen. Eisenhower's Staff) with responsibility for coal production, importation and allocation in N.W. Europe. Represented U.S. Bituminous Coal Industry to the Coal Mines Committee, I.L.O., London 1945, Geneva 1947, and Pittsburgh 1949. Tempy. Special Asst. to U.S. Ambassador to the U.K. 1947. Member, President's Committee on Foreign Aid (Harriman Cttee.) and Chairman (1948), National Bituminous Coal Advisory Council 1948–50; Actg. Dir., Industry Div., E.C.A. Apr.-May 1948; Special Consultant, E.C.A. Mission to U.K., Sept. and Oct. 1948. *Awards:* Legion of Merit (U.S.); Legion of Honour, Croix de Guerre with Palms (France); Order of the British Empire; Croix de Guerre with Palms (Belgium). Charles Rand Medal of A.I.M.E. for distinguished achievement in mining administration. *Member:* Amer. Inst. of Mining & Metallurgy; Institution of Mining & Metallurgy (London); Society of Economic Geologists; Council on Foreign Relations; Mining and Metallurgy Socy. of America; Trustee, Marine Historical Assn. Inc. *Publications:* An American Engineer Looks at British Coal (Foreign Affairs, 1948); Vertical Integration in Mining Industry, 1964 (The Sixth Sir Julius Wernher Memorial Lecture of the Instn. of Mining and Metallurgy, London); Ore, Avalanches and Water 1968 (Society of Mining Engineers of American Institute Mining, Metallurgical and Petroleum Engineers). *Clubs:* Harvard (N.Y.); Metropolitan (Washington); Seawanhaka Corinthian Yacht (Oyster Bay); New York Yacht; Mining (N.Y.). *Address:* 340 Cove Neck Road, Oyster Bay, N.Y. 11771, U.S.A.

**KOH, Prof. T. T. B.** Singaporean Diplomat & University teacher. *B.* 1937. *Educ.* Univ. of Singapore—LLB; Harvard Univ.—LLM; Cambridge Univ.—Diploma in Criminology. *M.* 1967, Siew Aing Poh. *S.* 2. *Career:* University Law teacher 1962–68; Ambassador to the UN & Canada 1968–71; Dean of Law Faculty, Univ. of Singapore 1971–74; Ambassador to the UN & Canada since 1974. *Member:* Advocate & Solicitor of the Supreme Court of Singapore. *Decorations:* Public Service Star. *Publications:* Articles in the Malayan Law Journal, the Malaya Law Review, etc. *Address:* 425 East 58th Street, New York, N.Y. 10022; and *office* 1 UN Plaza, 26th Floor, New York, N.Y. 10017, U.S.A.

**KOHL, Helmut.** German Politician. *B.* 1930. *Educ.* Universities of Frankfurt/Main and Heidelberg—Dr.Phil. *M.* 1960, Hannelore. *S.* 2. *Career:* Member of Landtag Rheinland-Pfalz 1959; Speaker of the CDU-Landtag-Group 1963–69; Chmn. of CDU-Rheinland-Pfalz 1966–74; Minister-President of Rheinland-Pfalz 1969–76; Dep. Chmn. of CDU-Germany 1969–73; Chmn. Admin. Board of German Television ZDF since 1970; Chmn.. Supervisory Board Landesbank Rheinland-Pfalz und Girozentrale 1970–77; Chmn. of CDU-Germany since 1973; Mem. of Bundestag 1976; Leader of Opposition in Bundestag since 1976. *Decorations:* Grand Cross 2nd Class of the Order of Merit of the Federal Republic of Germany; Grand Cross of the Order Sanctus Gregorius Magnus. *Publications:* Hausputz hinter den Fassaden (1971); Zwischen Ideologie und Pragmatismus (1973); (Ed.) Konrad Adenauer 1876–1976 (1976), *Address:* D-67 Ludwigshafen, Marbacher Strasse 11, Federal Republic of Germany; and *office* D-53 Bonn, Bundeshaus, F.R.G.

**KÖHLER, Dr. med. B. S. Lotte.** German. *B.* 1925. *Educ.* MD, BS; psychoanalytic training. *Career:* Generalbevollmächtigte G.C. Klebe GmbH., Darmstadt 1951–55; Board of Directors, Maschinenfabrik Goebel AG., Darmstadt. Managing Director, Psychoanalyst. Chairman of the Board, Maschinenfabrik Goebel GmbH, Darmstadt 1962—. Managing Director, Goeda-Vermögens-Verwaltungs-GmbH., Bad Wiesee 1962—. *Member:* Advisory Council, Society of Friends of Darmstadt Inst. of Technology (Dep. Chmn.); Adv. Council, Theodor-Hess-Preis e.V.: Deutscher Akademikerinnen Bund; Deutsche Gesellschaft für Psychotherapie, Psychosomatik und Tiefenpsychologie e.V.; International Psychoanalytic Assn. *Address:* Pienzenauerstrasse 58a, 8 Munich 81, Germany.

**KOHT, Paul.** Norwegian diplomat. *B.* 1913. *Educ.* University of Oslo (Law Degree 1937). *M.* 1938, Grete Sverdrup. *S.* Harald and Erik. *Dau.* Lise. *Awards:* Commander, Order of St. Olav (Norway); Commander, 1st Class, Order of Dannebrog (Denmark); Grand Cross, Order of Merit (FRG). *Career:* Entered Norwegian Foreign Service 1938; held posts at Bucharest, London, Tokyo, New York, Lisbon, Paris (with Norwegian Delegation to O.E.E.C. and N.A.T.O.; concurrently Norwegian Permanent Representative to Council of Europe) and Copenhagen; Ambassador to U.S.A.,

1957–63. Ambassador to Federal Republic of Germany 1963–68, to Great Britain 1968–75; Ambassador to Denmark since 1975. *Address:* Trondhjems Plads 4, DK 2100 København Ø, Denmark.

**KOIVISTO, Mauno Henrik,** PhD. Finnish, banker and politician. *B.* 1923. *Educ.* Turku Univ., PhD. 1956. *M.* 1952, Taimi Tellervo Kankaanranta. *Dau.* Assi. *Career:* Man. Dir., Helsinki Workers' Savings Bank 1959–67; Governor, Bank of Finland since 1968; Member Bd. Admin. of the Co-operative Union KK 1964—; Chmn. Bd. Admin. of the Co-operative Socy. ELANTO 1966—; Mortgage Bank of Finland Oy 1968—; Postipankki, 1970; Governor for Finland International Bank for Reconstruction & Development 1968–69, International Monetary Fund since 1970. Member of the Cabinet, Minister of Finance 1966–67; Prime Minister 1968–70; Minister of Finance, Deputy Prime Minister 1972. *Publications:* Social relations in Turku Harbour. Member, Social Democratic Party. *Address:* Pitkansillanranta 11 B. Helsinki 53; and *office* Suomen Pankki-Finlands Bank, Snellmaninaukio, 00170 Helsinki, 17, Finland.

**KOLB, Ernst.** Austrian politician. *B.* 9 Jan. 1912. *Educ.* University of Innsbruck (LLD). *M.* 1940, Irma König. *S.* 1. *Daus.* 2. *Career:* Elected to National Assembly 1945; Dir. Commerce, Federal Chamber of Commerce, Vienna 1946; Consultant of Minister for Trade and Reconstruction 1947; Minister for Trade and Reconstruction 1948–52; Minister for Public Education 1952–54; Lieut.-Governor of Vorarlberg 1954–59; Professor, Innsbruck University, Aug. 1959–77. *Address:* Schelderstrasse 16, Bregenz, Austria.

**KOLLER, Fortuné.** French executive. *B.* 1907. *Educ.* Modern Humanities. *M.* 1954, Paulette Liliane Desjardins. *Career:* Dir., Etablissements Henri Koller 1935–46. Director of Editions Mondaines; Chief Editor, Who's Who in Belgium 1956—; Director, International Register of Nobility 1955—; President, Armorial Universal 1951—. *Member:* Academy of Sciences, New York; Pres. Academie belgo-espagnole d'Historia. Institut de Coimbre; Society of the History of the Order of Malta: Hon. Member, Noble Association des Chevaliers Pontificaux, etc. *Club:* The Armorial. *Awards:* Donat 1st Cl. Order of Malta; Knight Const. Order of St. George; Officer, Order of Sainte Agathe (San Marino); Marianer Kreuz Teutonic Order; Gold Medal of Merit (Poland); Knight Order of St. Maurice and Lazare (Italy). *Publications:* Généalogie de la Famille ce Pape 1288–1939; Histoire de la Seigneurie de Paddeschoot; Les Belges dans les Ordres Militaires Espagnols; Histoire de la Famille Michault de Saint-Mars; Armorial Général de Belgique; Sceaux et Cachets Armories conservés dans les Dépôts d'Archives de Belgique; Who's Who in Belgium (in collaboration); Au service de la Toison d'or 1429–1971; more than 160 articles in the Belgian and foreign press. *Address:* 3 rue van Bemmel, 1030 Brussels, Belgium.

**KOLO, Sule,** High Commissioner for Nigeria. *B.* 1926. *Educ.* BSc (Econ); Imperial Defence College. *M.* 1957, Helen Patricia Kolo. *S.* 1. *Dau.* 3. *Career:* Counsellor, Nigerian High Commn. in London 1962; Permanent Secretary, Nigerian Ministry of Defence 1963, and to Nigerian Ministry of Trade 1966. Ambassador of Nigeria to Switzerland and Permanent Representative of Nigeria to the European Office of the United Nations 1966; Governor to the Int. Atomic Energy Agency 1969; High Commissioner in the United Kingdom 1970–75. Chmn., GATT, 1969–70; Vice-Chmn. U.N. First Cttee. (Political), 1970. *Awards:* Hon. degree FREconS; FRSA; awarded Franklin Peace Medal, 1969. *Club:* Lagos Island. *Address:* P.O. Box 185, Jos, Nigeria.

**KONTIOPÄÄ, Bjorn Harald Wilhelm.** Colonel (retired). *B.* 1916. *Educ.* Matriculation Oulun Lyseo; Military Academy, General Staff College. *M.* 1950, Hilkka Toropainen. *Career:* Officer of the Finnish Army, Second Lieut. 1939, Lieutenant 1940, Captain 1942, Major 1950, Lt. Colonel 1955. Colonel 1959; Company Cmdr. Finnish-Russian war, 1939–40, 1941–44, retired 1968. Managing Director, Finnish Road Assn., 1970—; Chief Editor Tie ja Liikenne (formerly Tielehti) 1970—. *Awards:* Cmdr. Order the Lion of Finland; Cross of Liberty III Class; IV Class with Oak Leaves and IV Class, Memorial Medals, 1939–40 and 1941–44 wars; German Order of the Eagle III class; Officer French Legion of Honour; Officer Swedish order of the Sword; UN Medal in the service of Peace; Member, Bd. of Directors, International Road Federation Geneva, 1969–72, and 1975, Cttee. of Representatives the European Road Assn. of IRF, 1968—. *Club:* Rotary Helsinki. *Address:* Pohjoinen Hesperiankatu 13 B 21, 00260 Helsinki 26, Finland.

**KOONTZ, John.** American accountant. *B.* 19 Oct. 1906. *M.* 1940, Margaret Elizabeth Bennett. *Career:* County Auditor 1934–43; Deputy State Auditor 1943–46; Secretary of State, State of Nevada since 1947. Pres., National Association of Secretaries of State since 1958–73; Appointed Dir. Nev. State Museum 1975. *Address:* 302 East John Street, Carson City, Nevada, U.S.A.

**KORHONEN, Gunnar Aleksander.** Finnish. *B.* 1918. *Educ.* BS Econ. *M.* (1) 1943, Elli Tamminen. (2) 1969, Seija Vapaa, née Niemi. *S.* 1. *Career:* Office Manager, Head, Dept. Ministry of Supply 1944–47; Secy. State Price & Wage Council 1947; Vice Pres. Oy Masalin & Co. 1947–50; Pres. Höyryvarustin Oy, 1950–51; Head, Price Dept., Ministry of Social Affairs, 1951–53; Director-in-Chief, Trade & Supply Sectn., Ministry of Commerce & Industry, 1953–60; Chmn. Bd. of Dirs. and Pres. of Finnair since 1960. *Member:* Bd. Dirs. State Licensed Bureau 1952–60; Treasure Balance of Prices Div. 1952–58; Delegate, Scandinavian Council 1956–59; Chmn. Finnish Group, Collaboration Cttee. on Scandinavian Economics 1957–59; Member Bd. AREA Travel Agency Ltd. 1960—; Bd. of Administration, Commercial Television of Finland 1963—; French-Finnish Chamber of Commerce 1963—; Tourism Development Fund of Finland 1965—; Int. Chamber of Commerce, Finnish Section 1966—; Finnish Aeronautical Assn. 1966–71, Finnish Employers General Group 1968—; Sampo-Tarmo Insurance Co. 1971—; Pres. Finnish Chapter, Finnish Amer. Chamber, Commerce 1972—; Minister, Social Affairs and Public Health 1970; Trade and Industry 1971. *Address:* Vänrikki Stoolinkatu 3A7, Helsinki 10; and *office* Mannerheimintie 102, 00250 Helsinki 25, Finland.

**KORHONEN, Keijo Tero,** PhD. Finnish Professor & Politician. *B.* 1934. *Career:* Asst. Teacher, Turku Univ. 1959–65; Freelance writer 1965–67; Officer at the Ministry for Foreign Affairs 1967–74 (Dep. Dir. for Political Affairs 1972–74); Prof. of Political History, Helsinki Univ. since 1974; Minister for Foreign Affairs 1976–77. *Member:* Historical Society of Finland; Paasikivi Society; International Inst. for Strategic Studies, London (Associate Member). *Publications:* Five books on Finnish–Russian & Finnish–Soviet Political Relations since the beginning of the 19th century; a book on nuclear-weapon-free Zones in International Politics. *Address: office* Institute for Political History, Hallitusk, 11–13 00103 Helsinki 10, Finland.

**KORNER, Eric.** British merchant banker. *B.* 1893. *Educ.* University of Vienna (LLD). *M.* 1935, Cacelie Bretz. *S.* 2. *Career:* Director: S. G. Warburg & Co. Ltd.; S. G. Warburg and Co. International Holdings Ltd.; Interbank A.G. (Vienna); Mercury Investment Trust Ltd.; British Reserve Insurance Co. Ltd.; Finanziaria Ernesto Breda S.p.A. (Italy); Selected Risk Investments S.A. (Luxembourg); Allianz International Insurance Co. Ltd. Chmn. Advisory Cttee. of Energy International N.V. (Curacao). *Address:* 22 Queen's Gate Gardens, London, S.W.7.

**KOROM, Mihály,** LLD. Hungarian. Lawyer and Politician. *B.* 1927. *Educ.* USSR Communist Party Univ.; Law School Budapest. *M.* 1949, Ilona Kövágó. *S.* 2. *Career:* Farmhand 1945; Various police posts, Head, Dept. Ministry of Interior 1945–60; Maj.-General and National Commander, Frontier Guard Force 1960–63; Secy. Central Cttee. Hungarian Socialist Worker's Party 1963–66; Minister of Justice since 1966. *Member:* Central Cttee. Hungarian Socialist Worker's Party. *Address:* Ministry of Justice, 1363 Budapest V., Szalay U. 16., Hungary.

**KOROMA, Sorie Ibrahim.** Sierra Leone politician. *B.* 1930. *Educ.* Govt. Model School Freetown; BO Govt. School and Co-op. Coll., Ibadan, Nigeria. *M.* 1955, Mabinti Kamara. *S.* 2. *Daus.* 3. *Career:* Co-operative Dept. 1951–58; private 1958–62; First Secy.-Gen. Sierra Leone Motor Transport Union 1958; MP 1962–65 and since 1967; Councillor, Freetown City Council 1964; Dept.-Mayor Freetown 1964; Minister Trade and Industry 1968–69; Min. Agric. and Nat. Resources 1969–71; Vice-Pres. since 1971; Prime Minister 1971–75; Min. of Interior 1971–73; Min. of Finance since 1975, & of Development & Economic Planning since 1977. Vice-Chmn. FAO Conference, Rome 1971; Repres. Sierra Leone at OAU Summit Conference, Addis Ababa 1971 and 1973, Morocco 1972. *Decorations:* Lebanon, People's Republic of China, Ethiopia and Liberia. *Address:* Office of Vice-President, Tower Hill, Freetown, Sierra Leone, and Hill Station 59, Freetown, Sierra Leone.

**KORTH, Fred.** American Counselor and Attorney at Law. *B.* 1909. *Educ:* Univ. of Texas (AB) and George Washington

Univ. (LLB) 1935, Hon LLD 1961. *M.* 1934, Vera Connell (*Div.* 1966). *S.* Fritz-Alan. *Daus.* Nina Maria (Cole) and Vera (Sheshunoff). *Career:* Attorney-at-Law 1935–42 (with Thompson & Barwise, Fort Worth); Mil. Serv., Lieut.-Col. U.S. Army Air Corps 1942–46; Attorney-at-Law, Wallace & Korth, Fort Worth 1946–51; Deputy-Counsellor, Department of the Army 1951; Assistant Secretary of the Army 1951–53; Secretary of U.S. Navy 1962–63; President, Continental National Bank of Fort Worth, Fort Worth, Texas 1959–61; Director: American Air Filter Co., Fischbach & Moore, Panama Canal Co., 1961–63 and First City National Bank of El Paso, Tex.; OKC Corp., Civilian Aide-at-Large to the Secy. of the Army 1961; Law Practice since 1963. *Awards:* Army's Exceptional Civilian Award; Army's Out-standing Civilian Service Award. *Member:* Amer. Bar Assn.; Amer. Law Inst. (Life Mem.) Reserve City Bankers' Assn., Democrat. *Clubs:* Ridglea (Fort Worth); Army & Navy (Washington); Confrere de Chevaliers du Tastevin; International (Wash.); San Antonio (Texas) Country. *Address:* El Retiro PO Box 13, Ecleto, Texas 78111; and *office* 401 Barr Building, Washington, D.C. 20006, U.S.A.

**KORVALD, Lars.** Norwegian M.P. *B.* 1916. *Educ.* Master of agricultural science. *M.* 1943, Ruth Borgersen. *S.* 1. *Daus.* 4. *Career:* Teacher of Agriculture 1943–48; Leader of Norwegian Agric. Clubs 1948–52; Rector of Tomb Agric. School 1952–61; M.P. 1961–72: Prime Minister 1972–73; Member of Parliament since 1973; Chmn. Christian Democratic Party since 1967. *Address:* 3050 Mjondalen, Norway; and *office* The Storting, Oslo, Norway.

**KOSAKA, Tokusaburo.** Japanese politician. *B.* 1916. *Educ.* Univ. Tokyo (Degree Economics, 1939). *M.* 1954, Asako Mitsui. *Daus.* 3. *Career:* Journalist, Asahi Shinbun Publish. Co. 1939–49; Shin-Etsu Chemical Industry Co. 1949–71, Vice-Pres. 1951–56; Pres. 1956–71; Lecturer, Univ. of Tokyo 1959–62; Lecturer Keiō Univ. 1960–62; Mem. of House of Represenatives since 1969; State Minister. Prime Ministers' Office and Okinawa Develop. Agency 1973–74; Dir. Shinano Mainichi Shinbun Publ. Co. since 1975. *President.* Assoc. of Inter. Education, Japan; Music Centre Japan. *Manager:* Japan Amateur Sports Assoc.; Japan Cttee. for Economic Development 1952–70, (Permanent) *Director* 1953–70. *Chairman* (special) Japan Federation Employers Assocs. 1962–67. *Publications:* Sangyojin Sengen (Industrialist Declaration); Ningen Daiichisyugi (Human Being First Policy). *Address:* 7-21-28 Fukazawa, Setagaya-ku, Tokyo, Japan; and *office* Room 717, Giin-kaikan, Nagatacho, Tokyo, Japan.

**KOSCIUSKO-MORIZET, Jacques.** French government official. *B.* 1913. *Educ.* Ecole Normale Supérieure. *M.* 1939. *S.* François, Jacques-Antoine. *Daus.* Marie-Catherine, Martine. *Career:* Was Asst. Prof. of Literature at Sorbonne and Columbia Univ.; Chef de Cabinet of Secretary-General, Prefecture of the Seine 1944; Directeur-Adjoint du Cabinet of President of Constituent Assembly 1946; Directeur-Adjoint du Cabinet of President of the Council Dec. 1946–Jan. 1947; Maître des Requêtes au Conseil d'Etat; Directeur du Cabinet of President of the Republic 1947–45; Director of Cabinet of Deleg. to Pres. of Council since Feb. 1956; Director of Cabinet of the Minister of State, June 1957; Permanent Delegate of France to Trusteeship Council of U.N., July 1957; Ambassador of France to Congo Kuishasa 1963–68; Director of Cultural and Technical Affairs to the Secretary of State of Foreign Affairs, Feb. 1968–Dec. 1968; Ambassador to the North Atlantic Council, 1970. Ambassador, Permanent Representative of France to the United Nations 1970–72; Ambassador of France to the United States since 1972. *Awards:* Officier de la Médaille de la Résistance; Commandeur de la Légion d'Honneur, Croix de Guerre; Knight Commander Royal Victoria Order (Great Britain). *Address:* 2535 Belmont Road N.W., Washington, D.C. 20008, U.S.A.; and 20 rue de Tournon, Paris 6.

**KOSYGIN, Alexei Nikolaevich.** Chmn. Council of Ministers of the U.S.S.R. *B.* 1904. *Educ.* Leningrad Co-op. Tech. Sch., Leningrad Textile Inst. *Career:* Siberian consumer co-op. system 1924–30; Foreman & Shop Superintendent, Zhelyabov Textile Works, Leningrad 1935–37; Mgr., October Spinning & Weaving Works, Leningrad 1937–38; Head of Dept., Leningrad C.P.S.U. 1938; Chmn., Exec. Cttee. of Leningrad Soviet of Workers' Representatives 1938–39; People's Commissar for the textile industry of the U.S.S.R. 1939–40; Dep. Chmn., Council of People's Commissars of the U.S.S.R. 1940–46 & Chmn., Council of People's Commissars of the R.S.F.S.R. 1943–46; Dep. Chmn., U.S.S.R. Council of Ministers 1946–March 1953, & U.S.S.R. Finance Minister 1948; Minister for Light Industry 1949–53, for Light and Food Industries 1953, for Consumer Goods 1953–54; Dep. Chmn., Council of Ministers Dec. 1953–56; First Dep. Chmn., Council of Ministers State Econ. Comm. for current econ. planning & Minister 1956–57; First Dep. Chmn., National Planning Bd. 1957; Dep. Chmn., Council of Ministers July 1957–60 & Chmn. National Planning Bd. 1959–60; First Dep. Chmn., Council of Ministers 1960–64, Chmn. since Oct. 1964; mem. C.P.S.U. since 1927, Central Cttee. of the C.P.S.U. since 1939; candidate mem. Politburo 1946–48, mem. Politburo 1948–52; candidate mem. Presidium of the Central Cttee. of the C.P.S.U. 1952–53 & 1957–60, mem. of the Presidium 1960–66; mem. Politburo of the Central Cttee of the C.P.S.U. since 1966; deputy of Supreme Soviet, 2nd–9th convocations, since 1946. *Decorations:* Twice Hero of Socialist Labour (1967, 1974); 6 Orders of Lenin; Order of the Red Banner; many medals. *Address:* The Kremlin, Moscow, U.S.S.R.

**KOTCHIAN, A. Carl.** U.S. citizen. Aerospace consultant. *B.* 1914. *Educ.* Stanford Univ., Stanford, Calif. (BS, MBA). *M.* 1940, Lucy Carr. *S.* Robert L. *Career:* Vice-Pres., Gen. Mgr., Lockheed-Georgia Co., Marietta, Ga., 1956–59; Group Vice-Pres. 1959–65 and Exec. Vice-Pres. 1965–67, Pres. 1967–75, Vice-Chmn. 1975–76 (Ret'd.), Lockheed Aircraft Corp. Dir., Consol. Equities Corp., Atlanta; Past Pres., Assoc. Industries Ga. CPA. *Clubs:* California, Los Angeles Country (both Los Angeles); Riviera Tennis; Palm Springs Tennis; Capital City (Atlanta, Ga.). *Address:* 283 Bel Air Road, Los Angeles, Calif. 90024; and *office* 2555 N. Hollywood Way, Burbank, Calif., U.S.A.

**KOTELAWALA, Rt. Hon. Sir John Lionel,** CH, KBE. Ceylonese politician. *Educ.* Christ College, Cambridge (BA); Royal College, Colombo. *Career:* entered Ceylon State Council as member for Kurunegela 1931; Acting Minister for Agriculture and Lands 1933; Minister for Communications and Works 1936; Minister for Transport and Works 1946; President, United National Party; Prime Minister and Minister of Defence and External Affairs 1953–56; Privy Councillor 1954. *Awards:* Grand Cross of following Orders: Legion of Honour (France), Merit (Italy), Merit (Germany), Rising Sun (Japan), White Elephant (Thailand), Lion (Netherlands). *Clubs:* The Orient (Colombo); Directors (London). *Address:* Ratmalana, Sri Lanka; and 'Brogues Wood', Biddenden, Kent.

**KOYAMA, Goro.** Japanese banker. *B.* 1909. *Educ.* Tokyo Imperial Univ. *M.* 1934, Atsu Koyama. *S.* Shogo and Shinji. *Dau.* (Mrs.) Aya Yokoyama. *Career:* With the Mitsui Bank Ltd., Dir. and Mgr.: General Affairs Dept. 1959–60, Tokyo Branch 1960–61, Osaka Branch 1961–63; Managing Dir. and Mgr.. Osaka Branch 1963; Man. Dir. 1963–65; Deputy-Pres. 1965–68. President, Mitsui Bank Ltd. 1968–74, Chmn. 1974; Director: Federation of Bankers' Assn. of Japan 1968—, Tokyo Bankers' Assn. 1968—. *Clubs:* Rotary (Tokyo-Higashi). *Address:* 3-15-10 Takaido-Higashi, Suginamiku, Tokyo, Japan.

**KRAG, Jens Otto.** Danish politician. *B.* 15 Sept. 1914. *M.* 1959, Helle Virkner. *Career:* Minister of Trade, Industry and Shipping 1947–50; member (Soc. Dem.) Randers, Folketing since 1947; Economic Counsellor, Embassy, Washington, 1950–52; Editor, Verdenes Gang (monthly) 1953; Min. Economics and Labour 1953–57; Minister of Foreign Economic Affairs 1957–58; of Foreign Affairs 1958–62; Prime Minister 1962–68; Prime Minister and Minister of Foreign Affairs 1966–68. Leader of the Social Democratic Party in Opposition, 1968–71; Prime Minister 1971–72; Head of the Delegation, Commission of the European Communities to the USA 1973–74. *Address:* Skodsborgparken 58, Skodsborg, 2942 Copenhagen, Denmark.

**KRAMER, Sidney B.** BS, LLB, JD. American. *B.* 1915. *Educ:* New York Univ. (BS); Brooklyn Law School; St. Lawrence Univ. (LLB. JD). *M.* 1939, Esther Schlansky. *S.* 1. *Dau.* 1. *Career:* Former Pres. & Dir. New Amer. Library; Senior Vice Pres. Secy. & Dir. Bantam Books Inc.; Dir. Canadian British subsidiaries; Man. Dir. Transworld Publisher Ltd. (Corgi Books); Man. Dir. Cassell & Collier Macmillan Publishers Ltd.; Man. Dir. Mews Books Ltd. (US and UK). *Member:* Connecticut Bar Association. *Club:* Overseas Press. *Address:* 25 Queensgate Gardens, London, S.W.7 and 20 Bluewater Hill, Westport, Conn. U.S.A. and *office:* 179 Main Street, Westport, Conn.

**KRAUT, Ralph John.** American engineer. *Educ.* Univ. of Wisconsin (BS in ME 1930). *M.* Virginia R. Dunn Smith. *S.*

Hans Beymer. *Daus.* Diane (Matson) and Karen (Annis). *Career:* Served as Lt.-Col. of Infantry, U.S. Army 1942–45. Production Engineer, A. O. Smith Corp,. Milwaukee 1931; successively student engineer, advertising, accounting and travelling auditor, General Electric Co., Schenectady, N.Y. 1931–35. With Giddings & Lewis Machine Tool Co.; Asst. Works Mgr. and Asst. to Pres. 1935–39; Dir. and Exec. Vice-Pres. 1939–42; Pres., Gen. Mgr., Dir. 1945–66; Chairman of the Board, Giddings & Lewis Inc., Fond du Lac, Wisconsin. Director: Great Northern Nekoosa Corp. N.Y. Port Edwards, Wis.; Twin Disc Clutch Co., Racine, Wis.; Harnischfeger Corp., Milwaukee; Marshall & Ilsley Bank, Milwaukee; Employers Insurance of Wasau, Wasau, Wisconsin. *Member:* Natl. Machine Tool Builders' Assn. (Past Pres.); Wisconsin Mfrs. Assn., Milwaukee; Amer. Ordnance Assn.; Univ. of Wisconsin Foundation; Amer. Socy. Mech Engrs.; Amer. Socy. Tool & Mfg. Engrs.; Amer. Management Assn.; U.S. Inf. Assn.; Amer. Legion Vets of Foreign Wars; Tau Beta Pi; Theta Chi. *Clubs:* Elks; Rotary International; Milwaukee Athletic; Green Lake Yacht. *Address:* 545 Illinois Avenue, Green Lake, Wis. 54941, U.S.A.

**KREISKY, Bruno.** Austrian Federal Chancellor. *B.* 1911. *Educ.* Univ. of Vienna (LLD). *M.* 1942, Vera Fuerth. *S.* Peter Staffan. *Dau.* Suzanne Christine. *Career:* Joined Austrian Social Democratic Party at 15 years of age; active in its Youth Movement until the Party was outlawed in 1934. Worked in the underground movement; arrested for political reasons and imprisoned for 18 months, and again arrested after the Nazi invasion of Austria 1938; escaped to Sweden, and in the period 1939–46 served as member of the scientific staff of the Stockholm Co-operative Society. Advised the Swedish Govt. on Austrian questions, and obtained right of political asylum for Austrians who deserted from the German forces. Joined Austrian Foreign Service 1946 and served in the Legation at Stockholm. Assigned to the Federal President's Office (where he was later nominated Assistant Director) 1951; Secretary of State for Foreign Affairs in the then Federal Chancellery, Dept. of Foreign Affairs 1953. Member of Austrian Delegations to the Berlin Conference 1954, and Moscow negotiations on the Austrian State Treaty 1955. Elected MP 1956; Federal Minister for Foreign Affairs 1959–66; Led Austrian Delegation to U.N. General Assembly 1959–65; Elected Chmn., Socialist Party Austria 1967; successful election campaign and sworn in as Federal Chancellor, 1970; re-elected 1971 and 1975. Vice-President, Theodor Koerner Foundation for the Promotion of the Arts and Sciences, Nov. 1959—, and Institute of Advanced Studies and Research, Vienna 1963; President, Vienna Institute for Development, May 1964—. *Publications:* numerous articles, chiefly on the international position of Austria and on economic subjects, in the Austrian and international press. Longer works include Veraussetzungen der Koexistenz (Verlag Rombach, 1960), Die österreichische Neutralität (Verlag des OGB 1960), Die Hereausforderung (ECON Verlag, 1963), Aspekte des demokratischen Sozialismus (LIST Verlag, 1974), Neutralilät und Koexistenz (LIST-Verlag, 1975), Brandt-Kreisky-Palme: Briefe und Gespräche (Europäische Verlagsanstadt). Numerous awards. *Address:* Armbrustergasse 15, Vienna XIX; and *office* Ballhausplate 2, Vienna I, Austria.

**KREKELER, Dr. Heinz L.** German diplomat. *Educ.* Universities of Freiburg, Munich, Goettingen, Berlin (PhD). *M.* 1931, Ilse Goebel (*Dec.* 1963). *S.* Jurgen. *M.* 1965, Helga Finke. *Career:* Chemical engineer with different firms 1930–46; member Lippe Diet 1946, Diet of North Rhine-Westphalia 1947–50, and of the First Federal Assembly 1949; partner Eilers-Schünemann Verlag (Publishers) Bremen 1948; Consul-General New York 1950–51; Chargé d'Affaires, Washington 1951–53; Ambassador since 1953; Ambassador Ex. and Plen. 1955–58; European Commissioner, European Atomic Energy Community 1958–64. *Member:* Max-Planck Gesellschft z. Forderung der Wissenschaften. *Awards:* Grand Cross 2nd Cl. of the Order of Merit (Fed. Republic of Germany); Grande Ufficiale dell'Ordine (Repub. Italy); Kt. Comdr. Order of St. Gregory (Holy See). Grand Officer Order of Leopold (Belgium). Hon. LLD Univ. of South Carolina 1956, and Xavier Univ. 1956. *Publications:* Diplomatie, (1965). Die Aussenpolitik (1967); Wissenschaft und Politik (1975). *Club:* Akademischer Segelverein (München). *Address:* Gut Lindemannshof 4902 Bad Salznflen 1. Germany.

**KRESS, Edward S.** American. *B.* 1931. *Educ.* B.S. Production Engineer, Univ. of Michigan. *M.* 1974, Rita S. Fales. *S.* 1. *Career:* USAF Navigator and Flight Engineer 1955–57, ret. Captain; Consultant Engineer 1958–65; Kress Automotive Engineering (Founded Slag Away Corp. 1965); President and Chmn. Kress Corporation since 1965. *Member:* A.S.M.E.; Phi Delta Theta Social Fraternity; Socy. Manufacturing Engineers. *Address:* Brimfield, Ill. 61517, U.S.A.; and *office* 400 Illinois Street P.O. Box 368, Brimfield, Ill. 61517.

**KRESS, Ralph H.** American professional consulting engineer. *B.* 1904. *Educ.* Graduate Certificate, Mechanical Engineer and Applied Mathematics, Lowell Institute; Massachusetts Inst. of Technology. *M* 1930, Edna L. Sheridan. *S.* Capt. Edward S., U.S.A.F. (Ret'd.; Pres. & Founder, Kress Corp., Brimfield, Ill.). Res. Retail Truck Salesman and Sales Manager 1922–39; Engineer and Technical Representative, Chevrolet Division, and Fleet Division, General Motors Corporation 1939–42 and 1946–50; Captain and Major AUS-TC 1943–46 (present title Major U.S.A.R.-T.C.); Legion of Merit; Executive Vice-Pres., Dart Truck Co., Kansas City 1950–55; Kress Automotive Engineering Count1955; Manager, Truck Division, Letourneau-Westing-Denm Co., Peoria, Ill. 1956–62; Manager, Truck Development Caterpillar Tractor Co., Peoria, Ill. 1962–69; Exec. Vice-Pres., Kress Corp., Brimfield, Ill. since 1969. Received 26 patents for motor vehicles & motor trucks. *Address:* 4444 Knoxville, Peoria, Ill., U.S.A.

**KRISTENSEN, Thorkil,** Cand polit, Dr Sc Pol hc (Ankara). Danish professor and politician. Director, Inst. for Development Research, 1969–72. *B.* 9 Oct. 1899. *Married* 1931. *S.* Niels Peder. *Dau.* Anne Marie. Inspector, Savings Bank 1928–35; Assistant Lecturer, Univ. of Copenhagen 1936–38; Professor, Business and Economics, Univ. of Aarhus 1938–45; Minister of Finance 1945–47 and 1950–53; MP (Lib.) 1945–60; Professor, Copenhagen School of Economics and Business Administration 1948–60; Secretary-General, Organization for Economic Co-operation & Development (OECD) 1960–69. *Publications:* Fixed and Variable Costs, 1939; The Economic World Balance, 1960. The Food Problem of Developing Countries, 1968: Development in Rich and Poor Countries, 1974. *Address:* 18 Odinsvej, 3460 Birkerod, Denmark.

**KRISTIANSEN, Erling (Engelbrecht).** Danish diplomat. *B.* 1912. *Educ:* Herning Gymnasium, Univ. of Copenhagen (MAEcon), and post-graduate studies, Economics and International Relations, Geneva, Paris, London 1935–37. *M.* 1938, Anne-marie Selinko (novelist). *Career:* Secretary-General 1935, President 1936, Fédération Universitaire Internationale pour la Société des Nations. Danish Civil Servant 1941; served with Free Danish Missions; Stockholm 1943, Washington 1944, London 1945. Joined Danish Diplomatic Service and stayed in London until 1947. Danish Foreign Ministry 1947–48; Head of Danish Mission to O.E.E.C. Paris 1948–50; Secretary to Economic Committee of the Cabinet 1950–51; Asst. Under-Secretary of State 1951; Deputy Under-Secretary of State for Economic Affairs, Danish Foreign Ministry 1954–64. Ambassador to the Court of St. James's, 1964–77; concurrently accredited in Ireland 1964–73. *Awards:* Grand Cross, Order of Dannebrog; GCVO (Hon); Grand Officier, Légion d'Honneur; Kt. Grand Cross Icelandic Falcon; Kt. Comdr. of St. Olav, White Rose of Finland, and the Star of Ethiopia; Commander, Order of Northern Star, Sweden. *Publications:* Folkeforbundet (The League of Nations), 1938. *Address:* 4 Granhojen, 2900 Hellerup, Denmark.

**KRISTIANSEN, Georg.** Norwegian diplomat. *B.* 1917. *Educ.* Royal Norwegian Military Acad., (Army Officer); Oslo Univ. (Studies in history and languages). *M.* 1962, Ann Mildrid Brinck. *Daus.* 2. *Career:* Army Service (Norway and U.K.) 1939–45; Secy. Norwegian Embassy Paris 1947–52; Secy., later Counsellor Ministry of Foreign Affairs 1952–57; Instructor Norwegian National Defence College 1957–59; Dir. (Later Dir.-Gen.) Political Affairs, Ministry of Foreign Affairs (Norway) 1959–63; Ambassador to NATO and OECD Paris 1963–70; Dir. Civil Defence and Emergency Planning 1970–74; Ambassador to OECD Paris since 1974. *Decorations:* Comm. St. Olav's Order, Comm. Etole Noire; Atlantic Star; 1939–45 Star; Chev. Legion of Honour (France); Comm. Dannesbrog; Grand Cross Agila Azleca Order; Grand Cross, Tunisian Order; Comm. Persian Sun and Lyon's Order. *Address:* 109 avenue Henri-Martin, Paris 75116, France.

**KROEGER, Arthur F.** American company director. *B.* 16 Feb. 1912. *Educ.* Brown Univ. (PhB); Harvard Graduate School of Business Administration (MBA). *M.* 1950, Alexa Copeland Daley. *Daus.* Alexa Gale and Joanne Trabue. *Career:* Director: Boorum & Pease Co. N.Y.; Keydata Corp. Wellesley, Mass.; Monroe Auto Equipment Co., Monroe, Mich.; Eriez Magnetics, Erie, Pa.; International Foodservice

Corporation, Los Angeles, Calif.; Standard Pressed Steel Co. Jenkintown, Pa.; Harbridge House, Boston, Mass.; Executrans, Greenwich, Conn.; CRC Chemicals Inc. (Jenkintown, Pa.); PMI Investment Corp. (San Fran., Cal.); PMI Mortgage Ins. Co. (San Fran.). *Address:* 535 Fifth Avenue, New York 10017, U.S.A.

**KRÖGER, Dr. Wilhelm,** LLD. German lawyer. *B.* 28 Feb. 1904. *M.* 1931, Frida Jensen. *S.* Uwe, Jens. Graduated 1934; Advocate; Senator for Justice, Hamburg 1950–53; Senator for Police and Regional Administration 1957–61; Judge of Constitutional Court of Hamburg 1962–72. *Address:* Raalandsweg 29, 2 Hamburg 56, Germany.

**KROHN, Dr. Hans-Broder.** German EEC Official. *B.* 1915. *Educ.* Univ. of Göttingen—Dr. Agricultural Science. *M.* 1941, Ilse Philipp. *S.* 2. *Dau.* 1. *Career:* Inst. for Agricultural Market Studies, Univ. of Göttingen; Private Secretary to the Minister of Food, Agriculture & Forestry, Bonn; Division Chief, FAO & OECE, studying farm economics and int'l agricultural policy; Official of the EEC Commission, helping to formulate common agricultural Policy 1958; Dir. of the Directorate of Agricultural Economics & Legislation of the Directorate General of Agriculture 1962; Deputy Dir.-Gen. of Agriculture 1968; Dir.-Gen. of the Directorate for Development of the Commission of the European Communities since 1970. *Member:* Int'l Conference of Agricultural Economists; American Agricultural Economist Assoc.; Gesellschaft für Wirtschafts-und Sozialwissenschaften WISOLA; AEPE—Association pour l'Etude des Problèmes de l'Europe, Paris. *Decorations:* Croix de fer G. M. II prem. et 2è cl.; Commander of the Order of Merit of the Italian Republic; Commandeur de l'Ordre National de Haute Volta, Benin, Tchad, Mali; Grand Officer de l'Ordre du Mono, Togo; Grand Officier de l'Ordre National de Madagascar, Senegal, Niger, Burundi, etc. *Publications:* Die Futtergetreidewirtschaft der Welt 1900–1954 (1957); Agrarpolitik in Europa (1962); The Common Agricultural Policy—in the International Manual on the EEC; Das Abkommen von Lomé zwischen der Europäischen Gemeinschaft und den AKP-Staaten (1975). *Address:* 12 Avenue des Cerfs—1950 Crainhem, Belgium; & *office* Commission of the European Communities, 200 rue de la Loi—1049 Brussels, Belgium.

**KRUEGER, Myron William.** International executive. Vice-President, Director, Chmn. Finance Cttee., Hercules Inc., 1968—. *B.* 1910. *Educ.* Univ. of Wisconsin (AB 1935, MA 1935). *M.* 1936, Dorothy Baillie Sterrett. *S.* 2. *Daus.* 2. *Career:* Kimberley Clark Corp., Neenah, Wis. 1936–39; Assistant Controller, Carnegie Illinois Steel Corp., Pittsburgh 1944–48; Exec. Vice-Pres., Treas., Director, Raymond International N.Y.C. 1948–60; President, M. W. Kreuger Associates 1960–68; Director, Commercial Union Fire Insurance Co. of N.Y., Columbia Casualty Co.; Trustee, Wisconsin Alumni Research Foundation. *Member:* National Association of Accountants (past National Vice-President), National Association of Manufacturers (Nuclear Energy Committee), American Arbitration Association, Newcomen Society, Phi Beta Kappa, Phi Kappa Phi, Artus, Delta Sigma Rho. *Clubs:* Bankers of America, University (N.Y.C.), Essex County Country Club (West Orange, N,J.) (Board of Governors), Wilmington Country. *Address:* 321 Hartshorn Drive, Short Hills, N.J.; and *office* 910 Market Street, Wilmington, Delaware, 19899, U.S.A.

**KRUSE-JENSEN, Carl.** Norwegian judge. *B.* 9 Aug. 1889. *M.* 1932, Ellen Rolfsen. *S.* 2. *Career:* Called to the Bar 1912; Secretary to Ministry of Foreign Affairs 1917; Consul-General, London 1921; Secy. to Norwegian Ambassadors, Paris and Copenhagen 1923; appointed Judge 1926; International Judge in Saar during the plebiscite 1934–35, and in conflict between France and Turkey concerning the Sandjak d'Alexandrette 1938; Norwegian Delegate, Expert Conference, Geneva 1947, and Diplomatic Conference, Geneva 1949; Judge of Supreme Court. *Publications:* The Geneva Conventions of 1949 (Gyldendal, Oslo 1952). *Address:* Gustav Vigelands veg 3A, Oslo, Norway.

**KUHN, Wayne E.** American. *B.* 1903. *Educ.* Reed College, Portland, Ore. (BA); Cornell Univ. (PhD); Registered Professional Engineer. *M.* 1929, Agnes J. Lakie. *S.* William E. *Career:* Citations: Army Ordnance, Navy Bureau of Ships, and Office of Research and Development; Asst. Instructor, Cornell Univ. 1925–29; with Texaco Inc. 1929–65. Executive and Professional Engineer 1965—. Formerly General Manager, Research and Technical Department, Texaco Inc. Former Dir.; Jefferson Chemical Co., Texaco Development Corp., Texaco Experiment Inc., Co-ordinating Research Council Inc., and Fifth World Petroleum Congress; Dir., Omark Industries; Kentnox Inc. Dir. Gillespie Petersen. *Member:* American Chemical Society (Past Chmn., Petroleum Chemistry Div.); American Institute of Chemists (Pres. 1959–60); American Petroleum Institute (Award); Chemical Society of London; Society of the Chemical Industry; Society of Automotive Engineers; Amer. Society of Testing Materials; American Rocket Society; AAIA; Commercial Chemical Development Association (Past Pres.). *Awards:* CCDA Hons. 1970; Honor Scroll, Gold Medal 1967; Fellow. American Inst. *Chemical* Engineers, American Petroleum Inst. Award. *Publications:* numerous patents and publications and publications in fields of petroleum, petro-chemicals, general research and management. *Clubs:* Chemists; Aero; International. *Address:* 1840 N.W. Ramsey Drive, Portland, Ore. 97229. U.S.A.

**KULKA, Marshall.** Canadian. *B.* 1911. *Educ.* Univ. of Alberta (BSc 1935, MSc 1936) and McGill Univ. (PhD 1942). *M.* 1939, Sophia Danyluk. *S.* David, William, MSc. *Dau:* Maria Louise, B.A. *Career:* High School teacher 1937–40; Research Chemist, Dominion Rubber Research Laboratories 1943–63. Manager, Organic Chemical Research; Senior Scientist, Uniroyal Research Laboratories, Guelph, Ontario 1963–76 (Ret'd.). *Publications:* about 30 patents and 60 papers on organic chemistry, published in Canadian Journal of Chemistry, Journal of Organic Chemistry and Journal of Amer. Chemical Socy. F.C.I.C. 1951, F.R.S.C. 1953. *Member:* Chemical Inst. of Canada; Amer. Chemical Socy.; Sigma Xi. First recipient of the Thomas W. Eadie Medal awarded by the Royal Society of Canada for contributions to Applied Science, June 1975. *Address:* 65 Metcalf Street, Guelph, Ontario; and *office* Uniroyal Research Laboratories, Huron Street, Guelph, Ontario, Canada.

**KUNERALP, Zeki,** GCVO. Turkish diplomat. *B.* 1914. *Educ.* Univ. of Berne (Dr. juris). *M.* 1943, Necla Ozdilci. *S.* Sinan and Selim. *Career:* Entered Diplomatic Service 1940; served Bucharest, Prague, Paris and at Ministry of Foreign Affairs, Ankara. Appointed Assistant Secretary-General in 1957 and Secretary-General in 1960. Ambassador to Berne, Sept. 1960. Ambassador to the Court of St. James's, Feb. 1964–66; Secretary-General of the Ministry of Foreign Affairs 1966–69; Ambassador to the Court of St. Jame's 1969–72; Ambassador to Madrid since 1972. *Address:* Embajada de Turquia, Calle de Monte Esquinza 48, Madrid, Spain.

**KÜNG-HÄUSLER, Heinrich,** Dr hc. Swiss bank director. *B.* 10 Jan. 1898. *Educ.* Basle University (Dr hc). *M.* 1922, Berta Häusler. *S.* 1. *Career:* A.G. Spörri & Co., Wald; Vice-Pres., Sandoz A.G.; previously: appren. to Schweiz Kreditanstalt, Glarus; served with A.G. Leu & Co., Zurich, a bank in Montreux, and Banca Unione di Credito, Lugano; Deputy, Schweiz Bankgesellschaft, Basle. *Publications:* numerous articles on banking and economic subjects. *Address:* 26 Beim Buremichelskopf, Basle, Switzerland.

**KURTH, Hans.** Swiss industrialist. *B.* 30 Oct. 1908. *Educ.* Commercial School; banking apprenticeship. *M.* 1940, Gertrud Buri. *Daus.* 2. *Career:* Former Director, CERTINA, Kurth Freres S.A. (watch manufacturers); joined company in 1929 (member of the Board 1932 and President of the Board 1937—; Cttee., General Watch Co. Ltd. 1971; Deputy FH (Fédération Horlogere) and Swiss Watch Chamber Cttee., Verband deutschschweizerischer Uhrenfabrikanten, Pres. 1963–66; member, Solothurn Rotary Club (Pres. 1961–62). *Address:* Gibelstrasse 22, Grenchen, Switzerland.

**KYPRIANOU, Spyros.** Cypriot Advocate & Politician. *B.* 1932. *Educ.* Barrister-at-Law (also studied Economics and Comparative law). *M.* 1956, Mimi Papatheoclitou. *S.* 2. *Career:* After completing his studies in London was appointed Representative in London of the Ethnarchy of Cyprus 1954; during his stay he attended conferences and gave many lectures on the Cyprus problem. Attended U.N. General Assembly in N.Y. as observer for the ethnarchy of Cyprus; returned to London Mar. 1957 until the signing of the Cyprus Agreements; accompanied Archbishop Makarios to Cyprus on latter's return from exile, Mar. 1959; represented the Greek Cypriot side at Athens Conf. to conclude the Tripartite between Cyprus, Greece and Turkey, Oct. 1959. Appointed Minister of Justice in first Cyprus Cabinet 16 Aug. 1960; was transferred to the Ministry of Foreign Affairs a few days later. Accompanied the President, Archbishop Makarios, on the latter's state visits to Greece, Turkey, U.S.A., West Germany, U.A.R., and India. Attended meetings of the Council of Europe, and represented Cyprus at meetings of Foreign Ministers of the Tripartite Alliance held in Paris, as well as other meetings and conferences; Represented Cyprus at Security Council of U.N. several times during 1964–65 and again in 1967 and 71, and at the Commonwealth Prime Ministers' Conferences held in London 1964 and 1965; served as Pres. of Cttee. of Foreign Ministers of Council of Europe 1967; resigned as Foreign Minister in May 1972 after serious dispute with the Military Regime in Athens and commenced practising law; after the coup in Cyprus and the Turkish invasion (July–Aug 1974) led Cyprus delegation to the U.N. and then took part—without any official capacity—in the talks between Greek Government & Pres. Makarios; ad hoc member of Cyprus delegation to Security Council meeting in New York, Feb. 1975; then continued practising law; President of Cyprus since 1977. *Awards:* Grand Cross, Order of George I of Greece 1962; Grand Cross of Fed. Rep. of Germany 1962; Grand Star of Rep. of U.A.R. 1961; Grand Cross, Order of Boyaca, of Colombia 1966; Grand Cross, Order of Merit, of Chile 1966; Grand Silver Cross of Austria 1973; Ecclesiastical Decoration of the Order of St. Aikaterini of Sinai 1966. *Address:* Kermia Bldgs, Office No. 202 (2nd Floor), 4 Diagoras Street, Nicosia, Cyprus.

**KYRIAZIS, Demetrius.** Greek. *B.* 1922. *Educ.* Technical Univ. of Athens. (E.M.P.). *M.* 1944, Angela Vayianos. *Career:* Man. Dir. Dexion Hellas S.A.; Chmn. Panotex S.A. *Member:* Technical Chamber of Greece; Greek Assn. Civil Engineers; Assn. Greek Mfrs.; Greek Mangt. Assn.; British Inst. of Management. *Address:* 8 Ermon Street, Athens, Greece.

# L

**LABOUISSE, Henry Richardson.** *B.* 11 Feb. 1904. *Educ.* Princeton (AB) and Harvard (LLB). *M.* (1) 1935, Elizabeth Clark (*Dec.* 1945). (2) 1954, Eve Curie. *Dau.* Anne (Peretz). *Career:* Practised law 1929–41; with Dept. of State 1941–51; Assistant Chief, Division of Defense Materials 1941; Chief of Division 1943; Chief, Eastern Hemisphere Division 1944; Minister, Economic Affairs, U.S. Embassy, Paris 1945; Special Assistant to Under-Secretary of State for Economic Affairs 1946; Special Asst. to Dir., Office of European Affairs 1946; Head, U.S. Dele., E.C.E. 1948; Coordinator for Foreign Aid and Assistance 1948; Director, Office of British Commonwealth and Northern European Affairs 1949, Chief, Special Mission to France of Economic Co-operation Administration 1951; Chief, Mutual Security Agency Special Mission to France 1952; Dir., U.N. Relief and Works Agency for Palestine Refugees 1954; Consultant, International Bank for Reconstruction & Development 1959; Director, International Co-operation Administration 1961; U.S. Ambassador to Greece 1962–65. Executive Director of UNICEF 1965—. *Address:* c/o UNICEF, United Nations, New York City, U.S.A.

**LABROUSSE, Andre Georges.** French telecommunications engineer. *B.* 1905. *Educ.* Ecole Polytechnique, Ingénieur des Ecoles Supérieures d'Electricité de Radio-electricité et des Télécommunications. *M.* 1932, Jeanne Marchand. *S.* Alain (*Dec.*). Comdr., Legion of Honour. Engineer, P.T.T. 1926; Central Dir. of P.T.T. in Algiers 1944–53; Gen. Engineer 1st Class of Telecommunications 1951; Secy.-Gen. Ministry of Posts, Telegraphs and Telephones (P.T.T.) 1953–58; Hon. Secretary-General 1958. *Address:* 10 Avenue Alphand, Paris 16e, France.

**LABRUYERE, Maurice.** French. Commandeur of the Legion of Honour. B. 1906. *Educ.* Diploma, Ecole des Hauts Etudes Commerciales. *M.* 1936, Elisabeth Bergeaud. *S.* Jean-Pierre and Vincent. *Daus.* Marie-Ange and Christine. *Career:* Economic Adviser. Chmn.: Comití d'expansion régionale; Syndicat National des Distributeurs Grossistes en Alimentations—Administrator of the Socy. Chairman, Société des Ateliers Bergeaud (métallurgie). Macon; Chairman STOGAZ (Gaz liquéfiés). Rotary Club. *Address:* 2I du Stand, Rue Enstein–71009 Macon, France; and *office* 37 Avenue d'Iena, Paris 16 éme, France.

**LACHER, Hans,** Dr. iur. Retired Swiss diplomat. *B.* 8 Aug. 1912. *Educ.* Univ. of Basle and Paris. *M.* 1941, Daisy E. Bubeck. *S.* 1. *Career:* Attaché 1944, 2nd Sec. 1946; 2nd Chief of Section 1947; 1st Sec. 1948; Counsellor 1954; Head of Swiss Delegation in Berlin 1954; Ambassador to the Philippines 1961; Consul General, New York City 1963; Ambassador to Federal Republic of Germany 1969–75. *Address:* Au Thovex, 1807 Blonay, Switzerland.

**LACHS, Manfred.** Polish Professor, Diplomat, Judge. *B.* 21 April 1914; LLM, U. Cracow (Poland), 1936; LLD. 1937; docteur de l'Université de Nancy (France), DSc Law, University Moscow (USSR); *Career:* Prof. Acad. Polit. Sc., Warsaw, 1952; legal adviser Polish Ministry Internat. Affairs, 1947–66, ambassador, 1960–66; Chairman legal com. UN gen. assemblies, 1949, 51, 55, vice chairman, 1952; Member Permanent Court of Arbitration, The Hague since 1956. mem. Polish delegations UN gen. assemblies, 1946–52, 55–60, 62–66; rep. Poland UN-Disarmament Com., 1962–63; repporteur, gen. colloque, Internat. Assn. Juridical Scis., UNESCO, Rome, Italy 1948, Internat. Law. Commn. UN, 1962; Chairman legal com. UN Peaceful Uses of Outer Space, 1962–66; lectr. throughout Europe, U.S. Pres. International Court of Justice, The Hague 1973–76. *Member:* Hon. Member, Mexican Academy of International Law; men. UN Internat. Civil Service Adv. Board, 1959–66, UN International Law Commision, 1962–66. Titular member. The Polish Academy of Science and Academy of Bologna; mem. Inst. Internat. Law; Vice-Pres., Curatorium Hague Academy Internat Law; Board of Trustees, UN Institute for Training and Research; hon. mem. Internat. Acad. Astronautics, Indian Soc. Internat. Law, American Soc. of Internat. Law. *Awards:* for ednl. achievements Polish Ministry Edn., 1956, award outstanding contbns. devel. rule of law outer space International Aeronautical Federation, 1962, gold medal, 1966; World Jurist Award (Washington 1975). Director Institute Legal Science, Polish Acad. Sc., 1961–67; LLD (hon) Budapest (1967); Algiers (1969); Delhi (1969); Nice; Bucharest; Brussels; Halifax; New York; Southampton; Howard U. (Washington); Sofia; Vancouver; London. *Publications:* War Crimes (1945); The Geneva Agreements on Indo-china (1954); Multilateral Treaties (1958); The Law of Outer Space (1969); Polish-German Frontier (1965); The Law of Outer Space, An Experience for Law Making (1972; Spanish edn., Madrid & Mexico 1977), and over a hundred essays and articles in eleven languages. *Address:* International court of Justice, The Hague, Holland.

**LACOSTE, Francis.** French diplomat. *B.* 1905. *Educ.* School of Political Science; liberal arts degree. *M.* 1929, Paulette Garat. *Daus.* 4. *Career:* Entered Diplomatic Service 1929; Secretary of Embassy Belgrade (1932–36) and Peking (1936–39); mobilised 1939–40; served in the Resistance and in First French Army; Minister-Counsellor of Embassy, Washington 1945; Delegate to Residence-General, Morocco 1948; Delegate to Security Council, U.N., 1950–1953; Resident General of France, Morocco, 1954; Ambassador to Canada 1955–62; to Belgium 1962–63; Spec. Rep. of UN Secy. Gen., Chief of UN Relief Operation in Bangladesh 1973. *Awards:* Comdr., Legion of Honour; Croix de Guerre; U.S.A. Medal of Freedom. *Address:* Ithurri Gaina, Urrugne. 64, France; and 3 square Malherbe, 75016 Paris.

**LACOSTE, Jacques Francois.** Belgian. *B.* 1924. *Educ.* Univ. of Brussels (Cand. en Droit). *M.* 1954, Christiane Jean-Haut. *S.* Bernard and Jean-Paul. *Daus.* Brigitte and Marie-Francoise. *Career:* Co-Manager, Doxometric Ltd. (market research) 1949–60. Dir. Sample Survey Department, Belgian Society of Economic and Applied Mathematics, SOBEMAP, S.A. 1960–68. Member of Board, Analis, S.A., Namur 1957—. Manager, 1969, Pres. 1971; Member of Bd. Onnium Scientifique et Industriel de France, OSI S.A., Paris, 1968; Pres., 1972. *Member:* European Society for Public Opinion and Market Research—ESOMAR; Association of Officers of the Air Force Reserve. *Awards:* Officer, Order of the Crown; Chevalier, Order of Leopold; Escapers' Cross; War Volunteers' Medal, Commemorative Medal of 1940–45; Defence Medal *Publications:* numerous professional articles and lectures. *Club:* Rotary (Brussels) Cercle Royal Gaulois. *Address:* 18 Avenue de l'Orée, 1640, Rhode St. Genèse, Brussels, Belgium;

and *office* 14 Rue Derwez, 5000 Namur, 141 Rue de Javel, 75 Paris, 15.

**LADAS, Stephen Pericles.** International lawyer. *B.* 1898. *Educ.* School of Law, Univ. of Athens (DCL); Ecole des Sciences Politiques, Paris (Diplome); Harvard Law School (LLB and SJD). *M.* 1929, Christine Douropulos. *Daus.* Natalie and Cornelia. *Career:* Attaché, Legation of Greece, Paris 1921–23; Secy., Bureau of International Research, Harvard Univ. 1926–30; Partner Ladas, Parry, von Gen. Goldsmith & Deschamps since 1930, (foreign patents and trademarks). *Member:* Commission for Industrial Property, International Chamber of Commerce (Hon. Chmn.); International Association for Protection of Industrial Property (Treasurer); Exec. Committee, International Patent & Trademark Assn. (Hon. Member); American Friends of Greece; Harvard Law Assn.; American Bar Assn. Trustee, Athens College and Anatolia College. *Awards:* Silver Cross of the Saviour, and Commander, Order of the Phoenix (Greece). Corresponding Member: Academy of Athens, and Instituto Argentino de Derecho Internationale. Democrat. *Publications:* The International Protection of Trademarks in American Republics (1929); The International Protection of Industrial Property (1930); The International Protection of Literary and Artistic Property (1938); The Exchange of Minorities: Bulgaria, Greece and Turkey (1933); Patents, Trade-Marks and Related Rights—National and International Protection (3 vols) (1975). *Clubs:* Harvard, Athletic (N.Y.C.). *Address:* 960 Fifth Avenue, New York City 10021; and *office* 10 Columbus Circle, New York City, 10019. U.S.A.

**LADJEVARDI, Ahmad.** Iranian. *B.* 1920. *M.* 1946, Banoo Akram Barzin. *S.* 2. *Daus.* 2. *Career:* Pres. Bd. Member Chmn. of many companies since 1944 including Arien Trading Co. Ltd.; Behshahr Ind. Co. Ltd.; Container Corp. Iran; Iran Steel Building Corp.; Paxan Corp.; The Behshahr Industrial Group; Founder of Akam Group of Companies. *Member:* Nat. Cttee., Standardization, Food and Agricultural Produce; President Association Inc.; Iran Management Assn.; (Assoc. Mem.) Stanford Research Inst.; Int. Imede Alumni Assn.; Gov., Iran-American Chamber of Commerce; Vice-Chmn., Irano-British Chamber of Commerce; Trustee, Iran Rehabilitation Centre. *Club:* Imperial Country. *Address:* 147 Farmanieh Avenue, Dezashib, Tehran, Iran; and *office* 56 Sepahbod Zahedie Avenue, Tehran, Iran.

**LAFLEUR, Henri Grier,** QC. Lawyer. *B.* 1908. *Educ.* McGill Univ. (BA 1929) and Oxford Univ. (Rhodes Scholar; BA 1931; BCL 1932); called to the Bar, Inner Temple, London 1932, and Quebec 1933. *M.* 1952, Celia Frances Cantlie. *S.* (twins, by former marriage) Henri P. and Anthony J. *Career:* with Cook & Magee, Montreal 1933–37; Mann, Lafleur & Brown 1937–49; Councillor, Montreal 1939–46; Kings Counsel 1946; Vice-Pres. and Dir.: Canadian Ingersoll-Rand Co. 1942–73; Mann, Mathewson, Lafleur & Brown 1949–50; Dir. Continental Can Co. of Canada Ltd. 1950—; Mathewson, Lafleur & Brown 1950–55; Lafleur, Brown & Pitcher 1955–57; Lafleur, Brown, Pitcher, Boulton & Lamb 1957–60; Lafleur, Brown, Pitcher, Boulton, Lamb, Culver & Chassé 1960–62; Partner, Lafleur & Brown, Montreal 1962–73. Rhodes Scholar 1929–32. *Member:* Canadian Bar Assn.; Quebec Bar; English Bar (Inner Temple). *Clubs:* Mount Royal, Montreal Racket; Canadian (N.Y.C.); Orleans Fish & Game. *Address:* 337 Metcalfe Avenue, Westmount, Quebec H3Z 2J2; and *office:* Box 214, Stock Exchange Tower, 800 Victoria Square, Montreal 115, Quebec H4Z IE4, Canada.

**LAIDLAW, Christopher Charles Fraser,** British oil co. dir. *B* 1922. *Educ.* Rugby; St. John's College Cambridge. *M.* 1952, Nina Mary. *S.* 1. *Daus.* 3. *Career:* War service in Europe and Far East (Major on Gen. Staff) 1939–45; Joined British Petroleum Co. Ltd. 1948; B.P. Representative in Hamburg 1959–61; Gen. Manager, Marketing Dept. 1963–67; Dir. B.P Trading 1967; Director, (Operations) 1971–72; Man. Dir., The British Petroleum Co. Ltd. since 1972; also Pres. B.P. Belgium 1967–71; Pres. B.P. Italiana 1972–73; Pres. Deutsche B.P.A.G. since 1972; Pres. Societe Industrielle Belge des Petroles since 1975. *Address:* 49 Chelsea Square, London SW3 6LH; and *office* British Petroleum Co. Ltd., Britannic House, Moor Lane, London E.C.2.

**LAINE, Jermu Tapani.** Finnish politician. *B.* 1931. *Educ.* Master of Law. *M.* 1954, Terttu Anneli. *Daus.* 3. *Career:* Notary, ombudsman, secy. and senior referendary, temp. asst. chief of bureau 1954–61; Sen. Govt. Secy. 1961–65; Commercial counsellor since 1961; Teacher of commercial law and theory of commerce, Valkeakoski Coll. 1965–69; Head Mänttä Commercial Coll. 1969–73; Polit. Secy. of Prime Minister 1972–73; Town counsellor, Valkeakoski 1968–69; Town counsellor Mänttä since 1973; Minister (Min. Trade and Industry & Foreign Affairs) 1973–75. *Chmn.* of several state cttees., and mem. or secy. of others. *Publications:* (in Finnish), Living in Work and Equality (1971); Basics of Economic Policy (1972); The Economic Policy Line of the Social Democratic Party (part-author); several technical articles. *Address:* Haapaneimenkatu 20 D 60, 00530 Helsinki 53.

**LAING, Hon. Arthur,** PC, MP, BSA. Canadian. *B.* 1904. *Educ.* BSc Agr. 1925. *M.* 1938, E. Geraldine Hyland. *Dau.* Mrs. Linda Laureen Billingsley. *Career:* Manager, Agricultural Chemicals Div., Buckerfield's Ltd., Vancouver 1933–51; MP Vancouver South 1949–53 and 1962—; Leader, British Columbia Liberal Party 1953–59; Member, Provincial Legislature 1953–56; Minister, Northern Affairs and National Resources 1963–66; Minister India Affairs; Northern Development 1966–68; Minister, Public Works 1968–72; Veterens Affairs 1972; Appointed to the Senate of Canada 1972. *Member:* Agricultural Inst. of Canada; United Church of Canada; Phi Kappa Pi; Sigma Tau Upsilon. *Address:* 5937 Angus Drive Vancouver 13, B.C.; and *office* The Senate, Ottawa, Ont., Canada.

**LAING, Sir (John) Maurice,** Kt 1965. Chmn., John Laing and Son Ltd.; John Laing Construction Ltd., Dir., Bank of England. *B.* 1918. *Educ.* St. Lawrence Coll., Ramsgate. *M.* 1940, Hilda Violet Richards. *S.* 1. *Career:* RAF 1941–45; U.K. Trade Mission to Middle East 1953, to Egypt, Sudan and Ethiopia 1955; Economic Planning Board 1961; Export Credits Guarantees Adv. Council 1959–63; Ministry of Transport Cttee. of Inquiry into Major Ports of Great Britain (Rochdale Cttee.) 1961–62; NEDC 1962–66. Vice-Pres., Federation of Civil Engineering Contractors 1960— (Chmn. 1959–60); President: British Employers Confederation 1964–65; Confederation of British Industry 1965–66; Export Group for the Constructional Industries 1976— (Chmn. 1957–59). Visiting Fellow, Nuffield Coll., 1965–70; Gov., Administrative Staff Coll., 1966–72; National Inst. of Economic & Social Research 1964—. Hon. LLD, Univ. of Strathclyde 1967. Commodore of the Royal Ocean Racing Club 1973–75, Admiral 1976—. *Clubs:* Royal Yacht Squadron; Royal Ocean Racing; Royal Burnham Yacht; Royal Southern Yacht. *Address:* Reculver, 63 Totteridge Village, London, N2O 8AG.

**LAIRD, Edgar Ord.** CMG, MBE, BA. British diplomat (Ret'd.). *B.* 1915. Educ. Rossall Emmanuel Coll. Cambridge (BA). *M.* 1940, Heather Lonsdale Forrest. *Davs.* 4. *Career:* Surveyor, Uganda Protectorate 1939; Served in Army (Major) 1939–46; Appointed, Malayan Civil Service 1947; Secy. to Govt. Federation of Malaya 1953–55; Secy. for External Defence 1956; Secy. Fed. of Malaya Constitutional Commission 1956–57; Deputy Secy. Prime Ministers Dept. Fed. of Malaya 1957; Appointed Commonwealth Relations Office 1958; First Secy. (Finance) British High Commission Ottawa 1960–63; High Commissioner in Brunei 1963–65; Deputy High Commissioner Kaduna, Nigeria 1965–69; Foreign & Commonwealth Office 1970–72; British Govt. Representative Assoc. States West Indies 1972–75. *Awards:* Companion Order of St Michael and St George; Order of the British Empire; Bachelor of Arts. *Clubs:* Royal Commonwealth Society. *Address:* Clarendon House, 33 The Strand, Topsham, Exeter EX3 0AY.

**LAIRD, Melvin R.** American Statesman. *B.* 1922. *Educ.* Marshfield, Wisconsin public schools; BA Carleton Coll., Northfield, Minnesota, 1944. *M.* 1945, Barbara Masters. *S.* John Osborn and David Malcolm. *Dau.* Alison. *Career:* U.S. Navy, 1942–46; Elected to the Wisconsin State Senate 1946–52; Chmn., Wisconsin Legislative Council; Mem. of Congress, 1952–69; Secy. of Defence 1969–73, Committee work in Congress, areas of national security, education and health; Served on the House Appropriations Committee, House Committee on Agriculture, various sub-Committees including Defense, Labor, Health, Education, Welfare and Military Construction. Chmn. of the House Republican Conference; member Coordinating Cttee; Counsellor to the President for Domestic Affairs 1973–74; Senior Counsellor for National and Internat. Affairs, Reader's Digest; Bd. of Dirs., Chicago Pneumatic Tool Co., Metropolitan Life Insurance Co., Northwest Airlines, Communications Satellite Corp., Purolator Inc., Investors Group of Companies, Phillips Petroleum Co. *Member:* Bd. of Trustees, George Washington Univ., & the Kennedy Center; Bd. of Dirs., Wolf Trap Foundation for the Performing Arts & Travel Program for

Foreign Diplomats, Chmn., American Enterprise Institute National Defense Project. *Publications:* Several books and articles dealing with public policy. *Awards:* Numerous honours including 15th Annual Albert Lasker Medical Research; Distinguished Service. American Political Science Assn. in the 90th Congress; Presidential Citation of the 21,000 members Amer. Public Health Assn. and the Distinguished Service Award of the National Education Association; John E. Fogarty Foundation for Mentally Retarded, Award, (1974); Medal of Freedom. *Address:* P.O. Box 279, Marshfield, Wis. 54449, U.S.A.

**LAKE, Francis Wilbur.** American oil executive. *B.* 1900. *Educ.* Cornell University. *M.* Mary E. Scaff Halbouty. *S.* Michael K. *Career:* Geologist, Standard Oil Co. of California in California, Texas and Mexico 1922; General Superintendent, Union Oil Co. of California, in California, to 1933; Consulting Engineer and Geologist in California, Texas, Colorado and Wyoming to 1942; Vice-Pres. and Dir., Wilshire Oil Co., Inc. to 1953; Executive Vice-Pres., Wilshire Oil Co. of Texas; Dir., Britalta Petroleums Ltd. (Calgary, Canada): Regional Vice-Pres., Cornell Alumni Class 22. *Member:* Wildcatter's Congress, Inc.; Independent Petroleum Assn.; New Mexico Oil & Gas Assn.; Cornell Soc. of Engineers; American Petroleum Institute; Mid-Continent Oil & Gas Assn.; Society of American Military Engineers. *Publications:* Petroleum Engineering; articles to various scientific journals. *Clubs:* Petroleum (Los Angeles); Petroleum (Midland); Midland Country; Voyagers Yacht. *Address:* 711 Sandy Mountain Drive, Sunrise Beach, Llano, Tex. 78643, U.S.A.

**LAKING, George Robert,** CMG. *B.* 1912. *Educ.* Auckland University & Victoria University of Wellington (LLB). *M.* 1940, Alice Evelyn Patricia Hogg. *S.* Robert George. *Dau.* Mary Alice. *Career:* Prime Minister's and External Affairs Department 1940–49; Counsellor, N.Z. Embassy, Washington 1949–54; Minister, Washington 1954–56; Deputy Secretary of External Affairs, Wellington 1956–58; Ambassador to European Economic Community 1960; High Commissioner for New Zealand (Actg.) in London 1958–61; Ambassador to U.S.A. 1961–67. Secy. of Foreign Affairs and Permanent Head of the Prime Minister's Department 1967–72; Business Consultant 1973–75; Ombudsman 1975–77; Chief Ombudsman 1977—; Privacy Commissioner 1977—. *Address:* 3 Wesley Road, Wellington, C.1, New Zealand.

**LAL, Muni.** Indian. *B.* 1913. *Educ.* Punjab University (MA Philosophy; BA History & Economics). *M.* 1939, Shivan. *S.* Akash, Jeevak. *Career:* Member, editorial staff, Civil & Military Gazette, Lahore, 1935–47; Joined Foreign Service, 1947; Press Attaché, Lahore, 1947–51; First Secretary (Information). Australia, 1951–54; Director, Information Services, Washington, 1954–56; Public Relations Officer: Djakarta, 1956–58; London, 1958–61; Deputy Secretary, Ministry of External Affairs, New Delhi, 1961–63; Director, Ministry of External Affairs, 1963–64; Controller-General of Emigration, 1964; High Commissioner in Trinidad, 1964–69; Member, Indian Delegation to Commonwealth Finance Ministers Conference 1967; Ambassador to the Republic of Somalia (retd.) 1971; with Consilium Private Limited since 1971. *Publications:* Schopenhauer—the Sage of Frankfurt (1936); Haryana—on High Road to Progress (1973); Profile of a Chief Minister—Biography of Bansi Lal (1974); Babar—Life & Times (1976); Humayun (1977); Crickinia (published annually 1936–47). *Club:* Delhi Gymkhana. *Address:* Street E-6/5, Vasant Vihar, New Delhi, 110057, India.

**LALKAKA, Rustan D.** Indian. *B.* 1928. *Educ.* BSc (India); BS and MS (Met. Eng.) Stanford University, U.S.A. *M.* 1955, Phiroza Billimoria. *S.* Dinyar. *Career:* Worked with U.S. Bureau of Mines on pilot plants for production of sponge titanium and ore benefication; joined IBCON. Industrial Consultants, 1953 and worked on steel-making and foundry problems, with special reference to layout and work simplification studies; Dir. and Project Manager, M. N. Dastur & Co. Private Ltd.; Consulting Engineers, Calcutta 1955–71; Regional Adviser, United Nations Economic Commission for Asia, Far East Bangkok since 1972. *Awards:* Scroll of Honour, Iron and Steel Insts. London (1963) and Latin-America (1968). *Member:* Indian Inst. of Metals; Institution of Engineers (India); Inst. of Indian Foundrymen; Iron and Steel Inst., London; Amer. Socy. of Metals; Amer. Inst. of Mining, Metall. & Petroleum Engrs.; Assn. of Iron & Steel Engrs., U.S.A.; German Iron & Steel Institute. *Publications:* a number of technical papers. *Club:* Calcutta. *Address:* Regional Adviser, United Nations Economic Commission, Asia & Far East, Bangkok, Thailand.

**LALL, Krishen Behari.** *B.* 1915. *Educ.* St. Stephen Coll., Delhi; School of Oriental Studies and Middle Temple Inn, London; and University Coll. Oxford. *M.* 1935, Indrani Lall. *S.* Ashok Behari and Rajiv Behari. *Daus.* Veenu and Ranjana. *Career:* Joined Indian Civil Service 1937. Servied in Madhya Pradesh until 1944; Dep. Secretary, Ministry of Commerce and Industry 1945–46, and Partition Secretariat; Member-Secy., Indian Deleg. to Post-Partition Inter-Dominion Conf. 1947–48; Secy. Delhi Emergency Committee; Administrator for former United States of Matsya 1948–49; Chief Secy., Madhya Bharat 1949–52; Chief Controller, Imports and Exports 1953–54; Alternate Delegate to 10th, 11th and 12th sessions of ECAFE; Member, Indian Delegation to Asia-Africa Conf., Bandung 1955; successively Joint Secretary, Additional Secretary, Min. of Commerce and Industry 1959–61 and Special Secretary, Min. of Finance Sept.–Dec. 1961; Ambassador of India to Belgium & EEC 1962–66; Secy., Min. of Commerce 1966–70; Principal Secy., Min. of Defence 1970–73; Ambassador to Belgium & Special Envoy for Economic Affairs to West Europe since 1973. Chairman, Foreign Trade Board 1957–60; Founder Chmn. State Trading Corp. 1956–59. Leader, Trade Delegations to United States 1958, U.S.S.R., German Democratic Repub. and Poland, Oct.–Nov. 1958; to West European countries Sept.–Oct. 1958, and to Nepal Sept. 1960; Chief of India Mission to the E.E.C. 1962–66; Chmn. Group of 77 1964; Permanent Representative of India to GATT, Chmn., GATT, 1966–67. Dep. Leader, Indian Delegation to UNCTAD II (1968), and to Third Asian Ministers Conference (1968); Chief Co-ordinator Indo-Iran Commission; Chief Consultant to ECAFE on Asian Regional Cooperation 1969. Chief Indian Delegate, Economic Cttee. Non Aligned Powers Conference, Lusaka 1970; and Algiers (1973) Chief Co-ordinator, Tripartite Ministers Meeting, Belgrade 1970; Founder Chmn., Trade Development Authority 1970. *Address:* Embassy of India, Avenue Molière 121, 1180 Brussels, Belgium.

**LALOR, Patrick Joseph,** TD. Parly. Sec. to the Taoiseach (Prime Minister) & to the Minister for Defence in the Govt. of Ireland. *B.* 1926. *Educ.* Patrician Brothers School, Abbeyleix; Knockbeg Coll., Carlow. *M.* 1952, Myra Murphy. *S.* Joseph. *Daus.* Frances, Helen and Veronica. *Career:* Member of Parliament for Laois Offaly since 1961; Parly. Secy. to the Minister for Agriculture & Fisheries, 1965–66; Transport & Power, Posts and Telegraphs, 1966–69; Minister for Posts & Telegraphs, 1969–70; Minister for Industry and Commerce 1970–73. *Address:* Main Street, Abbeyleix, County Laois; and *office* Government Buildings, Upper Merrion Street, Dublin, Eire.

**LALOVIC, Milos.** Yugoslavian. *B.* 1921. *Educ.* Faculté Economique. *M.* 1954, Borislava Nesovic. *S.* 2. *Daus.* 2. *Career:* Deputy Minister, Foreign Trade, 1947–51; Deputy Min., Pres. Cncl. Federal of Commerce (Interior) 1951–53; Envoy Extraordinary and Min. Plen. to Lebanon 1954–59; Ambassador in Tunisia 1960–64; Ambassador to the Secretariat of State for Foreign Affairs— au poste du Directeur Général de la Direction pour les relations économiques avec étranger—1964–67. Ambassador Extraordinary and Plenipotentiary of Yugoslavia to Belgium and Luxembourg 1967–71; Asst. Minister for Foreign Affairs 1971–74; Amb. Ex. & Plen., Perm. Rep. of the SFR of Yugoslavia to the Office of the UN, Geneva since 1974. *Publications:* A work on the foreign trade of Yugoslavia; many articles in economic and political journals. *Awards:* Medaille Commemorative 1941, and other Yugoslav and foreign honours. *Address:* 5 Chemin Thury, 1206 Geneva; & 22A Chemin du Bouchet, 1211 Geneva, Switzerland.

**LAMB, Albert.** British. *B.* 1929. *M.* 1953, Joan Mary Denise. *S.* Richard Llewelyn. Nicholas Maxwell. *Dau.* Jacqueline Victoria. *Career:* Northern Editor, Daily Mail, Manchester; Editorial Dir. News International Ltd; Editor of Sun since 1969. *Address:* 5 Durward House, 31 Kensington Court, London W8. and *office* 30 Bouverie Street, London, E.C.4.

**LAMB, Stewart Peter Paulsen.** Australian company director (broadcasting). *B.* 1917. *Educ.* Newcastle Boy's High School and Scots College, Sydney. *M.* 1940. Winifred McVittie. *Daus.* Elizabeth and Susan. *Career:* Chairman & Managing Director: Radio 2UE Sydney Pty. Ltd. 1957—; United Broadcasting Co. Pty. Ltd. 1947—; Radio 2KO Newcastle Pty. Limited 1947—; W.C.O. & Finance Co. Ltd. 1944—. *Clubs:* Australian; Royal Sydney Yacht Squadron; American National; Newcastle. *Address:* 10 Bangalla Street, Warrawee, N.S.W., 2074; and *office* c/o Radio 2UE Sydney Pty. Ltd., 237 Miller Street, North Sydney, N.S.W., 2060, Australia.

**LAMB, William Kaye.** Canadian government official, archivist. *B.* 11 May 1904. *Educ.* Univ. of British Columbia (MA); Univ. of London (PhD). *M.* 1939, Wessie M. Tipping. *Dau.* Barbara Elizabeth. *Career:* Provincial Librarian and Archivist, Provincial Library and Archives, Victoria, British Columbia 1934–40; Superintendent, Public Library Commission of British Columbia 1936–40, member, 1943–48; Librarian, Univ. of British Columbia 1940–48; Dominion Archivist, Public Archives of Canada 1948–69. National Librarian of Canada 1953–68. Hon. LLD, Univs. of British Columbia, Manitoba, Toronto, Assumption, Saskatchewan, York Univ., Univ. of New Brunswick and Univ. of Victoria; Hon. DLitt S, Victoria Univ. F.R.S.C. Officer, Order of Canada 1969; Tyrrell Medal (Royal Society of Canada) 1965. *Address:* 2055 Pendrell Street, Vancouver V6G 1T9, B.C., Canada.

**LAMBERT, Allen Thomas,** OC. Canadian. *B.*1911. *Educ.* Public and High School, Victoria. *Career:* Joined Toronto-Dominion Bank, 1927; Mgr. Yellowknife 1946, Insp. 1947, Gen. Mgr. 1956, Vice-Pres. and Dir., The Toronto-Dominion Bank 1956. Pres., The Toronto-Dominion Bank 1960, Chmn. of the Board 1961, Chmn. Chief Exec. Officer 1972; Chmn. of Bd. & Dir., The Toronto-Dominion Bank Trust Co.; Pacific Centre Ltd. Toronto-Dominion Centre Ltd.; Toronto-Dominion Bank Investments (U.K.) Ltd.; Toronto-Dominion Centre West Ltd.; Vice-Chmn. & Dir. International Consolidated Investments Ltd. Hong-Kong. Dir. Adela Investment Co. (SA); Arbuthnot Latham Holdings Ltd.; Canadian International Paper Co.; Canadian World Wildlife Fund; Continental Corp.; Dome Mines Ltd.; Dominion Insurance Corp.; Edmonton Centre Ltd.; Hiram Walker-Gooderham & Worts Ltd.; I.B.M. Canada Ltd.; Hudson Bay Mining & Smelting Co.; The International Nickel Co. of Canada Ltd.; London Life Insurance Co.; Union Carbide Corp.; Union Carbide Canada Ltd.; Westinghouse Canada Ltd.; Ontario Hydro; Toronto Dominion Bank; Midland and International Banks Ltd.; International Monetary Conf.; Private Investment Corp. of Asia; President & Director, Toronto Dominion Realty Col Ltd.; Member, Board of Governors, York University; Hon. Trustee, the Upper Canada College Foundation. *Clubs:* Toronto, Toronto Golf, Rosedale Golf, Granite, York, Mount Royal (Montreal); Toronto Hunt. *Address: office* 55 King Street West, Toronto M5K 1A2, Ont., Canada.

**LAMBERT, Baron Léon Jean Gustave.** Belgian Banker. *B.* 1928. *Educ.* Yale, Oxford and Geneva Universities and Inst. of International Studies, Geneva (Lic. Polit. Sc. Geneva Univ. and Inst. High International Studies Geneva). *Career:* Pres. Groupe Bruxelles Lambert S.A.; Compagnie de Constructions Civiles; La Concorde, S.A.; Manufacture Belge de Lampes et de Matériel Electronique; Institut de Médecine Social Baronne Lambert, A.S.B.L.; The Lambert Brussels Corp. New York; Artemis S.A. Luxembourg: *Administrateur* Magnum Fund Ltd.; GB Inno-BM S.A.; Compagnie Auxilaire Internationale de Chemin de Fer, Petrofina, Banca d'America e d'Italia, New Court Securities Corp. *Vice-President:* Banque Bruxelles Lambert S.A.; Electrobel S.A.; Member of general council of Assicurazioni Generali, Trieste. Director, Philharmonique de Bruxelles and Le Musée du Cinéma. *Awards:* Officer, Order of Léopold; Grand Ufficiale al Merito della Republica Italiana, Commander de l'Ordre de la Valeur du Cameroun, Das Grosse Goldene Ehrenzeichen (Austria). *Club:* Yale. *Address:* 24 Avenue Marnix 1050, Brussels, Belgium.

**LAMBERT, Walter Heath.** Australian. *B.* 1920. *Educ.* State Commercial High College (Brisbane); FAIM; FAMI. *M.* Joan Moriarty. *S.* Ian Heath. *Dau.* Kerry-Ann. *Career:* With Prudential Assurance: joined Brisbane Office 1936; Queensland Life Branch Manager 1952–61; Board of Head Office Management 1961—; Gen. Mgr. for Australia & New Zealand 1976—. President Brisbane Chamber of Commerce and member of Council of Management, Associated Chambers of Commerce of Australia 1960–61 and 1967–71; Dep. Pres., Australian Chamber of Commerce 1969–71; Pres., Sydney Chamber of Commerce, Aug. 1967–69. *Member:* Council of Taxpayers' Association, N.S.W. 1965–75, Convocation, Macquarie University, Sydney, 1966—. Council and Exec. of University of N.S.W. 1969–77. Exec. Council, Royal Flying Doctor Service, Queensland 1952–61. Sydney Group on the International Study and Training Programme on Metropolitan Problems. Mar. 1967–69. Exec. Member, Road Safety Council 1965–67; Chmn. Exec. Cttee., Life Offices Assn. Australia 1972–73. Justice of the Peace (Queensland and New South Wales). *Clubs:* Tattersall's (Sydney); Royal Sydney Yacht Squadron; N.S.W. Leagues; New Zealand; Warrawee Bowling. *Address:* 25 Greendale Ave., St. Ives, Sydney, N.S.W. 2075, Australia; and *office* 39–49 Martin Place, Sydney, N.S.W., Australia.

**LAMBO, Thomas Adeoye.** OBE, DPM, MD. Nigerian psychiatrist. *B.* 1923. *Educ.* Baptist High School, Abeokuta; Birmingham Univ., London University. *M.* 1945, Dinah Violet Adams. *S.* 3. *Career:* House Surgeon 1949, House Physician Birmingham 1950; Medical Officer Gen. Hospital Lagos 1950, (In Charge) Zaria 1951, General Hospital Gusav 1951–52; Special Grade 1953; Consultant Psychiatrist, Univ. Coll. Hospital Ibadan, Assoc. Lecturer, Univ. of Ibadan 1956; Specialist 1957, Senior Specialist Western Reg. Min. of Health 1960; Professor, Psychiatry, Head, Dept. Univ. of Ibadan 1963–74; Dean Medical School, Univ. of Ibadan 1966–68; Vice-Chancellor 1968–71; Asst. Dir.-Gen. 1971–73, Deputy Director-General, World Health Organization since 1973. *Member:* Adv. Scientific Panel. Centre, Advanced Study, Development Sciences; Hon. member Swiss Academy, Medical Sciences; Exec. Cttee. World Fed. Mental Health; Vice Pres. World Assn. Social Psychiatry; Co-Chmn. Int. Socy. Study Human Devel; Nigeria Medical Council; Pontifical Acad. of Sciences. *Awards:* Hon. DSC. Ahmadu Bellow Univ; Hon. LLD Kent State Univ. Birmingham Univ; Haile Selassie African Research; Doctor Honoris Causa, Univ. Dahomey; Univ. Aix-Marseille, France; Long Island Univ., N.Y.; Louvain Univ., Belgium. *Publications:* The Role of Cultural Factors in Paranoid Psychoses Among the Yoruba Tribe (1955); Traditional African Cultures and Western Medicine (1969), and numerous medical and Scientific monographs. *Address:* 27 chemin des Châtaigniers, 1292 Chambèsy-Geneva, Switzerland; and *office:* Deputy Director General, World Health Organisation, Geneva, Switzerland.

**LAMONT, Donald Breck.** American. *B.* 1919. *Educ.* Phillips Exeter Academy; Yale Univ. (BA); Harvard Business School (MBA). *M.* 1948, Patricia Rice (*Div.*). *Daus.* Pamela Jane and Susan Rice. *Career:* Vice-Pres. and Dir., United Canso Oil & Gas Co. 1959–64; President and Director, Pancoastal Inc. 1968–69; Vice-Pres. and Director: Pantepec International Inc. 1964–69, San Jose Oil Co. (Manila) 1959–69; Director: Canada Southern Petroleum Ltd. 1964–69, Magellen Petroleum Australia Ltd. 1965–69; Dir., Pan Ocean Oil Corp. 1970–72; Chmn. of the Board, Nepco Exploration Corp., an Affiliate of New England Petroleum Corp., Chmn., Interocean Oil Royalties since 1971. Major (retd.), U.S. Marine Corps. Member, Amer. Petroleum Inst. Republican. *Clubs:* Racquet and Tennis (N.Y.); Yale (N.Y.); Lunch (N.Y.); Country (New Canaan, Conn.). *Address:* 3 Taconic Road, Greenwich, Conn. 06830; and *office* 825 3rd Avenue, New York, N.Y. 10022, U.S.A.

**LAMONT, Norman Stewart Hughson,** MP. British Politician and Banker. *B.* 1942. *Educ.* Loretto Sch., Musselburgh, Midlothian (scholar); Fitzwilliam Coll., Cambridge—BA (Econ.). *M.* 1971, Rosemary White. *S.* 1. *Career:* Pres., Cambridge Union 1965; Merchant Banker, N. M. Rothschild & Sons since 1968; MP (Cons.) for Kingston-upon-Thames since 1972; an Opposition Spokesman on Prices & Consumer Affairs 1975–76, on Industry since 1976. *Member:* Chmn., Bow Group, 1972. *Publications:* Articles in The Times & other newspapers. *Club:* Carlton. *Address:* 30 Fentiman Road, London SW8.

**LAND, Gay Vallee.** American. Vice-President, Celanese Corp. *B.* 1924. *Educ.* Massachusetts Inst. of Technology (BS Chem.Eng.) and Wharton School of Finance, Univ. of Pennsylvania (MBA). *M.* 1945, Elizabeth Edna Cooper. *S.* David and Stephen. *Daus.* Eleanor and Cynthia. *Career:* Vice-Pres. American Metal Climax 1958; Pres. and Dir.; American Climax Petroleum Corp. 1958, and Camerina Petroleum Corp. 1959; General Partner, Lambert & Co. 1960; Chmn. of Board, Chatham Corp. 1960; Vice-Pres., Lambert Internl. Corp. 1963. Vice-Pres., Southern Natural Gas Co. 1969. *Member:* Amer. Inst of Mining, Metallurgical & Petroleum Engineers; Marine Technology Socy. *Clubs:* Cedar Point Yacht; N.Y. Yacht; Metropolitan; Windham Mountain. *Address: office* 1211 Avenue of the Americas, New York City, U.S.A.

**LAND, James Neville, Sr.** *B.* 1895. *Educ.* Daniel Baker Coll., Brownwood, Tex. (BA 1915) and Princeton Univ. (MA 1917). *M.* 1918, Frances Rebecca Hoon. *S.* Robert Edward and James Neville, Jr. *Daus.* Jane (Hudson) and Marjorie (Eshleman). *Career:* Teacher, Brownwood High School 1915–16. U.S. Navy 1918–19; except for this year in the U.S. Navy was with Guaranty Trust Co. of New York and its subsidiary, Guaranty Co. of New York 1917–34 (Manager, Public Utility Div. 1927; Second Vice-Pres., G. Co. of N.Y

1929); with Edward B. Smith & Co. 1934–37 (Partner 1935); Partner, Smith, Barney & Co. 1938; Vice-President, Mellon Securities Corp. 1938–46; with Mellon National Bank & Trust Co. as Vice-Pres. 1948–53, and Senior Vice-Pres. from 1953 to retirement in 1960. Supervisor, Colerain Township, Bedford County, Pa. 1962–68. Launched and was first Editor of Mellon National Bank & Trust Company's publication, Monetary Indicators. Director: Equitable Gas Co. 1950–73, Crucible Steel Co. of America 1959–63, The First Boston Corp. 1960–67; Consultant, Mellon National Bank & Trust Co. 1960–64. Trustee and Treasurer, Memorial Hosp. of Bedford County 1963—. *Address:* Route 4, Box 193, Bedford, Pa. 15522, U.S.A.

**LANDA, Alfonso.** Chevalier of the Order of St. Sepulchre; American business executive and attorney. *B.* 1897. *Educ.* Georgetown Univ. (U.S.A.); George Washington Univ. (LLB 1925); Oxford Univ., England. *M.* 1959, Alexandra Francesca. *S.* Alfonso. *Career:* Senior Partner: Davies, Richberg, Tydings Landa & Duff (began with law firm Joseph E. Davies 1926; partner 1935). Director: Florida Capital Corp. 1960–71. President and Director, Marquis Who's Who 1959–69; Vice-President and Director, Walker & Dunlop 1937; Director: American Inst. of Management 1948— (Pres. 1959–62), Fruehauf Trailer Co. 1942–71, Doehla Greeting Cards 1956–70. Formerly: Pres. & Dir.: Colonial Airlines 1951, Detroit & Cleveland Navigation Co. 1954; Dir.: Crane Co. 1959–60; General Fireproofing Co. 1961–62; Chmn. & Dir.: Baruch Foster Corp. 1955–62, Fairbanks Morse & Co. 1958–62; Chmn. Exec. Cttee. & Director: Fairbanks Whitney Corp. 1959–62; Atomics, Physics & Science Fund 1953–63; Shares in American Industry, Inc., 1950–63. *Clubs:* Brook, Racquet & Tennis (N.Y.C.); Everglades, Bath & Tennis, Seminole Palm Beach); Travellers (Paris). *Address:* 150 El Vedado Way, Palm Beach Fla.; and *office* 1125 Fifteenth Street, N.W., Washington 5, D.C., U.S.A.

**LANDA, Louis A.** Professor English Literature, Princeton University, 1954. *B.* 1901. *Educ.* Univ. of Texas (BA); Columbia Univ. (MA); Univ. of Chicago (PhD). *M.* 1928, Hazel Schaeffer. *Career:* Instructor of English, Univ. of Texas, 1926–28; Instructor and Asst. Professor of English, Univ. of Chicago, 1930–45; Associate Professor of English, Princeton Univ., 1946–53. Guggenheim Fellow, 1947–48; Fulbright Fellow and Lecturer at Oxford, 1952–53; Fellow of the Council of Humanities, Princeton Univ. 1956–57. Visiting Lecturer Australian Universities 1970. *Publications:* Swift and the Church of Ireland; English Literature, 1660–1800: A Bibliography; Gulliver's Travels and Other Writings; other books and articles on English literature of the 18th century. Edit. Adv. Board: Augustan Reprint Socy., Clarendon Press Edition of works of Henry Fielding, Huntington Library Quarterly, Essays in Literature. *Fellow:* Royal Historical Socy.; Modern Language Assn. of America; Amer. Assn. of University Professors. *Address:* 12 Regatta Row, Princeton, N.J.; and *office* 22 McCosh Hall, Princeton Univ., Princeton, N.J., U.S.A.

**LANDA, Maynard I.** Petroleum executive. *Educ.* Texas A. & M. (BS Elec. Eng.); graduate study in Business Administration, Economics and Corporation Finance at Columbia and New York Universities. *M.* 1934, Amanda V. Van Der Voort. *Career:* With Cities Services Co. 1919—; at Bartlesville, Okla. 1919–25; successively Junior Engineer Training Program, Operating Budget Engineer, Production Engineer, Oil Production Mid-Continent Field, Oil Operations Arkansas and Texas, Assistant to Manager of Oil Production Dept., N.Y.C. Headquarters 1925; Oil Operation Analyst 1925–35; Earnings Development Promotion—Marketing Companies 1936–41; Staff Engineer; Asst. to President of Petroleum Advisers 1941–51; Associate Petroleum Economics Co-ordinator 1951–53; Petroleum Economics Co-ordinator 1953–60; Vice-President 1960—. Asst. City Engineer, Cushing Okla.; rest of career entirely with Cities Service. Elected to Board of Dirs., Hudson Valley Assn. 1967. Chmn. of Finance since 1970. *Awards:* Certificate of Appreciation (Amer. Petroleum Inst.). *Member:* Amer. Legion; Amer. Inst. of Mining, Metallurgical & Petroleum Engineers; Amer. Economics Assn.; Amer. Marketing Assn.; Amer. Statistical Assn.; Amer. Petroleum Inst. (Statistical Adv. Cttee. 1940–57; Chmn. 1957); Chmn. Cttee. on Petroleum Statistics 1958–59; Marketing Research Cttee., Natl. Petroleum Council Technical Cttee. on Petroleum Storage; N.Y. Socy. of Security Analysts; Oil Analysis Group of N.Y.; Treas. Chmn. of Finance, Dir., National Sculpture Socy. since 1973. *Publications:* Major Oil Companies Pipeline Resumé; Corporate Structure Major Oil Companies; Resumé of Major Oil Companies; Major Interstate Natural Gas Transmission Companies; Oil Marketing Research; articles in trade papers and publications. *Clubs:* Bankers (of America); Texas A & M; Sixty. *Address:* 17 Stonehedge Drive South, Greenwich, Conn. 06830; and *office* 60 Wall Tower, New York City 5, U.S.A.

**LANDEGGER, Carl C.** American. *B.* 1930. *Educ.* Georgetown Univ. (BSoc Sc). *M.* 1951, Cecilla Elizalde. *S.* Carl M., Cary P. *Daus.* Christine E., Claudia M., Celia M. *Career:* Chmn., Parsons & Whittemore Inc. Pres., Black Clawson Company; Prince Albert Pulp Co. Ltd.; St Anne-Nackawi Pulp & Paper Co. Ltd. *Member:* Bd. of Regents, Georgetown University. *Clubs:* Explorers'. *Address: office* 200 Park Avenue, New York 10017, U.S.A.

**LANDIS, John William.** Industrial executive. *B.* 1917. *Educ.* Lafayette Coll. (BS in Engg. Physics 1939; Hon. DSc 1960); Grad. work in Physics: Univ. of Rochester 1940–41, and Princeton Univ. 1946–48. *M.* 1941, Muriel Trayes Souders. *Daus.* Maureen Lucille and Marcia Millicent. *Career:* Res. Eng., Eastman Kodak Co. 1939–43; Officer, U.S.N. 1943–46; Consultant in Guided Missiles, Navy Dept. 1946–50; Head of Science and Engineering Test Development, Educational Testing Service 1948–50; Reactor and Project Engineer, U.S. Atomic Energy Commission 1950–53: Head of Customer Relations, A.E. Div., Babcock & Wilcox 1953–55 (Asst. Manager 1955–62, Manager 1962–65); Gen. Manager, Washington Operations, Babcock & Wilcox, 1965–68; Regional Vice-Pres., Gulf General Atomic, 1968–69, Group Vice-Pres., 1969–70, Pres. since 1970. Director: Knickerbocker Growth Fund 1957—; Fidelity National Bank 1961—; Fidelity American Bankshares 1969—; Virginia Poly. Inst. Educational Foundation 1969—; Natl. Standards Inst. 1969—. Trustee: Lafayette Coll. 1962—, and Randolph Macon Women's Coll. 1963—, and Virginia Poly. Inst. 1966–70; Pres.-Elect and Dir., Amer. Nuclear Socy. Chairman: ANSI Nuclear Technical Advisory Board, 1967—, and Virginia State Adv. Bd. on Industrial Development and Planning 1962—. *Publications:* Nuclear Engineering (McGraw-Hill); and of some 60 papers and talks on nuclear power. Recipient of Commendation for Work on Operation Mulberry during Normandy Invasion; member, Phi Beta Kappa, Tau Beta Pi, Sigma Xi. Pi Delta Epsilon, and Omicron Delta Kappa. *Member:* Amer. Nuclear Socy.; Amer. Socy. of Naval Engineers; Amer. Inst. of Chemical Engineers; Amer. Management Assn.; Newcomen Socy. *Address: office:* P.O. Box 608, San Diego, Cal., U.S.A.

**LANE, David William Stennis Stuart.** British. *B.* 1922. *Educ.* Eton; Trinity Coll., Cambridge; Yale Univ. *M.* 1955, Lesley Anne Mary Clauson. *S.* 2. *Career:* Royal Navy 1942–45; British Iron & Steel Federation 1948 (Sec. 1956); Called to the Bar, Middle Temple 1955; Shell International Petroleum Co. 1959–67; Conservative MP for Cambridge 1967–76; PPS to Sec. of State for Employment 1970–72; Parly. Under-Sec. of State. Home Office 1972–74; Chmn., Commission for Racial Equality since 1976. *Clubs:* MCC. *Address:* 40 Chepstow Place, London W2 4TA; and 5 Spinney Drive, Great Shelford, Cambridge.

**LANG, Gordon.** Jeweller and silversmith. *B.* 1895. *Educ.* Denison University (BS 1918). *M.* 1927, Harriet Kendig (*Dec.*). *M.* 1965, Constance Bates. *S.* Gordon, Jr. *Career:* Served as 2nd Lieutenant and Instructor, Machine Gun Officers School in World War I. Successively sales correspondent, B.F. Goodrich Rubber Co. 1920; bond salesman for Borton and Borton; Manager, Bond Dept., Guarantee Tile and Trust Co.; Director of sales development, The Gorham Co. (silversmiths), Providence, R.I.; Vice-President and Gen. Mgr., Black Starr & Frost-Gorham (jewelers) New York; Pres., Spaulding-Gorham (jewelers), Chicago; Director, Spaulding Gorham Inc.; Black, Starr & Frost-Gorham (jewelers), New York; President, Spaulding-Gorham, Chicago; Gomanco Inc. President and Owner: Spaulding & Co., Chicago 1943–73, and Loring Andrews & Rattermann, Cincinnati 1953–64. Former Pres. and Owner of Spaulding & Tatman, Evanston & Tatman, Chicago; Pres & Owner Gordco Inc. (Investments) since 1973; Past Pres., Chicago Latin School for Boys; Dir. and Past Pres., Chicago Better Business Bureau; Past Dir., Chicago Area Project, Chicago Crime Commission, and Chicago Retail Merchants Assn. Past Chmn., City Planning Advisory Committee and member Exec. Cttee., Chicago Plan Commission; member and First Pres., North Michigan Avenue Assn.; V.P. and Dir., Chicago Cubs Baseball for Boys. Originator of the 'Place-Setting' method for sale of flat silver. Declined nomination for mayor of City of Chicago on Republican ticket 1950. *Clubs:* Racquet:

Chicago; Old Elm; Commercial; Commonwealth; Casino; Lyford Cay; Onwentsia; Everglades, Bath and Tennis, of Palm Beach. *Address:* 203 Bluffs Edge Drive, Lake Forest, Ill.; and *office* First National Plaza, Chicago, Ill. 60603, U.S.A.

**LANG, Otto Emil,** PC, QC, MP. Canadian. *B.* 1932. *Educ.* Cudworth, Englefield and Humboldt; Univ. of Saskatchewen, BA (1951), LLB (1953), Rhodes Scholar from Sask. 1953; Oxford Univ. BCL (1955). *M.* 1963, Adrian Ann Merchant. *S.* 3. *Daus.* 4. *Career:* Called to Sask. Bar 1956; College of Law, Univ. of Sask. Saskatoon 1956, Dean 1961–68; Liberal MP for Saskatoon-Humboldt since 1968 (re-elected 1972 and 1974); Cabinet member (spec. responsibility for Dept. Trade, Industry and Commerce) 1968–69; Acting Minister of Energy, Mines and Resources 1969; Reporting Assignment for Canadian Wheat Board 1969; Minister of Manpower and Immigration 1970–72; Minister of Justice and Attorney-General of Canada 1972–75; Minister of Transport since 1975. Made Queen's Counsel of Ontario and Saskatchewan 1972. *Publications:* (Editor) Contemporary Problems of Public Law in Canada; legal papers and articles. *President.* Assoc. of Canadian Law Teachers (1962–63). *Address:* House of Commons, Ottawa, Ont. K1A 0A6, Canada.

**LANG, Robert,** Dr jur. Swiss bank manager and lawyer. *B.* 30 Nov. 1909. *Educ.* Gymnasium, Zurich, and Universities of Zurich and Paris. *S.* 1. *Dau.* 1. *Career:* Assistant Secretary, Vertrauensstelle für Goldhypotheken, Zurich, 1934–37; Assistant of Delegierter für Arbeitsbechaffung, Berne 1942–45: Manager and General Manager of Swiss Credit Bank, Zürich 1946–75; Chmn. George Fischer Ltd. Schaffhouse; Gov. Atlantic Institute for International Affairs, Paris. Colonel-Brigadier. *Address:* General Guisan-Quai 22, 8002, Zürich, Switzerland.

**LANG, Rudolph.** American. *B.* 1908. *Educ.* Coll. of Engineering, N.Y. Univ. Business Administration, Law. *M.* 1934, Edna Clempner. *Career:* Administration and Purchasing, Smith, Barney & Co. 1928–42; Administrator General Services and National Director (Purchasing), American Red Cross 1942–49. National Business Show 1949–59; Managing Director of Exhibits, Office Equipment Manufacturers Exhibits Inc. 1959–61, and Business Equipment Manufacturers Exhibits 1961–62; Chairman of Board, President and Chief Executive Officer, Prestige Expositions Inc. since 1962. Consultant to World's Fair pavilions. *Publications:* At Trade Shows People are the Payoff; Effective Business Exhibiting; many articles. Recipient of awards by N.Y. Univ., Office Executives Association, Administrative Management Socy., American Ordnance Assn., Natl. Sales Executives, and other organizations. *Member:* Office Executives Assn. (2nd Vice-Pres., Dir., Secy.); Exposition Management Assn. (Dir., Past Pres.), Exhibitors Adv. Council (Dir. Treas.), Admin. Mgmt. Socy., Amer. Ordnance Assn., and Natl. Assn. Exposition Mgrs. Dir. Mason. *Clubs:* Sales Executives German Club. Advertising. *Address:* 165 Janes Lane, Stamford, Conn. 06903; and *office* P.O. Box 3084, Stamford, Conn 06905, U.S.A.

**LANGDON, James Lloyd.** Lieut.-Col. (Ret.) U.S.A.F.R. *B.* 1918. *Educ.* Univ. of North Carolina (BS). *M.* 1943, Madelyn Earl Pope. *Daus.* Madelyn Carol and Sheila Jeanne. *Career:* With U.S. Air Force 1941–45; Agricultural Development Agent for Carolina Power & Light Co. 1946–49; Manager, Farmers Supply Co. 1949–50; Exec. Vice-Pres. North Carolina Dairy Products Assn. 1950–59; Pres. Dairy Division-Pet Incorporated 1970–75; Group Pres. & Mem. of the Board, Pet Inc. since 1975. Light Co. 1946–49; Soil Conservationist, U.S. Dept. of Agriculture 1945–46; Former President: National Dairy Assn. Executives; Carolina Socy. of Assn. Executives; Raleigh (N.C.) Junior Chamber of Commerce; Ashville (N.C.) Agricultural Development Council; Bull & Bear Investment Club. *Member:* Public Relations Socy. of America; American Legion; Sales & Marketing Exec. International; Bd. of Dirs. Hamilton Bank (Johnson City, Tenn.); Tennessee Dairy Products Assn.; Johnson City Memorial Hosp.; U.S. Industrial Council, Milk Industry Foundation, International Assn. Ice Cream Manufacturers and National Dairy Council. *Clubs:* Johnson City Country; Hurstleigh; Sphinx. *Address: office* P.O. Box 0, Carroll Reece Station, Johnson City, Tenn., U.S.A.

**LANGE, Carvel.** American industrial & financial economist. *B.* Allenhurst, N.J. *Educ.* Columbia University (AB). *M.* Gloria Prudden Cluett. *S.* Murray Stuart, David Grenfeld. *Dau.* Caryn, Tina. *Career:* Financial and econ. advr. to Colgate Estates; retained by many leading worldwide corporations and several foreign governments. U.S.A. President, Industrial Commodity Corporation 1939—; J. Carvel Lange, Inc. and J. Carvel Lange International Inc. Owner, Industrial Commodity Co.; Director: Pine Street Fund, and Common Cold Foundation. Active in civic affairs in Greenwich, Conn.; Fellow, Royal Economic Society. *Member:* American Statistical Association; Econometric Society; National Industrial Conference Board; President's Council of American Institute of Management; Theta Delta Chi; Les Amis d' Escoffier (former Chairman). Inventor of salt tooth paste, marketed by Worcester Salt Company. *Publications:* The Dynamics of Commodity Prices (Econometrica, 1938); What's Ahead for Advertising (1945); Canadian Economic Outlook for 1955 on, and others. *Clubs:* University; Pinacle; Racquet & Tennis (N.Y.C.); Round Hill (former governor) (Greenwich, Conn.); Lyford Cay (Nassau); Field (Conn.); Fishers Island Country (N.Y.); Stanwich (Greenwich, Conn.); Maidstone (L.I., N.Y.); Old Baldy Club (Saratoga, Wyoming); Bath & Tennis (Palm Beach, Fla.); Windermere Island (Bahamas). *Address: office* 122 East 42nd Street, New York, N.Y. 10017, U.S.A.

**LANGFORD-HOLT, Sir John (Anthony),** MP. British Politician & Company Director. *B.* 1916. *Educ.* Shrewsbury School. *M.* 1971, Maxine Maxworthy. *S.* 1. *Dau.* 1. *Career:* Royal Navy, 1935–45; Conservative MP for Shrewsbury since 1945. *Clubs:* Whites. *Address:* House of Commons, London SW1A 0AA.

**LANGHAM, John Michael,** CBE, MA, CEng, FIMech E., FIMarE. British. *B.* 1924. *Educ.* Bedford School; Queen's Coll. Cambridge (MA). *M.* 1949, Elizabeth Morley. *S.* 2. *Dau.* 1. *Career:* Dir., Stone-Platt Industries Ltd.; Chmn., Stone Manganese Marine Ltd.; Stone-Wallwork Ltd.: Stone-Platt Australasia Pty. Ltd.; Stone Marine Singapore Pte. Ltd.; Brunton's Propellors Ltd.; Vacu-Lug Traction Tyres Ltd.; Casthorpe Developments Ltd.; LG Petroleum Services Ltd.; Winters Boatyard Ltd.; Pres., Le Grand Ltd.; Canadian Stone Marine Ltd.; Superston Corp.; Vice-Pres., Fonderies Phoceennes; Dir., Ferguson Propeller & Reconditioning Ltd.; Osborne Propellers Ltd.; Alcometaller AB; Far East Propeller Services Ltd.; BPB Industries Ltd.; Grantham Rubber Machinery Co. Ltd. Member, C.B.I. Council; Dep. Chmn. Quality Assurance Council. *Club:* Brook's. *Address: office* 21–24 Bury St., London, SW1Y 6AL.

**LANGTON, Alan Graham,** FAIM. Australian. Consultant in Executive Development. *B.* 1902. *Educ.* Swinburne, and R.I.T. Melbourne. *M.* 1929, Edith Isabel Dall. *Dau.* 1. *Career:* Engineer, Dept. of Aircraft Production 1941–44; Head, Department of Management, South Australian Institute of Technology 1944–53; Dir. of Industrial Development, Tasmania 1953–58; Dir., Secirtam International Ltd.; Chief Training Exec., Ampol Petroleum Ltd. 1958–68. Fellow and Past Pres., Australian Inst. of Management, Tasmania (F.A.I.M.). *Address:* 29 Pacific Boulevard, Beaumaris, Victoria, Australia.

**LANK, Herbert Hayman.** Executive. *B.* 1904. *Educ.* Univ. of Delaware (BA); Université de Nancy; Sorbonne; Ecole Libre des Sciences Politiques; Honorary degrees, Univs. of Montreal (LLD); Bishops' (DCL) and Delaware (LHD). *M.* 1927, Oriana Bailey. *S.* Ray, Alden and David. *Career:* With E. I. du Pont de Nemours & Co. 1925–27; La Société française Duco 1927–28; E. I. du Pont de Nemours & Co. 1928–31; Industrias Quimicas Duperial, Argentina 1931–42; Canadian Industries Ltd. 1942–54; Du Pont of Canada Ltd. 1954—. Hon. Director, Du Pont of Canada Ltd. Director of a number of other Canadian companies. *Member:* Founding Cttee., Canadian Chemical Producers Assn. *Clubs:* St. James's, Mount Royal, University, Forest & Stream (Montreal and area); Chemists (N.Y.C.); Union Interallée (Paris). *Address:* 168 Edgehill Road, Westmount, P.Q.; and *office* 555 Dorchester Boulevard West, 18th Floor, Montreal, H2Z 1B1, P.Q., Canada.

**LANTHIER, Ronald Ross.** Canadian. *B.* 1926. *Educ.* McGill Univ. (CA 1952). *M.* 1944, Jacqueline Barbara Dyment. *S.* Ronald Dyment and John Elliott. *Daus.* April Carolyn, Bonnie Alice and Andrea Elizabeth. *Career:* Controller, C.A.E. Consumer Products Div., 1954–56; Treasurer, Webb & Knapp (Canada) Ltd. 1956–62; Dir. of Admin., Greenshields Inc. 1962–67; Vice-Pres. & Dir. Emile Lanthier Ltd. 1962—; Vice-President Finance, Canadian Marconi Co., 1967–72; Dir. Vice Pres. Finance & mem. exec. cttee., MacDonald Tobacco Inc. 1972–75; Pres., Lanco Management Ltd. since 1975. *Member:* Inst. of Chartered Accountants of Quebec; Financial Executives' Inst.; Dir., Canadian National Inst. for the Blind Que. Div. *Club:* Royal Montreal

Golf; Montreal AAA. *Address:* 124 Highfield Avenue, Montreal, P.Q., Canada.

**LANZ, Kurt.** German. Executive Vice-President, Hoechst AG, Frankfurt/M-Hoechst. *B.* 1919. *Educ.* Abitur. *M.* 1955, Frau Sigrid Faust. *S.* 2. *Dau.* 1. *Address:* Im Waldhof 3. Kronberg/Taunus; and *office* Hoechst AG, Frankfurt/M-Hoechst, Germany.

**LAPHAM, Lewis A.** *B.* 1909. *Educ.* Yale. *Career:* Director: Federal Insurance Co., H.J. Heinz Co., Chubb Corp., Mobil Corp., Tri-Continental Corp., Vigilant Insurance Co., North American Philips Corp.; Bankers Trust New York Corporation, (former Pres.); Crane Co.; Chmn., Governing Cttee., United States Philips Trust; Former Vice-Chmn. of Bd. (Ret'd.), Bankers Trust Company. *Address:* 280 Park Avenue, New York City 10017, U.S.A.

**LAPIE ,Pierre-Olivier,** KBE, MC, D en D. French politician and lawyer, Dr. *Hon. Causa* Edinburgh Univ. *B.* 2 April 1901. *M.* Yolande Friedmann. *Dau.* Dominique. *Career:* Lawyer at Court of Paris; Deputy for Nancy, Nat. Assemb. 1936–58; Under-Secretary of State for Foreign Affairs 1946; Delegate to U.N.O., U.N.E.S.C.O. and Council of Europe; Minister of Education 1950-Aug. 1951; Vice-President of National Assembly 1956–58; Member of the High Authority of the European Coal and Steel Authority 1959–67; Chmn. of the French Com. for Franco-German Cooperation. Chmn., Association France-Grande Bretagne; Member of the Académie des, Sciences morales et Politiques. Commandeur de la Légion d'Honneur; Croix de Guerre avec palmes. *Publications:* Certitudes Anglaises; Cromwell; Aujourd'hui l' Angleterre; Herriot; De Leon Blum á de Gaulle. *Address:* 11 rue de Bellechasse, 75007 Paris, France.

**LAPOINTE, Col. Hon. Hugues,** PC, CD, QC. Lieutenant-Governor of the Province of Quebec, 22nd February 1966. *B.* 1911. *Educ.* Ottawa Univ. and Laval Univ.; BA, LLL; Hon. LLD Univ. of Ottawa. *M.* 1938, Lucette Valin. *Career:* Barrister. Elected to Canadian House of Commons (Lotbinière) 1940 (re-elected 1945–49–53). Delegate to General Assembly of U.N., Paris, Sept. 1948, Lake Success, April 1949 and Sept. 1950 (the last time as Vice-Chmn. of the Canadian Delegation). Parly. Asst. to Minister of National Defence, Sept. 1945, and to the Secretary of State for External Affairs, Jan. 1949. Sworn of the Privy Council and appointed Solicitor-General of Canada, Aug. 1949; Minister of Veterans Affairs, Aug. 1950; Agent-General for Quebec in London 1961–66. Served in World War II overseas with Le Régiment de la Chaudière. *Clubs:* Quebec Garrison; Royal Quebec Golf; Cercle Universitaire de Québec. *Address:* Residence of the Lieutenant-Governor, 1010 St. Louis Road, Quebec G1S 1C7, Canada.

**LAPUS, Major General Ismael D.** Filipino soldier-diplomat and Philippine Ambassador to Republic of China, Taipeh, Taiwan. *Educ.* Cabiao public schools; Univ. of Philippines, BSCE, Infantry School, Camp Murphy; Division Staff School, Baguio; Staff College Fort Leavenworth, Kansas (USA); Military Intelligence School, Camp Murphy; Inf. School, Fort Benning, Georgia (USA); US Army Defense School, Texas (USA). *M.* Pilar Castellano, 1941. S. 4. D. 3. *Career:* Chief of Staff, Guerilla Unit; Military service at Bataan & O'Dennel; after liberation Chief, Military Intelligence Service; RP Military Attache to Washington DC; Deputy Area Comdr Philippine Army; Commanding General and Vice-Chief of Staff AFP, Commanding General Phillipine Army until 1965; Dir. Nat. Intelligence Co-ordin. Agency 1966; Philippine Ambassador to Republic of China, Taipeh Taiwan. Delegate to 1954 Geneva Conference for the Unification of Korea; Tech. Adviser Phil. Delegation to London (N. Borneo); SEATO-London Conference; SEATO-Bangkok Conference; Pacific—Asian Co-operation Conference (Seoul); Council of Ministers, SEATO (Canberra). *Awards:* Dist. Conduct Star; Dist. Service Star/First Silver Anahaw Leaf Gold Cross; Phil. Leg. of Honour; Military Merit Medal, Silver Star (USA); Leg. of Merit (USA); Several Philippine awards and War Service medals (USA). *Clubs:* CEAGC Golf; Ramon Magsaysay Soc.; Manila Army and Navy. *Address:* 49 Annapolis St., Green Hills, San Juan, Rizal, Philippines.

**LARKIN, Felix Edward.** Executive. *B.* 1909. *Educ.* Fordham Univ. (AB; Encaenia Award 1961), New York Univ. School of Business (MBA; Business Man of the Year) and St. John's Univ. School of Law (J.D.). *M.* 1937, Evelyn M. Wallace. *S.* John Andrew and James Wallace. *Dau.* Nancy (Larkin Carr). *Career:* Investment and Securities business 1933–39; Law Secretary to Judge James G. Wallace of the Court of General Sessions of New York County 1939–47; Dept. of Defense, Washington 1947–51 (Certificate of Appreciation), Asst. General Counsel 1947–49, General Counsel 1949–51; joined W. R. Grace & Co., New York City 1951—. Executive Reserve, Office of the Secy. of Defense, Washington 1961–63. Mem., Nat. Advisory Cttee. to the Dept. of Labour under the Manpower, Development & Training Act 1962–66; Dir., W. R. Grace & Co. 1963. Director, GBA Alumni Assn. of N.Y. University 1966–69–; Marine Midland Banks Inc. since 1970—; Dir. of American Arbitration Assn. 1975; Pres., W. R. Grace & Co., New York 1971–74, Chmn. since 1974. *Member:* Friendly Sons of St. Patrick: Fordham Alumni Assn.; Member Bd. of Governors, New Rochelle Hospital Medical Center Assn.; Chmn. of the Board of Trustees, Fordham Univ. 1970–77, Mem. of the Board of Trustees since 1977; Mem. of the Board of Govs. of The Pinnacle Club 1974–76. *Publications:* Uniform Code of Military Justice. *Clubs:* Larchmont Yacht; Mid-Ocean; Winged Foot (Governor, Class of 1969 and 1976). *Address:* 1030 Old White Plains Road, Mamaroneck, N.Y.; and *office* 1114 Ave. of the Americas, New York, N.Y. 10036, U.S.A.

**LARKIN, Frederick G.,** Jr. American. *B.* 1913. *Educ.* University of Washington (BS); Stanford University (MBA). *M.* 1938, Frances D. Williams. *Dau.* Lucretia (Stephenson). *Career:* Joined Security Pacific National Bank as Research Asst., 1936; Vice-Pres. 1949; Senior Vice-Pres. in charge of investments & Bond Dept. 1960; Pres., Dir. & mem. of Managing Cttee. 1961; Chief Exec. Officer & Chmn. of Managing Cttee. 1967; Chmn. of the Board 1969. *Director:* Carnation Co.; Getty Oil Co.; Rockwell International Corp.; Southern Calif. Edison Co.; Banco Denasa de Investimento S.A., Rio de Janeiro (mem. of the Consultative Council); The Bank of Canton (Hong Kong) Ltd.; Security Pacific Interamerican Bank S.A., Panama; Tricontinental Corp. Ltd. (Australia); Western American Bank (Europe) Ltd., Chmn. of the Board. *Other Directorships:* Automobile Club of Southern Calif. (Vice-Chmn. of the Board); ACSC Management Services Inc.; Calif. Chamber of Commerce; Federal Reserve Bank of San Francisco; Highway Users Fedn. for Safety & Mobility; Hospital of the Good Samaritan Medical Center; Los Angeles Philharmonic Assn. (former Chmn. of the Board); Los Angeles World Affairs Council; National Safety Council, Greater Los Angeles Chapter; Southern Calif. Building Funds. *Trustee:* Calif. Inst. of Technology; The John Randolph Haynes & Dora Haynes Foundation; Industry-Education Council of Calif.; Occidental College (Chmn. of the Board of Trustees). *Member:* American Automobile Assn. National Advisory Council; Assn. of Reserve City Bankers; Advisory Cttee., Calif. Solar Energy Research Inst. Consortium; Calif. Inst. of Technology President's Council; Junior League of Los Angeles Advisory Board; Stanford Research Inst. Council; Univ. of Washington Advisory Board of the Grad. School of Business. *Clubs:* The Links (N.Y.); Men's Garden Club; California; Lincoln; Los Angeles Country; Pacific Union; Stock Exchange (Los Angeles); Sunset. *Address: office* Security Pacific National Bank, P.O. Box 2097, Terminal Annex, Los Angeles, California 90051, U.S.A.

**LARRY, Ralph Heath.** Lawyer, business executive. *B.* 1914. *Educ.* Grove City (Pa.) College (AB *cum laude*) and Univ. of Pittsburgh (LLB); Hon. LLD Grove City Coll.; Order of the Coif; Co-editor of Law Review. *M.* 1938, Eleanor Ketler. *S.* David Heath, Dennis Ketler and Thomas Richard. *Career:* Practised law, in public practice for one year 1938; joined law staff of National Tube Co., became Secy., General Attrny. and Dir. 1945; Asst. Gen. Solicitor to U.S. Steel Corp. 1952, and Admin. Vice-Press. 1958; and, Exec. Vice-Pres. & Assist. to Chmn. 1966; Vice Chairman, U.S. Steel Board of Directors, U.S. Steel Corp., Pittsburgh, Pa. 1969–77. Director, Pittsburgh National Bank and Textron Inc.; Board of Trustees, Grove City College, Pa.; member, Board of Visitors, University of Pittsburgh; Author of speeches reprinted in Challenge and Vital Speeches. *Member:* Pennsylvania and Allegheny County Bar Assocs.; Pres., National Assoc. of Manufacturers; Dir., Foreign Policy Assoc.; International Executive Service Corps; Presidential appointee to National Commission on Productivity. *Clubs:* Duquesne; Pine Valley Golf; Rolling Rock Club. *Address:* National Association of Manufacturers, 1776 F Street, N.W., Washington, D.C. 20006, U.S.A.

**LARSON, Dr. Clarence Edward.** *B.* 1909. *Educ.* University of Minnesota (BS 1932) and University of California (PhD 1937). *M.* 1957, Jane R. Warren. *S.* Robert E., E. Lawrence, and Lance S. *Career:* National Tb. Association. Fellow, Mt. Zion Research Lab. 1936–37; Research Assoc. 1936–37; Prof. of Chemistry, Coll. of Pacific 1937–40; Chmn.,

Chemistry Dept. 1940–42; Civilian, Office of Scientific Research & Development 1942; Chief Analytical Section, Radiation Lab., Univ. of California 1942–43; Asst. Supt., Tennessee Eastman Corp., Oak Ridge, Tenn. 1943–46; Dir. of Research & Development, electromagnetic plant, Carbide & Carbon Chemical Corp. 1946–48 (Plant Supt. 1948); Dir. Oak Ridge Nat. Lab. 1950; now member, Adv. Cttee. for Chemistry; Vice-Pres. Research, Natl. Carbon Co. (div. of Union Carbide & Carbon Corp.) 1955–59; Associate Manager, Research for Union Carbide Corp. 1959–61; Associate Manager, Research, Union Carbide Corp. President, Union Carbide Nuclear Division 1965–69. Gen. Mgr., Oak Ridge Operations 1961; Energy Consultant 1976. U.S.A.E.C. Commissioner 1969 and 1975; Dir., Oak Ridge Inst of Nuclear Studies; Official delegate. U.S. Delegation to Int. Conf. on Peaceful Uses of Atomic Energy, Geneva 1955. *Member:* Amer. Chemical Socy. (on Bd. of Dirs.); A.A.A.S.; Socy. of Experimental Biology & Medicine; Scientific Research Socy. of America; Fellow (and Member Bd. of Dirs.) Amer. Nuclear Socy. Inc. (Charter); Sigma Xi; Phi Lambda Epsilon; Tau Beta Pi; Nat. Academy, Engineering. US-USSR Joint Commission on Scientific & Tech. Co-operation. *Publications:* contributions to scientific journals. *Clubs:* Oak Ridge Rotary (Pres. 1953); Cosmos (Washington); Bethesda Country; Capitol Hill. *Address:* 6514 Bradley Blvd., Bethesda, Md., U.S.A.

**LARSON, (Lewis) Arthur.** American government servant, lawyer, educator and writer. *B.* 1910. *Educ.* Augustana College (AB); Univ. of South Dakota Law School; Oxford University (Hon. Fellow, Pembroke Coll.); BA and MA Jurisp. BCL and DCL. *M.* 1935, Florence Newcomb. *S.* Lex Kingsbury. *Dau.* Anna Barbara. *Career:* Law practice, Milwaukee, Wis. 1935–39; Asst. Prof. of Law Univ. of Tennessee 1939–41; Div. Counsel, Office of Price Administration 1941–44; Chief, Scandinavian Branch, Foreign Economic Admin 1944–45; Prof. of Law, Cornell Univ. 1945–53; Dean, Univ. of Pittsburgh Law School 1953–54; Dir. U.S. Information Agency 1956–57; Under Secy. of Labor 1954–56; Special Asst .to the President 1956–58; Special Asst. to the President 1957–58; James B. Duke. Prof. of Law and Dir. Rule of Law Research Centre. Duke Univ. 1958; Special Consultant to the Pres. of the U.S. 1958–61; Consultant to State Dept. to President Johnson, to Dept. of Health, Educ. and Welfare 1963–65, 1970–71; Vice-Pres. National Council of Churches 1966–69; Knapp Prof. Univ. of Wisconsin Law School 1968–69; Consultant to the Presidents Council of Economic Advisers 1968. *Publications:* Corporations (with R. S. Stevens) 1947, 2nd end. 1955; Towards World Prosperity (in collaboration) 1947 (2nd edn. 1955); The Law of Workmen's Compensation (8 vols) Yearly Supplement, 1952—; Know Your Social Security 1954 (2nd edn. 1958); A Republican Looks at His Party (1956); What we are *For* (1959); When Nations Disagree (1961); International Rule of Law (1961); Propaganda (1963); A Warless World (1963); Vietnam and Beyond (with Don Larson); Sovereignty Within the Law (1956); Eisenhower, The President Nobody Knew (1968); (with L. T. Lee) Population and Law; Workmen's Compensation for Industrial Injuries and Death (2 vols) (1972); The Law of Employment Discrimination (2 vols) Yearly Supplement (1975). Republican. *Address:* Law School, Duke University, Durham, N.C., U.S.A.

**LASKEY, Sir Denis Seward,** KCMG, CVO. British diplomat. (Ret'd). *B.* 1916. *Educ.* Marlborough Coll.; Corpus Christi Coll Oxford. *M.* 1947, Perronnelle Mary Gemma Le Breton. *S.* 1. *Daus.* 3. *Career:* with Foreign Office 1939–46; Berlin 1946–49; U.K. Delegation to U.N. New York 1949–53; Foreign Office 1953–60; Rome 1960–64; Cabinet Office London 1964–67; Bonn 1967–69; Ambassador Bucharest 1969–72; H.M. Ambassador Vienna Austria 1972–76. *Awards:* Knight Commander Order, St Michael & St. George; Commander Royal Victorian Order. *Address:* Loders Mill, nr. Bridport, Dorset.

**LASSENIUS, Tor-Erik.** Finnish lawyer. *M.* 1939, Britta Mathilda Rydh. *S.* Karl-Erik, Helge, Bertil. *Career:* Man. Dir.: Föreningen Konstamfundet r.f., 1964–73; Hufvudstadsbladets Förlags Ab, 1966–73. Member, Managing Cttee., Helsingfors Aktiebank, 1966–76. Director: Pargas Kalk Ab; Kymmene Ab.; Oy Stockmann Ab. Treasurer, Stiftelsen för Abo Akademi, 1948–63. *Address:* Bulevarden 19A Helsingfors 12; and *office* Hufvudstadsbladet, Mannerheimvägen 18, Helsingfors 10, Finland.

**LASSWELL, Harold Dwight.** Ford Foundation Professor Emeritus, Yale Law School, New Haven, Conn. *B.* 1902. *Educ.* Univ. of Chicago (PhB 1922; PhD 1926); graduate studies at Universities of Geneva, Paris, London, and Berlin. Unmarried. *Career:* Instructor, Asst. Prof. and Associate Prof. of Political Science, Univ. of Chicago 1922–38; Washington School of Psychiatry, Washington, D.C. 1938–39; Lecturer, New School for Social Research 1939–40; Visiting Sterling Lecturer, Yale Univ. 1941–46; Prof. of Law 1946–70; and of Political Science 1952–70; Yale Univ., Fellow, Center for Advanced Study in the Behavioural Sciences 1954—; Distinguished Prof. of Policy Sciences, John Jay Coll. of Criminal Justice, City Univ. of New York 1970–72; Distinguished Visiting Prof. History & Law Temple Univ. Philadelphia, Pa. 1972–76. *Publications:* Propaganda Technique in the World War (1927); Psychopathology and Politics (1930); World Politics and Personal Insecurity (1935); Politics: Who Gets What, When, How? (1936); World Revolutionary Propaganda: a Chicago Study (with D. Blumenstock) (1939); World Politics Faces Economics (1946); Analysis of Political Behaviour (1948); Power and Personality (1948); Language of Politics (with N. Leites) (1949); National Security and Individual Freedom (1950); Power and Society: A Framework for Inquiry (with A. Kaplan, 1950); World Revolution of Our Time (1951); Comparative Study of Symbols (with others) (1951); Comparative Study of Elites (with others) (1951); The Policy Sciences (with D. Lerner); In Defense of Public Order: The Emerging Field of Sanction Law (with R. Arens 1961); The Future of Political Science (1963); Power, Corruption and Rectitude (with A. Rogow) (1963); The Public Order of Space (with others) (1963); World Handbook of Political and Social Indicators (with others); World Revolutionary Elites (with D. L. Lerner), Sharing of Power in a Psychiatric Hospital (with R. Rubenstein) (1966); Formosa, China and the United Nations (with L. C. Chen) (1967); Interpretation of Agreements and World Public Order (with others) (1967); Political Communication (with Satish K. Arora) (1969); Pre-view of Policy Sciences (1971); The Policy Orientation of Political Science (1971); Policy Sciences & Population (with others) (1975); Values & Development (with others) (1976). *Awards:* Prize and Citation from the American Council of Learned Societies, 1960. Hon. LLD, Univ. of Illinois; Univ. of Chicago; Columbia Univ. N.Y.; Hon. LittD. Jewish Theological Seminary (Columbia Univ., N.Y.); Hon. ScD, Univ. of Pennsylvania; Hon. LHD, Temple Univ. *Member:* American Political Science Association (Pres. 1955–56); Amer. Acad. of Arts & Sciences; Amer. Sociological Socy.; Assn. of American Law Teachers; Amer. Socy. of International Law; Pres. American Society, International Law 1971–72; National Acad. of Sciences; World Acad. of Art & Science. *Clubs:* Cosmos (Washington); Univ. (N.Y.C.); Graduate (New Haven). *Address:* Policy Sciences Center, 1 Lincoln Plaza, New York, N.Y. 10023, U.S.A.

**LATHAM, Arthur Charles,** MP. British Politician. *B.* 1930. *Educ.* Romford Royal Liberty Sch.; Garnet Coll. of Educ. *M.* 1957, Ruby Margaret Green. *S.* 1. *Dau.* 1. *Career:* Councillor, Romford Borough Council since 1952, Leader Labour Group 1963–70; Chmn., Romford Labour Party 1958–70; Alderman, London Borough of Havering since 1961; mem., North East Metropolitan Regional Hospital Board 1966–72; Teacher in Further Education 1967–69; MP (Lab.) for Paddington North 1969–74, & for City of Westminster, Paddington since 1974; Chmn., Tribune Group 1975–76; Chmn., London Labour Party since 1977. *Club:* Paddington Labour. *Address:* House of Commons, London SW1A 0AA.

**LATHAM, Sir Joseph,** CBE. British. *B.* 1905. *Educ.* Stand Grammar School. *M.* 1932, Phyllis Mary Fitton. *S.* Anthony Piers. *Dau.* Althea Christine. *Career:* Director and Secretary, Manchester Collieries Ltd. 1941–46; various posts, finally Deputy Chairman, Nat. Coal Board, 1946–60; Dir., later Deputy Chmn. and Mng. Dir., Associated Electrical Industries Ltd., 1960–68. Chmn. Metal Industries Ltd. 1968–72, Wimpey Property Holdings Ltd.; Dir. Thorn Electrical Industries Ltd., George Wimpey & Co. Ltd. Holds Jt. Diploma in Management Accounting. *Fellow:* Inst. of Chartered Accountants, and British Inst. of Management; Companion, Inst. of Electrical Engrs. *Clubs:* Effingham Golf. *Address:* 25 Badingham Drive, Leatherhead, Surrey.

**LATYMER, Lord** (Thomas Burdett Money-Coutts). British banker. *B.* 1901. *Educ.* Radley College; Trinity College, Oxford (MA). *M.* 1925, Patience Courtenay-Thompson. *S.* Hugo. *Daus.* Joanna, Susan. *Career:* Chmn. London Committee, Ottoman Bank 1948–75; former Dir. several companies. *Address:* San Rebassa, Moscari, Mallorca.

**LAUDERMILK, Jack Irwin.** American consultant and business executive (engineering, geology and business administration). *B.* 1909. *Educ.* Univ. of Oklahoma (AB; BS Gen. Eng.; Petroleum Engineer). *M.* 1937, Mary Theresa

Gittings. *S.* John Irwin. *Dau.* Carolyn Theresa. *Career:* Owner-President of J. I. Laudermilk and Associates since 1954; Vice-Pres. & Director, Capital Finders Corp. 1961–63. Previously: production engineer, Gulf Oil Corp. 1936–39; petroleum engineer and co-ordinator of technical and college training 1947–54; Socony-Vacuum Oil Co., producing; Chief Storage Consultant, Panhandle Eastern Pipe Line Co. 1956–60; Instructor, Univ. of Texas, 1939–41; Captain and Major, American Army, World War II, 1941–46; Professor and Head of Dept. of Petroleum Engineering, N.M. School of Mines 1946–47. *Awards:* American Defence Service Medal; American Theatre of Operations; E.T.O. Ribbon with four combat stars; Army of Occupation Medal; Armed Forces Medal; Victory Medal; Texas Service Medal. Phi Beta Kappa; Tau Beta Pi; Sigma Tau; Sigma Xi; Sigma Gamma Epsilon; Pi Mu Epsilon; Pi Epsilon Tau; Phi Eta Sigma; Pi Epsilon; Tau Omega; President's Council, American Institute of Management 1959–61. *Publications:* numerous technical and general articles dealing with petroleum, geology, military science and business in various journals and newspapers since 1941. *Address:* 406 Mendel Lane, Titusville, Florida 32780; and *office* J. I. Laudermilk and Associates, P.O. Box 6392, Titusville, Florida 32780, U.S.A.

**LAUGHLIN, Edwin Bower.** Lt.-Comdr. U.S.N.R. (Retd.). *B.* 1920. *Educ.* Brown Univ. (AB 1942). *M.* 1944, Barbara Ann Paine. *Daus.* Carolyn Taber, Elisabeth Parmele and Whitney Longendyke. *Career:* Laboratory technician, American Cyanamid Corp. 1946; Secretary, Laughlin Textile Mills 1947–50; President, Half Moon Synthetic Yarns Inc., Waterford 1950–61 (absorbed by Laughlin Textile Mills 1961). President, Treasurer and Director: Laughlin Textile Mills Inc., Waterford, N.Y. 1950—. Director: Workshop Inc., Menands, N.Y. 1960—; Newsvision Co., Bridgeport, Connecticut 1967—; Dir. & Exec. V.P., Jacksonville Broadcasting Corp., Jacksonville, Fla. since 1971; Chmn. of the Board, Narrow Fabrics Institute; Dir. ACI Corp., Nashua N.G. since 1973. Member, Advisory Board of Quartermaster of U.S. Army Research and Development Command. Republican. *Clubs:* Schyler Meadows Country; Loudonville Albany County, N.Y.; Deerwood Country, Hidden Hills Country (Jacksonville, Fla.); Sawgrass, Ponte Vedra Beach, Fla. *Address: office* P.O. Box 100, Waterford, N.Y. 12188; and P.O. Box 772, Ponte Vedra Beach, Fla. 32082, U.S.A.

**LAUN, Louis F.** American. *B.* 1920. *Educ.* Yale Univ. (BA). *M.* 1947, Margaret West. *Daus.* Nancy, Margaret and Kathryn. *Career:* Lt.-Col. USMCR (retd.); Asst. to Pres., Bates Mfg. Co. 1946–55; Advt. Dir., Burlington Industries 1955–57; Gen. Merchandising Mgr., Celanese Corp. 1957–60; Marketing Dir., Celanese Fibers Co. 1960–67. Pres., Celanese Fibers Marketing Co. 1964–71; Vice-President, Celanese Inc. 1967–71; Dir.: Fiber Industries Inc. 1963–71, Cel-Cil Fibers Ltd. 1965–71. Chmn. Republican Industry Workshop Program 1971–72, Mgmt. Consultant since 1971, Associate Administrator, Small Business Administration 1973; Deputy Admin. 1973–77. *Publications:* Sketches 'Small Wonder' (Broadway musical 1948). Chmn., Manmade Fibres Assn.; Secy., Color Assn. of U.S.; Director: Better Business Bureau of N.Y. and Fashion Inst. of Technology. *Awards:* Bronze Star (U.S. Republican. *Clubs:* Mid-Ocean; Sleepy Hollow Country; Union League; Yale Club of N.Y.C.; Capitol Hill. *Address:* 25 Spring Lane, Chappaqua, N.Y. 10514; and *office* 260 Madison Avenue, New York, N.Y. 10016, U.S.A.

**LAURE, Maurice Fernand.** French banker. *B.* 1917. *Educ.* Lycée Saint Louis; Polytechnique. *M.* 1955, a Melle Marie Claude Girard. *S.* 3. *Career:* Deputy Permanent Secy. Dept. Taxes, Ministry of Finance 1952–55; Govt. Commissioner, Moroccan State Bank, Chmn. Cttee. Governors, Central Fund, Overseas France 1955–58; Dir. Financial Services & Programmes Min. for the Armies 1958–60; Dir. Crédit National 1960–67; Man. Dir. Société Générale 1967–73; Chmn. Societe Générale since 1973. Chmn. Sogebail; Sogen Swiss International Dir. European Amer. Banking Corp;. Credit National; Ciments Français; Dir. Vallourec; Cit-Alcatel B.E.C. *Awards:* Commandeur de la Légion d'Honneur; Medaille des Evadés. *Publications:* The Value Added Tax; Taxes and Productivity; Treaties of Competition; Revolution, the last chance for France; A Treaty of Tax Policy; V.A.T. in danger. *Address:* 26 Boulevard la Saussaye, 92200 Neuilly sur Seine; and *office* Societe Generale, 29 Boulevard Haussmann, 75009 Paris, France.

**LAURITZEN, John Ronnow.** American bank executive. *B.* 1917. *Educ.* Princeton Univ. and Graduate School of Banking, Univ. of Wisconsin. *M.* 1939, Elizabeth Ann Davis. *S.* Bruce Ronnow. *Dau.* Ann Davis. (Pape). *Career:* Chmn. Bd. Chmn. Exec. Cttee. and Dir. First National Bank of Omaha 1956; President and Director: Emerson (Ia.) State Bank 1947, First State Bank, Loomis (Neb.) 1955, Washington County Bank, Blair (Neb.) 1956; Farmers and Merchants State Bank, Bloomfield (Neb.) 1957; and Burt County State Bank, Tekamah (Neb.); President: Blair Insurance Agency Inc., Burt County Insurance Agency Inc., Emerson Insurance Agency Inc., and Farmers' and Merchants' Co. of Bloomfield. *Clubs:* Omaha, Omaha Country, Minnesouri Angling, University Cottage, Marco Island. *Address:* 6621 Underwood Avenue, Omaha, Neb., U.S.A.

**LAURITZEN. Knud.** Danish shipowner and company director. *B.* 12 April 1904. *S.* Ole, Jan. *Daus.* Grete, Inge-Lise, Marianne, Karen. *Career:* Man. Dir. J. Lauritzen A/S, D/S 'Vesterhavet'; Chairman, United Steamship Co., Copenhagen; Aalborg Shipyard, Aalborg, Atlas Engineering Works. Copenhagen, J.L.-Fund, Copenhagen. *Address:* Hammerensgade 1, DK-1291 Copenhagen, K, Denmark.

**LaVARRE, William.** American economic geographer (specializing in Pan America), author and editor. Director, American Foreign Service Council. Washington. D.C. 1950; Consultant on Latin American Affairs; Chief of Inter-American Intelligence, Washington, in World War II. *B.* 1898. *Educ.* Harvard Coll. and Harvard Univ. (Economic Geography). *M.* 1927, Alice Elliott. *Dau.* Yvette (Graham). Explorer for oil, gold and diamonds in South America (1920s); Special Latin American Correspondent, The North American Newspaper Alliance and Consolidated News Features (1930s); Contributor to U.S. and international magazines (1930s); Latin American Specialist in World War II service 1940–50. *Publications:* Up the Mazaruni for Diamonds; Gold, Diamonds & Orchids (English edition, Jungle Treasure); Southward Ho !; Dry Guillotine (memoir of Rene Belbenoit). Independent (Conservative). *Member:* Amer. Geographical Socy.; Royal Geographical Socy. (elected Fellow); Amer. Legion. *Clubs:* University (Washington); Harvard (N.Y.C.). *Address:* 1135 Sixteenth Street, N.W., Washington, D.C., U.S.A.

**LAVOIE, Léo.** Canadian banker. *B.* 1913. *Educ.* Advanced Management Program, Harvard University. *M.* 1940, Claire Maranda. *Dau.* Lise (Courville). *Career:* Joined Provincial Bank, 1930; Branch Mgr., Warwick, Quebec 1940, & then other branches; Manager, Main Office, Montreal, 1953; Assistant to President & Assistant General Manager, 1955; General Manager, 1957; Board of Directors, 1960; Vice-Pres. and Gen. Mgr., 1966; President 1967–76, Chief Exec. Officer 1967–77 & Chmn of the Board since 1974; Chmn. of the Board, Canadair Ltd., Ciné Monde Inc.; Dir.: Alliance Corp.; Mutual Life Insurance Co.; Compagnie France Film; Télé-Métropole Inc.; Canadian Reinsurance Co.; Canadian Reassurance Co.; Fondation J.A. DeSève; The Macdonald Stewart Foundation; & Director of several other corporations as well as of different social & cultural organizations. *Office* 221 St. James Street W., Montreal, Quebec H3Y IM7, Canada.

**LAWLER, Oscar Thom.** American banking executive. *B.* 1914. *Educ.* Yale Univ. (BA). *M.* 1937, Joan Day Pattinson. *S.* Daniel Day and Charles Frederick. *Dau.* Joan Day. *Career:* President and Director of the Farmers & Merchants National Bank of Los Angeles 1953–56. Chmn., Exec. Cttee. and Dir. Security Pacific National Bank, Los Angeles, Calif. 1956—: Dir., Union Pacific Corporation, & Security Pacific Corporation. *Member:* Newcomen Society in North America. *Clubs:* California, Stock Exchange, Lincoln (all in Los Angeles); India House, Yale (both in N.Y.C.). *Address:* 5224 West 2nd Street, Los Angeles 4, Calif., U.S.A.

**LAWRENCE, Joseph Dudley.** *B.* 1909. *Educ.* Liberia College (BA). *M.* 1941, Blanche Ottilee Cox. *S.* 2. *Daus.* 3. *Career:* Chairman, Liberian delegation to I.L.O. Cttee. on Works on Plantations, Bandung 1950; member, Liberian delegation to 6–7–8–9–11–12th Sessions, General Assembly of U.N. (Chmn. of delegation to 10th Session); member, Liberian delegation to 9th, 10th and 12th sessions World Health Assembly; Minister to Spain 1952–54; Ambassador 1954–56; Ambassador to France 1956–64. Ambassador of Liberia to the United Kingdom, and Minister to the Holy See 1956, and Ambassador to Switzerland 1961–67. *Awards:* Liberian —Knight Great Band, Kt. Commander, Order of African Redemption; Kt. Grand Commander, Order of Pioneers of Liberia; Grand Cross, Order of Civil Merit (Spain); Grand Officer, Legion of Honour (France); Grand Cross, Order of St. Gregory the Great Grand Cross Order (Holy See); Grand

Cross Order of Malta; Comdr. of the National Order (Madagascar); Grand Cross, Golden Order of Merit (Austria); Grand Cross, National Order of Merit (France). *Address:* c/o Ministry of Foreign Affairs, Monrovia, Liberia.

**LAWRENCE, Ruddick Carpenter.** American business executive. *B.* 1912. *Educ.* Univ. of Washington, Seattle (BA *cum laude* in journalism). *M.* 1937 (1) Barbara Dole (Div.). *S.* 2. *Daus.* 4. (2) 1973, Cherry McDonnell Swasey. *Step-daus.* 2. *Career:* Director of Publicity for Detroit Institute of Arts, and Assistant Director of World Adventure Series 1934 (Director 1962—); Western Mgr. for The American Boy magazine 1936; Time, Inc., Fortune magazine (Philadelphia and Southern Mgr.) 1939–44; Lieut. U.S. Navy, World War II, 1944–46; New York Manager of Fortune and Assoc. Advertising Manager 1946–50; Director of Sales Development for TV network, National Broadcasting Co. and Director of Promotion, Planning and Development for radio and TV network 1950–53; Vice-Pres., New York Stock Exchange 1953–68; Vice-President, Continental Oil Co., 1968–77; Pres., Lawrence Associates 1977—; Dir., International Film Foundation 1949—; Trustee, Sarah Lawrence College 1957–69 (Chmn. 1964–69) and Endowment Fund Corp. of Phi Kappa Psi Fraternity 1962—; Vice-Pres., Secy. & Dir. New York Board of Trade; Governor, Invest-in-America Natl. Cincl. Inc.; Board of Managers, New York Botanical Garden; Dir., Pres., U.S.-Arab Chamber of Commerce; Public Relations Socy. N.Y. *Member:* Phi Kappa Psi; Sigma Delta Chi; Pilgrims of U.S. *Award:* Star of Jordan (Jordan), Cedars of Lebanon (Leb.). *Clubs:* Economic, University (N.Y.C.); Hemisphere; Bronxville Field; Shelter Islands (N.Y.) Racquet Club. *Address:* 3 Wellington Circle, Bronxville, N.Y.; and *office* 30 Rockefeller Plaza, Suite 4515, New York, N.Y. 10020, U.S.A.

**LAWRENCE, Seymour.** American publisher. *B.* 1926. *Educ.* Harvard College (AB). *M.* 1952, Merloyd Ludington. *S.* Nicholas. *Dau.* Macy. *Career:* Editor & Publisher, Wake 1945–53; College Representative, D. Van Nostrand Co. 1948–50; Field Editor, The Ronald Press 1950–51; Special Assistant to the Editor, Atlantic Monthly 1952–54; Associate Editor 1954, and Dir. 1955–64, The Atlantic Monthly Press. Founded Seymour Lawrence Inc. 1965. President, Seymour Lawrence Inc. 1965—; Dir., Milford House Properties Ltd., Nova Scotia. *Member:* Signet Society (Cambridge, Mass.). *Clubs:* Harvard, Century Assn. (N.Y.C.); Union Boat Club (Boston). *Address:* 102 Chestnut Street, Boston, Mass.; and *office* 90 Beacon Street, Boston, Mass. 02108, U.S.A.

**LAWROSKI, Stephen.** American Chemical engineer. *B.* 1914. *Educ.* BS, MS, PhD. *M.* 1947, Helen Wilson. *S.* Stephen Wilson. *Dau.* Nancy Ann. *Career:* Research Assistant, Pennsylvania State University 1934–43; Research Chemical Engineer. Standard Oil Development Co. 1943–44, Asst. Section Head 1946; Reactor Trainee, Oak Ridge National Laboratory 1946–47; Chemical Engineering Division Director 1947–63, and Co-ordinator of Engineering Research 1959–63, Argonne National Laboratory; Associate Laboratory Director 1963–70. Senior Engineer since 1970. *Awards:* Evan Pugh Scholar, Louise Carnegie Scholarship; Fellow, Amer. Inst. Chemical Engineers. *Member:* Amer. Nuclear Society (Fellow; and Mem. Bd. of Dirs. 1956–59; Member, Nuclear Standards Bd. and Exec. Cttee.); Amer. Inst. of Chemical Engineers; Amer. Chemical Socy.; Amer. Assn. for Advancement of Science; Research Socy. of America; National Academy of Engineering; Member, General Adv. Cttee., U.S. Atomic Energy Commission; Advisory Cttee. on Reactor Safeguards since 1974. *Publications:* Chapter Editor for Nuclear Engineering Hand Book (McGraw-Hill); Editor, Quarterly Review of Reactor Fuel Processing (U.S. Atomic Energy Commission); contributor to miscellaneous textbooks on atomic energy. *Address:* 144 South Sleight Street, Naperville, Ill.; and *office* Argonne National Laboratory, Argonne, Ill., U.S.A.

**LAWSON-JOHNSTON, Peter O.** American. Business Director. *B.* 1927. *Educ.* University of Virginia (BA; Majored in Philosophy). *M.* 1950, Dorothy Stevenson Hammond *S.* Peter O., Jr. *Daus.*. Wendy, Tania and Mary. *Career:* Served in U.S. Army, Infantry, in Mediterranean Theatre 1945–47; Student, Univ. of Virginia 1947–51; Reporter on Baltimore Sun (also Yachting Editor) 1951–53; Executive Dir. Maryland Classified Employees Assn. 1953–54; Public Information Director of Maryland Civil Defense Agency 1954–56. Director and Chmn., Feldspar Corporation 1959, Kennecott Copper Corporation 1965—; Vice-Chmn. Pacific Tin Consolidated Corporation since 1972, Elgerbar Corporation 1963—, and Minerec Corporation 1964—; Dir. Anglo Co. Ltd., (Chmn.). Trustee (also Pres.), S.R. Guggenheim Foundation 1964—; Partner Guggenheim Brother since 1967. Dir. Nabors Drilling Co., Dir. Printex Corp.; Chmn. Harry F. Guggenheim Foundation since 1971, Now Dir.; Chmn Pacific Tin 1975; Dir. McGraw-Hill Inc. 1975; Pres. and Trustee Solomon R. Guggenheim Foundation. *Member:* Amer. Ceramic Socy. Republican. *Clubs:* Bankers; American (London); Beden's Brook (Princeton, N.J.); Green Spring Valley Hunt (Garrison, Md.); Pretty Brook Tennis; Edgartown Yacht. Maryland; River; Seminole Golf (Fla.); Jupiter Island (Fla.). *Address:* 215 Carter Road, Princeton, N.J. 08540; and *office* 120 Broadway, New York, N.Y. 10005, U.S.A.

**LAYH, William Oswald,** FCA British Company Director, *Career:* Chartered Accountant; member, Commonwealth Dairy Produce Equalization Cttee. Ltd. 1934; Local Dir, Sun Alliance Ins. Ltd. since 1939; Exec. Mem. Australian Red Cross Socy., Pres., Glenara Childrens' Homes, Fellow Inst. of Chartered Accountants of Australia. *Clubs:* Athenaeum (Melbourne); Launceston Northern (Launceston); Life Mem., Tasmanian Turf; Tamar Rowing; Nat. Agric. and Pastoral Socy. of Tasmania. *Address:* 1A Batman Avenue, Launceston, Tasmania (P.O. Box 1222, Launceston) 7250.

**LAYLIN, John Gallup.** American lawyer. *B.* 1902. *Educ.* Deep Springs Junior College; Cornell Univ. (AB 1925); Harvard Univ. (JD. 1928). *M.* (1) 1930, Dorothy Adams Lewis, and (2) 1942, Diana Morgan. *S.* John Gallup and David Lewis. *Daus.* Louise Elizabeth (Princess Firouz), Diana, and Laura. *Career:* Junior Legal Adviser, Ambassador Dwight Morrow, Mexico 1928; Associate, Sullivan & Cromwell, New York City 1929–33; Special Assistant to Under-Secretary of Treasury Dept., also Assistant General Counsel 1933–35. Member of Law Firm of Covington & Burling, 888 16th Street, N.W. Washington 20006, D.C. 1935—. Has served as legal adviser to various Latin-American, European, Middle Eastern and South Asian governments. *Member:* International Law Assn. (Exec. Cttee. Amer. branch); Amer. Law Inst., Amer. Bar Assn.; Inter-Amer. Bar Assn.; Amer. Socy. of International Law; Middle East Inst.; Washington Institute of Foreign Affairs (Executive Cttee.). *Awards:* Commander: Orders of the Lion (Finland) and of Dannebrog (Denmark), Sitari-i-Pakistan and Order of San Carlos Columbia). *Publications:* Legal: The Role of Adjudication in International River Disputes, The Lake Lanoux Case (co-author), American Journal of International Law; monographs: The Uses of the Waters of International Rivers, 1956; Principles of Law Governing Use of International Rivers, 1957; Development of the Law of State Responsibility—Equality of Treatment and the International Standard, 1961; Allocating Water on International Streams; Co-author Legal Climate for Private Enterprise under the Alliance for Progress, Renegotiation of Concession Agreements, Past, Present and Future Development of the Customary International Law of the Sea and Deep Seabed, Emerging Customary Law of the Sea; The International Lawyer, A.B.A.; Does Failure to Make Compensation for Expropriated Property Come Within the Act of State Doctrine, American Journal of International Law; The Legal Regime of the Deep Seabed Pending Multinational Agreement, Virginia Journal of International Law; Justiciable Disputes Involving Acts of State, The International Lawyer, A.B.A.; Memorable International Cases and Friendships with Lord O'Brian, Buffalo Law Review 1974. *Clubs:* 1925 F. Street, Metropolitan (Washington); Century Assn. (N.Y.C.); River Bend Golf and Country (Great Falls, (Va.). *Address:* Hidden Springs Farm, Great Falls, Va.; and *office* 888-16th Street, N.W. Washington, D.C., 20006, U.S.A.

**LAYTON, Lord,** 2nd Baron of Danehill (Michael John Layton. BA (Cantab), Ch. Eng. FIMechE; British executive *B.* 1912. *Educ.* St. Paul's School, and Gonville and Caius, Cambridge, (BA Mech. Sc.). *M.* 1938, Dorothy Cross. *S.* Geoffrey Michael. *Dau.* Diana Christine. *Career:* Works Manager: Ibbotson Bros., Sheffield 1939–43, and Commer Cars 1943–46: with Control Commission for Germany 1946–48; Head of International Relations Dept., British Iron & Steel Federation 1948–55; Sales Controller, Steel Co. of Wales 1956–67 (Director 1960; Asst. Mng. Dir. 1965–67; Mng. Dir. 1967); Bd. member British Steel Corp. since 1967; Dir. Economist Newspaper Ltd. since 1973; Pres. of Court of British Shippers' Council since 1974. *Address:* 6, Old Palace Terrace, The Green, Richmond, Surrey TW9 1LZ; and *office* 33 Grosvenor Place, London, SW1X 7JG.

**LAZAREANU, Alexandru.** Rumanian diplomat. *B.* 1913. *Educ.* Bucharest Faculty of Letters and Philology. *Career:*

Journalist 1931–36; Cultural and Press Counsellor, Washington 1946–48; Director, Ministry of Foreign Affairs 1949–51; First Counsellor, Chargé d'Affaires a.i., Paris 1951–53; Director, member of the Collegium of the Ministry of Foreign Affairs 1953–56; Deputy Minister of Foreign Affairs 1953–56; Deputy Minister of Foreign Affairs 1956–61; Minister to London 1961–64; Ambassador to London 1964–66: Director, member of the Collegium of the Ministry of Foreign Affairs 1966–68; Ambassador to Belgium & Luxembourg since 1968, also accredited to Upper Volta since 1971. Order of the Star of the Republic, Order of Labour, etc. *Address:* 105 rue Gabrielle, 1180 Brussels, Belgium.

**LAZZARONI, Giuseppe.** Italian Banker. *B.* 1931. *Educ.* Doctor in Commercial Sciences. *M.* 1956, Ernesta Fontana. *S.* 2. *Career:* Man. Dir., Credito Commerciale, Milan; Director: Finter Bank Zürich (Paris), Parigi; Instituto Centrale Banche e Banchieri; Mediocredito Regionale Lombardo. Member of the technical committee Associazione Nazionale Aziende Ordinarie di Credito. *Address: office* via Armorari 4, 20123 Milan, Italy.

**LEACH, Admiral Sir Henry Conyers,** KCB. British Naval Officer. *B.* 1923. *Educ.* St. Peter's Court, Broadstairs; Royal Naval Coll., Dartmouth. *M.* Mary Jean McCall. *Daus.* 2. *Career:* Specialised in Gunnery (Lieutenant) 1947; in command, HMS *Dunkirk* (Commander) 1959–61; Chief Staff Officer (Plans & Operations), Far East (Captain) 1962–64; in command, HMS *Galatea* & Captain (D) 27 Escort Squadron 1965–67; Dir. of Naval Plans (Captain) 1968–70; in command, HMS *Albion* (Captain) 1970–71; Asst. Chief of Naval Staff (Policy) (Rear Admiral) 1971–74; Flag Officer, First Flotilla (Rear & Vice Admiral) 1974–75; Vice Chief of the Defence Staff (Vice Admiral) 1976–77; Allied C-in-C Channel, C-in-C Eastern Atlantic, C-in-C Fleet (Admiral) since 1977. *Decoration:* Knight Commander of the Bath, 1977. *Club:* The Farmers, Whitehall. *Address:* Wonston Lodge, Wonston, Winchester; and *office* Admiralty House, Northwood, Middlesex.

**LEAHY, Robert James.** American international management consultant. *B.* 1908. *Educ.* Univ. of Wisconsin (BA 1932; LLB 1935 JD 1966); graduate work, law and chemistry 1937–41. *M.* 1936, Neva Gestland. *S.* Robert Gestland, James Wallace and John Lewis. *Career:* Man. Dir. Philip Morris (Aust.) Ltd., Australia 1956–61; Technical Service Manager, Philip Morris Inc., Richmond, Va. 1952–56; Legal Department, S. C. Johnson & Son Inc., Racine, Wis. 1946–52. Lieut., U.S.N.R. Manhattan Engineering District (atomic bomb project) 1943–46. Vice-Chairman Benson & Hedges (Canada) Ltd., Brampton, Ontario 1961–69; Director: Philip Morris (Australia) Ltd. 1956—; Man. Dir., Philip Morris (Australia) Ltd. 1956–61; Vice-Pres., Philip Morris Internl., N.Y.C. 1961. *Publications:* several articles in business and chemical journals. *Member:* Amer. Chemical Socy.; Amer. and Wisconsin Bar Assns.; Australian Inst. of Management (Fellow). *Clubs:* Chemists (N.Y.C.); St. Kilda Cricket, Victoria, Victoria Golf (all of Melbourne); St. George Golf & Country (Toronto), Mount Stephen (Montreal). *Address:* 208 Berkshire Road, Richmond, Virginia, 23221, U.S.A.

**LEAL, John Rowan.** South African. *B.* 1919. *Educ.* St. John Coll. Johannesburg. *M.* 1941, Sybil Anne Leal. *Career:* Chmn. Nat. Mining Co. Pty. Ltd.; Dir. 1952–58; Abercom Investments Ltd. (Sir George Ushers Group); Industrial Co. of C. W. Engelbard Group. S.A.; Robert Flemming & Co. Africa Ltd.; Spartan Engineering Ltd.; Alta Corp. Ltd.; General Dynamics Africa Ltd.; Firth Cleveland Africa Pty. Ltd. *Director:* Walter Runciman and Co. Ltd.; Tyre Equipment Mfg. Co. Ltd. (Part of Reed Paper Corp.); Mining and Finance Holdings Ltd.; Exploraton of Mining Syndicate Ltd.; National Underwriters Ltd., Schenker and Co. Ltd. Republic Oil Corp. Ltd.; Consolidated African Mines Ltd. *Clubs:* Rand R.A.C.; Country Johannesburg. *Address:* 14 Coronation Road, Sandhurst, Johannesburg, S. Africa; and *office* 136 Illovo Centre, 32 Central Ave., Illovo P.O. Box 8821, Johannesburg.

**LEANDER, Hugo Austin.** American business executive. *B.* 1894. *Educ.* Harvard Univ. (BS 1916); New York Univ. Graduate School. *M.* 1917, Marguerite R. McFarland. *S.* Hugh A. *Dau.* Jeanne. Special Accountant, Union Pacific System, N.Y. 1916–18; Auditor, Gen. Elec. Co., Schenectady, N.Y. 1918–21; Supervisor of Methods, Delaware & Hudson Co. N.Y. 1921–24; Manager, Arthur Anderson & Co., N.Y. 1924–26; Financial and Industrial Consultant and Dir., Amer. Rayon Products Corp., Consolidated Laundries Corp., General Laundry Machinery Corp. (all N.Y.C.) 1926–30; Vice-Pres., American Founders Corp., American Gen. Corp. 1930–36; Mgr., Industrial Dept., Van Alystyne Noel & Co. 1936–38; Vice-Pres., Dir., Reynolds Metals Co., Richmond Radiator Co.; Dir., U.S. Foil Co., Reynolds Corp., Robertshaw Thermostat Corp., Fulton Sylphon Corp., Reynolds Research Corp. 1938–41; Vice-Pres. and Dir.; Tobe Deutschman 1941–42, and Mu Switch Corp. 1941–43; Vice-Pres., Gen. Mgr., Dir., The W. L. Maxson Corp. 1944–47; President and Director, The W. L. Maxson Corp. 1947–59. Financial and industrial consultant, Chmn. Exec. Cttee., Avionics Investing Corp.; Pres., Avionics Management Corp. 1960; Director, Leetronics Inc. 1947—. *Member:* Harvard Engineering Society; The New England Society in the City of New York; N.Y. Chamber of Commerce. *Clubs:* Harvard (of New York); Union League. *Address:* 5 Old Parish Road, Darien, Conn.; and *office* 60 E42 Street, New York City 10017, U.S.A.

**LEARNED, Stanley.** American company director. *B.* 1902. *Educ.* Kansas Univ. (BSc 1924; Hon. Degree of CE 1936); Lawrence Univ. (D Eng. 1967). *M.* 1928, Mary Helms. *Dau.* Ann (Fitch). *Career:* Joined Phillips 1924; Chmn. Phillips Operating Cttee. July 1944; Vice-Pres., and Member Exec. Cttee. 1949, Dir. 1949–70; Exec. Vice-Pres. and Assistant to Pres. 1951; Pres. 1962; Pres. and Chief Exec. Officer Apr. 1964; Vice-Chmn. of the Board, 1967; Dir. Petroleum Inc (Wichita, Kansas) since 1970; Dir. Garvey Industries Inc. since 1973. *Award:* 1959, Kansas Univ. Alumni Assn. and Univ. joint citation for Distinguished Service to Mankind (this award is given annually by Kansas Univ. in lieu of honorary degrees). *Member:* Amer. Petroleum Inst. (Hon. Mem. Bd. Dirs.); Sigma Xi; Tau Beta Pi. *Clubs:* Hillcrest Country (Bartlesville); Sons of the American Revolution. *Address:* 821 Johnstone, Bartlesville, Okla. 74003; and *office* 201 Professional Bldgs., Bartlesville, Okla., U.S.A.

**LEATHAM, Louis Salisbury.** American. Lt.-Col., A.U.S. (Ret.). *B.* 1902. *Educ.* Salt Lake City Public Schools and University of Utah. *M.* 1930, Anna Grace Carn. *S.* Jon Paul and William Wallace. *Dau.* Janet (Lewis Penman). *Career:* Sec.-Treasurer, Park Fairfield Mining Company 1931–39; Cashier-Secretary, National Savings & Loan Association of American 1930–33; Examiner, State Banking Dept. 1933–35; Chief Cashier U.L.C.C. 1935–40; Bank Commissioner of the State of Utah 1951–56; President of State Depository Board 1951–56; Pres., Bank of Kearns 1956–59; Exec. Vice-Pres. and Dir., Beehive State Bank, Salt Lake City 1959–68; Treas. and Dir., World Trade Assn. of Utah 1962, Pres. 1972–73; Dir. Pro-Utah Inc. 1964–70; Exec. Vice-Pres. Commercial Security Bank 1968–70; Honorary Consul for Utah for the Republic of Senegal since 1970. Officer, U.S. Army, World War II, European theatre 1940–50; Chief of Financial Institutions Branch of Military Government, Hesse, Germany 1947–48; member, Eucom General Staff Heidelberg, Germany 1948–49; served as missionary for The Church of Jesus Christ of L.D.S. in Scotland and England 1927–29; Pres., Aberdeen (Scotland) Branch of L.D.S. Church 1928; Clerk of Sheffield (England) District 1929; member of Riverside Stake High Council (L.D.S. Church) 1955–57; member Kearns L.D.S. Stake High Council 1959–62; Charter Member, Great Salt Lake Yacht Club; member, Reserve Officers' Association of the U.S.; Chmn., Legislative Cttee. 1955, and member of the National Assn. of State Bank Supervisors 1955–58 (Hon. Member 1958–62). *Awards:* Lieut.-Col., U.S.A.R; World War II decorations; American Defense Medal; E.A.M.E. Medal (with 3 battle stars); American Area Campaign Medal; German Occupation W.W.II Medal; Victory Medal; U.S. Armed Forces Reserve Medal; Commendation from President Truman. Dir. and Treas., Kearns Chamber of Commerce 1956–59; Dir., Blue Shield of Utah 1964–71; Hon. Trustee, Nitcaps International Assn. 1966—; Salt Lake Area United Health Foundation. Treas. Salt Lake Area United Fund 1966–67. Patriarch, Ensign Stake 1966–73, Salt Lake Stake 1975, The Church of Jesus Christ of L.D.S. *Member:* American Bankers Association, Utah Bankers Ass. (Member, Executive Committee 1962–63). and Salt Lake Clearing House Association (Pres. 1965), Sons of Utah Pioneers International Club, Utah Historical Society, Salt Lake Chamber of Commerce; Public Representative Bd. Dirs. Utah Public Employers Assn. 1960–72; The Newcomen Society in North America, Robert Morris Associates, 1965–70. *Publications:* The Letham or Leatham Family Book of Remembrance (1955); Joshua Salisbury Family Book of Remembrance (1961); Karl S. Little, Utah's Mr. Credit Union (1963); many L.D.S. Church magazine articles, and newspaper articles on patriotic and religious subjects. *Clubs:* University, Salt Lake City. Lions

International Kiwanis International *Address:* 532-12th Avenue, Salt Lake City 84103, Utah; and *office* P.O. Box 1627, Salt Lake City, Utah 84110, U.S.A.

**LEATHER, Sir Edwin (Hartley Cameron).** KCMG, KCVO, Kt, K St J. *B.* 1919. *Educ.* Trinity Coll. School; Royal Military Coll. Kingston, Canada. *M.* 1940, Sheila A.A. *Daus.* 2. *Career:* served with Canadian Army 1939–45, U.K. and Europe 1940–45; Member of Parliament (Con.) N. Somerset 1950–64; Dir. of many companies; Chmn. and member many Associations and Cttees; Governor of Bermuda 1973–77. *Awards:* Hon. member, Nat. Inst. Social Sciences N.Y.; Medal of Merit, Royal Canadian Legion; LLD (hc) Bath (1975). *Address:* Mangrove View, Paget, Bermuda.

**LEATHERS, Viscount** (Frederick Alan Leathers). British. Chairman, Wm. Cory & Son Ltd., 30 Oct. 1951. *B.* 1908. *Educ.* Brighton Coll. and Emmanuel Coll., Cambridge (MA). *M.* 1940, Elspeth Graeme Stewart. *S.* 2. *Daus.* 2. *Career:* Member of the Baltic Exchange; an Underwriting Member of Lloyds Member of the Court of the Worshipful Company of Shipwrights; The Court of the Company of Watermen and Lightermen; Fellow, Inst. of Chartered Shipbrokers; Member: Inst. of Petroleum. *Address:* Hills Green, Kirdford, Sussex.

**LEAVEY, William Maxwell.** Australian company director. *B.* 1927. *Educ.* Univ. of Sydney (BEng-Civil). *M.* 1955, Margaret McKimm. *S.* David John. *Daus.* Sue Ellen and Katharine Mary. *Career:* Managing Director: Lend Lease Corp. Ltd. 1964—. Chmn. of Directors: Civil & Civic Pty. Ltd. 1963—, Elevators Pty. Ltd. 1964—, Richardson & Wrench 1965—, Bowman's Timber Pty. Ltd. 1961—, Autobric Pty. Ltd., Litecrete Pty. Ltd., and Unbehaun & Johnstone Pty. Ltd. 1964—. *Address:* 26 Willowie Road, Castle Cove, Sydney; and *office* c/o Lease Lend Corporation Ltd., Australia Square, Sydney, N.S.W., Australia.

**LEBER, Georg.** German politician. *B.* 7 Oct. 1920. *Educ.* Primary School, Commercial Coll. Commercial Teaching. *M.* 1942, Erna Maria. *S.* Manfred Willibald. *Career:* Private in German Army 1939–45; Sec. General, Building Workers Trade Union in the Limburg/Lahn area 1949–53; Member Exec. Cttee., Building Workers Trade Union 1953–57; First Pres., Building W.T. Union 1957–66; Federal Minister of Transport, Posts and Telecommunications 1966–72; Fed. Minister of Defence 1972—. Member, Fed. Exec. of the Fed. German Trade Unions 1957–66; Governing body Int. Fed. Building & Woodworkers T. Unions in the European Economic Community 1957–66. *Member:* West German Lower House of Parliament (Bundestag) 1957; Social-Democratic Party of Germany (SPD); Industrial Building Workers Union. *Publications:* Vermogensbildung in Arbeitnehmerhand Frankfurt, Main 1966, Europaische Verlaganstalt. *Address:* Bundesministerium der Verteidigung, P.O. Box 1328, 5300 Bonn, Germany.

**LEBON, Roger.** French banker. President, Union de Banques à Paris; Administrator, Economats du Centre. *B.* 1924. *Educ.* Licencié en droit; Diplôme de l'Institut Sciences Politiques. *M.* 1948, Suzanne Olivier (deceased). *S.* 3. *Dau.* 1. (2) 1971, Ariane Audouin-Dubreuil. *Awards:* Officer, Legion of Honour, Croix de Guerre (1939–45), Medal of the Resistance, and Medal of Freedom. *Address:* 22 place de la Madeleine, Paris, 8e, France.

**LECA, Dominique.** French. Commander, Legion of Honour. *B.* 1906. *Educ.* L'Ecole Normale Supérieure. *M.* 1947, Yvonne Dumas. *S.* François. *Daus.* Marie-Françoise and Marie Sabine. *Career:* Finance Inspector 1932; Director at Ministry of Finance 1939; Director on departmental staff of the Ministry of National Defence 1948; Financial Adviser to President of the Council 1953; Chmn. Union des Assurances de Paris; Société Sequanaise de Banque; Dir. Librairie Hachette; Northern Star Insurance Co. Ltd. Chairman, Union des Assurances de Paris (L'Union, L'Urbaine, La Séquanaise) 1968—. *Club:* Union Interalliée (Paris). *Address:* 109 rue de Courcelles, Paris, 17; and *office* 9 Place Vendôme, Paris 1, France.

**LECHIN-SUAREZ, Brigadier-General Juan.** Bolivian. *B.* 1921. *Educ.* Military in Bolivia and U.S.A. *M.* 1947, Ruth Varela. *S.* Kenneth. *Daus.* Maria Ruth, Claribel and Patricia. *Career:* Bolivian Military Academy, 1939–43; Chief of operations Bolivian Army H.Q. 1960–61; Military and Air Attaché, Bolivian Embassy, Bonn, 1962–63; Comdr. Bolivian Fifth Infantry Div. 1964; Pres. State Mining Corp. (Min. of State), 1964–68; Comdr. Third Infantry Div. 1969; Bolivian Ambassador to the Court of St. James's, accredited to the Court of the Hague 1970–74; Pres. Bolivian Delegation to the Int. Tin Council; Minister for Planning and Coordination in La Paz, Bolivia since 1974. *Awards:* Condor De Los Andes, Bolivia; Das Grosse Verdienstkreuz, German Fed. Republic; Guerrillero José M. Lanza Bolivia; Merito Aeronautico, Bolivia; Merito Naval, Bolivia. *Publications:* Several essays on Military History and Geopolitics. *Clubs:* Travellers, London. *Address:* Avenida Busch 2066, La Paz, Bolivia.

**LeCOUTEUR, George Sugden,** OBE. Australian company director. *B.* 1915. *Educ.* Newington Coll. Sydney, and Univ. of Sydney (BA 1937; MA 1946). *M.* 1939, Nancy Jean Oates. *S.* Michael George and Richard Andrew. *Dau.* Susan Jean. *Career:* With Australian Mercantile Land & Finance; Mgr. for Victoria & Riverina 1957–60; Asst. Gen. Mgr. for Australia 1961–63; Gen. Mgr. for Australia 1964–69; Dir. 1966–69; *Director:* Commercial Union Assurance Co. of Australia Ltd.; Containers Ltd. *Member:* Council Inst. of Public Affairs, Council, National Heart Foundation; Council Civilian Maimed and Limbless Association; *Fellow:* Aust. Inst. of Management (FAIM); Inst. Dirs. in Australia (F. Inst. D.A.). *Clubs:* Australian (Sydney), *Address:* 11 Avon Road, Pymble, N.S.W., Australia.

**LEDERER, Andre Albert Richard.** Belgian Naval Engineer. *B.* 1910. *Educ.* Civil Mechanical Engineer, and Civil Engineer for Naval Construction. *M.* 1941, Elisabeth Chardome. *S.* Francis, Philippe-Dominique and Jacques. *Dau.* Cécile. *Career:* Hon. Technical Director of Otraco; Member, L'Académie Royale des Sciences d'Outremer; Professor. Louvain University. Hon. Chmn., Reserve Officers of Belgium; Secretary-General, Union Belge des Ingénieurs Navals; member: Union des Ingénieurs de Louvain; Institution of Naval Architects (London). *Publications:* various publications on navigation of inland waterways. *Clubs:* Cercle Royal Africain; Cercle des Officiers de réserve, Brussels. *Address:* 15 rue de la Tarentelle, Brussels 1080, Belgium.

**LEDGER, Sir (Joseph) Francis.** Former Australian industrialist. *B.* 1899. *Educ.* Perth Boys Sch. *M.* 1923, Gladys Muriel Lyons. *S.* Colin Francis. *Daus.* Ethel June and Betsy Vilmai. *Career:* Governing Dir. Ledger Investments Pty. Ltd.; Pres. Mitchell Cotts Group of Companies W.A; W.A. Trotting Assn; Royal Commonwealth Socy.; Dir. Mitchell Cotts Aust; A.R.C. Engineers, Welshpool W.A. Past Chmn., Pres. and Dir. Chamber of Manufacturers Insurance Ltd; Past Chmn.of Dirs. J. & E. Ledger Pty. Ltd. J. & E. Ledger Sales Pty. Ltd; Ledger Electrics Pty. Ltd. Winget Moxey Pty. Ltd. (W.A.), South Aust. Insurance Co. W.A; W.A. Branch. Aust. Div. Inst. of Directors, London; Adv. Cttee. Dept. Industrial Development of W.A. Past Pres., Ironmasters Assn. W.A. Inst. of Foundrymen; Metal Ind. Fed. W.A. Employers Fed. W.A.; Chamber of Manufacturers; Past Vice Pres. Assoc. Chamber of Manfct., Canberra, Australia. *Clubs:* Weld; Cottesloe Golf; Royal Freshwater Bay Yacht; W.A. Turf; W.A. Trotting Assn; Royal Automobile; East Perth Football, W.A. *Address:* 2 The Esplanade, Peppermint Grove, Western Australia.

**LEDOUX, Albert Frédéric Edmond.** French diplomat. *B.* 5 June, 1901. *Educ.* Bowdon and Brighton Colleges; Lycée Jeanson de Sailly, Paris; École des Hautes, Études Commerciales, Paris. *M.* 1932, Geneviève Birot. *S.* Pierre. *Career:* Attaché, Constantinople 1927; Third Secretary, Rio de Janeiro 1928, Ministry of Foreign Affairs 1930, Madrid 1932, Brussels 1933; Second Secretary, Montevideo 1937, First Secretary 1939; resigned Oct. 1940 and joined Free French; General de Gaulle's Representative in South America 1941; French National Committee Delegate to Argentine, Brazil, Chile, Paraguay and Uruguay 1942; Counsellor 1943; in charge of staff and accounts to the Commissariat of Foreign Affairs, Algiers 1944; Minister 1944; Director 1945; Amb. Ex. and Plen. to Peru 1945; Amb. Ex. and Plen. to Uruguay 1949; Ministry Foreign Affairs 1952; member, Delegation to Economic and Social Council and to U.N. Assembly 1954; Ambassador to Norway 1955–57; Ministry of Foreign Affairs 1957–59; Diplomatic Counsellor to the Government 1959–62; Ambassador to Denmark 1962–66. Cmdeur. de la Légion d'Honneur, Médaille de la Résistance. *Address:* 11 Rue Lecerf, 06 Cannes, France.

**LEDWIDGE, Sir (William) Bernard (John),** KCMG. Retired British Diplomat. *B.* 1915. *Educ.* Cardinal Vaughan School, London; King's Coll. Cambridge, Princeton Univ. U.S.A. *M.* (1) 1948, Anne Kingsley, (2) 1970, Flora Groult. *S.* Francis. *Dau.* Diana. *Career:* major in British and Indian Armies

1940–46; Foreign Office 1947–49; British Consul, St. Louis U.S.A. 1949–52; First Secy. British Embassy Afghanistan 1952–56; Political Adviser, British Military Govt. Berlin 1956–61; Foreign Office Counsellor 1961–65; Minister, British Embassy Paris 1965–69; Ambassador to Finland 1969–72; Ambassador to Israel 1972–75; Chmn., United Kingdom Cttee. for UNICEF since 1976. *Clubs:* Travellers (London). *Address:* 54 rue de Bourgogne, 75007 Paris, France.

**LEE, Clarence Edgar.** American poultry and animal nutritionist, administrator and research director. *B.* 1893. *Educ.* Univ. of Connecticut (BS 1916); Graduate School, Cornell Univ. 1921–23. *M.* 1918, Muriel Louise Clark. *Daus.* Daphne Ann and Diane. Fellow, American Association for the Advancement of Science; Life member, New York Academy of Science. Member, Florida Acad. of Sciences. Vocational Agricultural Instructor, Concord High School (Mass.) 1916–17; Supervisor, War Garden Campaign 1917–18; Head Voc. Agricultural Department, Worcester (Mass.) High School 1918, and New Milford (Conn.) 1918–20; Instructor and Graduate School Student, Cornell University 1920–23; Head, Dept., of Poultry Husbandry, N.Y. State University Institute of Agriculture Farmingdale 1923–27; Lecturer, Columbia Univ., 1924–27; Poultry Specialist, The Beacon Milling Co. Inc., April 1927–35; Vice-President and Director, Poultry, Game Bird and Small Animal Research, The Beacon Milling Co. Inc., Cayuga, N.Y., 1935–58. Chmn., Nutrition Council, American Feed Manufacturers' Assn. 1941–42 (Life member 1958—); member, States Relations Committee 1940–51. Republican. International Torch (Pres., Auburn, N.Y., Chapter 1942); Life Member, American Poultry Historical Socy.; Committee of Fifty, Amer. Poultry Hall of Fame 1958—; Eugene Field Society (Hon.); U.S. Naval Institute (Associate); Poultry Science Association (North America); Empire State Society; New York Chapter, Sons of the American Revolution; Sewell Society Citation. 1948. *Publications:* Practical Poultry Husbandry for the Near East (1925); Profitable Poultry Management (20 editions 1928–52, with associates, 3 editions 1954–58); Profitable Broiler Battery and Laying Cage Management (6 editions 1936–51); Profitable Caged Layer Management (with J. M. Snyder (1958); scientific reports and magazine articles. *Address:* 2833, N.E. 26th Avenue, Lighthouse Point, 33064, Fla. U.S.A.

**LEE, Dong Whan.** Korean. *B.* 1916. *Educ.* Graduated from Seoul Commercial Coll. 1940, and from Tokyo Commercial Univ. 1942. *M.* 1943, Chung Duk Lee. *S.* 2. *Daus.* 3. Director, Postal Admin. Bureau, Ministry of Communications 1946–48; Special Member, Budget & Audit Cttee. House of Representatives, National Assembly 1954–57. Enrolled as Attorney-at-Law 1955. Director of Internal Affairs Bureau, Special City of Seoul 1958–59; Vice-Minister, Min. of Home Affairs 1960; En. Ex. and Min. Plen., Chief of Korean Mission to Japan 1961; Ambassador to Australia and New Zealand 1962. Leader, Korean Delegation to 14th Colombo Plan Consultative Cttee., Melbourne, Nov. 1962 (Leader of 15th meeting, Bangkok 1963); Leader, Korean Delegation to 21st Session of the Economic Commission for Asia and the Far East, Wellington, N.Z. 1965. *Club:* Royal Canberra Golf. *Address:* 333–67 Shindang Dong, Sundong-Ku, Seoul, Republic of Korea.

**LEE, Dwight Erwin.** American. *B.* 1898. *Educ.* University of Rochester (AB 1921; AM 1922); Harvard University (PhD 1928). *M.* 1928, Margaret Shipley. *Dau.* Lucinda Lee Thurston. Instructor in History, University of Rochester 1922–24; Asst. Prof. of Modern History, Clark University 1927–30 (Associate Prof. 1930–38); Professor of Modern European History 1938–67, and Chairman, Department of History, Government and International Relations 1943–62; Clark University. Administrative Secretary, War and Peace Studies Project 1942–43, and Research Secretary 1942–44, Council on Foreign Relations, New York; member: International Secretariat, U.N. Conf. on International Organization, San Francisco 1945, and Editioral Board, International Organization 1946–55; Dean of the Graduate School Clark Univ. 1962–67. LHD *hon. causa,* Clark 1967. *Member:* Phi Beta Kappa. *Publications:* Great Britain and the Cyprus Convention Policy of 1878 (1934); Ten Years; The World on the Way to War 1930–1940 (1942); Editor (with George E. McReynolds), Essays in History and International Relations in honour of George Hubbard Blakeslee (1949); and The Outbreak of the First World War ('Problems in European Civilization') 4th Ed (1975); Europe's Crucial Years: The Diplomatic Background of World War I 1902–14 (1974); Editorial Director, Problems in European Civilization 1961–71. *Address:* 14 Brookside Avenue, Worcester, Mass. 01602, U.S.A.

**LEE HOWARD, Leon Alexander.** British author and journalist. *B.* 1914. Editor, Sunday Pictorial, London, Jan. 1959–Mar. 1961; Editor, Woman's Sunday Mirror, London, June 1955–Jan. 1959. Editor, Daily Mirror, London Mar. 1961–71. *Publications:* four novels: Crispin's Day, Johnny's Sister, Blind Date, No Man Sings (under pseudonym). *Address:* Via San Damaso 51, Rome 00165, Italy.

**LEE KUAN YEW.** Prime Minister of Singapore. *B.* 1923. *Educ.* Raffles College, Singapore; Fitzwilliam, Cambridge, Middle Temple, London. BA Cantab Double First in Law with Star, Special Distinction; Barrister-at-Law, Middle Temple, London. *M.* 1950, Kwa Geok Choo. *S.* 2. *Daus.* 1. *Career:* Member, Cambridge Univ. Labour Club 1946–49; Advocate and Solicitor 1951; Legal Adviser to many Trade Unions 1952; Formed the People's Action Party, a democratic socialist party, affiliate of Socialist International, the first Secretary General 1954—; Assemblyman for the Tanjong Pagar constituency since 1955; Prime Minister since 1959. Won 4 subs. gen. elections 1963, 1968, 1972, 1976; One of 15 representatives from Singapore to Parlt. of Malaysia 1963–65 (when Singapore was asked to leave Federation); Elected to Bureau of the Socialist International 1967. LLD (honoris causa), Royal Univ. Cambodia; Fellow, Inst. of Politics, Harvard; Hon. Bencher, Middle Temple, London; Hon. Fellow, Fitzwilliam Coll. Cambridge; LLD (honoris causa) Hong Kong Univ.; Hoyt Fellow, Berkeley Coll. Yale; LLD (honoris causa) Univ. of Liverpool; LLD (honoris causa) Univ. Sheffield; Honorary Grand Cordon, Order of the Nile, U.A.R.; Grand Cross, Royal Order, Cambodia; First Class Order, Rising Sun Japan; Companion of Honour, United Kingdom; Hon. C.H., Hon. G.C.M.G. United Kingdom; Hon Fellow of R. Australasian Coll. of Surgeons (1973); Hon Fellow of R. Australasian Coll. of Physicians (1974); Bintang Republik Indonesia Adi Pradana (1973); Order of Sikatuna, the Philippines (1974). *Address:* The Prime Minister's Office, Singapore 6.

**LEE YONG LENG, Dr.** Singapore Diplomat. *B.* 1930. *Educ.* St Antony's Coll. Oxford; Univs of Singapore & Malaya; B Litt, MA, PhD. *Career:* University Teacher 1956–70: High Commissioner for Singapore in UK 1971–75; Ministry of Foreign Affairs 1975–76; Prof. & Head, Dept. of Geography, Univ. of Singapore since 1977. *Address:* c/o University of Singapore, Singapore.

**LEEDY, Haldon Arthur.** American. Educational administrator. *B.* 1910. *Educ.* Univ. of Illinois, MA (Physics) 1935; PhD (Physics) 1938. *M.* 1940, Margaret Rayner. *S.* Haldon John. *Daus.* Marilyn Sloan and Barbara Rayner. *Career:* Assistant in Physics, Univ. of Illinois 1933–38; Physicist, Armour Research Foundation 1938–44. Chairman, Physics Research Department 1944–48; Dir. 1948–50. Executive Vice-President & Director, Armour Research Foundation of Illinois Institute of Technology 1948–63; President, Nuclear-Chicago Corp. 1963–67. Industrial Executive; Vice-Pres. North Central Coll. since 1969. Trustee: N. Central Coll., Chicago Theolog. Seminary (Member, Exec. Cttee.), Dir. Stewart-Warner Corp.; Chmn. Illinois Educational Facilities Authority. *Member:* American Institute of Physics; American Society for Testing Materials: American Standards Society; National Research Council; and American Association for Advancement of Science. *Publications:* numerous articles on acoustics, noise vibration, research and development, automation, etc.; to various journals. *Clubs:* Economic Club of Chicago; University (Chicago). *Address: office* 30 Brainard Street, Naperville, Ill., U.S.A.

**LEENHARDT, Francis Emile Daniel.** French statesman. *B.* 1908. *Educ.* Lic. en droit; Lic. ès lettres. *M.* 1966, Anne Bayard. *Daus.* 2. *Career:* Chmn. of Finance Commission of National Assembly 1956–58; Chmn. of Socialist Parly. Group 1958–62; President of Marseilles International Fair 1967–72; Vice-Pres. and Dir-Gen. of Provençal; Pres. & Dir. Gen. of Var Matin/Republique; President of the Economic and Monetary Commission of the European Parliament 1975–76; Vice-Pres. of the National Assembly 1976–77. *Decorations:* Officer, legion d'Honneur; Croix de la Guerre; Rosette de la Resistance. *Address:* Le Cheverny, 1 La Cadenelle, Marseille 13008, France; and *office* Le Provençal, 248 Ave. Roger Salengro, Marseille 13015.

**LEGER, The Right Hon. Jules** CC, CMM, CD. Governor General of Canada. *B.* 1913. *Educ.* University of Montrea (Droit), and University of Paris (Literature). *M.* 1938, Gaby

Carmel. *Dau.* Hélène. *Career:* Served on editorial staff of *Le Droit*, Ottawa 1938–39; joined Department of External Affairs 1940; posted to Canadian Legation in Chile 1943; transferred to Canada House, London 1947; seconded to Prime Minister's Office, Ottawa 1949–50; Head, European Division, Department of External Affairs 1950–51; Asst. Under-Secretary of State for External Affairs 1951–53; Ambassador Ex. and Plen. to Mexico 1953–54; Under-Secy. of State for External Affairs Aug. 1954–58; Permanent Representative of Canada to the North Atlantic Council and the OEEC Nov. 1958–62; Ambassador to Italy 1962–64; to France, 1964–68. Under-Secretary of State, 1968–73; Ambassador to Belgium and Luxemburg 1973; Gov. Gen. since 1974. *Address:* Rideau Hall, Ottawa, Ontario, Canada KIA OA1; and *office*: Government House, Ottawa, Canada KIA OA1.

**LEGH-JONES, John Herbert.** British. industrial consultant. *B.* 1904. *Educ.* FCA; CPA. *M.* 1940, Elizabeth Anne Halford. *S.* Piers Nicholas. *Dau.* Dinah Victoria. *Career:* With Price Waterhouse & Co., U.S.A. 1928–36; Flintkote Co., U.S.A. 1936–37; Flintkote Co. Ltd., London 1938–69 (Chmn. & Man. Dir. 1948–69); Dir. Lucy Halford & Assoc. Ltd. since 1971. *Address:* Jordans, Bucks.

**LEHMANN, Ernst.** Dr.rer.pol.; Israeli. *B.* 1902. *Educ.* Universities of Berlin and Munich. *M.* 1926, Nelly Frank. *S.* Raphael. *Career:* On staff of Mitteldeutsche Bodenkreditanstalt, Berlin 1924; Gen. Mgr., Deutsche Realkreditbank A.G., Dessau-Berlin 1928. Manager FWI, Gesellschaft zur Forderung Wirtschaftlicher Interessen Deutscher Juden bei der Reichsvertretung Deutscher Juden, Berlin 1934–35. In Israel: Manager, The General Mortgage Bank of Palestine Ltd. 1935, of Issue Department Anglo-Palestine Bank Ltd., and Government Loans Administration 1948. Chmn. of Bd. of Dirs. Bank Leumi le-Istael B.M.; Chmn. Tel-Aviv Stock Exchange Ltd; Africa:Israel Investment Ltd.; IHUD Insurance Agencies Ltd.; General Mortgage Ltd.; Chmn., Migdal-Binyan Insurance Co. Ltd.; Director Bank Leumi (UK) Ltd., London; Chmn. Bank Leumi Le-Israel (France); S.A. Paris; Chmn. Bank Leumi Le-Israel (Switzerland) Zurich; Chmn., United Appeal (Keren Hayessod, Keren Kayemet Le-Israel); Chmn. of Council, 'Yad Itzhak Ben-Zvi', Jerusalem; Chmn. Council Otzar Hityashvuth Hayehudim; Chmn. Y Foerder Inst. for Economic Research (TA Univ.). *Member:* Bd. of Governors of the Technion, Israel Inst. of Technology, Board of the Hebrew Univ.; Advisory Council and Advisory Cttee. Bank, Israel. *Publications:* articles on financial and currency problems, and on real estate and housing. *Address:* 23 Benjamin Street, 52512 Rama-Gan, Israel; and *office* 26–32 Yehuda Halevy Street, Tel-Aviv, Israel.

**LEIGH-WOOD, Roger,** DL. British banker. *B.* 16 Aug. 1906. *Educ.* Winchester College and Trinity College, Oxford (MA). *M.* 1936, Norah Elizabeth Holroyde. *S.* 4. Partner, Brown, Shipley & Co. 1937–42; served in World War II, Royal Naval Volunteer Reserve (Lieut.-Commander) 1939–45; Chairman, Scott & Browne Ltd. since 1963. *Address:* Summerely, Bentworth, Alton, Hants.

**LEITCH, John Daniel.** Canadian. *B.* 1921. *M.* 1941, Margaret Beatrix Cartwright. *Daus.* Mary Frances and Hilda Jean. In Canadian Navy 1939–45. President, Upper Lakes Shipping Ltd. 1952—. Director: Canadian Imperial Bank of Commerce 1955—, Dominion Foundries and Steel Ltd. 1954—, Massey Ferguson Ltd. 1962—, Canada Life Ltd. 1964—, American Airlines, Canadian Oxygen Ltd., Maple Leaf Mills Ltd. *Clubs:* Toronto; York. *Address: office* 49 Jackes Avenue, Toronto, Ont., Canada.

**LEITO, Dr. B. M.** Governor of Netherlands Antilles. *B.* 1923. *Educ.* Curaçao; Univ. in Netherlands, Economist. *M.* 1951, Chr. A. M. Koot. *S.* 2. *Dau.* 2. *Career:* Junior Officer, Netherlands Antilles Dept. Social and Economic Affairs 1951; Officer, Gen. Affairs Div. of Island Territory of Curaçao 1952; Officer Finance Div. of Curaçao 1953; Member, Foundation for Technical Training in Netherlands Antilles 1952–54; Mem. Board of the Scientific Library Foundation 1953–70; Part-time Teacher Sec. School 1954–58; Mem. Curaçao Island Council 1955–63; Mem. Curaçao and Bonaire School Advisory Board 1956–62, Mem. Parlt. of the Netherlands Antilles 1959–62; mem. Antillean Parly. delegation visiting Netherlands at invitation of Netherlands Parliament 1960; Head, Finance Div. of Island Territory of Curaçao 1961–65; Mem. Working Cttee. advis. N.A. Govt.; Mem. Netherlands Antillean delegation to Surinam 1965; Dir. Netherlands Antillean Dept. Finance 1965–70; Pres. Supervisory Dirs. Bank of Netherlands Antilles 1965–70; Netherlands Antillean rep. at the Carib./L.A. Conference at Jamaica 1967; Chmn. Socio-Economic Council of Netherlands Antilles 1967–70; Mem. Netherlands-Antillean Govt. Delegation to Venezuela 1968; Acting Lieut.-Gov. of Island Territory of Curaçao 1968–70; Acting Gov. Neths. antilles 1969–70; Governor of Netherlands Antilles since 1970. *Patron:* Neth.-Antil. Branch Queen Wilhemina Fund Foundation (fight against cancer); Handicapped Children's Welfare Foundation (1970); *Trustee* (Acting) Prince Bernhard Fund (Neth-Antil) Foundation (culture); *Chairman* (Hon.) Neth/Antil Red Cross. *Member:* (Hon.) Board of Scientific Library Foundation (1971). *Decorations:* Officer in Order of Oranje Nassau (1970); Gran Cordon de la Orden del Libertador de Venezuela (1971); Gran. Cruz Placa de Oro de la Orden del Merito de Duarte, Sanchez y Mella, Dominican Rep. (1972); Knight in Order of Netherlands Lion (1973). *Address:* Governor's House, Fort Amsterdam No. 1, Willemstad, Curaçao, Netherlands Antilles.

**LEIVESTAD, Trygve.** Norwegian judge (Ret'd.) *B.* 29 Jan. 1907. *Married. S.* Erik, Torbjörn, Steinar. *Dau.* Vilgunn. *Career:* Secretary, Ministry of Justice 1937, Director 1945; Chief Justice, Court of Appeal of Northern Norway 1947; Justice, Supreme Court 1958; Chmn. of the Bd. Norwegian Broadcasting Co. 1968–72. *Publication:* The Basic Problem of Ethics. *Address:* H-Lövenskioldsvei 8, Oslo 7, Norway.

**LE MASSON, (Jules) Henri.** French public relations adviser, and writer on maritime subjects. *B.* 1900. *Educ.* Lic-en-D; Diplôme, Ecole des Sciences Politiques. *M.* 1925, Françoise Courtin. *S.* 4. *Daus.* 2. *Career:* With Cie. Générale Transatlantique (French Line 1920–28 and 1932–35; Usines Renault (Automobiles) 1928–32; P.L.M. Railway 1935–38; French National Railways 1938–55; Cie Française de Raffinage (TOTAL) Oct. 1955–65; (as Chief of the Advertising Department in each of these companies). Chief of Public Relations, French Shipbuilders' Association, since 1950; editor les Flottes de Combat (the French equivalent of Jane's Fighting Ships) 1943–74. *Publications:* Several books on maritime and naval problems, all of them dealing with the evolution of ships, mainly warships, including Forces sur la mer, Navires d'auiourd'hui, La France se bat sur mer, Le deuxième conflit mondial (jointly with four other authors, including Admiral Barjot); De la Gloire au Richelieu, Les lévriers de la mer, Porte-avions et sous-marins, Histoire du Torpilleur en France, 1872–1940 (first pub. 1967); Du Nautilus (1800) au Redoutable, (the first history of the French submarine service) (1969); Propos Maritimes (1970) Guerilla Sur Mer (1973); Contributor to Journal de Genève (naval correspondent) and others. *Awards:* Officer Legion of Honour; Chevalier du Mérite Maritime, and of Mérite Militaire. Pres., Académie de Marine, Member-founder, Association Francaise des Relations Publiques. *Address:* 9 avenue Sainte Foy 92200, Neuilly-sur-Seine (Seine), France; and *office* French Shipbuilders' Association, 47 rue de Monceau, Paris.

**LE MIEUX, Henry Fisher,** BE, BS. American. *B.* 1926. *Educ.* Tulane Univ. (BE Elec Eng), (BS Civil Eng). *M.* Marjorie E. Hunter. *S.* 1. *Daus.* 3. *Career:* Dir. Raycan Contractors Ltd.; Raymond Technical Facilities Inc.; Healy Tibbitts Construction Co.; Centriline Ltd.; Vice-Pres. Dir., Compania Raymond S.A.; Constructora Raymond C.A.; Pres. Dir., Raymond Concrete Pile Co. Ltd. of Liberia; Raymond Metal Products Co.; Pres. Man. Dir. Raymond Concrete Pile Co. Ltd.; Man. Dir., Raymond International (U.K.) Ltd.; Pres., Chmn. of the Bd., C.E.O., Dir. Raymond International Inc. Dir., Home Oil Co. Ltd., Calgary, Alta, Canada; Dir., Texas Commerce Bancshares Inc., Houston, Texas. *Member:* Amer. Socy. C.E.; Amer. Socy. Testing Materials; Moles; Beavers; Newcomen Socy. N.A.; Pan. Amer. Society. *Clubs:* Ocean Reef (Florida) American; Plimsoll (N. Orleans); River Oaks Country; Ramada; Houston; University (Houston); Sky (N.Y.). *Address:* 19 Courtlandt Place, Houston, Texas, 77006, U.S.A. and *office* 2801 South Post Oak Road, Houston, Texas 77027.

**LEMPRIERE, William Henry,** OBE. Australian. *B.* 1905. *Educ.* Geelong Grammar Sch. *M.* 1932, Kathleen Elizabeth Griffiths. *S.* Michael Raoul. *Dau.* Annette Rozel. *Career:* Chmn.: Australian Cncl. of Woolbuyers 1949–52, 1955–57, Victorian and South Australian Woolbuyers Assn. 1946–47, and Australian Wool Testing Authority 1958–64. Director, Lincoln Mills 1958–62. Chairman, Lempriere (Australia) Pty. Ltd. 1956—, Dir., Containers Ltd. 1963–70 and S. Pacific Canneries Pty. Ltd. 1966–76. *Publications:* Matthew Flinders Square, proposal for a Melbourne Civic Centre. *Clubs:*

Melbourne; Australian; Royal Melbourne Golf. *Address:* 33 Albany Road, Toorak, S.E.2, Vic.; and *office* Lempriere House, 35 Dryburgh Street, West Melbourne, Australia.

**LEONARD, Dick (R. L.),** MA. British politician. *B.* 1930. *Educ.* Ealing Grammar School, Univ. of London, Inst. of Education, Univ. of Essex. *M.* 1963, Irène Leonard Heidelberger. *Career:* School Teacher, 1953–55; Deputy Gen. Secy. of the Fabian Socy. 1955–60; Journalist and Broadcaster, 1960–68; Senior Research Fellow, Univ. of Essex 1968–70; Member of Parliament Labour for Romford 1970–74; Parly. Private Secy. to Rt. Hon. Anthony Crosland MP 1970–74; Chmn., Fabian Society 1977–78. *Publications:* Guide to the General Election (1964); Elections in Britain (1968); The Backbencher and Parliament (1972); Paying for Party Politics (1975); articles in Sunday Times, Guardian, Observer, New Society, Encounter; Assistant Editor of Economist since 1974. *Address:* 16 Albert Street, London, N.W.1.

**LEONARD, Nelson Jordan.** Professor of Chemistry. *B.* 1916. *Educ.* Lehigh University (BS in Chemistry 1937, Hon ScD 1963); Oxford University, England (BSc 1940); Columbia University (PhD 1942). *M.* 1947, Louise Cornelie Vermey. *S.* Kenneth Jan, James Nelson and David Anthony. *Dau.* Marcia Louise. *Career:* At University of Illinois: successively Fellow and Assistant, Instructor, Associate, Assistant Professor, Professor 1942–52, Head, Organic Division, 1954–63. Professor of Chemistry, Department of Chemistry, University of Illinois, Urbana, Ill. 1952—. Member, Center for Advanced Study, 1968—; Professor of Biochemistry since 1973; Investigator, Antimalarial programme, Committee of Medical Research, OSRD 1944–46; Scientific Consultant and Special Investigator, Field Intelligence Agency of Technology, U.S. Army and Department of Commerce 1945–46. *Publications:* contributions to professional journals; Editor, Organic Syntheses 1951–58 (Adv. Board since 1959; Bd. of Directors since 1969); member, Exec. Cttee., Journal of Organic Chemistry 1951–54 (Editorial Board 1957–61); Editorial Board, Journal of the American Chemical Society 1960–73 Editorial Advisory Bd., Biochemistry since 1973; Rockfeller Foundation Fellow 1950; Swiss-Amer. Foundation Lecturer 1953, 1970. John Simon Guggenheim Memorial Fellow 1959, 1967. Fellow, Amer. Acad. of Arts & Sciences. *Member:* National Acad. of Sciences; Amer. Chemical Socy.; Amer. Assn. for Advancement of Science; Chemical Socy. of London; Swiss Chemical Socy.; Gesellschaft Deutscher Chemiker; Amer. Socy. for Photobiology; Program Cttee. in the Basic Physical Sciences, Alfred P. Sloan Foundation 1961–66; Educational Advisory Board, John Simon Guggenheim Memorial Foundation, 1969—; Cttee. of Selection 1977—; Julius Stiegliz Memorial Lecturer, Chig. 1962; American Chemical Socy. Award for Creative Work in Synthetic Organic Chemistry, 1963; Synthetic Organic Chemical Manufacturers Award, 1970; Edgar Fahs Smith Award (Phild. Sect. of ACS, and Univ. of Penn. (1975). *Address:* 606 West Indiana Avenue, Urbana, Ill.; and University of Illinois, Urbana, Ill. 61081 U.S.A.

**LEONE, Giovanni.** President of the Italian Republic. *B.* 1908. *Educ.* Univ. of Naples—degrees in Law 1929 & Political Science 1930. *M.* 1946, Vittoria Michitto. *S.* 4 (one dec.). *Career:* Prof. of Law, Comenius Univ. 1933, Univs. of Messina 1936, Bari 1940, Naples 1948; Deputy, Constituent Assembly 1946; MP 1948–71; Chmn., Chamber of Deputies 1955–63; Prime Minister, June–Nov. 1963 & June–Dec. 1968; nominated Senator for Life 1967; Pres. of Italian Republic since Dec. 1971. *Address:* Palazzo del Quirinale, Rome, Italy.

**LEONHART, William.** American Diplomat. *B.* 1919. *Educ.* West Virginia Univ., BA; Princton Univ., MA, PhD. *M.* 1944, Florence Sloan Leonhart. *Daus.* 2. *Career:* U.S. Foreign Service—Buenos Aires 1943–46, Belgrade 1946–49, Rome 1948–50, Saigon, Phnom Penh, Vientiane 1950–51, Tokyo 1952–55; Member, Policy Planning Staff, Dept. of State & Alternate Rep., National Security Council Planning Board, Washington 1955–57; Student, Imperial Defence Coll., London 1958; Minister, sometimes Charge D'Affaires, U.S. Embassy, Tokyo 1959–62; U.S. Ambassador, Dar Es Salaam 1962–65; Special Asst. to the President, Washington 1966–67; Special Asst. to the President-Elect's Foreign Policy Rep., Washington 1968–69; U.S. Amb., Belgrade 1969–71; Deputy Commandant for Int'l Affairs, National War Coll., Washington 1971–75; Vice-Pres., National Defense Univ., Washington since 1975. *Awards:* Superior Honor Award, Dept. of State, 1966; Sec. of Defense Meritorious Civilian Service Award, 1974; Industrial College of the Armed Forces Distinguished Service Award, 1975. *Clubs:* Federal City Club, Washington D.C.; Princeton Club of Washington D.C. *Address:* Quarters 15, Fort McNair, Washington D.C. 20024, U.S.A.; and *office:* National Defense University, Washington, D.C. 20315, U.S.A.

**LEONTIEF, Wassily.** American citizen, Professor of Economics. *B.* 1906. *Educ.* High School, Leningrad; Univ. Leningrad, MA (1925); Univ. of Berlin, PhD (1928). *M*-Estelle Marks. *D.* 1. *Career:* Instructor Harvard University 1932–33; Asst. Prof. 1933–39, Assoc.-Prof. 1939–46; Professor of Economics Harvard University, 1946–53, Henry Lee Chair of Political Economy 1953–75; Prof. of Economics, New York Univ. since 1975. *Fellow* (Hon.) Royal Statistical Socy. London; (corresp.) Institut de France (1968). *Member:* American Philosophical Socy.; International Statistical Inst.; (Hon.) Japan Economic Research Centre, Tokyo; Nat. Academy of Sciences (U.S.) 1974; American Economic Association (President 1970); Hon. mem., Royal Irish Academy, 1976. *Decoration:* Officer French Legion of Honour (1968). *Awards:* Order of Cherubim, Univ. of Pisa (1953); Dr. (Hon. Causa) Univ. of Brussels (1962); Hon. Doctor of Univ., Univs. of York & Lancaster (1967); Bernard-Harms Prize, Economics, West Germany (1970); Doctor (Hon. Causa) Univ. Louvain (1971) and Paris, Sorbonne (1972); Nobel Prize in Economics (1973). *Publications:* The Structure of American Economy 1919–29 (1941, 1953); Studies in the Structure of the American Economy (1953); Input—Output Economics (1966); Essays in Economics (1966, 1967); The Future of the World Economy (1967). *Club:* Harvard (N.Y.C.). *Address:* Department of Economics, New York University, 518 Tisch Hall, Washington Square, New York, N.Y. 10003, U.S.A.

**LE PORTZ, Yves.** French financial executive. *B.* 1920. *Educ.* Univ. de Paris à la Sorbonne; Ecole des Hautes Etudes Commerciales; Econ. Libre des Sciences Politiques. *M.* 1946, Bernadette Champetier de Ribes. *Children:* 5. *Career:* Attached to Gen. Inspectorate of Finances 1943, Ministry of Finance & Econ. Affairs 1951; French Del. to Econ. & Social Council of UN 1957–58; Dir.-Gen. of Finance for Algeria 1958–62; Dir.-Gen., Bank for Devt. of Algeria 1958–62; Vice-Chmn., European Investment Bank 1962–70, Chmn. since 1970. *Address:* European Investment Bank, 2 Place de Metz, Luxembourg.

**LE QUESNE, Sir Charles Martin,** KCMG. *B.* 1917. *Educ.* Shrewsbury School, Exeter College, Oxford. *Career:* Served in H.M. Forces (Royal Artillery) 1940–45; Appointed Second Secretary, H.M. Foreign Service 1946; Baghdad 1947–48; Promoted, First Secretary 1948; Served in the Foreign Office 1948–51; Political Residency, Bahrain 1951–54; Attended NATO Defence College, Paris, 1954–55; Rome 1955–58; Foreign Office 1958–60; Ambassador, Bamako 1960–64; Councillor, The Foreign Office 1964–68; Ambassador Algiers 1968–71; Deputy Under Secy. of State, Foreign & Commonwealth Office 1971–74; High Commissioner Lagos 1974–76; Dir., Barclays Unicorn Group & Barclaytrust International (Channel Islands). *Clubs:* Reform (Chmn. 1973–74); M.C.C.; Royal Commonwealth Society; R.C.I.Y.C. *Address:* Beau Désert, St. Saviour, Jersey, Channel Islands.

**LERNER, Max.** American educationalist. *B.* 1902. *Educ.* Yale Univ. (AB 1923), Washington Univ. (AM 1925), and Robert Brookings Graduate School of Economics and Government (PhD 1927). *M.* (1) 1928, Anita Marburg (*Div.* 1940); and (2) 1941, Edna Albers. *Daus.* (by first marriage) Constance, Pamela (*Dec.*) and Joanna. *S.* (by second marriage), Michael, Stephen and Adam. *Career:* Asst. Editor, Encyclopedia of the Social Sciences 1927 (later Managing Editor); Member, Social Science faculty, Sarah Lawrence Coll. 1932–35; Prof. of Government, Harvard Summer School 1939–41; Editor, The Nation 1936–38; Prof. of Political Science, Williams Coll. 1938–43; Editorial Director PM 1943–48; Columnist, New York Star 1948–49; Professor of American Civilization and World Politics, Brandeis Univ. 1949—. World-wide syndicated columnist, New York Post 1949—. *Publications:* (books): Values in Education (1976); Tocqueville and American Civilization (1969); Tocqueville's Democracy in America (with J. P. Mayer 1966); Education and a Radical Humanism (1962); The Age of Overkill (1962); Essential Works of John Stuart Mill (1961); The Unfinished Country (1959); America as a Civilization (1957); Actions and Passions (1949); The Mind and Faith of Justice Holmes (1943), etc. *Address:* 445 East 84th Street, New York City; and *office* c/o New York Post, 210 South Street, New York City, U.S.A.

**LESAGE, Hon. Jean,** PC, CC, QC, LLD. Canadian *B.* 1912. *Educ.* Lic.-en-Droit, Laval, Univ. *M.* 1938, Corinne Lagarde

*S.* Jules, René and Raymond. *Dau.* Marie. *Career:* Practised Law 1934–45; Crown Attorney 1939–44; Deputy of Montmagny-L'islet in the House of Commons 1945–58; Parliamentary Secretary to the Secretary of State for External Affairs 1951–53, and to the Minister of Finance 1953. Minister of Resources and Development 1953, and Minister of Northern Affairs and National Resources 1953–57; Premier of Quebec 1960–66. Deputy of Louis-Hébert in the Legislative Assembly of Quebec June 1960–70. Leader of the Opposition in the Assembly June 1966 and 1970. Leader of the Liberal Party of Quebec May 1958 and 1970. *Awards:* Companion Order of Canada; Honorary degrees from the Universities: Laval, Bishop, Montreal, Mount Allison, Sherbrooke, McGill, Ottawa, Toronto, Western (London, Ont.), Sir George Williams, New Brunswick and Moncton; Dartmouth College (Hanover, N.H., U.S.A.) and School of Political Sciences (Athens, Greece). *Clubs:* Garrison (Que.); University (Que.); Reform (Que.). *Address: office* 150 St. Cyrille East, Quebec, Canada.

**LESCH, George H.** Director of Various Companies. *B.* 1909. *Educ.* Monmouth (Ill.) College and Univ. of Illinois (BS); Hon LLD Syracuse Univ. 1964. *M.* 1935, Esther Barrett. *Daus.* Elizabeth (Ramee, Jr.) and Georgette (Copeland). *Career:* Accountant: Arthur Andersen & Co., Chicago 1931–32, Colgate-Palmolive Co. 1932–36, and Colgate-Palmolive European Accounting Staff 1936–39; Office Mgr., Colgate-Palmolive S.A., Mexico 1939–48 (Exec. Vice-Pres. and Gen. Mgr. 1948–55); Vice-Pres., Colgate-Palmolive International 1955–57 (Pres. 1957–60); Pres., Colgate-Palmolive Co. 1960, Chmn. Bd. 1961–75. Member of Board of Dirs. of Bank of New York. Member, Board of Dir. America Sugar Co., Board of Dir., F. W. Woolworth Co.; Order of Merit of Republic of Italy (rank of Commander). *Club:* Candlewood Lake (Conn.). *Address:* 2817 Casey Key Road, Nokomis, Florida 33555, U.S.A.

**LESLIE, John Charles.** American aviation consultant. *B.* 21 July 1905. *M.* 1929, Jean Savage. *S.* John, Peter. *Daus.* Pauline (Lange), Susan (Munir Abu-Haidar). *Career:* Fokker Aircraft Corporation, Hasbrouck Heights, N.J. June 1928–Jan. 1929; Asst. to Chief Engr., Pan-Amer. Airways Inc. N.Y.C. Jan.–Nov. 1929, Assistant to Divisional Engineer of the Caribbean Division Nov. 1929–35, Divisional Engineer, Pacific Division 1935, Operations Manager, Pacific Division 1938, Divisional Manager, Atlantic Division 1941, Vice-President, Atlantic Division 1945, Vice-President, System Executive Offices, N.Y.C. 1946; Director and Administrative Vice-President, Pan-American World Airways Inc. 1950, Vice-President and Asst. to the President 1959, and to Chairman 1964–68; Senior Vice-Pres. International Affairs. 1968–70. Fellow, Amer. Inst. of Aeronautics and Astronautics; Royal Aeronautical Society. *Address:* 60 East End Ave., New York, NY 10028. and *office* 4502, Pan Am Building, New York City 10017, U.S.A.

**LESLY, Philip.** American public relations counsel. *B.* 1918. *Educ.* Northwestern University; BS (Hons. and Distinction). *M.* 1940, Ruth Edwards (*Div.* 1971). *S.* Craig. *Career:* Asst. News Editor, Chicago Herald Examiner 1935–36; Asst. Director of Public Relations, Northwestern University 1940–42; Vice-President, Theordore R. Sills & Co. 1942; Executive Vice-Pres. 1943–45; Exec. Vice-Pres., Harry Coleman & Co. 1945–49; founded Philip Lesly Co., U.S., Feb. 1949; Tisdall, Clark, Lesly & Partners, Canada 1958. President, The Philip Lesly Company. *Publications:* Public Relations: Principles and Procedures (co-author) (1945); Public Relations in Action (1947); Public Relations Handbook (1950, 2nd edn. 1962, 3rd edn. 1967); Lesly's Public Relations Handbook, 1971, most widely used book on the subject; Everything *and* the Kitchen Sink (co-author) (1955); The People Factor (1974). *Address:* 155 Harbor Drive, Chicago, Ill. 60601, U.S.A. (main office) 33 North Dearborn Street, Chicago, Ill. 60602, U.S.A. (other offices) 6 Crescent Road, Toronto, Ont., Canada.

**LESTER, Richard Allen.** U.S. Citizen. *B.* 1908. *Educ.* Yale University (PhB 1929), Princeton Univ. (MA 1930; PhD 1936) *M* .1937, Doris Margaret Newhouse. *S.* Robert Allen. *Daus.* Margaret Allyn (Wing) and Harriet Holmes (Tarver). *Career:* Trustee: Teachers Insurance & Annuity Assn. 1959–63, and Princeton Univ. Press 1958–60 (Vice-Pres., 1969–72). Asst. Prof. of Labor, Univ. of Washington 1938–40; Asst. Prof. and Associate Prof., Duke Univ. 1940–45; Prof. of Economics and Faculty Associate, Industrial Relations Section, Princeton Univ. 1948–74, Associate Industrial Relations Section; Chmn. N.J. Employment Security Council, 1954–64; Pres. Borough of Princeton 1960. Vice-Chmn.; President's Chmn. on the Status of Women, 1961–63; Chairman of Department of Economics 1948–55 and 1961–66. Dir. of the Graduate Program and Associate Dean, Woodrow Wilson School of Public and International Affairs 1966–68; Dean of Faculty 1968–73; Vice-Chmn., N.J. State Housing Finance Agency 1969–70; Bd. Dirs., Center for the Analysis of Public Issues 1971–76; Chmn., N.J. Public Employer-Employee Relations Study Commission (1975–76). *Member:* Amer. Economic Assn.; Royal Economic Assn.; Industrial Relations Research Assn.; Amer. Assn. of Univ. Professors. *Publications:* Monetary Experiments (1939); Economics of Labor (1941) 2nd Edn. 1964; Labor and Industrial Relations (1951); As Unions Mature (1958); Economics of Unemployment Compensation (1962); Manpower Planning in a Free Society (1966); Antibias Regulation of Universities (1974); Democrat. *Address:* 32 Maclean Circle, Princeton, N.J.; and *office* Industrial Relations Section, Princeton University, Princeton, N.J., U.S.A.

**L'ESTRANGE, Laurence Percy Farrer,** OBE, FRSA. British diplomat. *B.* 1912. *Educ.* Shoreham Grammar School; London University. *M.* 1933, Anne Catherine Whiteside. *S.* 2. *Career:* in Private Business 1932–39; H.M. Embassy, Venezuela 1939–42; R.A.F. 1942–46; H.M. Diplomatic Service in Spain, Salvador, Chicago, Philippines, Peru, Western Hemisphere Exports Council, Denver, Lagos, Ambassador in Honduras 1969–72; Consultant in the Export Trade since 1972; Elected Fellow RSA 1973. *Award:* Order of the British Empire. *Address:* 154 Frog Grove Lane, Wood Street Village, Guildford, Surrey GU3 3HB.

**LE SUEUR, Kenneth Lancelot.** British. *B.* 1906. *Educ.* Wellington (N.Z.) College. *M.* 1935, Edna Constance Reynolds. *Career:* Accountant, Commercial Bank of Australia, Auckland, N.Z. 1944; Sub Manager London 1948; Manager, International Dept., Melbourne 1951; Manager Wellington, N.Z. 1952, Manager for New Zealand, Wellington 1954, Manager, Head Office, 1963, Asst. Gen. Manager, 1964; Dep. Gen. Manager, Commercial Bank of Australia, 1964–69. Director and Gen. Manager The Commercial Bank of Australia, Ltd., Melbourne, 1969. *Clubs:* Athenaeum, Australian Savage, Melbourne Cricket (all of Melbourne). *Address: office* 337 Collins Street, Melbourne, Vic., Australia.

**LE TOCQ, Eric George,** CMG. British diplomat. *B.* 1918. *Educ.* Elizabeth Coll., Guernsey; Exeter Coll., Oxford (MA). *M.* 1946, Betty Esdaile. *S.* 2. *Dau.* 1. *Career:* Joined Commonwealth Relations, later Foreign & Commonwealth Office 1948; service in Pakastin, Irish Republic, Ghana, Uganda, ane Australia; High Commissioner in Swaziland 1972–75; British Govt. Rep. to the West Indies Associated States since 1975. *Address:* 18 Calvert Road, Dorking, Surrey; and *office* Foreign & Commonwealth Office, London, S.W.1.

**LEVARDI, Dr. Ferenc.** Hungarian. *B.* 1919. *Educ.* Esztergom Grammar School and Sopron Technical College (Diploma Mining Eng.). *Career:* Asst. Lecturer in geophysics and mine metrology, Sopron Technical College 1944–47; later successively mining engineer in Dorog coal mines, chief engineer, production manager, and eventually Dir. of Dorog Coal Mining Trust. Joined Communist Party 1947. Candidate in technical sciences; Pres., Mining Cttee., Hungarian Academy of Sciences; First Deputy Minister of Heavy Industry 1958–63, Minister 1963–71. *Address:* Bimbó ut 72, 1022 Budapest, Hungary.

**LEVEDAG, Edgar Peter.** *B* 1910. *Educ.* International School (Japan), University (Germany) and Hamilton Institute (U.S.A.). *M.* 1937, Agnes Margaret Cameron. *S.* Manfred Cameron and Robert Edgar. *Dau.* Rita Alice (Fischel). *Career:* President, Levedag & Co. Inc. 1963—. Branch Manager, John P. Herber & Co. Inc., Tokyo and New York 1948–54; Corporate Secretary and General Manager, Mol Shipping and Trading Inc. 1954–63; Import Manager, Sanyo Shokai Ltd., Tokyo 1931–40. *Member:* N.Y. Chamber of Commerce; Amer. Inst. of Mining & Petroleum Engineers; Japanese Chamber of Commerce (N.Y.C.); Far East Council of Commerce & Industry; Amer. Chamber of Commerce (Tokyo). *Clubs:* Downtown Athletic (N.Y.C.); American (Tokyo); Yokohoma Athletic (Y.C. and A.C.); Montclair Golf. *Address:* 19 Sunset Park, Upper Montclair, N.J.; and *office* 42 Broadway, New York City, N.Y. 10004, U.S.A.

**LEVERETT, Miles Corrington.** American nuclear engineer. *B.* 1910. *Educ.* Kansas State College (BS 1931); Univ. of Oklahoma (MSE 1932); Massachusetts Inst. of Technology (ScD 1938). *M.* 1938, Nancy Walker. *Career:* Senior Research Engineer, Humble Oil & Refining Co. 1938–42; Research

Associate, Univ. of Chicago 1942–43; Section Chief & Div. Dir., Clinton Laboratories (Manhattan District), Oak Ridge, Tenn. 1943–48; Research Associate, Humble Oil & Refining Co. 1948–49; Technical Director, Nuclear Energy for Propulsion of Aircraft 1949–51. Manager-Engineering & Manager-Development Laboratories, General Electric Co. Aircraft Nuclear Propulsion Dept. 1951–61; Manager Division Safety General Electric Co., San José, California; Consultant to several companies operating or building nuclear power reactors, 1976. *Member:* Amer. Nuclear Society (President); Amer. Physics Socy.; Amer. Inst. of Chemical Engineers; Amer. Assn. for Advancement of Science; Institution of Nuclear Engineers (British). *Address:* 15233 Via Pinto, Monte Sereno, Calif. 95030, U.S.A.

**LÉVESQUE, Joseph Adrien.** Canadian salesman. *B.* 1923. *Educ.* Bathurst Coll. (BA); Naval Univ. (BSA). *M.* 1949. Thérèse Tremblay. *S.* Jean Claude, Jacques, André. Bernard and Michel. *Daus.* Jocelyne, Denise, Louiselle and Hélène. *Career:* Agricultural Representative. Bathurst N.B. 1944–50; Asst. Agricl. Rep. Edmonton N.B. 1950–59; Agricl. Rep., Grand Falls, N.B. 1959; Liberal Minister of Agriculture, New Brunswick 1960–70. Hon PhD Social Sciences, Bathurst 1961; Ordre du Mérite Agricole, La Pocatiere, 1961. *Member:* Agricultural Inst. of Canada; N.B. Inst. of Agrologists; Knights of Columbus 4th. *Clubs:* Richelieu; Golf (Grand Falls, St. Leonard, Fredericton). *Address:* c/o House of Assembly, Fredericton, New Brunswick, Canada.

**LEVESQUE, René.** Canadian Politician. *B.* 1924. *Educ.* Laval Univ., Quebec. *Career:* Reporter-correspondent, attached to American Forces in Europe 1944–45; International Service of Canadian Broadcasting Co. 1946–51, war correspondent in Korea 1952, Chief of Radio-T.V. Reports 1952–56; Freelance T.V. Commentator 1956–59; elected to Quebec National Assembly as Liberal Mem. for Gouin 1960; Min. of Public Works & Hydraulic Resources 1961–65, & Min. of Natural Resources 1961–65; Min. of Family & Social Welfare 1966; Re-elected to constituency of Laurier 1962 & 1966; Co-founder of Souveraineté-Association, first Pres. of Parti Québécois 1968; returned to journalism 1970, daily articles on politics in the *Journal de Montréal* & the *Journal de Québec*; led Parti Québécois to victory in elections of Nov. 1976, mem., Quebec Legislature for Taillon 1976—; Premier of Quebec since 1976. Grand Officer, Legion of Honour; Grande Médaille de Vermeil. *Address:* 140 Port Royal, W. Montreal, P.Q., Canada.

**LEVIANT, Israël.** French. *B.* 1914. *Educ.* École Polytechnique; École Nationale des Ponts et Chaussées; Doctor-Engineer of the Faculty of Science of Paris. *M.* 1942, Andrée Cohen. *S.* Michel. *Dau.* Catherine. Chevalier Legion of Honour and Croix de Guerre 1939–45 (France); Medal of Freedom (U.S.A.); Duplat-Taylor Medal (British). *Career:* Engineer for Bridges and Roads 1938; Technical Adviser to M. Jean Monnet, Washington 1944; Asst. Director of Foreign Trade, French Ministry of National Economy 1945; President, French Supply Council, Washington 1946–47; Vice-Pres. Dir., Vacuum Concrete, Paris 1948, Pres. 1973–74; Gen. Mgr., Bechtel France, Paris since 1970. *Address:* 22 Avenue Bugeaud, Paris; and *office* 37 Avenue Pierre-ler-de- Serbie, Paris, 8, France.

**LEVINGS, Nelson Trimble.** Businessman, cotton planter, and former Commander U.S. Navy. *B.* 1903. *Educ.* Asheville (Prep.) School, N.C., and Univ. of Virginia (BS 1924; recipient Distinguished Service Award of Chi Psi). *M.* (1) 1925, Helen Hopkins (*Dec.*), (2) 1941, Mrs. Miriam Patterson Fairbank (*Dec.*). *S.* Nelson Trimble (Capt.) and Sanford H., *stepson,* Livingston Fairbank, Jr. (3) 1972, Mrs. Margaret Carr Howell, *stepsons,* Atlanta, Barrett Howell. *Career:* Commenced career with Central Trust Co. of Illinois (General Charles G. Dawes Bank) and became Asst. Vice-Pres. A delegate (conservative in politics) from Mississippi to every Democratic National Convention 1928–56 (excepting 1944, when he was in the Navy in the Pacific). Returned to Levingshire Plantation 1929, to develop the property; also became active in banking, newspapers, politics and civic affairs. In 1933 he took the lead (unsuccessfully at the time) in Mississippi for the repeal of the 18th Amendment. Colonel in the State Militia and *Aide-de-Camp* to the Governor (Hugh L. White) 1936–40. In 1939 defeated for Lieut.-Governor of Mississippi by a few hundred votes; and in 1946 was narrowly defeated for the U.S. Senate when he ran against Senator Bilbo. In 1942 he volunteered to serve in the U.S. Navy and was discharged with the rank of Commander (he hoisted the Mississippi State flag to the mainmast of the (third) U.S.S. Mississippi as they steamed into Tokyo Bay on surrender day to tie up in the same anchorage that the first Mississippi, under Commodore M. C. Perry, had used in 1853—the year Japan was opened up to world commerce). Vice-President and Director, Security-Columbian Banknote Co., New York; President and Director, 116 East 63rd Street Building Corp., New York; Owner, Levingshire Plantation, Moorhead, Miss.; Retired 1976. Honours: Admiral and/or Colonel on the Staff of Governors Chandler (Kentucky), Shivers (Texas), Ross Barnett (Mississippi) and numerous other Mississippi Governors. The Levings family went to America from the County of Fife (Scotland) in 1632. *Member:* St. Stephens Episcopal Church of Indianola, Miss. Chi Psi Fraternity (Pres.); St. Andrews Socy.; Southern Socy. of N.Y.; Naval Order of the U.S.; Military Order of Foreign Wars; American Legion; Veterans of Foreign Wars; Sons of the Confederacy; Sons of the American Revolution; Newcomen Socy. of England; Third Panel Sheriff's Jury of N.Y.; Royal Socy. of Arts; The Virginians. *Clubs:* Army & Navy (Washington); Metropolitan (Governor), The Church, Overseas Press, Broad Street, Adventurers, Economic (all of N.Y.C.); Greenwood Country (Miss.); Colonade, Farmington Country (Charlottesville, Va.); Tennessee (Memphis); Capitol City (Jackson, Miss.); Shinnecock Hills Golf, Bathing Corp., Ram Island Southampton Yacht, Meadow (all Southampton, L.I.); Chicago (Chicago); Deep Sea (Montauk, L.I.); Reading Room (Saratoga Springs, N.Y.); United Hunts Racing Association. *Address:* 680 West Wesley Road N.W., Atlanta, Georgia 30327, U.S.A.; 116 East 63rd Street, New York City; Levingshire Plantation, Moorhead, Miss.; Fairholme, Southampton, L.I., N.Y.

**LEVY, Walter James.** American economic consultant (oil); N.Y.C. *B.* 1911. *Educ.* Universities of Berlin, Freiburg, Munich, Hamburg, Heidelberg, Kiel. *M.* 1942, Augusta Sondheimer. *S.* Robert Allen. *Dau.* Susan Beatrice. *Career.* Assistant to Editor, Petroleum Press Bureau, London, 1937–41; Special Assistant and Chief, Petroleum Section, Office of Strategic Services. Member: Enemy Oil Committee under Joint Chiefs of Staff, 1942–44; U.S. Delegation on oil problems to United Kingdom and Sweden, 1945; Special Assistant, Office of Intelligence Research, Department of State, 1945–48; U.S. Delegation to Austrian Treaty Commission, June 1947; Consultant to President's Cttee. on Foreign Aid, Nov. 1947; Petroleum Adviser to U.S. Delegation to Council of Foreign Ministers, Dec. 1947; Foreign Economic Adviser, Socony-Vacuum Oil Company, and Consultant, Department of State, Mar.–July 1948; Consultant, Office of Deputy Administrator, Chief of Oil Branch, Economic Co-operation Administration, 1948–49; Consultant E.C.A., 1949–50; Consultant, President's Materials Policy Commission 1951; Adviser to Mr. Harriman, spec. rep. of President Truman on mission to Iran for the settlement of the Iranian oil problem, July–Sept. 1951; Consultant, National Security Resources Board, 1952, and Policy Planning Staff, Dept. of State, 1952–53. Consultant: Dept. of Defence 1951–54; International Co-operation Administration 1956–57; Consultant, Dept. of State Office of Under Secretary and Asst. Secretaries 1960—. Oil advisor to the Special Emissary of President Kennedy to the President of Indonesia, 1963; Consultant, European Economic Community since 1970. *Member:* Advisory Council, School of Advanced International Studies, The Johns Hopkins University; Council, Foreign Relations. *Awards:* President's Certificate of Merit, 1947; Dato Setia Laila Jasa (Brunei); Special plaque presented, Secy. of State for invaluable contribution to the welfare of the United States, 1963; Order of Taj-Iran 1969; Hon. C.M.G. Companion of St. Michael and St. George 1973. *Publications:* numerous articles and reports for periodicals. *Address:* 300 Central Park West, New York, 10024 and Westport, Connecticut; and *office* 30 Rockefeller Plaza, New York 10020, U.S.A.

**LEW, Dr. Yu-Tang, Daniel,** Professor & Director, Inst. of Sino-American Relations, College of Chinese Culture, Taiwan; Editor, *Sino-American Relations,* an International review in English. *B.* 1913. *Educ.* Yenching Univ., Peiping (BA 1937) and Harvard Univ. (MA 1940; PhD 1941). *M.* 1939, Yalan Chang. *S.* John, Anthony and Brian. *Career:* Chinese Delegate to Asian Relations Conference, New Delhi, & to Inst. of Pacific Relations Conference, Stratford-upon-Avon 1947; Private Sec. to Chinese Ambassador to Washington, 1943–46, & to Prime Minister of China, Nanking 1947–48; Prof. National Tsinghua Univ., Peiping 1948–49; Technical Counsellor, Chinese Mission to Japan 1950–51; Consul-Gen., Vancouver, B.C.; Minister to Brazil; Ambassador to New Zealand 1963–66, & to United Nations 1970–71. *Publications:* Manchurian Booty and International Law, 1946; Editor, First General Report of Joint Commission on Rural Reconstruction, Taipei 1950; Dimensions of Democratic Diplomacy, Ideology and the Bicentennial, a Forecast of Sino-American Relations. *Address:* College of Chinese Culture, Hwakang, Taiwan 113, R.O.C.

**LEWEN, John Henry**, CMG. British Diplomat. *B.* 1920. *Educ.* King's Coll., Cambridge—MA. *M.* 1945, Emilienne Galant. *S.* 3. *Career:* Royal Signals 1940–45; HM Foreign (later Diplomatic) Service: Foreign Office 1946–47; HM Embassy, Lisbon 1947–50, Rangoon 1950–53; Foreign Office 1953–55; HM Embassy, Rio de Janeiro 1955–59, Warsaw 1959–61; Foreign Office 1961–63; HM Embassy, Rabat 1964–67; Consul-Gen., Jerusalem 1967–70; Diplomatic Service Inspector 1970–73; Dir. in the Secretariat of the Council of Ministers of the European Communities 1973–75; HM Ambassador, Maputo since 1975. *Decoration:* Companion, Order of St. Michael and St. George, 1977. *Club:* Travellers'. *Address:* British Embassy, Maputo, Mozambique.

**LEWIS, Alexander, Jr.** American. *B.* 1916. *Educ.* Ursinus Coll. (BS); Univ. of Pennsylvania (MS); Univ. of Pittsburgh (PhD). *M.* 1942, Alice K. Lewis. *S.* Alexander III, Dennis James and Brady Mason. *Career:* Vice-Pres., Gulf Oil Corp. 1960–64; Dir., Manufacturing Chemists' Assn. 1964–68. Hon DSc Ursinus Coll. Governor's Science Advisory Cncl., State of Pennsylvania, 1965— President, Venezuela Gulf Refining Co. 1966—; Senior Vice-Pres. Gulf Oil Corp. 1967—; Vice-Chmn. U.S. National Cttee., World Petroleum Congresses, since 1971. *Member:* Amer. Chem. Socy.; Amer. Petroleum Inst.; Mfg. Chem. Assn.; Société de Chimie Industrielle (Amer. Sec.); Chemical Socy. (Amer. Sec.). *Clubs:* Longue Vue, University, Duquesne (Pittsburgh); Frosty Valley Country (Danville, Pa.); Chemists' (N.Y.). *Address:* 807 Valleyview Road, Pittsburgh, Pa. 15243; and *office* Gulf Oil Corp., Gulf Building, Pittsburgh, Pa. 15219, U.S.A.

**LEWIS, Arthur William John**, MP. British. *B.* 1917. *Educ.* Primary, Elementary & Technical College. *M.* 1940, Lucy E. Clack. *Dau.* Anita Wendy Jacqueline. *Career:* Engineer, 1933–38; Trade Union Official, 1938–47; Company Dir. & Consultant, Member of Parliament since 1945. *Address:* 1 Doveridge Gardens, Palmers Green, London N13 5BJ; and *office* Norman Shaw (North) G2., Embankment, London, S.W.1.

**LEWIS, David.** Canadian lawyer. *B.* 23 June 1909. *Educ.* McGill University (BA); Oxford (BA). *M.* 1935, Sophie Carson. *S.* Stephen Henry, Michael Edward. *Daus.* Janet, Nina. *Career:* National Secretary, Co-operative Commonwealth Federation 1937–50; National Vice-Chmn. 1950–54; National Chairman 1954–58; National President 1958–61; National Vice-President of New Democratic Party formed 1961; Member of Parliament 1962–63, re-elected 1965, 1968 and 1972; leader of N.D.P. resigned 1975; Prof. Pol Science Carleton Univ. *Publications:* (with F. R. Scott) Make This Your Canada: Le Canada Nouveau; Louder Voices, The Corporate Welfare, Bums. *Address:* 138 Rodney Crescent, Ottawa, Canada.

**LEWIS, David Sloan, Jr.** American. *B.* 1917. *Educ.* Georgia Inst. of Technology, Atlanta (BS Aero. Eng. 1939). *M.* 1941, Dorothy Sharpe. *S.* David Sloan III, Robert Sharpe, and Andrew Fielding. *Dau.* Susan Sloan. *Career:* From draftsman to Project Aerodynamicist, Glenn L. Martin Co., Baltimore, Md. 1939–46. With McDonnell: Chief, Aerodynamics 1946–50, Design Engineer 1950–52; Head, Preliminary Design Dept. Airplane Engineering 1952–55, Manager of Sales 1956–59, Vice-Pres. Project Management and Board of Directors 1957–59, Senior Vice-Pres. 1959–60, Senior Vice-Pres. Operations 1960–61, Exec. Vice-Pres. Jan.–Aug. 1961, Corp. Vice-Pres. Aug. 1961–July 1962, Pres. 1962–67; President, McDonnell Douglas Co. & Chmn. Douglas Aircraft Co. Div. 1967–70; Chmn., Pres. & Chief Exec. Officer General Dynamics Corp. since 1970. Member, Amer. Inst. of Aeronautics and Astronautics. *Clubs:* Old Warson Country; Racquet; Burning Tree; Conquistadores del Cielo. *Address: office* General Dynamics Corp., Pierre Laclede Center, St. Louis, Mo. 63105, U.S.A.

**LEWIS, Geoffrey Whitney.** retired. American diplomat. *B.* 1910. *Educ.* Harvard University (AB); Trinity College, Cambridge, England. *M.* 1936. Elizabeth M. Locke. *S.* Geoffrey W. Jr. *Dau.* Mrs. Robin Herbert. *Career:* U.S. Embassy, Karachi, 1956–58; U.S. Mission to NATO, Paris 1958–62; Counsellor, U.S. Embassy Amman, 1962–65; Ambassador to Mauritania, 1965–67, to Central African Republic 1967–70. *Address:* Cushing, Maine 04563 U.S.A.

**LEWIS, Kenneth**, DL, MP. British Politician. *B.* 1916. *Educ.* State Schools; Edinburgh Univ. *M.* 1948, Jane Pearson. *S.* 1. *Dau.* 1. *Career:* Labour Relations Manager, Row Hawthorne Leslie Ltd., Hebburn Shipyard, Co. Durham 1940–41; Flight Lieut., R.A.F. 1941–46; Chmn., Business & Holiday Travel Ltd. 1948–77; MP (Con.) for Rutland & Stamford since 1959. *Member:* Inst. of Travel & Tourism; Inst. of Marketing. *Publications:* Student Revolt (1963). *Clubs:* Junior Carlton; Pathfinder; RAF; St. Stephen's. *Address:* Dale Cottage, Preston, Rutland; and *office* 114 Grand Buildings, Trafalgar Square, London WC2.

**LEWIS, Robert Clyde.** *B.* 1910. *Educ.* Hampden Sydney Coll (BA); William & Mary Coll.; Atlanta Law School. *M.* 1948, Eve Newton. *Career:* Athletic Dir., Caroline County, Va. 1933–36. American Red Cross: Field Dir. 1936–40; Special Rep. to Great Britain 1941–42; Dir. Field Service, European Theatre Command 1942–43; Dir., China-Burma-India Command 1944–45; Commissioner, Far Eastern Command 1944–48; Deputy Manager, Southeastern Area 1948–50; Dir. of Operations, European Area 1951–56; Dir., Services to Armed Forces 1956–58; Vice-Pres., The American Red Cross since 1958. *Address:* P.O. Box 5724 Charlottesville, Virginia 22903; and *office* 17th and D Streets, Washington, D.C., U.S.A.

**LEWIS, Ronald Howard**, MP. Politician. *B.* 1909. *Educ.* Elementary. *M.* 1937, Edna Cooke. *S.* John and Colin. *Career:* Coal miner in Somerset. Moved to Derbyshire Coalfield, during the Thirties; Employed, L.N.E. Railway Co. 1936–64; Member of Parliament for Carlisle since 1964. *Member:* National Union of Railwaymen. *Address:* 22 Alandale Avenue, Langwith Junction, Mansfield, Notts.

**LEWIS, Ronello B.** American author and financial consultant. *B.* 1909. *Educ.* Univ. of Oregon (BA; Master of Business Administration). *M.* 1934, Margurette Troudt. *S.* Paul W. *Dau.* Phyllis (Mason). *Career:* Partner, E. F. Hutton & Co., Investment Brokers 1957–60; Vice-Pres. & Comptroller, Olin Mathiesen Chemical Corp. 1953–57; Controller, Radio Corp. of America 1949–53; various posts: Butler Bros. 1941–49, and Montgomery Ward & Co. 1932–41. *Publications:* Accounting Reports for Management (1957); Financial Analysis for Management (1959); Profit Planning for Management (1960); Financial Controls for Management (1961); Management Control Techniques for Improving Profits (1962) (all published by Prentice-Hall Inc.). *Member:* Phi Beta Kappa; Beta Gamma Sigma; Beta Alpha Psi; Financial Executives Inst. Producer and director of several hundred management seminars and financial forums for investment bankers and brokers since 1960. Republican. *Clubs:* Riverside (Conn.) Yacht; Whitehall (N.Y.C.); Rockefeller Center Luncheon (N.Y.C.). *Address:* Pecksland Road, Greenwich, Conn., U.S.A.

**LEWIS, Hon. Thomas Lancelot**, MLA. Australian Statesman. *B.* 1922. *Educ.* St. Peter's College, Adelaide. *M.* (1) *S.* 2. (2) 1971, Yutta Olivier. *Career:* Elected to N.S. Wales Parlt. as mem. for Wollondilly 1957; Served as Minister for Lands 1965–75; Minister for Mines 1965–67; Minister for Tourism 1973–75; Premier and Treasurer, State of N.S. Wales 1975–76. Member, Liberal Party of Australia, *Club:* Union (Sydney). *Address:* 'Redbraes,' Valetta Street, Moss Vale, N.S.W. 2577, Australia.

**LEWIS, Welbourne Walker, Jr.** American lawyer. *B.* 1915. *Educ.* Dartmouth Coll. (AB 1936) and Harvard Law School (LLB 1939). *Married. S.* W. Walker III, H. Hunter, and Berton B. *Career:* Partner, law firm of Smith & Schnacke 1945–76 (Associate, law firm of Smith, Schnacke & Compton 1939–45). General Counsel, The Mead Corp. 1955–75; Chmn. Bd. of Dirs., Master Consolidated Inc. 1950–67 (Dir. 1948–67). Director: Lion Uniform Inc. 1950— (Chmn. Bd. 1970—); Vulcan Tool Co. 1955—; Mead Investment Co. 1955–76; The Mead Corp. 1955–76; Dir., Dayton Aircraft Products Inc. since 1943. *Member:* Phi Beta Kappa; Dayton Bar Assn.; Ohio State Bar Assn.; Amer. Bar Assn.; Dayton Law Library Assn.; Dayton Cncl. on World Affairs (Trustee) since 1959; Dayton Private School Foundation (Trustee 1960–63); Cox Coronary Heart Inst. 1962–67 (Trustee) American National Red Cross (Dayton Area Chapter) 1965–71, since 1973; Trustee Diocese of Southern Ohio (Episc. Ch.) since 1974. *Clubs:* Ye Buz Fuz., Moraine Country, Dartmouth (Dayton), Harvard. *Address:* 765 Winding Way, Dayton, Ohio 45419; and *office* 2000 Courthouse Plaza N.E., Dayton, Ohio 45402, U.S.A.

**LEWIS, Wilfrid Bennett**, CC, CBE. Canadian citizen.; *B.* 1908. *Educ.* Gonville and Caius College, Cambridge Univ.

(BA 1930; MA 1934; PhD 1934) Hon. Fellow 1971. *Career:* Physics Research Cavendish Lab., Cambridge 1930–39; Univ. Lecturer in Physics, Cambridge, 1937–39; Radar Research with Air Ministry, Ministry of Aircraft Prod. and Min. of Supply 1939–46; Chief Superintendent, Telecommunications Research Establishment, Min. of Supply, Great Malvern 1945–46; Director, Atomic Energy Division, National Research Council of Canada, Chalk River, Ont. 1946–52, Vice-Pres. 1952–63; Senior Vice-President, Science, Atomic Energy of Canada Ltd. (Crown Company) 1963–73; Distinguished Professor of Science Queen's Univ. Kingston (Ont.); Canadian Representative, Scientific Advisory Committee to Secretary-General of United Nations 1955; renewed 1958—; Member, Scientific Advisory Committee to Director-General, International Atomic Energy Agency; also of U.N. Secretary-General's Committee of Experts on Implication of Nuclear Weapons, 1967. *Awards:* American Medal of Freedom (Silver Palms); First Award for Outstanding Achievement of Public Service of Canada, 1966. Atoms for Peace Award, 1967: Special 25th Anniversary Gold Medal, Canadian Assoc. of Physicists, 1970; Fellow, Royal Society (London) Royal Medal (1972); Fellow Royal Society of Canada: Fellow, Physical Society (London); Fellow American Physical Society; Fellow (1959) and President (1961), American Nuclear Society; Hon. Fellow Inst. Elec. Engs. 1974; Hon Fellow UMIST 1974; Foreign Associate, U.S.A. National Academy of Engineering 1976; Hon. DSc., Queens University, Kingston, Ont. 1960, Royal Mil. College, Kingston (Ont) 1974; University of Saskatchewan, McMaster University, Hamilton, Ontario and Dartmouth College, N.H., U.S.A.; Hon DSc McGill University, Montreal (1969), Laurentian Univ., Sudbury, Ont. (1977), Univ. of Birmingham, England (1977); Hon LLD Dalhousie University, Halifax, N.S., Carleton University, Ottawa, Trent University, Peterborough, Ontario, Univ. of Toronto 1972, Univ. of Victoria, BC (1975). *Publications:* Electrical Counting (Camb. Univ. Press, 1942); International Arrangements for Nuclear Fuel Reprocessing (ed. A. Chayes & W. B. Lewis, 1977); scientific papers in Proceedings of the Royal Society; Wireless Engineer; Journal of Scientific Instruments; Journal of Institution of Electrical Engineers; Proceedings of Physical Society; Proceedings of First, Second, Third and Fourth U.N. International Conferences on the Peaceful Uses of Atomic Energy. *Address:* 13 Beach Avenue, Deep River, Ont., Canada; and Physics Dept. Queens University, Kingston, Ont. Canada.

**LEYDENBACH, Joseph.** *B.* 1903. *Educ.* Licencié en sciences commerciales et financières Dr. en Droit; First Prize of the Conservatoire. *M.* 1963, Simone Massard. *S.* Théo. *Career:* Président: Banque Internationale à Luxembourg, S.A.; Banque Commerciale, S.A.; Banque Continentale du Luxembourg, S.A.; Société Electrique de l'Our, S.A., Luxembourg; Jeunesses Musicales, Luxembourg; S.E.L.F., Société des Ecrivains Luxembourgeois de Langue Française. Membre de l'Institut Grand-Ducal. Hon. Président de l' Université Internationale de Sciences Comparées, Luxembourg. *Awards:* Officier de l'Ordre de la Couronne de Chêne, Luxembourg; Commandeur avec Couronne de l'Ordre de Mérite Civil et Militaire d'Adolphe de Nassau; Commandeur de l' Ordre de Mérite du Grand-Duché de Luxembourg; Commandeur de l'Ordre de Léopold II; Grosses Verdienstkreuz des Verdienstordens der Bundesrepublik Deutschland; Croix de Commandeur, Ordre du Phoenix; Commandeur de l'Ordre de la République Tunisienne; Chevalier de la Légion d'Honneur. *Publications:* novels and works on the theatre. *Address:* rue des Cerisiers (Bellevue), Luxembourg.

**LEYDON, John.** Irish. Chairman. *B.* 1895. *Educ.* St. Mel's College, Longford, St. Patrick's College, Maynooth. *M.* 1927, Nan Layden (*Dec.*). *Dau.* Mary (Mrs. Barry O'Donnell). *Career:* Secretary: Department of Industry and Commerce 1932–39 and 1945–55, and Dept. of Supplies 1939–45. Chairman: Aer Lingus and Aer Rianta (Irish Airlines) 1937–49, First Pres. Inst. of Public Admin, 1957–60; Aerlinte (Irish Trans-atlantic Airline) 1958–61. National Bank of Ireland Ltd., Insurance Corporation of Ireland Ltd.; Irish Shipping Ltd. 1941–49; Mem. Council and Exec. Cttee, Irish Mgmt. Inst. 1957–65; Director: Cement Ltd. Member, Board of Governors, National Gallery of Ireland. *Awards:* Knight Commander of St. Gregory (Holy See); LLD (h.c.) Univ. of Dublin. *Club:* Stephen's Green (Dublin). *Address:* Our Lady's Manor, Bulloch Castle, Dalkey, Co. Dublin.

**LEYSEN, Vaast L. M.** Belgian university professor and banker. *B.* 1921. *Educ.* D.-en-D.; Lic en sciences not.; bacc. en philosophie. *M.* 1945, Maria L. Somers. *S.* Luc and Marc. *Dau.* Marie-Thérèse. *Career:* Extra-Mural Professor at Louvain University; Managing Director: Bank J. Van Breda & Co., Antwerp; Insurance Office J. Van Breda & Co., and Fiduciaire J. Van Breda & Co.; Hon. Pres., Vlaams Economisch Verbond. *Address:* 'Wilgendael', Bredabaan 43, Brasschaat, Antwerp; and *office* Plantin en Moretuslei 295–303 B-2200 Borgerhout, Antwerp, Belgium.

**LIDDELL, Donald Macy, Jr.** Lieut.-Col. U.S.A. Reserve. Investment counsellor. *B.* 1907. *Educ.* Princeton University (BSc 1928); graduate work at New York University and American Institute of Banking. *M.* 1940, Jane Hawley Hawkes. *S.* D. Roger Brooke. *Dau.* Jane (Bass). *Career:* Statistician: Bankers Trust Co. 1928–29, and White, Weld & Co. 1929–33 (both of N.Y.C.). Officer, U.S. Army 1933–35. Security Analyst, Fidelity Union Trust Co., Newark, New Jersey 1935–41; Officer, U.S. Army 1941–45. Investment Counsellor, Templeton, Dobbrow & Vance 1945— (Exec. Vice-Pres. 1951–61, Vice-Pres. 1945–51); Chmn. Bd. 1961–74, Chmn. Exec. Cttee. since 1974; Dir. 1946—, Templeton, Dobbrow & Vance Inc. New York City; Dir., member Exec. and Trust Cttee., National State Bank, Elizabeth, N.J.; Dir. and Treas., 930 Park Av. Corp.; Mem. Alumni Council, Princeton Univ.; Dir. NY School of Interior Design. *Awards:* U.S. Army Commendation Medal. Military Order of the Loyal Legion (Past C.-in-C.); Military Order of Foreign Wars; Socy. of Colonial Wars; (Treasurer-General); Sons of the Revolution; Pres., Order of Colonial Lords of Manors. *Publications:* contributor of articles to professional journals. *Clubs:* Union, University, Down Town, Badminton (N.Y.C.); Englewood; Englewood Field; *church:* Hillsboro; Lake Placid. *Address:* 930 Park Avenue, N.Y. City, U.S.A.

**LIDDEL, Urner.** American physicist. Consultant. *B.* 1905. *Educ.* Central Coll. (AB 1926) and George Washington Univ. (PhD 1941); Hon DSc Central Methodist Coll. 1963. *Career:* Physical Chemist, Fixed Nitrogen Research Lab., Washington, D.C. 1929–36; Physicist-in-Charge, Optics & Spectroscopy, Res. Labs. Amer. Cyanamid Co., Stamford, Conn. 1936–42; Head, Nuclear Physics Branch, Office of NavalRes., Navy Dept. 1946–51; Director, Physical Sciences Div. 1951–52; Chief, Physics & Mathematics Branch, Div. of Research, U.S. Atomic Energy Commission 1952; Director, Product Development, Bendix Aviation Corp., Detroit 1952–55; Biophysicist, Natl. Institutes of Health 1955–56; Director, Academic Year Institutes, Natl. Science Foundation 1956–57; Chief, Bionucleonics Lab. of Physical Biology, Natl. Insts. Health 1957–60; Asst. Dir.: General Research, Advanced Research Projects Agency 1960–61; Hughes Research Laboratories, Malibu, Cal., 1961–62; Assistant Director for Science, Lunar and Planetary Programs, National Aero and Space Administration, Washington, D.C. 1962–70. *Fellow:* The Physical Socy.; Amer. Physical Socy.; Amer. Assn. for Advancement of Science; Inst. of Radio Engineers; Washington Acad. of Sciences; Assoc. Fellow Amer. Inst. Aeronautics and Astronautics. *Member:* Optical Socy. of America; Philosophical Socy. of Washington (Vice-Pres. 1963–64; Pres. 1965). *Club:* Cosmos (Washington). *Publications:* numerous articles on molecular spectroscopy, hydrogen bonding, nuclear physics, etc. *Address:* 2939 Van Ness Street, N.W. Washington D.C., 20008, U.S.A.

**LIECHTENSTEIN, Prince Heinrich Hartneid.** Ambassador of Liechtenstein to Switzerland. *B.* 21 Oct. 1920. *Educ.* Schottengymnasium, Vienna and University of Political & Economic Sciences (Dipl. Kaufmann), Vienna. Chargé d'Affaires for Liechtenstein in Switzerland 1944–69, Ambassador since 1969. *Address:* Willadingwg 61, 3006 Berne, Switzerland.

**LIGHTFOOT, Howard Murray** OBE. Australian. *B.* 1904. *Educ.* FASA; ACIS. *M.* 1934, Elisabeth Archer Emmerson. *Daus.* 2. *Career:* Chmn. Nicholas Pty Ltd. 1953–67; Chmn. A. D. International Pty. Ltd. 1967—; Pres. Assn. for the Blind 1952–54, 1964–72; Member of Council, Inst. of Public Affairs. *Award:* Order of British Empire 1973. *Club:* Athenaeum; Peninsula Golf; M.C.C. *Address:* 4 Bonleigh Avenue, Brighton 3184, Vic., Australia.

**LIGHTFOOT WALKER, Angus.** American. *B.* 1909. *Educ.* Victoria Univ. Coll., Wellington, Canterbury University College, and Newcastle Schl. of Mines, Sydney. *M.* 1941, Amber Jacombe. *S.* 1. *Career:* With Broken Hill Pty. Ltd., Australia 1929–31; John Lysaght Ltd., Australia 1932–37, Gen.-Mgr., Rheem Australia Pty. Ltd. 1937, Exec. Asst. to President of Rheem Manufacturing Co. 1946, Vice-Pres. in charge, Rheem Int. Div. 1951, Dir., Rheem Manufacturing Co. 1955, Exec. Vice-Pres. 1956, Pres. Chief Exec. Officer

Sept. 1956 Chmn. Bd. and Chief Exec. Officer 1967–74 Chairman of the Board, City Investing Co.; Rheem Textile Systems Inc. New York; Rheem Canada Ltd., Ontario; Immobiliaria Rheem, S.A., Peru; Rheem Safim S.p.A., Italy; Rheem South Africa Pty. Ltd.; Vice-Pres. and Dir., Rheem Chilena S.A. Chile; Dir., City Investing Int. Inc.; Gen. Development Corp. Miami; Hayes International Corp. Birmingham, Ala.; International Marine Banking Co. Ltd. London; Marine Midland Bank New York; Rheem Blagden Ltd. England; Rheem. Hume Ptd. Ltd. (Singapore); Rheem Australia Ltd. (Aust); Rheem New Zealand Ltd.; Rheem Peruana S.A. Peru; Travail Mecanique de la Tole S.A. (Belgium); Sociedad Anomima Industrial Comercial de Aceros Rheem (SAIAR) Argentina; Fabricacion de Envases Metalicos S.A. (Spain); Honshu Rheem Co. Ltd. (Japan); Rassini Rheem S.A. de C.V. Mexico. Adv. Bd., Parmet-Participacoes Metalurgicas S.A. Brazil. *Member:* Council on Foreign Relations; Council on Latin Amer.; The Pan Amer. Society Inc.; The Newcomen Socy. in North America; Sales Exec. Club of New York; Trustee, U.S. Council Int. Chamber of Commerce. *Clubs:* Metropolitan; Pacific Union; Corinthian Seawanahaka Yacht; Deepdale, The Creek, Knickerbocker, Royal and Ancient, White's, Hon. Co. of Edinburgh Golfers. Buck's, Tryall. *Address:* 784 Par, Avenue, New York, N.Y. 10021; and *office* City Investing Co., 767 Fifth Avenue, New York, N.Y. 10022, U.S.A.

**LILIENTHAL, David Eli.** American. Chairman of the Board, Development and Resources Corporation, New York 1955—. *B.* 1899. *Educ.* DePauw Univ. (AB 1920) and Harvard Univ. (LLB 1923). *M.* 1923, Helen Lamb. *S.* David Eli, Jr. *Dau.* Nancy (Bromberger). *Career:* Chmn. U.S. Atomic Energy Commission 1946–50, and of U.S. State Dept. Board of Consultants on International Control of Atomic Energy ('Acheson-Lilenthal Report') 1946. Founding Director, Tennessee Valley Authority from 1933 and Chairman 1941–46. Member, Wisconsin Public Service Commission 1931–33. Practised law in Chicago 1923–31. Honours: Hon LLD; DePauw, Lehigh, and Boston Univ., Univ. of California and Indiana; Universidad de Los Andes (Colombia),and Michigan State Coll. D.P.A. Univ. of Illinois. *Awards*: Progressive Farmer Award for Services to Agriculture 1945; Catholic Committee of South Award 1946; Franklin D. Roosevelt Memorial Award—Government and Human Welfare, 1949; Page One Award, 1949; Freedom House Award, 1949; Public Welfare Medal of National Acad. of Sciences 1951. Comendador de la Orden El Sol del Peru, 1964; Brazilian Order of Rio Branco; Member, Amer. Acad. of Arts & Sciences; Amer. Philosophical Society. Council on Foreign Relations, Inc. (N.Y.); Asia Soc. (N.Y.). Trustee: Twentieth Century Fund; Committee on Economic Development. Democrat. *Clubs:* Century Association (N.Y.C.). *Address:* 88 Battle Road, Princeton, N.J.; and 1271 Ave. of Americas, New York City, U.S.A.

**LIM, Sir Han Hoe,** CBE, JP. British (Chinese) medical practitioner. *B.* 27 Apr. 1894. *Educ.* University of Edinburgh (MB, ChB). *M.* 1921, Chua Seng Neo. *S.* 2. *Daus.* 2. Resident, M.O., North Devon General Infirmary, Barnstaple 1918–19; Municipal Commissioner, Singapore 1926–32; member of Council, King Edward VII College of Medicine, Singapore 1930–41; member, Legislative Council, Straits Settlements 1933–42, Executive Council 1939–42; member, Advisory Council, Singapore 1946–48; member, Carr-Saunders Commission on Higher Education in Malaya 1947; member, Executive Council, Singapore 1948–50; Pro-Chancellor, University of Malaya 1949–59; Chairman of Board, Singapore Chinese Girls School; member, Public Service Commission, Singapore, 1951–56. LLD (Hon), Univ. of Malaya. *Address:* 758 Mountbatten Road, Singapore 15.

**LIMA, Dr. Francisco R.** Salvadorian Lawyer and Diplomat. *B.* 1917. *Educ.* Collège de St. Michel, Brussels; Lycée Lakanel, Paris; Quernmore School, London and Univ. of El Salvador (Doctor of Law and Social Sciences). *M.* Doña Edith Liebes de Lima; 3 children. *Career:* Postgraduate studies Univ. of Mexico, Rockefeller Foundation Fellowship: speaks Spanish, English and French; Practising lawyer 1945–56 (during this period represented, among others, the following international companies engaged in commercial activities in El Salvador: Lloyd's London; Texas Petroleum Co.; Standard Oil Co. of California; W. R. Grace & Co., Centro America Roebling & Co.; Jones Construction Co.). Delegate to 11th to 13th Sessions of U.N. General Assembly 1956–59; Conference of Plenipotentiaries on Maritime Law, Geneva 1958; Conference on Commercial Arbitration, U.N., N.Y. 1958; Vice-Chmn., Joint FAO/UNICEF Cttee., Rome 1958; U.N. Conf. on Commerce and Employment, Havana 1947; Social Security Seminar, Washington 1946; Conf. on Archaeology, Tegicigalpa, Honduras 1946. Previously: Dean of Faculty of Economics, and Professor of Labour and Commercial Law, Univ. of El Salvador; Head of Statistics Dept. Labour Office 1946; Head of the Social Security Commission 1947–49; Minister and Substitute Representative at U.N. 1956–59 Representative on the Executive Council of UNICEF 1957–59 Ambassador to U.S.A. and Representative of El Salvador to Organization of American States (Vice-Pres. of its Council and Chmn. of its Peace Commission) 1962–64; Vice-Pres. of El Salvador 1962–67; Pres., OAS Cttee. on Economic & Social Affairs 1964–65. *Member:* Int. Law Assn. (American branch); Academy of Human Rights; Child Welfare Organization; Friends of the Country; Assn. of Lawyers of El Salvador (Vice-Pres.). *Address:* c/o Ministry of Foreign Affairs, San Salvador, El Salvador.

**LIMERICK, Jack McKenzie,** M.Sc. FCIC. Canadian. *B.* 1910. *Educ.* Univ. N.B.; McGill; Queen's Univ. *M.* 1937, Elsie Anderson Wetmore. *Career:* Research Chemist, Fraser Companies, 1934–37; Chief Chemist, Bathurst Paper Co. 1937–41; Supt. of Control Dept. 1941–44, Technical and Research Dir. 1944–67; Company merged with Consolidated Paper Co. 1967 Associate Director of Research and Development, Consolidated-Bathurst Ltd. 1967–71; Consultant to the pulp, paper & packaging Industry since 1971 & to new mills under construction in Iran; Operations of Container Corp. of Iran, part of General Consulting Practice since 1972; Consultant on operations & organization, paper mills and container plants in Brazil, since 1973. Fellow: Canadian Inst. of Chemistry; Technical Assn. of the Pulp & Paper Industry. Amer. Chemical Socy.; British Paper & Board Makers Assn.; Tech. Sec., Canadian Pulp & Paper Assn. (Chmn. 1959); etc. *Publications:* many publications and patents in the field of pulp, paper and packaging. *Clubs:* Bathurst (N.B.) Golf (Past Pres.); Royal Montreal Golf; Engineers Club of Montreal. *Address:* 36 East Street, Suite PH4, Oakville, Ontario L6L 5K2, Canada.

**LIN, Chin-Ching.** Chinese Diplomat & Lawyer. *B.* 1923. *Educ.* Fu-Tan Univ., Shanghai; Taiwan Univ.—BL; Waseda Univ.—MA; passed Senior State Examination for Lawyer, Administrator and Diplomat. *M.* 1943, Wu, Ai-Kuei. *S.* 4. *Dau.* 1. *Career:* Dept. Chief of Civil Affairs, Taiwan Provincial Government 1950–57; Lawyer 1957–58; Asst., Japanese Section, Min. of Foreign Affairs 1958–59; 3rd Sec., Embassy of Republic of China 1959–62; Consul, Osaka, Japan 1962–66; Consul-General, Osaka 1966–67; Vice-Dir., Asian Dept., Min. of Foreign Affairs 1967–71; Counsellor of Embassy, Japan 1971–72; Adviser, Assoc. of East Asian Relations 1972–74; Vice-Rep. (Minister), Assoc. of East Asian Relations, Japan 1974–77. Holder of UN TAA Fellowship to study Administrative System in New Zealand. *Publications:* Criminal Anthropology on Criminal Law; Aboriginal Administration in Taiwan Province; Election System in New Zealand; United Nations Peace Force. *Address:* 8–11, Nishiazabu 3-chome, Minatoku, Tokyo, Japan; and *office* Association of East Asian Relations, 8, 1-chome, Higashi-Azabu, Minatoku, Tokyo, Japan.

**LIND, Albert William.** American investment banker. *B.* 1907. *Educ.* Harvard Univ. (AB 1929); Harvard Graduate Sch. of Business Administration (MBA 1931). *M.* 1941, Mary Helen Clark. *S.* Albert Clark, Hoxie Robert, Jon Aspegren and Thomas Martin. *Daus.* Mary Louise and Mignon Inez. *Career:* With First National Bank of New York 1931–38; with Sterling, Grace & Co. 1939— (General Partner 1942—; Limited Partner 1952–71). Partner, Bass Rocks Development Co. (Gloucester, Mass) *Director:* Seaboard Associates Inc., Welde Investors Inc.; Stuart National Bank (Fla); Port Salerno National Bank (Fla.); Mason (32nd Deg.); Shriner. *Clubs:* Jupiter Island, Hobe Sound Yacht (Hobe Sound, Fla.); Bass Rocks Golf, Bass Rocks Beach (Gloucester, Mass.); Le Mirador Country (Mont Pelerin, Switzerland). *Address:* Hobe Sound, Fla., U.S.A.

**LIND, Frithjof Andreas Dybwad.** Norwegian. Chairman of the Board: Kvaerner Brug A/S, Myrens Verksted A/S, Moss Verft & Dokk A/S, Mesnabrug A/S, Steen & Strøm A/S, Arendals Fosse Kompani A/S, and several other companies. Member of Board, Den Norske Creditbank, and Brage-Fram Insurance Co. *B.* 1899. *Educ.* Oslo Commercial High School. *M.* 1926, Lissi Eger. *S.* Frithjof, Jr., and Robert. Managing Director, Norske Esso 1936–62. Commander of the Orders of Dannebrog (Denmark), North Star (Sweden), and Lion (Finland); Golden Medal of Merit (Norway). Conservative. *Club:* Royal Norwegian Automobile (Hon. Member; Pres.

1947–57). *Address:* 13 Madserud Allé, Oslo 2; and *office* 126 Drammensveien, Oslo 2, Norway.

**LIND, Per.** Swedish Diplomat. *B.* 1916. *Educ.* Univ. of Uppsala (LLB). *M.* Eva Sandstrom. *Career:* Entered the Swedish Foreign Service as an Attaché, 1939; served in; Helsinki, 1939–41; Berlin, 1942–44; Second Secy., Stockholm Foreign Ministry, 1944–47; First Secy., Swedish Embassy, Washington, 1947–51; Personal Assistant to the Secy. Gen. of the U.N., 1953–56. Re-posted to Swedish Foreign Ministry: Chief of Div. of International Organisations, 1956–59; Dpty. Dir., Political Affairs, 1959–64; Ambassador with special duties (i.e. disarmament questions) and acting Chmn., Swedish Delegation in Geneva, 1964–66; Ambassador to Canada, 1966–69; Under-Secy. of State for Administration at the Foreign Ministry, Stockholm 1969–75; Chmn. Spec. Political Cttee of 29th session of Gen. Assembly of UN 1974; Ambassador to Australia since 1975. *Address:* Swedish Embassy, Canberra, Australia.

**LINDBERGH, Howard Vincent.** *B.* 1912. *Educ.* Boeing School of Aeronautics (Master Mechanic Dip., 1931) and Heald Business Coll. (Business Dip. 1933). *M.* 1937, Alma Chattin. *Dau.* Sherry Ann. *Career:* Purchasing Agent, Sales and Construction, Henry J. Kaiser Co. 1933–39; Sales Manager, Permanente Cement Co. 1939–40; Administration Manager, Sales Manager, Asst. Secretary, Executive Asst. to Vice-Pres. and President, Permanente Metals Corp. 1941–44; Director, Kaiser Community Homes 1945; Director of Experimental, Henry J. Kaiser Co. 1946; Sales Promotion Manager, Kaiser Fleetwings 1947; Vice-Pres. and Asst. Secy. and Manager of Styling Automobiles, and Vice-Pres. of Technical Assistance Aircraft, Kaiser-Frazer Corp. and Kaiser Motors Corp. 1948–53; Owners's Representative, Kaiser Hospitals 1953–54; Exec. Asst. to Pres. and Chmn. of Board, Kaiser Industries 1954–67, and to Founder Chmn. of Board 1957–67; Vice-President Kaiser Industries Corp., 1967–72; retired from corporate work 1973; engaged in own research, experimental and special projects 1973–77. *Address:* 2 Chapel Drive, Lafayette, Calif., 94549, U.S.A.

**LINDBLAD, Frederick Waldemar.** American. *B.* 1920. *Educ.* Worcester Polytechnic Inst. *M.* 1944, Vera G. Kingston. *S.* Craig W. and Ross F. *Career:* President, United States Diamond Wheel Co. 1944–68; Vice-President & General Manager, United States Diamond Wheel Division, United-Greenfield Corp. since 1968. *Publications:* Industrial Diamond Review, May 1968, Grinding & Finishing; U.S.A. and foreign patents (32). *Member:* ASTME, ASAM, IDA, Aurora C. of C. IMA, Aurora Foundation, etc. *Clubs:* St. Charles Country (Dir.); Svithiod; Detroit Athletic; Theta Chi; Elks; Moose; Y.M.C.A. *Address: office* 7 Hatherley Court, Prestbury, Aurora, Ill. 60507, U.S.A.

**LINDEBRAEKKE, Sjur,** LLD. Norwegian banker and politician. *B.* 6 Apr. 1909. *M.* 1936, Aagot Stoltz. *S.* 1. *Daus.* 2. *Career:* District Magistrate's Attorney 1932–33; Lecturer in Jurisprudence, University of Oslo 1933–36. Joined Bergens Privatbank, 1936; Chief General Manager, 1959–68, on leave from Bergens Privatbank, as Chairman of Post-War Economic Compensation Directorate. Member of Parliament (C.) 1945–53: Deputy Chairman, Conservative Party 1950–54; Chmn. 1962–70; Chmn. of Political Adv. Bd. of Conservative Party in Norway since 1970. Member of the Bd. Chr. Michelsens Institute for Science and Intellectual Freedom. Chmn. of the Bd. Bergens Privatbank 1968–75; Chmn. of the Bd. Bergen Bank (merger of Bergens Kreditbank & Bergens Privatbank) 1975–76 (Ret'd.). Chairman, Norwegian Bankers' Assn. 1954–60; Hon. Member of Royal Norwegian Academy of Science. Member, Institut International d'Etudes Bancaires. *Awards:* King of Norway gold medal; Knight 1st class St. Olav's Order. *Publications:* Negotiable Documents; Norwegian Indemnification Law; Documentary Credit Law: Ownership and Seizure in Bankruptcy Proceedings (thesis for the Doctorate); Confidence and Political Confidence; At a New Era (1956); Cooperative Society (1969); The Way Onward (1973). *Address:* Torvalmenning 2, 5000 Bergen, Norway.

**LINDELL, Karl Victor.** Canadian. *B.* 1905. *Educ.* BSc; Engineer of Mines 1928. *M.* 1930, Estelle Anita Jodouin. *S.* Karl, Jr., John, and Paul. *Daus.* Ruth, Claire and Victoria. *Career:* Engineer, Royal Tiger Mines, Colorado 1928; Mining Engr. to Underground Supt., International Nickel Co. of Canada Ltd., Ont. 1929–44; Underground Mine Supt. to Chmn. Canadian Johns-Manville Co. Ltd. 1945. Chairman of Board, Canadian Johns-Manville Co. Ltd. 1961–70; President, Asbestos and Danville Railway 1950–70; Chmn., Hazemag (U.S.A.) Inc. 1970–75; Vice-Chmn., Dir., Hazemag Canada Ltd. 1970–76; Pres., Karl V. Lindell Associates Ltd. Vice-President and Director, John-Manville Corporation 1967–70; Advocate Mines Ltd.; Consultant, Inst. of Occupational and Environmental Health, Montreal 1970–75; Vice-Pres. & Dir., Hazemag U.S.A. Inc. & Hazemag (Canada) Ltd.; in charge of the two subsidiaries of Hazemag, Dr. Andreas K. G. of Muenster (Westfalen), W. Germany. *Member:* A.I.M.E.; C.I.M.; Professional Engineer, Quebec. *Awards:* DSc *hon causa* Laval Univ. 1959, and Sherbrooke Univ. 1961. Michigan Technical Univ., DEng *hon causa* 1967; Michigan Technical Univ. Distinguished Alumnus 1972. *Clubs:* R. St. Lawrence Yacht; Asbestos Golf & Curling. *Address:* R.R.4. Danville, P.Q. JOA 1AO, Canada.

**LINDER, Harold Francis.** American. *B.* 1900. *Educ.* Columbia College. *M.* 1930, Bertha Rubin. *Daus.* Prudence (Steiner) and Susan. *Career:* Training in various businesses 1920–25; Cornell, Linder & Co. (industrial management & reorganization 1925–33; Partner, Carl M. Loeb, Rhoades & Co. (investment bankers and brokers) 1933–38; retired from active business and engaged in voluntary philanthropic work concerned with assistance to refugees 1938–42, 1945–48; Lt.-Comdr. and Comdr. in Navy with Bureau of Ordnance and in Secy's office of Procurement and Material 1942–45; Pres., Gen. Amer. Investors Co. Inc. (on leave of absence 1951–55) 1948–55; Dep. Asst. Secy. and Asst. Secy. for Economic Affairs, Dept. of State 1951–53; personal and family business affairs; Vice-Chmn. of General American Investors Co. and other corporate directorships; Treasurer and Chairman of Finance Committee, Institute for Advanced Study, Princeton; Director, Foreign Policy Association; Director, Institute of International Education 1938–Feb. 1961: Directorships in various corporations resigned upon taking oath of office on 2 Mar. 1961. Pres. & Chmn., Export-Import Bank of U.S. 1961–68. U.S. Ambassador to Canada, 1968–69. Chairman, Board of Trustees, Institute for Advanced Study, Priceton, 1969-73. Member, Cncl. on Foreign Relations. Dir., Inst. of Internl. Educ. Adv. Cncl., School of Advanced Intnl. Studies, Johns Hopkins Univ.; Finance Cttee. Smithsonian Institution; Hons. LLD Univ. of Pennsylvania 1972. *Clubs:* Cosmos, Century Assn., The Recess. *Address:* 10 E. 70th Street, New York, N.Y. 10021; and *office* 40 Wall Street, New York City, 10005, U.S.A.

**LINDLEY, Sir Arnold Lewis George.** British. *B.* 1902. *Educ.* Woolwich Polytechnic, DSc; CGIA (City & Guilds Insignia Award); Fellow, Woolwich Poly. *M.* (1) 1927, Winfred Cowling (*D.* 1961), and (2) (1963, Maud Rand. *S.* 1. *Dau.* 1. *Career:* Student apprentice, General Electric Co. Ltd. (G.E.C.) 1918; Chief Engineer, G.E.C. Ltd., South Africa 1933; Gen. Mgr., G.E.C. Turbine Works, Erith Kent, 1949; Director, General Electric Co. 1953, Man. Dir. 1958, Chmn. & Man. Dir. 1960–64. Chairman, Engineering Industry Training Board July 1964. Deputy-Chmn., Mortherwell Bridge (Holdings) Ltd. 1965—. Institute Mechanical Engineers, F.I.Mech.E.; President, British Electrical & Allied Manft. Assoc. 1962–63; International Electrical Assoc., 1962–64; Institution of Mechanical Engineers, 1968–69; Mem. Council City Univ. since 1969; Chmn. Council of Engineering Institutions 1972. *Publications:* Papers on Turbine Engineering. *Clubs:* Chislehurst Golf. *Address:* The Crest, Raggleswood, Chislehurst, Kent; and *office* Motherwell Bridge (Holdings) Ltd., P.O. Box No. 4, Motherwell, Lanarks. ML1 3NP.

**LINDO, Sir (Henry) Laurence,** OJ, GCVO, CMG. *B.* 1911. *Educ.* Jamaica College, Jamaica; and Keble College, Oxford. *M.* 1943, Holy Robertson Clacken. *Daus.* 2. *Career:* In Jamaica: Inspector of Schools 1935; Assistant Information Officer 1939–43; Assistant Secretary, Colonial Secretariat 1945 (Principal Asst. Secy 1950); Administrator, Dominica, Windward Islands 1952–59 (Acting Governor 1957 and 1959); Governor's Secretary, Jamaica 1960–62. High Commissioner for Jamaica in London 1962–73 and Ambassador to France, 1966–72 and Federal Republic of Germany, 1967–70. *Clubs:* Travellers'; West Indian. *Address:* c/o The Royal Bank of Canada, Cockspur Street, London, S.W.1.

**LINDO, Ralph J.** Panamanian. *B.* 1914. *Educ.* Menlo Coll. California. *M.* 1935, Marguerite Toledano. *S.* 1. *Dau.* 1. *Career:* Pres., Lindo & Maduro S.A.; Cia Nacional de Seguros S.A.; Primer Banco de Ahorros, S.A.; Cia. Panameña de Aceites, SA; Vice-Pres., Cia Sibros S.A.; Tolco S.A.; Colon Import & Export Ltd.; Director: Banco Internacional de Panama S.A.; Financiera Automotriz S.A. *Club:* Union. *Address:* Apartado 5300, Panama 5, Rep. de Panama.

**LINDOW, Wesley.** American economist and banker. *B.* 1910. *Educ.* Wayne State Univ. (AB 1931); George Washington Univ. (MA 1940). *M.* 1940, Eleanor Niemetta. *S.* John Frederick and Eric Anthony. *Career:* Economist with U.S. Govt. 1934–47; Asst. Dir. of Research and Statistics, Office of the Secy. of the Treasury 1944–47; Consultant to Secretary of the Treasury at various periods after 1947; joined Irving Trust Co. as Head of Economics Dept. 1947; Vice-Pres. 1948–61, Secy. 1959–70, Senior V. P. 1961–65; Head of Investment Admin. Div. Irving Trust Co. 1955–68, Exec. Vice-Pres. 1966–75; Exec. Vice-Pres. Charter N.Y. Corp 1966–70; Dir. 1968–76; Vice Chmn. 1970–72, Pres. 1972–75; Chmn. First Capital Inc. since 1975; Former Member, Advisory Cttee. on Banking, U.S. Bureau of the Budget; Advisory Cttee. on Tax Policies for Economic Growth, National Bureau of Economic Research; Assn. of Reserve City Bankers; Chmn. Research Cttee. Assn. of Registered Bank Holding Companies; Economic Adv. Cttee.; Amer. Bankers Association. *Publications:* Inside the Money Market, Determining the Business Outlook; (co-author) various Government and banking publications. *Address:* 23 Bellows Lane, Manhasset, N.Y. 11030, U.S.A.

**LINDSAY, George C(layton).** American editor. *B.* 1912. *Educ.* University of Illinois (BS in Commerce & Business Administration, 1933). *M.* 1935, Hazel D .Cook. *S.* George C., Jr. *Career:* Asst. Editor, Mechanization—The Magazine of Modern Coal, 1939–43 (Assoc. Editor 1943–46, Editorial Board 1946–47, Editor 1948–56). Co-Editor, Mechannual—The Book of Mechanization Progress, 1939–46 (Editor 1947–56); Editorial Board, Utilization, 1947–56. Editorial Director, Rock Products Magazine, Maclean-Hunter Publishing Corp., Chicago, Apr. 1956–64; Associate Manager, Concrete Products Magazine, Maclean-Hunter, Apr. 1956–64; Editorial Director, Coal Mining and Processing Magazine, and Metal Mining and Processing Magazine 1964–65. Gen. Mgr., Coal Mining & Processing 1965–69; Publisher since 1970. *Publications:* A Billion-Ton Year for Coal by 1975?, 1951; Coal Industry Expansion—A Must for Survival, 1952; Coal, Confidence, Capital, 1953; Aggregate Producers Battle Rising Costs, 1958; Aggregates Producers Invest for Profit, 1959; Will Expansion Bring Prosperity? (cement), 1960; Engineer Your Profits, 1960. Republican. *Member:* Amer. Business Press Inc.; Amer. Inst. of Mining; Metallurgical & Petroleum Engineers; Amer. Mining Congress; Illinois Mining Inst. *Clubs:* National Press; Rolling Green Country Club, Arlington Heights, Ill. *Address:* 2515 Farrell Avenue, Park Ridge, Ill. 50068; and *office* 300 W. Adams Street, Chicago, Ill. 60606, U.S.A.

**LINDSAY, Thomas Alfred.** Canadian executive. *B.* 1911. *Educ.* Univ. of Manitoba (BSc Elec Eng). *M.* 1942, Florence Edith Gibson. *S.* Dr. Ardis Brian and Dr. Peter Alfred. *Career:* Sales Engr., Phillips Elec. Works Ltd., Winnipeg 1934 and Canadian Telephones & Supplies, Winnipeg 1936 (Branch Mgr., Regina and Edmonton 1940); successively Branch Mgr., Ottawa 1942, Gen. Mgr., Toronto 1944, and Vice-Pres. and Gen. Manager 1951–53, Automatic Electric (Canada) Ltd.; successively Vice-Pres. 1953, Exec. Vice-Pres. 1954, and Pres. 1955, Phillips Electrical Co.; Pres. and Dir. Phillips Cables Ltd. 1955–75, Chmn. since 1975; Phillips CBA Conductors Ltd. (President 1969–70); Dir. Can. Standards Assn. 1957–75; Dir. BICC Intern. Ltd. 1974–76; Canadian Electrical Manufacturers Association 1958–61, President, 1969–70; Canadian Exporters Assn. 1960–65 (Governor 1966—); Canadian Electrical Assn. 1971–73; Pres., Brockville General Hospital 1958–60; Dir. Warnaco of Canada Ltd.; Dir. Black & Decker mnfg. Co. Ltd.; *Member:* Engineering Inst. of Canada; Assn. of Professional Engineers of Ontario; Canadian Standards Assn.; Canadian Red Cross Society; Newcomen Society; Institute of Directors (U.K.); Standards Council of Canada; Advisory Bd., Montreal Trust Co.; Trustee, Ontario Science Centre. *Clubs:* University (Toronto); Canadian (New York); Brockville Country; St. James's (Montreal). *Address:* 213 King Street East, Brockville, Ont., Canada.

**LINDSKOG, Claes Folke.** Swedish. *B.* 1910. *Educ.* Royal Inst. of Technology, Stockholm. *M.* Marguerite Thatcher. *S.* 2. *Dau.* 1. *Career:* Former Man. Dir., SKF Ball Bearing Co. Ltd., Johannesburg; Skefko Ball Bearing Co. Pty. Ltd. Man. Dir., Aktiebolaget SKF, Chmn. Bd. since 1971. *Address:* c/o SKF, S-415 50 Göteborg, Sweden.

**LINDSTRÖM, Bert Hjalmar.** Swedish. *B.* 1922. *Educ.* Licentiate in business administration. *M.* 1972, Viveka Vogel. *S.* 1. *Daus.* 2. *Career:* Manager, Swedish Wholesale Research Inst. 1948; studies in U.S.A. and France 1948–49; Management Secretary, Svenska Cellulosa AB 1951; Acting Manager, Finance Dept. of same company 1953. Financial Vice-Pres. 1954 and Exec. Vice-Pres. 1957; Financial and Administrative Vice-Pres. of Gränges 1959–63, Pres. of the Swedish Lamco Syndicate 1962–63. Managing Director of Götabanken 1964–71; Man. Dir., Dagens Nyheter-Expressen 1971–72; Dep. Admin. United Nations Dev. Program Jan. 1973. *Publications:* The Swedish Wholesale Trade (with Prof. Ulf af Trolle). *Address:* 500 East 77 Street, New York 10021, U.S.A. and *office* UNDP, 866 United Nations Plaza, N.Y., N.Y. 10017 U.S.A.

**LINDT, Dr. Auguste R.** Swiss diplomat (ret'd.). *B.* Switzerland 1905. *Educ.* Universities of Geneva and Berne (Law). *Career:* Special correspondent of several European newspapers in Manchuria, Liberia, Palestine, Jordan, Persian Gulf, Tunisia and Finland 1932–40; served in Swiss army 1940–45; special delegate of the International Red Cross at Berlin 1945; subsequently Press Attaché and Counsellor at Swiss Legation, London; Permanent Observer for Switzerland at U.N. 1953–56; U.N. High Commissioner for Refugees, Dec. 1956–Nov. 1960; has held a number of previous appointments connected with work of U.N.; has been Chairman both of the Executive Board of UNICEF and its Programme Committee; Pres., U.N. Opium Conference 1953; headed Swiss delegation to Conf. on the Statute of the International Atomic Agency, New York 1956; Ambassador to the U.S.A. 1960–62, to the Soviet Union since 1966; Delegate of the Swiss Federal Council for technical co-operation affairs, 1963–66; Ambassador to the Soviet Union 1966–69; Comm. Gen. Red Cross for Nigeria 1968–69; Ambassador to India and Nepal 1969–70, Pres. Internat. Union for Child Welfare since 1971. Adviser to the President of Rwanda 1973–75. *Address:* International Union for Child Welfare, rue de Varembé 1, 1211 Geneva 20, Switzerland.

**LINEN, James Alexander III.** *B.* 1912. *Educ.* Williams College (BA). *M.* 1934, Sara Scranton. *S.* James IV, Jonathan, Christopher and Worthington Warren. *Daus.* Ellen and Marion Margery. *Career:* Advertising Department, Time Magazine, 1934–38; Advertising Manager, Life Magazine 1940–42. Office of War Information (OWI) 1942–45; Head of OWI in Italy and the Balkans 1944–45, Publisher, Time Mag. 1945–60; Pres., Time Inc. 1960–69. Consultant, Time Inc. (publishers of Time, Life, Fortune, Sports Illustrated, and the international editions Time); Chmn., Linen, Fortinberry & Associates Inc. Hon LHD Long Island Univ. 1956, College of New Rochelle 1967. Hon LLD Adelphi Univ. 1966; Mem. Exec. Cttee. Nat. Urban League (past-pres.); Hon. Trustee, Adelphi Univ. (Past Chmn.). Trustee, Athen Coll. in Greece (Chmn.); Asian Inst. of Technology; Williams; Rockefeller U. (Chmn. Council); U.S. Council, International Chamber of Commerce (Member, Exec. Cttee.); Trustee, Asian Institute of Technology; Dir. Overseas Development Council; Joint Cttee. U.S. Japan Cultural & Educ. Cooperation, State Dept.; Member Japan–U.S. Friendship Commission, Advisory Cttee. of Japan Foundation and Vice-Chmn. U.S.-Iran Business Council; Grad. member, Business Council. *Awards:* Knight Commander, Knight Grand Cross (by the King of Thailand); Decoration of the Crown, Third Order of Iran; Rec'd Nararya Meritorious Dec. of Repub. of Indonesia (1974); Grand Cordon of Order of Star of Jordan (1975). *Clubs:* Blind Brook; Royal & Ancient (Scotland); Links (N.Y.C.); Stanwich, Round Hill Country (Greenwich); Mid-Ocean (Bermuda); Seminole (W. Palm Beach). *Address:* John Street, Greenwich, Conn.; and *office* Time, Inc. Time & Life Building, Rockefeller Centre, New York City, N.Y. 10020, U.S.A.

**LINK, Edwin Albert.** American aviation executive and oceanographic pioneer. *B.* 1904. *M.* 1931, Marion Clayton. *S.* 2. *Career:* inventor of the Link Aviation Trainer and Ocean Engineering Research and Development, small submersibles and other underwater safety gear; Consultant, Link, a Div. of the Singer Co. *Awards:* Potts Medal, Franklin Institute 1945); Wakefield Medal, Royal Aeronautical Society (1947); Exceptional Service Award, U.S. Air Force (1954); Frank G. Brewer Trophy (1957); Flight Safety Foundation—Aviation Week Award (1958); Nat. Aviation Club Award of Achievement, 1963; National Business Aircraft Assn. Award; Elisha Kent Kane Gold Medal—Geographical Socy. of Penna 1965; Arnold Air Socy. Paul T. Johns Trophy (1967); International Oceanographic Foundation, Gold Medal Award, Miami (1974); Aviation Hall of Fame (1976). Hon. Degrees: DComSc, Tufts Univ.; DEng College of Osteopathic Medicine & Surgery; LLD Hamilton Coll. Dr Sc from Syracuse Univ. 1966; Hon Dr Sc Florida Institute of Technology 1970. Hon. Trustee, Woods Hole Oceanographic Institution since 1974—;

Matthew Fontaine Maury Medal, Smithsonian Inst. 1971. *Publications:* Simplified Celestial Navigation (with P. V. H. Weems); A New Theory on Columbus's Voyage through the Bahamas (with M. C. Link); article. Man in Sea Project (National Geographic, 1963, 1964 and 1965); U.S. Naval Institute's Naval Review (with P. D. Gallery) 1967. *Address:* 10 Avon Road, Binghamton, N.Y., U.S.A.; and Link Port, Fort Pierce, Florida, U.S.A.

**LINNER, Dr. Carl Sture.** Swedish Int'l Civil Servant. *B.* 1917. *Educ.* Stockholm Univ., MA; Upsala Univ., D.Litt., Assoc. Prof. *M.* 1944, Clio Tambakopoulos. *S.* 2. *Career:* Dir., AB Electrolux, Sweden 1945–51; Dir., Swedish Employers' Confederation 1951–52; Exec. Vice-Pres., AB Bahco, Sweden 1952–57; Pres., Grangesbergsbolaget (mining), Sweden 1957–58; Exec. Vice-Pres./Gen. Mgr., Grangesbergsbolaget, Liberia 1958–60; Dir., Grangesbergsbolaget, Sweden 1960; Chief, UN Operation in the Congo 1960–61; Resident Rep., UN Development Program & Dir., UN INFO Centre, Greece 1962–64; Dir., UN INFO. Centre, London 1965–68; Resident Rep., UN Development Program, Tunisia 1968–71; Dir., Technical Advisory Div., UNDP, New York 1971–73; Resident Rep., UN Development Program, Egypt since 1973. *Member:* Royal Academy for Arts & Science; Sweden. *Decorations:* Star of Africa; Order of Phoenix; Prince Carl Medal. *Publications:* Syntaktische und Lexi, kalische Studien zur Historia Lausiaca des Pallidios (1943)- Giorgios Seferis (1963); Roms Konungahavder (1964); Fredrika Bremeri Grekland (1965); William Humphrey's First Journal on the Greek War of Independence (1967). *Address:* 2 Sharia El Nil, Giza, Cairo, Arab Republic of Egypt; and *office* 29 Sharia Taha Hussein, Zamalek, Cairo, Arab Republic of Egypt.

**LINSTEAD, Sir Hugh Nicholas,** OBE. British. *B.* 1901. *Educ.* City of London School; School of Pharmacy, Univ. of London; Birkbeck College. *M.* 1929, Alice Winifred Freke. *Daus.* Ruth Eleanor and Anne Marjorie. *Career:* Chmn. Macarthy's (Pharmaceuticals) Ltd.; Dir. Savory & Moore Ltd.; Secretary, Pharmaceutical Society of Great Britain 1926–64; Member of Parlt. (Putney) 1942–64. *Member:* Poisons Board 1933–57; Departmental Cttees. on Homosexual Offences and Prostitution, and on Experiments on Animals; Central Health Services Council 1948–66; General Advisory Council B.B.C. 1958–64; Medical Research Council 1960–64; Pres. Intnl. Pharmaceutical Fed. 1953–66. Chairman: Wandsworth Hospital Group, 1948–53, Parliamentary and Scientific Committee 1955–57, and Franco-British Parliamentary Relations Committee 1955–60, Conservative. *Awards:* Cmdr Legion of Honour; Cmdr. de Sanidad (Spain); LLD (h.c.) Univ. of BC, Univ. of Toronto. *Club:* Athenaeum. *Address:* 15 Somerville Hse, Manor Fields, Putney, London, SW15 3LX.

**LINTHORST HOMAN, J.** *B.* 17 Feb. 1903. *Educ.* Universities of Leiden and Dijon (LLD). *M.* 1928, (1) Jonkvrouwe E. Storm van's Gravesande (*D.*), (2) 1952, Maria Vittoria Senni. *S.* Jan Tymen. *Daus.* Louise Charlotte (Robertson), Jeannette Madeleine (Pels Rycken), Ernestine Amoene Sophie (van Schaijk). *Career:* Queen's Commissioner, Province of Groningen 1937–41; President, Government Office for Town and Country Planning 1947–53; President, Committee on European Recovery, International Federation of Agricultural Producers 1948–53; Vice-President, International Dairy Federation 1949–53; Director for European integration in the office for Foreign Economic Relations, Ministry of Economic Affairs 1952–58; President, National Olympic Committee 1951–58. Ambassador, Head of Netherlands Mission to European Economic Community and Euratom 1958–62. Mbr., High Authority of the European Community for Coal & Steel 1962–67; Chief Representative in the United Kingdom of the Commission of the European Communities 1968–71. *Awards:* Order of Netherlands Lion; Grand Cross, Order of the Oak Crown (Luxembourg); Grand Cross, Order of the Phoenix (Greece); Grand Officer, Order of Merit (Italy); Grand Cross, Leopold II; Cmdr. Mérite Agricole. *Publications:* European Agricultural Policy (1951); European Integration (1955), Memoire (1975). *Address:* 56, Via Cape le Casa, Rome, Italy.

**LIPPE, Freiherr Viktor (Hugo Rudolf) von der.** Dr. juris. Former Head of Division and Personal Adviser to the President, Deutsche Bundesbank, Frankfurt/Main (entered service in the Bank 1949). *B.* 1912. *Educ.* university studies in Vienna (Dr. juris.) and Consular Academy, Vienna (Diploma). *M.* 1944, Marie Irene Jantzen. *S.* Viktor. *Daus.* Theresia-Marie (Baronin Keyserlingk) and Clementine. *Career:* Attaché Foreign Office, Protocol and Legal Dept., Berlin 1938; at Consulate-General, Geneva 1939; Secretary of Legation, Berne 1940; with the Luftwaffe in World War II 1942; Defence Attorney at Nürnberg International Military Tribunal in the trials of Admiral Raeder, Krupp, and Under-Secretary Woermann (of the Foreign Office) 1945–48. *Publications:* Nurnberger Tagebuchnotizen 1945–46 (Verlag Knapp, Frankfurt/Main, 1951). *Address:* Landgraf Philipp Str. 19, Frankfurt/Main, Federal Republic of Germany.

**LIPSCOMB, Edward Lowndes.** Sales Promotion and Public Relations Counsellor, National Cotton Council and Cotton Producers Institute, 1967—. *B.* 1906. *Educ.* West Point (Grad.) and University of Mississippi. *M.* 1929, Cornelia Loper. *Daus.* Cornelia Blanche, Martha Ethel and Lynda *Career:* Asst. to Prof. of English, Univ. of Mississippi 1925–27; Editorial Staff, Gulf Coast Guide, Gulfport (Miss.) 1927–31 (Managing Editor 1931–36); Dir., Mississippi Advertising Commission, Jackson 1936–39; Director, Public Relations, National Cotton Council of America 1942–67 (Director, Sales Promotion Division 1939–67). President, Public Relations Socy. of Amer. (received their Distinguished Service Award 1957); Natl. Accreditation Bd. 1964–67; Pres., Agricultural Relations Council 1955; Pres., International Public Relations Assn. 1958–59; Chmn., Public Relations Cttee., People-to People Program 1956–57; Trustee, Foundation for Public Relations Research & Education Inc. 1956–58; member, National Defence Executive Reserve 1957–64, Adv. Board, Public Relations News (received their Annual Achievement Award 1950) 1953–55; Information Adv. Cttee., U.S. Dept. of Agriculture 1953–54; Consultant, U.S. Deleg. to International Cotton Textile Conf., Buxton. England 1952; Former Secy.: La.-Miss.-West Tenn. District Kiwanis International; and Gulf Coast Press Assn.; Somerset Chapter Magna Carta Barons; Sons of American Revolution; Pres., Tenn. State Socy., 1962–63, National Trustee 1964–65; Huegenot Society. *Awards:* Honour Medals by Freedoms Foundation, 1950–52–53–60. *Publications:* Grassroots Public Relations for Agriculture; The Personal Practice of Freedom; The Personal Search for Security; Public Relations or Peasantry; newspaper and mag. articles; booklets and sales literature. Public Relations Award, Advt. Fed of Amer., 1953. *Clubs:* Chicago Press; Memphis Advertising; Memphis Executives. *Address:* 94 North Goodlett, Memphis 17, Tenn.; and *office* Box 12285, Memphis, Tenn., U.S.A.

**LIPTON, Lt.-Colonel Marcus,** CBE, JP, MP. *B.* 1900. *Educ.* Oxford Univ., MA; Barrister-at-Law. *Career:* Alderman, Lambeth Borough Council 1937–56; Labour MP for Lambeth since 1945. *Decorations:* Commander Order of the British Empire. *Address:* 3 Wellington Court, Shelton Street, London W.C.2.

**LISTER, Sir (Charles) Percy,** KB, DL. British industrialist. *B.* 15 July 1897. *Educ.* Mill Hill and Royal Military College, Sandhurst (18th Q.M.O. Royal Hussars). Late Chairman and Managing Director, R. A. Lister & Co. Ltd., 1921–67; Chairman, Blackstone & Co. Ltd., 1936–67. Director of the following: Sir W. G. Armstrong (Engineers), Ltd. 1944, Harrison Lister Engineering Ltd. 1946, Broom & Wade Ltd. 1949. Hawker-Siddeley Group Board 1965. Joint Managing Director, United Kingdom Commercial Corporation, 1940–45; Capital Issues Committee 1946–67; Iron and Steel Board 1953–58. Dollar Exports Councils 1949–64. *Clubs:* Cavalry. *Address:* Stinchcombe Hill House, Dursley, Glos.

**LISTOWEL, Earl of,** (William Francis Hare) PC, GCMG. *B.* 28 Sept. 1906. *Educ.* Magdalene College, Cambridge. *M.* 1933, Judith de Marffy-Mantuano (marriage dissolved 1945). *Dau.* Diedre Mary Freda; member, L.C.C. 1937–46; Labour Party Whip in House of Lords 1941–44; Parliamentary Under-Secretary of State for India 1944–45; Postmaster General 1945–47; Secretary of State for India and Burma 1947; Minister of State of Colonial Affairs 1948–50; Jt. Parly. Sec., Min. of Agric. & Fisheries 1950–51; Governor-General of Ghana 1957–60; Chmn. of Committees, House of Lords, 1965–76. *Publications:* The Values of Life; A Critical History of Modern Aesthetics. *Address:* The House of Lords, London, S.W.1.

**LITHGOW, Sir William James,** Bt., FRINA, FBIM, MIPI (Patenter & Inventor). British. *B.* 1934. *Educ.* Winchester Coll. *M.* (1) 1964, Valerie Helen Scott (*D.* 1964); and (2) 1967, Mary Claire Hill. *Career:* Chairman, Lithgows Ltd., Lithgows (Holdings) Ltd., Scott Lithgow Drydocks Ltd., Campbeltown Shipyard Ltd., Western Ferries (Argyll) Ltd. Vice Chairman, Scott Lithgow Ltd. Director, Bank of Scotland. Member, Board of Nat. Ports Council; Queen's

Body Guard for Scotland (Royal Co. of Archers). *Clubs:* Western; Royal Scottish Automobile (Glasgow). *Address:* Drums, Langbank, Renfrewshire; Ormsary, By Lochgilphead, Argyll; and *office* Kingston Shipbuilding Yard, Port Glasgow, Renfrewshire, Scotland.

**LITRICO, Angelo.** Italian. *B.* 1927. *Educ.* High School. *Bachelor.* High Fashion Tailor and Designer. Grand Ufficiale della Repubblica Italiana. *Club:* Lion's. *Address: office* Via Sicilia 51, Rome 00187, Italy.

**LITTLE, Arthur Charles,** TD, BSc, FICE, FIOB, M Soc. CE (France). British. *B.* 1922. *Educ.* Univ. Coll. School; Cambridge Univ. Southampton University. *M.* 1944, Kathleen Mary Mills. *S.* 2. *Career:* Tech. Dir. Trollope & Colls Ltd. 1957–60; Man. Dir. Ronald Lyon Construction Ltd. 1961–65; Man. Dir. Hammond & Champness Ltd.; Hon. Treas. Concrete Society. *Clubs:* Army & Navy; Royal Naval; Royal Engineers Yacht. *Address:* Midlington House, Droxford, Hants.

**LITTLEFIELD, Edmund Wattis.** *B.* 1914. *Educ.* Stanford Univ. (BA 'with great distinction' 1936) and Graduate School of Business, Stanford Univ. (MBA 1938). *M.* 1945, Jeannik Mequet. *S.* Edmund Wattis, Jr. and Jacques Mequet. *Dau.* Denise Renée. *Career:* Trustee, San Francisco Bay Area Cncl. Mem., The Business Council; The Conference Board, Dir., Vice-Chmn., American Mining Congress; Member, Amer. Inst. of Mining, Metallurgical & Petroleum Engineers Inc. Officer, U.S.N.R. 1941–43. Special Assistant to Deputy Administrator, and Secy. to Domestic Operating Cttee., Petroleum Administration for War 1943–45. San Francisco Chamber of Commerce (Pres. 1956); Chmn. of the Bd. and Chief Exec. Officer, Member of Executive Committee, Director, Utah International Inc. 1961—. Chairman of the Board, Director, Marcona Corporation and its subsidiaries. Director: Cyprus Pima Mining Co., Wells Fargo Bank, Industrial Indemnity Co., General Electric Co., Southern Pacific Co., and Southern Pacific Transportation Co.; Phi Beta Kappa; Pres., Beavers, 1967; Chmn. Stanford Research Inst. *Clubs:* Bohemian, Burlingame Country Cypress Point, The Pacific-Union, San Francisco Golf; Augusta; Natl. Golf; Stock Exchange, Chi Psi Fraternity; The Links. *Address:* 1170 Sacramento Street, San Francisco, Calif. 94108; and *office* 550 California Street, San Francisco, Calif. 94104, U.S.A.

**LIU CHIEH.** Chinese diplomat. *B.* 1906. *Educ.* Oxford and Columbia Universities. *Career:* Secretary Legislative Yuan, Nanking 1929–31; Senior Secretary, Ministry of Foreign Affairs 1931–32; First Secretary and Counsellor, Embassy, London, 1932–40; Counsellor, Chinese Delegation to League of Nations 1932–39; Counsellor and Min. Plen., Washington, 1940–45; Vice-Minister, Foreign Affairs, Nat. Government of China, 1945–47; Chmn., Far Eastern War Crimes Commission 1946–47; U.N. Trusteeship Council 1943–49; President of the Council 1948; Delegate, 1st to 25th Sessions, U.N. General Assembly, 1946–68; Chief Delegate to a number of international conferences, including U.N. Conference on Law of the Sea, Geneva, 1958 and 1960; Ambassador to Canada 1947–63. Permanent Representative to U.N. 1963–71; Ambassador to the Philippines 1972–75. *Address:* c/o Ministry of Foreign Affairs, Taipei, Taiwan.

**LIVESEY, Stewart Ward.** British. *B.* 1905. *Educ.* Arnold School (Blackpool, Lancs.) and Manchester University (BA 1931). *Career:* With Calico Printers Association Ltd., Manchester 1924–36; Export Manager, Small & Parkes Ltd., Manchester 1936–39; Capt. R.A.O.C. 1939–40; Mgr., British Overseas Cottons Ltd. 1940–45; Production Director, William Yates & Sons Ltd., Boothstown, Manchester 1945–49; Man. Dir., Fothergill & Harvey Ltd., 1949–64, Chmn., since 1964. Dir., Plantation Holdings Ltd. (Former Chmn.); Sutcliffe Speakman & Co. Ltd.; Leigh, Lancs. Underwriting member of Lloyds. *Clubs:* Royal & Ancient Golf (St. Andrews); St. James's (Manchester); Pratts. *Address:* Rookwood, 68 Styal Road, Wilmslow, Cheshire; and *office* Sutcliffe Speakman & Co. Ltd., Guest St. Leigh, Lancs.

**LIZOTTE, Hon. Fernand.** Canadian. Former Minister of Transport, Government of the Province of Quebec. *B.* 1904. *Educ.* Doctor of Medicine. *M.* 1944, Claire Pelletier. *S.* Claudel, Pierre and André. *Daus.* Marie and France. *Awards:* decoration for voluntary service oversea. *Address:* Saint-Jean-Port-Joli, P.Q., Canada.

**LLESHI, Maj.-Gen. Haxhi.** Chairman of the Presidium of the Albanian People's Assembly 1953—. *B.* 1913. Fought with the resistance against the German and Italian occupations 1939–45; member of Provisonal Govt. 1944; Minister without Portfolio 1946. Member of the Central Committee of the Albanian People's Party. *Address:* Presidium of the People's Assembly, Tirana, Albania.

**LLEWELLYN, Lt.-Col. Sir Henry Morton,** Kt, CBE, MA, DL. British. *B.* 1911. *Educ.* MA Cambridge 1933. *M.* 1944, The Hon. Christine Saumarez. *S.* David St. Vincent and Roderic Victor. *Dau.* Anna Christina. *Career:* Managing Dir., C. L. Clay & Co. Ltd. (coal exporters and coal mine proprietors) 1936–47; Pres. Whitbread Wales Ltd.; Chmn. Davenco (Engineers) Ltd.; Chmn. S. Wales Board Eagle Star Ins.; Chmn. Nationwide Building Society Ltd. (Wales); Dir.: Whitbread International Ltd., Lloyds Bank (South Wales Region). Member Wales Tourist Board 1969–75. Chmn. Sports Council for Wales. President: Wales Branch Inst. of Directors 1963–65, Inst. of Marketing (Wales) 1965–67; Riding Captain British Show Jumping Team, winners Olympic Gold Medal, 1952. *Awards:* OBE (Mil.) 1943; U.S. Legion of Merit 1944; Royal Humane Socy. Medal 1956; Knight Bachelor 1977. *Club:* Jockey; Cavalry. *Address:* Llanvair Grange, Abergavenny, Gwent.

**LLEWELYN -DAVIES OF HASTOE, Baroness Patricia.** P.C. British politician. *B.* 1915. *Educ.* Liverpool Coll. Huyton; Girton Coll. Cambridge. *M.* 1943, The Lord Llewelyn-Davies. *S.* 3. *Career:* Civil Servant 1940–51, Min. of War Transport, F. office, Air Min., CRO, Contested Wolverhampton SW. (Lab.) 1951, Wandsworth Central 1955 and 1959; Member, Bd. Governors Hospital, Sick Children Gt. Ormond St. 1955–67, Chmn. 1967–69; Court Univ. of Sussex 1967–69; Dir. Africa Educ. Trust 1960–69; Hon. Secy. Labour Parly. Assn. 1960–69; A Baroness in Waiting Govt. Whip 1969–70; Chmn. Woman's Nat. Cancer Control Campaign 1972–74; Deputy Chief Whip, Opposition 1972–74; Privy Counsellor 1975; Government Chief Whip, House of Lords, Capt. Honourable Corps of Gentlemen-at-Arms since 1974; Co.-Chmn., Women's National Commission 1976. *Address:* House of Lords, Westminster, London, S.W.1.

**LLOYD of Dolobran, Lord** (Alexander David Frederick Lloyd), DL (Herts. 1963), MBE. *B.* 1912. *Educ.* Eton; Trinity Coll., Cambridge (MA). *M.* 1942, Lady Jean Ogilvy *Daus.* Davina Margaret, Laura Blanche Bridget. *Career:* served in World War II, in Palestine, Syria and N.W. Europe 1939–45; President, Navy League 1948–51; member, L.C.C. 1949–51; Lord in Waiting to King George VI and later to Queen Elizabeth II 1951–52; Under-Secy. of State for Welsh Affairs, Home Office 1952–54; for the Colonies Oct. 1954–Jan. 1957. Director, Lloyd's Bank; Dir., Lloyds Bank International; Chmn., National Bank of New Zealand; Member, Court of Governors, School of Hygiene and Tropical Medicine. Pres. Fed. of Commonwealth & British Empire Chambers of Commerce 1958–62; Member, White Fish Authority and Herring Bd. 1963–69. *Address:* Clouds Hill, Offley, Hitchin, Herts.

**LLOYD, Angus Selwyn.** British company director. *B.* 1935. *Educ.* Charterhouse School (G.C.E.). *M.* 1961, Wanda Davidson. *S.* James Selwyn, Christopher Robert Henry, Richard Gary. *Daus.* Virginia Elaine, Philippa Juliet. *Career:* Served with King's Royal Hussars, Malaya, 1955. Director: Oscar and Peter Johnson Ltd., Lowndes Lodge Gallery (Fine English pictures, 27 Lowndes Street, London, S.W.1) Henri-Lloyd Ltd. (Smithfold Lane, Walkden, Manchester); Chairman, Yachting and Angling Wear manufacturers, Henri-Lloyd (U.S.A.) Inc., (616 Third Street, Annapolis, M.D. 21403, U.S.A); Sealproof Ltd.; Craig-Lloyd Estates Ltd. (Property Company). Member, The Worshipful Company of Stationers & Newspaper Makers. *Clubs:* Cavalry; Royal St. Georges Golf; The Berkshire Golf; Walton Heath Golf; Royal West Norfolk Golf. *Address:* East Court, Beech Avenue, Effingham, Surrey; and *office* Oscar & Peter Johnson Ltd., Lowndes Lodge Gallery, 27 Lowndes Street, London, S.W.1.

**LLOYD, Prof. (William) Arnold de Gorges.** British. *B.* 1904. *Educ.* Sidcot School and Trinity College, Cambridge; PhD. *M.* 1952, Daphne Stella Harris. *S.* René Frederick Jonathan, Dafydd de Gorges. *Dau.* Dilys Mary. *Career:* Schoolmaster, Rhondda Technical School 1926; second Master, Halstead School 1927–32; Lecturer in Education, Selly Oak Colleges 1932–34; Director, Midland Adult Schools 1934–38; Sixth Form Master, Handsworth Grammar School 1939–44; research, Trinity College, Cambridge 1944–46; Lecturer in Education, University of Nottingham 1946–52; Professor of Education, University of Natal 1952–56; Professor of Education, Univ. of the Witwatersrand 1956-59. Travelling fellowship to Universities of Italy, France and Great Britain, 1956; and to Harvard, Columbia and Swarthmore 1957-58. Professor of Education, Cambridge University 1959-71; Fellow of Trinity College 1961—. Chairman, Nuffield Classics Project, Cambridge 1965-71. Fellow of Haverford College, Pennsylvania, 1959. *Publications:* God in the Experience of Men (1938); God in the Experience of Youth (1940); Quaker Social History (1950); Creative Learning (1952); Education and Human Relations (1957); The Old and the New Schoolmaster (1960); The Principals & Practice of Education, (1964); (Ed.) International Dictionary of Educational Terms, Vol. 1, England & Wales (1970). Editor: Pedagogica Europaea, (1964—); Journal of Conflict Resolution (Chicago 1957). *Address:* Trinity College, Cambridge; and Withersfield House, Withersfield, West Suffolk.

**LLOYD, Ian Stewart,** MA, MSc., MP. British. *B.* 1921. *Educ.* Michaelhouse (Natal). Univ. of the Witwatersrand; King's Coll. Cambridge; Administrative Staff College. *M.* 1951, Frances Dorward Addison. *S.* 3. *Career:* Pilot S. African Air Force, 1941-45; Post Grad. Work Cambridge Univ. 1945-49; Economic Adviser, Central Mining & Investment Corp. 1950-53; Member, Board of Trade & Industry S. Africa, 1953-55; Dir. Acton Society Trust London, 1955-56; Economic Adviser, British & Commonwealth Shipping Co. since 1957; Chmn. U.K. Cttee. I.C.H.C.A. 1960-64; and Isis Computer Services 1963-77; Member of Parliament, for Portsmouth Langstone 1964-74, for Havant & Waterlooville since 1974; Chmn. Select Sub-Cttee on Science since 1975; Member, Council of Europe and W.E.U. 1967-72; Dir. Bricomin Ltd. since 1970. Fellow, Royal Statistical Society. *Publications:* Articles in Econ. Journal; Jnl. of Industrial Economics; The Listener; The Spectator; The Times. *Clubs:* Brooks; Army & Navy; Royal Yacht Squadron; Royal Cork Yacht. *Address:* Bakers House Priors Dean, Petersfield, and *office* Cayzer House, 2 St. Mary Axe, London, EC3A 8BP.

**LLOYD, John Edward,** TD. British chartered accountant. *B.* 23 June 1901. *Educ.* Wycliffe College and St. John's College, Cambridge; Fellow of Institute of Chartered Accounts. *M.* (1) 1927 Marjorie Kidgell, and (2) 1949, Mavis Wise. *S.* 1. *Dau.* 1. *Career:* Member, Institute of Chartered Accountants (since 1926); served in Territorial Army 1921-51, and in World War II (Lt.-Col. H.Q., 21 Army Group 1944-45) 1939-45; Chmn., Assn. of Investment Trusts 1964-67. Chmn. St Martin's Property Corp. Ltd. 1967-72 & 1974; Commanded a T.A. Regiment 1947-51. Colon. T.A. (retd.). *Address:* 32 Hamilton Terrace, London, N.W.8.

**LLOYD, John Owen,** CBE, BA. Diplomat (retired). *B.* 1914. *Educ.* Marlborough Coll.; Clare Coll. Cambridge *M.* (1) *S.* 1. (2) 1972, Barbara Diana Clarke. *Career:* Vice Consul Tokyo 1937-42; Second Secretary Foreign Office 1943-46; First Secy. Commissioner General's Office Singapore 1946-48; First Secy. Foreign Office 1948-52; Canadian Defence College 1952-53; First Secy. (Commercial) Paris 1953-56; Counsellor Singapore 1957-60; Inspector Foreign Commonwealth Office 1960-63; Consul General Osaka 1963-67; Consul General San Francisco 1967-70; British Ambassador to Laos 1970-74; (retired 1974). *Awards:* Commander British Empire; B.A. (Cantab.). *Address:* 18 Reynolds Close. Hampstead Way, London, N.W.11.

**LLOYD, Trevor.** Canadian. Geographical consultant. *B.* 1906. *Educ.* Sidcot School; BSc, DSc (Bristol); PhD (Clark, U.S.); Cert. in Education (London); Collegiate Teaching Lic. (Manitoba). *M.* (1) 1936, Joan Glassco (*Div.*), and (2) 1966, Beryl Chadwick (*Dec.*). *S.* 1. *Dau.* 1. *Career:* Professor of Geography, Dartmouth College (Hanover, U.S.A.) 1942-59; H.M. Consul for Canada in Greenland 1944-45; Chief Geographer, Government of Canada 1947-48; Professor of Geography McGill University, Montreal 1959-77, Prof. Emeritus 1977—. Chmn. Dept. of Geography, McGill Univ., Montreal 1962-67; Dir. McGill Univ. Centre, Northern Studies & Research 1973-77; Exec. Dir., Assn. of Canadian Universities for Northern Studies, Ottawa 1977—. *Publications:* Canada and Her Neighbours; Southern Lands; Lands of Europe and Asia; A Geographer's World; and many articles in scientific journals. Canada Centennial Medal 1967; MA (Hon) Dartmouth, U.S. *Fellow:* Arctic Institute of North America, American Geographical Society, N.Y., and Royal Geographic Society; LLD (Hon.) Univ. of Windsor Canada 1973. *Member:* Association Amer. Geographers; Canadian Assn. Geographers (Ex-Pres.), Distinguished Service Award 1977; Arctic Institute of N. Amer. Former Chmn. Canadian Inst. International Affairs; Greenland Society; Pres. McGill Assn. University Teachers, 1969-71; Canadian-Scandinavian Foundation (Pres. 1975-77); Fellow, Royal Society of Canada (1976). *Clubs:* McGill Faculty (Montreal); Member, Society of Friends. *Address:* 120 Wurtemburg Street, Ottawa K1N 8M2; and *office* Suite 1208, 130 Albert Street, Ottawa K1P 5G4, Canada.

**LOCKE, Charles Herbert,** OBE. Australian. *B.* 1910. *Educ.* Wrekin Coll., Wellington Salop. *M.* (1) Lesley Alison Vine. *S.* 3. *Dau.* 1. (2) Mary Clare Gregory (Nee Luya). *Career:* Chairman: Tooheys Ltd., International Computers (Australia) Pty. Ltd., Lease Underwriting Ltd., Colonial Mutual Life Assurance Society (N.S.W. Board). Director, Lend Lease Corp. Ltd., Permanent Trustee Co. Ltd. Commercial & General Acceptance, Australian Equity Corp. Ltd.; Crothall Holdings Ltd.; Carpenters Investment Trading Co. Ltd. Man. Dir. Carpenter Locke Pty. Ltd. *Clubs:* Australian, Union; Royal Sydney Golf; Elanora Country; Tattersalls: Australian Jockey Club. *Address:* 11 Wyuna Road, Point Piper, N.S.W. and office 33 Bligh Street, Sydney, N.S.W., Australia.

**LOCKE, Edwin A., Jr.** American banker, diplomat and businessman. *B.* 8 June 1910. *Educ.* Phillips Exeter Academy; Harvard (AB, *cum laude*). *M.* (1) 1934, Dorothy Q. Clark (*Div.*); (2) 1952, Karin Marsh. *S.* Edwin A. 3rd, Benjamin Clark and Jonathan Winston. *Dau.* Elizabeth Eliane. *Career:* Associated with Chase National Bank, N.Y. City 1932-33, Paris branch 1933-35, London Branch 1935-36, N.Y. City 1936-40; Office of Coordinator of Purchases, Advisory Committee to Council of National Defense Nov. 1940 -Jan. 1941; Asst. Deputy Dir. Priorities Div., Office Production Management Jan.-Oct. 1941; Deputy Chief Staff Officer, Supply Priorities and Allocation Board Oct. 1941-Jan. 1942; Assistant to Chmn., War Production Board Jan. 1942-Sept. 1944; Exec. Assistant to Personal Rep. of the President Sept. 1944-May 1945; Personal Rep. of the President May 1945-Jan. 1947; also Special Assistant to the President Mar. 1946-Jan. 1947; Vice-President, Chase Nat. Bank, N.Y. City Jan. 1947-Nov. 1951; Special Rep. of the Secretary of State (with personal rank of Ambassador), to coordinate Economic and Technical Assistance in the Near East 1951-53; Pres. and Dir. Union Tank Car Co., Chicago 1953-63; Chmn. and Dir. Federal Home Loan Bank of Chicago 1956-63; Dir., Harris Trust & Savings Bank 1955-63; Pres. and Dir., Modern Homes Construction Co. 1963-67; Pres. American Paper Institute 1968-77; Pres., Economic Club of New York 1977—; Dir. Warner National Corp.; Stuyvesant Ins. Co.; Trustee, China Medical Board Inc. *Member:* Presidential Mission to Africa 1963; Advisory Cttee. on International Business Problems, U.S. Department of State 1960-64; Member, National Export Expansion Council, U.S. Dept. of Commerce 1959-63; Overseer, Harvard College (1956-62). *Address:* 522 Fifth Avenue, New York, N.Y. 10036, U.S.A.

**LOCKHART, Jack Herbert.** *B.* 1909. *Educ.* Pennsylvania State University 1927-29. *M.* 1935, Nina Doris Tall (Dec'd) *S.* Richard Anthony and Jeffery Herbert. *Dau.* Doris Jean. *Career:* The Commercial Appeal, Memphis, Tenn., newspaper work 1931-38; The Oklahoma News, Oklahoma City, Okla., Managing Editor 1938-39; TheCommercial Appeal, Memphis, Tenn., Managing Editor 1939-42; Asst. Director in charge of Press Division, U.S. Office of Censorship 1942-45. Assistant General Editorial Manager, Scripps-Howard Newspapers, New York, N.Y. 1945-75. Former member U.S. Nationa, Commission for UNESCO. *Address:* 30 Ridgedale Road, Scarsdale, N.Y., U.S.A.

**LOCKWOOD, Sir Joseph Flawith.** British company director. *B.* 1904. *Career:* Dir. E.M.I. Ltd. (chmn. 1954-74); Hawker-Siddeley Group, Smiths Industries Ltd., Laird Group; United Racecourses Ltd. Chmn. The Royal Ballet. *Member:* Council of Imperial Socy. of Knights Bachelor. *Publications:* Flour Milling (trans. into several languages), Provender Milling. *Address:* 33 Grosvenor Square, London, W.1.

**LODERMEIER, Ernst.** German banker; *Career:* former member, Bd. of Management, Bayerische Hypotheken- und Wechsel-Bank, Munich, currently mem. of Advisory Cttee.; mem. Bd. of Directors. Mainzer Baulandbeschaffungs-GmbH, Mainz. *Address:* Kardinal-Faulhaber-Strasse 10, 8 Munich, Germany.

**LODGE, John Davis.** American diplomat. *Educ.* Harvard (BA 1925), Ecole de Droit, Paris; LLB Harvard 1929. *M.* 1929, Francesca Braggiotti. *Daus.* Lily de Pourtales Lodge Marcus and Beatrice Anna Cabot Lodge de Oyarzabal. *Career:* Worked with Cravath, de Gersdorff, Swaine & Wood, N.Y

1929–31 (individually after 1931); Admitted to New York Bar 1932; employed by motion picture companies in U.S., England, France, Italy 1932–40; New York theatre 1940–42. Served with U.S. Navy 1942–46; liaison officer between French and U.S. fleets; public relations officer and press censor Sicilian Operation; landings at Salerno and Southern France. Member, Foreign Affairs Committee, 80th and 81st Congresses (4th District, Connecticut); Governor of Connecti cut 1951–55; member Exectiive Committee, National Governors Conference 1951–52; Chairman, New England Governors Conference 1953–55; Ambassador on special presidential missions to Porto Rico, Panama, Costa Rica 1953; Ambassador to Spain 1955–61 to Argentina 1969–74; Delegate to and asst. floor leader, Connecticut Constitutional Convention. *Member:* American Legion, Veterans of Foreign Wars and Reserve Officers' Assn.; National Order Polish Legion Amer. Veterans; Captain, USNR; New York Bar; Inter American Bar Assn.; Phi Beta Kappa (Hobart and William Smith. *Awards:* Hon. degrees; LLD Trinity, Middlebury, and Hobart and William Smith College; ScD Worcester Polytechnic. Dr. Humane Letters, Fairfield Univ. (Hororis Causa); Chevalier, Legion of Honour, Croix de Guerre with Palm (France); Grand Officer, Order of Merit of Republic (Italy); Grand Cross, Noble Order of Charles III, 1962 (Spain); Gold Medal and Hon. Citizenship of Madrid 1962; Order of Polonia Restituta, 1964; Gran Cruz al Merito de la Orden de Mayo, 1976; National Pres. Junior Achievement Inc. *Publications:* Magazine articles. *Clubs:* Harvard (N.Y.); National Press (Washington). *Address:* 129 Easton Road, Westport, Conn. 06880, U.S.A.

**LOEB, John Langeloth.** American investment banker. *B.* 1902. *Educ.* Harvard College (SB *cum laude*) LLD Hon) 1971. *M.* 1926, Frances Lehman. *S.* John Langeloth, Jr. and Arthur Lehman. *Daus.* Judith H. (Chiara), Ann M. (Bronfman) and Deborah F. (Davies). *Career:* With Amer. Metal Co., Pittsburgh office 1924–26; N.Y. office 1926–28; with Wertheim & Co. 1928–30; partner Loeb, Rhoades & Co., N.Y.C. 1935–55; Sen. Partner 1955—; Wartime Service; with Treasury Dept. and Office of War Mobilization, Washington 1942–44. Senior Partner, Loeb, Rhoades & Co.; Director: Dome Petroleum Ltd. 1950—; Arlen Realty Development Corp.; Governor, N.Y. Stock Exchange 1951–54; Distillers Corp. Seagrams Ltd. 1956—; Dir. General Instruments Corporation. Mem.: S.A.R. Council on Foreign Reins.; N.Y.C. Chamber of Commerce; Dir., Beekman-Downtown Hosp., N.Y.; Trustee: New York Univ.; Valeria Home, Oscawanna, N.Y.; mem.: Bd. of Govs. (Hon.), N.Y. Hosp.; Bd. of Overseers, Harvard Univ. 1962–68; Trustee, Mus. of Modern Art. *Clubs:* Harvard of Boston; Harvard of N.Y.; Recess; City Midday; Century Country; Economic Club of N.Y.; Lyford Cay; Regency; Sky and The Stanwich. *Address:* 730 Park Avenue, N.Y.C. 10021; and *office* 42 Wall Street, New York City 5, U.S.A.

**LOEFFLER, Henry Everett,** BA, DSc. American. *B.* 1906. *M.* 1946, Stella. *Career:* Former Dir. Mitchell Engineering Ltd.; Pres. Treas. Catoctin Trading Corp.; Former Exclusive Rep. for Stanley Aviation Corp.; Gamah Corp. both Denver. *Address:* 22 Eaton House, 40 Up. Grosvenor Street, London, W.1.

**LOESCH, Alfred,** D. en D. Luxembourg court official. *B.* 26 Oct. 1902. *M.* 1926, Fernande Metzler. *S.* Jean. *Daus.* Christiane, Jacqueline. *Career:* Formerly lawyer; Hon. Grand Marshal of the Court; Hon. Member, Council of State. *Awards:* Grand Croix, Ordre d'Adolphe de Nassau avec Palme en Or, Ordre de la Couronne de Chêne, Ordre de la Légion d'Honneur, Ordre de Léopold, Ordre de l'Etoile Polaire, Ordre du Danebrog, Al Merito della Repubblica Italiana, Ordre de St. Olav, Ordre de Pie IX. *Publications:* Le Contrôle Juridictionnel des Arrêtés-Lois; La Monnaie de Compte en Droit International Privé; La Responsabilité de l'Etat-Administrateur; Le Pouvoir réglementaire du Grand-Duc. *Address:* 17 Boulevard Joseph II, Luxembourg.

**LOFFMARK, Hon. Ralph Raymond,** MLA (Vancouver South, Sept. 1966); Canadian. *B.* 1920. *Educ.* Univ. of Toronto (BA Pol Sc and Econ 1942), Osgoode Hall (Barrister 1949) and Univ. of Pennsylvania (MBA 1951; Chartered Accountant, B.C. *M.* Barbara Grierson. *S.* 2. *Career:* Elected M.L.A. Vancouver-Point Grey Sept. 1963. Minister of Industrial Development, Trade & Commerce, Mar. 1964. Appointed to British Columbia Treasury Board. Professor on leave from Faculty of Commerce at Univ. of B.C. Appointed Minister of Health Services & Hospital Insurance, Apr. 1968. Appointed member of British Columbia Harbours Board, Mar. 1968. *Publications:* The British Columbia Corporation Manual (with A. H. Hall, Regst. of Companies); Estate Taxed; Tax and Estate Planning; Government Regulation of Business. *Member:* Ont. and Br. Columbia Bars; Law Socs. of British Columbia and Ontario; Chartered Accountants of B.C. Social Credit Party. *Clubs:* Faculty (Univ. of B.C.); Union (Victoria, B.C.). *Address: office* Parliament Buildings, Victoria, B.C., Canada.

**LOGAN, Sir Donald (Arthur),** KCMG. *B.* 1917. *Educ.* Solihull Sch. (W. Midlands.). *M.* 1957, Mlle. Irène Everts. *Daus.* Claire and Joya. *S.* Ian. *Career:* Fellow, Chartered Insurance Inst. 1939; Commissioned in Royal Artillery, Sept., 1939; Major 1942; British Army Staff, Washington 1942–43; Germany 1945. Joined H.M. Foreign Service 1945; Commercial Secretary, Tehran 1947–51; Asst. Political Agent at Kuwait 1954–55; Assistant Private Secretary to Secretary of State for Foreign Affairs 1956–58; Embassy, Washington 1959–60; Ambassador U.K. to Conakry, Guinea 1960–62: Head of Information Executive Dept., Foreign Office 1962–64; Vice-Pres. Int. Exhibitions Bureau, Paris 1964–68; Information Counsellor, Paris 1964–70; Ambassador, U.K. to Sofia, Bulgaria, 1970–73; Deputy Permanent U.K. Representative to NATO 1973–76; Amb. and Perm. Leader of U.K. Delegation to U.N. Law of the Sea Conf. 1976–77. *Clubs:* Brooks'; Royal Automobile. *Address:* 6 Thurloe Street, London, SW7 2ST.

**LOGAN, Harold Roy.** U.S. Corporate Executive. *B.* 1921. *Educ.* Oklahoma State University (BS 1942); post-graduate, Harvard 1943–44. *M.* 1941, Freda Townsend. *S.* Harold. *Dau.* Mary Betts. *Career:* Budget Director, Dept. of Defence, Washington, 1955–60; Senior Vice-President, Director, Grace Line Inc., N.Y.C., 1960–67; President, Chief Exec. Officer, 1967–68; Chairman Board, 1968–69. Exec. Vice-President W. R. Grace & Co.; Pres. & Dir. Grace Petroleum Corp. (N.Y.); Dir. W. R. Grace & Co. (N.Y.); Grace Ore & Mining Co. (N.Y.); Chemed Corp. (Cincinnati); Voyager Petroleums Ltd. (Canada). *Member:* A.I.M. Amer. Management Assn.; Pan. American Socy.; Newcomen Society. *Clubs:* Harvard (N.Y.C.); Aspetuck Valley Country (Weston, Conn.); Petroleum (Dallas); Army-Navy; Kenwood Country; Metropolitan (Washington). *Address: office* 1114 Avenue of the Americas, N.Y. 10036, U.S.A.

**LOMAS, Frederick Irvin.** Canadian executive. *B.* 1910. *M.* 1932, Alice Macfarlane. *S.* William Frederick. *Career:* Dir., Dack Shoes, Toronto 1954—. Executive Vice-Pres. and Gen. Mgr., Dack Corp. 1965— (Vice-Pres. 1958, Pres., 1969—). Man. Dir., Hartt Boot & Shoe Co. 1965—. Director and Exec. President, A. H. Marston Corp. 1964 (Vice-Pres. 1955–64). Pres., Church's English Shoes 1965—; Church & Co. (Canada), 1969—. Director: Church & Co. (England), 1969—; Church's British Shoes (New York), 1968—; C.E.S. Co. Ltd. (New York), 1969; Panam Corp. (U.S.A.), 1968—. Member, Toronto Board of Trade. *Clubs:* F.G.C.C.; B.T.G.C. (Westmount), Granite (Toronto). *Address: office* 595 Trethewey Drive, Toronto, Ont., Canada.

**LOMBARDI, Renato.** Italian Doctor in Engineering. *B.* 1906. *Educ.* High School diploma (1923) and degree in civil engineering, specializing in electrotechnics (1928). *M.* 1935, Anita Ragazzoni. *S.* Giancarlo. *Daus.* Giovanna and Gabriella. *Career:* After fulfilling military obligations, took up post of electrotechnical engineer with Società Romana di Elettricita; awarded Alessandro Volta scholarship 1930; spent one year at Stanford Univ.; worked in offices and laboratories of the Gen. Elec. Co., and became qualified Electrical Engineer (concerned principally in high tension field); returned to Italy under auspices of Compagnia Generale di Elettricità; worked successively with Ufficio Tecnico Raddrizzatori and Ufficio Centrali Elettriche e Cabine di Trasformazione (Dir. of the latter). In 1944, for family reasons left the electro-mechanics field and entered the wool industry. President & Managing Director, S.p.A. Filatura di Grignasco; Member of the Board: Credito Lombardo; Società Metallurgica Italiana SMI; Isituto Finanziario Italinano Laniero 'I.F.I.L.'. Past President and now member of the Boards of I.C.C., Confederazione Generale del' Industria Italiana, Associazione and Sindacato dell' Industria Laniera Italiana, and International Wool Textile Organization 'I.W.T.O.' *Awards:* Cavaliere del Lavoro and Gran Grce. of Merit of Republic; Commander Order of San Silvestro. Honorary President, Associazione fra le Societá Italiane per Azionic; Pres., Italian Association for Arbitration. *Publications:* numerous studies and memoirs in the field of electricity, the wool industry, economic and social problems. *Address:* 28570 Grignasco (Novara), Italy.

**LOMBARDO, Ivan Matteo.** Italian politician and company director. *B.* 22 May 1902. *M.* 1925, Maria Astorri. *Dau.* Ivana (*Dec.*). Editor of labour section of newspaper *Avanti.* Milan 1920–22; military service in Libya 1922–25; in trade and export business 1925–35; manager of various industrial plants 1935–45; Cmmr. for Industry in Lombardy May 1945; member, Consultative Assembly 1945–46; Under-Sec. of State for Industry and Commerce July 1945–46; Chief of Mission to Cotton Conf., U.S.A. May 1946; Chief, Ital. Dele. to negotiate between French and Italian Govts. in connection with the Peace Treaty 1946; member (Soc.), Constituent Assembly 1946–47; Secretary-General of the Socialist Party 1946; Ambassador Extraordinary leading Italian Delegation to U.S.A. in connection with negotiation of the Peace Treaty May–Aug. 1947; Chief of Italian Delegation for negotiation of Treaty of Friendship, Commerce and Navigation with U.S.A. Oct.–Dec. 1947; Min. of Industry and Commerce 1948–49; member (Soc.-Dem.), Milan and Naples, Chamber of Deputies 1948–53; Min. of Foreign Commerce 1950–51; Chief of Italian Delegation, Paris Conf. for European Community for Defence 1951–54; Pres. Lloyd Internazionale, Rome; Pres. Credito Commerciale Tirreno, Cava dei Tirreni (Salerno); Pres. Italian Cham. of Com. for the Americas, Rome; Italian Atlantic Cttee. (C.I.A.), Rome; European Freedom Council, Copenhagen; Hon. Governor of the Institut Atlantique, Paris. *Address:* Via Archimede 68, Rome, Italy.

**LONDON, Bishop of (Rt. Rev. & Rt. Hon. Gerald Alexander Ellison),** PC, MA, DD. British. *B.* 1910. *Educ.* Westminster School; New Coll. Oxford. *M.* 1947, Jane Elizabeth Gibbon. *S.* 1. *Daus.* 2. *Career:* Curate, Sherborne Abbey 1935–37; Domestic Chaplain, Bishop of Winchester 1937–39; Chaplain Royal Naval Volunteer Reserve 1937–43; Domestic Chaplain, Archbishop of York 1943–46; Vicar, St Mark, Portsea 1946–50; Bishop of Willesden 1950–55; of Chester 1955–73; Bishop of London since 1973. *Awards:* Hon. Bencher of the Middle Temple; Master of Arts. Oxford Univ.; Doctor of Divinity, Lambeth and London; Episcopal Canon of Jerusalem. *Clubs:* Leander. *Address:* London House, 8 Barton Street, London SW1P 3RX.

**LONG, Clarence Dickinson, Jr.** Member of Congress and university professor. *B.* 1908. *Educ.* Washington & Jefferson Coll. (AB 1932, AM 1933) and Princeton Univ. (AM 1935, PhD 1938). *M.* 1937, Susanna Larter. *S.* Clarence Dickinson. *Dau.* Susanna Elizabeth. *Career:* Instructor, Wesleyan Univ. 1936–39 (Asst. Prof. 1940–41, Assoc. Prof. 1941–45); Assoc. Prof., Johns Hopkins Univ. 1946; Labour Specialist, W.P.B. 1942. Member Research Staff, National Bureau of Econ. Research 1946–56, and of Senior Staff, Pres. Eisenhower's Council of Econ. Advisers 1953–54 (Consultant 1954—). Lt., U.S.N.R. 1943–46. Professor, Johns Hopkins University 1947–63; Acting Chairman, Maryland Democratic State Central Committee; Elected to 88th Congress as Representative for 2nd District of Maryland 1962; re-elected 1964, 1966, 1968, 1970, 1972 and 1974. *Publications:* Buildg. Cycles and the Theory of Invst. 1940; The Labor Force in Wartime Amer., 1944; (with Frederick C. Mills), Task Force Report on Statistical Agencies, Appendix D (Comm. on Organization of the Executive Branch of the Government); The Statistical Agencies, Appendix D (Comm. on Organization of the Executive Branch of the Government); The Statistical Agencies of the Federal Government (Natl. Bureau of Economic Research), 1949; The Labor Force in War and Transition, 1952; The Labor Force Under Changing Income and Employment, 1958; Wages and Earnings in the U.S. 1860–90, 1960. Fellow, Washington & Jefferson Coll. 1932–33; Sanxay Fellow, Princeton 1935–36; Fellow, John Guggenheim Memorial Foundation 1941–43; Citation and Board of Trustees, Washington & Jefferson Coll. 1959. *Member:* Inst. for Advanced Study Princeton 1941–46, 1948; A.A.A.S. (Fellow); Amer. Economic Assn.; Amer. Statistical Assn.; Econometric Socy.; Acad. of Political Science; Phi Beta Kappa; Alpha Tau Omega. Democrat. *Address:* Boyce Avenue, Ruxton, Md.; and *office* House of Representatives, Washington, D.C. 20515, U.S.A.

**LONG, Gerald.** Chief Executive, Reuters, since 1963 (Gen. Mgr. 1963–73, Man. Dir. 1973—); Chairman, Visnews Ltd. since 1968; Chairman of Executive Committee, International Institute of Communications Ltd. since 1973. *B.* 1923. *Educ.* St. Peter's Sch., York; Emmanuel Coll., Cambridge. *M.* 1951, Anne Hamilton Walker. *S.* 2. *Daus.* 3. *Career:* Army service 1943–47; joined Reuters 1948; served as Reuter Correspondent in Germany, France and Turkey 1950–60; Asst. Gen. Mgr. 1960–63. *Address:* 37 Wood Lane, Highgate, London N6 5UD; and *office* 85 Fleet Street, London EC4P 4AJ.

**LONG, Olivier.** Ambassador, Dir. General, GATT. *B.* 1915. *Educ.* Université de Paris, Faculté de Droit & Ecole des Sciences Politiques, Univ. de Genève. Ph.D. Law 1938; Ph.D. Pol. Sc. 1943. *Married. Children* 3. *Career:* Fellow, Rockefeller Foundation 1938–39; Swiss Armed Forces 1939–43; International Red Cross 1943–46; Swiss Foreign Affairs Dept., Berne 1946–49; Swiss Embassy, Washington 1949–54; Swiss Govt. Del. Trade Agreements 1955–66; Head. Swiss Del. European Free Trade Assn. (EFTA) 1960–66; Ambassador to U. Kingdom and Malta 1967–68; Dir. Gen., General Agreement Tariffs and Trade (GATT) since 1968; Professor, Graduate Inst. International Studies, Geneva since 1962. *Publications:* Several on Political Sciences and Trade Policy. *Address:* GATT, Centre William Rappard, rue de Lausanne 154, CH-1211 Geneva 21, Switzerland.

**LONG, Russell B.** U.S. senator. *B.* 3 Nov. 1918. *Educ.* Louisiana State University (AB, LLB). *M.* Carolyn Bason Long. *Daus.* 2. *Career:* Admitted to Louisiana Bar 1942; served World War II. U.S. Navy 1942–45; U.S. Senator from Louisiana since 1948; Chairman, Senate Finance Committee 1966; Senate Majority Whip 1965–69. Democrat. *Address:* Senate Office Building, Washington, D.C., U.S.A.

**LONGDEN, Sir Gilbert, (James Morley)** Kt., MA, LLB, MBE, British. *B.* 1902. *Educ.* Haileybury; Emmanuel Coll. Cambridge; The Sorbonne, *Career:* Secy. ICI (India) Ltd. 1930–37; Served, Durham Light Infantry, attained rank of Major, 1939–45, MBE (Mil. Div.). Member of Parliament for South West Hertfordshire 1950–74; U.K. Representative, Council of Europe, 1954–55; Delegate, United Nations, XII-XIII Sessions; Vice Chmn. The British Council 1965–74; Member: Council, British Atlantic Comm.; Vice-Pres., Conservative Group for Europe. *Publications:* A Conservative Philosophy; (part author) One Nation: Change is our Ally; A Responsible Society; One Europe. *Clubs:* Travellers'; Hurlingham. *Address:* 89 Cornwall Gardens, London SW7 4AX.

**LONGDEN, Henry Alfred,** BSc. British. *B.* 1909. *Educ.* Oundle; Birmingham Univ. (BSc Hons). *M.* 1935, Ruth Gilliat. *S.* 1. *Daus.* 4. *Career:* Production Dir. North E. Div. N.C.B. 1948–55, Gen. Prod. 1955–60; Chmn. West. M. Div. N.C.B. 1960–61; Dir. Trafalgar House Investments Ltd. 1970–76; Chmn. Chief Exec. of The Cementation Co. Ltd. 1961–70; *Fellow:* Inst. of Mining Engrs. (past Pres.). *Member:* Inst. Civil Engineers; Geological Society. *Club:* Brookes. *Address:* Raeburn, Northdown Road, Woldingham, Surrey.

**LONGFORD, Earl of (Francis Aungier Pakenham),** KG, PC. *B.* 1905. *Educ.* Eton; New Coll. Oxford, MA 1st Class in Modern Greats. *M.* 1931, Elizabeth Harman. *S.* 4. *Daus.* 3 (1 Dec.). *Career:* Tutor University Tutorial Courses, Stoke-on-Trent 1929–31; Cons. Party Economic Research Dept. 1930–32, Christ Church Oxford, Lect. in Politics 1934–46 and 1952–64; Prospective Parly. Labour Candidate for Oxford City 1938; Personal Asst. to Sir William Beveridge 1941–44; a Lord-in-Waiting to the King 1945–46; Parly. Under Secy. of State, War Office 1946–47; Chancellor, Duchy of Lancaster 1947–48; Minister, Civil Aviation 1948–51; First Lord of the Admiralty May-Oct. 1951; Lord Privy Seal 1964–65; Leader of the House of Lords 1964–68; Secy. of State for the Colonies 1965–66; Chmn. The National Bank Ltd. 1955–63; Sidgwick and Jackson since 1970. *Publications:* Causes of Crime (1958); Five Lives (1964); (with Thomas P. O'Neill) Eamon De Valera (1970); The Grain of Wheat (autobiog.); Abraham Lincoln; Jesus Christ (all 1974). *Address:* Bernhurst, Hurst Green, East Sussex.

**LONGLEY, Sir Norman,** CBE, DL, Hon DSc, FIOB. British. *B.* 1900. *Educ.* Clifton College. *M.* 1925, Dorothy Lilian Baker. *S.* Peter and Michael. *Dau.* Judith Wendy. Past Pres.: Nat. Fed. of Build. Trades Employers 1949–50, and of Inter. Fed. of Public Works & Building Contractors 1955–57. *Club:* R.A.C. (London). *Address:* 'The Beeches', East Park, Crawley; and *office* c/o James Longley & Co., Ltd., Crawley, Sussex.

**LONGO, Luigi.** Italian politician. *B.* 15 Mar. 1900. *M.* 1925. *S.* 2. Member, Central Committee, Italian Federation of Communist Youth, Communist Youth Internationale 1926–29; member, Central Executive, Communist Internationale 1932–34; Political Commissioner and Inspector-General, International Brigades in Spain 1936–39; Commander-General Garibaldi Assault Brigades 1943–45; member, National Italian Liberation Committee Alta Italia;

Deputy Commander, Volunteer Liberation Corps. 1944–45; member, Constituent Assembly 1946–47; Deputy Secretary-General, Italian Communist Party 1945–64; General Secretary, Aug. 1964 (on death of Sig. Togliatti), Chmn. 1972—. Member (P.C.I.), Italian Parliament 1948, '53, 58', '63, '68. *Publications:* Un popolo alla macchia (1947); Sulla via della insurrezione nazionale (1954); Le Brigate internazionali in Spagna (1956); Revisionismo nuovo ed antico (1957); Il Miracolo Economico e la Critica Marxista (co-author) (1962). *Address:* Via delle Botteghe Oscure 4, 00186 Rome, Italy.

**LOOMBE, Claude Evan,** CMG. British banker. *B.* 1905. *M.* 1936, Zoe Isabella Hotchkis. *Dau.* 3. *Career:* With Bank of England, Adviser and Adviser to the Governors, 1945–65. Director British Bank of the Middle East 1965–77 (Chmn. 1967–74). Vice-President, Middle East Association. *Club:* Oriental. *Address:* 64 Shepherds Way, Liphook, Hants.

**LÓPEZ MICHELSEN, Dr. Alfonso.** President of the Republic of Colombia. *B.* 1913. *Educ.* Lycée Pascal, Paris; Lycée Français, London. *M.* Cecilia Caballero Blanco. *S.* 4. *Career:* Lawyer at the National Univ. & at the Colegio Mayor de Nuestra Senora del Rosario, specializing in Constitutional Law; Senator of the Republic, Representative to Congress & mem. of the Advisory Commission of the Ministry for Foreign Affairs; a leader of the Movimiènto Revolucionario Liberal; Dir. of the weekly "La Calle"; held office under Pres. Carlos Lleras Restrepo as Governor of Cesar 1967–68, then Min. for Foreign Affairs 1968–70; worked at the creation of the Regional Andean Group & the campaign for the study of reforms to the Constitution of the U.N.; President of Colombia since 1974. *Address:* Office of the President, Bogotá, Colombia.

**LÓPEZ PORTILLO, José.** Head of State of Mexico. *B.* 1920. *Educ.* Escuela Nacional de Jurisprudencia, Nat. Univ. of Mexico; Univ. of Santiago, Chile; Licenciatura in Law, 1946. *M.* 1946, Carmen Romano y Nolk. *S.* 1. *Daus.* 2. *Career:* Prof. of the General Theory of the State, Law Faculty of the Nat. Univ. of Mexico, 1952–62; with the Ministry of National Patrimony, 1959; Dir.-Gen., Juntas Federales de Mejoras Materiales, 1960–65; Co-ordinator, Comisión de Desarrollo Urbano Fronterizo, 1961–64; Pres., Comisión de Administracion Publica in Presidencia, 1965–68; Dir.-Gen., Asuntos Jurídicos y Legislación, 1965–68; Under-Sec. of the Presidency, 1968–70; Under-Sec., Ministry of National Patrimony, 1970–72; Dir., Federal Electricity Comm., 1972–73; Minister of Finance 1973–76; Presidential candidate of the Partido Revolucionario Institucional (PRI), 1975; assumed office of President of the Republic of Mexico, 1976. *Address:* Palacio de Gobierno, Mexico, D.F., Mexico.

**LÓPEZ RODÓ, Laureano.** Spanish Lawyer & Politician. *B.* 1920. *Educ.* Univ. of Barcelona; Univ. of Madrid. *Career:* Prof. of Admin. Law, Univ. de Santiago de Campostela 1945–53, Univ. de Madrid 1953—; Tech. Sec.-Gen. Office of the President 1956–62; Minister without Portfolio 1965–73; Minister for Foreign Affairs 1973–74; Ambassador to Austria 1974–75; Member of the Cortes as Deputy for Barcelona. *Address:* c/o Cortes de España, Madrid, Spain.

**LORENTZEN, Helge Gustav.** Cand. jur.; Danish civil servant. *B.* 18 May 1905. *Career:* Asst. Prpl. Officer., Min. of Social Affairs 1931, Principal Officer 1938: Principal Officer, County of Faroe Islands 1935–37; Private Secretary to Minister and Deputy Asst. Secy., Ministry of Social Affairs 1942; Assistant Secretary, Ministry of Labour 1942 and Acting Chief, State Emigration Office 1945–48; Permanent Under-Secretary, Ministry of Labour 1948, Ministry of Labour and Social Affairs 1950; Lieutenant-Governor, County of Aarhus. 1951; At the disposal central administration of the government, 1970; retired 1975, appointed Chamberlain 1976; Chmn., different State Cttees. Comdr. and Silver Cross Order of Dannebrog. *Address:* Skaarup, Ebeltoft, Denmark.

**LORENZ-MEYER, (Ernst) Helmut.** German. *B.* 1908. *Career:* worked for Theodor Wille, Hamburg (founded 1844) since 1929, from 1930–35 in Brazil, a partner since 1942; Mem. of Board, Commerzbank AG since 1947 (now Vice-Chmn.); Plenary member, Hamburg Chamber of Commerce 1954—. Mem. of Board Bayer AG since 1974. Council of the Stock Exchange, Hamburg 1956—; Member of Board: Latin-American Association, Hamburg 1950—. *Awards:* Commander, Orders of Cruzeiro do Sul (Brazil); San Carlos (Colombia); Placa Aguila Azteca (Mexico); Andrés Bello (Venezuela). *Address:* Alter Wall 10, 2 Hamburg 11, Germany.

**LÖRINCZ-NAGY, Janos.** Hungarian Diplomat. *B.* 1931. *Educ.* Foreign Affairs Academy, Budapest; College of Political Sciences, Budapest. *M.* 1954, Ida Lörincz-Nagy. *Dau.* 1. *Career:* Press Attaché, Peking 1953–55; 2nd Sec., Djakarta 1957–61; Dep. Head of Personnel Dept. 1964–68; Ambassador to Ghana 1968–72; Head of Press Dept. 1972–74; Ambassador, Head of Hungarian Delegation to the International Commission of Control & Supervision in Saigon 1974; Ambassador to Sweden 1975–76; Ambassador to the Court of St. James's since 1976. *Decorations:* Golden Grade of Order of Merit for Labour. *Address:* 1 Lowndes Square, London SW1; and *office* 35 Eaton Place, London SW1.

**LOSONCZI, Pál.** Head of State of Hungary. *B.* 1919. *Career:* Mem. of Communist Party since 1945; mem. of Parliament since 1953; Minister of Agriculture 1960–67; Chmn., National Council of Co-operative Farms 1965–67; Pres. of Presidential Council of the Republic since 1967; mem., Central Cttee. of the Hungarian Socialist Workers' Party, & mem. Politbureau of the Central Cttee. since 1975. *Decorations:* Hero of Socialist Labour; Order of the Hungarian People's Republic. *Address:* The Presidential Council, H-1357 Budapest, Kossuth tér, People's Republic of Hungary.

**LOSSIUS, Hans Michael.** Norwegian; exporter of dried codfish; Vice-Consul of Spain since Apr. 1951. *B.* 1904. *Educ.* Commercial High School, and abroad. *M.* 1935, Grete Maalstad. *S.* 3. *Dau.* 1. At Norwegian Consulate General, Bilbao, Spain 1926–28; spent further four years there in private enterprise. Conservative. *Address:* Langveien 58, Kristiansund N., Norway.

**LOUDON, James Valentine,** OBE, F.Inst. FF, American. *B.* 1920. *Educ.* Univ. Calif., Los Angeles. *M.* 1947, Gloria Gene Hindin. *S.* 2. *Dau.* 1. *Career:* Pres. & Dir. James Loudon & Co. Inc.; H. B. Thomas & Co.; Van Cargo International; Partner Loudon Ziegler & Paul. *Member:* Los Angeles Chamber, Commerce; U.S. Naval Reserve; Mayor's Cttee. Int. Visitors, Los Angles; Pres. Cttee. Rotary Club Los Angeles; Japan Amer. Socy. Southern Calif.; Trustee & Dir. Combined British Charities; Past Pres. Foreign Trade Assn.; British-Amer. Chamber of Commerce; Secy.-Gen. Spain-U.S. Chamber of Commerce; Calif. Rep. Scottish Council (Development & Industry). *Address:* 125 Via Koron, Lido Isle, Newport Beach, Calif.; and *office* 110 West Ocean Boulevard, Suite 414, Long Beach, Calif. 90802.

**LOUDON, Jonkheer John Hugo,** KBE. Netherlands company director. *B.* 27 June 1905. *Educ.* Utrecht University (Doctor of Law). *M.* 1931, Baroness Marie Cornelie van Tuyll van Serooskerken. *S.* 3. *Career:* Dir., Orion Bank Ltd.; Chairman, Internat. Advis. Cttee. for Chase Manhattan Bank; Chmn., European Advisory Cttee, Ford Motor Co.; Chairman of the Board, Atlantic Institute, European Inst. of Business Administration, & Netherlands Economic Inst.; Pres., World Wildlife Fund International. *Address:* Lange Voorhout 48, The Hague, Holland.

**LOURIE, Arthur.** Israeli government official. *B.* 10 Mar. 1903. *Educ.* Cape Town Univ. (BA); Cambridge Univ. (MA, LLB); Choate Memorial Fellow, Harvard Univ.; Barrister-at-Law (Inner Temple). *M.* Jeannette N. Leibel. *S.* Daniel. *Dau.* Barbara. *Career:* Consul-General, New York and Dep. Representative of Israel to U.N. (with rank of Minister from 1950) 1948–53; Asst. Director-General, Ministry for Foreign Affairs 1954–57; Ambassador to Canada 1957–59; Ambassador to the Court of St. James's 1960–65. Dep. Dir.-Gen., Ministry Foreign Affairs 1965–72; Adviser to Foreign Minister since 1972. *Publication:* articles in diverse journals, the Book of Knowledge, and the Encyclopaedia Britannica. *Address:* Ministry of Foreign Affairs, Jerusalem, Israel.

**LOVE, George Hutchinson.** American industrialist. *Career:* Former Chmn. Bd. and Dir. Chrysler Corp.; former Dir. Union Carbide Corp.: General Electric Co.; Continental Oil Co.; Mellon National Bank. Bradford Computer & Systems Inc.; General Adjustment Bureau; Hanna Mining Co.; Honorary Chmn. & founder Consolidation Coal Co. Charter Trustee, Univ. of Pittsburgh and Princeton University. Member, Business Council. *Address: office* 3300 One Oilver Plaza. Pittsburgh 15222 Pa., U.S.A.

**LOVELAND, Samuel Crowley, Jr.** American marine transportation executive. *B.* 1910. *Educ.* Princeton University (BS 1933). *M.* 1938, Doris Crane. *S.* Samuel C., III, Crane Smith and Brian Hudson. *Daus.* Mary Dare and Cyrene. *Career:* Director of Small Vessel Operations, U.S. War

Shipping Administration, 1942–46; S. C. Loveland Co., Inc. since 1938, Chmn. since 1971; Pres. Inter-American Shipping Services, Inc. (1947); Loveland Enterprises, Inc. 1956; Director: Flanigan, Loveland Shipping Co., S.A. of Panama, R.P. 1947, and Tanker Owners S.A., of Panama, R.P. 1956. *Award:* Order of Alfaro. *Address:* Readbourne, Centreville, Queen Anne's Co., Md., U.S.A.

**LOVELL, Sir Bernard**, OBE, FRS. Professor of Radio *B.* 1913. *Educ.* Kingswood Grammar School, Bristol, and University of Bristol. *M.* 1937, Mary Joyce Chesterman. *S.* 2. *Daus.* 3. *Career:* Assistant Lecturer in Physics, University of Manchester 1936–39; Telecommunications Research Establishment 1939–45. Successively Lecturer, Senior Lecturer, and Reader in Physics, Physical Laboratories, Univ. of Manchester 1945–49. Astronomy, Univ. of Manchester, and Director, Jodrell Bank Experimental Station 1951. Reith Lecturer 1958, Condon Lecturer 1962, Guthrie Lecturer 1962, and Halley Lecturer 1964. Queen's Lecturer (Berlin) 1970. *Member:* (Hon. Foreign) Amer. Academy of Arts and Aeronautical Research Council, 1955–58; (Hon. Life), N.Y. Academy; Royal Swedish Academy 1962; Science Research Council 1965–70; Pres. Royal Astr. Society 1969–71; Vice-Pres., International Astronomical Union 1970–76; Visiting Montague Burton Professor, Int. Relations Univ. Edinburgh 1973; Pres. British Association 1974–75. *Awards:* Hon LLD Edinburgh; Hon DSc Leicester; Hon. LLD Calgary (1966): Hon DSc Leeds; Hon DSc London; Hon DSc Bath (1967); Hon DSc Bristol 1970; Hon D. Univ. Stirling (1974), Surrey (1975). Hon Fellow Inst. of Elect. Engrs.; Duddell Medal 1954, Royal Medal 1960, and Daniel and Florence Guggenheim International Astronautics Award 1961. Ordre du Mérite pour la Recherche et l'Invention 1962; Commander's Order of Merit of the Polish People's Republic (1975); Hon. Fellow Inst. of Physics (1976). *Publications:* Science and Civilization, (1939); World Power Resources and Social Development, (1945); Radio Astronomy, (1951); Meteor Astronomy, (1954); The Exploration of Space by Radio, (1957); The Individual and the Universe, (1958); The Exploration of Outer Space, (1961); Discovering the Universe, (1963); Our Present Knowledge of the Universe, (1967); The Story of Jodrell Bank, (1968); Out of the Zenith (1973); The Origins and International Economics of Space Exploration (1973); Man's relation to the Universe (1975); P. M. S. Blackett: A Biographical Memoir (1976); and numerous publications in professional journals. *Club:* Athenaeum. *Address:* The Quinta, Swettenham, Cheshire.

**LOVERIDGE, John Warren**, MP. British. *B.* 1925. *Educ.* St. John's Coll., Cambridge—MA. *M.* 1954, Jean Marguerite Chivers, JP. *S.* 3. *Daus.* 2. *Career:* Contested (C) Aberavon, 1951, & Brixton (LCC), 1952; Member of Hampstead Borough Council 1953–59; Treas./Trustee, Hampstead Conservative Assoc. 1959–74; JP West Central Div., since 1963; Conservative MP for Hornchurch Div. 1970–74, & for Upminster Div. since 1974; Vice-Chimn., Conservative Parly. Smaller Business Cttee.; Mem., Parly. Select Cttee. on Expenditure. *Member:* Fellow of the Royal Astronomical Society; member of the Royal Inst. of International Affairs. Freeman of the City of London; Liveryman of the Girdlers Company. *Clubs:* Carlton. *Address:* House of Commons, London S.W.1.

**LOVETT, Robert Abercrombie.** U.S. Banker. *B.* 1895. *Educ.* Yale University (BA 1918), Harvard Law School (Special Course) and Harvard Graduate School of Business Administration. *M.* 1919, Adele Quartley Brown. *S.* Robert Scott 2nd. *Dau.* Evelyn Lovett Brown (*Dec.*). *Career:* Special Asst. to Secy. of War 1940–41; Asst. Secretary of War for Air 1941–45; Under-Secretary of State 1947–49; The Deputy Secretary of Defense 1950–51; Secretary of Defense 1951–53. Partner, Brown Brothers Harriman & Co., New York City. Director: CBS Inc., June 1953–April 1977; Freeport Minerals Co., June 1953–70; New York Life Insurance Co., 1949–68, North American Aviation Inc., June 1953–69. Member, N.Y. Investment Committee, Royal-Globe Insurance Companies, Mar. 1953–Feb. 1975; Mbr., Exec. Cttee., Chmn. 1953–66 and Dir., since 1953, Union Pacific Railroad Co., Union Pacific Corp. *Publications:* Gilt-Edged Insecurity (Saturday Evening Post, 3 Apr. 1937). *Awards:* 1919 Navy Cross and 1945 D.S.M.; Presidential Medal of Freedom 1963; Grand Cross, Order of Leopold II (Belgium) 1950. Hon. LLD: Amherst Coll., Brown Univ., Columbia Univ., Harvard Univ., Long Island Univ. (C.W. Post Coll.), Princeton University, Sam Houston State Teachers College, Yale University (also MA Hon 1942), and Williams College; Corp. of Mass. Institute of Technology (Life Member Emeritus). *Clubs:* Century Association, The Links, Yale, Down Town Association (all of N.Y.C.); Metropolitan (Washington, D.C.); The Creek (Locust Valley). *Address:* Locust Valley, L.I., N.Y. 11560; and *office* 59 Wall Street, New York City, N.Y., 10005, U.S.A.

**LOVICK, Albert Ernest Fred.** British. *B.* 1912. *Educ.* Peter Symonds; Winchester. *M.* 1934, Florence Ena Jewell. *Career:* Chmn.: Co-operative Insurance Society 1964— (Director 1950—), and South West Wool Assn. 1963—. Director, C.W.S. Ltd. 1949—; Director. Shoefayre Ltd. since 1975; Chmn. Cumbrian CS Ltd.; Chmn. New Zealand Produce Assn. 1964, Centratour & Voyages Congress 1961–67. Member, various Government Cttees. 1939–45. Member, Export Guarantees-Advisory Cncl. 1968. *Fellow:* Co-operative Secretaries Assn.; Chartered Inst. of Secretaries; Inst. of Arbitrators. *Club:* Royal Commonwealth. *Address:* Coedway, Bristol Road, Stonehouse, Glos.; and *office* c/o C.I.S. Ltd., 1 Miller Street, Manchester, 4.

**LOW, Sir Alan Roberts**, Kt. 1977, MA. New Zealand. *B.* 1916. *Educ.* Canterbury Univ. Coll. New Zealand. *M.* 1940, Kathleen Mary Harrow. *S.* 1. *Daus.* 2. *Career:* Asst. Governor Reserve Bank of New Zealand 1960–62. Deputy Gov. 1962–67; Governor 1967–77 (Ret'd.). Chmn. Planning Advisory Group Nat. Development Council 1969–75. *Member:* N.Z. Assn. of Economists, former President. *Clubs:* Wellington. *Address:* 83 Penrose Street, Lower Hutt, New Zealand.

**LOWE, E. Nobles.** American. *B.* 1912. *Educ.* Univ. of Arkansas (BA 1932; LLB 1934); Cert of Dist. Alumnus 1972, *M.* (1) 1934, Catherine McDonald (*Div.* 1959) *S.* 1. *Dau.* 1. and (2) 1961. Margaret Breece *S.* 1. *Career:* Member, U.S. Supreme Court, New York, Federal Court (S. Dist. of N.Y,). Dist. of Columbia and Arkansas Bars. With Reid & Priest (Partner 1943) 1935–43; Electric Bond & Share Co. (Law Dept.), N.Y.C. 1934;–35; Arkansas State Bond Refunding Board, Little Rock, Ark 1934; with Westvaco Corp. (Formerly West Virginia Pulp & Paper Co.) N.Y.C., Vice-Pres. since 1966, General Counsel since 1943; Dir. Associated Industries of N.Y. since 1969. *Member:* Amer. Bar. Assn. (Past Chmn. Spec. Cttees.; on Corp. Lawyers Program, Vice-Chmn.; on Environmental Law & Membership Cttee.; Section on Corp., Banking and Business Law; organized Cttee. on Corp. Law Depts., 1952; chmn. Continuing Education Cttee. 1974); Bar Assn. of City of N.Y. (mem. Judiciary Cttee. since 1976; Past Vice-Pres. Member Exec. Cttee., Chmn. Cttee., Post-Admission Legal Education; Corp. Law Department and Trade Reg.) N.Y. State Bar Assn.; Amer. Socy. of Corporate Secretaries (Pres. N.Y. Group 1964); Assn. of General Counsel; World Soc. for Ekistics; Bd. of Mercantile Library of N.Y. (Pres. 1962–66); Chmn. Board of Directors, Arbitration Assn.; Past Chmn., Nat. Cncl. for Air and Stream Improvement; Fellow, Amer. Bar Foundation; Member Amer. Law Institute and Pres. Practising Law Inst. Sigma Nu; Arkansas State Socy.; Dir. Emeritus, Bronxville (N.Y.) Adult School; Secy., Fund for Modern Courts Inc. Fellow, Inst. of Judicial Admin. *Publications:* law review articles. Methodist, Republican. *Club:* University (Vice-Pres.). *Address:* 1170 Fifth Avenue, New York City 10029; and 299 Park Avenue, New York City 10017, U.S.A.

**LOWE, J. Austin.** British. *B.* 1923. *Educ.* Cleveley Coll.; Harris Institute. *M.* 1949, Marie J. Baldwin. *S.* 1. *Daus.* 2. *Career:* Dir. Thermic E. & E. Co. Ltd. 1955–60; Gibbons Bros. Ltd. 1962–68; Deputy Chmn. Gibbons Bros. Ltd.; Dir. Gibbons Dudley Ltd. *Clubs:* R.A.C.; Pall Mall, London; South Staffordshire Golf. *Address:* P.O. Box 20, Lenches Bridge, Brierley Hill, West Midlands.

**LOWE. Robson.** British. *B.* 1905. *M.* 1928, Winifred Denne. *Daus.* 2. *Career:* Dir., Robson Lowe Ltd.; Chmn. Regent Stamp Co. Ltd.; Chmn. Robson Lowe (Bermuda) Ltd.; Robson Lowe International Ltd.; Dir. Christie, Manson & Woods; Woods of Perth (Printers) Ltd. *Member:* British Philatelic Assn.; Socy. Postal Historians; Hon. Philatelic Advisor Nat. Postal Museum. *Clubs:* East India, Sports and Public Schools; Collectors, New York. *Address:* 16 St. James's Square, London, S.W.1.; and *office* 50 Pall Mall, London, S.W.1.

**LOWENSTEIN, James Gordon.** American Diplomat. *B.* 1927. *Educ.* Yale Coll.—BA. *M.* 1955, Dora L. Richardson (*Div.* 1977). *S.* 1. *Dau.* 1. *Career:* Economic Cooperation Admin., Paris 1950–51; Lieut. (jg), USNR 1952–55; Dept. of State, Washington, D.C. 1957–59; 3rd Sec., American Embassy, Colombo 1959–61; 2nd Sec., American Embassy, Belgrade 1962–64; Consultant, Senate Foreign Relations Cttee. 1965–74; Dep. Asst. Sec. of State for European Affairs 1974–77;

Ambassador to Luxembourg since 1977. *Member:* Council on Foreign Relations, New York; International Inst. for Strategic Studies, London. *Clubs:* Metropolitan (Washington); Century Assoc., Yale (New York); Travellers', Racing Club of France (Paris); Travellers' (London); Harbor (Seal Harbor, Maine). *Address:* American Embassy, 22 Boulevard E. Servais, Luxembourg.

**LOWNDES, Arthur George,** CBE. Australian land development consultant and company director. *B.* 1911. *Educ:* Sydney Univ. (MSc). *M.* 1941, Alison Adams. *S.* 3. *Career;* Economic Dept., Bank of New South Wales 1934–40; Australian Liaison Officer to U.N.R.R.A., China 1945–46. Consultant in Agriculture 1954—. Commissioner, Australian Broadcasting Commission, 1956, Vice Chmn. 1971–74; Chairman, Australian Institute of Political Science 1952–65; Fellow of Senate, University Sydney, 1969—. *Publications:* occasional contribution, political and agricultural journals; Editor, South Pacific Enterprise, C.S.R. *Club:* Australian (Sydney). *Address:* Derriwong Lane, Dural, N.S.W., Australia 2158.

**LOWY, Jacob Max.** Canadian. *B.* 1908. *Educ.* Public, elementary school and Talmudical Coll. in Bardejov, Czechoslovakia. *M.* 1968, Mrs. Clara Klein. *Daus.* (by first marr.) Ruth (Pollack) and Nellie (Stavisky). *Career:* President of the following Quebec Corporations with Head Office in Montreal: Pointe Claire Industrial Park Inc., Lowy Investment Corp. (1955—), Westshore Heights Inc., (all 1953—), Lakeshore Heights Inc. 1954—, Shoreland Realties Inc. 1956—; Century Investments Ltd. 1956; Dorval Leaseholds Inc. 1961—; Pointe Clare Leaseholds Inc. 1967. Pres., Zionist Organization, Bardejov 1933–39; Member, Bd. of Deputies, London 1944–49. Chmn. of Executive, Federation of Jewish Community Services of Montreal 1964–66. First Pres. of Allied Jewish Community Services of Montreal 1965–69. Pres., United Israel Appeal of Canada Inc. 1967–69; Chmn. Bd. of Hebrew Acad. Day Schools in Montreal 1966—; Chmn. of UJA of Canada Inc. 1968; Co-Chmn., Nat. Fund-Raising Cttee. United Israel Appeal and United Jewish Relief Agency in Canada 1962. *Member:* Bd. of Dirs., Cncl. of Jewish Federation and Welfare Funds Inc. (U.S.A. and Canada), N.Y.C. 1962–68 and of Bd. of Admin. Jewish Gen. Hosp. of Montreal 1966—. *Clubs:* Montefiore, Elm Ridge Country (both Montreal). *Address:* 5760 Deom Avenue, Montreal, Quebec; and *office:* 1117 St. Catherine Street West, Room 801, Montreal, Quebec, Canada.

**LOYD, Sir Francis Alfred,** KCMG, OBE. *B.* 1916. *Educ.* Eton and Trinity College, Oxford (MA). *M.* 1946, Katharine Layzell. *Daus.* 2. *Career:* In Kenya Government Service 1939–63; Provincial Commissioner 1956–62; Permanent Secretary, Governor's Office, Kenya 1962; HM. Commissioner for Swaziland, 1964–68; Director, London House for O'Seas Graduates, since 1969. *Club:* Royal Commonwealth Society. *Address:* London House, Mecklenburgh Square, London, WC1 and 53 Park Road, Aldeburgh, Suffolk.

**LOYDEN, Eddie.** MP. British Politician. *B.* 1923. *M.* 1944, Rose. *S.* 1. *Daus.* 2. *Career:* Pres., Liverpool Trades Council 1967–74; Metropolitan County Councillor since 1970; District Councillor 1960–74; Labour MP for Liverpool Garston since 1974. *Address:* House of Commons, London SW1A 0AA.

**LUBIN, Isador.** American economist. *B.* 9 June 1896. *Educ.* Clark College (AB, LLD); Brookings Institution Graduate Sch. (PhD); Brandeis Univ. (LLD). *M.* Carol Riegelman. *Daus.* Alice, Ann. *Career:* Asst. Prof. of Econs., Univ. of Michigan 1919–22; Associate Professor of Economics, University of Missouri 1924; Economic Adviser to Committee on Education and Labor, U.S. Senate 1928–29; U.S. Commissioner of Labor Statistics 1933–46; Chairman, Labor Advisory Board of Federal Emergency Administration, Public Works 1933–39; Vice-Chairman, U.S. Central Statistical Board 1933–38; member, Technical Board, President's Economic Security Committee 1934–35; U.S. Representative on Governing Body of the I.L.O. 1935, 1937, 1941, 1944, 1945; member, Temporary National Economic Committee 1938–41; Dep. Dir., Labor Div., Office of Production Management 1940–41; Special Statistical Assistant to the President of the U.S. 1941–45; Dir. of Statistical Analysis Branch, Munitions Assignment Board of the Combined Chiefs of Staff 1942–45; Associate U.S. Rep., Allied Commission of Reparations in Moscow, rank of U.S. Minister 1945; Special economic adviser to Dept. of Commerce 1946–47; U.S. Rep., Commission on Devastated Areas, Economic and Social Council, U.N. 1946; U.S. Rep., Advisory Cttee. on Korean Relief and Reconstruction Agency 1951–53; U.S. Rep. (with rank of Minister) to the U.N. Economic and Social Council 1950–53; Econ. Adviser to U.S. Dele to U.N. Gen. Assembly 1950 and 1951; alternate U.S. Delegate to 7th Session, U.N. Gen. Assembly 1952; U.S. Rep. to the U.N. Economic, Employment and Development Commission 1946–50; U.S. Representative, U.N. Conf. on Science and Technology 1962; member, Board of Trustees. Brandeis University 1947—; New School for Social Research 1947—; Consultant on Programs in Israel, United Israel Appeal Inc. 1960—: Economic Consultant, Twentieth Century Fund 1962–76; Chairman, President's Commission on Railroad Marine Workers 1962; Arthur T. Vanderbilt Professor of Public Affairs, Rutgers Univ. 1959–61; member, Natl. Commission on Money and Credit 1958–61; member, Board of Directors, Eastern Life Insurance Co. 1959–70; member, Economic Adv. Cttee., National Democratic Committee 1958–61. Board of Directors, United Nations Assn. of America. Industrial Commissioner, N.Y. State Dept. of Labor 1955–59; Chmn., Amalgamated Cotton Garment Industry Pension Fund; Columbia Univ. Seminar Associate. *Publications:* Government Control of Prices during the War (with Stella Stewart and Paul Gerratt); Miners' Wages and the Price of Coal; The British Coal Dilemma (with Helen Everett); The Absorption of the Unemployed by American Industry; The British Attack on Unemployment (with A. C. C. Hill, Jr.); The U.S. Stake in Foreign Trade; The U.S. Stake in the U.N. *Address:* 1095 Park Avenue, New York 10028, N.Y.; and *office* 515 Park Avenue, New York 22, N.Y., U.S.A.

**LUC, Robert Paul.** French diplomat. *B.* 1911. *Educ.* Lycée Heri Poincarré, Nancy; Lycée Louis Le Grand (Science); Paris Law School, Sorbonne, Bachelor of Law; Graduated, Ecole des Sciences Politques, Paris. *M.* 1940, Jane Holt. *Dau.* Valérie and Catherine. *Career:* Entered French Foreign Service, Attaché French Embassy at Shanghai, 1937–39; 3rd Sec., Athens, 1940; Joined Free French and sent on mission to France 1940–41; Attaché, Budapest 1942–43; 2nd then 1st Sec. London, 1943–50; Asst. French Dpty. to Austrian Treaty Conference 1947–50; Head, Near East Dept., Paris 1950–53; Counsellor, Berne 1953–55; Consul Gen., San Francisco 1955–61; Political Dir., Council of Europe, Strasbourg 1961–67; Minister Plenipotentiary, 1963; Consul Gen., Denver 1967–69; Foreign Office, Paris, 1969–70; Minister Plenipotentiary, Monaco, 1970–73; French Ambassador, Luxembourg 1973—. Officer, Legion of Honour, Medaille de la France Libre, Commandeur de l'Ordre de St. Charles. *Address: office* 2 rue Bertholet, Luxembourg.

**LUCE, Clare Boothe** (Mrs. Henry R. Luce). American author and former diplomat. *B.* 1903. *Educ.* St. Mary's College (Garden City, L.I., N.Y.) and The Castle (Tarrytown, N.Y.;) LittD, Colby College, Fordham Univ.; LLD, Creighton, Temple, Boston and Georgetown Universities, Mundelein Coll.; St. John's UDFa. *M.* 1935, Henry Robinson Luce (*Dec.* 1967). *Dau.* Ann Clare Brokaw (*D.*). *Career:* Associate Editor, Vogue Magazine, 1930; Associate Editor, Vanity Fair, 1931–32; Managing Editor, Vanity Fair Magazine, 1933–34; newspaper columnist 1934; playwright since 1934; member 78th and 79th Congresses (4th Connecticut District) 1943–47. U.S. Ambassador to Italy, Mar. 1953; resigned 1957; Member President's Foreign Intelligence Advisory Board; Board of Editors, Encyclopaedia Britannica. *Publications:* Stuffed Shirts (1933); Europe in the Spring (1940); plays: Abide with Me (1935); The Women (1937); Kiss the Boys Goodbye (1938); Margin for Error (1939); Slam The Door Softly (1970); collected and edited: Saints for Now (1952). Republican. *Address:* 4559 Kahala Avenue, Honolulu, Hawaii 96816, U.S.A.

**LUCE, Richard Napier,** MP. British. *B.* 1936. *Educ.* Cambridge Univ., degree in History; Oxford Univ., overseas civil service course. *M.* 1961, Rose Nicholson. *S.* 2. *Career:* Overseas Civil Service 1960–62; Brand Mgr., Gallaher & Co. Ltd. 1963–65; Marketing Mgr., Spirella Co. of GB 1965–68; Dir., National Innovations Centre 1968–71; Conservative MP for Arundel & Shoreham 1971–74 & for Shoreham since 1974; PPS to Minister for Trade & Consumer Affairs 1972–74; an Opposition Whip 1974–75; Chmn., Courtenay Stewart International Ltd. 1975—; Mem., European Adv. Bd. of Corning International S.A. 1975—. *Member:* Vice-Pres., Inst. of Patentees & Inventors. *Address:* House of Commons, London SW1A 0AA.

**LUCEY, Patrick J.** American Diplomat. *B.* 1918. *Educ.* Univ. of Wisconsin—BA (1946). *M.* 1951, Jean Vlasis. *S.* 2. *Dau.* 1. *Career:* Representative, State Assembly, State of Wisconsin

1948–50; Lt. Governor of State of Wisconsin 1964–66, Governor 1971–77; U.S. Ambassador to Mexico since 1977. *Member:* National Cttee. for Public Financing of Elections; Cttee. of One Hundred for National Health Insurance; Public Sector Cttee., National Comm. on Productivity & Work Quality; National Advisory Comm. for Balanced Growth; Democratic National Cttee.; Chairman: Nat. Governors' Conference Cttee. on Exec. Management & Fiscal Affairs; Great Lakes Governors' Caucus; Nat. Democratic Governors' Conference; Co-Chmn., Wisconsin delegation to Democratic Nat. Convention 1972, 1976; Campaign Advisor, Presidential Campaigns of Senator Robert F. Kennedy, Senator Eugene McCarthy, Senator John F. Kennedy; Chmn., State Democratic Party 1959–63. *Awards:* Hon. Degrees from St. Norbert's Coll., De Pere, Wis. & Northland Coll., Ashland, Wis.; decoration from Govt. of Nicaragua for Wisconsin's assistance in Nicaragua's recovery from national disasters. *Address:* 1015 Farwell Court, Madison, Wisconsin, U.S.A.; and *office* American Embassy, 305 Reforma, Mexico 5, D.F.

**LUCIOLLI, Dr. Mario.** Italian Diplomat. *B.* 1910. *Educ.* University of Rome (Law). *M.* Loredana Fritsch. *S.* 1. *Dau.* 1. *Career:* Foreign Service, Ministry of Foreign Affairs 1933–34; Vice-Consul in Zürich 1934–35; Vice-Consul in Paris 1935–38; Ministry of Foreign Affairs 1938–40; Italian Consul in Melbourne 1940; Secy, Embassy in Berlin 1940–42; Ministry of For. Affairs Italy, 1942–43; Consul in San Sebastian 1943–44; Ministry of For. Affairs 1944–48; Counsellor, later Minister, Italian Embassy in Washington 1948–55; Diplomatic Counsellor to the President of the Republic 1955–56; Ambassador in Santiago 1956–61; Ambassador in Ankara 1961–64; Italian Ambassador in Bonn 1964–76 (Ret'd.). *Decorations:* Grand Cross of Merit (Italy); Grand Officer of Merit (Germany); Comm. of Legion of Honour (France). *Address:* 8 bis Rue Margueritte, 75017 Paris, France.

**LÜCKER, Hans-August.** German Politician. *B.* 1915. *Educ.* Humanistisches Gymnasium (Abitur); Studium der Land— und Volkswirtschaft. *M.* 1940, Gertrud Lücker. *S.* 1. *Daus.* 2. *Career:* War Service, Lieutenant 1939–45; Head of Food Service, Munich/Freising 1945–46; Dir., Bavarian Regional Farmers' Board & Dep. Gen. Sec., Bavarian Farmers' Union 1947–53; mem. of Christian Socialist Union since 1947; mem. of German Federal Diet since 1953; mem. of Deliberative Assembly of Council of Europe since 1961; mem. of West European Union since 1961; mem. of European Parliament since 1958; Chmn. of CD Party of European Parliament 1969–75; Vice-Pres. of European Parliament since 1975. *Member:* List Society; IFO-Inst. for Economic Research, Munich; Chmn., Inst. for Structure Research, Univ. of Frankfurt; German Africa Society; Society for Foreign Policy. *Decorations:* Bavarian Order of Merit; Grand Cross of Merit of the German Federal Republic; Grand Officer of the Order of Merit of the Italian Republic; Order of San Carlos; Gold Medal of the Bavarian Free State. *Address:* 8000 Munich 90, Über der Klause 4, Federal Republic of Germany; and *office* 5300 Bonn, Bundeshaus.

**LUCKHOO, Sir Lionel Alfred,** KCMG, CBE, QC. Guyanese advocate. *B.* 1914. *Educ.* Barrister at Law (Middle Temple). *M.* Sheila Chamberlin. *S.* Lionel Michael, Mark Edward. *Daus.* Deborah, Sharman, Marina, Mala. *Career:* Member Georgetown Town Cncl. 1952–53, Exec. Cncl. and Min. without Portfolio 1954–57; Mayor City of Georgetown 1954–55–60–61; Chairman of a number of staturory boards, committees, commissions and enquiries. Commissioner for British Guinea in U.K. April 1965–May 1966. High Commissioner for Guyana (May 1966–70) and Barbados (Nov. 1966–70) in the United Kingdom. Ambassador Extraordinary and Plen. for Guyana and Barbados accredited to Paris, Bonn and The Hague 1967–70; retired from Diplomatic Corps. 1970 & returned to Legal Practice; listed in Guinness Book of Records as "The world's most successful advocate," having had 200 successive dismissals of accused on the capital charge of murder. *Publications:* The Fitzluck Theory of the Breeding of Racehorses; & many books on religion, incl. Life After Death; God is Love; Christ is Coming; Sense of Values; The Xmas Story; My Dear Atheist. *Member:* Hon. Secy. of the Middle Temple. *Clubs:* The 21; Crockfords; The Magic Circle. *Address:* Lot 1, Croal Street, Georgetown, Guyana.

**LUCKMAN, Charles.** American architect (registered in 27 States). Founder, Charles Luckman Associates. *B.* 1909. *Educ.* Univ. of Illinois (*magna cum laude* 1931); BA in Architecture. *M.* 1931, Harriet McElroy. *S.* Charles, Jr., James McElroy and Stephen Albert. *Member:* Pennsylvania Av. Comn.; Bd. of Trustees, Calif. State Coll., 1960—. President's Cttee. in Interntl. Trade Development 1961—; Governor's Commn. on Metropolitan Area Problems, California 1960—; Adv. Committee, National Rivers & Harbors Congress 1961—; Citizens Committee for International Development, Washington 1961—; Transit & Traffic Committee, Los Angeles Chamber of Commerce 1960—; Los Angeles World Affairs Council 1957—; Committee for Economic Development, Southern California Associates 1960—; Construction Cost Control Committee (Chmn. 1961—), American Institute of Architects. Colgate-Palmolive-Peet Co. 1931 (Manager Wisconsin district 1934; Divisional Manager Cincinnati H.Q. 1935). With Pepsodent Co.—later Pepsodent Division of Lever Bros. Co.—1935–50 Sales Promotion Manager, Sales Manager 1935–36; Vice-Pres. i/c Sales and advertising 1937; Vice-Pres. & Gen. Mgr. 1938; Exec. Vice-Pres. 1942–43; Pres. 1943–46; Exec. Vice-Pres., Lever Bros. Jan.–July 1946; Pres. 1946–50. President, partner, Pereira & Luckman, Los Angeles 1950–58. *Publications:* Future of Design, Humanation of Architecture, The Architect as Designer, Planning & Survival, Of Men & Materials, The Power of Knowledge. *Awards:* Star of Solidarity (Italy) 1948; Chevalier, Legion of Honour (France) 1948; U.S. Chamber of Commerce, 'Outstanding Young Man' award 1945; Horatio Alger Award, American Schools & Colleges Ass. 1940; Forbes Magazine, 'America's 50 Foremost Business Leaders' 1947; N.Y. Management Club, Outstanding Management Exec. 1945; LLD Univ. of Miami 1950; Dr. of Fine Arts, Calif. Coll. of Arts & Crafts 1958. Calif. Cncl., A.I.A., Distinguished Service Citation, 1962; A.I.A., Fellowship Award, 1963; Special Advisor, United States Del. to the 43rd Session, United Nations Economic & Social Council, Geneva 1967; Freedom Foundation George Washington Honor Medal 1964, 1967 and 1968. *Clubs:* Chevaliers du Tastevin. *Address:* 10730 Bellagio Road, Bel Air. Calif.; and *office* 9220 Sunset Boulevard, Los Angeles 69, Calif., U.S.A.

**LUDEWIG, Walter,** Professor, Dr.-Ing, Dr.-Ing. H.e. *B.* 1907. *Educ.* Technical University, Karlsruhe (Engineering; took Degree 1931). *Career:* Assistant in Gas Institute of the Technical University 1931–34; joined BASF 1934, Manager 1951, member of Board 1952–72; Member of the Boards of Klein, Schanzlin & Becker AG, Frankenthal; Züblin AG Stuttgart. Chairman: Forschungs Gesellschaft Verfahrens Technik; VDI, Düsseldorf, Research Assn. for Process Technology; and many other associations. Hon. Dr. Ing. TH Darmstadt, 1959; Hon. Senator 1963, Hon. Prof. TH Stuttgart, 1966. *Address:* c/o Badische Anilin-und Soda-Fabrik, Ludwigshafen-am-Rhein, Germany.

**LUGAR, Richard G.** United States Senator. *B.* 1932. *Educ.* Denison Univ., Granville, Ohio—BA; Rhodes Scholar, Pembroke Coll., Oxford—BA, MA. *M.* 1956, Charlene Smeltzer. *S.* 4. *Career:* Treasurer, Lugar Stock Farms, Inc., Indianapolis since 1960; Sec.-Treas., Thomas L. Green & Co., Inc., Indianapolis since 1968; Mayor, City of Indianapolis, Indiana 1968–75; Visiting Prof. of Political Science & Dir. of Public Affairs, Indiana Central Univ. 1975–76; U.S. Senator from Indiana since 1977. *Clubs:* Rotary; Columbia (both Indianapolis). *Address:* 5107 Dirksen Building, Washington, D.C. 20510, U.S.A.

**LUIKART, Fordyce W.** American. Member, Senior Staff, Brookings Inst., Washington, D.C. 1962—. Assistant Administrator for Personnel and Training, Federal Aviation Agency, U.S. Government 1959–62. *B.* 1910. *Educ.* Ohio Wesleyan University (AB *cum laude*, 1933); Graduate Work, Political Science, Ohio Wesleyan University 1933–34; Maxwell Graduate School, Syracuse University 1934–37. *M.* 1935, Margaret Clark. *S.* Clark Whitney, James Louis and John Ford. Director, Federal Aviation Organization Study, White House Staff of Asst. to President for Aviation 1957–59; Management Consultant, Principal Associate, Cresap, McCormick & Paget, New York 1955–57; Deputy Director and Director of Administration, Dept. of Health Education and Welfare, U.S. Govt. 1953–55; Staff Director, President's Committee on Government Organization, Nelson A. Rockefeller, Chairman, 1952–53; Special Consultant to Greek Govt. on Organization and Civil Service. Economic Co-operation Administration (U.S. Govt.) Mission to Greece 1949–50; Special Asst. to Arthur S. Flemming, Member, Commission on Govt. Organization (Hoover Commission) 1948–49; U.S. Civil Service Commission (Various positions, ending with Director), Executive Development 1939–53. Exec. Vice-Chairman, Federal Personnel Council 1951. *Publications:* Executive Development—Boundaries and Challenges Personnel Administration, Society for Personnel Administration,

May 1951) The Civil Service Commission's Inspection Programme (Personnel Administration May 1947). *Member:* Phi Beta Kappa; Board of Trustees, Ohio Wesleyan University, Delaware, Ohio. *Clubs:* Columbia Country, Chevy Chase, Maryland. *Address:* 3257 Beech Street, N.W., Washington 15, D.C.; and *office* The Brookings Institution, 1775 Massachusetts Avenue, N.W., Washington 25, D.C., U.S.A.

**LUKE, Desmond Edgar Fashole**, MA, BL. Sierra Leonean. Lawyer, Diplomat and politician. *B.* 1935. *Educ.* Freetown Secondary School; St. Edwards; Prince of Wales Sec. School; Kings Coll., Taunton; Keble Coll., Oxford Univ. (MA Hons); Magdalene Coll., Cambridge Univ. (MA Hons); Lincoln's Inn (BL); Called to the Bar in England 1962 and Sierra Leone 1963. *M.* 1961, Florence Valerie Whitaker. *Dau.* 1. *Career:* In Private Practice, Barrister & Solicitor, Legal Adviser to Leading Int. Co's. Mobil Oil (SL) Ltd.; B.P. (West Africa) Ltd.; Bata Shoe Co.; Singer Sewing Machine Co.; Legal Adviser, Co. Secy. Bata Shoe Co. & Allen & Elliot (SL) Ltd.; Dir. E. Osborne (SL) Ltd.; Legal Adviser, numerous Industries & Commercial Companies, 1963–1969; United Nations Human Rights Fellow, research in India, 1964; First Ambassador, Sierra Leone to the Federal Republic of Germany 1969; to Republic of Italy, Holland, Belgium & Luxembourg, 1970; to France and the Perm. Rep. to the EEC, 1971–73; Minister of External Affairs 1973–75. Leader, Sierra Leone's Delegation, Int. Atomic Energy Assn. Conference, Vienna 1970, to 20th African Economic Congress Milan 1971; to 21st Council of Ministers, O.A.U. Addis Ababa 1973; Deputy Leader O.A.U. 10th Heads of State Summit Conference Addis Ababa 1973. *Member:* Sierra Leone Bar Association; World Peace Through Law Centre Geneva; American Socy. Int. Law, Washington. *Awards:* Oxford Blue Athletics 1955–68; Finalist Empire Commonwealth Games (Long Jump) 1958; Public Schools, All England Schools Champion Record Holder (High Jump); Oxford & Cambridge Freshmen's Champion Record Holder, High Jump (1954); Grand Cross, Order of Merit, Federal Republic of Germany 1973. *Publications:* Republican Constitution, What Form? various articles. *Clubs:* Vincents, Oxford; Hawks, Cambridge; Embassy; Royal Commonwealth: Royal Overseas & Playboy; London; Rotary; Junior Diner & Aqua Sports, Freetown. *Address:* c/o Ministry of External Affairs, George Street, Freetown, Rep. of Sierra Leone.

**LUKE, The Rt. Hon. Lord**, of Pavenham, Ian St. John, KCVO, TD, DL, JP., British company director. *B.* 7 June 1905. *Educ.* Eton; Trinity College, Cambridge (MA). *M.* 1932, Barbara Anstruther-Gough-Calthorpe. *S.* Arthur Charles St. John, Ian Henry Calthorpe, George Andrew, Philip Richard. *Dau.* Caroline Jean (Bristow). *Career:* Chmn. Bd. of Dirs. Bovril Ltd. 1943–70; Chmn. Electrolux; Vice-Chmn. Gateway Building Society; Dir. Ashanti Goldfields Corp. Ltd.; and other companies; Chmn. Gov. Body, Queen Mary Coll. (Univ. of London) since 1963. *Member:* Beds C.C. 1943–52; Hon. Secretary Association of British Chambers of Commerce 1944–52; General Advisory Council of B.B.C. 1952; Chairman, National Playing Fields Association 1950–76; Chairman, Moorfields, Westminster and Central Eye Hospital 1947–56; Pres., Incorporated Sales Managers Assn. 1953–56; member for Great Britain, International Olympic Cttee.; Pres., Advertising Assn. (1955–58), Operation Britain Organization, London Chamber of Commerce (1952–55); President Institute Export since 1973; Pres. Recreation Mgrs. Assoc. of Gt. Britain. Hon. Col. 5th Bn. Beds. Regt.; Nat. Vice Pres. Royal British Legion; Lay Reader St. Albans Diocese since 1933. *Address:* Odell Castle, Odell, Beds MK43 7BB; and *office* 2nd Floor, 150 Southampton Row, London WC1V 6AA.

**LUKE, William Edgell.** British industralist. *B.* 1909. *Educ.* Kelvinside Academy, Glasgow; Old Hall, Wellington, Salop, and abroad. *M.* (1), 1933, Muriel Aske-Haley. *S.* 1. *Dau.* 1. (2) 1970, Constance Anne Reid. *Daus.* 2. *Career:* Successively Trainee, Sales Inspector, Sales Manager, The Linen Thread Company Ltd. 1927–38 (Sales Director, 1938–40); war service as Intelligence Officer (rank of Major) at home, in South Africa and in Central America 1940–46; Liaison Director to U.S.A. of Linen Thread Company Ltd. 1946–49; Managing Director 1949; Chmn. of the Board of Linen Thread Company Inc. (U.S.A.) 1952–59; Man. Dir. Lindustries Ltd. (and associated companies at home and abroad) 1949–73. Chmn since 1959: Dir. Powell Duffryn Ltd.; Past Master of the Worshipful Company of Makers of Playing Cards. *Member:* Confederation of British Industry (member of Council; formerly Chairman of Scottish Council); Council of Aims of Industry; Chmn., United Kingdom-South Africa Trade Association; Trustee, South Africa Foundation; former member, British National Export Council and Chairman, B.N.E.C. Southern Africa Committee; Mem., Advisory Council of British Overseas Trade Board. Conservative. *Clubs:* Travellers'. Royal Thames Yacht (London). *Address:* Trevor House, Knightsbridge, London, SW3 1EL.

**LUND, Joel Yowell.** *B.* 1902. *Educ.* Massachusetts Inst. of Technology (BS 1923); Hon DSc St. Louis College of Pharmacy 1957. *M.* 1931, Erle Hall Harsh. *Daus.* Erle Talbot (Lionberger) and Sarah Brandon (Donnem). *Career:* Asst. Superintendent, Lund-William Shoe Co. 1923–26; Industrial Engineer, International Shoe Co. 1926–28; St. Louis Manager, Lambert Pharmacal Co. 1928–32 (Vice-Pres., Production 1932–51, 1st Vice-Pres. 1951–52; Exec. Vice-Pres. 1952–55). Management Counsel, President, Edgefield Corp. Former Vice-Pres. Warner-Lambert Pharmaceutical Co., also Pres., Lambert-Hudnut Div. 1955–57; Vice-Pres. corporation manufacturing, engng. and control 1958–66. Member, City of Ladue (Mo.) District School Board 1940–55 (Pres. 1948–55). Trustee: St. Louis College of Pharmacy 1947–56, Morristown Memorial Hosp. and Morristown Community Chest. *Member:* Packaging Institute Board 1934–44 (Pres. 1942–44); The Proprietary Assn. Exec. Cttee., 1952–66 (Pres. 1960–64); Natl. Indust. Conf. Bd. (Bd. member); Defense Orientation Conference Assn.; Society of the Cincinnati. Consultant, U.S. Office of Emergency Planning; Trustee, America's Future; Neighborhood House; St. Louis Chamber of Commerce (Dir. 1948–50). *Clubs:* University Noonday (St. Louis); Morristown (Morristown); Morris County Golf; Union Club and M.I.T. (N.Y.C.). *Address:* 1 King Street, Charleston, N.C. 29401, U.S.A.

**LUND, Svend Aage.** Danish. *B.* 1900. *Educ.* Bach. Eng. 1925. *M.* 1929. Charlotte Bertelsen. *S.* Henrik and Kaj. *Daus:* Birgitte and Elsebeth. Berlingske Tidende: Sub-Editor 1929, Editor-in-Chief 1934–70, Chmn. 1970–73; A/S De Berlingske Virksomheder and A/S Det Berlingske Officin 1973. President: Federation of Danish Newspapers 1958–70; and of Danish-Swedish Co-operation, 1958–69. Conservative. *Address:* Carl Baggers alle 8, Charlottenlund, Denmark.

**LUNDBECK, G. Hilmer.** American shipping director. *B.* 10 Dec. 1900. *Educ.* Polytechnic Preparatory School, Brooklyn and Cornell Univ. *M. Daus.* Sigyn (Graham), Clare (Fraser, Jr.). *Career:* With Swedish American Line, New York since 1920, Vice-Pres. Dir. 1928–43; Resident Dir. 1944–66; Special Senior Rep. since 1966; Trustee, Empire Savings Bank; Dir.: Commercial Solvents Corp., Transportation Mutual Insurance Co., Quaker City Insurance Co., Travelers' Aid Socy. of N.Y., Swedish Cham. of Com. of the U.S.; Dir., Amer. Swedish News Exch., Swedish National Travel Office, The Folke Bernadotte Foundation; Chmn. Bd., Swedish Seamen's Welfare Fund. *Member:* Bd. of Governors, American-Swedish Historical Foundation, Phila.; Development Council; Gustavus Adolphus Coll., Minnesota. *Awards:* Order Honneur et Mérite (Haiti); Orden de Vasco Nuñez de Balbao (Panama). Order of Vasa (Sweden); Order of the Falcon (Iceland); Orden de Carlos Manuel de Céspedes (Cuba); Order of the Red Cross (Estonia); Order of the Finnish Lion; Order of the North Star (Sweden); Order of Dannebrog (Denmark); Order of Finnish Olympics; Swedish Patriotic Medal; New Sweden Medal; Order of Merit (Fed. Republ. of Germany); Commanderie du Boutemps-de-Medoc et des Graves (France); Medal of Merit (Spain); Knight, Order of Merit of the Italian Republic; Member, Confrérie des Chevaliers du Tastevin; LLD, Augustana Coll., and Upsala Coll. Swedish American of the Year, Stockholm, 1966. *Address:* 605 Park Avenue, New York, N.Y. 10021; and *office* 1270 Avenue of the Americas, New York, N.Y. 10020, U.S.A.

**LUNDBERG, Arne S.** Swedish Business Executive. *B.* 1911. *Married. S.* 1. *Dau.* 2. *Career:* Journalist 1929–44; Specialist, Min. of Communications 1944–47; Perm Sec, Min. of Communications 1947–51; Sec.-Gen., Min. of Foreign Affairs 1951–56; Man. Dir., Luossavaara-Kiirunavaara AB 1959–76; Chairman: Swedish Mine-owners Assoc. 1963–75; Byggherreföreningen 1964—; Norrbottens Järnverk AB 1967–70 (Board Member 1960–70); Sveriges Investeringsbank 1967—; AB Svensk Exportkredit 1962—; Oljeprospektering AB (OPAB) 1969—; Petroswede AB 1973—; Berol Kemi AB 1973—; Svenska Petroleum AB 1975—; Statsraff AB 1975—; Vice-Chmn., Post-och Kreditbanken 1966—. *Member:* Bd. of Swedish Ironmasters' Assoc. 1962–76; Swedish Academy of Engineering Sciences (IVA) 1962— (Pres. 1974–76). *Address:* LKAB, Fack, S-100 41 Stockholm, Sweden.

**LUNDBORG, Louis Billings.** Banker. *B.* 1906. *Educ.* Stanford Univ.; Hon LLD Rocky Mountain Coll. 1956. Occidental Coll.

1965. *M.* 1926, Barbara Wellington. *S.* Bradford Wellington. M.D. Vice-President, Stanford Univ. 1948–49; General Manager, San Francisco Chamber of Commerce 1943–48; Asst. General Manager, California State Chamber of Commerce 1939–43; other positions, California State C. of C. 1927–39. Former Chairman, Board of Directors, Bank of America N.T. & SA.; Chairman, Bank of America (Interntl.), and Bamerical Interntl. Finance Corp.; Bank America Corp. Republican. *Publications:* Public Relations and the Local Community (Harper's); Future without Shock; Up to Now (Norton). *Address:* 95 West Shore Road, Belvedere, California 94920; and *office* Bank of America Center, San Francisco, Calif., 94120, U.S.A.

**LUNDING, Franklin Jerome.** American corporation executive. *B.* 1906. *Educ.* Univ. of North Dakota and George Washington University (LLB 1929). *M.* 1933, Virginia Neil Hanna. *S.* Franklin Jerome Jr. and Christopher Hanna. *Dau.* Virginia (Coulter). *Career:* Research Department, U.S. Chamber of Commerce 1926–28; Attorney, Fed. Trade Commission 1929–31. Joined Jewel Tea Co. as Gen. Counsel 1931; later Asst. to Pres. and Exec. Vice-Pres.; Pres. 1942–51; Chmn. of Exec. Cttee. 1951–61; Chmn. Board of Directors 1954–65; Chairman: Executive Cttee., Lever Bros Co. 1950–57. Director Jewel Companies (formerly Jewel Tea Co. Inc.) 1942–77. Director: Illinois Bell Telephone Co. 1954–76; Thomas Industries Inc. 1955–72; G.B. Enterprises (Antwerp) 1960–70. U.S. Steel Corporation 1962–72; Chmn. Fed. Reserve Bank of Chicago 1949–53 and 1965–69. Penn Central Co. 1965–71. *Publications:* Sharing a Business (1951). Hon LLD Univ. of North Dakota 1949, and Marquette Univ. 1956. *Clubs:* The Chicago, The Commercial of Chicago; Indian Hill Country (Winnetka, Ill.); Old Elm Country (Fort Sheridan, Ill.). *Address:* 1630 Sheridan Road, Wilmette, Ill. 60091; and *office* Scoby, Biggam & Lunding, 180 North La Salle Street, Chicago, Ill. 60601, U.S.A.

**LUNKOV, Nikolai Mitrofanovich.** Soviet diplomat. *B.* 1919. *Educ.* Lomonosov Technical Inst. Moscow. *Career:* with Diplomatic Service 1943—; Asst. Minister of Foreign Affairs 1951–52; Deputy Political Counsellor, Soviet Control Commission, Germany 1952–54; Counsellor, Stockholm 1954–57; Deputy Head, Dept. International Organizations, Min. Foreign Affairs 1957, 3rd European Dept. 1957–59; Head, Scandinavian Dept. Min. Foreign Affairs 1959–62; Ambassador to Norway 1962–68; Head, Dept. Cultural Relations with Foreign Countries 1968–71; Head, 2nd European Dept. 1971–73; Ambassador to U. Kingdom and Malta since 1973. *Member:* Collegium Ministry Foreign Affairs 1968–73. *Awards:* Orders and Medals. *Address:* Embassy of the USSR, 13 Kensington Palace Gardens, London, W.8.

**LUNS, Joseph Marie Antoine Hubert,** GCMG, CH, DCL, LLD. Netherlands Secretary General of NATO. *B.* 28 Aug. 1911. *Educ.* Gymnasium at Amsterdam and Brussels; Law Study at Leiden and Amsterdam; courses in political and economic science, London; course at German Institute for Foreigners, University of Berlin. *M.* Baroness Elisabeth Cornelia van Heemstra. *S.* Hubert. *Dau.* Cornelia Sophie. *Career:* Attaché (1938), Second Secretary (1943), First Sec. of Embassy (1945) Couns. of Embassy (1949); Ministry for Foreign Affairs 1938–40; Legation, Berne 1940–41; Lisbon 1941–43; Netherlands Ministry for Foreign Affairs, London, 1943–44; Embassy, London, 1944–49; Perm. Delegation to U.N.O. 1949–52; Minister, Foreign Affairs 1952–71; Secy. Gen. of Nato since 1971. *Awards:* Officer, Order of Orange Nassau; Neth. Royal Silver Wedding Medal; Officer, Military Order of Christ, Portugal; Knight, Order of Leopold of Belgium; Commander, Order of Prakyat Trishakti Patti of Nepal; Grand Cross of following orders: St. Olav (Norway), Southern Cross (Brazil), Merit (Repub. of Italy), Georgios I (Greece), Leopold I (Belgium), Dannebrog (Denmark), Legion of Honour (France), Menelik II (Ethiopia), Polar Star (Sweden), White Elephant (Thailand), Oak Crown (Luxembourg), Merit (Austria), Boyaca (Colombia), Civil and Military Merits of Adolf of Nassau (Luxembourg), Merit for Special Services (Peru), Star of Africa (Liberia), Manuel Amador Guerrero (Panama), Vasa (Sweden), St. Michael & St. George (U.K.), Pius (Holy See), Rubén Darió (Nicaragua), Isabel la Católica (Spain), Carlos Manuel de Céspedes (Cuba), Cuarte Sánchez y Mella (Dominican Repub.), Homayou (Iran), Francisco Morazán (Honduras), Sun (Peru), Sardara Aala (Afghanistan), Merit (Germany), Liberator (Argentina). Officer of l'Instruction Publique (France); Order of Crown of Thailand; Aztec Eagle (Mexico); Order of Merit Bernardo O'Higgins (Chile); Order of Merit (Ecuador); Order of the Falcon (Iceland): Kt-Comdr. National Order of Republic of Senegal; Comdr. Order of Valour (Fed. Repub. of Cameroun); Grand Cross, Order of the Liberator of Venezuela; Grand Cross of the Order of Merit of Tunisia; Grand Cross of the Order of Gorkha Dashina Bahu of Nepal; Knight Grand Cross, Order of the Netherlands Lion; Hon. DCL Univs. of Oxford, Canterbury, Dublin & Harvard; Hon. Fellow, London School of Economics. *Address:* Secretary General of Nato, 1110 Brussels, Belgium.

**LUPKE, Oskar.** German banker. *B.* 1904. *Educ.* Banking. *M.* 1933, Johanna Thöl. *S.* Joachim. *Daus.* Elisabeth and Hildegard. Girozentrale, Hannover, Emden, and Bremen 1920–32; Sparkasse, Bremen (Member of the Management 1936—) 1932–45; Commercial Firms 1945–53; Bremer Landesbank and Staatliche Kreditanstalt, Oldenburg-Bremen (Member of the Management) 1953–58. General Manager, Norddeutsche Kreditbank, Aktiengesellschaft, Bremen 1959–69. *Club:* Rotary (Bremen). *Address:* Rockwinkler Landstr. 17, Bremen-Oberneuland, Germany.

**LURAGHI, Giuseppe Eugenio.** Italian. *B.* 1905. *Educ.* Doctor in Economics and Business Administration. *M.* 1927, Maria Maddalena Poli. *S.* Renzo and Dario. *Daus.* Liliana, Chiara and Marina. *Career:* Employed with the Pirelli Group (rubber industry); Gen. Mgr. and Dir. of Parent Company; Chmn. or Dir. of several Pirelli Subsidiaries 1930–50. Gen. Manager and Dir. of the Finmeccanica Group (I.R.I.); Deputy Chairman or Director of several Subsidiaries of affiliated companies such as Alfa Romeo, SIP and Vizzola (electricity) R.A.I. (National Radio Corp.), Siemens (communications). Ansaldo (shipyards, foundry and mechanics) etc. 1950–56, Chairman of Board of Lanerossi (textiles) 1956–60. Chairman of the Board: Alfa Romeo S.p.A. 1960–74; Alfa Romeo Alfasud S.p.A. 1968–74; SICA s.r.l (studies and automotive consultancy); Chmn. Fiera Campionaria (trade fair). Director, SIP (telephones), SIT-Siemens. *Publications:* Le Mac Chine della Liberta; Contributor on economic subjects to various Italian and foreign publications. *Address: office* 45 Via Gattamelata, Milan, Italy.

**LUTES, Lt.-General LeRoy.** American army officer; DSM (with oak leaf cluster), U.S.A.; Legion of Merit (U.S. Army); Bronze Star Medal (Europe); Commander of the British Empire; U.S. Typhus Commission Medal. *B.* 4 Oct. 1890. *Educ.* Wentworth Military Academy, Army Artillery School (Advanced Course), Command and General Staff School, and Army War College. *M.* (1) 1913, Martha M. Mulvihill. *S.* LeRoy, Jr. (Col., U.S. Army). *M.* (2) 1957, Mildred S. Speas. (3) 1973, Helen J. Kinney. *Career:* Officer 21st Infantry in California 1917–18; in N. Carolina and New Mexico 1919; Panama Canal Zone 1921–24; O.C., Submarine Mine Defence, Chesapeake Bay 1924–26; Adjutant, Post and Harbour Defence, Fort Monroe 1926–27; Plans and Training Officer, Hawaii 1931–34; on Staff Commanding General II Corps. 1939; Asst. Chief of Staff, G.4, Third Army 1940–41; General Staff Washington 1942; Dir. of Operations H.Q. Services of Supply; called to General Eisenhower's H.Q. to advise on plans of cross-Channel assault 1944; with Allied Expeditionary Forces on logistical operations at front 1944–45; Chief of Staff and Dep. Commanding General, Army Services Forces, Washington 1945; Commanding General, A.S.F. 1946; Director of Service, Supply and Procurement, Gen. Staff June 1946; Dir. of Staff, Munitions Board 1948; Commanding General, Fourth Army 1949–52; retired 1952. President, Pacific Tire and Rubber Co., and Vice-President Mamsfield Tire and Rubber Co. 1952–57. *Address:* Army-Navy Club, Washington, D.C., U.S.A.

**LUXTON, Lewis,** CBE. Australian executive. *B.* 1910. *Educ.* Melbourne C.E. Grammar School, and Pembroke College, Cambridge. *M.* 1938, Mary Varley Harry. *S.* Lewis Varley and James Varley. At Cambridge Univ. (Swimming Blue 1930–31; Rowing Blue 1932; BA Degree 1932, MA 1960) 1930–33; won Visitors Cup (1931) and Grand Challenge Cup (1932), Henley Royal Regatta; represented Great Britain in eight-oared crew at Olympic Games, Los Angeles 1932. *Career:* Joined Shell Co. of Australia Ltd. 1933; Chmn., Shell Group of Companies in Australia till 1968. War Service with A.I.F. in Middle East, Greece and Pacific Islands; discharged with rank of Lt.-Col.; awarded OBE. Director: McEwans Ltd., National Mutual Life Assn. Australasia Ltd., Australian United Corp. Ltd.; Elected member of International Olympic Committee 1951; Dept. Chmn. Organizing Committee for the XVI Olympic Games, Melbourne, 1956. *Clubs:* Melbourne, Australian; Leander (Henley-on-Thames); Victoria Racing; Barwon Heads Golf. *Address: office* 44 Market Street, Melbourne, Vic., Australia.

**LUYT, Sir Richard Edmonds,** GCMG, KCVO, DCM. Principal and Vice-Chancellor of the University of Cape Town 1968—. *B.* 1915. *Educ.* Univ. of Cape Town and Trinity Coll. Oxford (MA Rhodes Scholar); Hon LLD (Natal) 1972. *M.* (1) 1948, Jean Mary Wilder (*Dec.* 1951). *Dau.* 1 and (2) 1956, Eileen Betty Reid. *S.* 2. *Career:* Entered Colonial Service and posted to N. Rhodesia 1940; served in World War II 1940–45; with Mission to Ethiopia 1941, and with British Military Mission in that country until end of war. Returned to Colonial Service in N. Rhodesia 1945–53; transferred to Kenya 1953; later Labour Commissioner (1954–57), Permanent Secretary (1957–61), and Secretary to Cabinet of Kenya Govt. 1961–62; Chief Secretary, Northern Rhodesia 1962–64; Governor, British Guiana 1964–66. Governor General and Commander-in-Chief Guyana, May–Dec. 1966. *Clubs:* Royal Commonwealth Society; Nairobi; Civil Service, Cape Town. *Address:* Principal's Office, University of Cape Town, Rondebosch 7700, S. Africa.

**LYCHE, Jens Lange.** Norwegian. Managing Director of pulp and paper mills. *B.* 1909. *Educ.* Matriculated (baccalauréat ès sciences). *M.* 1938, Ella Marie Møller. *S.* Jens Fredrik. *Daus.* Inger Marie, Kari, Anne Lise. *Career:* Founder of firm of Jens Lange Lyche 1932; Sales Manager, A/S Hamang Papirfabrik 1936–42. Director of the Board of A/S Follum Fabrikker (with branch companies) 1946–75 Chairman, Council of The Norwegian Pulp and Paper Industry 1956–58, Member since 1958 Chairman, The Norwegian Papermakers' Association 1955–59; member of Board of The Federation of Norwegian Industries 1953–56; and from 1965–68; The Norwegian Council for Scientific and Industrial Research 1953–61 and of the Norwegian Export Council 1965–75. Conservative. *Awards:* Commander of the Finnish Lion Order. Knight of the Order of Dannebrog. *Address:* Ringåsen, Norderhov.

**LYDON, Martin James.** American. *B.* 1917. *Educ.* Harvard Coll. (AB 1940) and Harvard Graduate School (AM 1945); Hon DSc Lowell Technological Inst. 1954; Hon EdD Merrimack Coll. 1958. *M.* 1962, Maria Monti. *Career:* Instructor of English, Howe High School, Billerica, Mass. 1941–45. Instructor of Social Studies, Palm Beach Junior Coll., Palm Beach, Fla. 1945–46 and 1947–48. Successively Instructor, Asst. Prof. 1946–47 and 1948–49, Dean of Students 1949–50, Lowell Technological Inst. President, Lowell (Mass.) Technological Inst. 1950. *Publications:* contributor to various educational and technical journals. Dir., Washington Savings Institution; Amer. Council on Education; National Education Assn.; National Council for Textile Education; Amer. Socy. for Engineering Education; Amer. Assn. of Textile Chemists and Colorists; Lowell Tech. Associates Inc. (President). *Clubs:* Harvard, University, Vesper Country, Yorick. *Address:* c/o Lowell Technological Institute, Lowell, Mass. 01854, U.S.A.

**LYETH, Munro Longyear.** *B.* 1915. *Educ.* Harvard (AB 1937) and Harvard Law School (LLB 1940). *S.* Munro Longyear, Jr. *Dau.* Judith Good. *M.* (2) 1968, Marian Neal Rubey. *Career:* Law practice, New York City 1941; U.S. Navy 1941–46 (retd. as Comdr. U.S.N.R. 1948); Trust Officer, U.S. National Bank of Denver 1946–52; President, Cherry Creek Bank 1952–58 (Vice-Chmn. and Chmn. Exec. Cttee. 1958–61; Chmn. of Board 1961); Chairman of Board, Cherry Creek National Bank, Denver. Director: South Denver National Bank; First Trust Corp., Denver; Cyclo Mfg. Co., Denver (also Treasurer); Longyear Realty Co., Marquette, Mich.; Mountain Banks Ltd. *Member:* Newcomen Socy.; Trustee; Music Associates of Aspen; Fellow, Aspen Inst. for Humanistic Studies; Denver Symphony Orchestra; Central City Opera House Association (Director). *Clubs:* Denver; Denver Country; Garden of the Gods (Colorado Springs); Harvard (N.Y.C.). *Address:* 556 South Elizabeth Street, Denver, Colorado 80209; and *office* c/o Cherry Creek National Bank, East 1st Avenue at St. Paul Street, Denver 6, Colo., and P.O. Box 1860, Aspen Colorado 81611 U.S.A.

**LYKES, Joseph T., Jr.** American. *B.* 1918. *Educ.* Deerfield (Mass.) Acad. and Wasnington & Lee Univ. *M.* Marjorie Carrere. *S.* 5. *d.* 4. *Career:* Served in World War II with U.S. Navy (Europe, N. Africa and both the N. Atlantic Pacific theatres of operation). Joined Lykes Bros. S.S. Co. 1946; Member Board of Directors 1949, Vice-Pres. 1951, Senior Vice-Pres. 1957, Pres. 1962, Vice-Chmn. 1965. Chairman of the Board, Lykes Bros. Steamship Co. Inc. 1967—. Chairman and Director Lykes Lines Agency Inc. and Chmn & CEO Lykes-Youngstown Corp. 1969; Vice-Chmn. and Dir., Lykes Financial Corp.; Director: Gulf & South American S.S. Co. Inc.; Kennesaw Life & Accident Insurance Co.; Whitney National Bank; Louisiana & Southern Life Insurance Co.; and New Orleans S.S. Assn. *Member:* International Adv. Board of Chemical Bank New York Trust Co.; Bd. of Trustees Washington & Lee Univ.; Foreign Policy Cttee. of U.S. Chamber of Commerce; National Export Expansion Council; former Dir. and Member Exec. Cttee. of International House, and Chamber of Commerce of Greater New Orelans Area. Named Louisiana's Maritime Man of the Year for 1967 by New Orleans Propeller Club. *Clubs:* New Orleans Country; Pickwick; The Boston. *Address: office* Commercial Building, New Orleans, La., U.S.A.

**LYNCH, John.** Irish Politician. *B.* 1917. *Educ.* North Monastery C.B.S. (Cork), and University Coll., Cork; King's Inns, Dublin. *M.* 1946, Máirín O'Connor. *Career:* Entered Civil Ser. (Dept. of Justice) Dec. 1936; called to Bar 1945; resigned from Civil Ser. to become a member of Munster Bar and commence practice in Cork Circuit, Oct. 1945, T.D. Cork 1948—. Alderman, County Bor. of Cork 1950–57; member Cork Sanatoria Board and Cttee. of Management, North Infirmary, Cork 1950–51 and 1955–57; member, Cork Harbour Commissioners 1956–57; Parliamentary Secy. to the Government and to the Minister for Lands 1951–54; Minister for the Gaeltacht, Mar.–June 1957; Minister for Education 1957–59; Minister for Industry and Commerce 1959–65. Minister for Finance 1965–66; Prime Minister 1966–73; Leader of the Opposition 1973–77; Taoiseach (Prime Minister) 1977—. Vice-Pres. Consultative Assembly of Council of Europe 1958. President. Internat. Labour Conference 1962; Gov. Atlantic Institute for Intern. Affairs since 1974. *Awards:* LLD Honoris Causa, Univ. of Dublin, 1967; LLD Honoris Causa, National Univ. of Ireland, 1969; DCL Honoris Causa, Belmont Abbey Univ. N. Carolina 1971. Grande Cross of the Order of the Crown (Belgium) 1968. *Address:* 21 Garville Avenue, Rathgar, Dublin, Eire.

**LYNE, Eugene.** American attorney. Treasurer, Teradyne Inc. *B.* 1924. *Educ.* Harvard Coll. (AB 1946) and Boston Coll. Law School (LLD 1951). *M.* 1949, Ruth M. Lally. *S.* Daniel J. II. *Daus.* Susan, Barbara, Diane and Abigail. *Career:* First Lieut. U.S. Marine Corps 1943–46. Associate, Lyne, Woodworth & Evarts 1951–54, Partner, 1954–68; Chmn. Minico Systems Inc.; Dir. Rogerson House. Trustee, The Faulkner Hosp. 1959— (Vice-Pres., 1963–68); Trustee and Member Invest. Cttee., The Provident Instn. for Savings 1960—; Dir. Vice Pres. Boston Y.M.C.A. 1962—; Corporator: Boston Museum of Science 1959—, and Boston Legal Aid Socy. 1964—. Special Hearing Officer, U.S. Dept. of Justice 1967–68. *Member:* Boston Bar Association (Council, 1966–68). President's Council, Boston College. *Publications:* Annual Survey of Massachusetts Law (contributor 1960–63). *Clubs:* Longwood Cricket; Oyster Harbors; The Clover (Boston); Country (Brookline); Eire Society of Boston (Pres. 1967–68). *Address: office* 183 Essex Street, Boston 10, Mass. 02111, U.S.A.

**LYNG OLSEN, Burton Johan.** Norwegian liner-agent and shipbroker; sole owner of N. P. Olsen & Søn, Kragerø (estab. 1858). Vice-Consul of the Netherlands. *B.* 1908. *Educ.* Public High School. *M.* 1937, Anne Marie Schønberg. *S.* Johan Burton. *Dau.* Anne. *Address:* Dampskibskaien, Kragerø, Norway.

**LYON, Alexander Ward,** LLB, MP. British. politician and lawyer. *B.* 15 Oct. 1931. *Educ.* University Coll. London. Bachelor of Laws, Barrister. *Career:* Member of Parliament for York; Min. of State, Home Affairs 1974–76. *Address:* House of Commons, London SW1A 0AA.

**LYONS, Sir William,** RDI, DTech., FRSA, Hon. AMIAE. *B.* 4 Sept. 1901. *Educ.* Arnold School, Blackpool. *Career:* Founder-partner, Swallow Sidecar Co. 1922; the title of the firm was changed to Swallow Coachbuilding Co. Ltd. in 1928, and was acquired by S.S. Cars Ltd. (a private company) in 1933; the latter became a public company in 1935, and in 1945 its name was changed to Jaguar Cars Ltd. Chairman and Chief Executive, Jaguar Cars Ltd., Daimler Co. Ltd., Coventry; Chairman, Coventry Climax Engines Ltd.; A Deputy Chairman, British Leyland Ltd., Corp., ret. 1972; Pres. Jaguar Cars Ltd. since 1972. Appointed Royal Designer for Industry by the Royal Society of Arts 1964 (RDI); DTech; Fellow Royal Socy. Arts; Hon AMIAE; Past President: Fellowship of The Motor Industry (1957–59); The Society of Motor Manufacturers and Traders Ltd., Motor Industry Research Association, and Motor Trades Benevolent Fund (1950–51). *Address:* Wappenbury Hall, nr. Leamington Spa, Warwicks.

# M

**MABON, Dr. Dickson**, PC, MB, ChB, DHMSA, FInstPet, MP. *B.* 1925. *Educ.* University of Glasgow (MB, ChB, 1954). *M.* 1970, Elizabeth. *Career:* Labour Member of Parliament for Greenock 1955–74, for Greenock & Port Glasgow since 1974; Political columnist Scottish Daily Record 1955–64; Visiting Physician, Manor House Hospital, London; Minister of State for Scotland, 1964–70; Minister of State for Energy since April 1976; Member, Council of Europe and Assembly of Western European Union 1970–72 and 1974–76. *Chairman:* Labour Cttee for Europe; Manifesto Groups of Labour MPs; Trustees of Young Volunteer Force Foundation. Freeman, City of London. *Address:* House of Commons, London, S.W.1.

**MABROUK, Hédi.** Tunisian Diplomat. *B.* 1921. *Educ.* Annexe de l'Ecole normale d'instituteurs, & the Lycée Carnot, Tunis; Facultés des Lettres et de droit, Paris—Licencié ès Lettres, Law certificate. *M.* 1945, Essia Saadallah. *S.* 1. *Daus.* 3. *Career:* Administrator, General Secretariat of the Govt. 1941–50; Principal Private Sec. to Minister of Agric. 1951–54; Caid of Gabès 1955–56; Gov. of Sbeitla, of Gafsa & subsequently of Kef 1956–62; Pres. of Tunisian Marine Navigation & entrusted by Govt. with the administration & reconversion of the base at Bizerta 1962–67; General Commissioner for Textiles 1967–69; Vice-Chmn. of Economic & Social Council & Chmn., National Export Centre 1967–72; Dir., Central Admin. to Ministry of the Economy, Tunis 1973; Tunisian Ambassador to France since 1973. *Decorations:* Grand Officier de l'Ordre de la République tunisienne; Chevalier du Mérite Agricole; Grand Officier du Ouissam alaouite; Commandeur de la Légion d'Honneur; Commandeur de l'Ordre de l'Indépendance. *Address:* 25 Rue Barbet de Jouy, 75007 Paris, France.

**McADAMS, Edward Joseph.** American. *B.* 1902. *Educ.* Univ. of Chicago (PhD), Chicago Kent College of Law (LLB); C.P.A. State of Illinois. *M.* 1934, Catharine Healy. *S.* Edward J., Jr. and John A. *Daus.* Ann (Sheehan) and Catharine. *Career:* Treasurer, Armour & Co. 1958, Financial Vice-Pres., Treasurer and Secy. 1959, Pres. since 1965. *Clubs:* South Shore Country; Chicago (Chicago). *Address: office* 401 North Wabash Avenue, Chicago, Ill. 60611, U.S.A.

**McALEER, William Kearns.** BS, MS. American. *B.* 1921. *Educ.* Carnegie Inst. of Technology (BS); Univ. Pittsburgh (MS). *Married. S.* 1. *Career:* Asst. Sales Mgr. Plastics Div. Curtis Wright Corp. 1955–56; Dir. S. Amer. Div. N.B. Maynard & Co. Inc. 1957–60; Vice Pres. and Dir. Latin American Div. H.B. Maynard & Co. Inc. 1960–67; Pres. Peter F. Loftus Corp. *Member:* Amer. Socy. Mechanical Engineers; Sales & Marketing Execs. International *Clubs:* University, Pittsburgh; American Buenos Aires. *Address:* 651 Arden Road, Pittsburgh 16, Pa, U.S.A. and *office:* Chamber of Commerce Building, Pittsburgh, Pa.

**McALLISTER, Decker Gordon.** American. *B.* 1900. *Educ.* Massachusetts Inst. of Technology (BA). *M.* 1929, Martha C. Ransome. *S.* Decker Gordon Jr., and Bruce. *Career:* Pres., Pacific Scientific Co. 1955; Vice-Pres., Bendix Instrument Co. 1935; Director: Strategic Industries Assn. 1958; Chairman of the Board, Pacific Scientific Co. 1965—; Director: Varian Associates 1951—, and Oxford Laboratories 1960—; Chemetal Corp.; Vice Chmn. Oxford Laboratories. Hon. Trustee, California Academy of Sciences 1965—. California Roadside Cncl.; Arthritic Foundn. Fellow, California Acad. of Sciences; Chmn., Bd. of Trustees of California Acad. of Sciences 1956–64. *Member:* Strategic Industries Assn. *Clubs:* Hamoa Beach (Hawaii); Pacific-Union; Villa Taverna (San Francisco); Burlingame Country. *Address:* 700 Eucalyptus Avenue, Hillsborough, Calif. 94010; and *office* 541 Taylor Way, Unit 4, Belmont, Calif., 94002 U.S.A.

**McALPINE, Sir Edwin.** British. Co. Director. *B.* 1907. *Educ.* Oundle. *M.* Ella Mary Gardner. *S.* William Hepburn, Robert Alistair, David Malcolm. *Dau.* The Hon. Mrs. Robin Borwick. *Career:* Former Chmn. Dorchester Hotel Ltd.; Dep-Chmn. Brit. Nuclear Associates; Partner Sir Robert McAlpine & Sons Ltd. *Clubs:* Garrick; Caledonian; Buck's. *Address:* Benhams, Fawley Green, nr. Henley on Thames, Oxon; and *office* 40 Bernard Street, London WC1N 1LG.

**McALPINE, Hon. Sir John Kenneth,** KCMG. *B.* 1906. *M.* 1934, Lesley Ruth Hay. *Daus.* 2. *Career:* MP for Selwyn, N.Z., 1946–66; Member, Bd. of Canterbury Agricultural Univ. since 1959, Chmn. since 1967; Minister of Railways, Marine & Printing 1954–66, of Transport & Civil Aviation 1957–66, of Labour 1956–58; Chmn., New Zealand Ports Authority since 1969. *Member:* N.Z. National (Conservative) Party. *Club:* Christchurch. *Address:* 41 Innes Road, Christchurch 5, New Zealand.

**MACAPAGAL, Diosdado.** Former President of Republic of the Philippines. *B.* 1910. *Educ.* Univ. of Santo Tomás. Entered Philippine Diplomatic Service 1946; Second Secy., Washington 1948; member, House of Representatives 1949; Chairman Liberal Party 1957–61; Vice-President of the Republic 1957–61, President 1961–65; Pres. of Const. Convention 1971–73. *Address:* 92 Cambridge Circle, North Forbes Park, Makati, Rizal, The Philippines.

**MacARTHUR, Douglas II.** U.S. Consultant and Diplomatist. *B.* 1909. *Educ.* Yale University (BA); LLD Univ. of Maryland. *M.* 1934, Laura Louise Barkley. *Dau.* Laura. *Career:* Served as 1st Lt. O.R.C. 1933–35. Appointed Secy. Diplomatic Service, Dept. of State, 1935; Served Vancouver, B.C. 1935; Naples 1937; Paris 1938; Lisbon July–Oct. 1940; Vichy 1940–42; interned by Nazi authorities 1942–44; Asst. Political Adviser SHAEF, July–Oct. 1944; Secy. Embassy Paris 1944–48; Secy Embassy Brussels 1948–49; Chief, Div. Western European affairs. Dept, of State Mar. 1949; Dep. Dir., Office of European Regional Affairs 1949–51; Counsellor Embassy, Paris, Feb. 1951; Advisor to Genera Eisenhower, SHAPE, 1951–52; Counsellor, Dept. of State 1953–56; Ambassador to Japan 1957–61; to Belgium 1961–65. Assistant Secy. of State 1965–67; U.S. Ambassador to Austria, 1967–69; Ambassador to Iran, 1969–72; Bd Member of Belgian and American Cos. and of Ditchley Foundation; American Chamber of Commerce in Belgium; Belgo-Japanese Assn. and Chamber of Commerce. *Clubs:* Metropolitan, Chevy Chase. *Address:* Parc Longchamp, 65 Rue Langeveld (Bte-8), 1180 Brussels, Belgium.

**McARTHUR, Harvey King.** BSc. American. *B.* 1914. *Educ.* Okla. State Univ.; Oklahoma East Central State Coll. (BSc.). *M.* Patricia Toler. *S.* 1. *Daus.* 3. *Career:* Vice Pres. Welex Inc. 1957–61; Mgr. Eastern Hemisphere, Halliburton Co.; Man. Dir. & Pres. Halliburton Espanola; Dir. & Gen. Mgr. Halliburton Ltd. *Member:* Inst. of Petroleum; American Assn. of Petroleum Geologists; Socy. Pet. Engineers, A.I.M.M.E. Fellow Amer. Association Advancement of Science. *Clubs:* American; Highgate Golf; Houston. *Address:* 5523 Grape Street, Houston, Texas, U.S.A.

**MacARTHUR, Ian.** *B.* 1925. *Educ.* Oxford Univ. (Scholar; MA). *M.* 1957, Judith Mary Douglas Miller. *S.* 3. *Daus.* 3. *Career:* member Parliament (Con.) Perth and E. Perthshire 1959–Sept. 74; Asst. Govt. Whip 1962–63; Personal Asst. to Rt. Hon. Sir Alec Douglas-Home, Prime Minister, Kinross and W. Perthshire By-Election 1963; Govt. Scottish Whip and a Lord Commissioner of the Treasury 1963–64; Opposition Scottish Whip 1964–65, an Opposition Front-Bench Spokesman 1965–66 and 1969–70; Vice Chmn. Conservative Party in Scotland 1972–75. Associate Director, J. Walter Thompson Co., London 1958–63 and 1964–77; Dir., British Textile Confederation since 1977. *Publications:* various political pamphlets and articles. *Clubs:* Naval; New (Edinburgh); Puffins (Edinburgh); Royal County (Perth). *Address:* 42 Roehampton Gate, London SW15; and *office* 65 Victoria Street, London SW1.

**MACARTNEY, James Edward.** Australian. *B.* 1911. *Educ.* Hale School, Perth and University of West Australia. *M.* 1946, Margaret Cosson Bennett. *S.* 2. *Daus.* 2. *Career:* Managing Editor, W.A. Newspapers Ltd. 1951–62; between 1936 and 1951 held positions as editor, then Managing Director, of Perth Newspapers Ltd. Served as Pilot R.A.A.F. 1942–45. Managing Director, West Australian Newspapers Ltd., Perth, Western Australia, 1962–69. *Clubs:* Perth; Royal Perth Golf; Karrinyup Golf. *Address:* 99 Thomas Street, Nedlands, W.A., Australia.

**McAVITY, James Malcolm**, DSO, MBE. Canadian. *B.* 1909. *Educ.* Ridley College and Royal Military College. *M.* 1937, Margaret Temple. *S.* Ian. *Dau.* Virginia. *Career:* Pres., The House of Seagram Ltd. 1956–61. Canadian Export Association. *Publications:* Lord Stratheona's Horse—a Record of Achievement. *Clubs:* St. James's; Thistle Curling; Mount Bruno; Golf; Toronto Golf. *Address: office* Ste 1020, 1080 Beaven Hall Hill, Montreal, P.Q., Canada.

**McBAIN, Alexander McDougall.** Canadian. *B.* 1890. *Educ.* Williamstown High School. *M.* 1927, Margaret Laird. *S.* 1. *Dau.* 1. *Career:* Junior, Metropolitan Bank, Toronto 1909 (Metro. Bank merged with the Bank of Nova Scotia, 1914); Accountant, Bank of Nova Scotia, Dundas & Arthur Branch, Toronto 1914; Guelph 1915; Charlottetown 1916; absent on military duty, World War I 1916–19, Served with RFC; Accountant, Bank of Nova Scotia, Havana, Cuba 1923; Man., Havana 1925; Inspector, General Office, Toronto 1929; Supervisior, Foreign Dept., Toronto 1934; retired on pension 1953. Loaned to Canadian Government in World War II; served as Adviser to the Foreign Exchange Control Bd.; Pres,. Melander Homes Ltd.; Vice-Pres., Cluny Investment Co. Ltd.; member, War Finance Cttee.; and member, Interdepartmental Publicity Cttee; President, Canadian Handicraft Guild Ont., 1943–49; President, St. Andrew's Society of Toronto 1951–53; Honorary Vice-President Canadian Red Cross Society, Ontario Division; Member, Bd. of Managers, Rosedale Presb. Church; mem., Advisory Bd., Toronto Aged Men's and Women's Homes; Financial Adviser to the Bd. of Trustees, Presb. Church in Canada. *Member:* Advisory Council, Salvation Army; Financial Advisor, Girl Guides of Canada. Masons, Toronto: Island Chapter No. 1, Royal Arch Masons, Havana, Cuba. *Clubs:* Toronto Golf; Toronto; *Address:* 35 Cluny Drive, Toronto, Ont., Canada.

**MACBRIDE, Seán.** Irish barrister-at-law. *B.* 26 Jan. 1904. *Educ.* St. Louis de Gonzague (Paris) and Mount St. Benedict, Gorey, Ireland; National University, Ireland. *M.* 1926, Catalina Bulfin. *S.* 1. *Dau.* 1. *Career:* took a prominent part in Ireland's fight for freedom and was jailed many times by the British forces in Ireland; called to the Bar 1937, and to the Inner Bar 1943; founded political party Clann na Poblachta (Republican Party) 1946; member for Dublin County, Dail Eireann 1947–48 and Dublin S.W. since 1948; Minister for External Affairs Feb. 1948–51; President, Council of Foreign Ministers of Council of Europe 1950; Vice-President, O.E.E.C. (Organization for European Economic Co-operation) 1948–51; declined to accept portfolio in new Government, on ground of inadequate parliamentary representation, June 1954; Delegate to Council of Europe from Ireland and member of Economic Committee of Council of Europe, 1954; UN Commissioner for Namibia since 1973. Member, National Group for nominating candidates for membership of the International Court of Justice; Trustee, International Prisoners of Conscience Fund; Secy. Gen., International Commission of Jurists (Geneva, Switzerland) 1963–70, mem. 1971—, and Chmn. Amnesty International (London) since 1961; Member, Executive, Pan-European Union; Member, European Round Table; Chairman, Irish Section 'Amnesty'; Member, Ghana Bar; International Congress of Jurists, New Delhi (1958) and Rio de Janeiro (1962); Former Chairman, Irish Section International Commn. of Jurists; Vice-Chmn., Congress of World Peace Forces, Moscow 1973. Mem., Cttee. 1973—; Vice-Pres., World Fed. of UN Assocs. Joint Recipient of Nobel Peace Prize, 1974; Lenin Peace Prize, 1977. *Publication:* Civil Liberty. *Address:* Ruebuck House, Clonskea, Dublin 14, Ireland.

**MacCABE, Brian Farmer**, MC (and Bar). **British.** *B.* **1914.** *Educ.* Christ's Coll. *M.* 1940, Eileen Elizabeth Noel Hunter. *S.* Michael Murray. *Career:* Account Exec., C. R. Casson Ltd. 1934–40; Advertising Man., B.O.A.C. 1945–47. Served in World War II (Major, Tank Regt.). Chairman, Foote, Cone & Belding Ltd. 1948—. F.C.B. International Inc., 1967–74; Director, Foote, Cone & Belding, Communications Inc., 1953—. Recipient Royal Humane Society Medal for Saving Life at Sea; Olympic Games, 800 m finalist 1936. *Fellow:* Inst. of Practitioners in Advertising (Pres. 1963–65); Council Member Advertising Assn., 1952–69 *Member:* Committee on Marketing Studies, Ashridge Man. College; Appeal Committee, Olympic and Commonwealth Games; Publicity Panel, British Red Cross Socy. (1965–68); Bd. of Dirs. American Chamber of Commerce (UK); Fellow, Royal Socy. of Arts; Council of the Advertising Standards Authority 1969–72. *Clubs.* Boodles; Garrick: Thirty Club (London); London Athletic (Vice-Pres,); Bucks. A.A.A. (Vice-Pres.). *Address:* Somerford Penn Road, Beaconsfield, Bucks; and *office* 82 Baker Street, London W1M 2AE.

**McCABE, Louis C.** American geologist. *B.* 1904. *Educ.* Univ. of Illinois (BS, MS, PhD). *M.* 1936, Catherine Hessel. *S.* Michael J. and John C. *Daus.* Dorothy and Jean. Legion of Merit (U.S.); Order of the British Empire (OBE Mil.); Order of the Crown (Belgium). Illinois Geolog. *Career:* Surv. 1930–41; served in World War II (Capt. to Col., U.S. Army Engrs.) 1941–45; Chief of Coal Branch, U.S. Bur. of Mines 1946–47; Dir., Los Angeles County Air Polution Control District 1947–49; Chief, Office of Air and Stream Pollution, U.S. Bureau of Mines 1949–51; Chief, Fuels and Explosives Division 1951–55; Scientist Director, U.S. Public Health Service 1955; Dept. of State Representative to I.L.O. Coal Mining Committee 1947–51; Consultant to W.H.O. 1957—. President, Resources Research Inc. 1956–67; Chmn. of Board, Hazelton Laboratories Inc. 1963–67. Chairman and Chief Executive Officer, Environmental Development Inc. 1968–70. *Member:* Washington Academy of Science, American Chemical Society and American Institute of Mining and Metallurgical Engineers. *Fellow:* Geological Society of America, and American Association for Advancement of Science. Frank A. Chambers Award: Air Pollution Control Assn.; Diplomate of Amer. Academy of Environmental Engineers. *Publications:* more than fifty in fields of fuels, energy and atmospheric pollution. *Clubs:* Cosmos (Washington); Chemists (N.Y.C.); Sigma XI. *Address:* 7102 Pomander Lane, Chevy Chase 20015, Md., U.S.A.

**McCABE, St. Clair Landerkin.** Canadian. *B.* 1915. *M.* 1933, Elsie Dorothy Stricker. *S.* John Tomothy St. Clair. *Dau.* Mrs. J. Beatson. *Career:* Executive Vice-President and Chief Operating Officer and Director Thomson Newspapers Limited: Executive Vice-President and Director The Advocate Printing Co.; Atlantic Newspapers Limited; Canadian Newspapers Co. Ltd.; Carthage Publishing Co. Inc.; The Cordele Publishing Co.; The Courier Company; Douglas Dispatch, Inc.; Greenville Newspapers Inc.; The Independent Inc.; Key West Newspaper Corporation; Lock Haven Express Printing Company; Newburgh Beacon-News Co. Inc.; Ontario Newspapers Company Limited; Thomson-Brush-Moore Newspapers Inc.; Thomson Newspaper Publishing Co. Inc.; Thomson Newspapers Inc.; Thomson Newspapers (Florida) Inc.; Thomson Newspapers (Illinois) Inc.; Thomson Newspapers (Missouri) Inc.; Thomson Newspapers (New Hampshire) Inc.; Thomson Newspapers (Pennsylvania) Inc.; Thomson Newspapers (Wisconsin) Inc.; Thomson Publications of New York Inc.; Exec. Vice-Pres. and Man. Dir. and Dir. Thomson B.C. Newspapers Limited; Thomson International Corporation Limited; Thomwood Holdings Limited; Western Publishers Ltd. Pres. and Dir. The Evening Telegram Limited; The Northern Light Limited; Post Publishing Co. Ltd.; Replacement Sales Limited; Rocky Mount Publishing Company; Scotia Printers Limited; Thomson Newspapers (Ohio) Inc.; Vice-Pres. and Dir. Patriot Publishing Company Limited; The Punta Gorda Herald Inc.; San Gabriel Valley Tribune, Inc.; Western Printing and Publishing Limited; The Woodbridge Company Limited; Director The Advocate Company Limited; Central Canada Insurance Service Limited; The Guarantee Insurance Co.; Humboldt Newspapers, Inc.; Oxnard Publishing Company; Scottish & York Holdings Limited; Scottish & York Insurance Co. Limited; The Standard St. Lawrence Company Limited; The Thomson Corp. Ltd.; Thomson Equitable Corp. Ltd.; Victoria Insurance Company of Canada. *Member:* Canadian Daily Newspaper Publishers Association; Canadian Press; Commonwealth Press Union; Inland Daily Press Association; International Press Institute; Freemason (Scot. Rite). *Clubs:* Ontario; National; The Mississauga Golf and Country. *Address:* 1195 Greenoaks Drive, Mississauga, Ontario, L5J 3A1; and *office—Canada:* Thomson Newspapers Limited, 65 Queen Street West, Toronto, Ontario, M5H 2M8; *office—United States:* Thomson Newspapers Inc., 3150 Des Plaines Avenue, Des Plaines, Illinois, 60018.

**McCABE, Warren Lee.** American chemical engineer. *B.* 1899. *Educ.* University of Michigan (BSc Chem Eng 1922; MSc in Chem Eng 1923; PhD 1928). *M.* 1924, Lillian Hoag. *S.* Warren Lee, Jr. *Dau.* Barbara Louise Moran (Mrs.), *Career:* Instructor: Chemical Engineering, Massachusetts Inst. of Technology 1923–25; Instructor in Chemical Engineering, Univ. of Michigan 1925–28 (Asst. Prof. 1928–33; Assoc. Prof. 1933–36); Professor, Chemical Engineering, Carnegie Inst. of Technology 1936–47 (Head, Dept. of Chemical Engineering 1937–47); Director of Research, The Flintkote Co., Whippany, N.J. 1947–53 (Vice-Pres. 1949–53);

Administrative Dean, Polytechnic Institute of Brooklyn (N.Y.) 1953–64; Visiting Prof. N.C. State Univ., Raleigh, N.C. 1964–65; Reynolds Prof. of Engineering 1965–72, Prof. Emeritus since 1972. Fulbright Summer Lecturer, and Consultant Univ. of Taipei (Taiwan), Summer 1965—. *Member:* Amer. Inst. of Chemical Engineers (Pres. 1950); Amer. Chemical Socy.; Amer. Socy. for Engineering Education. *Awards:* Certificate of Merit, U.S.A. 1948; William H. Walker Award, American Institute of Chemical Engineers, 1937. Golden Key Award, National Education Assn., U.S.A. 1961; Warren K. Lewis Award (AICE) 1973. *Publications:* Elements of Chemical Engineering (with J. C. Smith) first ed. 1956, second ed. 1967, third ed. 1976, McGraw-Hill; and approximately forty papers on chemical engineering in technical and scientific journals. Independent. *Address:* 222 Ransom Street, Chapel Hill, N.C.; and *office* N.C. State University, Raleigh, N.C., U.S.A.

**MacCALLUM, Donald Charles.** Canadian professional engineer. *B.* 1916. *Educ.* McGill Univ. (BEng 1938). *M.* 1947, Marian Fenwick (Wilkinson). *Career:* Designer, Canadian Ingersoll-Rand Co. Ltd. 1938–40; Major, Royal Canadian Armoured Corps 1940–45; Director of Rehabilitation, Engineering Inst. of Canada 1945–46; Administrative Engineer & Purchasing Agent, Candair Ltd. 1946–48; Consultant to Corporation of Professional Engineers of Quebec 1948–49; Vice-Pres. & Managing Director, Charles Warnock & Co. Ltd. 1949–52; Secretary & Director, Construction Borings Ltd. 1949–52; Project Engineer on loan, Defence Construction (1951) Ltd. 1951–52. President & Director, Racey, MacCallum & Bluteau Ltd. *Member:* Order of Engineers of Quebec; Association of Professional Engineers of Ontario; Engineering Ins. of Canada; Montreal Board of Trade; Past Member & Pres., Montreal Port Cncl.; Montreal Citizens Committee; Past member and Chmn. Bd. of Governors, Lower Canada Coll.; Mayor, City of Westmount. *Clubs:* University (Montreal); Royal Montreal Golf; St. Maurice Fish & Game. *Address:* 4300 De Maisonneuve Boulevard, Westmount, Montreal 215; and *office* 8205 Montreal-Toronto Blvd., Montreal H4X 1NI, Canada.

**McCANCE, Sir Andrew,** DSc, LLD, FRS, DL. British company director. *B.* 30 Mar. 1889. *Educ.* Morrison's Academy; Allan Glen's School; Royal School of Mines, London. *M.* 1936, Joya Harriett Gladys Burford. *Daus.* Jean Nathalie, Margaret Charmian. *Career:* Assistant Armour Manager, Wm. Beardmore & Co. 1910–19; Founder and Managing Director, Clyde Alloy Steel Co. 1919–30; Past-President, The Iron and Steel Institute 1948–50, Glasgow and West of Scotland Iron and Steel Institute; Institute of Vitreous Enamellers; The Institution of Works Managers; Chmn. Colvilles Clugston Shanks Ltd. *Address:* 27 Broom Cliff, Newton Mearns, Glasgow, Scotland.

**McCANCE, Thomas.** American banker. *B.* 25 Aug. 1902. *Educ.* Yale University (PhB). *M.* 1932, Elizabeth Day Ferguson. *S.* Thomas. Henry Ferguson. *Dau.* Ellen Margaret (Parker III). *Career:* Associated with Brown Brothers Harriman & Co. since 1929, Partner since 1945. Member Bd. of Trustees of Foreign Parishes of the Protestant Episcopal Church in the U.S.A.; Trustee: Provident Loan Society of New York: Trustee, Seaman's Bank for Savings. *Address:* Brown Brothers, Harriman & Co., 59 Wall Street, New York 10005, New York, U.S.A.

**McCANN, Hugh James.** Irish diplomat. *B.* 8 Feb. 1916. *Educ.* Belvedere College, Dublin; London School of Economics, University of London (BScEcon). *M.* 1950, Mary Virgina Larkin. *S.* 4. *Dau.* 1. *Career:* Admin. Officer Dept. Industry and Commerce Dublin 1940–41; Private Secy. Minister, Industry and Comerce 1941–43; Superintending Officer, Dept. of Supplies 1943–44; Commercial Secy. Office, High Commissioner, Ireland, London 1944–46; First Secy. Dept. Foreign Affairs 1946–48; Counsellor, Irish Embassy Washington, D.C. 1948–54; En. Ex. and Min. Plen. to Austria and Switzerland 1954–56; Asst. Secy., Dept. of Foreign Affairs 1956–58; Amb. Ex. & Plen. to the Court of St. James's, 1958–63; Secy., Department of Foreign Affairs, Dublin 1963–74; Ambassador to France, Permanent Representative to OECD & Permanent Delegate to UNESCO since 1974, and concurrently Ambassador to Morocco since 1975. *Address:* 12 Ave Foch, Paris 16, France.

**McCARTHY, Donal John,** CMG. British Diplomat. *B.* 1922. *Educ.* Holloway Sch.; London Univ. *M.* 1951, Rosanna Parbury. *S.* 3. *Career:* Royal Navy 1942–46; Foreign Office 1946–47; HM Embassy, Jedda 1948–51; Brit. Middle East Office 1951–54; 1st Sec., Foreign Office 1955–58, Kuwait 1958–60, Ottawa 1960–63, Foreign Office 1963–64; Counsellor, Aden (Middle East Command) 1964–67; Head of Aden, then Arabian Depts., Foreign Office 1967–70; Imperial Defence Coll. 1970; Minister (Economic), UK Mission to UN, New York 1971–73; HM Ambassador, United Arab Emirates 1973–77. *Decorations:* Companion, Order of St. Michael & St. George, 1969; i.d.c. (1 year at Imperial Defence Coll.), 1970. *Clubs:* Travellers'; Royal Automobile; Ski of Great Britain; Lough Derg Yacht. *Address:* 29a Frognal, London NW3; and Glenculloo, Newport, Tipperary, Ireland; and *office* c/o Foreign & Commonwealth Office, London SW1A 2AH.

**McCARTHY, Eugene Joseph.** American Politician. *B.* 1916. *Educ.* St. John's Univ., Collegeville, Minn.; Minnesota Univ. (MA). *M.* 1945, Abigail Quigley. *S.* 1. *Daus.* 3. *Career:* Prof. of Economics, then Prof. of Education, St. John's Univ., Collegeville, Minn.; Civilian Tech. Asst., War Dept. Military Intelligence Div.; Acting Chmn., Sociology Dept., St. Thomas Coll., St. Paul, Minn.; Mem., U.S. House of Reps. 1948–58; Senator from Minnesota 1958–71; Candidate for the Democratic Nomination for the Presidency 1968; Independent Candidate for the Presidency 1976. *Awards:* Cardinal Newman Award, 1955; Hon. LLD St. Louis Univ., 1955. *Address:* 3053 Q Street, N.W., Washington, D.C. 20007, U.S.A.

**McCARTHY, Rt. Hon. Sir Thaddeus Pearcey.** PC, KBE, Past President, Court of Appeal in New Zealand. *B.* 1907. *Educ.* St. Bede's Coll., Christchurch and Victoria Univ. Coll., Wellington (LLM—1st Class Hons 1931). *M.* 1938, Joan Margaret Miller. *S.* John. *Daus.* Brigid and Mary. *Career:* Served in World War II (2 N.Z.E.F.), Middle East and Italy; DJAG 2 N.Z.E.F. 1945–46; Judge of Supreme Ct. of N.Z. 1957–63; Chmn. Royal Commission on State Services in New Zealand 1961–62; Judge of New Zealand Court of Appeal 1963–76, Pres. 1973–76; Privy Council 1968; Chmn., Royal Commissions on Salary and Wage Fixing Procedures in the State Services 1968 and 1972; Chmn. Winston Churchill Memorial Trust Bd. 1966–76; Chmn. Royal Commission on Nuclear Power Generation 1976—; Chmn. Policy Cttee. of New Zealand Computer Centre 1977—. Created Knight Bachelor 1964; Created Kt. Commander Brit. Empire 1974. Chmn. Royal Commission on Horse Racing; Trotting and Dog Racing, 1969; Royal Commission on Social Security, 1969; Vice-Pres. N.Z. Section, International Commission of Jurists. Honorary Bencher, Middle Temple 1974. *Clubs:* Wellington (Pres.); Wellington Golf (Capt. 1952, Pres. 1973–77). *Address:* 100 Donald Street, Karori, Wellington, New Zealand.

**McCAW, George Edwin,** ERD, DL, JP. British. *B.* 1903. *M.* 1934, Beatrix Anderson (*Dec.*) and (2) 1959, Amy Pennington. *Daus.* Shirlie (Brown) and Jeanne (Boydell). *Career:* Served in World War II (Capt. R.A. Retired. ERD. Mentioned in Dispatches) 1938–45; Managing Dir., McCaw, Allan & Co. Ltd., linen manufacturers, Lurgan, Nthn. Ireland 1950—; Chairman, Managing Committee, Lurgan College (25 years); High Sheriff, Co. Armagh (1964); Deputy Lieutenant, since 1967. *Clubs:* Ulster Reform; and various sporting clubs in Northern Ireland. *Address:* Taghnevan House, Lurgan, Northern Ireland.

**McCAW, Hon. Sir Kenneth Malcolm,** QC,. Australian. Barrister at Law. *B.* 1907. *Educ.* Matriculated privately. Evening School, Supreme Court Law Course. *M.* Valma Marjorie. *S.* Owen Kenneth. *Dau.* Margaret Thea. *Career:* M.L.A. (Lane Cove) continuously 1947–75 (retired); Solicitor, Sup. Ct. of N.S.W. Mar. 1933–May 1965; Attorney General, New South Wales 1965–75 (retired); *Member:* Cncl. of Law Socy. of N.S.W. (1945–48); N.S.W. Bar Council (*ex-officio* Member) 1965–75; Liberal Party of Australia; Appointed Queen's Counsel 1972. *Award:* Created Knight Bachelor, 1975; Coronation Medal. *Clubs:* Sydney; Lane Cove Businessmen's; Lane Cove Lions (Charter Member); Hon. Member Royal Automobile and Sydney Leagues; Tattersall's. *Address:* 'Woodrow House', No. 1 Charlish Lane, Lane Cove, N.S.W., 2066, Australia.

**McCLELLAND, Senator The Hon. Douglas.** Australian Parliamentarian. *B.* 1926. *M.* 1950, Lorna Belva McNeill. *S.* 1. *Daus.* 2. *Career:* Member, Labour Party Executive in New South Wales 1955–62; Hon. Dir., St. George Hospital, Sydney 1959–67; Senator for N.S.W. in the Australian Parliament 1962–76; Member, Senate Select Cttee on Television 1963–64; Mem., Senate Standing Cttee on Health & Welfare 1969–72: Minister for the Media 1972–75; Special Minister of State Jun.–Nov. 1975; Manager of Govt. Business in Senate 1974–75; Shadow Minister for Administrative Services & Manager of Opposition Business in Senate 1976–77; deputy leader of Australian Labor Party in Senate 1977. *Member:* Australian Journalists Assoc.; Fellow, Commercial Education Society of Australia. *Clubs:* City Tattersalls; St. George Leagues; Cronulla Workers. *Address:* Australian Parliament Offices, Sydney, N.S.W., Australia.

**McCLINTOCK, Eric Paul.** Australian. *B.* 1918. *Educ.* Univ. of Sydney (Dipl Pub Admin). *M.* 1942, Eva Trayhurn Lawrence. *S.* Lawrence Leigh and Eric Paul. *Dau.* Marjorie Vera. *Career:* First Asst. Secy., Department of Trade, Canberra 1956–61. Director: Development Finance Corp. Ltd.; Bestobell (Australia) Ltd. (Chmn.); William Adams Ltd.; Woolworths Ltd. *Member:* Australian Inst. of Dirs.; Sydney Univ. Appointments Bd.; *Fellow:* Australian Inst. Mgmt.; Aust. Inst. of Export. *Clubs:* Australian; Commonwealth (Canberra). *Address:* 71 Upper Pitt Street, Kirribilli, N.S.W.; and *office* Delfin House, 16 O'Connell Street, Sydney, N.S.W., Australia.

**McCLOSKEY, Paul Herbert,** MC. Canadian mining engineer and executive. *B.* 1914. *Educ.* Michigan Coll. of Mining & Tech. (BSc Mining Engineering, 1940). *M.* 1947, Helen Patricia Duncan. *S.* Richard. *Dau.* Anna May. *Career:* With Army Corps of Engins., 2nd Field Co. Engrs. 1942–46; Engineer to Mine Superintendent at Iron & Titanium property, Allard Lake Quebec, subsid. of Kennecott Copper Corp. 1946–52; Engr. and Officer with former Con. Howey Gold Mines Ltd. and Teck-Hughes Gold Mines Ltd. 1952–59; actively engaged in development and financing of Geco and Willroy Mines Ltd. 1953–59; Directing the investments and properties of Rock Realty & Investments Ltd., and other mining exploration work, 1959—. President: Rock Realty & Investments Ltd. (private corporation) 1954—, Madsen Red Lake Gold Mines Limited, 1967—, Matachewan Consolidated Mines Ltd.; Vice-President, Voyager Explorations Ltd. 1959—. *Awards:* MC in World War II; 1939–45 Star; French and German Stars; 3 Service Medals. *Member:* Canadian Inst. of Mining & Metallurgy. *Clubs:* Engineers' (Toronto), Big Bay Point Golf & Country; National St. George's Golf & Country; Boisclair Fish & Game. *Address: office* 365 Bay Street (Suite 705), Toronto 1, Ont., Canada.

**McCLOY, John J.** American lawyer, banker and administrator. *B.* 31 Mar. 1895. *Educ.* Amherst College (BA); Harvard Law School (LLB). *M.* 1930, Ellen Zinsser. *S.* John J. *Dau.* Ellen. *Career:* Member of Bars of New York, District of Columbia and U.S. Supreme Court; served World War I, U.S. Army (Captain); The Assistant Secretary of War 1941–45; Chairman, Civil Affairs Committee, Combined Chiefs of Staff 1943–45; President, International Bank for Reconstruction and Development 1947–49; former U.S. Military Governor and U.S. High Commissioner for Germany June 1949–Aug. 1952; Chairman of Board and Director, The Chase Manhattan Bank 1953–60 (Director 1953–67); Counsel Milbank, Tweed Hope & Hadley 1961–62; Partner, Milbank, Tweed Hadley & McCloy 1963—; Director, Dreyfus Corp.; Chmn. Exec. Cttee. Squibb Corp.; Dir. Olinkraft. Inc. Mercedes-Benz of North America Inc.; Trustee, John M. Olin Foundation; Adviser to President Kennedy on Disarmament Jan.-Oct. 1961; Hon. Chmn. of. Council on Foreign Relations, Inc., N.Y.C., and International House, N.Y.; Coordinating Cttee. of the U.S.A. on Cuban Crisis, 1962–63. Former Chmn. of the Bd. and Trustee, Ford Found.; Member, Bd. of Rockfeller Fondn. 1953–58; Former Dir.: Amer. Telephone & Telegraph Co., Metropolitan Life Insce. Co., Westinghouse Electric Corp.; Allied Chemical Corp.; Hon LLD Amherst, Brown, Colby, Columbia, Dartmough, Harvard, Franklin and Marshall, New York. Princeton, Yale, Pennsylvania, Syracuse, Trinity, Williams, Boston, Maryland, Middleburg, Wilmington, Leigh, Notre Dame Swarthmore, Haverford. Hon. DCL Washington Coll., Dr Ing Tech Univ. of Berlin. Hon. Chairman Board of Trustees Amherst Coll., Hon. Trustee Lenox Hill Hospital; Fellow of Bd, Johns Hopkins Univ.; Hon. Trustee, Deerfield Academy; Hon. Chm., Atlantic Institute (Paris); Treas., American School, Classical Studies Athens (Greece); Member exec. cttee. Salk Institute, Lajolla, Calif, Hon. member of Senat. Johann Wolfgang Goethe Univ., Frankgurt and Friedrich, Wilhelm Univ., Bonn, Hon. Citizen Ehrenburgher, Free University of Berlin, etc. *Address:* 1 Chase Manhattan Plaza, New York 10005, N.Y., U.S.A.

**McCLUSKEY, Lord** (Life Peer, cr. 1976) John Herbert McCluskey, QC, MA, LLB. Solicitor-General for Scotland. *B.* 1929. *Educ.* St. Bede's Coll., Manchester; Holy Cross Academy, Edinburgh; Edinburgh University. *M.* 1956, Ruth Friedland. *S.* 2. *Dau.* 1. *Career:* admitted to Faculty Advocates (Scotland) 1955; Standing Junior Counsel, Ministry of Power 1963–64; Advocate-Depute 1964–71; Chmn. Working Party in Forensic Pathology 1972–75; Medical Appeal Tribunals (Scotland) 1973–74; Sheriff Principal of Dumfries & Galloway 1973–74; Solicitor-General for Scotland since 1974. *Member:* Faculty of Advocates. *Awards:* Master of Arts; Bachelor of Laws. *Address:* 12 Moray Place, Edinburgh EH10 4RN.

**McCOLLUM, Leonard Franklin.** American. *B.* 1902. *Educ.* Univ. of Texas (BS Geol 1925). *M.* (1) 1927, Margaret Wilson. *S.* Leonard Franklin, Jr. *Dau.* Mrs. Olive McCollum Goldman. (2) 1975, Eleanor Searle Whitney. *Career:* Pres. Continental Oil Co. 1947–64; Co-ordinator production, Standard Oil Co. (New Jersey) 1943–47; Pres., Carter Oil Co. 1941–43. Chairman of the Board; Continental Oil Co. 1964–67, and Capital National Bank, Houston, Tex. 1965–76; Chmn. Emeritus 1976—. Director: Morgan Guaranty Trust Co., N.Y.; and Chrysler Corp. N.Y. Hon. Dr. Eng. Colarado School of Mines; Hon. LLD, Texas Technological Coll.; Forbes Magazine 'America's 50 Foremost Business Leaders' (1957); Distinguished Alumnus Award, Univ. of Texas Ex-Students Assn. *Member:* Amer. Petroleum Inst. (Chmn. of Board 1962–63); Chmn. of the Board, Fed. Capital Corp., Houston (Texas) 1974–76; Chmn. Emeritus, Mercantile Texas Corp. 1977—; National Petroleum Council; Independent Petroleum Assn. of America; Amer. Assn. of Petroleum Geologists; Amer. Inst. of Mining & Metallurgical Engineers. *Clubs:* Bohemian (San Francisco); Augusta (Ga.) National; Blind Brook (Port Chester, N.Y.); California (Los Angeles); Links, University, Fifth Avenue (N.Y.C.); Bayou, Ramada, Tejas & River Oaks Country (Houston, Tex.). *Address:* P.O. Box 2081, Houston, Tex. 77001, U.S.A.

**McCOLOUGH, C. Peter.** American. *B.* 1922. *Educ.* Osgoode Hall Law School, Dalhousie Univ. Law School, Halifax, N.S. (LLB 1947), and Harvard Graduate School of Business Administration (MBA 1949). *M.* 1953, Virginia W. *S.* 4. *Dau.* 1. *Career:* General Mgr. of Xerox's first reproduction service center in Chicago, later Asst. to Vice-Pres. i/c Sales; Mgr. of Marketing 1957; General Sales Mgr. 1959; Vice-Pres. i/c Sales 1960; Exec. Vice-Pres. of Operations 1963; Prior to joining Xerox in 1954, was Vice-Pres. i/c Sales for the Lehigh Coal & Navigation Co., Philadelphia. In Mar. 1966; Member Bd. Dirs. Rank Xerox Ltd. (London) 1963—; Pres. 1966—; Xerox Corporation Chief Exec. Officer 1968—; Member Bd. Dirs. Fuji-Xerox Co. (Tokyo) 1967—; Rank Organization, London 1967—; Dir. Citibank; Citicorp; Chmn. and Chief Exec. Officer Xerox Corporation Stamford since 1971; Board of Trustees: University of Rochester; Dir. Council, Financial Aid to Education; Dalhousie Univ. Foundation; Overseas Dev. Council; Trustee U.S. Council, Int. Chamber of Commerce; Member, Business Council, Council Foreign Relations; Chmn. Adv. Cttee. Woodrow Wilson Int. Center for Scholars; Chmn., Listed Company Adv. Comm., N.Y. Stock Exchange; Mem., Adv. Bd., Yale Univ. School of Organisation & Management. Mr McColough received a Presidential appointment to serve as a member of the United Service Organization Inc. for three year term. Democrat. *Clubs:* Harvard, The River (N.Y.C.); Greenwich Country; Belle Haven; Stanwich (Greenwich); Economic, N.Y. *Address: office* Xerox Corporation, Stamford, Connecticut, U.S.A.

**McCOMBS, Sir Terence Henderson,** OBE. New Zealand diplomat and educationalist. *B.* 1905. *Educ.* Christchurch and Waitaki Boys High School; Univ. of New Zealand. *M.* Christina Mary Tulloch. *S.* 4. *Dau.* 1. *Career:* Teaching 1931–35; Member N. Zealand Parliament 1935–51; Parly. Under Secy. to Minister of Finance 1945–47; Minister, Education, Science Ind. Research 1947–49; Teaching 1951–55; Headmaster Cashmere High School, Christchurch 1956–72; Chancellor Univ. of Canterbury 1969–73 High Commissioner for New Zealand in U. Kingdom, Ambassador in Ireland 1973–75; Chmn of Advis. Cttee on N.Z. Sec. Schools 1975–76. *Member:* Royal Society of New Zealand; N.Z. Inst. Educational Research. *Awards:* Fellow N. Zealand Inst. Chemistry; Mem. Royal Inst. Chemistry Gt. Britain & Ireland; Master, Science Univ. New Zealand; Efficiency Decoration. *Clubs:* University; Christchurch. *Address:* 7 Freeman Street, Christchurch 8, New Zealand.

**McCONNELL, James Edward.** Canadian executive. *B.* 1912 *Educ.* University of Western Ontario (BA; Business Admin.); Ridley Coll. *M.* 1943, Mary Priscilla Hazen. *S.* Malcolm Hazen and John Hazen. *Dau.* Mary Creaghan. *Career:* McConnell, Eastman Toronto Office; successively, Account Executive 1936; Director of Company 1937; Manager, Montreal Office 1945; Vice-President 1946; Man. Director and Manager, Toronto Office 1950, Pres. 1953; Chairman, 1965–68; Chmn. of the Bd. 1965–68; Pres. McConnell Leaseholds Ltd., 1965—. Pres., Chmn., Board of Governors, Ridley Coll., St. Catherine's, Ont.; Chmn. Bd. Central Neighbourhood House; Chmn. Bd. Trustees, Ridley Coll. Foundation. Conservative. *Member:* Delta Upsilon. *Clubs:* Georgian Peaks Ski; Granite; Hillside Tennis; London; National; Rocheleau Fish & Game; Rosedale Golf; R.C.Y.C.; St. James (Montreal); Mount Royal (Montreal); Trembec Fishing (Quebec); University (Toronto); Port Rowan; Devils Glen Ski; Alpine Ski; Long Point Company. *Address: office* Suite 801, 234 Eglinton Avenue, East Toronto 315, Ontario, Canada.

**McCONNELL, Joseph Howard.** American lawyer. *B.* 1906. *Educ.* Davidson (N.C.) College (AB); Univ. of Virginia (LLB). *M.* 1936, Elizabeth Bernard. *Daus.* 3. *Career:* Various executive positions with RCA 1941–49; President: National Broadcasting Co. 1949–52; Colgate-Palmolive Co. 1953–55. Dir.: British Aluminium Co. Ltd. 1963–76; Pres. Reynolds Metals Co. 1963–70; Dir. Basic Inc. 1963–76; Chmn. of the Bd. Directors Communications Satellite Corporation, 1970—. Member, Bd. of Visitors, Univ. of Virginia, 1968–76; Rector, 1970–76. *Address:* 200 N. Ocean Blvd., Delray Beach, Fla. 33444; *office* 950 L'Enfant Plaza, S.W. Washington, D.C. 20024, U.S.A.

**MacCORKLE, Stuart A.** American. Author & consultant in public administration. *B.* 1903. *Educ.* Washington & Lee Univ. (AB 1924), Univ. of Virginia (MA 1928) and Johns Hopkins Univ. (PhD 1931). *M.* 1942, L. Lucile Emerson. *Career:* Instructor in Government, Univ. of Texas 1930–31, Assoc. Professor of Government, Southwestern College, Memphis, Tenn. 1931–32; Assistant Professor University of Texas 1934–37; Assoc. Prof., Director of Bureau of Municipal Research 1937–41, Prof. and Director 1941–50; Special Lecturer, Univ. of Maryland, Spring Semester, 1942; Visiting educational Counsellor, National Institute of Public Affairs, Washington 1941–42; Special Consultant, U.S.A.A.F. 1942; Principal Civilian Mobilization Adviser, Office of Civilian Defense 1942–43; Lecturer, National Univ. of Mexico, summer 1944, and in Public Admin. summer 1968; Member summer session staff, Univ. of Illinois 1946; Prof. and Director, Inst. of Public Affairs 1950–51; Exec. Dir., Texas Economy Commission 1951–52 (on leave from Univ. of Texas); returned to Univ. of Texas, Sept. 1952–Mar. 1958; Principal Adviser in Public Administration, Seoul National Univ., Korea, Univ. of Minnesota Contract, Mar. 1958–April 1960 (on leave from Univ. of Texas); Visiting Lecturer, College of Europe 1964. Chairman, Governor Jester's Tax Study Commission 1949; elected to Austin City Council, April 1949, re-elected and Mayor *pro tem* April 1951–May 1953. Professor of Government and Director of the Institute of Public Affairs, The University of Texas, Sept. 1950–67. Elected Mayor, pro tem., City of Austin, 1969. Member: Board of Trustees St. Andrews Episcopal School, Austin 1968–71; Board of Directors, Western Republic Life Insurance Co., 1953–67. Chairman, Austin Airport Zoning Board 1955–67. *Member:* Southwestern Science Assn. (Secy.-Treas. 1934–37); Amer. Political Science Assn.; Amer. Socy. for Public Administration; International City Managers' Assn. (Hon. Life Member 1961—); National Municipal League; Hon. LLD Washington & Lee Univ. 1964; Phi Beta Kappa; Pi Sigma Alpha; Kappa Sigma. Member, Editorial Board, Public Administration Review 1942–44. *Publications:* The American Recognition Policy Toward Mexico (1933); Police and Allied Powers of Municipalities in Texas (1938); Municipal Administration (1948); American Municipal Government and Administration (1948); Texas Government (with Dick Smith; 1949, Supplement 1950, 2nd edn. 1952); Texas Civics (with Dick Smith, Thomas P. Yoakum, 1955); Texas Government (with Smith; 3rd edn. 1956, 4th 1960, 5th 1964, 6th 1968, 7th 1974); Austins Three Forms of Government (1973); Cities from Scratch (1974); numerous pamphlets and articles. *Clubs:* Headliners' (Austin); University (Washington); Rotary. *Address:* 3719 Gilbert Street, Austin, Tex. 78703, U.S.A.

**McCOTTER, Burney Richard,** AB. U.S. Citizen. *B.* 1920. *Educ.* Atlantic Christian College (AB). *M.* 1946, Margaret Palmer. *S.* 1. *Dau.* 1. *Career:* Senior Vice Pres., Administration, Occidental Life Insurance Co. North Carolina. *Member:* Amer. Socy. Chartered Life Underwriters; Kiwanis. *Clubs:* Raleigh Executives; Carolina Country. *Address:* 332 Buncombe Street, Raleigh, N.C. 27609, U.S.A. and *office* 1001 Wade Avenue, Raleigh, N.C. 27605.

**McCRINDLE, Robert Arthur,** MP. British Politician. *B.* 1929. *Educ.* Allen Glen's Coll., Glasgow. *M.* 1953, Myra Anderson. *S.* 2. *Career:* Conservative MP for Billericay 1970–74 and for Brentwood & Ongar since 1974. *Address:* House of Commons, London SW1A 0AA.

**MACDONALD, Chesborough Ranald.** Australian. *B.* 1938. *Educ.* Geelong Grammar School, Cambridge Univ. (MA Cantab) and Columbia Univ., N.Y. (MSc). *M.* 1973, Patricia Joan Kathleen Tryon. *S.* 1. *Dau.* 1. *Career:* Managing Director, David Syme & Co. Ltd., Oct. 1964—; Chmn. Australian Section, International Press Institute since 1971; Pres. Austr. Newspapers Council; Chmn. The Media Council of Australia; Chmn. Efftee Broadcasters Pty. Ltd. *Member:* Commonwealth Press Union. *Clubs:* Melbourne; Melbourne Cricket; Marylebone Cricket; St. Andrews; Royal Melbourne Golf, Sorrento Golf. *Address:* Avoca, 8 Gordon Grove, South Yarra, Vic.; and *office* 250 Spencer Street, Melbourne, Vic., Australia.

**McDONALD, Denis Ronald.** Irish diplomat. *B.* 1910. *Educ.* BA, HDipEd, National Univ. (UCC). *M.* 1941, Una Sheehan *S.* 1. *Dau.* 1. *Career:* Minister, later Ambassador, to Belgium, May 1954, concurrently Represenative to the European Economic Community, Dec. 1959; Ambassador to France, Sept. 1960–66; and Permanent Representative to O.E.C.D. and U.N.E.S.C.O.; Ambassador to Italy and Concurrently to Turkey 1966–75; Ambassador in Egypt 1975; retired 1976 *Awards:* Kt. Cmdr., Order of St. Gregory the Great; Kt. Grand Cross, Order of Merit of the Italian Republic. *Address:* c/o Ministry of Foreign Affairs, Dublin, Ireland.

**MACDONALD, Hon. Donald Stovel,** PC, MP, BA, LLM, LLD, DEng. Canadian Lawyer & Politician. *B.* 1932. *Educ.* Univ. of Toronto—BA; Osgoode Hall Law Sch.; Harvard Law Sch.—LLM; Cambridge Univ.—Diploma in International Law; LLD (h.c.), St. Lawrence Univ.; DEng. (h.c.) Colorado Sch. of Mines. *M.* 1961, Ruth Hutchison. *Daus.* 4. *Career:* Called to the Bar of Ontario 1955; Associate, McCarthy & McCarthy, Toronto 1957–62; mem. of Canadian Parliament since 1962; Parly. Sec. to Minister of Justice 1963–65, to Minister of Finance 1965, to Sec. of State for External Affairs 1966–68, to Minister of Industry 1968; Minister without Portfolio & Acting Min. of Justice April–July 1968; Pres. of Privy Council & Govt. House Leader 1968–70; Min. of National Defence 1970–72, of Energy, Mines & Resources 1972–75, & of Finance 1975–77 (resigned). *Member:* Law Soc. of Upper Canada; Canadian Bar Assoc.; Delta Kappa Epsilon. *Awards:* Prize in Insurance Law, Law Soc. of Upper Canada, 1955; Rowell Fellowship, Canadian Inst. of International Affairs, 1956. *Clubs:* Toronto Cricket, Skating & Curling; University (Toronto). *Address:* 15 Westward Way, Ottawa, Ontario K1L 5A8; and *office* Room 515-S Centre Block, Parliament Buildings, Ottawa, Ontario K1A OA7, Canada.

**MACDONALD, Keith Alexander.** Australian television executive. *B.* 1910. *Educ.* St. Peter's Coll., Adelaide, and St. Mark's Coll., Univ. of Adelaide (LLB). *M.* 1958, Sheila Sibyl Giles. *Career:* Practised Law at Adelaide Bar 1933–37; Radio Broadcasting with The Advertiser Broadcasting Network 1937–58 (Manager 1946–58); Gen. Mgr., Television Broadcasters Ltd., North Adelaide, Oct. 1958–66. Station Manager 1966–68. *Clubs:* Adelaide; Royal Adelaide Golf; Rotary. *Address: office* 'The Advertiser', Adelaide, South Australia.

**McDONALD, Lauren Hunter.** FIE Aust, MRINA, MIES. British. Consulting Engineer, Naval Architect. *B.* 1913. *Educ.* Brisbane State High School; Central Tech. College. Univ. of Queensland. *M.* 1938, Grace Elizabeth Pickering. *S.* 2. *Dau.* 1. *Career:* Chmn. of Dirs. Mephalene (Qld) Steel Treatment Pty. Group Ltd.. *Member:* Aust. Cttee. Lloyds Register of Shipping. Bd. Prof. Engineers, Queensland. *Clubs:* Royal Queensland Yacht Squadron; Queensland Cricketers; Brisbane. *Address:* 15 Gilmore Street, Ekibin, Brisbane Qld. Australia and *office* Box 99 P.O. Annerley, Queensland 4103.

**MACDONALD, Rt. Hon. Malcolm John,** PC. British diplomat. *B.* 1901. *Educ.* Bedales School, Petersfield; Queen's College, Oxford (MA). *M.* 1946, Audrey Fellowes Rowley, widow of Lt.-Colonel John Rowley. *Dau.* Fiona. *Career:* MP (Lab.) for Bassetlaw Division of Notts. 1929–31, (National Labour) 1931–35 and Ross and Cromarty 1936–45; Parliamentary Under-Secretary, Dominions Office 1931–35; Secretary of State for Colonies 1935 and 1938–40; Secretary of State for Dominion Affairs 1935–38 and 1938–39; Minister of Health 1940–41; United Kingdom High Commissioner in Canada 1941–46; Governor-General of the Malayan Union and Singapore May–July 1946; Governor-Gen. of Malaya, Singapore and British Borneo 1946–48; Special Ambassador to Indonesia Dec. 1949; Chancellor, University of Malaya 1949–61; Commissioner-General for the United Kingdom in South-East Asia 1948–55; High Commissioner for U.K. in India 1955–60; Leader of British Delegation, and Co-Chairman, at International Conference on Laos 1961–62; Governor and C.-in-C.. Kenya 1963; Visitor. Univ. Coll., Kenya; Gov. General of Kenya 1963–64, High Commissioner in Kenya 1965–66; Special Rep. in East and Central Africa 1966–67. Special Envoy: to Sudan, Oct. 1967; to Somalia, Dec. 1967; Special Representative in Africa 1967–69; Order of Merit 1969; Chancellor, Durham Univ. since 1970; Pres., Royal Commonwealth Society since 1971; Pres., Great Britain–China Centre since 1972; Pres., Voluntary Service Overseas since 1975; Pres., Caribbean Development Trust since 1977. *Publications:* Down North; The Birds of Brewery Creek; Borneo People; Angkor; Birds in my Indian Garden; Birds in the Sun; Treasure of Kenya; People & Places; Titans and Others. *Address:* Raspit Hill, Ivy Hatch, Sevenoaks, Kent.

**McDONNELL, James S., Jr.** American aerospace executive. *B.* 1899. *Educ.* Princeton University (BS 1921) and Massachusetts Institute of Technology (MS-Aero Engr 1925) *M.* (1 1934, Mary Elizabeth Finney (*Dec.* 1949). *S.* James Smith III and John Finney. *M.* (2) 1956, Mrs. Priscilla B. Forney. *S.* G. David. *Daus.* Susan Brush (Boyd) and Priscilla Young (Canny). *Career:* Aero. Engr. and Pilot, Huff Daland Airplane Co. 1924; Stress Analyst and Draftsman, Consolidated Aircraft Co. 1924–25; Asst. Chief Engr., Stout Metal Airplane Co. 1925; Chief Engr., Hamilton Aero Manufacturing Co. 1926–28; McDonnell & Associates 1928–30; Vice-Pres., Airtransport Engng. Corp. 1931–32; Chief Project Engr. for Landplanes, Glenn L. Martin Co. 1933–38.Chairman and Chief Executive Officer. Founder and Director, McDonnell Aircraft Corp., St. Louis, Mo. 1939–67; Chmn. & Chief Exec. Officer, McDonnell Douglas Corp. 1967–72, Chmn. & Chmn. Financial & Exec. Cttees. since 1972. Member Bd. of Directors Atlantic Council & Population Crisis Cttee. *Awards:* Hon Dr Engng., Missouri Sch. of Mines & Metall., 1957, and Washington Univ. 1958; Hon LLD. Princeton Univ. 1960, and Univ. of Arkansas 1965; Daniel Guggenheim Medal, 1963; St. Louis Award 1959; Forrestal Memorial Award 1972. *Member:* United Nations Assoc. (U.S.A.); Inst. of Aeronautics & Astronautics (Fellow); Air Force Assn.; Amer. Ordnance Assn. National (Security) Industrial Assn. *Clubs:* Metropolitan (Washington D.C.); University (N.Y. and St. Louis); Missouri, Athletic; St. Louis Country; Noonday; St. Louis; Old Warson Country; Bellerive country; Racquet. *Address: office* P.O. Box 516, St. Louis, Mo. 63166, U.S.A.

**MacDONNELL, Wilfred Donald.** American. *B.* 1911. *Educ.* St. Francis Xavier College (Antigonish, N.S., Canada) and Massachusetts Inst. of Technology (BS Metallurgy). *M.* (1) 1937, Evelyn E. Cronin (*dec'd*). *S.* Wilfred D., Jr. & Lawrence J. *Dau.* Sandra C. (Ryskamp). (2) Marian Olive Donaldson. *S.* 1. *Career:* College Trainee to Gen. Supt., Bethlehem Steel Co. (Lackawanna, N.Y.) 1934–49; Asst. Gen. Mgr. Bethlehem Steel Co. (Johnston, Pa.) 1949–57; Vice-Pres., Operations, Great Lakes Steel Co. (Ecorse, Mich.) 1957–59, Pres. 1959–62. Vice-Pres., Kelsey-Hayes Co. Aug.–Dec. 1962, Pres. and Chief Exec. Officer 1962–76, Chmn. & Chief Exec. Officer since 1976; Kelsey-Hayes Co., Romulus, Mich.; Chmn., Kelsey-Hayes Canada Ltd.; Manufacturers National Bank of Detroit, Mich.; Dir: Manufacturers National Corp., Detroit; Dir. Michigan Seamless Tube Co.; Dir., Taylor & Gaskin Inc.; Michigan State and Greater Detroit Chambers of Commerce; Member, Chamber of Commerce of the U.S. *Member:* Socy. Automotive Engineers; Engineering Socy. of Detroit; Amer. Inst.; National Academy of Engineering. *Clubs:* Bloomfield Hills Country; The Recess; The Economic of Detroit; Detroit Atheletic; Grosse Pointe Yacht; Old Club. *Address:* Suite 36, 1740 N. Woodward Ave., Bloomfield Hills, Michigan 48013, U.S.A.; and *office* 38481 Huron River Drive, Romulus, Mich., U.S.A.

**McDOUGALD, John Angus.** Canadian. *B.* 1908. *Educ.* Uppei Canada College, St. Andrew's Coll. *M.* 1934, Hedley Maude Eustace Smith. *Career:* Chmn. of the Bd. and President, Argus Corp. Ltd.; Pres. Ravelston Corp. Ltd.; Sugra Ltd.; Taymac Investments Ltd.; Thermax Ltd.; Chairman of Executive Committee & Vice-Pres., Hollinger Mines Ltd. Chairman of Board and Chmn. Executive Cttee., Dominion Stores Ltd.; Chmn. of Board & Chmn. Exec. Cttee., Avco of Canada Ltd.; Chairman of Board: Standard Broadcasting Corporation Ltd.; Standard Broadcast Sales (U.K.) Ltd. and Grew Ltd. Chmn. of Exec. Committee General Bakeries Ltd., Massey-Ferguson Ltd.; Chmn. Advisory Bd. Crown Trust Co. Vice-President. Taylor, McDougald Co. Ltd.; Vice-President, Director & Member of Executive Committee, Canadian Imperial Bank of Commerce; Director and Member of Executive Committee: Domtar Ltd., and St. Lawrence Corp. Ltd. Director: Canadian Mining & Finance Co. Ltd.; CFRB Ltd., Hinde & Dauch Ltd., Hollinger North Shore Exploration Co. Ltd.; Iron Ore Co. of Canada, Labrador Mining & Exploration Co. Ltd., Massey-Ferguson Holdings Ltd., Massey-Ferguson (Australia) Ltd., Massey-Ferguson Holdings (Australia) Ltd., Sangamo Co. Ltd., Standard Broadcast Sales Co. Ltd., Standard Broadcasting Corp. (U.K.) Ltd., Stone & Webster Canada Ltd. Member of Adv. Bd., First National Bank in Palm Beach, Fla., U.S.A.; Governor, Good Samaritan Hospital P.B. Florida; Member Bd. Trustees Ont. Jockey Club; Governor, Jockey Club of Canada. *Clubs:* (Toronto President) Toronto and North York Hunt; Eglinton Hunt; York (all Toronto); Mount Royal Montreal; Rolling Rock (Ligonier); Bucks; Turf; Whites (London, England); Bath & Tennis (vice-pres.); The Everglades (Pres.); Seminole Golf (all Palm Beach); Metropolitan; New York Yacht (both N. York). *Address:* 'Green Meadows', 5365 Leslie Street, Willowdale, Ont., M2J 2L1, Canada; (Winter residence: 640 South Ocean Ont., M2J 2L1, Canada; (Winter residence: 640 South Ocean Boulevard, Palm Beach, Fla. 33480 U.S.A.); and *office* 10 Toronto Street, Toronto, Ont. M5C 2B7.

**MacDOUGALL, Curtis D.** *B.* 1903. *Educ.* Ripon Coll. (BA), Northwestern Univ. (MSJ); Univ. of Wisconsin (PhD). *M.* 1942, Genevieve M. Rockwood. *S.* Gordon and Kent. *Daus.* Lois, Priscilla and Bonnie. *Career:* Reporter: Fond du Lac (Wis.) Commonwealth (1918–26), United Press (1926–27) and St. Louis Star-Times (1933–34); Editor: Evanston Daily News Index (1934–37), National Almanac & Year Book (1937–38), and News Map of the Week (1938–39); Illinois State Supervisor, Writers' Project 1940–42; Editorial Writer, Chicago Sun 1942. Professor Emeritus of Journalism, Northwestern University, Evanston, Ill.; member, Chicago Committee to United Nations 1945. *Member:* Amer. Sociological Assn.; Assn. for Education for Journalism; Amer. Civil Liberties Union; Investigative Reporters & Editors; Vice-Chmn., Chicago Cttee. to defend the Bill of Rights. *Publications:* Reporting for Beginners; Interpretative Reporting; Newsroom Problems & Policies; Covering the Courts; Hoaxes; Understanding Public Opinion; Greater Dead than Alive; The Press and its Problems; Gideon's Army; News Pictures Fit to Print; Reporters Report Reporters; Principles of Editorial Writing. *Address:* 537 Judson Avenue, Evanston, Ill., U.S.A.

**McDOUGALL, Cyril John.** Australian master builder. *B.* 1907. *M.* Violet May Richards. *S.* 1. *Dau.* 1. *Career:* Chairman, McDougall-Ireland Pty. Ltd. Director: Morton Investments Pty Ltd., Mulgrave Industries Pty. Ltd., New Oakleigh Motors Pty Ltd., Master Builders' Assn. Trust Guarantee Corp. *Member:* Aust. Inst. of Builders (Fellow); Inst. of Builders, London (Fellow); Victorian Employers Fed. (Past Pres.); Australian Council of Employers Federation (Past Pres.); Master Builders Association of Victoria (Past Pres.); Master Builders Federation of Australia (Past Pres.). *Clubs:* Melbourne Cricket; Royal Automobile (Victoria); Huntingdale Golf. *Address:* 17/1 Park Tower, 201 Spring Street, Melbourne Vic. 3000; and *office* 9 Morton Avenue, Carnegie, Vic. 3163, Australia.

**MacDOUGALL, Sir (George) Donald (Alastair),** CBE (1945); FBA (1966). British economist. *B.* 1912. *Educ.* Balliol Coll., Oxford (MA); Hon LLD, Strathclyde; Hon Litt D Leeds. *M.* (1) 1937, Bridget Christabel Bartrum (*Diss.* 1977). *S.* John Douglas. *Dau.* Mary Jean. (2) 1977, Laura Margaret (Lady) Hall. *Career:* Asst. Lecturer (later Lecturer), Univ. of Leeds 1936–39. At Statistical Branch of the First Lord of the Admiralty (Winston Churchill), 1939–40; at Statistical Branch of the Prime Minister (Winston Churchill) 1940–45 (Chief Asst. 1942–45) and 1951–53 (Chief Adviser). Econ. Dir., Natl. Econ. Development. Cncl., 1962–64; Dir. Gen., Dept. of Economic Affairs, 1964–68. Fellow at Wadham Coll., Oxford 1945–50; Hon. Fellow 1964; Professorial Fellow, Nuffield Coll. 1951–52 (a Reader in Internatl. Economics, Oxford Univ.); Official Fellow of Nuffield College 1952–64, and First Bursar 1958–64, Hon. Fellow 1967. Econ. Dir., O.E.E.C. Paris 1948–49; Visiting Prof., Australian Nat. Univ. 1959; M.I.T. Centre for Inter. Studies, New Delhi 1961; mem. Turnover Tax Comm. 1963–64. Head of Government Economic Service & Chief Economic Adviser to Treasury, 1969–73. Chief Economic Adviser Confederation of British Industry since 1973; Hon. Secy., Royal Economic Society 1958–70; Vice-Pres., 1970–72 & 1974. Pres. 1972–74 (member of Council since 1950). *Publications:* The World Dollar Problem (1957); The Dollar Problem: A Reappraisal (1960); Studies in Political Economy (2 Vols) 1975; Part author; Measures for International Economic Stability (1951); The Fiscal System of Venezuela (1959); contributions to: Britain in Recovery (1938); Lessons of the British War Economy (1951); articles in various economic and statistical journals. *Club:* Reform. *Address:* 86A Denbigh Street, London S.W.1.; and CBI, 21 Tothill Street, London, S.W.1.

**McDOWELL, Sir Frank Schofield.** Australian. *B.* 1889. *Educ.* Public School. *M.* 1912, Ethel Perrott, *S.* 6. *Dau.* 1. *Career:* Man. Dir. McDowells Ltd. 1935–67, Chmn. 1967, Pres., McDowells Holdings Ltd. 1971–72. Past Grand Master United Grand Lodge of N.S.W. Freemasons 1947–49; Past G.M. Mark Masons of N.S.W. 1946–48; Past Inspector-General Rose Croix Masons 33° Sydney S.E. Central District. *Clubs:* Sydney Rotary (Past Pres.); All Nations (Pres.); Retailers (Patron); South Cronulla Bowling (Patron); Created Knt. (Bach.) 1967, for services to Commerce and the Community. Masonic. *Address:* 'Melrose', 157 Ewos Parade, Cronulla, Sydney, N.S.W., Australia.

**MacEACHEN, Hon. Allan Joseph,** PC, MP. Canadian. *B.* 1921. *Educ.* St. Francis Xavier Univ., Antigonish, N.S. (BA); Dept. of Political Economy, Univ. of Toronto (MA); Dept. of Economics Univ. of Chicago, and Dept. of Economics and Social Science, M.I.T. Professor of Economics, St. Francis Xavier Univ. 1946–48 (and Head of Economics and Social Sciences Dept.). *Career:* Member Canadian House of Commons 1953–58 and 1962—. Parliamentary Observer to U.N. Gen. Ass. 1955. Alternate Delegate to U.N. Economic and Social Cncl., Geneva 1956. Special Asst. for economic affairs to Hon. Lester B. Pearson 1958–62. Minister of Labour, 1963–65. Minister of National Health and Welfare 1965–68. Minister of Manpower and Immigration, 1968–70; Pres. of the Privy Council 1970–74; Secy. of State for External Affairs 1974–76: Pres.. Privy Council & Govt. Leader in the Commons since 1976, Dep. Prime Minister since 1977. *Awards:* Hon LLD, St. Francis Xavier Univ.; Hon LLD Acadia Univ. 1966; Doctor of Humane Letters Honoris Causa. Loyola Coll., Baltimore, 1966; Hon LLD, St Mary's Univ. 1973 and Dalhousie Univ. 1974. *Address:* House of Commons, Ottawa, Ont., Canada.

**MacENTEE, Sean.** *B.* 1889. *Educ.* St. Malachy's College (Belfast) and Belfast Municipal College of Technology. *M.* Margaret Browne. *S.* 1. *Daus.* 2. *Career:* Easter Week Rising 1916; sentenced to death, afterwards commuted to penal servitude for life; imprisoned in Dartmoor, Lewes and Portland prisons; released under General Amnesty 1917; member, National Executive Committee, of Irish Volunteers and Irish Republican Army 1917–21; Minister for Finance 1932–39 and 1951–54; Minister for Industry and Commerce 1939–41; Minister for Local Government 1947–48; T.D. South Monaghan 1919–21, Monaghan 1921–22; Dublin County 1927–37, Dublin Townships 1937–48, and Dublin South (East) 1948—. (Deputy Prime Minister of Ireland) 1959–65; Minister for Health in the Government of Ireland 1957–65. Minister for Social Welfare 1958–61. Former Tanaiste. Member of Council of State, since 1948; Company director, electrical engineer and registered patent agent. Knight Grand Cross, 1st Class of Order of Pius, 1916; Medal with bar 1918 and 1921; Hon LLD, Nat. Univ. of Ireland; Author, Poems, 1918; Episode at Easter (1966). *Address:* Montrose, Trimleston Avenue, Booterstown, Co. Dublin, Eire.

**McERLEAN, Charles F.,** *B.* 1912. *Educ.* Georgetown U. (LLB). *M.* 1937, Theodora Emerson, *S.* Charles F., Jr., and Robert E., *Dau.* Mary Louise. *Career:* Attorney Harry Z. & Bernard Perel 1936–37; Attorney National Labor Relations Board 1937–45; Assistant to Pres., Director of Law, Vice President—Asst. to Pres., Senior V.P.—Law 1945–65; Exec. V.P. and Gen. Mgr. 1965–71; Exec. V.P. and Chief Operating Officer 1971–75, United Airlines, Chicago; Vice Chairman United Airlines 1975—; President UAL, Inc., 1975—; Board of Directors United Airlines and UAL, Inc. *Member:* Chicago, D.C. and American Bar Associations; Advisory Board Georgetown U. 1967–74, Director 1974–75. *Clubs:* University (Chicago) and Butterfield C.C., Hinsdale, Ill. *Address:* 166 Briarwood North, Oak Brook, Ill. 60521, U.S.A.

**McEWEN, Col. Ewen,** CBE. British. *B.* 1916. *Educ.* Merchiston Castle School; University Coll., London (BSc Eng, MSc Eng, DSc). *M.* 1938, Barbara Dorrien Medhurst. *S.* Andrew Patrick, and Colin Dougal. *Dau.* Bridget Mary Anne. *Career:* Asst. Dir., Tank Design (later Asst. Chief Engr. Fighting Vehicles Design) 1942–47; Professor, Agricultural Engineering, Newcastle upon Tyne, 1947–54; Dir., Royal Armament Research and Development Estab. 1955–58; Dir. of Engineering, Massey Ferguson Ltd. 1958–63; Deputy Mng. Dir. 1963–65 and Mng. Dir. 1965–67, Hobourn Group Ltd. Vice-Chairman, Engineering, Joseph Lucas Ltd. 1967—; Visiting Prof. Imperial Coll. London since 1970. *Fellow:* Royal Society of Edinburgh; Univ. Coll., London; Member of Cncl., Inst. of Mech Engrs 1961—; Vice-Pres. 1970–76; Pres. 1976–77; C Eng., FI Mech E., F Am SME. CBE 1975. *Publications:* papers and articles in technical press. *Clubs:* Army & Navy; Royal Thames Yacht; Parkstone Yacht. *Address:* 1 Howard Court, 21 Portland Road, Birmingham, B16 9HR; and *office* Joseph Lucas Ltd., Gt. King Street, Birmingham, B19 2XF.

**McEWEN, Rt. Hon. Sir John,** PC, GCMG, CH. Australian farmer and former politician. *B.* 29 Mar. 1900. *M.* (1) 1921, Annie Mills McLeod (*Dec.* 1967), (2) 1968, Mary Eileen Byrne. *Career:* Enlisted in Australian Imperial Force 1918; Engaged in Farming, Stanhope, Vic. 1919–76; mem. Aust. House of Reps. for Echuca 1934–37, Indi 1937–49, Murray 1949–71 (Ret'd.); Minister for Interior 1937–39; for External Affairs 1940; for Air and Civ. Aviation 1940–41; Member, War Cabinet 1940–41, & Advisory War Council 1941–45; Delegate, United Nations Conf. on International Organisation, San Francisco 1945; Dep. Leader Country Party 1943–58; led numerous dels. to GATT Talks, Geneva; Minister of State for Commerce and Agriculture 1949–56; for Trade 1956–63; for Trade and Industry 1963–71; Leader Aust. Country Party and Dep. Prime Minister 1958–71; Prime Minister 1967–68. *Awards:* Member Privy Council 1953; Companion of Honour 1969; GCMG 1971; Order of the Rising Sun, 1st Class (Govt. of Japan) 1973. *Club:* Melbourne. *Address:* 679 Orrong Road, Toorak, Vic. 3142, Australia; and *office* A.M.P. Tower, 535 Bourke Street, Melbourne, Vic. 3000, Australia.

**McEWIN, Hon. Sir (Alexander) Lyell,** KBE (1954), MLC. Australian politician. *B.* 29 May 1897. *Educ.* State School and Prince Alfred College, Adelaide. *M.* 1921, Dora Winifred Williams. *S.* 4. *Dau.* 1. *Career:* engaged in farming at Hart (near Blyth) since 1912; Sec., Blyth Branch, Agr. Bureau, 1920–26 (Pres. 1927–36); member, State Advisory Board of Agriculture 1930, Chairman 1935–37; member Agricultural Settlement Cttee. appointed by Hill Government 1931; member, Debt Adjustment Cttee. 1933; Producers' Representative for South Australia on Federal Advisory Committee for Export of Mutton and Beef in 1934 prior to appointment of Australian Meat Board; Councillor for Hart Ward of Hutt and Hill Rivers District Cncl. 1932–35, and for same Ward transferred to Blyth District Cncl. 1935–53; Chmn., S. Australian Rifle Assn. since 1948; Member, Commonwealth Council of State Rifle Assns. 1952–62 (Chmn. 1959–62); Chief Royal Caledonian Socy. (SA) 1959–68; Member, S. Australian Legislative Council for Northern District 1934–75; Chief Secretary and Minister of Health and Mines, South Australia, Aug. 1939–Mar. 1965. Leader of the Opposition in Leg. Council 1965–67; Pres. of Leg. Council, Mar. 1967–75. *Address:* 93 First Avenue, St. Peters, South Australia.

**McFADZEAN, The Rt. Hon. Lord** (William Hunter McFadzean, Kt. 1976). British Company Director. *B.* 1903. *Educ.* Stranraer Academy and High School; Glasgow University. *M.* 1933, Eileen Gordon. *S.* 1. *Daus.* 2 (one adopted). *Career:* Chartered Accountant 1927; joined British Insulated Cables Ltd. 1932, on amalgamation of British Insulated Cables Ltd. and Callender's Cable and Construction Co. Ltd. in 1945, appointed to the Board of British Insulated Callender's Cables Ltd. as Exec. Dir., Dep. Chmn., since 1947, Chief Exec. Dir. 1950, Man. Dir. 1954–71, Chmn. 1954–73. Hon. Pres. for Life 1973; Director, Midland Bank Ltd. since 1959 (dep. Chmn. 1968–77); Midland Bank Trust Co. Ltd. 1959–67; English Electric Co. Ltd. 1966–68; Steel Co. of Wales Ltd. 1966–67; Canadian Imperial Bank of Commerce 1967–74 (now director-emeritus); Dep. Chmn., RTZ/BICC Aluminium Holdings Ltd., 1967–73; Dir., Anglesey Aluminium Ltd., 1968–73; The Canada Life Assurance Co., 1969; Dep. Chmn., The Canada Life Assurance Co. of Great Britain 1971; Chmn., Canada Life Unit Trust Managers Ltd. 1971; Standard Broadcasting Corp. (UK) Ltd. 1972; Home Oil (UK) Ltd. 1972; Dir. Home Oil Co. Ltd. since 1972; Dep. Chmn.

National Nuclear Corp. Ltd since 1973; Chmn. Broadcast Marketing Services Ltd. 1974–76; Chmn. Scurry Rainbow (UK) Ltd. 1974; Dir., Standard Broadcasting Corp. Ltd. 1976. *Member:* Ministry of Labour Advisory Board on Resettlement of Ex-Regulars 1957–60; Board of Trade Advisory Council on Middle East Trade 1958–60; Pres., Federation of British Industries 1959–61; Chairman, Council of Industrial Federations of EFTA 1960–63; Founder Chmn., Export Council for Europe 1960–64 (Hon. Pres. 1964–71); Pres., British Electrical Power Convention 1961–62; Member, Ministry of Transport Shipping Advisory Panel 1962–64; Vice-Pres., British-Swedish C. of C. 1963–74; Pres., British Nuclear Forum 1964–66; Chmn., Commonwealth Export Council 1964–66; Chmn., British National Export Council 1964–66 (Pres. 1966–68); member, Court of British Shippers' Council 1964–74 (Pres. 1968–71); Vice-Pres., Middle East Assn. 1965; City of London Socy. 1965–72; Member, Council Anglo-Danish Socy. 1965–75 (chmn. 1969–75), hon. pres. 1975; Mem. Adv. Cttee. for the Queen's Award to Industry 1965–67; Chairman, Review Committee for the Queen's Award to Industry, for 1970; Member, Council Confederation of British Industry 1965–74; President CTBA 1967–68; Council Foreign Bond-holders 1968–74. President, The Electrical & Electronics Industries Benevolent Assn. 1968–69. *Awards:* Companion I.E.E. 1956; Knighted 1960; Commander, Order of Dannebrog 1964, Grand Commander 1974; JDipMA 1965; Grande Official da Ordem do Infante Dom Henrique Portugal 1972; Knight of the Most Ancient & Most Noble Order of the Thistle 1976. *Club:* Carlton. *Address:* Garthland, Woldingham, Surrey, CR3 7DH, and 114 Whitehall Court, London, SW1A 2EL.

**McFARLAND, Colonel Sir Basil Alexander Talbot,** Bt, CBE. British company director. *B.* 18 Feb. 1898. *Educ.* Bedford School; Neuwied am Rhein; Brussels. *M.* (1) 1924, Annie Kathleen Henderson (*D.* 1952). *S.* John Talbot. *Dau.* Annie Maureen (*Dec.*). *M.* (2) 1955, Mary Eleanor Dougan of Londonderry (*Dec'd* 1973). *Career:* Dir. Belfast Banking Co. Ltd. 1930–70; High Sheriff City of Londonderry 1930–38; of County of Londonderry 1952; Mayor of Londonderry 1939 and 1945–50; served in World War II, Middle East and Italy (dispatches) 1939–45; E.R.D., A.D.C. (Additional) to H.M. King George VI 1948–52; to H.M. Queen Elizabeth II 1952–60; H.M. Lieut. for Londonderry 1939–75. Chairman: Londonderry Port and Harbour Commissioners 1952–66. Dir. Lanes (Patent Fuels) Ltd.; J. R. Waterson Ltd.; R. C. Malseed & Co. Ltd.; Chmn. Lanes (Derry) Ltd.; Londonderry & Lough Swilly Railway Co.; J. W. Corbett & Sons; Sir Alfred McAlpine & Son (N.I.) Ltd.; Alexander Thompson & Co., Ltd.; Dir., Lanes (Fuel Oils) Ltd.; Lanes (Business Equipment) Ltd.; Londonderry Gaslight Co.; Holmes Coal Ltd.; Local Director, Commercial Union Assurance Co. Ltd.; member, Northern Ireland Air Advisory Council 1946–65. Trustee, Magee University College 1962–65. Chairman for Co. Londonderry, Territorial Army and Auxiliary Forces Assn. 1947–62; Pres., Territorial Auxiliary & Volunteer Reserve Assn. for Northern Ireland 1968–70. Commissioner of Irish Lights; member, London Midland Area of Board of British Transport Commission 1955–61. Command Brother of Order of St. John. *Address:* Aberfoyle, Londonderry, Northern Ireland.

**MACFARLANE, Charles Alston,** TD, DL. Formerly Deputy Chairman and Managing Director, J. Nimmo & Son Ltd.; Director, Dunblane Blending Co. Ltd. *B.* 1908. *Educ.* Mill Hill School and Balliol Coll., Oxford (BA). *M.* 1938, Kathleen Nimmo. *S.* 1. *Daus.* 2. *Club:* East India & Sports (London). *Address:* Eden Vale, Castle Eden, Co. Durham.

**MACFARLANE, David Neil,** MP. British Politician. *B.* 1936. *Educ.* Bancrofts School, Woodford. *M.* 1961, June King. *S.* 2. *Dau.* 1. *Career:* Army Service 1955–58; T.A. 1958–64; Shell-B.P. Executive 1961–70; BP Marketing Exec. 1970–74; Conservative MP for Sutton & Cheam since 1974. *Member:* National Trust. *Clubs:* Caledonian; MCC; Hintercombe GC; Surrey CCC. *Address:* 84A Worcester Road, Cheam, Surrey; & House of Commons, London S.W.1.

**MACFARLANE Sir James Wright.** British. *B.* 1908. *Educ.* Allan Glen's School, Glasgow University (PhD) and Royal Technical College D.R.T.C. Whitworth Scholar and Whitworth Senior Scholar. *M.* 1937, Claire Ross. *Career:* Apprentice, Engineer and Director, Macfarlane Engineering Co. Ltd. 1926–69; Chairman, The Macfarlane Engineering Co. Ltd., Cathcart 1967–69; Director, National Building Agency since 1964. *Member:* Royal Commission on the Police 1960–62; Holroyd Cttee. on the Fire Service 1969–71; Convener, County of Renfrew, Scotland to 1973. Hon. Warden, County of Renfrew, Ontario, Canada, Director of some 10 other companies. Past Pres., Association of County Councils in Scotland. Ex-Lt.-Col. T.A. for A.C.F. *Publications:* numerous papers in technical journals, Deputy Lieutenant and JP, Renfrewshire. FIEE; FIMechE; FRSE; FI Fire E. Conservative. Past Chairman E. Renfrewshire Unionist Assn. *Clubs:* Scottish Conservative; Royal Gourock Yacht. *Address:* Cartbank, Cathcart, Glasgow; and *office* Netherlee Road, Glasgow, G44 3YU.

**McFARLANE, Vincent Homer,** CBE, OBE. Jamaican. *B.* 1914. *Educ.* Cornwall Coll., Montego Bay, Jamaica; Rhodes House, Oxford; London Univ.; Economic Development Inst., Washington, D.C. (Fellow). *M.* 1944, Alice Joan McNeil-Smith. *S.* John Vincent. *Dau.* Hilary Anne. *Career:* Administrative Officer, Colonial Secretariat, 1948; Asst. Secy., Col. Secretariat 1950–53; Prin. Asst. Secy., Ministry of Agriculture and Lands 1953; and Perm. Secy. 1954–57; Perm. Secy., Premier's Office and Min. of Development 1957–62; Min. Counsellor, Jamaican Embassy, Washington, D.C. Aug. 1962; Chargé d'Affaires *ad interim* Aug.–Sept. 1962, also on a number of occasions during 1963–65. High Commissioner to Canada, 1965–70; and Ambassador (non-resident to the Republic of Panama. Ambassador Extraordinary and Plenipotentiary to the Federal Republic of Germany 1970; concurrently Ambassador (non-resident) to Belgium, the Netherlands and Luxembourg. *Awards:* Queen's Coronation Medal; Jamaican Independence Medal. *Clubs:* American Community Association. Men's Canadian (Ottawa). *Address:* c/o Ministry of External Affairs, Kingston, Jamaica.

**McFERRAN, William Robert,** MBE. Australian. *B.* 1890. *Educ.* Int. Correspondence School (Dipl.); Albury Superior Public School; Alfred Crescent School (Cert.). *M.* 1915, Alice F. Mitchell. *S.* Athol Robert. *Career:* Chmn. War Effort Publicity Board, Victoria, 1938–45; Federal Pres. Advertising Assn. of Australia 1923–25, 1950–52; Victorian Representative, Aust. Advertising Council (Commonwealth Govt.) 1948–67; Mng. Dir. McFerran Advertising Pty. Ltd. 1937–62. Former Director, Claude Mooney Advertising Pty. Ltd. Fellow Advertising Institute (Australia). *Member:* Advisory Council, St. Vincent's Hospital; Made in Australia Council. Holder of McFerran Award (A.A.A.A.). Liberal. *Clubs:* Royal Automobile (Vic.); Ad. Club of Victoria. *Address:* 10 Inglis Court, Doncaster, Vic. 3108, Australia.

**McGAUGHEY, Charles Eustace.** Canadian diplomat. *B.* 1917. *Educ.* Queen's University (BA; MA); Stud. Inter. Union, Geneva (Dip. in International Relations); Univ. of Chicago. *M.* 1941, Jessie Porter. *S.* Daniel Brien and Terrence Porter. *Career:* With Sudbury Star and North Bay Nuggett 1939; with Canadian Army in U.K., India, Malaya, Thailand, and Newfoundland 1941–47; Canadian Army Japanese Language School 1944–45; Vice-Consul, Chicago; Third Secretary, Embassy, Tokyo 1949; Second Secretary, Tokyo 1951; Dept. of External Affairs, Ottawa 1952–55; First Secretary, Canadian High Commission, New Delhi 1955; Acting High Commissioner, Wellington, N.Z. 1957–58; Dept. of External Affairs, Ottawa 1958–62; High Commissioner to Malaysia, and Amb. to Burma and Thailand 1962–65; High Commissioner to Ghana and Ambassador to Guinea, Togo, Upper Volta and Ivory Coast 1965–66. High Commissioner for Canada to Pakistan Oct. 1966–69; Ambassador to Afghanistan, Oct. 1968–69. Ambassador to Israel, 1969–72; High Commissioner to Cyprus, 1970–72; Deputy Commandant, National Defence College. *Address:* c/o Department of External Affairs, Ottawa, Ont., Canada; and National Defence College, Kingston, Ontario.

**McGEE, Dean Anderson.** American. Petroleum and geology. *B.* 1904. *Educ.* Univ. of Kansas, Lawrence, Kan. (BS Mining Engineering) 1926. *M.* 1938, Dorothea Swain. *Daus.* Marcia, Patricia. *Career:* Instructor, School of Engineering Geology, Univ. of Kansas 1926–27; petroleum geologist, Phillips Petroleum Co., Bartlesville, Okla. 1927 (exploration work 1927–37; Chief Geologist 1935–37); joined Kerlyn Oil Co. as Vice-Pres. in charge of production and exploration, Feb. 1937 (Exec. Vice-Pres., Pres. 1954–67; name of Company changed to Kerr-McGee Oil Industries Inc. Jan. 1946). Chief Executive Officer 1954—, and Chmn. 1963—, Kerr-McGee Corp. *Publications:* articles in Bull. of Amer. Association of Petroleum Geologists, Bulletin of American Petroleum Institute, Oil & Gas Journal, The Independent, and other oil industry publications; these include West Edmond Oil Field, Central Oklahoma (1946); Geology of the Oklahoma City Field (1932); Drilling & Production Practices (1950); Report on Exploration Progress in the Gulf of Mexico; The Petroleum Geologist in the Atomic Age (1953); Economics of

Offshore Drilling in the Gulf of Mexico (1954); Static Concepts and the Domestic Industry (1962); Problems, Challenges and Opportunities of the Domestic Producing Industry (1963); Our Giant Challenge (1968). Mines Magazine, The Earth—Our Provider 1968; Energy—Past, Present and Future (1968); Uranium Supply Situation (1967); Nuclear Industry, The Uranium Supply Situation (1966). *Address:* Kerr-McGee Center, P.O. Box 25861, Oklahoma City, Oklahoma 73125, U.S.A.

**McGHEE, George Crews.** American businessman & Government official. Owner, McGhee Production Co. *B.* 1912. *Educ.* Southern Methodist Univ., Dallas; DCL (Hon) 1953; Univ. of Oklahoma (BSc 1933); Oxford Univ. (Rhodes Scholar—D Phil 1937); Univ. of London, Hon LLD Tulane Univ. 1957, Univ. Maryland 1965; Hon Fellow, Queen's College, Oxford 1968; *M.* 1938, Cecilia Jeanne DeGolyer. *S.* George DeGolyer and Michael Anthony. *Daus.* Marcia Spruce. Dorothy Hart, Cecilia Goodrich and Valerie Foster. *Career:* Registered engineer, Texas 1941; indep. explorer for and producer of oil 1940—. Previously (in the period 1939–58), successively Geologist, Atlantic Refining Co.; Geophysicist, Continental Oil Co. and Cie Générale de Geophysique, Morocco; Vice-Pres., National Geophys. Co.; Partner, DeGolyer, MacNaughton & McGhee (consulting geologists); Dallas; Dir., Great National Life Insce. Co., American Security Trust Co. Govt. service between 1941–53; Snr. Liaison Officer, Stockpile & Import Shipping Branch, O.P.M. and W.P.B.; U.S.; Dir., Mobil Oil Corp. 1969–; Procter & Gamble since 1969; T.W.A. since 1976; American Security Bank. Dep. Exec. Secy., Combined Raw Materials Board; Director, U.S. Commercial Co.; Special Assistant to Under-Secy. for Economic Affairs; Coordinator, Aid to Greece and Turkey, Dept. State 1947–49; Special Rep. Secy. of State to Near East, Palestine Refugee Problem 1949; Special Asst. to Secy. State 1949; Asst. Secy. for Near Eastern, South Asian and African Affairs 1949–51; Senr. Adviser, N. Atlantic Treaty Cncl., Ottawa; U.S. Ambassador to Turkey; Chief, Jt. American Military Mission for Aid to Turkey, and Chmn., U.S. Educational Commission in Turkey 1951–53; Consultant to Nat. Security Council 1953—; Member of President's Cttee. to study the U.S. Military Assistance Program 1958–59; Chmn., Policy Planning Council, and Counselor, Dept. of State 1961; Senior Adviser, Ministerial Council Session, Central Treaty Organization, Ankara 1961; Senior Adviser, Ministerial Mtg., North Atlantic Council, Oslo 1961; Under Secy. of State for Political Affairs 1961–63. Member, Board of Trustees, or Director: Foreign Service Educ. Found. and School of Advanced International Studies, Johns Hopkins Univ.; Salonika Farm School; Vassar College 1959–61; Robert College, Istanbul; Board of Development, Southern Methodist University; Duke Univ. 1962; Ambassador: to the Federal Republic of Germany 1963–68; at-Large, 1968–69. Special Representative of the Chairman, The Urban Coalition. 1969–70; Chmn. of the Board. Business Council for International Understanding, 1969—; Dir., American Inst. for International Affairs 1977—; Resources for the Future 1977—. Served in U.S. Navy 1943–46; *Awards:* Legion of Merit, Asiatic Ribbon with three battle stars; Lt.Col., U.S.A.F. Reserve 1949—. Contrib. to State Dept. Bulletin, Foreign Affairs. Gewekschaft-Liche Rundschau, Werk und Wir. Europa Archiv Univ. Ruperto-Carola Weltraumfahrt; Holder of Patent for method of making dip determination of geological formations. Guest Lect. National Air & Naval War Colleges; Armed Forces Staff Coll.; Nato Defense Coll.; Salzburg Seminar, Salzburg, Austria; Univ. of Virginia; Ambassador-in-Residence 1971; Special Rep. of the Chmn. National Urban Coalition 1969–70; Chmn. Nat. Academy, Science's Advisory Cttee. to the Dept. Housing and Urban Development 1970; Advisory Council on Japan-U.S. Economic Relations, Vice-Chmn. 1970; Chmn. E.S.U. of U.S.A. since 1970; Vice-Chmn. International Council E.S.U. since 1974; Board Saturday Review/World 1973–77. *Awards:* U.S. Junior Chamber of Commerce Distinguished Service Award; Univ. of Oklahoma Distinguished Service Citation; Southern Methodist Univ. Distinguished Alumnus Award; Hon. Citizen of Ankara 1954; DSc Hon. Univ. Tampa, 1969. *Clubs:* City Tavern Assn. (Wash. D.C.); Metropolitan, Assn. The Brook, Century (N.Y.); Colonade (Univ. of Va.); Mill Reef (Antigua). *Address:* Farmers Delight, Middleburg, Va., U.S.A.; and 2808 N-Street, N.W.; Washington, D.C. 20007.

**McGILL, Robert Hampton Robertson.** MA. British. *B.* 1913. *Educ.* Oundle School; Trinity Hall, Cambridge (MA. Econ. & Law). *M.* 1936, Amelia May Robertson. *Dau.* 1. *Career:* Partner E. F. Turner & Sons, Solicitors 1945–55; Dir., Power Securities Corp. Ltd.; Balfour Beatty Ltd. 1956–70; Chmn., K.C.A. Drilling Group Ltd. 1972–74; Gen. Advisers Ltd.; Dir., Nigerian Electricity Supply Co. Ltd.; & Pensions & Charities Property Fund. Partner, Turner Peacock, Solicitors. *Clubs:* City of London; Army and Navy; Royal St. Georges; Cooden; Muirfield Golf; Hawks, Cambridge; Oxford & Cambridge Golfing. *Address:* 7 Princes Gate, London, S.W.7 and *office* 12 Bedford Row, London WC1R 4DN.

**McGLINN, Frank C. P.** Stella della Solidarieta (Italy). Banker and attorney. Exec. Vice-Pres., The Fidelity Bank. *B.* 1914. *Educ.* Univ. of N. Carolina (AB); Univ. of Pennsylvania (LLB), LLD Villanova University. *M.* 1942, Louise C. Lea. *Daus.* Marion Lea '(Lockwood), Louise Steuart (Preston), Alice Ashton (Connell) and Ann Croasdale. *Career:* Life Member Free Lib. of Phila.; Member, Advisory Cttee., World Affairs Cncl.; Hon. Trustee, Temple Univ. Chmn., Advisory Cttee. on Naval Affairs; U.S. National Commission for UNESCO (Philadelphia); Honorary Chmn., for Phila. National Con. of Christians and Jews, Order of Golden Fleece, Univ. of North Carolina; Pro Fide Medal, Catholic Communion Bankers. Republican (Member, Advisory Cttee.; Fin. Cttee. of Pa.); Exec. Cttee. Catholic Charities Appeal since 1960. *Member:* Philadelphia Bar Assn.; Public Relations Socy. of America; Philadelphia Public Relations Assn.; Phi Beta Kappa. *Club:* Midday; Union League. *Address:* 135 South Broad Street, Philadelphia, Pa., U.S.A.

**McGOVERN, Hon. George S.** U.S. Senator. *B.* 1922. *Educ.* Dakota Wesleyan Univ. (BA 1945) and Northwestern Univ. (MA 1951; PhD 1953). *M.* 1943, Eleanor Stegeberg. *S.* 1. *Daus.* 4. *Career:* Held teaching post and fellowship at Northwestern Univ. 1948–50; Prof. of History and Government, Dakota Wesleyan Univ. 1950–53; Exec. Secy., South Dakota Democratic Party 1953–56; elected to House of Representatives 1956; Dir., Food for Peace of the U.S. 1961–62; Senator from South Dakota 1963—; Candidate for President of U.S.A. 1972; served on the Agricultural Committee; sponsored a resolution reaffirming the need to establish a long-range national policy of food for peace; one of three Congressmen chosen to represent the U.S. at a world conference at Athens 1959; studied economic and political conditions in the Middle East (under a travelling fellowship given by the American Christian Palestine Committee) 1957; also one of the nine Congressmen selected to attend the NATO Parliamentarians' conferences in Paris (1958) and Washington (1959). Served in World War II (bomber pilot with 35 combat missions; awarded DFC and Air Medal with three oak-leaf clusters). *Publications:* War Against Want—America's Food for Peace Programme (Walker & Co., N.Y.); Agricultural Thought in the Twentieth Century (1967); A Time of War a Time of Peace (Random House, N.Y.) (1968); The Great Coalfield War (1972); An American Journey (1974). *Address:* U.S. Senate, Washington, D.C. 20510; and Mitchell, S.D., U.S.A.

**McGOWAN, Lionel J.** Canadian business consultant. *B.* 1900. *Educ.* Universities of Ottawa and Chicago. *M.* 1924, Mabel Christina Marquis. *Career:* Has engaged in various phases of engineering and construction work since 1919, principally in Canada, the U.S.A. and other countries in the Western Hemisphere. Consultant Taylor Woodrow Group. Director: Allied Chemical Canada Ltd., Regent Refining Ltd., St. John's Convalescent Hosp., Chmn. Arbitrators. Inst. of Canada Inc., fellow Inst. of Arbitrators (England). *Clubs:* National (Pst Pres.); Empire Canadian (Toronto), *Address:* 5 York Ridge Road, Willowdale, Ont., Canada. M2P 1R8.

**McGRATH, Sir Charles Gullan,** Kt (1968), OBE. Australian. *B.* 1910. *Educ.* Ballarat High School. *M.* 1934, Madge Louise. *S.* 1. *Daus.* 4. *Career:* Joined Replacement Parts Pty. Ltd., 1928; Gen. Manager, Tasmania, 1935–46; Melbourne, 1946–53; Managing Director, Repco Ltd., 1956–67; Chairman, Repco Ltd. since 1957; Vice Pres. Australian Industries Development Assn.; Dir. Aust. Foundation Development Corp., Aust. Industry Development Corp.; Capel Court Corp.; Ensign Holdings Ltd.; Union Fidelity Trustee Co. of Aust. Ltd.; Chmn. Petersville Australia Ltd.; Nylex Corporation Ltd. Vice Chmn. Defence (Industrial) Committee; Board of Management, Alfred Hospital, Melbourne. *Clubs:* Australian; Athenaeum; Kelvin, Melbourne; Commonwealth (Canberra). *Address:* 46 Lansell Road, Toorak, Vic. 3142, Australia.

**McGRATH, Denis,** CBE. New Zealand. Barrister and Solicitor of the Supreme Court of New Zealand (Admitted 1931). *B.* 1910. *Educ.* University of New Zealand (LLB). *M.* 1944, Margaret Milroy Fraser. *S.* John and Gordon. *Daus.* Caroline and Helen. *Career:* Practised law in Wellington since 1931. President, New Zealand Law Socy. 1968–71; Standing Committee New Zealand Law Society 1965–71; Council International Bar Association, 1970–72; Mercantile & General Inusrance Co. Ltd. Chmn. Equitable Building & Investment Co. of Wellington Ltd., McGowan & Magee Ltd.; W. & R. Smallbone Ltd. Member: Wellington City Council 1947–56 and 1962–68; Wellington District Law Society Cncl. 1957–68, President 1966–67. Victoria University of Wellington Council 1953–57 and 1965–68; National Art Gallery and Dominion Museum Board of Trustees 1965–68; Ornithological Society of N.Z. Council. 1962–66. Chairman, Karori Electorate National Party 1961–63; AIR. N.Z. Salaries Commission, 1969; Royal Commission, Parliamentary Salaries, 1970–71; Commission Equal Pay for Women 1971 Trustee: Calvary Hosp. and Wellington District Savings Bank; Dep. Mayor of Wellington 1952–65. *Clubs:* Wellington; Wellesey. *Address:* 14 Homewood Avenue, Karori, Wellington; and *office* 10 Woodward Street, Wellington, New Zealand.

**MACGREGOR, Sir Edwin Robert,** Bt. Canadian. *B.* 1931. *Educ.* University of British Columbia (MASc). *M.* 1952, Alice Jean Peake. *S.* Robert Lionel Frederick (*Dec'd.*), Ian Grant. *Daus.* Valerie Jean, Marlene Elizabeth. *Career:* Former Plant Manager, Union Carbide Canada Ltd., (later Mktg. Manager), Consulting Engineer 1973; Dir. of Projects, Dept. of Economic Development, British Columbia, 1975; appointed Asst. Dep. Minister, Mineral Resources, Ministry of Mines & Petroleum Resources, 1977. *Member:* Assn. of Professional Engineers of the Province of Ontario and BC. *Address:* 3189 Anders Place, Victoria, BC, V9B 4C5, Canada.

**MacGREGOR, Malcolm.** American accountant. *B.* Glasgow, Scotland, 1890, *Educ.* Glasgow public and private schools went to U.S. 1912; naturalized American 1935. *Career:* With Peat, Marwick, Mitchell & Co., New York City 1926–60; retired as a principal in 1960; now consultant to corporations. Certified Public Accountant, California, Maryland and New York State; admitted to practice Treasury Department, U.S.A. 1948. *Awards:* Alfaro Award Medal and Eloy Alfaro Medal. *Member:* American Institute of Accountants, American Philatelic Society; American Philatelic Congress, American Air Mail Society, American Topical Assn., Philatelic Library Assn. (contributor of articles on philately to magazines); Bureau Issues Assn.; Fundacion Internacional Eloy Alfaro; Republican. *Clubs:* Collectors (N.Y.C.), New York Athletic. *Address:* 4 Brooklands, Bronxville 8, New York, 10708, U.S.A.

**McGUIRE, Dominic Paul,** CBE. Knight Grand Cross of S. Sylvester; Commendatore nell' Ordine Al Merito della Repubblica Italiana (1967); Australian diplomat and author. *B.* 3 Apr. 1903. *Educ.* Univ. of Adelaide. *M.* 1927, Frances Margaret Cheadle. *Career:* Served in World War II in Royal Australian Navy; Deleg. to General Assembly, United Nations, 1953; En. Ex. and Min. Plen. to Italy from May 1954, Ambassador until Jan. 1959; Envoy Extraord. to Holy See on occasion of Coronation of H.H. Pope John XXIII. *Publications:* There's Freedom for the Brave (1949); Three Corners of the World (in U.S., Experiment in World Order) (1948); Australian Theatre (with B. P. Arnott and F. M. McGuire) (1948); Price of Admiralty (with F. M. McGuire 1944); Westward the Course (1942); Australian Journey (1939); The Two Men, and Other Poems; The Poetry of Gerard Manley Hopkins (Eng. Assoc.); Restoring All Things (with J. Fitzsimmons); Spanish Steps; Burial Service (in U.S.: Funeral in Eden); 'W.1.'; Cry Aloud for Murder; Born to be Hanged; Threepence to Marble Arch; 7.30 Victoria; The Tower; Three Dead Men; There Sits Death; Murder by the Law; Death Fugue; Murder in Bostall; Black Rose, etc. *Club:* Athenaeum (London); Navy, Army and Air Force (Adelaide). *Address:* 136 Mills Terrace, North Adelaide, S.A. 5006, Australia.

**MACHADO, Dr. Francisco Jose Vieira.** Portuguese lawyer and bank director. *B.* 8 Feb. 1898. *Educ.* University of Lisbon. *M.* Maria do Carmo Contreiras. *Dau.* 1. *Career:* Administrator then Vice Pres. Admin. Bd., Banco Nacional Ultramarino 1926–34; Dir. Anglo Portuguese Bank Ltd. London 1930–65; Pres. then Administrator, Banque Franco-Portugaise d'Outremer Paris 1930–63; Dir. Pres. do Banco Ultramarino Brasileiro 1954–61; Administrator, Companhia de Seguros, A Mundial 1943–68; Pres. General Assembly, several companies; Governor, Banco Nacional Ultramarino 1951–72; Under Secy. Colonial States 1934–35; Pres. Comissáo de Colónias da Uniao Nacional 1935–46; Minister of Colonies 1936–44. Member, Comissáo Central da Uniao Nacional; Imperial Portuguese Council; Câmara Corporative; Founding Member, Comissáo Portuguesa do Atlantico, Chanceler da Orden do Imperio. Ordem Cristo and Ordem do Império Colonial, Ordem de Cristo; Orden del Mérito Naval (Spain); Ordre de la Couronne (Belgium); Grã Cruz, Ordem do Cruzeire do Sul (Brazil); Grand Cross, Order of St. Sylvester (Holy See), Order of the British Empire. *Publications:* Grandes Emprestimos de Guerra; Degrêdo para Africa; Projectos de Decretos; Alguns discursos proferidos em Africa; O Doutor Manuel Rodrigues, O Estadista e o Honem; Cultura do Arroz em Portugal; Discursos em Mocambique no 1. Centenário do BNU. *Address:* Rua de S. Domingos, á Lapa 58, Lisbon, Portugal.

**MACHEL, Samora M.** Mozambique Politician. *B.* 1933. *Career:* Leader of Guerilla Army of Frente de Libertação de Moçambique (FRELIMO) since 1966; Sec. of Defence of FRELIMO since 1969; Pres. since 1970 & Pres. of Mozambique since 1975. *Address:* FRELIMO Party Headquarters, Maputo, Mozambique.

**MACHIZAUD, Jacques,** CBE, Leg of Hon, OM, LLD, DSc. French. *B.* 1922. *Educ.* Univ. of Paris (LLD, DSc.). *M.* 1948, Nicole Daille. *Daus.* 2. *Career:* Chmn. Roussel Laboratories, London; Chmn. Board of Mgmt. Rousel-Uclaf (Paris). *Address: office* 35 Boulevard des Invaliddes, 75007 Paris.

**McILRAITH, Hon. George J.,** PC, QC. *B.* 1908. *Educ.* Osgoode Hall, Toronto. *M.* Margaret Summers. *S.* 1. *Daus.* 3. *Career:* Barrister-at-Law (QC 1952). Served in World War II as Capt., Governor-General's Foot Guards. Member House of Commons 1940. Parliamentary Assistant to Rt. Hon. C. D. Howe (while latter was successively Minister of Reconstruction and Supply; of Trade and Commerce, and of Defence Production) 1945–53. Canadian Delegate to U.N. 1946; to Conf. of Commonwealth Finance Ministers (London 1950) and to Colombo Plan Confs. (London 1950; Karachi 1952); First elected H. of C. g.e. 1940, Re-elected 1945, 49, 53, 57, 58, 62, 63, 65 and 1968; Sworn of the Council, Min. of Transport 1963; Pres. Privy Council 1964; Min. Public Works 1965; Govt. House Leader 1964–67; Solicitor General of Canada 1968 resignation 1970; Appointed to the Senate 1972. *Address:* 300 Sandridge Road, Ottawa 7, Ont., KIL 5A3, Canada.

**McINTOSH, Sir Ronald (Robert Duncan),** KCB. British Civil Servant. *B.* 1919. *Educ.* Charterhouse Sch., Balliol Coll., Oxford—MA. Hon Dr. of Science, Univ. of Aston. *M.* 1951, Doreen MacGinnity. *Career:* Board of Trade 1947–57; Commercial Counsellor, New Delhi 1957–62; Dept. of Econ. Affairs 1964–67; Dep. Sec., Cabinet Office 1968–70, Treasury 1971–73; Dir.-Gen., National Economic Development Office since 1973. *Member:* Fellow, Brit. Inst. of Management; Fellow, Royal Soc. of Arts; Gov., National Inst. of Econ. & Social Research; Exec. Cttee., Political & Econ. Planning. *Decoration:* Knight Commander, Order of the Bath (1975). *Publications:* Lubbock Memorial Lecture (1974); Mercantile Credit Lecture (1976). *Club:* Royal Thames Yacht. *Address:* NEDO, Millbank Tower, London SW1.

**McKAY, Donald Norman,** MP (N.Z. Parliament) 1954–72. Minister of Health 1962–72, of Social Security 1962–72, and in charge of Child Welfare Dept. 1962–72; Chairman, Northland Harbour Board 1974—. *B.* 1908. *M.* 1934, Miriam Hilda Stehr. *S.* 2. *Dau.* 1. Member N.Z. National Party. *Clubs:* Whangarei; Northland. *Address:* Office of the Chairman, Northern Harbour Board, Northland, N.Z.

**MACKAY, Iver Edward Lavers.** British. International Civil Servant (retired). *B.* 1904. *Educ.* Marlborough Coll. and University Coll., Oxford (Hons. Modern History). *M.* 1946, Margaret Inglis. *S.* 2. Medal of Freedom (U.S.) 1947; Order of the Brilliant Star (Nationalist China) 1948. *Career:* Butterfield & Swire, merchants and ship-owning company, in China and Japan 1927–42; Ministry of War Transport, Representative in Equatorial and West Africa 1943–44, Paris 1945–46, and Singapore 1947. Secretary, Maritime Transport Committee, O.E.C.D., July 1948–70. *Publications:* various articles and reports on international maritime transport. Conservative. *Member:* St. Andrew's Society (France); Oxford Society. *Clubs:* Travellers', Junior Carlton (London); Travellers' (Paris); Walton Heath Golf. *Address:* Le/Siaresq Opio 06, Alpes Maritimes, France.

**McKEAG, Colonel The Hon. William John.** Canadian realtor. *B.* 1928. *Educ.* Graduated, Univ. of Manitoba 1949 (Bachelor of Commerce). *M.* 1950, Dawn Rue'Ann Campbell. *S.* 1. *Daus.* 3. *Career:* Joined family firm, Security Storage Co. Ltd. 1949, Gen. Mgr. 1952, Pres. 1956–69; Mem. Bd. of Dirs.,

Canadian Motorways Ltd. since 1960; Pres., McKeag Harris Realty & Development Co. Ltd. 1960, now McKeag Realty Ltd.; Mem. Bd. of Regents of United College (now Univ. of Winnipeg) 1963–67; Mem. Bd. of Govs., Balmoral Sch. for Girls 1963–71; Dir., Winnipeg Real Estate Bd. 1964–65; Dir., Winnipeg Chamber of Commerce 1965–66; Mem. of Bd. & Provincial Campaign Chmn., Manitoba Div. of Canadian Cancer Society 1965–69; Councillor for the Town of Tuxedo 1966–70; Exec. Mem., Winnipeg Blue Bomber Football Club 1968–70; Chmn., Greater Winnipeg Election Cttee. 1968–70; Lieutenant-Governor of the Province of Manitoba 1970–76; Mem. Bd. of Dirs., MEPC Canadian Properties Ltd. since 1974; Mem. Bf. of Dirs., The Investors Group since 1975; Vice-Pres., Winnipeg Jets Hockey Club 1975–76, Pres. since 1976; Mem. Bd. of Dirs., MEPC American Properties Ltd. since 1975; Mem. Bd. of Dirs., Johnson & Higgins Willis & Faber, Ltd. since 1976; Mem., Ducks. Unlimited (Canada) since 1976; Mem., Manitoba Medical Services Foundation since 1976; Mem. Bd. of Management, Grace General Hospital since 1976; Mem. Bd. of Govs., Manitoba Museum of Man & Nature since 1976. Active in Kinanis since 1951, served as District Gov. of the 67 Clubs in Western Canada in 1967; Mem. of the 1001: A Nature Trust since 1972. *Awards:* Knight of Grace in the Canadian Priory of the Most Venerable Order of the Hospital of St. John of Jerusalem 1971; Univ. of Manitoba Alumni Jubilee Award 1973; Hon. Colonel of Fort Garry Horse 1973; Hon. Dr. of Law, Univ. of Winnipeg 1976, Univ. of Manitoba, 1977; Hon. Councillor, Winnipeg Chamber of Commerce 1976; Hon. Life Mem., Winnipeg Rotary Club 1976; Hon. Life Mem., Manitoba Curling Assn. 1976. *Address:* 560 Park Boulevard West, Winnipeg, Manitoba R3P OH4; and *office* President McKeag Realty Ltd., 201–1311 Portage Avenue, Winnipeg, Manitoba R3G OV4, Canada.

**McKEEVER, Ronald Fraser.** CBE. British. *B.* 1914. *Educ.* George Watsons' College, Edinburgh, and Edinburgh University. *M.* 1944, Margaret Lilian Sabine. *S.* Frederick Brian. *Career:* Joined Foreign Service 1948; Vice-Consul Dakar (Senegal) 1948–50, and Chicago 1950–53; Consul Kansas City 1953–54; British Embassy, Bonn 1954–57; Consul Gdynia (Poland) 1957–59, and Brazzaville 1959–61, Chargé d'Affaires there 1960; Consul Tamsui (Formosa) 1962–66. Ambassador to Togo and Dahomey, Jan. 1967–70; H.M. Consul General, Naples 1971–74; Retired from H.M. Dipl. Service 1974. *Address:* Bowmillholm, St. Mungo by Lockerbie, Dumfriesshire.

**MacKEIGAN, Ian Malcolm,** Canadian. Chief Justice of Nova Scotia. *B.* 1915. *Educ.* Dalhousie Univ. (Masters degree, Philosophy); Graduat Dalhousie Law School; MA Public Admin. Univ. of Toronto. *M.* Jean Geddes. *Children:* 3. *Career:* Practiced Law in Halifax 1939–40; Deputy Enforcement Admin. Wartime Trade Board, Deputy Commissioner Combines Investigation Commission 1940–49; Law Practice, Halifax 1949; Active in Public Affairs, Chmn. Bd. Atlantic Research Centre; Gov. Nova Scotia Research Foundation; Canadian Welfare Council; Pres. Nova Scotia Barristers Socy.; Chmn. Atlantic Dev. Bd.; Member Economic Council of Canada; Dir. number of companies; Senior Partner, MacKeigan, Cox, Downie & Mitchell; Chief Justice. Province of Nova Scotia since 1973. *Award:* Hon. LLD (1975), *Address:* 833 Marlborough Avenue, Halifax, Nova Scotia B3H 3G7, Canada.

**McKELVIE, Donald.** Canadian telephone and mining company executive. *B.* 1913. *Educ.* Queen's Univ. (Kingston, Ont.). *M.* 1942, Aileen Laura Wright. *S.* Peter Donald. *Dau.* Julie Ann. *Career:* Office Mgr., Red Crest Gold Mines Ltd. 1936–37; Accountant, Northern Telephone Co. Ltd. 1937–41; served in World War II (Pilot Officer, R.C.A.F.) 1942–45; Secy.-Treas., Northern Telephone Co. Ltd. 1945–51. Chmn. Bd., Northern Telephone Ltd. since 1951; The Hudson Bay Mines, Combined Larder Mines. Director, Northern and Central Gas Co. Ltd. Liberal. *Address:* Box 1464, New Liskeard, Ont., Canada.

**McKENNA, Alexander G.** American. *B.* 1914. *Educ.* Grad. Crafton High School, Crafton, Pa. Carnegie Institute of Technology, Pittsburgh (BS 1938). *M.* 1949, Wilma Fitzmaurice. *S.* 1. *Daus.* 4. *Career:* Partner, McKenna Metals Co., Latrobe 1940–43; Vice-President, Director, Kennametal Inc., Latrobe 1943–51, Director, Exec. Vice-President, 1951–64. President, Director, Kennametal Inc., Latrobe, Pa. 1964—, Subterranean Tools Inc., Kenroc Tools Ltd.; Kennametal Co. of Ohio; Kennametal International S.A. Kennametal Tools Ltd.; Kenroc Western Ltd. Dir. Kennamex, S.A. de C.V. Mexico; Kennametal of Canada Ltd.; Kennametal Australia Pty. Ltd.; Kennametal Holdings Ltd.; Ca. Me. S., S.P.A. (Italy). *Member:* Amer. Socy. Mechanical Engineers; Amer. Socy. Tool Engineers. *Clubs:* University (Pittsburgh); Rolling Rock (Ligonier, Pa.); Country (Latrobe); Country (Ligonier). *Address:* Summit Avenue, Ligonier, Pa.; and *office* One Lloyd Avenue, Latrobe, Pa., U.S.A.

**MACKENZIE, Archibald Robert Kerr,** MA, BA, CBE. Retired British diplomat. *B.* 1915. *Educ.* Universities, Glasgow, Oxford, Chicago and Harvard. *M.* 1963, Virginia Ruth Hutchison. *Career:* British Embassy, Washington 1943–45; British Delegation, United Nations New York 1946–49; Foreign Office 1949–51; British Embassy Bangkok 1951–54; Governor's Staff, Cyprus 1954–55; Foreign Office 1955–58; O.E.E.C. Paris 1958–61; Commercial Counsellor, British Embassy, Rangoon 1961–64; British Consul Gen. Zagreb 1965–69; British Ambassador, Tunis 1970–73; H.M. Minister, Economic & Social Affairs at United Nations 1973–75. *Clubs:* Royal Commonwealth & Scottish RAC. *Address:* Strathcashel Cottage, Rowardennan G63 0AW.

**MACKENZIE, Hugh Sinclair,** QC. Canadian barrister and solicitor. Director of numerous companies. *B.* 1911. *Educ.* University of Toronto (BA 1932); Osgoode Hall Law School; Barrister-at-Law 1935. *M.* 1934, Eleanor Smythe Blair. *Dau.* Jean Blair (Dalton). *Career:* Practised law, since called to bar and admission as solicitor; with present firm, Mackenzie, Wood, Magill and Blakeman and predecessor firms since 1935; served in World War II, Canadian Infantry Corps; attached to 8th Royal Scots. 15th Scottish Division 1944; (wounded Normandy 1944) 1939–45; Queen's Counsel 1951. *Publications:* articles in legal periodicals. *Address:* 5 Summerhill Gardens, Toronto, M4T 1B3, Ont.; and *office* 330 University Avenue, Toronto, M5G 1R7, Ont., Canada.

**MACKENZIE, Rt. Hon. (James) Gregor,** PC, MP. British. *B.* 1927. *Educ.* Queens Park School, Glasgow; Glasgow Univ. School of Social Studies. *M.* 1958, Joan Swan Provan. *S.* Derek. *Dau.* Gillian. *Career:* Member and Magistrate, Glasgow Corporation, 1952–55, 56–64; Justice of the Peace since 1962; Member of Parliament, Labour, for Rutherglen since 1964; Parly. Private Secy. to Rt. Hon. James Callaghan MP 1965–70; Shadow Minister for Post & Telecommunications 1970–74; Parly. Under-Sec. of State for Industry 1974–75; Ministry of State for Industry 1975–76; Minister of State (Scotland) since 1976. Privy Councillor 1977. *Member:* Institute of Marketing. *Address:* 7 Carrick Court, Kennington Park Road, London, S.E.11 4EE; and 19 Stewarton Drive, Cambuslang, Glasgow; & *office* House of Commons, London, S.W.1.

**McKENZIE, John ,** CMG, MBE, PhD. British diplomat. *B.* 1915. *Educ.* Archbishop Holgates Grammar School York; Leeds University. *M.* 1943, Sigridur Olafsdōttir. *S.* Donald Olafur Andrew Alan. *Dau.* Rosalind. *Career:* Lecturer Univ. of Iceland 1938–40; Attache, British Legation Reykjavik 1940–47; Consul Helsinki 1948–50; First Secy. Foreign Office 1950–53; Sofia 1953–56; Economic Baghdad 1956–58; Foreign Office 1958–62; Asst. Secy. Cabinet Office 1962–64; Counsellor (Commercial) & Consul Gen. Helsinki 1964–67; Dep. High Commissioner Calcutta 1967–70; Ambassador Reykjavik 1970–75. *Address:* 60 Dome Hill, Caterham, Surrey.

**MACKENZIE, John Raymond.** Australian. *B.* 1911. *Educ.* Melbourne University. (BCEng) and Royal Melbourne Inst. of Technology (DiplCEng); DiplElecEng. *M.* 1939. Nancy Clair Trew (*Dec.*). *S.* Gary Raymond and Neil Kenneth. *Career:* Gen. Mgr. and Dir., The Gas Supply Co. 1958–64; and Gen. Mgr. Stothert & Pitt Coates Pty. Ltd. 1956–58; Senior Administrative Engineer and Executive Engr., Melbourne & Metropolitan Bd. of Works 1946–56. Chairman Australian-American Engineering Corp. Pty. Ltd. 1965—. Principal Partner J. R. Mackenzie & Associates (Consulting Engineers). Director: Ag Co. (Aust.) P/L, I.E.L. Burners Pty. Ltd. 1968–70, Applied Research & Development Pty. Ltd. 1967–73. Chairman, Australian Gas Conversion Association, 1966—. *Publications:* Bends as Flow Meters: The Commonwealth Engineer (1938); Engineering Management (1964). *Member:* Aust. Gas Assn. (Pres. 1965); Aust. Liquid Petroleum Gas Assn. (Vice-Pres. 1965); Inst. of Engrs., Australia (Chmn. Melbourne Div. 1954; Member Victoria Div. Committee and Federal Council 1950–65); Secy. and Treas., Science & Technology Careers Bureau of Victoria 1958–64; Melbourne Univ. Graduates Union. *Clubs:* Carlton Social: Carlton Football: East Ivanhoe Bowling. *Address: office* 991 Rathdowne Street, North Carlton, Vic. 3054, Australia.

**MACKENZIE, Maxwell Weir,** OC, CMG, LLD. Canadian business executive (Retd.). *B.* 30 June 1907. *Educ.* Lakefield Prep. School and Trinity Coll. Schl., Ontario; McGill Univ. (B Comm). *M.* 1931, Jean Roger Fairbairn. *S.* Hugh Blair, John Blair. *Daus.* Marion Roger, Alison Fairbairn. *Career:* Partner McDonald Currie & Co. Chartered Accountants 1935–44; Chairman of Management Committee, Foreign Exchange Control Board 1940; Deputy Chairman, Wartime Prices and Trade Board 1943; member of the Royal Commission on Taxation of Annuities and Family Corporations 1944; Deputy Minister of Trade and Commerce 1945–51; Dep. Minister of Defence Production 1951–52; Director: Canadian Imperial Bank of Commerce; Canron Ltd., International Maltifoods Corp. Member, Economic Council of Canada 1963–71 (2nd Term Expired); Joined Celamese Corp. of America in charge of its Canadian operations, as Exec. Vice-Pres., Canadian Chemical & Cellulose Co. Ltd. 1952–54; 1954–59. Chmn., Royal Commission on Security, 1966. Chmn. Federal Commission of Inquiry into Beef Marketing, 1975. *Address:* 383 Maple Lane, Rockcliffe Park, Ottawa, K1M 1H7, Canada.

**MacKENZIE, Professor Norman Archibald MacRae,** CC, CMG, MM and Bar, QC. Canadian. Appointed to the Senate of Canada, 1966. President Emeritus, Honorary Professor of International Law, Univ. of Brit. Columbia; Chmn., Board of Trustees, Carnegie Foundation for the Advancement of Teaching 1959; Director, Bank of Nova Scotia 1960. *B.* 1894. *Educ.* Pictou Academy (Nova Scotia), Dalhousie University, BA, LLB (Ibid.) Harvard (LLM), St. John's College, Cambridge (Post-graduate Diploma), Gray's Inn, London. *M.* 19 Dec. 1928, Margaret Thomas. *S.* Patrick Thomas. *Daus.* Susan Elizabeth, Sheila Janet MacRae. Called to Bar of Nova Scotia 1926; Legal Adviser, International Labour Office, Geneva 1925–27; Chmn. of Canadian Delegation to 10th Session of General Conference of UNESCO, Paris 1958; Assoc. Prof. of Law, Toronto Univ. 1927–33; Prof., International and Canadian Constitutional Law, Toronto Univ., 1933–40; Pres., Univ. of New Brunswick (1940–44) and Univ. of British Columbia 1944–62; delegate: Institute of Pacific Relations Conferences (Shanghai 1931, Banff 1933, Yosemite 1936, Virginia Beach 1939, Mont Tremblant 1942), and to British Commonwealth Conferences (Toronto 1933, Sydney 1938); Pres., Canadian Association for Adult Education 1957–59; member: Royal Commission on National Development in the Arts, Letters and Sciences 1949–51; Canada Council 1957–63; Pres., Canadian National Commission for UNESCO 1957–60, and 1962–63; member of numerous associations connected with learning, the law, world reconstruction, etc., in Canada, U.S., and Europe. Member, Board of Directors, Canadian Centennial Commission, 1963—; Chairman, Canadian Universities Foundation International Studies Commission, 1962–63; Member, Vancouver Advisory Board of Canada Permanent Trust Co. 1962—; Member, East African Commission on University Education, 1962; Chairman, Nova Scotia Grants Commission, 1963–69; Member, Fathers of Confederation Foundation, 1963—. *Awards:* John E. Read Medal in International Law, 1975; Hon. LLD Mount Allison University, and Universities of New Brunswick, Toronto, Ottawa, Bristol, Alberta, Glasgow, Dalhousie, McGill, Sydney, St. Francis Xavier, Alaska, University of British Columbia, University of California and Rochester; Royal Military College, Cambridge; DCL Whitman College and Saskatchewan; DSc Soc Laval; D Litt, Memorial University of Newfoundland. FRCS; Hon. Fellow, St. John's College, Cambridge. Served in World War I, 1914–19, with Nova Scotia Highlanders. *Publications:* Legal Status of Aliens in Pacific Countries; Canada and the Law of Nations (with L. H. Laing), Canada in World Affairs (with F. H. Soward, J. F. Parkinson, T. W. L. MacDermont); Challenge to Education (1953); First Principles (1954); A Canadian View of Territorial Sea and Fisheries (with Jacob Austin, 1956); The Work of the Universities (in Canadian Education—Today, 1956); contributor to American Journal of International Law, Canadian Bar Review, and other publications. *Address:* The University of British Columbia, Vancouver 8, and 4509 West Fourth Avenue, Vancouver 8, B.C., Canada.

**McKEON, Hon. Mr. Justice John Joseph.** *B.* 1906. *Educ.* Riverview Coll., N.S.W., Waverley Coll., and Sydney University (LL.B). *M.* 1938, Mary Margaret Gilmartin. *Career,* Barrister-at-Law 1934–55; Justice of the New South Wales Industrial Commission 1955–76; Pres., Intellectually Handicapped Persons Review Tribunal since May 1976. Chairman, Crown Employees Appeal Board, 1956–60. *Address:* 2 Lady Game Drive, Lindfield, N.S.W. 2070, Australia.

**MacKINLAY, Bruce,** CBE. Australian executive. *B.* 1912. *Educ.* Scotch College Claremont, W.A. *M.* 1943, Ruth Fleming. *S.* David and Alistair. *Career:* Dir., J. Gadsden Australia Ltd.; Whittakers Ltd.; Chamber of Manufacturers Insurance Ltd. Perth; Chmn., Inst. of Directors (W.A. Div.); Pres., Confederation W.A. Industry; Mem., Senate of W.A. Univ. 1970—; Keep Australia Beautiful Council (W.A. Div.) 1970—; Pres., W.A. Employers' Federation 1974–75; Pres., W.A. Chamber of Manufacturers, Perth, 1959–61; Vice-Pres., Assoc. Chamber of Manufacturers of Australia 1960; Commissioner, State Electricity Comm. 1961–75; Chmn., National Packaging Assn. (W.A. Div.) 1967–69; Pres., Fremantle (W.A.) Rotary Club 1956. *Member:* Scotch Coll. Council Claremont, W.A. 1954–74 & Chmn. 1969–74; Organizing Council, Commonwealth & Empire Games 1962; Commonwealth Manufacturing Industries Advisory Council 1962–71. Chmn., Duke of Edinburgh's Study Conference Finance Cttee. 1968. Leader: Aust. Trade Mission East & Central Africa 1968; W.A. Govt. Trade Mission Italy 1970. War Service AIF AASC Lieut. 1941–45. *Clubs:* Weld (Perth); Golf (Cottesloe, W.A.). *Address:* 50 Alexander Road, Dalkeith, W.A., Australia.

**MACKINNON, Angus,** DSO, MC. British banker. *B.* 20 Feb. 1911. *Educ.* Eton; Oxford University. *M.* 1947, Beatrice Marsinah Neison. *S.* Andrew and Robert. *Career.* Joined Gray Dawes & Co. 1932; with MacKinnon, MacKenzie & Co., Calcutta 1933–37; served in World War II, B.E.F., in France, Middle East, Home Forces, and B.L.A., commanded 7th Bn. Argyll and Sutherland Highlanders (despatches) 1944–45; joined Brown Shipley & Co. Ltd. 1946; member (Cons.) for City of London, L.C.C. 1947–48; Chairman, Brown Shipley & Co., Ltd. 1953–63; Chmn. Australia and New Zealand Bank; Inchcape & Co. Ltd.; an underwriting member of Lloyds; Chmn. Royal National Orthopaedic Hospital; Dir. Guardian Royal Exchange Assurance; Dep. Chmn. Guardian Assurance. *Address:* Hunton Manor, Sutton Scotney, Hants.

**MacKINNON, Hon. Graham Charles,** MLC. Australian. *B.* 1916. *Educ.* various State schools: won Scholarships and attended Northam, Collie and Bunbury High Schools. *M.* 1940, Mary Theresa Shaw. *S.* Craig and Scott. *Career:* Minister for Health and Fisheries and Fauna, 1965–71 Environmental Protection (also) since 1970; Minister for Education, Cultural Affairs and Recreation, WA, 1974–77; Leader of the Govt. in the Legislative Council & Minister for Fisheries & Wildlife, Tourism & Conservation & the Environment since March 1977; Member, Liberal Party of Australia. Commissioner, Boy Scouts Assn. to 1968, State Vice-Pres. Member, Council. *Clubs:* Commercial; Repertory, South-West. *Address:* 57 Stockley Road, Bunbury, W.A.; and *office* Parliament Place, Perth, W.A., Australia.

**MACKINTOSH, Hon. Lord,** Charles Mackintosh, MC. Scottish judge. *B.* 28 May 1888. *Educ.* Edinburgh Academy; Wadham College, Oxford and Edinburgh University. *M.* 1921, Mary Lawrie Prosser. *Daus.* 4. *Career:* Served in World War I with Royal Scots 1914–19; called to the Scottish Bar 1914, KC 1935; Sheriff of Argyll 1937–42, of Inverness, Elgin and Nairn 1942–44; Commissioner, General Board of Control for Scotland 1939–44; Senator, College of Justice in Scotland (with judicial title of Lord Mackintosh) 1944–64; Hon. LLD (Edinburgh); Hon. Fellow, Wadham College, Oxford. *Address:* 55 Northumberland Street, Edinburgh, Scotland.

**MacKINTOSH, Sir Angus (MacKay),** KCVO, CMG, DK (Brunei), NSAIV (Maldives). British. *B.* 1915. *Educ.* Fettes Coll., Edinburgh; University Coll., Oxford (MA; BLitt). *M.* 1947, Robina Marigold Cochrane. *S.* Eneas James. *Daus.* Helen Roberta, Anne Margaret and Elspeth Marigold Olivia. *Career:* Served in World War II (Adjutant, Cameron Highlanders, in Italy and Greece; dispatches; Major 1945) 1942–46. Entered Colonial Office 1946 P.P.S. to Secretary of State 1950; Asst. Secretary 1952. Seconded to Foreign Office as Deputy Commissioner-General for U.K. in S.E. Asia, Singapore 1956–60; Asst. Secretary, Cabinet Office 1961–63; High Commissioner for the United Kingdom in Brunei, 1963–64; Asst. Secy; Asst. Under-Secretary of State, Ministry of Defence 1965–66. Senior Civilian Instructor, Imperial Defence College 1966–68; Asst. Under-Secy. of State, Foreign & Commonwealth Office 1968–69. High Commissioner in Ceylon & Ambassador to the Republic of Maldives 1969–73. *Publications:* Advisory Bodies (Allen & Unwin, 1942); Open Air Dairying (1943); occasional papers. *Address:* 9 Leven Terrace, Edinburgh EH3 9LW; and Fenecreich, Gorthleck, Inverness IVI 2YS.

**MACKIW, Vladimir Nicolaus.** Canadian executive. *B.* 1923. Dip. Chemist; Professional Engnr. *M.* Bohdanna Irene Kebuz. *Educ.* Universities of Breslau and Erlangen, Germany, Dipl.-Chemist 1946; Post graduate studies, University of Louvain, Belgium 1948. *Career:* Chemist, Ligman Lake Gold Mines, Winnipeg 1948; Manitoba Provincial Bureau of Mines 1949; joined Sherritt Gordon Mines Ltd. as Research Chemist 1949—, Director of Research 1952. Director, Research & Development Division 1955–68; Director, Sherritt Gordon Mines Limited 1964, Vice-President, 1967, Vice-President Technology & Corporate Development 1968, Executive Vice-President 1972. *Member:* National Research Council of Canada 1971 to present; Co-Chairman National Advisory Committee on Mining & Metallurgical Research and Chairman Subcommittee on Extraction Metallurgy, Department of Energy. Mines & Resources, Ottawa 1972 to present. Fellow, Chemical Institute of Canada: Honorary Member, Shevchenco Scientific Society; American Institute of Mining Engineers; American Powder Metallurgy Institute; Association of Professional Engineers of Alberta; Canada Institute of Mining & Metallurgy. *Awards:* Inco Platinum Medal, Canadian Institute of Mining & Metallurgy 1966; Jules Garnier Prize, Metallurgical Society of France (co-recipient) 1966; R. S. Jane Memorial Award, Chemical Institute of Canada 1967; Airey Award (Noranda), Metallurgical Society of the Canadian Institute of Mining & Metallurgy 1972. *Publications:* Over 50 in chemical and metallurgical centres. *Club:* Board of Trade of Metropolitan Toronto. *Address:* 9 Blair Athol Crescent, Islington, Ontario, Canada; and *office* P.O. Box 28, Commerce Court West, Toronto, Ontario, Canada.

**McLACHLAN, Angus Henry.** Australian journalist. *B.* 29 Mar. 1908. *Educ.* Scotch College, Melbourne, and the University of Melbourne. *Career:* On literary staff of The Herald, Melbourne 1928–36; joined the Sydney Morning Herald 1936 (News Editor 1937–49); Joint Man. Dir., Australian Associated Press since 1953— (Chairman 1958–59, 1964–65, 1975–76); Director Reuters Ltd. London, 1964–71; Macquarie Broadcasting Holdings Ltd. 1965—; Amalgamated Television Services Ptd. Ltd. 1956—. General Manager, John Fairfax Ltd., proprietors of the Sydney Morning Herald and other publications 1949–64, Managing Director 1965–69; Director 1969—; David Syme & Co. Ltd.; (publishers The Age Melbourne); The Canberra Times. Member of Library Council of N.S.W. since 1965, Member, Sydney Univ. Extension Board. *Address:* Box 5303 G.P.O., Sydney 2001 N.S.W., Australia.

**McLAGAN, Thomas Rodgie,** OBE. *B.* 1897. *Educ.* McGill Univ. (BScMech). *M.* 1927. *S.* Peter William. *Career:* With Canadian Vickers Ltd. 1938–51; Dufresne, McLagan & Associates 1932–38; Consolidated Paper Corp. 1923–32. President: Canadian Manufacturers Assn. (1960–61); Canadian Industrial Preparedness Assn. (1960–61); Canadian Shipbuilding & Ship Repairing Association (1953–58). Hon. Dir. Canada Steamship Lines Ltd. *Clubs:* Mount Royal, St. James's, University (Montreal), Toronto (Toronto), Garrison (Quebec). *Address:* 36 Sunnyside Avenue, West-mount, Montreal, P.Q., Canada.

**McLAREN, Ian Francis,** OBE, MP. Australian Chartered Accountant. *B.* 1912. *Educ.* Melbourne Univ. (Dip Com); FCA. *M.* 1941, Eileen Adele Porter. *S.* 3. *Dau.* 1. *Career:* Dir., Kiwi International Co. Ltd., Kiwi Polish Co. Pty. Ltd., Nat. President, Australian Y.M.C.A. 1958–62; World Vice-President, Y.M.C.A. 1961–69; President Roy. Hist. Socy. of Victoria 1956–59; Chmn., Australian Wool Testing Authority 1964–65; Estate Agents Cttee. (Victoria) 1956–65. Fellow, Royal Institute of Public Administration 1956; member, Victorian Legislative Assembly 1945–47, 1965—. Councillor, Malvern City Council 1951–53; Pres., Caulfield Tech. Col. Cncl. 1951–52; Chmn. E. Malvern, Central Sch. Cttee. 1954–62; Victorian Chairman, Aust. Inst. of Political Science 1953–54; Pres., Youth Hostels Assn. of Victoria 1947–48; Chmn., Victorian Fed. of Co-operative Housing Societies 1946–49; Lieut., R.A.N.V.R. (G.H.Q., S.W.P.A.) 1942–45. Chmn., Wyperfeld National Park, 1946–57; Pres. Good Neighbour Council of Victoria 1955–58. Fellow, Royal Historical Socy. of Victoria. *Publications:* Local History in Australia (1954); History of Latrobe Valley (1957); Como (1957); Australian Aviation (1958); The Burke & Wills Tragedy (1960); C. J. Dennis (1961); McEvoy Mine Disaster (1962); Wm. Wills (1963); E. E. Pescott (1965); How Victoria Began (1968); In the Wake of Flinders (1974). *Address:* 235 Waverley Road, East Malvern, Vic., Australia.

**MacLAREN, Ian M.,** MC. KStJ. Canadian chemical engineer. *B.* 1896. *Educ.* St. Andrew's College, Aurora, Ont.; Univ. New Brunswick (BSc 1920, MSc 1922). *M.* 1922, late Hilda F. L. Gregory. *Career:* Served in World War 1915–19 as Lieut. with C.F.A. (awarded MC). Hon. LLD. Pres., Rochester & Pittsburgh Coal Co. (Canada) Ltd., 1927–61. (Chmn. of the Board July 1961); Associate Coal Controller, Dept. of Munitions and Supply 1943–47; Chief Chem. Engineer, Canadian Explosives Ltd. 1920–26; Dir., Rochester & Pittsburgh Coal Co. (Canada) Ltd. Conservative. *Member:* Assn. of Professional Engineers; Engineering Inst. of Canada. *Clubs:* University, Golf (Toronto); York; Board of Trade; Royal Canadian Inst.; St. Andrews Society. *Address:* Apt. 1203, 619 Avenue Road, Toronto, Ont., Canada.

**McLAUGHLIN, Thomas Oscar.** American sales executive, educator and lecturer. *B.* 1897. *Educ.* Phillips Univ. (AB 1916); Yale Graduate School; Edinburgh Univ.; Oxford Univ. (BA, BSc, MA, PhD) Scholarships in each, Rhodes Scholarship, Oxford. *M.* 1924, Tanya Ivanovna Evaskavich. *Career:* With Repatriation Commission, Europe 1922; with Mr. Herbert Hoover, American Relief Administration, Europe 1923–24; Representative of U.S. in British Isles, League of Nations 1924. Travelled extensively throughout Europe, Asia, Africa and the Americas; languages English, French, German and Russian. Joined Chevrolet Motor Division, General Motors Corporation, N.Y.C. 1924 (activities have included Sales Promotion Manager, North Atlantic Coast States; City Manager in Columbus, Philadelphia, Los Angeles and Detroit); engaged in various national sales activities, such as National City Manager, National Used Car Manager; Liaison work, General Motors and U.S. Government. Educational work and Armed Services 1942–45; Organizer and National Director, Post-Graduate School of Merchandising and Management 1938. Member of Rhodes Scholarship Panel 1952—. Served in World War I (U.S. Army A.E.F.) 1917–18; Elected to Wisdom Hall of Fame, Wisdom Award of Honor; Honorary Degree, Phillips Univ. Republican. Mason. *Clubs:* Western Golf & Country (Detroit); Phoenix Golf & Country; Hiram and Villa Monterey, Scottsdale. *Address:* 3014 N. Evergreen Street, Phoenix, Ariz., U.S.A.

**McLAUGHLIN, William Earle.** Canadian. Chmn. of the Board & Chief Exec. Officer of The Royal Bank of Canada. *B.* 1915. *Educ.* Queen's University (BA 1936). *M.* 1940, Ethel Wattie. *S.* William. *Dau.* Mary. *Career:* Joined The Royal Bank of Canada in Toronto May 1936; Asst. General Manager's Dept. 1938; Asst., Mgr., London (Ontario) 1942; at Head Office 1945; First Asst. Manager, Montreal Branch, 1946, Manager 1951; Asst. General Manager 1953; Asst. to President 1959; General Manager 1960; Pres. and Director 1960; Chairman and President 1962; Chmn. & Chief Exec. Officer 1977. *Director:* Algoma Steel Corp. Ltd.; l'Air Liquide; Metropolitan Life Insurance Co.; Power Corp. of Canada Ltd.; Ralston-Purina of Canada Ltd.; Genstar Ltd., Standard Brands Inc. (N.Y.), Shawnigan Industries Ltd.; Allied Chemical (Canada) Ltd.; Textron Canada Ltd.; Canadian Pacific Ltd.; General Motors Corp. (Detroit); The Royal Bank of Canada Trust Corp., Ltd.; Security Reinsurance Corp. Ltd.; Trustee of Sun Alliance & London Ins. Group, Canadian Staff Pension Plan; Chmn. Canadian Advisory Board, Sun Alliance & London Ins. Group; Chmn., Sun Alliance Insurance Co.; Chmn., Adela Investment Co. (S.A.). Trustee: Queen's Univ. Governor: Royal Victoria Hosp. Dir., Royal Victoria Hosp. Foundation. *Awards:* Hon. Dr. of Law: Bishop's Univ. 1964, Queen's Univ. 1976; Knight, Order of St. John of Jerusalem. *Clubs:* Canadian (N.Y.); Engineers (Montreal) Forest & Stream; Lyford (Nassau); Mt. Bruno Golf; Mt. Royal; Rideau (Ottawa); Royal Montreal Curling; Royal Montreal Golf; St. James's; Seigniory; Toronto; University (Montreal); York (Toronto); Mid-ocean (Bermuda). *Address:* 67 Sunnyside Avenue, Montreal, P.Q.; and *office* Royal Bank of Canada Building, 1 Place Ville Marie, Montreal H3C 3A9, P.Q., Canada.

**McLEAN, David Colin Hugh,** MA, CEng, MICE. British, *B.* 1922. *Educ.* Harrow School; Cambridge Univ. (M.A.). *M.* 1962, Deborah Packe. *Career:* Chmn., Control Systems Ltd; Dir., Lamson Industries Ltd.; Chmn., Lamson Engineering Co. Ltd. *Clubs:* Bath; M.C.C. *Address:* White Lodge, Monken Hadley, Barnet, Herts and *office* Lamson House, 75–79 Southwark Street, London, S.E.1.

**MACLEAN, Sir Fitzroy,** Bt, CBE, LLD, DLitt. British politician. *B.* 11 Mar. 1911. *Educ.* Eton; Cambridge Univ. (1st Cl. Hons MA). *M.* 1946, Hon. Veronica Fraser; dau. of Lord Lovat. *S.* 2. *Career:* entered Dipl. Service 1933; 3rd Secy., Embassy, Paris 1934–37; 2nd Secy. Moscow 1937–39; resigned Dipl. Service and enlisted in Cameron Highlanders; 2nd Lt. 1941; joined 1st Special Air Service Regt. 1942; Capt. 1942,

Lt.-Col. 1943, Brig. 1943; local Maj.-Gen. 1947; Cmd. British Military Mission to Yugoslav Partisans 1943–45; head of Special Refugee Commission (Germany, Austria, Italy) 1947; MP (Con.) Lancaster Division 1941–59; Bute & N. Ayrshire 1959–74; Lees Knowles Lecturer (Cambridge) 1953. LLD (Glasgow) 1969. Parliamentary Under-Secretary of State and Financial Secretary, War Office, 1954–57. *Awards:* CBE 1944; Croix de Guerre (France); Order of Kutuzov (USSR); Partisan Star 1st Class, Jugoslavia; Order of Merit (Jugoslavia). *Publications:* Eastern Approaches; Disputed Barricade; A Person from England; Back to Bokhara; Jugoslavia; A Concise History of Scotland; To the Back of Beyond; To Caucasus. *Address:* Strachur, Argyll.

**MacLEAN, Hon. John Angus**, PC, DFC, BSc, LLD, CD. Canadian. *B.* 1914. *Educ.* Local Schools; Summerside High School, Univ. of B.C.; Mount Allison Univ. BSc; LLD (Hon.). *M.* 1952, Gwendolyn Esther Burwash. *S.* Allan Duart and Robert Angus. *Daus.* Sarah Jean and Mary Esther, *Career:* Served with R.C.A.F. 1939–47; Honourably discharged with rank of Wing-Commander; Minister of Fisheries for Canada 1957–63; Delegate NATO Parly. Conf. Paris 1956; Led. Can. Del. Colombo Plan Con. Tokyo 1960, Rome 1961; Member Can. Japanese Ministerial Del. Tokyo 1963; Del. Commonwealth Parly. Conf. Wellington N.Z. 1965; Parly. Course Westminster Eng. 1969. Is a farmer. Progressive Conservative. Member, R.C.A.F. Association; R.A.F. Escaping Socy.; Mason. *Club:* Charlottetown United Services Officers. *Address:* Lewes, Belle River, R.R. 3, Prince Edward Island, Canada.

**McLEAN, John William.** *B.* 1922. *Educ.* Univ. of Oklahoma (BS in Bus. Admin. 1943). *M.* 1943, Eleanor J. Johnson. *S.* Lawrence W. and Scott Johnson. *Dau.* Margo. *Career:* Bronze Star, Commd. Medal and battle prom. to Capt., World War II. With Merrill Lynch, Pierce, Fenner & Beane, N.Y.C. Aug. 1946; Asst. Cashier May 1949; Asst. Vice-Pres. May 1950, The First National Bank & Trust Co., Tulsa, Okla. (Vice-Pres. 1951; served as commercial loan officer for nine years; served also as Secretary of Board of Directors). Pres. and Dir., Texas National Bank of Commerce, 1959–65. Banking, Senior Vice-President and Director of Marketing, Bank of America, San Francisco, Mar. 1965. Elected President, Liberty National Bank and Trust Co., of Oklahoma City, Okla. 1967—. Chmn. Bd. & Chief Exec. Officer since 1971. Director: Reading and Bates Offshore Drilling Co. Former Dir. Houston Branch, Federal Reserve Bank of Dallas; Dir. Lee Way Motor Feight Inc.; Oklahoma Natural Gas Co.; Oklahoma City Golf & Country Club; Liberty Nat. Corp.; Liberty National Bank & Trust Co.; Dir. member Exec. Cttee. Allied Bank International; Vice-Press Okla. City's Chamber of Commerce. *Member:* Amer. Bankers Assn. and Past Chmn. Credit Policy Cttee.; Assn. of Reserve City Bankers' Organization; member, Exec. Cttee. and Dir., Houston Chamber of Commerce 1961–62–63; Former exec. cttee., U.S. Golf Assn; Distinguished Service Citation (OU). *Clubs:* California; S.F. Golf; Houston; River Oaks Country (Pres.). *Address:* 6912 N.W. Grand Blvd., Oklahoma City, Okla. 73116; and *office* Liberty Tower, 100 Broadway, Okla. City, Oklahoma, U.S.A.

**McLEAN, Murdo Lauchlin.** Canadian corporation Treasurer. *S.* John Douglas. *Dau.* Mary Edith Ainslie. *Career:* Treas. and Dir. Connors Bros. Ltd. 1938—; Independent. *Member:* Chartered Institute of Secretaries (Fellow)—FCIS; Socy. of Industrial and Cost Accountants. *Clubs:* Union (Saint John, N.B.); Algonquin Golf (St. Andrews, N.B.); Ancient Arabic Order of the Mystic Shrine. *Address:* Black's Harbour, N.B., Canada.

**MACLEAN, Sir Robert (Alexander).** KBE. DL. LLD. (Glas). British industrialist. *B.* 11 Apr. 1908. *M.* 1938, Vivienne Neville Bourke. *S.* 2. *Daus.* 2. *Career:* Chmn., Stoddard Holdings Ltd.; Vice-Pres., Scottish Cncl. (Development & Industry); Member, Norwich Union Insurance Group, Scottish Adv. Board. *Address:* Woodend, Houston, Renfrewshire, Scotland.

**MacLELLAN, Robin Perronet.** CBE. OStJ, JP. British. *B.* 1915. *Educ.* Clifton Coll.; Ecole de Commerce, Lausanne. *M.* 1941. Margaret Robertson. *S.* 1. *Career:* Dir., Nationwide Building Society; Scottish Industrial Trade Exhibitions Ltd.; Chmn. Scottish Tourist Board; Board Member, British Tourist Authority; Gen. Advisory Cttee. of the IBA; Scottish National Trust Co. Ltd.; British Railways Scottish Regional Advisory Board; Ardvreck School Ltd.; Past Deputy Chmn. of Bd, British Airports Authority; Past Pres. Glasgow Chamber of Commerce. *Clubs:* Western, Glasgow; Caledonian, London. *Address:* 11 Beechwood Court, Bearsden, Glasgow.

**MacLENNAN, Charles Gilmore.** Canadian executive. *B.* 1904. *Educ.* Dalhousie Univ. (BA). *M.* 1932, Mary Jackson. *S.* Roderick Jackson (BSc, MBA). *Dau.* Heather Elizabeth (BSc; PDr). *Career:* Has been connected with the family-owned firm of Brookfield Creamery Ltd. (Sales Manager 1925–50; General Manager 1950—; President 1951—); Pres., Brookfield Dairy Products Ltd. Truro N.S.; Acadia Trust Co.; Dir., Bentleys Ltd.; Halliday Craftsmen Ltd. Progressive Conservative. Elder, First United Church, Truro. *Clubs:* Truro Curling; Kiwanis (service). *Address:* 40 Broad Street, Truro, N.S.; and *office* 91 Walker Street, Truro, N.S., Canada.

**McLENNAN, Sir Ian Munro,** KBE. Australian engineer. *B.* 1909. *Educ.* Melbourne Univ. (Bach El Eng). *M.* 1937, Dora Robertson. *S.* 2. *Daus.* 2. *Career:* With the Broken Hill Pty. Co. Ltd.; successively Asst. Mgr. Newcastle Steelworks 1943; Asst. Gen. Mgr. 1947, Gen. Mgr. 1950, Senior Gen. Mgr., 1955 and Chief Gen. Mgr., 1959–67; Man. Dir. 1967–71; Chmn., BHP-GKN Holdings Ltd. 1970—: Chmn. and Dir. of Administration, The Broken Hill Proprietary Co. Ltd. 1971–77; Australian Iron & Steel Pty. Ltd. 1971–77; Australian Wire Industries Pty. 1971–77; Chmn., Tubemakers of Australia Ltd. since 1973; Dir., ICI Australia Ltd. since 1976; Dir., Australia & New Zealand Banking Group Ltd. since 1976, Chmn. since 1977. Pres., Australian Acad. of Technological Sciences 1976—; Deputy Chmn., Immigration Planning Cncl. 1949–67; Chmn., Joint War Production Cttee. (Aust. Govt.) 1956–69; Chmn., Australian Mineral Development Laboratories 1959–67; remained as Member of Council; Chmn., Defence Cttee. Industrial 1969. *Member:* Australian Inst. of Management; Australian Inst. of Metals; Inst. of Engineers, Australia; Inst. of Directors, London; Australian Inst. of Mining & Metallurgy. President 1951, 1957 and 1972; International Council of Morgan Guarantee Trust Co. (N.Y.); Amer. Inst. of Mining, Metallurgical & Petroleum Engineers. *Clubs:* Australian, Athenaeum, Melbourne, Melbourne Cricket (all in Melbourne); Commonwealth (Canberra); Union (Sydney); Newcastle (Newcastle). *Address:* Apt. 3/112 Walsh Street, South Yarra, Vic.; and *office* 140 William Street, Melbourne, Vic., Australia.

**MACLENNAN, Robert Adam Ross,** MA. LLB. MP. British politician. *B.* 1936. *M.* 1968, Helen Cutter Noyes. *S.* 1 (+ 1 stepson). *Dau.* 1. *Career:* Barrister; Member of Parliament, Caithness and Sutherland 1966—; Member, House of Commons Select Cttee. on Estimates; P.P. Secy. to Rt. Hon. George Thomson, Minister without Portfolio 1967–69; Chancellor of Duchy of Lancaster 1969–70; Add. Opposition Spokesman, Scottish Affairs 1970–71; On Defence 1971–72; Under-Secretary Dept. Prices and Consumer Protection since 1974. *Member:* GMWU. *Club:* Reform. *Address:* House of Commons, SW1A 0AA.

**McLEOD, John Porter.** American manufacturer. *B.* 1913. *Educ.* Bowdoin College, Brunswick, Me. (BS). *M.* 1935, Mary Wallace Wall. *S.* Hugh Wallace and John Porter. *Dau.* Heather Ruth. *Career:* With R. B. Wall Co., Wilkes Barre, Pa. (wholesale electrical appliance distributors) 1935–41 (Wholesale Manager 1939–41); Porter-McLeod Machine Tool Co. Inc., Hatfield, Mass. (manufacturers of machine tools and other industrial machinery) 1941—. Pres. and Treasurer, Porter-McLeod Machine Tool Co. 1944—; Treasurer, Hatfield Machines Sales Corp. 1953. Pres., Leisure Time Industries 1961—. *Member:* National Machine Tool Builders Assn.; Associated Industries of Massachusetts; Clan McLeod Society of America; Psi Upsilon Fraternity. *Clubs:* Niantic Bay Yacht; Old Lyme Country; Hatfield Men's. *Address:* 21 School Street, Hatfield, Mass., U.S.A.

**McLINTOCK, George Gordon.** *B.* 1903. *Educ.* Sevenoaks School (England); LLD Adelphi Univ. 1954. *M.* 1929, Winifred Russell Kidner. *Dau.* Irene (*Dec.* 1940). *Career:* Cadet, Brit. Merchant Navy 1918–20; Qm. U.S. Merchant Service 1920; 3rd Officer Standard Oil Co. 1922; successively 2nd Officer, Chief Officer, Master, U.S. Steamship Inspector, Port of N.Y. 1930; Head, Exams. Div,. Washington 1937, and Casualty Investigation Div. 1940. Active service, USNR, Chief Inspection Officer, Bureau of Training, U.S. Maritime Commission 1941–46; Lieut.-Comdr. to Rear Admiral 1946. U.S. Delegate International Conference on Radio Aids to Marine Navigation, London, 1946, N.Y., New London 1947, Montreal 1946, to ILO Conf., Seattle 1946, and to Int. Meeting on Loran, Geneva 1949. Superintendent, U.S. Merchant Marine Academy, Kings Point, N.Y. 1948–70.

Pres. Int. Cargo Handling Co-ordination Assn. 1961–62; New York Chapter, Defense Supply Assn. of U.S. 1969–70; U.S. Institute of Navigation 1946–47–48; Hon. Life member Fellow, Royal Institute of Navigation; Benjamin Franklin Fellow; Royal Socy. Arts; Member, Middle States Accreditation Evaluation Cttee.; Society of Naval Architects and Marine Engineers; Regular mem. and Hon. Life Mem. Amer. Cncl. of Master Mariners; St. Andrews Scottish Socy. Congressional Panel to review the five U.S. Service Academies 1973–75. *Awards:* Commander, Order, Maritime Merit, France Legion of Honor medal Philippine Govt.; Dist. Service Medal Amer-Legion; Presidential Commendation promoted Vice-Admiral 1970. *Clubs:* India House, Princeton, Whitehall, Lotos, The Army and Navy. *Address:* 4605 Overbrook Road, Chevy Chase, Md. 20016, U.S.A.

**McLOUGHLIN, Hon. Henry Joseph.** *B.* 1911. *M.* 1941, Thelma A. Harris. *S.* 1. *Daus.* 3. *Career:* Tasmanian Minister for Transport 1961–69; Past Senior Vice-Pres., Hobart Trades Hall Council; Member, Australian Labour Party. *Clubs:* R.A.C.; City Bowls. *Address:* c/o House of Assembly, Hobart, Tasmania.

**McMAHON, Gerald J.** American lawyer. *B.* 1907. *Educ.* College of the City of New York (AB), and Columbia Univ. (JD 1932). *M.* 1943, Jane Morley Williams. *S.* Kevin C., Richard T., and Thomas Morley. *Dau.* Jane Scott. *Career:* Associate Counsel, American claimants against Germany in sabotage cases 1933–39. Lieut-Col. Staff Judge Advocate, 9th Armoured Div., A.U.S. 1943–46; Sec.-Gen., Intern. Bar Assn. 1956–76 (Asst. Secy.-Gen. 1947–53; Acting Secy.-Gen. 1953–56). *Award:* Decorated Bronze Star Medal for services in European Theatre of Operations. *Member:* Assn. of the Bar of the City of New York; American Bar Assn.; American Socy. of International Law; International Law Assn.; National Legal Aid Assn.; Selden Society; Fellow, American Bar Foundation. *Publications:* Restraints of Trade at Common Law (1932); International Assns. in United States Law (1956). *Clubs:* Town, Scarsdale Golf (Scarsdale, N.Y.); Squadron A. *Address:* 24 Walworth Avenue, Scarsdale, N.Y.; and *office* 180 E. Post Road, White Plains, N.Y. 10601, U.S.A.

**McMAHON, Rt. Hon. Sir William,** PC, CH, GCMG, LLB, BEC, Australian lawyer and politician. *B.* 1908. *Educ.* Sydney Grammar School and St. Paul's College, Sydney University. *M.* 1965, Sonia R. Hopkins. *S.* 1. *Dau.* 2. *Career:* Practised as a solicitor until 1939; enlisted in Australian Army Apr. 1940 (Lieut. 1st Infantry Battalion; discharged 1945 with rank of Major). Elected to the House of Representatives for Lowe, N.S.W. in general elections for 1949–51–54–55–58–61–63–66–69–72–74 & 75. Minister for the Navy and Minister for Air 1951–54; for Social Services 1954–56; for Primary Industry 1956–58; for Labour and Nat. Service 1958–66; Treasurer Commonwealth of Australia 1966–69; Minister, Foreign Affairs 1969–71; Prime Minister 1971–72. Acting Min. for Trade 1956; Acting Min. in charge C.S.I.R.O., 1956, for Labor & Nat. Service 1957, 1966, 1968, 1969; Acting Min. for Nat. Devel. 1959, for Territories 1961; Acting Attorny-Gen. 1960, 1961; Acting Treas. 1971; Vice-President of the Executive Council 1964–66; Deputy Leader Liberal Party 1966–71, Leader 1971–72. Leader of Austr. Dlgtn. to Commonwealth Parliamentary Conference to New Delhi, Nov. 1957–58; Pres. ILO Regional Conference Melbourne 1962; Visiting Minister to I.L.O. Conference, Geneva, 1960, 1964; Aust. Del. IMF and World Bank Conf. Washington 1966; Rio de Janeiro 1967; Washington 1968; Aust. Rep. at Commonwealth Finance Min. Confs. Montreal 1966, Trinidad 1967, London 1968; Chmn. Bd. Gov., Asian Development Bank 1968–69; Leader Aust. Del. ECAFE Bangkok, Conf. Foreign Ministers Djakarta, ASPAC Wellington, SEATO Manila, Troop Contributing Countries Conf. Saigon, Devt. Asst. Cttee. Tokyo, 25th U.N. Gen. Assembly 1970, Commonwealth Heads of Govt. Singapore 1971; as Prime Minister visited USA and Britain 1971, Indonesia and Malaysia 1972. *Clubs:* Union, Royal Sydney, Melbourne (Melbourne); Australian Jockey; Australian (Sydney). *Address:* 100 William Street, Sydney N.S.W. 2011; and *office* Parliament House, Canberra, A.C.T. 2600.

**McMANUS, Charles Edward, Jr.** American manufacturing executive. *B.* 1914. *Educ.* Bard College. *M.* 1938, Mary Schaffer. *S.* Charles III and David G. *Dau.* Eva M. *Career:* Vice-Pres.: Green Spring Dairy (1936–39) and Crown Cork and Seal Co. 1940–57; Pres., Crown Cork International Corp. 1945–52; Director, Crown Cork Co., Ltd. 1939–57; Chairman of Board, Multi-Krome Color Process Inc., 1957–62; Pres., Charlson Products Inc. 1957–62; Vice-Pres., CEM Securities Corp. 1957–73; Vice-Pres. & Dir., B. H. Hubbert & Son Inc. 1958–75; Currently Business Partner, Kalista Associates. Member, Governor's Commission on Civilian and Independent Colleges in Maryland; Society of Manufacturing Engineers. Holder of several patents relating to tin can manufacture, and steel products manufacture. *Clubs:* Kiwanis Club of Higlandtown; Baltimore Country. *Address:* 5908 Wilmary Lane, Baltimore 21210, Md., U.S.A.

**McMICKING, Joseph R.** Former American Co. Dir. and Chmn. *B.* 1908. *Educ.* Stanford University. *M.* 1931, Mercedes Zobel. *Career:* Chmn., Ampex Corp. 1948–55; Insular Life Assurance Co. 1948–63; FGU Insurance Group 1948–63; former Dir., Bank Philippine Islands; San Miguel Corp.; Ayala Securities Corp.; Maketi Development Corp.; Ayala Corp. Chmn., McMicking Foundation; Dir., Bank California; Partner, McMicking & Co. *Awards:* (Military) Legion of Merit, D.F.C.; Bronze Star D.S.M. Legion of Honor. Knt. Grand Cross Isabela Catolica (Spain). *Clubs:* Pacific Union; Bohemian; Cypress Point; Manila Polo; Manila Golf; Manila Yacht; Puerta de Hierro, Sotogrande, Spain, San Franciso; SF Golf; University; British; Filipino, Casino Español; Wack-Wack; Baguio Country; White's, Turf (London); R & A St Andrews (Scotland). *Address:* 351 California Street, Rm 900. San Francisco, Cal. 94104, U.S.A.

**McMILLAN, Edward Bellamy.** American consulting engineer. *B.* 1910. *Educ.* Annapolis (BSc 1933). *M.* 1952, Elizabeth Moore. *S.* Kirk Barry. *Dau.* Jean Moore. *Career:* Marine Corps Reserve Officer 1933–34; Naval Officer 1934–39; Inventor and licensor of techniques for electromagnetic wave radiation control, radio communications, geophysics, 1934—; Electronics Consultant to War Production Bd. 1943–45; Research Admin. and Physicist 1940—; Engng. Consultant 1946—; Pres., McMillan Laboratory Inc. 1951–64; Consultant, Electronics Cttee. Research and Development Bd. Office, Secy. of Defence 1951–53; Vice-Pres., McMillan Corp. of N. Carolina 1973—; Technical Director, Resources Development Inst. 1966—; Pres. Power and Transmission Corp. 1967–71; Pres., The Clan MacMillan Socyl of North America 1962–64. Publisher, The Clan MacMillan Magazine of North America 1958–62; Adviser Navy 1966–74; Vice-Pres. Wave Inc. since 1974. *Publications:* articles in Aviation magazines; McGraw-Hill, M.I.T. Radiation Laboratory Series, various papers on radar materials; manuscripts and development of data for U.S.A.F. engng. manuals. Senior Member: I.E.E.E. *Address:* P.O. Box 139, La Porte, Tx. 77571, U.S.A.

**MACMILLAN, Rt. Hon. (Maurice) Harold,** PC, OM, FRS. British statesman. *B.* 10 Feb. 1894. *Educ.* Eton; Balliol College, Oxford. *M.* 1920, Lady Dorothy Cavendish (*Dec.*). *S.* Maurice Victor. *Daus.* Ann Caroline (Faber), Catherine (Amery), Sarah Johanna (Heath) (*Dec.*). Served World War I in Grenadier Guards (Capt.) 1914–18; A.D.C. to Governor-General of Canada 1919–20; MP (Cons.) for Stockton-on-Tees 1924–29 and 1931–45, for Bromley 1945–64; Parliamentary Secretary to Ministry of Supply 1940–42; Under-Sec. for the Colonies 1942; British Minister Resident at Allied H.Q. in N.W. Africa 1942; Dipl. Representative with the French National Cttee. 1943; Acting President, Allied Commission, for Italy 1944; Sec. of State for Air 1945; Minister of Housing and Local Government 1951–54; of Defence 1954–55; Foreign Secretary Apr.–Dec. 1955; Chancellor of the Exchequer Dec. 1955–57; Prime Minister 1957–Oct. 1963. A Vice-Pres. Franco-British Society 1955; a Trustee: Historic Churches Preservation Fund 1957; Stationers' & Newspaper Makers' Co. 1957; Freeman of: Bromley, Kent, 1957; City of London 1961; Toronto 1962. Hon. Fellow Balliol College, Oxford, 1957; Hon DCL Oxford University 1958; DCL Oxford (by Diploma) 1960; LLD Cambridge 1961; Chancellor of Oxford University 1960. *Publications:* Industry and the State (in collaboration); Reconstruction; A Plea for National Policy; Planning for Employment; The Next Five Years; The Middle Way; Economic Aspects of Defence; Winds of Change; Tides of Fortune; Riding the Storm; The Blast of War; Pointing the Way; At the End of the Day (six volumes of Memoirs, 1966–73); The Past Masters (1975). *Address:* Birch Grove House, Chelwood Gate, Haywards Heath, West Sussex.

**MACMILLAN, Rt. Hon. Maurice Victor,** PC, MP. *B.* 1921. *Educ.* Eton; Balliol College, Oxford. *M.* 1942, Hon. Katherine Margaret Alice Ormsby-Gore. *S.* 3. *Dau.* 1. *Career:* served War with Sussex Yeomanry 1939–45; Member, Kensington Borough Council 1949–53; Member of Parliament (Con.) Halifax 1955–64; Economic Secy. to the Treasury 1963–64; Chief Secy. 1970–72; Member of Parliament Farnham since 1966; Former Chmn. and Dir. many companies; Secy. of

State, Employment 1972–73; Paymaster-Gen. 1973–74. *Clubs:* Turf; Beefsteak; Pratt's; Garrick; Carlton. *Address:* 12 Catherine Place, London, S.W.1; and Highgrove, Doughton near Tetbury, Glos.

**MacMILLAN, Norman John**, QC. Canadian. Chairman and President, Canadian National Railway Co. 1967–74. Director: Duluth, Rainy Lake & Winnipeg Ry. Co. (Pres.); Duluth Winnipeg & Pacific Railroad Co. (Pres.); Canadian National Railways Trust Co. (Pres.); Northern Alberta Railways Co. (Vice-Pres.); Shawinigan Falls Terminal Ry. Co. (Vice-Pres.); Toronto Terminals Ry. Co. (Vice-Pres.); The Northern Consolidated Holdings Co. (Pres.); Central Vermont Transportation Co. (Pres.). Chmn. and Pres.: Realties Ltd., Steamship Co. Ltd., Telegraph Co., Transfer Co., Transportation Ltd.; Canadian Northern Quebec Railway Co.; Great North Western Telegraph Co. of Canada; Mount Royal Tunnel & Terminal Co. Ltd.; Quebec & Lake St. John Railway Co.; Saint John & Quebec Railway Co.; Central Vermont Ry. Inc. (Chmn. Exec. Cttee.); Grand Trunk Western R.R. Co. (Chmn. Exec. Cttee.). *B.* 1909. *Educ.* BA and LLB. *M.* 1937, Doris Maude Horne. *S.* Ian Malcolm. *Dau.* Elizabeth Anne (Denyar). General Counsel, Trans-Canada Air Lines 1945–56; Canadian National Railways (Chmn. and Pres. 1967; Exec. Vice-Pres. 1955–56). Vice-Pres. and Gen. Counsel 1949–56; Gen. Counsel 1945–49; Asst. Gen. Solicitor, Montreal 1943–45; Solicitor Winnipeg 1937–43; Law Dept., Winnipeg Electric Co. 1930–37; with Guy, Chappell, DuVal and McCrea, Barristers and Solicitors, Winnipeg 1930–37. *Member:* Canadian Bar Assn.; Manitoba Bar Assn. Law Socy. of Manitoba; McGill Associates; Delta Upsilon. *Clubs:* Saint James's Mount Royal (Montreal), Canadian Railway. *Address:* 135 Lazard Avenue, Mount Royal, Montreal H3R 1N6, Canada.

**McMULLIN, Sir Alister Maxwell**, KCMG. *B.* 1900. *M.* 1945, Thelma Louise (*nee* Smith), *Dau.* of W. J. Smith of Sydney. *Dau.* 1. *Career:* Former Senator for New South Wales; President of the Senate 1953–71; Chancellor, University of Newcastle, N.S.W. since 1966; Grazier; Chairman, Commonwealth Parliamentary Assn. 1959–60, 1969–70; Member, Liberal Party of Australia. *Address:* St. Aubin's, Scone, N.S.W. 2337, Australia.

**McNAIR, F. Chaloner**, BS. American. *B.* 1904. *Educ.* Yale Univ. (BS. Hons.). *M.* 1948, Marie-Louise Walstrum. *S.* 1. *Daus.* 2. *Career:* Vice-Pres., Taylor Forge Inc. 1942, Senior Vice-Pres. 1961; Dir., Taylor Forge Ltd.; Welding Fittings & Flanges Ltd.; Industrias Tubulares y de Forja, S.A.; Chmn. & Man. Dir., Taylor Forge Inc. *Member:* Amer. Socy. Mechanical Engineers. *Clubs:* Union League; Chicago; Chicago Duquesne; Pittsburg; Indian Hill. *Address:* 1420 Sheridan Road, Wilmette, Illinois 60091, U.S.A.; and *office* P.O. Box 519, Wilmette, Illinois 60091, U.S.A.

**McNAIR, Hon. Sir William Lennox**, Kt Bach (1946), QC. Judge of the High Court of Justice 1950–66. *B.* 1892. *Educ.* Aldenham, Gonville and Caius Coll., Camb. (LLM); Barrister-at-law, Gray's Inn 1918, Bencher 1938, Treasurer, 1951; KC (1950); Legal Adv. to Min. of War Transport during World War II; served in World War I as Capt. Royal Warwickshire Regt. *Address:* 130 Court Lane, Dulwich Village, London, S.E.21.

**McNAIR-WILSON, Patrick**, MP. British politician. *B.* 1929. *Educ.* Eton. *M.* 1953, Diana Methuen Campbell. *S.* Guy. *Daus.* Jennifer Arabella, Ann, Kate. *Career:* Regular Army Officer, Coldstream Guards 1947–52; Exec. Louis Dreyfus et Cie. 1952–54; On Staff Political Centre, Conservative Central Office 1954–60; Dir. London Municipal Socy. and Editor, The Londoner 1960–62; Exec. with British Iron & Steel Fed. 1962–64; MP for West Lewisham 1964–66; Opposition Front Bench Spokesman on Power 1965–66; MP for New Forest since 1968; Parly. Private Secy. to Minister, Transport Industries 1970–74; Opposition Front Bench spokesman on Energy 1974–76. *Address:* 5 Kelso Place, London, W.8.; and *office* House of Commons, London, S.W.1.

**McNAIR-WILSON, Robert Michael Conal, MP.** British politician. *B.* 1930. *Educ.* Eton College *M.* 1974, Deidre E. Granville. *Career:* Director & Shareholder, Sidney Barton Ltd., Public Relations Consultants, since 1955; Member of Parliament for Walthamstow E. 1969–74, MP for Newbury since 1974. *Member:* Inst. Public Relations, *Clubs:* Royal Lymington Yacht. *Address:* 29 St. Luke's Street, London S.W.3; and *office* Sidney-Barton Ltd., 1 Lily Place, Saffron Hill, E.C.1.

**McNALLY, Jack Reginald**, MBE, JP. F.Comm.A, MASEE, FIWM, MBIM. British *B.* 1916. *Educ.* Plumstead Central Sec. School; Woolwich Polytechnic. *M.* 1939, Lena Medcraf. *Career:* Works Supt. Sunvic Controls Ltd. (AEI) 1946–50; Asst. Man. Dir., Bendix & Herbert Ltd. 1950–58; Works Mgr., Electrothermal Eng. Ltd. 1950–58; Chairman: Beckman (Holdings) Ltd., Beckman Insts. Ltd., Beckman-RIIC Ltd., Beckman SARL (France), Beckman Italiana; Chmn., Vivian Industries Ltd.; Chmn., Scientific Documentation Centre Ltd. *Member:* RAC; Inst. Directors; Liveryman Worshipful Co. Scientific Inst. Mfg. City of London. *Clubs:* English Speaking Union; City Livery; RAC. *Address:* Roseacre, Orchard Drive, Glenrothes, Fife, Scotland; and *office* Queensway, Glenrothes, Fife.

**McNALLY, James B. M.** American Judge. *B.* 5 Apr. 1896. *Educ.* St. John's University, Brooklyn (AB, LLD); Fordham University School of Law (LLB). *M.* 1943, Bessie Lahey. Practising Lawyer in New York City specializing in trial of civil cases 1920–43 Proefssor of Law, St. John's University 1925–38; Delegate to New York State Constitutional Convention 1938; United States Attorney for the Southern District of New York 1943–44; Justice, New York State Supreme Court, First Judicial District 1945; Associate Judge, Appellate Div., 1st Dept., N.Y. State Judicial Conference; Commander, U.S. Coastguard Reserve. Hon LLD, Fordham Univ., Manhattan and Assumption Colls. Democrat. *Address:* Appellate Division, Court House, 27 Madison Avenue, New York City, U.S.A.

**McNAMARA, Joseph Kevin**, MP. British Lecturer. *B.* 1934. *Educ.* St. Mary's Coll., Crosby; Hull Univ.—LLB; Graduate Diploma in Education. *M.* 1960, Nora Jones. *S.* 4. *Dau.* 1. *Career:* MP (Lab.) for Kingston upon Hull North 1966–74, for Kingston upon Hull Central since 1974. *Member:* Parly. Sec., Transport & General Workers' Union. *Address:* 128 Cranbrook Avenue, Hull; and *office* House of Commons, London SW1A 0AA.

**McNAMARA, Robert Strange.** *B.* 1916. *Educ.* Univ. of California (BA) and Harvard Univ. (MBA); Hon LLD Universities of Harvard, California, Columbia, Princeton, Notre Dame, Michigan, New York, and Amherst and Williams Colleges. *M.* 1940, Margaret Craig. *S.* Robert Craig. *Daus.* Margaret and Kathleen. *Career:* Lieut.-Colonel, U.S. Army Air Force (Legion of Merit) 1942–45: Professor, Harvard University 1940–42; Former President and Director, Ford Motor Co. Trustee: Ford Foundation; Brookings Institute, Urban Institute. Secretary of Defense of U.S.A. 1961–68; President, International Bank for Reconstruction and Development, International Development Assn., & International Finance Corp since 1968. *Awards:* Presidential Medal of Freedom with Distinction; Distinguished Service Medal from Department of Army, Navy & Air Force. *Publications:* The Essence of Security (1968); One Hundred Countries, Two Billion People: The Dimensions of Development (1975). *Address:* 1818 H Street, NW, Washington, D.C. 20433, U.S.A.

**McNEESE, Aylmer Green, Jr.** *B.* 1911. *Educ.* The Univ. of Texas (BA 1933; LLB 1937). *M.* 1938, Catherine Elsbury. *S.* Thomas Dwyer. *Dau.* Margaret Carter. *Career:* Admitted Texas Bar, 1937; with Fulbright, Crooker, Freeman, Bates & Jaworski 1939–43; Vice-Pres. and General Counsel, McCarthy Oil & Gas Corp. 1943–51; Admin. Asst. to the President, Houston Oil Co. of Texas 1951–53; Asst. President, Second National Bank of Houston (name changed to Bank of the Southwest in Jan. 1956) 1953–56. Chmn. of the Board, Bank of the Southwest, Houston 1967— (Director Jan. 1949—, Pres. 1956–67). Director: Fort Worth & Denver Railway Co., May 1959—; Natl. Airlines Inc.; Eastex Inc., since July 1958; Chmn. Board of Regents, Univ. of Texas 1973. *Member:* Amer. Bankers Assn.; Assn. of Reserve City Bankers; Texas Bar Assn.; Texas Industrial Commission (Vice-Chmn. 1958–59); Bd. of Regents, The Univ. of Texas; The Philosophical Socy. of Texas. *Awards:* Sons of the Amer. Revolution; Sons of the Republic of Texas, Knight's Cross, Order of the Crown (Belgium). *Clubs:* Coronado; Forest, Houston; Houston Country; Metropolitan N.Y.; Balboa, Matzalon, Mexico. Ramada. *Address:* 603 West Friar Tuck Lane, Houston 24, Tex.; and *office* Bank of the Southwest, P.O. Box 2629, Houston 1, Tex., U.S.A.

**McNICOL, David Williamson**, CBE. *B.* 1913. *Educ.* Kings Coll. Adelaide Univ. (BA). *M.* Elsa M. Hargrave. *S.* 1. *Career:* Australian Minister to Cambodia, Laos and Viet Nam 1955–56; Imperial Defence Col. 1957; Aust. Commissioner Singapore, Brunei, North Borneo and Sarawak 1958–60;

Asst. Secy., Dept. of External Affairs 1960–62; High Commissioner to Pakistan 1962–65; High Commissioner in New Zealand 1965–68, Australian Ambassador to Thailand, 1968–69; High Commissioner to Canada 1969–73; Deputy High Commissioner to London 1973–75; Aust. Ambassador to SA since 1975. *Clubs:* Naval & Military (Melbourne); Royal Canberra Golf. *Address:* c/o Dept. of Foreign Affairs, Canberra, ACT. Australia.

**MACPHERSON, Rt. Hon. Lord (James Gordon)**, JP, FRES, FZS, FRSA. British. *B.* 1924. *Educ.* Loretto. *M.* (1) 1947, Dorothy Ruth Coulter (dec'd 1974). *S.* The Hon. Thomas Ian. *Daus.* The Hon. Wendy and The Hon. Elizabeth; (2) 1975, Catherine Bridget MacCarthy. *Career:* Member of Council, London Chamber of Commerce 1958–74 (and of the General Purposes Committee 1959–74). Member, Executive Committee of the West India Committee 1959—, Chmn. 1973; Dep. Chmn., West India Cttee. 1971; Chmn. 1973,74,75. Chairman and Managing Director, Macpherson, Train & Co. Ltd.; Chairman: Gordon Mac Robin (Insurance) Ltd., 1965—; Allied Canners Ltd. 1952—, J. G. Macpherson Group Ltd. 1965—, Coastal Canners Ltd. 1953—. Macpherson Train (France) Ltd.; Chmn. A. J. Macpherson & Co. Ltd. (Bankers) 1973; Port of London Authority 1973–76. Freeman of the City of London, 1969. *Member:* East European Trade Council, 1969; Worshipful Company of Butchers, 1959; Governor, Brentwood School 1970–76; Hon. Game Warden for Sudan 1974; F.R.E.S. 1940; F.R.S.A. 1971; F.Z.S. 1966; Essex Magistrates Court Cttee. 1974; Dep. Chmn. Brentwood Bench 1973–75; Chief Scottish Clans Assoc. of London 1972–74. *Clubs:* Boodles (London). R.A.F. Bomber Command (Far East), 1939–45. Royal & Ancient Golf, St. Andrews, 1969. *Address:* Kyllachy, Tomatin, Inverness-shire and *office* 69–85 Old Street, London, E.C.1.

**McPHERSON, William Heston.** American. Professor Emeritus, economist, labour arbitrator. *B.* 1902. *Educ.* Harvard Univ. (AB); Ohio State Univ. (MA); Univ. of Chicago (PhD). *M.* 1930, Vivian Ratcliffe. *Daus.* Lucretia (Durrett), Janice (Fisch) and Charlotte. Member, Department of Economics; Dartmouth College, Western Reserve Univ., Oberlin College, 1929–40; Staff Member, Committee on Social Security, Social Science Research Council 1940–42; Principal Economist, War Manpower Commission 1942–43; Co-Chmn. and Chmn., Shipbuilding Commission, National War Labor Board, 1943–45; Labor Advisory Committee to Japan and Korea, U.S. War Dept. 1946. Professor of Economics, Institute of Labor and Industrial Relations, University of Illinois 1946–71; Umpire United Mine Workers & Illinois Coal Operators Assoc. 1973–76. *Publications:* Labor Relations in the Automobile Industry; Public Employee Relations in West Germany; Les Conseils de Prud'hommes (in Droit Social, 1962); Co-author, The French Labor Courts: Judgment by Peers; contributing author: How Collective Bargaining Works; Labor in Postwar America; Problems and Policies of Dispute Settlement and Wage Stabilization during World War II; Wege zum Sozialen Frieden. Lecturer, German Labor Academies 1952–53; Fulbright Research grant, France, 1960–61 Germany, 1969. *Member:* American Economic Association; Industrial Relations Research Assn. (Sec.-Treas. 1948–50; Exec. Board 1961–64); Nat. Acad. of Arbitrators (Bd. of Governors 1965–68); Amer. Assn. of Univ. Profs. (Nat. Council 1961–64, Chmn. Cttee. on Professional Ethics 1964–67); Internat. Socy. for Labour Law & Social Legislation (Exec. Cttee., U.S. Nat. Cttee., 1963—); Internat. Industrial Relations Assn.; Phi Delta Theta. *Address:* 62 Greencroft, Champaign, Ill.; and *office* 504 E. Armory Avenue, Champaign, Ill. 61820., U.S.A.

**MACQUAIDE, Charles Desmond**, TD, FCA. British. *B.* 1910. *Educ.* Lake House School; Bexhill-on-Sea; Cheltenham College. *M.* 1938, Olive Margaret Rhimes Frankland. *Dau.* 1. *Career:* various appointments with R.A. Lister & Co. Ltd. 1938–56; Finance Dir., Forestal Land, Timber & Rlys. Co. Ltd. 1957–65; Man. Dir., La Forestal Argentina S.A. 1959–62; Jt. Man. Dir., Forestal Land, Timber & Railways Co. Ltd. 1965–69; Dir., Hawker Siddeley Group Ltd., Chmn., Hawker Siddeley International Ltd., & Chmn. Hawker Siddeley Australia Pty. Ltd. 1969–77. *Address:* 4 Downsway, Merrow, Guildford, Surrey.

**McRAE, Eric George.** Australian. *B.* 1913. *Educ.* Shepparton High School (Victoria), University of Tasmania. *M.* Elma Weymouth. *S.* Scott Weymouth. *Daus.* Jennifer Anne & Elizabeth Nola. *Career:* Sales Manager, Commercial Broadcasters Pty. Ltd., 1940; Manager, Commercial Broadcasters Pty. Ltd. 1947–59. Dir.: TVT & 7HO Properties P/L, Macquarie Broadcasting Holdings Ltd., Macquarie Broadcasting Services P/L, 3AW Broadcasting Co. Pty. Ltd., Broadcasting Associates P/L, Artransa P/L. Canberra Broadcasters Ltd., Broadcasting Station 2GB/P/L.; Chmn. & Man. Dir., Tasmanian Television Ltd.; Chmn., Tasmanian Drive In Theatre Holdings Ltd.; Tasmanian Amusements Pty. Ltd.; Star Theatres (Holdings) Ltd. and subsidiary companies. *Member:* Australian Olympic Fedn.; National Parks & Wildlife Authority Adv. Council; Nat. Parks & Wildlife Cttee. (Tasmania); Exec. Pres., Tasmanian Olympic Council. *Clubs:* Athenaeum, Tasmanian; Royal Hobart Golf; Royal Yacht (Tasmania). *Address: office* 48–52 New Town Road, Hobart, Tasmania, Australia.

**MACTAGGART, William Alexander**, CBE, JP. British. *B.* 1906. *Educ.* Sedbergh School. *M.* 1932, Marjorie Laing Innes. *S.* William Bruce and Alan Harry. *Dau.* Mary Claire. *Career:* With Pringle of Scotland Ltd.: Director, 1932; Jt. Managing Director 1933–45; Sole Mng. Dir. 1945–66; Chairman, Pringle of Scotland Ltd., Knitwear Manufacturers, Hawick, 1960–70. Joint Mng. Dir. 1966–68 for New Zealand of BNEC 1965–68. *Address:* Bewlie House, Lilliesleaf, Melrose, Roxburghshire.

**MacTIER, Sir (Reginald) Stewart**, CBE. Comdr. Order of Maritime Merit (France); Medal of Freedom with Silver Palm (U.S.). *B.* 1905. *Educ.* Eton College and Magdalene College, Cambridge (BA). *M.* 1941, Mary Ling. *S.* 2. *Dau.* 1. *Career:* With Mansfield & Co. Ltd. (shipping agents), Singapore 1928–37; Glen Line Ltd., London 1937–55 (excluding war service); Deputy Director and subsequently Director, Port and Transit Control, Ministry of War Transport 1940–45. Director: Glen Line Ltd., 1939–67, Ocean Steamship Co. Ltd. 1955–67. Chairman: Liverpool Steamship Association 1960–61, and General Council of British Shipping 1960–61. President, Inst. of Marine Engineers 1966–67. *Address:* Scotnish Tayvallich, Lochgilphead, Argyll PA31 8PG.

**MacVEAGH, Lincoln.** American diplomat. *B.* 1890. *Educ.* Groton School; Harvard (AB); Sorbonne, Paris. *M.* (1) 1917, Margaret Charlton Lewis (*Dec.*); (2), 1955, Mrs. Virginia Ferrante Coats. *Dau.* Mrs. Samuel E. Thorne, step children. *S.* Colin L. *Daus.* Mrs. H. Reynolds, Gloria. *Career:* Secretary to the Director, Boston Art Museum, 1912–13; with U.S. Steel Products Co., 1914–15; Henry Holt Co., 1915–17, 1919–23; served in World War I, First Lieutenant, later Captain & Major, A.E.F.; cited by General Pershing for 'exceptionally meritorious and conspicuous services', 1918; Pres. Dial Press Inc., 1923–33; En. Ex. & Min. Plen. to Greece, 1933–41, to Iceland, 1941, to Union of South Africa, 1942; Amb. Ex. & Plen. to Greece & Yugoslavia, 1943, to Greece, 1944, to Portugal, 1948–52, to Spain, 1952–53. Represented Harvard at 700th anniversary of the Univ. of Salamanca, 1953; Grand Cross of George I (Greece), 1954; Hon. Citizen of Athens & Arcadia; DPhil, h.c., Univ. of Athens; Trustee, American School of Classical Studies; Hon. Fellow, Archaeological Socy. of Athens. *Member* (and former Trustee): Archaeological Socy. of America; Socy. of Mayflower Descendants; Stewart Socy. of Edinburgh; Council on Foreign Relations; Rotary (Hon. Lisbon); Phi Beta Kappa. *Publications:* New Champlin Cyclopedia for Young Folks (editor), 1924, 1925, 1930; Poetry from the Bible (1951); Greek Journey (1937), (with Margaret MacVeagh). *Clubs:* Jefferson Islands Country; Century, University (N.Y.C.); Metropolitan (Washington); New Canaan Country. *Address:* Avenida Biarritz 12, 1 Direito, Estoril, Portugal.

**McVITTIE, Wilfrid Wolters**, CMG. British diplomat. *B.* 1906. *Educ.* King's College, University of London. *M.* 1938, Harriett Morna Wilson. *S.* 1. *Daus.* 2. *Career:* Entered Japan Consular Service, 1930; Consul, Yokohama, 1938; 1st Secretary (Commercial) Buenos Aires, 1946; Counsellor (Commercial) Mexico City, 1948; Counsellor (Commercial) and Consul-General, British Embassy, Lisbon 1952–57. Ambassador to the Dominican Republic 1958–62. *Address:* White House, Itchenor, Sussex.

**McWHIRTER, William Buford.** American. *B.* 1918. *Educ.* Univ. of California (BA Econ *magna cum laude* 1939). *M.* 1956, Catherine E. Forbes. *Career:* With International Business Machines (26 years) 1940–65 (Field Mgr., San Francisco 1949, Field District Mgr., N.Y.C. 1956, Gen. Mgr. Supplies Div. 1957, Pres. Data Systems Div. 1959, Corporate Dir. of Organization 1962, Pres. Industrial Products Div. 1964). Corporate Executive till 1965; Consultant 1965—; Dir. Itel Corp. San Francisco; MHC Corp. New York; Amdahl Corp. Calif. *Member:* Phi Beta Kappa; Sales and Marketing Executives (Pres. San Francisco Club 1955–56); Trustee, Museum,

Northern Arizona. *Clubs:* Siwanoy (Bronxville, N.Y.); Phoenix (Ariz.); Desert Forest (Carefree); Army-Navy (Arlington, Va.); Pauma Valley (Calif.). *Address:* Box 981, Carefree, Arizona, 85331, U.S.A.

**MacWILLIAM, Robert Herman.** South African mining engineer. *B.* 1912. *Educ.* University of the Witwatersrand (BA, BSc, Eng.). *M.* 1937, Esmé Olga Muller. *Daus.* Jennifer and Diana. *Career:* mining engineer, Union Corp. Ltd. 1934–48; Gen. Mgr., St. Helena Gold Mines 1948–53; Consulting Engineer 1953–57, London Manager 1957–67, Dir., Union Corp. Ltd. 1960—; Chmn., Man. Dir., Union Corp. (U.K.) Ltd. 1967–72; Chmn., Union Corporation (U.K.) Ltd. since 1972. *Address:* Union Corporation (U.K.) Ltd., Princes House, 95 Gresham Street, London, E.C.2.

**MADARIKAN, Charles Olusoji.** *B.* 1922. *Educ.* St. Paul's Breadfruit School, Lagos; C.M.S. Grammar School; Higher College, Yaba. *Career:* called to Bar (Lincoln's Inn) 1948. Crown Counsel, Nigeria 1949–56; Senior Crown Counsel 1956–58; Acting Legal Secretary, Southern Cameroons 1957–58; Chief Registrar, Federal Supreme Court of Nigeria 1958–59; Director of Public Prosecutions, Western Region of Nigeria 1959–60; Judge, High Court of Western Nigeria 1960–67; Justice, Supreme Court of Nigeria. 1967–72; Pres. Western State Court of Appeal 1972–75; Justice, Supreme Court of Nigeria 1975–77; Part-time member, Police Service Commission since 1977. *Publications:* Selected Judgments of the Federal Supreme Court, Nigeria, 1957 and 1958; Brett and McLean's Criminal Law and Procedure of the six Southern States of Nigeria. *Address:* 6 Cole Street, Suru Lore, Yaba, Nigeria.

**MADDEN, Vincent Hamilton.** Irish. *B.* 1913. *Educ.* Mayfield College (Sussex, England) and Trinity College, Dublin (DPA). *M.* 1961, Phyllis Flynn. *S.* Gareth. *Dau.* Grainne. *Career:* Formerly employed in Comhlucht Siuicre Eireann, Dublin 1934–47. Marketing Director, Gateaux Ltd. Finglas, (Dublin) 1947–72. Director, Boulevard Foods Ltd., and R. W. Moore (Dublin) Ltd. 1960–72. Council Member, Irish Management Institute 1960–72; Exec. Cttee Member 1969–72, Consult. Cttee member 1970–72; Admin. Dir. Donald Davies Group of Cos. since 1972; Founder & Man. Dir., Integ International Ltd. 1976. *Member:* (Assoc.) Certified Accountants. *Club:* Rotary (Dublin). *Address:* 'Cloonagh', Leopardstown Road, Foxrock, Co. Dublin, Eire.

**MADDISON, Angus.** British economist. *B.* 1926. *Educ.* Cambridge University (BA 1947, MA 1951); Research Fellow; McGill University 1949–50, and Johns Hopkins University 1950–51. *Career:* Consultant with FAO, ECAFE, Twentieth Century Fund, and to governments of Pakistan, Ghana, Brazil and Greece. Lecturer in Economics, St. Andrews Univ. 1951–52; Senior Economist OEEC 1953–58. Head. Economics Div. OEEC 1958–62; Dir. OECD Development Dept. 1963; Fellow OECD Development Centre 1964–66; Research Director, Twentieth Century Fund Project on Economic Policy, 1966–69. Visiting Professor, Univ. of California Berkeley, 1968; Harvard Univ. 1969–71; Head, Central Analysis Division OECD. *Publications:* Economic Growth in the West (London 1964); Foreign Skills and Technical Assistance in Economic Development (Paris 1965); Foreign Skills and Technical Assistance in Greek Development (Paris 1966); Economic Growth in Japan and the U.S.S.R. (London 1969); Economic Progress and Policy in Developing Countries (London 1970); Class Structure and Economic Growth (London 1972). Contributor to several other books and numerous articles in academic and financial journals. *Address:* c/o OECD, 2 Rue Andre Pascal, Paris 16.

**MADDISON, Hon. John Clarkson.** Australian. *B.* 1921. *Educ.* University of Sydney (BA; LLB). *M.* 1953, Suzanne Berry-Smith. *S.* Richard. *Daus.* Deborah and Louise. *Career:* Solicitor, Supreme Court of N.S.W. 1948–75; Barrister since 1975. Dep. Leader of the Opposition in the State of N.S.W. since May 1976; Minister of Justice for N.S.W., May 1965–May 1976; Attorney-General for N.S.W., Jan. 1975–May 1976. Member, Legislative Assembly of N.S.W. Member Liberal Party of Australia; Macquarie Univ. Council. *Clubs:* Australian, Hornsby Bowling; Hornsby R.S.L. *Address:* 8 Bangalla Street, Warrawee, N.S.W.; and *office* Parliament House, Macquarie Sq., Sydney, N.S.W., Australia.

**MADGWICK, Sir Robert Bowden, OBE, MEc, DPhil, D.Litt, LLD, FACE.** *B.* 1905. *Educ.* N. Sydney Boys' High; Univ. of Sydney; Balliol Coll., Oxford; Rockefeller Research Fellow 1933–35; Harbison-Higginbotham Scholar Univ. Melbourne 1936. *M.* (1) 1937, Ailsa M. Aspinall (dec.). *Daus.* 3. (2) 1971, Mrs. Nance McGrath. *Career.* Lectr., Economic Hist. 1936; secy., Extension Board Univ. Sydney 1937; Dir. of Army Education 1941–46; Lt.-Col. 1941, Col. 1944, R. of O. 1946, Retd. List 1961, Col. Commdt. R.A.A. Educ. Corps. 1962–68; Vice-Chancellor Univ. of New England 1954–66; Chmn., Australian Broadcasting Commission 1967–73. Warden New England Univ. Coll. 1947–54. Chmn., N.S.W. Adv. Cttee. on Cultural Grants 1968–75. *Publications:* Immigration into Eastern Australia 1788–1851; Outline of Australian Economics (with E. R. Walker). *Clubs:* Killara Golf (Sydney). *Address:* 3 Collins Road, St. Ives, New South Wales 2075, Australia.

**MAEGRAITH, Prof. Brian Gilmore,** CMG, TD, MA. Australian emeritus professor of tropical medicine. *B.* 26 Aug. 1907. *Educ.* St. Peter's School, Adelaide; St. Mark's Coll., Adelaide Univ. (MB), Magdalen and Exeter Colls., Oxford (MA, BSc, D.Phil.); FRCP (London); FRCPE; FRACP; DSc. (Bangkok); MD (Athens). *M.* 1934, Lorna Langley. *S.* Michael Patrick. *Career:* Rhodes Scholar, Oxford 1930; Beit Memorial Fellow 1932–34; Medical Fellow, Exeter College, Oxford 1934–44; Dean of the Faculty of Medicine, Oxford 1938–44; Hon. Fellow, St. Mark's College, Adelaide 1956; Lt.-Col. R.A.M.C. 1939–45; O.C. Army Malaria Research Unit; Medical Research Council Committee on Malaria 1943–46; Perm. member (ex-Pres.) Council of Institutes of Tropical Med. of Europe. Prof. of Trop. Med., Sch. of Trop. Med., Liverpool Univ., 1944–72; Dean of School of Tropical Medicine, Liverpool Univ., 1946–75; Honorary Consultant Physician, Royal Infirmary, Liverpool; Nuffield Consultant in Tropical Medicine to British West Africa 1949–54; Tropical Medicine Research Board, Medical Research Council 1960–69; Maurice Bloch Lecturer Glasgow 1970; Heath Clark Lecturer London 1970; Craig (bicentennial) Lecturer, U.S.A. 1976; member, Council, Royal Society of Tropical Medicine and Hygiene since 1946; Vice-President, Royal Soc. of Trop. Med. 1949–51, Pres. 1969–71. *Awards:* Chalmers Gold Medal 1951; Le Prince Medal, American Soc. of Tropical Medicine 1954; Bernhard Nocht Medal (Germany) 1957. Mary Kingsley Medal, Liverpool School of Tropical Medicine 1973. Membre d'honneur de Soc. Belge de Med. Tropicale; Hon. Member, Society of Tropical Medicine, U.S.A. and Germany. *Publications:* Pathological Processes in Malaria and Blackwater Fever (1948); Clinical Tropical Diseases (with A. R. D. Adams, 6th edition 1975). Exotic Diseases in Practice (1965); One World (1973); numerous papers in technical and scientific journals on anthropology, physiology, medicine and tropical medicine. *Address:* 23 Eaton Road, Cressington Park, Liverpool 19.

**MAG, Arthur.** American lawyer. *B.* 1896. *Educ.* Yale University (AB 1918; JD 1920). *M.* (1) 1925, Selma Rothenberg (dec. 1930), and (2) 1932, Charline Weil. *Daus.* Josephine Selma (Randall) and Helen Louise (Wolcott). *Career:* Senior partner of firm of Stinson, Mag, Thomson, McEvers & Fizzell, Kansas City, Mo. 1924—. Member, National Advisory Mental Health Council for the U.S. Dept. of Health, Welfare, and Education, Washington, D.C. Oct. 1955–59; Pres. Greater Kansas City Mental Health Foundation 1952–56; Member, Exec. Cttee & Director; Host International Inc., Los Angeles; Chmn. Bd., Schutte Lumber Co., Kansas City. Director (companies located in Kansas City unless stated otherwise); The First National Bank of Kansas City, First National Charter Corp.; FLM Industries Inc.; Gold Inc. (Denver); Helzberg Diamond Shops; Hereford Redevelopment Corp.; The Marley Co.; Price Candy Co.; Rothschild & Sons Inc.; Standard Milling Co.; Rival Manufacturing Co.; Z Bar Cattle Company; Dir.-Sec., The L.B. Price Mercantile Co., St. Louis; Hon. Fellow, Amer. Coll of Hosp. Admin. Trustee: Univ. of Kansas City; The Menninger Foundn. (Topeka, Kansas); Carrie J. Loose Trust, Harry Wilson Loose Trust; Edward F. Swinney Trust; Kansas City Assn. of Trusts and Foundns.; Frederic Ervine McIlvain Trust; Sadie Danciger Charitable Trust; Carl W. Allendoerfer Memorial Library; Menorah Foundation for Medical Research; Menorah Medical Center (Hon. Chmn. Bd.); Midwest Research Inst.; Missouri Bar Foundation. *Member:* American, Missouri and Kansas City Bar Assns., Assn. of the Bar of the City of New York; Lawyers Association of Kansas City. Fellow, American Bar Foundation. *Awards:* Order of Coif (Hon., Univ. of Missouri) 1964; Mr. 'Kansas City' Award 1964; Brotherhood Citation, Nat. Conference of Christians & Jews, 1965; Missouri Academy of Squires; Law Day Award (Univ. Mo-Kansas City) 1966; Chancellor's Medallion 1966; Pro. Meritus Award (Rockhurst Coll., Kansas City) 1960; Hon. LLD (Univ. Mo-Kansas City) 1974. Civic Service Award 1975, Hebrew Acad. of Greater Kansas City; Greater Kansas City Mental Health Foundation Award, 1976.

*Publications:* Trusteeship—A/D (1948). Republican. *Clubs:* Yale, Lawyers (N.Y.C.); Kansas City Oakwood Country (Kansas City); Standard (Chicago); Graduate (New Haven); Reform (London). *Address:* Suite 2100, Ten Main Center, P.O. Box 19251, Kansas City, Mo. 64141, U.S.A.

**MAGEE, Bryan, MP.** British Politician. *B.* 1930. *Educ.* Christ's Hospital; Lycée Hôche, Versailles; Keble Coll., Oxford—MA (Open Scholar; Pres. of the Oxford Union); Yale. *M.* 1954, Ingrid Söderlund (Diss.). *Dau.* 1. *Career:* English Asst., Folk Univ., Lund, Sweden 1953–54; Visitor's Officer, British Council, Oxford 1954–55; Fellow in Philosophy, Yale Univ. 1955–56; Brewer, Arthur Guiness, Son & Co. 1956–57; Author, Critic & Broadcaster since 1957; Member, Critics' Circle (Music & Drama Sections) since 1970; Lecturer in Philosophy, Balliol Coll., Oxford 1970–71; Visiting Fellow, All Souls Coll., Oxford 1973–74; Regular Columnist on *The Times* 1974–76; Labour MP for Leyton since 1974. *Member:* Society of Authors; Critics' Circle (Council Member); British Soc. for the Philosophy of Science; Aristotelian Soc.; Oxford Philosophy Soc. *Publications:* Crucifixion & other Poems (1951); Go West, Young Man (1958); To Live in Danger (1960); The New Radicalism (1962); The Democratic Revolution (1964); Towards 2000 (1965); One in Twenty (1966); The Television Interviewer (1966); Aspects of Wagner (1968); Modern British Philosophy (1971); Popper (1973); Facing Death (1977). *Clubs:* Garrick; Savile; Reform; Elizabethan Club of Yale Univ. *Address:* 12 Falkland House, Marloes Road, London W8 5LF; and House of Commons, London SW1A 0AA.

**MAGINNIS, John Edward, JP.** British politician, farmer. *B.* 1919. *Educ.* Primary and Technical. *M.* 1964, Dorothy Rusk. *S.* 1. *Daus.* 4. *Career:* Served with Royal Ulster Constabulary, 1939–45; Group Sec. North Armagh Group, Ulster Farmers Union, 1956–59; Justice of the Peace, Co. Armagh since 1956; Member of Parliament, Ulster Unionist 1959–74. *Member:* Co. Armagh Agricultural Society; Commonwealth Parliamentary Assn. *Clubs:* Ulster. London. *Address:* Mandeville Hall, 68 Mullahead Road, Tandragee, Craigavon, Co. Armagh, N. Ireland.

**MAGISTRATI, Count Massimo.** Ambassador of Italy. *B.* 1899. *Educ.* Doctor of Jurisprudence. *M.* 1945, Cristiana Schütte. *S.* Pierandrea. *Daus.* Maria Luisa; Alessandra. Minister in Bulgaria 1940–43 and in Switzerland 1943–45; Vice-Deleg. for the Marshall Plan in Italy 1949–52; Dir.-General for Political Affairs in Foreign Office, Rome 1954–58; Amb. to Turkey 1958–61, to U.A.R. 1961–65; Administrator of the Banco de Roma, Rome; Chmn., of the Centro per la Riconciliazione Mn Terrazionale (Rome). *Publication:* Italia a Berlino (Mondadori, Milan, 1956). *Club:* Circolo della Caccia (Rome). *Address:* Via S. Nicola dei Cesarini 3, Rome, Italy.

**MAGNUSON, Warren Grant.** U.S. senator. *B.* 12 Apr. 1905. *Educ.* University of North Dakota; University of Washington. *Member* (Democrat), U.S. House of Representatives 1936–44; U.S. Senator from Washington since 1944. *Address:* 127 Senate Office Building, Washington, D.C. 20510, U.S.A.

**MAHGOUB, Mohamed Ahmed.** Sudanese. *B.* 1908. *Educ.* School of Engineering of the Old Gordon Memorial College. *Career:* Joined Govt. Service as Civil Engineer in Dept. of Public Works; joined School of Law and graduated as Legal Asst., and later became Provincial Judge; resigned from Judiciary and became an advocate. A founder of the Graduates Congress. Became Secy. of the Independence Front; toured European countries propagating the independence of the Sudan. Leader of the Opposition in the first Sudanese Parliament. Led delegation to U.N. to apply for membership. Minister of Foreign Affairs 1956-58, 1964–65; Prime Minister 1965–66, 1967–69. *Publications:* The Death of a World; Intellectual Trends in the Sudan; Story of a Heart; A Heart and Ordeals (the last two are books of verse; all were written in Arabic). *Address:* 60c Prince's Gate, Exhibition Road, London S.W.7.

**MAHLER, Dr. Halfdan T.** Danish Health official (WHO). *B.* 1923. *Educ.* High School, Randers, Denmark; Univ Copenhagen MD (1948); Univ Copenhagen EOPH (1956). *M.* 1957, Ebba Fischer Simonsen. *S.* 2. *Career:* Asst. Doctor Haellnaes Sanatorium, Sweden 1948, Amtssygehuset Gentofte, Copenhagen 1948–49; Planning Officer, Intern. TB campaign, Ecuador 1949–51; Sen. WHO officer, National TB Programme India 1958–60; Vis. Prof. WHO assisted post-grad. TB training courses Rome and Prague 1961; Chief Medical Officer TB WHO Geneva 1961–69; Dir. Project Systems Analysis, WHO, Geneva 1969–70; Asst. Dir. Gen WHO Geneva 1970–73; Dir.-Gen. WHO Geneva since 1973. *Awards:* Hon. Dr. of Laws, Univ. of Nottingham; Hon. Fellow: Faculty of Community Medicine of the Royal Colleges of Physicians of the UK., Royal Soc. of Medicine (London); Indian Soc. for Malaria & other Communicable Diseases (Delhi); Assoc. Mem., Belgian Soc. of Tropical Medicine; Membre d'honneur: Société Médicale de Genève, Union International Contre la Tuberculose; Jana Evangelisty Purkyne Medal (Presidential Award), Prague; Charles Univ. Medal, Prague; Comenius Univ. Gold Medal, Bratislava; Carlo Forlanini Gold Medal, Federazione Italiana Contro la Tubercolosi e le Malattie Polmonari Sociali, Rome. *Publications:* Essais d'application de la recherche operationnelle dans la lutte antituberculese; The Development of Models for TB Control; and articles relating to epidemiology, control of TB, Application of systems analysis to health care. *Address:* 12 chemin du Pont-Céard, 1290 Versoix, Switzerland; and *office* World Health Organization, Avenue Appia, 1211 Geneva 27, Switzerland.

**MAIONE, Salvatore.** Italian industrialist. Knight of the Italian Republic. *B.* 1920. *Educ.* Dr. in Economic and Commercial Sciences. *M.* 1948, Iside Ferretti. *S.* 1. *Dau.* 1. *Career:* President, Industrial Association of the Provinces 1950; member, Committee of the Chamber of Commerce, Industry and Agriculture (industrial section), Ragusa 1953; member, Council of the Provincial Association of Tourism 1953; Member, Discount Commission of the Banco de Sicilia 1955; Director, Molini & Pastifici Maoine (mills and pastry), Comiso. *Club:* Rotary (Ragusa). *Address: office* Via Milano /1428, Comiso, Italy.

**MAITLAND, Sir Donald (James Dundas),** GCMG, OBE. British Diplomat. *B.* 1922. *Educ.* George Watson's College; Edinburgh Univ.—MA. *M.* 1950, Jean Marie Young. *S.* 1. *Dau.* 1. *Career:* Army Service 1941–47; Joined Diplomatic Service 1947; Consul, Amara 1950; British Embassy, Baghdad 1950–53; Private Sec. to Minister of State, Foreign Office 1954–56; Dir., Middle East Centre for Arab Studies, Lebanon 1956–60; Counsellor, British Embassy, Cairo 1963–65; Head of News Dept., Foreign Office 1965–67; Principal Private Sec. to Foreign & Commonwealth Secretary 1967–69; Ambassador to Libya 1969–70; Chief Press Sec. to Prime Minister 1970–73; Perm. Rep. to UN 1973–74; Dep. Under-Sec. of State, FCO 1974–75; Member of British Overseas Trade Board 1974–75; UK Perm. Rep. to the European Communities since 1975. *Decorations:* Knight Grand Cross, Order of St. Michael & St. George; Knight Bachelor; Officer Order of the British Empire. *Clubs:* Travellers. *Address:* Avenue Henri Pirenne 21, 1180 Brussels, Belgium; and *office* Rond-Point Schuman 6, 1040 Brussels, Belgium.

**MAJERUS, Pierre.** Former Luxembourg diplomat. *B.* 29 Sept. 1909. *Educ.* University of Paris (D en D). *M.* 1945. Andrée Wagner. *S.* Paul, Marcel, Hubert. *Dau.* Gabrielle. *Career:* Practised as a barrister in Luxembourg 1933; Attaché, Ministry of Foreign Affairs 1936, Secretary of Legation 1944, Counsellor 1945; Chamberlain to H.R.H. the Grand Duchess of Luxembourg 1946; Chargé d'Affaires, Brussels 1944–47; Chief of the Political Section, Ministry of Foreign Affairs 1948; Delegate to U.N. General Assembly 1949 and 1950; En. Ex. and Min. Plen. to the Federal Republic of Germany and Chief of Luxembourg Military Mission to Berlin 1951; Ambassador to Italy 1961–74. *Publications:* Le Luxembourg Indépendants LÉtat Luxembourgeois; Principes élémentaires de droit public Luxembourgeois. *Address:* 44 rue Emile, Mayrisch, Luxembourg.

**MAJITHIA, Dr. Sir Surendra Singh,** Kt. 1946. Indian Industrialist. *B.* 4 Mar. 1895. *Educ.* Khalsa Collegiate High School & Khalsa College. Amritsar. *M.* 1921, Lady Balbir Kaur (*Dec.*). *Career:* Chairman: Saraya Sugar Mills Private Ltd.; Sardarnagar Block Development Cttee.; Senior Managing Partner: Saraya Surkhi Mill; Director: Punjab & Sind Bank Ltd., Amritsar. Member: Khalsa College Council, Amritsar; Akal College Council, Gursagar; UP Fruit Development Board, Lucknow. President: Chairman etc., of many educational foundations and social activities. Past member various Advisory and Consultative Cttees. Chairman: Lady Parsan Kaur Charitable Trust. Patron, Wrestling Federation of India; Patron, UP Badminton Assoc.; Life Member, International Soc. of Krishna Consciousness; Hon. Member, the Mark Twain Soc., U.S.A. Member, Garden Advisory Cttee, Gorakhpur. *Award:* Hon. DLitt, Gorakhpur, 1970. *Clubs:* Gorakhpur, Nipal (both in Gorakhpur). *Address:* P.O. Sardarnagar, Dist. Gorakhpur, Uttar Pradesh, India.

**MAJOLI, Mario.** *B.* 1906. *Educ.* Univ. of Bologna (Law degree 1927) and Univ. of Pavia (Pol. Sc. degree). *M.* 1934, Emma Viani della Mirandola. *S.* Massimo and Franco. *Dau.* Marina. *Career:* Consul-General Benghazi 1951; Minister Plenipotentiary 1957; Ambassador to Panama 1957; Chairman Fifth Committee, 15th Gen. Assembly, U.N. 1960; Deputy Director-General for Political Affairs, Ministry for Foreign Affairs, Rome 1963; Chairman, *ad hoc* Committee of Experts to examine the finances of U.N. and Specialized Agencies 1966; Ambassador to Canberra 1967–72; Member Adv. Cttee. on Administrative & Budgetary Questions of the United Nations. *Address:* Advisory Committee, Budgetary Questions, U.N. Headquarters, New York 10017, U.S.A.

**MAJOR, Randolph Thomas.** American professor, Research in field of plant and medicinal chemistry and Biochemistry. *B.* 1901. *Educ.* University of Nebraska (AB 1922, MSc 1924), Princeton Univ. (PhD 1927). *M.* 1928, Grace E. Lowe. *S.* Randolph T. Jr. *Daus.* Mary E., Anne C., and Jane W. *Career:* Teacher Albion (Neb.) High School 1922–23; Research Associate, Princeton Univ. 1927–30; Merck & Co., Inc., Dir. of Pure Research 1930–36, Dir. of Research and Development 1936–46, Vice-Pres. (Scientific) 1947–56. Scientific Adviser 1946–67; Adviser to Merck Inst. Therapeutic Research 1967–74; Research Professor of Chemistry Univ. of Connecticut since 1970. *Publications:* In Organic and Medicinal Chemistry. Hon. DSc. Univ. of Nebraska 1949. Medal of Industrial Research Institute 1951. Professor of Chemistry, Univ. of Virginia 1956–67. Research Professor of Chemistry, University of Virginia 1967–70. Republican. *Member:* Amer. Chemical Socy.; American Society of Biological Chemists; American Assn. for Advancement of Science, *Clubs:* Chemists (New York). *Address:* 393 Codfish Falls Road, P.O. Box 433, Storrs, Conn 06268; and *office* Dept. of Chemistry, University of Connecticut, Storrs, Conn., U.S.A.

**MAKINEN, Jussi.** Finnish Diplomat. *B.* 1929. *Educ.* Studies in Neuchâtel, Paris, The Hague and Helsinki; University of Helsinki (Master of Political Sciences). *Career:* Attaché, Ministry of Foreign Affairs of Finland 1950–51; Attaché, Finnish Embassy in Moscow 1951–53; 2nd Secy. Ministry of Foreign Affairs 1953–54; Private Secy. of Dr. Urho Kekkonen, Minister of Foreign Affairs 1954; Press and Cultural Attaché, Finnish Mission in Bonn 1954–59; Chief of Bureau, Ministry of Foreign Affairs 1959–60; Counsellor, Embassy in Paris 1960–63; Ambassador in Algeria, Morocco, Tunisia and Libya 1963–68; Ambassador in Vienna and to the Holy See, Perm. Rep. of Finland to IAEA and UNIDO. *Decorations:* Cmmdr. Finnish White Rose Order 1970; Officer of Finnish Lion Order 1961; Grand Cross of Republic of Tunisia 1965; Grand Cross of Pius IX 1971; Officer of Legion of Honour (France) 1962, Officer of Moroccan Order Ouissam Alaouite 1954; Cross of Merit (GFR) 1958, Grand Cross of Honour in Gold (Austria) 1972. *Publications:* Keskustelen Kekkosen Kanssa (speaking with Kekkonen, 25 years of dialogue) (1974); Several articles in foreign papers on politics including a study about Kissinger and Metternich. *Address:* Puistokatu 3 c 51, 00140 Helsinki 14, Finland; and *office* Untere Donaustrasse 13–15, 1020 Vienna, Austria.

**MALALASEKERA, Gunapala Piyasena,** OBE; Hon. PhD Moscow; Chairman, National Council of Higher Education in Ceylon. *Educ.* MA; PhD; DLitt. (London). *M.* 1933, Lyle Wijewardene. *S.* 3. *Daus.* 3. *Career:* Vice-Principal, Ananda Coll., 1921–23; Principal, Nalanda Coll., 1924–27; Prof. of Pali and Buddhist Civilization, Ceylon Univ. 1927–57; Pres.: Ceylon Socy. of Arts, Ceylon Congr. of Buddhist Assocs.; World Fellowship of Buddhists; Indian Philosophical Congress 1957; Chmn.: Central Adv. Bd. for Education, Ceylon, and National Council for the Welfare of the Deaf and Blind, Ceylon. Ambassador to U.S.S.R., Czechoslovakia, and Poland, and Minister to Roumania 1957–61; Permanent Representative of Ceylon to the United Nations and High Commissioner for Ceylon in Canada 1961–63, and in U.K. 1963–66. *Awards:* Officer, Order of the British Empire; Buddha Sasana Vepulla Hithadhara (Burma); Membre d'honneur de l'Ecole Française d'Extrême Orient (France); Commander, Order of Manisaraphon (Cambodia). *Publications:* The Pali Literature of Ceylon (R.A.S., Great Britain); The Dictionary of Pali Proper Names (2 vols. Humphrey Milford, Oxford); The Buddha and His Teachings (pub. Govt. of Ceylon); The Commentary of the Mahavamsa (Pali Text Soc., England); The Extended Mahavamsa (R.A.S., Ceylon Branch); Editor-in-Chief, The Encyclopedia of Buddhism (to consist of 10 volumes of 1000 pp. each). *Address:* National Council of Higher Education, 202 Buller's Road, Colombo 7, Sri Lanka and 12 Longden Terrace, Colombo 7, Sri Lanka.

**MALCOLM, Dugald,** CMG, CVO, TD. British diplomat. *B.* 1917. *Educ.* Eton and New Coll. Oxford (MA). *M.* 1957, Patricia Atkinson Clark. *Step-dau.* 1, *Dau.* 1. *Career:* Argyll & Sutherland Highlanders 1939–45. Third Secy. Foreign Office 1945; served in Peru, Germany, Korea (Chargé d'Affaires) 1956; Ambassador at the Court of Luxembourg 1966–70; Panama City 1971–75: Minister to the Holy See 1975–77. H.M. Vice-Marshal of the Diplomatic Corps 1957–65. Member of the Queen's Bodyguard for Scotland. *Member:* Oriental Ceramic Society (London). *Clubs:* Travellers'; M.C.C. (London). *Address:* c/o Foreign and Commonwealth Office, London, S.W.1.

**MALENBAUM, Wilfred.** U.S. Professor of economics. *B.* 1913. *Educ.* Harvard Univ. (AB 1934; MA 1935; PhD 1941). *M.* (1) 1950, Josephine Orenstein (dec.). *S.* Bruce T. and Ronald G. *Dau.* Roxanne F. (2) 1976, Gloria B. Balaban. *Career:* Dir., Chief Div. of Investment & Development, U.S. Dept. of State 1948—; U.S. Official Representative, Colombo Plan Conf., Karachi 1952; Director, India Project, Massachussetts Inst. of Technology 1953—; Director, M.I.T. Field Team, India 1954–55–56; U.S. Advisor to U.S. Delegations to UNNRA 1943; ECOSOC 1948–49–50; ECLA 1951; Professor of Economics Univ. of Pennsylvania since 1959; U.S. Delegate, SEATO Conf., Philippines 1960; Visiting Prof., Univ. of Hawaii, Summer 1961; Harvard Univ. 1963 and 1964; Prof. Univ. of Heidelberg, Süd Asien Institute 1966. Consultant, Government of India, 1962, and International Bank Coal Transport Study Team in India 1963–64; Ford Foundation Faculty Fellow 1964–65. Member, National Council, International Health; Nat. Science Foundation, Indian Council Scientific & Industrial Research, Exchange Scientist 1971; Health-Economic Mission, South Asia, July–Aug. 1972; Consultant, National Commission, Materials Policy 1972–73; Consultant, World Health Organisation, Geneva 1976, 1977; Member, Scientific Working Group on Epidemiology 1977—. *Member:* Phi Beta Kappa; Amer. Economics Assn.; Socy. for Economic Development; Assn. of Asian Studies; Asia Society. *Publications:* Books: The World Wheat Economy 1885–1939 (1953); India and China: Development Contrasts (1956); East and West in India's Development (1959); Prospects for Indian Development (1962); Modern India's Economy (1971); World Resources Requirements in the Year 2000 (1973); many articles in professional journals. Democrat. *Club:* Merion Civic. *Address:* 527 South 41st Street, Philadelphia, Pa.; and *office* Robert L. McNeil Building, University of Pennsylvania, Philadelphia, Pa., U.S.A.

**MALHERBE, Ernst Gideon.** South African educationist. Principal and Vice-Chancellor, Univ. of Natal, Pietermaritzburg and Durban (1945–65). *B.* 1895. *Educ.* Stellenbosch Univ. (BA Hons.; MA Philosophy); Columbia Univ. (MA; PhD); studied at Oxford, The Hague and Amsterdam; Hon. LLD, Cambridge; Queens; Melbourne; McGill; Cape Town; Rhodes; Natal; Witwatersrand; Hon. MA, Sydney; Hon. LLD St. Andrews 1972. *M.* 1922, Janie A. Nel. *S.* 3. *Dau.* 1. *Career:* Teacher, Cape Town Training College. Lecturer in Educational Psychology, University of Stellenbosch; Senior Lecturer in Education, University of Cape Town, 5 years; Chief Investigator, Education Section, Carnegie Poor White Commission of Research, 1928–32; member, Government to investigate Native Education in S.A., 1935; Director, National Bureau of Education and Social Research for S.A. 1929–39; Sec., Govt. Commission on Medical Training in S.A., 1938; Director of Census and Statistics for Union of S.A., 1939–40; Director of Military Intelligence, S. African Army, and Director, Army Education Services, 1940–45; member, Social and Economic Planning Council, 1946–52; of National Council for Social Research, 1946–50; Chairman, National War Histories Committee, 1945–49; President, S.A Association for the Advancement of Science, 1950–51; Member, Financial Relations Commission 1960–64; S.A. Institute of Race Relations, 1966–67. *Award:* Biesheuvel Medal for Study of Man 1969. *Publications:* Education in South Africa 1652–1922 (1925); Education and the Poor White (1929); numerous articles in educational and scientific journals; Carnegie Commission's Poor White Report on Education (1932); Education in a Changing Empire (1932); Educational Adaptations in a Changing Society (Editor) (1937); Entrance Age of University Students in Relation to Success (1938); Whither Matric? (1938); Educational and Social Research in South Africa (1939); Race Attitudes and Education (1946); Universities and the Advancement of Science (1951); Die Outonomie van ons Universiteite en Apartheid (1957); Education for Leadership in Africa (1960); Problems of School Medium in a Bilingual Country (1962). Into the 70's; Education and the

Development of South Africa's Resources (1966); The Need for Dialogue (1967); The Nemesis of Docility (1968); Bantu Manpower & Education (1969); Education in South Africa 1923–75 (1977). *Address:* By-die-See, Salt Rock, Natal, South Africa.

**MALIK, Charles Habib.** Lebanese philosopher, educator and diplomat. Distinguished Prof. of Philosophy (Emeritus), American Univ. of Beirut. *B.* 1906. *Educ.* Amer. Tripoli Boy's High School, Amer. Univ. of Beirut (BA 1927). Harvard (MA and PhD 1937) and Univ. of Freiburg (Germany). *M.* 1941, Eva Badr. *S.* Michael Habib Charles. *Career:* Teaching and Admin. positions, Amer. Univ. of Beirut 1927–76 (Dean, Graduate Studies 1955–60; Distinguished Prof. of Philosophy 1962–76); Visiting Prof. Dartmouth Coll. and Harvard Summer School 1960; Univ. Prof., Amer. Univ., Washington, D.C. 1961 and 1962. Fellow, Institute for Advanced Studies, Univ. of Notre Dame, 1969. En. Ex. and Min. Plen. to U.S.A. 1945–53, and to Cuba 1946–55; Ambdr. to U.S.A. 1953–55. Signatory for Lebanon: U.N. Charter 1945, Japanese Peace Treaty 1951. Mem. sometime Chmn., Lebanese Deleg. to U.N. 1945–54 (Chmn. 1956–58); Chmn. Third Cttee. U.N. Gen. Assembly 1948–49; Pres. 13th Session Gen. Assembly 1958–59; Mem. Security Cncl. 1953–54 (Pres. Feb. 1953 and Jan., Dec. 1954); Mem. ECOSOC 1946–49 (Pres. 1948); Mem. U.N. Human Rights Commn. 1947–54 (Chmn. Commn. 1951–52); Rep. Lebanon Internat. Bank Fund and UNESCO various times 1947–52; Delegation Bandung Conf. 1955. Minister for Foreign Affairs Lebanon 1956–58; for Natl. Education and Fine Arts 1956–57; Member of Parliament 1957–60;Pres., World Council of Christian Education 1967–71; Vice-Pres., United Bible Societies 1966–72. *Publications:* War and Peace (1950); Problem of Asia (1951); Problem of Coexistence (1955); Christ and Crisis (1962); Man in the Struggle for Peace (1963); The Wonder of Being (1973); author of many books in Arabic; contributor to parts of books and to numerous American, European and Near Eastern magazines. Decorated by governments of Lebanon, Italy, Jordan, Syria, Iraq, Cuba, Iran, Brazil, Dominican Repub., Austria, Greece and Nationalist China. Hon. Degrees: 50 Universities and Colleges, including Princeton, Notre Dame, Brown, Harvard, Yale, Columbia, Georgetown, California (L.A.), St. Mary's (Halifax, Canada), Freiburg, Fordham, Williams, Dartmouth, Boston, etc. *Fellow:* A.A.A.S., Amer. Geog. Socy. *Member:* Amer. Philos. Assn., Amer. Philos. Socy., Metaphysics Socy. of Amer., Amer. Pol. Science Assn., Amer. Socy. Internat. Law, Internat. Law Assn., Internat. Pol. Science Assn., Société Européenne de Culture, Assn. Mondiale de la Culture. Vice-Pres., United Bible Societies; Pres., World Council of Christian Education; Grand First Magistrate, Holy Orthodox Church. *Clubs:* Harvard, Century (N.Y.C.); Cosmos (Washington). *Address:* Harvard Club, 27 West 44th Street, New York City, U.S.A.; and American University, Beirut, Lebanon.

**MALIK, Gunwantsingh Jaswantsingh.** Indian Diplomat. *B.* 1921. *Educ.* Univ. of Bombay; Gujarat Coll., BSc; Univ. of Hamburg; Univ. of Zurich; Univ. of Cambridge, BA & MA. *M.* 1948, Gurkirat Kaur, née Singh. *S.* 2. *Career:* Physicist with British Industrial Plastics, Birmingham 1941–42; Technical Officer, RAF 1943–46; Joined Indian Foreign Service 1947; Second Sec. in Brussels 1948–50 & Addis Ababa 1950; Under-Sec., Min. External Affairs, Govt. of India 1950–52; First Sec. & CDA in Buenos Aires 1952–56 & Tokyo 1956–59; Commercial Counsellor and Asst. Commissioner, Singapore 1959–63; Dir., Min. of Commerce, Govt. of India 1963–64; Joint Sec., Min. of External Affairs 1964–65; Amb. to the Philippines 1965–68, to Senegal and concurrently to Mauretania, the Gambia, Ivory Coast and Upper Volta 1968–70, to Chile and concurrently to Peru, Ecuador and Colombia 1970–74; Amb. to Thailand since 1975; Member, Indian Delegation to ECAFE 1965, Group of 77 1971, Governing Body of UNDP 1971, UNCTAD III 1972, ESCAP 1975, and ESCAP 1976 when he was Chmn. of Technical and and Drafting Cttee. *Clubs:* National Liberal Club, London; Delhi Gymkhana Club, New Delhi; Royal Bangkok Sports Club, Bangkok. *Address:* 63 Soi Prompongse (39), Sukhumvit, Bangkok, Thailand; and *office* 139 Pan Road, Bangkok, Thailand.

**MALIK, Hon. Sri Bidhubhusan,** MA, LLD. Indian judge. *B.* 11 Jan. 1895. *M.* 1916, Leelavati Mitra. *S.* Sudhibhusan, Jyotibhusan. Advocate, High Court, Allahabad 1919. *Career:* Called to Bar, Lincoln's Inn 1923; Senior Advocate, Supreme Court of India; member, Judicial Committee, Benares State 1941–44; Special Counsel for Income Tax Department 1943–44; Puisne Judge, High Court, Allahabad 1944–47; Chief Justice, High Court, Uttar Pradesh (excepting Mar. and Apr. 1949 when he acted as Governor) 1947–55; member, Constitutional Commission for Fed. of Malaya 1956–57 and Air Transport Council of India 1955–Mar. 1962; Constitutional Adviser to Jomo Kenyatta and Kenya African National Union at Constitutional Conference, Lancaster House, London 1962; Commnr. for Linguistic Minorities 1957–62; Constitutional expert, U.N. Mission to the Congo 1962; Constitution Adviser to Govt. of Mauritius 1965; Vice-Chancellor, University of Calcutta 1962–68; Life member Calcutta Univ. Senate; Mem. Bd. of Dirs., Ewing Christian Coll., Allahabad; Pres., Iswar Saran Degree Coll., Allahabad; Pres., Jagat Tarran Degree Coll., Allahabad. *Address:* 23, Muir Road, Allahabad 1, 21101 Uttar Pradesh, India.

**MALIK, Yakov Alexandrovitch.** Soviet diplomat; *B.* 1906. *Educ.* Kharkov Institute of Economics; Institute of Diplomatic and Consular Staffs. *Career:* before 1935 worked in economic sphere in Ukraine; in People's Commissariat of Foreign Affairs 1937–39; Counsellor, U.S.S.R. Embassy, Tokyo 1939–42; Amb. Ex. and Plen. to Japan 1942–45; member, U.S.S.R. Delegation at Foreign Ministers' Conference 1945; Political Adviser to U.S.S.R. Representative on Allied Council for Japan 1946; Deputy Minister of Foreign Affairs 1946–53 and 1960–68; U.S.S.R. Permanent Delegate to Security Council of U.N.O. 1948–52; Amb. Ex. and Plen. to the Court of St. James's, May 1953–Jan. 1960; Perm. Rep. to the U.N., New York 1967–76. *Awards:* Order of Lenin (3 times); Order of October Revolution; Order of the Red Banner of Labour (twice); Medal 'For Valorous Services in War of 1941–45' and others. *Address:* c/o Ministry of Foreign Affairs, Moscow, U.S.S.R.

**MALLABY, Sir George,** KCMG, OBE. Extraordinary Fellow, Churchill College, Cambridge 1964–69. *B.* 1902. *Educ.* Merton Coll., Oxford (MA). *M.* Elizabeth, widow of J. Locker. *Stepson* 1. *Stepdaughters* 2. *Career:* Assistant, St. Edward's School. Oxford 1924–35; Headmaster, St. Bees School, Cumberland 1935–38; District Commissioner for Special Area of West Cumberland 1938–39; Deputy Regional Transport Commissioner, N.W. Region 1939–40; in World War II (Captain 1940; Major 1942; Lt.-Col. 1943; Col. 1945; in Military Secretariat of War Cabinet 1942–45), 1940–45; Secretary, National Trust 1945–46; Asst. Secy., Ministry of Defence 1946–48; Secy.-Gen., Brussels Treaty Defence Organization 1948–50; Under-Secretary, Cabinet Office 1950–54; Secy., War Council and Council of Ministers, Kenya 1954; Dep. Secy., University Grants Committee 1955–57; High Commissioner for United Kingdom in New Zealand 1957–59; First Civil Service Commissioner 1959–64; Chmn., Cttee. on Staffing of Local Govt. 1967; Hong Kong Govt. Salaries Commission 1971. *Publications:* Wordsworth—Extracts from the Prelude with other poems; Wordsworth—A tribute; From My Level; Wordsworth Poems; Each in his Office. *Address:* Down the Lane, Chevington, W. Suffolk.

**MALLALIEU, Joseph Percival William,** MP. British politician. *B.* 1908. *Educ.* Dragon School, Oxford; Cheltenham College; Trinity College, Oxford; University of Chicago. *M.* 1945, Harriet Rita Riddle Tinn. *S.* 1. *Dau.* 1. *Career:* On London newspapers 1933–41; Royal Navy 1942–45; Parliamentary Under Secretary of State for Navy 1964–66; Minister of Defence (Navy) 1966–67; Minister of State, Board of Trade 1967–68; Minister of State, Ministry of Technology 1968–70. Oxford Rugby Blue, 1927; President, Oxford Union, 1930; Commonwealth Fellow, Univ. of Chicago, 1930–32. *Publications:* Rats (1941); Passed to you, Please (1942); Very Ordinary Seaman (1944); Sporting Days (1955); Extraordinary Seaman (1957); Very Ordinary Sportsman (1957). *Club:* Press. *Address:* Village Farm, Boarstall, Aylesbury, Bucks.

**MALLALIEU, Sir Lancelot,** MA, QC. British. Queen's Counsel. *B.* 1905. *Educ.* Dragon School, Oxford; Cheltenham Coll.; Trinity Coll., Oxford. (Hons. Jurisprudence). *M.* 1934, Betty M. O. *S.* Huon Lancelot. *Daus.* Shuna (Askew); Lorraine (Joseph). *Career:* Member of Parliament for Colne Valley, 1931–35 and for Brigg since 1948; Chmn., Channel Tunnel Parly. Cttee. 1950–70; British Group, Inter-Parly. Union 1964–67, Franco-British Parly. Relations Cttee. 1964–71, Hon. Vice Pres. 1971; 2nd Church Estates Commissioner, 1964–70; Sec. Gen., World Assn. of World Federalists, 1965–67 and Parly. Adviser since 1967; 2nd Deputy Chmn. Ways & Means (Dep. Speaker) 1971–73, 1st Deputy 1973–74. *Member:* Inner Temple. *Award:* Chév Légion d'Honneur. *Club:* Royal Cruising. *Address:* 63 Woodstock Close, Oxford OX2 8DD.

**MALLART. José.** Spanish educationist and psychologist. *B.* 10 June 1897. *M.* 1929, Genoveva Palacios. *S.* Alberto.

*Daus.* Rosalia, Julia. *Career:* Educational Director, Institute for Re-education of Invalids 1926–33; Inspector-General of Workers' Education 1933–34; Secretary-General, National Committee of the Organization of Scientific Management 1928–48 (Director Revista de Organizacion Cientifica 1928–36); Chief of Department, Nat. Psychotechnic Institute, Madrid, since 1930; Prof., Social School, Madrid, since 1948; Prof., National Inst. for Rationalization of Labour 1948; Founder, Ibero-Americana Association for Efficiency 1951; Hon. Correspondent to National Institute of Industrial Psychology, London; and of Spanish Society of Hygiene; Council, International Assn. of Applied Psychology 1964—; Editor, Rev Psicologia Gral. y. Aplicada; Chief of Technical Assistance Mission of UNESCO in Ecuador 1957–59. *Publications:* La education activa; La escuela del trabajo; Colonias de educación; Colonias para formación general y profesional y para readaptación social; Elevación moral y material del Campesino; La Orientación profesional en España; La Organización económica internacional y el problema de la paz; El Mundo Economico-social que nace; Orientación funcional y formación profesional; Obras de dignificación humana; Cuadernos de organización cientifica del trabajo; Organización cientifica del trabajo agricola. *Address:* Calle San Julio 5, Madrid 2, Spain.

**MALLEN, Thomas Kevin.** American. *B.* 1905. *Educ.* Rockwell Coll. (Co. Tipperary, Ireland) and Skerry's Coll., Dublin. *M.* 1935, Jane Rice. *Daus.* Jane, Patricia, Janice, Margaret, Therese and Seana. *Career:* In Irish Air Force 1922–25; government service, Dublin 1925–28; represented D. Gestetner Ltd. in Ireland, England, Singapore and Fed. Malay States 1929–31; Department Manager, Heacock Co. Manila 1931–35; General Manager IBM, P.I. 1935–41, and Far East 1945–49. Partner, Ayala Associates, San Francisco 1949–53; Exec. Vice-Pres. and Gen. Manager, Ampex Corp. 1949–53 (Chmn. of Bd. 1953–56). Served in U.S. Army Air Forces 1942–45; Retd. Lt.-Col. USAF Dec. 1945; Vice Pres. Sutro & Co. San Francisco since 1961. *Awards:* Bronze Star (U.S.A.) and Presidential Citation. Regent: Univ. of San Francisco, and Coll. of Notre Dame (Belmont, Calif.). *Clubs:* Elks, Menlo Golf & Country, Palo Alto, University (all in California); American (London); United Services, Milltown Golf, Portmarnock Golf (Dublin). *Address:* 63 Crescent Drive, Palo Alto, Calif.; and *office* 460 Montgomery Street, San Francisco, Calif. 94104. U.S.A.; and Priorsland, Carrickmines, Co. Dublin, Ireland.

**MALLINSON, Frank Courtney.** American electronics executive; Senior Member, Institute of Radio Engineers (SMIRE); Electronics Consultant. *B.* 1909. *Educ.* Portsmouth (Eng.) Univ. (EE) and New York Univ. *M.* 1945, Jean Dorin Gossett. *S.* Frank Courtney, Jr. *Daus.* Constance Louise, Barbara Eugenie, Kathleen Victoria. *Career:* Pres. Dir., National Electronics Laboratories Inc., Washington, D.C. 1946–58; U.S.A.A. Electronics Engineer (developed sea rescue radio transmitter, 'Gibson Girl'; received U.S. Patent) and Communications Engineer (gliders and tow-planes, etc.) 1942–45; Radio Communications Engineer, pioneering in mobile and broadcast (developments include early police two-way radio communicating systems; and broadcast station design and installation) 130–42; since 1958, Consulting Electronics Engineer in U.S.A., South America and Middle East Spec. Communications. *Address:* 9100 Vernonview Drive, Alexandria, Va., U.S.A.

**MALLOUM, Brig.-Gen. Félix.** Chad Army Officer & Politician. *B.* 1932. *Career:* Army Chief of Staff 1971–72; Commander-in-Chief of the Armed Forces 1972–73; Head of State, Pres. of Council of Ministers and Minister of Defence since 1975. *Address:* Council of Ministers, Ndjaména, Chad.

**MALMROS, Frans Jacob.** Swedish. *B.* 1925. *M.* 1947, Eivor Nordenbeldt. *S.* Frans and Peter. *Career:* Managing Director: Malmros Rederi AB 1957—, The Frigoscandia-Group, AB Olson & Wright, AB Atlanttrafik, Munksjo AB, and Swedish Shipowners Association, Skånska Banken, Investment AB Öresund, Sveriges Ångfartygs Assurans Förening, Nordisk Skibsrederforening, Scandinavian Touring AB; Consul to Denmark 1966. *Address:* V. Vallgatan 22, 23100 Trelleborg; and *office* Algatan 27, Trelleborg, Sweden.

**MALONE, Brig. Richard Sankey,** OBE, ED. Canadian journalist. *B.* 1909. *Educ.* Bristol (Eng.), Ridley Coll. (Canada), Univ. of Toronto Schools, and Army Staff Coll. (Grad.). *M.* 1936, Helen Mary Cook. *S.* Robert Nesbit and Richard C. *Dau.* Deirdre Louise. *Career:* Past Pres., Winnipeg Chamb. of Com. Hon. Mgr. Imperial Press Conf. 1950. With Toronto Daily Star 1927–28, Regina Leader-Post 1929–33, Saskatoon Star-Phoenix 1934. Member, Parliamentary Press Gallery, Ottawa 1934–35; Winnipeg Free Press 1936–74; Hon. A.D.C. to Gov.-General of Canada 1946; Publisher & Ed-in-chief, The Globe & The Mail; Chmn. Winnipeg Free Press 1959—; Pres. and Mng. Dir., F.P. Publications Ltd. 1959—; Pres., Vancouver *Sun*; Chmn., Ottawa Journal. Director: Monarch Life Assurance Co., Lethbridge Herald, Victoria Times, Daily Colonist, Canadian Press, Free Press Weekly; Served in World War II; P.P.C.L.I. 1939; Staff Secretary to Ministry of Defence 1940; Staff College; successively Staff Capt. 5th Armoured Division and Brigade Maj. 1st Division; wounded and M.I.D. Sicily Invasion. Personal Liaison Officer to Gen. Montgomery in Italy; Asst. Dir. of Public Relations 21st Army Group and i/c Canadian Pub. Relations, Normandy campaign. Headed Canadian Mission to Gen. MacArthur's HQ Pacific. Among first to enter Paris, Brussels and Tokyo; present at peace signing on U.S.S. Missouri. Founder of Canadian Army newspaper Maple Leaf in Italy, France and Belgium. *Publications:* Missing from the Record. Trustee, Dafoe Foundation; Queen's Own Rifles Regimental Assn.; Hon. Colonel Royal Winnipeg Rifles. Liberal. *Clubs:* Manitoba, St. Charles Country (Winnipeg); Rideau (Ottawa); Toronto Club, Royal Military Inst. *Address:* 183 Dunvegan Rd., Toronto, Canada; and *office* The Globe & Mail, 444 Front St., W. Toronto, Canada.

**MALONE, Thomas Paul.** Canadian Diplomat. *B.* 1915. *Educ.* Univ. of Alberta—BA; National Defence Coll. of Canada. *M.* 1940, Deirdre Lavallette Ingram. *S.* 4. *D.* 1. *Career:* Commonwealth Press Union Exchange Fellowship, Great Britain (Yorkshire Evening News, London Times), Australia (Melbourne Argus, Sydney Sun) 1938–40; Canadian Wartime Information Board Rep. in Australia 1942–46; joined Dept. of External Affairs, Canada 1946; 1st Sec., Washington; Counsellor, The Hague; Ambassador, Iran; High Commissioner, Lagos; Ambassador, Israel; currently Ambassador, Finland. *Member:* Delta Upsilon Fraternity; Assoc. Mem., Inst. of Strategic Studies, London. *Clubs:* Rideau (Ottawa); Helsinki; Golf Club (Finland). *Address:* Rantapolku 22, 00330 Helsinki 33; and *office* P. Esplanadi 25B, 00100 Helsinki 10, Finland.

**MALTERUD, Otto Christian.** Norwegian Diplomat. *B.* 1915. *Educ.* University of Oslo (Nat. Econ.). *M.* 1945 Inger Naestvold. *S.* 1. *Dau.* 1. *Career:* Financial Editor Oslo 1938–41; Secy. Norwegian Embassy Stockholm 1942–45; Financial Attaché, Norwegian Embassy, Stockholm 1945–48; Counsellor Norweg. Deleg. to OEEC, Paris 1948–49; Counsellor Min. of Foreign Affairs, Oslo 1949–52; Counsellor Norwegian Embassy, London 1952–55; Dir.-Gen. the Export Council of Norway, Oslo 1955–71; Norwegian Ambassador to the Hague since 1971. *Awards:* Commander of Royal Order of St Olav; Grand Officer, Orange Nassau Order (Netherlands), Polar Star (Sweden), Order of Merit (Austria), Order of the Sun and the Lion (Iran); Commander, Dannebrog Order (Denmark), Leopold II Order (Belgium), Order of the Lion (Finland); British Coronation Medal (1953). *Publications:* The Economy of Norway during the Occupation (1942); Norway Independent and Occupied (1943). *Club:* Norske Selskab, Oslo. *Address:* Royal Norwegian Embassy, Andries Bickerweg 4, The Hague, Netherlands; and Royal Norwegian Embassy, Prinsessegracht 6a, The Hague, Netherlands

**MALVY, Pierre Gabriel.** *B.* 1909. *Educ.* BLitt.; BPhil. *M.* (1) 1935, Yvonne Brisset. *M.* (2) 1962, Francine Lucchini. *Career:* Chief of Cabinet, Prefecture, Algiers 1943; Sub-Prefect, Algiers, 1944; Sétif 1945; Dreux 1949, and Bastia 1953; Chief of Cabinet, Ministry of the Interior 1954; Prefect of French Guiana 1955; Meuse 1957; Tarn 1959; Conseilleur-pour l'interieur du Gouvernement de Monaco 1967–74; Officer, Legion of Honour (France); Commandeur de Saint-Charles (Monaco). *Address:* Le Giraglia, Ajaccio, Corsica.

**MAMO, Sir Anthony Joseph.** OBE, QC, LLD, BA, KStJ. Maltese Statesman. *B.* 1909. *Educ.* Royal Univ. of Malta. *M.* 1939, Margaret Agius. *S.* 1. *Daus.* 2. *Career:* Member, Statute Law Revision Commission, Malta 1936–42; Crown Counsel, Malta 1942–51; Professor, Criminal Law, Royal Univ., Malta 1943–57; Deputy Attorney-General 1952–54; Attorney-General 1955–57; Chief Justice & Pres. H.M. Court of Appeal 1957–71; Pres. H.M. Constitutional Court 1964–71; Governor General 1971–74; Pres. of the Republic of Malta 1974–76. *Awards:* Officer Most Excellent Order, British Empire: Queen's Counsel: Doctor of Laws; Bachelor of Arts; Knight of Grace, Most Venerable Order St. John of Jerusalem; Hon. D. Litt (Malta); Doctor, Literature (Honoris Causa) Malta; Hon. LL.D. (Libya); Doctor of Laws (Honoris

Causa) Libya. *Publications:* Lectures, Criminal Law, Criminal Procedure. *Clubs:* Casino Maltese; Malta Sports. *Address:* 49 Stella Maris Street, Sliema, Malta.

**MAMO DINGLI, Joseph.** Maltese. *B.* 1919. *Educ.* Lyceum Grammer School, Malta. Matriculated, Royal Malta University; Diploma, Economic & Social Admin., London School of Economics & Political Science, Univ. of London. *M.* 1944, Mary de Bono. *Daus.* 2, *Career:* Joined Malta Civil Service 1937; Private Secy. Minister, Work & Reconstruction, 1948–58; Secy. Gas Board, 1952–55; Asst. Secy. Economics Div. Ministry of Economic Planning & Finance, 1960–64; Member Malta Electricity Board, 1963–64; Deputy High Commissioner for Malta in London, 1964–67; Member, Malta Del. U.N. General Assembly, 1965, 66, 69; Envoy & Dep. Secy. Ministry, Commonwealth & Foreign Affairs, 1967–70; Permanent Rep. of Malta, Council of Europe, 1967–70; Ambassador, Sovereign Military Order of St. John of Jerusalem, of Rhodes and Malta, 1967–70; of Malta at the Holy See, 1968–70; Acting Secy, Ministry, Commonwealth & Foreign Affairs, 1969–70; High Comm. in Australia 1970–71. *Award:* Created Knight Grand Cross, Order of Pope Pius IX. *Clubs:* Civil Service Sports; Casino Maltese (Malta). *Address:* c/o Ministry of Foreign Affairs, Valletta, Malta.

**MAN, Morgan Charles Garnet,** CMG, DL. British. *B.* 1915. *Educ.* Cheltenham College: The Queen's College, Oxford, BA (Modern Languages). *M.* 1956, Patricia Mary Talbot. *Career:* British Ambassador to Saudi Arabia, 1964–68; Senior Civilian Instructor, Imperial Defense College, London, 1968–69; Retired H.M. Diplomatic Service 1970; Dir. Metallurgical Plant Makers Fed. since 1970. *Address:* 272 Earl's Court Road, London S.W.5; and *office* 7 Ludgate Broadway, London, E.C.4.

**MANCHAM, Hon. James Richard Marie.** F.R.S.A. Lawyer, *B.* 1939. *Educ.* Seychelles Coll., Seychelles; Univ. of Paris. France; Called to the Bar Middle Temple London, 1961. *M.* Heather Jean Evans. *S.* 1. *Dau.* 1. *Career:* Founded Seychelles Weekly newspaper 1963; Seychelles Democratic Party 1964; First Seychellois Chief Minister of Seychelles 1970–75; Prime Minister 1975–76; President, Republic of the Seychelles 1976–77. *Member:* Legislative Council 1963–70; Governing Council 1967–70; Legislative Assembly 1970–77; Council of Ministers 1970–77; Led Democratic Party Delegation, Seychelles Constitutional Conference London 1970. *Club:* Seychelles Yacht. *Address:* c/o Lloyds Bank Ltd., 81 Edgeware Road, London, NW2.

**MANCROFT, Lord** (Stormont Mancroft Samuel Mancroft), KBE, TD. *B.* 1914. *Educ.* Winchester and Christ Church Oxford (MA). *M.* 1951, Diana Lloyd. *S.* 1. *Daus.* 2. *Career:* Served with Royal Artillery 1939–46, Lieut.-Col. (despatches twice); MBE; Croix de Guerre. Col. Commandant R.A. Barrister-at-Law, Inner Temple 1938. Member Bar Council 1947–51; member, St. Marylebone Borough Cncl. 1947–53; Lord-in-Waiting 1952–54; Under-Secretary of State, Home Affairs 1954; Parly. Sec., Ministry of Defence Jan.-June 1957; Minister without Portfolio, 1957–58; Dir., Gus 1958–66; Inst. of Marketing 1959–62; Pres., London Tourist Bd., 1963–73; Pres., St. Marylebone Conservative Assn. 1961–67; Dep. Chmn., Cunard Line 1966–71. Chmn. Tote Board 1972–76; Chmn., British Greyhound Racing Federation. Member, Council on Tribunals 1972. *Address:* 29 Margaretta Terrace, London SW3 5NU.

**MANESCU, Corneliu.** Romanian politician and diplomatist. *B.* 1916. *Educ.* Law College, Bucharest. *Career:* Member: Democratic Students' Front, Romanian Communist Party 1936. Dep. Minister of Armed Forces 1948–55, Deputy Chairman, State Planning Committee 1955–60; Chief of Political Dept., Ministry of Foreign Affairs 1960; Ambassador to Hungary 1960–61. Minister, Foreign Affairs 1961–72; Head Romanian Delegation, U.N. Gen Assembly 1961–72; Member, Central Cttee. Romanian C.P. 1965—; Deputy to Grand Nat. Assembly 1965—; Chmn. 22nd Session, U.N. Gen. Assembly 1967–68; Mem., Academy of Social & Political Sciences 1970; Pres., Romanian Interparl. Group 1973—; Vice-Pres. of Nat. Council of Socialist Unity Front 1973–77; Ambassador to France since 1977. *Address:* 5 rue de l'Exposition, 75007 Paris, France; & Bulevardul Aviatorilor 46, Bucharest, Romania.

**MÁNESCU, Manea.** Chmn. Council of Ministers of the Socialist Republic of Romania. *B.* 1916. *M.* Maria. *Career:* member Communist Party 1936—; Gen. Dir. Central Statistical Office 1951–55; Minister for Finance 1955–57; Chmn. Labour and Wages State Cttee. First Vice Pres. State Planning Cttee. 1957; Member Central Cttee. R.C.P. 1960, Secy. 1965–72, alt. member Exec. Cttee. 1966–68, full mem. since 1968; Chmn. Economic and Financial Standing Cttee. Grand Nat. Assembly 1961–69; Mem. of Standing Presidium of Central Cttee of R.C.P. 1971–74; Vice-Pres. State Council 1969–72; Chmn Economic Council 1968–72; vice-chmn. Council of Ministers 1972–74, Chmn. since 1974; Chmn. State Planning Cttee 1972–74; vice-chmn. High Council of Econ. and Social Devel. 1973; vice-pres. Socialist Unity Front 1974. *Member:* Corresponding mem., Romanian Acad. of the S.R.R. 1955–74; mem., 1974—; Acad. Social and Political Sciences 1970—; Latin World Acad.; Hero of Socialist Labour 1971. *Address:* Central Committee of the Romanian Communist Party, Bucharest, Romania.

**MANGALDAS, Madanmohan.** Indian. *B.* 1917. *Educ.* BA (Hons.). *M.* Leena Mangaldas. *S.* 1. *Career:* Chmn., Victoria Mills Ltd., Bombay; till June 1976 was Chmn., Indo-Pharma Pharmaceutical Works Pvt. Ltd. & Dir. of various Cotton Textile Mills & Mahindra Ugine Steel Co. Ltd., National Machinery Manufacturers Ltd., Great Eastern Shipping Co. Ltd.; Pres., Ahmedabad Millowners' Assn., 1955, 1958; Ahmedabad Management Assn. 1959; Pres., Federation of Indian Chambers of Commerce & Industry, 1972–73; Chmn., The Indian Cotton Mills' Federation 1967–68, 1968–69; Rep. of Employers on Employees' State Insurance Corp.; was elected to Bombay Assembly 1951. *Clubs:* Willingdon Sports (Bombay); Gujarat Sports (Ahmedabad); Gymkhana (Ahmedabad), *Address:* Mangal Bag, Ellis Bridge, Ahmedabad 380006, India; and *office* Mangaldas Girdhardas Bungalow, Lal Darwaja, Ahmedabad 380001, India.

**MANGIERI, Robert P.** American politician and businessman. *B.* 1941. *Educ.* Queen's Coll.; The City College of New York; York College; Pohs Inst and US Marine Corps School. *Career:* Reporter, US Marine Corps; Special Consultant of Youth Affairs, Office of the Mayor; Legisl. Asst. New York City Council; Reporter, Leader-Observer Newspaper; Man. Editor, Sea History (magazine); Member of firm of Marsh and McLennan. *Member:* Advisory Cttee, Bicent. Cttee.; Community Planning Board (Exec. Secy.); Alumni Assn., The College of New York. *Decoration:* Honorary Fire Chief, N.Y. State Fire Fighters Assn. *Publications:* The Pictorial History of Richmond Hill, Kew Gardens, Woodhaven, Ozone Park; (Editor) Sea History (mag.). *Clubs:* Franklin Mint Socy.; South Street Seaport Socy. *Address:* 82–60 116th Street, Kew Gardens, NY 11418, U.S.A.; and *office* 1221 Ave. of the Americas, New York, NY 10020.

**MANGWAZU, Timon Sam.** Malawian Diplomat. *B.* 1933. *Educ.* BA, MA (Oxon.). *M.* 1958, Nelly Kathewera. *S.* 3. *Daus.* 4. *Career:* Joined Nyasaland Civil Service 1956; Sec.-Gen. Nyasaland African Civil Servants Assoc. 1961; Asst. Registrar of Trade Unions 1962–63; First Sec. (Trainee) British Embassy, Vienna 1964; Amb. of Malawi to German Fed. Republic, later Accred. to Norway, Sweden, Denmark, Netherlands, Belgium, Switzerland, Austria 1964–67; Malawi High Commissioner in UK 1967–69, concurrently Amb. to Holy See, Portugal, Netherlands and Belgium; Reading Econs. and Politics at Brasenose Coll., Oxford 1969–72; Malawi Amb. to EEC, concurrently Amb. to Belgium and Netherlands since 1973. *Decorations:* Malawi Independence Medal; Malawi Republic Medal; Knight Commander Cross of Order of Merit of Fed. Republic of Germany. *Address:* 283 Chaussée de Bruxelles à Kraainem, Belgium; and *office* 13–17 rue de la Charité, 1040-Bruxelles, Belgium (Boite 3).

**MANHEIM, Paul E.** American. *B.* 1905. *Educ.* Univ. of Virginia. *M.* Simone Gardner. *S.* Anthony A. *Daus.* Mrs. Martha Green, and Mrs. Emily Goldman. *Career:* Partner, Lehman Brothers, New York City. Chairman of Board, Vertientes-Camaguey Sugar Co. Director; Brascan Co. Ltd.; Media General Incorporated and One William Street Fund. Trustee, Brooklyn Museum; Board of Sponsors, Univ. of Virginia Graduate School of Business; Art Advisory Cttee.; Metropolitan Museum; Boston Museum of Fine Arts; Dartmouth College, University of Notre Dame. *Club:* Century Country. *Address:* 2 East 67th Street, New York, N.Y.; and *office* 1 William Street, New York, N.Y. 10004, U.S.A.

**MANLEY, Hon Michael.** Prime Minister of Jamaica. *B.* 1924. *Educ.* London Univ., BSc(Econ.). *M.* 1972, Beverly Anderson. *Dau.* 1. *Career:* Royal Canadian Air Force Pilot Officer 1943–45; Freelance Journalist BBC 1950–51; Assoc.-Editor 'Public Opinion' (Jamaica) 1951; Member People's National Party Exec. 1952; Sugar Organiser, National Workers' Union 1953; NWU Island Supervisor and First Vice-Pres. of Caribbean Bauxite and Mineworkers' Union 1955; Senator 1962–67; MP for Central Kingston 1967; President of the

People's National Party since 1969; Leader of the Opposition in the House of Representatives 1969–72; Prime Minister since 1972. *Decorations:* Order of Liberator (Venezuela) 1973; Doctor of Laws, Morehouse College, Atlanta 1973; Order of Mexican Eagle 1975; Order of Jose Marti (Cuba) 1975. *Address:* Prime Minister's Office, 1 Devon Road, Kingston 6, Jamaica; and Jamaica House, Hope Road, Kingston 6, Jamaica.

MANLEY-WALKER, **Edward.** British. *B.* 1919. *Educ.* Berkhampsted School. *M.* 1952, Anne Handley Page. *Daus.* 3. *Career:* With British-American Air Services Ltd. 1938–39; Served in British Army 1939–46; Area Sales Manager, Masson Seeley Ltd. 1946–51; Route Manager, Commercial Manager, Silver City Airways Ltd. 1952–58; Managing Director, Handley Page (Reading) Ltd. 1958–63; Director, Handley Page Ltd. 1958–68: Chairman Otmerplace Developments Ltd. 1962–66 and Win-a-Bet Ltd. since 1962. *Clubs:* Carlton; Royal Southern Yacht. *Address:* Stratton House, Cirencester, Gloucestershire.

**MANN, Colin Henry.** British. Vice-Chairman Hill and Knowlton (U.K.) Ltd. (International Public Relations), London. *B.* 1914. *Educ.* Oundle School and King's College Cambridge (MA). *M.* (1) 1939, Marie-Elise Gosling; (2) 1961, Jane de Pury Langridge. *S.* 1. *Daus.* 2. *Career:* With British Council 1938–41; Royal Navy 1942–46; P.R.O. of the Conservative Party 1947–52; Head of Lintas Information Services Ltd. 1952–53; Chief Exec. E. D. O'Brien (P.R. Consultants) 1954–55; Head of Publicity and Advertising, J. Lyons & Co. Ltd. 1956–57; Head of P.R. and Information Dept., H. J. Heinz Co. Ltd. 1957–63. Dir., Infoplan Ltd. 1964–66. Personal Asst. to Sir Anthony Eden (Prime Minister) 1955 General Election. Member L.C.C. 1952–58. A Governor of Birkbeck Coll. 1955—. *Member:* Inst. of Public Relations (*Fellow;* President 1964), and International Public Relations Assn. Conservative. *Address: office* Hill and Knowlton (U.K.) Ltd., 10 Wardour Street, London, W1V 3HE.

**MANN, Donald Jack,** CBE, MA. British. *B.* 1910. *Educ.* Bristol Grammar School; Merton Coll. Oxford (MA). *M.* 1939, Audrey Blacklin (*Dec'd.* 1973). *Dau.* 1. *Career:* Chmn., Lintas Ltd. 1955–59; Dir., Unilever Ltd., Unilever N.V. 1960–71; Chmn., Food, Drink and Tobacco Industry Training Board. *Club:* United Oxford & Cambridge University. *Address:* Heronwood, Beckley, Rye, Sussex; and *office* Barton House, Barton Street, Gloucester GL1 1QQ.

**MANN, Philip Ahsley,** TD (with clasp). British. Chairman, Mann & Son (London) Ltd. *B.* 1919. *Educ.* Harrow School. *M.* 1941, Marjorie Elizabeth Eldridge. *S.* Christopher, Peter and Alexander. *Dau.* Jennifer. *Career:* Engaged in commercial banking 1937–39; War Service (G.S.O. II) 1939–45. Engaged in shipping director of various shipping companies since 1945. *Clubs:* Vintage Sports Car, and Veteran Car Club of Great Britain. *Address:* The Manor House, Crooms Hill, Greenwich, London, S.E.10.

**MANN, Ronald.** British. *B.* 1908. *Educ.* Cranleigh School, Surrey. *M.* 1935, Beatrice Elinor Cröwell Wright. *S.* Nicholas Ronald (B.Sc. GI.Mech.E; grad. RAe.S). *Daus.* Sara Louise, Marilyn Elinor and Ione Carina Jane. *Career:* Assistant in Ceylon of The Eastern Produce and Estates Co. Ltd. 1930–35 (Manager in Ceylon 1935–46; Managing Director in London 1947–71); Chmn. Eastern Produce (Holdings) Ltd. 1957–71; Standard Tea Holdings Ltd. and subsidiaries 1958–74; Deputy Chairman, Grindlays Bank Ltd. 1964–77; Dir. Butlers Warehousing and Distribution Ltd. Chairman, The Ceylon Estates Proprietary Assn. 1942. *Member:* The Ceylon Assn. in London (Pres. 1952–53). *Club:* Oriental. *Address:* Fernhurst Place, Fernhurst, nr. Haslemere, Surrey.

**MANN, Sam.** British. *B.* 1917. *Educ.* Graduate Advanced Management Programme, Harvard Univ. *M.* 1940, Carol Carroll. *Dau.* Margaret Carol. *Career:* Controller and Treasurer, Bowater's North America, 1955, Vice-Pres., Finance, 1963; Comptroller, Bowater Paper Corp. 1965. Dir. of Financial Planning 1967. Director of The Bowater Paper Corporation Ltd.; and Pres. Bowater Incorporated U.S.A. since 1970. FCA; Fellow Inst. Chartered Accountants Eng. and Wales; CA Canada. Member, Financial Executives Inst., U.S.A. *Club:* St. James, Montreal, Canada; Canadian (New York). *Address: office* 1500 East Putnam Avenue, Old Greenwich, Conn., U.S.A.

**MANN, William Allen.** American. *B.* 1901. *Educ.* Kansas City Junior College and Univ. of Illinois, (BSEE). *M.* 1946, Lonnie Payne. *S.* William E. *Dau.* Majorie (Wallace). *Career:* With General Electric since 1923, first in Schenectady, N.Y. three years later transferred to Industrial Sales Div., Chicago; apptd. Assistant District Manager of Industrial Sales, Chicago 1943; apptd. Manager G.E's Apparatus Sales Office, Milwaukee 1948; transferred to Chicago as District Manager, same Div. 1955; Regional Vice-President, General Electric Co., St. Louis, Mo. 1955–66. *Member:* Missouri State, Chambers of Commerce; St. Louis Electrical Board of Trade (Director); Jefferson National Expansion Memorial Assn. (Trustee); Board of Aldermen, City of Huntleigh; Missouri Baptist Hospital Assn.; Univ. of Illinois Foundation. *Clubs:* Old Warson Country, (St. Louis). *Address:* 39 Huntleigh Woods, St. Louis, Mo. 63131, U.S.A.

**MANNING, Rt. Hon. Ernest Charles,** PC, CC. Canadian company director & politician. *B.* 20 Sept. 1908. *M.* 1936, Muriel Preston. *S.* Keith, Preston. *Career:* Provincial Secretary and Minister of Trades and Industry, Alberta Government 1935–43; member of Legislative Assembly (Social Credit), Alberta, 1935–68; Provincial Treasurer, 1944–55; Minister of Mines & Minerals, 1952–62; Attorney-General, 1955–68. Premier 1943–1968; Pres., M. & M. Systems Research Ltd.; Director: Canadian Imperial Bank of Commerce; Steel Co. of Canada Ltd.; Canadian Pacific Airlines; Manufacturers Life Insurance Co.; Melton Real Estate Ltd.; McIntyre Porcupine Mines Ltd.; Burns Foods Ltd. Member Canadian Senate; Companion, Order of Canada 1970 *Address:* P.O. Box 2317, Edmonton, Alberta, Canada T5J Y61.

**MANNING, Herbert L.** American professional engineer. *Educ.* Pennsylvania State Univer. (BS in ME; and graduate work in Industrial Engineering). *M.* 1937, Anne M. Myhill. *S.* Glenn, H. *Dau.* Virginia A. *Career:* Supervisor of Time Standards, Consolidated Molded Products Corp. 1935; Time Study Engineer, General Electric Co. 1936; Instructor in Industrial Engineering, Cornell Univ. 1936–39; Wage and Salary Administrator, United Aircraft Corp. 1939–48. Professor and Head of Industrial Engineering, Virginia-Polytechnic Institute, Blacksburg, Va. 1948–66; Asst. Dean of Enging. 1966–70; Prof., Industry Enging., and Operation Res., Virginia Polytechnic Ins., Blacksburg, Va. 1971–77, Prof. Emeritus 1977—; Consultant to General Electric Co., C. & O. Railway Co., J. P. Stevens Corp., U.S. Navy & others. *Member:* Amer. Socy. for Engineering Education; Amer. Inst. of Industrial Engineers; Tau Beta Pi; Alpha Pi Mu. *Address:* 320 Bravado Lane, Palm Beach Shores, Riviera Beach, Fla. 33404, U.S.A.

**MANNING, Hon. Sir James Kenneth.** *B.* 1907. *Educ.* Sydney Grammar School. *M.* 1957, Sheila Alison Barker. *Career:* Admitted as Solicitor 1930; admitted to Bar of New South Wales 1940, appointed Queen's Counsel 1953; Challis Lecturer in Bankruptcy at Sydney Univ. Law School 1952–55; Justice of the Supreme Court of New South Wales Court of Appeal (Ret. 1973); Former Chairman, N.S.W., Law Reform Commission. Hon. Treas. N.S.W. Bar Assn. 1949–53; served with R.A.A.F. 1941–46; mentioned in despatches for services in New Guinea; later appointed Deputy Director of Personal Services with rank of Wing Commander. *Publications:* (joint author) Law of Banker and Customer in Australia (1947); Australian Bankruptcy Law and Practice (3rd ed.) (1953). *Deceased, 11th August 1977.*

**MANNIO, Niilo Anton.** Finnish government official. *B.* 5 Nov. 1884. *Educ.* University of Helsinki (MA, LL.B). *M.* (1) 1913, Greta Langerstroom. *S.* Mikko Ilmari, Veikko Olavi, Niilo Pekka. *M.* (2) 1963, Eila Koponen. *Career:* Attached High Court of Justice, Turku 1910, Supereme Court 1912–16; Minister for Social Affairs 1928–29; Secretary-General, Ministry for Social Affairs 1917–51; member, Governing Body, I.L.O. 1922–25 and 1934–37, member, Government Group I.L.O. Conference 1919–51; Correspondent in Finland 1950–54. *Awards:* Commander 1st Class, Order of White Rose of Finland, Commander 1st Class, Order of Dannebrog (Denmark); Commander 1st Class, Order of North Star (Sweden); Commander 1st Class, Order of St. Olav (Norway). *Publications:* Industrial Peace; International Labour Legislation; The Position of Professional Workers; Social Development in Finland; Unemployment of Young Persons and Women. *Address:* Kirhosalmentie 3g107, Helsinki 84, Finland.

**MANNIX, Frederick Philip.** Canadian. *B.* 1942. *Educ.* Ridley Coll.; Univ. of Alberta (B.Comm.). *M.* 1968, Gloria Jean MacDonald. *Career:* various previous appointments with

Mannix Co. Ltd.; Rep., Loram Co. Ltd. 1966–67, Vice-Pres., Gen. Mgr. 1968–69; Pres. Loram Co. Ltd 1969–75; Chmn. Bd. Loram Co. Ltd. and Dir. of Loram Co. Ltd., Loram International Ltd., Pembina Pipeline Ltd., Manalta Coal Ltd., Manark Industrial Sales Ltd., Loram Maintenance of Way Inc., Dir. of the Investors Group, Siemans Canada. *Clubs:* Ranchmen's; Glencoe; Calgary Golf & Country. *Address:* 320 7th Avenue, S.W., Box 2550, Calgary, T2P 2M7, Alberta, Canada.

**MANSAGER, Felix Norman.** American. *B.* 1911. *Educ.* Colton High School. *M.* Geraldine Larson. *S.* Douglas Norman. *Daus.* Donna Hogsven (Harlan) and Eva Kay Sieverts (Walter). *Career:* Joined Hoover Co. as Vacuum Cleaner Salesman 1929. From Field Representative through various posts to Vice-Pres. (Sales) 1931–1959. Exec. Vice-Pres. and Director: The Hoover Co. 1961, and Hoover Group 1963. President-Chairman, The Hoover Company and Hoover Worldwide Corporation 1966–75; Chairman Exec. Cttee., The Hoover Co. 1975. Director, Harter Bank & Trust Co. (Canton, Ohio) 1967—. *Member:* National Business Council, Consumer Affairs Ohio Foundation of Independent Coll. Inc., member Bd. of Trustees; The Pilgrims of the U.S.; Association of Ohio Commodores Rotary International; Newcomen Socy. in North Amer. Honorary, World League of Norsemen; Trustee at Large Exec. Cttee., Chmn., Independent Coll. Funds of Amer. (Dir.); Council on Foreign Relations; Ditchley Foundation) Governor). *Awards:* Masonic Shrine. Chevalier, Order of Leopold (Belgium); Order of St. Olav. Knight First Class Norway 1971; French Legion of Honor; Hon. Commander, Most Excellent Order, The British Empire; Marketing Award British Inst. Marketing; Hon LLD, Capital University (Columbus, Ohio). Hon LLD, Strathclyde Univ., Scotland; Hon. Doctor Humane Letters, Malone College Vaasa Univ. (Finland) Medal of Honour (1972); Univ. Coll. Fellow (Wales) Cardiff (1973); Walsh College (Canton, Ohio) Hon. Dr. Pedagogy (1974); Univ. Akron (Ohio) Hon. Mem. Beta Sigma Gamma (1974). *Clubs:* Metropolitan (N.Y.C. & Wash., D.C.); Capitol Hill (Wash. D.C.); Congress Lake Country. *Address:* The Hoover Company, North Canton, Ohio 44720.

**MANSFIELD, Hon. Sir Alan James,** KCMG, KCVO, KStJ. Hon. LLD (Queensland). Australian judge. *B.* 1902. *Educ.* Univ. of Sydney (LLB). *M.* 1933, Beryl Susan Pain. *S.* Charles James. *Dau.* Rachel Margaret. *Career:* Barrister 1924–40; Lecturer in Law, University of Queensland 1938–40; Chairman, Land Appeal Court 1942–45; Chairman, Aliens Tribunal 1942–45; Chairman, Royal Commissions on Sugar Industry 1942, 1950; member, Board of Enquiry into Japanese War Atrocities 1945; Australian Representative, United Nations War Crimes Commission, London, 1945, 1946; Chief Australian Prosecutor, International Military Tribunal for the Far East, Tokyo 1946–47; Chmn., Central Sugar Cane Prices Board 1955–56; Judge of Supreme Court of Queensland since 1940; Senior Puisne Judge of Supreme Court of Queensland 1947–56; Chief Justice 1956–66; Administrator of the Government of Queensland 1957–63–65. Warden, Univ. of Queensland 1956–66; Chancellor of Univ. of Queensland 1966–76; Governor of Queensland 1966–72. Hon. Col. 2/14 Queensland Mounted Infantry 1966–72; Hon. Air Commodore, citizen Air Force 1966–72. *Address:* 81 Monaco Street, Surfers Paradise, Queensland 4217, Australia.

**MANSFIELD, John Michael Roger.** New Zealand Diplomat. *B.* 1931. *Educ.* Univ. of Canterbury, Christchurch, N.Z.—BA. *M.* 1960, Annemarie Niesje Hootsen. *S.* 1. *Dau.* 1. *Career:* Commissioned in British Regular Army 1954–56; entered Ministry of Foreign Affairs, Wellington 1957; 3rd Sec., N.Z. Embassy, Bangkok 1961–62; 1st Sec., N.Z. Embassy, Bonn 1966–69; Counsellor, N.Z. High Commission, Apia (W. Samoa) 1970–72; Minister, N.Z. Mission to the UN, New York 1973–76; High Commissioner to Papua New Guinea, Port Moresby since 1976. *Address:* c/o Ministry of Foreign Affairs, Private Bag, Wellington, New Zealand; and *office* New Zealand High Commission, P.O. Box 1144, Boroko, Port Moresby, Papua New Guinea.

**MANSFIELD, Michael Joseph.** American Politician. *B.* 16. Mar. 1903. *Educ.* University of Montana, BA (MA). *M.* 1931, Maureen Hayes. *Dau.* Anne. *Career:* Served in U.S. Navy Feb. 1918–Aug. 1919, U.S. Army Nov. 1919–Nov. 1920, U.S. Marine Corps. Nov. 1920–Nov. 1922; Miner and Mining Engineer Dec. 1922–30; University Professor Sept. 1933–Dec. 1942; member, House of Representatives 1943–53; Senator for the terms 1953–59; 1959–65; 1965–71; 1971–76; Majority Whip 1957–61; Majority Leader 1961–76. Ambassador to Japan since 1977. *Address:* U.S. Embassy, 10-5 Akasaka 1-chome, Minato-ku, Tokyo, Japan.

**MANUELLI, Ernesto.** Italian. Dr. Prof., Cavaliere del Lavoro, Cav. Gr. Groce Repubblica Italiana. *B.* 1906. *Educ.* Degree in commercial sciences, master degree in economics. financial politics. *M.* 1931, Beatrice Paternostro. *S.* Manlio and Franco. *Daus.* Mirella and Orietta. *Career:* Gen. Secy., Sofindit, Italian Industrial financial co. 1932–35; Gen. Inspector, Min. of Exchange and Currencies 1935–40; Gen. Mgr., Vice-Chmn. Ansaldo S.p.A. Genova 1940–45; Gen. Mgr., Finsider S.p.A. 1945–58. Chairman, Finsider S.p.A., Rome, 1958–75; Director: Cemintir S.p.A., Rome, 1967—; Societe Financiere Italo-Suisse, Geneva 1958—; Italsider S.p.A. Geneva, 1961—; Chmn. EGAM-Rome (1975). *Publications:* Nuovi aspetti della bilancia dei pagamenti (Milan, 1939); Pan-americanismo economica (Noepli, 1939) and several minor papers on economic matters. Member, Board, Internat. Iron and Steel Inst., Brussels; Hon. Deputy Chmn., British Iron and Steel Inst., London; Member Bd. ASSONIME Italian corporations assn.; Assobancaria, Italian bankers' assn.; Int. Chamber of Commerce. *Address:* Viale della Camilluccia 495, Rome; and *office* Via Boncompagni 6, 00187, Rome, Italy.

**MANZINI, Raimondo.** Italian diplomat. Cavaliere di Gran Groce all'Ordine della Repubblica, GCVO. *B.* 1913. *Educ.* Univ. of Bologna (LLD); Clark Univ., Mass (MA); Univ. of California. *Career:* Entered Diplomatic Service, 1940; Secretary to Legation, Lisbon, 1941–43; Ministry of Foreign Affairs; Brindisi, 1943; Salerno, 1944; Secretary, Embassy, London, 1944–47; Consul-General, Congo Nigeria, 1947–50 and Baden Baden, 1951–52; Head, Information Service, C.E.D., Paris, 1952–53; Ministry of Foreign Affairs, 1953–55; Adviser to Minister for Foreign Trade, 1955–58; Chef de Cabinet, Minister for Foreign Affairs, 1958; Dip. Adv. to Prime Min., 1958–59; Adv. to Minister of Industry, 1959–64; Ambassador to O.E.C.D., Paris, 1965–68, to the Court of St. James's 1968–75. Secy. Gen. at Min. of Foreign Affairs, Rome, since 1975. *Address* : Ministry of Foreign Affairs, Rome.

**MANZITTI, Francesco.** Italian average adjuster. *B.* 1908. *Educ.* Doctor in Law and Doctor in Economics and Business Administration. *M.* 1934, Maria Carla Zarri. *S.* Beppe and Andrea. Grand Officer, Al Merito (Republic of Italy); Chevalier, Legion of Honour (France). *Career:* Pres.: Chamber Commerce, Genoa 1945–54; Higher Council of the Merchant Marine 1948–52; du Comité International des'Echanges (Paris) 1949–53; Società Finanziaria FINMARE, Rome 1951–59. Chairman: Italian Committee of Lloyd's Register of Shipping, and Board of Ausiliare Ltd. Director: Istituto Bancario S. Paolo di Torino, Cieli Ltd., Morice Tozer & Beck (London) Ltd., Sifir Ltd., and Ceresio Ltd. *Publications:* several contributions on economics and legal matters, mainly in the following reviews: Diritto Marittimo, La Marina Mercantile Italiana, and La Marina Italiana. *Clubs:* Rotary, Union (both of Genoa). *Address:* Via Privata Piaggio 38, Genoa, Italy.

**MARAIS, Walter.** BCom. British. *B.* 1930. *Educ.* Wynberg Boys School, Cape Town; Univ. Cape Town (BCom.). *M.* 1956, Barbara Brown. *Career:* Man. Dir., Bishopsgate Steels Ltd.; Dir., Windgrange Property Co. Ltd.; Chartdene Ltd.; Marwalt Investments Ltd.; Marka Metals Ltd.; Panex (International) Ltd. *Clubs:* Brooks'; Lansdowne. *Address:* Garden House, Cornwall Gardens, London, S.W.7; and *office* 53 Grosvenor Street, London, W.1.

**MARBURY, William Luke.** American lawyer. *B.* 1901. *Educ.* Univ. of Virgina (BA 1921) and Harvard Univ. (LLB 1924). *M.* 1935, Natalie Jewett Wheeler. *S.* Luke. *Daus.* Anne Jewett and Susan Fendall. *Career:* Engaged in practice of law in Baltimore Md. and member of the firm of Piper & Marbury (and predecessor firms) 1925—; Assistant Attorney-General of Maryland 1930–31; Expert Consultant to Secretary of War in matters related to procurement contracts 1940–41; Chief Counsel to War Department (in same capacity) 1942–45; Chairman, Commission on Higher Education in the State of Maryland 1945–47. Member of Cncl., Amer. Law Inst. 1946—; Maryland Commission, Judicial Disabilities since 1971; Dir. National Institute for Trial Advocacy since 1971. Member, U.S. Delegation to 2nd Session of Signatories of GATT, Geneva 1948; Member of Harvard Corp. 1948–70, Gen. Cnsl., Maryland Port Auth. 1955–67; Chmn., Bd. of Trustees, Peabody Inst. 1957–67. *Member:* Phi Beta Kappa; Amer. Acad. of Arts & Sciences; American College of Trial Lawyers; Chancellor of the Diocese of Maryland 1962–71; Member, Amer. Bar Assn. Cttee. on Standards of Judicial

Conduct; Amer. Bar Foundation. *Awards:* Medal for Merit 1945; LLD Harvard, 1970; DMA Peabody Institute, 1967. *Clubs:* Elkridge; 14 W. Hamilton Street (Baltimore); Harvard; Century Assn. (N.Y.). *Address:* 43 Warrenton Road, Baltimore 21210, Md.; and *office* 2000 First Maryland Building, 25 South Charles Street, Baltimore, Maryland 21201, U.S.A.

**MARCELLIN, Raymond.** French politician. *B.* 19 Aug. 1914. *Educ.* D en D; advocate Paris Appeal Court; Under-Sec. of State for the Interior 1948–49; Sec. of State for Information 1952–53; Deputy since 1946; Delegate to U.N. 1951–52; Under Secretary of State for Industry and Commerce 1949; Secretary of State, Prime Minister's Office January 1952; Secretary of State for Civil Servants 1958, Minister of Health and Population 1962. Ministre de l'Industrie, 1966–67; Ministre Chargé du Plan et de l'Aménagement du Territoire 1967–68. Ministre de l'Intérieur, 1968–74; Ministre de l'Agriculture March–May 1974; Senator for Morbihan since 1974. Officer, Croix de Guerre; Knight Commander of the Royal Victorian Order. *Address:* 71 Avenue de Breteuil, Paris 15e.

**MARCHANT, Sir Herbert Stanley,** KCMG, OBE; British Foreign Service. *B.* 1906. *Educ.* First Class Honours in Modern Languages; MA (Cantab). *M.* 1937, Diana Selway; *S.* 1. *Career:* Assistant Master, Harrow School 1928–39; entered Foreign Service 1940; Ambassador to Cuba 1960–63, and to Tunisia 1963–66; Associate Director, Institute of Race Relations, 1966–68; British Representative U.N. Cttee. on Elimination of Racial Discrimination 1969–73. *Publication:* Scratch a Russian (1938). *Club:* Travellers' (London). *Address:* 32 Buckingham Ct., Kensington Park Road, London, W.11.

**MARCONI, Dr. Prof. Mario.** Italian industrialist. *B.* 1896. *Educ.* Nat. Coll. of Genoa; Univ. of Genoa; graduated in Econ. and Commerce (major) and Pure Maths. (minor). *M.* 1931, Maria Brunelli. *S.* Dr. Ettore. *Dau.* Dr. Maria Rosa (Countess A. Archinto). *Career:* Professor of Political Economy until 1933. General Manager: Ansaldo Co., Genoa 1929–34, and Aquila Petroli, Trieste 1936–44. Managing Director: Whitehead Co., Fiume, and of Moto Fides Corp., Leghorn, until 1946; Franco Tosi Co., Legnano 1946–57. Past President, now Hon. President, ANIMA (National Association of Mechanical Industries); President, Italian-Argentine Chamber of Commerce in Italy 1956–62; Honorary Chairman of Board: Compagnia Italiana Westinghouse, Nebiolo; Chmn. Rexim Bugnone (Turin); Member, Bd. of S.p.A. Reinach S.p.A.; Ercole Marelli & C., S.p.A.; Oerlikon Italiana (all of Milan), etc. *Awards:* Cavaliere di Gran Groce della Repubblica Italiana; Cavaliere del Lavoro; Papal decoration of St. Gregorio Magno; Chevalier, Legion of Honour (France); Gran Oficial de la Republica Argentina. *Clubs:* Clubino Milan; Societè del Casino (Genoa). *Address:* S. Angelo Pauzo, 06081 Assisi, Perugia, Italy.

**MARCOS, Ferdinand Edralin.** Head of State of the Philippines. *B.* 1917. *Educ.* Univ. of the Philippines. *M.* Imelda Romualdez. *S.* 1. *Daus.* 2. *Career:* Special Asst. to Pres. Manuel Roxas 1946–47; mem. House of Reps. 1949–59, & Senate 1959–66 (Pres. 1963–65); President of the Republic of the Philippines since 1965, re-elected 1969, & Prime Minister since 1973. *Address:* Malacañang Palace, Manila, Philippines.

**MAREE, Johan Christiaan Holm.** Ambassador of the Republic of South Africa. *B.* 1915. *Educ.* BA: LLB. *M.* 1942, Elzabé Wepener van den Heever. *S.* 1. *Daus.* 2. *Career:* Chargé d'Affairs Athens 1954; Chief of Protocol, South Africa 1958; Ambassador: to Argentina 1960; to Australia, 1965–69 and to Spain 1969–73. *Club:* Real de Puerta De Hierro, Madrid. *Address:* c/o Ministry of Foreign Affairs, Pretoria, South Africa.

**MARELLI, Alfredo** (also known as Fermo). Italian engineer. *B.* 1900. *Educ.* University of Milan (Dr Ing 1928). *M.* 1935, Rosa Ronzoni. *S.* Ferdinando. *Dau.* Maddalena. *Career:* President & Man. Dir., Ercole Marelli & Co., S.p.A. 1946—; Consigliere; Istrumenti di Misura C.G.S., Monza; Fabbrica Italiana Magneti Marelli; Vice-Pres., Società Anonima Elettrificazione, Milan. *Club:* Rotary. *Address: office* Via Borgonuovo 24, Milan, Italy.

**MAREMONT, Arnold.** American industrialist. *B.* 1904 *Educ.* Univ. of Chicago (Ph.B 1924; JD 1926. *Career:* Chairman Executive Committee, Maremont Corporation, 1969–71, Dir. since 1971, (President, 1953–69); Chairman Exec. Cttee., Allied Paper Corp., 1963–66; Chmn. of Board. Eckmar Corporation (formerly Phillips-Eckhardt Electronic Corp.) 1961–69. Distinguished Service Award, 1951). Trustee: Lyric Opera of Chicago Community Music Centre of the North Shore. Governing Life Member, Art Inst. of Chicago; Trustee: Bard Coll.; Southern Ill. Univ.; Natl. Assocn. for Mental Health (also First Vice-Pres.); Member, Board of Directors and Vice-Pres., Planned Parenthood World Population; Member, Board & Exec. Cttee., Western Hemisphere Gov. Body International Planned Parenthood Federation; Civil Liberties Educational Fund Foundation; Former Chmn., Ill. Public Aid Commn.; Charter Member, Board of Governors of Medical Research Institute of Michael Reese Hospital and Medical Center; member of Board, Inst. for Psychoanalysis; Dir., Mental Health Socy. of Greater Chicago; Bd. Member, N.Y. City Centre of Music & Drama; Trustee, N.Y. Center Opera and Ballet Company; Trustee, Hull House. *Awards:* Order of the Coif, Univ. of Chicago (1926); Chicago Human Relations Award (1946); Dist. Serv. Award Univ. of Chicago (1951); Man of Year award (Mentally Retarded Socy. of Ill). Knight Order of Merit of the Republic of Italy. Hon LLD, Southern Illinois Univ., 1968. *Clubs:* Lotos (N.Y.C.); Tavern; Arts (Chicago). *Address:* 30/31 Chesham Place, London SW1X 8DL; and Crystal Springs, St. James, Barbados, West Indies; and 330 Cocoanut Row, Palm Beach, Fla. 33480; *office* 200 East Randolph Drive, Chicago, Ill. 60601.

**MARGETTS, Walter Thomas, Jr.** American attorney and executive. *B.* 1905. *Educ.* St. Lawrence Univ. (LLB, LLM); Fairleigh Dickinson Univ. (LLD); Columbia Univ. (Advanced Agronomy); New York Univ. (Finance). *M.* 1935, Josephine Sharon. *S.* Walter T. III. *Daus.* Mrs. Richard E. Doremus, Mrs. Charles Robinson, Mrs. Charles Connell. *Career:* With Brooklyn (N.Y.) Trust Co. 1923–29; Associated with Beekman, Bogue & Clarke, N.Y.C. 1929–35; Partner, Bainton, McNaughton & Douglas 1935–43; Partner, McLanahan, Merritt & Ingraham 1943–55; Appointed by Pres. Roosevelt, Industry Member of the Natl. War Labor Board 1942–45. Appointed Chmn., N.J. State Board of Mediation, 1945. Re-appointed in 1948. Treas., State of New Jersey 1949–53. Chmn. of Board and Pres., Bright Star Industries, 1954; Counsel for Forstmann Woolen Co. 1957. Chairman of Board, Laytham Foundry Inc. 1957–70; Chairman, Exec. Committee, Franklin Bank, Paterson, N.J.; Former Chairman and Treasurer, New Jersey Republican Finance Committee; President and Treas. Hudson & Manhattan Corp.; Director: U.G.I. Corp., Philadelphia; S.F.M. Corp.; Plainfield N.J.; Newark, N.J.; Tec Torch Co., Inc., Carlstadt, N.J.; Automatic Data Processing; Vornado Inc.; Vice-President Finance, Foundation Life Assurance Co. of America; Member: New York Advisory Board, American Mutual Liability Insurance Co.; Member U.S. Dept. of Commerce, Economic Development Adv. Board. Republican. *Member:* Alpha Chi Epsilon; Delta Theta Phi; Elks, Mason; St. Andrew's Socy.; Patrolman's Benevolent Assn., Chairman, New Jersey Camp for Blind, Inc.; Pres., Frost Valley Assn. (Y.M.C.A.). *Clubs:* Downtown Athletic (Life Member); National Press, Capitol Hill, Metropolitan (all of Washington); Essex; Morristown (N.J.); Morris County Golf. *Address:* Holly Hill Farms, New Vernon, N.J., U.S.A.

**MARGOLIN, Leo Jay.** American public relations counsel, attorney-at-law and adjunct professor of public administration. *B.* 1910. *Educ.* Long Island Univ. (BS 1932); Brooklyn Law School of St. Lawrence Univ. (JD 1935). *M.* 1960, Eve Wolf. *Career:* Reporter-writer, Brooklyn Daily Times (1962–29), N.Y. Times (1929–34) and N.Y. Herald-Tribune 1934–38; Public Relations and Legal Consultant to Columbia Univ., Cooper Union, Philco Corp., Amer. Chemical Society, Ethyl Gasoline Corp., Amer. Inst. of Architecture 1938–40; Assoc. Editor P.M. (newspaper) 1940–43; Senior field representative and Editor, U.S. Office of War Information (assigned to Psychological Warfare Brance, A.F.H.Q., N. Africa, Italy, Balkans; propaganda broadcaster, U.N. radio Algiers; organizer-news editor, A.N.S.A. Italian co-op. press association) 1943–45; Assoc. Dir. of Public Information U.N.R.R.A. and Chief of Operations 1946–47; Public Relations Counsel and U.S. Director, Times of India Publications 1948–51; in practice of public relations 1951–55; Dean and Professor of Business Administration, Borough of Manhattan Community Coll. 1964—. Vice-Pres., Martial & Co. Inc. (public relations counsellors) 1956–62; Vice-Pres., A. J. Armstrong Co. Inc. Commercial Finance 1962–64; Adjunct Professor of Public Administration, New York University 1951—; Attorney-at-Law, State of New York 1938—. *Publications:* Paper Bullets, 1946; Fundraising Made Easy (co-author), 1954; contributor of special series articles on India, North American Newspaper Alliance 1949–50; Christian Science Monitor 1946–47; N.A.N.A. 1953–58; Traffic Quarterly, 1952; special broadcasts from Europe and Africa for National Broadcasting 'Monitor' Service 1958–59; seekly columnist 'Your Public Relations IQ', Civil Service Leader 1961—. Trustee, Brookdale Hospital Center, Brooklyn, N.Y., 1957—. *Member:* Public Relations Socy. of America; Socy. of the Silurians (N.Y.). *Clubs:* National Press (Washington); Overseas Press (N.Y.). *Deceased.*

**MARIAS, Ernst Jacobus.** South African scientist. *B.* 1921. *Educ.* University of Stellenbosch (DSc 1945). *M.* 1946, Ruth Esther Beetge. *S.* 1. *Daus.* 3. *Career:* Associated with N.P.R.L. as research scientist until appointed as Director Dir. 1955–62, Vice-Pres. 1962—, South African Council for Scientific and Industrial Research. Vice-Chancellor and Principal, Univ. of Port Elizabeth 1964—; Dir. Sanlam. *Publications:* various scientific works and articles. *Address:* University of Port Elizabeth, P.O. Box 1600, Port Elizabeth 6000, Republic of South Africa.

**MARIE, Jean Henri Théophile,** Hon. Pres., Compagnie Générale Transatlantique (French Line) 1961—. *B.* 1891; *Educ.* Ecole Polytechnique and Ecole du Génie Maritime; LLD (Honoris Causa), Temple University; DSc (Honoris Causa), Lafayette College, Easton, Pa.; Ingénieur Général du Génie Maritime. *M.* 1921, Madeleine Villard. *Daus.* Françoise (Mme Pierre Calvet) and Micheline (Mme Dominique Pedinielli). *Career:* As Marine Engineer, loaned to Ministry of Merchant Marine 1921; Director, Commercial and Operational Fleet 1938–40; President, Société des Services Contractuels des Messageries Maritimes 1940–44. *Member:* Adadémie de Marine, and Académie des Sciences d'Outremer; Ancien Vice-President, Comité Central des Armateurs de France. Hon. Pres., Association Technique Maritime et Aéronautique. Grand Croix de la Légion d'Honneur; Commandeur du Mérite Maritime et du Mérite Touristique; numerous other decorations. *Publications:* numerous; dealing with the technique and safety of ships, sea and air transport, and the art of the sea. *Clubs:* Automobile Club de France; Yacht Club de France; Club des Cent. *Address:* Tour Atlantique, La Défense, Paris, France.

**MARIN GASTON, Gheorghe.** Engineer. *B.* 1918. *Educ.* graduate of Grenoble (France) Polytechnical Institute 1937–40. *Career:* Assistant lecturer at Grenoble Institute 1940–44. Fought with the French patriots in the resistance movement against the Nazi invaders. Returned to Rumania and became member of the Rumanian Communist Party. General Secy., then Deputy Minister, Ministry of Industry 1947–49; Minister of Electric Power 1949–54. First Vice-President, then President, State Planning Cttee. 1954–65. Vice-Pres. Council of Ministers 1962–69; Pres. State Cttee. for Prices. *Address:* Str. Doamnei No. 8, Bucharest 4, Romania.

**MARIS, Albert Branson.** American judge. *B.* 19 Dec. 1893. *Educ.* Drexel Univ.; Temple University (LLB). *M.* (1) 1917, Edith M. Robinson (*Dec.* 1967). *S.* William Robinson, Robert Wood; (2) 1968, Mildred C. Butler. *Career:* Practised law in Chester, Pennsylvania 1918 and in Philadelphia, Pa., 1919–36; Editor, 'The Legal Intelligencer,' Philadelphia 1933–36; Member of Council, Borough of Yeadon, Pa., 1935–36; Judge, U.S. District Court, Eastern District of Pa., 1936–38; Judge U.S. Court of Appeals, 3rd Circuit 1938–58; Senior Circuit Judge, 3rd Circuit, since Jan. 1959; Adjunct Professor of Law, Temple University, Philadelphia 1941–55; Chief Judge, U.S. Emegency Court of Appeals 1943–62; Chmn., Committee on Rules of Practice and Procedure, Judical Conf. of U.S. 1959–73. *Awards:* Hon LLD Drexel Univ. Haverford College, Swarthmore College, Temple Univ. and Villanova Univ.; Hon. Fellow American Bar Foundation 1974; Virgin Islands Medal of Honour 1954. *Address:* 18613 United States Courthouse, Independence Mall West, Philadelphia 19106, U.S.A.

**MARJORIBANKS, Sir James Alexander Milne,** KCMG. *B.* 1911. *Educ.* Edinburgh University (MA 1st Cl Hons) *M.* 1936, Sonya Patricia Stanley-Alder. *Dau:* Patricia Mary (Baillie Strong). *Career:* At British Embassy, Peking 1935–38; Consulate-General Hankow 1938; Marseilles 1939–40; H.M. Consul, Jacksonville, Florida, U.S.A. 1941–42; Vice-Consul, New York 1942–44; Assistant to British Political Representative in Rumania 1944–45; in Foreign Office, London 1945–49; Deputy to Secretary of State for Foreign Affairs for Austrian Treaty 1947–49; Official Secretary, U.K. High Commissioner, Canberra 1950–52; Deputy Head of United Kingdom Delegation to High Authority of European Coal and Steel Community 1952–55; Cabinet Office 1955–57; Minister (Economic), British Embassy, Bonn 1957–62; Assistant Under-Secretary of State, Foreign Office 1962–65. Ambassador and Head of British Delegation to the European Communities 1965–71; Dir. Scottish Council (Development and Industry) and Chmn. EEC Cttee.; Dir. Distillers Co. Ltd.; General Council Assessor, Edinburgh University Court. *Address:* 13 Regent Terrace, Edinburgh 7, and Lintonrig, Kirk Yetholm, Roxburghshire.

**MARKS, Albert Aubrey. Jr.** MBA, BS, Econ. American. *B.* 1912. *Educ.* Williams Coll; Univ. of Pennsylvania (BS.(Econ.) MBA). *M.* 1939, Elizabeth. *S.* 2. *Dau.* 1. *Career:* Gen. Partner, Newburger & Co.; Dir. Guarantee Bank & Trust Co.; Anchor Savings & Loan Assn.; Famous Players Int. *Member:* Newcomen Socy; Investment Bankers Assn.; Assn. New York Exchange Firms; Int. Platform Association. *Clubs:* Explorers; Williams; Marco Polo. *Address: office* 20 S. Tenn Avenue, Atlantic City, N.J. 08401, U.S.A.

**MARKS, Sir John Hedley Douglas,** CBE. British. Chartered Accountant. *B.* 1916. *Educ.* Sydney C. of E. Grammar School; FCA (Aust.); Fellow, Inst. Chartered Accountants in Australia. *M.* 1941, Judith Norma Glenwright. *Daus.* Anthea (Ryrie) and Gail (Storey). *Career:* Chairman: Development Finance Corporation Ltd. 1953—, Development Holdings Ltd., Delfin Australian Fund Incorporated and Garrett's Ltd. Commissioner of the Electricity Commission of New South Wales 1966—. Director: Brambles Industries Ltd. (Dep. Chmn.); CHEP International Finance S.A.; CHEP International Investments S.A.; West Lakes Ltd.; Dickson Primer Consolidated Ltd.; R.D.C. Holdings Ltd.; Dir. & Chmn. Reinsurance Co. of Australasia Ltd.; Dir. Borg-Warner (Australia) Ltd.; Japan Australia Investment Co. Ltd.; Canada Aust. Investment Co. Ltd.; Alcan Australia Ltd.; Dir. & Chmn. Acmil Ltd.; Dir. Dev West Ltd.; Chmn. Emeritus, Prince Henry Hospital, Eastern Suburbs Hospital and Prince of Wales Hospital. *Member:* Inst. of Chartered Accountants in Australia; Aust. Socy. of Accountants; Inst. of Directors. *Clubs:* Royal Sydney Yacht Squadron; Australian; American National; Elanora Country; Manly Golf. *Address:* 6b Raglan Street, Mosman, N.S.W.; and *office* 16 O'Connell Street, Sydney, N.S.W., Australia.

**MA'ROUF, Taha M.** Iraqui. *B.* 1924. *Educ.* Law Coll. Univ. of Baghdad. *Career:* Lawyer 1949; Joined Diplomatic Service and appointed to Iran, Spain, U.A.R., U.K. 1964; D.G. Public Relations Dept. Min. for Foreign Affairs, Baghdad 1968; Min. Plen. Charge d'Affaires, Embassy of Iraq, London 1968; after July Revolution appointed Minister of State Iraqui Cabinet, Min. of Works and Housing Mar. 1970; Ambassador to Italy July 1970; Vice-Pres. of the Republic since 1974. *Address:* c/o Ministry of Foreign Affairs, Baghdad, Iraq.

**MARPLES of Wallasey, Baron, (Alfred) Ernest,** PC, FCA, FRSA. British. *B.* 1907. *Educ.* Stretford Grammar School. *M.* 1956, Ruth Dobson. *Career:* Chartered Accountant 1928. Joined London Scottish July 1939; 2nd Lieut., R.A. 1941; Captain 1941. Member, Parliament (Con.) Wallasey 1945–74; Parly. Sec., Ministry of Housing & Local Government 1951–54; and Ministry of Pensions & National Insurance 1954–55; Postmaster-General 1957–59; Minister of Transport 1959–64; Shadow Minister of Technology, 1964–66; Sponsor Conservative Party Public Sector Research Unit, 1967–70; Created Life Peer, Baron Marples of Wallasey in County of Merseyside (1974). International Dir. Purolator Services Inc. (U.S.A.) 1970–76; Purolator Services (UK) 1970–76. *Award:* Hon. Freeman, The Borough of Wallasey 1970. *Publication:* The Road to Prosperity (1947). *Address:* c/o Lloyds Bank International, Monaco.

**MARRE, Sir Alan (Samuel),** KCB Former British Parliamentary Commissioner. *B.* 1914. *Educ.* St. Olave's and St. Saviour's Grammar School, Southwark; Trinity Hall, Cambridge. *M.* 1943, Romola Mary Gilling. *S.* 1. *Dau.* 1. *Career:* Asst. Principal, Ministry of Health 1936, Principal 1941; Asst. Secy. 1946; Under Secy. 1952–63; Under Secy., Ministry of Labour 1963–64; Deputy Secy., Ministry of Health 1964–66; Min. Labour, Dept. of Employment and Productivity 1966–68; Second Perm. Secy. Dept. of Health and Social Security 1968–71; Parliamentary Commissioner for Admin. 1971–76; Member of Councils on Tribunals 1971–76; Health Service Commissioner for England, Scotland, and Wales 1973–76. *Club:* Athenaeum. *Address:* 44 The Vale, London, NW11 8SG.

**MARRIAN, Peter Derek,** MLC. British farmer. *B.* 1916. *Educ.* Shrewsbury and Trinity College, Oxford (MA Hons). *M.* 1948, Susan Vogel. *S.* 3. *Career:* In Colonial Admin.

Service 1939–42 (resigned); Capt. R.A. 1940–45; farming at Mweiga Estate, Kenya 1948–61; member of Legislative Council for the Central Rural Constituency, Mar. 1961–63. Pres., Kenya National Farmers' Union 1959–60; Minister of Tourism 1961; Parliamentary Secy., Ministry of Local Government 1962–63; Ministry of Lands and Settlement 1963–64; Specially Elected Member, Kenya National Assembly 1963–64. Resigned from all political activities 1964. *Clubs:* Vincents; Muthiaga. *Address: office* P.O. Box 30221, Nairobi, Kenya.

**MARRINER, Kenneth William.** American wool textile manufacturer. *B.* 1899. *Educ.* Cheltenham College (England). *M.* 1929, Mary Keyes. *S.* Kenneth William, Jr.; Thomas Eaton and John Sterling. Chmn. Pres. Marriner Import Export Co. *Clubs:* The Country (Brookline, Mass.); Nashua (N.H.) Country. *Address:* Marriner Import Export Inc., 201 Clarlemont St., Newton, Mass. 02161, U.S.A.

**MARRYATT, Henry William.** Australian. *B.* 1907. *Educ.* University of Melbourne (BCom), MAppSc. *M.* 1937, Anne Rowe. *S.* Ian HenryHalford. *Dau.* Heather Anne. *Career:* Dir. and General Manager, Wormald Brothers (Aust.) Pty. Ltd., and associated companies 1953 until retirement in 1965; Chmn. Melba Memorial Conservatorium of Music 1965–72; Chmn. Australian Fire Protection Assoc. 1960—, Standard Chemical Co. Pty. Ltd. 1966—; President, Building Industry Congress of Victoria 1966–67 and 1969–71; Chmn. Volclay Standard Pty. Ltd. 1971—; Durachem Pty. Ltd. since 1971. *Member:* Grad. Cncl., Univ. of Melbourne1959–68 Subscriber's Committee of Melbourne Symphony Orchestra 1960–67. *Fellow:* Institute of Management, and Institute of Directors. Charter *Member:* Society of Fire Protection Engineers (U.S.A.). Associate Member National Fire Protection Association (U.S.A.), and Fire Protection Association (England). *Publications:* numerous articles on fire protection and fire prevention in various Australian publications; Fire-Automatic Sprinkler Performance in Australia and New Zealand, 1886–1968. *Clubs:* Australian, Athenaeum, Savage, Kingston Heath Golf, Melbourne Cricket, Waldara Golf, Wangaratta, Wangaratta Rotary, (all of Melbourne). *Address:* Harborough, Brosters Road, East Wangaratta, Vic. 3678 and *office* 1st Floor, 51 William Street, Melbourne, 3000, Vic., Australia.

**MARS, Louis.** Grand Cross, Order of Honour and Merit, Ambassador of Haiti. *B.* 1906. *Educ.* Doctor of Medicine. *M.* 1943, Madeleine Targète. *S.* Maurice and Louis-Henry. *Dau.* Emmeline. *Career:* Professor of Psychiatry, Faculty of Medicine, Port-au-Prince 1937–46 (Dean of the Faculty 1946–51); President, University of Haiti 1957; Minister of Foreign Affairs 1958–59, and June 1958–Dec. 1959; Ambassador to Paris 1960–61, to United States 1961. Doctor *h.c.* (Law) Univ. of Liberia. *Member:* Academy of Medicine of New York; Academy of Medicine, Rome; American Psychiatric Assn. *Address:* Ministry of Foreign Affairs, Port-au-Prince, Haiti.

**MARSH, Donald Bailey,** MA, PhD. *B.* 1911. *Educ.* Univ. of New Brunswick (BA), Louisiana State Univ. (MA), and Univ. of Illinois (PhD). *M.* 1939, Kathleen Idel Moore. *S.* Denis Michael. *Daus.* Susan Melinda, Elizabeth Mavity and Donna Lee. *Career:* Teaching Fellow, Louisiana State Univ. 1935–36; Assist. in Economics, Univ. of Illinois 1936–37; Acting Prof. of Economics, Univ. of New Brunswick 1937–38; Fellow in Economics, Univ. of Illinois 1938–40; Instructor in Economics, Barnard Coll., Columbia Univ. 1940–46; Economic Specialist, Dept. of Finance and Business Research, The Chase National Bank, N.Y. 1945–47; Rapporter, Committee on Flow of Capital, U.S. Associates, The International Chamber of Commerce, N.Y. 1946, Economist 1947–54, Director of Economic Research 1952–54, The Royal Bank of Canada, Montreal; Prof. of Economics 1947–54, Bronfman Prof. of Economics 1954–58, Chmn., Social Studies & Commerce Group 1954–58, Chmn. Dept. of Economics and Political Science 1955–58, McGill University, Montreal; Asst. General Manager (Economic Research), The Royal Bank of Canada, Montreal 1958–72. *Publications:* Taxes without Tears (1945); World Trade and Investment (1951); Chapter on Canada in B. H. Beckhart (ed.) Banking Systems (1954); miscellaneous articles and reviews in professional journals. *Clubs:* Faculty of McGill University; University (Montreal). *Address:* 510 Lakeshore Drive, Dorval, Quebec, Canada.

**MARSH, Frank.** American Career Politician. *B.* 1924. *Educ.* University of Nebraska (BSc; ED); Hon. Degree, Lincoln Sch. of Commerce. *M.* 1943, Shirley M. McVicker. *S.* 4. *Daus.* 2. *Career:* Served in U.S. Army (European theatre; in battles of St. Lo, Rhineland and Ardennes) 1943–46; Univ. of Nebraska 1946–50; Businessman, teacher 1950–53; Secretary of State, State of Nebraska. Jan. 1953–71; Lieutenant-Governor 1971–75; State Treasurer 1975–79; Member, Past Pres., COSERV; Amer. Legion; Veterans of Foreign Wars; Disabled American Veterans; Central States Corrections Assn.; Nebraska Correctional Assn.; Gateway Sertoma; Mayor's Cttee. for International Friendship; Combined Organization of Police Service; International Trustee, American Field Service; Bd. of Dirs., American Youth Hostels; Bd. of Dirs., Midwest Intern. Trade Assn., Symphony United Nations; *Member:* State Hist. Socy.; Senior Vice-Pres., Nat. Assn. State Treasurers; Board of State Canvassers; Natural Disaster Fund; Board of Equalization and Assessment; Native Sons and Daughters of Nebraska; Nebraska Beef Promotion Foundation; American Correctional Assn.; Nebraskaland Foundation; Lincoln Chapter. Amer. Field Service; Ak-Sar-Ben; Scottish Society of Nebraska; C.R.O.P. (Church World Relief); State Claims Board. Consul-Gen. Nebraska for Guatemala; Alpha Phi Omega, National Service Fraternity; Life Mem., Nebraska Alumni Assn.; Lincoln Gem & Mineral Soc.; Chmn., Admin. Bd., Trinity Methodist Church. *Clubs:* Lincoln Stamp; Lincoln Polemic; Lincoln University. *Address:* 2701 South 34th Street, Lincoln, Nebraska 68506, U.S.A.

**MARSH, (Henry) John,** CBE. British. *B.* 1913. *Educ.* China Inland Mission School (Chefoo), Wimborne Grammar School, Birmingham Central Tech. Coll. *M.* 1950, Mary Costerton. *S.* 2. *Daus.* 2. *Career:* Commercial apprentice, Shanghai 1930–32; Engineering apprentice 1932–35; Apprentice Supervisor, Austin Motor Co. 1936–39; Personnel Officer, British Overseas Airways Corp. 1946–47. Dir. Inst. of Personnel Management 1947–49, and Industrial Welfare Society 1950–61; Dir. Gen. The British Inst. of Management 1961–73; Asst. Chmn. Counsellor 1973–76; Chmn. W. D. Scott (U.K.). Served in World War II R.A.S.C. (T.A.), Singapore Fortress; B.E.F. France 1940; Malaya 1941–42 (despatches twice); Prisoner-of-war 1942–45; released with rank of Major 1946. *Member:* Voluntary Service Overseas (Chmn. 1957–61); B.B.C. General Adv. Cncl. (1959–64); U.K. Council on Education for Management, 1961–65; Governing Body, Univ. of Surrey, 1963–69; Council for Technical Education & Training for Overseas Countries; Member, Russell Cttee. on Adult Education 1969–72; Part-time member, National Coal Board, 1968–74; Member, Commonwealth Team of Industrial Specialists 1976—. *Award:* Hon. DSc. *Publications:* People at Work (1957); Partners in Work Relations (1959); Work and Leisure Digest (1960); Ardeshire Dalal Memorial Lecture (1953); Clarke Hall Lecture (1957); E. W. Hancock Lecture (1960); McLaren Memorial Lecture (1962). *Club:* Reform. *Address:* 13 Frank Dixon Way, Dulwich Village, London, S.E.21; and Management House, Parker Street, London, W.C.2.

**MARSH, Robert Thornton, Jr.** American commercial banker. *B.* 1901. *Educ.* Univs. of Richmond (BA) and Virginia (MA). *M.* 1928, Thelma Hill. Rector, Univ. of Richmond 1958—. Treas., Dominion Securities Corp. 1929–38; Chairman of the Board (1962–66), President (1952–62) and Director (1948–67), First and Merchants National Bank, Richmond, Va.; Dir.: Life Insurance Co. of Virginia 1952–68, Dan River Mills 1953—, Richmond, Fredericksburg & Potomac Railroad Co. 1952—; Ethyl Corp. 1962—; Lawyers Title Insurance Co.; Chmn. of Board, Richmond Life Insurance Co., 1969. Virginia Public School Authority 1962—. Phi Beta Kappa; Beta Gamma Sigma; Omicron Delta Kappa. Democrat. *Clubs:* Commonwealth; Country (Virginia); Farmington Country; Virginia Boat. *Address: office* P.O. Box 6-R, Richmond 17, Va., U.S.A.

**MARSHALL, Dr. Edmund Ian.** MP. British Politician. *B.* 1940. *Educ.* Magdalen Coll., Oxford (Double First Class Honours, MA); Liverpool Univ., (PhD). *M.* 1969, Margaret Pamela Antill. *Dau.* 1. *Career:* University Lecturer in Mathematics 1962–66; Mathematician in Industry 1967–71; Labour MP for Goole since 1971; Parliamentary Private Sec. to the Sec. of State for Northern Ireland 1974–76; PPS to the Home Secretary since 1976. *Club:* Reform. *Address:* House of Commons, London SW1A 0AA.

**MARSHALL, Sir Frank Shaw,** MA, LLB, FRSA. British Solicitor. *B.* 1915. *Educ.* Queen Elizabeths Wakefield; Downing Coll., Cambridge (Scholar). *M.* 1941, Mary Barr. *Daus.* 2. Freeman of the City of Leeds. *Career:* Dir. Leeds & Holbeck Building Society 1963—, (Pres. 1967–69); Chmn. Association, Municipal Corps. England, Wales, N. Ireland. Chmn. Local Govt. Information Office, England & Wales 1968–73; Chmn. Leeds Grand Theatre & Opera House Ltd.

1970–73; Steering Cttee. Local Authority Management Structures 1970–72; Man. Trustee, Municipal Mutual Insurance Ltd. 1970—; Member, Uganda Resettlement Board 1971–73; Local Govt. Conditions of Service Adv. Board 1971–73; Vice-Chmn. Centre, Environmental Studies 1971—; Member Yorks & Humberside Economic Planning Council 1971–74; Chmn. Maplin Development Authority 1973–74. Dir. several companies. *Member:* Mangt. Cttee. The Automobile Association. Fellow, Royal Society of Arts. *Clubs:* Carlton; Leeds. *Address:* Wigton Manor, Manor House Lane, Leeds 17 and *office* Guildford Chambers, 111 The Headrow, Leeds LS1 5JP.

**MARSHALL, J. Howard II.** American executive and lawyer. *B.* 1905. *Educ.* Haverford Coll. (AB 1926) and Yale Univ. (LLB *magnum cum laude*, 1931). *M.* (1) 1931, Eleanor Pierce. *S.* J. Howard III and E. Pierce. *M.* (2) 1961, Bettye M. Bohanon. *Career:* Inst. and Asst. Cruise Dir. Floating University 1926–27 (Cruise Director 1928–29); Assistant Dean and Assistant Professor of Law, Yale University 1931–33; member Petroleum Administrative Board, U.S. Department of Interior 1933–35; Special Asst. to Attorney-General of U.S. and Asst. Solicitor, U.S. Dept. of the Interior 1933–35; Special Counsel, Standard Oil Co. of California 1935–37; partner, Pillsbury, Madison & Sutro, San Francisco 1938–44; Chief Counsel, Petroleum Administration for War 1941–44; also Asst. Deputy Administrator 1943–44; General Counsel, U.S. Delegation to Allied Commission on Reparations 1945; Pres., Dir., Ashland Oil & Refining Co., and subsidiary corporations 1944–51; Member Military Petroleum Advisory Bd. to Joint Chiefs of Staff since 1944; Director: National Bank of Commerce, Houston; Consultant to Secy. of Interior on petroleum defence programme 1950–52. Exec. Vice-Pres. and Dir., Signal Oil & Gas Co. 1952–60; Director: Frontier Refining Co. 1953–67; Great Northern Oil Purchasing Co. 1953–62; Dir.: Great Northern Oil Co. 1953–70; Analog Technology Corp.; Chmn. of the Bd. The Petroleum Corp.; President & Director, Union Texas National Gas Corp. & affiliated Corps. 1961–62; President, Union Texas Petroleum, 1962–67; Dir. Allied Chemical Corp. 1965–67; Chmn. of the Bd. Great Northern Oil Co. since 1970. *Member:* Twenty-five Year Club of the Petroleum industry, American Petroleum Inst. (Vice-Pres. and Dir. 1948–50), National Petroleum Cncl., Amer. Inst. of Mining & Metallurgical Engineers; Amer. California and Kentucky Bar Associations; Bd. of Managers Haverford College; Beta Rho Sigma (Haverford); Order of Coif (Yale). *Club:* Bohemian (San Francisco); River Oaks Country (Houston). *Address:* 11100 Meadowick, Houston, Texas 77024 and *office* 1320 Esperson Building, Houston, Texas 77002, U.S.A.

**MARSHALL, Rt. Hon Sir John Ross,** GBE, CH, BA, LLM, Hon. LLD. New Zealand barrister and solicitor. *B.* 5 March 1912. *M.* 1944, Margaret Livingston. *S.* 2. *Daus.* 2. *Career:* Commenced practice as Barrister and Solicitor 1936; attended World Conf. of Christian Youth, Amsterdam 1939; served World War II with 2nd N.Z.E.F., Pacific Islands and Italy 1941–46 (Infantry Major): MP (National) for Mount Victoria 1946–54; for Karori 1954–75; Lecturer in Law, Victoria Univ. College 1948–51; Minister, Asst. to Prime Minister, in charge of State Advances Corp., Public Trust Office and Census and Statistics Dep. 1949–54; Minister of Health 1951–54, and Information and Publicity 1951–57; Attorney-General and Minister of Justice 1954–57; Deputy Prime Minister 1957; Deputy Leader of the Opposition, Dec. 1957–60; Dep. Prime Minister, Minister of Ind. and Com. 1960–69 and Overseas Trade 1960–72; Minister of Customs 1960–61. Minister of Labour & Immigration 1969–72; Attorney-General, 1969–71; Prime Minister 1972; Leader of Opposition 1973–74; N.Z. Representative at Colombo Plan conference, New Delhi 1953. Visited U.S. on Foreign Leader Grant, Apr. 1958. Represented N.Z., GATT Ministerial Conf. 1961, 1963, 1966; ECAFE Conf. 1962, 1964, 1966, 1968 and 1970 (Chmn., Wellington Conf. 1965), Commonwealth Prime Ministers' Conf. 1962, and Commonwealth Trade Ministers' Conf. 1963 and 1966; Commonwealth Parliamentary Conf. 1965. Privy Councillor 1966. Chmn. National Development Council 1969–72; New Zealand Commission for Expo 70; Chmn. of Cttee. on Teacher Registration, 1976–77. Visiting Fellow, Victoria Univ. of Wellington; Consultant partner Buddle, Anderson, Kent & Co.; Hon. Bencher Gray's Inn London. Mem. Advisory Council, World Peace through Law; Chmn. of Dirs. Nat. Bank of NZ, Norwich Winterthur Insurance (NZ) Ltd., Philips Electrical Industries, Contractors Bonding Corp; Dir. Norwich Union Ins. Socy., DRG (NZ), Fletcher Holdings and Hallenstein Bros. *Publication:* The Law of Watercourses. *Address:* 22 Fitzroy Street, Wellington, New Zealand.

**MARSHALL, Sylvan Mitchell.** American Attorney & Consul of Finland. *B.* 1917. *Educ.* Townsend Harris High School; Coll. of the City of New York (BA); Harvard Univ. Law School (Doctor of Laws). *M.* 1951, Mara Byron. *S.* 2. *Career:* Practice of Law, New York and Washington 1946—; Special Deputy Attorney Gen. New York State 1946–50; Hon. Deputy Police Commissioner, New York City 1950–51; Special Asst. to the Chief Counsel, Office, Price Stabilization, Washington 1950–52; National Broadcasting Co. T.V. Prod. Public Affairs Programming 1953–58; Chmn. Bd. Dirs. International Gem and Mineral Show Inc. since 1968; Amb., Rep. of the Pres. of the U.S. to the Inaugural of the Pres. of Mexico, 1976. Sen. Partner Marshall, Leon, Weill & Mahony. *Member:* Nat. Academy, Television Arts & Sciences. *Awards:* Knight Commander, Order, Vasco Nunez De Balboa (Panama); Comm. Order of the Lion (Finland); Order of the Crown (Iran); Knight, Order of the Southern Cross (Brazil); Commander, Order of Ruben Dario (Nicaragua); Knight Commander Order of the Falcon (Iceland); Commander, Order of Aztec Eagle (Mexico). *Clubs:* Cosmos; International (Washington). *Address:* 2929 Ellicott Street, N.W. Washington, D.C. 20008, U.S.A.

**MART, Marcel.** Luxemburger. Minister. *B.* 1927. *Educ.* Doctor of Law. *M.* 1955, Margaret Vogeley. *S.* Daniel. *Dau.* Caroline. *Career:* Lawyer 1953–55; Journalist 1955–60; Spokesman ECAC 1960–64; Head, EEC Information Office, New York 1964–66; Head Information Service for countries outside EEC in Brussels 1967–69; formerly Minister, National Economy, the Middle Classes and Tourism, Minister, Transport and Power, Luxembourg; currently Luxembourg Rep. to EEC's Court of Audit, Luxembourg. *Address: office* 19 Boulevard Royal, Luxembourg.

**MARTIN, Archer John Porter,** CBE. British *B.* 1910. *Educ.* Bedford School and Peterhouse, Cambridge (MA, BA, PhD). *M.* 1943, Judith Bagenal. *S.* 2. *Daus.* 3. *Career:* With Nutritional Lab., Cambridge 1933–38; Wool Industries Research Assn., Leeds 1938–46, Research Dept., Boots Pure Drug Co., Nottingham 1946–48; National Inst. of Medical Research 1948–56; Chemist Consultant 1956–59; Dir. Abbotsbury Laboratories Ltd. 1959—; Extraordinary Prof. at the Technological Univ. of Eindhoven (Netherlands) 1965–73; Consultant, Wellcome Research Laboratories 1970–73; Professional Fellow, Univ. of Sussex since 1973; Welch Professor of Chemistry, Univ. of Houston, Texas since 1974. *Awards:* F.R.S. 1950; Hon. DSc (Leeds University) 1968; Hon. LLD (Glasgow Univ.) 1973; Berzelius Gold Medal, Swedish Med. Society 1951; Nobel Prize (jointly) 1952; John Scott Award 1958; John Price Wetherill Medal 1959; Franklin Inst. Medal 1959; Royal Society's Leverhulme Medal 1963; Koltoff Medal of Academy of Pharmaceutical Science, 1969; Callendar Medal, Inst. of Measurement and Control 1971. *Member:* Royal Socy.; Biochemical Society; Society for Analytical Chemistry; American Society of Biological Chemists Incorporated. *Club:* Chemists (N.Y.C.). *Address:* Abbotsbury, Barnet Lane, Elstree, Herts.

**MARTIN, Byron Samuel.** American management consultant. *B.* 1922. *Educ.* Univ. of Chicago (BA Politics; MA Int. Law). *M.* 1961, Julia Jane Moninger. *Career:* Pathfinder navigator/bombardier 15th USAF 1943–44; OSS attached staff Supreme Allied Cmdr. SEAC 1944–45; Operations Officer U.S. Army General Staff 1948–49; Exec. Asst. Chief Historian U.S. Army. Gen. Secy. American Military Inst. Editor Military Affairs 1949–50; Intelligence Officer U.S. Army Gen. Staff 1950–51; Liaison Group, Staff C in C, U.N. Command, Korean War 1951–53; Faculty U.S. Army General School 1953; Man. Editor Steelways 1954–56; Hill and Knowlton Inc. 1956–65; Management Consultant since 1965; Dir. Combined Agencies Corp. since 1970; IB Securities Corp 1969–74; Hardenburgh Securities Corp. *Member:* Registered Principal, Nat. Assn. of Securities Dealers Investment Adviser. *Awards:* Distinguished Flying Cross (USA); Air Medal with two Oak Leaf Clusters (USA); Purple Heart (USA); Wharang Order of Military Merit with Gold Star (Republic of Korea). *Publications:* The American Mexican Claims Commission of 1947 (1948); The Stock Exchange the SEC and Your Financial Public Relations (1962); Numerous articles topics relating to management. *Clubs:* British United Services (Los Angeles); Continental Country (Flagstaff). *Address:* 5241 East Hickory Drive, Flagstaff, Arizona 86001, U.S.A.

**MARTIN, Edmund Fible.** American steel executive (Ret.). *B.* 1902. *Educ.* Stevens Inst. of Technology (BS 1922); DEng., Univ. of Buffalo 1961; LLD, Moravian College 1964; LLD, Lehigh Univ. 1966; EngD, Stevens Institute of Technology,

1967; LLD, Valparaiso Univ., 1967. *M.* 1926, Frances Taylor. *Daus.* C. Bettie and Barbara T. (Stout). *Career:* Chairman and Chief Executive Officer, Bethlehem Steel Corp. 1964–70; Member Bd. of Directors: Morgan Guaranty Trust Co. of New York (Subsidiary of J. P. Morgan & Co. Ltd.); American Iron & Steel Institute. *Trustee:* Lehigh University; St. Luke's Hospital; Stevens Institute of Technology; Chairman: Amer. Iron & Steel Inst. 1967–69; Member: Pennsylvania Socy. Director: Bethlehem Chamber of Commerce; Director, Bethlehem Area Foundation; National Industrial Conference Board (Trustee). *Awards:* Knight Comdr.: Royal Order of the North Star (Sweden); of Southern Cross (Brazil); Grand Band Order of Star of Africa (Liberia); Elbert H. Gary Memorial Medal (AISI); The Pennsylvania Society Gold Medal; Benjamin F. Fairless Award (AIME). *Clubs:* Pennsylvania; Bethlehem; Bethlehem Steel; Links, Sky, (all of N.Y.C.); Laurel Valley Golf, Rolling Rock (both of Ligonier, Pa.); National Golf Links of America; Augusta (Ga.) National Golf; Lyford Cay, Nassau, Bahamas; Saucon Valley Country; Skytop. *Address: office* Suite 310, 437 Main Street, Bethlehem, Pa. 18018, U.S.A.

**MARTIN, Georges Gérard.** Belgian insurance executive. *B.* 1903. *Educ.* Military School (Engineering); Diplomé Belgian and French Staff Colleges. *M.* 1927, Louise Boël. *S.* Georges, Louis and Michel. *Dau.* Lucy-Monique. *Career:* Officer, Belgian Army 1927–45; Belgian Staff College 1936; French Staff College 1939, Chairman of Board & Man. Dir., Royal Belge Life and Accident Insurance, and Royale Belge Fire Insurance Lloyd Belge. *Awards:* Officer, Order of Leopold; Commandeur, Order of the Crown (Belgium); Chevalier, Légion d'honneur; M.B.E. (England); Bronze Star Medal (U.S.A.). *Clubs:* Chateau Ste-Anne; Cercle Gaulois; Mars et Mercure. *Address:* 82 Boulevard Saint-Michel, Bte. 6, Brussels; and *office* 25 Bd. du Souverain, 1170 Brussels, Belgium.

**MARTIN, Guy.** American. *B.* 1911. *Educ.* Oxford University (BA 1934, MA 1944) and Yale Univ. (LLB 1937). *M.* 1946, Edith Kingdon Gould. *S.* Guy III, Jason Gould, and Christopher Kingdon. *Dau.* Edith Maria Theodosia Burr. *Career:* Partner, Martin, Whitfield, Thaler & Bebchick and predecessors, Washington, D.C. 1952—. Dir. & Chief Exec. Officer, Financial Mortgage & Realty Corp.; Dir., International Bank, and International Trust Co., Liberia. *Member:* American, District of Columbia and New York City Bar Associations; Phi Beta Kappa; Sigma Alpha Epsilon. *Award:* U.S. Legion of Merit. *Clubs:* Metropolitan, City Tavern, Arts (Washington), Yale, The Brook (N.Y.C.). *Address:* 3300 'O' Street, N.W., Washington, D.C. 20007; and *office* 1701 Pennsylvania Avenue, N.W., Washington, D.C. 20006, U.S.A.

**MARTIN, Sir Leslie Harold,** CBE. Australian professor (emeritus); physicist; Dean of Military Studies, Professor of Physics, Royal Military College, Duntroon, Canberra. *B.* 1900. *Educ.* Melbourne and Cambridge Universities; PhD (Cantab.). *M.* 1923, Gladys Bull. *S.* Leon (*Dec.*); Raymond. *Career:* Professor of Physics, University of Melbourne 1945–59. Chairman, Australian Universities Commission 1959–66; Commissioner, Australian Atomic Energy Commission 1958–68; Scientific Adviser Department of Defence, Australia 1948–67. Prof. of Physics, Royal Mil. Coll., Duntroon, Canberra 1967–70; DSc (Melbourne; Australian Natl. Univ.; Queensland; New South Wales; Adelaide); LLD (W. Aust.); LittD Sydney; FAA; FRS Fellow; Royal Society, London; Australian Acad. of Science; Inst. of Physics. *Address:* 11 Wedge Court, Glen Waverley, Victoria 3150, Australia.

**MARTIN, Leslie Keith.** Australian newspaper publisher. B. 1902. *Educ.* Malvern School, Sydney. *M.* 1941, Joan Quinan. *S.* Peter. *Career:* Formerly Sales Manager, N.S.W., Ford Motor Co. of Australia; Asst. Managing Director, Australian Consolidated Press Limited. Director, Conpress Printing Limited; Golden Press Ltd., Sydney; F. Muller Ltd., London; Australian Newsprint-Mills Ltd. *Publications:* Australian Women's Weekly, Sydney Daily Telegraph, Sydney Sunday Telegraph. Member United Australia Party. *Address:* 13 Wentworth Street, Point Piper, Sydney, N.S.W., Australia.

**MARTIN, Hon. Sir Norman Angus.** Australian grazier and company director. *B.* 1893. *M.* 1919, Gladys Violette Barrett. *S.* Neil Angus. *Dau.* Della. *Career:* Minister of Agriculture, State of Victoria 1942–45; Agent-General for Victoria in London 1945–50; Chmn., Ball & Welch Ltd., Victorian Inland Meat Authority, Australia Day Council. Resident Dir. in Australasia for Thomas Cook & Son. *Address:* Longleat, 133 Alexandra Avenue, South Yarra, Vic. 3141, Australia.

**MARTIN, Hon. Paul,** PC, CC, QC, Canadian Lawyer & Politician. *B.* 1903. *Educ.* St. Alexander's Coll., Quebec; St. Michael's Coll., Toronto (MA); Osgoode Hall Law School; Harvard Univ. (LLM); Trinity Coll., Cambridge; Geneva School of Internatl. Studies. *M.* 1936, Eleanor Adams. *S.* Paul. *Dau.* Mary Ann. *Career:* Barrister, 1931; Lecturer in Political Science, Assumption College, Univ. of Western Ontario 1931–34; Chairman, Canadian Delegation to World Youth Congress, Geneva 1936; King's Counsel 1937; Canadian Delegate to Assembly of League of Nations 1938; Parliamentary Assistant to Minister of Labour 1943; Chmn., Canadian Delegation, International Labour Conference, Philadelphia 1944; Secretary of State 1945; Canadian Delegate to sessions of General Assembly, United Nations, London 1946, New York 1946 and 1949 and each year from 1952 to 1955, and Head of Canadian Del. to U.N. General Assembly from 1963 to 1968. Canadian Representative to Economic and Social Council, London 1946, New York 1946 and 1947; MP (Lib.) 1935–68; Appointed to Senate April 1968. Minister of National Health and Welfare 1946–57; Secy. of State for External Affairs, Govt. of Canada 1963–68; Senior Minister & Govt. Leader in the Senate 1968–74; High Commissioner for Canada in the U.K. since 1974. *Member:* Parliamentary Delegation to Czechoslovakia, 1969; Canadian Delegation to Council of Europe, Strasbourg, 1969; Pres., N. Atlantic Council, 1965. Hon. LLD, Michigan, Dalhousie, Toronto, Ottawa, Laval, Assumption, Queen's, Montreal, Dartmouth, St. Thomas, Loyala (Los Angeles), and John Carroll Universities; DCL, Univ. of W. Ontario, and Bishop's Univ.; Hon. Dr. Hum., Wayne State Univ., Ont., Canada; Degree, Univ. of B.C., Univ. of N.B. and Waterloo Lutheran Univ. *Address:* Canadian High Commission, Macdonald House, 1 Grosvenor Square, London W.1.

**MARTIN, Robin Geoffrey.** MA, MIQ. British. *B.* 1921. *Educ.* Cheltenham College; Jesus Coll. Cambridge. *M.* 1946, Marjorie Chester Yates. *S.* 2. *Dau.* 1. *Career:* Dir. Tarmac Ltd. 1955; Man. Dir. Tarmac Roadstone Ltd. 1958; Former Man. Dir. Tarmac Group of companies. Chmn. and Chief Exec. 1971—; Dir. Serck Ltd. since 1971, Dep. Chmn. since 1974, Chmn. since 1976; Dir., Burmah Oil Co. 1975; Mem. Midlands Advisory Board, Legal & General Assurance Society Ltd. 1977; Dir., Ductile Steels Ltd. 1977. *Club:* East India & Sports. *Address:* The Field, Wergs Hall Road, Tettenhall, Staffs and *office* Ettingshall, Wolverhampton.

**MARTIN, Wade Omer, Jr.** American attorney at law. *B.* 18 April, 1911. *Educ.* Southwestern Louisiana Institute (BA); Louisiana State University (LLB). *M.* 1938, Juliette Bonnette. *S.* Wade O., David Mills, Wallace Thurston, Gregory Bonnette. *Daus.* Merle Mary, Marcelle Adrienne. *Career:* Assistant Attorney-General of Louisiana 1935–40; Attorney at Law 1940–44; Secretary of State (1944–75) and Insurance Commissioner of Louisiana 1944–56; Past President, National Association of Secretaries of State and National Association of Insurance Commissioners. Democrat. *Address:* 210 L.S.U. Avenue, Baton Rouge, Louisiana, U.S.A.

**MARTIN, Walter Edwin.** Professor of Biology, University of Southern California. *B.* 1908. *Educ.* Northern Illinois State Univ. (BEd 1930) and Purdue Univ. (MS 1932; PhD 1937). *M.* 1934, Ruth Butler. *S.* John and David. *Daus.* Carol and Judith. *Career:* Insturctor, Purdue Univ. 1934–37; Asst. Prof. 1937–41, Assoc. Prof. 1941–46, and Prof. 1946–47, De Pauw Univ.; Assoc. Prof. 1947–48; Prof. and Head of Zoological Dept. 1948–54, and Head of Biological Dept. 1954–58, Univ. of Southern California. Naval Technologist to Egypt 1953 and 1955, and to Japan, Taiwan and Philippines 1957; attended Sixth International Congress on Tropical Medicine and Malaria, Lisbon 1958. Sabbatical at Neuchâtel, Switzerland 1963–64; Brisbane Australia 1970–71. *Member:* Amer. Assn. for Advancement of Science (Fellow); Amer. Socy. of Zoologists; Amer. Micro Socy.; Amer. Socy. of Parasitologists; Southern California Acad. of Science (Fellow); Indiana Acad. of Sciences (Fellow); Western Socy. of Naturalists; Sigma Xi; Phi Sigma. *Publications:* approximately 80 scientific papers on parasitology, helminthology, and experimental embryology; includes works on life cycles, pathology, physiology and nucleic acid metabolism, using radio isotopes and antimetabolites; Distinguished Alumnus Award (Ill.), 1969. *Address:* 2185 Warmouth Street, San Pedro, Calif.; and Biology Dept., University of Southern California, Los Angeles 7, Calif., U.S.A.

**MARTIN, William Frederick.** American executive. *B.* 1917. *Educ.* University of Oklahoma (BS). *M.* 1941, Betty Jean

Randall. *S.* William Scott. *Dau.* Sharol Ann. *Career:* With Phillips Petroleum; Finance Clerk 1939. Secy. and Asst. Treas. 1959, Treasurer 1960, Secy. and Treas. 1962, Member Board of Directors 1964, Senior Vice-President, 1965, Exec. Vice-Pres. 1968–71; Pres. since 1971, Pres. and Chief Exec. Officer 1973, Chmn. of Board and Chief Exec. Officer since 1974, Dir.: Amer. Petroleum Inst.; Dir.: National Bank of Tulsa and First Nat. Bank in Bartlesville. *Address:* 615 East 16th Place, Bartlesville, Okla. 74003; and *office* 18 Phillips Building, Bartlesville, Okla. 74004, U.S.A.

**MARTIN ARTAJO, Alberto.** Spanish statesman. *B.* 2 Oct. 1905. *Educ.* Cardinal Cisneros High School (Extr. Prize in Matriculation); University of Madrid (Extr. Prize in Licentiate Exam.); LLD (Hons.). *M.* 1931, dona Maria Jesus Saracho e Ibanez de Aldecoa. *S.* 6. *Daus.* 2. *Career:* On taking Law degree was apptd. Asst. Prof., Chair of Administrative Law, Univ. of Madrid; held Chair of Social Policy, Faculty of Economic and Political Sciences 1944–45; represented Spanish universities at many congresses and assemblies abroad elected Secretary-General, Council of State, 1940; during Civil War was legal adviser to Labour Commission of the Technical Junta of the State, and later to Ministry of Labour; was editor of Catholic daily El Debate: Minister for Foreign Affairs 1945–57; Member, Real Academia de Ciencias Morales y Politicas 1961. *Publications:* several social books and many newspaper articles in Spain and abroad. *Awards:* 32 Spanish and foreign Orders. *Address:* General Sanjurjo, 34, 5°, Madrid 3, Spain.

**MARTIN-BATES, James Patrick,** JP. British company director. *B.* 1912. *Educ.* Perth Academy; Glenalmond; Worcester Coll. Oxford (BA 1933; MA 1944). *M.* 1939, Clare Miller. *S.* 1. *Daus.* 2. *Career:* With Lamson Industries 1933–36; Dorman Long & Co. Ltd. 1936–38; P.E. Group 1938–61; Managing Director Production Engineering Ltd. 1953–59; Vice-Chmn. P. E. Holdings 1959–61; Principal, Administrative Staff College Henley-on-Thames, 1961–72; Director Hutchinson's Ltd., 1957—. Averys Ltd., 1970—; W. S. Atkins Group Ltd. since 1972; Charringtons Industrial Holdings Ltd. since 1972. *Member:* U.K. Adv. Cncl. on Educ. for Management 1961–66, Cncl. Glenalmond 1963—, Econ. Development Cttee for the Rubber Ind. 1965–69; Cncl. for Technical Education & Training for Overseas Countries 1962–73; and Council of University College, Nairobi 1964–68; High Sheriff of Buckinghamshire 1974–5. Justice of the Peace 1962. *Award:* Burnham Medal (BIM) 1974. *Publications:* various articles on management, etc. Fellow: British Inst. of Management: International Acad. of Management; Member, Inst. of Chartered Secretaries & Administrators (F.C.I.S.) 1965–74. *Clubs:* Caledonian (London); Royal & Ancient (St. Andrews). *Address:* Ivy Cottage, Fingest, Henley-on-Thames, Oxon, England.

**MARTIN-JENKINS, Dennis Frederick,** TD. British. *B.* 1911. *Educ.* St. Bede's School; Marlborough College; Lausanne and Bonn. *M.* 1937, Rosemary Clare Walker. *S.* 3. *Career:* Chairman of Ellerman Lines Ltd.; Past Chmn. London General Shipowners' Society; Past President Chamber of Shipping of the U.K.; Past Chmn. International Chamber of Shipping. *Member:* Council of the Chamber of Shipping; British Transport Docks Board; Inst. of Transport. *Club:* United Oxford and Cambridge University. *Address:* Oriel Cottage, Shamley Green, Surrey; and *office* 12–20 Camomile Street, London, EC3A 7EX.

**MARTINEAU, John Edmund.** Director of Whitbread & Co. Ltd., Brewers, London. *B.* 1904. *Educ.* Eton, New College, Oxford (MA). *M.* 1936, Catherine Makepeace Thackeray Ritchie. *S.* 2. *Daus.* 2. Fellow of the Society of Antiquaries; President, The Institute of Brewing 1954–56; Master of Brewers' Company 1955–56. *Address:* Walsham-le-Willows, Bury St. Edmunds, Suffolk.

**MARTINELLI, Hon. Mario.** Member of the Italian Parliament (Senate). *B.* 1906. *M.* Francesca Vergottini. *S.* 3. *Dau.* 4. *Career:* Member of the Resistance 1944; Secretary, Christian Democratic Party for Province of Como, 1945–46; elected Member of the Italian Parliament 1946; member, National Council, Christian Democratic Party since 1949; Under-Secretary of State to the Treasury 1951; Under-Secretary of State for Foreign Trade 1953; Minister for Foreign Trade Feb. 1954–July 1955. Chmn., Commission of Transports, European Parliament in Strasbourg, 1958. Chmn., Finance and Treasury Cttee., Chamber of Deputies 1958–60; Minister of Foreign Trade 1960–62; Minister of Finance 1963; Vice-Pres. (1964) and President (1968) of the Finance and Treasury Cttee. Senate; Pres. Fiscal Reform Cttee. 1972; Confirmed Senator 1972; Chmn. Senate Transport Comm. 1972–75; Min. of Transport, 4th Moro Govt. 1975; Member of European Parliament 1976, Vice-Pres. of Cttee. on External Economic Relations; Member, Chamber of Deputies following 1976 election. *Address:* Via Dante, 100 Como, 22100 Italy.

**MARTONMERE, Rt. Hon. Lord** (John Roland Robinson), PC, GBE, KCMG, KStJ, Kt 1954, MA, LLB. *B.* 1907. *Educ* Trinity Hall, Cambridge; Barrister-at-Law (Certificate of Honour and Buchanan Prize, Lincoln's Inn 1928) 1929. *M.* 1930, Maysie Gasque. *S.* 1. *Dau.* 1. *Career:* MP: Widnes Div. of Lancs. 1931–35, Blackpool 1935–45; South Blackpool 1945–64. Wing Comdr. R.A.F.V.R. 1940–45. Former Chmn. Conservative Party Commonwealth Affairs Cttee., and of General Council Commonwealth Parliamentary Assn. (1961–62); Dep. Chmn. U.K. Branch of latter; Governor and Commander-in-Chief Bermuda 1964–72; Past Pres.: Royal Lancashire Agriculture Socy., Assn. of Health and Pleasure Resorts and Residential Hotels Assn. of Great Britain. Officer, Legion of Merit (U.S.A.); Hon. Freeman, Town of St. George and City of Hamilton (Bermuda). *Clubs:* Carlton: Royal Lytham St. Annes Golf; Royal Yacht Squadron; Royal Bermuda Yacht; Mid-Ocean (Bermuda); Lyford Cay (Bahamas). *Address:* Romay House, Tuckers Town, Bermuda; and El Mirador, Lyford Cay, Bahamas.

**MARVIN, Philip.** American executive. *B.* 1916. *Educ.* Rensselaer Polytechnic Inst. (B. Ind.E. 1937). Illinois. Inst. of Technology (Industrial Research Management): Oak Ridge Inst. of Nuclear Studies (special training course); Ind. Applications of Nuclear Energy, Univ. of Indiana; MBA 1951; DBA 1951; La Salle Univ. (LLB 1954); Institute of Chartered Financial Analysts (CFA 1963). *M.* 1942, Grace E. Meerbach. *Career:* Commercial Research and Engineering, General Electric Co. 1937–42; Dir., Chemical and Metallurgical Engineering, Marine Div., Bendix Aviation Corp. 1943–44; Dir. of Research and Development, Milwaukee Gas Speciality Co. 1945–51; Management Consultant, Booz, Allen & Hamilton Feb.–July 1952; Vice-Pres. and Dir., Commonwealth Engineering Co. 1952–54; Economist, American Viscose Corp. 1955–56; Division Manager, American Management Assn. 1956–62; Pres., Clark, Cooper, Field & Whol 1964–65; Dean, Univ. of Cincinnati 1965—; Lecturer, Management Centre Europe 1963—. Lecturer: University of Michigan 1966—; Rensselaer Polytechnic Institute, 1968—; California Institute of Technology 1970; Univ. of Colorado 1970; Univ. of Waterloo Canada since 1971. Consultant, National Aeronautics and Space Admin., 1966—. Fellow Inst. of Directors (London). *Publications:* Books: Top Management and Research (1953); Administrative Management (1954) (second edition 1954); Planning New Products, Vol. I, 1958; Planning New Products, Vol. II, 1964; Management Goals, 1968; articles: Management Strategy for Product Pioneering; Profit Opportunities in the Atomic Energy Industry; Planning New Products (1958; 2nd edn. 1964); Multiplying Management Effectivness (1971); Developing Decisions for Action (1971); Man in Motion (1972); Effective Mgmt. of Research and Development (1973). *Clubs:* Princeton (N.Y.C.); Number 10 (London); Cincinnati. *Address:* 2750 Weston Ridge Drive, Cincinnati, Ohio 45239; and *office* University of Cincinnati, Cincinnati, Ohio 45221, U.S.A.

**MARZOUK, Ahmed Wageeh.** Egyptian. Ambassador of Arab Republic of Egypt. *B.* 1920. *Educ.* Faculty of Commerce, Cairo Univ., BEcon. (1946). *M.* Enayat S. Nasr. *Children:* 2 *Career:* Diplomatic Attaché, Ministry of For. Affairs, Cairo 1948; 3rd Session, Gen. Assembly, Paris, 1948; Seminar of International Law, The Hague, 1950; 6th Session U.N. Gen. Assembly, Paris 1951; 3rd Sect. Permanent Delegation of Egypt to U.N. (New York) 1952; mem. of 7th, 8th and 9th sessions of Gen. Assembly in N.Y. (Egypt. Delegation); Vice-consul, Genoa 1954; Consul in Tripoli (Libya) 1955–57; 1st Secy. Embassy of Egypt in Madrid 1957–59; 1st Secy. to Dept. of Inspection, Min. of Foreign Affairs 1959–61; Counsellor of Embassy of Egypt in Canberra 1961–65; Counsellor in Protocol Dept., Min. of Foreign Affairs in Cairo 1965–68; Minister Plenipotent. of Embassy of Egypt in Algeria 1968–71; Director of Inspector's Dept. Min. of Foreign Affairs, Cairo, 1971–73. Am bassador Extraordinary & Plenipotentiary of the Arab Republic of Egypt to Australia, New Zealand & Fiji 1973–76. *Awards:* Order of Republic (2nd Cl.) Egypt; Order of Merit (2nd Class) Spain. *Clubs:* Gezira; Automobil; Tahrir (Cairo); C'wealth, Royal Golf (Canberra); Melbourne Club (hon. mem.). *Address:* c/o Ministry of Foreign Affairs, Cairo, Arab Republic of Egypt.

**MASEFIELD, Sir Peter Gordon.** *B.* 1914. *Educ.* Westminster School; Chillon Coll., Switzerland; Jesus College, Cambridge (MA). *M.* 1936, Patricia Doreen Rooney. *S.* Charles Beech, Richard William, Oliver Peter. *Dau.* Susan Victoria. *Career:* Design Staff, Fairey Aviation Co. Ltd. 1935–37; Technical Editorial Staff, The Aeroplane 1937–43; War and Air Correspondent, The Sunday Times 1940–43; Personal Adviser on Civil Air Transport to Lord Privy Seal and Secretary of War Cabinet Air Transport Committee 1943–45; British Civil Air Attaché, Embassy, Washington, D.C. 1945–46; Director-General of Long Term Planning and Projects, Min. of Civil Aviation 1946–48; Chief Executive and member of Board, B.E.A. 1949–55; Mng. Dir., Bristol Aircraft Ltd. 1955–60; Director, Pressed Steel Co. and Beagle Aircraft Ltd., 1960–67; Chairman, British Airports Authority 1965–71; Chairman, Beagle Aircraft Ltd., 1968–70; Chmn. Project Management Ltd.; Dir. Worldwide Estates Ltd.; Nationwide Building Society since 1973; Part-Time Member, London Transport Exec. since 1973; Caledonian Airways Ltd. since 1975. *President.* Brit. Inst. of Transport 1955–56; *Member:* (Chmn). Royal Aero Club 1968–70; Pres., Royal Aeronautical Society 1959–60; Vice-President, Air League; Chmn. Imperial War Museum 1977–78; Chmn., Royal Society of Arts, 1977–79. *Awards:* CEng., FRAeS, MInstT, Hon. AIAA (U.S.A.), Hon. FCASI (Canada); Knighted 1972; Hon. DSc (Cranfield); Hon DTech (Loughborough). *Address:* 'Rosehill', Doods Way, Reigate, Surrey.

**MASHOLOGU, Mothusi Thamsanga.** Lesotho ambassador. *B.* 1939. *Educ.* Basutoland High School, Maseru; University College of Forth Hare (BA, Rhodes, 1958); University College of Rhodesia and Nyasaland; Queen's University, Belfast, BA (Hons. 1963); London School of Economics (Certificate in International Relations, 1965). *Career:* Teacher at Basutoland High School and at Basutoland Training College, 1960 and 1963–64; joined Ministry of Internal and External Affairs, 1965; served as Assistant Secretary in the Cabinet Office before taking up assignment as Counsellor in the Permanent Mission of Lesotho to the United Nations; member of Lesotho Delegation to 21st, 22nd, 24th, 25th and manent Secretary for Foreign Affairs, 1968–69; Ambassador to the U.S.A. 1969–73, Perm. Rep. to the UN 1969–71; Sec. to Cabinet 1974–75; Pro-Vice- Chancellor, National Univ. of Lesotho 1975–76, Vice-Chancellor since 1976. *Address:* National University of Lesotho, Roma, Lesotho.

**MASHOLOGU, Teboho J.** Lesotho Diplomat. *B.* 1942. *Educ.* Lehigh Univ. *Career:* Perm. Sec., Ministry of Foreign Affairs 1973; Perm. Rep. of Lesotho to the U.N. 1974–75; Ambassador to the U.S.A. 1975–76. *Address:* c/o Ministry of Foreign Affairs, Maseru, Lesotho.

**MASI, Fausto.** Italian industrialist. *B.* 1904. *Educ.* Diploma in mechanical engineering. *M.* 1931, Bianca Molteni. *Daus.* 2. *Career:* Engineer, Società Nazionale delle Officine di Savigliano (structural steel), Turin 1927–32, and A. Badoni Co. (structural steel), Lecco 1933–38; General Manager, Officine Bossi Co., Milan 1939–53 (structural steel—boilers). *Publications:* La pratica delle costruzioni metalliche; Case in acciaio; Conoscere l'acciaio; Acciaio. *Member:* C.T.A. Collegio Tecnici Acciaio; Touring Club Italiano, Lions Club. *Address:* Via Filomarino, 13, Rome, Italy.

**MASON, Alexander Gray.** Irish company director. *B.* 1910. *Educ.* High School, Dublin and Trinity College, Dublin (BSc). *M.* 1942, Nora McConnell. *S.* Jonathan Gray. *Dau.* Margaret Tennant. *Career:* Entered family firm 1932. Served in Ordnance Corps, Irish Army 1940–46; retired with rank of Captain and returned to family firm. Chairman Thomas H. Mason & Sons Ltd. 1958—. Author of papers and notes on ornithological subjects. *Address:* Eaton Brae Cottage, Shankill, Co. Dublin; and *office* 29 Parliament Street, Dublin 2.

**MASON, Alpheus Thomas.** *B.* 1899. *Educ.* Dickinson Coll. (AB 1920) and Princeton Univ. (PhD 1923); LittD Dickinson Coll. 1947; Phi Beta Kappa; DLitt Univ. of Louisville 1956; LLD Dickinson School of Law 1963; LHD Washington College, 1969; LHD Brandeis Univ. 1973; LLD Princeton 1974; ScD Utah State Univ. 1976; DLitt Centre College of Kentucky 1977; Guggenheim Fellow 1952; American Library Assn. Liberty & Justice Book Award 1956. *M.* 1934, Christine Este Gibbons. *Dau.* Louise Este (Bachelder III). *Career:* Asst. Prof. of Political Science, Duke Univ. 1923–25; Member, Inst. for Advanced Study, 1938; McCormick Prof. of Jurisprudence Princeton Univ. 1947–68; Lecturer, Northwestern Univ. 1961; Casper P. Bacon Lecturer, Boston Univ. 1953; Messenger Lecturer, Cornell Univ. 1955; Edward Douglass White Lecturer, Louisiana Univ. 1958. Vice-President, American Political Science Assn. 1959; Ford Research Professor in Governmental Processes 1960; W. W. Cook Lecturer, University of Michigan, 1962; Prof. of Government & Law Univ. of Virginia 1968–70; Visiting Prof. of Government Harvard 1st Semester 1970–71; Political Science Winter quarter Univ. of California Santa Barbara 1971; Government Dartmouth Coll. Spring quarter1971; Political Science Univ. of Minnesota Full quarter 1971; History Univ. of Michigan 1971; Spring Robb. Prof. Barnard Coll. Fall 1972; Visiting Prof. Johns Hopkins Univ. 1973, Pomona Coll. 1974, Utah State Univ. 1975, Claremont Men's Coll. 1976, Centre Coll. of Kentucky 1977. *Publications:* Organized Labour & The Law (1925); Brandeis & The Modern State (1935); Bureaucracy Convicts Itself (1941); Brandeis: a Free Man's Life (1946); Free Government in the Making (1949); Security through Freedom (1955); Harlan Fiske Stone: Pillar of the Law (1956); The Supreme Court from Taft to Warren (1958); The Supreme Court: Palladium of Freedom (1962); The States Rights Debate (1964); William Howard Taft: Chief Justice (1965); and many other books and articles. *Member:* American Political Science Assn.; American Academy of Arts and Sciences (Fellow). *Clubs:* Authors' (London); Nassau; P.E.W. *Address:* 8 Edgehill Street, Princeton, N.J., U.S.A.

**MASON, Birny, Jr.** American. *B.* 1909. *Educ.* Hill School. Pottstown, Pa.; Cornell Univ. (BS in chemical engineering), *M.* Elizabeth Brownson Smith. *S.* Jerome Acheson. *Career:* Joined Union Carbide, 1932; Manager, Industrial Relations Dept., 1952; Secretary to the Corporation, 1955; Vice-President, 1957; executive vice-president & member, board of directors, 1958; president. 1960; chief exec. officer, 1963; Chairman, Board of Directors, 1966–71; Chmn. Exec. Cttee. 1971–74. Director: North Amer. Philips Corp.; Metropolitan Life Insurance Co.; Bradford Computer & Systems Inc. *Trustee:* Presbyterian Hosp., N.Y.C.; Member, Business Council, Washington, D.C. *Clubs:* Larchmont Yacht; Blind Brook. *Address:* *office* 270 Park Avenue, New York City 10017, U.S.A.

**MASON, Charles John,** FCA. Canadian chartered accountant. President: Mason-Barkey Ltd., Omega Sand & Gravel, Ltd., Rossfrank Ltd., and Mabar Ltd.; Director, E. F. Hanscombe Ltd. *B.* 1902. *Educ.* St. Olave's Grammar School and London School of Economics. *M.* 1932, Mary Ross. *S.* Ross Hoadley. *Career:* Five years Articles, Edward Blinkhorn Lyon & Co., London (Eng.); 5 years with Fred Page, Higgins & Co., Toronto; 9 years with H. R. Bain & Co. Ltd., Toronto. Major Canadian Army Overseas for 4½ years; in practice 13 years. *Member:* Institute of Chartered Accountants (England and Ontario); Mason (Cornhill Lodge, Eng.). *Clubs:* Royal Canadian Military Inst.; Granite, Board of Trade (Toronto). *Address:* *office* 862, Eglinton Av. E. Toronto, 17 Ont., Canada.

**MASON, David Richard.** British. *B.* 1930. *Educ.* Beverley Secondary School (New Malden, Surrey). Unmarried. *Career:* Asst. News Editor, Radio 2WL, Wollongong, N.S.W. 1955–57; Asst. Editor, The Fiji Times, Suva, 1957–58. Editor, Advertising News, and Advertising in Australia 1961—. Member Australian Journalists' Association. *Address:* 2 Wirringulla Avenue, Elvina Bay, via Church Point, N.S.W.; and *office* Butt & Clisdell Streets, Surry Hills, N.S.W., Australia.

**MASON, Sir Frederick Cecil,** KCVO, CMG. British. *B.* 1913. *Educ.* City of London Sch. & St. Catharine's Coll., Cambridge (BA). *M.* 1941, Karen Rorholm. *S.* John Frederick, Richard Stephen. *Dau.* Janet. *Career:* Commercial Counsellor. Embassy Athens, 1955–57; Econ. counsellor, Tehran, 1957–60: Head. Economic Rel. Dept., Foreign Office, 1960–64; Under-Secretary: Ministry of Overseas Development, 1965; Commonwealth Office, Jan.–July 1966. H.M. Ambassador to Chile, 1966–70; UK Permanent Representative, U.N. Geneva 1971–73; Dir. New Court Natural Resources Ltd. since 1973. *Clubs:* Travellers; Canning. *Address:* The Forge, Ropley, Hants.

**MASON, Sir Paul,** KCMG, KCVO. Retired British diplomat. *B.* 11 June 1904. *Educ.* Eton; King's College, Cambridge. *Career:* Hon. Attaché at Berne 1926–28, resigned 1928; entered Diplomatic Service 1928; Third Secretary, Brussels 1928, Prague 1930; Second Secretary 1933; Assistant Private Secretary to the Secretary of State 1934–36. Private Secretary to Parliamentary Under-Secretary of State 1936–37; on staff of U.K. High Commissioner at Ottawa 1937–39; Acting First Secretary 1939; Acting Counsellor 1945; former Head of Refugees Dept. and of North American and U.N. Depts. of Foreign Office; En. Ex. and Min. Plen. to Bulgaria

1949–51; Assistant Under-Secretary of State 1951–54; Amb. Ex. and Plen. to the Netherlands 1954–60; British Representative on North Atlantic Council, May 1960–64; and at Geneva Disarmament Conference 1964; Treasurer, Univ. of Nottingham since 1972. High Sheriff of Notts 1970. *Awards:* Grand Cross, Order of House of Orange; Chevalier, Ordre de Léopold (Belgium). *Address:* Morton Hall, Retford, Notts.

**MASON, Rt. Hon. Roy**, PC, MP. British politician. *B.* 1924. *Educ.* Carlton Junior School; Royston Senior School; London School of Economics (T.U.C. Scholarship). *M.* 1945, Marjorie Sowden. *Daus.* 2. *Career:* miner (underground 14 yrs of age) 1938–53; Member, Parliament for Barnsley (Labour) 1953—; Spokesman, Defence and Post Office Affairs 1960–64; Minister of State (Shipping), Board of Trade, 1964–67; Minister of Defence (Equipment), 1967–68; Postmaster-General, April–June 1968; Minister of Power 1968–69; Entered Cabinet President, Board of Trade, 1969–70; Official spokesman, Civil Aviation Shipping, Tourism, Films and Trade Matters 1970–74; Sec. of State for Defence 1974–76; Sec. of State for Northern Ireland since 1976; Vice Chmn. Miners Group, MPS. *Member:* Council of Europe and Western Union 1973. *Address:* House of Commons, London SW1A 0AA; & 12 Victoria Avenue, Barnsley, Yorkshire.

**MASRI, Taher Nashat.** Jordanian Politician & Diplomat. *B.* 1942. *Educ.* North Texas State Univ.—Bachelor of Business Administration. *M.* 1968, Samar Bitar. *S.* 1. *Dau.* 1. *Career:* Member of Parliament 1973–74; Minister of State for Occupied Territories Affairs 1973–74; Ambassador in Spain since 1975. *Decorations:* Jordanian Al-Kaukab 1st Grade; Gran Cruz del Mérito Civil (Spain). *Address:* Santiago Bernabeu no. 5, Madrid 16; and *office* Paseo del General Martinez Campos no. 41, Madrid 10, Spain.

**MASSAND, Bhagvan Khemchand.** Ambassador of India. *B.* 1913. *Educ.* BSc (Hons.), LLB. Married. Three daughters. *Career:* Practised at Bar for about a year and later entered business in an executive capacity. Attaché, High Commission of India, Karachi 1947–48; joined Indian Foreign Service, Nov. 1948; First Secretary, High Commission of India, Karachi 1948–49. Officer on special duty, Ministry of Commerce, Jan. 1950; First Secretary (Commercial) High Commission, Colombo 1950–53; Chargé d'Affaires, Ankara May–Oct. 1954, First Secretary 1954–55; First Secretary, Washington 1956–57; Counsellor, Cairo 1957–59, and Budapest 1959–62 (also Chargé d'Affaires); High Commissioner in Australia 1962–65, and concurrently accredited to New Zealand in same capacity 1962–63. Ambassador to Chile, Peru and Colombia 1965–67; Joint Sec. to Ministry of Foreign Affairs 1967–69; Ambassador to Mexico, Cuba and Panama 1969–71. *Address:* 5 Reshma Apartments, 13 Pali Hill, Bandra, Bombay 4000 50, India.

**MASSEY, Sir Harrie Stewart Wilson.** British. *B.* 1908. *Educ.* Melbourne University (BA 1929; MSc 1929) and Trinity College, Cambridge (PhD); Aitchison Travelling Scholar, Melbourne University 1929–31. *M.* Jessica Elizabeth Barton-Bruce. *Dau.* Pamela (Duncanson). *Career:* Goldsmith Prof. of Mathematics, Univ. Coll. London 1938–50; Quain Professor of Physics, University College, London 1950–75; Hon. Fellow, University Coll., London 1976; Hon. Res. Fellow, Dept. Phys. & Astron., Univ. Coll., London 1975; Emeritus Prof. of Physics, Univ. of London 1975; Hon. Fellow, Inst. Physics 1976. Chairman: British National Committee for Space Research 1959—, and Council for Scientific Policy 1964–70; Vice-Provost Univ. Coll. London 1969–73; Member of Council: Royal Society (1949–51 and 1959–60) and Physical Society 1949–54; (Pres. 1954–56); Vice-Pres. Royal Astronomical Society 1950–53; Physical Sect. and Vice-Pres., The Royal Society 1969—. Pres. Atomic Scientists Assn. 1956–57; Mem. Governing Board, National Inst. for Research in Nuclear Science 1957–64; Pres. European Preparatory Commission for Space 1964. Mbr., Central Advisory Council for Science and Technology 1967–70. Assessor, Sc Res. Council since 1974; Mem. Royal Commission for Exhib. of 1851, since 1972; Amer. Phil. Socy.; Chmn. Prov. Space Science Adv. Bd. for Europe since 1974; Mem. Anglo-Austr. Telescope Bd. since 1975; Corres. mem. Acad. of Sci. Liege since 1974; Mem. American Philosophical Soc. 1975; Corres. Mem. Australian Acad. of Sci. 1976. *Publications:* approximately 200 published articles and 15 books, including New Age in Physics, 2nd edn. (published in London, Toronto, Rumania, and New York); Electronic & Ionic Impact Phenomena (2nd edn. 1969) (Vol. I and II), 1971 (Vol. III), 1974 (Vol. IV and V). *Awards:* F.R.S. 1940; Hon. LLD Melbourne and Glasgow; Hon. DSc (Belfast and Leicester), Hull, 1968, Melbourne, Adelaide Univ. (1974), Heriott-Watt Univ. (1975), Liverpool Univ. (1975), Western Ontario 1970; Hughes Medal 1955, and Royal Medal 1958 (both from Royal Society). *Club:* Athenaeum (London). *Address:* 'Kalamunnda', Pelham's Walk, Esher, Surrey; and *office* Physics Department University College, London, W.C.1.

**MASSIE, Rantun Albert Benjamin,** LLD. Indonesian. Banker. *B.* 25 Sept. 1922. *Educ.* Graduate in Law, Gadjah Mada University. *M.* 1956, Els Kawengian. *S.* Herling. *Career:* Employee of Ministry of Justice 1943–55; Judge 1955–57; Banker since 1957; Pres. Bank Bumi Daya (State owned Commercial Bank) since 1970. *Awards:* Guerrilla Medal of Merit; Symbol of Freedom I and II. *Address: office* Dji Kebonsirih No. 66, 70, Djakarta, Indonesia.

**MASTEN, John Eugene.** Retired American business executive. *B.* 1912. *Educ.* Dartmouth Coll. (AB *summa cum laude* 1933); Yale Univ. (LLB 1936). *M.* 1940, Laura Cass Wood. *S.* John Hall. *Dau.* Elizabeth Lawrence (Hammill). *Career:* In law practice with Davis, Polk, Wardwell, Gardiner & Reed (N.Y.C.) 1936–42; Visiting Lecturer in Law, Yale School of Law 1940; Counsel, Metals Reserve Co., Washington, D.C. 1942–45; Asst. Counsel, Joint Congressional Committee on the Pearl Harbor Attack, Washington 1945–46; practice of law with Davis Polk, Wardwell, Sunderland & Kiendl (N.Y.C.) 1946–51; Consultant on government corporations, Hoover Commn. 1947. Member, Cncl. of Alumni, Dartmouth Coll. 1957–60; Secy., Internatl. Copper Research Assn. (N.Y.C.) 1960–67; Asst. Vice-President & Secretary 1951–62, Vice-President and Secretary 1962–76, Vice-Pres. 1976–77, Phelps Dodge Corp. Director, Vice-Pres. and Secy., Foreign Bondholders Protective Cncl. Inc. *Member:* Phi Beta Kappa; Council on Foreign Relations. *Clubs:* University (N.Y.C.). *Address:* 81 Oakland Beach Avenue, Rye, N.Y., U.S.A.

**MATANZIMA, Chief Kaiser.** Transkei Lawyer & Politician. *B.* 1915. *Educ.* Lovedale Missionary Inst.; Fort Hare Univ. Coll. *Career:* Chief, Amahale Clan of Tembus, St. Mark's District 1940; Member, United Transkeian Gen. Council 1942–56; Perm Head, Emigrant Tembuland Regional Authority & Member, Exec. Cttee., Transkeian Territorial Authority 1956–58; Regional Chief of Emigrant Tembuland 1958–61; Presiding Chief Transkeian Territorial Authority 1961–63; Chief Minister of Transkei 1963–76; Prime Minister since Independence, Oct. 1976. *Awards:* Order of Good Hope, 1976. *Address:* Office of the Prime Minister, Umtata, Transkei.

**MATHER, Sir William (Loris).** OBE, MC, TD, VL, MA, ChEng., FIMech.E, FBIM. British. *B.* 1913, *Educ.* Oundle School and Trinity College, Cambridge (MA in Engineering and Law). *M.* 1937. Eleanor Ames George. *S.* 2. *Daus.* 2. *Career:* Chairman, Mather & Platt Ltd. (Dir. 1955—, Chmn. 1960—; A.D.C. 1961–66). Director: National Westminster Bank Ltd. 1963—, Chmn. North Reg. Bd. 1973—; Manchester Ship Canal Co. 1970—; Strip Mills, Div. British Steel Corp. 1970–73; Dir. Compair since 1973; Past Pres. Manchester Chamber of Commerce and Industry 1964–66; Vice-Pres. Assoc. British Chamber of Commerce; Chmn., North-West Reg. Economic Planning Cncl. 1968–75; Member, Court of Manchester Univ., Salford Univ.; Pres. Manchester Univ. Inst. of Science and Technology, and Council of Manchester Business School 1964—; Chmn. British Pump Manufacturers Assn. 1970–73; Member, Council, Russo-British Chamber of Commerce 1959–75; Past Chmn. Institute of Directors, Manchester 1967–71; Pres. Manchester Scouts; Pres. Manchester Guardian Soc. for Protection of Trade; Governor: Manchester Grammar School; Feofee, Chetham's Hosp. Sch.; Trustee, Civic Trust, London Chmn. Civic Trust for the North-West; Manchester Y.M.C.A.; Advisory Council, The Granada Trust. *Member:* Council, Institute of Directors; Manchester Chamber of Commerce; Council of Industrial Design 1960–72; Council, North-West Arts Assn.; Chmn. BBC Manchester Local Radio Council 1970–75; Governor, Royal College of Art; High Sheriff of Cheshire 1969–70; Hon. Fellow, Manchester College of Art & Design. *Clubs:* Bath (London); St. James's (Manchester). *Address:* Whirley Hall, Macclesfield, Cheshire; and *office* Park Works, Manchester, M1O 6BA.

**MATHESON, Wallace Alexander,** BA. Canadian. *B.* 1931. *Educ.* Acadia Univ. (BA Hist. & Pol. Sci.). *M.* 1957, Martha Ann Driscoll. *S.* 1. *Daus.* 2. *Career:* Vice-Pres. Prentice-Hall of Canada Ltd. 1961–65, Pres. & Dir. since 1965; Dir. of Prentice-Hall Inc. since 1976. *Member:* Univ. Lodge 496 AF & Am., Canadian Book Publishers' Council (Pres. 1972), Canadian Library Exhibitors' Assn. (Pres. 1966–68), Dir. of Montreal International Book Fair, Dir. of Canadian Book

Design Cttee. *Address:* 8 Palomino Crescent, Willowdale, Ont., M2K 1W1, Canada; and *office* 1870 Birchmount Road, Scarborough, Ontario M1P 2J7, Canada.

**MATHEWS, Frank Dawson.** British executive. *B.* 1906. *Educ.* Norwood High School, Adelaide, South Australia. *M.* 1934, Zoe Nell Penrose. *S.* James Penrose. *Career:* Engaged in retail merchandising through Myer Emporium, Adelaide 1930–35, Foy & Gibson Pty. Ltd., Adelaide 1936–40; Buckley & Nunn Ltd., Melbourne 1941; Chairman of Dirs. Buckley & Nunn Ltd., 310 Bourke Street, Melbourne, Australia. *Clubs:* Athenaeum; Victoria Golf; Victoria Racing; Victoria Amateur Turf; Moonee Valley Racing. *Address:* 8 Woorigoleen Road, Toorak, Melbourne, 3142; and *office* 310 Bourke Street, Melbourne, Vic., Australia.

**MATHEWS, Ralph Howard Groves.** American marketing executive, engineer, and sales training and public relations director. *B.* 1897. *Educ.* Armour Inst. of Technology, Chicago (Elec. Eng.). *M.* 1936, D. Elizabeth Ebrenz. *Career:* Served as Lieutenant (j.g.) and Lieut.-Comdr., U.S. Navy 1918–21; Comdr., U.S.N.R. 1940–57; retired 1957. Chief Engineer and Partner, Chicago Radio Laboratory 1919–22; Chief Engineer i/c Broadcasting Station and Sales Promotion, Zenith Radio Corp. 1922–26; Vice-Pres., Amer. Broadcasting Corp. 1926–29; Partner, R. H. G. Mathews & Associates, Sales Engineering Consultants 1929–33; Partner i/c new business, Ford, Browne & Mathews Advertising Agency, Chicago, 1933–40; Pres., Mathews Supply Corp. Ind. 1945–47; Sales Promotion and Advertising Mgr., Ind. Tractor Sales 1947–49; Self-employed Sales Training Consultant and Member of Faculty of Purdue University Ext. Div., Ind. 1949–50; General Sales Manager, Honan-Crane Corp. 1950–52; Vice-President i/c new business, Burton-Browne Advertising Agency 1953–54; Dir., High Fidelity Div.; Dir., Public Relations, Asst. to Vice-Pres. and Gen. Mgr., The Magnavox Co., Fort Wayne, Ind. 1954–57. Vice-Pres. (Marketing), Pyrotronics Div., Baker Industries Inc., Newark, N.J. 1962–64; Dir. of Marketing, Blonder-Tongue Labs. Inc., Newark, N.J. 1960–62; Manager, High Fidelity Division, of National Accounts, of Sales Training and of Publicity, Westinghouse Electric Corp., Metuchen, N.J. 1957–60. Dir. of Marketing & Consultant to Pres., Diamond Electronics, 1964–67; President, Coltech Corp., N.J. since 1964. *Member:* Inst. of Radio Engineers (Senior Member), Mid-West Badminton Assn. (Past Vice-Pres.),Umpires Cttee., Amer. Badminton Assn. (Chmn.); Chicago Tennis Assn. (Past Vice-Pres.), American Legion (Past Post Vice-Cmdr.); Military Order of World Wars (Past State Cmdr.), DeForest Pioneers, Eta Kappa Nu (Hon. Electrical Fraternity), Retired Officers Assn.; Past Pres. Lake Chapala (Mexico Chapter). Naval Reserve Assn. (Past State Vice-Pres.). Mason. *Address:* Apartado Postal 38, Ajijic, Jalisco, Mexico.

**MATHEWSON, William A.** Consult. Engineering Standards & Freelance writer. *B.* 1904. *Educ.* New York Univ., City Coll. of New York, and American Inst. of Banking. *M.* 1939, Gertrude Elizabeth Einig. *S.* William Joseph. *Dau.* Susan. *Career:* Head Statistician, Remington Rand Inc., N.Y.C. 1941–43; Methods Engineer, Bell Telephone Labs., N.Y.C. 1943–46; Technical Writer, Air Reduction Co., N.Y.C. 1946–48; Course Co-ordinator, City College of New York 1948–49; Exec. Secretary-Treasurer, Amer. Socy. of Architectural Hardware Consultants, N.Y.C., 1949–56. Standards Editor, Apollo Space Program, G.E.C. Daytona Beach Fla. 1956–69. *Publications:* Drawings & Constructional Details; Hardwaer Metals & Finishes; Hardware Data Sheets; Door Butts & Hinges (these four publications received Honourable Mention Awards in Annual Best Industry Publications of the Year Contests sponsored jointly by American Inst. of Architects & Producers Council of America). *Address:* (home and office) 713 Heritage Blvd. Winter Park, Fla. U.S.A.

**MATTHESS, Walter.** German publisher and advertising executive. *B.* 1903. *Educ.* High School; trained as book dealer. *M.* 1949. Lydia Höfner. *S.* Thomas, Peter and Michael. *Dau.* Jutta. *Career:* Previously Advertising Manager for publishing houses; Advertising Manager with Ullstein AG, Berlin for journal Querschnitt; and for the German edition of the American magazine Vogue 1929–30; Business Manager, Dorland Advertising Agency in Berlin; Chief Partner and General Manager, Dorland Werbeagentur (advertising agency), Berlin and Munich; Owner and General Manager, Dorland Werbeagentur, Berlin. Founder of Verlag Walter Matthess & Co. 1930—. *Club:* Rotary. *Address:* 20 Dohnenstieg. Berlin-Dahlem; and *office* 1 Berlin 30 Keithstr, 2-4 (Dorland Werbeagentur) Dorland-Haus, F.R.G.

**MATTHEWS, Albert Bruce,** CBE, DSO, ED, CD. Canadian. *B.* 1909. *Educ.* Upper Canada Coll., Toronto. *M.* 1937, Victoria Thorne. *S.* Bryn and Victor Bruce. *Dau.* Harriet. *Career:* Entered investment business 1928, moved to New York 1930, returned to Toronto 1931, and in 1932, became a general partner in firm of Matthews & Co. Commissioned 3rd Field Brigade, R.C.A. 1928; on active service Sept. 1939 with First Canadian Div., commanding 15th Field Battery, R.C.A.; promoted to rank of Lieut.-Col. 1941, and Brigadier and C.R.A. of First Canadian Div. 1943; became Maj.-Gen. as G.O.C. Second Canadian Div. Nov. 1944. Director The Excelsior Life Insurance Co., Toronto; Director, Economic Investment Trust Ltd. (to conserve space the suffix 'Ltd' is omitted); Director: Canada Permanent Trust Co.; Chmn. & Director Dome Mines; Dir. Dome Petroleum, Dominion Stores, Standard Broadcasting; Third Canadian General Investment Trust, Domtar, Aetna Life & Casualty, Massey-Ferguson; Hollinger Mines; Exec. Vice-Pres. and Dir., Argus Corp.; Hon. Vice-Pres. Toronto Dominion Bank; Hon. Vice-Pres., Art Gallery of Ontario. *Awards:* Legion of Honour, Croix de Guerre with Palm, and Grand Officer, Order of Orange Nassau. *Clubs:* Toronto, York, National Toronto Golf & Country, Royal Canadian Military Institute, Granite, Mount Royal (Montreal), Rideau (Ottawa), The Brook (N.Y.C.). *Address:* 19 Riverview Drive, Toronto M4N 3C6, Canada.

**MATTHEWS, Brigadier Sir (Harold Lancelot) Roy,** CBE, FRICS. British. *B.* 24 April 1901. *Educ.* The Leys School. *M.* 1927, Violet Mary Wilkinson. *S.* William Roy. *Dau.* Mary Patricia. *Career:* Chmn. Manx Local Bd. Sun Alliance & London Insurance Group; Dir., Vannin International Securities Ltd.; Julian Hodge Bank (Isle of Man) Ltd. *Awards:* Officer, Legion of Merit (U.S.A.); Commander, Order of Orange Nassau (Netherlands). *Address:* Road End, Ramsey, Isle of Man.

**MATTHEWS, Paul Whiteside,** MBE, MA. Canadian investment banker. *B.* 1905. *Educ.* Upper Canada Coll. and McMaster Univ. (BA; MA). *M.* Elva Christina Brooks. *S.* Christopher H. and Roger W. *Career:* Served with R.C.A.F.: Canada 1940, U.K. 1941–43, and Middle East 1944–45; retired with rank of Wing Commander; Associate Matthews Office A.E. Ames & Co. Ltd.; Excelsior Life Insurance Co.; General American Oil Co. of Texas. *Member:* Advisory Board, Metropolitan Toronto Y.W.C.A., British Sailors' Society (Canada), Beta Theta Pi Fraternity, Toronto Commanderie Order, St Lazarus of Jerusalem. *Clubs:* Toronto, Toronto Golf, Toronto Hunt, Rosedale Golf, The York. Eglinton Hunt (Past Pres.); Everglades, Bath & Tennis, Palm Beach (Fla.). *Address:* The Lonsdale, 619 Avenue Road, Toronto, Ont.; and (summer) Sans Souci, P.O., Georgian Bay, Ont., Canada.

**MATTHEWS, William Stephen,** CBE. Australian. *B.* 1899. *Educ.* Normal State-Controlled Education. *M.* 1925, Jessie Marguerite Stevenson. *S.* 2. *Dau.* 1. *Career:* Manager, Perpetual Trustee Co. Ltd. 1952–64; Chairman of Directors, Deposit & Investment Co. Ltd. 1964–68. Director: Reed Consolidated Industries Ltd. 1966–72; President 1969–71. Fed. Cncl.. Royal Flying Doctor Service of Australia (Pres. N.S.W. Section, 1964–66) and 1971–74. *Clubs:* Union; Warrawee Bowling. *Address:* 36 Dalrymple Avenue, Chatswood, N.S.W., Australia.

**MATTHIAS, Russell Howard,** AB, JD. American. *B.* 1906. *Educ.* Northwestern Univ. (AB, JD). *M.* 1932, Helene Seibold. *S.* 3. *Career:* Assoc. & Partner Meyers & Matthias; Dir. Old Orchard Bank & Trust Co.; Bankers Mutual Life Insurance Co.; United Founders Life Insurance of Illinois; United Founders Life Ins. Co. Oklahoma City; *Director:* Great Central Insurance Co.; Mattco Inc. (and Pres.); Lutheran Gen. Hosp.; Secy. Treas. and Dir. Supervised Investors Income Fund Inc.; Supervised Investors Summit Fund Inc.; Technology Fund Inc.; Vice-Pres. & Dir. Lutheran Brotherhood. *Award:* Northwestern Univ. Alumni Service 1973. Bd. Trustees, Valparaiso Univ. Law School; Bd. Assoc. Carthage College. *Clubs:* Mid-Day Chicago; Minneapolis; Citius, Orlando (Country); Indian Hills University Club of Chicago. *Address:* 1500 Sheridan Road, Wilmette Ill., U.S.A.; and *office* 230 W. Monroe Street, Chicago Ill. 60606,

**MATTHIESSEN, Harald (Peter Wilhelm),** Dr. jur. German Attorney-at-Law. *B.* 1901. *Educ.* Universities of Munich and Kiel. *M.* 1930, Gerda Ferlin. *S.* Christian and Axel. *Dau.* Benedicta. *Career:* Judge, Altona Court of Appeal until 1929; Managing Director, Deutsche Waren-Treuhand AG, Hamburg 1930–70. Chairman, Supervisory Board; Bodenseewerk Perkin-Elmer & Co. GmbH, Uberlingen, Bodenseewerk Geratetechnik GmbH., Überlingen; member Supervisory Board, Gislaved Gummifabriken AB Vertriebsgesellschaft mbH. *Publications:* various publications on the subject of bank and company law. *Club:* Anglo-German (Hamburg). *Address: office* Ferdinandstrasse 59, Hamburg, Germany.

**MATTILA, Olavi Johannes.** Finnish Statesman. *B.* 1918. *Educ.* MSc in Technology; MSc in Science of Commerce. *M.* 1956, Annikki Vestinen. *S.* Juha OlliTapio. *Dau.* Annasirkku. *Career:* Commercial counsellor, Finnish Embassy in Peking 1952–56; Embassy Secy. Buenos Aires 1957–60; Head of Dept. Min. of Trade and Industry 1960–62; Acting Head, Industrial Dept. 1961–62; Head of Trade Political Dept. Min. Foreign Affairs 1962–64; Pres. Valmet Oy 1965–73; Chmn. of Valmet Oy since 1973; Second Min. in Prime Ministers Office and Foreign Affairs 1962; Minister Trade and Industry Second Min. Foreign Affairs 1964; Min. of Trade and Industry 1970; Second Min. Prime Ministers Office and Min, of Foreign Trade 1970–71; Min. of Foreign Affairs 1971–72. Chmn. Enso-Gutzeit Osakeyhtiö since 1973; Min. of For. Affairs 1975. *Member:* Assn. of Finnish Metal Working Industries Finland; Finnish Industrial Association; Central Assn. of Finnish Forest Industries. *Awards:* Grand Cross of Cruzeiro do Sul of Brazil; Grand Cross order San Carlos of Columbia; Grand Cross order Merito Civil of Spain; Grand Officer order of May of Argentine; grand cross North Star of Sweden; Grand Cross order of Lion and Sun of Iran. *Club:* Rotary. *Address:* Puistokatu 3A 12, 00140 Helsinki 14, Finland; and *office* Valmet Oy, Punanotkonkatu 2, 00130 Helsinki 13, Finland and Enso-Gutzeit Osakeyhtiö, Kanavaranta 1, 00160 Helsinki 16, Finland.

**MATTOON, Henry Amasa, Jr.** American advertising marketing, direct mail consultant. *B.* 1914. *Educ.* Yale University (Sheffield Scientific School), BS 1935. *M.* 1936, Dorothy Ann Teeter. *S.* David Scott. *Daus.* Ann Brooks (Wofford), Sara Halsey (Sparks) and Judith Scott. *Career:* Vice-President, Creative Director, various Adv. agencies, 1935–52; Pres., Dir., Reach, Yates & Mattoon, Inc., 1953–56; Chmn., Marketing Plans Board-Home Office, McCann-Erickson 1956–61; Vice-President, General Manager, Los Angeles & Houston offices, 1962–67; Sen. Vice-Pres., 1965–68; Dir. Adv. & Pub. Relations Yardley of London Inc., 1968–69; Partner, Walter Weintz & Co., 1969–70. Principal, Otto Man Associates; Pres., The Hamandot Co. *Clubs:* Yale, The Sky (N.Y.C.); Aspetuck Valley C.C. *Address:* 11 October Drive, Weston, Conn. 06883; and *office* 60 Wilton Rd., Westport, Conn. 06880 U.S.A.

**MAUDE, Angus Edmund Upton,** TD, MA, MP. British. author journalist, politician. *B.* 1912. *Educ.* Oxford Univ. (MA Hons.). *M.* 1946, Barbara Sutcliffe. *S.* 2. *Daus.* 2. *Career:* Deputy Dir. PEP, 1948–50; Dir. Conservative Political Centre, 1951–55; MP, Ealing South, 1950–58; Editor Sydney Morning Herald, 1958–61; Member of Parliament Cons. Stratford-on-Avon since 1963. *Publications:* The English Middle Classes (1949); Professional People (1951); Biography of a Nation (1955); South Asia (1965); The Common Problem (1969). *Address:* South Newington House, Banbury Oxon; and *office* House of Commons, London, S.W.1.

**MAUDLING, Rt. Hon. Reginald,** PC, MP. British politician. *B.* 1917. *Educ.* Merchant Taylor's School; Merton College, Oxford. *M.* 1939, Beryl Laverick. *S.* Reginald Martin, Edward Christopher, William Anthony. *Dau.* Caroline Mary. *Career:* Member, Parliament (Cons.) for Barnet, Herts. 1950–74; for Barnet, Chipping Barnet since 1974; Parliamentary Secretary, Ministry of Civil Aviation 1952; Economic Secretary to the Treasury 1952–55; Minister of Supply 1957–59; President, Board of Trade, 1959–61. Secretary of State for the Colonies 1961–62; Chancellor of the Exchequer 1962–64; Secretary of State for the Home Department, 1970–72. *Address:* Bedwell Lodge, Essendon, Herts.

**MAULL, Baldwin.** American banking executive. *B.* 1900. *Educ.* Princeton Univ. (AB 1922); Univ. of Pennsylvania (LLB 1925). *M.* 1929, Flora Davis. *S.* Baldwin, Jr. *Dau.* Diana. *Career:* Admitted to New York Bar 1926; practised with Sullivan & Cromwell (N.Y.C.) 1925–34; Vice-Pres., The Marine Midland Trust Co. of N.Y. 1935–51; Exec. Vice-Pres., Marine Midland Corp. 1952–54. Director: Marine Midland Grace Trust Co. of New York 1952–70; Marine Midland Corp. 1951–70; Marine Midland Trust Co. of Western New York 1952–69, Vice-Chairman of Board, 1962–69; Pres., Marine Midland Banks Inc., 1955–65, Chmn. 1966–68, Vice-Chmn., 1969–70; Hon. Member, Association of Registered Bank Holding Cos.; Dir., Lehigh Valley Railroad Co.: Niagara Mohawk Power Corp.: Kreutoll Realization Co.; Amer. Re-Insurance Co.; St. Regis Paper Co.; Graphic Arts Mutual Ins. Co.; Trustee English Speaking Union (Princeton); Trustee Princeton Battlefield Assn.; Hon. LLD Univ. Delaware (1966); Hon. Dr. Com. Sc., Niagara Univ. (1969); Former Pres., Western N.Y. Socy. of Archaeological Inst. of America, *Member:* Council American Numismatic Socy., Socy. of Colonial Wars (N.Y.); Sons of the Revolution; Friends of Lafayette; Swedish American Socy.; Pilgrims of U.S.; Trustee of Archaeological Inst. of America. *Member:* Citizens Adv. Cttee. on Services New York State Department, Social Services; State Board Social Welfare; Bd. of Mgrs., State Communities Aid Assn.; Trustee Welfare Research Inc. *Publications:* John Maull and Descendants (1941); various articles in banking and genealogical magazines. *Clubs:* Downtown Association, University, Badminton, Princeton, Squadron A (N.Y.C.); Nassau, Springdale Golf, Pretty Brook Tennis (Princeton, N.J.). *Address:* 25 Alexander Street, Princeton, N.J.; and *office* 250 Park Ave., New York, 10017, U.S.A.

**MAURER, Ion Gheorghe,** D. IUR. Romanian jurist and politician. *B.* 1902. *Educ.* Craiova Military School; Bucharest University. *Career:* joined Romanian Comm. Party 1936; Under Secy. of State for Transport 1944–46; Min. of Nat. Economy 1946–47; Member Central Cttee. Worker's Party 1945–74; Grand National Assembly 1948–75; Dep. Min. Industry and Trade 1948; Dir. Inst. of Juridical Research 1954–58; Member Acad. of Socialist Republic 1955—; Minister, Foreign Affairs 1957–58; Chmn. Presidium Grand Nat. Assembly (Head of State) 1958–61; Chmn. Council of Ministers 1961–74; Member, Political, Bureau 1960–65, Exec. Cttee. and of Perm. Presidium Central Cttee. Romanian Comm. Party 1965–74; Defense Council 1969–74; Acad. of Social and Political Science since 1970. *Awards:* Hero of Socialist Labour; Order Victoria Socialismului; Hero, Socialist Republic of Romania. *Address:* Academia R.S. România, Calea Victoriei 125, Bucharest, Romania.

**MAURER, Richard S.** *B.* 1917. *Educ.* Ohio Wesleyan Univ. (AB) and Yale Univ. School of Law (LLB). *M.* Lella Levine. *S.* Ske and Lyle. *Daus.* Mary and Nancye. *Career:* Asst. to General Counsel, Chicago & Southern Airlines (now Delta) 1943; Secy. and Asst. Gen. Counsel 1945; General Counsel 1946; Vice-Pres., Legal (Delta Air Lines and C. & S. merged in 1953) 1950. Vice-President, General Counsel, and Director 1954—, and Secretary 1960—, Delta Air Lines, Atlanta, Ga. *Member:* American, Federal, Georgia and Atlanta Bar Associations. Corp. Counsel, Assn. of Greater Atlanta. *Clubs:* Lawyers, Capital City, and Chamber of Commerce (all of Atlanta); National Aviation (Washington, D.C.). *Address:* 2601 Arden Road, N.W., Atlanta, Ga.; and *office* Delta Air Lines Inc., Atlanta Airport, Atlanta, Ga., U.S.A.

**MAURY, Reuben.** Editorial Writer. *B.* 1899. *Educ.* Public Schools (Butte, Mont.) and Univ. of Virginia (LLB). *M.* 1928, Thomasine Lafayette Rose. *Career:* Attorney-at-Law 1923–26; Chief Editorial Writer, New York Daily & Sunday News 1926–72; Editorial consultant (same newspaper) since 1972. *Awards:* Pulitzer Prize for newspaper editorials (N.Y. Daily & Sunday News), 1941; Christopher Editorial Award, 1954; Catholic War Veterans Citation, 1961; Nationalist Chinese Order of the Golden Knights, 1961; Assembly of Captive European Nations award 1965; George Sokolsky award of American-Jewish League Against Communism 1965: Order, Brilliant Star, Nationalist China: Freedoms Foundation, Valley Forge Editorial Honor Certificate; N.Y.C. Deadline (journalistic) Club's Hall of Fame 1977. *Member:* Sigma Delta Chi journalistic fraternity; Silurian Society. *Publications:* articles and short stories in various U.S. magazines. Books: The Wars of the Godly (1928); Americans to Remember (1958); Effective Editorial Writing (with Prof. Karl Pfeiffer) (1960). *Club:* Dutch Treat (N.Y.C.). *Address:* Box 305, Saugatuck, Conn. 06880, U.S.A.

**MAXWELL, Ian Robert,** MC. British. *B.* 1923. Self-educated. *M.* 1945, Elisabeth Meynard. *S.* 3. *Daus.* 4. *Career:* Chmn., Robert Maxwell & Co. Ltd. 1948—; Publisher and Chairman of the Board of Pergamon Press Ltd. (Oxford, London); Chmn., President, Pergamon Press Inc., New York, since 1949; Dir., Gauthier-Villars (Publishers) Paris 1961–70. Chmn., Nat. Fund Raising Foundation 1960–70; Treas. The Round House Trust Ltd. (formerly Centre 42) 1965—; Director, Computer Technology Ltd. 1966–77; Chairman, Labour Working Party on Scieoce, Government and Industry 1963–64; MP (Lab.) Buckingham, 1964–70. Member Estimates Committee 1964–67. Chmn. & Chief

Exec., International Learning Systems Corp. Ltd. 1967–69. member Council Europe; Vice Chmn. Cttee. Science & Technology 1968; Kennedy Fellow Harvard Univ. 1971; Hon. mem. Int. Acad. of Astronautics; Co-produced films: Mozart's Don Giovanni, Salzburg Festival 1954; Bolshoi Ballet, 1957; Swan Lake, 1968. *Publications:* Information U.S.S.R. (1963); (Ed); Economics of Nuclear Power (1965); Public Sector Purchasing (1968); (Jnt. Author) Man Alive (1968). *Address:* Headington Hill Hall, Oxford.

**MAXWELL-HYSLOP, Robert John (Robin),** MP. British. *B.* 1931. *Educ.* Stowe; Christ Church, Oxford—MA. *M.* 1968, Joanna Margaret McCosh. *Daus.* 2. *Career:* Rolls-Royce Ltd., Aero-Engine Division 1954–60; Conservative MP for Tiverton Division of Devon since 1960; Vice-Chmn., Anglo-Brazilian Parliamentary Group; Sec., Conservative Parliamentary Aviation Cttee; Mem., Trade & Industry Sub-Cttee of Public Expenditure Cttee. *Clubs:* Steering Wheel; Devon Farmers' Club. *Address:* White House, Silverton, Devon; House of Commons, London SW1A 0AA.

**MAY, Geoffrey Richard,** OBE. Australian business executive. *B.* 1910. *M.* 1940, Myra Edgoose. *S.* David. *Daus.* Joan and Patricia. *Career:* Joined Gollin & Co. Ltd. 1927. Managing Director, Gollin & Co. Ltd., Sydney, N.S.W. 1951–71; Deputy Chairman, Export Development Council (appointed by Commonwealth Government) 1958–61; Leader, Australian Government Trade Mission to U.S.A. and Canada 1959. *Clubs:* Australian, Riversdale Golf. *Address: office* 50 Clarence Street, Sydney, N.S.W., Australia.

**MAYALL, Sir (Alexander) Lees,** KCVO, CMG (retired). British diplomat. *B.* 1915. *Educ.* Eton Coll. and Trinity Coll. Oxford (MA). *M.* (1) 1940, Renee Eileen Burn. *Dau.* Elizabeth. (2) 1947, Mary Hermonie Ormsby Gore. *S.* Robert George Lees. *Daus.* Cordelia Isobel and Alexandra Beatrice. *Career:* Counsellor H.M. Embassies: Tokyo 1958–61, Lisbon 1961–64, and Addis Ababa 1964–65. Her Majesty's Vice-Marshal of the Diplomatic Corps; Head of the Joint Protocol and Conference Department, Foreign and Commonwealth Office. 1965–72; H.M. Ambassador Caracas 1973–75. *Awards:* Hon. Comdr. Order of Menelik II (Ethiopia); Decoration of Honour for Services to the Republic of Austria (Hon. Comdr. Silver); Hon. Comdr.: Order of Al Kawkab (Order of the Star) (Jordan); Order of the White Rose (Finland); Order of Merit Italian Republic; Order, The Sacred Treasure (3rd Class) Japan and others. *Clubs:* Travellers', Beefsteak, Pratts (all London). *Address:* Sturford Mead, Warminster, Wilts.

**MAYBERRY, William Maurice,** DSO. British company executive. *B.* 1915. *Educ.* Rugby School (England). *M.* 1942, Rosemary Mortimer Mathew. *S.* Robert Edmond and Ian Paul. *Dau.* Deborah Elizabeth Peta. *Career:* Served in World War II (Australian Imperial Forces; Lt.-Col., D.S.O.) 1939–46. With Edward Lumley & Sons Pty. Ltd., Melbourne, London, Sydney 1947–51; General Manager, Vanguard Insurance Co. Ltd. 1951–57; Director: Whale Industries Ltd., Sydney 1951—; Australian Fixed Trusts Ltd., Sydney 1955—; Chairman, Functional Holdings Ltd., Sydney 1962—; also director of a number of private companies interested in plantations, hotels and light industry in Papua and New Guinea, real estate in Victoria and primary production in Australia. *Address:* Flat 1, 5 Gladswood Gardens, Double Bay, Sydney, N.S.W., Australia.

**MAYBORN, Frank Willis.** Newspaper Editor, Publisher. *B.* 1903. *Educ.* Univ. of Colorado (BA). *Career:* With Dallas News, 1926; North Texas Traction Co., Fort Worth 1927–29; Business Manager, Temple Telegram 1929–45; Editor Pres. Publisher 1945—; Founder, Pres. Operator 1936–70; Radio Station KTEM. Temple; Founder Pres. 1953, since operator KCEN-TV, Temple; Owner Sherman (Tex) Democrat 1945–77; Pres. Part owner operator Killeen (Tex.) Herald 1952—; Taylor Press, Taylor Texas 1959–74; Founder, operator Radio Station WMAK, Nashville 1947–54; Pres. Dir. Bell Publishing Co. Temple 1945—; Bell Broadcasting Co. Temple 1936–70; Sherman Democrat Co. 1945–77; Kileen (Tex.) Publishing Co. 1952—; FWM Properties 1956—; Community Enterprises Inc. 1959–75; Taylor (Texas) Publishing Co. 1959–62; Channel 6, Inc. 1962; The Frank W. Mayborn Foundation since 1964; County Developers Inc. 1967—; Dir. 1st National Bank Temple; Dir. Temple Ind. Foundation, Pres. 1963. *Member:* Baylor Univ., Broadcast Council. 1964–65. Texas Council Higher Education; Pres. Chamber Commerce 1939–40, member Bd. Dirs. 1953–55, 1959–61, 1970–73; member Texas Democratic Exec. Cttee. 1948; Southern Newspaper Pub. Assn. Dir. 1951–54, 1956–59, Pres. 1962, Chmn. Bd. 1963; Amer. Socy. Newspaper Editors 1953—; Adv. Dev. Bd. Texas Industria Commission 1958–64; A & M Adv. Council Dept. of Journalism 1958–59; Fort Hood Civilian Adv. Cttee. 1963—; Member Adv. Council Univ. Texas Journalism Foundation 1964–66; Chmn. Scott and White Dev. Bd.; Member Texas State Historical Survey Cttee. 1966–69; Bd. Dirs. Waco Symphony Assn. 1968—; Temple Boys Choir 1969; Bd. Trustees, Peabody Coll. Tennessee 1970—; Trustee, Central Texas Medical Foundation 1970—; Pres. Kinsolving Youth Center 1971—; *Member:* Retail Merchants Assn.; Temple; Texas Daily Newspaper Assn. (past Pres.); Texas Daily Press League; Military Affairs Cttee.; Texas Ind. Commission; Amer. Newspaper Publishers Assn.; (Federal Laws Cttee.) Phi Kappa Psi; Sigma Delta Chi; Presbyterian Elder; Mason; member Broadcast Pioneers 1972; Served from pvt. to Major AUS 1942–45. *Awards:* Decorated Bronze Star Medal; Outstanding Citizens Award Temple; Texas Award, Outstanding Service Veterans Foreign Wars; AUSA Certificate of Achievement, Outstanding Service, U.S. Army; Soil Conservation Service, Contribution, Soil & Water Conservation; Jnr. Chamber of Commerce Citizenship; Jaycee, Man of the Year, Outstanding Service to 4-H clubs. *Clubs:* National Press; Advertising; Forth Worth; Dallas Athletic; Country; Headliners (Austin); Lancers (Dallas). The Presidents, 1966–69; Rotary (Hon. member). *Address:* Highway 36, Temple, Tex.; and *office* 17 South Third Street, Temple, Tex., U.S.A.

**MAYBRAY-KING, Rt. Hon. Lord,** PhD, BA, FKC, DL. British. Peer of the Realm. *B.* 25 May 1901. *Educ.* King's Coll. Univ. of London (BA First Class Hons.; Doctor of Philosophy). *M.* 1967, Una (second wife). *Dau.* Hon. Margaret Wilson. *Career:* Head, English Dept. Taunton's School, Southampton; Headmaster Regents Park School, 1947–50; Member of Parliament, 1950–70; Deputy Speaker House of Commons 1964–65; Speaker, House of Commons. 1965–70; Baron Maybray-King since 1970. Chmn., Spina Bifida Assn. 1970—; Hon. Treas., Help the Aged 1971—; Dep. Lieutenant, Hampshire 1976. (Hon.) *Member:* National Union of Teachers. *Awards:* Hon. DCL Durham; Hon. LLD Southampton; Hon. LLD Bath; Hon. DSoc.Sci. Ottawa; Hon. LittD. Loughborough; Fellow, Royal Coll. Preceptors; Freeman of Southampton and Stockton on Tees. Fellow, King's Coll. London. *Publications:* Selections from Macaulay; Selections from Homer; Parliament & Freedom; State Crimes, Before Hansard; Life of Oglethorpe; Songs in the Night; The Speaker and Parliament. *Address:* House of Lords, Westminster, London, S.W.1.

**MAYER, Daniel.** French politician and journalist. *B.* 29 April 1909. *M.* 1931, Claire Livian. *Career:* Formerly Secretary-General Socialist Party; Minister of Labour 1947–49; Deputy (Soc.) for Paris 1945–58. *Awards:* Chevalier de la Legion d'Honneur: Croix de Guerre; Médaille de la Résistance. Pres. former French League for the Rights of the Man; Pres., International Federation of Human Rights. *Address:* 27 rue Jean Dolent, Paris, 14e, France.

**MAYER, Frederick Miller.** Business executive; Lawyer. *B.* 1898. *Educ.* Heidelberg Coll., Tiffin. Ohio (BA 1920) and Harvard Univ. Law School (JD 1924). *M.* 1926, Mildred Katharine Rickard. *S.* Frederick Rickard. *Dau.* Elizabeth Ann (Boeckman). *Career:* Admitted Ohio Bar 1924; practice of law, Akron 1924–26, and Youngstown 1926–32, Treas., Continental Supply Co., Dallas 1932–33 (Vice-President 1933–45, President 1946–56, at which time company became Continental-Emsco Co.); Retired in 1964 as President of Continental-Emsco and its English, Canadian, Mexican and Venezuelan subsidiaries, which he had headed since 1945, and as Vice-Pres. of the Youngstown Sheet and Tube Co. 1956–64; Dir., Chicago, Rock Island & Pacific R. R. Co. 1947–59 and 1961–74; Gen. Amer. Oil Co. of Texas 1953–57 and 1961—; Hon. LLD Heidelberg College 1948 (he has been a Trustee since 1948). Chmn., Dallas Art Assn. *Member:* American Petroleum Institute; Mid-Continent Oil & Gas Association; Petroleum Equipment Suppliers Assn . (Dir., past Pres.); Independent Petroleum Assn.; Huguenot Socy. of Pennsylvania; Sons of American Revolution; Pi Kappa Delta. *Clubs:* Acacia, Petroleum, Idlewild, Brook Hollow, Hunting & Fishing (all of Dallas). *Address:* 3131 Maple Avenue, Dallas 9, Tex.; and *office* Mercantile Continental Building, Dallas 1, Tex., U.S.A.

**MAYER, Joseph E.** Professor of Chemical Physics. *B.* 1904. *Educ.* California Inst. of Technology (BS 1924); Univ. of California (Berkeley). PhD 1927. *M.* (1). 1930, Maria Goeppert. *S.* Peter Conrad. *Dau.* Maria Ann Wentzel. (2) 1972, Margaret Griffin. *Career:* Editor, Journal of Chemical Physics 1940–52;

Fellow, Int. Education Board, Göttingen, Germany 1929–30; Associate Johns Hopkins Univ. 1930–35 (Assoc. Prof. 1935–39); Assoc. Prof., Columbia Univ. 1939–45; Prof., Univ. of Chicago 1946–55 (Carl Eisendraht Prof. 1955–60); Pres., Commission on Thermodynamics & Statistical Mechanics, Int. Union of Pure & Applied Physics 1951–56; Chmn., Div. of Physical & Inorganic Chemistry, National Research Council 1954–58; Editor-in-Chief, International Encyclopedia of Physical Chemistry & Chemical Physics 1958–68; Professor of Chemical Physics Univ. of Calif. San Diego since 1960. *Publications:* Statistical Mechanics (with Maria Goeppert Mayer (1940); Phase Transformations in Solids (with Smoluchowski and Weyl 1951); various papers on research in chemical physics. *Member:* Natl. Acad. of Sciences; American Philosophical Society corresponding member, Heidelberg Academy; American Academy of Arts & Sciences; Faraday Society; New York Academy of Sciences; Amer. Chemical Society; Member Scientific Adv. Cttee. Ballistics Research Laboratories, U.S. Ordnance Dept. 1946—; Visiting Cttee. National Bureau of Standards 1957–60; Member, Solvay Institute 1960—; Adv. Cttee. for Chemistry, Oak Ridge National Laboratory 1965–68. *Awards:* Gilbert Newton Lewis Medal and Peter Debyl Award; James Flack Norris Award. American Physical Society (Fellow), Vice-Pres. 1972, Pres. 1973. *Address:* 2345 Via Siena, La Jolla, California 92037; and *office* Department of Chemistry, University of California, La Jolla, California, U.S.A.

**MAYFIELD, Gene.** American. *B.* 1915. *Educ.* Missouri University (AB 1936; LLB 1938). *M.* 1941, Winifred Neill Horner. *S.* Douglas Eugene and Allan Horner. *Career:* In law firm of Bartley & Mayfield 1938–42; U.S. Naval Reserve 1942–46. Joined Pet Inc. as General Attorney 1946, Asst. Secretary 1952, General Counsel 1956; Vice-President and General Counsel, Pet Inc., Nov. 1966—. *Member:* American, Federal, Missouri and St. Louis Bar Associations. Beta Theta Pi. *Address:* 2 Maryhill Drive, Ladue, Mo. 63124; and *office* 400 South Fourth, St. Louis, Mo. 63166, U.S.A.

**MAYHEW, Christopher Paget,** British politician, writer and director. *B.* 12 June 1915. *Educ.* Haileybury; Christ Church, Oxford (MA). *M.* 1949, Cicely Elizabeth Ludlam. *S.* 2. *Daus.* 2. *Career:* Served World War II, Army (despatches) 1939–45; MP (Lab.) for South Norfolk 1945–50; Parly. Private Secretary to Lord President of Council 1945–46; Parly. Under-Secretary of State for Foreign Affairs 1946–50; Minister of Defence for the Navy from 1964 until his resignation in 1966. MP (Soc.) for East Woolwich 1951–74; Resigned Labour Party and joined Liberal Party 1974; Liberal Parly. Candidate for Bath since 1974; Chmn., Liberal Action Group for Electoral Reform; Middle East International (Publishers) Co.; Chmn. ANAF Foundation. *Publications:* Those in Favour; Men Seeking God; Coexistence Plus; Britain's Role Tomorrow, Party Games; Publish It Not; The Disillusioned Voter's Guide to Electoral Reform. *Address:* 39 Wool Road, Wimbledon, London S.W.20.

**MAYHEW, Patrick Barnabas Burke,** QC, MP. British Barrister. *B.* 1929. *Educ.* Tonbridge School; Balliol Coll., Oxford. MA. *M.* 1963, Jean Elizabeth Gurney. *S.* 4. *Career:* Called to the Bar, Middle Temple 1955; Appointed Queen's Counsel 1972; Conservative MP for Royal Tunbridge Wells since 1974. *Address:* House of Commons, London SW1A 0AA.

**MAYNARD, Harry Edgar.** American communications expert. *B.* 1918. *Educ.* Wilbraham Academy (Grad. 1936), Colgate Univ. (AB 1940), and Harvard Univ. (Advanced Management). *M.* 1960, Natalie Ryshna Hook. *Daus.* Melanie Dawn and Amy Anne. *Career:* Regional Sales Mgr., Columbia Records 1940–42; Field Dir., retail rep. program for Life 1945–46; N.Y. Advtg. Mgr. Life International Editions 1952–53 (U.S. Advtg. Mgr. 1953–59); Publishing Mgr., Special publications, Time-Life International Editions 1967–68. Founder and Pres., General Semantics Found. 1965—; Vice-Pres. and Dir., Foto-Cube; Contributing Editor Audio-Video Magazine; Producer-Moderator of Radio programmes, 'Men of Hi-Fi' and 'Sound Advice'. *Awards:* Presidential Citation with Cluster; Air Medal (Army). Teacher of general semantics at New York and Columbia Universities, Cooper Union, Graduate School, City Coll. of City Univ. of N.Y., management training courses, etc.; Bd. Member, Internatl. Society for General Semantics; Inst. of General Semantics (Trustee), Pres. 1972; N.Y. Socy. for Gen. Semantics (Bd. of Dirs.); Internatl. Communications Conf. (Chmn. 1963); Amer. Marketing Assn.; Phi Kappa Psi. *Publications:* articles in Audio Video, Popular Science, Popular Mechanics, Gramophone, Hi-Fi Stereo Buyer's Guide, Radio Electronics. *Address:* 14 Charcoal Hill, Westport, CT 06880, U.S.A.

**MAYNE, Richard.** British writer, international Civil Servant. *Educ.* St. Paul's School and Cambridge Univ. (MA; PhD). *M.* (1) Margaret Lyon, (2) Jocelyn Ferguson. *Career:* Army service 1944–47; successively Styring, Senior, and Research Scholar, and Earl of Derby Student, of Trinity College, Cambridge 1947–53; Leverhulme European Scholar 1953–54; Rome Correspondent, New Statesman 1953–54; Assistant Tutor, Cambridge Institute of Education 1954–56. Official of the High Authority of the European Coal and Steel Community 1956–58; Official of the Commission of the European Economic Community 1958–68; Director of Documentation Centre, Action Cttee. for the United States of Europe 1963–66; Dir. of the Federal Trust for Education and Research (London) 1970–73; Dir. U.K. office, Commission of the European Communities. *Publications:* The Community of Europe (1962); The Institutions of the European Community (1968); The Recovery of Europe (1970); Ed. Europe Tomorrow (1972); The Europeans (1972); Editor, the New Atlantic Challenge (1975); Translator, the Memoirs of Jean Monnet (1977); contributions to various periodicals in Europe & the U.S. *Address:* 67 Harley Street, London NW1.

**MAYOBRE, José Antonio.** Venezuelan economist, lawyer and diplomat. *B.* 1913. *Educ.* Colegio Sucre, Cumana; Liceo Andrés Bello Caracas; Central University of Venezuela; Dir. Econ. Social Sc. 1944; LLD 1945. *M.* 1941, Experanze Machedo. *S.* José Antonio and Eduardo. *Career:* Asst. Chief, Economic Investigations, Banco Central de Venezuela 1940–45; Alternate Governor for Venezuela, International Monetary Fund 1947–49; Director, Agriculture & Livestock Bank of Venezuela 1949; General Manager, Industrias Azucareras, S.A. 1949–51; Asst. Dir., Economic Commission for Latin America, United Nations 1951–53; Chief Div. Economic Development, U.N. Economic Commission for Latin America, Santiago, Chile 1954–57; Professor, Economic Analysis School of Economy, Univ. of Venezuela 1956–60; Dir., Venezuelan Development Corp. 1958; Minister of Finance of Venezuela 1958–60. Executive Director for Venezuela 1958–60. United Nations Under-Secretary, Commissioner for Industrial Development, June 1962–63; Ambassador to the United States, Dec. 1960–May 1962, and to the Organization of American States, Dec. 1960–May 1962; Executive Director, International Monetary Fund 1960–62; President, Society for International Development 1960—; Executive Director for Venezuela, Mexico, Guatemala, El Salvador, Honduras, Nicaragua, Costa Rica and Cuba to the International Monetary Fund 1960—. United Nations Executive Secretary, Economic Commission for Latin America, Santiago, Chile, 1963–66; Minister of Mines & Hydrocarbons, Caracas, Venezuela 1967–69; Adviser, Banco Central de Venezuela; Dir. H. L. Boulton & Co. S.A. Caracas 1969–70. *Publications:* La Paridad del Bolívar (1945); La Situation Economique Actuelle de Venezuela (1945). Hon. Prof. Univ. of Merida; Member College of Economists of Venezuela. *Awards:* Orders: Orden del Libertador, Venezuela; Matías Delgado, El Salvador; del Cóndor de Los Andes, Bolivia; de las Fuerzas Armadas de Cooperación, Venezuela. *Address:* 1A Avenida Montecristo 9, Caracas, Venezuela.

**MAZUROV, Kirill Trofimovich.** Soviet statesman. Member Central Committee of C.P.S.U. since 1956 (candidate member of the Presidium of the Central Committee 1957–65); member of the Presidium of the Central Committee 1965–66. Member, Political Bureau, Central Cttee., C.P.S.U., 1966—. Deputy of the Supreme Soviet; the U.S.S.R.; the B.S.S.R. (Belorussian Republic); the R.S.F.S.R. (Russian Soviet Federative Socialist Republic). *B.* 1914. Graduated from the Road transport technical school in Gomel in 1933, and the High Party School of the Central Committee of the C.P.S.U. in 1947. Engineer, then chief of the Road transport department, Komarinsky district, B.S.S.R., 1933–36; served in the Soviet Army 1936–38; worked in the Political Department of the Belorussian railways and then in the Gomel regional committee of the B.Y.C.L. (Komsomol of the Belorussian Republic) 1938–39; Secretary of Gomel City Komsomol Committee and Brest regional committee 1940–41. During the war (1941–45) served in the Soviet Army (in 1941—at the front; 1942–43—in partisan detachments). Secretary and then First Secretary of the Central Committee of B.Y.C.L. 1942–47; Second and then First Secretary of Minsk City Committee of the Belorussian C.P. 1948–49; First Secretary of Minsk regional Committee C.P. of the Bellorussia 1950–53; Chairman of the Council of Ministers of the Belorussian Republic 1953–56; First Secretary of the Central

Committee of the Communist Party of the Belorussian Republic 1956–65; Member of the Presidium of the U.S.S.R. Supreme Soviet 1958–65. Since April 1965, First Deputy Chairman of the Council of Ministers of the U.S.S.R. *Awards:* Order of Lenin three times, and is the recipient of the Order of Red Banner and Order of the Great Patriotic War (1st Class) and several medals. *Address:* Council of Ministers of the U.S.S.R., the Kremlin, Moscow, U.S.S.R.

**MAZZOCCHI, Gianni.** Italian publisher. *B.* 1906. *Educ.* Doctor of Law Grand Officer, Order of Merit of the Republic of Italy; Knight, Sovereign Military Order of Malta. Sole Director of Editoriale Domus S.p.A. Publisher of Domus 1928—. Editor of Quattroruote 1956—. *Club:* Rotary (Milan). *Address: office* Via Monte de Pietà 15, Milan, Italy.

**MBAH, Jules.** Ambassador of the Gabonese Republic. *B.* 1928. *Educ.* Secondary Studies at Brazzaville; won Diploma at the Overseas Institute for Higher Studies, Paris. *M.* 1956, Helene Gningone. *S.* Martial Feliz and Henri Jules. *Daus.* Radegonde Cecile and Patricia Therese. *Career:* After completion of his secondary education, he served in the Finance Administration until 1958; Prefect, later Technical Adviser to the Minister for Home Affairs Department of the Gabonese Public Administration 1960; Ambassador to United States 1961–65. *Address:* c/o Ministry of Foreign Affairs, Libreville, Republic of Gabon.

**MEACHER, Michael Hugh,** MP. British Politician. *B.* 1939. *Educ.* Berkhamsted School; New Coll., Oxford—Greats, Class 1; London Sch. of Economics. *M.* 1962, Molly Christine Reid. *S.* 2. *Daus.* 2. *Career:* Sec., Danilo Dolci Trust 1963–64; Research Fellow in Social Gerontology, Univ. of Essex 1964–66; Lecturer in Social Admin., Univ. of York 1966–69 & LSE 1970; Labour MP for Oldham West since 1970; Parliamentary Under-Sec. of State, Dept. of Industry 1974–75, DHSS 1975–76, & Dept. of Trade since 1976. *Member:* Fabian Society; Child Poverty Action Group. *Publications:* The Care of the Old (1969); Taken For a Ride; Special Homes for the Elderly Mentally Infirm, a Study of Separatism in Social Policy (1972); numerous articles in journals, newspapers etc. on economic & social policy. *Address:* 45 Cholmeley Park, London N.6; & House of Commons, London S.W.1.

**MEAGHER, Blanche Margaret,** OC. Canadian diplomat. *B.* 1911. *Educ.* Dalhousie University (MA). *Career:* Junior High School Teacher, Halifax, N.S. 1932–42; Wartime Assistant, Department of External Affairs, Ottawa 1942–45; Second Secretary (Third Secretary 1945–47), Canadian Embassy, Mexico 1947–49; Officer, Dept. of External affairs 1949–53; Counsellor (First Secretary 1953–55), Canadian High Commission, London, 1955–56; Chargé d'Affaires, Tel Aviv 1957; Ambassador to Isreal Oct. 1958 to Dec. 1961; High Commissioner to Cyprus (concurrently with assignment in Israel) Aug.–Dec. 1961; Ambassador to the Republic of Austria, 1962–66; and to Sweden since 1969. Canadian Governor on the Board of Governors of the International Atomic Energy Agency, Mar. 1962–66; Chairman, Board of Governors, International Atomic Energy Agency, Sept. 1964–65; Head, Canadian Delegation to Trade and Development Board (UNCTAD), U.N. Headquarters, New York, Apr. 1965. Member Canadian Delegation to U.N. General Assembly, New York, Oct.–Dec. 1965 and Sept.–Dec. 1966; High Commissioner for Canada to Kenya and Uganda, 1967–69; Ambassador to Sweden 1969–73; For. Service Visitor, Dalhousie Univ. 1973–74; Retired 1974; Mem. Board of Trustees, Nat. Museum of Canada since 1974. Adviser to Canadian delegations to UNESCO Assembly, Mexico 1947, I.T.U., Mexico 1948, U.N. Econ. & Soc. Council (New York 1950, Geneva 1950, Santiago 1951, Geneva 1951, New York 1952), Disarmament Sub-Committee, London 1954–55–56. *Address:* 6899 Armview Ave. Halifax, Nova Scotia, Canada.

**MEARS, Robert Bruce.** American. *B.* 1907. *Educ.* Pennsylvania State Univ. (BS); Cambridge Univ. (PhD). *M.* 1929, Margaret Hart. *S.* Dana Christopher. *Dau.* Diana (Marquis). *Career:* Member of Technical Staff, Bell Telephone Laboratories, 1928–32; Research Student, Cambridge Univ. 1932–35; Chief Chemical Metallurgy Div., Alcoa Research Laboratories, 1935–46; Director, Applied Research Laboratories, 1946–60; Asst. Vice-Pres., Applied Research 1960–63, U.S. Steel. Vice-President, New Product Development, U.S. Steel 1964–72, Volunteer Executive, Fundacao Centro Tecnologico De Minas Gerais, Belo Horizonte, MG, Brasil. *Publications:* Numerous Technical Papers, Transactions, Faraday Socy; Proceedings, Royal Socy; Carnegie Scholarship Memoirs; Industrial and Engineering Chemistry; Journal Electrochemical Socy.; Mechanical Engineering, etc. Carnegie Scholar, British Iron & Steel Inst.; Whitney Award, National Assn. Corrosion Engineers; Consultant, Manhattan Project. *Member:* Amer. Socy. for Metals. *Clubs:* Oakmont Country. *Address:* 628 California Avenue, Oakmont, Pa., 13519, U.S.A.

**MECKE, Theodore Hart McCalla, Jr.** *B.* 1923. *Educ.* LaSalle High School and LaSalle College (Hon. LLD 1964) both in Philadelphia. *M.* 1956, Mary Eleanor Flaherty. *S.* William Moyn, Theodore Hart McCalla III, John Chetwood and Stephen Campbell. *Career:* Man. Editor, Germantown (Pa.) Courier 1942 and 1946–49; Served in H.Q. Third U.S. Infantry Div. in Europe, World War II. Joined Ford Motor Co. Dearborn Mich. Feb. 1949; served in several posts, including General Public Relations Manager and Vice-Pres. Public Relations. Vice-President Public Affairs since 1969. *Member:* Public Relations Socy. of America; Economic Club of Detroit. *Clubs:* Detroit, Athletic, Press, Cardinal, Country, Yondotega (all of Detroit); International (Washington); Windermere Island (The Bahamas). *Address:* 296 Cloverly Road, Grosse Pointe Farms, Mich.; and *office* The American Road, Dearborn, 48121 Mich., U.S.A.

**MEDBOE, Odd Harald.** Norwegian. *B.* 1914. *Educ.* Special studies in journalism, public relations, history social sciences and psychology. *M.* 1938, Katja Riosianu. *S.* Harald. *Daus.* Eva, Wenche (actress at Norwegian Theatre of Oslo), and Katja (of National Theatre of Oslo). *Career:* Chmn. Norwegian Public Relations Socy. 1955–60; Pres. International Public Relations Assn. 1957–58. Director of Public Relations, Scandinavian Airline System, Region Norway, 1950; Pres. Norwegian Artists Assoc. since 1974. *Awards:* Commander Order de Merito (Argentine), Order de Rio Branco (Brazil), Order Al Merito (Chile), Order Al Merito (Italy); Grand Cross of Honour (Austria); Kt. 1st Cl. Order of the Crown (Iran), and of the Order of the White Elephant (Thailand); Officer, Order of the Flag (Yugoslavia); Silver Medal, Norwegian Aero Club. *Publications:* Himmeltårnet (1963); Stakkars Jørgen (1964); Kong Oavs ferd til Østerland (royal saga 1965); Spillet (dramatic play, 1966); De heldige Tré Konger (1969); many poems, "Because you made me a man", inspired Egil Hovland to compose his 3rd symphony. World Premier Aula of Oslo Univ. (1970); Jørgen Kommer Hjem (1972). *Awards:* Medal of Honour of League of Norwegians; Hon. Member, Technical Museum of Norway; Grand Cross of Norwegian Artists Association. *Address:* Sondreveien 4, Oslo 3; and *office* SAS Building, Ruseløkkvn 6, Oslo, Norway.

**MEDICI, Prof. Giuseppe.** Chairman of Montedison S.p.A., Milan; Professor, University of Rome. Senator. *B.* 24 Oct, 1907. *Educ.* Degree of Doctor, Agricultural-Economics. Milan, 1929. *M.* Grazia Fiandri. *S.* Franco. *Dau.* Paola. Awarded Chair of Agricultural Economics, Perugia 1933; called later to Turin University, in 1952 to Naples University, and in 1960 to Rome University. Italian Delegate to Marshall Plan Conference; In response to foreign university invitations, has lectured in U.K. (Oxford and London), U.S.A., Germany, India, Bulgaria, etc.; Minister of Agriculture and Forests 1954–55; Treasury Minister 1956–58; Minister for the Budget 1958–59; Minister for National Educn. 1959–60; Delegate to U.N.O. Minister for the Reform of Public Administration 1962–63; Minister for the Budget 1963; Minister for Industry and Trade 1963–65; Minister for Foreign Affairs 1968 and 1972–73. *Publications:* L'Azienda Agraria Tipica (The Typical Farm) (1945); L'Agricoltura e la Riforma Agraria (Agriculture & Agrarian Reform) (1946); Italy (1950); Politica Agraria (Agrarian Policy) (1952); Perizie e Pareri (Valuations & Opinions) (1954); Principi di Estimo (Estimate Principles) (1954); Lezioni di Politica Economica (Lessons of Political Economy) (1967). *Address:* Via Stoppani 10, Rome, Italy.

**MEDINA, Harold R.** American judge. *B.* 16 Feb. 1888. *Educ.* Princeton University (AB), Columbia University (LLB). *M.* 1911, Ethel Forde Hillyer. *S.* Harold Raymond, Standish Forde. Admitted to New York Bar 1912; practised law 1912–47; Lecturer in law, Columbia 1915–17; Assoc. in law 1917–25; Associate Professor of Law 1925–40; Judge, U.S. District Court, Southern District of New York 1947–51; Judge, U.S. Court of Appeals, 2nd Circuit July 1951; retired and became a Senior Circuit Judge March 1, 1958. Democrat. *Address:* U.S. Court House, Foley Square, New York, 10007, U.S.A.

**MEDLICOTT, Ronald Francis.** FCA. British. *B.* 1911. *Educ.* Eton. *M.* (1), 1936, Marie Theodora Moncheur (D. 1967). *S.* 3,

*Daus.* 3. (2), 1968, Doris Wootton (D. 1973). (3) 1976, Diane de Montpellier D'Annevoie. *Career:* Dir. Tanganyika Concessions Ltd.; Union Minière S.A.; Kleinwort, Benson (Europe) S.A. *Clubs:* Traveller's; Rand Johannesburg. *Address:* Beechwood House, Great Hockham, nr. Thetford, Norfolk; and *office* 6 John Street, London, WC1N 2ES.

**MEECH, Sir John Valentine,** KCVO. JP. New Zealand. *B.* 1907. *Educ.* Hutt Valley High School, and Public Service College. *M.* 1938, Rachel Crease Anderson. *Career:* N.Z. Secretary to the Queen and Director of Royal Visit, July 1962–Feb. 1963. Secretary for Internal Affairs, Secretary of Civil Defence and Clerk of the Writs 1959–67; Council of Duke of Edinburgh Award Scheme 1963–69 Chmn. Bd. of Trustees, National School of Ballet 1966—; Member, Music Advis. Committee, Queen Elizabeth II ·Arts Council, 1967—; Deputy Chairman, Electricity Distribution Commission 1968—. *Clubs:* Civil Service; Miramar Golf. *Address:* 205 Barnard Street, Highland Park, Wellington 1, New Zealand.

**MEERS, Henry Weber.** American business excutive. *B.* 1908. *Educ.* University of Illinois (BA 1930). *M.* 1945, Evelyn Huckins. *S.* Henry Weber, Jr., Albert Huckins and Robert. *Career:* Dir. Securities Investor Protection Corp.; Dukane Corp.; Kroehler Manufacturing Co.; Illinois Tool Works; International Minerals & Chemical Corp.; Mutual Broadcasting Corp.; Reliance Insurance Co.; Federal Express Corp.; Reliance Group Inc.; Vice-Chmn. White Weld & Co. Incorporated, Chicago. *Member:* Midwest Stock Exchange. *Clubs:* Commercial, The Links (N.Y.C.); Chicago, Onwentsia, Economic; University; Casino; Bohemian (San Francisco); Capitol Hill (Washington). *Address: office* 30 West Monroe, Chicago, Ill. 60603 U.S.A.

**MEHTA, Dr. Jivraj Narayan.** Indian physician and statesman. *B.* 1887. *Educ.* Amreli High School, Grant Medical College, Bombay, and London Hospital (Sandhurst Gold Medal, Bombay University, and University Gold Medal, London University, and Sir Mangaldas Nathoobhoy Travelling Fellowship, Bombay University). *M.* Shrimati Hansa Mehta. *S.* Harsharaj. *Dau.* Kumari Anjani. *Career:* Consulting physician, Bombay, 1915; Dean, Gordhandas Sunderdas Medical College and King Edward Memorial Hospital 1925–42; Chief Medical Officer Baroda State, 1923–1924, and Physician to H.H. Maharaja of Baroda 1921–24; Secretary and Director-General, Health Services, Govt. of India 1947–48; Chairman, Executive Council, Kamala Nehru Memorial Hospital Allahabad, 1940—. Central Salt and Marine Research Institute, Bhavnagar 1967—; Vice-President, All India Prohibition Council New Delhi 1968—. President, chairman or member of many medical and research assocs.; Examiner, Medical Faculty, Bombay University 1916; and 1926–30; delegate at several conferences, Chairman of Govt. Committee on the working of Bombay Medical Practitioners' Act 1938, and of the Administrative Enquiry Committee to provide efficient and economic administrative machinery in the Bombay Govt. 1946; elected to Bombay Legislative Assembly 1946, and in 1951 and 1957; Dewan of Baroda State (prior to its integration in the State of Bombay) 1948–49; joined Bombay Cabinet as Minister for Public Works 1949; Minister of Finance, Bombay State 1952–60; Chief Minister, Gujarat State 1960–63. High Commissioner for India in U.K. 1963–66. *Member:* Medical Council of India; Council of Scientific & Industrial Research 1959–62. Chairman, Bombay Gandhi Smarak Nidhi 1967–70. Managing Committee, Motilal Nehru, Memorial Rural Inst., Allahabad 1968–69. Member, Exec. Cttee., Mahatma Gandhi Memorial Coll. of Medical Sciences. *Publications:* Studies regarding presence of glycogen in suprarenal Bodies (Lancet, London 1915); Height, Weight and Chest Measurements enquiry relating to some children (males) in Bombay (Journal of Indian Medical Association 1941). *Address:* Everest House, 14 Carmichael Road, Bombay 26, India.

**MEIGHEN Maxwell Charles Gordon,** OBE. Canadian. *B.* 1908. *Educ.* Royal Military College (Kingston, Ontario) and Univ. of Toronto (BASc). *M.* 1934, Catherine Jane McWhinnie. *Career:* Engaged in various engineering projects until he joined Canadian General Investments Ltd. and Third Canadian General Investment Trust Ltd. in 1939; served in World War II (2 Canadian Corps H.Q. as Deputy Director of Mechanical Engineering) 1939–45. Past Pres. Dir. (1939), Chmn. & Dir. 1970—, Canadian Gen. Investments Ltd.; Chmn. of the Bd., Dir. & Mem. of Exec. Cttee., Domtar Ltd.; Dir. & Mem. of Exec. Cttee., The Algoma Steel Corp. Ltd., Dominion Stores Ltd., Hollinger Mines Ltd., Massey-Ferguson Ltd.; Vice-Pres., Dir. & Chmn. of Exec. Cttee., Argus Corp. Ltd.; Director, C.F.R.B., Standard Broadcast Sales, Standard Broadcasting Corp. Ltd., Canadian General Electric Co. Ltd., Labrador Mining & Exploration Co. Ltd., Massey-Ferguson Ltd. (London, U.K.); Vice-Pres. & Dir., The Ravelston Corp. Ltd.; Chmn., Toronto Advisory Bd., Vice-Pres. & Dir., The Canada Trust Co.; Vice-Pres. & Dir., Canada Trustco Mortgage Co.; Mem. & Dir., Canadian Advisory Bd., Sun Alliance & London Insurance Group, England. *Member:* Bd. of Management, Grace Hospital, Toronto; Chmn., Advisory Bd., The Salvation Army. *Awards:* Order of the British Empire (Mil.); Croix de Guerre avec Palme; Order of Leopold with Palm (mentioned in despatches). *Club:* Toronto. Conservative. *Address:* 102 Binscarth Road, Toronto, Ont., Canada M4W 1Y4.

**MEIJER, Albert.** Dutch. *B.* 1928. *Educ.* Technol. Univ. Delft. *M.* 1955, Johanna B. van Nus. *S.* 2. *Career:* various appointments with Wilton-Fijenoord; Dir. N.V. Koninklijke, Nederlandse Vliegtui-genfabriek Fokker; Cincinnati-Nederland N.V.; Zentralges VFW/Fokker m.b.H.; Van Gelder Papier N.V.; Member Exec. Bd. Verenigde Machinefabrieken N.V.; Fearnley International NV; Stoomvaartmaatschappij Oostzee. *Member:* Royal Inst. Engineers, The Hague; Royal Inst. Naval Architects; Assoc. member, Inst. Mech Engineers, London. *Address:* Meresteyn 17, Maasland, Netherlands.

**MEIKLEJOHN, David S.** Financial executive. *B.* 1908. *Educ.* Williams Coll., Williamstown, Mass. (BA 1931). *M.* 1945, Mary Jeanne Faulkner. *Dau.* Shirra Belvoir. *Career:* Credit Analyst, Bankers Trust Co. 1933–36; Assistant to President, The Dorr Co. 1936–40; Director, New York City Dept. of Commerce 1940–42; Lieut.-Comdr. U.S. Navy 1942–45; Exec. Secretary to Hon. F. H. LaGuardia, Mayor of N.Y. City 1946; American Machine & Foundry Co. 1946—; Vice-President 1958—, Treasurer 1951— and Director 1954—, American Machine & Foundry Co. resigned 1970; Exec. Vice-Pres. Finance and Dir. Integrated Resources Inc. since 1970; Treasurer & Dir., American Property Investors. *Member:* Phi Beta Kappa; St. Andrews Socy. *Clubs:* Williams; Stanwich Golf; Belle Haven (Greenwich, Conn.); Union League. *Address:* 23 Clapboard Ridge Road, Greenwich, Conn.; and *office* 295 Madison Avenue, New York City 10017, U.S.A.

**MEINANDER, Nils,** PhD. Finnish economist. *B.* 4 Aug. 1910. *M.* 1947, Anita Meinander. *S.* Martin, Tor, Göran, Nils Torkel. *Dau.* Juni. *Career:* Bank clerk 1929–33; Journalist 1935–42; Lecturer, Swedish School of Economics, Helsingfors since 1942, Professor in Economics 1953–73; MP (Swedish People's Party) 1945–62; Deputy Minister of Finance 1950–51, 1953; Minister of Finance 1957. *Publications:* En krönika om vattensågen; Virkeshushållning och sågverksrörelse i Torne. Kemi och Simo älvdalar; Ränteeffekten; Det tillbakahållna vålståndet; Penningpolitik under etthundrafemtio år; Gränges en krönika om svensk jarnmalm; Ekonomerna och verkligheten; Penningen i den Ekonomiska Politiken. *Address:* Kallbäck, Immersby, Finland.

**MEIR Golda.** Former Prime Minister of Israel. *B.* 1898. *Educ.* Teachers' Seminary, Milwaukee, U.S.A. Leading member Poalei Zion (Zionist Labour Party) Milwaukee; Delegate of United States section, World Jewish Congress until 1921; emigrated to Palestine 1921; with Solel Boneh, Labour Federation (Histadruth) Contracting and Public Works Enterprise, 1924–26; appointed Secy., Women's Labour Council of Histadruth 1928; member of Exec. and Secretariat, Federation of Labour, 1929–34; Chairman, Board of Directors, Workers' Sick Fund, and Head, Political Department, Fed. of Labour, and Mapai (Labour Party) delegate, Actions Committee, World Zionist Organization, 1936; member, War Economy Advisory Council of Palestine Government, and leading member of the Hagana struggle, 1939; Head, Political Dept., Jewish Agency for Palestine, Jerusalem, 1946–48; Minister to Moscow, Aug. 1948–April 1949; Minister of Labour and Social Insurance in Israeli cabinet, 1949–52; Minister of Labour, 1952–56; Minister for Foreign Affairs, 1956–66; Secy. General Labour Party 1966–69; Prime Minister 1969–74. *Address:* 8 Habaron Hirsch Street, Ramat-Aviv, Israel.

**MEIRING, Jacobus Gerhard.** South African educationalist & author. *B.* 1898. *Educ.* Stellenbosch Univ. (BSc; BEd) and Leipzig (PhD). *M.* 1925, Hester Magdalena Erasmus. *S.* 3. *Daus.* 2. Lecturer Normal Coll., Potchefstroom, Transvaal 1925–35; Head of the Training Coll. for Teachers, Wellington, Cape Province 1936–39; Professor of Educational

Psychology, University of Stellenbosch 1940–53; Superintendent-General of Education in the Cape Province July 1953–Dec. 1959. Rector, University College, Western Cape, Republic of South Africa, Jan. 1960–Dec. 1967. *Publications:* various works and articles on educational and psychological matters in Afrikaans; regular contributions to educational journals in South Africa. *Address:* Waveren, Durbanville C.P., South Africa.

**MEIRY, Meir Ben-Zion,** FCCS, FAIA. Israeli certified public accountant. *B.* 1905. *Educ.* High School of Commerce. *M.* 1933, Rivka Reitman. *Dau.* 1. *Career:* Sec., Accountant, General Accountant, and Dir., Haifa Marine, Ltd. 1927–33; studied and graduated as Fellow of Corpn. of Certified Secretaries (F.C.C.S.) 1934–36; Director, Finance Information Dept. of Jewish Agency, Jerusalem 1937–48; Asst. Accountant-General of Govt. of Israel, Hakirya 1948–49; Dir.-General of State Comptroller's Office, Jerusalem 1949. Controller, World Zionist Organization, The Jewish Agency for Israel, 1962. *Address:* 12 Feival Street, Tel-Aviv, Israel.

**MEISCH, Adrien Ferdinand Joseph.** Luxembourg diplomat. *B.* 1930. *Educ:* Luxembourg schools; Univ. Grenoble and Paris; Univ Oxford. Doctor of Law; B.Litt (Modern and Contemporary History). *M.* 1963, Solange Prégermain. *S.* 2. (adopted). *Career:* Attorney, member of Luxembourg Bar 1953; Attaché of Legation in Ministery of Foreign Affairs in Luxembourg 1956; Deputy Perm. Rep. of Luxembourg to UN in New York 1958–59; Deputy Perm. Rep. to European Communities in Brussels 1960; Deputy Perm. Rep. to NATO and OECD in Paris 1961–67; Political Director of Min. of Foreign Affairs in Luxembourg, and Perm. Rep. of Luxembourg to European Council in Strasbourg 1968–70; Ambassador of Luxembourg to USSR and Poland (residing in Moscow) 1971–74, to Finland 1972–74, to USA and Mexico 1974 and Canada 1975. *Decorations:* Luxembourg, Belgium, Netherlands, Yugoslavia, Senegal and Italy. *Address:* 2200 Massachusetts Ave. NW, Washington, DC 20008, U.S.A.

**MELANDER, Johan Arnt.** Norwegian banker. *B.* 1910 *Educ.* Oslo University (Cand. jur.). *M.* 1939, Tatiana Prestin. *S.* Haakon and Johan Andreas. *Dau.* Ella. *Career:* Secy. Norwegian Legation, London 1939–40; Secretary to Board of Directors, Bank of Norway, London 1941–43; Adviser to Norwegian Ministry of Foreign Affairs, London 1944–45; Commercial Counsellor, Norwegian Embassy, London 1945–48; member, Norwegian Delegation to First General Assembly, United Nations and First Session, Economic and Social Council of United Nations, London 1946; member, Norwegian Delegation, International Trade Organization Conferences, London 1946, Geneva 1947, Havana 1947–48, Organization of European Economic Co-operation. Paris 1948; Chairman of Contracting Parties to the General Agreement on Tariffs and Trade (G.A.T.T.) 1951–53; Head, Economic Department, Ministry of Foreign Affairs 1949–53; Managing Director and member of the Board of Den norske Creditbank since 1954; member, Institut International d'Etudes Bancaires since 1955, Chmn. 1967–68. In period Feb. 1957–Oct. 1958, on part time basis, was Chmn. of O.E.E.C. Cttee on European Free Trade Area Treaty. Chmn., Supervisory Bd., Shipping Companies Snefonn, Bergehus & Sigmalm (Sig. Bergesen d.y. & Co.). Chmn. Norwegian Bankers Assoc. 1963–66. *Awards:* Commander, 1st Class of the following Orders: North Star (Sweden), Lion (Finland), Dannebrog (Denmark), Orange Nassau (Netherlands) and St. Olav (Norway). *Address:* Den norske Creditbank, Oslo, Norway.

**MELCHIOR, Mogens Gustav Ivar.** Danish diplomat. *B.* 1904. *Educ.* Gl. Hellerup Gymnasium and Univ. of Copenhagen LLD. *M.* 1935, Karen Westenholz. *S.* Peter Ivar. *Daus.* Anne Patricia (Scott) and Siri Veronica. *Career:* Entered diplomatic service 1930; served in the Netherlands, China, Belgium, Switzerland, Finland, USSR, Norway, New Zealand, and in the Ministry of Foreign Affairs, Copenhagen, where Deputy Under-Secretary of State (Director-General Political Affairs) 1957; Ambassador to Turkey 1959–60; to Yugoslavia 1960; to Switzerland 1968–74. *Awards:* Knight Commander with cross of honour, Order of Dannebrog; medal for merit, and foreign decorations. *Address:* 3115 Gerzensee, Berne, Switzerland.

**MELDRUM, Hon. Wendell Wynne.** Canadian. *B.* 1924. *Educ.* Dalhousie University (LLB 1948). *M.* 1944, Dorothy F. Downey. *S.* Wynn Wendell and Kirk Walter. *Career:* Attorney-General 1965–1966. Minister of Education, New Brunswick, Canada, April 1966–70. Judge of the County Court of New Brunswick. *Member:* Nova Scotia, New Brunswick and Canadian Bar Society. Mason. *Clubs:* Sackville Country; Rotary; Canadian Herefore Assn. *Address:* P.O. Box 38, Sackville, N.B., Canada.

**MELGAR CASTRO, Brig.-Gen. Juan Alberto.** Head of State, Republic of Honduras. *B.* 1930. *Educ.* Military Academy. *M.* Señora Alba Nora Gunera. *S.* 3. *Daus.* 3. *Career:* Joined the Army in 1947; 2nd Lieut. 1951, Lieut. 1954, Infantry Captain 1956, Infantry Major 1961, Lieut.-Colonel 1965, Infantry Colonel 1968 & Brig.-Gen. 1975; positions held include: Exec. Officer & C.-in-C. of the 1st Battalion 1964–65; Chief of the Second Military Zone & Commander of the 3rd Infantry Battalion 1965–71; C.-in-C. of the Special Forces (Police) 1972; appointed by decree Minister for Home Affairs & C.-in-C. of the 5th Infantry Brigade, then C.-in-C. of the Armed Forces & in April 1975 Head of State. *Decorations:* Gold Medal for Conduct; Medal for Distinguished Services; La Orden del Quetzal (Guatemala). *Address:* Office of the Head of State, Tegucigalpa, Republic of Honduras.

**MELLISH, Rt. Hon. Robert Joseph,** MP. British politician. *B.* 1913. *Educ.* St. Joseph's School, Deptford. *M.* 1938. *S.* 5. *Career:* Parliamentary Private Secretary: to Civil Lord of Admiralty, 1947–49; to Ministry of Supply, 1950–51; Parliamentary Secretary, Ministry of Housing & Local Government, Oct. 1964–Aug. 1967; Minister of Public Building & Works, 1967–69; Govt. Chief Whip to Gen. Election, 1969–70; Parly. Secy. to Treasury 1969–70; Minister, Housing and Local Government, 1970; Opposition Chief Whip 1970–74; Govt. Chief Whip 1974–76. *Address:* c/o House of Commons, London, S.W.1.

**MELLON, Paul.** American. *B.* 1907. *Educ.* Choate School (Wallingford, Conn.), Yale Univ. (BA) (Hon LHD 1967); Cambridge Univ. (Clare Coll.), Eng. (BA, MA); Oxford Univ., Eng. (Hon DLitt 1961); Carnegie Inst. of Technology (Pittsburgh) Hon. LLD. 1967. *M.* (1) 1935, Mary Conover (D. 1946). *S.* Timothy. *Dau.* Mrs. Ashley Carrithers. (2) 1948, Rachel Lambert. *Career:* President and Trustee National Gallery of Art, Washington D.C.; Trustee A.W. Mellon Educational and Charitable Trust (Pittsburgh), The Andrew W. Mellon Foundation, N.Y.C. (merged Old Dominion & Avalon Foundation); Virginia Museum of Fine Arts (Richmond Va.). *Awards:* Yale Medal 1953; Associate Fellow, Berkeley Coll., Yale; Hon. Fellow; Clare Coll., Cambridge, and St. John's Coll., Annapolis, Md.; Horace Marden Albright Scenic Preservation Medal, 1957; Award for Distinguished Service to the Arts, National Inst. of Arts and Letters, 1962; Benjamin Franklin Medal, Royal Society of Arts, London, 1965. Benjamin Franklin Fellow, Royal Society of Arts, 1969; Member Amer. Philosophical Socy. Phila. 1971; Skowhegan Gertrude Vanderbilt Whitney Award 1972.; Hon. KBE, 1974. Republican. *Clubs:* Jockey, Knickerbocker, Links, Racquet & Tennis, River, Yale, Grolier, National Steeplechase & Hunt Assn. (all in N.Y.C.); Metropolitan, 1925 F. Street (both in Washington). *Address:* 1729 H Street, N.W., Washington, D.C. 20006 and Oak Spring, Upperville, Va., U.S.A.

**MELMOTH, Christopher George Frederick Frampton,** CMG. British. *B.* 1912. *Educ.* Chartered Secretary, Cost Accountant. *M.* 1946, Maureen Joan Brennan. *Daus.* 3. *Career:* Coordination of Supplies Office, Malta 1942–45, Hong Kong Government 1946–55; Minister of Finance, Uganda 1956–62; South Asia Department, Wold Bank 1962–75 (Retired). *Address:* Hoptons Field, Kemerton, Tewkesbury, Glos.

**MELVILLE, Sir Eugene,** KCMG. British. *B.* 1911. *Educ.* Queen's Park School, Glasgow; St. Andrews University (Harkness Residential Scholar; 1st cl. Honours Classics; 1st cl. Honours Economics). *M.* 1937, Elizabeth Strachan. *S.* 2. *Dau.* 1. *Career:* Financial Adviser, Control Commission for Germany 1949–52; Asst. Under Secy. Colonial Office 1952–61; Foreign Office 1961–62; Minister (Economic) British Embassy, Bonn 1962–65; Permanent U.K. Delegate to EFTA and GATT 1965; Ambassador, Permanent U.K. Representative to the United Nations and other International Organizations at Geneva 1966–71; Special Adviser to British Government on Channel Tunnel 1971–73; Dir.-Gen. British Property Fed. since 1974; Chmn. Aldeburgh Festival—Snape Maltings Foundation; Hon. Treasurer, British Sailors' Society; Dir., Metropolitan Housing Trust. *Club:* Reform (London). *Address:* Longcroft, Aldeburgh, Suffolk.

**MELVILLE, Sir Leslie Galfreid,** KBE. Australian economist. *B.* 26 March, 1902. *Educ.* Sydney Church of England Grammar School: University of Sydney (BEcon). *M.* 1925,

Mary Maud Scales. *S.* 2. Public Actuary of South Australia 1924–28; Professor of Economics, University of Adelaide 1929–31; Economic Adviser, Commonwealth Bank 1931–49; member of committees on Australian Finances and Unemployment 1931 and 1932; Financial Adviser to Australian Delegates, Imperial Economic Conference 1932, World Economic Conference 1933; member, Australian Financial and Economic Advisory Cttee. 1939; Chmn., Australian Deleg. United Nations Monetary Conference, Bretton Woods 1944; member, Advisory Council of Commonwealth Bank 1945–51; Chairman, United Nations Sub-Commission on Employment and Economic Stability 1947–50; Assistant Governor (Central Banking), Commonwealth Bank of Australia 1949–53; Executive Director, International Monetary Fund and International Bank for Reconstruction and Development 1950–53. *Member:* Commonwealth Bank Board 1951–53; Reserve Bank Board 1959–63, 1965–75; Vice-Chancellor, Australian Natl. Univ. 1953–60; Chmn., Australian Tariff Board 1960–63. Development Advisory Service, I.B.R.D., 1963–65; Chmn. Commonwealth Grants Commission 1966–74. *Address:* 71 Stonehaven Crescent, Canberra, A.C.T. 2600, Australia.

**MENDES-FRANCE, Pierre.** D. en D. French statesman, lawyer and financial expert. *B.* 11 Jan. 1907. *M. S.* 2. *Career:* Was admitted to the Paris Bar as the youngest lawyer in France; elected deputy from the Eure (Radical-Socialist) 1932; Under-Sec. of State for Finance (Blum Cabinet) 1938; mobilized Sept. 1939, served as Lieut. in French Air Force in Syria; returned to France concurrently with the German invasion; endeavoured unsuccessfully to prevent armistice with Germany; arrested and imprisoned; escaped June 1941 and reached London in Feb. 1942, where he served as captain-observer with the Free French bomber group, 'Lorraine'; appointed by General de Gaulle as Finance Commr. of the French Cttee. for National Liberation (Algiers), Nov. 1943; headed French delegation to Bretton Woods Conf.; Minister of National Economy (co-ordinating Production, Agriculture, Housing and Supply), Sept. 1944–April 1945; headed French delegation to Savannah Financial Conf., March 1946; later, Exec. Dir. for France in the Int. Bank for Reconstruction and Development in Washington until Oct. 1947; also served as French administrator of the Int. Monetary Fund and as French rep. to U.N. Economic and Social Concl.; elected Deputy to Second Constitutent Assembly 1946; re-elected to Nat. Assembly 1946, 1951, 1956 and 1967; called to form a Cabinet in June 1953, failed by 13 votes to obtain the investiture of the Natl. Assy.: Prime Minister June 1954–Feb. 1955; Minister of State 1956. *Awards:* Commandeur, Légion d'Honneur; Croix de Guerre; medals of Escaped Prisoners and the Resistance, many others. *Publications:* L'oeuvre Financière du governement Poincaré (1927); The Pursuit of Freedom (1942); Gouverner, c'est Choisir (1949); La science économique et l'action (co-author) (UNESCO); Rencontres (with A. Bevan and P. Nenni) (1958); La République Moderne (also in English, 1962); Dialogues avec l'Asie d'aujourd'hui (1972); Science Economique et lucidite politique (1973); Choisir (1974); La Verité Guidait leurs Pas (1976). *Address:* Les Monts, Louviers, France.

**MENDEZ, Dr. Aparicio.** Uruguayan lawyer. *B.* 1904. *Educ.* Faculty of Law & Social Sciences, Montevideo. *M.* Blanca Alonso González. *Career:* Teacher of history at secondary schools 1925–33; Called to the Bar 1930, practised as a lawyer, specializing in Administrative Law, 1930–70; progressed from Tutor to Acting Professor to holding the Chair of Administrative Law at the Faculty of Law & Social Sciences, 1930–55; Asst. Sec. to the Law Faculty 1930–34; Legal Adviser & Head of the Montevideo Law Dept. 1934–38; Minister for the Electoral Court 1943–46; headed various Uruguayan delegations to international congresses; with the Ministry of Public Health 1961–64; appointed Counsellor of State 1973, First Vice-Pres. of the Council 1974–76, then temporarily its President; held the office of Pres. of the Council of the Nation for an interim period in 1976; President of Uruguay, Sept. 1976. *Awards:* Hon. Dr. in the Faculty of Law, Univ. of Río Grande do Sul (Brazil). *Address:* Oficina del Presidente, Montevideo, Uruguay.

**MENDIS, Vernon Lorraine Benjamin.** Diplomat of Sri Lanka. *B.* 1925. *Educ.* Prince of Wales Coll. Moratuwa; Royal Coll. Colombo; Univ. of Ceylon, 1944, BA (Hist) 1948; Lond Univ. M Philosophy 1966. *Married. Son.* 1. *Career:* Ceylon O'seas service 1949; 3rd. Secy. Ceylon Embassy, Washington 1951–55; Chargé d'Affaires, Ceylon Embassy, France 1956–58; 1st Secy. Embassy of Ceylon, Moscow 1958–60; Chief of Protocol, Min. of External Affairs, Colombo 1960–61; Counsellor For. Relations, Min. of Defense & Ext. Affairs, Colombo; Counsellor, Ceylon High Commission, London 1963–66; Deputy High Commissioner, Ceylon HC, New Delhi 1966–69; Dir. Foreign Relations (Western Affairs) 1969–70; Dir.-Gen. of Foreign Affairs, Min. of Def. & F.A., Colombo; High Commissioner for Sri Lanka in Canada & concurrently Ambassador to Cuba 1974; High Commissioner for Sri Lanka in the U.K. 1975–77; Sec.-Gen. of 5th Non-Aligned Summit Conference, Colombo, Aug. 1976. *Publication:* The Advent of the British to Ceylon. *Address:* c/o Ministry of Foreign Affairs, Colombo, Sri Lanka.

**MENEMENCIOGLU, Turgut.** Turkish Diplomat. *B.* 1914. *Educ.* Robert Coll., Istanbul; Faculty of Law, Geneva. *M.* Nermin Moran. *S.* 2. *Career:* Joined Turkish Min. of Foreign Affairs 1939; Various posts—Bucharest, Geneva, Washington, New York, etc.; Turkish Amb. to Ottawa 1960; Perm. Rep. of Turkey to U.N., New York 1960–63; Amb. in Washington 1963–67; Sec.-Gen. of CENTO, Ankara 1967; Political Adviser to Minister of Foreign Affairs, Ankara 1972; Turkish Amb. to Court of St. James's since 1972. *Address:* 69 Portland Place, London W.1; and *office* 43 Belgrave Square, London, S.W.1.

**MENICHELLA, Donato.** Italian banker. *B.* 1896. *Educ.* Laureat in Political Science. Director-General: Institute for Industrial Reconstruction 1933–43, and Banca d'Italia, 1946–48 (Governor, 1948–60). President, Ufficio Italiano Cambi, 1948–60. Honorary Governor, Banca d'Italia; Alternate Governor for Italy, I.B.R.D. 1961–65; member, Board of Directors. Bank for International Settlements. *Address:* Banca d'Italia, Via Nazionale, 91, Rome, Italy.

**MENKE, John Roger.** American director and consultant, *B.* 1919. *Educ.* Columbia University (BS Physics 1943; BS mech. Eng. 1945). *M.* 1945, Betty Bayer. *S.* David John. *Dau.* Ellen R. *Career:* Senior Scientific Staff, S.A.M. Laboratories, Columbia Univ. 1942–46; Principal Physicist, Oak Ridge National Laboratories, 1946–48; Pres. Nuclear Development Associates, 1948–55; Nuclear Development Corp. of America 1955–61. Director: United Nuclear Corporation; Standard Shares; Verde Exploration Ltd.; Hudson Inst.; Dir. Consultant United Nuclear Corp. *Member:* Amer. Socy. of Mech. Engrs.; Amer. Nuclear Socy.; Atomic Industrial Forum; Council on Foreign-Relations. *Publications:* Co-editor (with J. Gueron, J. A. Lane, and I. R. Maxwell), The Economics of Nuclear Power; Series VIII of Progress in Nuclear Energy (London, Pergamon Press. 1956). *Address:* 44 Ogden Road, Scarsdale, N.Y. 10583; and *office* 2 Overhill Road, Scarsdale, N.Y. 10583, U.S.A.

**MENNELL, Peter,** CMG, MBE, MA. British diplomat. *B.* 1918. *Educ.* Oundle School; Cambridge Univ. King's College. *M.* 1946, Prudence Helen Vansittart. *S.* Simon Nicholas, Jonathon Piers. *Daus.* Lindsay Katherine, Alexandra Helen. *Career:* Royal Artillery 1939–46; Vice-Consul New York 1946–49; U.K. Delegation GATT, Finance Cttee. Brussels, Treaty Secy. Various Bilateral Economic Cttees. 1949–51; First Secy. British Embassy Moscow 1951–53; United States Regional Adviser, Foreign Office (Information Policy Dept.) 1953–57; First Secy. Head of Chancery, Brit. Embassy Madrid 1957–62; H.M. Consul Gen. Cleveland Ohio U.S.A. 1962–65; Inspector, H.M. Diplomatic Service 1965–67; Counsellor Kinshasa, Chargé d'Affaires Congo (K) and Burundi 1967–69; H.M. Ambassador, Quito Rep. del Ecuador 1970–74; British High Commissioner to C'wealth of the Bahamas, Nassau since 1974; Leader of UK Delegation to ECLA 1973 & 1977. *Member:* Pilgrims Socy.; Hon. Life member English Speaking Union (Cleveland Branch); Livery, Worshipful Company Grocers; Freeman City of London; Hon. member Ecuadorean Branch Int. Law. Assn.; Keys to Cleveland, Toledo Louisville, New Orleans & various U.S. cities; Kentucky Colonel. *Clubs:* Oxford & Cambridge University; Lyford Cay Club. *Address:* 7 Sheen Common Drive, Richmond upon Thames and *office* Foreign and Commonwealth Office, London SW1A 2AH.

**MENON, Parakat Achutha,** BA (Hons.) Madras University. Indian diplomat. *B.* 2 Jan. 1905. *S.* of late Sir M. Krishnan Nair, one-time Dewan of Travancore and Law Member, Madras Government. *Educ.* Presidency College, Madras; New College, Oxford. *M.* 1930, Palat Padmini Menon. *S.* Govind. *Dau.* Kalyani. *Career:* Joined Indian Civil Service 1929; Sub-Collector, South Arcot, Madras Presidency 1931–33; Vice-Pres. Indian Council of World Affairs (New Delhi); Member Exec. Council, Ind. Inst. of Public Administration (New Delhi); Under-Secretary, Public Works Department, Madras Government 1934–37; Under-Secretary Home Department, India Government 1938–41; member (nominated)

Indian Legislative Assembly 1938 and 1939; Member of the Syndicate, Andhra Univ. 1942; Collector and District Magistrate, Guntur, Madras 1941–43; Deputy Secretary and Secretary to India Supply Mission, Washington, U.S.A. 1943–47; Adviser to Indian Delegation to United Nations Organization, San Francisco 1945; Delegate on United Maritime Executive Board, U.S.A. 1945–46; Alternate Delegate, Fourth Session of U.N.R.R.A. Council, Atlantic City, U.S.A. 1946; Adviser to Indian Delegation to United Nations Assembly, New York 1946; member, Indian Delegation to International Emergency Food Council, U.S.A. 1946; member, Indian Delegation to Far Eastern Commission, U.S.A. 1946–47; Joint Secretary to the Government of India, Ministry of External Affairs 1947–49; Envoy and Minister of India in Portugal Nov. 1949-July 1951; Ambassador of India to Belgium and Minister of India to Luxembourg 1951–54; Ambassador of India to Thailand 1954–56; High Commissioner of India to Australia and New Zealand 1956–59; Ambassador to Argentina Nov. 1959–60; and to Federal Republic of Germany, Jan. 1961–Nov. 1964; Chmn. Fertilizers and Chems. Travancore Ltd; Kerala 1965–70; Chairman, Madras Industrial Linings Ltd.; Director, Cochin Refineries Ltd.; Premier Breweries Ltd.; State Bank of India 1965–73; Pres., Madras Musical Assn.; Chmn. Indo-German Chamber of Commerce, Southern Region Council, Kerala Samaj Education Socy.; Pres. Federation of Indo-German Societies in India, New Delhi; Vice-Pres. Indian Inst. of Public Admin. Regional Branch Madras, Chmn. Madras Literary Socy. (Madras). *Clubs:* New Delhi Gymkhana; Madras; Madras Gymkhana. *Address:* Padmaja, 4-A Tank Bund Road, Madras 34, India.

**MENSFORTH, Sir Eric**, CBE, DL, MA, Hon. DEng, DSc, FIMechE, FRAeS, FIProdE. British company director. *B.* 17 May 1906. *Educ.* Altrincham County High School; University College School; King's College, Cambridge (MA). *M.* 1934, Betty Francis. *Daus.* 3. *Career:* Formerly engaged in engineering work at Woolwich Arsenal, Mather & Platt Ltd., Bolckow Vaughan Ltd., Kloecknerwerke A.G., Dorman Long & Co. Ltd., Westland Aircraft Ltd. (managing Dir. 1939–43), Chmn. 1953–68; Thos. Firth & John Brown Ltd. 1943–50; Chief Production Adviser to Chief Executive, Min. of Aircraft Prod.; Deputy Chmn., John Brown & Co. Ltd. Dir., Firth Brown Steels Ltd., Canada; F. Issels & Son Ltd., Bulawayo; Boddy Industries Ltd.; Westland Aircraft Ltd.; Chmn. Electronics E. D. C. 1968–70. Member, Royal Ordnance Factories Board to 1972; Chmn. Council of Engineering Institution 1970–71; Hon. Fellow, Sheffield Poly. (1975). Vice Lieut. S. Yorks. *Address:* 3 Belgrave Drive, Fulwood, Sheffield, S10 3LQ, S. Yorks.

**MENTULA, Tuure Adam**, LLB, LLM. Finnish diplomat. *B.* 1915. *Educ.* Graduated Commercial High School Finland, 1935; Bachelor of Law, Helsinki Univ. 1941; Master of Law, 1954. *M.* 1947, Marjatta Ikavalko. *S.* Arto K. *Dau.* Ritva P. *Career:* Employed, Pohjoismaiden Yhdyspankki, 1936–37; Military Service 1939–40; Bank of Finland, 1940–41; Military Service, World War II, 1941–44; Attorney of Law, 1944–46; Finnish Foreign Service since 1946; Ministry, Foreign Affairs, 1946–47; Vice-Consul, New York, 1947–50; Secy. of Bureau, Ministry, Foreign Affairs, 1950–52; Consul New York, 1952–55; Secy of Embassy, The Hague, 1955–57; Chief of Bureau, Ministry, Foreign Affairs, 1958–60; Consul Gen. of Finland, San Francisco, 1961–69; Ambassador, Finland to Australia and New Zealand 1969–75; Special Adviser, Ministry of Foreign Affairs 1975–77; Ambassador, Finland to Indonesia since 1977. *Awards:* Knight First Class, The Order of The Lion of Finalnd; Commander, The Order of The Lion of Finland. *Cluvs:* Bohemian, World Trade, Commonwealth of California (all San Francisco). *Address:* Haapaniemenk. 20 D 56, 0530 Helsinki 53, Finland.

**MENZIES, Arthur Redpath.** Canadian Diplomat. *B.* 1916. *Educ.* Toronto Univ. (BA); Harvard Univ. (MA). *M.* 1943, Sheila Isabel Halliday Skelton. *S.* Kenneth Skelton. *Dau.* Norah Jane. *Career:* Joined Dept. of Extnl. Affairs 1940; Second Secy., Havana 1945–46; Head, Canadian Liaison Mission, Tokyo 1950–53: Chargé d'Affaires (after Peace Treaty); Head, Far Eastern Div., Dept. of External Affairs, Ottawa 1953–58. Canadian High Commissioner to The Federation of Malaya 1958–61; concurrently Canadian Ambassador to the Union of Burma 1958–61. Head, Defence Liaison Div., Dept. of External Affairs; and External Affairs member of Canada-U.S.A. Permanent Joint Bd. on Defence 1961–1965. High Commissioner to Australia 1965–72 and concurrently to Fiji 1970–72; Representative & Ambassador to the North Atlantic Council 1972–76; Ambassador to the People's Republic of China since 1976. *Address:* Canadian Embassy, 10 San Li Tun Road, Peking, People's Republic of China.

**MENZIES, Henry Copeland**, ISO. Australian. Export Consultant. *B.* 1910. *Educ.* Melbourne Univ. *M.* 1937; Edna May Kerr. *S.* Hugh Douglas. *Dau.* Gillian Ruth. *Career:* With Australian Dept. of Commerce 1935; Officer-in-Charge, Eastern Trade Div. 1937; Asst. Dir., Food Manufacture 1943–46; Comm. Counsellor, Australian Embassy, Tokyo 1948–52; Trade Commnr., Hong Kong 1953–56; Dept. of Trade, Canberra 1956–58; Sen. Trade Commnr., Wellington, N.Z. 1958–61, N.Y. 1961–66; Commercial Counsellor. Australian Embassy, The Hague, 1966–70. *Club:* Hong Kong. *Address:* 8-33 Moruben Road, Mosman, N.S.W. Australia.

**MENZIES, James Gordon.** Australian. *B.* 1909. *Educ.* Canterbury (N.S.W.) High School, and University of Sydney (BEc, LLB); FASA, FCIS, ABIA. *M.* 1937, Jean Mann. *S.* Ian Donald. *Dau.* Margaret Robertson. *Career:* Deputy Governor, Central Bank of Malaysia 1962–66; Chief. Accountant, Reserve Bank of Australia 1960–62; Asst. Chief Superintendent, Commonwealth Savings Bank of Australia 1952–59. Manager for Victoria, Reserve Bank of Australia 1966–70; Dir., Thos. Cook Pty. Ltd. 1970—. Trustee, Presbyterian Church of N.S.W. 1972—; (Chmn. 1977—); Chmn. The Scottish Hospital since 1972. *Publications:* Study of Postal Savings System (1953). *Award:* J.M.N. (Johan Mangku Negara) from Malaysian Govt. *Member:* Economic Socy. of Australia and New Zealand. *Clubs:* Royal Commonwealth Socy. (Sydney). *Address:* 40 Stafford Road, Artarmon, N.S.W. 2064, Australia.

**MENZIES, Sir Peter Thomson.** British. *B.* 1912. *Educ.* Edinburgh Univ. (MA; 1st Cl. Hons. Mathematics and Natural Philosophy). *M.* 1938, Mary M. A. Menzies (née Menzies). *S.* 1. *Dau.* 1. *Career:* Dir. Imperial Chem. Ind. Ltd. 1956–67; Dep. Chmn. 1967–72; Dir. Imperial Metal Industries Ltd. 1962–64 Chmn. 1964–72; Part-time Member, Central Electricity Generating Board 1960–72; Dir. Commercial Union Assurance Co. Ltd. 1962—; National Westminster Bank Ltd. 1968—; Chmn. The Electricity Council 1972–77. President UNIPEDE 1973–76; Fellow Inst. of Physics (FInstP); Companion IEE; Fellow Inst. Directors. *Club:* Caledonian. *Address:* Kit's Corner, Harmer Green, Welwyn, Herts.; and *office* 30 Millbank, London, S1WP 4RD.

**MENZIES, Rt. Hon. Sir Robert (Gordon)**, KT, AK, CH, FRS, QC, LLM. Constable of Dover Castle and Lord Warden of the Cinque Ports. *B.* Jeparit, Victoria, 20 Dec. 1894. *Educ.* Jeparit State School, Humffrey Street State School, Ballarat (headed Scholarship list for Victoria), Grenville College, Ballarat (Exhibitioner), Wesley College, Melbourne (English Exhibition), Univ. of Melbourne (1st Class Final Honours in Law, Winner, Dwight Prize in Constitutional History, the Sir John Madden Exhibition, Jessie Leggatt Scholarship, Bowen Essay Prize, and the Supreme Court Judges' Prize); *M.* Pattie (G.B.E. 1954), daughter late Senator J. W. Leckie. *S.* 2. (1 Dec'd). *Dau.* 1. *Career:* Called to Victoria Bar and High Court of Australia 1918. K.C. 1929. Elected to Legislative Council. East Yarra province 1928–29; M.L.A. for Nunawading 1929–34; Honorary Minister McPherson Government 1928–29; Attorney-General, Minister for Railways and Deputy Premier of Victoria 1932–34; Federal Attorney-General 1934–39, M.H.R. for Kooyong, Vic. 1934–66; Prime Minister, 1939–41; Leader of Federal Opposition 1943–49; Prime Minister 1949–66; original member of the Australian Advisory War Council; Leader of Mission to Pres. Nasser in Cairo to discuss Suez Canal affairs, Aug.–Sept. 1956. Scholar-in-Res., Univ. of Virginia 1966. Chancellor, University of Melbourne 1967–72. *Awards:* Honrary Master of the Bench at Gray's Inn, London; Honorary LLD Melbourne; Bristol; British Columbia; Queen's College, Belfast; Sydney; McGill, Montreal, Royal Univ. of Malta, Laval Univ., Tasmania, Cambridge, Harvard 1960, Adelaide 1961, Brisbane 1961, Leeds 1961, Aust. Nat. Univ. 1966, Sussex 1966; Edinburgh 1963, Birmingham 1964. Drury Coll., Missouri 1966; Univ. of Calif. 1967. Hon. DSc, Univ. of N.S.W.; Hon. D.C.L., Oxford 1959; Univ. of Kent, 1969; Hon. DLitt W. Aust. 1964, Hon. Fellow, Royal College of Physicians, Royal Australian College of Physicians, Royal Australian Inst. of Architects, Roy. Socy. of Arts; Royal Coll. of Surgeons, Edinburgh; Royal Australian Coll. of Surgeons, Honorary Fellowships: Institute of Meat 1957; Academy of Sciense 1958; Royal College of Obstetricians and Gynaecologists 1961; Zoological Socy. of London 1963; Inst. of Builders (London) 1964; Australian Coll. of General Practitioners 1964. Freedom of the Cities of Edinburgh, Swansea, Athens, London, Oxford, Melbourne,

Hastings, Sandwich, Deal; Chief Commander Legion of Merit (U.S.); 1st Class Order of the Rising Sun (Japan). *Publications:* The Rule of Law during War; To the People of Britain at War; The Forgotten People: Speech is of Time; Afternoon Light Central Power in the Australian Commonwealth; The Measure of the Years; and joint-author of Studies in Australian Constitution. *Clubs:* Australian, Savage (Melbourne); Melbourne Scots; Savage, M.C.C., Pratts (London); Commonwealth (Canberra); Athenaeum (London & Melbourne); West Brighton (Melbourne). *Address:* 2 Haverbrack Avenue, Malvern 3144, Vic.; and *office* 95 Collins Street, Melbourne 3000, Vic., Australia.

**MERA, Boris Edouard.** French. *B.* 1914. *Educ.* Higher Studies of Public Law and Political Economy, Institut des Sciences Politiques. *M.* 1949, Suzanne Béraldi. *S.* Patrick, Alain and Yves. *Dau.* Lise. *Career:* Administrator and Director-General, Union Française des Banques 1959—. Chairman, Locabail 1963—. Assistant General Manager, Compapnie Bancaire 1968–69; Member Directoire, Compagnie Bancaire 1969. Chevalier of the Legion of Honour; War Cross. *Address:* 12 Boulevard Jean Mermoz 92200 Neuilly; and *office* 25 Avenue Kléber, 75016 Paris, France.

**MEREDITH, L(ewis) Douglas.** American *B.* 1905. *Educ.* Bucknell Univ.; Syracuse Univ. (AB *cum laude* 1926; AM 1927); Yale University (PhD 1933); Keystone Junior College Alumni Association. Honor Award 1949; Phi Beta Kappa. *M.* 1935, Laura J. Parker. *Career:* Instructor Syracuse University 1925–27; Asst. Prof. of Econs., Univ. of Vermont 1927–35; Univ. Fellow, Yale Univ. 1930–31; Contrib. Editor, Burlington (Vt.) Free Press 1933–35; Vermont Comr. on Banking and Insurance 1934–35; Investment Analyst, National Life Insurance Co. 1935–38 (member, Finance Cttee. 1938–68; Asst. to Pres. 1939–42; Treas. 1940–44; Vice-Pres. 1944–47); Director, Vermont Electric Power Co. Inc.; Director, Connecticut Valley Electric Co. Inc.; Vermont Mutual Fire Insurance Co., Northern Security Co., Inc., Rutland Railway Corp. (1955–60), Ogdensburg Terminal Corp. (1959–60), Chittenden Tr. Co. (Burlington) 1964—, Alleghey Airlines since 1965; Pres. and Chief Executive Officer, Central Vermount Public Service Corp. Rutland Vt. 1968–72, Chmn. since 1972; Hon. Mem. Vermont Bankers Assn. 1964—. Chmn., Cttee. to Study Question of Taxation, State of Vermont 1951–52; Alumni Trustee, Syracuse Univ. 1960–56, and 1959–60; Trustee at Large 1966–73; Charter Trustee, Middlebury (Vt.) Coll. 1962–75 Chmn. of Bd. Middlebury Coll 1968–75; Mem., Residential Real Estate Credit Advisory Cttee. (Fed. Reserve Bank) 1950–52. National Planning Cttee. of New England 1950–54; participated in Life Round Table on Housing 1948 and 1952; Commissioner Vermont Housing Authority to 1975; Pres., New England Council 1957–59; Universidad International, Santander, Spain 1958; Summer Study 1969–74; Lecturer, Universidad de Puerto Rico1960; member, Fiscal Adv. Cttee., State of Vermont 1959; Governor's Blue Ribbon Re-apportionment Com., State of Vt. 1964. Dir., Natl. Life Insurance Co. Consultant to State Department AID Program, Ecuador, June 1965. *Publications:* Merchandising for Banks, Trust Companies and Investment Houses (Bankers Publ Co.) (1935); How to Buy a House (Harper & Bros.) (1947); contributions to various publications. *Member:* Amer. Econ. Assn. Mason. Republican. *Clubs:* Metropolitan (Washington, D.C.); University (N.Y.C.); Algonquin (Boston); Lake Mansfield Trout; Ethan Allen (Burlington). *Address:* 1500 Spear Street, South Burlington, Vt. 05401, U.S.A.

**MERIFIELD, Russel Roy,** QC (1961). *B.* 1916. *Educ.* McGill Univ. (BA, BCL); Associate Chartered Inst. of Secretaries. *M.* 1943, Helen Margaret Kydd. *S.* Russell, Thomas, *Dau.* Elizabeth. *Career:* Admitted Quebec Bar 1941 Royal Canadian Navy 1942–46. Private law practice, Montreal 1946–48. Joined Shawinigan Chemical Ltd. (patent dept.); transferred to Shawinigan Water & Power Co. (i/c legal dept.) 1951, Asst. Secy. 1952. Secy. 1954. Joined Royal Trust Co. as Exec. Asst. 1964, and appointed Secy. same year; Vice-President and General Manager, Victoria and Grey Trust Co. 1967—. *Publications:* Canadian Secretarial Practice (Pitman, Toronto). Former Lecturer in Company Law, Faculty of Law. McGill Univ.; Treas. The Presbyterian Church in Canada, Montreal; Past Chmn., Canadian Div., Chartered Inst. of Secretaries. *Clubs:* University (Montreal); Hermitage Country (Magog, P.Q.); National; Donalda (Toronto). *Address: office* 2990 Commerce Court West, Toronto, Ont M5L 1H5, Canada.

**MERIKOSKI, Veli Kaarlo.** *B.* 1905. *Educ.* Univ. of Helsinki (LLD). *M.* 1940, Margit Winge. *Children* 3. *Career:* Professor of Administrative Law, Helsinki Univ. 1941–69; Chairman, Finnish Society of Lawyers 1946/51 and 1956–58; and Finnish People's Party 1958–61. Minister of Foreign Affairs of Finland, Apr. 1962–63; Pres. International Association of Universities 1970–75, Hon. Pres. since 1975; Chancellor Turku School of Economics since 1974; Member, High Court of Impeachment 1950–69; Hague Int. Court of Arbitration since 1966. *Address:* The University, Helsinki, Finland.

**MERMIS, Leo Fidelis.** BS. American. *B.* 1918. *Educ.* St. Benedict's Coll. Atchison, Kansas (BS. Bus. Admin.). *M.* 1942, Florence Adeline Kutina. *Career:* Gen. Mgr. International Operations, Halliburton Services 1965–69, Vice Pres. 1969–74, Exec. Vice-Pres. since 1974. *Clubs:* Nomads (Tulsa Chapter); Elks Golf & Country. *Address:* 1113 Crescent Drive, Duncan, Okla. U.S.A. and *office* P.O. Drawer 1431, Duncan, Oklahoma 73533.

**MERONI, Charles F.** American patent lawyer and professional engineer. *B.* 1905. *Educ.* Graduate, Plant Engineering School, Western Electric A.T. & T. 1922; Chicago Kent College of Law (LLB 1924; DePaul Univ. (LLM 1927); Northwestern Univ. Graudate School of Business Administration. *M.* 1928, Kathryn O'Brien. *S.* Charles F., Jr. and Thomas J. *Dau.* Marilyn K. Weidler. *Career:* In Patent Law Dept., Western Electric Co. ed. A.T. & T. 1922–24; Associate of Patent Law firm of Brown Jackson,, Biettcher & Dienner, Chicago 1924–27; with present firm since 1927. Has lectured on patent law at De Paul Univ. and John Marshall Law School, Chicago. Associate. Senior Partner of patent law firm of Hill, Sherman, Meroni, Gross & Simpson 1943—. *Member:* Chicago Patent Law Assn; Life member Illinois & National Society of Professional Engineers; Hon. Pres. Postal History Society of the Americas; Phi Alpha Delta; (awarded Gold Honour Award (on origin of posts), London International Philatelic Exhibition 1950, and Canada International Exhibition 1951); Amer. Philatelic Socy.; Society of Philatelic Americans; Chicago Philatelic Socy. (Hon. Member); Peoria (Ill.) Philatelic Socy. (Hon. Member); Life member Union League Club of Chicago; Collectors Club of N.Y.; Collectors Club of Chicago. *Publications:* contributions to philatelic and postal history organs. *Address:* 160 Canal St., Tavernier, Fla 33070; and *office* Sears Tower, Chicago, Ill. 60606, U.S.A.

**MERRIFIELD, Hon. Samuel.** British surveyor. *B.* 1904. *M.* 1936, Margaret Lillian Smith. *Career:* Member of Australian Labour Party (Victorian branch) 1922–77; survey or with late H. C. Crouch in private practice 1920–27, with Melbourne and Metropolitan Tramways Board 1927–28 and 1935–39; with County Roads Board 1928–30; with Forests Commission of Victoria 1928, Commonwealth Dept. of Interior 1940–43, and State Electricity Commn. of Victoria 1939–40; Minister of Public Works, Victoria 1952–55. Former Member of Parliament of Victoria 1943–55 & 1958–70; Justice of Peace since 1952. *Award:* Doctor of Letters (Monash Univ.) 1973. *Address:* 81 Waverley Street, Moonee Ponds, 3039 Victoria, Australia.

**MERRILL, Hon. Charles Merton.** U.S. Circuit Judge. *B.* 1907. *Educ.* University of California (AB) and Harvard University (LLB). *M.* 1931, Mary Luita Sherman. *S.* Charles McKinney. *Dau.* Julia Booth (Jackson). *Career:* Admitted to Bar of California 1931, and Nevada 1932; Private practice, Reno 1932–50; elected to Nevada Supreme Court 1950; member of the Court 1951–59; Chief Justice 1955–56. Appointed U.S. Court of Appeals, 9th Circuit, Sept. 1959. Member, Executive Board, National Conference of Chief Justices 1956–57. Member, Council of American Law Institute. *Address:* 2243 North Point Street, San Francisco, Calif. 94123, U.S.A.

**MERRY, Donald Henry,** OBE. Australian economist. *B.* 1909. *Educ.* University of Melbourne (BCom) and London School of Economics (post-graduate studies). *M.* (1) 1937, Barbara B. Church (*D.* 1954) and (2) 1956, Alison B. Mitchell. *S.* 3. *Dau.* 1. *Career:* Economic Staff, Bank of New South Wales, Sydney and London 1933–45; Asst. Secy., Commonwealth Price Control 1940–42; Secy., Army Inventions Directorate 1942–43; Deputy to Treasury Representative, Dept. of Defence 1943–45; Financial Editor, Melbourne Argus 1945–47; Economist, Union Bank of Australia 1947–1951, A.N.Z. Bank 1951–54. Chief Economist 1955–68, Asst. Gen. Manager 1968–70. Member: Australian Government Ctts. of Enquiry into (1) Decimal Currency 1959–60, and (2) into Wool Marketing 1961–62. Assistant Gen. Mgr. and Economic Adv., Australia & New Zealand Banking Group, Melbourne 1970–72; Ind. and Pastoral Holdings Ltd. 1972; Barclays (Austr.) Ltd. since 1973; Mem Vict. Govt. Dairy

Industry Enq. 1974–77; Vict. Govt. (Westonport Bay) Env. Study Review Cttee 1974; *Member:* Economic Socy. of Aust. and N.Z. (Victorian Branch, Past Pres.); Univ. of Melbourne, Archives Bd. of Management; Advisory Bd., Graduate Sch. of Business Admin.; Business Archives Council of Aust., Victorian Branch (Chmn.); Pres. Cttee. for Economic Development of Australia; Council Melbourne Chamber of Commerce 1950–75. *Publications:* Investment in Australia (Penguin; co-author G. R. Bruns); General Editor, Australia 1974–75: A survey of Business & Economic Trends; contributions to economic journals and to Australian and New Zealand Association for the Advancement of Science. *Clubs:* Australian, Athenaeum (Melbourne); West Brighton. *Address:* "Parklands", Riddell's Creek, Vic. 3431; and *office* 140 Queen Street, Melbourne, Vic., Australia.

**MERRY, Ellis B.** American. *B.* 1907. *Educ.* Univ. of Michigan College of Literature, Science and Arts (AB) and Law School (JD). *M.* (1) 1937, Lorraine Armstrong (*D.* 1955). (2) 1956, Elizabeth Austin. *S.* James Thomas Whitehead II. *Dau.* Mary (Warren). *Career:* Practised law with Bulkley, Ledyard, Dickinson & Wright, Detroit, 1931–44; Asst. Attorney General of Michigan 1938. At National Bank of Detroit: Vice-Pres. 1944, Senr. Vice-Pres. 1958, Exec. Vice-Pres. 1964, Chmn. Exec. Cttee. 1966. Chmn. of Board and Director of National Bank of Detroit 1968–72; Chmn. and Dir. of International Bank of Detroit; Western American Banks (Europe) Ltd. London, Adela, Lima, Peru; Dir.: Douglas & Lomason Co., McLouth Steel Corp., and Sheller Manufacturing Co. (all of Detroit). *Member:* Assn. of Reserve City Bankers; Amer. Bar Assn.; State Bar of Michigan. *Clubs:* Detroit, University, Athletic, Country (all of Detroit). *Address:* 161 Lothrop Road, Grosse Pointe Farms, Mich. 48236. U.S.A.

**MESSMER, Pierre Auguste Joseph.** Former Prime Minister of France. *B.* 1916. *Educ.* Graduated, National School of Overseas France; Doctor of Law; Degree School Oriental Languages. *Career:* Sub-Lieutenant Colonial Infantry 1939; Free French Forces 1940; Active service Syria, Libya, Bir-Hakeim, El Alamein and Tunisia 1940–44; Landed in Normandy 1944; Commanded French Mission in Calcutta, made prisoner by Viet-Minh, escaped rejoined French Mission 1944–45; Demobilized 1946; Private Secy. High-Commissioner, Indochina 1947–48; Commanding Officer Atar District Mauritania 1950–51; Governor, Mauritania 1952–54; Ivory Coast 1954–56; High Commissioner, French Republic in Cameroon 1956–58, French Equatorial Africa Brazzaville 1958, H. C. General, French West Africa Dakar 1958–59; Minister. Armies 1960–69; Member Parliament 1968, re-elected 1969, 1974—; Member General Council Dept. of Moselle 1970; Min. of State in charge Overseas Depts. Territories 1971; Prime Minister 1972–74. *Awards:* Knight Commander, Legion of Honour; Companion, National Order of Liberation; War Cross with Six Bars; Resistance Medal; Excapee's Medal; Officer, American Legion. *Address:* 1 rue du Général Delanne, 92200 Neuilly-sur-Seine, France.

**METCALF, Arthur George Bradford.** American mathematical physicist. *B.* 1908. *Educ.* Massachusetts Institute of Technology; Boston Univ. (SB), LLD; Harvard Univ. (SM); Franklin Pierce Coll. (ScD). *M.* 1935, Mary G. Curtis. *S.* 1. *Daus.* 4. *Career:* Asst. Prof., Boston Univ. 1935–37; Pres., Electronics Corp. of Amer. 1937–42; served in World War II (Lieut.-Col. U.S. Army; Officer-in-charge, Procurement, Boston Ordnance Dist.; also Duty, Office; Under-Secy. of War and General Staff Corps: Legion of Merit; Commend. Medal) 1942–45; Founder, Chmn., Pres., Electronics Corporation of America (Cambridge, Mass.); Founder, Chmn., United States Strategic Institute, Washington, D.C.; Associate Fellow, Royal Aeronautical Society (London) 1934; Associate Fellow, Institute of Aeronautics and Astronautics 1936; Benjamin Franklin Fellow, Royal Society of Arts (London) 1972; recipient, George Washington Medal Award, Freedoms Foundation 1972; Chmn., Board of Trustees, Boston Univ.; Member, Trustee Council, Boston Univ. Medical School; Trustee, Symmes Hospital (Arlington, Mass.); Member, Research Laboratory Committee, Museum of Fine Arts, Boston; Dir., American Defense Preparedness Association; Dir. and Vice Pres., American Security Council Education Foundation; Strategic Studies Editor, American Security Council; Member, National Board of The International Security Studies Program, The Fletcher School of Law and Diplomacy. *Clubs:* Harvard (Boston and New York); Harvard Faculty Club, Algonquin (Boston), Athletic (New York), Winchester (Mass.) Country, Edgartown (Mass.) Yacht, Royal Canadian Yacht (Toronto), Army & Navy (Washington, D.C.). *Address:* 45 Arlington Street, Winchester Mass., U.S.A.

**MEYER, Sir Anthony John Charles,** MP. British. *B.* 1920. *Educ.* Eton; New Coll., Oxford. *M.* 1941, Barbadee Violet. *S.* 1. *Daus.* 3. *Career:* Scots Guards 1941–45; H.M. Treasury 1945–46; Joined H.M. Foreign Office 1946; H.M. Embassy, Paris 1951; H.M. Embassy, Moscow 1956; Conservative MP for Eton & Slough 1964–66, and for West Flint since 1970. *Clubs:* Beefsteak. *Address:* Cottage Place, Brompton Square, London S.W.3; and House of Commons, London S.W.1.

**MEYER, John Mount Montague.** CBE. British. *B.* 1915. *Educ.* Sherborne School. *M.* 1942, Denise Georgina Saunders. *S.* 2. *Career:* Dir. Montague L. Meyer Ltd. 1938; Asst. Man. Dir. & Gen. Mgr. 1939, Vice-Chmn. 1951–61, Chmn. Man. Dir. since 1961; Man. Dir. MacMillan Bloedel Meyer Ltd.; Dir. MacMillan Bloedel Ltd. (Vancouver) since 1972; Dir., Hallam Group of Nottingham Ltd.; Vice-Chmn., Port of London Authority; Pres. British-Soviet Chamber of commerce. *Club:* M.C.C. *Address:* 52 Northgate, Regent's Park, London, NW8 7EH and *office* Villiers House, 41–47 Strand, London, WC2N 5JG.

**MEYER, Oscar Gwynne,** OBE, ED, MIE (Aust.), FAIM. Australian. *B.* 1910. *Educ.* Diploma Mechanical Engineering Sydney; Harvard Graduate School of Business Admin (1956) *M.* 1938, Marion Bohle. *S.* Jonathon. *Dau.* Alison. *Career:* War service. AIF. Royal Aust. Engrs. 1940–46 (Col.); MID (twice) Commissioner, Victoria Rlys, 1950–58 Dep. Chmn. 1956–58; and Commonwealth Serum Laboratories 1961–67; Pres. Australian Inst. Management (Vic. Div.) 1965–67, Nat. Pres. 1970–71; Managing Director, Australian Carbon Black Pty. 1958–73, Chmn. 1973–75; Chmn. West Gate Bridge Authority since 1965; Chmn. E. A. Watts Holdings Pty. Ltd. since 1974; Director: Colonial Mutual Life Assurance Socy. Ltd., Nylex Ltd.; Valvoline (Aust.) P/L; Aust. Innovation Corp. Ltd. Dep. Chmn., Export Development Cncl. 1966–69; Council Member 1962; Chmn. Aust. Interstate Pipe Line Co. L5d.; Dir. Spencer Stuart & Associates; Perpetual Executors & Trustee Assoc. of Aust. Ltd.; National President, Australian Institute Management, 1970. Member, Inst. of Engineers (Aust.); Fellow, Inst. of Management. *Clubs:* Australian: Naval & Military; Royal Melbourne Golf; Royal Sydney Yacht Squadron. *Address:* 2 Cross Street, Toorak, Vic., Australia 3142; and *office* Suite 4, 14th Floor, 50 Queen Street, Melbourne 3000, Vic. Australia.

**MEYER, (Raymond) Roger.** French industrialist metallurgist. *B.* 1897. *Educ.* Diplômé, Lycée Technique de Nancy; member, Society of Civil Engineers of France. *M.* 1932, Jacqueline Gunsbourg. *S.* Guy-Raoul. Past Vice-President, Syndicat Général des Fondeurs de France; President: groupe national des Fondeurs de fontes sur modèles, and commission des Industries Mécaniques et Electriques au Comité National des Conseillers du Commerce Extérieur, etc. *Awards:* Officer, Legion of Honour; Cmdr., Ordre National du Mérite; numerous French and foreign decorations. General Secretary (1914), then Partner (1927) in the Sté de Produits Métallurgiques (Fonderies Havraises et Fonderies de Roncherolles), Paris; member of various industrial organizations; engaged in numerous official missions in France and abroad. *Clubs:* Lions-Club de Monaco (Pres., 1959–60 Neuilly). *Address:* Le Palmier-46 Boulevard des Moulins, Monte-Carlo.

**MEYER-LOHSE, Dr. Heinz-Werner.** German Diplomat. *B.* 1914. *Educ.* Salem Coll., Law Studies Universities Berlin, Lausanne. Dr. Jur.—Foreign Service. Exam. *M.* 1952, Marion Schniewind. *S.* 1. *Daus.* 3. *Career:* Lawyer 1950; Joined Foreign Service 1951; Counsellor of Legation, Caracas 1952–55; Foreign Ministry, Bonn 1955–58; Consul in Naples 1958–60; Foreign Ministry, Bonn—Head of Atomic Section 1960–63, Head of Latin American Section 1963–69; Minister Counsellor, Embassy Madrid 1969–75; Ambassador to Luxembourg since 1975. *Dedorations:* Commander, Orden del Libertador, Venezuela; Orden del Aquilar Azteca, Mexico; Orden al Merito, Chile; Cruz do Sur, Brazil; Al Merito, Argentina; Knight Commander, Orden al Merito Civil, Spain. *Club:* German Soc. for Foreign Affairs. *Address:* D-5300 Bonn-Bad Godesberg, Deutschherrenstrasse 3, Federal Republic of Germany; and *office* 20–22 Av. Emile Reuter, Luxembourg.

**MEYNEN, Johannes.** Dutch executive. *B.* 1901. *Educ.* Free University of Amsterdam (LLM). *M.* 1930, Nelia Laura Westerhuis. *S.* Wessel Wille D. and Johannes Jacob Frits. *Daus.* Sarina Dorothea, Wilhelmina Laura and Carla Eveline. *Career:* Chmn. Bd. Dirs. (formerly President),

Algemene Kunstzijde Unie N.V., Arnhem, Holland; member of Board of its affiliations: British Enkalon Ltd.; American Enka Corp. (U.S.A.); La Seda de Barcelona S.A. (Spain); Perlofil S.A. (Spain); Erste Oesterreichische Glanzstoff Fabrik A.G., Vienna; Bemberg S.p.A., Milan. Member of Board: National Bank of the Netherlands, Amsterdam (Vice-Chairman); Amsterdam-Rotterdam Bank, Amsterdam; Iron Foundry Ubbink, Doesburg; Overseas Gas & Electricity Works, Rotterdam; Elsevier Publishing Co., Amsterdam; Albert Heijn N.V. (Zaandam) and many other companies, as; Bank voor Handel en Scheepvaart; Wessanen's Koninklyke Fabrieken N.V.; Kon. Tapytfabricken, Bergors, N.V. Vice-Chmn.: Christian Manufacturers Association; European League for Economic Co-operation (E.L.E.C.); European Council for the Netherlands of the European Movement. Chairman, University-Industrial Contacts; Assistant Sec., Chamber of Commerce, Arnhem 1925–26; with Hercules Powder Co. Inc., Wilmington (U.S.A.), in charge of sales at their European office, The Hague, from 1930, Asst. General Manager of this European office, 1927–40; General Manager in charge of sales of cinema apparatus, measuring apparatus, etc., N.V. Philips. Radio and Lamp Factories, Eindhoven 1940–45; Major in the Dutch Army Staff of H.R.H. Prince Bernhard of the Netherlands, Chief Commander of Dutch Forces 1944–45; Secretary-General, War Office 1945; Minister of War (in the first Dutch Cabinet after the liberation of the country) 1945–46. Knight, Order of the Netherlands Lion; Commander, Order of Orange Nassau; Officer in the Order of the British Empire; Medal of Freedom with silver palms (U.S.A.). Recipient of Peter Stuyvesant Award. Elected Fellow of the Royal Society of Arts, London 1973. *Address:* Pinkenbergseweg 33, Velp (Gld.), Netherlands; and *office* Velperweg 76, Arnhem, Netherlands.

**MHUN, Henry André.** Canadian consulting economist. *B.* 1914. *Educ.* University of Paris (D en D) and University of Montreal (D ès Sc Soc et Econ). *M.* 1954, Francine Lacroix. *Daus.* Catherine, Françoise and Sophie. *Career:* Probationary period in the Indo-China Bank 1938–39; Economist at the Economic Documentation Centre of the Ministry of Industrial Production, Paris 1945; President Mhun Associates Ltd.; correspondent and collaborator in the production of several European and Canadian publications; commentator on Canadian radio and television; Dir. Economic Research, The Provincial Bank of Canada. Economic Adviser 1950—; journalist. *Publications:* Le Commerce Imperial, Paris (1946); Inventaire Economique du Canada, Montreal (1950); L'Economie Sans Douleur (1968). *Member:* Canadian Economics Assn.; Institut Canadien des Affairs Internationales; Montreal Economics Assn.; Community Planning Assn. of Canada. La Chambre de Commerce Française au Canada. *Club:* Cercle de la Place d'Armes. *Address:* 4954 Ponsard Avenue, Montreal; and *office* 221 St. James Street West, Montreal, Que., Canada.

**MIALARET, François Bernard Marie Georges.** French *B.* 1914. *Educ.* Stanislas College, Paris; Student Polytechnic School (1933–35); National Superior Mining School, Paris (1936–38). *M.* 1938, Marguerite-Marie Giraudon de Mazaubert. *S.* Laurent and Benoit. *Daus.* Nicole (Mrs. Genès), Anne (Mrs. Jeanteur) and Catherine. *Career:* Engineer Corps des Mines; Légion d'Honneur; Croix de Guerre (1939–45). Previously: Ministry of Public Works, Ministry of Labour, Crédit Lyonnais and Banque Mobilière Privée (1948–67). President Banque Industrielle et Mobilière Privée; Vice-Pres. Providence IARD; Vice-Pres. Providence SA; Vice-Pres Sopabra; Director: Banque de Bretagne, Soyer-Margerie S.A., Financia, Brasseries du Cameroun, Secours SA, Secours IARD, SOPAIC. *Address:* 63 rue Notre-Dame-des-Champs, 75006 Paris.

**MICHAELS, Ronald Guy.** Australian executive. *B.* 1915 *Educ.* Fairfield State School and Melbourne Grammar School. *M.* 1941, Beryl Ellen Newby. *Daus.* Wendy, Diane and Linda. *Career:* Chmn., United Artists Australasia Pty. Ltd. (motion picture distributors) June 1953—. Dir., United Artists Television International (Far East Div.); Vice-Pres., United Artists Television International Inc. since 1975. Previously associated with the same company in various capacities dating back to 1931, when he joined as office boy in Victorian branch offices. *Clubs:* American National; Film; Masonic; Green Room. *Address:* Unit 20 Kalamunda, 74–76 Upper Pitt Street, Kirribilli N.S.W. 2061; and *office* 8–24 Kippax Street, Sydney, N.S.W., Australia.

**MICHAELSEN, Edward Hugo.** American. *B.* 1917. *Educ.* Danish-English College, Ealing, England (BBA). *M.* 1941, Fritze Pihl. *S.* John Edward. *Daus.* Carol Ann and Linda Phil. *Career:* With Holger Morvile, Copenhagen 1936–38; Svenska Handelsbanken, Sweden 1938–39; Lazard Frères, N.Y.C. 1939–40. President, Phelps Dodge Copper Prods. International Corp. 1962–68; Vice-President and Director, Phelps Dodge Industries Incorporated 1966–67: Exec. Vice-Pres. 1967. Pres. & Chief Exec. Officer, Phelps Dodge Industries Inc., 1968—. Chmn. of Bd.; Phelps Dodge Copper Products Corp.; Phelps Dodge Pycsa S.A., Mexico; Dir. Phelps Dodge Corp.; Asian Cables Corp. India; Consolidated Aluminium Corp.; Lee Brothers Corp.; Phelps Dodge Int. Corp.; Phelps Dodge Magnet Wire Corp.; Phelps Dodge Puerto Rico Corp.; Phelps Dodge Steel Corp.; Inc.-Puerto Rico; Societa Tecnica Industriale Siciliana S.p.A. (Italy); Viohalco-Cables, S.A. Greece; Adv. Cttee. Bankers Trust Co. (N.Y.C.). *Member:* Lucas Point Association. *Awards:* Order Agrl. and Industrial Merit (Cuba). *Clubs:* Rockefeller Center Luncheon; Innis Arden Golf; Board Room. *Address:* South Crossway, Old Greenwich, Conn. 06870, U.S.A.

**MICHALOWSKI, Jerzy.** *B.* 1909. *Educ.* Graduated at Warsaw University Law Faculty. Married. *S.* 2. *Career:* Engaged at the Institute of Social Affairs (Warsaw) and at the Association of Workers Settlements 1935–39. As a reserve officer, was called to the army, and during an engagement with the German enemy was taken prisoner, and remained one until the end of the war. Appointed Head of the Housing Department in the Warsaw local government 1945; at the end of that year he joined the Polish Foreign Service and was appointed Counsellor of the Embassy in London; in 1946 he became Deputy Delegate to the U.N., and at the end of the year was nominated Ambassador to the United Kingdom; appointed Vice-Minister of Educ. 1954; on his return to the diplomatic service he held the post of Director of the Department of International Organizations in the Ministry of Foreign Affairs. Appointed Representative of Poland at the International Commission for Supervision and Control in Vietnam, 1955; in 1956 he became Ambassador and Permanent Representative of Poland to U.N. in New York. From 1960 he was Director-General of the Ministry of Foreign Affairs and member of the Council of the Ministry; in 1962 he was elected Chairman of the U.N. Economic and Social Council; Ambassador of the Polish People's Republic to the United States 1967–71. *Address:* Al. 1 Armii W.P. 16–20, Warsaw, Poland.

**MICHAUD, Paul Galt,** QC. Canadian barrister and solicitor *B.* 1906. *Educ.* LLB; BSc; BA; MPolSc. *M.* 1949, Géraldine Gervais. *Career:* Called to Canadian Bar 1926; Queen's Counsel 1959. (with firm Michaud & Calder); Director: Guard-X Inc.; Perfection Dairy Ltd.; Pan-American Insurance Co. Ltd.; Trans Atlantic Insurance Co. Ltd.; Rosemount Industries Ltd.; Levis Mushroom Co. Ltd.; Super Industries Ltd., etc. Director: Montreal Translation Socy.; Chambre de Commerce française du Canada; Société de géographie du Canada. Past President: Union des Latins d'Amérique; Chambre de Commerce de Montréal. Liberal. *Clubs:* Reform; Mount Stephen; University. *Address:* 3495 Mountain Street (Apt. 205), Montreal 109, P.Q.; and *office* 620 Catheart (Suit 752), Montreal H3B 1M1, P.Q. Canada.

**MICHELI, Pierre.** Swiss diplomat. *B.* 1905. *Educ.* Universities of Oxford, Berlin and Geneva; Lic. en Droit. *M.* Marie-Rose Chappuis. *S.* Jean-Léopold and Jacques. *Dau.* Anita, *Career:* Secretary to the President of the port and waterways of Dantzig; entered Federal Political Department 1933; served successively in the Swiss Legations in Paris, The Hague and Rio de Janeiro; Consul, Batavia 1941; First Secy. of Legation, Tokyo 1942; promoted Counsellor of Legation 1945; Secretary-General of the Diplomatic Conference, Geneva 1949; Minister Plenipotentiary 1952, Chief of the Division, International Organisation, Berne; Minister to France 1956; Ambassador to France 1957–61; Secretary General, Federal Political Dept. of Switzerland 1961–71; Member The International Red Cross Committee. *Address:* 3 Plateau De Frontenex, 208 Geneva, Switzerland.

**MICHENER, Rt. Hon. Roland,** CC, CMM, CD. *B.* 1900. *Educ.* Univ. of Alberta (BA 1920); Rhodes Scholar for Alberta 1919; Oxford Univ. (BA 1922; BCL 1923; MA 1929). *M.* 1927, Norah Evangeline Willis. *Daus.* Joan (Rohr), Diana (Schatz) and Wendy (Lawrence, dec.). *Career:* Barrister, Middle Temple (England) 1923, Ontario 1924, KC 1943; Practising lawyer in Toronto 1924–57, with firm Lang, Michener and others. Member Ontario Legislature for St. David, Toronto 1945–48, and Provincial Secretary and Registrar for Ontario 1946–48. Elected to House of Commons

Aug. 1953; re-elected 1957 and 1958; Elected Speaker, House of Commons 1957 and 1958; Sworn of the Privy Council Oct. 1962. Member Council Commonwealth Parly. Assn. 1959–61; High Commissioner to India & Ambassador to Nepal 1964–67; Gov. General, Commander in Chief 1967–73. Barrister (Counsel) with Lang, Michener, Cranston, Farquharson & Wright (Toronto) since 1974; Hon. Chmn. of Board, Metropolitan Trust Co.; Chmn. Teck Mining Corp. Ltd.; Dir. E-L Financial Corp. & Pamour Mines Ltd.; Chancellor Queen's University. *Awards:* Hon. LLD; Ottawa, 1948; Queen's 1958; Laval, 1960; Univ. of Alberta 1967; St. Mary's University, Halifax 1968; University of Toronto, 1968; Royal Military Coll. of Canada 1969; Mount. Allison Univ. Sackville 1969; Brock Univ. St. Catherines Ont. 1969; Univ. Manitoba Winnipeg 1970; McGill Univ. Montreal 1970; York Univ. Toronto 1970; Univ. of Brit. Col. Vancouver 1971, Jewish Theol. Seminary of America 1972; Univ. of New Brunswick 1972; Univ. of Dalhousie 1974; Hon. Fellow, Hertford College, Oxford, 1961; Academy of Medicine Toronto 1967; Royal College of Physicians and Surgeons of Canada, 1968; Royal Architectural Institute of Canada, 1968; Trinity College, Toronto, 1968; Frontier Coll. Toronto 1972; Royal Socy of Canada 1975. Chancellor and Principal Companion of the Order of Canada, 1967. Prior for Canada and Knight of Justice of the Most Venerable Order of the Hospital of St. John of Jerusalem, 1967; Chancellor and Cmdr. Order of Military Merit 1972. Hon. DCL Bishops Univ. Lennoxville, 1968; Univ. of Windsor 1969, Oxford 1970; Hon. Member, Canadian Medical Assoc. 1968. Hon. Bencher, Law Society of Upper Canada 1968. *Member:* Board of Governors, Toronto Stock Exchange 1974–76; Law Soc. of Upper Canada (Hon. Bencher 1968); Gen. Secy. for Canada for Rhodes Scholarship 1936–64. Formerly: Governor Toronto Western Hospital; Pres. Lawyers Club; The Empire Club and the Board of Trade Club (all of Toronto); Hon. Counsel Chairman Exec. Cttee. (now Pres.), Canadian Inst. of International Affairs; Hon. Counsel, Red Cross Ontario Div.; Chmn. of the Executive, Canadian Assn. for Adult Education; Officer and Director of various Canadian mining and financial companies. *Club:* University (Toronto). *Address:* 24 Thornwood Rd., Toronto, Ont. M4W 2S1, Canada; and *office* First Canadian Place, Toronto, Ont. M5X 1A2.

**MICKLETHWAIT, Sir Robert Gore,** QC. *B.* 1902. *Educ.* Clifton College and Trinity College, Oxford (MA; 2nd Class Honours LitHum). *M.* 1936, Philippa Jennette Bosanquet. *S.* Anthony Robert, Peter Bernard and Brian Hugh. *Dau.* Daphne Louisa (Watkins). *Career:* Barrister (Middle Temple) 1925; Bencher 1951; Reader 1964; Deputy Treasurer, 1970; Treas., 1971; Recorder of Worcester 1946–59; Deputy Chairman Staffordshire Quarter Sessions 1956–59. A Deputy Commissioner for the National Insurance and Industrial Injuries Acts 1959–61. The Nat. Ins. Commissioner & Industrial Injuries Commissioner 1961–66; The Chief National Insurance Commissioner of Great Britain 1966–75; *Awards:* Hon LLD Newcastle upon Tyne; Hon. Knight Honourable Socy. of Knights of the Round Table. *Publications:* The National Insurance Commissioners (Hamlyn Lectures, 1976). *Address:* 71 Harvest Road, Englefield Green, Surrey TW20 0QR.

**MICKLEY, Harold Somers.** Chemical engineer. *B.* 1918. *Educ.* Calif. Inst. of Tech. (BS; MS) and Mass. Inst. of Tech. (ScD). *M.* 1941. Margaret W. Phillips. *S.* Steven P. and Richard S. *Career:* Chemical Engineer, Union Oil Co. of Calif. 1941–42; Research Engineer, M.I.T. 1942–46 (Asst. Prof. Chem. Eng. 1946–48, Assoc. Prof. 1948–55); President, Tyron Inc. 1955–57; Professor Chemical Engineering 1957–61; Ford Prof. of Engineering 1962–70; Chmn. of Faculty 1962–63; Dir. Center, Advanced Engineering 1963–70; Grad. School Study Cttee. Mass. Inst. Tech. 1966–67; Dir. Stauffer Chemical Co. 1967—; Vice Pres. Technical 1971; Exec. Vice Pres. since 1972. *Award:* Naval Ordnance Development Award, 1946. *Member:* Amer. Inst. of Chemical Engineers; Amer. Chemical Socy.; Amer. Acad. of Arts & Sciences; Amer. Assoc. Adv. of Science Socy. of Chemical Ind.; Tau Beta Pi; Sigma XI. *Publications:* Applied Mathematics in Chemical Engineering, over 30 technical articles. *Address:* 11 Pequot Trail, Westport, Ct. 06880; and *office* Stauffer Chemical Co., Westport Ct. 06880. U.S.A.

**MIDDELBURG, Duco Gerrit Eduard.** Netherlands. *B.* 1907. *Educ.* Thorbecke School, The Hague; Netherlands School of Economics (Rotterdam); Academy of International Law (The Hague). *M.* 1931, Stephanie Elizabeth Sprajc. *S.* 1. *Dau.* 1. *Career:* Assistant Netherlands Association of Labour Exchanges, Paris 1927–28; Assistant, Consulate-General, London 1928; Aspirant Vice-Consul, London (1931–32) and Hong Kong (1933–35); promoted Vice-Consu 1934; Vice-Consul Kobe (1935) and Hong Kong (1935–38); Actg. Consul-General, Paris 1938–39; promoted Consul 1939; Actg. Consul-General, Hong Kong 1939–42; Japanese internment Hong Kong and Shanghai (diplomatic exchange via Lourenço Marques) 1942; Netherlands Ministry for Foreign Affairs, London 1942–44; Netherlands Government representative in Italy (Bari, Naples Rome) 1944; successively Consul-General Montreal (1944–45), Shanghai (1946–48), Antwerp (1948–54) and Singapore (1954–58); Ambassador to Poland (1959–62) and Chile (1963–67); Permanent Representative to the United Nations, 1967–70; Ambassador to Portugal 1970–72. *Awards:* Chevalier Order of the Netherlands Lion; Officer, Order of Orange-Nassau; Cdr., Order of Homayoon; Cdr., Order of Leopold II; Grand Cross Order of Merit of Chile; Grand Cross Henry the Navigator. *Publications:* articles and brochures on geographic and genealogical subjects. *Address:* Apartado 22, Estoril, Portugal, and c/o Coutts & Co., 1 Old Park Lane, London, W.1.

**MIDDLEMISS, Stewart Carlyle,** OBE. Australian First-Class Airline Transport Pilot. *B.* 1912. *Educ.* Brighton (Vic.) and Melbourne Technical Coll. *M.* 1941, Ethel Hope Holmes. *S.* 2. *Dau.* 1. *Career:* On leaving school, joined Commercial Bank of Australia Ltd.; after eight years resigned to join Aviation Dept., Queensland Insurance Co. Joined R.A.A.F. Sept. 1939; demobilized, with rank of Squadron Leader, April 1946. Was Chief Flying Instructor No. 5 S.F.T.S. Uranquinty, C.O. 11 Squadron (Catalina); O.C. Ferry Detachment, San Pedro Calif.; Movements Officer, R.A.A.F., New York (as member of R.A.A.F. Staff Mission to Washington); Founded Barrier Reef Airways 1946–50, Man. Dir. 1950–53; Director, Ansett Airways 1953—; Manager, Ansett Flying Boat Division; General Mgr., Butler Air Transport Ltd. (now Airlines of New South Wales, a subsidiary of Ansett Transport Industries Ltd.) 1958—; Gen. Man. Dir. Ansett Airlines, Papua, New Guinea since 1971. Member, Institute of Transport. *Clubs:* Papua; Australian Jockey. *Address:* Ansell Airlines of Papua New Guinea, P.O. Box 1213 Boroko, Papua New Guinea.

**MIDDLETON, Sir George Humphrey,** KCMG. British. *B.* 21 Jan. 1910. *Educ.* Magdalen Coll., Oxford (BA). *Career:* Vice-Consul, Buenos Aires 1933–34; Vice-Consul and Third Secretary, Asunción 1934–36; Vice-Consul, New York 1936–39, Lwow, Poland 1939, Cluj, Rumania 1940–41; Funchal, Madeira 1941–43; Second Secretary, Foreign Office, London 1943–44; Second Secretary 1944 and First Secretary 1945–47, Washington, D.C.; First Secretary, Foreign Office 1947–49, Counsellor and Chargé d'Affaires, Teheran 1950–52; Deputy High Commissioner for the United Kingdom (with rank of Minister) in India 1953–56; Ambassador to the Lebanon 1956–58; British Political Resident in Bahrain 1958–61; Ambassador to the Argentine 1961–64; to United Arab Republic 1964–65; Industrial Reorganisation Corp., 1967–68; Chmn. Mears Bros. Holdings Ltd.; Dir. various international companies; Chief Exec. British Industry Roads Campaign 1969–76; U.K. Rep on U.N. Financial Cttee. Member British Elec. Section. Fellow Royal Socy of Art.. *Address:* 53 Albert Hall Mansions, London, S.W.7.

**MIETTUNEN, Martti Juhani.** Finnish Politician. *B.* 1907. *Educ.* Agricultural Institute. *M.* 1962, Henna Salovaara. *S.* 1. *Daus.* 2. *Career:* Mem. of Parliament 1945–58; Sec., Agrarian Party 1946–50; Minister of Communications 1950–51, 1954–56, of Agriculture 1951–53, 1956–67, 1958, of Finance 1957; Gov. of Lappland 1958–73; Prime Minister 1961–62; Minister of Agriculture 1968–70; Prime Minister 1975–77. *Member:* Dir., Central Union of Agricultural Producers 1947–58; Chmn., Administrative Council of Kemijoki Oy 1956—; Pres., Provincial Assn. of Municipalities of the Province of Lappland 1959–72; Chmn., Bd. of Administration of the Central Bank of the Cooperative Banks of Finland Ltd. 1971–75. *Decorations:* Grand Cross, Order of the White Rose of Finland; Cross of Merit, in Gold, of Finnish Sport; Grand Cross, Order of the North Star; Knight Grand Cross of the Order of the British Empire; Das Grosskreuz des Verdienstordens der Bundesrepublik Deutschland. *Address:* Ohjaajantie 30 F, Helsinki 40; and *office* Aleksanterinkatu 3D, Helsinki 17, Finland.

**MIKI, Takeo.** Japanese Politician. *B.* 1907. *Educ.* Graduated from Faculty of Law, Meiji Univ., Tokyo. *M.* 1940, Mutsuko Mori. *S.* 2. *Daus.* 1. *Career:* Elected to House of Representatives 1937; Minister of Posts & Telecommunications 1947–48; Minister of Transport 1954–55; State Minister & Dir.-Gen. of Economic Planning Agency 1958; State Min. & Dir.-Gen.

of Science & Technology Agency & Chmn. of Atomic Energy Commission 1958–62; Min. of Int'l. Trade & Indus55–try 19 66; Min. of Foreign Affairs 1966–68; Dep. P.M. & Dir.-Gen. of Environment Agency 1972–74; Prime Minister & Pres. of Liberal Democratic Party 1974–76. *Decorations:* Gross Kreuz I Klasse Ehrenreichen für Verdienste um die Republike Osterreich (Austria); Grand Cross of the Yugoslav Star; Grand Cross of St. Michael and St. George (England); Al-Nahda 1st Class (Japan); Hon. Doctor of Laws, Univ. of Southern California and Columbia Univ. *Address:* 18–20 Nampeidai-Machi, Shibuya-ku, Tokoyo 150, Japan; and *office* 2-3-1 Nagata-cho, Chiyoda-ku, Tokyo, Japan.

**MIKOYAN, Anastas Ivanovich.** Soviet statesman. Chairman of the Presidium of the U.S.S.R. Supreme Soviet 1964–65; Member of Presidium 1965–75. A Deputy to all convocations of the Supreme Soviet of the U.S.S.R. 1937—. *B.* 1895, in Sanain, Tumanjan district of Armenia. *Educ.* Secondary school and Armenian Theological Seminary, Tbilisi. Joined the Communist Party (C.P.) 1915; took an active part in the October (1917) revolution. Engaged in the Bolshevik organizations of the Transcaucasus and in the establishment of Soviet power in Azerbaijan; was a member of the bureau of the Baku Committee of the Party and a member of the Political Bureau of the Central Committee of the Azerbaijan C.P. Sent by the Central Committee of the Party to Nizhny Novgorod (now Gorky) to direct the party organization in the province 1920; and (Spring 1922) to Rostov-on-Don, where he was at first Secretary of the Central Committee's Bureau for the South-East and subsequently (until 1926) Secretary of the Party's North Caucasus Territory Committee. Moved to Moscow and appointed People's Commissar for Foreign and Home Trade 1926–30; Commissar for Supplies 1930–34 and for the Food Industry 1934–38. Vice-Chairman of the Council of People's Commissars 1937–46 and concurrently (1938–46) Commissar for Foreign Trade; Vice-Chmn. of Council of Ministers and concurrently (1946–55) Minister of Foreign Trade, and Minister of Trade 1953–55; First Vice-Chmn. of Council of Ministers 1955–64. In 1922 was elected an alternate member of the Central Committee of the Russian C.P. (Bolsheviks) and in 1923 elected a member of the Central Committee; in 1926 elected an alternate member of the Political Bureau of the Central Committee of the All-Union C.P. (Bolsheviks) and in 1935 member of the Political Bureau of the Central Committee of the All-Union C.P. Elected member of the Presidium of the Central Committee of C.P.S.U.; and in 1919, to the All-Russian Central Executive Committee, and subsequently to the Central Executive Committee (of Soviets) 1919. During the war, 1941–45, was a member of the State Committee for Defence. From 1942, for special services in organizing supplies of food, fuel, clothing, etc. for the Red Army in difficult wartime conditions, the title of Hero of Socialist Labour was conferred upon him; he has also been awarded the Order of Lenin four times, and is the recipient of other Orders and medals. *Address:* Presidium of the U.S.S.R. Supreme Soviet, The Kremlin, Moscow, U.S.S.R.

**MILANO, John.** President & Chief Executive Officer, Byer-Rolnick, a division of Koracorp Industries Inc. *B.* 1928. *M.* 1955, Maria L. Wedlin. *S.* 2. *Career:* Joined Byer-Rolnick as retail salesman 1956; rose through ranks to manager of retail stores in New York 1958; Vice-Pres. & Dir. of National Retail Div. of Byer-Rolnick 1967, Pres. 1973; Pres. of Corporate Divisions Churchill Hats Ltd., Cavanagh Hats, Ecuadorian Panama Hats, Dobbs Hats, Knox Hats, Kevin McAndrew Hatmakers; Pres., Resistol Sales Inc. Horatio Alger Award 1976. *Clubs:* Brookhaven Country Club (Dallas); Cherokee Club (Longview, Tx): Merchandise Mart Club (Chicago, Ill.); Rotary Int'l. *Address: offices* 601 Marion Drive, Garland, Texas 75040, U.S.A.; & 350 Fifth Avenue, N.Y.C.; Merchandise Mart Building, Chicago, Ill.; 110 E. Ninth Street, Los Angeles, Ca.

**MILBRATH, Robert Henry,** Comdr. U.S.N. (Ret.); petroleum executive. *B.* 1912. U.S. Naval Acad. (BS). *M.* 1940, Margaret Ripperger. *S.* Robert S. *Daus.* Constance and Susan. *Career:* With Standard Oil Co. 1934–38; Vice-Pres., Gen. Mgr., Esso Sociedad Anonima Petrolera Argentina 1938–42 and 1946–50; area contact, East Coast of South America, marketing coordination 1950–52; Internatl. Petroleum Co. Ltd. 1952, Dir. 1954, Vice-Pres. 1956; Vice-Pres. and Dir., Esso Export Corp. 1957; Chairman, Esso Export Ltd., London (Eng.) 1958; Exec. Vice-Pres., Esso Export Corp. 1959; President, Esso International Inc. (formerly Esso Export Corp.) 1961–66.; Exec. Vice Pres. Esso Europe Inc. 1966–68; Logistics Co-ordinator, Standard Oil Co. (N.J.), 1968–69; Director & Senior Vice-Pres. EXXON Corp. (formerly Standard Oil Co., N.J.), 1969–73. *Award:* Secretary of Navy Commendation plus ribbon for outstanding performance of dury as Chief of the Latin American Section of the Army-Navy Petroleum Board throughout the war. *Member:* Amer. Petroleum Inst.; Trustee, Inst. of International Education; Institute of Int. Education. Republican. *Clubs:* University; Navy League of U.S.; U.S. Naval Adad. Alumni Assn. *Address:* 185 San Juen Drive, Ponte Vedra, Fla. 32082, U.S.A.

**MILES, John Perry.** American. *B.* 1917. *Educ.* Bellaire High School Ohio; Ohio State University. *M.* 1966, Pamela Duffey. *S.* 3. *Career:* Asst. Mgr. Asian & Eastern Div. Goodyear International Corp. 1952; Asst. to Man. Dir. Goodyear Tyre & Rubber Co. (Aust.) 1954, Sales Mgr. 1955, Sales Dir. 1958; Vice-Chmn. & Man. Dir. 1965—; Vice-Pres. Goodyear International Corp. 1967–71; Vice-Chmn. and Man. Dir. Goodyear Tyre and Rubber Co. (Aust.) Ltd.; Dir. Australian Synthetic Rubber Co., *Member:* Aust.-Amer. Assn.; Inst. Directors; Past Dir. Amer. Chamber Commerce Australia. *Clubs:* Amer. National; Elanora Country; Royal Sydney Yacht Squadron; Royal Motor Yacht Squadron. *Address:* 55A Wunulla Road, Point Piper, Sydney, N.S.W. Australia and *office* 4 Yurong Street, Sydney, N.S.W.

**MILI, Mohamed Ezzedine.** Tunisian Telecommunication Engineer. *Educ.* Graduate of Ecole Normale Supérieure, Saint-Cloud, and Ecole Nationale Supérieure des Telecommunications, Paris; Qualified as a Telecommunications Engineer in 1946. *M.* 1950, Najiba Zouhir. *S.* 3. *Daus.* 2. *Career:* Joined Tunisian Posts Telegraphs & Telephones Administration 1948; Chief Engineer 1957–64; Dir.-Gen. of Telecommunications at the PTT 1964–65; Elected Deputy Sec.-Gen. of the ITU, Geneva 1965, elected Sec.-Gen. 1967; Vice-Chmn. Plan Cttee. for Africa 1961, Chmn. 1964–65; represented Tunisia to Admin. Council of ITU 1960–65; Chmn., ITU Admin. Council 19th Session 1964. *Member:* Senior Member, Inst. of Electrical & Electronics Engineers (IEEE). *Decorations:* Officer of the Order of Independence of Tunisia; Commander of the Order of the Tunisian Republic; Commander of the Swedish Order of Vasa; Grand Cross of the Order of Duarte, Sanchez y Mella with Silver Star (Dominican Republic); Order of Merit Medal (Paraguay); Grand Star of the Order of Merit of Telecommunications (Spain); Commander of the Order of Leopold (Belgium). *Address:* 5 Route de Mon Idée, CH-1226 Thônex, Geneva, Switzerland; and *office* International Telecommunication Union, Place des Nations, 1211 Geneva 20, Switzerland.

**MILLAN, Bruce,** PC, MP. *B.* 1927. *Educ.* Harris Academy, Dundee. *M.* 1953, Gwendoline May Fairey. *S.* 1. *Dau.* 1. *Career:* Member, Parliament (Lab.) Glasgow Craigton 1959—; Under-Secy. of State for Defence for the R.A.F. 1964–66; Joint Parly. Under-Secy. of State for Scotland 1966–70; Minister of State for Scotland 1974–76; Secy. of State for Scotland since 1976; Privy Councillor since 1975. *Member:* Inst. of Chartered Accountants of Scotland. *Address:* 46 Hardy Road, London, S.E.3.

**MILLARD, Sir Guy Elwin,** KCMG, CVO. British diplomat. *B.* 1917. *Educ.* Charterhouse; Pembroke College, Cambridge. *M.* (1) 1946, Anne Mackenzie. *S.* 1. *Dau.* 1. (2) Judy Dugdale. *S.* 2. *Career:* Former Ambassador to Hungary; Minister, Washington 1970–71; Ambassador to Sweden 1971–74; Ambassador to Italy 1974–76. *Club:* Boodle's. *Address:* Fyfield Manor, Southrop, Lechlade, Glos.

**MILLARD, Mark J.** American. *B.* 1908. *Educ.* Heidelberg; phD (Econ.). *M.* Liselotte. *Dau.* Marsha Antonia. *Career:* Vice-Chmn., Loeb, Rhoades & Co. Inc., investment bankers, New York City. Director: Apco Oil Co., Gulf Interstate Corp; Halcon Chemicals Co.; Florida Gulf Trust. *Address:* 907 Fifth Avenue, New York City; and *office* 42 Wall street; New York City, U.S.A.

**MILLER, Arjay.** American. *B.* 1906. *Educ.* Univ. of California at Los Angeles (BA with highest honors 1937) and graduate student at Univ. of Calif. at Berkeley 1938–40. *M.* 1940, Francis Marion Fearing. *S.* Menneth Fearing. *Dau.* Ann Elizabeth Olstad. *Career:* Teaching Asst., Univ. of Calif. at Berkeley 1938–42; with Federal Reserve Bank of San Francisco 1941–43; Captain U.S. Air Force 1943–46; Asst. Treasurer, Ford Motor Co. 1947–53 (successively Controller, Vice-Pres. and Controller, Vice-Pres., Finance, and Vice-Pres. Staff Group 1953–63), Director 1962, President 1963–68, Vice-Chmn. 1968–69; Dir., Ford Motor Co., Wells Fargo Bank, Utah International Inc., Levi Straus & Co., Washington Post. Dean, Grad. Sch. of Business Admin., Stanford Univ. since

1969. *Trustee:* The Brookings Institution (Washington, D.C.) June 1964—, International Executive Service Corps, The Conference Board, Eisenhower Exchange Fellowship, Urban Institute. *Member:* Board of Dirs., SRI International; Economic Policy Council of UNA; The Trilateral Commission. *Publications:* (with Arthur G. Coons) An Economic and Industrial Survey of the Los Angeles and San Diego Areas. Hon. LLD: Univ. of Calif.; Whitman Coll.; Univ. of Nebraska. *Clubs:* Bohemian; Pacific Union. *Address:* Graduate School of Business, Stanford University, Stanford, Calif. 94305, U.S.A.

**MILLER, Hon. Brian Kirkwall.** Australian. *B.* 1921. *M.* 1947, Eunice Joyce Cashion. *S.* Stephen Alexander and John Andrew. *Career:* Member Legislative Council Div. Newdegate since 1957; Deputy Leader of the Government in the Legislative Council 1959; Chief Secretary for the State of Tasmania 1964–69; Leader of Govt. Legislative Council; Attorney-Gen. and Minister for Police and Emergency Services; Patron & Life Member Multiple Sclerosis Socy. of Tasmania; Cttee., Royal Tasmanian Socy. for the Blind and Deaf; Chmn. Tas. Div. Aust. Chest & Tuberculosis Assn Patron, Tasmanian Caledonian Socy.; Patron, St. Andrews Socy.; Patron South Tas. Badminton Assn.; Fox Terrier Club; Life member Aust.-Italian Club; Exec. member Commonwealth Parly. Assn. (Tas. Branch). *Clubs:* North Hobart Rotary; Journalists'; Derwent Bowling. *Address:* 11 McGuinness Crescent, Lenah Valley, Tasmania; and *office* c/o Public Buildings, Franklin Square, Hobart, Tasmania.

**MILLER, Donald Herbert, Jr.** American magazine executive. *B.* 1914. *Educ.* Dartmouth College (AB 1937). *M.* Claire Strauss Kaufman. *S.* Donald III, Bruce and Geoffrey. *Daus.* Meredith, Sheila and Linda. *Career:* Ex. Asst. to the Director-General Canadian Dept. of Munitions & Supply, Washington, D.C., 1941–45; Asst. Circulation Mgr., Honolulu Advertiser 1940–41, and Honolulu Star-Bulletin 1937–40; Director, Vice-President, Secretary and General Manager, Scientific American Inc since 1947; Publisher of magazine Scientic American. Dir.: American Electronic Laboratory, Inc. Philadelphia; Educational Foundation for Nuclear Science, In Publisher of magazine Bulletin of the Atomic Scientists, Chicago. Dir., W. H. Freeman and Co.. San Francisco; Le Scienze, Spa. Milan. Italy. *Clubs:* Dartmouth, University (N.Y.C.). *Address:* 31 Seneca Drive, Chappaqua, N.Y. 10514; and *office* 415 Madison Avenue, New York, N.Y. 10017, U.S.A.

**MILLER, Prof. E. Willard.** Geographer. *B.* 1915. *Educ.* Clarion State Coll. (BS 1937), Univ. of Nebraska (AM 1939) and Ohio State Univ. (PhD 1942). *M.* 1941, Ruby Skinner. *Career:* Geographer, Office of Strategic Service 1944–45; Asst. Prof., Western Reserve Univ. 1943–44; Instructor, Ohio State Univ. 1942–43. Author of some 70 articles to professional publications. Certificate of Merit, Office of Strategic Service 1945; Professor, and Head, Department of Geography, Pennsylvania State University 1945–63; Asst. Dean, Resident, Coll. of Earth and Mineral Sciences 1964–72; Associate Dean since 1972; Dir., National Science Foundation Academic Year Institute, Earth Service 1967–71. Programme Chmn., Assn. of American Geographers, Pittsburgh 1959; U.S. Member, Committee on National Resources, Commission on Geography, Pan-American Inst. of Geography and History 1959—. *Member:* Sigma Xi; Pi Gamma Mu; President: Amer. Socy. Professional Geographers; Penna. Council for Geography Education; Penna. State Univ. Chapter, Amer. Assn. Univ. Professors; Penna. Acad. of Science. *Member:* Amer. Inst. of Mining, Metallurgical and Petroleum Engineers; Natl. Cncl. for Geographic Education; Int. Geographical Union; Royal Canadian Geographical Socy.; Assn. of American Geographers; Geographical Assn. (United Kingdom). *Awards:* Fellow: American Association for Advancement of Science; Ray Hughes Whitbeck Award, outstanding Article on economic Geography; National Council for Geographic Education; Int. Inst. of Arts & Letters; Amer. Geographical Society; Penn. Dept. of Commerce Secretary's Meritorious Services Award 1975; Gov. of Penn. Citation for service to the Commonwealth. *Publications:* Global Geography (1957); A Geography of Manufacturing (1962); The World's Nations, an Economic and Regional Geography (1958); An Economic Atlas of Pennsylvania (1964); Exploring Earth Environment: A World Geography (1964). Mineral Resources of the United States (1967); Energy Resources of the United States (1967); A Geography of Industrial Location (1970); Socioeconomics Patterns of Pennsylvania: An Atlas (1975); Manufacturing: A Study of Industrial Location (1977); Associate Editor, Journal of Geography; Contributing Editor, Producers Monthly; Geographic Adviser to Thomas Y. Crowell Co. National Science Foundation Travel Grant to attend Internationa Geographical Congress. Stockholm 1960 and New Delhi, India 1968. *Address:* 845 Outer Drive State College, Pa.; and *office* 104 Mineral Sciences Building, University Park, Pa., U.S.A.

**MILLER, Sir Ian Douglas,** FRCS, FRACS. Neurosurgeon. *B.* 1900. *Educ.* Univ. of Sydney (MB) and Royal Coll. of Surgeons, England (Fellow). *M.* 1939, Phyllis Laidley Mort. *S.* John, David and Adrian. *Daus.* Katharine and Christina. *Career:* Member, Council of Royal Australian College of Surgeons 1948–60 (Pres. 1957–59); Hon. Neurosurgeon, St. Vincent's Hosp. 1929–60. Lieutenant-Colonel Royal Australian Medical Corps 1941–46; Hon. Consulting Surgeon Repatriation Hospital 1946—; Chairman, Board, St. Vincent's Hospital, Sydney 1967–74 and Hon. Consulting Neurosurgeon 1960— (Dean of Clinical School 1932–62). Chairman, Editorial Board, Modern Medicine in Australia, and of Editorial Cttee. Australian and New Zealand Journal of Surgery; Hon. President, Asian-Australian Neurological Society 1965–67. Hon. Member; Acad. of Medicine, Singapore; Australian Medical Assn.; International Society of Surgery. President, Academy of Forensic Sciences, 1970; Hon. D. Litt Singapore 1973. *Publications:* Treatment of Tic Douloureux (1956); Study of Subdural Haematoma (1960); Sciatica Due to Intervertebral Disc Lesions (1962); Australian and New Zealand Journal of Surgery. *Clubs:* Australian; Royal, Sydney. *Address:* Coronation Avenue, Balmoral, N.S.W.; and *office* 149 Macquarie Street, Sydney, N.S.W. 2000, Australia.

**MILLER, James Derrick.** BEng.(Hons.) CEng., FIMechE, FIProdE, FBIM. British. *B.* 1924. *Educ.* Clare Coll.; Cambridge Univ.; Sheffield University. *M.* 1947, Florence. *S.* 2. *Dau.* 1. *Career:* Chmn. & Chief Exec. Harris & Sheldon Group Ltd.; Chmn. following H. & S. Group subsidiaries. Antler Ltd.; Joseph Billingham Ltd.; Castle Products Ltd.; Churchill Atkin Grant and Lang Ltd.; Desmo Ltd.; English Rose Kitchens Ltd.; Evertaut Ltd.; Formula Contracts Ltd.; Fibatube Ltd.; Hardy Bros (Alnwick) Ltd.; Chmn. of Harris Sheldon Display Ltd.; Jet Filters Ltd.; Presto Lock International Ltd.; Sedgemoor Eng. Ltd.; Alfred Stewart Ltd.; A.S. Toone & Sons Ltd.; Wm. Wadsworth & Sons Ltd.; Dir. & Deputy Chmn. H. & S. Group Subsidiary Evans Lifts Ltd.; Pres. Birmingham Branch Inst. of Marketing 1968–69; Chmn. Midland Branch Inst. Directors 1972–74; Chmn., Midland Regional Adv. Bd. British Inst. Management 1972–76. *Address:* North Court Packington Park, Meriden, Warwickshire.

**MILLER, James F(ranklin).** American research chemist. *B.* 1912, *Educ.* Franklin & Marshall Coll. (BS Chem.) and Pennsylvania State Univ. (PhD and MS— Analytical chemistry). *M.* 1938, Nellie Virginia Weadon. *Dau.* Caryl Jean. *Career:* Head, Dept. of Analytical Chemistry, Mellon Institute 1951–59 (Senior Fellow 1944–51); Post-Doctoral Fellow, Purdue Univ. 1943–44; Instructor in Chemistry, Pennsylvania State Univ. 1939–42. Manager, Applied Research, Chemical and Physical Laboratories, Corporate Research and Development Dept., Continental Can Co. 1959–68; Exec. Secy. Editor Alpha Chi Sigma Fraternity since 1968. *Publications:* A New Reagent for Detection of Cerium (1937); The Determination of Thalium with Phosphomolybdic Acid (1939); Determination of Hydrogen in Fluorine-Containing Halohydrocarbons (with H. Hunt, H. B. Hass and E. T. McBee (1947); Decomposition and Analysis of Organic Compounds Containing Fluorine and Other Halogens (with Hunt and McBee 1947); Spectrophotometric Determination of Aliphatic Sulfides in Crude Petroleum Oils and Their Fractions (with H. V. Drushel 1955); Polarographic Determination of Elemental Sulfur in Petroleum and Its Fractions (with Drushel, R. Clarke and W. Hubis 1956); Anodic Polarography of Sulfur Compounds in Petroleum and Its Fractions (with Drushel 1956); Anodic Polarographic Estimation of Aliphatic Sulfides in Petroleum (with Drushel 1957); Polarographic Estimation of Thiophenes and Aromatic Sulfides in Petroleum (with Drushel 1958). Holder of two patents: Emulsifying Apparatus (with M. C. Jaskowski), and Apparatus for Fractionating Finely Divided Material. *Member:* Phi Beta Kappa, Socy. of Sigma Xi; Phi Kappa Phi; Phi Lambda Upsilon; Alpha Chi Sigma (Vice-Pres. 1962–66); Pres. 1966–68, Grand Recorder (Exec. Secy. 1968—). American Chemical Socy.; American Institute of Chemical Engineers; Mason. *Address:* 11 S. Kitley Avenue, Bldg. # 1, Indianapolis, Ind. 46219, U.S.A.

**MILLER, John Robinson, Jr.** Publisher. *B.* 1914. *Educ.* St. Paul's School (Garden City, N.Y.) and Goldey Business

Coll. (Wilmington, Del.). *M.* 1935, Helen Elizabeth Fulton *S.* John Robinson III and Mark Fulton. *Dau.* Dale Dunlap. *Career:* With Hearst Magazines 1934–73; Dir. and Secy., Vice-Chmn. Audit Bureau of Circulations 1958–74;, Natnl. Better Business Bureau 1962–72 (Chmn. of Bd. 1966–68); Natnl. Magazine Co. Ltd. (London), and of Central Registry 1957–58 (Chmn. of Board 1958). Dir., Secy., Treas., Audit Bureau of Marketing Services 1967–69; Vice-President and General Manager, Hearst Magazines 1962–67; Exec. Vice-President and General Manager 1967–73; Exec. Vice-Pres. Hearst Corp. 1973–75; Pres. Hearst Corp since 1975. (Vice-President and Director of Circulation 1955–62; Assistant General Manager 1945–55); President and Director, Periodical Publishers' Service Bureau, Sandusky, Ohio 1963–70; Chairman of Board, 1970–71; (Vice-President 1953–63), and of Popular Mechanics Co. 1958–63; Director, Hearst Corporation 1960—; Vice-President, Science Co. 1958–59; Vice-President & Director Omega Pub. Corp., Miami, Fla. *Club:* Cherry Valley Golf (Garden City). *Address:* 18 Wellington Road, Garden City, N.Y.; Ginger Quill, Buck Hill Falls, Pa.; and *office* 959 Eighth Avenue, New York City 10019, U.S.A.

**MILLER, Joseph Irwin.** Manufacturer and banker. *B.* 1909. *Educ.* Yale Univ. (BA) and Oxford Univ. Balliol Coll. (MA). *M.* 1943, Xenia Simons. *S.* Hugh Thomas II, and William Irwin. *Daus.* Margaret Irwin, Catherine Gibbs and Elizabeth Ann Garr. *Career:* Lieut. U.S.N.R. 1942–45. Chairman: Cummins Engine Co. Inc. 1951—, Irwin-Union Bank & Trust Co. 1952–75; Chmn. of Exec. Cttee., Irwin Union Corp. since 1975. Director: American Telephone & Telegraph Co. The Urban Institute since 1969. Chmn., President's Special Committee on U.S. Trade Relations with East European Countries and the Soviet Union, 1965; National Advisory Commission for Health, Manpower, 1966–67. President, National Council of Churches 1960–63; Member Exec. Cttee. of Central Cttee. World Council of Churches, 1961–68. *Member:* The Business Council; Trustee, Ford Foundation; Yale Univ. Museum of Modern Art; Member, Commission on Money and Credit 1958–61; President's Cttee. on Postal Reorganization, and on Urban Housing 1966–67. *Awards:* Hon. LLD: Bethany Coll. Texas Christian Univ., Indiana Univ., Oberlin Coll., Princeton Univ., Hamilton Coll. Columbia Univ., Michigan State Univ. LLD, Dartmouth Coll. 1971. Hon LHD Case Inst. 1966; Hon MA, Yale Univ.; LLD. Notre Dame Univ. 1972; LLD Ball State Univ. 1972; LHD Manchester Coll. 1973. Republican. *Clubs:* Links, Yale (N.Y.C.); Chicago. Columbia (Indianapolis). *Address:* 2760 Highland Way, Columbus Ind.; and *office* 301 Washington Street, Columbus, Ind., U.S.A.

**MILLER, Raymond Wiley.** American consultant. *B.* 21 Jan. 1895. *Educ.* San Jose State Coll.; LLB La Salle Ext. Univ., Hon LLD, St. John's Univ., Collegeville, Minn. *M.* 1919, Florence E. Burk. *S.* Robert W. *Dau.* Ruth Genevive (Powell). *Career:* Consultant to Food and Agriculture Organization of U.N. 1949–56; Visiting Lecturer, Harvard Graduate School of Business Admin. (Public Relations and World Affairs) 1948–64; Lecturer, Graduate School of Public and Int. Affairs, Univ. of Pittsburgh; developed and operated walnut grove, Linden, Calif. since 1919; Pres., World Trade Relations Inc. since 1944; President, Public Relations Research Associates, Inc.; President and General Counsel American Inst. of Co-operation 1944–48; Public Relations consultant to many North American business firms since 1930; Lecturer on public relations since 1935, Consultant, Technical Co-operation Admin., Dept. of State 1952–53; Consultant, International Rice Commission, Bangkok 1949; Technical Meeting on Co-operatives in Asia and Far East, Lucknow 1949, and Kandy 1954; Int. Fed. of Agricultural Producers (Guelph, Ont. 1949; Stockholm 1950; Mexico City 1951); Consultant Office of Facilitation U.S. Dept. of Transportation 1971—; Ecumenical Commission on European Co-operation, Germany 1952; member, International Planning Team, Ford Foundation, New Delhi 1954; member: White House Conf. on Rural Education (Washington 1944). *Member:* Bd. of Dirs. Transportation Assn. of America 1947–71; Bar of Supreme Court of U.S.; Amer. Bar Assn.; Cttee. on Education About Communism and its Contrast with Liberty under the Law. Hon. Member, Phi Alpha Delta Fraternity 1968—.; Scottish Rite of Freemasonry 33°; York Rite KT; Republican; Methodist; *Awards:* Distinguished Service Award, Natl. Catholic Rural Life Conf., five awards from Freedoms Foundation, Valley Forge; American Council on Public Relations; Hall of Fame Award, Boston Conf. on Distribution; Silver Buffalo Boy Scouts of Amer.; Federal Land Bank Outstanding Contribution Award; GC Masons. *Publications:* Keepers of the Corporate Conscience (1946): The Corporation—A Brotherhood of Service (1947); Take Time for Human Engineering (1948); Humanizing the Corporate Person (1949); Public Relations (with Wm. Nielander) (1951); Our Economic Policy in Asia (1951); The Layman's Orbit (1958); Can Capitalism Compete? (1959); Co-operative—Catalysts for Freedom in the Community of Nations (1960); Communism, Capitalism, Co-operation (1961); A Conservative Looks at Co-operatives (1964); We Funny Methodists (1965); A Look Back and a Look Ahead on Foreign Aid, (1966); Men or Beasts? (1967); Balancing Food and People (1975); The Pope's County Agent (1975); contributor to agricultural fraternal, educational, legal, economic, religous, public relations, and marketing journals. 11 papers on inflation 1969–72. *Clubs:* Cosmos, (Washington, D.C.); Commonwealth (San Francisco). *Address:* 2121 Massachusetts Avenue, N.W., Washington, D.C. 20008, U.S.A.

**MILLIKEN, Roger.** Textile executive. *B.* 1915. *Educ.* Yale Univ. (AB). *M.* 1948, Justine Van Rensselaer Hooper. *S.* Roger, Jr., David Gayley and Weston Freeman. *Daus.* Justine Van Rensselaer, and Nancy. *Career:* Pres. & Dir., Milliken & Co. 1947– (Formerly Deering Milliken Inc.). Director: Mercantile Stores Co. Inc. 1939—; Citibank, N.A. 1947— (Formerly First National City Bank of N.Y.); Westinghouse Electric Corp. 1962—; W. R. Grace & Co. 1953—; Milliken Research Corp. 1955— (Formerly Deering Milliken Research Corp.). Chmn., Greenville/Spartanburg Airport Commission 1959—. Chmn. of the Board, Inst. of Textile Technology 1948— (Charlottesville, Virginia). Member: The Business Roundtable 1973—; The Business Council 1965—. Member, Board of Trustees: Wofford Coll., Spartanburg; South Carolina Foundation of Independent Colleges. *Clubs:* Union League; Augusta National Golf; Links. *Address:* 627 Otis Boulevard, Spartanburg, S.C.; and *office* 234 South Fairview Avenue, Spartanburg, S.C., U.S.A.

**MILLIKEN, William G.** American State Governor. *B.* 1922. *Educ.* Yale (Degree). *M.* Helen Wallbank. *S.* 1. *Dau.* 1. *Career:* State Senate 1960–64; Lieut.-Gov. 1964–69; Governor of the State of Michigan since 1969. *Decorations:* Purple Heart; Air Medal (2 Oak Leaf Clusters); European Theatre Ribbon with 3 battle stars. *Address:* Office of the Governor, State Capitol, Lansing, Michigan 48909, U.S.A.

**MILLIKIN, Severance Allen.** *B.* 1895. *Educ.* University School; Princeton Univ. (LittB). *M.* 1952, Marguerite Steckerl Manville. Personal investments. Member Board of Directors: Cleveland Trust Co. 1925—. *Trustee:* Cleveland Museum of Art 1947—, John Huntington Art & Polytechnic Trust 1936—, and University Hospitals of Cleveland 1948—. *Clubs:* Union, Tavern (Cleveland); Union, Recess (N.Y.C.); Chagrin Valley Hunt (Gates Mills, O.); Kirtland Country (Willoughby, O.). *Address: office* 480 The Arcade, Cleveland, Ohio, U.S.A.

**MILLS, John Brent.** South African. *B.* 1921. *Educ.* Rondebosch Boys' High School; Univ. of Cape Town, MA. *M.* 1948, Pamela Elizabeth. *S.* 1. *Daus.* 2. *Career:* Consul Gen. San Francisco 1962–68; Under Secy. Dept. Foreign Affairs 1968–71: Ambassador Republic of South Africa to Australia 1971–77, to Italy since 1977. *Address:* Embassy of South Africa, Philips Building, Piazza Monte Grappa 4, Rome 00195, Italy.

**MILLS, Joseph Roger.** Canadian civil engineer. *B.* 1916. *Educ.* Mount Allison University; Nova Scotia Technical College (BE). *M.* 1941, Jane Evelyn Stairs Roscoe. *S.* Peter. *Daus.* Roberta and Nancy. *Career:* Field Engineer, Foundation Maritime Ltd., Halifax, N.S. 1941; Engineer, Geocor Ltd., Montreal 1943; Vice-Pres. and Gen. Mgr. 1946; Secy., The Foundation Co. of Canada Ltd., Montreal 1951; Vice-Pres. 1956; Director, Voluntary Economic Planning Province of Nova Scotia Dept. of Development 1963–71; Director, Dept. of Devel., Province of Nova Scotia since 1971. *Clubs:* Halifax; Royal Nova Scotia Yacht Squadron. *Address:* 5901 Chain Rock Drive (P.O. Box 519) Halifax, N.S. B3J 2R7 Canada.

**MILLS, Peter McLay.** MP. *B.* 1921. *Educ.* Epson; Wye College. *M.* 1948, Joan Weatherley. *S.* 1. *Dau.* 1. *Career:* Farmer since 1943; Member, Parliament (Con.) Torrington 1964–74, for Devon West since 1974; Parly. Secy. Min. of Agriculture, Fisheries & Food Apr–Nov. 1972; Parly. Under-Secy. of State Northern Ireland Office 1972–74; Mem., European Legislation Cttee., EEC, 1974. *Address:* House of Commons, London SW1A 0AA; & Priestcombe, Crediton, Devon.

**MILLS-OWENS, Hon. Mr. Justice Richard Hugh,** C.B.E. British. *B.* 1910. *Educ.* Rhyl Grammar School. Solicitor 1932

(Clifford's Inn Prizeman). *Career:* Barrister-at-Law (Middle Temple) 1956; practised in Wales until 1949. Joined Colonial Legal Service as Registrar of Titles; Principal Registrar, Crown Counsel and Legal Draftsman, Kenya 1952; Magistrate 1956, District Judge 1958, Puisne Judge 1961, Hong Kong. Chief Justice, Fiji 1964–67; Puisne Judge. Hong Kong 1967–71. *Address:* Westwood, Hangersley, Ringwood, Hants.

**MILNE, Edward James.** British. *B.* 18 Oct. 1915. *Educ.* Robert Gordons Coll., Aberdeen. *M.* 1939, Emily Constable. *Daus.* 3. *Career:* Lecturer, T.U.C. Educational Dept. 1942–47; Area Official, Union of Shop Distributive & Allied Workers, 1951–60; Member of Parliament for Blyth, Northumberland 1960–74; Parly. Private Secy. (Sir Frank Soskice H. Office), 1964–66; Secy. Anglo-Norwegian Parly. Group 1965–71, Anglo Swedish 1965–71; Elected to Blyth Valley Council, May 1976. *Award:* Grand Order of the Star of Africa, (Gold Band). *Publication:* No Shining Armour (1976). *Address:* Strathearn, Alston Grove, Seaton Sluice, Northumberland.

**MILNE-WATSON, Sir Michael Milne,** Kt CBE, MA. *B.* 1910. *Educ.* Eton and Balliol College, Oxford (MA). *M.* 1940, Mary Lisette Bagnall. *S.* Andrew. *Career:* Joined Gas Light & Coke Co., London 1933; War-service RNVR 1943–45; Mng. Dir. Gas, Light & Coke Co. 1945; Governor 1946–49; Chmn., North Thames Gas Board, 1949–64; Richard Thomas & Baldwins Ltd., 1964–67; Dep. Chmn., B.S.C., 1967–69. (Mem. Organising Cttee., 1966–67); Iron and Steel Advisory Cttee., 1967–69. Chairman, The William Press Group of Companies 1969–74; Dir. Marine Oil Industry Repairs Ltd.; Salveson Offshore Holdings Ltd.; Dir. Commercial Union Assurance Co. Ltd., Industrial and Commercial Finance Corp., Finance Corp. for Industry Ltd. *Member:* Vice-Pres. Council of Reading Univ.; Pres. The Society of British Gas Industries 1970–71; Pres. the Pipeline Industries Guild 1971–72; Liveryman of Grover's Co. 1947; Chmn., The British United Provident Assn.; Gov., Nuffield Nursing Homes Trust. *Clubs:* Athenaeum; Leander. *Address:* 39 Cadogan Place, London, SW1X 9RX, and Oakfield, Mortimer, Berks.

**MILWARD, Sir Anthony (Horace),** CBE, OBE 1945. British. *B.* 1905. *Educ.* Rugby and Clare Coll., Cambridge (BA). *M.* 1931, Frieda Elizabeth Anne von der Becke. *S.* Ian Newton. *Dau.* Clare Anthony (Gray). *Career:* With Glazebrook, Steel & Co., Manchester 1926–40. Served Fleet Air Arm, R.N.V.R. as Pilot, reaching rank of Lieut.-Comdr. 1940–45. With B.E.A. in various capacities 1946–70; Chairman, British European Airways, Apr. 1964–70. Member (part-time) of Board of British Overseas Airways Corp. 1964–70. Member of the Air Registration Board 1964–70; Chmn. London Tourist Board 1971–76, Pres. 1976—. *Member:* Fellow of Chartered Inst. of Transport. *Club:* Royal Automobile. *Address:* Dene House, Lower Slaughter, Gloucestershire.

**MINETT, Irving Jerome.** American executive. *B.* 1914. *Educ.* Purdue Univ. (BEng). *M* 1942, Dorothy Elaine Scott. *Dau.* Susan Scott. *Career:* With Chrysler Corp. Group Executive Defence: Head, Defence, Space and Missiles Operations 1958–61; Gen. Mgr. Defence, Operations Div. 1955–57: Operating Mgr., Delaware Tank Plant 1954–55; Director and Group Vice-President, Chrysler Corp. (U.S.A.) 1961–74. President 1967—, Director 1962—, Chrysler International (Switzerland); Director: Société des Automobiles Simca (France) 1962—, Rootes Motors Ltd. (England) 1964—, Barreiros Diesel S.A. (Spain) 1964—, and Fabricas Automex S.A. (Mexico) 1966—. *Member:* Amer. Defence Preparedness Assn. (Nat. Pres.); Detroit Bd. of Commerce; Detroit Economic Club; Detroit Cttee. on Foreign Relations; Trustee of Detroit Inst. of Arts.. *Clubs:* Knickerbocker (N.Y.C.); Bloomfield (Mich.) Country; The Detroit; Detroit Athletic. *Address:* 535 North Williamsbury Road, Birmingham Mich.; and *office* Chrysler Corp., 341 Massachusetts Avenue, Detroit, Mich., U.S.A.

**MINNIS, Wesley.** Chemist. *B.* 1895. *Educ.* Univ. of Washington (BSc 1916; MSc 1916) and Univ. of Michigan (DPh 1922). *M.* (1) 1919, Nola E. Sauer (*D.* 1946). *Dau.* Marjorie Lee. *M.* (2) 1947, Janette E. Moore. *Career:* Research Chemist: National Aniline & Chemical Co. 1918–20, Semet Solvay Corp. 1922–23, National Aniline Div., Allied Chemical Corp. 1923–31 (successively Asst. Dir. of Research and Development 1931–51, Director of the Division 1951–58, Asst. to Dir. of Corporate Res. and Dev. 1958–60, Consultant, 1962–65). Special Lecturer, Newark College of Engineering 1961–67. Consultant, New Jersey State Department of Higher Education, 1968–70. *Publications:* Organic Syntheses; holder of several U.S. Patents. *Awards:* Citation, Univ. of Buffalo 1959; Outstanding Alumnus Achievement Award. Univ. of Michigan 1960. *Member:* Amer. Chemical Socy.; Amer. Inst. of Chemists. *Address:* 501 Gardens Parkway, Ocean City, N.J., 08226, U.S.A.

**MINTOFF, Hon. Dominic.** Maltese statesman, architect and civil engineer. *B.* 6 Aug. 1916. *Educ.* Royal Univ. of Malta, and Oxford Univ. (Rhodes Scholar); MA; BSc; BE & A; A & CE. *M.* 1947, Moyra Bentinck. *Daus.* 2. *Career:* Gen. Sec. Malta Labour Party, 1936–37; Civil Engineer in U.K. 1941–43; set up in practice as architect in Malta; re-joined Malta Labour Party 1944; elected to Council of Government and Member of Exec. Cttee. 1945; elected to Malta Legislative Assembly (Lab.) and as Dep. Leader of Labour Party was Deputy Prime Minister, also Min for Works and Reconstruction 1947; resigned his Ministry over divergence of opinion with Prime Minister, and elected Leader of Labour Party 1949; Prime Minister and Minister for Finance 1955; resigned office in 1958 to lead the Maltese Liberation Movement. Leader of Opposition in the House of Representatives 1962–71; Prime Minister. Minister of Commonwealth and Foreign Affairs since 1971 & Minister of the Interior since 1976. *Publications:* scientific, literary and artistic works. *Address:* Auberge de Castille, Valletta; and "Olives," Xintill Street, Tarxien, Malta, G.C.

**MIRABITO, Paul S.** American business executive. *B.* 1915. *Educ.* City Coll., N.Y.C. (BA 1935); Columbia Univ. 1935–37; N.Y. Univ. (MBA 1938). *M.* 1940, Virginia Ellen Woodstock. *S.* 2. *Daus.* 2. *Career:* Controller's Div. of City of N.Y. 1936–39; with Haskins & Sells, Certified Public Accountants. N.Y.C. 1939–42; Director of Budgets, Controller, Control Instrument Co. (subsidiary of Burroughs) 1942–52; Asst. Controller, Burroughs Corp., Detroit 1951–55, General Manager, Defence Contracts Organization 1955–60, Vice-Pres. 1960–62, Vice-President Administrative 1962–65. Vice-President and Group Executive, Federal and Special Systems Group, Burroughs Corp. 1965–68; Exec. Vice Pres. 1968–73; Pres. and Chief Operating Officer since 1973; Dir. Economic Club of Detroit; the Detroit Bank Corp. and its chief subsid. Detroit Bank and Trust Co.; Computer Business Equipment Manf. Assn. (CBEMA). *Member:* Chamber of Commerce of Greater Philadelphia (Dir.); National Security Industrial Assn.; Detroit Symphony Orchestra. *Clubs:* Detroit; Philadelphia Country; Bloomfield Hills Country (Michigan); Lost Tree (Florida). *Address:* 2687 Indian Mound South, Birmingham, Mich., 48010; and *office* Burroughs Corporation, 6071 Second Avenue, Detroit, Michigan 48232, U.S.A.

**MISRA, Sirdar Iswary Raj.** Nepalese diplomat. *B.* 1917. *Educ.* Patan High School, Katmandu; St. Zavier's College; Scottish Church College, Calcutta; Calcutta University (BL, MA). *M.* Indira Devi Khanal. *S.* Raman. *Dau.* Renu. *Career:* Sectional Head, Department of Law, 1942; Head, Buying Agency to Government of Nepal in Calcutta, 1943; Dept. of Law, Katmandu, 1945; First Secretary, Nepalese Embassy in London, 1947; Dep. Sec. Ministry of Foreign Affairs Katmandu, 1956; Registrar, Supreme Court of Nepal, 1960; Judge: Western High Court of Nepal, 1960; Supreme Court, 1961. Ambassador to France, 1965–67; Ambassador to the Court of St. James's, 1965–69; to Italy, 1967–69; to Greece, 1968–69; to Pakistan, concurrently accredited to Iran & Turkey 1969–73; Judge of Supreme Court of Nepal since 1974. *Awards:* Suprasidha Prabal Gorkha Dakshin Bahu (Nepal); Grand Officer of Merit (France); Knight Commander of the Order of Orange-Nassau (Netherlands); Officer, Legion of Honour (France). *Clubs:* Hurlingham; Combehill Golf; Royal Automobile. *Address:* 1/97 Kopundol, Lalitpur, Kathmand, Nepal.

**MITCHELL, Austin (Vernon),** MP. British Journalist & Politician. *B.* 1934. *Educ.* Woodbottom County Sch., Bingley Grammar Sch., Manchester Univ., Oxford Univ.—MA, D.Phil. *M.* (1) Patricia Dorothea Jackson. (2) Linda Mary McDougall. *S.* 1. *Daus.* 3. *Career:* Lecturer in History, Univ. of Otago, N.Z. 1959–62; Senior Lecturer in Politics, Univ. of Canterbury 1962–67; Official Fellow, Nuffield Coll., Oxford 1967–69; Journalist, Yorkshire TV, Leeds 1969–71; Presenter, BBC 1972–73; Journalist, Yorkshire TV, Leeds 1973–77; MP (Lab.) for Grimsby since 1977. *Member:* Political Studies Assoc.; National Union of Journalists. *Publications:* New Zealand Politics in Action (1962); Government by Party (1966); Politics & People in New Zealand (1969); The Whigs in Opposition (1969); The Half Gallon Quarter Acre Pavlova Paradise (1972); Yorkshire Jokes (1973); Teach Thissen Tyke. *Clubs:* Grimsby Labour Club; AEU Club, Saltaire,

Yorks. *Address:* 1 Abbey Park Road, Grimsby, Yorks.; and *office* House of Commons, London SW1A 0AA.

**MITCHELL, Lieut.-Colonel (Retd.). Colin Campbell.** British politician. *B.* 17 Nov. 1927. *Educ.* Whitgift School; Graduated Camberley Staff Coll. 1955. *M.* 1956, Jean Hamilton Susan Phillips. *S.* Lorne and Angus. *Dau.* Colina. *Career:* Served British Army, Argyll & Sutherland Highlanders, Italy 1944, Palestine 1945–48; Korea 1950–51; Cyprus, 1958–59, Borneo 1964 (Brevet Lt.-Col.), Aden 1967 (Dispatches) Service from 1943–68; Correspondent Vietnam, Writer & Journalist, 1968–70; Member of Parliament for West Aberdeenshire 1970–74; Parly. Private Secy. to Secy. of State Scotland 1972–73; Chmn. Garrison (Research and Procurement Services) Ltd.; Vice-Pres., Royal Scottish Country Dance Society; Hon. Pres. Scottish Military Collectors Society. *Publications:* Having Been A Soldier (1969). *Clubs:* Caledonian Garrick; East India; Sports & Public Schools. *Address:* 710 Hood House, Dolphin Square, London SW1V 3NJ.

**MITCHELL, David Bower,** MP. British parliamentarian. *B.* 1928. *Educ.* Aldenham School. *M.* 1954, Pamela Elaine Haward. *S.* 2. *Dau.* 1. *Career:* Farming, 1945–51; Wine Merchant since 1951; Member of Parliament, Conservative for Basingstoke since 1964; Opposition Whip, 1965–67; Secy. M.P. Cttee. Industrial Relations, 1968–70; Parly. Private Secy. to Rt. Hon. Sir Keith Joseph 1970–74; Chmn. Cons. Smaller Business Cttee. since 1973. *Address:* 46 Eaton Terrace, London, S.W.1; and *office* 1 Hare Place, London, E.C.4.

**MITCHELL, James William,** TD. South African. *B.* 1920. *Educ.* Hull Grammar School. *M.* 1939, Beatrice Phoebe Smith. *Dau.* Wendy. *Career:* Chmn. Transcape Steels Pty. Ltd., Valley Earth Moving Pty. Ltd., and Melody Investment Trust. *Club:* Western Province Sports (Cape Town). *Address:* Ken Heights, Hout Bay, Cape; and *office* 2516, Trust Bank Centre, Heerengracht, Cape Town, South Africa.

**MITCHELL, Richard Charles,** MP. British. *B.* 1927. *Educ.* Southampton Univ., BSc (Econ); Postgraduate Certificate in Education. *M.* 1950, Doreen Gregory, *S.* 1. *Dau.* 1. *Career:* Schoolmaster & Deputy Headmaster 1953–66; Member, Southampton City Council 1955–67; Labour MP for Southampton Test 1966–70, for Southampton Itchen since 1971; PPS to Sec. of State for Prices & Consumer Affairs 1974–76; Member of European Parliament since 1975; Member, Bureau of Socialist Group in European Parliament. *Member:* National Union of Teachers; Municipal & General Workers Union; Fabian Society. *Address:* 49 Devonshire Road, Polygon, Southampton.

**MIYAMOTO, Kenji.** Japanese Politician. *B.* 1908. *Educ.* Tokyo Imperial Univ. *Career:* Member, Communist Party of Japan since 1931, Central Cttee. since 1933, Gen. Sec. of Central Cttee. since 1958, Chmn. Presidium Central Cttee. since 1970. *Address:* Central Committee of the Communist Party of Japan, Sendagaya 4-chome 26, Shibuya-ku, Tokyo, Japan.

**MOBERLY, John Campbell,** CMG. British Diplomat. *B.* 1925. *Educ.* Winchester Coll.; Magdalen Coll., Oxford—BA. *M.* 1959, Patience Proby. *S.* 2. *Dau.* 1. *Career:* War Service Royal Navy 1943–47; entered HM Foreign (later Diplomatic) Service 1950; served in Bahrain, Kuwait, Qatar, Greece & London 1950–68; Canadian Nat. Defence Coll., Kingston, Ont. 1968–69; Counsellor, British Embassy, Washington D.C. 1969–73; Dir., Middle East Centre for Arab Studies, Shemlan, Lebanon 1973–75; HM Ambassador, Amman since 1975. *Decorations:* Mentioned in Despatches, 1945; Companion, Order of St. Michael & St. George, 1976. *Clubs:* Travellers'; RAC; Leander (Henley-on-Thames). *Address:* c/o Foreign & Commonwealth Office, London, SW1.

**MODALSLI, Jakob.** Norwegian civil servant. *B.* 1 April 1911. *Educ.* Agricultural High School (Cand. agric.). *M.* 1943, Helga Hansen. *S.* 1. *Career:* Secy., Norwegian Agricultural Price Central 1936–41; Secretary, Ministry of Supply 1941–45; Manager of Office, Min. of Supply 1945–47; Gen. Sec., Norwegian Farmers' Union 1947–49; Dir., Export and Import Department, Ministry of Trade 1949–52; Permanent Secretary of Defence 1952–66; Director, The Directorate of Construction & Property 1960–61; Permanent Secy. of Defence 1962–66; County Governor, Ostfold since 1966. *Address:* Dronningensg, 1 Moss, Norway.

**MODREY, Joseph.** *B.* 1916. *Educ.* Columbia Univ. (BS; MS in ME; RPI; DEng.). *M.* 1944. Evelyn Tabery. *S.* Jon Tabery. *Dau.* Laurie. *Career:* Design engineer (aircraft engines and gas turbines) Wright Aeronautical Corp. 1938–47; Professor in charge of Machine Design, Polytechnic Institute of Brooklyn 1947–55; Professor of Mechanical Engineering, Purdue University, June 1965—. Chmn., Department of Mechanical Engineering, Union College, Schenectady, N.Y. 1955–63; National Chmn. Mechanical Engineering Division, American Society for Engineering Education, June 1960—. *Publications:* Creative Engineering; Analysis of Highly Complex Kinematic Systems; Crankshaft Stresses and Deflections. Awarded National Science Foundation Faculty Fellowship, 1959. Visiting Lecturer Imperial Coll. 1962–63. *Member:* Amer. Socy. for Engineering Education; Amer. Socy. of Mechanical Engineering; Socy. of Automotive Engineers; Sigma Xi; Pi Tau Sigma. *Address:* Department of Mechanical Engineering, Purdue University, West Lafayette, Ind. 47907, U.S.A.

**MOHLMAN, Robert Henry.** AB, JD, MBA. American. *B.* 1918. *Educ.* Univ. of Chicago (AB JD); Harvard Graduate School, Business Admin (M.B.A.). *Career:* Vice Pres. Inland Container Corp. since 1966; Dir. & Corp. Vice Pres. Finance & Admin. Ball Corp.; Dir. Kent. Plastics UK; Avery Laurence (Singapore) Pte. Ltd.; Ball Bros. Research Corp.; Co-Man. Dir. Ball A.G. *Address: office* 345 South High Street, Muncie, Ind., U.S.A.

**MOHR, Milton Ernst.** American. *B.* 1915. *Educ.* Univ. of Nebraska (BS 1938). *M.* 1938, Vyvian Crane. *S.* Lawrence H. and Douglas C. *Career:* Department Head, Radar Laboratory, Hughes Aircraft Co., California 1950–54; Vice-Pres. and Gen. Manager, TRW Computer Div., TRW Inc. 1954–64. With Bunker-Ramo Corp.: Vice-President, General Manager Industrial Systems Division 1964–65, and Defense Systems Div. 1965–66 (Pres. 1966–68). Chairman of the Board, The Bunker-Ramo Corp., July 1968–69, President & Chief Exec. 1969–70; Pres. and Chief Exec. Officer Quotron Systems Inc. (formerly Scantlin Electronics, Inc.) since 1971. Hon. DEng. Univ. of Nebraska 1959; Honourable mention outstanding young electrical engineer award, Eta Kappa Nu, 1948. *Member:* Inst. of Electrical and Electronic Engineers (Fellow); Amer. Inst. of Aeronautics and Astronautics; Pi Mu Epsilon; Sigma Tau; Eta Kappa Nu. *Address:* 5454 Beethoven Street Los Angeles, Calif., U.S.A.

**MOLDEN, Fritz P.** Austrian publisher. *B.* 1924. *Educ.* High School, Vienna, and Universities of Vienna and Innsbruck. *M.* Hanna Bernhard. *S.* 2. *Daus.* 3. *Career:* Military Service in World War II; Personal Secy. to Austrian Minister of Foreign Affairs 1945–46; journalistic activity with Die Presse 1946–48; diplomatic service, New York 1948–49; Man. Dir., Die Presse 1950; Chmn.: Neue Wiener Presse Druck- und Verlagsgesellschaft m.b.H. 1953–61, Express Verlagsgesellschaft m.b.H. 1958–60 1962–70 and 1965–70. Verlag Fritz Molden Grossdruckerei u. Verlag G.m.b.H. Publisher: Die Presse 1953–56; Wochen-Presse 1953–61; Express 1958–60. Publisher: "Wiener Wochenblatt"; Chairman, Fritz Molden Verlag, Vienna; President Verlag Fritz Molden A.G. (book publishing) Zurich, and Verlag Fritz Molden Ges. m.b.H. (book publishing) Munich; Pres., Eroica Ges. m.b.H., Vienna. *Awards:* Officer, Order of Christ (Portugal); Medal of Freedom (U.S.); Hon. Major, Passeirer Schützen. *Publications:* "Ungarns Freiheitskampf", Vienna 1956; "Fepolinski & Waschlapski auf dem Berstenden Stern", Vienna 1976; frequent articles and editorials in Die Presse and Wochen-Presse. *Address:* Eroicagasse 1, Vienna XIX, and *office* Sandgasse 33, Vienna XIX, Austria.

**MOLLER, Dr. George.** Canadian (naturalized) Chartered Accountant and business consultant. *B.* 1903. *Educ.* University of Prague (Dr. Juris.); Institute of Chartered Accountants of Ontario (FCA) (Past Member of Cncl.); Society of Industrial & Cost Accountants (RIA) (Past member, Board of Directors). *M.* 1931, Edith Berger. *S.* Wayne Brian. *Career:* Law practice in Prague; Manager, Bohemian Union Bank, Prague, 1928–39; Office Manager, Tru-Lite Ltd., Toronto, and Armaco Ltd., Toronto and Acton, Ontario, 1939–42; Former Chartered Accountant, George A. Touche & Co., Toronto; Vice-Pres. H. H. Robertson & Co. Ltd. (Hamilton, Ont.) 1949–70; Past Treas. and Dir. Financial Executives Inst. of Canada; Secy.-Treas. IAFEI Int. Assoc. Fin. Execs. Insts. (Zurich); Governor, Hamilton Philharmonic; Consultant and Dir., H. H. Rerobtson Co. Ltd., Robertson Building Systems Ltd.. Pres., Hansada Ltd.: Dir., Mayfield Investments Ltd.; Consultant, Dom. Auto Accessories Ltd., Buck Bros. Ltd., & Assoc. Companies. Special Sen. Lect. Univ. of Toronto. *Publications:* numerous articles on taxation cost accountancy and management in Financial Executive,

Cost & Management, The Canadian Chartered Accountant, The Tax Review, Tax Bulletin, Burlington Gazette, etc. *Address:* 3164 Princess Boulevard, Burlington, Ont., Canada.

**MØLLER, Hans Severin.** Danish Diplomat. *B.* 1918. *Educ.* Univ. of Copenhagen—LLM. *M.* 1951, Ursule Dufort. *S.* 3. *Career:* Joined Danish Foreign Service 1945; Sec. Legation, Moscow 1948; Private Sec. to Foreign Minister 1953, & to Prime Minister 1955; attended negotiations with leading Soviet politicians during Prime Minister's visit to USSR, 1956; Chargé d'Affaires, Athens 1958; Minister, Chief of Protocol, Copenhagen 1963; Ambassador in Prague 1969; Ambassador in Algiers & Tunis 1974; Ambassador in the German Democratic Republic since 1976; mem., Delegation to the UN 25th (1970), 28th (1973) & 32nd (1977) General Assemblies. *Decorations:* Various Danish & Foreign Decorations. *Publications:* Articles in the Danish Press. *Clubs:* Assoc. of Royal Hussars; Assoc. of Cavalry Officers out of active service. *Address:* Gotlandstrasse 16, 1071 Berlin; and *office* Unter den Linden 41, 108 Berlin-Mitte, German Democratic Republic.

**MOLLER, Maersk Mc-Kinney.** Danish. *B.* 1913. *M.* 1940, Emma Marie Neergaard Rasmussen. *Daus.* 3. *Career:* Partner, A. P. Moller since 1940; Chmn. and Chief Exec. Officer, A. P. Moller, Copenhagen comprising Steamship Company of 1912 Ltd., Steamship Company Svendborg Ltd., Maersk Line A/S, *Chairman,* Odense Steel Shipyard Ltd., Disa A/S, Tanganyika Planting Co. Ltd., Danish Shipping Board. *Director:* International Business Machines Corp. *Member:* International Council of Morgan Guaranty Trust Co. *Address:* 8 Kongens Nytorv, DK-1098 Copenhagen K, Denmark.

**MØLLER, Orla Reinhardt.** Danish Politician. *B.* 1916. *Educ.* Master of Divinity. *M.* 1940. Minna Cecilie Hansen Aarrebo. *S.* 4. *Dais.* 2. *Career:* Vicar in Borum-Lyngby 1942–46; Perpetual curate at the Church of Ansgar, Aarlborg 1946–51; Sec.-Gen. of the Danish YMCA & YWCA 1951–56; Vicar in Hasseris 1956–65; Perpetual curate in Hasseris 1965–66; Minister for Ecclesiastical Affairs 1966–68; Minister of Defence, Sep.-Dec. 1973; Political spokesman & Chmn. of the Social Democratic Parly. group 1971–73; Chmn. of the Defence Commission & mem. of the Broadcasting Council 1971–73 & 1973–75; Minister of Justice & Defence 1975–77. *Member:* Hasseris parish council 1958–63; Bd. of Danish Youth Council 1950–57; Bd. of Reps. of the Ecumenic Joint Council in Denmark 1952–56; Joint League of National Church Orgs. 1952–56; Bd. of the Home Mission 1952–56; Chmn. of the Bd., YMCA & YWCA Athletic League & mem. of the Bd. of the Danish Athletic League 1959–61. *Publications:* Various books & articles on theological subjects. *Clubs:* Masonic Lodge. *Address:* Slotsholmsgade 10, 1216 Copenhagen K, Denmark.

**MOLSON, Rt. Hon. Lord** (Hugh Molson), PC (Unionist). *B.* 1903. *Educ.* Naval Colleges of Osborne and Dartmouth; Lancing, New College, Oxford. *M.* 1949, Nancy Astington. *Career:* Doncaster 1931–35, High Peak Div. of Derbyshire 1939–61; Parly. Sec. Min. of Works, 1951–53; Joint Parly. Secretary, Ministry of Transport and Civil Aviation 1953–57; Minister of Works 1957–59; Member of the Monckton Commission on Rhodesia and Nyasaland, 1960; Chmn., Commn. of Privy Councillors on the dispute between Buganda and and Bunyoro, 1962; Chmn. Council Protection of Rural England 1968–71, Pres. since 1971. *Clubs:* Athenaeum, Carlton. *Address:* 14 Wilton Crescent, London, S.W.1.; and Cherrytrees, Kelso, Roxburghshire.

**MOLTKE, Carl Adam Christian.** Danish administrator. *B.* 17 Feb. 1907. *Educ.* University of Copenhagen (Cand. jur.). *M.* 1940, Hélène Huyssen van Kattendyke. *S.* 2. *Daus.* 2. *Career:* With Ministry of Justice 1932; Ministry of Interior 1933; Secretary, Danish Country Municipalities Association 1942–46; Prefect of Copenhagen and Chairman, Port of Copenhagen Authority 1945–77; Chmn. Copenhagen Free Port Co. Ltd. 1975–77; Member of Executive Board Danish anti-Tuberculosis Association since 1946 (Vice-Chmn. 1960); President, Danish Mental Health Association 1948–71; Member Exec. Bd. 1971–73; Member, Exec. Board, Danish Boy Scouts 1946–70: Hon. Treas. Danish Royal Orders 1970, Chamberlain since 1977. *Awards:* Commander (1st Class) Order of Dannebrog, Order of St. Olav (Norway), Order of North Star (Sweden), Order of Crown (Thailand), Order of Merit (Italy). *Address:* Nyropsgade 24, Copenhagen, Denmark.

**MONAHAN, DeLong Haviland.** *B.* 1904. *Educ.* Dartmouth College (AB) and Tuck School of Administration and Finance. *M.* 1950, Barbara L. Greenwood. *Career:* With New England Telephone & Telegraph Co. 1925–28; with Scudder, Stevens & Clark, N.Y.C. 1928–32; with Provident Mutual Life Insurance Co. 1932–67. Retired Financial Vice-President, Provident Mutual Life Insurance Co. of Philadelphia 1946–67. *Club:* Merion Golf. *Address:* The Regency Creek Drive, St. Davids, Pa. 19087, U.S.A.

**MONDALE, Walter Frederick.** American Politician. *B.* 1928. *Educ.* Univ. of Minnesota; Univ. of Minnesota Law Sch. (LLB). *Career:* Attorney-Gen., Minnesota 1960–64; Senator from Minnesota 1964–76; Democratic nominee for the Vice-Presidency 1976; inaugurated Vice-Pres. of the U.S.A. Jan. 1977. Former member: President's Consumer Advisory Council; Exec. Bd., National Assn. of Attorneys General, etc. Democrat-Farmer-Labor. *Address:* The White House, Washington, D.C., U.S.A.

**MONEY, Robert,** OBE, JP. Australian. *B.* 1904. *M.* 1928, Florence Minerva. *Career:* Director, The Equity Trustees Executors & Agency Co. Ltd., and 6 subsidiaries; Chairman: Reg Hunt-Rhodes Group; Dir. Slough Estates (Australia) Ltd. *Fellow:* Australian Institute of Accountants, and Institute of Directors; Fellow of Exec. & Trustee Institute. *Clubs:* Athenaeum; R.A.C.V.; Commonwealth Golf (all Melbourne). *Address:* 3 Hertford Crescent, Balwyn, Australia.

**MONICK, Emmanuel,** L. en D., L. ès L. General-Inspector of Finance; French banker. *Educ.* Sorbonne. *M.* 1920. *Daus.* 2. *Career:* Financial Attaché, Embassy, Washington 1930–34, London 1934–40; General-Secretary of the French Residency in Morocco 1940–41; General Secretary of the French Treasury 1944; Governor, Bank of France 1944–49; Chairman, Banque de Paris et des Pays-Bas S.A. 1950–61; Hon. Chairman 1962—. *Address:* Banque de Paris et des Pays-Bas S.A., 3 Rue d'Antin, 75002 Paris, France.

**MONNET, Jean.** French. *B.* 1888. *Educ.* Cognac Coll. Dep. Secy.-Gen. League of Nations 1918. Chmn. Franco-British Economic Co-ordination Cttee. 1939; helped in organization for common defence programme 1940; Member British Supply Cncl., Washington 1940–43; Commissioner for Supplies, French National Liberation Cttee. 1943–44. Created the Monet Plan 1947; Gen. Commissioner, Plan for French modernisation and equipment of France 1947. Pres.: preparatory conference of Schuman Plan 1950, and of European Coal and Steel Community 1952–55. Chairman Action Committee for a United States of Europe 1956–75. Hon. G.B.E. 1947 Hon. CH 1972. Recipient doctorates and awards, including Wateler Peace Prize 1951, Charlemagne Prize 1953, Freedom Award 1963, Emile Cornez Prize 1963 U.S. Presidential Medal of Freedom 1963; Family of Man Award for Peace (1965); Robert Schuman Prize (1966); Socy. for the Family of Man Award (1967); Comite D'Action pour Les Etat-Unis D'Europe. *Publications:* Les Etats Unis d'Europe ont commencé. *Address:* Houjarray, par Montfort l'Amaury, Seine et Oise, France.

**MONNIN, Hon. Mr. Justice Alfred Maurice.** *B.* 1920. *Educ.* BA; LLB; QC. *M.* 1942, Denise Pelletier. *S.* 5. *Career:* Served in World War II (Canadian Infantry Corps) 1942–45; general practice of law 1946–57; formerly with Mr. J. T. Beaubien (lately until his death Mr. Justice Beaubien); Law firm of Monnin, Grafton, Deniset, Dowhan, Betournay & Muldoon until appointment to present post. Judge of the Court of Queen's Bench of Manitoba 1957–1962, when elevated to Manitoba Court of Appeal. *Address:* Judges' Chambers, The Law Courts, Winnipeg, Man., Canada.

**MONSEN, Thorleif.** Canadian. President, Aall & Co. Ltd. 1950—. *B.* 1910. *M. S.* Mads Erik and Thomas John. *Daus.* Tove and Guri. *Award:* Sankt Olavs (Norway). Hon. Consul General to Norway in Japan. *Clubs:* Royal Norwegian Yacht (Oslo); Layford Cay (Bahamas); Three Hundred, Tokyo (Japan). *Address: office* Hatobacho, Ikuta-ku, Kobe, Japan.

**MONSON, Sir William Bonnar Leslie,** KCMG, CB. K.St.J. British Diplomatic Service (ret.). *B.* 1912. *Educ.* Edinburgh Academy and Hertford College, Oxford; BA (Oxon). *M.* 1948, Helen Isobel Browne. *Career:* Chief Secy., West African Council 1947–51; Asst. Under-Secy. of State, Colonial Office 1052–64; British High Commissioner, Zambia 1964–66;; Asst. Under-Secy. of State, Commonwealth Office 1966–67; Deputy Under-Secy. of State, Foreign & Commonwealth Office, London, Sept. 1967–72; Director Overseas Relations, St. John Ambulance H.Q. since 1975. *Club:* United Oxford & Cambridge University (London). *Address:* Golf House, Goffers Road, Blackheath, London, S.E.3.

**MONTAGNE, Adhemar.** Peruvian diplomat. *B.* 1911. *Educ;* in Peru & Italy. *M. Dau.* 1. *Career:* Entered Diplomatic Service, 1932; Vice-Consul, Milan, 1932–37; Consul, Milan, 1937–42. Concul-General, Havana, 1942–44; First Secretary, Washington, 1944–47; Consul-General, Genoa, 1947–57; Minister Plenipotentiary, Beirut, 1957–62; Chief of Protocol, Ministry of Foreign Affairs, Lima, 1962–64; Ambassador: To Rabat, 1964–67; to Montevideo, 1967–69; to the Court of St James's, 1969–77. *Address:* c/o Ministry of Foreign Affairs, Lima, Peru.

**MONTAGU, Alexander Victor Edward Paulet.** Formerly Earl of Sandwich, the title he has disclaimed. *B.* 1906. *Educ.* Eton; Cambridge (MA Nat Sc). *M.* 1934, Rosemary Peto (marriage dissolved 1958). *S.* 2. *Daus.* 4. *Career:* Served in World War II, in France from 1940 (Major 1942); MP (as Viscount Hinchingbrooke) (Con., S. Dorset) 1941–62; Contested Accrington Divn. of Lancashire 1964; Private Secy. to Rt. Hon. Stanley Baldwin 1932–34; Treasurer, Junior Imperial League 1934–35; Chairman, Tory Reform Cttee. 1943–44. President, Anti Common Market League, 1962—; Chmn. Conservative Trident Group since 1973. *Address:* Mapperton, Beaminster, Dorset.

**MONTAGU, Hon. David Charles Samuel.** British banker. *B.* 1928. *Educ.* Eton and Trinity College, Cambridge (BA). *M.* 1951, Christiane Françoise Dreyfus. *S.* Charles Edgar Samuel. *Daus.* Fiona Yvonne and Nicole Mary. *Career:* Chairman & Chief Executive Orion Bank Ltd.; Dir. Orion Pacific Ltd.; Drayton Commercial Investment Co. Ltd., London Weekend Television; Rothmans International Ltd.; Carreras-Rothmans Ltd., United British Securities Trust, Second United British Securities Trust, Derby Trust Ltd. (Chairman), Ashdown Investment Trust Ltd., Trades Union Unit Trust Managers Ltd. *Clubs:* Turf, Portland, Pratt's (all of London). *Address:* 25 Kingston House, South Ennismore Gardens. London, S.W.1; and *office* 1 London Wall, London, E.C.2, and The Kremlin, Newmarket.

**MONTEITH, Alexander Crawford.** USA Citizen. Electrical engineer. *B.* 1902. *Educ.* Queen's Univ., Kingston, Ont., Canada (BS in EE; Hon LLD). *M.* 1930, Evelyn Smith. *S.* Alexander Henry and William Frederick. *Dau.* Susanne Elizabeth. *Career:* Registered Engineer, Pennsylvania; Senior Vice-President, (Retd.) Westinghouse Electric Corporation, Pittsburgh, Pa. Hon. degrees: LLD, Queen's Univ., Kingston, Ont.; DSc Lafayette Coll. (Easton, Pa.); DEng Drexel Institute of Technology (Philadelphia); and Carnegie Institute of Technology (Pittsburgh). *Awards:* Westinghouse Order of Merit 1940; Award to Executives, Amer. Socy. for Testing Metals 1962; Washington Award 1962; Edison Medallist for 1962. Fellow, Inst. Electrical and Electronic Engineers; *Hon. Member:* Amer. Socy. Mechanical Engrs.; Natl. Electrical Mfrs. Assn. (Pres. 1964–65); National Academy of Engineering. *Address:* South Orleans Box 557, Mass. 02662, U.S.A.

**MONTEITH, Hon. Jay Waldo,** PC, FCA. Canadian Privy Councillor. *B.* 1903. *Educ.* Stratford Public Schools and Collegiate Institute; Trinity College, University of Toronto (CA Degree). *M.* 1936, Mary B. Strudley. *Daus.* Sally (Wismer), Nancy (Freeman) and Mary (Jardine). *Career:* Senior Partner, Monteith, Monteith & Co., Chartered Accountants, Stratford, Ont. 1938. Alderman, Stratford 1939–41; Mayor of Stratford 1944–45; Member, Public Utilities Commission, Stratford 1946–50 (Chmn. 1947–50); President, Ontario Municipal Electrical Association (Dist No. 6) 1950; Secretary and Director, Farquharson-Gifford Ltd., Stratford 1951–57; President and Director, James Lloyd & Son, Ltd., Stratford 1946–57; Minister of National Health and Welfare Aug. 1957–63; Member of Parliament (Progressive Conservative) for Perth constituency 1953–72; Chmn., Perth County Historical Foundation, 1964–67; Bd. Governors, Stratford Shakespearean Festival Foundation of Canada, 1967–73. Hon. Dr. of Laws, Univ. of Western Ontario. Fellow Chartered Accountant. *Clubs:* Rideau (Ottawa); Stratford Golf and Country; Mason. *Address:* 145 Kemp Crescent Stratford Ontario N5A 5C2, Canada.

**MONTGOMERY, Jeff.** American. *B.* 1920. *Educ.* Graduated from High School 1937; Texas A & M College (BS Petroleum Eng. 1941); Harvard Graduate School of Administration; George Washington University Law School (LLB 1948). *M.* 1944, Leonora Ryan. *S.* Franklin Jefferson and John Noland. *Daus.* Bethany Rebecca and Catherine Melinda. *Career:* Major U.S.A.A.F.—Military Service 1942–45. Practised Law (Klapproth, Hamilton & Montgomery), Midland, Tex. 1948–50; Manager, Texas Crude Oil Co., Fort Worth, Tex. 1950–53; Vice-Pres. and Dir., Murmanill Corp., Dallas, Tex. 1954–56. Editor: Texas A & M Engineer and George Washington Law Review; President and Director, Kirby Petroleum Co., Houston, Tex. 1956—. Director, Florida Gas Co., Winter Park, Fla. 1966—. Chairman, Welfare Committee, Salvation Army Advisory Board 1965. Director, Planned Parenthood of Houston 1967–73. Trustee, First Unitarian Church, Houston 1961–65. *Member:* Order of the Coif; Tau Beta Pi; Amer. Inst. Mining, Metallurgical & Petroleum Engineers; Texas Mid-Continent Oil & Gas Assn. (Dir.); Independent Petroleum Assn. of America (Dir.); Amer. Inst. Management (mem. President's Council); Young Presidents Organization; Amer .Bar Assn., and Member State Bar of Texas. Republican. *Club:* Ramada (Houston). *Address:* 2212 Del Monte Drive, Houston, Texas 77019, U.S.A.

**MONTGOMERY, Robert Alexander Arnulf.** Investment broker. *B.* 1911. *Educ.* Harvard Univ. (AB *cum laude* 1933). *M.* (1) 1948, Sonya Paris. (Div.) *S.* Robert Leaming. *Dau.* Alexandra (Dial). (2) 1972, Murray McIlvaine (Taylor) Schoettle. *Career:* Pres., Pennsylvania Planning Assn. 1953–54; Chmn., Southeastern Penna Planning Commission 1954–58; Alternate Delegate, Republican National Convention 1952–56–60; Chmn., Young Republicans, Delaware County 1950–52. Lieut.-Commander U.S.N.R. (retired 1953). Member of Janney Montgomery Scott Inc. of Philadelphia. Member: Board of Managers, Episcopal Hospital, Philadelphia (Pres. 1953–55); Board of Trustees, Temple University, Philadelphia; Curator, Ordnance Museum, Valley Forge Military Academy (Wayne, Pa.). *Clubs:* Philadelphia, Midday (both of Philadelphia). *Address:* Newtown Road, Villa Nova, Pa.; and *office* Five Penn Center Plaza, Philadelphia, Pa. 19103, U.S.A.

**MONTI, Attilio.** Italian Industrialist (petrol refining). *B.* 1906. *Dau.* Marisa Signor Bruno Riffeser. *Career:* Founded and administered commercial and industrial concerns since 1922; Deputy Administrator: Sarom S.p.A. 1951—; Pres. Pibimare S.p.A., de Navigazione 1963—; Poligrafici 'Il Resto del Carlino' S.p.A. 1966—; Società Editoriale 'Il Resto del Carlino' S.p.A. 1967—; Società Editoriale 'La Nazione' S.p.A. 1967—; Società Editrice 'Il Telegrafo'-S.E.I.T.-S.p.A. 1967—; Eridania Zuccherifici Nazionali S.p.A. 1967—; S.I.S. Società per Azioni 1968—; Galfa S.p.A. 1968—; Il Giornale d'Italia, S.p.A. 1969—; Hon. Chairman: Mediterranea S.p.A. Raffineria Siciliana Petroli 1966—. Vice-President: Sariaf S.p.A. 1956; Counsellor of Administration: BP Italiana, S.p.A. 1959—; Gruppo Industrie Alimentari S.p.A. 1961—; Industrie Agricole Ligure Lombarda S.p.A. 1966—; Ligure Lombarda per I.M.C.A. 1968—. *Awards:* Cavaliere del Lavoro, Cavaliere di Gran Croce al merito della Republica Italiana; Cavaliere de Grazia Magistrale (Gran Priorato di Roma); del Sovrano; Militare Ordine di Malta. *Address: office* Grattacielo 'Galfa', Via-Gen. Fara 41, Milan, Italy.

**MONTROSE, Maynard E.** American business executive; *B.* 1903. *Educ.* General Electric Engng. School (Elec. Eng.). *M.* 1926, Mary E. McGrath. *Career:* Petroleum Industry Specialist; Gen. Electric Co. 1925–29; Manager, General Electric Co., Shreveport, La., 1929–35; Director, Vice-President, Lane-Wells Co. 1935–45; President, General Manager, Director, Marion Power Shovel Co. 1945–47; Senior Vice-Pres., Hughes Tool Co., Pres., Hughes Oil Tool Div. 1945–68; Director, American Petroleum Inst. 1953–57; and 1966–67; Hughes Tool Co. Ltd., London; Hughes Tool Co., Houston, Texas; Rosemont Enterprises Inc. Nevada. Texas-National Bank of Commerce, Houston; Dir. and Past-Pres., Petroleum Equipment Suppliers Assn; mem. Natl. Petroleum Council 1956; Director, Welex Jet Services 1948–75; Director Energy Research & Education Foundation, 1969–75. *Address:* P.O. Box 1342, Rancho, Santa Fe, California 92067, U.S.A.

**MOODIE, Colin Troup.** Australian Diplomat. *B.* 1913. *Educ.* St. Peter's Coll., Adelaide; Univ. of Adelaide—LLB. *M.* 1954, Hilaire Davenport. *S.* 1. *Daus.* 2 *Career:* Joined Dept. of External Affairs, Canberra 1937; Private Sec. to Hon. R. L. Casey, Treasurer 1938–39; Australian Military Forces 1941–43; Official Sec., Aust. High Comm, India 1944–47; served Washington, London, Rangoon (Minister, from 1956 Ambassador) 1950–57; Dept. of External Affairs, Canberra 1957–66 & 1970–72; Ambassador to the Netherlands 1966–70, to South Africa 1972–75; High Commissioner to New Zealand since 1975. *Club:* Commonwealth (Canberra). *Address:* 12

Fowlers Road, Glen Osmond, South Australia; and *office* Australian High Commission, Wellington, New Zealand.

**MOONMAN, Eric.** MP. British. *B.* 1929. *Educ.* MSc Management Science. *M.* 1962, Jane. *S.* 2. *Dau.* 1. *Career:* Northern Mgr., Daily Mirror 1954–56; British Inst. of Management, Human Relations Adviser 1956–62; Senior Research Fellow, Univ. of Manchester 1964–66; Labour MP for Billericay 1966–70, and for Basildon since 1974. *Member:* British Inst. of Management; British Inst. of Personnel Management. *Publications:* The Manager & the Organization (1960); European Science & Technology (1966); Communication in an Expanding Organization (1968); Reluctant Partnership (1969). *Address:* 1 Beacon Hill, London N.7.; and House of Commons, London SW1.

**MOORE, Earle T.** Canadian business executive. *B.* 1907 *Educ.* Strathcona Academy, Montreal. *M.* 1930. Nora G. Lehane. *S.* Earle C. *Dau.* Geraldine E. *Career:* Chairman of the Board, Moore Brothers Machinery Co. Ltd., 1942—. Past Pres. Boy Scouts of Can. (Que.) 1957–67; internat. commissioner 1952–63; Mem. Exec. Cttee. Montreal Bd. Trade, 1961–62; Dir. E. F. Walter & Co.; Past Pres. Royal Commonwealth Socy. Montreal; Life Governor & Member, Executive, Antiguan & Numismatic Society, Montreal; Alderman T.M.R. 1951–54. Baie d'Urfé, Que. 1956–57; Candidate for Prog. Con. Party, 1951; Gov. Mtl. Diocesan Theological Coll.; Member, Anglican Synod.; Newcomen Socy.; Heraldic Socy.; Scottish Rite; Life member Masonic Order; National Dir. English Speaking Union & Chmn. Montreal Branch; Past Pres., Que. Museum's Association. (Past-pres.) Comm. Travellers' Assn.; Vintage Auto Club; Antique Aeroplane Assn.; Dir. Canadian Heritage Socy., (Past-Pres.) Down-Town Citizens' Assn.; Mem. Bd. of Governors Dioc. Theol. Coll. and Provincial Synod; Dir. E. W. Walter Ltd and other Assns. and Cos. Hon. Pres., Rawdon Art Circle. Owner of Canadian Restored Village, Rawdon, Quebec. *Awards:* Silver Wolf, Boy Scouts Can. 1953; Centennial medal awarded by Fed. Govt. for Services to Canada 1967. *Clubs:* Mount Stephen; Montreal Rotary (Past Pres.); Farmers', Montreal (Pres.). *Address: office* 8455 Decarie Boulevard, Montreal, P.Q., Canada.

**MOORE, Lyle Howard,** CBE. Australian company director. *B.* 8 Dec. 1899. *Educ.* Sydney Grammar School. *M.* (1) 1923, Phyllis Evans Goulding, (2) Patricia Lillian Rickards. *S.* Robert Lyle. *Daus.* June Isabel Louise, Shirley Phyllis, Margaret Ruth. *Career:* Jointly founded real estate firm, Moore Bros., 1927; Alderman, Municipal Council, Hunter's Hill 1931–35, Woollahara 1936–47, Mayor of Woollahara 1940–41; President, Real Estate Institute of N.S.W. 1945–49; Created Life-Fellow Real Estate Institute N.S.W. 1966; Mem. Bd. Dir. of Real Estate Institute 1942 to present day and still serving; Mem. of the Australian Executives of the Real Estate & Stock Institute of Australia 1944–74; Pres. and Fellow 1947–56 inclusive; Director, H. W. Horning & Co. Pty. Ltd. since 1945; Foundation Mem., Liberal Party of Australia; State President for N.S.W. Liberal Party 1950–56, and member of Federal Executive Council 1949–66; Federal Pres., Liberal Party of Australia 1956–60; Fed. Trustee, Liberal Party of Australia 1956—; Mem., Auctioneers & Agents Council of N.S.W. 1949—, elected Chmn. 1966; Dir., Eagle Star Insurance Co., N.S.W. until 1971, (Chmn. 1966); Chmn. of Dirs., Red Cedars Motels Pty. Ltd.; Life Member & Pres., Sydney Grammar School O.B. Union 1954–56. *Clubs:* Sydney; Killara Bowling; Chatswood Bowling; Executive Dir., Real Estate and Stock Institute of Australia, 1969—. *Address: office* 72, Pitt Street, Sydney, N.S.W., Australia.

**MOORE, Maurice Thompson.** American lawyer. *B.* 16 Mar. 1896. *Educ.* Trinity Univ., Texas (AB); Columbia Univ. (MA, LLB). *M.* 1926, Elisabeth Luce. *S.* Maurice Thompson, Michael Moore. *Career:* Partner, Cravath Swaine & Moore 1926—; Dir., Time Inc. 1939–70, Chmn. of the Bd. 1942–60, Advisory Dir. 1970–76; Dir. Chemical Bank, New York Trust Co., 1949–68; (Advisory Dir. 1968–74); Chmn. of Trustees, Columbia University 1955–67; Trustee Emeritus Columbia Univ.; Trustee, Trinity Univ. 1944–67; Advisory Trustee, Trinity Univ. *Address:* 1000 Park Avenue, New York; and *office* 1 Chase Manhattan Plaza, New York, N.Y. 10005, U.S.A.

**MOORES, The Hon. Frank Duff,** MHA. Premier of Newfoundland. *B.* 1933. *Educ.* United Church Academy Carbonear; St. Andrew's Coll. Aurora, Ontario. *M.* 1973, Janice Johnson. *S.* 2 (1 by previous marriage). *Daus.* 6 (by previous marriage). *Career:* Pres. North Eastern Fish Industries Ltd. 1965–68; Elected to House of Commons, P.C. Member for Bonavista, Trinity-Conception 1968–71; Pres. P.C. Party in Canada 1969–70; Elected member, Humber West 1971–72, Re-elected 1972, 1975; Sworn in, First Progressive Premier, Newfoundland and Labrador since 1972. *Member:* Fisheries Council of Canada; Frozen Fish Trades Assn.; Governor, College of Fisheries, Navigation, Marine Engineering and Electronics. Hon. LLD, Memorial Univ. *Clubs:* Masonic Order and Kiwanis; Harbour Grace Recreation Centre. *Address;* Confederation Building, Ss. John's Newfoundland, Canada.

**MOOTHAM, Sir Orby Howell.** British lawyer. *B.* 17 Feb. 1901. *Educ.* private; London University (MScEcon). *M.* (1) 1931, Maria Augusta Elisabeth Niemöller (*deceased*). *S.* Dolf Cecil. *Dau.* Beatrix Eirene. (2) 1977, Beatrix Douglas, widow of Basil Ward, FRIBA. *Career:* Called to the Bar, Inner Temple 1926; Honorary Bencher, 1958; practised as Advocate of the Rangoon High Court 1927–41; Deputy Judge Advocate-General, Army in Burma, June 1941–May 1942; Assistant Judge Advocate-General, G.H.Q. (India) 1942–43; Chief Judicial Officer, British Military Administration, Burma, Jan. 1944–Nov. 1945 (dispatches); Judge, Rangoon High Court from Dec. 1945–Apr. 1946; Judge, High Court of Judicature, Allahabad 1946–55; (Chief Justice, Jan. 1955–61); Chmn., Allahabad Univ. Enquiry Cttee. 1953–54; Chmn., Medical Appeals Tribunal, London 1963–73; Dep. Chmn., Essex Quarter Sessions 1964–71; Kent Quarter Sessions 1965–71; Surrey Quarter Sessions 1970–71; A Recorder 1972. Member Gov. Body. Froebel Educational Inst. 1965. *Publication:* Burmese Buddhist Law. *Address:* 3 Paper Buildings, Temple, London, E.C.4.

**MOQUETTE, Henri Ernest.** Netherlands banker. *B.* 1909. *M.* 1944, Gloria R. Cosgrave. *S.* 2. *Daus.* 2. *Career:* With Nationale Handelsbank N.V. (with service in the Netherlands Indies, Singapore, Hong Kong, China, Philippines) and subsequently Man. Dir. in Amsterdam 1927–56; served in World War II (Royal Netherlands Air Force in Singapore, Java, Australia and New Guinea; retired as Lieut.-Col.). Pres. Mercantile Bank of Canada 1953–64; North American Trust Co., Montreal 1964–67; Vice-Pres. and Representative for Europe and Middle East, Banco De Comercio, S.A., Mexico, for U.K. and Europe, 1970—. *Awards:* Officer Order of Orange-Nassau (Netherlands); Netherlands D.F.C. *Address:* 85 Gracechurch Street, London EC3V ODY.

**MORAN, Lord,** CMG. **(Richard John McMoran).** British Diplomat. *B.* 1924. *Educ.* Eton; King's Coll., Cambridge. *M.* 1948, Shirley Rowntree Harris. *S.* 2. *Dau.* 1. *Career:* Joined Foreign Office 1945; 3rd Sec., Ankara 1948, Tel-Aviv 1950; 2nd Sec. Rio de Janeiro 1953; 1st Sec., Foreign Office 1956, Washington 1959, Foreign Office 1961; Counsellor, South Africa 1965; Head of West African Dept., FCO 1968–73; HM Ambassador to Chad 1970–73, to Hungary 1973–76, to Portugal since 1976. *Decoration:* Companion, Order of St. Michael & St. George, 1973. *Publication:* CB: a life of Sir Henry Campbell-Bannerman (1973; Whitbread Award, 1973). *Clubs:* Beefsteak; Flyfishers'. *Address:* 26 Church Row, Hampstead, London NW3; and Llewelyn House, Aberedw, Radnorshire; and *office* c/o Foreign & Commonwealth Office, London SW1A 2AH.

**MORE, Jasper,** MP. British politician. *B.* 31 July 1907. *Educ.* Eton; Kings Coll., Cambridge. *M.* 1944, Clare Mary Hope Edwards. *Career:* Member, Salop County Council, 1958–70; and 1973—; Member of Parliament Ludlow since 1960; Government Whip 1964; Opposition Whip, 1964–70; Vice-Chamberlain of the Household 1970–71. *Publications:* Land of Italy (1949); The Mediterranean (1955). *Clubs:* Travellers; Brooks's. *Address:* Linley Hall, Bishop's Castle, Shropshire; and *office* House of Commons, London, S.W.1.

**MOREL-JOURNEL, Hugues,** Hon. OBE. French industrialist. *B.* 1907. *Educ.* Baccalauréat (Latin Sciences-Philosophy), Lyons; Diplomé Political Economics, Oxford University (Wadham College). *M.* 1931, Alyette de la Garde de Saignes. *S.* Bernard, Régis, Guy, Didier and Christian. *Daus.* Albine, Chantal, Anne and Claire. *Career:* Pres. Morel-Journal et Cie. S.A., Lyons. Hon. President, Lyons Chamber of Commerce. Hon. Pres., International Silk Association. Treasurer, Académie del Sciences, Belles Lettres et Arts de Lyon. Formerly President; Lyons Political Economy Society. *Award:* Hon. Officer of British Empire. *Club:* Lyons Rotary. *Address:* 21 Route de Dardilly, Ecully (Rhône); and *office* 20 rue Joseph-Serlin, Lyons 1, France.

**MORELL, Rodney Telford.** Australian solicitor and company director. *B.* 1910 (*S.* of late Sir Stephen Morell). *Educ.*

Melbourne Grammar School and Melbourne University. *M.* (1) 1936, Honor Strutt. *Daus.* 2. *M.* (2) 1947, Naomi Mears. *Career:* Local Director, Commercial Banking Company of Sydney 1954—. Director: Carlton & United Breweries Ltd. *Club:* Athenaeum. *Address:* 231 Domain Road, South Yarra, Vic., Australia.

**MORENO, Dr. Luis.** Ecuadorian Diplomat. *B.* 1936. *Educ.* University & Graduate Studies. Lawyer, Dr. in Jurisprudentia Dr. in International Law. *M.* 1971, Edith de Moreno. *S.* 1. *Dau.* 1. *Career:* Prof., Universidad Central, Quito 1968–73, Universidad Catolic, Quito 1970–73, & Military Academy. Quito 1972–73; Dir. of Legal Affairs, Ministry of Foreign Affairs. Quito 1971–73; Consul of Ecuador in Hamburg 1973–74; Chargé d'Affaires a.i., Bonn since 1977. *Member:* Assoc. des Anciens Auditeurs de l'Academie de Droit International de L'Haye; International Law Assoc.; International World Assoc.; University Professors' Assoc.; etc. *Awards:* Gold Medallion of the Universidad Central; Laureate, Doctoral Thesis; Best Student Award, Universidad Gran Colombia. *Publications:* United Nations & The Organisation of American States; Territorial Justice; Dominican Republic Affair; Special Law; etc. *Clubs:* Lawyers' Club, Quito; Press Club, Bonn; Juniors Club, Bonn. *Address:* Andagoya 320, Quito, Ecuador; and *office* Botschaft von Ecuador, 53 Bonn-Bad Godesberg, Koblenzer Strasse 37–39, Federal Republic of Germany.

**MORENO-SALCEDO, Luis.** Filipino diplomat. *B.* 1918. *Educ.* Royal Univ. of Santo Tomás (LLB *magna cum laud* 1940). *M.* Hermelinda Ycasiano. *S.* Alexis and Ramón María. *Daus.* Maria Luisa and María Esmeralda. *Career:* Professional Lecturer: in Commercial Law and in Political Science, Far Eastern Univ. 1946–59; in Political Science, St. Theresa's Coll., Manila 1958–59; and in International Law, Univ. of Santo Tomás 1959. Lieutenant Philippine Army 1941–46. Joined the Department of Foreign Affairs as Assistant 1946; Career Minister 1957–62; Chief of Protocol 1948–54; Secretary to Philippine Delegation to the Korean Political Conf., Geneva 1954; Second Secretary and Consul, Mexico City 1955; Second Secretary and Consul, Washington, D.C. 1956–57; Minister-Counsellor to the Holy See 1957–58; Diplomatic Observer, Fourth Session, Executive Council of Union Latina, Rome 1958; Counsellor on Political and Cultural Affairs, Dept. of Foreign Affairs, Manila 1958–59; Minister-Counsellor, Buenos Aires 1959–62; Ambassador: to Argentina and concurrently to Chile 1962–64; to Viet-Nam 1965–68 to France since 1969. *Awards:* Knight, Sovereign Military Order of Malta; Knight's Cross, Order of Malta; Commander, Order of Isabel the Catholic (Spain); Grand Cross, Order of the Liberator General José de San Martin (Argentina); Grand Officer, National Order of Viet-Nam. *Publications:* A Guide to Protocol (1949, revised edition 1959); Selected Readings on the Foreign Policy of the Philippines (1959); The Philippines and its Foreign Policy (in preparation). *Address:* Embassy of the Philippines, Avenue Georges-Mandel 26, Paris 16E, France.

**MORETON, Sir John (Oscar),** KCVO, KCMG, MC. British diplomat (Ret'd.). *B.* 1917. *Educ.* St. Edwards School; Trinity College, Oxford (MA). *M.* 1945, Margaret Katherine Fryer. *Dau.* 3. *Career:* With Colonial Office, 1948–53; Government of Kenya, 1953–55; Private Secy. to Secretary of State for the Colonies, 1955–59; Commonwealth Relations Office, 1960; Counsellor, British High Commission, Lagos, 1961–64; Imperial Defence College, 1965; Assistant Under-Secretary, Commonwealth Office (later Foreign and Commonwealth Office), 1965–69; Ambassador to South Viet-Nam, 1969–71; British High Commissioner Malta 1972–74; Deputy Perm. Rep. U.K. Mission to United Nations (N.Y.) 1974–75; H.M. Minister, British Embassy, Washington 1975–77. *Club:* Travellers. *Address:* Woodside House, Woodside Road, Cobham, Surrey.

**MOREY, Albert Anderson.** Industrial engineer. *B.* 1903. *Educ.* BBA Boston Univ. 1925; Spl. studies Industrial Engineering Westinghouse Electric Corporation. *M.* 1930, Margaret D. Ice. *S.* Albert A. *Career:* With Employer's Liability Assurance Corp., Boston, 1925–29; with Marsh & McLennan, Inc., Chgo., 1929—; Partner, 1946; Asst. V.P. 1938–47; V.P. 1947–59; Sr. V.P. 1959–62; Exec. V.P. 1962–66; Chmn. 1966–69; member Exec. Cttee. 1961–70; Chmn. Exec. Cttee. 1969–70; Chmn. Marsh & McLennan Securities Corp. 1969–70; Chmn. Marsh & McLennan National Marketing Corp. 1969–70; also Dir. Marlennan Corp., Chmn. 1969–70; Chmn. Exec. Cttee. 1970—; also Dir. Chmn. Natkin & Company 1971–72; Chmn. Exec. Cttee. 1972—; Dir. of Oak Electro/Netics Corp.; American Bakeries Company; Marsh & McLennan Limited, Canada; Marsh & McLennan Pty., Australia; William M. Mercer Limited (Canada); Chicago Association of Commerce and Industry; Rehabilitation Institute of Chicago. Member, Lloyd's of London 1972—. Partner, Justice Associates, Inc.; Elector, Insurance Hall of Fame; member Board of Fellows, Boston University 1970—; Midwest-Japan Assn.; Safety Code, Chem. Warfare Div. AUS, World War II; Wisdom Socy.; Chmn. Cook County March of Dimes, 1949. *Awards:* Outstanding Public Service Award, Boston Univ., 1963; Honorary Degree Doctor of Humane Letters, Boston Univ. 1969; Golden Plate Award, American Academy of Achievement, 1970; Three Million Miler airlines plaque; Registered profl. engr., Ill.; Mo.; *Member:* Amer. Society of Mechanical Engineers (Life membership); Amer. Socy. Military Engineers; Army Ordnance Assn. Amer. Socy. of Safety Engineers; Socy. of Automotive Engineers; Amer. Socy. of Civil Engineers; Amer. Institute of Mining & Metallurgical Engineers; Illinois Socy. of Engineers; National Aeronautic Assn.; Western Socy. of Engineers; Amer. Socy. of Heating & Ventilating Engineers; Institution of Mechanical; Engineers, England; National Socy. of Professional Engineers; Veterans of Safety; Verein Deutscher Ingenieure, West Germany; U.S.A. Civil Service Chief Inspector DPPS; Societe Des Ingenieurs Civils de France; Japan Society of Mechanical Engineers; Pioneer Airman (OX5) 7335; Ao Conselho Deliberative Do Instituto De Engenharia, Brazil; Engineering Institute of Canada (L'Institute Canadien Des Ingenieurs); The Institution of Nuclear Engineers; Societe Suisse Des Ingenieurs Et Des Architectes; member Newcomen Soc.; Chgo. Council Foreign Relations; English Speaking Union; Indiana Society Chgo.; Citizens Board of the Univ. of Chicago; The British-American Chamber of Commerce; The Chicago Cttee.; Navy League of the United States. *Clubs:* Chicago; Executives'; Union League; Mid-America; The 900 Club; Marco Polo (N.Y.); Westmoreland (Wilmette, Ill.); Bob O'Link (Highland Park, Ill.). Contbr. articles engineering magazines. *Address: office* 222 South Riverside, Chicago, Illinois 60606, U.S.A.

**MORGAN, Cecil.** American lawyer. *B.* 1898. *Educ.* Louisiana State Univ. (LLB 1919); Order of the Coif. Law School, Tulane Univ.; Hon ODK. Louisiana State Univ., Hon LLD, Centenary Coll., 1956. *M.* 1932, Margaret Geddes. *S.* Cecil, Jr. *Dau.* Margaret G. *Career:* United States Commissioner for Western District of Louisiana 1922–25; member, Louisiana House of Representatives 1928–32, Louisiana State Senate 1932–34; Judge, First Judicial District Court, Louisiana 1934–36; Louisiana Civil Service Commission 1944–48; Exec. Asst. to Chmn. for Public Affairs, Standard Oil Co. (N.J.) 1955–63; Dean Emeritus and Professor of Law, School of Law, Tulane University, New Orleans. Pres., Natl. Municipal League 1956–58. Served in World War I (2nd Lieut.). *Address:* 1435 Jackson Avenue, New Orleans, Louisiana 70130, U.S.A.

**MORGAN, Dafydd Elystan.** British. Barrister at Law. *B.* 1932. *Educ.* Bachelor of Law (Hons.). *M.* 1959, Alwen. *S.* Owain Elystan. *Dau.* Eleri Elystan. *Career:* Solicitor, Partner in Firm North Wales 1958–68; became Barrister at Law 1971; Member of Parliament for Cardigan 1966–74; Under Secy. of State Home Office, 1968–70; Pres. Welsh Local Authority Assn. 1967–74; Chmn. Welsh Parly. Party, 1968–69 and 1971–74. *Address:* Carreg Afon, Dolau, Bow Street, Dyfed.

**MORGAN, David E.** American. *Educ.* Massachusetts Institute of Technology (M.I.T., BS in Petroleum Eng.); University of Liege, Belgium; Columbia University Graduate School. *S.* Nicholas. *Daus.* Leslie, Alexandra and Fern. *Career:* Pres. Aero Technology; Pres. and Chmn. Exodus House, New York; Member Rhode Island Council of Environmental Quality; President, Peerless Precision Products, Pawtucket, R.I., 1950—. *Publications:* Petroleum Industries of Poland; American Institute of Mining & Petroleum Engineers. *Clubs:* Le Club; City Athletic; (all N.Y.). *Address: office* 122 Bacon Street, Pawtucket, R.I. 02860, U.S.A.

**MORGAN, Graham J.** *B.* 1917. *Educ.* Carleton College, Northfield, Minn. (BA). *M.* 1952. Vernile Murrin. *Dau.* Heather Lynn. *Career:* Dir. United States Gypsum Co. 1958; B.P.B. Industries Ltd. 1962; American Hospital Supply Corp. Evanston Illinois 1963; Illinois Central Industries 1967; Illinois Central Railroad Chicago 1967; International Harvester Co. Chicago 1969; Illinois Bell Telephone Co. Chicago 1969; Columbia Corp. Portland Oregon 1969; Pres. Member of Exec. Cttee. 1960, Chief Exec. Officer since 1965 United States Gypsum Co. Elected Chmn. of the Bd. since 1971. *Member:* Bd. of Dirs. Bd. of Trustees, Northwestern

Univ. Evanston; Advisory Bd. Kemper Insurance Co. Chicago; Council on Medical & Biological Research, Univ. of Chicago; Mayor's Cttee. on Economic and Cultural Development. *Clubs:* Old Elm (Chicago); The Glenview (Golf, Ill.); Chicago (Chicago); The Commercial; Mid-America; Seminole Golf, Palm Beach Florida. *Address: office* 101 South Wacker Drive, Chicago 60606, Ill., U.S.A.

**MORGAN, Hugh Travers,** CMG. British diplomat. *B.* 1919. *Educ.* Winchester Coll.; Magdalene Coll. Cambridge. *M.* 1959, Alexandra Belinoff. *S.* Nicholas Travers, Andrew Travers. *Dau.* Victoria Louise. *Career:* War service with R.A.F. (Prisoner of war 1941–45) 1939–45; Diplomatic appointments, New York, United Nations Delegation; Moscow; Canada, Defence College; Mexico; Geneva, Disarmament Delegation; Peking; Berlin 1945–67; Head, Western Dept. Foreign Office London 1967–70; British Ambassador, Peru 1970–74; Asst. Under-Sec. of State in Foreign & C'wealth Office 1974–75; Ambassador, Austria since 1976. *Address:* British Embassy, Reisnerstrasse 40, 1030 Vienna, Austria.

**MORGAN, Rt. Hon. William James,** PC, JP. *B.* 1914. *M.* 1942, Dorothy Eileen Brennan. *S.* 2. *Dau.* 1. *Career:* Transport contractor. MP (U.) Oldpark Div. of Belfast, N. Ireland Parliament 1949–58, and Clifton Div. of Belfast 1959–69. Minister of Labour & National Insurance 1964; Minister of Health & Social Services 1965. Minister of Health & Local Government, Northern Ireland 1961–68. *Address:* Rhanbuoy, Carrickfergus, Co. Antrim, Northern Ireland.

**MORGAN-GILES, Rear Admiral (Morgan Charles)** (Ret.), DSO, OBE, GM, MP. British. *B.* 1914. *Educ.* Clifton Coll. Royal Navy (Public School Entry). Joint Services Staff College. *M.* (1) 1946, Pamela Bushell (*D.* 1966). *S.* 2. *Daus.* 4. (2) 1968, Marigold Steel. *Career:* Entered Royal Navy, 1932; War Service, Atlantic, Mediterranean, Western Desert, Malta, Yugoslavia, Far East, 1939–45; Captain R.N. Chief, Naval Intelligence, Far East 1954; Dartmouth Training Squadron (in command), 1956–57; H.M.S. Belfast, 1960–62; Promoted Rear Admiral, 1962; Admiral President, Royal Naval Coll. Greenwich, 1962–64; Retired at own request, 1964; Member of Parliament Conservative for Winchester since 1964. *Member:* Royal United Service Institution; Cttee. of Management, Royal National Lifeboat Institution; Chmn. H.M.S. Belfast Trust. *Clubs:* Carlton; Royal Yacht Squadron; Australian (Sydney). *Address:* Upton Park, Alresford, near Winchester, Hants.; and *office* House of Commons, London, S.W.1.

**MORI, Haruki.** Japanese diplomat. *B.* 1911. *Educ.* Univ. of Tokyo. *M.* 1940, Tsutako Masaki. *S.* 4. *Career:* Ministry, Foreign Affairs, Tokyo 1935; Head, Economic Section, Dept. Political Affairs 1950–53; Counsellor Italy 1953–55, Asian Affairs Bureau 1955–56; Private Secy. to Prime Minister 1956–57; Dir. American Affairs Bureau 1957–60; Minister Plenipotentiary U. Kingdom 1960–63, France 1963–64; Ambassador Ex. and Plen. O.E.C.D. Paris 1964–67; Deputy Vice- Min. for Foreign Affairs 1967–70, Vice Minister 1970–72; Ambassador Ex. and Plen. to the Court of St. James's 1972–75; Adviser to Ministry of Foreign Affairs since 1975. *Address:* Ministry of Foreign Affairs, Tokyo, Japan.

**MORIN, Claude.** Canadian Economist. *B.* 1929. *Educ.* Université Laval; Columbia Univ. of New York. *M.* 1955, Mary Lynch. *S.* 2. *Daus.* 3. *Career:* Prof., Faculté des Sciences sociales (économique), Université Laval 1956–63; Dep. Minister of Intergovernmental Affairs. Quebec 1963–71; Prof., Univ. du Québec (Ecole nationale d'administration publique) 1971–76; Minister of Intergovernmental Affairs, Quebec, since 1976. *Member:* Assoc. canadienne des économistes; Assoc. canadienne de science politique. *Publications:* Le Pouvoir Québécois (1972); Le Combat Québécois (1973); Quebec vs Ottawa (in English) (1975). *Address:* 1225 Place Georges V, Québec, Canada.

**MORLEY, Ian Webster,** ISO, BME, BMetE. Australian mining engineer. *B.* 1904. *Educ.* Melbourne University (Bachelor of Mining Engineering and Bachelor of Metallurgical Engineering, 1922–26). *M.* (1) 1937, Evelyn Mary Marshall (*D.* 1948), and (2) 1950, Janet Emily Innes (*D.* 1975). *S.* Donald Marshall. *Dau.* Colyn Mairi. *Career:* Assistant Surveyor, Underground, Broken Hill South Ltd., N.S.W. 1927–28; Surveyor-Party Leader, Imperial Geophysical Experimental Survey, Tasmania, Victoria and South Australia 1929; Chief Surveyor, Central Mine Sulphide Corp. Ltd., Broken Hill 1930; Chief Sampler, New Guinea Goldfields Ltd. 1931–32; Inspector of Mines, Assistant Warden, Department of Mines, Wau, New Guinea 1933–34; Acting Superintendent Gold Mines of Australia Ltd., Mount Coolon, Qld. 1935; General Manager Georgetown Gold Mines W.L. 1935–36; Mount Kasi Mines Ltd., Fiji 1936; Foreman, Wiluna Gold Mines Ltd., W.A. 1937–38; Inspector of Mines, Dept. of Mines, Kalgoorlie 1938; Assistant State Mining Engineer, Qld. 1939; State Mining Engineer and Chief Inspector of Mines, Queensland. Chairman: Board of Examiners, Department of Mines 1940–69; Queensland Energy Resources Advisory Council 1966–69. Member, I.L.O. (International Labour Office) Panel of Consultants on Safety in Mines, 1967–71; Consultant, Minerals, Petroleum since 1969. *Publications:* papers to Inst. of Mining and Metallurgy, Australasian Inst. of Mining & Metallurgy, and Queensland Government Mining Journal. Fellow, Institution of Mining & Metallurgy (London), and Member, Australasian Inst. of Mining & Metallurgy, Geological Socy. of Australia. *Club:* Johnsonian and University Staff (Brisbane, Qld.). *Address:* 7 Wongabel Street, Kenmore, Brisbane, 4069, Qld.; and *office* I. W. Morley & Associates, Consultants, Minerals Petroleum, 7 Wongabel Street, Kenmore, Brisbane, 4069, Qld., Australia.

**MORO, Aldo.** Italian statesman. *B.* 1916. Lawyer; Professor of Criminal Law, University of Bari, where, since 1940, he was also Reader of Philosophy of Jurisprudence. National President, Italian Catholic Federation of University Students (FUCI) 1939–42 and later Pres. of the Movement of Catholic University graduates. For many years Editor of Studium and author of many scholarly studies. When elected to the Constituent Assembly for Bari, took an active part in the drafting of the Italian Constitution; at the same time he was also Vice-Pres. of the Christian Democratic Parliamentary Group (CDPG). Returned to the Chamber of Deputies in 1948 for Bari-Foggia, was appointed Under-Secretary for Foreign Affairs in 5th Gasperi Cabinet, May 1948–Jan. 1950. In 1953 elections was re-elected for Bari. Having become Pres. of the CDPG, his position was confirmed in July 1954 and Jan. 1955. Minister for Justice in the first Segni Cabinet, July 1955–May 1957, and Minister for Education in the Zoli Cabinet, May 1957–June 1958; returned at the 1958 election was again appointed Minister of Education in the Fanfani Cabinet, July 1958–Feb. 1959. Political Secretary of Christian Democratic Party, 1959–63. Returned to the Chamber in 1963, for the same constituency. Prime Minister 1963–68, 1974–76; Minister of Foreign Affairs 1965–66, 1969–72, 1973–74; Pres., Foreign Affairs Commn., Chamber of Deputies 1972–73, Chmn., Council of Ministers of the Common Market July–Dec. 1971. Elected Pres., Christian Democrat Party, 1976. *Address:* Camera dei Deputati, Rome, Italy.

**MORRA, Giuseppe.** Italian. *B.* 1926. *Educ.* AA and BA in Liberal Arts; AA in Foreign Affairs. *Career:* Staff Member of UNRRA in Rome 1945–47; Staff Member of the Italian Technical Delegation in Washington 1948–54; Editorial Asst. in the Office of Information, International Bank for Reconstruction and Development, Washington, D.C., Jan. 1956–. Editorial Assistant with the Information Dept., I.B.R.D 1959–64; Administrative Head of I.B.R.D. Permanent Mission in Eastern Africa (Nairobi) 1965–67; Office, Director-Projects since 1968. *Publications:* articles on the World Bank and the International Finance Corporation in various journals (including encyclopaedias and the U.N. Year Book). *Club:* Italian Sports Social (Washington). *Address: office* 1818 H. Street, Washington, D.C., U.S.A.

**MORRIS, Alfred,** MA, MP. British politician. *B.* 1928. *Educ.* Ruskin and St. Catherine's Coll. Oxford; Univ. of Manchester (post Grad. studies). *M.* 1950, Irene Jones. *S.* 2. *Daus.* 2. *Career:* Schoolmaster in Manchester 1954–56; Industrial Relations Officer Electricity Supply Industry 1956–64; Member of Parliament, Manchester, Wythenshawe since 1964; Parly. Private Secy. Minister Agriculture, Fisheries & Food 1964–67; Parly. Private Secy. Lord President of the Council, Leader, House of Commons 1968–70; Opposition Front Bench Spokesman, Social Services 1970–74; Parly. Adv. Police Fed. England & Wales 1972–74; Britain's First Minister for the Disabled, since 1974. *Member:* Gen. Adv. Council BBC 1968–74; Rep. Privy Council, Council Royal Coll. Vet. Surgeons 1968–74; Exec. Cttee. Central Council, Disabled 1970–74; Nat. Fund, Research Crippling Diseases 1971–74; Patron, Disablement Income Group. *Awards:* Master, Arts Univ. Oxford; Field Marshal Lord Harding; Nat. League of the Blind; Grimshaw Memorial. *Publications:* Human Relations in Industry (1959); VAT, A tax on the Consumer (1970). *Clubs:* Royal Coll. Veterinary

Surgeons; Royal Norwegian. *Address: office* House of Commons, London, S1WA 0AA.

**MORRIS, Rt. Hon. John.** PC, QC, MP. British politician. *B.* 1931. *Educ.* Ardwyn, Aberystwyth; Univ. Coll. of Wales; Gonville & Caius Coll. Cambridge; Acad. of Int. Law. The Hague. *M.* 1959, Margaret. *Daus.* 3. *Career:* member, Parliament Aberavon 1959—; Parliamentary Secretary, Ministry of Power, 1964–66; Joint Parl. Sec., Ministry of Transport, 1966–68. Chmn., Joint Enquiry into 'Finances and Management of British Rail', 1966–67. Minister of Defence (Equipment), 1968–70. Privy Counsellor, 1970. Member North Atlantic Assembly 1970–74; Secy. of State for Wales since 1974. *Address:* House of Commons, London, S.W.1.

**MORRIS, Michael Wolfgang Laurence,** MP. British Politician. *B.* 1936. *Educ.* Bedford Sch., St. Catharine's Coll., Cambridge —MA. *M.* 1960, Dr. Ann Morris. *S.* 2. *Dau.* 1. *Career:* Dir., Benton & Bowles International Advertising Agency since 1971; MP (Cons) for Northampton South since 1974; Chmn., Roy Friedlander & Ptnrs, Ad. Agency, since 1975. *Member:* Inst. of Practitioners in Advertising; Inst. of Marketing. *Publications:* (Jointly) Helping the Exporter (1968); (Jointly) Below the Line Marketing (1970). *Club:* Carlton. *Address:* Caesar's Camp, Sandy, Bedfordshire; and *office* c/o Benton & Bowles Ltd. 197 Knightsbridge, London, SW7.

**MORRIS, Sir Philip Robert,** KCMG, CBE. *B.* 1901. *Educ.* Tonbridge School; St. Peter's, York; Trinity Coll., Oxford (MA). *M.* 1926, Florence Redvers Davis Green. *S.* Richard Walford and Robert Davis. *Dau.* Helen Daphne. *Career:* Lecturer in History and Classics, Westminster Training Coll. 1923–25; successively Admin. Officer (1925–32), Asst. Director (1932–38) and Director (1938–44), Kent Education Committee; Director-General of Army Education 1944–46; Vice-Chancellor, Univ. of Bristol 1946–66; Vice-Chmn., Board of Governors of B.B.C. 1954–60. Life Trustee Carnegie U.K. Trust. Member of Exec. Cttee. of British Council 1947–64; member of Cttee. on Higher Education 1961–64. Chairman: Bristol Old Vic Trust Ltd. 1946–71, Pres. since 1971. Commonwealth Education Liaison Cttee. 1959–62. *Publications:* articles and published addresses on educational subjects. *Club:* Athenaeum (London). *Address:* Bryncoedifor Vicarage, Rhydymain, Dolgellau, Gwynedd, LI40 2AN.

**MORRIS, Sir Willie,** KCMG. British diplomat. *B.* 1919. *Educ.* St. John's College, Oxford (MA). *M.* 1959. Ghislaine Margaret Trammell. *S.* 3. *Career:* Head, Eastern Department, Foreign and Commonwealth Office, 1963–67. Fellow, Centre for International Affairs, Harvard University, 1967–68; Ambassador to Saudi Arabia, 1968–72; to Yemen Arab Republic 1971; to Ethiopia 1972–75; to Egypt since 1975. *Clubs:* Travellers', Pall Mall. *Address:* c/o Foreign & Commonwealth Office, King Charles Street, London, S.W.1.

**MORRIS, Yaakov.** Israeli Diplomat. *B.* 1920. *M.* 1941. Sarah. *S.* 1. *Dau.* 1. *Career:* Consul, New York 1957–61; Dep. Dir., Information Div., Min. of Foreign Affairs, Jerusalem 1965–69; Head of Israel Mission, India 1969–71; Counsellor. Embassy of Israel, Stockholm 1972; Spokesman, Perm. Mission of Israel to UN 1972–76; Ambassador of Israel to New Zealand since 1977. *Publications:* Masters of the Desert; Israel; On the Soil of Israel; Israel's Struggle for Peace. *Address:* Embassy of Israel, Williams Centre, Wellington, New Zealand.

**MORRIS OF BORTH y GEST, Rt. Hon. Lord** (John William Morris), CH, PC, CBE, MC, DL. British judge. *B.* 11 Sept. 1896. *Educ.* Liverpool Inst.; Cambridge Univ. (MA, LLB); Harvard Law School, Harvard Univ., U.S.A. *Career:* called to the Bar in England Nov. 1921; Bencher of the Inner Temple 1943, and Treasurer 1967; appointed King's Counsel 1935; Judge of Appeal, Isle of Man 1938–45; Judge of the High Court of Justice (King's Bench Division) 1945–51; a Lord Justice of Appeal Apr. 1951–Jan. 1960; Lord of Appeal in Ordinary 1960–75. Pro-Chancellor of the Univ. of Wales 1958–74. Hon. LLD, Univs. of Wales, British Columbia, Liverpool, and Cambridge. *Address:* House of Lords, London, S.W.1.

**MORRISON, Paul Leslie.** Educator and corporate director. *B.* 1899. *Educ.* De Pauw University (BA 1921) and Northwestern Univ. (MBA 1922; DPh 1927). *M.* 1924, Carolyn Rosemeier. *S.* Paul, Jr. and James F. *Career:* Prof. of Finance, Northwestern Univ. (member of Faculty) 1923–58; Chief, Central Fiscal Office, China Theatre, U.S. Army 1944–45; Asst. Comptroller (rank of Colonel, Gen. Staff Corps.), International Affairs, U.S. Army 1950–52; Asst. Director, Bureau of the Budget, Office of the President of the U.S. 1953–54. Member, American Advisory Board, Zürich Insurance Co., and Director of its American subsidiaries, Zürich, Switzerland. Director: California Cold Storage & Distributing Co. (Chmn. of Exec. Cttee.), Long Beach, California. *Publications:* Principles of Accounting (with E. L. Kohler); numerous articles in professional publications. *Awards:* LLD De Pauw Univ. 1949; Legion of Merit, Commanding General, China Theatre, U.S. Army 1945. *Member:* Investment Analyst Socy. (Past Pres.); Phi Beta Kappa; Amer. Economic Assn. *Clubs:* University (Chicago); Westmoreland Country (Wilmette, Ill.). Lauderdale Yacht, Fort Lauderdale Fla.; Tower. *Address:* 32 Knox Circle, Evanston, Ill. 60201, U.S.A.

**MORRISON, Robert Ian.** Irish. *B.* 1929. *Educ.* Fellow, Inst. of Chartered Accountants of Ireland. *M.* 1953, June Nesbitt. *S.* William Ian. *Dau.* Wendy. *Career:* Qualified in 1952. Previously a partner in Peterson, Morrison & Co., Chartered Accountants, Advisory Partner until 1971, Consultant since 1971; Lecturer in Accountancy, University College, Dublin 1952–64; Chairman, Dublin Society of Chartered Accountants 1964–65. Group Managing Director of the Bank of Ireland 1966, (Deputy Governor 1964–67). *Member:* Irish Management Inst.; Inst. of C.A.s in Ireland. *Clubs:* Royal Irish Yacht, Royal Ocean Racing. *Address:* Spindrift, Baily, Dublin, and *office* Bank of Ireland, Dublin.

**MORRISON-JONES, Derek Hassell,** FCA. British chartered Accountant. *B.* 1908. *Educ.* Cranleigh School, Surrey. *M.* 1961, Elaine Frances Robinson. *S.* Roger Derek and Jack Richard. *Dau.* Diana. *Career:* Articles with Price Waterhouse & Co.; Chief Accountant, Higgs & Hill 1941–46; Chief Accountant, Sir Robert McAlpine & Sons Ltd. 1946–58, Secy. 1958–65. Financial Adviser 1966–71; Edger Investments Ltd. since 1955; Financial Consultant since 1971. Conservative. *Clubs:* Bath (London); Royal St. George's Golf (Sandwich); MCC. *Address:* Hazeldene, 6 Russell Close, Heath Drive, Walton-on-the-Hill, Tadworth, Surrey.

**MORROW, Clarence Joseph.** Canadian business executive. *B.* 1895. *Educ.* High School. *M.* 1925, Beulah Jean Smith. *S.* 2. *Dau.* 1. *Career:* Dir.: National Sea Products Ltd., Halifax, N.S.; Director of the following: North Eastern Corporation Ltd., Halifax, Great Eastern Corporation Ltd., President, The Morrow Investment Co. Ltd., Lunenberg, (Nova Scotia); President Isleview Investments Ltd. Lunenberg (N.S.); Bens Holdings Ltd. (Halifax, N.S.), N.S. *Address:* P.O. Box 127 Lunenburg, Nova Scotia, Canada.

**MORROW, Sir Ian Thomas,** CA, FCMA, JDipMa, FBIM. British co. dir. & deputy-chmn. *B.* 1912. *Educ.* Dollar Academy. *M.* (1) 1940, Elizabeth Mary Thackray (Diss.). *S.* 1. *Dau.* 1. (2) 1967, Sylvia Jane Taylor. *Dau.* 1. *Career:* Chartered Accountant 1936; FCMA 1945; Asst. Accountant, Brocklehurst-Whiston Amalgamated Ltd. 1937–40; Partner, Robson, Morrow & Co., 1942–51; Financial Dir., 1951–52, Dep. Man. Dir., 1952–56, Joint Man. Dir. 1956–57 The Brush Electrical Engineering Co. Ltd. (now the Brush Group Ltd.) of which he was Man. Dir., 1957–58; Jt. Man. Dir. H. Clarkson & Co. Ltd., 1961–72; Chairman Associated Fire Alarms Ltd., 1965–70; Rowe Bros. & Co. (Holdings) Ltd., 1960–70; Crane Fruehauf Trailers Ltd., 1969–71; Dep. Chairman Rolls Royce Ltd., 1970–71; Dep. Chairman Rolls Royce (1971) Ltd., 1971–73 (Managing Director 1971–72); Led Anglo-American Council on Productivity Team on Management Accounting to U.S., 1950; Dep. Chmn. & Man. Dir. UKO International Ltd.; Chmn. of subsidiary cos.; Dep. Chmn. Siebe Gorman Holdings Ltd.; Chmn. Lion International Ltd.; Chmn. J. H. Vavasseur Group Ltd.; Dir., Chmn., The Laird Group Ltd.; Dir Hambros Ltd.; International Harvester Co. of Gt. Britain Ltd.; Lindustries Ltd.; Martin-Black Ltd. *Council Member:* British Electrical & Allied Manufacturers' Assoc., 1957–58; British Internal Combustion Engine Manufacturers Assoc., 1957–58; Grand Council, FBI, 1953–58; Production Engineering Research Assoc., 1955–58; Inst. of Cost and Mgmt. Accountants, 1952–70 (Pres. 1956–68; Performing Right Tribunal 1968–74; Council, Inst. of Chartered Accountants of Scotland 1968–72 (Vice-President 1970–72), Press Council since 1974. *Awards:* Freeman, City of London; Liveryman, Worshipful Co. of Spectacle-makers; Comp IEE(Hon). *Publications:* Papers and addresses on professional and management subjects. *Clubs:* R.A.C.; National Liberal; Royal & Ancient St. Andrews. *Address:* 23 Chester Terrace, Regent's Park, London, N.W.1. and *office* 41 Bishopsgate, London, E.C.2.

**MORSE, David Abner.** American administrator and lawyer. *B.* 31 May 1907. *Educ.* Rutgers University (LittB, Hon. LLD); Harvard Law School (LLB); Hon. LLB Geneva;

Docteur *Hon. Causa.* Strasbourg; Hon. Doctor, Social Sciences, Laval Quebec; Doctor of Humanities, Brandeis Univ. Boston Mass. *M.* 1937, Mildred. Hockstader. *Career:* Formerly Special Assistant to U.S. Attorney-General; General Counsel National Labour Relations Board; Chief Counsel, Petroleum Labour Policy Board; Impartial Chairman, Milk Industry, Metropolitan area of New York; Assistant Secretary of Labour, later Under-Secretary and Acting Secretary; Director-General, International Labour Office 1948–70; Law Firm of Surrey, Karasik Morse & Seham, N.Y.C., Washington D.C., Paris & Beirut; Impartial Chmn. Coat and Suit Industry (Metropolitan New York). *Awards:* Legion of Merit; Order of Merit of Labour of Brazil; Grand Officer, The Federal Rep. of Cameroon. Cmdr. de l'Etoile Equatorial (Gabon); Grand Officer (Simon Bolivar) Republic of Columbia; Grand Officer of Italy; Grand Officer French Legion of Honor. *Member.* Bd. Trustees Rutgers Univ.; U.S. Cttee. Dag. Hammarskjold Foundation; Bd. Dirs. World Rehabilitation Fund Inc.; Chmn. Cttee. on Policy & Planning; New York Foundation; National Council, United Nations Assn. of the U.S.A.; Amer. Arbitration Assn.; Adviser to the Admin. United Nations Development Programme; Chmn. Adv. Panel, Programme Policy, U.N. Dev. Programme. *Address:* 14 East 75th Street, N.Y. 10021, U.S.A.

**MORSE, Kenneth Pratt.** American industrialist and mechanical engineer. *B.* 1905. *Educ.* Chauncey Hall School (Boston, Mass.) and Massachusetts Inst. of Technology, *M.* 1931, Florence May Stillwell. *S.* Kenneth P., Jr., and Peter S. *Career:* Previously: Asst. Chief Engineer, Lanston Monotype Machine Co., Philadelphia; with The Standard Register Co.: successively Development Engineer, Chief Engineer, Chief Engineer & Works Supt., Asst. General Manager, Exec. Vice-Pres. and General Manager, President and Director, The Huebner Co., Dayton. Director and former Pres., Office Equipment Manufacturers Institute. President & Director, The Standard Register Co., Dayton, Ohio, 1969; Chmn. of Bd., 1970–71; Chmn. Emeritus since 1971; Dir. & Pres., Goodwill Industry, Dayton; Dir., The Third National Bank & Trust Co., Dayton 1966–76. Dir. & Campaign Chmn., Community Chest of Dayton; Trustee, Miami Valley Hosp., Dayton. Trustee, University of Dayton, 1968–72. *Member:* Nat. Defense Executives Reserves D.B.S.A., U.S. Dept of Commerce; President, Education Council of the Graphic Arts Industry Inc., Washington. *Clubs:* Racquet (Dayton); Cincinnati (Cincinnati). *Address:* 5885 Folkestone Drive, Dayton Ohio, 45459; and *office* 626 Albany Street, Dayton, Ohio 45401, U.S.A.

**MORSE, Robert Hosmer III.** Canadian business executive, *B.* Indianapolis, Ind., U.S.A. 6 Aug. 1921. *Educ.* Phillips Exeter Academy; Princeton University (BS 1943). *M.* (1) 1950, Lucille Conkey (*D.* May 1961). *S.* Henry Conkey. *Dau.* Virginia Phillips. *M.* (2) Anne Laura Coates. *S.* Colin Robert and Ian Coates. *Career:* Gen. Mgr. Beloit (Wis.) Works, Fairbanks, Morse & Co., 1952–54, Vice-Pres. Sales, Chicago 1956–57, Vice-Pres. Budgets & Planning, 1957–58; Pres., Chief Exec. Officer, Dir. Robert Morse Corp. Ltd. (Formerly Canadian Fairbanks-Morse Co. Ltd.), Montreal 1958–72; Chmn. Vanmor Holdings Ltd., Vancouver 1972—. Ensign to Lieut., U.S.N.R. 1943–46. *Clubs:* Chicago Club (Chicago); Everglades, Bath & Tennis (Florida); Forest & Stream, Mount Royal, St. James's (Montreal); Shaughnessy Golf & Country, Royal Vancouver Yacht, Vancouver Lawn Tennis & Badminton, Vancouver Club (Vancouver). *Address:* 5695 Newton Wynd, Vancouver V6T 1H6; and *office* Suite 3213, 595 Burrard Street, Vancouver V7X 1L2, Canada.

**MORSKI, Albert.** Director, Political Department, Ministry of Foreign Affairs, Warsaw. *B.* 1909. *Educ.* BA; also Postgraduate course for the Candidate of Science in Modern History. *M.* 1939, Nancy Packowski. *S.* Edwin, Casimir, and Maciej. *Career:* Chief of Division, Political Dept., Ministry of Foreign Affairs, Warsaw 1947; Consul-General in London (Eng.) 1948; First Counsellor, Polish Embassy, London 1949–51; Chief (with rank of Min. Plen.), Polish Delegation to the Neutral Nations Supervisory Commission in Korea 1955–56; Ambassador to Norway, 1957–61; concurrently Minister in Iceland 1961–62; Chief, Polish Delegation, Internatl. Control Commn., Laos (with rank of Ambassador; Director II Dept., Ministry of Foreign Affairs. *Address:* Ministry of Foreign Affairs, Warsaw, Poland.

**MORTIMER, Gerald James.** MBE, BSc. British. *B.* 1918. *Educ.* Caterham School; Royal School of Mines (BSc. ARSM). *M.* 1942, Connie Dodd. *S.* 2. *Daus.* 2. *Career:* War Service Royal Engineers 1939–46; Mining Official, Gold Fields Group Mines 1946–55; Manager, Exec. Dir. & Dep. Chmn., Consolidated Gold Fields Ltd. 1959–75, Dep. Chmn. & Group Chief Exec. since 1976; Chmn., Gold Fields Mining & Industrial Ltd.; Director: Associated Minerals Consolidated Ltd., Azcon Corp., Commonwealth Mining Investments Ltd., Consolidated Gold Fields Australia Ltd., Gold Fields American Corp., Gofmil Inc., Gofmil Development Corp., Gold Fields Mining & Development Ltd., Gold Fields of South Africa Ltd., Newconex Holdings Ltd., Sand & Gravel Association Restoration Guarantee Fund Ltd., Waterval (Rustenburg) Platinum Mining Co. Ltd. Member of Council, African Welfare Ltd. Fellow & Pres. Inst. of Mining & Metallurgy; Member, Inst. of Quarrying; Fellowship of Engineering; Assoc. Member, Assn. of Mine Managers, South Africa; County Councillor of Surrey since 1973. *Address:* 40 Harestone Valley Road, Caterham, Surrey and *office* 49 Moorgate, London, E.C.2.

**MORTON, Henry Vollam,** FRSL. British author and journalist; *B.* 1892. *M.* (1) Dorothy Vaughton. *S.* 2. *Dau.* 1, and (2) Violet Mary Greig. *S.* 1. *Career:* Commenced on staff of Birmingham Gazette and Express, 1910 (Asst. Ed. 1912); Ed., Empire Magazine, London, 1913; sub-ed., Daily Mail, 1913–14 served in World War I; editorial staff, Evening Standard, 1919; Daily Express, 1921; special writer, Daily Herald, 1931–42. *Publications:* The Heart of London (1925); The London Year (1926); London (1926); The Spell of London (1926); The Nights of London (1926); In Search of England (1927); The Call of England (1928); In Search of Scotland (1929); In Search of Ireland (1930); In Search of Wales (1932); Blue Days at Sea (1932); In Scotland Again (1933); In the Steps of the Master (1934); Our Fellow Men (1936); In the Steps of St. Paul (1936); Through Lands of the Bible (1938); Ghosts of London (1939); Women of the Bible (1940); H. V. Morton's London (1940); Middle East (1941); I, James Blunt (1942); I Saw Two Englands (1942); Atlantic Meeting (1943); In Search of South Africa (1948); In Search of London (1951); In the Steps of Jesus (1953); A Stranger in Spain (1954); A Traveller in Rome (1957); This is Rome (1960); This is the Holy Land (1961); A Traveller in Italy (1964); Fountains of Rome (1966); A Traveller in Southern Italy (1969); H. V. Morton's Britain (1970); H. V. Morton's England (1975); The Splendour of Scotland (1976). *Awards:* Order of Merit (Italy) and Phoenix (Greece). *Address:* P.O. Box 67. Somerset West, C.P., South Africa.

**MORTON, William Gilbert.** Banker. *B.* 1906. *Educ.* Dartmouth College (BSc 1928; MComSc (Amos Tuck School) 1929). *M.* 1936, Barbara Link. *S.* William G., Jr. and Albert Harry. *Dau.* Linda Coté. *Career:* Bond Dept., Bankers Trust Co., N.Y.C. 1929–33; Bond Dept., L. F. Rothschild & Co., N.Y.C. 1933–34. With Onondaga Savings Bank: Asst. to Pres. 1934–37, Asst. Treasurer 1937–39, Treasurer 1939, Trustee 1947—, Vice-Pres. 1948–54, Exec. Vice-Pres. 1954–58, Pres. 1958—; Chmn. since 1973; Dir. Great Bear Spring Co. N.Y.C.; Syracuse Transit Co.; Metropolitan Dev. Corp. Pres. 1970; Chmn. 1969; New York Higher Educ. Assit. Corp. Treas. 1958–74; Savings Banks Assn. Pres. 1971–72; Council of Administration, Savings Bank Assn. of N.Y. State; mem. N.Y. State Banking Board 1973–76; Dir. Lab. of Ornithology, Cornell Univ., since 1972. *Clubs:* Century; Onondaga Golf & Country; University; Dartmouth Club of N.Y. *Address:* 307 Hurlburt Road, Syracuse, N.Y. 13224 and *office* 101 South Salina Street, Syracuse 13201 N.Y., U.S.A.

**MOSES, Sir Charles Joseph Alfred,** CBE. British. *B.* 1900. *Educ.* Oswestry Grammar School; Royal Military College, Sandhurst. *M.* 1922, Kathleen O'Sullivan. *S.* 1. *Dau.* 1. *Career:* Vice-Pres., Royal Agric. Soc. of N.S.W.; Vice-pres. Elizabethan Trust; Trustee of Remembrance Driveway, President: Austrian/Australian Cultural Society; Vice-Chmn., International Inst. of Communications, London; Councillor, Royal Inst. for Deaf/Blind Children of N.S.W.; Member, Prix Jeunesse Foundation (Munich); Vice-Chmn., Asian Mass Communication and Information Centre (Singapore); Hon. Dir. Post-Graduate Medical Foundation; Lieutenant 2nd Border Regiment 1918–22; Fruitgrower, Bendigo 1922–24; Motor Salesman and Sales Manager. Melbourne 1924–30; Radio Announcer A.B.C. Melbourne 1930–32; Radio Talks and Sporting Editor, A.B.C. Sydney 1933–34; Federal Talks Controller, A.B.C. 1934–45; General Manager, Australian Broadcasting Commission (A.B.C.) 1935–65; Secy. General Asian Broadcasting Union 1965–77, now Hon. Councillor. War Service; Lieutenant 45th Battalion. A.M.F. 1940; Captain 2/20 Battn., A.I.F. 1940; Major A.I.F. (Malaya) H.Q. 1941–42; Lieut.-Col. commanding 2/7 Division Cavalry Regiment, New Guinea 1942–43; mentioned in dispatches. *Address:* 78 New Beach Road. Darling Point,

Sydney; and *office* A.B.U. 203 Castlereagh, Sydney, N.S.W., Australia.

**MOSLEY, Sir Oswald Ernald,** Bt. English politician and former Army Officer. *B.* 1896. *Educ.* Winchester and R.M.C. Sandhurst. *M.* (1) 1920, Lady Cynthia Curzon (*D.* 1933). *S.* 2. *Dau.* 1. (2) 1936, Hon. Diana Mitford. *S.* 2. *Career:* Served 1914–18 war with R.F.C. and 16th Lancers. Conservative MP 1918; Independent MP 1922–24; Labour MP 1924–30 Minister in Labour Govt. as Chancellor of the Duchy of Lancaster (resigned) 1929–30. Founded New Party, later merged in British Union; imprisoned for opposition to 1939 war; after the war, founded the Union Movement. *Publications:* The Greater Britain, (1932); Tomorrow we Live, (1938); My Answer, (1947); The Alternative, (1947); Die Europäische Revolution (also published in Germany); Policy & Debate. (1954); Europe: Faith & Plan, (1958); Europa Una Fede e Una Programma, (1960); Mosley—Right or Wrong? (1961); Ich Glaube an Europa, (1962); La Nation Europe, (1962); My Life (1968); Weg und Wagnis: ein Leben für Europa (1973) Mi Vida (1973). *Club:* White's. *Address:* 1 rue des Lacs, 91400 Orsay, Essonne, France; Secretariat, 76A Rochester Row, London, S.W.1.

**MOSS, Alfred.** Australian company director. *Educ.* Sydney Grammar School. *M.* Joyce Myers. *S.* 1. *Dau.* 1. *Career:* Dir. Pick-Me-Up Condiment Co. Ltd. 1950–58; Chmn. 1958–61; Vice Pres. Pick-Me-Up Food Products Pty Ltd. 1962–67; Dir. Torrens & Strata Investments Pty. Ltd.; Alfred Moss Investments (Real Estate) Pty. Ltd.; Aljoy Investments Pty. Ltd.; Bamco Pty. Ltd.; Man. Dir. Alfred Moss Investments Pty. Ltd. *Clubs:* Tattersall's; Masonic. *Address:* 4a Wentworth Street, Point Piper, Sydney, N.S.W. Australia and *office* 154 Castlereagh Street, Sydney, N.S.W.

**MOSSÉ, Robert.** *B.* 1906. *Educ.* DEcon; Fellow, Economic Sciences; Dr hon c. Univ. Lisbon. *M.* 1934, Ruth Galewski. *S.* Sacha, Georges and Olivier. *Dau.* France. *Career:* Founder Dir. Documentation economique since 1934; Prof. of Economics, Univ. of Washington 1942–43; Prof. of Political Science, Univ. of Illinois 1944; Asst. Financial Attaché, Washington 1945; Economic Officer, U.N. 1946–48; Professor of Economics, University of Grenoble, France; Member of Council, International Economic Association 1950—; Consultant, International Monetary Fund. Member, National Committee for Scientific Research, France 1955–65; Member, French National Committee for UNESCO; Director, Bilans de la Connaissance Economique. French Delegate to Bretton Woods Conf.; Secretary-General, European Community for Municipal Credit 1957–67. *Awards:* Officer, Legion of Honour; Commander of the Public Instruction; Cavaliere Republic of Italy. *Member:* Academy of Sciences, Turin; Association Française de Science Economique; Chmn. Monetary Group; American Economic Association; Econometric Society; Institut international de sociologie; Institut International de Finances Publiques, etc. *Publications:* L'assurance obligatoire contre le chômage, Paris (1929); L'économie collectiviste, Paris (1939); Economie et législation industrielles, (1940); La France devant la reconstruction économique, New York (1946); Le système monétaire de Bretton Woods, Paris (1948); La monnaie, Paris, (1950); Les salaires, Paris (1953); Bibliographie d'économie politique, 4 Vols, (1946–68); Les Problèmes Monétaires Internationaux, 3rd Ed., (1970); L'Economie Socialiste, (1968); Introduction à l'Economie, (1968) La politique Monitaire (1972). *Address:* Les Gémeaux, 12 Avenue Rochambeau, Grenoble, France.

**MOSSIGE, Erling.** Norwegian. *B.* 1907. *Educ.* Univ. of Oslo (Grad. Law 1928). *M.* 1936, Hanne Rode. *S.* Erling. *Career:* Assistant District Judge 1929–33; Secretary, Norwegian Ministry of Finance 1933–39; Manager, Norwegian Ministry of Supply 1939–40; Financial Manager (1940–45) and Director (1945–46), Norwegian Shipping and Trade Mission, London; Managing Director of the Mission in Oslo 1946–48; Manager, Christiania Bank og Kreditkasse, Oslo 1948–57; Manager, Den norske Creditbank, Oslo 1957–58; Deputy Man. Dir., Den norske Creditbank, Oslo Feb. 1958–1974 (retired). *Awards:* King Haakon VII Commemoration Medal (Norway); Medal of War Participation (Norway); The King's Medal for service in the cause of freedom (Britain). *Publications:* various articles on finance and banking. *Address:* Den norske Creditbank, Kirkegaten 21, Oslo, Norway.

**MOTTE, Jacque Edouard.** French industrialist. *B.* 1920. *Educ.* College of Notre Dame des Victoires, Roubaix; and Douai School, Woolhampton, England; Baccalauréat 1st and 2nd. *M.* 1942, Adèle Coisne. *S.* Jacques. *Daus.* Donatienne, Bénédicte, Marie-Adèle, Marie-Sophie, and Laurence. Member Lions Club, Roubaix. Associate Director, Motte-Bossut, S.A. Roubaix; Past-President, Roubaix Chamber of Commerce; Administrateur Societé Ugimo & Societé Soprimnor. *Member:* Cons. Surveillance Origmy-Desvroise. *Address:* 2 rue Anatole France, Roubaix; and *office* Boulevard Lecere, Roubaix (Nord), France.

**MOUNTBATTEN OF BURMA, Earl, Admiral of the Fleet** (Louis Francis Albert Victor Nicholas Mountbatten), KG, PC, GCB, OM, GCSI, GCIE, GCVO, DSO. *B.* 1900. *Educ.* Royal Naval Colleges Osborne and Dartmouth; Christ's Coll. Cambridge. *M.* 1922, Hon. Edwina Ashley, CI, GBE, DCVO, LLD (*D.* 21 Feb. 1960). *Daus.* Patricia (Baroness Brabourne, Heiress by special remainder to the Earldom), Pamela. *Career:* Naval Cadet 1913; Midshipman 1916; Lieut. 1920; Lieut.-Commander 1928; Commander 1932; Captain 1937; Commodore 1st Cl. 1941; Acting Admiral 1943; Rear-Admiral 1946; Vice-Admiral 1949; Admiral 1952; Admiral of the Fleet 1956; Hon. Lieut.-Gen. 1942; Hon. Air Marshal 1942; served in Grand Fleet, World War I, specialized in wireless and became chartered elect. eng.; served in World War II, Commanding 5th Destroyer Flotilla (dispatches twice, DSO) 1939–41; commanding aircraft carrier Illustrious 1941; Commodore, Combined Operations 1941; Chief of Combined Operations and member of British Chiefs of Staffs committee 1942; Supreme Allied Commander, South-East Asia (KCB 1945, KG 1946) 1943; last Viceroy of India (GCSI, GCIE) 1947; 1st Governor-General of India 1947; commanding 1st cruiser squadron 1948; Fourth Sea Lord of the Admiralty 1950; C.-in-C., Mediterranean 1952; C.-in-C., Allied Forces, concurrently 1953; First Sea Lord, 1955–59; Chief of the Defence Staff and Chairman, Chiefs of Staff Committee, 1959–65. Personal Naval A.D.C. to King Edward VIII, King George VI and Personal A.D.C. to Queen Elizabeth II; Grand Pres., British Commonwealth Ex-Service League, Royal Overseas League, Royal Life Saving Society; Pres., Soldiers', Sailors' and Airmen's Families Assn., Royal Auto. Club, King George's Fund for Sailors; Comm. of the Sea Scouts; Royal Thames Yacht Club; Elder Bro. of Trinity Ho.; Hon. Fellow, Christ's College, Cambridge; received Sword of Honour and Freedom of City of London 1946; first Freeman of Romsey 1946; Freeman, City of Edinburgh 1954; FRS 1966; Hon. LLD (Cambridge, Edinburgh, Southampton, London, and Sussex); Hon. DCL (Oxford); Hon. DSc (Delhi and Patna). Foreign *Awards:* for War Service: Grand Cross, Order of George I and Military Cross (Greece); Legion of Merit and Distinguished Service Medal (U.S.A.); Special Grand Cordon of the Cloud and Banner (China); Grand Cross, Legion of Honour and Croix de Guerre (France); Grand Cross of the Star of Nepal, Order of the White Elephant (Siam), and of the Lion (Netherlands). Other Foreign Decorations: Order of the Nile (Egypt); Grand Cross of Isabella the Catholic (Spain), the Crown and Star of Roumania, and of the Military Order of Aviz (Portugal); Knight, Order of the Seraphim (Sweden); Agga Maha Thiri Thudhamma (Burma); Grand Cross, Order of Dannebrog (Denmark). *Address:* Broadlands, Romsey, Hants.; and Classiebawn Castle, Co. Sligo, Ireland; and 2 Kinnerton Street, London, S.W.1.

**MOURSUND, Tor.** Norwegian Banker. *B.* 1927. *Educ.* Univ. of Oslo, Graduated in law 1950. *M.* 1954, Guri Nilsson. *Dau.* 1. *Career:* Barrister 1955–65; Man. Dir., Romsdals Fellesbank 1966–70; Dep. Man. Dir., Christiania Bank og Kreditkasse 1970–77, Man. Dir. since 1977. *Address:* Heggeliveien 65, Oslo 3, Norway.

**MOWATT, Allan Quimby.** American. *B.* 1913. *Educ.* Mass. Institute of Technology (BSEE). *M.* 1953, Doreen Elizabeth Simpson. *S.* Peter Quimby and Christopher Simpson. *Daus.* Pamela Ann and Melissa Robertson. *Career:* Gen. Mgr. West India Chem. Ltd. Inagua, Bahamas, 1935–39; Sub-Contract Supv. Westinghouse Elec. Corp. Pittsburgh 1939–46; Education Dir. Eastern Co-operatives, N.Y.C. 1946–49; Supv. Buyer, Raytheon Co. Waltham Mass. 1949–51; Pres. Gen. Mgr. Atlee Corp. Winchester Mass. 1951–63; Vice Pres. Gen. Mgr. Astrodyne Inc. (Burlington Mass.) 1965–72; Pres. Chief Exec. Officer Mass. Flex Research Inc. (Waltham Mass.) 1973; Treas., Mass. Flex Research Inc. 1973–74; Pres. Gen. Mgr. Theta, J. Relays, Inc. (Reading, Mass) since 1975. *Publications:* Heat Dissipating Tube Shields, (1959); A New Trimmer Capacitor, (1959). *Member:* Inst. Electrical & Electronic Engineers. *Address:* 61 Beaumont Avenue Newtonville. Mass. 02160; and *office* 2 Linden Street, Reading, Mass, 01867, U.S.A.

**MOWBRAY, Geoffrey. Alwyn.** BSc. AIM. British. *B.* 1932 *Educ.* Chigwell School; London University. *Career:* Dir.

Industrial Powder-Met (Consultants) Ltd.; Prod. Mgr. S.M.C. (Sterling) Ltd. 1958–62; Man. Tabletting Equipment Dept. F. J. Stokes Ltd. 1962–66; Man. Dir. Höganäs (Gt. Britain) Ltd.; Man. Dir. Container Trucking Co. Ltd.; New Sales Mgr., J. & J. Mauin Ltd. *Address:* Lambourne House, Hotley Lane, Prestwood, Gt. Missenden Bucks and *office* Wallhead Mill, Rochdale, Lancs.

**MOXON, John.** *B.* 1906. *Educ.* Univ. of Paris (Certificat); School of Political Science, Paris; Dartmouth College (AB *magna cum laude*), 1929; Tuck School of Business Administration (MCS 1930). *M.* 1933, F. Rosamond Sawyer. *S.* John Sawyer. *Dau.* Fredericka Sawyer (Heller). *Career:* Clerk, Guaranty Co. of New York 1930–32; Clerk 1932–37, Assistant Trust Officer 1937–44, Guaranty Trust Co. of New York. With Carpenter Technology Corp., Reading: successively Secretary, Treas. and Dir. 1944–53; Vice-Pres., Secy., Treas. & Dir. 1953–56; Exec. Vice-Pres. & Dir. 1957–59, Pres. and Dir. 1959–71; Chmn. of the Bd. Director, Carpenter Technology Corporation, Reading, Pa., July 1959–71; Director: American Bank and Trust Co. of Pennsylvania; Titanium Technology Corp., Pomona, Calif. 1968–71. *Member:* Member American Iron & Steel Institute (Director 1964–71), New York; Life Member, American Socy. for Metals. Hon LLD Albright Coll. *Clubs:* Wyomissing, Berkshire Country, Moselem Springs G.C., (Reading); Dartmouth College (Philadelphia). *Address:* R.D.I., Oley (Berks County), Pa.; and *office* 35N 6th Street, Reading, P.a., U.S.A.

**MOYER, Frederick Weaver.** American. *B.* 1917. *Educ.* Ohio State Univ. (BS, MA, PhD). *M.* 1939, Mary Carolyn Keller. *Career:* Professor of Finance, The Univ. of Akron since 1970; Trustee, Sumnit County Red Cross. *Address:* 104 South Meadowcroft Drive, Akron, Ohio 44313; and *office* 304 E. Buchtel Avenue, Akron, Ohio 44325, U.S.A.

**MOYLE, Roland Dunstan,** MA, LLB, MP. British politician. *B.* 1928. *Educ.* Llanidloes County School; Univ. Coll. of Wales, Aberystwyth (LLB); Trinity Hall, Cambridge (MA, LLB); Grays Inn. *M.* 1956, Shelagh Patricia Hogan. *S.* 1. *Dau.* 1. *Career:* Legal Assistant Wales Gas Board 1953–56; Snr. Industrial Relations Exec. with H.Q. Gas Industry (1956–62) and Electricity Supply Industry (1962–66); Member, Parliament North Lewisham 1966–74; Parly. Private Secy. Chief Secy. to the Treasury 1966–69; Parly. Private Secy. Home Secretary 1969–70; Vice-Chmn., Parly. Labour Party Defence Group 1968–72; Hon. Sec., British American Parly. Group 1971–74 & currently an Exec. Cttee. Member of the Group; Labour Spokesman on Higher Education 1972–74; Member, Parliament East Lewisham since Feb. 1974, Parly. Secy. Ministry of Agriculture from March to June 1974, Min. of State N.I. Office 1974–76; Min. of State, Dept. of Health since 1976. *Member:* Grays Inn. *Address: office* House of Commons, London, S.W.1.

**MOYNIHAN, Daniel Patrick.** American Academic & Politician. *B.* 1927. *Educ.* City Coll. of New York, Tufts Univ. & Fletcher Sch. of Law & Diplomacy (BA, MA, PhD). *M.* 1955, Elizabeth T. Brennan. *S.* 2. *Dau.* 1. *Career:* U.S. Navy 1944–47; Fulbright Fellow, London Sch. of Economics 1950–51; Dir. of Public Relations, Int. Rescue Comm. 1954; Asst. to Sec., Asst. Sec., then Acting Sec. to Gov. of N.Y. State 1955–58; Mem. N.Y. Tenure Comm. 1959–60; Dir., N.Y. State Govt. Research Project, Syracuse Univ. 1959–61; Special Asst. to Sect. of Labor 1961–62, Exec. Asst. 1962–63, Asst. Sec. of Labor 1963–65; Fellow, Centre for Advanced Studies, Wesleyan Univ. 1965–66; Dir., Joint Center Urban Studies, Mass. Inst. of Technology & Harvard Univ. 1966–69; Prof. of Educ. & Urban Studies and Mem. of the Faculty, Kennedy Sch. of Govt., Harvard Univ. 1966–73, Prof. of Govt., Harvard Univ. 1972–76; Asst. to Pres. of U.S.A. for Urban Affairs 1969, Counsellor to Pres. (with Cabinet Rank) 1969–70; Consultant to the Pres. 1971–73; U.S. Rep. to U.N. General Assembly 1971; Ambassador to India 1973–75; Perm. Rep. to UN 1975–76; Senator from New York since 1977 (Democratic). Fellow American Acad. of Arts & Sciences. *Member:* Amer. Philosophical Soc.; Council of Amer. Assn. for the Advancement of Science (former Vice-Pres. & Mem. Bd. of Dirs.); National Acad. of Public Administration. Hon. Degrees from 25 Colleges & Universities. *Address:* Senate Office Building, Washington, D.C. 20510, U.S.A.

**MOYNIHAN, Martin John,** CMG, MC. British Diplomat (Ret'd.). *Career:* Consul-General at Philadelphia 1966–70; Ambassador in Liberia 1970–73; British High Commissioner in Lesotho, SA 1973–76. Council Mem., Hakluyt Society, 1976; U.S.P.G., 1976; Africa Cttee., Oxfam, 1976; Pres., The Lesotho Diocesan Assn. 1976; Fellow, International Scotist Congress, Padua 1976; Administering Officer, Kennedy Memorial Trust 1977; Assoc. Mem. in Southern African Studies, Clare Hall, Cambridge 1977. *Award:* Knight Grand Band of the Humane Order of African Redemption. *Publications:* The Strangers (1946); South of Fort Hert (1956). *Clubs:* Athenaeum; Travellers. *Address:* 5 The Green, Wimbledon Common, London SW 19.

**MOYNIHAN, Maurice.** *B.* 1902. *Educ.* Univ. College, Cork (BCom, 1923); DEcon Sc Hon. Causa, National Univ. of Ireland. 1955. *M. S.* 2. *Daus.* 3. Knight Commander, Order of St. Gregory the Great. *Career:* Entered Dept. of Finance 1925; Secretary to Government 1937–60; Civil Service Commissioner 1937–53; Director, Central Bank of Ireland 1953–60; Governor, Central Bank of Ireland and Alternate Governor for Ireland, International Monetary Fund 1961–69; Member of Commissioners of Charitable Donations and Bequests for Ireland. *Publication:* Currency and Central Banking in Ireland 1922–60 (1975). *Address:* 48 Castle Avenue, Clontarf, Dublin 3.

**MPOTOKWANE, Lebang Mogaetsho.** Botswana diplomat. *B.* 1944. *Educ.* Moeng Coll.; Kisii Higei School; Univ of East Africa, Nairobi, BA. *M.* 1970, Lillian Reobonye Maphanyane. *Dau.* 1. *Career:* Asst. Secy. Office of the President 1968–69; 2nd Secy. Botswana High Commission, London 1969–70; Private Secy. to President 1970–73; Sen. Private Secy. to the President 1973–74; High Commissioner of Botswana to United Kingdom 1974–75; Administrative Sec., Office of the President, Botswana since 1975. *Clubs:* Notwane, Gabarone (Botswana); Le Petit Club Francais. *Address:* c/o Office of the President, Gaborone, Botswana.

**MUIR, Sir David John,** CMG, FCIS, FASA, FAIM, AAUQ. Queensland government official. *M.* 1942, Joan Haworth. *S.* Peter David. *Dau.* Beverley Joan. *Career:* Entered Queensland Public Service June 1933; served in Lands Dept. and Chief Secretary's Dept.; Investigation Officer, Cane Prices Board 1943; Secretary to the Premier 1946; Under-Secretary to the Premier and Chief Secretary's Department 1948; Agent-General for Queensland in London and Australian Representative on the International Sugar Council 1951 (Chmn. of the Council 1958). Dir., Industrial Development 1964–77; Chmn. Public Service Board of Queensland 1977—. Pres., Chartered Inst. of Secretaries 1964. Chmn., Queensland Theatre Co. since 1969. *Address:* Public Service Board, Box 59, P.O., Brisbane North Quay, Queensland, Australia 4000.

**MUIR, Sir John Harling,** Bt, TD, DL. British company director. *B.* 1910. *Educ.* Stowe School. *M.* 1936, Elizabeth Mary Dundas. *S.* 5. *Daus.* 2. *Career:* Director, James Finlay & Co. Ltd.; Consolidated Tea & Lands Co. (Bangladesh) Ltd.; Amalgamated Tea Estates Co. Ltd., African Highlands Produce Co. Ltd.; Royal Insurance Co. Ltd.; London & Lancashire Insurance Co. Ltd.; Liverpool & London & Globe Insurance Co. Ltd.; National & Grindlays Bank (Holdings) Ltd.; Scottish United Investors Ltd.; S. H. Lock & Co. (Holdings) Ltd. Member, Queen's Bodyguard for Scotland (Royal Company of Archers). *Clubs:* Oriental (London); Tollygunge (Calcutta); Western (Glasgow). *Address:* Blair Drummond, Perthshire, by Stirling; and *office* 22 West Nile Street, Glasgow, C.1.

**MUIRHEAD, Sir David Francis,** KCMG, CVO. British diplomat. *B.* 1918. *Educ.* Cranbrook School. *M.* 1942, The Hon. Elspeth Hope-Morley. *S.* David Nicholas, Mark. *Dau.* Mary. *Career:* Regular Army Major, A/Lt.-Colonel 1939–46; First Secy. British Embassy, La Paz 1947–49; Buenos Aires 1950; Brussels 1950–53; Foreign Office 1953–55; Washington 1953–59; Counsellor, Foreign Office 1959–65; Asst. Under-Secy. Foreign Office 1966–67; H.M. Ambassador to Peru 1967–70; to Portugal 1970–74; to Belgium since 1974. *Award:* Kt. Grand Cross of Military Order of Christ (Portugal). *Clubs:* Travellers', Special Forces. *Address:* 16 Pitt Street, Kensington, London, W.8 and *office* British Embassy, Brussels, Belgium.

**MUIRSHIEL, Rt. Hon. Viscount (John Scott Maclay).** KT, PC, CH, CMG. British politician. *B.* 29 Oct. 1905. *Educ.* Winchester; Trinity College, Cambridge. *M* 1930, Betty L'Estrange Astley. *Career:* Member, Parliament (Nat. Lib. and Cons.) for Montrose Burghs 1940–50, for Renfrewshire West 1950–64. Head, British Merchant Shipping Mission, Washington 1944; Chmn., British National Cttee. of Internat. Chamber of Commerce 1947–51; Parl. Sec., Min. of Prod. May–July 1945; Min. of Transport and Civil Aviation Oct. 1951–May 1952; Minister of State for Colonial Affairs 1956–57; Secretary of State for Scotland 1957–62; Chmn. Joint

Exchequer Board (Northern Ireland) 1965—73; Pres., Assembly of Western European Union 1955–56. Lord Lieutenant of Renfrewshire 1967. Hon. LLD Edinburgh 1963, and Strathclyde 1966, Glasgow, 1970. *Address:* Knapps, Kilmacolm, Renfrewshire.

**MULDOON, Rt. Hon. Robert David,** PC, MP. New Zealand Politician. *B.* 1921. *Educ.* Mount Albert Grammar School. *M.* 1951. Thea Dale Flyger. *S.* 1. *Daus.* 2. *Career:* Pres., N.Z. Inst. of Cost Accountants 1956; MP for Tamaki since 1960; Parly. Under-Sec. to Minister of Finance 1963–66; Minister of Tourism 1967, of Finance 1967–72; Dep. Prime Minister, Feb.–Nov. 1972; Dep. Leader. National Party & Dep. Leader of the Opposition 1972–74; Leader of the National Party since 1974; Leader of the Opposition 1974–75; Prime Minister & Minister of Finance since 1975. *Member:* FCANZ; CMANZ; FCIS; FCWA. *Awards:* Companion of Honour 1977. *Publication:* The Rise & Fall of a Young Turk (1974). *Clubs:* Wellington; Professional. *Address:* 290 Kohimarama Road, Auckland 5, New Zealand.

**MULLENS, Sir Harold (Hill).** British. *B.* 1900. *Educ.* Merchant Taylor's School and Durham University (BSc). *M.* 1932, Winifred McConnell. *S.* 1. *Dau.* 1. *Career:* Joined North Eastern Electrical Supply Co. Ltd. 1924; held various appointments from Assistant Engineer to Deputy General Manager with the Company until nationalization of the electricity supply industry. First Chairman, North Eastern Electricity Board 1948–54; resigned to become Managing Director of A. Reyrolle & Co. Ltd. 1954; relinquished this post to become Chairman of the Company 1958; Chmn. C. A. Parsons & Co. Ltd. 1959; President: British Electrical & Allied Mfrs. Assn. 1962–63, and British Electrical Power Convention 1963–64. President, Reyrolle Parsons Ltd. 1969; Deputy Chairman, The Nuclear Power Plant Co. Ltd. Author of various technical papers. Fellow, Institution of Electrical Engineers. *Clubs:* Northern Counties (Newcastle). *Address:* 4 Westfield Grove, Gosforth, Newcastle-upon-Tyne; and *office* Reyrolle Parsons Ltd., Cuthbert House, All Saints Precinct, Newcastle-upon-Tyne.

**MÜLLER, Charles.** Swiss Diplomat. *B.* 1922. *Educ.* Univs. of Zürich & Geneva—Graduate in Political Science & International Affairs. *M.* 1950, Marlise Brügger. *Career:* Swiss Foreign Service, posts in Berne, Cairo & Moscow 1946–60; Secretariat, European Free Trade Association (EFTA) 1960–65 (Dept. Sec.-Gen. from 1965); Swiss Foreign Service 1966–76; First Counsellor, Swiss Embassy, Washington D.C. 1966–70; Swiss Ambassador to Indonesia 1970–73; Head of Europe—North America Division of Swiss Federal Political Dept. 1973–76; Sec.-Gen. of EFTA since 1976. *Address:* 2 Rue des Granges, 1204 Geneva, Switzerland; and 9–11 Rue de Varembé, 1211 Geneva 20, Switzerland.

**MULLER, Gebhard,** Dr jur. German politician. *B.* 17 Apr. 1900. *M.* 1940, Marianne Lutz. *S.* Wolfgang, Peter, Thomas. *Career:* Judge at Württemberg Courts 1929–45; Attorney-General, Stuttgart 1945; Ministerial Director, Ministry of Justice, Tübingen 1946; President, Land Württemberg-Hohenzollern since Aug. 1948; Minister of Finance since 1949 and Minister of Justice, Land Württemberg-Hohenzollern since 1950; Minister-President Land Baden-Württemberg, 1953–58; member of Bundesrat 1953–58; President, The Federal Constitutional Court of Karlsruhe 1959–71. *Awards:* Hon. Senator, University of Tübingen; Hon. Doctor, University of Freiburg; Hon. Professor, Univ. Tübingen. *Publications:* Empfehlungen des juristischen Ausschusses der Ministerpräsidenten; Die Revision des Besatzungsrechtes; Die Rechtsvorschriften der Besatzungsmächte; Wirtschaftsverfassung und Bundesverfassung-Gericht; Sozial Sicherheit in einer demokratischen Gesellschaft. *Address:* Friedrich-Ebertstrasse 112, Stüttgart, Germany.

**MULLER, Dr. Hilgard,** MP. *B.* 1914. *Educ.* University of Pretoria (BA, MA, DLitt); Oxford University (BLitt); University of South Africa (LLB). *M.* 1943, Nita Dyason. *S.* Cornelius Johannes. *Career:* Elected Rhodes Scholar for Transvaal Province 1937; research work in Ancient History at University College and obtained BLitt degree and gained Oxford University Rugby Blue; Senior Lecturer in Latin, Univ. of Pretoria 1940; practised as lawyer in Pretoria since 1947; member, City Council of Pretoria 1951; elected Deputy Mayor and served two terms as Mayor 1953–55; elected MP for Pretoria East, 1958; High Commissioner in the U.K. Jan.–May 1961. Ambassador of Republic of South Africa to the Court of St. James's, May 1961–63; Foreign Minister of South Africa 1964–77; lawyer and director of companies; Councillor, City of Pretoria since 1951; Trustee, National Development Foundation (1954); member of Council and President of Convocation, University of Pretoria (1952); Chairman, Weskoppies Hospital Board (1952); Director, Dunlop South Africa Ltd. (1956). Chancellor of Pretoria Univ. 1965. *Awards:* Received hon. degree DPhil from Stellenbosch Univ. 1968; Grand Cross, Order of Merit, Paraguay; Grand Cross, Order of Christ of Portugal; Grand Cross of the Order of Infante Dom Henrique of Portugal (1973); Grand Officer of the Order of Merit of the Central African Republic (1976); Decoration for Meritorious Service (South Africa, 1976). Member, Royal Society of Arts. *Publications:* Relations of Christians and Pagans from Constantine the Great until 410 A.D. (2 vols.); several works and papers in the Afrikaans language. *Address:* P.O.B. 793, Pretoria, South Africa.

**MULLER, Dr. Thomas Frederik.** *B.* 1916. *Educ.* University of Witwatersrand (BSc, and Gold Medal and Research Fellowship of Chamber of Mines); MSc (Birmingham); DComm (h.c. Potchef). *M.* (1) Susanna Elizabeth Jordaan (*Dec.* 1968). *Daus.* 2. (2) 1970, Nicolette Van Schalkwyk. *S.* 1. *Career:* With Anglo Transvaal Group of mines in Transvaal and O.F.S. 1949–55; Federale Mynbou Beperk 1957, Managing Director 1963. Managing Director: General Mining & Finance Corporation Ltd. Federale Mynbou Beperk. Chairman and director of other companies in the General Mining Group until 1971; Chmn. South African Iron and Steel Industrial Corp. Ltd. (ISCOR); Amcor Ltd.; Mektor Investments Ltd.; International Pipe & Steel Investments S.A. (Pty) Ltd. *Publications:* papers on mining matters. Past President: Chamber of Mines of S.A.; Afrikaanse Handelsinstituut. Member: Prime Minister's Economic Adv. Cncl. *Clubs:* The River; Royal Johannesburg: Rand; Country; R.S.A.; Randpark and Zwartkop. *Address:* 17 Molesey Avenue, Auckland Park, Johannesburg; and *office* Iscor P.O. Box 450, Pretoria, South Africa.

**MULLEY, Rt. Hon. Frederick William,** PC, MP (Park (Sheffield) 1950—). *B.* 1918. *Educ.* MA (Oxon) 1st Cl. Hons. in Philosophy, Politics and Economics; MA (Cantab); BSc Econ (London). *M.* 1948, Joan Phillips. *Daus.* Deirdre and Corinne. *Career:* Deputy Secretary of State for Defence and Minister of Defence for the Army 1964–65; Minister of Aviation 1965–67. Minister of State, Foreign Office, 1967–69; Minister of Transport, 1969–70 and 1974–75; Sec. of State for Education & Science 1975–76; Sec. of State for Defence since 1976. Fellow St. Catharine's Coll. Cambridge 1948–50. *Publications:* The Politics of Western Defence, (1962). *Address:* House of Commons, London, S.W.1.

**MULLIGAN, Col. Hugh Waddell,** CMG. British. *B.* 1901. *Educ.* Univ. of Aberdeen, MB, ChB (1923); MD (Hons., 1930); DSc (1934). *M.* 1929, Rita Armstrong. *S.* Andrew and John. *Dau.* Shelagh. *Career:* Consultant Malariologist, G.H.Q., Persia and Iraq Command, 1941–43; Dir., Central Research Institute, Kasauli, India, 1943–47; West African Institute for Trypanosomiasis Research, 1947–54; Director, Wellcome Research Laboratories, Beckenham, Kent, 1954–66; Visting Lecturer, University of Salford, 1967–76. *Publications:* numberous scientific papers on tropical medical subjects; Editor-in-Chief, The African Trypanosomiases (1970). Member of Royal Society of Medicine; Royal Society of Tropical Medicine and Hygiene; British Medical Association. North Persian Forces Memorial Medal, 1929; Commonwealth Fund Fellow, University of Chicago, 1933–35; Mentioned in Dispatches, 1941. *Address:* 5 Thorngrove Road, Wilmslow, Cheshire SK9 1DD.

**MULLIKEN, Robert Sanderson.** American. *B.* 1896. *Educ.* M.I.T. (BS), and Univ. of Chicago (PhD). *M.* 1929, Mary Helen von Noé (Dec'd). *Daus.* 2. *Career:* Junior Chemical Engr. Bureau of Mines, U.S. Dept. of Interior 1917–18; Assistant, rubber research, N.J. Zinc Co. 1919. Fellowship, Natl. Research Cncl. Chicago and Harvard 1921–25; Asst. Prof. Physics, Washington Square Coll. 1926–28; Assoc. Prof. Chicago 1929–31 (Prof. 1931–61); Distinguished Service Prof. of Physics & Chem. since 1961; Distinguished Research Prof. of Chemical Physics (Florida State Univ.) 1965–71; Guggenheim Fellow, Germany 1930–32. Directed educational work and information, Plutonium Project, Chicago 1942–45; Fulbright Scholar, Oxford 1952–53; Scientific Attaché, U.S. Embassy, London 1955; Baker Lecturer, Cornell 1960; Distinguished Service Professor of Physics and Chemistry, Univ. of Chicago 1961—, and (winters) at Florida State Univ. 1965–70. Silliman Lecturer, Yale 1965; Visiting Prof., Bombay 1962; I.I.T. Kanpur 1962; Jan va Guens, Amsterdam 1965 and 1971; Univ. Calif, Sante Barbara 1968; Univ. Paris

1968; Univ. Texas, Austin 1970. *Awards:* Hon. Fellow, London Chemical Socy.; Hon. Member Sté. de Chimie Physique, Royal Irish Academy, Japanese Chemical Soc.; Hon. Fellow, Indian Academy of Science; Foreign Member, Royal Socy. London; Hon, ScD: Columbia, Marquette and Cambridge; Hon. PhD Stockholm; Bronze Medal, Liège; G. N. Lewis Gold Medal, Calif, Section, Amer. Chem. Socy.; T. W. Richards Gold Medal, Northeastern Section, A.C.S.; Peter Debye Award, A.C.S.; J.G. Kirkwood Award, New Haven Section, A.C.S., and Willard Gibbs Gold Medal, Chicago Section, Nobel Prize Winner in Chemistry 1966. *Member:* U.S. Natl. Acad. Sciences; Philosophical Socy.; Amer. Chem. Socy; Amer. Physical Socy.; Amer. Acad. of Arts & Sciences; American Assoc. for Advancement of Science; Int. Acad. of Quantum Molecular Science. *Publications:* over 200 scientific papers in professional journals. *Clubs:* Quadrangle (Chicago); Cosmos (Wash.). *Address:* 5825 Dorchester Avenue, Chicago Ill. 60637; and University of Chicago, Chicago, Ill. 60637, U.S.A.

**MUMFORD, Milton Christopher.** American. *B.* 1913. *Educ.* Univ. of Illinois (AB). *M.* 1942, Louise Greene. *S.* Christopher Greene. *Daus.* Emily Stearns and Letitia Bronson. *Career:* Joined Marshall Field & Co., Chicago 1935 (Vice-Pres 1948–54; Gen. Mgr., Fieldcrest Mills Div. 1950–53; Pres. Fieldcrest Mills Inc. 1953–54). Joined Lever Bros. Co., N.Y. 1954 (Vice-Pres. 1954–55; Dir. 1955—; Exec. Vice-Pres. 1955–59; Pres. and Chief Exec. Officer 1959–65; Chmn. 1964–72). Commander, U.S. Navy in World War II (awarded Legion of Merit). Appointed in 1947, Housing and Redevelopment Co-ordinator in Chicago, supervised a slum clearance and housii g programme and development of underground parking garages; Chairman: Lever Brothers Co. 1964–72, Educational Facilities Laboratories (Ford Foundation 1959–72. Director: Lever Bros. Ltd. Canada) 1964–76, Thomas J. Lipton Inc. 1964—, Equitable Life Acsurance Society 1962—, Crown Zellerbach Corp. 1965—, Federal Reserve Bank of New York 1966–72, National Merit Scholarship Corp. 1965–70, and The Stamford Hospital, Conn., 1964–76. Trustee: Consolidated Edison Co. of N.Y. Inc. 1964—The Presbyterian Hospital 1967–77. Advisory Director, Unilever Ltd. since 1965. *Awards:* Chicago (III) Junior Chamber of Commerce and Industry Service Award as Chicago's Outstanding Young Man of 1948; Hon. LLD Long Island Univ. 1969. *Clubs:* Commercial, University, (Chicago); River, Blind Brook (N.Y.); Pine Valley (N.J.); Cypress Point (Calif.); Augusta National Golf (Ga.); Wee Burn Golf (Darien, Conn.); Racquet & Tennis (N.Y.). *Address:* 514 Hollow Tree Ridge Road, Darien, Conn. 06820; and *office* 390 Park Avenue, New York, N.. 10022, U.S.A.

**MUNCH, Prof. James Clyde.** American pharmacologist and toxicologist. *B.* 1896. *Educ.* Illinois Wesleyan Univ. (BS and MS); George Washington Univ. (PhD). *M.* 1927, Soula Robinson. *S.* James Clanton. *Dau.* Margaret Clyde (Mrs. H. J. McWhinnie). *Career:* Pharmacologist, U.S. Food and Drug Admin. 1917–27; U.S. Fish and Wildlife Service 1928–44; War Food Admin. 1943–44; Prof. of Physiology and Pharmacology, Temple Schools of Dentistry and Pharmacy 1932–54; Lecturer and Asst. Prof., Dept. Pharmacology, Hahnemann Medical College and Hospital 1940–65; Pharmocologist. Sharp & Dohme 1928–36; Wyeth 1936–38; Medical Dir., Strong, Cobb & Co. 1951–53; Professor of Human Pharmacology, Hahnemann Medical College 1940–65; U. Miami Med. School, 1965–72 Consultant Pharmacologist 1938—; Medical Dir., Vaponefrin Co. 1938–70; Key Pharm. 1958–72; Consultant Secy., Health and Welfare, Commonwealth, Penn. Member, Attorney-General's Committee, Narcotics & Dangerous Drugs; Consultant to several branches of U.S. Govt. in Pharmacology and Toxicology Adv. Committee, U.S. Federal Bureau of Narcotics. *Member:* American Acad. Allergy Fellow; International Narcotic Enforcement Officers Assoc.; American Pharmaceutical Assn. (Life Member and former Vice-Pres.); AAAS (Life Member); Assn. of Military Surgeons of U.S. (Life Member); American College of Cardiology (Fellow); American Statistical Assn. (Life Member); American Medical Assn.; College of Physicians of Philadelphia (Assoc. Member); Member, Pan-American Congresses Pharm. Biochem. of Lima 1951, Brazil 1954; Sec., Pharmacology, Washington, D.C. 1957; Secretary, Pharmacology, Pan American Assn. (life member), Mexico 1960; Socy. of Toxicologists; Forensic Medicine & Toxicology (London); European Socy. for Study of Drug Toxicology, Inter-American Conference Toxicology Occup. Med. Republican. *Publications:* over 200 in pharmacology, toxicology and bioassays in various scientific journals in Great Britain, Peru, U.S.. Cuba and Germany, three books on bioassays and on pharmacology; another, on inhalational therapy. *Clubs:* Union League (Phila.); Cosmos (Washington D.C.); Chemists (N.Y.C.); Mason (Past Master); Rotarian; Optimist (Life Member). *Address:* 271–C, 15001 Westholm Court, Silver Spring, MD. 20906, U.S.A.

**MÜNCHEMEYER, Alwin,** Dr. Jur. (h.c.). German banker. *B.* 1908. *Educ.* High School (Abitur). *M.* 1934, Gerturde Nolte. *S.* 1. *Daus.* 4, *Career: Chairman:* Advisory Board, Schröder, Munchmeyer, Hengst & Co., Hamburg. Frankfurt, Offenbach.; Chairman: Allgemeine Kreditverischerung AG, Manz; Nord- Deutsche Versicherungs AG, Hamburg; Philips GmbH, Hamburg; Nord-Deutsche Lebensversicherungs-AG, Hamburg; Vereins-und Westbank AG, Hamburg; Hamburg-Mannheimer Sachvers AG; Mem. of Bd. Nordwestdeutsche Kraftwerke Bayerische Vereinsbank, Munchen; Maizena Gesellschaft mbH, Hamburg; Member, Adv. Bd., Hamburger Sparkasse, Hamburg; Hermes-Kreditversicherungs-AG, Hamburg; Hamburg, Landeszentralbank in der Freien und Hansestadt Hamburg; Hamburg-Mannheimer Vers. AG; Hon. Pres. Permanent Conference, Chambers of Commerce and Industry, EEC countries. Hon. member Bd. Deutscher Industrie-und Handelstag, Bonn; Esec. Ctte. German Section, International Chamber of Commerce. Chmn. Foreign Trade Advisory Bd. Ministry of Economy, Bonn; Council Int. Chamber of Commerce Paris; Deutsch-sowjetische Kommission für wirtschaftliche und wissenschaftlich-technische Zusammenarbeit. *Address:* 2000 Hamburg 56, Tinsdaler Kirchenweg 219, and *office* Schröder Munchmeyer, Hengst & Co., 2 Hamburg 1, Ballindamm 33, Germany.

**MUNCHMEYER, Louis W.** Retired American executive chemical engineer. *B.* 1904. *Educ.* West Virginia University (BS Chem Eng). *M.* 1934, Margaret Gordon. *S.* Louis W. (MD). *Dau.* Margaret M. Lehman. *Career:* With E. I. du Pont de Nemours & Co. (Parlin, N.J., and Richmond, Va.) 1927–42; U.S. Army Army-Navy Munitions Bd., Chem. Corps; Colonel 1942–45; Legion of Merit. Vice-President, Michigan Chemical Corp. 1945–48; Assistant General Mgr., Ansco Div., General Aniline & Film 1948–55. Asst. General Manager, M.A. Div. 1955–58; Vice-President, Wyandotte Chemicals Corp. 1958–66; Dir. McCormick Theological Seminary. Associated with Kenower MacArthur & Co., Investment Securities, 1967–70. *Member:* National Pres. Armed Forces Chemical Assn. 1952–54; American Institute of Chemical Engineers; American Chemical Society; Amer. Ordnance Assn.; Engineering Socy. of Detroit. *Address:* Box 212 Cruz Bay, St. John, U.S. Virgin Islands, 00830; (summer) 555 N. Taylor Place, Ithaca, N.Y. 14850, U.S.A.

**MUNKKI, Olavi.** Finnish foreign service official. *B.* 8 July 1909. *Educ.* University of Helsinki (LLM). *M.* 1946, Eila Martta Korkela. *S.* 1. *Career:* Attached Ministery of Foreign Affairs 1937; Attaché and Vice-Consul, London 1937–42; with Ministry of Foreign Affairs, Helsinki (various posts) 1942–45; First Secretary, Legation Washington 1945–50; Chief of Bureau, Ministry for Foreign Affairs, Helsinki 1950–52; Counsellor 1951: Trade Commissioner of Finland at Cologne since 1952 (Consul-General since 1954); Asst. Dir., Commercial Div., Ministry of Foreign Affairs 1957–59; Director, Commercial Division, Ministry of Foreign Affairs 1959–62. En. Ex .& Min. Plen. 1960. Ambassador to Switzerland 1962–65, to U.S. 1965–72; Ambassador to Norway since 1973. *Awards:* Cmdr. Order of White Rose (Finland). Commander, Order of the Lion (Finland); Grand Cross, Order of the Phoenix (Greece); Grand Cross with Star, Order of Merit of Fed. Republic of Germany; Kt. Comdr., Order of St. Olav (Norway); Das grosse goldene Ehrenzeichen mit den Stern (Austria); Grande Ufficiale nell'Ordine Al Merito della Repubblica Italiana. *Address:* Embassy of Finland, Thomas Heftyes gate 1, Oslo 2, Norway.

**MUNRO, Hon. John Carr.** PC (Can.). Canadian politician. *B.* 1931. *Educ.* Central Public School; Westdale Composite School; Univ. of Western Ontario (BA). *M.* 1956, Marguerite Harriet Clay. *Daus.* Susan, Ann. *Career:* Barrister and solicitor; Hamilton City Council, 1955; Member of Parliament for Hamilton East, 1962; re-elected 1963, 1965, 1968; Parly, Secy. to Minister of Citizenship & Immigration, 1963, to Min. of Manpower and Immigration 1966; Made Privy Councillor (Canada) 1968; Min. without Portfolio 1968; Min. of Nat. Health and Welfare 1968–72; Apptd. Min. of Labour 1972 and 1974. *Address:* 340 Laurier West, Ottawa, Canada.

**MUNSON, Charles Sherwood.** American. *B.* 1888. *Educ.* Yale University (BA 1912). *M.* 1912, Marjorie Jean Oatman. *S.* Charles Sherwood, Jr. *Career:* Began with Amoskeag Mfg.

Co. 1912; joined what is now Air Reduction Co. in 1917 (became Vice-Pres. 1924, Pres. 1937, Chmn. of Board 1948–64). Chmn. Chemical Industry Advisory Committee of the Munitions Board 1944–48; In the period 1946–51 served continuously as Pres., Chmn. and Dir. of the Manufacturing Chemist's Assn.; Hon. Chmn. Bd. of Airco Inc.; Member, Directors Advisory Council, Morgan Guaranty Trust Co. of N.Y. Director and Member Exec. Cttee.: Greyhound Corp., Greyhound Lines, Michigan Gas Utilities, Warnaco Inc., Director: General Fire & Casualty Co., Greyhound Food Management Inc., National Distillers & Chemical Corp., Baxter Laboratories, and Greyhound Lines of Canada Ltd.; Dir. Main Street Fund Inc.; Compass Ins. Co. Was the 1953 Medallist awarded by the Society of the Chemical Industry. Is a director and/or trustee of numerous institutions and, in addition, devotes considerable time to civic affairs and philanthropic activities. *Clubs:* Links (Pres.), Yale (Council), Cloud (Gov.), Union, Church (all N.Y.C.); Pilgrims of U.S.; Fairfield (Conn.) Country; The Pinnacle of N.Y.C. (Organizer and first Pres.). *Address:* 893 Sasco Hill Road, Southport, Conn. 06490, U.S.A.

**MURDOCH, John Edward Victor.** Australian chartered accountant and company director. *B.* 1907. *Educ.* Albany High School. *M.* 1931, Evelyn Isobel Harle. *S.* John Geoffrey. *Dau.* Jocelyn Isobel. *Career:* Commissioner, Australian National Airlines Commission, which runs Trans-Australia Airlines, 1957–70. Director of several public and private companies. *Member:* Institute of Chartered Accountants in Australia; Australian Society of Accountants; Chartered Institute of Secretaries; Institute of Directors Australia. *Clubs:* Weld; *Address:* 66 Jutland Parade, Dalkeith, W.A.; and *office* 16 Altona St. West Perth, W.A., Australia.

**MURDOCH, Lawrie George,** LLB. British. *B.* 1911. *Educ.* The Hutchins School and Univ. of Tasmania (LLB). *M.* 1937, Marie Jean Dakin. *Daus.* Diana Jane and Angela Sue. *Career:* Notary Public, Chmn. Hobart Building Society, Tasmanian Government Insurance Office; Dir. The Mercury newspaper; Tasmania Television Ltd.; Frank Hammond Pty. Ltd. *Address:* 42 Fisher Avenue, Sandy Bay, Hobart, Tasmania.

**MURDOUGH, Thomas Gorden.** American. *B.* 1904. *Educ.* Dartmouth College (BA 1926). *M.* 1931, Grace Clark. *S.* Samuel Clarke, Charles Pratt, and Thomas Gorden. *Career:* Vice-President and Director, American Hospital Supply Corp. 1947–54, Pres. and Dir. 1954–64; Vice Chairman of Board, American Hospital Supply Corp., July 1964–69. Director: Illinois Tool Works 1961, Northern Trust Co., and Universal Oil Products, 1962; Hon. Dir., American Hospital Supply Corp. Hon. LLD, Dartmouth Coll., 1976. *Clubs:* Glen View Golf (Illinois); Chicago, Commercial, University (all in Chicago). *Address:* 2825 Lincoln Street, Evanston, Ill. 60201, U.S.A.

**MURPHY, Charles Haywood, Jr.** Investor. Petroleum company official. *B.* 1920. *Educ.* El Dorado High Schools and studied with private tutors. *M.* 1939, Johnnie Walker. *S.* Michael Walker, Charles Haywood III, and Robert Madison. *Dau.* Martha Wilson. *Career:* President, Murphy Oil Corp. (El Dorado, Ark.) 1950, Chmn. Bd. 1972—; Chairman of Board: Ocean Drilling & Exploration Co. (New Orleans) 1953—. *Member:* Amer. Petroleum Inst. (Dir.); Ark. State Bd. of Higher Education. National Petroleum Council. LLD (Hon.) Univ. of Arkansas, 1966. *Address:* 200 Jefferson, El Dorado, Ark., U.S.A.

**MURPHY, Dr. Franklin David.** American publisher & educator. *B.* 1916. *Educ.* Univ. of Kansas (AB); Univ. of Pennsylvania (MD); Hon. DSc, Univ. of Pennsylvania, and Univ. of Nebraska; LLD, Univ. of S. California, Park Coll., Temple Univ., Occidental Coll., and Bucknell Univ.; LHD, Kansas Wesleyan and Univ. of Judaism. *M.* 1940, Judith Joyce Harris. *S.* Franklin Lee. *Daus.* Judith Joyce (Dickey), Martha Alice (Crockwell) and Carolyn Louise (Milner). *Career:* Dean, School of Medicine, Univ. of Kansas 1948–51 (Chancellor 1951–60); Chancellor, University of California, Los Angeles, 1960–68; Chairman of the Board, Times Mirror Co. since 1968. *Publications:* reports and articles in numerous medical journals. Fraternities; Phi Beta Kappa, Sigma Xi, Alpha Omega Alpha, Beta Theta Pi, Nu Sigma Nu. *Address:* 419 Robert Lane, Beverly Hills, Cal. 90210; and *office* Times Mirror Square, Los Angeles, California 90053, U.S.A.

**MURPHY, John Fitzjames,** Irish. *B.* 1909. *Educ.* Downside School (Somerset, England) and Royal Military Academy (Woolwich, Eng.). *Career:* Served in British Army 1929–47 (retired with rank of Lt-Col.) Joined James J. Murphy, Cork 1947. James J. Murphy & Co. Ltd., Ladyswell Brewery, Cork 1957—. Dir.: The Munster & Leinster Bank Ltd., Cork 1957—; and The West Cork Bottling Co. Ltd., Bandon, Co. Cork since 1947. *Address:* Burlington, River Bank, Douglas Rd, Cork; and *office* Ladyswell Brewery, Cork, Ireland.

**MURPHY, Michael Joseph.** Irish. *B.* 1919. *Educ.* Christian Brothers College, Dun-Laoghaire. *M.* 1941, Joan Huggard. *S.* Joseph and James. *Daus:* Christine, Annajane, Micheline and Marguerite. *Career:* Director: Joseph Murphy (Ballina) Ltd. 1942—, Chmn. 1973; Ulster Bank Ltd., Belfast since 1969. President, Golfing Union of Ireland 1963–65; Member, Ballina Golf Club, Sligo G.C., and Portmarnock G. C., and Royal & Ancient Golf Club of St. Andrews. Chairman, Council of National Golf Unions, 1969. *Clubs:* Hibernian United Service; Fitzwilliam L.T.C.; R.I.A.C. *Address:* 'Hilltop', Sligo Road, Ballina, Co. Mayo; and *office* Lord Edward Street, Ballina, Co. Mayo, Ireland.

**MURPHY, Robert D.** *B.* 1894. *Educ.* Marquette University; George Washington Univ. (LLB, LLM). *M.* 1921, Mildred Claire Taylor. *Daus.* Catherine Taylor, Rosemary, Mildred Margaret. *Career:* joined State Dept. 1920; Vice-Consul, Zürich 1921, Munich 1921; Consul, Seville 1925; State Department 1926; Consul, Paris 1930; First Secretary, Paris 1936, Counsellor 1939; Chargé d'Affaires, Vichy 1940; Personal Representatives of the President in North Africa with rank of Minister 1942; U.S. Political Adviser on German affairs with rank of Ambassador, S.H.A.E.F. 1944; Acting Director, Office of German and Austrian Affairs 1949; Amb. Ex. and Plen. to Belgium 1949–52; to Japan 1952–53; Asst.-Sec. of State for U.N. Affairs, Mar. 1953; Dept. Under-Sec. of State 1953–59; Under-Secretary of State for Political Affairs, July 1959–Dec. 1959. Hon. Chairman, Corning Glass International since 1960. *Address:* 717 Fifth Avenue, New York City 22, U.S.A.

**MURRAY, Sir (Francis) Ralph (Hay),** KCMG, CB. British diplomat. *B.* 3 Mar. 1908. *Educ.* St. Edmund Hall, Oxford. *M.* 1935, Mauricette Kuenburg. *S.* 3. *Dau.* 1. *Career:* B.B.C. 1934–39; Foreign Office 1939–45 and 1948–51; A.C.C. Austria 1945; Special Commissioner's Staff, S.E. Asia 1946–47; Counsellor, Embassy, Madrid 1951–54; Minister, Embassy, Cairo 1954–56; Under-Secretary, Foreign Office 1957; Ambassador to Greece 1962–67; Governor B.B.C. 1967–73; Chmn. Sea Tank Co. (U.K.) Ltd.; Dir. of other Companies. *Address:* The Old Rectory, Stoke Hammond, Bletchley.

**MURRAY, James Dalton,** CMG. British. *B.* 1911. *Educ.* Stowe School and Magdalene College, Cambridge (BA Hons 1932). *M.* (1) Denny Carter (*D.* 1958). *S.* 1. *Daus.* 2; and (2) 1959, Merriall Rose Eden (*S.* 1, and one adoptive son). *Career:* Entered Consular Service 1933; served in San Francisco, Mexico City, and Washington; First Secy. La Paz, 1943–44; and Foreign Office 1945–48, and Singapore 1948–50. Promoted Counsellor and appointed to Foreign Office 1950; Deputy High Commissioner in Karachi 1952–55; Foreign Office 1955–59; Embassy Lisbon 1959–61; Minister to Rumania 1961, and first British Ambassador there 1963. High Commissioner in Jamaica, May 1965–70; and concurrently (non-resident) Ambassador to Haiti 1966–70; Retired and re-employed as First Secy. and Consul resident Port-au Prince, Haiti 1970–76. *Club:* Travellers' (London). *Address:* British Embassy, P.O. Box 1302 Port-au Prince, Haiti and c/o Foreign and Commonwealth Office, London, S.W.1.

**MURRAY OF NEWHAVEN, Lord,** KCB (Keith Anderson Hope Murray). *B.* 1903. *Educ.* Edinburgh Univ. (BSc); Cornell Univ. (PhD); Oxford Univ. (MA, BLitt); Cambridge Univ. (MA); Hon. Fellow, Oriel and Lincoln Colleges, Oxford Downing College, Cambridge and Birkbeck Coll. London; Visitor, Loughborough Univ. of Technology; Hon. DLitt Keele; Hon. DCL Oxford; Hon. LLD, Western Australia, Bristol, Cambridge, Hull, Edinburgh, Southampton, Liverpool, Leicester, California, Strathclyde and London Universities; Hon. D Univ., Stirling and Essex. *Career:* Commonwealth Fund Fellowship 1926–29; Agricultural Economics Research Institute, Oxford 1929–39; Ministry of Food 1939–40; Royal Air Force 1940–42; Dir. of Food and Agriculture, Middle East Supply Centre 1942–45; Chmn. University Grants Committee 1953–63; Dir. Leverhume Trust Fund 1964–72; Fellow and Bursar, Lincoln College, Oxford 1937–44; Rector and Bursar 1944–53; Chairman: Australian Universities Cttee. 1957; World Univ. Service, 1957–63; Dartmouth Review Cttee., 1958; Chmn., Royal Commission, 1851 Exhibition, 1962–71; Cttee., of Enquiry into the Governance of London Univ. 1970–72; Chancellor Southampton Univ. 1964–74. *Address:* c/o Drummonds Branch, Royal Bank of Scotland, 49 Charing Cross, London, S.W.1.

**MURTO, Olavi Kalervo.** Finnish diplomat *B.* 1911. *Educ.* Helsinki University (Lic. ès lettres). *M.* 1943, Anne Speranza. *S.* Kaarlo Charles. *Career:* Entered Min. of Foreign Affairs 1938; Attaché Moscow 1939; Attaché and Secy. Bucharest 1941–43; First Secretary Prague 1947–49 and Brussels 1949–52; Chief of Bureau, Min. Foreign Affairs 1952–54; Chargé d'Affaires Mexico (with Colombia and Venezuela) 1955–59; Adjoint Director, External Commerce, Min. Foreign Affairs 1959–63; Ambassador of Finland to Belgium and to Luxembourg 1963. Chief of Finnish Mission at the European Communities 1964. Minister to Ireland whilst resident in Brussels 1963–64. *Awards:* Cross of Liberty (Finland); Comdr., Order of the Lion (Finland); Grand Cordon of The Phoenix (Greece), and of the Aztec Eagle (Mexico); Comdr., Order of Merit (Austria); Officer, Orders of Leopold (Belgium) and the Crown (Rumania). *Address:* Munkkiniemen Puistotie 11, Helsinki, Finland.

**MUSGRAVE, Sir (Frank) Cyril,** KCB. British administrator (Ret'd.). *B.* 21 June 1900. *Educ.* St. George's Coll., London. *M.* (1), Elsie Mary Williams. *S.* 1. *Dau.* 1; (2), Jean Elsie Soulsby. *S.* 2. *Career:* Entered Civil Service 1919; Inland Revenue 1920–37; Air Ministry 1937–40; Ministry of Aircraft Production 1940–46; Ministry of Supply 1946–59; Under-Secretary i.c. Air Div., 1946–51; Deputy Secretary 1951–53; Second Permanent Secretary, 1953–56; Permanent Secretary 1956–59; Chairman, Iron & Steel Board 1959–67; Part time member, British Steel Corp., 1967–70; Director, various Companies 1960–76. *Address:* Willows House, Walsham-le-Willows, Bury St. Edmunds, Suffolk IP31 3AH.

**MUSGRAVE, Merrill N.** professional technical engineer. *B.* 1895. *Educ.* Public Schools; Doctor *Tempus Aires. M.* 1922, Selma O. Westberg. *Career:* With U.S. Army Corps 1917–19; Boeing Aircraft Co. 1919–24; Instructor U.S. Air Corps Univ. of Washington 1924–27; Owner Merrill N. Musgrave & Co. 1927–57. Owner, Merrill Musgrave & Associates, Consulting Engineers, Seattle, Wash. President and Treasurer, The MAVE Co., Newberg, Ore.; President and Chairman, Board of Directors, Sanitherm Engineering Ltd., Vancouver, B.C.; Vice-Pres., Treas. and Chmn. Dot-Sel Inc. of Hawaii Hilo Hawaii; Partner, Malco, Environmental Polution Control Engineers Washington. *Member:* National Socy. of Professional Engineers; Amer. Socy. of Heating Refrigerating & Air-Conditioning Engineers; American Legion, Royal Socy. of Health (London); Internat. Platform Assn. *Clubs:* Washington Athletic; OX-5; Automobile. *Address:* 1610 East Boston Terrace, Seattle, Wash., 9812; and *office* Merrill N. Musgrave & Associates, 1610 Boston Terrace, Seattle, Wash., 98112 U.S.A.

**MUSK, Albert Charles Edward,** CVO. British. *B.* 1903. *Educ.* privately. *M.* 1931, Kathleen Nita Wright. *Career:* Joined Coutts & Co. 1920; Principal Officer 1946, Secretary 1952; Director, Coutts & Co., Bankers, London, 1956–73; Trustee A.T.S. and W.R.A.C. Benevolent Fund; Hon. Treas. The Royal Albert Hall; The Royal Life Saving Society 1957–73. *Address:* 46 Queensberry House, Richmond, Surrey.

**MUSKIE, Edmund Sixtus.** American Lawyer & Politician. *B.* 1914. *Educ.* Bates Coll., Maine; Cornell Law Sch., Ithaca, N.Y. (AB, LLB). *M.* 1948, Jane Gray. *S.* 2. *Daus.* 3. *Career:* Practised as Lawyer since 1940; U.S. Navy 1942–45; Mem., Maine House of Reps. 1947–51; Democratic Floor Leader 1949–51; District Dir. for Maine, Office of Price Stabilisation 1951–52; City Solicitor Waterville, Maine 1954–55; Gov., State of Maine 1955–59; Democratic Senator from Maine since 1959–; Senate Asst. Majority Whip since 1966; Chmn., Senate Sub-Cttees. on Environmental Pollution, Intergovt. Relations; Chmn., Dem. Senatorial Campaign Cttee. 1967–69; Candidate for Vice-Presidency of U.S.A. 1968; Chmn., Senate Budget Cttee. *Member:* Exec. Cttee., Nat. Governors Conference; American Acad. of Arts & Sciences; Roosevelt Campobello Int. Park Comm. *Awards:* Hon. LLD, Bates, Lafayette, Bowdoin and Colby Colls., Marine, Portland and Suffolk Univs. *Address:* Senate Office Building, Washington, D.C. 20510, U.S.A.

**MUSSA-IVALDI-VERCELLI, Carlo.** Italian scientist. *B.* 1913. *Educ.* Dr. Physics, Dr. Electro-Technical Engineering; Libero Docente. *M.* 1947, Franca Sciolla. *S.* Ferdinando. *Dau.* Anna. *Career:* Has devoted himself chiefly to scientific research applied to industry. With T. I. Brown-Boveri 1938–40; S.A. Microtecnica (manufacture of precision instruments) 1940–44. Director of a Research Branch on the Physical Chemistry of High Polymers for Montecatini Ltd. (in co-operation with Turin Univ. and Milan Polytechnical High School) 1946–64; Professor of Applied Physical Chemistry, Turin University, 1960; Vice-Pres. of the society S.I.P., running the telephone system of Italy. Member of Parliament 1963–72. Played an active part in the anti-fascist underground movement, Giustizia e Libertà from 1931; arrested in 1934, and exiled for two years; Veteran of the Resistance, of which he was one of the organizers; awarded Silver Medal V.M. *Publications:* many articles in Italian and foreign (mostly U.S.A.) scientific reviews, chiefly related to physical chemistry and problems concerning macro-molecular compounds. Former member of Partito d'Azione; at present member of P.S.I. *Address:* Corso L. Einaudi 30, Turin; and Istituto Chimico dell'Università C. M. d'Azeglio 48, Turin, Italy.

**MUSSI, Dr. Ingo.** Austrian Diplomat. *B.* 1935. *Educ.* Univ. of Vienna—PhD; postgraduate studies at Georgetown Univ., Washington, D.C. *M.* 1960, Renate Distler. *S.* 1. *Dau.* 1. *Career:* Federal Chancellery, Vienna 1959–62; Press Attaché, Austrian Embassy, Washington 1962–66, & London 1966–70; Acting Chef de Cabinet & Spokesman, Federal Chancellery, Vienna 1970–73; Minister Counsellor, Austrian Embassy, London 1973–76; Austrian Ambassador to Israel since 1976. *Member:* Künstlervereinigung Sezession, Vienna (Corresponding mem.). *Decorations:* Member of the Royal Victorian Order; Order of Merit, German Federal Republic; Order of the Hungarian Flag; Commander, Order of Bintang Jasa, Indonesia. *Publications:* Numerous contributions on literature & the Arts in various Austrian newspapers & magazines. *Club:* Brooks' (London). *Address:* Gassen 35, Stockenboi, 9714 Austria; and *office* 11 Hermann Cohen Street, Tel Aviv, Israel.

**MUTHIA, Annamalai Chidambaram.** Indian. *B.* 1941. *Educ.* Madras Univ. (BEngMech). *M.* 1965, Devaki. *Career:* Engineer. South India Corporation (Agencies) Private Ltd., Madras, Mar. 1965—; Dir. Exec. Vice-Pres. Southern Petrochemical Industries Corp. Ltd. Madras. *Clubs:* Polo, Boat, Rifle, Cricket, Gymkhana (all in Madras). *Address:* Adayar Villa, Madras 85; and *office* South India Corporation (Agencies) Private Ltd., South India House, 99 Armenian Street, Madras 1, India.

**MUTTUKUMARU, Major-General Anton Marian,** OBE, ED. *B.* 1908. *Educ.* BA (Oxon); Barrister-at-Law (Gray's Inn). *M.* 1944, Margaret Ratnarajah. *S.* Anton, Philip and Christopher. *Career:* Practised as Advocate of the Supreme Court of Ceylon 1934–39 and 1946–48. Army Commander 1955–59; A.D.C. to H.M. The Queen 1954–59; Commanded Ceylon contingents at Victory Parade 1946, at funeral of King George VI (1952), and at the Coronation of Queen Elizabeth (1953). High Commissioner in Pakistan 1960–62; Ambassador to Iraq 1961–62, and to Iran 1962. High Commissioner in Australia and New Zealand 1963–66. Ambassador of Ceylon in the U.A.R. and concurrently to Yugoslavia, Lebanon, Jordan and Sudan 1967–69; Pres. Ceylon Institute of World Affairs; Chmn., Sri Lanka Foundation. *Address:* 2 Skelton Place, Colombo 5, Sri Lanka.

**MYAING, U. Chit.** Ambassador of Burma. *B.* 1922. *Educ:* Univ. of Rangoon. *M.* 1944, Daw Khin Yu. *S.* 2. *Dau.* 1. *Career:* Joined Liberation movement under General Aung San 1942; Bn. Comd. 1945; Burma Army 1946; Lt.-Col. Inf. Bn. Comd. 1948, Dy. Spl. Commissioner S. Burma; Inf. Bde. Comd. 1950; Minister, Foreign Trade 1963; Ambassador Jugoslavia 1968; Ambassador Gt. Britain 1971–75. *Award:* SITHU (Burma). *Address:* c/o Ministry of Foreign Affairs, Rangoon, Socialist Republic of the Union of Burma.

**MYNORS, Sir Humphrey Charles Baskerville,** Bt. British banker. *B.* 28 July 1903. *Educ.* Marlborough; Corpus Christi College, Cambridge. *M.* 1939, Lydia Marian Minns. *S.* 1. *Daus.* 4. *Career:* Deputy Governor, Bank of England 1954–64; Chmn. Finance Corporation for Industry 1964–73. *Address:* Treago, St. Weonards, Hereford HR2 8QB.

**MYRDAL (née Reimer), Madame Alva.** Swedish. *B.* 1902. *Educ.* Stockholm (BA 1924); Uppsala (MA 1934); Hon. LLD, Holyoke, Leeds, Edinburgh, Columbia, Temple, Gothenburg, East Anglia, Brandeis University; Doctor of Divinity, Gustavas Adolphus, Minn. *M.* 1924, Gunnar Myrdal. *S.* Jan. *Daus.* Sissela and Kaj. *Career:* Dir. Dept. of Social Sciences, U.N.E.S.C.O., Paris, 1951–55; Principal Dir., Dept. of Social Affairs, U.N., New York, 1949–50; Social Pedagogical Institute, Stockholm, 1936–48; mebr. chmn. or secy. numerous Government committees preparing social and educational reforms in Sweden 1935–73; Ambassador to India and Ceylon 1955–61, and to Nepal 1960–61. Member of Swedish Parliament 1962–70; Leader of Swedish Delegation to U.N. Disarmament Conference. Geneva 1962–73; Minister of Disarmament and of Church Affairs 1967–73; Visiting Prof. MIT 1973–75 and Wellesley 1976. *Publications:* Crisis in the Population Problem; City Children; Nation and Family; Contact with America; Social Progress in Great Britain; Comments on World Affairs; Post-War Plans; Are we too many?; America's Role in International Social Welfare (with Dean Rusk, A. Altmeyer); Women's Two Roles (with Viola Klein); The Control of Proliferation (in Adelphi Papers 1966); The Game of Disarmament (1976); editor, Via Suecia (multilingual refugee magazine 1945–47; numerous articles on Social, Educational and Political Problems; member Swedish Social Democratic Party; Chmn. Programme Cttee. on Equality since 1968. *Address:* Vaester-Langgatan 31, Stockholm 11129, Sweden.

**MYRDAL, Karl Gunnar.** Swedish Politician and Economist. *B.* 1898. *Education:* Stockholm Univ. Law School, law degree (1923), Juris dr. degree in economics (1927); Studied in Germany & Britain; Went to USA as a Rockefeller Fellow 1930–31. *M.* Alva Reimer. *S.* 1. *Daus.* 2. *Career:* Associate Professor in Post-grad. Inst. of Intern. Studies Geneva 1931–32; Professor (Lars Hierta Chair) of Political Economy and Public Finance at Univ. of Stockholm 1933; Elected to Senate as mem. of Swedish Social Democratic Party 1934; Studied American Negro Problem (Carnegie Corp of NY) 1938; Re-elected to Swedish Senate 1942, also member of Board of Bank of Sweden and Chmn. Post-war planning Comm; Minister of Commerce for Sweden 1945–47; Later Exec. Secy. UN Economic Commission for Europe until 1957; Studied economic trends in S. Asia 1957–67; Professor of International Economics at Stockholm 1961; Founded Inst. for Intern. Economic Studies at Stockholm 1961 (still on directorate); Chmn of SIPRI 1967 (still on Board); Vis. Res. Fellow at Center for Study of Democratic Institutions (Santa Barbara) 1973–74; Dist. Vis. Prof. NY City Univ. 1974–75. More than 30 (hon) degrees from Europe and America; Many Prizes, most recently Malinowski Award, 1975 (Socy. of applied Antropology). *Member:* British Academy; American Acad. of Arts and Sciences; Vetenskapsakademien (R.S. Acad. of Scs.); American Economic Assn (Hon.). *Fellow:* Econometric Socy. Nobel Prize for Economics, 1974. *Publications:* The Cost of Living in Sweden 1830–1930, (1933); Monetary Equilibrium, (1939); An American Dilemma: The Negro Problem and Modern Democracy (1944); The Political Element in the Development of Economic Theory (1953); An International Economy: Problems and Prospects (1956); Economic Theory and Underdeveloped Regions (1957); Value in Social Theory (1958); Beyond the Welfare State: Economic Planning and its International Implications (1960); Challenge to Affluence (1963); Asian Drama: An Inquiry into the Poverty of Nations (1968); Objectivity in Social Research (1969); The Challenge of World Poverty: A World Anti-Poverty Program in Outline (1970); Against the Stream: Critical Essays on Economics (1973). *Address:* Vasterlanggatan 31, 111 29 Stockholm, Sweden.

# N

**NA POMBEJRA, Vivadh.** Thai Diplomat. *B.* 1915. *Educ.* Vajiravudh Coll. Bangkok; Thammasat Univ. Bangkok; LSE, Univ. of London. *M.* 1952, Momrajawongs Nivatvar Sonakul. *S.* 2. *Career:* British Army (Lieut.) Force 136, 1940–45; Editor of Thai Section, BBC Overseas Service London 1947–48; 1st. Secy. Royal Thai Embassy Cairo 1957; 1st Secy. Royal Thai Embassy Paris 1961; Dir. SEATO Div. Dept. of Intern. Organisation 1965; SEATO Council Rep. for Thailand; Ambassador (Extra and Plenipot.) in Denmark and Norway 1967–71; Ambassador in Australia and Fiji 1971–75. *Decorations:* Order of Crown of Thailand (K.G. Commd.); Order of Chula Chom Klao, Thailand (Gr. Comp); Order of the White Elephant, Thailand (Knight. Commd.); Order of Dannebrog, Denmark (K. G. Commd.); Order of Merit, France (Commd); Order of Al Istiklal, UAR (Commd.). *Clubs:* Siam Socy; Royal Canberra Golf. *Address:* c/o Ministry of Foreign Affairs, Bangkok, Thailand.

**NABULSI, Omar.** Jordanian Politician. *B.* 1936. *Educ.* Cairo Univ. Egypt, LLB, LLM Master's Degree in Public and International Law. *M.* 1966, Haifa Alkhas Hatough. *S:* 2. *Career:* Legal Adviser Sasco Oil Co., Libya 1958–60; Political Attaché, League of Arab States, Cairo 1960–70; Head Admin. Dept. Royal Palace Amman, 1970; Minister Nat. Economy Govt. Jordan, Amman, 1970–72; Ambassador of Jordan to Court of St James's 1972–73; Minister Agriculture 1973; Minister Nat. Economy 1973–75. *Award:* Star of Jordan, First Order. *Address: office* c/o Ministry of National Economy, Amman, Jordan.

**NAESSENS, Maurice.** Belgian banker. *B.* 1908. *Educ.* Lic en Sc Com, Lic en Sc Pol and Lic Sc Econ. *M.* 1931, Yvonne Verhasselt. *S.* Fritz. *Dau.* Nora. *Career:* Dir., Caisse Générale d'Epargen et de Retraite 1947–50. President Honoraire, Banque de Paris et des Pays-Bas, Brussels; Lecturer, Universitaire Instelling Antwerpen; Pres. Mercatorfonds; Royal Commission for Site and Monument Protection; Pres. of Honour, Vereniging voor Economie (Flemish Economic Assn.). *Publications:* conferences and publications of a scientific nature. *Address:* 30 avenue d'Hoogvorst, Meise; and *office* 31 rue des Colonies, Brussels, Belgium.

**NAGANO, Shigeo.** Japanese executive. *B.* 1900. *Educ.* Faculty of Jurisprudence, Tokyo Imperial University (LLB). *M.* 1927, Setsu Otsuka. *S.* Tatsuo, Shigemasa and Tetsuzo. *Dau.* Kuniko. *Career:* Man. Dir., Japan Iron & Steel Co. Ltd. 1934–46. Mng. Dir. 1946–50: Pres., Fuji Iron & Steel Co. Ltd. 1950–70; Councellor, The Japan Development Bank 1963—; The Bank of Japan 1970—, Chmn. 1970—, Dir. Hon. Chmn. Nippon Steel Corp since 1973. Hon. Pres., Japan Iron Steel Federation 1965—; President, Japan and Tokyo Chambers of Commerce and Industry 1969; Chmn. Prime Minister's Council, Foreign Economic Aid 1969—; Vice-Pres., Pacific Basin Economic Co-operation Council, 1970—. *Awards:* Government's Medal of Honour with a Blue Ribbon, 1959; Decorated, His Majesty, Emperor of Japan, First-Order, Sacred Treasure. *Club:* Japan Industry. *Address:* 34-4, Matsubara, 4-chome Setagaya-ku, Tokyo; and *office* 6-3, Otemachi 2-chome, Chiyodaku, Tokyo, Japan.

**NAGEON DE LESTANG, Sir Clement.** *B.* 1910. *Educ.* St. Louis' College, Seychelles, and King's College, London (LLB Hons.); Barrister-at-Law (Middle Temple). *M.* 1933, Danielle Sauvage. *S.* Bernard. *Daus.* Marie-Jose, Michelyne, Anne-Marie. *Career:* Private practice, Seychelles 1932–35; Crown Prosecutor and Legal Adviser, Seychelles 1935–39; Actg. Chief Justice 1939–44; Resident Magistrate, Kenya 1944–47; Puisne Judge, Supreme Court of Kenya 1947–56; Federal Justice, Federal Supreme Court, Nigeria 1956–58; Chief Justice, High Court of Lagos 1958–64, and of Southern Cameroons 1958–60; Justice of Appeal. Court of Appeal for E. Africa 1964–66, Vice Pres. 1966–69. *Address:* 10 Court Drive, Shillingford, Oxford.

**NAIR, Vallillath Madhathil Madhavan.** Indian Diplomat. *B.* 1919. *Educ.* BA (Hons.) Madras; MA Oxford; MA Cambridge; Barrister-at-Law, Inner Temple. *M.* 1945, Krishnakumari. *S.* 1. *Dau.* 1. *Career:* Joined Indian Civil Service 1942; High Commissioner of India in Malaya 1957–58; Ambassador of India to Cambodia 1958–60, to Norway 1960–63; Joint Sec., Ministry of External Affairs, New Delhi 1964–67; Ambassador of India to Poland 1967–70, to Morocco & Tunisia 1970–74, & to Spain since 1974. *Clubs:* Delhi Gymkhana (New Delhi); Real Club Puerta de Hierro (Madrid). *Address:* Calle Penalba 5, Somosaguas, Madrid; and *office* Embassy of India, Velazquez 93, Madrid, Spain.

**NAJAR, Amiel Emile.** Israeli Ambassador. *B.* 1912. *Educ.* Licencié en Droit de la Faculté de Droit de Paris; Diploma, Higher Studies of Public Law and Political Economics. *M.* 1935, Aviva Weisman. *Career:* President, Zionist Federation of Egypt 1943–47; Delegate to Zionist Conference London 1945, Zionist Congress Basle 1946; Came to Israel 1947; Dir. Western European Division, Ministry for Foreign

Affairs 1952–57; Observer Suez Conference London 1956; Asst. Dir. Gen. Ministry of Foreign Affairs 1957–58; Israel Minister in Japan 1958–60; Ambassador to Belgium and Luxembourg and Head, Israeli Missions to E.E.C. and other European Communities, 1961–68. Member, Israelian Delegation to U.N. 1948–51–52–53–55–56–57–61–64–67; Ambassador to Malta 1968–71, to Italy 1971–73. Author of various articles. *Address:* c/o Ministry of Foreign Affairs, Jerusalem, Israel.

**NAKAMURA, Sadao,** M. Agric. Japanese. *B.* 1906. *Educ* Tokyo Imperial Univ. (M. Agric). *M.* 1936, Sumiko Tominaga. *S.* 1. *Daus.* 2. *Career:* Man. Dir. Daicel Ltd. 1960–68; Man. Dir. & Mgr. Central Research Institute Japan Monopoly Corp. 1958–60; Man. Dir. Daiichi Bussho Co.; Pres. P.T. Indonesia Japan Tobacco. *Address:* 5-2 Higashinakano 5-chome, Nakano-ku Tokyo, Japan; and *office* 21, Honshio-cho, Shinjuku-ku, Tokyo, Japan.

**NALDER, Hon. Sir Crawford David.** Australian. *B.* 1910. *Educ.* W. A. General State School & Wesley College, Perth. *M.* (1) 1934, Olive May Irvin, (*D.* 1973). *S.* 1. *Daus.* 2. (2) Brenda Wade. *Career:* Entered Parliament, 1947; Dep. Leader, Country Party, 1956; Minister for War Service Land Settlement, 1959–66; Minister for Agriculture 1959–71; Minister for Electricity 1962–71; Leader, West Aust. Country Party 1962–73; Retired as MP in 1974. *Vice-President:* Methodist Conference, W. Australia, 1974; Chmn. Ladies Coll. Council, 1974. *Member:* Board, British and Foreign Bible Socy. (W. Austr. Div.). *Address:* 7 Morriett Street, Attadale, W. Australia 6156.

**NALLINGER, Fritz,** Prof. Dr Ing eh Dipl Ing. German executive. *B.* 1898. *Educ.* Tech. High School, Tech. Coll., Karlsruhe (Dipl Ing). *M.* 1925, Frohmut Panther. *S.* 1. *Daus.* 3. *Career:* Designer, Benz. & Co., Rhein. Automobil und Gasmot Fabr., Mannheim 1922–24; First Research Engineer, Daimler-Benz, Stuttgart 1924; Head of Research Dept. and Asst. to the Tech. Mgr. 1928; granted procuration 1932; Tech. Mgr. and Head of Dept. for development of high powered engines 1935; Construction, Research and Development Mgr., and Deputy Member of Exec. Bd. 1940; Member of Exec. Bd. and Chief Engr. for development of motor vehicles. Chief Engineer and Member of Executive Board, Daimler-Benz AG., Stuttgart-Untertürkheim, I.R. Consulting Engineer. Member: Max-Planck Socy. for Promotion of Science, Göttingen; German Museum in Munich. Management Councils of the Reunion of Friends of Karlsruhe and Darmstadt Tech. Coll., and Stuttgart Tech. Coll.; Management Committee of the DVL. Member: Council of Economic Research at the Baden-Württemberg, Min. of Economics; DirIng (Hon.) Tech. Coll. of Karlsruhe 1951; Title of Professor by the State Government of Baden-Württemberg 1955. *Publications:* Gottlieb Daimler-Karl Benz (biography; pub. Ullstein); numerous publications on the development of vehicles and engines, and the promotion of roadbuilding as a demand of modern traffic. *Awards:* Lilienthal Commemorative Medal 1937; VDI Ring of Honour 1938; Grand Order of Merit 1954; Gold Diesel Medal from German Inventors' Society 1956; Gold Diesel Ring by Assn. of Journalists 1961. Star for the Distinguished Federal Service Cross 1963. *Club:* Stuttgart Golf (Pres.). *Address:* Albrecht-Dürerweg 5, Stuttgart-N; and *office* Daimler-Benz AG., 7 Stuttgart-Untertürkheim, Germany.

**NANCE, James J.** American industrialist-banker. *B.* 1900. *Educ.* Ohio Wesleyan Univ. (AB 1923), Ohio State Univ. (grad. studies); LLD Lawrence College, St. Lawrence Univ. & CSU (1975). *M.* 1925, Laura Battelle. *S.* James Battelle. *Dau.* Marcia (Mrs. William E. Atcheson). *Career:* National Cash Register Co., Dayton, O. 1924–27; Frigidaire Div., General Motors Corp., Dayton, 1927–40; Vice-Pres., Zenith Radio Corp., Chicago 1940–45; Pres., Chief Exec. Officer & Dir.; Hotpoint Inc., Chicago 1945–52; Packard Motor Car Co., Detroit 1952–54; and Studebaker Packard Corp. 1954–56; Vice-Pres. Ford Motor Co. 1956–59; Pres., Chief Exec. Officer, Central National Bank of Cleveland 1960–62, Chmn. & Chief Exec. Officer, 1962–67, Dir. 1960–71, Hon. Chmn. 1967–71, Hon. Dir. 1971—; Chmn. & Chief Exec. Officer, First Union Real Estate Investments 1967—; Dir., Standard Oil of Ohio 1953–60; Dir. & Chmn. Exec. Cttee., Montgomery Ward & Co. 1962–70; Dir. & Chmn. Exec. Cttee., Globe Refractories 1964–70; Dir., Exec. Cttee., Oglebay Norton Co. 1967—; Dir., Marcor Inc. 1968–70; Dir., Montgomery Ward Life Insurance Co. 1966–75; Dir., Chmn. Exec. Cttee., Pioneer Trust & Savings Bank, Chicago 1968–74; Chmn. Bd. of Trustees, Cleveland State Univ.; Trustee: Northwestern Univ., Univ. Hospitals of Cleveland; Member-at-Large, Cleveland State Univ. Development Foundation. *Awards:* Horatio Alger Award 1951; Ohio Sesquicentennial Award 1953; Governor's Award Ohio 1957; Appliance Manufacturers' Industry Leadership Award 1960; Sales Marketing Execs. of Cleveland Man-of-the-Year Award 1966; Finance Banker of the Year Award 1966; American Acad. Achievement Award 1967; Gold Medal Pub. Service, Cleveland C. of C. 1969; Named to Hall of Fame-Distbn. 1953. *Member:* Phi Delta Theta, Omicron Delta Kappa; Beta Gamma Sigma; Newcomen Socy. Republican. Mason. *Clubs:* Union, Pepper Pike, Kirtland, Chagrin Valley Hunt (Cleveland); University (N.Y.C.); Commercial, Athletic (Columbus); Lost Tree, Quail Ridge (Fla.). Chicago (Chicago); *Address:* Fairmount Boulevard, Hunting Valley, Chagrin Falls, Ohio 44022; and *office* 55 Public Square, Cleveland, Ohio 44113, U.S.A.

**NAPIER, Hon. Sir (John) Mellis,** KCMG, Kt St J. Australian. Lieutenant Governor of South Australia 1942–73. *B.* 1882. *Educ.* Adelaide Univ. (LLB). *M.* 1908, Dorothy Bell Kay (*Dec.* 1959). *S.* 2. Judge, Supreme Court S.A. 1924–42; Chief Justice, South Australia, 1942–67; Chancellor, Univ. of Adelaide, 1948–61. *Address:* Glenwood, Stirling East, South Australia 5152, Australia.

**NARAYANAN, Kocheril Raman.** Indian Diplomat. *B.* 1921. *Educ.* Travancore Univ. (MA); London Sch. of Economics (B.Sc Hons.). *M.* 1950, Usha. *Daus.* 2. *Career:* Worked in Editorial Dept. of 'Hindu', Madras 1944–45; Reporter, 'Times of India' 1945; entered Indian Foreign Service 1949, served at Indian Missions in Rangoon, Tokyo & London, and also at Headquarters in New Delhi, until 1960; Acting High Commissioner, Canberra 1961–62; Consul-General, Hanoi 1962–63; Dir. (China Div.), Min. of External Affairs, New Delhi 1963–67; Ambassador to Thailand 1967–69; Joint Sec. (Policy Planning Div.), Min. of External Affairs, New Delhi 1964–70; Ambassader to Turkey 1973–75; Additional Sec. (Policy Planning & Asia & Africa Div.), Min. of External Affairs, New Delhi 1975–76; Sec. (East), Min. of External Affairs, New Delhi April–May 1976; Ambassador to People's Rep. of China since July 1976. *Member:* India International Centre; Inst. of Strategic Studies & Analysis; Indian Council of World Affairs. *Awards:* Jawaharlal Nehru Fellowship 1970–72; Hon. Prof., Jawaharlal Nehru Univ. 1970–72; Hon. Fellow of LSE since 1972. *Publications:* various articles on International Relations. *Address:* Kocheril House, Ozhavoor, P.O., Kottayam District, Kerala, India; and *office* Embassy of India, Peking, c/o Ministry of External Affairs, New Delhi, India.

**NARITA, Tomoni.** Japanese Politician. *B.* 1912. *Educ.* Tokyo Univ. *Career:* Former Pres., Kagawa Prefectural Fed. of Socialist Party; Mem., House of Reps.; successively, Mem. Central Exec. Cttee. of Socialist Party; Chmn., Control Cttee., Left Wing Socialist Party; Chmn., Policy Bd., Socialist Party 1961–62, Sec.-Gen. 1962–67, Chmn. of Party 1968–77. *Address:* Socialist Party of Japan, 1-8-1 Nagata-cho, Chiyoda-ku, Tokyo, Japan.

**NASH, Benjamin Capwell.** American. *B.* 1922. *Educ.* Rensselaer Polytechnic Institute, Troy, N.Y. (BME). *M.* 1943, Anne Riggs. *S.* Douglas E. II and Daniel R. *Dau.* Georgia A. *Career:* With Nash Engineering Co.: Designer 1949–51; Sales Engineer 1951–57; Asst. Works Mgr. 1957–58; Dir. of Manufacturing 1958–62. President: Nash Engineering Co., 1975—; Pres. Nash Engineering Co. of Canada Ltd., 1975—; Chmn., Nash Engineering Co. (Great Britain) Ltd., June 1962—; Geschaeftsfuehrer, Nash International G.m.b.H., Sept. 1964—; Director, Nash Hytor AB, Nov. 1963—; Chairman, Nash International 1969—. *Member:* Society of Sigma Xi; Pi Delta Epsilon; Young Presidents Organizational Amer. Management Assn. Republican. *Club:* Noroton Yacht. *Address: office* Wilson Avenue, South Norwalk, Conn., U.S.A.

**NASIR, Ibrahim,** RBK, NGIV. President of the Republic of Maldives. *B.* 1926. *Educ.* in Ceylon. *M.* 1969, Naseema Mohamed Kalegefaan. *S.* 4. (3 by previous marriage). *Dau.* 1. *Career:* Under-Secretary to Minister of Finance and to Minister of Public Safety, 1954; Minister of Public Safety, 1956; Minister of Home Affairs, 1957; Prime Minister (First Term), 1957; Prime Minister (Second Term) and Minister of Home Affairs, Finance, Education, Trade, External Affairs and Public Safety, 1959; Prime Minister (Third Term) and Minister of Finance. Education. External Affairs and Public Safety, 1964. Pres. of Republic of Maldives (First Term) 1968; President of the Republic of Maldives (Second Term) 1973.

*Address:* Velaanaage, 22 Amir Ahmed Magu, Henvaru, Malé; and *office:* The Office of the President, Marine Drive, Malé, Republic of Maldives.

**NASLUND, Hans Sture Alexander.** Swedish engineering Co. Exec. *B.* 1916. *Educ.* Grad. High School. *M.* 1946, Marianne. Nystrand *S.* 2. *Career:* with Birger Carlson & Co. AB 1937–39; AB Atlas Diesel 1939–44; Market Investigator S. Africa, India, Middle East 1944–46; Pres. Delfos Ltd. S. Africa 1947–50; Luxor Radio AB 1950–59; Luxor Industri AB 1959–66; Pres. Monark-Crescent AB and daughter companies 1966–74; Consultant to the Board since 1974; Finnish Consul Varberg 1971–75; Chmn. The International Motor Cycle Fair, Stockholm since 1972. *Member:* Industrial Council, The Royal Swedish Academy of Engineering Sciences; Swedish Assn. Engineers, Architects. *Awards:* Commander Royal Order of Vasa. *Clubs:* Rotary International, Varberg; American of Stockholm; Automobile, Royal de Suéde. *Address: office* 15 Kyrkogatan, 43200 Varberg, Floragatan 7, Stockholm, Sweden.

**NASON, Howard King,** AB. American. *B.* 1913. *Educ.* Univ. of Kansas (AB Chemistry); Washington Univ. (post Grad.); Harvard Univ. (AMP Course). *Career:* various appointments with Monsanto since 1936; Planetarium Commission since 1966; Atomic Energy Comm.'s Ad. Cttee on Isotopes & Radiation Development 1964–68; Atomic Energy Labor-Mgmt. Adv. Cttee. since 1965; President's Comm. on Patent System 1965–8; Patent Advisory Cttee. (USA) 1968–72; Chamber of Commerce (US Cttee. on Sc. & Tech.) 1968–71; Chmn. of Board St Louis Res. Coun. 1971–73; Trustee-at-large Univ. Res. Assoc. since 1971; Dir. & mem. Exec. Cttee. St Louis Reg. Commerce & Growth Assoc. 1971–74; Vice-Pres. & mem. Exec. Cttee. Atomic Industrial Forum Inc. 1971–73; Aerospace Adv. Panel since 1972; Chmn. since 1973; Nat. Materials Adv. Board (Cttee.) 1972; Mftg. Chemists Assoc. Nuclear Cttee. since 1962; Trustee Charles F. Kettering Foundation since 1973; Nat. Materials Advisory Board of Nat. Acad. of Eng. since 1973; Pres. Monsanto Research Corporation. *Member:* Amer. Chemical Socy.; Amer. Socy. Chemical Industry; Amer. Mineralogical Socy.; Amer. Inst. Aeronautics & Astronautics; Amer. Inst. Chemists; Inst. Aeronautical Sciences; Scientific Research Socy of America; Amer. Nuclear Socy.; Am. Soc. for Testing & Materials; Am. AASci.; N.Y. Acad. of Sciences; Am. Inst. Chem. Engs.; American Nuclear Socy; Socy. of Rheology. *Clubs:* St. Louis; Quiet Birdmen; Cosmos Washington. *Address:* 800 N. Lindbergh Boulevard, St. Louis, Mo. 63166.

**NATHAN, Sir Maurice Arnold,** KBE. *B.* 1914. *Educ.* Geelong Church of England School, Corio (Victoria). *M.* 1942, Margaret McKay. *S.* David R. *Career:* Enlisted A.I.F. Dec. 1941; overseas service 18 months; Captain R.A.O.C.; Reserve of Officers, Sept. 1945. Councillor of City of Melbourne (Australia) 1952–72. Lord Mayor 1961–63. Chmn. and Manag. Dir., Patersons (Australia) Ltd. and Associated Companies. Chairman: Olympic Civic Committee; Founder and Chmn. Vict. Promotion Cttee. and Australian World Exposition Project; Pres. Victorian Football League; Chmn. Olympic Park Cttee of Mgmt.; Cttee. Mem., Victoria Amateur Turf Club. *Address:* 152 Bourke Street, Melbourne 3000, Vic.; and 20 St. George's Road, Toorak, 3142, Vic., Australia.

**NATVIG, Nils Einar.** Norwegian shipbroker. *B.* 1907. *Educ.* Matric. 1925; Commercial School 1926. *M.* 1934, Else Egeborg Ottesen (*Div.* 1958); and *M.* 1960, Fanny Mørch. *Dau.* 1. *Career:* In shipbroker's office, Oslo, until autumn of 1928, and in London 1928–39; Manager of shipbroking firm in Oslo until May 1945; member, Norwegian U.M.A. Delegation in London, June 1945–Feb. 1946; Established and managing own shipbroking business in Oslo 1946. *Address:* P.O. Box 1627, Vika, Oslo 1, Norway.

**NAUDE, Dr. Stephanus Jacobus,** D.Com. South African bank director. *B.* 26 June 1905. *M.* 1930, J. B. Nel. *Career:* Dir., Federale Volksbeleggings Ltd., Volkskas Limited, and other companies. Chmn. Council, O.F.S. University. *Address:* 1 College Avenue, (P.O. Box 399), Bloemfontein 9300, South Africa.

**NAUDÉ, Willem Christiaan.** D.Com. South African. *B.* 5 May 1909. *M.* 1932, Maud Josephine Gill. *Daus.* Gilliann Maud, Rinda Suzanne. *Career:* Economic Adviser to South African High Commissioner, London 1946–47, Political Secretary and Economic Adviser 1947–49; Consul-General, Lourenço Marques 1951–54; Delegate, U.N. Assembly 1953–59–63–65; Leader South African Delegations to G.A.T.T., 1954–56, 1966–68, 1970–72, to UNCTAD-II, New Delhi, 1968; Minister to Switzerland 1956–57; Under Secy. for External Affairs, 1959–60; Ambassador to U.S.A., 1960–65; Principal Deputy Secretary for Foreign Affairs, 1965–66; Ambassador, Permanent Representative, Geneva, 1966–71; Ambassador Chief of Mission to European Communities, Brussels 1971–75; Chmn., Massey-Ferguson (S.A.) Ltd., Mem. of S.A. Electricity Control Bd. *Address:* 1 Quendon Road, Sea Point, Cape Town 8001, South Africa.

**NAVE, John Lionel.** Australian. *B.* 1906. *Educ.* Associate in Commerce, University of Adelaide. *M.* 1936, Lois Dean Afford. *S.* Peter and Robert. *Daus.* Janet and Wendy. *Career:* The National Bank of Australasia Ltd. Chief Man. 1965–70; Dir. The Trustees, Executors & Agency Co. Ltd. President, Melbourne Chamber of Commerce. *Clubs:* Australian; Melbourne; Union (Sydney); Royal Melbourne Golf. *Address:* 11 Monomeath Avenue, Canterbury, Vic.; and *office* 83 William Street, Melbourne, Vic., Australia.

**NAVES, Yves René.** French. Knight Legion of Honour (France). *B.* 1902. *Educ.* Chemical Engineer: D ès Sc. *M.* 1945, Lise-Monique Yersin. *Dau.* Renée-Georgette (by previous marriage). *Career:* Chemist with Antoine Chiris Co., Grasse (France) 1927–35. Head, Research and Analytical Dept. 1930–35; Chemist with Société Biotix, Pantin (France) 1936–37, and Givaudan 1938–67. (Scientific Dir. 1954–67). Lecturer Univ. of Geneva 1944–52. Professor, Faculty of Science, University of Neuchâtel 1965–71. *Publications:* Les Parfums Naturels, Paris 1938 (translation into English, New York 1947); Technologie et Chimie des Parfums naturels (Paris 1974); some 460 original articles in various scientific journals. *Awards:* Fritszche Prize (American Chemical Society, 1952). Member: Sté. Chimique de France; Sté. Suisse de Chimie; Sté Technique des Parfumeurs de France; Sté. Chimique de Genève. *Address:* 14 Chemin des Erables, 1213 Petit-Lancy, Geneva, Switzerland.

**NAYLOR, Franklin Llewellyn, Jr.** American registered professional engineer and business consultant. *B.* 1910. *Educ.* Univ. of Calif. (ME). *M.* 1932, Edna Anabel Woglom. *S.* Franklin L., III. *Daus.* Marjorie E. (Glidden) and Virginia I (Wolf). *Career:* With Ind. Div. of S.S. White Dental Mfg. Co. 1928–32; Consulting Engineer under own name 1932–37 and 1946–51; Vice-President, Industrial Engineering Division, Baker & Weikel 1948–50; Chief Engineer, Waldrip Engineering Co. 1948–49; Consulting Engineer, Bendix Aviation Corp. 1951–52; Pres. Dir. Chmn. Bd. Naylor Engineering & Research Corp. 1952; Chief Engineer, Grand Central Aircraft Co. 1953–54; Owner, Arizona Chemical & Engineering Co. 1953—; Naylor & Associates (Consultants) 1956—; Man. Gen. Agent, National Old Line Insurance Co. Little Rock, Ark 1965—; Pres. American Pacific Life Insurance Co. Ltd. since 1968; Registered Financial Adviser with the Securities & Exchange Commission in Washington D.C. since 1970. In World War II: War Production Board, Office of Production Management; Trainer, Training-Within-Industry Div. of WPB; Chairman Trade Adv. Committee for Sheet Metal Workers, and Employer-Representative, Trade Cttee. for Drafting, Lofting and Pattern Makers 1943–45. Assoc. Member, Amer. Inst. of Management. Life Member, Amer. Socy. Mech. Engineers. Member, SCORE, Washington, D.C. 1964— (Vice-Chmn. SCORE Small Business Executives Clearing House, Arizona 1952—). Member: Internat. Executive Service Corps. N.Y.; Aeronautical Affairs Cttee. of Hawaii Chamber of Commerce. Member National Panel, American Arbitration Assn. 1952—. Qualified instructor in engineering and management at secondary schools and colleges in California and Arizona. *Publications:* Aluminium and its Alloys; co-author books and courses on supervisory development, instruction, planning and presentation, Estate & Tax Planning, Estate Preservation, departmental training, organization of management. *Clubs:* Presidents; Nat. Travel; Executive; Phoenix. *Address:* 1334 W. Mulberry Drive, Phoenix, Arizona 85013, U.S.A.

**NEAME, Lieut.-General Sir Philip,** VC, KBE, CB, DSO, DL (Kent). British officer. *B.* 12 Dec. 1888. *Educ.* Hawtrey's; Cheltenham College; Royal Military Academy, Woolwich. *M.* 1934, Berta Drew. *S.* 3. *Dau.* 1. *Career:* Entered Army 1908; served World War I, Royal Engineers and Staff (dispatches 5 times) 1914–18; Directing Staff, Staff College, Camberley 1919–23; served with King George's Own Bengal Sappers and Miners, India 1925–29; Chief of Staff, Waziristan, North-West Frontier 1932–33, Eastern Command, India 1934–38; member of Mission to Lhasa, Tibet 1936; Commandant, Royal Military Academy, Woolwich 1938–39; World War II Deputy Chief of General Staff, France 1939–40;

Commander, 4th Indian Division, Western Desert 1940; G.O.C., Palestine, Transjordan and Cyprus 1940; G.O.C.-in-C. and Military Governor, Cyrenaica 1941 (dispatches twice); Lieut.-Governor, and C.-in-C., Guernsey and its Dependencies 1945–53; Colonel Commandant, Royal Engineers 1945–56; President, Institution of Royal Engineers 1954–56; Hon. Col. 131 Airborne Reg. R.E. (T) 1948–58, and of Kent AC.F. Regt., R.E. 1952–58; F.R.G.S. Vice Pres. National Rifle Association. *Awards:* Knight, Order of St. John of Jerusalem; Knight, Order of White Lion of Czechoslovakia; Chevalier de la Légion d'Honneur; French and Belgian Croix de Guerre; Olympic Gold & Bronze, Medals, Rifle Shooting 1924. *Publications:* German Strategy in the Great War, 1914–18; Playing with Strife (autobiography). *Address:* The Kintle Selling Court, Faversham, Kent.

**NEAVE, Airey Middleton Sheffield,** DSO, OBE, MC, TD, MP. British politician. Director, Clarke Chapman Ltd. *B.* 1916. *Educ.* Eton and Merton Coll., Oxford (BA Hons. jurisprudence 1938; MA 1955); called to the Bar (Middle Temple) 1943. *M.* 1942, Diana Josceline Barbara Giffard. *S.* 2. *Dau.* 1. Member, Parliament (Con.) Abingdon Div. of Berkshire 1953—. Served in World War II (R.A.; France; wounded and captured; escaped 1942; MI9 1942–44; G.S.O. 1944–45; dispatches; MC; DSO); Lt.-Col. A.A.G., British War Crimes Executive 1945–46; served indictments on Goering and other high-ranking Nazi war criminals 1945; Commissioner for Criminal Organization. International Military Tribunal, Nuremberg 1946. P.P.S. to Minister of Transport and Civil Aviation 1954, and to Secretary of State for the Colonies 1954–56; Joint Parly. Secy., Ministry of Transport and Civil Aviation 1957–59; Parliamentary Under Secretary of State for Air Jan.–Oct. 1959. Chmn., Conservative Party Cttee. on Space Research, 1962; Vice-Chmn., Conservative Party Parliamentary Atomic Energy Committee 1955 and 1959, Party Cttee. on Science and Technology 1960, Transport 1962, Aviation 1964 and Chmn. Select Cttee., Science & Technology 1970–74; Head of Private Office of Leader of the Opposition and Shadow Spokesman for Northern Ireland 1975. *Awards:* Croix de Guerre (France); Bronze Star (U.S.A.); Officer Orange Nassau (Netherlands). *Publications:* They Have Their Exits (1953); Little Cyclone (1954); Saturday at M19 (1969); The Flames of Calais (1972). *Address:* House of Commons, London, S.W.1.

**NEF, Dr. Victor.** Swiss diplomat. *B.* 9 Feb. 1895. *Educ.* Cantonal School; Institute of Political and Social Sciences, St. Gall; University of Berne (Dr Sc econ). *M.* 1920. *S.* Edward. *Dau.* Irene. *Career:* Entered Political Dept. and attached to Consulate as Vice-Consul, New York 1920, Consul 1928, Acting Consul-General 1929, Consul-General 1933–46; Swiss High Commissioner to New York World's Fair 1939–40; Chmn., Swiss Delegation, Internatl. Telecommunications Confs. Atlantic City 1947, and of Swiss Delegation, International Red Cross Confce., Toronto 1952; En. Ex. and Min. Plen. to Canada 1946–56; Ambassador 1957–61. Chmn., Board of Dirs., Credit Suisse (Canada) Ltd., Montreal 1961–74; member, Board of Dirs. and Directing Trustee, Sandoz Ltd., Montreal and New York 1961–70. Hon. Citizen of New York and Cornwall (Ont.) Canada. Swiss Commissioner-General to World Exhibition, Montreal 1967. *Address:* 33 Templar Way, Summit, N.J., 07901, U.S.A.; and St. Gall, Switzerland.

**NEFF, Alfred,** Dipl rer pol, Dr rer pol. Federal Cross of Merit 1st Cl.; German manufacturer. Owner and principal: Neff-Werke, Carl Neff GmbH, Bretten; Neff-Werke, Vertriebs-KG. Dr. A. Neff, Bretten; Carl Neff Ges.m.b.H., Vienna. President, Industrie- und Handelskammer, Karlsruhe. *B.* 1906. *Educ.* Mannheim University (Dipl.) and Cologne (DPol Econ). *M.* 1933, Ellen Nauen. *Daus.* 2. *Career:* Entered father's business 1931; sole owner and principal 1940. Mayor of Bretten and District Magistrate, Karlsruhe district; member, Provisional Diet of Baden-Württemberg (regional parliament) 1946. Lecturer in Sociology and Psychology, Technical College, Karlsruhe. Hon. Senator, Univ. of Karlsruhe. *Award:* Federal Grand Order of Merit. *Publications:* Das Führerproblem in der Wirtschaft (The Problem of Management in Industry, 1930); Das produktive Schaffen in der Wirtschaft (Productive capacity in industry, 1932), Uber die Psychologie des Schaffens und die produktive Geistestätigkeit (On the psychology of production and productive intellectual activity 1946); Beruf und Vorbild (Vocation and Example, 1954); Technischer Fortschritt als Aufgabe und Verantwortung in Handel und Industrie (Technical Progress as Task and Responsibility in Trade and Industry, 1955); Absatzwerbung und Kundenwerbung (Market Publicity and Canvassing of Customers, 1957); Der Stifter heute (The Founder of Today, 1957); Der initiative Mensch (The man of initiative, 1957); Die Freiheit des Handelns und ihre Grenzen (Freedom of Trade and its limitations, 1959); Freiheit und Neubeginn (Freedom and a Fresh Start, 1959); Der Mensch als Persönlichkeit im industriellen Zeitalter (Man as a personality in the Industrial age, 1960). *Club:* Lions (Karlsruhe). *Address:* Leibnizstrasse 2, Bretten, Germany.

**NEHMER, Stanley.** American. *B.* 1920. *Educ.* City College of New York (BSS 1941); Columbia Univ. (MA 1942); attended George Washington and American Univs. *M.* 1946, Phyllis Fleischman. *S.* 1. *Dzu.* 1. *Career:* Economist, Dept. of State 1945–57; Senior Economist, International Bank for Reconstruction & Development Dec. 1957–Sept. 1961; Dep. Director, Office of International Resources, Dept. of State 1961–64, Director 1964–65. Deputy Assistant Secretary of Commerce of the U.S. 1965–73; Dir. Econ. Consulting Services, Wolf and Co. since 1973. *Member:* American Economic Assn. *Publications:* contributor to Encyclopedia Britannica, Encyclopedia Americana, Current History, and Far Eastern Survey. *Awards:* Commendable Service Award, Dept. of State 1956; Superior Honor Award, Dept. of State 1964; Gold Medal Award, Dept. of Commerce 1971. *Address:* 9007 Kirkdale Road, Bethesda, Md.; and *office* 1101-17 Street N.W., Washington, D.C., U.S.A. 20036.

**NEHRU, Braj Kumar.** *B.* 1909. *Educ.* University of Allahabad (BSc), London School of Economics (BSc Econ), Balliol College, Oxford, and Inner Temple, London (Barrister-at-Law); Hon LLD Missouri Valley Coll.; Hon LittD Jacksonville (Fla.) Univ. *M.* 1935, Magdelena Friedman. *S.* 3. *Career:* Asst. Commissioner, Govt. of the Punjab 1934–39; Under-Secy., Dept. of Education, Health and Lands, Govt. of India 1939; Under-Secy., Deputy Secy., Joint Secy., Ministry of Finance, Govt. of India 1940–49; Exec. Director, World Bank, and Minister, Embassy of India, Washington, D.C. 1949–54; Joint Secy., Department of Economic Affairs, Govt. of India 1954–57; Economic Secy. 1957–58; Commissioner-General for Economic Affairs 1958–61. Ambassador of India to the United States, 1961–68; Governor of Assam and Nagaland, 1968–73 also of Meghalaya and Tripura and Manipur 1972–73; High Commissioner to the United Kingdom 1973–77. Representative: Reparations Conf. 1945, Commonwealth Finance Ministers Conf., UN Gen. Assembly 1949–52, 1960, FAO Confs. 1949–50, Sterling Balances Confs. 1947–49, Bandung Conf. 1955; deputed to enquire into Australian Fed. Finance 1946; Mem. UN Advisory Cttee. on Admin. & Budgetary Questions 1951–53; mem. UN Investments Cttee. 1961—, & Chmn. 1977. Hon. Fellow, London School of Economics. *Publications:* Australian Federal Finance; Speaking of India. *Clubs:* Gymkhana (New Delhi), Travellers, Oriental, Hurlingham. *Address:* India House, London W.C.2.

**NEILAN, Edwin Peter.** American *B.* 1905. *Educ.* Rice Inst. (BA) 1928; Univs. of Omaha and Texas; S. Texas School of Law; Amer. Inst. of Banking; Stonier Graduate School of Banking, Rutgers Univ. *M.* 1929, Julia Ellen Motheral. *Career:* With Bank of Delaware: Vice-Pres., Secy. and Chmn. Trust Cttee. 1946–52, Exec. Vice-Pres. 1952–56. President and Chairman of the Board 1959–70; and Director 1945–70; Bank of Delaware (formerly Security Trust Co.). Director: Chanslor Western Oil & Development Co. 1956–72; H. P. Cannon Inc. 1965–71; Delaware Economic Development Board 1960—, Delaware Safety Council 1966–70; (Vice-Pres. Finance 1965), Delaware Industrial Development Foundation 1960—, Greater Wilmington Development Council Inc. 1963–70; U.S. Chamber of Commerce 1962–70. Employer Delegate and Member Governing Body, I.L.O. 1966–75; Vice-Pres. 1970 and 74; Pres. Int. Organization, Employers 1970–71. Dir. United Community Fund 1951–70; Adviser, Rice University Fund Council since 1973; Mem. Finance Cttee and Admin. Bd. 1st United Methodist Church (Corpus Christi); Director Carriage Park Condominum since 1975, Pres. 1977–78. *Awards:* Hon DSc Bryant Coll. 1963; Hon. LLD Univ. of Omaha 1964; Manager of the Year (Socy. Advancement of Management) 1961; Gold Medal for Outstanding American of the Year (E. Side Assn. of N.Y.C.) 1963; Leonard Ayres Award of Leadership (Stonier Graduate School) 1964; Good Citizenship Gold Medal (Sons of Amer. Revolution). *Member:* Amer. Bankers Assn. (State Bank Div.; Pres. 1964–65); Delware Bankers Assn. (Pres. 1952–53); U.S.C. of C. (Pres. 1963–64; Chmn. of Bd. 1964–65; Chmn. Exec. Cttee. 1965–66); National Industrial Conf. Board; Bd. Int. Centre, Advanced Technical & Vocational Training, Turin 1958–72; Business Adv. Cttee. Brookings Institution 1964–78. Republican. *Clubs:* Pharaoh Country (cc Texas),

*Address:* 62 Town House Lane, Corpus Christi, Texas 7842. U.S.A.

**NEILL, Gordon Webster McCash,** DSO. British. Croix de Guerre, silver gilt and silver stars (France). *B.* 1919. *Educ.* Edinburgh Academy. *M.* 1950, Margaret Mary Lamb. *S.* John Victor. *Dau.* Fiona Margaret. *Career:* Legal apprenticeship 1937–39. Served with R.A.F. 1939–46. Qualified as Solicitor 1947; became Partner in Neill & Gibb 1947. Amalgamated business to form Neill & Mackintosh, S.S.C. in 1967. Principal of Firm of Neill & Mackintosh, S.S.C., Arbroath. Notary Public. Chairman, Dundee Area Board of British Law Insurance Co. Ltd.; Interim Chmn., Scottish Gliding Assn. Appointed Notary Public 1947. Elected Fellow of the Institute of Directors 1958. *Member:* Society of Solicitors in Supreme Courts of Scotland; Law Society of Scotland; Scottish Law Agents' Society; Secretary, Arbroath Chamber of Commerce. *Club:* Rotary (Arbroath) (President 1968). *Address:* Fortree, Salisbury Place, Arbroath; and *office* 93 High Street, Arbroath, Angus, Scotland.

**NEILSON, Hon. William Arthur.** Premier and Treasurer Tasmania. *B.* 1925. *Educ.* Ogilvie High School, Hobart. *M.* 1948, Jill Benjamin. *S.* Andrew William Hansen. *Daus.* Christine Mary, Carolyn Gay, Robin Maxwell. *Career:* Elected Mem. of House of Assembly for Franklin 1946; Parlmnty. Labour Party Whip 1946–55; Minister for Tourism Forests, and Immigration, 1956–58; Attorney-General (Tasmania) July–Oct. 1958; Minister for Education 1958–69 and 72–74; Dep. Premier, Attorney-General, Minister for Police & Licensing & Environment, Tasmania, 1974–75; Premier and Treasurer since 1975; *Address:* 40 Cornwall Street, Rose Bay, Hobart, Tasmania.

**NELLI, Andrew Edward,** BS, MA, AMP. American. *B.* 1916. *Educ.* Fordham Univ. (BS); Columbia Univ. (MA); Harvard Univ. (AMP). *M.* 1944, Hope A. Merian. *S.* 3. *Dau.* 1. *Career:* Exec. Vice Pres. Carnation International, Div. Carnation Co.; Chmn. Far East Broadcasting Co. *Member:* Amer. Inst. C.P.A.; State, Cal. C.P.A.; New York State C.P.A. *Award:* Hon LLD, S. Calif. Coll. 1974. *Address:* 2905 Elvido Drive, Bel Air, California 90049, U.S.A.

**NELSON OF STAFFORD, Lord** (Henry George Nelson). Chairman, General Electric Co. Ltd. *B.* 1917. *Educ.* Oundle and King's College, Cambridge (MA; Exhibition 1935); Hon. D.Sc, Aston, Keele, Cranfield; Hon. LLD, Strathclyde; Fellow of Imperial College. *M.* 1940, Pamela Roy Bird. *S.* 2. *Daus.* 2. *Career:* Practical training: English Elec. Co. 1934–37, Société des Construction de Batignolle (Paris), Renault Cie (Paris), Sulzer Bros. Ltd. and Brown Boveri (Switzerland) 1937–39. Joined English Elec. 1939 (successively Supt., Asst. Works Manager, Dep. Works Manager 1939–42); Managing Dir., D. Napier & Son Ltd. 1942–49; Executive Dir., Marconi's Wireless Telegraph 1946–48; Outside Lect. Univ. of Cambridge 1947–49; Deputy Managing Director English Electric 1949–56. Dir. 1943—; Man. Dir. 1956–62, Chmn. Chief Exec. English Electric Co. Ltd. 1962–68; Chmn. General Electric Co. Ltd. since 1968. Dep. Chmn. British Aircraft Corp. Holdings Ltd. 1960–77. Dir., Bank of England; National Bank of Australasia (London Adv. Bd.); International Nickel Co. of Canada Ltd. Awarded Benjamin Franklin Medal 1959 by R.S.A. (with approval of the Duke of Edinburgh). Membership; Engineering Advisory Council; Engineering Employers' Federation (various committees). Fellow Institution of Civil Engineers; Royal Aeronautical Society. Hon. Fellow, Institution of Mechanical Engineers: Institution of Electrical Engineers, Pres. 1970–71; International Electrical Assn. (Chmn. 1955); Middle East Assn. (Vice-Pres. 1959–62); World Power Conference (Chmn. Brit. Natl. Cttee. 1971–74); President: S.B.A.C., 1961–62; L.A.M.A. 1964; B.E.A.M.A. 1966; B.E.P.C. 1966; Orgalime 1969–70; Sino-British Trade Council since 1973; Lord High Steward Borough of Stafford 1966–71; Chancellor Univ. Aston in Birmingham since 1966; Liveryman, Worshipful Company of Coachmakers and Coach Harness Makers of London, Worshipful Company of Goldsmiths; The Civic Trust (Trustee 1962–72); City and Guilds of London Institute (Hon. Member). *Clubs:* Carlton, Hurlingham. *Address:* 8 Carlton Lodge, 37 Lowndes Street; London SW1X 9HX.

**NELSON, Bertram,** CBE, LLD, JP, FCA. British. *B.* 1905. *M.* 1954. Eleanor Kinsey. *S.* Edward. *Dau.* Louise. *Career:* Chmn., Liverpool Chamber of Commerce; Pro-Chancellor, Univ. of Liverpool; Bd. Mem.. Merseyside & North Wales Electricity Bd.; Chmn., Liverpool Daily Post & Echo Group; Mem., Council of the Inst. of Chartered Accountants of England & Wales. *Clubs:* Reform; Athenaeum; University Staff House. *Address:* Tyddyn Rossa, Prion, Denbigh, Clwyd L16 4RP; and *office* 42 Castle Street, Liverpool, L2 7LF.

**NELSON, Charles E.** American executive. *B.* 1904. *Educ.* Univ. of Wisconsin (PhBEcon). *M.* 1928, Mary Haven. *S.* Spencer Charles. *Dau.* Sylvia (Moldenhauer). *Career:* District Representative, Jessie A. Smith Auto Co. 1927–29; Asst. to General Manager, Waukesha Motor Co. 1929–33; Secy. and Treasurer, Fageol Truck & Coach Co. (subsidiary of Waukesha Motor Co.) 1933–34; Asst. to Gen. Mgr., Waukesha Motor Co. 1935–36 (successively Director of Purchasing 1936–47; Asst. to President 1947–49; Vice-Pres. 1949–55; Secy. and Treasurer 1955–57; Exec. Vice-Pres. 1957–60; Pres. 1960–68; Dir. Bangor Ponta Corp. 1st Holding Co.; Dir. 1st Nat. Bank of Waukesha; Dir. Alloy Products Co. *Awards:* Silver Beaver Award, Boy Scouts of America; Scroll and Merit Award Key, National Office Management Association. *Member:* Wisconsin Manufacturers Assn.; Society of Automotive Engineers; Internal Combustion Engine Inst. *Clubs:* University (Milwaukee); Merrill Hills Country. *Address:* 2526 Highway ZD, Dousman, Wis., U.S.A.

**NELSON, George J.** American investment banker. *B.* 1905. *Educ.* MA (Econ). *M.* 1940, Ilse Netter. *S.* Gerald Raymond. *Daus.* Irene Sylvia and Ingrid Maria. *Career:* Economist with Laird Bissell & Meeds (1939–50) and Shields & Co. (1950–55); President: Nelson Fund Inc. (Investment Trust), Nov. 1955–Dec. 1976; Snr. Partner, Nelson Fund Assoc. since 1976. *Member:* American Economic Assn., Chamber of Commerce of State of New York, St George Society, New York Society of Security Analysts, N.Y. Assn. of Business Economists; Japan Socy.; Asia Socy.; France-Amerique Socy.; National Council Metropolitan Opera Co. *Award:* Knight of Malta. *Clubs:* Church of New York; Mid-Ocean; Paris-American; Laymen's of the Cathedral; The Pilgrims; American (London); Baur-an-Lac (Zurich); National Economist (Washington D. C.). *Address:* 12 East 93rd Street, New York 10028, N.Y., U.S.A.

**NELSON, (Richard) Anthony,** MP. British Politician. *B.* 1948. *Educ.* Harrow; Christ's Coll., Cambridge—MA (Hons) in Economics & Law. *M.* 1974, Caroline Victoria Butler. *Career:* Merchant Banker 1969–75; Conservative Candidate for East Leeds at General Election, Feb. 1974; Conservative MP for Chichester since 1974; Member of Select Cttee on Science & Technology since 1975; Jt. Sec., All Party Penal Affairs Group; Sec. to Conservative Industry Cttee since 1975. *Publications:* various papers on Economic & Int'l Affairs. *Clubs:* Coningsby Club. *Address:* The Old Vicarage, Easebourne, Sussex; and House of Commons, London SW1.

**NELSON, W. Linton.** Rear Admiral, U.S.N.R. (Retired). Legion of Merit, Bronze Star Medal, Commendation Ribbon. *B.* 1900. *Educ.* Univ. of Pennsylvania. *M.* 1934, Mrs. Grace E. Solly. *Career:* Served in U.S. Navy in both World Wars. With Fidelity-Philadelphia Trust Co. 1922–29; Investment Corporation of Philadelphia 1929–41; Dir., Operations Office of Foreign Liquidation, U.S. Dept. of State 1945–46, Rowing Championships: National Quadruple Sculls 1921. National Doubles 1924–26; and Canadian Singles 1926. Mutual fund executive. Director: Delaware Fund; Decatur Income Fund; Delta Trend Fund; Delchester Bond Fund; OMC Tax-Free Income Trust, Pa.; Chmn. of Bd. & Dir., Delaware Management Co.; Senior Partner, Delaware Co. *Member:* Investment Company Inst.; Past Bd. Govs. Securities Industry Assn.; Financial Analysts Club (N.Y.C.); Navy League of U.S. (Past Nat. Dir.). Republican. *Awards:* Hon LLD Wash. and Jefferson Coll. 1975. *Clubs:* Racquet; British Officers; Philadelphia Country, Union League, Undine Barge (Philadelphia). *Address:* 1124 Stony Lane, Gladwyne, Pa. 19035; and *office* Seven Penn Center Plaza, Philadelphia, Pa. 19103, U.S.A.

**NERDRUM, Johan.** Norwegian lawyer. *B.* 1912. *Educ.* Univ. of Oslo (cand jur 1935); law and languages studies in England, France, Germany and U.S.A. 1936–38. *M.* 1955, Inger Lise. *S.* Odd and Johan M. *Dau.* Ingrid. *Career:* Practising lawyer 1938–47; Attorney (høyesterettsadvokat), Supreme Court of Norway 1955. Military service Norway 1940–44, Norwegian Legation Stockholm 1944, and Norwegian High Command, Special Forces Headquarters London 1945. Joined Norwegian Airlines 1947 as Assistant to Management with first SAS (Overseas) as special field of duty; Asst. to Management of SAS in Stockholm 1949–51: Deputy Regional Manager (regionalsjef) SAS Region, Norway 1951–60; Vice-Pres. and Gen. Manager SAS, Norway Region 1960–68; Gen. Mgr. and Bd. Member Norwegian Airlines (DNL), parent company of SAS, 1968—. Awarded King's Medal for Courage (British). *Address: office* DNL, Oslo Airport, Norway.

**NESMEYANOV, Alexandre Nikolaevich.** Russian. Member of the Presidium of the Academy of Sciences, U.S.S.R.; Director, Inst. of Elemento-organic Compounds; Professor of Organic Chemistry, University of Moscow. *B.* 1899. *Educ.* Moscow University 1917–22; Postgraduate 1924; Doctor of Chemistry, Professor 1934. *M.* Nina Vladimirovna Nesmeyanova. (2) Marina Anatolivena Vinogradova. *S.* Nikolai Alexandrovich. *Dau.* Olga Alexandrovna. *Career:* Asst. 1924–30, docent 1930–34, and professor 1934–54, Professor of Organic Chemistry, Univ. of Moscow; Dir., Inst. of Organic Chemistry, Academy of Sciences 1939–54; Dir. of the new Inst. of Elemeto-organic Compounds (hetero-organic comp.) 1954; Rector, Univ. of Moscow 1948–51; Pres., Acad. of Sciences 1951–61; Head of Chair (Prof.) of Organic Chemistry Univ. of Moscow 1945—. Author of 1,000 papers in scientific journals, and of a 4-vol. of collected works (1959) condensed to one volume published in England 1963; Series Methods of Elemento-organic Chemistry, Handbook of Magnesium-Organic Compounds (with S.T. Joffe). Foreign Member: The Royal Society (Eng.); Royal Society of Edinburgh; Indian National Institute; American Academy of Arts & Sciences; New York Academy. Hon. Member, Academies of Poland, Hungary, Czechoslovakia, Bulgaria, Rumania, and The Chemical Society of Industry. Dr. *h.c.* University of Paris, Bordeaux, Calcutta and Jena. *Awards:* State Prize 1943; Lomonsov Gold Medal 1961; Lenin Prize 1965, Hero of Socialist Labour; Six Orders of Lenin and one of Red Banner. *Address:* University Corpus K (Apt. 105), Institute of Elemento-organic Chemistry, Uliza Vavilova 28, Moscow, U.S.S.R.

**NETHERTHORPE** (of Anston), **Lord** (Sir James Turner), LLD, BSc. British farmer. *B.* 6 Jan. 1908. *Educ.* Leeds University (BSc Agric). *M.* 1935, Margaret Lucy Mattock. *S.* 3. *Career:* President, National Farmers' Union of England & Wales 1945–60. Trustee, Royal Agricultural Society of England; President British Productivity Council 1965; Member, Council, Animal Health Trust, and Pres. Royal Association of British Dairy Farmers, 1964. Director Fisons Ltd. (Chmn. 1961–73) Lloyds Bank Ltd., Abbey National Building Society, The Steetley Co. Ltd.; Rank Group Holdings; Rank Foundation Ltd.; Unigate Ltd. (Vice-Chmn. 1976—); J. H. Fenner & Co. (Holdings) Ltd.; The National Bank of New Zealand Ltd. *Awards:* Freeman of the City of London and Liveryman of the Painter Stainers, and Farmers Companies. Pres., Int. Fed. of Agricultural Producers 1946–48. *Address:* Hadley Hurst, Hadley Common, Barnet, Herts. EN5 5QG.

**NETHERSOLE, Harrison John Hastings.** South African engineer and company director. *B.* 1903. *Educ.* St. Andrew's Coll., Grahamstown, and University of the Witwatersrand (BSc pure science; BSc Eng); CEng, FRSA, FIEE, FIMechE, MIEEE, MSAIEE, FInstD, MILocoE. *M.* 1930, Dorothy Joyce. *S.* 1. *Daus.* 2. *Career:* Apprentice with Metropolitan-Vickers Electrical Co. Ltd., England 1926–29; Asst. Engineers, Merz & McLellan, England 1930–35; Electrical Engineer and later Chief Engineer, Trinidad Leaseholds Ltd., W.I. 1936–45; Engineer, The English Electric Co., Stafford, England 1945–46; Managing Director, English Electric Co. of South Africa (Pty.) Ltd. 1947–59; Managing Director, English Electric Co. (Traction) Ltd., General Manager, Traction Division, English Electric House, London, Jan. 1960—. Member of the Board: Vulcan Foundry Ltd. May 1960—; The English Electric Co. of South Africa (Pty.) Ltd.; Marconi (S.A.) Pty. Ltd. 1947—. *Address:* c/o The English Electric Co. Ltd., English Electric House, Strand, London, W.C.2.

**NEUBERT, Michael Jon,** MP. British Politician/Travel Consultant. *B.* 1933. *Educ.* Queen Elizabeth's Sch., Barnet; Bromley Grammar Sch.; Royal Coll. of Music; Downing Coll., Cambridge—MA, Modern & Medieval Languages. *M.* 1959, Sally Felicity Bilger. *S.* 1. *Career:* Operations Mgr., Wings Ltd., 1960–73; Conservative MP for Romford since 1974. *Publications:* Running Your Own Society (1967). *Club:* Romford Conservative & Constitutional Club. *Address:* 12 Greatwood, Chislehurst, Kent; and House of Commons, London SW1A 0AA.

**NEUKOM, John Goudey.** American. *B.* 1912. *Educ.* University of Chicago (PhB 1934). *M.* 1937, Ruth Horlick. *S.* William Horlick, Davidson Raymond and Daniel Ingraham. *Dau.* Barbara Anne (Bohn, Jr.). *Career:* with James O. McKinsey & Co., and McKinsey, Kearney & Co., Chicago 1934–45; on leave to Office of Price Administration, Washington; Director of Fuel and Automotive Rationing Division, Local Board Operations 1942–45; Dir. Kaiser Aluminium & Chemical Corp.; Transamerica Corp. and Univar. Corp; Trustee Univ .of Chicago; Former Director, McKinsey & Co., Inc., Management Consultants. *Award:* Hon. LLD, (Yankton) Golden Gate Univ. *Publications:* various articles relating to professional interests. *Clubs:* Burlingame Country; Cercle de L'Union; Rotary; Bohemian; Villa Taverna; Eldorado Golf (Palm Desert). *Address:* 1805 Floribunda Avenue, Hillsborough, 94104 Calif.; and *office* 311 California Street, San Francisco, Calif., U.S.A.

**NEUMANN, Robert Gerhard.** American educationalist, consultant & diplomat. *B.* 1916. *Educ.* Amherst College (MA); University of Minnesota (PhD); Geneva School of International Studies; University of Rennes. *M.* 1941, Marlen Eldredge. *S.* Ronald Eldredge, Gregory Woodsmall. *Dau.* Marcia Woodsmall (*Dec.*). *Career:* Professor, Political Science, University of California, 1949–69; Ambassador to Afghanistan 1967–73; to Morocco 1973–76; Senior Associate, Center for Strategic & International Studies, Georgetown Univ. 1976—; Program Dir. & Professional Lecturer, Georgetown Univ. 1977—. *Awards:* Chevalier, Legion of Honor, France (1957); Officer's Cross, Order of Merit, FRG (1963); Order of Star, First Class, Afghanistan (1973); Commander's Cross, Order of Merit, FRG (1974); Grand Officer, Order & Star of Ouissam Alaoui, Morocco (1976). *Publications:* European Government (4th Ed. 1968); The Government of the German Federal Republic, (1967). *Member:* American Political Science Association; American Society of International Law; International Studies Association; American Foreign Service Association. Republican. *Address:* 4986 Sentinel Drive, #102, Washington, D.C. 20016, U.S.A.

**NEVELL, Thomas G.** Consultant in design, engineering, and styling of products, packages, interiors, exhibitions and graphics. Patentee in field. *B.* 1910. *Educ.* New York Univ. College of Fine Arts, and Columbia Univ. *M.* 1942, Raye Inez Babcock. *S.* Richard William. *Dau.* Nancy Barbara. *Career:* Designer, Hampton Shops, New York, Charles Robeson of London (2 years); Cushing & Nevell; junior partner 1934, senior partner 1939. Partner, Cushing & Nevell, N.Y.C., and Secretary-Treasurer of subsidiary companies in New York City, Los Angeles, Canada, and of Cushing & Nevell Technical Design Corp., N.Y.C. *Awards:* Modern Plastics Award, 1939; Electrical Manufacturing Award, 1940; Industrial Designers Institute Award, 1951. *Member:* Industrial Design Society of America; Amer. Socy. of Mechanical Engineers; Socy. of Amer. Military Engineers. *Clubs:* Riverside Yacht (Past Rear Commodore); New York Yacht. *Address* and *office:* 101 Park Avenue, New York City, N.Y. 10019, U.S.A.

**NEWCOMB, Robinson.** American executive. *B.* 1901. *Educ.* Univ. of Ohio, Univ. of North Carolina, Oberlin College (AB, MA *summa cum laude*), and Brookings Graduate School (PhD 1928). *M.* 1929, Carolyn Jones. *S.* Anthony Mead. *Dau.* Sara Robinson. *Career:* Consulting economist, Dept. of Commerce, and Dept. of the Interior; Director of construction research, War Production Board 1940–45; Director, office of economic research, Federal Works Agency 1945–47; Economist, President's Council of Economic Advisers 1947–50, and 1953–55; Office of Secy. of Commerce 1950–51, Office of Defense Mobilization 1951–53; consultant and technical adviser on highways, Committee of Economic Development 1947–55; committee on construction statistics, Business Research Advisory Council, Dept. of Labor 1955–59; member, Adv. Committee on Construction Statistics, U.S. Census 1959. Principal, Robinson Newcomb Associates, Washington, consultants to Ammann & Whitney, Baker-Wibberly, AID, Standard Oil of N.Y.B., C & O, B & O, Ry. *Publications:* Construction (for Committee of Economic Development); Modern Economic Organization (translator); contributor of articles to professional and business journals. *Member:* Chmn. Building Research Advisory Board, National Academy of Sciences, 1957–73. *Clubs:* Cosmos (Washington); International (Washington). *Address:* 1328 Beulah Road, Vienna, Va. 22180, U.S.A.

**NEWELL, John Rogers.** Retired shipbuilding executive. *B.* 1912. *Educ.* Phillips Acad. (Prep.); Massachusetts Inst. of Technology (BS). *Career:* With Bethlehem Steel Co. (Shipbuilding Div.) 1935–Asst. Gen Mgr. 1938–44, Vice-Pres. 1947–50, Bath Iron Works. Lieut. U.S. Navy 1944–47. Pres., Bath Iron Works Corp., Bath, Maine 1950–65: Trustee, Bates College. Hon. LLD. Univ. of Maine, Bowdoin Coll.; Hon. DEng, Stevens Inst. of Technology. *Member:* Society of Naval Architects & Marine Engineers (Past Pres.). *Address:* 241 N.E. Spanish Trail, Boca Raton, Fla., 33432, U.S.A.

**NEWENS, Arthur Stanley**, MP. British. *B.* 1930. *Educ.* Univ. Coll., London—BA (Hons) in History; Westminster Coll.—Postgraduate Certificate in Education. *M.* (1) 1954, Ann Sherratt (*Dec.* 1962). (2) 1966, Sandra Christina Frith. *Daus.* 4. *Career:* Coal Miner 1952–56; Secondary School Teacher 1956–64, 1970–74; Labour MP for Epping 1964–70 (Sponsored by Nat. Union of Teachers), for Harlow (Sponsored by Co-operative Movement) since 1974. *Member:* National Union of Teachers; Chmn. of Liberation (formerly Movement for Colonial Freedom); Dir. of the London Co-operative Society since 1971, Pres. since 1977; Chmn., Eastern Group of Labour MPs; Vice-Chmn., Eastern Regional Council of the Labour Party; Vice-Chmn., Parly. Labour Party Foreign Affairs Group; Mem., Central Executive of the Co-operative Union. *Publications:* (Pamphlet) the Case against NATO (1972); (Collection of Writings etc.) Nicolae Ceauçescu (1972). *Address:* House of Commons, London SW1.

**NE WIN, General U Shu Maung.** President Socialist Republic of Burma. *B.* 1911. *Educ.* Government High School, Prome and Rangoon University. Commander-in-Chief of Burma Independence Army 1943; in command of Resistance Forces against the Japanese in the Delta region and later joined the Allied Forces 1945; Major-General 1948; Deputy Prime Minister 1949–50; General 1956; Prime Minister during Caretaker Government 1958–60; Chief of General Staff 1962–72; Prime Minister & Minister of Defence, & Chmn. of Revolutionary Council 1963–74; Chmn., Exec. Cttee., Burma Socialist Programme Party since 1973; Pres. of Burma since 1974. *Address:* Office of the President, Rangoon, Socialist Republic of the Union of Burma.

**NEWMAN, Augustus James.** British electrical engineer. *B.* 1901. *Educ.* St. Mary Redcliffe and Merchant Venturers, Bristol. *M.* 1953, Frances Moody, dau. of James Russell. *Career:* Founder, Chairman and Managing Director, Newman Industries Ltd. (estab. 1936; makers of electric motors and rotating electrical machinery; special purpose machine-tool manufacturers and rebuilders, ironfounders and makers of light alloy castings), Bristol. Chairman: Newman Electric Motors Inc., U.S.A.; and Higgs Motors Ltd., Birmingham. Director, Machine Tools, Ministry of Aircraft Production. Conservative. Church of England. *Clubs:* East India and Sports (London); Bankers; New York Athletic (New York City); Petroleum (Houston, Tex.). *Address:* 9 Alford House, Park Lane, London, W.1; 17 West 54th Street, New York City; and *office* Yate, Bristol.

**NEWMAN, Sir Jack**, CBE, JP, FCIT. New Zealand. *B.* 1902. *Educ.* Nelson College. *M.* 1926, Myrtle O. A. Thomas. *Daus.* 4. *Career:* Chairman of Directors of TNL Group Ltd. & Newmans Holdings Ltd. Director: Zip Holdings Ltd., NZ Motor Bodies Ltd. & Moller Holdings Ltd.; N.Z. Travel Association (Life Member). Represented N.Z. Cricket, also Canterbury and Wellington 1931–36; also represented Nelson Cricket, Rugby (past Pres. Nelson Rugby Union), Golf and Bowls. Past-Pres. & Life Member N.Z. Cricket Council; Pres., N.Z. Cricket Foundation. *Clubs:* Wellesley (Wellington) and Nelson (Nelson). *Address:* 36 Brougham Street, Nelson; and *office* TNL Group Ltd., Private Bag, Nelson, New Zealand.

**NEWMAN, James Wilson.** *B.* 1909. *Educ.* Clemson Coll, (BS), and New York Univ. Law School (JD). *M.* 1934. Clara Collier. *S.* James Wilson, Jr., and Charles Carter II. *Daus.* Clare (Blanchard) and Mildred (Thayer) B. *Career:* Started as reporter with Dun & Bradstreet 1931; Pres. of the Co. 1952, and Chmn. of Bd. 1960–68. Chairman Finance Committee, Dun & Bradstreet Companies Inc. New York, 1968—. Trustee: Atlantic Mutual Insurance Co.; Mutual Life Insurance Co. of N.Y.; Committee on Economic Development. Director: General Foods Corp.; International Paper Co.; Fidelity Union Trust Co.; Chemical Bank New York Trust Co.; Lockheed Aircraft Corp., also Chmn. Special Review Cttee.; Chmn. President's Task Force, Improving Prospects of Small Business 1969; Mem. Commission on Bankruptcy Laws of U.S.; member Price Commission. Author of various speeches and pamphlets. Hon. LLD, Clemson Univ. *Member:* Economic Club of N.Y.; American Bar Association; National Industrial Conference Board. *Clubs:* University; Downtown Association. *Address:* 21 Lake Road, Short Hills, N.J. 07078; and *office* 99 Church Street, New York City, U.S.A.

**NEWMAN, Robert Jacob.** American. Officier de L'Ordre de L'Etoile Noir. *B.* 1904. *Educ.* Tulane Univ. (New Orleans). *M.* 1948, Claire Poe. *S.* Robert, Jr. and Christopher. *Dau.* Leslie. *Career:* Senior Partner, Newman, Harris & Co., Investment Bankers 1932–40; Associated with Newman Brown & Co. 1942–66; Gen. Partner Kohlmeyer & Co.; Member New York Stock Exchange; Dir. Royal Orleans Hotel Inc.; Owner Vineyards, Latriciers Chambertin Mazys, Chambertin Bonnes Mares, Burgandy. *Awards:* Chevalier de la Confrérie du Tastevin; Commanderie de Bordeaux; Chevalier de la Chaine des Rotisseurs; Compagnons de Bontemps Bordeaux); Pres. Bd. Trustees, Isaac Delgado Museum of Art, New Orleans 1964–65–67, 1970–71. *Clubs:* Kitzbuhel Golf; Metairie Country (New Orleans); Pass Christian Yacht (Mississippi); Arlberg Ski (St. Anton, Austria); Kitzbuhel Ski; Silver Snow Flake, Kitzbuhel; Charter member, Yachting Club of America; Plimsoll (New Orleans). *Address:* 1111 Falcon Road, Metairie, La. 70005; and *office* 1947 Carondelet Street, New Orleans, La. 70130, U.S.A.

**NEWNS, Sir Alfred Foley Francis Polden**, KCMG, CVO, British administrator. *B.* 1909. *Educ.* Christ's Hospital and St. Catherine's Coll., Cambridge (MA). *M.* 1936, Jean Bateman. *S.* Peter. *Dau.* Marie. *Career:* Administrative Officer, Nigeria 1932; Actg. Principal Asst. Secy., Central Secretariat 1950; Resident 1951; Secy. to the Council of Ministers 1951–54; to the Governor-General and the Council of Ministers 1955–59; Deputy Governor Sierra Leone, Jan. 1960–61 (Actg. Governor during (1960); Adviser to Govt. of Sierra Leone 1961–63. Secretary to the Cabinet, Govt. of Bahamas 1963–71. *Address:* Cedar House, Caxton Lane, Foxton, Cambridgeshire, England.

**NEWSOM, David Dunlop.** American diplomat. *B.* 1918. *Educ.* University of California (AB); Columbia University N.Y. (MS). *M.* 1942, Jean Craig. *S.* John, Daniel, David. *Dau.* Nancy, Catherine. *Career:* Dir., Office of Northern African Affairs, U.S. Dept. of State, 1962–65; Ambassador to Libya, 1965–69; Assistant Secretary of State for African Affairs, 1969–74; Ambassador to Indonesia since 1974. *Address:* American Embassy, Jakarta, Indonesia.

**NEWSON, Ernest Alfred Reeve**, QC. Canadian Barrister-at-Law and Solicitor. *B.* 1900. *Educ.* Osgoode Hall, Toronto (Deg. Barrister-at-Law). *M.* 1925, Josephine Rachel May Wagg. *Daus.* Gloria Sheard and Elizabeth Helen McLean. *Career:* Called to Bar of Ontario 1924; Partner, Roebuck & Newson, 1924–30; practised alone 1930–54; partner, Newson & Sheard 1954–73, Practising alone since 1973; Director of other Corporations. Progressive-Conservative. *Address:* 53 Widdicombe Hill Blvd., Apt. 808 East, Weston, Ontario, Canada M9R 1Y3.

**NEWTON, Lord** (Peter Richard Legh). *B.* 1915. *Educ.* Eton and Christ Church, Oxford. *M.* Priscilla, widow of Viscount Wolmer (and daughter of late Capt. John Egerton-Warburton). *S.* 2. *Career:* Second Lieut., Grenadier Guards 1937, Capt. 1941, Major 1945. MP (Con.) Petersfield Div. of Hants. 1951–60; Parly. Private Secy. to Financial Secy. to the Treasury 1952–53; an Asst. Govt. Whip 1953–55; Lord Commissioner of Treasury 1955–57; Vice-Chamberlain of the Household 1957–59, Treasurer 1959–60; Capt. of the Yeoman of the Guard and Govt. Asst. Chief Whip, House of Lords 1960–62; Joint Parliamentary Secy., Ministry of Health 1962–64; Minister of State for Education and Science Apr.–Oct. 1964. *Clubs:* Carlton, Pratt's Constitutional, and Hampshire (Winchester). *Address:* Vernon Hill House, Bishop's Waltham, Hants.

**NEWTON, John Mordaunt**, CB. British. *B.* 1913. *Educ.* Cambridge University (BA 1st Cl. Hons.). *M.* 1939, Pamela Frances Maude. *Daus.* 5. *Career:* Asst. Secretary, British Post Office 1949; Principal: Home Office 1942–45, H.M. Treasury 1945–47. Dir., British Post Office 1957–73. *Address:* Thames Bank, Chiswick Mall, London, W.4 2PR.

**NEWTON, Theodore Francis Moorhouse.** *B.* 1903. *Educ.* McGill Univ. (BA 1925; MA 1927); Harvard, M.A. *M.* 1943, Margaret E Cameron. *Stepson* John Fraser Cameron. *Career:* Instructor, Harvard Univ. 1928–37; Assoc. Professor of English, McGill Univ. 1937–43; Canadian Wartime Information Board, New York 1943–47; First Secretary, Canadian Embassy, Washington 1947–48; Consul, Boston (Mass.) 1948–50; Director, NATO Information Service, London 1950–52; Paris 1952–53; Head, Information Div., Dept. of External Affairs, Ottawa 1953–54; Minister-Counsellor, Tokyo 1954–57; Ambassador to Indonesia 1958–60. Ambassador of Canada to Colombia and Ecuador, July 1961–64. Dept. of External Affairs, Ottawa 1964–68. *Publications:* monographs on early English journalism and Daniel Defoe. *Address:* 149 Manor Avenue, Ottawa, Ont., Canada.

**NIARCHOS, Stavros Spyros.** Greek shipowner. *B.* 1909. *Educ.* Univ. of Athens (LLD). *M.* (1) 1947, Eugenie Livanos (*D.* 1970). *S.* Philip Spyros and Constantine. *Dau.* Maria-Isabella. *M.* (2) Charlotte Ford (*Diss.* 1967). *Dau.* Elena. (3) 1971, Tina Livanos (*D.* 1974). *Awards:* Grand Cross, Order of the Phoenix; Cmdr., Order of St. George and St. Constantine; Cmdr., Order of George I. *Career:* On leaving the University joined the family grain and shipping business; started independent shipping concern 1939; joined Royal Hellenic Navy 1941; served as Lieut. on destroyer engaged on North Atlantic convoy duty; demobilized 1945; returned to shipping business. Pioneered super-tankers. Head of Niarchos Group of companies, which control 4 million tons of shipping (in operation and on order). *Publications:* articles in various technical journals. *Clubs:* Metropolitan (N.Y.C.): Royal Bermuda Yachting; Royal Hellenic Yachting, Athenian (Athens); Corviglia Ski. *Address:* c/o 41 Park Street, London W1A 2JR.

**NICHOLLS, Frank Gordon.** Australian scientist. *B.* 1916. *Educ.* Melbourne High School; Univ. of Melbourne (MSc). *M.* 1940, Yvonne Isabel Miles. *Career:* Radio research with Commonwealth Council for Scientific & Industrial Research (C.S.I.R.) 1936–40; in charge of Aust. Scientific Research Liaison Office, London 1941–44; Asst. Secy., C.S.I.R. and C.S.I.R.O. (Commonwealth Scientific & Industrial Research Organization) 1945–52; Secy. (Gen. Admin.) 1952–60, Research Secy. C.S.I.R.O. 1952–63; member, Pakistan Scientific Commission 1959; United Nations Appraisal of Scientific Activities Expert advising Govt. of Thailand 1960–61; United Nations Chief Advisor, Applied Research, Special Governor, Applied Scientific Research Corp. of Thailand 1963–70; Deputy Dir. Gen. International Union for Conservation of Nature & Natural Resources Morges Switzerland 1970–76; Dep. Gen. Mgr., Australian Innovation Corp. Ltd.; Jt. Man. Dir., Trans Knowledge Associates Pty. Ltd. since 1977. *Member* Exec. Nat. Assn. Testing Authorities 1949–60, Standards Assn. 1949–60; Secy. National Standards Comms. 1952–63; Radio Astronomy Trust 1956–63; Organizing Cttee. Melbourne Film Festival 1952–63; Melbourne Film Socy. 1956–60; Chmn. Govs. Aust. Film Institute 1958–63. Member, Royal Australian Chemical Inst. (Associate); Illuminating Engineering Socy. of Australia (Fellow); Public Relations Inst. of Australia; International Public Relations Assns.; Australian Inst. of Physics (Associate); Intern. Council of Environmental Law. *Award:* Most Noble Order, Crown of Thailand. *Publications:* scientific papers; Editor, I.E.S. Lighting Review; U.N. Report, A Programme for the Development of Scientific Research in Thailand 1961. *Address:* 61/4 Sydney Street, Armadale, Vic. 3181, Australia.

**NICHOLS, Clement Roy,** CMG, OBE. Australian company director and textile technologist. *B.* 1909. *Educ.* Scotch College, Melbourne. *M.* 1933, Margareta Pearse. *S.* 1. *Dau.* 1. *Career:* Chmn. Alpha Spinning Mills Pty. Ltd., Alphington, Vic. Chairman, National Wool Committee (Vice-Pres. IWTO) 1967–75; Pres. Victorian Chamber of Mnfs 1970–72; Pres. Assoc. Chamber, Mnfs. of Australia 1971–74. Member: World Committee of World Conference of the Boy Scout Movement 1959—65, 1967–73; Far East Scout Adv. Committee 1962–65; Chief Commissioner, Australian Boy Scouts Assn. 1963–66, National Chmn. 1973—. Fellow Australian Inst. of Management; Aust. Inst. of Directors; Associate, Textile Institute (England), Governor 1961–62. District 280, Rotary International. Pres., Australian Wool Textile Manufacturers' Assn. 1965–68. *Clubs:* Australian (Melbourne); Rotary (Heidelberg, Vic.). *Address:* 82 Studley Park Road, Kew, Vic. 3101, Australia.

**NICHOLS, Thomas Steele.** American. *B.* 1909. *Educ.* Cambridge (Md.) High School, Temple Univ. and Univ. of Pennsylvania. *M.* 1971, Mrs. Tatiana A. McKenna. *S.* 1. *Dau.* 1. *Career:* With E. I. duPont, deNemours & Co. 1926–37; Vice-Pres. Prior Chemical Corp. 1937–46; Pres. Mathieson Chemical Corp. 1948–54; Pres. Olin Mathieson Chemical Corp. 1954–57, Chmn. of the Board 1957–63; Chairman of Exec. Committee, Olin Corp. 1963–74. *Awards:* Hon. DSc Southwestern Coll., Winfield, Kansas; LLD Polytechnic Inst. of Brooklyn, N.Y.; Hon. Dr. Humanities, Washington Coll., Chestertown, Maryland; Grand Officer, Legion of Honor of the Italian Republic. *Clubs:* The Brook, Links, River (all of N.Y.C.); Bath and Tennis; Everglades; Palm Beach (Fla.); Maidstone (East Hampton, N.Y.); Ristogouche Salmon (Matapedia, Canada); Metropolitan (Washington, D.C.); Lyford Cay (Bahamas); Seminole Golf (Palm Beach, Fla); Beach, National Golf Links of America (Southampton, N.Y.). *Address:* P.O. Box 253, Owings Mills, Maryland 21117, U.S.A.

**NICHOLS, William Ichabod.** American. Editor Publisher, Library Executive. *B.* 1905. *Educ.* Harvard Coll. (BA, mcl); Balliol Coll., Oxford (Rhodes Scholar, 1926–27); Freshman Dean, Harvard College, 1927–29. *M.* 1942, Marie Therese Brollova. *Career:* Director, Harvard University News Office, 1932–34; Adv. Publicity Mgr., Nat. Electric Power Co., N.Y.C., 1929–32; Dir. Electric Development, Tennessee Valley Authority 1934–37; Editor, Sunset Magazine, San Francisco, 1937–39; Mgr. Ed., This Week Magazine, N.Y.C., 1939–43; Editor-in-Chief and Publisher 1943–70; Pres., American Library in Paris, 1970–72; Chmn., Nat. Book Cttee. 1967 and 1968; Hon. Consultant in Journalism & Communications, Library of Congress, 1970–72. Founder, Nat. Library Week; Member: Adv. Bd. Hoover Inst. on War, Revolution and Peace; Adv. Cncl. School of Internatl. Affairs, Columbia Univ., etc. Freedom Foundation Public Address Award 1962; Amer. Legion Fourth Estate Award 1963; Irita van Doren Book Award 1967. *Publications:* Edited: Words to Live By; A New Treasury of Words to Live By; The Third Book of Words to Live By; also On Growing Up and Fishing for Fun, by Herbert Hoover. *Clubs:* National Press; Dutch Treat; Coffee House; P.E.N.; Century Assn., Pilgrims of U.S.; Overseas Press; hon. mem. Sigma Delta Chi. *Address:* 21 rue de Verneuil, 75007 Paris, France.

**NICHOLSON, Ian Edmond.** Australian diplomat. *B*, 1932. *Educ.* Camberwell Gr. School; Univ. of Melbourne LI B. *M.* 1956, Judith Ann Wyatt. *S.* 1. *Daus.* 3. *Career:* Third Secy. S. Africa 1957–59; Second Secy. Egypt 1959–60; First Secy. Cambodia 1963–65; Consul, New Caledonia 1965–67; Deputy High Commissioner, India and Nepal 1971–73; Head Papua, New Guinea and Inform. Branches. Dept of Foreign Affairs, Canberra 1974–75; High Commissioner Malta 1975; Ambassador, Chile since 1976. *Clubs:* Melbourne Cricket; Prince of Wales Country Club. *Address:* Casilla 14427, Santiago de Chile.

**NICHOLSON, Sir John Norris,** Bt. British shipowner. *B.* 19 Feb. 1911. *Educ.* Winchester College; Trinity College, Cambridge. *M.* 1938, Vittoria Vivien Trewhella. *S.* 2. *Daus.* 2. Served World War II, Capt., 4th Bn. Cheshire Regt. (T.A.) 1939–41 (despatches); employed Ministry of War Transport 1942–46; *Director:* Ocean Transport and Trading Co.; Barclays Bank Ltd.; Royal Insurance Co. Ltd. *Address:* Mottistone Manor, Isle of Wight.

**NICHOLSON, Hon. John R.,** PC, OBE, K St J, QC. Canadian. *B.* 1901. *Educ.* Dalhousie Univ., Halifax, N.S. (BA 1921; LLB 1923; Hon. LLD 1967); Hon. LLD (UBC), 1970. *M.* 1924, Charlotte Jean Annand. *S.* (Dr.) John Robert Nicholson. *Career:* Practised law in Vancouver, B.C. 1924–41; Deputy Controller of Supplies, Department of Munitions & Supplies 1941–42; General Manager and later Executive. Vice-President, Polymer Corp. Ltd., Sarnia, Ont. 1942–51; Chief Executive Officer in Brazil. Brazilian Light & Power Co., 1951–56. Resumed practice of law Vancouver (Guild Nicholson & Co.) 1957–60; President, Cncl. of the Forest Industries of British Columbia 1960–61; elected as MP for Vancouver Centre, June 1962; re-elected and entered Canadian Cabinet as Minister of Forestry Apr. 1963; Postmaster-General 1964–65. Minister of Citizenship & Immigration, 1965; Minister of Labour, 1965–68; Lieut. Governor of British Columbia, 1968–75. *Awards:* OBE, FRAI (Can.), Medal of Honour (Boy Scout Association of Brazil). *Clubs:* Vancouver; Union (Victoria; B.C.). *Address:* 5, 2002 Robson Street, Vancouver B.C., Canada.

**NICKERSON, Albert Lindsay.** American oil company executive. *B.* 1911. *Educ* Noble and Greenough School, and Harvard (BS 1933); Hon. LLD, Hofstra Univ. 1965, Harvard Univ. 1976. *M.* 1936, Elizabeth Perkins. *S.* Albert W. *Daus.* Christine (Morgen), Elizabeth (Davis), Victoria. *Career:* Began a service station attendant, Socony Mobil Oil Co. (then Socony-Vacuum Oil Co. Inc.) 1933; district manager 1940, division manager 1941; Director, Placement Bureau War Manpower Commission 1943; Asst. Gen. Mgr. Eastern Marketing Division, elected to Board of Directors, London, England 1945, Chmn. of Board, 1946; Vice-President, Director 1951; President Socony Mobil Oil Co. Inc. 1955–61; Chmn. Exec. Cttee. 1958, name of Co. changed 1966; Chief Exec. Officer 1958–69. Chmn. 1961–69 Mobil Oil Corporation; Dir. Federal Reserve Bank N.Y. 1961–66; Chmn. Bd. Fed.

Reserve Agent 1969–71; Dir. Metropolitan Life Insurance Co.; Raytheon Co.; State Street Investment Corp.; Federal Street Fund Inc.; General Partner, State Street Exchange Fund 1977. *Member:* Corporation Harvard Univ., 1965–75; The Business Council, Business Cttee. for the Arts. Trustee, Rockefeller Univ.; Boston Symphony Orchestra; Member of Corp. Woods Hole Oceanographic Inst. (Mass.); Peter Bent Brigham Hospital. Former Chmn. The Business Council; Balance of Payments Adv. Cttee.; U.S. Dept. of Commerce; Member Exec. Bd. National Alliance of Businessmen, Nat. Petroleum Council; Member, Council Foreign Relations; Nat. Foreign Trade Council; Dir. Amer. Mgt. Assn.; First Nat. City Trust Co.; Trustee. Amer. Museum, Natural History; International House N.Y.C.; Cttee. Economic Development; Rye Country Day School; Overseer Harvard College. Pres. 25-year Club, Petroleum Industry; Dir. Treas. Amer. Petroleum Institute. Republican, Episcopalian. *Clubs:* Harvard Varsity, Thames Rowing; Harvard Club of N.Y. City; 25-year club of Petrol Industry; The Country, Brookline Mass.; Cambridge Boat Mass. *Address:* Lexington Road, Lincoln, Mass., 01773; and *office* 150 East 42nd Street, New York N.Y. 10017 U.S.A.

**NICKLIN, Hon. Sir George Francis Reuben,** KCMG, MM, LLD (Hon.), MLA. Premier and Minister for State Development of Queensland 1957–68. *B.* 1895. *Educ.* Highfield Coll., Turramurra, North Sydney. *Career:* Engaged in tropical fruit culture; Pres., North Coast Branch, Surf Life Savings Assn. of Australia 1921—; member, Queensland State Parliament 1932–68; Parly. Secy. of Country Party 1935–38; Leader of Opposition 1941–57; Hon. Councillor, Royal National Association 1957—. Councillor, Royal National Agricultural and Industrial Association 1951–57. Military Medal. *Address:* 13 Upper Gay Terrace, Caloundra, Qld. 4551, Australia.

**NICOLAREISIS, Demetrios J.** Ambassador of Greece. *B.* 1908. *Educ.* Univ. of Athens (Law, Political Science and Economics); studied history of Art in Florence. *M.* Yola Georgopoulos. *Daus.* Bianca and Ioanna. *Career:* Entered Diplomatic Service 1946; Vice-Consul and Political Counsellor to the Military Governor of Northern Epirus at Argyrocastro 1940; served in Crete, London and Cairo 1941. Head of Mission concerned with repatriation of prisoners of war and hostages, Rome 1944–46; Head, First Political Section of Min. for Foreign Affairs 1947–48. Consul in Hamburg and Chargé d'Affairs at Bonn 1948–52; Head NATO Dept., Min. for Foreign Affairs 1952–53 Asst. delegate for Greece at NATO, Paris 1953–56; Chargé d'Affairs and Counsellor of Embassy, London 1956–58; Asst. Chairman, Greco-Yugoslav Commission 1959; Minister Plen. 1959; Ambassador to Yugoslavia 1960–64, to the Court of St. James's 1964–67. *Member:* Royal Order of the Saviour; Kt. Cmde. Order of Phoenix, and of the Yugoslav Flag; Commander: Order of George I, of Civil Merit (Italy) and Verdienst Kreuz (Germany). *Address:* c/o Ministry of Foreign Affairs, Athens, Greece.

**NICOLIN, Curt (Rene),** tech.dr.(h.c.), KVO. Swedish executive. *B.* 1921. *Educ.* Graduated, Royal Inst. of Technology. *M.* 1946, Ulla Sandén. *S.* Clas René, Tomas René and Magnus René. *Daus.* Ulla Marie and Ulla Charlotte. *Career:* Man. Dir.: STAL 1955–59, Turbin AB de Laval Ljungström 1959–61, ASEA 1961–76, Chmn. since 1976; President (for temporary. mission), Scandinavian Airlines System July 1961–Apr. 1962. *Address:* Mariebergs, Säteri, Grödinge, Sweden.

**NICOLL, Alexander Scrimgeour,** TD. British. *B.* 1912. *Educ.* Trinity College Glenalmond. *M.* (1) 1938, Catherine Elizabeth Grant Robbie (*D.* 1963). *Dau.* Elspeth Margaret (Collins). (2) 1970, Beryl Wallace (Bain). *Career:* Territorial Army Commission 1938; war service, finishing with rank of Major. Partner, Jas. Nicoll & Co., Stockbrokers (now Parsons & Co., Glasgow, Edinburgh, Dundee, Aberdeen & London) 1933—. *Member:* Dundee Stock Ex. Assn. 1933—; Secy. 1945–56. Scottish Stock Exchange; The Stock Exchange; Dundee Chamber of Commerce. Conservative. *Clubs:* Scottish National Angling Clubs (Pres. 1965-67, Secretary, 1968–); Intern. Fly Fishing Assoc. (Pres., 1966; Secy., 1968—), Dundee Rotary (Pres. 1964–65); Dundee Angling (Hon., Secy. 1939–74, Pres. 1956). *Address:* 10 East Grange Street, Monifirth, Dundee DD5 4LB; and *office* 51 Meadowside, Dundee, Scotland.

**NICOLSON, Nigel,** MBE, FSA, FRSL. British. Director, Weidenfield & Nicolson Ltd. (Publishers). *B.* 1917. *Educ.* Oxford University. *M.* 1952, P. Tennyson-d'Eyncourt (*Div.*). *S.* Adam. *Daus.* Juliet and Rebecca. *Career:* Conservative MP for Bournemouth East, 1952–59; member of British Delegation to Council of Europe 1953–56; Chmn. of United Nations Association of Gt. Britain, 1960–67. *Publications:* People and Parliament; Lord of the Isles; Great Houses of Britain; Great Houses of the Western World; Alex (Field Marshal Alexander of Tunis); Portrait of a Marriage; the Himalyas; Mary Curzon; Editor, Letters of Virginia Woolf (Vol. 1); and editor of three vols. of Harold Nicolson's Diaries and Letters. *Member:* Royal Institute of International Affairs; National Trust; Royal Society of Antiquaries. Fellow, Royal Society of Literature. *Clubs:* Beefsteak. *Address:* Sissinghurst Castle, Kent.

**NICULESCU-MIZIL, Paul.** Romanian politician. *B.* 1923. *Educ.* Academy of Higher Commercial and Industrial Sciences. *Career:* Professor, Bucharest Univ.; Stefan Gheorghiu Acad. of Social and Political Sciences, Bucharest; Deputy to Grand Nat. Assembly 1957; mem. Central Cttee RCP 1955— & Sec. 1965–72; mem. exec. cttee. of CC of PCP since 1965; Member Perm. Presidium, Central Cttee. 1966–74; Nat. Council Socialist Unity Front 1968—; Defence Council Romania 1969–74; Dep. Prime Minister and Minister of Education 1972–76. Hero of Socialist Labour. Award 1971. *Address:* Central Committee of the Romanian Communist Party, Bucharest, Romania.

**NIELSEN, Arthur Charles, Sr.** American. *B.* 1897. *Educ.* Univ. of Wisconsin (BS Eng), Sc.D. (Hon.) *M.* 1918, Gertrude B. Smith. *S.* Arthur Charles, Jr. and Philip Robert. *Daus.* Margaret Ann, Barbara Harriet and Virginia Beatrice. *Career:* A pioneer in marketing research, he developed Nielsen Food, Drug, Pharmaceutical, Confectionery, Variety, Tobacco, Household, Radio, Television and Station Index Services and the world's largest marketing research organization. Served in World War I (Ensign, U.S. Navy; transport duty in N. Atlantic); Electrical Engineer, Isko Co., Chicago (one year); research worker for H. P. Gould Co., Chicago (three years). Chairman of Exec. Cttee., A. C. Nielsen Company (market research organization), Northbrook, Ill. with offices in Chicago, New York, Menlo Park (Calif.) & others Chairman of the Board, A.C. Nielsen International Inc. & subsidiary companies at Amsterdam, Toronto, Sydney and Wellington, Argentina, Milan, Paris, Lucerne and Frankfurt/Main, Vienna, Tokyo, Mexico City, Lisbon, Madrid, Johannesburg. Director, A. C. Nielsen Co. Ltd., Oxford, A. C. Nielsen of Ireland Ltd., A.C. Nielsen Co.( Belgium) S.A. *Awards:* Silver Medal by the Annual Advertising Awards Committee 1936; Chicago Federated Advertising Club Award 1941; Paul D. Converse Award (by American Marketing Association), 1951; Citation by Wisconsin Alumni Association for distinguished contributions to the welfare of the Univ. of Wisconsin; Parlin Memorial Award 1963. Knight, Order of Dannebrog (by King of Denmark) 1961; Man of the Year Award, distinguished services Int. marketing & Advertising; National Lawn Tennis Hall of Fame. *Address:* 720 Ardsley Road, Winnetka, Ill. 60093; and *Office* Nielsen Plaza, Northbrook, Illinois 60062, U.S.A.

**NIETO-CALDERON, Dr. Eduardo.** Colombian banker. *B.* 1920. *Educ.* Gimnasio Moderno, Bogatá; Lawyer, Colegio del Rosario Bogotá; London School of Economics. *M.* 1963, Beatriz Jaramillo de Nieto. *S.* Luis Eduardo. *Dau.* Maria Isabel. *Career:* Pres. Banco Popular 1958–74; Pres., Banco Tequendama. *Member:* Sociedad Econónómica Amigos del Pais; Incoida; Asociación Bancaria de Colombia; Bolsa Agropecuaria; Seguros Tequendama; Thomas de la Rue de Colombia. *Clubs:* Country Jockey; de Ejecutivos. *Address:* Carerra 18 84–11, Bogotá, Colombia; and *office* Diagonal 27 6–70, Air Box 5552, Bogotá, Colombia.

**NIKPOUR, Senator Mohammad Ebrahim.** Iranian. *B.* 1921. *Educ.* Iran and Germany (Economics); speaks German, English and French. *M. S.* 1. *Dau.* 1. Chose a business career; now owns several commercial concerns; former Managing Director of a local oil distribution Co., Charghe Insurance Co., and Iran Glass Factory; Pres. Bank Pars 1960, Chmn. Bd. Chief Exec. of Bank Pars Tehran. Former Dep. Chmn. of Teheran Chamber of Commerce and Industry; Elected Senator of Teheran, 1975. Former Member of Parliament & Former Dep. Chmn. of Iranian Bankers' Assn. *Address:* Bank Pars, Head Office, 193 Takhte Jamshid Avenue, Teheran. Iran.

**NILERT, Tore (Henrik).** Airline executive. *B.* 1915. *Educ.* Univ. of Commerce (Gothenburg, Sweden), B.A. *M.* (1) 1948, Catharina Bernadotte af Wisborg. *S.* Jan. Carl Henrik Svante and Fredrik Tore. *Dau.* Charlotta Catharina and Ann

Marie Catharina; (2) 1969, Ebba Wachtmeister. Knight, Orders of Dannebrog (Denmark): Vasa (Sweden), and St. Olav 1st Cl. (Norway); XV Olympiad Commemorative Medal (Finland); Expeditor of Swedish air interests in Washington 1941–45; organized United States office for Scandinavian air carriers 1945. President, Scandinavian Airlines System, Inc. (Airlines of Denmark, Norway and Sweden) New York City 1946–70. *Clubs:* California (Lod Angeles); Piping Rock (Locust Valley, L.I.); Racquet and Tennis (N.Y.C.); Royal Swedish Yacht (N.Y.C.); Seawankhaka Corinthian Yacht (Oyster Bay, L.I.); Wings, N.Y.C. (Pres. 1968–69). *Address:* Centre Island Road, Oyster Bay, N.Y. 11771, U.S.A.

**NILSEN, Oliver John,** CBE. British. Pres. Oliver J. Nilsen (Australia) Ltd. and its subsidiaries. *B.* 1884. Widower. *S.* Oliver Victor Alexander. *Dau.* Jean Christina. *Career:* JP 1937—. Melbourne City Councillor 1934–64, Lord Mayor 1951–52; Commission, Melbourne and Metropolitan Board of Works 1939–64. Founder and Chmn., Neon Electric Signs Ltd. until 1962; Foundation Dir., General Television Corp. (resigned 1957). Served on: Metropolitan Fire Brigades Board 1954–64, and Victorian Civil Ambulance Board 1937–64. *Clubs:* Melbourne Rotary; Victoria Racing; Victorian Amateur Turf; Moonee Valley Racing; Danish; West Brighton; Royal Automobile (of Aust. and of Victoria); Royal Commonwealth Society. *Address: office* 45 Bourke Street, Melbourne, Vic., Australia.

**NILSSON, Harald Torsten Leonard.** Swedish politician. *B.* 1 Apr. 1905. *Educ.* in Sweden and Germany. *M.* 1935, Vera Mansson. *Career:* Secy., Soc. Democrat Youth Organization, Chairman 1934–40; Secy., Soc. Democrat Party 1940–48; Member (Soc. Dem.), Andra Kammaren, Riksdag, 1941; Minister of Communications 1945–51; Minister of Defence 1951–57; Minister of Social Affairs, Labour & Housing 1957–62; Minister of Foreign Affairs, 1962–71. *Address:* Parliament Buildings, Stockholm, Sweden.

**NILSSON, Sven-Eric S.,** Swedish diplomat. *B.* 1925. *Educ.* B.Laws. *M.* 1926, Anna-Britt Svensson. *S.* 1. *Career:* Secy. of district court 1952–54; Secy. of circuit court 1954–56; borough magistrate 1956–57; Secy. of labour court 1957–60; Assoc. Judge of appeal 1960–61; legal expert of Min. of Finance 1961–62; head of Division of the legal dept. of Min. of Finance 1962–64; Cabinet Minister 1964–73; Swedish Ambassador in Switzerland since 1973. *Address:* Thunstrasse 67, CH 3006 Berne; and *office* Swedish Embassy, Case Postale 36, CH 3000 Berne 6, Switzerland.

**NIMEIRI, Gaafar Mohammed.** President of the Democratic Republic of the Sudan. *B.* 1930 *Educ.* El Hijra Elementary Sch., Omdurman; Wad Medani Government Sch., Gezira; Hantoub Secondary Sch., Medani. *Married. Career:* Graduated as 2nd Lieut from Military Coll., 1952, & transferred to Western Command; various courses in Egypt, Federal Rep. of Germany & U.S.A.; joined first batch of officers to establish the Northern Command at Shendi, 1957; Southern Command, Juba 1959; with the Free Officers Group played leading role in the October Revolution of 1964; after its setback transferred to Western Command, El Fasher, subsequently to Eastern Command, Gedaref; Officer in Command of troops at Torit, Southern Command, transferred to Infantry Sch. at Gebeit as 2nd Commanding Officer & Senior Lecturer, then Officer in Command until the May Socialist Revolution, 1969, when he became Chairman of the Revolutionary Command Council, C-in-C of the Armed Forces & Minister of Defence; elected by plebiscite first Pres. of the Republic, 1971; unanimously elected Pres. of the Sudanese Socialist Union by the First National General Congress, 1974. *Decorations:* Insignia of Honour; Grand Cordon of Honour; Order of the Revolution; Order of Loyal Son of the Sudan; Order of Bravery (1st Class); Long Meritorious Service Medal; Evacuation Medal; Independence Medal; Duty Medal (1st Class). *Address:* Office of the President, Khartoum, The Democratic Republic of the Sudan.

**NITESCU, Trajan.** Canadian, Petroleum Consultant. *B.* 1902. *Educ.* Polytechnical School of Bucharest (grad. Mining Engineer 1924). *M.* 1929, Florica Constantineanu. Previously: College of Engineers, Romania; Romanian Economic Institute; former Pres. Assn. of Engineers & Technicians of the Romanian Mining & Petroleum Industry. Engaged in the oil industry in Romania since graduation in 1924 until 1948, when he was forced to escape the Communist régime. Formerly Consul of Belgium. Chmn. and Chief Executive Officer, Canadian Fina Oil 1950–67. *Clubs:* Ranchmen's (Calgary); Calgary Golf & Country. *Address: office* 723 Riversdale Avenue S.W., Calgary, Alta., Canada T2S 0Y4.

**NIXON, Hon. Peter James.** Australian politician. *B.* 1928. *Educ.* Orbost & Wesley Coll., Melbourne. *M.* 1954, Jacqueline Sally Dahlsen. *S.* 2. *Dau.* 1. *Career:* Member of Federal Parliament for Gippsland 1961–67; Minister for the Interior 1967–71; Minister for Shipping & Transport 1971–72; Opposition Spokesman on Transport 1973–75; Minister for Transport & Postmaster General (in caretaker government) Nov.–Dec. 1975; Minister for Transport since 1975. *Club:* Melbourne. *Address:* Macclesfield. P.O. Box 262, Orbost, Victoria; and *office* Parliament House, Canberra, A.C.T. Australia.

**NIXON, Richard M.** *B.* 9 Jan. 1913. *Educ.* Whittier Coll. (AB); Duke Univ. Law School (LLB). *M.* 1940, Patricia Ryan. *Daus.* Patricia (Finch Cox), Julie (Eisenhower II). *Career:* Practised law in Whittier, Calif., 1937–42; on Active Duty with U.S. Navy 1942–46; member, U.S. House of Representatives 1947–50; U.S. Senator from California 1950–53; Vice-Pres. of the United States 1953–61; Republican Candidate for the Presidency 1960; Republican Candidate for Governor of California 1962; President 1969–74. Republican. *Address:* La Casa Pacifica, San Clemente, California, U.S.A.

**NIXON, Stanley Elkin.** Canadian. Corporate Dir. and Financial Consultant. *B.* 1912. *Educ.* Public School graduated High School 1928. *M.* 1941, Marie Elizabeth Wilson. *S.* David Brooks. *Dau.* Martha Elizabeth. *Career:* Entered Dominion Securities Corp. 1928; Partner Dominion Securities Co. 1946–72; Past Vice-Chmn. Dir. Bristol Aeroplane Co. of Canada Ltd. 1964—; Dir. Canadian Pacific Investments Ltd. 1962—; Cominco Ltd. 1966—; Rolls Royce Holdings (North America) Ltd. 1968—; Trizec Corp. 1971; Celanese Canada Ltd. (past Chmn.) 1971; Canadian Pacific (Bermuda) Ltd. 1973; Continental Illinois (Canada) Ltd.; Montreal City & District Savings Bank; Member, Royal Commission Dominion-Provincial Relations, Specialist Public Finance, 1938–39; Bank of Canada & Dept. of Finance, Government of Canada, 1940–46; Canadian Securities Cttee., Investment Bankers Assn. of America (Chmn. 1949); Montreal Stock Exchange (Vice-Chmn., 1956–57); Montreal Board of Trade (Council 1966–68); Investment Dealers Assn. of Canada (Pres. 1968–69). *Clubs:* Mount Royal; Hermitage (Past Pres.); Magog (P.Q.); Riddell's Bay Golf and Country; Coral Beach, (Bermuda). *Address:* 3468 Drummond St., APT 606, Montreal, H3G 1Y4 P.Q. Canada, and *office* 1155 Dorchester Boulevard West, Montreal H3B 2L6 P.Q., Canada.

**NJOROGE, Ng'ethe.** The High Commissioner of Kenya in Gt. Britain since 1970. *Address:* 45 Portland Place, London, W1N 4AS.

**NKWETA, Lucas Zaa.** Cameroonian. Minister Plenipotentiary *B.* 1929. *Educ.* BSc (Agric) London. *M.* 1959, Fernanda Oluremilkun. *S.* Taji Efesoa, Zaa. *Daus.* Clementine, Esmeralda and Mariette. *Career:* Field Asst., Cameroon Development Corp. 1955–58; Agricultural Officer, Southern Cameroon, 1958–59; Senior Agricultural Officer, Southern Cameroon, 1960; Prin. Agricultural Officer, West Cameroon, 1961–62; First Secretary, London 1963–64; Consul-General, Lagos 1964–65; Ambassador Extr. and Plen. to the U.K. 1965–73; Dir. of International Organisations, Ministry of Foreign Affairs, Yaounde. *Awards:* Officer de l'Ordre de Valeur. *Club:* Cameroon National Union. *Address:* c/o Ministry of Foreign Affairs, Yaounde, United Republic of Cameroon.

**NOBELS, Francois C. B. A.** Steel construction. *B.* 1900. *M.* 1926, Simone de Nobele. *S.* 4. With Nobels-Peelman S.A. since 1919; Pres. of the Bd.; Dir. Nometal S.A. Knight, Order of the Crown; Silver Medal, Order of the Crown; Officer, Order of Leopold II; Medal of the Resistance 1940–45; Industrial decoration 1st Class; Lauréat du Travail de Belgique, Insigne d'argent. *Member:* Fabrimétal; Marchands de fer de Belgique. *Clubs:* Rotary; Syndicat d'Initiative de Bruxelles. *Address:* Chateau Paddeschoot, St. Niklaas; and *office* Rue du Gazomètre 101, St. Niklaas, Belgium.

**NOBLE, Cdr. Rt. Hon. Sir Allan (Herbert Percy),** RN, PC, KCMG, DSO, DSC, DL. *B.* 1908. *Educ.* Radley Coll. *M.* Barbara Janet Margaret Gabbett. *Career:* Entered Royal Navy 1926; A.D.C. to Viceroy of India 1936–38; commanded destroyers 1940–42; Commander 1943; attended Quebec and Yalta Conferences; served in World War II (despatches;

DSC, DSO); retd. 1945; Member, Parliament (Con.) Chelsea 1945–59; Govt. Observer, Bikini Atomic Bomb Test ,1946; Parly. Private Sec. to Mr. Anthony Eden 1947–51; Parliamentary and Financial Secretary, Admiralty 1951–55; Under-Sec. of State, Commonwealth Relations 1955–56; Minister of State for Foreign Affairs 1956–59; Special Ambassador, Ivory Coast Aug. 1961; Advisory Cttee. on Service Parliamentary Candidates 1963–74. *Club:* White's. *Address:* 3 Culford Gardens, London, S.W.3 and Troston Cottage, Bury St Edmonds, Suffolk, 1P31 1EX.

**NODA, Uichi.** Japanese politician. *B.* 10 Sept. 1903. *Educ.* Tokyo Imperial University (LLB). *M.* 1931, Mitsu Shima. *S.* Minoru Shima. *Career:* Deputy-Minister of Finance 1948–49; Vice-Pres., Japan Monopoly Corporation 1949–50; Minister of Construction 1951–52; Minister, Hokkaido Development Agency 1951–52; Minister Administrative Management Agency 1952; member, Lib.-Democratic Party; House of Councillors 1950–53; House of Representatives since April 1953; President, Japan-Sri Lanka Association since 1956; Minister Economic Planning Agency. Nov. 1976. *Address:* 14-2, 4-chome, Otsuka, Bunkyoku, Tokyo, Japan.

**NOEL, Philip William.** American politician. *B.* 1931. *Educ.* Brown Univ. (Providence RI) BA (Econ) 1954; Georgetown Univ. (Washington DC) LLB in Law (1957). *M.* 1956, Joyce Anne Sandberg. *S.* 2. *D.* 3. *Career:* Attorney at Law 1958–67; Councilman from Warwick Rhode Island 1960–66; Mayor of Warwick, RI 1967–72; Pres. of RI League of Cities and Towns 1970–72; Governor of Rhode Island 1973–77; State Co-Chmn. of New England Regional Commission 1974; Vice-Chmn. Democratic Governors' Conference 1974–75, Chmn. 1975–76; Member of Advisory Commission on Intergovernmental Relations (U.S.A.) since 1975. *Member:* American Bar Assn.; Rhode Island Bar Assn.; Kent County Bar Assn.; American Judicature Socy. *Decorations:* Man of the Year: Jun. Ch. of Commerce (1972), Kiwanis Club of Roger Williams (1973) and Providence Journal-Bulletin (1973). *Clubs:* Elks Lodge 2196; Knights of Columbus 2295; Aurora Civic Assn.; University. *Address:* 21 Kirby Ave., Warwick, R. I. 02889, U.S.A.

**NOEL-BAKER, Rt. Hon. Lord (Philip John).** PC, British politician. *B.* Nov. 1889. *Educ.* Bootham School, York; Haverford, Pa.; King's College, Cambridge (MA). *M.* 1915, Irene Noel (*D.* 1956). *S.* 1. *Career:* Vice-Principal, Ruskin College, Oxford 1914; member, League of Nations Section of British Delegation in Peace Conference 1919, League Secretariat 1919–22; Sir Ernest Cassel Professor of International Relations, London Univ. 1924–29; Member Parliament (Lab.) for Coventry 1929–31, South Derby 1936–70; Parly. Private Secy. to Secretary of State for Foreign Affairs 1929–31; Principal Assistant to President of Disarmament Conference, Geneva 1932–33; Dodge Lecturer, Yale University 1934; Parliamentary Secretary, Ministry of War Transport 1942–45; Minister of State, Foreign Office 1945–46; Secretary of State for Air 1946–47; Secretary of State for the Commonwealth 1947–Feb. 1950; Minister of Fuel and Power Mar. 1950–Oct. 1951; Chmn., Foreign Affairs Group. Parly. Labour Party 1964; Pres., Internat. Cncl. of Sport and Physical Education (UNESCO) 1960. *Awards:* Croix de Guerre. *Publications:* Geneva Protocol; Disarmament; League of Nations at Work; Disarmament and the Coolidge Conference; The Private Manufacture of Armaments, Vol. I; J. Allan Baker, MP, a Memoir (with E. B. Baker); The Juridicial Status of British Dominions in International Law; The Arms Race: A Programme for World Disarmament, 1958. Hon. Degrees from Univs. of Birmingham,Nottingham, Manchester, Colombo, Queen's (Ontario); Haverford Coll., and Brandeis Univ. (U.S.A.); Hon. Fellow King's Coll. Cambridge 1961; Awarded 1959 Nobel Peace Prize; Olympic Diploma of Merit 1975; Officier, Legion of Honour 1976; Papal Knight, Order of St. Sylvester 1977; Life Peer, June 1977. *Address:* 16 South Eaton Place, London, S.W.1.

**NOEL-BROWN, Sidney James.** Management consultant. *B.* 1898. *M.* 1941, Eileen Maw Casey. *Career:* Chairman, S. J. Noel-Brown & Co. Ltd. 1947—. Director: Productivity Ltd. 1961—; Lankester & Crook Ltd. 1950—; Hon. Vice-Pres., Association of International Accountants Ltd. 1932—, Past Council Member European Work Study Federation 1961–69; Secretary, General Aircraft Ltd., and Director of several associated flying training schools 1934–42. Associate Member, Royal Aeronautical Society, and of Chartered Institute of Secretaries. Fellow: Institute of Work Study Practitioners, and of The Institute of Marketing; Nat. Joint Cncl. on Materials Handling, Past Chmn. *Publications:* Economics of Air Transport; Costing and Its Application to Government Contracts; Handbook for M.A.P. and M.O.S. Contractors. *Address:* 1 Darby Crescent, Sunbury-on-Thames, Middlesex.

**NOKIN, Max.** Belgian. *B.* 1907. *Educ.* University of Liège (Civil Mining Engineer) and Institut Montefiore (Electrical Engineer). *M.* 1933, Denise Malfeson. *S.* 2. *Daus.* 3. *Career:* Engineer, Sté. Générale de Belgique 1935–48, Director 1949–61, Governor 1962–75, Hon. Governor since 1976. Chairman and Managing Director Cimenteries CBR Cementbedrijven. Chairman SIDMAR, Mines et Fonderies de Zinc de La Vieille Montagne; Vice-Chmn. Cockerill, ARBED. Metallurgie Hoboken Overpelt. Dir.: SIBEKA, Westinghouse Electric Corp. Pittsburgh, Genstar Ltd. (Montreal). *Awards:* Comdr. Ordre du Chéne (Luxembourg); (Hon) KBE; Grand Officer Order Leopold II; Comdr. Order of Léopold Croix de Guerre with palm. *Member:* Fondation Industrie-Université pour le Perfectionnement des Dirigeants d'Entreprises (Chairman); Fondation Francqui (Director); Member Royal Golf Club of Belgium. *Address* and *office:* rue Royale, 30, 1000 Brussels, Belgium.

**NOLDE, George V.** Electrical Engineer, Doctor of Science. Consulting Engineer, Berkeley, Cal. 1965 (on U.S. Navy & Air Force programmes with advanced technology establishments in California). *B.* 1900. *Educ.* Moscow (U.S.S.R.) Technical School of Higher Learning, Dipl Engr (Elec Eng.) 1923; DSc (Chem. Eng.) 1929. *M.* 1936, Eugenia Poliakova. *Career:* Engineering engagements in industrial installations and research institutions, Moscow 1923–33; Consulting Engr., Los Angeles 1934–36; Research Assoc., Photometry Lab., Univ. of California 1937; Development Engr., Butte Electric & Mfg. Corp., San Francisco 1938–40; Research Engr. Marchant Calculators Inc., Oakland, Calif. 1940–44; Consulting Engr., Dalmo Victor Inc., San Carlos, Calif. 1945–46, and Marchant Calculators Inc. 1946–48 (Research Dir. 1949–52); Development Engr. & Mgr., Computing Devices Unit, R.C.A., Camden, N.J. 1952–54; Prof. of Elec. Engr., Univ. of Calif., Berkeley 1955–57; Project Engr., Missile & Surface Radar Div., R. C. A. Van Nuys 1957–62; Senior Stf. Eng. Aerospace Corp., El Segundo 1963–64. *Publications:* many monographs in the field of automatic systems and radar technology: Radar Visibility of Submarine Snorkels (with Nance ,1959); Study & Development of Counter-measures Against Guided Missiles (with Berfield and Chamberlain, 1960); On Kinetics of Flexible Leaves (1952); Synthesis & Optimization of Continuous Wave Systems for Terminal Guidance of Space Vehicles (1964); Influence of Format on Information Entropy (1967); On Statistical Precision in Availability of Systems (1968); On Telegraphic Information-Fields, Their Entropies & Legibilities (1972); Awarded 16 U.S. Letters Patents in the field of electron computers, automatic control systems, magnetometric devices, calculating machines and techniques; accredited with design of electronic computing equipment in the Logistic Data Processing System created by R.C.A. for the Ordnance Tank & Automotive Center, Detroit 1955. *Member:* Amer. Socy. of Mech. Engineers; Inst. of Radio Engineers (Senior member); Calif. Acad. of Sciences; Amer. Assn. for Advancement of Science (Life member). *Address:* 537 San Vicente Boulevard, Santa Monica, Calif.; and *office* 910 Great Western Building, Berkeley, Calif. U.S.A.

**NORBERG, Charles Robert.** Attorney and Counsellor-at-Law (specializing in international legal matters). *B.* 1912. *Educ.* University School (Cleveland), Cornell Univ. (BS Admin. Eng. 1934), Univ. of Grenoble (France), Univ. of Pennsylvania (MA Internat. Economics 1937) and Harvard Univ. Law School (LLB 1939); *Career:* With Willard Storage Battery Co., Cleveland 1934–35; Assoc. Attorney, Norris, Lex, Hart Eldridge, Philadelphia 1939–42. Military service (Reserve Office 1934; called to active duty as Lieut. U.S.A.F. 1942; combat duty in the China-Burma-India Theatre; participated in China Defense and offense campaigns; aide in preliminary negotiations for surrender of the Japanese in China; many decorations; promotions 1st Lieut. to Major) 1943–45; at HQ. U.S.A.F. Washington 1945–46; now Member U.S. Air Force Reserves (retired) with rank of Colonel. With Office of Asst. Secy. of State for Public Affairs 1948–51: Executive Office of the President 1952–53; National Security Council (as Consultant) 1954. Staff member, U.S. Delegation to U.N.G.A., Paris, France 1951; Adviser, U.S. Delegations to U.N.E.S.C.O. Conference, Montevideo, Uruguay 1954, and attended other internat. conferences. Chief, A.I.D. Special Mission to Uruguay and I.C.A. Consultant Mission to Ecuador 1961. *Member:* American Law Inst., and of the following Bar Associations: Philadelphia; Pennsylvania; American; Federal; Inter-American; and International. Admitted to practice in Pennsylvania 1940, the District of Columbia 1947 and before the U.S. Supreme Court 1946. General Counsel, Inter-American Commercial Arbitration Commission. Founder, President, Director and member of Exec. Cttee., Inter-American Bar Foundation. Corresponding member, Academia Colombiana de Jurisprudencia. Member Board of Directors of the Academia Interamericana de Derecho Internacional y Comparado. Author of Various articles in legal journals and two official government reports on foreign economic development. *Clubs:* Metropolitan (Washington); Midday (Phila.); Harvard (N.Y.C.). *Address: office* 310 Federal Bar Building, West, 1819 H Street, N.W., Washington D.C., 20006, U.S.A.

**NORD, Hans Robert,** LLD. Dutch lawyer. *B.* 11 Oct. 1919. *Career:* Practised at Bar, The Hague 1943–46; member of International Committee, European Movement, Brussels 1949–61; President of the European Movement in the Netherlands 1958–61; Chmn., Netherlands Atlantic Cttee. 1954–61; Vice-Pres., North Atlantic Treaty Assn., London 1955–57; Secy.-General, European Parliament since 1961. *Address:* 15 Rue Conrad I, Luxembourg, Luxembourg.

**NORDAL, Dr. Johannes.** Icelandic. *B.* 1924. *Educ.* BSc (Econ), PhD (London). *M.* 1953, Dora Gudjonsdottir. *S.* Sigurdur. *Daus.* Bera, Gudrun, Salvor, Olof, Marta. *Career:* Economic Adviser, Natl. Bank of Iceland, 1953–58; Editor: Fjarmalatidindi (Financial Review), 1954—; Nytt Helgafell (Literary Journal) 1955–59; Chmn. Humanities Div. Science Fund of Iceland 1957—; General Manager, National Bank of Iceland, 1959–61; Governor, Central Bank of Iceland (Sedlabanki Islands) 1961— (Chmn. 1964—); Governor for Iceland, International Monetary Fund 1965—; Chmn. National Power Company since 1966. *Member:* Icelandic Scientific Society, 1958—. *Address: office* Central Bank of Iceland, Austursdltraeti Reykjavik, Iceland.

**NORDENFALK, Baron Johan Axel Erland.** Swedish judge (retired). *B.* 12 Nov. 1897. *Educ.* University of Stockholm (LLB). *M.* 1920, Baroness Stina Rålamb. *S.* Sigfrid Rålamb Erik Johan. *Daus.* Marie Louise, Hedvig Christina Madeleine, Ingegerd Gunvor Thérèse. *Career:* Assistant Judge, Court of Appeal 1931, Judge 1937; Man. Dir. Norstedt & Soner Publishing Co. Ltd. 1942–48; Managing-Dctor, Swedish Printing Corp. Ltd., 1948–63; Commander, 1st. Cl. Order of Vasa; Knight, Order of North Star; Cmdr. Order of St. Olav. (Norway); Grand Officer, Order of Chevalier of Merit (Italy); Commander, 1st Cl., Order of the Lion (Finland). *Address:* Strandvaegen 51, Stockholm, Sweden.

**NORDMEYER, Hon. Sir Arnold,** KCMG. New Zealand politician; *B.* 1901. *Educ.* Otago University. *Career:* Member (Labour Party) House of Representatives for Oamaru 1935–49; for Brooklyn 1951–54; for Island Bay 1954–69; Minister of Health 1941–47; of Industries and Commerce May 1947–49; National Pres., N.Z. Labour Party 1950–55; Minister of Finance 1957–60; Leader of Parly. Labour Party 1963–65. Knight Commander of St. Michael & St. George 1975. *Address:* 53 Milne Terrace, Wellington, New Zealand.

**NORGARD, John Davey.** Australian engineer. *B.* 1914. *Educ.* Adelaide Univ. (BE); FSASM. *M.* 1943, Erena Mary Doffkont. *S.* 1. *Daus.* 3. *Career:* War service with the Royal Australian Air Force (Flight-Lieutenant) (Ret.). Executive General Manager, Operations, Broken Hill Proprietary Company Ltd. (B .H.P.), Melbourne, 1970; Chairman, Metric Conversion Board, Australia 1970—; Deputy Chancellor, La Trobe University 1972–75; Chmn., Cttee. of Enquiry into Child Care Services in Victoria. *Publications:* Coal Utilization in Modern Steelworks Practices; Magnesium and its Alloys. *Member:* Australian Inst. of Mining & Metallurgy; The Metals Socy. *Clubs:* Australian (Melbourne); Newcastle. *Address:* 29 Montalto Avenue, Toorak, Vic.; and *office* 450 St. Kilda Road, Melbourne, 3000, Vic. 3004 Australia.

**NORLIN, Per A.** Director of the Axel Johnson Group since 1955. *B.* 23 Jan. 1905. *Educ.* Faculty of Commerce, Stockholm. *M.* 1933, Eva de Champs. *S.* Christoffer, Malcolm. *Dau.* Ewa. *Career:* with Swedish Air Lines (A.B.A.) 1924; represented A.B.A. in Amsterdam 1925–26; Vice-Pres. 1927–42; President, Swedish-Inter-continental Air Lines (S.I.L.A.) 1943–49, and 1955—; President, S.A.S. 1946–54; Exec. Vice-Pres., A.B.A. 1948, President 1949–51. Vice-Chairman Royal Swedish Aero Club 1949–70; Chairman, Assembly of Representatives of S.A.S.; Chairman of the Board: AB Linjebuss, the National Maritime Museum; Vice-Chairman of the Board AB Nynäs-Petroleum; Member of the Board Rederiaktiebolaget Nordstjernan AB. Has been awarded numerous decorations and medals. *Address:* Johannesgatan 20, 11138 Stockholm; and *office* A Johnson & Co. HAB, Stureplan 3, 10380, Stockholm 7, Sweden.

**NORMAN, Isaac Richard,** CBE. Australian banker. *B.* 1913. *M.* 1941, Eileen Margaret Ashton. *S.* Roger Richard. *Career:* Chief Manager for Tasmania, Commonwealth Bank of Australia 1954–59; Staff Inspector Commonwealth Banking Corporation 1959–60. General Manager, Commonwealth Savings Bank of Australia, Sept. 1960—. *Clubs:* Killara Golf; Tasmanian. Awarded CBE in Queen's Birthday Honours List, June 1977. *Address:* 26 Rosebery Road, Killara, N.S.W.; and *office* Commonwealth Savings Bank, Martin Place & Pitt Street, Sydney, N.S.W., Australia.

**NORMAN, Sir Mark Annesley,** Bt. British, farmer and director of companies (home and abroad). *B.* 1927. *Educ.* Winchester College. *M.* 1953, Joanna Camilla Kilgour. *S.* Nigel James and Antony Rory. *Dau.* Lucinda Fay. *Clubs:* White's; M.C.C.; and St. Moritz Tobogganing Club. *Address:* Wilcote Manor, Charlbury. Oxfordshire.

**NORMAN, Willoughby Rollo.** British. *B.* 1909. *Educ.* Eton and Magdalen College, Oxford (MA). *M.* 1934, the Hon. Barbara Jacqueline Boot. *S.* Jeremy Nicholas. *Daus.* Sarah Jessica and Tessa Roselle. *Career:* Chmn. The Boots Company Ltd.; Dir. National Westminster Bank Ltd.; Chmn. Eastern Region; Dir., English China Clays Ltd.; Guardian Royal Exchange Assurance Ltd. Dir. Sheepbridge Engineering Ltd.; National Westminster Bank Ltd.; Underwriting Member of Lloyds. *Club:* White's (London). *Address:* English China Clays Ltd., John Keay House, St Austell, Cornwall.

**NORMAN-WALKER, Sir Hugh Selby,** KCMG, OBE. British *B.* 1916. *Educ.* Sherborne School and Corpus Christi College, Cambridge (M.A.). *M.* 1948, Janet Baldock. *Career:* In Indian Civil Service 1938–48; Colonial Administrative Service 1949; Development Secretary, Nyasaland 1954; Secretary to the Treasury, Nyasaland (Malawi) 1959; H.M. Commissioner for Bechuanaland 1965, KStJ (1967). Governor and Commander-in-Chief, Seychelles, and Commissioner, British Indian Ocean Territory 1967. Colonial Secretary. Hong Kong, 1969–74. *Clubs:* East India & Sports (London); Island Sailing (Cowes, I. of W.). *Address:* Houndwood, Farley, Wilts.

**NORODOM SIHANOUK,** H.R.H. Prince. *B.* 1922. *Educ.* Lycée Chasseloup-Laubat, Saigon. Crowned King of Cambodia 1941; Launched Royal Crusade for Independence 1952 and achieved it in 1953; took command of the Army, abdicated 1955. Prime Minister & Minister of Foreign Affairs Oct. 1955, March 1956, Sept. 1956, April 1957; Perm. Rep. to UN Feb.–Sept. 1956; Elected Head of State June 1960, deposed March 1970 & exiled; Head of State Sept. 1975–April 1976.

**NORRIS, Sir Eric (George),** KCMG. British diplomat. *B.* 1918. *Educ.* Cambridge University (BA). *M* .1941, Pamela Crane. *Daus.* 3. *Career:* First Secretary: British Embassy, Dublin, 1948–50; British High Commission, Pakistan, 1952–55. Counsellor, New Delhi, 1956–57; Deputy High Commissioner: Bombay, 1957–60; Calcutta, 1962–65; Imperial Defence College, 1961; Asst. Under Secy. of State, Commonwealth Office, 1965–68. High Commissioner, Kenya, 1968–72; High Commissioner, Malaysia 1974–77. *Club:* East India. *Address:* Melton Half, Newdigate, Surrey.

**NORSTAD, General Lauris.** *B.* 1907. *Educ.* U.S. Military Academy, West Point; graduated, Air Corps School 1931; commissioned 2nd Lieut. of Cavalry 1930. *M.* 1935, Isabelle Helen Jenkins. *Dau.* Kristin. *Career:* Commander 18th Pursuit Group, Hawaii, July 1933; O.C. 9th Bombardment Group Navigation School, Dec. 1939; member, Advisory Council to Commanding General of the Army Air Force, Washington, Nov. 1940; Assistant Chief of Staff for Operations 12th Air Force (with which he went to England) July 1940; moved to Algiers, Oct. 1942; Director of Operations, Mediterranean Allied Air Forces, Dec. 1943; moved with it to Caserta, Jan. 1944; Chief of Staff, 20th Air Force (with additional duty of Deputy Chief of Air Staff, Army Air Force H.Q.), Washington, Aug. 1944; Director, Plans and Operations Division, War Department, Washington, June 1946; Lieut.-General, Oct. 1947; Deputy Chief of Staff, Operations of U.S. Air Force, Washington, Nov. 1947; commanded 'Exercise Swarmer' (joint Army and Air Force manœuvre to test service capabilities of establishing and maintaining sustained military operation entirely by airborne operations), Feb. 1950; Actg. Vice-Chief of Staff, Air Force, May 1950; C.-in-C., U.S. Air Forces Europe, Oct. 1950; C.-in-C. Allied Air Forces Central Europe (additional to his duties as C.-in-C. USAFE), Mar. 1951; Air Deputy to Supreme Allied Commander Europe, July 1953. Supreme Allied Commander Europe, and C.-in-C., U.S. European Command 1956–63. Director: Owens-Corning Fiberglas Corp. (Pres. Dec. 1963–67, Chmn. 1967–72, Hon. Chmn.); United Air Lines. Abitibi Paper Co.; Director, English-Speaking Union. *Awards:* DSM; Silver Star; Legion Merit; Air Medal; Commander, Order of the British Empire; Commander, Legion of Honour (France); Commander, Croix de Guerre avec palme (France); Grand Officer, Order of Ouissam Alaouite Cherifien (Morocco); Royal Order of King George I (Greece); Grand Cross, Order of Avis (Portugal) and many others. *Address:* 717 Fifth Avenue, New York, N.Y. 10022, U.S.A.

**NORTH, Rt. Hon. Sir Alfred Kingsley,** PC, KBE. *B.* 17 Dec. 1900. *Educ.* Canterbury Coll., New Zealand (LLM). *M.* 1924, Thelma Grace Dawson, *S.* John Derek Kingsley, Kenneth Alfred Kingsley. *Dau.* Margaret Kingsley. *Career:* Formerly practised as a barrister in City of Auckland; appointed one of H.M.'s Counsels May 1947; Judge of the Supreme Court 1951–57; Judge of the Court of Appeal, 1957–72. Knighted 1959. President of Court of Appeal 1963–72. First Chmn., NZ Press Council since 1972. *Address:* 28 Mahoe Avenue, Remuera, Auckland, New Zealand.

**NORTH, Nelson Luther.** American. *B.* 1918. *Educ.* Wesleyan Univ., Middletown, Conn. (BA 1940) and Rutgers Univ. Graduate School of Banking. *M.* 1942, Carolyn Willis. *S.* Nelson L. Jr. and Bruce W. *Career:* Served with Army of U.S. in World War II (Major; Croix de Guerre; Bronze Star); Chmn. Bd. of Finance Town of Easton Conn. 1966–73; Trustee, Fairfield Conn. Univ. 1966–73; Pres. Connecticut Financial Services Corp. 1969—; Chmn. Bd. Chief Exec. Officer The City National Bank of Connecticut 1971; CFSC Leasing Corporation since 1972. *Director:* Southern Connecticut Gas Co.; Connecticut Family Health Care, Inc.; Bridgeport Economic Dev. Corp. and Bridgeport Hosp., *Member:* Board of Trustees of Connecticut Public Expenditure Council Inc.; Chmn. of Board, CFSC Mortgage Corporation. *Clubs:* Brooklawn Country; Alonguin (of Bridgeport) Waterbury; Pequot Yacht (Southport, Conn.); New York Yacht; Ex-members Assn. of Squadron A (N.Y.C.). *Address:* 8 Cedar Hill Lane, Easton, Conn 06612; and *office* 961 Main Street, Brideport, Conn., 06602. U.S.A.

**NORTHROP, John Knudsen.** American aeronautical engineer. *B.* 10 Nov. 1895. *Educ.* High School. *M.* (1) 1918, Inez Maybelle Harmer (Diss.). *S.* John Harmer. *Daus.* Bette (Johansing), Ynez (Koch); (2) 1950, Margaret Bateman. *Career:* Designer Loughead Aircraft Co., Santa Barbara. California 1916–17 and 1919–20; served World War I, U.S. Army 1918; designer, Douglas Aircraft 1923–26: joined in formation of Lockheed Aircraft Co. 1927; Pres. and Chief Engineer, Northrop Aircraft Co. (1929–32) and Douglas El Segundo Div. (1932–38); self-employed in research, 1938–39. Designed and built various Northrop airplanes; Co-founder Pres., and Dir., Northrop Aircraft Inc. (now Northrop Corp.) 1939–52; Consulting Engineer since 1953; Hon DSc, Occidental Coll.; Hon DSc, Northrop Inst. of Technology; Fellow, Royal Aeronautical Society; Fellow, Institute of Aeronautics and Astronautics (Pres. 1948). Co-founder Trustee, Northrop University. *Address:* 1046 Fairway Road, Santa Barbara, Ca 93108, U.S.A.

**NORUP, Bengt Samuel Bengtsson.** Swedish statesman. *B.* 1896. *Educ.* Farm School. *M.* 1921, Signe Henricson. *Daus.* 2. *Career:* Member of Parliament 1940–60; Dir.-Gen., National Board of Agriculture 1957–62; Minister, Ministry of Agriculture 1951–57; member, Agriculture Marketing Board 1935–39 (Deputy Chmn. 1946–47); Chmn., Swedish Dairy Assn. 1944–51; Chairman, Federation of Swedish Farmers 1944–51; Chairman, Federation of Swedish Farmers 1949–51. *Awards:* Commander, Order of North Star (Sweden); Knight, Order of Vasa (Sweden); Commander, Grand Cross, Order or Boyaca (Columbia); Knight, Order of White Rose (Finland); KSLA (member, Swedish Academy of Agriculture and Forestry). *Address:* Knislinge, via Stockholm.

**NOTENBOOM, Dr. Harry A.C.M.** Dutch politician. *B.* 1926. *Member:* European Parliament. *Address:* Postbus 347, Venlo, Netherlands.

**NOTOWIDIGDO, Moekarto.** Indonesian diplomat. *B.* 1 Nov. 1911. *Educ.* Law Faculty of Djakarta (LLB). *M.* 1938, Martaniah Notowidigdo. *S.* 2. *Career:* Official of Dept. of Finance during Dutch occupation; during that period organized a nationalist group; during Japanese occupation was Secretary of the Indonesian Study Club, a cultural and educational arm of the nationalist revolution; imprisoned twice by Japanese; on proclamation of Indonesian independence (1945) was member of P.N.I. Indonesian Nationalist Party Exec. Cttee., and Vice-Chmn. of its International Affairs Cttee.; as Inspector-General of Indonesian Foreign Service visited all of Asia (except China), Western Europe and United States; Deputy Chief Delegate to U.N. 1950; Foreign Minister in Wilopo Cabinet 1952; Ambassador to United States 1953–60; to India 1960–64; to Canada 1964–65. *Publications:* Various articles in miscellaneous newspapers in Indonesia. *Address:* Ministry of Foreign Affairs, Djakarta, Indonesia.

**NOTT, John William Frederic,** BA, MP. British politician and former company director. *B.* 1932. *Educ.* Bradfield Coll. Trinity Coll. Cambridge Univ. (Bachelor of Arts Hons. degree in Law & Economics). Inns of Court, Inner Temple Barrister at Law. *M.* 1959, Miloska Sekol. *S.* Julian, William. *Dau.* Alexandra. *Career:* Captain Regular Army 2nd Gurkha Rifles, 1951–56; Camb. Univ. 1956–59; Gen. Manager, S. G. Warburg & Co. Ltd. Merchant Bankers (London), 1959–65; Dir. S. G. Warburg Finance & Developments Ltd. 1965–67; Member of Parliament Conservative St. Ives Div. of Cornwall since 1966; Sec. Con. Parly. Party Finance Cttee. 1968–70; Former Chmn. Imperial Eastman (U.K.) Ltd., Dir. Imperial-Riv. Turin, (Italy) Flexoger SA. Lyon, (France), Clarkson Int. Tools Ltd. (U.K.); ITE Int. Sales NV. (Antwerp); Minister of State, HM Treasury 1972–74; Conservative Party Spokesman for Trade. *Member:* Inns of Court (Inner Temple). *Address: office* House of Commons, London, S.W.1.

**NOUIRA, Hedi.** Prime Minister of Tunisia. *B.* 1911. *Educ.* Sousse Lycée, Paris Univ (Law Degree). *Career:* Called to the Bar (Tunis) 1937; As member of Neo-Destour Party was Secretary General of Tunisian Trade Union Confederation; Integrated union action in national movement; Arrested and imprisoned for work in organizations and contributions to 'L'Action Tunisienne' 1938–1943; Assist-Gen Secy & mem. of Political Bureau 1948–52; Imprisoned, exiled or held under surveillance 1952–54; In charge of Dept. of Trade in first independent govt. 1954–55; Minister of Finance in second govt. 1955–58; Gov. of Central Bank of Tunisia 1958–1971; Set up Institut d'Emission and became its head; Pres. of World Bank Conference 1970; Was re-elected mem. of Party Political Bureau at Sfax Congress (1955), Sousse Congress (1959) and Bizerta Congress (1964); Assist. Secy-Gen to Neo-Destour Party and Minister of State 1969, mem of Sen. Commission (Const. and Party Congress) 1970; Head of Dept. for Nat. Economy 1970; interim Prime Minister, then Prime Minister from 1970; during the first year he combined this post with that of Minister of the Interior; Re-elected member of Central Cttee (Monastir Congress) and mem. of Political Bureau 1971, also Sec-Gen to the Party from 1971. *Decorations:* Grand Cordon of Order of Independence (1962); Order of Republic (1966) and Order of Bourguiba (1973). *Address:* c/o Dir. of Political Affairs, Office of Prime Minister, Republic of Tunisia.

**NOYES, Guy Emerson.** Economist. Senior Vice-President and Economist, Morgan Guaranty Trust Co. 1965—. *B.* 1913. *Educ.* Univ. of Missouri (AB 1934); Yale Univ. *M.* 1943, Patricia Hartnett. *S.* Guy L. *Dau.* Pamela A. *Career:* Instructor, Yale Univ. 1937–41; Lieut.-Colonel, U.S. Army 1942–45: Dir., Research Div., State Dept. 1946–48; Asst. Dir., Adviser, Federal Reserve Board 1949–65. Director of Research and Statistics, Federal Reserve Board of the U.S. 1960–65. *Publications:* various articles on economic subjects. *Awards:* U.S. Bronze Star; Legion of Honour (France). *Club:* Cosmos (Washington). *Address: office* 23 Wall Street, New York, N.Y. 10015, U.S.A.

**NSEKELA, Amon James.** High Commissioner for Tanzania in the U.K. *Address:* 43 Hertford Street, London, W.1.

**NTLHAKANA, Thabo Ephraim.** Lesotho Diplomat. *B.* 1935. *Educ.* BA (South Africa). *M.* 1961, Regina 'Maselometsi. *S.* 1. *Daus.* 4. *Career:* Secondary School Teacher 1957–62; Information Officer and Broadcaster 1965–70; Counsellor, Lesotho High Commission, London 1970–74; Chief of Protocol 1974–75; Dir. of Information and Broadcasting May–Sept. 1975; High Commissioner of Lesotho in London Oct. 1975–Aug. 1976; Ambassador to Belgium since Sept. 1976. *Address:* Embassy of Lesotho, Brussels, Belgium.

**NÚÑEZ V., Amado Humberto.** Honduran lawyer. *B.* 1918. *Educ.* post graduate studies in France, Degree in Legal & Social Sciences. *M.* 1960, Saltía Ennabe. *S.* 3. *Daus.* 3. *Career:* teacher Maraita primary school 1942–43; Teacher & Headmaster Gold Mines (Minas de Oro) School 1943–46; Danli School and Schools in Tegucigalpa 1946–55; Justice of the Peace Tegucigalpa Criminal Court 1951–52; Lect. Introductory Course, Univ. Law Studies 1955—; Gen. Mgr. of Labour 1956–57; Prof. in the Faculty of Law 1958–60 (1964–65); Asst. Min. Labour & Social Security 1957–63; Minister 1963 and 1965–71. *Member:* Coll. of Lawyers; Nat. Foundation Rehab. of the Invalid. *Awards:* Diploma de Buen Hondureño; Hon. member Nat. Assn. Lawyers of Mexico. *Publications:* The Master's Messenger; Liberal Youth, various articles. *Address: office* 20 piso Sucursal Muebles Contesa, Tegucigalpa, Republic of Honduras.

**NURIEV, Ziya Nurievich.** Soviet statesman. Member, C.P.S.U. Central Committee. Member, Presidium of the Supreme Soviet 1954–69; Deputy to Supreme Soviets of U.S.S.R. and Bashkir A.S.S.R.; Member, C.P.S.U. 1939—. *B.* 1915. *Educ.* graduated from a pedagogical secondary school; finished the Higher Party School at the C.P.S.U. Central Committee 1951. *Career:* Engaged in pedagogical activities 1933–38; served in Soviet Army 1938–40; worked in the public education system 1940–42; engaged in Party work 1942–48 and 1951–52 (Head of the Political Dept. of a Machine and Tractor Station; Secretary of a District Committee of the C.P.S.U.; Head of a department of the Regional Committee of C.P.S.U.); Secretary, Bashkir Territorial Committee of C.P.S.U. 1952–53 (Secretary and Second Secretary of Regional Committee 1953–57 and First Secretary 1957–69); Minister of Agricultural Procurements of U.S.S.R. 1969–73; Dep. Chmn. of Council of Ministers since 1973. Awarded Order of Lenin and Order of the Red Banner of Labour. *Address:* U.S.S.R. Council of Ministers, The Kremlin, Moscow, U.S.S.R.

**NUTTING, Rt. Hon. Sir. Anthony,** Bt. PC. Politician and writer. *B.* 1920. *Educ.* Eton and Trinity College, Cambridge. *M.* 1941, Gilliam Leonora Strutt (*M. Dis.* 1959). *S.* 2. *Dau.* 1. *M.* 1961, Anne Gunning Parker. *Career:* Served with Leicestershire Yeomanry (invalided) 1939–40; served in H.M. Foreign Service 1940–45; MP (Con.) for Melton 1945–56; Chmn. Young Conservative Movement 1945–46; Conservative National Union and National Executive 1950–52; Parliamentary Under-Secretary of State for Foreign Affairs 1951–54; Minister of State for Foreign Affairs Oct. 1954; Leader U.K. Delegation to U.N. Assembly 1954–56; resigned Oct. 1956. Special writer for New York Herald-Tribune 1956–58. *Publications:* I Saw for Myself (1958); Disarmament (an outline of the Negotiations, 1945–59); Europe Will Not Wait (1960); Lawrence of Arabia (1961); The Arabs (1964); Gordon, Martyr and Misfit (1966); No End of a Lesson, The Story of Suez (1967); Scramble for Africa (1970); Nasser (1972). *Address:* 1½ Disbrowe Road, London W6.

**NYBOE ANDERSEN, Poul.** Danish politician and professor. *B.* 1913. *Educ.* Graduate in Political Science, Doctor of Economics. *M.* 1938, Edith Raben. *S.* Svend, Bent and Anders. *Dau.* Bodil. *Career:* Journalist; Tutor, Univ. of Aarhus; Teacher, Krogerup Folk High School, 1939. Study visit to U.S.A., 1947; Asst. Professor, Political Economy at Copenhagen Graduate School of Economics & Business Administration, 1948; Full Professor, 1950–62 and 1966–68; Chmn. of the Bd. for Technical Co-operation with Developing Countries 1962–68; Minister for Economic Affairs, European Integration and for Nordic Affairs in the Baunsgard Cabinet (a Liberal Coalition Government) 1968–71; Member Parliament since 1971; Minister for Economic Affairs & Commerce 1973–75; Chief Gen. Mgr., Andelsbanken A/S Danebank 1976. *Publications:* Money and its Value (1941); Danish Exchange Policy 1914–1939 (1942); From Gold Standard to Clearing (1942); Bilateral Exchange Clearing Policy (Doctors Thesis, 1946); Loan Interest (1947); Interaction of Economic Forces (1947); Brief Textbook on Political Economy (1948); Country and Town (1949); International Economic Relations (1955). *Address:* Gl. Strandvej 19, 3050 Humlebaek, Denmark; and *office* 4a Vestersbrogade, 1620 Copenhagen V, Denmark.

**NYERERE, Julius Kambarage,** President of the United Republic of Tanzania. *B.* 1922. *Educ.* Tabora Secondary School, Makarere Univ. Coll., and Edinburgh Univ. (MA; DipEd); several honorary degrees. *M.* 1953, Maria Magige. *S.* 5. *Daus.* 3. Began career as Teacher; later Pres., African Association, Dar es Salaam 1953; formed Tanganyika African National Union. Abandoned teaching and campaigned for the Nationalist Movement 1954; addressed Trusteeship Council 1955 and Committee of U.N. Gen. Assembly 1956. M.L.C. Tanganyika July–Dec. 1957; resigned in protest. Elected Member for E. Province in first elections 1958, and for Dar es Salaam 1960. Chief Minister 1960; Prime Minister of Tanganyika 1961–62, President, 1962–64. President Tanzania 1964—, and Tanganyika African National Union 1954—. First Chancellor University of East Africa 1963–70. Univ. of Dar es Salaam 1970—. *Publications:* Freedom & Unity (Uhuru na Umoja); Freedom & Socialism (Uhuru na Ujamaa). *Address:* State House, Dar es Salaam, United Republic of Tanzania.

**NYGAARD, Marius.** Norwegian judge. *B.* 1 June 1902. *Educ.* Oslo University. *M.* Eva Julie Johanne Christensen. *Daus.* 3. Chief of Division, Ministry of Justice and Police 1936–45, Director 1945–49; Judge of Supreme Court 1949–72. *Address:* Gustavs gate 4, Oslo 3, Norway.

**NYKOPP, Johan Albert.** Finnish diplomat and industrialist. *B.* 1906. *Educ.* University of Helsinki (AM). *M.* 1930, Marianne Achilles. *S.* Erik, Torsten. *Dau.* Fritzi (Mrs. Erkki Salmi). *Career:* Entered foreign service 1930; Attaché, Finnish Legation, Moscow, 1931–35; Vice-Consul, Leningrad 1935–37; reassigned to Foreign Ministry (political division) 1937–40; Secretary and later Counsellor, Moscow 1940–41; Foreign Ministry (commercial division) 1941–45; Deputy Director, Commercial Division, Foreign Ministry 1945–47; Dir. 1947–51; Pres., Export and Import License Board of Finland 1949–51; Governor for Finland of Interntl. Bank for Reconstruction and Development 1950–51; served as Chmn. of several commercial delegations to foreign countries 1947–51; Amb. Ex. and Plen. to United States 1955–58 (previously En. Ex. and Min. Plen. from June 1951); was also En. Ex. and Min. Plen. to Cuba and Mexico 1951–58, and to Venezuela and Colombia 1954–58; Director Gen., Central Organization of Finnish Employers 1958–61. President, Tampella Ltd. 1962–72. *Awards:* Cmdr., Order of the Lion (Finland); Knt., Order of the White Rose (Finland); Cmdr., Order of St. Olav (Norway); Cmdr., Polonia Restituta (Poland); Cmdr., Legion of Honour (France); Grand Officer. Finnish War 1939–40. *Address:* Vatakuja 2c, Helsinki, 20, F nland.

# O

**OAKES, Gordon James,** MP. British Politician. *B.* 1931. *Educ.* Wade Deacon Grammar Sch., Widnes; Univ. of Liverpool—BA (Hons). *M.* 1952, Esther O'Neill. *S.* 3. *Career:* Widnes Borough Councillor 1952–66; Mayor of Widnes 1963–64; Labour MP for Bolton West 1964–70; PPS Home Office 1966–68, Education 1968–70; Labour MP for Widnes since 1971; Opposition Spokesman on the Environment 1972–74; Under Secretary of State, Dept. of Environment 1974–76, and Dept. of Energy 1976; Minister of State, Dept. of Education since 1976. *Member:* Vice-Pres., Urban District Assoc. 1972–74; Rural District Assoc. 1972–74; Vice-Pres., Environmental Health Officers since 1973. *Publications:* Various articles. *Address:* Upton Bridle Path, Widnes, Cheshire WA8 9HB.

**OAKES, John Bertram.** American. *B.* 1913. *Educ.* Princeton Univ. (AB *magna cum laude* 1934 (Rhodes Scholar)), and Queen's Coll., Oxford (AB, AM 1936). *M.* 1945, Margery Hartman. *S.* John George Hartman. *Daus.* Andra Nan, Alison Hartman and Cynthia Jane. *Career:* Reporter,

Trenton Times 1936–37; Political Reporter, Washington Post 1937–41; served in U.S. Army 1941–46. Editor, Review of the Week, Sunday New York Times 1946–49; member Editorial Board 1949–61; Editor of Editorial Page, New York Times 1961–77; Snr. Editor, N.Y. Times 1977—. *Awards:* LLD Univ. of Hartford 1960; LHD, Chatham College, 1969. Carnegie Foundation Travel, Award Europe and Africa 1959; Columbia-Catherwood Award 1961; U.S. Dept. of Interior Conservation Service Award, 1963; George Polk Memorial Award (for outstanding journalistic achievement) 1965. Silurian Society Award, 1969; Francis K. Hutchinson Award, Garden Club of America, 1969: Woodrow Wilson Award, Princeton Univ. 1970; John Muir Award, Sierra Club (1974); Audubon Medal, Nat. Audubon Society (1976); Decorated Bronze Star (US); Order Brit. Empire; Croix de Guerre, Medaille de Reconnaissance (France). *Member:* Amer. Assn. Rhodes Scholars (dir.); Nature Conservancy (Dir.); Amer. Socy. Newspaper Editors; Phi Beta Kappa Assn.; Council Foreign Relations; Vice-Pres. Temple Emanu-El. N.Y.C. Trustee, Fisk Univ. and Chatham Coll.; Secy. Interior's Advisory Bd. National Parks 1955–62; member President's Commission on White House Fellows 1964–68. *Publications:* The Edge of Freedom (Harper 1961). *Clubs:* The Century Assn. (N.Y.C.); The Coffee House (N.Y.C.); Cosmos (Washington D.C.); Nassau (Princeton U.S.A.); Sierra. *Address:* 1120 Fifth Avenue, New York, N.Y. 10028; and *office* 229 West 43rd Street, New York, N.Y. 10036, U.S.A.

**OBASANJO, Lt. Gen. Olusegun.** Head of the Federal Military Government, Commander-in-Chief of the Armed Forces of the Federal Republic of Nigeria. *B.* 1937. *Educ.* Abeokuta Baptist High School; training courses at the Mons Officers Cadet School, Royal College of Military Engineering, Newbury School of Survey & Royal College of Defence Studies (all UK), Indian Staff College, Indian Army Engineering School. *Married. Children:* 4. *Career:* Joined Nigerian Army 1958, commissioned 1959; served with the 5th Battalion joining UN Peace Keeping Force, Congo 1960; promoted to Captain 1963, Major 1965, Lt-Col. 1967 & Colonel 1969, appointed General Officer Commanding 3 Infantry Div.; promoted to Brigadier 1972; appointed Federal Commissioner for Works & Housing, Jan. 1975; appointed Chief of Staff, Supreme Headquarters, with the rank of Lt.-Gen., July 1975; Head of the Federal Military Government & C.-in-C. of the Armed Forces since 1976. *Address:* SupremeHeadquarters, State House, Dodan Barracks, Lagos, Nigeria.

**OBERLÄNDER, Theodor.** *B.* 1905. *Educ.* Dr. agr., Dr.rer.pol., Professor of Political Economy. *M.* 1935, Erika Bucholz. *S.* Erwin, Dieter, Klaus. *Career:* Toured Russia, China Japan, and U.S.A. to study methods of rationalization in agriculture 1930–31; a further visit to Russia 1932 and 1934; Asst. Univ. of Königsberg 1934; Dir., Institute of Economy in East Europe, and Prof. agarian policy, Danzig 1934; Prof. Univ. of Konigsberg 1937, and at Prague Univ. 1940; Captain, German Army (Caucasus and Ukraine) 1940; discharged by order of Himmler on account of resistance to Gestapo methods against Slav population 1943; arrested in Prague; U.S. prisoner 1945; discharged 1946; State Secretary for Refugees in Bavaria Dec. 1950; Federal Minister for Expellees, Refugees and War Victims 1953–60; Member of Parliament from 1953–65, since 1971 with Messerchmitt-Bölkow. Christian Democrat Party. *Publications:* The Exodus from the Country Regions in Germany: Its Causes and the Measures taken against it; The Agrarian Over-population of Poland; and many political articles in newspapers and journals. *Address:* Luisentr. 6, Bonn, Germany.

**OBERLY, James Richard.** American international trade executive. *B.* 1921. *Educ.* Univ. of Wisconsin (BA); Yale Univ. School of Law, JD 1948. *M.* (1) 1947, Lucille M. Kraus (decd. 1961). *S.* James Warren. *Dau.* Kathryn Ann. (2) 1963, Marjorie J. Shearer. *Career:* USNR 1942–46; Admitted to Bar (Illinois) 1949; US Tax Court 1950; US Supreme Court 1951, Wisconsin 1971; Pope and Ballard (Chicago) 1948–51; Pres. Admiral Intern. Corp. 1953–60; Vice-President, Admiral Corp. 1955–60; President, Admiral International Corp. 1953–60; Pres. Sunbeam International A.G., 1961—, Sunbeam-Oster S.A. 1961–68; President's Export Expansion Council 1964–68; Schwartz & Oberly Ltd. since 1974. *Member:* Bar Associations: American, Wisconsin, Chicago, Manitowoc County; Exec. Cttee. Bay-Lakes Boy Scout Council (Vice-Pres.); Rotary International; Manitowoc Elks; Legal Counsel, Bd. of Trustees Manitowoc Hosp.; Manitowoc Industrial Devel. Comm. (Chmn.); Nat. Panel of Arbitrators, Am. Arb. Assn.; Phi, Delta Theta; Phi Eta Sigma; Phi Kappa Phi; Beta Gamma Sigma. *Address: office* 926 S 8th St., Manitowoc, Wis., U.S.A.

**O'BRIEN, John William Alexander,** DSO, ED. Australian Engineer. *B.* 1908. *Educ.* Royal Melbourne Technical Coll. (Dipl. Civ. Eng.). *M.* Gwendolyn V. Britton. *S.* John Goddard. *Dau.* Jill Goddard (Borthwick). *Career:* Civil and mechanical Engr., Dorman Long Ltd., Melbourne 1925–28; Structural Engr., Melbourne Tramways 1929, and American Bridge Co., U.S.A. 1930; Consulting Engr., specializing in mechanical handling and marine engineering, United Stevedoring Pty. Ltd., Melbourne 1931–39; co-founder and General Mgr., Fleet Forge Pty. Ltd. (marine and general engineers) 1939. Commissioned Lieut., Australian Military Forces 1928; military history studies in U.S.A. 1930; attached Royal Artillery, U.K. 1931. Advanced through ranks to Brigadier (at 33 years) 1942; Comdr. 2nd/5th F.A. Regt in Egypt and Palestine and in operations in Western Desert and Syria 1942; commanded 3rd Divisional Artillery 1942; Director of Artillery for Australian Army 1942–43; Dept. Master-General Ordnance 1943–45; special duty in U.S. and in U.K. 1944; present at operations in Pacific 1942–43–44 and in Western Europe, Italy, and Burma 1944. Leader, Aust. Scientific Mission to Japan 1945–46; Chief Scientific and Technical Div., General MacArthur's SCAP HQ., Tokyo 1946–51; Member, Economic Policy Board for Japan 1947–51; detached for duty as Pres., G.H.Q. War Crimes Tribunal, trial of Adm. Toyoda, former C.-in-C. Japanese Navy and Chief Naval General Staff 1948–49; represented Japan at ECAFE/UNESCO International Conferences, Thailand 1950. Transferred to Reserve of Officers and apptd. Maj.-Gen. and Senior Supply & Defence Production Rep. for Australia, Washington 1951–54; represented Australia at Triennial Assembly, International Standards Organization New York 1952. Mng. Dir., Howard Industries Pty. Ltd., Sydney 1955–59; established Contract Tooling Pty. Ltd. as owner, Chmn. and Man. Dir. 1959–73. *Awards:* D.S.O. 1941; ED 1948; MID 1941; recommended by Gen. MacArthur for U.S. Legion of Merit 1950. Fellow, Inst. of Engineers of Australia; Fellow, Inst. of Arbitrators, Aust.; Alderman, Woollahra Municipal Council, 1968—; Mayor 1971–72, 1975–76; Councillor, Royal Blind Socy. (NSW); Advisory Board, St. Margaret's Hospitals (Sydney); Justice of the Peace, 1970. *Publications:* Guns and Gunners (1950); contributor of articles on military equipment, engineering, Japan. *Clubs:* Australian (Sydney); Royal Sydney Golf. *Address:* 73 Yarranabbe Road, Darling Point, N.S.W. 2027 Australia.

**O'BRIEN of Lothbury, Baron (Leslie Kenneth),** PC, GBE. British. *B.* 1908. *Educ.* Wandsworth School. *M.* 1932, Isabelle Gertrude Pickett. *S.* Michael John. *Career:* With Bank of England 1927–73; Deputy Chief Cashier 1951–55; Chief Cashier 1955–62, Executive Director 1962–64, Deputy Governor 1964–66. Director, Commonwealth Development Finance Co. Ltd. 1962–64. Governor of the Bank of England 1966–73. One of Her Majesty's Lieutenants for the City of London 1964—; Hon. Fellow & Vice-Pres. Inst. of Bankers; Pres. O'seas Bankers' Club. *Director:* The Prudential Assurance Co. Ltd. since 1973; The Rank Organisation since 1974; Bank for International Settlements since 1974; Saudi International Bank since 1975. *Chairman:* Cttee. of Inquiry into export of animals for slaughter 1973; Intern. Council of Morgan Guaranty Trust Co. of N.Y. since 1974. *Member:* Adv. Bd. of Unilever Ltd. since 1973; Consultant to J. P. Morgan & Co. since 1973; Adv. Coun. Morgan Grenfell & Co. Ltd. 1974; Finance & Appeal Cttee. Royal Coll. of Surgeons since 1973; Counc. of Royal Coll. of Music since 1973; Board of Nat. Theatre since 1973; Coun. of Marie Curie Foundation since 1963; Investment Advisory Cttee. of Mercers' Co. since 1973; City of London Savings Cttee. since 1966; Trustee Glyndebourne Arts Trust since 1974; Press. United Banks Lawn Tennis Assoc. since 1958. *Awards:* Freeman, City of London in Co. of Mercers; Hon. Liveryman Leathersellers Co. Created Baron 1973; Hon. Dr. Laws (Univ. Wales) 1973. Hon. Doctor Science, City Univ., 1969. Cavaliere di Gran Croce, Al Merito Della Republicca Italian, 1975; Grand Officier de l'Ordre de la Couronne, Belgium 1976. *Clubs:* Athenaeum; Garrick; Boodle's; Grillions; All England Lawn Tennis; M.C.C. *Address:* 33 Lombard Street, London EC3P 3BH.

**O'BRIEN, Terence John,** MC, CMG. British diplomat. *B.* 1921. *Educ.* Gresham's School Holt; Merton Coll. Oxford. *M.* 1953, Rita Emily Drake Reynolds. *S.* Roderick David. *Daus.* Sally Ann, Harriet Emily. *Career:* Dominions Office, Commonwealth Relations Office 1947–49; Second Secy.

British High Comm. Ceylon 1949–52; First Secy. Commonwealth Relations Office 1952–54; Principal Treasury 1954–56; Financial Secy. Brit. High Comm. Australia 1956–58; Planning Officer Commonwealth Relations 1958–60; First Secy. Brit. High Comm. Malaya 1960–62; Secy. Inter-Governmental Cttee. on Malaysia 1962–63; Counsellor Head Chancery, Brit. High Commission, India 1963–66; Student, Imperial Defence Coll. 1967; Head, Economic Relations Dept. Foreign Office 1968; Head, Financial Policy & Aid Dept. Foreign & Commonwealth Office 1969; British Ambassador, Nepal 1970–74; Brit. Ambassador Burma 1974–78. *Clubs:* Reform; Royal Commonwealth. *Address:* Beaufort House, Woodcutts, Salisbury, Wilts. and British Embassy, Rangoon, Burma.

**O'CONNOR, Edmund.** British. Organizer of Extramural Studies, School of Oriental and African Studies, Univ. of London. *B.* 1924. *Educ.* St. Andrews Univ. (MA Hons. 1949), London University (Teacher's Diploma 1950) and Oxford Univ. *M.* 1949, Vivien Oldaker. *Daus.* 5. *Career:* Temp. Sub-Lieut., Royal Navy Volunteer Reserve 1942–45. In H.M. Overseas Civil Service (Ministry of Education, Kenya; retired as Senior Education Officer, April 1964). Formerly Conf. Organizer, Commonwealth Inst. London. *Address:* St. Anthony's, Cavendish Road, Weybridge, Surrey; and *office* School of Oriental and African Studies, London, W.C.1.

**O'CONNOR, Hon. Raymond James,** MLA. Australian. *B.* 1926. *M.* 1950, Vesna Francis *S.* Craig, Lance, Thomas Raymond James. *Daus.* Kim, Nola, Tomazina. *Career:* Business proprieter 1950–59; Member for North Perth 1959–62, and for Mount Lawley 1962—; Minister for Transport Railways and Police, Government of Western Australia 1965–71; Minister of Police, Traffic and Transport 1974–76. Member Liberal Party of Australia. *Clubs:* numerous. *Address:* Mandalay, Middle Swan Road, Caversham, W.A.; and *office* Parliament House, Perth, W.A., Australia.

**O'CONNOR, Lieut.-Col. Thomas Patrick.** Canadian lawyer. *B.* 1911. *Educ.* De La Salle College, Toronto; St. Michael's College, Toronto; Univ. of Toronto (BA 1932); Osgoode Hall, Toronto (Grad. 1935). *M.* 1938, Agnes Christine Bernard. *S.* Terrence Patrick and Dennis Rory. *Dau.* Shelagh Louise. *Career:* Read Law with firm of MacMurchy & Spence (C.P.R. Solicitors), Toronto; called to Bar of Ontario 1935; created Q.C. 1955; Senior Solicitor, Ontario Securities Commission 1946–49. Lieut.-Col. First Canadian Army 1940–45. Partner, O'Connor, Coutts, Crane, Ingram, Barristers and Solicitors, Toronto. *Member:* Canadian Bar Association; County of York Law Association. *Clubs:* Rosedale Golf; Engineers; Toronto Lawyers; Canadian. *Address:* 11 The Bridle Path, Willowdale, Ont.; and *office* 330 University Avenue, Toronto, Ont., Canada.

**Ó DÁLAIGH, Cearbhall.** Former President of Ireland. *B.* 1911. *Educ.* Nat. School, Bray; Christian Brothers' School, Dublin; Univ. Coll., Dublin; BA (Celtic Studies); BL (King's Inns, 1934); LLD (Hon. Causa) Dublin Univ.; D.Litt. Celt. (Hon. Causa) Nat. Univ. of Ireland; MRIA; FRCSI (Hon. Causa); Fellow, Inst. of Engineers of Ireland (Hon. Causa); Studied Irish—An Rinn, An Blascaod, Dún Chaoin, Comineoil; Studied Italian, Univ. Per Stranieri, Perugia. *M.* 1934, Máirín Nic Dhiarmada. *Career:* Irish Editor (Irish Press) 1931–40; Called to Bar 1934; Admitted to Inner Bar 1945; Attorney-General 1946–48, 1951–53; Judge of the Supreme Court 1953; Chief Justice and President of the Supreme Court 1961–73; Judge of Court of Justice of European Communities, Luxembourg 1973; President of First Chamber of Court of Justice of European Communities 1974; President of Ireland 1974–76 (Resigned). *Awards:* Commendatore (al Merito) della Repubblica Italiana. *Address:* Cuan Anna, Cathair Saidhbhin, Co. Kerry, Ireland.

**ODD, Richard Sidney,** BSc, ACGI, CEng, MICE, MIEE, F. I. Prod. E. British. *B.* 1906. *Educ.* Imperial Coll. of Science & Technology; London School of Economics. *M.* 1936. *S.* 4. *Dau.* 1. *Career:* former Dir. Senior Exec. Urwick Orr & Partners; Dir. Gen. Mgr. Wilmot Breeden Ltd.; Telehoist Ltd.; Dir. The Kaye Organization; Lansing Bagnall Ltd. *Clubs:* Oriental; Anglo-Belgian. *Address:* Coldharbour Farm, Goring Heath, Reading RG8 7SY.

**O'DEA, Hon. Fabian A.,** QC, KStJ (both 1963). Canadian. Barrister & Solicitor. *B.* 1918. *Educ.* St. Bonaventure's Coll., St. John's; Memorial Univ. of Nfld.; St. Michael's Coll., Univ. of Toronto (BA 1939); Dalhousie Univ., Halifax; and Christ Church, Oxford Univ. (Rhodes Scholar; BCL 1948); called to the Bar of England (Inner Temple, London) 1948 and to the Bar of Newfoundland 1949; Hon. LLD. Memorial Univ. Newfoundland 1969. *M.* 1951, Constance *Career:* Practised law in London for a short while in 1948; engaged in practice of law in St. John's from 1949 until appointment as Lieut. Governor. Vice-Pres. for Nfld. of Canadian Bar Assn. 1961–63. Mbr., Board of Regents, Memorial Univ. of Nfld. 1959–63; commission in R.C.N.V.R. Sept. 1940, discharged Sept. 1945. On loan to Royal Navy 1943–44; Commanding Officer, H.M.C.S. Cabot 1953-56. Commander R.C.N.R. (Retd.). Hon. Aide-de-Camp to Governor-General of Canada 1949–52; and to Lieut.-Governors of Nfld. 1949–61. Consular Agent for France in Nfld. 1957–62. Secy., Selection Committee, Rhodes Scholarships for Nfld. 1950–63. Hon. Solicitor of the Nfld. Provincial Command of the Royal Canadian Legion 1950–63; Lieutenant-Governor of Newfoundland 1963–69. *Address:* 12 Winter Place, St. John's, Newfoundland, Canada.

**ODEY, George William,** CBE 1945. Hon. Pres. Barrow Hepburn Group Ltd., Tanners & Leather Merchants, since 1974 (Chmn. 1937–74). *B.* 1900. *Educ.* Faversham Grammar School and University College, London (BA). *M.* (1) 1926, Dorothy Christian Moir (*D.* 1975). *S.* 1. (2) 1976, Mrs. Doris Harrison-Broadley. *Career:* Asst. Secy., Univ. of London Appointments Bd. 1922. Joined Barrow Hepburn & Gale, London 1925 (Dir. 1929, Managing Director 1933, Chairman 1937); Chairman, Barrow Hepburn Group Ltd., London 1937–74; Hon. Pres. since 1974. Represented Ministry of Supply in Washington on joint purchase of hides between U.K. and U.S.A. 1941; Member U.K.-U.S.A. Mission on Hides and Leather to South America 1943. Delegate from British National Committee of International Chambers of Commerce to International Business Conf. in New York 1944. Hon. Air Comdre., R.Aux.A.F. 1961. Fellow, Univ. Coll.. London 1953. President: Intnl. Cncl. of Tanners 1954–67, Hon. Pres. 1967; British Leather Mfrs. Research Assn. 1964, and Gelatine & Glue Research Assn. 1950; Vice-Pres.: Fed. of Gelatine & Glue Mfrs. 1957, and Natl. Assn. of British Mfrs. 1956. Pres., British Leather Fed. 1965. Chmn., Bd. of Governors, National Leathersellers College 1951; Member of Lloyds. *Member:* East Riding County Council 1964–74; Lloyds; Livery, Leathersellers' Company 1939. *Clubs:* Carlton; Royal Automobile; Royal Yorkshire Yacht. *Address:* Keldgate Manor, Beverley, North Humberside; and *office* Barrow Hepburn Group Limited, 73 South Audley Street, London, W17 6JR.

**ODGERS, James Rowland,** CBE. Australian. *B.* 1914. *M.* 1939, Helen Jean Horner. *S.* 2. *Dau.* 1. *Career:* Deputy Clerk of the Australian Senate 1955–65; Usher of the Black Rod 1950–55. Clerk of the Australian Senate, since 1965. *Publications:* Australian Senate Practice (5th edn. 1976). *Address:* 11 La Perouse Street, Canberra; and *office* Parliament House, Canberra, A.C.T., 2000, Australia.

**ODINGA, Ajuma Oginga.** Kenyan politician. *B.* 1911. *Educ.* Alliance High School (Kikuyu) and Makerere College (Uganda). *Career:* Teacher at Maseno School and Maseno Veterinary Training College. Founder Luo Thrift and Trading Corp. Member Central Nyanza African District Council 1947–49; for Nyanza Central, Kenya Legislative Council 1957–63; Chmn, African Elected Members' Organization; Vice-Pres., Kenya Africa National Union (KANU) 1960. Member for Bondo, Kenya House of Representatives 1963—. Minister for Home Affairs, Kenya May 1963–64; Vice-Pres. Republic of Kenya 1965–66, Resigned from Govt; Pres. Kenya Peoples Union 1966–69; In Detention 1969–71; Out of Detention, Farmer and Mem. K.A.N.U. since 1971. *Address:* c/o KANU, P.O. Box 12394, Nairobi, Kenya.

**ÖDNER, Sture Paul Erik.** Swedish. *B.* 1920. *M.* 1950, Eva Brotherus. *S.* Bengt. *Dau.* Lena. *Career:* Managing Director of Saléninvest AB, Stockholm, and Chmn. of main affiliated companies; Director of Atlas Copco AB; Hansa Insurance Co.; J. S. Saba AB, all of Stockholm, Chmn. of Swedish Ship Owners' Association. *Address:* Strandvägen 23, 7 tr. S-114 56 Stockholm, Sweden; and *office* c/o Saléninvest AB, POB 14018, S104 40 Stockholm, Sweden.

**OEHLERT, Benjamin Hillborn, Jr.** American attorney, executive and business consultant. *B.* 13 Sept. 1909. *Educ.* University of Penna. (BS in Econ., JD). *M.* 1937, Alice Greene. *S.* Benjamin Hilborn. *Dau.* Alice Ann (Jenkins). *Career:* In law practice, Philadelphia 1933–35; Attorney, Mexican Claims Agency, U.S. Dept. of State, Washington, D.C. 1935–38; Assistant Counsel, Assistant to President and Vice-President, The Coca-Cola Co., Wilmington, Atlanta, Georgia. and New York 1938–48; Vice-President and

Director, W. R. Grace & Co., New York 1948-53; Vice-Pres. The Coca-Cola Co. New York and Atlanta 1953-65; Pres. and Chmn. Minute Maid Co. Fla. 1962-65; Senior Vice-Pres. and Dir. The Coca-Cola Co. Atlanta 1965-67; U.S. Ambassador to Pakistan 1967-69; Member Town Council Palm Beach. *Publications:* The Restatement in the Courts; Eminent Domain in Pennsylvania. *Address:* Everglades Club, 356 Worth Avenue, Palm Beach, Fla. 33480, U.S.A.

**OELMAN, Robert Schantz.** American business executive. *B.* 1909. *Educ.* Dartmouth Coll. (AB *summa cum laude* 1931) and Univ. of Vienna; Hon. HHD University of Dayton, 1959; Hon. LLD Miami University 1960; Hon. LHD, Wilmington College 1965; Hon MA Dartmouth College, 1963; Hon. LLD Wright State, 1976. Delta Kappa Epsilon, Phi Beta Kappa. *M.* 1936, Mary Coolidge. *S.* Bradford Coolidge and Robert Schantz Jr. *Daus.* Kathryn Peirce and Martha Forrer. *Career:* With the NCR Corp. since 1933 (Assistant to President 1942; Assistant Vice-President 1945; Vice-Pres. 1946; Executive Vice-Pres. 1950; Pres. 1957, Chairman 1962, and Director since 1948); Chairman, Exec. Cttee. 1974; NCR Corp., Dayton, Ohio. Director: Koppers Co. Inc., Pittsburgh: The Ohio Bell Telephone Co., Cleveland; The Procter & Gamble Co., Cincinnati; The Winters Natl. Bank & Trust Co., Dayton; Ford Motor Co., Detroit. *Member:* United Appeal Board of Trustees, Dayton; Trustee Community Research Inc., Dayton. *Clubs:* Moraine Country; Augusta National Golf; County Club of Florida. *Address:* 2846 Upper Bellbrook Road, Bellbrook, Ohio 45305; and *office* NCR Corp. 2485 Winters Bank Tower, 45402, Dayton, Ohio, U.S.A.

**OFFIELD, Wrigley.** American. *B.* 1917. *Educ.* Choate School and Yale. *M.* 1941, Edna Jean Headley. *S.* James Sanford and Paxson Headley. *Dau.* Dorsse. *Career:* Engineer: Douglas Aircraft 1942-44, and Memo-Vox Co. 1944-45; President & Director, Aims Inc., of Chicago. Director, Wm. Wrigley Jr. Co., Santa Catalina Island Co., Catalina Island Sightseeing Lines, Catalina Operations Co. *Clubs:* Tavern. *Address:* Box 395, Harbor Springs, MI 49740, U.S.A.

**OFSTAD, Einar-Frederik.** Norwegian Diplomat. *B.* 1916. *Educ.* Lawyer. *M.* 1948, Beate Paus-Knudson. *S.* 1. *Daus.* 2. *Career:* Army Service (Lieut.) 1940-45; Secy. Min. of For. Affairs 1945-46; Attaché, Norwegian Embassy, London 1946-48; Norwegian Consul, Chicago 1948-51; Counsellor, Norwegian Ministry For. Affairs 1951-53; Counsellor Norwegian Embassy, Ankara 1953-56; Counsellor Norwegian Embassy, The Hague 1956-60; Head of Division, Min. of For. Affairs 1960-64; Deputy Head of Mission, Bonn 1964-68; Dir.-Gen. Legal Dept. Ministry of Foreign Affairs 1948-72; Norwegian Ambassador in Bonn since 1973. *Decorations:* Knight 1st Class, Royal Order of St. Olav., War Medal 1945; Commander Dutch Oranje Nassau Order; Commander Islandic Falcon Order; Commander Verdienst Kreuz (German) Order; Knight, Order of Malta. *Address:* Norwegian Embassy, 53 Bonn-Bad Godesberg 1, Germany.

**OFTEDAL, Torfinn.** Ambassador of Norway. *B.* 1909. *Educ.* University of Trondheim (BSc). *M.* 1942, Gloria Grosvenor (*D.* 1972). *S.* Olav Tonnes. *Dau.* Elsie Doersam. *Career:* Entered Norwegian Foreign Service 1938; served subsequently with Embassy in Washington 1938-46; Ministry of Foreign Affairs 1946-49; Norwegian Deleg. to O.E.E.C. 1949-51; Embassy, Washington 1951-60; Ambassador to Vienna and Minister to Prague and Budapest 1960-65; Special Counsellor in Foreign Ministry 1965-66; Ambassador to Canada 1966-72; Ambassador to Prague and Bucharest 1973-75. Member of Norwegian delegations to the Monetary Conference, Bretton Woods 1944; UNRRA Conf., Montreal 1944; U.N. Conf. San Francisco 1945; Tariff negotiations, Geneva 1947; Conf. on International Trade Organization, Havana 1947-48; U.N. Gen. Assembly, N.Y. 1965; E.C.E., Geneva 1966; Alternate Executive Director, World Bank 1956-57; Permanent Representative, International Atomic Energy Agency, Vienna 1960-65. *Awards:* Commander, Order of St. Olav (Norway); Grand Cross, Order of Merit (Austria). *Clubs:* Norske Selskab (Oslo); Chevy Chase (Washington). *Address:* 3900 Cathedral Avenue N.W., Washington, D.C. 20016, U.S.A.

**OGDEN, Chester Frank.** *B.* 1911. *Educ.* Univ. of Michigan (Mech. Engineering & Business Administration—MBA 1934). *M.* 1935, Jane LaChapelle. *S.* David James and John Hall. *Dau.* Jill A. *Career:* Consultant War Production Bd., Administrator of Utilities Order U-9, 1941-45; Asst. Dir. Office Defence Mobilization, Executive Office of the President 1955-56; U.S. State Department (A.I.D.), India Power Survey Team. 1963; Exec. Vice-Pres. Admin. The Detroit Edison Co. 1964-74 (Retired); Dir. Vice-Pres. Edison Illuminating Co. Detroit 1964—; Vice-Pres. Dir. Essex County Light and Power Co. Ltd. 1972—; Vice-Pres. The Peninsular Electric Co. 1972—; St. Clair Edison Co. 1972—; The Washtenaw Light and Power Co. since 1972. Member Exec. Cttee. and Trustee, Children's Hospital of Michigan, Chmn. Bd. of Dirs., Michigan Cancer Foundation, Trustee Village of Grosse Pointe Shores. Past Pres. Jun. Achievement of Southeastern Michigan, Inc.; United Community Services; Belter Business Bureau of Detroit (Past Pres.); Past Pres., Grosse Pointe War Memorial Association. *Publications:* various articles to magazines and trade publications. Shipman Medallist, National Association of Purchasing Agents, 1960. *Member:* N.A.P.A. (Past Natl. Pres.); Edison Electric Inst. (Past Chmn. Purchasing & Stores Committee); Engineering Socy. of Detroit. *Clubs:* Economic; Lochmoor; Detroit Athletic. *Address:* 20 Hawthorne, Grosse Point Shores, Mich. 48236; and *office* 2000 Second Avenue, Detroit 48226, Mich., U.S.A.

**OGILVY, David Mackenzie,** CBE. British advertising agent. Chairman, Ogilvy & Mather International, 1965-75. *B.* 1911. *Educ.* Fettes College, Edinburgh; and Christ Church, Oxford University. *S.* David Fairfield. *Career:* British Security Coordination 1942; Second Secretary, British Embassy, Washington 1944. Trustee, World Wildlife Fund. *Club:* Brook (N.Y.C.). *Address:* Chateau de Touffou, 86 Bonnes, France.

**O'HALLORAN, Michael Joseph,** MP. British/Irish. *B.* 1928. *Educ.* Elementary School. *M.* 1956. Stella Beatrice Macdonald. *Daus.* 3. *Career:* Railway worker 1948-63; Building worker (Office manager) 1963-69; Labour MP for Islington North since 1969. *Clubs:* Challoner; Irish; Irish Centre. *Address:* 40 Tytherton Road, Islington N.19; and House of Commons, London SW1.

**OHIRA, Masayoshi.** *B.* 1910. *Educ.* Tokyo University of Commerce; married. *S.* 3. *Dau.* 1. *Career:* Entered Ministry of Finance 1935; served in Tax Offices in Yokohama and Sendai, and in Japanese Government Offices in Changchiakow, Manchuria, etc. Private Secretary to Minister of Finance 1949. Elected to House of Representatives 1952; Secretary-General of the Cabinet 1960. Minister of Foreign Affairs, Japan 1962-64; Chmn. Policy Bd., Liberal Democratic Party 1967-68; Minister of Int. Trade and Industry 1968-70, of Foreign Affairs 1972-74, of Finance 1974-76. *Address:* 105 Komagome Hayashicho, Bunkyo-ku, Tokyo, Japan.

**OHNO, Katsumi.** Japanese diplomat. *B.* 1905. *Educ.* Kyoto Imperial University (Dept. Economics). *M.* 1931, Misako Kikuchi. *S.* Kiyoshi and Naomi. *Daus.* Yoriko (Hanabusa) and Keiko (Takabatake). *Career:* Passed Higher Diplomatic Service Exam. 1928; Attaché, Berlin, 1930; Vice-Consul, Hamburg, 1932, Sec. of Foreign Office 1936; Third Sec., Washington, D.C., 1939; Chief of Second Section, Bureau of American Affairs Foreign Office, Tokyo, 1941; First Secretary, Nanking, 1943; Personal Secretary to Foreign Minister, 1945; Director, Bureau of Control, Foreign Office, 1947; Director, Bureau of General Affairs, F.O., 1948; of Bureau of Political Affairs 1949; En. Ex. and Min. Plen. to Philippines, 1953; to Austria 1955; Ambassador to Germany 1956; Vice-Minister for Foreign Affairs 1957. Amb. Ex. and Plen. to U.K. 1958-64; Adviser to Foreign Minister 1964; Exec. Vice-Pres. Arabian Oil Co. Ltd. 1967-71; Auditor Imperial Hotel 1971; Pres. Imperial Hotel since 1972. *Awards:* KBE. *Address:* Ministry of Foreign Affairs, Tokyo, Japan.

**OHTA, Saburo.** Japanese diplomat. *B.* 1905. *Educ.* Tokyo Imperial Univ. ('Hogakushi'). *M.* 1935, Chizuko Shinagawa. *S.* 1. *Daus.* 2. *Career:* Attaché, Japanese Embassy, London 1930; Vice-Consul, Sydney 1931; Information Officer, Information Board 1936; 3rd Sec., Embassy, Moscow 1937; Chief, Third Section, Bureau for European & West Asiatic Affairs, Ministry for Foreign Affairs 1940; Chief, Third Section, Bureau for Research & Documentation, Min. for For. Affs. 1943; Director, Third Department, Central Liaison Office 1945; Mayor, Yokosuka City 1947; member, Transport Council, Ministry of Transport 1949; Special Assistant to the Minister for Foreign Affairs 1954; Ambassador to Burma 1955-58; to Poland 1958-61; Ambassador Ex. and Plen. to Australia 1961. *Award:* Order (IV Cl.) of the Sacred Treasure. *Address:* c/o Ministry of Foreign Affairs, Tokyo, Japan.

**OITTINEN, Reino. Henrik,** MA, DEhc Finnish politician. *B.* 1912. *M.* 1935. *S.* Heikki Juhani. *Career:* Director-General, National Board of Schools 1950—. Minister of Education

1948–50, 1951–53. Minister of Education and Deputy Prime Minister 1957–58, 1963–64 and 1966–68; Chmn. Finnish National Commission for UNESCO 1957–65, Member 1966–68. Member of the Finnish deleg. at the general conferences of UNESCO 1949 to 1968. Finnish deleg. at conferences of the Intnl. Conference on Public Education 1954 to 1963. Secretary, Workers' Educational Assn. 1938–45, member of the board 1947–65. Member of Finnish delegation to Pohjoismaiden Kulttuuritoimikunta—Scandinavian Cultural Commission 1948–67. Administrative Council of the Finnish National Opera (Chmn. 1952—); Bd. of Dirs. of Nordiska Folkhögskolan, Geneva 1943–50; Administrative Bd., International Fed. of Workers' Educational Associations 1955–62. Työväen Näyttämöiden Liitto—Union of Workers' Theatres (Chmn. 1949—); Historian Ystäväin Liitto—League of Friends of History (Chmn. 1953—). *Award:* Rank and Title Minister by the President Republic of Finland 1971. *Publications:* Jyväskylän Työväenyhdistys 50-vuotias (1938); Työväenkysymys ja työväenliike Suomessa (1948); The Finnish Workers' Institutes (1947); The Ideological Development of Democratic Socialism in Finland (1957); Die ideologische Entwicklung des demokratischen Sozialismus (1958); The Finnish School System and its Present Problems, Moscow (1958); The Finnish Theatre & Community (1959); The Finnish School System (UNESCO) (1960); Man and His Work, article in anniversary publication dedicated to K. A. Fagerholm; 100 Years of Finnish Primary School, Moscow 1966; Tasks and aims in the field of Labour Movement (1970); numerous articles in Finnish and foreign journals, newspapers and bulletins. *Address:* Etelä Esplanadikatu 16, Helsinki 13, Finland.

**OKAWARA, Yoshio.** Japanese Diplomat. *B.* 1919. *Educ.* Tokyo Univ.—LLB. *M.* 1948. Mitsuko Terajima. *S.* 3. *Career:* 1st Sec. 1962, Counsellor 1963–65, Embassy of Japan, U.S.A.; Dir., Personnel Div. 1965–67, Dep. Dir.-Gen., American Affairs Bureau 1967–71, Ministry of Foreign Affairs, Tokyo; Envoy Extraordinary & Minister Plenipotentiary, Embassy of Japan, U.S.A. 1971–72; Dir.-Gen., American Affairs Bureau 1972–74, Dep. Vice-Minister for Administration 1974–76, Ministry of Foreign Affairs, Tokyo; Ambassador Ex. & Plen. of Japan to Australia, concurrently Ambassador to Fiji & to Republic of Nauru since 1976. Fellow, Center for International Affairs, Harvard Univ. 1962. *Clubs:* Commonwealth (Canberra); Royal Canberra Golf; Melbourne (Melbourne); Metropolitan Club of the City of Washington (U.S.A.). *Address:* 114 Empire Circuit, Yarralumla, A.C.T. 2600; and *office* Embassy of Japan, 112 Empire Circuit, Yarralumla, A.C.T. 2600, Australia.

**OLAFSSON, David.** Icelandic. *B.* 1916. *Educ.* Kiel Univ. (BSc Econ.). *M.* 1941, Augusta Gisladottir. *S.* Olafur. *Dau.* Sigrün. *Career:* Delegate to F.A.O. Conference (Copenhagen 1946 and Geneva 1947); delegate to first Marshall Aid Plan Conference, Paris 1947; subsequently representative to various conferences of the O.E.E.C. and O.E.C.D.; delegate to the International Council for the Exploration of the Sea (I.C.E.S.). 1951–68, Vice-Pres. 1964–67. Delegate to the Permanent Commission under the Intnl. Fisheries Convention (1946) 1953–63; to North-east Atlantic Fisheries Commission 1963–69 (and First Vice-Pres.), Pres. 1966–69. Icelandic representative to various conferences on European fisheries; Icelandic representative to the U.N.O. International Technical Conference on the Conservation of the Living Resources of the Sea, Rome, 1955; Icelandic Representative to U.N. Conf. on the Law of the Sea, Geneva, 1958 and 1960. Icelandic repres. to F.A.O. Fisheries Cttee. 1965–67; Member Bd. of Governors of the Central Bank of Iceland 1967—; Chmn. Bd. Dirs. Fisheries Fund of Iceland 1967—; Bd. Fish Industry Price Equalization Fund since 1969. Elected Member of Althing (Parliament) for Independence Party, 1963–67. Pres., Fisheries Assn. of Iceland 1940–67 (since 1944 the title is Director of Fisheries); Editor of monthly publication on fisheries Aegir from 1955–67. *Publication:* Yearly survey of Icelandic Fisheries 1940–51 in monthly publication Aegir. *Address:* Hoergshlid 26, Reykjavik, Iceland.

**OLDENBURG, Troels V. A.** *B.* 1915. *Educ.* University of Copenhagen (Master degree in Law). *M.* 1942, Marie Gasmann. *S.* Christian and Claus. *Dau.* Merete. *Career:* Ministry of Foreign Affairs, Copenhagen 1940–45; Attaché and Second Secy., Danish Embassy London 1945–47; Min. Foreign Affairs 1947–50; Consul, Flensburg, Germany 1950–54; Head of Dept. Min. Foreign Affairs 1957; Dep. Danish Permanent Rep. at NATO, Paris 1958–62; Asst. Under-Secretary for Political Affairs, Copenhagen 1962–65. Danish Ambassador to the People's Republic of China 1965–68. Ambassador, Deputy Under-Secy. for Political Affairs in the Foreign Ministry, Copenhagen 1968–74; Danish Ambassador in the Fed. Republic of Germany since 1974. *Awards:* Commander: (1st Class) Order of Dannebrog (Denmark); St. Olav (Norway); of Merit (1st Class) Austria, Italy & Netherlands; Grand Cross of Order of Merit, FR Germany; Officer, Order of Vasa (Sweden). *Address:* Royal Danish Embassy, Bonn am Rhein Pfalzer Strasse 14, F.R. of Germany.

**OLIPHANT, Professor Sir Mark (Marcus Laurence Elwin).** KBE, FRS, FAA. Governor of South Australia 1971–76. *B.* 1901. *Educ.* High Schools, South Australia; Univ. of Adelaide (B.Sc. First class hons.); Awarded an 1851 Overseas Scholarship, Cambridge, England, 1927. *Career:* Asst. Dir. of Research Cavendish Laboratory 1935–37; Elected to Fellowship St. John's Coll. Cambridge 1934, Royal Society of London 1937; Professor and Head, Physics Dept. Univ. of Birmingham, England 1937–50; Established Research School, Physical Sciences, Aust. National Univ. Canberra 1950; (First Director); With Rutherford and others discovered deuterium reactions used later in the Hydrogen Bomb; Lecturer and writer on atomic energy in war and peace. *Awards:* Hon. D.Sc., Toronto, Belfast. Melbourne, Birmingham, A.N.U., N.S.W., Adelaide, Flinders; Hon. LLD, St. Andrews. *Publication:* Rutherford—Recollections of the Cambridge Days (1972). *Address:* 37 Coluin Street, Hughes, A.C.T., Australia.

**OLIVER, Peter Richard,** CMG. British H.M. diplomatic service (ret'd.). *B.* 1917. *Educ.* Felsted School, Hanover, Berlin; Trinity Hall Cambridge. *M.* 1940, Freda Evelyn Gwyther. *S.* 2. *Daus.* 2. *Career:* Indian Civil Service (Punjab and Bahawalpur) 1939–47; 2nd Secy. British High Commission Karachi, Pakistan 1947–49; 1st Secy. Foreign Office 1950–52; The Hague, Netherlands 1952–56, Havana, Cuba 1956–59, Foreign Office 1959–61; Counsellor Djakarta, Indonesia 1961–64; Bonn, Germany 1965–69; Deputy High Comm. Lahore, Pakistan 1969–72; Ambassador Montevideo, Uruguay 1972–77. *Award:* Companion, Order of St. Michael and St. George. *Clubs:* United Oxford and Cambridge Universities; Hawks and Union (Cambridge). *Address:* c/o Grindlays Bank Ltd., 13 St James's Square, London, SW1Y 4LF.

**OLIVER, Sir William Pasfield,** GBE, KCB, KCMG, DL. (Lieut.-General; retired). *B.* 1901. *Educ.* King's College School, Cambridge; Radley College; RMC, Sandhurst. *M.* 1938, Elisabeth Marjorie Brind. *S.* 1. *Dau.* 1. *Career:* Commissioned into Queen's Own Royal West Kent Regt. Major-General, Chief of Staff, Middle East 1945–46; Brigade Commander 1948; Instructor, Imperial Defence College 1949–50; Chief of Staff, Eastern Command 1951–52; Principal Staff Officer to High Commissioner Malaya 1953–54; Commandant, British Sector, Berlin 1954–55; Vice-Chief, Imperial General Staff 1955–57; retired 1957; Princ. Staff Officer to Secretary of State, Commonwealth Relations 1957–59; High Commissioner for United Kingdom in Australia 1959–65;. Commissioner-General for Britain to the 1967 Montreal Exhibition, 1965–67; Adv. Cttee. on Rhodesian Travel Restrictions 1968; Colonel, Queen's Own Royal West Kent Regiment 1949–59; Deputy Lieutenant, County of Kent 1959. *Awards:* D.C.L. (Hon.) Bishops Univ., Quebec. Knight Grand Cross, Order of the Phoenix (Greece); Comdr., Legion of Merit. *Governor:* Corps of Commissionaires. *Address:* Little Crofts, Sweethaws, Crowborough, East Sussex.

**OLLIVIER, Gabriel Florentin Juste.** *B.* 1908. *M.* 1934, Antonia Marchesi, Member l'Institut de France. Technical Councillor in the Government of Monaco. Head Keeper, National Museum of Monaco. Consul-General for Greece. 1947—. Ambassador Ex. & Plen. with the Council of Europe & Superintendent of Museums & Monuments of the Sovereign Order of Malta. Corresponding member of: l'Académie d'Athènes-Beaux Arts et Lettres, l'Académie Royale Des Beaux Arts de San Fernando d'Espagne, l'Académie Nationale des Beaux Arts du Portugal. Member, Free Academy of Belgium. Correspondent, U.N.O. Information Centre. *Awards:* Officier de l'Ordre de Saint-Charles (Monaco); Commandeur: Légion d'Honneur, Order of the Phoenix (Greece), Order of George 1st of Greece; Grand Croix de Grâce Magistrale avec Cordon & Grand Croix au Mérite de l'Ordre Souverain de Malte; Grand Officier de l'Ordre du Saint Sépulcre de Jerusalem, l'Ordre de la Couronne de Belgique, l'Ordre Pontifical de Saint-Sylvestre, l'Ordre du Mérite de La République Italienne, l'Infant Henri de Portugal. Hon. Member, Rotary, Lions Clubs (Monaco). *Publications:* Le Vrai Visage de Monaco (The True Face of Monaco); Le Personnel Touristique dans le Monde (World Tourist Personnel); Les Quatre Villes de Monaco (The Four Towns of Monaco); En parcourant la Côte d'Azur (Passing Through the Blue Coast). *Address:* Musée National de Monaco, 17 avenue Princesse Grace, Monte-Carlo, Principality of Monaco.

**OLMSTEAD, Ralph Webb.** American. *B.* 1911. *Educ.* Univ. of Idaho (AB 1933) and Geo. Washington Univ. (JD 1935). *M.* 1937 Jeanne Charrier. *S.* Frederick Law. *Dau.* Carol Emilie. *Career:* Secy. to U.S. Senator 1933–39; office of Secy. of Agriculture, 1939; Office of Personnel, 1940; Asst. to Secy. 1941; Asst. Administrator Agricultural Marketing Administration and Food Distribution Administration, 1941–45. Director of Supply War Food Administration; Vice-Pres. and Director Commodity Credit Corp.; Pres. Federal Surplus Corp.; Exec. Officer combined Food Board; U.S. Army Lt.-Col. 1942–45, Legion of Merit; Operations Director UNRRA (China) Nov. 1945; Adviser Premier of China; Gen. Mgr. Henningsen Produce Co. 1946 to 1950; joined Morrison-Knudsen Co. Boise, Idaho 1950; Vice-President and Director Morrison-Knudsen Company until 1971; Director, Triangle Industries and Ionics, Inc.; President, The H. K. Ferguson Company, Cleveland, Ohio. Member, National Advisory Committee on Regional Economic Development. *Address*: RT1, Box 41, Jackson Springs, N.C. 27281, U.S.A.

**OLMSTED, George H.** American. *B.* 1901. *Educ.* U.S. Military Academy (West Point); Maj.-Gen. USAR (Retd.). *M.* 1949, Carol Shearing. *S.* George H., Jr. and Jerauld L. *Dau.* Alice Louise (Burt). *Career:* Chairman and Chief Exec. Officer, International Bank of Washington, D.C. Hon. Chmn., Financial General Bankshares; Chmn., United Services Life Insurance Co. (both of Washington, D.C.). Director, Transorient Bank (Beirut, Lebanon), Credit Européen (Luxembourg), Europa Bank (Saarbrucken, Germany), and International Bank of Washington (Bahamas) Ltd. (Nassau). *Awards:* U.S. Distinguished Service Medal; Legion of Merit; Bronze Star; Comdr. Order of British Empire; Legion of Honour (France); Order of Sacred Tripod (China). The 1967 World Trade Award (by Metropolitan Washington Board of Trade). *Trustee:* Drake University (Des Moines, Iowa); The American University (Washington, D.C.); Pres. appointee to Bd. of Visitors to U.S. Mil. Acad. West Point; Assn. Mason (32°). (W.P. Alumni). *Clubs:* Army & Navy (Washington); Washington Golf & Country; Des Moines. *Address:* 2775 North Quebec Street, Arlington, Va. 22207; and *office* 1701 Pennsylvania Avenue, N.W., Washington, D.C. 20006, U.S.A.

**OLSEN, Edward Gustave.** American Professor of Education. *B.* 1908. *Educ.* Pacific University (AB); Union Theological Seminary (BD); Columbia University (MA and EdD). *M.* 1948, Pauline Walsh. *S.* Marvin Elliott and Douglas Walsh. *Dau.* Marcia Evelyn. *Career:* Chmn. Department of Education, Colgate Univ. 1935–41; Dir., School of Education, Russell Sage College 1941–45; Dir., School & Community Relations, Washington State Office of Public Instruction 1945–50; Associate Professor of Educational Administration, Univ. of Texas 1950–51. Dir. of Educ., Nat Conference of Christians & Jews, Chicago Region 1951–66; Professor of Education, California State Univ. at Hayward, 1966–73; Professor Emeritus of Education since 1973. *Awards:* Thomas H. Wright Award, City of Chicago. 1957; Fulbright Lecturer, Univ. College of Rhodesia and Nyasaland, 1958; Distinguished Service, Nat. Community School Education Assn. 1969. *Member;* Natl. Education Assn. (Life Member); Rotary International. *Publications:* School & Community, 1945 (rev. 1954; Japanese and Spanish edns.); School & Community Programmes, 1949; The Modern Community School, 1953; The School and Community Reader, 1963; (with Phillip Clark) Life Centering Education, 1977; about 100 magazines articles and book reviews. *Address:* 317 Memory Lane, Brookings, Oregon, 97415, U.S.A.

**OLSON, Harry F.** Staff Vice-President Acoustical and Electro-mechanical Research, R.C.A. Laboratories. *B.* 1902. *Educ.* Univ. of Iowa (BS; MS; EE; PhD). *M.* 1935, Lorene E. Johnson. Holder of 100 U.S. Patents. *Awards:* Hon. DSc Iowa Wesleyan Univ. Recipient of many awards. Republican. *Fellow:* Inst. of Radio Engineers; Audio Engineering Socy. (Pres.); Amer. Physical Socy.; Socy. of Motion Picture & Television Engineers; Natl. Acad. of Sciences; and Acoustical Socy. of America (Pres. 1952–53); Andio Engineering Socy. (Pres. 1962–63). *Publications:* Dynamical Analogies; Musical Engineering; Acoustical Engineering; Modern Sound Reproduction; over 120 articles in technical journals; over one hundred U.S. Patents. *Address:* 71 Palmer Square West, Princeton, N.J. 08540; and *office* R.C.A. Laboratories, Princeton, N.J., U.S.A.

**OLSSON, Sture Gordon.** *B.* 1920. *Educ.* University of Virginia (BS Mech. Eng. 1942). *M.* 1957, Anne Shirley Carter. *S.* 1. *Daus.* 3. *Career:* service Engineer, Sperry Gyroscope Co. Inc. 1943–44; U.S. Naval Reserve 1944–46; Plant Engineer 1946–50; Vice-Pres. i/c Mfg. 1951; Exec. Vice-Pres. and Gen. Manager Jan.–Oct. 1952; President & Director, The Chesapeake Corp. of Virginia 1952–68, Chmn. of the Board since 1968; Foudrinier Kraft Board Institute since 1952; Chmn. of the Board 1975–77; Bd. of Dirs., American Paper Inst.; President and Trustee, Elis Olsson-Chesapeake Foundation 1956—. *Member:* Virginia Manufacturer Assn.; Virginia State Chamber of Commerce. *Clubs:* Country of Virginia, Commonwealth; West Point (Va.). Country. *Address:* Romancoke, West Point, Va., U.S.A.

**OLSZOWSKI, Stefan.** Polish politician. *B.* 1931. *Educ.* Lodz Univ. (Master's degree, Philology). *Career:* on the Main Board Polish Youth Union 1954–56; Chmn. Supreme Council, Polish Students Assn. 1956–60; Secy. Poznan Voivodship Cttee. Polish United Workers Party 1960–63; Headed Press Bureau Party's Central Cttee. 1963–68; Central Cttee. Secretary 1968; Minister of Foreign Affairs 1971–76; Mem. Party Secretariat. *Awards:* Order, Banner of Labour, First Class; Officers' Cross, Order of Polonia Restituta. *Address:* 23 Al. 1 Armii, W. P. Warsaw, Poland.

**OLVER, Sir Stephen John Linley,** KBE, CMG. Retired British diplomat. *B.* 1916. *Educ.* Stowe School. *M.* 1953, Maria Morena. *S.* 1. *Career:* with Indian Police 1935–41; Indian Political Service 1941–47; British Foreign Service, Karachi 1947–49; Foreign Office 1950–53; Berlin 1953–56; Bangkok 1956–58; Foreign Office 1958–61; Consul General Washington D.C. 1961–64; Foreign & Commonwealth Office 1964–66; Counsellor, The Hague 1967–69; High Commissioner Freetown 1969–72; High Commissioner Nicosia 1973–75. *Awards:* Knight Commander of the Order of the British Empire: Commander, Order of St. Michael and St. George. *Club:* Marylebone Cricket. *Address:* Tanglewoods, Heath Ride, Wokingham, Berks.

**O'NEAL, Edward Asbury.** American company executive. *B.* 1905. *Educ.* Davidson College, North Carolina (AB). *M.* 1928, Mildred Pruet. *S.* Edward Asbury, Jr. *Daus.* Mildred (Palmer), Julia Ann (Gould), Nancy. *Career:* Director: Monsanto Co., St. Louis, Mo.; Trustee, Washington Univ., St. Louis, Mo. Director, Foreign Policy Assn., New York, N.Y. *Member:* American Chemical Socy. and Socy. of Chemical Industry (American Section). *Address:* 665 South Skinker Blvd. Apt. 12F, St. Louis, Missouri 63105; and *office* 665 South Skinker Blvd. Ste. 2-B, St. Louis, Missouri 63105, U.S.A.

**O'NEIL, Hon. Desmond,** MLA (East Melville 1962—). Australian. *B.* 1920. *Educ.* Teachers' College, W.A. *M.* 1944, Nancy Jean Culver. *Daus.* Marilyn Anne and Wendy Lee. *Career:* Elected to W.A. Parliament 1959; Government Whip 1962; Minister for Housing and Minister for Labour, Govt. of Western Australia 1965–71; Deputy Leader Opposition 1972–74; Minister for Works, Water Supplies and Housing Govt. of WA Feb. 1974–June 1975; Dep. Premier, Minister for Works, Water Supplies & the North-West June 1975–Feb. 1977; Dep. Premier, Chief Sec., Minister for Police & Traffic, Minister for Regional Admin. & the North West since Feb 1977. *Member:* Executive W.A. Branch of Commonwealth Parliamentary Assn.; Parly. Public Acs. Committee; Liberal Party of Australia. *Address:* c/o Legislative Assembly, Perth, Western Australia, Australia.

**O'NEILL, Sir Con Douglas Walter,** GCMG. *B.* 1912. *Educ.* Eton College and Balliol College, Oxford (MA). *M.* 1954. Baroness M. Marschall von Bieberstein (*D.* 1960). *S.* 1. *Dau.* 1 (by previous marriage). Fellow, All Souls' College, Oxford 1935–45. *Career:* called to Bar (Inner Temple) 1936; entered diplomatic service 1936; in World War II 1940–43; at Foreign Office 1943–46; journalist 1946–47; rejoined Foreign Service 1948; served in Germany 1948–52; Imperial Defence College 1953; Head, Foreign Office News Dept. 1954–55; Chargé d'Affaires, Peking 1955–57; Asst. Under-Secretary, Foreign Office, 1957–60: Ambassador to Finland, Jan. 1961–63; to European Communities, Brussels 1963–65; Deputy Under-Secretary of State, Foreign Office 1965–68, Resigned 1968. Dir., Hill Samuel & Co. Ltd., 1968–69; Deputy Under Secy. of State Foreign Office, Leader Official U.K. Delegation negotiate entry European Community 1969–72; Chmn. Intervention Bd. Agricultural Produce 1972–74; Director, Britain in Europe (for Referendum Campaign) 1974–75; Director Unigate Ltd. since 1974. *Address:* 37. Flood St., London, S.W.3.

**O'NEILL OF THE MAINE. The Rt. Hon. Lord (Terence Marne)**, PC, DL (Co. Antrim). *B.* 1914. *Educ.* Eton. *M.* 1944, Katherine Jean Whitaker. *S.* Patrick Arthur Ingham. *Dau.* Penelope Anne. *Career:* Served in World War II (Irish Guards) 1939–46; Mem. Parliament (Unionist) for Bannside Div., Co. Antrim 1946–69; Parly. Sec., Ministry of Health and Local Government 1948–53; Chairman of Ways and Means and Deputy Speaker 1953–55; High Sheriff 1953; Parly. Sec., Ministries of Health and Local Government and Home Affairs 1955–56; Minister of Home Affairs April–Sept. 1956 (when he became joint Minister of Finance and Home Affairs until end of Oct. 1956); Minister of Finance 1956–63. Prime Minister of N. Ireland 1963–69. *Address:* Lisle Court, Lymington, Hants.

**OOSTENS, Emile Elie Eugène.** Belgian chemist. Brussels, Brabant. *B.* 1911. *Educ.* Degree in Chemistry. *M.* 1948, Eliane Vanhee. *Daus.* 3. Knight, Order of Leopold II and Order of the Crown; Industrial Medal 1st Class; Labour Decoration (Technical Engineer). Counsellor A.K.Z.O. Coatings Belgium S.A. *Member:* Belgian Association of Paint & Varnish Technicians and Related Industries—A.T.I.P.I.C. Past Pres.); Federation of Associations of European Paint & Varnish Technicians (Past Pres.); Brussels Chamber of Commerce (Award as expert on paints and varnishes); Royal Belgian Federation of Rowing Clubs (Past Chmn., Judges' Panel); Internatl. Rowing Judge. *Clubs:* Brussels, Ostend and Ghent Royal Water Sports (Rowing). *Address:* 48 Avenue Jean de Bologne, 1020 Brussels, Belgium.

**OPITZ, Hans-Joachim,** Dr. rer. oec. German. Director-General. *B.* 1921. *Educ.* Dresden, Leipzig. Tübingen, Fribourg (Suisse), London School Economics, Paris Universities. *M.* 1957, Lottie. *S.* 2. *Dau.* 1. *Career:* Director-General European Parliament since 1959. *Award:* Bundesverdienstkreuz (First class); Commandeur de l'Ordre nat. de la Répub. de Côte d'Ivoire. *Publication:* Der Verwaltungsbegriff in der Betriebswirtschaftslehre. *Address:* European Parliament, Plateau du Kirchberg, Luxembourg.

**OPPENHEIM, Sir Duncan Morris.** British solicitor and company director. *B.* 6 Aug. 1904. *Educ.* Repton School. *M.* 1936, Susan May Macnaghten (died 1964). *S.* Nicholas Anthony. *Dau.* Sarah Jane. *Career:* In private practice as Solicitor 1929–34; Solicitor to British-American Tobacco Co. Ltd. 1934–36; Director, British-American Tobacco Co. Ltd., 1943–72; Deputy-Chmn. 1947, Vice-Chmn. 1949, Chairman 1953–66; President 1966–72, Advisor 1972–74; Director: Lloyds Bank Ltd. 1956–75; Equity Law Life Assurance Society 1966—. Deputy Chairman, Commonwealth Development Finance Co. Ltd. 1968–74. Chairman: Royal College of Art 1956–72; Council of Industrial Design 1960–72 (member 1959–72); British National Committee, International Chamber of Commerce 1963–74; Royal Inst. of International Affairs 1966–71; Tobacco Securities Trust Co. Ltd., 1969–74. *Address:* 43 Edwardes Square, London, W2 6HH.

**OPPENHEIM, Sally (Mrs.).** M.P. British. *Married:* S. 1 *Daus.* 2. *Career:* Member of Parliament (Con.) for Gloucester since 1970; Front Bench Spokesman on Prices and Consumer Protection 1974–75; Shadow Cabinet since 1975; Former Exec. Dir. Industrial & Investment Services Ltd.; Social Worker, School Care Dept. Inner London Educ. Authority; Member, Clergy Rest House Trust. *Member:* Former Mem. Exec. Cttee. Nat. Council, Single Woman, Her Elderly Dependants Ltd.; Mangt. Cttee. National Vice-Pres. Nat. Mobile Home Residents Assn.; Nat. Union Townswomen's Guilds; Chmn. Cons. Party; Parly. Consumer Protection Cttee.; Pres. Gloucester District Branch, British Red Cross Socy.; Vice-Pres. South Wales, West Fire Liason Panel; Western Centre of Public Health Inspectors; National Vice-Pres. Royal Socy. Prevention of Accidents. *Address:* 1 Ardmore Close, Tuffley, Gloucester; and *office* House of Commons, London, S.W.1.

**OPPENHEIMER, Franz Martin.** Partner, Leva, Hawes, Symington, Martin & Oppenheimer. *B.* 1919. *Educ.* Univ. of Chicago (BS 1942); Univ. of Grenoble, 1938–39; LLB (cum Laude), Yale, 1945. *M.* 1944, Margaret Spencer Foote. *S.* 2. *Daus.* 1. Dir., International Student House. *Member:* American Bar Assn.; Federal Bar Assn.; American Society of International Law (Treas. 1967–76); American Psychological Assn.; Cttee. of 100 on the Federal City, also Trustee; Chatham Hall (Trustee); Inst. Empirical Econ. Research, Berlin (Trustee). *Publications:* articles on legal matters. *Clubs:* Yale (N.Y.C.); Federal City; City Tavern (Washington); Metropolitan (Washington). *Address:* 3248 O Street, N.W., Washington, D.C. 20007; and *office* 815 Connecticut Ave., N.W., Washington, D.C. 20006, U.S.A.

**OPPENHEIMER, Harry Frederick,** MA. South African company director. *B.* 1908. *Educ.* Charterhouse (England) and Christ Church, Oxford. *M.* 1943, Bridget McCall. *S.* 1. *Dau.* 1. *Career:* Represented Kimberley City in Parliament of Union of South Africa 1948–57. Chairman: Anglo American Corp. of S.A. Ltd., Anglo American Investment Trust Ltd., and other companies in the Anglo American Group. Chmn.: De Beers Cons. Mines Ltd. (and other producing, marketing and investment companies in the De Beers Group), A.E. and C.I. Ltd.; Director, Chartered Consolidated Ltd.: Barclays Bank, D.C.O., General Mining & Finance Corp. Ltd. Commonwealth Development Finance Co. Ltd., and other investment, mining, colliery and development companies. Served with 4th S.A. Armoured Car Regt. 1940–45. Chancellor of Univ. of Cape Town. *Clubs:* Rand, Kimberley, Inanda (S.A.); Salisbury; Brooks (London). *Address:* Brenthurst, Federation Road, Parktown, Johannesburg, South Africa.

**OPPERMAN, Hon. Sir H. F.,** OBE, OStJ. Australian director. *B.* 1904. *M.* 1928, Mavys Paterson Craig. *S.* 1. *Dau. Dec. Career:* Served in World War II RAAF, Flt. Lieut. (Adjutant) 1945. Member, House of Representatives for Corio 1949–67 (Government Whip 1955); Minister of State for Shipping and Transport, February 1960–63; Minister for Immigration 1963–66; Acting Minister for Navy, 1960; High Commissioner to Malta 1967–72. Life Governor, Alfred Hospital, Prince Henry's Hospital, Royal Children's Hospital, Royal Melbourne Hospital, Grace McKellar Homes, Geelong, Assn. for Blind, and Royal Women's Hosp. Internationally known as former champion cyclist 1924–40; Medal Council of Paris 1971. Convener Commonwealth Jubilee Sporting Committee 1951. *Award:* Order. Knight Commander, St. John of Jerusalem (Hospitaller). *Publication:* Pedals Politics & People (Autobiog.) (1977). *Clubs:* R.A.A.F. (Melbourne); U.S.I. Geelong (Vic.). *Address:* 6A/121 Marine Poe, St. Kilda, Vic. 3182, Australia.

**OPPLER, Kurt,** Dr. jur. German diplomat. Ret. *B.* 1902. *Educ.* Johannes Gymnasium, Breslau, and University of Breslau. *M.* 1932, Rosa Winkler. *Career:* Commercial activity 1921–27; Advocate in practice, Gleiwtiz/OS 1932–37; emigrated (Netherlands and Belgium) 1938–44; Chief, Dept. of Hessian Ministry of Justice 1946–47; Dir. ,Bipartite Personnnel Office, Economic Council (subsequently Liquidation Agency), Frankfurt A/M. 1947–52; at Foreign Office, Bonn 1952; En. Ex. and Min. Plen. to Iceland, Dec. 1952. Ambassador to Iceland 1956, to Norway, Oct. 1956; to Belgium 1953-63, to Canada 1963. *Awards:* Grand Cross, Order of Icelandic Falcon, Order of St. Olav, Order of Merit (Germany), Order of the Crown (Belgium), Grand Cordon, Order of Leopold (Belgium), Hon. Citizen of Ostend and of Winnipeg. *Publications:* concerning questions of labour, administration and public law; between 1950–52 especially concerning reform of the public services in Germany and the civil service in foreign countries. *Address:* 757-Baden-Baden, Staufenbergstr. 46A, Germany.

**ORBACH, Maurice,** MP. British. *B.* 1902. *Educ.* Cardiff & New York City. *M.* 1935, Ruth Beatrice Huebsch. *S.* Laurence. *Dau.* Susan. *Career:* Member, London County Council, St. Pancras, 1937–46; Gen. Sec., Trades Advisory Council since 1940; MP. Willesden East, 1945–59; Member of Parliament, Stockport South since 1964; Chmn. & member various Hospital Mgt. Cttees. Central Middlesex Hospital over 12 years. Vice-Pres., Socialist Medical Association. Exec. British O.S.E.; *Publications:* Austria 1946; Programme for Progress; Anti-Semitism in Great Britain; Does Eichmann Matter ?; Mission. *Clubs:* Royal Overseas League. *Address:* 76 Eton Hall, Eton College Road, Hampstead, London, N.W.3.; and *office* T.A.C., 169–171 Cricklewood Broadway, N.W.2.

**ORCHARD, Peter Francis.** MA. British. *B.* 1927. *Educ.* Downside School; Magdalene Coll., Cambridge (MA). *M.* 1955, Helen Sheridan. *S.* 2. *Daus.* 2. *Career:* Chief Executive: The De La Rue Co. Ltd.; *Director:* Thomas De La Rue International Ltd.; Thomas De La Rue AG, Switzerland; De La Rue Giori SA, Switzerland; Crosfield Business Machines Ltd.; Crosfield Electronics Ltd.; Crosfield Electronics—France SA, France; Crosfield Graphic Equipment Ltd.; Westwood Instruments Ltd.; Security Express Ltd.; Courier Express Ltd.; Federated Banknote Printing Co. Ltd.; Thomas De La Rue Int. Services Ltd.; Anglo-Swiss Engineering Ltd.; *Chairman:* Thomas De La Rue (Security Systems Print) Ltd.; Thomas De La Rue Holdings Ltd.; Thomas De La Rue & Co. Ltd.

*Member:* Inst. of Directors. Fellow, British Inst. Management; Liveryman Drapers Co. *Address:* Willow Cottage, Little Hallingbury, Bishop's Stortford, Herts and *office* De La Rue House, 84–86 Regent Street, London, W1A 1DL.

**O'REILLY, Francis Joseph.** Irish. *B.* 1922. *Educ.* St. Gerard's (Bray), Ampleforth Coll. (York) and Trinity College, University of Dublin (BA, BAI 1943). *M.* 1950, Teresa. *S.* 3. *Daus.* 7. *Career:* Served with H.M. Forces (Lieutenant, Royal Engineers, 7th Indian Division, S.E.A.C.) 1943–46; Chairman, Irish Distillers Group Ltd.; Irish Raleigh Industries; Player & Wills (Ireland) Ltd.; Deputy-Chmn. Ulster Bank Ltd.; Dir. Bostik (Ireland) Ltd. President, National Equestrian Federation of Ireland (F.E.I.); Member, Committee of Agriculture and Horse Show Committee of Royal Dublin Socy.; Director and Steward, Fairyhouse Race Club; Member, Managing Committee and Steward, Kildare and National Hunt Races (Punchestown); Chmn., Kildare Hunt Club. *Clubs:* Turf; The Kildare Street (Dublin). *Address:* The Glebe, Rathmore, Naas, Co. Kildare; and *office* Bow Street Distillery, Dublin 7, Eire.

**ORESCANIN, Bogdan,** Yugoslav Diplomat. *B.* 1916. *Educ.* Grammar Sch., Zagreb; Univ. of Zagreb; Belgrade Higher Mil. Acad. *M.* 1947, Dr. Sonja Dapcevic. *Career:* Corps Commdr. & Gen., Nat. Liberation Struggle, 1941; Asst. & Dep. Chief of General Staff & Asst. Defence Sec. 1945; Mil. Attaché to the U.K. 1952–54; Mem. Parl., Fed. Council, Chmn. Cttee. for Nat. Defence, Foreign Affairs Cttee., Exec. Bd. of Yugoslav Group of Interparl. Union; Ambassador to People's Republic of China, Democratic People's Republic of Korea & Democratic Republic of Vietnam 1970–73; Ambassador to the U.K. 1973–76. *Awards:* Order of the Nat. Hero & many other Decorations. *Address:* c/o Ministry of Foreign Affairs, 1100 Belgrade, Yugoslavia.

**ORKOMIES, Osmo Lennart,** MA, LLB. Finnish diplomat. *B.* 8 Oct. 1912. *Educ.* Suomalainen Normaalilyseo and Helsinki University. *M.* 1942, Sirkka Liisa Weckman. *S.* Esko Kaarlo Lennart and Juha Osmo Alexis. Entered Foreign Service 1943; Press Attaché, Stockholm 1943; 2nd Secretary 1946; 1st Secretary, Ministry for Foreign Affairs 1946; Consul, Frankfurt am Main 1950; Cologne 1951; 1st Secretary, London 1952; Counsellor 1953; Head of Dept., Ministry for Foreign Affairs 1955; Deputy Director 1957; Director of Political Affairs 1959; Ambassador to Berne 1959; to Cairo 1962, concurrently Ambassador to Khartoum, and Minister to Addis Ababa, Amman, Beirut, and to the Holy See; Director of Political Affairs 1966. Ambassador to Warsaw 1967; Inspector General, Foreign Service 1972; Ambassador to Algiers since 1975, concurrently Ambassador to Tunis. *Awards:* Commander 1st Class, Order of White Rose of Finland, Order of Lion of Finland. Grand Cross, Order of St. Gregory The Great (Holy See), also of U.A.R.; Comdr., Order of Dannebrog (Denmark), Order of North Star (Sweden); Chevalier 1st Cl. Order of Vasa (Sweden). *Address:* c/o Ministry for Foreign Affairs, Helsinki, Finland.

**ORME, Rt. Hon. Stanley,** PC, MP. British Politician. *B.* 1923. *Educ.* Elementary & Technical Schools; National Council of Labour Colleges & Workers' Educational Association Classes. *M.* 1951, Irene Mary Harris. *Career:* AUEW Shop Steward 1949–64; Councillor (Labour) Sale Borough Council 1957–65; Labour MP for Salford West since 1964; Minister of State, Northern Ireland Office 1974–76; Dept. of Health & Social Security 1976; Minister for Social Security since 1976. Current Chmn., AUEW Parliamentary Group of Labour Members. *Clubs:* A.S.E., Altrincham; Ashfield Labour Club, Salford. *Address:* 47 Hope Road, Sale, Cheshire; and House of Commons, London SW1.

**OROSA, Sixto Luna, Jr.** Filipino. *B.* 1916. *Educ.* De La Salle Coll. (BSc Valedictorian 1935), Univ. of the Philippines (post-grad. courses in Banking and Finance); Philippine Law School (Valedictorian 1947); Member Philippine Bar. *M.* 1937, Edita do Santos. *S.* Sixto S. III. Jose S., Ramon S., and Roberto *S. Daus.* Christina O. (Naylor) and Socorro S. *Career:* Previous senior appointments: Exec. Vice-Pres. & Dir., Prudential Bank & Trust Co.; Vice-Pres. & Secy., Equitable Banking Corp.; Asst. Vice-Pres. and Credit Mgr., The Philippine Bank of Commerce; President, General Manager, and Director, Philippine Commercial and Industrial Bank. Chairman of Board: Industrial and Management Associates Inc., Belgor Investments Inc., and Mercantile Insurance Corp. Director: Visayan Packing Corp., Taggat Industries Inc., Sta. Mesa Market Corp. Philippine Prudential Life Insurance Co., and Construction and Development Corp. of the Philippines. *Publications:* various publications and lectures on economics, banking and finance in Manila newspapers and journals. Chosen: Banker of the Year 1960 and 1961 (Business Writers' Assn. of the Philippines); Outstanding Alumnus (De La Salle Coll.) 1961; Outstanding Alumnus in field of banking and finance during last fifty years ending 1962 (Occidental Negros High School); Outstanding Batangueño (Press Assn. of Batangas Province). *Member:* Philippine Columbian Assn.; Natl. Assn. Bank Auditors & Comptrollers (Past Pres. Philippine Chapter); Natl. Assn. Bank Auditors & Comptrollers, U.S.A. (Past State Vice-Pres. for Philippines and Far East); Management Assn. of Philippines (Past Pres.); Bankers' Assn. of the Philippines (Dir.). *Clubs:* Manila Golf; Wack Wack Golf & Country; Filipino; Casiño Español de Manila; Army-Navy (Manila); First Friday; Manila Polo; Philippine-British and Philippine-Italian Assns. *Address: office* Philippine Commercial & Industrial Bank, T.M. Kalaw Street, Manila, Philippines.

**ORR, Clarence Montague.** British. Chartered Accountant and Chartered Secretary. *B.* 1899. *Educ.* University of Sydney (BEcon); Fellow, Institute of Chartered Accountants in Australia (F.C.A.); Fellow & Life Member, Australian Socy. of Accountants (F.A.S.A.) and Fellow, Chartered Institute of Secretaries (F.C.I.S.); Fellow & Life Member, Taxation Inst. of Australia; Life Governor, Balmain Hospital. *M.* 1926, Vera Ruth Bridson. *S.* Dr. K. B. Orr, MB, BS, FRCS (Eng.), and Dr. Colin M. Orr, MB, BS, DA. *Career:* Manager, Offner, Hadley & Co., Public Accountants 1921–27; Secretarial duties, Farmer & Co. Ltd., Sydney 1927–33; Secretary, Accountant and Co-Attorney in Australia and New Zealand of Fassett & Johnson, Ltd. 1933–49; Manager, MacRobertson (N.S.W.) Pty. Ltd. 1949–59, and retained by that company as adviser 1959–60; Director: Shepherd & Newman Pty. Ltd. 1960–75; Prudential Co-operative Building Society, Nos. 1 & 2; Director, Paddington-Woollahra Starr-Bowkett Building Societies, Nos. 9 to 15; member, Council N.S.W. Division, Australian Society of Accountants; member, N.S.W. Council, Taxation Institute of Australia; General President, Taxation Institute of Australia 1950–52; Vice-President, Federal Institute of Accountants 1952, and of Australian Society of Accountants 1955–57; Member of Council, Federal Institute of Accountants 1940–52, and of N.S.W. Taxpayers' Association 1938–42. *Publications:* Federal & State Income Tax Instructor (N.S.W. and Queensland editions); author of a number of articles in Australian Accountant. *Clubs:* University Union (Life member); N.S.W. Masonic (Life member); Double Bay Bowling (Hon. Treas. 1960–68 & Life member); Royal Automobile of Australia; South Sydney Rotary; N.S.W. Rostrum; Bowlers of N.S.W.; Canberra Yacht. *Address:* 7 Yamba Road, Bellevue Hill, Sydney, N.S.W., Australia.

**ORR, George Wells Jr.** American business executive *B.* 1913. *Educ.* Duke Univ. (AB) and Harvard Univ. Schoo of Business Administration (AMP 1960). *M.* 1939, Evelyn Louise Baker. *Dau.* Jane Harris. *Career:* With Vick Chemical Co., N.Y., 1935–38, The Wm. S. Merrell Co., Cincinnati 1938–51, and Ames Co. Inc. 1951–67. President and Director: Ames Co. Division Miles Laboratories, Inc., Elkhart Ind. 1956–67, and Ames Co. of Canada Ltd., Toronto 1958–67, Vice-President, Miles Laboratories Inc., Elkhart 1959–67. Exec. Vice-President, Miles Laboratories, Inc., Elkhart, Ind. 1971–73; Miles Sankyo Company Ltd., Tokyo 1967–73; Serral, S.A., Mexico City, 1967–71; Dir. Miles Laboratories Inc., Elkhart 1963—; Pelam Inc., Chicago, 1968–70; Miles Seravac Pty. Ltd., Capetown, S. Africa; Miles-Yeda Ltd., Rehobot, Israel 1971; St. Joseph Valley Bank, Elkhart, Ind. since 1973; Blue Cross of Indiana Inc., Indianapolis, since 1976. Pres. Miles Laboratories since 1973. Member Executive Cttee., Miles Labortories, Inc., Elkhart 1965—. *Publications:* Structure of a Pharmaceutical Firm (1959); The President's Job is Easier: Management Accounting (1975). *Member:* National Pharmaceutical Council (U.S.A.); Pharmaceutical Manufacturers Assn. (U.S.A.). Dir. 1969—; The Newcomen Socy. in North America. Republican. *Clubs:* Rotary; City, Elcona County (Elkhart). *Address:* 5 Holly Lane, Elkhart, Ind.; and *office* Miles Laboratories, Inc., 1127 Myrtle Street, Elkhart, Ind., U.S.A.

**ORR, James Hunter.** American. *B.* 1899. *Educ.* Northeastern Univ. and Harvard (AB 1920; Law Degree 1924);. *M.* Ida Lee Hayes. *S.* JamesHunter, Francis Atlee. Past Director, Pitney-Bowes, Inc. 1932–71; The First Boston Corp. 1939–71; Draper Corp. 1953–57; State Mutual Life Assurance Co. of America 1969–74; Terra Chemicals Int'l Inc. 1965–75; Pilot Insurance Co. 1958–74; Chmn. Bd. Dir., Colonial Management Associates, Inc. 1971–75; Present Directorships; The

Colonial Fund, Inc. 1934—: Colonial Growth Shares, Inc. 1949—; Colonial Income Fund, Inc. 1969—; Colonial Convertible & Senior Securities Inc. 1971—; Accounting Service Corp 1941—; Suffolk Corp. 1941—. *Member:* Massachusetts Bar Assn. *Clubs:* The Links, The Wall Street (N.Y.C.); Eastward Ho! Country (Chatham, Mass.); Algonquin Club of Boston, Down Town Club (Boston, Mass.); The Country Club (Brookline, Mass.); Hole-in-the-Wall Golf (Naples, Fla.); Agawam Hunt (Providence, R.I.). *Address:* 330 Beacon Street, Boston, MA 02116, U.S.A.; and *office* 75 Federal Street, Boston, Mass. 02110, U.S.A.

**ORR-EWING, (Lord Charles). Ian** (Life Peer U.K. cr. 1971) OBE, MA, CEng, FIEE. British politician, Electronic Engineer & Director. *B.* 1912. *Educ.* Harrow and Trinity College, Oxford (MA). *M.* 1939, Joan McMinnies. *S.* 4. *Career:* served in World War II (R.A.F.V.R.: N. Africa, Italy, France and Germany; Wing Comdr. 1941; Chief Radar Officer, Air Staff of SHAEF 1945; dispatches) 1939–46; B.B.C. Television 1946–48; Member, Parliament (Con.) North Hendon 1950–70; P.P.S. to Minister of Labour and National Service 1951–55; Junior Minister, Air Ministry 1957–59; Civil Lord of the Admiralty 1959–63; Member, Parly. Select Cttee. on Science and Technology 1966–68; Pres., Chmn., Electronic Eng. Assn. 1969–70; Chmn. Ultra Electronics Ltd. and Clayton Dewandre Ltd.; Dir. Richardsons Westgarth, Dowty, MK Electric, Johnson's Wax; Chmn. Metrication Board 1972–77; Created Baronet 1963; became Life Peer 1971. *Clubs:* Founder Lords and Commons Ski; Pres. National Ski Fed. Great Britain. *Address:* Old Manor, Little Berkhamstead, near Hertford.

**ORTEGA-URBINA, Alfonso.** Nicaraguan diplomat. *B.* 1925. *Educ.* Granada, Madrid & Dallas, Texas; Doctor of Law. *M.* Norma Guerrero de Ortega. 5 children. *Career:* Entered Nicaraguan diplomatic service; successively Sec. of Legation, Spain; Chargé d'Affaires, Costa Rica; Counsellor & Consul-Gen., El Salvador; Counsellor & Chargé d'Affaires, Dominican Republic & Haiti; Minister-Counsellor, Mexico, El Salvador & U.S.A.; Ambassador to Honduras; Dep. Foreign Minister 1961–62; Foreign Minister 1962–67; Ambassador to Mexico, Ecuador, Paraguay, Brazil & Bolivia. Head of Nicaraguan delegations to many international conferences. *Address:* c/o Ministry of Foreign Affairs, Managua, Nicaragua.

**ORTON, Dwayne.** American. *B.* 1903. *Educ.* University of Redlands (AB 1926) and University of Pacific (MA 1933); Hon. Degs.: University of Redlands, Tusculum Coll., St. Lawrence University, Clarkson Coll., Pace Coll., Nasson Coll., Western New England Coll. Univ. of Tampa and Pratt Institute. *M.* 1926, Edna Marie Olson. *S.* Lawrence Dwayne. *Daus.* Jean Elizabeth (Hilchey) and Nancy Marie (Littauer). *Career:* Instructor, Baylor Coll. 1926–29; Asst. Prof., Univ. of Pacific 1929–33 (Assoc. Prof. and Dir. of Chapel 1930–35); Dir., Univ. of Pacific Junior Coll. 1933–34; Dean Gen. Coll., Univ. of Pacific 1934–36; Pres., Stockton Coll. 1936–42; Dir. of Education, International Business Machines Corp. 1942–54; Former Chairman Editorial Board, Think magazine 1964–68, Editor 1954–64. Educational consultant, IBM till 1968. U.S. Rep. to International Management Council 1957. President, Council for International Progress in Management 1957–60 (Chmn. 1960–63). *Member:* Natl. Cncl. Student Christian Assn. 1930; Assoc. Hazen Foundation 1933–39; Cttee. on Guidance Award, 1947–50; Calif. State Commn. on Needs of Post High School Youth 1939–41; Calif. State Cncl. on N.Y.A. 1941; Dir., N.Y. State Citizens Cncl. 1944–50; Consultant, Civil Aeronautics Admin. 1941–43, and U.S.A.F. 1952–53; Asst. Administrator, U.S. Fed. Civil Defense Admin. 1951; Dir. and Exec. Cttee., Amer. Arbitration Assn.; Chmn. Board for Exec. Development for Church Leadership; Dir., Freedom House; Trustee and Exec. Cttee., Pratt Inst. Fellow, Int'l. Academy of Management. Member, National Cttee., Student Div., Natl. Cncl. of Y.M.C.A., and Natl. Cncl. of Churches Cttee. on Church and Economic Life. Dir., World Neighbors. Distinguished Alumni Award, Univ. of Redlands 1962; Trustee, Univ. of Redlands, 1968—. Chmn. of the Board of Overseers Johnston College; Lecturer, Univ. of Santa Clara. *Award:* George Washington Honor Medal, Freedoms Foundation; Hon. Counsellor C.I.O.S. Wallace Clark Award in International Management, 1969; Fellow, Int. Academy of Management. *Member:* S.A.M. and A.A.A.S.; Phi Delta Kappa; Pi Kappa Delta; Pi Gamma Nu. *Clubs:* University (N.Y.C.); Commonwealth (Calif.); Rotary; Circumnavigators. *Address: office* 590 Madison Avenue, New York City 10022, U.S.A.

**OS, Lars Øystein.** Norwegian. *B.* 1914. *Educ.* University of Oslo (Law). *M.* 1941, Elsa Julie Bjørn Hansen. *S.* Arne and Lars. *Daus.* Kari and Ragna. *Career:* Educational Supervisor, Brage Life Insurance Co. 1939–41, and Christinia General Insurance Co. Storebrand 1941–47. Man. Dir., The Insurance Information Office, Norway 1947—. Editor, Forsikringstidende (the trade insurance periodical in Norway) 1947—. *Member:* Norwegian Assn. of Trade Journals (Dir. 1949–54, Chmn. 1955–58); International Public Relations Assn. *Member:* Norwegian Assn. of Trade Journals (Dir. 1949–54, Chmn. 1955–58); International Public Relations Assn. (Member of Council 1960–71); International Fed. of Periodical Press (Dir. 1955–58); Norwegian Public Relations Assn. 1950— (Pres. 1960–64). *Address:* Myrvollveien 5, 1322, Høvick; and *office* Hansteens gt. 2, Oslo 2, Norway.

**OSADEBAY, Dennis Chukude,** FRGS. Nigerian Barrister-at-Law, politician and journalist. *B.* 1911. *Educ.* Government School, Asaba; Sacred Heart School and Hope Waddel Institute, Calabar; LLB Barrister (Lincolns Inn) 1948. Broadcaster, B.B.C. London 1946–49; Dir. of Information. *Career:* West African Students Union 1947; Solicitor and Advocate, Supreme Court of Nigeria 1949; Elected to the Western House of Assembly 1951; elected to Federal House of Representatives, Lagos 1952 (also Legal Adviser to the N.C.N.C.); Leader of Opposition, Western House 1956; appointed Privy Councillor, W. Nigeria 1955; Deputy Speaker, Western House 1960; President, Senate of the Fed. of Nigeria 1960–64; acted for Governor-General June-Aug. 1961; Administrator, Midwestern Nigeria 1963–64, Premier 1964–66; Solicitor to Eastern Nigerian Development Corp. for some years. Formerly: Secretary responsible for organization to bring together all Ibo unions in Nigeria into the Ibo Federal Union (now Ibo State Union). Prior to his visit to U.K. was supervisor of Customs and Excise. As a politician was one of the founder-members and legal adviser of N.C.N.C. under Dr. Nnamdi Azikiwe's leadership. Attended the London Constitutional Conferences 1954–57–58; elected Leader of the Midwest State Movement, an organization formed to fight for the creation of a fourth region in Nigeria, 1956; led the Nigerian Parliamentary Delegation to U.K., U.S.A. and Canada 1962. Fellow, Royal Geographical Society (1949); Life Member, Red Cross Society; Chairman, Girl Guides Association at Aba, Eastern Nigeria; Chairman, Parliamentary Guild of Old Scouts 1961–64. *Awards:* LLD. Univ. Nigeria 1964; Grand Commander Order of the Niger 1964. *Publications:* Africa Sings (book of 100 poems); contributor to Daily Times, and West African Pilot. *Address:* 88 Pentney Road, London, S.W.12.

**OSBORNE, Brian Gumley,** JP. *B.* 1921. *Educ.* Friends School; St. Virgil's College. *Career:* Secy. Australian Newspapers Council 1962—; of International Press Institute (Australian Section) 1966—; The Commonwealth Press Union (Australian Section) 1966—, Joint National Cttee. for Disparaging Copy since 1965; Media Council of Australia 1967—. Secy. until 1963: Royal Agricultural Society of Tasmania, and Tasmanian Racing Club, Printing & Allied Trades Employers' Assn., Botanical Gardens Trustees, Society for Care of Crippled Children, Bloodhorse Breeders' Assn. (Tasmanian Div.), Junior Farmers' Clubs, State Fodder Conservation Competitions, Working Sheepdog Association, Wrapping Paper Merchants Association, Paper Bag Association Member, Tasmanian Advisory Board of Australian Broadcasting Commission; Australian Representative for Odham's Press Ltd. (Horse & Hound Section). Previously Secretary: Tasmanian Turf Club, Agricultural Show Council, and Northern Club; Judge, Racing Club and Registered Clubs 1941–45; former Director, Hobart Rotary. *Member:* Government Betting Control Board; Hon. Treas., Australian Goat Breeders Socy. (Tasmanian branch); Hon. Treas., Royal Hobart Regatta Assn. 1960–61. Contributor to English and Australian periodicals. *Address:* 8/85c Ocean St., Woollahra, Sydney, N.S.W., Australia.

**OSBORNE, Hon. Frederick Meares,** CMG, DSC (and Bar), VRD. *B.* 1909. *Educ.* North Sydney Boys School High, Sydney Church of England Grammar School, and St. Andrew's College, Sydney University (BA; LLB). *M.* 1944, Elizabeth Drake. *S.* Alick C. D., and Michael D. *Daus.* Imogen E. D., and Penelope J. D. *Career:* Admitted as Solicitor, New South Wales 1934; served with the Royal Australian Navy and Royal Navy 1939–46; Commanded H.M. Ships *Gentian* 1941, *Vanquisher* 1943, *Peacock* 1945, (Commander, R.A.N.V.R. 1955); resumed legal practice in Sydney 1946; elected to Australian Federal Parliament in 1949; Minister for Customs and Excise, Jan. 1956, and Minister for Air, Oct. 1956; Minister for Repatriation Dec. 1960–Dec. 1961; represented Australia at Ghana Independence celebration, 1957; lost seat General Election Dec. 1961. Member, Dudley Westgarth & Co., solicitors, Sydney; Gen. Counsel for Lloyds of London 1963–75; Chmn. Mauri Bros. & Thompson Ltd.; Hardboards Australia Ltd.; Sandoz Australia Pty. Ltd.; Dir. Burns Philp & Co. Ltd.; H. B. Selby Australia Ltd.; Mortgage Guaranty Ins. Corp. of Aust. Ltd.; Member NSW Board of Advice, National Bank of Australasia Ltd. Member, Liberal Party of Australia (Former Pres. N.S.W. Division). *Clubs:* Union University; Royal Sydney Yacht Squadron. *Address:* 9 Mary Street, Longueville, N.S.W., Australia.

**OSBORNE, Henry Gerard Alexander.** Australian. *B.* 1908. *Educ.* Scotch College (Melbourne) and Melbourne University (BAgrSc). *M.* 1938, Beryl Somerville Corbett. *S.* Dr. William A. Osborne. *Dau.* Mrs. Peter Brockhoff. *Career:* Former Chmn. and Dir. Kraft Foods Inc. *Member:* Australian Inst. of Agricultural Scientists; National Museum of Victoria (Trustee); Australian Inst. of Management (Fellow); Victoria Promotion Cttee. *Clubs:* Athenaeum; Melbourne; Rotary (Melbourne); Frankston Golf. *Address:* 'Lowestoft', Warrandyte, Vic. 3113, Australia.

**OSBORNE, Stanley de Jongh.** American business executive. *B.* 1905. *Educ.* Phillips Academy (Andover Mass.); Harvard Coll. (AB *cum laude* 1926); Harvard Business School. *M.* 1929, Elizabeth Ide. *S.* Richard de Jongh. *Daus.* Mary Ide (Mrs. M. Osborne Downing) and Cynthia Adams (Hewett). *Career:* Director of Publicity, Harvard Athletic Association 1927–28; Old Colony Corp., Boston, Mass. 1928–29; successively Asst. to Pres., Treasurer, Secy., Vice-Pres., Atlantic Coast Fisheries Co. 1929–43; Special Asst. to Rubber Director, Washington 1942–43; Vice-President, Eastern Air Lines Inc. 1944–50; Financial Vice-President, Mathieson Chemical Corp. 1950–54; Exec. Vice-President 1954–57 and President and Director 1957–63, Chairman 1963–64; Olin Mathieson Chemical Corp.; Special Adviser to President of U.S. for Supersonic Transport 1963–66; Consultant to Natl. Aeronautics and Space Admin. 1967–68; Member, Board of Directors: A.M.F., Inc., N.Y.; Lone Star Industries Corp., N.Y.; New England Fish Co., Seattle, Wash.; Chmn. Private Investment Corp. for Asia, Singapore. Limited Partner, Lazard Frères & Co., N.Y.C. 1964—. *Member:* Socy. of the N.Y. Hosp. (member, Bd. of Governors and Pres.); Council on Foreign Relations. *Clubs:* The Brook, River, Harvard (N.Y.C.); Bucks (London). *Address:* One East End Avenue, New York City 10021; and *office* 1 Rockefeller Plaza, New York City 10020, U.S.A.

**O'SHEA, Alexander Paterson,** CMG. *B.* 29 Dec. 1902. *Educ.* Otago High School; Victoria University College (BCom). *M.* Vera Isabell Cooper. *Dau.* 1. *Career:* Dominion Secy., New Zealand Farmers Union since 1935; General Secretary, Federated Farmers of New Zealand 1946–64; North American Dir., New Zealand Meat Producers Board, 1964–68. M.L.C. 1950. Fellow Chartered Accountant. *Publication:* The Public Be Damned. *Address:* Apt. 3B, Herbert Gardens, The Terrace, Wellington, New Zealand.

**OSMAN, (Abdool) Raman (Mahomed),** GCMG, CBE. Mauritian Governor-General and Commander in Chief. *B.* 1902. *Educ.* Royal Coll., Mauritius; Inns of Court, London. *Career:* called to the Bar 1925; District Magistrate 1930–38; Additional Substitute Procureur and Advocate General 1938–50; Acting Procureur and Advocate General 1950–51; Puisne Judge 1950–59; Acting Chief Justice April–Nov. 1958; Ret. as Senior Puisne Judge 1960; Chmn. Wages Council, Agricultural Workers, Sugar Industry 1965–72; Termination, Contracts of Service Board; Electoral Boundaries, Electoral Supervisory Commission; Commission, Prerogative of Mercy 1968–72; Acting Governor General, 3 occasions 1970–72; Governor General since 1972. *Awards:* Knight Grand Cross, Most Distinguished Order of St. Michael and St. George; Commander, Civil Div. Most Excellent Order, British Empire; Hon. Dr. of Civil Law, Univ. of Mauritius 1975. *Club:* Port Louis Gymkhana. *Address:* Government House, Le Réduit, Mauritius.

**OSTBYE, Rolf.** Norwegian. *B.* 1898. *Educ.* Tech. Univ. of Norway. *M.* (1) 1923, Richm Berg. *S.* Niels Johan. *Dau.* Elisabeth. (2) 1933, Ellen Martinsen. *S.* Kjell. *Dau.* Mette. *Career:* Man. and Dir. of breweries and flour mills 1921–47; Member Bd. Standard Telefon og Kabelfabrik 1947—; President 1956–66, Former chairman of the Board, Norsk Hydro. Former Chmn. Bd., Norsk Spraengstofindustri A/S; Norsk Atlas Copco, Asea-Per Kure; Chairman of Shareholders' Cttee. of Dennorske Creditbank: Det norske Luftfartselsk apt A/S. Chairman, Shareholders' Committee, Norden Forsikrings A/S, Shareholders' Committees DE-NO-FA og Lilleborg Fabriker A/S, with Wilhelmsens & Norges Eksportråd. Consul-General of Denmark. Commander: Order of St. Olav with star (Norway) and Homayun (Iran); Kungl. Vasaorden (Sweden); Order of Dannebrog (Denmark); Cruzeiro do Sul (Brazil); Officer, Legion of Honour; IDR.M.; N.I.F. Medal. *Honorary Member:* Royal Norwegian Society of Science (Trondheim); Norwegian Technical Academy of Science (Oslo); Academy of Engineer Science (Stockholm); and Academy of Technical Science (Copenhagen). *Clubs:* Norske Selskab; Association of Norwegian Engineers. *Address:* Hoffsjef Lövenskiolds vei 55, Ullernåsen, Oslo; and *office* Bygdöy alle 2, Oslo, Norway.

**OSTERRIETH, Frédéric.** Belgian merchant and company director. *B.* 14 July 1903. *M.* 1929 Rosie Grütering. *S.* 4. *Career:* Head of Belgian Economic Mission, Dec. 1944–Oct. 1946; Belgian Representative, E.C.I.T.O. 1945–47; Hon. Chmn., Antwerp Chamber of Commerce, O.R.E. (Office de Récupération Economique), Office Belge du Commerce Extérieur; Vice-Chmn., Belgian National Committee of the International Chamber of Commerce; member of Council, International Chamber of Commerce; Vice-Chmn., Director and member of the Permanent Committee, Belgian National Railways; Director, Banque de Bruxelles, Banque Belge d'Afrique SCRL; Banque de Commerce, S.A.; Compagnie Maritime Belge, S.A.; Chairman, Société Anglo-Belge des Ferryboats; Cockerill Yards Hoboken S.A.; member of Tribunal de Commerce, and of different Committees, Marshall Plan, etc. *Awards:* Grand Officer, Ordre de Léopold II; Commander: Ordre de la Couronne; Order of Orange Nassau, and Couronne de Chêne (Luxembourg); Knight Légion d'Honneur (France); Commander Merito (Italy). *Address:* Markgravestraat 12, Antwerp, Belgium.

**OSTERWIND, Heinz.** Deputy Chmn. Supervisory Board of the Deutsche Bank AG; member Supervisory Boards of a number of major companies. *B.* 1905. *Address:* Junghofstr. 5–11, Frankfurt am Main, Germany.

**OSWALD, Thomas.** Scot. Politician. *B.* 1904. *Educ.* Yardheads & Bonnington Elementary Schools. *M.* 1933, Colina MacAskill MacAlpine. *S.* 3. *Dau.* 1. *Career:* Trade Group Secy. Scottish Region, Transport & General Workers Union, 1941–69; Member of Parliament for Edinburgh Central 1951–74; Secy. Treas. Scottish Parly. Labour Group, 1956–66; Parly. Private Secy. to the Secy. of State for Scotland, 1966–70; Nat. Pres. Scottish Old Age Pensions Assn. since 1975. *Clubs:* Edinburgh Trades Council. *Address:* 28 Seaview Terrace, Edinburgh EH15 2HD, and *office* 53 George IV Bridge, Edinburgh EH1 1EJ.

**OTHMER, Donald Frederick,** BSc, MS, PhD. American chemical engineer. *B.* 1904. *Educ.* Universities of Nebraska (BS 1924) and Michigan (MS 1925, PhD 1927); Hon. Dr. Eng., Univ. of Nebraska 1962; Hon. Prof., Univ. of Concepcion, Chile 1951. *M.* 1950, Mildred Jane Topp. *Career:* Licensed chemical engineer in New York, New Jersey, Pennsylvania and Ohio; Licensor of over 125 process patents since 1931 to companies and governmental departments throughout the world in Refrigeration, Evaporation, Distillation, Petrochemicals, Acetic Acid, Sugar, Extractive Metallurgy, Wood & Pulping Technology, Desalination, Pipe Line Heating, Sewage Treatment, Solar & other energy production, etc. Consultant to U.N., W.H.O., Nat. Sc. Foundation, U.S. Army & Navy, Dept. of State and other U.S. Government depts., Member Nat. Materials Adv. Bd. and designer of processes and plants for numerous corporations in U.S. and foreign countries. Previously Development Engineer, Eastman Kodak Co. and Tennessee Eastman Corp., 1927–31; Instructor (1932–33); Professor (1933—), Head of Department of Chemical Engineering (1937–61), Secy. Graduate Faculty 1948–58, and Distinguished Professor (1961—), Polytechnic Institute of New York; lecturer sponsored by American-Swiss Foundation for Scientific Relations 1948, Chemical Institute of Canada 1950, India 52–68, 71; Japan 55; lecture tours for American Chemical Socy. 1944–69; ACHEMA, Frankfurt/Main; Hon. Delegate 1958–76; Lecture Sympos., European Feed. Chemical Engineering, Athens, Greece, 1962; 1970; Plen. Lect. Intl. Cong. Chem. Eng., Equip., Design & Automation, Czechoslovakia 1962–75; Lect. Congr. Soc. de Chimie Ind., Belgrade, 1963, 70; Lect. Congr. Chem. Ind. Warsaw, 1964, 67, 69; Plen. Lect. IX Congr. Latinamericano, Puerto Rico, 1965; Lectures: U.S. Army War College 1964; Moderator, U.N. Sympos. Economics of Water Desalination 1965; ASTM 1966; TAPPI 1966; U.N. World Health Org., Poland (1967);

Chmn., Amer. Program Société de Chimie Ind., Paris 1968–74; Lecture Tour Argentine Universities 1969; Plen. Lect. 38 Congr. Soc. de Chimie Ind. Istanbul 1969; 1st Int. Congr. Thermodynamics, Warsaw 1969; 7th Arab Petroleum Congress, Kuwait (1970); 8th, Algeria 1972; 9th, Dubai UAE, 1975; 10th, Abu Dhabi, UAE 1976. *Fellow:* Amer. Assn. for Advancement of Science; N.Y. Acad of Sciences, Chmn. Eng. Div. 1972–73; Hon. Life Member (1975); American Institute of Chemists (Dir. 1950), Honor Scroll 1970, Pioneer Award 1977, Hon. Life Fellow 1977; Amer. Inst. of Chem. Engrs.; (Mem. Prof. Devel. Comm. & Intrnl. Relat. Comm.; Dir. 1956–59; received Tyler Award 1958); Amer. Socy. of Mechanical Engrs Chmn. Process Industries Div. *Member:* Amer. Inst. of Consulting Engrs., Engineers Jt. Cncl. (Dir. 1957–59), Amer. Chem. Socy. (Murphree Award 1978), Socy. of the Chem. Industry, Amer. Socy. for Engineering Education (Barber-Coleman Award 1958); Japanese Socy. of Chemical Engineering; Société de Chimie Industrielle, Pres. (Amer. Section) 1973–74; Chemurgic Council, (Dir. 1963—); Assn. of Consulting Chemists & Chemical Engineers, 1st Distinguished Service Award, 1975; Hon. Mem. Deutsche Gesel. für Chem. Appar.; Newcomen Socy.; Sigma Xi, Tau Beta Pi, Phi Lambda Upsilon, Iota Alpha, Alpha Chi Sigma, Lambda Chi Alpha; member, Nat. Panel of Arbitrators, American Arbitration Association; Life member, Norwegian Club (N.Y.C.), Chemists Club Pres. 1974–76; Rembrandt, N.Y.C.; Trustee & Regent several hospitals, univs. and foundations. *Publications:* more than 315 articles on chemical processes, thermodynamics Chemical & Power engineering etc. in American and foreign technical journals; co-author, Fluidization and Fluid Particle Systems; member, Advisory Board, Perry's Chemical Engineer's Handbook; Adv. Industrial Waste Water Control, Delaware River Basin Comm. 1970—; Tech. Editor U.N. Report, Technology of Water Desalination; Editor, Fluidization 1956; Co-editor, Kirk-Othmer Encyclopedia of Chemical Technology 1st Ed. (17 vols.) 2nd Ed. 24 vols. 1947–72. *Address:* 333 Jay Street, Brooklyn 11201, N.Y., U.S.A.; also 140 Columbia Heights, Brooklyn, New York, 11201; also Coudersport, Pa. 16915.

**OTTO, George John.** *B.* 1904. *Educ.* Univ. of California (AB College of Letters & Science). *M.* 1933, Marie Kendrick. *Daus.* Marie Luise, Elizabeth Ann and Susan Katherine. *Career:* Partner, Irving Lundborg & Co.; Vice-Chmn., Clark Dodge & Co. Inc.; Senior Vice-Pres. Kidder Peabody and Co.; Members of New York Stock Exchange (Brokers), American Stock Exchange, Pacific Coast Stock Exchange. *Clubs:* Bohemian; San Francisco Golf; Menlo Country; Stock Exchange. *Address:* 2701 Pierce Street, San Francisco; and *office* 555 California Street, San Francisco, Calif., U.S.A.

**OTTO, Robert Henry.** International advertising executive. *B.* 1904. *Educ.* Univ. of Washington (BBA 1926) and Cambridge Univ., England (post-graduate 1927). *M.* 1935, Lydia A. Maguire. *Daus.* Helen M. (Greeley III) and Susan M. (Spicer, Jr.). *Career:* Exec. Vice-Pres., Export Advertising Agency, Chicago 1941–46. Chmn. Bd. LPE-Robert Otto Inc., N.Y.C. 1962–70; Director: L.P.E. International, London (Eng.) 1962–70; President: LPE-Robert Otto & Co., Argentina 1946–70; Robert Otto & Co. S. A., Mexico 1946–70, and LPE-Robert Otto & Co. (Puerto Rico) Inc. 1959–70. *Member:* Sigma Alpha Epsilon; Alpha Delta Sigma; International Advertising Assn. (active A.R.C.; Pres. 1946); Assn. of International Adevrtising Agencies (Pres. 1955). Republican. *Clubs:* University, Wings (N.Y.C.); American (London); American (Buenos Aires); Club de Industriales A.C. (Mexico City); Pelham Country, Men's (Pelham). *Address:* 555 Pelham Manor Road, Pelham Manor, N.Y. 10803, U.S.A.

**OUBRIDGE, Victor William,** FIMechE, FIPE, FBIM. British. *B.* 2 April 1913. *Educ.* Oundle School and Jesus College, Cambridge, University (BA Eng.). *M.* 1937, Ruth Louise Carpenter. *S.* John Victor. *Dau.* Gillian Ruth. *Career:* Joined the British Piston Ring Co., Ltd., as Technical Assistant 1935 (elected Director 1937 and appointed Man. Dir. and Deputy Chairman British Piston Ring Co., and British Aero Components, April 1941; Chairman 1956). Elected Director of Group Company Associated Engineering Holdings, now Associated Engineering Ltd., on its formation 1947. Resigned as Chairman and Managing Director British Piston Ring Co., Ltd., and British Aero Components on appointment Director, Personnel Planning of Associated Engineering Group of companies 1966. Resigned directorship of Associated Engineering Ltd. on secondment to Dept. of Economic Affairs as Industrial Adviser 1967–69. Visiting Research Fellow, Aston Univ., Birmingham; Warks Area Health Authority. *Address:* 21 Wasperton, Warwick.

**OUELLET, Hon. André.** PC, MP, LL L. Canadian Lawyer & Politician. *B.* 1939. *Educ.* Univ. of Ottawa—BA; Univ. of Sherbrooke—Law degree. *M.* 1965, Edith Pagé. *S.* 2. *Daus.* 2. *Career:* MP for Papineau Riding since 1967; Pres. Quebec Liberal Caucus 1968–70; Parly. Sec. to Minister of External Affairs 1970–71;, to Minister of National Health & Welfare 1971–72; Postmaster-General of Canada 1972–74; Minister of Consumer & Corporate Affairs 1974–76; Minister of State for Urban Affairs since 1976. Mem. of the Quebec Bar. *Club:* Cercle Universitaire, Ottawa. *Address:* 2285 Virginia Drive, Ottawa, Ontario K1H 6R9; and *office* Room 105-A, House of Commons, Ottawa, Ontario K1A 0A6, Canada.

**OURY, Vivian Libert.** British company director. *B.* 17 Dec. 1912. *Educ.* St. George's College, Weybridge and Beaumont College, Old Windsor. *M.* 1936, Mary Cecilia Vincent. *S.* 2. *Career:* Chmn. or Dir. of various companies, including Trans-Zambesia Railway Co., Ltd., Sena Sugar Estates, Ltd., Beira Town Sites, Ltd., the Thames Corporation Ltd. *Award:* Commander, Ordem do Cristo (Portugal). *Address:* 1/3 Great St. Thomas Apostle, London EC4V 2BH.

**OUTZE, Børge.** Danish. *B.* 1912. *Educ.* Public School (became a journalist 1928). *M.* 1935, Ruth Lillevang. *Daus.* Annemarie (Jensen) and Eva. *Career:* Journalist: Fyns Venstreblad, Odense 1928–36, and Nationaltidende, Copenhagen 1936–43. Head of Danish underground news service agency, 'Information', August 1943 (arrested by the Gestapo Oct. 1944; escaped six weeks later and became one of the leaders of the Danish underground news service in Stockholm until May 1945). Editor-in-Chief the independent daily Information from the day of the liberation of Denmark. Member of the Board and Editor-in-Chief, daily newspaper Information, Copenhagen 1945—. *Publications:* Denmark during the German Occupation (in English, 1946); Spidser (with Erik Seidenfaden), 1946; Danmarks Frihedskamp (with Ebbe Munck); Danmark under den anden verdenskrig I–IV, 1962–68; has made translations of British and American books on the invasion of France, the war in Norway, and in Greenland. Commended for bravery by the Supreme Headquarters of the Allied Expeditionary Force and awarded la Croix de Guerre avec Etoile d'Argent. *Member:* Association of Editors (Copenhagen); Danish Publicists; Danish P.E.N. *Clubs:* Rotary (Copenhagen); Royal Automobile Club of Denmark; World Veterans Federation in Denmark. *Address:* 164 Amager Strandvej, 2300 Copenhagen, Denmark; and *office* 40 Store Kongensgade, 1264 Copenhagen, K.

**OVERALL, Sir John Wallace,** (Knight Bachelor 1968), CBE, MC (and Bar). Australian. *B.* 1913. *Educ.* Sydney Technical College; Holder N.S.W. Board of Architects Overseas Travelling Scholarship 1939. *M.* 1943, Margaret J. Goodman. *S.* 4. *Career:* With A.I.F. 1940–46 (C.O. 1st Aust. Parachute Battalion A.I.F.; Lieut.-Col.); Chief Architect, South Australian Housing Trust 1946–48; Private Practice as Architect and Town Planner 1949–51; Chief Aust. Govt. Architect, Cwealth Dept. of Works 1952–57; Chmn., Olympic Games Fine Arts Architecture and Sculpture Exhibition, Melbourne 1956; Commissioner, National Capital Development Commission, Canberra 1958–72. Chmn., National Capital Planning Cttee., Canberra 1958–72. Commissioner, Cities Commission 1972–73; Principal, John Overall and Partners, since 1973; Dir. CSR Ltd. since 1973; Dir. Lend Lease Corp. Ltd. since 1973; Dir., Alliance Holdings Ltd. since 1975; General Property Trust. *Member:* Canberra Legacy Club (past-Pres.); Pres. and Chmn. Austr. Inst. of Urban Studies 1970–71; *Publications:* Observations on Redevelopment of Western Side of Sydney Cove (1967). *Awards:* Sydney Luker Memorial Medal, 1964; The Sir James Barrett Medal, 1970; Life Fellow: RAIA, FAPI, AMTPI. *Clubs:* Australian (Sydney); Sydney Royal Golf. *Address:* 10 Wallaroy Road, Double Bay, N.S.W. 2028, Australia.

**OVERBY, Andrew N(orris).** American. Legion of Merit, U.S.A.; Order of the Rising Sun, Japan. *B.* 1909. *Educ.* Univ. of Minnesota and Columbia Univ. (BS 1930; MS 1940). *M.* 1928, Annette Picus. *Career:* with Irving Trust Co. N.Y.C. 1930–41; Foreign banking, Asst. Vice Pres. i/c portfolio investments 1936–41; Lt.-Col. Gen. Staff Corps. U.S. Army 1942–46; Special Asst. to Vice Pres. 1942, Asst. Vice Pres. Federal Reserve Bank of N.Y. 1946; Special Asst. to Secy. of the Treasury i/c of international finance, U.S. Treas. Dept. 1946–47; Deputy Managing Dir. 1949–52, U.S. Exec. Dir. 1947–49, International Monetary Fund; Asst. Secy. of U.S. Treasury 1952–57. U.S. Exec. Dir.: International Bank for Reconstruction and Development 1952–57, and International Finance Corp. 1956–57. Director 1957—, Member Executive Committee 1963–74, and Vice-

Chmn. of the Board 1965–74 (Vice-Pres. 1957–64), The First Boston Corp. Director: International Executive Service Corps; and Liberian Iron Ore Ltd.; Chmn. Exec. Cttee., The First Boston Corp. 1971–72; Dir. Japan Socy. Inc. (Pres. 1977—). *Member:* Council on Foreign Relations: Japan Socy.; National Honor Award, Beta Gamma Sigma Alumi 1947. *Clubs:* India House, Univ.; Century Assoc. (N.Y.C.); Army and Navy, Alfalfa and Metropolitan (Washington, D.C.). *Address:* 200 East 66th Street, New York City 10021; and *office* 20 Exchange Place, New York City 10005, U.S.A.

**OVERHOLSER, J. Homer Harold.** American aircraft executive. *B.* 1914. *Educ.* Wittenberg College 1932–34. *M.* 1939, Marian Lee Whelan. *S.* James Alan. *Dau.* Sharyl Ann. *Career:* Real Estate, President, Vice-President and Chairman of numerous companies; Chairman of the Board, numerous financial, international, catering companies; President numerous international and national companies; Designer and pioneer airplanes, rocket engines, including Lunar Excursion Module, and Saturn Rocket Craft. Developed first Sonic Altimeter; and pioneered adoption of the Decca Navigator System in Canada. *Member:* A.S.M.E., A.I.M., American Helicopter Society, American Ordnance Association, American Society Air Affairs, Inst. Aero Sciences, Society Automotive Engineers, Chamber of Commerce, Association of the U.S. Army; Los Angeles World Affairs Council; Nat. Voter Adv. Bd. Amer. Security Council; Chmn. Bd. Govs. San Fernando Wine and Food Socy.; Patron member, Los Angeles Country Museum of Art. *Publications:* Diversification in Business-ASME Journal; Anti Skid Braking System-Aero Digest and Aviation Engr., Bendix-Decca Navigation System applies to Helicopter Operations. Western Aviation and Flying. Certificate of Appreciation—The Nat. Fdn. of Infantile Paralysis. *Awards:* Honorable Order of Kentucky Colonels; Freedom Season Pioneer Award; Million Miler Awards—United Airlines; Certificate of Merit Distinguished Service Business Development; Certificate of Appreciation, The National Foundation of Infantile Paralysis; Hold patents, Hydraulic Valves, Hydraulic Fluid Transmission & Tire Warning Device. *Clubs:* Lakeside Golf; Deanville Golf; Woodland Hills Shrine; Al Malaikah Shrine; Free and accepted Masons Lodge of Perfection 32°. *Address:* 4961 Palomar Drive, Tarzana, Calif.; and *office* 18321 Ventura Blvd., Suite 480, Tarzana, Ca. 91356, U.S.A.

**OVERTON, William Ward, Jr.** American banker. *B.* 1897. *Educ.* Private Schools, Kansas City and Texas Universities. *M.* 1924. *S.* Thomas N. *Dau.* Nancy (Lemmon). *Career* Chmn. of the Board, W. W. Overton & Co., Investing Co. 1961—, (President 1931–61). Chairman of the Board, 1947—, Director 1936—, President 1961–65, Texas Bank & Trust Co. of Dallas. Dir.: Southland Corp., Dallas Texas Corp., Dallas Clearing House Assn. (President 1962–65); Pilot Institute for the Deaf Advisory Cttee., Theatre Center, Zoological Socy., Cncl. on World Affairs (Chmn. 1957–58), Chamber of Commerce (Past Pres.) (Salary Cttee.), Services for the Blind. Chmn., Dallas Citizens Cncl. Governor Dallas Foundation. Officeholder: Southern Methodist Univ. and Board of Development; Southwestern Medica Foundation; American Bankers Assn.; Greater Dallas Planning Council; former Vice-Chmn., American National Red Cross; Mem. Dallas Cncl. on World Affairs; Dallas Associates of Cttee. for Economic Development; Dir. 1966–67–68, Finance Cttee. 1966–67–68, Southwestern Insurance Cttee.; State Fair of Texas; Central Business Dist. Assn.; Dallas Cttee. for Economic Development Associates; Business Executives Res. Committee; Texas Mid-Continent Oil & Gas Assn.; Dallas Museum for Contemporary Arts. *Member:* Methodist Clubs; Texas Historical Society; Garden of the Gods (Colorado Springs); Dallas Crime Commission; National Bible Week (National Chairman); Nat. Industrial Conference Board (Councelor); Texas Safety Assn. (Chmn. of Board of Dirs.). Recipient of Service Certificate, American National Red Cross Board of Governors, 1952–58; and of Distinguished Service Plaque, Dallas County Chapter, American National Red Cross; Kudos College Award, Dallas; Testimonial Luncheon, Citizens of Dallas; Texas Safety Association; Metropolitan Opera Board of Dallas (Board member). *Clubs:* Brook Hollow Golf; Little Sandy Hunting & Fishing (Hawkins, Tex.); Broadmoor Coutry (Colorado Springs); City; Conferie des Chevaliers du Tastevin; Dallas; City; Imperial; Court (Dallas). *Address: office* Texas Bank & Trust Co. of Dallas, 1 Main Place, Dallas, Tex. 75226, U.S.A.

**OVERVAD, Marius.** Danish. *B.* 1899. *Educ.* Univ. of Copenhagen (Exam in Philosophy 1917) and Royal Polytechnic, Copenhagen (Civil Engineer). *M.* 1929, Gertrud Nécom. *S.* Gert. *Daus.* Lykke (Mrs. Henning Madsen) and Lene. *Career:* Civil Engineer: Det Danske Hedeselskab, Slagelse 1921–24, and Port of Aarhus Authority 1924–58. *Member:* Council Under International Organisation for Prevention of Pollution of Sea by Oil (Danish Ministry of Commerce) 1958–69; Gen. Manager, Port of Aarhus Authority 1958–69. The Harbour Law Commission (Danish Ministry of Public Works) 1962–69. Alternate Dir. Internat. Assn. of Ports & Harbours 1965–68, Dir. 1968–69; Knight Order of Dannebrog. Member Inst. of Civil Engineers. *Address:* Strandparken 36, 8000 Aarhus C, Denmark.

**OWE, Aage Willand.** Norwegian company director. *B.* 9 Oct. 1894. *Educ.* University of Oslo; Technical University of Norway. *M.* 1922, Marie Mathiesen. *S.* Christofer. *Daus.* Bergljot, Else. *Career:* Asst. Professor, Technical University of Norway, Trondheim 1920–23; Research Chemist, O. Mustad & Son, Oslo 1923–27, Chief Chemist 1927–35; Technical Dir., A/S Margarinsentralen, Oslo 1935–47; President, Association of Norwegian Engineers 1937–46; Director, Industrial Supply, Ministry of Supply, Oslo 1945; Chairman of the Board, A/S Nordisk Lettmetall 1945–47; Chairman, Government Fuel Commission 1940–42 and 1945–50; Chairman of the Board, Norsk Brenselimport A/S 1940–59; member of Board, O. Mustad 1957–59; member, Royal Norwegian Council for Scientific and Industrial Res. 1946–54; Chmn. 1964–67; Managing Dir. and Vice-Chairman of the Board of A/S Ardal og Sunndal Verk 1947–64; Pres., Norwegian Chemical Society 1950–54; Chmn., Committee of Industrial-Educational Relations, The Technical University of Norway 1959–68; King Haakon's Gold Medal for Technical and Scientific Work; Knight, Order of North Star (Sweden), Order of White Rose of Finland; Cmdr., Order of St. Olav (Norway); The Norsk Hydro Prize, Assn. of Norwegian Engineers, for achievements in Research and Industrial Development 1957; Hon. member, Assn. of Norwegian Engineers; Norwegian Chemical Socy. *Member:* Royal Norwegian Acad. of Science & Letters (at Trondheim and Oslo); Norwegian Acad. of Tech. Science. *Publications:* The Determination of Iodine Value (in collaboration); The Corrosion of Canning Tinplate; Research and the Research Worker. *Address:* Övre Ullern Terrasse 25, Oslo 3, Norway.

**OWEN, Rt. Hon. Dr. David Anthony Llewellyn.** MA, MB, BChir, MP. British. Medical practitioner. *B.* 1938. *Educ.* Cambridge Univ. and St. Thomas's Hospital London. *M.* 1968, Deborah Schabert. *S.* Tristan Llewellyn, Gareth Schabert. *Career:* Neurological Registrar, St. Thomas's Hospital 1964–66; Member of Parliament for Plymouth (Sutton) 1966–74; M.P. for Plymouth (Devonport) since 1974; Research Fellow Medical Unit St. Thomas's Hospital, 1966–68; Governor Charing Cross Hospital, 1967–68; Under Secy. of State, Royal Navy, 1968–70; Opposition Defence Spokesman 1970–72; Resigned over E.E.C.; Chmn. Decision Technology International 1970–72; Parly. Under-Secy., Dept. Health & Social Security 1974–76; Minister of State, Foreign & Commonwealth Office 1976–77, Sec. of State since 1977. Privy Counsellor, June 1976. *Member:* Royal Socy. of Medicine; Institute, Strategic Studies. *Publications:* A Unified Health Service (1968); Social Service for all (1968); The Politics of Defence (1972); In Sickness and in Health (1976); and articles in Lancet Clinical Science. *Clubs:* Royal Western Yacht. *Address:* 78 Narrow Street, London E14 8BP; and *office* House of Commons, London, S.W.1.

**OWEN, Peter Lothar.** Book publisher. *B.* 1927. *Educ.* King's School, Harrow-on-the-Hill. Middlesex. *M.* 1953, Wendy Desmoulins (Wendy Frances Julie) (*Div.*). *S.* Benedict. *Daus.* Antonia Beatrice Desmoulins and Georgina Alexis. *Career:* Apprentice publisher, The Bodley Head, commenced 1946; Managing Director and Managing Editor, Peter Owen Ltd., Publishers, London since 1951. Editor of two anthologies of prose and poetry: Springtime Two—Current Trends in Prose and Poetry; Springtime Three. *Address:* 20 Holland Park Avenue, London, W11; *office* 73 Kenway Road, London, S.W.5.

**OWEN, Ralph.** Banker. *B.* 1905. *Educ.* Vanderbilt University. *M.* 1929, Lulu Estelle Hampton. *S.* Ralph, Jr. *Dau.* Melinda (Rogers). *Career:* With Fourth and First National Bank, Nashville, Tenn. 1928–30; Equitable Securities Corp. 1930–70 (Pres. 1950–70). Independent. American Express Co.; Holiday Inns of America, Inc., Murphy Oil Corp. *Clubs:* Links, Blind Brook (N.Y.C.); Belle Meade Country; Nashville; Twenty Nine (N.Y.C.). *Address:* 104 Lynwood Boulevard, Nashville, Tenn. 37205, U.S.A.

**OWEN, Col. the Hon. Walter Stewart,** QC, LLD, Kt.St.J. Canadian. *B.* 1904 .*Educ.* Vancouver Law Schl. *M.* (1) 1929,

Jean Margaret Dowler (*D.* 1970). *S.* David Stewart and Philip Walter. (2) 1972, Shirley Woodward Grauer. *Daus.* Margaret Ann Barbeau and Daphne Muriel Francis. *Career:* Barrister-at-Law and Solicitor, Vancouver. Chmn., of Bd., Monsanto Canada Ltd. Chmn. Emeritus, The Foundation for Legal Research in Canada; Dir. The East Asiatic Co. (Canada) Ltd. Imperial Life Assurance Co. of Canada; Canada Security Assurance Co., Western Broadcasting Co. Ltd.; Radio OB Ltd.; Radio ML Ltd.; Radio QR Ltd.; Radio NW Ltd.; Greyhound Lines of Canada Ltd., Greyhound Computer of Canada Ltd.; Brewster Transport Co. Ltd.; Eastern Canadian Greyhound Lines Ltd.; Alaskan Coachways Ltd.; Canada Permanent Morgage Corp.; Canada Permanent Trust Co., Act. Oils Ltd. Cascade Gas Utilities Ltd.; Western Productions Ltd.; Atlin Investments Ltd.; Saturna Investments Ltd.; Alouette Estates Ltd.; N.W. Sports Enterprises Ltd.; Vancouver Hockey Club Ltd.; Canucks Publishing Ltd., Treasurer, Law Socy. of British Columbia 1964–66. Pres., Canadian Bar Assn. (1958–59); Crown Prosecutor, County of Vancouver 1933–42; Lieut.-Governor Province of British Columbia since 1973. *Member:* Law Society of B.C.; Canadian Bar Assn.; North West Territories Bar. Federation of Insurance Counsel, Amer. College of Trial Lawyers, Canadian Maritime Law Assn., Newcomen Socy., International Commission of Jurists; Exec. International Bar Assn., World Peace Through Law. Canadian Tax Foundation; Hon. member: American, Manitoba, Minnesota, and Washington Bar Associations. Liberal. Member of Advisory Board, Young Mens' Christian Association of Greater Vancouver; The Salvation Army; Vancouver Grace Hospital. Hon. Governor, Canadian Association for Retarded Children (Vancouver). *Address:* 28th Floor, Bental Centre Three, 595 Burrand Street, Vancouver, B.C., Canada and *office* Government House, Victoria, B.C., Canada.

**OWTRAM, Godfrey Herbert.** AIMechE, MIPetroleum. British. *B.* 1907. *Educ.* Shrewsbury School; Brasenose Coll., Oxford. *M.* 1958, Gwen Barden Barden. *S.* 1. *Daus.* 2. *Career:* Dir. Horrockses Crewsdon & Co., Ltd. 1938–39; Chmn. Man. Dir. Petrochemicals Ltd. 1952–55; Chmn. E. H. Bentall & Co., Ltd. 1956–63. Chmn. Peter Crook Ltd.; Vice-Pres. Chas. Page & Co. Inc.; Dir., Davers Stretton Co. Ltd. *Member:* Council Inst. of Directors. *Club:* Boodles. *Address:* Oak Lodge, Matfield, Kent and *office* Petteridge Lane, Matfield, Kent.

**OXENFELDT, Alfred Richard.** Economist. *B.* 1917. *Educ.* Columbia Univ. (MA 1938; PhD 1942), and Univ. of Pennsylvania (BS in Econ. 1937). *M.* 1941, Gertrude Eisenbud. *Daus.* Joan Beth and Alice (Div. 1967). *Career:* Statistician in charge of Surveys, Dun & Bradstreet 1940–41; Principal Economist, War Production Board 1941–43; U.S. Navy 1943–46; Assoc. Prof. and Chmn., Dept. of Economics, Hofstra Coll. 1946–51; Assoc. Prof., Dept. of Economics, College of City of N.Y. 1951–52; Exec. Vice-Pres., Boni, Watkins, Mountier & Co. 1952–56; Prof. of Economics, Sarah Lawrence College 1956. Professor of Marketing, Graduate School of Business, Columbia University. *Publications:* New Firms & Free Enterprise (1943); Industrial Pricing & Market Practices (1951); Economic Systems in Action (1952); Economics for the Citizen (1953); Make or Buy, Factors in Executive Decision (with M. W. Watkins) (1956); Economic Principles & Public Issues (1958); Pricing for Marketing Executives (1961); Insight into Pricing (1961), with others; Models of Markets (ed. 1963); Marketing Practices in the T.V. Set Industry (1964); Management of the Advertising Function (with Carroll Swan, 1964). Executive Action in Marketing (1946). *Member:* Amer. Economic Assn.; Amer. Marketing Assn.; Amer. Assn. of University Professors. *Address:* 464 Riverside Drive, New York City, N.Y. 10027, U.S.A.

**OXLEY, Alan John.** *B.* 1919. *Educ.* Univ. of South Africa (BA). *S.* 1. *Dau.* 1. *M.* (2) 1970, Vicki Claasen. *Career:* Legation Secretary, Cairo, 1949; Athens 1949–54; Consul, Elisabethville, 1954–57. Asst. Chief of Protocol, Pretoria 1958, Head, Political Div., Ministry 1959–60; Political Counsellor, South African Embassy London, 1961–65, and Consul-General, United Kingdom 1962–65. South African Consul-General in New Zealand 1965–69; Under Secy. (Africa) 1969–70; Ministry, Promoted Ambassador 1970; Consul-General, Tehran 1970–73; Under-Secy., Ministry 1973–77; Ambassador, Australia since 1977. *Address:* c/o Department of Foreign Affairs, Pretoria, South Africa.

# P

**PAASIO, (Kustaa) Rafael.** Finnish. *B.* 1903. *M.* 1936, Mary Wahlman. *S.* Pertti and Antti. *Dau.* Maija-Liisa. *Career:* Editor-in-Chief of Turun Päivälehti 1942–64; Pres. of the Parliamentary Cttee. for Foreign Affairs 1949–66; Minister of Social Affairs 1951 and 1958–59. Prime Minister of Finland, 1966–1968, 1972. Speaker of the Parliament 1966. Member of the Social Democratic Party; Member of Parliament 1948–75. Member of Turku Municipal Council 1945—. Chairman of the Social Democratic Party 1963–75. Speaker of the Parliament 1970. *Address:* Kannuskatu 8G 95, 20880 Turku 88, Finland.

**PACE, Frank, Jr.** *B* 1912. *Educ.* Princeton Univ. (AB 1933) and Harvard Law School (LL.B. 1936)). *M.* 1940, Margaret Morris Janney. *Daus.* Paula (Smith), Priscilla (von Matthiessen) and Margaret. *Career:* Admitted Arkansas Bar 1936; Asst. District Attorney (12th Dist. Arkansas) 1936–38; Gen. Counsel, Arkansas State Dept. of Revenue 1938–41; member law firm of Pace, Davis & Pace, Little Rock, Ark. 1941–42. Second Lieut. to Major, Air Transport Command of Army Air Corps 1942–46 (now reserve Lieut.-Col. in Air Force). Post-war: Special Asst. (taxation div. of Dept. of Justice) to Attorney-General of U.S., Exec. Asst. to Postmaster-General 1946–48; Asst. Director 1948–49, Director, Bureau of the Budget 1949. Secretary of the Army 1950; Chmn., Defense Ministers' Conf. of NATO, Dec. 1950; Delegate to NATO Confs., Ottawa and Rome 1952; Secy. of the Army until June 1953. President, International Executive Service Corps. Director: The Bullock Fund, Carrier & General Corp., Colgate-Palmolive Co., Continental Oil Co., Dividend Shares Inc., Nation-Wide Securities Co., Putman Trust Co., Time Inc., Monthly Income Shares Inc.; Institute for the Future: Pres., Natl. Inst. of Social Sciences 1962–77; Council for Latin America. Named by Pres. Eisenhower as Vice-Chmn. of Commission on National Goals 1960; named by Pres. Kennedy, member of Foreign Intelligence Advisory Board 1961–73; other appointments include member of Cttee. of American Bar Assn. on legal aspects of national defence 1947–49; Vice-Pres., U.P.U. 1947; Chief, U.S. Delegation to U.P. Congress, Paris 1947; representative of U.P.U. at U.N. 1947–48. *Member:* President's Adv. Cttee. on management improvement, Cttee. on Contributions, U.N., and joint Congressional Cttee. on reduction of non-essential federal expenditures 1949–50; Adv. Bd. of Renewable Natural Resources Found.; Dir., Intern. Mgmt. and Devel. Inst.; Council for Progress of Non-trad. Education; Adv. Cttee. of Edna McConnell Clark Foundation; Advisory Board of the Strategic Studies Center at Stanford Res. Inst.; Advisory Cttee. of the Congressional Asst. Program of the Conference Board; Former Trustee, Calif. Inst. of Technology; Trustee, Taft Inst. of Government. *Awards:* Arkansan of the Year' 1950; MA Princeton Univ. 1950; Hon LL.D, Univs. of Louisville, Arkansas; Temple, Syracuse, West Virginia, Columbia, Norwich Univs.; Dartmouth, Northland and Adelphi Colls.; Sc.D., Lafayette and Clarkson Colls.; LHD, Washington Coll. *Awards:* United Shareholders of America Annual Meeting Award 1960, Eighth Annual Gold Medal Award (AAU) 1961. 'Great Living Arkansan' 1961, George Catlett Marshall Medal 1976. *Member:* Amer. Legion (Post 1, Little Rock), Assn. of U.S. Army, Natl. Security Industrial Assn. (Hon. Life Member). *Address:* 622 Third Avenue, New York City 10017, U.S.A.

**PACE, Stanley Carter.** American. *B.* 1921. *Educ.* U.S. Military Academy (BS) and California Ins. of Technology (M.Sc.); *M.* 1945, Elaine Marilyn Cutchall. *S.* Stanley Dan, Lawrence Timothy and Richard Yost. *Career:* Executive Vice-President and Director TRW Inc. Director: Lamson & Sessions; Pres. Area 5, East Central Region, Boy Scouts of America. Trustee,

National Assn. of Manufacturers. *Member:* Amer. Inst. of Aeronautics and Astronautics; Society for Automotive Engineers; Republican. *Clubs:* The Country; The Pepper Pike; Union. Tavern. *Address:* 2750 Chesterton Road, Shaker Heights, Ohio 44122; and *office* 23555 Euclid Avenue, Cleveland, Ohio 44117, U.S.A.

**PACKARD, David.** American. *B.* 7 Sept. 1912. *Educ.* Stanford University (BA); 1934 and 1939 (Elect. Eng.). *M.* 1938, Lucile Laura Salter. *S.* David Woodley. *Daus.* Mrs. Robin Burnett; Mrs. Franklin. *M.* Orr and Julie Elizabeth *Career:* Gen. Electric Co. Vacuum Tube Engin. Dept. 1936–38; Co-founder-partner, Hewlett-Packard Co.; Calif. 1939–46, Pres. 1947–64, Chmn. Bd. Chief Exec. Officer 1964–69; Dir. Palo Alto Nat. Bank 1945–58; Adv. Bd. Anglo Calif. Nat. Bank 1948–57; Dir. Crocker-Anglo Nat. Bank 1957–59; Pacific Gas and Electric Co. 1959–69; National Airlines Inc. 1962–64; Gen. Dynamics Corp. 1964–69; U.S. Steel Corp. 1964–69; Deputy Secy. of Defense 1969–71; Chmn. Bd. Hewlett-Packard Co. since 1972; Dir. Standard Oil of Calif. 1972—; member Sen. Exec. Council, The Conference Bd. since 1972; Dir. Caterpillar Tractor Co. 1972—; TWA 1972–77; Trustee Stanford Univ. 1954–69; Dir. Granger Assoc. 1957–66; Bd. Dirs. Stanford Research Inst. 1958–69, Exec. Cttee. 1958–69; Nat. Merit Scholarship Corp. 1963–69; Univ. Research Assn. 1966–69; Trustee Colo. Coll. 1966–69; Dir. State Chamber Commerce since 1972. *Member:* Alpha Delta Phi; Phi Beta Kappa; Tau Beta Pi; Sigma XI; IEEE; Inst. Radio Engrs.; Chmn. S.F. Secy. Fellow 1948 N.Y. Acad. of Science; Adv. Bd. Hoover Inst. on War, Rev. and Peace; *Awards:* Amer. Way of Life; Herbert Hoover; Hon. ScD. Colo. Coll.; Hon LLD. Univ. Calif.; Hon. LLD Catholic Univ.; Business Statesman; Harvard Bus. School Club; James Forrestall Memorial; Very Dis. Public Service and many others. Member, Amer. Acad. Pol. & Social Science; Amer. Assoc. Adv. of Science; Nat. Acad. Eng.; Wildlife Society. *Club:* Bohemian. *Address:* P.O. Box 1330, Los Altos Hills, Ca. 94022, U.S.A.; and *office* Hewlett Packard Company, 1501 Page Mill Road, Palo Alto, California 94304.

**PACHECO ARECO. Jorge.** Former President of the Republic of Uruguay. *B.* 1920. *Educ.* Studied Law and Social Sciences. *S.* Ricardo, Jorge. *Dau.* Maria Isabel. *Career:* Teacher of Spanish Language and literature in Secondary Schools, 1940–45; Later joined daily newspaper El Dia as Journalist, Assist. Editor, 1958; Editor in Chief, 1961; Member of Parliament (Colorado Party), 1962; Vice-President of the Republic, 1967. President 1967–72; Ambassador in Spain since 1972. *Awards:* Grand Chair, Order of Liberator General San Martin, Argentine Republic; Order of the Silver Cross, Brazil; Shining Star, Special Grand Cord Class, Chinese Republic; National Order of Paraguay; Bernardo O'Higgins Order of Merit, Republic of Chile. *Address:* Embassy of Uruguay, Paseo del Pintor Rosales 32, Madrid, Spain.

**PACKETT, Charles Neville,** MBE, JP (City of Bradford). *B.* 1922. *Educ.* Bradford Grammar School, Queen Elizabeth's Grammar School (Kirkby Lonsdale) and Ashville Coll. (Harrogate). *M.* 1969, Audrey Winifred Clough. *Career:* Served Royal Army Ordnance Corps (Middle East and North Africa) 1941–46. Dir., Sydney Packett & Sons Ltd., Incorporated Insurance Brokers, Bradford and London 1941—. Past-Pres., Royal Socy. of St. George (Bradford Branch); National Assembly Representative and Yorkshire Regional Cttee. Member: National Savings Movement; Chmn., Bradford Met. Savings Cttee., Nat. Savings Movement. President, Bradford Savings Guild. Member, Examiners Cttee., Chartered Insurance Institute. Vice-Pres. (a Past Pres.) Bradford Insnce. Inst. Past Chmn., Yorkshire Area Cttee., Corp of Insurance Brokers. Appointed Governor of Ashville Coll., Harrogate 1970; Member City of Bradford Watch Cttee. 1971–74; In the period 1948–76 actively engaged as officer and/or member with the following associations: British Drama League, Bradford Amateur Operatic & Dramatic Socy., Ashvillian Socy., Bradford Mental Health and Hospital Management Cttees., Royal National Lifeboat Institution. Chairman, Insurance Advisory Section, Bradford Chamber of Com. (and Member of the Council of the Chamber) 1963–65. Nat. Pres. United Kingdom Commercial Travellers Assoc. 1975–76; also Hon. Pres. Bradford Branch and past-pres. Yorkshire Federation; Area Commissioner (Midland Area), St. John Ambulance; Master, Ionic Lodge No. 3210 1964–65 and 1966–67. *Awards:* St. John British; St. Agatha (San Marino), St. Lazarus (Jerusalem), St. Dennis (Zante), FRSA; FRGS; FCIB; ACII; Liveryman & Member, Court of Assistants of Worshipful Company of Tin Plate Workers alias Wire Workers of London, & Under Warden of the Worshipful Company of Woolmen, London; Freeman of London by Redemption Mem.: Socy. of Genealogists, League of Dramatists (Socy. of Authors) and British Drama League (Life Member). *Publications:* The Story of the Order of St. Denis of Zante; Guide to Republic of San Marino; Guide to Tongatapu Island, Kingdom of Tonga; the 1962 Year Book of the City of Bradford Local Savings Cttee., Guide To The Republic of Nauru; A History and A to Z of Her Majesty's Lieutenancy of Counties. *Clubs:* National Liberal (London); City of London Livery; Otley Golf; The Bradford. *Address:* 'San Marino', 15 Fairway, Tranmere Park, Guiseley, Yorkshire LS20 8JT; and *office* Lloyds Bank Chambers, Hustlergate, Bradford, Yorkshire, BD1 1PA.

**PADELFORD, Norman J.** *B.* 1903. *Educ.* Denison Univ. (AB 1925) and Harvard Univ. (AM 1928; PhD. 1929). *M.* 1929, Helen Proctor. *Career:* Prof. International Law, Colgate Univ. 1933–36; Fletcher School of Law & Diplomacy 1936–44; Consultant and Special Asst., U.S. Dept. of State 1942–59; member, Dumbarton Oaks Conf. on International Organization 1944; U.N. Conf. of Jurists to revise Statute of International Court of Justice 1945; San Francisco U.N. Conf. 1945; U.S. Delegate, Inland Transport Conf. 1945; Council of Foreign Ministers 1945, Massachusetts Institute of Technology 1945–74. Member Board of Editors, International Organization; Journal of Maritime Law and Commerce. Member, Board of Trustees, Denison Univ. 1954—. Presidential Task Force on Oceanography 1969–70. *Publications:* International Law and Diplomacy in the Spanish Civil War (1939); The Panama Canal in Peace & War (1942); International Politics (with Col. G. A. Lincoln), (1954); The Dynamics of International Politics (with Col. G. A. Lincoln) (1967); Africa and World Order (1963); The United Nations in the Balance (with L. M. Goodrich) (1965); Public Policy and the Use of The Seas (1968); New Dimensions of U.S. Marine Policy (1971); Maritime Commerce and the Future of the Panama Canal (1974). *Awards:* Hon LLD, Denison Univ., Hon. Phi Beta Kappa, Tufts Univ.; awarded Faculty Research, Social Science Research Council 1963–64. Fellow, American Academy of Arts and Sciences. *Member:* American Political Science Assn.; American Society of International Law, Marine Technology. *Address:* 654 West 10th St., Claremont, Calif. 91711, U.S.A.

**PADLEY, Walter Ernest,** MP. *B.* 1916. *Educ.* Chipping Norton Grammar School and Ruskin Coll. Oxford. *M.* 1942, Sylvia Wilson. *S.* 1. *Dau.* 1. *Career:* Pres. Union of Shop, Distributive and Allied Workers 1948–64. MP. (Lab. Ogmore 1950—). Minister of State for Foreign Affairs 1964–67. Member National Executive of Labour Party since 1956 (Chmn. 1965–66); Represented Labour Party, the Socialist International 1956–72. *Publications:* The Economic Problem of the Peace; Am I My Brother's Keeper?; Britain: Pawn or Power?; U.S.S.R.: Empire of Free Union? *Address:* 73 Priory Gardens, Highgate, London, N.6.

**PAGAN, Brigadier Sir John Ernest,** Kt. 1971., CMG, MBE, C St J, ED. Australian. *B.* 1914. *Educ.* Collegiate School of St. Peter, Adelaide, S.A. *M.* 1948, Marjorie Hoskins. *S.* John Grant. *Daus.* Clarissa and Nichola. *Career:* Served RAA, AIF, Middle East, Papua/New Guinea 1939–45; Citizen Military Forces 1948–62; Hon ADC to Govr. of N.S.W. 1950–55; Dist. Scouts Commsnr. N.S.W., 1952–58; Australian Council Boy Scouts Assoc. 1969—. *Member:* Bd. N.S.W. Crippled Children's Socy. 1967—; Chmn. Council Big Brother Movement 1947–70; Mem. Bd. Church of England Retirement Villages 1961—; Commonwealth Immigration Advisory Council; Liberal Party, President N.S.W. Division 1963–66, Federal Pres. 1966–70; Agent General for New South Wales in London 1970–72. Freeman, City of London 1973. *Clubs:* Boodle's, White's, (London); Imperial Service; Union, Australasian Pioneers, Sydney; Royal Sydney Golf; Royal Sydney Yacht. *Address:* 2 Lincoln Place, Edgecliff (Sydney), NSW 2027, Australia.

**PAGE, Rodney Graham,** PC, MBE, MP. *B.* 1911. *Educ.* Magdalen College School, Oxford and London University, LL.B., Hon. FIPA, FIWSP, FCCS. *M.* 1934. Hilda Agatha Dixon. *S.* Timothy Graham. *Dau.* Margaret Anne. *Career:* Solicitor 1934—. Privy Council Appeal Agent 1946–70 & since 1974; MP for Crosby since 1953; Minister of State, Housing and Local Government 1970; Min. Local Government and Development 1970–74; Chmn. of select cttee. of Parlt. on Statutory Instruments 1964–70 and since 1974; Member of the Law Society. *Publications:* Law Relating to Flats; Rent Act (1965); Author and promotor of following Acts of Parliament & Bills; Cheques Act 1957; Pawnbrokers Act 1960; Stock Transfer Act 1963; Payment of Wages Bill; several Road Safety Bills; National Sweepstake Bill;

Lotteries Bill, and others. *Address:* 21 Cholmeley Lodge, Highgate Hill, London N6.

**PAGE, Walter Hines.** American. *B.* 1915. *Educ.* Harvard College (BA 1937). *M.* 1942, Jane N. Nichols. *S.* Walter Hines, Jr. and Mark Nichols. *Dau.* Jane N. *Career:* With J. P. Morgan & Co. Inc. 1937–59; Bank merged with Guaranty Trust Co. of New York 1959; Vice-Pres. Morgan Guaranty Trust Co. 1959–64, and Senior Vice-Pres. 1964–65, Exec. Vice-Pres., 1965–68. Director 1967—, Morgan Guaranty Trust Co., New York. Pres. since 1971. Director: Kennecott Copper Corp., and Merck & Co. Inc. Dir. Foreign Policy Association; Trustee Carnegie Inst. of Washington D.C.; Dir.: Cold Spring Harbour N.Y. Laboratory; N.Y. Urban Coalition. *Member:* Council on Foreign Relations. *Club:* New York Yacht. *Address:* Cold Spring Harbor, N.Y. 11724; and *office* 23 Wall Street, New York, N.Y. 10015, U.S.A.

**PAGET, Richard M.** Management consultant. *B.* 1913. *Educ.* Northwestern Univ. (BS 1934). *M.* 1936, Inez Bouvea. *S.* Richard J. *Dau.* Nancy L. *Career:* In President's Office, Northwestern Univ., Evanston, Ill. 1934; Staff member, then Partner, Booz, Allen & Hamilton 1934–42. Management Engineer, Navy Dept.; commissioned Lieut. (j.g.) U.S.N.R.; returned to inactive duty as Captain (Legion of Merit) 1942–46; Partner in present firm 1946—; President Association of Consulting Management Engineers 1958–59, President, Cresap, McCormick & Paget, Inc., New York, Chicago, Washington, San Francisco, Sao Paulo, Melbourne. and London; Director: Skandia Re-Insurance Company: N.L. Industries Inc.; ICI America Wilmington Del; Company Trustee: Union Dime Savings Bank (N.Y.C.); Metropolitan Museum of Art, N.Y.C.; Northwestern U; Dir. The Washington Post Co. (Wash. D.C.); Liggett & Myers Inc. N.Y.; Simplicity Pattern Co. Inc., N.Y.; Member President's Advisory Council on Executive Organization 1969–70; Trustee, New York Univ. Medical Center, and Saint Barnabas Medical Center, Livingston, N.J. *Award:* Gilbreth Medal 1973. *Clubs:* University, Recess, Pinacle, Links, (N.Y.C.); Metropolitan (Washington, D.C.); Chicago (Chicago). *Address:* 32 Lakeview Ave., Short Hills, N.J. 07078; and *office* 235 Park Avenue, New York City 10017, U.S.A.

**PAGET-COOKE, Richard Anthony,** MBE, MA. Australian Public Relations Consultant. *B.* 1919. *Educ.* Eton Coll. (Scholar) and Christ Church, Oxford (MA). *M.* 1944, Dorothy Horbal. *Daus.* 2. *M.* 1975, Mary Wilkinson. *Career:* With Grenadier Guards 1940–46. Public relations appointments in fields of electricity supply, the printing industry, and International Advertising Conf. (Gt. Britain) 1951; Dir. of Public Relations, Foote, Cone & Belding Ltd. 1951–56; Chief P.R.O., Bowater Paper Corp. Ltd. 1956–58; joined Voice & Vision Ltd. (Public Relations Consultants) 1959; Executive Dir., Voice & Vision Ltd. 1963—68. Managing Director, Communications and Marketing 1968–70. Managing Dir. Charles Barker Aust. Pty. 1971–75; Dir. of Spec. Assignments, Charles Barlow Aust. Pty since 1975; Sec. to the Trustees, The Fleming Memorial Fund for Medical Research 1962–68; Mbr.: International Public Relations Association Inst. of Public Relations, Great Britain (Fellow and Past Pres.); Worshipful Company of Grocers, City of London (Liveryman). Fellow Public Relations Inst. of Australia. *Publications:* various articles on public relations in Britain, France, U.S.A., etc. since 1948. *Address:* 11th Floor Union Carbide Building 157-167 Liverpool Street, Sydney, N.S.W. 2000, Australia.

**PAGH, Mogens.** Chairman of the Board and Managing Director of The East Asiatic Company Ltd., Copenhagen. *B.* 1911. *Grad.* Fredericia High School 1929. Apprentice The East Asiatic Company Ltd., Copenhagen, Denmark 1929–31; overseas service Shanghai, Hong Kong, Canton 1931–39; Manager Hong Kong Office 1939–48; San Francisco Office 1949–52; Head Office, Copenhagen 1953; General Manager ibid. 1954–56; Managing Director 1956—; Chairman of the Board 1964—; Honorary Board Member ADELA Investment Co. S.A., Luxembourg; alternate Chairman of the Assembly of Representatives of Scandinavian Airlines System; Director A/S Net Danske Luftfartsselskab (Danish Air Lines); Chairman of the Board, The East Asiatic Co. Inc., USA; The West Indian Co., Ltd., St. Thomas, VI, USA; Tahsis Co. Ltd., Vancouver, Canada; The East Asiatic Co. (Canada) Ltd., Vancouver; and Plumrose A/S, Copenhagen; Vice-Chairman of the Board Den Danske Bank af 1871 A/S, Copenhagen; Board Member East Asiatic Company affiliated companies. Memberships: Academy of Technical Sciences; Chemical Bank International Advisory Board; General Motors European Advisory Council; Swiss Bank Corporation, Council of International Advisers; Foreign Policy Society; Danish Overseas League. *Awards:* Decorated Commander Order of Dannebrog; Second Class Order of the Sacred Treasure of Japan; Commander of the Most Noble Order of the Crown of Thailand. *Address:* 128 Taarbaek Strandvej, DK-2930 Klampenborg Denmark; and *office:* 2 Holbergsgade, DK-1099 Copenhagen K Denmark.

**PAGLIAL, Bruno.** Mexican Industrialist. *B.* 1902. *Educ.* Engineering studies in Italy. *S.* Bruno II. *Dau.* Francesca. *Career:* Pres.: Tubos de Acero de México S.A. 1952—; Alumino S.A. de C.V. 1963—; Organizacion Editorial Novaro S.A. 1964—; Industrias de Baleros Intercontinental 1966—; Lomas Verdes, S.A. de C.V.; Director: Industrial Minera México S.A. 1965—, Capital National Bank, Houston, Texas. Hon. Degree in Engineering, Univ. of Veracruz, Mexico. Commendatore and Grand Officiale dell' Ordine al Merito della Repubblica Italiana. Member Board of Trustees: San Carlos Museum; Member of Visiting Cttee.; Graduate School of Business Administration, Univ. of California. *Clubs:* Bankers; Jockey (of Mexico); Industriales. *Address:* Paseo de Lomas Atlas 164, Mexico 10 D.F.; and *office* Paris 15, Mexico 4 D.F., Mexico.

**PAHR, Willibald P.,** Dr. jur. Austrian. Minister for Foreign Affairs. *B.* 1930. *Educ.* Univ. of Vienna—Dr. jur. 1953; College d'Europe (Bruge). *M.* 1961, Inge Varga. *S.* 1. *Dau.* 1. *Career:* Scientific Asst. at the Inst. of International Law & International Relations at the Univ. of Vienna 1952–55; Constitutional Service at the Federal Chancellery of the Republic of Austria 1955–76 (Head of International Section 1968, Head of Dept. 1973, Dir.-Gen. 1975); Federal Minister for Foreign Affairs since 1976. *Member:* Austrian Assoc. for Administrative Sciences & for Political Sciences; Osterreichische Juristentag; Osterreichische Gesellschaft für Aussenpolitik; Vice-Pres., International Inst. for Human Rights. *Decorations:* Insigne d'Honneur en Or pour services rendus à la République d'Autriche; Grand Cross of the Greek Order of Phoenix. *Address:* 1130 Wien XIII, Granichstaedtengasse 31; and *office:* 1014 Wien 1, Ballhausplatz 2, Austria.

**PAHUD, Jean-Louis.** Swiss diplomat and advocate. *B.* 26 Oct. 1909. *Educ.* D.-en-D. *M.* 1968 Anne-Marie de Bousies. *Career:* With Federal Political Dept., Berne, 1938–40; Attaché, Legation, Cairo 1940–42 (2nd Secretary 1943–46, 1st Secretary 1946–47); with Commercial Division, Berne 1948–49; Chargé d'Affaires Sofia 1949; Counsellor, Legation, Madrid 1950–55; Chargé d'Affaires, Addis Ababa 1955–56; Ambassador: Cairo 1957–62; Brussels 1963–67, Mexico 1967. *Address:* Ministry of Foreign Affairs, Berne, Switzerland.

**PAI, Ei Whan.** Korean. Diplomat. *B.* 1907. *Educ.* Commercial High School, Pusan; Business College, Northeastern Univ. Boston, Mass., U.S.A.; Graduate School of Business Admin. New York Univ. (grad. 1937). *Career:* With Bank of Chosun, 1923–28; Straw Stock Brokerage Co., U.S.A., 1938–42; Dept. of Justice, U.S.A., 1942; Far Eastern Div., Office of Censorship and of Foreign Economic Admin., Washington, 1943–45; Asst. Dir. Financial Dept. Military Govt., Seoul, 1946–49; Pres. Korean Chamber of Commerce, 1950–60; Governor, Bank of Korea, 1960; Ambassador Extraordinary and Plenipotentiary to: Japan, 1961–64; Argentina, Chile, Paraguay, Uruguay, and Bolivia, 1965–67. Ambassador to the Court of St. James's, 1967–71; and concurrently to Malta and The Gambia, 1967–71; Ambassador at Large, Special Emissary of the President 1972–73; Pres. Overseas Economic Research Inst. since 1973; Member of the President's Council of Economic and Scientific Advisers 1974. *Address:* CPO Box 5864, Seoul, Republic of Korea.

**PAINE, Peter Standish.** American company director. *B.* 5 July 1909. *Educ.* Kent School; Princeton (AB). *M.* 1933, Ellen Cabeen Lea. *S.* Peter Standish. *Career:* Chmn., Nypen Co. since 1953; Chmn. Exec. Comm., Great Northern Nekoosa Corp; Chairman, Essex County Champlain National Bank; Director, Irving Trust Company, Consolidated Edison Co. of N.Y., The Continental Corp.; Chmn., The Juilliard School; Trustee, Lincoln Center for the Performing Arts. *Address:* 522 Fifth Avenue, New York, N.Y. 10036, U.S.A.

**PAISLEY, Rev. Ian Richard Kyle,** MP. Minister, Martyrs Memorial Free Church Belfast. *B.* 1926. *Educ.* Ballymena Model School; Tech. High School; S. Wales Bible Coll.; Reformed Presbyterian Theol. Coll. Belfast; Ordained 1946. *M.* 1956, Eileen Emily Cassells. *S.* 2. *Dau.* 3. *Career:* Minister Martyrs Memorial Free Church 1946—; Moderator, Free Presbyterian Church, Ulster 1951; Editor, The Revivalist

1950—; Published, The Protestant Telegraph 1966; Contested (Prot. U.) Bannside N.I. Parly. 1969; Member, Parliament (Prot. U.) North Antrim 1970—; Bannside Co. Antrim Parliament of N. Ireland 1970–72; Founder member, Ulster Democratic Unionist Party & elected Leader 1972; Leader of Opposition in House of Commons N.I. & Chmn. of Public Accounts Cttee. *Awards:* Hon. D.D. Bob Jones Univ.; SC. FRGS. *Publications:* History of the 1859 Revival (1959); Christian Foundations (1960); Exposition of the Epistle to Romans (1968); Billy Graham and the Church of Rome (1970); the Massacre of St. Bartholomew (1974); America's Debt. to Ulster (1976). *Address:* 'The Parsonage', 17 Cyprus Avenue, Belfast, Northern Ireland.

**PALAR, Lambertus Nicodemus.** Ambassador of Indonesia. *B.* 1902. *Educ.* Univs. of Djakarta and Amsterdam. *M.* 1935, Johanna Petronella Volmers. *S.* Bintoar. *Daus.* Noni and Maesi. *Career:* Represented Republic of Indonesia at U.N. Security Council Sept. 1947–Oct. 1950; Permanent Rep. (with rank of Ambassador) at U.N. 1950–53; Ambassador to India May 1953–Feb. 1956; to Federal Germany and U.S.S.R in 1956 (each for 10 weeks during visits of President Sukarno) to Canada 1957–62; Amb. & Perm. Rep. of Indonesia at U.N. 1963. *Address:* c/o Ministry of Foreign Affairs, Djakarta, Indonesia.

**PALEWSKI, Gaston.** French politician. *B.* 20 March 1901. *Educ.* Sorbonne (L. ès L.); Ecole des Sciences Politiques; Oxford University. *Career:* Attached to Political Office of Marshal Lyautey Resident-General in Morocco 1924–25; Chief de Cabinet, Min. of Justice and Colonies, later Director du Cabinet, Min. of Finance 1929–39; Dir. of Political Affairs of Free France 1940; Commander, Free French East African Forces 1941–42; Directeur du Cabinet of General de Gaulle 1942–46; member (in charge of international questions), Executive Committee, Rassemblement du Peuple Français since 1947; Deputy (6th Sector, Seine) since July 1951; 1st Vice-Pres., Natl. Assembly; member, Committee for Foreign Affairs; Minister-Delegate to Presidency Council Feb.–Oct. 1955; Ambassador to Italy 1957–62; Minister of State for Scientific Research and Atomic and Spatial Questions Apr. 1962–65. President of the Constitutional Council 1965–74; Membre de l'Institut (Académic des Beaux-Arts) since 1968. *Awards:* Grand Cross of the Legion of Honour; Compagnon de la Liberation; Hon. Fellow Worc. Coll. Oxford since 1974. *Address:* 1 Rue Bonaparte, Paris 6e, France; and H9 rue de Valois, Paris 1 and Château du Marais par Saint-Chéron, 91–Essonne.

**PALLISER, Sir (Arthur) Michael,** GCMG. British diplomat. *B.* 1922. *Educ.* Wellington Coll.; Merton Coll. Oxford. *M.* 1948, Marie Marguerite Spaak. *S.* 3. *Career:* served Cold. stream Guards 1942–47, Capt. 1944; Entered H.M. Diplomatic Service 1947; Ambassador Head U.K. Delegation European Communities Brussels 1971–73; Ambassador and Permanent Rep. to European Communities 1973–75; Perm. Under Secy. of State and Head of Dipl. Service since 1975. *Award:* Chevalier, Order of Orange Nassau; Legion d'Honneur. *Address:* Foreign and C'wealth Office, London, S.W.1.

**PALMAR, Derek James.** British Chartered Accountant. *B.* 1919. *Educ.* Dover Col. *M.* 1946, Edith Brewster. *S.* 1. *Dau.* 1. *Career:* With Peat, Marwick, Mitchell & Co., Chartered Accountants, 1937–57. Served in Royal Artillery and Staff 1941–46; Lt.-Col. 1945; Dir. Hill Samuel Group Ltd. 1957–70. Industrial Adviser to the Department of Economic Affairs 1965–67; Member British Railways Bd. 1968–72; Dover Harbour Board 1964–75; Chmn., Bass Charrington, Rush & Tompkins Group Ltd., British Railways London & South-Eastern Board; Dir., Grindlays Bank, Hall-Thermotank Ltd., Howard Machinery Ltd. *Club:* Boodles. *Address:* The Old Forge, nr. Bore Place, Chiddingstone, Kent; and *office* 7 Grosvenor Gardens, London S.W.1.

**PALME, Olaf.** Swedish politician. Chmn., Swedish Social Democratic Labour Party; Vice-Pres., Socialist International. *B.* 1927. *Educ.* Stockholm Univ. Law Degree (Jur. Kand); Kenyon Coll. Ohio (BA). *M.* 1956, Lisbeth Beck-Friis. *S.* Joakim, Marten and Mattias. *Career:* Member of Parliament since 1957; Minister without Portfolio, 1963–65; of Communications 1965–67; of Education, 1967–69; Prime Minister 1969–76. *Awards:* Honorary Doctors Degree, Kenyon College. *Address:* Lövångersgatan 31 Vällingby Sweden, and *office* Riksdagen, 10012 Stockholm 46.

**PALMER, Arthur Montague Frank,** MP. British Chartered Engineer and Member of Parliament. *B.* 1912. *Educ.* Grammar School and Technological University. *M.* 1939, Dr. Marion Woollaston. *Daus.* 2. *Career:* Student Engineer, Met. Elec. Supply Co., London 1932–35; Junior Transmission Engr. 1933–36; Tech. Asst., Head Office, London Power Company 1936–45; National Officer, Electrical Power Engineers' Assoc. since 1945; Labour MP for Wimbledon 1945–50, Labour and Co-op MP for Cleveland Div. of Yorks 1952–59, for Bristol Central 1964–74, for Bristol North East since 1974; sometime Front Bench Spokesman for Parliamentary Labour Party (Energy Matters) 1957–59; Chmn., Parliamentary Scientific Cttee. 1964–66; Chmn., Select Cttee. of House of Commons on Science and Technology 1966–70, 1974—. *Member:* Inst. of Electrical Engineers; Inst. of Fuel; Royal Society of Arts; Royal Institution; Fabian Society. *Decorations:* Defence Medal; Queen's Coronation Medal. *Publications:* Future of Electricity Supply; Nationalisation of the British Electricity Supply Industry; Modern Norway; Law and the Power Engineer; and many articles on technical, economic and political subjects. *Clubs:* R.A.C. *Address:* 14 Lavington Court, 77 Putney Hill, London SW15 3NU; and *office* EPEA, 140 Lower Marsh, London SE1 7AE.

**PALMER, Hon Gordon William Nottage,** OBE, TD, DL. JP, MA. British. *B.* 1918, *Educ.* Eton Coll.; Christ Church, Oxford (MA). *M.* 1950, Lorna Eveline Hope Bailie. *S.* 2, *Career:* former Man. Dir. Huntley & Palmers Ltd.; Dir. Huntley Boorne & Stevens Ltd.; Chmn. and Man. Dir. Associated Biscuits Ltd.; Vice-Chmn. Assoc. Biscuit Manufacturers Ltd. *Member:* Inst. of Directors; British Inst. Management; Chmn. Council Royal Coll. of Music; former Pres. Council Reading Univ.; former Hon. Colonel, Royal Yeomanry; Vice Lord-Lieutenant for the County of Berkshire. *Club:* Cavalry. *Address:* Harris House, Mortimer, Berks.; and *office* 121 King's Road, Reading, Berks.

**PALMER, Philip.** Ambassador of Sierra Leone to the U.S.A. *B.* 1940. *Educ.* Durham Univ.; trained as Examiner for W. African Exams Council. *Career:* Ambassador to Ethiopia 1970; engaged in OAU cttees; Ambassador to U.S.A. since 1972 and High Commissioner to Trinidad and Tobago and Jamaica since 1973; Permanent Rep. of Sierra Leone to United Nations (1974); Ambassador to Brazil 1976; High Commissioner to Canada 1977. *Address:* 1701 19th Street, N.W. Washington, D.C. 20009, U.S.A.

**PALMER, Richard Creighton.** American business executive (Ret'd). *B.* 1903. *Educ.* Denison Univ. (Ph.B. 1926); Univ. of Denver (LL.B *cum laude* 1929); Oxford Univ., England (special law subjects) 1929–30. *M.* 1933, Jeanette Ripley. *S.* Brooks Ripley. *Daus.* Hollis Ann and Linda (Bostchen). *Career:* Reporter, Cleveland (O.) News 1920–26. Admitted Colorado Bar 1929; partner law firm of Lewis & Bond, Denver 1929–36; Sec. to Congressman Lawrence Lewis, Denver 1932–36; Attorney, Office of General Counsel Bureau of Internal Revenue, Washington, D.C. 1936–39; Secy. to Senator Alva R. Adams 1939–40, and to Senator Eugene D. Millikin 1940–42; Asst. Director, National Aircraft War Production Council, Washington 1943–44; Gen. Mgr. 1944–45; Asst. to Pres., Fairchild Engine & Airplane Corp. 1945–58; Vice-Pres.: Stromberg Carlson of General Dynamics, 1958–62: Mack Trucks Inc., 1962–65; U.S. State Dept. Overseas Private investment Corp. (a Govt. Agency) 1965–71. Pres., National Security Industrial Assn.; N.S.I. Forrestal Award Committee. Member, Board of Trustees, Temple Buell College; Trustee, Woodside Methodist Church, Silver Spring, Md. *Member:* American Ordnance Assn., Lambda Chi Alpha, Ph. Delta Phi, Tau Kappa Alpha, Fourth Estate. *Clubs:* National Aviation; Aero (Washington); Wings (N.Y.C.); Metropolitan (Washington, D.C.); Columbia Country (Chevy Chase, Md.). *Address:* 15 King Ave., Jekyll Island, Georgia 31520, U.S.A.

**PALTHEY, Georges Louis Claude.** French. *B.* 1910. *Educ.* Institution des Chartreux; Faculté catholique, Lyon; and Sorbonne, Ecole libre des Sciences politiques, Paris (Doctor in Law 1934). *M.* (1) 1938, Marie-Louise Bourdin. *S.* François. (2) 1967, Jacqueline De Roll. *Career:* Finance Officer, Control of Expenditure Commitments, Ministry of Finance, France 1934; Chief of Secretariat, General Dept. of Economic Control 1942; Deputy Financial Comptroller of French Missions in Great Britain 1945; Secy.-Gen., French Supplies Board in Great Britain 1947; Director of Personnel, United Nations 1948. Deputy Director-General of the United Nations Office at Geneva 1954–75 (Retired). *Publications:* Le contrôle préalable des finances publiques. *Address:* 2 rue des Granges, Geneva; and *office* Palais des Nations, Geneva, Switzerland.

**PANA, Gheorghe.** Romanian politician. *B.* 1927. *Educ.* Academy of Economic Sciences Bucharest. *M.* Antoaneta. *Dau.* 1. *Career:* First Secy. Brasov Regional Cttee. 1966–68; County Cttee. R.C.P. 1968–69; Chmn. Exec. Cttee. Brasnov County People's Council 1968–69; Member Exec. Cttee. Permanent Presidium 1969–74; Secy. Central Cttee. R.C.P. 1969–75; Deputy to the Grand National Assembly; Member, Nat. Council, Front Socialist Unity 1968—; State Council 1969–75; Chmn., General Trade Union Confed. 1975—. Hero of Socialist Labour. *Address:* General Trade Union Confederation, 14 Aleea Stefan Gheorghiu, Bucharest, Romania.

**PANCER, Louis.** Canadian consulting mining engineer. *B.* 1918. *Educ.* Univ. of Toronto (BASc. 1941). *Career:* Pres. and Man. Dir., Apollo Porcupine Mines Ltd.; Director: Canadian Dyno Mines Ltd., International Lithium Mining Corp. Ltd.; Pres.: Cerpan Financial Corp. Ltd.; Basalt Bay Mines Ltd., New Goldvue Mines Ltd.; Duvex Oils & Mines Ltd.; Director: Canadian Manganese Mining Corp. Ltd. On Staff of Department of Mining Engineering, University of Toronto 1941–46. *Address:* 121 Richmond Street West, Toronto, Ont., Canada.

**PANT, Yadav Prasad,** KCVO. Nepali Diplomat. *B.* 1928. *Educ.* Banaras Hindu Univ., India—BA, MA, PhD, D.Litt. *M.* 1942, Rama Devi Pant. *S.* 3. *Dau.* 1. *Career:* Prof. of Economics, Tri-Chandra Coll. 1951–57; Mem., Nepal's First Planning Commission 1954–56; Economist, UN Economic Comm. for Asia & Far East 1957–59; Chief Economic Advisor to His Majesty's Govt. 1959–61; Mem., National Planning Board 1959–61; Sec., Ministry of Finance & Economic Affairs 1961–66, Ministry of Finance & Economic Planning 1966–68; Visiting Prof., UN Asian Inst. of Economic Development & Planning 1965, 1969; Guest Prof., Inst. of Social Studies 1970; Snr. mem., Nat. Planning Comm. 1968–72; Gov., Nepal Rastra (Central) Bank 1968–73; Ambassador to Japan since 1974. *Member:* Pres., Nepal Assoc.; Fellow, Royal Economic Soc., London; Former Vice-Pres., Nepal Red Cross Soc.; Former Pres., Nepal UN Assoc.; Fellow, International Bankers' Assoc. *Decorations:* Knight Commander, Victorian Order (1961); Gorkha Dakshin Bahu Class 1 (1963); Mahendra Bidya Bhushan (1963); Tri Sakti Patta Class 1 (1964); Janapada Sewapadak (1967). *Publications:* Principles of Economics (1955); Planning in Underdeveloped Economies (1957); A Study in Industrial Location (1957); Planning for Prosperity in Nepal (1957); Nepal's Development on International Basis (1957); Economic Development of Nepal (1965); Fiscal & Monetary Problems in Nepal (1970); Development Problems of Smaller Countries (1974). *Clubs:* Foreign Correspondents' Club of Japan; International House of Japan. *Address:* 25-6, Minami-Azabu 1-chome, Minato-ku, Tokyo; and *office* 16-23, Higashi-Gotanda 3-chome, Shinagawa-ku, Tokyo, Japan.

**PANYARACHUN, Anand.** Thai. Diplomat. *B.* 9 Aug. 1932. *Educ.* Bangkok Christian Coll.; Dulwich Coll. London; BA (Hon) Univ. of Cambridge, England. *M.* 1956, Sodsee Chakrabandh. *Daus.* Nanda, Daranee. *Career:* Joined Min. Foreign Affairs Bangkok 1955; Secy. to Minister of Foreign Affairs 1959–64; First Secy. Permanent Mission of Thailand to the United Nations 1964–66; Counsellor and Charge d'Affaires a.i. Permanent Mission of Thailand to the United Nations 1966–67; Ambassador Ext. and Plenipotentiary of Thailand to Canada and to the United Nations 1967–72, Permanent Representative 1972–75, concurrently Ambassador Extra. and Plenipotentiary to the U.S.A. 1972–75; Under-Secy. of State for Foreign Affairs 1975–76; Ambassador-designate to Federal Republic of Germany 1977. *Member:* Delegation of Thailand International Conference on Settlement of the Laotian Question 1961–62, at Geneva; Del. of Thailand to Several SEATO Council Meetings; Rep. of Thailand, 15th Session, from 18th to 26th Session, United Nations/Gen. Assembly also (Thailand) in other United Nations bodies. *Clubs:* Royal Bangkok Sports. *Address:* c/o Ministry of Foreign Affairs, Bangkok, Thailand.

**PANZERA, Dr. Alfred.** Austrian government official. Counsellor. *B.* 1921. *Educ.* High School and Univ. of Vienna; Univ. of Aberdeen and Berlin. *M.* 1956, Anni Jaeger. *S.* Alfred, Jr. *Dau.* Ingrid. *Career:* Lecturer in English, Univ. Extension of Vienna 1945.; With Central Office of Statistics 1949—Counsellor Central Branch for Austrian Companies 1964; Secretary General since 1972. *Member:* Austrian Statistical Society, Society for the National Economy; Biometric Society, and other associations. *Publications:* Modern International Bank and Currency Arrangements and their Significance in National and World Economy, (1948); Austrian Companies in 19th and 20th Centuries, (1960); Source of Austrian Housing and Building Statistics, (1961); The Housing Situation and the Building Industry in Europe, (1968); Management of Small Timber Firms (1973). *Address:* Gentzgasse 57–14, A-180 Vienna, Austria.

**PAPADOPOULOS, Achilles Symeon,** MVO, MBE. British Diplomat. *B.* 1923. *Educ.* The English Sch., Nicosia. *M.* 1954, Joyce Martin Stark. *S.* 1. *Daus.* 2. *Career:* British Military Administration, Eritrea 1943–52; HM Overseas Civil Service, Cyprus 1953–59, Tanganyika 1959–61; Dir., British Information Services, Malta 1961–64; HM Diplomatic Service: Malta 1964–65; 1st Sec., Nairobi 1965–68; Asst. Head of UN Dept., FCO 1968–71; Head of Chancery, Colombo 1971–74; Counsellor, Washington 1974; Counsellor & Head of Chancery, Havana 1974–77; HM Ambassador, San Salvador since 1977. *Decorations:* Member of the Royal Victorian Order (4th Class), 1972; Member of the Order of the British Empire, 1954. *Address:* 5 Lansdowne Close, Wimbledon, London SW20; and *office* c/o Foreign & Commonwealth Office, London SW1A 2AH.

**PAPADOPOULOS, Christakis Georghiou.** Company director. *B.* Jan. 1916. *Educ.* Greek Gymnasium, Famagusta; American Academy, Larnaca. *M.* 1947, Marie Alex. Diab. *Career:* Chmn. Man. Dir., The Cyprus Shipping Co., Ltd., The United Sea Transport Co. Ltd., The Cyprus Bonded Warehouses & Shipping Co. Ltd, Famagusta. Dir. Middle East Agents Ltd.; Seafarer Navigation Co. Ltd, Famagusta; Cyprus Freighters Co. Ltd, Famagusta; Cyprus Merchants Shipping Co. Ltd, Famagusta; Chmn. The Cyprus Development Bank Ltd, Nicosia; Pres. Fed. of Trade and Industry 1955–56; The Rotary Club 1962–63; Municipal Port Cttee. 1962–64 (all Famagusta); Chmn. The Cyprus Shipping Assn. 1968–69; Dir. Salamis Shipping Lines Ltd; Kourion Shipping Lines Ltd (Shipowning Companies). *Address:* Democratias Avenue, 63 Famagusta; and *office* P.O. Box 73, Limassol, Cyprus.

**PAPADOPOULOS, George.** Greek politician. *B.* 1919. *Educ.* Military Cadet School; High Acad. of War; High Naval Academy; Artillery School; Officers Training School in Middle East; Special Forces Training School. *M.* (twice). *S.* 1. *Daus.* 2. *Career:* Graduated from Military School, 1940 and rose to rank of Brigadier General, 1967. Fought throughout Greek-Italian war (1940) and, following German-Italian occupation of Greece, joined National Resistance Units. Served against Guerilla Forces as Commander of Artillery Battery. Subsequently, Artillery School Instructor, Battery Commander, Intelligence Burea. Chief of Staff in Artillery Div., Head of National Security and Counter-Intelligence, Commander of F.A. unit, Staff Bureau of Army General Staff, and served with other military units; Prime Minister 1967–73. Imprisoned since 1975. *Awards:* Decorated, Gold Cross for Gallantry; six Military Crosses; Distinguished Services Medal; George I Silver Cross with crossed swords; George I Gold Cross; Medal of Military Merit; Cross of Commander of the Royal Order of the Phoenix, and many other military awards.

**PAPPAS, Costas Ernest.** American aeronautical engineer. *B.* 1910. *Educ.* New York Univ. (BS 1933; MS 1934); Recipient Wright Bros. Award, Socy. of Automotive Engineers 1943; Award, Rep. Aviation Corp. 1944; Certificate of Distinction, N.Y. Univ. Coll. of Engineering 1955. *M.* 1940, Thetis Hero. *S.* Conrad. *Dau.* Alceste. *Career:* Successively Stress Analyst, 1935–39, Chief of Aerodynamics 1939–54; Chief of Aerodynamics & Thermodynamics 1954–57, and Asst. Director of Scientific Research 1957–59, Republic Aviation Corp. Consultant to Aerospace Industry 1964—. Assistant to Vice-President Research and Development, Secretariat for Advanced Planning, Republic Aviation Corporation 1959–64; Chairman, Vehicle Design Panel 1960— and Member, Membership Cttee. 1955—, Member, Advisory Board, San Francisco Section, 1970; Chmn. Work-Shop for Professional Employment AIAA; Pres. San Francisco Peninsula Alumnus Tau Beta Pi; Member Air Force Assn; National Socy. of Professional Engineers; California Socy. of Professional Engineers. American Institute of Aeronautics and Astronautics. Member New York Univ. Alumni Visiting Committee; member Natl. Adv. Cttee. for Aeronautics (Sub-Cttee. High-Speed Aero. 1947–53; Special Sub-Cttee. Research Problems, Transonic Aircraft Design 1948). *Member:* Ramjets Panel, American Rocket Socy. Professional Engineer, licensed in State of New York & California. *Award:* AIAA (San Francisco), Award for contributions to section, 1974 .*Publications:* The Determination of Fuselage Moments, (1944); The Effects of a Fuselage upon the Stability of an Airplane, (1944); Compressibility Calls a

Challenge, (1944); Effect of Temperature Lapse Rate on Recovery from Compressibility Dives, (1945); Analysing the Aspects of Future Flight, (1945); An Investigation of the Aerodynamics of Sharp Leading Edge Swept Wings at Low Speeds, (1954); Design Concepts and Technical Studies of an Aerospace Plane, (1961), etc. *Member:* Tau Beta Pi, Iota, Alpha, Assoc. Fellow AIAA; British Interplanetary Socy.; Amer. Assn. for Advancement of Science; Amer. Geophysical Union. Consultant, Scientific Advisory Board U.S.A.F.—Aero Space Vehicles Panel. *Club:* Commonwealth (Calif.). *Address:* 2 Admiral Drive, 477 Emeryville, Calif. 94608.

**PARARAJASINGAM, Sir Sangarapillai.** Ceylonese businessman and planter. *B.* 25 June 1896. *Educ.* St. Thomas' College, Mt. Lavinia, Ceylon. *M.* 1916, Padmavati, daughter of Sir Ponnambalam Arunachalam. *S.* 1. *Dau.* 1. *Career:* Senator (United National Party) 1954–59; JP since 1923; formerly Chmn. Bd. of Dirs., Agricultural & Industrial Credit Corp., Ceylon; Chairman, Education Cttee., Ceylon Social Service League; Chairman, Low Country Products Assn. 1943–44 and 1944–45; Past President, Board of Directors, Manipay Hindu College (Manager 1929–60); Chairman, Ceylon Coconut Board and Coconut Commn.; member, Textile Tribunal; Ceylon Tea Propaganda Board; Coconut Research Scheme; Radio Advisory Board; Excise Advisory Cttee.; Central Board of Agriculture; Income Tax Board of Review; Rice Advisory Board; Services Standing Wages Board; National Savings Cttee.; Motor Tribunal of Appeal; Commn. on Broadcasting; Member, Board of Governors, Ceylon Inst. of Scientific and Industrial Research; Former Chmn., Colonial Motors. (1961–74). Holds Coronation Medals of King George VI and Queen Elizabeth II. *Address:* 50 Pathmalaya, Flower Road, Colombo 7, Sri Lanka.

**PARDO, Prof. Arvid.** Maltese Diplomat and Academic. *B.* 1914 *Educ.* Collegio Mondragone, Frascati, Italy; Univ. of Rome; Univ. of Tours, France. *M.* 1947, Margit Claeson. *S.* 2. *Dau.* 1. *Career:* Archivist, UN 1945–46; Trusteeship Dept., UN 1946–60; UN Development Programme 1961–64; Perm. Rep. of Malta to the UN 1964–71; Amb. of Malta to the U.S. 1967–71; High. Comm. of Malta to Canada 1968–71; Amb. of Malta to Soviet Union 1968–70; Amb. of Malta for Ocean Affairs 1971–73; Fellow, Centre for Study of Democratic Institutions, Santa Barbara 1971–72; Dir. Ocean Programme, W. Wilson International Centre for Scholars, Washington D.C. 1972–75; Prof. of Political Science & International Law, Fellow Inst. of Marine & Coastal Studies, Univ. of Southern California since 1975. *Awards:* Hon. Doctor of Science (Iowa, Wesleyan). *Publications:* Il Trattato di Locarno (1939); The Common Heritage (1974); (co-author) The New International Economic Order & The Law of the Sea (1976). *Address:* 11972 Kiowa Avenue, West Los Angeles, California 90049, U.S.A.; and *office* University Southern California, Political Science Dept., V.K.C. 327, Los Angeles.

**PARDOE, John Wentworth,** MA, MP. British politician. *B.* 1934. *Educ.* Master of Arts (Cantb.) in Economics & English. *M.* 1958, Joyce Rosemary Peerman. *S.* Rupert Adam Corin and Jonathon Francis. *Dau.* Tanya Kate. *Career:* Executive, Television Audience Measurement Ltd. London, 1958–60; with Osborne Peacock Co. Ltd. London, 1960–61; Gen. Manager, Liberal News (weekly newspaper) 1961–66; Member of Parliament for North Cornwall since 1966; Treas. of the Liberal Party 1968–69; Dir. Gerald Metals Ltd. London (Int. Metal Merchants); Sight & Sound Ltd., London. *Member:* London Metal Exchange. *Publications:* Crusade Against the Selfish Society; Integration and Choice; We Must Conquer Inflation. *Address:* House of Commons, London, S.W.1.

**PARIS, Jacques-Emile.** French. Ambassador of France. *B.* 1905. *Educ.* Licencié ès lettres et en droit. *M.* 1934, Monique de Romrée. *S.* Marc. *Dua.* Gilda. *Career:* Minister to Bulgaria 1945; Ambassador to Syria 1950, Iran 1954, Rumania 1955, and Ireland 1960–64, to Luxembourg 1964. Commander Legion of Honour (France); Medal of the Resistance. *Address:* 12 Avenue Paul-Doumer, Paris 16e.

**PARISEAULT, Philippe,** BA, BSA, LSA. Canadian agronomist. *B.* Québec City, 11 March 1915. *Educ.* Assumption College; Univ. of Ottawa (BA 1937); Agricultural Inst. of Oka (BSA and LSA 1941); Univ. of Montreal. *M.* 1942, Marguerite Poulin. *S.* Claude. *Daus.* Lise, Monique, Ginette. *Career:* Former General Manager, Agricultural Co-operative. of Granby 1955–76; Dir., Dairy Division Co-operative Fédérée de Québec; Pres. and Dir.-Gen. Quebec-Lait Inc.; Vice-Pres.: Sino Canadian Dairy & Co. Ltd.; Centres Agricoles of Quebec. Dir., General Investment Corporation; Legrade Inc.; David Lord Ltd.; Chmn., Advisory Cttee., Canadian Dairy Commission; Dir. National Dairy Council of Canada, and Canadian Agronomist Association. *Address:* 40 Elm Avenue, Granby, Shefford County, Canada.

**PARK, Chung Hee.** Korean. President of Republic of Korea. *B.* 1917. *Educ.* Taegu Normal School; Military Acad. of Manchukuo; Japanese Imperial Military Academy; R.O.K. Military Acad.; U.S. Artillery School Advanced Course; R.O.K. Command and General Staff Coll. *M.* 1950, Yook Young Soo (*D.* 1974). *S.* 1. *Dau.* 2. *Career:* Teacher Mungyong Pr. School, N. Kyronsang Province, 1937–40; First Lieut. Japanese Army 1945; Capt. R.O.K. Army 1946, Brigadier-General 1953; Commandant Artillery School and Commander Artillery R.O.K. Army 1954; Comm.-General 5th R.O.K. Infantry Div. 1955; Deputy-Com.-General VI R.O.K. Corps. 1957; Comm.-General 7th R.O.K. Infantry Div. 1957; Major-General, Chief of Staff 1st R.O.K. Army 1958; Comm.-General 6th Military District Command 1959; Comm.-General Logistics Base, 1st Military District, Deputy-Chief of Staff for Ops. R.O.K. Army Headquarters, Deputy-Comm.-General 2nd R.O.K. Army all 1960; Led Military Revolution May 1961; Chmn. S.C.N.R. and General R.O.K. Army 1961; Acting President, concurrently Prime Minister (June 18–July 10) 1962; Elected President of Republic of Korea 1963, re-elected 1967, 1971 and 1972 (under new constitution). *Publications:* Leadership: In the midst of the Revolutionary Process (1961); People's Path to the Fulfilment of the Revolutionary Tasks: Direction of National Movement (1961); Our Nation's Path (1962); The Country, the Revolution and I (1963); To Build a Nation (1971); Toward Peaceful Unification (1976). *Address:* Ch'ong Wa Dae (Executive Mansion), Seoul, Korea.

**PARK, Samuel Culver, Jr.** American. *B.* 1903. *Educ.* Yale Univ. (Ph.B.) and Harvard Univ. (MBA). *M.* 1930, Katharine Anderson. *Career:* Director: Great Northern Paper Co. 1942–47, Hewitt-Robins Inc. 1944–65; Partner, J. H. Whitney & Co. 1946–59; Vice-Pres. & Dir. Interior Design 1949–59; Dir. Scientific American Inc., 1946–54; Vice-President & Director, San Jacinto Petroleum Corp. 1950–59. Dir., Southern General Insurance Co. 1954–59; N.Y. Airways Inc. 1954–68. Field Adviser, Small Business Administration 1955–60; N.Y. Herald Tribune S.A. 1958–67; Partner, Whitcom Investment Co. 1967–68; Vice-Pres. Dir. Greentree Stud Inc; Chmn. of Finance Cttee. and Dir. Whitney Communications Corp; Financial Associate, John Hay Whitney; Pres. and Dir. Greenwood Seed Co.; Vice-Pres. and Dir., Kern House Enterprises Ltd. 1965–74; Trustee, U.S. Trust Co. of New York 1954–75, Hon. Trustee 1975—; Trustee, John Hay Whitney Foundation 1950—; Gov., New York Hospital 1963–75, Life Gov. 1975—; Dir.: Talcott National Corp., 1968–73; James Talcott Inc., 1963–73; Geovision Inc., I.H.T. Corp. (formerly N.Y. Herald Tribune), Parade Publications 1968–73. *Clubs:* Links, River, Union, University (all N.Y.C.); Piping Rock (Long Island). *Address:* 850 Park Avenue, New York, N.Y. 10021; and *office* 110 West 51st Street, New York, N.Y. 10020, U.S.A.

**PARKER, Gordon Davenport.** British. *B.* 1914. *Educ.* Preparatory and private tutor. *M.* 1935, Sybil Louise Dormer. *Dau.* Carole Ann. *Career:* Clerk, Basic Slag and Phosphate Companies Ltd., London 1930–34; Asst. Secretary, Kimolo Manufacturers Ltd. 1935–44; General Manager, British Uralite Ltd. 1944–48. Chmn. since 1948. *Address:* British Uralite Ltd., Higham, Rochester, Kent.

**PARKER, James Roland Walter,** OBE, CMG. British diplomat. *B.* 1919. *Educ.* Southall Grammar School. *M.* 1941, Deirdre Mary Ward. *Career:* Ministry of Labour 1938–57; H.M. Forces 1940–41; Labour Attache Tel Aviv 1957–60; Labour Adviser Accra 1960–62, to Lagos 1962–64; Seconded to Foreign Office 1965–66; Ist Secy. Lagos 1966; Deputy High Commissioner Enugu 1966–67; Foreign and Commonwealth Office 1968–70; Head, Chancery British High Comm. Suva 1970–71; British High Commissioner to the Gambia 1971–75; HM Consul-General, Durban 1976; Gov. and C. in C. of the Falkland Islands since 1977. *Clubs:* Travellers'; M.C.C. *Address:* 1 St. Edmund's Court, St. Edmund's Terrace, London, N.W.8, and *office* Government House, Stanley, Falkland Islands.

**PARKER, John,** CBE, MA, MP. Politician. *B.* 1906. *Educ.* Marlborough College; History Scholar, Oxford. *M.* 1943, Zena Mimardiere. *S.* Michael John. *Career:* Assistant to Dir. Merseyside Social Survey, Liverpool Univ. 1929–32; Gen. Sec. New Fabian Research Bureau, 1933–39; Gen. Secy.

Fabian Socy. 1939–45; MP for Romford, 1935–45; Parliamentary Sec. Dominions Office, 1945–46; Member, Parliament, Labour, Dagenham, 1945—; Publisher, 1947–67. *Member:* National Trust E.C. since 1970; Historic Buildings Council since 1974; Inland Waterways Amenity Adv. Council since 1969; Member Speaker's Conferences 1944, 1965/6, 1973–74; Trade Union Transport & General. Yugoslav Red Star 1975. *Publications:* The Small Business; 42 Days in Soviet Union; Newfoundland; Harold Wilson; Willy Brandt. *Clubs:* Arts. *Address:* 4 Essex Court, Temple, London, E.C.4; and *office* House of Commons, London, S.W.1.

**PARKER, Hon. Mr. Justice Glenn.** Instructor and Lecturer, Wyoming Law School 1935–75. *B.* 1898. *Educ.* University of Wyoming (AB 1922; LLB 1927); Rhodes Scholar 1922 (Exeter 1923); graduate work, University of Chicago, 1922. *M.* (1), 1924, Ruth Beggs (D. 1971), *S.* William Robert (West Point grad. class 1946). *Dau.* Marilyn Ruth (Mrs. William T. Reeder; (2), 1972, Sarah J. Weitz. *Career:* Instructor of English, Laramie High School (Wyo.), 1922–23; Principal and Superintendent of schools, Casper (Wyo.) 1923–26; admitted to Wyoming State Bar 1927; Attorney, Laramie City, 1930–32, and Albany County 1932–42; Colonel, Judge Advocate General's Dept. (J.A.G.D.), U.S.A., 1942–46; Liaison Officer to U.S. Dept. of State; now Colonel, J.A.G.D. Retired. Judge of Second Judicial District, Wyoming, 1949–55; Justice of Supreme Court, Wyoming, 1955–75, Chief Justice 1963–67; Chief Justice, Wyoming Court 1973–75. Now lawyer with Hirst & Applegate. Was a rancher, Big Horn, Wyoming, until 1917 (i.e. until first year at Univ. of Wyoming). *Awards:* Univ. of Wyoming Outstanding Alumnus Honor Award 1958; U.S. Army Special Commendation; Rotary Pres. 1935 & 1967; 33° Mason. *Address:* 100 W. 29th Street, Cheyenne, Wyo., 82001 and *office* 200 Boyd Building, P.O. Box 1346, Cheyenne, U.S.A.

**PARKER, Ralph Douglas.** *B.* 1898. *Educ.* University of California (B.Sc. Mining); Hon. LL.D. Laurentian University of Sudbury; University of California. *M.* 1930, Mina Bayne Todhunter. *Career:* Placer Mining in Butte county, California, then to Cherry Creek Mining Co., Vernon, B.C., Canada 1920–21. Asst. Mine Superintendent: McIntyre Porcupine Mines, Schumacher, Ont. 1921–28; International Nickel Co. of Canada, Copper Cliff, Ont. (Supt. Creighton Mine 1928–29); Supt., Frood Mines 1929–31; Supt. of Mines 1931–35; General Supt. Mining and Smelting Div. 1935–47, Asst. Vice-Pres. 1947–54; Asst. Vice-Pres. and Gen. Mgr., Canadian Operations 1954–55 (Vice-Pres. and Gen. Mgr. 1955–57; elected a Director 1957; Vice-Pres. 1958; Senior Vice-Pres. May 1960); retired as Senior Vice-Pres. and continues as a Consultant, Apr. 1963, retired 1967. Served in U.S. Army (Machine Gun Corps and Officers Training Camp) 1917–18. Honorary Chairman, Board of Governors, Laurentian Univ. of Sudbury. *Member:* Canad. Institute of Mining & Metallurgy; American Institute of Mining, Metallurgical & Petroleum Engineers. *Clubs:* Idylwylde Golf and Country (Sudbury); Hunt, Toronto, Rosedale, York (Toronto). Protestant. *Address:* Apt. 503, 235 St. Clair Street West, Toronto, Ont. M4V 1R4, Canada.

**PARKER, Thomas James.** Australian company director. *B.* 1888. *Educ.* Australia; Germany; Charterhouse, England; *M.* 1922, Phyllis McWilliam. *S.* 2. *Daus.* 3. Joined Huddart Parker Ltd. 1906; served World War I, R.F.A., France, Flanders and Italy 1915–19; member, British Military Mission to Austria 1918; Hon. Consul for Austria 1929–38. *Address:* 19 Wentworth Road, Vaucluse, N.S.W., Australia.

**PARKES, Geoffrey,** CMG. British company director. *B.* 24 April 1902. *Educ.* Clifton College; L'Institut Technique, Roubaix. *M.* 1925, Marjorie Syddal (*D.* 1976). *Career:* Director, Narrow Fabrics, Ministry of Supply and Hon. Advisor to Board of Trade 1939–44; Director-General, Textiles and Light Industries Branch. Control Commission for Germany 1944–46, Deputy Chief, Trade and Industry Division 1946; Director: Small & Parkes Ltd. 1927–64; Geigy (Holdings) Ltd. 1943–66; District Bank 1948–69; National Provincial Bank 1963–69; Deputy Chairman, National Westminster Bank, North Region. 1969–72; Member, Court, Manchester Univ. 1949–69; FTI, JP City of Manchester 1949–65. MA (*h.c.*) Manchester Univ. 1966. *Address:* Berth-y-Coed, Colwyn Bay, North Wales.

**PARKHURST, George Leigh.** Lawyer and chemical engineer. *B.* 1907. *Educ.* Illinois Inst. of Technology (BS) and De Paul Univ. (JD). *M.* 1932, Margaret Sarles. *S.* Peter, Perry and Paul. *Career:* Chemist, chemical engineer, senior patent attorney, Standard Oil Co. (Indiana) 1927–41; Asst. Director of Refining, and Contract Executive, Petroleum Administration for War 1941–45; Pres., Oronite Chemical Co. 1946–49. Vice-President 1949–72, and Director 1955—, Standard Oil Co. of California. Director: Arabian American Oil Co. 1955–72, Trans-Arabian Pipeline Co. 1955–72, and Iran-Californian Oil Co. (Chairman and Director 1959–72. Consultant since 1972); Dir., Natomas Co. 1976—. Author of miscellaneous articles and patents. *Member:* Amer. Chemical Socy.; Amer. Inst. of Chemists (Fellow); Amer. Assn. for Advancement of Science (Fellow); Socy. of Chemical Industry; Manufacturing Chemists Assn. (Director 1955–58, 1960–63); Société de Chimie Industrielle (Dir. 1960–71). *Clubs:* Bohemian (San Francisco); Chemists. *Address:* 150 Val de Flores Drive, Burlingame, Calif. 94010, U.S.A.

**PARKIN, Leslie Wedgwood.** Australian. *B.* 1916; *Educ.* University of Adelaide (M.Sc.) and Sydney Technical College (Diploma in Mining Engineering A.S.T.C.). *M.* 1940. Molly Jean Wilson. *S.* 4. *Dau.* 1. *Career:* Exploration and Mine Geologist, North Broken Hill Ltd. 1939–50; Chief Geologist, S.A. Dept. of Mines 1950–55; Dep. Dir. 1956–70; Mem., Natural Gas Pipeline Authority of South Aust., 1967—; Dir. South Australian Dept. of Mines 1970–71; Deputy Chmn. Aust. Mineral Development Laboratories 1971—; Dir. Aust. Mineral Foundation Incorporated 1972–76; Consultant Geologist 1977—. *Member:* Aust. Inst. of Mining & Metallurgy; Geological Socy. of Aust.; Socy. of Economic Geologists; Royal Socy. of S. Australia, Pipeline Authority of S. Australia, Board of Advanced Education of S. Australia, Chmn. National Parks & Wildlife Advisory Council. *Publications:* Handbook of South Aust. Geology (Editor); Geology of South Australia (Editor with M. F. Glaessner); numerous technical papers in scientific journals. *Address:* 6 West Terrace, Beaumont, S.A., Australia.

**PARKINSON, Cecil Edward,** MP. British Politician. *B.* 1931. *Educ.* Royal Lancaster Grammar Sch.; Emmanuel Coll., Cambridge—MA. *M.* 1957, Ann Mary Jarvis. *Daus.* 3. *Career:* Partner, Chartered Accountants 1961–71; Chmn., own group of companies since 1967; MP (Cons.) for Enfield West 1970–74, & for Hertfordshire South since 1974; PPS to Minister for Aerospace & Shipping 1972–74; Conservative Whip 1974–77; Opposition Front Bench Spokesman on Trade since 1977. *Member:* Fellow, Inst. of Chartered Accountants. *Clubs:* Hawks (Cambridge). *Address:* House of Commons, London SW1A 0AA.

**PARKINSON, Charles J.,** (C. Jay). *B.* 1909. *Educ.* University of Utah (BS 1931), University of Utah Law School (LL.B. 1934); Montana Coll. Mineral Science and Technology 1969, Hon. LL.D. *M.* 1936, Edith Williams. *S.* Dennis Jay. *Dau.* Christine Mitchell. *Career:* With Draper, Romney, Boyden & Parkinson 1934–37; Stewart, Stewart & Parkinson 1937–39; Stephens, Brayton & Lowe 1939–40, (Law firms). Counsel and Asst. Secy. Basic Magnesium Inc.; Law firm, Van Cott; Cornwall & McCarthy; Stauffer Chemical Co.; Amer. Gilsonite Co.; Manganese Inc.; U.S. Lime Products Corp. and others, 1945–46; Vice-Pres., Anaconda Aluminium Co. 1955—; Gen. Counsel The Anaconda Co. 1957–64; Vice-Pres. 1958, Exec. Vice-Pres. 1960—; Pres., Anaconda Co., Chile Copper Co., Chile Exploration Co., Andes Copper Mining Co.; Vice-Pres., Mines Investment Corp. 1964—; Chmn. Bd. Dirs., Chief Exec. Officer, The Anaconda Co. and certain subsidiaries 1969–71; Former Chmn., now Dir., Anaconda Int. Corp., Anaconda Jamaica Inc., Chile Copper Co., Chile Exploration Co., Int. Smelting & Refining Co.; Dir., Stauffer Chemical Co. 1968—; First Bank System Inc., Anaconda Aluminium Co., Anaconda American Brass Co., Anaconda Wire & Cable Co., Anaconda Aust. Inc. 1965, Speech Rehabilitation Inst., United Cerebral Palsy Research & Education Foundation Inc., Muscular Dystrophy Assn. of Amer. Inc., Chamber Commerce New York, Council of the Americas. *Member:* Finance Cttee. Economic Development Council New York; Exec. Cttee Amer. Bureau, Metal Statistics; Amer. Inst. Mangt.; Governors, Fed. Hall Memorial Assoc. Inc.; University of Utah Alumini Assn.; Amer. Bar Assn.; Bar Associations, States of Utah, Nevada, Calif. and New York; Assn. Bar of the City of New York. *Awards:* Sylvan Gotshal World Trade Arbitration Medal 1969; Achievement Award, Univ. Utah Coll. of Business. *Clubs:* Alta (Salt Lake City); The Lawyers; Pi Kappa Alpha; Owl and Key; The University (New York); The Creek. *Address:* Post Office Box 591, Glen Cove, New York 11542 (Home) Creek House, West Island, Clen Cove, New York 11542; and *office* The Anaconda Company, 25 Broadway, New York, New York 10004, U.S.A.

**PARKINSON, Nicholas Fancourt.** Australian Diplomat. *B.* 1925. *Educ.* The King's School, Parramatta, N.S.W.; Univ.

of Sydney—BA (1st Class Hons.). *M.* 1952, Roslyn Sheena Campbell. *Daus.* 2. *Career:* Australian Dept. of Foreign Affairs, served in Canberra, Cairo, Hong Kong, Moscow, Wellington, Kuala Lumpur 1951–70; Australian High Commissioner to Singapore 1970–74; Deputy-Sec., Dept. of Foreign Affairs, Canberra 1974–76; Australian Amb. to the U.S. 1976–77; Sec., Dept. of Foreign Affairs, Canberra since 1977. *Clubs:* Commonwealth Club, Canberra. *Address:* 19 Beagle Street, Red Hill, A.C.T.; and *office* Department of Foreign Affairs, Canberra, A.C.T., Australia.

**PARKINSON, Thomas I., Jr.** American. *B.* 1914. *Educ.* Harvard College (BA) and University of Pennsylvania (LLB). *M.* 1937, Geralda E. Moore. *S.* Thomas I., III and Geoffrey Moore. *Dau.* Cynthia Moore. *Career:* Partner, Milbank, Tweed, Hope & Hadley (lawyers) 1946–56 (previously associated with same firm). President, Breecom Corp. 1951—. Director, Pine Street Fund, N.Y.C. 1963—. *Member:* Pilgrims of U.S.A.; Amer. Bar Assn.; Assn. of Bar of City of New York; Milbank Memorial Fund N.Y.C.; State Communities Aid Assn.; N.Y.C.; British War Relief Socy. N.Y.C. *Clubs:* Knickerbocker, Union, Down Town Assn. (all of N.Y.C.); Piping Rock. *Address:* 215 Lakeview Avenue West, Brightwaters, N.Y.; and *office* 25 Broadway, New York City 10004, U.S.A.

**PARLIN, Charles C.** Lawyer. *B.* 1898. *Educ.* Univ. of Pennsylvania (BS and Ec) and Harvard (LLB). *M.* 1924, Miriam Boyd. *S.* Charles C., Jr. and Blackwood B., *Dau.* Camilla (Smith). *Career:* Member in law firm of Shearman & Sterling, New York City 5 (lawyers; specializes in banking, corporate finance, taxation and international law). Compania Ontario S.A.; Guerlain Inc.; Potash Import & Chemical Corp.; Schlumberger Ltd. Hon. LLD.: Bethune-Cookman, Lycoming, Florida Southern, Iowa Wesleyan Wofford and Albright Colleges; and Drew and American Universities. Past-Pres., World Methodist Cncl., Pres., World Cncl. of Churches. Member, New York and American Bar Associations. Republican. *Clubs:* Harvard, Brook, Links, Wall Street Downtown (N.Y.C.). *Address:* 123 Hillside Avenue, Englewood, N.J. 07631; and *office* 399 Park Avenue, New York City 10022, U.S.A.

**PARMELEE, Alfred Franklin.** American business executive. *B.* 1907. *Educ.* Ripon Coll.; Univ. of Wisconsin. *M.* 1932, Dorothy Helen Osgood. *Dau.* Susan. *Career:* Chmn. & Director: Parmelee Industries Inc.; U.S. Safety Service Co., Parmelee Plastics Co., Parmelee Products Div.; Cesco Safety Products, Flood Safety Products Co.; Parmelee Ltd. (England), Parmelee Ltd. (Canada), Société Française Pour La Securité Du Travail (France), Parmelee Foundation Inc.; Chmn. & Dir. Parmelee Tool & Mold Div.; Dir.: Columbia Union National Bank, Kansas City, Overland Park State Bank; National Safety Council; Past-Pres., Veterans of Safety, Greater Kansas City Area Safety Council. Consul for Denmark. Knight of the Order of Danneborg. Trustee, Univ. of Kansas City, Kansas City Art. Inst. and Midwest Research Inst.; Trustee, Ripon Coll. *Clubs:* Kansas City; Carriage; Ocean Reef; Rotary, Indian Hills; River; University (U.S.A.); American (London). *Address:* 1535 Walnut Street, P.O. Box 1237, Kansas City, Mo. 64141, U.S.A.

**PARNESS, Victor Henry.** British. Chairman and Managing Director, Victor Industrial Group of Companies. *B.* 1939; *Educ.* City of London School. Member, Inst. of Directors. *Club:* Royal Automobile. *Address:* 45 Eaton Place, London, S.W.1.; and *office* 1–11 Hay Hill, Berkeley Square, London. W.1.

**PARODI, Alexandre,** L. ès L. *B.* 1901. *M.* 1931, Annie Vautier. *S.* Jean-Luc, Jacques. *Career:* Auditor, Council of State 1926; Deputy Secretary-General, National Economic Council 1929–38; Maître des Requêtes, Council of State 1938; Director-General of Work and Manual Labour, Ministry of Labour 1939–40; Délégue Général, Provisional Government in occupied France March-Aug. 1944; Minister of Labour and Social Security Sept. 1944-Nov. 1945; Councillor of State 1945; Ambassador and Delegate to Consultative Council for Italian Affairs 1946; Permanent Represenative, United Nations Security Council 1946; Secretary-General, Ministry of Foreign Affairs 1949–55; Permanent Representative on the North Atlantic Council; Ambassador to Morocco 1957–60. Vice-President of the Council of State of France, 1960–71. Representative, Administrative Council, Internatl. Bureau of Labour. *Member:* l'Académie des Sciences Morales et Politiques. *Address:* 102 rue de Grenelle, Paris 7e, France.

**PARODI, André Gustave.** Swiss diplomat. *B.* 1909. *Educ.* Univ. of Geneva (Lic. ès Sc. Econ.) and Johns Hopkins Univ., Baltimore (MA). *M.* 1940, Andrée Piretti. *S.* Pierre-Christian. *Dau.* Alix-Chantal. *Career:* Entered Federal Department of Public Economy 1932; transferred to Political Department 1945; Counsellor of Legation, Rome 1947; Chargé d'Affaires, Rumania 1954; Ambassador to Colombia and concurrently Minister to Ecuador 1956. Ambassador Plenipotentiary and Extraordinary Envoy to Czechoslovakia 1961. Ambassador to the U.A.R., Cairo, the Democratic Republic of Sudan, Khartoum, and the Democratic Republic of Somalia, Mogadiscio 1967; Ambassador to Spain, Madrid 1971–75. (Retired). *Publication:* The Moving Pictures Industry in the U.S.A. (Johns Hopkins University Press 1932). *Address:* Le Coin de Chausse, chemin des Hauts-Crêts No. 70, 1253, Vandoeuvres, Geneva, Switzerland.

**PARRALES-SANCHEZ, Ricardo.** Ambassador of Nicaragua *B.* 1931. *Educ.* BS (Econ); MS (Econs & Finance). *M.* Leda. *S.* 3. *Career:* Counselor (Econ) Embassy, Washington, 1955–61; Dir. Tech. Co-operation, (Center of Ind. Bank) 1961–63; Under-Sec. Min. of Economy, 1963–65; Under-Sec. Min. of Finance 1965–67; Gen. Mgr. Coffee Institute 1968–70; Ambassador to London 1970; Ambassador to the Netherlands 1973. *Address:* c/o Ministry of Foreign Affairs, Managua, Nicaragua.

**PARRISH, Wayne William.** Editorial Consultant. *B.* 1907. *Educ.* Columbia Univ. School of Journalism (BLit.), and Columbia Univ. Graduate School (MS). *M.* 1935, Frances Knight. *Career:* Staff writer, New York Herald Tribune 1928–30 and 1931–33; staff writer, Literary Digest 1933–35; Editor, National Aeronautics Magazine 1935–37; Founder president and editor, American Aviation Publications, 1937–69; Spec. Rep. of Chmn., Pan-Am World Airways. *Award:* Hon. LL.D. Missouri Valley College. *Address:* 2221 30th Street, N.W. Washington, D.C. 20008 and *office* 1800K St., N.W., Washington 20006 D.C., U.S.A.

**PARROTT, Sir Cecil (Cuthbert),** KCMG, OBE, MA. (Cantab.) Hon. F.I.L. *B.* 1909. *Educ.* Cambridge Univ. (MA). *M.* 1935 Ellen Julie Matzow. *S.* 3. *Career:* at British Embassy Legation Oslo 1939–40; Legation Stockholm 1940–45; British Embassy Prague 1945–48; Foreign Office 1948–50; Head, U.N. Dept. Foreign Office 1950–52; Principal Political Adviser, British Delegation, Gen. Assembly 1951–52; Counsellor, Brussels 1952–54; Minister Moscow 1954–57; Librarian, keeper of the Papers, Dir. of Research Foreign Office 1957–60; Ambassador, Prague, 1960–66. Professor of Russian and Soviet Studies, Lancaster Univ. 1966–71; Dir. of the Comenius Centre 1968; Prof. of Central and South Eastern European Studies Lancaster Univ. 1971–76. Vice-Chmn., D'Oyly Carte Opera Trust. *Publications:* First complete translation into English of The Good Soldier Svejk (1973); The Tightrope (1975); The Serpent & the Nightingale (1977); The Bad Bohemian (1977); numerous broadcast talks & features. *Address:* c/o The University, Lancaster, England.

**PARRY, John Hywel,** OBE. *B.* 1913. *Educ.* Brighton Coll. (England) and Gonville and Caius Col., Cambridge (BA Hons.). *M.* 1941, Evelyn Florence Upton. *Daus.* 3. *Career:* Features Editor, Johannesburg Daily Express 1938; Secretary-Announcer, Southern Rhodesia Broadcasting Station 1941; Studio Controller 1945; Controller, Federal Broadcasting Service 1960–64. Director-General, Rhodesia Broadcasting Corp. 1964–66; Dir. Gen. Malawi, Broadcasting Corp. 1967–70; Broadcasting Officer Audio Visual Services Rhodesia 1971. Retired. Author & Broadcaster. *Address:* "Chestnuts," South Repps, Norfolk.

**PARRY-OKEDEN. William Nugent,** DSO, Lieut.-Col. (R. of O.); The Director, Royal Agricultural Society of New South Wales, May 1961. *B.* 1910. *Educ.* Toowoomba Grammar School, Queensland. *M.* 1940, Mary E. Moseley. *S.* David, Ian, and Simon. *Career:* Secy., Australian Jockey Club 1946–60. Served with Australian Imperial Forces (Infantry and Divisional Staff) in Middle East, India and New Guinea; DSO and mentioned in dispatches (New Guinea campaign). *Clubs:* Union (Sydney); Queensland (Brisbane). *Address:* Rawson, Showgrounds, Moore Park, Sydney, Australia.

**PARSONS, Geoffrey.** American. Commander, Legion of Honour (France). Vice-President and European Representative, Northrop Corp., Beverly Hills, Calif. *B.* 1908; *Educ.* Phillips Exeter Academy and Harvard University. *M.* 1945, Dorothy Blackman Tartière. *S.* Geoffrey III. *Career:* Journalist Boston Globe 1931–38; Mid-Western correspondent, New York Herald Tribune (H.Q. Chicago) 1937–41; War Correspondent, London 1941; Chief of London Bureau

1943–44; Editor, European edition, New York Herald Tribune in Paris 1944–50; Chief of Press and Public Relations and Deputy Director of Information, NATO 1950, Director of Information 1954–57; Vice-Pres. for Europe, Northrop Corp. since 1957. *Member:* Anglo-American Press Assn. Paris: Assn. of U.S. Aerospace Industries in Europe. *Publications:* articles in Reader's Digest, Saturday Evening Post, etc. *Clubs:* Century (N.Y.C.); American (Paris). *Address:* 18 Quai d'Orleans, Paris, France.

**PARSONS, Sir Maurice Henry,** KCMG. *B.* 1910. *Educ.* University College School, London. *M.* Daphne Idina Warner. *S.* 1. *Dau.* 1. *Career:* Entered Bank of England 1928; Private Secretary to Governor (Montagu Norman) 1939–43; Alternate Executive Director for U.K. on International Monetary Fund 1946–47; International Bank 1947; Director of Operations, International Monetary Fund 1947–50; Alternate Governor 1957–66; Deputy Chief Cashier, Bank of England 1950; Assistant to Governors 1955; Exec. Dir. 1957–66, Dep. Governor, Bank of England 1966–70; Chmn. Bank of London and S. America July-Dec. 1970; Dir. John Brown & Co. Ltd. 1970–72; Chmn. Billing & Sons Ltd. since 1971; London Regional Industrial Group National Savings Cttee. since 1971; Hon. Treas. Socy. International Development since 1971. *Clubs:* St. James's; National. *Address:* Clifford House, Shalford, Surrey.

**PARSONS, Richard Edmund.** British Diplomat. *B.* 1928. *Educ.* Bembridge Sch.; Brasenose Coll., Oxford—BA. *M.* 1960, Jenifer Jane Mathews. *S.* 3. *Career:* Member of British. Diplomatic Service since 1953; 3rd Sec., Washington 1953–56; 2nd Sec., Vientiane 1956–58; Foreign Office 1958–60; 1st Sec., Buenos Aires 1960–63; Foreign Office 1963–65; 1st Sec., Ankara 1965–67; Foreign Office 1967–69; Counsellor, Lagos 1969–72; Head of Personnel Dept., FCO 1972–76; Ambassador to Hungary since 1976. *Clubs:* Travellers'. *Address:* c/o Foreign and Commonwealth Office, King Charles Street, London, S.W.1.

**PARSONS, Robert Wade.** American investment banker. *B.* 1900. *Educ.* Wesleyan Univ., Middletown (BS 1922). *M.* 1931, Irene Johnson. *S.* Robert W., Roger B., and Stanley G. (*Dec.*). *Career:* Formerly: with Bankers Trust Co., N.Y.C. 1922–60 (Sales Mgr. 1929–44, Asst. Vice-Pres. 1944–54, Vice-Pres. 1954–60; retired). Former Dir. Seatrain Lines Inc.; Director and Chairman, Charles E. Pettinos Graphite Corp.; Chairman Board Directors, International Advisory Corp. Ltd.; Former Dir. Previews Inc.; New England Socy.; and member Policy Cttee. Waddell & Reed Inc. Former Trustee New York Skin and Cancer Hospital; Stuyvesant Square Hospital, N.Y.C.; Overlook Hospital; New York Univ.; and Treasurer, Inst. for Science and Technology, and Elizabethtown Historical Foundation; Former Pres., Mantoloking Borough Council N.J. Chmn. and Trustee, The Lillia Babbitt Hyde Foundation; Chmn. Dirs. The John Jay and Eliza Jane Watson Foundation, The Charles E. and Joy C. Pettinos Foundation; Dir. Summit & Elizabeth Trust Co. Trustee: New Jersey Historical Socy.; Gen. Proprietors, Eastern Div. N.J.; Emeritus, Wesleyan Univ. Middletown; Psi Upsilon Foundation. Member: Finance Cttee. Overlook Hospital Summit, N.J.; Sons of the Amer. Revolution; Squadron A Ex-Members Assn.; Skull and Serpent Socy.; Exec. Council, Psi Upsilon Fraternity; Trustee, Historic Deerfield Inc., Mass; Governor's New Jersey American Revolution Bicentennial Celebration Commission; Trustee, Foundation of New Jersey Coll. of Medicine & Dentistry. *Clubs:* Baltusorol Golf; Bay Head Yacht; Nassau; Spring Lake Golf (all N. Jersey); The University (N.Y. City). *Address:* 44 Lenox Road, Summit, N.J. 07901 and *office* 507 Westminster Avenue, Elizabeth, N.J., 07208, U.S.A.

**PART, Sir Antony (Alexander),** GCB, MBE. British. Chmn., The Orion Insurance Co. & a director of other companies. *B.* 1916. *Educ.* Harrow School; Trinity College, Cambridge (First Cl. Hons., Modern Languages Tripos). *M.* 1940, Isabella Bennett. *Career:* Under-Secretary, Min. of Education, 1954; Deputy Secretary, 1961; Deputy Secretary, Min. of Public Buildings and Works 1963 and Perm. Secy. 1965. Permanent Secretary, Board of Trade, 1968–70; Dept. of Trade & Industry 1970–74; Dept. of Industry 1974–76. *Awards:* Hon. D.Tech., Brunel Univ. 1966; Hon. D.Sc., Univ. of Aston 1974, Hon. D.Sc., Cranfield 1976. *Clubs;* United Oxford & Cambridge Univ., M.C.C. *Address:* Flat 5, 71 Elm Park Gardens, London, S.W.10.

**PARTRIDGE, Sir (Ernest) John, KBE, 1971. British. *B.* 1908. *Educ.* Queen Elizabeth's Hospital, Bristol. *M.* (1) 1934, Madeline Fabian (*Dec.* 1944), and (2) 1949, Joan Johnson.** *S.* 2 (one by each marriage). *Daus.* 2 (one by each marriage). *Career:* With Imperial Group, Secretary 1946–57, Director 1949–75, Deputy Chairman 1960–64. Chmn. 1964–75; Director, British-American Tobacco Co. Ltd. 1963–75; Tobacco Securities Trust Ltd. 1964–75; National Westminster Bank Ltd. 1968; General Accident Fire & Life Assurance Corp. Ltd. 1973; Dunlop Holdings 1973; Delta Metal Co. Ltd. 1973; Finance for Industry Ltd. 1975; Chairman, Council of Industry for Management Education, 1967–71; Pres. Confederation of British Industry 1970–72; Pres. Foundation for Management Education since 1972; Chmn., CBI Education Foundation since 1976. *Member:* National Economic Development Council 1967–75; British National Export Council, 1968–72; Governor, London Graduate School of Business Studies, 1968–75; Member, Council of Industrial Society, 1968–75; Int. Adv. Bd. of Chemical Bank U.S.A. since 1972; The Queen's Silver Jubilee Appeal Council 1976—; Fellow, British Institute of Management; Pres. Nat. Council of Social Service since 1973. *Awards:* Hon. LL.D. Bristol Univ., 1972; Hon. DSc. Cranfield Inst. of Tech. 1974. *Club:* The Athenaeum (London). *Address:* Wildwood, Haslemere, Surrey; and 601 Carrington House, Hertford St., London W1; *office* Imperial House, 1 Grosvenor Place, London, SW1.

**PARTRIDGE, Jack Herbert.** British executive. *B.* 1913. *M.* 1939, Mary Agnes Maclean. *Dau.* Margaret Maclean (Clarke). *Career:* AMF-AIF. 1941–46; R.A.A.S.C. Captain, Retired List. First Chairman of Australian Hire Purchase Conf. (N.S.W. Div.) 1958–60; Managing Director: Alliance Holdings Ltd. and subsidiary companies; Chief Executive Officer of Alliance Acceptance Co. Ltd. since formation 1951. *Member:* Manufacturing Industries Advisory Council 1962–73; Federal Chairman, Australian Hire Purchase and Finance Conference, 1963–64, 1975–76; Fellow, Australian Institute of Management. Member, Inst. of Directors. *Clubs:* Tattersall's, Royal Automobile (of Australia); Double Bay Bowling, Rotary (Sydney). Commonwealth (Canberra A.C.T.). *Address:* Box 2872 G.P.O. Sydney, N.S.W., 2001, and *office* Alliance Holdings House, 19–31 Pitt Street, Sydney, N.S.W., 2000, Australia.

**PASCOE, Frank,** CBE. Australian. *B.* 1919. *Educ.* Maryborough Technical College. *M.* 1945, Edna Jean Nattrass. *S.* 1. *Daus.* 2. *Career:* With Australian National Airways: Asst. Secy. 1941, Chief Accountant 1950, Asst. New South Wales Manager, 1955. With Ansett-A.N.A.; New South Wales Manager 1957, Commercial Manager 1958. General Manager, Ansett-Airlines of Australia 1959—; Dir., Ansett Transport Industries Ltd. 1972, Exec. Gen. Man. since 1973. *Member:* F.A.S.A., F.C.I.T. and FAIM. *Clubs:* Huntingdale Golf; Victorian Amateur Turf; Moonee Valley Racing. *Address:* Ansett-Airlines, 489 Swanston Street, Melbourne, Vic., Australia. 3000.

**PASSOT-BIÉ, Henri René.** French banker and company director. *B.* 29 June 1913. *M.* 1945, Suzy Bié. *S.* Paul Louis, *Daus.* Frédérique, Raphaelle, Jocelyne. *Career:* Director, Société Anonyme Franco-Suisse des Conserves Lenzbourg. Vice-Pres., Société Lyonnaise de Depôts et de Crédit Industrial, Compagnie des Salins du Midi et des Salimes de l'Est and other companies. Formerly Secretary Member, Lyon Chamber of Commerce. Member, Chevalier de la Légion d'Honneur. *Address:* Château de la Roüe, Chalamont, Ain, France.

**PĂTAN, Ion.** Romanian economist and politician. *B.* 1926. *Educ.* Economic Studies Acad. Bucharest. *Career:* Several posts, Ministry of Light Industry 1952–56; Dir. Min. Light Industry 1956–62, Gen. Secy. 1962–64; Deputy Minister 1964–65; Member Central Cttee. R.C.P. 1969—; Alt. member Exec. Cttee. 1972—; Minister Home Trade 1968–69; Vice-Chmn. Council of Ministers 1969—; Minister Foreign Trade since 1972; Member Exec. Cttee. 1974 and Permanent Bureau; Member of Parliament 1975. *Address:* Council of Ministers, Bucharest, Romania.

**PATERNOTTE de LA VAILLEE, Baron Alexandre.** Belgian diplomat. *B.* 6 May 1923. *Educ.* Univs. of Lyons and Brussels (D. en D.). *M.* 1946, Eliana, Countess Orsolini-Cencelli. *S.* Alexandre. *Daus.* Marianita, Aline. *Career:* Joined Min. of Foreign Affairs 5 Oct. 1945; Attaché at Washington, D.C. Aug. 1946; Head, Section of the Cncl. of Europe, Min. of Foreign Affairs 1949–1952; 2nd Sec. July 1952; Cultural and Press Attaché, Embassy, Paris; member of H.Q. Committee of U.N.E.S.C.O. and of the International Bureau of Expositions, Paris, Sept. 1952; First Secretary Jan. 1956; at Nato

Defence College Sept. 1956–March 1957; Counsellor of Embassy, Rio de Janeiro, April 1957, Chargé d'Affaires Jan. 1958; Director, Scientific Policy, Brussels 1962; Vice-Pres., European Conference on Satellite Telecommunications, and Council of European Launcher Development Organization 1964. Minister Plen. 1965; Chmn., Council of ELDO 1966; Ambassador to Lebanon, Jordan, Cyprus and Kuweit 1967–70. Ambassador to Brazil since 1970; Delegate to Euro-Arab dialogue, 1975 *Awards:* Croix de Guerre avec Etoile d'Argent (France); Knight of the Sovereign Military Order of St. John of Jerusalem; Croix de Guerre (with Palm) and Decoration Militaire (with Palm) of Belgium. Comdr. Order Leopold (Belgium). Grand Cross Rio Brenco (Brazil); Cruzeiro do Sul (Brazil); Cedar of Lebanon; Al Istiklal (Jordan). *Address:* Ministère des Affaires Estrangères, Brussels, Belgium.

**PATERSON, Donald Savigny,** DFC. Canadian grain merchant. *B.* 22 April 1918. *Educ.* Ashbury Coll. Ottawa, and Bishop's Univ. (BA Arts). *M.* 1947, Jane Lynch. *S.* 4. *Dau.* 1. *Career:* With Royal Canadian Air Force in Canada and England 1940–45 (Distinguished Flying Cross); Dir., Grain Insurance & Guarantee Co.; Grain Insurance Brokers Ltd., Fidelity Trust Co.; Techniscan Systems Ltd.; Voyager Explorations. Chmn., Norfab Homes Ltd. Vice-Pres., N. M. Paterson & Sons Ltd.; Pres. Stall Lake Mines Ltd.; Seagreen Air Transport, Pres. Traders' Building Association; Pres. Canadian Protein Pellets Ltd. *Address:* 131 Ridgedale Crescent, Winnipeg, Manitoba, Canada.

**PATIENCE, John Delmont.** Australian. *B.* 1910. *Educ.* Sydney University (LLB). *M.* 1941, Rhoda King. *S.* 2. *Dau.* 1. *Career:* Partner, Parish, Patience & McIntyre, Solicitors, Sydney 1938–51. Chmn., Argus & Australasian Ltd. Melbourne 1954–57; Reed Consolidated Industries Ltd. Dep. Chmn. Blue Metal Industries Ltd. Director: Ready Mixed Concrete Ltd., Australian Newsprint Mills Holdings Ltd.; Mercantile Mutual Insurance Co. Ltd., United Dominions Corp. Ltd., and other companies. *Clubs:* Union, Atheneaum (Melbourne). *Address:* Unit 8, 4 Marathon Road, Darling Point, N.S.W.; and *office* 8th Floor, 60 Martin Place, Sydney, N.S.W., Australia.

**PATON, Sir George Whitecross.** British. *B.* 1902. *Educ.* MA (Melbourne); BA, BCL (Oxford); Hon. LLD Glasgow, Brisbane, Sydney, Tasmania, Monash, Melbourne and London. Hon. DCL, Univ. of Western Ontario. *M.* 1931, Alice Watson. *S.* Frank Watson, C.B.E. *Daus.* Mrs. K. Mills, Mrs. M. Winneke and Mrs. G. Jacobs. Professor of Jurisprudense, Melbourne 1931–50; Chmn. Australian Vice-Chancellor's Committee 1957–60; Vice-Chancellor, University of Melbourne 1951–68. *Club:* Melbourne. *Address:* Dunraven Ave., Toorak, Victoria 3142, Australia.

**PATON, Sir Leonard Cecil,** CBE, MC. Director, Harrisons and Crosfield Ltd., East India Merchants (1844). *B.* 1892. *Educ.* Geo. Watson's College, Edinburgh; Edinburgh Univ. (MA 1st Class Honours Classics); Christ Church, Oxford (Exhibitioner). *M.* 1917, Muriel Searles. *S.* 1. *Dau.* 1. *Career:* Deputy U.K. Timber Controller, 1939–45; A Man. Dir., U.K. Commercial Corp. Ltd., 1940–45. *Address:* 63 Woodland Court, Dyke Road Avenue, Hove, Sussex; and *office* 1–4 Great Tower Street, London, E.C.3.

**PATTERSON, Dwight Fleming.** American. *B.* 1907. *Educ.* Wofford Coll., Spartanburg, S.C. (AB); Graduate School of Banking, Rutgers Univ. (Dipl.); Hon. LLD, Wofford Coll. *M.* 1935, Mary M. Smith. *S.* Dwight F., L. Leon, Drayton Smith. *Career:* With First National Bank, Spartanburg 1929–31; joined Palmetto Bank 1931. Dir. Independent Bankers' Association of America. Palmetto Bank, Laurens, S.C. 1952—. Mem. Bd. of Trustees of Wofford College, Spartanburg, S.C. 1946–58, and 1966—. *Publication:* Financing of Cotton Farmers in the South, (1940). *Member:* Phi Beta Kappa (scholastic); Pi Kappa Phi (social); Blue Key Fraternity (leadership). *Club:* Piedmont (Spartanburg). *Address:* 701 West Main Street, Laurens, S.C., U.S.A.

**PATTERSON, Ellmore Clark.** American. *B.* 1913. *Educ.* Lake Forest (Ill.) Academy (Grad. 1931) and University of Chicago (BS 1935). *M.* 1940, Anne Hyde Choate, *S.* 5. *Career:* With J. P. Morgan 1935–39; Morgan Stanley 1939; again with J. P. Morgan: successively in Investment Department, Assisjant Vice-Pres., Vice-Pres., Senr. Vice-Pres. 1939–62 (J. P. Morgan merged with Guaranty Trust Co. of N.Y. and changed name to Morgan Guaranty Trust Co. of N.Y.) Exec. Vice-Pres., 1962–65, Vice-Chmn. & Chmn., Exec. Cttee., 1955–69. President and Director, Morgan Guaranty Trust Co. of N.Y. 1969–71, Chmn. since 1971; Chmn. & Pres. J. P. Morgan & Co. Director; Atchison Topeka & Santa Fé Railway, Canada Life Assurance (mem. Inv. Cttee.), Standard Brands Inc., General Motors Corp., Downtown-Lower Manhattan Association, Fishers Island Development Corp., Schlumberger Ltd., Bethlehem Steel Corp., Federal Reserve Bank of New York. Trustee: Memorial Sloan-Kettering Cancer Center, Mass Inst. of Technology, Univ. of Chicago, Alfred P. Sloan Foundation; Bd. of Mgrs. Memorial Hosp. for Cancer and Allied Diseases. Member: Council on Foreign Relations; National Inst. of Social Sciences; The Pilgrims of the U.S. *Clubs:* Bedford Golf & Tennis; Bond (N.Y.); Chicago; Fishers Island Country; Hay Harbour; The Links; Links Golf. *Address:* Hook Road, Bedford Village, N.Y.; and *office* 23 Wall Street, New York City, U.S.A.

**PATTERSON, George Robert Brown,** OBE. Australian. *B.* 1903. *Educ.* Melbourne Church of England Grammar School. *M.* 1943, Margaret Best. *S.* 1. *Dau.* 1. *Career:* With Elder Smith & Co. Ltd., Melbourne 1921–26; Hume Pipe Co. (Australia) Ltd. 1926–38; James Hardie & Co. Ltd., Sydney 1938–39; A.I.F. Royal Australian Engineers 1939–45; Australian Government Trade Commissioner (South and Eastern Africa) 1947–53; Aust. Govt. Senior Trade Commissioner, London 1953–58, and Hong Kong 1959–63. With Jardine Matheson & Co. (Australia) Pty. Ltd. 1963–76 (Local Chmn. 1965–75). *Clubs:* Union, Imperial Services (both in Sydney). *Address:* 19 Warrabina Avenue, St. Ives, N.S.W.; and *office* Macquarie House, 167 Macquarie Street, Sydney, N.S.W. 2000, Australia.

**PATTERSON, Jere Wescott.** American. *B.* 1917. *Educ.* Princeton Univ., Magdalen College, Oxford (Rhodes Scholar), Univ. of Paris, and London School of Economics (studied international trade and finance). *M.* 1941, Betty Muggleton. *Children:* Jere, Jr., Bettina (Sands), Dean, Knight. *Career:* Formerly Exec. Vice-Pres. of Erwin Wasey and Erwin Wasey, Ruthrauff & Ryan; Asst. to Pres. of Foote, Cone & Belding International; Foreign Sales Dir. of Parker Pen Co.; Pres., Jere Patterson & Associates. Partner, Patterson & Wood. *Publications:* Marketing: On Target; and Marriage in Marketing (for German edition of Reader's Digest, Verlag das Beste). *Member:* International Management Assn.; Interntl. Exec. Assn.; Amer. Marketing Assn.; Internatl. Advertising Association (Director and President); Society of Professional Management Consultants; Inst. of Management Consultants. *Clubs:* Princeton, Union, University, Rotary, Norfolk, (Conn.); Mid-Ocean, Coral Beach (Bermuda); Travellers' (Paris). *Address:* 480 Park Avenue, New York City, N.Y. 10022; and *office* 1 Rockefeller Plaza, New York City, U.S.A.

**PATTIE, Geoffrey Edwin,** MP. British Politician. *B.* 1936. *Educ.* Durham Sch.; St. Catharine's Coll., Cambridge—MA (Hons.); Barrister-at-Law, Gray's Inn. *M.* 1960, Tuëma Eyre-Maunsell. *S.* 1. *Dau.* 1. *Career:* Dir., Collett, Dickenson, Pearce, International 1966–69, 1973— (Joint Man. Dir. 1969–73); Mem., GLC Lambeth 1967–70; MP (Cons.) for Chertsey & Walton since 1974; Mem. of the General Synod 1970–75. *Member:* Fellow, Inst. of Practitioners in Advertising. *Publications:* Towards a New Defence Policy; (with James Bellini) A New World Role for the Medium Power: The British Opportunity. *Clubs:* St. Stephen's; Royal Green Jackets. *Address:* Terrington House, 15 College Road, London SE21 7BG; and *office* House of Commons, London SW1A 0AA.

**PATTISSON, John Harmer.** British company director. *B.* 1931. *Educ.* Radley and Trinity College, Oxford (MA). *M. S.* 2. *Career:* Dir. Hanson Trust Ltd. 1959–74; Man. Dir. Dawnay Day & Co. Ltd. 1965—; Dir. 1962—, Dawnay Day Group Ltd. Man. Dir. since 1969; Dir. Target Trust Group Ltd. since 1973. *Address:* 31 Gresham Street, London, EC2V 7DT. and 28 Cresswell Place, London, SW10 9RB.

**PATTON, Stuart Lynn.** *B.* 1912. *Educ.* Newark School of Fine Arts, and Univ. of Southern California. *M.* 1935, Elizabeth Prall(Dec.). *Career:* Reporter, Honolulu Star-Bulletin, Hawaii 1935–36, San Francisco News 1936, San Francisco Chronicle, 1937; Art Dept., Universal Pictures, Hollywood 1937; Associated Art Director 1937–39; Editorial and Advertising, Southern California Association of Newspapers 1939–41; Comdr., U.S. Maritime Commission 1941–49; successively Director, West Coast Public Relations, Editor of Mast magazine, Exec. Officer, Pacific Coast Operations, Promotion Director, Brooklyn Eagle 1949–55. Commander, U.S. Maritime Commission (R.). President, Southern Arts Syndicate,

Ocala, Fla. Publisher, All Florida magazine 1955–60; Publisher, Private Campgrounds and R V Parks Buying Guide; Pres., Campground Marketing Associates Inc. *Awards:* Two citations from Commandant, U.S. Maritime Commission 1943. *Member:* National Newspaper Promotion Assn. (Pres., N.Y. Chapter 1953–55). *Clubs:* Golden Hills Golf and Turf. *Address:* Barcliff Avenue, Chatham, Mass.; and Palos Verdes Estates, Calif., U.S.A.

**PAUL VI, His Holiness Pope** (Giovanni Battista Montini). *B.* Concesio, Brescia, 26 Sept. 1897. *Educ.* Arici Institute, Brescia, Diocesan Seminary and Gregorian University, Rome. *Career:* Ordained priest 1920. Entered Vatican Secretariat of State; Attaché in Apostolic Nunciature in Warsaw for a short period. Recalled to the Secretariat of State in Rome. Substitute of Secretariat in 1937 and Pro-Secy. 1952; Appointed Archbishop of Milan 1954; created Cardinal 1958; elected Pope 21 June 1963, and crowned 30 June 1963. *Address:* The Vatican, Vatican City.

**PAUL, Dr. Frank.** German diplomat. *B.* 1918. *Educ.* Study of econ. Zurich (Switz), Freiburg (Germany), Fribourg (Switz.), Dr. rer. pol. *M.* 1950, Irma Sutter. *S.* 2. *Career:* Federal Foreign Office 1950; Head of Political Dept. 1968–70; State Secretary since 1970; Chief of the Office of the President of FRG since 1974. *Address:* Bundesprasidialamt, 53 Bonn, Kaiser-Friedrich-Str. 16, F.R. Germany.

**PAUL, Sir John Warburton,** GCMG, OBE, MC. *B.* 1916. *Educ.* Weymouth Coll., Dorset and Selwyn Coll., Cambridge Univ.; MA (Cantab.). *M.* 1946, Kathleen Audrey Weeden. *Daus.* 3. *Career:* Regular soldier (Royal Tank Regt.) 1938–47; in Colonial Administrative Service 1947–73; District Commissioner, Sierra Leone 1952; member of Board, West African Airways Corp. 1954–56; Permanent Secretary, Sierra Leone, 1956. Provincial Commissioner 1959, Secretary to the Cabinet 1960; Governor and C.-in-C., The Gambia 1962–64. Governor-Gen .1956–66; Gov. and C.-in-C. British Honduras 1966–72; Governor and C.-in-C. The Bahamas 1972–73 & Gov. Gen. 1973; Lt.-Governor, The Isle of Man 1974. K.St.J. Barrister-at-Law (Inner Temple). *Clubs:* Athenaeum; Royal Dorset Yacht (Weymouth). *Address:* Government House, Isle of Man.

**PAULEY, Edwin Wendell.** American industrialist. *B.* 7 Jan. 1903. *Educ.* Georgia Military Academy; University of California. *M.* 1937, Barbara Jean McHenry. *S.* Edwin Wendell, Stephan McHenry, Robert van Petten. *Dau.* Susan Jean. *Career:* President, Independent Petroleum Association 1934–38; Special Representative of California Government on Natural Resource Commission 1939, and Interstate Oil and Compact Commission 1940; Organizer of State of California Defense Council 1941; Treasurer, Democratic National Committee, Secretary 1941–43; Petroleum Co-ordinator for European War on petroleum lend-lease supplies for Russia and the U.K. 1941; U.S. Representative on Allied Commission on Reparations (with Rank of Ambassador) 1945–46; Industrial and Commercial Adviser, Tri Parte Potsdam Conf.; Special Adviser on Reparations to Secretary of State 1947–48; Special Assistant Secretary of Army 1947; Regent, University of California since 1939 (Chairman. Board of Regents 1956–58 and 1960–72); and currently Chairman of the Board, Pauley Petroleum Inc., California, Texas, New Mexico and Mexico. *Address:* 9521 Sunset Boulevard, Beverly Hills, Calif. 90210; and *office* 10,000 Santa Monica Boulevard, Los Angeles 67, Calif., U.S.A.

**PAULS, Rolf Friedemann.** Ambassador of the Federal Republic of Germany. *B.* 1915. *Educ.* University of Hamburg (Doctor of Law 1950). *M.* 1951, Lilo Serlo. *S.* Rolf; Christian; Andreas. *Career:* Consul and Secretary, German Legation in Luxembourg, 1951–52; Personal Asst. to State Secretary, Prof. Walter Hallstein, Foreign Office, Bonn, 1952–55; Head of Political Dept., German Embassy, Washington, 1956–60; Counsellor & Deputy Chief of Mission in Athens, 1960–62; Deputy Chief of Economic Development Policy, German Foreign Office; First German Ambassador to Israel, 1965–68; Ambassador-at-Large, Foreign Office, Bonn; Ambassador to U.S.A. 1969–73, Ambassador to People's Republic of China 1973–75; Ambassador & Perm. Rep. to NATO since 1976. Hon. Doctor at Law, Illinois College, Jacksonville, U.S.A. *Address:* Permanent Mission of the Federal Republic of Germany, NATO, Brussels, 1110, Belgium.

**PAULSON, Boyd Colton.** American executive. *Educ.* Univ. of Utah, Montana School of Mines, and Univ. of Illinois (BS Civil Eng.). *M.* 1945, Barbara McKinstry. *S.* Boyd, Jr. *Daus.* Virginia, Beth. Kathryn and Patricia. *Career:* with U.S. Civil Engineering Corps. 1943–46; Project Constructor Supervisor, Project Engineer, and Project Manager on various large construction projects throughout the U.S. 1946–1961. Project Manager of £21 million Snowy Mountains Hydro Electric Authority project, Australia, 1961–64; Vice-Pres. and Man. Dir. Utah Construction and Engineering Pty. Ltd. 1964–66; Vice-Pres. Construction Utah Construction & Mining Co. 1966–69; Vice Pres. Gen. Mgr. Fluor Utah Inc. 1969–72; Exec. Vice-Pres. since 1972; Vice-Pres. Utah International Inc. since 1973; Registered Professional Engineer, Canada; *Member:* Instn. of Engineers of Australia. Receipient of Honour Award of American Society of Civil Engineers. Sigma, Rho; Sigma Tau; Chi Epsilon; B.S.C.E.; Sigma Chi. *Club:* Peninsula Golf and Country. *Address: office* 177 Bovet Road, San Mateo, California, 94402 U.S.A.

**PAULUS, Dr. John Douglas.** American. Corporate Vice-Pres. of Public Relations & Public Affairs. *B.* 1917. *Educ.* Univ. of Pittsburgh (BA). *M.* 1937, Mildred Hankey. The Baron Von Paulus— title unused—is a great-grandson of the Baron Ghermani von Paulus of Wallachia. *Career:* General Editorial Executive, The Pittsburgh Press 1934–44; Sports Editor, The Washington Post 1936–40; Associate Publisher, the Brooklyn Eagle 1944–51; Dir. of Public Relations & Advertising, Jones & Laughlin Steel Corp. 1951–58; Lecturer in Journalism & Public Relations, Univ. of Pittsburgh 1951–58; Book Editor, Pittsburgh Press 1940–54; Trustee Point Park Coll. Pittsburgh, Mercy Hospital, Duquesne Univ., Seton Niel Coll., American Red Cross, Pittsburgh Council of International Visitors; Corporate Vice-Pres. Public Relations & Public Affairs, Allegheny Ludlum Ind. Inc. mem. Am. Iron & Steel Inst.; Mem. Int. Iron & Steel Inst.; Chmn. of Public Relations & Public Affairs Cttee. 1971–74. *Publications:* The Dollar in Danger, (1958); Rome Wasn't Bilked in Day, (1961); For Whom the (Steel) Bell Tolls, (1962); Jack Shall Pipe and Jill Shall Dance, (1965) Carrying Kumquats to Khartoum (1973); Curious Case of the Busted Buck (1973); (all monographs); Pittsburgh in Music, (1949); Pittsburgh sings, (1950) (both musical festivals); The Still Samovars of Samarkand (1976); Caliphs & Calipers (1976); Energy, Synergy & Political Hanky-Panky (1977). *Awards:* The Putman Award for Industrial Advertising, 1954; Pittsburgh Press Club; Sigma Delta Chi (professional journalism); Omicron Delta Kappa (hon. scholarship). *Clubs:* Duquesne, University, Press, Chartiers Country; Trustee, Seton Hill Coll. and Mercy Hospital (all of Pittsburgh). *Address:* 826 North Meadowcroft Avenue, Pittsburgh, Pa. 15216; and *office* (personal) 2319 Oliver Building, Pittsburgh, Pa. 15222; (corporate) 2 Oliver Plaza, Pittsburgh, Pa. 15222, U.S.A.

**PAVLOWITCH, Kosta Stevan.** Yugoslav diplomat. *B.* 1905. *Educ.* Lycée Janson de Sailly, Paris; Belgrade (LLM); MA (Cantab.). *M.* 1931, Mara Dioukitch. *S.* Stévan Kosta and Dimitri Kosta. *Career:* Attaché, Foreign Office, Belgrade 1928; Private Secretary to Minister of Foreign Affairs 1928–32. Participated in the Little Entente Conference and the League of Nations Assemblies and Councils 1929–32; The Hague Reparations Conferences 192—30, and the Paris Reparations Conference 1930; meetings of the Cttee. of European Union 1930–31; Disarmament Conference 1932; Lausanne Reparations Conf. 1932. Secy. in the Political Dept. of the Foreign Office 1932–35; Secretary Legation, Brussels 1935–36. Chargé d'Affaires 1935; First Secretary, Embassy, Bucharest 1936–41, Chargé d'Affaires 1939; Principal Private Secretary to Prime Minister 1941–43; First Secretary, Embassy, London 1943–45; Secretary General, Yugoslav National Committee in Exile 1945–56. Member, Faculty of Modern and Medieval Languages, University of Cambridge 1957, Librarian, Dept. of Slovonic Studies, Senior Member of the University 1961, and Member of the Selwyn College 1962. *Member:* Académie Internationale des Sciences et des lettres; Polish Soc. of Arts & Sciences Abroad; Soc. of Serbian Writers & Artists Abroad; Institut Français du Rogaume-Uni. *Publications:* The Struggle of the Serbs, (1943); The World's Verdict, (1947); Voyislav Marinkovich and his Times (5 vols. in Serbian) 1955–60; Lady Paget (in Serbian 1959); Serbian, Ragusan and Croatian Reader (2 vols.) 1962); (Yovan Doutchitch (in Serbian) (1967); Conversations with Slobodan Yovanovitch (2 vols. in Serbian) 1969–72; The Marriage of King Peter II as seen from British Sources (in Serbian) 1975. *Awards:* Orders from Belgium, Czechoslovakia, France, Greece, Italy, Poland, Romania and Yugoslavia. *Club:* United Oxford & Cambridge Univ. *Address:* 6 Larchfield, Gough Way, Cambridge.

**PAYNE, John Jr.** American mining engineer and executive. *B.* 1908. *Educ.* Texas Western College, El Paso, Tex. (BS Mining Eng.). *M.* 1944, Marjorie E. Chubb. *Career:* Mine

Geologist, Chief Geologist, Patino Mines & Enterprises. Llallague, Bolivia 1931–36; Geologist, Consolidated Mines Inc. Manilla 1937–38; Chief Eng. Chief Geologist, Surigao Consolidated Mines Inc. Philippines 1938–40; Mining Engineer Amer. Metal Co. Ltd. 1940–44; Lieut. U.S. Navy 1944–46; Asst. Manager and Mgr. Mining Dept. AMAX 1946–55; Pres. Exploration & Mine Development Dept. (AMAX) 1955–68; Vice-Pres. Amer. Metal Climax Inc. 1955–73; Group Vice-Pres. Overseas Mining Activities for AMAX 1967–73; Dir. Amer. Metal Climax Inc. (AMAX) 1969–73; Vice-Pres. & Dir. Ivoryton Minerals Inc. *Award:* Outstanding Graduate Texas Western Coll. 1951. *Member:* American Institute of Mining, Metallurgical & Petroleum Engineers; Mining & Metallurgical Society of America; Canadian Inst. Mining & Metallurgical; Geological Society of America. *Clubs:* Mining; Westchester Country; Explorers; University. *Address:* 1070 Park Avenue, New York 10028; and *office* AMAX Center, Greenwich, Conn, 06830, U.S.A.

**PAYTON, Stanley Walden,** CMG. British executive. *B.* 1921. *Educ.* Monoux School (Essex) and privately. *M.* 1941, Joan Starmer. *S.* Robert Walden. *Dau.* Rosemary Anne Walden. *Career:* Service with the Fleet Air Arm 1940–46; varied experience and overseas missions for Bank of England 1946–57; United Kingdom Alternate on Managing Board of European Payments Union and European Monetary Agreement 1957–59; Governor, Bank of Jamaica 1960–64; First Deputy Chief Overseas Dept. Bank of England 1965–71; Senior adviser to the Bank of England 1971–75; Chief of Overseas Dept. since 1975. *Clubs:* Naval; Overseas Bankers. *Address:* Pollards Park House, Chalfont St. Giles, Bucks.

**PAZ ESTENSSORO, Victor.** *Educ.* Universidad Mayor de San Andrés. *M.* Carmela Cerrute. *S.* Ramiro. *Dau.* Miriam; *M.* (2) Teresa Cortez. *Daus.* Patricia, Moira, and Silvia Valentina. *Career:* Senior Official of Finance 1932–33; Deputy for Tarija 1938–39; Pres., Banco Minero 1939; Natl. Deputy for Tarija 1940–43; Professor of Economic History, La Paz Univ. 1939–41; Min. of Finance 1943–46; Head of Natl. Revolutionary Movement; Pres. of the Republic 1952–56; Ambassador to Court of St. James's 1956–59; Pres. of the Republic of Bolivia 1960–64. Lect. in Economics Nat. Eng. Univ. of Lima 1966–71. *Publications:* Esquema de la Organización Politica y Administrative de Bolivia; Aspectos de la Economia Boliviana; Revolución y Contrarrevolutión; Processo y Sentencia de la Oligarquia Boliviana; La ultima carta de la oligarquia boliviana; Como Presidente de la Republica ha llevado a cabo en dos años de gobierno la Nacionalización de las Minas; Reforma Agraria; Voto Universal; Reorganización del Ejército; Desarrollo y Diversificación de la Economia Boliviana, y el mejoramiento del nivel de vida de las masas obreras y campesinas. *Address:* Casilla 1301, Lima, Peru.

**PEACHEY, Roy Albert.** Australian. *B.* 1917. *Educ.* University of Tasmania (BCom); Columbia Univ. (MA). *Career:* Australian Imperial Forces, 1940–45; Dept. of External Affairs, Canberra, 1945–48; Australian Mission to U.N., 1948–53; Chmn., U.N. Mission to West Africa, 1952; Acting High Commissioner in Colombo, 1955–56; Counsellor, Bangkok, 1958–61; Ambassador to Republic of Korea, 1964–68. Ambassador to Sweden, and Finland 1968–72 and Norway 1970–72; Ambassador to Turkey since 1976. *Address:* Australian Embassy, Ankara, Turkey.

**PEACOCK, Hon. Andrew Sharp.** Australian Politician. *B.* 1939. *Educ.* Scotch Coll., Melbourne and Melbourne Univ.—Bachelor of Laws. *Career:* Former Partner, Rigby and Fielding, Solicitors; Pres., Victorian Liberal Party 1965–66; Chmn., Peacock & Smith Pty Ltd. 1962–69; Liberal MP (Australia) for Kooyong since 1966; Minister for the Army and Minister assisting the Prime Minister 1969–71; Minister assisting the Treasurer 1971–Feb. 1972; Minister for External Territories, Feb.–Dec. 1972; Member, Opposition Executive 1973–75; Minister for Foreign Affairs since 1975. *Clubs:* Melbourne Cricket; Sorrento Golf. *Address:* 30 Monomeath Avenue, Canterbury, Victoria 3126, Australia; and *office* 4 Treasury Place, Melbourne, Victoria 3002.

**PEAKE, Sir Harald.** British banker. *B.* 1899. *Educ.* Eton; Trinity College, Cambridge (MA). *Career:* Served in World War I, Coldstream Guards and World War II, Auxiliary Air Force (Air Cdre.) Chmn. Lloyds Bank Ltd. 1962–69, Lloyds & Scottish Ltd., Lloyds Bank Unit Trust Managers Ltd. Yorkshire Bank Ltd.; National Bank of New Zealand Ltd. *Address:* 2 Shepherds Close, Shepherds Place, Upper Brook Street, London W1Y 3RT; and Court Farm, Tackley, Oxon, OX5 3AQ.

**PEAKE, Henry James,** OBE. Australian publisher and editor. *B.* 1925. *Educ.* Primary and Secondary, Mount Barker, S.A. *M.* 1946, Helen Margaret Langley. *S.* Richard James. *Daus.* Christine Anne and Susan Marie. *Career:* Justice of the Peace 1952—; South Aust. Provincial Press Exec. 1955—; Chmn. of Directors, S.A. Country Newspapers Ltd. 1966—. Dir. South East Telecasters 1964–73; Pres., Adult Education Centre, Naracoorte 1966–77. Pres., Naracoorte and District Promotional Group 1970–71; Pres. Rotary (1971–72). President: Australian Provincial Press Association 1962–65 (Life Mem., 1977), SA. Provincial Press Assn. 1959–62 (Life Mem., 1977), Naracoorte Chamber of Commerce 1962–63, Mount Barker R.S.L. 1957–58, Naracoorte R.S.L. 1962–63, & Naracoorte Youth Centre 1972–75 (Life Mem. 1977); Naracoorte Justices Assn. 1967–77; Commonwealth Immigration Publicity Council 1962–68; Australian Provincial Press Executive 1959–68; Publisher and Editor Naracoorte Herald; Legatee (1974). *Club:* Naracoorte Rotary. A Founder, Naracoorte Community Club (Public Officer); Life member, R.S.L., 1968. *Address:* 92 Gordon Street, Naracoorte, S.A.; and *office* 93 Smith Street, Naracoorte, S.A., Australia.

**PEARCE** (*of Sweethaws*), **Lord** (Edward Holroyd). Lord of Appeal; *B.* 1901. *Educ.* Charterhouse; Corpus Christi College, Oxford (MA). *M.* 1927, Erica Priestman. *S.* 2. *Career:* Called to the Bar 1925; King's Counsel 1945; Bencher of Hon. Society of Lincoln's Inn 1948; Judge High Court of Justice, 1948–57, Lord Justice of Appeal 1957–62. Lord of Appeal in Ordinary 1962–69; Chmn. Commission on Rhodesian Opinion 1971–72; Chmn. of Press Council 1969–74; Landscape Painter. Hon. Fellow of Corpus Christi College. *Address:* Sweethaws Crowborough, Sussex.

**PEARKES, Hon. George Randolph,** VC, PC, CC, CB, DSO, MC. *B.* 1888 (Watford, England). *Educ.* Berkhamsted School (England). *M.* 1925, Constance Blytha Copeman. *S.* John Andre. *Career:* Went to Canada 1906; served 2½ years with Royal North West Mounted Police in Yukon; enlisted in Canadian Mounted Rifles as Pte. Jan. 1915 (successively Lieut. (1916), Capt., Maj. and Lieut.-Col. commanding 116th Bn., C.E.F.); won VC at Passchendaele 1917; wounded in action five times; awarded MC, DSO and Croix de Guerre (France). After World War I remained on permanent force as officer of Princess Patricia's Canadian Light Infantry; graduated from British Army Staff College 1919; staff appointments in various H.Q. Dir. of Military Training and Staff Duties at Army H.Q. Jan. 1935; graduated from Imperial Defence College 1937; promoted to rank of Brigadier to command M.D. No. 13, Calgary. Went overseas in Dec. 1939 as O.C. 2nd Canad. Inf. Brigade; Major-General July 1940, to command 1st Div., G.O.C., Pacific Command Sept. 1942–Feb. 1945. Created Companion Order of the Bath (U.K.) and Commander, Legion of Merit (U.S.A.); Companion of the Order of Canada 1967; Hon. LLD, Univ. of Victoria, Hon. LLD, Simon Fraser Univ., Hon. LLD, University of British Columbia. First elected to House of Commons (Canada) at Gen. Election 1945; re-elected 1949–53–57–58. Canadian Minister of National Defence 1957–60. Lieut.-Governor of British Columbia Oct. 1960–68. Progressive Conservative. *Club:* Union (Victoria, B.C.). *Address:* 1268 Tattersall Drive, Victoria, B.C., Canada.

**PEARSON, Rt. Hon. Lord** (Colin Hargreaves Pearson), C.B.E. *B.* 1899. *Educ.* St. Paul's School; Balliol College, Oxford. *M.* 1931, Sophie Grace Thomas. *S.* 1. *Dau.* 1. *Career:* Served in World War I, Army 1918; called to the Bar 1924; Junior Common Law Counsel to Ministry of Works 1930–49; KC 1949; temporary member, Treasury Solicitor's Department 1939–45; Recorder of Hythe 1939–51; Judge of High Court 1951–61; Member, Supreme Court Rule Committee 1957–65. President, Restrictive Practices Court 1960–61; Lord Justice of Appeal 1961–65, Chmn., Law Reform Committee 1963–73; Chmn. of Court of Inquiry into a dispute in the Electrical Industry 1964; Lord of Appeal 1965–74; Chmn. of Court of Inquiry into certain matters concerning the Shipping Industry 1966, Chmn. of Court of Inquiry into the dispute between the British Overseas Airways Corp. and the British Airlines Pilots Assn. 1968. Chmn. Court of Inquiry into dispute between British Steel Corp. and certain of its employees, 1968; Chmn. Court of Enquiry, Dock Strike 1968; Arbitral body, Teachers Renumeration 1971 and 1972; Royal Commission, Civil Liability and Compensation for Personal Injury since 1972. *Address:* House of Lords, London, S.W.1.

**PEARSON, Sir (James) Denning,** JP. British. *B.* 1908. *Educ.* Canton Secondary School and Cardiff Technical Coll. (BScEng; Whitworth Scholar). *M.* 1932, Eluned Henry. *Daus.* 2. *Career:* Joined Rolls-Royce 1932, appointed to

Board 1949. I/C Aero Engine Div. 1954–65; Chief Executive & Deputy Chairman Rolls Royce Ltd. 1957–68. President Society of British Aircraft Constructors 1963–64. Member Natl. Economic Development Council 1964–67. Member of Council, Manchester Business School; Member of Governing Body London Graduate School of Business Studies. 1968–70. Chairman & Chief Executive, Rolls-Royce Ltd. 1969–70; Consultant Chmn. Gamma Assn. 1973—. *Member:* Governing Body of Administrative Staff College, Henley 1968–73; Member of Council of Voluntary Service Overseas. *Awards:* Dr Ingeh Brunswick Univ. 1962; Hon. FRAeS; CEng; Hon. FIMechE; FBIM; FRSA, and various honorary degrees and fellowships; Benjamin Franklin Roy. Soc. of Arts Gold medal 1971. *Publications:* The Development and Future of Turbine Engines for Airline Aircraft (1955); Management of Managers (1961); A Review of the Aero Engine Industry in the West since the end of World War II (1962); The Present State of Engineering—Bridge between Science and Industry (1965); Application of Modern Management and Organizational Techniques to Engineering Activities (1965). *Address:* 'Greenacres,' Holbrook, Derbyshire.

**PEARSON, Nathan Williams**, *B.* 1911. *Educ.* Dartmouth College (AB) and Harvard Univ. (MBA). *M.* 1947, Kathleen Patricia McMurty. *S.* Nathan Williams, Jr. *Career:* With U.S. Steel Corp. 1939–42. On Active duty U.S. Navy, released to inactive duty as Commander U.S.N.R. 1942–46. Manager, Research, Matson Navigation Co. 1946; Controller, The Carborundum Co. 1947; Financial Exec. for Paul Mellon, 1947—; Vice-Pres. and Governor T. Mellon & Sons Pittsburgh 1957–71; Dir. Ampex Corp; The Carborundum Co.; The Hanna Mining Co.; Aluminium Company of America; Gulf Oil Corp.; Koppers Co. Inc.; Mellon N.A. Bank; Mellon National Corp. *Clubs:* Allegheny Country; Duquesne; Edgeworth; Harvard-Yale-Princeton; Laurel Valley Golf; Racquet & Tennis; Rolling Rock. *Address:* 10 Woodland Road, Sewickley, Pa. 15143; and *office* Mellon Square, Pittsburgh, Pa.15230, U.S.A.

**PEART, Lord** (T. Frederick), PC. *B.* 1914. *Educ.* Wolsingham Gr. School; Henry Smith Sec. Hartlepool; Bede Coll. Durham Univ. B.Sc.; Inner Temple, Inns of Court. *M.* 1945, Sarah Elizabeth Lewis. *S.* 1. *Career:* Councillor, School-teacher, and war-service 1937–45; Parly. Private Secy. to Minister of Agriculture 1945–51; British Delegate to Council of Europe 1952–55 (rep. Agric. Cttee. and Cttee. for Culture and Science, Vice-Pres.); Min. of Agriculture, Fisheries and Food 1964–68; Leader of the House of Commons 1968–70; Apr.–Oct. 1968, Lord Privy Seal; Lord President of the Council 1968–70; Leader of British Labour Delegation, Council of Europe and Western European Union 1973–74; Min. of Agriculture, Fisheries and Food 1974–76; created Life Peer 1976; Lord Privy Seal and Leader of the Lords. Privy Council Rep. on Council of RCVS; Dir. F.M.C. 1971–74. *Address:* House of Lords, London, S.W.1.

**PECK, Sir Edward Heywood**, GCMG. British Diplomatic Service (Ret'd.). *B.* 1915. *Educ.* Clifton College Bristol and The Queen's College Oxford (MA Oxon). *M.* 1948, Alison Mary MacInnes. *S.* Donald. *Daus.* Rosamund and Sylvia. *Career:* In Consular and Diplomatic Service since 1938. Served in Barcelona, Ankara (and elsewhere in Turkey), Greece and Delhi. Deputy Commandant British Sector, Berlin, 1955–58; Counsellor in office of Commissioner-General for South-East Asia, Singapore 1959–60; Asst. Under-Secretary, Foreign Office, London 1961–66; British High Commissioner in Kenya 1966–68. Deputy Under-Secretary of State, Foreign Office, Apr. 1968–70; U.K. Permanent Representative to North Atlantic Council 1970–75; Hon. Visiting Fellow in Defence Studies at Aberdeen Univ. since 1976. *Club:* Alpine. *Address:* Easter Torrans, Tomintoul, Banffshire.

**PECK, Sir John Howard**, KCMG. *B.* 1913. *Educ.* Wellington College and Corpus Christi College, Oxford. *M.* 1939, Mariska Caroline Somlo. *S.* 2. *Career:* Entered Civil Service (Admiralty) 1936; Asst. Private Secy. to First Lord of the Admiralty 1937–39, to Minister for Co-ordination of Defence 1939–40 and Prime Minister 1940–46. Transferred to Foreign Service 1946; British Embassy, The Hague 1947–50; Head, Information Research Dept., Foreign Office 1951–54, and Political Div., British Middle East Office 1954–56; Director-Genera, British Information Services, New York 1956–59; U.K. Permanent Representative on the Council of Europe 1959–62; Ambassador to Senegal 1962–66 and Mauritania 1962–65. Assistant Under-Secretary of State, Foreign Office, 1966–70. H.M. Ambassador Dublin 1970–73. *Address:* 4 Eglinton Park, Dun Laoghaire, Co. Dublin.

**PECK, William Charles.** British chemical engineer. *B.* 1897. *Educ.* University of London (MSc). *M.* 1922, Winifred Emily Fox. *S.* Geoffrey Charles Alan and Raymond Frederick Julian. *Career:* Technical Director and Chemical Engineer, Burgoyne Burbidges & Co. Ltd., London 1918–32; Lecturer in Chemical Engineering, University of London (Battersea Polytechnic) 1931–46. Chairman, Apex Construction Ltd. (Chemical, Pharmaceutical and Special Process Engineers), Kent; Senator Univ. of London since 1946. *Member:* Institution of Chemical Engineers, Fellow Royal Socy, of Health, Inst. of Food Sciences and Technology (Fellow), Royal Institute of Chemistry (Fellow), Institution of Mechanical Engineers (Fellow), Society of Chemical Industry, Institute of Metals American Chemical Society. *Publications:* many scientific articles in Manufacturing Chemist, Pharmaceutical Journal, Food Manufacture, Chemical Age, Industrial Chemist, Chemical Products, Thorpe's Dictionary of Chemistry (1940), Chemistry and Industry, Dechema-Monographien Band, etc. *Address:* 18 The Grove, Bexleyheath, Kent.

**PEDERSEN, Inger Helga**, Cand jur. Judge of the Supreme Court of Denmark. *B.* 1911. *Career:* Secy., Ministry of Justice 1936; Minister's Private Secy. 1940–46; Attorney 1945; Leading Attorney 1949; Judge, Town Court, Copenhagen 1949–50 and 1953–56; Judge, Court of Appeals 1956–64. Pres., Danish Women's Council 1949–50; Minister of Justice 1950–53. Member of Parliament 1953–64. Delegate: UNESCO Conferences 1949–50–56–60–62–64–66–68–72 & 74; U.N. Conference General 1958 and 1959, and to Parliamentary Union Natl. Board 1953. U.N. Status of Women Commission 1950. Pres., Danish National Cttee. of UNESCO, 1970–74; Steering Bd. Red Cross 1971–76; Chmn., Danish Press Board 1971; Danish State's Controlling Bd. Inst. of the Press since 1973. Judge of the European Court of Human Rights since 1971. Vice-Pres. Court of revision of Crime Cases since 1972; Pres., Foundation for Trees and Environment 1974. *Publications:* Celine and Denmark (1975); and articles on legal and political subjects. *Address:* Statholdervej 19, Copenhagen, N.V.

**PEDERSEN, Victor August.** Norwegian. *B.* 1923. *Educ.* Oslo University (Graduate in Law 1949); Supreme Court Barrister 1962. *M.* 1952, Audhild Moen. *S.* Thor Henning. *Career:* Deputy Judge 1949–51; Secy., Ministry of Justice and Police 1951–52; Legal Adviser to Norwegian Savings Banks Association 1952–58. Joined Fellesbanken A/S, Oslo as Legal Adviser 1959. Dep. Man. Dir. 1960, Managing Director since 1964. *Address:* Torjusbakken 11, Oslo 3; and *office* Kirkegt. 14–18, Oslo 1, Norway.

**PEDLER, Sir Frederick Johnson**, Kt 1969. British. *B.* 1908. *Educ.* Watford Grammar School and Gonville & Caius College, Cambridge (MA). *M.* 1935, Esther Ruth Carling. *S.* Robin and Martin. *Dau.* Mrs. R. A. W. Sharp. *Career:* Civil Servant 1930–47. Director, Unilever Ltd. and N.V. 1956–68. Deputy Chairman, The United Africa Co. Ltd. 1965–68; Chairman of The Council for Tech. Educ. and Training for Overseas Countries 1962–73. Director, William Baird & Co. Ltd. 1969–75, Treasurer, School of Oriental and African Studies, 1969, and Hon. Fellow 1976. *Publications:* West Africa (Methuens); Economic Geography of West Africa (Longmans), The Lion and the Unicorn in Africa (Heinemann). *Clubs:* Reform; Royal Commonwealth. *Address:* 36 Russell Road, Moor Park, Northwood, Middlesex.

**PEDROSA, Pio.** Philippine banker. *B.* 4 May 1900. *Educ.* University of the Philippines (BSc, MA). *M.* 1927, Luisa Noble Acebedo. *S.* Ramon, Alberto, Fernando, Augusto, Carlos. *Daus.* Lourdes Maria, Ana Josefina, Victoria Leticia. *Career:* Dir. and Pres.: Prudential Bank and Trust Co., Philippine Capital Management, Inc.; Chairman of the Board, Capital Insurance Co.; Insular Sugar Refining Corp.; Dir.: Philippine-American Life Insurance Co., Commonwealth Insurance Co., Philippine-American Assurance Co., Inc.; Philippine-American Accident Insurance Co., Inc.; Philippine Home Assurance Corp.; Formerly: Sec. of Finance; Presiding Officer, Monetary Board, Central Bank of the Philippines; Commissioner of the Budget; President, Philippine National Bank; Chairman, Board of Governors, Agricultural Credit and Co-operative Financing Administration; President, Manila Railroad Co.; Member, Council of State; Chairman: National Economic Council, Central Board of Tax Appeals; Chairman, Boards of Directors of Philippine Air Lines, Inc.; National Development Co.; De La Rama Steamship Co.; Regent, University of the Philippines; Governor: Philippine National Red Cross, Philippine Tuberculosis Society; Vice-Chairman, 1948 Conference on General

Agreements on Tariffs and Trade, Torquay, England; Delegate of Bankers Association of the Philippines to the Far East American Council on Commerce and Industry, New York City, 1958, 1959; Philippine delegate to the 1959 and 1961 meetings of the International Bank for Reconstruction and Development, the International Monetary Fund, and the Development Loan Fund, Washington, D.C., and Vienna, Austria. *Address:* 137 Hoover Street, San Juan, Rizal, Philippines.

**PEEBLER, Charles D. (Jr.)** *Educ.* Drake Univ. *Career:* Production Dept. Assist. and Account Exec. Bozell andJacobs Inc. 1958–59; Vice-Pres. and mem. Plans Board (New Business Development Dept) 1960–65; President Bozell and Jacobs Inc. 1965–67; Chmn. of the Board, Pres. and Chief exec. officer Bozell and Jacobs International since 1967. *Dir.* Junior Achievement Inc. since 1964 (Pres. 1973–74); Nat. Conference of Christians and Jews 1962–65; United Community Funds of America (1968); also chmn. P.R. adv. cttee and mem. Nat. Exec. Cttee; American Association of Advertising Agencies; Nat. Outdoor Advertising Assoc.; Stonar cos. *Member:* United Community Services Finance Campaign (gen. chmn. 1966); Bd. of Trustees of Regional Health Care Corp.; Drake Univ. Devel. Program Alumni Bd.; *President:* Bd. of Trustees Brownell-Talbot Sch. (Pres. 1975–76); International Young Presidents' Org. *Awards:* Relig. Heritage of America Man of the Year (1971). *Address:* Bozell and Jacobs Inc., Advertising and PR., One Dag Hammarskjold Plaza, New York, N.Y. 10017, U.S.A.

**PEECH, Neil Malcolm.** British industrialist. *B.* 27 Jan. 1908. *Educ.* Wellington College, and Magdalen College, Oxford. *M.* 1932, Margaret Josephine Smallwood. *S.* Malcolm Richard Alan. *Dau.* June Jennifer. *Career:* Pioneered the production of magnesia from seawater and dolomite. Chairman, The Steetley Co. Ltd. 1935–76, President 1976; Dir. Sheepbridge Engineering Ltd. since 1949; Treas. Dir. Solway Chemicals Ltd. 1952; Chairman, Steetley of Canada (Holdings) Ltd. 1952–75; Chairman, Steetley Industries, Ltd. 1953–75. Director, Albright & Wilson Ltd. since 1958; and other companies, Underwriting Member of Lloyd's 1950–69. Vice-Consul for Sweden since 1949, Consul 1974–76. Chmn., Ministry of Power Solid Smokeless Fuel Committee 1959. High Sheriff of Yorkshire 1959. *Address:* Gateford, Worksop, Notts.

**PEEL, Bruce Braden.** Canadian librarian. *B.* 1916. *Educ.* Univ. of Saskatchewan (MA 1946) and Univ. of Toronto (BLibSc 1946). *M.* Margaret Fullerton. *S.* 1. *Dau.* 1. *Career:* Canadiana Librarian, Univ. of Saskatchewan 1946–50; Chief Cataloguer 1950–54, and Asst. Librarian 1954–55, Univ. of Alberta, Chief Librarian since 1956. *Publications:* The Saskatoon Story 1882–1952 (with Eric Knowles); Editor, Librarianship in Canada, 1946–67. Steamboats on the Saskatchewan (1972); Bibliography of the Prairie Provinces (enlarged ed. 1972, first published 1956); Early Printing in the Red River Settlement (1974). *Member:* Canad. Library Assn. Pres. 1969–70; Historical Socy. of Alberta; Bibliog. Socy. of Canada; Pres. 1970–72; Study of Canadian Academic Libraries Dr. Robert Downs, Chmn. 1966–70. Recipient of the Bibliographical Soc. of Canada's Tremaine medal "for outstanding service to bibliography in Canada, 1975". *Address:* 11047— 83 Avenue, Edmonton, Alta.; and Cameron Library, University of Alberta, Edmonton 7, Alta., Canada.

**PEERS, Roy Gillespie,** MBE. Canadian executive. *B.* 1900. *Educ.* Parkdale Collegiate Institute, Toronto. *M.* 1925, Madeline Rogers. *S.* 2. *Dau.* 1. *Career:* Exec. Dir., Joint War Production Cttee. U.S.—Canada 1941–44; Gen. Mgr., War Supplies Ltd., Washington, D.C. 1941–43; Vice-Pres., Canadian Commercial Corpn., Ottawa 1951–53; Dir. Canadian Arsenals Ltd. 1951–53. *Awards:* Order of the British Empire; Medal of Freedom with Palms (U.S.); Order of Brilliant Star (China). *Address:* P.O. Box 98, Paget, Bermuda.

**PEERSEN, Kaare (Rudolf Dostad).** Norwegian wholesaler. *B.* 1907. *Educ.* Commercial College *M.* 1938, Agnes Gerrard. *S.* Sven Rudolf. *Dau.* Ragnhild Margrethe. *Career:* Chmn., Kristiansand Handellstand Forening 1954–57; First Vice-Chairman, Norges Grossistforbund 1957–59. Member of Board, Norges Colonialgrossisters Forbund 1957–59. Chairman, Kristiansand Colonialgrossisters Forening 1954–58. Member of Board, Kristiansand Commercial College 1955—; and of N.H.F. (Norwegian Fed. of Commercial Associations) 1957–60. Member of Liberal Party. *Address:* Bellevue 25, Kristiansand S., Norway.

**PEIN, Franz,** LLD. Austrian diplomat. *B.* 1924. *Educ.* University of Graz (Law and Political Science); Commerce University, Vienna; University of Grenoble, Georgetown University Law School, Washington. *M.* 1947, Dorothea. *Career:* Social Administration, Graz, 1947–51; Federal Ministry of the Interior, Vienna, 1952–55; Entered Foreign Service, 1956; Federal Ministry for Foreign Affairs, Legal Div., 1956–59; Embassy, Washington, 1959–62; Consul, later Consul-General, New York, 1962–65; Federal Ministry for Foreign Affairs, Counsellor, Political Div. 1965–68. Ambassador to Australia and New Zealand 1968–73. Member, Austria's U.N. Delegations, 1963–68 and 1971; Minister, Federal Ministry, Foreign Affairs (Legal Div.) 1973–75; Ambassador, Head of Legal Div. since 1976. *Address:* Min. of Foreign Affairs, Vienna 1, Ballhausplatz, 2, Austria.

**PELL, Claiborne de Borda.** American Politician and Captain, U.S. Coast Guard Reserve. *B.* 1918. *Educ.* Princeton University (AB *cum laude*) and Columbia University (MA). *M.* 1944, Nuala O'Donnell. *S.* Herbert C. III, and Christopher T. H. *Daus.* Dallas and Julia L. W. *Career:* U.S. Coast Guard 1941–45; U.S. State Dept. and Foreign Service Officer 1945–52; Consultant, Democratic National Committee 1953–60; National Democratic Registration Chairman 1956; Vice-Pres., International Rescue Committee 1957–60; U.S. Delegate, Intergovernmental Maritime Consultative Organization 1959; 25th United Nations Gen. Assembly 1970; Formerly Vice-Pres., North American Newspaper Alliance; Senator from Rhode Island 1961–76. Democrat. *Clubs:* Hope (Providence, R.I.); Reading Room (Newport, R.I.); White's (London); Travellers (Paris); Knickerbocker, Brook, Racquet & Tennis (N.Y.C.); Metropolitan (Washington, D.C.). *Address:* 'Pelican Ledge', Newport, R.I., U.S.A.

**PELL, John Howland Gibbs.** American historian and trustee. *B.* 1904. *Educ.* St. Paul's School; Harvard Univ. LLD; Adelphi Coll.; Chung-ang Univ.; Fairleigh Dickinson Univ. LHD; Russell Sage College. *M.* 1929, Pyrma Tilton. *S.* John Bigelow. *Dau.* Sarah Gibbs (Dunning). *Career:* Engaged in Historical Research 1925–29; Estate Mangt. 1930–32; Organizer Partner John H. G. Pell & Co. 1932—; served from Lt. to Commander, 1941–45. Trustee, Dime Savings Bank N.Y.; Former Chancellor L.I.U.; Former Member Interstate Comm. on Lake Chaplain Basin; Commissioner of Education's Cttee. on New York State Museums; Former Chmn. Fed. Hudson-Champlain Celebration Commission; Pres. Ft. Ticonderoga Assn. 1950—; Trustee, N.Y. State Board, Historic Preservation 1966—; Member N.Y. State History Assn., Trustee 1950—; Chmn. N.Y. State Amer. Revolution Bicentennial Comm. 1968—; Dir. N.Y.C. Amer. Bicentennial Corp. 1971—; Trustee, Estate and Property, Episcopal Diocesan Convention, New York, New York Historical Society since 1973. *Awards:* Commendation from the Secy. of the Navy; Order of Orange Nassau (Holland); Chevalier Legion of Honor (France); Chauncey Depew Medal, Citation and Gold Medal S.A.R.; Garden Club of America Medal. *Publications:* Ethan Allen (a biography; Houghton Mifflin Co.), 1929; Chapter on Philip Schuyler in General Washington's Generals; articles on historic and economic subjects. *Clubs:* Knickerbocker; Downtown Association; Piping Rock; Seawanhaka Corinthian Yacht; Century, Metropolitan (Washington). *Address:* 870 Fifth Avenue, New York City, N.Y. 10021; Pelican Point, Centre Island, Oyster Bay, Long Island, N.Y. 11771, and *office* One Wall Street, New York City, N.Y.10005, U.S.A.

**PELLA, Giuseppe,** MP, DEcon, DComm. Italian politician. *B.* 18 Apr. 1902. *M.* 1935, Ines Cardolle. *Dau.* Wanda. *Career:* Member, (P.D.C.), Turin-Novara-Vercelli, Constitutent Assembly June 1946; Secretary, Parliamentary Commission on Finance and the Treasury; Under-Secretary of State for Finance Oct. 1946–June 1947; Minister of Finance June 1947–May 1948; Minister of the Treasury and the Budget May 1948–51; Minister of the Budget 1953–54 and Pres., Cncl. of Ministers, and Min. for For. Affs. Aug. 1953–54; Pres., General Assembly CECA, 1954–56; Deputy Prime Minister and Minister for Foreign Affairs 1957–58; Minister for Foreign Affairs. Feb. 1959–60; Minister of the Budget 1960–62; Member, Italian Senate 1968—; Chmn. Commission for Foreign Affairs, Minister of Finance Feb.–July 1972. *Address:* Via Ludovisi n. 35, Rome, Italy.

**PELLY, Blake Raymond,** OBE, MA. Group Captain, R.A.A.F. (Retd.). Australian company director. *B.* 1907. *Educ.* Wellington and Emmanuel College, Cambridge (BA 1928; MA 1950); Graduate, Air Staff Course, Fort Leavenworth, U.S.A. 1945. *M.* 1938, Mary Pamela Laidley Dowling. *S.* Andrew Douglas Blake and Michael Francis Blake. *Dau.*

Mrs. Angela Mary Compton. *Career:* Personal A.D.C. to Governor of N.S.W. 1937–38; R.A.A.F. 1937–46 (served in World War II; Western Desert and Pacific 1939–45); Group Capt. 1944, Commanded 451 Sqdn. 1941; R.A.A.F. Station Canberra 1942; 73 (F) Wing 1943; 71 (B) Wing 1944; Senior Air Staff Officer (Plans) R.A.A.F. Command 1944; Diploma, U.S.A. Air Staff Course 1945; Director of Tactics and Operational Requirements 1945; Director of Operations, R.A.A.F. HQ 1945–46; Managing Partner, Currawong Pastoral Estate 1938–66; Chmn. Mary Kathleen Uranium Ltd. 1956–72; Sun Alliance Life Assurance Ltd. 1959—; Vice-Chmn. Conzinc Rio Tinto of Australia 1962–67; Chmn. Sun Alliance Insurance Ltd. since 1972. Member Liberal Party of Australia; Member of Parliament N.S.W. 1950–57 (resigned). *Member:* Royal Agricultural Society of N.S.W.; member Committee, Australian Jockey Club since 1959 (Hon. Treas., 1960–74), Vice-Chmn since 1974. Deputy Chairman, Universities Board, N.S.W. & Member Higher Education Board (N.S.W.) 1976. Chmn. Australian Nat. Cttee. of United World Colleges. *Clubs:* Union (Sydney); Royal Sydney Golf; Australian Jockey; Sydney Turf. *Address:* 22 The Crescent, Vaucluse, 2030 Sydney; and *office* c/o Sun Alliance Life Assurance Ltd., 22–30 Bridge Street, Sydney, N.S.W. Australia.

**PENDLETON, Morris B.** American executive. *B.* 1901. *Educ.* Pomona Coll. (BA); Pepperdine Coll. LLD. *M.* 1924, Gladys Shepard. *S.* John M *Dau.* Barbara (Wittenberg). *Career:* Chmn. Bd. Emeritus'. Pendleton Tool Industries Inc. Dir. Federal Home Loan Bank; Trustee, Pomona Coll.; Dir. Los Angeles Y.M.C.A., and of Southern California Council on Economic Education; member, National Council of Boy Scouts of America; Director, Quarter Century Metals Club, and of All Year Club of Southern California; Life Member, Chamber of Commerce of the Philippines. Republican. *Clubs:* Jonathan; San Gabriel Country; San Marino City; Balboa Bay. *Address:* 1433 St. Albans Road, San Marino, Calif. 91108; and *office* Box 3519 Terminal Annex, Los Angeles 54, Calif., U.S.A.

**PENNEY, Lord William George** (created Life Peer, 1967), OM, KBE, FRS. British Scientist. *B.* 24 June 1909. *Educ.* Imperial College, London Univ. (BSc, PhD, DSc), Wisconsin Univ. (MA), and Cambridge Univ. (PhD). *M.* (1) 1935, Adele Minnie Elms (*D.*); (2) 1945, Eleanor Joan Quennell. *S.* Martin Charles, Christopher Charles. *Career:* Asst. Prof. of Mathematics, Imperial Coll. 1936–45; Prin. Scientific Officer, Dept. of Scientific Research, Los Alamos Lab., New Mexico, 1944–45; Chief Superintendent, Armaments Research Establishments, Min. of Supply 1946–52; Director, Atomic Weapons Research Establishment, Aldermaston, 1953–59; Member for Weapons Research & Development, U.K. Atomic Energy Authority 1954–59, member for Scientific Research, U.K. Atomic Energy Authority 1959–61; Deputy Chairman, U.K. Atomic Energy Authority 1961–64, Chairman 1964–67, Rector, Imperial College of Science and Technology 1967–73. *Publications:* articles on Quantum Theory and Hydrodynamics in various scientific journals. *Address:* Orchard House, East Hendred, Wantage, Oxon.

**PENNOCK, Donald William.** American professional engineer. *B.* 1915. *Educ.* College of Engineering, Univ. of Kentucky (BSc Mech Eng 1940; ME in Mech Eng 1948). *M.* 1951, Vivian Claire Kern. *S.* Douglas William. *Career:* With Scheeley Corp. 1935–39; Mechanical Equipment Design Eegineer, Univ. of Kentucky 1939; Experimental Test Engineer, Wright Aeronautical Corp. 1940–41; Investigative and Advisory Engineer to Wright Personnel Div. 1941–43; Industrial Engineer, Eastern Aircraft, Division of General Motors Corp. 1943–45; Factory Engineer 1945–55, Facilities Planning Engineer 1955–58, Senior Facilities Planning Engineer 1958–60, Corporate Staff Engineer 1960–64, Manager Facilities Engineering 1964—, Carrier Corporation. Member, Bd. of Material Handling Products Corp. 1950–55; member, Munitions Bd., SHIAC 1950–52; Exec. Cttee., National Material Handling Conf. 1951; ASMEAMHS Handbook Cttee. 1951–58; Chmn. of Bd. and Pres., American Material Handling Soc. 1950–53; National Vice-Pres., Society for Advancement of Management 1953–55; *Member:* A.S.M.E.; A.I.P.E.; N.S.P.E.; S.A.M.; N.J.S.P.E.; S.A.M.E.; Tau Beta Pi; Life member, All-A.M.A. Council, American Management Assn.; Induction, The Executive and Professional Hall of Fame 1966. *Publications:* contributions to U.S. and foreign technical journals. Editorial Advisory Bd., Modern Materials Handling (magazine) 1949–52; Managing Editor, magazine section, Materials Handling Engineering 1949–50. Bd. of Contributing and Consulting Editors, The 1958 Ronald Press Materials, Handling Handbook. *Address:* 24 Pebble Hill Road, Dewitt, N.Y., U.S.A.; and *office* Carrier Parkway, Syracuse, N.Y., U.S.A.

**PENROSE, Charles, Jr.** Association executive. *B.* 1921, *Educ.* Episcopal Academy, Overbrook, Pa. *M.* 1943, Ann Lucille Cantwell. *S.* James Cantwell, Thomas, John. *Career:* Exec. Secy., Newcomen Socy. in N.A., Philadelphia 1946–48; Philadelphia District Sales Manager, Fitchburg (Mass.) Paper Co. 1948–50 and 1952–53; Sales Manager, A. M. Collins Mfg. Co., Philadelphia 1953–54 (Vice-Pres. Sales 1954–55; Sales Mgr., A. M. Collins division of International Paper Co., N.Y.C. 1955; Asst. to Sales Mgr., fine paper and bleached board division 1956–57). Pres. Chief Exec. Officer and Trustee, Newcomen Society in North America Inc. 1961—, and of Newcomen Publications in North America Inc. 1958–61; Senior Vice-President for N.A., Newcomen Society, London 1957—; President and Director, Rocaton Inc., Darien, Conn., 1960–61. Served to Captain in both USAAF (S.W. Pacific 1940–46) and Army of U.S. (Germany 1950–52). *Publications:* They Live on a Rock in the Sea—The Isles of Shoals in Colonial Days, (1957). *Member:* Newcomen Societies in N.A. and London: Royal Socy. of Arts (Benjamin Franklin Fellow 1960); Pilgrims of U.S.; Franklin Inst. (Vermilye Medal Committee); First Troop Philadelphia City Cav. (Hon.); English-Speaking Union; Socy. of Amer. Military Engineers; National Inst. of Social Sciences; Chi Psi; Socy. of Amer. Historians; Marine Historical Assn.; Historical Societies of Pennsylvania, New Hampshire, and Portsmouth (N.H.); Amer. Philatelic Socy. Republican. *Clubs:* Philadelphia; Metropolitan (N.Y.C.); Tokeneke (Darien). *Address:* 6 Tory Hole Road, Darien, Conn. 06820; and *office* 412 Newcomer, North Ship Road, Exton, Pa. 19341 U.S.A.

**PEPER, Christian Baird.** American lawyer. *B.* 1910. *Educ.* Harvard (AB); Washington Univ. (LLB); Yale Univ. (LLM). *M.* 1935, Ethel Kingsland. *S.* Christian Baird. *Daus.* Mrs. K. B. Larson and Mrs. J. W. M. Perkins. *Career:* Lecturer on Law, Washington Univ. 1943–63; Partner, Peper, Martin, Jensen, Maichel & Hetlage (law firm); Chmn., St. Louis Steel Casting, Inc.; Hydraulic Press Brick Co.; Dir., St. Louis Preparatory School for Boys Inc. Member, Board of trustees, City Art Museum, St. Louis 1965–76. *Publications:* various articles in legal journals. *Clubs:* Noonday, University, Harvard (St. Louis), East India (London). *Address:* 1454 Mason Road, St. Louis County, Mo., U.S.A. and *office* 24th Floor, 720 Olive Street, St. Louis, Missouri 63101, U.S.A.

**PEPIN, Hon. Jean-Luc**, PC, CC. Canadian. *B.* 1924. *Educ.* BA; LPh (Philosophy); LLL (Law); DESD (Diploma in Higher Studies of Law). *M.* 1952, Mary Brock-Smith. *S.* 1. *Dau.* 1. *Career:* Professor 1951–56 and 1958–63; Dir. Dept. of Political Science, Faculty of Social Sciences, Univ. of Ottawa 1961–63. Minister of Energy, Mines and Resources, 1965–68; Min. of Industry and Minister of Trade & Commerce 1968–69. Minister of Industry, Trade & Commerce, Canada, 1969–72; Consultant on Trade, Pres. Interimco Ltd. 1972–75; former mem. Bd. of Dirs., Bombardier Ltd., Power Corp. of Canada Ltd., Collins Radio Co. of Canada Ltd., Celanese Canada Ltd., Crédit Foncier Franco-Canadien, Sidbec & Sidbec-Dosco Ltée., until 1975 when appointed Chmn. of Anti-Inflation Board; Co-Chmn., Task Force on Canadian Unity since 1977. *Awards:* Companion of the Order of Canada; Doctorates in Public Administration (h.c.) from Univs. of Sherbrooke & Laval (Quebec). *Address:* 16 Rothwell Drive, Ottawa; and *office* Task Force on Canadian Unity, 171 Slater Street, Ottawa, Ont. K1P 5R4, Canada.

**PEPPERCORN, Trevor Edward.** *B.* 1904. *Educ.* Beaumont and Balliol Coll., Oxford (BA Hons.). *M.* 1935, Sheila Ayre (*D.* 1972). *S.* Michael Anthony John. *Career:* Joined Dunlop Rubber Co. Ltd. as a trainee in 1928; served with Dunlop in India and South Africa. Appointed Director of Dunlop 1957: retired 1967; Chmn. Triplex Holdings Ltd. 1966–75; Overseas Development Inst. 1967–72; Weldall Engineering Ltd.; Fibreglass Pilkington Ltd. *Club:* Boodles. *Address:* The Grange, Yattendon, Newbury; and *office* Selwyn House, Cleveland Row, London, S.W.1.

**PERCIVAL, Sir Anthony**, Kt 1966, CB 1954. British. *B.* 1910. *Educ.* Manchester Grammar School and Cambridge Univ. *M.* 1935, Doris Cuff. *Dau.* 1. *Career:* Secretary, Export Credits Guarantee Department 1962–71; President, Union D'Assureurs des Credits Internationaux 1966–68; Chmn. Gordon & Gotch Holdings Ltd.; Dir. Simon Engineering Ltd.; Bank of Adelaide; Switzerland General Insurance Co.; Trade Indemnity Company. *Club:* Overseas Bankers. *Address:* 16 Hayes Way, Beckenham, Kent.

**PERDUNN, Richard Francis.** American. *B.* 1915. *Educ.* Lehigh University (BS in EE 1939). *M.* 1941, Eugenia Morel. *Dau.* Justine Réneau. *Career:* Principal, Stevenson, Jordan & Harrison Inc. 1954; Manager of Admin., Chemical Control Division, Merck & Co. 1949; Engineer, U.S. Steel Corp. and Glenn L. Martin 1939; Supt. of Machining and Assembling, U.S. Time Corp. 1943; President & Chief Executive Officer, Parcel Delivery Service Inc. 1961—; First Bank of Colonia, N.J. 1962—. President, Executive President, Stevenson, Jordon & Harrison 1964—; Vice-President, Golightly & Co., International 1967—. President, Eldunn Co. Inc.; and Woodunnel Co. *Publications:* Small Lot Planning, (1962); Profit Planning, (1962). *Member:* Newcomen Socy. of North America; A.M.A.; Systems & Procedure Assn. of America; S.A.M.; Council for Economic Development. International Platform Assoc. *Clubs:* Echo Lake Country (Westfield, N.J.); University. *Address:* 407 Kenli Lane, Brielle, N.J.; and *office* 1 Rockefeller Plaza, New York, N.Y. 10020, U.S.A.

**PEREDA APARICIO, Fernando Maria.** Spanish company director and lawyer. *B.* 26 June 1904. *Educ.* University of Deusto (L en CE). *M.* 1934, María Dolores Perez Herrera. *S.* 6. *Daus.* 5. *Career:* Pres., Colégio de Consignatarios de Buques; Pres. Naviera Montañesa, S.A.; Naviera de Castilla S.A.; Transportes de Petroleos S.A.; Transportes Frigorificos Maritimos S.A.; Financiera Montañesa S.A.; Consejero de Electra de Viesgo, S.A.; Pres. de Recuperaciones Submarinas, S.A.; Frigorificos de Santana, S.A.; Procurador en Cortes Españolas. *Address:* Reina Victoria 115, Santander .Spain.

**PEREIRA, Horace Felix de Courcy.** American. Financial Consultant. *B.* 1906. *Educ.* Oxford Univ. (BA 1929, MA 1950) and Harvard Univ. (EdM 1954). *M.* 1930, Beatrice Marie Bowie. *S.* Peter David Mandell. *Dau.* Penelope (Mrs. C. R. Johnson). *Career:* Asst. Vice-Pres. 1943, First National Bank of Boston, Vice-Pres. 1962–72; Dir. Chmn. Finance Cttee. Ryder Systemic Assoc. Transport Inc; Member, Mass, Advisory Council on Education; Trustee, The Putney School. *Publications:* Business Loans of American Commercial Banks (co-author). *Clubs:* Union (Boston); The Country (Brookline, Mass.); Weavers (N.Y.C.); Overseas Bankers (London); Gresham (London). *Address:* 943 High Street, Dedham, Mass. 02026, U.S.A.

**PERERA, Leslie Simon Bernard.** Ceylonese. *B.* 1910. *Educ.* Royal College (Colombo), London Univ. (BSc) and Cambridge Univ. as Ceylon Govt. Scholar. *M.* 1941, Nimal De Fonseka. *S.* Cecil. *Dau.* Indrani. *Career:* In Ceylon Civil Service 1935–63 (held senior executive positions during this period, including posts of Permanent Secretary in the Ministries of Health, Commerce and Trade, Industries and Home Affairs); Ceylon High Commissioner in Canada, 1965. *Clubs:* Sinhalese Sports (Colombo); Royal Colombo Golf; Nuwara Eliya Golf; Rideau (Ottawa). *Address:* c/o Ministry of Foreign Affairs, Colombo, Sri Lanka.

**PEREZ DE CUELLAR, Javier.** Peruvian lawyer and diplomat. *B.* 1920. *Educ.* Law. *M.* 1947, Yvette Roberts-Darricau. *S.* 1. *Dau.* 1. Entered Foreign Ministry 1940; served in France, Britain, Bolivia and Brazil 1944–60; Director: Personal, Protocol and Political Depts. 1961–64; Ambassador to Switzerland 1964–66. Prof. of Diplomatic Law, Peruvian Diplomatic Academy 1962–63, and of International Relations, Air War Academy of Peru 1963–64. Secretary-General Peruvian Foreign Ministry June 1966–69; Ambassador to the U.S.S.R. 1969–71; Perm. Rep. to the UN 1971–75; Special Rep. of UN Sec.-Gen. in Cyprus since 1975. *Publications:* Manual de Derecho Diplomàtico (1964). *Member:* Sociedad Peruana de Derecho Internacional (Peruvian Socy. of International Law); Sección Peruana de la Comisión Internacional de Juristas. Instituto Interamericano de Estudios Jurídicso Internacionales (Interamerican Institute for Juridicial International Studies). Several national and foreign decorations. *Address:* Office of the Special Representative, UN Peace Keeping Force, Nicosia, Cyprus.

**PEREZ MORALES, Col. Jesus Manuel.** Ambassador of Venezuela. *B.* 1917. *Educ.* Venezuela Military School, and Superior College of War, Brazil. *M.* Irma Amoroso Blanco; four children. Chief of Staff of the Venezuelan Armed Forces 1958. Military Attaché: Washington 1958–59, and Italy 1960. Ambassador to Portugal 1960–63, and to Turkey 1963–65. Special foreign missions: Member of delegation to inauguration of monument to Bolivar in Mexico 1946; to Colombia, by invitation of the Armed Forces; to Peru. As Min. Plen. forming part of the delegation of service over the repatriation of the ashes of Don Simón Rodriguez, and General José Trinidad Morán 1954. Member of delegation of OEA for demilitarization of the border between Nicaragua–Honduras during the conflict opposing those countries in 1956; Ambassador to Japan 1966. *Awards:* Grand Officer, Order of the Liberator; Order of General Rafael Urdaneta (2nd Cl.); Comdr. Order of Vasco Nunez de Balboa; Mil. Order of Ayacucho (Official) Peru; 'Honor al Mérito' (Chile); Cross of Military Merit (Guatemala); Order of Merit General José Mariá de Cordoba, Colombia; Military Order of Merit, Brazil; Medal of the Peacemaker (Brazil); Cross of the Land Forces 2nd Cl. (Venezuela). *Address:* c/o Ministry of Foreign Affairs, Caracas, Venezuela.

**PEREZ RODRIGUEZ, Carlos Andrés.** Venezuelan politician. *B.* 1922. *Educ.* Univ. Central de Venezuela. *Career:* Private Sec. to Pres. Betancourt 1945; Deputy 1947–48; in exile 1949–58; Chief Editor, La République, San José 1953–58; Deputy since 1958; Minister of the Interior 1963–64; Sec.-Gen., Acción Democrática 1968; President of Venezuela since 1974. *Address:* Palacio de Miraflores, Caracas, Venezuela.

**PERKINS, Richard S.** American banker. *B.* 27 June 1910. *Educ.* Greenwich, Conn. *M.* (1) Adaline Havemeyer (*Div.* 1976). *S.* 2. *Daus.* 2. (2) 1977, Audrey Walker Newell. *Career:* With Thompson Fenn & Co., Hartford, Conn. 1929; Wood Struthers & Co., New York City 1932; Partner, Harris Upham & Co. 1936; Exec. Vice-Pres., City Bank Farmers Trust Company Mar. 1951; Pres. First National City Trust Co. 1951–59, Chmn. 1959–66; Chairman, Exec. Committee, First National City Bank of New York, 1959–70; Dir., Allied Chemical Corp., New York Life Insurance Co., International Telephone & Telegraph Corp., and Southern Pacific Company; Dir. New Court Equity Fund & Hospital Corp. of America; Trustee: The Seeing Eye Inc., Y.M.C.A., Carnegie Institutions of Washington, Consolidated Edison Co. of N.Y., Metropolitan Museum of Art, and Vincent Astor Foundation. *Address:* 399 Park Avenue, New York 10022, N.Y., U.S.A.

**PERLOFF, Harvey Stephen.** American. Dean, School of Architecture and Planning, UCLA. Fellow, American Academy of Arts and Sciences. *B.* 1915. *Educ.* Univ. of Pennsylvania (AB); Graduate Study, London School of Economics; Harvard Univ. (PhD). *M.* 1944, Miriam Seligman. *S.* 2. Economist, Fed. Reserve Board 1941–43; Consultant, Govt. of Puerto Rico 1946–47 and 1950–51; Prof. of Social Sciences, Univ. of Chicago 1947–55, Head, Planning School 1951–55; Consultant, President's Water Resources Policy Commission 1950; TVA 1953–54; Member U.S. Mission to Turkey and Israel 1954; Member Cttee. of Nine, Alliance for Progress 1961–64; Consultant Dept. of State 1963–64; Economic Development Admin., Dept. of Commerce 1965–66. Dir. Program of Regional and Urban Studies, Resources for the Future, 1955–68. *Publications:* many books and articles on city and regional planning, economy and finance. *Member:* Phi Beta Kappa; Pi Gamma Mu; Amer. Econ. Assn.; Regional Science Assn.; Amer. Socy. of Planning Officials; Amer. Socy, for Public Administration. *Address:* 930 Manning Ave., Los Angeles, Calif. 90024; and *office* School of Architecture and Planning, UCLA.

**PERRET du CRAY, Jean Comte.** Assurance executive. *B.* 1909. *Educ.* Licencié en Droit; Diplomé of the Free School of Political Sciences. *M.* 1932, Nicole de Tourville de Buzonnière. *S.* Alain François, Bertrand and Gerard. *Daus.* Eliane (Comtesse Geoffray de Montenay) and Ghislaine (Chabert). Administrator, Union Nationale des Caisses d'Allocations Familiales. President, Caisse d'Allocations Familiales de la Haute Garonne 1963–68. Hon. Consul for the Philippines 1959–62; Director, Union Assurance Companies 1936–74; Regional President, Federal Council of the Federation of General Assurance Agents 1954–70. Administrator, Société Centenaire Blanzy 1963–73. Vice-Président de l'Union Régionale des Professions Libérales 1969–74. *Awards:* Honoraire Lieutenant-Colonel; Chevalier, Legion of Honour; Officier Ordre National du Mérite; Croix de Guerre (1939–45); Croix de Combattant Volontaire; Officer du Mérite Militaire. *Club:* Automobile du Midi (member Directors' Committee). Conseiller de l'Enseignment Technique 1964–70. *Address:* Château de Chanzé, par Pontcharra (Rhône); and 10 rue Ninau, Toulouse, France.

**PERROTT, Sir Donald (Cyril Vincent),** KBE. Chairman and Director of a number of industrial companies. *B.* 12 Apr. 1902. *Educ.* Taunton's School, and University Coll., Southampton. *M.* (1) 1925, Marjorie May Holway. *S.* John Anthony. (2) 1969, L. L. Byre. *Career:* Entered Inland Revenue 1920; Ministry of Aircraft Production 1941; Ministry of Supply 1942; Dep. Sec., Ministry of Food 1947–49; Deputy Chmn., Overseas Food Corp. 1949–51; Chmn., Queensland British Food Corp. 1950–53; British

Ministry of Supply, European Purchasing Commission 1951–52, and Inter-departmental Cttee. Woolwich Arsenal 1953; Paymaster-General's Office, Preparatory work transfer Atomic Energy Sept. 1953; Secretary, Dept. of Atomic Energy 1954; member for Finance and Admin. of Atomic Energy Authority 1954–60; member, Governing Board, National Institute for Research in Nuclear Science 1957–60. *Clubs:* Royal Automobile; *Address:* 5 Plane Tree House, Duchess of Bedford's Walk, London W8 7QT.

**PERRY, Claud William.** *B.* 1897. *Educ.* King Edward VI Grammar School (Stourbridge). *M.* 1934, V. K. Pyke. *Daus.* Ann Gillian and Valerie Ruth. *Career:* Chairman: Blackheath Stamping Co. Ltd. 1921—, South Wales Forgemasters Ltd. 1948—, Bescot Drop Forgings Ltd., Deritend Drop Forgings Ltd., Midland Electric Installation Co. Ltd., E. J. Wilcock Ltd. 1958—, Hotfoil Ltd. 1962—. Mechanised Assembly Ltd., since 1974, Deritend Aluminium Castings Ltd., since 1974, Deritend Stamping Group Sales Ltd. since 1976; Executive Chairman, The Deritend Stamping Co. Ltd. Chairman: Brass & Alloy Pressings (Deritend) Ltd., Deritend Precision Castings Ltd. 1958—; Chmn. Harold F. Ward Ltd. since 1970; Chmn. Yeovil Precision Castings Ltd. 1973, Bralloy Fittings Ltd., 1976, Deritend Advanced Technology Ltd. 1976, Deritend Vacuum Castings Ltd. 1976. Governor, Halesowen College of Further Education 1941–54. *Club:* Rotary (Rowley Regis). *Address:* 'Springwell', Racecourse Lane, Stourbridge, West Midlands DY8 2RF; and *office* The Deritend Stamping Co. Ltd., Bridge House, Station Road, Rowley Regis, Warley, West Midlands B65 0LW.

**PERRY, Glen Crossman Hayes.** Public relations consultant *B.* 1903. *Educ.* Princeton Univ. (AB 1926). *M.* 1937, Sylvia Louise Wallau. *S.* Christopher Lawrence. *Career:* Asst. Space Buyer, H. E. Lesan Advertising Agency, N.Y.C. 1926–27; City Staff, New York Sun (covering ship news, City Hall, Police Headquarters; general reporting and rewrite, except for summers, when he covered yachting) 1927–37; Asst. Washington Correspondent, New York Sun 1937–44. Asst. Dir. Public Relations Dept. E. I. du Pont de Nemours & Co. Oct. 1944–Mar. 1965. Director, Public Relations Department, E. I. du Pont de Nemours & Co., 1965–68. *Member:* Civilian Public Relations Adv. Cttee. to Superintendent U.S. Military Acad. West Point 1961–74; Public Relations Socy. of America; (Accredited) Public Relations Seminar Cttee. 1962–70; Chmn. 1968; Trustee, Foundation for Public Relations Research and Education 1963–68; Pres. 1967–68; Trustee National Cathedral Assn. 1971–73. *Publications:* Watchmen of the Sea (Scribners 1937); collaborated with Roscoe Drummond on articles for Look magazine, and Saturday Evening Post 1942–44; contributor of articles to popular magazines 1927–44. U.S. Navy Commendation for work as correspondent 1945. Accredited Republican. *Clubs:* Gridiron, National Press (Washington); Princeton (N.Y.C.); Quadrangle; Nassau (both Princeton). *Address:* 10 Lighthouse Way, Darien, Conn. 06820, U.S.A.

**PERTH, Rt. Hon., Earl of** (John David Drummond) PC. First Crown Estate Commissioner June 1962—. Director: Royal Bank of Scotland, Tate & Lyle. *B.* 1907. *Educ.* Downside; Cambridge University. *M.* 1934, Nancy Seymour Fincke. *S.* 2. Minister of State for Colonial Affairs 1957–62. *Address:* Stobhall, by Perth, Scotland.

**PERUTZ, Gerald Eric Alexander.** British. *B.* 1929. *Educ.* Gadebridge Park; Loughborough College. *M.* 1953, Dinah Fyffe Pope. *S.* 2. *Dau.* 1. *Career:* Project Engineer Foster Wheeler Ltd. 1950–56; Exec. positions with Rank Organization 1956–62; Dir. Bell & Howell A. B.; Chmn. Bell & Howell France S.A., Benelux S.A.; Bell & Howell Italia S.A.; Corporate Senior, Vice-Pres. Bell & Howell Co. Gen. Mgr. Eastern Hemisphere. *Member:* Inst. of Petroleum; Inst. Marketing & Sales Management. *Address:* 20 Clarendon Road, London, W.11 and *office:* Alperton House, Bridgewater Road, Wembley, Middlesex.

**PESMAZOGLU, Georges J.** Greek economist. *B.* 18 Oct. 1890. *Educ.* Universities of Athens, Paris, Naples and Siena. *M.* 1912, Irene T. Theologo. *S.* John. *Dau.* Helly. *Career:* With Bank of Athens 1908–14; Deputy for Athens 1915–36; co-founder, Greek Populist Party 1915. Co-founder, with his brother Stephen, of newspaper Proia 1925; Deputy Chairman, Balkan Union 1926; Counsellor for State Budget 1927; Minister of National Economy 1932–34; Foreign Minister, a.i. 1934; Minister of Finance 1935; member, Governing Council and Deputy Governor, National Bank of Greece 1940–43; Governor, National Bank of Greece 1945–51; Governor, National Mortgage Bank of Greece 1945–51; Deputy Chairman, Société Générale Hellénique Co. Ltd. 1950; Chairman, Mortgage Bank of Greece 1951; Chairman, Ethniki Insurance Co. 1950; National Bank of Greece 1951; Ambassador to Turkey 1957. *Awards:* Grand Cross of the Greek Phoenix; Grand Officer, Royal Order of George I; Commander, Order of the Redeemer; Grand Croix, Ordre de Léopold (Belgium); Grand Cross, Order of the White Eagle (Poland); Order of the White Lion (Czechoslovakia); Order of the North Star (Sweden); Order of St. Sava (Yugoslavia); Order of Merit (Rumania); Commandeur de la Légion d'Honneur; Grand Officer, order Al Merito delle Rep. Italiano. *Publications:* L'Union monétaire Balkanique; The Greek Economy; The Problem of Productive Works; The Reform of land tax in Greece; Les causes des crises périodiques; The Greek problem and the Marshall Plan; The monetary problem in Greece; Directives for Economic Policy; Around the restoration of the throne in 1935; The Problem of Europe; The History of my Country during 1967–76 (in Greek). *Address:* Pesmazoglu Street 23, Kifissia, near Athens.

**PETERLIN, Aurelio E.** Italian. *B.* 1901. *Educ.* Acad. of Commerce (Trieste). *M.* 1931, Luigia Kainer, Dir., Professional Union of Trieste, 1937–45. Administrative Secretary, the Syndicate of Writers of Trieste; Consultant to the Free Trade Unions of Trieste; Int. Pres. of the Columbus Assoc., 1945—. *Publications:* Absolute Reality, The Unquenched Flame— Franciscan Portraits (in Italian). Fellow, the Inst. of Commerce (London). *Awards:* Pontifical Cross of Lateran (1st Class); Silver Medal, Red Cross of Japan; Red Cross Medal, Spain; Prix Humanitaire, France; Medaille d'Honneur Société d'Encouragement au Bien (Paris 1973). *Member:* Union et Maintien (Paris); Academia Tiberina (Rome); Authors and Writers (Trieste); Assn. of Criminology. Christian Democrat. *Address:* 9, Via S. Michele, Trieste, Italy.

**PETERS, Lovett Chase.** Vice-President, Transportation and Supplies, Continental Oil Co., Houston, Tex. *B.* 1913. *Educ.* Yale University (BA 1936). *M.* 1938, Ruth Elizabeth Binkerd Stott. *S.* Charles Adams II, Daniel Stott, and Samuel Kittredge. *Dau.* Ruth Binkerd. *Career:* With Bankers Trust Co., N.Y.C. 1936–49 (Asst. Treas. 1945–49); Financial Vice-Pres., Laclede Gas Co., St. Louis, Mo. 1949–53; Continental Oil Co.: Financial Vice-Pres. and Treas. 1953–59; Vice-Pres., Co-ordination and Supply 1959–60; Vice-Pres., Transportation and Supllies 1961—. *Publications:* A Way to Finance Higher Education (Freeman Mar. 1959—pub. The Foundation for Economic Education Inc.). *Member:* Phi Beta Kappa; National Fed. of Financial Analysts Societies; Houston Society of Financial Analysts. *Clubs:* The Houston; Houston Country; Downtown; Pipeliners. *Address:* 3714 Chevy Chase Drive, Houston 19; and *office* P.O. Box 2197, Houston 1, Tex., U.S.A.

**PETERS, William,** MVO, MBE. British Diplomat. *B.* 1923. *Educ.* King Edward VI Grammar Sch., Morpeth; Balliol Coll., Oxford—MA; London School of Economics. *M.* 1944. Catherine Bailey. *Career:* War Service, Queen's Royal Rifles, King's Own Scottish Borderers, & 9th Gurkha Rifles 1942–46; joined HM Overseas Service 1950; Asst. Commissioner, Gold Coast; also served in Cape Coast, Bawku & Tamale 1950–59; Asst. Principal in Commonwealth Relations Office 1959; 1st Sec., Dacca 1960–63, Nicosia 1963–67; Head of Zambia & Malawi Dept., CRO 1967–68; Head of Central African Dept., FCO 1968–69; Dir., Int. Affairs Div., Commonwealth Secretariat 1969–71; Conference Sec., Commonwealth Heads of Govt. Meeting 1971; Counsellor & Head of Chancery, Canberra 1971–73; Dep. High Commissioner, Bombay 1974–77; HM Ambassador, Montevideo since 1977. *Member:* Diplomatic Service Assoc.; Royal Commonwealth Soc. *Decorations:* Royal Victorian Order (member Class IV). 1961; Member of the Most Excellent Order of the British Empire, 1959. *Publications:* Diplomatic Service: Formation & Operation; & contributions to *Journal of African Administration, Illustrated Weekly of India,* etc. *Clubs:* United Oxford & Cambridge University; Jockey Club of Montevideo. *Address:* 12 Crown Court, Deal, Kent; and *office* c/o Foreign & Commonwealth Office, King Charles Street, London SW1.

**PETERSEN, Howard Charles.** *B.* 1910. *Educ.* De Pauw Univ. (AB 1930, LLD 1953); Univ. of Michigan Law School JD 1933; DSC Drexel Institute 1962; Swarthmore Coll. 1968; Univ. of Pa 1974. *M.* 1936, Elizabeth Anne Watts. *Dau.* Elizabeth. *Career:* Member of President's Cttee. for Education Beyond the High School 1957; Dir., The Panama Canal Co. 1953; elected to Board of Trustees Committee for Economic Development, and later Vice-Chairman of Board and

Chairman of the International Economic Policy Sub-Committee of its Research and Policy Committee; appointed Special Assistant to President on trade policy 1961; member: Council on Foreign Relations, Philadelphia Committee on Foreign Relations, American Philosophical Society; University (of Pennsylvania) Museum; Director and Past Pres., The World Affairs Council of Pennsylvania; Harvard Economics Visiting Cttee.; 1933–41; Associate of law firm of Cravath, deGersdorff, Swaine & Wood (now Cravath, Swaine & Moore), New York; as member of National Emergency Committee of Military Training Camp Association was one of the principal drafters of the Burke-Wadsworth Bill which became the Selective Service Act of 1940, (1940); Counsel of Committee appointed by President Roosevelt to draft initial regulations; Special Executive Assistant to Under-Secretary of War, 1941–45; Assistant Secy of War 1945–47; headed U.S. delegation to Commonwealth Nations Conference, London (on subject of most-favoured-nation treatment to Japan during U.S. military occupation) 1948; National Finance Chairman for Eisenhower pre-convention campaign 1952; Trustee, Carnegie Endowment for International Peace Chairman of the Board, The Fidelity Bank, Philadelphia, Apr. 1966. Advisory Committee of Export-Import Bank of Washington 1965–67; Director: Insurance Co. of North America, Rohm & Haas Co. 1967–76, Banque Europeenne de Financement; Chairman, Univ. of Pennsylvania Museum. Chairman, Adela Investment Co. S.A., 1969–71 UN Assoc. Nat. Policy Panel Chmn. on Org. of US Govt for Effective Partic. in Intern. Orgs 1973; ABA Govt. Borrowing Cttee.; Pres. International Monetary Conf. 1973; Harvard O'seas Visiting Cttee. to Economics Dept. (1967–73). Member ABA Govt. Borrowing Cttee.; Chmn. Bd. of Trustees, Inst. for Advanced Studies (Princeton). *Awards:* Medal for Merit, Exceptional Civilian Service Award, and the Selective Service Medal. 1945, *Address:* Radnor, Pennsylvania, U.S.A.

**PETERSEN, Jeffrey Charles**, CMG, British ambassador. *B.* 20 July 1920. *Educ.* Westcliff High School; London School of Economics. *M.* 1962, Karin Kristina Hayward. *S.* 1. *Daus.* 3. *Career:* Royal Navy (Lieut. RNVR) 1939–46; Foreign Office Second Secy. 1948—; Second Secy. H.M. Embassy Madrid 1949–51; First Secy. H.M. Embassy Ankara 1951–53; Brussels 1953–56; Nato Defence Coll. Paris 1956–57; First Secy. Foreign Office 1957–62, Djakarta 1962–64; Counsellor H.M. Embassy Athens 1964–68; Minister, H.M. Embassy Rio De Janeiro 1968–71; H.M. Ambassador at Seoul, Republic of Korea 1971–74; H.M. Ambassador at Bucharest, S. Rep. of Romania 1975–76; H.M. Ambassador at Stockholm, Sweden since 1977. *Clubs:* Travellers; Pall Mall (London). *Address:* 32 Longmoore Street, London, S.W.1. and *office:* c/o Foreign & Commonwealth Office, King Charles Street, London, S.W.1.

**PETERSON, Arthur G(oodwin)**, American Economist and Author. *B.* 1904. *Educ.* Univ. of Minnesota (BS; MS); Harvard Univ. (AM; PhD). *M.* Ruby Kettles. *Stepson* Jerry B. Roach. *Career:* Economist, statistician and historian, U.S. Dept. of Agri. 1927–44; Asst. Dir. of Research, Industrial College of the Armed Forces 1944–47; Chief, Statistics Div., National Economic Board, South Korea 1948; Chief, Textiles, Forest and Agricultural Products Div., Office of Secretary of Defense 1949–54; Economist, U.S. Public Health Service 1955–62.; Adviser, Bureau of Commercial Fisheries 1962–64; Past Pres., Agricultural History Society. *Publications:* Historical Study of Prices Received by Producers of Farm Products in Virginia 1801–1927 (V.P.I. 1929); Salt and Salt Shakers (1960); 400 Trademarks on Glass 1968; Glass Salt Shakers: 1000 Patterns (1970); Glass Patents and Patterns (1973). *Club:* Cosmos (Washington, D.C.). *Address:* 16 Madera Road De Bary, Florida, 32713, U.S.A.

**PETERSON, Hon. Leslie Raymond**, QC, LLB, LLD, EdD, FRSA. Canadian. *B.* 1923. *Educ.* McGill Univ., London (Eng.) Univ., and Univ. of B.C. (grad. 1949). *M.* 1950, Agnes Rose Hine. *S.* Raymond Erik. *Dau.* Karen Isabelle. *Career:* With Royal Canadian Artillery; served in England and the Continent. Called to the Bar of B.C. July 1949; Appointed Q.C., Dec. 1960. Elected M.L.A. for Vancouver Centre, Jan. 1956 (re-elected, 1956, 1960, 1963; elected to represent Vancouver—Little Mountain, 1966); Minister of Education Sept. 1956–68; Minister of Labour, 1960–71; Attorney-General, 1968–72, Province of British Columbia. *Member:* Vancouver Bar Assn., and of Law Socy. of B.C.; Fellow, Royal Socy. of Arts. In public service holds high office in societies devoted to child welfare, rehabilitation, education and the arts. Hon. President, Grandview Branch, Royal Canadian Legion; Hon. Vice-President, Provincial Council of St. John Ambulance; Hon. President, B.C. Historical Association; Hon. Vice-Pres., Vancouver Art Gallery. Founding Member of Convocation: Simon Fraser Univ. and Univ. of Victoria (B.C.). *Clubs:* Twenty (Past Pres.); Scandinavian Business Men's (Past Pres.); Canadian (Victoria); Union (Victoria); Seymour Golf & Country (Vancouver). *Address:* 814 Highland Drive, West Vancouver, B.C. V7S 2G5, Canada; and *office* 6th Floor, 890, West Pender Street, Vancouver, B.C. V6C 1K4, Canada.

**PETERSON, Russell Wilbur.** American. *B.* 1916. *Educ* University of Wisconsin (BSc; DPhil). *M.* 1937, E. Lillian Turner. *S.* 2. *Daus.* 2. *Career:* With du Pont Co.: Research Chemist 1942–46; various posts to Dir. New Production Div. 1959–63; Dir. Research and Development Div. Dev. Dept. 1963–68; Governor of Delaware 1968–73. *Member:* Textile Research Inst. 1956–59, Chmn. Exec. Cttee. 1959–61, Chmn. Bd. Dirs. 1961–63; Pres. Three S. Citizens Campaign 1961–64; Bd. Dirs. Greater Wilmington Development Council 1961–68; United Fund, Community Services Council Del. 1962; Chmn. for Del. Republican Finance Cttee., nominated Republican Pres. Elector 1964; Regional Vice-Pres. National Municipal League 1968—; Vice-Pres., Council State Governments 1970–71; Chmn. Cttee. on Law Enforcement, Justice and Public Safety, Nat. Governors Conference 1970–73; Cttee. nuclear energy and space technology, South Govs. Conference 1970–71; Education Commission of the States 1970; Chmn. Presidents Council on Environmental Quality 1973–76; Pres. of New Directions (public interest citizens' lobby focusing on global issues) since 1976; Commission on Critical Choices for Americans, Chmn. Exec. Cttee. 1973, member since 1973; Deputy Chmn. U.S. Delegation to World Population Conference 1974; Dep. Chmn. U.S. Delegation to World Conference on Human Settlements 1976; Chmn., Bio-Energy Council; Dir., Alliance to Save Energy, World Wildlife Fund, Population Crisis Com., U.S. Assoc. of the Club of Rome; special advisor to the Aspen Inst. for Humanistic Studies. *Member:* Amer. Assn. Advancement of Science; Chemical Ind. (Eng.); Textile Inst. (Eng.); Phi Beta Kappa; Sigma Xi. *Awards:* Gold Medal, World Wildlife Fund; Annual Award, Commercial Development Assn.; Conservationist of the Year, Nat. Wildlife Fed.; Gold Plate, National Academy of Achievement, Honorary Doctor of Science, Williams Coll., Parsons Award, American Chemical Soc. *Publications:* include among others: Engineering of Fabrics from Blends with Synthetic Fibres (with R. M. Hoffman, 1958); New Venture Management in a Large Company (1967); The Quest for Quality of Life, *Bioscience* (March 1975); A Perspective on the Population Problem, Conference Board *Record* (July 1975); Let's Not Gamble with our Public Forests, *American Forests* (Jan. 1976); Threats to World Security—A Chemist's View, *Chemical & Engineering News* (June 1977). *Club:* Cosmos (Washington, D.C.); Kiwanis (Wilmington, Past Pres.). *Address:* 616 South Royal Street, Alexandria, Virginia 22314, U.S.A.; and *office* 722 Jackson Place, Washington DC, 20006, U.S.A.

**PETERSON, Val (demar) (Frederick) (Erastus).** U.S. diplomat. *B.* 18 July 1903. *Educ.* Wayne (Neb.) State College (AB); Univ. of Nebraska (AM). *M.* 1929, Elizabeth Howells Pleak. *Career:* Teacher, public school, Carroll, Neb. 1925–26, public school, Madison, Neb. 1927–29; taught at Kimball, Neb. 1929–30; Instructor in political science, Univ. of Nebraska 1930–33; Supt., Elgin, Neb. 1933–39; Publisher, Elgin Review 1936–46; Secretary to Governor Dwight Griswold of Nebraska 1941–42; served in World War II (Lt.-Col.) in China, Burma and India 1943–45; Governor of Nebraska 1947–53; Chairman, Governor's Conference 1952; Pres., National Council of State Governments 1952; member, Missouri Basin Inter-Agency Commission 1947–53; Chairman, Missouri River States Cttee. 1948–52; Adminstrator, Federal Civil Defence Administration; Administrative Assistant to President Eisenhower 1953; Ambassador to Denmark June 1957–Mar. 1961. Chmn., Nebraska State Centennial Commn., 1961–62; Vice-Chmn. of Board, J. M. McDonald Co. 1961–66; Vice-Pres. & Administrator, J. M. McDonald Foundation, Inc. 1961–64; Chmn., Board of Dirs., Life Investors of Nebraska, 1963–69; Omaha; Dir., First National Bank of Hastings, Neb. 1963–69; Ambassador to Finland 1969–73; Distinguished Professor, Political Science Public Affairs Wayne State Coll. 1973. Dir. State National Bank and Trust Co.; Pres. Wayne State Foundation; Regent, Univ. of Nebraska 1963–65 (Pres. 1965); Trustee People to People Int. former Vice-Chmn. Board of Trustees, and member of the Exec. Cttee. *Member:* American Legion, Veterans of Foreign Wars, Airforce Assn. Republican. *Clubs:* Omaha: National Press, (Washington, D.C.). *Address:* 710 E 7th Street, Wayne, Neb. 68787, U.S.A.

**PETERSSON, Karl Barry,** OBE. Australian. Commissioner of Patents 1959—. *B.* 1912. *Educ.* Univ. of Western Australia (BSc, FAIM). *M.* 1941, Mim Tribe. *S.* Ross, John and Karl. Previously: Deputy Commissioner of Patents 1951. *Publications:* Information Systems in Documentation; Rating Systems. *Member:* Professional Officers' Assn.; Royal Inst. of Public Admin.; Australian Inst. of Management; Royal Commonwealth Society. *Clubs:* Royal Canberra Golf. *Address:* 38 Stonehaven Crescent, Deakin, A.C.T.; and *office* Patent Office, Canberra, A.C.T.

**PETRI, Lennart.** Swedish Diplomat. *B.* 1914. *Educ.* cand. phil., cand. jur. *M.* 1949, Carin Buchberger. *S.* 1. *Daus.* 2. *Career:* Joined Swedish Foreign Service 1938; Attaché, Swedish Legation, Madrid 1939–41, Washington 1941–42; Sec., Swedish Legation, Buenos Aires 1942–43, Lima 1943–45; Ministry of Foreign Affairs, Stockholm 1946–49; Sec., Swedish Embassy, Paris 1949–55; Counsellor, Swedish Embassy, Moscow 1955–58; Swedish Ambassador, Rabat 1958–63, Peking 1963–69, Vienna 1969–76, & Madrid since 1976. *Decorations:* Knight Commander, Order of the North Star (Sweden); Grand Cross, Order of Merit (Austria); etc. *Address:* Mjövik, 290 17 Everöd, Sweden; and *office* Embajada de Suecia, Zurbano 27, Madrid 4, Spain.

**PETTERSSON, Filip Daniel.** Finnish. Chief General Mgr.: Bank of Helsinki Ltd. 1967—. *B.* 1920. *Educ.* MSc (Econ). *M.* 1944, Doris Skutnabb. *S.* 2. *Dau.* 1. *Career:* Manager of the marine insurance department of the Fennia Insurance Co. 1952–60. Man. Dir., Fennia Insurance Co. Ltd. 1960–67, Patria Life Insurance Co. Ltd. 1963–67, Norma Reinsurance Co. Ltd. 1960–67. *Publications:* two text-books on marine insurance. Member of various societies. *Club:* Rotary. *Address:* Kalliolinnävagen 16 c 14, 00140 Helsinki 14; and *office* Bank of Helsinki Ltd., Aleksanterink, 17, Helsinki.

**PETTIGREW, Donald George.** Australian insurance executive. *B.* 1918. *Educ.* Fort Street Boys' High School, Sydney. *M.* 1942, Llyris M. Noad. *S.* Alan G. *Dau.* Bronwyn M. *Career:* R.A.A.F. 1941–45 (Flt. Lieut.); New South Wales Manager, The Employers Liability Assurance Corp. Ltd. 1951–56; General Manager, Australian Equitable Insurance Co. Ltd. 1956–61; Manager for Australia, The London Assurance 1961–66; Manager for Australia, Sun Alliance & London Insurance Group, 1966–71; Man. Dir. Sun Alliance Insurance Ltd. since 1972. *Publications:* various technical papers in British and Australian insurance journals. *Clubs:* Concord Golf; Royal Sydney Yacht Squadron; Australian. *Address:* 11 Mirrabooka Avenue, Homebush, N.S.W.; and *office* 22 Bridge Street, N.S.W., Australia.

**PETTINGELL, Sir William Walter,** CBE. Australian. *B.* 1914. *Educ.* Univ. of Sydney (BSc 1st Class Hons.). *M.* 1942, Thora M. Stokes, *S.* 1. *Daus.* 2. *Career:* Research Dir. Australian Gas Light Co. Sydney 1974—; Member Bd. of Reserve Bank of Australia 1961—; Chmn. National Coal Research Adv. Cttee. 1965—; Dep. Chmn., Australian Consolidated Industries Ltd., Manufacturers Mutual Insurance, Hanimex Pty. Ltd., Higher Education Authority of N.S.W.; Chmn. Sydney Cove Redevelopment Authority; Dir., Howard Smith Ltd., Coal & Allied Industries Ltd. Past Pres., Associated Chamber of Manufacturers of Australia; Fellow, International Academy of Management. Fellow Inst. of Fuel, and of Australian Inst. of Management. Member Inst. Gas Engineers. *Clubs:* Union; Royal Prince Alfred; Royal Yacht Squadron; American; Eleanora Country. *Address:* 54 Linden Way, Castlecrag, N.S.W. 2068; and *office* 477–487 Pitt Street, Sydney, N.S.W., Australia.

**PETTY, Hon. Sir Horace Rostill.** Agent-General for Victoria (Australia) in London, May 1964–69. *B.* 1904. *Educ.* Melbourne University (BCom). *Married. S.* 2. *Daus.* 2. *Career:* Fellow Australian Socy. of Accountants. Served in Australian Army 1940–44. Member (Lib.-Country) of Legislative Assembly for Toorak in Victorian Parliament 1952–64; Minister of Housing 1955–61; Minister of Immigration 1956–61; Minister of Public Works 1961–64. *Address:* 593 Toorak Road, Melbourne, Victoria 3142, Australia.

**PEW, George Thompson.** American. *B.* 1917. *Educ.* The Hill School; Mass. Inst. Tech. *M.* 1940, Constance D. Clarke. *S.* G. Thompson Pew Jr. *Dau.* Margaret (Moorhouse Jr.). *Career:* Chairman, Aero Design Eng. Inc. 1950–60; Pres., 1958–60. President, George T. Pew Enterprises. *Member:* Aerospace Industries Assn. of Amer.; Amer. Inst. of Aeronautics and Astronautics. *Clubs:* Merion Cricket; Union League; Racquet (Phila.); Aviation C.C.; Corinthian Y.C. of Phila.; Bay Head Y.C.; Keylargo Anglers'. *Address:* 231 Cheswold Hill Road, Haverford, Pa. 19041, U.S.A.

**PEYTON, Rt. Hon., John Wynne William,** PC, MA, MP. British. Politician. *B.* 1919. *Educ.* Oxford (Law MA). *M.* 1966, Mary Wyndham. *S.* Thomas. *Dau.* Sarah. *Career:* Called to the Bar, 1945; Member of Parliament for Yeovil, Somerset, since 1951; Parly. Secy. Ministry of Power, 1962–64; Chmn. Texas Instruments Ltd., since 1974; Minister, Transport June–Oct. 1970; Minister, Transport Industries, Dept. of the Environment 1970–74; Shadow Leader of the House of Commons 1974–76; Chief Opposition Spokesman on Agriculture since 1976. *Clubs:* Boodles. *Address:* 6 Temple West Mews, West Square, London SE11; and The Old Malt House, Hinton St. George, Somerset.

**PFLEIDERER, Otto,** Dr sc pol. German banker. *B.* 17 Jan. 1904. *Educ.* Universities of Tübingen, Hamburg and Kiel. *M.* 1937, Hildegard Hoffmann. *Career:* Lecturer, University of Heidelberg 1947–61; Professor by title (Honorarprofessor), Univ. of Heidelberg 1961—; Pres., Landeszentralbank von Württemberg-Baden, Stuttgart 1948–52; Landeszentralbank von Baden-Württemberg 1953–57; Landeszentralbank in Baden-Württemberg 1957–72; member, Board of Directors, Bank deutscher Länder, Frankfurt-am-Main 1948–57; Board of Directors, Deutsche Bundesbank, Frankfurt-am-Main 1957–72. Alternate Member, Managing Board, European Payments Union, Paris 1950–51; Exec. Dir., International Monetary Fund, Washington 1952–53. *Address:* D–7 Stuttgart, Rosengartenstr 88, Germany.

**PFLIMLIN, Pierre,** D en D. French politician. *B.* 5 Feb. 1907. *M.* 1939, Marie Odile Heinrich. *S.* Etienne. *Daus.* Antoinette, Odile. *Career:* Deputy for Lower Rhine, First and Second Constituent Assemblies 1945–46; Under-Secretary of State for Population and for National Economy 1946; Minister of Agriculture 1947–49; Municipal Councillor, Strasbourg since 1945; Deputy (M.R.P.), Lower Rhine National Assembly 1946–67; Minister of Agriculture July 1950–Aug. 1951; Minister for Commerce and Foreign Economic Relations, Pleven Cabinet Aug. 1951–Jan. 1952; Minister of State for European Affairs, Faure Cabinet Jan.–Mar. 1952; Minister of Overseas Territories, Pinay Cabinet Mar. 1952–Jan. 1953; Minister of Finance and Economic Affairs 1955–56, and again, Nov. 1957–58; Pres., Cncl. of Ministers 1958; Minister of State in the De Gaulle cabinet 1958–59; Minister of State for Co-operation, Pompidou cabinet 1962. Mayor of Strasbourg 1959—; Pres., Consultative Assembly, Cncl. of Europe 1963–68. *Publications:* L'Industrie de Mulhouse; La Structure Economique du Troisième Reich; L'Europe Communautaire; L'Alsace-Destin et Vononté. *Address:* 24 avenue de la Paix, 67 Strasbourg, France.

**PHAM VAN DONG.** Vietnamese Politician. *B.* 1906. Member of Communist Movement 1925— (imprisoned by the French for political activities 1929–36; supporter of Ho Chi-Minh, with whom he founded the Viet-Minh guerilla movement); Foreign Minister 1954–61. Prime Minister, Democratic Republic of Vietnam 1955–76, Socialist Republic of Vietnam since July 1976. *Address:* Office of the Prime Minister, Hanoi, Vietnam.

**PHANOS, Titos.** Cypriot Politician & Diplomat. *B.* 1929. *Educ.* Pancyprian Gymnasium, Nicosia; Middle Temple, London—Barrister-at-Law. *M.* 1958, Maro Phierou. *S.* 1. *Daus.* 2. *Career:* Advocate 1952–66; Mem., House of Representatives 1960–66; Mem., Consultative Assembly of Council of Europe 1963–65; Minister of Communications & Works 1966–70; Head of Mission to European Communities & Ambassador to Belgium since 1971; concurrently Ambassador to Luxembourg & to the Netherlands & Perm. Delegate to the EEC since 1973. *Address:* 83 Rue de la Loi (4th floor), 1040 Brussels, Belgium.

**PHELAN, Arthur J.** American. *B.* 1915. *Educ.* American Inst. of Banking; N.Y. Univ. *M.* 1939, Mary Frances Ryan. *Daus.* 3. *Career:* Webb & Knapp Inc. Dir., Treasurer, Vice-Pres., Treasurer & Snr. Vice-Pres. 1949–65; Financial Vice-Pres. Lefrak Organisation (& Trustee, Employee Retirement Fund) since 1966; former Dir. Gulf-States Land & Industries Inc., Univ. American Corp.; Roosevelt Field Inc.; Zeckendorf Hotels Corp.; Exec. Vice-Pres. & Dir. David Greenewald Assocs. Inc. 1965–66. *Club:* North Hempstead Country (Port Washington, N.Y.). *Address:* 88 Summit Road, Port Washington, N.Y.; and *office* 97–77 Queens Boulevard, Forest Hills, N.Y., U.S.A.

**PHELPS, Brig. Douglas Vandeleur,** TD, DL, JP. Glass manufacturer. *B.* 1904. *Educ.* Harrow School and Magdalen

College, Oxford (MA Oxon). *M.* 1953, Hon. Rosemary Cozens-Hardy. *S.* John Edward Vandeleur. *Dau.* Laura Douglas (both adopted). *Career:* With Pilkington Brothers Ltd. since 1927. Service in Territorial Army from 1928–54; attained rank of Brigadier, and was A.D.C. to King George VI and to Queen Elizabeth II; Dir. Pilkington Brothers Ltd. until 1973. National Westminister Bank Ltd. (Northern Board) until 1973. *Clubs:* Boodle's (London); Norfolk (Norwich). *Address:* Bayfield Hall, Holt, Norfolk; 7 Egerton Place, London SW3; and *office* Pilkington Brothers Ltd., St. Helens, Lancs.

**PHELPS, Dudley Francis.** American engineering Consultant. *B.* 1904. *Educ.* Cornell University (ME 1926). *M.* 1934, Marguerite Elizabeth Sullivan. *S.* Richard Francis. *Career:* Design Engineer, Assistant Purchasing Agent, E. L. Phillips & Co. 1926–32; Traffic Engineer & Sales, various motor freight companies 1932–38; taught mechanics, heat and electricity, Pratt Institute (evenings) 1938–44; Evaluation Engineer, Long Island Lighting Co. 1938–40; with The J. G. White Engineering Corp.: successively Asst. Mechanical Engineer, Chief Mechanical Engineer, Engineering Manager, elected Vice-Pres. and Chief Executive Officer (also Director of the Corp.) 1940–56; Dir. 1956–74; Pres., and Chief Executive Officer, The J. G. White Engineering Corp. 1957–69. Vice-President and Director, Whitengeco Venezolana S.A. 1957–62; Director, White Securities Corp. 1963–71; Dir., Ninth Federal Savings & Loan Association of New York City 1964—; Dir., Nineco Corp., Nanuet, N.Y. 1977—. Member Process Selection Board, Office of Saline Water, U.S. Dept. of the Interior 1959–62. Licensed Professional Engineer; N.Y. 1943—, and New Jersey 1950—. Newcomen Society in N. America; Fellow, American Society of Mechanical Engineers; Vice-Pres., Reg. 11, 1965–67 (Chmn., Metropolitan Section 1954–55; Chmn., Vice-Chmn. and member of various Cttees. 1951—; and Adviser, Nuclear Energy Div., Program Committee 1955–57). *Clubs:* India House, Cornell (N.Y.C.). *Address:* 2 Fenimore Road, Port Washington, N.Y. 11050, U.S.A.

**PHELPS, Phelps.** American administrator and Executive Editor, Chelsea Clinton News, N.Y.C. *B.* 4 May 1897. *Educ.* Williams College (AB); Fordham Law School (LLB); Hon. LLD, Univ. of San Domingo; served in World Wars I and II; member, New York State Assembly 1924–28 and 1937–38; member, New York Senate 1940–42; Governor of American Samoa 1951–52; Ambassador to Dominican Republic July 1952–June 1953; Delegate, Democratic Natl. Conventions 1936, 1956 and 1960; New Jersey State Constitutional Convention, 1966; member, Palisades Interstate Park Commission since 1956. Knight Commander, Order of King George I (Greece). Winner of the Annual Award of the Urban League of Essex County, N.J.. 1966. George Washington Carver Award, 1962. *Address:* 315 Pacific Avenue, Jersey City, N.J. 07304, U.S.A.

**PHELPS, Thomas William.** American economist, Partner, Scudder, Stevens & Clark, investment counsel firm. 1960–70. *B.* 1902. *Educ.* Univ. of Minnesota (BA *cum laude*). *M.* (1) 1933, Rosalie Bailey Phelps (*Dec.* 1965). *S.* Thomas William, Jr. *Daus.* Rosalie Greenleaf (Mrs. Robert L. Thomas), Lucinda Bradford (Mrs. James C. S. Buckley). *M.* (2) 1966, Christine Reed Cameron. *Career:* Manager, Economics & Special Studies Dept., Socony Mobil Oil Co. Inc. 1958–60 (Asst. to the Chmn. of the Bd. 1949–58); Partner, and Economist in charge of research, Francis I du Pont & Co. 1938–49; Editor, Barron's Business and National Financial Weekly 1936–38: News Editor and Chief of the Washington Bureau of Wall Street Journal 1929–35. *Awards:* Univ. of Minnesota Outstanding Achievement 1955. *Publications:* Your Securities Under Social Security, a Handbook of the Labor Factor in Investments (1936); Fortune Magazine article, 1929 Upside Down (1949); Atlantic Monthly Article Hazards of the Stock Market (1962); 100 to 1 in the Stock Market (1972). Life Trustee, American Schools of Oriental Research. *Member:* New York Society of Security Analysts, Inc.; Academy of Political Science. *Clubs:* Deadline; Explorers; University, Pilgrims (N.Y.C.); Nantucket Yacht; Nantucket (Mass.). (Nassau) Princeton, N.J.). *Address:* 19 Orange Street, Nantucket, Mass. 02554, U.S.A.

**PHILIPPE, André J.** Luxembourg Diplomat. *B.* 1926. *Career:* Barrister-at-Law Luxembourg 1951–52; Joined Diplomatic Service 1952; Deputy-Dir. Political Affairs, Min. of Foreign Affairs 1952–54; Deputy Perm. Rep. to NATO 1954–61 and to OECD 1959–61; Dir. of Protocol and Legal Adviser Min. of Foreign Affairs 1961–68; Ambassador and Perm. Rep. to U.N. and Consul-Gen. New York 1968–72 (Vice-Pres. of 24th Session Gen. Assembly UN 1969); Luxembourg Ambassador in Gt. Britain, Ireland and Iceland and also Perm. Rep. to Council of Western European Union since 1972. *Member:* Bd. of Dirs. Societé Internationale de la Moselle 1961–68; Bd. of Directors Soc. Elec. de l'Our 1961–68; Intern. Moselle Navig. Commission 1961–68 (Chmn. 1965 and 68). *Awards:* Commander Order of Adolphe Nassau (Luxem), GCVO (Hon) and other foreign decorations. *Address:* The Luxembourg Embassy, 27 Wilton Crescent, London, SW1X 8SD.

**PHILIPPS, Hon. James Perrott.** British. *B.* 1905. *Educ.* Eton; Christ Church, Oxford (MA). *M*. 1930, Hon. Elizabeth Joan Kindersley. *S.* Peter Anthony. *Daus.* Penelope Doune (Lake), Daphne Deirdre (Lewes). *Career:* Served World War II, Leicestershire Yeomanry and Shropshire Yeomanry in Middle East, Italy (despatches) 1939–45. Chmn. & Man. Dir. Dalham Farms Ltd. & Dir., Dalham Stud Farms Ltd.; *Address:* Dalham Hall, Newmarket, Suffolk. CB8 8TB.

**PHILLIPS, Edgar Hereward.** British. Public Relations and Fundraising Consultant in London. *B.* 1905. *Educ.* King Edward's School (Birmingham). *M.* 1954, Mary Monaghan. *Dau.* Cherrie. *Career:* Journalist: Yorkshire Evening Post 1926–27; Press Assn. 1927–30; London Evening Standard (Parliamentary Correspondent) 1930–35; Public Relations Adviser, Govt. of India 1935–39. Responsible for Public Relations and fund-raising for National Cancer Day, I'm Backing Britain, Royal National Life-Boat Institution, U.N.I.C.E.F., Field Studies Council, National Institute of Hardware, Lincoln Cathedral and others. *Publications:* Fund-raising Techniques & Case Histories. Fellow, Inst. of Public Relations; member, Inst. of Journalists. *Club:* Press. *Address: office* 11, Ravenscroft Park, Barnet, Herts EN5 4ND.

**PHILLIPS, Sir Fred Albert,** CVO. British. Special Representative of Cable & Wireless in the Caribbean. *B.* 1918. *Educ.* Barrister-at-Law; LLB 1957. *Career:* Commissioner of Carriacou (Windward Islands) 1953–56; Actg. Administrator, Grenada 1958; Senior Asst. Secy. 1958–60, and Cabinet Secy. 1960–62, West Indies Federation; Senior Lecturer, University of the West Indies 1962; Administrator, St. Kitts, Nevis and Anguilla 1966. Governor of the State of St. Christopher, Nevis and Anguilla (West Indies), 1967–69. *Publications:* The Foreign Service of a Small Independent Country (1962); Trials in and out of Court (1954); Developments in West Indian Constitutions (1958); Constitution of the Windward and Leeward Islands (1959); Training for the New Diplomacy (1964); A West Indian looks at Canadian Federalism (1965); Politics and the Administration of Justice in newly independent countries (1966). In course of publication: Federalism and the West Indies, The Structure and Functions of the Supreme Court in four federal jurisdictions, A Decade of West Indian Constitutionalism 1957–1967, and Ministerial Government in the Eastern Caribbean. *Address:* Chambers, Kingstown, St. Vincent, West Indies.

**PHILLIPS, Sir Horace,** KCMG. British Diplomat (Ret'd.). *B.* 1917. *Educ.* Hillhead High School, Glasgow. *M.* 1944, Idina Doreen Morgan. *S.* Michael. *Dau.*, Maureen. *Career:* First Secretary and Chargé d'Affaires, Jedda (Saudi Arabia) 1953–56; Protectorate Secretary, Aden 1956–60; Counsellor, Tehran 1960–64; Deputy Political Resident in Persian Gulf, at Bahrain 1964–66; British Ambassador to Indonesia 1966–68; High Commissioner in Tanzania 1968–72; Ambassador to Turkey 1973–77. Hon. LLD (Glasgow) 1977. *Address:* 34A Sheridan Road, London SW19 3HP.

**PHILLIPS, John Fleetwood Stewart,** CMG. British Diplomat (Ret'd.). *B.* 1917. *Educ.* Worcester Coll. Oxford—M.A. (Litt. Hum.) *M.* 1948, Mary Gordon. *Career:* War Service, Palestine, W. Desert & Crete, 1st Bn. Argyll & Sutherland Highlanders, 1939–45; Asst. Dist. Comm. Sudan Political Service 1946–51; District Comm. Kordofan & Blue Nile Provinces 1951–55; 1st Sec. Foreign Off. 1955–57; Oriental Sec. Libya 1957–60; H.M. Consul-General Muscat 1960–63; Counsellor at Amman 1963–66; IDC 1967; Dep. High Commissioner Cyprus 1968; Amb. to S. Yemen 1969; Amb. to Jordan 1970–72; Ambassador to Sudan 1973–77. *Clubs:* Travellers; Royal Commonwealth Society. *Address:* Southwood, Gordon Rd., Horsham, W. Sussex.

**PHILLIPS, Sir John Grant,** KBE. Australian Banker. *B.* 1911. *Educ.* Univ. of Sydney (BEc). *M.* 1935, Mary Willmott Debenham. *S.* 2. *Daus.* 2. *Career:* Research Officer, N.S.W. Retail Traders' Assoc. 1932–35; Economic Assistant, Royal Com. on Monetary and Banking System 1936–37; Economic

Dept., Commonwealth Bank of Australia 1937–51, Investment Adviser 1954–60; Deputy Governor and Deputy Chmn. of Bd. Reserve Bank of Australia 1960–68, Governor and Chmn. 1968–75. *Member:* of Council, Macquarie University since 1967; Board, The Howard Florey Inst. of Exp. Physiology & Medicine since 1971, Advisory Cttee. The Australian Birthright Movement, Sydney Branch since1971, Board, Lend Lease Corp. Ltd. since 1976; Chmn., Australian Statistics Advisory Council since 1976. *Address:* 2/25 Marshall Street, Manly, N.S.W. 2095, Australia.

**PHILLIPS, Neil Franklin.** QC, BA, LLB, BCL. Canadian. *B.* 1924. *Educ.* Westmount High School; Williams Coll. Williamstown Mass. (BA); Yale Univ. (LLB); McGill Univ. (BCL). *M.* 1957, Sharon Whiteley Greer. *S.* 1. *Dau.* 1. *Career:* Partner, Phillips & Vineberg, Member of the Bar, Province of Quebec; Canadian Bar Association. *Clubs:* Mount Royal; University; Elm Ridge Golf; *Address:* 634 Clarke Avenue, Westmount, P.Q. Canada and *office* Room 930, 1 Place Ville Marie, Montreal, Quebec H3B 2A5.

**PHILLIPS, Percy.** British. *B.* 1900. Educ. City of London College. *M.* 1924, Gertrude Nelken. *Daus.* 2. *Career:* An Accountant in practice; Dir. of many public and private companies. *Fellow:* Assn. of Certified Corporate Accountants, and of Chartered Institute of Secretaries. *Address:* 'Bracken Knoll', Courtenay Avenue, London, N.6; and *office* 76 New Cavendish Street, London, W.1.

**PHILLIPS, Warren Henry.** American. *B.* 1926. *Educ.* Queen's College, Flushing, N.Y. (BA). *M.* 1951, Barbara Anne Thomas. *Daus.* Lisa, Leslie and Nina. *Career:* Copy editor, The Stars & Stripes, Germany, early 1949; successively copy editor 1947–48, correspondent in Germany 1949, Manager, London Bureau 1950–51, Foreign Editor 1952, News Editor 1953–54; Managing Editor, Mid-West edition 1954–59, Managing Editor, 1957–65; Exec. Editor 1965–70, The Wall Street Journal. Vice-Pres., and General Manager of Dow Jones & Co., Inc., publishers of the Wall Street Journal and other publications and news services 1970–72; Pres. & Dir. since 1972, Chief Exec. Officer since March 1975. *Address:* 22 Cortlandt Street, New York, N.Y. 10007, U.S.A.

**PHILLIPS, William George.** Company Chmn. *B.* 1920. *Educ.* Antioch College, Yellow Springs, O. (AB); Certified Public Accountant (Ohio). *M.* 1943, Laverne Anne Evenden. *S.* Scott William. *Daus.* Karen Anne (Berry) and Connie Allynette (Tressel). *Career:* First Lieut. Army of U.S. 1942–45. With Price Waterhouse & Co. 1945–48; Tax Accountant 1948–52, Assistant Treasurer 1952—. Glidden Co., Treasurer 1953, Director 1953, Vice-President, Planning 1962, Administrative Vice-President 1962–64, and President 1964–68. The Glidden Co., Cleveland, O.; Glidden Ltd., and Glidden International C.A; Chief Executive, International Multifoods (formerly International Milling), Minneapolis 1968—, Chmn. Bd since 1970; Chairman & Trustee, Educational Research Council of America; Trustee Baldwin-Wallace Coll; Consultative Council Univ. of Minnesota Coll. of Business Administration; Bd. Dirs., North-western National Bank of Minneapolis: Soo Line Railroad Co.; Data 100 Corps; North American Life & Casualty Co.; Grocery Manufacturers of America; U.S. Chamber of Commerce; Minnesota State Council on Economic Education. Vice-Pres. & Dir. Greater Minneapolis Chamber of Commerce. *Member:* Adv. Bd., Inst. of International Education; The Conference Board; Adv. Bd., Nat. Alliance of Businessmen; Nat. Corp. Adv. Cttee., United Negro Coll. Fund; U.S. Section of Canada–U.S. Cttee. & Mem., International Policy Cttee., Chamber of Commerce of the U.S.; Exec. Cttee., U.S.–Iran Joint Business Council; YMCA Investment Cttee.; Exec. Bd., Viking Council, Boy Scouts of America; Exec. Cttee., Minneapolis Foundation; Bd., Downtown Development Corp. Minneapolis; Ohio Socy. Certified Public Accnts.; Wayzata Community Church. *Award:* Bronze Star & 5 Campaign Medals (Eur.). *Member:* Ohio Society of Public Accountants. Republican. *Clubs:* Minneapolis; Lafayette; Woodhill Country. *Address:* 2610 West Lafayette Road, Shorehills, Excelsior, Minn. 55331; and *office* 1200 Multifoods Building, Minneapolis 55402, U.S.A.

**PHIPPS, Dr. Colin Barry,**MP. British politician. *B.* 1934. *Educ.* University Coll., London—BSc (1st Class Honours) Geology; Birmingham Univ.—PhD, Geology. *M.* 1956, Marion May Lawry. *S.* 2. *Daus.* 2. *Career:* Justice of the Peace since 1972; Labour MP for Dudley West since 1974; Member, Council of Europe since 1975; Member, Western European Union since 1975. *Member:* Fellow, Geological Society of London; Fellow, Inst. of Petroleum. *Clubs:* Reform. *Address:* Mathon Court, Mathon, Malvern WR13 5NZ; and House of Commons London S.W.1.

**PHIRI, Hon. Amock Israel.** *B.* 1932. *Educ.* Chewa Native Authority; Chisali River School; Munali Sec. School, (Sen. Cambridge School Cert.); A levels, Univ. Hamburg, W. Germany (MA, Sociology); Special Course, Regional Planning. *M.* 1967, Jennifer M. *Children* 5. *Career:* With Rhokana Corp., Industrial PRO 1957–59; Lect. in Sociology, University of Zambia 1967–69; Member Parliament Zambia 1968; Min. of State, of National Guidance, 1969; Min. Information, Broadcasting and Tourism 1970; High Commissioner in London and Ambassador to the Holy See 1970–74; Cabinet Minister, North Western Province 1974–75. *Awards:* Knight Grand Cross order of Pius, 1st Class. *Address:* PO Box 100, Solweze, Zambia.

**PIATIER, André Sylvain.** French. *B.* 1914. *Educ.* Doctorates of Law and Economic Science; Graduate at the School of Political Science; Fellow (Agrégé) Faculties of Law and Economic Science. *M.* 1940, Line Werling. *Dau.* Nicole. Rockefeller Fellow. *Career:* Asst. Prof., Faculty of Law, Paris 1937; Deputy Lecturer, Strasbourg Univ., Clermont-Ferrand 1941; Director of Naval Economic Services 1940–45, and of Foreign Economic Services, Ministry of National Economy 1945–47. Dir. National Institute of Statistics and Economic Studies 1947–55; Centre d'Etude des Techniques Economiques Modernes (C.E.T.E.M.). Professor: Ecole Pratique des Hautes Etudes, Sorbonne (School for Higher Education) 1947; Institut d'Etudes Politiques (Institute of Political Studies) University of Paris 1941; Ecole d'Application de la Statistique (School of Instruction in Statistics) 1947; Institut d'Etude de Dévelopement économique et social (Institute for the study of economic and social development) 1958. Member, National Cttee. of Scientific Research 1950; Vice-Pres., Cttee. of Economic Science and Development at the General Delegation for Scientific Research 1959; member, Committee of four experts commissioned to study the national accounts 1949–51; Scientific Director for the period of Unesco studies on economic development 1959; member, Committee of O.E.E.C. experts on Rising Prices and Inflation 1959–60. Chairman of Cttee. on Economic Science of General Services of Scientific Research 1962–68. UNO Expert, Population and Development Cairo 1973–74; Special Counsellor of the European Community on scientific information. *Publications:* Sur le contrôle des changes (The Control of Exchange); Les Finances publiques (public finance); L'economie de guerre (war economy); La statistique etles fluctuations économiques (statistics and economic fluctuations); Les méthodes de prévision, la psychologie économique, les pays sous développés, l'étude des marchés (methods of forecasting, economic psychology, the underdeveloped countries, the study of markets); Handbook on Statistics, Econometrics, business cycles, and national accounting, Demography & Development, Scientific Information, etc. Founder of the journals Etudes et Conjoncture Documentation Economique and Problèmes Economiques. Member, Committee of the French Association of Economic Science, member of the Cttee. on the History of the Second World War. Officer, Legion of Honour. *Address:* 11-*bis*, rue Vauguelin, 75005 Paris, France.

**PICARD, Fernand Louis.** French engineer. *B.* 1906. *Educ.* Ingenieur des Arts et Metiers. *M.* 1928, Marguerite Châtre. *Daus.* 4. *Career:* Tool Designer 1928, and Chief of Servicing 1931, Delage Automobiles. Joined Renault, successively Experimental Engineer 1935, Chief of Motor Study 1940, Chief of Studies 1942, Director of Studies 1946, Director of Studies in Research for Renault Motors 1951—. Presidentr Ingenieurs Civil de France (1970). Pres. de l'Association pou; le Developpment de la Production Automatic (ADEPA), *Publications:* Scientific collaborator, Larousse du XX Siècle. numerous conferences in France and abroad; articles in Ingenieurs de l'Automobile, and Société d'Encouragement à l'Industrie Nationale; communications to World Petrol Congress (1951) and to U.N.O. (1949). *Member:* Federation International des Sociétés d'Ingenieurs et de Techniciens de l'Automobile (President); Société des Ingenieurs de l'Automobile (Pres. 1956–59); Société des Ingenieurs Civils (Pres. 1970); Société des Ingenieurs Arts et Métiers (President); Society of Automotive Engineers (U.S.A.). Officer, Legion of Honour. *Address:* 17, Boulevard de Picpus 75012, Paris, France.

**PICK, Alfred John.** Canadian diplomat. *B.* 1915. *Educ.* McGill Univ. (BA, MA, BCL). *M.* 1946, Patricia Ross. *S.* Lawrence.

*Daus.* Paula and Frances. *Career:* Canadian Ambassador to Peru 1958–62, to Tunisia, 1966–69; Ambassador in the Netherlands 1969–72; Ambassador and Permanent Observer to the Organization of American States 1972. *Address:* c/o Department of External Affairs, Ottawa, Canada.

**PICKARD, Sir Cyril Stanley,** KCMG. British. *B.* 1917. *Educ.* Alleyns School, Dulwich, and New College, Oxford (1st Class in School of Modern History 1939). *M.* 1941, Helen Elizabeth Strawson. *S.* 3. *Dau.* 1. *Career:* Under-Secretary, Commonwealth Relations Office 1962–66; Deputy High Commissioner in New Zealand 1958–61; Asst. Sec., Commonwealth Relations Office 1955–58; Counsellor, Office of United Kingdom High Commissioner in Canberra, Australia 1952–55, High Commissioner Pakistan 1966–71; High Commissioner Nigeria 1971–74. *Address:* Sommer House, Oak Lane, Sevenoaks, Kent.

**PICKERSGILL, Hon. John Whitney,** PC. *B.* 1905. *Educ.* University of Manitoba (BA; MA) and Oxford University (BLitt). *M.* (1) 1936, Beatrice Landon Young (*D.*). *M.* (2) 1939, Mary Margaret Beattie. *S.* Peter and Alan. *Daus.* Jane and Ruth. *Career:* Lecturer in History, Wesley College, Univ. of Manitoba 1929–37; Third Secretary, Dept. of External Affairs 1937; served in various capacities in Prime Minister's Office 1937–52 (then holding title of Special Assistant to the Prime Minister); Clerk of the Privy Council and Secretary to the Cabinet, June 1952; joined the Government as Secretary of State of Canada, June 1953; elected Member (Lib.) of Parliament for Newfoundland Riding of Bonavista-Twillingate at General Election, Aug. 1953; resigned as Secretary of State and appointed Minister of Citizenship and Immigration 1954–57; resigned with Liberal Administration 1957; re-elected to House of Commons 1957–58, 1962, 1963 and 1965. Secretary of State 1963; Minister of Transport 1964; resigned as Minister of Transport and MP for Bonavista-Twillingate, Newfoundland 1967; Pres. of Canadian Transport Commission 1968–72. *Publications:* The Mackenzie King Record 1939–44; The Liberal Party; Le parti libéral (1963); My Years with Louis St. Laurent (1975). *Address:* 550 Maple Lane East, Rockcliffe Park, Ottawa, Canada.

**PICKLES, Stephen Hartley.** British business executive. *B.* 1923. *Educ.* Oundle School. *M.* 1949, Valerie Joyce Bracewell. *S.* 1. *Dau.* 1. *Career:* Dir. of the 12 companies within the S. Pickles & Sons group 1949—; Dir. Fryer & Co. (Nelson) Ltd. 1962–65; Man. Dir. Manufacturing Bradfield Brett Holdings Ltd. since 1965. Served in World War II (Royal Engineers in U.K. and Middle East, reaching rank of Major; on General Staff at GHQ Middle East until demobilization, having served in Field Companies in the Western Desert and Tunisia. Commissioned 1942). Won Silver Medal for Cotton Manufacture, London City & Guilds 1948; fifth year First Prize. Associate of the Textile Institute. *Address: office* Barnsey Shed, Barnoldswick, Colne, Lancs. BB8 6BW.

**PIEL, Gerard.** American publisher. *B.* 1915. *Educ.* Harvard College (AB *magna cum laude* 1937); Hon. DSc: Lawrence College 1956, Colby Coll. 1960, Univ. British Columbia 1965, and Brandeis University 1965. Hon. LittD: Rutgers University 1961; Bates Coll. 1974; Hon. LHD, Columbia Univ. 1962, Williams Coll. 1966. Hon. LLD: Tuskegee Institute 1963, Bridgeport University 1964; Brooklyn Polytechnic Inst. 1965; Carnegie-Mellon Univ. 1968. *M.* 1955, Eleanor V. Jackson. *S.* Jonathan Bird and Samuel Bird (*Dec.*). *Dau.* Eleanor Jackson. *Career:* Science Editor, Life Magazine 1939–46; Assistant to Pres., Henry J. Kaiser Co. and associate companies 1946–48; Publisher and Pres., Scientific American (monthly magazine of science) since 1948; Overseer Harvard Coll.; Trustee, Radcliffe College; Phillips Academy; American Museum of Natural History; New York Botanical Garden; Henry Kaiser Family Foundation; Mayo Foundation. *Awards:* Fellow Amer. Acad. of Arts and Sciences, American Philosophical Society; Council on Foreign Relations; Institute of Medicine 1962, Kalinga Prize. *Publication:* Science in the Cause of Man (Alfred A. Knopf, New York 1961); The Acceleration of History (1972). *Clubs:* Harvard of N.Y. City; Century; Cosmos. (Washington DC); Somerset (Boston); Duquesne (Pittsburgh). *Address:* 415 Madison Avenue, New York N.Y. 10017 U.S.A.

**PIERCE, Samuel Riley, Jr.** Lawyer. *B.* 1922. *Educ.* Cornell Univ. (AB 1947), Cornell Law School (LL.B 1949), New York Univ. School of Law (LLM in Taxation 1952); Ford Foundation Fellow, Yale Law School 1957; New York Univ. LLD (1972). *M.* 1948, Dr. Barbara P. Wright. *Dau.* Victoria Wright. *Career:* Asst. Dist. Attorney, County of N.Y. 1949–53; Asst. U.S. Attorney for South. Dist. of New York 1953–55; Asst. to Under-Secretary of Labor, U.S. Dept. of Labor 1955–56; Gen. Councel of U.S. Treasury 1970–73; Partner in law firm of Battle, Fowler, Lidstone, Jaffin, Pierce & Kheel since 1973; Member: New York State Banking Board 1961—, Faculty of New York University School of Law 1958—, National Panel of Arbitrators of the American Arbitration Association and of the Federal Mediation and Conciliation Service 1957—, Board of Directors of New York 1964–65 World's Fair Inc. 1961–65; U.S. Industries Inc. 1964—; Prudential Insurance Co. of America; International Paper Co.; International Basic Economy Corp.; Dir. General Electric Co.; Consultant to Fund for International Social and Economic Education 1961—. U.S. Delegate to Conference on Cooperatives in the Caribbean, Georgetown, British Guiana 1956; Counsel to Sub-committee on Anti-Trust of the Committee on the Judiciary, U.S. House of Representatives 1956–57; Fraternal Delegate to All-African People's Conf., Accra 1958. Judge, Court of General Sessions 1959–60; Chairman, N.Y. State Minimum Wage Board for the Hotel Industry 1961; member, New York City Board of Education 1961. Trustee: Hampton Inst., Mt. Holyoke Coll. Cornell Univ. *Awards:* Junior Chamber of Commerce Annual Distinguished Award for 1958; Annual Award of the Bible Soc. 1959; C.I.D. Agents Assn. Distinguished Service Award 1959; City College Newman Club Award 1960, Alexander Hamilton Award 1970. *Member:* Amer. Bar Assn.; Amer. Judicature Socy.; Assn. of Bar of City of New York; New York Country Lawyers Assn. (Dir. 1961—); Cornell Law Assn. (Exec. Cttee. 1962—); N.Y. Univ. Law Assn. Inc. (Dir. 1961—). *Publications:* Manpower in the Atomic Age (1956); Legal Problems in Private Layoff Plans (1956); The New Look in Collective Bargaining Agreements; A Study of Supplemental Unemployment Benefit Plans (1957); Organized Professional Team Sports and the Anti-Trust Laws (1958); Mental Illness and Due Process (Cornell Univ. Press 1962). Phi Beta Kappa; Phi Kappa Phi; N.Y. City. *Address:* 16 West 77th Street, New York, N.Y. 10024; and *office* 280 Park Avenue, New York, N.Y. 10017, U.S.A.

**PIERCE, Sydney David,** OBE. Canadian diplomat. *B.* 1901. *Educ.* Lower Canada College, Montreal and McGill Univ. (BA; BCL) Hon. LLD. *M.* 1927, Jean Mather Crombie. *S.* 1. *Daus.* 3. *Career:* Previously member, Canadian Olympic Team 1924; Reporter, Montreal Gazette 1925–26; Lecturer, Dalhousie University 1926; with Associated Press 1937; in private buisness 1928–39; with Dept. of Munitions and Supply, Washington 1940–44 (serving on Combined Production and Resources Board; Joint War Production Committee); Director-General 1944; joined Dept. of External Affairs 1944; Ambassador to Mexico 1947–49; on special duty, Paris 1948–49; Associate Deputy Minister, Dept. of Trade and Commerce, Ottawa 1949–50; Canadian Representative to O.E.E.C., Paris 1950–51; Canadian member, Military Production and Supply Board, N.A.T.O.; Minister and Director of Washington Office of Dept. of Defence Production 1951–53; Ambassador to Brazil 1953–56; Deputy High Commissioner for Canada in London 1956–59. Canad. Amb. to Belgium and Luxembourg and European Communities, 1959–65. Chief negotiator for Canada, Kennedy Round, Geneva. 1965–67; Chmn .Manpower and Immigration Council 1969–72. *Address:* 50, Rideau Terrace, Ottawa, Canada.

**PIERCE, Wallace Lincoln.** American Investment Trustee. *B.* 1912. *Educ.* Harvard Coll. (BS). *M.* 1936, Mary Markle Bannard. *Career:* Chmn. Bd. Dir. S.S. Pierce Co.; Pres. Pierce Co. Inc.; S.S. Pierce Realty Co.; Dir. New England Merchants National Bank; Trustee, William Underwood Co.; Suffolk Franklin Savings Bank; Incorporator Boston Children's Friend Society, Dir. National Amer. Wholesale Grocers Assn. 1958–63; Amer. Socy. Friendship with Switzerland; Robert B. Bingham Hospital. *Clubs:* Country, Brookline; Union; Merchants; Harvard; Wardroon (all Boston); Leash (N.Y.C.). *Address:* 60 Fernwood Road, Chestnut Hill, Mass. 02167, U.S.A.

**PIETTE, André Auguste.** Officer, Ordre de la Couronne; Chevalier, Ordre de Léopold; Belgian technical engineer. *B.* 1910. *Educ.* Ingenieur des Arts et Métiers, 1930. *M.* 1933, Marie L. Simeon. *S.* Jean-Marie and Raymond. *Dau.* Andrée. Member of the Board Chrysler Belgique since 1972. *Address:* Rue Roberts Jones, 32, Brussels 1180, Belgium.

**PIGOTT, Stanley Capel.** British. *B.* 1918. *Educ.* Cheltenham College. *M.* 1942. Alix Mawhinny. *S.* 1. Executive. Mather &

Crowther Ltd. 1956–65; Secretary, Ogilvy & Mather International Inc. 1965–72 *Publications:* Hollins—A Study of Industry 1784–1949; OBM 125 Years (1976). *Address:* c/o Williams & Glyn's Bank Ltd., 25 Millbank, London SW1.

**PIKE, Rt. Hon. Baroness.** *B.* 1918. *Educ.* Hons. BA-Economics and Social Psychology. *Career:* Man. Dir., Clokie & Co. Ltd., Castleford 1946–59; Member Parliament (Cons.) Melton Mowbray 1956–74; P.P.S. Under Secretary of State, Home Office 1957; Asst. Postmaster-General 1959; Under-Secretary of State, Home Office 1963. Member of the Shadow Cabinet and Spokesman on Social Security for the Conservative Opposition 1966–67. Director: Dunderdal Investments, and Watts, Blake, Bearne Ltd. since 1964. *Clubs:* Hurlingham. *Address:* 25 Chester Row, London SW1; and House of Lords, London, S.W.1.

**PILAVACHI, Aristide N.** Greek. *B.* 1913. *Educ.* Lausanne Univ. (Economics) and Grenoble and Athens Univs. (Law). *M.* 1947, Frosso Zarifi. *S.* 2. *Dau.* 1. *Career:* Entered Diplomatic Service 1939; served at Min. of Foreign Affairs and with the Government-in-Exile until Oct. 1944 (during this period took part, as a corporal, in the campaign against the Axis—Oct. 1940–Apr. 1941—and undertook a secret mission to occupied Greece—Sept. 1943–June 1944). Chargé d'Affaires and Actg. Consul-General, Addis Ababa 1944; apptd. to Min. of Foreign Affairs, and became Head of U.N. Section 1946; First Secy. Greek Legation, Berne 1949, and Greek Embassy, London 1950; Head, Balkan Section and later Chef de Cabinet of the Foreign Minister 1955; Counsellor of Embassy, Cairo 1956, and First Counsellor, Washington 1958; Head, 4th Political Div. (including affairs of Turkey and Cyprus) 1962. Member of Greek Delegations: Paris Peace Conf. 1946, London Conf. on external debts of Germany (Dep. Head), NATO Council meetings 1963–64–65, and Gen. Assembly UN 1964–65 and 1968–69. Ambassador of Greece to Canada, June 1965–70; First Deputy Dir.-Gen., R. Ministry of Foreign Affairs 1970–72. Ambassador to Paris 1974–76; Sec.-Gen. to the Presidency of the Republic since Dec. 1976. *Awards:* Silver Cross Order of the Redeemer; Order of George I; Order of the Phoenix; Order of Merit for Gallant Action (mil.) World War II; and Military Medal for Outstanding Acts. *Address:* Menandrou and Irodou Attikou, Kifisia, Greece.

**PILCHER, Sir John Arthur, GCMG.** British. *B.* 1912. *Educ.* Shrewsbury; Clare Coll., Cambridge (BA); and in France, Austria and Italy. *M.* 1942, Delia Margaret Taylor. *Dau.* 1. *Career:* Served in Japan 1936–39 and China 1939–41; Ministry of Information and Foreign Office 1941–48; Press Attaché, Rome 1948–51; Head of Japan and Pacific Department, Foreign Office 1951–53; Counsellor, Madrid 1954–59; Ambassador to Philippines 1959–63; Assistant Under-Secretary of State, Foreign Office 1963–65; Ambassador to Austria 1965–67 and to Japan 1967–72. *Awards:* Grand Crost (Gold) of the Austrian Order of Merit; Order of the Rising Sun (First Class); Grande Ufficiale of the Order Al Merito della Repubblica Italiana. *Club:* Brooks's, London. *Address:* 33 The Terrace, London, S.W.13.

**PILKINGTON, Lawrence Herbert Austin, CBE, JP.** British. *B.* 1911. *Educ.* Bromsgrove School; Magdalene College, Cambridge (MA). *M.* 1936, Nora Holden. *Daus.* 2. *Career:* Dir. Pilkington Brothers Ltd., 1935—. *Member:* Council of British Glass Industry Research Assn., 1954–75; Society of Acoustic Technology. Chairman, British Coal Utilization Research Association, 1963–68. *Awards:* Hon. LLD, Sheffield Univ. 1956; Hon. DSc, Salford Univ. 1970. *Address:* Coppice End, Colborne Rd., St. Peter Port, Guernsey, C.I.; and *office* Pilkington Brothers Ltd., St. Helens, Lancashire.

**PILKINGTON, Lord.** British glass manufacturer. *B.* 19 Apr. 1905. *Educ.* Cambridge Univ. (BA and MA). *M.* (1) 1930, Rosamund Margaret Rowan (*D.* 1953). *S.* 1. *Daus.* 2. *M.* (2) 1961, Mavis Joy Doreen Wilding. *Career:* Chairman, Pilkington Brothers Ltd. 1949–73; President, Council of European Industrial Federations 1954–57; President. Federation of British Industries 1953–55; Chancellor, Loughborough Univ. of Technology; Chmn., N.W. Sports & Recreation Council; Vice Lord Lieut. of Merseyside. *Address:* Windle Hall, St. Helens, Lancs.

**PILLSBURY, John Sargent, Jr.** American. Insurance executive. *B.* 1912. *Educ.* Yale Uni,v. (BA 1935) and Univ. of Minnesota (LLB 1940). *M.* 1936. Katharine Harrison Clark. *S.* John Sargent III, Donaldson Clark and Lynde Harrison. *Dau.* Katherine Clark Wood. *Career:* At Pillsbury Mills 1936–37; with law firm of Faegre & Benson 1940–56, Pres. 1956–69; Chmn. & Chief Exec. Officer since 1969; Northwestern National Life Insurance Co. *Member:* American Bar Assn. *Clubs:* The Minneapolis; Woodhill Country; Minnetonka Yacht; Yale (N.Y.C.). *Address:* 315 Woodhill Road, Wayzata, Minnesota 55391; and *office* 20 Washington Avenue South, Minneapolis, Minn. 55440, U.S.A.

**PINCKERNELLE, Hans G. E.,** Dr jur. German lawyer. *B.* 1903. *Educ.* High School and University, Dr jur. *M.* 1928, Doramarie Passow. *S.* Ulf and Klaus. *Daus.* Karin and Heide, *Career:* Hon. Chmn. Board of Directors, Haftpflichtverband der Deutschen Industrie VaG, Hanover since 1973; Member, Board of Directors, Werner & Pfleiderer, Stuttgart-Feuerbach. *Address:* Habichtweg 5, 433 Mülheim-Ruhr-Speldorf; and *office* Böninger Strasse 35 (Postfach 10 13 04), 41 Duisburg. Germany.

**PINDLING, Rt. Hon. Lynden, PC.** *B.* 1930. *Educ.* Western Senior School; Government High School; University of London (LLB); LLD (Hon.), Middle Temple (Barrister-at-Law). *M.* 1956, Marguerite M. McKenzie. *S.* Lynden Obafemi, Leslie Oscar. *Daus.* Michelle Marguerite, Monique Marguerite. *Career:* Practised as a lawyer, 1952–67; joined Progressive Liberal Party, 1953; elected to Bahamas House of Assembly. 1956; 1962; 1967 and 1968; Parliamentary Leader of Progressive Liberal Party, 1956; Leader of the Opposition, 1964; Member, Delegations to United Nations Special Cttee. of Twenty-four, 1965 and 1966; Premier, and Minister of Tourism and Development, 1967; led Bahamian Delegation to Constitutional Conference, London, 1968, to Independence Conference London 1972; Prime Minister of the Commonwealth of the Bahama Islands since 1969. *Address:* Office of the Prime Minister, Rawson Square, Nassau, Bahamas.

**PINE, Cecil Cady.** American. Engineering manager. *B.* 1910. *Educ.* Int. Correspondence School; Capital Radio Engineering Institute; Alexander Hamilton Institute; Univ of Washington (special course); Long Island A and T (special course). *M.* (1) 1933, Mary E. Angle (*Div.* 1963); (2) 1966. *Career:* Engineering Section Head for flight tests, Sperry Gyroscope Co. 1948–56; Project Engineer, same company 1945–58; Aircraft Radio Maintenance Supervisor, Pan American World Airways 1943–45; Aircraft Radio Mechanic, same company 1941–43; U.S. Naval Reserve (special assignment; inactive duty) 1942–44; Adviser to the Special Committee No. 18, Radio Technical Commissioner for Aeronautics 1950–56. Engineering Facilities Supervisor, Sperry-Phoenix Co. 1956–61; Man. Engineering Shops, Sperry Flight Systems Div. of Sperry Rand since 1961. *Publications:* Your Other You, (1973); papers and articles in Proceedings of Radio Engineers, Electronics, Aviation Age, Radio News, Engineering Review (Sperry Gyroscope Co.); paper published in Aero/Space Engineering (publ. of Inst. Aero Sciences); paper on Design Considerations of a Climate Control Laboratory for Asthma and Allergy Research; holder of five U.S. patents on aircraft electronic control systems. *Member:* Scientific Research Council for Children's Asthma Research Institute and Hospital 1956–63; Careers for Youth 1960–61; Member, Past Pres. Valley Artists League; Arizona Academy of Science. *Address:* 1015 West Mission Lane, Phoenix, Arizona, 85021 U.S.A.

**PINKER, Martin Wallis, OBE.** British Methodist Minister. *Educ.* private study, and Hartley Victoria College, Manchester. *M.* 1922, Lilian H. Eccles. *S.* 1. *Dau.* 1. After training for a business career, was commissioned in Lancs. Fus. in World War I; Ordained Methodist Minister 1922; released from pastoral work to become Organizing Secy. of Discharged Prisoners' Aid Society, at Strangeways Prison, Manchester 1929; first General Secy. of National Association of Discharged Prisoners' Aid Societies (Inc.), London 1936–58 (elected Vice-Pres. 1958); Dir., Central Association for the Aid of Discharged Convicts 1944–48; Dir. for England and Wales, Central After-care Association (men's division) 1948–58; appointed by Home Secretary member of Joint Committee to review work of voluntary prisoners' aid societies and their relationship with statutory authorities (Maxwell Committee) 1951; British Representative to International Prisoners' Aid Association (Vice-Pres. 1951; Pres. 1955); at request of U.N. High Commissioner for Refugees, visited Germany to report on position of displaced persons in German prisons. and to advise on rehabilitation 1954; Founding Hon. Secy., Commonwealth Association of

Prisoners' Aid Societies 1952; appeared before Select Cttee. of the Legislature, Ontario 1953; Chmn.: Training Schools Advisory Board 1958–63, and Minister's Advisory Council on the Treatment of the Offender 1959–73, Government of Ontario. *Address:* 88 Don River Boulevard, Willowdale, Ontario, Canada.

**PINOCHET UGARTE, General Augusto.** Chilean Soldier & Politician. *B.* 1915. *Educ.* Military Sch.; Infantry Sch.; War Academy; National Defence Academy. *M.* Maria Lucia Hiriart Rodriguez. *S.* 2. *Daus.* 3. *Career:* After joining the Military School in 1933, rose to the rank of Major, 1953; Infantry Regiment. No. 4 "Rancagua" Operations Officer 1953; Adjutant in Under-Secretariat of War & teacher at the War College 1954; Chilean Military Mission to USA & Service Commission as Military Prof. of War Acad. of Army of Republic of Ecuador 1956; HQ I Army Div., 1959; Commanding Infantry Regiment No. 7 "Esmerelda", with rank of Lt.-Col., 1961; Exec.-Dir. of War Academy 1964; Chief of Staff of II Army Div., 1968; Commander in Chief of VI Div. (Brigade General) 1969; GOC Army Garrison, Santiago (General of Division) 1971; Chief of Army GHQ 1972; Service Commission attending celebration of CLXII Anniversary of Mexican Independence 1972; Acting Commander in Chief of Army 1972; Promoted General & Commander in Chief of Army 1973; on 11th Sept. 1973, formation of the Council of Government: appointed Pres. of the Council; on 27th June, 1974, adopted as Supreme Head of the Nation in accordance with decree; on 17th Dec. 1974, appointed Pres. of the Republic by decree. *Decorations:* many Chilean, incl. Grand Star for Military Merit (30 years); Distinguished Service Decoration (1st class), "11 de Septiembre" Medal; "Diosa Minerva" Medal (Title of Prof. of the Acad.); etc. & many foreign, incl. "Abdón Calderón Parra" Decoration, 1st class (Ecuador); General José Maria Córdova "Order of Military Merit", with rank of Commander (Colombia); Military Order of St. Saviour & St Brigitte of Sweden, Supreme Grand Chain Class; Grand Diamond Cross of the Order of Ayacucho (Peru); Decoration of Mayo Order of Military Merit, Grand Cross Class (Argentina); Grand Cross of Military Merit (Spain); etc. *Publications:* Intelligence Service—Quito (1958); Military Geography—Military Interpretation of Geographical Factors (1967); Geopolitics—various stages for the Geopolitical study of the States—The Geography of Chile.—The Geography of Argentina, Peru & Bolivia—the 1879 War of the Pacific—First Land Operations (1968). *Address:* Secretaria de Prensa, Presidencia, Santiago, Republic of Chile.

**PINSENT, Roger Philip.** British. *B.* 1916. *Educ.* Downside School, Lausanne, London (BAHons 1940) and Grenoble (Dipl. Phonetique 1939) Universities. *M.* 1941, Suzanne Smalley. *S.* Philip John. *Daus.* Prudence and Charlotte (Malvezzi). *Career:* H.M. Forces (Capt. Gloucester Regt.) 1940–46; entered Foreign Service 1946; Legation, Havana 1947 (1st Secretary 1948); Consul, Tangier 1950–52; 1st Secretary, Madrid 1952–53; Foreign Office 1953–56; 1st Secy., Embassy, Lima 1956–59; Deputy Head of U.K. Delegation to European Communities, Luzembourg 1959–63; Ambassador to Nicaragua 1963–67. Commercial Counsellor, Embassy, Ankara, 1967–70. H.M. Consul-General, Sao Paulo 1970–73. *Club:* Canning (London). *Address:* Cranfield Cottage Maugersbury, Stow-on-the-Wold, Glos. GL54 IHR.

**PIPER, W. T., Jr.** *B.* 1911. *Educ.* Harvard College (AB). *M.* 1940, Margaret Bush. *Career:* With Piper Aircraft Corp. 1934–73. Former Dir. Piper Aircraft Corp.; Former Vice-President, First National Bank (now Fidelity) Lock Haven. Former Director, Pennsylvania State Chamber of Commerce. *Member:* Quiet Birdmen; Aviation Council of Pennsylvania. Republican. *Clubs:* Anglers (N.Y.C.), Spruce Creek Rod and Gun, Harvard Central Penna., Clinton Country. *Address:* 411 W. Water Street, Lock Haven, Pa., U.S.A.

**PIRACHA, Riaz.** Pakistani Diplomat. *B.* 1924. *Educ.* Univ. of the Punjab, Lahore—BA (Hons.), MA; Fletcher School of Law & Diplomacy, Boston, U.S.A. *M.* 1949, Masuda. *S.* 1. *Daus.* 2. *Career:* 2nd Sec., Pakistan Mission to UN, New York 1951–55, Embassy of Pakistan, Cairo 1955–57, & Khartoum 1957–58; Under-Sec., Ministry of Foreign Affairs, Karachi 1958–59; 1st Sec., Pakistan Mission to UN, New York 1959–61, & Pakistan High Commission, Kuala Lumpur 1961–63; Pakistan Trade Commissioner, Hong Kong 1963–65; Dir.-Gen., Ministry of Foreign Affairs, Islamabad 1966–68; Ambassador of Pakistan to Belgium, Luxembourg & the EEC 1968–70, to Burma & Singapore 1970–75, & to Australia, New Zealand and Fiji since 1975. *Club:* Royal Canberra Golf Club. *Address:* 15 Canterbury Crescent, Deakin, ACT 2600; and *office* 59 Franklin Street, Forrest, ACT 2603, Australia.

**PIRIE, Gordon.** FCIB. British. *B.* 1903. *Educ.* Felsted School. *M.* (1) 1939, Lucille Carterette Gruchy (D. 1970). (2) 1971, Peggy Louise des Salles d'Epinoix. *Career:* Alternate Dir. The Trade Indemnity Co. Ltd. 1946–57; Head Office Exec. The London & Lancashire Insurance Co. Ltd. 1948–57; Dir. Hogg, Robinson & Gardner Mountain Ltd.; Hogg Robinson & Gardner Mountain (Reinsurance) Ltd.; Hogg Robinson & Gardner Mountain (Overseas) Ltd., Credit Indemnity Co. Ltd., Agostini Bros. (Insurance) Ltd. Trinidad; Vice-Pres. Dir. Hogg, Robinson & Capel-Cure (Canada) Ltd.; Corredores de Seguros S.A. (Caracas); Bain Sons & Golmick Ltd.; Gallo-Britannique Pour L'Assurance S.A. (Paris). *Member:* Lloyd's Corp. of Insurance Brokers; Inst. of Dirs.; Chartered Insurance Institute. *Club:* Reform. *Address:* Priory Lake Cottage, Park Lane, Reigate, Surrey.

**PIRIE, John Charles.** Lawyer. *B.* 1907. *Educ.* Univ. of Nebraska (AB 1929) and Oxford Univ. (BA Juris 1934; Ma 1964). *M.* 1935, Edith Ferguson-Murdoch. *Career:* Assoc., law firm of Root, Clark, Buckner & Ballantine 1934–43. Joined Pan Amer. World Airways 1943, Asst. Gen. Cncl. 1946, Assoc. General Counsel 1956, Vice-Pres. 1958 and General Counsel 1968; Senior Vice-President and General Counsel & Dir., Pan American World Airways Inc. 1970–72; Dir., Con Rail 1976. *Member:* American and N.Y. State Bar Assns.; Bar Assn. of City of New York; Maryland State Bar Assn.; Anne Arundel County Bar Assn. *Clubs:* Sky; Wings (N.Y.C.); Burning Tree; Annapolis Yacht. *Address:* 1910 Carrollton Rd., Annapoli, Md 21401, and *office* 222 Severn Avenue, Annapoli, Md 21401, U.S.A.

**PIRRUNG, Gilbert Robinson.** Colonel U.S.A.R. (Retd.); corporation executive. *B.* 1911. *Educ.* Yale Univ. (BSc 1934). *M.* 1947, Joan Dorothy Harrison Burgess. *S.* Clifford Mark and Timothy Burgess. *Daus.* Lynette R. H. and Henriette Christine. *Career:* Owner, Manager of Pirrung Racing Team, Indianapolis, Inc. 1934–36. With Gaylord Container Corp., St. Louis, Mo.: Production Sales Dept. 1936–39, Budget Director and Asst. to Treasurer 1939–41. Owner and Manager, Aragon Farms, Bainbridge, Ga. 1945—. Director 1950–55. Officer, Boy Scouts of America, Chmn., Region Six, 1960–63 (member, National Exec. Board 1961—), International Commissioner 1968–72; Pres., Inter-American Council of the World Bureau 1962. Member, General Council Presbyterian Church in the U.S. 1962. Trustee, Aiken Preparatory School (Aiken, S.C.) 1962–72; Vice-Pres. Dir., United States Foundation, Int. Scouting; Chmn., Georgia Foundation for Independent Colleges 1970–72. *Awards:* Silver Star, Bronze Star with two Oak Leaf Clusters and Croix de Guerre avec Etoile Vermeil; Recipient Silver Beaver, Antelope, and Buffalo Awards. A.I. Merit Award from Boy Scouts of Chile; Silver Hawk, Boys Scouts of Japan; Fleur de Lis de Plata, Boy Scouts of Paraguay; Bronze Wolf, by 23 World Scout Conference. *Clubs:* Racquet, St. Louis Country (St. Louis); St. Anthony (N.Y.C.); Yale (N.Y.C.); Capitol City (Atlanta). Little Harbor (Mich.). *Address:* Aragon Farms, Bainbridge, Ga. 31717, U.S.A.

**PIRSON, André-Xavier.** Belgian. B. 1923. *Educ.* Master's Degree in Commercial, Consular, Financial Sciences. *Career:* Entered service of Ministry of Foreign Affairs 1945; Head of Civil Aviation Dept. of the Ministry 1949; Belgian Representative on Council of International Civil Aviation Organization 1954–60; Director, International Organizations Division, Political Department, Belgian Ministry of Foreign Affairs 1960. Representative on the Council of the International Civil Aviation Organization 1962–74; Minister Plenipotentiary, Belgian Mission to U.N. since 1975. *Publications:* Study of International Loans to Europe; various articles on economy and development of air transportation. *Address:* 809, United Nations Plaza, New York, N.Y. 10017, U.S.A.

**PISTERMAN, Walter Waldemar.** Swiss. *B.* 1914. *Educ.* Berne Gymnasium and Geneva School of Commerce. *M.* 1946, Jean H. Tinkler. *S.* David Howard. *Daus.* Wendy Pamela and Ann Carolyn. *Career:* Managing Director: Swiss Textile Machine Industries 1944—, and Simplon Distributing Co. 1946—. Chmn. Australian Board, Switzerland General Insurance Co. Ltd.; Chairman: Dun & Bradstreet (Aust.) Pty. Ltd. 1959—, Switzerland Life Assurance Society Ltd.,

Australia; Director: World Travel Service Holdings Pty. Ltd. 1973, Edward Keller Ltd., Zurich, 1967; Stewart Moffat Travel Group 1969—. Director: Valchem (Aust.) Pty. Ltd., 1969—, and Australian Representative of the Credit Suisse 1969—; Bruck (Aust.) Ltd. since 1972. *Member:* Institute of Directors. *Clubs:* Athenaeum; Australian Golf; Sorrento Golf; Victorian Racing; Victorian Amateur Turf. *Address:* 16/77 Caroline Street, South Yarra, Vic.; and *office* 31 Queens Street, Melbourne, Vic., Australia.

**PITMAN, Benjamin Franklin, Jr.** Investment banker. *B.* 1898. *Educ.* University of Nebraska 1914–17; Sorbonne 1918–19; Univ. of Washington 1919–20. *S.* Benjamin Franklin, III. *Dau.* Peggy (Mays). *Career:* Secretary, Chadron (Nebraska) Building & Loan Assn. 1920–22; Pitman & Co., real estate, Sarasota, Fla. 1921–24; Manager, El Paso (Tex.) branch, Henry L. Doherty & Co., investment bankers 1924–29. President, Pitman & Co., San Antonio, Texas 1929—; Stock Broker, Rotan Mosle Inc.; Republican. *Clubs:* San Antionio Country; St. Anthony; Argyle. *Address:* 5425 N. New Braunfels Avenue, San Antonio, Texas, 78209; and *office* 100 National Bank of Commerce Bldg., San Antonio, Tex. 78205, U.S.A.

**PITMAN, Sir (Isaac) James,** KBE, Educator & Former British Publisher & MP (Con.) Bath. *B.* 14 Aug. 1901. *Educ.* Eton Coll. and Ch. Ch., Oxford (MA—History, 2nd Cl. Honours); DHum Litt (Hon), Hofstra N.Y. DLitt Hum (Hon) Strathclyde; DLitt Hum (Hon); Bath. *M.* 1927, Hon. Margaret Beaufort Lawson-Johnson. *S.* Peter John, Michael Ian, David Christian. *Dau.* Margaret. *Career:* Bursar, Duke of York's and King's Camp 1933–39. Inventor and Introducer, Pitman's Initial Teaching Alphabet. Chmn. and Man. Dir. Sir Isaac Pitman & Sons Ltd. 1934–66; Director, Bank of England 1941–45; Member of Parliament for Bath 1945–64. Bovril Ltd. 1949–71; Dir. Boots Pure Drug Co. Ltd. 1951–72: Equity & Law Life Assurance Society 1954–77. Chmn., the Initial Teaching Alphabet Foundation. Vice-Pres., British and Foreign Schools Society; Charter Pro-Chancellor, Bath Univ.; Mem. Management Cttee., Institute of Education, London Univ.; Vice-Pres., Inst. of Office Management. *Publications:* Alphabets and Reading (with John St. John); Thoughts and Theories; Modern Course in Pitman's Shorthand; Student's Review of Pitman's Shorthand (jointly with Miss E. D. Smith); The Employer and the New Education Act (jointly with R. A. Miles); Chapter on Games and Recreations in 'The Character of England' (O.U.P.); Management Efficiency in Nationalized Undertakings. *Address:* 58 Chelsea Park Gardens, London, S.W.3.

**PITTERMANN, Dr. Bruno,** PhD, LLD; *B.* 1905. *Educ.* Landstrasser Gymnasium; Vienna University (PhD *summa cum laude*). *M. Dau.* 1. *Career:* After teaching in the former Vocational School of Machine Construction and Electrical Engineering, appointed Secretary of Chamber of Labour, Klagenfurt, Aug. 1929 (first in Dept. of Education and later in Dept. of Social Welfare); dismissed for political reasons in Feb. 1934, resumed teaching, and passed degree of LLD *summa cum laude*; but for political reasons was refused admission as a candidate for graduation, which was deferred until 1946; was also denied permission to work as a lawyer, and 'went underground'. On restoration of the Republic, entered the service of the Provisional Government's Department of Social Welfare and Administration as Secy. to the head of the department; here he organized the re-establishment of the Chambers of Labour and became Secy.-Gen. of the Vienna Chamber of Labour; Deputy, National Assembly 1945; subsequently Exec. Floor-leader of Socialist Parliamentary Party (Klub der Sozialistischen Abgeordneten und Bundesräte). After election of Dr. Schärf as Federal President he was appointed Vice-Chancellor, Chairman of Austrian Socialist Party, and Minister of Nationalized Industries. Member, Committee for Political Affairs, Strasbourg; and Council of European Consultative Assembly (later Depty. Chmn.). Elected Pres. of the Socialist International 1964. After the general elections, Mar. 1966, the coalition between the Soc. Party and the Catholic People's Party was discontinued. Former leader of Soc. Opposition & Chmn. of the Soc. Parliamentary Party; Chmn. Socialist International. *Address:* The Socialist International, Vienna, Austria.

**PIXLEY, Sir Neville (Drake),** Kt 1976, MBE, KStJ, VRD. Australian. *B.* 1905. *M.* 1938, Lorna Stephens. *Daus.* 3. *Career:* Commander, Royal Australian Naval Reserve World War II; A.D.C. to H.M. King and Queen 1951–54. Former Chmn. P & O Lines of Australia Pty. Ltd.; Director, Burns Philp & Co. Ltd., Mauri Bros. and Thomson Ltd.; Board of advice National Bank of Australasia Ltd.; Chmn. Australian Cttee. Lloyds Register of Shipping; Chmn., Royal Humane Society of N.S.W. *Address:* 335 New South Head Road, Double Bay, Sydney, N.S.W. 2028, Australia.

**PLAJA, Eugenio.** Italian Diplomat. *B.* 1914. *Educ.* Univ. of Palermo—Doctor of Jurisprudence. *M.* 1939, Elena Pagliarello. *S.* 3. *Career:* Joined Italian Foreign Service 1937; served in France, Argentine & Chile 1938–1952; Ministry of Foreign Affairs, Rome 1952–55; Deputy Perm. Rep. to UN, New York 1955–61; Dir.-Gen., Emigration, then Dir. Gen., Personnel 1961–69; Amb. to Egypt 1969–73; Perm. Rep. to UN 1973–75; Dir.-Gen., Political Affairs, Min. of Foreign Affairs, Rome 1975–76; Perm. Rep. to the European Communities since 1976. *Clubs:* Circolo degli Scacchi, Rome. *Address:* Avenue Victoria 27–1050 Brussels, Belgium; and *office* Rue de la Loi 74–1040 Brussels, Belgium.

**PLANT, Sir Arnold.** British. Professor Emeritus at University of London. LLD (Hon) Cape Town 1968. *B.* 1898. *Educ.* University of London (BCom 1922; BSc Econ 1923). *M.* 1925, Edith Render, BA. *S.* 2. *Career:* Engineering Management 1915–20 (interrupted by war service in Army); Professor of Commerce and Dean of Faculty, University of Cape Town 1924–30; Professor, London Sch. of Econ. 1930–66 (interrupted by service as Temporary British Civil Servant 1940–46). Member of Council and Vice-President, Royal Economic Society, etc. *Address:* 19 Wildwood Road, London, N.W.11.

**PLANTEY, Alain.** French Diplomat. *B.* 1924. *Educ.* Licencié ès Lettres, Docteur en Droit, Lauréat des Facultés de droit de Bordeaux et de Paris; Ecole Nationale d'Administration. *M.* 1955, Christiane Wioland. *Daus.* 4. *Career:* Auditeur, then Maitre des Requêtes of the Council of State 1949; Mem., French Delegation to the U.S. 1950–51; Technical Counsellor to the Min. of Overseas Territories 1958–59; Sec.-Gen., Conseil Supérieur de l'A.F.P.; Counsellor to the Presidency of the Republic 1959–67; Ambassador to Madagascar 1967–72; Asst. Sec.-Gen., Western European Union since 1972; Counsellor of State since 1974. *Member:* Hon. Pres., Association des Anciens Elèves de l'Ecole Nationale d'Administration; Council Mem., National Museum of Natural History; Vice-Pres., l'Institut International de droit d'Expression Française; Société des Gens de Lettres. *Decorations:* Officier de la Légion d'Honneur; Officier de l'Ordre National du Mérite et des Palmes Académiques; Commandeur des Arts et des Lettres; Grand Croix de l'Ordre National Malgache; Grand Officier de l'Ordre National de Côte d'Ivoire et de l'Etoile équatoriale; Commandeur des Ordres nationaux du Sénégal, du Congo, du Tchad, du Niger et du Mauritanie; Officier du Ouissam Alaouite. *Publications:* La Réforme de la Justice Marocaine; La Justice Répressive et le Droit Pénal Chérifien; Traité Pratique de la Fonction Publique; La Formation et le Perfectionnement des Fonctionnaires; La Communauté; Indépendance et Coopération; Prospective de l'Etat; Droit et Practique de la Fonction Publique Internationale. *Address:* 6 avenue Sully Prud'homme—75007 Paris, France; and *office* Union de l'Europe Occidentale, 43 Avenue du Président Wilson, 75775 Paris.

**PLAQUET, Jules L.** *B.* 1896. *Educ.* Classical High School Law and Technical Science. *M.* 1925, Germaine Planquart (*Dec.*). *S.* Jacques (Engineer). *Daus.* Térèse (Mme. Louis Janssens van der Maelen) and Christiane. *Career:* Belgian company director, President: S.A. Compagnie des Ciments Belges 'CCB'. Gaurain-Ramecroix; La Cimenterie Belge 'CIMBEL', Brussels; Comité Interconsulaire du Hainaut Occidental; Assurances ABEILLE-PAIX, Brussels. *Director:* Financière d'Anvers BUFA; GB-INNO-BM SA; Société Intercommunale de Dèveloppement Economique et d'Aménagement du Territoire due Hainaut Occidental SIDEHO; Conférence Permanente des Chambres de Commerce et d'Industrie frontalières françaises et belges, etc. Union des Centrales Electriques de Liège-Namur-Luxembourg-Hainaut S.A. à Liège; Ciments Liégeois S.A., Haccourt; Ciments de Visé S.A., Brussels, etc. Previously: Burgomaster. Provincial Councillor. Féd. Industrie Cimentière Belge. Member, Society of History and Archæology. *Awards:* Commander, Order of Leopold, Order of the Crown; Officer, Order Black Star; Doyen d'Honneur du Travail, etc. *Address:* Château de Froidmanteau, Maulde (Barry), Belgium.

**PLASTO, Leonard Patrick.** Australian company director. *B.* 1896. *Educ.* Ryde Catholic School, and Ryde Public School. *M.* 1922, Rita Fay Harper. *S.* Leonard John and

Geoffrey Drummond. *Dau.* Fay Ursula. *Career:* Governing Dir. L. P. Plasto Pty. Ltd., Hampden Hotel Pty. Ltd., L. P. & R. F. Plasto Pty. Ltd.; Chmn.-Trustee, L. P. Plasto Trust. With New Zealand Insurance Co. 1910–15; served in World War I (A.I.F. Lieut. 13th Bn.) 1915–19; Licensed Victualler 1919–56; Vice-Chairman, Western Suburbs Ambulance 1934–61; Patron, Returned Soldiers League (Ashfield Sub-branch). *Address:* 55 Wolsley Road, Point Piper, N.S.W., Australia.

**PLATOU, Ragnar Stoud.** Norwegian. *B.* 1897. *Educ.* High School and Commercial School. *M.* 1939, Annette Schultz. *Career:* Conrad Boe, shipbroker since 1915; partner in firm 1918–36; Hon. Chmn. R. S. Platou A/S, Shipbrokers, Oslo. *Awards:* Knight of the following Orders: Dannebrog (Denmark); Comdr., St. Olav (Norway), Vasa (Sweden); Officer, Order of Orange-Nassau (Netherlands); service medal for service with the Home Guards in Norway. *Address:* Jonsrudveien 5, Oslo 2; and *office* Dronning Maudsgt 3, Oslo (Vika), Norway.

**PLATT, Joseph B.,** PhD. *B.* 1915. *Educ.* Univ of Rochester (BA physics) and Cornell Univ. (PhD experimental physics). *M.* Jean Ferguson Rusk. *Daus.* Ann and Elizabeth. *Career:* Teaching Asst., Cornell Univ. 1937–41; Instructor, Univ. of Rochester 1941–43; Staff member and section chief, Radiation Lab. at M.I.T. (on leave from Univ. of Rochester), where he worked especially on radar devices, with U.S. Air Force as civilian introducing these devices into combat use in European and Pacific theatres 1943–46; Asst. Prof., Assoc. Prof., Univ. of Rochester 1946–49; Chief of Physics Branch, Research Div., Atomic Energy Commission (on leave from Rochester) 1949–51; Assoc. Prof., Prof., Assoc. Chairman, Dept. of Physics, Univ. of Rochester (helped to design and construct 240-million volt cyclotron; directed research team which produced mesonic atoms from which X-rays were discovered) 1951–56. Consultant: National Defense Research Committee 1941–45, National Science Foundation 1953–56, and U.S. Office of Ordnance Research 1953–56. Member: Mine Advisory Committee, Natl. Acad. of Sciences, Natl. Research Committee 1955–61; Consultant .1962. Nat. Acad. of Sciences Pac. Sci. Bd. 1964–70. Governor's Committee, Study of Medical Aid and Health (California), 1959. President Harvey Mudd College, Claremont, Calif. 1956–76; Pres., Claremont University Center 1976—. member: Southern California Industry Education Council 1957–69, Panel on Special Projects in Science Education, National Science Foundation 1957–63, Committee on International Organizations and Programmes, National Academy of Sciences, National Research Council 1962–64, Panel on International Science, The President's Science Advisory Cttee. 1961–64, and Advisory Cttee, Study of Medical Education Needs, Coordinating Council for Higher Educ. (Calif.) 1962–63; & currently: Trustee Analytic Services Inc. 1959— Chmn. 1962—); Trustee, China Foundation for the Promotion of Education & Culture 1966—; Mem., Board on Science & Technology for International Dept., Nat. Acad. of Sciences 1969— (ex-officio 1974—) (Chmn. Sub-Cttee. on Sino-American Science Cooperation); Trustee, Carnegie Foundation for the Advancement of Teaching 1970—; Dir., Los Angeles World Affairs Council 1970—; Trustee Aerospace Corp. 1971— (Vice-Chmn. 1975—); Dir., Automobile Club of Southern California 1973—; Mem., Carnegie Council on Policy Studies in Higher Education 1975—. *Member:* Amer. Physical Socy. (Fellow); Amer. Optical Socy. (Assoc.); Twilight, Pasadena; Amer. Assn. of Physics Teachers; Soc. of Sigma Xi; Phi Kappa Phi; Phi Beta Kappa. *Clubs:* Bohemian Club, San Francisco; Cosmos (Washington); California, Sunset (Los Angeles). *Address:* President's House, Claremont University Center, Claremont, Calif., U.S.A.

**PLAYER, Willis.** American. Public relations executive. *B.* 1915. *Educ.* Univ. of Michigan (AB). *M.* 1938, Doris Wisner. *Daus.* Nan and Jill. *Career:* Reporter, Wall Street Journal 1935; Chicago Daily News 1937; writer, Booth Newspaper Inc. 1937–43; Dir., Public Relations, Pan American World Airways 1946–53; Vice-Pres., Public Relations, Northwest Airlines 1953–54; Special Asst. to Asst. Secy., Navy for Air 1954; Vice-Pres., Public Relations, Air Transport Assn. 1954–57, and American Airlines Inc. 1957–64. Vice-President, Public Relations, Pan American World Airways 1964. *Member:* Phi Beta Kappa; Phi Beta Phi; Phi Eta Sigma; Public Relations Socy. of America; Air Service Post 501 of American Legion. *Clubs:* National Press, The Wings, Lotos, Sky, National Aviation. *Address: office* Pan Am. Building, 200 Park Avenue, New York City, 10017, U.S.A.

**PLAYFAIR, Sir Edward Wilder,** KCB. *B.* 1909. *M.* 1941, Dr. Mary Lois Rae. *Daus.* 3. *Career:* Appointed to Inland Revenue 1931; H.M. Treasury 1934–46 and 1947–56; Control Office for Germany, Austria 1946–47; Permanent Under-Secy. of State for War 1956–59; Permanent Secretary, Ministry of Defence 1960–61; Chmn. I.C.T. Ltd. 1961–65. Director, National Westminster Bank Ltd.; Equity & Law Life Assurance Society Ltd.; Glaxo Holdings Ltd.; and Tunnel Holdings Ltd. *Address:* 12 The Vale, Chelsea, London, SW3 6AH.

**PLAYFORD, Hon. Sir Thomas,** GCMG. Australian politician. *B.* 5 July 1896. *Educ.* Norton Summit Public School. *M.* 1928, Lorna Beaman Clark. *S.* Thomas. *Daus.* Margaret, Patricia. *Career:* Served in World War I, A.I.F. in Gallipoli and France 1914–18; MHA (Lib.) for Murray, South Australia 1933–38; Minister of Lands, Repatriation and Irrigation 1938; MHA (Lib. Country) Gumeracha, South Australia 1938–66; Premier, Treasurer and Minister of Immigration, South Australia 1938–65; Leader of the Opposition 1965–66. *Address:* Norton Summit, S.A. 5136, Australia.

**PLEN, Leon,** FICD. South African. *B.* 1915. *Educ.* Boys' High School Pretoria; Matriculated. *M.* 1942, Hannah Nathalia Pastoll. *S.* Nigel Julian. *Dau.* Ethné Ann. *Career:* Served in World War II (Natal Mounted Rifles, East Africa, Western Desert) 1940–43; Director Smigil Investments (Pty.) Ltd.; Hon. Life Vice-Pres. (Founder and first Chmn.), Pinetown Chamber of Com.; previously (for 3 years) member, Natal Chamb. of Industries; member, Exec. Cttee, Durban Centenary Industrial Exhibition and Fair 1954; member (and first Chmn.) Pinetown Division, Natal Chamber of Industries (for two years was one of Natal members of Federated Chamber of Industries Executives Committee) 1966; Chmn., Umhlanga Rocks Commercial Assoc.; Patron (and Hon. Life Member), Pinetown Rugby Club; Past Pres., Pinetown Rotary Club; Rotary District Governor (230) 1973–74. *Address:* 204 Villa Pax, Ocean Way, Umhlanga Rocks, 4320, Natal, South Africa.

**PLIMPTON, Francis T. P.** American lawyer and diplomat. *B.* 1900. *Educ.* Phillips Exeter Acad.; Amherst Coll. (BA *magna cum laude* 1922); Harvard Law School (JD 1925); Hon. LLD Colby Coll. 1960, Lake Forest Coll. 1964; N.Y. Univ. 1970; Yale Univ. 1972; Hon. LHD Pratt Inst. 1967. Adelphi Univ. 1972. Amherst Coll. 1973. *M.* 1926, Pauline Ames. *S.* George Ames, Francis T. P., Jr., and Oakes Ames. *Dau.* Sarah. *Career:* Associated with Root, Clark, Buckner & Ballantine, N.Y.C. 1926–32 (in charge of Paris office 1930–31); Gen. Solicitor, Reconstruction Finance Corp., Washington, D.C. 1932–33. Partner, Debevoise, Plimpton, Lyons & Gates, and predecessor firms, 1933–61, 1965—. Deputy Representative (with the rank of Ambassador Extraordinary and Plenipotentiary) of the U.S. to the U.N. 1961–65; U.S. Delegate to the 15th (resumed), 16th, 17th, 18th and 19th General Assemblies; member U.N. Administration Tribunal 1966—; State Dept. Adv. Com. on Intl. Orgs. 1966–69; Chmn. N.Y.C. Board of Ethics 1973—; Mayor's Commission on Distinguished Guests 1976—; Trustee, Bowery Savings Bank 1948–75, United States Trust Co. of N.Y. 1936–68, (now Hon.), Teachers Insurance & Annuity Association 1946–69, Amherst College 1939–73 (now Emeritus), Barnard College 1936—, Union Theological Seminary 1936–75 (now Emeritus), Athens College (Greece) 1933—, Lingnan Univ. (China) 1937—, Roosevelt Hosp. 1960–75 (now Advisory), Metropolitan Museum of Art 1965–75 (now Honorary); Overseer, Harvard Univ. 1963–69; Director: Philharmonic Symphony Socy, 1950—, America-Italy Socy, 1949—, Fédération des Alliances Françaises 1962—, U.N. Association of U.S.A. 1965, Theodore Roosevelt Assn.; Formerly Dir. or Trustee: Phillips Exeter Academy (Pres. of Board 1956–62); Greater New York Fund, Practising Law Institute, Graduate Faculty of New School for Social Research (University in Exile), Municipal Art Society, Dalton School, Morningside Heights Inc., Foundation for Youth and Student Affairs, Church Peace Union, Judson Health Centre, etc. Contributor to various periodicals. Independent. Distinguished Public Service Award, New England Socy. of N.Y. 1963, Fed. Bar Assn., N.Y., N.J., & Connecticut 1964, St. Nicholas Soc. 1974, Inst. on Man & Science 1975, N.Y. City (Bronze Medal) 1975, N.Y. State Bar Assn. (Gold Medal) 1977; Chevalier Legion of Honor (France), Cmdr., Order of Merit (Italy); Assoc. Knight. Order of St. John of Jerusalem. *Fellow:* Amer. Acad. of Arts and Sciences, Amer. Bar Foundation; Royal Society Arts (Franklin Fellow). *Member:* American (mem. House of Delegates) N.Y. State, and N.Y. City (Pres. 1968–

70) Bar Associations; Union Internationale des Advocates (Vice-Pres., 1969—); American Society of Intl. Law; American Law Inst.; Society of Mayflower Descendants; Colonial Society of Massachusetts; Pilgrims; Council on Foreign Relations, Washington Institute Foreign Affairs, Foreign Policy Assn. (Dir. 1935–49), Econ. Club of N.Y., Delta Kappa Epsilon, Phi Beta Kappa. *Clubs:* Union, Century, Brook, River, Grolier, Coffee House, Down Town (N.Y.C.); Piping Rock, Cold Spring Harbor (Long Island); Metropolitan (Wash.); Ausable (Adirondacks); Mill Reef (Antigua). *Address:* 131 E. 66 St., New York City 10021; and 168 Chichester Road, West Hills, Huntington, N.Y. 11743; *office* 299 Park Avenue, New York City 10022, U.S.A.

**PLIMSOLL, Sir James**, Kt 1962, CBE 1956. Australian diplomat. *B.* 1917. *Educ.* Sydney High School and University of Sydney. *Career:* Economic Department, Bank of New South Wales 1938–42; Australian Army 1942–47; Australian Delegation, Far Eastern Commission 1945–48; Australian Representative, U.N. Commission for the Unification and Rehabilitation of Korea 1950–52; Asst. Secy. Dept. of External Affairs, Canberra 1953–59; Aust. Permanent Representative at the United Nations 1959–63; Aust. High Commissioner in India, and Amb. to Nepal, 1963–65. Secretary, Australian Department of External Affairs, 1965–70; Aust. Ambassador to the United States 1970–74; Aust. Amb. to USSR & to Mongolia 1974–77; Aust. Amb. to Belgium, Luxembourg & the European Communities since 1977. *Address:* Australian Embassy, 52 Avenue des Arts, 1040 Brussels, Belgium.

**PLOURDE, Gérard.** French Canadian. *B.* 1916. *Educ.* Brebeuf College, Montreal (BA 1936) and Univ. of Montreal (MCom 1939). *M.* 1943, Jeannine Martineau. *S.* Pierre and Marc-André. *Dau.* Monique. *Career:* With Soap Co. 1940; United Auto Parts Inc. 1941—; Manager, International Electric Co. Ltd. (subsidiary of UAP) 1945–51. Pres., UAP Inc. (formerly, United Auto Parts Inc.) 1951–70, Chmn. Bd. since 1970. Vice-Pres. and Dir., Alliance Mutual Life Ins. Co. 1957—; Toronto Dom. Bank since 1963; Dir. Bell Canada 1973—, Gulf Oil Canada Ltd. 1965—; Anglo-French Drug Co. Ltd. 1960—, Northern Telecom Ltd. 1962—, Rolland Paper Co. Ltd. 1964—, Steinberg's Ltd. 1963—, Editions du Renouveau Pédagogique Inc. 1966—, Molson Industries Ltd. 1969—. *Member:* La Chambre du Commerce de Montreal; Montreal Board of Trade; Canadian Chamber of Commerce; Society of Automotive Engineers. Automotive Industries Association of Canada. *Clubs:* Laval-sur-le-Lac; Saint-Denis; Mount Bruno. *Address:* 6065 De Vimy, Montreal, H3S 2R2 Quebec; and *office* 7025 Ontario Street East, Montreal, HIN 2B3 Quebec, Canada.

**PLOWDEN, Lord** (Sir Edwin Noel Plowden), KCB, KBE. *B.* 6 Jan. 1907. *Educ.* Switzerland; Pembroke College, Cambridge. *M.* 1933, Bridget Horatia Richmond; *S.* William Julius Lowthian, Francis John. *Daus.* Anna Bridget, Penelope Christina. *Career:* Ministry of Economic Warfare 1939–40; Min. of Aircraft Production 1940–46; Chief Exec. Aircraft Supply Council, 1945–46; Chief Planning Officer and Chmn., Econ. Planning Bd. 1947–53; Vice-Chmn., Temporary Cncl. Cttee. NATO 1951–52; Adviser, Atomic Energy Administration 1953–54; Chmn.; Atomic Energy Authority 1954–59; Cttee. of Inquiry into Treasury Control of Public Expenditure 1959–61; Cttee. of Enquiry into Organization of Representational Services Overseas 1962–63; Cttee. of Enquiry into U.K. Aircraft Industry 1964–65; Cttee. Enquiry into Structure Electricity Supply Industry 1974–75. Pres. Tube Investments Ltd. since 1976 (Chmn. 1963–76); Chmn., Equity Capital for Industry Ltd. since 1976; Chmn., Standing Advisory Cttee. on Pay of Higher Civil Service 1968–70; Pres., Governing Body and Council London Grad. School Business Studies since 1976 (Chmn. 1964–76); Dir., Com. Union Assurance Co. Ltd.; National Westminster Bank Ltd. 1960–77. Visiting Fellow, Nuffield College Oxford 1956–64. *Awards:* Hon. Fellow, Pembroke College, Cambridge; Hon. DSc. Pennsylvania State Univ. 1958; Univ. of Aston 1972; Hon. DLitt Loughborough 1976. *Address:* 7 Cottesmore Gardens, London, W.8; and Martles Manor, Dunmow, Essex.

**PLOWMAN, E. Grosvenor.** American Educator and author. *B.* 1899. *Educ.* Dartmouth (BS *cum laude*); Univ. of Denver (MS Com); Univ. of Chicago (PhD): Hon. DSc. Univ. of Maine 1971. *M.* 1924, Genifred Homer. *Daus.* 2. *Career:* Asst. Secy. Manufacturers Assn. 1924–29; Dir. Bureau, Business Research and Dean, Ext. Dir. Univ. of Denver 1930–33; Manager, Denver Municipal Water System 1933–36; Traffic Manager Colorado Fuel & Iron Corp. 1937–43; Steel Div., War Production Board 1942–43; Vice-President, Traffic, United States Steel Corporation 1944–62. Deputy Under Secretary of Commerce for Transportation 1963–64. Lecturer on Business Administration, Univ. of Maine, 1965—. Chairman, Maine Transportation Cttee. 1965–68, Maine Aeronautical Comm. 1966–68, Pres. 1968–70, Chmn. 1971–72, Transportation Research Foundation. *Award:* Certificate of Appreciation for Distinguished Public Service to the Dept. of Defense 1952. *Publications:* Business Organization and Management (co-author); Elements of Business Logistics; Transportation Coordination, (Editor), numerous magazine articles. *Member:* Phi Beta Kappa (Associate); Amer. Statistical Assn. (Fellow); National Defense Transportation Assn. (Past Pres.); American Society of Traffic & Transportation (Past Pres.). *Address:* 48 Partridge Circle, Portland, Maine, 04102, U.S.A.

**PLUMLEY, H. Ladd.** *B.* 1902. *Educ.* Williams Coll. (AB 1925). *M.* Christine A. Larsen. *Daus.* Nancy (Ljungberg) and Susan (Arruda, Jr.). *Career:* Underwriter, Regional Sales Supervisor, Asst. Superintendent of Sales, Travelers Ins. Co. 1925–42. Lieut.-Colonel, U.S.A. 1942–45. Chairman of Board, and Chief Executive Officer, State Mutual Life Assurance Co. of America 1956–71, Hon. Chmn. of Board since 1971, Chmn. of the Board Emeritus since 1976. Past Pres. Past Dir., Chamber Commerce U.S.A. 1962–63; Hon. Chmn. Bd. State Mutual Life Assurance Co. Amer. since 1971. Trustee, Worcester Foundation Experimental Biology, Arts Council of Worcester Inc.; Dir., Worcester County Music Assn. Worcester; Worcester Polytechnic Inst. and Becker Junior Coll.; Adv. Bd. Greater Area Chapter, Nat. Conf. Christians and Jews; Chmn. of the Bd., Nat. Council on Crime and Delinquency; Trustee, The Bank of New York; Member Adv. Council, Assumption Coll.; Corporator Worcester Boys Club; Corp. member, United Church Bd. for Homeland Ministeries. *Member:* Phi Delta Theta; Chartered Member; Clark Univ. President's Council. *Awards:* Supreme Knight, Comdr. of Justice, Sovereign Order of St. John of Jerusalem, Knights of Malta. LLD, LaSalle College; Hon. LLD, Clark Univ., Williams Coll.; ScD, Worcester Polytechnic Inst.; SCD, Assumption Coll., Coll. of Holy Cross. *Publication:* Budgeting the Cost of Illness. *Clubs:* Bald Peak Colony: The Bohemians; Tatnuck Country; National Press; Wall St.; The Pilgrims; Worcester Art Museum. *Address:* Worcester 01609, Mass.; and *office* 440 Lincoln Street, Worcester 01605, Mass., U.S.A.

**PLUMMER, William Edwin.** American electronic engineer and telecommunication executive. *B.* 1905. *Educ.* Johns Hopkins University (BE Elec Eng 1929). *M.* 1933, Margaret Fairchild Torsch. *S.* Dr. William Torsch and Edwin Fairchild. *Career:* Member, Technical Staff, Bell Telephone Laboratories, N.Y.C. 1929–32; Torsch Canning Co., Baltimore 1932; Radio Station WFBR, Baltimore 1932–33; Senior Engineer with Glenn D. Gillett, Consulting Radio Engineer, Washington, D.C. 1933–41; Office of Chief Signal Officer, U.S. Army (Asst. Chief and Chief, Communication Liaison Branch, 1st Lieut. to Col.) 1941–46; Partner, Glenn D. Gillett and Associates 1946–50; member, Technical Staff, President's Communications Policy Bd. 1950–51. With U.S. Government 1951; Asst. for Engineering, staff of Telecommunications Advisor to the President 1951–53; Asst. for Engineering, Telecommunications, ODM 1953–58; OCDM 1958–59; Deputy Dir., Telecommunications, OCDM 1959–61; O.E.P. 1961–64. Acting Chief & Chief, Frequency Management Division, O.E.P., 1964–65; Assoc. Dir. of Telecommunications Management (Frequency Management), Exec. Office of the Pres., 1965–69; Acting Asst., Dir., OEP; Acting Dir., Telecommunications Management, 1969–70. Assoc. Dir., Telecommunications International; Office of Telecommunications Policy, Executive Office of the Pres. 1970. Retd. Chmn. Interdepartment Radio Advisory Cttee. (IRAC), Aug. 1953–64. *Publications:* As member of Technical Staff, President's Communications Policy Board, wrote part of Telecommunications—a Program for Progress (1951); mentioned in Electro-Surgery by Drs. Howard A. Kelly and Grant E. Ward for assistance in preparing chapter on Physics of High Frequency Currents; The Radio Frequency Spectrum, United States Use and Management (1969); United States Response to its Telecommunication Responsibilities (1970); The Interdepartment Radio Advisory Cttee.—Fifty Years Service in Radio-communication (1972). *Member:* United States National Cttee., International Union of Radio Science (U.R.S.I.), 1968–70. *Club:* The Johns Hopkins. *Address:* 2804 Military Road, N.W., Washington 20015, D.C., U.S.A.

**PLUMPTON, Jack.** Canadian chartered accountant. *B.* 1912.

*Educ.* Chartered Accountant. *M.* 1938, Vera May Cornell. *S.* Jack Edward and Stephen Richard. *Dau.* Barbara Ann. *Career:* Vice-Pres. Comptroller, Dominion Foundries & Steel Ltd. Director, National Steel Car Corp. Ltd., Hamilton, Ont.; Dir., Int'l Portable Pipe Mills Ltd. *Fellow:* Institute of Chartered Accountants. Chartered Inst. of Secretaries (F.C.I.S.). *Member:* Canadian Inst. of Chartered Accountants; Canadian Manufacturers Assn.; Institute of Profit Sharing. *Clubs:* The Hamilton; Hamilton Golf & Country; The Canadian. *Address:* 3140 Princess Boulevard, Burlington, Ont.; and *office* Dominion Foundries & Steel Ltd., P.O. Box 460, Hamilton, Ont., Canada.

**PODGORNY, Nikolai Viktorovich.** Soviet (Ukrainian) statesman. *B.* 1903. *Educ.* Kiev Technological Institute of the Food Industry. Took his first job at the age of 15, in the machine shops; active in setting up Young Communist League organizations in the Poltava Region; entered a workers' faculty 1923; after graduation was successively engineer, Asst. Chief Engineer and Chief Engineer at sugar refineries and trusts in the Ukraine 1931–39; Deputy People's Commissar of the Food Industry of the Ukrainian S.S.R. 1939–40 and 1944–46, and Food Industry of U.S.S.R. 1940–42; Director, Moscow Technological Institute of the Food Industry 1942–44; Permanent Representative of the Council of Ministers of the Ukrainian S.S.R. at U.S.S.R. Government 1946–50; First Secy., Kharkov Regional Committee of the C.P. of the Ukraine 1950–53; Second Secretary, Central Committee of the C.P. of the Ukraine 1953–57 (First Secy. 1957–63).; Alternate Member 1958–60, and Member 1960–66; Member of the Bureau and then Member of the Presidium of the Central Committee of the Ukraine 1957–63; also Member of the following: Central Auditing Commission of C.P.S.U. 1952–56; Secy. of the Central Cttee., C.P.S.U. 1963–65; Chmn., U.S.S.R. Supreme Soviet 1965–77; Member C.P.S.U. Central Cttee. 1960–66; Member of the Central Committee of the C.P.S.U. Praesidium (later Politburo) 1966–77; Deputy to Supreme Soviets of the U.S.S.R. and the Ukrainian S.S.R. Orders of Lenin (5) and the Red Banner; Medals of the U.S.S.R. Hero of Socialist Labour 1973. *Address:* c/o The Kremlin, Moscow, U.S.S.R.

**POINTET, Prof. Dr. Pierre Jean.** Swiss lawyer and university professor; Dr h c University of Lyon (France). *B.* 19 July 1910. *Educ.* Universities of Neuchâtel, Berlin and Heidelberg (D-en-D). *M.* 1947, Marianne Nicati. *S.* 3. *Daus.* 2. *Career:* Practised law 1936–38; Prof., University of Neuchâtel; Chmn. Swiss Assn. of Arbitration; Past Chairman, Swiss Group, International Association of Industrial Property. *Publications:* La neutralité de la Suisse et la liberté de la presse; Du défaut d'exploitation des brevets d'invention; La protection de la marque; La Protection des Inventions; Problèmes actuels de la protection internationale des marques de fabrique et de commerce; La Convention de N.Y. sur la reconnaissance of l'exécution des sentences arbitrales; La Convention de Genève sur l'arbitrage commercial international; numerous other publications dealing with industrial property and arbitration. *Address:* Les Marpies, 38 Ch. de la Planaz, 1807 Blonay, Switzerland.

**POITRAS, Herman Arthur.** American. Consultant in Chemical Production and Engineering. *B.* 1912. *Educ.* Tufts Univ. (BS in ChE 1935). *M.* 1953, Gertrude M. Van Kampen. *S.* Robert H. *Dau.* Gail M. *Career:* Chemical Engineer, Barrett Div., Allied Chemical & Dye Corp. 1936–42; Chief Process Engineer, Heyden Chemical Corp. 1942–45. With Chas. Pfizer & Co. Inc.; Asst. Dept. Head 1945–48; Vice-Pres. Manufacturing and Engineering 1949–69, Dir. 1950–69; Plant Superintendent (Terre Haute, Ind.) 1948–49; General Production Manager, Jan.–Sept. 1949; Dir. Pfizer International Inc. 1951–69; Consultant since 1969. Holds U.S. Patent No. 2,420,496 (Recovery of Products from Aldehyde Condensations) and 2,420,497 (Process for the Purification of Tripentaerythrital). *Member:* Amer. Chemical Socy.; Amer. Inst. of Chemical Engineers; Parmaceutical Manufacturers Assn.; Amer. Management Assn.; Armed Forces Chemical Assn.; Hon. society Tau Beta Pi. *Clubs:* Ridgewood Country; Saddle River Valley; Ridgewood Rifle; Plantation Country. *Address:* 41 Baynard Park Road, Sea Pines Plantation, Hilton Head Island, South Carolina 29928, U.S.A.

**POLYANSKY, Dmitry Stepanovich.** U.S.S.R. politician. *B.* 1917. *Married. Educ.* Kharkov Agricultural Institute Ukraine; Higher Party School, Central Committee of the Communist Party of the Soviet Union, Moscow *S.* 2. *Daus.* 2. Manager, Agricultural Dept., Kharkov Provincial Cttee. LKSMU, 1939–40; Military Service; Head, Political Dept., Khoroshensk Machine & Tractor Service Station, and subsequently First Secy., Karasuksk Party Cttee. Novosibirsk Region; responsible for work in staff administration in the Central Cttee. of the Communist Party of the Soviet Union, and then Inspector of the Central Cttee. since 1945; Second Secy., of the Crimean Provincial Party Cttee. for 10 years and then Chmn., Crimean Provincial Executive Cttee. of the Council of Workers' Representatives; after assignment in Crimea, First Secy., Orenburg Provincial Party Cttee., First Secy., Krasnodarsk Regional Party Cttee., 1948–58; Dpty. Member, Politburo, Central Cttee. of the Communist Party of the Soviet Union, 1958–60; Chmn., Council of Ministers of the Russian Federation for 5 years; Dpty. Chmn., Council of Ministers of the U.S.S.R., 1962–65; Member, Politburo, Central Committee of the Communist Party of the Soviet Union, 1960–76; First Vice-Chairman, Council of Ministers of the U.S.S.R., 1965–73; Minister of Agriculture of the U.S.S.R., 1973–76; Ambassador Ex. & Plen. of the Union of Soviet Socialist Republics in Japan since 1976. Mem., Central Cttee. of the C.P.S.U.; Deputy, Supreme Soviet of the U.S.S.R., all sessions commencing in 1954. *Publications:* Pearl of Russia (1958); The Great Plan of Economic and Cultural Progress of the Russian Federation (1959); articles in newspapers and journals. *Awards:* Four Orders of Lenin & many medals, Member, Communist Party, 1939—; Professional Union of Workers in State Institutes. *Address:* U.S.S.R. Embassy, 1-1, Azabudai 2-chome, Minato-ku, Tokyo, Japan.

**POLLARD, Alfred Hurlstone.** Australian consultant & company director. *B.* 1916. *Educ.* MSc (Sydney); MSc (Econ), PhD (London); FIA, ASA, FASSA. *M.* 1941, Pearl Cross. *S.* 4. *Dau.* 2. *Career:* Asst. Director, Radio Physics Training 1942–44; General Secy. M.L.C. Assurance Co. 1954–61, Dep. Gen. Mgr. 1961–66; Director of several companies. Professor of Economic Statistics & Director of Actuarial Studies, Macquarie Univ. 1966–76. Consultant Economist, Development Finance Corp. 1966—; Head, School of Economics and Financial Studies 1971–73; Commissioner Commonwealth Enquity, Superannuation Pension Updating 1973. Member Adv. Cttee. on Crime Statistics and Research, Medical Benefits Fund Council, Committee of Inquiry into Taxation. Director of several public companies. President: N.S.W. Statistical Socy. 1951–52; and Actuarial Socy. of Australasia 1953–54. *Awards:* Rhodes Prize by Inst. of Actuaries (London) 1947, and Messenger & Brown Prize 1967; Awarded Silver Medal by same Institute 1975; H.M. Jackson Award by Institute, Actuaries of Aust. and N.Z., 1969 and 1970; Fellow, Academy of Social Sciences, Australia. *Member:* Inst. of Actuaries (London); Inst. of Actuaries of Australia and New Zealand; Royal Statistical; Eugenics Socy. *Clubs:* Australian; Royal Sydney Yacht Squadron. *Address:* 51 Cliff Road, Northwood, N.S.W.; and *office* Delfin Discount Co., 16 O'Connell Street, Sydney, N.S.W., Australia.

**POLLOCK, David Linton,** MA. British. *B.* 1906. *Educ.* Marlborough College; Trinity College, Cambridge (Hons. degrees in Modern Languages and Law). *M.* (1) Diana Turner; *S.* Adam. (2) Margaret D. Mackintosh. *Career:* Partner, Freshfields (Solicitors), 1938–51; British Treasury, 1939–40; Commander (RNVR), 1940–45; Member, British Government Economic Mission to Argentine, 1946. Chairman, Societe Civile du Vignoble de Chateau Latour: Director, S. Pearson & Son Ltd. 1951–77. *Member:* The Council of Marlborough College 1950–71; Council of Royal Yachting Association, 1950–65. *Clubs:* Royal Thames Yacht Club; Itchenor Sailing Club. *Address:* The Old Rectory, Wiggonholt, Pullborough, Sussex; and *office* Millbank Tower, Millbank, London, S.W.1.

**PONIATOWSKI. Prince Michel Casimir.** French Minister of State of the Interior 1974–77. *B.* 1922. *M.* 1946, Gilberte de Chavagnac. *S.* 3. *Dau.* 1. *Address:* 22 Boulevard Jean Mermoz, 92200 Neuilly-sur-Seine, France.

**PONOMARYOV, Boris Nikolayevich.** Soviet politician. *B.* 1905. *Educ.* Moscow State Univ.; Red Professors' Inst. *Career:* Volunteered for Red Army 1919, joined first the Komsomol, later the Communist Party & served as functionary in home town; graduated from Moscow Univ. 1926; Party work in Donbas & Turkmenia 1926–28; graduated from Red Professors' Inst. 1932; Dir., Red Professors' Inst. 1933–36; Dir., Moscow Inst. of Party History 1934; Exec. Cttee., Communist International 1936–39; Asst. Dir., Marx-Engels-Lenin Inst. 1943–45; Central Cttee., CPSU 1944–46; First Dep., Chief, Soviet Information Bureau, USSR Council of Ministers 1947–49; Head of Dept., Central Cttee. CPSU 1949–61, Mem. of Central Cttee. since 1956, Secretariat since

1961, alt. mem. of Political Bureau since 1972 (in charge of Central Cttee's relations with non-ruling foreign communist parties); Deputy to USSR Supreme Soviet since 1958. Corres. Mem., Acad. of Sciences of USSR 1958, mem. since 1962. *Decorations:* Order of Lenin (twice); Order of Red Banner of Labour (twice); etc. *Address:* c/o Central Committee of the Communist Party of the Soviet Union, 4 Staraya Ploshchad, Moscow, USSR.

**PONSONBY, Sir Ashley Charles Gibbs**, Bt, MC, DL. British. *B.* 1921. *Educ.* Eton and Balliol College, Oxford. *M.* 1950, Lady Matha Butler. *S.* 4. *Career:* Second Lieut. Coldstream Guards 1941; served in World War II (N. Africa and Italy; wounded; Captain 1943); on Staff, Bermuda Garrison 1945–46. Dir.: Romney Trust Ltd., Dec. 1958; Malton Investments Ltd., 1959—; Dir. Colville Estates Ltd. 1958–; Aust. and International Investment Trust Ltd. (Chairman, April 1968), Trans-Oceanic Trust Ltd., July 1963—(Chairman Mar. 1964—), J. Henry Schroder Wagg & Co. Ltd., April 1962; Church Commissioner 1963; Dir. Fundivest Ltd. 1965—; Dir.: Triplevest Ltd. Jan. 1966—, City & Commercial Investment Trust Ltd., 1969—, Equitable Life Assurance Society since 1969; DL Oxon (1974). *Club:* Brooks. *Address:* Grims Dyke Farm, Woodleys, Woodstock, Oxon.; and *office* 120 Cheapside, London EC2V 6DS.

**PONTE, Maurice.** French. *Educ.* École Normale Supérieure; Doctor of Science; Professor of University. *M.* 1925, Nelly Andrews. *S.* Jean. *Daus.* Nicole and Françoise. Comdr., Legion of Honour; Grand Cross, Natl. Order of Merit, various foreign Orders. *Career:* Studied in London with Sir William Bragg 1926–27; Paris Univ. 1927–29, Career with CSF Group 1929–68 (successively Research Engineer; Director, Dept. of Tubes and Advanced Research Labs.; Technical Director and Asst. Director-General; and Chmn. and Dir.-Gen.). Dir., Institut Pasteur 1967. Hon. Director. Agence Nationale de Valorisation de la Recherche (A.N.V.A.R.), 1968–71; Chairman and Director-General, CSF (Electronique) 1950–68; Scientific Adviser to Commissarat à l'Enérgie Atomique; adviser to and member of various committees concerning French government. Member: Académie des Sciences, Paris. *Publications:* various publications on scientific subjects and electronics; lectures. *Awards:* Blondel Medal; Science Academy Prize; Christopher Columbus Prize (Communications) 1964. *Member:* Sté. Française des Electriciens; Sté. Française des Electroniciens et Radioélectriciens; Fellow, Inst. of Radio-Engineers (U.S.A.); Hon. Fellow British I.E.R.E. *Address:* 5 Square Mozart, 75016 Paris, France.

**PONTOH, Sandruddin Yahya.** Indonesian diplomat. *B.* 1915. *M.* 1943, Ramla Moleng Manoppo. *S.* 4. *Daus.* 2. *Career:* Joined Indonesian Foreign Service 1945; Head, Information Section 1945–47; Vice-Head, Asia Desk 1950; 2nd Secy., Karachi 1950–53; Head, S. Asian Div., Foreign Ministry 1954–55; Consul Bombay 1956–57; Chargé d'Affaires Kabul 1957–59; Dep. Chief Protocol, Djakarta 1960–63; Counsellor, Warsaw 1963. *Address:* Foreign Ministry, Djakarta, Indonesia.

**POOLE, Arthur Bensell.** American. *B.* 1894. *Educ.* University of Minnesota (BA 1917); Harvard University (MBA 1927); Certified Public Accountant. *M.* (1) 1925, Mildred Loyal Wood (*D.* 1957); (2) 1963, Helen Walburn. *S.* Gordon Leicester, Roger Stanley and Warren Gray. Officer, U.S. Navy 1917–20; in Public Accounting 1920–27; in Motion Picture Industry 1927–37. Director, American President Lines Ltd., San Francisco 1938–71; Financial consultant, Natomas Co., San Francisco, 1961–72; Director American Mail Line Ltd., Seattle, 1954–73; Dir. Eocom. Corp. Newport Beach, Calif. since 1971—. *Member:* American Institute of Certified Public Accountants. Republican. Episcopalian. *Club:* Bohemian (San Francisco). *Address:* 360 Everett Avenue, Palo Alto, Calif., 94301, U.S.A.

**POPA, Pretor.** Romanian Ambassador in England. *B.* 1922. *Educ.* Grad. Academy for High Commercial & Industrial Studies in Bucharest. *M.* Ileana. *Dau.* 1. *Career:* Dir. Ministry for Oil Extraction and Processing 1950–66; Gen. Dir. Ministry Foreign Trade 1966–70; Deputy Minister, Ministry Foreign Trade, Vice Chmn. Chamber of Commerce 1970–73; Ambassador Extraordinary & Plenipotentiary of Socialist Republic of Romania to the Court of St. James's since 1973. *Award:* The Star of Socialist Republic of Romania, Order of Labour and other medals. *Address:* 1 Belgrave Square, London, S.W.1; and *office* 4 Palace Green, Kensington, W.8.

**POPAL, Dr. Ali Ahmad.** Ambassador of the Republic of Afghanistan in U.S.S.R. *B.* 1916 *Educ.* Nedjat College, Kabul; and Univ. of Jena (Dr Phil). *Married. S.* 2. *Daus.* 3. *Career:* Recipient of Medal of Education and the title of Sardar-i-A'li. Teacher of Psychology and Teaching Methods, Teachers' Training School; Dir. Teacher of Geography, Nedjat Coll., Kabul 1942–46; Educational Dir., Teachers' College 1946–49; General Dir. of Educ. 1949–51; Deputy Minister, Education 1951–55, Minister 1955–63; (by new Cabinet, second time) Minister of Education and Second Deputy Prime Minister 1963–64; Ambassador to Fed. Republic of Germany & non-resident Ambassador to Sweden & Switzerland 1964–66; Ambassador to Turkey 1966–67; again Minister, Education, First Deputy Minister 1967–69; Ambassador to Pakistan Islamabad 1969, non-resident to Thailand and Sri Lanka (Ceylon) 1969–74; Ambassador to Japan and non-resident Ambassador to Australia, Philippines and S. Korea 1974–76; Ambassador to the U.S.S.R. & non-resident Ambassador to Romania, Finland & Mongolia since 1976. Official visits to U.S.A. to study educational system and inspect schools 1951–52; & visits to India, West Germany & many other parts of Europe, Turkey, Iran, Burmah, Pakistan, U.S.S.R., United Arab Republic, The Lebanon and the People's Republic of China. Led the Afghan delegation to the Annual Conference of the International Bureau of Education, June 1955. *Publications:* Several articles published in Afghanistan, Turkey and W. Germany. *Address:* Embassy of the Republic of Afghanistan, 25 Skatertny Per., Moscow, U.S.S.R.

**POPAL, Dr. Sultan Ahmad.** *B.* 1913. *Educ.* High Gymnasium, Kabul; University of Kabul (Faculty of Medicine); Universities of Berlin, Frieberg/Sachsen, and Gottingen (Dr. Rerum Naturalium). *M.* Habiba Khodadad (*Dec.* 1943); (2) Ruhafza Khodadad, 1953. *S.* 2. *Daus.* 3. *Career:* Fieldologist at the Ministry of Mines, 1943. Director, Geological Survey Dept., 1950. Director General, Geological and Mineralogical Survey Dept., 1953. President, Mines Dept., Ministry of Mines and Industries, 1957–60. Vice-President, Industries and Mines, 1960–65. Ambassador Extraordinary and Plenipotentiary of Afghanistan to Czechoslovakia and Hungary, Mar. 1965–70; Senator, Meshrana Jerga (Senate) since 1971. *Member:* German Geological Society; American Petroleum Geologic Assn.; Encyclopedia Afghanica Society. Five times 'Takdirnama'; Gold Medal 'astor' (3rd Grade); Gold Medal 'Minapal' (Both 1962); Gold Medal 'Astor' (1st Grade), 1967. *Publications:* Beiträge zur näheren Kenntnis der Hils-Mulde; Lapis-Lazuli Mines in Afghanistan; Geology of Afghanistan (both in Persian); and many articles in Afghan scientific magazines. *Address:* 1375 Shersha-Mina, Kabul, Afghanistan; and *office* Meshran Jerga, Kabul, Afghanistan.

**POPE-HENNESSY, Sir John Wyndham**, CBE. British museum director. *B.* 1913. *Career:* Victoria and Albert Museum 1938–73, Keeper of Dept. Archit. and Sculpture 1954—66, Dir. and Secy. 1967–73: Director British Museum 1974–76; Consultative Chmn., Dept. European Paintings, Metropolitan Museum of Art, New York 1977—; Prof. of Art History, Inst. of Fine Arts, New York Univ. 1977—. *Fellow:* British Academy; Socy. of Antiquaries; Royal Socy. of Literature; Royal Socy. of Arts. *Member:* (Foreign) American Philosophical Socy. *Awards:* Knight (1971); Commander of British Empire (1959). *Publications:* Giovanni di Paolo, (1937); Sassetta, (1939); Sienese Quattrocento Painting (1947); A Sienese Codex of the Divine Comedy, (1947); The Drawings of Domenichino at Windsor Castle (1948); A lecture on Nicholas Hilliard (1949); Paolo Uccello, (1950, rev. ed. 1969); Fra Angelico (1952 rev. ed. 1974); Italian Gothic Sculpture, (1955, rev. ed. 1972); Italian Renaissance Sculpture (1958, rev. ed. 1971); Italian High Renaissance and Baroque Sculpture (1963, rev. ed. 1970); Catalogue of Italian Sculpture in the V & A Museum (1964); Renaissance Bronzes in the Kress Collection (1965); The Portrait in the Renaissance (1967); Essays on Italian Sculpture (1968); The Frick Collection, Sculpture (1970); Raphael (1970). *Address:* 1130 Park Avenue, New York, N.Y. 10028, U.S.A.

**POPOVIĆ, Koča.** Former Deputy of the Federal Assembly; *B.* 1908. *Educ.* Belgrade secondary school and the Sorbonne (grad. in philosophy 1932). *Career:* Engaged in literary and political writing. An active member of the progressive movement and the Communist Party of Yugoslavia (arrested on occasions) 1932–37; served (from ordinary soldier to commander of an artillery unit) with the International Brigade in the Spanish civil war. Returned from France to Yugoslavia at the outbreak of World War II and took an active part (as detachment commander to Commander of the Second Army) in the People's Liberation war 1941–45. Chief ot General Staff 1945–53; Secretary of State for Foreign Affairs 1953–65. After the war was elected to the Anti-fascist People's Liberation Council (the first Federal parliament), to the Constituent Assembly, and to the Federal People's Assembly; member, Federal Committee of the Socialist Alliance of the Working People of Yugoslavia and of the Central Committee of the League of Communists of Yugoslavia. Chief of delegation to a number of sessions of U.N. General Assembly accompanied Marshal Tito on state visits to several countries; he himself paid official visits to 28 States. Member of the Central Committee of the League of Communists of Yugoslavia; Head of its Commission for International Socio-Economic and Political Relations 1965; Vice Pres. of Yugoslavia 1966; Member Federation Council 1969–71; Mem. of the Presidency of the Socialist Fed. Republic of Yugoslavia. *Award:* Order of Liberty (highest Yugoslav decoration) and others, including numerous foreign awards. *Address,* Lackovićeva 1A, Belgrade, Yugoslavia.

**PORRITT, The Lord (Sir Arthur Bart.)**, GCMG, GCVO, CBE. British. *B.* 1900. *Educ.* Oxford (MCh; FRCP; FRCS; FRCOG; Hon. MD; Hon. LLD; Hon. DSc). *M.* 1946, Kathleen Peck. *S.* Jonathon and Jeremy. *Dau)* Joanna. *Career:* Sergeant Surgeon to H.M. the Queen 1952–67. President: Royal Coll. of Surgeons of England 1960–63, British Medical Assn. 1960–61, and Royal Society of Medicine 1966–67. Master, Socy. of Apothecaries 1964–66; Consulting Surgeon to the Army 1950–67; Gov.-General N. Zealand 1967–72. *Publications:* Athletics (Longmans), 1928; Essentials of Modern Surgery (Livingstone 1939, and 6 editions); also numerous articles in medical journals. *Awards:* Hon. MD (Bristol); Hon. DSc (Oxford); Hon. FRCS (Edin.); Hon. LLD (St. Andrews, Otago University, New Zealand and Birmingham); Hon. FRCS (Edinburgh, Glasgow, Ireland, Australasia, South Africa and Canada); Hon. FACS; Hon. FRCOG; Hon. FRCP, FRACP; Officer, Legion of Merit (USA. Knight of St. John. *Member:* Académie de Chirugie (France); Amer. Assoc. of Surgeons; Surgical Clinical Society (U.S.A.); Hunterian Society. *Clubs:* Bucks. (London). *Address:* 57 Hamilton Terrace, London, N.W.8.

**PORTARLINGTON, The Earl of** (George Lionel Yuill Seymour Dawson-Damer); British. *B.* 1938. *Educ.* Eton College (Windsor, Eng.). *M.* 1961, Davina Windley. *S.* Charles George Yuill Seymour Dawson-Damer, Viscount Carlow. *Career:* Dir., G. S. Yuill & Co. Pty. Ltd., Sydney; Australian Stock Breeders Co. Ltd., Brisbane; Queensland Trading & Holding Co. Ltd., Brisbane; Cold Storage Holdings Ltd., London; Island Investments Pty. Ltd., Sydney. Pres., Australia-Malaysia-Singapore Assn. *Club:* Union (Sydney). *Address:* 19 Coolong Road, Vaucluse, N.S.W. 2030; and *office* G. S. Yuill & Co. Pty. Ltd., Box 524, G.P.O., Sydney, N.S.W., Australia.

**PORTER, Hon. Dana Harris.** Former Chief Justice of Ontario. *B.* 14 Jan. 1901. *Educ.* University of Toronto (BA); Oxford University (MA); Osgoode Hall. *M.* 1929, Dorothy Chaplin Ramsey Parker. *S.* Dana George Channel, Julian Harris. *Career:* Called to the Bar 1926; specialized for a number of years in litigation; Pres. of the Empire Club of Canada 1933–34; Minister of Education for the Province of Ontario 1948–51; Attorney-General 1949–55; Treasurer of Ontario 1955–58; Chief Justice 1958–68. Chmn., Federal Commission to Report on Banking and Finance in Canada 1961. Chancellor, Univ. of Waterloo, 1960–66; LLD, Queen's Univ., McMaster Univ., Univ. of W. Ontario and Univ. of Waterloo; member, Board of Governors Univ. of Toronto. *Address:* 10 Pinehill Road, Toronto, Canada.

**PORTER, Professor Sir George.** British Scientist. *B.* 1920. *Educ.* Leeds Univ. BSc; Cambridge, MA, PhD, ScD; FRIC, FRS. *M.* 1949, Stella Jean Brooke. *S.* 2. *Career:* Asst Dir. of Research in Phys. Chem, Univ. of Cambridge 1952–54; Asst. Dir. of the British Rayon Research Assn. 1954–55; Professor of Physical Chemistry, Univ. of Sheffield 1955–63; Firth Prof. and Head of Dept. Univ. of Sheffield 1963–66; Dir. and Fullerian Prof. of Chem., The Royal Institution of Gt.B. since 1966; Dir. of Davy Faraday Research Lab. of the Royal Institution since 1966. *Fellow:* Royal Society (1960); Chemical Socy. (Pres. 1970–72). *President:* Faraday Div. of Chemical Socy. 1973–74; The National Assn. for Gifted Children 1975—. *Trustee:* British Museum (1972–74). *Member:* BBC Science Consultative Group 1967–75; Science Advisory Cttee of Nat. Gallery since 1968; Comite International de Photobiologie (Hon) (Pres. 1968–72); Science Research Council, Council 1976—, Science Board 1976—. *Awards:* Hon. DSc from 14 univs.; Corday-Morgan Medal of Chemical Socy. (1955); Nobel Prize for Chemistry (1967); Hon. Mem. New York Academy of Sciences (1968); Hon. Mem. Leopoldina Academy (1970); Davy Medal of Royal Society (1971); jointly awarded Kalinga Prize (1976); Foreign Assoc. Nat. Acad. of Sc. Washington; Member of Pontifical Academy of Sciences; Corresp. Mem. Academy of Science (Gottingen); Fairchild Distinguished Scholar, Cal. Inst. Tech. (all 1974). *Club:* Athenaeum. *Address:* The Royal Institution of Gt. Britain, 21 Albemarle Street, London W1X 4BS.

**PORTER, Ivor Forsyth.** CMG, OBE. Diplomat. *B.* 1913. *Educ.* Barrow Grammar School; Leeds University (BA, PhD). *M.* 1961, Katerina Cholerton. *S.* 1. *Dau.* 1. *Career:* Second Secretary Bucharest 1946; Second Secy. 1947, First Secy. Foreign Office 1948; First Secy. Washington 1951, Foreign Office 1953; Counsellor UK Delegation to Nato 1956; Deputy High Commissioner Cyprus 1959; Permanent Representative, Council of Europe (with personal rank of Minister) Strasbourg 1962–65; Deputy High Commissioner, Eastern Region, Calcutta India 1965–66; Minister U.K. Delegation Disarmament Conference Geneva 1967; Ambassador, Permanent U.K. Delegate 1967–71; Ambassador to Senegal concurrently Ambassador (non-resident) to Guinea, Mali and Mauritania 1971–73. *Awards:* Commander, Most Distinguished Order of St. Michael and St. George; Order of the British Empire (Military). *Publications:* The Think Trap (1972). *Address:* 17 Redcliffe Road, London SW10; and *office* Foreign and Commonwealth Office, King Charles Street, S.W.1.

**PORTER, Hon. Sir Murray Victor.** Former Agent-General in London for Victoria. *Educ.* Brighton Grammar School. *M.* Edith Alice Johnson. *Daus.* 2. *Career:* Government Whip, 1955–56; Asst. Minister 1956–58; Minister of Forests 1958–59; Minister for Local Government 1959–64; Minister for Public Works, 1964–70; Agent-General 1970–76. Member Liberal Party. *Clubs:* Melbourne Cricket, Royal Automobile of Victoria; Royal Melbourne Golf; East India, Sports & Public Schools. *Address:* Victoria House, Melbourne Place, Strand, London, WC2B 4LG.

**PORTER, Paul Robert.** American diplomat and business executive. Officer, Grand Cross, Royal Order of the Phoenix (decoration by King Paul of Greece). *B.* 1908. *Educ.* Univ. of Kansas (BA 1928). *M.* 1940, Hilda Roberts. *S.* Daniel Robert, John Samuel and Kendall Ross. *Dau.* Kathleen Ann. *Career:* Chmn. Shipbuilding Stabilization Committee, War Production Board, Washington 1941–45; Deputy Chief and Chief, U.S. Mission for Economic Affairs, London 1945–47; Chief, U.S. Delegation, U.N. Economic Commission for Europe, Genev 1947–49, and of U.S. Aid Mission to Greece 1949–50 Asst. Administrator, E.C.A. 1951; U.S. Special Representative in Europe, Paris 1951–52. President and Director, Porter International Co. 1953—. Director, Doxiadis Associates Inc. 1960—; Trustee, Meridian House Foundation 1961—. *Publications:* Multilateral Protection of Foreign Investment; various magazine articles. Democrat. *Address:* 11164 Saffold Way, Reston, Va. 22090, U.S.A.

**PORTER, Richard William.** Consultant, engineering. *B.* 1913. *Educ.* Univ. of Kansas (BS in Elect. Eng. 1934; Alumni Award) and Yale Univ. (PhD 1937; Hon. ScD); Coffin Award. General Electric Co. *M.* 1946, Edith Wharton Kelly. *S.* Thomas Andrew. *Daus.* Susan Jane and Mary Elizabeth, *Career:* With General Electric Co.; successively Design Engineer, Group Leader, Project Manager, and Gen. Mgr. Missiles Dept. 1937–55, Consultant Corp. Engineering Staff 1955–69, Mgr. Sci. & Tech. Affairs Aerospace Gr. 1969–75; Independent Consultant Aerospace, Energy & Environment 1975—. Chmn., Technical Evaluation Group for Guided Milles, Research and Development Board, U.S. Dept. of Defence 1948–49; Chmn., Technical Panel on Earth Satellite Program, U.S. National Committee for I.G.Y., U.S. National Academy of Sciences 1955–59. Chairman, International Relations Committee, Space Science Board, U.S. National Academy of Sciences 1959—; Vice-President, Committee on Space Research, International Council of Scientific Unions 1959–71. Author of Introductory Remarks, Symposium on Scientific Effects of Artificially Introduced Radiation at High Altitudes (1959); 1959 Preview of Scientific Progress (1959); What the Future Holds; Weather Modification and Space Exploration; Adventures in Energy Conversion; Das Amerikanische Erdsatellitenprogram; Recovery of Data in Physical Form; Rocket and Satellite Programs; Book Reviews; Manual on Rockets and Satellites; Fundamentals of Advanced Missiles; Sounding Rockets; Soviet Space Science; The Versatile Satellite (1977). *Member:* Amer. Rocket Socy. (awarded Goddard Medal; Fellow; Pres. 1955);

Amer. Inst. Aeronautics & Astronautics; Amer. Inst. of Radio Engineers; Amer. Geophysical Union; Tau Beta Pi; Sigma Xi; Eta Kappa Nu (Outstanding Electrical Engineer 1944 Award). *Clubs:* Cosmos (Washington); Yale (N.Y.C.); Mohawk (Schenectady); Indian Harbour Yacht (Greenwich, Conn.). *Address:* 164 Cat Rock Road, Cos Cob, Conn.; and *office* 1154 East Putnam Avenue, Riverside, Conn. 06878, U.S.A.

**PORTER, Robert Keith.** Canadian. *B.* 1918. *Educ.* Univ. of British Columbia (BCom). *M.* 1942, Agnes Merle Turnbull. *S.* Lawrence, Robert and William. *Dau.* Barbara. *Career:* Pres. Harriett Hubbard Ayer Inc., New York 1951–54; Exec. Vice-Pres. Thomas J. Lipton Ltd., Toronto 1955–63. Dir., Lever Brothers Ltd. President, Thomas J. Lipton Ltd., Toronto 1963—; Vice-Pres. & Dir. Canadian Council Int. Chamber of Commerce, Chmn. Board & Dir. Dineen Construction Ltd. *Member:* Tea & Coffee Association of Canada (Dir.); Grocery Products Manufactureres of Canada (Vice-Chairman and Director); Tea Council of Canada (Director) *Member:* Beta Theta Pi; Sigma Tau Chi. *Clubs:* Rosedale Golf, Granite, Toronto (all of Toronto); Canadian (N.Y.C.); Lyford Cay (Nassau). *Address:* 7 Valleyanna Drive, Toronto M4N 1J7, Ont.; and *office* 2180 Yonge Street, Toronto M4S 2C4, Ont., Canada.

**PORTER, Robert Maxwell.** Australian. Insurance executive. *B.* 1918. *Educ.* Associated Chartered Inst. of Secretaries; Associate. Australian Socy. of Accountants; Associate Australian Insurance Inst. *M.* 1945, Shirley Biggs. *S.* Robert and Ian. *Dau.* Helen. *Career:* Gen. Mgr., Government Insurance Office of N.S.W. 1964—. Pres. Insurance Institute of N.S.W. 1965—. Vice-Pres. Australian Insurance Institute 1966—. *Member:* ACIS; AASA; AAII. *Clubs:* Royal Sydney Yacht Squadron; Imperial Service; Pymble Golf Club. *Address: office* Box 3999, G.P.O., Sydney, N.S.W., Australia.

**PORTER, Rt. Hon. Sir Robert Wilson,** Kt 1971, QC. *B.* 1923. *Educ.* Model School, Londonderry; Foyle College, Londonderry; Queen's Univ. Belfast. *Married. S.* 1. *Dau.* 1. *Career:* Royal Air Force Volunteer Reserve 1943–46; Royal Artillery (T.A.) 1950–56; Called to Bar of N. Ireland, 1950; Junior Crown Counsel for Co. Londonderry, 1960–63, and Co. Down, 1964–65; Counsel to Attorney-General for Northern Ireland, 1963–65. M.P. (U) for Queen's University, Northern Ireland, 1966–69, and Lagan Valley, Northern Ireland, 1969–73; Parliamentary Secretary to Ministry of Home Affairs, Jan. 1969. Minister of Health and Social Services, Jan.–Mar. 1969. Minister of Home Affairs, Northern Ireland, 1969–70. *Address:* Ardkeen, 86 Marlborough Park North, Belfast BT9 6HL.

**POSEL, Max Michael,** MD, MRCP (London). South African consultant physician. Honorary Consulting Physician to Johannesburg Hospital. Regent, American College of Chest Physicians. *B.* 1903. *Educ.* Univ. of London (MD; MRCP) and St. Bartholomew's Hospital, London. *M. Daus.* 2. Medical Specialist, Union Defence Forces 1939–45. *Publications:* various contributions to South African and British medical journals. *Address:* P.O. Box 5868, Johannesburg, South Africa.

**POSNETT, Richard Neil,** CMG, OBE, MA. British diplomat. FCO Adviser on dependent territories. *B.* 1919. *Educ.* Kingswood School; St. John's Coll. Cambridge (BA, MA); Barrister, Society of Grays Inn. *M.* 1959, Shirley Margaret Hudson. *S.* 2. *Dau.* 1. (*S.* 2. *Dau.* 1 by previous marriage) *Career:* District Officer Uganda 1941–51; Resident Magistrate Uganda 1952; Clerk, Legislative & Exec. Councils 1953–55; Ministerial Secretary Uganda 1956–57; Colonial Office London 1958–60; Judicial Adviser Uganda 1960–61; Perm. Secy. Ext. Affairs and Trade Uganda 1961–63; British Foreign Service London 1964–66; UK Mission, United Nations New York 1966–70; Foreign Office London, Head, West Indian Dept. 1960–71; Governor of Belize 1972–76; Special Mission to Ocean Island 1977. *Member:* Royal Inst. Int. Affairs London. *Awards:* Companion of St. Michael & St. George; Order of the British Empire; Knight of St. John of Jerusalem. *Clubs:* Royal Commonwealth; Achilles; Ski of Gt. Britain. *Address:* Timbers, Northway, Godalming, Surrey.

**POST, Allen.** Lawyer. *B.* 1906. *Educ.* University of Georgia (A.B. *summa cum laude*) and Oxford University (BA in Jurisprudence, with First Hons.; BCL with Second Hons.; Master of Arts); PhD. *M.* 1934, Mary Chastaine Cook. *S.* Allen W. Williams. Jr. *Career:* Lieut.-Comdr., U.S.N.R. in World War II 1943–45. Dir., The Constitution Publishing Co. 1934–51; Democratic Presidential Elector from Georgia 1956; Cttee., Political Organization of Democratic National Cttee.; member, Committee to Revise Election Laws of Georgia 1956–58, Georgia Income Tax Revision Committee 1956–58, Governor's Staff 1955–58, and State Democratic Executive Committee 1955–58. Special Attorney-General of Georgia 1934; President, Atlanta Estate Planning Council 1960. Commander, American Legion 1956. Senior Partner in law firm of Hansell, Post, Brandon & Dorsey, Atlanta, Ga., Dir. First National Bank Atlanta, First National Holding Corp., Atlanta Gas Light Co. American Cast Iron Pipe Co.; W. L. Hailey & Co., Thomaston Mills, Georgia Highway Express Inc.; Atlantic American Corp.; H.S.F. Co. Inc., Inc. Trustee: Howell Fund, W. N. Banks Foundation Trustee & Exec. Cttee., Atlanta Arts Alliance, Inc. Pres., Old War Lawyers Club. Chmn. First Methodist Church. *Publications:* Numerous legal publications. Fraternities: Phi Beta Kappa; Phi Kappa Phi; Phi Delta Phi; Pres., Atlanta Alumni Socy., Kappa Alpha Order. *Member:* Atlanta (member Exec. Cttee 1940–45 and 1947–53. Pres. 1956), Georgia, and Amer. Bar Associations; Lawyers Club of Atlanta; American Judicature Society; American College of Trial Lawyers; American College of Probate Counsel; American Assn. of Rhodes Scholars; Sons of American Revolution; Navy League; Reserve Officers of the Naval Service (President 1946); Atlanta Chamber of Commerce; Univ. of Georgia Alumni Socy. (Dir.); Atlanta Claims Assn.; Law Forum. Military Order of World Wars. *Clubs:* Piedmont Driving; Capital City; Commerce; Sphinx; Gridiron; Rotary. *Address:* 620 Peachtree Battle Avenue, N.W., Atlanta, 30327; and *office* 33rd Floor, First National Bank Tower, Atlanta, Ga., 30303, U.S.A.; *European office:* 6th Floor, Bartlett House, 9 Basinghall Street, London EC2V 5BQ.

**POSWICK, Baron Prosper Charles Marie Joseph Ghislain.** Belgian diplomat. *B.* 1906. *Educ.* University of Louvain (D.-en-D. 1930); Institute of St. Louis, Brussels (Cand. en Phil. et Lettres 1925); matriculated in Thomiste Philosophy. *M.* 1935, Baroness de Dieudonné de. Corbeek-over-Loo. *S.* 2. *Daus.* 2. *Career:* Entered diplomatic service 1932; Attaché of Legation 1934; Secretary of Legation 1937; at Berne 1937; Chargé d'Affaires a.i. 1937; Secretary of Conference and Secretary of the Belgian Delegation, Conference of Brussels 1937; at Cairo 1939; Secretary of Legation 1st Cl. 1941; at Ankara 1941 (Counsellor 1944); at Central Administration 1945; Sec.-Gen. of Belgian delegation, Peace Conf. Paris 1946; at The Hague 1947; Chief of Cabinet 1951; member of Belgian delegations to: Japanese Peace Conf., San Francisco 1951, North Atlantic Pact Conf., Ottawa, Lisbon, Paris and Rome; at U.N. Paris 1951, New York 1952; European Defence Community; European Coal and Steel Community; Council of Europe (Strasbourg); European Political Community; Council of Ministers of O.E.C.E., Minister to Luxembourg 1953 (Amb. 1955), Amb. to Holy See 1957; Ambassador to Spain 1968; Hon. Ambassador 1972 & Delegate, Sovereign Order of Malta, to Belgium since 1975; Knight of Honour and Devotion, Sovereign and Military Order of Malta. *Awards:* Grand Officer, Order of the Crown; Grand Officer, Order of Leopold II; Commander, Order of Léopold; Grand Cross, Order Adolphe de Nassau (Luxembourg); Grand Cross, Order of the Oak Crown (Luxembourg); Grand Cross Order of Pius IX; Grand Cross, Isabel la Catolic; Grand Cross, "Pro Merito Melitense" (Order of Malta); Grand Officier, Phenix (Greece); Cdr. Militari Order of Christ with Star (Portugal); Cdr. of Orange Nassau (Netherlands). *Address:* Château de Tihange, 5201 Tihange, Belgium.

**POTE SARASIN.** Thai lawyer, Barrister-at-Law. *B.* 1906. Ambassador to U.S.A. 1952–57; Representative of Thailand to U.N. Gen. Assembly 1952–57; Prime Minister of Thailand Sept. 1957–Jan. 1958; Secy.-General of SEATO 1956–63; Minister of Econ. Affairs & Nat. Devt. 1963–68; Minister of Econ. Affairs 1968–69; Vice-Chmn., United Thai People's Party 1968—; Dep. Prime Minister & Minister of Nat. Devt. 1969–71; Mem., Nat. Exec. Council & Dir. Econ., Finance & Industry Affairs 1971–72. Rector, University of Kern Kaen 1966. *Address:* Saha-Pracha-Thai, 1/226, Sri Ayudhya, Dusit, Bangkok, Thailand.

**POTTER, Sir (William) Ian.** Knight Bachelor; British. *B.* 1902. *Educ.* Univ. of Sydney (BEcon). *M.* (1) 1955, Patricia Anne Fitzgerald. *Daus.* Robin Bernice, Carolyn Anne. (2) Primrose Catherine Dunlop. *Career:* Economist to Federal Treasurer 1933–35; Comm. Rep. on Rural Debt. Adjustment Cttee., 1934; Mem. Commonwealth Immigration Planning Council 1956–62; Principal, Ian Potter & Co., which he founded, until 1967. Chairman: Australian United Investment Co. Ltd.; Tricontinental Corp. Ltd.; Atlas Copco Australia Pty. Ltd.; ASEA Electric (Aust.) Pty. Ltd.; McIlwraith McEacharn Ltd.; Associated Steamships Ltd.; Petrochemical Holdings Ltd.; CIBA-Geigy, Australia, Ltd.; R. W. Miller (Holdings) Ltd.; Bulkships Pty. Ltd.; Australian Elizabethan Theatre Trust; Ian Potter Foundation; Dir.; Commercial Union Ass. Co.; Consolidated Goldfields Australia, Email Ltd. Group; Boral Limited; Boral Basic Industries Ltd.; Union Steam Ship Co. of New Zealand Ltd.; The Bellambi Coal Co. Ltd.; Thomas Nationwide Transport Ltd.; Trans Freight Lines Inc. *Member:* Royal Society of Victoria; Victorian Arts; Centre Building Cttee. *Publications:* Various articles contributed to the press on economic and financial subjects. *Clubs:* Melbourne; Australian; Royal Melbourne Golf; Royal Yacht Victoria; Links (New York). *Address:* 30 Sargood Street, Toorak, Victoria 3142 Australia; and *office* 460 Bourke Street, Melbourne, Victoria 3000, Australia.

**POTTLE, Herbert Lench.** Canadian social scientist. *B.* 16 Feb. 1907. *Educ.* Mount Allison (BA); University of Toronto (MA, PhD). *M.* 1937, Muriel Ethel Moran. *Daus.* Helen Louise, Kathryn Elaine. *Career:* On staff of University of Toronto, Dept. of Psychology 1934–37; Psychologist, Infants' Home, Toronto 1937–38; Executive Officer, Department of Education, Newfoundland 1938–43; Director of Child Welfare and Judge of St. John's Juvenile Court 1943–47; Commissioner for Home Affairs and Education 1947–49; Minister of Public Welfare, Province of Newfoundland 1949–55; Acting Minister of Natural Resources 1949–51; Secretary, Bd. of Information and Stewardship, The United Church of Canada, Toronto, 1955–63; on leave of absence to United Nations for one year as Social Welfare Adviser to Government of Libya 1961–62; Rapporteur, Interregional (United Nations) Expert Meeting on Social Welfare Organization & Administration, 1967; Principal Research Officer (International Welfare and Special Projects), Dept. of National Health and Welfare 1963–72. *Address:* 175 Island Park Drive, Ottawa, Canada.

**POULSON, John Wilson.** *B.* 1901. *Educ.* Public Schools; unmarried. *Career:* Salesman, Fruit of the Loom Corp. 1925–31; Sales Manager, Pepperell Mfg. Co. 1932–42; Lieut.-Comdr., U.S. Navy, South Pacific 1942–45; with Fruit of the Loom: Vice-Pres. 1945–48; Exec. Vice-Pres. 1948–52; Pres. & Director 1953–61. President & Director. Bates Fabrics Inc., New York, May 1961—; Vice-President & Director, Bates M.F.G. Co. Lewiston, ME 1962—; Chairman, V.I.P. Fabrics Inc. 1964—. *Clubs:* Merchants (N.Y.C.). *Address: office*, 112 West 34th Street, New York City, U.S.A.

**POULSSON, Annar Baard.** Norwegian. *B.* 1911. *Educ.* Oslo University (full Law exam.). *M.* 1938, Else Johanne Møller. *S.* Haavar and Dag Einar. *Career:* Assuranceforeningen Skuld 1936; insurance studies abroad 1937–38; Assistant Director Assuranceforeningen Skuld 1943. Managing Director, Skuld Protection and Indemnity Insurance Association since 1947. Member, Comité Maritime International; Board Member Norwegian Maritime Law Assn. Member Institute Norwegian Insurance Companies and Employers' Assn., Norwegian Veritas; International Tanker Owners' Pollution Federation Ltd. *Publications:* Lectures on Protection and Indemnity Insurance, University of Bergen, (1943). Conservative. *Awards:* Knight of the Royal Norwegian Order, St. Olav; Resistance Medal. *Address:* Hundsundv 15, Snarøya, Baerum, Norway.

**POULTON, Harold William, OBE. Australian.** *B.* **1918.** *Educ.* Melbourne (BA; LLM) and Yale (JSD). *M.* **1952,** Dorothy H. Partington. *S.* 5. *Dau.* 1. *Career:* Assistant Commonwealth Crown Solicitor 1950–57; First Assistant Director-General (Policy), Department of Civil Aviation 1957–64; Exec. Gen. Mgr. Policy & Legal; Ansett Transport Industries Ltd.; Member, Faculty Board, Monash Law School; Commissioner Nat. Airline Comm. Papua New Guinea since 1973. *Awards:* Fellow, Royal Aeronautical Socy.; Chartered Inst. of Transport. *Publications:* Various articles in law journals and periodicals. *Clubs:* Savage (Melbourne). *Address: office* P.O. Box 1629 M, 489 Swanston Street, Melbourne, Vic., Australia.

**POWELL, Benjamin Harrison.** BA, LLB, LLM. American. *B.* 1915. *Educ.* Virginia Military Inst. (BA); Univ. of Texas (LLB); Harvard (LLM). *M.* 1939, Kitty King Corbett. *S.* 1. *Daus.* 3. *Career:* Exec. Vice-Pres. Dir. Gen. Counsel Brown & Root Inc. and affiliated companies; Chmn. American Nat. Bank of Austin; Dir. Mercantile Texas Corp. (Dallas); Brown & Rook Wimpey Highlands Fabricators Ltd. *Member:* Amer. Bar Association. *Award:* Legion of Merit. *Clubs:* Ramada; River Oaks Country; World Trade (all Houston.) *Address:* 3451 Del Monte Drive, Houston, Texas 77019, U.S.A. and *office* P.O. Box 3 Houston, Texas 77001.

**POWELL, Irwin Augustus.** American. *B.* 1905. *Educ.* Princeton Univ. (*cum laude* 1928). *M.* 1954, Edith Harlan. *S.* Irwin A., Jr. *Daus.* Patricia, Pamela (Bermudez-Ruiz), and Helen (O'Brien); stepdaughter, Edith Myles Countess Lannes de Montebello. F.R.C. (*Frater Rosa Crucian*). *Career:* Buyer, R. H. Macy & Co. 1929–32; Asst. to Operating Vice-Pres. of International Tel. and Tel. 1933–36; Purchasing Mgr. Rumanian Telephone Co. 1937–40; Supply Supt. Intl. Tel. & Tel. Corp. Sud America 1941–49; Special Supply Supt., Brazilian Traction, Light & Power Corp. 1950–52. Account Executive, Merrill Lynch, Pierce, Fenner & Smith 1952–68. Exec. Dir. Foundation for Advancement of Arts & Letters, 1969—. *Member:* American Academy of Political and Social Science. Arcane Society; English-Speaking Union; International Society General Semantics; Atlantic Union; United World Federalists; Anthroposophical Socy. Democrat. *Publications:* Fundamental Principles of Life (Princeton Univ. Thesis); One Universe and Further Knowledge of It; Parascience (Treatise); The Science of Man. *Clubs:* Piping Rock (Locust Valley, L.I., N.Y.); Princeton (N.Y.C.), *Address:* 40 Frost Creek Drive, Locust Valley, Long Island, New York, and *office* 955 Lexington Avenue, Penthouse, New York City 10021, U.S.A.

**POWELL, Jerome Vladimir.** American. *B.* 1915. *Educ.* Institute of Technology, Prague; Univ. of Calif. Berkeley; Dipl. Engr.-E.E. *M.* 1940, Virginia Foulds. *S.* Jerome Evan. *Dau.* Linda Elizabeth. *Career:* Engineer, General Electric Co., Schenectady, N.Y. 1940–41; Standard Oil Co. of California (last assignment President, California Crude Sales Co.) 1941–63; Mobil Chemical Co. (Regional Vice-President, Europe) 1964–70; Regional Vice-President, Mobil Chemical Co. Vice-President and Director, Mobil Chemical International Ltd. Executive Vice-President and Director, Mobil Inner Europe Inc.; General Superintendence Co. Ltd.; Vice-Pres . & Dir. of Petroleum and Petrochemical Division; Pres. Redwood International S.A. *Address: office* 1 Place Des Alpes, 1211, Geneva, Switzerland.

**POWELL, Brig. John Enoch,** PC, MBE, MA, MP. *B.* 1912. *Educ.* King Edward's School, Birmingham; Trinity College. Cambridge (Craven Scholar; First Chancellor's Classical Medallist; Porson Prizeman; Browne Medallist; Craven Travelling Student); Fellow, Trinity College, Cambridge; MA (Cantab.) 1937. *M.* 1952, Margaret Pamela Wilson. *Daus.* 2. *Career:* Professor of Greek, Univ. of Sydney; served in World War II (Private, 2nd Lieut., Capt., Major, Lt.-Col., Col., Brigadier); MP for Wolverhampton SW 1950–74 (cons.) and for Down South (UU) since 1974; Parly. Secy., Ministry of Housing & Local Government, 1955–57; Financial Secy. to H.M. Treasury, 1957–58; Minister of Health, July 1960–63. *Publications:* Has written many books, including The Social Services, Needs and Means; (co-author) One Nation; Saving in a Free Society; Medicine and Politics: A Nation Not Afraid; The House of Lords in the Middle Ages; Freedom and Reality; Common Market, the case against; Still to Decide; No Easy Answers; Joseph Chamberlain (biography); Wrestling with the Angel. *Address:* 33 South Eaton Place, London, S.W.1.

**POWELL, Lewis Franklin, Jr.** Lawyer and Judge. *B.* 1907. *Educ.* Washington & Lee Univ. (BS; LLB) and Harvard Law School (LLM). *M.* 1936, Josephine Rucker. *S.* Lewis Franklin III. *Daus.* Josephine McRae (Smith), Ann Pendleton (Carmody), and Mary Lewis (Sumner). *Career:* With United States Air Force (various ranks from Lieutenant to Colonel) 1942–46. Member of firm of Hunton, Williams, Gay, Powell & Gibson, Richmond, Va.; U.S. Supreme Court Justice since 1972. *Member:* Amer. Bar Ass. (Pres. 1964–65); Bar Assn. of City of New York; Amer. Law Inst.; Amer. Coll. of Trial Lawyers (Pres., 1969–70); Amer. Bar Foundation (Pres. 1969–71); Natl. Commn. on Law Enforcement and Administration of Justice 1965–67. *Awards:* Legion of Merit, Bronze Star, Croix de Guerre with Palms (France). Hon LLD Washington & Lee Univ., Univ. of Florida, William and Mary Coll., and Hampden-Sydney College; Blue Ribbon Defense Panel, appointed by Pres. Nixon 1969–70; Hon. Bencher, Lincolns Inn. *Clubs:* Century; University (N.Y.C.). *Address:* 1238 Rothesay Road, Richmond, Va. 23221; and *office* U.S. Supreme Court, Washington, D.C. 20543, U.S.A.

**POWELL, Sir Richard (George Douglas),** Bt. MC. *B.* 1909. *Educ.* Eton College. *M.* 1933, Elizabeth McMullen. *S.* 1. *Daus.* 2. *Career:* Served in World War II (Welsh Guards; M.C. and Bar; Croix Militaire, 1st Cl. Belgium) 1939–45;

Asst. Military Attaché. Brussels 1946–48; Dir. Gen. Inst. of Directors 1954–74; Director, Bovis Ltd.; Pierson Heldring & Pierson (UK) Ltd.; Russell-Garratt Ltd.; Cornwall Daborn Garratt Ltd.; BUPA Medical Centre Ltd.; THinc Group (U.K.) Ltd. *Address:* Smalls House, Brightwell-cum-Sotwell, Oxfordshire OX10 0SJ.

**POWELL, Sir Richard Royle,** GCB, KBE, CMG. British. Merchant banker & Director of industrial companies. *B.* 1909. *Educ.* Queen Mary's School, Walsall and Cambridge University; BA 1930. *Career:* At Admiralty 1931–46; Under-Secy., Ministry of Defence 1946–48; Deputy Secy., Admiralty 1948–50; Deputy Secy., Ministry of Defence 1950–56; Permanent Secy., Ministry of Defence 1956–59; Permanent Secy., Board of Trade 1960–68; Dep. Chmn., Perm. Cttee. on Invisible Exports 1968–76; Chmn., Alusuisse (U.K.) Ltd. & subsidiary companies since 1969. *Address:* 56 Montagu Square, London, W1H 1TG.

**POWELL, Stanley, Jr.** American. *Educ.* University of California (BA). *M.* 1942, Betty Winstead. *S.* Robert. *Daus.* Katherine, Nancy and Georgia. *Career:* With Matson Navigation Co. since 1941, in various capacities, principal ones being Assistant Treasurer 1955–57, Asst. Treasurer 1957, Treasurer 1958–59, Secy.-Treas. 1959–61, Vice-Pres. Freight Div. 1961–62 and Exec. Vice-Pres. Pres. 1962–70; Vice-Pres. 1965–66 Alexander & Baldwin Inc.; Pres. 1966–70 Director: United States Leasing International Co. *Member:* Bd. of Managers, Amer. Bureau of Shipping; Commis. Commission, Amer. Shipbuilding; Member, Nat. Defense Transportation Assn.; Trustee, San Francisco Maritime Museum; Bd. Governors, San Francisco Symphony Assn. *Clubs:* Pacific-Union, Bohemian (all in S. Francisco); Meadow (Fairfax, Calif.); *Address:* 130 Barber Avenue, San Anselmo, California, U.S.A.

**POWELL-JONES, John.** British Diplomat. *B.* 1925. *Educ.* Charterhouse; Oxford Univ (1st Cl. Hons Modern History). *M.* 1968, Pamela Sale. *S.* 2. *Dau.* 1. *Career:* Foreign Office 1949; 3rd Secy. and Vice-Consul Bogota 1950–52; 2nd Secy. Foreign Office 1952–55; 2nd and later 1st Secy. Athens 1955–59; 1st Secy. For. Office 1959–60; 1st Secy. Leopoldville 1961–62; Assist. head of UN Dept. Foreign Office 1962–67; Counsellor, Political Adv. Office, Singapore 1968–69; Counsellor and Consul-Gen. Athens 1970–73; Ambassador in Phnom-Penh 1973–75; Ambassador in Dakar since 1976. *Decoration:* Companion of St. Michael and St. George. *Club:* Travellers. *Address:* Gaston Gate, Cranleigh, Surrey; and *office* Foreign and Commonwealth Office, London, S.W.1.

**POWER, Donald Clinton.** American. *B.* 1899. *Educ.* Ohio State Univ. (BS 1922; JD 1926; MA 1927). *M.* 1927, Catherine Hamilton. *Daus.* Jane (Mykrantz) and Charlotte (Kessler). *Career:* Instructor, Asst. Prof., Associate Prof., Ohio State Univ. 1922–39; Asst. Attorney-General of Ohio and Attorney for Ohio Public Utilities Commission 1933–36; Secy. to the Governor of Ohio 1939–43; Pres., General Telephone Corp. 1951–59. Chmn. of Board and Chief Exec. Officer, General Telephone & Electronics Corp., New York City, 1959–66. Chmn., Bd., General Telephone & Electronic Corp. 1966–72; Mr. Power has maintained law offices in Columbus, Ohio, since 1926. Director, American Manufacturers Mutual Insurance Company; Surveyor Fund, Inc.; Norton Simon, Inc.; Brown Steel Company; The Ohio State Life Insurance Company; The Jeffrey Company; Hon. LLD. Uppsala College; Hon. DBA, Rio Grande Coll. *Awards:* Distinguished Service Award, Ohio State Univ.; Business Executive of the Year 1959; citation from U.N. We Believe Cttmee.; National Honor Award; Beta Gamma Sigma; Heart & Torch Award (Amer. Heart Assn.). *Member:* Amer. Bar Association; National Industrial Conference Board; Committee for Economic Development (Trustee); National Security Industrial Association (Trustee); etc. *Publications:* Law of Contracts Condensed, (1939); many articles on various public utility subjects. *Clubs:* Athletic, Sigma Chi, University, Faculty (Colombus). *Address:* Route 1, 9291 W. Broad St., Galloway, Ohio 43119, U.S.A.

**POWER, John Francis,** JP. Manager, South Australian Country Newspapers Ltd.; Secretary, Provincial Press Association of South Australia (INCORP). *B.* 1910. *Educ.* St. Anthony's, Port Pirie; private tutor. *M.* 1932, Rose Ella May Murray. *S.* Colin John, Neil Francis, and John Joseph. *Daus.* Patricia Ann, Judith Rose and Ann Maria. *Member:* Gawler Municipal Council for eight years. Served five-and-a-half years in R.A.A.F. *Publications:* Country Story. *Clubs:* Air Force Association; I.E.F.T.S. (R.A.A.F.); Contact: The Commerce Club Incorporated. *Address: office* 130 Franklin Street, Adelaide, S.A. 5000, Australia.

**POWERS, Aaron Bates.** American electronic scientist. *B.* 1916. *Educ.* Univ. of Washington (Seattle). BS in Electrical Engineering; U.S. Naval Ordnance Development Award, 1945. *Career:* Electrical Engineer, U.S. Bonneville Power Administration (1941–42) and U.S. Navy Degaussing Office, Seattle, 1942–43; Research Scientist, Office of Scientific Research and Development, Harvard Univ., 1943–45; Electronic Scientist, U.S. Navy Underwater Sound Lab., New London, Conn., 1946–51; member, Nat. Research Council special study group on Mine Warfare, 1951; Electronic Scientist, U.S. National Bureau of Standards, Corona, 1951–53; U.S. Naval Ordnance Laboratory, Corona, 1953–64; Technical Director, U.S. Naval Fleet Missile Systems Analysis and Evaluation Group, Corona, California 1964–73; Management Consultant 1974—. *Address:* P.O. Box 2097, Laguna Hills, Calif. 92653, U.S.A.

**POWERS, Robert Bruna.** American publisher and writer; *B.* 1904. *Educ.* Michigan State University (AB). *M.* 1935, Josephine Sibley. *S.* Robert Sibley and Roger Kenyon. *Dau.* Cheryl. *Career:* Assoc. Editor, China Weekly Review (Shanghai) 1926–27; Head of Department of Journalism, University of Detroit, 1927–28; Art Director, Brooke, Smith & French, Inc., 1928–37; Editor and Business Manager, The F.T.D. News, 1940–45; Executive Editor. The Tool Engineer, 1947–53. Chmn., Ward's Communications Inc. (1946); Chmn., The Social Secretary (1976). Republican. *Address:* (winter) 4160, Cresta Drive, Santa Barbara, Calif. 93110; and (summer) 274 Provencal, Grosse Pointe Farms, Mich. 48236, U.S.A.

**POWLES, Sir Guy Richardson,** KBE, CMG, ED. New Zealand *B.* 1905. *Educ.* Victoria Univ., N.Z. (LLB); Hon LLD (1969). *M.* 1931, Eileen Nicholls. *S.* Charles Guy and Michael John. *Career:* Barrister and Solicitor, Supreme Court, N.Z. 1929; served in N.Z. Military Forces to rank of Colonel 1939–45; Counsellor, N.Z. Legation, Washington 1946–48; High Commissioner of Western Samoa 1949–60; High Commissioner for New Zealand in India, concurrently in Ceylon and Ambassador in Nepal 1960–62. Ombudsman 1962–75, Chief Ombudsman 1975–77; Commissioner of International Commission of Jurists 1975—; Commissioner of Churches, Commission of International Affairs of World Council of Churches 1970—; President, New Zealand Institute of International Affairs 1967–71; Race Relations Conciliator 1971–73. *Publications:* Articles and Speeches on Internat. Affairs, Race Relations & Administ. Law. *Address:* 34A Wesley Road, Wellington C.1, New Zealand.

**PRAG, Derek N.** British consultant on European affairs. *B.* 1923. *Educ.* Bolton School, Emmanuel Coll., Cambridge (MA) and London Univ. (School of Slavonic and E. European Studies). *M.* 1948, Dora Weiner. *S.* Nicholas, Jonathan and Stephen. *Career:* Served in British Army, Intell. Corps. in Egypt, Italy and Austria 1943–47. Journalist with Reuters News Agency 1950–55 (London, Brussels, Madrid), and Manager of Comtelsa—subsidiary of Reuters and Spanish News Agency EFE—1954–55; joined Information Service of the High Authority of the European Coal and Steel Community 1955; Chief of Publications Division, E.C. Information Service 1960–65; Dir., European Commission's London Press and Information Office 1965–73. *Publications* include brochures and articles on European integration; (with E. D. Nicholson) Businessman's Guide to the European Community (1973). *Address:* 27 Longton Avenue, London, SE26 6RE.

**PRAIN, J. Murray,** DSO, OBE, TD, DL. Member Queen's Bodyguard for Scotland Royal Company of Archers since 1950. *B.* 1902. *Educ.* Charterhouse School and Clare College, Cambridge (BA 1924). *M.* 1934, Lorina Helen Elspeth. *S.* Philip James. *Dau.* Tessa Helen (Fane). *Career.* Chmn., James Prain & Sons, Dundee 1945–64; Director, Tayside Floorcoverings Ltd. 1946–69; Alliance Trust Co. Ltd., Dundee 1946–73; 2nd Alliance Trust Co. Ltd. 1946–73; The Scottish Life Assurance Ltd. 1949–72; Royal Bank of Scotland 1955–71; William Halley & Sons Ltd.; Vice-Chmn., Caird (Dundee) Ltd. 1956–64. *Member:* Jute Working Party (1946–48), and of Scottish Committee, Industrial & Commercial Finance Corp. (1946–55); Chmn., Jute Importers Assn. (1947–49), and Assn. of Jute Spinners and Manufacturers (1950–52); Chmn., Dundee District Cttee., Scottish Board for Industry 1948–62; part time member Scottish Gas Board (1952–56); member, Employers' Panel, Industrial Disputes Tribunal 1952–59; Employers Panel Industrial Court 1959–71; Industrial Arbitration Bd. 1971–73; Deputy

Lieut., County of Fife. Served in World War II (Fife and Forfar Yeomanry; wounded; dispatches, D.S.O.; Lieut.-Col.) 1939-45. *Address:* Mugdrum-by-Newburgh, Fife, KY14 6EH, Scotland.

**PRAIN, Sir Ronald Lindsay**, Kt 1956, OBE 1946. *B.* 1907. *Educ.* Cheltenham Coll. (Eng.). *M.* 1938, Esther Pansy Brownrigg. *S.* Graham Lindsay and Angus Lindsay. *Career:* Controller, Diamond Die & Tool Control 1940-45; Quartz Crystal Control 1943-45; Chief Exec. 1943-68, Roan Selection Trust (RST) Int. Group Mining Companies Chmn. 1950-72; First Chmn., Merchant Bank of Central Africa Ltd. 1956-66, Merchant Bank (Zambia) Ltd. 1966-72, Agricultural Research Council of Rhodesia & Nyasaland 1959-63; Pres., British Overseas Mining Assn. 1952, Inst. of Metals 1960-61; Chmn., Council of Commonwealth Mining & Metallurgical Insts. 1961-74, Botswana RST Group 1959-72, Past Director: International Nickel Co. of Canada Ltd. 1951-72, Wankie Colliery Co. Ltd. 1953-63, Metal Market & Exchange Co. Ltd. 1943-65, San Francisco Mines of Mexico Ltd. 1944-68, Barclays Bank International 1971-77, etc.; & currently: Foseco Minsep Ltd., Minerals Separation Ltd., Monks Investment Trust Ltd., Pan-Holding S.A., Selection Trust Ltd. & other companies. Hon member Metals Socy. & BNF Metals Technology Centre; Hon. Pres. Copper Development Assoc.; Hon Fellow Inst. of Mining & Metallurgy; Pres. Cheltenham Coll. Council; Mem. of Council, Overseas Development Inst.; Trustee, Inst. for Archeao-Metallurgical Studies. *Award:* Copper Club of New York ANKH Award 1964; Inst. of Mining & Metallurgy Gold Medal 1968; Inst. of Metals Platinum Medal 1969. *Publications:* Selected Papers (4 vols.); Copper . . . the Anatomy of an Industry. *Clubs:* Brooks's; White's; M.C.C. (London). *Address:* Waverley, St. George's Hill, Weybridge, Surrey KT13 0QJ; and 43 Cadogan Square, London SW1X 0HX.

**PRALL, Bert R.** Corporation executive. *B.* 1895. *Educ.* High School Graduate. *M.* 1919, Luella Powell. *S.* Bert Apperson. *Career:* Chairman of Board: Midwest Variety Inc., Winnetka, Ill.; The Chicago-Tokyo Bank, Chicago; 1964-75; Director: Universal Oil Products (Chmn., Finance Cttee.), Chicago 1956-75; McCrory Corp. (Member Exec. Cttee.) N.Y.C.; Pres.; McCory Credit Corp. 1965-75; Vice-Pres., Dir., Montgomery Ward & Co., Chicago 1919-46; President Butler Bros., Chicago 1948-56. Chairman of Board: Phillips & Buttorf Corp., Nashville Tenn. 1956-57; Federal Reserve Bank of Chicago 1953-60; Hosho Overseas Trading Co. (Tokyo, Japan) 1966-68; H. L. Green Co. Inc. (and Pres.), N.Y.C. 1960-61. *Member:* Japan-America Socy. of Chicago (Hon. Dir.); Chicago Assn. of Commerce & Industry; Senior Council. *Awards:* Order of Sacred Treasure 3rd Class, Japan. Republican. *Clubs:* Chicago, Executives, Bankers (Chicago); Mid-America; Westmorland Country (Wilmette, Ill.). *Address:* 558 Ridge Road, Winnetka, Ill.; and *office* 40 North Dearborn Street, P.O. Box 457, Chicago, Ill., 60690, U.S.A.

**PRANTNER, Robert.** Dr. theol, Dr. rerpol. Austrian diplomat. *B.* 1931. *Educ.* Humanistic Gymnasium Vienna; Univ. of Vienna, DD; D. pol. science. *M.* 1960, Johanna Sandler-Taubinger. *S.* 1. *Dau.* 1. *Career:* Lecturer, Catholic Academy of Vienna 1955; Publicist Consultant OVP (Wirtschaftsbund), Personal Secy. Fed. Chancellor Ing. Julius Raab 1956-63; Scient. Consultant, Dr. Alfred Maleta, Pres. of the Austrian Nat. Parliament 1964-71; Dir. Studies Political Academy, Vienna 1972; Asst. Professor, Political Science, Phil. Theol. Institute, Stift Klosterneuburg near Vienna since 1974. *Member:* Catholic Academy Vienna; Political Academy; Gorres Gesellcshaft zur Pflage der Wissenschaften, Fed. Republic of Germany. *Awards:* Minister of the Sovereign Order of Malta; Papal Pilgrim Cross of Jerusalem in Gold; Grand Cross of St. Pauls Order; Yugoslav Flag Order with Golden Star; Knight of St. Georges Order, Austria and many others. *Publications:* Christlichcoziale Partei und Katholische Kirche im Spiegel der Presse; Weins unter Kardinal piffl und Bundeskanzler (1955); Malteserorden und Völkergemeinschaft (1974). *Address:* Parkstrasse 19, A-2371 Hinterbrühl b. Wien and *office*: Johannesgasse 2, A-1010 Wien, Austria.

**PRATE, Alain Marie André.** French Finance Official. *B.* 1928. *Educ.* Collège Saint-Joseph, Lille; Faculty of Law, Paris—Licencié en droit, Diplômé d'Études Supérieures d'Économie Politique, Diplômé de l'Institut d'Etudes Politiques; Ecole Nationale d'Administration. *M.* 1956, Marie-José Alexis. *S.* 2. *Dau.* 1. *Career:* Inspection of Finances 1953-56; Dep. Dir. of overseas economic affairs 1956-58; Sec. of the Monetary Cttee. of EEC 1958-61; Dir. of the Commission of EEC 1961-65; Dir.-Gen. of the Marché Intérieur 1965-67; Counsellor on Economic & Financial Affairs to the Presidency of the Republic 1967-69; Head of Dept. of the Inspector General of Finances 1969-71; Dir.-Gen. of Customs 1971-75; Dir. of the Crédit National since 1975. *Director:* Crédit Naval, Banque Française du Commerce Extérieur, Société Centrale pour l'Equipement du Territoire, COGEMA; Chmn., Société Financière pour l'Innovation "SOFINNOVA". *Member:* Conseil Supérieur du Pétrole. *Decorations:* Chevalier de la Légion d'Honneur; Officier de l'Ordre de Mérite. *Address:* 4 Square Thiers—75116 Paris, France; and *office* Crédit National, 45 Rue Saint-Dominique—75700 Paris, France.

**PRATT, Henry Reginald Clive.** British chemical engineer. *B.* 1911. *Educ.* Lower School of John Lyon, Harrow; Birkbeck College, Univ. of London (BSc 1st Class Hons. in chemistry; PhD, DSc). *M.* 1939, Phyllis Denton. *S.* Robert David. *Dau.* Margaret Christina. *Career:* Research Chemist, I.C.I. (General Chemicals) Ltd., Widnes, Lancs. 1934-45; Chief Chemical Engineer, BX Plastics Ltd., Essex 1945-49; Deputy Chief Scientific Officer, Chemical Engineering Section, Atomic Energy Research Establishment, Harwell 1949-58; Chief of Div. of Chemical Engineering, Commonwealth Scientific and Industrial Research Organization, Melbourne 1958-73; Visiting Professor, Dept. Chemical Engineering, Univ. of Melbourne 1973-74 & 1976, & Newcastle upon Tyne 1975. *Fellow:* Inst. of Chemical Engineers (former Vice-Pres., Mem. of Council & of Examinations & Publications Cttees.); Royal Institute of Chemistry; Royal Australian Chemical Inst.; Institution of Engineers, Australia. *Publications:* about 40 papers in chemical engineering journals on aspects of heat transfer, distillation, absorption and extraction; Counter-current Separation Processes (Elsevier Publ. Co.). Contributor to book, Separation of Isotopes (edited by H. London and published by George Newnes Ltd.). *Address:* 209 Dendy Street, East Brighton, Vic.; and *office*, Department of Chemical Engineering, Univ. of Melbourne, Parville, Vic., Australia.

**PRATTEN, David Autton.** British. *B.* 1910. *Educ.* Sydney Church of England Grammer School. *M.* 1934, Violette Whitley. *S.* 1. *Dau.* 1. *Career:* Chmn. Comeng Holdings Ltd. & Group; Chmn. Man, Dir. Turee Pty. Ltd. Hon. Vice-Pres. Royal Agric. Socy. N.S.W. *Clubs:* Australian, Sydney; Eleanora Country; Cabbage Tree, Palm Beach. *Address:* Bombery, 7 Michell Rd., Palm Beach, NSW, Australia.

**PREBLE, Robert Curtis.** American publishing executive. Retired President, Encyclopaedia Britannica, Inc. *B.* 1897. *Educ.* Univ. of Illinois; Kent Coll. of Law (BSc, Industrial Administration). *M.* (3) 1963, Beatrice Dowsett Ross. *S.* Robert C. Jr., William W. *Dau.* Patricia Ann. Encyclopaedia Publishing 1920—. *Publications:* World Language Dictionary. *Clubs:* Chicago; Executives; Chicago Press; Lake Shore; Tavern. *Address: office* 425 North Michigan Avenue, Chicago 11, Ill., U.S.A.

**PRENTICE, John Gerald.** Canadian. *B.* 1907. *Educ.* Textile Engineering School (Reutlingen, Germany) and University of Vienna (LLD 1930). *M.* 1932, Eve Schlesinger-Acs. *Daus.* Elizabeth (Jarvis) and Marietta (Longstaffe). *Career:* Signing Officer, E. G. Pick (Obersleutendorf, Czechoslovakia) 1926-38; Partner Pick & Co. (Wiener Neustadt, Austria) 1936-38. President, Pacific Veneer & Plywood Co. (New Westminster, B.C.) 1938-44; Vice-President, Canadian Forest Products Ltd. (Vancouver) 1944-50; Pres. 1950-70; Chairman of the Board, Canadian Forest Products Ltd. Canfor Ltd.; North Canadian Forest Industries Ltd. Vice-Pres. and Director: West Coast Woollen Mills Ltd. Director: Bank of Montreal, Prince George Pulp & Paper Co. Ltd., Intercontinental Pulp Co. Ltd. Member Executive Board, Canadian Pulp and Paper Assoc.; Member British North Amer. Cttee.; Hon. Life Pres., Playhouse Theatre Co.; Dep-. President, Fed. Internationale Des Echecs (FIDE); Member Exec. Cttee. Canada Cttee. for Unesco; Conference Bd. Canadian Council; Canad. Cncl. of Christians & Jews; Convocation Founder, Simon Fraser Univ. (Burnaby, BC.). *Clubs:* Men's Canadian; Southlands Riding & Driving; Vancouver Lawn Tennis & Badminton; Manhattan Chess (N.Y.C.); Capilano Golf & Country. *Address: office* 505 Burrard Street, Vancouver, B.C. V7X 1B5, Canada.

**PRENTICE, Rt. Hon. Reginald Ernest**, PC, JP, MP. *B.* 1923. *Educ.* BSEcon London 1949. *M.* 1948, Joan Godwin. *Dau.* 1. *Career:* On staff of Transport & General Workers Union (Head of the Union's advice and service bureau) 1950-57; Member of Parliament East Ham N. 1957-74, & for Newham NE since 1974; Minister of State for Education & Science 1964-66. Minister of Public Building and Works 1966-67. Minister of Overseas Development 1967-69, and 1975-76;

Member, Shadow Cabinet, Opposition spokesman on Employment 1972–74; Sec. of State for Education 1974–75. *Member:* Fabian Society; Royal Inst. of International Affairs; United Nations Association; Transport and General Workers Union. *Publications:* Social Welfare and the Citizen (1957). *Address:* 5 Hollingsworth Road, Croydon, Surrey, CRO 5RP.

**PRESTON, Sir Kenneth Huson.** *B.* 1901. *Educ.* Rugby and Trinity College Oxford. *M.* 1922, Beryl Wilmot Wilkinson. *S.* 1. *Dau.* 1. President, Stone-Platt Industries Ltd. *Clubs:* Royal Yacht Squadron; Royal Thames Yacht. *Address:* Ilsom Farm, Tetbury, Gloucestershire.

**PRETORIUS, Johan Frederick.** South African Diplomat. *B.* 1929. *Educ.* Univ. of South Africa—BA 1950, B.Econ. 1954. *M.* 1961, Almuth Erika Hofmann. *S.* 1. *Dau.* 1. *Career:* Vice Consul, S.A. Consulate-General, Lourenço Marques 1955–59; Second Sec., S.A. Embassy, Lisbon 1959–62; First Sec., Dept. of Foreign Affairs (Africa Division), Pretoria 1962–66; Counsellor, S.A. Embassy, Paris 1966–71; Under Sec., Dept. of Foreign Affairs (Africa Division), Pretoria 1972–75; Ambassador Extraordinary & Plenipotentiary, Brasilia since 1976. *Address:* South African Embassy, 6 Avenida das Nações, Brasilia D.F., Brazil.

**PREW-SMITH, Harry.** British company director. *B.* 1905. *Educ.* Public School. *M.* 1942. Joyce May Beattie. *S.* Paul Trevor and Harry Edward. *Daus.* Diana Patricia and Jane Elizabeth. *Career:* Dir. Harry Prew-Smith Ltd. since 1940, Durowear Ltd. (1939), Prew-Smith (Bolsover) Ltd. (1950), Prew-Smith Knitwear Ltd. (1957), Meridian Ltd. (1968) and I. R. Morley Ltd. (1968). *Member:* National Hosiery Manufacturers Federation. *Club:* Nottingham and Union Rowing. *Address:* Ravenscourt, Blidworth Way, Linby, Notts.

**PRICA, Srdja.** Republic of Yugoslavia diplomat. *B.* 1905. *Educ.* Graduate, Faculty of Law, Zagreb. *M.* Vukica Prica. *Career:* Lived as political emigrant in Vienna, Prague and Paris 1935–37, and in the U.S.A. 1937–45 (where he was mostly engaged as a journalist, writing for various newspapers and magazines of Yugoslav settlers in America); Editor, Yugoslav Trades Union paper in Belgrade 1945–47; Head of Department in Ministry of Foreign Affairs in Belgrade 1947–49; Assistant to Minister 1949–51; Ambassador in Paris 1951–55; Under-Secretary of State for Foreign Affairs 1955–60; Ambassador to London 1960–65, to Rome 1967–71, to Malta 1968–72; Member, Council, Federation of Socialist Federal Republic of Yugoslavia since 1972; Council for Foreign Affairs of the Presidency of the Republic of Yugoslavia since 1971. *Awards:* A number of Yugoslav and foreign decorations (French, Egyptian, Greek, Italian, Swedish). Member of Central Committee of League of Communists of Yugoslavia 1953–64. *Address:* Council of the Federation of the S.F.R., Belgrade, Yugoslavia.

**PRICE, Christopher,** MP. British Journalist & Politician. *B.* 1932. *Educ.* Oxford Univ.—MA. *M.* 1956, Annie Grierson Price. *S.* 2. *Dau.* 1. *Career:* Labour MP for Birmingham, Perry Barr 1966–70, & for Lewisham West since 1974; PPS to Sec. of State for Education 1966–67, 1975–76; Education Correspondent, New Statesman 1968–74; Chmn., Council of the National Youth Bureau. *Publications:* (Ed.) Your Child & School (1970); articles in New Statesman, etc. *Address:* House of Commons, London, S.W.1.

**PRICE, Douglas Gordon.** BE. Australian civil engineer. *B.* 1927. *Educ.* Sydney High School; Univ. of Sydney. *M.* 1950, Eileen Boardman. *S.* 1. *Daus.* 3. *Career:* With Royal Aust. Air Force 1945; Engineer, Snowy Mountains Hydro-Electric Authority 1950–70; Assistant Dir., Snowy Mountains Engineering Corporation 1970–75, since when Dir. *Member:* Amer. Socy. Civil Engineers; Councillor Aust. Professional Consultants Council; Fellow Inst. Engineers, Australia. *Club:* Cooma Golf; Royal Automobile Club of Australia, Sydney. *Address:* 9 Moonbi Street, Cooma North 2630 N.S.W., Australia; and *office* Box 356, Cooma North 2630.

**PRICE, John Robert,** FCA, FCIS, FCWA, MBIM. South African company director. *B.* 8 April 1908. *Educ* .Univ. of North Wales. *M.* 1932, Gertrude Doris Doxey. *S.* 1. *Dau.* 1. *Career:* Vice-Pres. Greaterman Stores Group of Department Stores (South Africa & Rhodesia). Past Pres., Durban Chamber of Commerce; Past Chmn., Durban Distributive Employers Assn.; Past Treas., Commercial Employers of S. Africa; Past Vice-Pres., S.A. Assn. of Chambers of Commerce; Past Chmn. Southern Africa Div. Chart. Inst. of Secretaries. Past President, Durban Wings Club: Past Commissioner, Boy Scouts; Mayor, Borough of Westville 1957–58. *Member:* N.A.A. (U.S.A.); Pres., S.A. Inst. of Management. *Publications:* Factory Administration, Solicitors' Accounts and other technical works. *Address:* 26 Federal Road, Sandhurst, Johannesburg, South Africa.

**PRIESTMAN, John David.** British European Civil Servant. *B.* 1926. *Educ.* Private School in Paris; Westminster School: Christ Church, Oxford—Honour Moderations & Literae Humaniores. *M.* 1951, Nada Valić. *S.* 2. *Daus.* 2. *Career:* Coldstream Guards, finishing as T/Captain on British Military Mission in Paris 1944–47; 3rd (subsequently 2nd) Secretary, British Embassy, Belgrade 1950–53; Asst. Private Sec. to Rt. Hon. Anthony Eden 1953–55; joined Secretariat of Council of Europe 1955; Head of Sec.-General's Private Office 1961; Sec. of the Cttee. of Ministers 1966; Deputy Clerk of Parliamentary Assembly 1968; Elected Clerk of Assembly 1971, re-elected for a second five year term from 1st Jan. 1977. *Clubs:* Buck's; Guards & Cavalry. *Address:* 53 Allée de la Robersau, 67000 Strasbourg, France; and *office* Council of Europe, Strasbourg 67000, France.

**PRINDIVILLE, Bernard Francis,** JP, FASA, FISM, FInstD. Australian. *M.* 1938, Mary Agnes O'Mahoney. *S.* 3. *Daus.* 2. *Career:* Chmn. of the following limited Companies: Commercial Finance Houghton Motors Pty; Houghton Holdings; Lynford Motors; *Director:* Equitable Life and Gen. Ins. Co. Ltd. (local); Glenway Corp., Penrith Pty; Swan Television; Town and Country Perm. Bldg. Socy.; Wallace Sassoon Securities; Westralian Plywoods Hearn Industries; Lynas Motors Pty.; Queensland Insurance Co. (Local Director). *Fellow:* Australian Inst. of Management; Australian Society of Accountants; Institute of Sales & Business Management (Past Pres.); Chartered Inst. of Directors, London. Past Pres. and Life member, W.A. Socy. for Crippled Children. *Clubs:* Tattersalls (W.A.); Celtic (Past Pres. and Life member); Royal King's Park Tennis; Lake Karringyup Country; Royal Automobile (Victoria); Royal Perth Golf; W.A. Football League; W.A. Cricket Assn. *Address:* 8 Stone Street, South Perth, W.A., Australia.

**PRIOR, Rt. Hon. James Michael Leathes,** PC, MP. *B.* 1927, *Educ.* Charterhouse, Pembroke Coll. Cambridge. *M.* 1954, Jane Primrose Gifford. *Career:* Member of Parliament, Lowestoft Div. Suffolk since 1959; P.P.S. to Pres. Bd. of Trade 1963, to Minister of Power 1963–64; Leader of the Opposition 1965–70; Minister, Agric. Fisheries and Food 1970–72; Lord Pres. of the Council 1972–74; Opposition Spokesman on Employment since 1974. *Address:* Old Hall, Brampton, Beccles, Suffolk, and 36 Morpeth Mansions, London, S.W.1.

**PRITCHARD, The Rt. Hon. Lord (Derek Wilbraham).** British. *B.* 1910. *M* 1941, Denise Arfor Huntbach. *Daus.* Rosemary Gail, Diana Gillian Amanda. *Career:* Chmn., British National Export Council, 1966–68; Chairman, Allied Breweries Ltd., 1968–70 Carreras Ltd. 1970–72; Rothmans International Ltd. 1972–75. President: Inst. of Directors 1968–74; Abbeyfield Society; Vice-Pres., Wine & Spirit Assn. of G.B.; Chmn., Dorchester Hotel 1976. D.L. of Northants. *Address:* West Haddon Hall, Northampton NN6 7AU.

**PRITCHARD, Sir Neil,** KCMG. Ambassador to Thailand 1967–70. *B.* 1911. *Educ.* Liverpool College, Worcester College, Oxford (First Class Honours—History 1932). *M.* 1943, Mary Devereux Burroughes. *S.* 1. *Career:* Entered Dominions Office 1933; Private Secy. to Permanent Under-Secretary 1936–38; Assistant Secretary, Rhodesia-Nyasaland Royal Commission 1938; Secretary, Office of the U.K. High Commissioner, Pretoria 1941–45; Assistant Secretary, Dominions Office 1946; Principal Secretary, Office of U.K. Representative, Dublin 1948–49; Asst. Under-Secretary of State, Commonwealth Relations Office 1950–54; Deputy U.K. Commissioner: Canada 1954–57, and Australia 1957–60; Acting Deputy Under-Secretary of State, C.R.O. 1961; British High Commissioner in Tanganyika 1961–63; Deputy Under-Secretary of State, C.R.O. 1964–67. *Address:* Little Garth, Daglingworth, Cirencester, Glos.

**PROBST, Raymond R.** Swiss Diplomat. *Educ.* Gymnasium, Bienne; University of Berne—Dr. Jur. *M.* 1945, Annemarie Probst. *S.* 1. *Dau.* 1. *Career:* Attaché, Min. of Foreign Affairs 1942–47; Second Sec., Swiss Embassy, Athens 1947–52; First Sec., Swiss Embassy, Washington, D.C. 1952–56; Office of the Legal Adviser, Min. of Foreign Affairs 1957–58; Dep. Head of Political Affairs, Min. of Foreign Affairs 1959–66; Minister Plenipotentiary, Delegate of Swiss Govt. for Trade Agreements 1967–68; Ambassador, Deleg. of Swiss

Govt. for Trade Agreements 1969–75; Amb. to the U.S. since 1976. *Member:* Schweiz. Vereinigung für Internat. Recht; Schweiz. Gesellschaft für Aussenpolitik; Schweiz. Gesellschaft für Luftrecht; Schneiz. Vereinigung für Politische Wissenschaft. *Publications:* Zwischenstaatl, Abgrenzung der Wehrplicht (1955); Rechtliche Probleme des Raumflugs (1958); Die Schweiz. und die Internat. Schiedsgerichtsbarkeit (1960); Die Guten Dienste der Schweiz (1963); Aussenwirtschaftsbeziehungen Gegenuberden Staatshandelsländern (1975). *Clubs:* International Club, Washington, D.C. *Address:* Embassy of Switzerland, 2900 Cathedral Avenue, N.W., Washington, D.C. 20008, U.S.A.

**PROCHNOW, Herbert Victor.** American banker. *Educ.* University of Wisconsin (BA, MA): Northwestern University (PhD). *M.* Laura Virginia Stinson. *S.* Herbert Victor. *Career:* Formerly Assistant Professor, Indiana University; Advertising Manager, Union Trust Company, Chicago; formerly Lecturer at Loyola University and Northwestern Universities, Chicago; Secretary, Federal Advisory Council since 1945; Pres., Bankers Club of Chicago 1952; Chicago Assn. of Commerce and Industry 1964–66; Chicago Council Foreign Relations 1966–68; Treasurer National 4-H 1962–69. Director, summer Graduate School of Banking, University of Wisconsin, Madison, Wisconsin since 1945; First National Bank of Chicago, Asst. Cashier 1933; Asst. Vice-Pres. 1936; Vice-Pres. 1947; Exec. Vice-Pres. 1960; Pres. 1962–68; Dir. 1960–68; Hon. Dir. 1968–73; Financial Columnist, Chicago Tribune 1968–70; Deputy Under-Secretary of State for Economic Affairs, 1955–56; Alternate Governor for the U.S. of the International Bank and I.M.F., 1955–56; member, U.S. Delegate to Colombo Conf., Singapore 1955; and to the Organization for Economic Cooperation, and Development, Paris 1956; Chmn., U.S. Deleg., General Agreement on Tariffs and Trade, Geneva, 1956. *Awards:* Hon LLD, Ripon Coll., Ripon Wisconsin, 1950, Univ. of Wisconsin 1956, Northwestern Univ. 1963, Lake Forest Coll., 1964, Thiel Coll. 1965, Monmouth Coll. 1965; Univ. North Dakota 1966; DLett, Millikin Univ. 1952; Ayres Leadership Award; Commander's Cross Order of Merit, Federal Republic of Germany; Cmdr., Order of Vasa, Royal Government of Sweden; Business Statesmanship Award, Harvard Business School Assn., Chicago; Silver Plaque, Highest Award, Nat. Conference of Christians & Jews. *Publications:* (Co-author) The Next Century is America's; Practical Bank Credit; The Public Speaker's Treasure Chest; Great Stories from Great Lives; Meditations on the Ten Commandments; The Toastmaster's Handbook; Term Loans and Theories of Bank Liquidity; The Successful Speaker's Handbook; Meditations on the Beatitudes; 1001 Ways to Improve your Conversation and Speeches; Speaker's Treasury for Sunday School Teachers; The New Guide for Toastmasters and Speakers; Determining the Business Outlook; Speaker's Handbook of Epigrams and Witticisms; American Financial Institutions (Editor); The Federal Reserve System (Editor); Meditations on the Lord's Prayer; A Family Treasury of Inspiration and Faith; The New Speaker's Treasury of Wit and Wisdom; The Complete Toastmaster; A Treasury of Stories, Illustrations, Epigrams & Quotations for Ministers and Teachers; A Dictionary of Wit, Wisdom, and Satire; World Economic Problems and Policies (Editor); The Speaker's Treasury of Stories for all Occasions; Speaker's Book of Illustrations; A Speaker's Treasury; 1000 Quips, Stories & Illustrations; The Eurodollar; (with Herbert V. Prochnow Jr.) A Treasury of Humorous Quotations; The Changing World of Banking. *Address:* 2950 Harrison Street, Evanston, Ill., U.S.A.; and *office* One First National Plaza, Chicago, Ill., U.S.A. 60670.

**PROCTOR, Sir Philip Dennis,** KCB. *B.* 1905. *Educ.* Harrow and King's Coll., Cambridge (MA). *M.* (1) 1936, Dorothy Varda, and (2) 1953, Barbara née Adam. *S.* 2. *Dau.* 1. *Career:* Entered Civil Service 1929; served in H.M. Treasury 1930–50; resigned from Civil Service 1950; joined firm of A. P. Møller, Copenhagen, becoming Man. Dir. of the Maersk Co. Ltd. 1951–1953; re-entered the Civil Service as Dep. Secy., Ministry of Transport and Civil Aviation 1953. Director, Williams Hudson Ltd. 1966–71; Perm. Secretary, Ministry of Power 1958–65; Chairman of Trustees, Tate Gallery 1953–59. Hon. Fellow King's College, Cambridge, 1968. *Publications:* Hannibal's March in History; The Autobiography of G. Lewis Dickinson. *Address:* 43 Canonbury Square, London, N.1.

**PROUVOST, Jean.** French administrateur. Anonyme Lainiere de Roulaix, Prouvost Mazurel. *B.* 1885. *Educ.* Beaumont College, Old Windsor (Great Britain). *M.* 1905, Germaine Lefebvre. *S.* Jacques *(Dec.)*. *Career:* Dir.-General Paris-Midi, Paris-Soir and Match, 1932–39; Minister of Information, 1940; Pres.Dir.-Gen. and Editor-in-Chief, Paris-Match and Marie Claire (1949), La Maison de Marie Claire (1967), Parents (1969), Télé 7 Jours (1960). General Administrator, Radio-Télé-Luxembourg (1966); Pres. Dir. Gen. de la Société du FIGARO; La Sté. Nouville d'Information et Publicité; Editions Robert Laffont. Mayor of Yvoy-Le-Marron, 1951. *Clubs:* Safari (Mt. Kenya); Automobile (Paris). *Address:* 216 rue de Rivoli, Paris; and *office* 51 rue Pierre Charron, Paris 8, France.

**PROXMIRE, William.** American politician. *B.* 1915. *Educ.* Yale & Harvard Univs. (MA). *Career:* U.S. Army Intelligence Service 1941–46; State Assemblyman for Wisconsin 1951–52; Democratic Senator from Wisconsin since 1957. Chmn., Senate Banking Cttee. 1975. *Address:* Senate Office Building, Washington, D.C. 20510, U.S.A.

**PRYKE, Graham Ernest,** AASA, FEAA, FAIM, AIPM, JP. Australian executive. *B.* 1920. *Educ.* Stott's and Muirden Colls. *M.* 1943, Marjorie C. Casey. *S.* Christopher. *Dau.* Jennifer. *Career:* Industrial Officer, State Cttee. of Overseas and Interstate Shipping Companies 1943–52; Industrial Director and Chief Industrial Advocate of the South Australian Employers' Federation, 1952–71; Lect. Industrial Law and Relations; Employers' delegation adviser I.L.O., Geneva 1955 and 1965; Commissioner, Industrial Commission, South Australia since 1972. President: Aust. Paraplegic & Quadriplegic Council; Paraplegic Assn. of S.A.; Aust. Sports Council for the Handicapped. *Publications:* Automation and You; Industrial Negotiations Abroad and our Pattern; Handbook to Workmen's Compensation, S.A. *Member:* Rotary. *Address: office* 33 King William Street, Adelaide, S.A. 5000, Australia.

**PUGH, Sir Idwal Vaughan,** KCB. British. *B.* 1918. *Educ.* St. John's College, Oxford (MA). *M.* 1946, Mair Lewis. *S.* David *Dau.* Elinor. *Career:* Civil Air Attaché, British Embassy, Washington, 1957–59; Under Secy. Ministry of Transport & Ministry of Housing & Local Government, 1959–66; Dep. Secy. Ministry of Housing & Local Government 1966–69. Permanent Under Secretary of State, Welsh Office 1969–71; Second permanent Sec. Dept. of the Environment 1971–76; Parly. Commissioner for Administration, Health Service Commissioner since 1976. *Club:* Brooks's. *Address:* 81 Raleigh House, Dolphin Square, London S.W.1; & Nant-y-Garreg, Bontddu, Gwynedd.

**PUMPHREY, Sir (John) Laurence,** KCMG. British diplomat (Ret'd.). *B.* 1916. *Educ.* Winchester College and New College, Oxford (First Class Hon Literae Humaniores). *N.* 1945, Jean Buchanan-Riddell. *S.* Matthew, Charles, Jonathan and James. *Dau.* Laura. *Career:* Formerly High Commissioner, Lusaka; Ambassador to Islamabad. *Address:* Caistron, Thropton, Morpeth, Northumberland.

**PUNGAN, Vasile.** *B.* 1926. *Educ.* Doctor in Econ. Sciences and Univ. Prof. *M.* 1951. *Dau.* 1. *Career:* Dean of Faculty, Agronomical Institute 'Nicolae Balcescu', Bucharest 1954; General Director, Ministry of Agriculture & Forestry 1955–58; Counsellor, Rumanian Embassy, Washington 1959–62; Director, Member, Foreign Ministry College 1963–66. Ambassador of the Socialist Republic of Rumania to the Court of St. James's 1966–72; Counsellor to the Pres. of the Socialist Rep. of Romania on Economic Affairs since 1973. Alternate Member Central Cttee., Rumanian Communist Party, 1969, Member 1972—. *Awards:* Order of Star of the Republic; Order of Labour; Order Tudor Vladimirescu. *Address:* c/o State Council, Bucharest, Romania.

**PURCELL, Robert William.** *B.* 1911. Business Consultant. *Educ.* Cornell Univ. (AB, LLB). *M.* 1939, Hazel Becker. *Career:* Vice-Pres. Dir. Vice-Chairman, Allegheny Corporation 1945–53; General Counsel, Vice-President, Director, C. & O. Railway 1946–53; Chmn. of Board, Pathe Industries Inc. 1945–50; Vice-Pres.-Dir., White Sulphur Springs Co. 1946–53; Dir., Cleveland Cliffs Iron Co. 1946–53; Chmn. of Bd., Investors Diversified Services Inc., Minneapolis, Minn. 1953–57; Director: The Investors Group; International Basic Economy Corp.; Bendix Corp., Seaboard World Airlines, International Minerals, and Chemical Corp.; S. S. Kresge Co.; C.I.T. Financial Corp., Caneel Bay Plantation Inc.; Mauna Kea Beach Hotel Corp.; National Bank of North America; Rockefeller Center Inc.; Chmn. Board of Trustees, Cornell Univ. Member, Board of Trustees, Cornell University. Chairman, Exec. Cttee., International House. Mem.

Bd. of Governors, New York Hosp. Dir. Basic Resources Intern. SA 3. Dir. The Pittston Co.; Bus Conslt. Rockefeller Family & Assocs. *Member:* Psi Upsilon. *Clubs:* University, Cornell (N.Y.C.); New York Yacht. *Address:* 765 Park Avenue, New York City 10021; and *office* 30 Rockefeller Plaza, New York City 10020, U.S.A.

**PURDY, Ken William.** American writer and editor; free-lance writer. *B.* 1913. *Educ.* Univ. of Wisconsin (ex-1935). *M.* 1946, Lucille Grossman von Urff. *S.* Geoffrey Hale. *Dau.* Tabitha Maria. *Career:* Editor, The Free Press, Oshkosh, Wis. 1935; Associate Editor, Radio Guide 1936–37; Managing Editor, Radio Digest 1939; Assoc. Editor, Click 1938, and Look 1939–41; Editor-in-Chief, Victory 1941–45; Parade 1946–49, True 1949–54, and Argosy 1954–55. *Publications:* (books) Kings of the Road (1952); Bright Wheels Rolling (1954); Wonderful World of the Automobile (1960); All But My Life (with Stirling Moss (1963); (magazines) Atlantic Monthly, Harper's, Esquire, Look, MacLean's, Saturday Review, Saturday Evening Post, The Motor, The New York Times Magazine, Town & Country, Vogue, etc. *Member:* Society of Magazine Writers; The Guild of Motoring Writers (England). *Clubs:* The Century Association (N.Y.C.); Bugatti Owners, Vintage Sports Car (both in England); Delta Kappa Epsilon. *Address:* The Steering Wheel, Curzon Street, London, W.1.

**PURSGLOVE, Joseph, Jr.** American engineer consultant. *B.* 1909. *Educ.* Cornell Univ. (CE 1930). *M.* (1) 1931, Josephine Knapp Lester (*div.* Apr. 1961). *S.* Paul David. *M.* (2) 1961, Mrs. Prescott Smith, widow. *Career:* Former Dir., Pitt-Consol Chemical Co., Atomic Power Development Associates Inc. Detroit). Vice-President (Chemicals), Consolidation Coal Co. to 1968. President, Pitt-Consol Chemical Co. to 1968–70; Trustee (Director) St. Joseph Lead Co., New York until 1971; Consultant on all matters pertaining to coal since 1968. *Address:* R.D. 1, Country Club Road, Sewickley, Pa. 15143, U.S.A.

**PURVIS, Arthur Blaikie.** Canadian financier. *B.* 1924. *Educ.* McGill Univ. (BA 1949) and Harvard Business School (MBA 1951). *M.* 1951, Margaret Mary Wright. *S,* Michael, Christopher and Audrew. *Dau.* Lois Mary. *Career:* Lieut., Scots Guards 1943–46. Assistant Vice-President and Secretary (1956—), Vice-Pres. 1963—, Managing Director 1968—, Pres. 1972—; Calvin Bullock Ltd., Montreal; Secretary, 1956—, Vice-President 1968—, Canadian Investment Fund Ltd.; Chmn. & Pres. Acrofund Ltd., Montreal; Asst. Secy., Canadian Fund Inc., New York City, 1952—, Vice-President since 1969. Governor & Past Chmn. Investment Funds Inst. of Canada. *Club:* University (Montreal). *Address:* 1745 Cedar Avenue, Montreal; and *office* C-I-L House, Montreal H3B 1X1, Canada.

**PUTMAN CRAMER, Pieter Veecken.** Netherlands Diplomat. *B.* 1913. *Educ.* Univ. of Leiden—Master Degree in Law; Univ. of Geneva; Institut des Hautes Etudes, Geneva. *M.* 1947, Esther Elizabeth Keller. *S.* 2. *Daus.* 2. *Career:* 1st Lieutenant, Netherlands Army 1944–46; 2nd Sec. of Embassy Bogota 1946–48; 2nd Sec. of Embassy, Canberra 1949–52; 1st Sec. of Embassy, Ottawa 1952–54, & Belgrade 1954–57; Councellor of Embassy, Stockholm 1958–64; Ambassador at Addis Ababa 1965–69, Bucharest 1970–74, & Copenhagen since 1975. *Decorations:* Knight, Order of the Netherlands Lion; Officer, Orange-Nassau; Commander, Polar Star of Sweden; Grand Officer, Order of Merit of Luxembourg; Grand Cross, Order of Dannebrog of Denmark; Grand Cross, Star of Honour of Ethiopia; Grand Cross, Tudor Vladimirescu of Rumania. *Address:* Royal Netherlands Embassy, Amaliegade 42, 1256 Copenhagen K, Denmark.

**PUTNAM, Carleton.** American air line executive and author. *B.* 19 Dec. 1901. *Educ.* Princeton University (BS); Columbia University (LLB). *M.* (2) 1944, Lucy Chapman (*div.* 1956). *M.* (3) 1956, Esther Willcox (Auchincloss). *Career:* Adviser, U.S. Delegation to International Civil Aviation Conference, Chicago 1944; Founder and President of Chicago and Southern Air Line 1933–48, Chairman of the Board 1948–53; Chairman of Board, Delta Air Line 1953–54; at present Director, Delta Air Lines. *Publications:* High Journey, a decade in the Pilgrimage of an Air Line Pioneer; Theodore Roosevelt—The Formative Years; Race and Reason: a Yankee View; Race and Reality; a Search for Solutions. *Address:* 1465 Kirby Road, McLean, Va., U.S.A.

**PUTNAM, David Frederick.** BS. American. *B.* 1914. *Educ.* Phillips Andover Dartmouth Coll. (BA). *M.* 1938, Rosamond C. Page. *S.* 4. *Daus.* 2. *Career:* Chmn. Bd. and Dir. Markem Corp.; Milford Astor Ltd.; Dir. Waters Associates Inc. Milford; The First National Bank of Boston; Ludlow Corp. Pres. and Dir. Milford-Astor Ltd. *Member:* Inst. Directors, London. *Clubs:* University, New York; Algonquin, Boston. *Address:* 150 Court Street, Keene, N.H. 03431, U.S.A.

**PUYAT, Hon. Gil J.** Filipino banker, statesman, civic leader, educator, parliamentarian & nationalist. *B.* 1907. *Educ.* BS (Bus. Admin.), Univ. of the Philippines 1929. *M.* Eugenia Guidote. *S.* 5. *Daus.* 2. *Career:* Prof. of Economics, Univ. of Philippines; Dean, Coll. of Business Admin.; elected to Phil. Senate (re-elected 3 times); elected Pres. of the Senate 1967 up to declaration of Martial Law; Chmn. several Senate cttees., mem. several cttees.; Chmn. Technical Panel to study proposals for revision of the Trade Agreement with the U.S., 1954; Vice-Chmn. Economic Mission to the U.S. that negotiated the Laurel-Langley Agreement, 1954; Presiding Officer, National Economic Council 1956; Chmn. Joint Legislative-Executive Tax Comm. 1959–61; SEATO Lecturer in Pakistan & Thailand 1959; Dir., Phil. National Bank 1945–49. First Vice-Pres. Rotary International 1947–48; Pres. Manila Rotary 1940, re-elected 1945; elected Rotary District Governor 1946; Pres. Chamber of Commerce of the Philippines 1945–49. *Awards:* Dr. of Laws (h.c.) Angeles Univ. 1976; Dr. of Education (h.c.) Phil. Normal Coll. 1968; awarded the Diplomatic Service Merit Changhwa Merit, Highest Korean Decoration for Diplomacy by Pres. Park Chung Hee 1971; Dr. of Economics (h.c.) Kyung Hee Univ. Seoul, Korea 1971; nominated Regent's Lecturer, Center for South & Southeast Asian Studies, Univ. of California, Berkeley 1972; several awards from Univ. of the Philippines as Outstanding Alumnus; award for "Outstanding service as one of the founders, first President, & first fund campaign Chairman", Community Chest 1953; Presidential Award for Devoted Service as a pioneer in the Community Chest, 1959; Presidential Award for Economic Leadership 1966. Pres. & Chmn. of the Bd., The Manila Banking Corp.; Chmn. of the Bd., Loyola Group of Companies, Manila Bankers Life Insurance Corp., Phil. Century Resorts Inc., Group Developers Inc.; Pres. Batulao Vil. Club; Pres. & Chmn. of the Bd., Manila Mngt. & Invt. Assoc. Inc.; Chmn. Bd. of Trustees, Small Business Development Foundation Inc.; Foundation for Youth Development in the Philippines. *Address:* # 6 D. Tuazon, Quezon City, Philippines; and *office* 10th Floor. Manilabank Building, Ayala Avenue, Makati, Metro Manila, Philippines.

**PYLE, Howard Carter.** American petroleum engineer. *B.* 1904. *Educ.* Univ. of California (BS 1926); and University of Southern California (MS 1939; PE (Professional Degree of Petroleum Engineering) 1941); Hon. DEng, Colorado School of Mines 1959. *M.* 1930, Linda Elfrida Klamroth. *S.* Carter. *Dau.* Jane (Jones). *Career:* Geological exploration in Venezuela, California and Canada 1927–32, Petroleum Engineer in California 1932–42; Chief Production Engineer 1939–42, Union Oil Co. of California; Petroleum Officer on Gen. Eisenhower's Staff 1943–45, Lieut.-Col. 1944–45, U.S. Army; Vice-Pres., Bank of America, Los Angeles 1945–47; Pres., Continental Consolidated Corp., Los Angeles (oil producers) 1947–50; Consulting Petroleum Engineer, Los Angeles 1950–51; President, Director and Chairman of Executive Committee, Monterey Oil Co. 1951–61; Director, Reserve Oil & Gas Co. 1962—, Santa Fé International Corp. 1964–74. Partner, Lacal Petroleum Co. 1961–68. *Publications:* numerous technical articles relating to oil production published in technical journals. *Member:* Sigma Chi; Theta Tau; Sigma Xi; Hon. Member, Pi Epsilon Tau. *Clubs:* California, Pauma Valley Country, San Diego Country. *Address:* Pauma Valley, Calif. 92061, U.S.A.

**PYM, The Rt. Hon. Francis Leslie,** MC, DL, MP. British politician *B.* 1922. *Educ.* Eton Coll. and Magdalene Coll. Cambridge. *M.* 1949, Valerie Fortune Daglish. *S.* 2. *Daus.* 2. *Career:* Parly. Private Secy. Mr. R. Maudling MP, 1962; Asst. Whip, 1962–64; Opposition Whip, 1964–67; Opposition Deputy Chief Whip, 1967–70; Parly. Secy. to the Treasury & Govt. Chief Whip 1970–73; Secy. State N. Ireland 1973–74; Opposition spokesman on Agriculture 1974–75 and 1976, on Devolution & House of Commons Affairs since 1976. *Clubs:* Bucks; Cavalry. *Address:* Everton Park, Sandy. Bedfordshire.

**PYM, Lisle Angelo.** British petroleum engineer. *B.* 1900. *Educ.* Marist Brothers, Western Australia; University of Western Australia; BE; BSc (Eng.); AMIE (Aust.); AMIPT. *M.* 1935, Elizabeth Margaret Drake-Brockman. *S.* 1. *Dau.* 1. *Career:* Chief Petroleum Engineer, British Petroleum Co.

1930; Deputy Fields Manager, B.P. Co. 1946; General Mgr., Australasian Petroleum Co. 1948–61. Director: Frome Broken Hill Pty., Ltd. since 1949; Oil Search Ltd., Australasian Petroleum Co., Island Exploration Co. 1961—. *Publications:* The Measurement of Gas-Oil Ratios and Saturation Pressures and their Interpretation (Proceedings of World Petroleum Congress) 1933; Bottom Hole Pressure Measurement (Science of Petroleum) 1938; Oil Exploration in Papua (Chemical Engineering & Mining Review) 1955. *Address:* 27 Waldemar Road, Heidelberg, Melbourne, Australia.

# Q

**QUASHA, William Howard.** American lawyer. *B.* 1912. *Educ.* New York Univ., BSME, MA; St. John's Univ. N.Y., LLB. *M.* 1946, Phyllis Grant. *S.* 3. *Career:* New York Bar 1936; Philippine Bar 1945, U.S. Supreme Court 1947; Practised law in N.Y.C. 1936–42; Practiced law in Philippines since 1946; Member ICC World Congress Istanbul (1969), Vienna (1971), CAFEA-ICC World Congress Bangkok (1970), World Peace Through Law Congress Washington D.C. (1967) and Bangkok (1969); Sen. Member Quasha, Asperilla, Ancheta, Valmonte, Peña & Marcos; Dir. Marcopper Mining Corp. *Member:* Ramon Magsaysay Memorial Soc., Am. Chamber of Commerce (Phils.); Am. Soc. International Law; Intern. Chamber of Commerce; Dept. Comdr. American Legion, YMCA and Masonic Hospital for Crippled Children; Bd. of Trustees, Jose P. Laurel Memorial Foundation; Philippine Constitution Assn.; Pres., St. Luke's Hospital Inc.; Mem., Integrated Bar of the Philippines; Past Pres. & Charter Mem., Propeller Club of the Philippines; Navy League U.S. (Judge Advocate & Charter Mem.); Boy Scouts Philippines, Hon. Life-Pres., Nat. Exec. Bd., Vice-Pres.-Treas. *Awards:* Bronze Star, Phil. Legion of Honour (Officer rank); Sp. award and citation City of Manila; Knight Cmdr. Knights of Rizal; Medals and awards World War II; Several Boy Scout Awards from Philippines, America and Austria. *Clubs:* National Sojourners; Manila Rotary; Nat. Lawyers (Washington D.C.); Am. Nat. Sydney, Australia; Creek L.I., Univ. N.Y.; Army and Navy, Manila; Manila Polo; Manila Golf and Country. *Address:* 22 Molave Place, P.O. Box 210 MCC, Makati, Rizal, Philippines; and *office* Don Pablo Bldg., 114 Amorsolo St., Makati, Rizal, Philippines.

**QUELLMALZ, Frederick.** Association executive and editor. *B.* 1912. *Educ.* Princeton Univ. (AB 1934) and Woodrow Wilson School of Public and International Affairs. *M.* 1942, Jayne Elysabeth Osten. *Daus.* Barbara Jayne, Carol Grant, Patricia Ellen, Sandra Lee and Tracy Louise. *Career:* Kentucky Colonel, 1934; Special Asst. Pepperell Mfg. Co. 1934–40; Dir., Photographic Activities, New York World's Fair 1940; Asst. to Chief Engineer, Naval Ordnance Plant, York, Pa. 1942–45; Exec. Secy., Photographic Society of America. 1940–42; Editor, PSA Journal 1939–52; Exec. Vice-Pres., Professional Photographers of America, Des Plaines, Ill. 1953–74; Editor, Publisher, Prof. Photographers Magazine 1953–74; Exec. Dir., Photo Art & Sci. Foundation Inc., Des Plaines 1972—, Sec. 1965—. Hon. Master of Photography; Life Member, Royal Photographic Socy. of Great Britain; Hon. Member and Assoc., Photographic Society of America. *Member:* Natl. Assn. Exhibit Managers (Dir. 1959); Amer. Socy. of Association Executives, Dir. 1963–66; Wisconsin Socy. of Assn. Executives, (Pres. 1965); Amer. Socy. Photographers; Natl. Press Photographers Assn.; Winona School of Photography Board of Trustees (Secy.). Republican. *Clubs:* Princeton (Chicago); York Camera (Hon.). Hon. Bachelor of Professional Arts. Brooks Inst., 1968. Kappa Alpha Mu. Fellow, Royal Society of Arts. *Address:* 111 Stratford Road, Des Plaines, Ill., 60016, U.S.A.

**QUICK, Joseph Haslam.** American industrialist. *B.* 1909. *Educ.* Pennsylvania State College, and University of Pennsylvania (commercial courses). *M.* 1949, Salome (Jacques) Swift. *Daus.* Patricia Nina and Victoria Stephanie (*Dec.*). Remarried Winifred K. Humphrey. *S.* Kenneth McKay. *Daus.* Sally Jayne aud Susan Knight. *Career:* Supervisor time study and methods, Philco Radio Corp., Philadelphia 1932–38; originated and developed Work-Factor System and Mento Factor System, predetermined time systems, 1934; Asst. Chief Industrial Engineer, Radio Corporation of America (Camden, N.J.) 1938–46; Assistant to President, Milton Bradley Co. (Springfield. Mass,) 1946; organized Work-Factor Co., industrial management consultants 1947 (remains as Partner 1947–62); Exec. Vice-President, Colonial Radio Corp. 1949–51; Pres., Gen. Mgr., Harrington & Richardson Inc. (Worcester, Mass.) 1951–54; Dir., Natl. Co. (Malden, Mass.) 1953; Pres. and Gen. Mgr., 1954–62; Vice-Pres. and Treas., Wofac Corp. (now Wofac Co., a Division of Science Management Corp.); Sen. Vice-Pres., Treasurer, W.F. Company & Science Management Corp. 1963–71; Chmn. Bd. 1971–73; Cooperator, Westboro Savings Bank 1976. *Member:* Inst. of Electronic and Electrical Senior Engineers; Amer. Inst. of Industrial Engineers. *Award:* Gilbreth Medal of 1971. *Publications:* articles on motion time standards for labour measurement, business systems, section in Industrial Engineering Handbook, McGraw-Hill (1962). Co-author of Work-Factor Time Standards (McGraw-Hill 1962); Brief Work-factor Manual; Mento Factor Manual; Detailed Work-factor Manual (Science Management Corp.). *Address:* Fellowship Road, Moorestown, N.J., 08057; and (home) West Main Street, Westboro, Mass. 01581, U.S.A.

**QUICK-SMITH, G. W.** CBE. British Barrister-at-Law. *B.* 23 Aug. 1905. *Educ.* London University (LLB); Chartered Secretary (FCIS). *M.* 1934, Ida Muriel Tinkler. *Career:* Deputy Chairman, National Freight Corporation 1968–71. Chief Exec., Transport Holding Co. 1962–71 (created under the Transport Acts, 1962–68); Director, various transport companies; held various positions in national & international organizations connected with road transport; Secretary of National Road Transport Federation 1935–48; Secretary and Legal Adviser to Road Haulage Executive (British Road Services) 1948–53; member of Board of Management of British Road Services 1953–59; Adviser (Special Projects), British Transport Commission, 1959–62; Past Vice-President Inst. of Transport. Liveryman of the City of London, Past Master, Worshipful Company of Carmen; Past Vice-Pres. and Fellow Chartered Inst. of Transport (FCIT); Transport Tribunal since 1973. *Address:* 6 Martello Towers, Ravine Road, Canford Cliffs, Poole, Dorset.

**QUIJANO, Raul Alberto.** Argentine Diplomat. *B.* 1923. *Educ.* Colegio de la Salle, Buenos Aires; Univ. of Buenos Aires, Faculty of Law—Lawyer, Dr. of Law. *M.* 1963, Mercedes Santander Raddatz. *Dau.* 1. *Career:* Secretary of Embassy—UN, India, Pakistan, South Africa 1947–58; Counsellor of Embassy—Foreign Office, Mission to UN 1959–62; Minister, Dep. Perm. Rep. to UN 1963–66; Ambassador, Dir.-Gen. of the Political Dept. 1967–69; Ambassador, Perm. Rep. to OAS, Washington 1969–74; Chmn., International Civil Service Commission, UN 1975–76; Minister of Foreign Affairs, Buenos Aires, Jan.–Apr. 1976; Rep. to Security Council & ECOSOC; Pres., Perm. Council of OAS 1972; Pres., International Civil Service Advisory Board 1974. *Decorations:* from many countries, incl. Chile, Italy, Japan, Brazil, Norway, Spain, Bolivia, etc. *Address:* 160 East 38th Street, Apt. 35E, New York, N.Y. 10016. U.S.A.; and *office*, United Nations, Room BR 1032, New York 1017, U.S.A.

**QUILLEN, James Henry.** *B.* 1916. *Educ.* Dobyns-Bennett High School, Kingsport, Tenn. *M.* 1952. Cecile Cox. *Career:* Elected member, minority floor leader twice nominated for Republican speaker, Tennessee House of Representatives; member, Tennessee Legislative Council. Delegate-at-large, Republican National Conventions of 1956, 1964, 1968, 1972 & 1976 from Tennessee. Hon. LLD, Steed College of Technology (Johnson City. Tenn.). Republican. U.S. Representative, 88th–95th Congresses, First District, Tennessee; Ranking Minority Member, Rules Cttee.; Standerds of Official Conduct Cttee. *Clubs:* Lions International; American Legion; VFW; Chamber of Commerce; SAR; Ridgefields Country.

*Address:* 1601 Fairidge Place, Kingsport, Tenn. 37664; and *office* Room 102, Cannon House Office Building, Washington, D.C. 20515, U.S.A.

**QUINLAN, William Allen.** American lawyer, trade association representative. *B.* 1909. *Educ.* University of Chicago (PhB 1932; JD 1933). *M.* (1) 1936, Grace Elizabeth Anderson (*dec'd.* 1967). *S.* William Allen, Jr., John Raymond and Michael Andrew. (2) Elizabeth Mary Welty (née Hayes). *Step Daus.* Patricia Mary Welty, Mrs. D. Zahn. *Career:* Member of staff, National Bakers Council (NRA Code Authority for the baking industry) 1933–35; member of staff (editor, public and industrial relations, government affairs, general counsel), American Bakers Association 1935–43. Member of Bar of Illinois (since 1936), District of Columbia (1942), and Maryland (1957); in private practice of Law since 1943; General Counsel, Associated Retail Bakers of America 1943—; Special Counsel, Private Truck Council of America, Inc. 1943—; General Counsel, Nat. Candy Wholesalers Assn. Inc. 1945—; *Member:* County Board of Appeals for Montgomery County Md. 1953–60. Republican. *Address:* 3045 Riva Road, Annapolis, Maryland 21401, U.S.A.

**QUINN, William J.** *B.* 1911. *Educ.* St. Thomas Coll., St. Paul, Minn. (BA 1933); Univ. of Minneapolis (LLB 1935; Hon LLD 1959). *M.* 1942, Floy I. Heinen. *S.* William J., George M., Patrick J., and Richard T. *Daus.* Floy, Maureen, Michaele and Shannon. *Career:* Practised Law in St. Paul 1935–37; Asst. U.S. Attorney, Dist. of Minnesota 1937–40; Attorney Soo Line R.R., Minneapolis, 1940–42; Special Agent, Federal Bureau of Investigation (F.B.I.) 1942–45. Asst. Commerce Counsel 1945; Commerce Counsel 1945–52; Asst. Gen. Counsel 1952; General Counsel 1952–53; Vice-Pres. and General Counsel 1953–54 (all with Soo Line R.R.); General Solicitor C.M.St. P. & P.R.R., 1954–55; Vice-Pres. and General Counsel 1955–58, Pres. 1958–66; Pres. C.B. & Q.R.R., 1966–70. Chairman of Board & Chief Executive Officer, Chicago, Milwaukee St. Paul & Pacific R.R. Co., 1970—.; Chmn. Bd. and Pres. Chicago Milwaukee Corp. since 1972. *Clubs:* Commercial; The Metropolitan; The Chicago, Mid-Amer., Skokie Country (Glencoe, Ill.). *Address:* 1201 Chatfield Road, Winnetka, Ill. 60093; and *office* 874 Union Station Building, Chicago 60606, Ill., U.S.A.

**QUINTANILLA, Luis.** Mexican diplomat. *B.* 22 Nov. 1900. *M.* (1) 1923. *S.* Luis. *Dau.* Jane (de Debler). (2) 1949, Sara Cordero. *S.* Ian and Leonardo. *Career:* Entered Foreign Service 1922; Amb. Ex. and Plen. to U.S.S.R. 1942, Columbia 1945, Organization of American States, Washington 1945; Delegate, San Francisco Conf. 1945, United Nations Second Assembly 1947; Chmn., Inter-American Peace Commn. 1948, Fact Finding committee in Central American 1948, Council of Organisation of American States, Washington 1949; Professor of Political Science, George Washington University. Professor of Political Science and International Law, National University of Mexico. Delegate, 9th Inter-American Conf., Bogotà 1948 and the 10th, Caracas 1954: Delegate, 4th meeting, Council of Foreign Ministers, Washington, 1951; Acting Chief Delegate, 7th General Assembly, U.N. 1952. Consultant to the Center for the Study of Democratic Institutions, Santa Barbara, Calif. Medalla al Mérito Militar; Grand Cross of Boyaca (Colombia), Carlos Manuel de Céspedes (Cuba), Miranda (Venezuela), Cruzeiro do Sul (Brazil), Orden de Francisco Morazan (Honduras), Orden de la Liberación de España (Spain); Honneur et Mérite (Haiti); Al Mérito (Argentina), Condor de los Andes (Bolivia), Al Mérito (Chile), Lanuza (Cuba), Juan Pablo Duarte (Dominican Republic), Ruben Dario (Nicaragua), Vasco Nuñez de Balboa (Panama), Al Mérito (Paraguay), Sol (Peru); Grand Officer Orden de Quetzal (Guatemala), Orden al Mérito (Ecuador); Officer, Order of Golden Sheaf (China); Commandeur de la Légion d'Honneur; Official de la Orden Instruction Publique (France). *Publications:* A Latin American Speaks; Pan Americanism and Democracy (1952); Democracia y Panamericanismo (1952); Bergsonismo y Politica; (in collaboration) The Caribbean; Contemporary Trends (1953); Control of Foreign Relations (1957); The Greatness of Woodrow Wilson (with preface by Pres. Eisenhower) (1957). Pintura Moderna (1968). *Address:* Reyna 199, San Angel Inn, Mexico 20, Mexico, D.F.

**QUIRKE, Arthur Gerrard,** MA, LLB. Executive Director, The National Bank of Ireland Ltd., Dublin. *B.* 1909. *Educ.* Ampleforth College and Dublin University; MA; LLB; TCD. *M.* 1942, Brenda Moira Scroope. *S.* 1. Assistant Solicitor, The National Bank Ltd. 1934–54. *Clubs:* Kildare Street, University (Dublin). *Address: office* The National Bank of Ireland Ltd., College Green, Dublin 2, Ireland.

**QUITMAN, Harold Channing.** *B.* 1918. *Educ.* Malvern College. *M.* 1950. J. Jacqueline Lawrence. *S.* Jeremy Roland. *Dau.* Annabel Susan Maude. *Career:* Served in World War II (Major) 1939–45. Fellow, Royal Society of Arts; Court of Assistants, Haberdashers' Company; Veteran, Hon. Artillery Company. Presidential Council, City of Westminster Chamber of Commerce 1957 (Chmn. 1965–67). Executive Cttee.—London Tourist Board—General Commissioner of Taxes. Chairman and Managing Director, Aquis Securities Ltd. and subsidiary companies. *Clubs:* Hurlingham; M.C.C. *Address:* Rookley Farmhouse, Upper Somborne, Hants. SO20 6QX.

# R

**R. De LUZURIAGA, Claudio, Jr.** Filipino. *B.* 1931. *Educ* Manila (LLB); Columbia Univ., N.Y. *M.* 1955, Violeta G. Saguin. *Daus.* 3. *Career:* Pres. Bd. member, Victorias Milling Co. Inc.; Pres. Dir. Victorias Insurance Factors Corp. Dir.: Pacific Airways Corp.; V-M-C Rural Electric Service Co-operative, V-M-C Sugar-Plants Co-op. Marketing Assn. Inc.; V-M-C Sugarcane Planters Co-op. Assn. Inc. Rural Bank of Dipolog Inc.; Chmn. of the Bd., Prince Investment Corp., Insular Sugar Refining Corp.; Dir. & Pres., Sugar Prospects, Inc.; Dir. & Pres. Victorias Chemical Corp.; North Negros Marketing Corp.; Trustee & Vice-Pres. M. J. Ossorio Pension Foundation Inc.; Dir. Philippine Sugar Refiners' Inst. *Member:* Chmn., Financial Advisory Council, Diocese of Bacolod, Negros Occidental; Trustee, Philippine Sugar Assn.; Bd. of Trustees, Philippine Business for Social Progress. *Clubs:* Casino Espanol de Manila; Filipino; Baguio Golf & Country; Philippine Sugar Technologists; Vicmico Golf. *Address:* Vicmico Victorias, Negros Occidental, Philippines and *office* Vicmico, Negros Occ. 6037, Philippines.

**RAAB, Carl Philip Sven Hugo Ossian.** Swedish. *B.* 1901. *Educ.* Doctor of Law. *M.* 1932, Maj Zielfelt. *S.* Erik. *Dau.* Ingrid. *Career:* Attorney, Deputy Manager, Stockholms Garanti AB 1930–34; Deputy Manager, Manager, Deputy General Manager, Gotabanken Bank, Göteborg 1941–53; Managing Director 1954–64; Chmn. Board of Directors 1964; Chairman or Board Member of a number of Swedish companies. *Award:* Commander, 1st Class, Order of Vasa (Sweden). *Clubs:* Royal Bachelor's (Gothenburg); Overseas Bankers (London). *Address: office* Gotabanken Bank, Gothenburg, Sweden.

**RAADE, (Tauno) Uolevi.** MS. Engineering. BS.Econ. *B.* 5 July 1912. *Educ.* Institute of Technology, Helsinki; School of Economics, Turku. *M.* 1941, Toini Maria Charlotta Jäämeri. *S.* Olli. *Daus.* Kristiina, Maarit. *Career:* Dir. of Research Dept., State Aeroplane Factory 1937–39; Head of Purchasing Office, State Aeroplane Factory 1939–40; Engineer in Charge, Metallurgical Dept., Lokomo Oy, 1940–42; Head of Home Market Industry Bureau, Ministry of Commerce and Industry, 1942–44; Head of Industrial Dept., Ministry of Commerce and Industry 1944–55; Acting Managing Director, Finnair Oy, 1946; Vice-Chmn., Finnair Oy 1944—; Vice-Chairman, State Metal Works 1946–50; Chairman, Typpi Oy 1946–55. Vice-Chairman, Otanmäki Oy 1946–55; Chmn. Suo Oy 1947–55; Managing Director of Neste Oy the State Oil Refinery. Petrochemical and Shipping Company 1955—; Chmn. 1959; Chmn., Pekema Oy 1969–73, Vice-Chmn. 1974, Chmn. 1975—; Man. Dir., Neste Exploration Ltd. since 1972. *Member:* of the Royalty Committee of The Bank of Finland 1953–54; Member of Licence Committee 1953–55; Board Member of State Technical Research Institute 1953–

55; Member of the Executive Committee of the of The Board Confederation of Finnish Industries 1957—; Finnish Employers' General Group 1957—; Central Chemical Assn. 1960–65; Finnish Aeronautical Assn. 1963—; Ordinary & Hon. Mem. of the Acad. of Technical Sciences 1963—; Vice-Chmn. 1966–69, Chmn. 1970–73; Finnish Shipowners' Assn. 1968—; Council Inst. of Technology 1961—; Council, Helsinki School of Economics 1961—; Bd. Supervisors, Finnish Cultural Foundation 1963—; Kansallis-Osake-Pankki 1964—, mem. of the Inspection Cttee. 1976—; Tourism Development Fund 1965–72; Foundation Medical Sciences 1966—; Vice-Chmn. Urho Kekkonen's Vocational School Foundation 1970–75; Mem. of Board of Stymer Oy since 1970, Vice-Chmn. 1973–75; Council for Technical & Commercial Sciences, Higher Education 1971–73; Bd. World Wildlife Fund, Finnish Section 1972–75; Chmn., The Federation of Finnish Chemical Industry 1976—. *Address:* Neste Oy, Keilaniemi, 02150 Espoo 15, Finland.

**RABAEUS, Bengt.** Swedish Diplomat. *B.* 1917. *Educ.* Univ. of Uppsala, MA. *M.* Birgitta Svensson. *S.* 3. *Career:* Entered Foreign Service 1946, served Prague, Paris, Swedish delegation to UN, New York; Swedish del. to OEEC; Political Div., Foreign Office, Stockholm; Ambassador to Algeria 1963–66; Dep. Sec.-Gen. EFTA 1966–72, & Sec.-Gen. 1972–75; Dep. Perm. Under-Sec. of State since 1976. *Decorations:* Various Swedish & Foreign decorations. *Address:* Karlavägen 111, 115 26 Stockholm, Sweden; and *office* Box 16 121, 103 23 Stockholm, Sweden.

**RABIN, Yitzhak,** Israeli Politician. *B.* 1922. *Educ.* Kadoorie Agricultural School, Lower Galilee. *M.* Lea. *S.* 1. *Dau.* 1. *Career:* Army 1940–67 as Chief of General Staff, also Commander of Israel Defense Forces (Six Day War); Ambassador of Israel to Washington 1968–73; Jerusalem 1973–74; Minister of Labour 1974; Prime Minister of Israel 1974–77. *Address:* c/o The Knesset, Jerusalem, Israel.

**RADEBAUGH, William Henry.** American industrial public relations consultant, in TV, Radio and Motion Pictures. *B.* 1909. *Educ.* Ohio State University (Journalism Major). *M.* 1936, Marie Rose Herman. *S.* William H., Jr. (Dec.). and Patrick Walsh. Winner of 1945 Award of American Public Relations Association for Best Industrial Public Relations. *Career:* In charge of Food Publicity, The Great Atlantic & Pacific Tea Co. 1938–40; and Radio Publicity, National Association of Manufacturers 1940–41; Founder and Exec. Dir., South Jersey Manufacturers Assn., Oct. 1941–May 1952; Founder and Exec. Secy., South Jersey Industrial Safety Council, Oct. 1941–May 1952. Regular Panel Consultant to WCAU TV. 1949–52 with E.I. du Pont de Nemours & Co. Inc. 1952–74. *Member:* Public Relations Society of America; Radio & TV News Directors Assn. *Publications:* weekly newspaper column in Camden (N.J.) Courier-Post 1950–52; collaboration with wife on children's books, including The Fishy A-B-C; also illustrator of other works; Associate Editor of Journal of Industry & Finance, 1942; articles on labour relations and public relations; Contributing Editor 1971 *Delaware* Magazine; Motion Picture Productions; History of Du Pont Company; Geo. Washington Didn't Sleep Here, Product Safety. *Clubs:* Poor Richard; Pen & Pencil (both of Philadelphia). *Address:* Marshall Bridge Road, Box 99, R.D. No. 3, Kennett Square, Pa. 19348, U.S.A.

**RADJI, Parviz Camran.** Iranian Diplomat. *B.* 1936. *Educ.* Trinity Hall, Cambridge—MA (Econ.). *Career:* National Iranian Oil Co. 1959–62; Ministry of Foreign Affairs, Private Sec. to the Minister 1962–65; Prime Minister's Office, Private Sec., later Personal Asst. to the PM 1965–72; Special Adviser to the PM 1972–76; Amb. to the Court of St. James since 1976. *Address:* 26 Princes Gate, London SW7; and *office* 16 Princes Gate, London SW7.

**RADULESCU, Gheorghe.** DSc (Econ.). Romanian economist and politician. *B.* 1914. *Educ.* Acad. of Higher Commercial and Industrial Studies, Bucharest. *M.* 1938, Dorina. *S.* 1. *Career:* Member, Romanian C.P. 1933—; Gen. Secy., Deputy-Minister of Trade and Minister Home and Foreign Trade 1957–63; Member, Central Cttee. C.P. 1960—; Deputy-Chmn., Council of Ministers 1963—; Member Exec. Cttee., Central Cttee.. C.P. 1965; Perm. Presidium, Central Cttee. C.P. 1969–74; Deputy to Grand Nat. Assembly 1961—; Member, Acad. of Social and Political Sciences since 1970. *Publications:* Numerous Economic studies on Home and Foreign Trade. *Address:* Central Committee of the Romanian Communist Party, Bucharest, Romania.

**RAE, John,** FIM. Metallurgist and company director. *B.* 1913. *Educ.* Bromsgrove School. *M.* 1939, Hannah Heath. *S.* Andrew and John Douglas. *Dau.* Elizabeth Margaret. *Career:* Joined McKechnie Bros. Ltd., 1931, Dir. (1949); Chmn. Macdem (Pty.) Ltd.; Chmn. McKechnie Delta Holdings (Pty.) Ltd.; Eachairn Investment Co. (Pty.) Ltd.; Uitkyk. Plantations (Pty.) Ltd.; Maksal Tubes (Pty.) Ltd.; Dir., McKechnie Brothers Ltd., Widnes; Huletts Aluminium of S.A. Ltd.; Republic Aluminium Co. (Pty.) Ltd. *Address:* Brook House, 17 Fricker Road, Illovo, Johannesburg, South Africa.

**RAEDER, Johan Georg Alexius.** Norwegian diplomat. *B.* 23 April 1905. *Educ.* University of Oslo (Law). *M.* 1940, Gudrun Dorothea Martius. *S.* Peter Nicolay. *Dau.* Ingrid Elisabeth. *Career:* Entered Diplomatic Service 1928; Commercial Counsellor, Embassy, London 1940–45; Head, Economic Department, Foreign Ministry 1945–48; En. Ex. and Min. Plen. to Belgium and Luxembourg 1948–51; Head, Political Dept. Foreign Ministry 1951–53; En. Ex. and Min. Plen. to Spain 1953–57; Ambassador 1957–58; Secy.-General, Foreign Ministry 1958–65; Ambassador to Italy and Greece 1966: also to Malta, 1969. Grand Officer, Order of St. Olav; Grand Cross, Dannebrog (Denmark); North Star (Sweden); Crown of Belgium; Crown of Oak of Luxembourg; Isabel la Católica (Spain); Finnish Lion; Siamese White Elephant; Persian Sun and Lion; Republic (Tunisia); Aquila Azteca (Mexico); Merit (Austria); Flag (Yugoslavia); Merit (Italy); S. Silvestro (Vatican); Commandeur de la Légion d'Honneur. *Address:* c/o Ministry of Foreign Affairs, Oslo, Norway.

**RAFAEL, Gideon.** Israeli diplomat. *B.* 1913. *Educ.* Univ. Law and Economics. *M.* 1940, Nurit Weissberg. *S.* 1. *Dau.* 1. *Career:* Emigrated from France 1934; Member Kibbutz 1934–43; War Services, Haganah 1939–42; Jewish Agency, Political Dept. 1943; Nuremberg War Crimes Trial 1946; Member, Jewish Agency Comm., Anglo Amer. Comm. UN Special Comm. for Palestine 1946–47; Israel Perm. Del. to UN 1951–52, Alt. Rep. 1953, Rep. UN Gen. Assemblies, 1947–66; Counsellor, Middle East, UN Affairs, Min. for Affairs 1953–57; Ambassador, Belgium and Luxembourg 1957–60; European Econ. Comm. 1959; Deputy Dir. Gen. Ministry, Foreign Affairs 1960; Head, Israel Del. Int. Conf. Law of the Sea, Geneva 1960; Deputy Dir. Gen. Min. Foreign Affairs 1960–65; Perm. Rep. UN Geneva 1965–66; Special Ambassador, Adviser to Foreign Minister 1966–67; Perm. Rep. Israel to UN 1967; Dir. Gen. Min. For. Affairs 1967–71; Senior Adviser, Foreign Minister 1972; Head, Israel Del. to UNCTAD III 1972; Head, Del. Rep. most UN General Assemblies 1947–67; Ambassador to U.K. 1973–77, concurrently Israel's First Ambassador (non-resident) to Ireland 1975–77; Ambassador at Large & Senior Political Adviser, Foreign Ministry, Jerusalem since 1977. *Address:* Kiryath Yovel, Jerusalem, Israel.

**RAHIMTOOLA, Sir Fazal Ibrahim,** CIE, BA, JP. Honorary Consul-General for Thailand in Bombay. Ex. Honorary Magistrate. Economic Advisor to the Junagadh State. Director, Anmedabad Advance Mills, Ltd., Tata Power Co. Ltd., Tata Iron & Steel Co. Ltd., Bharat lines, Ltd. (Chmn.), The Swadeshi Mills, Ltd., New Swadeshi Sugar Mills Ltd., Dhrangadhra Chemical Works Ltd., Overseas Communications Service (Indian Govt.) and other companies. *B.* 21 Oct. 1895. *Educ.* St. Xavier's High School and Coll., Bombay; Bombay Univ. (BA); Poona Law Coll. (LLB). *M.* Jainabai. *S.* 3. *Daus.* 5. Member, Bombay Municipal Corp. 1919–30; Member, Advisory Cttee.: Bombay Development Department 1922; on liquor shops in Bombay City 1922; Government Securities Committee; Representative of Bombay, Munic. Corp. on B.B. and C.I. Railways Advisory Cncl. until 1930; member (Ind.) Central Legislative Assembly 1925–30; Haj Inquiry Cttee. 1929; Pres., Urdu Newspapers Assn.; member, Central Broadcasting Advisory Committee until 1930; Acting President, Indian Tariff Board 1932, President 1935; member (Ind.), Bombay Legislative Assembly 1937 and 1948; Chairman and member of many committees and boards during World War II; Indian Delegate to U.N.E.S.C.O. Conference, 1950 and 1952; Sheriff of Bombay 1950; Delegate, International Engineering Conference 1951; as Pres. of India Tariff Board, conducted enquiries in connection with industries 1930–38. Chairman, Com. of Hosts, 38th International Eucharistic Congress. Chairman of Deep Sea Fisheries Station Bombay. Member of Central Board of Fisheries. Member, Post War Reconstruction Committee for Agriculture; Industrial Planning Committee; All India Council for Technical Education.

Delegate, Fourth Commonwealth T.B. & Health Conference. Fellow, Royal Society of Arts (London). *Address:* Ismail Building, Hornby Road, Fort, Bombay, India.

**RAHMAN PUTRA, Tunku (Prince) Abdul,** CH. *B.* 1903. *Educ.* Alor Star, Penang, Bangkok, and St. Catherine's Coll., Cambridge (BA 1925); entered Inner Temple, London, but his studies were interrupted, and he was not called to the Bar until 1949; LLD Univ. of Malaya. *M.* 1939. Puan Sharifah Rodziah binte Syed Mohamed Alwi Barakbah (third wife); by his first wife he had one son and one daughter, and he has since adopted another boy and girl. *Career:* Joined Kedah State Civil Service 1931; District Officer in Kuala Nerang, Langkawi Islands, Sungei Patani and Kulim; during the occupation, when the Japanese 'returned' Kedah to Thailand, he served as Supt. of Education and Director of Passive Defence until the re-occupation in Sept. 1945. Opposed the British Government's fusion of the pre-war Federated States (Perak, Pahang, Selangor, and Negri Sembilan), the unfederated States (Johore, Kelantan, Trengganu, Kedah, and Perlis and the two colonies of Penang and Malacca to form the Malayan Union; took a leading part in the formation of the United Malay National Organization (UMNO); when the Malayan Union gave way to the Federation of Malaya (1948), became Chairman of UMNO in Kedah. After being called to the Bar of the Inner Temple, he returned to Kedah and was seconded to the Federal Legal Dept. as a Dep. Public Prosecutor, 1949; became Pres. of UMNO 1951; resigned from the Civil Service and a year later was appointed unofficial member of the Fed. Exec. and Legislative Councils; leader of Alliance Party (UMNO), Malayan Chinese Association, Malayan Indian Congress, 1954; elected to Fed. Legislative Council 1955; became Chief Minister and Minister for Home Affairs (in re-shuffle of 1956 also took portfolio of Minister for Internal Defence and Security). Headed Alliance deleg. to London to negotiate independence for the Federation, Dec. 1955; received the independence of Malaya and became first Prime Minister, 31 Aug. 1957 (also holding Min. of External Affairs and continuing as Chmn. of the Emergency Operations Council which decides the broad policy in fighting the Malayan Communist Party); resigned as Prime Minister, Feb. 1959 to prepare for the general elections in Aug.; became P.M. for the second time (when the Alliance was returned with 73 seats out of 104). Holds Kedah Order of Merit and various foreign Orders. Received Freedom of the City of London, thus becoming the second Asian Prime Minister to be conferred this very distinguished award, after the late Pandit Nehru. As representative of the Federation of Malaya (then the newest member of the Commonwealth) attended the Commonwealth Prime Ministers' Conference in London, April 1960 (where he criticized the South African policy of apartheid). After the Conference he was made State Guest of Federal Germany, Belgium, Netherlands and France. In the following October and November toured Canada, U.S. U.K. and the Netherlands. In 1961 the Tunku agreed with President Garcia of the Philippines to go ahead with the establishment of the Association of South-East Asia (A.S.A.); in March 1961 he attended the Commonwealth P.M.s Conference in London (when South Africa decided to withdraw from the Commonwealth). In May he announced that Malaya should have an understanding with Britain and the peoples of Singapore, N. Borneo, Brunei and Sarawak—the genesis of the Malaysia Plan. In July A.S.A. was formally launched by joint agreement of Malaya, Thailand and the Philippines and the signing of the Bangkok Declaration; in November the talks between the Tunku and the British Government resulted in agreement to go ahead with the Malaysia concept; further discussions in London resulted in the decision to establish the new nation on or before August 1963. Visited Pakistan and India in Oct. 1962. On Aug. 9 1965 the Malaysian House of Representatives approved the separation of Singapore from Malaysia; Secy. Gen. Islamic World Organization Sec. Gen. Islam 1969–73; Chmn. Islamic Dev. Bank 1974; President of Asian Football Confederation since 1963. *Awards:* Hon LLD: Universities of Cambridge, Malaya, Sydney, Araneta (Philippines), Saigon, and Aligrarh Muslim Univ. (India); DCL (Oxford). *Publications:* two historical Malay plays, Mahsuri and Raja Bersiong. *Address:* 1 Jalan Tunku, Kuala Lumpur, Malaysia.

**RAHNEMA, Majid,** D. en D. Iranian. Ambassador-at-large. *B.* 1924. *Educ.* Doctor of Law; Univ. Paris; Diploma d'Etudes Superieures en Economie Politique, LLB Univ. St Joseph, Beirut. *M.* 1946, Maryam Rahnema. *S.* 2. *Dau.* 1. *Career:* Joined Foreign Service, various posts 1945–67. Iranian Embassy, Paris 1945–48; Beirut 1948–49; Moscow 1950–54; Mission to U.N., New York 1957–58; Consul General, San Francisco 1959–62; Professor, Univ. of Tehran 1962; National Univ. of Iran 1962; Dir., Dept. Int. Affairs, Vice-Minister for Foreign Affairs, International & Economic Affairs 1962–65; Ambassador to Switzerland 1965–67; Minister, Science and Higher Education 1967–71; Pres., Iranian Central Council Education 1968–71; Ambassador-at-Large detached to UNESCO 1971. Special Advisor to Prime Minister and Imperial Organization of Social Services. Member, Int. Comm. Dev. Education 1971–72. Fellow, Adlai Stevenson Inst. for International Affairs (Chicago, U.S.A.) 1972–73. Representative, Human Rights Comm. 1957–58, 1965–67; United Nations Gen. Assembly 1965–71; 1st UNCTAD Conf., Geneva 1964, United Nations Comm. for Ruanda-Urundi 1960–62; Member, U.N. Economic and Social Council 1962–67. Chmn., U.N. Trusteeship Cttee. XXth Session 1965. Vice-Pres., U.N. Economic and Social Council 1967; Conference on Application of Science & Technology in Asia (CASTASIA) 1967. Director, Department of International Organizations, Ministry of Foreign Affairs Dec. 1962–June 1964. Representative: General Assembly (16th-21st Sessions); ECAFE (19th Session), Manila, March 1963; General Assembly (4th Special Session), May 1963; ECAFE (20th Session), Tehran, March 1964; U.N. Conf. on Trade & Development, Geneva, March–June 1964; UNESCO (13th General Conference), Oct. 1964; Economic & Social Council (39th Session), Geneva, June 1965. Head, Iranian Deleg. to Meeting of Ministers to prepare for Second Afro-Asian Conf., Djakarta, Apr. 10–15, 1964 (Rapporteur, Geneva, June 1964). *Publications:* Problems of Afro-Asian Countries 1965 and 1971; Introduction to Some Problems of Planned Economy and Economically Backward Countries (1948); Education for a Complete Man (1970); Aspects d'un humanisme en voie de developpement (1971); co-author Learning to Be. *Address:* Golabdareth, Kaveh Street, No. 39, Tehran, Iran.

**RAISMAN, Sir (Abraham) Jeremy,** GCMG, GCIE, KCSI. British company director. *B.* 19 March 1892. *Educ.* Leeds High School; Leeds University; Pembroke College, Oxford (MA). *M.* 1925, Renée Mary Kelly. *S.* John Michael, Jeremy Philip. *Career:* Joined Indian Civil Service 1916; Commissioner of Income Tax, Punjab and N.W. Frontier Province 1928–31; Joint Secretary of Commerce Dept., Government of India 1931–34; member, Central Board of Revenue 1934, Secretary of Finance Dept., Government of India 1938–39; Finance member, Exec. Council of Governor-General of India 1939–45; retired 1945; Chmn. British-Indian Delegation to International Monetary Conference, Bretton Woods 1944; Public Works Loans Board; Deputy-Chairman, Lloyds Bank Ltd. 1953–63; Chairman, Lloyds Bank (Foreign) Ltd.; Foreign Investments Commission, International Chamber of Commerce. Hon. Fellow, Pembroke College, Oxford; Hon. LLD (Leeds). *Address:* Fieldhead, Shamley Green, near Guildford, Surrey.

**RAJAH, Arumugam Ponnu.** Singapore Citizen. High Commissioner for the Republic of Singapore . *B.* 1911. *Educ.* Oxford University (BA); Barrister-at-Law (Lincoln's Inn). *M.* 1943, Vijaya Lakshmi, (D. 1971). *S.* Chelva Retnam. *Dau.* Nirmala. *Career:* City Counsellor of Singapore, 1949–57; Speaker, Parliament 1964–66; First High Commissioner for the Republic of Singapore in United Kingdom 1966–71; High Commissioner in Australia 1971–73; Practising Lawyer in Singapore since 1973. *Member:* Board of Trustees, Singapore Improvement Trust, 1949–57; Raffles College Council & University of Malaya Council, 1955–63. Chairman, Public Accounts Cttee., 1956–63; Singapore Legislative Assembly & Parliament 1959–66. *Address:* c/o Ministry of Foreign Affairs, Singapore.

**RAMGOOLAM, Dr. the Rt. Hon. Sir Seewoosagur,** Kt, LRCP, MRCS, PC, MLA. Mauritian. Prime Minister of Mauritius. *B.* 1900. *Educ.* Royal College, Curepipe; University College and University College Hospital, London (LRCP, MRCS). *M.* Sahoduth Ramjoorawon. *S.* Nuvin. *Dau.* Sunita. *Career:* Elected Municipal Councillor, 1940–53; re-elected 1956; Deputy Mayor, Port Louis, 1956; Mayor, 1958; Entered Legislative Council, 1940, elected Member Legislative Council for Pamplemousses-Riviere du Rempart, 1948; re-elected, 1959; re-elected for Triolet, 1959; Member of Executive Council 1948, 1953; Liaison Officer for Education, 1951–56; Ministerial Secretary to Treasury, 1958; Leader of the House since 1960; Chief Minister and Minister of Finance, 1961; Premier, 1965; Prime Minister, Minister of External & Internal Affairs since 1968, Minister of Information & Broadcasting since March 1969, Minister of Defence & Internal Security since Dec. 1969. Chmn., OAU 1976–77. *Awards:* Knighted, 1965; Grand Croix de l'Ordre National de la Republique Malagasy; Doctor in Law 'Honoris Causa' of the University of New Delhi; Fellow, University College; Grand Croix, Ordre National de Lion de la Republique du Senegal; Citoyen d'Honneur de la Cité de Port Louis; 1st Hon. Mem., African Psychiatric Assn.; Medaille de l'Assemblée Nationale Francaise; Grand Croix de l'Ordre du Merite de la Republique Centrafricaine; Grand Croix National de Benin (Togo); Grand Officier de la Legion d'Honneur de la Republique Francaise; UN Prize for Outstanding Achievements in the Field of Human Rights. President Indian Cultural Association; Editor, Indian Cultural Review; Chairman Board of Directors Advance. *Address:* 87 Desforges Street, Port Louis, Mauritius; and Prime Minister's Office, Port Louis, Mauritius.

**RAMO, Simon.** *B.* 1913. *Educ.* University of Utah (BS, EE 1933); California Institute of Technology (PhD) *magna cum laude* 1936); Hon D.Eng. Case Inst. of Technology 1960; Hon DSc Univ. of Utah 1961, Union Coll. 1963; Hon. D.Eng. Univ. Michigan 1966; Hon D.Sc Worcester Polytechnic Inst. 1968; Hon. DSc. Univ. of Akron 1969; Hon. LLD Carnegie-Mellon Univ. 1970; Hon. D.Eng. Polytechnic Inst. N. York 1971; Hon. LLD. Univ. Southern California 1972. *M.* 1937. Virginia May Smith. *S.* James Brian and Alan Martin. *Career:* Teaching Fellow, Calif. Inst. of Tech., 1933–36; Dir. Physics Section, Electronics Research Lab. General Electric Co. 1936–46; Vice-Pres. Dir. Operations Hughes Aircraft Co., 1946–53; Exec. Vice-Pres. Co-founder The Ramo-Wooldridge Corp. 1953–58; Scientific Dir. U.S. Intercontinental Ballistic Missile Program 1954–58; Pres, Space Technology Lab. Div. of Ramo-Wooldridge Corp. 1957–58, Exec. Vice-Pres. TRW. Inc. 1958–61, Vice Chmn. Bd. 1961–69. Vice Chmn. Bd. Chmn. Exec. Cttee. TRW. Inc. since 1969. Dir. TRW. Inc.; Union Bank; Union Bancorp Inc.; Los Angeles World Affairs Council; Southern Calif. Symph. Hollywood Bowl Assn.; Music Center Opera Assn.; Times Mirror Co.; Chamber Commerce U.S.A.; Trustee, Educ. Foundation Inc.; Nat. Symphony Orchestra Assn.; Calif. Inst. Technology; City of Hope, Member; Trustee Emeritus Calif. State Univs.; Fellow Am. Acad. Arts & Sciences; American Assn. for Adv. of Science; Am. Astron. Soc.; Am. Inst. Aeronautics & Astronautics; Physical Soc. IEEE; IAE; Amer. Philosophical Socy.; Nat. Acad. Engineering; Consultant Presidents Science Adv. Cttee.; Nat. Acad. of Scs.; Eta Kappa Nu; Epsilon Eta Sigma; Phi Kappa Phi; Sigma Pi Sigma; Sigma Xi; Tau Beta Pi; Theta Tau; Phi Beta Kappa; Mem. White House Energy R. & D. Adv Council; US State Dept. Cttee. on Science & For. Affairs; Numerous Advisory Councils & Cttees. (intern.); Adv. Council School, Engineering Stanford Univ.; Adv. member Bd. Dirs. Mangt. Dev. Center Univ. Houston Coll. Business Admin.; Senior Exec. Adv. Council Nat. Ind. Conference Bd.; Exec. Cttee. United Way Inc.; Campaign Chmn. 1971 United Crusade Awards: Outstanding young elect Engineer Fta Kappa Nu; Electronic Achievement; Inst. Electrical & Electronic Engineers, Paul T. Johns Arnold Air Society, Man of Hope; Eminent Mem. Eta Kappa Nu; Charles M. Schwab Memorial Lecture; Farfel Lecture, Armed Forces Dist. Service Gold Medal; WEMA Medal; USC Sch. of Business Mgmt. award; Los Angeles Jewish Awards; Col. Univ. Kayan Medal. *Publications:* Fields and Waves in Communication Electronics (with John R. Whinnery and Theodore Van Duzer) 1965; Cure for Chaos (1969); Century of Mismatch (1970); Extraordinary Tennis for the Ordinary Player (1970); The Islands of E. Cono & My (1973); editor and contributor: other textbooks, numerous articles, technical publications. *Address:* One Space Park, Redondo Beach, Calif. 90278, U.S.A.

**RAMPHAL, Shridath Surendranath,** Kt 1970, CMG 1966, QC 1965, SC. Guyanese Barrister-at-Law. *B.* 1928. *Educ.* Queen's Coll. (Georgetown, Guyana); King's Coll. (London); Gray's Inn; Harvard Law School. *M.* 1951, Lois Winifred King. *S.* 2. *Daus.* 2. *Career:* Govt. of British Guiana: Crown Councel, Asst. to Attorney General & Legal Draftsman 1952–59, Solicitor General 1959–61; Federal Govt. of the West Indies: Legal Draftsman 1958–59, Asst. Attorney General 1961–62; Govt. of Guyana: Attorney General 1965–73, Member of Nat. Assembly 1965–75, Attorney General & Min. of State for External Affairs 1966–72, Min. of Foreign Affairs & Attorney-General 1972–73, Min. of Foreign Affairs & Justice 1972–75; Commonwealth Secretary-General 1975–(1980). *Member:* Hon. Advisory Cttee., Center for International Studies, New York Univ. 1966—; International Comm. of Jurists 1970—; Board, Vienna Inst. of Development 1973—; International Hon. Cttee. of the Dag Hammarskjold Foundation 1977—; Governing Body of the Inst. of Development Studies, Sussex Univ. 1977—. *Awards:* Gray's Inn: Arden & Atkin Prize 1952: John Simon Guggenheim Fellowship 1962; Order of the Republic (First Class), Arab Rep. of Egypt 1973; Grand Cross of the Order of the Sun of Peru 1974; Grand Cross of the Order of Merit of Ecuador, 1974; Hon LLD, Panjab Univ., Chandigarh, India 1975 & Southampton Univ. 1976; Fellow, King's Coll., London 1975. *Publications:* Contributions in various Legal & Political Journals incl. Int'l & Comparative Law Quarterly; Caribbean Quarterly; Public Law; Guyana Journal; Foreign Policy; Round Table. *Address:* Commonwealth Secretariat, Marlborough House, Pall Mall, London SW1Y 5HX.

**RAMPTON, Calvin L.** US Lawyer-Politician. *B.* 1913. *Educ.* Davis County, Utah public schools; Davis HS. Graduated (1931); Univ. of Utah, B.S. (1936); George Washington Univ. (Washington DC) and Univ of Utah Law Schools, Juris Doctor Degree (1940). *M.* 1940, Lucybeth Cardon. *S.* 2. *D.* 2. *Career:* Enlisted in Utah National Guard in 1932, held all enlisted ranks. Entered full-time military service in World War II as Lieutenant. Served in France, Holland Germany. At war's end, served as Chief of Senior United States Army Claims Commission in Paris. Now retired Reserve Colonel in Army Field Judiciary Service; Administrative Assistant to Congressman 1936–38; Davis County Attorney 1939–40; Assistant Attorney General of Utah 1941–42 and 1946–48; Governor of Utah 1965–76. Attorney Utah State Bar; U.S. Supreme Court (practiced before); International Academy of Trial Lawyers; Interstate Commerce Commission (and other regulatory agencies) (practiced before). *Governor:* Chairman-National Governors' Conference, 1974–75; President-Council of State Governments, 1974–75; Chairman-Federation of Rocky Mountain States, 1970–71; Chairman-Western Governors' Conference, 1969–70; Chairman-Education Commission of the States, 1967–68. *Member:* Nat. Governors' Conference Cttee. *Awards:* World War II; Outstanding Public Administrator of the year (1971) (Brigham Young Univs. Assn.); Nat. Conf. of Christian and Jews Award (1973). *Address:* 1270 Fairfax Rd., Salt Lake City, Utah 84103, U.S.A.

**RAMSAY, Sir Thomas (Meek).** Kt CMG. Australian. *B.* 1907, *Educ.* Melbourne University (BSc); Malvern Grammar, Scotch College. *M.* 1941, Catherine Anne Richardson. *S.* 4. *Dau.* 1. *Career:* Joined The Kiwi Polish Co. Pty. Ltd. 1926; C.M.F. Lieut. 1940–41; Assistant Controller, Min. Munitions 1941–45; Jnt. Man. Dir. 1945, Man. Dir. Kiwi Polish Co. Ltd. 1956–72; Chmn. The Kiwi International Co. Ltd., Melbourne 1967—; Norwich Union Life Insurance Society (Australian Bd.); Director: ACI-Nylex Pty. Ltd.; Australian Consolidated Industries Ltd., Group; Collie (Aust.) Ltd., Group Alex Harvey Industries Group, New Zealand; Anzac Fellowship Selection Cttee. *Member:* Victorian Chamber of Manufacturers (President 1962–64); Associated Chambers of Mfrs. of Aust. (Pres. 1962–63); Victoria Promotion Cttee.; Selection Cttee., Sir Winston Churchill Industrial Fellowships. *Awards:* Fellow, Royal Historical Society of Victoria; British Institute of Management; Aust. Inst. of Management; Scottish Antiquarian Socy.; Royal Hist. Socy. of Queensland; Knighted 1972. *Clubs:* Athenaeum (Melbourne); Melbourne (Melbourne); Commonwealth (Canberra); Oriental (London); Australian (Melbourne). *Address:* 23 Airlie Street, South Yarra, Vic. 3141, Australia.

**RAMSBOTHAM, Hon. Sir Peter Edward,** GCVO, GCMG. British Diplomat. *B.* 1919. *Educ.* Eton Coll.; Oxford Magdalen College. *M.* 1941, Frances Blomfield. *S.* 2. *Dau.* 1. *Career:* H.M. Forces in Europe 1943–46; Regional Political Officer, Hamburg with British Control Commission 1946–48; Second Secretary Berlin 1948–50; First Secy. Foreign Office 1950–53; Head of Chancery, Delegation to UN New York 1953–57; Counsellor to Foreign Office 1957–62; Head of Chancery, Paris 1962–67; With Institute, Strategic Studies, London 1967–68: British High Commissioner, Cyprus 1969–71; Ambassador to Iran 1971–1973; Ambassador to the United States 1974–77; Governor & Commander-in-Chief, Bermuda since Sept. 1977. *Awards:* Grand Commander, Royal Victorian Order; Grand Commander, Order St. Michael and St. George; Croix de Guerre and Palme. *Address:* East Lane, Ovington, Nr. Alresford, Hampshire; and *office* c/o Foreign and Commonwealth Office, King Charles Street, London, S.W.1.

**RAMSDEN, George Edward Warwick.** Australian. *B.* 1910 *Educ.* Sydney C. of E. Grammar School. Chartered Accountant (Australia). *M.* 1938, Phyllis Elsie Swan. *S.* Jonathan Warwick. *Career:* Director of the Shell Group of Companies in Australia 1957–70. President, Australian Rugby Football 1963–68. Director, Trustees Executors and Agency Co. Ltd.

1969—; Yellow Express Carriers Ltd. 1969–72, Chmn. 1970–72; Dir. and Chmn., Renold Australia Pty. Ltd. since 1972; Dir. The Colonial Mutual Life Assurance Soc. Ltd. since 1974; Dir. Actrol Ltd. since 1974. *Clubs:* Australian; Royal Melbourne Golf; Rugby (Sydney). *Address:* 20 Church Street, Toorak, Vic. 3142, Australia.

**RAMSDEN, Patrick John Vance.** Australian. *B.* 1906. *Educ.* Melbourne C. of E. Grammar School. *M.* 1933, June Angwin. *S.* Andrew Patrick and Richard Anthony. *Career:* Senior Partner, Wilson, Danby & Giddy (Chartered Accountants), Melbourne (Ret'd.). Chmn., Australian Paper Manufacturers Ltd. Dir.: Lamson Industries (Australia) Ltd., Georges (Australia) Ltd. (also Chmn.) and National Bank of Australasia Ltd. Fellow Inst. of Chartered Accountants in Australia. *Clubs:* The Australian; The Melbourne; Metropolitan Golf. *Address:* Flat 1, 18 Huntingtower Road, Armadale Melbourne; and *office* 461 Bourke Street, Melbourne, Vic., Australia.

**RAMSEY OF CANTERBURY. The Rt. Rev. and Rt. Hon. Lord (Arthur Michael),** PC, MA, BD; Hon. D.D. Durham, Leeds, Edinburgh, Cambridge, Hull, London, Manchester, Toronto, Huron Coll., Virginia Theological Seminary, Kings, Coll., Novia Scotia, Pacific Lutheran Univ., Episcopal Theol. School, Cambridge, Mass. Dr. Theology, Institut. Catholique, Paris Hon. LLD Canterbury, N.Z. Occidental College, Los Angeles. Hon. DLitt., University of Newfoundland, University of Keele, Hon. DCL, Oxford, Kent, Nashotah Ho., Wis, Hon. Dr. of Humane Letters, Woodstock Coll., N. York; Hon. Dr. of Sacred Theology, Columbia Univ. and General Theological Seminary New York. Hon. Fellow Magdalene College, Cambridge 1952—, Merton College, Oxford 1974—. *B.* 1904. *Educ.* Repton and Magdalene College, Cambridge. Ordained 1928. *M.* 1942, Joan, daughter of Lieutenant-Colonel F. A. C. Hamilton. *Career:* Curate, Liverpool Parish Church 1928–30; Subwarden Lincoln Theological College 1930–36; Examining Chaplain to Bishop of Chester 1932–39, of Durham 1940–50, and of Lincoln 1951–52; Select Preacher, Cambridge 1934–40–48–59, Oxford 1945–46. Lecturer, Boston Parish Church 1936–38; Vicar, St. Benedict, Cambridge 1939–40; Canon, Durham Cathedral, Prof. of Divinity, Univ. of Durham 1940–50; Regius Prof. of Divinity Univ. of Cambridge 1950–52; Canon and Prebendary, Lincoln Cathedral 1951–52; Bishop of Durham 1952–56; Archbishop of York, 1956–61; and Canterbury 1961–74. Hulsean Preacher, Cambridge 1969–70. *Award:* Royal Victorian Chain 1974. *Publications:* The Gospel & the Catholic Church (1936). The Resurrection of Christ, 1944; The Glory of God & the Transfiguration of Christ, 1949; F. D. Maurice and the Conflicts of Modern Theology, 1951; Durham Essays and Addresses, 1956; From Gore to Temple, 1960; Introducing the Christian Faith, 1961; Canterbury Essays and Addresses, 1964; Sacred and Secular, 1965; God, Christ and the World 1969; The Christian Priest Today, 1972; Canterbury Pilgrim, 1974; Through the Year with Michael Ramsey, 1975; Holy Spirit, 1977. *Address:* 50 South Street, Durham, Darlington.

**RAND, Rex.** *B.* 1922. *Educ.* London and Oxford Universities (England). District Manager, Broadcast and TV for South-eastern U.S. for Radio Corp. of America 1946–51 President, Rand Broadcasting Co., operating Radio and TV stations WINZ (Miami), WINQ (Tampa), WEAT, and Radio and WEAT TV (Palm Beach). *Clubs:* Yacht de Monaco, Monte Carlo, Marco, Polo, Le Club, Cat Cay. *Address: office* 100 Biscaynes Towers, Biscayne Boulevard, Miami, Fla., U.S.A.

**RANDERS, Gunnar.** Norwegian scientist. *Educ.* Univ. of Oslo (MSc 1937). *M.* 1939, Engelke Irgens Rynning Koren. *S.* Jørgen and Jan Gunnar. *Dau.* Karen. *Career:* Instructor, Univ. of Chicago 1940–41; Scientific Officer, Ministry of Supply 1940–41; Director, Astrophysics Inst., Oslo Univ. 1946–47; Chief Scientist, Norwegian Defence Research Establishment 1947–51; Director, Dutch-Norwegian Joint Establishment for Nuclear Energy Research 1951–59; Mng. Dir., Inst. for Atomic Energy, Kjeller, Norway 1959—; Chmn., Norwegian Atomic Energy Council 1955—; Norwegian Development Agency 1963–68. President, European Atomic Energy Society 1966—. Special adviser on atomic energy matters to the Secy.-Gen. of U.N. 1954–56; and to Dir.-Gen., International Atomic Energy Agency (Norwegian Governor 1964), Vienna 1958. Managing Director, Norwegian Institute for Atomic Energy 1960–68; Asst. Secy. Gen. for Scientific Affairs, NATO 1968–73; Pres., Scandpower Inc., Norway, since 1976. *Publications:* scientific papers in U.S. and Norwegian astronomical journals; two books (in Norwegian) on atomic energy; & Memoirs (Norwegian) 1975. *Member:* Norwegian Acad. of Science, Oslo; Royal Astronomical Socy., London; Technical Acad., Trondheim. *Address:* Trosterudstien 4, Slemdal, Oslo 3, Norway.

**RANDOLPH, Cyril George.** British banker. *B.* 1899. *Educ.* Christ's Hospital. *M.* 1927, Betty Dixey. *Dau.* Christian Elizabeth (Macpherson). Director: Glyn, Mills & Co. 1941–69, Sun Life Assurance Society Ltd. 1943— (Chairman 1953–71); General Funds Investment Trust Ltd. 1964— (Chmn. 1965–73. *Clubs:* Brooks's (London); New Zealand Golf (West Byfleet). *Address:* 3 Castle Court, Castle Hill, Farnham Surrey.

**RANDOLPH, Jennings.** U.S. Senator from West Virginia 1958–76. *B.* 1902, *Educ.* Salem Academy and Salem College. *M.* 1933, Mary Katherine Babb. *S.* Jennings, Jr. and Frank. *Career:* Pres., West Virginia Intercollegiate Press Association 1922–23; Editor, The Message, Salem, W.Va., 1922–25; member, editorial staff, Clarksburg (W. Va.) Daily Telegram, 1924–25; Assoc. Editor, West Virginia Review 1925–26; Assoc. Editor, Randolph Enterprise Review, Elkins; Prof.. Dept. of Public Speaking and Journalism, Davis & Elkins Coll. 1926–32; former instructor (effective speaking), South-western Univ. and Dean of Coll. of Business and Finanacial Administration; faculty mem., Leadership Training Inst.; Asst. to Pres. and Dir. of Public Relations, Capital Airlines 1947–58; Trustee, Salem Coll.; Bd. of Governors, Natnl. USO 1958–59; member, Adv. Board, National Council for Advancement of Small Colleges; elected to U.S. House of Representatives 73rd Congress; re-elected six consecutive terms; elected Delegate-at-Large for W. Virginia to Democratic National Convention 1948–52–64–68. *Publications:* Going to Make a Speech? Mr. Chairman, Ladies and Gentlemen. Hon LLD, Davis and Elkin Coll.; Univ. of Pittsburgh; Alderson-Broaddus College; West Virginia University, Milton College, Waynesburg College, West Virginia Wesleyan College; LittD, Southeastern University; Aeronautical Science, Salem College; Dr. Hum. W. Virginia State College; Humane Letters, Maryville College. *Member:* National Aeronautic Assn. (former Vice-Pres. & Dir.); Transportation Assn. of America (Bd. of Dirs. Alumni); Amer. Road Builders Assn. (former Treas. and Pres. Airport Div.); President's (U.S.) and Governor's (W.Va) Committee on Employment of Handicapped; W.Va Press Assn.; International Platform Assn.; City of Elkins and West Virginia Chambers of Commerce. *Clubs:* National Press; Kiwanis; Rotary; Lions; Lions International (Counsellor and formed Governor, W.Va. branch). *Address:* 4608 Reservoir Road, N.W. Washington, D.C. 20007, U.S.A.

**RANGEL, Rafael.** MS. Mexican. *B.* 1915. *M.* 1941, Ma Enriqueta Gomez. *S.* 3. *Daus.* 3. *Career:* Man. Dir. Sociedad Electro Mecánica, S.A. de C.V.; Chmn. Cutler Hammer Mexicana S.A.; Dir. Cleaver Brooks de Mexico S.A.; Super Diesel, S.A.; Industrial Electricia S.A. *Member:* I.E.E.E.; A.M.I.M.E. *Club:* de Golf Mexico. *Address:* Manuel Ma, Contreras 25, Mexico, 4DF.

**RANKI, Matti Lauri.** Finnish Banker. *B.* 1926. *Educ.* Univ. of Helsinki—MA (Econ.). *M.* 1952, Irma Fredman. *S.* 1. *Daus.* 2. *Career:* Clerk & Head Clerk, Kansallis-Osake-Pankki 1950–53; Consultant, the Finnish Savings Banks Assn. 1953; Inspector, the Finnish Savings Banks Inspectorate 1954–56; Manager, the Finnish Savings Banks Assn. 1957–61; Gen. Mgr., Skopbank 1961–67; Dep. Chief Gen. Mgr., Skopbank 1967–77; Chief Gen. Mgr., Skopbank since April 1977. Board mem. in various associations & companies. *Address:* Toppelundintie 5A, SF-02170 Espoo 17; and *office* Aleksanterinkatu 46, SF-00100 Helsinki 10, Finland.

**RANKIN, Bruce Irving.** Canadian diplomat. *B.* 1918. *Educ.* Univ. of Alberta (BCom 1941); National Defence College (n.c.c. 1954). *M.* 1949, Mona Miller. *Daus.* Janet, Marilyn and Susan. *Career:* Asst. Commercial Secy., Australia 1946–48; Consul, China, 1948–51; Commercial Secy., Australia, 1950–51 and India 1951–53; First Secy. (Comm.) Spain 1954–56; Commercial Counsellor, Switzerland, 1956–59; Deputy Consul General, New York, 1959–64; Alternate Representative, 22nd to 28th United Nations General Assemblies, Chmn. 2nd Cttee. (Economic & Financial) of 27th Gen. Assembly; Representative, Economic & Social Council, 1966 & 67; Ambassador to Venezuela and concurrently Ambassador to Dominican Republic 1964–70; Consul-General of Canada in New York 1970–76; Ambassador to Japan since 1976. Pres., UNDP Pledging Conference, 1968. *Club.* Country (Caracas). *Address:* Canadian Embassy, 3–38, Akasaka 7-chome, Minato-ku, Tokyo, Japan.

**RANKIN, Hon. Dame Annabelle Jane Mary,** DBE. Australian. *Educ.* Glennie Memorial Girls' School. Toowoomba. *Career:* Opposition Whip in Senate 1947–49; Government Whip in Senate 1951–66. Federal Minister for Housing, Commonwealth of Australia, 1966–71; Aust. High Commissioner to New Zealand 1971–74. Retired. *Address:* 79 Captain Cook Parade, Deception Bay, Qld., Australia.

**RANOV, Theodor.** American. Professor of Engineering, *B.* 1910. *Educ.* Tech. Univ., Berlin (Dipl. Ing., Dr. Ing.). *M.* 1941, Frances Joy Craig. *S.* Peter Henry. *Daus.* Jeannie Elizabeth and Stephanie Anne. TKX Award for Pedagogical Achievement. *Career:* With Anglo-Danubian Transport Co., London 1937–39; C.M.C. Chemicals Mfg. Co., Wellington, N.Z. 1939–41; Radio Corp. of N.Z. 1941–46; Wellington (N.Z.) Technical College 1946–48; Faculty of Engineering and Applied Sciences; State University of N.Y. at Buffalo 1949–76; Engineering Consultant, Buffalo Forge Co. 1952—. *Publications:* author and co-author of numerous papers, dealing with stress analysis, fluid mechanics, lubrication, etc. Fellow American Society of Mechanical Engineers. *Address:* 414 53rd Street, West Palm Beach, Florida 33407, U.S.A.

**RASKY, Frank John.** Canadian. *B.* 1923. *Educ.* Univ. of Toronto (BA 1945). *M.* 1958, Brenda Dolin. *S.* Franklyn. *Dau.* Deena. *Career:* Formerly Editor-in-Chief: Liberty Magazine of Canada; and of Toronto News-Observer weekly. Senior Writer, The Canadian (Canada's largest magazine, with a circulation exceeding two million), Jan. 1967—; Staff Writer, Toronto Star since 1974; Teacher of Magazine Journalism, University of Toronto since 1965. *Publications:* The North Pole or Bust; The Polar Voyagers; The Taming of the Canadian West; Roy Rogers—King of Cowboys; Great Olympic Athletes. Gay Canadian Rogues, Great Canadian Disasters. Winner of the James Polk Memorial Award of the U.S. for Fearless Journalism. *Member:* Arctic Institute of North America; Historical Societies of Alberta, Saskatchewan, and British Columbia. *Address:* 445 Eglinton Avenue, E. (suite 506), Toronto, Ont.; and *office:* The Toronto Star, 1 Yonge Street, Toronto, Ontario, M5E 1E6, Canada.

**RASMINSKY, Louis,** CC, CBE. Canadian banker. *B.* 1 Feb. 1908. *Educ.* Univ. of Toronto (BA and Hon. LLD); London School of Economics. *M.* 1930, Lyla Rotenberg. *S.* Michael. *Dau.* Lola. *Career:* Attached Economic and Financial Section, League of Nations 1930–39; Executive Director, International Monetary Fund, 1946–62; International Bank for Reconstruction and Development, 1950–62; Deputy-Governor, Bank of Canada 1956–61, Governor, Bank of Canada 1961–73; Chmn. Bd. Governors International Devel opment Research Center since 1973. *Address:* 440 Roxborough Road, Rockcliffe Park, Ottawa, Ontario K1M OL2, Canada.

**RASMUSON, Elmer Edwin.** *B.* 1909. *Educ.* Harvard (BS *magna cum laude* 1930; AM 1935) and University of Grenoble 1930. *M.* (1) 1939, Lile Vivian Bernard (*D.* 1960). *S.* Edward Bernard. *Daus.* Lile Muchmore and Judy Ann. *M.* (2) 1962, Colonel Mary Louise Milligan. *Career:* Chief Accountant, National Investors Corp., New York City 1933–38; Principal, Arthur Andersen & Co., N.Y.C. 1935–43. Chairman, National Bank of Alaska 1965–74 (Pres. 1943–65, Chmn. Exec. Cttee. since 1975); Member, City Council of Anchorage 1945; Chmn., City Planning Commission 1950–53; Consul for Sweden 1955—; Mayor of City of Anchorage 1964–67. Member, Board of Regents, University of Alaska (Pres. 1956–69) 1950–69; Civilian Aide for Alaska to the Secretary of the Army 1959–67; Commissioner, Int. North Pacific Fisheries Commission 1969—; member, Int. Cttee. United States-Japan Cultural & Educational Cooperation since 1972. Dir. Coast Guard Academy Foundation. *Publications:* Economic Threshold of Alaska; How to Know Alaska. Certified Public Accountant, New York, Texas and Alaska. Phi Beta Kappa, Officer Order of Vasa (Sweden). *Clubs:* Explorers; Anchorage Rotary (Past President); Harvard (N.Y.C. Boston); Washington Athletic; Explorers; Seattle Yacht; Ranier, Harbor (Seattle); Petroleum (Anchorage). *Address:* Box 600, Anchorage, Alaska 99501, U.S.A.

**RASMUSSEN, Einar Normann.** Norwegian shipowner. *B.* 1907. *M.* 1934, Jenny Tjøm. *S.* Einar Johan. *Dau.* Rannfrid. *Career:* Chairman, Board of Directors: Kristiansands Tankreder, II, A/S Kristiansands Taukrederi III, Aksjeselskapet Avant Aksjeselskapet Skjoldheim, Aksjeselskapet Songvaar; A/S Froland Vaerk, Kristiansands Fiskegarnsfabrik A/S, A/S Trolla Brug, Kristiansands & Oplands Privatbank A/S, Christianssands Assuransekontor A/S. Member of the Board of Directors of Falconbridge Nikkelverk A/S, A/S Vigeland Brug, A/S Norges Skipshypotek J Christiannsands Skibsassuranceforening. Chairman of the Board of Representatives of A/S Norske Alliance, Redernes Skibskredittforening. Member of the Board of Representatives of Bank of Norway, Livsforsikringsselskapet B rage. *Address:* Wergelandsveien 20 A, Kristiansand S., Norway.

**RASMUSSEN, Viggo J.,** BComm. Danish company director. *B.* 20 Jan. 1915. *M.* 1939, Lydia Hansen. *S.* Hans Peter. *Dau.* Marianne. *Career:* Commercial Apprentice 1931; Traffic Officer, Danish Airlines 1934; Trainee, Imperial Airways Ltd., London 1937; Senior Traffic Officer, Danish Airlines 1938, Secretary 1942, Assistant Traffic Manager 1945, Deputy Managing Director 1947; General Manager, Scandinavian Airlines System, European Division 1949; Executive Vice-President and General Manager, Region Denmark, Scandinavian Airlines System 1950; Managing Director, United Breweries Ltd. and Tuborg Breweries Ltd. 1962–71; Bd. Member United Breweries Ltd. 1972–74; Advisor to the Danish Breweries since 1974. Member, Danish Academy of Technical Sciences. *Awards:* Knight, Orders of Dannebrog 1st Degree (Denmark) and Vasa (Sweden); Comdr. Order of Merit (Italy). *Address:* Store Kongensgade 130, DK-1264 Copenhagen K; and *office* Tuborg, 2900 Hellerup, Denmark.

**RATCLIFFE, Myron Fenwick.** American business executive. *B.* 1902. *Educ.* Univ. of Illinois (BSc). *M.* 1945, Margaret Archibald. *Dau.* Elizabeth Robertson (Heinze). *Career:* Goldman, Sachs & Co. 1925–33; National Recovery Administration (Administrator, Financial Codes) 1934–35; Lehman Bros. 1936–49; Partner, Bache & Co. 1949–56; President and Director: Miami Corporation, Chicago, Ill., 1956—; Cutler Oil & Gas Corp., Chicago, 1956—. Chairman, Board of Directors, National Boulevard Bank of Chicago 1956—. Dir.: National Standard Co., Niles, Mich., 1956—. Trustee, Ill. Children's Home and Aid Society. Member, Board of Governors, Midwest Stock Exchange (1949–56); Served Lt. Col. Aus. 1942–46. *Award:* Legion of Merit. *Clubs:* Chicago; Casino; Mid-America; Bond (all Chicago): Indian Hill Country; Old Elm Club; Birnam Wood Golf (Santa Barbara, Calif.). *Address:* 82 Indian Hill Road, Winnetka. Ill. 60093; and *office* 410 North Michigan Avenue, Chicago, Ill. 60611, U.S.A.

**RATHBONE, John Rankin (Tim),** M.P. British Politician & Company Director. *B.* 1933. *Educ.* Eton; Christ Church, Oxford; Harvard Business School. *M.* 1960, Margarita Sanchez y Sanchez. *S.* 2. *Daus.* 1. *Career:* Robert Benson Lonsdale & Co., Merchant Bankers 1956–58; Trainee to Vice-Pres., Ogilvy & Mather Inc., New York 1958–66; Chief Publicity & Public Relations Officer, Conservative Central Office 1966–68; Charles Barker ABH International since 1968; Man. Dir., Ayer Barker Hegemann 1970–73 & Dep. Chmn. since 1973; Conservative MP for Lewes since 1974. *Member:* Advertising Association (Council Mem.); Inst. of Practitioners in Advertising; Marketing Society; Market Research Society. *Clubs:* Brooks's; The Sussex Club; Society of Sussex Downsmen. *Address:* 30 Farringdon Street, London EC4A 4EA.

**RAUBENHEIMER, Abraham Jakobus.** South African Politician. *B.* 1920. *Educ.* Univ. of Pretoria—BSc (Agric.). *M.* Charmaine Raubenheimer. *Daus.* 5. *Career:* Mem. of the Citrus Board of S.A.; mem., Exec. Comm. of the Head Cttee. of the Ruling National Party of Transvaal; mem., Council of Univ. of Pretoria; Chmn., Tobacco Council of S.A.; mem. of the House of Assembly for Nelspruit; Chmn., Bantu Affairs Comm.; Dep. Minister of Bantu Development; Minister of Water Affairs & Forestry. *Club:* Rapportryers. *Address:* 850 New Government Avenue, Pretoria; and *office* P/B X313, Pretoria, South Africa.

**RAUM, Hon. Judge Arnold.** Judge, Tax Court of the United States since 1950. *B.* 1908. *Educ.* Harvard University (AB (*summa cum laude*) 1929; LLB (*magna cum laude*) 1932); Travelling Fellowship to Cambridge University, England, 1932. *M.* (1) 1944, Muriel Leidner Slaff. (2) 1957, Violet Gang Kopp. *Career:* Special Assistant to the Attorney-General of U.S. 1934–50; Asst. to the Solicitor-General of U.S. 1939–50 (now Deputy Solicitor General) from time to time Acting Solicitor-General of U.S.; member of Faculty: Yale Law School (1938) and Harvard Law School (1947). *Publications:* contributions to various legal periodicals. *Address:* United States Tax Court, Washington, D.C. 20217. U.S.A.

**RAWLINSON, Rt. Hon. Sir Peter Anthony Grayson.** PC, QC, MP. English barrister. *B.* 1919. *Educ.* Downside School; Christ's Coll., Cambridge. *M.* 1954. Elaine Angela Dominguez.

*S.* 2. *Dau.* 1. *Career:* Major in H.M. Irish Guards 1939–46; Barrister, Inner Temple 1946; Member of Parliament for Epsom 1955—; Queen's Counsel 1959—; Recorder of Salisbury 1961–62 and for Kingston upon Thames since 1975; Solicitor-General 1962–64; Privy Counsellor 1964—; Attorney-General 1970–74; Vice-Chmn. General Council of Inns and Bar 1974–75, Chmn. 1975–76. *Member:* Inner Temple Bencher; Bar Council; Senate. Hon. Fellow American College of Trial Lawyers; Hon. Member, A.B.A. *Clubs:* White's; Pratt's; M.C.C. *Address:* 4 Paper Buildings, Temple, London, EC4 and *office:* 12 King's Bench Walk, Temple, EC4.

**RAWSON, Christopher Selwyn Priestley,** British. Chairman and Managing Director, Christopher Rawson Ltd. *B.* 1928. *Educ.* The Elms School (Colwall, nr. Malvern) and the Nautical College (Pangbourne). *M.* 1959, Rosemary Ann Focke. *Daus.* 2. *Career:* Navigating apprentice. Merchant Service 1945–48; Livery of Clothworkers Company 1952; Freeman, Company of Watermen & Lightermen 1966; member, Court of Assts. 1974; Sheriff of the City of London 1961–62; Member of the Common Council of City of London 1963–72; Alderman of City of London (Ward of Lime Street) since 1972; Chmn. Port & City of London Health Cttee. 1967–70; Chmn. Billingsgate & Leadenhall Markets Cttee. 1972–75; Chmn. of Governors, The Elms School, since 1966. *Awards:* Silver Medallist, City & Guilds of London Institute 1951. Associate Member: Inst. of Marine Engineers (AIMarE). Associate of the Textile Institute. *Clubs:* Royal Automobile; City Livery; Royal Thames Yacht; Royal Corinthian Yacht. *Address:* 56 Ovington Street, London, S.W.3; and *office* Clarence House, Arthur Street, London, E.C.4.

**RAWSON, Merle Richard.** American Businessman. *B.* 1924. *Educ.* Univ. of Illinois; Northwestern Univ.—BS degree in Accounting. *M.* 1947, Jane Armstrong. *S.* 2. *Dau.* 1. *Career:* Asst. to Plant Controller, John Wood Co. 1949; Asst. Controller, Easy Laundry Appliances 1958; Controller, O'Bryan Bros. 1961; Budget Dir., The Hoover Co. 1961; Controller 1962, Controller & Asst. Treas. 1963, Vice-Pres. & Treas. 1964, Vice-Pres. Finance 1965, Hoover Worldwide Corp.; Dir., Hoover Industrial y Comercial S.A. (Colombia) 1967; Dir., The Hoover Co., Hoover Worldwide Corp. & The Hoover Co. Ltd. (Canada) 1968; Snr. Vice-Pres., Hoover Worldwide Corp. & Snr. Vice-Pres. & Treas., The Hoover Co. 1969; Exec. Vice-Pres., Hoover Worldwide Corp. 1971; Dir., Hoover Ltd. (U.K.) 1972; Chmn. of the Bd. & Chief Exec. Officer, The Hoover Co. & Hoover Worldwide Corp. 1975; Dir., Hoover Mexicana S.A. de C.V. 1975; Dir., Hoover Holland B.V. & S.A. Hoover (France) 1976. *Member:* Bd. of Trustees, Walsh Coll.; Advisory Council, Pace Univ.; Bd. of Trustees, Ohio Foundation of Independent Colleges; Aultman Hospital Assoc.; Aultman Hospital Development Foundation. *Clubs:* Union League Club of New York; Congress Lake Country Club. *Address:* 101 East Maple Street, North Canton, Ohio 44720, U.S.A.

**RAY, Dixy Lee.** American Scientist & Administrator. *B.* 1914. *Educ.* Mills Coll., Oakland, Calif.; Stanford Univ. (MA. PhD.). *Career:* Teacher 1938–42; John Switzer Fellow. Stanford Univ. 1942–43, Van Sicklen Fellow 1943–45; Assoc. Prof. of Zoology, Univ. of Washington 1945–72; Exec. Cttee., Friday Harbour Laboratories 1945–60; Special Consultant, Biological Oceanography, Nat. Science Foundation 1960–62; Dir., Pacific Science Center, Seattle 1963–72; Mem., Atomic Energy Commission 1972–75, Chmn. 1973–75; Asst. Sec. of State 1975; Gov., Washington State since 1977—. Democrat. *Member:* Marshall Fellowship Cttee.; Foreign Mem., Danish Royal Soc. for Natural History 1963. *Awards:* Hon. Degrees: Mills Coll. 1967, St. Martins Coll. 1972, Hood Coll. 1973, Seattle Univ. 1973, Ripon Coll. 1974, St. Mary's Coll. 1974, Puget Sound Univ. 1974, Michigan State Univ. 1974, Union Coll. 1974, Northern Mich. Univ. 1974; Seattle Maritime Award 1966; William Clapp Award in Marine Biology 1959; Florence K. Hutchison Medal for Service in Conservation 1973; Francis Boyer Science Award 1974; YWCA 1974 Gold Medal Award; Outstanding Women of Science Award, ARCS Foundation 1974. *Address:* Office of the Governor, Legislative Building, Olympia, Washington 98504, U.S.A.

**RAY, George Washington, Jr.** American. *B.* 1898. *Educ.* Univ. of Texas (AB 1920); Columbia Univ. (MA, JD 1922); Piedmont Coll. (LLD 1969). *M.* 1946, Bonnie Dowd Van Dyk. *S.* George Carleton Ray and James Van Dyk. *Daus.* Nancy Trimble Armstrong and Bonnie Van Dyk Ray. Admitted: New York Bar, 1923; Conn. Bar, 1962; Vermont Bar 1968; U.S. Supreme Court 1933; member, Legislative Drafting Research Bureau, Columbia 1921–22; prosecuted claims by U.S. on behalf of American nationals against Germany, before Mixed Claims Commission, U.S. and Germany 1922–24; Counsel Texas Co. 1922–42; Gen. Attorney 1942–47. General Counsel, Arabian American Oil Co., Trans-Arabian Pipe Line Co., and Aramco Overseas Co. 1947–61; Agent for Arabian-American Oil Co. in the International arbitration between Saudi Arabia and Arabian-Amer. Oil Co. 1955–58; past Dir. & Chmn., International Economic Affairs Cttee., National Association of Manufacturers; Chairman, Advisory Board, International & Comparative Law Center 1963–66 (now Member of that Board). Served with Air Flying Corps. 1918–22. Republican. *Club:* University (N.Y.C.). *Address:* E. Thetford, Vermont, 05043, U.S.A. and *office* 24N. Main Street, White River Junction, Vermont 05001, U.S.A.

**RAY, Gordon Norton.** President, John Simon Guggenheim Memorial Foundation. *B.* 1915. *Educ.* Univ. of Indiana (AB 1936; AM 1936) and Harvard University (AM 1938; PhD 1940); unmarried. *Career:* Instructor in English, Harvard Univ. 1940–42. Lieut. U.S. Navy (duty chiefly in the Pacific (seven battle stars; Presidential unit citation; 1942–46. Professor of English, Univ. of Illinois 1946–60 (Head of Dept. of English 1950–57; Vice-Pres. and Provost 1957–60, same University Berg. Prof. of English and American Literature, N.Y. University 1952–53; Adviser in Literature, Houghton Mifflin Co. Boston Mass. 1954–71; Professor ,of English, New York Univ. 1962—; Associate Secy. 1960–61, Secy. General 1961–63, Guggenheim Foundation, Pres. since 1963. Trustee, Foundation Library Center 1962–68 (Chmn. of Bd. 1965–68); Center for Applied Linguistics 1965–69; Modern Language Association of America 1968—; Adv. Cncl., Smithsonian Inst., 1968—; Chmn. 1970—; Trustee, Pierpont Morgan Library 1970—; Rosenbach Foundation 1972; New York Public Library 1975—; Dir. & Treas., American Council of Learned Societies 1973—; Trustee, Columbia Univ. Press 1977—; Trustee, Winterthur Museum 1977—. *Publications:* Letters and Private Papers of William Makepeace Thackeray (4 vols. 1945–46); The Buried Life (1952); Thackeray: The Uses of Adversity (1955); Thackeray: The Age of Wisdom (1958); Henry James and H. G. Wells (1958); Contributions, 'Morning Chronicle'; Wells, Desert Daisy & History of Mr. Polly, H. G. Wells & Rebecca West (1974); The Illustrator & the Book in England from 1790 to 1914 (1976). Member, American Philosophical Society 1977—. *Fellow:* Royal Socy. of Lit., 1948, and of Amer. Acad. of Arts and Sciences, 1962, LittD, Monmouth Coll., 1959, Syracuse Univ., 1961, Duke Univ. 1965. LLD: N.Y. Univ., 1961; Tulane Univ., 1963; Columbia Univ., 1969; Univ. of Calif., 1968. LittD, University of Illinois 1968; LHD Indiana Univ., 1964; LLD, Univ. of S. Calif., 1974; LittD, Northwestern Univ., 1974. *Clubs:* Grolier (Pres. 1965–69); Century Association, Harvard (N.Y.C.); Athenaeum (London). *Address:* 25 Sutton Place South, New York, N.Y. 10022, U.S.A.; and *office* 90 Park Avenue, New York, N.Y. 10016.

**RAY, Linton G. Jr.,** AB, MS, PhD. American. *B.* 1917. *Educ.* Emory Univ. (AB, MS); Columbia Univ. (PhD). *M.* 1964, Doris Pfennig. *S.* 1. *Daus.* 2. *Career:* Vice-Pres. Deering Milliken Inc. 1959–60; Pres. Deering Milliken Research Corp. 1960–63; Vice-Pres. Indian Head Inc.; Pres. Joseph Bancroft & Sons, Co. 1964–74; Vice-Pres. Borg Textile Corp., a subsidiary of Bunker Ramo Corp. 1975. *Member:* Textile Research Institute. *Clubs:* Union League; N.Y.C.; Weavers. *Address:* 420 East 51st Street, New York, N.Y., U.S.A.; and *office:* 104, W. 40th Street, New York, N.Y. 10018, N.Y.

**RAY, William F.** American banker. *B.* 1915. *Educ.* University of Cincinnati (AB 1935); Harvard University (MBA 1937). *M.* 1939, Helen Payne. *S.* William F., III. *Daus.* Katharine (Sturgis); Barbara (Stevens), Mary (Struthers, Jr.). Margaret (Gilbert), Deborah, Susan. *Career:* Joined Brown Brothers Harriman & Co. 1937; Asst. Manager 1944–49; Manager 1950–67, Partner since 1968; Trustee, Atlantic Mutual Ins. Co., New York; Dir. Centennial Insurance Co., New York. *Member:* Phi Beta Kappa; Pres., Harvard Business School Assn. 1963–64; Vice-Pres. & Dir., American Australian Assn.; Dir. and Vice-Pres. Robert Brunner Foundation; President, Bankers Association for Foreign Trade (1966–67). Member: Robert Morris Associates (New England President, 1962–63); The Pilgrims of the United States. Republican. *Clubs:* Harvard, Union, Links Golf (New York); Country (Brookline), Apawamis (Rye); Skating Club of Boston (Pres., 1956–58): Woods Hole Golf (Mass.). *Address:* One East End Avenue, New York 10021; and *office* 59 Wall Street, New York, 10005.

**RAYMOND, Hon. Jean,** QC. Canadian. *B.* 1907. *Educ.* Montreal Coll. (BA), and Univ. of Montreal (LLB). *Career:*

Commenced with Alphonse Raymond 1930. Chairman and President, Alphonse Raymond Ltd. (food products); Vice-President: Banque Canadienne Nationale, Montreal, Refrigeration & Storage Ltd., and Provident Assurance Co. Director (to conserve space, 'Ltd.' has been ignored): Bennett, British American Bank Note Co., Canadian Arena Co., Canadian International Paper Co., Canadian Petrofina, Canada Salt Co., Canadian Vickers, Chemcell (1963),Dominion Coal Co., Executive Fund of Canada, Federal Commerce & Navigation Co., Gaspe Copper Mines, General Steel Wares, Holt Renfrew & Co., International Bronze Powders, Laurentide Financial Corp., Noranda Mines, Provincial Transport Co., Quebec Natural Gas Corp., Ritz-Carlton Hotel of Montreal, Sogemines, Warnock Hersey International, Scott LaSalle, Toronto & London Investment Co., and Trust General du Canada. Dir.: Canadian Inst. for the Blind, Montreal Boys' Assn., Canad. Mental Health Assn., Zoological Socy. of Canada, Montreal Museum of Fine Arts, Montreal Symphony Orchestra, and Notre-Dame Hospital. *Clubs:* Mount Royal, Bonaventure, Mount Bruno Country (Montreal); Garrison (Quebec); Lyford Cay (Nassau). *Address: office* 1830 Panet Street, Montreal, P.Q., Canada.

**RAYMOND, Rodrigue Louis.** Haiti Diplomat. *B.* 1925. *Educ.* Doctorate in Economic Science, Paris. *Divorced. S.* 3. *Dau.* 1. *Career:* Ambassador-at-Large, 1962; Ambassador Ex. & Plen. to the EEC since 1969. *Member:* Cercle Royal des Nations. *Decorations:* Ordre National, Honneur et Merite; Ordre Peton et Bolivar. *Publications:* Perspectives d'Haiti. *Club:* Club International de la Courtoisie Française. *Address:* Avenue Louise 524, 1050 Brussels, Belgium.

**RAYMOND, Sir Stanley Edward.** British. *B.* 1913. *Educ.* Orphanage and Hampton Grammar School. *M.* 1938, Enid Buley. *S.* Peter. *Career:* Entered Civil Service 1930; Assistant Secretary, Society of Civil Servants 1939–45. War Service in Royal Artillery 1942–45, Lt. Col. on demobilization. London Passenger Transport Board 1946; British Road Services 1947; Chief Commercial Manager, Scottish Region, British Rlys. 1957 and Asst. General Manager, 1959; Traffic Adviser B.T.C. 1961; General Manager, Western Region, B.R. 1962 and additionally Chmn. Western Railways Board 1963; Member, British Railways Board, Oct. 1963; Vice-Chmn. B.R.B. 1964. Chairman, B.R.B. 1965–67. Chairman: Gaming Board for Great Britain, 1968–77; Chmn. Horse Race Betting Levy Board 1972–74. Governor Thames Polytechnic. *Address:* 26 Cavendish House, King's Road, Brighton, Sussex.

**RAYNE, Edward.** British. *B.* 1922. *Educ.* Harrow. *M.* 1952, Phyllis Cort. *S.* 2. *Career:* Chmn. and Man. Dir. H. & M. Rayne Ltd. since 1951; Chmn of Rayne-Delman Shoes Inc., since 1961; Member, Board of Governors, Genesco Inc., 1967–72; Chairman of Incorporated Society of London Fashion Designers, 1960—: Dir. Debenhams Ltd., since 1975; Pres. Debenhams Inc. since 1976. Member of Export Council for Europe, 1962–71, European Trade Cttee since 1972. President, Royal Warrant Holders Association 1964; President, British Footwear Manufacturers Federation (1965). Fellow, The Royal Society of Arts 1971; Pres. British Boot & Shoe Institution since 1972, Hon. Treas. Royal Warrant Holders Assn. since 1974. *Clubs:* White's; Portland; Travellers' (Paris). *Address:* 15 Grosvenor Square, London, W.1; and *office* H. & M. Rayne Ltd., Tileyard Road, London, N.7.

**RAZAFIMBAHINY, Jules Alphonse.** Malagasy. Ambassador of the Malagasy Republic. *B.* 1922. *Educ.* Lawyer and Economist; MA in Economic and Social Sciences; Graduated at the Inst. for Law and Financial Sciences at the Faculty of Law, Paris. *M.* 1930, Razafy Ravaoarisca. *S.* 1. *Dau.* 1. *Career:* Pres. Commission of Associated Overseas Countries of the Economic and Social Cttee. of the European Economic Community, Brussels, 1958–59. Technical Adviser to the Minister of National Economy, Antananarivo, and Chmn. of the Board of Management, Sté, d'Energie de Madagascar 1960–61. Secy.-Gen., African and Malagasy Organization for Economic Cooperation (with H.Q. in Yaounde, Cameroun). Director-General, Ministry of Foreign Affairs in charge of External Relations Oct. 1964–May 1965; Ambassador to Great Britain & concurrently (non-res.) to Italy, Greece & Israel 1965–67; Sec. of State for Foreign Affairs, Tananarive 1967–70; Amb. to U.S.A., Washington 1970–72; Amb. to Belgium, Holland, Luxembourg, Democratic Republic of Germany, Switzerland & the Holy See, & Perm. Rep. to the EEC, Brussels since 1973. Founder & Dean of the Malagasy Career Diplomatic Coll., 1973. *Publications:* Les sociétés d'économie mixte et leur intervention dans les pays en voie de dévelopment. *Awards:* Grand Cross Orders of St. Sylvester & the Italian Republic; Comdr. National Orders of Chad, Mauretania, Comoros, Zaire & the Malagasy Republic; Officer, National Orders of Gabon and of Upper Volta. *Member:* Board of Directors, Pan-African Development Inst., Douala, Cameroun (Pres.). *Address:* 276 Avenue de Tervueren, 1150 Brussels, Belgium.

**REA, W. Harold.** Canadian. Professional Dir. and Corporate Executive. *B.* 1907. *Educ.* Kincardine (Ont.) public and high schools, and at the Port Colborne (Ont.) High School. *M.* Marion Josephine Currie. *Daus.* Marilyn and Barbara. *Career:* Entered as junior the firm of Thorne, Mulholland, Howson & McPherson, Chartered Accountants, Toronto, 1926; obtained his degree as Chartered Accountant 1931; joined Canadian Oil as internal auditor, 1933; transferred to sales department and became engaged chiefly in sales promotion; loaned to Canadian Government (as Liaison Officer between the Oil Controller and the Armed Services in Ottawa), 1942; Executive Assistant (in charge of supply and transportation) to the Oil Controller, 1944; returned to Canadian Oil as Executive Assistant to the President, 1945 (Pres. Apr. 1949) until company was acquired by Shell Canada Ltd., 1963. Chmn. of Board, Great Canadian Oil Sands Ltd. 1964–77. Vice-Pres. and Dir. Mutual Life Assurance Co. of Canada, 1968—; Governor of the Univ. of Western Ontario, London, Ontario 1968–73; Director A. Johnson & Co. (Canada) Ltd. 1969—. Bank of Nova Scotia, Interprovincial Pipe Line Co., Kerr-Addison Mines Ltd., Canadian & Foreign Securities Ltd., Mutual Life Assurance Co. of Canada, Moore Corp. Ltd., Dominion Foundries and Steel Ltd.; Chmn. Bd. A. Johnson & Co. (Canada) Ltd. since 1972; Dir., Wellesley Hosp., Toronto. Elected Fellow, Inst. of Chartered Accountants of Ontario; Mem. Adv. Committee, University of Western Ontario's School of Business Administration. Hon. LLD, Univ. of Western Ontario. *Clubs:* York, Granite, Toronto, Rosedale Golf (Toronto); *Address:* Suite 1505, 44 King Street West, Toronto M5H 1E2, Ont., Canada.

**READ, Leonard Edward.** *B.* 1898. *Educ.* Hubbardston High School, and Ferris Institute, Big Rapids (Grad.). *M.* 1920, Gladys Emily Cobb. *S.* Leonard Edward and James Baker. *Career:* Pres., Ann Arbor Product Co. 1919–25; Secy., Burlinghame (Calif.) Chamber of Commerce 1927; Mgr., Palo Alto (Calif.) Chamber of Commerce 1928; Asst. Mgr., Western Div., U.S. Chamber of Commerce 1929–32, Mgr. 1932–39; Gen. Mgr., Los Angeles Chamber of Commerce 1939–45; Dir. and Mgr., Western Conference for Commercial and Trade Executives, Stanford Univ. 1929–40; Dir., National Association of Commercial Organization Secretaries 1942–44; Exec. Vice-Pres., National Industrial Conference Board, N.Y. 1945–46. Trustee, College of Artesia, New Mexico: President, Foundation for Economic Education, New York 1946—. Honn. LittD, Grove City Coll. 1964. Member, Amer. Economic Association. *Publications:* Romance of Reality (1937); Pattern for Revolt (1945); Students of Liberty (1950); Outlook for Freedom (1951); Government: An Ideal Concept (1954); Why Not Try Freedom! (1958); Elements of Libertarian Leadership (1962); Anything That's Peaceful (1964); The Free Market and Its Enemy (1965); Deeper than you Think (1967); Accent on the Right (1968); The Coming Aristocracy (1969); Let Freedom Reign (1969); Talking to Myself (1970); Then Truth Will Out (1971); To Free or Freeze (1972); Who's Listening (1973); Having My Way (1974); Castles in the Air (1975); The Love of Liberty (1975); Comes the Dawn (1976); Let's Awake for Freedom's Sake (1977). *Clubs:* Canadian (N.Y.C.); St. Andrews Golf. *Address: office* 30 South Broadway, Irvington, N.Y., U.S.A.

**READ-BARRERAS, Lic. Eduardo.** Dominican diplomat. *B.* 1904. *Educ.* Univ. of Santo Domingo (Lin.-in-Law). *M.* Zoraida Ramona Delgado. *S.* Federico, Roberto, Victor and David. *Daus.* Rosa Maria, Frances and Ramona. *Career:* Under-Secy. of State for Labour, 1957–59; for Foreign Relations Jan.–May 1959; and again for Labour May–Nov. 1959. Secretary of State for Justice Nov. 1959–Jan. 1960; for Labour 1960–61. President of the Supreme Court 1961–62; First Vice-President, Council of State Jan.–Feb. 1962; Pres., Supreme Court Aug. 1962–Feb. 1963. Amb. to U.K. 1963–64. Ambassador to Italy 1964. *Address:* c/o Ministry of Foreign Affairs, Santo Domingo, Dominican Republic.

**REAGAN, Charles Michael.** American business executive. *B.* 1896. *Educ.* Univ. of Notre Dame (BS 1917). *M.* 1923, Lucile Ann McKim. *Dau.* Ann Reagan Hafer. *Career:* President, Greater Indianapolis Amusement Co. Inc.; Vice-President; 540-15th Street Corp., Empire Theatres Corp.,

Theatreama Ltd. Vice-Pres. and General Sales Manager, Loew's Inc., N.Y.C. 1952–57; Vice-President and General Sales Manager, Paramount Pictures Co., N.Y.C. 1944–49; Knight of Malta; Knight of the Grand Cross, Equestrian Order of the Holy Sepulchre. *Address:* 2 Sutton Place South, New York, N.Y. 10022, U.S.A.

**REAGAN, Ronald.** American Politician. *B.* 1911. *Educ.* Eureka, Ill. (AB). *M.* (1) 1940, Jane Wyman (*Div.* 1948). *S.* 1. *Dau.* 1. (2) 1952, Nancy Davis. *S.* 1. *Dau.* 1. *Career:* Sports announcer, WHO, Des Moides 1932–37; Motion Picture & T.V. Actor 1937–66 (served as Captain, USAAF 1942–43); Gov., State of California 1967–74; Chmn., Republican Governors' Assn. 1969; Candidate for Republican nomination for the Presidency 1976. *Address:* 10960 Wilshire Boulevard, Los Angeles, Calif. 90024, U.S.A.

**REARDON, Harriman Apsley.** American insurance agent and broker. *B.* 1895. *Educ.* Cushing Academy. *M.* 1917, Flora A. Duran. *Career:* Dir., Hudson Co-operative Bank 1926–70; Pres., 1931–65; Chmn. Bd. 1965–71, Hon. Life Director; Corporator Hudson Savings Bank 1926–74; Trustee 1931–62; Director Hudson National Bank 1925–76; Consultant and Dir., Harriman A. Reardon & Co. Inc. since 1968. *Trustee:* Benevolent Funds of Hudson (Mass.) 1935–62; First Methodist Church of Hudson 1929–62; member, Alumni Cncl. of Cushing Academy; President and Director, Lewis Dewart Apsley Fund for the Aged and Indigent, Inc. President: Insurance Brokers Assn. of Massachusetts (1948–52), Old English Game Club of America (1943–58), Hudson Chamber of Commerce (1931 and 1932), Hudson Industrial Commission (1956); Trustee, Cushing Academy (1952–58); Treas., Boston Poultry Exposition (1938–43; Dir. 1938–53). President and Treasurer, Harriman A. Reardon & Co. Inc. (1914–67). *Awards:* Named Man of the Year, by Boston Bd. of Underwriters 1952. *Publications:* Editor, Lines for Brokers (1948–55); former member, Editorial Advisory Board of New England Poultrymen; Editor, Northeastern Fantail News. Republican. *Member:* American Pigeon Club; Dir., North-eastern Fantail Club; Pres. 1968–69; American Poultry Assn., American Legion, Sons of Union Veterans of Civil War, Life Member Hudson Historical Soc. *Clubs:* Hudson Rotary (Pres. 1959–60); Old English Game Club of America. *Address:* 2 Brigham Street, Hudson, Mass., U.S.A.

**RECTOR, Luther Griffith.** Canadian. *B.* 1909. *Educ.* Cornell College (Mt. Veron, Ia.) and Armour Inst. of Technology (Chicago). *M.* 1935, Eileen Margaret Riddell. *S.* Donald James and Darcy Griffith. *Dau.* Mrs. Sally Janet Coulter. *Career:* Chmn. of the Board. The Griffith Laboratories Ltd. Dir.; Griffith Laboratories Inc., U.S.A.; Past Chmn. Institute of Profit Sharing; Past Chmn. United Community Fund of Metropolitan Toronto. *Clubs:* Granite Rosedale Golf. *Address:* 1 Valleyanna Drive, Toronto, M4N 1J7, Ont.; and *office* 757 Pharmacy Avenue, Scarborough M1L 3J8, Ont., Canada.

**RECTOR, William George.** American manufacturing exec. *B.* 1916. *Educ.* University of Minnesota, Northwestern University and Univ. of Arizona (BS). *M.* 1940, Kathleen Spriggs Wager. *S.* Walter William. *Daus.* Barbara Kathleen (Morken) and Susan Elizabeth (Boynton, Jr.). *Career:* Trainee, Montgomery Ward & Co. 1940–45; Works Manager, Evansville Tool Works 1945–49, and Kelly Axe Works 1949–53 (Exec. Vice-Pres., True Temper Corp. 1953, Pres. 1953–64, Consultant 1964—). President, Lufkin Rule Co., Saginaw, Mich. Pres., True Temper Corp. 1953—; Crescent Niagara Corp., Jamestown, N.Y.; Vice Pres. Dir. Cooper Industries Inc., Houston, Texas. *Clubs:* Cleveland Union; Chicago Athletic; McGregor Downs Country Club (Raleigh, North Carolina); Tucson Country Club; Old Pueblo Club. *Address:* Rt. 2 Box 737 M Tucson, Arizona 85715; and *office* Cooper Industries, Inc., Pres. Hardware Group PO Box 728 Apex, North Carolina 27502, U.S.A.

**REDCLIFFE-MAUD, Lord (John Primatt Redcliffe).** GCB, CBE. British academic. *B.* 3 Feb. 1906. *Educ.* Eton; New College, Oxford (MA); Harvard College (AB). *M.* 1932, Jean Hamilton. *S.* Humphrey John Hamilton. *Daus.* Caroline Mary Stewart, Virginia Jean Furse. Fellow and Dean, University College, Oxford 1929–39, Hon Fellow 1956; Hon. Fellow of New College 1964, Hon LLD, Witwatersrand and Natal Universities S. Africa, Leeds and Nottingham Universities, Hon. DSoc Sc Birmingham University; *Career:* University Lecturer in Politics, Oxford 1938–39; Master of Birkbeck College, Univ. of London 1939–43; Dep. Secretary, Ministry of Food, later Second Secretary 1941–44; United Kingdom delegate to Conferences on Food and Agriculture, Hot Springs, 1943, U.N.R.R.A., Atlan ic City 1943, General Conferences of U.N.E.S.C.O. 1946–50; Second Secretary, Office of Minister of Reconstruction 1944–45; Secretary, Office of Lord President of Council; member, Executive Board of U.N.E.S.C.O. 1947–49, Chairman 1949–50; Permanent Secretary Ministry of Education 1945–52; Perm. Sec., Min. of Power 1952–58; High Commissioner for U.K. in Union of South Africa 1959–61; Ambassador to Republic of South Africa 1961–63, and High Commissioner for Basutoland, Bechuanaland Protectorate and Swaziland 1959–63. Master of Univ. Coll., Oxford, 1963–76; Chairman, Royal Commission on Local Government in England, 1966–69; Chmn. of Council Royal Coll. of Music 1965–73; Pres. Queen Elizabeth House Oxford; For. Associate Venezuelan Acad. of Science 1973; Chmn. P. Minister's Cttee. on Local Govt. Rules of Conduct 1973–74. *Publications:* English Local Government; City Government; The Johannesburg Experiment; Johannesburg and the Art of Self-Government; English Local Government Reformed (1974). *Address:* 221 Woodstock Road, Oxford.

**REDDAWAY, George Frank Norman,** CBE. British Diplomat. *B.* 1918. *Educ.* Oundle Sch.; King's Coll., Cambridge—MA; Staff Coll., Camberley—psc. *M.* 1944, Jean Brett. *S.* 2. *Daus.* 3. *Career:* British Army 1939–46; Foreign Office 1946–49; HM Embassy, Rome 1949–52; UK High Commission, Ottawa 1952–55; Foreign Office 1955–59; Imperial Defence Coll., 1960; HM Embassy, Beirut 1961–65; Political Advisor's Office, Singapore 1965–66; HM Embassy, Khartoum 1967–69; Foreign & Commonwealth Office 1970–74; HM Ambassador, Warsaw 1974–77. *Decorations:* Member, Order of the British Empire (Military), 1946; Commander, Order of the British Empire, 1965. *Clubs:* Oxford & Cambridge; Royal Commonwealth Soc. *Address:* 51 Carlton Hill, London NW8; and *office* Foreign & Commonwealth Office, King Charles Street, London SW1.

**REDDING, James Deyo.** American aeronautical engineer. International Consultant. *B.* 1906. *Educ.* Wittenberg College (AB 1930); Univ. of Michigan (BS-Aero Eng. 1930; MSE 1931). *M.* 1934, Hildegarde I. Poppenberg. *S.* James H., Robert R., and John L. *Career:* Dir. International Development, Univac Defense Systems Division of Sperry Rand Corp., 1961–71. Dir. Military Applications, Univac Div. 1959–61. Marketing Manager 1957–59, Manager Headquarters Sales 1956–57, and Staff Assistant to Chief Engineer 1954–56, Westinghouse Aviation Gas Turbine Division, Kansas City, Mo.; Executive Director of Committee on Aeronautics, Research and Development Board, Dept. of Defense; later Technical Assistant to Deputy Asst. Secretary of Defense 1949–54; Manager, Aeronautical Dept., Society of Automotive Engineers 1941–49; Asst. Chief of Aircraft Airworthiness Section, Civil Aeronautics Administration 1936–41; Aircraft Stress Analyst, Consolidated Aircraft Corporation 1931–36, Republican. *Fellow:* Royal Aeronautical Socy. (London, Eng.); Associate Fellow, American Institute of Aeronautics & Astronautics. *Member:* Socy. of Automotive Engineers. *Clubs:* International (Washington); National Aviation; Shrine; Abdallah Temple; Washington, D.C. *Address:* 5100 Lawton Drive, Washington, D.C. 20016, U.S.A.

**REDDISH, Sir Halford (Walter Lupton),** FCA. *B.* 1898. *Educ.* Rugby School. *M.* 1946, Valerie Campbell Smith. (D. 1971.). *Career:* In professional practice (Chartered Accountant) 1922–33. Chairman and Chief Executive, The Rugby Portland Cement Co. Ltd. 1933–76. Director: Granada Group Ltd.; Meldrum Investment Trust Ltd.; Warburg Investment Management Ltd.; Underwriting Member of Lloyd's. Mem.: Bd. of Referees (Inland Revenue); Patron Rugby Conservative Association; Freeman of the City of London in the Livery of the Patternmakers. *Awards:* First Place and Institute Gold Medal. Final Examination, Institute of Chartered Accountants, 1920; Hon. FRCP 1977. *Publications:* sundry articles on industrial and economic subjects. *Club:* Carlton (London). *Address:* Welton House, nr. Daventry, Northants; and *office* Crown House, Rugby, Warwicks.

**REDDROP, Sydney.** Australian. *B.* 1897. *Educ.* State Schools. *M.* 1923, Elsie Marion Jeppesen. *Daus.* 2. *Career:* Chairman, Kolotex Holdings Ltd.; Director: Frank G. O'Brien Ltd.; Culivulla Co-op Building Society; Lift Slab, Australasia; Willis, Faber & Nicholls Pty. Ltd. Formerly State Manager for N.S.W., The Commercial Bank of Australia Ltd. *Address:* c/o 2 Burleigh Street, Lindfield, Sydney, Australia.

**REDELE, Charles Hendrik Julien.** Dutch. *B.* 1900. *Educ.* Technical High School. *M.* 1908. Johanna H. Van Mesdag. *S.* Julien Geert and Alexander Charles and Geert. *Career:* Member, Board of Directors: Amfas Assurance Co., Rotterdam 1943–72; Prinsenstee Orchards, Brielle 1962–72. *Member:* My v. Nyverheid en Handel (Pres. Dordrecht Section) 1935–44, Member of the National Management Committee 1938–42; Weizigt Sanatorium (President 1944–56); A.N.W.B. (Automobile Assn.)Board of Directors 1935–60;Pres,Victoria Biscuit Co. 1926–52. *Club:* Rotary. *Address:* Luryer, 1807 Blonay, Switzerland.

**REDPATH, Albert Gordon.** Banker. Member, Auchincloss Parker & Redpath; Director: Marine Studios Inc., Marineland, Fla.; and Northwest Airlines, St. Paul, Minn.; Photometric Corp. *B.* 1896. *Educ.* Columbia Coll. (AB 1918); Phi Beta Kappa and Columbia University Law School (LLB 1922). *M.* 1936, Arthemise Baldwin Ottmann. Special Assistant to Secretary of the Treasury, Washington, D.C. 1927–31; Lawyer, 37 Wall Street, New York City 1922–27; Trustee, Columbia Universitiy, N.Y.C. 1946–52. Trustee & Secretary, Columbia Univ. Press, N.Y.C.; Director & Secy.-Treas., Columbia Law Review Assn., N.Y.C.; Trustee & Chmn. of Board, Foxhollow School, Lenox, Mass. *Member:* Medieval Acad. of America; Acad. of Political Science; Amer. Bar Assn.; Assn. of Stock Exchange Firms; Amer. Judicature Socy.; Assn. of the Bar of City of New York; New York County Lawyers Assn. *Clubs.* The Brook; Circumnavigators; The Creek; Chevy Chase (Md.); Columbia Univ.; Downtown Assn.; Faculty (Columbia Univ.); Harbor View; Lawyers; University; Metropolitan (Washington). *Address:* 40 East 67th Street, New York City, N.Y. 10021; and *office* 60 Broad Street, New York City, N.Y. 10004, U.S.A.

**REDROW, Samuel L., Jr.** American. Financial and Tax Consultant & Writer. *B.* 1905. *Educ.* Univ. of Cincinnati (Business Admin. 1928–29), and International Accountants Socy. 1930–33. *M.* 1924, Margaret Louise Reif. *Dau.* Margaret Jeanne (Willson). *Career:* With a stock and bond securities broker 1920–25. Joined Cincinnati Milling Machine Co. (now Cincinnati Milacron Inc.) Feb. 1926 (early positions in accountancy, publicity and administrative capacities) offices held were—Secretary: Public and Financial Relations, The Cincinnati Milling Machine Co. 1956–70, Cincinnati Milling & Grinding Machines Inc. 1952–70. Secretary and Director: The Factory Power Co. 1954–70, and Cincinnati Grinders Inc. 1956–70. Director, Cincinnati Lathe & Tool Co. 1956–70. Manager, Cincinnati Milling Machine Foundation 1961–70. *Member:* Amer. Ordnance Association; Council on World Affairs; Amer. Socy. Corporate Secretaries. Mason. Republican. *Address:* 8950 Old Indian Hill Road, Cincinnati, Ohio 45243, U.S.A.

**REECE, David Chalmer.** Canadian diplomat. *B.* 1926. *Educ.* Cambridge Univ. MA; Called to Bar 1951. *M.* 1958, Mima Stone, *S.* 1. *Daus.* 2. *Career:* Dept. of External Affairs since 1952; Minister and Deputy Permanent Representative of Canada to United Nations NY 1969–71; High Commissioner of Canada to Trinidad and Tobago and Barbados 1972–74; High Commissioner of Canada to Ghana, and Ambassador of Canada in Togo and Dahomey 1974. *Clubs:* Tesano (Accra); Ghana (Accra). *Address:* c/o Department of External Affairs, Ottawa, Canada.

**REECE, Hon. Eric Elliott.** *B.* 6 July 1909. *Educ.* State and technical schools. *M.* 1935, Alice Lucy Hanigan. *S.* 2. *Daus.* 2. *Career:* Minister for Housing, Tasmania 1946–47; Minister for Lands, Works and Mines, Tasmania 1947–58; President, Tasmanian Section, Australian Labour Party 1948–56 and 1958–59; Federal Executive Member, Australian Labour Party 1948–59; Senior Vice-President 1950–52; Federal President 1952–53 and 1954–55. Premier of Tasmania. 1958–69, Leader of the Opposition, Tasmania, 1969–72; Premier 1972–75. *Award:* Companion of the Order of Australia, 1975. *Address:* 59 Howard Road, Glenorchy 7010, Tasmania, Australia.

**REED, Albert Mount.** American. *B.* 1912. *Educ.* Wharton School, University of Pennsylvania (BSEcon 1936). *M.* (1) 1941, Ruth L. Hullfish (*D* 1976). (2) 1977, Erma A. Livirrie. *Career:* Joined Bethlehem Steel Corp. Accounting Dept. Loop Course for Coll. graduates; Asst. Comptroller 1956; elected comptroller and Dir. 1963; Vice-Pres. Accounting comptroller 1965, Senior Vice-Pres. 1977. Member, Exec. Cttee., finance Cttee., employee Compensation Cttee, Investment Cttee., Savings Plan Cttee., General Pension Bd., Insurance Bd.-Social Insurance Plan. *Member:* Beta Gamma Sigma. *Member:* American Iron & Steel Inst.; Financial Executives Inst.; Pennsylvania Economy League. *Clubs:* Saucon Valley Country, Bethlehem (both of Bethlehem). *Address:* 1906 Homestead Avenue, Bethlehem, Pa. 18018; and *office* Bethlehem Steel Corporation, Bethlehem, Pa. 18016, U.S.A.

**REED, David.** *B.* 1945. *M.* (1) 1970, Jackie Woodley, (2) Susan L. Garrett. *Career:* Reporter, The Northern Echo; Public Relations Officer, North East Development Council; P.R.O. Vickers Ltd. Member of Parliament for Sedgefield, 1970–74; Public Affairs Manager Hewlett-Packard Ltd. *Address:* 37 Damer Gardens, Henley on Thames, Oxon RG9 1HX; and *office* King Street Lane, Winnersh, Wokingham, Berkshire, RG11 5AR.

**REED, Firmin Preece.** British. *B.* 1914. *Educ.* Alsop High School (Liverpool) and Liverpool (England) University (BSc (Hons 1st Cl.); PhD); ARIC. *M.* 1938, Isabel Wilson Woollam. *S.* John Wilson. *Dau.* Elaine Wilson. *Career:* Research Chemist, Dyestuffs Div., I.C.I., Manchester 1936–45; Control Officer I, Control Commission for Germany (British Element) 1945–48. With I.C.I. Dyestuffs Div.: Plant Supt., Head of Dept., and Asst. Works Manager 1948–54. With I.C.I. (Organics), Providence, R.I., U.S.A.: Research Manager 1954–55. Technical Vice-President 1955–58, Exec. Vice-Pres. 1958—; Executive Vice-President and Director, I.C.I. (Organics) Inc. 1958—. Director, I.C.I. (New York) Inc. 1962—. *Publications:* Research contributions to Journal of the Chemical Society 1936–38. *Member:* American Chemical Society; American Association of Textile Chemists & Colorists; Society of the Chemical Industry; Royal Institute of Chemistry. *Clubs:* Bristol (R.I.) Yacht; Turks Head (Providence); Chemists (N.Y.C.). *Address:* *office* 55 Canal Street, Providence, R.I., U.S.A.

**REED, Gordon Wies.** American executive. *B.* 1899. *Educ.* Univ. of Illinois (ME). *M.* (1) 1928, Naomi Bradley (*Dec.*). *S.* Thomas. *M.* (2) 1967, Genevieve Funston. Asst. Dir. W.P.B. 1941–44; Chmn., Glass Fibers 1946–54; Vice-Pres. Hanley Co. 1925–41; Asst. Dir. Al & Mag. Div. W.P.B. 1941–44: Chmn. Texas Gulf Producing Co., 1941–65. Special Asst. Chief of Staff, U.S.A.F. 1950–60. Dir. American Metal Climax (now Amax Inc.); Dir. Putman Trust Co. Greenwich. *Publications:* Reed Cttee. Report on Military Air Transport Service (MATS) 1960, Republican. *Clubs:* Links; Metropolitan; Chicago; Round Hill; Blind Brook; Indian Harbor Yacht, Clove Valley Rod & Gun. *Address:* 100 Clapboard Ridge Road, Greenwich, Conn.; and *office* AMAX Center, Greenwich, Conn. 06830 U.S.A.

**REED, Lieut.-Commander John Cameron.** British company director and naval officer (retired). *B.* 11 Feb. 1898. *Educ.* Royal Naval Colleges, Osborne and Dartmouth; Emmanuel College, Cambridge. *M.* 1943, Zelia Teixeira de Lemos. *S.* John. D. *Dau.* Marie-Louise. Served in World War I, with the Royal Navy 1914–18; retired from Royal Navy 1922; entered oil industry in 1923, and served in various capacities in Persia, India, South America and the United Kingdom; served in World War II with the Royal Navy; Former Dir. The Carioca Property Co. Ltd., The Strattan Shipping Co. Ltd., Société Immobilière Niagara. *Address:* La Californie, Avenue du Roi Albert, Cannes, A.M., France.

**REED, Lawrence Stevens.** *B.* 1905. *Educ.* Univ. of Illinois. *M.* (1) 1938, Sarah Gaffney (Dec.). *Dau.* Polly. (2) 1974, Mary C. Kempner. *Career:* Engineer, Hanley Co. Summerville, Pa. 1927–33; Contractor, New York City and Bradford, Pa. 1933–36; Manager, Reed Oil Co., Garnett, Kansas 1936–42. Pres. & Dir.; Texas Gulf Producing Co. 1942, Compania de Petroleo Ganso Azul Ltda. 1953, and Libyan American Oil Co. 1955. (These companies were sold in 1964 to Sinclair Oil Corporation, and Mr Reed resigned as President and Director in each company.) Past Dir., Planned Parenthood, Vice Chmn. Amax Petroleum Corp. *Member:* American Inst. of Mining & Metallurgical Engineers; and Independent Petroleum Assn. of America (Director). *Clubs:* Eagle Lake Rod & Gun; Texas; Houston Country; Texas Corinthian Yacht. *Address:* 3688 Willowick Drive, Houston, Texas 77019. and Room 506, Bank of the Southwest Building, Houston, Tex. 77002, U.S.A.

**REED, Philip Dunham.** American. Director: *B.* 1899. *Educ.* Univ. of Wisconsin (BSc in Elec. Engineering); Fordham Univ. (LLB *cum laude*). *M.* 1921, Mabel Mayhew Smith. *S.* Philip Dunham Jr. *Daus.* Kathryn V. (Wilson Smith). *Career:* Various appointments with General Electric Co. 1926–59. Chmn. Bd., 1940–42 & 1945–58; Dir. Emeritus, 1968—. Chairman, International Gen. Electric Co. 1945 until merger with parent company in 1952; Chief, Bureau of Industries, War Production Board, 1942; Chief, U.S. Mission for Economic Affairs, London, 1943–45. Chairman, U.S. Side, Anglo-American Council on Productivity 1948–52; Member, U.S. Adv. Cttee. on Information 1948–61; Spl. Amb. to Mexico, 1958. Dir. Bankers Trust Co. 1939–58 and 1966–72; Metropolitan Life Insurance Co. 1940–73; Otis Elevator Co. 1956—72; Tiffany & Co. 1956—; Krafto Corp. 1958–70; American Express Co. and Amer. International Corp. 1958–72; Bigelow Sanford Inc. since 1959; Red. Res. Bank of N.Y. 1959–65, Chmn. 1960–65; Eurofund 1959–71; Bankers Trust New York Corp. 1966–72; Elfun Trusts 1966–72; U.S. Financial 1970–72; Cowles Communications Inc. since 1972. offices in other civic and cultural organizations. *Member:* Pilgrim Trust of U.S., Amer. Ditchley Foundation, English-Speaking Union, etc. Republican. *Clubs:* University, Links (N.Y.C.); Apawamis. (Rye, N.Y.); Blind Brook (Port Chester, N.Y.); Augusta (Georgia); National Golf; Bohemian (San Francisco); Mill Reef (Antigua, W.I.). *Address:* Sunset Lane, Rye, New York, 10580; and *office* 375 Park Avenue, New York, N.Y. 10022.

**REED, Sir Reginald Charles**, CBE. Australian executive. *B.* 1909. *Educ.* Public School. *M.* 1934, May Moore. *S.* Kenneth Reginald. *Career:* Associated with James Patrick & Co. Pty. Ltd. and Patrick Stevedoring Co. since 1930, in stevedoring and shipping. Appointed by Commonwealth Govt. to Australian Stevedoring Industry Authority in 1949 and served until 1956; Governing Dir.: Patrick Operations Pty. Ltd./Patrick Agencies (Sydney, Melbourne, Brisbane, Adelaide, Fremantle); Patrick Stevedoring Co. (Sydney, Brisbane, Melbourne); Patrick Bulk Stevedoring (ACT) Pty. Ltd. (Sydney); Man. Dir.: Smith Patrick Stevedoring Co. Pty. Ltd. (Adelaide); Smith Patrick Stevedoring (W.A.) Pty. Ltd. (Fremantle); Director, Universal Charterers Pty. Ltd.; J. Meloy Ltd. Chmn., Australian Shipbuilding Bd. 1966; Dir., Sims Consolidated Ltd.; Dep. Chmn. Australian National Line; Chmn. Glebe Island Terminals Pty Ltd. *Member:* Council Aust. Chamber of Shipping; Royal Commonwealth Society. Created Kt. Bachelor 1971. *Clubs:* Tattersall's; American National; Royal Automobile (of Australia); Royal Sydney Yacht Squadron; Australian. *Address:* 11 Montah Avenue, Killara 2071, N.S.W.; and *office* Patrick Operations Pty. Ltd., 33 Pitt Street, Sydney, N.S.W., Australia.

**REES, Leslie.** Australian author and previously radio editor-producer. *B.* 1905. *Educ.* BA (Western Aus.). *M.* 1931, Coralie Clarke (author). *Daus.* Megan and Dymphna. *Career:* As Federal Drama Editor to the A.B.C., as co-founder and chairman. from its inception (1937) of the Playwrights' Advisory Board, and as author of various books and hundreds of articles on the drama, he has worked continuously for the development of the Australian drama and theatre. Produced many plays for the A.B.C. and recordings of some of these have been broadcast in programmes of the B.B.C. and almost every other English-speaking country. Dramatic critic in London, 1931–36. *Publications:* Thirty books published include The Making of Australian Drama (1973), a historical-critical work usually acknowledged as the standard work on its subject, several collections of Australian plays; four books of travel (written in collaboration with Coralie Rees)—Spinifex Walkabout (hitch-hiking in remote Australia), Westward from Cocos (Indian Ocean travels), Coasts of Cape York (travels around Australia's pearl-tipped peninsula); and People of the Big Sky Country (characters of North & Central Australia); also many books for children, including Shy the Platypus, Two Thumbs the Koala, Mates of the Kurlalong, A Treasury of Australian Nature Stories, Digit Dick (some of these have been translated into foreign languages; and total sales have reached two million copies). *Address:* Unit 4, 5 The Esplanade, Balmoral Beach, N.W.S., Australia.

**REES, Rt. Hon. Merlyn,** PC 1974, MP. *B.* 1920. *Educ.* Goldsmiths' Coll., London School of Economics (MScEcon). *M.* 1949 Colleen Faith Cleveley. *S.* 3. *Career:* Parly. Private Secy. to the Chancellor of the Exchequer 1964–65; Under-Secy. of State for Defence for the Army 1965–66. Under-Secy. of State for Defence for the Royal Air Force 1966–68. Member of Parliament (Lab.) Leeds South; Joint Parly. Secretary, Home Office, 1969–70. Member Cttee. to examine Section 2, Official Secrets Act, 1971; Front Bench Spokesman on Northern Ireland 1972; Elected Shadow Cabinet 1972; Sec. of State N.I. 1974–76; Home Secretary since 1976. *Address:* House of Commons, London, S.W.1.

**REES, Peter Wynford Innes,** QC, MA. British. Queen's Counsel, *B.* 1926. *Educ.* Stowe School; Christ Church Oxford. *M.* 1969, Anthea Maxwell Hyslop. *Career:* Lieutenant Scots Guards, 1945–48; Practice in Law (Revenue Bar) since 1953 Member of Parliament for Dover since 1970. *Club:* Boodles. *Address:* 39 Headfort Place, London, S.W.1; and *office* 11 New Square, Lincolns Inn, W.C.2.

**REES, Raymond Griffith,** JP, FCA. Australian. *B.* 1916. *Educ.* Fellow Inst. of Chartered Accountants. *M.* (1) 1940, Mary Roberts (died 1956). *S.* 1. *Daus.* 2. *M.* (2) 1965, Theresa Doeppel. *Career:* Senior Partner in firm of A. E. H. Evans & Co., Chartered Accountants, Adelaide, S.A.; South Australian Consultant-Dir. of Aust. Eagle Insurance Co. Ltd.; Chmn. S.A. Trotting Control Board; Mem. & Treas., Australian Trotting Council and Inter-Dominion Trotting Council; Mem. Grand Council; Mem. S.A. Totalizator Agency Board; State Councillor, Old People's Welfare Council of S.A.; Member of Boards of several companies; Regd. Taxation Agent and Licensed Company Auditor and Liquidator. *Clubs:* Stock Exchange (Adelaide); Adelaide Bowling; S.A. Cricket Assn. *Address:* 19 Grove Street, Unley Park, S.A. 5061; and *office* Da Costa Building, 68 Grenfell Street, Adelaide, S.A. 5000, Australia.

**REES-MOGG, William.** British. Editor of The Times (London), Jan. 1967. *B.* 1928. *Educ.* Charterhouse and Balliol College, Oxford (Brackenbury Scholar). *M.* 1962, Gillian Shakespeare Morris. *S.* Thomas Fletcher, Jacob William. *Daus.* Emma Beatrice and Charlotte Louise. *Career:* With Financial Times 1952–60 (Chief Leader Writer 1955–60, Asst. Editor 1957–60). With Sunday Times 1960–67 (City Editor 1960–61, Political and Economic Editor 1961–63, Deputy Editor 1964–67). *Publications:* The Reigning Error: the crisis of world inflation (1974); An Humbler Heaven (1977). *Club:* Garrick. *Address:* Ston Easton Park, Bath, Avon; 3 Smith Square, London, S.W.1; and *office* The Times, Gray's Inn Road, Printing House Square, London, WC1X 8E2.

**REESE, Addison Hardcastle.** American. *B.* 1908. *Educ.* University School, Riderwood, Maryland; Johns Hopkins University, Baltimore. *M.* 1936, Gertrude Craig. *Career:* President and Chairman of the Board, County Trust Co., Maryland, 1947–51; Director: Federal Reserve Bank of Richmond, Va. 1961–63; Chairman of the Board, North Carolina National Bank 1967–73; Chmn., NCNB. Corp. 1968–73; Director: Ruddick Corp., 1968—, Duke Power Co. 1974—, Engraph Corp. 1975—; Dir. Research Triangle Foundation 1964–67. *Trustee:* University of North Carolina, 1964–72; Chairman, Board of Trustees, Charlotte College 1964–65; Dir. Int. Monetary Conference 1971–73; Chmn. of Trustees, Univ. of N.C. Charlotte since 1972. Hon. LLD University of N. Carolina. Pres.: Assn. of Reserve City Bankers, 1965–66. *Clubs:* Charlotte Country; Quail Hollow Country; City; Elkridge (Baltimore); Sankaty Head Golf (Nantucket). *Address:* 441 Eastover Road, Charlotte, North Carolina; 28207; and *office* North Carolina National Bank, Box 120; Charlotte, North Carolina 28255, U.S.A.

**REESE, Everett David.** American banker. *B.* 1898. *Educ.* Ohio State University (BS). *M.* (1). 1924, Martha Grace Miller. (D. 1970.). (2) 1971, Mrs Pendery Haines. *S.* John Gilbert and David Everett. *Daus.* Phoebe (Lewis); Thekla (Shackelford). *Career:* Chmn. Bd. Park National Bank of Newark Ohio; Emeritus. The City National Bank & Trust Co., Columbus, Ohio; Park National Bank, Newark, Ohio, and First National Bank, Cambridge, Ohio; Director and Chmn., First Federal Savings and Loan Association, Newerk, O.; Director, Suburban Motor Freight Inc., Liqui Box Corp., Columbus, O.; Member of Board: Coshocton, O; Dir. First Bancgroup of Ohio, Inc. *Trustee* (Emeritus): Denison Univ., and Denison Univ. Research Foundation, Granville, O.; Columbus Gallery of Fine Arts, Children's Hospital, Mt. Carmel Hospital (all of Columbus, O.); Dawes Arboretum, Newark, O.; Chairman of Trustees, Piney Woods Country Life School, Miss.; Chairman, Park National Bank (Pres. 1926–62); Pres. Ohio Bankers Assn. (1942) and Amer. Bankers Assn. (1953); Vice-Pres. 1952; Past-Pres., Newark. Ohio, Chamb. of Com.; Chairman, Executive Committee, The Presidents Club, The Ohio State University. *Address:* 320 N. Parkview Avenue, Columbus, Ohio 43209; and *office* Suite 1100, 88 East Broad Street, Columbus, Ohio 43215, U.S.A.

**REEVES, Frank Andrew,** CBE. New Zealand citizen. *B.* 1910. *Educ.* Auckland Grammar School and Auckland Univ. Registered Member of N.Z. Socy. of Accountants (A.R.A.N.Z.). *M.* 1939, Florence Settle. *S.* Graeme Frank, John Settle, and Ralph Andrew. *Dau.* Jillian. *Career:* In shipping, export and import depts. (reaching post of Manager of export division), A. S. Paterson & Co. Ltd. 1927–35; Primary Products Marketing Dept. (responsible for establishing shipping and accounting procedures) 1936–39. On outbreak of World War II joined R.N.Z.A.F.; served 6 years. South Pacific War Theatre, attaining rank of Sqdn.-Leader, then posted to active Reserve of Officers, R.N.Z.A.F. Joined the New Zealand Airline, then named TEAL as Supply Manager 1946; Commercial Manager 1949; Asst. Gen. Mgr. Technical) 1954; Gen. Man. 1958–69. Member Auckland Univ. Council; Area Co-ordinator Duke of Edinburgh Award; Royal Commission on Container Shipping; New Zealand Ports Authority. General Manager and Chief Executive, New Zealand's International Airline Air New Zealand Ltd. (previously named Tasman Empire Airways Ltd.) June 1958–74. *Member:* Royal Comm. on Containerization; N.Z. National Ports Authority; Royal Aero Socy. (N.Z. Div.); Inst. of Transport (N.Z. Div.); N.Z. Socy. of Accountants; Rotary movement. *Clubs:* Northern, Officers. *Address:* "Greenhill", Pakuranga, Auckland, E.2, New Zealand.

**REEVES, Hazard Earle.** Chairman of the Board, Reeves Telecom Corp. & Realtron Corp. *B.* 1906. *Educ.* Georgia Institute of Technology (BS 1928). *M.* 1944, Annette Brown. *S.* Hazard Earle Jr. and Dr. Alexander Garden. *Career:* Pres. Reeves-Ely Laboratories Inc. 1942–45; Founder and Pres., Audio Devices Inc. 1937–43; and Cinerama Inc. 1950–60. Founder President Chmn. Reeves Industries Inc., 1947–67. *Awards:* 1957 Alumni Distinguished Service Award, Georgia Inst. of Technology. *Member:* Fellow, Society of Motion Picture and Television Engineers; member, Anak Society (Georgia Inst. of Technology); Mem., Technical Advisory Cttee. of New York Inst. of Technology; Mem., Acad. of Motion Picture Arts & Sciences; Dir. St. John's Art Gallery (Wilmington, N.C.). *Trustee:* Amer. Foundation for the Blind (N.Y.); Psychiatric Research Foundation Inc.; Georgia Tech. Foundation (Atlanta). *Clubs:* Economic, Metropolitan, Union League, Tuxedo (Tuxedo Park), Coral Ridge, North Carolina Socy. of N.Y. (Trustee). *Address:* Tuxedo Park, N.Y. 10987; and *office* 708 Third Avenue, New York City 10017, U.S.A.

**REFSHAUGE, Maj.-Gen. Sir William Dudley,** CBE., ED. Australian. *B.* 1913. *Educ.* Melbourne University, MB, BS (1938); FRCOG (1961); FRACS (1962); FRACP (1963); MRCOG (1947); Hon. FRSH (1967); Fellow: Australian College of Medical Administration (FACMA), 1967; Hon. Life Mem., Australian Dental Assn. (ADA) 1976. *M.* 1942 Helen Allwright. *S.* 4. *Dau.* 1. *Career:* Dir. Gen. Army Medical Services A.M.F. 1955–60 (Deputy-Director 1951–55); Medical Superintendent, Royal Women's Hospital, Melbourne 1948–51. Commonwealth Director-General of Health, Canberra, 1960–73; Sec. Gen. World Medical Assn. 1973–76. Chairman: National Health & Medical Research Council of Australia, 1960–73; Commonwealth Council for National Fitness, 1960–73; Chief Delegate for Australia at World Health Assemblies of World Health Organization 1961–68; Chmn., Exect. Board, 1969–70. Pres. 24th World Health Assembly 1971; Chief Censor ACMA since 1971. National Trustee, RSL 1960–73, 1977—; Mem., Walter & Eliza Hall Inst. of Medical Research Bd. 1977—. *Publications:* Organization of the Medical Services in Mass Management of Burns (1952); National Use of Antibiotics and Public Health Problems Created by their Use (1964); Bricks Without Straw (1965). Queen's Honorary Physician 1955–64. *Clubs:* Naval & Military (Melbourne); University (Sydney); Commonwealth (Canberra); Thirty Niners' Assn. *Address:* 26 Birdwood Street, Hughes, A.C.T. 2605, Australia.

**REGIRER, Walter W.** Lawyer, Health Executive & Consul for Mexico & El Salvador in the U.S.A. *B.* 1913. *Educ.* Law schools at Lille (France) Warsaw and Cracow LLM; Richmond (Virginia) JD; *M.* (1) 1948, Geneva J. Clark (*D.* 1961), (2) 1964, Maria Teresa Afonso Pires. World War II: U.S. Army Engineer—China, Burma, India Theatre; 2nd Asst. Engineer, Merchant Marine 1942–45; Adm. Asst., U.S. Economic Mission to Monrovia, Liberia 1945. *Career:* Export Dept. Montgomery Ward, Chicago 1947; Attorney-at-Law since 1949; Lecturer, International Law, RPI of College of William and Mary, Richmond (Va) 1955–59; Aide-de-Camp to Virginia Governors Harrison and Godwin since 1958; U.S. Exhibition Mgr., U.S. Dept. of Commerce with Embassies in Rio, Guatemala, San Salvadore, Montevideo, and U.S. Consulates Gen. in Zurich and Barcelona 1963–66; Pres. & Gen. Counsel, Health of Virginia managing Plyler's, Windsor & University Park; Instructor, International Law, the Judge Advocate Gen. School, Charlottesville, Va. 1966–70; Lt. Col. Army of the U.S., retired 1974. Director-General, International Consular Academy. Chairman, Diplomatic & Consular Law, American Bar Assn.; Chmn. Cooperation with Foreign Bar, Member: Bar Council (1960–64) Virginia State Bar; Fed. Bar Assn. (Past Vice-Pres.); Rotary International. *Decorations:* U.S. Army Commendation Medal, British Star (1939–45), Order of Consular Merit, Gran Oficial, Instituto Consular Interamericano 1977, Distinguished Service Award, Puerto Rico Consular Corps. 1977. *Publications:* Editor Consular Review. *Clubs:* National Lawyers (Wash. D.C.); Downtown (Richmond, Va.). *Address:* 9 Roslyn Hills Drive, Richmond, Va. 23229, U.S.A.; and *office* 1002 Mutual Building, Richmond, Va. 23219, U.S.A.

**REIBER, Ernst,** Dr. rer. pol. Former Swiss Government Councillor; Head of Department of Education and Health. *B.* 23 Sept. 1901. *Educ.* Gymnasium and Universities of Berne, Zurich, Geneva, and Hamburg. *M.* 1931, Elisabeth Bolliger. *Daus.* 2. Formerly editor of Schweizerische Bodensee-Zeitung (Romanshorn). *Publication:* Die gewerbsmässige Nachrichtenvermittlung 1926. *Address:* 48 Talackerstrasse, Frauenfeld, Switzerland.

**REICHSTEIN, Tadeus.** Dr. ing. chem. *B.* 1897. Senior Secondary School (matura 1916) and Federal Institute of Technology (ETH), Zürich (Dr. ing. chem. 1922). *M.* 1927, Luise Henriette Quarles van Ufford. *Dau.* Ruth. Dr. h.c. Sorbonne, University of Basle, Genève, Abidjan and ETH Zurich; London, Leeds; Nobel Prizewinner 1950; Cameron Prize 1951. Scientific Assistant 1922–30, Professor for Organic Chemistry 1930–37, ETH; Head of Pharmaceutical Institute 1938–45, and of Organic Chemistry Department 1946–60, Basle University; Professor for Organic Chemistry, University of Basle 1946–67. *Awards:* Royal Soc. Copley Medal 1968, Endocrinol Soc. Dale Medal 1975. *Publications:* over 500, dealing mainly with glycocides and the steroids. *Member:* Royal Society, Chemical Society (London); National Acad. of Science (Washington); Naturalists Society (Basle); Royal Irish Academy; American Acad. of Arts & Sciences; Royal Academy of Medicine (Belgium); Corresponding Member, Museums of Natural History (Paris). Hon. Member: Indian Pharmaceutical Assn.; Pharmaceutical Socy. of Japan; Amer. Socy. of Biological Chemists; Linnean Socy. (London); Leopoldina; Brit. Pteridol. Soc.; Amer. Fern Soc.; Basler Botan. Ges.; Deutsche Botan. Ges. *Address:* Weissensteinstrasse 22, Basle, Switzerland.

**REID, Bryan, S. Jr.** *B.* 1925. *Educ.* North-western Univ. (Bachelor of Lib. Arts, 1945). *M.* 1949, Marian Vilas. *S.* Bryan S. III, Andrew V., and Alexander B. *Dau.* Nancy M. *Career:* Salesman, Bacon, Whipple & Co. 1947–57 (Partner 1957–63); Dir. Caicos Co. Ltd. 1961—; Chmn. Bd., Paxall, Inc. since 1963. Member, Nat. Exec. Bd., and Treas. Boy Scouts of America; Dir. Member Exec. and Finance Cttees. Northwestern Memorial Hospital; Trustee, Vice Chmn. The Art Inst. of Chicago; Trustee, Chicago Historical Socy.; Dir. La Salle National Bank; The John Crerar Library. *Clubs:* Wayfarers: Commonwealth: Chicago Commercial; Mid-day; Geneva Golf; Dunham Woods Riding. *Address:* 4N844 Burr Road, St. Charles, Ill. 60174; and *office* 100 W. Monroe, Chicago, Ill. 60603, U.S.A.

**REID, Escott Meredith.** C.C. *B.* 21 Jan. 1905. *Educ.* Universities of Toronto and Oxford. *M.* 1930, Ruth Herriot. *S.* Patrick, Timothy. *Dau.* Morna. *Career:* National Secretary, Canadian Institute of International Affairs 1932–38: Department of External Affairs 1938–62; High Commissioner in India 1952–57; Ambassador to Germany 1958–62; Director, World Bank's operations for South Asia and the Middle East 1962–65. Principal, Glendon College, York University, Toronto, 1965–69; Consultant Canadian International Development Agency 1970–72; Skelton-Clark Fellow, Queens Univ. Kingston 1972–73. *Publications:* Strengthening The World Bank (1973); Time of Fear & Hope: The Making of the North Atlantic Treaty 1947–49 (1977). *Address:* R.R.2 Ste-Cécile de Masham, Quebec, Canada, JOX 2WO.

**REID, George Newlands,** MP. British Politician. *B.* 1939. *Educ.* Tullibody Sch.; Dollar Acad.; Univ. of St. Andrews—MA(Hons.); various American Univs. *M.* 1968, Daphne Ann MacColl. *Daus.* 2. *Career:* Reporter, Scottish TV 1962–64; Producer, Granada TV 1964–68; Head of News & Current Affairs, Scottish TV 1968–73; MP (SNP) for Clackmannan & East Stirlingshire since 1974; SNP Spokesman on Constitutional & EEC Affairs since 1974; mem., Select Cttee. on Direct Elections to European Assembly 1975–76; mem., UK Delegation to Council of Europe & Western European Union since 1977. *Club:* Caledonian (London). *Address:* 21 Hamilton Drive, Glasgow G12 8DN; and *office* House of Commons, London SW1A OAA.

**REID, Hon. Sir George Oswald,** QC. *B.* 1903. *Educ.* University of Melbourne (LLB). *M.* (1) 1930, Beatrix Waring

McCay (LLM). (Dec.). *Dau.* Dr. Madeleine Sophie Reid. (2) 1973 Dorothy Maitland Ruttledge. *Career:* Admitted to practice as barrister and solicitor by Supreme Court of Victoria, May 1926; served in World War II in Royal Australian Air Force with rank of Wing-Commander; MLA for Box Hill, Vic. 1947–52, & 1955–73; Min. Vic. Cabinet 1955–73, having held portfolios of Attorney Gen. (1967–73) and at other times Labour & Industry; Electrical Undertakings Fuel & Power, Immigration, Ch. Sec.; Member Liberal Party. Knight Bachelor 1972. *Address:* Nilja, Alexander Road, Warrandyte, Victoria, Australia.

**REID, Patrick Robert,** MBE, MC, British. *B.* 1910. *Educ.* King's Coll., London Univ. (BSc Hons Eng.); MICE. *M.* 1943, Jane Rush Cabot. *S.* Michael Christopher, and Henry. *Daus.* Diana and Christina. *Career:* Pupilage, Sir Alexander Gibb & Partners 1934–37; civil engineering contracting 1937–39. War service 1939–46 (P.O.W. Germany 1940; escaped to Switzerland 1942; A.M.A. British Legation, Berne 1943–46). First Secy., British Embassy, Ankara 1946–49; Chief Administrator, O.E.E.C., Paris 1949–52; politics, farming and writing 1952–59; engineering company director 1959–64. Director; Windett, Reid, Burrows & Bonar Law Ltd. 1963–68, Aidco Properties Ltd. 1963—, and Kem Estates Ltd. 1967—. *Publications:* The Colditz Story; The Latter Days; From Nile to Indus; Winged Diplomat; My Favourite Escape Stories. *Member:* Institution of Civil Engineers; Anglo-Swiss Socy.; Anglo-Turkish Socy. *Clubs:* Lansdowne. *Address:* The Well House, Eastbourne Road, Uckfield, Sussex.

**REIDARSON, Per.** Norwegian. *B.* 1934. *Educ.* MA in Business Administration & Political Science. *M.* 1964, Nina. *S.* 1. *Dau.* 1. *Career:* Sales Manager 1959–70; Asst. Dir. 1970–75; Exec. Pres. (Man. Dir.) since 1975, Norges Grossistforbund. *Member:* Poly Teknisk Forening; Oslo Handelsstands Forening; Norske Finansanalytikeres Forening. *Awards:* Fulbright Scholarship. *Publications:* A Series in Finance, Franchising & Distribution. *Clubs:* Rotary, p.t. president. *Address:* Jonsokveien 9, 1320 Stabekk, Norway; and *office* Norges Grossistforbund, Drammensveien 30, Oslo 2, Norway.

**REIERSON, Raymond,** MLA. Canadian. *B.* 1919. *Educ.* High School. *M.* 1949, Joyce Eleanor Stewart. *S.* 2. *Daus.* 2. *Career:* First elected to the Alberta Legislature at the General Election of 5 Aug. 1952; re-elected 1955, 1959, 1963 and 1967. Joined the Army as Gunner 1941; served for five years, and obtained discharge with rank of Captain. Settlement Supervisor for the Veterans' Land Act, 1946–49; subsequently a salesman for an investment firm, and more recently a salesman of automobiles and farm machinery in St. Paul (Alberta). Minister of Industries and Labour 1955–59; of Telephones 1959–67. Minister of Education 1967–68; Government of the Province of Alberta; Minister of Labour and Telephones 1968–73. Past Master, St. Albin's Lodge A.F. & A.M. and past Zone Commander Canadian Legion of St. Paul. Member, Social Credit Party. *Address:* c/o Legislative Assembly, Edmonton, Alta., Canada.

**REIERSON, Roy Lester.** American economist. *B.* 1906. *Educ.* St. Olaf Coll., Northfield, Minn. (AB); Northwestern Univ. School of Commerce (MBA), Northwestern Univ. Graduate School (PhD); Univ. of Minnesota (summer session) and Oxford Univ. (summer session). *M.* 1935, Doris Hiney (*Dec.*). *M.* (2) 1963, Maria Alber. *S.* Lars Andreas, Kristofer. *Dau.* Kaari Maria. Instructor at St. Olaf Coll. 1926–28; Instructor, Asst. Prof., Northwestern Univ. 1929–34; Research Asst., Wisconsin Public Service Commission 1931–32. Senior Vice-President and Chairman Advisory Committee, Bankers Trust Co., New York City 1934–75 (interruption for military service 1942–45; Commander U.S. Naval Reserve); Snr. Vice-Pres. & Economic Adviser Crocker Int. Bank, 1972–74. *Publications:* numerous articles on business and financial subjects. Awards CPA (Silver Medal), Illinois; Commendation, Secretary of the Navy; Hon. LLD St. Olaf Coll.; Merit Award, Northwestern Univ. *Member:* Amer. Economic Assn.; Amer. Finance Assn.; Amer. Statistical Assn. (Fellow). *Clubs:* University (N.Y.C.); Cosmos (Washington D.C.); Reform (London). *Address:* Box F, Granite Springs, N.Y. 10527, U.S.A.

**REIGATE, Rt. Hon. The Lord. Baron of Outwood Surrey. (John Kenyon Vaughan-Morgan).** PC. *B.* 1905. *Educ.* Eton; Christ Church, Oxford. *M.* 1940 Emily Cross. *Daus.* 2. *Career:* Member, Chelsea Borough Council, 1928, L.C.C. 1946–52; Member of Parliament (Con.), Reigate Div. of Surrey 1950–70; Minister of State, Board of Trade 1957–59. Served in World War II (Welsh Guards; dispatches). Chmn. of the Board of Governors, Westminster Hospital 1963–74. Parliamentary Secretary, Minister of Health 1957–64; Created Life Peer 1970; Hon. Freeman, Borough of Reigate 1971. *Clubs:* Brooks's, Hurlingham. *Address:* 36 Eaton Square, London, S.W.1.

**REILLY, Sir (D'Arcy) Patrick,** GCMG, OBE. British. *B.* 1909. *Educ.* Winchester and New College, Oxford; 1st class Hon Mods. 1930, Lit. Hum. 1932; Laming Travelling Fellow, Queen's College 1932; Fellow of All Souls College 1932–39; and since 1969; Hon. Fellow New College 1972. *M.* 1938, Rachel Mary Sykes. *Daus.* 2. *Career:* Entered Diplomatic Service 1933; 3rd Sec. Tehran 1935–38; Min. of Econ. Warfare 1939–42; 1st Sec. Algiers 1943; Paris 1944; Athens 1945; Counsellor at Athens 1947–48; Imperial Defence Coll. 1949; Asst. Under-Sec. of State F.O. 1950–53; Minister in Paris 1953–56; Dep. Under-Sec. of State, F.O., 1956; Ambassador to U.S.S.R. 1957–60; Deputy Under-Sec. of State, Foreign Office 1960–64. Ambassador to France, Feb. 1965–68. Chairman: Banque Nationale de Paris Ltd., Pres. London Chamber of Commerce 1972–75, Vice-Pres. 1975—. *Address:* Hampden Cottage, Ramsden, Oxford OX7 3AU.

**REILLY, James Dunn.** American executive. Chevalier, Legion of Honour (France). *B.* 1908. *Educ.* Public Schools of West Terre Haute, Ind. *M.* 1934, Alice Hankins. *Career:* Worked in dairy at Terre Haute 1923; various coal mining jobs, advancing from coal loader to fire boss at Terre Haute; became section foreman 1937, Asst. Superintendent at Hanna Coal Co. Piney Fork No. 1 Mine 1940; Superintendent 1942; General Superintendent 1945; Gen. Manager of Underground Mines, Hanna Coal Co. 1946. Vice-Pres. (Operations), Hanna Coal Co. 1947— (President 1961, Hanna Coal Co., Div. of Consolidated Coal Co.). Vice-President, Consolidated Coal Co. 1967—; Chairman of Board, Pike Natural Gas Co. 1957—, St. Clair Oil Co. 1957—, and of Reilly Chevrolet-Cadillac Co. 1958—. *Member:* American Inst. of Mining Engineers. Chmn. Coal Div., Amer. Inst. of Mining & Metallurgical Engineers; Dir. Ohio Coal Assn. President, emeritus of Mining Inst. of America; Chmn., emeritus of National Safety Cncl. (Pres. 1975); Pres. Socy. Mining Engineers, American Institute of Mining, Metallurgical & Petroleum Engineers. *Address:* Rand Avenue, St. Clairsville, Ohio 43950; and *office* St. Clair Oil Company, 219 E. Main Street, St. Clairsville, Ohio 43950, U.S.A.

**REILLY, Sir Paul.** British. *B.* 1912. *Educ.* Winchester; Hertford College, Oxford (MA); London School of Economics. *M.* (1) 1939, Pamela Wentworth Foster. *Dau.* Victoria Wentworth. (2) 1952, Annette Stockwell. *Career:* Venesta Ltd., Salesman and Sales Manager 1934–36; Leader Page Editor, Feature Editor News Chronicle 1936–40; Royal Army Corps. 1940–41; Royal Naval Volunteer Reserve 1941–45; Co.-Edit. Staff Modern Plastics, New York 1946–47; Co-Editor British Plastics Encyclopedia 1947–48; Chief Inf. Officer, Council of Industrial Design (now Design Council) 1948–57, Deputy Director 1954–60, Director 1960–77. *Awards:* Master of Arts; Snr. Fellow, Royal College of Art. Hon. Fellow Royal Inst. British Architects; Socy. Ind. Artists and Designers. *Publication:* An Introduction to Regency Architecture (1948). *Clubs:* Athenaeum; United Oxford and Cambridge University Arts. *Address:* 3 Alexander Place, London, SW7 2SG.

**REINHART, Paul Albert.** Swiss industrialist. *B.* 4 Sept. 1894. *Educ.* Zurich University (Dr. rer. cam.). *M.* 1922, Lili Ganzoni. *S.* 3. *Dau.* 1. President, Zum Lenzengraben Real Estate Co., Ltd. *Publication:* Die Lohn und Arbeitsverhältnisse der Winterthurer Metallgrossindustrie während des Krieges 1914–18. *Address:* Leimeneggstrasse 24, Winterthur, Switzerland.

**REINIER, Glenn H.** American. Consultant to Pharmaceutical Industry, 1969—. *B.* 1905. *Educ.* Lake Forest College (AB) and Harvard Business School (AMP). *M.* 1927, Marguerite Lindhout. *S.* G. Hobart, Peter D., and Christopher N. *Daus.* Katherine J., Marguerite L. and Susan L. *Career:* With Abbott Laboratories: Chemist 1927, Inventory Control 1929, Accountant 1931, Buyer 1934, Asst. Dir. of Purchase 1949 (Director 1949), Manager of Operations, Abbott Laboratories, Sarl (Suisse) 1961. *Publications:* Purchasing Handbook (McGraw-Hill, 1950, 1965). Outstanding Alumnus, Lake Forest College. Dir. of Corporate Procurement, Abbot Laboratories, April 1965–68. President, Lake County Civic League, May 1965—; Mem., Lake County Public Building Commission (Chmn. 1975–76). *Member:* National Assn. of

Purchasing Agents; Chicago Drugs and Chemical Associations. President, Rotary International Waukegan, 1970—. Republican; Ancient Order of Freemasons. *Address:* 1117 Paxton Drive, Zion, Ill. 60099, U.S.A.

**REINTGES, Heinz,** LLD. German Solicitor. *B.* 1914. *M.* 1975, Emmy Joanna Best. *Career:* With IG Farbenindustrie and Farbenfabriken 'Bayer' 1941–51; Ruhrgas, Essen 1951–58; Managing Member of the Board, General Assn. of the German Coal-Mining Industry, Assn. of Ruhr Mining Enterprises, Essen; Chairman, Rationalisation Association of Coal Mining, Essen; General Manager, Mining Assn. Bonn; Member of Board of Assn. of the Industrial Power Industry, Essen; Supervisory Board Member, Ruhrkohle Aktiengesellschaft, Essen; Member of the Advisory Council, Max Planck Institute for Coal Research, Mulheim-Ruhr; Vice-Chmn. of the Advisory Council, Trustee Agency for the housing of Miners in the Coal-Mining area of Rhineland-Westphalia, (Ltd. Co.), Essen; Mining Research and Development (Ltd. Co.), Essen; Manager Assn. for the Chemistry of Olefines, Essen. *Address:* Bahrenbergring 16, 4300 Essen-Heisingen; and *office* Friedrichstrasse 1, Glückaufhaus, 4300, Essen, West Germany.

**REISCHAUER, Edwin O.** American professor and diplomat. *B.* 1910. *Educ.* BA, MA, PhD. *M.* 1935. Adrienne Danton. *S.* Robert D. *Daus.* Ann (Heinemann) and Joan. *M.* 1956, Haru Matsukata. *Career:* Instructor ,Assoc. Prof., Prof. (1953) and 1966—, Harvard Univ. 1939—. Special Asst., War Dept. 1942–43; Major-Lieut.-Col. U.S. Army 1943–45; Special Asst. to Dir. of Far-Eastern Affairs, Dept. of State 1945–46; Dir., Harvard-Yenching Institute 1956–63, Ambassador to Japan 1961–66. *Publications:* Japan Past and Present; The United States and Japan; Wanted: An Asian Policy; Ennin's Travels in T'ang China; Ennin's Diary; Translations from Early Japanese Literature (with Joseph Yamagiwa); East Asia: The Great Tradition (with J. K. Fairbank); East Asia: The Modern Transformation (with Fairbank and Craig); Beyond Vietnam; The United States and Asia, 1967; Japan. The Story of a Nation, 1970; East Asia, Tradition and Transformation (with Fairbank and Craig) 1973; Toward the 21st Century, Education for a Changing World (1973); The Japanese. *Awards:* Hon LittD, and Hon LLD; Grand Cordon, Order of the Rising Sun, Japan. *Member:* Assn. for Asian Studies; Amer. Historical Socy.; Japan Socy. New York and Boston. *Address:* 1737 Cambridge Street, Cambridge, Mass. 02138 U.S.A.

**REITEMEYER, John Reinhart.** American. *B.* 1898. *Educ.* Trinity College, Hartford (BA), Hon. Degree Dr. of Laws, Wesleyan Univ. June 1968. *M.* 1923, Gertrude Bullis. Did newspaper work for Elizabeth Daily Journal during high school vacation periods: after leaving Trinity College joined The Courant as reporter, subsequently Assistant City Editor, Sunday Editor, City Editor, and after serving in Army 1941–46, returned to The Courant as Executive Vice-President; elected President, The Hartford Courant Co. and publisher of The Hartford Courant 1947; Formerly Chairman, President and Publisher, The Hartford Courant, Hartford, Connecticut; Former Director: Connecticut Mutual Life Insurance Co., Connecticut Bank & Trust Co., Central Vermont Railway Inc.; former Director, Associated Press; Trustee: Trinity College (Hartford); Hon. Trustee Society for Savings; Director, Inter-American Press Association. Served in Tank Corps, U.S. Army, World War I, 1918–19; World War II: Colonel, Military Intelligence, First Army and Eastern Defence Command; now Colonel, Military Intelligence Reserve, Retired. Member, Connecticut Commn. for Higher Education. *Awards:* Tom Wallace Award 1963. Legion of Merit; Army Commendation Ribbon; Grand Officer, Order of Duarte, Sanches y Mella (Dominican Republic); Yankee Quill Award, on basis of sustained distinction in journalism and enrolled as member of Academy of New England Journalists. Republican. *Address: office* 285 Broad Street, Hartford, Conn., U.S.A.

**REKSTEN, Hilmar August.** Norwegian shipowner. *B.* 1897. *Educ.* University of Cologne (Dipl.). *M.* 1952, Carol Montgomery. *S.* 3. *Daus.* 4. *Award:* Knight, First Class, Order of St. Olav (Norway). *Address:* Fjösanger pr. Bergen, Norway.

**RELYEA, Thomas Arnold.** Canadian. *B.* 1907. *Educ.* Univ. of Toronto (BCom). *M.* 1939, Margaret Eva Collins. *S.* Brian. *Dau.* Diane. *Career:* Secy. Treas., Canadian & Foreign Securities Co. Ltd. 1937–47, Vice-Pres. and Managing Director 1947–62. President: Canadian & Foreign Securities Ltd. 1962—, and Canadian Northern Prairie Lands Co. Ltd. 1962—. Vice-Pres., Debenture & Securities Corporation of Canada 1958—; Vice-Pres. E-L Investment Management Ltd. Conservative. *Clubs:* National; Granite; Board of Trade. *Address: office* 165 University Avenue, Toronto 1, Ont., Canada.

**REMEZ, Aharon.** Israeli. *B.* 1919. *Educ.* Harvard Business School; Public & Int. Affairs, Woodrow Wilson School, Princeton. *M.* 1951, Rita Levy. *S.* 1. *Daus.* 3. *Career:* R.A.F. fighter Pilot 1942–47; Member Kibbutz Kfar Blum 1947; Commander, Israel Air Forces 1948–51; rank of Brig. General; Studies in U.S.A. 1951; Dir. Supply Mission Ministry of Defence U.S.A. 1952–53; Man. Dir. Solel Boneh Koor Industries & Crafts Co. Ltd. 1954–58; M.K. (Mapai) 1955–58, 1958–59; Admin. Dir. Weizman Inst. of Science; Dr. Int. Cooperation Dept. MFA, 1960–65; Ambassador to the Court of St. James 1965–70; Dir.-Gen., Israel Ports Authority since 1970; Chmn. of the Board, Israel Airports Authority since 1977. *Address:* 8 San Martin Street, The Cottages, Jerusalem, Israel.

**RENAUD, Edmond Charles.** French company director. *B.* 1903. *Educ.* Ingénieur des Arts de Métiers. *M.* 1926, Gabrielle Lancioni. *Career:* Pres. Dir.-Gen.. Société Novatrans, Paris. President d'Honneur, Fédération Nationale des Transport Routiers de France 1952—; and of the Chamber of Commerce, Nice et des Alpes-Maritimes; Member, Economic & Social Cttee., the European Commonwealth Development Corporation 1953–73. Fellow Automobile Club de Nice. *Awards:* Officier, Légion d'Honneur; Comm. de l'ordre du Merite. *Address:* 3 Place General de Gaulle, Nice (A/M/), France.

**RENCHARD, George Willmot.** American diplomat. *B.* 1907. *Educ.* Princeton University (BS). *M.* 1941. Stellita Stapleton. *S.* George Ronald, Randolph William. *Daus.* Stella Mae; Roberta Stapleton. *Career:* Asst. to Secretary of State Cordell Hull, 1936–44; Secretary of Embassy: Paris, 1944–45; The Hague, 1945–48; Vienna, 1948–49; Bonn. 1950–53; Consul-General, Bermuda, 1960–67; Ambassador on Special Mission, 1967; Ambassador to Burundi 1968–70; Dir. Int. Student House Washington; Deafness Research Foundation New York; Washington Inst. of Foreign Affairs. *Award:* Knight Commander, Order of St. Gregory the Great. *Clubs:* Metropolitan; Chevy Chase; F. Street (Washington); Princeton (N.Y.); Mid Ocean (Bermuda). *Address:* 1743 22nd Street, N.W., Washington, D.C., U.S.A.

**RENDELL, Sir William.** British *B.* 1908. *Educ.* Winchester and Trinity College, Cambridge (Economics Tripos I and II). *M.* 1950, Annie Henriette Maria Thorsen. General Manager, Commonwealth Development Corporation 1953–73. Fellow Institute of Chartered Accountants (FCA). *Address:* 10 Montpelier Place, London, S.W.7.

**RENÉ, France Albert.** Seychelles barrister, economist & politician. *B.* 1935. *M.* (1) Karen Handley (*Div.*). (2) Geva Adam. *S.* 1. *Daus.* 3. *Career:* Called to the Bar 1957; practised law 1958–75; Minister of Works & Land Development 1975–76; Prime Minister 1976–77; President since 1977. Founder & Pres. of the Seychelles People's United Party since 1964. Founder of newspaper *The People*. *Member:* Middle Temple, Inns of Court. *Publications:* Philosophy of a Struggle; A Vision of the Future; New Horizons. *Address:* L'Exil, Mahé, Seychelles; and *office* State House, Victoria, Mahé, Seychelles.

**RENGER, Annemarie.** German Politician. *B.* 1919. *M.* (1) 1938, Emil Renger (*Dec'd.*). *S.* 1. (2) 1965, Aleksandar Loncarevic (*Dec'd.* 1973). *Career:* Private Sec. to Dr. Kurt Schumacher 1945–52; Mem. of the Bundestag since 1953; SPD Parly. Group Mgr. 1969–72; Pres. of the Bundestag 1972–76. *Member:* SPD Presidium; former mem., Advisory Ass. of European Council & Ass. of West European Union; Vice-Pres. Int. Council of Social Democratic Women of the Socialist International. *Address:* 53 Bonn, Deutscher Bundestag, Federal Republic of Germany.

**RENNAU, Heinz Helmut.** *B.* 1913. *Educ.* High School; Commercial Univ., Vienna; and Sorbonne, Paris; Doctor in Commercial Sciences. *M.* 1940, Herta Mühlbacher. *S.* Horst Dieter. *Career:* Expert in tourist traffic; SOL bus excursions, Salzburg 1930–31, active with Austrian Tourist Traffic Agency, Vienna 1931–32, Touring Club, Salzburg 1932, and Provincial Tourist Dept., Linz, Upper Austria 1935. Commercial and tourist activities; Paris 1932–33; Cairo, Alexandria, Khartoum 1934–35; Balkan countries 1936–38; Turkey, 1939; Italy 1947–51; Spain, Scandinavia, South

Africa 1952; Director, Salzburg (Austria) City Tourist Centre 1953—. *Publications:* articles on economics and tourism in various journals. *Member:* American Socy. of Travel Agents Inc. (ASTA); Confederacion de Organizaciones Turisticas de la America Latina (COTAL); Austrian Traffic Society; Universal Federation of Travel Agents' Assn. (UFTAA), Fédération Internationale des Centres Touristiques (FICT) Pres.; American Field Service (Hon. Member); Cavalliere Order of Merit (Italy). *Clubs:* Skål (Past Pres. & Hon. Pres.); Lions (Hohensalzburg); Salzburg Press; Union of Graduates of the Commercial University (Past Pres.). *Address:* Fichtenweg 43, 5026 Salzburg-Aigen and *office* Auerspergstrasse 7, 5024 Salzburg, Austria.

**RENNE, Roland Roger.** Professor of agricultural economics. *B.* 1905. *Educ.* Rutgers Univ. (BSc 1927; LittD 1947), Univ. of Wisconsin (MS 1928; PhD. 1930); LLD Univ. of Philippines, 1953; Doctor *honoris causa*, National Univ. Asuncion, 1962; LHD, Montana State Univ., 1969. *M.* 1932, Mary K. Wisner. *S.* Roger L. and Paul W. *Daus.* Karen S. and Joan E. *Career:* Agric. Economist, Montana State Univ. 1930–43; President, Montana State Univ. 1943–64, on leave 1963, to serve as Asst. Secy. of Agriculture for International Affairs, Wash. D.C.; Chief U.S. Economic and Tech. Miss. to the Philippines 1951–53; Int. Bank FAO Agricultural Survey Peru 1958–59; Consultant, Land Development to U.S. Mission to Ethiopia 1960; Dir. Office of Water Research U.S. Dept. of the Interior 1964–69; Prof. of agriculture economics Associate Dean Coll. of Agriculture Univ. Illinois 1969–74; Consultant AID Agricultural Univs. Programme in Indonesia Nov–Dec. 1974; Dir. Foreign Trade Studies, Montana State Univ. 1974–77 (retired). Chief Agricultural Universities Development Division USAID, Delhi India under Univ. Illinois contract with AID. *Publications:* Land Economics (Harpers) 1947, 1958; The Government and Administration of Montana (Crowell 1959); The Montana Citizen (State Publishing Co.), 1937, 1940, 1960, (with J. W. Hoffmann junior author). *Member:* Amer. Economic Assn.; Amer. Agricultural Economics Assn.; International Assn. of Agricultural Economics; Western Farm Economics Assn.; Fellow Amer. Assn. for Advancement of Science. *Club:* Rotary. *Address:* Route 3, Box 1, Bozeman, Montana 59715, U.S.A.

**RENNELL, Lord** (Sir Francis James Rennell Rodd), KBE, CB (mil.), MA (Oxon.), LLD (Manchester), JP; sometime Visiting Fellow, Nuffield Coll., Oxon.; British banker. *B.* 1895. *M.* 1928, Hon. Mary Constance Vivian Smith. *Daus.* Joanna Phoebe, Juliet Honor, Mary Elizabeth Jill, Rachel Georgiana. Served World War I (despatches) 1914–18; joined Diplomatic Service 1919; Foreign Office 1923–24; member of the Stock Exchange 1926–29; Bank of England 1929–32; served World War II, Major-General, Civil Affairs Administration in Middle East, East Africa and Italy (dispatches) 1939–44; Former mem. Advisory Cttee., Morgan Grenfell & Co. *Address:* The Rodd, nr. Presteigne, Powys; and *office* 23 Great Winchester Street, London ,E.C.2.

**RENNIE, Charles Henry,** CBE. Australian. *B.* 1913. *Educ.* University High School, Melbourne. *M.* 1940, Joan H. Castell (*D.* 1976). *Daus.* 2. *Career:* Dir., Marsh & McLennan Pty. Ltd., Laporte Australia Holdings Ltd., Utah Mining Australia Ltd., Bradmill Industries Ltd., Marrickville Holdings Ltd., Sperry Rand Australia Ltd.; Man. Dir., Australia & New Zealand Banking Group Ltd. 1973–76; Chmn., Australian International Finance Corp. Ltd. 1973–76. *Clubs:* Melbourne; Australian; Athenaeum (Melb.). *Address:* 6 Sylvan Court, Kew, Victoria 3101, Australia.

**RENNIE, Sir John Shaw,** GCMG, OBE. British. *B.* 1917. *Educ.* Glasgow University (MA) and Balliol College, Oxford (Dip. Anth.). *M.* 1946, Mary Winifred McAlpine Robertson. *S.* 1. *Career:* District Officer, Tanganyika 1940–51; Deputy Colonial Secretary, Mauritius 1951–55; British Resident Commissioner, New Hebrides 1955–62. Governor and Commander-in-Chief, Mauritius 1962–68; Governor-General 1968. Deputy Commissioner General, U.N.R.W.A., 1968–71; Commissioner General 1971–77. *Club:* Royal Commonwealth Society. *Address:* via Roma 33, 06050 Collazzone (PG), Italy; and 26 College Cross, London, N.1.

**RENOOIJ, Dirk Cornelis.** Dutch. *B.* 1908. *Educ.* Higher Commercial School and Nederlandse Economische Hogeschool Rotterdam (DEcon.). *M.* 1934, M.J. voor de Poorte. *S.* 2. *Dau.* 1. Officer, Order of Orange-Nassau; Ridder Order Nederlandsche Leeuw; N.V. Extraordinary Professor in Economics, Free University of Amsterdam. *Publications:* Beschouwingen over een tolunie tusschen Nederland en Belgie-Luxembourg; Het vraagstuk van een tolunie tusschen Nederland en Belgie-Luxemburg (De Economist 1935); De Nederlandse emissiemarkt van 1904–1939 (thesis); Structuurveranderingen in het Nederlandse algemene bankwezen en de monetaire politiek. *Club:* De Groote-Doctrina et Amicitia. *Address:* Prinses Margrietlaan 2, Amstelveen, The Netherlands.

**RENSHAW, John Brophy.** Australian. Member, Legislative Assembly of New South Wales since 1941; Treasurer of N.S.W. since 1976. *B.* 1909. *Educ.* Holy Cross Coll., Ryde, N.S.W. *M.* 1966, Marjorie Renshaw. *S.* Anthony. *Stepsons:* Christopher, Anthony, Mark S. John. *Career:* Leader of the Opposition, N.S.W. May 1965–68; Premier Treasurer and Minister for Industrial Development and Decentralisation, N.S.W. 30 April 1964–65. Deputy Premier and Treasurer 1959–64; Minister for Local Government and Highways 1957–59; Minister for Public Works and Local Government 1953–57; Minister for Public Works and Asst. Minister for Local Government 1952–53; Minister for Lands 1950–52. Member Australian Labor Party. *Address:* Parliament House, Sydney, N.S.W., Australia.

**RENSHAW JONES, Roy,** TD, JP (1951). British. *B.* 1915. *Educ.* William Hulme Grammar School (England). *M.* 1939, Charlotte Chambers. *Career:* War service with British Army, various theatres: commissioned Lieut.-Col. 1939–46. Director, Sterling Offices Ltd., International Reinsurance Brokers 1955–61; Attorney for: L'Union Fire, Accident & General Insurance Co. Ltd. of Paris 1949–61, and Irish National Insurance Co. Ltd. & Hibernian Insurance Co. Ltd. of Dublin 1949–61. General Manager: The Automobile Fire & General Insurance Co. of Australia Ltd. 1961–69, and Regent Insurance, Ltd. 1961–69. Secretary, British Medical Insurance, Co. of Victoria Ltd. 1961–65. Hon. Consul of Iceland 1958; Consul General 1966—; Manager, Australia-Vesta Insurance Co. Ltd., Bergen, Norway, since 1969. *Awards:* Fellow Chartered Insurance Institute; Australian Insurance Institute; Australian Institute of Management; Knight of the Icelandic Falcon 1972. *Member:* English Public Schools Association, Melbourne. *Clubs:* Athenaeum, Savage, Victoria Golf (all Melbourne); Australian (Sydney); R.A.C. (Victoria). *Address:* 2 Montalto Ave., Toorak Vic. 3142; and *office* 570 Bourke Street, Melbourne, Vic., Australia.

**RENTON, Rt. Hon. Sir David Lockhart-Mure,** PC, KBE, TD, QC, DL, MP. *B.* 1908. *Educ.* Oundle and Univ. Coll., Oxford (MA; BCL). *M.* 1947, Claire Cicely Duncan. *Daus.* 3. *Career:* Called to the Bar (Lincoln's Inn) 1933 (Bencher 1962). Commissioned (T.A.) 1938; served in World War II (Middle East; Capt. 1941; Major 1943); returned to law practice 1945; Member, Parliament (Cons.) Huntingdonshire since 1945; Parliamentary Secretary to Ministry of Power, 1955–58; Joint Parly. Under-Secretary of State, Home Office 1958–61; Minister of State, Home Office, 1961–62; Recorder, 1963–71; Vice Chmn. Council Legal Education 1969–73; Chmn. Cttee. Preparation of Legislation 1973–75. *Member:* Commission on the Constitution 1971–73; Pres. Conservation Society 1970–71; Hon. Treas., National Society for Mentally Handicapped Children since 1976. *Address:* House of Commons, London, S.W.1.

**RENTON, Ronald Timothy,** MP. British. *B.* 1932. *Educ.* Eton (King's Scholar); Magdalen Coll., Oxford (Roberts Gawen Scholar)—MA. *M.* 1960, Alice Fergusson. *S.* 2. *Daus.* 3. *Career:* Joined C. Tennant Sons & Co. Ltd., London 1954; with Tennants' subsidiaries in Canada 1957–62; Dir., C. Tennant Sons & Co. Ltd. & Man. Dir. of Tennant Trading Ltd. 1964–73; Dir., Silvermines Ltd. since 1967; Dir., Australia & New Zealand Banking Group 1967–76; Conservative MP for Mid-Sussex since 1974; Mem., Select Cttee. on Nationalised Industries since 1974; Vice-Chmn., Conservative Parliamentary Trade Cttee. since 1974. *Publications:* articles in Financial Times, Bankers' Magazine, Contemporary Review, The Statist, Times, etc. *Clubs:* Brooks's; Coningsby. *Address:* Mount Harry House, Offham, Lewes, East Sussex.

**RENTSCHLER, William Henry.** American. *B.* 1925. *Educ.* Princeton Univ. (BA). *M.* (1) 1948, Sylvia G. Angevin. *S.* Peter Ferris. *Daus.* Sarah Yorke, Mary Angevin and Phoebe Mason. *M.* (2) 1967, Martha Snowdon Kinney. *Dau.* Hope Snowdon. *Career:* Newswriter, assistant to executive editor, Minneapolis & Tribune 1949–53; President: Martha Washington Kitchens, Inc. (manufacturers and distributors of packaged and bulk candies) 1957–68. Second Vice-President. The Northern Trust Co., Chicago, until Dec. 1956. Candidate or Republic nomination for U.S. Senator 1960 and 1970;

Director, United Republican Fund of Illinois 1958–69; President, Young Republicans of Illinois 1957–59; Chmn., Illinois Citizens for Richard Nixon 1968; Special Advisor, National Program for Voluntary Action, 1969; Entrepreneur-investor in closely-held coys. 1970–73; Independent business financial consultant since 1974; Free-lance writer. *Member:* Republican Committee on Program and Progress 1959. Trustee, Rockford College. Dir. Better Boys Foundation; Trustee, Goodwill Industries. *Address:* 361 Cherokee Road, Lake Forest, Ill., U.S.A.

**REPO, Eino Sakari.** Finnish. *B.* 1919. *Educ.* Licencié ès lettres (BA). *M.* 1947 Eva Tellervo Välisalo. *S.* Risto. Petri and Anssi. *Daus.* Kristiina, Susanna and Nina. *Career:* Literary Editor with Aura (publishers) 1945–46; Man. Dir., Kudosteollisuus Oy 1957–58; Literary Editor, *Apu* (journal) 1959–63; Programme Director, Mainos TV Advertising Co. (Mainos-TV) Reklam Oy Ab 1964; Director-General, The Finnish Broadcasting Co., (Oy. Yleisradio Ab) Jan. 1965—. *Publications:* has written among others the following: Toiset pidot Tornissa (1954); Urho Kekkosen juhlakirja (1960); Ny finsk lyrik (1960); Urho Kekkonen idässä ja lännessä (1962); additionally, critical works and essays in various journals. *Awards:* Cross of Liberty (Classes 3 and 4). *Clubs:* Sté. Paasikivi; Sté. Eino Leino. *Address: office* Oy Yleisradio Ab, Unioninkatu 16, Helsinki 13, Finland.

**RESOR, Stanley R.** American Lawyer. *B.* 1917. *Educ.* Groton, Yale Univ. and Yale Univ. Law School (AB; LLB). *M.* 1942, Jane Lawler Pillsbury. *S.* 7. *Career:* Second Lieutenant to Major of Artillery in World War II, Feb. 1942–Jan. 1946; Began practice of law in 1946; partner in firm of Debevoise, Plimpton, Lyons & Gates 1946–65, 1971–73; Secretary of the Army, U.S. July 1965–71 (Under-Secretary Apr. 1965–July 1965); Ambassador, Negotiations for Mutual & Balanced Force Reductions, Central Europe 1973—. Member American Bar Assn. and Assn. of Bar of City of New York; Bd. Trustees, Inst. for Defence Analyses; Visiting Cttee. and Adv. Bd. The Brookings Institution Council on Foreign Relations. *Clubs:* Yale, Links, New Canaan Country, New Canaan Winter, Metropolitan, Chevy Chase. *Address:* 809 Weed Street, New Canaan, CT 06840, U.S.A.

**RESTA, Nicola.** Italian building contractor. *B.* 1907. *Educ.* Degree in Economy and Commerce, Rome. *M.* 1934, Lea Longarini. *Daus.* Rosalia and Piera. *Career:* President, Taranto Manufacturers & Artisans Association. *Member:* Exec. Cttee. Institute of Foreign Commerce (I.C.E.); Assn. for Increasing Industrial Area of Taranto; Deputy Pres. & mem. Gen. Council, Medio Credito Roma; Vice-Pres., Fédération Internationale des Petites et Moyennes Enterprises Industrielles, Paris; Member, Council of Administration, Institut International d'études des classes Moyennes, Brussels; Vice-Presidency of the General Confederation of Italian Industry; Nat. Pres., Small Industry; Mem. of Presidential Cttee., National Building Contractors' Assn.; Vice-Pres. I.N.A.I.L.; President, Taranto Rotary Club 1957–58. Grand Officer of Republica Italiana; Vice-Pres. I.C.C., Princ. Ital. Section; Mem. of Executive Council Gen. Confed. of Landed Property Owners. *Club:* Circolo Nautico Taranto. *Address: office* Via Amedeo No. 8, Taranto, Italy.

**REUSCHEL, Dr. Heinrich**, Dipl-Kfm. Partner in the banking firm of Reuschel & Co., Munich. *B.* 1922. *Educ.* Secondary School, Munich Univ. Doctorate. Economics, 1951. *Career:* Chmn., Advisory Board, WKV-Teilzahlungsbank GmbH (Hire Purchase Co.), Munich; Member Bd. Directors, Union Investment-GmbH, Frankfurt; Thosti Bauaktiengesellschaft, Augsburg; Awitag Munich; Advisory Board, Vereinigung für Bank-betriebsorganisation e.V. (Association for Banking Organization) Frankfurt; Manager, Organ Organizationsgesellschaft für Konsumkredite mbH, Munich; Member Competitive Commission, German Banks Fed. Assn.; Working Cttee. Bavarian Banking Fed. Munich; Commercial Judge. *Address: office* 8000 München 2, Maximiliansplatz 13, Federal Republic of Germany.

**REUSCHEL, Dr. Wilhelm.** Hon. Pres. Verwaltungsrates des Bankhauses, Reuschel & Co. 1971. *B.* 1893. *Educ.* High School. *M.* 1917, Maria Ringer. *Career:* Dir. at Head Office: Bayerische Hypotheken und Wechsel-Bank, Munich, 1919–45; Partner, Bankhauses, Neuvians, Reuschel & Co., 1948–67. Hon. Pres. Advisory Bd. F. Bruckmann KG, Munich. *Awards:* Holder of Gr.BVK with Star, and the Bavarian Order of Merit, Commendatore dell'Ordine al Merito della Repubblica Italiana. Hon. PhD (University of Würzburg). *Address:* 6 Hornstein-Str., Munich 80; and *office* 13 Maximiliansplatz, Munich 2, Germany.

**REUTERSKIOLD, Gustaf.** Swedish. *B.* 1907. *Educ.* Univ. of Stockholm (LLB 1931). *M.* 1938, Brita Erikson. *S.* 2. *Dau.* 1. *Career:* Served in District Courts 1932–34; Asst. Secretary, Swedish County Council Corporation 1935–42; Captain Artillery Reserves 1942; Director, Uppsala County Council 1943–49, and of Uplandsbanken 1949. Managing Director, Uplandsbanken, Uppsala, 1952–73; Member of Boards of Swedish Banks' Association 1952–73; Uppsala County Council 1952–70; and County Labour Board 1963–75. *Address:* Banergatan 11, 75237 Uppsala, Sweden.

**REYES, Narciso G.** Filipino. *B.* 1914. *Educ.* University of Sto. Tomas (AB 1935). *M.* Apolonia Mendoza. *S.* Narciso Jr., Antonio, Reynaldo, Gregorio. *Dau.* Teresa. *Career:* Member: English Faculty, Univ. of Sto. Tomas, 1935–36; National Language Faculty, Ateneo de Manila, 1938–41; Associate Editor: Philippines Commonweal, 1935–41; Manila Post, 1945–47; Evening News (Manila), 1947–48; Managing Director, Philippine Newspaper Guild; Director: Philippine Information Agency, 1954–55; Cultural Foundation of the Philippines, 1954–57. Hon. Pres., British-Philippine Society, 1967–70. Adviser, Economic & Social Affairs, Philippine Mission to U.N., 1948–54; Adviser on information & community development, Office of the President, Manila, 1954–55; Minister Counsellor, Embassy Bangkok, 1956–58; Minister (later Ambassador) to Burma, 1958–62; Ambassador to Indonesia, 1962–67. Ambassador of the Philippines to the Court of St. James's 1967–70; and concurrently Ambassador to Denmark, Norway & Sweden; Permanent Representative of the Philippines to the United Nations since 1970. *Member:* numerous special missions and Philippine delegations to international conferences; Chmn., U.N. Social Commission; Chmn. Unicef Exec. Board; Pres. U.N.D.P. Gov. Council; Vice-Pres. U.N. Environ. Program Gov. Council. *Awards:* Bintang Mahaputera, Class II (by Pres. Sukarno of Indonesia); Order, Diplomatic Service, Merit Class 1, Republic, Korea; Outstanding Alumnus, Univ. City, Santo Tomas (1968); Dir. of Laws (h.c.) Philippine Women's Univ. 1977. *Publications:* Essays, poems and short stories (First Prize, 1943, national short story competition in Filipino). *Address:* Philippine Mission to the United Nations, 556 Fifth Ave, New York, NY 10036, U.S.A.

**REYNOLDS, Richard S., Jr.** American. *B.* 1908. *Educ.* Univ. of Pennsylvania, Wharton School of Finance (BS 1930); Hon. DComSc, Univ. of Richmond. *M.* Virginia Sargeant. *S.* R.S. III. *Career:* Former Civilian Aide to Secretary of the Army for the State of Virginia; and C.A. for the 15-state 1st U.S. Army Area. Member, N.Y. Stock Exchange 1930; Asst. to Pres., Reynolds Metals Co. 1938 (Treas. 1938–44 Vice-Pres. and Treas. 1944–48; Pres. Aug. 1948–Feb. 1963): Chmn. Bd. 1963–71: Chmn. Bd. & Pres. 1971–75; Chmn. Bd. 1975–76; Chmn. Exec. Comm. 1976–77; Hon. Chmn. of Bd. 1977—; Chairman of Board, Robertshaw Controls Co. Director: British Aluminium Co. Ltd., London; Lawyer's Title Insurance Corp.; Central National Bank, Richmond, Va. *Member:* The Business Council; Richmond Chamber of Commerce (Past Pres.); The Aluminium Assn. (Past Pres.); Virginia Museum of Fine Arts (Trustee); Univ. of Richmond (Member of Bd.); Union Theological Seminary (Finance Cttee.); Boy's Clubs of America (Director). *Clubs:* N.Y. Yacht, The Brook (both in N.Y.); Metropolitan (Washington); Bucks (London); Country of Virginia; Commonwealth; Deep Run Hunt (Former Joint M.F.H.). *Address:* 4509 Sulgrave Road, Richmond, Va.; and *office* Reynolds Metals Co., 6601 West Broad Street, Richmond, Va., U.S.A.

**REZZARA, Aldo.** Italian. *B.* 1900. *Educ.* University entrance (classics). *M.* 1932, Iris Giraud. *Career:* Press Office Manager: Illustrazione Italiana, Rome 1928, and E. Mondadori 1937–45. Opened three companies and acted in the capacity of Chairman and Managing Director: Rezzara Pubblicità; Omnia Pubblicità; and Pubblicità Grandi Periodici, 1945; set up Pubblicità Stampa S.p.A. (of which he is also Chairman), Pres. since 1960. Inaugurated the Bruno Rezzara national award (in conjunction with his brother) 1952. Founder member of FIP (Italian Advertising Federation), and of Press Advertising Association. Member Collegio Periti-AIRP Italian Public Relations Association). *Clubs:* Rotary (Milan); Press; Italian Yacht. *Address:* Viale Argonne 51, Milan, Italy.

**RHYL, Rt. Hon. the Lord (Evelyn) Nigel (Chetwode) Birch**, PC, OBE. British politician. *B.* 18 Nov. 1906. *Educ.* Eton. *M.* 1950, Hon. Esme Glyn, daughter of 4th Baron Wolverton. *Career:* Partner in Cohen, Laming, Hoare until May 1939, when retired to study politics; Territorial Army Officer before World War II: served with K.R.R.C. and General Staff in

Great Britain and Italy; Lieut.-Col. 1944; MP (Con.) Flintshire 1945–50 and West Flint 1950–70. Parliamentary Under-Secretary of State, Air Ministry 1951–52; Parliamentary Secretary, Ministry of Defence 1952–54; Minister of Works 1954–55; Secretary of State for Air 1955; Economic Secretary to the Treasury Jan. 1957; resigned Jan. 1958. *Publication:* The Conservative Party. *Address:* 73 Ashley Gardens, London, S.W.1, and Hollywell House, Swanmore, Southampton.

**RHYNE, Charles S.** American lawyer. Senior Partner, Rhyne & Rhyne; *B.* 1912. *Educ.* Berryhill High School (North Carolina); Duke University; George Washington J.D. (1937); Duke University Law Hon. LLD, Duke Univ. 1958, Loyola 1958, Dickinson 1960; Ohio Northern 1966. DCL, George Washington Univ. 1958; De Paul 1968; Centre 1969; Richmond 1970; Howard Univ. 1975. *M.* 1932, Sue M. Cotton. *S.* William. *Dau.* Mary. *Career:* Formerly consultant to National Defense Advisory Commission, Office of Civilian Defense, and other Fed. Depts. and agencies; General Counsel Federal Commission on Judicial and Congressional Salaries 1954–55; member, International Commn. on Judicial Procedure 1958–61; Presidents Commission, United Nations, 1970. Special Consultant to the President U.S. 1959–60; Ambassador, Special Rep. Pres. of U.S., U.N. High Commission for Refugees since 1972. Member of Bars of District of Columbia; Supreme Court of U.S.A.; Interstate Commerce Commn.; Fed. Communications Commn.; U.S. Tax Court; U.S. Court of Claims, and other Fed. Bds. and Agencies; Pres. Bar Assn. of District of Columbia 1955–56; Natl. Chmn., Junior Bar Conf. 1944–45; Pres. Amer. Bar Assn. 1957–58, Amer. Bar Fdn. 1957–58, World Peace through Law Center, 1963–73; Vice-Pres., Intl. Bar Assn. 1957–58, Inter-Amer. Bar Assn. 1957–58; Chmn., House of Delegates of the Amer. Bar Assn. 1956–57; Lecturer on Federal State and City Relations, Graduate School, Amer. Univ. 1945; Professional Lecturer on Aviation Law, George Washington Univ. Law School 1948–54; Trustee, George Washington Univ. 1960–66, Duke Univ. 1961–68; member of Practitioners' Assns. of: Interstate Commerce Commn.; Federal Power Commn.; Federal Communications Commission; Internatl. Bar Assn. (Patron member: Amer. Bar Assn. Deputy 1948–60; Council Member 1958–60); Amer. Socy. of International Law; The Barristers; member, Amer. Judicature Socy. (Director 1951–58); Editorial Advisory Board, Journal of Air Law and Commerce 1953–56; Delta Theta Phi Legal Fraternity; activities in American Bar Assn.: Chmn.: Administration Cttee., Bd. of Governors; Cttee. on Rules and Calendar; Cttee. on Draft House of Delegates: Aeronautical Law Cttee.; Special Cttee. on Federal Legal Education Requirements, Section of Legal Education and Admissions to the Bar; Cttee. to sponsor Federal Act Prohibiting Picketing of Courts; Cttee. to erect monument to Magna Carta at Runnymede (Chmn. and member sole 1955–57); Cttee. on World Peace through Law Center Pres. since 1963; Gen. Counsel, National Inst. of Municipal Law Officers; Dir. National Savings & Trust Co. Washington D.C. member of other committees. *Awards:* Grotius Peace Award 1958; George Washington Alumni Achievement Award 1959; Amvets Americanism 1965; Leader Washington Bar Association 1965; Gold Medal, American Bar Association 1966; First Whitney Young Jr. Award 1972. Fellow, American College of Trial Lawyers Freedoms Award for Founding Law Day U.S.A. 1958; Fellow Amer. Bar Foundation 1959–60. Leadership Award, National Bar Association 1962. *Publications:* Civil Aeronautics Act Annotated (1939); Airports and the Courts (1944); Labour Unions and Municipal Employee Law (1946); Aviation Accident Law (1947); Airport Lease and Concession Agreements (1948); The Law of Municipal Contracts (1952); Cases on Aviation Law (1950); Municipal Law (1957); International Law (1971). *Clubs:* Congressional Country; Aero; Metropolitan; National Press; Easton (Md.) Country; National Lawyers. *Address:* 2621 Foxhall Road, N.W., Washington 20007 D.C.; and *office* 400 Hill Building, 839 17th Street N.W., Washington 20006, D.C., U.S.A.

**RHYS WILLIAMS, Sir Brandon Meredith,** Bt. MP. British. *B.* 1927. *Educ.* Eton. *M.* 1961, Caroline Susan Foster. *S.* Arthur Gareth Ludovic. *Daus.* Elinor and Miranda. *Career:* Imperial Chemical Industries Ltd. 1948–62; Assistant Director, Spastics Society, 1962–63; Consultant, Management Selection Ltd., 1963–71; Member, Parliament (Con.) for South Kensington 1968–74; M.P. for Kensington since 1974. Member, British Delegation to Council of Europe, 1970–72, and to European Parliament since 1973 (Vice-Chmn. Economic & Monetary Affairs Cttee.). *Publications:* The New Social Contract; Redistributing Income in a Free Society; More Power to the Shareholder? *Clubs:* White's; Cardiff & Country (Cardiff). *Address:* 32 Rawlings Street, S.W.3; and Miskin Manor, Pontyclun, Mid-Glamorgan.

**RIBICOFF, Abraham A.** United States Senator from Connecticut. *B.* 1910. *Educ.* Univ. of Chicago (LLB *cum laude* 1933); Hon. Degrees from Trinity Coll. (Hartford, Conn.), Wesleyan Univ. (Middletown, Conn.), Hillyer Coll. (Hartford, Conn.), Heshiva Univ. (New York, N.Y.), Boston College (Boston, Mass.), Dropsie College (Philadelphia, Pa.), Coe Coll. (Cedar Rapids, Ia.), Univ. of California Medical School (San Francisco, Calif.), Bard Coll. (Annandale-on-Hudson, N.Y.), Bryant Coll. (Providence, R.I.), Amherst Coll. (Mass.), New York Univ. (N.Y.), Jewish Theological Seminary (N.Y.), DePaul Univ. (Chicago, Ill.), American International Coll. (Springfield, Mass.), Fairfield Univ. (Conn.), Hebrew Union Coll. (Cincinnati, O.). *M.* Lois Mathes. *S.* Peter. *Dau.* Jane. *Career:* Admitted to Connecticut Bar 1933; Member of Connecticut Legislature 1938–42; Judge, Hartford Municipal Court 1941–43, and 1945–47; elected to U.S. House of Reps. 1948 & 1950; elected Governor of Connecticut 1954 & re-elected 1958; received national prominence as Governor by Auto Safety campaign; by reorganizing state government; abolishing county governments; & providing leadership enabling Connecticut to survive & then rebuild following disastrous flooding that left the state devastated in 1955; as Governor was first elected official who publicly advocated the candidacy of Senator John F. Kennedy for President; was a principal adviser to Senator Kennedy in his successful campaign for the Presidency in 1960, including being floor manager for the Kennedy forces at the 1960 Democratic National Convention; selected by Pres. Kennedy to serve in the Cabinet as Sec. of the Dept. of Health, Education & Welfare Jan. 1961–July 1962; elected to U.S. Senate from Connecticut to 1962, 1968 & 1974; Chmn. of Senate Governmental Affairs Cttee. & of International Trade subcttee. of Senate Finance Cttee.; mem. of Joint Economic Cttee. & Senate Ethics Cttee. Democrat. *Address:* Room 337, Russell Senate Office Building, Washington, D.C. 20510, U.S.A.

**RICART, Alfredo A.** Dominican Diplomat. *B.* 1938. *Educ.* Villanova Univ., Pennsylvania. *Career:* First Sec. at the Embassy of the Dominican Republic in Great Britain 1962–64; Consul General, London 1964; Special Asst. to the Pres. of the Dominican Republic 1965–66; Counsellor, Embassy, U.S.A. 1966–69; alternate delegate, Dominican Delegation to OAS, Washington, D.C. 1966–69; delegate to FAO Second World Fishing Congress, London 1963; delegate to Inter-American Economic & Social Cttee. (CIES) 1967, '68, '69; delegate to Intergovernmental Conf. on the Convention on Dumping of Wastes at Sea, London 1972; del. to International Conf. on Marine Pollution, London 1973; Minister Counsellor at Embassy, Great Britain 1971–75; Ambassador of the Dominican Republic to the Court of St. James since 1975; Perm. Rep. of the Dominican Republic to the International Sugar Organization in London since 1975 & to the International Coffee Organization since 1975. *Clubs:* Travellers; Annabel's. *Address:* 62D Princes Gate, London SW7; and *office* Embassy of the Dominican Republic, 4 Braemar Mansions, Cornwall Gardens, London SW7.

**RICCARDI, Riccardo Roberto.** Italian professor and Doctor. *B.* 1918. *Educ.* Doctor in Law; Doctor in Economics (Honoris causa). *Career:* Mgt. consultant; former Director of Administration and Services, the International Civil Aviation Organization, Montreal, Canada; former Dir. of Organization and Personnel, the European Space Technological Centre, Noordarjk, Holland. Professor: Deusto Univ., Bilbao, Spain, 1957; International Univ. Pro Deo, Rome 1957; Catholic Univ. of Cordoba, 1967; Catholic Univ. of Buenos Aires, 1969. Previously: Indus. Exec., Labour and Personnel Dept., Montecatini Ltd., Milan; Director I.A.I. (Institute per Addestramente Industria), Milan. Doctor *Honoris causa,* Deusto Univ., Bilbao, Spain, and Catholic Univ., Buenos Aires. *Member:* A.M.A.; B.I.M.; S.A.M.; C.I.D.A.; A.S.T.D.; C.O.F.C.E.; C.N.I.O.S.; C.E.A.; Association de licenciados de Deusto; A.I.C.O. *Publications:* in Italian and Spanish: Management Dynamics; Job Relations; Job Instructions; How to make a Speech; Job Analysis; Rating Personnel; Theory and Practice of Training in Industry; Safety for Top Management; Theory of Communications in Industry; How to Interview. *Address:* Av. Aristides Rojas, Res. Terrazas del Avila P.H. 41-A, San Bernardino, Caracas, Venezuela.

**RICE, Oscar Knefler.** Kenan Professor of Chemistry, University of N. Carolina. *B.* 1903. *Educ.* Univ. of California, Berkeley (BS 1924; PhD 1926). *M.* 1947, Hope Ernestyne Sherfy *Daus.* Margarita and Pamela. *Career:* Associate in

Chemistry, Univ. of California 1926–27; National Research Council Fellow, California Inst. of Technology 1927–29, and at Univ. of Leipzig 1929–30; Instructor in Chemistry, Harvard 1930–35; Research Associate in Chem., Univ. of California 1935–36; Associate Professor of Chemistry 1936–43 and Professor of Chemistry 1943–59, Univ. of North Carolina; Kenan Prof. of Chemistry 1959–75; Emeritus since 1975; Principal Chemist, Oak Ridge National Laboratory 1946–47; Chemistry Panel, Army Research, Durham 1967–72; Visiting Professor, Virginia Polytechnic Institute, 1968; Seydel-Woolley Visiting Professor of Chemistry, Georgia Institute of Technology, 1969. Member, Advisory Panel on Chemistry, National Science Foundation 1958–61, and N.C. Governor's Scientific Advisory Committee 1961–64. O. M. Stewart Lecturer, Univ. of Missouri 1948; Reilly Lecturer, Univ. of Notre Dame 1957; Member, 12th Solvay Congress on Chemistry, Brussels, 1962. Barton Lecturer, Univ. of Oklahoma 1967; Distinguished Lecturer Howard Univ. 1971; Robert A. Welch Foundation Lecturer 1971. *Awards:* American Chemical Society in Pure Chemistry, 1932; Cert. of Appreciation for war research, U.S. Army and Navy, 1947; Southern Chemist 1961; North Carolina in Science 1966. Florida Section, Amer. Chemical Society 1967; Peter Debye, Physical Chemistry (Amer. Chemical Society) 1970; Charles H. Stone, Carolina Piedmont Section, Amer. Chemical Society 1972. *Member:* Amer. Chemical Society (Secy.-Treas., Vice-Chmn., Chmn. Division of Physical and Inorganic Chemistry 1942–44; Chairman N.C. Section 1946); American Physical Society (Fellow); American Assn. for Advancement of Science (Fellow); National Academy of Sciences; Faraday Div. of the Chem. Socy., London; N.C. Acad., of Science; Sigma Xi; Fed. of Amer. Scientists (member Bd. of Sponsors); Amer. Assn. of Univ. Professors; Amer. Civil Liberties Union. *Publications:* Electronic Structure and Chemical Binding (1940); Chapter, Critical Phenomena, in Thermodynamics and Physics of Matter (1955); Statistical Mechanics, Thermodynamics and Kinetics (1967); numerous articles in scientific journals. *Address:* 311 Clayton Road, Chapel Hill, N.C.; and *office* University of North Carolina, Chapel Hill, N.C., U.S.A.

**RICE, Walter Lyman.** American. *Educ.* University of Minnesota (AB); Harvard University (LLB). *M.* 1960, Inger Vestergaard. *S.* John Eric. *Dau.* Lisa Milda. *Career:* Ambassador to Australia 1969–73; former Vice-President, Director, Reynolds Co.; President, Director, Reynolds Mining Corp., Reynolds Jamaica Mines Ltd., Reynolds Haitian Mines, Caribbean Steamship Co. S.A., Reynolds Surinam Mining Corp., Reynolds Pacific Mines Property Ltd., Director, Reynolds Aluminium Co., Eskimo Internat. Inc. Allied Aluminium Fabricators Inc.; Vice-Pres. Dir. & Chmn. Policy Cttee. U.S. Chamber of Commerce. Vice-Pres. (ret.) U.S. Chamber of Commerce. Drafted Federal Anti-Racketeering Act, 1934. *Clubs:* Harvard Club: Congressional Country Club (Washington). *Address:* Lock Island, 1000 Lock Island, Richmond, Va. 23226, U.S.A.

**RICH, Steven.** Australian company director. *B.* 1926. *Educ.* New York University (BA); University College School, London; Columbia University. *M.* 1956, Gayl Beatrice. *S.* John David. *Dau.* Nicolet. *Career:* Dir. Hunter Douglas Ltd. 1955—; Chairman of Directors: A.N.G. Holdings Ltd., 1963—; Pacific Islands Corporation Ltd., 1964—; Traveland International Ltd., 1963—; Tasman Pacific Pty. Ltd., 1963—; Beaulieu Holdings Pty. Ltd., 1963—; Australia New Guinea Corp. Ltd. 1964—; Executive Vice-President in charge of operations, Hunter-Douglas Group, 1956–62. *Member:* Manufacturing Industry Advisory Council; Chmn. Medical Foundation, Univ. N.S.W.; Salvation Army; Chmn. Ascham School Project. *Clubs:* Royal Sydney Yacht Squadron; Royal Motor Yacht; American; Papua. *Address:* 4 Carthona Avenue, Darling Point, N.S.W. 2027; and *office* 12th Floor, 22 Sir John Young Crescent, Woolloomooloo, N.S.W. 2011, Australia.

**RICHARD, Ivor Seward,** QC, MA. British politician and Lawyer. *B.* 1932. *Educ.* MA Oxon; Barrister at Law. *M.* 1962, Alison Mary. *S.* 2. *Dau.* 1. *Career:* Parly. Private Secy. to Secy. of State for Defence 1966–69; Parly. Under Secy. of State for Defence 1969–70; Opposition spokesman Posts and Telecommunications 1970–71; Member of Parliament for Barons Court 1964–74; Opposition Spokesman Foreign Affairs 1971–74; U.K. Perm. Rep. United Nations since 1974; Chmn., Rhodesia Conference, Geneva 1976. *Member:* Inner Temple; Royal Inst. International Affairs; Inst. of Strategic Studies. *Publications:* various articles; Europe or the Open Sea (1971). *Clubs:* Reform. *Address:* 47 Burntwood Grange Road, S.W.18; and *office* 845 3rd Ave., New York, N.Y. 10022, U.S.A.

**RICHARD-DESHAIS, Jean.** French. Président d'Honneur de l'Automobile Club de France, Premier Vice-Pres. de la Federation Internationale de l'Automobile, Administrator & Hon. Pres.: Générale de Transport & d'Industrie-Sté. de Transports S.T.A.; Administrator: Société de Contrôle et d'Exploitation de Transports Auxiliaires; Cie. Air-Transport. Hon. President, International Road Transport Union (I.R.U.) Cmdr., Legion of Honour; Croix de Guerre; Grand Officier dans l'Ordre du Mérite. *Address:* 1 Avenue Rodin, Paris 16; and *office* ACF. 6 place de la Concorde, 75008 Paris, France.

**RICHARDS, Sir (Francis) Brooks,** KCMG. British diplomat. *Educ.* Stowe School; Cambridge, MA. *M.* 1941. Hazel Myfanwy Williams. *S.* 1. *Dau.* 1. *Career:* 3rd and later 2nd. Secy. British Embassy, Paris 1945–48; Foreign Office 1948–52; 1st Secy. (Inf.) British Embassy, Athens 1952–54; 1st Secy. and Head of Chancery, Political Residency, Bahrain 1954–57; Foreign Office 1957–58; Asst. Private Secy. to Secy. of State for Foreign Affairs 1958–59; Counsellor (Inf.) British Embassy, Paris 1959–64; Head of Information Policy Dept., F.O. 1964–69; Minister, British Embassy, Bonn 1969–72; Ambassador, British Embassy, Saigon 1972–74; Ambassador, British Embassy, Athens since 1974. *Member:* Royal Inst. of International Affairs; International Inst. of Defence Studies; Society for Nautical Research. *Decorations:* Knight Commander of Order of St. Michael and St. George; DSC and Bar; Chevalier Legion d'Honneur; Croix de Guerre. *Clubs:* Travellers'; Royal Ocean Racing Club (both London). *Address:* The Rangers' House, Farnham, Surrey; and *office* British Embassy, Athens, Greece.

**RICHARDS, James Alan.** Australian Diplomat. *B.* 1913. *Educ.* Unley High School, South Australia; Coll. of Business Admin., Univ. of Hawaii. *M.* 1939, Mabel Joyce Cooper. *S.* 3. *Dau.* 1. *Career:* with Ampol Petroleum Ltd. 1946–75; Sales Mgr., South Australia 1952–53; State Mgr., Western Australia 1954–75; Agent General for Western Australia since 1976. *Member:* Western Australian Cricket Assoc. *Clubs:* East India Sports & Public Schools, Perth, W. Aust. *Address:* 22 Lincoln Avenue, Wimbledon SW19; and *office* Western Australia House, 115 Strand, London WC2R 0AJ.

**RICHARDS, James C.** American. *B.* 1913. *Educ.* Kansas State Univ. (BS in ChE 1934). *M.* 1938, Erma Miller. *S.* James C. III. *Dau.* Jane (Leipper). *Career:* Vice-Pres. (Sales) B. F. Goodrich Chemical Co. 1952–58; Vice-Pres. (Sales) B. F. Goodrich Industrial Products Co. 1958–61, Vice-Pres. Marketing 1961–62, Pres. 1962–72. Recipient Distinguished Service Award, Kansas State Univ. *Member:* Amer. Chemical Socy.; Amer. Inst. of Chemical Engineers; Amer. Management Assn. *Clubs:* Portage Country (Akron, Ohio). *Address:* *office* 500 South Main Street, Akron, Ohio 44318, U.S.A.

**RICHARDS, Mervyn Whitmore.** South African *B.* 1901; son of late Sir Henry Richards, KC, KBE. *Educ.* MA (Cantab.) LLD (Hon.) (Witwatersrand). *M.* 1940, Jean Mackenzie. *S.* 2. *Daus.* 2. *Career:* Director, Union. Liquid Air & Northern Trust Co.; connections with Union Corp.; former industrial, mining & financial exec. *Member:* Council of Education, Witwatersrand; Council, University of Witwatersrand; Pres., English Acad. of Southern Africa. Director, Roedean School, South Africa. *Address:* 40 Jameson Avenue, Melrose, Johannesburg, 2001, South Africa.

**RICHARDS, Reginald Baron Julius.** British. General Counsel, International Finance Corp. 1960. *B.* 1916. *Educ.* St. Paul's School (London) and Trinity Coll. Cambridge (MA). *M.* 1939, Nora Ellaline Marsden. *Publications:* contributions to professional journals. Member The Law Society of London. *Clubs:* Lansdowne, Oriental (London). *Address:* *office* International Finance Corporation, 1818 H Street N.W., Washington, D.C. 20433, U.S.A.

**RICHARDS, William Thomas Griffith.** Australian journalist. Editor-in-Chief, The West Australian newspaper, Perth 1956–72; Consult. West Australian Petroleum Ltd. since 1972. *B.* 1908. *Educ.* Univ. of Western Australia. *M.* 1933, Leila Leach. *Daus.* Margot Lang and Jane Hocking. *Clubs:* Lake Karrinyup; Anzac. *Address:* 96 Victoria Avenue, Dalkeith, W.A. 6009, Australia.

**RICHARDSON, Arthur Raymond Edouard.** De la Société, Richardson Frères (founded by his grandfather, Charles Francis Green Richardson in 1850); Founder-President of the Franco-Spanish Chamber of Commerce of South and South-East France 1938; of the Franco-Latin American Chamber of Commerce of South East France 1947; and of the Franco-Portuguese Chamber of Commerce of South South East France 1942; Life President and Founder of the Franco-British Club of Marseilles 1945; Consul of the United States of Mexico for the Departments of Aveyron, Basses Alpes, Bouches du Rhône, Lozère, Var, and Vaucluse. *B.* 1901. *Educ.* Reverend Marist Brothers College, Barcelona. *M.* 1929, Giuliana Marie-Anne de Andreis. *S.* John and Georges (*D.* 1958). Commander, Order of Elizabeth the Catholic of Spain. Adjunct President, Hippique Club (Aix en Provence). *Address: office* 2 Place Gantès, Marseilles, France.

**RICHARDSON, Burton Taylor.** Canadian writer and editor. *B.* 1906. *Educ.* Universities of Manitoba (BA 1929) and Syracuse, N.Y. (MA 1930); graduate student London School of Economics, London 1934–35. *M.* 1931, Wanda Agnes Davidson. *Career:* Reporter: Regina Leader-Post 1929–35, Winnipeg Free Press 1936–46. Correspondent: Ottawa 1940–44, South Pacific 1943, Washington and London 1945–46. Editor: Saskatoon Star-Phoenix 1946–48, Winnipeg Citizen 1948; Associate Editor, Ottawa Citizen 1949–51. Secretary Royal Commission on South Saskatchewan River 1951–53; Leader, Canadian Deleg. to Commonwealth Relations Conf., N.Z. 1959. Special assistant to Rt. Hon. John G. Diefenbaker, House of Commons, Ottawa, 1963–66. Editor. The Telegram, Toronto 1953–63. Consulting Associate, P.S. Ross & Partners 1967–74. Hon. Pres., Canadian Institute of International Affairs. Fellow, Royal Canadian Geographical Society. Founding partner, Yonge Street Press 1976, five books. *Clubs:* Albany (Toronto); Arts & Letters (Toronto); Toronto Press. *Address:* 581 Avenue Road, Toronto, Canada.

**RICHARDSON, The Hon. Sir Egerton (Rudolf),** OJ, CMG. Jamaican. *B.* 1912. *Educ.* Oxford University. *Married* (widower). *S.* Michael Alexander Schumann. *Dau.* Noelle Esther Ann. Ambassador of Jamaica to the United States of America 1967–72. Perm. Representative of Jamaica to U.N. 1962–67; Financial Secy. of Jamaica 1956–62. *Address:* P.O. Box 244, Kingston 6, Jamaica.

**RICHARDSON, Elliot Lee.** United States diplomat. *B.* 1920. *Educ.* Harvard BA (cum laude); Harvard Law School LLB (cum laude) 1947. *M.* 1952, Anne F. Hazard. *S.* 2. *Dau.* 1. *Career:* War Service (Europe); law clerk in Court of Appeals and Supreme Court 1947–49; associate of Boston Law firm (Ropes, Gray, Best Coolidge and Rugg 1949–53 and 1955–56; Assist to Senator Saltonstall (Mass.) 1953–54; Assist Secy for Legislation, Dept. Health, Education and Welfare 1957–59 (Acting-Secy. April-July 1958); U.S. Attorney for Mass. 1959–61; Spec Assist. to Attorney-Gen. of U.S. 1961; Partner, Ropes and Gray 1963–64, (Headed Greater Boston United Fund Campaign 1963); Lieut.-Gov. of Massachusetts 1964–66; Attorney-Gen Mass. 1966–69; Under-Secy. of State (U.S.A.) 1969–70; Secy. Health, Education and Welfare 1970–73: Secy. of Defense 1973; Attorney-Gen. U.S.A. 1973; Fellow at Woodrow Wilson Intern. Center for Scholars & Chmn. of Advisory Group at Center for program in State & Local Govt. 1974. Ambassador to the Court of St. James's 1975; U.S. Secretary of Commerce, Feb. 1976–Jan. 1977; Ambassador-at-Large & Special Rep. of the President for the Law of the Sea Conference since 1977. Director and on Exec. Cttee. of Nat. Council on Crime and Deling.; Nat. Civil Service League Board; Salzburg Seminar in Am. Studies; Harvard Alumni Assoc. *Trustee* (former) Radcliffe College and Mass. Gen. Hosp. *President.* World Affairs Council of Boston. *Member:* Council on Foreign Relations; Trilateral Commission; Comm. on U.S./Latin American Relations, American Bar Foundation, American Acad. of Arts and Science; Board of Overseers of Harvard Coll. (1968–70) (re-elected until 1980); Overseas Cttee. to visit school of Govt. (John F. Govt.). *Awards:* Hon. Degrees Mass. (Coll. of Optometry), Springfield, Emerson, Univ. of New Hampshire, Lowell Tech. Inst.; Harvard Univ.; Univ. of Pittsburgh; Yeshiva; Brandeis; Ohio State; Lincoln; Temple; Whittier Coll.; Cincinnati, East Mich. State Univ.; St. Anselm's; Georgetown Univ.; Worcest. Polytech. Inst.; Rose-Hulman Inst. of Tech; Western State Univ. Coll. of Law; Providence Coll; Univ. Mass.; SE Mass. Univ. *Decorations:* Bronze Star Medal; Purple Heart with Oak Leaf Cluster, and other war awards. *Address:* c/o Department of State, Washington, D.C. 20520, U.S.A.

**RICHARDSON, Sir George Wigham,** Bt. British. *B.* 1895. *Educ.* Rugby School. *M.* 1944, Barbara. *Daus.* 3. *Career:* Served in European War in Flanders and France 1915–18, and with Army of Occupation in Germany 1918–19 (despatches). Member Worshipful Co. of Shipwrights (Prime Warden 1943); Pres. Wigham Poland Ltd. *Clubs:* Carlton, Constitution City of London. *Address:* H3 Albany, London, W.1.; and *office* Bevington House, 24–26 Minorities, London EC3N 1BY.

**RICHARDSON, Gordon** (William Humphreys), MBE. British. Governor, Bank of England. *B.* 1915. *Educ.* Nottingham High School and Gonville and Caius College, Cambridge (BA in Law, LLB). *M.* 1941, Margaret Alison Sheppard. *S.* 1. *Dau.* 1. *Career:* Commissioned South Notts. Hussars Yeomenry 1939; Staff Coll., College, Camberley 1941. Called to Bar (Gray's Inn) 1946; member Bar Council 1949–55. With Industrial & Commercial Finance Corp. Ltd. 1955–57; Dir., J. Henry Schroder & Co. 1957; member Company Law Amendment Committee (Jenkins Committee) 1959–62; Chmn. Committee on Turnover Taxation 1963–64; member Court of London University 1962–65; Director Lloyds Bank Ltd. 1960–67 (Vice-Chmn. 1962–66); Dir., Legal & General Assurance Society Ltd., 1956–70; (Vice-Chmn., 1959–70). Chairman Schroders Ltd. 1965–73; and J. Henry. Schroder Wagg & Co. Ltd. 1962–72. Chairman of Board Schroders Incorporated New York 1968–73; Chairman, Schroders AG, Zurich 1967–73; Dir. Rolls-Royce (1971) Ltd. 1971–73; Imperial Chemical Industries Ltd. 1972–73; Dir. 1967—; Governor of the Bank of England since 1973. *Member:* NEDC 1971–73; Chmn. Industrial Development Adv. Board 1972–73. *Club:* Brooks's (London). *Address:* Bank of England, London, E.C.2.

**RICHARDSON, Sir (Horace) Frank.** Australian company director. *B.* 1901. *Educ.* Kerang State and High Schools; All Saints Grammar, Melbourne; Tasmanian Univ. *M.* 1949, Marjorie Amy Hislop. *S.* 4. *Daus.* 2. Member Council, Australian National Univ., Canberra, A.C.T.; Life Governor Retail Trades Assn. of Victoria. *Clubs:* Athenaeum; Kingston Heath Golf; Melbourne Cricket; V.R.C.; West Brighton; Sydney Cricket. *Address:* 40 Heyington Place, Toorak, Melbourne.

**RICHARDSON, Hon. James Armstrong,** PC, MP. Canadian. *B.* 1922. *Educ.* St. John's Ravenscourt, Winnipeg and Queen's Univ. Kingston, Ont. (BA). *M.* 1949, Shirley Anne Rooper. *S.* James Armstrong, Royden Rooper. *Daus.* Carolyn Anne, Serena Susan, Sara Jane. *Career:* Former pilot with No. 10 B.R. Squadron; Entered family firm James Richardson & Sons Ltd. Winnipeg 1945, Chmn. and Chief Exec. Officer, resigned to enter public life 1968; Elected Member, Parliament 1968; Minister without Portfolio, Canadian Federal Cabinet 1968; Minister, Supply and Services 1969; Re-elected, House of Commons Oct. 1972, Minister National Defence 1972–76 (resigned). Re-elected House of Commons 1974. *Address:* 5209 Roblin Boulevard, Winnipeg, Manitoba, R3R OG8 and *office* House of Commons, Ottawa, Ontario, K1A OA6.

**RICHARDSON, Sir (John) Eric** Kt., CBE, PhD, BEng, CEng. British educationist. *B.* 1905. *Educ.* Birkenhead Higher Elementary School; Liverpool University. *M.* 1941, Alice May Wilson. *S.* 1. *Daus.* 2. *Career:* Apprentice Electrical Engineer 1920–26, J. H. Wooliscroft & Co., Liverpool, Journeyman 1926–28; Chief Lecturer Elec. Eng. Hull Tech. College 1933–37; Head Engineering Dept. 1937–41; Principal Oldham Technical College 1941–44; Royal Tech. Coll. Salford 1944–47; Northampton Polytechnic London 1947–56; Dir. National Coll. of Horology London 1947–56; Education The Polytechnic, Regent Street, London 1957–69; The Polytechnic of Central London 1969–70; Chmn. London Bible College 1970–77; Leprosy Mission since 1974; Gen. Optica Council since 1975. *Fellow:* Inst. Electrical Engineers; British Horological Institute; Physical Socy.; Royal Socy. of Arts. *Address:* 73 Delamere Road, Ealing, London, W5 3JP.

**RICHARDSON, Sir Leslie Lewis,** Bt. British director of companies. *B.* 1915. *Educ.* Harrow. *M.* 1946, Joy Patricia Rillstone. *S.* 2. *Dau.* 1. *Career:* Served with South African Artillery in World War II. *Club:* Port Elizabeth (Port Elizabeth). *Address:* Old Vineyard, Constantia, Cape 7800, South Africa.

**RICHEBÄCHER, Dr. Kurt.** German. *B.* 1918. *Educ.* Diplom-Kaufmann; Dr. rer. pol. *M.* 1949, Anna Maria Bienen. *S.* Thomas and Axel. *Dau.* Sabine. *Career:* Financial journalist 1947–52. Dir., Economic Department, Berliner Bank, Berlin 1958–60; Director Association of Private Banks of Germany 1960–64. Executive Manager, Dresdner Bank AG. Frankfurt

1964—. *Publications:* Börse und Kapitalmarkt; Das Bankwesen im gemeinsamen Markt; and various articles in The Banker (London) and in German periodicals and newspapers. *Address: office* Dresdner Banb AG, Gallusanlage 7, Frankurt a. M Germany.

**RICHMOND, Frederick William.** American. *B.* 1923. *Educ.* Harvard and Boston University (BA). *Career:* Chairman of Board, President, Walco National Corp. (N.Y.C.). Pres. F. W. Richmond & Co. Inc., and Frederick W. Richmond Foundation Inc. Chmn. Executive Committee and Dir., National Valve & Mfg. Co. (NAVCO); Chairman of Board, Carnegie Hall Corp. *Awards:* Distinguished Service Award as Outstanding Young Man of New York (N.Y.C. Jr. Chamber of Trade), 1955; Stephen S. Wise Award for 1962 for 'Exemplifying Individual Achievement'; Brotherhood Award for 1965, by Concord Baptist Church, Brooklyn, N.Y.; Business and the Arts Award, N.Y. Board of Trade, 1967. Member New York City Commission Human Rights; Dir., Chmn., Governors Cttee., Scholastic Achievement; New York State Council on the Arts; Trustee Brooklyn Institute Art & Sciences. *Address:* 34 Pierrepoint Street, Brooklyn, N.Y. 11201; and *office* 743 Fifth Avenue, New York City, U.S.A.

**RICHTER, Hon. Sir Harold.** Australian. *B.* 1906. *Educ.* Ipswich (Qld.) Grammar School. *M.* 1933, Gladys Barbara James. *S.* Graham James and Howard James. *Daus.* Justine Noelette and Suzanne Mary. *Career:* State President, Australian Country Party (Qld.) 1956–60; M.L.A. for Somerset 1957–72; Minister for Public Works & Local Government (in State of Queensland) 1961–63; Minister for Local Government and Conservation 1963–69; Chmn. Boonah Shire Council 1942–48. Pres. Boonah Show Society 1944–57, *Address:* 20 Wills Street, Coorparoo, Brisbane, Qld. 4000, Australia.

**RICKETT, Sir Denis Hubert Fletcher,** KCMG, CB. *B.* 1907. *Educ.* Rugby and Balliol College, Oxford. *M.* 1946, Dr. Ruth Pauline Armstrong. *S.* 2. *Dau.* 1. Fellow, All Souls Coll., Oxford 1929–49. *Career:* staff of Economic Advisory Council 1931; office of War Cabinet 1939; P.P.S. to Minister of Production (Mr. Oliver Lyttelton) 1943–45; Personal Assistant (work on atomic energy) to Chancellor of Exchequer (Sir John Anderson) 1945; transferred to Treasury 1947; P.P.S. to Prime Minister (Mr. Attlee) 1950–51; Economic Minister, Washington, and Head of U.K. Treasury and Supply Delegation 1951–54. Head of U.K. delegation at British-Egyptian payments settlement 1959. Second Secretary to H.M. Treasury, 1960–68; Vice-Pres., International Bank for Reconstruction & Development 1968–74; Dir., De La Rue Co. 1974–77; Dir., Schroder International since 1974; Adviser, J. Henry Schroder Wagg & Co. since 1974. *Address:* 30 Warwick Avenue, London W.9; and Broomball, East Anstay, N. Devon.

**RIDLEY, Hon. Nicholas,** MP. British Politician. *B.* 1929. *Educ.* Eton; Balliol Coll., Oxford. *M.* 1950, Clayre Campbell (*Div.*). *Daus.* 3. *Career:* MP (Cons.) for Cirencester & Tewkesbury since 1959; Junior Minister, Dept. of Trade & Industry 1970–72; Del. to Council of Europe 1961–66. *Member:* Inst. of Civil Engineers. *Club:* Pratts. *Address:* 50 Warwick Square, London SW1; and *office* House of Commons, London SW1A 0AA.

**RIEBER, Christian.** Norwegian. *B.* 1925. *Educ.* Bergen Secondary School of Commerce (BA). *M.* 1949, Ragna Sofie Berle. *S.* Paul Christian. *Daus.* Vibeke and Jannike. *Career:* Chairman of the Board (1962—) and Man. Dir., G.C. Rieber & Co. A/S and daughter companies 1958—. Member of the Board: Bergens Bank, Bergen 1965—. *Address:* Skjoldberg, nr. Nesttun per Bergen; and *office* Damsgårdsgt. 131, 5031 Laksevåg, Norway.

**RIEBER, Fritz Carl.** Norwegian. *B.* 1903. *Educ.* Bergen Higher School of Commerce and St. John's Coll., Oxford Univ. *M.* 1930, Tordis Anderson. *S.* Bjarne. *Career:* Chairman of Board of Rieber & Son A/S (wholesale business and industrial undertaking), Bergen (founded 1839; with branch offices at Oslo, Trondheim, London, Copenhagen, Gothenburg and Roven) 1928–73. *Awards:* Commander of St. Olav, 1957; Knight of Dannebrog. *Address:* Hordnes i Fana, 5047 Stend, Norway.

**RIEDER, Rudolph Charles.** American. *B.* 1915. *Educ.* Univ. of Michigan (BSc); General Electric Bus. Trng. School. *M.* 1938, Marion V. Fitzgerald. *Career:* Office Mgr. and Cost Accountant. General Electric Co., Niles, 1939–41; Industrial and Management Engnr., Goodyear Aircraft Corp., Akron, 1941–46; Vice-Pres. and Works Mgr., Dir., Baker Perkins Inc., Saginaw, 1946–61; Joined Continental-Emsco Co. as Vice-Pres. mfg. and Engng. 1961. Executive Vice-Pres. 1963–64; President and Chief Executive Officer, Continental-Emsco Co. (a division of Youngstown Sheet & Tube Co.) 1964–77, Chmn. 1977—; Vice-President, Youngstown Sheet & Tube Co. 1964–70; Dir. 1970—; Sen. Vice-Pres. Mfg. 1971–72, Exec. Vice-Pres. 1973–77, Chmn. of the Board & Chief Exec. Officer 1977—; President: Fibrecast Co. 1964–74, (Chmn. since 1974), Timberline Equipment Co. 1965—. President and Director, Continental-Emsco Co. Ltd. and Contental-Emsco Co. C.A. (Venezuela) 1965—; Chairman of the Board, Continental Emsco Co. (G.B.) Ltd., England, 1965–71; Dir. Lykes Corp. 1971—, Vice-Pres. 1974–77, Exec. Vice-Pres. & member Exec. Com. 1977—; Exec. Vice-Pres. and Dir. Nippon-Conemsco Ltd. Japan since 1972; Dir. Conemsco Ltd. (England) since 1973; Pres. & Dir. Conemsco Marine Systems S.A. (France) since 1975. *Member:* Amer. Petroleum Inst. Independent Petroleum Assn., Texas Mid-Continent Oil & Gas Assn. (Dir.); Dir. & Past Pres., Petroleum Equipment Supplies Assoc.; Member, Natl. Ocean Industries Assn.; Member & Dir., American Iron & Steel Inst. & International Iron & Steel Inst. *Clubs:* Brook Hollow Golf; Dallas Petroleum; Sigma Phi. *Address:* 7106 Currin Drive, Dallas, Texas, 75230; and *office* Continental-Emsco Co., Mercantile Cont. Bldg., 1810 Commerce St., Dallas, Texas 75201, U.S.A.

**RIELLE, (Fernand) Paul.** French industrialist (carpentry and joinery). *B.* 1916. *Educ.* Baccalauréat (Philosophy) Law studies at Nancy; Diplomé in Russian language, Faculty of Nancy. *M.* 1948, Monique Desandre du Bouvot. *Dau.* Monique. *Career:* Captain of Reserve. Chairman and Managing Director, Ets. Rielle, Saint-Dié 1941;— Administrator, G.Q.G. Andrez-Brajon, Saint-Dié 1941—; President, Syndicate of Master Joiners from Vosges to Epinal 1947—; Vice-President, National Union of Syndicates of master-carpenters, joiners and parquet workers, Paris 1951—; Counsellor, Bank of France 1955—; Pres. French Federation of the Heavies Wood Industries; European Fed. of Industrial Joinery (FEMIB); Knight of Legion of Honour. *Club:* Rotary of Saint-Dié (Pres. 1960–61). *Address:* 14 Rue des Sablons, 75116 Paris; 30 Avenue Marceau, Paris 8; and *office* 1 rue des Folmard, Saint-Dié (Vosges), France.

**RIFA'I, Zaid Al-.** Jordanian. *B.* 1936. *Educ.* Harvard University, U.S.A. (BA Political Science); Columbia University, U.S.A. (MA, International Law and Relations). *M.* Muna Talhouni. *S.* Samir. *Dau.* Alia. *Career:* Attaché, Jordan Embassy, Cairo, 1957; Third Secretary, Jordan Embassy, Beirut, 1958; Political Secy., Jordan Mission to U.N., 1959–60; Director, International Organization Dept., Foreign Ministry, 1960–61; First Secy., Jordan Embassy, London, 1962–63; Chief of Royal Protocol, 1963–64; Director Political Dept., Foreign Ministry, 1965; Assistant Chief of Royal Court, 1966; Director General of Royal Court, 1967; Personal Secy. to H.M. the King, 1968; Chief of Royal Court 1969–70; Ambassador to United Kingdom 1970–71; Political Adv. to His Majesty the King 1971–73; Prime Minister of Jordan, Portfolio of Foreign Affairs and Defense 1974–76. *Awards:* Grand Cordon of Al-Istoqlal of Jordan; and other decorations from Lebanon, Libya, Morocco, Ethiopia, China and Spain. *Address:* c/o The Secretary, Office of the Prime Minister, Amman, Jordan.

**RIFKIND, Malcolm Leslie,** MP. British. *B.* 1946. *Educ.* George Watsons Coll., Edinburgh Univ.—LLB, MSc. *M.* 1970. Edith Amalia Steinberg. *Dau.* 1. *Career:* Conservative MP for Edinburgh Pentlands since 1974; Opposition Front Bench Spokesman on Scottish Affairs 1975–76; Hon. Pres., Scottish Young Conservatives 1976–77. Admitted to the Scottish Bar 1970. *Address:* 8 Old Church Lane, Duddingston Village, Edinburgh.

**RIFKIND, Simon H.** American attorney. *B.* 5 June 1901. *Educ.* C.C.N.Y. (BS); Columbia Law School (LLB). *M.* 1927, Adele Singer. *S.* Richard Allen, Robert Singer. *Career:* Secretary to U.S. Senator Robert F. Wagner 1927–33; member of law firm of Wagner, Quillinan & Rifkind 1930–41; United States District Judge 1941–50; Adviser on Jewish Affairs to General Eisenhower 1945; member of law firm of Paul, Weiss, Rifkind Wharton & Garrison since 1950; Board of Higher Education, New York City 1954–66; member, N.Y. State Commission on Governmental Operations of the City of New York 1959–61; Special Master, Supreme Court of U.S., Colorado River Case 1955–61; Chairman, Presidential Railroad Commission 1961–62; Co. Chmn. President's Commission on Patent System 1965–66;

Chairman, Board of Directors, Jewish Theological Seminary of America 1963–73; Dir.: Revlon Inc., and Sterling National Bank, New York. Medal of Freedom (U.S.), Doctor of Letters (Jewish Theological Seminary of America); LLD Hofstra College & Brandeis Univ. *Address:* 345 Park Avenue, New York, N.Y., U.S.A.

**RIGAUT, Pierre.** French banker. Deputy Foreign Manager, Banque Nationale de Paris 1943; Conseiller du Commerce Extérieur de la France. *B.* 1898. *Educ.* Lycée Condorcet and Ecole Commerciale de Paris. *M.* 1937. *S.* Jean-Paul. *Career:* Asst. Manager in the Far East of Banque Franco-Chinoise 1926–31; Gen. Manager, Société pour le Commerce d'Outre-Mer, Paris 1932–39; Director of several national boards (market organization of potatoes, onions, potato seed, linseed) 1939–43; Chief Inspector Comptoir National d'Escompte 1943–51; Dir. London Branch 1951–53. *Publications:* various translations, particularly Victorious Troy by John Masefield. Awarded Military Medal. *Club:* Yacht de France. *Address:* 2 Boulevard Pereire, Paris 17; and *office* 16 Boulevard des Italiens, Paris 9, France.

**RIJPSTRA, H.** Dutch administrator. *B.* 1919. *Educ.* Zutphen gymnasium; Amsterdam (to study laws). *Career:* Queen's Commissioner of province of Friesland since 1970. *Address:* Provincial Residence, Leeuwarden, Friesland, Netherlands.

**RINGADOO, Sir Veerasamy, MLA.** Mauritian politician. *B.* 1920. *Educ.* London School of Economics and Middle Temple; LLB. *M.* 1954, Lydie Vadamootoo. *S.* 1. *Dau.* 1. *Career:* Municipal Councillor since 1956. Member Legis. Council for Moka/Flacq. 1951–67; Ministry of Labour and Soc. Sec. 1959–64; Min. of Education 1964–67; Min. of Agric. and Natural Resources 1967–68; Min. of Finance since 1968; Chmn. Board of Govs., African Development Bank & African Development Fund 1977—78. *Decorations:* Officer de l'Ordre National Malgache 1969; Knight Bachelor 1975; Dr. in Law (h.c.) Univ. of Mauritius 1975; Hon. Fellow, London School of Economics 1976. *Address:* Cnr. Farquhar and Sir Selincourt Antelme Avenues, Quartre Bornes, Mauritius; and *office* Ministry of Finance, Government House, Port Louis, Mauritius.

**RIPLEY, Sir Hugh,** Bt. Director, John Walker & Sons Ltd. *B.* 1916. *Educ.* Eton. *M.* (1) 1946, Dorothy Mary Dunlop Bruce Jones. *S.* Hugh. *Dau.* Caroline. (2) 1972, Susan Hilary Parker *Dau.* Katherine. *Career:* Regular soldier, King's Shropshire Light Infantry; retired as Major 1946 (Despatches twice; American Silver Star). Farming interests on Bedstone Estate, Bucknell, Shropshire. *Member:* C.L.A.; N.F.U. *Club:* Boodles. *Address:* 20 Abingdon Villas, London W.8; and *office* 63 St. James's Street, London, S.W.1.

**RIPPON, Rt. Hon. Geoffrey, PC, QC, MP.** *B.* 1924. *Educ.* Kings College (Taunton) and Brasenose College, Oxford. Hon. Fellow. Barrister-at-Law, QC 1964. *M.* 1946, Ann Leyland Yorke. *S.* 1. *Daus.* 3. *Career:* MP (Con.) Norwich South 1955–64, Parliamentary Secy.: Ministry of Aviation 1959–61, and Min. of Housing and Local Govt. 1961–62. Created P.C. July 1962. Minister of Public Building and Works, July 1962–64; (Cabinet Oct. 1963–64). Member Parliament for Hexham since 1966; Minister of Technology 1970; Chancellor of the Duchy of Lancaster 1970–72; Secy. of State for the Environment 1972–74: Admiral of the Manx Herring Fleet 1971–74; Shadow Foreign and C'wealth Secretary 1974–75; Leader, Conservative Group in the European Parliament 1977—. Pres., British Section, Council of European Municipalities; British Section European League for Economic Co-operation; *Clubs:* White's, Pratts, M.C.C. (London). *Address:* House of Commons, London, S.W.1.

**RISSO, Massimo.** Italian Industrialist. *B.* 1916. *Educ.* Degree in Jurisprudence 1938. Positions held: Chmn. & Mem. Exec. Cttee., C.E.I. (Compagnia Elettrotechnica Italiana); Chmn., SpA Sanac, Genoa; Chmn., SpA Plinthos, Genoa; Vice-Chmn., SpA SCIS (Foreign Trade), Head Office Mogadiscio. *Director:* SpA Italsider, Genoa (Mem. of Exec. Cttee.); SNAM, S. Donato Milanese (Eni Group); Generalfin, Milan (Mem. of Exec. Cttee.); Generalfin International Ltd. S.a., Head Office Panama; SpA S.A.I.S., Milan (Mem. of Exec. Ctte.); SpA C.E.I.-Sud, Milan; SpA Romana, Head Office Mogadiscio; SATAP (Società Autostrada Torino-Alessandria-Piacenza); Società per il Traforo Bargagli-Ferriere; S.S.S. (Servizio Segnalazioni Stradali), Milan; Fondazioni Gaslini, Genoa. Other Duties: Pres. Genoa Chamber of Comm. and Ligurian Chambers of Comm.; Vice-Pres. Comité de Direction du Bureau Internat. d'Information des Chambres de Commerce; Hon. Chmn., Nat. Assn. of Brick and Tile Industrialists, Rome; Hon. Chmn., Eur. Brick and Tile Fed.; *Member:* Resident Ctte., Union of Ital. Chambers of Comm., Rome; Internat. Council, Internat. Chamber of Comm. and Ital. Council of C.C.I.; Managing Ctte., Eur. Refractories Assn.; Bd. of Federceramica, Milan; Bd. of Genoa Univ. *Address:* Presidente Camera di Commercio, Via Gariboldi 4, 16124 Genova, Italy.

**RITCHIE, Albert Edgar,** CC. Canadian. *B.* 1916. *Educ.* Mount Allison Univ. (BA); Oxford Univ. (BA, Rhodes Scholar). *M.* 1941, Gwendoline Perdue. *S.* Gordon and Donald. *Daus.* Heather (Zourdoumis) and Holly (Dale). *Career:* Deputy Under-Secy. of State for External Affairs 1964–66. Ambassador to the United States 1966–70; Under-Secy. of State, External Affairs 1970–74; Ambassador to the Republic of Ireland since 1976. LLD, Mount Allison Univ. and St. Thomas Univ.; Companion of the Order of Canada 1975. *Clubs:* Rideau (Ottawa); Stephen's Green (Dublin). *Address:* Canadian Embassy, 65 St. Stephen's Green, Dublin 2, Ireland.

**RITCHIE, Charles Stewart Almon.** Canadian. *B.* 1906. *Educ.* Trinity Coll. School, Port Hope, Ont.; Univ. of King's Coll., Halifax, N.S.; Oxford Univ. (MA 1929); Harvard Univ. (MA 1930); Ecole Libre des Sciences Politiques, Paris. *M.* 1948, Sylvia Catherine Beatrice Smellie. *Career:* Joined Dept. of External Affairs, Ottawa, as Third Secretary 1934; Third Secretary, Washington 1936; Second Secy., London 1939; First Secretary 1943; Ottawa, Jan. 1945; Counsellor, Paris 1947; Asst. Under-Secretary of State for External Affairs, Ottawa, Jan. 1950, Deputy Under-Secretary of State 1952; Ambassador to Fed. Republic of Germany, Bonn, and Head of Military Mission, Berlin, May 1954; Ambassador and Permanent Representative of Canada to U.N., Jan. 1958. Ambassador to the United States, May 1962, to NATO 1966; High Commissioner to U.K. 1967–70. Hon. DCL, University of King's College, Halifax, N.S. *Clubs:* Brook's (London); Rideau (Ottawa). *Address:* 216 Metcalfe Street, Ottawa, Ont., Canada.

**RITCHIE, Sir James Edward Thomson,** Bt., TD, FRSA. Chairman: M. W. Hardy & Co. Ltd., associated companies. Director: Wm. Ritchie & Son (Textiles) Ltd. *B.* 1902. *Educ.* Rugby and The Queen's College, Oxford. *M.* 1936, Rosemary Streatfeild. *Daus.* 2. *Career:* Joined Inns of Court Regt. 1936; commissioned 1938; served 1939–45 (C,M,F, 1944–45); Lt.-Col. 1945; recommissioned 1949 to command 44 (Home Counties) Div. Provost Co. R.C.M.P. (T.A.); retired 1953, Selected Military Member and County Welfare Officer, Kent T.A. & A.F.A. (Mem. Gen. Purposes Cttee.) 1953–68. Pres. Ashford (Kent) Royal Btirish Legion 1952–75. Member Court of Assistants, Merchant Taylors' Company (Member 1963–64). Patron Ashford & Dist. Caledonian Socy.; Chmn. Finance and Gen. Purposes Cttee. (1953–68) and joint Hon. Treas.; London School of Hygiene and Tropical Medicine, Univ. of London 1951–61 (Co-opted mem. Bd. of Mgement. 1964–67). *Fellow:* Royal Society of Arts. *Club:* Army and Navy. *Address:* Kirkbank House, High Halden, Kent TN26 2JD; and *office* 44–45 Chancery Lane, London, W.C.2.

**RITTER-ZWEIFEL, Dr. Robert Johann,** Dr oec publ. Swiss lawyer and President of Board of Administration Weberei Sirnach. *B.* 18 Dec. 1891. *Educ.* Maturitat Zurich and University of Zurich. *M.* 1928, Rosa Margrit Zweifel. *S.* 1. *Daus.* 2. Member, School Commission, Sirnach; formerly auditor, District Court of Zurich, and later successively Secretary and Head of the Taxation Office of Town of Zurich, and President, Board of Administration Sirnach Weaving Works. *Publication:* (Thesis) Die Bank in Glarus. *Address:* Fischingerstrasse, Ehrenburger von Sirnach, Switzerland.

**RITZ, Charles.** *B.* 1891. *Educ.* Public and High School, Mitchell, Ont., and Stratford Business College, Stratford, Ont., Canada. *M.* 1924, Evelyn Millicent Herron. *S.* Gordon Herron. *Dau.* Norma Elizabeth (Mrs. Edmund J. Phelps, Jr.). *Career:* Private Secy., Temiskaming Ontario Railway, North Bay, Ont. 1908–10; Stenographer and Sales Correspondent, Robin Hood Multifoods Ltd., Moose Jaw, Sask. 1910–12 (Sales Mgr. Calgary 1912–14; Eastern Mgr., Montreal 1914–31; General Mgr., Montreal 1931–37); Dir., International Multifoods Corp., Minneapolis 1934— (Vice-Pres. 1937–43); Pres., RHM Ltd., Montreal 1937–61; Exec. Vice-Pres. IM 1942–43 (Pres. 1943–55); Chmn., Exec. Cttee., RHM Ltd. 1961–69; Chairman of Board, IM 1955–65, Hon. Chmn. 1965—. Hon. Chairman of the Board, International Multifoods Corp., Minneapolis; *Clubs:* Minikahda (former Pres.), Minneapolis (Minneapolis); Thunderbird

Country (Palm Springs, Calif.). *Address:* 510 Groveland Avenue, Minneapolis, Minn.; and *office* 850 Baker Building, Minneapolis, Minn. 55402, U.S.A.

**RITZENTHALER, Arthur B.** American. *B.* 1901. *M.* 1927, Edna Gullen. *S.* Bruce. *Dau.* Sallie. *Career:* Past-Pres., Institute of Appliance Manufacturers (1948–49–50, three terms); Dir.; American Gas Assn., Liquefied Petroleum Gas Assn., and Gas Appliance Mnfrs. Assn. Senior Vice-Pres., The Tappan Co., Mansfield, Ohio, since 1945 (Director 1945); Pres., Tappan-Detroit Inc.; Chmn, Exec. Cttee., L.P. Gas Council; Director, Canadian Tappan Stove Co., Montreal, since 1955; First National Bank, Mansfield 1950; Richland Development Co. Inc. *Clubs:* Buffalo Athletic; Oak Hill Country (Rochester, N.Y.); Westbrook Country (Mansfield, O.); Union (Cleveland, O.); Coral Ridge Country (Ft. Lauderdale, Fla.). *Address:* 1400 South Ocean Boulevard, Pompano Beach, Fla., U.S.A.

**RIVERDALE, Lord** (Robert Arthur Balfour). *B.* 1901. *Educ.* Aysgarth and Oundle. *M.* (1) 1926, Nancy Marguerite Rundle (*D.* 1928). *S.* 1. (2) 1933, Christian Mary Hill. *S.* 1. *Dau.* 1. *Career:* Joined Arthur Balfour & Co. Ltd. 1918 (Director 1924), Asst.Man. Dir. 1934, Man. Dir. 1949, Chmn. & Man. Director 1957–61, Director of subsidiary Companies of the Group; Exec. Chmn. Balfour Darwins Ltd., 1961–69, President 1969–75; Director, Tinsley Rolling Mills Co. Ltd. 1936–66, Chmn. 1950–66; Director, Newton Chambers & Co. Ltd. 1958–69; Director, High Speed Steel Alloys Ltd. 1953–69, Dep. Chmn. 1959–63; Chmn. 1963–69; Director, Hadfields Ltd. 1961–67; Director, National Provincial Bank Ltd., (Local Board 1949–69), (Main Central Board 1964–69); National Westminster Bank Ltd. (Eastern Region Board) 1969–71; Director, Yorkshire Television Ltd. 1967–73; Director, The Sheffield Steelmakers Ltd. 1952–74, Chmn. 1958; Director, Light Trades House Ltd., 1956–65, Chmn. 1960–65; Governor, Sheffield Savings Bank 1948–58, Patron since 1958; Deputy Lieut. South Yorkshire County (formerly West Riding of Yorks) since 1959; Master Cutler 1946–47; Trustee of the Sheffield Town Trust since 1958; Town Collector, Sheffield since 1974; Justice of the Peace, City of Sheffield, 1950–66; President, Magistrate's Assocn. South Yorks Branch, since 1971; Guardian of Standard of Wrought Plate within City of Sheffield, since 1948, Belgian Consul for Sheffield area since 1945. The Association of British Chambers of Commerce—Member Executive Council, since 1950, Chmn. Overseas Comm. 1953–57, Vice-Pres. 1952–54, Deputy Pres. 1954–57, President 1957–58; Member, Federation of Commonwealth & British Chambers of Commerce, U.K. Comm. 1961–62; Pres., Nat. Fed. of Engineers' Tool Mnfrs. 1951–57, Hon. Vice-President since 1957, Rep. on the Gauge & Tool Advisory Council 1o46–64; President Sheffield Chamber of Commerce, 1950, Joint Hon. Sec. since 1957; Member, Australian British Trade Assn. (formerly Austr. Assn. of Brit. Man.) 1946–54, Chmn. 1954–57, Vice-Chmn. 1957–64, Hon. Member since 1965; Pres., Milling Cutter & Reamer Trade Assn. 1936–54, Vice-Pres. 1954–57, Hon. Vice-Pres. 1958 to date; President, Twist Drill Traders' Assn. 1946–55; Member, High Speed Steel Assn. Management & Technical Comm. 1947–65; Member, British National Comm. Int. Chamber of Commerce Adv. Council, 1957–58; *Member:* The National Production Advisory Comm. 1957–58; Consultative Comm. for Industry, 1957–58; Crucible & High Speed Steel Conference, Standing Comm. 1951–64; Western Hemisphere Exports Council (formerly Dollar Exports Council), 1957–61; Member, Royal Cruising Club, since 1937, Rear Comdr. 1958–59, Commodore 1961–66; Royal Yachting Assn. since 1960; Royal Naval Sailing Association since 1960; Pres. Amateur Yacht Research Soc. since 1966; Assoc. of Royal Inst. of Naval Archs.; Pres. Derwent Fly Fishing Club since 1974. *Awards:* Chevalier De L'ordre de la Couronne (Belgium); La Médaille Civique, Prèmiere Classe: Officer De L'ordre De Leopold II. *Clubs:* Sheffield (Sheffield); Bath; Royal Cruising. *Address:* Ropes, Grindleford, via Sheffield S30 1HX.

**RIZIKA, Jack Wilford.** BA, MSc. American. *B.* 1927. *Educ.* St. Lawrence Univ. (BA); Mass. Inst. of Technology (BSc, MSc). Post Grad. work Harvard University. *M.* 1961, Mary Karen Serumgard. *S.* 2. *Daus.* 2. *Career:* Project Analyst, Glenn L. Martin Co. 1953; with Aircraft Gas Turbine Div. & Management Consulation Services Div. General Electric Co. N.Y. 1954–57. Pres. Dir. Northern Research & Engineering Corp.; Northern Research & Engineering Corp. International 1974–75; Pres. Rizika Realty Trust. *Member:* Nat. Academy of Economics & Political Science; Amer. Socy. Mechanical Engineers; Amer. Inst. Aeronautics & Astronautics; Sigma Xi. *Clubs:* Harvard (Boston); Harvard (N.Y.C.); M.I.T. Faculty; M.I.T. (N.Y.C.). *Address:* 36 Edgehill Road, Brookline, Mass. 02146, U.S.A.

**ROBARTS, Hon. John Parmenter,** PC, CC, QC, LLD, DCL. Barrister & Solicitor. *B.* 1917. *Educ.* Univ. of Western Ontario, and Osgoode Hall Law School; BA. *M. S.* 1. *Dau.* 1. *Career:* Member of the Ontario Legislature 1951–71; Minister of Education, 1959–62; Prime Minister of Ontario, Canada 1961–71; Partner in law firm of Stikeman, Elliott, Robarts & Bowman, Toronto. Member Progressive Conservative Party of Ontario. *Clubs:* Albany; York; London Hunt and Country; London Club (London, Ont.). *Address:* Box 85, Commerce Court West, Suite 4950, Toronto, Canada, M5L 1B9.

**ROBBINS, George V.** Business consultant. *B.* 1902. *Educ.* Rennselaer Polytechnic Institute, Mechanical Engineer, 1925, Hon. Degree, 1960. *M.* 1971, Elayne Brill. *Daus.* Robin, Elizabeth C. *Career:* With Arbuckle Bros. 1925–29; Manager Yuban Coffee, Inc. 1930–32; with California Packing Corp. 1932–47, Manager, Coffee Department 1932–36, Gen. Mgr., Coffee Division 1936–47, Bd. of Drs. 1942–47. With General Foods Corp., Director, Green Coffee Operations 1947–65; Consultant to Department of Agriculture 1944–47. Trustee, founder member, Nutrition Foundation, Inc. 1941–47; member adv. committee, Organization of American States; Adviser to U.S. State Dept. since 1957; Adviser to Brown Bros. Harriman & Co. (Bankers); Consultant to General Foods Corp. Board of Directors, Grace National Bank 1961–65; Chmn., Board of Directors, Corporate Equities 1964—. Board of Directors: General Foods de Mexico S.A. 1962—. *Awards:* Comdr., Order of Southern Cross (Braqil) 1959; Award for recognition of Service from Govt. of Columbia, S.A. 1952; Grand Cross, Order of San Carlos 1957; Comdr. Ordem Militar de Cristo (Portugal) 1960; Chevalier, Ordre de la Légion d'Honneur (France) 1961; Officer, Order of Crown (Belgium) 1961; Comdr., Nat. Order of Ivory Coast 1961; Chevalier, Order of Republique de Malagasy, 1964; Comdr., National Order of Jose Matais Delgado of El Salvador, 1965; Comdr. National Order of Merit of the Republic of Cameroun, 1965. Member Pan American Socy. of U.S.A. since 1949; National Coffee Assn., Vice-Pres. 1943–44, Pres. 1945–49, Bd. of Directors 1933–65. Foreign Affairs Committee 1957–65; American Brazilian Assn. 1958—, Pres. 1960–62; Board of Directors, Columbian-American Chamber of Commerce 1961—; Board of Governors, India House 1961—; Chmn., Treasurer, 1970—; Member Exec. Committee, Adv. Council, Brazilian Inst. of N.Y. Univ.; and Steering Committee, N.Y. Univ. Brazil Conf. 1958; member, Committee on Latin America of Business Advisory Council 1959–63; Executive and Professional Hall of Fame 1966; Life F.I.B.A. Elected Member, Exec., Advisory Cttee., Metall-Beteiligungen A.G., 1969; Founder Member, U. S. Naval War Coll. 1971. Theta Xi, Cum Laude Society. Republican. Episcopalian. *Publications:* Contributor, articles on coffee. *Clubs:* Westchester Country, Goldens Bridge Hounds, India House, Boca Raton (Fla.). *Address:* Lawrence Farms East, Mount Kisco, New York; and *office* 80 Pine Street, New York, N.Y. 10005, U.S.A.

**ROBBINS, John Dennis.** OBE, TD, FCA. British. *B.* 1915. *Educ.* Aldenham School. *M.* 1942, Joan Mary Mason. *S.* 1. *Daus.* 2. *Career:* Director: Smith & Nephew Associated Cos Ltd.; The National Bank of Australasia Ltd.; (London Bd. of Advice) Technical Utilities (London) Ltd.; British Metal Canada Investments Ltd.; Norddeutsche Affinerie. British Metal International Ltd.; British Metal Corp. (Canada) Ltd.; Amalgamated Metal Corporation Ltd.; Chmn., Gulf Public Relations (Europe) Ltd. *Clubs:* Gresham. *Address:* Inworth Hall, Kelvedon, Essex.

**ROBBINS, Sidney Martin.** Economist. Chase Manhatten Professor of Financial Institutions. *B.* 1912. *Educ.* City College of New York (BS 1932; MBA 1933); Columbia Univ. (Student) and New York Univ. (PhD 1943). *M.* 1939, Anne Strax. *S.* Seth and Mark. *Daus.* Lois. Joan and Kim. *Career:* Research Asst. to National Bureau of Economic Research 1933–34; Economist, National Retail Tobacco Dealers of America 1935; Security Analyst, Bache & Co. (stockbrokers, N.Y.C.) 1936–40. Economist: U.S. Treasury Dept. 1941–42, U.S. Federal Public Housing Authority 1943, and U.S.A.F. 1946–47. Lecturer 1948, Prof. of Finance and Chmn., Dept. of Finance 1948–57, Univ. of Toledo. Visiting Prof. U.S. Air Inst. of Technology (Wright Patterson Air Base, Dayton, O.) 1947; Special Consultant, U.S.A.F. 1948–49. Served with U.S. Army 1943–45; Economic Consultant 1948—; Professor of Finance Columbia Univ. 1957. *Publications:* Managing Securities (1954); The Securities Markets; The Financial

Manager; Money Metropolis (co-author); Investment Analysis & the Securities Markets; articles and book reviews in professional journals. *Member:* Amer. Economics Association; Amer. Finance Assn.; National Assn. of Accountants. *Address: office* Graduate School of Business, Columbia University, New York, N.Y. 10027, U.S.A.

**ROBENS, Rt. Hon. Lord**, PC, DCL, LLD. British. *B.* 1910. *Educ.* Secondary School, Manchester. *M.* 1937, Eva Powell. *Career:* Trade Union Official 1935; MP (Labour) for Wansbeck, Div. of Northumberland 1945–50, for Blyth, Northumberland 1950–60; Parliamentary Private Secretary to Minister of Transport 1946; Parliamentary Secretary to Ministry of Fuel and Power 1947–51; Minister of Labour and National Service April–Oct. 1951; Deputy Chairman, National Coal Board, Oct. 1960, Chairman 1961–71; Dir. Times Newspapers Ltd. 1966—; Bank of England 1966—; Dir. Trust Houses Forte Ltd.; Chmn. Vickers Ltd. 1971—; Johnson Matthew Ltd. 1971—; M. L. H. Consultants Ltd. since 1971; Chmn. St. Regis International Ltd. since 1976; Dir. St. Regis Paper Co. since 1976. *Member:* National Economic Development Council 1962–71; Pres., Advertising Assn. 1963–68. Chancellor, University of Surrey 1966–77. Chmn. Board of Governors of Guy's Hospital 1965–74, Guy's Medical & Dental Sch. since 1974; Member Exec. Cttee., Queen Elizabeth's Foundation for the Disabled; Member, Royal Commission on Trade Unions and Employers Associations 1965–68. Dir.: Chmn. Joint Steering Cttee. for Malta 1967; former Chmn. Committee on Safety & Health at Work. *Publications:* Human Engineering (1970); Ten Year Stint (1972). *Club:* Reform (London). *Address:* Vickers Ltd. Vickers House, Millbank Tower, Millbank, London SW1P 4RA.

**ROBERTHALL, Lord (Robert Lowe)**, KCMG, CB. British economist. *B.* 6 Mar. 1901. *Educ.* University of Queensland (BEng), Hon. DSc; and Oxford University (MA). *M.* (1) 1932, Laura Margaret Linfoot (*Div.* 1968). (2) 1968, Perilla Thyme Nowell-Smith. *Daus.* Felicity and Anthea. Fellow, Trinity College, Oxford 1927–50; Fellow of Nuffield College, Oxford 1938–47 (Visiting Fellow 1961–64); Temporary Civil Servant 1939–47; Director, Economic Section, Cabinet Office, London 1947–53; Economic Adviser to H.M. Government Nov. 1953–May 1961; Principal, Hertford College, Oxford 1964–67; President, Royal Economic Soc. 1958–60, Society of Business Economists, 1968–73. *Publications:* Earning and Spending (1934); The Economic System in a Socialist State (1937). *Address:* 7A Carey Mansions, Rutherford Street, London S.W.1.

**ROBERTS, Albert**, JP, DL, MP. British Politician. *B.* 1908. *M.* 1932, Alice Ashton. *S.* 1. *Dau.* 1. *Career:* Mines Safety Board Inspector 1941–51; Labour MP for Normanton Div. of West Riding of Yorkshire since 1951; Chmn., Inter Parliamentary Union 1968–71. *Decorations:* Encomenda de Numero de Isabel la Catolica; Justice of the Peace, 1946; Deputy Lieutenant, West Yorks 1967. *Address:* Cordoba, 14 Aberford Road, Oulton, Leeds; and House of Commons, London SW1A 0AA.

**ROBERTS, Bonny Kaslo.** American lawyer. *B.* 1907. *Educ.* Univ. of Florida (LLB 1928; Univ. of Miami LLD 1954). *M.* 1937, Mary Newman. *S.* Thomas Frederick. *Dau.* Mary Jane. *Career:* Admitted to Florida Bar 1928; in general practice of law in Tallahassee, Florida, 1928–49; Business Executive since 1928; Past President of Capital Lincoln-Mercury, Inc., Shoppicenter, Inc., Vice-President and Director of Tallahassee State Bank and Trust Co.; Dir.-Secy. of Radio Station WTNT; U.S. Shipping Commissioner for Port of Jacksonville, Florida during war 1943–45; served as Lt.-Cmdr. of the U.S. Coast Guard 1942–45; Assigned Headquarters Legal Officer 6th Naval District, also on staff District Coast Guard Officer 1944–45: Justice of the Supreme Court of Florida 1949–76; Chief Justice of the Florida Supreme Court 1953–54, 1961–63 and 1971–72; Deputy Chmn. Nat. Conference Chief Justices 1972–73; Partner, law firm of Roberts, Miller, Baggett & Laface since 1977; appointed by Florida Legislature as the senior member of the 1977 Constitution Revision Commission. *Member:* American, International, Florida (past Vice-Pres.), and Tallahassee (past Pres.) Bar Associations, American Law Institute, American Judicature Society. Newcomen Society of England in North America; Florida State Improvement Commission in 1949; Chmn., Florida Judicial Council; Chmn., Board of Trustees, Florida State Univ. Foundation Inc. Member of Alpha Kappa Psi, Blue Key, Gold Key, Phi Alpha Delta, Delta Chi, Mason (Shriner), Elk, Odd Fellow; Society of Wig and Robe. *Awards:* Stetson Law Coll. Distinguished Citizen: Fellow Amer. Bar Foundation. Democrat; Presbyterian. *Address:* P.O. Box 1752, Tallahassee, Florida 32302, U.S.A.

**ROBERTS, David Arthur**, CMG. British diplomat. *B.* 1924. *Educ.* Hereford Cathedral School; Jesus Coll. Oxford. *M.* (1) 1951, Nicole Marie Fay (*D.* 1965). *Daus.* 2. (2) 1968, Hazel Faith Arnot. *Career:* with Army 1943–46; H.M. Foreign Service 1947 serving in Baghdad, Tokyo, Alexandria, Khartoum, F. Office, Dakar, Damascus to 1966; Political Agent in the Trucial States 1966–68; Head Accommodation Dept. F.C.O. 1968–71; High Comm. Barbados 1971–73; H.M. Ambassador, Damascus 1973–76; High Comm. to Sierra Leone 1976–77. *Address:* c/o Foreign and Commonwealth Office, London, S.W.1 and 15 Basingstoke Close, Fleet, Hampshire.

**ROBERTS, Sir Frank Kenyon**, GCMG, GCVO. British Advisory Director of Unilever, Adviser to Lloyd's on International Affairs and Director, Dunlop. *B.* 27 Oct. 1907. *Educ.* Rugby and Trinity College, Cambridge. *M.* 1937, Celeste Leila Beatrix Shoucair. *Career:* Apptd. 3rd Sec., Foreign Office, Oct. 1930; after serving at Paris (1932) and Cairo (1935), transferred to Foreign Office 1937; Chargé d'Affaires to Czechoslovak Govt. in London 1941; Minister Counsellor, Moscow 1945 (Chargé d'Affaires there 1945–47); Principal Private Sec. to Secretary of State 1947; Assistant Secretary of State 1949; seconded to Commonwealth Relations Office and apptd. Deputy U.K. High Commissioner in India 1949; returned to Foreign Office 1951; Deputy Under-Secretary of State 1951; Ambassador to Yugoslavia 1954; U.K. Permanent Representative on the North Atlantic Council 1957; Ambassador to the U.S.S.R., Oct. 1960–Nov. 1962 and the Federal Republic of Germany, Feb. 1963–April 1968. Member, Review Cttee. on Overseas Representation, 1968–69; President, British Atlantic Cttee.; Vice-Pres. and Former President Atlantic Treaty Assoc., Pres. European Atlantic Group. Gov. Atlantic Inst.; Mem. of Council of the Royal Inst. for Intern. Affairs; Vice-Pres. (former-Pres.) German Chamber of Commerce; U.K.; Pres. Anglo-German Assn.; Vice-Pres. GB-USSR Soc.; Former Chmn. of Governors, Bedales School. *Awards:* Grand Cross German Order of Merit. *Address:* 25 Kensington Court Gardens, London W8 5QF.

**ROBERTS, Frank Leonard**, OBE, FAIM. Australian. *B.* 1896. *Educ.* St. Andrew's College and Bendigo School of Mines. *M.* 1922, R. Edna Leggo. *S.* Frank Arthur. *Dau.* June Edna. Founded V.I.A. Ltd. 1935 (Managing Director 1935–65), Chmn., 1964–69. Served in World War I (Lieut. Aust. Flying Corps—in France) 1917; Squadron Leader R.A.A.F. 1943. Fellow, Australian Inst. of Management (F.A.I.M.); Piloted and organized First Air Mail in Australia. *Clubs:* Royal Victorian Aero (Hon. Life Member); Naval & Military (Melbourne); Melbourne Cricket; Returned Soldiers (Caulfield). *Address:* 24 Kooyong Road, North Caulfield, S.E.7, Vic., Australia.

**ROBERTS, George A.** *B.* 1919. *Educ.* Carnegie Institute of Technology (DSc). *Married. S.* Thomas, William. *Dau.* Mary. *Career:* Metallurgist and President, VASCO Metals Corp., 1940–66 (VASCO merged with Teledyne in 1966); President: American Society for Metals 1954–55 (A.S.M. Foundation 1955–56) and Metal Powder Industries Federation 1957–61. Chairman of Board, Metallurgy-Ceramics Foundation 1960–65. Member of Board of Directors: Latrobe Municipal Authority 1957–62; Latrobe School District 1959–66; and Material Advisory Board, Washington, D.C. 1959–64; Pres. and Dir. Teledyne Inc. since 1966. Trustee, Carnegie-Mellon Univ. (formerly Carnegie Institute of Technology). *Member:* A.S.M. and A.I.M.E.; American Society of Tool Engineers; Amer. Iron and Steel Institute. Fellow, The Amer. Socy. for Metals and A.I.M.E. *Publications:* Tool Steels, A.S.M. 1944; numerous articles and scientific papers. *Address:* Teledyne, Inc., 1901 Avenue of the Stars, Los Angeles, Calif. 90067, U.S.A.

**ROBERTS, Sir Peter Geoffrey**, Bt. *B.* 1912. *Educ.* Harrow, and Trinity College, Cambridge; Barrister-at-Law. *M.* 1939, Judith Randell Hempson. *S.* Samuel. *Daus.* Jane, Catherine, Deborah and Rebecca. *Career:* Member of Parliament, Ecclesall Div. of Sheffield 1945–50; Heeley Div. of Sheffield 1950–66; Chairman, Conservative Power Committee, House of Commons 1960–62. Chairman: Wellman Engineering Corp. Ltd., 1952–72; Newton Chambers & Co. Ltd. 1954–72; Curzonia Knitwear Co. Ltd.; The Wombwell Investment Co. Ltd.; Hadfields Ltd. 1961–67; Director, Williams & Glyn's Bank Ltd.; Guardian Royal Exchange Assurance Ltd. Master Cutler, Sheffield 1957; High Sherriff of Hallamshire, 1970–71; Hon. Freeman City of Sheffield 1970; Town Collector of Sheffield 1971–74. Major, Coldstream Guards. *Publications:* Coal Act (1938). *Clubs:* Brooks's; Carlton; Sheffield

(Sheffield). *Address:* Stubbin House, Carsick Hill Road, Sheffield S10 3LU and 11 Mount Street, London, W1Y 5RA.

**ROBERTSON, Hon. Alexander Bruce,** QC. Justice of Court of Appeal for British Columbia, Canada. *B.* 1904. *Educ.* Shawnigan Lake School; Trinity College School; Univ. of Toronto (BA); called to B.C. Bar 1928. *M.* 1924, Jean Keefer Campbell. *S.* Harold Barnard. *Dau.* Joan Marjorie. *Career:* Practised Law with Robertson, Douglas & Symes 1928–46. Joined B.C. Electric Railway Co. Ltd. as General Solicitor; Vice-President of that Company, British Columbia Power Corporation, and British Columbia Electric Co. Ltd. 1948; Vice-President & General Counsel, Mar. 1959; Senior Vice-President Dec. 1960. Chairman and President, British Columbia Power Corp. Ltd., Aug. 1961–63; Chairman of Board, Wilshire Oil Co. of Texas 1965; Appointed to the Bench 1967. *Clubs:* Vancouver (Vancouver); Union (Victoria); Vancouver Lawn Tennis and Badminton (Vancouver). *Address:* 1999 Cedar Crescent, Vancouver V6J 2R5; and (Chambers) Law Courts, Vancouver V6C 1P6, B.C., Canada.

**ROBERTSON, Norman Napoleon.** Australian company director. *B.* 1909. *Educ.* Trinity Grammar School and Melbourne University. *M.* 1934, Joan Robinson. *S.* 1. *Daus.* 2. *Career:* Previously: Gen. Manager, Colorprint Pty. Ltd. (1934) and MacRobertson Pty. Ltd. (1943); Governing Director, Colorprint Pty. Ltd. 1945–67; Man. Dir. MacRobertson (Australia) Ltd. (1950–59). Chairman of Directors, MacRobertson (Australia) Ltd., 1950–70; Dir. National Mutual Life Association of A/asia Ltd. 1960—. *Member:* Council, Inst. of Public Affairs 1960—, Decimal Currency Board (1963–68), and of Federal Executive of Associated Chambers of Manufactures of Australia 1955—. Defence Business Adviser, 1969—. Metric Conversion Board, 1970–73; Pres.: C'wealth Chocolate & Confectionery Manufacturers' Association. (1948–49, 1950–51, 1955–56 and 1958–59); President: Victorian Chamber of Manufactures (1958–60); The Associated Chambers of Manufactures of Australia (1959–60). Member Export Development Council (1958–66); Pres., Aust. Inst. of Advanced Motorists (1961–66). *Awards:* Fellow Aust. Inst. of Management; Cr., C.B.E. 1968. *Address:* c/o Vanauto Accessories Pty. Ltd., 288 Normanby Rd., Port Melbourne, Victoria 3207, Australia.

**ROBERTSON (Robert) Gordon.** Canadian government official. *B.* 1917. *Educ.* Univ. of Saskatchewan (BA, LLD); Oxford Univ. (BA Juris); Univ. of Toronto (MA. LLD); McGill Univ. (LLD). Laval Univ. (D. de l'Univ.). *M.* 1943, Beatrice Muriel Lawson. *S.* 1. *Dau.* 1. *Career:* Entered Public Service of Canada as Third Secretary, Dept. of External Affairs 1941; Assistant to Under-Secy. of State for External Affairs 1943–45; Secy., Office of the Prime Minister 1945–49; member of Cabinet Secretariat (Privy Council Office) 1949–51; Assistant Secy. to the Cabinet 1951–53; Deputy Minister of Northern Affairs and National Resources 1953–63; Commissioner of the North-West Territories 1953–63; Clerk of the Privy Council and Secretary to the Cabinet, Ottawa 1963–75; Sec. to Cabinet for Federal-Provincal Relations since 1975. *Address:* 20 Westward Way, Ottawa K1L 5A7, Canada.

**ROBERTSON, Robert William,** EM. Australian. *B.* 1916. *Educ.* Geelong Grammar School and Univ. of Melbourne (BCom). *M.* 1947, Rona Dorothy Benton. *Daus.* Margaret and Barbara. *Career:* Dir. of Studies, Hemingway Robertson Inst. 1947; Director, Hemingway Robertson Pty. Ltd. 1949. Chairman and Managing Director, Principal, Hemingway Robertson Institute 1961–69. *Publications:* Money, Banking and Exchange (with A. Adamson (1949); Statistical Method Applied to Business (with J. S. Egan 1949); Budgetary Control (1957). *Member:* Chartered Inst. of Secretaries (Chmn. Vic. Branch 1967–68). *Clubs:* Naval & Military; Victoria Racing; Toorak Services; Peninsula Golf. *Address:* 7–11 Albany Road, Toorak, Vic.; and Benwerrin, Piries, via Mansfield, Vic., Australia.

**ROBICHAUD, Hon. Hédard-J.,** PC, BA, DC, LLD. *B.* 1911. *Educ.* Ste. Famille Academy; Sacred Heart University, Bathurst, N.B., and St. Joseph's University (BA). *M.* Gertrude Léger. *Children.* 9. *Career:* Fisheries Inspector 1938–47; Director of Fisheries for New Brunswick 1947–52. Member Canadian House of Commons 1953; re-elected 1957–58–62–63–65. Minister of Fisheries, Canada 1963–68; Canadian Senate 1968; Lieut. Governor, New Brunswick since 1971. *Address:* Government House, Fredericton, Canada.

**ROBICHAUD, Louis Joseph.** Canadian government official. *B.* 1925. *Educ.* Sacred Heart Univ. Dr. Polit. Science; Postgrad. Laval Univ.; LLD, U.N.B. 1960; St. Joseph's Univ. 1961; Univ. Montreal 1961; Ottawa 1962; St. Dunstan's Charlottstown 1964; St. Thomas 1965, McGill 1967; Dalhousie 1969; D.C.L. Mt. Allison University 1961. Moncton University. *M.* 1951, Loraine Savoie. *S.* Jean-Claude, Paul, Louis-Rene. *Day.* Monique. *Career:* admitted to N.B. Bar; Practice of Law, Sichibucto N.B. 1952–60; Commd. Queen's Counsel 1960; Member N.B. Legislature 1952–71; Financial Critic 1957–58; Leader, Opposition 1958–60, 70–71; Attorney-Gen. N.B. 1960–65; Premier 1960–70; Mem. Privy Council since 1967; Chmn. Canadian Sec. Int. Joint Comm. 1971–73; Summoned to the Senate of Canada 1973. Leader Liberal Party NB., 1958–71; Nom. N.B. Barristers Society. *Awards:* Invested Companion, Order of Canada; Gold Medal, Laval Univ. Alumni Association. Roman Catholic. *Address:* 2365 Georgina Drive, Ottawa, Ont., Canada and *office:* The Senate of Canada, Parliament Buildings, Ottawa, Ontario, K1A 0A4.

**ROBINSON, Sir Albert Edward Phineas.** *B.* 1915. *Educ.* Durban High School (Matric) and Trinity Coll., Cambridge (MA); Barrister-at-Law (Lincoln's Inn). *M.* (1) 1944, Mary Judith Bertish (*D.* 1973). *Daus.* Peta, Paulle, Robyn and Beverley. (2) 1975, Mrs. M. L. Royston-Pigott. *Career:* With Imperial Light Horse, Western Desert and N. Africa 1940–43. Member Johannesburg City Council and Leader of United Party in Council 1945–48. MP (United Party) in S. African Parliament 1947–53. Became permanant resident in S. Rhodesia 1953. Director in Rhodesia of various banks, building societies and companies 1953–61. Chmn. Central African Airways Corp. 1957–61; Johannesburg Consolidated Investment Co. Ltd.; Rustenburg Platinum Mines Ltd. 1971—; Director: Anglo-American Corp. of South Africa Ltd.; Dir. Anglo-American Corp. (Rhodesia) Ltd., Director of various other companies in South Africa & Rhodesia. Mem. Monckton Commission to review the Constitution of Fed. of Rhodesia and Nyasaland 1960. High Commissioner for the Federation in the United Kingdom 1961–63. *Clubs:* Salisbury, New (Rhodesia), Carlton (London), City (Capetown). *Address:* P.O. Box 590, Johannesburg, 2000, South Africa; and Rumbavu Park, P.O. Box 2341, Salisbury, Rhodesia.

**ROBINSON, Calvin.** American educator, lawyer and author. *B.* 1905. *Educ.* Lowell (Mass.) High School; Northeastern University (LLB), and Boston University (LLM). *M.* 1936, Sylvia Berman. *S.* Richard B. *Dau.* Marjorie D. (Oolie). *Career:* Admitted Massachusetts Bar 1927, and Federal Bar 1929. Founder, Robinson Bar Review (School), Boston 1929 (Director 1929—). Lecturer in Practical Psychology 1930—; Lecturer in Business Law, Amer. Inst. of Banking 1944–46; Admitted to U.S. Supreme Court 1963. *Member:* Amer. Bar Assn.; Amer. Judicature Socy.; Bigelow Assn. of Masters of Law; Boston Univ. Law School Assn.; Academy of Political Science; Bd. Trustees, Lowell (Mass.) City Library. *Publications:* Give Yourself One Day (Crowell Co.); (in collaboration) The World's Work (Sidgwick & Jackson, London, Eng.); contributor to articles to popular magazines; publications on legal subjects. *Address:* 193 Lincoln Parkway, Lowell, Mass.; and *office* 174 Central Street, Lowell, Mass., U.S.A.

**ROBINSON, Denis Morrell.** American. *B.* 1907. *Educ.* King's Coll. London (Siemen's Prize, 1st Cl Honours in Electrical Engineering, BSc 1927), Univ. of London (PhD 1929); Commonwealth Fund Fellowship, MIT SM Elec Eng 1931. *M.* 1932, Alix A. Casagrande. *S.* 2. *Career:* Research Engineer: Callender's Cable & Construction Co. Ltd. 1931–35, and Scophony Television Labs. London 1935–39; Telecommunications Research Estab., Min. of Aircraft Production 1939–41; Staff Member, Radiation Lab., M.I.T. and British Air Commission Representative of same 1941–45; Prof. Elec. Eng. and Head of Dept., Univ. of Birmingham, England 1945–46. President, High Voltage Engineering Corp., Burlington, Mass. 1946–70; Chmn. Bd. HVE since 1970. *Member:* National Academy of Arts & Sciences; National Academy of Engineering; U.S. National Commission for UNESCO; Chmn. Bd. Trustees Marine Biological Lab. Woods Hole; Secy. Amer. Academy of Arts & Sciences. *Awards:* Order of the British Empire; U.S. Medal of Freedom with Bronze Palm. *Fellow:* Amer. Physical Socy; Institution of Electrical Engineers (London) and of Amer. Academy of Arts & Sciences. *Publications:* Dielectric Phenomena in High Voltage Cables (1936); and articles in professional journals. *Address:* 19 Orlando Avenue, Arlington, Mass.; and *office* High Voltage Engineering Corp., South Bedford Street, Burlington, Mass., U.S.A.

**ROBINSON, Dwight P., Jr.** American. *B.* 1900. *Educ.* Noble & Greenough School. Harvard Coll. and Harvard Business School. *M.* 1943, Mary Gass. *Career:* Dir. Overseer, Boys' Clubs of Boston; Member of Corpn.: Peter Bent Brigham Hosp.; Museum of Science; Trustee and Member of Corp. Northeastern Univ. Previously: Overseer of Harvard Coll. for six years (Chmn. of Cttee. to Visit Mathematics Dept., and of Committee to Visit the Economics Department); also member of Committee to Visit the Divinity School; the Division of Engineering and Applied Physics; the Business School; and the University Resources Committee; Chairman Harvard Fund Council. Salesman, Amory Browne & Co. 1923–24; Bureau of Business Research, Harvard Business School 1925–26; Statistician, Lee Higginson & Co. 1926–29; Lee Higginson Trust Co. 1929–31; in World War II in Navy Dept., Office of Procurement & Material, Washington, D.C. 1942–44. Joined Massachusetts Investors Trust 1932 (Trustee 1937, Vice-Chmn. 1950); Chairman, Board of Trustees Masachusetts Investors Trust Jan. 1954–65, and Chairman, Board of Directors, Massachusetts Investors Growth Stock Fund Inc.; Consultant, Massachusetts Financial Services, Inc., Investment Adviser to MIT, MIGSF, MCD, MFD and MID 1969—. Formerly Cambridge Chairman and Industry and Finance Chairman, Greater Boston Community Fund Campaigns of 1939 and 1940, respectively; Pres., Boston Council of Social Agencies 1941–42; member, Harvard Business School Alumni Assn. (Pres. 1929–30; member of Executive Council 1926–33, 1934–41, 1945–48; Chmn. Tercentenary Program); Associated Harvard Clubs (Treas. 1941–49; Pres. 1950–51). Director American Research & Development Corp. 1962–76; Texaco, Inc. (N.Y.C.) 1958–72; former director United States Smelting Refining & Mining Co.; Illinois Central Railroad; and Central and South West Corp. 1951–71; Fellow, Amer. Acad. of Arts & Sciences. Republican. *Clubs:* Harvard (N.Y.C.), Harvard, Somerset, Commercial (all of Boston). The Country (Brookline, Mass.). *Address:* 34 Welch Road, Brookline, Mass.; and *office* 200 Berkeley Street, Boston, Mass. 02116, U.S.A.

**ROBINSON, Geoffrey,** MP. British Politician. *B.* 1938. *Educ.* Emanuel Sch.; Cambridge & Yale Univs. *M.* 1968, Marie-Elena Giorgio. *Dau.* 1. *Career:* Labour Party Research Asst., Transport House 1965–68; Snr. Exec., Industrial Reorganisation Corp. 1968–70; Financial Controller, British Leyland 1970–72; Man. Dir., Leyland Innocenti 1972–73; Chief Exec., Jaguar Cars, Coventry 1974–75; MP (Lab.) for Coventry North-West since 1976. *Member:* Fabian Soc.; Industry Group 1972; NEC Industry Group; NEC Industry Policy Sub-Cttee. *Publications:* Contributor to *The Guardian, Engineer, & Spectator*; author of Fabian Pamphlet. *Address:* House of Commons, London SW1.

**ROBINSON, Harold Wenham,** CBE, JP. Australian. *B.* 1902. *Educ.* Wollongong High School (Secondary); M.(Aust.) IMM.; MID. *M.* 1956, Kathleen Aimée Wyndham, *S.* 1. *Dau.* 1. *Career:* Man. Dir.: Blue Metal Industries Ltd. 1952–64, and N.S.W. Associated Blue Metal Quarries Ltd. 1941–66, and subsidiary companies. President: Australian Council of Employers Federations 1959–62; Building Industry Congress of N.S.W. 1955—57 and 1964—65; Blue Metal Quarry Masters Assn. of N.S.W. 1938–64. Chairman: Consolidated Quarries Ltd. (Victorian company) 1955–56; *Member:* Parole Board, New South Wales; Australian Council of Employers' Federations (also Treasurer); Council and Executive Employers' Federation of N.S.W.; National Employers Policy Committee of Australia; Institute of Quarrying, Australia; and Vice-Pres., Parent Branch, England 1952–67. Employers' Delegate, International Labour Organization, Geneva 1960, 1966 and 1968; Melbourne (Australia) Asian Conference 1962, Pres. Inst. of Quarrymen of England 1969–70; *Member:* A/Asian Inst. of Mining & Metallurgy; Fellow of Inst. of Quarrying, Chairman of Australian Branch and Vice-Pres. of Parent Institute (England); Inst. of Directors. *Clubs:* Royal Sydney Yacht Sqdn.; New South Wales; Newcastle; Warrawee Bowling. *Address:* 32/10 Etham Avenue, Darling Point, N.S.W., Australia.

**ROBINSON, John Minor.** American lawyer. *B.* 1910. *Educ.* Harvard University (AB; LLB). *Career:* Partner, Musick, Peeler & Garrett (attorneys), 1947—. Engaged in oil and mining operations. Formerly Vice-President, Consolidated Western Steel Division of United States Steel Corporation. Director: Mapco Inc.; St. John del Rey Mining Co. Ltd. *Clubs:* California, Los Angeles Country (Los Angeles); Pacific Union (S. Francisco); The Union (N.Y.C.); Metropolitan (Washington, D.C.); Cypress Point (Pebble Beach). *Address:* California Club, 538 South Flower Street, Los Angeles, Calif. 90017, U.S.A.

**ROBINSON, Joseph Lawrence.** Professional engineer (N.Y. State). National Certification by State Boards of Engineering Examiners. *B.* 1900. *Educ.* Dartmouth, and Cornell University (MME 1926). *M.* 1928, Jeannette Palmer. *S.* Palmer H. and Jeremy C. *Daus.* Beryl Ann (Fox) and Molly J. *Career:* Successively office boy 1916–18, Mining Engineer 1923–25 and 1926–28, Phelps Dodge Corp.; Structural Engineer, McClintic Marshall Co. 1928–30. With Jabez Burns & Sons Inc.: Sales Engineer 1930–38; Director 1938; Vice-Pres. 1944–57. Contributor to trade publications in the fields of coffee, chocolate, nuts and confectionery; President and Director, Jabez Burns & Sons Inc. 1957–64. Chairman of Board (since 1959) of three wholly-owned subsidiary companies; B. F. Gump Co., Temp-Vaine Mfg. Co., and Tempo-Steel Corp., Vice-Pres., Blaw-Knox Co. 1964–67; Director of Marketing, The Lummus Co., 1967–71; Engineering Consultant since 1971. *Member:* Amer. Assn. of Industrial Management (Pres. N.Y. and N.J. Branch) 1952–54; member Administrative Council 1953–54; National Pres. 1954–57); Sigma Alpha Epsilon Fraternity. Republican. *Clubs:* Columbia University; Canoe Brook Country; Plainfield Country; Buffalo Athletic; Wanakah Country, Hanover C.C. *Address:* P.O. Box 963 Hanover, N.H. 03755, U.S.A.

**ROBINSON, Rt. Hon. Kenneth.** PC. British. *B.* 1911. *Educ.* Oundle School. *M.* 1941, Helen Elizabeth Edwards. *Dau.* Hester. *Career:* Member, Parliament (Lab.) St. Pancras North 1949–70; Minister of Health 1964–68; Minister for Planning & Land 1968–69; Man. Dir. Personnel, British Steel Corp. 1970–74; Chmn. London Transport Exec. since 1975; Chmn. English National Opera 1972–77; Chmn. Arts Council since 1977. *Publications:* Wilkie Collins: a Biography (1951); Policy for Mental Health (1958); Patterns of Care (1961); Look at Parliament (1962). *Address:* 12 Grove Terrace, London, N.W.5; and *office* 55 Broadway, London, S.W.1.

**ROBSON, Sir Thomas Buston,** MBE. British. *B.* 1896. *Educ.* University of Durham (BA Hons in Modern History 1920; MA 1923). *M.* 1936, Roberta Cecilia Helen Fleming. *Daus.* 2. *Career:* Partner in firm of Price Waterhouse & Co., Chartered Accountants, London, 1934–66. Chairman: Paper and Board E.D.C. under N.E.D.C. 1964–67 and Board of Trade Accountancy Advisory Cttee. under Companies Act of 1948 (1955–68). Member of Transport Tribunal, 1963–69. Chmn. of Renold Ltd. 1967–72. Institute of Chartered Accountants in England and Wales (Member of Council 1941–66; Vice-President 1951–52; President 1952–53); Vice-President Greater London Central Scout Council. *Publications:* Consolidated and Other Group Accounts; Garnsey's Holding Companies and their Published Accounts (3rd edn.); numerous papers for accounting bodies at home and abroad. F.C.A. (Ontario); *Club:* Athenaeum (London). *Address:* 23 Brompton Square, London, SW3 2AD; and *office* Southwark Towers, 32 London Bridge Street, London SE1 9SY.

**ROBSON, Walter Guy.** British. *B.* 1904. *Educ.* St. Andrews School (Eastbourne) and Malvern College. *M.* 1938, Florence Le Beau. *S.* Edward Guy. *Career:* Chairman and Managing Director, Lafayette Trading Corporation Ltd. President & Managing Director, Adamex S.A.; Pres. Man. Dir. Archivos Modernos S.A. Member Lloyds of London. Conservative. *Club:* Royal Aero. *Address:* Barrilaco 375, Lomas de Chapultepec, Mexico 10 D.F.; and *office* Apartado 278, Tlnapantla Edo de Mexico.

**ROCHE, James Michael.** American. *B.* 1906. *Educ.* Elgin (Ill.) High School (graduated) and LaSalle University (Chicago). *M.* 1929, Louise McMillan. *S.* James M., Jr., and Douglas D. *Dau.* Joan (Quinlan). *Career:* Gen. Mgr. Cadillac Motor Car Div. 1957–60; Vice-President, Distribution, General Motors Corp. June 1960–Sept. 1962 (Exec. Vice-Pres. Sept. 1962–June 1965); Pres. 1965–67; Chmn. Bd. Chief Exec. Officer 1967–72; Dir. General Motors Corp.; Pepsico Inc.; Chicago Bd. of Trade; New York Stock Exchange; Dir. Jack Eckerd Corp. (Clearwater, Fla.). *Awards:* Honorary Degrees: Doctor of Laws: John Carroll University (Cleveland, O.), and Fordham University (Bronx, N.Y.); Michigan State University Doctor of Science, Judson College (Elgin); Coll. of Holy Cross (Worc., Mass.); E. Michigan Univ. (Ypsilanti); Dr. Comm. Science, Niagara Univ. (Niag. Falls, N.Y.); Dr. Bus. Mgmt., Hillsdale Coll. (Mich.). *Member:* Socy. of Automotive Engineers; Engineering Society of Detroit. *Clubs:* Detroit Athletic; Bloomfield Hills Country; Orchard Lake Country; Detroit; Links; University Club. *Address:* 425 Dunstan Road, Bloomfield Hills, Mich. 48013; and *office* General Motors Building, Detroit, Mich. 48202, U.S.A.

**ROCHETA, Manuel Farrajota,** GCVO. Portuguese. *B.* 1906. *Educ.* University of Lisbon (LL). *M.* 1933, Maria Luiza Belmarço. *Dau.* 1. *Career:* Foreign Ministry Lisbon 1931; Consul Hamburg 1934, Copenhagen 1935–39; Secretary of Legation (2nd Cl.) Foreign Ministry 1939; 1st Cl. 1943; Chargé d'Affaires, Bucharest 1943–45; Chargé d'Affaires, Dublin 1945 and Washington (Nov. 1946–Mar. 1947, and May–June 1947); Counsellor Embassy, Washington 1947; Minister (2nd Cl.) Washington 1950; Deputy of Director-General for Foreign Policy and Internal Administration 1951; Vice-Pres., organizing committee for meeting of N. Atlantic Council and Pres. of its Executive Committee, Lisbon 1952 accompanied President of State on his visit to Spain, May 1953; Min. Plen. (1st Cl.) 1954; Dir.-Gen. for Foreign Policy and Internal Administration 1954; accompanied President of State on his official visit to U.K., Oct. 1955; Minister to Federal Germany and Plen. to Rio de Janeiro 1959–61; Special Envoy to Installation in Office of President of Mexico 1958; accompanied President of Brazilian Republic, Dr. Kubitschek de Oliveira on state visit to Portugal Aug. 1960; Ambassador to the Court of St. James 1961–68 and to Madrid 1968–74 (Ret'd.). *Awards:* Grand Officer of following Orders: Militar de Cristo (Portugal), al Mérito (Chile), the Crown (Belgium), Cruzeiro do Sul (Brazil), George I (Greece); Grand Cross: do Mérito Civil (Spain), Orange-Nassau (Netherlands); Hon. Kt. Grand Cross, Victorian Order (U.K.); Grand Cross, Order of Merit (Federal Republic of Germany). *Address:* c/o Ministry of Foreign Affairs, Lisbon, Portugal.

**ROCKEFELLER, David.** American. *B.* 1915. *Educ.* Lincoln School of Teachers College, New York City; Harvard University (BS 1936); University of Chicago (PhD 1940); LLD (Hon) Columbia University 1954; LLD (Hon) Bowdoin College, 1958; LLD (Hon) Jewish Theological Seminary, 1958; LLD (Hon) Williams College, 1966; LLD Wagner Coll. 1967; LLD Harvard Univ. 1969; LLD Pace Coll. 1970. *M.* 1940, Margaret McGrath. *S.* David, Jr., and Richard. *Daus.* Abby, Neva (Kaiser), Margaret and Eileen. *Career:* Secretary to Mayor LaGuardia, New York City 1940–41. Assistant Reg. Director, U.S. Office of Defense, Health and Welfare Service 1941–42; enlisted as Private U.S. Army 1942; demobilized as Captain 1945; served two years N. Africa and France; seven months as Asst. Mil. Attaché, Paris; Vice-Chmn. Bd. The Chase Manhattan Bank, New York 1961 69; Chief Exec. Officer 1969—; Vice-Chmn., Rockefeller-Brothers Fund; Director, Rockefeller Center, Inc.; Chairman, Rockefeller University; Trustee: Rockefeller Family Fund; Chmn., Museum of Modern Art, New York; Dir. Center for Inter-American Relations, Inc.; Downtown-Lower Manhattan Association; Director International Executive Service Corps; Trustee Council of the Americas. Dir. and Chmn. Council on Foreign Relations. *Publications:* Creative Management in Banking; Unused Resources and Economic Waste. *Member:* Advisory Committee on International Monetary Arrangements, Near East Emergency Donations. Founding Dir. Business Committee for the Arts. *Awards:* Order, Southern Cross Brazil; Order, Cross of Boyaca Colombia; Order, Vasco Nunez de Balboa Panama; Order of Merit Italy and many others; Order of White Elephant (Thailand) 1955, Legion of Honour (France). *Address:* 1, Chase Manhattan Plaza, New York, N.Y. 10015, U.S.A.

**ROCKEFELLER, James Stillman,** American. *B.* 1902. *Educ.* Yale University (BA). *M.* 1925, Nancy Carnegie. *S.* James Stillman, Jr. and Andrew. *Daus.* Nancy R. (Copp) and Georgia (Rose). *Career:* Dir. National Cash Register Co.; Pan American World Airways; Trustee, American Museum of Natural History. Member, Board of Managers, Memorial Hospital for Cancer and Allied Diseases. *Awards:* Orders of the Lion (Finland), St. Olav (Norway) and Boyaca (Colombia). Republican. *Clubs:* Down Town Association, Univ., Union League, Links (all of N.Y.C.); Metropolitan (Washington, D.C.); Field (Greenwich, Conn.). *Address:* Indian Spring Road, Greenwich, Conn. 06832; and *office* Room 2900, 399 Park Avenue, New York, N.Y. 10022, U.S.A.

**ROCKEFELLER, John Davison 3rd.** Philanthropist. *B.* 1906. *Educ.* Browning School, New York City, and Loomis School, Windsor, Connecticut; Princeton (BS 1929). *M.* Blanchette Ferry Hooker (1932). *S.* John D. IV. *Daus.* Sandra, Hope (Spencer) and Alida. *Career:* Trustee, Colonial Williamsburg, 1934–54. Chmn., 1939–53; trustee General Education Board, 1932–71, Chairman 1952–71; Director Rockefeller Center, Inc., 1932–63. Consultant Dulles Mission to Japan on peace settlement, 1951; advisor U.S. delegation, Japanese peace treaty conference, San Francisco. 1951. Served as Lt.-Cmdr., USNR, 1942–45, working with Combined Civil Affairs Com. and State-War Navy Coordinating Com.; special assistant to under-secretary of Navy, October–December 1945. Hon. Chairman Board of Trustees: Rockefeller Foundation; Hon. Chmn., Lincoln Center for the Performing Arts. Founder and Chmn.: Population Council; Agricultural Development Council; Asia Society. Founder and Pres. The JDR 3rd Fund; Chairman, Japan Society. Trustee, Rockefeller Brothers Fund. Board member; Educational Broadcasting Corporation; Trustee Emeritus, Princeton University; Chmn. Commission, Population Growth and the American Future 1970–72. *Awards:* Grand Cordon, Order of the Sacred Treasure, Japan 1954; Most Nobel Order of the Crown of Thailand, First Class 1960; Special Tony Award, American Theatre Wing, 1960; Commander, Order of the Thousand Elephants and the White Parasol, Laos, 1961; Lasker Award in Planned Parenthood, 1961; Gold Baton, American Symphony Orchestra League, 1963; Presidential Citation, President Johnson, 1967; Order of Sikatuna, rank of datu, the Philippines, 1967; Margaret Sanger Award for Public Service in Family Planning, 1967; and others. *Address:* 30 Rockefeller Plaza, New York City, 10020, U.S.A.

**ROCKEFELLER, Laurance S.** Business executive and conservationist. *B.* 1910. *Educ.* Princeton (BA 1932). *M*.1934, Mary French. *S.* Laurance. *Daus.* Laura Chasin, Marion (Weber), Dr. Lucy R. Waletzky. *Career:* Served Lt.-Comdr. USNR, 1942–45. Chairman, U.S. Outdoor Recreation Resources Review Co. 1958–65, White House Conf. on Natural Beauty 1965. Chairman: Rockresorts, Inc., Grand Teton Lodge, Caneel Bay Plantation, Inc., Little Dix Bay Hotel Corporation, The Woodstock Resort Corporation. Director: Fountain Valley Corporation, Rockefeller Center, Inc .Chairman: President's Citizens Advisory Committee on Environmental Quality 1969–73, Member New York State Council of Parks and Recreation. President, Palisades Interstate Park Commission. National Recreation and Park Assn.; National Geographic Society. Trustee and President: Jackson Hole Preserve, Inc., American Conservation Assn. Hon. Chmn., New York Zoological Society; Member National Park Foundation; Chmn., Rockefeller Bros. Fund. Memorial Sloan-Kettering Cancer Center. Director, Community Blood Council of Greater New York; Trustee Alfred P. Sloan Foundation; Charter Trustee, Princeton Univ.; Advisory Council of the Department of Philosophy, Princeton University; Life Member of the Corporation Massachusetts Institute of Technology; Member, National Cancer Adv. Board. Del. to Conference U.N. Conference on the Human Environment. *Awards:* Commandeur de l'Ordre Royal du Lion, Belgium, 1950; Conservation Service Award, 1956 and 1962; Horace Marden Albright Scenic Preservation Medal, Gold Medal, Nat. Inst. of Social Sciences, 1959 and 1967; Distinguished Service Medal, Theodore Roosevelt Assn. 1963; Medal of Freedom 1969. *Address:* 30 Rockefeller Plaza, N.Y.C., 10020.

**ROCKEFELLER, Nelson Aldrich.** *B.* 8 July 1908. *Educ.* Lincoln School of Teachers Coll., Dartmouth College AB. *M.* 1930, Mary Todhunter Clark (*Div.* 1962). *S.* Rodman, Steven, Michael (*D.*). *Daus.* Ann (Coste), Mary (Morgan). (2) 1963, Margaretta Fitler Murphy. *S.* Nelson Aldrich, Jr., Mark Fitler. *Career:* Dir. Rockefeller Center Inc. 1931–58, Pres. 1938–45, Chmn. 1945–53, 1956–58; Pres. Museum Modern Art 1939–41, 1946–53, Chmn. 1957–58; Member Nat. Foreign Intelligence Adv. Bd. Coordinator of Inter-Am. Affairs 1940–44; Asst. Secy. of State for Amer. Republic Affairs 1944–45, Chmn. Int. Development Adv. Bd. 1950–51 (Point 4 program); Pres. International Basic Economy Corp. 1947–53, 1956–58, Dir. 1947–53, 1956–58, Chmn. 1958; Founder Govt. Affairs Foundation 1953–58; Chmn. President's Adv. Cttee. Govt. Organization 1953–58; Special Asst. to Pres. 1954–55; Under Secy. of Health, Education and Welfare 1953–54; Chmn. Human Resources Cttee; Gov. Conf. Pres. Museum Primitive Art, Trustee 1954–74; Pres. Rockefeller Brothers Fund 1956–58; Governor of New York 1959–73; Chmn. Commission Critical Choices for Americans 1973–75; Chmn. National Comm. on Water Quality 1973–76; Vice-Pres. U.S.A. 1974–77; Member President's Adv. Cttee. on Intergovernment Relations 1956–69. *Awards:* Order of Merit Chile; Nat. Order, Southern Cross Brazil; Order, Aztec Eagle Mexico; Ramon Magsaysay Award Philippines; Gold Medal Nat. Planning Assn.; Mangt. Great Lakes Commission; Medal of Freedom 1977; and many others. *Clubs:* Century Assn.; Dartmouth (N.Y.C.); Cosmos (Washington); Phi Beta Kappa. *Publications:* The Future of Federalism (1962); Unity, Freedom and Peace (1968); Our Environment Can Be Saved (1970). *Address: office* 30 Rockefeller Plaza, New York, N.Y. 10020, U.S.A.

**ROCKEFELLER, William.** American. *B.* 1918. *Educ.* Yale Univ. (AB 1940), Univ. of Wisconsin, and Columbia Univ. (LLB 1947). *M.* 1947, Mary D. Gillett. *Daus.* 3. *Career:* Served in U.S. Navy to Lieut.-Cmdr. Partner in law firm of Shearman & Sterling, New York. Director or Trustee: American Society for Prevention of Cruelty to Animals (Pres. 1956–64); Memorial Sloan-Kettering Cancer Center; Metropolitan Opera Assn. (Pres.) Chmn. Geraldine Dodge Foundation; miscellaneous industrial corporations. *Member:* Amer. and New York Bar Assocs.; Assn. of the Bar of the City of New York; Natl. Inst. of Social Sciences. *Award:* Bronze Star Medal; Fellow Amer. Bar Foundation. *Clubs:* Amer. Yacht, Manursing Island, Rye, N.Y.; Metropolitan (Washington); The Anglers, Church, Down Town Assn., Links, Metropolitan Opera, N.Y. Yacht, Pilgrims, Racquet & Tennis, Westminster Kennel, Yale (N.Y.C.). *Address:* 84 Grandview Avenue, Rye, N.Y. 10580; and *office* 53 Wall Street, New York, N.Y. 10005, U.S.A.

**ROCKWELL, Willard F., Jr.** American Manufacturing Executive. *B.* 1914. *Educ.* Pennsylvania State University (BS and technical degree of Industrial Engineering for post-graduate work); Hon LLD, Grove City, Pa. College; Hon Dr Engrg, Tufts Univ. Hon Dr Engrg Science, Washington & Jefferson College. Hon Dr of Laws, Lambeth College, Jackson, Tenn. *M.* Constance Templeton. *S.* Willard F., III, Steven Kent, George Peter and Russell Alden. *Dau.* Patricia Lynn (Boorn). *Career:* After graduation in 1935, employed by Pittsburgh Equitable Meter Co. (which became Rockwell Mfg. Co. in 1945); with Timken-Detroit Axle Co. 1936–37; returned to Pittsburgh Equitable 1938 and became Vice-Pres. & Controller 1939, Director 1940, Vice-Pres. & Gen. Manager 1945; Elected Pres. of Rockwell in Feb. 1947, and Vice-Chairman in 1964, Chmn. 1971–73; Dir., Rockwell-Standard Corp. 1942–67, Pres. 1963–67; Chmn., North American Rockwell Corp. 1967–70, Chmn. & Chief Exec. Officer (co. name changed to Rockwell International Corp., 1973) 1970–74; Chmn., Rockwell International Corp. since 1974; Dir. El Paso Co., El Paso, Texas; Pittsburgh Symphony; World Affairs Council of Pittsburgh; Mellon Bank NA; Allegheny Ludlum Industries Inc.; Realty Growth Co. all of Pittsburgh; Kearney & Trecker Corp. Wisconsin. Trustee: Amer. Enterprise Institute for Public Policy Research, Washington; Ducks Unlimited Inc. Chicago; Council of the Americas, New York; United States Council of the International Chamber of Commerce Inc.; Chmn. Tax Foundation Inc., N.Y.; Southwest Research Inst., San Antonio, Tex.; Midwest Research Inst., Kansas City; Grove City (Pa.) College; Trustee, Univ. of Southern California. *Clubs:* Laurel Valley Golf Club, Ligonier, Pa.; Duquesne, University, Longue Vue, Pittsburgh Athletic, Allegheny (all of Pittsburgh); Rolling Rock; University (N.Y.C.); Bath, Indian Creek (all of Miami Beach, Fla.); Chicago; Detroit Athletic; International (Washington), California (Calif.), Cat Cay Club Ltd., Cat Cay (Bahamas). *Address:* Chatham Center Apartment Tower, Pittsburgh, Pa. 15219; and *office* 600 Grant Street, Pittsburgh, Pa. 15219, U.S.A.

**RODD, John Miller,** CBE. Australian solicitor and company director. *B.* 1911. *Educ.* Scotch Coll., Melbourne and Univ. of Melbourne (Articled Clerks Law Course). *M.* 1943, Joan Patricia Berry. *S.* Michael John. *Dau.* Diana Patricia. *Career:* Law Clerk and Solicitor with firm of Arthur Robinson & Co. 1931–39; admitted to practice as barrister and solicitor, Victoria 1935—. A.I.F. Middle East and New Guinea (ment. in despatches) 1940–44. President, Law Institute of Victoria 1952–53; admitted to partnership in firm of Arthur Robinson & Co. 1944; Solicitor and Company Director 1944—. Director, Conzinc Riotinto of Australia Ltd.; C.D.F.C. Australia Ltd.; Vice-Chmn., Mary Kathleen Uranium Ltd.; Dir., Reckitt & Colman Aust. Ltd.; Vice-Chmn., Asea Electric (Aust.) Pty. Ltd.; Chmn. Engelhard Industries Pty. Ltd.; Dir., Folkestone (Aust.) Pty Ltd.; Grosvenor International (Aust.) Holdings Pty. Ltd.; Hutchinson Group (Aust.) Pty. Ltd.; and other companies. Consul for Sweden in Melbourne, 1967—; Appointed Consul General 1971. Member, Council of Law Inst. of Victoria 1945–67; Chairman, Companies Auditors Board 1959–64. Member Australian Company Law Adv. Cttee.; 1967–73; Victoria Law Foundation. *Clubs:* Melbourne; Athenaeum; Queensland. *Address:* 13 Chastleton Avenue, Toorak; Vic. and 447 Collins Street, Melbourne, Vic., Australia.

**RODERICK, Howerd Franklin.** Chemical Manufacturer. *B.* 1908. *Educ.* Univ. of Michigan (BSc Chem Eng). *M.* 1934, Emily Olmsted. *S.* James Howard. *Daus.* Grace, Sarah, Emily, Judith and Constance. *Career:* Chemist, Michigan Alkali Co.; 1931–34, Dir., research 1934–48; Prodn. Sales Mgr., Gen. Sales Mgr., Wyandotte Chem. Corp. 1948–50, Dir. Sales 1950–54; Vice-Pres., International Minerals and Chemicals Corp., Chicago, 1954–5; Dir., Miles Laboratories Inc., 1959–62; Pres., Miles Chemical Co. 1960–62; Dir., Quimica Mexama, S.A., and Miles Chemicals Ltd., 1960–62; Pres., and Dir., Exambia Chemical Corp., N.Y.C., 1964–67. Vice-Pres., Hooker Chemical Corp., 1967—. *Member:* Amer. Chemical Socy.; Amer. Inst. of Chemical Engineers; Chemical Market Research Assn. Dir., Chemurgic Cncl., adv. cncl., National 4-H Club Fdn. *Clubs:* Chemists; University (Chicago); Indian Hill (Winnetka, Ill.); Epixoplean Clubs, Farmington Country (Charlottesville, Va.), Nutmeg Curling (Darien, Conn.); Presidents Assn., The Union League (N.Y.C.). *Address: office* Hooker Farm Chemical Holding Corp., 277 Park Avenue, N.Y., N.Y. 10017, U.S.A.

**RODGER, Geoffrey James.** Australian forester. *B.* 4 July 1894. *Educ.* University of Adelaide (BSc in Forestry). *M.* 1929, Alice Valerie Armstrong (*Dec.*). *S.* John Geoffrey. Joined the service of the Woods and Forests Department, South Australia 1915; served in World War I, with 25th Battalion Australian Imperial Forces, Overseas 1916–19; served with N.S.W. Forestry Commission and the Forests Department of Western Australia from 1919 until appointed Chief Forestry Officer, Australian Capital Territory 1926; Chief Working Plans Officer, N.S.W. Forestry Commission 1928; Conservator of Forests, South Australia 1935; Director-General, Forestry and Timber Bureau, Commonwealth of Australia, April 1946; appointed Royal Commissioner on Forestry and Timber in Western Australia 1951; Chairman, 7th British Commonwealth Forestry Conference, Australia-New Zealand 1957; appointed Royal Commissioner on Bush Fires in Western Australia 1961. Dir. Softwood Holding Ltd., since 1960; Consultant in Forestry since July 1960. *Publications:* A Forest Survey of Tasmania; Softwoods in Australian Forestry; Forest Finance in Australia. *Address:* 38 Lynington Street, Tusmore, S.A., Australia.

**RODGERS, Sir John (Charles), Bart,** MA, DL, MP. British Politician. Company Director & Author. *B.* 1906. *Educ.* St. Peter's, York; in France and Keble Coll. Oxford (MA Hons in Modern History). *M.* 1931, Betsy Aikin-Sneath. *S.* John Fairlie Tobias and Andrew Piers Wingate. *Career:* Sub Warden, Mary Ward Settlement 1930–31; Lecturer, Administrative Asst. Hull University, 1931–32; J. Walter Thompson Co. Ltd. 1932–70, Dir. 1936–60, Dep. Chmn. 1960–70; Vice-Chmn., Cocoa Merchants Ltd. since 1970; Chmn. British Market Research Bureau Ltd. 1933–55; Dir. other companies; High Administrative Offices Dept, Overseas Trade, Ministries of Information, Production and Foreign Office. 1939–45; Member of Parliament for Sevenoaks Div. of Kent since 1950; Parly. Private Secy. to Viscount Eccles, Ministry of Works, Trade & Education 1950–56; Minister, Board of Trade, 1958–61; U.K. Delegate (and Leader of Conservatives) and Chmn. Political Affairs Comm., Council of Europe; U.K. Delegate and Vice-Pres. Western European Union since 1969; Vice-Pres. European League for Economic Co-operation; Member U.K. Exec. Interparliamentary Union; Deputy Lieutenant for Kent; Fellow Royal Socy. Arts; British Inst. Management; Pres. Institute of Statisticians; Council of the City University, Univ. of Kent at Canterbury & Royal Coll. of Arts. *Member:* Royal Institute of Foreign Affairs; Hon. Treas., Royal National Inst. for the Deaf (RNID). *Awards:* Knight Grand Cross, Order of Civil Merit (Spain); Grand Cross of Lichtenstein; Commander Order of Infante Dom Henrique (Portugal); Defence Medal; Coronation Medal. *Publications:* The Old Public Schools of England; The English Woodland; English Rivers; One Nation; Change is our Ally; Stress and Strain of Capitalism; One Europe, etc. *Clubs:* Brooks's, Pratt's, Royal Thames Yacht. *Address:* The Dower House, Groomsbridge, Kent; and *office* The House of Commons, London, S.W.1.

**RODGERS, Rt. Hon. William Thomas,** PC, MP. Politician. *B.* 1928. *Educ.* Magdalen College, Oxford (MA). *M.* 1955, Silvia Szulman. *Daus.* Rachel, Lucy and Juliet. *Career:* Member of Parliament (Labour) since 1962. Parliamentary Under-Secretary for Economic Affairs, 1964–67; Parliamentary Under-Secretary for Foreign Affairs, 1967–68; Leader U.K. Delegation to Council of Europe 1967–68; Minister of State, Board of Trade, 1968–69; Minister of State, Treasury, 1969–70; Chmn. House of Commons Select Cttee .Trade and Industry 1971–74; Min. of State for Defence 1974–76; Sec. of State for Transport since 1976. *Publications:* The People into Parliament (1966); Editor, Hugh Gaitskell (1964). *Address:* 48 Patshull Road, London, N.W.5; and House of Commons, London, S.W.1.

**RODRIGUEZ, Carlo.** Italian. *B.* 1910. *Educ.* Industrial Technical School, Messina, and Electrical Univ. Brussels. *M.* 1946, Lilly Savoia. *S.* Leopoldo and Riccardo. *Daus.* Rosa and Maria. *Career:* Served as Captain in Italian Artillery; Owner and President, Cantiere Navaltecnica SpA; Messina; Pres., Lido di Mortelle, S.p.A. Founder Industrie Meccaniche Soc. Anonima S.p.A. *Awards:* Grande Ufficiale al Merito, and Cavaliere del Lavoro (both Italian). *Member:* Italian Chamber of Commerce (representing shipbuilding industry); Rotarian. *Address:* 22 Via S. Raineri, 98100 Messina, Sicily.

**RODRIGUEZ, Mario.** Chilean diplomat. *B.* 1908. *Educ.* University of Chile (LLM—Admitted to Chilean Bar 1930) and School of Foreign Service, Georgetown Univ., Washington, D.C. (MSc). *M.* 1935, Marjorie Talman. *S.* Roberto Mario. *Dau.* Adela Elizabeth. *Career:* Entered Chilean Ministry of Foreign Affairs 1925; Second Secretary, Washington 1931–36; First Secretary, Lima (Peru) 1936–38, Rio de Janeiro 1938–39; Counsellor, Washington 1939–43; Chief of Diplomatic Dept., Ministry of Foreign Affairs 1944–45; Minister Counsellor and then Minister Plenipotentiary, Washington 1945–53; Alternate Representative of Chile in the Council of the Organization of American States 1946–53; Head of Political Dept., Ministry of Foreian Affairs 1953–55; Ambassador to United States 1956–57 and to Canada 1959–65; Head of Juridical Department, Ministry of Foreign Affairs 1965–73; Juridical Adviser Min. of Foreign Affairs 1973–75; Ambassador to Denmark since 1975. *Publications:* Consular Law (in Spainish, 1930); The First Permanent International Tribunal: The Central American Court of Justice (1934). *Awards:* by the Governments of Brazil, Peru, Italy, Ecuador, Bolivia and Dominican Republic. Hon. Member, Pan American Society of N.Y. *Clubs:* de la Unión (Santiago de Chile); Chevy Chase (Washington, D.C.); Rideau, Country (Ottawa). *Address:* Chilean Embassy, Copenhagen, Denmark.

**RODRIGUEZ-PORRERO Y DE CHÁVARRI, Fernando.** Spanish Diplomat. *B.* 1917. *Educ.* Doctor of Law; former Prof. of Madrid Univ. *M.* 1945, Maria Isabel Miret. *S.* 1. *Daus.* 2. *Career:* Sec., Spanish Embassy, Brussels 1945–47, Lisbon 1947–53, Athens 1953–56; Dir. of European Political Affairs, Ministry of Foreign Affairs, Madrid 1957–59; Minister-Counsellor, Spanish Embassy, Paris 1959–65; Ambassador of Spain in Tripoli 1965–70; Dir.-Gen. of Political Affairs, Ministry of Foreign Affairs, Madrid 1970–73; Ambassador of Spain in Athens 1973–76, and in Lisbon since 1976. *Decorations:* Grande Croix: Merito Civil (Spain), Id. Cristo (Portugal), Benemerencia (Portugal), Etoile (Ethiopia), Fenix (Greece), Au Merite (Germany), O'Higgins (Chile), etc.; Commandeur: Santiago (Portugal), Legion d'Honneur (France), Uissam el Alauita (Morocco); Grand Officier: Leopold II (Belgium), Ordre de Mai (Argentina), etc.; Chevalier: Carlos III (Spain), etc. *Address:* Embassy of Spain, Lisbon, Portugal.

**RODZINSKI, Dr. Witold.** Polish diplomat. *B.* 1918. BA, MA, Columbia Univ. (history); PhD Warsaw. Formerly worked in U.N. Secretariat, and Polish Ministry of Foreign Affairs; Counsellor of Embassy, Peking 1956–57; Senior Lecturer in History, Warsaw Univ. 1957–71 (Ret'd.); Ambassador of Poland to the Court of St. James's 1960–64, to the People's Republic of China 1966–69; Visiting Scholar, East Asian Inst., Columbia Univ., N.Y. 1975; Visiting Fellow, Clare Hall, Cambridge 1976–77. *Publication:* A History of China (Polish edn. 1974, English edn. 1978). *Address:* ul. Zimorowicza 4, Warsaw, Poland.

**ROEBLING, (Mrs.) Mary G.** American. *B.* 1905. *Educ.* New Jersey Public Schools, University of Pennsylvania and New York Univ.; Hon Degrees by Ithaca College (Ithaca, N.Y.) and Bryant College (Providence, R.I.); Muhlenberg College (Allentown, Pa.); Wilberforce (Ohio) University; Rider College (Trenton, N.J.); St. John's Univ. (N.Y.). *M.* 1933. Siegried Roebling (*Dec.*). *S.* Paul. *Dau.* Mrs. David Hobin. *Member:* N.J. State Investment Council. *Trustee:* U.S. Council, Int. Chamber of Commerce, Advisory Council on Naval Affairs (4th Naval District); National Bd. Medical Coll. of Pennsylvania; Economic Ambassador for State of N.J.; Member Advisory Council, N.J. State Museum. Comptroller, Trenton Parking Authority; Chairman of Board, National State Bank, Trenton, New Jersey, U.S.A.; Dir. Companion Life Ins. Co. & Tattersall Co.; Civilian Aide to The Secy. of the Army for New Jersey. *Address:* 777 West State Street, Trenton, N.J., U.S.A.

**ROGERS, Evan Benjamin.** Canadian diplomat. *B.* 1911. *Educ* Dalhousie Univ. (BA) and London Univ. (MSc Econ.). *M.* 1939, Frances Morrison. *S.* David. *Career:* On Staff, Royal Inst. of International Affairs, London 1935–36; Canadian Inst. of International Affairs 1937–38. Appointed Third Secretary, Dept. of External Affairs, Ottawa 1938; served in Ottawa 1938–39, 1948–50, 1952–55; and in diplomatic missions at Canberra 1939–43; Washington 1943–44, Rio de Janeiro 1944–48. Chargé d'Affaires a.i. Prague 1950–52; Ambassador to Peru 1955–58, to Turkey 1958–60; Deputy High Commissioner in London1960–64; Ambassador to Spain and Morocco, 1964–69. Ambassador to Italy and High Commissioner to Malta, 1970–72; Chief of Protocol Dept. of External Affairs Ottawa 1972–75 (Ret'd.). *Publications:* Canada Looks Abroad (with R. A. MacKay). *Address:* 450 Piccadilly Avenue, Ottawa K1Y OH6, Canada.

**ROGERS, Louis.** Canadian diplomat. *B.* 1919. *Educ.* Univ. of Toronto (BA). *M.* 1949, Elisabeth June Wrong. *S.* 3. *Dau.* 1. *Career:* Foreign Service Officer since 1946. Last appointments, Deputy Permanent Representative of Canada to the North Atlantic Council; Canadian Ambassador to Israel 1965–69; Deputy High Commissioner for Canada in Britain 1969–72; Ambassador to Yugoslavia, Romania and Bulgaria 1972–75; Canadian High Commissioner to India and Ambassador to Nepal 1977. *Publication:* History of the Lincoln and Welland Regiment. *Address:* Canadian High Commission, Shanti Path, Chanakyapuri, New Delhi 110021, India.

**ROGERS, Paolo N.** Italian executive. Member, Board of Directors, Underwood Corp. U.S.A. *B.* 1910. *Educ.* Univ. of Milan (LLD). *M.* 1948, Lucille Johnson Seratt. *Career:* Employee and then executive of Mann & Rossi (a company specializing in foreign trade) 1930–44; Senior Italian Executive Officer with Allied Commission in Rome in charge of liaison with Italian Government 1944–46; in same capacity with Italian Mission to U.N.N.R.A. 1946; Deputy Chief, Italian Technical Delegation, Italian Embassy, Washington 1946–55; Italian Delegate in various international organizations in the economic field 1946—; Dir. Foreign Relations Olivetti Co. Rome since 1955; Member Bd. Dirs. Underwood Corp. U.S.A. *Publications:* lecturer and author of various articles on international economics. Kt. Comdr., Order of Italian Republic and Ordem Nacional do Cruzeiro do Sul. Member of various commissions, International Chamber of Commerce, Italian Section. *Address: office* Piazza di Spagna 15, Rome, Italy.

**ROGERS, Sir Philip James,** CBE. British. Chairman Tobacco Research Council 1963—. *B.* 1908. *Educ.* Blundell': School. *M.* 1939, Brenda Mary Sharp, CBE, 1965. *Career:* served in World War II 1940–44; Chmn. M.L.C. Nigeria 1947–51; Pres., Nigeria Chamber of Comm. 1948 and 1950; Member, Nigerian Executive Cttee., Road Transport Board 1948–51; Mem., Central Council of Red Cross Society of West Africa 1950–51; Pres., Amateur Athletic Association of Nigeria 1951; Mem., Trades Advisory Committee, Nigeria, 1950 and 1951; Director, Nigerian Electricity Corporation 1951; Governor, Nigerian College of Technology 1951; East African Tobacco Co. Ltd., 1951–63, and Rift Valley Cigarette Co. Ltd. 1956–63. *Member:* Wages Advisory Board, Kenya 1957–62; Legislative Council Kenya, 1957–63; E.A. Air Advisory Council 1956–60; Chairman of E.A. Road Federation, 1954–56; President of Nairobi Chamber of Comm. 1957 (Vice-Pres. 1956); Chmn. of African Teachers' Service Board 1956–63; Rep. of Assoc. Chambers of Commerce and Industry of Eastern Africa; Mem. Gov. Council Royal Technical College of E.A., 1957–58 (Chairman 1958–59–60); Chairman of Council, The Royal College, Nairobi 1961–63; member, Provincial Council, Univ. of East Africa 1961–63; Chmn., Kenya Cttee. on Study and Training in the U.S.A., 1958–63; Mem. E.A. Air Licensing Appeals Tribunal, 1958–60; Trustee, Outward Bound Trust of Kenya, 1959–63; Chmn. Board of Governors, The College of Social Studies 1960–63; Chairman, Nairobi Special Loans Cttee. 1960–63; elected Representative, Kenya, E.A., Central Legislative Assembly 1962 and 1963; Chmn. Tobacco Research Council 1963–71; Member, Industrial Tribunals, England & Wales, 1966—; East Sussex Education Cttee. Governor, Plumpton Agricultural Coll. 1967—; Chmn., Federation of Sussex Amenity Societies 1968—; Member Financial Cttee. University Coll. London since 1972; Chmn. Age Concern, E. Sussex since 1974. *Address*: Brislands, Newick, Sussex.

**ROGERS, Thomas Edward.** CMG, MBE, BA. *B.* 1912. *Educ.* Bedford School; Emmanuel Coll. Cambridge (Exhibitioner); School of Oriental Studies, London University. *M.* 1950, Eileen Mary Speechley. *Career:* in India and Iran, Indian Civil Service, Indian Political Service 1937–48; Foreign Office 1948–50; First Secretary, Bogota 1950–53;

Counsellor, Madrid 1954–58, Belgrade 1958–63; Minister, Buenos Aires 1963–66; Deputy High Commissioner, Canada 1966–70; Acting High Commissioner 1967, 1968. Ambassador to Colombia, Bogota 1970–73. *Awards:* Companion, Order of St. Michael and St. George; Order of the British Empire; Grand Cross Order of San Carlos (Colombia); Bachelor of Arts (Honour). *Address:* Chintens, Firway, Grayshott, Hants.

**ROGERS, William Pierce.** American lawyer & politician. *B.* 1913. *Educ.* Colgate University (AB); Cornell University (LLB). *M.* 1936, Adele Langston. *S.* Anthony Wood, Jeffrey Langston, Douglas Langston. *Dau.* Dale (Marshall). *Career:* Admitted to the New York Bar, 1937; Asst. District Attorney, New York County, 1938–42 & 1946–47; Lieut.-Cmdr. U.S. Navy, 1942–46; Counsel to Senate War Investigating Cttee., 1947–48; Chief Counsel, Senate Investigations Sub-Cttee., Executive Expenditures Cttee., 1948–50. Member, Dwight, Royall, Harris, Koegel & Caskey, 1950–53; Deputy Attorney-General, U.S.A., 1953–57; Attorney General, 1957–61. Partner, lawfirm, Royall, Koegel, Rogers & Wells, 1961–69; Secretary of State. 1969–73; Partner, law firm Rogers & Wells 1973—. *Awards:* Hon. LLD: Duquesne Univ. 1957; Loyola Univ., 1958; Columbia Univ., 1959; St. Lawrence Univ., 1959; Washington-Jefferson College, 1960; Middlebury College, 1960; LHD, Clarkson College, 1957; DCL, Colgate Univ., 1958. *Address:* 7007 Glenbrook Road, Bethesda, Md. 20014, U.S.A.

**ROGSTAD, Per.** Norwegian civil servant and lawyer. *B.* 21 May 1905. *Educ.* Oslo University (Cand. jur.). *M.* 1939, Lise Augusta Mogensen (*D.* 1955). *S.* Daniel Emil. *Daus.* Anne, Tone Lise. *M.* (2) 1957, Aase Behrens Lie. Associate Judge in Fosen 1929–33; Consultant, Ministry of Trade Affairs 1933–38; Chief of Fisheries Division 1938–45; Judge, Court of Appeal of Southern Norway 1945–46; Gen. Dir., Commercial Dept., Ministry of Fisheries, Oslo 1946–75; Chmn. and/or member of various committees and boards. *Publication:* Fiskerikalenderen (editions 1–11). *Address:* Gjennomfaret 14, Oslo, Norway.

**ROISELAND, Bent.** Norwegian farmer and politician; Chairman of Venstre 1952–70 (Liberal Party); member, Audit Department 1954–74. *B.* 1902. *Educ.* Matriculated. *M.* Bertha Langeland. *S.* Bent, Anders, Oddvar, Sigurd and Øystein. *Dau.* Brynhild. *Address:* Mandal, Norway.

**ROLL, Lord** (of Ipsden), KCMG, CB. Merchant banker and director of companies. Formerly British civil servant. *B.* 1907. *Educ.* Univ. of Birmingham (BCom, PhD), Gladstone Memorial Prize, 1928; Hon DSc, Birmingham, Hull, 1958, Hon. LLD Southampton 1974. *M.* 1934, Winifred Taylor, *Daus.* Joanna and Elizabeth. *Career:* Lecturer, later Professor of Economics, University of Hull 1930–39; Rockefeller Fellow, U.S.A. 1939–41; successively U.K. Exec. Officer, Combined Food Board, British Food Mission in North America; Asst. Secretary, Ministry of Food; Under-Secretary, Treasury; Deputy Head, U.K. Delegation to O.E.E.C. and NATO; Exec. Director, Internl. Sugar Council; Deputy Secretary, Ministry of Agriculture, Deputy Leader, United Kingdom Delegation for negotiations with the European Economic Community. Head of U.K. Treasury and Supply Delegation, and Economic Minister, British Embassy, Washington; Executive Director, I.M.F. and I.B.R.D. 1963–64. Permanent Under-Secretary of State, Department of Economic Affairs 1964–66; Chmn. S. G. Warburg & Co. Ltd.; Dir. Bank of England 1968–77, Times Newspapers Ltd., etc. since 1967; Chancellor Univ. of Southampton 1974. *Publications:* An Early Experiment in Industrial Organization (1930); Spotlight on Germany (1933); About Money (1934); Elements of Economic Theory (1935); A History of Economic Thought (1973); The World After Keynes (1968). *Clubs:* Athenaeum, Brooks's. *Address:* D2, Albany, Piccadilly, London, W.1.

**ROMERO, Hon. José E.** Philippine diplomat. *B.* 3 Mar. 1897. *Educ.* University of the Philippines (AB, LLB). *M.* (1) 1923, Pilar Sinco (*D.* 1927). *S.* 1. (2) 1930, Elisa Villanueva. *S.* 4. *Daus.* 3. *Career:* Member, Provincial Board of Negros Oriental 1925–31; member, House of Representatives 1931–35; Chmn. House of Representatives Cttee. on Public Instruction and ex-officio member, Bd. of Regents, Univ. of the Philippines 1934–35; Floor Leader, Constitutional Convention 1934–35; Floor Leader, National Assembly 1936–38; Chairman, House of Representatives Committee on Foreign Relations, and Chairman, Joint Congressional Committee on Rehabilitation and Reconstruction 1945–46; elected to Senate 1946; En. Ex. and Min. Plen. to the Court of St. James's 1949–54, and concurrently accredited as Minister to Norway, Sweden and Denmark; Washington Representative, Philippine Sugar Assn. 1954–57; Sec.-Treas., Philippine Sugar Assn. 1957–59; Secretary of Education 1959–61; Secy.-Treas., Philippine Sugar Assn. 1961–75, Snr. Consultant since 1975. *Address:* 15 Galaxy, Bel Air, Makati, Philippines.

**ROMULO, General Carlos Pena.** Philippine officer, government official and diplomat, author. *B.* 1901. *Educ.* Univ. of the Philippines (AB); Columbia Univ. (MA). *M.* 1924, Virginia Llamas. *S.* Carlos Llamas, Gregorio Vicente, Ricardo José, Roberto Rey. *Career:* Editor-in-Chief, T.V.T. Publications, Manila 1931; Publisher, D.M.H.M. Newspapers 1937–41; served in World War II, Gen. MacArthur's A.D.C. at Bataan, Corregidor and in Australia, later accompanying him in the invasion of Leyte and the recapture of Manila; Sec. of Information in President Quezon's War Cabinet, Washington, D.C. 1943–44; Resident Commissioner to U.S.A. 1944–46 Acting Secretary of Public Instruction 1944–45; President; U.N. General Assembly Sept. 1949–Sept. 1950; Chief of Philippine Mission to U.N. since 1946; Chief, Philippine Delegation to Far Eastern Commission, Washington, D.C. since 1946; President, U.N. Conference on Freedom of Information, Geneva Mar.–April 1948; Secretary of Foreign Affairs 1950–52; Chairman, Philippine Delegation to Japanese Peace Treaty Conference Sept. 1956; Amb. to U.S.A. Dec. 1951–52, 55–61; Chairman, Philippine Delegation to Asian-African Conference, Bandung, Indonesia, April 1955; President: Univ. of the Philippines 1962–68; The Philippine Academy of Sciences and Humanities. Secretary, Department of Education 1964–68. Chmn., Philippine Delegation, 10th Commemorative Session of the U.N., twice President of the U.N. Security Council; Chairman Philippines Delegation to UNESCO 14th Gen. Conference, Paris, 1966; Secy. of Foreign Affairs since 1969, Member Foreign Policy Council. *Awards:* Pulitzer Prize for Journalism 1942; Hon LLD, University of the Philippines, Arellano Univ., Univs. of Maine, Notre Dame, Harvard, Akron, California (Berkeley), Carnegie Inst. Technology, Pittsburgh; Hon DHL, Carnegie Inst. of Technology; Boston Coll., Georgetown Univ., Hon PhD, University of Athens. Distinguished Service Cross of the Philippines; Cultural Heritage Award for 1965 (Philippines); Gold Cross; Commander, Philippine Legion of Honour; Philippine Congressional Gold Medal; Commander, Legion of Merit (U.S.A.); Presidential Unit Citation with two Oak Leaf Clusters (U.S.A.); Grand Cross, Order of the Phoenix (Greece); Gran Cruz, Orden de Carlos Manuel de Céspedes (Cuba); Four Freedoms Award. Republic Cultural Heritage Award, 1965; Grand Cross Award, Univ. of Santo Tomas 1967, & many others; recipient of 66 honorary degrees from universities in Asia, America, Europe & Latin America. *Publications:* include I Saw the Fall of the Philippines; Mother America (1943); My Brother Americans (1945); I See the Philippines Rise; The United (1951); Crusade in Asia (1955); The Meaning of Bandung; The Magsaysay Story; Friend to Friend (1958); I Walked With Heroes (biography 1961); Mission to Asia, The Dialogue Begins; Contemporary Nationalism and the World Order (1964); Identity and Change; Towards a Definition (1965); Evasions and Response (1966); The University and External Aid (1968); The Asian Mystique (1970); In the Mainstream of Diplomacy (1971). *Address:* 74 McKinley Road, Forbes Park, Makati, Rizal, Philippines; and *office* Department of Foreign Affairs, Padre Faura Street, Manilla.

**RONAN, Sean Gerard.** Irish Diplomat. *B.* 1924. *Educ.* National Univ. of Ireland, Dublin—MA, LLB (Hons.). *M.* 1949, Brigid Teresa McGuinness. *S.* 1. *Daus.* 3. *Career:* Dept. of Finance, Dublin 1942–47; Dept. of Foreign Affairs, Dublin 1949–72; Consul General, Chicago 1955–60; Asst. Sec.-Gen. in charge of Political, Information & Cultural Affairs, Dublin 1960–72; Ambassador to the Federal Republic of Germany 1972–73; Dir.-Gen. for Information, Commission of European Communities, Brussels 1973–77; Ambassador to Greece since 1977. *Member:* Statistical & Social Enquiry Society of Ireland; Irish Inst. of Public Administration. *Decorations:* Grand Order of Merit with Star of the Federal Republic of Germany. *Clubs:* United Arts, Dublin. *Address:* Hilton Hotel, Athens; and *office* 7 Vas. Constantinou, Athens Greece.

**ROOK, John William.** Canadian. *B.* 1925. *Educ.* Univ. of Toronto (BA Sc, Chem Eng); Harvard School of Bus. Admin. (MBA with distinction). *Career:* Time and motion study engineer, Procter & Gamble Mfg. Co. Ltd. 1946–47; Harvard Business School 1947–49; Bank of Canada, Ottawa, Economic Research 1948; Industrial Development Bank, Montreal and Vancouver 1949–52; Assistant to the President (securities research and sales) Yorkshire Securities Ltd.,

Vancouver, 1952–53; Asst. to Vice-Pres., Cochran, Murray & Co. Ltd. 1953–55; Gen.-Mgr., Power Corp. of Canada Ltd. 1956–62; member, Bd. of Management, Queen Elizabeth Hospital of Montreal. *Address:* R.R. 16 Ste. Adele. Quebec, Canada.

**ROOS, Rudolf Frederick.** Dutch banker. *B.* 1911. *Educ.* University of Groningen (Law). *M.* 1939, Henriëtte Enk. *S.* Anton. *Dau.* Ariane. *Career:* Entered Rotterdamsche Bank 1939; Manager at Winschoten 1940; District Manager: Leeuwarden 1948, and Groningen 1952; Man. Dir. at Amsterdam 1960. Managing Director Amsterdam-Rotterdam Bank, Amsterdam, 1965–73. Member of the Board of the Amsterdam Stock Exchange; Chamber of Commerce. Hon. Consul of Federal Republic of Germany at Groningen. Recipient First Class Order of Merit( Federal Republic of Germany) and Officer Oranje Nassau. *Club:* De Groote Club (Amsterdam). *Address:* de Cuserstraat 21, Amsterdam-Buitenveldert; and *office* Herengracht 595, Amsterdam, Netherlands.

**ROOSEVELT, Julian Kean.** American investment banker. *B.* 1924. *Educ.* Phillips Exeter Academy and Harvard College (AB). *M.* 1946, F. Madeleine Graham (*Div.* 1955). *S.* Nicholas Paul, George Emlen III, and Robin Addison. *M.* Dec. 1957, Margaret F. Schantz *Dau.* Fay Satterfield. *Career:* Vice Pres. Sterling Grace & Co. Inc.; Trustee, United Mutual Savings Bank; Member Naval War Coll. Foundation; served U.S. Coast Guard and discharged as gunner's mate 1943–46; now discharged 1st Lieut. F.A. active Reserve 1955; mbr., Investment Assn. of New York (Vice-Pres. 1952); Bond Club of New York; Amer. Seamen's Friend Socy. (Trustee); Treasurer, U.S. Olympic Committee; Trustee, Museum of City of New York, Member of Council, N.Y. State Maritime College. Republican. Episcopalian; Member of Int. Olympic Cttee. for U.S.A. *Clubs:* New York Yacht; Seawanhaka Corinthian Yacht; Cruising of America; Royal Norwegian Yacht; Royal Bermuda Yacht; Royal Swedish Yacht. Union; Imperial Poona; The Piligrims; member, U.S. Olympic Team 1948–52; Gold Medal 1952; Manager, U.S. Olympic Yachting Team 1956, 1960 and 1964. *Address:* Bonnie Brae, Centre Island, Oyster Bay, N.Y.; and *office* 39 Broadway N.Y. 10006, U.S.A.

**ROOTES, Lord** (of Ramsbury—William Geoffrey Rootes). Company Director. *B.* 1917. *Educ.* Harrow and Christ Church, Oxford. *M.* 1946, Marian Hayter. *S.* 1. *Dau.* 1. *Career:* World War II 1942–46 (Act.-Maj.); re-joined Rootes Motors 1946; Man. Dir. 1962–67, Deputy Chmn. 1965–67, Chmn. 1967–70; Dir. Joseph Lucas (Industries) Ltd.; Rank Hovis McDougall Ltd. since 1973; Pres. of Socy. of Motor Manufact. and Traders 1960–61; Chmn. Exec. Cttee. 1972–73; Pres. Motor Industry Research Assn. 1970–71; Pres. of Inst. of the Motor Industry 1973–75; Pres. Motor and Cycle Trades Benev. Fund 1968–70; *Member:* Council, Cranfield Inst. of Technology; Chmn. of the Council, Game Conservancy. *Address:* North Standen House, nr. Hungerford, Berks.; and Glenalmond House, Glenalmond, Perthshire.

**ROPER, John Francis Hodgess,** MP. British. *B.* 1935. *Educ.* Wm. Hulme's Grammar School, Manchester; Reading School, Reading; Magdalen Coll., Oxford; Univ. of Chicago. *M.* 1959, Valerie Hope Edwards. *Dau.* 1. *Career:* Lecturer, Univ. of Manchester 1961–70; Labour MP for Farnworth since 1970; Mem., Council of Europe Assembly since 1973; Chmn., Cttee. on Defence Questions and Armaments, Western European Union since 1977. *Member:* Royal Economic Society; Royal Inst. of International Affairs; International Inst. of Strategic Studies; Manchester Statistical Society; Inst. for Fiscal Studies. *Publications:* (with Lloyd Harrison) Towards Regional Co-operatives (1967); The Teaching of Economics at University Level (1970). *Club:* Farnworth & Kearsley Labour Club. *Address:* 137 Hampstead Way, London NW11 7JN; and House of Commons, London SW1A 0AA.

**ROPNER, John Raymond.** British company director. *B.* 1903. *Educ.* Harrow and Clare Coll., Cambridge (BA Econ). *M.* 1928, Joan Redhead. *S.* William and Jeremy. *Dau.* Susan. *Career:* Dir.: Ropner Holdings Ltd., London American Finance Corp. Ltd. (formerly BOECC (Holdings) Ltd.); (Chmn.), Hartlepools Water Co. (Chmn.) and other companies. *Awards:* Order of Orange-Nassau (Netherlands) and Mérite Maritime (France). *Club:* Bath (London). *Address:* Middleton Lodge, Middleton Tyas, Richmond, Yorks.; and *office* P.O. Box 18, 140 Conniscliffe Road, Darlington, Co. Durham.

**ROQUES, Pierre Eugene.** French banker. *B.* 1925. *Educ.* Institut d'Etudes Politiques de Paris (Lec en Droit); Ecole National d'Administration. *M.* 1951, Madeleine Metge. *S.* Francis, Bernard. *Career:* Inspector of Finance, 1953; Technical Adviser to the Office of the Minister of Finance, French Equatorial Africa, 1958–59; Dir., Administration, Finance and Organization, Commune and Region of the Sahara, 1959–60; Dir. Economic and Financial Affairs, Ministry for Co-operation, 1961–65. President, Banque Internationale pour l'Afrique Occidentale (B.I.A.O.), 1965—. Vice-President Compagnie Cotonnière Franco Tchadienne, 1968. President Directeur-Général de la Société Cotonnière Franco-Tchadienne, 1970, Vice-President de la Société d'Etudes de Travaux et de Gestion, 1976. *Publications:* Course at the Institute of Political Studies, Paris, on the Economic Problems of Development. President. French National Council for the Employment of Labour. *Address: office* 157 avenue Charles de Gaulle, 92521 Neuilly-sur-Seine, France.

**ROSA, Andre Joseph.** *B.* 1905. *Educ.* Lycée Marseille; Academie d'Aix (BM). *M.* 1926, Renee Valensi. *S.* 2. *Dau.* 1. *Career:* Chmn. & Man. Dir. La Concorde Insurance Co. Ltd.; Dir. Compagnie du PLM; La Federation Continentale Insurance Co. Ltd.; Northern Star Insurance Co. Ltd.; *Clubs:* Polo (Paris); Union Interalliee; Golf Club de la Boulie. *Address:* 24 Ave. Raphael, Paris 16eme, France; and *office* La Concorde, 5 Rue de Londres, Paris 9eme.

**ROSARIO, Ernesto del.** Filipino. Journalist, columnist, *B.* 1915. *Educ.* Univ. of Santo Tomas (Manila); Law and liberal arts. *M.* 1935, Feliciana del Rosario y Ramos. *S.* Julio. *Daus.* Lourdes Maria and Laura Maria. *Career:* Journalist for more than thirty years, commencing as a reporter, Cofounder and Business Manager; Manila Post, Feb. 1945, and Manila Chronicle, April 1945; Editor-in-Chief, Manila Chronicle 1948–65. Previously connected with the Philippines Herald, Manila Tribune, Commentator, Fookien Times, Asia Philippine Examiner. Public Relations Practitioner, Member, Editorial Board, Manila Chronicle 1963—. Public Relations Director, Manila Electric Co., 1965—. *Awards:* Gained for the Manila Chronicle the Press Club Award as Outstanding Newspaper in the Philippines, 1957; Philippine Civil Liberties Union Award for Defence of Civil Liberties, 1948. *Member:* International Press Institute, Zurich; Philippine National Committee (former Chmn. 1954–57); National Press Club of the Philippines (Emeritus); Overseas Press Club. Pres., Public Relations Society of the Philippines (1968). *Address: office* Manila Electric Co., P.O. Box 451, Manila, Philippines.

**ROSE, Edward Michael,** CMG. British diplomat. *B.* 1913. *Educ.* Rugby School and St. John's College, Cambridge Univ. (BA 1st Cl. Honours 1935; MA 1959); unmarried. *Career:* At British Embassy, Copenhagen 1945–48; Foreign Office 1949–52; Deputy Commandant, Berlin 1952–55; Foreign Office 1955–58; Fellow, Center for International Affairs, Harvard Univ. 1958–59; Minister, Embassy, Bonn 1960–63. H.M. Ambassador to the Republic of the Congo Leopoldville), 1963–65; Asst. Under-Secy., Foreign Office, Sept. 1965–67; Deputy Secretary of the Cabinet 1967—; Director and Secretary East Africa and Mauritius Association, 1969—; Chmn. Internat. Div., British Council of Churches 1974. *Club:* Travellers'. *Address:* 2 Godfrey Street, London, S.W.3 and Ovington Grange, Clare Sudbury, Suffolk.

**ROSE, Lindsay John,** CVO, OBE. Australian. Retired Public Servant. Official Secy. to the Gov. N.S.W. 1957–76. *B.* 1911. *Educ.* University of Sydney (Dipl. Public Admin.). *M.* 1937, Margaret Fletcher. *S.* 2. Is a great-great-grandson of Thomas Rose, one of the first free settlers to arrive in Australia, 1793. *Career:* N.S.W. Public Service 1926; Private Sec. to Premier 1937–39; N.S.W. Agent-General's Office, London 1939–40; A.I.F., New Guinea and Solomons, in World War II, 1941–45; First Officer, Cabinet Section, Premier's Dept. 1945–57. Official Secretary to the Governor of New South Wales 1957–76. Member Royal Commonwealth Society. *Publications:* The Framework of Government in New South Wales. *Address:* 17/44 Lauderdale Avenue, Fairlight, N.S.W., Australia.

**ROSE, Paul Bernard, LIB, AIL, MP.** British. *B.* 1935. *Educ.* Manchester University, Bachelor of Laws. Grays Inn. *M.* 1957, Eve Marie Therese Lapu. *S.* Howard Imre, Danie-Sean. *Dau.* Michelle Alison. *Career:* Legal Advisor Cooperal tive Union Ltd. 1958–61: Lect. Salford University, 1961–63; Practising Barrister since 1962; Deputy Circuit Judge since 1975. Member of Parliament for Blackley since 1964; P.P.S. to Ministry of Transport, 1966–68; Chmn. N.W. Sports Council, 1966–69, Campaign for Democracy in Ulster 1966–73; Member, Council of Europe 1967–69; Home Office Group

1968–71; Front Bench Opposition Spokesman Dept. of Employment 1960–71; Chmn. PLP Employment Group 1971-75; Vice-Chmn. Labour Cttee. for Europe 1974–76; Vice-Pres. Manchester European Movement. Chmn. Family Action Information & Rescue. *Member:* Inst. of Linguists. *Publications:* Industrial and Provident Societies Acts; Weights and Measures Law; The Manchester Martyrs. *Clubs:* Moston & Crumpsall Labour. *Address:* 47 Lindsay Drive, Harrow, Middlesex; and *office* 10 King's Bench Walk, Temple, E.C.4.

**ROSE, Wilfred Andrew.** National of Trinidad and Tobago. *B.* 1916. *Educ.* Imperial College of Tropical Agriculture, Trinidad (Diploma); Associateship of Chartered Auctioneers & Estate Agents' Institute, London; Royal Society of Health (Sanitary Science Diploma); First Examination Certificate in Estate Management, London Univ. *M.* 1944, Pamphylia Marcano. *S.* Peter Rose. *Career:* Agricultural Technologist, Food Control Dept., Trinidad, during World War II; Cane Farmers' Superintendent, and Estate Manager, both in Trinidad. Housing Manager, Planning & Housing Commission, Trinidad & Tobago; Directorships with Colonial Development Syndicate Ltd., and Trinidad Industries Ltd. 1943–48. Minister of Communications & Works, Federal Govt. of the West Indies 1958–62; High Commissioner in Canada 1962–64. High Commissioner for Trinidad and Tobago in U.K., 1964–69; Ambassador to the EEC 1965–69, & Ambassador to UN Agencies, Europe, & Perm. Rep. to GATT 1965–68; Ambassador to Brazil 1969–72; Chmn. Commonwealth Rhodesia Sanctions Cttee. 1968–69; Vice-Chmn. UNCTAD II, New Delhi 1968. *Publications:* articles on agriculture in the Trinidad Press; Editor, Journal of the Agricultural Socy. of Trinidad & Tobago. *Member:* Royal Socy. of Health, London; Agricultural Socy. of Trinidad & Tobago (Life membership); West Indies Committee; Chartered Auctioneers' & Estate Agents' Inst., London; Royal Inst. of International Affairs, Member, People's National Movement. Freeman of the City of London 1967. *Clubs:* Travellers'; United Services; West Indian; Hurlingham. *Address:* 15 Charlotte Street, Port of Spain, Trinidad.

**ROSENBAUM, Tibor.** Swiss banker; Ambassador Extraordinary and Plenipotentiary of the Republic of Liberia. *B.* 1923. *Educ.* Dr rer pol (Econ. and Political Science), Univ. of Graz, Austria. *M.* 1948, Stéphanie Stern. *S.* Charles, Eric. *Dau.* Evelyn Léa. *Career:* Dir., Jewish Agency for Palestine, Immigration Dept., Geneva 1950–65. President Helvis S.A. (Geneva) 1951—, International Credit Bank Geneva 1959—; Member Bd. Mossad Harav Kook (Jerusalem) 1961; Bd. Dirs. Israel Corp. Ltd. (New York) 1970—; Zim Israel Navigation Co. Haifa 1971—; Chmn. ATA Textiles Co. (Haifa); Lodzia Textile Works, Holon 1964; Member Bd. London & General Insurance Co. (London) 1965; Economic Adv. El Al Israel Airlines 1966—; Commercial Attaché, Liberian Embassy Rome 1957–63; Perm Del. Republic of Liberia to UNESCO 1964; Ambassador Extra. & Plen. to UNESCO 1968; to Austria since 1973. *Member:* Gov. Council, Co-Treas. World Jewish Congress 1966–70, Member Bd. Govs. Bar-Ilan Univ. (Ramat-Gan) 1968—; Member, Gov. Council of Jewish Agency 1971—; Praesidium of Exec. of World Mizrachi Organization 1973; Praesidium, World Conference, Jewish Organizations 1973; Exec. Cttee. Prime Ministers Third Economic Conf. (Jerusalem) 1973. *Awards:* Grand Band of Human Order of African Redemption and Great Band of Star of Africa (both Liberian). *Publications:* International Investments in Under-Developed Countries (1959) (also translated into German); Eleh Divrei Shmuel (Hebrew, 1961); Towards New International Banking Organization (1968); regular contributor to various European and overseas periodicals on economics. *Address: office* 9 Conseil Général, Geneva, Switzerland.

**ROSENTHAL, Milton Frederick.** American. *B.* 1913. *Educ.* College of City of New York (BA); Columbia Univ. LLB. *Married. Dau.* 1. *Career:* Admitted to the Bar, State of N.Y. 1935; Research Asst., N.Y. Law Revision Commn. 1935–37; Law Secy., Federal Judge Wm. Bondy, U.S. Dist. Court, S. Dist. of N.Y. 1937–40; Associate Attorney Leve Hecht & Hadfield 1940–42; U.S. Army 1st Lt. Judge Advocate Gens. Department 1942–45; with Hugo Stinnes Corp.: Secy. Treas. 1946–48, Exec. Vice-Pres. & Treas. 1948–49, Pres. 1949–64; Pres., Minerals & Chemicals Philipp Corp., N.Y., 1964–67; President, Engelhard Minerals & Chemicals Corp., New York, 1967—. Member Bd. Dirs. Engelhard Minerals & Chemicals Corp.; European-American Banking Corp; European-American Bank & Trust Co.; Ferro Corp.; Midlantic Banks Inc. Foreign Policy Association; Mem. Bd. Schlering-Plough Corp. Romanian-U.S. Economic Council U.S., U.S.S.R. Trade and Economic Council. *Member:* Assn. of the Bar of the City of N.Y.; Chicago Bar Assn.; Judge Advocate's Assn. *Address:* Woodlands Road, Harrison, New York 10528; and *office* 299 Park Avenue, New York City.

**ROSKILL, Sir Ashton Wentworth,** QC. British. Chairman of the Monopolies Commission 1965–75. Bencher, Inner Temple. *B.* 1902. *Educ.* Winchester College and Exeter College, Oxford (Scholar); 1st Class Honours, School of Modern History; MA; Barrister-at-Law; Certificate of Honour, Council of Legal Education. *M.* (1) 1932, Violet Willoughby, dau. of Charles Waddington, CIE, (*D.* 1964), and (2) 1965, Phyllis Sydney, dau. of Sydney Burney, CBE. *S.* 1. *Dau.* 1. *Club:* Reform (London). *Address:* Cox's Newtown, Newbury, Berkshire; and 8 Kings Bench Walk, Temple, London, E.C.4.

**ROSS, Adrian E.** Manufacturer and contractor. *B.* 1912. *Educ.* Mass. Inst. of Technology (BS and MS in Elec Eng 1934 and 1935). *M.* 1934, Ruth Thelma Hill. *S.* James Adrian and Daniel Robert. *Career:* Professional Engineer, Pennsylvania. Materials Engineer, U.S.N. 1935–37; Development Engineer, Electrolux Corporation 1937–41. Lieut.-Col. U.S.A.A.F. 1941–46. Chief Engineer and Assistant to President, Sprague & Henwood Inc. 1946–53. Dir., James A. Ross Foundation, 1950—: President, 1970—; Sprague & Henwood, Inc., 1951—; President, 1953–74; Sprague & Henwood Foundation, 1952—; Pres., 1952—; Director, N.E. Pa. Nat'l. Bank & Trust Co., 1957—; Scranton Lackawanna Building Co., 1959—; Chmn. of Board Sprague & Henwood Inc. since 1963. Dir., Chmn., Hands-England Drilling Ltd., 1968—; Sprague & Henwood de Venezuela (Caracas, Venezuela) 1969—. *Publications:* Cementing in Deep Diamond Drill Holes (1952); Oriented Diamond Bits Cut Drilling Costs (1953); Experiments with Oriented Diamonds Indicate 42% Savings in Bit Cost (1954). *Member:* Diamond Core Drill Manufacturers Assn. (past Pres.); Amer. Inst. of Mining & Metallurgical Engineers; Amer. Socy. of Civil Engineers; Industrial Diamond Assn. of America (Past Pres.); U.S. National Council of Soils Mechanics; Amer. Socy. for Testing Materials; Pres. Industrial Diamond Association. Trustee Keystone Jun. Coll.; Chmn. of Bd. Johnson School of Technology. Republican. Mining, M.I.T. (N.Y.C.); Scranton (Pa.). *Address:* 5 Overlook Road, Clarks Green ,Pa.; and *office.* 221 West Olive Street, Scranton, Pa. 18501, U.S.A.

**ROSS, Sir Alexander, Kt 1971.** New Zealand. *B.* Auckland, N.Z. 1907. *Educ.* Mount Albert Grammar School and Auckland University College. *M.* (1) 1933, Nora Bethia Burgess. *S.* 2. *Daus.* 2. (2) 1975, Cynthia Alice Barton. *Career:* Joined Reserve Bank of N.Z. on its establishment 1934 (Deputy Governor 1948–55). Represented New Zealand on numerous occasions overseas, including the sterling area Conference in Australia 1954. Chairman: United Dominions Trust Ltd. 1963–74; Deputy Chairman, Eagle Star Insurance Co. Ltd. Chairman, Australia & New Zealand Banking Group Ltd. 1970–75; Director: Whitbread Investment Trust Ltd., Drayton Far East Investment Trust, Power Components Ltd. Member British Nat. Export Council 1965–69, and of Nat. Research Development Corp. 1966–74; Chmn.: British Commonwealth Games Fed. 1968—; East European Trade Council, 1967–69; Vice-President, British Export Houses Association, 1968–71; President N.Z. Society 1965, and of Motor and Cycle Trades Benevolent Fund. Council of Dominion Students' Hall Trust; Pres., Fellowship of Motor Industry 1969–71; Council, Royal Overseas League. Represented N.Z. rowing at the Empire Games 1930; managed N.Z. team to the Games at Vancouver 1954; N.Z. rowing selector for various Olympic and Empire Games. *Clubs:* Brooks's. *Address:* 36 Fairacres, Roehampton Lane, London, S.W.15.

**ROSS, Sir Archibald David Manisty,** KCMG. British. *B.* 1911. *Educ.* Winchester and New College, Oxford (First Class, Honour Mods. and Lit Hum; MA). *M.* 1939, Mary Melville Macfadyen. *S.* John Melville Archibald. *Dau.* Susan Dallas. *Career:* Entered Diplomatic Service 1936; Counsellor, Foreign Office 1950–53; Minister, Rome 1953–56; an Asst. Under-Secy. of State for Foreign Affairs 1956–61. Ambassador to Lisbon, 1961–66. Ambassador at Stockholm, Sept. 1966–71. Chmn. Alfa Laval Co. Ltd. and UK Cos. of Saab Scania Group since 1972, Datasaab since 1975. *Clubs:* Travellers'; Leander. *Address:* 17 Ennismore Gardens, London, S.W.7.

**ROSS, Claude Gordon Anthony.** American diplomat. *B.* 1917. *Educ.* University of Southern California (BS in Foreign Service). *M.* 1940, Antigone Andrea Peterson. *S.* Christopher, Geoffrey. *Career:* Entered U.S. Foreign Service, 1940; First Secretary. Beirut, 1955–56; National War College,

1956–57; Political Counsellor, Cairo, 1957–60; Counsellor, Conakry, 1960–62; Dept. of State, 1962–63; Ambassador to Central African Republic, 1963–67, Haiti, 1967–69 and Tanzania 1969–72; Deputy Asst. Secy. of State 1972–74; Snr. Foreign Service Inspector 1974, Consultant to Dept. of State since 1975. *Member:* Phi Beta Kappa; Phi Kappa Phi: Delta Phi Epsilon. *Address:* 3257 Worthington Street, N.W. Washington D.C. 20015 and Bureau of African Affairs, Department of State, Washington, D.C. 20520, U.S.A.

**ROSS, Donald Hamilton.** Engineer. *B.* 1901. *Educ.* Universities of Michigan and Illinois (BSc in Engineering). *M.* 1930, Grace Pajeau (*Dec.*). Treasurer: Ross Carrier Co. 1924–53, Michigan Power Shovel Co. 1930–53, and Ross Carrier Inc., Hoboken, N.J. 1929–53. President, Donald H. Ross Inc. 1959—; Director: F & M National Bank 1958—, and Clark Equipment Co., Buchanan 1956—. Republican. *Clubs:* Berrien Hills Country, Point of Woods Country (Benton Harbor, Mich.); Union League (Chicago); Pickwick (Niles, (Mich.); Biscayne Bay Yacht (Florida); St. Joseph (Mich. River Yacht. *Address:* Great Hopes Farm, Roslin Road, RR No. 4, Benton Harbor, Mich., 49022, U.S.A.

**ROSS, Rt. Hon. William, PC, MBE, MA, MP.** *B.* 1911. *Educ* Ayr Academy and Glasgow University (MA). *M.* 1948, Elizabeth Jane Elma Aitkenhead. *Daus.* Fiona and Sheila. *Career:* Member, Parliament (Lab.) Kilmarnock; Secy. of State for Scotland 1964–70; Member, Labour Shadow Cabinet 1970–74; Sec. of State for Scotland 1974–76. *Awards:* LLD, St. Andrews Univ.; LLD Strathclyde Univ.; F.E.I.S. Inst. of Scotland. *Address:* House of Commons, London SW1A 0AA; & 10 Chapelpark Road, Ayr.

**ROSSI, Hugh Alexis Louis,** LLB, MP. British. Solicitor and Politician. *B.* 1927. *Educ.* Finchley Grammar School and Kings Coll. Univ. of London, Batchelor of Laws. *M.* 1955, Philomena Jennings. *S.* 1. *Daus.* 4. *Career:* A Senior Partner in Solicitors Practice since 1955; Councillor, Hornsey Borough Council, 1956–65, Middlesex County Council, 1961–65, London Borough of Haringey, 1964–67; Member of Parliament, Hornsey since 1966; Assistant Govt. Whip 1970; Europe Whip 1971–73; Lord Commissioner of the Treasury 1972–74; Deputy Leader, Govt. Delegation to Council of Europe and W.E.U. 1972–74; Parly. Under-Secy. State Dept. of Environ. Jan.–Mar. 1974; Official Opposition Front Bench Spokesman for Environment (Housing & Land) since Mar. 1974. *Member:* Law Society. *Awards:* Knight of the Holy Sepulchre. *Address:* House of Commons, London SW1A 0AA.

**ROSSI, Taru Reino Kai,** PhD. Finnish Minister. Comdr. Order of the White Rose, Comdr., Order of the Lion (Finland). General Manager, Finnish Sugar Corp., 1970—. *B.* 1919. *Educ.* Univ. of Helsinki (PhD); Rockefeller Fellowship. *M.* 1944, Brita Juhas. *S.* Jukka and Pekka. *Daus.* Kirsi and Laura. Joined Inst. for Economic Research, Bank of Finland 1946; Head of Department 1955; Chief 1956. Professor of Economics, Helsinki School of Economics 1957–58; Member, Board of Management, Bank of Finland, 1958–70; Deputy Governor, 1967–70; Ambassador at large for EEC Negotiations 1970–72, Minister of Foreign Trade 1971–72. *Publications:* The interest rate policy of the Bank of Finland in 1914–38 (1951); The Finnish Credit System and the Lending Capacity of the Monetary Institutions (1956). *Address:* Uimarinpolku 2, Helsinki 33; and *office* Mannerheimintie 15, Helsinki 25, Finland.

**ROSSIDES, Zenon G.** Cypriot diplomat and barrister-at-law. *B.* 1895. *Educ.* Barrister-at-Law, Middle Temple, London (Hons. Bar Exam.). *M.* 1929, Teresa Michaelides. *Career:* In legal practice 1924–55; member of National delegation of Cyprus to London 1929; represented National Organization of Cyprus in London 1930–31; member, Ethnarchy Council of Cyprus 1943–45, and of the Council under Archbishop Makarios 1950–59; Observer of Cyprus at the U.N. General Assembly 1954–55; with the Archbishop, attended the Bandung Conference in Indonesia 1955; member of the Greek delegation to U.N. 1956–57–58; actively engaged in the cause of Cyprus in London, Athens, and U.S.A. 1954–59. Vice-Pres. 16th and 18th sessions of U.N. General Assembly, 1961, 1963. Chairman, U.N. Special Committee on Territories under Portuguese Administration, 1962; Ambassador to the United States, and Permanent Representative of Cyprus to the United Nations, Oct. 1960—; Chairman of Cyprus Delegation to U.N. General Assembly; Member, U.N. Admin. Tribunal since 1966; International Law Comm. since 1972; Chmn. Legal Cttee. Gen. Assembly 1971; Cttee. Definition of Aggression 1972; Cttee. on Security and Host Country Relations 1972. *Publications:* Self-determination and Other Aspects of the Question of Cyprus (A Rejoinder to Lord Passfield), London 1930; The Island of Cyprus and Union with Greece, Nicosia (1951 2nd edn. 1953); The Problem of Cyprus, Athens (1958); articles on the subject of Cyprus in the leading British, American and Greek press. *Member:* Bar Assn. of Cyprus. *Clubs:* Union (Limassol); Metropolitan (Washington). *Address:* Embassy of Cyprus, 2211 R Street N.W., Washington, D.C.; and Cyprus Mission to U.N., 820 Second Avenue, New York City 10017, U.S.A.

**ROSSINI, Frederick Dominic.** American scientist and educator. *B.* 1899. *Educ.* Carnegie Inst. of Technology, Pittsburgh, Pa. (BS 1925; MS 1926) and Univ. of Calif., Berkeley (PhD 1928). *M.* 1932, Anne K. Landgraff. *S.* Frederick Anthony *Career:* Teaching Assistant, Mathematics, Carnegie Inst. of Technology 1925–26; Teaching Fellow in Chemistry, Univ. of Calif., Berkeley 1926–28; Chemist 1928–36, Chief of the Section on Thermochemistry 1936–50, Natl. Bureau of Standards, Wash. D.C.; Silliman Professor of Chemistry, Head of Dept. of Chemistry, and Dir. of the Chemical and Petroleum Research Laboratory, Carnegie Inst. of Technology 1950–60. Dean of the College of Science, Associate Dean of the Graduate School, and Professor of Chemistry, University of Notre Dame, Indiana, 1960–67; Vice-President for Research 1967–71; Professor of Chemistry, Rice Univ. Houston, Texas since 1971. *Awards:* Hon. DSc Carnegie Inst. of Technology, 1948; Univ. of Notre Dame, 1959, Loyola Univ., 1960, Univ. of Portland 1965; Hon. D Eng Sc, Duquesne Univ., 1955; Hon. LittD, St. Francis College, Pa. 1962; PhD (hon causa) Univ. Lund (Sweden) 1974; Hillebrand Award (Chemical Socy. of Washington) 1934; Reilly Lecturer (Univ. of Notre Dame) 1949; Gold Medal Exceptional Service Award (U.S. Dept. of Commerce) 1950; Marburg Lecturer (Amer. Socy. for Testing Metals) 1953; Award in Chemistry (Jr. Chamber of Commerce, Pittsburgh) 1957; Indian Science Congress Lecturer (Indian Science Congress Assn. and Govt. of India) 1958; Hon. Membership, Phi Lambda Upsilon, National Honour Chemical Socy. 1958; Pittsburgh Award (Pittsburgh Section, Amer. Chem. Socy.) 1959; Lactare Medal. Univ. of Notre Dame 1965; John Price Wetherill Medal, Franklin Inst. 1965; William H. Nichols Medal (N.Y. Section, Amer. Chem. Socy.) 1966; Priestley Medal American Chemical Society 1971; Redwood Medal, Institute of Petroleum London 1972; Carl Engler Medal, Deutsche Gesellschaft fur Mineralölwissenschaft und Kohlechemie, 1976. *Publications:* 258, including 11 books. principally in the areas of thermodynamics and thermochemistry, data for science and technology, and physical chemistry of hydrocarbons and petroleum. *Club:* Cosmos (Washington). *Address:* 3614 Montrose Blvd., Houston, Texas, 77006; and Rice University, Houston, Texas 77001, U.S.A.

**ROSTOW, Walt Whitman.** *B.* 1916. *Educ.* Yale Univ. (BA 1936, PhD 1940) and Balliol Coll., Oxford (Rhodes Scholar 1936–38). *M.* 1947, Elspeth Vaughan Davies. *S.* Peter Vaughan. *Dau.* Ann Larner. *Career:* Instructor of Economics, Columbia Univ. 1940–41; Asst. Chief, German-Austrian Div., Dept. of State 1945–46; Harmsworth Professor of American History, Oxford Univ. 1946–47; Asst. to the Exec. Secretary, Economic Commission for Europe, Geneva (Switzerland) 1947–49; Pitt Professor of American History, Cambridge (Eng.) Univ. 1949–50; Professor of Economic History, Massachusetts Inst. of Technology 1950–61, Staff Member, Center for Internl. Studies M.I.T. 1951–61. Professor of Economic History. Special Assistant to the President for National Security Affairs, The White House, Apr. 1966–69. Professor of Economics & History, University of Texas, 1969—. Counsellor and Chmn., Policy Planning Council, Department of State 1961–66. U.S. Mem., Inter-American Cttee. on the Alliance for Progress 1964–66. *Publications:* The American Diplomatic Revolution (1947); Essays on the British Economy of the Nineteenth Century (1948); The Process of Economic Growth (1952); The Growth & Fluctuation of the British Economy, 1790–1850 (with A. D. Gayer and A. J. Schwartz, 1953, 1975); The Dynamics of Soviet Society (with A. Levin and others, 1953); The Prospects for Communist China (with others, 1954); An American Policy in Asia (with R. W. Hatch, 1955); A Proposal: Key to an Effective Foreign Policy (with M. F. Millikan, 1957); The Stages of Economic Growth 1960, (2nd Ed. 1971); The United States in the World Arena: An Essay in Recent History (1960); View from the Seventh Floor (1964); The Economics of Take-Off into Sustained Growth (Ed. 1963); A Design for Asian Development (1965); Politics and the Stages of Growth (1971); The Diffusion of Power (1972); How

It All Began (1975). *Address:* 1 Wildwind Point, Austin, Texas 78746, U.S.A.

**ROTBLAT, Joseph,** CBE. British scientist. *B.* 1908. *Educ.* MA, DSc (Warsaw); PhD (Liverpool); DSc (London); *Career:* Editor, Physics in Medicine & Biology; Secy.-General, Pugwash conferences; Assistant-Dir., Atomic Physics, Warsaw 1937–39; Senior Lecturer, Dept. of Physics, Univ. of Liverpool 1940–49; work on atom bomb at Liverpool and Los Alamos 1940–45; Director of Research in Nuclear Physics, Liverpool University 1945–49. Professor of Physics in the University of London at St. Bartholomew's Hospital Medical College since 1950; Physicist to St. Bartholomew's Hospital since 1950; Vice-Dean Faculty of Science London Univ.; Men., Governing Bd. of SIPRI (Stockholm International Peace Research Inst.) 1966–71; Mem., Advisory Cttee. on Medical Research, WHO 1972–75. *Member:* Polish Acad. of Sciences; Hon. Member Amer. Academy, Arts and Sciences; President, Hospital Physicists Assoc., Pres. British Institute of Radiology; Pres. Int. Youth Science Fortnight. *Award:* Hon. DSc. (Bradford). *Publications:* Radioactivity and Radioactive Substances; Atomic Energy, A Survey; Atoms and the Universe; Science and World Affairs; Aspects of Medical Physics; Pugwash—the First Ten Years; Scientists in the Quest for Peace; papers on nuclear physics and their medical applications in various journals. *Address:* 8 Asmara Road, London NW2 3ST.

**ROTH, Frederic Hull.** American Certified Public Accountant (CPA). *B.* 1914. *Educ.* Wooster College (AB 1935); Harvard Graduate School of Business Administration (MBA 1937). *M.* 1936, Emmy Alice Braun. *S.* Frederic Hull, Jr., and Robert Allan. *Career:* With Scovell, Wellington & Co. since 1938 (successively junior, semi-senior, senior, supervisor, special partner 1952). General Partner, Scovell, Wellington & Co. (Certified Public Accountants and Management Consultants) 1956–62; Partner, Lybrand, Ross Bros. & Montgomery 1962— (after merger of Scovell and Lybrand); company name changed to Coopers & Lybrand 1973. Republican. *Member:* American Institute of Certified Public Accountants; Ohio Society of C.P.A.s; National Assn. of Accountants; Inst. of Internal Auditors; American Inst. of Management; and Tax Club of Cleveland. Fraternal: Lake Erie Lodge, Al Sirat Grotto; Lake Erie Conservatory; Al Koran Shrine. *Clubs:* City; Mid-Day; Chamber of Commerce; University; Harvard (Cleveland); Cleveland Yacht; Commodore 1969; Union; Westwood Country; Cleveland Rotary; Newcomen Society of North America; Beaver Creek Hunt; Catawba Island; Play House; Forty Club; Al Koran Mariners; Pres. District 9th International Order Blue Gavel 1975, Eastern Vice-Pres. 1976; CYC Blue Gavel Chapter. *Address:* 20661 Avalon Drive, Rocky River, Ohio 44116, U.S.A.

**ROTH, William Matson.** *B.* 1916. *Educ.* Yale Univ. (AB 1939). *M.* 1946, Joan Osborn. *Daus.* Jessica, Margaret and Anna. *Career:* With United Press 1941; Colt Press 1941–42; U.S. Office of War Information 1942–45; Prentice-Hall 1946; Barber Oil Corp. 1947; Honolulu Oil Corp. 1948–50; Treasurer, Matson Navigation Co. 1952–57 (Vice-Pres., Finance 1957–59). Office of the Special Representative for Trade Negotiations, Executive Office of the President, U.S. Govt., (with rank of Ambassador) 1963–69. Dir. Norton Simon Inc.; Crocker National Bank; Atheneum Publishers; Regent University of California; Trustee: Institute for Advanced Study, Princeton University; Cttee. for Economic Development; Carnegie Institution of Washington; Pres. & Dir. San Francisco Museum of Art. *Clubs:* Pacific-Union; Burlingame Country; Bohemian; Cypress Point. *Address:* 2721 Pacific Avenue, San Francisco, Calif. 94115, U.S.A.

**ROTHBERG, Joseph.** American executive. *B.* 1909. *Educ.* Massachusetts Inst. of Technology, and Boston Univ. (Faculty Member). *M.* 1931, Dorothy Evelyn Cohen. *S.* Marvin H., Ira B. and Howard M. *Career:* Sound Recording Consultant 1930–33; Research Asst., Harvard Univ. 1932; Audio Visual Asst., Northeastern Radio 1933–38. Newsreel Cameraman: Paramount News 1935, C.B.S. Television 1950–58, T.V. Station WPIX 1956, and Graphic Films 1938–48. War Correspondent, News-Reel Pool W/R.A.F. 1943–44; President, Dekko Film Productions Inc. Director, United Broadcasting Corp. President, Ballantyne Radio Corp.; Manager of Operations S.P.H.-O.I.D. Harvard Univ. since 1971. *Member:* Audio Engineering Socy.; Socy. of Motion Picture & Television Engineers (mem. Bd. of Managers); Broadcast Executives Club; Delta Kappa Club. *Address:* 29 Harold Street, Sharon, Mass.; and *office* 295 Huntington Avenue, Boston, Mass. 02115, U.S.A.

**ROTHERMERE, Viscount,** Esmond Cecil Harmsworth, Bt. British newspaper proprietor. *B.* 29 May 1898. *M.* (1) 1920, Margaret Hunam Redhead (marriage dissolved 1938). *S.* 1. *Daus.* 2; (2) 1945, Lady Ann Geraldine Mary, widow of Baron O'Neill (marriage dissolved 1952); (3) 1966, Mary Murchison Ohrstrom (of Texas). *S.* 1. *Career:* Served in World War I, Royal Marine Artillery 1917–18; A.D.C. to Prime Minister, Paris Peace Conference 1919; MP (Unionist) for Isle of Thanet 1919–29; Chmn. Daily Mail & General Trust Ltd.; Pres. & Dir. of Group Finance, Associated Newspapers Ltd. since 1971 (Chmn. 1932–71). Chairman, Newspaper Proprietors' Association 1934–61; member, Advisory Council, Ministry of Information 1939; Chancellor of the Memorial University of Newfoundland 1952–61. *Address:* 11 South Audley Street, London W.1.

**ROTHMAN, Sydney.** British. Freeman of the City of London. *B.* 1897. *Educ.* Highgate School, London. *M.* 1929, Jeannette Tropp. *S.* Louis James. *Dau.* Virginia. *Career:* Chairman, Rothmans Tobacco (Holdings) Ltd., London (Chmn., Rothmans Ltd., cigarette manufacturers and predecessor of above) 1929—. *Member:* Worshipful Company of Pipe Makers and Tobacco Blenders. *Address:* c/o National Westminster Bank, 227c City Road, London EC4.

**ROTHNIE, Alan Keir,** CMG. British diplomat. *B.* 1920. *Educ.* Montrose Academy; St. Andrews Univ. *M.* 1953, Anne Cadogan Harris. *S.* 2. *Dau.* 1. *Career:* Royal Navy 1939–45; Foreign Office 1945–46; 3rd Secy. Vienna 1946–49; 2cd Secy. Bangkok 1949–50; Foreign Office 1950–53; 1st Secy. Madrid 1953–56; Asst. Polit. Agent, Kuwait 1956–58; Foreign Office 1958–60; MECAS 1960–62; Charge d'Affaires, Kuwait 1961; Counsellor (Commercial) Baghdad 1963–65; Counsellor (Commercial) Moscow 1965–68; Consul-General, Chicago 1969–72; H.M. Ambassador Jedda 1972–76; H.M. Ambassador Berne since 1976. *Decoration:* Companion of the Order of St. Michael and St. George. *Clubs:* White's; MCC. *Address:* Little Job's Cross, Rolvenden Layne, Cranbrook, Kent TN17 4PP; and *office* British Embassy, Berne, Switzerland.

**ROTHSCHILD, Lord** (Nathaniel Mayer Victor Rothschild, Bt), GBE, GM, FRS. British scientist. *B.* 31 Oct. 1910. *Educ.* Harrow; Trinity College, Cambridge (MA, PhD, ScD); Hon. DSc: Newcastle; Manchester; Technion, Haifa; City Univ. London; Hon. PhD Tel Aviv Univ.; Hebrew Univ. Jerusalem. *M.* (1) 1933, Barbara Hutchinson (marriage dissolved 1946). *S.* Nathaniel Charles Jacob. *Daus.* Sarah, Miranda; (2) 1946, Teresa G. Mayor. *S.* Amschel Mayor James. *Daus.* Emma Georgina, Victoria Katherine. *Career:* Served in World War II, Army Intelligence Corps 1939–45;. Chairman, Agricultural Research Council 1948–58; Asst, Director of Research, Department of Zoology; Cambridge, 1950–70; Vice Chmn. Shell Research Ltd. 1961–63, Chmn. 1963–70; Research Co-ordinator Royal Dutch Shell Group 1965–70; Dir. Shell Chemicals U.K. Ltd. 1963–70; Shell Internationale Research Mij 1965–70; Chmn. Shell Research N.V. 1967–70; Dir. Gen. First Perm. Under-Secy. Central Policy Review Staff, Cabinet Office 1970–74; Chmn., Rothschilds Continuation since 1976; Dir. N. M. Rothschild & Sons (Chmn. 1975–76); Chmn. Royal Comm. on Gambling since 1976. *Awards:* Fellow of Trinity College, Cambridge 1935–39 (Hon. Fellow 1961); Hon. Fellow Bellairs Research Inst. of McGill University, Barbados (1960); Weizmann Institute of Science, Rehovoth, (1962). University College Cambridge (1966) Institute, Biology (1971) and of Imperial Coll. of Science & Technology (1975). *Address:* c/o House of Lords, London S.W.1.

**ROTHSCHILD, Robert,** KCMG (Hon.). Belgian diplomat. *B.* 1911. *Educ.* Dr Rer pol, (Brussels). *Dau.* Anne. *Career:* Entered Foreign Office Jan. 1937; Secy. of Legation, Lisbon, Oct. 1941; First Sec., Chungkin Embassy, July 1944; Consul-General, Shanghai, 1945–50; Counsellor, Embassy, Washington, 1950–52; Chief of Cabinet, Ministry of Foreign Affairs, 1954–58; Head of Delegation to Interim Commission of the Common Market and Euratom, May 1957; Ambassador to Yugoslavia 1958–60; Deputy Head, Belgian Diplomatic Mission to the Republic of Congo 1960; Chief of Cabinet, Ministry of Foreign Affairs 1961–64; Ambassador to Switzerland 1964–66, to France 1966–73; Ambassador to the Court of St. James 1973–76. *Clubs:* Travellers' (London); Cercle Gaulois' Brussels). *Address:* 51 Avenue Général de Gaulle, Brussels, Belgium; and 43 Ranelagh Grove, London SW1.

**ROUAMBA, Tensore Paul.** Ambassador of Upper Volta. *B.* 1933. *Educ.* Sorbonne, Paris L es L) .*M.* 1961, Jeanne Zongo.

*S.* Alexandre and Christian. *Daus.* Beatrice and Daniele. *Career:* Asst. Ecole Pratique des Hautes Etudes, Sorbonne, 1960; Professor, Ecole Normale d'Instituteurs, Ouagadougou, Upper Volta; Professor, Lycee Kabore; Member, Cour Supreme Ougadougou, 1964; Assistant Professor Univ. of Abidjan, 1965; Perm. Rep. of Upper Volta to the UN & Ambassador to the U.S.A. & Canada 1966–72; Ambassador to Nigeria 1972 & to Ghana since 1972. *Publications:* Several studies on African problems in West Africa. *Address:* Embassy of Upper Volta, House No. 772/3, Asylum Down, off Farrar Avenue, P.O. Box 651, Accra, Ghana.

**ROUDYBUSH, Franklin.** American. U.S. Foreign Service of Department of State. *B.* 1906. *Educ.* MA and PhD. *M.* 1941, Alexandra Brown, *dau.* of Constantine Brown. *Career:* Dean of a Foreign Service School 1931–42 and 1957–78; U.S. Government 1942–57; Director, Pan American Institute, Editor of Affairs 1938–42; Professor of International Economic Relations, Southeastern University 1938–45. With Foreign Service Institute, stationed at Strasbourg, Council of Europe 1948–54; American Embassy, Paris; Lahore (Pakistan); American Embassy, Dublin (Ireland). *Member:* American Society of International Law; Delta Phi Epsilon; Assn. des Amis du Salon d'Automne. Royal Dublin Society. *Publications:* An Analysis of the Educational Background and Experience of 828 United States Foreign Service Officers; Evaluative Criteria for Foreign Service Schools and Foreign Service Training; Training for the Foreign Service (in French); XX Century Diplomacy; La Situation Actuelle du Capitalism Occidental (in French); Art and Diplomacy; The Twentieth Century; Diplomatic Language. Democrat. *Clubs:* Hamilton (London); Royal Aberdeen Golf, Scotland; Harvard; National Press (Washington); National Yacht; Portmarnock Golf; Fitzwilliam (Dublin); Dunloughaire Golf; Miramar Golf (Oporto, Portugal). *Address:* 15 Avenue President Wilson, Paris 16; and Sauveterre de Rouergue, l'Arveyron, France, and Villa St. Honoré, Moledo do Minho, Minho, Portugal.

**ROUHANI, Mansour.** Iranian civil Engineer. *B.* 1921. *Educ.* Civil Engineering (MS), Tehran Univ.; Water Eng. Specialization, London Univ. College. *M.* Parvin Shakib. *S.* Dariush. *Dau.* Nasrin. *Career:* Technical Asst. Tehran Water Authority; Tehran Water Authority Man. Director; Minister Water and Power 1963, Minister of Agriculture & Natural Resources since Oct. 1971 and in charge of Ministry of Cooperatives & Rural Affairs since Nov. 1976, and Minister of Agriculture & Rural Development since July 1977. *Member:* Iran Engineers Assn.; National Resurrection Party; English Coll. Engineers Association. *Awards:* Grosse Goldene Ehrenzeichen Am Bande Austria; Croix de Commandeur of France; Medal Legion d'Honneur from the French Govt.; Ordinul, Tudor Vladimirescu, Romanian Govt.; First Class Medal of Land Reform, Coronation, Taj Homayoun Medals awarded by His Imperial Majesty. *Publications:* Policies Relating to Water Resources; Development in Iran; Policy for Agricultural Development in Zones of Water and Soil Resources. *Address:* Shemiran, Farmanieh, Rouhani Avenue, Tehran, Iran; and *office* Ministry of Agriculture & Rural Development, Elizabeth Boulevard, Tehran, Iran.

**ROUNTREE, Maj. Charles Nelson Meredith,** OBE. British. *B.* 1916. *Educ.* Royal School, Dungannon; and Queen's Univ., Belfast; Solicitor. *M.* 1942, Sylvia Catherine MacFarland. *S.* 4. *Career:* Under-Sheriff, Co. Tyrone 1949–64. High Sheriff Co. Tyrone, 1958. Clerk of the Crown and Peace for County Tyrone Dec. 1964—, Secretary to the Lieutenancy 1976—. Vice-Chairman, Ulster Savings Committee 1958–74. Chairman, C Tyrone Savings Committee 1954–74; Ulster Savings cttee since 1974; Governor Rotary Int. Ireland 1974–5. Local Director Ulster Bank Ltd.; Incorporated Law Society of Northern Ireland; Area Council, British Legion (N.I. Area) & Chmn. No. 5 District. *Clubs:* Tyrone County; Omagh Rotary. *Address:* The Laurels, Hospital Road, Omagh, Co. Tyrone, and *office* County Court Court House, Omagh, Co. Tyrone, Northern Ireland.

**ROUNTREE, William Manning.** *B.* 1917. *Educ.* Columbus Univ., Washington (LLB). *M.* 1946, Suzanne McDowall. *Dau.* Susan. *Career:* At U.S. Treasury 1935–41; Official, Lend-Lease Admin. 1941–42; General Assistant to U.S. Representative on Middle East Supply Centre, Cairo, and to Director, U.S. Economic Operations in the Middle East 1942–45; Special Asst. for Economic Affairs to Dir. Office of Near Eastern, South Asian and African Affairs, Dept. of State, Washington 1946–48 (Deputy Asst. Secy. of State 1955–56); Administrative Asst., Anglo-American Committee of Inquiry on Palestine and Related Problems 1946; Member, American Economic Mission to survey Greek requirements in connection with inauguration of American Aid 1947; Special Asst. to U.S. Ambassador to Greece 1948–49; Deputy, and later Director, Office of Greek, Turkish and Iranian Affairs, Dept. of State 1949–52; Counsellor and Dep. Chief, U.S. Embassy, Ankara 1952–53; Minister-Counsellor and Dep. Chief, Teheran 1953–55; Asst. Secy. of State 1956–59; Ambassador to Pakistan 1959–62; to the Sudan 1962–65. Ambassador of the U.S.A. to the Republic of South Africa 1965–70; and to Brazil 1970–73. *Address:* 2220 S.W. 34th Street, Gainsville, Fla., 32608, U.S.A.

**ROUSE, Edmund Alexander.** Australian. *B.* 1926. *Educ.* Paramatta King's School and Leeds University (BSc-Hons. 2). *M.* 1951, Dorothy Jane, Dau. of Lady Rolph and late Sir Gordon Rolph. *S.* 1. *Daus.* 3. *Career:* Chairman and Managing Director Examiner-Northern TV Ltd. and subsidiary companies April 1959, Chairman 1970. Member, Board of Northern Tasmanian Home for Boys; Chairman Exec. Committee, Launceston Church Grammar School. Foundation member, Australian Press Council. *Clubs:* Launceston; Tasmanian. *Address: office* 71/75 Paterson Street, Launceston, Tasmania.

**ROUSSEAU, Pierre Etienne.** South African. *B.* 1910. *Educ.* Univ. of Stellenbosch (MSc); FIChemE. *M.* 1936, Magdalena Elizabeth Loubser. *S.* 1. *Daus.* 4. *Career:* Chairman Federale Group (Federale Volksbeleggings Bpk); Director: Barlow Rand Ltd.; Federale Chemiese Beleggings Bpk; General Mining & Finance Corp. Ltd.; Federale Mynbou Bpk; S.A. Coal Oil & Gas Corp. Ltd. (Sasol); Safmarine Ltd.; S.A. Manganese Amcor Ltd.; Sanlam; S.A. Reserve Bank. *Awards:* DMS 1975, Commander Homayoun 1976; Hon. DSc Univ. of Stellenbosch 1966; Hon. DSc. Univ. of O.F.S. 1962; PhD (h.c.) RAU 1976; William McNab Medal in Associateship Exam. of Inst. of Chemical Engineers. Chancellor Univ. of Fort Hare. Hon. Pres. S.A. Foundation. *Clubs:* Rand, R.S.A. and Country (all of Johannesburg); Here XVII (Cape Town). *Address:* P.O. Box 2911, Johannesburg 2000, South Africa.

**ROW, Sir John Alfred.** *B.* 1905. *Educ.* Senior Public Examination. *M.* (1) 1929, Gladys Mary Hollins (*Ded.* 1952). *Dau.* Lorraine Anne. *M.* (2) 1966, Irene Gough. *Career:* Australian Minister for Primary Industries, Queensland, June 1963–72; Member of Parliament in the State of Queensland, representing Hichinbrook Electorate 1960–72; Created Knight Bachelor 1974; Member Australian National Party (Queensland). *Club:* North Queensland (Townsville). *Address:* 10 Gort Street, Ingham, Qld. 4850, Australia.

**ROWALLAN, Rt. Hon. Lord,** KT, KBE, MC (Thomas Godfrey Polson Corbett). *B.* 1895. *Educ.* Eton. *M.* 1918, Gwyn Mervyn Grimond (*D.* 1971). *S.* 4 (and one killed in action). *Dau.* 1. Served in World War I (wounded; MC); commanded Bn. of Royal Scots Fusiliers in France 1940; retired Lt.-Col. 1944. Chief Scout of the British Commonwealth and Empire 1945–59; Governor, National Bank of Scotland 1951–59; Governor of Tasmania 1959–63. Member of The Pilgrims Socy.; Hon. LLD McGill, Glasgow and Birmingham Univs. Freeman, City of Edinburgh. KStJ 1959. *Club:* Brooks's. *Deceased 30th Nov. 1977.*

**ROWAT, Donald Cameron.** Canadian Professor of Political Science. *B.* 1921. *Educ.* Saskatchewen & Ontario; Toronto (B.A. 1943); Columbia (M.A. 1946, Ph.D. 1950). *Married. Children:* 2. *Career:* Research Asst., Dept. Finance, Ottawa 1943–44; Admin. Officer, Dept. Nat. Health and Welfare 1944–45; Lect. Political Science, N. Texas State Teachers' Coll. 1947; Dir. Research, Inst. Public Affairs & Lect. Political Science, Dalhousie Univ. 1947–49; Lect. Political Science, Univ. B.C. 1949–50; Asst. Prof. Political Science, Carleton Coll. Ottawa 1950–53; Assoc. Prof. 1953–58; United Nations (T.A.A.) Expert on Public Admin. Ethiopia 1956–57; Acting Dir. School of Public Admin. Carleton Univ. Ottawa 1957–58; Prof. Dept. Political Science since 1958; Canada Council Senior Fellow, govts. Western Europe 1960–61; studied Ombudsman plan, Scandinavia and France 1962; Chmn. Dept. Political Science 1962–65; Supervisor Grad. Studies Political Science 1965–66; Canada Council Senior Fellow, Federal capitals 1967–68; Memb. Editorial Cttee. and Group Chmn. 32nd. American Assembly on Ombudsman 1967; Vis. Prof. Univ. of California, Berkeley, 1972; Exchange Fellow Univ. of Leningrad 1974; Canada Council Leave Fellow editing volumes on admin. secrecy and local govt. reform 1974–75. *Member:* Cttee. on Univ. Govt., Canadian

Assoc. Univ. Teachers (Chmn. 1959–60, Exec. Cttee. 1965–67); Co.-Dir. 8th Annual Seminar, Canadian Union of Students, 1965; Comm. on Relations between Univs. and Govts., 1968–69; Policy Cttee. Parly. Internship Programme (Chmn. since 1971); Canadian Political Science Assoc. (Pres. 1975–76). *Publications:* The Reorganisation of Provincial-Municipal Relations in Nova Scotia (1949); The Public Service of Canada (1953); Your Local Government (1955, 1975); Basic Issues in Public Administration (1961); The Ombudsman: Citizen's Defender (1965, 68); The Canadian Municipal System (Essays, 1969); The University, Society and Government (1970, and Editor of studies of same); The Government of Federal Capitals (1973); The Ombudsman Plan (1973); Provincial Government and Politics: Comparative Essays (1972, 1973); editor, The Finnish Parliamentary Ombudsman, by Mikael Hiden (1974); joint editor, The Provincial Political Systems (1976), & Political Corruption in Canada (1976). *Address:* Department of Political Science, Carleton University, Ottawa, Canada.

**ROWDEN, Henry Wells,** CBE. British. *B.* 1908. *Educ.* Wellington College and University of New Zealand; BCom; FCA (N.Z.). *M.* 1933, Mary Davies Wiggins. *S.* 2. *Daus.* 2. *Career:* Senior Partner in firm of Vickery, Rowden & Starke, Public Accountants, Wellington, New Zealand 1931–53. Director: Acmil Ltd. and Subsidiaries since 1947; Director Feltex New Zealand Ltd. 1941—, Australian Paper Mfrs, Ltd.; Aldus Ltd.; Mem. of Board, Reserve Bank of Australia 1961–73; Chairman, Consultative Council, Export Payments Insurance Corp. 1965–70; Vice-Chmn., Council of Australian Administrative Staff College 1962–75. Member, New Zealand Taxation Inquiry Committee 1951. *Awards: Fellow:* N.Z. Socy. of Accountants; Australian Inst. of Management; Inst. of Directors; Royal Horticultural Socy, C.B.E. 1972. *Clubs:* Wellington (N.Z.); Melbourne; Australian. *Address:* 53 Eckersley Avenue, Buderim, Qld. 4556, Australia.

**ROWE, Hon. F. W.** *B.* 1912. *Educ.* Memorial Univ. Coll. (1st Class Hons. 1936); Mt. Allison Univ. (BA 1941; awarded O. E. Smith Scholarship): Univ. of Toronto; B Paed (Hons.) (1949) and D Pedagogy (1951) Univ. of Toronto. *M.* Edith Laura Butt. *S.* 4. *Career:* Principal of various schools; Supervising Inspector of Schools 1942–43; first Principal Curtis Acad., St. John's 1943; lectured in English and Education, Memorial University. Summer sessions 1938–46; gave weekly talks over C.B.C. network on Newfoundland social welfare, life and culture; engaged by Toronto Y.M.C.A. for research 1948–49. Member, Council of Higher Education 1945–48; First Deputy Minister of Public Welfare 1949–52; member, United Church Education Council 1952–56; elected by acclamation Member of House of Assembly to represent District of Labrador 1952; Minister of Mines & Resources 1952–56, Public Welfare 1955–56, and Education 1956–59; Minister of Highways 1959–64; Minister of Finance 1964, and of Community and Social Development 1966. Minister of Education 1967–71 in the Government of Newfoundland and Minister of Labrador Affairs 1967–71; Minister of Finance 1971. Elected representative of: District of White Bay South, Oct. 1956; (re-elected 1959 and 1962); District of Grand Falls, Sept. 1966. *Publications:* Political History of Newfoundland (Encyclopedia of Canada); History of Education in Newfoundland (Ryerson Press 1952); Blue-print for Education in Newfoundland, 1958; The Development of Education in Newfoundland (Ryerson 1964); articles on Newfoundland and Labrador in the World Book Encyclopedia. *Address:* c/o Legislative Assembly, St. John's, Newfoundland, Canada.

**ROWE, Henry Stuart Payson.** American executive. *B.* 1900. *Educ.* Harvard Univ. (AB 1922). *M.* 1927, Florence van Arnhem Cassard. *Daus.* Barbara C. (de Marneffe) and Pamela O. (Peabody, Jr.). *Career:* Second Vice-President, Massachusetts Mutual Life Insurance Co. (Springfield, Mass.) 1934–45; Manager, Boston Office, Bankers Trust Co., New York 1927–34. Previously associated with Merrill, Oldham & Co., Boston; Financial Vice-President and Director, John Hancock Life Insurance Co., Boston. Mass. 1945–65; Pres. Brookline Savings Bank 1965–73, Chmn. 1973–75, Hon. Trustee since 1975; Director: State Street Bank & Trust Co. 1949–72, Norfolk & Western Railway 1961–72; United Telecom Inc., Missouri Public Service Co., Boston Gas Co. Trustee, Eastern Gas & Fuel Associates. Member, Advisory Board, Investment Trust of Boston. Republican. *Clubs:* Union, Harvard, Harvard Varsity (Boston); Badminton & Tennis; Longwood Cricket; Dublin Lake; Cambridge Tennis. *Address:* 110 Coolidge Hill, Cambridge, Mass. 02138; and *office* 160 Washington Street, Brookline, Mass., U.S.A.

**ROWE, William Stanhope.** American banker. *B.* 1916. *Educ.* Harvard (AB 1939). *M.* 1939, Martha Phyllis Whitney. *S.* George Whitney. *Daus.* Mrs. Nancy Sherlock Rowe Conner, Jennifer Stanhope and Mrs. Martha Whitney Rowe Long. *Career:* Joined Fifth Third Bank 1939; Asst. Vice-Pres. 1945; Credit Manager 1948; Vice-Pres. Jan. 1949; Exec. Vice-Pres. Jan. 1962; Pres. since 1963. *Address:* 4766 Burley Hills Drive, Cincinnati, Ohio 45243; and *office* Fifth Third Bank, Cincinnati, Ohio 45201, U.S.A.

**ROWLAND, John Russell.** Australian. *B.* 1925. *Educ.* Sydney University (BA). *M.* 1956, Moira Armstrong. *S.* Andrew James. *Daus.* Katherine and Philippa. *Career:* Australian Ambassador to the USSR, 1965–68; First Assistant Secretary, Department of External Affairs, 1969; High Commissioner to Malaysia 1969–72; Ambassador to Austria 1973–74; Dep. Secy. Dept. of Foreign affairs since 1975. *Publications:* The Feast of Ancestors, Snow (verse, 1965, 1971). *Address:* Dept. of Foreign Affairs, Canberra, A.C.T., Australia.

**ROWZEE, Edwin Ralph.** Canadian chemical engineer. *B.* 1908. *Educ.* Massachusetts Inst. of Tech. (MChem Eng); Hon. DSc, Laval Univ. *M.* 1935, Mary Elizabeth Hudson. *Daus.* Susan Anne (Rowcliffe); Mary Elizabeth (Williams) and Nancy Lee (Pullen). *Career:* Rowzee Chemical Engineer (1931–35), in charge of Synthetic Rubber development (1935–42), Goodyear Tire & Rubber Co., Akron, O.; on loan to Canadian Synthetic Rubber Ltd. (establishment of Copolymer plant) 1942–44; Director of Research, Polysar Ltd., Sarnia, Ont. 1944–47. Special temporary commission of Lieut.-Colonel in Canadian Army 1945. Manager (1947–51), Director of the Board (1950), Vice-Pres. and Manager (1951–57), Pres. Man. Dir. 1957–71, Polysar Ltd. Chmn. Bd. since 1971; Urban Trans. Development Corpn. Toronto since 1973; Pres. Soc. Chemical Industry 1969–70. *Publications:* Sarnia, the Birthplace of Canada's Petro-chemical Industry (1949); Polysar Kyrnol, Nouvelle Etape des Caoutchoucs Artificiels (1952); Synthetic Rubber Comes of Age (1951); Investigation of German Synthetic Rubber Industry (1946); Synthetic Rubber Research in Canada (1946) Polysar Ltd—Its Research & Development Organization; Your Profession and You (1954); L.Avvenire Della Gomma Sintetica (1944); Rubber, Research and Human Resources (1960); New Horizons in Synthetic Rubber (1963); The World of Rubber and Its Future (1963). *Member:* Board of Governors Univ. of Windsor; Amer. Chemical Socy.; Pres., Socy. of Chemical Industry 1969–70; Chemical Int. of Canada; Board of Governors, Ontario Research Foundation 1961; Science Council of Canada 1966–68; Board of Directors, Canadian Chemical Producers' Assn.; Pres. Chem. Inst. of Canada 1954–55. *Clubs:* Toronto; Detroit Athletic Club; London Hunt and Country Club. *Address:* 580 Woodrowe Avenue, Sarnia, Ont. N7V 2W2 Canada.

**ROXAS, Ruben L.** Filipino lawyer. *B.* 1927. *Educ.* Ateneo de, Manila; De La Salle College; Univ. of Philippines, LLB. *M.* 1949, Lourdes Quisumbling. *S.* 5. *Daus.* 2. *Career:* Specialises in Counter-Intelligence & in trial and appellate advocacy; Past Governor, Rotary International, District 380. *Member:* Philippine Soc. of International Law; Philippine Bar Assn.; Integrated Bar; Philippine Constitution Assn.; Filipino-Korean Soc.; Tarlac Rotary Club; Rotary Foundation Paul Harris Fellow. *Address:* 58 Samar Avenue, Quezon City, Philippines.

**ROY, Kiran Kumar,** MSc. Indian aeronautical engineer. Managing Director, Air Survey Co. of India, Pte. Ltd., Veegal Engines & Engineering Ltd.; Director: Airways (India) Ltd., Shillong Hydro-Electric Co. Ltd. Past President Aeronautical Society of India; Bengal Nat. Chamber of Commerce & Industry. *Address:* P-9 Gariahata Road, Calcutta 29, India.

**ROY, Suresh Chandra,** MA, BL. Indian industrialist. *B.* 1902. *M.* 1932, Pratima Lahiri. *Dau.* Basabi. *Career:* Member, Insurance Legislation Consultative Committee, Government of India 1936; Chairman, Textile Control Advisory Committee, Government of Bengal 1943–45; President, Bengal Millowner's Association 1948; President, Indian Life Assurance Offices Association 1951; Chmn. Indian Statistical Institute; 1971–72; Dir., India Steamship Co. Ltd.; Sheriff of Calcutta 1956–57 and 1957–58; Member Senate, Calcutta Univ., 1957–69. *Awards:* Padma Bhusan by President. *Address:* 36 New Road, Alipore, Calcutta 27, India.

**ROYLE, Sir Anthony,** KCMG, MP. British Politician. *B,* 1927. *Educ.* Harrow; Sandhurst Military Acad. *M.* 1957. Shirley Worthington. *Daus.* 2. *Career:* Conservative MP for Richmond, Surrey since 1959; Conservative Whip 1967–70; Vice-Chmn., Cons. Parliamentary Foreign Affairs Cttee. 1965–67; Under-Sec. of State or Foreign Affairs 1970–74; Vice-Chmn., Cons. Parliamentary European Affairs Cttee. since 1974. Mem., Lloyd's of London. *Director:* Brooke Bond Leibig Ltd.; Wilkinson Match Ltd.; Sedgwick Forbes Overseas Ltd. *Decorations:* Knight Commander of St. Michael & St. George; Most Esteemed Family Order of State of Brunei, 1st Class. *Clubs:* White's; Pratt's. *Address:* The Chapter Manor, South Cerney, Glos.; and 47 Cadogan Place, London SW1; and House of Commons, London SW1.

**ROYLE, John David Fanshawe.** British. Chmn. & Managing Director, Mono Containers Ltd., Eastcote, Middlesex. *B.* 1915. *Educ.* Harrow School. *M.* 1945, Sarah Margaret Ireland. *S.* John Fanshawe. *Dau.* Mary Christina. *Career:* Trainee, Continental Can Co., New York City 1937–39. Capt. Royal Artillery, World War II (Africa, India, Burma, U.K.) 1940–45. With Mono Containers since 1936. *Member:* Inst. of Directors. *Club:* Norwegian. *Address:* Stonedean House, Jordans, Bucks.; and *office* Mono Containers Ltd., Eastcote, Middlesex.

**ROYLE, Sir Lancelot Carrington,** KBE. British Company Director. *B.* 31 May 1898. *Educ.* Harrow School and Royal Military Academy, Woolwich. *M.* 1922, Barbara Rachel Haldin. *S.* Anthony Henry Fanshawe, KCMG, MP (Richmond, Surrey), Timothy Lancelot Fanshawe. *Dau.* Penelope Barbara (Oldham). *Career:* Served in both World Wars; appointed member Marcharg-Royle Committee by Treasury 1940; Chmn. Navy, Army and Air Force Insts. 1941–53; Chmn. and Managing Director, Allied Suppliers Ltd. 1947–59; Chairman, Lipton Ltd. 1952–59; Lipton (Overseas) Ltd. 1959–63; Director: British Match Corp. Ltd. 1961–68; Liebigs Extract of Meat Co. Ltd. 1961–68; Oxo Ltd., 1961–68; Bryant & May Ltd. 1961–71. Governor of Harrow School 1947–62. *Address:* 31 Elsworthy Road, Primrose Hill, London, N.W.3.

**ROZELL, Walter H.,** Jr. American Banking Consultant. *B.* 27 Feb. 1910. *Educ.* Amherst College (AB) and Rutgers University (Graduate, School of Banking). *M.* 1936, Gunhild Nicholson. *S.* 1. *Dau.* 1. Governor, State Bank of Ethiopia 1953–56. Vice-Pres., Federal Reserve Bank of New York 1957–67; Consultant, Bank of Thailand 1968–69. Adviser to Governor, Central Bank of Nigeria 1970; UN Consult. to Nat. Bank of Vietnam 1974–75. *Address:* Brookhollow, Plainfield, Massachusetts 01070, U.S.A.

**RUBLOFF, Arthur.** American. Head of one of the largest real estate and development firms in the U.S.A. *Educ.* Public Schools, Chisholm, Minn. *M.* 1934, Josephine Catherine Sheehan (*Dec.*). *Career:* Established Arthur Rubloff & Co., Chicago, Aug. 1930; Chmn. of the Exec. Cttee., Arthur Rubloff & Co., Chicago. Pres. & Dir.: North Kansas City Development Co. (Mo,), Evergreen Park Shopping Plaza, Rubloff Investments, New Hyde Park Inc. (all of Chicago); Developer, Carl Sandburg Village, Univ. Gardens, 69 W. Washington Building; Magnificent Mile North Michigan Avenue Old North Town Dev. and Fort Dearborn Projects, all Chicago; Parner, Bayshore Properties, San Francisco, Cal., comprising: Southland, Hayward, Cal.; Sun Valley, Concord, Cal.; Eastridge, San Jose, Cal. (also Builder). Former Real Estate Consultant, New York Port Authority World Trade Center; Trustee Roosevelt Univ. Chicago; Dir. & Vice-Pres., Chicago Boys' Clubs; Trustee, Goodwill Industries. *Member:* Amer. Socy. Real Estate Counsellors; Dir. Civic Fed. (Chicago); State Street Council (Chicago) and many other bodies. Chicago Assn. of Commerce & Industry (Mem. S. R. Council); Chicago Univ.—Citizens Bd., Loyola Univ.-Citizens Bd. & Dir., Lyric Opera of Chicago, Nat. Conference of Christians and Jews National Bd., N.Y.; Chmn. & Dir., United Cerebral Palsy of Metropolitan Chicago, and many other bodies. *Publications:* many papers on real estate (latest: Let's Tax our Slums to Death—Look magazine, Dec. 1960). *Awards:* Stella Della Solidarieta Italiana, 1956; Horatio Alger Award (Amer. Schools & Colleges Assn.) 1955; North Side Civic Committee Award 1955; Award of American Planning & Civic Assn.. Columbus, O., 1954; Chicagoan of the Year 1972; B'na B'r'th International Humanitarian Award 1975. Member: Roosevelt Univ.; Bd. Governors, Michael Reese Hospital & Medical Center; Chicago Real Estate Board; National Association of Real Estate Boards; American Chapter, Int. Real Estate Federation; National Association of Housing & Re-development Officials; Chicago Plan. Commn.; Cttee. on Economic & Cultural Development; Chamber of Commerce of U.S. *Clubs:* Economics; Internl.; Variety Clubs International; Mid-America; Mid-Day; Executives; Downtown; Oil Men's; Arts; Standard; Monroe; Metropolitan; Harmonic; Hemisphere (N.Y.C.); Lambda Alpha. *Address:* 1040 Lake Shore Drive, Chicago, 60611; 781 5th Avenue, New York, N.Y.; and *office* 69 W. Washington Street, Chicago 60602, Ill., U.S.A.

**RUDEL, Thomas Ryder.** American machine tool executive. *B.* 1905. *Educ.* Lawrenceville School and Princeton Univ. (AB). *M.* (1) 1934, Doris Taylor (*Dec.* 1970). *Dau.* Barbara (Wendt), (2) 1971, Margaret Murchison. *Career:* Began business career with Eberhard Pencil Co. and became its President and Chairman (1949–52); Chmn. Rudel Machinery Co. Inc. 1941—. Chairman, Rudel Machinery Co. Ltd. 1944–60; V. & O. Press Co., Inc. Chairman of the Board, American SIP Corp. 1950; Dir. Lynch Corp.; Trustee, Lincoln Savings Bank. United States Government Service 1951–52. Goucher College; The Lawrenceville School. *Member:* American Machine Tool Distributors Association (Dir. & Pres. 1953–54): National Machine Tool Builders' Assoc. (Chmn. & Dir.); Academy of Political Science (Life Member); American Society of Tool Engineers, American Arbitration Assn., and Newcomen Socy. *Clubs:* University, Union League (N.Y.C.); New York Yacht; Kanawaki Golf, Montreal (Honorary Life Member); Pinehurst C.C.; (founder mem.); U.S. Seniors' Golf. *Address:* 2 Sutton Place South, New York City. 10022; and *office* 100 East 42nd Street, New York City 10017, U.S.A.

**RUDHART, Dr. Hans-Wilhelm,** Dr rer pol. German industrial merchant. *B.* 1902. *Educ.* Diplom-Volkswirt, Dr rer pol. Auditor. *M.* 1938, Dr. Marta Rudhart-Kaltenbach (Dental Surgeon). *S.* Hendrik. *Dau.* Heidemarie. *Career:* Apprentstudent 1921–27; auditor in an industrial combine and a trust co. 1927–35; Man. Dir. of an indus. combine 1934–45; independent auditor 1946–48; Manager, Commerzbank AG 1949–54; Vice-President in an industrial combine 1954—. Member of Board, UTMAL, Uktal Machinery Ltd., Bombay; Haniel AG, Basel, Schweiz; Zahräderfabrik Renk AG, Augsburg; Vereinigte Aluminium-Werke AG, Bonn; Maschinenfabrik Hennecke, GmbH, Birlinghoven; Eisenwerke Nürnberg AG. vowm J. Tafel & Co., Nurnberg. *Member:* Schmalenbach-Gesellschaft, Duisberg (industrial administration); Gesellschaft der Freunde von Bayreuth; Max-Planck-Gesellschaft; Museum Folkwang; Kungstring Folk wang, Essen; Kulturkreis im Bundesverband der Deutschen Industrie. *Publication:* On Credit Policy of Prussian State Bank. *Club:* Rotary. *Address:* 43 Essen-Bredeney, Am Tann 7, Federal Republic of Germany.

**RUEGGEBERG, Walter Herman Carl.** American. *B.* 1915. *Educ.* Johns Hopkins Univ. (PhD 1941); Graduate Rifle and Heavy Weapons Course, Infantry School, U.S. Army, Fort Benning, Ga. 1942. *M.* 1942, Gertrud E. H. Evers. *S.* Frederick Allen. *Daus.* Margaret Elise and Christine Luise. *Career:* Second Lieut. to Major, Army of U.S. 1942–46; Asst. Scientific Director, Chemical Corps., U.S. Army 1946–50; Faculty, Johns Hopkins Univ. 1948–49; Director of Organic Research, Tennessee Corp., Atlanta, Ga. 1950–55; Vice-President and Director, Research and Development, ICI, United States Inc., Wilmington, Del. 1961–76 (Dir. Chemical Research 1955–61); retired 31st Jan. 1976. *Publications:* 24 published articles in scientific journals; 11 U.S. and foreign patents. Commendation Ribbon, U.S. Army; Phi Beta Kappa; Sigma Xi (Honorary Societies). *Member:* Amer. Chemical Socy. *Address:* 1205 Red Leaf Road, Carrcroft, Wilmington, Del. 19803, U.S.A.

**RUETE, Dr. Hans Hellmuth.** German diplomat. *B.* 1914. *Educ.* Dr. of Law. *M.* Ruth Arfsten. *S.* 1. *Daus.* 2. *Career:* Second Law Examination 1949; Ministry of Justice of Fed. Rep. of Germany 1950–52; entered Foreign Service 1952; Embassy in Tokyo 1952–56; Foreign Office, Bonn 1956–60; Inst. for International Affairs, Harvard Univ. 1960–61; Consul-General in Calcutta 1961–64; Under-Sec. of State, Foreign Office 1964–66; Dep. Sec. of State 1966–70; Ambassador in Paris 1970–72, in Warsaw 1972–77 and in London since April 1977. *Address:* Embassy of the Federal Republic of Germany, 22 Belgrave Square, London SW1X 8PZ.

**RUFFIN, William Haywood.** Textile manufacturing executive. *B.* 1899. *Educ.* Porter Military Academy (Charleston, S.C.) and Univ. of North Carolina (BS Com). *M.* 1929, Josephine Craige Kluttz. *S.* William Haywood, Jr. and Burton Craige. *Dau.* Josephine (Adamson). *Career:* Doctor of Textile Science, North Carolina State College, Raleigh, N.C.

Vice-Pres., Burlington Industries. Chmn., Wachovia, Durham Board, Erwin Mills Inc., Durham, N.C. 1948—. Director: Wachovia Bank & Trust Co., Winston Salem, N.C.; General Telephone of the S.E.; Durham & S. Railway. *Award:* Freedom Foundation Award for one of the best speeches of the year. Previously: President: N.C. Cotton Mfrs. Assn. 1942, N.C. Industrial Council 1948, National Assn. of Manufacturers 1951 (Chmn. of Bd. 1952), Univ. of N.C. Alumni Assn. 1949, N.C. Citizens' Assn., Laymen's Assn., Episcopal Diocese of N.C. 1947 (served as member of Diocesan Council, and as Chmn. of Finance Dept.), American Cotton Manufacturers Institute. *Clubs:* University, Weavers (N.Y.C.); Augusta (Ga.) National Golf; Hope Valley Country; Country of N.C.: Rotary-Durham (Past Pres.); Key Largo Anglers (Florida). *Address:* 25 Oak Drive, Forest Hills, Durham, N.C.; and *office* West Durham Station, Durham, N.C., U.S.A.

**RUIA, Madanmohan Ramnarian.** Indian industrialist and millowner. *B.* 24 Aug. 1914. *Educ.* Marwari Vidyalaya; St. Xavier's College, Bombay. *M.* Miss Kantabai. *S.* Shyam. *Daus.* Nandini, Uma. *Career:* Ex-President, The East India Cotton Assn.; Ex-Pres., Fed. of Indian Chambers of Commerce and Industry, and Ex-Vice-Pres., Indian Central Cotton Committee. Director of several cotton firms, mill, and companies in Bombay, M. Ramnarain Pvt. Ltd. *Address:* Eucharistic Congress Bldg. 5 Convent Street, Bombay, India.

**RUIA, Radhakrishna Ramnarain.** Indian millowner and merchant. *B.* 1916. *Educ.* Marwari Vidyalaya; St. Xavier's College, Bombay (BA). *M.* Miss Rajkumari. *Career:* Chmn. Man. Dir. The Phoenix Mills Ltd.; Director: Malabar Steamship Co. Ltd., and Coorla Spinning & Weaving Co. Ltd.; Bombay Textile Research Association; Uttar Pradesh Straw & Agro Products Ltd.; Rishab Ispaat Ltd.; Chmn. Bombay Textile Research Assn. *Address:* State Bank, Building, Bank Street, Fort, Bombay 1, India.

**RUIA, Ramniwas Ramnarain.** Indian banker. *B.* 4 Oct. 1910. *Educ.* Marwari Vidyalaya, Tombay and privately. *M.* Miss Kamlabai. *S.* Nirmalkumar Ramniwas Ruia. *Dau.* Veena Ramniwas. Director in many leading firms in Bombay. *Address:* Ramnarain Sons, Private, Ltd., State Bank Building, Bank Street, Fort, Bombay 1, India.

**RUIZ GALINDO, Antonio.** Mexican company director. *B.* 1897. *Educ.* secondary and commercial schools. *M.* Serafina Gómez Sariol. *Career:* Chmn. of the Bd., D.M. Nacional, S.A. Hoteles y Turismo, S.A., Cal Hidratada-Veracruzana, S.A., Industrias Ruiz Galindo, S.A., Fortín de las Flores, S.A. Cía. Urbanizadora, Cía. Comercial e Industrial Veracruzana, S.A. de C.V.; Café Fortín S.A. Member Bd., Tubos—de Acero de México, S.A., Aluminio, S.A., Banco Veracruzano, S.A.; Hon. Life Pres. Mexican Hotel Association; Minister of Commerce and Economy 1946–48; Theodore Brent Inter-American Award 1961. *Address:* Paseo de la Reforma 90, Mexico City, Mexico.

**RUIZ-GIMENEZ CORTES, Joaquin,** LLD. Spanish professor and politician. *B.* 2 Aug. 1913. *Educ.* Colégio Alfonso XII; Faculty of Law, Universidad Madrid. *M.* Mercedes Aguilar Otermin. *Career:* Professor of Philosophy of Law, University of Madrid; former Dir. Institute of Spanish Culture; former Ambassador to Holy See; Minister of Education 1951–56; Pres., International Catholic Movement for Intellectual and Cultural Affairs, Pax Romana; Leader, Spanish Christian Democrat Party. *Awards:* Gran Cruz Orden de Isabel la Católica; Gran Cruz de la Orden El Sol de Perú; Gran Cruz al Mérito del Ecuador; Gran Cruz de la Orden Piana. *Publications:* Introducción a la Filosofía Juridica; Concepción Institucional del Derecho; Derecho y Vida Humana; Derecho y Dialogo. *Address:* Velazquez 51, Madrid, Spain.

**RUMBOLD, Sir (Horace) Anthony (Claude),** Bt. KCMG, KCVO, CB. British. *B.* 1911. *Educ.* Eton College, Magdalen College, Oxford (BA); Fellow Queens College, Oxford. *M.* (1) 1937, Felicity Ann Bailey. *S.* Henry. *Daus.* Serena (Lancaster), Venetia, and Camilla (Swayne). (2) 1974 Pauline Tennant. *Career:* Principal Private Secretary to the Foreign Secretary 1954–55 Assistant Under-Secretary of State 1957–60; Minister, Paris 1960–63; Ambassador, Bangkok 1965–77. Ambassador, Vienna 1967–70. *Club:* Travellers' (London). *Address:* Var House, Stinsford, Dorset.

**RUMBOUGH, Stanley Maddox, Jr.** American manufacturer. *B.* 1920. *Educ.* Yale (BA 1942) and N.Y. University Graduate School of Business Administration. *M.* (1) 1946, Nedenia Marjorie Hutton (*Div.* 1966). *S.* Stanley Hutton and David Post (*Dec.*). *Dau.* Nedenia Colgate; (2) Margaretha Wagstrom 1967. *Career:* Military Career. Capt. USMCR, Pilot 1942–45; Pres. 1960–61; Vice-Pres. Dir. Willis Air Service N.J. 1946–47; Pres. & Dir., Metal Container Corp. 1950–59; Pres. Dir. Amer. Totalisator 1956–58; Dir. C. P. Clare & Co. Chicago 1956–58; General Register Co. 1956–58; Co-Founder, Dir. Promocion Technica, S.A. 1958–60; Dir. Employee Relations Inc. 1958–60; Chmn. Bd. Extrusion Dev. Corp. 1959–61; Co-Founder Chmn. Bd. Elect. Engineering Ltd. 1960–69; Co-Founder, Dir. Trinidad Flour Mills Ltd. 1961–72; Dir. Wallace Clark Inc. 1962–72, Chmn. Bd. 1962–69; Co-Founder Dir. Jamaica Flour Mills Ltd. 1963–66; Dir. Avis Industrial 1965–68. Self-employed, Investments & Business Development 1956—; Dir. Dart Industries Inc. 1961—; Bowmar Instrument Corp. 1961—; International Flavors & Fragrances 1964—; New Company Ltd. since 1966; Comp-U-Card of America, Inc. since 1976. Co-founder, Citizens for Eisenhower 1951; Special Asst. to Secy. of Commerce 1953; Special Asst. White House, in charge of Exec. Branch liaison 1953–55; member, Davis Cup Committee 1955–57, and 1969–70. Dir., Young Presidents' Organization 1956, 1958–60 and 1962–65. Chmn., U.S. Cttee. for the U.N. 1957–58; Dir. New York World's Fair 1961–70; Foreign Policy Assn. 1961–70; Trustee, Library for Presidential Papers 1966–70. Member, People to People Sports Council 1957—; Adv. Cttee. Eastern Tennis Patrons Foundation 1958—; Defense Orientation Conf. Assn. 1959—; Trustee, Amer. Health Foundation 1972–76; Dir. Nat. Conference on Citizenship since 1973. *Awards:* two Distinguished Flying Crosses and eight Air Medals. Republican. *Clubs:* Bath and Tennis; Everglades (Fla.); Int. Lawn Tennis Club of the U.S.; Madison Square Garden; Maidstone (East Hampton, N.Y.); Racquet & Tennis (N.Y.C.); Sailfish; Seminole (Fla.). Zeta Psi Fraternity. *Address:* 318 Caribbean Road, Palm Beach, Florida; and *office* 339 Royal Poinciana Plaza, Palm Beach, Florida 33480, U.S.A.

**RUMOR, Mariano.** Italian Statesman. *B.* 1915. *Educ.* Laureato in Lettere. *Career:* Parliamentary Deputy since 1948; Minister of Agriculture 1960–63; Minister of the Interior 1963–64, 1971–73; Sec.-Gen., Christian Democrat Party 1964–68; Pres. of the Council of Ministers 1968–69, 1973–74; Minister of Foreign Affairs 1974–76; Pres., European Union of Christian Democrats 1965–76, Hon. Pres. since 1976. *Awards:* Sovrano Ordine Militare di Malta; Grand Cross Order of Orange-Nassau (Netherlands); Grand Star of Somalia 1963; Grand Cross, Order O'Higgins 1965 (Chile); Grand Cross of Gold 1971 (Austria); Grand Cross II (Fed. Rep. of Germany ); Grand Ribbon, Abdul Aziz (Saudi Arabia); Grand Ribbon, Order of Leopold (Belgium); Cavaliere Grazia Magistrale (Malta); Gran Croce Ordine Piano (Vatican); Grand Cross, Order of Bolivar (Venezuela). *Address:* Via Kenia 58, Rome; and *office* Via Gregoriana 54, Rome, Italy.

**RUNCIMAN of DOXFORD, Viscount** (Walter Leslie Runciman), OBE, AFC. British shipowner and company director. *B.* 26 Aug. 1900. *Educ.* Eton; Trinity Coll., Cambridge (MA). *M.* 1932, Katherine Schuyler Garrison. *S.* Walter Garrison. *Career:* Chairman, North of England Shipowners' Association 1931; Director-General, B.O.A.C. 1940–43; Air Commodore and Air Attaché, British Embassy, Teheran 1943–46; Chairman, Walter Runciman & Co. Ltd. 1946–76; Dpty. Chmn., Lloyds Bank, Ltd. 1962–71; President, Chamber of Shipping of United Kingdom 1952; President, Royal Institution of Naval Architects 1951–61. Chairman of Trustees, National Maritime Museum 1962–72. Hon. DCL, Durham University; an Elder Brother of Trinity House. *Address:* Doxford, Chathill, Northumberland.

**RUNDALL, Sir Francis Brian Anthony,** GCMG, OBE. British Diplomatic Service Officer. *B.* 1908. *Educ.* Marlborough Coll.; Peterhouse, Cambridge. *M.* 1935, Mary Syrett. *S.* 1. *Dau.* 1. Vice-Consul, Antwerp 1930; Colon 1932; Panama, 1933–35; transferred to Boston, Apr. 1935; Acting Consul-Gen. there in 1935 and 1938; Consul, Piraeus, 1940; Vice-Consul, New York, 1941; Consul, Sept. 1944; Foreign Office, Aug. 1946; Inspector of Foreign Service Establishments, Sept. 1949; Chief Administrative Officer, Wahnerheide, Jan.–Oct. 1953; Consul-General New York, Oct. 1953–57; Ambassador to Israel 1957–59; Deputy Under-Secretary, Foreign Office 1959–63. Ambassador to Japan 1963–67. *Address:* Travellers' Club, Pall Mall, London, S.W.1.

**RUSCK, John Ake.** *B.* 1912. *Educ.* Royal Inst. of Technology, Stockholm. *M.* 1938, Ilse Monica Weber. *S.* Jan Yngve, Leif

Arne, John Olof. *Career:* Entered Swedish State Power Board 1934, Operating Manager 1939, Manager of Local Administration 1944, Vice-Pres. of the Bd. 1946; Pres., Swedish State Power Bd. 1948; member, Royal Swedish Academy of Engineering Sciences; Pres., Scandinavian Airlines 1958–61; Dir. & Project Manager, Industrial Studies & Development Centre, Tanzania, 1965–69. Senior Inter-regional Adviser, United Nations Industrial Development Organization (UNIDO), 1969–72; Chmn. AB Scandinavian Eng. Corp. Consulting Engineers 1961–72. *Awards:* Kt. Cmdr., 1st Class, Order of the North Star; Kt. Cmdr., 1st Class, Order of Dannebrog (Denmark), Comdr. Order of Cedar (Lebanon), and Legion of Honour (France). *Address:* Bergbacken 9, Saltsjö-Duvnäs, Sweden; and Monte Rojo 27A, Sunwing San Agustin, Gran Canaria.

**RUSH, Kenneth.** American. Director: El Paso Co. and its affiliates, El Paso Natural Gas Co. and El Paso Products Co.; Alliance to Save Energy; The Atlantic Council. *B.* 1910. *Educ.* Univ. of Tennessee (AB 1930) and Yale Univ. School of Law (JD 1932). *M.* 1937, Jane Gilbert Smith. *S.* George Gilbert (*D.*), David Campbell (*D.*), Malcolm, John Randall, and Kenneth. *Dau.* Cynthia Shepherd (Rush Monahan). *Career:* Admitted to New York Bar 1934; associate Chadbourne, Stanchfield & Levy (now Chadbourne, Parke, Whiteside & Wolff) 1932–36; Assistant Professor of Law, Duke Univ. Law School 1936–37; joined Law Dept., Union Carbide Corp. 1937, Vice-Pres. 1949–61, in charge of international, nuclear and ore groups, 1954–64, Exec. Vice-Pres. 1961–66; Pres. & member Exec. Cttee. 1966–69, Dir. 1958–69, U.S. Ambassador to Federal German Republic 1969–72; U.S .Deputy Secy. of Defence 1972–73; U.S. Dep. Secy. of State 1973–74; Secy. of State ad interim, Sept. 3–22, 1973; Counsellor to the President of the U.S. for Economic Policy, with Cabinet rank, May 29–Oct. 18, 1974, & as such was designated as Primary Adviser to the President for & Coordinator of Foreign & Domestic Economic Policy; Mem. of National Security Council 1973, 1974; U.S. Ambassador to France 1974–77; Chmn., Travel Program for Foreign Diplomats; Mem. of the Advisory Board, The Citadel; Hon. Co-Chmn., The International Foundation for Cultural Cooperation & Development. Former Mem. of Cttee. on Energy; Former Chmn. of Council on International Economic Policy, of the President's Cttee. on East–West Trade Policy, of the Presidnt's Food Cttee., of the Council of Wage & Price Stability, & of the Joint Presidential-Congressional Steering Cttee. for the Conference on Inflation. *Member:* Development Cncl., Univ. of Tennessee, 1963—; Member Exec. Cttee. Yale Law School Assn. 1952–62; Dir., 1965–67, and Chmn. of Bd., 1966–67, Manufacturing Chemists' Assn. Inc.; Director: Amer. Sugar Co. 1962–69, Bankers Trust Co., 1966–69, Bankers' Trust New York Corp., 1966–69, Institute of International Education 1968–69, and Foreign Policy Association 1964–69. Trustee and Secretary-Treasurer, Grand Central Art Galleries, New York City 1951–69; Trustee, U.S. Cncl., International Chamber of Commerce 1955–69. Public Advisory Cttee. on U.S. Trade Policy of Pres. L. B. Johnson 1968–69; Trustee, The Taft School, Watertown, Conn., 1957–62. *Awards:* Hon. LLD, Tusculum College, 1961; Grand Cross, Order of Merit (Germany) 1972; Dept. of Defense Medal, Distinguished Public Service 1973. *Address:* c/o Department of State, Washington, D.C. 20520, U.S.A.

**RUSHTON, William James.** U.S. Life Insurance Executive. *B.* 1900. *Educ.* Washington and Lee Univ., Lexington, Va.—BS 1921; Southwestern Univ., Memphis—HHD 1959. *M.* 1926, Elizabeth Perry (*D.* 1972). *S.* William James III, James. *Career:* Asst. Mgr., Birmingham Ice & Cold Storage Co. 1922–27, Vice-Pres. 1927–32, Pres. 1932–38, Vice-Chmn. Bd., Sec. 1938–57; Pres., Protective Life Ins. Co. 1937–67, Chmn. Bd. Dirs. 1967–76, Chmn. Emeritus since 1976, Dir. since 1927; Mem. Adv. Bd., Investment Co. of America (Cal.); Chmn. Bd., Franklin Coal Mining Co. 1927–42; Past Dir., First Nat. Bank of Birmingham 1927–73, Alabama Power Co. 1937–70, Gulf Mobile & Ohio R.R. Co. 1940–72, Moore-Handley Hardware Co. 1948–63, Ill. Central Gulf R.R. 1972–74; Chief, Birmingham Ordnance Dist., U.S. Army 1946–61. Vice-Chmn., Trustee, Southern Research Inst.; Pres., Birmingham Boy Scout Council 1927–30 (Dir. 1925–55); Mem., Nat. Citizens Cttee. of United Community Campaigns of America 1961–75; Dir., Birmingham Community Chest since 1937, Vice-Pres. 1942–43, 1948–52, Pres. 1954, Mem. Exec. Cttee. since 1945; Dir., Trustee (Life), Birmingham Museum of Art; Local Dir., Salvation Army, Y.M.C.A.; Trustee, Children's Hosp., Agnes Scott Coll., Decatur, Ga. 1935–45. Served to Col., U.S. Army, World War II. Decorated Legion of Merit. *Member:* Amer. Ordnance Assn. (Past Vice-Pres.), Nat. Assn. Ice Industries (Dir. since 1928, Pres. 1936–37), Nat. Assn. Refrigerated Warehouses (Pres. 1933–35, Mem. Nat. Code Authority), Amer. Warehousemen's Assn. (Pres. 1935–36), Life Ins. Assn. of Amer. (Dir. 1955–61), Health Ins. Assn. of Amer. (Dir. 1964–67), Amer. Life Conv. (Ala. Vice-Pres.), Inst. Life Ins. (Dir. 1963–69), Assoc. Industries Ala. (Dir. 1956–63), Beta Gamma Sigma, Beta Theta Pi, Omicron Delta Kappa, Delta Sigma Rho. Presbyn. (Mem. Bd. Deacons, Chmn. Bd. Trustees, Elder; Mem. Bd. Annuities & Relief, Presbyn. Church in U.S. 1959–65). Birmingham Rotary Club. *Clubs:* Mountain Brook, Country, Downtown, The Club, Relay House (Birmingham); Chaparal (Dallas, Texas). *Address:* 2848 Balmoral Road, Birmingham, Alabama 35223; and *office* Protective Life Insurance Co., P.O. Box 2606, Birmingham, Alabama 35202, U.S.A.

**RUSHTON, William James III.** U.S. Life Insurance Executive. *B.* 1929. *Educ.* Princeton Univ.—BA *magna cum laude* (Math) 1951. *M.* 1955, LaVona Price. *S.* William James IV, Deakins Ford, Tunstall Perry. *Career:* Assoc. Actuary, Protective Life Ins. Co. 1954–59, Agent 1959–62, Vice-Pres. 1962–63, Agency Vice-Pres. 1963–67, Pres. since 1967, Pres. & Chief Exec. Officer since 1969. Mem., Million Dollar Round Table 1962. Fellow, Soc. of Actuaries 1962. *Director:* Protective Life Ins. Co. 1956—, Alabama Power Co. 1970—, The Southern Co. 1971—, First Nat. Bank of Birmingham 1973—, The Economy Co. of Oklahoma 1974—. *Trustee:* Southern Research Inst. 1973—, Children's Hospital 1964—, Birmingham-Southern College 1977—, Baptist Hospital Foundation 1967—. Director, Moore-Handley Hardware Co. 1956–62, Birmingham Fire Ins. Co. 1956–62, Industrial Health Council 1966; Trustee, Highland Day School 1975. Adv. Bd., Samford Univ. School of Business 1971—; Bd. of Visitors, College of Commerce & Business Admin., Univ. of Alabama 1972—; Birmingham Co-ordinating Council of Social Agencies 1975—; Dir., United Way Appeal 1974—; Chmn., United Way Campaign 1977. Former State Vice-Pres., Amer. Life Convention; State Vice Pres., American Life Ins. Assn. 1975. Captain of Artillery, U.S. Army, active duty Korean War. Decorated Bronze Star. Dir., Birmingham Chamber of Commerce. Deacon, First Presbyterian Church. *Clubs:* Rotary (Bd. of Dirs. 1973–74), Mountain Brook Country, Relay House, Birmingham Country, Redstone. *Address:* 2900 Cherokee Road, Birmingham, Ala. 35223; and *office* Protective Life Insurance Co., 2801 Highway 280 South, Birmingham, Ala. 35223, U.S.A.

**RUSK, Hon. Dean.** Professor of International Law University of Georgia. *B.* 1909. *Educ.* Davidson Coll., N.C. (AB 1931), St. John's Coll., Oxford (Rhodes Scholar; BS 1933, MA 1934), and Mills Coll. (Hon. LLD 1948); Hon. LLD Davidson Coll. 1950, Univ. of California 1961, Princeton 1961; Emory Univ. 1961, Louisiana State Univ. 1965, Amherst Coll. 1962, Columbia Univ. 1963, Harvard Univ. 1963, Rhode Island Univ. 1963, Hebrew Union Coll. 1963, Valparaiso Univ. 1964, Williams Coll. 1964, Univ. N. Carolina, George Washington Univ., Oberlin Coll.; Hon. LHD, Westminster Coll. 1962; Dr. of Civil Law, Oxford Univ. 1962. *M.* 1937, Virginia Foisie. *S.* David and Richard. *Dau.* Margaret. *Career:* Associate Professor of Government (later, also Dean of the Faculty) at Mills Coll., Oakland, Calif. 1934–40; also studied at Univ. of California 1937–40; Asst. Chief, Div. of International Security Affairs, U.S. Dept. of State 1946; Special Asst. to Secretary of War 1946–47; Director, Office of United Nations Affairs, Dept. of State 1947–49; Asst. Secretary of State Feb. 1949 (Deputy Under-Secretary 1949–50); Asst. Secy. of State for Far Eastern Affairs 1950–51; President, Rockefeller Foundation 1952–61; Secretary of State of the U.S. 1961–69. Served in World War II, 1940–46 (Legion of Merit; Oak Leaf Cluster). Received Cecil Peace Prize 1933; Hon. Knight Commander of the British Empire (KBE). *Member:* American Society of International Law. Distinguished Fellow, Rockefeller Foundation, 1969. *Address:* University of Georgia, Athens, Georgia 30602, U.S.A.

**RUSSELL, Donald Joseph.** Railway executive. *B.* 3 Jan. 1900. *Educ.* Stanford University: Hon. LLD, Loyola Univ. 1955. *M.* 1921, Mary Louise Herring. *Dau.* Mary Ann (Miller). *Career:* Engineering, construction, maintenance and operating departments, Southern Pacific Co. 1920–41; Asst. to the President 1941; Vice-President 1941–51; Exec. Vice-Pres. 1951–52; Pres. 1952–64; Chmn. 1964–72; Hon. Dir. Southern Pacific Co.; Director Emeritus: Tenneco Inc.; Founding Dir., Stanford Research Institute. Member Tulane Univ. Bd. of Visitors; Hon.-member, The Business Council,

*Address:* One Market Street, San Francisco, Calif. 94105, U.S.A.

**RUSSELL, Francis Henry.** American diplomat. *B.* 1904. *Educ.* Tufts Univ. (AB 1926, LLD 1959); Harvard Law School (LLB 1929). *M.* 1932, Ruth A Libbey. *S.* Paul L. *Dau.* Alene J. (Hochschild). *Career:* Practised law in Boston, Mass. 1929–41; Chief, Div. of World Trade Intelligence, State Department 1941–45; Director, Office of Public Affairs, State Department 1945–52; Chargé d'Affaires, Tel-Aviv 1952–54; Special Assistant to Secretary of State 1954–57; Ambassador to New Zealand 1957–60; Ghana 1960–61; to Tunisia 1962–69. Fletcher School of Law & Diplomacy, Tufts Univ., 1970—. *Address:* Fletcher School, Tufts Univ., Mass., U.S.A.

**RUSSELL, George.** American. *B.* 1905. *Educ.* University of Minnesota (BS). *M.* 1936, Mary-Love Rose. *S.* George, Jr. *Dau.* Mary-Love (Harman). *Career:* With General Motors Corp.: Finance Manager, G.M. Overseas Operations 1949, Treas. 1951–56, Vice-Pres. 1956–58, Exec. Vice Pres. 1958 67; Vice Chmn. 1967–70, Mbr. of the Bd. of Dirs. and of the Finance and Public Policy Cttees., Gen. Motors Corp. 1958–74; Kennecott Copper Corp., and S.S. Kresge Co. National Bank of Detroit 1970–77; First National Bank in Palm Beach. *Awards:* Outstanding Achievement Award, Univ. of Minnesota; Sir William Wallace Award; Hon. Degree, Univ. of Strathclyde, Meharry Medical Coll. Trustee: Founders Socy.; Detroit Inst. of Arts. *Clubs:* Univ. Links (N.Y.C.) Detroit; Bloomfield Hills Country. Yondotega, Detroit; Lost Tree, Seminole and Everglades (Florida); Royal and Ancient St. Andrews (Scotland). *Address:* 11741 Lake House Ct., North Palm Beach, Florida 33408, U.S.A.

**RUSSELL, George Vernon.** *B.* 1905. *Educ.* Univ. of Washington, Seattle (BA Arch); Diplomé Arch., L'Ecole des Beaux Arts, Fontainebleau, France; M.I.T. Prize, Prix J.P. Alaux 1928. *M.* London, 1942, Mary Adelaide Younie. *S.* Colin and Ian. *Dau.* Kirsty. *Career:* Travel in Europe 1929, Architect, New York 1930–32. Travel in Mexico 1933; Partner, Honnold and Russell, Architects, Los Angeles 1934–42; Architect for air bases in United Kingdom for Lockheed and USAF 1942–44. Resumed practice in Los Angeles 1946. *Awards:* 17 national and regional architectural awards.; Fellow Amer. Inst. of Architects, Sociedad de Arquitectos Mexicanos (Hon. Colegio Nacional de Arquitectos Mexicanos (Hon). Faculty, University of Southern California, Graduate School of Architecture 1953–64; Past Pres., Southern California Chapter American Institute of Architects; Director, Calif. Council of Architects 1956–60; Assoc. Nat. Academy of Design. *Awards:* Co-Winner International Town Planning Competition, Bratislava, Czechoslovakia; member, Rancheros Visitadores, Santa Barbara, E. Clampus Vitus. *Clubs:* California (Los Angeles); Valley Hunt (Pasadena, Calif.). *Address:* 475 Orange Grove Circle, Pasadena, Calif., U.S.A.

**RUSSELL, Sir John Wriothesley,** GCVO, CMG, MFH. British Diplomat (retired) & Foreign Affairs Adviser, Rolls-Royce (1971) Ltd. *B.* 1914. *Educ.* Cambridge Univ. (MA). *M.* 1945, Aliki Diplarakos. *S.* Alexander. *Dau.* Georgiana. *Career:* Entered Foreign Service 1937; 3rd Secy. Foreign Office 1937, Vienna 1937, Foreign Office 1938; Moscow 1939; Second Secy. Washington 1942; First Secy. Warsaw 1945, Foreign Office 1948, Secretary-General, Brussels Treaty Permanent Organization, 1948; Rome 1950; Counsellor 1953, and Dir. General, British Information Services N.Y.; Counsellor, Embassy, Teheran 1956–59; Head of News Department, Foreign Office 1959–62; Ambassador to Ethiopia 1962–66; to Brazil, 1966–69. Ambassador to Spain, 1969–74. Jt. Master West Street Fox Hounds. *Awards:* Coronation Medal 1953; Order of the Throne Iran; Order of the Star Ethiopia; Order of the Southern Cross Brazil. *Clubs:* White's, Beefsteak. *Address:* 80 Chester Square, London, S.W.1; The Vine Farm, Northbourne, Kent.

**RUSSELL, Kenneth William.** Australian. *B.* 1920. *Educ.* Brisbane Grammar School; AASA. *M.* 1943, Molly Alexandra M. Hansen. *S.* 1. *Dau.* 1. *Career:* Post war; various managerial appointments with Adelaide S.S. Group; General Manager, The Adelaide Steamship Co. Ltd. 1967—; Dir. 1972—; Man. Dir. 1977—. Dir. of a number of subsidiary companies of Adelaide Steamship; North Aust. Cement Ltd.; Harbour Lighterage Pty. Ltd. Sydney; Standard Steamship owners Protection & Indemnity Assn. (Bermuda) Ltd. *Clubs:* Adelaide; Naval, Military & Air Force (of S.A.); Stock Exchange (Adelaide). *Address: office* 123 Greenhill Road, Unley, South Australia, 5061.

**RUSSELL, Sir (Sydney) Gordon,** CBE, MC. British industrial design consultant. *B.* 20 May 1892. *Educ.* Campden Grammar School. *M.* 1921. Constance Elizabeth Jane Vere Denning. *S.* Michael, Robert Henry, Oliver John (*Dec.*). *Dau.* Katherine. Chmn., Gordon Russell Ltd., and of The Lygon Arms Ltd. (Broadway). Member, Utility Furniture Advisory Committee and Furniture Production Committee (Board of Trade) 1942; Chairman, Board of Trade Design Panel 1943–47; original member of Council of Industrial Design 1944; Director 1947–59; member 1960—; member Crafts Advisory Cttee. 1971–74; original member of Executive Committee, Festival of Britain 1951; member of Council, Royal College of Art 1948–51, and 1952–63; member, Design Panel, British Railways Board 1956–66; Pres. Design and Industries Assn., 1959–62; Member: Art Workers Guild 1926, Master 1962; Nat. Council for Diplomas in Art and Design 1961–68; Arts Advisory Cttee. of UNESCO National Commission for the U.K. 1960–66; RDI 1940; FSIA 1945; Hon. Des. RCA 1952; Hon. ARIBA 1953; Hon. FRIBA 1965; Hon. AILA 1955; Hon. LLD Birmingham 1960; Senior Fellow RCA 1960; Albert Medal, Royal Socy. of Arts 1962; Hon. Dr., Univ. of York 1969; Member Hon. Cttee. for international exhibition of architecture and industrial design, Halsingborg, Sweden 1955; Higher Jury XIIth Milan Triennale Exhibition 1960; Officer, Order of Vasa (Sweden); Com., Order of St. Olav (Norway). *Publications:* The Story of Furniture, Puffin Book (1947); Looking at Furniture (Lund Humphries) (1964); autobiography Designer's Trade (Allen & Unwin 1968); and articles, lectures and broadcasts on design and country life. *Address:* Kingcombe, Chipping Campden, Gloucestershire.

**RUSSELL, Thomas,** CBE. Governor of the Cayman Islands. *B.* 1920. *Educ.* Hawick High School; St. Andrews' Univ., MA; Peterhouse Coll., Cambridge—Dip. in Anthropology. *Married. S.* 1. *Career:* Entered Colonial Admin. Service as District Officer in British Solomon Islands Protectorate 1948; Asst. Sec. to Western Pacific High Comm., Fiji 1951, Solomon Islands 1952 (District Commissioner 1954); Seconded to Colonial Office 1956–57; Senior Asst. Sec. (Personnel), Solomon Is., 1958; Dep. Financial Sec., Western Pacific High Comm. 1962. Financial Sec. 1965; Chief Sec. to Western Pacific High Comm. 1970–74, acting as High Commissioner on 3 occasions; Governor of Cayman Is. since 1974. Fellow, Royal Anthropological Inst. *Publications:* Monographs in Oceania and the Journal of the Polynesian Society; papers on constitutional development in The Parliamentarian and the Papua New Guinea Law Journal. *Address:* Governor's Office, Grand Cayman, Cayman Islands, B.W.I.

**RUSSELL, Thomas Dameron.** American. *B.* 1903. *Educ.* Univ. of Alabama (AB 1925, LLD 1970). *M.* 1929, Julia Walker. *Daus.* Mrs. E. C. Gwaltney, Mrs. R. W. Goree, and Mrs. Jorge Caoenes. President: Russell Mills Inc., Alexander City Manufacturing Co. (all of Alexander City, Ala.); Chairman of Board: First National Bank, Russell Lands Inc. (both of Alexander City); Dir. First National Bank Montgomery, Ala.; First Alabama Banshanes Birmingham, Ala. *Member:* Board of Trustees, Univ. of Alabama, Samford Univ., Tuskegee Institute, Southern Research Institute, and National Foundation. *Clubs:* Marco Polo, Weavers, Empire State (N.Y.C.); The Club, Relay House (Birmingham, Ala.). *Address:* Russwood, Alexander City, Ala. 35010; and *office* Russell Mills Inc., Alexander City, Ala., U.S.A.

**RUSSELL, William George Ainge.** British Chartered Accountant; Pres.: Glynwed Ltd. Director: Hoskins & Horton Ltd., Legal & General Assurance Society Ltd., and other companies; Past President, Birmingham & District Society of Incorporated Accountants; Fellow, Royal Society of Arts; Life Governor and Member of Council, University of Birmingham. *B.* 1903. *Address:* Pinfield House, Cherry Hill Road, Barnt Green, Worcs.

**RUSSELL, William Robert.** British. *B.* 1913. *Educ.* Wakefield Road Central School, East Ham. *M.* 1940, Muriel Faith Rolfe. *S.* John. *Dau.* Pamela. *Career:* Manager, Shaw Savill & Albion Co. Ltd., 1959 (Gen. Mgr. 1961; Dep. Chmn. 1966). Chairman & Managing Director, Shaw Savill & Albion Co. Ltd., 1969–73; Chmn Committee of European National Shipowners Association 1969–76; British Council Australian British Trade Association; Australian & New Zealand Trade Advisory Cttee. (B.O.T.B.) Director: Bank of New Zealand Ltd. (London Board). *Club:* R.N.V.R. *Address:* Westland, Uvedale Road, Limpsfield, Oxted, Surrey; and *office* St. Mary Axe House, St. Mary Axe, London, E.C.3.

**RUSSEY, Edward Swain.** *B.* 1906. *Educ.* Muncie Public Schools. *M.* 1931, Kathryn Mae Wolfe. *S.* James William. *Dau.* Phyllis Kay. *Career:* Employed by Warner Gear in sales department 1925; Vice-Pres. & Gen. Manager 1944–52; Pres. & General Manager July 1952–67; V. P. Borg Warner 1952–60; Chmn. Borg Warner Ltd. (England) 1960–67; Snr. V. P. Borg Warner Corp. 1967–68; Dir. Ball Memorial Hospital, Muncie, and Merchants National Bank of Muncie.; Trustee YMCA (Muncie) since 1960. *Member:* Society of Automotive Engineers; Mason (Shriner). Elks. *Clubs:* Columbia (Indianapolis); Deleware Country (Muncie). *Address:* 20 Meadow Lane, Muncie, Ind. 47304, U.S.A.

**RUTLEDGE, Philip Casteen.** Professor, Doctor; Consulting Engineer. *B.* 1906. *Educ.* Harvard SB 1927; ScD 1939; Mass. Inst. Technology (SM 1933); Hon. DEng, Purdue Univ. 1957. *M.* 1934, Dorothy Loomis. *S.* John Loomis. *Dau.* Cecily Loomis. *Career:* Consultant, heavy foundations and dams; Treasurer International Conf. on Soil Mechanics, Cambridge, Mass. 1936; Chmn., Conf. on Soil Mechanics, Purdue Univ. 1940; Prof. of Soil Mechanics, Purdue Univ. 1937–43; Prof. of Civil Engineering, Northwestern Technological Inst. 1943–52; Consultant, member Bd. of Consultants on airfield pavements. Office Chief Engineers, U.S. Army 1943—; Partner Moran, Proctor, Mueser, Rutledge 1952–64; Partner, Mueser, Rutledge, Wentworth & Johnston since 1964. Recipient of War Dept. Certificate of Appreciation for Services during World War II. *Member:* Amer. Socy. of Civil Engineers; Amer. Inst. of Consulting Engineers; Amer. Geophysical Union; Sigma Xi; The Moles. *Publications:* contributions to Proceedings (Amer. Socy. of Civil Engineers). to Engineering New Record, and other scientific journals. *Clubs:* Wee Burn Country (Darien, Conn.); Harvard, Engineers (N.Y.C.). *Address:* 415 Madison Avenue, New York, N.Y. 10017, U.S.A.

**RUTTEN, Franciscus Josephus Theodorus,** D Litt, PhD, D Psych, MB. Dutch politician and professor. *B.* 15 Sept. 1899. *M.* 1927, E. C. H. Leen. *S.* Frans. *Daus.* Liesbeth, Jos, Maria, Hildegard. Formerly Teacher, Amsterdam; Professor of Psychology, University of Nijmegen 1931; Minister of Education 1948–52. *Publications:* Felix Timmermans; Psychology of Observation; Education and Instruction of the Abnormal Child; Human Relations (with others), Vols I and II (1956–57) etc. *Address:* Pater Brugmanstraat 1, Nijmegen; and *office* Berg en Dalseweg, 105, Nijmegen, Netherlands.

**RUTTENBERG, Stanley H(arvey).** American. Consultant in economic research & manpower utilization. *B.* 1917. *Educ.* Massanutten Military Academy (Woodstock, Va.) and University of Pittsburgh (BS 1937). *M.* 1940, Gertrude Bernstein. *S.* Joel and Charles. *Dau.* Ruth. *Career:* Dir. Department of Research, American Federation of Labour and Congress of Industrial Organizations 1955–62 (Dir. Economic Policy Cttee. 1956–62); Dept. of Education and Research of C.I.O. 1948–55 (Assoc. Dir. of Research 1939–48, except for 1943–46 in U.S. Army); C.I.O. Organizer and field representative in Ohio Valley prior to 1939 (1937–38); Asst. to Dir., Hull House 1938. Member, Board of Directors of Resources for the Future Inc., Labour Cttee. of National Planning Assn.; public member, Foreign Service Selection Board 1950; Special Adviser to Amer. Deleg. of 4th and 5th International Confs. of UNESCO; public adviser to GATT negotiation, Geneva 1956 and 1958; Labour Specialist, U.S. Dept. of State Educational Exchange Programme, Oct.–Dec. 1959. Member, Commn. on Money and Credit 1958–61; Labor Observer, Special Meeting of Inter-American Economic and Social Council, Punta del Este, Uruguay, 1961; Assistant-Secretary for Manpower, and Manpower Administrator, U.S. Department of Labor 1965–69. Special Assistant to the Secretary of Labour, U.S. Department of Labour 1963–65; Pres. Ruttenberg, Friedman, Kilgallon, Gutchess & Associates Inc. since 1969. *Member:* Amer. Economic Assn.; Amer. Statistical Assn.; Industrial Relations Research Assn. *Publications:* Manpower Challenge of the 1970s; Institutions and Social Change (1970); The Federal-State Employment Service, A Critique (1970). *Address:* 6310 Maiden Lane, Bethesda 14, Md.; and *office* 1211 Connecticut Avenue, N.W. Washington, D.C. 20036, U.S.A.

**RUZEK, Miloslav.** *B.* 1923. *Educ.* Charles University, Prague (PhD 1950). *M.* 1949, Věra Černohlávková. *S.* Jan, Václav. *Daus.* Miloslava and Ludmila. *Career:* Held various Local Government posts 1945–49; Ministry of Education and Culture 1949–50; Ministry of Foreign Trade 1950–54; Ministry of Foreign Affairs 1954—; Counsellor of Embassy, London 1954–57; Ambassador to United States 1959–63; to Great Britain 1966–71; Deputy Minister of Foreign Affairs 1971–75; Perm. Rep. to UN at Geneva since 1975. *Address:* Mission of Czechoslovakia to the UN at Geneva, Palais des Nations, 1211 Geneva 10, Switzerland.

**RYAN, John Edmund.** OBE Australian diplomat. *B.* 1923. *Educ.* St. Patrick's College, Goulburn; Sydney Univ. BA. *M.* 1950, Patricia Mary Wall. *S.* 1. *Daus.* 2. *Career:* High Commissioner in Ghana 1965–67; Ambassador to Laos 1968–69; Minister, Washington 1969–71; 1st Asst. Secy. Dept. of Foreign Affairs, Canberra 1971–74; Ambassador in Italy since 1974. *Clubs:* Commonwealth (Canberra); Federal Golf (Canberra). *Address:* Australian Embassy, 215 Via Alessandria, Rome 00198, Italy; and *home* 42 Salita dei Parioli, Rome.

**RYAN, John Thomas. Jr.** American Business executive. *B.* 1912. *Educ.* Pennsylvania State Univ. (BS 1934); Harvard Univ. (MBA 1936); Hon. DSc, Duquesne Univ. 1959; Hon. D. Laws Univ. Notre Dame 1973. *M.* 1939, Irene O'Brien. *S.* John III, Michael, Daniel and William. *Daus.* Irene Ryan Shaw and Julia. *Career:* With Mine Safety Appliances Co.; Engineer 1936–38; Asst. Gen. Mgr. 1938–40; General Mgr. 1940–48; Exec. Vice-Pres. and Director 1948–53; Pres. and Dir. 1953–63; Chmn. & Dir. since 1963; Director; M.S.A. foreign subsidiaries, International Minerals & Chemicals Corp., H. J. Heinz Co., Allegheny-Ludlum Industries Inc., Mellon Bank N.A.; Trustee, Thomas A. Edison Foundation. Chmn. Allegheny Conf. of Community Development 1961–64. Member, Exec. Cttee., United Way, Pittsburgh Educational TV Station, Children's Hospital. Chmn. Univ. Health Center, Pgh., Vice-Chmn., Regional Industrial Development Corp., Trustee, Univ. of Notre Dame. *Publications:* A Businessman Views the Gordon-Howell and Pierson Studies (1960); How Will Hospitals Meet Their Capital Needs During the Next Twenty Years? (1958). *Award:* Leadership in Management Award 1953; Hon. Fellowship in Amer. College of Hospital Administrators, 1953; 1959 Professional Mgr. Award; Penn. State Distinguished Alumnus Award 1961; Erskin Ramsey Award 1974. *Member:* Amer. Inst. of Mining & Metallurgical Engineers; Amer. Socy. of Mechanical Engineers; Cncl. on Foreign Relations; American Chemical Socy. *Clubs:* Pittsburgh Athletic; University; Fox Chapel; Rolling Rock; Duquesne; Union League; N.Y. Yacht; Chicago; Metropolitan. *Address:* West Woodland Road, Pittsburgh, Pa., 15232, U.S.A.; and *office* Mine Safety Appliances Co., 600 Penn Center Blvd, Pittsburgh Pa 15235.

**RYAN, Royal Winston.** *B.* 1899. *Educ.* Univ. of Cincinnati. *M.* 1925, Ruth Durrell (*Dec.*). *S.* Winston D. *Daus.* Nancy Ruth and Mary Elizabeth. *M.* 1964, Margaret Guetschow. Reporter, Cincinnati Commercial Tribune 1919–22 (City Editor 1922–28; Managing Editor 1928–30); special writer on Business, Cleveland Plain Dealer 1930–31; Director of Publicity, National Hotel Management (Ralph Hitz Hotels) 1933; Director of Sales & Advertising, Netherlands Plaza Hotel, Cincinnati 1933–39; Vice-Pres., Swafford & Koehl Advertising Agency 1939; Pres., Ryan & Thrasher Advertising Agency 1940–41; Director of Sales and Advertising, Hotel New Yorker 1941–45. Executive Vice-President, New York Convention & Visitors Bureau 1945–65; Advisor to Foreign Govt, Business travel promotion since 1965. *Awards:* Special Award of Merit, National Association of Travel Agents 1955; Man of the Year, Hotel Sales Management Association, N.Y. 1955; Travel Agency Man of the Year, N.Y. 1959. *Member:* Int. Assn. of Convention Bureaus (Past Pres.); Natl. Assn. of Travel Organizations (Past Pres.); Travel Adv. Council, U.S. Department of Commerce. *Club:* New York Athletic. *Address:* Walker Brook Road, New Milford, Connecticut, U.S.A.

**RYDBECK, Olof.** Swedish Diplomat. *B.* 1913. *Educ.* BA, 1934; LLB, 1939. *M.* 1940, Monica Schnell. *S.* 1. *Dau.* 1. *Career:* Attaché, Ministry for Foreign Affairs 1939; in Berlin 1940, Ankara 1941, Stockholm 1942, Second Sec. 1943, First Sec. of Embassy in Washington 1945, Bonn 1950; Head of Press Section of Min. for Foreign Affairs 1952; Dir.-Gen., Swedish Broadcasting Corp. 1955–70; Perm. Rep. of Sweden to the UN 1970–76; Ambassador to the Court of St. James's since 1976. Chmn., Advisory Cttee. on Outer Space Communications of UNESCO 1966–70; Chmn., Working Group on Direct Broadcast Satellites of UN Cttee. on Peaceful Uses of Outer Space since 1969; Chmn., Cttee. of Trustees for UN Fund for South Africa; Chmn., Preparatory Cttee. for World Food Conference; Chmn., Second Cttee. 30th General Assembly 1975; Rep. of Sweden to the Security Council since 1975; Special Rep. of the Sec-Gen. on the

Question of Western Sahara 1976. *Member:* Pres., European Broadcasting Union 1961–64 (thereafter Hon. Pres.); Chmn., International Broadcasting Inst., London 1967–70; Chmn., Assoc. of the Royal Swedish National Defense College 1957–70; Royal Swedish Acad. of Music 1962; Swedish Inst. of International Affairs 1967—; National Swedish Preparedness Commission for Psychological Defense 1954–70. *Decorations:* Royal Order of the North Star, Commander First Class (Sweden); Order of the White Rose, Commander First Class (Finland); Order of the Falcon, Grand Knight with a Star (Iceland); Commander of the Order of the Dannebrog (Denmark): Grosscreutz, Grand Class (Fed. Rep. of Germany). *Address:* Royal Swedish Embassy, 23 North Row, London W.1.

**RYDER, Lord,** of Eaton Hastings, ((Don) Sydney Franklin Thomas); Chmn. & Chief Exec. National Enterprise Board 1975–77. *B.* 1916. *M.* Eileen Winifred Dodds. *S.* 1. *Dau.* 1. *Career:* Editor, Stock Exchange Gazette 1950–60; Jt. Man. Dir. Kelly Iliffe Holdings and Assoc. Iliffe Press Ltd. 1960–61, and Sole Man. Dir. 1961–63; Dir. International Publishing Corp. 1963–68; Man. Dir. Reed International Ltd. 1963–68; Chmn. and Chief Exec. Reed International Ltd. 1968–74; Industrial Adviser to H.M. Govt. since 1974. Life Peer 1975. *President:* National Material Handling Centre. *Fellow* (and Dep. Chmn.) British Institute of Management. *Member:* British Gas Corp. *Address:* Eaton Hastings House, Eaton Hastings, nr. Farington, Berkshire.

**RYDGE, Sir Norman Bede,** CBE. Australian company director. *B.* 1900. *Educ.* Fort Street High School. *M.* 1950, Phoebe McEwing. *S.* Norman, Richard, Alan. *Career:* Pres.: Greater Union Organization Pty. Ltd., Carlton Hotel Ltd., Carlton Investments Ltd., Manly Hotels Ltd., Amalgamated Holdings, Ltd., Wests Ltd.; Deputy Chmn. City Mutual Life Assurance Socy. Ltd. 1960–76; Commissioner, Rural Bank of New South Wales 1961–76. Founder of Rydge's Business Journal; Hon. Life Govnr., Royal Prince Alfred Hosp., Sydney, Royal Children's Hospital, Melbourne, Australian Inst. of Management; Royal Life Saving Society (N.S.W.) Member Cttee. Review of Parly. Salaries 1971. *Publications:* Federal Income Tax Law; Federal Land Tax Law; The Law of Income Tax in N.S.W.; Employers' Endowment Tax; Commonwealth Income Tax Acts; Australasian Executorship Law and Accounts; The N.S.W. Income Tax Management Act; Australasian edition of Stevens' Mercantile Law. *Address:* 55 Wunulla Road, Point Piper, N.S.W., Australia.

**RYDMAN, Bengt (Ivan Axel).** Swedish company director. *B.* (in Finland) 1907. *Educ.* Secondary School, Military School and London County School of Lithography. *M.* 1930, Ragna Anita Roering. *S.* Georg, Finn, Mikael, Sten. *Career:* served with Oy Tilgmann Ab 1924 (Sales Manager 1944–45; Asst. Director 1945–46); Asst. Director, Oy Karl Fazer Ab and Managing Director, Oy Hangö Kex Ab 1946–53; Managing Director, Oy Stockmann AB Department Stores, Helsinki 1953–57; Man. Dir. AB Turitz & Co. Gothenburg 1957–70; Consul Gen. of Finland in Gothenburg 1967–70. *Awards:* Knight Comdr. Order of Vasa (Sweden); Knight Comdr. Order of the Lion (Finland); several military orders. International pilot's certificate and military air-scout certificate. *Address:* Palazzo Eden Roc 6612, Ascona, Switzerland.

**RYMILL, Hon. Sir Arthur (Campbell).** Barrister and Solicitor. *B.* 1907. *Educ.* Queen's School, St. Peters School and Univ. of Adelaide. *M.* 1934, Margaret Earle, dau. of Roland Cudmore. *Daus.* Rosemary (de Meyrick) and Annabel (Greaves). *Career:* Barrister and Solicitor 1930. Chairman of Directors, The Bank of Adelaide 1953—. Director of a number of Public Companies in South Australia. Lord Mayor of Adelaide 1950–54. Member Adelaide City Council 1932–38 and 1946–64; Principal Bd. Aust. Mutual Provident Society; Legislative Council South Aust. 1956–75; Pres. S.A. Liberal and Country League 1953–55; Vice-Pres. Adelaide Children's Hospital; First Pres. National Trust of S.A. 1955–60; Vice-Pres. Australian Elizabethan Theatre 1954–63; Foundation member Bd. Govs. Adelaide Festival of Arts. Won Australian Unlimited Speedboat Championship 1933; represented S.A. in Australasian Polo Championships 1938 and 1951. Served in World War II; 2nd Australian Imperial Force; enlisted Private 2/7 Field Regt.; later commissioned. *Clubs:* Adelaide (Adelaide); Melbourne (Melbourne); Royal Adelaide Golf; Royal S.A. Yacht Squadron. *Address:* 39 Brougham Place, North Adelaide, S.A. 5006, Australia.

# S

**SAAD, Ahmed Zaki.** Egyptian. Special Counsellor to the King of Saudi Arabia. *B.* 1900. *Educ.* Egypt Univ. Cairo, LLB; Univ. of Paris, LLD and degrees in Economics and Public Law. *M.* 1940, Hoda Ruffet. *S.* 2. *Career:* Asst. Attorney-Gen. of Egypt 1922–29; Egypt. consul, Genoa (Italy), 1929–31; Hamburg (Germany) 1931–33; L'pool (England) 1933–37; Dublin (Ireland) 1933–37; Chargé d'affaires Bagdad, Iraq 1937–38; First Secy. Egyptian Embassy, London 1938; Dir. Dept. for alien affairs, Cairo 1939–44, Postmaster-general 1944; Under-Secy. State Min. of Finance, Egyptian Govt. 1945–51; Gov. Nat. Bank of Egypt 1951–52, 55–57; Exec. Dir. International Monetary Fund 1946–70, Gov. IMF 1946–52, and since 1958; Gov. Int. Bank for Reconstruction and Development 1946–52, and since 1955, Chmn. Board of Governors 1955 and 1962; Principal Representative of Saudi Arabia, with rank of Ambassador to International Monetary Fund since 1964. *Address:* International Monetary Fund, 19 Street, N.W., Washington, D.C. 20431, U.S.A.

**SACASA, Alfredo José.** Nicaraguan. *B.* 1919. *Educ.* San Ramon School, Leon; Purdue Univ. Lafayette, Indiana; School of Chemical Engineering; Univ. of Michigan. *M.* 1944, Ann Margaret Murphy. *S.* 2. *Dau.* 1. *Career:* Gen. Mgr. Cía Cervecera de Nicaragua; Dir. Banco Nicaraguense, Embotelladora Nacional; Vehiculos Importados, S.A.; Corporacion Nicaraguense de Inversiones; Inversiones Nicaraguense de Desarrollo, S.A. *Member:* American Inst. Chemical Engineers; Socy. Interamericana de Planificacion; Assn. de Ingenieros y Arquitectos de Nicaragua. *Address:* Km 9½ Carretera León, Qta. Samur, Nicaragua.

**SACHS, Mendes H.** American banker. *B.* 1907. *Educ.* Univ. of California at Berkeley (BS). *M.* Celia Zelitan. *S.* 2. *Career:* Citrus grower foreman, Citrus Groves Calif. 1928–31; Mgr. Gan Chaim 1931–; Pardness Syndicate 1947–51; Man. Dir. Mehadrin Ltd. 1951–; Dir. Bank Leumi Le Israel, B.M.; General Mortgage Bank; Bank Leumi Investment Co.; Citrus Marketing Bd.; Citrus Control Bd.; Pardness Syndicate; Man. Dir. Mehadrin Ltd.; Chmn. First Israel Bank & Trust Co. New York. Governor, Hebrew Univ.; Nat. Univ. of Agriculture. *Publications:* miscellaneous articles on technical and economic aspects of the citrus industry in Israel. *Address:* *office* c/o Citrus Marketing Board of Israel, P.O.B. 2590, Tel Aviv, Israel.

**SADAT, Anwar El.** President of Egypt since 1970. *B.* 1918. *Educ.* Military Coll., Cairo. *M.* Jihan Sadat. *S.* 1. *Daus.* 3 (+ 3 by previous marriage). *Career:* Minister of State 1955–56; Vice-Chmn., National Assembly 1957–60, Chmn. 1960–68; Gen. Sec., Egyptian National Union 1957–61; Speaker, UAR National Assembly 1961–69; mem., Presidential Council 1962–64; Vice-Pres. of Egypt 1964–66, 1969–70, Pres. since 1970, Prime Minister 1973–74; Chmn., Arab Socialist Union since 1970. *Address:* The Office of the President, Cairo, Egypt.

**SAFFAR, Dr. Salman Mohamed Al-.** Bahraini Diplomat. *B.* 1931. *Educ.* Univ. of Baghdad—BA; Univ. of Paris—Ph.D. *M.* Monique Jeanselme. *Career:* Teacher, Elementary & Secondary School, Bahrain 1954–59; Officer in Charge of Political Affairs, Min. of Foreign Affairs, Bahrain 1970–71; Ambassador, Perm. Rep. of Bahrain to UN since 1971. *Address:* Ministry of Foreign Affairs, Manama, Bahrain, Arabian Gulf; & Permanent Mission of Bahrain to the UN, 747 Third Avenue, New York, N.Y. 10017, U.S.A.

**SAINSBURY, Lord (Alan John).** British. Jt. Coy. President. *B.* 1902. *Educ.* Haileybury. *M.* (1) 1925, Doreen Davan Adams (*Div.*). *S.* 3. (2) 1944 Anne Elizabeth Lewey. *Dau.* 1.

*Career:* Joined firm of J. Sainsbury Ltd., 1921, President since 1967. Served on Ministry of Food committees during World War II: Member, Williams Committe on Milk Distribution, 1947–48; Member, Food Research Adv. Cttee., 1960–70; Member, N.E.D.C. Committee for Distributive Trades, 1964–68; Chmn. Cttee. of Inquiry into Relationship of Pharmaceutical Industry with Natl. Health Service, 1965–67; President, Multiple Shops Fed., 1963–65; The Grocers' Inst., 1963–66; International Assocn. of Chain Stores 1965–68; Royal Inst. of Public Health and Hygiene, 1965–70; Pestalozzi Children's Village Trust, 1963—; Vice-Pres., Assocn. of Agriculture, 1965–73; Royal Society for the Encouragement of Arts, Manufactures and Commerce, 1962–66; Member, Court of Univ. of Essex 1966—; Exec. Cttee. P.E.P.; Chmn. Trustees Overseas Students Adv. Bureau; Governor, City Literary Inst. 1967–69; Hon. Fellow Institute of Food Science & Technology; Chmn. of Trustees, Uganda Asian Relief Trust 1972–74; Pres. Distributive Trades Education & Training Council since 1975; Liberal Candidate, Sudbury Div. of Suffolk, Gen. Elections, 1929, 1931 and 1935. Joined Labour Party, 1945. *Address:* J. Sainsbury Ltd., Stamford House, Stamford Street, S.E.1.

**SAINSBURY, John Ronald**, AM, ERD. British. *B.* 1912. *Educ.* St. Benedict's (Ealing, London) and Cardiff Technical College; Fellow, Institution of Civil Engineers (London) by examination. *M.* 1939, Joan Eastham. *S.* John Douglas Joseph and David Andrew. *Daus.* Elizabeth Mary and Margaret Rose. *Career:* Asst. Chief Engineer, Tyne Improvement Commission (Newcastle-upon-Tyne, England) 1949–58; Chief Engineer 1958–61, Gen. Mgr. 1961–67, The South Australian Harbors Board; Dir. Marine & Harbors, South Australia 1967–76 (Ret'd). *Awards:* Member of the Order of Australia; Knight Officer, Order of Orange-Nassau (Netherlands); Lieut. Col. R.E. (Mentioned in Dispatches) 1939–45. FICE; MIE (Aust.); FCIT. *Clubs:* Naval, Military and Air Force (Adelaide); Legacy. *Address:* 18 Bandon Terrace, Kingston Park, S.A., Australia.

**ST. ALDWYN, The Rt. Hon. the Earl**, PC, KBE, TD (Sir Michael John Hicks Beach, Bt) K.St.J. *B.* 1912. *Educ.* Eton; Christ Church, Oxford. *M.* 1948, Diana Mary Christian Mills. D.St.J. *S.* 3. *Career:* Joint Parliamentary Secretary Ministry of Agriculture and Fisheries 1954–58. Chief Whip, House of Lords, and Capt. Hon. Corps of Gentlemen-at-Arms 1958–64; Opposition Chief Whip 1964–70; Chief Whip, House of Lords; Captain Honourable Corps of Gentlemen-at-Arms 1970–74; Opposition Chief Whip since 1974. *Address:* Williamstrip Park, Cirencester, Glos. and 13 Upper Belgrave Street, London, S.W.1.

**SAINT BRIDES, Rt. Hon. Lord** (Sir Morrice James), PC, GCMG, CVO, MBE. *B.* 1916. *Educ.* BA (Oxon.). *M.* (1) 1948, Elizabeth Margaret Roper Piesse (*Dec.*). *S.* 1. *Daus.* 2; (2) 1968, Genevieve Sarasin. *Career:* Served in World War II (Royal Navy and Royal Marines) 1940–45; Deputy High Commissioner for United Kingdom in Lahore, Pakistan (1952–53). Karachi, Pakistan (1955–56); Assistant Under-Secretary of State, Commonwealth Relations Office 1957–58; Deputy High Commissioner in India 1958–61; High Commissioner in Pakistan 1961–66; Deputy Under-Secy. Comm. Office, 1966–68. Permanent Under-Secy. of State, Commonwealth Office, March–Oct. 1968; High Commissioner in India, 1968–71; and in Australia 1971–76. Created Life Peer 1977. *Club:* Oriental. *Address:* Cap Saint-Pierre, 83990 Saint-Tropez, France.

**ST. JOHN-STEVAS, Norman Antony Francis.** MP. British author, barrister and journalist. *B.* 1929. *Educ.* Ratcliffe; Fitzwilliam, Cambridge; Christ Church, Oxford; Yale Scholar. Clothworkers Exhibnr, 1946, 1947; BA Cambridge (1st class Hons in Law) 1950, MA 1954. *Career:* Contested Dagenham Gen. Election 1951; Barrister Middle Temple 1952; Lecturer, Southampton Univ. 1952–53, King's Coll. London 1953–56; Tutored in jurisprudence Christ Church 1953–55 and Merton 1955–57, Oxford; Lecture tours of U.S.A. 1958–68; joined The Economist, to edit collected works, Walter Bagchot; legal, ecclesiastical and political correspondent 1959; Member of Parliament (Conservative) Chelmsford 1964—; Regents' Prof. Univ. of California, Santa Barbara 1969; Founder member Christian Social Inst. of Culture Rome 1969; Secy. Parly Home Affairs Cttee. 1969. Parly. Under-Secretary of State Dept. Education and Science; 1972, Minister 1973–74; Shadow Secy. of State for Ed. and Science and Opposition Spokesman for the Arts since 1974. *Member:* Fulbright Commission 1961; Parly Select Cttee. Race Relations & Immigration 1970, on Civil List 1971; Cons. Nat. Adv. Cttee. on Policy 1971. Hon. Secy. Fed. Cons. Students 1971. *Awards:* Fellow Yale Law School 1957; Fulbright Award; Fellow 1958, Dr. of Science & Law (Yale); Ph.D. London; Yorke Prize Cambridge Univ.; K. St. Lazarus of Jerusalem; Cav. Order of Merit (Ital. Republic); FRSL. *Publications:* Obscenity and the Law (1956); Walter Bagehot (1959); Life, Death and the Law (1961); The Right to Life (1963); Law and Morals (1964); The Collected Works of Walter Bagehot Vols. I–VIII. *Clubs:* Garrick; Beefsteak. *Address:* 34 Montpelier Square, London, SW1.

**SALAS, Rafael M.** BA, LLB, MPA, PhD (h.c.), DHL (h.c.). *B.* 1928. *Educ.* Negros Occidental Prov. High School; graduated Bachelor of Arts, Bachelor of Law (*magna cum laude*), Univ. of the Philippines (*cum laude*). *M.* Carmelita Rodriguez. *S.* 1. *Career:* Member Phil. Bar 1953; Master Public Administration, Littauer Center Harvard Univ. 1955; Professorial Lect. in Pol. Science and Economics Univ. of Philippines 1955–59; Economics Grad. School Far Eastern Univ. 1960–61; Law Univ. Philippines 1963–66 (Asst. Vice-Pres. 1962–63, Member Bd. Regents 1966–69 of the Univ.); Gen. Mgr. Manila Chronicle, Asst. to President Meralco Securities Corp. 1963–65; Exec. Secy. of the Philippines 1966–69; Action Officer, Philippine Rice and Corn Sufficiency Programme, Green Revolution 1967–69; Senior Consultant to the Administrator UNDP 1969; Exec. Dir. United Nations Fund for Population Activities since 1969. Rank elevated to Under-Secretary-General since 1973. *Publications:* People: An International Choice (The Multilateral Approach to Population) (1976); and numerous articles for professional journals. *Address:* United Nations Fund for Population Activities, 485 Lexington Avenue, New York, N.Y. 10017, U.S.A.

**SALCEDO, Dr. Juan Sanchez, Jr.** University President, administrator and scientist. *Educ.* College of Liberal Arts, Coll. of Medicine, Univ. of the Philippines (MD); Univ. of Chicago, John Hopkins Univ. and Columbia Univ. (MA). *M.* Elvira Galvez. *S.* 2. *Daus.* 4. *Career:* Adviser to Philippine Delegate to UNRRA. Montreal 1944, Washington 1946, Shanghai 1947; Dir. Public Welfare 1945; Rep. of the President, UNRRA 1945–47; Exec. Officer, PPRA 1945–47; Dir. Nutrition, Philippines 1948–50; Chief Del. 4th Int. Congress on Tropical Medicine & Malaria, Washington 1948 and 5th & 6th World Health Assemblies, Geneva 1952–53; Member, FAO-WHO Expert Cttee. on Nutrition Geneva 1949 and 1954; Alternate Del. 5th Conf. FAO Washington 1949, Rice Conf. Rangoon 1950; Secy. of Health Philippines 1950–53; Chmn. Bd. of Nutrition 1951–58; Philippine National Red Cross 1951–54; Pres. 5th WHO Assembly 1952–53; Prof. of Biochemistry, Coll. of Medicine and Dean of Graduate School, Univ. of Philippines 1954–58; Chmn, Adv. Bd. Institute, Science & Technology 1954–58; Member. National Civil Defence Council 1955–58; Dean Coll. of Medicine, Ramon Magsaysay Memorial Medical Center, Univ. of the East 1958–62; Prof. and Head, Dept. Physiological Hygiene & Nutrition Inst. of Hygiene 1954–58; Chmn. Council of Deans, Philippine Medical Schools Inc. 1960–52; Leader, Philippines Delegation, Pacific Science Congress 1961 and 1971; and at the U.S. Philippine Workshops on Scientific & Technological Co-operation & Development 1965, 66, 67 and 69; and at UNESCO-CASTASIA 1968; Presidential Assistant, Science & Technology 1962–63; Chmn. National Science Development Bd. Manila 1963–70; First Vice-Chmn. Asian Conference, Children & Youth in National Planning & Development, Bangkok 1966; Chmn. National Research Council of the Philippines; Meals for Millions Foundation (Philippines) Inc. Pres. Science Foundation Philippines; Chmn. President, Nutrition Foundation of the Philippines. Pres. Araneta Univ. Foundation. Malabon, Rizal Philippines since 1970. *Member:* Phi Kappa Phi Sigma XI, Phi Sigma Biological Socy. American Inst. of Nutrition. Fellow N.Y. Academy of Sciences; Fellowships, Univ. of the Philippines, in Vitamins & endocrines; Columbia Univ. William J. Giles, in Biochemistry of Philippine Public Health Assn.; Philippine Socy. of Gastroenterology and Charter Diplomate, Philippine Bd. of Preventive Medicine and Public Health. Rockefeller Foundation Travel Grantee in Public Health Nutrition 1954 and 1955 and in science development 1966; N.Y. Acad. of Sciences travel grantee 1961. Guest, Governments of Australia, Federal Republic of Germany and Israel to visit their Scientific institutes and laboratories, 1966. *Awards:* 1966 Republic Cultural Heritage Award in Science; Presidential Pro Patria Award 1969; Certificates of Honour, Hon. DSc. and DLL. 30 plaques of Merit. *Publications:* Road to National Progress; some239 publications on Biochemistry, health, medical education, nutrition and science development. *Address:* 160 Grace Road, Pasay City, Philippines.

**SALIBA, Jacob.** Industrial engineer and business executive. *B.* 1913. *Educ.* Boston University (CLA, BS). *M.* 1942, Adla Mudarri. *S.* John and Thomas. *Dau.* Barbara. *Career:* Senior Supervisory Engineer, Thompson & Lichtner 1942–46; Pres. J. Saliba & Assoc. 1946–54; Exec. Vice Pres. Brockway Motors Inc. 1954–56; Pres. Sawyer-Tower Inc. 1956–59; Pres. Fanny Farmer Candy Shops Inc. 1963–66; President: W. R. Grace & Co. (Frozen Foods Div.) 1967–68; W. F. Schrafft & Sons Corp. Jan.–Aug. 1967; President, Northeast Industries Inc.; Pres. Katy Industries Inc. since 1969. *Director:* Katy Industries Inc., Elgin, Ill.; Missouri-Kansas-Texas Railroad, Dallas, Texas; Bush Universal Inc., New York; HMW Industries Inc., Stamford, Conn.; A. M. Castle & Co., Franklin Park, Ill.; Midland Insurance Co., New York; First National Stores Inc., Somerville, Mass. Trustee, Boston Univ.; Mem. of the Corp., Mass. General Hospital Museum of Science. *Award:* Meritorious Citation by Secretary of U.S.A.F. for consulting services to U.S. Government. *Publications:* Welding Controls for Ship Construction (Marine Engineering). *Member:* Socy. of Naval Architects and Marine Engineers; Bostonian Socy. *Clubs:* Union League (N.Y.C.); University, Algonquin (Boston). *Address: office* Prudential Tower, Suite 4368, Boston, Massachusetts 02199, U.S.A.

**SALISBURY, Franklin Cary.** *B.* 1910. *Educ.* Yale Univ. (BA); Western Reserve Univ. (LLB); JSD. *M.* 1955, Tamara Voloshin. *S.* Franklin and John Gregory. *Daus.* Elizabeth Tamara, Elaine Nadine and Claire Louise. *Career:* Asst to Commissioner, Fed. Communications Commission 1939–40; Office, Chief of Ordnance 1940–45; Judge Advocate-General's Dept. (JAG); Dir., Legal Div., Office of Foreign Liquidation, U.S. Embassy, Brazil 1945–46; Pres. and Trustee. Latin-American Institute, Washington, D.C. 1946–76. Vice-Pres. and Gen. Counsel, Radio St. Louis Inc. 1953–58; Sec. and Gen. Counsel, Atlantic Research Inc. 1949–64; Chmn., Orbit Industries Inc. 1961–68; Chmn., Wire Conveyor Belts, Inc. Inc. 1968—; Sec. Treas. Multi-Tech Inc., 1969—. Americans United. Gen. Counsel 1963–72; Exec. Dir. Bethesda Nat. Foundation 1972–76; Dir., International School of Law 1975—. Nat. Foundation for Cancer Research since 1972. Maior U.S. Army 1942. *Publications:* Speaking of Politics (1956). *Clubs:* University (Wash., D.C.); Army-Navy Country (Wash.); (N.Y.C.); Morys (New Haven, Conn.); Yale. *Address:* 10811 Alloway Drive, Potomac, Maryland, U.S.A.

**SALK, Dr. Jonas Edward.** American physician and scientist. Developer of the Salk Vaccine in prevention of poliomyelitis. *B.* 1914. *Educ.* College of the City of New York (BS 1934) and New York University College of Medicine (MD 1939). *M.* 1939. *Career:* Fellow in Chemistry 1935–36, Christian A. Herter Fellow in Chemistry 1936–37, Christian A. Herter Fellow in Experimental Surgery 1937–39, and Fellow in Bacteriology 1939–40, N.Y. Univ. Coll. of Medicine. Intern, Mt. Sinai Hospital, N.Y.C. 1940–42. Fellow in the Medical Sciences of the National Research Council 1942–43, Research Fellow in Epidemiology 1943–44, Research Associate in Epidemiology 1944–46 and Asst. Prof. of Epidemiology 1946–47, Dept. of Epidemiology, School of Public Health, Univ. of Michigan. Associate Research Professor of Bacteriology 1947–49; Consultant to Secy. of War 1944–47 and to Secy. of the Army 1947–54 in Epidemic Diseases, Member of Commn. on Influenza, Army Epidemiological Bd. Consulting Staff Municipal Hospital for Contagious Diseases, Pittsburgh, Pa. 1948–56, Presbyterian Hospital, Pittsburgh 1949–62; Member, Expert Advisory Panel on Virus Diseases, World Health Organization 1951—. Research Prof. 1949–55, Commonwealth Prof. of Preventive Medicine 1955–57, and Commonwealth Prof. of Experimental Medicine 1957–62, Director of Virus Research Laboratory. School of Medicine, Univ. of Pittsburgh 1947–63; Prof. at Large, Univ. of Pittsburgh 1963–64; Fellow, The Salk Inst. for Biological Studies, San Diego, Calif. 1963— (Dir. 1963–75, Founding Dir. 1975—); Adjunt Prof. of Health Sciences Dept. of Psychiatry, Community Medicine and Medicine, Univ. of Calif. San Diego since 1970. *Member:* Assn. of Amer. Physicians; Amer. Socy. for Clinical Investigation; Amer. Epidemiological Socy.; Amer. Assn. of Immunologists; Amer. Assn. for Advancement of Science (Fellow); Amer. Public Health Assn. (Fellow); Amer. Coll. of Preventive Medicine; Amer. Medical Assn.; Socy. for Experimental Biology & Medicine; Socy. of Amer. Bacteriologists; Phi Beta Kappa; Alpha Omega Alpha; Sigma Xi; Delta Omega. *Publications:* Man Unfolding (1972; British edn.: How Like an Angel); The Survival of the Wisest (1973); & 90 published papers and articles. *Address:* P.O. Box 1809, San Diego, Calif. 92112, U.S.A.

**SALMAN, Dr. Salah D.** Lebanese Physician. *B.* 1936. *Educ.* American Univ. of Beirut—BS (with distinction). MD (Penrose Award). *M.* Wadad Assad Najjar. *S.* 2. *Career:* Physician, Aramco, Saudi Arabia 1961–62; Resident in Otolaryngology, American Univ. Hospital, Beirut 1962–65; Resident in Surgery, Johns Hopkins Hospital, Baltimore 1965–66; Fellow in Otolaryngology, Johns Hopkins Hospital 1966–68; Research Asst. in Environmental Medicine, Sch. of Hygiene & Physical Health 1968–69; Instructor, Dept. of ENT, American Univ. Hospital 1968–69; Asst. Prof. Dept. of ENT & Acting Chmn. 1969–74; Assoc. Prof. & Chmn. since 1974. *Member:* Lebanese Order of Physicians; Lebanese ENT Soc.; American Acad. of Ophthalmology & Otolaryngology; Alpha Omega Alpha Honor Medical Soc.; American Coll. of Surgeons. *Awards:* Penrose Award, 1961. *Clubs:* Sigma-Xi; Eagles. *Address:* Lyon Street, Assa'd Najjar Building, Beirut; and *office* American University Hospital, Beirut, Lebanon.

**SALMON, Eric Percy,** OBE, JP. New Zealand. *B.* 1903. *Educ.* Univ. of Auckland. *M.* 1942, Joyce Harbutt Winstone. *S.* 2. *Dau.* 1. *Career:* Previously Company Director, several companies in the printing industry. Pres., Fed. of Master Printers of N.Z. 1963–66; Past Pres.: Auckland Master Printers' Assn., Auckland Chamber of Commerce 1961–62; Auckland Provincial Employers Assn., 1964–69; and N.Z. Inst. of Management 1967–69; Pres.: N.Z. Inst. of Printing 1965–70; N.Z. Employers Fed. 1969–71; Deleg. to I.L.O. Conf., Geneva 1966 & 1969, Tehran 1971. Councillor, Auckland City Council 1968—, Chmn., several cttees.; Council of the Auckland Technical Insts. 1974—; Auckland Metropolitan Fire Board 1975—; Chmn. N.Z. Museum of Transport & Technology; Area Patron, Scout Assn.; FCIS, FCA (N.Z.), F.N.Z.I.M. *Address:* 20 Gardner Road, Epsom, Auckland, New Zealand.

**SALMON, Sir Samuel.** British. *B.* 18 Oct. 1900. *Educ.* Jesus College, Cambridge (MA). *M.* 1937, Lallah Wendy Benjamin. *S.* 1. *Dau.* 1. *Career:* Chairman, J. Lyons & Co., Ltd. 1965–68. President J. Lyons & Co. Ltd. 1968–72. Member, London County Council since 1949; Greater London Council 1964–67. Mayor of London Borough of Hammersmith 1968–69; Chmn. Metropolitan Water Board 1971. *Address:* 14 Carlos Place, London, W.1.

**SALO, Tuure Olavi H.** Finnish town Governor. *B.* 1921. *M.* 1950, Raija Sirkka Koch. *S.* Petri and Pirkka. *Daus.* Merja, Terhi and Kirsti. *Career:* Lawyer 1947–50; Manager, Rovaniemi Savings Bank July 1950–May 1963. Appointed Vice-county judge. Town Governor of Rovaniemi. June 1963—. Member of Parliament 1962–70. Major in the reserve of the Finnish Army. Finnish Minister of Justice since 1977. *Awards:* Cross of Freedom (3, viz., Class 3, Class 4 (with oak leaves), Class 4); Memorial Medal of the Winter Campaign; Memorial Medal of the Continuation of the War; Iron Cross; Polonia Restituti; Order of Merit (Jugoslavia). *Member:* Finnish Jurists Soc., Liberal Party of Finland. *Clubs:* Lions. *Address:* Katajaranta, 7, Rovaniemi: and *office* Valtakatu 18, Rovaniemi, Finland.

**SALOMON, Irving.** American industrialist, diplomat, author. *B.* 1897. *Educ.* Northwestern Univ.; Hon LHB, Calif.. Western Univ.; Hon LLD Georgetown Univ. 1972, Brandeis Univ. 1973. *M.* 1937, Cecile Leibowitz. *Dau:* Abbe. *Career:* Chmn., U.S. Delegation to UNESCO, Paris 1953; member, U.S. Deleg. to ECOSOC, Geneva 1953; Pres., Royal Metal Mfg. Co. 1926–42 (Chmn. of Board 1942–58); Member of Board of Georgetown, Brandeis, Calif.-Western and Atlanta Universities, and Clairmont University of Theology; Inst. of International Education; U.S. Commission to UNESCO; Foreign Policy Association; UNICEF Board and Executive Committee; U.N. Association of the U.S.; Hon. Chairman of the Board of United Nations Association of San Diego; member of Executive Board of American Jewish Committee; and former Chairman, Executive Committee, World Federation of U.N. Association, Geneva; Member of Board of several industrial firms, Charity & Civic Organizations, including the Y.M.C.A.; San Diego Symphony, Old Globe Theatre; San Diego Ballet Assn., President, World Affairs Council, and Children's Hospital, San Diego; Chairman U.N.A. delegation to Moscow 1958; Consultant, Ford Foundation, Fund for the Advancement of Education, Fund for Adult Education, and Member Bd. Institute on Man and Science; Member San Diego Park Board; Former U.N. Under-Secretary and foundation executive, rancher and lecturer. U.S. Delegate to 13th General Assembly of U.N. Professor of Political Science, University of San Diego. *Publications:* Retire and be Happy (1951); Management Surveys in Colleges and Universities (1955); numerous newspaper and magazine articles and broadcasts on world affairs, N.B.C. Republican. *Clubs:* Harmonie (N.Y.C.); Standard (Chicago); Kona Kai Cuyamaca; University (San Diego, Calif.). *Address:* Rancho Lilac, Valley Center, Calif.; and 3200 6th Avenue, San Diego, Calif., U.S.A.

**SALTES, Jean François Charles Louis.** French banker. *B.* 1906. *Educ.* Ecole Polytechnique. General Inspector of Finance 1959; Chairman, Board of Directors, Crédit National. Commandeur Légion d'Honneur; Croix de Guerre 1939–40; Commandeur National Order of Merit; Commandeur Order of Arts and Letters. *Address:* 45 rue St.-Dominique, Paris, 7e.

**SALTZMAN, Charles E.** American investment banker. *B.* 1903. *Educ.* Cornell Univ.; U.S. Mil. Acad. (BS); Oxford Univ. (BA, MA). *M.* (1) 1931, Gertrude Lamont. *S.* Charles McKinley; (2) 1947, Cynthia Southall Myrick. *S.* Richard Stevens (*Dec.*). *Daus.* Cynthia Myrick and Penelope Washburn. *Career:* Served U.S. Army, 2nd Lt., Corps of Engineers 1925–30; with New York Telephone Co. 1930–35; with New York Stock Exchange 1935–49; served World War II, Lt.-Col. to Brig.-Gen. 1940–46; Assist. Secy. of State 1947–49; Maj.-Gen. U.S.A.R. 1955–60; Under-Secy. of State 1954–55; Partner, Henry Sears & Co. 1949–56; Gen. partner, Goldman Sachs & Co., investment bankers 1956–72; limited partner since 1973; Dir., American Council on Germany; Assn. Am. Rhodes Scholars, Downton-Lower Manhat. Assn. ESU of USA (nat. pres. 1961–66); Federation des Alliances Francaises; Fed. Protestant Welfare Agencies, Milbank Memorial Fund. *Member:* Bd. of Mgrs.: American Bible Soc., Seamen's Church Inst. of N.Y.; Bd. of Trustees: Assn. of Graduates U.S. Mil. Acad. (vice-pres. 1940–41 and 1959, pres. since 1974), Christ Ch. United Methodist N.Y.C. (Pres. Bd. of Trustees since 1976), George C. Marshall Research Foundation, U.S. Council of Intern. Chamber of Commerce; Member Center for Inter-American Relations; Council on For. Relations; Japan Soc.; Mil. Order of World Wars; Nat. Inst. Soc. Sciences; Pilgrims of U.S.A.; Society of Cincinnati (hon.); Kappa Alpha Soc.; The Most Ven. Order of Hosp. of St. John of Jerusalem (Knight); St. George's Soc. N.Y. *Awards:* DSM, Legion of Merit (U.S.); Hon. OBE; Croix de Guerre with gold star (France); Cross of Merit (Poland); Bronze Medal (Italy); Grand Officer Order of the Crown of Italy; War Medal (Brazil); Ouissam Alaouitte, Deg. of Commander (Morocco). *Address:* 55 Broad Street, New York 10004, U.S.A.

**SALZBERG, Paul Lawrence.** Chemist. *B.* 1903. *Educ.* Knox Coll. (BS 1925; Hon ScD 1958) and Univ. of Illinois (PhD 1928). *M.* 1929, Grace Ella Johnson. *S.* Robert Harris and John Paul. *Dau.* Claire Grace. *Career:* With E. I. du Pont de Nemours 1928–67 (successively chemist, res. supervisor, assistant dir. of res.). Former Dir. Central Research Department. E. I. du Pont de Nemours & Co. Inc., Wilmington, Del. (1953–67); Trustee Knox Coll. U.S. since 1963. Patentee in field of activity. Recipient Industrial Research Institute Medal. *Member:* Amer. chemical Socy.; Amer. Assn. for Advancement of Science; Socy. of Chemical Industry; Phi Beta Kappa; Sigma Xi; Alpha Chi Sigma; Phi Lambda Upsilon. Hon Member, Chemists Club, N.Y. *Address:* 1525 Foulk Road, Wilmington, Del. 19803, U.S.A.

**SAMPAIO, Paulo de Oliveria.** Brazilian aviation expert and air line executive. *B.* 26 July 1907. *Educ.* Polytechnic University, Rio de Janeiro; Ecole de Travaux Publiques, Paris. *M.* 1934, Gilda de Oliveira Sampaio. *S.* Luiz Paulo, Octavio. *Daus.* Sonia María, María Luiza. *Career:* Reserve Officer, Brazilian Naval School 1930–33; Man. Dir. Aviação Sul-Americana and President of Aerobrasil Ltda. 1934–37; Director, Companhia Agrícola e Pastoril de São Paulo and Administradora Imobiliária Ltda. 1937–40; President, Panair do Brasil S.A. 1943–55, and 1961—; Pres. Companhia Paulista de Energia Nuclear (COPEN); Pres., Petróleo Guarani S.A. (PEGASA), Petroles Andino S.A. (PETROLANSA), and Consórcio Cabo Frio Busios; Vice-Pres., Kenranda Pesquizas Minerais S.A. Officier de la Légion d'Honneur; Officer, Order of Cedar (Lebanon); Al Mérito de Cisneros (Spain); Al Mérito Bernardo O'Higgins (Chile); Ordinis Sancti Gregorii Magni (Holy See); Mérito Aeronáutico and Pioneiro da Aviação (Brasil); Chevalier Order of Malta; Comendador, Órdem Nacional do Mérito; Medalha de Serviços Relevantes-Para; Cidadão Paulistano, Baiano, de Manaus, de Petrópolis. *Address:* 454 Avenida Rui Barbosa, Rio de Janeiro, Brazil.

**SAMPHAN, Khieu.** Cambodian Soldier & Politician. Former Commander-in-Chief of the Khymer Rouge; Dep. P.M. & Defence Min. 1975; Head of State following resignation of Prince Sihanouk 1976. *Address:* Peoples' Assembly, Phnom-Penh, Democratic Cambodia.

**SAMPLES, Reginald McCartney,** CMG, DSO, OBE. British Diplomatic Service. *B.* 1918. *Educ.* Rhyl Grammar School and Liverpool University (BCom). *M.* 1947, Elsie Roberts Hide. *S.* Graeme McCartney and William Paul McCartney. *Stepdaughter,* Murcia Valentine Mears. *Career:* Served in World War II 1940–46; Air Branch, R.N.V.R.; Observer Lieut.; DSO 1942; Econ. Editor, Overseas Newspapers, Central Office of Information 1946–48; Commonwealth Relations Office: Economic Information Officer, British Information Services, Bombay 1948–52; Editor-in-Chief, B.I.S., New Delhi 1952–53 (Deputy Dir. 1953–56); Director, B.I.S.: Pakistan, Karachi 1956–59; Counsellor (Information) & Dir., B.I.S. Canada 1959–65. Counsellor (Information), British High Commission, New Delhi, and Dir., British Information Services, India, Nov. 1965–68; Assistant Under Sec. of State, Commonwealth Office 1968–69; Senior British Trade Commissioner, Toronto 1969; British Consul-General, Toronto 1973—. *Clubs:* The Naval (London). *Address:* British Consulate-General, 200 University Avenue, Toronto, Ontario, M5H 3E3, Canada.

**SAMPSON, William Stephen Bertram,** FCA, J. Dip., MA, FCIS, CPA (U.S.A.). British. *B.* 1911. *Educ.* Queen Elizabeth's Grammar School, Mansfield. *M.* 1947, Rowena Cook Jordan. *S.* 3. *Daus.* 2. *Career:* with Deloitte & Co. 1936–40, 1945–55; British Purchasing Comm. New York 1941–44; Financial Adv. to Chmn. Great Universal Stores Ltd. 1956; Chief Accountant Int. Finance Corp. 1957–61. Finance Dir. Baker Perkings Holdings Ltd. 1962–75, Dir. Baker Perkins Far East A.G. Zug. Switzerland. *Clubs:* Canning; The Pilgrims. *Address:* 13 Rutland Terrace, Stamford, Lincs.

**SAMSAMI, Gholam-Ali.** Persian diplomat. *Educ.* University of Teheran (BSc, LLB); University of Paris (D en D Dr oec pol). *Married. Dau.* 1. *Career:* Member, Third Political Department, Ministry of Foreign Affairs 1922–26; Attaché, later Third and Second Secretary, Moscow 1926–31; member, Second Political Department, Ministry of Foreign Affairs 1931–33; Second Secretary, Paris 1933–36; Director, Personnel Status Dept., Ministry of Foreign Affairs 1936–37; First Secretary of Legation, Rome 1937–41; Premier Member, Legal Department, Ministry of Foreign Affairs Nov. 1941–Jan. 1942, Premier Member, Second Political Department Jan.–Sept. 1942, Director, Nationality Bureau Sept. 1942–May 1943, Legal Consultant May 1943–Mar. 1944, Chief of Department for U.N.O. Affairs and Specialized Agencies 1944–48; Counsellor and Chargé d'Affaires, a.i., Damascus 1948–Oct. 1949; Chargé d'Affaires, a.i., Beirut Oct.–Dec. 1949; Chargé d'Affaires, Cairo July–Sept. 1950; Counsellor of Embassy, Cairo since Dec. 1949; Head of Cultural Relations Section, Ministry of Foreign Affairs, April 1951–52, Min. Plen. to Afghanistan, April 1952; Member of the Supreme Political Council in the Ministry of Foreign Affairs, June 1956; retired Oct. 1958. Lawyer, first class since 1963; President, Freemantle Chamber of Commerce; First Freeman, City of Freemantle. Order of Homayoun (Iran) and of Merit (Syria). *Publication:* United Nations and Specialized Agencies. *Address:* 37 Kuye Ahar, Shemran Road, Bissim, Kasr, Teheran, Iran.

**SAMUEL, OF WYCH CROSS, Lord. (Harold Samuel),** Kt. FRICS, Baron cr. 1972 (Life Peer). *B.* 1912. *Educ.* Mill Hill School; College of Estate Management. *M.* 1936, Edna Nedas. *Daus.* 3 (1 *Dec.*). *Career:* Dir. Railway Sites Ltd. British Rail 1962–65; Chmn. The Land Securities Investment Trust Ltd., Central London Housing Trust for the Aged. *Member:* Covent Garden Market Authority 1961–74; Crown Estate Commissioners Regent Street Cttee. 1963—; Land Commission 1967–70; Special (Rebuilding) Cttee. The Royal Inst. of Chartered Surveyors; Courts of Univs. of Sussex and Swansea; Court of Patrons Royal College of Surgeons; Vice-President, British Heart Foundation; Trustee, Mill Hill School. *Awards:* Hon. Fellow Magdalene Coll. Cambridge 1961; University Coll. London 1968. *Club:* Devonshire. *Address:* 75, Avenue Road, Regent's Park, London NW8 6JD; & Wych Cross Place, Forest Row, East Sussex.

**SAMUEL, Hon. Peter Montefiore,** MC, TD. British banker. *B.* 1911. *Educ.* Eton; New College, Oxford (BA). *M.* 1946, Elizabeth Adelaide Pearce-Serocold (née Cohen); *S.* Nicholas Alan, Michael John. *Dau.* Sarah Virginia (Fitzwilliams). *Career:* Served in World War II, with Warwickshire Yeomanry in Middle East, Italy and Great Britain 1939–45; Dep. Chmn. Director, Hill Samuel Group Ltd. 1935—; Dir. Shell Transport Trading Co. Ltd. 1938—; Chairman: Dylon

International Ltd. 1958—, Samuel Properties Ltd. 1961—, Samuel Properties (Developments) Ltd. 1962—, Moorgate Investment Co. Ltd. 1960—, Trades Union Trust Managers Ltd. 1960—, Norcros Ltd. 1961–77, Samuel Properties (Services) Ltd. 1962—, Chmn. HS & Co. (Ireland) Ltd. 1964—, Mayborn Products Ltd. 1946—, Computer & Systems Engineering Ltd. (CASE) 1971–77, General Consolidated Investment Trust Ltd. 1975—; President Norwood Home for Jewish Children 1962—; Chmn. of Council of Royal Free Hospital School of Medicine 1973— (Mem. since 1948); Hon. Treas., Nat. Assn. for Gifted Children 1968—. *Address:* Farley Hall, Farley Hill, Reading, Berks RG7 1UL; and *office* Hill Samuel Group Ltd., 19 St. James's Square, London SW1Y 4JQ.

**SAMUELS, Nathaniel.** U.S. business executive. *B.* 1908. *Educ.* Harvard—BS 1930. *M.* 1952, Mary Elizabeth Hyman, MD. *S.* 2. *Career:* Read law privately in Chicago law office 1931–35; admitted to Ill. bar 1935; practised in Chicago 1935–42; Dir., Soc. Financière de Transports et d'Enterprises Industrielles (SOFINA), Brussels 1949–67; with Kuhn, Loeb & Co. 1955–69, 1972—, gen. partner 1960–66, 1972—, managing partner 1966–69, Chmn. Bd. of Advisory Dirs. 1977—; Chmn., Louis Dreyfus Holding Co. Inc. 1974—, Dir. Banque Louis Dreyfus et Cie., Paris 1974—; Dir., Erste Allgemeine Versicherungs-Aktiengessellschaft, Vienna 1972—; Dir., Transocean Holding Corp. 1972—; Dir., Internat. Basic Economy Corp., N.Y.C. 1963–69, Chmn. 1972–77; mem. Council on Foreign Relations N.Y.; Chmn. Exec. Comm. Center for Strategic & International Studies, Washington; Dir. Atlantic Council of the U.S.; Gov. Atlantic Inst., Paris; Dir. Center for Inter-American Relations, N.Y.; mem. Cttee. on Changing International Realities, National Planning Assn., Washington; Dir. the French-American Foundation, N.Y.; mem. the International Inst. for Stategic Studies, London; mem. Exec. Comm., U.S. Council, International Chamber of Commerce, N.Y.; mem. Comm. on U.S./Latin American Relations, Center for Inter-American Relations, N.Y.; Dir. Industria Electrica de Mexico, S.A., Mexico City 1963–69; Dep. Under-Sec. of State for Econ. Affairs 1969–72; U.S. Alt. Gov. IMF, International Bank for Reconstruction & Development, Inter-American Devel. Bank, Asian Devel. Bank 1969–72; mem. Bd. Dirs., Overseas Private Invest. Corp. 1971–72; Special Adviser, Dir. Div. Indsl. Resources Mut. Security Agency, Paris 1952–53; Served to 1st Lt. AUS 1942–46; ETO. *Clubs:* Harvard, University, Recess, Sky (N.Y.C.); Metropolitan, Federal City (Washington). Contributor to professional journals. *Address:* 775 Park Avenue, New York City, N.Y. 10021; and *office* 40 Wall Street, New York City, N.Y. 10005, U.S.A.

**SANBAR, Moshe.** Israeli economist and banker. *B.* 1926. *Educ.* Hebrew University MA, Economics, Statistics and Sociology. *M.* Bracha Rabinowich. *Career:* Project Director, Israel Inst. Applied Social Research, Jerusalem later Deputy Director 1951–58; Dir. Research Dept. Internal State Revenue Div. Ministry, Finance 1958–59; Deputy Dir. Internal State Revenue Division 1960–63; Dir. Budgets and Economic Adviser, Ministry of Finance 1963–68; Deputy Chmn. Bd. Dirs. Industrial Dev. Bank of Israel Ltd. 1968–69; Chief Economic Adv. Minister of Finance 1969–71; Chmn. Bd. Dirs. Ind. Dev. Bank of Israel, Acting Deputy, Minister Commerce & Industry 1970–71; Governor, Bank of Israel 1971–76; Chmn. Bd. Dirs., Electrochemical Industries (Frutarom) Ltd. since 1977; Prof. of Economics, Tel-Aviv Univ. since 1977. Chmn. Bd. Trustees, The Coll. of Administration; Chmn. Bd. Dirs. Habimah Nat. Theatre; Chmn. Economic Dev. Refugee Rehabilitation Trust; Pres. Israel Assn. of Graduates in the Social Sciences & Humanities; Hon. Pres. World Fedn. of Hungarian Jews. *Publications:* My Longest Year; articles research studies economic subjects. *Address:* 44 Pincas Street, Tel-Aviv; and Electrochemical Industries (Frutarom) Ltd., P.O.B. 1929, Haifa, Israel.

**SANBORN, Theodore S.** American. *B.* 1921. *Educ.* University of Minnesota. *M.* 1949, Dorothy Louise Cammack. *S.* Bruce C. and David S. *Daus.* Conradine W. and Margaret Ann. *Career:* Agent, Minnesota Mutual Life Ins. Co. 1945–46; Agency Supervisor, 1946–48, Vice-President 1948, Executive Vice-President 1949–50, Modern Life Ins. Co.; Pres. The North Central Companies Inc. 1960—. Pres. North Central Life Insurance Co. 1950—. Director: American National Bank 1964—. Former National Vice-Pres. & Chmn. Twin City Chapter Young Presidents' Org.; Mem., Chief Executives' Forum; Past State Chmn. of Life Underwriters' Training Council; Past Pres. & Chmn., National Consumers Credit Insurance Assn.; Trustee, Hamline Univ.; Elder, House of Hope Presbyterian Church. *Clubs:* St. Paul Athletic; Town & Country; The Minnesota; White Bear Yacht. *Address:* 13 Manitou Island, White Bear Lake, Minn. 55110, U.S.A.; and *office* 275 E. Fourth Street, St. Paul, Minnesota 55101.

**SANBURN, Richard Louis,** OBE. Canadian. Retired Editor-in-Chief, The Calgary Herald, Calgary. *B.* 1912. *Educ.* University of Alberta. *M.* 1941, Isabel Jean McCurdy. *Career:* Reporter: Shaunavon (Sask.) Standard 1931–35, Regina (Sask.) Leader Post 1935–40, and Winnipeg (Man.) Tribune 1940–42; R.C.A.F., Public Relations 1942–43, Pilot Officer; War Correspondent, Southam Press Ltd. 1943–45; Southam Press Correspondent, Parliamentary Press Gallery, Ottawa 1945–49; Chief, London (U.K.) Bureau, Southam Press 1949–51; Associate Editor, Calgary Herald 1951–54, Editor 1954–57; Editor-in-Chief 1957–76. *Member:* Canadian War Correspondents Assn. *Address:* 6912 Lowes Court S.W., Calgary, Alta. T3E 6G7, Canada.

**SANCHEZ-GAVITO, Vicente.** Mexican Diplomat. *B.* 1910. *Educ.* Mexico, B. of Laws. *Career:* Mexican Foreign Service Officer since 1935; Dir. Mex. Dip. Services 1947–51; Mem. U.N. Tribunales in Lybia & Erithrea 1951–55; Min. Counsellor Mex. Embassy Washington 1956–59; Ambassador to the Org. of American States (UAS) 1959–65; Amb. to Brazil 1965–70; Amb. to Court of St. James 1970–73; Amb. to Iceland 1970–73; Amb. to F.R. of Germany 1974–75; Adviser to the Min. of Foreign Affairs since 1975. *Awards:* Order of the Liberator (Venezuela); Order of Southern Cross (Brazil); GCOV (G.B.). *Address:* Av. Ruben Dario 17, Mexico City, Mexico.

**SANCHEZ-HERNANDEZ, Colonel Fidel.** *B.* 1917. *Educ.* El Divisadero; San Miguel; Military Academy, San Salvador; School of Armoured Weapons, Fort Knox, U.S.A.; School of General Staff, Madrid (1951–54). *M.* Marina Uriarte. *S.* Manuel Vicente, Fidel Angel. *Dau.* Arely, Marina, Teresa. *Career:* Military Attaché, Paris; General Inspector, Armed Forces; Air & Military Attaché, Washington, 1960. Entered politics, 1966; candidate of National Conciliation Party for Presidency; President of the Republic of El Salvador, 1967–72. *Awards:* Legion of Merit (U.S.A.); Order, Aztec Eagle (Mexico); Grand Cord, Order of the Quetzal (Guatemala); Special Cord of the Propitious Clouds (National Repc. of China); Grand Order, Foundation of the Republic (South Korea); Condecoración de la Gran Cruz de la Orden de Mérito en Grado Especial, otorgado porel Gobierno de la Repúplica Fed. de Alemania; Orden Nacional Rubén Dario Gran Cruz Placa de Oro, otorgada por el Gobierno de Nicaragua. *Address:* Partido de Conciliacion Nacional, Calle Arce 1128, San Salvador, El Salvador.

**SANCHEZ SANTAMARIA, Jacinto E. T.** Ambassador of Argentina. *B.* 1917. *Educ.* University of Buenos Aires (Law); International University of Social Studies Pro-Deo, Rome. *M.* 1940, Lelia Ana Faggionato. *S.* 1. *Daus.* 2. *Career:* On staff of the Argentine National Bank 1933–48; Official, Industrial Bank of Argentina 1948–50; Counsellor of Embassy, London 1955; Counsellor of Embassy and Chargé d'Affaires the Vatican 1956; Minister Counsellor 1958; Minister and Chargé d'Affaires, Embassy, Rome 1959 (late in the year En. Ex. & Min. Plen.); Ambassador to Republic of South Africa 1961–63; General Director, Personnel, Ministry of Foreign Affairs, Buenos Aires. Consul-General of Argentina in London 1964–67; Ambassador to Australia, 1967–69, to Turkey 1969. *Awards:* Cross, Order of Merit (Italy); Grand Cross of Merit with Bars, Order of Malta; Grand Cross with Bars, Order of St. Gregory Magnus—Civil Class (Holy See). *Clubs:* Jockey (Buenos Aires); Canning (London); Commonwealth (Canberra). *Address:* c/o Ministerio de Relaciones Exteriores, Buenos Aires, Argentina.

**SANCHEZ-VILELLA, Roberto.** President, People's Party. *B.* 1913. *Educ.* BS in Civil Engineering, Ohio State Univ. 1934. *M.* (1) 1936, Conchita Dapena Quinoñes (*Div.*). *Daus.* Vilma Josefina (Marquez), Evelyn Guadalupe (Monserrate); (2) 1967, Jeannette Ramos-Buonomo. *S.* Roberto José. *Career:* Civil Engineer, Insular and Fed. Governments 1934–41; Asst. Commissioner of Interior 1941–42; Director, Puerto Rico Transportation Authority 1942–45; Mayor of San Juan, P.R. 1945–46; Special Assistant to President of Senate 1946–47; Executive Secretary of Puerto Rico 1949–51; Commissioner of the Interior 1951–52; Secretary of Public Works 1952–59; Secretary of State, July 1952–Jan. 1965; Governor 1965–69. *Member:* Puerto Rico Coll. of Engineers; American Soc. of Public Administrators. Hon. LLD Ohio

State Univ. 1966. *Address:* 156 F.D. Roosevelt Avenue, Hato Rey, Puerto Rico 00918.

**SANDELSON, Neville Devonshire,** MP. British Barrister-at-Law. *B.* 1923. *Educ.* Westminster School; Trinity Coll., Cambridge—MA. *M.* 1959, Nana Karlinski. *S.* 1. *Daus.* 2. *Career:* Mem., London County Council 1952–58; Labour MP for Hayes & Harlington 1971–74, for Hillingdon, Hayes & Harlington since 1974; Mem. of Defence & External Affairs Sub-Cttee (Expenditure Cttee) since 1972; Mem. of Court of Brunel University since 1975; Treasurer of Manifesto Group (Parly. Labour Party) since 1974; Executive, Labour Cttee for Europe since 1972; Sec. of British-Greek Parly. Group since 1975; Called to the Bar, Inner Temple 1946. *Member:* Society of Labour Lawyers; Fabian Society; General & Municipal Workers Union. *Publications:* various Political Articles. *Clubs:* Reform. *Address:* Wetherby, Burleigh Lane, Ascot, Berks.; & House of Commons, London SW1.

**SANDERS, Donald Neil.** Australian Banker. *B.* 1927. *Educ.* Wollongong High Sch.; Univ. of Sydney—BEc. *M.* 1952. Betty Elaine Constance. *S.* 4. *Dau.* 1. *Career:* Commonwealth Bank of Australia 1943–60; Australian Treasury 1956; Bank of England 1960; Reserve Bank of Australia since 1960: Superintendent, Credit Policy Div., Banking Dept. 1964–66; Dep. Mgr., Banking Dept. 1966–67; Dep. Mgr., Research Dept. 1967–70; Australian Embassy, Washington D.C. 1968; Chief Mgr., Securities Markets Dept. 1970–72; Chief Mgr., Banking & Finance Dept. 1972–74; Adviser & Chief Mgr., Banking & Finance Dept. 1974–75; Dep. Governor & Dep. Chmn. of the Bd. since 1975. *Address: office* Reserve Bank of Australia, 65 Martin Place, Sydney, N.S.W. 2000, Australia.

**SANDILANDS, Sir Francis Edwin Prescott,** Kt 1976, CBE, MA. British. *B.* 1913. *Educ.* Eton, Corpus Christi Coll. Cambridge (MA), (Hon. Fellow). *M.* 1939, Susan Gillian Jackson. *S.* 2. *Career:* Dir. Trafalgar House Investments Ltd.; Finance For Industry Ltd.; Imperial Chemical Industries Ltd.; Plessey Co. Ltd.; Kleinwort Benson Lonsdale Ltd.; Royal Opera House, Covent Garden; Chmn. Commercial Union Assurance Co. Ltd.; Royal Trust Company of Canada; Cttee. on Invisible Exports. *Member:* British Overseas Trade Board; Cambridge Univ. Appts. Board 1963–66; Chmn. British Insurance Assn. 1965–67; Treas. Univ. Coll. London 1973—; Gov. Admin. Coll. Henley since 1973. *Address:* 53 Cadogan Square, London S.W.1; and *office* St. Helen's, London, E.C.3.

**SANDON Viscount,** (Dudley Danvers Granville Coutts Ryder), TD. *B.* 1922. *Educ.* Eton. *M.* 1949, Jeannette Rosalthé Johnston-Saint. *S.* Hon. Dudley Adrian Conroy. *Dau.* Hon. Rosalthé Frances. *Career:* Served 1939–45 War in N.W. Europe (wounded), India and Java. Hon. Treasurer: Staffordshire Society 1947–51; TA (City of London) Regt. R.A. (56 Armoured & Inf. Div.). Lieut.-Col. comm. 1962–64; Member Exec. Cttee. London Area Conservative Assn., 1949–50; Kensington Borough Council (Chmn. G.P. Cttee. 1957–59) 1950–65; Hon. Treas. Family Welfare Assn. 1951–65; Dir., Dinorwic Slate Quarries Co. Ltd. 1951–69; Hon. Treas. S. Ken. Cons. Assn. 1953–56. Central Council for Care of Cripples 1953–60; Manager of Fulham and Kensington Hospital Group 1953–56; Gen. Comm. for Income Tax 1954–71; Member, Bd. Governors, Univ. of Keele, N. Staffs., 1956–68; Pres. Staffordshire Society 1957–59; Pres. Wolverhampton S.W. Cons. Union. Assn. 1959–68; Dir. National Provincial Bank 1964–69; Member Kensington & Chelsea Council 1965–71 (Chmn. Finance Cttee. 1968–71); Deputy Chmn. Teaching Hospitals Assn. London Post-Graduate Cttee. 1968–69; Dir. Olympia Group 1968–73 (Chmn. 1971–73). Chmn. International Westminster Bank Ltd. since 1977; Dep. Chmn., Coutts & Co. since 1970 (Man. Dir. 1949); National Westminster Bank since 1971 (Dir. 1968); Dir. U.K. Provident Institution since 1955 (Dep. Chmn. 1956–64); Dir., Powell Duffryn Group since 1976; Sheepbridge Engineering Ltd. since 1977. *Member:* Goldsmiths Company Court of Assistants since 1972; Cttee. of Mgmt., Inst. of Psychiat. 1953–73 (Chmn. 1965–73); Bd. of Govs. Bethlem Royal & Maudsley (Post-Grad. Teaching) Hosps. 1955–73 (Chmn. 1965–73); Chmn. National Biological Standards Board since 1973; Lord Chancellor's Advisory Investment Cttees. for Court of Protection 1965–77 & for Public Trustee 1974–77. *Address:* 5 Tregunter Road, London SW10 9LS; and Sandon Hall, Stafford.

**SANDWELL, Percy Ritchie,** BASC, MEIC, P Eng. Consulting engineer. *B.* 1912. *Educ.* Grad. Univ. British Columbia, Hons. Mech. Eng.; Brock Scholarship Convocation Prize. *M.* (1) 1938. Lillian Patricia Scott. *Daus.* 3. (2) 1961, Inge Agnete Poulsson. *Stepsons* 3. *Stepdau.* 1. *Career:* Founded Sandwell & Co. Ltd. consulting and engineering services 1949; Dir. Athabasca Columbia Resources Ltd: British Columbia Medical Research Council; Glencannon Corp; Ritchie Developments Ltd.; Royal Bank of Canada; Pacific Basin Economic Council (Canadian Exec. Cttee.); Placer Development Ltd.; Hernando Island Holdings Ltd.; Lucerne Investments Ltd.; Ritchie Services Ltd. Chmn. Sandwell and Company Ltd. *Member:* Eng. Institute of Canada; Assn. of Consulting Engins. of Canada; CPPA; TAPPI; BPMA; APPITA. Member Atlantic Inst. Canadian Del. Int. Conference, Tokyo 1971, Brussels 1972. *Clubs:* Vancouver; Union (Victoria); Mount Royal (Montreal) Rainier (Seattle); Royal Vancouver Yacht (Vancouver); Royal Swedish Yacht (KSS); Transpacific Yacht (Los Angeles). *Address: office* 1550 Alberni Street, Vancouver, B.C. V6G 1A4, Canada.

**SÄNGER, Fritz.** Journalist. *B.* 1901. *Educ.* High School, Teaching Seminary, University, and Academy of Management. *M.* 1936, Susanne Kühne. *S.* 1. *Daus.* 2. Entered General-Anzeiger, Stettin, 1921; Press Secy. German Civil Servants' Union, 1923; Editor-in-Chief, Preussische Lehrerzeitung, and Press Secy., Prussian Teachers' Union, 1977; dismissed 1933; Editor, Frankfurter Zeitung, 1935, and Neues Wiener Tagblatt, 1943; Editor-in-Chief, Braunschweiger Neue Presse 1945; Sozialdemokratischer Pressedienst 1946; and Deutscher Pressedienst 1947–49; Deutsche Presse-Agentur 1949–59. Adviser, North German Broadcasting, 1950; German Press Cncl., 1957; German Broadcasting 1961. Member of Parliament (Deutscher Bundestag) 1961–69; Member, German Social Democratic Party since April 1920. *Publications:* German Parliamentary Handbook (1949–53–57); Soziale Demokratie, Commentary of the Programme of the SPD, 1960; Erich Ollenhauer. Reden und Aufsätze, 1964. Politek der Täuschungen, Missbrauch der Presse im Dritten Reich, 1975. *Address:* Erlenweg 28, Wedel (Holstein), Germany.

**SANGER, Gerald Fountaine,** CBE, JP. British. *B.* 1898. *Educ.* Shrewsbury School and Keble College, Oxford (MA, Oxon.). *M.* 1922, Margaret Hope Munroe. *S.* 2. *Dau.* 1. *Career:* Lieut. Royal Marine Artillery 1917–18; Secretary to Hon. Esmond Harmsworth, MP (present Viscount Rothermere) 1921–29; Editor, British Movietonews Ltd. 1929–53; Chairman, London General Cab. Co. 1951–57; Director: Daily Mail & General Trust Ltd., British Movietonews Ltd. Hon. Production Adviser, Conservative Films Association 1948–59; Director, Associated-Rediffusion Ltd. 1955–57. Appointed JP County of Surrey (Woking Bench). *Member:* Dorking Division of Surrey Conservative Assn. (Chmn. 1949–52; Pres. 1958–62), Old Salopian Club (Hon. Secy. 1948–55; Chmn. 1955–57; Pres. 1963). Pres., Keble Assn. 1965. Institute of Directors; member, Surrey County Council 1965–74. *Clubs:* Garrick. *Address:* Willingham Cottage, Send, Surrey.

**SANNESS, John (Christian Munthe).** Norwegian journalist and historian. *B.* 1913. *Educ.* Univ. of Oslo (Cand. Philol; Dr. Philos). *M.* 1939, Dagny Goa. *S.* Stian. *Daus.* Toril and Kari. *Career:* Pres., Norwegian Students Union 1940; Foreign Office and Norwegian Army in Britain 1942–45; International Secy., Norwegian National Trade Union Organization 1945–46; Foreign Editor, Arbeiderbladet, Oslo 1946–50, and 1955–59; Asst. Teacher, Lecturer, Univ. of Oslo 1940, and 1950–54; Dr. Philos., Univ. of Oslo 1959. Director, Norwegian Institute of International Affairs, 1959—. Professor of Modern History, Univ. of Oslo 1965—. *Publications:* Stalin og vi (Stalin & Ourselves), 1952; Aschehougs Verdenshistorie (Aschehougs World Hictory), Vol. V of Verden blir en 1850–1914 (The World Becomes one World); parts of vols. VII and VIII, Oslo 1953–57; Patrioter, intelligens og skandinaver (Patriots, Intelligentsia and Scandinavians), diss. 159; a large number of pamphlets, articles, etc. Member Det norske arbeiderparti (Norwegian Labour Party). Member Institute of Strategic Studies (London). Nobel Cttee., of Norwegian Storting, 1970. *Address:* Langerudsvingen 18, Oslo; and Norwegian Institute of International Affairs, Parkveien 19, Oslo, Norway.

**SANTA CRUZ, Marques de.** *B.* 1902. *Educ.* Madrid University (Law) and Oxford University; Hon. Fellow, New College, Oxford 1959. *M.* Casilda de Silva, Marquesa de Santa Cruz (Duquesa de San Carlos); *S.* Marqués del Viso, José Carlos F. Villaverde, Rafael F. Villaverde. *Dau.* Casilda F. Villaverde de Eraso. *Career:* Permanent Under-Sec. of State for Foreign Affairs 1955; Ambassador, Cairo 1953; Minister, The

Hague 1950 and Copenhagen 1948: Minister-Counsellor in London 1944: Ambassador of Spain to Court of St. James's, 1958–72; Permanent Councillor of State since 1972. *Awards:* Grand Cross: Order of Carlos III, Order of Isabel la Católica, El Mérito Naval (Spain), Dannebrog (Denmark), Orange-Nasau (Netherlands), de Cristo (Portugal), Cruzeiro do Sul (Brazil); Caballero de la Orden Militar de Calatrava. *Clubs:* Nuevo (Madrid); White's, Beefsteak (London). *Address:* San Bernardino 14, Madrid, Spain.

**SANTA-CRUZ, Alfonso.** Chilean. *B.* 1907. *Educ.* Law, Political and Social Sciences, University of Chile 1930; Graduate work in economics, Harvard University 1944–45. Professor, Catholic University of Chile 1935—. *M.* 1947, Irene L. de Santa Cruz; *S.* Diego and Cristobal. *Daus.* Francisca, Guadalupe, Fernanda and Carmen. Economic Affairs Officer UNO 1947; Secy. of the Commission and Exec. Asst. to Exec. Secy. of ECLA (UN Economic Commission for Latin America) 1951, Dir. Mexico office 1959; Dep. Exec. Secy. ECLA 1962; Ambassador to Austria, Hungary, Czechoslovakia and Permanent Representative to International Atomic Energy Organization 1965; Chief Chilean Deleg. to U.N. ECOSC 1966; Ambassador of Chile to Belgium, Luxembourg and the European Economic Community, 1967–71. *Awards:* Austria Goldene Ehrenzeichen am Bandi. Is a Christian Democrat. *Club:* de la Union (Santiago, Chile). *Address:* c/o Ministry of Foreign Affairs, Santiago, Chile.

**SANTER, Dr. Jacques.** Luxembourg Politician. *B.* 1937. *Educ.* Secondary Studies, Athénée of Luxembourg; University Studies in Law. Strasbourg & Paris; Institut d'Etudes Politiques, Paris (Economic & Financial Dept.). *M.* 1967, Danièle Binot (Prof.). *S.* 2. *Career:* Barrister, Luxembourg 1961–64; Attaché, Min. of Works 1963–66; Parly. Sec., Christian Socialist Group 1966–72; Sec.-Gen., Christian Socialist Party 1972–74; Sec. of State for Social & Cultural Affairs 1972–74; Elected Deputy 1974; Pres., Christian Socialist Party since 1974; Vice-Pres., European Parliament 1975; Alderman of the Town of Luxembourg since 1976. *Decorations:* Grand Cross of Leopold II (Belgium); Order of G. Vladimirescu (II) (Romania); Grand Cross, Orange-Nassau (Netherlands); Grand Cross of Merit (Fed. Rep. of Germany). *Address:* 7 rue Tockert, Luxembourg; and *office* 37 rue de Curé, Luxembourg.

**SANTESSON, Per V.** Swedish judge. *B.* 22 April 1892. *Educ.* University of Stockholm (LL.B). *M.* 1942, Elsa Fischer. *Dau.* Mona; Deputy Circuit Judge 1918; Acting Secretary, Court of Appeal 1920; Assistant Under-Secretary Ministry of the Interior 1926–30, Ministry of Justice 1930–32; Judge of Appeal 1930; member, Committee for Reform of Legal Procedure 1932–38; Chairman, Board for Legal Aid to Poor People, Stockholm 1936–67; Judge, Supreme Court 1939–57; Chairman, Restitution Court 1945–58; Knight Grand Cross, Order of North Star. *Address:* Strandvägen 55, 11523 Stockholm, Sweden.

**SANTOS, Emmanuel Tiu.** Philippine statesman. *B.* 1938. UP College of Liberal Arts (AA, AB); UP College of Law, LLB. *M.* Carmelita Soriente-Santos. *S.* 1. *Daus.* 2. *Career:* Manager, Corporate Secy. and Legal Counsel, Cabanatuan City Devel. Bank 1961–66; Instructor, Phil. Wesleyan College 1963–66; Corp. Secy. and Legal Counsel, Cabanatuan City Dev. Bank 1966–74; Tech. Asst. Mfctrs. Bank and Trust Co. 1966–67; Lecturer of Business Laws, UP College of Business Admin, 1967–70; Head, Dept. of Business Development and Economic Research, Manufacturers Bank and Trust Co. 1967–68; Partner, Santos, Santos & Assocs. Law Office 1966—, Seminar. Dir. Prof. Training and Review Academy 1967–68; Man. Dir. Empress Handicrafts Inc. 1968–69; Instr. of Business and Finance, UE College of Bus. Admin. 1968–70; Asst. Vice-Pres. Manufacturers Bank & Trust Co. 1968–74; Dir. Perfect Realty & Invest. Co. 1968—; Corp. Secy. Hotel Filipinas Inc., Hotel Mabuhay Inc., Empress Trading Corp., Intern. Supermarket Inc. 1968—; Pres. E. T. Santos Realty Co. 1969—; Legal Counsel Mead Johnson Labor Union and Manila Times Publ. Co. 1970–71; Delegate Const. Convention, Rep. of Philippines 1971–73; Dir. Vice-Pres and Asst. Corp. Secy. Manufacturers' Bank and Trust Co. 1973–74; President MAHOITI (Manila House of Intern. Trade Inc. 1974—; Mem. Phil. Delegation, ASEAN Seminar on Collective Bargaining & Labour Arbitration. Observation Tours of M. East, Europe and U.S.A. (1966) and Southeast Asia (1967 & 1977). *Awards:* Medals and Diplomas UP, YMCA. *Founder:* Nueva Ecija Bankers Assn. (Past-Pres. 1963–64); *President:* St. Scholastrica's PCA 1973; Phil. Soc. of Constitutional Law; Phil. Acad. of Professional Arbitrators; *Chmn.* Cttee on Public Information, Philconsa, 1974. *Mem.* Nat. Pres. Club 1961–66: Development Bankers' Assn. of Philippines 1961–66; Philconsa 1971–74; Phil. Soc. Intern. Law 1973—; Intern. Law Assn., London, 1974; Am. Soc. Intern. Law 1974—; ASEAN Soc. of Labour 1977—. *Sec.-Gen.* Phil. Chamber of Shoe Mftrs. Inc. 1961; Phil. Org. for Human Rights 1977—. Vice-Chmn. Cttee. on Mgmt. NE YMCA 1962–63. *Secy.* NE Rice-Traders and Millers' Assn. 1967–68. *Publications:* numerous contributions magazines and journals, columnist, The Manila Chronicle 1961; Business writer, The Manila Daily Bulletin 1966–67; Features Writer, Variety Magazine 1967–68; Man. Editor, Philippine Journal of Business and Finance 1967–68; Columnist "Law & You", in Bulletin Today; Author, Philippine Business Laws (1969); Constitution of the Philippines: Notes & Comments. *Address:* 268 Escolta, Manila, Philippines.

**SANTOS MATIAS, Albertino dos.** Portuguese diplomat. *Educ.* Lic. in Law, University of Coimbra. *M.* 1935, Capitolina Pinto dos Santos. *Career:* Lawyer 1932–45; Ministry Foreign Affairs, Lisbon 1945; Consul, Durban 1946; Foreign Office 1953; 2nd Secretary of Legation and Chargé d'Affaires, Tokyo 1954; 1st Secretary and Chargé d'Affaires, Bangkok 1956; Foreign Office, Lisbon 1958; Counsellor of Embassy and Chargé d'Affaires, Dublin 1960 and Copenhagen Feb. 1962. Minister to Ecuador May 1962–65. Office of Secy. Gen. of Foreign Affairs 1965–67; Ambassador to Pakistan 1967, to Greece 1974; Secy. Gen. of Foreign Affairs since 1975. *Address:* Avenue Infante Santo, 4–3-Dir., Lisbon, Portugal.

**SANZ-BRIZ, Angel.** Spanish diplomat. *B.* 1910. *Educ.* Licencié en Droit. *M.* 1942, Adela Quijano. *S.* Juan. *Daus.* Adela, Paloma, Pilar and Angela. *Career:* Chargé d'Affaires in Cairo 1939–41 and Budapest 1943–44; Ambassador, Guatemala 1960–62; Delegate Gen. Assembly U.N. 1960–64; Consul General, New York 1962–64; Ambassador Lima 1964–67; The Hague 1967–72; Brussels 1972–73; Peking 1973–76; Holy See since 1976. *Awards:* Gran Cruz: Mérito Civil (Spain), Couronne (Belgium); Quetzal (Guatemala); S. Gregorio Magno (Holy See); Orange Nassau (The Netherlands); del Sol (Peru); Officer Leg. d'Honneur (France). *Clubs:* Real Club de Puerta de Hierro (Madrid). *Address:* Embassy of Spain to the Holy See, Palazzo di Spagna, Piazza di Spagna 57, 00187 Rome, Italy.

**SANZ, Luis Santiago.** Ambassador of Argentina. *B.* 1920. *Educ.* University of Buenos Aires (Doctor Jur.). *M.* 1946, Lucia de Urquiza Estrada. *S.* 3. *Daus.* 3. *Career:* Director. S. American Dept., Ministry of Foreign Affairs 1955; Director-General of Policy 1958–61 and 1965–67. Argentinian Representative at 14th General Assembly of U.N. 1959. Counsellor and technical adviser of delegation to 5th meeting of American Ministers of Foreign Affairs 1959, Secy.-General at the 11th meeting 1967. Ambassador on special mission to Brazil and Paraguay 1960. Chmn. of delegation on negotiation of boundary limits between Argentina and Uruguay 1961. Ambassador to Denmark 1961–65; Belgium and Luxembourg, 1967–70. Chief of delegation to 3rd Consultative Meeting on the Antarctic Treaty 1964. Representative at the 2nd Extraordinary Inter-American Conference 1965, and Secretary-General of the 3rd Conf., 1965. Representative at 3rd and 4th meetings of Preparations Commission on denuclearization of Latin America 1966–67. Under-Secy. of State, a.i. 1966. Professor of Economic and Social History 1947–60, and Prof. of Diplomatic History, Univ. of Buenos Aires 1952, of Argentinian International Policy at High School of War 1960 and 1967. Ambassador to Uruguay 1970–73; Adviser, Antarctic National Direction 1976, and in Strategic Center Studies of the Navy 1975. *Member:* Inst. of Law History, Inst. of International Law, Inst. of Diplomatic History, Inst. of International Studies (Argentina). Corresponding Member, Royal Hispano-America Acad. of Cadiz. Grand Cross Orders from Peru, Denmark, Belgium, Italy, Bolivia, Brazil, Paraguay, Malta, Japan; Grand Official, Austria and Ecuador. *Publications:* La Cuestion de Misiones su historia diplomatica (1957); Historia diplomatica desde la Presidencia de Mitre hasta (1930). *Club:* Jockey (Buenos Aires). *Address:* Diego Palma 1755, Buenos Aires, Argentina.

**SAOUMA, Edouard.** Lebanese. Director-General, FAO. *B.* 1926. *Educ.* Ingénieur Agronome—Ecole Supérieure d'Ingénieurs de l'Université de Montpellier, France. *M.* 1951, Ines Forero. *S.* 1. *Daus.* 2. *Career:* Dir. of the Tel Amara Agricultural School 1952–53; Dir. of the National Centre for Farm Mechanization 1954–55; Dir.-Gen., National Inst. for Agric. Research 1955–62; Minister of Agric., Fisheries & Forestry, Lebanon 1970: FAO—Dep. Regional Rep. for

Asia & Far East, New Delhi 1962–65; FAO—Dir. of Land & Water Development Div., Rome 1965–75; FAO—Dir.-Gen. since 1976. *Decorations:* Order of the Cedar (Lebanon); Said Akl Prize (Lebanon); Merite Agricole (France). *Address:* FAO, Via delle Terme di Caracalla, 00100 Rome, Italy.

**SARABHAI, Gautam.** Indian industrialist. *B.* 4 March 1917. *Educ.* Cambridge University (MA). *M.* 1947, Shrimati Kamalini Khatau. *Daus.* 2. *Career:* Chmn. Karamchand Premchand Pvt. Ltd. (Sarabhai Chemicals) and Dir., Calico Mills, Bakubhai & Ambalal Ltd. (London). *Address:* The Retreat, Shahibag, Ahmedabad, India.

**SARAGAT, Giuseppe.** Italian Statesman. *B.* 1898. Is a University graduate in Economics. Joined the Socialist Party in 1922 and was appointed to the Party Executive 1925. In 1926 went into exile with other members of the Party Executive—in Austria and France, to take part in the anti-Fascist movement. On the collapse of the Fascist régime returned to Italy to organize the Socialist Party. During the German occupation arrested in Rome, but helped to escape and to carry on, underground, his activities as member of the Party Executive. After the liberation of Rome became Minister without Portfolio in first Bonomi Cabinet, June-Dec. 1944; later appointed Ambassador to France and member of Italian Deleg. to Peace Conf. 1945–46. On June 2, 1946, the first elections of the post-war and post-Fascist period were called to elect a Constitutional Assembly and to draft a new Italian Constitution; Saragat was elected to the Assembly and became its President on June 25, 1946. Towards the end of 1946 difficulties arose within the ranks of the Socialist Party between those supporting unit of action with the Communists and those who believed in the party's autonomy and independence; led by Saragat the latter left the Socialist Party to form the Italian Workers' Socialist Party, later named Italian Social Democratic Party. In the De Gasperi Cabinet Saragat was Vice-Pres. of the Cncl. of Ministers 1947–48. Re-elected to Parl. in 1948–53–58–63, Saragat held various posts; was re-appointed to his previous post in the 4th and subsequent De Gasperi Cabinets; was also Min. of Merchant Marine. Later was re-appointed in the Scelba Cabinet, Feb. 1954–July 1955, and again in the first Segni Cabinet, July 1955–May 1957. Having resumed the secretariat of the Party, which he had resigned owing to his ministerial responsibilities, he held that office from Nov. 1957 until he became Minister of Foreign Affairs in the first and second Moro Cabinets. President of the Republic of Italy 1964–71; Pres., Social Democratic Party 1975–76 and since 1976. *Address:* c/o Partito Socialista Democratico, Via Santa Maria in Via 12, 00187 Rome, Italy.

**SARAIYA, Ramanial Gokaldas.** OBE, BA, B.Sc. Sem. Indian cotton merchant. *B.* 16 Jan. 1898. *M.* 1920, Padmavati. *S.* 3. *Career:* Chairman, All-India Co-operative Planning Committee 1945–46; Leader, Indian Delegation, International Cotton Advisory Committee, Cairo 1948, Brussels 1949, Washington 1950 and 1962, Mexico City 1960; Chmn., ICAC meeting 1963; member, Indian Delegation, Tech. Meeting on Co-operatives in Asia and the Far East under the aegis of the F.A.O., Lucknow 1949; Chairman, Narandas Rajaram & Co. Pvt. Ltd.; Vice-President, Indian Central Cotton Cttee. 1947–52 Pres., Federation of Indian Chambers of Commerce and Industry (1953–54), and All-India Co-op. Union 1952–54; President, Indian Merchants Chamber 1950; Hon. Export Promotion Adviser to Govt. of India 1959–68; Chmn., Maharashtra State Rd. Transport 1954–74; Chairman, Banking Commission (Govt. of India 1969–62); Director, Sutle, Cotton Mills Ltd. and other companies; Acting Head of International Chamber of Com. delegate to U.N. Conf. on Int. Commercial Arbitration, May-June 1958. Awarded Padma Bhushan 1963. *Address:* Navsari Chambers, Outram Road, Fort, Bombay and 'Casa Grande', Little Gibbs Road, Bombay 6, India.

**SARBANES, Paul.** American Senator & Lawyer. *B.* 1933. *Educ.* Princeton Univ.—AB *magna cum laude*; Oxford Univ., Rhodes Scholar; Harvard Law Sch.—LLB *cum laude*. *M.* 1960, Christine Dunbar Sarbanes. *S.* 2. *Dau.* 1. *Career:* Law clerk, Judge Morris Soper, U.S. Court of Appeals 1960–61; Associate in law firm of Piper & Marbury 1961–62; Asst. to Chmn. of Pres. Kennedy's Council of Economic Advisers 1962–63; Exec. Dir., Baltimore Charter Revision Comm. 1963–64; Associate, law firm of Venable, Baetjer & Howard 1965–70; mem., Maryland House of Delegates 1966–70; mem., U.S. House of Reps. 1970–76; U.S. Senator from Maryland since 1977. Democrat. *Address:* 2327 Dirksen Senate Office Building, Washington, D.C. 20510, U.S.A.

**SARELL, Sir Roderick Frances Gisbert,** KCMG, KCVO. *B.* 1913. *Educ.* Radley and Magdalen College, Oxford. *M.* 1946, Pamela Muriel Crowther-Smith. *S.* 3. *Career:* Counsellor and Consul-General, Rangoon 1953–56; Consul-General, Algiers 1956–59; Head of Southern Dept., Foreign Office 1959–61, and Head of General Dept., F.O. 1961–63; Ambassador to Libya, 1964–69; to Turkey 1969–73. *Awards:* KCMG 1968; KCVO 1971; C.M.G. 1958; Coronation Medal 1953. *Clubs:* Oriental, Royal Overseas League; Leander. *Address:* The Litten, Hampstead Norreys, Newbury, Berks.

**SARGENT, Sir Donald,** KBE, CB, British Civil Servant. *B.* 1906. *Educ.* King Edward's School, Birmingham Trinity College, Cambridge (B.; Classical Tripos 1st Cl.). *M.* 1944, Dorothy Mary Raven. *S.* 1. *Career:* Asst. Principal, G.P.O. 1929; Private Secretary to Director-General 1935–37 Principal 1937; Home Office (A.R.P. Dept.) 1938–41; Principal Private Secretary to Postmaster-General 1941–44; Asst. Secretary, G.P.O. 1944; Deputy Chief Administrative Officer, Control Commission, Germany 1946–47; Imperial Defence College 1948; Director of Personnel and Accommodation, G.P.O. 1949–53; Director of Postal Service, G.P.O. 1953–55; Deputy Director-General, G.P.O. 1955–59; Chairman, Executive and Liaison Cttee. of Universal Postal Union 1957–59; Secy., Natl. Assistance Bd. 1959–66. Secretary of the Supplementary Benefits Commission, and Dep. Secy. Ministry of Social Security 1966–68. Director, Abbeyfield Society, 1968–70. Chairman, Civil Service Retirement Fellowship 1968–74; Chairman, Society of Pension Consultants since 1970. *Clubs:* M.C.C.; United University. *Address:* 1 Croham Valley Road, South Croydon, Surrey, and *office* 6–7, Buckingham Street, London, W.C.2.

**SARGENT, Joseph Denny.** American. *B.* 1929. *Educ.* Yale Univ. (BA 1952). *M.* 1955, Mary A. Tennant. *S.* Robert and Thomas. *Daus.* Mary Diane and Suzanne. *Career:* Managing Partner, Conning & Co., Hartford, Conn. 1957—; Chairman of Board' and Treasurer Sherburne Corp. 1957—; Treasurer and Dir.' Minnesota National Life Insurance Co. 1964–71; Director Terry Steam Turbine Co.; Beekley Corp.; Am-Cam Industries Inc. 1972—; Pres. & Dir. Fox-Pitt, Kelton, London. Trustee: Wadsworth Atheneum 1965—, Children's Services of Connecticut 1962—; Dir., Hartford Hospital; Dir., Hartford Symphony Soc. 1966–68; Trustee, Westledge School 1968–72. *Clubs:* Hartford Golf, University, Hartford Yale (all of Hartford). *Address:* 25 Colony Road, West Hartford, Conn. 06117; and *office* 41 Lewis Street, Hartford, Conn., U.S.A.

**SARIDIS, Eleftherios.** Greek. *B.* 1907. *Educ.* Freres des Ecoles Chretiennes Constantinople; School of Commerce, Freres Maristes, Athens. *M.* 1934, Susan Giovan. *Career:* Gen. Mgr. Saridis S.A. *Member:* Interior Decorators & Designers Assn. Ltd., London; Union, Societies Anonymes; Union of Greek Industrialists. *Award:* Gold Cross, Royal Batralia of the Phoenix. *Clubs:* Greek Jockey; Greek Golf. *Address:* 3 Neofitou Douka Street, Athens 138, Greece and *office* 11G Frangoudi Street (Syngros Avenue), Athens 404.

**SARKIS, Elias.** Lebanese Banker & Politician. *Career:* Pres., Management Cttee. of Intra Bank 1967; Gov., Bank of Lebanon 1968; Pres., Comm. Supérieure des Banques; President of Lebanon since 1976. *Awards:* Medal of Independence 1st Class, Jordan. *Address:* Office of the Presidency, Palais de Baabda, Beirut, Lebanon.

**SARTRE, Pierre Emile.** French naval engineer. *B.* 10 May 1909. *Educ.* École des Beaux-Arts, Marseilles; École Poly technique; École Supérieure Nationale du Génie Maritime. *M.* Marguerite Gardet. *S.* 1. *Dau.* 1. *Career:* Engaged in repairing destroyers and cruisers and in building minesweepers, Lorient Arsenal 1935–40; with Research Dept. of Construction of the Fleet and Arsenal Installations, Ministry of the Navy 1940–44; engaged in recuperation of enemy material and its adaptation to the needs of the Fleet and arsenals 1944–45; Head of Naval Section of the Minister's Department, Ministry of Armament 1946–47; supervised work and construction of Navy and Merchant Navy at Marseilles 1947–49: Manager, Compagnie des Messageries Maritimes 1948–76; Counsellor of "Compagnie Maritimes" (Ret'd. 1977). Officier de la Légion d'Honneur; Commandeur du Mérite Maritime. *Address:* 135 Bd. Raspail, Paris 6, France.

**SASAKI, Tadashi.** Japanese banker. *B.* 1907. *Educ.* Graduated, Dept. Economics, Tokyo Imperial Univ. (now Tokyo University). *M.* 1934, Kusuko Tsukasaki (*Dec.*). *S.* Hajime. *Dau.* Eiko (Hatano). *Career:* Joined the Bank of Japan

1930; Chief Personnel Dept. 1946–47; Chief Coordination Dept. 1947–51; Chief Business Dept. 1951–54; Exect. Director 1954–62; Vice-Governor 1962–69; Chmn. Policy Bd. and Governor of the Bank of Japan 1969–74. *Address:* 5-34-10 Yoyogi, Shibuya-ku, Tokyo 151, Japan.

**SATTERTHWAITE, Joseph C.** American diplomat. Consultant to the Department of State, Washington 1966—. *B.* 1900. *Educ.* University of Michigan (AB and AM); LL.D. Univ. of Michigan 1958. *M.* 1947, Leyla Libars. *Dau.* Ruth Eva. *Career:* Entered Foreign Service 1924, served first at Stuttgart; Department of State 1926; Guadalajara 1927; Mexico City 1929; Buenos Aires 1934; Baghdad 1937; Ankara 1940; Damascus 1944; Dept. of State 1945; Personal Representative of the President with rank of Minister, Special U.S. Diplomatic Mission to Nepal 1947; Deputy Dir., Office of Near Eastern and African Affairs 1947 (Dir. 1948); Ambassador to Ceylon 1949; Diplomatic Agent at Tangier 1953; Ambassador to Burma 1955; Director-General of the Foreign Service 1957; Asst. Secy. of State for African Affairs, 1958; Ambassador to Repub. of South Africa 1961–66; Pres. DACOR (Diplomatic & Consular Officers. Retired) since 1974. *Address:* 5120 Upton Street, N.W., Washington, D.C. 20016, U.S.A.

**SAUCIER, John James,** QC. Canadian barrister and solicitor. *B.* 15 May 1903. *Educ.* University of Alberta (BA, LL.B). *M.* (1) 1933, Lillian DuBois. *Daus.* Suzanne, Mary, Carolyn. (2) 1974, Margaret Kayler. *Career:* Assistant Private Secretary to the Prime Minister of Canada, Jan. 1934–June 1935; President, Calgary Chamber of Commerce 1947; Associate, Jones, Black & Co.; Past President, Canadian Bar Assn.; Past Pres., Law Society of Alberta. *Address:* 2725 Carleton St. S.W., Calgary, Alberta T2T 3LI, Canada.

**SAUERWEIN, Georges.** French. Officer Order National du Mérite; Chevalier Legion of Honour; Officer du Mérite Militaire; Chevalier des Palmes Academiques. Management Consultant. *B.* 1904. *Educ.* BS. *M.* 1929,. Marcelle Paillard. *Dau.* Marie-Claude (Mrs. P. C. Holzberger) *Career:* Merchant Marine (French Naval Reserve) 1922–26; Secretary, later Asst. General Manager *Le Matin* 1926–39; Commanding Officer of admiral flagship, French Mediterranean Naval Forces 1939–40; Manager, Regional French Relief Organization (Lyons) 1941–44, Agence Havas 1945–48, and Information Dept. Esso-France 1949–66; Lecturer at Social Sciences Faculty, Sorbonne, Paris. Management Consultant 1967—. *Publications:* many articles and lectures, dealing mostly with the social importance of information and communications. *Address:* 78 Feucherolles, France.

**SAUNDERS, Sir John (Anthony Holt),** CBE, DSO, MC, British banker. *B.* 1917. *Educ.* Bromsgrove School. *Married. Daus.* Elisabeth Ann and Diana Mary. *Career:* Chmn. London Adv. Cttee. The Hong Kong and Shanghai Banking Corp; International Commercial Bank Ltd.; Dir. British Bank of the Middle East London; P & O S.N. Co.; World Shipping and Investment Co. Ltd. Hong Kong; World Maritime Ltd. Bermuda; World Finance Int. Ltd. Bermuda. *Clubs:* M.C.C., Oriental (London). *Address:* 17 Hyde Park Gate, London, S.W.7 and The Dairy House, Maresfield, Sussex.

**SAUNDERS, Joseph Benjamin, Jr.** American. *B.* 1901. *Educ.* two years at university, and one year at business college. *M.* (1) 1926, Gladys LaVerne Edmondson (*Dec.*). *S.* Joseph B. III. *Dua.* Eleanor Suzanne (Mrs. L. M. Inkley, Jr.). *M.* (2) 1968, Georgia J. Comegys. *Career:* Pres. Dir. Triangle Refineries (Houston, Tex.) 1946–62, and Withers & Wellford Oil Co. (Memphis, Tenn.) until 1950. Vice-Pres. and Dir.: Atlas Processing Co. (Shreveport, La.) until 1966, Transcentral Oil Corp. (Chicago) until 1955, and Triangle Pipeline Co. (Shreveport) until 1954. Dir., Moran Shoe Co. (St. Louis, Mo.) until 1966. Vice-Pres., Texas Eastern Transmission Co. (Houston) until 1958. Vice-Chairman of the Board, Kerr-McGee Corp. Chairman, Triangle Refineries, 1962—. Director: The Liberty National Bank and Trust Co., Southwest Title and Trust Co., and Oklahoma City Chamber of Commerce. Trustee, Oklahoma City University. *Honours:* Hon. LL.D. Okla. City Univ., 1967; Legion of Honor—Order of DeMolay. *Member:* Amer. Petroleum Inst.; National Petroleum Refiners' Assn.; Independent Petroleum Association. *Clubs:* Sleepy Hollow Country (N.Y.C.); Seigniory (Quebec); Oklahoma Golf & Country, Tower, Petroleum, Beacon (Oklahoma City); River Oaks Country, Lakeside Country, Coronado, Houston Cork and International (Houston; St. Louis; Missouri Athletic (St. Louis); Kona Kai (San Diego. Cal.); Shreveport (Shreveport, La.). *Address:* 3435 Westheimer Road, Houston, Texas 77027; and *office* P.O. Box 2944, Houston, Texas 77001; Kerr-McGee Building, Oklahoma City, Okla. 73102, U.S.A.

**SAUNDERS, Peter Paul,** B.Comm. Canadian. *B.* 1928. *Educ.* Vanouver College, and University of British Columbia (B. Comm. 1948). *M.* 1956, Nancy Louise McDonald. *Daus.* Christine Elizabeth and Paula Marie. *Career:* Chmn., President and Dir. Cornat Industries Ltd.; Chmn. & Pres., Cornat Corp.; Chmn., Bralorne Resources Ltd.; Versatile Manufacturing Ltd.; Coronation Credit Corp. Ltd.; Chmn. & Dir. Johnston Terminals & Storage Ltd.; Dir. Campeau Corp.; Western Broadcasting Company Ltd.; British Columbia Television & Broadcasting System Ltd.; Wajax Ltd.; B.C. Ice and Cold Storage Ltd.; Burrard Dry Dock Co. Ltd.; Quadra Steel Ltd.; Bennett Pollution Controls Ltd.; Bank of British Columbia; Northwest Sports Enterprises Ltd.; Canfor Investments Ltd. *Member:* Canadian Chamber of Commerce, Vancouver Bd. of Trade; Board, Governors York House School. Vancouver; Dir. Vancouver Symphony Socy.; Pres. & Dir., Canadian Cancer Socy. (BC and Yukon Reg.); Member, Vancouver Advisory Board of Nat. Trust Co. Ltd. Roman Catholic. *Clubs:* University; Shaughnessy Golf and Country; Vancouver Lawn Tennis and Badminton; Royal Vancouver Yacht. *Address:* 2186 S.W. Marine Drive, Vancouver, B.C. V6P 6B5, Canada.

**SAUNDERSON, Alexander John Raeburn.** South African. *B.* 1915. *Educ.* Durban High School. *M.* 1946, Doreen Sylvia Wise. *S.* Michael, Derek, Robin. *Career:* Member, Natal Chamber of Industries; responsible for developing a new method in connection with the use of porcelain enamel tiling in architectural enamelling; Works Manager, Union Enamel Co. Ltd., 1933–45; Managing Director, Enamel Products (Pty.) Ltd., Neon Electric Products (Pty.) Ltd., and Abbottsgarth (Pty.) Ltd. *Address:* Gardens Road, Hill-Crest, Natal, South Africa.

**SAUVAGNARGUES, Jean.** French diplomat. *B.* 1915. *Educ.* Higher Normal School; Agrégé de l'Université. *M.* 1948, Lise Marie L'Evesque. *S.* Philippe and François. *Daus.* Sylvie and Anne. *Career:* Attaché, Embassy, Bucharest 1941; served with the Free French Forces 1943; Cabinet of the High Commission, Beirut 1943; M. Massigli 1944; in the Army, June 1944–May 1945; Cabinet of General de Gaulle 1945–46; Specialist on German questions, Quai d'Orsay 1947–55; in Cabinet of M. Pinay 1955; in negotiations concerning the Saar, Jan.–June 1956; Ambassador to Ethiopia 1956–60; to Tunisia, 1962–70; Director, African and Middle-Eastern Affairs, Ministry of Foreign Affairs 1960–62; Ambassador to the Federal Republic of Germany, Bonn, 1970–74; Minister of Foreign Affairs 1974–76; Ambassador to the Court of St. James's since 1977. *Awards:* Officer, Legion of Honour; Croix de Guerre avec palme; Commandeur de l'Ordre du Merite. *Address:* The French Embassy, 58 Knightsbridge, London, SW1 7JT.

**SAUVÉ, Hon. Maurice,** PC, BA, LL.B, Ph.D. *B.* 1923. *Educ.* St. Mary's Coll., Montreal (BA): Univ. of Montreal (LL.B), London School of Economics, and Univ. of Paris (Ph.D). *M.* 1948, Jeanne Benoit. *S.* Jean-François. *Career:* Tech. Adviser to Canadian and Catholic Confed. of Labour 1952–55; Asst. Sec., Royal Com. on Canada's Economic Prospects 1955–58; Dir. of Public Relations for Quebec Liberal Party 1958–62: Member of Parliament for Magdalen Island, P.Q. 1962 (re-elected 1963 & 1965); appointed to Privy Council and Minister of Forestry 1964–66; Ministry of Forestry & Rural Developments 1966–68; Vice-Pres. Administration-Consolidated-Bathurst, 1968—; Dir. B.P. Canada; Benson & Hedges (Canada) Ltd.; The Halifax Insurance Co.; The Commercial Life Assurance Co. of Canada; Automobiles Renault Canada Ltée; Liberal. *Address:* 281 McDougall Avenue, Montreal, P.Q., and 800 Dorchester Boul., W. Montreal, H3B 1Y9, Quebec.

**SAVAGE, Sir Alfred William Lungley,** KCMG. British administrator. *B* 5 May 1903. *Educ.* Owens School, London. *M.* 1931, Doreen Hopwood. *S.* 1. *Dau.* 1. *Career:* Entered Civil Service 1920; Assistant Treasurer, Northern Rhodesia 1928; Deputy Treasurer, Fiji 1935; Deputy Treasurer, Palestine 1939; Deputy Financial Secy., Palestine 1940, Nigeria 1946; Financial Secretary, Nigeria 1948; Governor and Commander-in-Chief, Barbados 1949–53; of British Guiana 1953–55; Second Crown Agent 1955–63. Chairman, West African Currency Board 1956–69. *Address:* 19 Caledonia Place, Clifton, Bristol B58 4DJ.

**SAVAGE, Everard Richards.** South African director of companies. *Educ.* Durban High School. *M.* 1950, Molly Kathleen Schoentjes. *S.* 2. *Daus.* 1. *Career:* Man. Dir. Thomson Savage & Co. (Pty.) Ltd., Thomson Supply Co. (Pty.) Ltd., Thomson Savage Land Co. (Pty.) Ltd., Savage Properties (Pty.) Ltd. Director: Felt & Textiles (S.A.) Ltd., Coronation Brick & Tile Co. Ltd., and other companies. Past President, South African Federated Chamber of Industries; Chairman, Industrial Council for the Clothing Industry (Natal) 1941–60; Chairman, National Co-ordinating Council for the Clothing Industry of South Africa 1945; President, Natal Chamber of Industries 1952; Chairman, Natal Clothing Manufacturers Association 1942–52. *Address:* Chrisleigh, Lee Drive, Westville, Durban, South Africa.

**SAW, Evan Staples,** FCA, FCIS. Chartered Accountant. Australian company director. *B.* 20 Sept. 1900. *Educ.* Hale School, Perth and Melbourne Grammar School. *M.* 1928, Eileen Tindale. *S.* Brian, David. *Career:* Secretary, Perth Chamber of Commerce 1928–57; Secretary of the Stock Exchange of Perth 1934–65. Chairman of Directors, Perth Arcade Co. Ltd.; Consultant Binder Hamlyn and Co.; Fellow Aust. Society of Accountants. *Address:* c/o Binder Hamlyn & Co. (Chartered Accountants), 12–14 St. George's Terrace, Perth, Western Australia, 6000.

**SAWARD, Dudley,** OBE, Comp. IEE F.B.I.S. Group Capt. R.A.F. (retd.). *B.* 1913. *Educ.* Bishops Stortford College; R.A.F. Coll. (Cranwell); R.A.F. Elec. and Wireless School, Officers' Technical Signals Course (qualified for symbol 'S'). *M.* 1951, Janet Mulford. *Daus.* Peta Anne and Michele. *Career:* Cadet, R.A.F. College, Cranwell 1932–34; served as pilot in England aud India 1934–38; with British Expeditionary Force in France 1939–40; with Wireless Investigation and Development Unit, England (promoted Squadron Leader) 1940; at Air Ministry in Directorate of Operational Requirements (promoted Wing-Commander) 1941; Chief Radar Officer, R.A.F. Bomber Command (awarded OBE Military Div.; promoted Group Capt.; twice mentioned in Despatches) 1942–45; Controller of Navigation and Telecommunications, British European Airways 1946–48. Director, International Aeradio Ltd. and Barratt & Co. Ltd., London 1948–51 (Dep. Chmn. and Man. Dir. 1952–56). Man. Dir. Texas Instruments Ltd. 1956–61. and Rank-Bush-Murphy Ltd. 1961–65; Chmn. Bullock & Turner Ltd. 1972–76; Dir. British Space Development Co. Ltd. 1961–75; Kraus-Thomson Organization 1968–71; General Technology Systems Ltd. 1973—; HJH & S Holdings Ltd., since 1973. Inst. of Directors. *Publications:* The Bomber's Eye; What of Tomorrow? *Address:* c/o Williams & Glyn's Bank, Ltd., Columbia House, 69 Aldwych, London WC2B 4JJ.

**SAWYER, William E.** American pharmaceutical executive. *B.* 1912. *Educ.* Univ. of Buffalo (BA 1934). Student Sales Training, LaSalle Univ.; Sales Analysis Inst., F.B.I. Academy. *M.* 1942, Eleanor Booth. *S.* William Eddy and Stephen Thomas. *Career:* With General Electric Co. (in various capacities, including advertising, promotion manager, editor radio magazine, Bandwagon, and with radio div., home laundry division, electric cleaner div., General Electric home bureau) 1934–42; Special Agent, F.B.I. 1942–45; joined Johnson & Johnson 1946; Dir. of Education 1946–53. Director of merchandising services, Johnson & Johnson (New Brunswick, N.J.) 1953—. *Publications:* Co-author (motion picture and book) Sell—As Customers Like It (1949); Make Point of Purchase Point-of-Sale (1950); Know Your Sales People, also textbook on Salesmanship (1951); co-author: Design for Selling (motion picture and book) (1953); Orientation of Merchandising Personnel (book) (1955); Bandages and Bullets (motion picture) (1954); The Newest in Bandaging, Best Foot Forward (motion pictures) (1955); Success Story in Modernization (book) (1956); It's Time to Take Stock—motion picture on stockroom modernization and inventory improvement programmes for retailers (1960); Space Project (motion picture on retail management) 1965. Speaker to advertising groups, clubs and associations. *Associations:* Point of Purchase Advt. Inst. (Dir.), Industrial Audio-Visual Assn., Assn. of Natl. Advertisers, Sales Promotion Execs., Assn. of Sales Executives, National Visual Presentation Assn., Soc. of Former F.B.I. Agents, Inc. *Clubs:* New York; Ad. Club (N.J.). *Address:* 1542 Deer Path, Mountainside, N.J.

**SAXTON, Andrew E.** Canadian. *B.* 1929. *M.* Carlyn Kaiser. *S.* Richard L. D., and Andrew Elliot *Daus.* Shelley Susan and Anne Marie. *Career:* Chmn. Bd. Grouse Mountain Resorts. Ltd. Director: B.C. Television Broadcasting System Ltd.; Derston Investment Corp. Ltd.; B.C. Heart Foundation; Pacific Undersea Gardens Ltd.; Canyon Aerial Tramways Ltd. Member Phi Kappa Pi Fraternity. *Clubs:* Royal Vancouver Yacht Club; Vancouver Lawn Tennis & Badminton; The University (Vancouver). *Address:* 3637 Angus Drive, Vancouver, B.C.; and *office* 1030 West Georgia Street, Vancouver 5, B.C., Canada.

**SAYEM, Abusadat Mohammad.** Bangladesh Advocate. *B.* 1916. *Educ.* Rangpur Zilla School; Presidency College, Calcutta; Carmichael Coll., Rangpur Univer. Law Coll., Calcutta. *M.* 1949. Khojesta. *Dau.* 1. *Career:* Advocate Calcutta High Court 1944; joined Dacca High Court Bar 1947; Examiner in Law, Dacca Univ., Mem. State Bank of Pakistan until 1956; Sponsor, Gen. Secy. and Vice-Pres. East Pakistan Lawyers' Assn.; former Secy. and Vice-Pres. High Court Bar Assn. Advocate and Sen. Advocate 1956–62; Mem. Bar Council until 1962; Judge, High Court Dacca 1962–72; First Chief Justice, High Court of Bangladesh 1972; Chief Justice, Supreme Court of Bangladesh 1972–75; President of Bangladesh 1975–77. *Address:* 105 Azimpur Road, Dacca, Bangladesh.

**SCAMBLER, Harry McEwin.** Australian Company Director. *B.* 1910. *Educ.* Scotch College, Melbourne; Associate, Australian Society of Accountants; Associate, Chartered Institute of Secretaries. *M.* 1936, Valerie Isabelle Carter. *S.* John McEwin and David Ian. *Dau.* Diana Valerie. *Career:* General Manager, The English Scottish and Australian Bank Ltd., 1964–70; Chmn. Australian Resources Development Bank Ltd. 1967–73; Man. Dir. Australia & New Zealand Banking Group Ltd. 1969–73; Dir. Alcoa of Aust. Ltd.; IBM Aust. Ltd.; Bowater-Scott Australia Ltd.; The Colonial Mutual Life Assurance Society Ltd. *Address:* 29 Berkeley Street, Hawthorn, 3122, Vic., Australia.

**SCARLETT, Sir Peter William Shelley Yorke,** KCMG, KCVO. Retired British diplomat; Chairman Cathedrals Advisory Committee of Gt. Britain 1967—. *B.* 1905. *Educ.* Eton and Christ Church, Oxford. *M.* 1934, Elisabeth Dearman Birchall. *S.* 1. *Daus.* 3. 3rd Secretary, Foreign Office 1929; Cairo 1930; Baghdad 1932; Lisbon 1934; Riga 1936 (Chargé d'Affaires 1937 and 1938); attached to Latvian Representative at Coronation of King George VI 1937; Brussels 1938; Acting 1st Secretary 1940; captured by enemy forces in France May 1940; resumed duty at Foreign Office Dec. 1941; Paris 1944; British Political Adviser at Allied H.Q. Caserta, July 1946; Counsellor, Foreign Office 1947; Inspector of Foreign Service Establishments 1950; Consul-General, Strasbourg and Permanent U.K. Deputy on Council of Europe (with personal rank of Minister), Oct. 1952; Ambassador to Norway 1955–60; Minister to the Holy See 1960–65. *Address:* Rudhall, Ross-on-Wye, Herefordshire.

**SCELBA, Mario,** L. giur. Italian lawyer and politician. *B.* 5 Sept. 1901; joined the Partito Popolare Italiano (P.P.E.) 1919; retired from political life during the Fascist régime but kept in contact with Signor De Gasperi. Counsellor, National Christian Democratic Party since 1944. Minister of Posts and Telecommunications June 1945; Deputy of Parliament since 1946; Minister of the Interior 1947–53 and 1960–62; Prime Minister 1954–55; Deputy European Parliamentary Assembly 1958—. Pres. European Parliament 1969–71. *Address:* Via Barberini 47, Rome, Italy.

**SCERRI, A. J.** The High Commissioner of Malta to Great Britain. *B.* 1921. *Educ.* St. Mary's Coll. Cospicua; dockyard Tech. School. *M.* Ruby Howell. *Dau.* 1. *Career:* Draughtsman GEC Elliot 1950–70; Draughtsman Procon (London) Ltd. 1970–71; Dip. Work Study, Stats. & Engl. 1971; High Commissioner for Malta in London since 1971; High Commissioner in Cyprus and Ambassador Moscow and Tehran (non-resident basis). *Member:* Rep. Malta Labour Party in Britain; Chmn. Hampstead Labour Party (also Secy.); Movement for Colonial Freedom (Secy. Medit. & ME Cttee.). *Publ.:* London Corresp. of Voice of Malta. *Address:* 24 Haymarket, London, SW1Y 4DJ.

**SCHACHT, Lawrence.** U.S. Business executive. *B.* 1905. *Educ.* Stevens Institute of Technology (M.E. Deg.). *M.* 1934, Aleen Ginsberg. *S.* Michael. *Dau.* Barbara Marshall. *Career:* President, Schacht Steel Construction Inc. 1933—, Schacht Foundation Inc. 1951—, Director: Royal National Bank of New York 1952–70 (Chairman Exec. Comm. 1966–68); Standard Dredging Corp. 1967–72; (Chairman of the Board 1968–72); Director, Industrial Development Bank of Israel 1962–66. B'nai B'rith; Pi Lambda Phi; Chmn., New York City State of Israel Bonds, 1954; Chmn. & Pres. Essex County Israel Bonds Cttee., 1956–58; Hon. Chmn., 1958; Board of Trustees, Hillside Industrial Foundation, 1953–60;

Jewish Community Council of Essex County, New Jersey. Member, Exec. Cttee., American Israel Public Affairs Cttee., Society, Founders, Albert Einstein Medical. Coll., Vascular Research Foundation; Amer. Israel Chamber of Commerce; American Technion Society, Director 1958—; Board of Governors, 1967; President, 1969–70; Dir. Amer. Friends of Tel Aviv Univ.; American Associates Ben Gurien Univ.; Member Bd. Gov. Israel Inst. of Technology; Tel Aviv University. *Clubs:* Green Brook Country; Boca Rio Country. *Address:* 216 Crestwood Drive, South Orange, N.J.; 1200 Ocean Blvd., Boco Raton, Fla.; *office* 200 East 57th Street, New York, U.S.A.

**SCHADDELEE, Hubert Richard.** *B.* 1905. *Educ.* Univ. of Michigan (BA 1927). *M.* 1930, Dorothy Dee Denman. *S.* Richard Denman. *Dau.* Anne Louise (Juell). *Career:* With Otis & Co., Chicago 1928–30; Iowa-Nebraska Light & Power, Lincoln, Neb. 1931–36; Managing Partner, Schaddelee & Co. 1936–60. Director Emeritus: American Natural Gas Co., Michigan Consolidated Gas Co., and Michigan-Wisconsin Pipe Line; Dir., Amer. Nat. Gas Production Co.; Amer. Nat. Gas Service Co. *Clubs:* Lauderdale Yacht; University (Grand Rapids); Macatawa Bay Yacht (Past Commodore); Grand Rapids Yacht (Past Commodore); Cruising (of America). Past Commander, Grand Rapids U.S. Power Squadron; Lago Mar Country. *Address:* 1700 South Ocean Drive, Fort Lauderdale, Fla. 33316, U.S.A.

**SCHAEFER, Julius Earl.** *B.* 1893. *Educ.* U.S. Military Academy. *M.* 1918, Catherine Rockwell. *S.* Robert J. *Dau.* Mrs. Charles Bartlett. *Career:* One of the first Army officers commissioned at West Point to request assignment to aviation before graduation; made pioneer flight from Fort Sill (Okla.) to Wichita, June 1919; officer in charge of flying and training 1919; flew one of the first De Havilland bombers Aug. 1919 (an item of interest in this machine was SCR-64, the first adaptation of radio to aviation, and forerunner of air-to-ground and air-to-air communication). After World War I, in collaboration with Laird, Stearman and Weaver, produced the Laird Swallow airplane. Joined Stearman Aircraft Co. (predecessor of Boeing facility at Wichita) 1928; Secy.-Sales Manager, Stearman Aircraft Divn., United Aircraft & Transport Co. 1929–38; Gen. Manager, Stearman Aircraft Divn., Boeing Aircraft Co. 1938–40 (Wichita Divn. 1941–57); Consultant and first Director Emeritus, Boeing Co. (Vice-Chairman 1957–61); former Vice-President, Boeing Airplane Co. G.M. Wichita Div.; Director, Fourth National Bank, Wichita (Kan.). Former Vice-President, Eisenhower Foundation. *Awards:* Citation of Honor by the Air Force Association for 'distinguished public service through his dedicated and effective efforts on behalf of the men and women of the Armed Forces to make military service a more attractive and respected career' 1956; cited for 'distinctive service and contributions to the aircraft industry' by Institute of Aeronautical Sciences 1959; Hon. Member, Alpha Kappa Psi, Univ. of Wichita 1961. *Clubs:* University, Rotary, Wichita Country (Wichita). *Address:* The Hillcrest, Apt. 6A, 115 S. Rutan, Wichita, Kan.; and *office* Boeing Co., Wichita, Kan., U.S.A.

**SCHAEFFER, Robert F.** Luxembourg diplomat. *B.* 1930. *Educ.* Paris, Diplome HEC (1953); Fulbright Scholar, Univ. of Kansas Graduate School. *M.* 1955, Barbara M. Krug. *S.* 1. *Dau.* 1. *Career:* Hon Consul, State of Missouri since 1972; Hon. Consul (for Luxembourg), States of Arkansas, Colorado, Kansas, Minnesota, Nebraska, and Oklahoma (in addition to Missouri) since 1975. *President* (past) National Assn. of Litho Clubs; (past) Kansas City Ballet Assn. *Member:* Consular Corps of Greater Kansas City; Consular Corps Coll. of Richmond, Virginia; Exec. Cttee. of Trustees—Conservatory of Music (Univ. of Missouri); (past) Luxembourg Olympic Track Team, Helsinki (1952). *Decorations:* Man of the Year Award, Nat. Assoc. of Printers & Lithog. 1973; Elmer G. Voight Award, Educ. Council of the Graphic Arts Industry 1969; Numerous awards by Graphic Arts local and nat. assns. for merit. *Publications:* in various Graphic Arts mags. in U.S.A. *Address:* 3805 NW 63rd Terrace, Kansas City, Missouri 64151 U.S.A.; and *office* 1429 Atlantic Street, N. Kansas City, Missouri 64116, U.S.A.

**SCHAETZEL, J. Robert.** American Diplomat. *B.* 1917. *Educ.* Pomona College—AB; Univs. of Mexico & Harvard; Pomona LLB. *M.* 1944, Imogen Spencer. *Daus.* 2. *Career:* Bureau of the Budget, Washington D.C. 1942–45; Dept. of State, Washington D.C. 1945–72: Office of Economic Affairs, Bureau of Economic Affairs, Office Sec. of State Atomic Energy, Special Asst. to Under-Sec. of State, Dep. Asst. Sec. for Atlantic Affairs, Ambassador to European Communities; Writer-Consultant since 1973. *Member:* Council on Foreign Relations; Vice-Chmn., Atlantic Inst.; Vice-Pres., Atlantic Visitors Association; Board, Atlantic Council. *Awards:* Rockefeller Public Service Award. *Publications:* The Unhinged Alliance; & Articles in Fortune, Foreign Affairs, Foreign Policy, Daedelus, Readers Digest, etc. *Address:* 2 Bay Tree Lane, Washington D.C. 20016, U.S.A.; & *office* 7900 Westpark Drive, 12th Floor, McLean, Va. 22101, U.S.A.

**SCHAFFNER, Hon. Hans.** Swiss advocate. *B.* 1908. *Educ.* Law studies, Berne University; advocate 1934; Hon. Doctorate in Economics, Berne Univ. *M.* 1936, Ruth Rudolph. *S.* Thomas and Andreas. *Career:* Lawyer to Directorate of Federal Industry, Trade and Labour Office 1939–41; Head, Central Office for War Economy 1941–45; Dir., Div. of Commerce, Federal Dept. for Public Economy 1954–61; Pres. Swiss Clearing Institute, of the Clearing Commission and of the Inter-departmental Permanent Board for Co-ordination of Foreign Economic Policy; Head of Swiss Delegs. to OEEC, GATT and EFTA 1954–61; Swiss representative at the Commercial Conf. in Paris 1960; Member, Steering Board for Trade of OEEC 1953–61; Federal Councillor. Head of the Federal Department of Public Economy 1961–69. Pres., GATT Ministerial Meeting, Geneva 1964; President of the Swiss Confederation 1966. Member Liberal Democratic Party of Switzerland. *Address:* Junkerngasse 59, Berne, Switzerland.

**SCHAFFNER, Robert.** Minister of Public Works, Sport and Physical Education in the Grand Duchy of Luxembourg 1959–64. *B.* 1905. *M.* 1933, Marie Sophie Berthe Berblé. *Dau.* Madeleine. Mayor of Echternach 1946–47; Minister of Public Works, and of Reconstruction of Transport and Electricity 1947–51; President, Commission of E.C.E., Geneva 1947–48, Deputy 1951–59; Councillor and Alderman of Echternach 1952–59. President, Union Internationale des Forgerons-Constructeurs 1953; Commissioner-General, Fédération des Eclaireurs de Luxembourg. Grand Cross Order of Orange Nassau, and Commander, Order of Civil and Military Merit of Adolphe of Nassau (Luxembourg); Commander, Order of the Crown (Luxembourg); Grand Cross with Star and Sash, Order of Service (Germany); Grand Cross, Orders of Leopold, and of Crown (Belgium), and the King of Thailand. Member Democrat Party. *Club:* Panathlon. *Address: office* 4 Boulevard Roosevelt, Luxembourg.

**SCHAIRER, George Swift.** Engineer. *B.* 1913. *Educ.* Swarthmore College (BS 1934) and Massachusetts Inst. of Technology (MS 1935). *M.* 1935, Pauline Tarbox. *S.* George E. and John O. *Daus.* Mary E. and Sally H. *Career:* With Bendix Products Corp. 1935–37; Consolidated Aircraft Corp. 1937–39; commenced with the Boeing Co. 1939. Vice-President, Research, The Boeing Co., Seattle, U.S.A. Member: Panel on Scientific & Technical Manpower to the President's Science Adv. Cttee. 1962–64; International Academy of Astronautics; Trustee: A Contemporary Theatre. Cornish Sch. of Allied Arts. Member: Scientific Adv. Bd., U.S.A.F. 1944–45 and 1955–60, and of many N.A.C.A. (Natl. Adv. Cttee. for Aeronautics) 1945–61. Hon. D.Eng., Swarthmore Coll.; Sylvanus Albert Reed Award, Inst. of Aerospace Sciences; Spirit of St. Louis Medal, Amer. Socy. of Mechanical Engineers; Daniel Guggenheim Medal 1967. Member: Amer. Inst. of Aeronautics & Astronautics (Hon. Fellow), Amer. Helicopter Socy., National Academy of Sciences, National Academy of Engineering, Soc. of Naval Architects and Marine Engineers. *Address:* 4242 Hunts Point Road, Bellevue, Washington 98004; and *office* The Boeing Co. Box 3707, Seattle, Washington 98124, U.S.A.

**SCHARFFENBERGER, George Thomas.** U.S. Business Executive. *B.* 1919. *Educ.* Columbia University (BS 1940); C.P.A., New York State. *M.* 1948, Marion A. Nelson. *S.* George Thomas Jr., John E., Thomas J., and James N. *Daus.* Ann Marie, Joan Ellen. *Career:* General Auditor 1943–44; with Arthur Anderson & Co. 1943–44; Asst. Comptroller, Federal Telegraph and Telephone Corp. 1944–47, Comptroller 1947–50; Asst. to Pres. International Telegraph and Telephone Corp. 1950–53; Vice-Pres. Fed. Telephone and Radio Co. 1953–55; Vice-Pres. 1955–56, Pres. Kellogg Switchboard & Supply Co. 1956–59; Vice-Pres. 1959–62, Senior Vice-Pres. Litton Industries Inc. 1962–66: Exec. Vice-Pres. Litton Systems Inc. 1961–66; Chmn., Chief Exec. Officer & Director, City Investing Co., N.Y.C., Jan. 1966—; Dir. I. C. Industries; Litton Industries, Inc.; Georgetown Univ.; Trustee Univ. of So. Calif. *Member:* American Arbitration Assn. Member. Financial Institute of America. Amer. Management Assn.; Amer. Arbitration Assn. Republican. *Club:* Columbia University. *Address:* 4 Appaloosa Lane, Rolling Hills, Calif.; and *office* 9100 Wilshire Blvd., Beverley Hills, California, U.S.A.

**SCHAUS, Emile.** Politician, Luxembourg. *B.* 1903. *Educ.* Lycée classique, Diekirch; and Univs. of Paris, Munich and Berlin; Doctor of Philosophy and Philology. Assistant, Lycée classique 1931–33, Diekirch (Professor 1933–35); Professor, Athénée, Luxembourg 1935–41 (removed by Nazi occupation); Director, Teachers' Training College, Luxembourg 1945–59; member of Advisory Council 1945; Journalist 1933–68; editor of Internal Politics in Luxemburger Wort 1944–45; Town Councillor, Luxembourg 1951–58; Asst. to Mayor 1958–59. Created the Family and Popular Front, 1946. First President of the Municipal Organization of the Christian Social Party 1951–59. Minister of Education and Agriculture 1959–64, Deputy 1964–68. Representative of Council of Europe and European Parliament, 1964–69. Political prisoner in Wittlich, Hinzert and Dachau concentration camps 1941–42; deported to Ehrenbreitstein until Aug. 1944. *Publications:* Cahiers de Redressement, Politique Familiale (1945); Schne'g, story of a cat (1946); Memoiren eines Douaniers (1948); Rougette, story of a cow (1954); Paul-ü-Zorro (1967); Tieresgeschichte und Resistenzgeschichte; Origin and achievement of Conservative and Christian Social Party 1914–74; Poems (1977). *Decorations:* Officer, Order of the Oak Crown (Luxembourg); Grand Cross, Order of the Crown (Belgium); Verdienstorden mit Stern und Schulterband (Germany); Cmdr. Cross of Agricultural Merit (France). *Address:* Val-Ste-Croix 188, Luxembourg.

**SCHAUS, Eugéne,** D. en D. Luxembourg politician. *B.* 11 May 1901. *M.* 1926, Alice Arend. *S.* Raymond. *Daus.* Evelyne, Yvette. *Career:* Lawyer, Luxembourg Bar 1924—; member (Dem.), Chamber of Deputies 1937—; Minister of the Interior and Justice and of Physical Education 1945–51; Vice-Pres. of Government and Minister of Foreign Affairs and the Armed Forces March 1959–64; Vice-Pres. Government; Min. of Justice Interior and Public Force 1969–74. *Address:* 56 Grand Rue, Luxembourg.

**SCHEEL, Walter.** President of Federal Republic of Germany. *B.* 1919. *Educ.* Reform-Gymnasium, Solingen. *M.* 1969, Dr. Mildred Wirtz. *S.* 2. *Daus.* 2. *Career:* Head of Market research organization; Member Landtag North Rhine-Westfalia 1950–54; Member Bundestag 1953–74, Vice-Pres. 1967–69; Federal Minister for Economic Cooperation 1961–66; Chmn. of Free Democrats 1968–74; Federal Minister Foreign Affairs, Vice-Chancellor 1969–74; Elected Pres. of Federal Republic 1974. *Publications:* Konturen einer neuer Welt (1965); Formeln deutscher Politik (1969); Reden und Interviews (1972, 1976); Vom Recht des Anderen (1977). *Address:* 5300 Bonn, Haus des Bundespräsidenten, Germany.

**SCHEICHELBAUER, Heinz, J.** Austrian advertising and public relations consultant. *B.* 1921. *Educ.* Commercial Coll., Vienna. *Career:* In head office of the Aplenelektrowerke, Vienna 1945, and head office of the Austrian Advertising Agency, Vienna 1945; Manager of the Agency 1954–65; engaged in independent advertising activity 1955; Austrian Rep. Swedish Fair Gothenburg 1957—; Owner, Teamservice H. J. Scheichelbauer Public Relations Agency 1958–65; Managing Partner, Busskamp & Koch, Scheichelbauer Advertising Agency 1965–74; Chmn. Bd. Kontakt Adv. Agency 1973–74; Media-Mix Space Broker Agency 1974 (all Vienna). *Publications:* various minor articles in commercial and technical publications. *Clubs:* Freemasons Lodge 'Zukunft', Vienna; Quatuor Coronati Lodge, No. 2076, London. *Address:* Argentinierstr 22/2/13, A-1040 Vienna IV, Austria.

**SCHELBERGER, Prof. Herbert,** Dr. jur. h.c., German industrialist, mem. of [illegible] y Bd. of Ruhrgas AG. *B.* 1908. *Ed*[illegible] bitur and law studies at Univer[illegible] rg and Kiel. *M.* 1937, Anne[illegible] Barbara and Ursula. *Career:* [illegible] n Gas-, Wasser- u. Elek[illegible] Bd. Nordrheinische Erdgas[illegible] che Erdgas-Transport [illegible] Trans-Europa-Natur[illegible] d. Dirs. Gas-Union [illegible] GmbH; Süddeutsche [illegible] Dirs. Concordiaberg [illegible] enag AG. *Award:* [illegible] tern. Senator E.h. [illegible] dustrieclub (Dussel[illegible] *dress:* 43 Essen-(1) Bredeney, Brucker Holt 41, Federal Republic of Germany; and *office* 43 Essen 1, Huttropstr. 60.

**SCHEPERS, Lykle.** *B.* 6 Sept. 1903. *Educ.* mining engineer, Delft. *M.* 1928, Charlotte E. Wigersma. *S.* Menno. *Daus.* Martha Elizabeth, Nynke Jetske, Elisabeth Charlotte. *Career:* Joined Royal Dutch/Shell Group Oct. 1926; Exploit. Eng. in Rumania, Java, California and the Argentine; Chief. Exploit. Eng. and Field Supt., Shell Caribbean Petroleum Co. 1938; Prod. Manager for Group in Balikpapan and Manager of N.N.G.P.M. in New Guinea 1939; Prod. Mgr., Shell Caribbean Petroleum Co. 1947; returned to Holland 1948; Head of Prod. Dept., Shell Petroleum N.V., The Hague Jan. 1949; Co-ordinator for Explor. and Prod. 1951–52; Man. Dir., Royal Dutch/Shell Group of Companies 1952–64; Director, Royal Dutch Shell Petroleum N.V., and The Shell Petroleum Co. Ltd. 1964–74. *Address:* Flat 16, Stoeplaan 9, Wassenaar, Netherlands.

**SCHEUFELEN, Karl-Erhard,** Dr. rer. pol. hc. German. *B.* 1903. *Educ.* Univs. of Munich, Leipzig and Hamburg. *M.* Elli Köpfer. *Dau.* 1. *Career:* Chairman, Executive Board, der Papierfabrik Scheufelen. (Hon.) Pres. Verband Deutscher Papierfabriken E.V. (VDP) in Bonn; Director A. Stotz AG; Deutsches Museum; Munchen Chmn. Baden-Wurttembergische Papierverbande; Society of Friends of State Museum of Natural History, Stuttgart; Vice-Pres. IHK Mittlerer Neckar, Stuttgart; Rotarian. *Awards:* Grand Cross of Meritorious Service (Germany); Hon. Senator: TH Darmstadt 1953, and Stuttgart 1955; Freeman of the City of Oberlenningen; Dr. rer. pol. h.c., University of Tübingen. *Address:* Adolf-Scheufelen-Strasse 20 Oberlenningen; and Papierfabrik Scheufelen, 7318 Lenningen 1, Germany.

**SCHIEFFELIN, George McKay.** American publisher. *B.* 1905. *Educ.* St. Paul's School; Princeton Univ. *M.* 1929, Louise Winterbotham; *S.* George Richard and John Winterbotham. *Career:* With Charles Scribners' Sons, N.Y.C. 1928—; successively Asst. to Mgr., Scribner Press, Asst. Mgr., Mfg. Dept., Dir. Asst.-Treas., Treas. 1932–42. Served as Commander, U.S.N.R. 1942–47; Pres. Dir. Model Fireproof Tenement Co. 1947–65; Exec. Vice-Pres. Treas. and Dir. Charles Scribners Sons 1955, Chmn. of the Bd. since 1970. *Clubs:* Groiler, Players, Somerset Hills. *Address:* Whitehouse Station, N.J. 08889; and *office*, 57 Fifth Avenue, New York N.Y. 10015, U.S.A.

**SCHIEFFELIN, William Jay III.** American. *B.* 1922. *Educ.* Yale Univ. (AB 1945). *M.* 1947, Joy Williams Proctor. *S.* 5. *Dau.* 1. *Career:* Chairman of Board, Schieffelin & Co. 1962—; Almay Inc. N.Y. Former Dir. Penn Surgical Manufacturing Co; New York Bd. of Trade; Former Trustee The Cisqua School Mount Kisco; Columbia Coll. of Pharmacy; Dir. Chamber of Commerce & Industry of New York Inc; National Assn. Alcholic Beverage Importers Inc; America-Italy Socy; Past Pres. Hundred Year Assn. of New York (Member Exec. Council); Member Italy-Amer. Chamber of Commerce; New York Chamber of Commerce; Adv. Bd. La Maison Francaise; Ad. Cttee. European Inst. Business Administration (INSEAD); Bd. Trustees Tuskegee Institute; Bd. Dir. The British-Amer. Chamber of Commerce; Exec. Vice-Pres. French Chamber of Commerce in United States; Past member, Commerce & Industry Assn. of N.Y. Life Member, Amer. Pharmaceutical Assn. *Clubs:* Union Yale, N.Y. Yacht (all of N.Y.C.). *Address:* 30 Coopor, Square, New York, N.Y. 10003, U.S.A.

**SCHIEWECK, Erich.** German refining and chemical industrialist. *B.* 1897. *Educ.* Training of Technical Chemist. *M.* 1922, Helene Kleinholz. *S.* Wolfgang (killed in war 1945) and Dieter. *Dau.* Inge. *Career:* Chmn. of Council Max-Planck Inst. (Aeronomie), Linday; Member of Council: Hubertussprudel GmbH, Bad-Hönningen; Main proprietor and manager: Kleinholz & Co., Essen; Ascalia GmbH; AKS Aussenhandelskontor Schieweck GmbH; Münder & Jentzshe GmbH; Synko-Chemie GmbH all Hamburg; EBF Beratungs- und Forschungs-gesellschaft für Energiefragen mbH; Mineralöl-und Filtertechnik GmbH both Essen. *Publications:* Christ-Inform oder Kom-Inform, 1949; Die überholte Weltrevolution—Neue Perspektiven für die Beziehungen zwiszhen Ost und West, 1959. *Member:* Max-Planck-Gesellschaft, Munich; Stifer-Verband für d. deutsche Wissenschaft, Essen; Mineralöl-Wirtschafsverband, Hamburg: Arbeitsgemeinschaft Selbständiger Unternehmer, Bonn. *Address:* Waldfrieden, 1, Essen; and *office* Kleinholz & Co., Huyssenallee 68, Essen, Germany.

**SCHIFF, Emile Louis Constant.** Netherlands Diplomat. *B.* 1918. *Educ.* Univ. of Leiden—Law Degree. *M.* 1944, Jeannette Van Rees. *S.* 1. *Dau.* 1. *Career:* Second Sec., Netherlands Embassy, Washington 1945–49; Second/First Sec., Netherlands Legation, Madrid 1949–52; Private Sec., Minister of Foreign Affairs 1952–54; Counsellor, Perm. Mission, New York 1955–59; Minister at Embassy, Washington D.C. 1959–64; Ambassador to Indonesia 1964–68; Sec.-Gen., Ministry of Foreign Affairs since 1968. *Decorations:* Knight, Order of Netherlands Lion; Officer, Order of Orange Nassau; and many Foreign Awards. *Clubs:* The Hague Golf & Country Club. *Address:* Neuhuyskade 28, The Hague, Netherlands.

**SCHIFF, John M.** American. Director: C.I.T. Financial Corporation, Great Atlantic & Pacific Tea Co., Madison Fund Inc., Getty Oil Co. Uniroyal, Inc., Westinghouse Electric Corp. and Kennecot Copper Corp. *B.* 1904. *Educ.* Yale University (AB 1925) and Oxford University (New College; BA; MA). *M.* (1) 1934, Edith Baker (*Dec'd.*). *S.* David T. and Peter G. (2) 1976, Mrs. Josephine Fell. *Clubs:* Creek; Grolier Links Golf; Meadow Brook; Metropolitan; Wash., D.C., National Golf; Piping Rock; River; Turf & Field. *Address:* Berry Hill Road, Oyster Bay, L.I., N.Y. 11771; and *office* 40 Wall Street, New York, N.Y., U.S.A.

**SCHILLER, Prof. Dr. Karl August Fritz.** German economist and politician. *B.* 1911. *Educ.* Univs. of Kiel, Frankfurt, Berlin and Heidelberg (Dr rer. pol.). *Divorced. S.* Michael-Tonio. *Daus.* Barbara, Bettina, Christa. *Career:* Director Research Team, Institut für Weltwirtschaft, Kiel 1935–41. Teacher at University of Kiel 1939; served in World War II in German Army 1941–45; Professor of Economics and Director of the Institute for Foreign Trade and Overseas Economy and Social Economic Seminary, University of Hamburg since 1947; Member of Scientific Adv. Cncl. to the Federal Ministry of Economics since 1947; Senator for Economy and Transport of the Hansestadt Hamburg 1948–53; Member, Hamburg Parliament 1949–57; Rector, Univ. of Hamburg 1956–58; Senator of Economics, Berlin 1961–65; Deputy Chmn. Economic Policy Cttee. of Exec. Board of S.P.D. 1962–64; Chmn. of this committee since 1964; *Member:* Exec. Board of S.P.D. 1964–72; of the Bundestag 1965–72; and of Select Board of S.P.D. 1966–72. Minister of Economics, Federal Republic of Germany 1966–71; Minister Economics and Finance 1971–72. *Publications:* Marktregulierung and Marktordnung in der Weltagrarwirtschaft; Wirtschaftspolitik (in Handwörterbuch der Sozialwissenschaften); Preisstabilität durch globale Steuerung der Marktwirtschaft; Der Ökonom und die Gesellschaft; Berliner Wirtschaft und deutsche Politik; Reden zur Wirtschafts- und Finanzpolitik. *Address:* 2 Hamburg 55, Kuulsbarg 26, Germany.

**SCHINDLER, Hans Max.** Swiss company director. *B.* 22 Nov. 1896. *Educ.* Eidgenössische Technische Hochschule; Cambridge University (PhD). *S.* Werner, Peter, Hans. *Daus.* Annemarie, Elisabeth, Ruth. Former Chairman, Swiss Foundation for Technical Assistance (Swisscontact). *Address:* Hohenbuhlstrasse, 8032, Zürich, Switzerland.

**SCHIOTTZ-CHRISTENSEN, Alf Krabbe.** Danish. *B.* 1909. *Educ.* Univ. of Copenhagen (BA 1927), and Columbia Univ., New York (LittB 1931). *M.* (1) 1944, Ebba Jorgensen (*D.* 1964) and (2) 1967, Inger Larsen. *Career:* On Staff of Seattle Times 1931; Correspondent to Danish newspapers at the League of Nations, Geneva 1932–33; Editorial staff of present newspaper, April 1933; Director and Chief Editor Aalborg Stiftstidende (newspaper) 1940—(Publisher of the same 1950—). Director: Aalborg Stiftsbogtrykkeri (printing works) since 1940. *Awards:* Officier Legion of Honour (France), and of Dannebrog (Denmark); Officer Merito Civil (Spain); Order of Benignitate Humana Finland; Commander, Order of the Finnish Lion; Chevalier of the Order of Vasa (Sweden); Commander, Order of the Falcon (Iceland). Vice-Pres. Danish Newspaper Publishers' Assn.; Vice-Pres. Exec. Cttee., Federation International des Editeurs de Journaux 1961; Dir. Board INCA-FIEJ Research Assn. 1970; Past Pres. Aalborg Rotary Club, and of Aalborg Aero Club. *Address:* 48B Klostermarken, Aalborg, Denmark.

**SCHLAGETER, Herman.** Swiss importer. *B.* 26 Sept. 1903. *Educ.* Commercial schools in Basle. *M.* 1930, Josefina Charlaix. *S.* 2. *Dau.* 1. Proprietor of Casa Herman H. Schlageter (import and export); Swiss Consul 1945–68; Hon. Member, San Salvador Rotary Club Aug. 1953—. *Address: office* P.O. Box 1994, San Salvador, El Salvador.

**SCHLESINGER, James Rodney.** American Economist. *B.* 1929. *Educ.* Harvard Univ. (MA, Ph.D). *M.* 1954, Rachel Mellinger. *S.* 4. *Daus.* 4. *Career:* Asst. Prof. & Assoc. Prof., Univ. of Virginia 1955–63; Snr. Staff Mem., RAND Corp. 1963–67, Dir. Strategic Studies 1967–69; Asst. Dir., Office of Management and Budget 1969–71; Chmn., U.S. Atomic Energy Commission 1971–73; Dir., Central Intelligence Feb.–May 1973; Defense Sec. May 1973–Nov. 1975; White House Adviser on Energy since 1977. *Address:* 3601 N. 26th Street, Arlington, Va. 22207, U.S.A.

**SCHLIEMANN, Erich (Ernst Karl).** German. *B.* 1924. *Educ.* Univ. of Hamburg (Junior Barrister). *M.* 1958, Inger Bugge. *S.* Johann Christoph, Henrik Oliver and Claas Benjamin. *Dau.* Katharina. *Career:* Man. Dir. Burmah Castrol Europe Ltd. London & Hamburg; Dir. The Burmah Oil Co. Ltd. Glasgow; Castrol Ltd. London; Chmn. Bd. Burmah Castrol España S.A. Madrid; Burmah Castrol Nederland; Burmah Trading N.V.; Castrol AB, Stockholm; Castrol AS Copenhagen; Castrol Austria GmbH, Vienna; Castrol Italiana, Milan; Norge AS Oslo; Portuguesa Ltd. Lisbon; Switzerland A.G. Zurich; Deutsche Castrol GmbH, Hamburg; S.A. des Huiles Castrol Paris; AB UNO-X Skövde; Albatros S.A. Antwerp; ARAL BELGIQUE S.A. Brussels; Borg Service GmbH, Dusseldorf; Ets Matthys, Rouen; Tabbert Wohnwagenwerke GmbH; Bad Kissingen. *Clubs:* Hamburger Golf; Lyford Cay, Nassau, Bahamas. *Address: office* Burmah Castrol Europe Ltd., 2 Hamburg 39, Bellevue 27, Germany.

**SCHMID, Karl (Carlo).** German politician. *B.* 3 Dec. 1896. *Educ.* Gymnasium; Univ. of Tübingen (Dr. jur.). *M.* 1921, Lydia Hermes. *S.* Hans, Martin, Raimund. *Dau.* Beate. *Career:* Pres., Direktorium des Landes Württemberg-Hohenzollern 1945; Pres., Social Democratic Party in Württemberg-Hohenzollern 1946; member (S.P.D.), Landtag, Württemberg-Hohenzollern 1946; Minister of Justice and Deputy President 1947–50; member, Parliamentary Council, Bonn 1948–49; Professor of International Law, University of Tübingen since 1929; Professor of Political Sciences of Frankfurt; Vice-President of Bundestag 1949–66 and 1969–72; Minister for Federal Affairs 1966–69. Member Central Committee of Social Democratic Party 1949–72; member of Praesidium, German Red Cross; member, Consultative Committee of Council of Europe; Pres. Assembly, Western European Union 1963–66. *Publications:* Römisches Tagebuch; translation of Les Fleurs du Mal (Baudelaire) Pièces sur l'Art (Valéry); L'Autre Sommeil (Julien Green); Antimémoires; Les chênes qu'on abat (André Malraux); Politik und Geist (1961): Tätiger Geist-Gestalten aus Geschichte und Politik (1964); Politik als Geistige Aufgabe (1973), Europa und die Macht des Geistes (1973; Band I & II der Gesammelten Werke). *Address:* 5340 Bad Honnef 6, Paul-Keller-Strasse 34, Federal Republic of Germany.

**SCHMIDT, Adolph William.** Financial and foundation executive. *B.* 1904. *Educ.* Princeton (AB 1926); Harvard (MBA); certificates from the Universities of Dijon, Berlin and Paris (Sorbonne). *M.* 1936, Helen Sedgeley Mellon. *S.* Thomas. *Dau.* Helen. *Career:* With Mellon National Bank & Trust Co. (or affiliated or predecessor institutions) 1929–38. Associated with A. W. Mellon interests, Pittsburgh, Pa. 1938–42; with U.S. Army 1942–46; Governor T. Mellon & Sons 1946–69. Pres. and Chmn., Allegheny Conference on Community Development 1956–61. U.S. Delegate, Conference on North Atlantic Community, Bruges 1957, and Atlantic Congress, London, June 1959; member U.S. Citizens Commission on NATO 1961–62; U.S. Delegate, Atlantic Convention of NATO Nations, Paris, Jan. 1962; Governor, Atlantic Institute, Paris; Director, Atlantic Council of the U.S., Washington D.C. 1962; Adviser U.S. Deleg., Economic Commission for Europe 1967; Ambassador of the United States to Canada 1969–74. *Awards:* Hon. LLD of Pittsburgh, 1954. Hon. LHD Chatham Coll. 1965; Hon. LLD Univ. of New Brunswick 1973, Princeton Univ. 1977. Trustee: The A. W. Mellon Educational and Charitable Trust; Old Dominion [illegible]oundation; Carnegie Institute. Chairman, Pennsylvania S[illegible]e Planning Board. Member, Council on Foreign Relat[illegible] N.Y.C. *Clubs:* The Links Century Association, Anglers [illegible]; Duquesne, Pittsburgh Golf, Rolling Rock, Laurel [illegible]f (Pittsburgh); Metropolitan (Washington). *Add*[illegible] Ligonier, Pa. 15658, U.S.A.

**SCHMIDT, Benno Cha**[illegible]13. *Educ.* Public & High Schools, Abilen[illegible]A, LLB. Member of Delta Kappa Ep[illegible] (Abbot), Grand Chancellor Order of t[illegible]ief of the Texas Law Review. *M.* Na[illegible]mann. *S.* 5 (1 *dec.*). *Career:* Prof. o[illegible]6–40; Thayer Teaching Fellow, Ha[illegible] Staff of the

General Counsel, War Production Board 1941–42; U.S. Army 1942–45, retiring as Colonel; Bronze Star, Legion of Merit, Legion d'Honneur, Croix de Guerre with Palms, French Medal of Merit, Four battle stars, European theatre of operations; General Counsel, Office of the Foreign Liquidation Comm., State Dept., Washington, D.C. 1945–46; Partner, J. H. Whitney & Co. (venture capital investment firm) since 1946, Managing Partner since 1960; Chmn., Freeport Minerals; Director: Schlumberger, Global Marine, Merichem, Memorex, Esperance Land & Development Co., Orleans Farms and 12 other U.S. and foreign corporations; Former Dir., Transco Companies and General Signal Corp. Chmn. of the Bd., Memorial Hospital for Cancer & Allied Diseases; Vice-Chmn., Memorial Swan-Kettering Cancer Center; Trustee, Whitney Museum; Chmn., Bedford-Stuyvesant Development & Services Corp.; Chmn., Senate Panel on the Conquest of Cancer 1970–71; Chmn., President's Cancer Panel since 1971; mem., President's Biomedical Panel 1975–76. *Awards:* American Cancer Soc. Award for Distinguished Service in Cancer Control; Clement Cleveland Award for Distinguished Service in the Crusade to Control Cancer from N.Y.C. Div. of the American Cancer Soc.; Papanicolaou Award; James Ewing Award; Distinguished Alumnus, Univ. of Texas 1969; Dr. of Humane Letters (h.c.), N.Y. Medical Coll. 1972; Dr. of Laws (h.c.), Columbia Univ., 1976; Alfred P. Sloan Jr. Memorial Award, N.Y. Div., American Cancer Soc. 1977; Stanley P. Reimann Medal, The Fox Chase Cancer Center, Philadelphia 1977. *Address:* 630 Fifth Avenue, New York City, N.Y. 10020, U.S.A.

**SCHMIDT, Helmut.** Chancellor of the Federal Republic of Germany. *B.* 1918. *Educ.* Volksschule Grammar School; High School, Oberschule; Univ. of Hamburg, economics; Dipl.-Volkswirt, 1948; Newberry College S.C., U.S.A. LL.B (1973). *M.* 1942, Hannelore Glaser. *Dau.* 1. *Career:* Member Social Democratic Party, Germany 1946—; Mgr. Transport Admin., State of Hamburg 1949–53; Member German Bundestag 1953–62 and since 1965; Senator (Minister) for Domestic Affairs, Hamburg, 1961–65; Chmn. S.P.D. Parliamentary Group 1967–69, Deputy Chmn. 1968—; Federal Minister of Defence 1969–72, Finance & Economics July–Dec. 1972, Finance 1972–74; Chancellor Federal Republic of Germany since May 1974. *Member:* Deutsche Gesellschaft für Auswärtige Politik Bonn; Int. Inst. for Strategic Studies London; Hudson Inst. N.Y. *Publications:* Defence or Retaliation (1962); Balance of Power (1971); Bundestagsreden (1974): Auf dem Fundament des Godesberger Programms (1973). *Address:* Bundeskanzleramt, 5300 Bonn 12, Adenauerellee 139–141, W. Germany.

**SCHMIDT, Dr. Otto,** LLD. German politician. *B.* 1 Aug. 1902. *Educ.* Secondary; University. *M.* Marie Knoch. *S.* Gerhard, Hans-Jürgen. *Daus.* Sigrid, Christa. *Career:* Advocate; syndic at father Publishing House since 1928, later Manager; Lord Mayor of Wuppertal 1948–49; Minister for Recons., Nordrhein-Westfalen 1950–54; Min. for Labour, Soc. Affs. and Recons. 1953–54. Member of Bundestag 1957–72. *Publications:* German Taxes Review; Court Decisions on Limited Companies; Afrika im Aufbruch, Türkei-Iran. Ostafrika (1964); Impressionen einer Sud-strasienreise; many essays on political, sociological and philosophical subjects. *Address:* Am Walde 26, 56 Wuppertal-Elberfeld, Germany.

**SCHMITT, Geoffrey Joseph.** New Zealander. Professor of Management Studies. *B.* 1921. *Educ.* Christian Brothers' Coll., Waverley, N.S.W., Australia; St. Patrick's Coll., Wellington, N.Z.; Victoria Univ. College, Wellington (MA Hons Econ; BComm, Dip in Public Admin); Prof. Acct., Prof. Cost Acct., 38th Advanced Management Programme, Harvard 1960. *M.* 1942, Joanne Mitchener. *S.* 2. *Dau.* 1. *Career:* Treasury Department, Wellington 1937–41. Sub-Lieut. (Radar), R.N.Z.N.V.R. 1941–43; Dept. of Scientific and Industrial Research 1943–44; Treasury Dept. (Research Officer) 1944–53; Secy. Tasman Pulp & Paper Co. Ltd. 1953–55 (Secy. & General Sales Manager 1955–56; Commercial Manager & Secretary 1956–57; General Manager 1962–63; Managing Director, July 1963–Dec. 1967); Consultant 1968–69; Chmn. National Development Conference Cttee. Education Training and Research 1968–69; Professor of Management Accounting Victoria Univ. Wellington 1968–70; Prof. Mangt. Studies Univ. of Waikato since 1970 and Dean of Mangt. Studies since 1971; Mem., Bd. of Research, New Zealand Soc. of Accountants since 1971. *Address:* Newell's Road, Hamilton RD3, New Zealand; and *office* University of Waikato, Hamilton, New Zealand.

**SCHMITT, Harrison H.** American. *B.* 1935. *Educ.* Calif. Inst. of Technology—BS; Univ. of Oslo, Norway; Harvard Univ. —Doctorate in Geology. *Career:* Fullbright Fellowship 1957–58, Kennecott Fellowship in Geology 1958–59, Harvard Fellowship 1959–60, Harvard Travelling Fellowship 1960, Parker Travelling Fellowship 1961–62, Nat. Science Foundation Postdoctoral Fellowship, Dept. of Geological Sciences, Harvard 1963–64; with U.S. Geological Survey Astrogeology Dept. until 1965; project Chief on Photo and Telescopic Mapping of Moon & Planets; Selected as Scientist-Astronaut by NASA, June 1965; completed Flight Training 1966; Lunar Module Pilot, Apollo XVII, Dec. 1972; Chief, Astronaut Office, Science & Applications, Johnson Space Center 1974; Asst. Admin., Energy Programs, NASA, Washington, D.C. 1974–76; Republican Senator from New Mexico since 1977. *Member:* Geological Soc. of America; Amer. Geophysical Union; Amer. Assn. for the Advancement of Science; Amer. Assn. of Petroleum Geologists; Amer. Inst. of Aeronautics & Astronautics; Sigma Xi; Navy League. *Address:* Room 1251, Dirksen Senate Office Building, Washington, D.C. 20510, U.S.A.

**SCHMITT, Henry J.** American newspaper editor and publisher. *B.* 1909. *Educ.* College of Science, North Dakota, *M.* 1937; Viola D. Oyhus. *S.* Peter. *Career:* Pres. Aberdeen News Co., Aberdeen, South Dakota; Editor, American News; Director: Aberdeen National Bank; Grand Forks (N.D.) Herald; Dir. Bd. Chmn. Boulder Pub. Co. Boulder, Colorado. *Address:* 1415 North Washington Street, Aberdeen, S.D., U.S.A.

**SCHMITT-VOCKENHAUSEN, Dr. (Karl) Hermann.** German Publisher and Politician. *B.* 1923. *Educ.* Goethe Gymnasium Frankfurt/Main; Univ. of Frankfurt. *M.* 1951, Ruth Schulz. *Dau.* 1. *Career:* Departmental Head, Hessen Ministry of the Interior 1945–48; mem., SPD since 1945; Chmn., Mainz-Taunus Subdistrict of the SPD 1950–71; mem., District Cttee. of Main-Taunus District 1948–52; Chmn., District Council 1952–77; mem. Bundestag since 1953; Chmn., Internal Cttee. of the Bundestag 1961–69; Vice-Pres. of the Bundestag since 1969; Vice-Pres., German Municipal Council 1966–73; Pres., German Town & Municipalities League since 1973. *Member:* Central Cttee. of German Catholics; German Forests Protection Assoc., Hessen District Fed. (Chmn.); German-Ibero-American Soc. (Pres.). *Decorations:* Diplomatic Distinguished Service Order (Rep. of Korea), 1971; Freiherr von Stein-Plakette, 1973; Grand Medal in Gold, with ribbon, for distinguished services (Austria), 1975; Medal: "To the Patron of the German Book Trade," 1975; Hon. Dr., Nat. Univ. of Seoul, 1975; Grand Cross of the Fed. German Republic for Distinguished Services, with Star & Sash, 1976. *Publication:* Die Wahlprüfung in Bund und Ländern unter Einbeziehung Österreichs und der Schweiz (Dissertation, 1969). *Address:* Oranienstrasse 20, 6232 Bad Soden/Ts; and *office* Bundeshaus, 5300 Bonn, Federal Republic of Germany.

**SCHMITZ, Dr. Wolfgang.** Austrian economist and central banker. *B.* 1923. *Educ.* University of Vienna (LLD, 1948); University of Freiburg (Switzerland); Catholic University of Washington D.C. *M.* 1951, Dr. Elisabeth Mayr-Harting. *S.* Stefan. *Daus.* Johanna, Dorothea, Therese and Veronika. *Career:* Federal Chamber of Commerce, 1950–64; Chmn., Beirat für Wirtschafts und Sozialfragen, 1964; Federal Minister of Finance, 1964–68; President of the Austrian National Bank, Feb. 1968–73; Governor for Austria of the International Monetary Fund, 1968–73; Lecturer on Economic Policy, Univ. of Vienna; Pres., Institute for Advanced Studies, Vienna; Hon. Pres. Austro-American Soc., Austro-Japanese Soc. *Publications:* Books & numerous articles on economic (mainly monetary) and legal topics. *Address:* Gustav Tschermakgasse 3, A-1180 Vienna; and *office* c/o Austrian Federal Economic Chamber, 10 Biberstrasse, A-1010 Vienna, Austria.

**SCHMOLLER, Hans Peter,** RDI 1976. British book designer. *B.* 1916; educated in Germany. M. (1) 1947, Dorothée Wachsmuth (*D.* 1948) and (2) 1950, Tatyana Kent. *S.* Sebastian. *Dau.* Monica. *Career:* Joined Penguin Books Ltd. 1949, Dir. 1960–76, Consultant since 1976. Contributions to The Times, The Times Literary Supplement, The Penrose Annual, Signature, Imprimatur, Der Druckspiegel, Graphis. Contributed to publication: Essays in the History of Publishing (Longman 1724–1974). *Awards:* British gold medallist, International Book Design Exhib. Leipzig 1971; Royal Designer for Industry (Royal Soc. of Arts) 1976. *Clubs:* Arts (London); Double Crown (London, President 1968). *Address:* Steading, Down Place, Windsor, Berks.

**SCHNABEL, Frank.** American. *B.* 1926. *Educ.* Univ. of Washington (BA Pol Sc) and Univ. of Calif., Los Angeles (BA Geography). *M.* (1) 1952, Hylma Freer (Div.) *S.* Frank Lorne. *Dau.* Gina Maria (2) 1972, Marthe Picard. *Career:* President, Schnabel & Associates Ltd. (San José, Costa Rica) 1950–52. Editor, Hemophilia To-day (handbook); Vice-President and Director: Canabam Ltd. Research Analyst, Imperial Trust Co., Montreal, Director, Kativo Chemical Industries Ltd., San José Costa Rica; Pres., World Federation of Haemophilia; Hon. Consul, Costa Rica, Montreal, Canada. Trustee: National Haemophilia Foundation. *Director:* Wesley Investments Ltd. *Member:* Phi Delta Theta. Anglican. *Address:* 505 Habitat 67, Montreal; and *office* Suite 2912, 1155 Dorchester Boulevard West, Montreal H3B 2L5, Canada.

**SCHNYDER, Felix.** Swiss diplomat. *B.* 1910. *Educ.* University of Berne. *M.* Sigrid Bucher. *Dau.* Barbara. *Career:* With Foreign Service of Federal Political Department, since 1940. Served in Moscow, Berlin & Washington. Minister Plenipotentiary to Israel, 1957; High Commissioner of the United Nations for Refugees, 1961–65; Ambassador to the U.S.A. 1966–75; Pres., Swiss National Cttee. for UNESCO & Swiss Soc. for Foreign Policy since 1976. *Address:* Via Navegna 25, 6648 Minusio, Switzerland.

**SCHOBER, Karl Herbert.** Austrian diplomat. *B.* 1916. *Educ.* Consular Academy, Vienna, Dip 1938; Univ. of Vienna, LLD 1947. *M.* 1950, Ebba Kleinwächter. *S.* 3. *Dau.* 1. *Career:* Secy. of Embassy, Washington DC 1949–54; Counsellor, Foreign Office, Vienna 1954–57; Chargé d'Affaires in Denmark 1957–59; Envoy Extr. and Plen. in Denmark 1959–61; Ambassador Extr. and Plen. in Denmark 1961–62; Dir. Dept. for bilateral economic affairs, F.O. Vienna 1962–65; Ambassador, Chief of Austrian Mission to E.C. Brussels 1965–69; Ambassador Extr. and Plen. in Sweden 1969–74; Ambassador, Dir.-Gen. for economic affairs, F.O. Vienna 1974–76; Ambassador Ex. & Plen. in the U.S.A. since 1976. *Vice-President:* Hindemith Foundation. *Decorations:* Grand Cross of the Danish Order of Danebrog; Grand Cross of the Swedish Order of the Northern Star; Grand Cross of the Egyptian Decoration of Merit; Knight Commander of the Polish Decoration of Merit; Iranian Tadj Decoration II Class. *Address:* 2419 Wyoming Avenue, N.W., Washington, D.C. 20008, U.S.A.

**SCHOCH, Herman Constantijn, CVO. Dutch** diplomat. *B.* 1910. *Educ.* Lyceum (Gymnasium) Amsterdam; University of Utrecht. LLD. *M.* 1946, Carla Francoise van der Wyck. *S.* 2. *Dau.* 1. *Career:* Secretary British-American Tobacco Co. (Java) Ltd. 1937–46. Served in Netherlands Indies Forces, World War II. Joined Netherlands Foreign Service 1946; Embassy, Paris 1946–47; Ministry of Foreign Affairs, The Hague 1947–49; First Secy. & Counsellor, Embassy, London 1949–54; Counsellor, Embassy, Pretoria 1954–57; Madrid 1957–59; Consul-General in Hong Kong 1959–62; Ambassador to Costa Rica, Nicaragua and Panama 1963–65; Ambassador to Hungary 1965–70; Ambassador to Argentina 1970–72. *Awards:* Knight Order, Netherlands Lion; Officer, Order of Orange-Nassau; Grand Cross Order de Mayo (Argentine); Grand Cross Order of Vasco Nuner de Balboa (Panama); Commander, Royal Victorian Order (U.K.); Commander, Order of Civil Merit (Spain). *Address:* 20 Avenue des Figuiers, 1067 Lausanne, Switzerland.

**SCHOEMAN, Barend Jacobus.** South African Politician (Ret'd). *B.* 1905. *Educ.* Matric. and two years' study for degree. *M.* Herculina Pauline van Kooyen. *S.* 1 (adopted). *Career:* Former Minister of Labour, of Public Works, of Forestry; Minister of Transport 1954–74. Member South African National Party. *Address:* Bryntivion 11, Pretoria, South Africa.

**SCHOFIELD, Edward Guy.** British. Director, United Newspapers Ltd. *B.* 1902. *Educ.* Leeds Modern School. *M.* 1937, Ellen Clark. *Dau.* 1. With Leeds Mercury 1918–25; Daily Dispatch (Manchester) 1925–28; Evening Chronicle (Manchester) 1928–29; Chief Sub-Editor, Evening Standard (London) 1931–38; Editor: Yorkshire Evening News 1938–43, Evening News (London) 1943–50, Daily Mail (London) 1950–54. Director, Associated Newspapers Ltd. 1947–54; Director of Publicity, Conservative Party 1956–57. *Publications:* The Purple and the Scarlet (1959); Crime Before Calvary (1960); In the Year '62 (1962); Why Was He Killed? (1965); The Men that Carry the News (1975). Fellow Inst. of Journalists; Chairman, British Committee, International Press Inst. (1953–54); Founder Member of the Press Council. *Club:* National Liberal (London). *Address:* Pear Tree Cottage, Sinnington, York.

**SCHOLEFIELD, Jack Hardy Bree.** British. barrister and solicitor. *B.* 1909. *Educ.* Cheltonia Coll. (London); Lansdowne School and Wairarapa Coll., Masterton, N.Z. (*dux* 1927); and Victoria Univ. of Wellington, N.Z. (LL.M 1936); Bowen Prize (World Affairs) 1935. *M.* 1935, Patricia May Taplin. *S.* Guy William Hardy. *Daus.* Annette Patricia (Taylor) and Jacqueline (Murie). *Career:* Practising law in Invercargill since 1939; City Solicitor, Invercargill Corporation, New Zealand 1950–66; Partner, Scholefield & Skipworth, Solicitors, Invercargill. *Member:* Cncl., Southland Dist. Law Socy. 1940–58 (including term as Pres.); Council N.Z. Law Society. Lecturer in law, Timaru Technical Coll., and later Southland Tech. Coll. Former Pres., Wellington Law Students' Socy.; Exec., University Club (Wellington) and South Canterbury Junior Chamber of Commerce (Timaru) 1937–39. Exec. and Hon. Life Member, Southland Lawn Tennis Assn. 1939–54 and 1957–60 (represented Southland tennis 1942). Pres., Southland Lawn Tennis Umpires Assn. and Vice-Pres. N.Z. Assn. 1958—. Foundation, Exec. Member, Southland Provincial Council of Sport, and Foundation Pres., Southland Fed. of Home and Schools Associations. *Address:* 13 Kauri Terrace, Invercargill; and Scholefield & Skipworth, Commercial Bank Chambers Invercargill, N.Z.

**SCHOLTEN, Willem, MP.** Dutch politician. *B.* 1927. *Educ.* Master of Law. *M.* 1954, Cornelia Maria van der Eijk. *S.* 1. *Dau.* 1. *Career:* Insp. of Taxes (Finance Dept.) 1951–63; MP (Second Chamber) 1963–71; Secy. of State of Finance (Taxation) 1971–73; MP and Member European Parlt. 1972–76; Mem., Council of State since 1976. *Mem.* Intern. Assoc. of Fiscal Law; Commissaris Ennia, Nationale Investerings Bank Bam en Nutsspaarbank; board of Bronovo en Papefonds. *Awards:* Ridder Nederlandse Leeuw, Grootkruis orde van verdienste van Luxembourg. *Publications:* Editor, (weekly) Fiscal Law; various publications on fiscal rights. *Address:* Kievitlaan, 2 Leidschendam, Netherlands; and *office* Binnenhof, 1 den Haag, Netherlands.

**SCHOTT, Stuart.** U.S. Consultant. *B.* 1913. *Educ.* Univ. of Kentucky (BS), and Univ. of Cincinnati (MA; PhD). *M.* 1939, Laurene Davis. *Daus.* Susan and Nancy. *Career:* Research Chemist, Lemanco Laboratories 1937–39; Asst. Chemist, U.S. Public Health Service 1939–41; Major, Sanitary Corps. U.S. Army 1941–45. With National Distillers & Chemical Corp.: Research Chemist 1946–49, Asst. Research Director 1949–54, and Research Director 1954—; Vice-Pres., Research, U.S.I. Chemicals Co., Div. of Natl. Distillers & Chemical Corp. 1957–73; Visiting Lecturer Marine Sciences Dept. of South Florida, Chemical Consultant since 1973; Technical Consultant, Bayfront Medical Center, St. Petersburg, Fla. since 1977. Awarded 30 patents (and a number pending) in the fields of petrochemicals, polymer chemistry, alkali metals and metal organic compounds. *Member:* Amer. Chemical Socy,; Socy. of the Chemical Industry (American Section). *Address:* 515 55th Avenue, St. Petersburg Beach, Florida 33706, and *office* 801 S. 1st Street, St. Petersburg, Florida 33701, U.S.A.

**SCHRAMM, James Siegmund.** Lieut.-Col., U.S.A.; Legion of Merit; businessman, merchant, art collector. *B.* 1904. *Educ.* Amherst College (LHD) and Coe College (LLD); DFA Grinnell College. *M.* 1931, Dorothy Daniell. *Daus.* Mrs. E. C. Martin and Mrs. Charles I. Doughty. *Career:* Executive of J. S. Schramm & Co. 1946—; Pres., Des Moines Art Center, 1963—; Chairman, Amherst College Advisory Cttee. on Contemporary Art; Republican State Chairman of Iowa and member of National Committee 1952–54; member, National Planning Association 1952–63; Director, Committee for International Trade Organization 1950–51; member, U.S. Foreign Trade Missions to Japan 1958; and to France 1960; at U.S. Office of Civil Defense 1941–42; member, Army of the U.S. 1942–45, and American Association for the United Nations; Dir. member Exec. Cttee. National Trade Policy 1950—; Bd. Dirs. Chicago Museum of Contemporary Art 1968. *Member:* Natl. Retail Merchants Assn. (Director 1950—; Amer. Federation of Arts (Trustee 1950— Exec. Cttee. 1954—; Pres. 1956–58). *Awards:* Distinguished Service Award Univ. of Iowa 1971. Royal Society of Arts (Benjamin Franklin Fellow); Foreign Policy Association. *Publications:* numerous addresses on art on foreign trade. *Clubs:* Rotary International; Des Moines; American Collectors; Century Assoc.; des Compagnons du Bontemps-Medoe (Bordeaux, France). *Address:* 2700 South Main Street, Burlington, Iowa 52601; and *office* P.O. 727 Burlington, Iowa, 52601 U.S.A.

**SCHREIL, Per Johan Edvard.** Swedish. *B.* 1916. *Educ.* Royal Tech. Univ. Stockholm. *M.* 1944, Elisabet Smedinger. *S.* 1. *Daus.* 2. *Career:* Dir. Marinverkstaderna 1951–61; Karlskronavaret AB 1961–62; Deputy Man. Dir. Fernstroms Granitindustrier & Fernstroms Rederier 1962–63. Man. Dir. Uddevallavarvet Aktiebolag 1964–75; Dir. The Statsforetag Group of Sweden 1975–77. *Member:* Swedish Assn. Engrs. & Architects. *Address:* Ringvägen 8, 37100 Karlskrona, Sweden.

**SCHREUDER, Johannes.** Dutch. *B.* 1915. *M.* 1942, Elisabeth Margaretha van Overeem. *S.* Gilles Jan. *Daus.* Henriette Elisabeth Margaretha, Antoinette Maria. Manager Coöperateve Centrale Raiffeisen-Bank 1958–73. *Award:* Knight, Order of Netherlands Lion. *Address:* Jan Steenlaan 32, Bilthoven, Netherlands.

**SCHRÖDER, Dr. Gerhard.** Chairman, Foreign Affairs Committee of the German Parliament. *B.* 1910. *Educ.* Königsberg, Edinburgh, Berlin, Bonn and Cologne (Doctorate). *Career:* Worked as assistant in the legal faculty of Bonn Univ. and the Kaiser-Wilhelm Institute in Berlin, and passed his final state examinations 1936; commenced law practice in Berlin 1936; member of the Bekennende Kirche (confessing church). Served as a soldier throughout World War II; joined the civil service and was engaged in administrative work in North Rhine-Westphalia; appointed Deputy member of the Zonal Council (in which the States of the British occupation zone consulted on joint political and economic questions); returned to law practice in Düsseldorf 1947. When the German mining and steel industry was reorganized he was appointed departmental director in the Association of Steel Trustees; attracting the attention of the Christian Democratic Union, he was asked to stand for the Bundestag (Lower House of Parliament); Member (C.D.U.) of Bundestag, since 1949; elected Deputy-Leader, Christian Democratic and Christian Socialist parliamentary group in Bundestag 1952; Federal Minister of Interior 1953–61. Minister of Foreign Affairs 1961–66 Minister of Defence in the Federal Republic of Germany 1966–69. Chairman, Protestant Group of Christian Democratic and Christian Socialist Union. *Address:* Bonn-Bad Godesberg, Pappelweg 25a, Germany.

**SCHRODERUS, Eero (Wilhelm).** Finnish banker. *B.* 1914. *Educ.* MA. *M.* 1940. Anita Grönlund, DDM. *S.* Timo and Martti. *Career:* With Oy Pohjoismaiden Yhdyspankki: Assistant Manager, Pori 1946–49, and Vaasa Branches 1949–55, Manager of the latter Branch 1955–56; Assistant General Manager 1956–59. Member, Board of Management 1956—, and Deputy Chief General Manager, Oy Pohjoismaiden Yhdyspankki, Helsinki 1959—. Member, Bd. Dir. Industri alization Fund of Finland Ltd., Vakuutus Oy Fennia, The Industrial Bank of Finland. Oy Finlayson Ab., Oy. L.M-Ericson Ab. and Oy Suomen Bayer Ab, Oy Agfa-Gernert Ab, Sponsor Oy, Medals: Vap. mit. i, K.SL. Member, Board of the Chamber of Commerce of the City of Vaasa 1954–56; Bd. Dlrs. Finnish Bankers Association. *Address:* Pormestarinrinne 3. Helsinki; and Oy Pohjoismaiden Yhdyspankki, Aleksanteriokatu 30, Helsinki, Finland.

**SCHROTH, Erich.** German industrialist. Member of the Board of Didier-Werke AG, Wiesbaden 1954—. *Member:* Technical Board, Research Institute of the Feuerfest-Industrie of Germany; Supervisory Board of Sintermag, S.A., San Sebastian (Spain), and of Didier-Mersa S.A., Lugones (Spain). *B.* 1902. *Educ.* Technical High School, Breslau (Civil Engineer). With various fire-proofing works: Stellawerk, Ratibor; Möncheberger Gewerkschaft, Kassel; Scheidthauer & Giessing, Duisburg 1926–31; Works Director, Mainzlar Division of Didier-Werke 1931–39; Head of West Work-Group, of Didier-Werke 1939–45; Technical Director of main administration 1945–54. *Member:* German Ceramic Society, and of the Association of German Iron Foundry Works. *Club:* Golf (Wiesbaden). *Address: office* Lessingstr. 16, Wiesbaden, Germany.

**SCHUBERT, Hans.** German executive. *B.* 1917. *M.* 1943, Anni Gerda Lefin. *Daus.* 2. *Career:* Consul for the Dominican Republic 1956—. Owner of the Sportfilm and Weltvertrieb Hans Schubert, Munich. Filmed: the Football World Championships at Berne, 1954, at Stockholm, 1958, and in Chile, 1962; has World Distribution rights for films of Olympic Games. *Address:* Mauerkircherstrasse 37, Munich 80; and *office* Pacellistrasse 7, Munich 2, Germany.

**SCHÜLER, Franz.** German businessman (with dipl.), Lecturer (dipl.) and Dr. Phil. *B.* 1910. *Educ.* technical studies (physics, chemistry, anatomy, and zoology); Diplom-Kaufmann; Diplom-Handelslehrer; Dr. Phil. *M.* 1946, Toni Risse, *S.* 3. *Daus.* 4. *Career:* Previously: with Hildebrand Sohn Rheinmühlenwerk, Mannheim; Karl Bob (Manager), Staufen-Breisgau; Bonames AG leather factory (member of Board), Frankfurt; Rothe AG leather factory (Chairman), Bad Kreuznach; and Auer-Mühle-Konzern (Advisor), Cologne. Manager: Labona GmbH (oil distribution), Baden-Baden; and Kairos Publications GmbH, Baden-Baden. *Publications:* books on the local history of Baden-Baden; free-lancing in various electro-technical works. *Address:* Yburgstr. 25, Baden-Baden, Germany.

**SCHULTZ, Whitt Northmore,** LittD. American public relations executive, lecturer, writer, director of special education projects and consultant to business. *B.* 1920. *Educ.* Washington and Lee University 1938–40, North-western University 1940–42 (BS Public Speaking, Journalism), Webber Coll. (LittD), University of Buffalo (Hon. awards). *M.* (1) 1948, Patricia Reynolds Will (*Dec.*). *S.* Hunter Northmore. *Dau.* April Northmore, Dawn Marie. *M.* (2) 1969, Mary Ann Adams. *Career:* U.S. Army (Official Army War Correspondent; Editor Stars & Stripes, Pacific Area) 1942–45; Chief Exec. Officer, Northmore's (mail order firm with over one hundred thousand customers) 1948–53; Former Director, Public Relations and Adveristing, Encyclopaedia Britannica, Educational Corporations' Reference Division, and of National Marketing, Great Books Division (1965–67). P.R.E., Bell Telephone System 1953–65. Owner, How to Book Co. 1955—; Chief Executive Officer, Perry & Schultz, Publishers, and the Knowledge News and Feature Syndicate 1960—; WKNRB International; International operating consultants to management; Pres. Management Consultant Publishers Inc. Lake Forest, Ill. *Member:* Advisory Board Creative Education Foundation Inc., Buffalo; Evening School faculties at New Trier High School, Central College, North-western University; University of Chicago, Mallinckrodt College; Sigma Delta Chi. *Publications:* How you can make more money by Mail Order Clinic: Creative Salesmanship; How to start, build and operate your own mail order business; How to start, build and operate your own franchise business; over 2,000 magazine and newspaper articles. *Clubs:* University (Chicago); Exmoor Country (Highland Park, Ill.). *Address:* 1245 Richmond Lane, Wilmette, Ill. 60091; and *office* c/o How to Company, P.O. Box 100, Kenilworth, Ill. 60043, U.S.A.

**SCHULTZE, Charles Louis.** American Economist. *B.* 1924. *Educ.* Georgetown Univ. & Univ. of Maryland (Ph.D). *Career:* U.S. Army 1943–46; Admin. Asst., Democratic Nat. Cttee. 1948; Research Specialist, Army Security Agency 1948–49; Instructor, Coll. of St. Thomas (St. Paul, Minn.) 1949–51; Economist, Office of Price Stabilisation 1951–52, Council of Econ. Advisers 1952–53, 1955–59; Machine & Allied Products Inst. 1953–54; Assoc. Prof. of Economics, Indiana Univ. 1959–61; Prof. of Economics, Univ. of Maryland 1951–52, 1968–76; Asst. Dir., Bureau of the Budget 1962–65, Dir. 1965–68; Senior Fellow, Brookings Institution; Chmn. Council of Econ. Advisers since 1977. *Address:* 5826 Nevada Avenue, N.W., Washington, D.C. 20015, U.S.A.

**SCHULZ, Alfred Ernst-August.** German industrialist, *B.* 1906. *Educ.* practical studies in banking, auditing and industry. *M.* 1965, Irene von Siemens, (*dec'd*). *S.* 1. *Daus.* 3. *Career:* Banking and auditing until 1936, mining 1939, Member of the Board: Henschel (aircraft and motor works), Kassel, and of Henschel & Sohn GmbH, Kassel. German Commissioner General for EXPO 70, Osaka, Japan, Member of Board of Export Committee of BDI, Köln; Senior Member, Board of VDMA, Frankfurt/M; Member of Board, Councillors of Gerling Corp., Northrhine-Westfalia. Chairman of Supervisory Board of Aug. Gundlach GmbH, Grossalmerode; *Publications:* articles in German and foreign trade papers on development aid problems in German export. *Clubs:* Ubersee; Ibero-Amerik: Verein, Hamburg. *Address:* Haldenstr. 6, CH 8700 Kusnacht ZH, Switzerland.

**SCHULZ, Klaus-Peter,** Dr. German politician, medical doctor and writer. *B.* 1915. *Educ.* French coll. Berlin; Universit. in Greifswald and Berlin; Dr. Medicine. *M.* Sigrid Blumer. *S.* 3. *Daus.* 7. *Career:* Military Service 1937–45; Journalist in radio and later studio-director, Berlin 1945–65; Mem. of Regional Diet of Baden-Württemberg 1952–56; Mem. of Berlin Chamber of Deputies 1962–65; mem of German Bundestag, the Assembly of Council of Europe, Assembly of Western European Union and European Parliament 1965–77. *Member:* SPD (Germany) 1931–71; CDU (Christian

Dem. Union) 1971–76; European Union since 1950; German-Israeli Assn.; Assn. for Human Rights. *Decoration:* (Declined FDSO); 1974 Medal of Council of Europe. *Publications:* Sorge um die Deutsche Linke (1954) (Anxiety about the German Left); Opposition als Politishes Schicbsal? (1958) (Opposition as political destiny?); Tucholsky Monograph (1959) (Tucholsky was a German Communist poet); Berlin zwischen Freiheit und Diktatur (1961) (Berlin between freedom and dictatorship); Auftakt zum Kalten Krieg (1965) (Prelude to the Cold War); Der Reichstag gestern—morgen (1969) (The Reichstag yesterday–tomorrow); Ich warne (1972) (I issue a warning); Die Ehrbaren Erpresser (1976); Berlin und die Berliner (1977). *Address:* 1 Berlin-19, Eichkampstrasse 16, Germany.

**SCHUMANN, Christian Gustav Waldemar.** South African. *B.* 1898. *Educ.* BSc (Stellenbosch) and DComm (Rotterdam). *M.* 1928, Hester Winifred Perks. *S.* 1. *Daus.* 3. *Career:* Prof. of Commerce, Univ. of Stellenbosch 1932–60 and Dean of Faculty 1936–60 (retired). Director, South African Reserve Bank 1956–65 (resigned); Pres. Economic Socy. of South Africa 1957–58. Economic Advisor, Bureau for Economic Research, Univ. of Stellenbosch. Director: Trust Bank of Africa Ltd., and several other companies. *Member:* Economic Socy. of South Africa. Member Nationalist Party. *Publications:* Die Kredietmark in Suid Afrika (1928); The World Depression, South Africa and the Gold Standard (1932); Structural Changes and Business Cycles in South Africa 1806–1936) (1938); Ekonomie—in Inleidende Studie (with Dr. Franzen and Dr. de Koch) 1944 (twice revised); Economic Diagnosis and Business Forecasting (1954); many articles in South African and overseas publications. *Clubs:* Stellenbosch Golf; Here Seventien (Capte Town). *Address:* 5 Rowan Street, Stellenbosch, C.P., South Africa; and *office* Bureau for Economic Research, University, Stellenbosch, C.P., South Africa.

**SCHUMANN, Maurice.** French politician. *B.* 10 Apr. 1911. *Educ.* Lycée Janson de Sailly (L. ès L.). *M.* 1944, Lucie Daniel. *Daus.* Christine Laurence, Béatrice. *Career:* Editor, Havas Agency and Asst. Dir. in London 1933–35; attached to Diplomatic Section, Havas Agency, Paris 1935–39; Liaison Officer to the British Army 1939–40 and 1944–45; Spokesman for the Free French in London 1940–44; landed in Normandy with Commandos, 6 June 1944, and entered Alençon, Paris and Strasbourg 1944–45; Deputy (M.R.P.) for Nord since 1945; President of M.R.P. 1945–49; Chief French Delegate to U.N.O. 1948–50; Secretary of State for Foreign Affairs 1951–54; Pres., Foreign Affairs Cttee. of Nat. Assembly 1959; Minister of State (Prime Minister's Office) April–May 1962; Minister of State, in charge of Scientific Research & Atomic Questions 1967–68; Minister of State for Social Affairs 1963–69; Minister for Foreign Affairs 1969–73; Senator from Department of The Nord since 1974. Member, Académie Française since 1974. *Awards:* Hon. LLD Cambridge 1972, St. Andrews 1974; Chevalier de la Légion d'Honneur; Compagnon de la Libération; Croix de Guerre avec palmes. *Address:* 53 Avenue du Marechal-Lyautey, 75016 Paris, France.

**SCHUURMANS, Constant.** Belgian diplomat. *B.* 1914. *Educ.* D.law, D.Litt (classical philology); Lic.Phil. (St. Thomas Sch. Louvain). Entered dipl. service 1946; Held posts in Amsterdam 1947–48; Held posts in Paris 1948–52; Secy. to Secy. Gen. Min. Foreign Affairs 1953–58; Chief of Cabinet, Min. of Foreign Affairs 1958–61; Ambassador to Greece 1962–65; Perm. Repres. to U.N. 1965–69; Ambassador to Federal Republic of Germany 1970–76; Perm. Repres. to NATO since 1976. *Decorations:* Civic Cross (1st class) 1977; Grand Officer of Order of Leopold II 1967; Grand Officer Order of Leopold 1977; Grand Officer of Order of the Crown 1971; Officer of the Order of the Legion of Honour 1954; Commander 1st Class of l'Ordre Etoile Brillante, 1958; Grand Officer of the Order of Couronne de chêne, 1959; Grand Officer of Order d'Orange Nassau 1959; Cmmd. Cruzeiro de Sul, 1959; Comdr. of the Order of St. Gregory the Great; Comdr. of the Order of Isabelle the Catholic 1960; Grand Officer of the Order of the Crown of Thailand 1960; Commd of the order of St Sepulchre 1961; Grand Cross of the Order of the Phoenix 1961; Grand Officer of the Order of l'Homayoun, 1962; Grand Cross of the Order of George Ier, 1965; Grand Cross of the Order of Merit of the Federal Republic of Germany 1971. *Address:* Leeuwerukendreef 20, 1900 Overijse (B); & *office* NATO, 1110 Brussels, Belgium.

**SCHWAB, Reynold Jean.** Swiss executive. *B.* 1924. *Educ.* Mercantile School. *M.* 1950, Hedwig Huber. *S.* Jean-François Reynold and Yves Alexandre. *Dau.* Catherine Denise. *Career:* Extensive education in banking, insurance, commerce and industry. Gen. Mgr. Swissair in Germany 1967, of Swissair Germany and Northern Europe 1975, of Swissair North America since 1976. Board member, Swiss Center Inc., New York & American-Swiss Assn. New York. *Clubs:* Rotary, Skal, N.Y. Athletic, Wings (New York). *Address:* 300 East 56th Street, Apt. 27f, New York, N.Y. 10022; & *office* 608 Fifth Avenue, New York, N.Y. 10020, U.S.A.

**SCHWARTZ, Alan Earl.** American attorney. *B.* 1925. *Educ.* Western Michigan College, Harvard Business School, University of Michigan (BA with distinction 1947) and Harvard Law School (LLB *magnum cum laude* 1950). *M.* 1950, Marianne Shapero. *S.* Marc and Kurt. *Dau.* Ruthanne. *Career:* Previously: Associate of Kelley, Drye & Warren, New York City 1950–52; Special Assistant Counsel, N.Y. State Crime Commission 1951; on Board of Directors: Kaiser-Frazer Corp., Inc. and Willys Motors Inc. 1953; Visiting Teecher, Wayne State Univ. Law School 1953; Snr. Partner, Honigman, Miller, Schwartz & Cohn, Detroit; member, Board of Directors: Cunningham Drug Stores Inc., Detroit Edison Co., Michigan Bell Telephone Co., Burroughs Corp., SOS Consolidated Inc., Detroitbank Corp., Detroit Bank & Trust Co., Tesoro Petroleum Corp., Handleman Co., Pulte Home Corps., Howell Industries, Inc. Director: United Hosps. of Detroit, March of Dimes, Detroit Renaissance, Inc., Jewish Home for Aged, Cranbrook Sch.; Economic Club of Detroit, Michigan Cancer Foundation, Dir. & Vice-Chmn. United Foundation; Dir. Jewish Welfare Federation of Detroit. Trustee: Detroit Grand Opera Assn., Oakland Univ., Thomas Alva Edison Foundation, Interlochen Arts Academy; Vice-Pres. & member Exec. Cttee. Detroit Symphony Orchestra; Chmn. Governor's Council for Economic Expansion for Michigan; Hon. Trustee, Kalamazoo Coll.; Council of Advisers, Walsh Coll.; Vice-Pres., Mich. Efficiency Task Force Inc. *Publications:* Medical Expert Testimony. *Member:* Michigan and American Bar Associations. *Clubs:* Standard City, Franklin Hills Country. *Address:* 4120 Echo Road, Bloomfield Hills, Michigan 48013; and *office* 2290 First National Building, Detroit 48226, Mich., U.S.A.

**SCHWARZENBERGER, Georg.** British. Director, London Institute of World Affairs 1943—; Emeritus Professor 1975; Professor of International Law, Univ. of London 1962–75; Barrister-at-Law, Gray's Inn. *B.* 1908. *Educ.* PhD (London); Dr. Jur. (Tübingen). *M.* 1931, Suse Schwarz. *S.* Rolph Ludwig Edward. *Career:* Secy., London Institute of World Affairs (formerly New Commonwealth Institute) 1934–43; Lecturer and Reader in International Law & Relations 1938–62, Sub-Dean and Tutor of the Faculty of Laws 1942–49, Vice-Dean, Faculty of Laws 1949–55, 1963–65, Dean 1965–67, University College, London. *Publications:* The Library of World Affairs, The Year Book of World Affairs. and Current Legal Problems. Das Völkerbunds-Mandat für Palästina (1929); Die Kreuger-Anleihen (1931); Die Internationalen Banken für Zahlungsausgleich und Agrarkredite (1932); Die Verfassung der Spanischen Republik (1933); William Ladd, (1935) (2nd ed. 1936); The League of Nations & World Order (1936); Making International Law Work (with G. W. Keeton), 1939 (2nd ed. 1946); Power Politics, 1941 (3rd ed. 1964; transl. into German and Spanish); International Law as Applied by International Courts and Tribunals (International Law, Vol. I, 1945, 3rd ed. 1957; Vol. II, 1968; Vol. III (1976)); A Manual of International Law (1947) (6th ed. 1976, together with E. D. Brown; transl. into German); The Fundamental Principles of International Law (Recueil, Hague Acad. ofInt. Law, 1955— Vol. 87); The Legality of Nuclear Weapons (1958); The Frontiers of International Law (1962); The Inductive Approach to International Law (1965); Foreign Investments & International Law (1969); International Law and Order (1971); The Dynamics of International Law (1976). *Member:* Permanent Finnish-Netherlands Conciliation Commission. *Address:* 4 Bowers Way, Harpenden, Herts.

**SCHWARZMANN, Maurice.** Canadian business consultant. *B.* 1920. *Educ.* Mill-Hill School, London; Univ. of Toronto, BA (Hons), MA (Polit Sc. and Econ.); Univ. of McGill, Montreal. *M.* (1) *S.* 3. *Dau.* 1. (2) 1975, Patricia Finlayson. *Career:* Canadian Army Overseas (Intelligence) 1943–45; Dept. of Trade and Commerce, Ottawa 1949; Asst. Deputy Minister (Trade Policy) 1964–72; Minister (Economic) Canadian Embassy Washington 1959–63; Minister, CDN Delegation, Geneva 1964–67; Chmn. of Canadian delegation to International wheat conferences 1968–72; Ambassador of Canada in Mexico and Guatemala 1972–75; Ambassador of Canada in Venezuela and Dominican Republic 1975–77; Private Business Consultant. *Decorations:* Service Medals: Breuls

Gold Medal (Polit. Sc.) Canada Medal. *Publications:* Background Factors in Spanish Economic Decline (1950–MA Thesis); numerous official publications. *Clubs:* Bankers' (Mexico City); University (Mexico City). *Address:* Calle Amsterdam No. 162, Mexico 11, D.F.; P.O. Box M-2876, Mexico 1, D.F.

**SCHWEIG, Karl Franz,** OBE. German City Tourist Director. *B.* 1906. *Educ.* High School, Commercial School, Commercial Academy. *M.* 1943, Gretel Schmidt. *Career:* Head of German Congress Centre, Berlin 1928–45; Publicity Manager with Fihumin, Hamburg 1945–50; Director, Düsseldorf Bureau of Publicity and Tourism 1950. Vice-President, German Language Cttee. of Académie Internationale de Tourisme. Colonel on Staff of Governor John J. McKeithen, Louisiana, and Aide-de-Camp, Governor's Staff. Hon. Member, International Cultural Centre, Amsterdam; member, Expert Cttee. Académie Internationale du Tourisme, Monaco; member, Cultural Committee 'Malkasten,' Düsseldorf. *Publications:* Archives for the Right of International Organisations (in two languages); How to Organise a Congress (in five languages). Dusseldorf is worth more than just one visit. *Awards:* Cavaliere Uff. al merito della repubblica (Italy); Officer, Order of Leopold II (Belgium); Gold Medal (for Int. Tourist Promotion) N.Y. World's Fair 1964–65. First Class Decoration of the Royal Harmony (Maastricht, Netherlands); Offizier des höchsten Ordens des British Empire (OBE); Great Badge of Honour for special merits (Austria); Cavalier of the Sovereign Military Order of St. George of Carinthia (Grand Officer); Medal of Honour (German Red Cross) Ring of Honour and Certificate of the International Tobacco Scientific Assn. in Rome; Hon. Commodore of the Home Lines Fleet; Praetor, Neronie Order of Knights, Antia, Italy; Chevalier de l'Ordre National du Mérite (France); Chevalier de la Chaine des Rotisseurs; Order of the Alaska Walrus. Member Clipper Club Pan. Amer. World Airways; Compagnon de Bordeaux, L'Académie du Vin. *Member:* Commandeur de la Confrérie des Chevaliers du Tastevin, and of recruiting committee of the German Red Cross. Max Reinhardt Medal, Salzburg. Hon. Citizen of Texas. Diploma, Europe à Montecatini (European philatelic exhibition). *Address:* Jägerhofstrasse 18, Düsseldorf, Federal Republic of Germany.

**SCHWEIKER, Fritz.** German banker; Member, Board of Management Bayerische Hypotheken- und Wechsel-Bank, Munich; Chairman, Vereinigte Fränkische Schuhfabriken, A.G., Nurenberg; member, Committee on Minor Business Relations of the Federal Assn. of Private Banks (E.V.), Cologne, *Address:* Theatinerstrasse 11, Munich, Germany.

**SCHWEIKER, Richard S.** United States Senator. *B.* 1926. *Educ.* Pennsylvania State Univ.—BA (1950); Phi Beta Kappa. *M.* 1955, Claire Joan Coleman. *S.* 2. *Daus.* 3. *Career:* Served with US Navy, World War II; Founder and Two-Term Pres. (1952–54), Montgomery County Young Republican Club; Elected to Congress 1960 (re-elected '62, '64, '66); served on House Government Operations & Armed Services Cttees.; Co-authored plan for mutual de-escalation of Vietnam War; sponsored "Schweiker Act" for cash awards to Military Service Personnel for cost-cutting ideas, 1965; Elected Senator from Pennsylvania 1968 (re-elected 1974): serves on Appropriations Cttee., Human Resources Cttee., Select Cttee. on Nutrition & Human Needs. *Member:* Lions; Navy League; Pa. Society; American Legion; VFW (life); AMVETS (life); Rotary (hon.); Kiwanis (hon.); YMCA; Sons of the American Revolution; Anthracosilicosis League of Pennsylvania (hon.); Dir., Schwennkfelder Library. *Awards:* Hon. Dr. of Public Service, Temple Univ. (1970); Hon. LLD: Ursinus (1963), Pennsylvania Medical (1972), Dickinson (1972), Allbright (1973), LaSalle (1973) and Widener (1973) Colleges; Distinguished Alumnus Award, Pennsylvania State Univ. (1970) and many others. *Publications:* (co-author) How to End the Draft: The Case for an All-Volunteer Army. *Address:* Senate Office Building, Washington, D.C. 20510, U.S.A.

**SCHWEITZER, Pierre-Paul.** French. *B.* 1912. *Educ.* Lic. en Droit; Diplomé, School of Political Science. *M.* Catherine Hatt. *S.* 1. *Dau.* 1. *Career:* Inspector of Finance 1936; Central Finance Administration 1941; Deputy Dir. Directorate of External Finances 1946; Alternate Executive Dir., International Monetary Fund 1947; Secretary-General, Inter-ministerial Committee, European Economic Co-operation 1948; Financial Attaché, Washington 1949; Director of the Treasury, Ministry of Finance 1953; Deputy Governor, Bank of France 1960; Managing Director and Chairman of Executive Board, International Monetary Fund, Washington, D.C. 1963–73; Chmn. Bank of America Intern. SA, Luxembourg & Banque Petrofigaz; Adv. Dr. Bank of America, New York & Unilever NV. Rotterdam; Dir. Robeco Group, Rotterdam 1974. *Awards:* Grand Officer, Legion of Honour; Croix de Guerre (1939–45); Medal of the Resistance; LLD Yale Univ., Harvard Univ., 1966; Leeds Univ., New York Univ., 1968; George Washington, Univ., Univ. of Wales 1972; Williams Coll. 1972. *Address:* 31 rue Danielle Casanova, 75001, Paris, France.

**SCHWEIZER, Dr. jur., Dr. phil. h.c. Samuel.** Swiss banker. *B.* 1903. *Educ.* Universities of Basle and Geneva (Dr. jur.). *M.* 1939, Angela Maria Michelini. *S.* 3. *Daus.* 3. *Career:* Hon. Chmn. Swiss Bank Corp. Basle; Chmn. Sté Internationale Pirelli S.A. Trustee World Wildlife Fund (International); Vice-Chmn. Comité de Direction de l'Institut Suisse à Rome. *Address:* 34 Via Leoni 6932 Breganzoma, Switzerland; and *office* Aeschenvorstadt 1, 4002 Basle, Switzerland.

**SCHWENDLER, William Theodore.** Ret'd Aerospace Mfg. Exec. (Chmn. of Exec. Ctte.), now Director. *B.* 1904. *Educ.* New York University (BS Mech Eng 1924). *M.* 1933, Mabel R. Jorden. *S.* William Theodore, Jr. *Daus.* Olga E. and Hazel A. *Career:* Engineer, Loening Aeronautical Engineering Corp. 1924–25; Project Engineer (1926–27) and Asst. General Manager 1928–30; Chief Engineer, Grumman Aircraft Engineering Corp. 1930–50; Director 1939–69; Vice-Pres. 1940–46; Exec. Vice-Pres. 1946–56; Senior Vice-Pres. 1956–60; Chmn. Exec. Cttee. 1960–69. Chairman of Executive Cttee. Grumman Corp. 1969–73, Dir. 1969–76, Dir. Emeritus since 1976; Consultant since 1974; Vice-Chmn. of the Board, Grumman Aerospace Corp., 1969–71; Senior Exec. 1971–73; Dir. 1969–74 (Ret'd); Dir. Sunrise Federal Savings and Loan Association; *Director* (Ret'd 1974); Grumman Allied Industries, Inc.; Grumman International Inc.; Grumman Data Systems Corp. Inc.; Paumanock Development Corp., formerly Montauk Aero Corp.; Grumman Ecosystems Corp; Grumman American Aviation Corp.; Paumanock Ins. Co. Ltd.; Paumanock Leasing Services Ind. *Awards:* Hon. Dr. Eng, New York University College of Engineering; Fellow, American Institute of Aeronautics and Astronautics; Emeritus Member, Adv. Bd., Acad. of Aeronautics. *Member:* Socy. of Automotive Engineers; Nassau County Council Boy Scouts of America; Board of Trustees, N.Y. Univ. (Life Member); Pi Tau Sigma, Tau Beta Pi, Phi Kappa Tau; Newcomen Socy. in N. America. Presidential Citation from N.Y. Univ. 1965. *Clubs:* New York Yacht; Ocean Reef. *Address:* Merritt Road, Farmingdale, N.Y. 11735, U.S.A. and *office* Grumman Corp., Bethpage, N.Y. 11714, U.S.A.

**SCHWENGEL, Hon. Frederic Delbert.** *B.* 1907. *Educ.* Sheffield (Iowa) High School, N.E. Missouri State Teachers' Coll. (BS) and Univ. of Iowa; Hon. LLD Parson Coll. (Fairfield, Iowa), Lincoln (Ill.) Coll., Sullivan Award Winner. *M.* 1931, Clara Ethel Cassity. *S.* Franklin Dean. *Dau.* Dorothy (Neale Cosby). *Career:* State Representative to the Iowa Legislature 1945–54. Previously High Schoolteacher and coach, and insurance agent. Representative (Republican) to U.S .Congress 1954–64, 1967–72. (Member, Pub. Works Cttee. and House Admin. Chmn.; Bd. of Governors of Lincoln Group of D.C. (also past Pres.); Joint Cttee. on Arrangements for 100th Anversity of the First Inauguration of Abraham Lincoln, and Jt. Cttee. on Arrangements for the 150th Anniversity of the Birth of Abraham Lincoln. Vice-Chairman, National Civil War Centennial Commission. Exec. Dir. Joint Committee for Second Inauguration. *Publications:* Lincoln for The Ages; various historical papers for special occasions. Hon. Member, Lincoln Sesquicentennial Commission. *Member:* U.S. Capitol Historical Society (Pres.); Civil War Centennial Commission; Zeraphath Consistory, Kaaba Shrine, Royal Order of the Moose, DeMolay Legion of Honor, Phi Sigma Epsilon and Blue Key fraternities. *Address:* 3232 N. Ohio, Arlington ,Va.; *office* 200 Maryland Avenue, N.E. Washington, D.C. 20515, U.S.A.

**SCOPES, Sir Leonard Arthur,** KCVO, CMG, OBE. *B.* 1912. *Educ.* Gonville and Caius College, Cambridge (MA). *M.* 1938, Brunhilde Slater Rolfe. *S.* 2. *Daus.* 2. *Career:* A member of the British Consular, Foreign and Diplomatic Services 1933–67; United Nations Joint Inspection Unit 1968–71. *Address:* Salcombe, Devon.

**SCOTT, Sir David Aubrey,** KCMG. British diplomat. *B.* 1919. *Educ.* Charterhouse and Birmingham University. *M.* 1941, Vera Kathleen Ibbitson. *S.* Robert and Andrew. *Dau.* Diana. *Career:* Royal Artillery 1939–47 (Major); Chief Radar Adviser to the Egyptian Army 1945–47; Commonwealth Relations Office 1948; in the Union of South Africa 1951–53;

seconded to Cabinet Office, London 1954–56; Secretariat to Prime Ministers' Meeting 1955, and Constitutional Conferences on Malta 1955, West Indies 1956, Federation of Malaya 1956; Singapore 1956–58; Secretariat, Monckton Commission 1960; Deputy High-Commissioner in Fed. of Rhodesia and Nyasaland 1961–63; member of Mr. Butler's Team of Advisers on Central Africa 1962; Deputy High Commissioner, New Delhi 1965–67. British High Commissioner, Kampala 1967–70, and Ambassador (non-resident) to Rwanda; Assistant Under Secretary of State, Foreign & Commonwealth Office 1970–72; British High Commissioner Wellington, Governor Pitcairn Island 1973–75; British Ambassador to South Africa since 1976. *Clubs:* Royal Overseas League (London); Pretoria; City & Civil Service (Cape Town). *Address:* 23 Petersham Mews, London, S.W.7.

**SCOTT, Harry (Albert).** Canadian diplomat. Consul-General of Canada, New York 1956–66. *B.* 1899. *Educ.* Queen's University (Kingston, Ont.); BA 1922. *M.* 1924, Agreeta Denness. *Career:* Ambassador to Cuba 1951–56 (concurrently Ambassador to Haiti and the Dominican Republic 1955–56); Consul-General, San Francisco 1948–51; Commercial Counsellor, Embassy, Washington, D.C. 1941–48; Canadian Foreign Trade Service 1925; successively in Liverpool, Buenos Aires, Shanghai (1938), London (1939) and Washington (see above) 1941; seconded to Commonwealth Air Training Plan, as Secretary to Supervisory Board, Ottawa, 1940; Foreign Dept., Ford Motor Co. of Canada Ltd. (Windsor, Ont.) 1922–24; served in World War I in United Kingdom (Royal Naval Air Service 1917 and the Royal Canadian Navy 1918). *Address:* 12 Church Street, St. Catherines, Ont., Canada.

**SCOTT, John Vivian.** Diplomat, Foreign Service Officer. *B.* 1920. *Educ.* LLB (New Zealand). *M.* 1946, Marguerite Cachemaille Boxer. *Daus.* Hilary Judith, Susan Veronica and Deborah Mary. *Career:* First Secy., N.Z. Permanent Mission to U.N., N.Y. 1951–55; Councillor, N.Z. High Commission, London 1958–62; Head, Economic Div., Dept. of External Affairs, Wellington 1962–65; Acting Asst. Secy. 1964; Ambassador to Japan & Republic of Korea, 1965–68; Permanent Representative of New Zealand to United Nations 1969–73; Dep. Secy. For. Affairs, Wellington, N.Z. since 1973. *Address:* Ministry of Foreign Affairs, Wellington, N.Z.

**SCOTT, Laurence Prestwich.** British newspaper publisher. *B.* 1909. *Educ.* Rugby School; Trinity College, Cambridge (BA). *M.* (1) 1939, Constance Mary Black (*D.* 1969). *S.* Martin and Jonathan. *Dau.* Susan. (2) Jessica Mary Crowther Thompson. *S.* Laurence Jo. Chairman, Manchester Guardian and Evening News Ltd. 1949–73; Director, Anglia Television Ltd. since 1958. *Address:* Redes House, Siddington, Macclesfield, Cheshire.

**SCOTT, Nicholas Paul.** MBE. JP. British politician. *B.* 1933. *Educ.* Clapham College. *M.* Elizabeth Robinson (*diss.* 1976). *S.* 1. *Daus.* 2. *Career:* served Holborn Borough Council 1956–59; Contested (C) S.W. Islington 1959 and 1964; Nat. Chmn. Young Conservatives 1963; Member Parliament (Con.) South Paddington 1966–74; and for Chelsea since 1974; Vice Chmn. Cons. Party Employment Cttee. 1967–72; Parly. Private Secy. to Chancellor Exchequer 1970; to Home Secretary 1972–74; Parly Under Secy. State Dept. of Employment. 1974; Shadow Cabinet (Housing Spokesman) 1974–75; Dir. A. S. Kerswill Ltd.; Eastbourne Printers Ltd.; Juniper Studios Ltd.; Cleveland Offshore Fund; Ede & Townsend Ltd.; Midhurst White Holdings Ltd.; Bonusplan Ltd.; Creative Consultants. *Member:* Cttee. MCC; Chmn. Westminster Comm. Relations Council; Paddington Churches Housing Assn.; Brit. Atlantic Group, Young Politicians; Nat. Pres. Tory Reform Group; Gov. British Inst. Human Rights. *Club:* Turf. *Address:* House of Commons, London SW1A 0AA.

**SCOTT, Thomas Peat.** *B.* 1905. *Educ.* Scotch College, Melbourne (Matriculation); Fellow Australian Insurance Institute. *M.* 1930, Frances Joyce Elliston. *S.* 2. *Career:* Commissioner, State Electricity Commission of Victoria 1959; Director, Trustees Executors & Agency Co. Ltd. 1971; Dir. (formerly Gen. Man.). National Mutual Life Association of Australasia Ltd., sinee 1970. Dep. Chmn., Melbourne Underground Rail Loop Authority 1971. Past-Pres., Insurance Inst. of Victoria. *Publications:* articles on Australian insurance in various journals and periodicals. *Address:* 21 Irving Road, Toorak, Melbourne, Australia.

**SCOTT. Sir Walter,** Kt, CMG. Australian management consultant. *B.* 1903. *M.* 1931. Dorothy Ransom. *S.* Brian Walter and Ronald Malcom. *Career:* Governing Director, W. D. Scott & Co. Pty. Ltd., and subsidiary and associated companies throughout the world since 1938. Chancellor (and Fellow) Int. Academy of Management; Pres. Fed. Commonwealth Chamber Commerce 1968–70; Pres. (Hon. Pres.) Int. Cttee. for Scientific Mangt. (CIOS) 1958–60; Chmn. Aust. Industrial Design Council 1961–66. Chmn. Australian Productivity Council 1963–68; Australian Decimal Currency Board 1963–69; Pharmaceutical Benefits Cttee. 1964—; Deputy Chmn. N.S.W. Ministry of Munitions 1940–45. Member: Australian Secondary Industries Commission 1944–52, and Collinsville Royal Commission 1954–56; Chmn. Australian Decimal Currency Cttee. 1959–60. Pres. Australian Institute of Cost Accountants 1950–52, Aust. Institute of Management 1955–56. Leader, Australian Management Delegation to Stockholm 1947 and São Paulo 1954. *Awards:* Wallace Clark Award (U.S.A.) for services to international management 1957; Henry Robinson Towne Lecturer 1961 (Amer. Socy. Mechanical Engineers); John Storey Award 1962; Frank & Lilian Gilbreth Award 1963; C.I.O.S. Gold Medal 1966. Leffingwell Award (Amer. Society); Fellow Aust. Socy. of Accountants; Chartered Inst. of Secretaries. *Publications:* Budgetary Control (1937); Cost Accounting (1944); Greater Production (1951); Australia and the Challenge of Change (1960). *Clubs:* Union; Royal Sydney Yacht Sqdn.; American; Sydney Rotary. *Address:* 44 The Anchorage, 5 Milson Road, Cremorne Point, N.S.W. 2090; and *office* 100 Pacific Highway, North Sydney, N.S.W., Australia.

**SCOTT, Willard Philip.** Lawyer and corporation executive *B.* 1909. *Educ.* Ohio State Univ. (AB (Hons.) 1930) and Columbia University (LLB; Dean's Scholar 1933). *M.* 1936, Lucille Westrom. *S.* Robert Willard and David Winbourne. *Dau.* Anne Lucille. *Career:* partner, Oliver & Donnally 1938–65; Vice Chmn. Gen. Counsel and Dir. American Potash & Chemical Corp. 1951—; Bd. of Appeals, Scarsdale N.Y. 1957–68; Vice Pres. and Gen. Counsel, Kerr-McGee Corp. 1968–72, Financial Vice Pres. 1973; Senior Vice Pres. since 1973; Dir. First National Bank & Trust Co. Oklahoma City; Transocean Drilling Co. Acting Mayor and Police Commissioner 1953–55; Mayor of Scarsdale 1955–57. Trustee 1951–55. Editor, The Business Lawyer 1958–59. *Member:* Phi Beta Kappa; Pi Sigma Alpha; Phi Alpha Theta. Fellow, Amer. Bar Foundation. Member: American Law Institute; Research Fellow, The Southwestern Legal Foundation; American Bar Assn. (House of Delegates 1961–62; Secy., Chmn.-Elect. and Chmn. of Section of Corporation, Banking and Business Law 1958–61); New York State Bar Assn.; Chairman, Committee on Corporate Laws, 1966—; Assn. of the Bar of the City of New York; International Bar Assn. (Patron); Phi Delta Phi. *Publications:* various articles on corporate law. *Clubs:* Madison Square Garden N.Y.C.; Union League (N.Y.C.); Metropolitan, University (Washington); California (Los Angeles); Scarsdale Golf (Scarsdale, N.Y.); Oklahoma City Golf and Country; Beacon and Whitehall (Oklahoma City). *Address:* 1812 Drury Lane, Oklahoma City, Oklahoma; and *offices* Kerr-McGee Building, Oklahoma City, Oklahoma 73125, and 99 Park Avenue, New York City 16, U.S.A.

**SCOTT, William Dallas,** ARCS, BSc, DIC, PhD, FRIC, FIRI. British. *B.* 1907. *Educ.* Imperial Coll. of Science & Tech. (ARCS, BSc, DIC, PhD); London School, Economics; Harvard Business School (AMP). *M.* 1933, Phyllis May. *S.* 1. *Dau.* 1. *Career:* Research and Process Engineer, Anglo Iranian Oil Co. 1929–35; Research to Deputy Min. Dir. Monsanto Chemicals Ltd. 1935–51; Overseas Development Dir. Monsanto Chemical Co. (U.S.A.) 1951–54; Dir. Man. Dir. B.T.R. Industries Ltd. 1954–64; Dir. Air Products Ltd. *Member:* Chemical Socy.; Socy. Chem. Ind.; Amer. Chem. Socy.; Plastics Institute; Deputy Chmn. Governing Body, Imperial Coll. Science & Technology. *Clubs:* Harvard Business School; Savage. *Address:* Kirkhill House, Colmonell, Ayrshire.

**SCOTT, Hon. William John.** New Zealand. *B.* 1916. *Educ.* Mount Albert Grammar School. *M.* 1945, Mary Jackson. *Career:* Minister of Broadcasting 1963–66; Senior Government Whip 1961–63; Dep. Chairman, Commonwealth Parliamentary Association 1963–64. Postmaster-General, Minister of Marine, and Minister in Charge of Government Printing Office 1964–69; Director, Seatrans Consolidated (NZ) Ltd., 1970— Chmn. Lakewood Trading Co. Ltd.: Chmn. N.Z. Historic Places Trust, 1970–73; Dir., North Shore Ferries; Man. Dir., Glen Eden Travel Centre, Devonport Travel Centre. Leader N.Z. Delegation Commonwealth Parliamentary Assoc., Conference Malaysia 1963, Trinidad, 1969; N.Z. Delegation Colombo Plan Conference British Columbia (Canada) 1969, Colonel of Kentucky (U.S.A.);

Freeman of City of Louisville, Kentucky; Trustee Museum of Transport & Technology. Member National Party. *Club:* Auckland (Auckland). *Address:* 31 A. Stanley Point Road, Devonport, Auckland, New Zealand.

**SCOTT-HOPKINS, Major James Sidney Rawdon, MP.** British. *B.* 1921. *Educ.* Eton & New Coll., Oxford. *M.* 1946, Geraldine Elizabeth Hargreaves. *S.* 3. *Dau.* 1. *Career:* Served Second World War with Gurkha Rifles & from 1946–50 with Kings Own Yorkshire Light Infantry; contested Bedwellty Div. for House of Commons 1955; won North Cornwall Div. 1959, member 1959–66; PPS to Joint Parl. Under-Sec. of State, Commonwealth Relations Office 1961–62; Joint Parl. Under-Sec. of State, Min. of Agric., Fisheries & Food 1962–64; Conservative Member for Derbyshire West since 1967; Mem. of European Parly. since 1973; Dep. Leader European Conservative Group & Spokesman on Agriculture; Vice-Pres. of European Parliament since 1976. *Clubs:* Carlton. *Address:* Edensor House, Edensor, Baslow, Derbyshire; & House of Commons, London SW1A 0AA.

**SCRANTON, William Warren.** *B.* 1917. *Educ.* Yale Univ. and Law School. *M.* Mary Lowe Chamberlin. *S.* William Worthington, Joseph Curtis, and Peter Kip. *Dau.* Susan. *Career:* Served in World War II (4 years as Pilot Captain) in Army Air Force, in Africa, the Middle East and South America. Associated with International Textbook Co. and Haddon Craftsmen Inc., rising to rank of Vice-Pres. 1947–52. Pres., Scranton-Lackawanna Trust Co. 1954–56; Chmn. of Board, Northeastern Pennsylvania Broadcasting Inc. 1953–59. Special Asst. to Secy. of State Christian. A Herter and represented the U.S. Government at international conferences in Europe, Latin America, and at U.N. during 1959–60; mem. U.S. House of Reps. 1961–63; Gov. of Pennsylvania 1963–67; Special Envoy to Middle East on behalf of Pres.-elect Nixon Dec. 1968; Chmn., President's Comm. on Campus Unrest 1970; President's Price Comm., 1971–72; U.S. Railway Assn., 1973–74; Special Consultant to the President 1974; Perm. Rep. to the UN 1976. Board member: American Express Co., Cummins Engines, Bethlehem Steel, IBM, New York Times, Scott Paper Co. Republican. *Address:* P.O. Box 116, Dalton, Pennsylvania, U.S.A.

**SCRIPPS, Edward Willis.** American. *B.* 1909. *Educ.* Pomona College (founded by the Scripps family). *M.* 1950, Betty Knight McDonnell. *S.* Edward Wyllis III and Barry Howard. *Career:* Board member: Inter-American Press Assn.; Pres., IAPA Tech. Center. Chairman of the Board and President of Scripps League of Newspapers. *Clubs:* Ranier (Seattle); Villa Taverna (San Francisco); St. Francis Yacht (San Francisco); Lyford Cay Nassau. Bahamas. *Address:* 850 Hayne Road, Hillsborough, Calif.; and *offices* 400 El Camino Real, San Mateo, Calif. 94401, U.S.A.

**SCRIVENER, Ronald Stratford,** CMG. *B.* 1919. *Educ.* Westminster School; St. Catharine's College. Cambridge. *M.* 1962, Mary Alice Olga Sofia Jane Hohler. *Career:* Exec. Dir., British-Soviet Chamber of Commerce since 1977; formerly H.M. Diplomatic Service; Served in Berlin, Buenos Aires, Vienna, Caracas, Berne, Bangkok; Ambassador to Panama 1969–70, to Czechoslovakia 1971–74; Asst. Under-Secy. of State, FCO 1974–76. *Clubs:* White's; Anglo Belgian. *Address:* 72 Bedford Gardens, London, W.8.

**SCRIVENOR, Sir Thomas Vaisey,** CMG. British civil servant (retd.). *B.* 1908. *Educ.* King's School, Canterbury and Oriel College, Oxford (MA). *M.* 1934, Mary Elizabeth Neatby *S.* 1. *Daus.* 3. *Career:* Temporary Asst. Principal, Colonial Office 1930–33; Asst. District Officer, Tanganyika 1933–37; and Palestine 1937–43; Asst. Lieut.-Governor, Malta 1943–44; Temporary Principal, Colonial Office 1944–45; Principal Asst. Secy., Palestine 1946–48; Civil Service Commissioner, Nigeria 1948–53; Deputy High Commissioner, Basutoland, Bechuanaland Protectorate and Swaziland 1953–60; Commonwealth Relations Office 1960–61. Secretary, Commonwealth Agricultural Bureaux 1961–73. *Address:* Vine Cottage, Minster Lovell, Oxon.

**SEABORN, James Blair.** Canadian public servant. *B.* 1924. *Educ.* Univ. of Toronto (BA, MA; Pol. Econ.). *M.* 1950, Carol Allen Trow. *S.* Geoffrey Blair. *Dau.* Virginia Allen. *Career:* On post (embassies) The Hague 1950–54, Paris (First Secy.) 1957–59; Moscow (Counsellor) 1959–62; Dept. of External Affairs, Ottawa (Head, Eastern European Section) 1962–64; Canadian Commissioner, International Commission for Supervision and Control, Vietnam, June 1964–65; Head, Eastern European Section, 1966–67; Head, Far Eastern Division, 1967–70; Asst. Deputy Minister (Consumer Affairs), Department, Consumer and Corporate Affairs, 1970–74; Deputy Minister, Dept. Evironment Ottawa since 1975. *Address:* 79 MacKay Street, Ottawa, Ont.; and Department of the Environment, Fontaine Building (Hull), Ottawa, Ontario K1A OH3, Canada.

**SEABROOK, John Martin.** American corp. executive and Professional Engineer. Chmn., Chief Exec. Officer and Pres., IU International Corporation. *B.* 1917. *Educ.* Princeton University (BS, Ch.E. 1939); Hon. LLD Gettysburg Coll. 1974. *M.* (1) 1939, Anne Schlaudecker (*Div.* 1951). *Daus.* Carol Ormsby and Elizabeth Anne. *M.* (2) 1956, Elizabeth Toomey. *S.* John Martin Jr. and Bruce Cameron. *Career:* Engineer Deerfield Packing Corp. 1939–41; Vice-Pres. Dir. Seabrook Farms Co., Seabrook, N.J., 1941, became executive V.P., Director 1950, Pres. 1954–59, Chief executive officer 1955–59; Pres. & Dir. Salem Farms Corp (N.J.) 1948—; Cumberland Automobile & Truck Co., 1954–59; Cumberland Warehouse Corp. 1954–59; Dir. New Jersey Bell Telephone Co. Newark 1951—; Pennsylvania Reading Seashore Lines 1958–64; South Jersey Gas Co. (Folsom) 1959—; Frick Co. (Waynesboro, Pa) 1959–69, Chmn. 1959–68; Frick Canada Ltd. (Toronto Ont.) 1960–69; Brown Bros. Contractors Inc. 1960–67, Pres. 1960, Chmn. 1965–67; American Portable Irrigation Co. (Eugene, Oregon) 1961–68, Pres. 1961, Chmn. 1966–68; Amvit Corp. 1962–69, Chmn. 1964–68; Walworth Co. (Phila.) 1964–70; New York Central Railroad 1964–68; Penn Central Co. (Phila.) 1968–70; Southwest Fabricating & Welding Co. Inc. (Houston), Dir. & Chmn. 1964–68; Frick India Ltd. (New Delhi) 1965–69; Home Town Foods Inc. (Jackonsonville) 1964–69; Ryder Truck Lines Inc. 1965–69; Northwestern Utilities Ltd. (Edmonton) 1965–72; Gotaas-Larsen Inc. (New York) 1965—; McCord Corp. (Detroit) 1965—; Provident National Bank (Phila.) 1966–71; P.A.T.H. (Australasia) Ltd. U.K. 1966–68; Australasian Travel Holdings Ltd. (U.K.) 1966–68; I.U. International Corp., Consultant 1959, Vice-Pres. 1960, Dir 1963—, Pres. 1965–73, 1974—, Chief Exec. 1967—, Chmn. 1969—; Provident National Corp. (Phila.) 1969–71; Toronto & London Investment Co. Ltd. (Toronto, Ont.) 1968–72; Canadian Western Natural Gas Co. Ltd. 1966–72; Divcon Inc. (Houst. Texas) 1967–71, Chmn. 1967–69; Northland Utilities Ltd. (Edmonton) 1968–72; Brascan Ltd. (Toronto) 1968–70; Power Corp. of Canada Ltd. (Montreal) 1968–73; Shawinigan Ind. Ltd. (Montreal) 1968–73; Canadian Utilities Ltd. (Edmonton) 1968—; Adela Investment Co. (Luxembourg) 1969–71; C. Brewer and Company Ltd. (Hawaii) 1969—; South Jersey Industries Inc. (Folsom) Dir. since 1970; Gen. Waterworks Corp. (Phil.) 1959–71 (v-p, dir. pres. & chmn.); G.W.C. Incorp. (Phil.) Chmn. & Dir. 1971–73; Consolidated-Bathurst Ltd. (Montreal) since 1975; I.U. Overseas Capital Corp. (Wilmington, Del.). Pres. & Dir. 1966—, Chmn. 1970—; Lenox Inc. (Trenton, N.J.), Dir. 1976—. *Member:* N.J. State Migrant Labor Board 1945–67 (Chairman 1955–67) and N.J. State Board of Higher Education 1967–70; Trustee Eisenhower Exchange Fellowships since 1974; Dir., Brandywine Conservancy Inc. since 1972; President's Air Quality Advisory Board, 1968–70; Licensed Professional Engineer N.J. and Delaware. Phi Beta Kappa. *Clubs:* Racquet & Tennis (N.Y.C.); Racquet (Phila.); Wilmington (Del.); Buck's (London, Eng.); Toronto Club (Ontario); The Philadelphia. *Address:* R.D.I., Griscom Road, Salem, N.J. 08079; and *office* 11 West Avenue, Woodstown, N.J. 08098; and 1500 Walnut Street, Philadelphia, Pa. 19102, U.S.A.

**SEAGRAM, Lt.-Col. Joseph Edward Frowde,** ED. Canadian manufacturer and executive. *B.* 1903. *Educ.* Waterloo Public Schools; Upper Canada College and Prep. School; McGill University. *M.* 1929, Marjorie Houson. *S.* 1. *Dau.* 1. *Career:* Pres. and Dir., Jos. E. Seagram & Sons Ltd., Waterloo, Ont. since 1937; Chmn. and Director, Canbar Products Ltd., Waterloo; started with Company 1924; Hon. Director The Seagram Co. Ltd., Montreal, P.Q.; Dir., The Canada Trust Co. London, Ont.; The Economical Mutual Insurance Co., Kitchener, Ont., Missisquoi and Rouville Insurance Co. Frelighsburgh P.Q., Vice-Pres. and Trustee The Ontario Jockey Club, Toronto. *Address:* 50 Albert Street, Waterloo, N2L3S2, Ont.; and *office* Box 635, Waterloo, N2J 4B8 Ont., Canada.

**SEAMAN, Keith Douglas,** OBE 1976, BA, LLB. Governor of South Australia since 1977. *B.* 1920. *Educ.* Unley High School; Univ. of Adelaide. *M.* 1946, Joan Birbeck. *S.* 1. *Dau.* 1. *Career:* South Australian Public Service 1937–54 (RAAF Overseas HQ London 1941–45, Flight Lieutenant); entered Methodist Ministry 1954, Renmark 1954–58, Adelaide Central Methodist Mission 1958–77; Sec., Christian Television Assn.

of South Asutralia 1959–73; Mem., Executive World Assn. of Christian Broadcasting 1963–70; Dir., 5KA, 5AU & 5RM Broadcasting Companies from 1960, Superintendent Adelaide Central Mission & Chairman 5KA, 5AU & 5RM 1971–77; Mem., Australian Govt. Social Welfare Comm. 1973–76; Governor of South Australia since 1st Sept. 1977. *Club:* Adelaide. *Address:* Government House, Adelaide, S.A. 5000, Australia.

**SEARLE, John Gideon.** Pharmaceutical manufacturer. *B.* 1901. *Educ.* University of Michigan (BS 1923); (Honorary Doctor of Science 1967); Honorary Doctor of Laws, Northwestern Univ., 1970. *M.* 1925, Frances Louise Crow. *S.* Daniel Crow and William Louis. *Dau.* Suzanne (Dixon, Jr.). *Career:* Buyer 1923–25, Treasurer 1925–36, Pres. 1936–66, Chmn. Bd. since 1942; G. D. Searle & Co., Chairman of the Board, G. D. Searle & Co., Skokie, Ill.; Former Dir., Harris Trust & Savings Bank of Chicago. Citizen Fellowship, Institute of Medicine of Chicago; Life Trustee, Northwestern Univ. Former (Pres.) Field Museum of Nat. Hist., and Searle Foundation. Director: Evanston Hospital, Hobe Sound Co. Republican. *Clubs:* Chicago, Commonwealth, Commercial, Casino, Old Elm, Shoreacres, Owentsia (all of Illinois); Seminole, Jupiter Island, Everglades, Hobe Sound Yacht (Fla.). *Address: office* Searle Parkway, Skokie, Ill., U.S.A.

**SEATH, Hon. David Coutts.** New Zealand Politician. *B.* (Musselburgh, Scotland) 1914. *Educ.* Waihi (N.Z.) and Edinburgh. *M.* 1940, Kathleen Elizabeth Rose. *S.* 1. *Dau.* 1. *Career:* Pres. Taumarunui Chamber of Commerce 1946–51, and Rotary 1954; Mayor, Taumarunui Borough Council 1953–55; Member of Parliament for Waitomo 1954–72; Minister of Internal Affairs, Local Government and Civil Defence 1963–72. Parliamentary Under-Secretary to Minister of Finance 1960–62; Associate Minister of Finance 1962–63. *Member:* Assn. of Corporate and Certified Accountants (Great Britain); FPANZ; FNZIA. Member National Party of N.Z. *Clubs:* Wellington; Wellesly; Taumarunui. *Address:* 3 Ashdown Way, Chatsworth, Silver Streat, Upper Hut, New Zealand.

**SEBALD, William Joseph.** American diplomat. *B.* 5 Nov. 1901. *Educ.* U.S. Naval Academy (BS); School of Law, University of Maryland (JD, LLD). *M.* 1927, Edith Frances de Becker, *Career:* Commissioned Officer, U.S. Navy 1922–30; Language Officer attached to Embassy, Tokyo 1925–28; practised law, Kube, Japan 1933–39; Washington 1939–41; Lieut.-Commander, U.S.N.R. 1942; Chief, Pacific Division, Combat Intelligence, U.S. Navy; returned to inactive duty as Captain 1945; Auxiliary Foreign Service Officer, Department of State 1945; Foreign Service Officer 1947; Chief, Diplomatic Section, GHQ, SCAP 1947–52; Deputy for the Supreme Commander, Chairman and member for the U.S., Allied Council for Japan 1947–52; Minister Plenipotentiary of U.S. 1948; Acting U.S. Political Adviser for Japan 1947–50; U.S. Political Advisor for Japan with personal rank of Ambassador 1950–52; U.S. Amb. Ex. and Plen. to Burma 1952–54; Deputy Asst. Secretary of State for Far Eastern Affairs 1954–57; Ambassador to Australia 1957–61. *Publications:* Translations and annotations of various Japanese laws and legal codes 1934–45; With McArthur in Japan (1965); Japan: Prospects, Options and Opportunities (1967). Legion of Merit, First Class Order of the Rising Sun with Grand Cordon (Japan). *Address:* 245 Spring Line Drive, Naples, Fla. 33940, U.S.A.

**SEDDON, Norman Richard,** CBE. British. *B.* 1911. *Educ.* Sherborne School, Dorset; Balliol College, Oxford (MA). *M.* 1937,, Barbara Mary Hogg. *S.* 3. *Career:* Deputy Chmn. & Man. Dir. British Petroleum Co. of Australia Ltd., 1963–67; Chmn. Lucas Industries Australia Ltd.; President, Council of Trustees, National Gallery of Victoria, 1965–76; Deputy Chmn., Victorian Arts Centre Building Cttee.; Chmn. Australian Ballet Foundation; Member, Board of Dirs.: Australian Elizabethan Theatre Trust; Dir., Woodside Petroleum Ltd.; and other companies. *Clubs:* Melbourne; Australian (Melbourne); East India & Sports (London). *Address:* 11 Como Avenue, South Yarra, Victoria 3141, Australia.

**SEEBOHM, of Hertford, The Rt. Hon. Lord (Frederic), TD,** LLD (Hon.). British Banker. *B.* 1909. *Educ.* Leighton Park School, Reading; Trinity College, Cambridge. *M.* 1932 Evangeline Hurst. *S.* Richard Hugh. *Daus.* 2. *Career:* Joined Barclays Bank Ltd., 1929; local executive director, Sheffield, York & Birmingham; Dep. Chmn., Barclays Bank Ltd., 1968–74; Dir.: Barclays Bank Limited, Barclays Bank International Ltd., Technical Development Capital Ltd., Ship Mortgage Finance Co. Ltd., Finance for Shipping Ltd., Estate Duties Investment Trust Ltd., Equity Capital for Industry Ltd., Friends' Provident Life Office, Gillett Bros. Discount Co. Ltd.; Chmn. of Finance for Industry Ltd., Industrial & Commercial Finance Corp. Ltd., Finance Corp. for Industry Ltd.; Pres.: Age Concern, National Institute for Social Work, Royal African Society, Institute of Bankers 1966–68; Chmn.: Joseph Rowntree Memorial Trust, London House, Export Guarantees Advisory Council 1967–72, Cttee. on Local Authority and Allied Personal Social Services (Seebohm Cttee.) Dec. 1965–July 1968, Committee set up to examine the R.N. Welfare Services 1971–73; Governor: London School of Economics and Political Science, Haileybury and Imperial Service College, The Volunteer Centre. *Member* (of Council): Design Council, Chmn. Finance and General Purposes Committee; Centre for Studies in Social Policy. Fellow: Royal Society of Arts and Institute of Bankers. *Awards:* Fellow, Institute of Bankers (Pres. 1966–68); High Sheriff of Hertfordshire 1970; Hon. LLD Notts. Univ. 1970; Hon. DSc. Aston Univ. 1976; Knight Bachelor 1970; Life Peer 1972. *Clubs:* Brooks's; Carlton; Political Economy. *Address:* 5 Lowndes Lodge, Cadogan Place, London, S.W.1; Brook House, Dedham, Nr. Colchester, Essex; and *office* Finance for Industry Ltd., 91, Waterloo Road, London SE1 8XP.

**SEEFELDER, Matthias,** Prof. Dr. rer nat. German. *B.* 1920. *Educ.* Humanistisches Gymnasium and Univ. München (Chemistry, Physics & Physiology). *Career:* Joined BASF 1951. Deputy Mem. of Board 1971, Mem. of Board 1973, Chmn. since 1974. *Member:* Senat der Max-Planck-Gessellschaft, Heidelberg; Hon. Prof. Univ. of Heidelberg 1974. *Address:* BASF Aktiengesellschaft, 6700 Ludwigshafen, Federal Republic of Germany.

**SEELIGER, Ulrich, Dr Jur.** *B.* 1904. *Educ.* Gymnasium; and Univs. of Freibrug, Munich, Berlin and Tübingen (Dr Jur at advanced level for higher judicial service). *M.* 1941, Gertrude Wild, DPh. *Daus.* 2. *Career:* Junior barrister, Stuttgart Court of Justice 1927–31; lawyer 1931–34; Officer in German Army 1934–45 (P. of W. 1943–46); Personal Adviser to Lord Mayor of Stuttgart 1946–48. Dir., Official Tourist Office, Stuttgart 1949—. *Publications:* Investigation into possibilities of increasing tourist travel to United Kingdom of Libya; Four year plan to increase tourism in Libya; numerous articles on tourism. *Member:* Acad. Internationale de Tourisme, Monaco; Féd. Internationale de Centres Touristiques, Lausanne; Assn. Int. d'Experts Scientifiques du Tourisme, Berne; Beirat der Deutschen Zentrale für Fremdenverkehr, Frankfurt/M. *Club:* Scal (Stuttgart). *Address: office* Lautenschlagerstr. 5, Stuttgart-N, Germany.

**SEGALAT, André.** Former Councillor of State of France. *B.* 1910. *Educ.* Charlemagne & Louis-le-Grand Lycées; Paris Faculty of Law; graduated in law, diploma from the Ecole Libre des Sciences Politiques. *Career:* Commissioner 1937, then Rapporteur 1944, of the Council of State; Government Secretary-General 1946–58; Pres., Bd. of Dirs. of the S.N.C.F. 1958–75; Councillor of State 1960–75; mem., Bd. of Admin. of the Ecole Polytechnique 1945–74; Dir., Fondation des Sciences Politiques since 1945; mem., Bd. of Advanced Studies of the Institut d'Etudes Politiques since 1945, then mem. of the Management Council; mem., Council of the Order of the Legion of Honour since 1973; Pres. & Dir.-Gen., Groupement de l'Industrie Chimique since 1976; Pres., Interinfra (Compagnie Internationale pour le Développement d'Infrastructures) since 1976. *Decorations:* Grand Officier de la Legion d'Honneur; Grand Officier de l'Ordre national du Mérite. *Address: office* 16 rue de la Baume, 75008 Paris, France.

**SEGRE, Marco Claudio.** Italian engineer and industrialist. Member: I.N.P.D.A.I., and the Probiviri Committee of the General Confederation of Italian Industry. *B.* 1893. *Educ.* Doctor of Civil and Electro-Technical Engineering. *M.* 1926, Rosa Guastalla. *S.* Giuseppe and Claudio. *Dau.* Renata. *Career:* Army Major, Italian Military Air Corps 1915–18; Asst. Machine Mechanics, University of Rome 1919–23; Counsellor, Compagnia Italina Reti Telefoniche (Italian Telephone Network Co.), C.I.R.T. since 1926; Counsellor, Società Sacchi Cemento e Affini (Cement Bag Co. and allied trades) from 1929. Deputy, Counsellor, Società Anonima Nazionale Immobili (National Real Estate Co.) 1932; member, Italian Thermo-Technical Committee 1933; Vice-President: National Insurance Association for Accidents at Work 1948, and Italian Section of the International Chamber of Commerce 1948; Consiglio Superiore di Statistica (Higher Council of Statistics) 1957—. *Publications:* Corso di Esercitazioni sul collaudio dei motori (Course of Exercises on the Testing of Motors) 1918; Un Nuovo Freno Dinamometrico (A new dynamo-metric brake) 1920; Sulla misura a distanza del liquido contenuto in un serbatoio. (On the measuring at a distance of a liquid contained in a tank) 1920; I tormenti vibratori dei motori aeronautici (Vibratory stresses of aeronautical motors) 1921; Industria e Confidustria (Industry and The General Confederation of Italian Industry) 1949. Iniziativa pubblica ed iniziativa privata di fronte alla disoccupazione dei Paesi sovrapopolati 1952; Considerazioni sul piano Vanoni 1955; Una politica di libertà economica per il progresso sociale 1957; Evoluzione delle condizioni di lavoro nell'industria e prospettive future 1959; L'organizzazione scientifica ed il suo divenire 1963; L'economia italiana nel dopoguerra ed i suoi sviluppi futuri 1963. Grand Cross of the Republic; Knight of Labour; Veteran of Italian Activity. Hon. Pres., Union of Industrialists of Lazio; member, Order of Italian Engineers; Pres., C.N.O.S. (National Committee for Scientific Organization). *Club:* Rotary (Rome). *Address:* Via Taramelli 15, Rome, Italy.

**SEIN, U Mya.** Burmese diplomat. *B.* 1917. *Educ.* Univ. of Rangoon (Honours Graduate). *M.* 1943, Daw Nu Nu. *S.* 4. *Dau.* 1. *Career:* Member of Constituent Assembly 1946–47; joined Burma Foreign Service 1947; Minister Resident to France 1948–51; Counsellor Chargé d'Affaires, Djakarta 1951–55; Head of U.N. and Political Divisions, Foreign Office, Rangoon 1955–59; Minister Chargé d'Affaires, Kuala Lumpur 1959–62 (Ambassador 1962–63). Ambassador of Burma to Australia and New Zealand, Nov. 1963. *Awards:* Chat a Sangha Yana Medal 1958; Mawgun 1961; Thiri Pyanchi title 1962; Legion of Honour (France) 1951. *Address:* c/o Ministry of Foreign Affairs, Rangoon, Burma.

**SEIN, U On.** Burmese diplomat. *B.* 1910. *Educ.* BA; LLB. *M.* 1933, Ma Khin Pu. *S.* Tin Ohn. Government Advocate 1946–52; Member of Parliament and Parliamentary Secretary in Ministry of Foreign Affairs 1952–56: Ambassador to Pakistan 1956–59, to United States 1959. Member, Anti Fascist People's Freedom League. Represented Burma at the Asian African Conference at Bandung, Indonesia, 1955 and at U.N. General Assembly 1953–55–56–58–59–60–61–62–63; appointed Permanent Representative to U.N. 1961–62. *Address:* Ministry of Foreign Affairs, Rangoon, Burma.

**SEITZ, Howard A.** American lawyer. *B.* 1907. *Educ.* Fordham University (BA 1930) and Columbia University (LLB 1933). *M.* 1932, Mary V. Cunningham. *S.* Howard Gerard. *Dau.* Mary V. Gallagher. *Career:* Partner: Paul, Weiss, Rifkind, Wharton & Garrison (lawyers), New York City 1943—. Trustee: The Aquinas Fund 1954—. Coll. of Mt. St. Vincent, New York 1970—. Chmn. Bd. Community Council of Greater New York; Dir. Field Enterprises Inc.; Field Enterprises Educational Corp.; Cttee. Religion and Art in America; The Akbar Fund Inc. *Awards:* Knight of Malta; Knight of the Holy Sepulchre. *Member:* American and New York Bar Associations. Association of the Bar of the City of New York. *Clubs:* Metropolitan (N.Y.C.); Chicago (Chicago, Ill.); Westhampton Country (Westhampton Beach, N.Y.); National Golf Links of America (Southampton, N.Y.); Lost Tree (N. Palm Beach, Fla.). *Address:* 1088 Park Avenue, New York, N.Y. 10028; and *office* 345 Park Avenue, New York, N.Y. 10022, U.S.A.

**SELBY, Ralph Walford.** MA, CMG. *B.* 1915. *Educ.* Eton, Christ Church Oxford; Heidelberg, Ecole des Sciences Politiques, Paris. *M.* 1945, Julianna Snell. *Daus.* 3. *Career:* Foreign Office London 1938–39; Grenadier Guards 1939–45; Foreign Office, 1945–47; First Secretary, UK High Commissioner New Delhi, 1947–50, The Hague, 1950–53; Foreign Office 1953–56; Counsellor British Embassy Tokyo 1956–58, Copenhagen, 1958–61, Djakarta, 1961–63, Warsaw, 1964–66; H.M. Consul General, Boston, Massachusetts 1966–69; Minister British Embassy, Rome, 1969–72; Ambassador in Oslo 1972–75. *Clubs:* The Turf: MCC; Royal Yacht Squadron. *Address:* Mengeham House, Hayling Island, Hamp.

**SELIGMAN, Sir Peter Wendel,** CBE, British company director. *B.* 16 Jan. 1913. *Educ.* King's College School, Wimbledon; Harrow School; Kantonschule, Zurich, Switzerland; Cambridge University. *M.* 1937, Elizabeth Lavinia Mary Wheatley. *S.* Peter J. B. W., Bruce H. J. W. *Daus.* E. Hildagrace, Lavinia M. A., Johanna Joy, Gabrielle Christine. *Career:* Joined the A.P.V. Company Ltd. as Assistant to Joint Managing Directors in 1936, Dir. 1939, Man. Dir. since 1943: Deputy Chairman & Managing Director, 1961–65; Chairman, 1965–77. Chmn., Kandahar Ski Club; Chmn. designate, National Ski Federation of Great Britain. *Address:* Dagmar House, Birmingham Road, Cowes, Isle of Wight.

**SELKIRK, Earl of,** Lord (George) Nigel Douglas Hamilton, Kt, PC, GCMG, GBE, AFC, AE. *B.* 4 Jan. 1906. *Educ.* Eton; Balliol Coll., Oxford (MA); Edin. (LLB). *M.* Audrey Drummond Sale-Barker. *Career:* Admitted Faculty of Advocates 1935; Command 603 Squadron A.A.F. 1934–38; member of Edinburgh Town Council 1935–40; Commissioner, General Board of Control, Scotland 1936–39: Commissioner for Special Areas in Scotland 1937–39; Commander, 603 Squadron A.A.F. 1934–38; served World War II R.A.F. (O.B.E. dispatches twice), Gp. Captain A.A.F. 1939–45; Scottish Representative Peer 1945–63; Lord-in-Waiting to H.M. King George VI and H.M. Queen Elizabeth II 1951–53; Paymaster-General 1953–55; Chancellor of the Duchy of Lancaster 1955–57; First Lord of the Admiralty 1957–59; U.K. Commissioner in Singapore and Commissioner-General for S.E. Asia, 1959–63. Freeman of Hamilton. Pres.: National Ski Federation of Great Britain 1964–68; Building Societies Assn.; Pres. Royal Society for Asian Affairs 1965–76; Anglo-Swiss Society 1964–74; Victoria League 1971–77. *Address:* Rose Lawn Coppice, Wimborne, Dorset; 60 Eaton Place, London, S.W.1.

**SELLERS, Rt. Hon. Sir Frederic Aked,** PC, MC. *B.* 1893. Barrister, Gray's Inn 1919, Bencher 1938, King's Counsel 1935; Recorder of Bolton 1938–46; Justice of the High Court, Queen's Bench Division 1946–57; Court of Appeal 1957–68; Chairman, Criminal Law Revision Committee 1959–69, member until 1972. *Address:* Highwood Lodge, Mill Hill, London NW7.

**SELLERS, George Henry,** AFC, CStJ. Canadian. *B.* 1914. *Educ.* Ridley College (St. Catharines, Ont.) and University of Manitoba. *M.* 1936, Margaret Ann. *S.* David H. A. (PhD, MSc, PEng). *Daus.* Margaret Ann (Harvey) and Joan Irene. *Career:* Associated with Federal Grain Ltd. 1933–36; Dir. 1945, Asst. to Pres. 1947, Vice Pres. 1956–63; Melady Sellers & Co. Ltd. 1936–39, 1945–52; Commissioned Pilot Officer in 112th Aux. Sqdrn., R.C.A.F. June 1933 and served overseas 1940–41; Served in Canada as Chief Flying Instructor, Station Commander and Senior Air Staff Officer, Commanding Officer 39th Reece Wing, Tactical Air Force Europe 1944–45. Transfd. to R.C.A.F. reserve with rank of Group Captain. C.O. Reserve Wing H.Q., Winnipeg Apr. 1951–Mar. 1952; Pres. Central Northern Airways Ltd. 1946–56; Selburn Oil Co. Ltd. 1948–52; Bailey Selburn Oil & Gas Ltd. 1952–62; Melady, Sellers Securities & Grain Corp. Ltd. 1952–61; Sellers, Dickson Securities Ltd. 1961—; Chmn. Bd. Transair Limited 1956–68; Pres. Riverwood Investments Ltd.; Pres. and Chief Exec. Officer, Federal Grain Ltd., Winnipeg, Manitoba 1963–73; Dir.: Bank of Montreal, Canada Malting Co. Ltd., Greater Winnipeg Gas Co., Royal Trust Co. (Winnipeg Adv. Board), and Heritage Craftmen Incorp.; Appointed Hon. A.D.C. to Governor-General of Canada (Viscount Alexander) 1946. Past-Pres., St. John Ambulance Assn. (Division for Manitoba). *Clubs:* Manitoba; Ranchman's (Calgary). *Address:* and *office* 2210 One Lombard Place, Winnipeg R3B OX3, Man., Canada.

**SELLEY, David Colin.** British. *B.* 1927. *Educ.* Saltus Grammar School (Bermuda), Mount Hermon School (U.S.A.) and Wharton School, Univ. of Pennsylvania. *M.* 1951, Ann Erol Walker. *S.* Mark, Craig and Douglas. *Daus.* Susan and Linda, *Career:* Staff Announcer, Bermuda Radio Station ZBM. 1948–49; Asst. Manager (1950–53), Manager (1953–62), Bermuda News Bureau. On secondment, Government P.R.O. 1963–64. Publicity Dir., 1965–67. Deputy Director, Bermuda Dept. of Tourism & Trade, 1967–69. Director of Public Relations, Officer of Executive Council, Bermuda Government, 1969–71; Dep. Dir. and Marketing Manager, Bermuda Dept. Tourism, Bermuda Govt. Appointment 1971, Dir. of Tourism since 1976. Press Officer of international conferences held in Bermuda 1953–57–61 also (Heath-Nixon) 1971. Royal visits H.R.H. Prince Philip 1959, H.R.H. Prince Charles 1970. H.M. The Queen and H.R.H. Prince Philip 1975. *Member:* Saltus Old Boys Association (Past President); Trustee of Saltus Grammar School. *Clubs:* Royal Bermuda Yacht; Riddells Bay Golf; Coral Beach Tennis Bd. of Governors; Bermuda Lawn Tennis Assn. (Past Pres., Tournament Dir., B.L.T.A. Grand Prix Tennis Tournament, 1976); Castle Harbour Golf (Past Pres.); Skal (past-pres.). *Address:* 'Finiterre', Point Shares, Pembroke, Bermuda; and *office* Department of Tourism, Old Town Hall, Front Street, Hamilton, Bermuda.

**SELTZER, Leon Zee.** *B.* 1914. *Educ.* Univ. of Illinois (PhC) and Univ. of Michigan (BSE); Registered Professional Engineer 1950. *M.* 1940, Mary Jane Kehoe. *S.* Thomas Lee. *Career:* Aeronautical Engineer, Douglas Aircraft Co. 1940; Prof. and Head, Aeronautical Engineering, Virginia Polytechnica Institute 1944 Chairman, Department of Aero Space Engineering, West Virginia Univ., Morgantown 1949–63, and concurrently Professor of Aero Space Engineering, Aero Space Engineer, West Va. Univ. Engineering Experiment Station. Dean, Parks College of Aeronautical Technology, St. Louis University Aug. 1963—. *Publications:* Spanwise Airload Distribution—An Approximate Method; Design and Calibration of a Wind Tunnel Balance System; Blade Profile Properties in the Low Reynolds Number Range of Compressor Operation; Roughness Effects on Blade Performance at Low Reynolds Numbers; Experiment in Contact-Instrument Flight Training; Elementary Instrument Flight Training of Certificated Pilots. Gemmel Scholar, Donovan Scholar, Sheehan Aeronautical Scholar, Univ. of Michigan. Sigma Xi; Tau Beta Pi; Alpha Eta Rho; Alpha Phi Omega; Pi Tau Sigma; Sigma Gamma Tau (Natl. Pres. 1961–70 and 1964–67); Pi Mu Epsilon. Chmn., Engineering Preparations Cttee., National Society of Professional Engineers Assoc. Fellow, of Int. Aero-space Sciences; Awarded Aeronautics & Astronautics St. Louis for 1972 (AIAA). *Member:* Amer. Socy. for Engineering Education; National, Missouri, and West Va. Societies of Professional Engineers; University Aviation Assn.; Socy. of Automotive Engineers (Vice-Pres. St. Louis Section); Guidance Cttee. of Engineers Council for Professional Developments; Scientific Adv. Group Army Aviation Systems Command; Hon. Member, Army Aviation Assn. of Amer. Dir., Southwest Civic Memorial Airport Assn.; Assn. United States Army Dir. since 1967; Vice-Chmn.: St. Louis Section A.I.A.A.; Conf. of Jesuit Schools of Engineering; Chmn. Education Committee, St. Louis Section, A.I.A,A. Licensed Airplane Pilot; Dir. East St. Louis Chamber of Commerce. *Club:* Forest Hills Country; Dir. since 1970. Engineers; Aero (St. Louis). *Address: office* Parks College of St. Louis University, Cahokia, Ill., 62206, U.S.A.

**SELVAAG, (Jens) Olav (Walaas).** Norwegian civil engineer. Knight, Order of St. Olav 1st Cl.; war medal. *B.* 1912. *Educ.* Civil Engineering. *M.* 1937, Andrea (Dea) Brøvig. *S.* Ole Gunnar. *Daus.* Cecilie and Kari Lene. *Career:* In 1936 Olav Selvaag commenced work in the contracting firm in which he was admitted as a partner a few years later. The firm was named Ringnes & Selvaag, of which he became sole owner in 1957; now named Selvaag-Bygg, and its purpose is house building. Mr. Selvaag is recognized as a pioneer in this field, in which new and rational designs have been employed to produce modern housing. Mr. Selvaag is also active in matters of public benefit. Owner: Selvaag-Bygg 1920—, Sameiet Selvaag 1958—, A/S Docko 1959—, and A/S Selvaagbygg 1961—. Director: Bergen Bank, and Gjensidige Life Insurance Co. *Publications:* Do we have a social policy in Norway?; Liberty; Houses for everybody or for the few?; Practical Housing. *Member:* of several public and professional organizations. *Club:* Gimle Rotary. *Address:* Hoffsjef Løvenskiolds vei 57, Oslo 3; and *office* Holmenveien 19, Oslo 3, Norway.

**SELWYN-LLOYD, Rt. Hon. Lord,** PC, CH, CBE, TD, DL, QC. British politician. *B.* 1904. *Educ.* Fettes; Magdalene Coll., Cambridge; President, Cambridge Union 1927; Hon LLD Sheffield Univ. 1955, Liverpool Univ. 1957, Cambridge 1975; Hon. DCL Oxford 1960. *Career:* Barrister, Gray's Inn and Northern Circuit 1930; served in World War II, Army (Brigadier) 1939–45; M.P. (Cons.) for Wirral 1945–71; Minister of State Foreign Office 1951–54; Minister of Supply Oct. 1954–Apr. 1955; Minister of Defence Apr. 1955–Dec. 1955; Secretary of State for Foreign Affairs 1955–60; Chancellor of the Exchequer 1960–62; Lord Privy Seal 1963–64; Speaker of the House of Commons & MP for Wirral 1971–76. *Awards:* Cmndr. Legion of Merit (U.S.A.); Life Peer 1976. *Address:* Hilbre House, Macdona Drive, West Kirby, Wirral, Merseyside L48 3JD.

**SEMEGA-JANNEH, Bocar Ousman.** MBE. High Commissioner of the Gambia in London & Ambassador to Western Germany, Belgium, Sweden, Switzerland, France and Austria since 1971. *Address:* Gambia High Commission, 60 Ennismore Gardens, London SW7.

**SEMENENKO, Serge.** Financier, Corporate Director and Financial Consultant. *B.* Russia, 1903, *Educ.* Classical College (AB); Robert College, Istanbul (BS); Harvard (MB) DS in BA (Hon.) Bryant College. *M.* 1948, Virginia Boyd. *Dau.* Christine. *Career:* In Credit Dept., The First National Bank of Boston, 1926, Assistant Vice-President, 1928, Vice-Pres., 1932–47, Senr. Vice-President, Director, Vice-Chairman to 1967; Director, Jan. 1956—, and Vice-Chairman, Oct. 1959—, The First National Bank of Boston. Director: The American New Co. Inc., Antiquities Inc., Chemway Corp. (member Exec. Cttee.), City Stores Co., French & Co. Inc., Hilton International Co., The 721 Corp. (Bonwit Teller Corp. N.Y.C.), 795 Fifth Avenue (Hotel) Pierre (N.Y.C.)), United Carr Fastener Corp., and Warner Bros. Pictures Inc. Trustee: Children's Hospital, Boston. Chairman: Atwood Richards Inc., Director: 721 Corp., (Bonwit Teller Corp); Chairman: Tilden Yates Laboratories, Director, Vice-Chairman, Columbia Pictures Corporation. *Clubs:* Harvard Union (Boston); Wianno (Cape Cod, Mass.). *Address:* 32 Embankment Road, Boston, Mass. 02114, U.S.A.

**SEMYONOV, Nikolai Nikolaevich.** Russian. Member of the Academy of Sciences of the U.S.S.R. Director of the Institute of Chemical Physics (of the Academy). *B.* 1896. *Educ.* Leningrad University. *M.* Lidiya Grigorievra Scherbakova. *S.* 1. *Dau.* 1. *Career:* Formerly Assistant Director of the Physico-Technical Institute of the Academy of Sciences. *Member:* Royal Socy. of London (Foreign Member), Indian Acad. of Sciences (Hon.), German Acad. of Naturalists (Leopoldina), Hungarian Acad. of Sciences (Hon.), New York Acad. of Sciences (Hon.). Royal Society of Edinburgh Hon.); member-correspondent of the Berlin Academy of Sciences, D.D.R. Dr *h.c.* Oxford University, and Brussels University. Foreign Member, National Acad. of Sciences of U.S.A., Rumanian Acad. of Sciences (Hon.), Czechoslovakian Acad. of Sciences, Bulgarian Acad. of Sciences. Doctor *h.c.* Milan Polytechnic Inst., Budapest Techn. Univ. (Dr *h.c.*); Carlovy Univ. C.S.S.R. (Dr *h.c.*). London Univ. (Dr *h.c.*)., Humboldt Univ. Berlin 1973. Member, Chemical Socy, of England ,and of the Mendeleev Chemical Socy, of the U.S.S.R. Awarded State Premium of the U.S.S.R., 1941–49, and the Nobel Prize, 1956. *Publications:* about 200 scientific papers; main monographs: Chain Reactions (Moscow-Leningrad, ONTI, 1934; English edition, Oxford 1935); Some problems of Chemical Kinetics and Reactivity (Acad. Sc. M. 1958, English edition and U.S. edition 1959; also translated into German, Hungarian and Chinese). Member of the Communist Party of the U.S.S.R. since 1947. *Address:* Vorobyevskoye chaussee 2-b Institute of Chemical Physics, 117334, Moscow, U.S.S.R.

**SEN, Sri Samar.** Indian Diplomat. *B.* 1914. *Educ.* BA (Calcutta), BSc (London), Oxford and Lincoln's Inn (London). *M.* 1950, Sheila Lal. *S.* Jupiter and Julius. *Daus.* Ariana and Sevaly. *Career:* Indian Civil Service, London 1938; various administrative posts in Bengal (Asst. Magistrate and Collector 1939–40, Sub-divisional Officer 1941–44, Regional Controller of Procurement, Dept. of Civil Supplies 1944–46) 1939–46; appointed to the Indian Political Service 1946; Government of Indian Liaison Officer with U.N., New York 1946–48; Head of Chancery, High Commission of India in London, 1949–50; Consul-General in Switzerland 1953–55; Chairman, International Commission for Supervision and Control, Laos 1953–55; High Commissioner in Australia and New Zeland 1959–62; Ambassador to Algeria 1962–64; to Lebanon, Jordan and Kuwait, and High Commissioner to Cyprus 1964–66; High Commissioner for India in Pakistan 1966–68; U.N. Rep. 1969–74; High Commissioner of India in Bangladesh 1974–76; Ambassador to Sweden since 1977. Decorated Kaiser-i-Hind and Padma Sri. *Address:* Embassy of India, Box 1340, Stockholm, Sweden.

**SENANAYEKE, Hon. Maithripala.** Ceylonese landed proprietor and Member of Parliament. *B.* 1916. Parliamentary Secretary, Ministry of Home Affairs, 1950; Minister of Transport and Works, 1956; Minister of Transport, Works and Cultural Affairs, 1958; Minister of Industries, Home Affairs & Cultural Affairs, 1960; Industries Trade and Commerce, 1963; Leader of the House 1964; Member of Parliament, Deputy Leader of the Opposition, 1965; Minister, Irrigation, Power and Highways; Leader of the House since 1970. Member of Parliament for Medawachchiya, since inauguration of Parliament of Ceylon in 1947; Member, Sri Lanka Freedom Party. *Address:* 121 McCarthy Road, Colombo 7, Sri Lanka; and Harischandra Mawata, New Town Anuradhapura, Sri Lanka.

**SENDALL, Bernard Charles,** CBE. British. *B.* 1913. *Educ.* Magdalen College, Oxford (BA Final Honour School of Modern History); Harvard Univ. (U.S.A.). *M.* 1963, Barbara Mary Coviello. *S.* Anthony Robert Scott (stepson). *Career:* Entered Admiralty 1935. Principal Private Secretary to Minister of Information 1941–45; Controller (Home), Central

Office of Information 1946–49; Controller, Festival of Britain 1949–51; Asst. Secy., Admiralty 1951–55: Deputy Dir. General, Independent Broadcasting Authority 1955–77. *Address:* Lynton Cottage, Chearsley, Bucks HP18 0DD.

**SENGHOR, Léopold Sédar**, President of Republic of Senegal. *B.* 1906 *Educ.* Dakar Lycée; Louis-le-Grand lycée (Paris); Passed concours d'agregation exam. 1935. *Career:* Teacher of French, Latin and Greek in French Lycées 1935–45; Professor of African Negro languages and civilizations at French O'seas Nat. School (Paris) 1945; Elected Senegal Deputy to French Nat. Assembly (mem. of Socialist Party Group) 1945; Mem. Mgmt. Cttee French Section Workers International (S.F.I.O.) 1945; Left S.F.I.O. during war in Indochina and founded 1st African Socialist Party (B.D.S. or Sengalese Democratic Bloc) 1948; The B.D.S. gained power in elections 1951; Persuaded M. Lamine Gueye to join P.R.A., 1958; New Constitution following failure of Mali federation, and Mr. Senghor elected President of Republic of Senegal 1960; Remained Secy.-Gen. of U.P.S. 1960; Chmn. of Cttee. OUA (African Unity Organization). *Decorations:* Grand Cross Legion of Honour; Commander of Academic Palms; Franco-Allied Medal of Recognition; Serviceman's Cross 1939–45; Comm. Medal (with bar) 1939–45; Grenoble Gold Medal 1972; Cravat of Comdr. of Order of French Art and Letters 1973. *Awards:* Dr. Hon. Causa. Univ. Paris (1962), Ibadan, Nigeria (1964); Bahia, Brazil (1965); Strasbourg (1965); Cath. Univ. of Louvain Belgium (1965); Lebanese Univ. of Beirut, Lebanon (1966); Howard, Washington (1966); Laval, Quebec, Canada (1966); Al Azar, Cairo, Egypt (1967); Algiers (1967); Bordeaux-Talence (1967); Vermont (U.S.A.) 1971; California, Los Angeles (1971); Harvard, U.S.A. (1971); Ethiopia-Haile Selasse I (1971); Abidjan, Ivory Coast (1971); Lagos, Nigeria (IFE) (1972); Oxford, Gt. Britain (1973); Corresp. mem. of Bavarian Academy (1961); International French Friendship Prize (1961); French Lang. Prize (Gold Medal) (1963); International Grand Prize for Poetry (1963); Dag Hammarskjoeld International Prize, Gold Medal for Poetic Merit (1965); Marie Noël Poetry Prize (1965); Red and Green International Lit. Grand Prix (1966); German Bookshops' Peace Prize (1968); Assoc. mem of Acad. of Moral & Polit. Sciences (1969); Knokke Biennial Intern. Poetry Grand Prix (1970); Mem. of Acad. of O'seas Sciences (1971) and Black Academy of Arts & Sciences (U.S.A.) 1971; Haile Selasse Prize (Ethiopia) (1973). *Publications:* Many works of prose, poetry, philosophy including: 5 collections of poetry: Chants d'Ombre; Hosties noires; Ethiopiques, Nocturnes and Lettres d'Hivernage; essays (2 Vols) Liberté; basic work, Nation et Voie Africaine du Socialisme. *Address:* Office of the President, Dakar, Senegal, W.Africa.

**SENIOR, Sir Edward (Walters)**, CMG. British company director. (Ret.). *B.* 29 Mar. 1902. *Educ.* Repton School and Sheffield Univ. *M.* 1928, Stephanie Vera Heald. *S.* 1. *Dau.* 1. *Career:* Vice-Consul for Sweden in Sheffield 1930; JP, 1937–1950; Major, R.A., T.A. 1938; Gen. Dir. Alloy Special and Steels, Iron and Steel Control 1941; Director, Steel Division, Raw Materials Mission to Washington 1942; Controller of Ball and Roller Bearings 1944; Master of the Cutlers' Company of Hallamshire in the County of York 1947; Vice-President, Sheffield Chamber of Commerce 1948; Chairman, Steel, Re-armanent Panel 1951. *Address:* Hollies, Church Close, Brenchly, Tonbridge, Kent TN12 7AA.

**SENSEN, Friedrich.** German. Service Cross, First Class, Service Order of the German Federal Republic; Grosses Verdienstkreuz des Verdienstordens der Bundesrepublik Deutschland. *B.* 1906. *Educ.* High School. *M.* 1944, Elfriede Vietheer. *S.* 1. *Career:* Formerly apprentice shipbroker, and Export-Import Agent between Hamburg and England. With Ahlmann-Carlshütte KG, Rendburg, since 1936; Chmn., Land Assn. of Schleswig-Holstein Employers, Rendsburg. Member of the Board: Assn. for the Advancement of Trades in Schleswig-Holstein, Kiel; and of the Federal Association of German Employers, Cologne. Chairman: Iron Foundry Industry Trade Assn., Schleswig-Holstein. Member, Association for World Trade e.V. (Hamburg). *Club:* Ubersee. *Address:* Kanalufer 12, 237 Rendsburg, Germany.

**SEOUD, Abdel Hamid Ibrahim.** Diplomat of the United Arab Republic. *B.* 23 Dec. 1906. *Educ.* Cairo University (Grad. Faculty of Law); joined Foreign Service Jan. 1929; posted as Attaché to Consulate-General Marseilles; has held appointments in U.S.A., Germany, Belgium, France, Haifa, Liverpool and London; Amb. Ex. and Plen. to Pakistan 1955; to Canada 1959–64. *Address:* 265 Avenue de l'Armée, Glymenopolen, Alexandria, Egypt.

**SEPPÄLÄ, Richard Rafael.** Finnish diplomat. *B.* 1905. *Educ.* University of Helsinki (Law degree); Attorney-at-Law. *M.* 1953, Patricia Erkko. *Dau.* Rafela. *Career:* Entered Ministry for Foreign Affairs, 1930; served in Riga, Rio de Janeiro, London; Chief of Bureau, Ministry for Foreign Affairs 1942–44; Assistant Director and Director, Political Dept. 1944–48; Consul-General and Permanent Observer at U.N. 1948–53 Secy.-Gen., Min. for For. Affs. 1953; Secretary of State 1954; Amb. to France 1956–58, to U.S.A. 1958–65; Ambassador to France 1965–72; Permanent Delegate: to U.N.E.S.C.O., 1967–72, to O.E.C.D. 1968–69. *Awards:* Cross of Liberty 3rd Cl. with Swords (Finland); Grand Cmdr. White Rose (Finland); Grand Cross Lion of Finland; Grand Cross of Falcon (Iceland); Grand Cross Order, Merit of France; Grand Cmdr. Legion of Honour; Grand Cmdr. Crown of Belgium; Officer of Orange-Nassau (Netherlands), and of Polonia Restitua; Chevalier, Southern Cross of Brazil; Coronation Medal (George VI). *Clubs:* Pörssiklubi Helsinki, Yt Puistotie 11Y18, Finland.

**SEPPELT, John Rothwell.** Australian vigneron. *B.* 1913. *Educ.* St. Peters Coll., Adelaide; Montpellier (France); Pasteur Institute. *M.* 1956, Elizabeth Anne Johnson. *S.* Anthony Johnson and Hugh Johnson. *Dau.* Sarah Annabel. *Career:* Served in R.A.A.F. in New Guinea and over Europe 1941–46. Dir. 1939—. B. Seppelt & Sons Ltd. Dep. Chmn. since 1974; Sales Adv. Manager since 1946. *Member:* Australian Association of National Advertisers (State Chmn. 1958–59; Federal Deputy Chmn. 1958–59): International Advertising Assn. A.I.M. S.A. Marketing Cttee. 1960–61. *Awards:* Fellow Inst. Sales and Marketing Executives; Fellow, Inst. of Directors. *Publication:* The House of Seppelt 1851–1951. *Address:* 25 Davenport Terrace, Hazelwood Park, S.A.; and office 27 Gresham Street, Adelaide, S.A., Australia.

**SERRATE REICH, Carlos.** Bolivian. *B.* 1932. *Educ.* Colegio Nacional Ayacucho, La Paz 1945–50; graduated Bachiller in Humanidades; lawyer, Univ. San Andrés, La Paz 1957. *M.* Marta Valdivia. *Career:* Under-Secretary of Cultural Affairs 1959–60; and of Education 1960–61; Member Advisory Council for Foreign Affairs 1961–62; Private Secretary to the President of Bolivia 1962–63; Minister of Education and Cultural Affairs 1964; Minister Mining and Metallurgy 1971; Hugo Banzer Suarez Government; Dean of Social Sciences Faculty, Univ. "San Andrés", La Paz 1972–75; Political leader in the Nationalistic Revolutionary Movement and leading columnist in the newspaper "Hoy"; writes essays on political and economic topics. *Publications:* How to keep a Democratic Revolution; Critical analysis of the educational problems in Bolivia. Hon. Member, Bolivian Journalists' Association. *Address:* Law and Economics Studio, Box 5810, La Paz, Bolivia.

**SERUP, Dr. Axel.** Danish diplomat. *B.* 1911. *Educ.* Univ. of Copenhagen (Master of Law 1935) and Geneva (Doctor of Political Science 1938). *M.* 1962, Monique Carette. *Career:* Vice-Consul Hamburg 1941–43; Ministry of Foreign Affairs 1943–46; Senior Officer, Secretariat of the United Nations, New York 1946–54; Ministry of Foreign Affairs 1954–59; Counsellor of Embassy, Washington 1959–62; Ambassador to New Zealand 1962–66, to Venezuela 1966–74, concurrently to Haiti & Dominican Republic 1967–74; Delegate to UN General Assemblies 1968, 1969, 1974, 1975, 1976; Head of Danish Delegation to Diplomatic Conference in Geneva on Humanitarian Law 1975, 1976, 1977. *Publication:* Article 16 du Pacte de la SDN (thesis). Knight, Order of Dannebrog: and other Orders. Member American Society of International Law. *Clubs:* Harvard (New York). *Address:* c/o Ministry of Foreign Affairs, Copenhagen, Denmark; & "Altamira", Les Hauts du Plascassier, Mourns-Sartaux, Alpes Maritimes, France.

**SETTE, Pietro.** Italian lawyer. Chevalier Grand Cross of Merit (Italy); Cavaliere del Lavoro. *B.* 1915. *Educ.* Liceo University, Bari (Degree in Law); Degree *honoris causa* in mining Engineering, Univ. of Cagliari. *M.* 1956, Renata Pes. *S.* Francesco and Alessandro. *Career:* Chmn. Finanziaria E. Breda and assoc. companies 1951–76; Società M.C.S. 1957–75; INSUD-Nuove Iniziative per il Sud 1963–76; Chmn. EFIM-Ente Partecipazion; e Finanziamento Industria Manifatturiera 1963–75; Presently: Chmn., ENI-Ente Nazionale Idrocarburi; Director, EFIM, Finanziaria E. Breda, INSUD, Banco di Roma. *Member:* Arbitration Board of Italy; I.B.M. Europe, European Advisory Council, CEEP (Communauté Economique Européenne Publique). *Address:* Via Puccini 9, Rome; and *office* P. le Enrico Mattei, 00144 Rome, Italy.

**SEVILLA SACASA, Guillermo.** Nicaraguan diplomat, statesman, jurist and congressman. *B.* 1908. *Educ.* Instituto Nacional de Occidante; University of Leon. *M.* Lillian Somoza-Debayle. *Children* 9. *Career:* Amb. Ex. and Plen, to U.S.A. since 1943; Permanent Representative to U.N. and Ambassador Representative to the Organization of American States; Dean of the Diplomatic Corps accredited to the White House; Ambassador to Canada; former Representative of the Nicaraguan House and Senate; President of the National Congress 1936; former Professor of Civil Law and International Law in the universities of Nicaragua; delegate to San Francisco Conference 1945; has attended all General Assemblies of U.N.; has represented Nicaragua in more than 150 international conferences; President, Council of the Organization of American States; elected Chairman of the Political-Juridical Committee, 10th Inter-American Conference, Caracas, 1954; Chmn., Inter-Amer. Commission of 21; First Chmn., Inter-Amer. Commission on Nuclear Energy; Chief of Nicaraguan delegation to U.N. Conference (1955 and 1965), San Francisco; Vice-Pres. Gen. Assembly 1968 and 1974; Pres. Security Council U.N., July 1970 and Oct. 1971; Special Mission Security Council U.N. to Senegal 1971. Hon. Pres., Pan-American Society of the United States; Governor for Nicaragua, I.M.F., and the World Bank. Hon. member of numerous international institutions. *Awards:* from more than 50 countries. *Publication:* Exporpriación. *Address:* Nicaraguan Embassy, 1627 New Hampshire Avenue, N.W., Washington, D.C. 20009, U.S.A.

**SEWARD, George C.** American. partner of Seward & Kissel, Attorneys, N.Y.C. *B.* 1910. *Educ.* Louisville (Ky.) Male H.S. (1929), Univ. of Virginia (BA 1933; LLB 1936), (JD 1936). *M* .1936, Carroll Frances McKay. *S.* Gordon Day and James Carroll. *Career:* Trustee, Benson Iron Ore Trust & Edwin Gould Foundation for Children; Pres. Phi Beta Kappa Associates 1969–75; Founder & Hon. Life Pres., Business Law Section and life member of Council of International Bar Assn.; Chmn. 1958–59, (life member) Council of Section of Corp. Banking and Business Law of Amer. Bar Assn.; House of Delegates Amer. Bar Assn. (1959, 1963–74); Member Joint Cttee. on Continuing Legal Education of the American Law Inst. and The American Bar Assn. (1965–76); Chmn. Cttee. on Corporate Laws of ABA 1952–58; Chmn. Amer. Bar Foundation Cttee. on Model Business Corporation Acts 1956–65; Chmn. Banking Cttee. of ABA 1960–61. *Member:* Phi Beta Kappa; Raven Society, Delta Sigma Rho; Order of the Coif; Cum Laude Society. Fellow, Amer. Bar Foundation; Amer. Law Institute; Assn. of Bar of City of New York; New York State, Kentucky. Virginia & Dist. of Columbia Bar Associations. *Publications:* Basic Corporate Practice; co-author, Model Business Corporation Act Annotated. *Clubs:* Knickerbocker; Down Town, N.Y. Yacht (N.Y.C.); University (Chicago); Metropolitan (Washington, D.C.); Scarsdale Golf; Shelter Island Yacht; Mashomack Preserve. *Address:* 48 Greenacres Ave, Scarsdale, N.Y. 10583; and *office* 63 Wall Street, New York, N.Y. 10005, U.S.A.

**SEWELL, James Leslie.** American engineer and executive. *B.* 1903. *Educ.* Texas Agricul. & Mech. College (BS MechEng) 1927. *M.* 1929, Charlotte Barnard. *S.* George B., Frederic D., James M. and John C. *Career:* Pres. Dir., Taylor Oil & Gas Co. 1952–55; President, Texas Mid-Continent Oil & Gas Assoc. 1963–65; Vice-Pres., Taylor Refining Co. 1946–52; Vice-Pres. Member of Eexcutive Cttee. & Director, Petroleum Heat & Power Co. 1946–50; General Supt., Taylor Refining Co. 1939–46, Refinery Supt., Coastal Refineries Inc. 1935–39, and Taylor Refining Co. 1933–35. President & Director, Delhi-Taylor Oil Corp., Dallas Texas., Jan. 1955–68. Mid-Continent Oil & Gas Assn. 1967–69. Dir. & Pres. Standard Lumber Co. 1968—; Dir.: Delhi Australian Petroleum Ltd. 1958—. American Petroleum Institute 1966—; Aztec Oil & Gas Co., 1969–76; *Member:* Amer. Socy. of Mechanical Engineers; Socy. of Automotive Engineers; Texas Socy. of Professional Engineers; National Socy. of Professional Engineers; The Newcomen Socy. of N. America; Tau Beta Pi. *Clubs:* Dallas Country; Dallas Petroleum; Petroleum (Houston). *Address:* 5338 Meaders Lane, Dallas, Tex.; and *office* Fidelity Union Life Bldg., Dallas, Texas, U.S.A.

**SEXTON, Maurice Colin.** New Zealand chartered accountant. *B.* 1925. *Educ.* Palmerston North Boys High School and Canterbury Univ. (BCom); Fellow, Chartered Inst. of Secretaries; Associate, N.Z. Society of Accountants, and Australian Inst. of Cost Accountants. *M.* 1947, Lorna Isobel Campbell. *S.* Michael Anthony. *Dau.* Linda Christine. *Career:* Cost Accountant, N.Z. Woolpack & Textiles Ltd. 1947–51; Chartered Accountant Palmerston North, N.Z. 1951—. Councillor, City of Palmerston North 1962–71; Chairman, N.Z. National Party, Palmerston North Electorate 1946–72; Director, International Hotel Reservations 1960—; Managing Secretary, Manawatu Creditmens Assn. Ltd. 1953—; Secretary, Society of Friends of the Aged 1951—; Manawatu-Wanganui Provincial Council 1962—; and Palmerston North Hotel Assn. 1954—; Pres., Manawatu Lawn Tennis Assn. 1958; Vice-Pres., N.Z. Lawn Tennis Assn. 1958–68. Member P.N. Licensing Committee 1956–62; Pres., P.N. Jaycee Inc. 1956. World Chairman, Extension and Membership, Junior Chamber International 1957 (Vice-Pres. 1958, World Pres. 1959; visited 60 countries on its behalf 1959–60; attended World Congresses; Wellington (N.Z.) 1956, Tokyo 1957, Minneapolis 1958, Rio de Janeiro 1959, Paris 1960; promoted world-wide Jaycee relief programme for Tibetan refugees in India 1959–60). Deputy Chmn., Council for Development of University Education in Manawatu 1961–62. Editor, Review, Canterbury University 1946. Vice-President, New Zealand Library Association 1967, Pres. 1968–69; Vice Pres. Assoc. Credit Bureaux of N.Z. Inc. since 1968, Pres. since 1975; Trustee, Palmerston North Showgrounds Board of Control 1974—; Treas., Manawatu West Coast Agricultural & Pastoral Assn. 1974—; Mem. Palmerston Hosp. Bd. 1977—. *Member:* Junior Chamber International (Life); P.N. Jaycee Inc. (Life); Chamber of Commerce: Manawatu Society of Arts; N. Zealand Travel & Holiday Assn.; Pacific Area Travel Assn. *Awards:* Medaille D'Argent (Paris). Hon. Citizen: Duluth, Minn.; Jacksonville, Fla.; Winnipeg, Canada; New Orleans, La.; Hon. Mayor, Lake Charles, La.; l'Ordre de Bon Temps, Nova Scotia. Member National Party of N.Z. *Clubs:* Manawatu (P.N.). *Address:* 134 Featherston Street, Palmerston North, New Zealand.

**SEYBOLT. George Crossan.** American executive. *B.* 1914. *Educ.* Valley Forge Military Academy, Wayne, Pa. (Grad. 1932). *M.* 1947, Hortense E. Kelley. *S.* George Crossan, Jr. and Calvert Horace. *Daus.* Reva Blanche and Edwina Porter. *Career* With brokerage firm, Orvis Bros. & Co. 1933–35; American Can Co., 1935–37, Salesman 1937–39; Assigned to Boston sales office 1939–42; United States Naval Int. commissioned an Ensign 1942; served at U.S.N.A.S., Quonset Point, U.S.N.A.B.D. Rhode Island 1942–43; Op. Int. Officer U.S.N.A.S. South Weymouth 1943; U.S. Naval Attache London England, Op. Int. Officer Comm. Gen. European Theatre of Operations 1943–44; Admin. Officer Alsos Mission 1944–45; Amer. Can Co. New York, For. Dept. 1945–46; Asst. Regional Sales Man. 1946–47, New England Sales Man. 1947–50; William Underwood Co. Mass. and Assoc. Cos. 1950—; Marketing Planning Div. 1950–54; Vice Pres. 1954–56, Exec. Vice-Pres. 1956–57; Pres. and Dir. Wm. Underwood Co. Mass. and Maine since 1957; Pres. and Trustee Mass. Vol. Assoc. since 1957; served Chmn. Pres. Treas. and Dir. Wm. Underwood Canada since 1957, Chmn. and Dir. 1972; Pres. and Dir. Richardson & Robbin's Co. 1959–61; Treas. Dir. Sell's Speciality Inc. 1960–63; Pres. Treas. and Dir. Diablitos Venezolanos, C.A. Caracas 1960—; Pres. Dir. The Burnham & Morrill Co. 1965–66; Dir. J. H. Senior & Co. Ltd. 1967–68; C. Shippam Ltd. 1968—; Cinta Azul 1969—; Ac'cent International Inc. since 1971, Pres. since 1973. Dir. Nat. Canners Assn. Chmn. Legislative Cttee.; Consumer Service Cttee.; Member Admin. Council Finance Cttee. Int. Trade Cttee.; Chmn. Maine Sardine Industry Research Cttee., Pres. Maine Sardine Packers Assn.; Chmn., Sardine Council and many responsible Interests. Member, Valley Forge Military Academy, Bd. of Trustees 1966–73; Trustee Suffolk Univ.; Past Chmn. Adv. Council, Vice Chmn. Bd. Trustees, Chmn. Bd. Trustees; Served many Cttees. with Government Interests 1951–67; Dir. M.F.T.A. since 1967; Trustee George Robert White Fund; Chmn. Economic Development & Industrial Corp. of Boston; Member, Nat. Adv. Council of the Episcopal Church Foundation; Dir. & Member Exec. Comm., Business Cttee. for the Arts Inc; Hon. Member, Smithsonian Council. Pres. Emeritus & Trustee, Museum of Fine Arts, Boston; Chmn. Trustees Comm. & Legislative Comm., American Assn. of Museums; Member, National Council on the Arts, U.S.A.; Overseer, Old Sturbridge Village, Sturbridge, Mass., U.S.A. *Awards:* Member Anthony Wayne Legion; Hon. Doctor Conm. Science Suffolk Univ.; U.S. Naval Commendation with Ribbon; Order, British Empire. *Publications:* several articles including The Widening World of Wm. Underwood. *Clubs:* Tennis & Racquet, The Brook (N.Y.C.); Country (Brookline, Mass.); Union, Somerset; St. James (London). *Address: office* Wm. Underwood Co., Westwood, Mass. 02090, U.S.A.

**SEYDOUX, Roger Jacques Charles,** L en D. French diplomat. *B.* 28 Mar. 1908. *Educ.* Ecole des Sciences Politiques. *M.*

1944, Jacqueline Doll. *S.* Eric, Pierre. *Career:* Assistant to Financial Attaché at Embassy, London 1931–32; Asst. to Directeur du Cabinet of Résident Général, Morocco 1934–35; Secretary, Ecole Libre des Sciences Politiques 1936; Dir., Ecole des Sciences Politiques 1942, Institut d'Etudes politiques, University of Paris 1945; member, Executive Council, U.N.E.S.C.O. since Dec. 1948; Counsellor of Embassy in charge of Consulate-General, New York since Nov. 1950; Min. Plen., French Embassy in Washington 1951; Deputy Minister, Tunis, Sept. 1954; High Commissioner, Tunis 1955; Ambassador of France in Tunis 1956–57; Director-General of Cultural and Technical Affairs, Ministry of Foreign Affairs 1957; Ambassador to Morocco 1960–62; Ambassador and Permanent French Rep. to the United Nations, New York 1962–67; North Atlantic Treaty Organization, Brussels 1967. Ambassador to U.S.S.R. 1968–73; Ambassador of France since 1970. Pres., Banque de Madagascar et des Comores 1973—, Grand Officer de la Légion d'Honneur; Croix de Guerre. *Address:* 60 Rue de Varenne, Paris 7e, France.

**SEYDOUX de CLAUSONNE, François.** Ambassador and Counsellor of State of France. *B.* 1905. *M.* 1930, Beatrice Thurneyssen. *S.* Jacques. *Daus.* Liliane (Mme. Pierre Peugeot), Laurence (Mme. Daniel Fries), Anne (Mme. Tristan d'Albis), Yolande (Mme. Louis Roncin). *Career:* Ambassador to Austria 1955–58; to Fed. Republic of Germany Aug. 1958–62; to N.A.T.O. 1962–65; to Fed. Republic of Germany 1965–70. Grand Officer, Legion of Honour. *Address:* 14 Rue des Sablons, 75116 Paris France.

**SEYMOUR, Raymond B.** Chemical educator, consultant and researcher. *B.* 1912. *Educ.* University of New Hampshire (BS 1933; MS 1935) and University of Iowa (PhD 1937), post-doctoral studies, Rensselaer Polytechnic Institute, Institute of Paper Chemistry, University of Utah. *M.* 1936, Frances B. Horan. *S.* David R., Peter J. and Philip A. *Dau.* Susan J. (Mrs. Howard F. Smith). *Career:* Instructor in Chemistry Univ. of Hampshire 1933–35; Univ. of Iowa 1935–37; Research Chemist, Goodyear Tire and Rubber Co. 1937–39; Chief Chemist Atlas Mineral Products Co. 1939–41; Research Group Leader Monsanto Co. 1941–45; Dir. Research Univ. of Chattanooga 1945–48; Dir. Special Products Research Johnson and Johnson 1948–49; Pres. aud Dir. Atlas Mineral Products Div. Electric Storage Battery Co. 1949–55; Chmn. Bd. and Pres. Loven Chemical of California 1955–60; Chmn. Science Div. and Prof. of Chemistry, Sul Ross State Coll. Alpine Texas 1960–64; Prof. Chem. Dept. Univ. of Houston 1964–76; Distinguished Prof. of Polymer Science, Univ. of Southern Mississippi 1976—. Member, Exec. Reserves. U.S. Dept. of Defense 1958; Western Plastics Award, 1960. Fellow, American Assn. for Advancement of Science and Texas Academy of Science. *Member:* American Chemical Society; American Institute of Chemical Engineers; Houston Society of Engineers and Scientists; Amer. Assoc. of Oceanography; Alpha Chi Sigma; Phi Lambda Upsilon; Gamma Sigma Epsilon; Sigma Xi. *Publications:* Hot Organic Coatings, (1959); Plastics for Corrosion Resistant Applications, (1955); Plastics in Building, (1955); National Paint Dictionary, (1948); Polymer Chemistry, (1968); General Organic Chemistry, (1970); Experimental Organic Chemistry, (1970); Modern Plastics Technology (1972); Chemistry and You (1974); Contributor to Chapters in Engineering Materials Handbook (1958); Testing of Plastics (1966); Encyclopedia of Chemistry (1966); Treatise on Analytical Chemistry (1966); Annual Plastics Review, Industrial and Engineering Chemistry, 1948–72; over 400 articles in scientific journals and over 50 U.S. and foreign patents. *Club:* Hattlesborg C.C. *Address:* Lakeshore Drive, RT 10, Hattiesburg, MS 39401; and *office* USM, Southern Station, Box 276, Hattiesburg, MS 39401, U.S.A.

**SHACKFORD, Roland Herbert.** Journalist. *B.* 1908. *Educ.* Antioch College, Yellow Springs, Ohio (BS). *M.* 1936, Augusta McMurray. *S.* John Steven and James Leon. *Dau.* Kristin (Ruckdeschel). *Career:* With United Press Assn.: Correspondent, New York 1935–37 and Washington 1937–43; Diplomatic Correspondent, Washington 1943–48 General European News Manager, London (Eng.) 1948–52. Foreign News Analyst, Scripps-Howard Newspapers 1952—. European Correspondent, Scripps-Howard Newspapers, London 1952–54. Foreign News Analyst, Scripps-Howard Newspapers, Washington, 1954–66; Asian Correspondent, Scripps-Howard Newspapers, Hong Kong, 1967–68; Foreign News Analyst, Scripps-Howard Newspapers, Washington, 1969–73; Snr. Fellow, Woodrow Wilson National F'ship Foundation since 1973; Pres., Harbour Square Owners, Inc. 1970; Editor, Harbour Square News 1969. *Awards:* Journalism Award of National Headliners Club. 1946; Lawrence S. Mayers Peace Award, 1955; William the Silent Award for Journalism, 1960. *Publication:* The Truth about Soviet Lies (1962). Bi-weekly Report on Red China 1964–68. *Clubs:* Overseas Writers (Washington). *Address:* Harbour Square Apts. S. 405, 530 N. Street S.W., Washington, D.C. 20024, and *office* 777 Fourteenth St., N.W., Washington, D.C., U.S.A.

**SHACKLETON, The Rt. Hon. The Lord Edward Arthur Alexander,** KG, PC, OBE, MA. *B.* 1911. *Educ.* Radley College; Magdalen Coll., Oxford (MA). *M.* 1938, Betty Homan. *S.* 1. *Dau.* 1. Created Baron (Life Peer) of Burley, 1958. *Career:* Member of Cabinet, Minister of Defence, R.A.F. 1964–67; Minister without Portfolio, 1967–68; Paymaster-General, Deputy Leader of the House of Lords, Leader of the House of Lords Privy Seal, 1968; Minister in charge Civil Service Department. Leader of the Opposition, House of Lords, 1970–74; Dep. Chmn. R.T.Z. Corporation Ltd. (Personnel/Admin); Dir. Woodrow Wyatt Holdings Ltd.; Chmn., R.T.Z. Development Enterprises. *Member* of Council Industrial Society; Pres., Royal Geographical Society 1971–74 (formerly Vice-Pres.); Pres. Parly & Scientific Cttee. 1975—; Fellow B.I.M. *Awards:* Cuthbert Peek Award (Royal Geographical Society), 1933; Ludwig Medallist (Munich Geographical Society), 1938; LLD (Hon), Univ. of Newfoundland. *Publications:* Arctic Journeys; Nansen the Explorer; Borneo Jungle (part author). *Address:* Long Coppice, Canford Magna, Dorset; and House of Lords, London, S.W.1.

**SHAH, Idries** (The Saiyid Idries Shah, el-Hashimi). Author. Director, several electronic, import-export and publishing companies. *B.* 1924. *M.* Kashfi Khanum. *S.* 1. *Daus.* 2. Author of numerous works on Eastern thought and affairs (several awards); Fellow, Royal Socy. of Arts; Guest Professor Univ. Geneva 1972–73; Prof. Nat. Univ. (La Plata) Argentina, since 1974; Visiting Prof., Univ. of California 1976. Adviser to Heads of State and others in the Middle East. Governor, Royal Humane Society (London); Royal Hospital & Home for Incurables (London). Life Governor, Inst. for Advanced International Studies, New Jersey; Royal National Life Boat Inst. Lectures, New School of Social Research, New York. *Member:* Society of Authors; Folklore Society; The Royal Commonwealth Society (London); Club of Rome. Life Member, Brit. Assn. for the Advancement of Science; The National Trust. Adviser: Internat. Center for Educational Advancement 1975—; Human Nature Journal; Internat. Business News; Philosophy Publications Adviser, Harcourt Brace Jovanovich Inc. *Awards:* Gold Medal, Cambridge Poetry Festival 1973; Award (Services to Human Thought) Inst. for the Study of Human Knowledge, Stanford 1975. Subject of Festschrift: Sufi Studies: East & West, Papers in Honour of Idries Shah, Edited by Prof. L. F. Rushbrook Williams (London and N.Y., 1973/4); Contributor: The Oxford Companion to the Mind (1978); VI World Congress of Psychiatry, 1977. *Clubs:* Athenaeum; The Authors (London). *Address:* c/o Jonathan Cape Ltd. (Publishers), 30 Bedford Square, London, W.C.1.

**SHAH, Shantilal Harjivan,** BA, LLB. Indian politician. *B.* 30 July 1898. *Educ.* Gujerat College; Ahmedabad; Elphinstone College, Bombay. *M.* Hiralaxmi. *S.* Sharad. *Daus.* Usha, Bindoo. Member, Bombay Legislative Assembly; Congress Worker in Bombay Suburban District, jailed for 18 months in 1932, for nine months in 1941 and in 1942 arrested and detained for two years and nine months; Minister Government of Bombay 1952–60; Minister, Government of Maharashtra 1960–66. Elected to Parliament 1967; Managing Trustee, Saurashtra Trust (Janmabhoomi Group of Newspapers) Bombay. *Address:* Near Laxmi Nagar Hall, Junction of 8th and 10th Roads, KHAR, Bombay 052.

**SHAHMIRI, Khawaja Muzaffar-ud-Din Ahmad.** *B.* 1898. *M.* 1925, Zuhra Bano. *S.* Rafique Ahmad, BA, Hamid Ahmad, BCom (Accounts Mgr., Grindlays Bank Ltd. H.O. Calcutta), Javid Ahmad, BSc, ME (Exec. Engineer, Kashmir Eng. Service), Iqbal Ahmad, BE (Kashmir Eng. Service). *Dau.* Tahira Shahmiri, MA (Dir., Women s Education, J & K State). *Educ.* LLM King's College, London University; specialised in Constitutional, International, and Hindu and Mohammedan Law; BA (Honours), LLB 1st Class, Punjab University; Barrister-at-Law, Middle Temple; Lord Hardinge Gold Medallist and Mannersmith Gold Medallist, S.P. College 1921; Punjab Government Scholar; Foster Campbell Prize; *Career:* Practised at law 1923–29; Vakil, High Court 1925; Public Prosecutor, Mirpur 1928–29; Deputy-General Secretary to Jammu and Kashmir Govt. Feb.-Apr. 1932; Sessions Judge, Naushera and Mirpur (for trial of riot cases 1931-32); Deputy-Gen. Secy. to Govt. and Secretary to Civil Service Recruiting and Scholarship Selection Board 1933-35; Revenue Secy. 1935-36; Additional District Magistrate and Senior Subordinate Judge of Jammu Province, and later of Kashmir Province 1936-41; Federation Secy. 1938-39; permanent District and Sessions Judge 1941; Law Secy. and Legal Remembrancer 1942-43; Chief Secy. to Govt. 1942 and again in 1945; Administrator of Poonch (with powers of revenue and judicial minister) 1943-44; Governor, Jammu Province 1944-45; Director-General Civil Supplies and Supplies Sec. 1945-47; Governor Kashmir Province 1947-48; Sessions Judge, Kashmir and Jammu Provinces 1948-49; held concurrently the following posts: Judge, High Court of Judicature, Jammu and Kashmir Constitutional Adviser to Jammu and Kashmir State, Constitutional Adviser to Jammu and Kashmir Constituent Assembly, Senator and Syndic of Jammu and Kashmir University 1949-58. Chmn., Anti-Corruption Tribunal 1954-56. Member, University Council Kashmir Univ. since 1970. Vice-Chairman, Backward Classes Ctte.. 1969: Legal Adv. to Jammu and Kashmir 1958-62; Tribunal for trial of Leh embezzlement cases 1959; member, Aligarh Muslim Univ. Enquiry Cttee. 1960; Chmn., Delimitation Commission 1950 & 1961. *Address:* 'Chaman'. Aerodrome Road, Srinagar, 5, India 190005.

**SHAKESPEARE, Rt. Hon. Sir Geoffrey Hithersay**, Bt, PC. British politician. *B.* 23 Sept. 1893. *Educ.* Highgate School; Emmanuel College, Cambridge (MA, LLB). *M.* (1) 1926, Lady (Aimée) Fisher, née Loveridge (*D.* 1950). *S.* William Geoffrey. *Dau.* Judith Anne (*D.* 1949); (2) 1952, Elizabeth, dau. of Brig.-Gen. Hare, of Norwich. *Career:* Served World War I with 5th Bn. Norfolk Regt. 1914-19; called to the Bar Middle Temple 1921; Private Secretary to Prime Minister 1921-22; MP (Nat. Lib.) for Wellingborough (Northants.) 1922-23, Norwich 1929-45; Junior Lord of the Treasury and Chief Whip (Lib.-Nat. Pty.) 1931-32; Parliamentary Secretary to Ministry of Health 1932-36, and the Board of Education 1936-37; Parliamentary and Financial Secretary to Admiralty 1937-40; Parliamentary Secretary to Department of Overseas Trade 1940; Under-Secretary of State for Dominion Affairs 1940-42; Chairman, Industrial Copartnership Assn. 1958-68; Chmn. Council of the Baronetage 1972-75. *Publication:* 'Let candles be brought in.' *Address:* 6 Greatash, Lubbock Road, Chislehurst, Kent.

**SHAMMAS, Shukri Hanna.** Lebanese. *B.* 1909. *Educ.* American University of Beirut—AUB (BA and Normal Certificate); BSc in Civil Engineering, AUB and London Univ. *M.* 1943, Olga Khoury. Children Hiyam, Issam, Muram, Nizam and Siham. *Career:* Past Teacher: Elementary School, AUB 1923-25; Secondary School, Shweir, Lebanon 1925-26; Gordon College, Khartoum 1927-32; Engineer Building Construction Dept. Iraq Petroleum Co. Ltd. 1932-36; Teachers College, Baghdad 1937-39; Is Mayor of Rabiya; Partner, Man. Dir. Contracting & Trading Co. C.A.T.; Chairman, President, Tourism & Hotel Development Corp. Sal.; Engineering Contractors Ltd. Managing Director, Shammas Economic Institute SARL; Mothercat Ltd. (Scotland). Director: MEOS; Vice-Pres. Banque de l'Industrie et du Travail S.A.L.; Bailey's (Electrical) Ltd. Société des Grand Hotels du Levant S.A.L. *Member:* Bd. of Trustee, AUB 1963—; Chairman Adv. Council, Lebanese Management Assn. *Publications:* Some problems of science and engineering education in the Middle East 1961); Al-Rabiya—a residential project in the Lebanon (1962); Pipelines in the service of the Petroleum Industry; Storage Tanks, Oil Control, Cutbacks. *Clubs:* Alumni (AUB); Rabiya; Lions; Automobile; Propeller; Diners'. *Address:* Residence Shammas, Rabiya, El-Metn, P.O.B. 2265 Lebanon; and *office* C.A.T. Building, Al-Arz Street, Saifi Qtr., P.O.B. 11 1036, Beirut, Lebanon.

**SHANLEY, Bernard Michael.** Knight of Malta. Lawyer. *B.* 1903. *Educ.* Columbia Univ. 1925, and Fordham Univ. Law School 1928; LLD Seton Hall Univ. *M.* 1936, Maureen Virginia Smith. *S.* Seton, Kevin, Brendan. *Daus.* Maureen Virginia, Brigid. *Career:* Admitted to Bar of State of New Jersey 1929. Special Counsel to the President of the U.S. 1953-55; Secretary to the President 1955-58. Member; Shanley & Fisher (Newark, N.J.); Member: Republican National Committee and its Exec. Cttee. 1959—, and Membership Cttee. of the U.S. States Chamber of Commerce 1959—. War Department Citation; Man of the Year Award (Advertising Council of New Jersey), 1954. *Clubs:* Union (N.Y.C.); Metropolitan, Capitol Hill (Washington); Somerset Hills Country (Bernardsville); Essex (Newark); National Golf Links of America (Southampton). *Address:* Bernardsville, N.J.; and *offices* 550 Broad Street, Newark 1, N.J., U.S.A.

**SHANN, Keith Charles Owen**, CBE. Australian diplomat. *B.* 22 Nov. 1917. *Educ.* Univ. of Melbourne (BA Hons.). *M.* 1944, Betty Evans. *S.* 2. *Dau.* 1. *Career:* With Commonwealth Bureau of Census and Statistics 1939-40; with Australian Department of Labour and National Service 1940-46; with Australian Department of External Affairs since 1946; with U.N. Division, Dept. of External Affairs 1946-48; Australian Mission to U.N., New York, 1949-52; Counsellor i/c U.N. Branch, Canberra 1952-55; member, Australian Delegation to Gen. Assembly of U.N. 1948-49-50-51-52-53-57-67-74; En. Ex. and Min. Plen. to Philippines 1955; Ambassador 1956-59; Rapporteur, U.N. Special Committee on the Problem of Hungary 1957; Senior External Affairs Representative, London May 1959-62; Ambassador to Indonesia 1962-66; Leader of Australian Delegation to the Development Assist. Committee of O.E.C.D., Paris, 1966-67, 1968-69; First Assistant Secretary, Dept. of External Affairs, Canberra 1966-70, Deputy Secy., Dept. of Foreign Affairs, 1970-74; Ambassador to Japan 1974-76; Chmn., Aust. Public Service Board 1977. *Award:* Coronation Medal 1953. *Address:* Public Service Board, Canberra, A.C.T., Australia.

**SHANNON, Robert Henry.** Canadian *B.* 1923. *Educ.* Univ. of Western Ontario BA, Hons., Business Admin. *M.* 1948, Adrienne Ann White. *Daus.* 3. *Career:* Exec. Vice-Pres., Viceroy Manufacturing Co. Ltd. 1958-61; Sales Manager, Canadian Aniline and Extract 1951-58; Secy. Treas., Milko Products Ltd. 1948-51; Lieutenant, Royal Canadian Navy four years. Manager, Chemical Products Dept., Corporation of Canada Ltd. 1961—. Warden of County of Halton 1955; Reeve of Town of Burlington 1951-56; Governor and Chairman of Finance; Joseph Brant Memorial Hospital 1955-58. *Clubs:* Lambton Country; Chinguacousy Country. *Address: office* 48 St. Clair Avenue West, Toronto 7, Ont., Canada.

**SHANNON, William Vincent.** American diplomat. *B.* 1927. *Educ.* Clark Univ., Worcester, Mass.—AB *magna cum laude* 1947, DLitt 1964; Harvard Univ.—MA 1948; Boston Univ.—DLitt 1971. *M.* 1961, Elizabeth McNelly. *S.* 3. *Career:* Research Associate, Mass. Inst. of Technology 1949; Freelance writer 1949-51; News Correspondent, The New York Post 1951-64; Editorial Board, The New York Times 1964-77; U.S. Ambassador to Ireland since 1977. Member, Sigma Delta Chi. Trustee, Clark Univ. *Publications:* The American Irish (1964); The Heir Apparent (1967); They Could Not Trust the King (1974). *Clubs:* Cosmos (Washington, D.C.); Century (N.Y.). *Address:* American Embassy, 42 Elgin Road, Dublin 4, Republic of Ireland.

**SHAPIRO, Isadore.** American research chemist and professional engineer. *B.* 1916. *Educ.* Univ. of Minnesota; PhD (1944); BChE with High Distinction (1938); Research Fellow, Univ. of Minnesota 1944-45. *M.* 1938, Mae Hirsch. *S.* Stanley Harris and Jerald Steven. *Career:* Pres. Aerospace Chemical Systems Inc. 1964-66; Universal Chemical Systems Inc. 1962-66. Head of Chemistry, Hughes Tool Co., Aircraft Div., Culver City, Calif. 1959-62. Dir. Research Lab., Olin Mathieson Chemical Corp., Pasadena, Calif. 1952-59. Dir. Chemical Lab., U.S. Naval Ordnance Test Station 1947-52. Research Chemist, E. I. du Pont de Nemours & Co., Philadelphia 1946, Director of Contract Research, HITCO, Gardena, Calif., 1966-67. Principal Scientist, McDonnell Douglas Astronautics Co. of McDonnell Douglas Corporation, Santa Monica, Calif., 1967-70; Consultant 1970; Mgr. Materials & Processes, Airesearch Manufacturing Co. Torrance Calif. since 1971. *Awards:* Fellow, American Institute of Chemists; Associate Fellow, American Institute of Aeronautics & Astronautics. *Member:* American Chemical Socy., American Ceramic Socy., Natl. Inst. of Ceramic Engrs, Amer. Physical Socy., Socy. for the Advancement of Materials and Process Engineers, American Assn. for the Advancement of Science, N.Y. Acad. of Science, Amer. Inst. of Physics, Socy. of Rheology, Amer. Ordnance Assn., Amer. Assoc. Contamination Control, International Plansee Socy. for Powder Metallurgy, Amer. Inst. of Management Sigma Xi, Tau Beta Pi, Phi Lambda Upsilon. *Publications:* Numerous patents and over 70 publications in various scientific journals; presented over 30 papers before scientific orgs. incl. the XVI (Paris, 1957), XVII (Munich, 1959), and XIX (London, 1963), International Congresses of Pure and Applied Chemistry. Discoverer of the Carborane Series of Compounds, Developer, process to make high-strength, high-modulus carbon fibres from coal-tar pitch. *Address:* 5624 West Sixty-second Street, Los Angeles, Calif. 90056, U.S.A.

**SHARMA VICHITRA NARAIN, Vichitra Bhai.** Indian politician. *B.* 10 May 1898. *M.* 1933, Maitreyee Devi. *S.* Ramesh Narain, Umesh Narain, Akhilesh Narain. *Daus.* Indira, Usha. Founded, with Acharya Kriplani, Gandhi Ashram, U.P. 1920; jailed for boycotting the visit of the Prince of Wales 1921; jailed again in 1932 and 1942; Secy., Shri Gandhi Ashram 1920–72; member of Legislative Council, U.P. 1947 elected to State Legislative Assembly 1952; member, All-India Khadi and Village Industries Board 1952–72; (Chairman, Certification Cttee. 1954–72); Minister for Transport 1952; Minister for Public Works 1954–57; Min. for L.S.G. Apr. 1957–60; elected third time to State Legislative Assembly 1962, Minister for L.S.G. 1962–63; Chmn. Khadi Swaraj since 1967. *Address:* 3 La Place, Lucknow, India.

**SHARP, Hon. Mitchell W.,** PC. *B.* 1911. *Educ.* Univ. of Manitoba (BA 1934) and London School of Economics (1937–38). *M.* (1) Daisy Boyd (*Dec.*). *S.* 1. *M.* (2) Jeannette Dugal. *Career:* Officer 1942 Director, Economic Policy Division, Canadian Dept. of Finance since 1947; Associate Deputy Minister of Trade and Commerce 1951–57, Deputy Minister 1957–58. Vice-President Brazilian Traction, Light & Power Co. 1958–62. Elected to House of Commons 1963; Minister of Trade and Commerce 1963–65; Minister of Finance, Canada 1965–68. Secretary of State for External Affairs, Canada 1968–74; Pres. of Privy Council and Leader of House of Commons Canada 1974–76. *Awards:* Hon. LLD Univ. of Manitoba 1965; Hon. Dr. of Social Science Univ. Ottawa 1970; Hon. LLD Univ. of Western Ontario 1977. *Address:* c/o Parliament Building, Ottawa, K1A OA3, Ont., Canada.

**SHARPE, Henry Dexter, Jr.** *B.* 1923. *Educ.* Brown Univ., Providence (AB). *M.* 1953, Peggy Boyd. *S.* Henry Dexter III and Douglas Boyd. *Dau.* Sarah Angell. *Career:* Chmn. & Chief Exec. Officer, Brown & Sharpe Manufacturing Co. (manufacturers of machine tools, cutting tools, industrial hydraulics and precision tools). Director, Providence Journal Co., Pres.: National Machine Tool Builders Assn. 1970–71; Machinery & Allied Products Institute (member Executive Committee). *Address:* Pojac Point Road, North Kingstown, R.I.; and *office* Brown & Sharpe Manufacturing Co., Precision Park, North Kingstown 02852 R.I., U.S.A.

**SHAVE, Lionel Kenneth Osbourn,** OBE, ED. British company director. *B.* 1916. *Educ.* Scotch College, Melbourne, and Scots College, Sydney. *M.* 1942, Phyllis Evelyn Knight. *Daus.* Margaret Wendy and Jillian Louise. *Career:* Served in World War II (Infantry and General Staff; Lt.-Col. 1942) 1939–46. General Manager: Whale Industries Ltd.; Whale Products Pty. Ltd., Gurley Station Pty. Ltd., Feed Lots Pty. Ltd. 1952–63. Director, Whale Industries Group 1961–63; Gen. Mgr. McDonald Industries Ltd. Group of Companies 1965–71; Chief Exec. Robe River Ltd. since 1971. Fellow, Australian Inst. of Management (Councillor, Queensland Division 1954–63); Queensland Chamber of Manufacturers (Cnclr. 1958–62); Queensland Lawn Tennis Assn. (Cncl. 1958–62); Chmn. Old Tate Theatre since 1970. Adviser, Australian Govt. Delegation, Conservation of Sea Stocks Conf., UNFAO, Rome 1955. *Clubs:* Naval & Military (Victoria); Queensland, Union (Sydney); Australian Golf. *Address:* 24 Darling Point Road, Edgecliff, Sydney, N.S.W., Australia.

**SHAW, Edward Stone.** American. Professor of economics; economist. *B.* 1908. *Educ.* Stanford Univ. (AB 1929, AM 1930, PhD 1936); Social Science Research Fellowship, England 1937–38. *M.* 1935, Elizabeth Ashworth. *Dau.* Janet Stone. *Career:* Successively Asst. Instructor, Asst. Prof., Assoc. Prof. Stanford Univ. 1929–41–74. Exec. Head, Dept. of Economics, Stanford 1941–43, 1948–53 and 1960–61; Ford Faculty Fellow 1959–60; Consultant: U.S. Dept. of the Treasury 1961, U.S. Army Engineering Corps 1961, and California Division of Savings and Loan 1962. Research Associate, Brookings Institution. Washington, D.C. 1954; Visiting Professor, University of Hawaii 1962; Visiting Lecturer, Bank of Japan 1962. Alexander Baldwin Professor, Univ. of Hawaii 1969–70; Lecturer, Bank Markezi (Iran) 1969; Consultant Harvard Univ. Dev. Adv. Service Ghana 1970, Malaysia 1971; Agency for Int. Development, Afghanistan 1973; Visiting Scholar, Federal Reserve Bank of San Francisco 1974–75; Prof., Univ. of California 1975; Consultant, Banco de Portugal 1976. U.S. Naval Reserve 1943–46. At times consultant to Board of Governors of Federal Reserve System, Bank of America, The Rand Corp., The Ford Foundation, and Commission on Money and Credit. Fellow, American Academy of Arts & Sciences. Trustee, Teachers Insurance & Annuity Assoc., 1963–67. *Publications:* Money, Income and Monetary Policy (1950); Co-author: Money in a Theory of Finance (1960); Mobilizing Resources for War (1961); Commodity Stockpiling (1949); The Allocation of Economic Resources (1960); various articles in professional journals. Ford Faculty Research Professorship, 1959–60. Financial Deepening in Economic Development (1973). *Member:* Amer. Economic Assn. *Address:* 525 Los Arbolos Avenue, Stanford, Calif.; and *office* Department of Economics Stanford University, Calif., U.S.A.

**SHAW, John Dennis Bolton.** British diplomat. *B.* 1920. *Educ.* Manchester Gr. School; Balliol College, Oxford, MA. *M.* 1955, Isabel Lowe. *S.* 2. *Career:* War-time service in N. Africa, Italy and India 1940–46; Colonial Office 1948–55; District Commissioner and Deputy Financial Secy. Sierra Leone 1955–57; 1st Secy. British High Commission, Karachi, 1958–61; 1st Secy. British Embassy Washington 1961–62; C'wealth Relations Office 1962–65; Head of Chancery. Brit. High Commission Nairobi 1965–67; Brit. Rep. on UN Trusteeship Council and Cttee on Colonization 1967–71; Head of Gibraltar and Gen. Dept, For. & C'wealth Office 1971–73; British Ambassador in the Somali Democratic Republic 1973–76; Dep. High Commissioner, Kuala Lumpur since 1976. *Decoration:* MVO. *Address:* c/o Foreign and Commonwealth Office, King Charles St., London S.W.1.

**SHAW, Michael Norman,** JP, MP. British Politician. *B.* 1920. *Educ.* Sedbergh. *M.* 1951, Joan M. L. Mowat. *S.* 3. *Career:* Partner, Robson Rhodes; MP for Brighouse & Spenborough 1960–64; PPS to Minister of Labour 1962–63; MP (Cons.) for Scarborough & Whitby 1966–74, & for Scarborough since 1974; PPS to Sec. of State, Dept. of Trade & Industry 1970–72, & to Chancellor of the Duchy of Lancaster 1973; mem., British Del. to European Parliament, Strasbourg since 1974. Fellow, Inst. of Chartered Accountants. JP Dewsbury, 1953. *Club:* Junior Carlton. *Address:* Duxbury Hall, Liversedge, West Yorkshire; and *office* House of Commons, London SW1A 0AA.

**SHAW, Roland Clark.** American. *B.* 1921. *Educ.* Princeton University (BA) and London School of Economics. *M.* 1952, Baroness Felicitas von Frankenberg und Proschlitz. *Daus.* Alexandra P.M. and Victoria H. D. *Career:* Pilot to Captain U.S.A.F. 1940–45; Diplomatist, United States Department of State, High Commission, Germany, and Second Secy., U.S. Embassy, London 1950–55; Vice-Pres. Cornell Oil Co., Foster Petroleum, and Foster Investment Corp. 1955–59; Pres., Dir.-Gen., Transworld Petroleum, Paris 1959–62. Vice-Pres., Eastern Hemisphere, Transnational Oil Producers 1963–65. Petroleum Consultant 1963–70; Chmn. & Man. Dir., Ball and Collins (Oil & Gas) Ltd. 1970—; Heritage Oil Ltd.; Premier Consolidated Oilfields Ltd.; Intep (U.K.) Ltd.; Tartan Drilling Co. Ltd. *Member:* Socy. of Petroleum Engineers; A.I.M.E.; Assn. Française des Techniciens du Petrole. *Clubs:* Travellers (Paris). *Address:* Pound Cottage, Headley Bordon, Hampshire; and *office* 23 Lower Belgrave Street, London SW1W 0NR.

**SHAW, Thomas Richard,** CMG. *B.* 1912. *Educ.* Repton School and Clare College, Cambridge (MA). *M.* 1939, Evelyn Frances Young. *S.* 4. *Career:* Probationer Vice-Consul, Istanbul 1934; Vice-Consul, Bushire 1937; Acting Consul Gr. II, Tientsin 1938; Vice-Consul, Trieste 1939, Leopoldville 1940, Elisabethville 1942, Casablanca 1943, Rabat 1943; Foreign Office 1944; Consul, Bremen 1949; Deputy Consul-General, New York 1953; Consul-General, Izmir 1955; Inspector of Foreign Service Establishments 1957, Senior Inspector 1961, Ambassador to Ivory Coast, Upper Volta and Niger 1964; Minister, Tokyo, 1967; H.M. Ambassador Rabat 1969–71. *Address:* Upton, Harrow Road, West Dorking, Surrey.

**SHAWCROSS (of Friston), Rt. Hon. Lord** (Sir Hartley Shawcross), GBE, PC, QC, LLM. Master of the Bench, Grays Inn. *B.* 1902. *Educ.* Dulwich College and Geneva; LLM Liverpool; LLD *Hon. Causa*, Columbia, Michigan, Lehigh (U.S.A.) and New Brunswick (Canada), Bristol and Sussex Univs. Hon. LLD, Liverpool and Hull Univs. *M.* 1944, Joan Mather (dec'd.). *S.* William Hartley Hume, and Hume. *Dau.* Joanna. *Career:* KC 1939; Recorder of Salford 1939–45; Deputy Regional Commissioner 1940; Chief Reg. Commr. for N.W. England 1942–45; Chmn., Catering Commn. 1943–45; mem., Home Secy's. Adv. Cttee. on Delinquency 1943–45; MP (Lab.) for St. Helens 1945–57; Chief Prosecutor for U.K. at Nuremberg Trial of War Criminals 1945–46; one of the principal delegates for the U.K. to the Assembly of the United Nations 1945–50; Attorney-General of England

1945–51; Privy Councillor 1946; Recorder of Kingston-upon-Thames 1946–61; President of the Board of Trade, Apr.–Oct. 1951; Chairman, General Council of the Bar of England 1952–57; Friends of Atlantic Union Organization 1953–58; Chmn.: Upjohns Ltd.; Thames Television Ltd. 1970–74; City Panel on Company Take-overs & Mergers; Morgan Bank International Advisory Council; London & Continental Banks Ltd.; The Press Council. Director: Times Newspapers Ltd. 1968–74. Shell Transport and Trading Co. Ltd. 1968–72, Shell Kuwait Co. Ltd., E.M.I. Ltd., Ranks, Hovis, Macdougall Ltd., Caffyns Ltd. Chmn.: Dominion-Lincoln Assurance Co. Ltd. Director, Morgan Et Cie SA; Morgan Et Cie International SA France; European Enterprises Development Co. S.A. (Luxembourg) since 1973. Special Adviser to Morgan Guaranty Trust Co. of New York. U.K. Representative on the International Commission of Jurists; member of Court of London Univ. since 1955; Chairman of 'Justice'; Chmn., Public International Law Section, British Institute of International & Comparative Law. Member, Board of Trustees of American University of Beirut. Pres. British Hotels & Restaurants Assn. 1958–71; Chmn, Royal Commission on Press 1961; British Medical Research Council, 1961–65; Chmn., Int. Chamber of Commerce "Commission of Eminent Persons on Unethical Practices". *Awards:* Knight Grand Cross, Imperial Iranian Order of Homayoun (1st class); Hon. Fellow, American Law Foundation 1961; Hon. Member, New York (1946) and American (1956) Bar Assns. Chancellor, University of Sussex. *Address:* Friston Place, Sussex.

**SHEARER, Rt. Hon. Hugh Lawson,** PC, MP. *B.* 1923. *Educ.* St. Simon's College (Jamaica). Trade unionist and politician. Honorary Doctor of Laws, Howard University, Washington, D.C. Councillor, Kingston and St. Andrew Corporation, 1947–50; Assistant General Secretary, Bustamante Industrial Trade Union, 1947–53; Island Supervisor, BITU, 1953–67, Vice-Pres. since 1960 (on leave of absence 1967–72); Member: House of Representatives, 1955–59; Legislative Cncl., 1959–62. Min. without Portfolio and Leader of Govt. Business in the Senate, 1962–67; Dep. Chief of Mission for Jamaica at the U.N. General Assembly, 1962–66. Prime Minister of Jamaica, Minister of External Affairs and Minister of Defence 1967–72. *Awards:* Hon. Dr. of Laws, Howard Univ., Washington, D.C. 1968. *Address:* c/o Bustamante Industrial Trade Union, Kingston, Jamaica.

**SHEARES, Dr. Benjamin Henry,** MD, LMS, MS, FRCOG, FACS. Singapore Head of State. *B.* 1907. *Educ.* St. Andrew's School, Raffles Inst., Edward VII Coll. of Medicine. *M.* Yeo Seh Geok, *S.* 2. *Dau.* 1. *Career:* Asst. Medical Officer, Outram Hospital 1929–31; Head of Dept. Obstetrics and Gynaecology, Kandang Kerbau Hospital also Medical Superintendent 1942–45; Acting Prof. at King Edward VII Coll. of Medicine, 1945; Hon. Consultant, British Military Hospital 1948; Prof. Obstetrics & Gynaecology Univ. of Malaya Singapore 1950–60; Private practice 1960—; Hon. Consultant Kandang Kerbau Hospital 1960—; President of the Republic of Singapore since 1971. *Awards:* GCB; Litt.D.(h.c.); Star of the Republic of Indonesia Adipurna; Ancient Order of Sikatuna. Hon. Fellow, Royal Soc. of Medicine 1975, Royal College of Obstetricians & Gynaecologists 1976. *Publications:* Many Articles on obstetrics and gynaecology in professional journals. *Address:* The Istana, Singapore 9.

**SHEDDEN, Kenneth Newton,** FAIM, FInstSME, FIBA. Australian. *B.* 1918. *M.* 1948, Lily Joyce Peters. *S.* 2. *Dau.* 1. *Career:* Dir., Berger Jenson & Nicholson Ltd., London; Chairman: Berger Jenson & Nicholson (Aust.) Pty. Ltd.; Berger Paints (Australia) Pty. Ltd.; British Paints Ltd., Australian Branch; Celchem Ltd.; British Paints (New Zealand) Ltd.; Berger Paints NZ Ltd.; Par Paints Malaysia Sdn. Bhd.; Par Paints Singapore Private Ltd.; Kobe Paints Ltd., Japan. *Clubs:* Amer. National (Sydney); R.A.C., Avondale Golf; Ku-Ring-Gai Motor Yacht. *Address:* 8 Rawson Crescent, Pymble, N.S.W. 2073; and *office* P.O. Box 210, Pymble, N.S.W. 2073, Australia.

**SHEETS, Herman E.** American mechanical engineer. *B.* 1908. *Educ.* University of Dresden (ME 1934); University of Prague (Doctor of Technical Sciences in Applied Mechanics). *M.* 1942, Norma Elinor Sams. *S.* Lawrence S., Michael R. and Arne H. *Daus.* Diane E., Elizabeth J. and Norma K. *Career:* Dir. of Research, Chamberlin Research Organization, East Moline, Ill. 1939–42; Dir. Research St. Paul Engineering & Manufacturing Co., St. Paul, Minn. 1942–44; Project Engineer Elliott Co. Jeannette, Pa. 1944–46; Engineer Manager Goodyear Aircraft Corp. Akron O. 1946–53; Vice-President, Electric Boat Division, General Dynamics Corpn., June 1953–69; Professor, Chmn. Dept of Ocean Engineering, Univ. of R.I., Kingston, R.I. since 1969. *Award:* Citation for Work on Manhattan Project 1945. *Publications:* Underwater Propulsion (1961); The Engineering of Submarines (1962); Aluminaut (with R. R. Loughman, 1963); The Mixed-Flow Vaneaxial (with K. Lawrence, 1963); The Aluminaut (with R. R. Loughman, 1964); Residual Stresses due to Surface-rolling or Pressing (1938); Die Verbesserung der Dauerfestigkeit durch Eigenspannungen (1939); The Flow Through Centrifugal Compressors and Pumps (1950); High Energy Spark Ignition Systems for Jet Engines (co-author with M. A. Zipkin and C. N. Scott) (1951); Electric Ignition System for High-Altitude Starting of Jet Engines (co-author with J. W. Cross and N. E. Whitchurch, 1951); Non-dimensional Compressor Performance for a Range of Mach Numbers and Molecular Weights (1952); the Slotted Blade Axial-Flow Blower (1956); Hydronautics (1970). *Member:* National Academy of Engineering, New York Academy of Sciences, Amer. Socy. of Mechanical Engineers, Institute of the Aeronautical Sciences, American Association for the Advancement of Science. *Address:* 87 Neptune Drive, Mumford Cove, Groton, Conn., U.S.A.

**SHEFELMAN, Harold S.** Assoc. Commander, Order of St. John of Jerusalem (1970). American lawyer. *B.* 1898. *Educ.* Brown Univ. (PhB); Yale Univ. (LLB); Hon. LLD, Brown University, Seattle Pacific College. *M.* 1924, Madolene Whitehead (*D.* 1955). *M.* (2) 1958, Sylvia Rogers (*Div.* 1964). *S.* Thomas Whitehead. *Dau.* June Henderson (Hensley). *Career:* Member of firm of Roberts, Shefelman, Lawrence, Gay, & Moch; member (former President), Board of Regents, University of Washington 1957–75; Trustee, Brown University 1962–69; Director, National Conference on Metropolitan Area Problems 1956–62; Council, National Municipal League 1956–76; Chairman, Seattle Civic Center Commission 1956–71; member (former Chmn.), Seattle Planning Commission 1948–71; Cncl., National Planning Assn. 1955–65; Chmn., State Planning Advisory Council 1964–66; Pres., Pacific Science Centre Foundation 1968; Exec. Committee, Yale Law School Assn.; Chancellor, Episcopal Diocese of Olympia 1951—. Phi Beta Kappa; Order of the Coif; Distinguished Citizen Award of National Municipal League 1957; Outstanding Citizen Award of Seattle Municipal American Inst. of Architects; Brown Univ. Alumni Citation for Achievement 1959; 'Others' Award of Salvation Army, 1963; Univ. of Washington Recognition Award 1977; American Assembly participant 1955, 1960 and 1966. Pres., Seattle Bar Assn. 1937–38; Chmn., Section of Municipal Law, American Bar Assn. 1952–54; member, House of Delegates, American Bar Assn., 5 years; Council on Legal Education, American Bar Assn. 1938–40; member, Washington State Board of Education 1951–57; Chmn., Washington State Deleg. to White House Conference on Education 1955; Washington State Little Hoover Commission 1951–55; Governor's Cttee. on Metropolitan Problems 1956–57; Washington State Tax Council 1957–59; Governor's Constitutional Revision Commission 1968–70; Lecturer, University of Washington School of Law 1930–57; member, Yale Alumni Board 1953–57; Pres., Amer. Socy. of Planning Officials 1959–61; Vice-President, Yale Law Sch. Assn. 1966–69. Municipal League of Seattle 1956–58. *Member:* American Law Inst., since 1930; Fellow, American Bar Foundation; Municipal Forum of New York, American Acad. of Social and Political Science. *Clubs:* Lawyers (N.Y.C.); College (Seattle); Washington Athletic (Seattle). *Address:* 1818 IBM Bldg., Seattle, Washington 98101, U.S.A.

**SHELDON, Robert Edward,** PC, BSc, MP. British. *B.* 1923. *Educ.* Grammar School; Technical Colleges; Engineering Diploma; External Grad. London University. *M.* 1971, Mary Shield. *S.* 1. *Dau.* 1. *Career:* Member Parliament for Ashton-under-Lyne since 1964; Member Fulton Cttee. on Civil Service 1966–68; Chmn. Economic and Finance Group Parly. Labour Party 1966–67, Vice-Chmn. 1971–74; Front Bench Spokesman, Parly. Party on Civil Service Machinery of Government 1970–74; Min. of State, Civil Service Dept. since 1974; Chmn. North West Group Labour MPs 1971–74; Front Bench Spokesman, Treas. matters 1971–74; Chmn., General Subs-Cttee. of Expenditure Cttee. 1972–74; Minister of State Civil Service Dept. March–Oct. 1974, of Treasury Oct. 1974–June 75, since when Financial Secy. to the Treasury. *Address:* 27 Darley Avenue, Manchester 20; and *office* 2 Ryder Street, London, S.W.1.

**SHELLENBERGER, John Owen James.** American. *B.* 1907. *Educ.* Lafayette Coll. (BS in Ch). *M.* 1943, Nancy Bertolet. *S.* John O. J. III and James Alexander. *Daus.* Nancy Bertolet and Ann Virginia. *Career:* Development Chemist,

Proctor & Gamble Co. 1929–32; Pres. Eastern Herald Corp. 1932–35; Chemist Asst. Sales Mgr. Amer. Chemical Paint Co. 1935–41; Lieut. Commander U.S. Navy 1941–45; Dir. International Div. Amchem Products Inc. 1945–55; Vice Pres. Dir. Marketing Amchem Products Inc. 1955—; Vice-Pres. Rorer-Amchem Inc. 1968–72; Pres. Herald Enterprises Ltd. since 1972; Director, Industrial Chemical Products Ltd. (S. Africa), Tecnimetal S.A. (Belgium). *Publications:* Articles on international business practice in various magazines. *Clubs:* Philadelphia Cricket; Ex-members Squadron A (New York); Yank Anuck (Canada). *Address:* 700 St. Andrews Road, Chestnut Hill, Philadelphia 19118, U.S.A.

**SHELLY, Warner Swoyer.** American advertising executive. *B.* 1901. *Educ.* University of Pennsylvania; Fordham University Law School; LLD Ursinus Coll., 1969. *M.* 1931, Kathrine G. Seckel. *Career:* Joined N. W. Ayer & Son, Inc. 1923; Vice-President and Manager of New York Service 1938; President and Director 1951; Chairman of Board, N. W. Ayer & Son, Inc. (210 West Washington Square, Philadelphia, Pa.) Apr. 1965–73; Chmn., Automotive Safety Foundation, Washington, 1968–72; Pres., W. M. Armistead Foundation Inc., 1967–74; Pres. N. W. Ayer Foundation since 1974. *Clubs:* Racquet and Tennis (N.Y.); Racquet (Philadelphia); Pine Valley Golf (N.J.); Ekwanok C.C. (Vermont); Prestwick (Scotland); Royal and Ancient Golf (St. Andrews); The Hon. Co. of Edinburgh Golfers; Royal Johannesburg Golf (Hon.), River (Hon.), Kimberley (South Africa). *Address:* Pine Valley, Clementon, N.J. 08021; and *office* c/o N. W. Ayer & Son, Incorporated, 210 West Washington Square, Philadelphia, Pa. 19106, U.S.A.

**SHELTON, Talbot.** American. *B.* 1914. *Educ.* Stanford Univ. (ABEcon; Phi Beta Kappa 1937), and Harvard Law Schl. (LLB 1940). *M.* 1941, Helen Margaret Laros. *S.* Talbot, Jr. and Peter L. *Career:* U.S. Delegate, Steel Cttee. meetings of Economic Commission for Europe, Geneva 1962–63–64. Chairman of Committee on Foreign Relations of American Iron and Steel Institute 1962–64. Member, Board of Directors, Bethlehem Steel Corp. Jan. 1958–April 1965; First Vice-President, Smith Barney & Co. Inc., New York City, since 1967. *Member:* American Bar Assn.; State Bar of California. *Clubs:* Racquet & Tennis (New York, N.Y.); Saucon Valley Country (Bethlehem Pa.); Lyford Cay (Nassau); Seminole Golf, Everglades (Florida). *Address:* Bath Pike, near Macada Road, Bethlehem, Pa. 18017; and *office* 1345 Avenue of the Americas, New York, N.Y. 10019, U.S.A.

**SHEN, James Chien-Hung.** *B.* 1909. *Educ.* Yenching Univ. of Peiping, China (BA) and Univ. of Missouri, Columbia, Mo. (MA). *M.* 1939, Winifred Wei. *S.* Carl. *Daus.* Joyce and Cynthia. *Career:* Secy. of the Pres. 1956–59; Spokesman, Min. Foreign Affairs 1959–61; Director Govt. Information Office, 1961–66; Ambassador of the Republic of China to Australia 1966–68. Vice-Minister of Foreign Affairs, Republic of China, 1968–71; Ambassador to the United States since May 1971. Member, Nationalist Party of China. *Address:* Embassy of Taiwan, 2311 Massachusetts Avenue, N.W., Washington, D.C. 20008, U.S.A.

**SHEN, Sampson Chi.** Chinese. Ambassador. *B.* 1917. *Educ.* Chengch University, China (BA); Benares Hindu University, India (DLitt). *M.* 1948, Faye Peng. *S.* Bing. *Dau.* Anne. *Career:* Chief, Public Relations Office, Taiwan Provincial Government, 1949; Press Adviser, Chinese National Aviation Co., 1949–50; Chief, First Section, Government Spokesmen's Office, 1951–52; Secretary to President Chiang Kai-Shek, 1952–56; Director, Government Information Office, 1956–61; Ambassador to Congo (Brazzaville) 1961–64; Minister, Chinese Embassy, Washington, U.S.A., 1964–65. Political Vice-Minister of Foreign Affairs, 1965–68; Ambassador Ext. and Plen. to Australia, Western Samoa and the Kingdom of Tonga 1968. *Awards:* Has high decorations from 21 countries including China, Argentina, Thailand, Brazil, Peru, Venezuela, Colombia, Jordan, Viet-Nam, Korea, and Malawi. Hon. Citizen: State of Texas; La Paz, Bolivia; San Salvador, and of Pergemino, Argentina. *Publications:* Confucius & Tagore (in English). *Clubs:* Royal Canberra Golf; Commonwealth (Canberra). *Address:* c/o Ministry of External Affairs, Taipei, Taiwan.

**SHENK, William Edwin,** SM. American. *B.* 1906. *Educ.* Mass. Inst. of Technology. *M.* 1935, Priscilla Heindlhofer. *S.* 2. *Daus.* 2. *Career:* Senior Research Eng. (Physics) United States Steel Corp. 1929–43; Mgr. Quality Control American Transformer 1943–44; Gen. Engineering Mgr. 1944–48, Tech. Dir. 1948–50; Chief Elect. Engineer McKay Machine Co. 1950–56, Dir. Electrical Eng. 1956–61; Vice Pres. Abbey Etna Machine Co. *Member:* Amer. Socy. for Metals; Assn. of Iron & Steel Engineers; Ordnance Assn.; Inst. Electrical & Electronic Engineers. *Address:* 7154 Stockport Drive, Lambertville, Mich., U.S.A.; and *office* East Indiana Avenue, Perrysburg, Ohio.

**SHEPARD, David Allan.** *B.* 1903. *Educ.* Massachusetts Inst. of Technology (BS 1926; MS 1927). *M.* 1927, Katherine B. Fisher. *S.* David Allan, Jr. *Dau.* Berney (Freeman). *Career:* Research Engineer, Standard Oil Co. Louisiana, Baton Rouge 1927–29; Chem. Engr., Hydro Engng. Co., Bayway, N.J. 1929–30, and S.O. Devmt. Co., Bayway 1930–32, and S.O. Devmt. Co., N.Y. and N.J., and S.O. of N.J. 1932–33; Sales Engr., S.O. of N.J. 1933–34; European Rep., S.O. Dev. Co., Paris 1934–35; Consultant and European Rep., International Co. (Vaduz), Paris 1935–36; Chmn., Foreign Products Cttee., Int. Assn. (Pet. Ind.) Ltd., London 1936–40; Technical Advisor, S.O. Co. (N.J.), N.Y. 1940–42; Petroleum Attaché, U.S. Dept. of State, U.S. Embassy, London 1942–43; Shareholders Rep., S.O. Co. (N.J.), London 1943–45; Chmn. of Board, Anglo-American Oil Co. Ltd. 1945–49; Exec. Asst. to Pres, S.O. Co. (N.J.), N.Y. Sept. 1949–51; Member, Bd. of Dirs., S.O. Co. (N.J.) 1951–66; Executive Vice-President 1959–66. Trustee, The Rand Corporation 1959–63, and 1965–73; Member and Trustee, System Development Corporation 1965–67. Chairman of the Rand Corporation 1967–70. Trustee M.I.T. 1951—. Member Exec. Cttee. 1958–71; Trustee, New York Public Library 1958—; Member Exec. Cttee. 1965–71; Trustee & Chmn. of Exec. Cttee., Carnegie Corpn. of N.Y. 1962–71, Chmn. Bd. 1971–75. *Member:* Tau Beta Phi; Phi Gamma Delta; Amer. Association for Advancement of Science; Society of Automotive Engineers; American Institute of Chemical Engineers; American Chemical Society; Royal Horticultural Society. *Clubs:* University, Century Association, Pilgrims. *Address:* Creamer Road, Greenwich, Conn.; and *office* 1 Rockefeller Plaza, New York City 10020, U.S.A.

**SHEPARDSON, Wallace Lloyd.** American advertising executive. *B.* 1919. *Educ.* Dickinson College, and Harvard Business School (AMP). *M.* 1939, Janet M. Rice. *Daus.* Laurinda and Christina. *Career:* With Photo Reflex Studios 1938–42; Pilot, U.S. Army Air Force 1943–45; with B. F. Goodrich Co. 1945–47; with James T. Chirurg Co. 1948— (Account Exec. Cairns Inc. 1955–68, Chmn. Bd. since 1968; Vice-Chmn., LKP International since 1977. *Member:* National Industrial Advertisers Assn.; Harvard Business School Assn.; Young Presidents Assn.; American Assn. of Advertising Agencies. Chief Executive Forum, World Business Council. *Clubs:* Broadcasting Executives; Advertising (Boston); Weston Golf; Truro Fish & Game; Cape Cod Tuna; Longwood Cricket; Rolling Hills Tennis; Caribbean Game Fishing Association. *Address:* LKP International, 767 Fifth Avenue, New York, N.Y. 10022, U.S.A.

**SHEPHERD, George William, Jr.** American. professor. *B.* 1926. *Educ.* Univ. of Michigan (BA 1949), and Univ. of London (PhD 1952). *M.* 1948, Shirley Brower. *S.* 2. *Daus.* 2. *Career:* Visiting Lecturer, Univ. of Khartoum 1964–65; Temporary Staff Associate, Rockefeller Foundation 1964–65; Editor, Africa To-day 1966—; Professor Graduate School of International Relations, University of Denver 1968—; Director, Center on International Race Relations, Univ. of Denver. *Awards:* Anisfield Wolf Award, 1956. *Member:* American Political Science Association; International Studies Assn.; African Studies Assn.; Rocky Mountains open space Council; Secy. American Cttee on Africa. *Publications:* They Wait in Darkness (1956); The Politics of African Nationalism (1962); Non aligned Black Africa (1970); Racial Influence in U.S. Foreign Policy (1970). Independent Democrat. *Club:* Colorado Mountain Climbers. *Address:* 6053 S. Platte Canyon Road, Littleton, Colo.; and G.S.I.S., University of Denver, Denver, Colo., U.S.A.

**SHEPHERD, Rt. Hon. Lord Malcolm Newton,** PC. British. *B.* 1918. *M.* Lady Allison Shepherd, JP. *S.* 2. *Career:* Dpty. Opposition Chief Whip, 1959–64; Opposition Chief Whip, 1964; Government Chief Whip, 1964–67. Minister of State, Foreign and Commonwealth Office, July 1967–70; Deputy Leader, House of Lords, Oct. 1967–70; Deputy Leader Opposition House of Lords 1970–74; Lord Privy Seal & Leader House of Lords 1974–76 (Resigned); Dep. Chmn., Sterling Group of Companies. Member of the Labour Party. *Address:* 29 Kennington Palace Court, London, S.E.11; and *office* 8 Heddon Street, London, W.1.

**SHERBROOKE-WALKER, Col. Ronald Draycott.** CBE, TD. British. *B.* 1897. *Educ.* Sherborne School. *M.* 1925, Ruth Bindley. *Career:* Partner in Carter & Co., Chartered Accountants 1924–39. Served European War 1914–19, Lieut. Dorset Regt. and R.F.C.; Lieut. to Major, 8th Bn. Middlesex Regt. T.A. 1925–31. Second war: 1939–45; Lt.-Col. to Col. Middx. Regt. and R.A.F. Member Middx T. and A.F.A. (Vice-Chmn. 1951–56) 1930–63. Comdt. Middx. Army Cadet Force 1948–54; Member Amery Cttee. 1956–57. Dep. Lieut. Middx. 1947–65 (Vice-Lieut. 1963–65). Director, Securicor (Southern) Ltd. 1945–72; Deputy Lieutenant of Greater London 1965–76. Vice-Pres., Army Cadet Force Association 1966—. *Publications:* Khaki and Blue. Fellow, Inst. Chartered Accountants (FCA). *Club:* Naval and Military. *Address:* 22, Bathwick Hill, Bath, Avon BA2 6EW.

**SHERER, Albert William Jr.** United States diplomat. *B.* 1916. *Educ.* Yale Univ. AB (1938); Harvard LLB (1941). *M.* 1944 Carroll Russell. *S.* 2. *Dau.* 1. *Career:* Foreign Service, officer in Morocco, Hungary, Czechoslovakia and Poland, 1946 onwards; Ambassador to Togo 1967–70: Ambassador to Guinea 1970–72; Ambassador to Czechoslovakia 1972–75 & concurrently Chief of U.S. Delegation to Conference on Security & Co-operation in Europe, Geneva 1974–75; Mem., U.S. Mission to U.N. 1975—; U.S. Rep., Security Council 1975—. *Decoration:* DFC (twice). *Clubs:* Metropolitan, Washington D.C.; Yale (N.Y.C.). *Address:* U.S. Mission to the U.N., 799 U.N. Plaza, New York, N.Y. 10017; and c/o Dept. of State, Washington, D.C., 20520, U.S.A.

**SHERFIELD, Lord** (Roger Mellor Makins), GCB, GCMG. *B.* 3 Feb. 1904. *Educ.* Winchester; Christ Church, Oxford; Fellow, All Souls College, Oxford, Hon. DCL Oxford; Hon DL London; D.Litt. Reading. *M.* 1934, Alice Davis. *S.* 2. *Daus.* 4. *Career:* Called to Bar (Inner Temple) 1927; entered Foreign Office 1928; served in Washington 1931–34, Oslo 1934; Foreign Office 1934; Assistant Adviser on League of Nations Affairs 1937; Secretary, Inter-governmental Committee on Refugees from Germany 1938–39; Adviser on League of Nations Affairs 1939; Adviser to British Delegation, International Labour Conference, New York 1941; on staff of Resident Minister in West Africa 1942; Assistant to Resident Minister at Allied Force Headquarters, Mediterranean 1943–44: Minister at British Embassy, Washington 1945–47; Assistant Under-Secretary of State, Foreign Office 1947–48; Deputy Under-Secretary of State for Foreign Affairs 1948–52; Amb. Ex. and Plen. to U.S.A. 1953–56; Joint Permanent Secretary to the Treasury 1956–59; Chairman U.K. Atomic Energy Authority, Jan. 1960–64. Chairman, Finance for Industry 1973–74, Industrial and Commercial Finance Corp. 1964–74; Ship Mortgage Finance Co. 1966–74; Estate Duties Investment Trust 1966–72; Technical Development Capital Ltd. 1966–74; A. C. Cossor Ltd.; Wells Fargo Ltd.; Chancellor, University of Reading; Pres. Centre for Intern. Briefing; Chairman, Governing Body, Imperial College of Science and Technology; Chmn. Marshall Aid Commemoration Commission 1966–74; President, Parliamentary & Scientific Cttee. 1969–73; Pres., British Standards Institution 1969–73; Fellow and Warden of Winchester College; Hon. Student, Christ Church, Oxford. *Address:* Sherfield Court, near Basingstoke, Hants.; and 8 Southwick Place, London, W.2.

**SHERMAN, Joseph Vincent.** American consulting economist and writer. *B.* 1905. *Educ.* Columbia College, N.Y.C. (AB 1928). *M.* 1944, Viola Signe Maria Lidfeldt. *Career:* Manager, Investment Dept., National Newark & Essex Banking Co., Newark, N.J. 1929–36; Statistician, Case Pomeroy & Co., N.Y. 1936–38; Vice-Pres., Economic Analysts, Inc., N.Y. 1938–42; Associate, Herbert R. Simonds (consulting engineer) 1943–45. Served in U.S. Army 1942–43. *Member:* Amer. Assn. for the Advancement of Science, American Economic Assn., Amer. Statistical Assn. *Publications:* Research as a Growth Factor in Industry (1940); The New Plastics (1945); Plastics Business (1946); The New Fibers (1946); contributor of numerous articles to Barron's National Business and Financial Weekly, and various other publications. *Address:* 160 Columbia Heights, Brooklyn, N.Y. 11201; and 280 Broadway, New York, N.Y., 10007, U.S.A.

**SHERRARD, Thomas James,** OBE, MSM, JP. New Zealand. Cl. *B.* 1895. *Educ.* Pongaroa and Banks College, Wellington. *M.* 1933. Rona Hould. *Dau.* 1. *Career:* Secy., Public Service Appeals Board 1924–27; Private Secy.: to Sir Frank Heath during the official tour of New Zealand 1926, and to the Leader of the Legislative Council 1927. Asst. Clerk of the Executive Council 1945–48, Clerk 1948–67. Clerk of first Privy Council meeting held in N.Z. during the Royal Tour (presided over by H.M. the Queen) 1954; First Chief of the Clan Sherrard formed in 1960. *Address:* 43 Hobson Street, Wellington, N.Z.

**SHERSBY, (Julian) Michael,** MP. British Politician. *B.* 1933. *Educ.* John Lyon Sch., Harrow-on-the-Hill. *M.* 1958, Barbara Joan Barrow. *S.* 1. *Dau.* 1. *Career:* Mem., Paddington Borough Council 1959–64; mem., Westminster City Council 1964–71; Dep. Lord Mayor of Westminster 1967–68; Sec., Assoc. of Specialised Film Producers 1958–62; Dir., British Industrial Film Assoc. 1962–66; Dir., British Sugar Bureau 1966–77, Dir.-Gen. since 1977; MP (Cons.) for Uxbridge 1972–74, & for Hillingdon, Uxbridge since 1974; PPS to Minister of Aerospace & Shipping, Dept. of Trade & Industry 1974; Jt. Sec., Conservative Party Parly. Industry Cttee. 1972–74; Chmn., Cons. Party Trade Cttee. 1974–76, Vice-Chmn. 1977; mem., Commonwealth Parly. Assoc. Delegation to Caribbean 1975; promoted Private Member's Bills: Town & Country Amenities Act, 1974, Parks Regulation (Amendment) Act, 1974, Stock Exchange (Completion of Bargains) Act, 1976. Mem. of Court, Brunel Univ. 1975; Pres., Abbeyfield Uxbridge Soc. 1975—; Jt. Sec., Parly. & Scientific Cttee. 1977. *Member:* Fellow, Inst. of Directors; mem., Inst. of Public Relations. *Clubs:* Junior Carlton; Conservative (Uxbridge). *Address:* Anvil House, Park Road, Stoke Poges, Slough SL2 4PG; and *office* House of Commons, London SW1A 0AA.

**SHERWIN, John.** *B.* 1901. *Educ.* Hotchkiss School, Lakeville, Conn., and Sheffield Scientific School, Yale University (BS 1923). *M.* 1924. Frances Bunts Wick. *S.* John, Jr. *Daus.* Susan (Bushnell Keeler) and Martha (Stewart). *Career:* Director: Moore McCormack Resources Inc., Brush Wellman Inc. Hon. LLD, John Carrol University, 1958, Case Institute. Chmn., Cleveland Foundation; Trustee: Cleveland Clinic Foundation; Republican. *Clubs:* Union, Kirtland Country, Chagrin Valley Hunt, Tavern (all of Cleveland); St. Anthony, Links (both of N.Y.C.). *Address:* 1721 Diamond Shamrock Building, Cleveland, Ohio 44114, U.S.A.

**SHERWOOD, Arthur Murray.** Lawyer. *B.* 1913. *Educ.* Harvard College (BSc 1936) and Columbia University School of Law (JD 1939). *M.* 1947, Marjorie F. Catron. *S.* Philip Townsend aud Thomas Catron. *Dau.* Evelyn Wilson. *Career:* Associate Attorney, Shearman & Sterling, New York City 1939–41 and 1946–54. Counsel 1954–55, Assistant Secretary 1955–56, Mobil Oil Corporation, Secy. 1956–72. Associate Attorney, Smith Stratton Wise & Heher since 1972; Enlisted as Private, U.S. Army, Mar. 1941; rose through ranks to Lieut.-Colonel 1944. Asst. Chief of Staff, G-1, 2nd Infantry Div. 1944–45. Awarded 5 battle stars. Legion of Merit (U.S.), Bronze Star (U.S.), Croix de Guerre avec Palme (France), Military Cross (Czechoslovakia). *Club:* Fly (Cambridge, Mass.). *Address:* 19 Cleveland Lane, Princeton, N.J. 08540, U.S.A.

**SHIBATA, Tatsuo.** Japanese. Comdr. Order of Sowathara (Cambodia). *B.* 1910. *Educ.* University of Washington, Seattle, Washington, U.S.A. (BA in Journalism). *M.* 1937, Seiko Morimoto. *S.* Takeshi. *Daus.* Tomoko and Masako. *Career:* Managing Editor, Mainichi Daily News 1952–64. Editor-in-Chief, 1964–70. Advisory Editor Mainichi Daily News, 1970—. (Published in Tokyo and Osaka, English language edition of The Mainichi Shimbun); Adv. Dir. Superior Public Relations. Dir. Japan Socy. of Translators; Hon. Advisor, Ikebana International. *Member:* Sigma Delta Chi (U.S. professional journalistic society); Japan Association of Current English; America-Japan Society. *Clubs:* Foreign Correspondents, of Japan; Transportation. *Address:* 31–3 Kamitakata, 5-chome, Nakano-ku, Tokyo; and *office* The Mainichi Newspapers, 1-1-1 Hitotsubashi, Chiyoda-ku, Tokyo, Japan.

**SHIBEIKA, Izz Eldin Mekki.** Sudanese diplomat. *B.* 1928. *Educ.* BA 2nd Cl (London); Diploma of Public Administration, Khartoum University. *M.* 1958, Louyja Hassan. *S.* 2. *Career:* District Officer 1952–53; District Commissioner Kermak 1953–54, and Akobo (South) 1955–56; First Secy., Foreign Affairs June 1956; Bagdad (Irak) 1956–58; Consul-General, Uganda and Kenya 1958–60; Counsellor, United Nations 1961; Minister (Actg. Under-Secy. Foreign Affairs) 1961–64; Ambassador to Somalia 1964. *Publications:* various papers and lectures on the history and economy of the Sudan (in course of publication). *Club:* Rotary (Baghdad and Mogadishu). *Address:* c/o Ministry of Foreign Affairs, Khartoum, Sudan.

**SHIDELER, Ross Odor.** American chemical engineer. *B.* 1922. *Educ.* Purdue Univ. (BS Chem Eng); graduate work, Business Administration, Indiana Univ. *Career:* Apprentice Seaman, U.S. Navy 1943; Lieut. (j.g.); discharged 1946; Chemical Engineer, Plant Development, Eli Lilly & Co., Indianapolis 1946–48; Administrative Asst., Eli Lilly International Corp. 1948–50; Owner, Beauty-Seal Plastics Co. 1950–52; Pres. United States Equipment Corp., Indianapolis, Ind. 1952—. Owner of patents, copyrights and trademarks. *Member:* Amer. Chemical Socy.; Amer. Inst. of Chemical Engineers; Sigma Nu Fraternity; Alpha Phi Omega Honorary (Past Pres.): Catalyst Club. *Club:* Indianapolis Athletic. *Address:* P.O. Box 22303, Dallas, Texas 75222, U.S.A.

**SHIELDS, James Getty, Jr.,** BS, LLB. American. *B.* 1918. *Educ.* Univ. of California (BS, LLB). *M.* 1947, Valerie Moore. *S.* 1. *Daus.* 2. *Career:* Exec. Vice Pres. Dir. Industrial Indemnity Co. 1946–64; Chmn. & CEO, California Canadian Bank 1964–72; Pres. & CEO Great State Financial since 1972; Exec. Vice-Pres. Crocker National Corp 1972–75, Financial & Management Consultant since 1975. *Clubs:* Bohemian; Pacific Union; Stock Exchange (San Francisco); California (Los Angeles). *Address:* 120 Santa Paula Avenue, San Francisco, Cal. 94127, U.S.A. and *office* 235 Montgomery Street, San Francisco, California.

**SHIELDS, Robert Hazen.** American Attorney. *B.* 1905. *Educ.* Univ. of Nebraska (AB 1926); Harvard (LLB, JD. 1929). *M.* 1927, Ruth Elizabeth Wood. *Daus.* Jane Louise and Sarah Lowe. Cmdr. Order of Carlos Manuel de Cespedes (Cuba). *Career:* Private Practice, New York 1929–34; Admitted to Bar of New York 1931; Senior Attorney, Office of Gen. Counsel, Agric. Adjustment Administration, Washington D.C. 1934–35; Supreme Court, U.S. 1935; District of Columbia 1947; Head Attorney and other positions, Officer of Solicitor, Dept. of Agriculture 1935–41, Asst. to Secy of Agriculture, and Chief Judicial Officer 1941–42; Solicitor 1942–46; War Food Administration 1943–45; President and Member Board of Directors, Commodity Credit Corp., and of Federal Crop Insurance Corp.; Administrator, Production and Marketing Administration; member, General Administrative Board, Graduate School, Dept. of Agriculture 1946; Adviser, U.S. Delegation, F.A.O. 1946; Executive Vice-President and General Counsel, U.S. Beet Sugar Association, Washington 1946–48, Pres. and General Counsel 1948–72; Chairman, Sugar Advisory Committee, Dept. of Agriculture 1947–49; Pres., New York Sugar Club 1960–66; Vice-Chairman, Information and Standards Committee, Sugar Industry 1948; Dir. and Vice-Pres. Sugar Research Foundation Inc. N.Y.C. 1946–68; Industry Adviser, U.S. Delegations to International Sugar Council 1950–68; Dir. and Vice-Pres. Sugar Information Inc. and Sugar Assn. Inc. 1949–72; Exec. Vice-Chmn. Amer. Sugar Beet Industry Policy Cttee. 1949–65; Dir. Int. Sugar Research Foundation Inc. Bethesda 1968–72; Dir. Viatech Inc. Syosset L.I.N.Y. 1967–75. *Member:* American, D.C. and Federal Bar Association (Pres., Federal Bar 1945–46); American Trade Association Executives (Director 1952–53); Washington Trade Association Executives (President 1952–53); Group Health Association, Inc. (Trustee 1940–46; President 1944–48). Mason. *Publications:* Contributor of legal and agricultural articles, law reviews, and other publications, including Federal Statutory Provisions Relating to Price Support for Agricultural Commodities (1944); Maximum Prices with Respect to Agricultural Commodities (1945); (co-author with Edward M. Shulman) Federal Price Support for Agricultural Commodities (1949). *Clubs:* Metropolitan; Congressional Country. *Address:* 9523 East Stanhope Road, Rock Creek Hills, Kensington, Md., 20795, U.S.A.

**SHINNAR, Felix Elieser,** Dr jur. Former Israel Ambassador Ex. & Plenipotentiary to Federal Republic of Germany. *B.* 1905. *Educ.* Heidelberg University (Dr jur). *M.* 1941, Alisa Oppenheim. *S.* 2. *Career:* Economic adviser and expert to Chamber of Industry and Commerce, Berlin, until 1934; economic adviser in Israel 1934–37; Man. Dir. of Haaretz (daily newspaper), Tel-Aviv, 1937–49; Controller of Fuel 1948; Economic Counsellor, Embassy London Nov. 1949–Jan. 1951; Head of Department, Ministry of Finance, Jan.–June 1951; adviser to Israel Foreign Office in all matters concerning claims against Germany, 1951; head of delegation (with Dr. Josephthal) for negotiation of reparations agreement with Fed. Republic of Germany, Mar.–Sept. 1952; head (with personal rank of Ambassador) of Israel Mission to implement the Reparations Agreement 1953. Chairman of 'Delek' The Israel Fuel Corp. Ltd. *Publications:* Bericht eines 'Beauftragten', book on the development of Israel-German relations from 1951–66—published in Hebrew and German (1967). Articles and brochures on economic subjects. *Address:* Tel Ganim, Israel.

**SHINWELL, Rt. Hon. Lord (Emmanuel),** PC, CH, DCL. British politician. *B.* 18 Oct. 1884. MP (Lab.) Linlithgow, 1922–24 and 1928–31, Seaham (Durham) 1935–50, Easington 1950–70; Financial Secretary, War Office 1929–30; Parliamentary Secretary to Dept. of Mines 1924 and 1930–31; Minister of Fuel and Power 1945–47; Chmn. Labour Party 1947–48; Secretary of State for War 1947–50; Minister of Defence 1950–Oct. 1951; Chmn. Parly. Party 1964–67. Hon. DCL Durham, 1969. *Publications:* The Britain I Want; When the Men Come Home; Conflict without Malice; The Labour Story; I've Lived Through It All. *Address:* House of Lords, London, S.W.1.

**SHIPLEY, Linwood Parks.** American. *B.* 1905. *Educ.* Univ. of Maryland (BA 1927). *M.* 1930, Emily Catherine Herzog. S. L. Parks, Jr., Frederick H., and Walter V. II. *Dau.* Emily Jane. *Career:* Partner, Brown Brothers Harriman & Co., New York City 1933— (various executive positions 1933–52). *Clubs:* Union League, India House (both N.Y.C.); Baltusrol Golf (Springfield, N.J.). *Address:* 81 Oakridge Avenue, Summit, N.J. 07901; and *office* 59 Wall Street, New York, N.Y. 10005, U.S.A.

**SHIRES, Sir Frank.** British company director. *B.* 10 Aug. 1899. *Educ.* West Leeds High School. *M.* 1929, Mabel Tidds. *S.* 1. *Dau.* 1. *Career:* Served in World War I (Major); Director and Deputy Managing Director, H. J. Heinz & Co. Ltd. 1940–55. Director: Marsh & Baxter Co. Ltd., and C. & T. Harris (Calne) Ltd. 1958–65; Chmn. Dell Foods Ltd. 1965—; Vice Pres. Inst. of Food Science and Technology 1967–69; Chmn. Bd. National Coll. of Food Technology since 1969. *Member* of Executive Committee of Canners' War-Time Association 1942–49; President, Food Manufacturers' Federation Inc. 1950–52; member of Council, British Food Manufacturing Industries Research Association 1947–64. Chairman, Governing Body, National College of Food Technology 1950–66. Food Hygiene Advisory Council 1955–73; Monopolies Commission 1957–61; Council of Reading Univ. 1966—; Fellow of the Institute of Food Science & Technology 1965. *Address:* Redholt, Linksway, Northwood, Middlesex.

**SHISTER, Joseph.** Chairman and Professor, Dept. of Industrial Relations, State Univ. of New York at Buffalo; Labour Arbitrator and Consultant. *B.* 1917. *Educ.* Univ. of Montreal (BS); Harvard Univ. (MA; PhD). *M.* 1941, Edna Louise Tuck. *S.* Neil Barry. *Daus.* Jayne Ellen, Gail Marilyn and Diane Marjorie. *Career:* Selected as one of Buffalo's Ten Outstanding Citizens. Moderator, Univ. of Buffalo Round Table of the Air, WBEN-TV, and WBEN. Member, N.Y. State Minimum Wage Board in Amusement and Recreation Industry; Chmn., Buffalo Full Employment Cttee.; Chmn., Erie County Grievance Board; Labour Arbitrator in disputes involving Union Carbide Corp., Goodyear Tire & Rubber Co., Curtiss-Wright Corp., Bell Aircraft Corp., and others. Referee, National Railroad Adjustment Board. Consulting Economist, National War Labour Board 1944; member, Nat. Wage Stabilization Bd. 1951–52; Member of White House Conferences on National Economic Issues 1962; Member White House Conference, Industrial World Ahead 1972; Chmn., Presidential Labor Dispute Emergency Boards 1961–62, 1964; Special Consultant on labour matters to Governor of Connecticut 1948–50; Member N.Y. State Board of Mediation 1966—. Research Associate, Rockefeller Foundation Study of Trade Unionism 1944–45; Instructor in Economics, Cornell University 1942–43; Assistant Professor of Economics, Syracuse University 1945–46; Asst. Prof. and Dir. of Research, Yale Univ. 1946–49; Visiting Prof. of Economics: Tufts Univ., Wesleyan Univ., Univ. of Montreal; member, Social Stratification Committee, Social Science Research Council 1952–53. *Publications:* Economics of the Labor Market; Labor Economics & Industrial Relations; Insight into Labor Issues; Job Horizons; A Decade of Industrial Relations Research; Conflict & Stability in Labor Relations; Public Policy and Collective Bargaining; numerous articles on economic and labour relations in various professional journals. *Member:* National Acad. of Arbitrators; American Economic Assn.; Federal Mediation & Consiliation Service; N.Y. State Board of Mediation; American Arbitration Assn.; Phi Beta Kappa; Beta Gamma Sigma. *Clubs:* University (Buffalo); Harvard. *Address:* 310 Brantwood Road, Snyder, N.Y. 14226, U.S.A.

**SHOLL, Hon. Sir Reginald Richard.** Australian legal consultant and company director. Formerly Australian judge and diplomat. *B.* 8 Oct. 1902. *Educ.* Queen's College; Melbourne Grammar School; Trinity College, Univ. of Melbourne (MA); New College, Oxford (MA, BCL, Rhodes Scholar). Formerly Official Law Fellow, Brasenose College, Oxford. *M.* (1) 1927, Hazel Bradshaw (*D.* 1962). *S.* 2. *Daus.* 2; (2) 1964, Anna McLean. *Career:* Called to the Bar, Middle Temple, London 1927, to the Bar of Victoria 1928, New South Wales and Tasmania 1935. Served World War II, A.M.F. and A.I.F. 1940–44; KC 1947; Justice, Supreme Court of Victoria 1950–66. Consul-General, New York, 1966–69. Federal Pres., English-Speaking Union (Australia) (Ret. 1973). Board Member and Deputy National Pres. Winston Churchill. Memorial Trust in Australia, and former Chmn. of its National Fellowship Cttee.; Advocate, Anglican Diocese of Melbourne. *Address:* 257 Collins Street, Melbourne, Australia.

**SHOMAN, Khalid Abdul Hameed.** Jordanian. *B.* 1931. *Educ.* St. George's School, Jerusalem; Victoria Coll., Alexandria; Jesus Coll., Cambridge England; Dip. Grad. in Economics (1955), BA, MA. *M.* 1973. *Career:* Dep. Gen. Mgr. & Dep. Chmn. Arab Bank (1974). *Member: of the Board:* Alia (Royal Jordanian Airlines); Arab Morgan Grenfell Finance; UBAE (Union de Banques Arabes et Europ.) Luxembourg & Frankfurt; Arab Bank (Overseas) Ltd., Switzerland 1975; Arab Bank (Morocco) Ltd. 1975; Jordanian World Airlines 1975; Arab Insurance Co., Lebanon 1975; Royal Jordanian Air Acad. 1975; Pension Funds, Jordan 1976. Dep. Gen. Mgr. & Dep. Chmn., Arab Computing Co., Jordan 1976. Mem., Amman City Council 1974. *Address:* Arab Bank Ltd., P.O. Box 68, Amman, Jordan.

**SHONE, Sir Robert (Minshull),** CBE. *B.* 27 May 1906. *Educ.* Sedbergh School; Liverpool University (MEng); Chicago University (MA Econ); Commonwealth Fellow, U.S.A. 1932–34. *Career:* Lecturer, London School of Economics 1935–36; British Iron & Steel Federation 1936–39 and 1945–53, Dir. 1950–53; Dir., Prices, Costs, Statistics Iron & Steel Control 1940–45; Joint Chairman, U.K. and E.C.S.C., Council of Association Steel Committee 1954–62; Executive Member, Iron & Steel Board 1953–62; Director-General, National Economic Development Council 1962–66; Visiting Professor, City University, London 1967. Director, Rank Organization since 1965; White Drummond 1966; A.P.V. Holdings 1970–76; Honorary Fellow, London School of Economics. *Publications:* Problems of Investment (1971); Price and Investment Relationships (1975); articles in journals. *Address:* 7 Windmill Hill, London, N.W.3.

**SHORE, Rt. Hon. Peter David,** PC, MP. *B.* 1924. *Educ.* King's College Cambridge (BA). *M.* 1948. *S.* 2. *Daus.* 2. *Career:* Head, Labour Party Research Dept. 1959–64; Member, Parliament (Lab.) for Stepney since 1964; member Select Committee on Estimates 1965–66, and of the Select Committee on Publications 1965–66, Parliamentary Secretary Ministry of Technology 1966–67; Secy. of State for Economic Affairs 1967–69; Deputy Leader, House of Commons 1969–70; Member, Shadow Cabinet, Labour Party Spokesman on Europe 1971–74; Secy. of State for Trade 1974–76; Secy. of State for the Environment since 1976. Exec. Member of the Fabian Society. *Publications:* Entitled to Know (1966). *Address:* House of Commons, London SW1A 0AA.

**SHORES, Arthur Davis.** American Negro. *B.* 1904. *Educ.* Birmingham Public Schools, Talladega College, Univ. of Kansas; AB; LLB; Hon. LLD, Daniel Payne College, Miles Coll. (1971). *M.* 1938, Theodora Helen Warren. *Daus.* Helen Glynn, Barbara Sylvia. *Career:* Teacher, Dunbar High School 1927–34 (Principal 1935–39); Secy., Alabama Teachers Assn. 1933–34; Vice-Pres., National Teachers Assn. 1933–34; Secretary-Director, Browne-Belle Bottling Co. 1941–47; Secy.-Treas., Hollins & Shores Realty Co. 1943–49; admitted to the Ala. Bar; and to U.S. Supreme Court Bar. Has been counsel in most outstanding Civil Rights cases over past 20 years. Commissioner, Birmingham Housing Authority. President, Jones Valley Finance Co. since 1945; Mem. Birmingham City Council since 1968. Pres. (Pro Tem) since 1971. Appointed by President Carter to serve on the Judicial Commission, April 1977. Vice-Pres. General Counsel, Citizens Federal Savings & Loan Association; and Citizens Drug Co.; Director, American National Bank. *Awards:* Negro Lawyer at the Bar—South. Alpha Chi Chapter, Omega Psi Phi Fraternity (for outstanding achievement in field of civil rights) 1948; Southern Beauty Congress Inc. (award for eminent leadership in field of civil rights) 1949; Alpha Chi Chapter award as Birmingham's Man of the Year 1954; Omicron Lambda Chapter, Alpha Phi Alpha Fraternity Award (outstanding citizen and champion of civil rights) 1956; Alpha Phi Alpha Medal of Honour (for outstanding lawyer and leader in field of civil rights) 1956; Cook County Illinois, Bar Association, 25 years outstanding Service in Legal Profession; Russwarm Award; elected to Council for Social Action of Congregational Christian Churches 1958; LHD Univ. of Alabama 1975. President, Progressive Democratic Political Organization. Trustee, Talladega College, Alabama. Life Member, N.A.A.C.P. Shriner. Elk. Democrat. *Address:* 1021 North Center Street, Birmingham 4, Ala., U.S.A.

**SHORLAND, Francis Brian,** OBE (1959). British (N.Z.). Hon. Lecturer, Biochemistry Victoria University. *B.* 1909. *Educ.* Univ. of New Zealand (MSc 1st Cl. Hons. Chem 1932) DSc 1970 and Liverpool Univ. (PhD 1937; DSc 1950); awarded the Sir George Grey, Jacob Joseph and D.S.I.R. Scholarships and a Univ. Free Passage. *M.* 1971. *Career:* Cadet, Chemistry Section, Dept. of Agriculture 1927. On completion of studies at Liverpool Univ. 1937, returned to the Agricultural Chemical Lab. In 1946 he was made Officer-in-Charge, and later Director of newly established D.S.I.R. Fats Research Lab. (1946–66); Dir., Food Chemistry Division, D.S.I.R. 1966–69. *Publications:* about 200 scientific papers mainly in the field of fats and other lipids; has also contributed by invitation to chapters in the following: Progress in Chemistry of Fats and Other Lipids (1955); Annual Review of Biochemistry (1956); Biochemists' Handbook (1961); Comparative Biochemistry (1963) Chemical Plant Taxonomy. Delivered 11th Liversidge Lecture to A.N.Z.A.A.S.; a Vice-Pres. of 1st International Congress on Food Science and Technology, London 1962. Fellow and I.C.I. Medal, N.Z. Inst. of Chemistry 1951. Fellow and Hector Medallist 1955, Royal Society of N.Z., and N.Z. Assoc. Scientists Medal for outstanding service to Science 1970, Senior Fulbright Fellow & Visiting Prof., Michigan State Univ. 1974–76. *Address:* P.O. Box 2447, Wellington, N.Z.; and 267 Karaka Bay Road, Wellington, E.5, New Zealand.

**SHORT, Jeffrey Robson, Jr.** American. *B.* 1913. *Educ.* Phillips Exeter Academy, and Harvard University (SB). *M.* 1937, Barbara Allen. *Career:* With J. R. Short Milling Co. 1936–43; U.S. State Department, Ankara, Turkey, 1944–46; J. R. Short Canadian Mills Ltd., Toronto, 1946–52. Pres., J. R. Short Milling Co., Chicago, since 1955. *Address:* 233 South Wacker Drive ,Chicago, Ill. 60606, U.S.A.

**SHOUPP, William Earl.** American. *B.* 1908. *Educ.* Miami Univ. (BA 1931) and Univ. of Illinois (MA 1933; PhD 1938). *M.* 1932, Kathryn Torbeck. *S.* William Joseph. *Career:* With Westinghouse Electric Corp. 1938–73; Research Fellow and Section Head, Electronics and Nuclear Physics 1938–43; Mgr. Electronics and Nuclear Physics Dept. Research Labs. 1943–48; Dir. of Research and Development. Assist Manager-Development of Bettis Atomic Power Lab. 1948–54; Technical Dir. Atomic Power Div. 1954–61, Astronuclear Laboratory 1961–62; Vice-Pres. Research Westinghouse Electric Corp. 1962–73, Consultant since 1973. *Member:* Nat. Acad. of Engineering, Vice-Pres. since 1973; Past Chmn. Marine Board (NAE); Member and Past Pres. Marine Technology Socy; Past Bd. member and Fellow Amer. Inst. of Physics and Inst. Electrical and Electonic Engineers; Chmn. Nuclear Standards Board of U.S. Standards Institute; Member, Commission, Natural Resources of NRC (Nat. Research Council) 1973–74; Member U.S. Navy Oceanographers Advisory Cttee since 1974. Fellow past Pres. Amer. Nuclear Socy.; Amer. Socy. Mechanical Engineers; Amer. Inst. Aeronautics & Astronautics. *Awards:* Hon. DSc., Miami Univ. 1956; The Order of Merit (highest achievement award by Westinghouse) 1953; named 'Man of the Year in Science' (Pittsburgh, Pa., Junior Chamber of Commerce 1949). Industrial Research Inst. medal, 1973; Hon. DSc. Indiana Inst. of Technology 1972. *Publications:* many on nuclear power, approx. 50 in atomic physics, electronics, nuclear power for military, and civilian and space use. *Address:* 343 Maple Avenue, Pittsburgh, Pa. 15218, U.S.A.

**SHOWERING, Keith Stanley.** British. *B.* 1930. *Educ.* Cathedral School, Wells. *M.* 1954, Marie Sadie. *S.* 4. *Daus.* 2. *Career:* Chmn. & Chief Exec. Allied Breweries Ltd., since 1975, John Harvey and Sons Ltd.; Vice Chmn. Guardian Royal Exchange Assurance since 1975. *Clubs:* Buck's; Bath; Arts. *Address:* Allied House, 156 St. John Street, London EC1P 1AR.

**SHPEDKO, Ivan F.** *B.* 1918. *Educ.* Kharkov Pedagogical Institute (graduated 1939). *Married. Daus.* 2. *Career:* Joined Diplomatic Service of the U.S.S.R. 1941; served in Iran until 1945; Counsellor at Afghanistan 1949–53; Ambassador to Pakistan 1956–60; later Deputy Head of the South Asian Div., the U.S.S.R. Foreign Ministry 1961–63; Ambassador to Canada 1963–68; Deputy Head, Second European Div., U.S.S.R. Foreign Ministry 1968–70; Head Second Far Eastern Division since 1970. *Awards:* Four decorations by the Soviet Government. *Address:* Ministry of Foreign Affairs, Smolenskaya-Sennaya Ploschad 32–34, Moscow, U.S.S.R.

**SHRIVER, Robert Sargent.** American Attorney. *B.* 1915 *Educ.* Yale University (BA, LLB). *M.* 1953, Eunice Mary Kennedy. *S.* Robert Sargent III, Timothy Tayloe Perry, Mark Kennedy, Anthony Paul. *Dau.* Maria Owings. *Career* With Winthrop, Stimson, Putnam & Roberts, 1940–41; U.S. Navy 1941–45; Newsweek Magazine 1945–46; Joseph P. Kennedy Enterprises, 1946–48; Merchandise Mart, 1948–61; Director, Peace Corps. 1961–66; Special Assistant to the President, 1965–68; Office of Economic Opportunity, 1964–68; Ambassador to France 1968–70; Senior Partner, Fried Frank, Harris, Shriver & Jacobson since 1971; Vice-Presidential Candidate (Democrat) Nov. 1972. Executive Director, Joseph P. Kennedy Jr. Foundation; President: Chicago Board of Education, 1955–60; Catholic Interracial Council of Chicago, 1955–60; Chairman, Yale Alumni Board 1958–60; Director, Chicago Council of Foreign Relations. Hon. LLD at more than twenty universities. *Address:* c/o Fried, Frank, Harris, Shriver & Jacobson, 120 Broadway, New York. N.Y. 10005, U.S.A.

**SHULMAN, Marshall Darrow.** American university professor and writer. *B.* 1916. *Educ.* Univ. of Michigan (AB) and Columbia University (MA, PhD). *M.* 1960, Colette Schwarzenbach. *S.* Michael Thomson. *Dau.* Lisa Sears (both by previous marriage). *Career:* Special assistant to Secretary of State 1950–53; Military Service 1942–46; Reporter, The Detroit News 1937–39 and 1940. Associate Dir., Russian Research Center, Harvard University 1954–62, and Professor of International Politics, Fletcher School of Law and Diplomacy 1961–67. Professor of Government and Director of Russian Institute, Columbia University 1967—. *Publications:* Stalin's Foreign Policy Reappraised (Harvard University Press, 1963); Beyond the Cold War (Yale University Press, 1966); various articles. *Award:* Rockefeller Public Service Award, 1953. Visiting Research Scholar, Carnegie Endowment for International Peace 1967. *Member:* American Political Science Assn.; International Political Science Assn.; Fellow, Amer. Academy of Arts and Sciences; Institute for Strategic Studies (London). Democrat. *Club:* Harvard (N.Y.C.). *Address:* 450 Riverside Drive, New York City, N.Y. 10027, U.S.A.

**SHULMAN, Max L.** American lawyer and department store executive. *B.* 1908. *Educ.* National University (LLB). *M.* 1939, Sylvia C. Weinstein. *S.* Lloyd J. *Dau.* Gail P. Lawyer, Washington, D.C. 1930–39. Served in World War II (Maj.; Army Commendation Medal with oak leaf clusters) 1941–46. Chairman, President and Director, J. W. Mays. Inc. (Brooklyn, N.Y.) since 1963. Director, Equitable Savings & Loan Association since 1959. *Address:* 510 Fulton Street, Brooklyn 1, N.Y., U.S.A.

**SHULTZ, George P.** American. *B.* 1920. *Educ.* Princeton University (Cum Laude 1942); Massachusetts Institute of Technology (PhD 1949). *M.* 1946, Helena M. O'Brien. *S.* Peter and Alexander. *Daus.* Margaret Kathleen and Barbara. *Career:* U.S. Marine Corps, 1942–45; M.I.T. faculty, 1948–57; senior staff economist, President's Council of Economic Advisers, 1955–56; Professor of Industrial Rleations, University of Chicago's Graduate School of Business, 1957–62; Dean, Chicago University Graduate School of Business, 1962–69; Secretary of Labor, 1969–70. Dir., Office of Management and Budget. Executive Office of the President, 1970–72; Sec. of the Treasury 1972–74: Exec. Vice-Pres. & Dir., Bechtel Corp. 1974–75; Pres. & Dir. since 1975. *Publications:* Pressures on Wage Decisions; The Dynamics of a Labor Market; Causes of Industrial Peace Under Collective; Management Organization and the Computer; Strategies for the Displaced Worker, and Guidelines, Informal Controls and the Market Place; Workers and Wages in an Urban Labor Market; as well as numerous articles, reports and book chapters. *Address:* Office of the President, Bechtel Corporation, 50 Beale Street, San Francisco, Calif. 94105, U.S.A.

**SHUTE, John Lawson,** CMG, OBE. *B.* 1901. *Educ.* Parramatta High Schl. *M.* 1937, Constance Winifred Mary Douglas. *S.* Douglas John, and Robert Grant. *Career:* Asst. Secretary, Primary Producers' Union of N.S.W. 1923–33. General Secretary 1933–43; Deputy-Controller of Meat Supplies, N.S.W. 1943–45; Chmn., Australian Meat Board 1946–70. Animal Production Cttee. 1947–70; Australian Cattle and Beef Research Cttee. 1960–66, and of Australian Meat Research Cttee. 1966–70. Dir., Yates Seeds Ltd. First Secretary, Australian Dairy Farmers' Federation, and Foundation Director, Commonwealth Diary Produce Equalization Committee; First Secretary, Federated Co-operative Bacon Factories of N.S.W., and the N.S.W. Potato Growers' Council. *Member:* N.S.W. Rural Reconstruction Board 1942–71, Export Development Council 1958–66, Overseas Trade Publicity Cttee. 1955–70, and Australia-Japan Business Co-operation Cttee. 1962–70; Chmn., Committee, Belmont Brian Pastures Research; Member, Council Egg Marketing Authority of Australia; Member, Egg Marketing Bd., N.S.W.; Member Industry Co-operative Programme (F.A.O.). *Clubs:* Eastwood Rugby Union; Commercial Travellers'. *Address:* 2, Woonona Avenue, Wahroonga, N.S.W., Australia.

**SIBSON, Arthur Robert,** MLM, MA(h.c.), Hon. RCM. CEng, FIMechE, MIEE. British Chartered electrical and mechanical engineer. *B.* 9 Feb. 1906. *M.* (1) 1927, Alice Edith Couldridge (*D.*). *Dau.* 1. *M.* (2) 1957, Dorothy Williams. *Career:* City Electrical Engineer, Bulawayo, S. Rhodesia, 1946–62; Past Pres., Association of Municipal Electricity Undertakings of Southern Africa; Past Pres., Rhodesian Institution of Engineers; Past Hon. Vice-Pres., South African Inst. of Electrical Engineers; Chmn., Byo Tech. College Adv. Cncl. 1956–72: Dep. Dir.. Bulawayo Philharmonic Orchestra; Dir. Rhodesian Academy of Music 1962–76, now Chairman. Member various cttees. concerned with education and training. *Award:* Civic Honours 1972; Legion of Merit (mem.) 1973. *Publications:* Technical papers in professional journals. *Address:* P.O. Box 9074, Bulawayo, Rhodesia.

**SICH, Sir Rupert,** CB. British barrister-at-law. Registrar of Restrictive Trading Agreements 1956–73. *B.* 1908. *Educ.* Radley College and Merton College, Oxford (MA). *M.* 1933, Elizabeth Mary Hutchison. *S.* 1. *Daus.* 2. Board of Trade, Solicitor's Department, 1932–48; Principal Assistant Treasury Solicitor 1948–56. *Address:* Norfolk House, The Mall, Chiswick, London, W.4.

**SIDNAM, Alan Northcote.** American business Consultant. *B.* 1916. *Educ.* Kalamazoo College, Mich. (AB 1937). *M.* 1947, Shirley Lazo Steinman. *Step-son* Robert DeWitt Clinton Meeker, Jr. *Step-daughter* Pamela Meeker Thye. *Dau.* Caroline Northcote. *Career:* with Staake & Schoonmaker Kalamazoo 1937–38; Winternitz & Cains N.Y.C. 1938–40, Acct, Exec, Robert Winternitz 1940–42; Dir. 1158 Fifth Av. Corp. 1954–69, 1969–72, Pres. 1957–59; Sen. Vice Dir. Ogilvy, Benson & Mather & Mather Inc. N.Y.C. 1963–66; Dir. Ogilvy & Mather Int. 1965–68; Vice Chmn. Ogilvy & Mather Inc. 1966–68; Dir. Lancaster Newspapers Inc.; Steinman Devel. Co.; Steinman Stations; Intelligencer Printing Co. (Lancaster, Pa.); Nigel Sitwell Ltd. (London) 1969—; Private business Consultant 1969—; Dir. Moonraker Pub. Corp. 1970—; Airwick Ind. Inc. N.J. since 1971. *Award:* Air Medal (U.S.A.A.F. 1942–45). *Trustee:* John Frederick Steinman Foundation (Lancaster, Pa.), The Day School, New York City; Board of Managers, Jacob A. Riis Neighbourhood Settlement House (N.Y.C.). *Clubs:* Waccabuc (N.Y.) Country; University (N.Y.C.). *Address: office* 2 East 48th Street, New York, N.Y. 10017, U.S.A.

**SIEGEL, Milton P.** U.S.A., Educator, Management Consultant. *B.* 1911. *Educ.* Drake University. *M.* 1934, Rosalie Rosenberg. *Dau.* Betsy Lee. *Career:* Director of Finance and Statistics, Iowa Emergency Relief Administration, Des Moines 1933–35; Regional Finance and Business Manager, Farm Security Administration, U.S. Dept. of Agriculture, Washington D.C. 1935–41; Chief Fiscal Officer 1942–44; Dir., Office for the Far East, and Asst. Treas., U.N. Relief and Rehabilitation Administration, Washington 1944–45; Asst. Dir., Fiscal Branch, Production Marketing Administration, Dept. of Agriculture, Washington 1945–47. Assistant Director-General, World Health Organization, Geneva 1947–71; Visiting Professor, Univ. of Michigan 1967; Consultant Univ. of North Carolina, Chapel Hill 1970; Professor of International Health, Univ. of Texas, Health Science Center, School of Public Health Houston 1971–75. Member, Permanent Scale of Contributions Commission, L.R.C.S. since 1967; Chief Exec. Officer, Fed. World Health Foundation. *Address:* 1 rue Viollier, 1207 Geneva, Switzerland.

**SIEGEL, Seymour Nathaniel.** American. *B.* 1908. *Educ.* Univ. of Pennsylvania (BSEcon) and Columbia Univ. (MA). *M.* Frances Ladd. *Stepson,* John Meade Hanan. *Stepdaughters,*

Deborah Hanan and Sarah Hanan. *Career:* Chief Statistician, Morris & Smith 1929–34; Program Dir., Radio Station WNYC 1934–37; Lecturer, College of the City of New York 1948–50. Director of Communications Service for the City of New York; Vice-Pres., Broadcasting Foundation of America; Director, WNYC-TV UHF Channel 31 and WNYC-WNYC-FM; Chairman, Government-Industry Committee on all channel broadcasting station operations. Treasurer, American International Music Fund; Fellow, Public Communications Seminar, Columbia Univ. *Publications:* Censorship on the Air; Cities on the Air; and articles in professional journals. Member, National Republican Club, and Overseas Press Club. *Address:* 870 UN Plaza, New York City, N.Y. 10017, U.S.A.

**SIEVEKING, Kurt.** German politician and lawyer. *B.* 1897. *Educ.* Univs. of Heidelberg, Munich and Marburg (Dr jur). *M.* 1925, Ellen Ruperti. *S.* Kai. *Dau.* Sabine. *Career:* Lawyer in Hamburg 1925–35; Gen. Representative, Bankhaus Brinckmann Wirtz & Co., Hamburg 1935–45; Syndic, Senate of Freie und Hansestadt Hamburg and Chief of Senate Chancellery 1945–51; Minister, Stockholm 1951–53; Pres. of Senate and First Burgomaster of Freie und Hansestadt 1953–57. *Address:* Alsterarkaden 27, Hamburg, Germany.

**SIFNEOS, Panayotis.** Greek. *B.* 13 June 1903. *Educ.* Downing College, Cambridge (MA, LLB). *M.* 1931. *Dau.* Mary. King's Medal for Courage in the Cause of Freedom. *Publications:* Considerations on Life and Man. *Address:* 41 Ypsilantou Street, Athens 140, Greece.

**SIGMON, Loyd Claunts.** Broadcasting executive and consultant. *B.*1909. *Educ.* Wentworth Military Academy; Massachusetts Institute of Technology and Milwaukee School of Engineering (Hon. Degree). *M.* Patricia Lynn. *S.* James W. and David L. *Career:* Former Lt.-Col. U.S. Army Signal Corps. Executive Vice-Pres. & Consultant, Golden West Broadcasters—radio stations KMPC, Los Angeles, KSFO, San Francisco, California; KVI, Seattle,Washington; KEX, Portland, Oregon; KTLA-TV, Los Angeles, Calif. Sigalert & Airwatch, Inc. Dir.: National Association of Broadcasters; California State Broadcasters; Southern California Broadcasters; Armed Forces Communications and Electronics Assn.; Chairman of Board, Sigmon Enterprises, Techno Products, Los Angeles. *Awards:* Order of the British Empire; U.S. Legion of Merit; Hon. Member, French Signal Corps. *Member:* Los Angeles and Hollywood Advertising Clubs; Hollywood American Legion. *Clubs:* Lakeside Country; O'Donnel Golf Club, Palm Springs; Balboa Bay. *Address:* 3800 Alomar Drive, Sherman Oaks, Calif., 91423, U.S.A.

**SIGURDSSON, Niels Parsberg.** Diplomat. Ambassador of Iceland. *B.* 1926. *Educ.* Univ. of Iceland (Law). *M.* 1953, Olafia Rafnsdottir. *S.* 2. *Dau.* 1. *Career:* joined Diplomatic Service 1952; First Secy. Paris Embassy 1956–60; Dir. Int. Policy Div. Ministry, Foreign Affairs, Reykjavik 1961–67; Ambassador to Belgium, NATO and EEC 1968–71; Ambassador to the Court of St. James's 1971–76; Ambassador to the Federal Republic of Germany since 1976. *Address:* Isländische Botschaft, Kronprinzenstrasse 6, 53 Bonn Bad Godesberg, Federal Republic of Germany.

**SILBER-BONZ, Gert.** German businessman. *B.* 1930. *Career:* Managing Director, Veith-Pirelli AG, Breuberg-Sandbach; Veith International GmbH. Höchst: J.J. Schlayer GmbH, Pfullingen; Germatex GmbH, Michelstadt. Mem. Bd. of Govs., Drahtcord Saar GmbH and Co. KG, Merzig. Chmn. Bd. of Dirs., Polydress-Plastic GmbH, Michelstadt; Polydress-Plastiques S.A., Ste. Marie-Aux-Mines, France; Gemeinnützige Baugesellschaft mbH, Erbach. Mem. Bd. of Govs., "Canada IV" Lehndorff Vermögensverwaltung GmbH & Co., Hamburg. Mem. Adv. Bd., Deutsche Bank AG, Frankfurt/Main, Frankfurter Versicherungs AG, Frankfurt/Main. Bd. Member, Wirtschaftsverband der Deutschen Kautschukindustrie e.V., Frankfurt/Main. *Club:* Rotary (Aschaffenburg). *Address:* Erbacherstrasse 41, Michelstadt i. Odw.; and *office* Veith-Pirelli AG, Höchst i. Odw., Germany.

**SILHA, Otto Adelbert.** Publishing Executive. *B.* 1919. *Educ.* University of Minnesota (BA *magna cum laude*). *M.* 1942, Helen Elizabeth Fitch. *S.* Stephen Fitch, David William (*dec.*) and Mark Albert. *Dau.* Alice Barbara. *Career:* Copyreader, Mpls. Star, 1940–41; Served from Pvt. to Major USAAF 1942–46; Promotion Dir. Mpls. Star and Tribune, 1947–51; Promotion and Personnel Dir. 1951–54; Bus. Man. 1954–65; Gen. Man. 1965–68; Exec. Vice-Pres. and Pub. 1968–73, Dir. 1954—, Vice-Pres. 1956–68, Pres. 1973—; Vice-Pres., Dir., North Star Research Inst. 1963–75; Trustee Midwest Research Inst. since 1975, of Univ of Minn. Foundation, since 1974; Dir. Northwestern National Bank since 1975, of Midwest Radio-Television Inc. since 1974; Bd., Regents U. Minn., 1961–69; Dir., Tyrone Guthrie Theatre Found., 1960–62; Minn. Theatre Co. Found., 1962–72; Chmn., Steering Comm., Minn. Experimental City Project, 1966—; Dir. Newspaper Advertising Bureau Inc. 1970–73, Vice-Chmn. since 1974, Harper & Row Publishers Inc. since 1972. *Member:* Gov. Minn. Adv. Com. Dept. Bus. Devel. 1955–63; Chmn., 1957–59, Nat. Newspaper Promotion Assn. (Pres. 1953–54); Pres. Mpls. Aqua tennial Assn. 1956; Am. Newspaper Publishers Assn., Research Inst. (Dir. 1960–70, Treas. 1963–65, Vice-Pres. 1965–67. Pres. 1967–69); Mpls. C. of C. (Director, Vice-Pres.), U. Minn Alumni Assn. (Dir. 1959–63); Dir. Gtr. Mpls. Meltrop Housing Corp. since 1971. Phi Beta Kappa, Delta Tau Delta (Regional v.p. 1947–52), Sigma Delta Chi. *Awards:* Named one of 100 outstanding young men, Mpls. 1953; Boss of the Year Award 1971; Amer. Adv. Federation Silver Medal 1972; Univ. of Minn. Outstanding Achievement Award 1974. *Clubs:* Minneapolis, Minikahda. Mpls. Althletic, 5:55 (Pres. 1956–57) (Mpls.); Minnesota (St. Paul) Players (N.Y.C.). *Address:* 6708 Point Dr., Mpls. 55435; and *office* 425 Portland Ave., Mpls. 55488 U.S.A.

**SILKIN, Rt. Hon. Samuel Charles,** QC, MP. British Attorney-General & Barrister. *B.* 1918. *Educ.* Dulwich Coll.; Trinity Hall, Cambridge—BA. *M.* 1941, Elaine Violet Stamp. *S.* 2. *Daus.* 2. *Career:* Barrister (Middle Temple) 1941; mem. 1952–58, Dep. Leader 1952–56, Chmn. Planning Cttee. 1953–57, Camberwell Borough Council; Queen's Counsel 1963; MP (Lab.) for Camberwell, Dulwich 1964–74, & for Southwark, Dulwich since 1974; Chmn., Council of Europe Legal Cttee. 1966–69; Leader, British Delegation to Council of Europe & Western European Union 1967–69; Opposition Front-Bench Spokesman (Legal Matters) 1970–74; Attorney-General since 1974. *Member:* United Nations Assn.; Justice; European Movement; American Bar Assn. (Hon. Mem.). *Awards:* BA (Cantab.) (First Class Honours Parts I & II Law Tripos); Open Scholar Dulwich Coll.; Trinity Hall, Cambridge; Harmsworth Law Scholar, Middle Temple; Certificate of Honour, Bar Final Examination. *Address:* House of Commons, London SW1A 0AA.

**SILLER, Charles William,** MBE. Australian. *B.* 1930. *Educ.* Univ. of Queensland (BScGeol). *M.* 1953, Beverley Barbara Neill. *S.* 3. *Dau.* 1. *Career:* Vice-Pres., Lucky Strike Drilling Co. and subsidiaries 1954–60; Director, Oil Drilling and Exploration Ltd. 1960—. Chairman of Directors: Oilmin N.L. 1962—, Transoil N.L. 1964; Petromin N.L. 1969—. Chairman, Geological Services Pty. Ltd. *Member:* American Assn. of Petroleum Geologists; Royal Socy. of Queensland. *Address:* 38 Carroll Street, Bardon, Brisbane; and *office* 27 Turbot Street, Brisbane, Qld., Australia.

**SILLOWAY, Charles Thompson.** Corporation executive. *B.* 1913. *Educ.* Princeton Univ. (AB *cum laude* 1934). *M.* 1943, Greta Burgess. *S.* Charles Thompson, Jr. and Robert L. *Career:* With Guaranty Trust Co., N.Y.C. 1934–36; Eastman Dillon & Co., N.Y.C. 1936–39; Salesman to Vice-Pres. & Director, Maltine Co. (merged with and name changed to Warner-Lambert Pharmacal Co.) 1939–45. Pres., Chemway Corp. and subsidiaries 1955–62; Ex. Vice-Pres., Ciba Pharmaceutical Co. 1962–63; Pres. 1964–69; Pres., The Ridge Group, Inc. since 1969; Chmn., Primary Medical Communications Inc. since 1971. *Clubs:* University (N.Y.C.); Canoe Brook C.C. (Short Hills, N.J.). *Address:* Van Beuren Rd., Morristown, New Jersey 07960, U.S.A.

**SILVA, Manuel R.** Espirito Santo, Grand Cross, Ordre Isabelle-la-Catholique. Portuguese. *B.* 1908. *M.* 1928, Isabel Pinheiro. *S.* Manuel, Antonio, Bernard Jorge, Jose & Pedro. *Daus.* Matilde, Mafalda, Ana, Madelena and Isabel. *Career:* Chmn., Banque Espirito Santo e Comercial de Lisboa. President: The Bank Espirito Santo and Commercial of Lisbon; Sociedade Agricola do Cassequel; Fundacao Ricardo Espirito Santo. *Address: office* R. do Comercio 95, Lisbon, Portugal.

**SILVER, Francis, 5th.** American consulting engineer (air pollution; air-borne toxicity). *B.* 1916. *Educ.* BEng in Gas Engineering. *M.* 1965, Nevelyne Wyndham. *Career:* Heavy Chemical management and engineering, Standard Lime & Co. 1937–42; U.S. Army (Ordnance) 1942–46; Engineering and Management (wholesale and retail business, flour and feed mfg.), John W. Bishop & Co. and Grafran Inc. 1947–50; Aircraft Engineering, Fairchild Aircraft and Boeing 1951–57; member, City Planning Commission, Martinsburg 1950–57; engaged in independent research and writing during periods not listed. *Member:* Amer. Socy. of Mechanical Engineers; Amer. Chemical Socy.; Amer. Speleological Socy.; Institute of General Semantics; Amer. Assn. for Advancement of Science; Sixma Xi; Fellow, Royal Socy. for Health. Registered Professional Engineer, West Virginia. *Publications:* Storage & Handling of Pulverized Materials (1951); A Teaching Trick for General Semantics (1951); Levels of Living—An abridged Scheme for Estimating Conditions of Various Parts of the Nervous System (1959). *Address:* 501 South Queen Street, Martinsburg, W. Va. U.S.A.

**SILVERMAN, Hirsch Lazaar.** Professor of Education and Psychology. *B.* 1915. *Educ.* Coll. of City of N.Y. (BS in Soc Sc 1936); City Coll. of N.Y. (MScEduc 1938); N.Y. Univ. (MA 1948); Seton Hall Univ. (MA Superv 1957); PhD Yeshiva University 1951; DSc Lane College 1962; LLD Florida Memorial College 1965, LHD, Ohio Coll. of Podiatric Medicine 1972. *M.* 1942, Mildred Friedlander. *S.* Morton Maier and Stuart Edward. *Dau.* Hyla Susan. *Career:* Held various posts in psychology at Yeshiva Univ., Nutley (N.J.) Bd. of Education, Rutgers Univ., Stevens Inst. of Technology, State Univ. of N.Y. 1946–61. Intelligence Officer and Psychologist, U.S. Army, World War II 1942–46. Earlier posts with City of Newark Bd. of Education and Dept. of Public Affairs. Lecturer various colleges and universities 1936–71; Chmn. Dept. of Educational Admin. and Superv, Clinical Psychologist, West Orange N.J. 1950—; School of Educ. Seton Hall Univ. S. Orange N.J. 1965—; Consulting Research Psychologist N.Y. Medical Coll. 1961–65; Visiting Prof. of Psychology, Lane Coll. of Tennessee and Florida Memorial Coll. (North Miami Beach) 1961—; Vocational Consultant, U.S. Dept. of Health, Educ. and Welfare, Wash. D.C. 1962—; Research Clinical Psychologist, Columbus Hospital, Newark, N.J. 1963—; Medical Staff, Psychiatry Psychology Div., St. Vincent's Hospital Montclair since 1972. *Fellow:* World Academy of Art & Science International Council of Psychologists; American Psychological Association; N.J. Academy of Science (Vice-President 1963–66); Amer. Assn. on Mental Deficiency; Gerontological Socy.; N.Y. Acad. of Science; Amer. Assn. for Advancement of Science; A.A.M.D. Fellow: Philos. Socy. of England, Royal Socy. of Arts, and Royal Socy. of Health. Fellow, College of Preceptors, of England. Titular de La Cruz de Eloy Alfaro. Diplomate, American Board of Professional Psychology; Certified Clinical Psychologist, States of N.Y., N.J., Maine, Hawaii and Pennsylvania; Former Chmn., New Jersey State Bd. of Marriage Counselor Examiners; Member N.J. State Board of Psychological Examiners since 1975. *Publications:* Humanism, Psychology and Education (1969); Moments of Eternity (1964); Psychiatry and Psychology (1963); Psychology and Education (1961); Education Through Psychology (1954); Relationships of Personality Factors and Religious Background Among College Students (1954); Marital Counselling (1967); Marital Therapy (1971); Dimensions of Education & Psychology (1975); and many other books. *Address:* 123 Gregory Avenue, West Orange, N.J. 07052; and *office* Seton Hall University, South Orange, School of Education, N.J. 07079, U.S.A.

**SILVERMAN, Robert.** South African Civil Engineer. *B.* 1920. *Educ.* Wynberg Boys High School, Cape Town; University of Cape Town; BSc (Eng.). *M.* 1951, Bella Joffe. *S.* Alan and William. *Dau.* Bertha. *Career:* Served with S.A.A.F. in Italy, World War II. Chmn. South West Africa Fishing Industries Ltd.; West Point Fishing Corporation, Saldanha Bay Canning Co.; Vice-Chmn. Willem Barendsz Ltd.; Mayor, Saldanha Bay 1956–66; Dir. Peltours International & Federal Marine Ltd.; Trustee, South Africa Foundation and S.A. Jewish Board of Education; Member Cape Board of Standard Bank of S.A. & Cape Board of United Building Society; Ex. Member of Cape Jewish Board of Deputies. *Address:* P.O. Box 255, Cape Town, South Africa.

**SILVESTER, Frederick John,** MP. British Politician. *B.* 1933. *Educ.* Sir George Monoux Sch., London; Sidney Sussex Coll., Cambridge—BA; Gray's Inn—Barrister-at-Law. *M.* 1971, Victoria Ann Lloyd Davies. *Daus.* 2. *Career:* Teacher 1955–57; Political Education Officer 1957–60; Snr. Assoc. Dir., J. Walter Thompson Co. since 1960; MP (Cons.) for Walthamstow West 1967–70, & for Manchester, Withington since 1974. *Member:* Inst. of Practitioners in Advertising. *Address:* House of Commons, London SW1.

**SIM, Sir George Alexander Strachan.** British. *B.* 1905. *Educ.* Winchester College; Chartered Accountant (Edinburgh). *M.* 1938, Florence May Smith. *Dau.* Margaret Alexandra. *Career:* Formerly: Dir., Andrew Yule & Co. Ltd. (Dep. Chmn. 1947–48, Chmn. 1953–56) President: Bengal Chamber of Commerce & Industry 1955–56 (Vice-Pres. 1954–55), and of Associated Chambers of Commerce of India 1955–56; Dir. Yule Catto & Co. Ltd. 1956–76; Chairman, Horserace Totalisator Board 1961–70. Director, Tote Investors Ltd. 1962–70; Deputy Chmn. The Cementation Co. Ltd. 1963–70; Dir. Peirce Leslie & Co. Ltd. 1964–68. Member, Horserace Betting Levy Board 1961–70. *Clubs:* Oriental (London); Bengal (Calcutta); Royal Calcutta Turf. *Address:* East View, Iden, Rye, Sussex.

**SIMMONDS, Claude Christopher John.** British. *B.* 1905. *Educ.* Repton, and Corpus Christi College, Cambridge (BA 1st Cl. Hons.). *M.* 1933, Nancy Trusted. *Dau.* Elizabeth. *Career:* With Pritchard, Wood & Partners (Director) 1932–46. War service: Lieut. Suffolk Regt. 1939–46. Director of Public Relations, Board of Trade 1942–46; Sales Director, Harris Lebus Ltd. 1946–50. Managing Director, Editorial Services Ltd. 1950–59; Chmn., Managing Dir., C.S. Services Ltd. 1959–67; Chairman Burson-Marsteller Ltd. (London) 1967–77, Public Relations Consultants. Fellow: Inst. of Public Relations; Member, Church Information Advisory Cttee., 1948–75; Publicity Cttee., Conservative Party, 1952–68. Conservative. *Clubs:* Buck's; Cambridge Union. *Address:* Bay House, Porlock Weir, Minehead, Somerset; and *office* 25 North Row, London, W.1.

**SIMON, Frank Herbert,** American company director. *B.* 1909. *Educ.* Massachusetts Institute of Technology (BS; MS). *M.* 1951, May Rose Aymer. *Career:* Exec. Dir., Metropolitan Rapid Transit Commission, N.Y. 1954–59; Asst. Chief Operating Officer 1951–54, and General Manager 1950–51, Long Island Rail Road; Director: English China Clays Ltd. 1959—; John Brown (S.E.N.D.) Ltd. 1959–70; British Smelter Construction Ltd., 1968–73; John Brown Engineering (Clydebank) Ltd., 1969–75; John Brown & Co. (Overseas) Ltd., 1970–75. *Publications:* Planning for Rapid Transit in the New York Metropolitan Area. Fellow Institute of Directors. *Clubs:* University N.Y.C.)· American, Hurlingham (both London). *Address:* 24 Lowndes Square, London, S.W.1.

**SIMON of Glaisdale, Rt. Hon. Lord (Jocelyn Edward Salis)** PC, DL. *B.* 1911. *Educ.* Gresham's School and Trinity Hall, Cambridge (Exhibitioner); called to Bar, Middle Temple (Blackstone Prizeman), 1934. *M.* (1) 1934, Gwendolen Helen Evans (*D.* 1937); (2) 1948, Fay Elizabeth Leicester, Pearson, JP (Inner Area, Greater London). *S.* 3. *Career:* Served in World War II (C.O. Special Service Sqdn., R.A.C., Madagascar; Burma Campaign, Lieut.-Col. 1945); resumed practice at Bar 1946; KC 1951; MP (Con.) Middlesborough W. 1951–62; Parliamentary Under Secretary to the Home Office 1957–58; Financial Secy. to the Treasury 1958–59. Solicitor-General, Oct. 1959–62; President, Probate Divorce and Admiralty Division, High Court, Feb. 1962–71; Lord of Appeal in Ordinary since 1971. Elder Brother, Trinity House 1975. Hon. Fellow, Trinity Hall, Cambridge 1963. DL NR Yorks 1973. *Member:* Royal Commission on the Law Relating to Mental Illness and Mental Deficiency, 1954–57. *Publications:* part author, Change is Our Ally, (1954); Rule of Law, (1955); The Church and the Law of Nullity, (1955). *Address:* Carpmael Building, Temple, London, E.C.4.; and Midge Hall, Glaisdale, Whitby, Yorks.

**SIMON, Viscount (John Gilbert Simon),** CMG. *B.* 2 Sept. 1902. *Educ.* Winchester College; Balliol College, Oxford (BA). *M.* 1930, James Christie Hunt. *S.* 1. *Dau.* 1. *Career:* Joined P. and O. Steam Navigation Co. in 1936 as Assistant Manager, after 12 years in service of Messrs. Mackinnon Mackenzie & Co. of Calcutta, India; served as Assistant Director, Deputy Director and Director of Liner Division and latterly as Shipping Adviser, Ministry of War Transport 1940–46; Managing Director, P. & O. Steam Navigation Co. 1947–58; President, Chamber of Shipping of U.K. 1957; Chairman of Port of London Authority 1958–71; Pres.: International Assn. of Ports and Harbours 1965–67; International Cargo Handling Co-ordination Assn. 1963–67; Inst. of Marine Engineers 1960–61; Royal Inst. of Naval Architects 1961–71. Officer, Order of Orange Nassau. *Address:* 51 The Strand, Topsham, Exeter EX3 0AS.

**SIMON, Kenneth Cyril.** South African Attorney. *B.* 1917. *Educ.* Forest High School. *M.* 1944, Phyllis Alice Beatrice la Grange. *S.* 1. *Dau.* 1. *Career:* Served in Union Defence Force in South, East and North Africa 1940–45 (Captain on release from service). Partner in law firm of Dumat, Pitts & Blaine 1946–72; Partner in law firm Webber Wentzel and Co. since 1972. *Director:* Dumb Driller Services (Pty.) Ltd.: Sesco

Security (Pty.) Ltd.; Agport (Pty.) Ltd., Ifafa Trust Pty. Ltd.; Ifafa Marina Pty. Ltd.; (alternate) shares and Investments Pty. Ltd.; Terenure Farming Estate Pty. Ltd.; Tudor Nurseries and Landscape Co. (Pty.) Ltd.; Century Land and Investment Co. Ltd.; Advance Transformer Co., S. Africa (Pty.) Ltd., Revlon S. Africa (Pty.) Ltd. *Awards:* 1939–45 Star, African Star with Eighth Army Clasp; War Medal and Africa Service Medal. *Address:* 42 Oaklands Road, Orchards, Johannesburg, South Africa.

**SIMONS, Dolph Collins.** American. *B.* 1904. *Educ.* Univ. of Kansas (AB 1925). *M.* 1929, Marie Nelson. *S.* Dolph Collins, Jr., and John Nelson. *Career:* Editor, Journal-World, Lawrence, Kansas since 1944; Director, The Associated Press, U.S.A. 1950–61; Vice-Pres., Eisenhower Foundation since 1951; Trustee (former President), William Allen White Foundation since 1960; Former Pres. Univ. of Kansas Endowment Association (Trustee) since 1936. Director Lawrence National Bank 1956–61; Director, Chairman, Federal Reserve Bank, 10th District, 1962–71; Chmn. Kansas 4-H Foundation 1971–75. *Publications:* Germany and Austria (May–June 1947); A Globe Circler's Diary (1949). *Awards:* Citation for Distinguished Service to Mankind, Univ. of Kansas 1956; Univ. of Minnesota Award for Distinguished Service in Journalism 1966; Fred Ellsworth Award for Significant Service to Univ. of Kansas 1975; Special Citizenship Award from Baker Univ. 1976. *Address:* 444 Country Club Terrace, Lawrence, Kansas; and *office* 6th and New Hampshire Street, Lawrence, Kansas, U.S.A.

**SIMPSON, Alfred Moxon,** CMG. Australian manufacturer. *B.* 1910. *Educ.* BSc; Associate of Commerce of the Univ. of Adelaide. *M.* 1938, Elizabeth Robson Cleland. *S.* 1. *Career:* Director, Bank of Adelaide, Elder Smith Goldsborough Mort Ltd., Simpson Pope Holdings Ltd., Adelaide Steamship Co. Ltd., SA Telecasters Ltd. and associated companies, QBE Insurance Co. Ltd. Pres.: Adelaide Chamber of Commerce 1950–52; Metal Industries Assn. of S. Australia 1952–54. Member: Hulme Cttee, on Rates of Depreciation 1954–55; Associated Chambers of Manfrs. of Australia 1957–58; South Australian Chamber of Manufacturers 1956–58. *Address:* 135 Waymouth Street, Adelaide, 5000 S.A., and 31 Heatherbank Terrace, Stonyfell, S.A., 5066, Australia.

**SIMPSON, James Joseph Trevor,** KBE. Ugandan (formerly British). *B.* 1908. *Educ.* Ardingly College (Sussex England). *M.* 1940, Enid Florence Danzelman. *Career:* With the African Mercantile Co. Ltd. 1925–32, Vacuum Oil Co., 1932–46, Uganda Co. Ltd. (General Mgr. 1947–52) 1946–52 Political activities: Uganda Exec. Cncl. 1952–55, Uganda Legislative Cncl. 1950–58; East Africa Legis. Assembly 1957–60 and 1962–63. Minister of Econ. Affairs, Uganda Government 1962–63. Pres., Uganda Chamber of Commerce 1941 and 1946–50; E.A. Railways and Harbours: Transport Advisory Council 1948–61; Uganda Electricity Board 1955–60, etc.; Chairman Uganda Development Corporation Ltd. 1952–64 when Director of 37 companies in East Africa; Chmn., East African Airways Corp. 1958–73; Member of Uganda Parliament for Kyagwe N.E. until 1964, Min. Econ. Affairs 1962–63. *Clubs:* Kampala Uganda, Muthaiga (Kenya); East India & Sports (London). *Address:* P.O. Box 48816, Nairobi, Kenya.

**SIMPSON, John Wistar.** *B.* 1914. *Educ.* U.S. Naval Acad. (BSEng 1937) and Univ. of Pittsburgh (MS Elec Eng 1941). *M.* 1948, Esther Slattery. *S.* John W., Jr., and Carter Berkeley. *Daus.* Patricia and Barbara. *Career:* Manager, Switchboard Engineering, Switchgear Division, Westinghouse Electric Corp. 1937–46; Daniels Pile Group, Oakridge National Laboratory 1946–48; Westinghouse Electric Corp., Bettis Atomic Power Laboratory; Asst. Engineering Mgr. 1949–52; Asst. Division Mgr. 1952–54; Mgr., Shippingport Project 1954–55; General Manager 1955–58; Vice-Pres. and Gen. Mgr. 1958–59; Vice-President and General Manager, Atomic Power Divisions (including Astronuclear Laboratory) 1959–62; Vice-President, Engineering & Research 1962–63. President, Power Systems, Westinghouse Electric Corp., (Group Vice-Pres., Electric Utility Grp., 1963–69). Member, Board of Directors: Westinghouse Canada; Westinghouse Electric Europe S.A. and Westinghouse S.A. (Madrid); Navy Commendation for switchboard production during World War II, 1946; Westinghouse Order of Merit (Company's highest award to employee), 1952); Delegate (Speaker in 1955) to 1st and 2nd International Conference on Peaceful Uses of Atomic Energy, Geneva 1955 and 1958. Member, National Academy of Engineering. *Publications:* Nuclear Propulsion Plant of the U.S.S. Nautilus, (1954); Description of the Pressurized Water Reactor (PW)R at Shippingport, Pa. (1955). *Clubs:* University, St. Clair Country (Pittsburgh); Farmington Country (Charlottesville, Va.); Laurel Valley Golf; Rolling Rock. *Address:* 2055 Outlook Drive, Trotwood Acres, Pittsburgh 15241, Pa., U.S.A.

**SIMPSON, Robert Edward.** American Economist & Civil Servant. *B.* 1917. *Educ.* Amherst Coll. (AB 1938); U.S. Natnl. War Coll., Washington, D.C. 1961–62; AM George Washington Univ. 1964. *M.* 1954, Anna-Margaret Nelson. *S.* John. *Daus.* Karen and Heather. *Career:* U.S. Naval Reserve CDR 1942–46; Assistant Director, European Division, U.S. Dept. of Commerce 1948–50; Dep. Asst. Director, Office of International Trade 1951–53; Director, Office of Economic Affairs 1953–60. Director, Office of International Regional Economics, U.S. Department of Commerce, Washington, D.C. 1961–70; and Commercial Relations 1970–73; Counselor for Economic and Commercial Affairs Amer. Embassy since 1973. Member, American Economic Association. *Clubs:* Commonwealth, Royal Canberra Golf. *Address:* American Embassy, Canberra, A.C.T. 2600, Australia.

**SIMPSON, Samuel Leonard,** FRCP. *B.* 1900. *Educ.* Cambridge Univ. (MA; MD), London Univ. (FRCP) and Mayo Clinic, U.S.A. *M.* 1940, Heddy Monique de Fanto. *Dau.* Georgina. *Career:* Chmn. S. Simpson Ltd., and Simpson Piccadily, Ltd., London; Invertère Ltd. Pres.: Simpson Imports Inc., Daks U.S.A. Inc., N.Y.C.; and Daks Canada Ltd. Research Fellow, Mayo Clinic 1929–30; Research Worker, Dept. of Experimental Endocrinology, Lister Institute, London, 1930–33; Member: Grand Cncl., F.B.I., 1948–52, and currently Council C.B.I.; Overseas Cttee., F.B.I. 1962. Hon. member, Machine Gun Corps Officers Club. Fellow: Royal Society of Medicine and Royal College of Physicians; Scientific member, Zoological Society; Cncl. Member; Council of C.B.I.; British-American Chamber of Commerce; Natl. Inst. Industrial Psychology, Pres. and Founder, Simpson Services Club; Founder member, Nat. Equestrian Centre. Conservative. Walter Hagen 1976 Award for Anglo-American Friendship. *Publications:* numerous papers on Adrenal Gland; Major Endocrine Disorders (Oxford Univ., Press—3rd edn. 1959). *Clubs:* Carlton (London); Sunningdale Golf. *Address:* 28 Hyde Park Gate, London, S.W.7; Grouselands, Colgate, Sussex.

**SIMS, Ivor Donald.** *B.* 1912. *Educ.* Lehigh Univ. (BS Bus. Admin. 1933); Honorary Doctors of Laws Degree, University of Liberia, 1967; Hon. Doctor of Law Degree, Lehigh Univ., 1970. *M.* 1937, Christine Buchman. *Dau.* Christine. *Career:* Former Dir. International Nickel Co. of Canada, Ltd.; Former Exec. Vice-President and Director, Bethlehem Steel Corporation. Trustee Lehigh Univ.; Member, Amer. Iron & Steel Inst. (N.Y.C.). *Awards:* Kt.-Comdr. Human Order of African Redemption (Liberia); Star of Equatorial Africa from President of Gabon 1969; L-in-Life Award, Lehigh Club of New York 1970; Knight Grand Band Humane Order of African Redemption. *Clubs:* Saucon Valley Country (Bethlehem); University (N.Y.C.). *Address:* 1723 Cloverleaf Street, Bethlehem, Pa. 18017, U.S.A.

**SIMS, Roger Edward,** MP. British Politician and Export Manager. *B.* 1930. *Educ.* City Boys' Grammar Sch., Leicester; St. Olaves' Grammar Sch., London. *M.* 1957, Angela Mathews. *S.* 2. *Dau.* 1. *Career:* Export Mgr., Dodwell & Co. Ltd., London since 1962; Justice of the Peace 1960; Chmn., Bromley Juvenile Court 1970–72; Mem., Chislehurst & Sidcup Urban District Council 1956–62; Conservative MP for Chislehurst since 1974. *Member:* Inst. of Marketing. *Address:* 68 Towncourt Crescent, Petts Wood, Orpington, Kent; and *office* Dodwell & Co. Ltd., 18 Finsbury Circus, London EC2; and House of Commons, London SW1A 0AA.

**SIMSON, Walter H.** American executive. *B.* 1906. *Educ.* Columbia Univ. *M.* (1) Merle Ott Sandifer (*Dec.*). *S.* Alfred R. *Daus.* Patricia (Mays), Gwendolyne (Hazel) and Virginia. *M.* (2) Jean Catherine Birdsall. *Career:* President and Member, Board of Directors, Duro-Test Corp., N. Bergen, N.J. Director: Cornwall (N.Y.) Electric Corp.; Luxor Lighting Products Inc., N.Y.C.; Arc-Ray Electric Corp., N.J.; Tungsten Products Corp.; Jewel Electric Products Inc. (all of U.S.A.); Fabbrica Italiana Lampadine Electtriche, Lecca, Italy; Duro-Test Electric Ltd., Toronto, Canada; Duro-Test International Corp., San Juan, P.R. *Clubs:* White Beeches Golf & Country (Haworth, N.J.); Westhampton Country (Westhampton Beach, L.I., N.Y.). *Address:* Duro-Test Corporation, North Bergen, N.J., U.S.A.

**SINCLAIR, D'Alton Lally.** Canadian executive. *B.* 1925. *Educ.* Upper Canada Coll. (Snr. Matric.) and Univ. of Toronto (BASc Engineering and Business). *M.* 1960, Diana Harris.

*S.* Robert Ian. *Dau.* Susan Elizabeth. *Career:* With Canadian Gypsum Co. Ltd. May 1949–Nov. 1955. Pres. (Nov. 1962—) and General Manager (Dec. 1960—), Charterhouse Canada Ltd. Dir. Charterhouse Group Canada Ltd., Charterhouse Canada Ltd., Charterhouse Canada Securities Ltd., Armoured Floor Co. Ltd., Bow Valley Industries Ltd., John Millen & Son Ltd., Manoir Industries Ltd. (Secy.), Hardee Farms International Ltd., Riley's Reproductions Ltd., and First Toronto Corp. Ltd. *Clubs:* Badminton & Racquet, University, Toronto Golf (Toronto); University (Montreal). *Address: office* 60 Yonge Street, Toronto 1, Ont., Canada.

**SINCLAIR, Ernest Keith,** CMG, OBE (Mil.), DFC. Australian Journalist & Company Director. *B.* 1914. *Educ.* Hampton and Melbourne High Schools. *M.* 1949, Jill Nelder. *S.* Andrew. *Career:* Editor, The Age, Melbourne 1959–66; Chmn. Australian Associated Press 1965–66 (Director 1959–66). Director, General Television Corp. 1959–66. Consultant to Prime Minister of Australia and Prime Minister's Department 1967–72; Deputy Chmn., Australian Tourist Commission 1969–74; Observer National Capital Planning Cttee. 1967–72; Dir., Australian Paper Manufacturers 1966—; Hecron (Aust.) Ltd. 1971–76; Hecla-Rowe Ltd. 1971–76; Deputy President, Library Council of Victoria since 1969. Associate Commissioner, Industries Assistance Commission since 1974; Chmn. Schools Board for the Humanities, Victoria Institute of Colleges, 1969–72; Commissioner, Australian Heritage Comm. 1976—. *Clubs:* Melbourne; Commonwealth (Canberra); Press (London). *Address:* 138 Toorak Road West, South Yarra, Vic., Australia.

**SINCLAIR, Sir George Evelyn,** CMG, OBE, MP. British. *B.* 1912. *Educ.* Abingdon Sch.; Pembroke Coll., Oxford where he was a Scholar and read Classics. *M.* (1) 1941, Katherine Jane Burdekin (*Dec'd*). (2) 1972, Mary Violet, widow of G. L. Sawday. *S.* 1. *Daus.* 3. *Career:* Colonial Administrative Service 1936–61: Gold Coast 1936–55 (Regional Officer 1952–5); war service, Royal West African Frontier Force (Major) 1940–43; seconded Colonial Office 1943–45; Cyprus Dep. Gov. 1955–1960 (ret'd 1961); Political Consultant on Developing Countries 1960–63; Wimbledon Borough Council 1962–65; Conservative MP for Dorking since 1964. Parliamentary Select Cttees on: Procedure 1955–6, Race Relations 1967–70, Overseas Aid 1969–70, Race Relations & Immigration 1970–74, Abortion Amendment Bill 1975–6, Members Interests 1975—, Cyprus 1975; Conservative Parly. Cttees on: Commonwealth Affairs 1966–68 (Secretary), Education Cttee (Vice-Chmn.) 1974–76. *Member:* Vice-Pres., Intermediate Technology Development Group, 1968—; Birth Control Campaign; Trustee: Runnymede Trust 1968–74, Human Rights Trust 1972–74, Physically Handicapped & Able Bodied (PHAB); Council of Christian Aid; Chmn. Governors, Abingdon Sch.; Direct Grant Joint Cttee; Assoc. of Governing Bodies of Public Schools. *Decorations:* Officer Order of the British Empire, 1950; Companion of St. Michael & St. George, 1956; Knight Bachelor, 1960. *Publications:* contributor to The Growth of Parliamentary Scrutiny by Committees: A Symposium, ed. Alfred Morris MP (1970). *Clubs:* The Athenaeum; Royal Commonwealth; Aldeburgh Golf Club; Aldeburgh Yacht Club. *Address:* Carlton Rookery, Saxmundham, Suffolk; & House of Commons, London SW1A 0AA.

**SINCLAIR, Ian McCahon,** PC. Australian member House of Representatives. *B.* 1929. *Educ.* Knox Grammar School, Wahroonga, and Sydney University (BA; LLB). *M.* (1) 1956, Margaret Anne Tarrant (*Dec.* 1967). *S.* 1. *Daus.* 2. (2) 1970, Rosemary Edna Fenton. *S.* 1. *Career:* Barrister since 1952; Grazier and Man. Dir., Sinclair Pastoral Co. 1953—; Director, Farmers' and Graziers' Co-op Co. Ltd. 1962–65; Member of Legislative Council, New South Wales 1961–63; Member for New England 1963—; Minister for Social Services 1965–68; Minister Asst. Min. for Trade and Industry 1966–71; Minister for Shipping and Transport 1968–71; Minister for Primary Industry 1971–72; Deputy Leader, National Country Party of Australia 1971—; Opposition Leader in House of Reps. 1972–75; Minister for Agriculture & Minster for Northern Australia 11th Nov.–22nd Dec. 1975; Minister for Primary Industry 1975—; Govt. Leader in House of Reps. 1975—. *Clubs:* Killara Golf; Tamworth; American; Union; Australian. *Address:* 'Glenclair', Bendemeer, N.S.W. 2352, Australia.

**SINCLAIR OF CLEEVE, Lord** (Sir Robert John Sinclair), KCB, KBE, Hon. LLD (Bristol). British tobacco manufacturer. *B.* 29 July 1893. *Educ.* Glasgow Academy, Oriel College, Oxford Univ. (BA 1914 MA 1918; Hon. Fellow 1959). *M.* 1917, Mary Shearer Barclay. *S.* John Robert Kilgour, David Barclay (killed in action 1942). *Career:* Served World War I; commissioned King's Own Scottish Borderers, Aug. 1914, wounded, Gallipoli 1915; seconded to Ministry of Munitions 1916; Deputy Director of Munitions Inspection 1917–19; appointed member of Prime Minister's Advisory Panel of Industrialists, Jan. 1939; Dir.-Gen. of Army Requirements, War Office 1939–42; member, Ministry of Supply Council 1939–42; member, Army Council 1940–42; Deputy for Minister of Production as member of Combined Production and Resources Board, Washington 1942–43; Chief Executive, Ministry of Production 1943–45; Board of Trade 1945; President, Federation of British Industries 1949–51; Chairman, The Imperial Tobacco Co. (of Great Britain and Ireland) Ltd. 1947–59, President 1959–67. Director: British-American Tobacco Co. Ltd. 1944–63, Bristol Waterworks Company 1946— (Chmn. 1960–71), Tobacco Securities Trust Co. Ltd. 1948–69, Finance Corporation for Industry Ltd. 1945–49 and 1951–69 (Chmn. 1960–64); Dollar Exports Board 1949–51; Dollar Exports Council 1951–54; Commonwealth Development Finance Co., Ltd. 1953–69; National Provincial Bank Ltd. 1953–69; Debenture Corp. Ltd. 1959–72; General Accident, Fire & Life Assurance Corp. Ltd. 1959–73; member, Chemical Bank, New York Trust Company's Advisory Board on International Business until 1969. Pro-Chancellor, University of Bristol 1946–70; High Sheriff of Somerset 1951–52; United States Medal of Freedom with Gold Palm (1947). *Address:* Cleeve Court, nr. Bristol.

**SINGH, Kewal.** Indian Diplomat. *B.* 1915. *Educ.* former Christian Coll., Lahore—BA (Hons.); Law Coll., Lahore—LLB; Balliol Coll., Oxford. *M.* 1942, Shamie Grewal. *Dau.* 1. *Career:* Asst. Commissioner, Ferozepur, Punjab 1939–40, & Hissar 1940–42; Sub-Divisional Magistrate, Dalhousie 1942–44; Colonization Officer, Neelibar, Montgomery 1944–46; Dep. Commissioner, Shahpur 1946–47, & Simla 1947–48; First Sec., Indian Embassy, Turkey 1948–49; First Ses., Indian Military Mission, Berlin 1949–51; Chargé d'Affaires, Embassy of India, Lisbon 1951–53; Consul-General of India to French Establishments in India at Pondicherry 1953–54; with merger of French possessions with India, took over from French Governor as Chief Commissioner of India 1st Nov. 1954–56; Ambassador of India to Cambodia 1956–58, & to Sweden, Denmark & Finland with residence at Stockholm 1958–62; Dep. High Comm. of India, London 1962–65; High Comm. of India in Pakistan 1965–66; attended Tashkent Conference 1966; Amb. of India to Moscow 1966–68; Sec. to Govt. of India in Foreign Office 1968–70; Amb. of India to Fed. Rep. of Germany, Bonn 1970–72; Foreign Sec. to Govt. of India 1972–76; Amb. of India to the U.S.A. since 1976. *Decorations:* Awarded National Award of "Padma Shree" for the 'historic role played in the merger of the French possessions with India'. *Address:* c/o Ministry of External Affairs (P.A.–I. Section), New Delhi, India.

**SINGH, Khadga Man.** *B.* 1908. Nepalese Ambassador Extraordinary and Plenipotentiary to Pakistan & also to Iran & Turkey. *M.* 1951, Praja Rajya Laxmi Shah (*Dec*). *S.* 1. *Career:* Ministry Parly. Affairs 1951; H.M.'s Counsellor for Foreign Affairs, Forest & Revenue 1952; Commissioner 1961–64; Rt. Hon. member standing Cttee of Raj Sabha; Royal Nepalese Ambassador to Islamic Rep. of Pakistan and simultaneously acredited to Iran and Turkey since 1974. *Award:* Suprasidha Prabal Gorkha Dakshin Bahu (1st Class). *Address:* Royal Nepalese Embassy, No. 506 84th Street, Ramna 6/4, Islamabad, Pakistan.

**SINGH, Sardar Swaran.** Indian Politician. *B.* 19 Aug. 1907. *Educ.* Government College, Lahore MSc, Physics, LLB, Law College, Lahore. *M.* Sardani Charan Kaur. *Daus.* 4. *Career:* Member, Punjab Legislative Assembly 1946; Minister for Development, Food and Civil Supplies 1946; Member, Security Council; Member of Partition Cttee. to divide assets of the Punjab 1947; re-elected to Punjab Legislative Assembly 1952; resigned ministership in Punjab and was included in the Central Cabinet as Minister of Works, Housing and Supply 1952; Led Indian Deleg. to Session of Econ. and Social Council of U.N., Geneva 1954, 1955, 1970 and 1974, to U.N. Gen. Assembly ten times 1964–74; Rep. India Comn. Conference London 1966; Singapore 1971; Ottawa 1973; Minister of Steel, Mines and Fuel 1957–62; re-elected to Lok Sabha Feb. 1962; Minister of Railways 1962–63; Food and Agriculture 1963–64; Industry and Supply 1964; Minister of External Affairs 1964–66; Minister of Defence 1966–70; re-elected to Lok Sabha 1971; Min. of External Affairs 1970–74; Min. of Defence 1974–75; Pres. Indian Council of World Affairs, Sapru House, New Delhi s ince 1976. *Address:* Link Road, Jullundur City, Punjab; and New Delhi, India.

**SINGHANIA, Sir Padampat.** Indian industrialist. *B.* 1905. *M.* Anusuiya Devi Loalka. *Career:* Founded Merchants' Chamber of Uttar Pradesh; former President, Federation of Indian Chambers of Commerce and Industry, Employers' Assoc. of Northern India; Member, First Indian Parliament; Former member Central Advisory Board of Forest Utilization, Cotton Textile Advisory Cttee.; Indian Council of World Affairs; Indian Standards Institution; Nat. Industrail Development Corp. Ltd.; Former Chmn., Bd. of Governors, Indian Inst. of Technology; Member: Advisory Council, Industries (A) Department, Rajasthan. *Address:* Kamla Tower, Kanpur, India.

**SINGHATEH, Alhaji Sir Farimang,** KCMG, JP. Governor-General, The Gambia 1965–70. *B.* 1912. *Educ.* Catholic, Methodist and Armitage Secondary Schools. *M.* 1941, Ajaratu Lady Fanta. *S.* 3. *Daus.* 4. *Career:* Civil Servant, 1935–63; chemist and druggist, 1956. Member, Public Service Commission, 1963–65; Gov. Gen., The Gambia 1965–70. *Club:* Bathurst. *Address:* 48 Grant Street, Banjul, The Gambia.

**SIRIWARDANE, Codippiliarachchige Don Stanislaus.** Ambassador of the Republic of Sri Lanka. *B.* 1911. *Educ.* London Univ. BA. *M.* 1941, Telina de Silva. *S.* 3. Daus. 2. *Career:* Advocate of the Supreme Court of Sri Lanka; Lecturer, Ceylon Law Coll. 1962–70; Senator 1962–70; Ambassador to the U.S.S.R.; G.D.R.; Poland; Czechoslovakia; Hungary and Romania 1970–74; Ambassador to Pakistan since 1974. *Address:* Embassy of Sri Lanka, 468-F, Sector G6/4, Islamabad, Pakistan.

**SIRNA, Anthony Alfred III.** American company director. *B.* 1924. *Educ.* Harvard Coll. (BS *cum laude* 1944); Harvard Univ. (Researcher 1944–46); Columbia Univ. (post-graduate 1946–47); N.Y. Inst. of Finance 1953. *M.* (1) 1946, Jane Allison Porter; *S.* Anthony Alfred IV. *Daus.* Meredith Allison and Corinne Hart; (2) 1972, Therese Cooper. *S.* James. *Dau.* Rebecca. *Career:* Pres., East 55th Street Corp.. N.Y.C. 1946–50; Writer and Editor, New York City, Medical Economics. Unicorn Press 1950–53. With American Securities Corp. 1953—. Director: American Securities Corp., N.Y.C. 1956—, Western Union International Inc., N.Y.C. 1963—, Mangood Corp., Chicago 1968—; Union Stock Yards of Omaha 1969—, and other U.S. and international corporations. Trustee, N.Y. College of Music. Lecturer, Corporate Mergers and Acquisitions 1962—. *Publications:* The Wanderings of Edward Ely (with Allison Sirna, 1945); numerous articles to science and business publications. Lt.-Col. N.Y.C. Auxiliary Police; Captain Riverview Manor Hose Company No. 3, Hastings-on-Hudson, N.Y. Member N.Y. Socy. of Security Analysts. *Clubs:* Harvard (N.Y.C., Westchester County, N.Y. & Boston, Mass.); New York Plaza; American (London); Riverview Manor Tennis; Chequessett Country (Cape Cod, Mass.); Westchester Country. *Address:* 784 Park Avenue, New York, N.Y. 10021; Long Pond, Wellfleet, Cape Cod, Mass.; and *office* 122 East 42nd Street, New York, N.Y. 10017, U.S.A.

**SISSENER, Wilhelm.** Norwegian business executive. *B.* 1901. *Educ.* Univ. of Economics, Leipzig (MSc 1924), and Univ. of Frankfurt/Main (AM 1925). *S.* 2. *Dau.* 1. *Career:* Business training in England and Norway; started own business in pharmaceutical and medical fields 1928; Chairman of Board of Apothekernes Laboratorium for Specialpræparater 1937—; President, March 1939—, and Chairman of the Board Sept. 1959—, A/S Apothekernes Laboratorium for Specialpræparater. A/S Plantevern-Kjemi, Sandvika since 1946; member, Board of Directors, Norgesplaster A/S, Kristiansand S. 1938—. *Award:* Freedom Cross of Finland 1939. *Address:* 6315 Oberægeri (ZG), Switzerland.

**SIX, Robert Forman.** American. *B.* 1907. *Career:* Student flying instructor, Stockton and Frisco. Stockton, Calif. 1929–33; District Circulation Manager, San Francisco Chronicle, 1933–35; owner-partner, Mouton & Six 1935–37; Pres. and Dir., Continental Air Lines 1938–75; Chmn. & Ch. Exec. Officer since 1975; Lieut-Colonel, U.S. Army Air Force 1942–44; Chmn. and Dir., Continental Air Service 1966—; Dir. United Bank of Denver, Chmn. Bd. Mutal Computer Services. *Address:* 350 Trousdale Place, Beverley Hills, Calif. 90210; and *office* Continental Air Lines Inc., Los Angeles International Airport, Los Angeles, Calif. 90009, U.S.A.

**SJOQUIST, Sigurd Preben,** JP, FIBM. British. *B.* 1914. *Educ.* St. Jorgens Coll.; Commercial Coll., Copenhagen *M.* 1940, Kirsten Marie. *S.* 2. *Career:* Man. Dir. Schlegel Pty. Ltd. *Member:* Bd. Danish Overseas League; Hon. Member, Assn. Denmark, Sydney; American Chamber of Commerce in Australia. *Award:* R of D (Knight of Dannebrog). *Clubs:* Scandinavian Businessman's; Rotary. *Address:* 12A, 26 Etham Avenue, Darling Point, N.S.W. 2027; and *office* 565-577 Harris Street, Ultimo, N.S.W. 2007, Australia.

**SJOWALL, Hilding Einar Joachim.** Swedish judge. *B.* 15 Sept. 1908. *Educ.* Stockholm University (Cand. jur.); *M.* 1939, Birgitta Bruno. Advocate 1933–48; member of Board Swedish Advocates' Association 1940–46; Judge of Supreme Court 1948–58 and 1967—; Member, Permanent Court of Arbitration at The Hague 1961—. Knight Grand Star, Order of Pole Star (Sweden), and of Order of St. Olav (Norway); Cross of Liberty (Norway). *Address:* 164 Valhallavägen, Stockholm, Sweden.

**SKERMER, Victor John William,** CBE. Australian. *B.* 1908. *M.* 1935, Lilian Ruby Wilson. *Daus.* Jennifer Anne and Susan Edwina. *Career:* Secretary and Chief Inspector, Commonwealth Auditor-General's Office 1951–61; Auditor-General for the Commonwealth of Australia, 1961–73; Gov., Rotary International, District 270, 1974–75; Hon. Treas., Winston Churchill Memorial Trust 1975—; Member, Administrative Appeals Tribunal, Dec. 1976—. Company Director. Fellow: Australian Society of Accountants (FASA), Chartered Institute of Secretaries (FCIS), and Australian Inst. of Management (FAIM). *Clubs:* Royal Canberra Golf; Sydney Cricket; Commonwealth (Canberra). *Address:* 90 Strickland Crescent, Deakin, Canberra, ACT, Australia.

**SKROMME, Lawrence H.** American. *B.* 1913. *Educ.* Kelly (Iowa) High School (Valedictorian) and Iowa State College (BS in Agric. Eng., Hons.). *M.* 1939, Margaret Gleason. *Daus.* 3. *Career:* Designer and Test Engineer, Goodyear Tyre & Rubber Co., Akron 1937; Project Engineer and Asst. Exec. Engineer, Harry Ferguson Inc., Detroit 1941; joined New Holland Division of Sperry Rand Corp. as Chief Engineer in 1951; Vice-President for Engineering, Sperry New Holland Division of Sperry Rand Corp. since 1961. Appointed by Secretary of Agriculture to serve on U.S. Department of Agriculture Research and Advisory Committee; and by Governor of Pennsylvania to serve on his Committee on Agriculture. *Member:* Amer. Socy. Agricultural Engineers (Vice-Pres. 1952–55, Pres. 1959–60); Amer. Socy. Engineering Education; Amer. Socy. Automotive Engrs.; Amer. Assn. Advancement of Science; National Professional Engrs. Socy.; ASAE Rep. and mem. Mgmt. Bd., Commission Internationale du Genie Rural; Vice-Pres. and Pres. of Power and Machinery Section, Conestoga Valley Assn. (Bd. Dirs.); Farm & Home Foundation of Lancaster County (Vice-Pres.); ASAE Rep. to Eng. Joint Council-Technology Assessment Panel and Bd. of Dirs. *Award:* Professional Achievement Citation, Iowa State University; ASAE John Deere Gold Medal (Dist. Achievement in Applic. of Science & Art to Soil). *Publications:* The Challenge and Rewards of a Design Career; Extending our Horizons. *Address:* 2150 Landis Valley Road, Lancaster, Pa. 17601; and *office* Sperry New Holland, New Holland, Pa., U.S.A.

**SLADE, Richard Gordon,** OBE, FRAeS. Group Captain (rtd.). *B.* 1912. *Educ.* Dulwich College. *M.* 1948. Eileen Frances Cooper. *S.* Patrick and Jonathan. *Daus.* Elisabeth and Mary Ann. *Career:* Royal Air Force 1933–46. With Fairey Aviation Company: Chief Test Pilot 1946–57, Superintendent of Flying 1957–59. Director, Fairey Aviation Ltd. 1959–60. Managing Director, Fairey Hydraulics Ltd., Heston, Middlesex 1965–75, Chmn. 1975—; Chmn., Fairey Hydraulics Inc., Cleveland 1973—; Director, Fairey Surveys Ltd., Maidenhead, Berks. 1959–72; Fairey Filtration Ltd., 1970–72. Member of Council of SBAC & of London & S.E. Regional Council of C.B.I. *Awards:* OBE, and American Silver Star. Liveryman of the Guild of Air Pilots and Air Navigators. *Clubs:* Naval & Military; Royal Aero; Royal Air Force. *Address:* Mickledore, Maidenhead Thicket, Berks.; and *office* Fairey's, Heston, Hounslow, Middlesex.

**SLATER, James Derrick,** FCA. British company chairman. *B.* 1929. *Educ.* Preston County Grammar School. *M.* 1965, Helen Goodwyn. *S.* 2. *Daus.* 2. *Career:* articled to firm of Accountants 1946–53; Accountant, later Gen. Mgr. group Metal-finishing companies 1953–55; Secy. Park Royal Vehicles Ltd. 1955–58; Dir., A.E.C. Ltd. 1959; Deputy Sales Dir., Leyland Motor Corp. 1963; Acquisition interest in H. Lotery & Co. Ltd., re-named Slater Walker Securities Ltd.,

Chmn. 1964–75 (Man. Dir. 1964–72). Fellow Inst. Chartered Accountants. *Publication:* Return to Go (1977). *Address:* High Beeches, Blackhills, Esher, Surrey.

**SLATER, Joseph Elliott.** President, Aspen Institute for Humanistic Studies. *B.* 1922. (B.A. hons., Univ. Cal. at Berkeley, 1943, grad. student, 1943; Hon. LLD Colorado Coll., Denver Univ. & Univ. of New Hampshire; Hon. LL.D., Kung Hee Univ., Korea, 1966; Order of Merit, Federal Republic of Germany. *M.* Annelor Kremser, 1947. *Daus.* Bonnie Karen Hurst, Sandra Marian. *Career:* Teaching asst., reader Univ. Cal. at Berkeley, 1942–43; U.S. secretary, economic directorate Allied Control Council, asst. U.S. sec. econ. and financial affairs Allied Control Council, Berlin, 1945–48; member, UN planning staff State Department, Washington, 1949; sec.-general, Allied High Commander for Germany, U.S. sec. Office High Commission, Bonn, Germany, 1949–52; executive secretary U.S. Spl. Representative in Europe, U.S. secretary to U.S. delegation to NATO and Orgn. European Econ. Coop., 1952–53; chief economist Creole Petroleum (Standard Oil Co. N.J.), Caracas, Venezuela, 1954–57; Mem. Internat. affairs program Ford Found., 1957–60, officer charge Office Internat. Relations, 1966–67, study Dir. special comm., to establish policies and programs, 1960–61; asst. Man. Dir. Development Loan Fund, Dep. asst. secy. Department of State for Education and Cultural Affairs, 1961–62. Delegation Atlantic Congress, London, 1959; secretary, Presidents Commission on Foreign Assistance (Draper Com.), 1959; Mem. Devel. Assistance Panel President's Sci. Adv. Cttee., 1960–61; Chmn., Vice-President's Cttee. on U.S.-European, East-West Relations; consultant Department State, 1961–68 and Ford Foundation, 1967—; Director, member Bd. Creole Foundation, 1956–57; Amer. Council on Germany and Overseas Dev. Council; Trustee: The Salk Inst.; International Broadcast Institute; Asian Society; Aspen Institute; adv. Center for Advanced Study, Univ. of Illinois; Visiting Professor Univ. of Colo, Member visiting cttee. Dept. of Philosophy MIT. Served to Lt. USNR, 1943–46; mil. Govt. planning officer, London, Paris, Berlin; Pres. The Salk Institute 1967–72, Special Fellow 1972—. *Member:* Inst. Strategic Studies, Soc. Intntl. Devel. Center for Inter-Amer. Relations Inc. Council Foreign Relations, Nat. Planning Assn., Com. Internat. Edn. Exchange, Phi Beta Kappa. *Clubs:* Century Assn., University (NYC); Cosmos (Washington). *Address:* 870 UN Plaza, N.Y. NY 10017, U.S.A.; and *office* Aspen Institute, 717 Fifth Avenue, N.Y. N.Y. 10022.

**SLATER, Richard Mercer Keene,** CMG. British. *B.* 1915. *Educ.* Eton and Magdalene College, Cambridge (BA). *M.* 1939, Barbara Janet Murdoch. *S.* 4. *Career:* Counsellor: Foreign Office 1962–66, Rangoon 1959–62, Foreign Office 1958–59. H.M. Ambassador in Havana, 1966–70; High Commissioner, Uganda 1970–73; Asst. Under-Secy. of State Foreign and Commonwealth Office 1973; Adviser to Commercial Union Assurance Co. since 1973. *Address:* Vicary's, Odiham, Hampshire.

**SLATTERY, Sir Matthew Sausse,** KBE, CB. British company director. *B.* 1902. *Educ.* Stonyhurst College and Royal Naval Colleges of Osborne and Dartmouth; Queens (Belfast) Univ. (DSc *Hon. Cau.*); FRAeS. *M.* 1925, Mica Mary Swain. *S.* 2. *Dau.* 1. *Career:* Joined R.N. 1916; Director, Air Material, Admiralty 1939–41; Cmdd. H.M.S. Cleopatra 1941–42; Dir.-Gen. of Naval Aircraft Development and Production, Min. of Aircraft Production 1941, and Chief Naval Representative 1943; Vice-Controller (Air) and Chief of Naval Equipment at Admiralty, and Chief Naval Representative on Supply Council, Ministry of Supply 1945–48; Retired List 1948; Managing Director, Short Bros. & Harland Ltd. 1948–52 (Chmn. & Man. Dir. 1952–60); Chmn.: S.B. (Realisations) Ltd. 1952–50, and Bristol Aircraft Ltd. 1952–60; Director, Bristol Aeroplane Co. Ltd. 1957–60; Special Adviser to the Prime Minister on Transport of Middle East Oil 1957–59; Chmn., British Overseas Airways Corp. 1960–63, BOAC-Cunard 1962–63; Dir., Williams & Glyn's Bank Ltd. 1970–72; Hawthorn Leslie & Co. Ltd. (Dir.) 1964–77. *Award:* Commander, Legion of Merit (U.S.A.). *Address:* Harvey's Farm, Warninglid, Sussex.

**SLAVENBURG, Pieter.** Dutch banker. *B.* 1916. *Educ.* University of Leyden (LL.D). *M.* 1942, Catharina A. Backer. *S.* 2. *Daus.* 2. *Career:* Joined Slavenburg's Bank, 1942; Manager, Rotterdam Office, 1947; General Manager, 1950. President and Ch. Exec. Officer, N.V. Slavenburg's Bank, 1963—. Director: Netherlands' Bankers' Association; Rotterdam Bankers' Association, N.V. Bank-Giro Centrale. *Member:* Netherlands Organization of Reserve Officers; Chamber of Commerce Rotterdam: Institut International d'Etudes Bancaires. *Clubs:* Overseas Bankers (London); Netherlands (New York); 'de Maas' (Rotterdam). *Address:* Waldeck Pyrmontlaan 6, Rotterdam, and Kon. Astrid Boulevard 32, Noordwijkaan Zee; and *office* Coolsingel 63, Rotterdam (P.O. Box 1045), The Netherlands.

**SLEIGH, Peter Harold.** British. *B.* 1930. *Educ.* Geelong Church of England Grammar School. *M.* 1953, Brenda Jean McRoberts. *S.* 1. *Daus.* 2. *Career:* Dir. H. C. Sleigh Ltd. & Assoc. Companies; Australian Lubricating Oil Refinery Ltd.; Wooltana Industries Ltd.; Man. Dir. The Botany Bay Tanker Co. (Aust.) Pty. Ltd.; Chmn. Flinders Shipping Co. Ltd.; Dir., Firestone Australia Pty. Ltd.; Chmn. & Chief Exec., H. C. Sleigh Ltd.; Hon. Consul for Finland in Melbourne. *Member:* Assoc. Inst. Chartered Shipbrokers. *Clubs:* Australian (Melbourne); Australian (Sydney). *Address:* 117 Walsh Street, South Yarra, Melbourne, Vic., Australia; and *office* 160 Queen Street, Melbourne, Victoria.

**SLIMMINGS, Sir William Kenneth MacLeod,** CBE,D.Litt. British chartered accountant. *B.* 1912. *Educ.* Dunfermline High School. *M.* 1943, Lilian Ellen Willis. *S.* 1. *Dau.* 1. *Career:* Partner, Thomson McLintock & Co. Chartered Accountants 1946; Member of Govt. Cttees: Committee of Inquiry on Costs of Housebuilding 1947–53, Committee on Tax-paid Stocks 1952–53; Committee on Cheque Endorsement 1955–56. Chmn. Board of Trade Advisory Committee 1957–66, Council of Institute of Chartered Accountants (Scotland) 1962–66 Pres. 1969–70). Member. Performing Right Tribunal 1963—; Scottish Tourist Board, 1969–76; Chmn. Review Bd. for Government Contracts since 1971; Mem., Review Body on Doctors' & Dentists' Remuneration since 1976; Chmn., Accounting Standards Cttee. since 1976. *Award:* D. Litt. Heriot-Watt Univ. 1970. *Club:* Caledonian (London.) *Address:* 62 The Avenue, Worcester Park, Surrey.

**SLINGENBERG, Hillebrand Jacob.** Dutch banker. *B.* 1911. *M.* 1939, Mrs. H. S. C. Slingenberg-Mouthaan. *S.* 1. *Dau.* 1. *Career:* Has served in the Bank in various capacities; seven years with Royal Dutch Shell. Managing Director, Shell Italiana and Managing Director, Rotterdam-Rhine Pipeline Company; Member of Board of Managing Directors, Amsterdam-Rotterdam Bank N.V., in Rotterdam. Chevalier, Order of Merit of the Italian Republic. Liberal Member Party for Freedom and Democracy. *Address: office* Amsterdam Rotterdam Bank N.V., Rotterdam, Netherlands.

**SLITOR, Richard Eaton.** American economic consultant. *B.* 1911. *Educ.* Harvard Coll. (S.B. *magna cum laud*); MA, Colgate Univ. Harvard Univ. (PhD); attended Univ. of Wisconsin. *M.* 1937, Louise H. Bean. *S.* Nicholas Wentworth and Christopher Wells Eaton. *Daus.* Prudence van Zandt (Crozier, Jr.) and Deborah Beckwith (Christiana). *Career:* Instructor and tutor Harvard Univ. and Radcliffe Coll. 1934–41; Assoc. Prof. and Chmn., Dept. of Economics and Bus. Admin., Mt. Union Coll. 1941–42; Economist of U.S. Treasury in various capacities 1942—; Assistant Director, Tax Analysis, Office of the Secretary, U.S. Treasury Department 1963–72; Federal Exec. Fellow, Brookings Inst. 1963–64; Visiting Professor of Economics, Grad. Faculty, Univ. of Mass. 1967–68; Consultant, Rand Corp. U.S. Dept. of Housing & Urban Labour Dev. and Nat. Science since 1972; Foundation Advisory Comm. on Intergovernmental Relations. *Publications:* Numerous articles on taxation and public finance; recent publications include: The Value- added Tax as an Alternative to Corporate Income Tax (1963); The Tax Treatment of Research and Innovatine Investment (1965); Corporate Tax Incidence: Economic Adjustments to Differentials Under a Two-Tier Tax Structure (1966); Federal Income Tax in Relation to Housing (1968). *Member:* Phi Beta Kappa; Phi Eta Sigma; Amer. Econ. Assn.; Royal Econ. Socy.; Amer. Statistical Assn.; Natl. Tax Assn.; Int. Inst. for Public Finance; Acad. of Political Science. *Club:* Harvard (Washington). *Address:* 9000 Burning Tree Road, Bethesda, Maryland 20034; and *office* 726 Jackson Place NW, Washington, D.C. 20575, U.S.A.

**SMALES, Fred Benson.** American. *B.* 1914. *M.* 1965. Constance Brennan. *S.* Fred Benson III. *Daus.* Catherine Malia, Patricia Anne (Pilkington) and Nancy Alice (Clark). *Career:* Vice-President, Champion International 1933–68; President: Lewers & Cooke, Inc. 1966–68; Geothermal Resources International 1961–66; Dir. Oahu Development Conference; Dir., Hawaii Chamber of Commerce; Trustee, Hawaii Pacific Coll., Dir., Big Brothers; Pres., Cyprus Hawaian Cement Corp. since 1970. Republican. *Clubs:* Yacht Waikiki: Transpacific, Kaneohe; Oahu CC; Pacific Club.

*Address:* 46-422 Hulupala Place, Kaneche, Hawaii 96744; and *office* 700 Bishop Street, Suite 610, Honolulu, Hawaii 96813.

**SMALLPEICE, Sir Basil,** KCVO, FCA, BCom. British chartered accountant. *B.* 1906. *Educ.* Shrewsbury Schl. *M.* (1) 1931, Kathleen Brame (*dec'd.*); (2) 1973, Rita Burns. *Career:* Articles to Bullimore & Co., Chartered Accountants 1925–30. Accountant, Hoover Ltd. 1930–37; Chief Accountant and later Secretary, Doulton & Co. Ltd. 1937–48; Dir. of Costs and Statistics British Transport Commission 1948–50; With British Overseas Airways Corporation: Financial Comptroller 1950–56, Member of Board 1953–63, Deputy Chief Exec. 1954–56, Man. Dir. 1956–63; Man. Dir. BOAC-Cunard Ltd. 1962–63; Admin. Adviser in Her Majesty's Household 1964—; Dir. The Cunard Steam Ship Co. Ltd. 1964–71; Chmn. and Chief Exec. 1965–71; Chmn. Cunard Line Ltd. 1965–71; Assoc. Container Transportation (Aust.) Ltd. 1967—; ACT(A)/Australian National Line Coordinating Board 1969—; Offshore Marine Ltd. 1969–70; Cunard Cargo Shipping Ltd. 1970–71; Dir. Barclays Bank London Local Board 1966–74; a Dep. Chmn. Lonrho Ltd. 1972–73. *Member:* Inst. Chartered Accnts. Council 1948–57, Inst. Transport Council 1958–61, British Inst. Management Council 1959–64 and 1965—; Chmn. 1970–72, Vice Pres. since 1972; Member Cttee. for Exports to U.S.A. 1964–66; Chmn. English Speaking Union of the Commonwealth 1965–68; Chmn. The Air League 1971–74; Pres., Inst. of Freight Forwarders 1977–78. *Award:* Order of Cedar Lebanon 1955. *Clubs:* Boodle's. Athenaeum, Melbourne (Aust.). *Address:* Reed Thatch, 25 Clare Hill, Esher, Surrey KT10 9NB; and *office* A.C.T. (Australia) Ltd., 136 Fenchurch Street, London, EC3M 6DD.

**SMALLWOOD, Hon. Joseph R.** Canadian politician. *B.* 24 Dec. 1900. *M.* 1925, Clara Isobel Oates. *S.* Ramsay, William. *Dau.* Clara. *Career:* Launched and led the movement to have Newfoundland become a Province of Canada 1947–49; Premier of Newfoundland 1949–72; Retired from Newfoundland Legislature, June 1977; Founder of Liberal Party of Newfoundland; has practised journalism in Newfoundland, U.S.A. and England; Member of Privy Council of Canada 1967. *Address:* 119 Portugal Cove Road, St. John's, Newfoundland A1B 2N1, Canada.

**SMEDLEY, Sir Harold, K.** CMG, MBE(Mil). British Diplomat. *B.* 1920. *Educ.* Aldenham Schl. and Pembroke Coll., Cambridge (Major Scholar) 1939–40 and 1945–46; Classical Tripos Part I, Class I, 1946; M.A. 1948. *M.* 1950 Beryl Brown. *S.* 2 *Daus.* 2. *Career:* War service in Royal Marine Commandos. Entered Dominions Office, later Commonwealth Relations Office, 1946; served in New Zealand 1948–50, S. Rhodesia 1951–53, and India 1957–60. Principal Pte. Secy. to Secretary of State for Commonwealth Relations 1954–57. British High Commissioner in Ghana, 1964–67. British Ambassador in Laos, 1968–70; Secy. Gen. Commission on Rhodesia Opinion 1971–72; Asst. Under-Secretary of State, Foreign and Commonwealth Office, 1970–72; British High Commissioner in Sri Lanka & Ambassador (non resident) to the Republic of Maldives 1973–75; British High Commissioner in New Zealand, & concurrently Governor of the Pitcairn Islands, since 1976 & British High Commissioner (non-resident) in Western Samoa since 1977. *Clubs:* Athenaeum; United Oxford & Cambridge University (London); Wellington (N.Z.). *Address:* Sherwood, Oak End Way, Woodham, Weybridge, Surrey.

**SMELLIE, Robert Gordon,** QC. Canadian. *B.* 1923. *Educ.* Univ. of Manitoba (LLB 1950). *M.* 1946, Lois Evelyn Cochrane. *Daus.* Susan, Carol and Linda. *Career:* Minister of Municipal Affairs, Manitoba, Feb. 1963–July 1966. Chairman, Local Government Boundaries Commission, 27 July 1966–70; Partner Aikins, MacAulay & Thorvaldson. *Member:* Canadian and Manitoba Bar Assns.; Pres. Manitoba Heart Foundation. Progressive Conservative. *Clubs:* Royal Canadian Legion (Past-President, Dominion Command). *Address:* *office* 300–333 Broadway Avenue, Winnipeg 1, Man., Canada.

**SMETS, Francois Alexandre.** Belgian banker. *B.* 1907. *Educ.* Université libre de Bruxelles (Dr.Sc.Ec.). *M.* 1929, Madeleine Mathieu. *S.* Paul. *Dau.* Nadine. *Career:* Except for a break in 1938, when he became Attaché au Cabinet of the Minister of Finance, he has spent all his career in the banking profession. Now Dir. & Hon. Vice-Chmn. Banque Bruxelles Lambert; Hon. Chmn. Exec. Cttee. Banque de Bruxelles; Hon. Chairman, Banque de Commerce; Hon. Vice-Chmn. Union Zairoise de Banques; Vice-Chmn. Banco Espanol en Bruselas. Past Chmn. Association Belge des Banques; Hon. Chmn. Caisse Interprofessionnelle de Depôts et de Virements de Titres (C.I.K.); Former Member, Council and Commission on Monetary Policy, International Chamber of Commerce. *Awards:* Commandeur l'Ordre de Léopold Officier de l'Ordre de la Couronne and various other foreign awards. *Publications:* Le Statut Légal des Banques et des Banquiers en Belgique (edited in collaboration with M. Luc Hommel); articles in economic periodicals. *Address:* 51 avenue de l'Horizon, Brussels 1150, Belgium.

**SMETS, Jacques J. C. C.** Belgian Ambassador. *B.* 1912. *Educ.* Univ. of Louvain (Com. Econ. Pol. Diplomatic Sc.). *M.* 1945, Mary Smets. *S.* 2. *Daus.* 3. *Career:* Served in China 1939–44, U.S.A. 1944–45, Yugoslavia 1945–48, Brussels 1948–50, The Hague 1950–54, France 1954–58, Caracas 1958–62, Repub. of South Africa 1963–68; Republic of Ireland 1968–71; Ministry of Foreign Affairs 1971–74: Ambassador to Denmark since 1974. *Club:* Limburg Golf; Rotary Copenhagen. *Address:* Oster Alle 23, DK 2100 Copenhagen, Denmark.

**SMIRNOVSKY, Mikhail Nikolaevich.** Soviet diplomat. *B.* 1921. *Educ.* Moscow Aviation Institute. *M.* Liudmila A. *S.* 1. *Daus.* 2. *Career:* Member Soviet Foreign Service 1948; Deputy Head, American Div. Ministry, Foreign Affairs 1957–58; Counsellor 1958, Minister-Counsellor Soviet Embassy Washington 1960–62; Head U.S. Div. Member Collegium, Ministry, Foreign Affairs 1962–66; Ambassador to the Court of St. James's 1966–73; Ambassador (non-resident) to Malta 1967–73. Member, Central Auditing Comm. of the C.P.S.U. since 1966. *Address:* c/o Ministry of Foreign Affairs, 32–34 Smolenskaya Sennaya Ploschad, Moscow, U.S.S.R.

**SMIT, Jan Ulrich.** Dutch shipping executive. *B.* 1918. *Educ.* Durham University, and Kings College (England) 1937–39. *M.* 1941, Johanna G. Varkevisser. *S.* Johan, Cornelis Fop and Jan Steven. *Career:* With Shipyard de Noord, Alblasserdam; Asst. Dir. 1940–41; Dir. 1941–62; Part-owner 1957–62. Managing Director, Van der Giessen-de Noord N.V. (merger of Shipyard de Noord and Shipyard C. van der Giessen Krimpen a/d IJssel) 1962—. Director: Reederij de Noord, and Gebrs. Smit Reederij. Served as Sergeant in Dutch Army 1940; 2nd Lieut. 1945; Head, local underground 1940–1944; prisoner-of-war, Germany 1944–45. Royal decoration (Officer). *Address:* *office* 23 Schaardijk, Krimpen a/d IJsell, Netherlands.

**SMITH, Arnold Cantwell.** C.H., First Secretary-General of the Commonwealth. *B.* 1915. *Educ.* University of Toronto (BA Hons. PolSc and Econ. 1935) and Oxford Univ. (MA Jurisprudence 1937; BCL 1938; Rhodes Scholar); Hon. DCL (Michigan 1966, Oxford 1975); LL.D (Ricker, Queen's, UNB, UBC, Toronto, Leeds). *M.* 1938, Evelyn Hardwick Stewart. *S.* Stewart Cantwell and Matthew Cantwell. *Dau.* Alexandra Hardwick. *Career:* Ed., Baltic Times (Tallinn, Estonia) 1939–40; Asst. Prof. of Economics Tartu (Estonia) Univ. 1939–40; Attaché, Brit. Embassy, Cairo 1940–43; Secy., Canadian Embassy, Kuibyshev (1943) and Moscow 1943–45; Dir., Natl. Defence Coll. of Canada 1947–49; Alternate Reptve. of Canada on U.N. Security Cncl. and to Atomic Energy Commn., and Principal Adv. to Canadian Delegation, Lake Success 1949–50; Counslr., Embassy, Brussels 1950–53; Special Asst. to Secy. of State for External Affairs, Ottowa 1953–55; Commissioner, International Truce Commission, Cambodia 1955–56; Canadian Minister, London 1957–58; Ambassador to U.A.R. 1958–61; to U.S.S.R. 1961–63; Asst. Under Secretary of State for External Affairs, Ottawa 1963–65; First Secy. Gen. 1965–75; Lester Pearson Professor International Affairs, Carleton University. Ottawa since 1975; Chmn. of Boards of Dirs., North-South Inst. of Canada, International Peace Acad. (UN Plaza, N.Y.), Hudson Inst. of Canada; Pres., Canadian Bureau for International Education; Trustee, Hudson Inst. (New Jersey, U.S.A.); Life Vice-Pres. Royal Commonwealth Society. *Clubs:* Cercle Universitaire (Ottawa); Athenaeum, Travellers' (London). *Address:* 300 Queen Elizabeth Driveway, Ottawa; and *office* Norman Paterson School of International Affairs, Carleton University, Ottawa, Canada.

**SMITH, Arnold Nigel,** MA, FICeram. British. *B.* 1926. *Educ.* Leeds Grammar School; St. John's Cambridge (MA). *M.* 1948, Moira Anne Robson. *S.* 2. *Career:* Man. Dir. Pilkington's Tiles Holdings Ltd.; Chmn. Pilkington Tiles Ltd., Carter & Co. Ltd., Pilkington Tiles (S.A.). (Pty.) Ltd., Pilkington Tiles (Australia) Pty. Ltd., Pilkington Tiles (W.A.) Pty. Ltd., Dir. Building Adhesives Ltd.; British Ceramic Tile Council Ltd., Somany-Pilkington's Ltd.

*Address:* Lake House, Legh Road, Knutsford, Cheshire; and *office* Clifton Junction, Manchester.

**SMITH, Bruce Henry.** Australian business executive. *B.* 1925. *Educ.* Sydney Church of England Grammar School. *M.* 1949, Olive Hazel Green. *S.* Timothy Peter. *Dau.* Adrienne Denise. *Career:* Senior Partner and Co-founder B. O. Smith and Son 1955—; Chmn. Cemac Associated Ltd. 1956—; Receiver: Lanray Industries Ltd., 1957–58; Production Plant Ltd., 1963–67; an official Liquidator, State of New South Wales 1963; Receiver Chevron Sydney Ltd. 1965; Official Manager, Anglo Pacific Securities Ltd., 1964 (now Dane Industries Ltd.); Liquidator: Caldwells' Wines Ltd., 1958 (now Calderman Ltd.) Mort's Dock & Engineering Co. Ltd., 1965 (now Favelle Mort Ltd.); Receiver operating subsid. A. L. Vincent Industries Ltd. 1963; Chairman, United Australian Industries Ltd., 1960–63; Project Development Corp. Ltd., 1966–69; Tangible Securities Ltd. 1965–70; Vokes Australia Pty. Ltd. 1965–71; Neville Jeffress Holdings Pty. 1966–75; Project Mining Corp., Ltd., 1968–69; International Footwear Industries Ltd. 1969–76; (Dir. 1965—); F. T. Wimble & Co. Ltd. 1969–75 (Dir. 1965); Stott Datagraphics Ltd., 1969–75; Shepherd Mercantile Agency Pty. Ltd. 1969; Hawley Credit Service Pty. Ltd. 1969; R. M. Tyson Pty. Ltd. 1969; Acting Chmn. Buckle Investments Ltd., 1961–64; Dir., Frederic Ash Ltd., 1968–69 Official Manager Epstein Ltd. 1968 Chmn. 1974; Dep. Chmn. W. P. Martin Pty. Ltd. 1969; Forest Developments Aust. Ltd. 1971–74; Dir. Pacific Mining Ltd. 1971; Chmn. Assoc. Business Consultants Pty. Ltd. 1971; Transport Distributors International Pty. Ltd. 1972; Suncoast Group 1972; Manzitti Corsi & Nisbet Pty. Ltd. 1972 (now MCN Australasia Pty. Ltd.); Vam Limited (Prov. Liquidator) 1971–73, Scheme Trustee 1973; Perkins Shipping & Mining Corp. Pty. Ltd. 1973; Smith's General Contracting Pty. Ltd. 1973; Arnhem Transport Services Pty. Ltd. 1974. *Clubs:* Australian Tattersall's; Royal Automobile; Roseville Golf; Australian Jockeys; Sydney Turf. *Address:* 32 North Arm Road, Middle Cove, New South Wales; and *office* 20th Floor, A.N.Z. Bank Building, 68 Pitt Street, Sydney, N.S.W., Australia.

**SMITH, Sir Carl Victor,** CBE, Hon LLD-OU. New Zealand company director. *B.* 19 April 1897. *Educ.* George Watson's College, Edinburgh. *M.* 1919, Catherine Elizabeth Gettings Johnston. *S.* Brian Hamilton, Ronald Gordon Hamilton. *Dau.* Catherine Fullwood Hamilton. *Career:* Pres. N.Z. Manufacturers Federation 1940–43; member, Economic Stabilisation Committee 1941; Chairman, Cadbury-Fry, Hudson, N.Z. 1939–1963, and Director of other companies; member, Royal Commission Railways 1952; Chairman Finance Cttee., Otago University Council; Royal Commission on Parliamentary Salaries 1955 and 1958. *Address:* Rowheath, Dudley Place, Dunedin, New Zealand.

**SMITH, Charles Franklin.** Canadian Co. Director. *B.* 1918. *M.* 1941, Constance Charlotte Munroe. *S.* 1. *Dau.* 1. *Educ.* Queens Univ., Kingston (Ontario), BSc. MSc. *Career:* Vice-Pres. Europe, Sperry Vickers, Sperry Rand Corp.; Dir. Sperry Rand of France Ltd., Lucifer S.A. Geneva; Vice-Pres. & Dir. Vickers Sperry Div., Sperry Rand of Canada Ltd. 1955–66. *Member:* RAC, RYA, Island Sailing; Cruising Assn.; Inst. of Dirs.; English Inst. of Canada; Soc. of Genealogist; Royal Inst. of International Affairs; Registered Prof. Eng., Province of Ontario. *Clubs:* Royal Ocean Racing. *Address:* Wycliffe, Pine Walk, Cobham KT11 2HJ.

**SMITH, Charles Henry, Jr.** Business executive. *B.* 1920. *Educ.* Mass. Inst. of Technology (BS 1942). *M.* 1943, Rhea Day. *S.* Charles H., III, and Hudson D. *Dau.* Deborah S. *Career:* President, The Steel Improvement & Forge Co., Cleveland, now SIFCO Industries Inc., 1943–70. Chairman, Chief Executive Officer, 1970—. Chmn.: Custom Tool & Manufacturing Co., Minneapolis 1957—; Sifco Metachemical Co., Cleveland 1959—; and Sifco do Brasil, Sao Paulo 1959—; Pres., Canadian Steel Improvement Ltd., Toronto 1951–54; Dir.: Metachemical Machines Ltd. 1961–65, Metachemical Processes Ltd. 1959–65 (both of Crawley, Sussex, U.K.); Bharat Forge Co. Ltd., Poona, India 1962—; Industries Kaiser Argentina, Buenos Aires 1958–65. Pres., Forging Industry Education & Research Foundation, U.S.A. 1962–65. Trustee: The Defiance College, and Cleveland Y.M.C.A. Adviser to U.S. Employer-Delegate, I.L.O. Conf., Geneva 1953 and 1962 (U.S. Employer-Delegate Geneva 1956 and Buenos Aires 1961). Named One of America's Ten Outstanding Men, 1955; Vice-Pres., Chamber of Commerce of the United States, 1970–72; Treasurer 1973, Chmn. 1974–75; U.S. Employer Delegate to Int. Labor Conference Geneva 1975, 1976; Member of Governing Body International Labor Organization 1975–78; Chmn., Advisory Bd., Salvation Army. *Member:* Amer. Socy. for Metals; Cleveland Engineering Socy. *Clubs:* The Union (Cleveland); Shaker Heights Country; Burning Tree, Capitol Hill (both Washington D.C.); Pine Lake Trout (Chagrin Falls, Ohio). *Address:* 22500 McCauley Road, Shaker Heights, Ohio 44120; and *office* 970 East 64th Street, Cleveland 3, Ohio, U.S.A.

**SMITH, Cyril,** MBE, O St. J. MP. British Politician & Company Director. *B.* 1928. *Educ.* Rochdale Grammar Sch. for Boys. *Career:* Man. Dir., Smith Springs (Rochdale) Ltd. since 1963; Mayor of Rochdale 1966–67; Liberal MP for Rochdale since 1972. *Decorations:* Member of the Order of the British Empire, 1966; Officer of the Order of St. John of Jerusalem. *Clubs:* National Liberal Club. *Address:* 14 Emma Street, Rochdale, Lancs.; & House of Commons, London SW1A 0AA.

**SMITH, Donald MacKeen.** Canadian. President, J. E. Morse & Co. Ltd., Halifax 1956—. *B.* 1923. *M.* 1949, Helen Elizabeth Guildford. *Daus.* Felicity, Ann and Sally. Member Progressive Conservative Association. *Clubs:* The Halifax; Royal Nova Scotia Yacht Squadron. *Address:* 5758 Inglis Street, Halifax, N.S. B3H 1K6, Canada.

**SMITH, Dudley (Gordon),** MP. British politician, management consultant and journalist. *B.* 14 Nov. 1926. *Educ.* Chichester High School, Sussex. *M.* (1) 1958, Anthea Higgins (*Diss.* 1974). *S.* Russell Dudley. *Daus.* Charlotte Jane Dudley, Antonia Louise Dudley. (2) 1976, Catherine Amos. *Career:* Worked for various provincial and national newspapers, as journalist & senior exec. 1943–66; Div. Dir. Sen. Exec. Beecham Group 1966–70; M.P. Brentford & Chiswick (Con.). 1959–66; Parly. Private Secy. to the Secy. for Technical Co-operation 1963–64; Opposition Whip 1964–66; Member Parliament for Warwick and Leamington since 1968; Parly. Under Secy. of State Dept. of Employment 1970–74; Under Secy. State for the Army Jan.–March 1974; Vice-Chmn. Parliamentary Select Cttee. on Race Relations & Immigration, since 1974; promoted Town & Country Planning (Amendment) Act, 1977, as a private member; Chmn. United and Cecil Club since 1975. *Publications:* Harold Wilson: A Critical Biography (1963); etc. *Address:* Hunningham Hill, Hunningham, nr. Leamington Spa, Warwickshire.

**SMITH, Elsdon Coles.** American lawyer and onomatologist. *B.* 1903. *Educ.* University of Illinois (BS 1925) and Harvard University (LLB 1930). *M.* 1933, Clare I. Hutchins. *Dau.* Laurel Gleda. *Career:* Admitted to Illinois Bar 1930; member, Faculty, Chicago Law School 1933–35; associated with Follansbee, Shorey & Schupp, 1933–48; member, Blumberg & Smith, 1948–58, Blumberg, Smith, Wolff & Pennish 1958, and Pennish & Steel 1961–63. Founder and first president American Name Society, 1951–54; member, International Committee on Onomastic Sciences. *Publication:* Naming Your Baby (1943); The Story of our Names (1950); Personal Names: an Annotated Bibliography (1952); The Dictionary of American Family Names (1956), revised & enlarged, 1972. Treasury of Name Lore (1967). American Surnames (1969). *Address:* 8001 Lockwood Avenue, Skokie, Ill. 60076, U.S.A.

**SMITH, G. E. Kidder.** Order of the Southern Cross (Brazil); architect, author. Lecturer at numerous U.S. and European universities and in South America and Asia for U.S. Department of State. *B.* 1913. *Educ.* Princeton Univ. (AB 1935) and Princeton School of Architecture (MFA 1938). *M.* 1942. Dorothea F. Wilder. *S.* Kidder, Jr., and Hopkinson K. Visiting Professor, Massachusetts Inst. of Technology 1955–56; Critic Yale Univ. 1948–49. *Publications:* A Pictorial History of Architecture in America (1976); The New Architecture of Europe; Italy Builds; Sweden Builds; Switzerland Builds; Brazil Builds (with P. L. Goodwin): The New Churches of Europe; Contributor to Encyclopedia Britannica (Religious Architecture) and to New Catholic Encyclopedia; Exhibitions with or by: Museum Modern Art, Amer. Federation of Arts, Smithsonian Institution. Photographs in collection of Museum of Modern Art. Fellow, Amer.-Scandinavian Foundation 1939–40; Guggenheim Found. 1945–46; (President's Fellow), Brown Univ. 1949–50; Research Fulbright Fellow 1951–52; Brunner Fellow 1959–60; Research Fulbright Fellow to India 1965–66. National Foundation on Arts and Humanities and Graham Foundation for Advanced Studies in the Arts (joint grants) 1968–70. Natl. Foundation, Arts and Humanities and Ford Found. (Joint grants) 1970–71; Ford Found. grant 1972. *Member:* Amer. Inst. of Architects (Fellow); Socy. of Architectural Historians; Coll. of Art Association, etc.; General Committee and Commission on Architecture, National Council of Churches, Council on Architecture, New York State. *Clubs:* Century Assoc., Princeton, Church (all of N.Y.C.); Coopertown Country. *Address:* 163 East 81st Street, New York City 28, U.S.A.

**SMITH, Hon. George Isaac,** MBE, ED, QC, DCL, LLD Canadian. *B.* 1909. *Educ.* Bachelor of Laws. Queen's Counse 1950. *M.* 1938, Sarah Hobart Archibald. *S.* John Robert and George Isaac. *Dau.* Ruby Alison. *Career:* Lieut.-Colonel; Mentioned in Dispatches; Member Order of Orange-Nassau with Crossed Swords (Netherlands); Deputy Asst. Adjutant-General, First Canadian Army 1944–45; Asst. Adjutant-General, Canadian Military Headquarters, London 1945; Commanding Officer, North Nova Scotia Scottish Highlanders 1946–49. Minister of Highways, Nova Scotia 1956–62; Provincial Secretary, Govt. of Nova Scotia 1956–60; Minister in Charge of N.S. Liquor Control Act 1956–58; Minister under the Water Act, Govt. of N.S. 1959–62. President, Canadian Good Roads Assn. 1960–61; Member, House of Assembly, Nova Scotia 1949–74, Member of Executive Council 1956–70, Minister of Finance and Economics 1962–68. Chairman, Nova Scotia Power Commission 1959–70; Premier of Nova Scotia 1967–70; Summoned to Senate of Canada 1975. Pres., Nova Scotia Barristers' Soc. 1976–77; Mem., Canadian Barr Assn. Progressive Conservative. Snr. Partner Patterson, Smith, Matthews & Grant, Solicitors. *Club:* Royal Canadian Legion. *Address:* 116 Burnyeat Street, Truro, N.S.; and *office* 10, Church Street, Truro, N.S., Canada.

**SMITH Harry.** Chmn. wire, wire rope and fibre manufacturer. *B.* 1917. *Educ.* Oundle School, Peterborough. *M.* 1943, Margaret Eileen Churcher. *S.* 2. *Career:* Works Mgr., Templeborough Rolling Mills Ltd., Rotherham 1940; General Manager, William Cooke & Co. Ltd., Sheffield 1942. Chairman 1958— and Joint Managing Director 1953—, Bridon Ltd.; Chairman; Templeborough Rolling Mills Ltd.; Dir. Tinsley Wire Industries Ltd., United Steel Companies Ltd., Wire Rope Indus. Ltd.; Depy. Chmn., The Steetley Co. Ltd.; Depy. Chmn., The Rank Organization Ltd.; Haggie Rand Ltd., The Steetley Industries Ltd., Steetley of Canada (Holdings) Ltd.; *Fellow:* British Institute of Management and The Institution of Works Managers. *Clubs:* Royal Solent Yacht Club (Yarmouth I.O.W.); *Address:* Flat 11, 2 Mansfield St. London W1M 9FF. and *office* Bridon Ltd., 77 South Audley Street, London W1Y 5TA.

**SMITH, Sir Howard Frank Trayton,** KCMG. British diplomat. *B.* 1919. *Educ.* Sidney Sussex College, Cambridge. *M.* 1943, Winifred Mary Cropper. *Dau.* Amanda (Mrs. Roderic Lyne). *Career:* Second Secretary (Information) Washington, 1950; First Secy., Dec. 1950; First Secy. and Consul, Caracas, 1953; Foreign Office, 1956; Counsellor, Moscow, 1961–63; Head of Northern Dept., Foreign Office, 1964–68. Ambassador in Prague, 1968–71; United Kingdom Representative in Northern Ireland 1971–72; Deputy Secretary, Cabinet Office 1972–75; Ambassador in Moscow 1976–78. *Club:* Travellers. *Address: office* c/o F.C.O., King Charles Street, London, S.W.1.

**SMITH, Ian Douglas.** Rhodesian Politician. *B.* 1919. *Educ.* Rhodes Univ., Grahamstown, S. Africa—BCom. *M.* Janet Watt. *S.* 2. *Dau.* 1. *Career:* RAF 1941–45; Farmer; mem., Southern Rhodesia Legislative Assembly 1948–53, & Parliament of the Fed. of Rhodesia & Nyasaland 1953–61; Chief Govt. Whip 1958; foundation mem. & Vice-Pres. Rhodesian Front, 1962, Pres. since 1965; mem., Legislative Assembly since 1962; Dep. PM & Minister of the Treasury Dec. 1962–April 1964, Minister of Defence April 1964–May 1965, Minister of External Affairs April–Aug. 1964, Prime Minister since April 1964; delivered Rhodesia's Unilateral Declaration of Independence Nov. 1965. *Decorations:* Independence Decoration (1970). *Address:* 8 Chancellor Avenue, Salisbury, Rhodesia.

**SMITH, John, MA, LLB, MP. British.** *B.* **1938.** *Educ.* **Dunoon** Grammar School; Glasgow University. *M.* 1967, Elizabeth Margaret Bennett. *Daus.* Sarah, Jane and Catherine. *Career:* Solicitor in Glasgow 1963–66; Advocate of the Scottish Bar since 1967; Member of Parliament for North Lanarkshire since 1970; Chmn. Glasgow Univ. Labour Club 1960; PPS to Secy. of State for Scotland Feb.–Oct. 1974; Parly. Under-Secy. of State for Energy 1974–75; Minister of State for Energy 1975–76; Minister of State, Privy Council Office (responsibility for devolution) since 1976. *Award:* Observer Mace Nat. Debating Tournament 1962. *Address:* 44 Craiglea Drive, Edinburgh, EH10 5PF; and *office* House of Commons, London, S.W.1.

**SMITH, J(ohn) B(ertie). Art and art education. Chairman** Department of Art, Baylor University, Waco, Tex. *B.* 1908 *Educ.* Baylor Univ. (AB 1929), Univ. of Chicago (AM 1931) and Columbia Univ. (EdD 1946). *M.* 1933, Ellen M. Capes. *Dau.* Elaine (Mrs. Elaine Parke, Jr.). *Career:* Principal, Rural School, Athens, Tex. 1926–27, and Malakoff (Tex.) High School 1927–29. Head of Art Department: Adams State Coll., Alamosa, Colo. 1931–36 and 1937–39; Univ. of Wyoming, Laramie 1939–45; Univ. of Alabama, Tuscaloosa 1946–49. Dean, Kansas City Art Institute 1949–54; Head of Art Dept. and Humanities. Hardin-Simmons Univ., Abilene, Tex. 1954–60. *Member:* Alpha Chi, Kappa Delta Pi, Phi Delta Kappa, Kappa Pi; Texas Fine Arts Assn. (Pres. 1960–61); Texas Art Education Assoc. (Pres. 1969); College Art Assn.; Amer. Socy. for Aesthetics; National Art Education Assn.; regional and local societies. *Publications:* 25 articles for various journals; Editor, Texas Trends in Art Education. Exhibited in regional and national art exhibitions since 1933; represented in permanent collection at Denver Art Museum. *Address:* 2109 Charboneau Drive, Waco, Texas 76710; and *office* Department of Art, Baylor University, Waco, Tex. 76703, U.S.A.

**SMITH, John Herbert.** Canadian. Consulting Engineer & Chairman, de Havilland Aircraft of Canada Ltd. *B.* 1909. *Educ.* Univ. of New Brunswick (BSc Elec; MSc Elec). *M.* 1937, Eldred Marian Shaidle. *Career:* 'Test Course', Canadian General Electric Co. Ltd., Peterborough, May 1932; Sales Engineer, Hamilton 1936; Manager, Supply Sales, Toronto 1945; Manager, Apparatus Div., Toronto 1948; General Manager, Wholesale Dept., Toronto 1952; Vice-Pres., Toronto 1953; General Manager, Appliance Dept., Montreal 1955; General Manager, Apparatus Dept., Peterborough 1955; President, Toronto 1957; Chairman, Toronto 1970–72, Director: Acres Consulting Services Ltd.; Banister Continental Ltd.; Heitman Canadian Realty Investors; Ontario Press Council; Rio Algom Ltd.; Rio Tinto Holdings Ltd.; Canadian Imperial Bank of Commerce; CIBC (mem. Exec. Cttee.); Sun Life Assurance Co. of Canada; Lornex Mining Corp. Ltd.; Wellesley Hospital. Hon. DSc. Univ. of New Brunswick (Fredericton) and Assumption Univ. (Windsor, Ont.). Member: Assn. of Professional Engineers of Ontario (Pres. 1953); Engineering Inst. of Canada; Inst. of Electrical & Electronics Engineers (Fellow). *Clubs:* York; National; Toronto; Board of Trade of Metropolitan Toronto; Toronto Hunt. *Address:* 48 Forest Hill Road, Toronto, Ontario, Canada.

**SMITH (Maurice) Frederik.** American conservationist and business executive. *B.* 1908. *Educ.* Univ. of Michigan (special student) and College of William & Mary 1928–32. *M.* 1942, Catherine Hanley. *S.* Christopher, Frederick, Mark. *Daus.* Michaele, Drusilla, Francesca. Annual Award, Contribution to Conservation, Boston, 1957; Hon. Fellow, Rochester (N.Y.) Museum of Science. *Career:* Asst. to Secy, of U.S. Treasury 1944–45; Assistant to Pres., Bretton Woods International Conference 1945; Asst. Chmn., National Labour-Management Conference called by President Truman 1947. Associate, Rockefeller Family & Associates. Consultant to Prudential Insurance Co. and to National Aeronautics & Space Admn. Associate Office of Rockefeller Family and Associates. Director: (Fin. Comm.); American Motors Corporation, Detroit, Mich.; Mallinckrodt Chemical Workss St. Louis, Mo.; Howard Johnson Co., D.Y.; Perini Corporation (Exec. Cttee.), Boston, Mass. United Nations Development Corp. Council of Conservationists; Chairman, Graphic, Group. Member: Advisory Board on National Parks, Monuments & Historic Sites, U.S. Department of Interior, and National Outdoor Recreation Resources Review Commission; Chairman, State Park Commission for the City of New York, Advisory Committee, N.Y. State Dept. of Conservation; Chairman Adv. Cttee., N.Y. State Recreation Council; Hudson River Commission; Chmn. & Member, Bus. Commn., National Planning Assn. Trustee, Jackson Hole Preserved Inc. *Publications:* Contributions to national magazines. Republican. *Clubs:* Explorers'; Sky (N.Y.); Boone & Crockett; Missouri Athletic (St. Louis). *Address:* 20 Sutton Place South, N.Y. 10022, U.S.A.; and Shelter Island, N.Y., U.S.A.

**SMITH, Monroe Githens.** American business executive. *B.* 1910. *Educ.* University of Pennsylvania (BSc Econ). *M.* 1936, Lois Alberta Wade. *S.* Charles Monroe and Wade Monroe. *Dau.* Judith Ann. *Career:* Group Vice-President, E.S.B. Inc., Philadelphia 1957—. President, Diagnostic Data Inc., 1968—. *Member:* Material Handling Inst. (Past Pres.); National Security Industrial Assn. (Past Pres.); Industrial Truck Assn. (Director); Society of Former Special

Agents of F.B.I.; Financial Executives Inst.; Newcomen Socy.; Amer. Ordnance Socy.; Amer. Socy. Naval Engineers. *Clubs:* United Million Mile; Franklin; Jeff Davis; Canadian; Vesper; Brooklyn; Manufacturers Country; Merchants & Manufacturers; Seaview Country; Honorary First Defenders; Sharon Heights Country. *Address:* 201 Family Farm Drive, Woodside-Cal., 94062; and *office* 518 Logue Avenue, Mountain View, Calif. 94040, U.S.A.

**SMITH, Morton.** American. *B.* 1903. *Educ.* Stationers' Company's School (London, Eng.) and Temple University, Philadelphia (LL.B). *M.* 1926, Guida Williams. *Dau.* Jeannette. Vice-Pres., Girard Trust Bank 1942. *Member:* Philadelphia Bar Assn.; Chartered Financial Analysts. Senior Vice-Pres., Girard Trust Bank, Philadelphia, Pa. 1967–68. *Clubs:* Union League (Phila.); St. Davids Golf. *Address:* 242 West Valley Road, Strafford, Pa. U.S.A.

**SMITH, Nelson Lee.** American economist. *B.* 15 Feb. 1899. *Educ.* Dartmouth College (AB); Amos Tuck School of Administration and Finance (MCS); University of Michigan (PhD). *M.* 1924, Dorothy Gertrude Leonard. *S.* Nelson Lee, Leonard Wayne. *M.* (2) 1955, Terry Niles. Instructor in Economics, Dartmouth College 1921–24; graduate student and instructor in Economics, University of Michigan 1922–24; Assistant Professor of Economics, Dartmouth College 1924–34; Professor of Economics, Dartmouth College 1934–37; admitted to practice before Interstate Commerce Commission 1934; member, New England Governors' Railroad Committee 1929–31, New Hampshire Public Service Commission 1933–41, Chairman 1934–41, Board of Investigation and Research, Transportation, Chairman 1941–43, New England Assocation of Utilities Commissioners, President 1935–36; President, National Association of Railroad and Utilities Commissioners 1938–39; N.A.R.U.C. Executive Committee 1936–55; N.A.R.U.C. Committee on Co-operation between State and Federal Commissions 1936 and 1940; Chairman, N.A.R.U.C. Committee of Depreciation 1939–44; member of Federal Power Commission 1943–55; Vice-Chairman 1946, Chairman Jan. 1947–May 1950; Vice-Pres., American Airlines, Inc. 1955–61; Professor of Business, Columbia Univ. Graduate School of Business 1962–67. *Address:* 80 Hilltop Place, New London, N.H. 03257, U.S.A.

**SMITH, Noel George.** British. *B.* 1912. *Educ.* Haberdashers Askes School. *M.* 1959, Monique Helburg. *Career:* Articled to a London firm of chartered accountants 1931; qualified 1937. With Price Waterhouse Peat & Co., Brazil 1938–41; Military Service (Europe, Burma; Major R.A.S.C.) 1941–46. After a year with Price Waterhouse, joined John M. Winter & Sons; Partner 1953; resigned partnership at end of 1953 to join Edmundsons as Secretary; made Director 1954, Joint Managing Director 1957, Managing Director 1966; Deputy Chmn. Ventas Distribution Ltd. 1971–73; Dir. Edmundson Distribution Ltd. (late Ventas) 1973–74 (Ret'd). Dir. THV International Contr. & Eng. Ltd. since 1973. Fellow, Inst. of Chartered Accountants. *Clubs:* Naval & Military, Anglo-Belgian. *Address:* 14A Kensington Court Gardens, W.8; and *office* 199–201 High Street, Orpington, Kent BR6 0PF.

**SMITH, Olcott Damon.** American attorney. *B.* 1907. *Educ.* Kent School 1925, Yale Univ. (BA 1929) and Harvard Univ. (LLB 1932). *M.* 1933, Lucy B. Brainerd. *S.* 3. *Dau.* 1. Hon LLD Trinity College. *Career:* Chairman, Aetna Life & Casualty 1963–72. Director: Morgan-Guaranty Trust Co., Hartford National Bank & Trust Co.; United Aircraft Corp.; Hartford Courant Co., Emhart Corp. *Member:* Connecticut and Hartford County Bar Associations. *Clubs:* Links; Yale (N.Y.C.); Harford; Farmington Country. *Address: office* One Constitution Plaza, Hartford, Conn., U.S.A.

**SMITH, Patrick.** Irish politician and farmer. *B.* 1901. Battalion Commandant, I.R.A. 1920, later Brigade Officer Commanding; Parl. Secy. to the Taoiseach and to Minister for External Affairs Sept. 1939–43, to Minister for Finance 1943–46; Parliamentary Sec. to Minister for Agriculture 1947; Minister for Agriculture 1947–48; TD for Co. Cavan 1923–77; Minister for Local Government 1951–54; Minister for Local Government, and Minister for Social Welfare Mar.–Nov. 1957; Minister for Agriculture 1957–64; Deputy for Cavan, 1964–69 and 1969–72, Re-elected 1973, Retired June 1977. *Address:* Drumman, Cootehill, Co. Cavan, Ireland.

**SMITH, Sir Raymond Horace,** KBE. British. Chairman, Hawker Siddeley and other British Cos. in Venezuela. *Educ.* Salesian College, London; Barcelona University; London University, BSc. *M.* 1943, Dorothy Hart. *S.* Raymond, Richard, Robert. *Career:* During 2nd World War with Intelligence Corps. in: France, Burma, Malaya, Indonesia, U.S.A., and South America; Attaché, Brit. Embassy, Caracas; Rep. of London Reinsurers in Venezuela, 1954–60; Representative: Rolls-Royce Ltd.; British Aircraft Corp.; Cammell Laird; Hawker Siddeley Aviation; Provincial Insurance Co. Ltd., etc. Director: Britanica de Seguros (Insurance); Daily Journal. Board Director: British Venezuelan Cultural Institute; Anglo-Venezuelan Trade Assn. President, Brit. Commonwealth Assn. of Venezuela, 1955–57. Companion, Royal Aeronautical Socy. *Award:* Venezuelan Air Force Cross. *Clubs:* Royal Aero (London); Caracas Country (Caracas). *Address:* Edificio Las Americas, Calle Real de Sabana Grande, Caracas, Venezuela.

**SMITH, Robert Guy Carington.** Canadian Foreign Service Officer. Ret. 1973. *B.* 1908. *Educ.* Bishop's Coll. Schl., Royal Military Coll., Kingston, Ont. (Hons), and McGill Univ. *M.* 1932, Constance Isobel Price (*D.* 1944), and 1945, Jean Alexandra McCraig. *Daus.* Vallière Ann (Van Alstyne), Susan Pamela (McCarter) and Penelope Joan (Younger). *Career:* Junior Trade Commissioner, Department of Trade and Commerce 1930; Asst. Trade Commissioner, Buenos Aires 1931, and New York 1936. Enlisted in R.C.A. as Lieut. with 94th Anti-Tank Battery; Captain 1941; Major O.C. 18th Anti-Tank Battery (Second Regiment) 1942; returned to Canada following a serious motor-cycle accident and posted Lieut.-Col., Directorate, Military Operations and Planning, N.D.H.Q., Ottawa 1943; discharged with rank of Lieut.-Col. 1945 (Defence Medal, C.V.S.M. and Clasp, War Medals 1939–45); Cdn. Centennial Medal; Commercial Secretary, Havana 1946, Rome 1948, London 1950; seconded Dept. of Defence Production; Commercial Counsellor 1951; member of Canadian Delegation to NATO and OEEC, Paris, as Representative of D.D.P. 1953; Commercial Counsellor, Paris; Washington 1953; Minister (Commercial) 1957–58; Commissioner for Canada to The West Indies, Mar. 1958–June 1962; Department of Trade & Commerce Head Office, 1962–63; Minister (Commercial) in Tokyo 1963–65; Consul-Gen., New York 1966–70. *Clubs:* Royal Military College (Canada); East India & Sports (London). *Address:* 10 Cliff Side Crescent, Brockville, Ont., Canada.

**SMITH, Robert J(ames).** *B.* 1899. *Educ.* Jefferson School of Law (AB and LLB 1929); Northwestern Univ. (Spec. Economics and Business Administration—summers 1926–28). Admitted to practise before Supreme Court of the U.S. *M.* 1920, Jean Whittle. *S.* Robert J., Jr. *Dau.* Elsie Jean (Lauratis). *Career:* U.S. Army 1917–18; U.S. Army Air Force 1942–46 (Lt.-Col. 1942; Col. 1942), Brigadier-General 1948, Maj.-Gen. U.S.A.F.R.,1957; Dir., First National Bank Dallas, 1948–52, Dir. and Chmn. of the Bd., Fed. Reserve Bank of Dallas, 1952–60, Dir. and Mem. of Advisory Cttee., Export-Import Bank of Wash., D.C. 1960–62; and Dir. and Mem. of Exec; Cttee., DPA, Inc.; Pres., Pioneer Texas Corp. 1953–68; Dir., Continental Air Lines Inc. 1955—; Space Corp. 1958–70. *Awards:* Legion of Merit, Air Medal, Commendation Medal and Victory Medals of World Wars I and II; Comdr., Order of Nishan Iftakar (Tunisia), Amer. European and Asiatic Theatre Ribbons, Command Pilot. *Member:* American, Texas and Dallas Bar Associations; Air Force Assn.; Dallas Chamber of Commerce (Dir. 1965–67); Dallas Council on World Affairs; Vice-Chmn., National Security Resources Bd., Wash., D.C.; Mem.: Task Force on Defence Dept. Personal Administration, Hoover Commn., 1954–55; Assoc., National Industrial Conference Bd.; 5th Circuit Root-Tilden Scholarship Selection Cttee. (New York Univ. Sch. of Law); Dallas Citizens Cncl. Mem. Federal and State Legislation Cttee.; Trustee, Southwest Legal Fdn.; Chmn., Air Force Academy Liaison Cttee., of the Dallas Chamber of Commerce. *Clubs:* Army & Navy (Washington); Town & Gown, City (Dallas). *Address:* Apt. 812, 6335 West Northwest Highway 2, Dallas, Texas 75225; and *office* 619 Meadows Building, Dallas, Tex. 75206, U.S.A.

**SMITH, Hon. S. Bruce.** Canadian. *B.* 1899. *Educ.* Univ. of Alberta (BA and LL.D). *M.* 1925, Doris Gertrude Charlesworth. *S.* David Bruce and Sidney Gerald Denis. *Career:* Chmn., Bd. of Transport Commissioners of Canada 1958; Justice of the Trial Div. of the Supreme Court of Alberta, Jan. 1959, and of the Appellate Div. of the Supreme Court of Alberta, April 1960. A member of the Appellate Division of the Supreme Court of Alberta and *ex-officio* a member of the Trial Division of the same Court. Chief Justice of Alberta & Chief Justice of the Court of Appeal for the Northwest Territories Mar. 1, 1961–Dec. 5, 1974. Member of Council, Canadian Bar Assn. 1947–59; Vice-Pres., Alberta, of Canadian Bar Assn. 1947–49 (Member of Executive 1957–59);

formerly Chmn. Legal Education and Training Section of C.B.A.; formerly Pres., Conference of Governing Bodies of the Legal Profession in Canada; Bencher. Law Socy. of Alberta 1946–58 (Pres. 1956–58); Chmn. Rhodes Scholarship Committee for Alberta 1959–64; Chancellor, Anglican Diocese of Edmonton 1959–71. LL.D Univ. of Alberta 1962. *Clubs:* Edmonton, Edmonton Petroleum. *Address:* 2 Riverside Crescent, Edmonton, Alta., Canada; and The Law Courts, Edmonton, Alta., Canada.

**SMITH, Solomon Byron.** American banker. *B.* 1905. *Educ.* Yale Univ. (BA 1928). *M.* 1932, Barbara Neff. *S.* Solcmon Albert II. *Career:* With The Northern Trust Co. 1928–70; successively Assistant Cashier 1931, Second Vice-President 1933; Dir. 1937, Exec. Vice-President 1949, Vice-Chairman 1957, Chmn. Exec. Cttee. 1963–70; Dir., The Northern Trust Co.; Nortrust Corp.; U.S. Gypsum Co.; Illinois Tool Works; John Crerar Library; Trustee, Museum of Science and Industry; Treas., Glenwood School for Boys; Trustee, Rush-Presbyterian, St. Luke's Hospital; James C. King Home; Yale Univ. Art Gallery Associates; Treas. Chicago Sunday Evening Club; Protestant Foundation of Greater Chicago. Republican. *Clubs:* River Brook (N.Y.C.); Yale; University; Racquet, Chicago, Casino (Chicago): Onwentsia, Old Elm, (Lake Forrest); Shoreacres. *Address:* 255 Mayflower Road, Lake Forest, Ill. 60045; and *office* 50 South La Salle Street, Chicago, Ill. 60690, U.S.A.

**SMITH, Timothy John,** MP. British Industrialist & Politician. *B.* 1947. *Educ.* Harrow Sch.; St. Peter's Coll., Oxford—MA. *Career:* Pres., Oxford Univ. Conservative Assoc. 1968; Chmn., Coningsby Club 1977–78; MP (Cons.) for Ashfield, Notts. since 1977. *Member:* Associate, Inst. of Chartered Accountants. *Clubs:* Sutton-in-Ashfield Conservative Club; Hucknall Conservative Club. *Address:* 17 Norman Court, Lordship Lane, London SE22; and *office* 1 North Court, Great Peter Street, London SW1.

**SMITH, Hon. Mr. Justice Thomas Weetman.** Australian judge. *B.* 28 Sept. 1901. *Educ.* North Sydney Grammar School; Melbourne University; called to the Bar 1926; King's Counsel 1948; Justice, Supreme Court of Victoria 1950–73; Law Reform Commission since 1974. *Address:* 155 Queen Street, Melbourne, Australia.

**SMITH, Mrs. Turner E.** (Leila Bunce). American education publisher. *Educ.* Columbia Univ. (BS 1925; AM 1929). *M.* 1934, Turner E. Smith (*D.* 1947). *Career:* Pres. and Mgr., Turner E. Smith & Co. 1947; selected Atlanta's Woman of the Year in Business 1949; Supervisor, Home Economics, Fulton County High Schools, Atlanta 1917–34; mem., White House meeting—Child Health and Protection 1930 and 1931; Amer. Home Econ. Assn. (counsellor at large, life member); Georgia Home Econ. Assn. (pres., counsellor, life member), Georgia Dietetics Assn.; Natl. Educ. Assn. (Chmn., Dept. Home Econ.; Life Member); National League of Amer. Pen Women; American Vocational Assn. (Life Member); Georgia Vocational Assn.; Atlanta Chapter, American Red Cross (Chmn. Nutrition Vol.); Better Homes in America (State Chmn.); Georgia Parent-Teacher Assn. (Chmn. Edn.); Georgia Federation of Women's Clubs (Chmn. Edn.); Georgia Council Ch. Women; Young Matrons Circle. Tallulah Falls School (life member) Atlanta Art Assn. (life member); Ga. Textbook Publishing Assn.; Jos. Habersham Chapt., D.A.R.; Atlanta Chapt. U.D.C.; The National Society, Daughters of the American Colonies; The National Society, Magna Charta Dames; English-Speaking Union. *Clubs:* Atlanta Woman's (Life Member); Capitol City (wid. members); Mem. Bd. St. Mark Ch. *Publications:* History of Home Economics in Georgia (1933); Survey of Home Economics in Georgia (1929); A History of Fulton Co. Schools (1930); Better Nutrition Through Better School Lunches (1930); First Course in Home Making and Workbook (with Maude Calvert) (1939); History of Georgia Home Economics Association for 25th Anniversary (1944); Advanced Course in Home Making and Workbook (with Maude Calvert) (1946); cited for Service by Alabama Future Farmers of America 1955; Awarded 1961 Plaque 'In Appreciation of Outstanding Service to the Future Farmers of America'; also Georgia Future Homemakers 1955; Ga. Vocational Education Assn. (Home Economics) 1963; listed in national magazine (Fortune) as one of 3 doz. top American business women (1956). *Address:* 1428 Peachtree Street, N.E., Atlanta 09, U.S.A.

**SMITH, Victor Colston.** British insurance executive. *B.* 1899. *Educ.* Fairfield and Bristol University; Fellow, Australian Insurance Institute (FAII), Fellow, Royal Commonwealth Society (FRCS). *M.* 1924, Ivy Kathleen (Betty) Ball. *S.* 2. *Dau.* 1. *Career:* Pres., Australian Insurance Inst. 1954–55; Lieutenant, Royal Engineers 1917–18; Manager, Phoenix Assurance Co. Ltd., Leicester, England 1936–47; President, Leicester Insurance Institute 1939–41; Vice-Pres., Council of Fire & Accident Underwriters 1954–55; Chairman, Leicester Boy Scouts Assn. 1945–47; Brighton & Hove Round Table 1935–46, and Leicester Round Table 1939–45; Manager for Australia, Phoenix Assurance Co. Ltd. 1949–63; Gen. Mgr. 1949 and Chmn. Bd. 1960–68, Southern Insurance Co. of Australia Ltd.; Controller, State Emergency Service and Civil Defence Organization, City of Sydney 1966—; President, Council of Fire and Accident Underwriters Association of Australia 1956–57; Dir., Indpendent Theatre, Sydney 1964–68. *Clubs:* Pymble Golf; Imperial Services; Central Coast League; Bowers (N.S.W.); Combined Services (Sydney); Motor Yacht (Newport, N.S.W.). *Address:* 18 The Marquesas, Ocean Street, Narrabeen, N.S.W., Australia.

**SMITH, Waldo Edward.** Hydraulic engineer and geophysicist) *B.* 1900. *Educ.* Univ. of Iowa (BEng 1923 and MSc 1924. and Univ. of Illinois (work toward PhD 1927–28). *M.* 1927, Martha Althaus. *S.* David W. E. (MD). *Dau.* Martha Carol (Nance). *Career:* Engaged by consulting engineers on water supply and power, flood control, and other engineering works, chiefly hydraulic 1924–27; Instructor in Theoretical and Applied Mechanics, Univ. of Illinois 1927–28; Assoc. Prof. of Civil Engineering and Acting Head of Dept., Robert College, Istanbul 1928–31; Asst. Prof. of Civil Engineering, North Dakota State Univ. 1931–35, Hydraulic Engineer, Muskingum Watershed Conservancy District of Ohio (flood control and water conservation), 1935–39; Hydraulic Engineer, U.S. Government service (hydraulic and hydrologic works and projects) 1939–44; Executive Dir., American Geophysical Union 1944–70, Exec. Dir. Emeritus 1970–; Editor, Transactions (of A.G.U.) 1945–68; Professional Lecturer (part-time), George Washington Univ. 1946–60; Managing Editor, Geophysical Monograph Series 1956–70; Lect. and consultant geophysical and environmental problems since 1970. Honours: Fellow, Univ. of Iowa 1923–24; Tau Beta Pi; Sigma Xi; Sigma Tau; U.S. Delegate, VIII–XVI General Assemblies of the International Union of Geodesy and Geophysics; Delegate to The Ocean World, Tokyo 1970, and other international science congresses and gatherings in Honolulu, Mexico City, Madrid, Heidelberg & elsewhere. *Member:* Amer. Geophysical Union (Fellow); Amer. Assn. for Advancement of Science (Fellow); Amer. Socy. of Civil Engineers (Fellow; Past Pres. National Capital Section; National Dir., 1961–64). *Publications:* scientific and technological papers in various journals, including: Some Observations on Water Levels and Other Phenomena along the Bosporus (1946); The Hydraulic Behaviour of Agricultural Watersheds (1944); Byzantine Aqueduct Still in Use; Resources and Long-Range Forecasts (1973). *Club:* Cosmos (Washington). *Address:* 3907 Jocelyn Street, N.W., Washington 20015, U.S.A.

**SMITH, Wilfred Cantwell.** Canadian. *B.* 1916. *Educ.* Toronto Univ. (BA) and Princeton (MA, PhD); Westminster College, Cambridge (Theology); DD(hon.) McGill and United Theological College. *M.* 1939, Muriel McKenzie Struthers. *S.* 3. *Daus.* 2. *Career:* Lecturer in Indian & Islamic history, Forman Christian Coll., Lahore 1941–45; Prof. of Comparative Religion, McGill Univ. 1949–63; Dir., Inst. of Islamic Studies, McGill 1951–63; Professor of World Religions 1964–73, and Director, Center for the Study of World Religions 1964–73, Harvard University. Advisory Editor: Muslim World (Hartford), The Middle East Journal (Washington), Religious Studies (Cambridge), Studies in Religion (Toronto), Dionysius (Halifax), Fellow Royal Society of Canada, Pres. Humanities & Social Sciences Section 1972–73; Fellow of Amer. Acad. of Arts and Sciences; President: American Society for the Study of Religion (1966–69); McCulloch Professor of Religion, Chmn. Dept. Religion, Dalhousie University. *Publications:* Meaning and End of Religion (1963); The Faith of Other Men (1962–1972 also in Swedish); Islam in Modern History (1957 also in German, French, Swedish, Indonesian, Japanese and Arabic), Modern Islam In India (1943, 1947, 1964, 1972); Modernisation of a Traditional Society (1966); Questions of Religious Truth (also in Japanese) (1967); Religious Diversity (1976); Belief & History (1977). *Address:* Dalhousie University, Halifax, N.S., Canada.

**SMITH, William Reece, Jr.** American. Lawyer. *B.* 1925. *Educ.* University of S. Carolina (BS 1946). University of Florida (JD with high honours 1949) and Oxford University, England (Rhodes Scholar); Univ. South Florida. LL.D(Hon.). *M.* 1963, Marlene Medina. *S.* William Reece III,

*Career:* Chmn., Carlton, Fields, Ward, Emmanuel Fields & Ward, Attorneys; Interim Pres., University of South Florida 1976–77; City Attorney, Tampa, Florida 1963–72; Secretary, American Bar Association 1967–71; Pres., American Bar Endowment 1976–78; Past President, The Florida Bar, The Florida Bar Foundation, Florida Legal Services Inc., Florida Gulf Coast Symphony; Bar Association of Hillsborough County. Member, House of Delegates, Amer. Bar Assn. Fellow, American Law Institute, American College of Trial Lawyers, International Academy of Trial Lawyers. Hons.: Junior Chamber of Commerce Award as Outstanding Young Man of Tampa 1960; Fla. Jaycee Award for Outstanding Service in Field of Good Government 1965; Fla. Young Lawyers Award as Most Outstanding Past Member 1965; Phi Kappa Phi; Omicron Delta Kappa; Fla. Blue Key; Sigma Alpha Epsilon. *Clubs:* Ye Mystic Krewe of Gasparville; University; Yacht & Country (all of Tampa). *Address:* 11 Ladoga, Tampa, Fla.; and *office* 20th Floor, Exchange Bank Tower, Tampa, Fla., U.S.A.

**SMITHERS, Robert Brinkley.** American. *B.* 1907. *Educ.* Johns Hopkins Univ. *M.* 1930 Gertrude Finucane. *S.* Francis Christopher. *Dau.* Marian (Moore). *Career:* President, Christopher D. Smithers Foundation 1952—. Vice-Pres. and Administrator, and its representative to U.N., International Council on Alcohol and Alcoholism 1964—. Member N.Y. State Adv. Council on Alcoholism 1962–72; Treas. 1955–58, Pres. 1958–62, and Chmn. 1962–64, National Council on Alcoholism; Vice-Pres., Risitigouche Salmon Club; Vice-Chmn. Adv. Council, Alcoholism to Health Services Admin. New York City; Sec.-Treas., The E.M. Jellinek Memorial Fund, Inc.; Member Emeritus, Community Council of Greater New York. *Publications:* Pamphlets of the Smithers Foundation, Alcoholism in Industry; Arresting Alcoholism; Experimentation; Alcoholism Complex; Basic Outline for Company Program; Understanding Alcoholism and 'The Key Role of Labor in Employee Alcoholism Programs' (Scribner's). Hon. LL.D Rutgers Univ. 1964. *Clubs:* Racquet & Tennis (N.Y.C.); Ristigouche Salmon; Piping Rock, Creek (Locust Valley). *Address: office* Box 67, Mill Neck, N.Y. 11765, U.S.A.

**SMYTHE, Hugh H.** American educationalist & diplomat. *Educ.* Virginia State College (BA, 1936); Atlanta University (MA); Fisk University of Chicago; North-western University (PhD); Woodstock School, Vermont; Columbia University. *M.* Mabel Hancock Murphy. *Dau.* Karen Pamela. *Career:* Researcher, American Youth Commission of American Council on Education, 1937–38; Research Assistant, Fisk Univ., 1938–39; Research Associate, Atlanta Univ., 1942; U.S. Army, 1942–44; Professor of Sociology: Morris Brown Univ., Atlanta, 1944–45; Tennessee State Agricultural & Industrial Univ., 1945–46; Deputy Director, Special Research, National Association for Advancement of Coloured People, New York, 1947–49; Director of Research, W. B. Graham & Associates, New York, 1949–50; Visiting Professor of Sociology & Anthropology, Yamaguchi National Univ., Japan, 1951–53; Professor of Sociology, Brooklyn College, City Univ., New York, since 1953; on leave special assignments; Director of Research, New York State Senate Finance Cttee., 1956; Senior Adviser, Economic & Social Affairs, U.S. Mission to United Nations, 1961–62; Special lecturer, Foreign Service Institute, U.S. Dept. of State, 1960–65; Senior Adviser, Economic & Social Affairs, U.S. Mission to the United Nations, member many delegations to sessions of the UN, 1961, 1962; Senior Adv. National Research Council of Thailand, Fulbright Professor at Chulalongkorn Univ., Bangkok 1963–64; U.N. Correspondent, Eastern World Trade & Development 1964—; Lect. Special Forces, U.S. Army North Carolina 1964; Chief Consultant, Youth in Action, Poverty Program N.Y. 1965; White House Conference, Race Relations 1966; Ambassador to Malta, 1967–69, Special Lect. Armed Forces Staff Coll. 1969–70; Examiner on Panels Bd. of Examiners N.Y. City Bd. of Educ. 1970–71, 1972–74. Special Lect. Foreign Service Inst. U.S. Dept. of State since 1970. Ambassador to Syrian Arab Republic, 1965–67; Consultant to Ford Foundation, Phelps Stokes Fund. U.S. Office, Education. Fellow: African Studies Assoc.; Society of Applied Anthropology; American Anthropological Assn. *Member:* Eastern Sociological Socy.; Assn. of Asian Studies; Japan Socy.; American Assn. of Teachers of Chinese Language & Culture; Institute of Race Relations (Great Britain); Siam Socy.; American Assn. of University Professors; Middle East Inst.; The Atlantic Council; Washington Task Force on Africa; Freedom House; Common Cause; Malta-U.S. Alumini Assn.; Professional Staff Congress, City Univ. of New York; American Cttee. on Africa; etc. Bd. memberships include: Near East Foundn.; United Service Org.; African Student Aid Fund; Museum of African Art (Washington, D.C.); UN Assn. of the U.S.A.; Trustee, Luther Coll. (Iowa); Ralph Bunche Fellowship Sel. Cttee. of UNA, U.S.A. *Publications:* (with L. Crow W. & Murray) Educating the Culturally Disadvantaged Child (1966); (with M. M. Smythe) New Nigerian Elite (1960); (with W. E. B. Dubois) Negro Land Grant Colleges Social Studies Project (1944). Member, Editorial Board: Journal of Human Relations, 1954—; Africa Today 1955—. *Awards:* Recipient of many Scholarships & Academic awards, most recently; LLD Virginia State Coll. 1968; Distinguished Alumnus & Citation for Distinguished Service to International & Public Affairs, Atlanta Univ. 1972; Guest Fellow Member, Columbia Univ. Seminars 1974–76; Phelps-Stokes Fund Visiting Scholar 1975. Mem., Sixma Xi, Sigma Lambda, Alpha Kappa Delta, Alpha Pi Zeta. Knight of the Grand Cross of the Royal Crown of Crete 1968; Knight of the Grand Cross of the Sovereign Military Order of Saint Agath 1969. *Address:* 345 8th Avenue, New York 10001, U.S.A.

**SNEATH, William S.** Chairman of the Board, Union Carbide Corporation. *Address:* Union Carbide Corp., 270 Park Avenue, New York, N.Y. 10017, U.S.A.

**SNEDDEN, Rt. Hon. Sir Billy Mackie,** QC, MP. Australian. *B.* 1926. *Educ.* LLB. *M.* 1950, Joy Forsyth. *S.* 2. *Daus.* 2. *Career:* Barrister, Supreme Ct. W.A. 1951, Supreme Ct. Victoria 1955; Australian Govt. Attorney-Gen. 1963–66; Minister for Immigration 1966–69; Leader of the House 1966–71; Minister for Labour & National Service 1969–71; Treas. Commonwealth of Australia 1971–72; Party Leader and Leader of Opposition 1972–75; Speaker of House of Reps. since 1976. Federal Member of Parliament for Bruce (Vic.) since 1955. *Awards:* KCMG 1978. *Clubs:* Melbourne Scots. (Councillor); Naval and Military (Melbourne). *Address:* 22 Pine Crescent, Ringwood, Vic. 3134, Australia.

**SNELL, Foster Dee,** PhD, ScD. American. Chairman: Emeritus, Foster D. Snell, Inc. (Consulting Chemists—Engineers), New York City 1966—. *B.* 1898. *Educ.* Colgate Univ. (BS 1919), and Columbia Univ. (AM 1922, PhD 1923). *M.* 1921, Cornelia A. Tyler. *Dau.* 1. *Career:* Licensed Chemical Engineer in the State of New York. Consulting Chemist and chemical engineer 1919—. Asst. Chemistry Instructor, Columbia Univ. 1919–20; Instructor, Coll. of the City of New York 1920–23; in charge Technical Chemistry, Pratt Institute, 1923–28; Pres. Foster D. Snell Inc. 1931–66. Holds high offices in many scientific organizations. *Awards:* Life Fellow of the Chemical Socy. of London, and Royal Socy. of Arts (London), and Fellow of Amer. Assn. for Advancement of Science, and of Amer. Inst. of Chemists. Honours: Sigma Xi; Phi Lambda Upsilon; Alpha Chi Sigma (Pure Science Award Cttee.; Chmn. 1946–62); Phi Beta Kappa (Alumnus Member); DuPont Fellow (Colgate Univ. 1919); Gold Medal of Socy. of Chemical Industry (England 1949); Honor Scroll of Amer. Inst. of Chemists (N.Y. Chapter 1952); Acceptance Address published in the Congressional Record; Hon. ScD, Colgate; Alumni Medal, Columbia Univ. 1964; Chemical Pioneer Award, Amer. Inst. of Chemists, 1970; John F. Kenblar award, Alpha Chi Sigma 1971. *Publications:* about 200 published articles, 20 books, and 50 patents. *Address:* 860 U.N. Plaza, New York, N.Y. 10017; and *office* 245 Park Avenue, New York, N.Y. 10017, U.S.A.

**SNELLING, Sir Arthur Wendell,** KCMG, KCVO. *B.* 1914. *Educ.* University College, London (BSc Econ). *M.* 1939. Frieda Barnes. *S.* 1. *Career:* British High Commissioner in Ghana 1959–61. Deputy Under-Secretary of State, Commonwealth Office, London, S.W.1, 1962–69; British Ambassador to South Africa 1970–72; Dir. Gordon & Gotch Holdings Ltd. *Club:* Reform. *Address:* 19 Albany Park Road, Kingston-upon-Thames, Surrey KT2 5SW.

**SNELLING, Harold Alfred Rush,** CBE, LLB. QC. Australian Barrister. *B.* 1904. *Educ.* Fort Street High School and Sydney University (LLB). *M.* 1932, Ruth Neilley. *Daus.* Carole (Wise), Julia (Crawford) and Priscilla (Flemming). *Career:* Admitted Solicitor 1927; Admtd. Bar 1933; QC 1952. AIF 1942–45; Asst. Dir. Ordnance Services 1944, Lieut.-Col.; Snr. Vice-Pres., Australian Branch, International Law Assn. and Correspondent for United Nations on Prevention of Crime and Treatment of Offenders; Solicitor General for the State of New South Wales 1953–74. Vice Pres. Australian Academy of Forensic Sciences. *Club:* Sydney (Vice-Pres.). *Address:* 32 The Crescent, Vaucluse, N.S.W. 2030, Australia.

**SNITOW, Charles.** American. *B.* 1907. *Educ.* Cornell Univ. (AB, LLB, Doctor of Laws). *M.* Virginia. *S.* 1. *Dau.* 1. *Career:* Pres. Charles Snitow Organization Inc.; Exhibition Publications Inc.; Exhibition Suppliers Inc.; Fair Management Corp.; International Photography Fair; National Fancy Food & Confection Show; Consumer Electronics Management Inc.; National Hardware Show; United States World Trade Fair Corp. *Member:* Phi Beta Kappa; Alpha Kappa Delta; Dir. Bill of Rights Foundation; Colonel Commonwealth of Kentucky. *Awards:* Knight Order of Merit Republic of Italy. *Address:* 81 Walworth Avenue, Scarsdale, N.Y. 10583, U.S.A.; and *office* 331 Madison Avenue, New York, N.Y. 10017, U.S.A.

**SNYDER, Hon. John Wesley.** American financier and banker. *B.* 1895. *Educ.* Jonesboro Schools and Vanderbilt Univ. *M.* 1920, Evelyn Cook (*D.*). *Dau.* Edith Cook (Horton). *Career:* Banker in Arkansas and Missouri 1919–30; Bank Receiver & Conservator, Office of Comptroller of the Currency, St. Louis 1931–37; Mgr., St. Louis Loan Agency of the R.F.C. 1937–43; Exec. Vice-Pres. and Dir., Defense Plant Corp. Washington 1940–43; Asst. to Bd. of Dirs. of R.F.C. 1940–44; Vice-Pres., First Natl. Bank of St. Louis, Mo. 1943–45; Fed. Loan Admintr. 1945; Dir., Office of War Mobilisation and Reconversion 1945; Sec. of Treasury 1946–53; Chmn., Natl. Advisory Council on International Monetary and Financial Problems 1946–53; U.S. Governor of International Monetary Fund and International Bank for Reconstruction 1946–53; Snr. U.S. Financial representative in administration of Anglo-American Financial Agreement 1946, financial rehabilitation programme for the Philippines 1946, interim assistance programme for France, Italy and Austria 1947 U.S. aid programme for Turkey and Greece 1947, financial reconstruction activities in Germany 1948, and Japan 1949–50, and Marshall Plan operations 1948; instrumental in working out U.S.-Mexican currency stabilisation agreements 1947–49; member of presidential invitation U.S. National Security Council 1951–52; member N.A.T.O. Council 1949–53; delegate to International Financial Conferences: Mexico City 1945–52, Rio de Janeiro 1947, London 1947, Paris 1950–52, Ottawa 1951, Rome 1951, Lisbon 1952, Washington. Served in World War I (Capt. Field Artillery, 57th Brig.; retired Colonel 1955); Dir. and member Exec. Cttee. of Overland Investment Corp. Toledo, Ohio. *Member:* Omicron Delta Kappa, Alpha Tau Omega, American Legion, Reserve Officers' Assn. (past Pres. Missouri Dept.); Former Pres. Rotary Club, Toledo, Ohio, 1966–67. *Address:* 8109 Kerry Lane, Chevy Chase, Md. 20015, U.S.A.

**SNYDER, William Cordes, Jr.** American company executive. *B.* 1903. *Educ.* Lehigh University (Class of 1926). *M.* 1932, Virginia Harper. *S.* William Cordes III. *Dau.* Virginia (McGraw). *Career:* In charge Chemical Lab., Wheeling Mold & Foundry Co. 1923–27; Metallurgist, Lewis Foundry & Machine Div. of Blaw-Knox 1927–34 (Vice-Pres. and Gen. Mgr. 1934–45); Pres., Continental Foundry & Machine Co. 1945–46; Vice-Pres. i/c Engineering Construction of Koppers Co. 1947–51 (i/c of steel plant construction for Compania de Acero del Pacifico at Santiago, Chile); Pres. and Chief Exec. Officer, Blaw-Knox, Nov. 1951; elected Chmn. of Bd., Pres. and Chief Exec. Officer Dec. 1958–June 1963: relinquished Presidency but remains Chmn. Officer. *Awards:* Horatio Alger Award April 1956; Hon. DEng. Lehigh University June 1963. *Member:* American Iron & Steel Inst.; American Inst. Mining & Metallurgical Engineers; Assn. Iron & Steel Engineers; Engineers' Socy. of W. Pa.; American Ordnance Assn. Republican. *Clubs:* Duquesne; Allegheny Country: Union League; Pinnacle; Rolling Rock; and Carlton, Metropolitan (Washington, D.C.); Pine Valley Golf; Laurel Valley Golf. *Address:* Pine Road, Sewickley, Pa. 15143; and *office* One Oliver Plaza, Pittsburgh, Pa. 15222, U.S.A.

**SOAMES, The Rt. Hon. Sir (Arthur) Christopher (John),** GCMG, GCVO, CBE. *B.* 1920. *Educ.* Eton and R.M.C. Sandhurst. *M.* 1947, Mary Churchill. *S.* 3. *Daus.* 2. *Career:* 2nd Lieut. Coldstream Guards 1939, Capt. 1942; served in World War II (Middle East, Italy and France); Asst. Military Attaché British Embassy, Paris 1946–47; MP (Con.) Bedford Div. of Bedfordshire 1950–66; Parliamentary Private Secy. to the Prime Minister 1952–55; Parliamentary Under-Secretary of State, Air Ministry 1955–57; Parly. and Financial Secy., Admiralty 1957–58; Secretary of State for War 1958–60. Minister of Agriculture, July 1960–64; Dir. Decca Ltd. 1964–68; James Hole & Co. Ltd. 1964–68. Ambassador to France. September 1968–72; Member, Vice Pres. Commission of the European Communities 1973–77; non-exec. Dir., N. M. Rothschild & Sons since 1977. *Awards:* Croix de Guerre (France) 1942; Grand Officier de la Legion d'Honneur 1972; Hon. LLD, St. Andrews 1974; Grand Cross of St. Olav 1974. *Clubs:* White's; Portland. *Address:* c/o White's Club, St. James's Street, London SW1.

**SOARES, Dr. Mário.** Portuguese politician. *B.* 1924. *Educ.* Degrees in History & Philosophy & Law. *M.* 1949, Maria Barroso. *S.* 1. *Dau.* 1. *Career:* Took part in the Movement of Antifascist National Unity (MUNAF) & the Young People's Democratic Unity Movement (MUDJ); mem., Central Cttee. of the Democratic Unity Movement (MUD) 1946–48; law practice in Lisbon; co-founder, Portuguese Socialist Action movement (ASP) 1964 (transformed into the Socialist Party 1973); Democratic Opposition candidate for National Assembly, Lisbon 1965 & Electoral Cttee. of Democratic Unitv (CEUD) candidate, Lisbon 1969; arrested 12 times, deported once, finally exiled in Paris 1970–74, teaching at the Univ. of Paris (Vincennes & Sorbonne) & the Faculty of Arts of Haute Bretagne (Rennes); returned to Portugal after coup & reorganised Socialist Party, Sec.-Gen. since 1973; Minister of Foreign Affairs 1974–75, negotiating agreements with the PAIGC & FRELIMO guaranteeing recognition of independence of Guinea-Bissau & Mozambique; Minister without Portfolio March–Aug. 1975; Prime Minister since July 1976. Member, Portuguese Assn. of Writers. *Address:* Serviço do Primer Ministro, Largo das Cortes, Lisbon 2, Portugal.

**SOBHI, Mohamed Ibrahim.** Egyptian International Civil Servant. *B.* 1925. *Educ.* Cairo Univ.—Bachelor of Engineering; Vanderbilt Univ., Nashville. *M.* 1950, Laila Ahmed. *S.* 2. *Dau.* 1. *Career:* Engineer Corps, Road & Airport Construction 1950; Tech. Sec. on Communications Commission, Perm. Council for Development & National Production 1954; one-year Fellowship Studying Transport & Communications Services, Vanderbilt Univ., Nashville, Tenn. 1955–56; Tech. Dir., Office of Min. of Communications for Posts, Railways & Coordination between means of Transport & Communications 1956–61; attended UPU Congress, Ottawa 1957; attended UPU CCPS session, Brussels 1958; Dir.-Gen. of Sea Transport Authority, while remaining Mem. of Tech. Cttees. of the Postal Organization, Egypt 1961–64; Under Sec. of State for Communications & Mem. of Board of the Postal Org., Egypt 1964–68; Chmn. of Board, Postal Org. of Egypt & Sec.-Gen. of African Postal Union 1968–74; attended, as Head of Egyptian delegation, the UPU Tokyo & Lausanne Congresses & the sessions of the CCPS set up by the former Congress, 1969–74; Dir. of Exec. Bureau in charge of Egyptian projects in Africa 1963–74; Dir. Gen., International Bureau of the Universal Postal Union, Berne since 1975. *Decorations:* Order of Merit, 1st class, of Egypt (1974). *Address:* Jupiterstr. 29, CH-3015 Berne, Switzerland; & *office* Weltpoststrasse 4, CH-3000 Berne 15, Switzerland.

**SODAY, Frank John.** American chemist and chemical engineer. *B.* 1908. *Educ.* Grove City Coll., (BSChE 1929); Ohio State Univ. (M.S. 1930; PhD 1932); (Hon. SD Grove City Coll. 1955). *M.* 1932, Myrtle Rose Fry. *Career:* Group Leader, Penn. Grade Crude Oil Assn. 1933–34; Senior Group Leader, Research Laboratories, Monsanto Chemical Co. 1934–37; Asst. Laboratory Manager, United Gas Improvement Co. 1937–42; Technical Dir., Copolymer Corp. 1943–46; Director of Research & Development, Devoe & Raymonds 1946–47; Director, Research Division, Lion Oil Co. 1947–51; Vice-President, Research & Development, Chemstrand Corp. 1951–58; Vice-President, Research & Development, Liquid Carbonic Division, General Dynamics Corp. 1959—; Pres., Industrial Development Research Council 1961—; Vice-Pres., Chemicals, Skelly Oil Co. 1961—; Pres., Sesa Inter-american S.A. (Panama) 1974—, Sesa Homes S.A. (Panama) 1977—. Director: Chembond Corp. 1965—, Yong-Nam Chemical Co. Ltd. (Korea) 1965—, Chemplex Co. 1966—, Vancouver Plywood Co. 1966—; Tongsun Petro-Chemical Corp. Ltd. (Korea) 1968—; Chembond, British Columbia since 1968. Pres., Soday Research Fdn.; Trustee, Midwest Research Institute, Kansas City, 1963—. *Award:* Herty Medal 1955. Republican. *Member:* American Chemical Socy. (Councillor); American Inst. of Chemical Engineers (Chmn. Baton Rouge Sect.); Alabama, N.Y. and Illinois Academies of Science; Southern Assn. of Science & Industry (Pres. 1954–57; Chmn. 1957–59); some 180 archaeological and anthropological societies. *Publications:* 150, on chemicals, fibres, rubber, plastics, southern developments, archaeology, anthropology; 125 U.S. Patents. *Clubs:* Explorers; Decatur Country; Decatur Yacht; Decatur Rotary. *Address:* 5709 E. 61st Court, Tulsa, Okla.; and *office* Oil Center Building, Tulsa, Okla., U.S.A.

**SÖDER, Karin Anne-Marie.** Swedish Politician. *B.* 1928. *M.* 1952, Gunnar Söder. 3 Children. *Career:* Mem., Communal Council of Täby 1963—; County Council of Stockholm Region 1969—; Mem. of Swedish Parliament since 1971; Second Vice-Pres., Center Party since 1971; Minister of Foreign Affairs since 1976. *Address:* Riksdagshuset, 100 12 Stockholm 46, Sweden.

**SODERHJELM, Johan Otto.** Finnish industrialist. *B.* 3 Sept. 1898. *Educ.* University of Helsinki (LLD). *M.* (1) 1922, Anna Brigitta Ehrensvärd (*D.* 1956). *S.* Johan Ulrik. *Daus.* Mary Brigitta, Sigrid Annie Olivia. (2) 1958, Helvi Maria Leppaluoto (*D.* 1970). *Career:* Partner, Serlachius & Ryti 1928–40; 'Ombudsman', of Finnish Diet 1929–30; MP (Swedish People's Party) 1933–39, 1944–51 and 1962–66. Minister of Justice 1939–40, 1957, 1958, 1962–63 and 1964–66. General Manager, Central Assn. of Finnish Woodworking Industries 1940–60; member, Govt. Foreign Trade Agreement Commn. 1940–64; member, Government Econ. Adv. Commission 1951–58; Diet-appointed Supervisor, Bank of Finland 1945–62; Chairman and Director of various companies. Commander 1st Class. Order of White Rose of Finland; Grand Cross Order of North Star (Sweden); Grand Order of Dannebrog (Denmark). *Publication:* Demilitarisation et Neutralisation des Iles d'Aland en 1856 et 1921. *Address:* O. Brunnsparken 11, Helsinki, Finland.

**SODERLUND, Gustaf.** Swedish banker. *B.* 20 Jan. 1890. *Educ.* University of Upsala (LLB); Stockholm School of Commerce. *M.* 1917, Elvan Johanna Andersson. *S.* Hans Gustaf Ulf. *Dau.* Ylva Ingrid. *Career:* Under-Secy. of State. Finance Dept. 1924; Civic Director of Finance, Stockholm 1926; Managing Director, Confederation of Swedish Employers 1931, Chairman 1943; Chairman and Managing Director, State Industrial Commission 1939; General Manager, Skandinaviska Banken 1946–57; Chairman 1957–61; Chairman, The Swedish Cellulose Association, 1958–68. Knight Commander, Grand Cross, Order of North Star; Knight Commander, Order of Vasa, Order of White Rose of Finland; Grand Officer, Ordre de la Couronne (Belgium); Cross of Liberty 1st Class (Finland); Grande Ufficiale dell'Ordine 'Al Marito della Repubblica Italiana'. Hon MD, 1960. *Address:* Kungsholmstorg Stockholm, Sweden.

**SODERSTROM, Olof Anders Viktor.** Swedish. *B.* 1903. *Educ.* BA, LLB. *M.* 1930, Karin Nyström. *S.* Sverker, Göran and Peter. *Daus.* Margareta, Katarina and Anna Maria. *Career:* Deputy Judge, Svea Court of Appeal 1931–36; Assoc. Judge of Appeal 1936–43; Judge of Appeal 1943–50. Expert, Ministry of Agric. 1936–39; Head, juridical section, State Food Commission 1939–44; Vice-Chmn. 1945; Chmn. 1946–50; Dir.-Gen. Head Swedish Agric. Marketing Board 1950–57; Chmn. AB Statsgruvor (State Mining Co.) 1951–65, and AB Sara 1954–58. Bd. Member, Swedish Tourist Traffic Assn. 1961–63; Managing Director, Swedish Tobacco Co., Stockholm 1957–70; Chairman: Djupfrysningskommittén (Deep Freezing Committee) 1953–75; Swedish Tobacco Co. Medical Advisory Board 1957–70; Sveriges Kreditbank 1958–74; Swedish Hotesl & Restaurants Assn. 1960–76; Uddevalla Shipyard 1963–71; AB Naringslivets Planinstitut (Swedish Inst. for Planning of Industry & Commerce) 1964–75; Stiftelsen Svensk Konserveringsforskning (Fdn. for Food Preservation Research) 1970–75; ICL Data AB, Sverige (International Computers) 1970–74; Uddcomb Sweden AB 1973–77; Steam Generators Sweden AB 1973–77; Kalmar Verkstads AB since 1973. Member of the Board: Wenner-Gren Center 1959–77, Chmn. 1977; National Office for Administrative Rationalization & Economy 1961–69; AB Findus 1962–74; Postbanken Swedish Post Office Bank 1970–74; Postverksstyrelsen (Swedish Post Office Administration) 1970–74: AB Pripps Bryggerier (Breweries) 1975–77. Chmn. of several government inquiry committees; delegate in a number of trade negotiations and international conferences, Chairman Malmfonden (Fdn. for Technical Research Development) 1961–68; Inst. for Utilization of Research Results 1965–68. Kt. Grand Cross, Order Polar Star; Kt. Cmdr.; Vasa, Greek Phoenic, and Colombian Boyaca. *Member:* Royal Swedish Acad. of Agric. & Forestry 1946—; Finnish and Greek Red Cross Orders of Merit. Delegate, Stockholm Chamber of Commerce. *Publications:* Several Govt. official reports; articles in various agricultural and economic journals. *Address:* 54 Norr Mälarstrand, S-112 20 Stockholm; and *office* P.O. Box 17007 6 Maria Bangata, S-104 62 Stockholm, Sweden.

**SOEHARTO, General.** President of the Republic of Indonesia. *B.* 1921. *Educ.* Army Staff College. *M.* 1947, Siti Hartinah. *S.* 3. *Daus.* 3. *Career:* Deputy Chief of Staff of the Army (Brigadier General), 1960; Major General, Comm. East Indonesian Terr., 1962, Commander of the Army Strategic Command, 1963: Cabinet Minister, Commander of the Army, 1965; Deputy Prime Minister for Defence & Security, 1966; Lieutenant General of the Army, February 1966; Chairman Presidium of the Cabinet, Presidium Minister for Defence and Security, Commander in Chief of the Army, July 1966; Acting President of the Republic of Indonesia, March 1967; Pres. since 1968. *Awards:* from Yugoslavia, Japan, Philippines, Cambodia, Malaysia, Thailand, thd Netherlands and West Germany. *Club:* Djakarta Golf Club. *Address:* Djalan Tjendana 8, Djakarta, Indonesia; and *office* Merdeka Palace, Djakarta, Indonesia.

**SOHL, Hans Günther,** Dr-Ing. E.h. German. *B.* 1906. *Educ.* Qualified Engineer (Mining). *M.* 1938, Annelis Freiin von Wrede. *S.* 1. *Dau.* 1. *Career:* Chmn. Supervisory Bd.: THYSSEN AKTIENGESELLSCHAFT vorm. August Thyssen-Hütte, Allianz Versicherungs-AG. Supervisory Bd.: Dresdner Bank AG; Rheinishe-Westfälisches Elektrizitätswerk AG; Thyssen Industrie AG; Thyssen Edelstahlwerke AG; Thyssen Handelsunion AG; Vice-Pres., Bundesverband der Deutschen Industrie. *Publications:* various publications. Honorary Member: British and American Iron & Steel Institutes, International Iron & Steel Inst., The Metals Socy., London. *Club:* Rotary (Duisburg). *Address:* Am Gartenkamp 12, 4000 Düsseldorf-Gerresheim; and *office* THYSSEN AKTIENGESELLSCHAFT vorm. August Thyssen-Hütte AG, Postfach 8006, 4000Düsseldorf, Germany.

**SOKORAC, Aleksandar.** Yugoslavian Diplomat. *B.* 1923. *Educ.* Higher School for Political Studies. *Married. Children:* 2. *Career:* Participated in National Liberation War 1942–45; one of the editors of Daily Newspapers 'Narodni List', 'Vjesnik' & 'Borba' 1945–49; Counsellor at Yugoslavian Embassy, London 1949–53; Counsellor, Federal Secretariat for Foreign Affairs, Belgrade 1953–55; Head of Press Div., Secretariat for Information at the Federal Exec. Council 1956–58; Sec. International Dept. of the Socialist Alliance of the Working People of Yugloslavia 1958–60; Chargé d'Affaires, Yugoslavian Embassy, Peking 1960–63; First Asst. Head, later Head of the Office of Mr. E. Kardelj, Member of the Presidency of the SFR of Yugoslavia 1963–72; Head of Office of the President 1973–76; Ambassador to Australia since 1976. *Address:* Embassy of the SFR of Yugoslavia, 11 Nuyts Street, ACT, Australia.

**SOLANDT, Omond McKillop,** CC, OBE, MD, DSc, MA LLD, DEng, FRCP, FRSC, FAAAS. Canadian. *B.* 1909, *Educ.* Toronto (BA 1931; MA 1933; MD 1939); Cambridge (MA 1939). *M.* 1941, Elizabeth McPhedran. (D. 1971). *S,* Andrew. *Daus.* Sigrid and Katharine. *M.* 1972, Vaire Pringle. *Career:* Dir. S.W. London Blood Depot 1939–41; Army Operation Research Group 1941–46; Chmn. Defence Research Bd., Canada 1946–56; Vice-Pres. Research and Development, Canadian National Railways 1956–63; formerly Director of EXPO '67; Former Chairman, Science Council of Canada; Dir., Huyck Corp., Wake Forest N.C. Trustee, International Center for Agricultural Research in Dry Areas —Syria & Iran 1976; Trustee, Cimmyt (Centro Internacional de Mejoramiento de Maiz y Trigo-Internation Maize & Wheat Improvement Center) 1976; Trustee, ICIPE (International Centre of Insect Physiology & Ecology) 1977. *Awards:* DSc Univ. of British Columbia, Laval Univ., Univ. of Manitoba, McGill, St. Francis Xavier, Montreal, R.M.C. Canada. LLD: Sir George Williams, Dalhousie, Saskatchewan, and Univ. of Toronto; DEng, Waterloo. U.S. Medal of Freedom with Bronze Palm 1947; Gold Medal, Professional Institute of Canada 1956; Civic Award of Merit, City of Toronto; Companion of the Order of Canada. Honorary Member Engineering Institute of Canada. Former President: Canadian Operation Research Socy. Vice-Pres. American Management Association. *Member* and former President Royal Canadian Geographical Society. *Clubs:* The Rideau (Ottawa); The Athenaeum (London, Eng.). *Address:* RR 1, Bolton, Ont., Canada LOP 1AO.

**SOLDATOV, Aleksandr Alekseyevich.** Soviet Diplomat. Awarded the Order of Labour Red Banner (1965). *B.* 1915. *Educ.* Moscow Teachers' Training Institute. Graduated in Hist. Sciences 1939, Candidate of Science (History). *M. Daus.* 2. *Career:* Entered Soviet Foreign Office 1941; Counsellor of the U.S.S.R. Mission to the Commonwealth of Australia 1944–46; Senior Counsellor, Soviet Delegation to U.N. and Representative at the Trusteeship Council 1948–53; Head of U.N. Div. 1953–54 and American Div. 1954–59 in Soviet Foreign Office. Member, Soviet Delegation to Geneva Conferences on Germany (1959) and Laos (1961). Ambassador of the U.S.S.R. to the Court of St. James's 1960–66; Dep.-Minister for Foreign Affairs of the U.S.S.R. 1966–68; Mem., CPSU Central Auditing Commn. 1966–71;

Ambassador to Cuba 1963–70; Rector, Moscow State Inst. of International Relations since 1970. *Address:* Ul. Metrostroevskaya 53, Moscow, U.S.S.R.

**SOLE, Donald Bell.** South African Diplomat. *B.* 1917. *Educ.* Kingswood Coll., Rhodes Univ., Grahamstown, South Africa. *M.* 1950, Elizabeth Dorothy Wookey. *S.* 3. *Dau.* 1. *Career:* Joined South African Foreign Service 1938; S.A. Perm. Rep. to the UN 1956–57; Chmn. of Bd. of Govs., Int. Atomic Energy Agency 1959–60; Minister, S.A. Embassy, Vienna 1958–61; Under-Sec., subsequently Dep. Sec., Dept. of Foreign Affairs 1962–68; S.A. Ambassador, Bonn; currently S.A. Ambassador, Washington, D.C. *Decorations:* Grand Cross First Class, Order of Merit of the Federal Republic of Germany. *Address:* Embassy of the Republic of South Africa, 3051 Massachusetts Avenue, N.W., Washington, D.C. 20008, U.S.A.

**SOLOMON, George Charles.** Canadian. *B.* 1913. *M.* 1932, Doris Ilene Dean. *Daus.* Sharon, Vaughn, Adrian. *Career:* President; Western Ltd. Director: Bank of Montreal; Canadian Hydrocarbons Ltd.: International Paints (Canada) Ltd.; Carling O'Keefe Ltd.; Ocelot Industries Ltd. *Member:* CKCK Children's Fund; The Canadian Council, Christians and Jews; The Salvation Army; Chamber of Commerce; United Church of Canada. *Club:* Assiniboia. *Address:* 2600 19th Avenue, Regina, Sask.; and *office* Western Tractor Ltd. P.O. Box 1730, Regina, Sask., Canada.

**SOLOMON. Dr. Patrick Vincent Joseph.** High Commissioner for Trinidad and Tobago in London 1971–77, also Ambassador to Switzerland, France, Germany, Austria, Luxembourg, Finland. Denmark, Norway, Sweden, Italy & Netherlands. *Address:* c/o Ministry of External Affairs, Port of Spain, Trinidad & Tobago.

**SOLOMON, Samuel Joseph.** American aviation and insurance executive. *B.* 1899. *Educ.* George Washington Univ. (LLB). *M.* 1923, Alma Marie Garber. *S.* Robert Franklin, Richard Joseph, William Samuel. *Career:* Dir. Avemco and subsidiary Avemco Insur. Co. Jan. 1960—, American Mercury Ins. Co., and Life Insurance Securities Corp., Washington Baltimore Helicopter Airways; Manager, Washington National Airport 1933–41; Vice-President, National Airport Corp. 1932–33; Vice-President, Northeast Airlines Inc. and predecessor cos., National Airways Inc. and Boston-Maine Airways 1933–41; President, Northeast Airlines Inc. 1941–44, Chairman 1944–45; President, Airlines War Training Inst. 1942–45; Chairman, Airlines Committee for U.S. Air Policy 1943–44; Pres. and Dir., California Eastern Airways Inc. 1949–59; Dir., TACA Airways S.A., TACA Airways Agency Inc. 1947–57; Chmn., Air Carrier Service Corp. 1954–55, and also (Pres.). Land-Air Inc. 1954–55. President's Certificate of Merit 1947. *Address:* 9101 Colesville Road, Silver Spring, Md., U.S.A.

**SOLTMANN, Dr. Otto.** German diplomat. *B.* 1913. *Educ.* Gymnasiums Berlin and Switzerland; Univs Berlin, Rostock. *M.* 1949. Margaret Oakleigh-Walker. *Daus.* 2. *Career:* War Service 1939–45; Local Govt. 1947–52; Foreign Office, Bonn 1952–55; Consulate General Montreal, Canada 1955–58; Sen. Consul Seattle, U.S.A. 1958–61; Ambassador to Brazzaville (Congo) 1961–63; Ambassador to Nairobi (Kenya) 1963–67; Foreign Office, Bonn 1967–70; Consul-General Bombay, India 1970–74; Ambassador to Wellington (New Zealand). *Decorations:* Iron Cross (World War 2); Officer's Cross of Order of Merit (FRG). *Award:* German Ice Hockey Champ. Medal 1936/37. *Clubs:* Mittelrhein Golf (Bad Ems); Wellington Golf (Heretaunga). *Address:* Embassy of FRG, 23rd Floor, Williams City Centre, PO Box 1687, Wellington, New Zelaland; and *home:* 5411 Neuhausel, Stebenbirken, Federal Republic of Germany.

**SOLZHENITSYN, Aleksandr Isayevich.** Russian writer. *B.* 1918. *Educ.* Student Philology Moscow Inst. History, Philosophy Literature; Degree in Maths. Physics Univ. Rostov. *Career:* Officer Russian Army World War II; Imprisoned under Premier Stalin unnamed political charges 1945–53; in exile, Siberia 1953–57; Rehabilitated & took up teaching of mathematics, Ryazan 1957; expelled from Writers' Union of U.S.S.R. 1969; expelled from U.S.S.R. Feb. 1974; Hon. U.S. Citizen 1974. *Publications:* One Day in the Life of Ivan Denisovich (1962); The First Circle (1968); The Cancer Ward (1968); In the Interests of the Cause (1970); August 1914 (1971); The Gulag Archipelago, Vol. 1 (1973), Vol. 2 (1974), Vol. 3 (1977); Letter to Soviet Leaders (1974); Candle in the Wind (1975); Lenin in Zurich (1975). *Award:* Nobel Prize for Literature 1970; Hon. Fellow of Stanford Univ. *Address:* Stapferstr. 45, 8033 Zurich, Switzerland.

**SOMARE, Michael Thomas,** PC. Papua New Guinean Politician. *B.* 1936. *M.* Veronica Somare. *S.* 3. *Daus.* 3. *Career:* Schoolteacher 1954–64; Broadcasts Officer 1963–66; Journalist 1966–68; Member of House of Assembly since 1968; Chief Minister of National Coalition Government 1972, becoming Prime Minister after Independence in 1975. *Publications:* Sana: an Autobiography. *Address:* Office of the Prime Minister, P.O. Box 2501, Konedobu, Papua New Guinea.

**SOMERSET, Sir Henry Beaufort,** CBE. Australian executive. *B.* 1906. *Educ.* St. Peter's College, Adelaide; Melbourne University (MSc); Univ. Tasmania DSc (Hon). *M.* 1930, Patricia Agnes Strickland. *Daus.* 2. *Career:* Chancellor, University of Tasmania, 1964–72; Chmn. of Directors; Humes Ltd., Goliath Cement Holdings Ltd., Perpetual Execs. Trustees; Director: Assoc. Pulp and Paper Mills Ltd., E.Z. Industries Ltd., Australian Fertilizers Ltd., Tioxide Australia. *Member:* Advisory Council, C.S.I.R.O. 1955–60, and Member of Executive 1965–74. President: Australasian Inst. of Mining and Metallurgy 1958 and 1966; Australian Pulp & Paper Industry Technical Association (Past Pres.); Council, National Museum Victoria. Royal Australian Chemical Inst. (Fellow & Leighton Medallist). *Clubs:* Melbourne; Australian; Tasmanian. *Address:* 193 Domain Road, South Yarra, Victoria; and *office* 459 Collins Street, Melbourne, Vic., Australia.

**SOMMARUGA, Dr. Jur. Cornelio.** Swiss Diplomat. *B.* 1932. *Educ.* Maturita Classica, Rome; studied Law at Univs. of Paris, Rome & Zurich—Dr. in Law of Univ. of Zurich. *M.* 1957, Ornella Marzorati. *S.* 2. *Daus.* 4. *Career:* Attaché, Swiss Embassy, The Hague 1960–61; Sec., Swiss Embassy, Cologne/Bonn 1962–64; First Sec., Swiss Embassy, Rome 1965–68; Counsellor (Dep.-Head), Swiss delegation to EFTA. GATT, UNCTAD, Geneva 1968–72, Asst. Sec.-Gen. of EFTA 1973–75; Minister Plenipotentiary in the Division of Commerce of the Federal Dept. of Public Economy, Berne 1976; Pres. of the UN/Economic Commission for Europe 1977–78; Ambassador Plenipotentiary, responsible for economic relations of Switzerland with Western & Eastern Europe since 1977. *Address:* 15 rue de l'Hôpital, CH-1700 Fribourg, Switzerland; and *office* CH-3003 Berne, Palais Fédéral, Switzerland.

**SOMMERFELT, Christian.** Norwegian. *B.* 1916. *Educ.* Univ. of Oslo. *M.* 1950, Else Tjersland. *S.* 1. *Daus.* 4. *Career:* Chmn. Elkem Spigerverket A/S; Dir. Fed. Norwegian Industry; Chmn. Norwegian Export Council. *Address:* Jegerveien 12, Oslo 3, Norway; and *office* Stortingsgaten 30, Oslo 1.

**SOMOZA DEBAYLE, General Anastasio.** President of the Republic of Nicaragua. *B.* 1925. *Educ.* La Salle Military Academy of New York & Military Academy of West Point. *M.* Doña Hope Portocarrero de Somoza. *S.* 3. *Daus.* 2. *Career:* Enlisted in the Army 1941; promoted to General of Division 1964; President of Nicaragua 1967–72, & since 1974. *Awards:* Dr. (h.c.), Hahnemann Medical College of Philadelphia (1972), & the Instituto Centroamericano de Administracion de Empresas (1972). *Address:* Palacio Presidencial, Managua, Nicaragua.

**SONGER, Wesley Ansel.** American business executive. *B.* 1918. *Educ.* University of Kansas (B.S. 1940) and Harvard University (MBA 1947) *M.* 1939, Lois Elaine Holloway. *S.* Steven Wesley. *Dau.* Shirley Elaine. *Career:* Asst. to Gen. Sales Mgr. J. A. Folger & Co. 1940–42; Appliance and Merchandise Dept. General Electric Co. 1947–48; Staff Exec Dept. 1948–50; Principal, Songer & Associates 1961–62; President, Crane Co., 1959–60, Director 1060–61; Management Consultant 1958–59; Exec. Vice-Pres. (1953–57) and Vice-Pres. and Gen. Mgr. Operations (1952–53), A.S.R. Products Corp. Pres. Ingraham Div., McGraw-Edison Co., Bristol, Conn. 1967–74 (Exec. Vice-Pres. 1962–63 and Pres. and Dir. 1963–67, The Ingraham Co.; Pres. and Dir., Ingraham Canadian Clock Co. Ltd. 1963–69; Dir., United Bank & Trust Co. since 1963 and Bristol Brass Corp. since 1963; Chmn. of Bd. and Dir., New England Council (Pres. 1973–74); Dir., Manufacturers Assn. of Hartford County 1963–74 (Pres., 1970–72). *Publications:* Conducting a Self-Appraisal of Management; Streamlining to Meet Competition; Qualifications of the Manager; Flexibility in Line-Staff Relationships; Organizing for Growth and Change; A Management Appraisal of Trade Associations (1962). *Member:* American Management Assn. *Clubs:* Harvard Business School, Harvard (both of N.Y.). Pi Kappa Alpha. Masonic Lodge (A.F. & A.M.). *Address:* 28 Village Road, Southington, Conn. 06489, U.S.A.; and *office* 2074 Park Street, Hartford, Conn. 06106, U.S.A.

**SONNEMAN, Robert Charles.** American. Vice-Pres. and Secretary Bethlehem Steel Corporation. *B.* 1911. *Educ.* Swarthmore Coll. (AB 1932) and Yale Law School (JD 1935). *M.* 1939, Katherine Rea. *Career:* With law firm Cravath, Swaine & Moore 1935–54; with Bethlehem Steel 1955—; Asst. Gen. Counsel 1963–75; Secy. 1965, Vice Pres. since 1975. *Member:* Phi Beta Kappa; Pi Delta Epsilon; Amer Bar Assn.; Amer. Iron and Steel Institute; Amer. Socy. of Corporate Secretaries. Republican. *Clubs:* Saucon Valley Country (Bethlehem); Univ. (N.Y.C.); Port Royal Beach; Royal Poinciana Golf (Naples, Fla.). *Address:* R D 4, Bethlehem, Pa. 18015; and 2401 Gulf Shore Blvd. N., Naples, Fla. 33940; and *office* Bethlehem Steel Corporation, Bethlehem, Pa. 18016, U.S.A.

**SONNEMANN, Theodor Hans Karl Adolf.** Dr der Staatswissenschaften; Dr agr hc. *B.* 2 Sept. 1900. *Educ.* Universitätsstudium. *Career:* Officer in Imperial German Navy 1918; Economic Assistant Chamber of Industry and Commerce, Hanover Jan.–June 1923; Syndikus, Reichslandbund July 1923–33; Chief of Staff, Reichsnährstand 1934; served in World War II with German Navy 1939–45; Deputy Landrat, Kreis Gifhorn July–Dec. 1945; Secretary, Land Food Office, Hanover 1946–1947; Chief Secretary, Verband des Niedersächsischen Landvolkes, Hanover 1947–1949; Secretary of State, Ministry of Good, Agriculture and Forest, 1949–1961; Pres. Deutscher Raiffeisenverband Bonn 1961–73, Ehrenpresident since 1974; Deutschen Gonossenschafts-und Raiffeisenverbandes e.V.; Deutscher Raiffeisenverband e.V. *Address:* 9 Wolkenburgweg 53 Bonn-Beuel 1, Germany.

**SOPWITH, Sir Thomas Octave Murdoch,** CBE. British company director. *B.* 1888. *M.* (1) 1914, Hon. Beatrix Hore-Ruthven (*D.* 1930): (2) 1932, Phyllis Brodie Gordon; *S.* 1; founded Sopwith Aviation Co. Ltd.; former Chairman, Society of British Aircraft; President, Hawker Siddeley Group Ltd. *Address:* Compton Manor, Kings Somborne, Hants.

**SORAVUO, Ernst Ossian,** CBE. Finnish diplomat. *B.* 3 Dec. 1904. *Educ.* University of Helsinki (L. ès L.). *M.* 1934, Elsa Annikki Waldén. *S.* Ernest Lauri, Gustaf Henri. *Dau.* Mirja Anneli Katarina (*D.* 1967). *Career:* Entered Diplomatic Service 1929; posts in Buenos Aires, Berlin, Paris, Stockholm; En. Ex. and Min. Plen. to Argentina 1947–52, to Chile 1948–52, to Uruguay 1949–52; En. Ex. and Min. Plen. to the Court of St. James's 1952–55; Director, Finland S.S. Co. Ltd., Helsinki 1955–63. Chairman Suomen Tupakka oy 1960–76. Mng. Dir., Finnish Board Mills Assn. 1963–69; Chmn. Finnish Petroleum Federation since 1970. *Awards:* Com. de Honneur, Order del Merit Civil (Spain); Commander, Order of the White Rose of Finland, Gran Official, Orden al Mérito (Chile); Orden del Mérito (Argentina); Officer de la Légion d'Honneur. *Address:* 10 Toolonkatu, Helsinki, Finland.

**SØRENSEN, Svend O.** Danish. Commander of the Order of the Dannebrog (Denmark). *B.* 1914. *Educ.* Copenhagen Schl of Economics & Business Administration (Dipl. in Banking); studied banking in Switzerland, U.S.A., France and Gt. Britain. *M.* 1949, Karen Vontillius. *Daus.* Aase and Birgit. *Career:* With Management of Den Danske Bank af 1871: Secretary Jan. 1947; Manager 1950; Asst. Gen. Manager 1954; Deputy Gen. Manager 1959; Man. Dir. 1962—. *Address:* Hambros Alle 11 A, 2900 Hellerup, Copenhagen; and *office* Den Danske Bank af 1871, Holmens Kanal 12, 1092 Copenhagen K, Denmark.

**SORN, Hon Lord.** James Gordon McIntyre, MC. Scottish judge. *B.* 21 July 1896. *Educ.* Winchester; Balliol College, Oxford (BA) and Glasgow University (LLB); LLD Glasgow Univ. (1957). *M.* 1923, Madeline Scott Moncrieff (*D.* 1954). *S.* 1. *Dau.* 1. Served World War I with Ayrshire Yeomanry 1914–18; called to the Scottish Bar 1922; KC 1936; Dean of the Faculty 1939–44; Senator of College of Justice in Scotland (with judicial title of Lord Sorn) 1944–63. *Address:* Sorn Castle, Ayrshire, Scotland.

**SORSA, Taisto Kalevi.** Finnish Politician. *B.* 1930. *Educ.* Journalists' Exam, School for Social Sciences 1957, Tampere Univ., Master of Social Sciences (1963). *M.* 1953, Elli Irene Lääkäri. *Career:* Journalist 1948–55; Editor in Publ. Co. 1956–59; UNESCO official 1959–65; Secy. Gen. of Finnish Nat. Commission for UNESCO 1965–69; Deputy-Dir. Ministry of Educ. 1967–69; Secy.-Gen. of Social Dem. Party 1969–75, Chmn. since 1975; Minister of For. Affairs 1972 (Par); Prime Minister 1972–75; Minister of Foreign Affairs 1975–76; Prime Minister since 1977. M.P. since 1970, and chmn. of its foreign Affairs Cttee. 1970–72. *Address:* Haapaniemenkatu 20 D64, 00530 Helsinki and *office* Aleksanterinkatu 3 D, 00170 Helsinki 17 Finland.

**SOSSIDI, John N.** Greek diplomat. *B.* 1924. *Educ.* Diploma of Law, Political & Economic Sciences, Univ. of Thessaloniki. *M.* 1955, Danae Kyrou. *S.* Nicolas. *Dau.* Christine. *Career:* appointed Attache of the R. Ministry of Foreign Affairs 1952; Diplomatic Secy. of the Prime Minister, Principal Private Secy. of the Minister of Foreign Affairs 1952–55; Asst. Dir. NATO Div. Ministry Foreign Affairs 1956–57; Head, Greek Military Mission, Berlin 1957–61; Charge d'Affairs of Greece in Morocco 1961–64; Head, Diplomatic Office of the Prime Minister 1964–65; Dir. Gen. Political Office of the Prime Minister 1965–66; Dir. 3rd Political Div. Div. of European Cooperation 1967–70; Dir. 10th Div. Min. Foreign Affairs 1970–71; Ambassador to Argentina, Chile, Bolivia, Peru, Paraguay and Uruguay since 1971. *Awards:* Distinguished Service Cross; Medal of St. Marc; Knight Comdr. Order of Phoenix; Comdr., Order of George I (all Greek); Knight Commdr. Order of Christ (Portugal); Knight Commdr. Order of Vladimirescu (Roumania); Commdr. Order of Merit (Italy) and many others. *Clubs:* Royal Hellenic yacht; Nautical of Thessaloniki; Athens Lawn Tennis; Jockey of Argentina. *Address:* Greek Embassy, Avda. Pte. Roque Sáenz Peña 547, 4 Buenos Aires, R. Argentina.

**SOTERIADES, Antis Georghiou.** Ambassador of Cyprus. *B.* 1924. *Educ.* Barrister-at-Law; BSc Econ (Inter.). *Career:* Practised Law 1951–56; freedom fighter 1956–59; Chmn. of first political party, EDMA, in Cyprus since independence of Cyprus; resigned on assuming appointment of High Commissioner for Cyprus in the United Kingdom, 1961–66; Ambassador in Egypt since 1966, & accredited to Lebanon & Syria since 1967, Sudan since 1971, Iraq since 1973. *Address:* 16 Cleopatra Road, Heliopolis, Cairo, Egypt.

**SOUBRY, Emile Edmund.** American. *B.* 1896. *Educ.* Acton Commercial College, Acton (England). *M.* 1919, (1) Jennie Bennett (*D.* 1970); *S.* Kenneth William Stephen. *Dau.* Moira Barbara Esdaile. (2) 1971, Renee McCredy Mayberry. *Career:* With Anglo-American Oil Co. Ltd., London (now Esso Petroleum Co. Ltd.) 1911–41 (Chmn. of Board 1939–41); with Standard Oil Co. (New Jersey) 1941–61 (Exec. Vice-Pres. 1955–61). Liaison between British Trade Cttee. and the U.S. Government 1940–43; Member of the Foreign Petroleum Committee of the U.S. Petroleum Administration 1951–56. Director 1958— and Chairman of the Board 1962–69, Foreign Policy Association (U.S.A.); Director, U.S. Committee for the United Nations 1962–73, now member of National Council. Member, Council of Foreign Relations. *Clubs:* R.A.C. (London, Eng.); Hermitage Country (Magog. Canada). *Address:* 620 Fifth Avenue, New York, N.Y. 10020, U.S.A.

**SOUFFLET, Jacques,** French. *B.* 1912. *Educ.* St. Cyr. *Career:* Pres. Directeur Général de la Generale de Transport & D'industrie nouvelle denomination de la Sté Gle des Transport, Départmentaux; Senator for Yvelines; Minister of Defence 1974–75. *Address:* 14 rue Saint-Dominique, Paris 7. France.

**SOUTHAM, Gordon Hamilton.** *B.* 1916. *Educ.* Univ. of Toronto (BA 1939) and Oxford Univ. (Modern History, 1939). *M.* (1) 1940, Jacqueline Lambert-David (diss. 1968). *S.* Peter, Christopher and Michael. *Dau.* Jennifer. (2) 1968, Gro Mortensen. S. Gordon. *Dau.* Henrietta. *Career:* Officer Cadet, Royal Artillery; Lieut. Royal Canadian Artillery 1940; served in U.K., Italy and Northwestern Europe; discharged as Capt. 1945. Reporter, The Times, London 1945–46; Editorial Writer, The Citizen, Ottawa 1946–47, Joined Dept. of External Affairs 1948; Third Secretary Stockholm, Aug. 1949; Second Secretary Dec. 1949; Chargé d'Affaires Warsaw, March 1959; Ambassador 1960; Head of Information Division 1962–64; Co-ordinator, National Arts Centre 1964–67. Director-General, National Arts Centre, Ottawa since 1967. *Clubs:* Reform (London). *Address:* National Arts Centre, Ottawa, Ont., Canada K1P 5W1.

**SOUTHARD, Frank A. Jr., OBE (Mil.)** *B.* 1907. *Educ.* Pomona College (BA 1927) and University of California (PhD 1930). *M.* 1941, Mary I. Hay. *Career:* Instructor in Economics, University of California 1930–31; Asst. Prof. and Professor of Economics, Cornell Univ. 1931–48 (Chairman Dept. of Economics 1946–47); Senior Economic Analyst,

U.S. Tariff Commission 1935; Director, Office of International Finance, Treasury Dept. 1947–48; Associate Director of Research and Statistics, Board of Governors of Federal Reserve System 1948–49. Lieut., Lieut.-Commander, Commander, U.S. Naval Reserve 1942–46; Deputy Managing Director, International Monetary Fund 1962–74; U.S. Executive Director, I.M.F. and Special Assistant to the Secretary of the Treasury 1949–62; Snr. Assoc. Kearns International; Pres., Per Jacobsson Foundation; Dir., Atlantic Council, Population Crisis Cttee. *Publications:* American Industry in Europe; Canadian-American Industry; Foreign Exchange Practice and Policy; The Finances of European Liberation; Some European Currency and Exchange Experiences 1943–46; various articles in journals and encyclopaedias in the field of international economics. Guggenheim Fellow, 1940; Social Science Research Fellow, 1940. *Member:* Amer. Economic Assn.; Council on Foreign Relations; Phi Beta Kappa. *Club:* International (Washington, D.C.). *Awards:* Officer, Legion of Merit; Officer, Legion of Honour (France); LLD (Pomona 1976). *Address:* 4620 No. Park Ave., Chevy Chase, MD 20015, U.S.A.; and *office* 1701 Pennsylvania Ave., NW Washington, D.C. 20006, U.S.A.

**SOUTHBOROUGH, Lord** (Francis John Hopwood); (Retd.) company director. *B.* 7 Mar. 1897. *M.* 1918, Audrey Evelyn Dorothy Money. *S.* 1. *Daus.* 1. *Educ.* Westminster School. *Career:* Served European War, 1914–18, Sub-Lieut., R.N.V.R., Admiralty and Foreign Office; seconded, 1917, to staff of Irish Convention in Dublin and later was Sec. to War Trade Advisory Cttee. Joined Royal Dutch Shell Group of Companies, 1919; Pres. Asiatic Petroleum Corporation, U.S.A. (also represented Petroleum Board), 1942–46; Managing Director the Shell Petroleum Co., and Bataafse Petroleum Maatschappij N.V., 1946–57, retired. Managing Director 'Shell' Transport & Trading Co. 1951–70 (Director 1946–70). *Awards:* Knighted 1953. Commander of the Order of Orange-Nassau. *Club:* Brooks's. *Address:* Bingham's Melcombe, nr. Dorchester, Dorset.

**SOUTHEY, Sir Robert (John)**, Kt 1976, CMG, MA. Australian. *B.* 1922. *Educ.* Geelong Grammar School; Magdalen Coll. Oxford (First Class PPE, MA). *M.* 1946, Valerie Janet Cotton Clarke (*D.* 1977). *S.* 5. *Career:* Dir. Wm. Haughton & Co. 1953—; Dir. British Petroleum Co. of Australia Ltd.; Buckley & Nunn Ltd.; Internat. Computers (Aust.) Pty. Ltd.; Kinnears Ltd.; Timbersales Ltd.; Chmn. Wm. Haughton & Co. Ltd. Member: Aust. Adv. Council, General Accident Fire & Life Assurance, Corp. Ltd.; Chmn. Council Geelong Grammar School 1966–72; Aust. Adv. Cttee. Nuffield Foundation 1970—; Federal Pres. Liberal Party, Australia 1970–75. *Clubs;* Melbourne; Australian Melbourne; Union; Sydney; Cavalry & Guards London; M.C.C.; Melbourne Cricket. *Address:* Denistoun Avenue, Mount Eliza, Vic. 3930, Australia; and *office* 627, Chapel Street, South Yarra, Vic., Australia.

**SOUVANNA PHOUMA, Prince Tiao.** Laotian Statesman. *B.* 1901. *Educ.* Paul Bert College and Albert Sarraut Lyceum (Hanoi) Higher Studies at Paris (Dipl. Engineer-Architect) and Grenoble (Dipl Eng-Electrician). *S.* 2. *Daus.* 2. *Career:* Ambassador to France 1958–60 and Minister Plenipotentiary to Borun, Brussels, Rome and Jerusalem. Engineer, 1940–50. Minister of Public Works, 1950–51; Prime Minister, Pres. of the Cncl., and Ministry of Public Works and Planning 1951–54; Vice-President of the Council and Minister of National Defence of Ex-Servicemen 1954–56; Prime Minister 1960–74. Entered Dept. of Public Works, Indo-China 1931; at Bureau of Architecture (Division of the Ministry of Public Works), Vientiane 1931–40; in the period 1932–35 assumed the functions of Chief of the Bureau, and directed the water and electricity services of Vientiane; under the auspices of the French School of the Far East, he assumed the direction of the work of restoring Vat phrakeo, Vientiane; Sub-Divisional Engineer of the new works at Phoukhoun 1940–41; Sub-Divisional Engineer at Luangprabang 1941–44; Engineer Chief of Technical Bureau, Territorial Division of Public Works, Vientiane 1944–45; Principal Engineer of the 1st Class, Ministry of Public Works, Indo-China. *Address:* Vientiane, Laos.

**SOZZANI, Antonio.** Italian banker. *B.* 1918. *Educ.* Doctorate in Economic Science, University of Milan. *M.* 1948, Duchess Emanuela De Dampierre. *Career:* Chairman, Banque de Suez-Italia; Vice-Chairman, Società Cisalpina Impieghi Mobiliari, Finanziaria Indoseuz; Dir. Associazione Nazionale Aziende Ordinarie di Credito; Istituto Centrale di Banche e Banchieri, Milfid-Fiduciaria di Milano; Camera di Commercio Internazionale; Sezione Italiana. Italia. *Clubs:* Nuovo Circolo degli Scacchi (Rome). *Address:* 4, via dei Bossi, 20121 Milan; 3, Piazza Campitelli, 00186 Rome; and *office* 2, via Mengoni, 20121 Milan, Italy.

**SPÁČIL, Dr Dušan.** Czechoslovak diplomat. *Educ.* Charles Univ. Prague; Schevcenko Univ. Kiev; Lomonosov Univ. Moscow, LLD 1954. *M.* 1953, Růžena Koubová. *S.* 2. *Career:* with Ministry of Foreign Affairs 1954—; Second Secy. Czechoslovak Mission, U.N. 1956–60; Deputy Resident Rep. to IAEA, Vienna 1962–64; Counsellor, Embassy Moscow 1964–67; Head, Dept. Int. Organizations, Ministry Foreign Affairs 1967–72; Ambassador, Czechoslovak Socialist Republic to United States 1972–75; Dep. Foreign Minister, Prague. *Address:* c/o Ministry of Foreign Affairs, Prague, Czechoslovakia.

**SPADA, Massimo.** Italian banker. Chairman, Banca Cattolica del Veneto S.p.A. *Address:* Banca Cattolica del Veneto, Vicenza, Italy.

**SPAETHEN, Rolf.** German. *B.* 1909. *Educ.* Matriculation at Humanist Grammar School; studies Law, Economics and History in Munich, Leipzig, Berlin and Hamburg. *M.* 1954, Lieselotte Peters. *Dau.* 1. *Career:* On Sales Staff (with full negotiating powers) 1935–37; Business Teacher and employed by a Chartered Accountant 1937–40; five years military service; Business Teacher and Interpreter 1945–46; entered Head Office of DAG 1947 (elected Chmn. Sept. 1960). Former Chmn., German Salaried Staff Trade Union, and of the Board of Directors, Deutscher Ring Insurance Co. (member of Scientific Committee). Member: Atlantic Committee of the German Atlantic Society; Association for Social Progress; Streseman Society; German Committee of the European Movement Bonn; Board of Trustees, Friends of Israel Development. Chairman, Representative Body of the Federal Insurance Institute for Salaried Staff. *Publications:* Editor of the DAG booklets on economic, social and cultural politics; numerous publications on these subjects in professional journals. *Address:* Hamburg 3, St Benedict Str. 37, Germany.

**SPAGHT, Monroe E.** American. *B.* 1909. *Educ.* Stanford University (AB 1929; AM 1930; PhD 1933—all in Chemistry). Entire professional career, since 1933, has been with Shell companies; Man. Dir. Royal Dutch Shell Group, Chmn. Bd. Shell Oil Co. 1965–70; Director Royal Dutch Petroleum Co. since 1965; Shell Oil Co. since 1953, Dir. additional coys. since 1970. *Member* of scientific and professional societies and social clubs. *Awards:* Citations and honorary degrees in the United States and Europe. *Publications:* Various articles, reviews, book sections, and patents of a scientific and professional nature. *Address:* Shell Centre, London, S.E.1.

**SPARKMAN, John Jackson.** American politician. *B.* 1899. *Educ.* University of Alabama (AB, LLB, AM); LLD, Univ. of Alabama, Spring Hill College, and Auburn Univ. *M.* 1923, Ivo Hall. *Dau.* Julia Ann (Shepard). *Career:* Practised law at Huntsville, Alabama 1925–37; Member U.S. House of Representatives (Democrat) 1937–46; U.S. Senator from Alabama since 1946; U.S. Delegate to United Nations Fifth General Assembly. Democratic nominee for Vice-President in 1952. Chmn., Senate Foreign Relations Cttee. 1975—. *Address:* Room 3203, Senate Office Building, Washington, D.C. 20510, U.S.A.

**SPARLING, H(erbert) Alan, CBE, DSO, CD.** Canadian. Maj.-General (Retd.). Member Ontario Police Commission; *B.* 1907. *Educ.* Graduate Royal Military College of Canada. *M.* 1935, Edith B. Hunter. *S.* Timothy Alan Hunter. *Career:* Vice-Chief of General Staff, Canadian Army 1950–55; Chmn., Canadian Joint Staff, Washington, D.C. 1956–58; General Officer Commanding Central Command, Canadian Army 1958–62. World War II: Commander Corps Royal Artillery, 1st Canadian Corps (Retd. 1963). Col. Commandant, Roy. Regt. of Canadian Artillery 1969–74. *Club:* Toronto Golf. *Address:* 1236 Cumnock Crescent, Oakville, Ont. L6J 2N5, Canada.

**SPEARMAN, Clement.** British Diplomat. *B.* 1919. *Educ.* Cardiff High Sch. *M.* 1950, Olwen Regina Morgan. *S.* 1. *Daus.* 2. *Career:* Royal Navy 1942–46; entered HM Diplomatic Service 1948; 3rd Sec., Brussels 1948–49; 2nd Sec., Foreign Office 1949–51; HM Consul, Skoplje 1951–53; Foreign Office 1953–56; 1st Sec., Buenos Aires 1956–60; Foreign Office 1960–62; Dep. Sec.-Gen., Central Treaty Org. 1962–65; Reykjavik 1965–69; FCO 1969–71; Manila 1971–74; Toronto 1974–75; HM Ambassador to the Dominican Republic since 1975. *Clubs:* Travellers'; Naval; Roehampton. *Address:* c/o Foreign & Commonwealth Office, London SW1A 2AH.

**SPEAS, Robert Dixon.** American executive. *B.* 1916. *Educ.* Mass. Institute of Technology (BS 1940). *M.* 1944, Manette Lansing Hollingsworth. *S.* Robert Dixon, Jr. and Jay Hollingsworth. *Career:* With American Airlines Inc.: Engineer 1940–44; Asst. to Vice-Pres.-Engr. 1944–47; Director, Maintenance and Engr., Cargo Division 1947–48; Special Asst. to President 1948–50. U.S. Manager, A. V. Roe & Co., Canada 1950–51; Pres. Chmn. Bd. R. Dixon Speas Associates Inc. since 1951. *Publications:* Airplane Performance and Operations; Pilots' Technical Manual; Airline Operation; Technical Aspects of Air Transport Management; many technical papers. *Awards:* First Award—Annual National Boeing Thesis Competition; Research Award—Air Transport Assn. of America. Fellow (and Past Treasurer) Amer. Inst. of Aeronautics and Astronautics; Associate Fellow Royal Aeronautical Society; Past Vice-Pres. Society of Automotive Engineers. *Clubs:* Wings (Past President and Member of Council); Port Washington Yacht. *Address:* 1615 Northern Boulevard, Manhasset, N.Y. 11030; and *office* 47 Hillside Avenue, Manhasset, N.Y. 11030, U.S.A.

**SPECHT, Charles Alfred.** American business consultant. *B.* 1914. *Educ.* Univ. College, Rutgers University (BBA) and New York University Graduate School of Business Administration. *M.* 1940, Gertrude A. Morris. *Daus.* Sara Ann, Sandra Morris. *Career:* Clerk, bookkeeper, American Surety Co., N.Y.C. 1933–37; Credit Analyst, Irving Trust Co. 1937–42; Staff Accountant, Price Waterhouse & Co. 1942–44; Chief Accountant, DeLaval Steam Turbine Co., Trenton, N.J. 1944–45; Works Controller, Joy Mfg. Co., Franklin, Pa. 1945–50; Controller, Chas. Pfizer & Co. Inc., Brooklyn 1950–52 (Dir. 1952–55, also Pres. Foreign Trade subsidiaries 1952–55); Pres., Dir., Horizons Titanium Corp. 1955–57; Vice-Pres., Dir., Horizons Inc. 1955–56; Pres., Dir.: Minerals & Chemicals Philipp Corp., 1956–63; Mac-Millan Blocdel Ltd., 1963–68; President and Chief Executive Officer, Consolidated Packaging Corporation, Chicago, 1968–72. *Member:* Financial Executive Inst.; Amer. Management Association. *Publication:* Financing Foreign Chemical and Pharmaceutical Operations (1955). *Clubs:* The University, Broad Street (N.Y.C.); Union League; Midday Chicago; The Englewood, The Englewood Field (Englewood, N.J.): Vancouver; Mission Valley Golf. *Address:* 628 Armada Road, S. Venice, Florida 33595, and *office* 4N. Michigan Ave., Chicago, Ill., U.S.A.

**SPEED, (Herbert) Keith,** RD, MP. British Politician. *B.* 1934. *Educ.* Greenhill Sch., Evesham; Bedford Modern Sch.; Royal Naval Coll., Dartmouth. *M.* 1961, Peggy Voss Clarke. *S.* 2. *Dau.* 1. *Career:* Regular Officer, Royal Navy 1947–56; Admin. Asst., H. J. Heinz Co. Ltd. 1956–57; Sales Mgr., Amos (Electronics) Ltd. 1957–60; Mktg. Mgr., Plysu Products Ltd. 1960–65; Conservative Research Dept. 1965–68; MP (Cons.) for Meriden 1968–74, & for Ashford since 1974; Government Whip 1970–72; Parly. Under-Sec. of State, Dept. of Environment 1972–74; Opposition Spokesman on Local Government since 1975. *Decoration:* Reserve Decoration 1967. *Publication:* Blueprint For Britain (1964). *Clubs:* St. Stephen's; Elwick (Ashford); Tenterten. *Address:* Strood House, Rolvenden, Cranbrook, Kent; and *office* House of Commons, London SW1A 0AA.

**SPEIDEL, General Hans.** German military officer. *B.* 1897 *Educ.* Gymnasium of the Humanities; University (History): Dr Phil; Military Academy with Brevet rank to General Staff. *M.* 1925, Ruth Stahl. *S.* 1. *Daus.* 2. *Career:* Grenadier Regt., König Karl (5 Württemberg) 123, 1914; Western Front, 1915–18; entered Reichswehr (three years at Military Academy; promotion; exchange availability between Front and General Staff); during second World War was successively Chief of Staff of Corps, of Army (both on Eastern Front), and then Army Group of General Field Marshal Rommel (Western Front); arrested on Himmler's orders Sept. 1944; released from Gestapo imprisonment at the end of the war; Instructor at Tübingen University and Leibniz Univ. College; Military Adviser, Federal Government, 1951; Military Delegate-in-Chief to E.V.G. and N.A.T.O. negotiations, 1951–55; entered Bundeswehr as Commander-in-Chief of Combined German Forces 1955; Commander, Allied Land Forces Central Europe 1957–63, and 1963–64. Adviser on Defence to Govt. of Federal Republic of Germany 1964—. Pres. Science and Policy (Wissenschaft und Politik) Foundation 1964—; Professor h.c. 1971. *Publications:* Invasion 1944 (a contribution to the fate of Rommel and the Reich) (1949); Ludwig Beck 'Studien' (1955); Zeitbetrachtungen (1969). Essays on Ernst Jünger, Theodor Heuss, Eugene Bircher, Gneisenau and Beck. *Awards:* Knight, Württemberg Order of Merit; Knight, Iron Cross; Grosses Verdienstkreuz mit Stern und Schulterband. Freeman of Metzingen 1972. *Address:* Am Spitzenbach 21, 534 Bad Honnef, Germany.

**SPELLACY, Frederick John,** OBE, JP. British. Road transport executive. *B.* 1901. *Educ.* Dulwich College (London) and London University (Matriculation). *M.* 1927, Aileen Maude Bradstreet. *Career:* Managing Director, Blue Mountains Transport Pty. Ltd.; Alderman, Katoomba, N.S.W., Municipal Council 1932–35; Chmn. of Dirs., Blue Mountains, N.S.W. District Hospital 1962–65. Pres., N.S.W. Omnibus Proprietors Assn. 1950–56. Chmn. (Bus Section) Motor Traders Assn. of N.S.W. 1952–61, and (Passenger Section) Australian Road Transport Fed. 1954–56. Vice-Pres., Australian Road Transport Fed. 1954–56 (Pres. 1956–58, 1960–62, 1965–68). Australian Employer Delegate to I.L.O. Conference, Hamburg, Germany 1957. Awarded OBE New Years Honours List 1968. *Publications:* Various papers and articles on road transport. Fellow, Chartered Inst. of Transport (N.S.W. Section). *Clubs:* Pitt (Sydney). *Address:* Redleaf, Leura, N.S.W., Australia.

**SPENCE, Ernest John Hamilton,** OBE. Canadian. Professor and Consultant. *B.* 1915. *Educ.* Univ. of Manitoba (BA), Queen's Univ. (BCom), and Northwestern Univ. (MBA; PhD). *M.* 1938, Mary Jane Gotschall. *S.* Michael Randall and Murray. *Career:* Lecturer Northwestern Univ. (Chicago) 1939–42; Asst. to Chmn. Wartime Prices and Trade Bd. Dominion Govt. (Ottawa) 1942–47; Asst. Gen. Mgr. Fur Trade Dept. Hudson's Bay Co. Ltd. (Winnipeg) 1947–49; Pres. and Dir. Canadian Food Products Ltd. (Toronto) 1949–59; Exec. Vice-Pres. and Dir. Triarch Corp. (Toronto) 1960–65; Consultant, Economic Council of Canada 1965–70; Prof. of Business, York Univ. 1966–73; Dir. Bovis Corp. Ltd; Reed Paper Ltd.; Chmn. & Dir., Signet Food Systems Inc. since 1973. *Member:* Newcomen Socy. of N. America. *Publications:* Canadian Wartime Price Control Policy (1946); Scale & Specialization in Canadian Industry (1968). *Clubs:* National, Granite (all of Toronto); Princeton (N.Y.C.). *Address:* 6 Forest Laneway, Willowdale, Ontario, Canada.

**SPENCE, John Deane,** MP. British industrialist. *B.* 1920. *Educ.* Queens Univ., Belfast. *M.* 1944, Hester Nicholson. *S.* John Deane, Jr. *Dau.* Diana Elizabeth Ann. *Career:* Member of Parliament Heeley Div. of Sheffield 1970–74, MP for Thirsk & Malton since 1974; PPS to Minister for Local Government and Development 1971–74; Hon. Secy. Cons. Backbenchers Agric., Fisheries & Food Cttee. 1974; Nat. Ind. Select Cttee. 1974; appointed Member, Panel of Chmn. of Ctte's. 1974; Elected Exec. British American Parliamentary Group 1974. Former National President, United Kingdom Commercial Travellers Association; Secy. Yorkshire Conservative Members Group. *Member:* National Farmers' Union; Country Landowners' Assn.; Yorkshire Derwent Trust; Anglo-Israel Friendship Socy. Conservative. *Clubs:* Junior Carlton; Constitutional; Royal Automobile. *Address:* Greystones, Maltongate, Thornton Dale, Nr. Pickering, Yorks.; and *office* House of Commons, London, SW1.

**SPENCER, William Marvin.** American transportation executive. *B.* 1892. *Educ.* Princeton University (BA). *M.* 1924, Gertrude White; *S.* Edson White and William Marvin, Jr. *Dau.* Suzanne. *Career:* Asst. to Secy., Hammermill Paper Co., Erie, Pa. 1915–21; Pres. Erie Brass & Copper Co. 1921–23; Spencer, Kamerer & Co., Erie 1924–29; Partner, Jackson Bros. Boesel & Co., Brokers, Chicago 1930–34; Pres. and Dir., Bruke Electric Co., Erie (1934–35) and Inland Car Lines, Inc., Chicago (1935–40); Vice-Pres. & Dir., Perry Spencer & Co., Investment Banking, Chicago 1939–40; Director, North American Car Corporation 1941—(Chmn. 1941–59); Director, La Salle National Bank, Chicago 1970–72; Trustee: Chicago Boys' Clubs; Illinois Children's Home & Aid Socy. 1944— (Pres. 1948–52); Fourth Presbyterian Church, Chicago 1948—; Pres., Chicago Latin School Board of Trustees 1938–46; member, Chicago Plan Commission 1947–57 (Chmn. 1951–57); Lyric Opera of Chicago, Chicago Orchestral Assn., Northwestern Univ. Republican. *Address:* 1430 Lake Shore Drive, Chicago, Ill. 60610, U.S.A.

**SPENCER-STRONG, George Henry.** American. Technical Consultant. *B.* 1906. *Educ.* B Ceramic Eng 1928, MS 1931, PhD 1934; Ceramic Engineer (professional degree) Distinguished Alumnus, College of Engineering, 1970. Ohio State Univ. *M.* 1936, Anita Barbara Koenig. *S.* William Henry II; and *Dau.* Marianna (James, Jr.). *Career:* Director of Research 1942–47, and Vice-President and Dir. of Research 1947–60, The Pemco Corporation, Baltimore, Md. Technical Director, Pemco Div., The Glidden Company 1961–65; Ceramic Group Glidden-Dunkee Div., S.C.M. Corp. 1965–71;

Secretary, Committee C22, American Society for Testing and Materials 1949–70; 1st Vice-Chairman, 1970–71; Chairman, Standards Committee, Porcelain Enamel Inst. 1944–71. *Member:* Amer. Ceramic Socy. (Trustee 1949–52; Amer., Ceramic Socy., Distinguished Lecturer, 1968–69, Honorary Life Member, 1970. President 1960–61); National Institute of Ceramic Engineers; American Society for Metals (Hon. Mem. 1975); Hon. Mem., American Society for Testing & Materials 1974; Canadian Ceramic Society; Baltimore Torch (President 1968–69); Maryland Historical Society; Fellow, American Association for Advancement of Science. *Publications:* approximately 70 publications in field of ceramics and vitreous enamels. Sigma Xi; Keramos: Award of Merit, Amer. Socy. for Testing and Materials 1965. *Address:* 109 Witherspoon Road, Baltimore, Md. 21212, U.S.A.

**SPENDER, Hon. Sir Percy Claude,** KCVO, KBE, QC, KStJ. Australian statesman; Judge of the International Court of Justice 1958–67. President of the Court 1964–67. *B.* 1897. *Educ.* Fort Street High School; University of Sydney (BA, LLB). *M.* 1925, Jean Maud Henderson (dec'd 1970). *S.* Peter Beaufort, John Michael. *Career:* Called to N.S.W. bar 1923, King's Counsel 1935; Acting Treasurer of Commonwealth 1939; Chairman, Australian Loan Council 1940; Treasurer of Commonwealth 1940; Minister for Army 1940–41; mem., War Cabinet 1940–41. War Council 1940–45; member, Parliamentary Ctte. of Privileges, Parliamentary Committee on Broadcasting 1947–49; Chairman, Australian Delegation, Conference of British Commonwealth Foreign Ministers, Colombo (at which he put forward a plan for economic aid to S. and S.E. Asia, subsequently known as the Colombo Plan) 1950; Vice-President of the General Assembly of U.N. 1950–51; Chmn., Australian Delegation to U.N. 1952–56; Australian Rep. at signing of Regional Security Treaty between U.S.A., N.Z., and Australia, San Francisco 1951 (which he negotiated as Minister of External Affairs); Australian Governor, Internat. Monetary Fund and Internat. Bank 1951–53; Australian Governor of International Monetary Fund 1954–57; Vice-President, Japanese Peace Treaty Conference, San Francisco 1951; M.H.R. (Lib.), Warringah 1937–51; Minister of State for External Affairs and External Territories 1949–51; Amb. Ex. and Plen. to U.S.A. 1951–58; Chmn., Australian Delegation, Internat. Sugar Conf. May–June 1956; negotiated nuclear power agreement with U.S. on behalf of Australian Govt.; Director, Fulbright Foundation in Australia 1949–51. Mem. Council of Assicurug. Gen. (Italy); Chmn. of Cttee. to create National Index of Austr. Birds. *Awards:* Hon. degrees at several univs; Grande Ufficiale of the Order of Merit of the Republic of Italy, 1976. *Publications:* Company Law and Practice; Foreign Policy—The Next Phase; Exercises in Diplomacy; Politics and a Man. *Address:* 11 Wellington Street, Woollahra, 2025 N.S.W., Australia.

**SPICER, Hon. Sir John Armstrong.** Australian Lawyer. *B.* 1899. *Educ.* Torquay (England); Hawksburn (Vic.); University of Torquay (England); Hawksburn (Vic.); University of Melbourne; Admitted as Barrister and Solicitor 1921; KC 1948. *M.* 1924, Lavinia Webster. *S.* John. *Career:* Chmn., Senate Committee on Regulations and Ordinances 1940–43; Senator in Commonwealth Parliament 1940–44 and 1949–56; Attorney-General, Commonwealth of Australia, 1949–56; Chief Judge Australian Industrial Court 1956–76. *Clubs:* Australian; Constitutional. Deceased, 3rd January 1978.

**SPICER, (William) Michael (Hardy),** M.P. British Politician. *B.* 1943. *Educ.* Cambridge Univ.—MA (Econ.). *M.* 1967, Ann Hunter. *S.* 1. *Daus.* 2. *Career:* Asst. to Editor of *The Statist* 1964–66; Conservative Research Dept. (organizing Party's contacts with academics and business consultancies) 1966–68; Dir., Conservative Systems Research Centre 1968–70; Man. Dir., Economic Models Ltd. & Pres., Economic Models Corp. (Delaware) since 1970; MP (Cons.) for South Worcestershire since 1974. *Address:* House of Commons, London SW1A 0AA.

**SPIERENBURG, D. P.** Dutch administrator. *Career:* Director-General, Directorate-General for Foreign Economic Relations, Ministry of Economic Affairs, The Hague, to 1952; member of the High Authority of the European Coal and Steel Community, Luxemburg, 1952–58; Vice-Pres., European Coal and Steel Community 1958–62; Ambassador, Head of the Permanent Netherlands Delegation to the European Communities in Brussels. 1963–70; to Nato in Brussels 1970–73. *Address:* Ministry of Foreign Affairs, The Hague, Netherlands.

**SPINDLER, Gert Paul.** Public Relations Consultant. *B.* 1914. *M.* 1942, Wiltrud Fischer. *S.* 1. *Dau.* 1. *Career:* At Textile Schl., Zürich, Switzerland 1933–34; with T. F. Firth & Sons, London 1934–35; Military Service 1935–37; Paul-Spindler-Werke KG 1938 (Partner and Vice-Pres. 1939; Pres. 1949–72). Member, Adv. Bd., Gerling Konzern since 1958. *Publications:* Die menschenwürdige Tat; Mitunternehmertum; Partnerschaft statt Klassenkampf; Neue Antworten im sozialen Raum; Praxis der Partnerschaft; Public Relations—Aufgabe für Unternehmer. *Clubs:* Rotary. *Address:* 4006 Erkrath-Hochdahl, Heinrich-Heine-Str. 31; and Public Relations Office, Schalbruch 45, 4010 Hilden, Germany.

**SPINELLI, Altiero.** Italian politician. *B.* 1907. *Educ.* Univ. of Rome. *M.* 1944, Ursula Hirschmann. *Daus.* 3. *Career:* Political prisoner in Italy 1927–43; Partisan in Italian Resistance 1943–45; Leader of European Federalist Movement 1945–61; Vis. Professor Johns Hopkins Univ. Center for Advanced International Studies in Bologna 1961–64; Founder and Dir. of Inst. of International Affairs in Rome 1965–70; Mem. of the Commission of the European Communities 1970–76 Mem. of Italian & European Parliaments 1976—. *Publications:* Dagli Stati Sovrani agli Stati Uniti d'Europa 1952; L'Europa non cade dal cielo, 1960; Tedeschi al bivio, 1960; The Eurocrats, 1966; The European Adventure, 1973; Il lungo Monologo, 1970. *Address:* Clivo Rutario 5, 00152 Rome; & *office* via Uffici del Vicario 21, 00186 Rome, Italy.

**SPINKS, John William Tranter,** CC, MBE. Canadian. President Emeritus, University of Saskatchewan. *B.* 1908. *Educ.* London Univ. (BS 1928, PhD 1930); DSc 1957, post-doctoral study in Germany 1933. *M.* 1939, Mary Strelioff. *Career:* Asst. Prof. of Chemistry, Univ. of Sask. 1930; Operations Research, R.C.A.F. 1943–44; Canadian Atomic Energy Project 1944–45; Head, Dept. of Chemistry 1948, Dean of Graduate Studies 1949 (Univ. of Sask.), Pres. 1959–74. *Publications:* Translations of Herzberg, Atomic Spectra and Molecular Spectra; Introduction to Radiation Chemistry (with Woods); over 200 publications in the scientific literature. Hon. LLD: Carleton, and Assumption; Fellow, King's Coll., London. *Member:* Royal Socy. of Canada; Chemical Inst. of Canada; Inst. of Chemistry; Faraday Socy.; Canadian Operations Research; Amer. Chemical Socy. *Clubs:* Saskatoon; Arctic Circle. *Address:* University of Saskatchewan, Saskatoon, Sask. S7N 0W0, Canada.

**SPINOLA, General Antonio Sebastiao Ribeiro.** *B.* 1910. *Educ.* Military College; Military (cavalry) School. *Career:* Army, rising from 2nd Lieut. (1933) to General (1969); National Republican Guard, Azores 1945–61, Lieut.-Gen. N. Angola 1961–64; Military Commander Guinea & Governor of the Province 1968–73; Vice-Chief of Gen. Staff of Armed Forces 1973–74; President of Junta April–Sept. 1974; retired from the Army Nov. 1974; in exile since 1975. *Publication:* Portugal and the Future. *Awards:* Grand Officer of Tower & Sword, with palm; Gold & Silver medals (military valour); DSM; Officer & Commander of the Military Order of Aviz; Military Medal; Cross of Order of Military Merit, other medals.

**SPIRIDONOV, Ivan Vasilyevich.** Soviet statesman. *B.* 1905; first job as fitter in a Leningrad plant. Graduated at Volgograd secondary engineering school 1925; worked as foreman and shop superintendent at Leningrad plant for 14 years; after graduation at the corresponding dept. of the Leningrad Industrial Inst. (1939) was appointed Director, Oryol Textile Machinery Plant. Dir.: Kuznetsk Plant 1941–44, and Leningrad Gosmetr Plant 1944–50. Went into Party work 1950; First Secy., Moskovsky District Committee of C.P.S.U., Leningrad; Assistant Head, Dept. of Leningrad Regional Communist Party Committee; Secretary 1954–56; First Secy. Leningrad City Committee 1956–57, and of Leningrad Regional Committee 1957–62; Secretary, C.P.S.U. Central Committee 1961–62; Member, Presidium, U.S.S.R. Supreme Soviet 1958–62; Member, C.P.S.U. Central Committee 1961–71; Deputy to U.S.S.R. Supreme Soviet of 5th, 6th, 7th and 8th convocations; Chairman of the Soviet of the Union of U.S.S.R. Supreme Soviet 1962–70; C.P.S.U. member 1928; Member, Foreign Affairs Commission of the Soviet of the Union; Cttee. U.S.S.R. Parly. Group. *Awards:* Orders of Lenin (twice), Red Banner of Labour, Patriotic War (1st Cl.), Badge of Honour, and Medals of the U.S.S.R. *Address:* The Presidium, The Supreme Soviet, The Kremlin, Moscow, U.S.S.R.

**SPIRO, Sidney.** MC 1945. *B.* 1914. *Educ.* Law Degree, Cape Town Univ. Royal Artillery in Middle East & Italy 1939–45. *Career:* Joined Anglo American Corp. 1953, Exec. Dir. 1961–77; Man. Dir. & Dep. Chmn., Charter Consolidated 1969, Chmn. 1971–76; Director: De Beers Consolidated Mines Ltd.,

Barclays Bank International Ltd., The Rio Tinto-Zinc Corp. Ltd., member of the International Advisory Council of the Canadian Imperial Bank of Commerce; Chmn., Societe Miniere de Tenke-Fungurume. *Clubs:* White's; MCC; Sunningdale; Rand. *Address:* 43 Lowndes Square, London, SW1.

**SPITZER, Arthur Hoermann.** American. Knight, Order of Orange-Nassau (Netherlands). Consul of the Netherlands (Hon.), Honolulu, Hawaii, May 1953—. *B.* 1917. *Educ.* Univ. of Wisconsin (AB 1937) and Harvard (LLB 1940). *M.* 1949, Blanche Helen van Oort' *S.* John Arthur, Robert Joseph, and Allan Thomas. *Daus.* Louise Justine and Lynne Selma. *Career:* Attorney-at-Law; Pres., Standard Shoe Store, Honolulu 1941—. Associate, M. B. Henshaw 1941—, and Heen & Kai 1951; Partner, Spitzer and Hustace 1955–56; private practice 1956—. Judge, tax appeals Court of Hawaii 1953–60; Consul of the Netherlands (Hon.) Honolulu Hawaii 1953—; Dean, Consular Corps of Honolulu 1962; Deputy City, County Attorney (Honolulu) 1946. Major, Army of U.S. 1941–45 and 1950–52 (Bronze Star, Asian-Pacific Meda with bronze arrowhead and 3 stars; Victory Medal, Philippine Liberation, 2 stars), Hon. LLD Jackson Coll. Member: Amer. and Hawaii Bar Assns.; Consular Corps. of Honolulu. Republican. *Clubs:* Pacific, Oahu Country, Outrigger Canoe; Honolulu Amateur Radio; New Zealand Assn. of Radio Transmitters Inc. Deceased.

**SPITZER, Frederick O.,** BSc. British Company Director. *B.* 1919. *Educ.* Carlsbad School; Univ. of Birmingham (BSc). *M.* 1954, Jane S. Eylenbosch. *Daus.* 2. *Career:* Dir. Audco Serck S.A. (France); Ets. Charrieras & Petit S.A., France; Audco-India Ltd.; Serck Ltd.; Audco-Rockwell Italiana; Chmn. Serck AG; Serck Audco S.A. (Belgium); Serck Audco N.V. (Netherlands); Serck Audco (Pty.) Ltd. (Australia); Serck Southern Africa (Pty.) Ltd. *Address:* Regina, Davos Platz, Switzerland; and *office* Gubelstrasse 15, Zug, Switzerland.

**SPONNER, Hans-Walter.** Diplom-Kaufmann; German. *B.* 1926. *Educ.* Maturity graduation from Landsberg High School 1948, and Hamburg Univ. (Diplom-Kaufmann 1952), *M.* 1956, Gisela Lange. *S.* Bernhard and Wolfgang. *Dau.* Irene. *Career.* With Kersten Hunik's International Transportbedrifj N.V., Rotterdam 1951–52; with Deutsche Philips GmbH, Hamburg Jan. 1953–Sept. 1958 (Sales Planning Export 1953–54; Market Research 1955–58). Market Research Manager of BP Benzin and Petroleum Aktiengesellsschaft, Hamburg, Oct. 1958—; Member: Vice-Pres., Vereinigung Betrieblicher Marktforscher (VBM German Company Market Researchers' Association), Oct. 1963–65. *Member:* Federal Parents Council Bundeselternrat; Vice-Pres. Bd. of Parents Chamber of Hamburg; Depty. of Christian Democratic Union in School Authority of Hamburg. *Member:* VBM (Regional Group Manager North 1961–66; Vice-Pres. 1963–65); BVM Berufsverband Deutscher Marktforscher. Founder of the new BVM Bundesverband Deutscher Marktforscher 1965. *Publications:* Wie Plane ich Meinen Absatz Praktikum des Industriellen Vertriebes (1960). *Clubs:* KD St. V. Wiking im CV; Amerika Gesellschaft (Hamburg). *Address:* 2104 Hamburg 92 Neugraben Flschbek, Wettloop 14a, Germany; and *office* Deutsche BP AG, Überseering 2, 2000, Hamburg 60, Germany.

**SPOONER, Archibald Wilberforce.** Australian industrialist and pastoralist. *B.* 1910. *Educ.* Scotch College, Melbourne, Vic. *M.* 1933, Violet Valentine. *S.* 3. *Dau.* 1. *Career:* Served in R.A.A.F. (Pastoral holdings: Dalmore Park, Scoresby, Vic., and Wellington Park, Sale, Vic.). Founder & Chairman Dalmore Preserving Co., Tom Piper Ltd., International Plastics (Aust.) Pty. Ltd., and International Marine Australasia Pty. Ltd. Chairman: Bertram Yacht Co. (Australia) Pty. Ltd., Tom Piper Exports Pty. Ltd., and United Cattle Corp. Ltd. Director, Alliance Acceptance Ltd. Australasian Chairman, Hanover Fire Insurance Co. of New York. Victorian member, Export Payments Insurance Corp. since 1957. Leader, Australia's First Food Survey Mission (Government sponsored) to Japan, 1963. *Clubs:* Australian, Danish (Melbourne). *Address: office* c/o Tom Piper Ltd., Williamstown Road, Garden City, S.C.7, Vic., Australia.

**SPRAGUE, John Louis.** American. *B.* 1930. *Educ.* Princeton Univ. (AB Chm) and Stanford Univ. (PhD Chem). *M.* 1952, Mary-Jane Whitney. *S.* John Louis, William Whitney, and David Hyatt. *Dau.* Catherine (van Zelm). *Career:* With Sprague Electric: Snr. Vice-Pres., Engineering Jan. 1964–July 1965; Senr. Vice-Pres., Co-Director of Engineering 1962–64; Senior Vice-President, Research and Development, 1965–67, Senior Vice-Pres., Semiconductor Div. 1967–75, Senior Vice-Pres., Semiconductor Div. & Ceramics Div 1975–76, President since 1976 and Director 1962—, Sprague Electric Co., North Adams, Mass.; Director: Mostek Corp., Carrollton, Tex.; Hybrid Systems, Burlington, MA.; & State Mutual Life Assurance Co. of America, Worcester, MA. *Member:* Electro-chemical Socy.; Amer. Chemical Socy.; Industrial Research Inst.; N.Y. Acad. of Sciences; Inst. of Electric and Electronic Engineers; Amer. Management Assn. *Publications:* several works on Electrochemical Technology, Physical Electricians, Physical Statua Solidi. *Clubs:* Chemists, Princeton (N.Y.C.); Mayflower Historical Socy.; Confrerie des Chevaliers du Tastevin; Confrerie de la Chaine des Rotisseurs. *Address: office* Sprague Electric Co., 87 Marshall Street, North Adams, Mass. 01247, U.S.A.

**SPRAGUE, Robert Chapman.** American. Founder of Sprague Specialties Company (now Sprague Electric Company) *B.* 1900. *Educ.* Hotchkiss School; U,S. Naval Academy; U.S. Naval Post-Graduate School; Massachusetts Institute of Technology; Hon. DSc Mass Univ. 1975. *M.* 1921, Florence Antoinette van Zelm. *S.* Robert C. Jr. and John Louis. *Career:* Continued his career as Naval Architect; was member of staff which superintended design and construction of Aircraft Carrier U.S.S. *Lexington*; Dir., Telegraph Condenser Co. Ltd., London, Eng. 1960–65. Pres. Sprague Specialties Co. 1926–53 (Treas. 1954–65). Chmn. OPA Industry Adv. Cttee. for Electronic Components and Parts 1944–45; Member Exec. Cttee. Massachusetts Cttee. on Post-War Reconversion 1942–45; Member Munitions Bd. Electronics Equipment Adv. Cttee. 1950–53; Pres., Radio Electronics Television Mfgrs. Assn. 1950–51; Chmn. Bd. 1950–52 and 1953–54; Pres., Associated Industries of Massachusetts 1951–53; Chmn. Sprague of Wisconsin 1948–68; Consultant on Continental Defence to Natl. Security Council (appointment by President Eisenhower) 1954; Chmn. Fed. Reserve Bank of Boston 1955–60. Consultant to Technological Capabilities Panel of Science Adv. Cttee. to Office of Defence Mobilization, 1954–55. Dir. United Carr 1953–68. Chairman Board of Directors, Sprague Electric Co. 1953–71; Chmn. Exec. Cttee. 1976; Hon. Chmn. of the Board & Dir. 1976—. Director, Sprague Products Co., North Adams, Mass. (wholly-owned subsidiaries of Sprague Electric Co.); Director, The First National Bank of Boston 1961–73; Member of Board, Mitre Corp., 1958—, Chmn., 1969–72. *Member:* Assoc. Ind. Mass. *Awards:* Hon DEng, Northeastern Univ. 1953; Hon DSc, Williams College 1954, and Lowell Technical Institute 1959; Hon. LLD Tufts Univ. 1959; Hon. DSc North Adam State Coll. 1972 & Univ. of Mass. 1975; Hon. LLD, Univ. of New Hampshire 1967, 'Outstanding Service' Award, North Adams Chamber of Commerce; Medal of Honour Award, Radio-Electronics-Television Manufacturers Association; 'Man-of-the-Year' Award, Hotchkiss Alumni Association; 'Distinguished Citizenship' Award, Bates College; Fellow, American Academy of Arts & Sciences. Life Member, Corp. of M.I.T. *Clubs:* Algonquin (Boston); Chemists' (N.Y.); Engineers (N.Y.); Union (Boston); Metropolitan (Washington). *Address:* 34 Bulkley Street, Williamstown, Mass., U.S.A.

**SPRIGG, Reginald Claude.** Australian. Consultant Geologist. *B.* 1919. *Educ.* Adelaide Technical High School (Matriculation 1936) and Adelaide University (BSc Hons Geology and Zoology 1941; MSc Geology 1943) Tate Medalist 1941. *M.* 1951, Griselda Agnes Findlay Paterson. *S.* Douglas Paterson. *Dau.* Margaret. *Career:* Army Engineer 1940; Shift Chemist Supervisor, Munitions, Salisbury, S. Aust. 1941–42; Asst. Research Officer, C.S.I.R.O. Division of Soils 1942–43; Asst. Govt. Geologist (SA) 1943–54; Established the Radium Hill Project 1943–49; Verco Medal 1970. Managing Director: Geosurveys of Australia Pty. Ltd. 1954–75; Geoseismic (Aust.) Pty. Ltd. 1954–75; Geotechnical & Engineering Services Ltd. 1956–65; South Australian Oceanographic Research Institute 1963–75; Foundation Chmn., Australian Petroleum Exploration Assn. 1961, Chmn., 1961–67, Councillor 1967—. Chmn., Australian Marine Science Assn. 1972. Dir., Petroleum Industry Environmental Council Executive 1973–74; Man. Dir., Beach Petroleum N.L.; Tasman Petroleum (N.Z.); Turkish Beach Petroleum N.L.; Chmn., Science Aids Pty. Ltd.; Dir., Southwestern Mining Ltd.; Nickel Mines of Aust. Ltd. *Publications:* (with wife) Arkaroola Mount Painter in the Flinders Ranges, S.A. (1976); & over 100 scientific & technical publications. Inventor of the "Aerodyne" wind generator. Co-owner (with wife) of Arkaroola Mount Painter Sanctuary since 1968. *Address:* Arkaroola Tourist Resort & Wildlife Sanctuary, via Copley, South Australia 5732; and *office* Arkaroola Travel Centre, 50 Pirie Street, Adelaide, South Australia 5000.

**SPROUL, Allan.** American banker. *B.* 9 Mar. 1896.

*Educ.* University of California (BS). *M.* 1921, Marion Meredith Bogle. *S.* Allan, Gordon John, David Saffell. *Career:* Head, Division of Analysis and Research, Federal Reserve Bank of San Francisco 1920–24, Assistant Federal Reserve Agent and Secretary 1924–30; Assistant Deputy Governor and Secretary, Federal Reserve Bank of New York 1930–34, Assistant to Governor and Secretary 1934–36, Deputy Governor 1936, First Vice-President 1936, President 1941–56; member, Tri-partite Economic Mission to India and Pakistan 1960; Chairman, President's Committee on Balance of Payments and Domestic Economic Situation of United States, 1961; Consultant, Wells Fargo Bank, San Francisco; Emeritus Trustee, Committee for Economic Development; Hon LLD, New York, Colgate, California and Columbia Universities. *Address:* Kentfield, Calif., 94904, U.S.A.

**SPROULL, Robert L.** *B.* 1918. *Educ.* Cornell University (BA; PhD). *M.* 1942, Mary Louise Knickerbocker. *S.* Robert F. *Dau.* Nancy M. *Career:* With RCA. Laboratories 1943–46; Professor of Physics Cornell Univ. 1946–68; Oak Ridge National Laboratory 1952; European Research Associates 1958–59; Editor, Journal of Applied Physics 1954–57; Director, Laboratory of Atomic and Solid State Physics, Cornell Univ. 1959–60 (Dir., Materials Science Center 1960–63). Vice-President for Academic Affairs, Cornell Univ. 1965–68. Director, Advanced Research Projects Agency, U.S. Department of Defence 1963–65; Chmn., Defence Science Board, U.S. Dept. of Defence, 1968–69; Vice-President and Provost, Univ. of Rochester, 1968–70. President, Univ. of Rochester, since 1970; Dir. John Wiley & Sons; Security Trust Co.; Sybron Corp; United Technologies Corp.; Xerox Corp. *Awards:* Fellow American Academy of Arts and Sciences; Amer. Physical Society. *Publication:* Modern Physics (John Wiley & Sons, 1956). *Clubs:* Cosmos, Genesee Valley. *Address:* 692 Mt. Hope Ave., Rochester, N.Y., 14620; and *office* University of Rochester, Rochester, N.Y., 14627, U.S.A.

**SPÜHLER, Willy.** Dr oec. publ. *B.* 1902. *Educ.* Universities of Zürich and Paris. *Career:* Worked in banks and at I.L.O. and as Secretary, International Union of Food Workers. Entered Statistical Office, Zürich 1931. Director, Zürich Employment Office 1935–42; Head, Central Office of War Economy 1939–48; Municipal Councillor (Head of Public Health and Public Economy Office) 1942–59; Pres., Swiss Broadcasting Corp.; National Councillor 1938–55; States Councillor 1955–59; elected to Federal Council, Dec. 1959; President of the Swiss Confederation 1963 and 1968 (Vice-Pres. 1962 and 1967); Minister of Transport, Communications, and Power. Minister of Federal Political Department (Foreign Affairs) 1966–70; Pres. Cultural Foundation Pro Helvetia since 1971. *Address:* Hirschengraben 20, 8000 Zürich, Switzerland.

**SPURLING, The Hon. Sir Arthur Dudley,** Kt, CBE, JP. British (Bermudian) barrister and attorney. *B.* 1913. *Educ.* Saltus Grammar (Bermuda); Rossall Sch. (Lancs., England) Bermuda Scholar; Trinity College Oxford (Rhodes Scholar); Lincoln's Inn, London. *M.* 1941, Marian Taylor (nee Gurr). *S.* 3. *Career:* Member of English Bar (Lincoln's Inn) since 1937; member of Bermuda Bar since 1938; Chmn. Board of Trade, Bermuda 1945–46; Senior Partner Messrs. Appleby, Spurling and Kempe, Bermuda since 1948; Chmn. Board of Immigration, Bermuda 1946–57; Common Councillor, Corporation of St. George, Bermuda, 1953–63; Chmn. Board of Public Works, Bermuda 1957–63, Member Executive Council 1957–68; Member Cabinet, Bermuda 1968–69, Minister of Education 1968–69; Chmn. Law Reform Cttee., Bermuda since 1969; Member, House of Assembly, Bermuda 1943–76 & Speaker 1972–76. *Chairman:* Board of Education, Bermuda 1963–68; St. George's Gr. School, Bermuda (and Trustee) 1958–63. *Director.* Numerous in Bermuda. *Trustee:* Bermuda Biological Station for Research since 1955. *Decorations:* Knight Bachelor 1975; Commander British Empire 1963. *Clubs:* St. George's Dinghy and Sports, St. David's County Cricket, ESU, Royal Bermuda Yacht (all Bermuda); Royal Hamilton Amateur Dinghy; Mid-Ocean. *Address:* Three Chimneys, Wellington, St. George's, Bermuda; and *office* Reid House, Church Street, Hamilton (P.O. Box 1179), Bermuda.

**SPYCHALSKI, Marian.** Polish. Marshal of Poland. *B.* 1906. *Educ.* Warsaw Technological University. *Career:* Chief of Staff of the People's Polish Army; First Mayor of Warsaw 1944–45; Assistant Commander-in-Chief of the Polish Army 1945; First Deputy Minister of National Defence 1945–48; Minister of National Defence 1956–68; Marshal of Poland 1963—; Pres. of Council of State, Polish People's Republic 1968–70. Member, Political Bureau of the Central Cttee., Polish United Workers' Party 1948–49, 1956–70; Deputy, National Home Council and afterwards to the Seym (1947–49 and 1957–72). Retired. Grand Prix award 1937 for development of the capital project. *Awards:* Grunwald Cross, Second Class (1945); Order of the Banner of Labour (1959); Order of Builders of People's Poland. *Address:* 4/6 Wiejska, Warsaw, Poland.

**SREENIVASAN, Mandayam A.** Indian Administrator & industrialist. *B.* 1897. *Educ.* Madras University. *M.* 1916. Srimathi Singamma. *S.* 3. *Daus.* 3. *Career:* Entered Mysore Civil Service 1918 and served in various departments; on Mysore State business in London and New York 1928–30; on special duty to reorganize and manage Sri Krishnarajendra (Textile) Mills, Mysore 1931–34; Deputy Commissioner and President, City Municipal Council, Mysore 1935–39; Chmn. and Government Director of various industrial concerns 1939–40; services lent to the Government of India during the war as Controller of Supplies, South India 1940; Minister for Food, Industries, Civil Supplies, Forests and Mining, Mysore State; Chairman, Mysore Iron and Steel Works, Board of Industrial Research 1943–45; Minister for Agriculture, Local Self-Government, Army, etc. 1945–46; Vice-President, Executive Council, Gwalior State, and Member, Constituent Assembly, States Negotiating Committee, Union Constitution Committee, etc. 1947–48; Dir. Southern Veneers Ltd.; Sifco Ltd.; Indian Oxygen Ltd. Chmn., Consolidated Coffee Ltd., Coffee Lands Ltd.; Shivmoni Steel Tubes Ltd. *Address:* Rajamahal Extn., Bangalore, India.

**SRIVASTAVA, Chandrika Prasad,** Padma Bhushan 1972. Indian. *B.* 1920. *Educ.* Lucknow, India; BA (1st class) 1940, BA (Hons 1st class) 1941, MA (1st class) 1942, LLB (1st class) 1944; gold medal for proficiency in Eng. Lit. & Polit. Sci. *M.* 1947, Nirmala Salve. *Daus.* 2. *Career:* Under-Sec. to the Govt. of India, Ministry of Commerce 1948–49; City Magistrate, Lucknow 1950; Additional District Magistrate, Meerut 1951–52; Officer on Speical Duty, Directorate General of Shipping 1953; Dep. Dir.-Gen. of Shipping 1954–57; Dep. Sec., Ministry of Transport, & Private Sec. to the Minister of Transport & Communications/Minister of Commerce & Industry 1958; Senior Dep. Dir.-Gen. of Shipping 1959–60; Man. Dir., Shipping Corp. of India Ltd., Bombay 1961–64; Joint Sec. to the Prime Minister of India 1964–66; Chmn. of the Board of Dirs. & Man. Dir. Shipping Corp. of India Ltd. 1966–73; Dir., Central Inland Water Transport Corp. 1967; Chmn. of the Board of Dirs., Mogul Line Ltd. 1967–73; Dir., Central Board, Reserve Bank of India 1972–73; Sec.-Gen., Inter-Governmental Maritime Consultative Org. since 1974. *President:* Indian National Shipowners Assn. 1971–73; Inst. of Marine Technologists, India; UN Plenipotentiary Conference on Code of Conduct for Liner Conferences. *Chairman:* Cttee. of Invisibles including Shipping, Insurance & Tourism, 3rd UN Conference on Trade & Development 1972. *Vice-President:* Sea Cadet Council. *Member:* National Shipping Board 1959–73; Merchant Navy Training Board 1959–73; National Welfare Board for Seafarers 1966–73; American Bureau of Shipping 1969; Governing Body, Indian Inst. of Foreign Trade 1970; State Board of Tourism 1970; National Harbour Board 1970–73; General Cttee., Bombay Chamber of Commerce & Industry 1971; Governing Body, Indian Inst. of Management, Ahmedabad. *Publications:* articles on shipping in newspapers & journals. *Clubs:* Willingdon Sports (Bombay); Anglo-Belgian & Curzon House (London); Delhi Symphony Society. *Address:* 56 Ashley Gardens, London SW1.

**STABELL, Peter Platou.** Norwegian lawyer. *B.* 1908. *Educ.* Oslo University (LLB) and London School of Economics (International Law). *M.* 1948, Dorothy Nicholson Bates (diss. 1972). *S.* Bredo Peter. *Career:* Cand. Jur. 1932; Legal Assistant 1932–34. Secretary to Agricultural Federation of Employers 1937–40; Secretary in Norwegian Ministry of Justice (in exile in London) 1940–41, Chief of Division of same Ministry 1941–45. Has practised Law in Oslo since 1945; became Supreme Court Advocate 1949. Member of firm of Wilhelm Bugge, Peter P. Stabell Erling Christiansen & F. M. Bugge 1949–65; Chairman of the Board: Odda Smelteverk A/S 1952—, and Skaland Grafitverk A/S 1952—, Norsk A/S Christiani & Nielson since 1972, Robert Bosch Norge A/S since 1975, A/S Tyssefaldene since 1975. Member of the Board: Harald A. Møller A/S 1961—, and A/S Norsk Marconikompani 1962—. Member Committee of Surveillance, A/S Andresens Bank 1959—; Member of firm of Peter F. Stabell, Otto Chr. Ottesen and Niels M. Heiberg 1965—. *Member* of Board, Norwegian Branch of the International Law Assn. Conservative. *Club:* Det Norske Selskab. *Address:* Dalsveien 51,

Slemdal, Oslo; and *office* Drammensveien 40, Oslo 2, Norway.

**STACE, Francis Nigel.** N.Z. *B.* 1915. *Educ.* Canterbury Univ., Christchurch (BEng in both Elec.-Mech. and Mech.); Certificate of Proficiency in Journalism. *M.* 1939, Margaret Jean Fitch. *S.* 1. *Daus.* 4. *Career:* Editor: N.Z. Energy Journal since 1939, and of N.Z. Engineering 1946—; Secy. Electric Supply Authority Engineers Inst. of N.Z. 1946—; Man. Ed. 1947–61, Man. Dir. and Editor in Chief, Technical Publications Ltd. 1961—; Dir. Technical Books Ltd. 1948—; Senate Investments Ltd. 1960—; N.Z. Institution, Engineers Conf. (Wellington 1964) 1962–64; D. A. White & Sons (1975) Ltd. Life Member (Senator) Junior Chamber International 1955— (Chmn. of Dirs. J.C.I. XI World Congress, Wellington 1956; N.Z. Deleg., Mexico City Congress 1954); apptd. by N.Z. Govt. to Special Committee on Moral Delinquency in Children and Adolescents 1954, and by French Embassy in N.Z. to represent N.Z. Press at First Paris Technical Fortnight 1962, and by Australian National Committee at Sixth World Power Conf. 1962 (similarly by Japan 1966, U.S.S.R. 1968, Romania 1971, U.S.A. 1974), and by British Information Service in N.Z., to tour U.K. as technical Press representative 1964. Member: N.Z.I.E. (member Publications Committee 1944–67, Council member 1963–69, Vice-Pres. 1967–69, Chmn. Wellington Branch 1962–63); Instn. Elec. Engineers, London; Amer. Socy. Engineering Education; Amer. Inst. Electrical and Electronic Engineers; Inst. of Scientific and Technical Communications; Wellington Ratepayers' & Citizens' Assn. (Dep. Chmn. 1960–66). *Publications:* Technical Exposition—Principles & Practice (1940); The Iron Curtain between Science & the Community in N.Z. (1947); Technical Man v. Librarian (1948); Technical Tedium (1973). *Clubs:* Rotary; J.C.I. Senators; University. *Address:* 118 Cecil Road, Wadestown, Wellington 1, New Zealand.

**STACK (STACHIEWICZ), Bogdan R.** American. *B.* 1924. *Educ.* Univ. of Bristol (BSc Elec Eng) and McGill Univ. (MEng-Electronics). *M.* 1955, Mathilde Moore Norvell. *S.* Thomas R. *Daus.* Elisabeth Ann, Joanna and Christina. *Career:* Engineer Radio Engineering Products Ltd. Montreal 1947–52; Senior Engineer Leukurt Electric Co. (San Carlos) 1952–55; Asst. Section Head, Stromberg Carlson Co. (Rochester N.Y.) 1955–57; Associate Director, Communication Lab., International Telephone & Telegraph Corp. 1957–62; Manager Communications Sciences Dept. Western Development Labs. Philco Corp. 1962–64; Mgr., Systems Development Department, Stanford Research Institute (Menlo Park Calif.) 1964–68; Mgr. Systems Design Dept. Philco-Ford Corp. 1968–71; Program Manager Space Systems Philco-Ford Corp. 1971–73; Man. Internat. Commun. Satellite Systems, Ford Aerospace & Communications Corp. (formerly Aeronutronic Ford Corp.) since 1973. *Publications:* Several papers on electronics and telephony. Holder of seven U.S. patents, Senior Member, I.E.E.E. (N.Y.C.). *Address:* 358 Toyon Avenue, Los Altos, Calif. 94022; and *office* Ford Aerospace & Communications Corp. W.D.L. M/S G-83 Palo Alto, Calif. 94303, U.S.A.

**STACKELBERG, Count Fritz Carl Louis,** LLB. Swedish diplomat. *B.* 21 May 1899. *M.* 1937, Marianne Schumacher. *S.* Claes-Erik. *Daus.* Katarina, Madeleine. En. Ex. and Min. Plen. to Venezuela 1948–53; Chief of Protocol 1953–56; Ambassador to Greece 1956–62; Ambassador to Switzerland 1962–65. *Address:* Engelbrektsgaten 21, Stockholm, Sweden.

**STADLER, Marinus.** German. *B.* 1928. *Educ.* Munich University (Dr. phil) and Salzburg Seminar in American studies. *M.* 1954, Eva Pruss. *S.* Manuel. *Daus.* Marina and Felicitas. *Career:* Manager of a Publishing House 1954–57. Executive Vice-President, SAW Werbeagentur GWA (advertising agency) 1958–70; Owner, Stadler & Kemnitz Marketing Promotion (agency) 1970—. *Publications:* articles on marketing, management and organization, in various professional journals. *Address: office* Steinlestrabe 9, 6 Frankfurt/Main, Germany.

**STAGG, Ronald Gurr.** American actuary and life insurance executive; *B.* 1904. *Educ.* University of Toronto (BA with Hons. in Mathematics) 1925; member (Fellow) Institute of Actuaries (Great Britain), Society of Actuaries (member, Bd. of Governors and past Vice-Pres. of the latter). *M.* 1929, Bernice L. Jacobs. *S.* Michael J. *Career:* With Canada Life Assurance Co. 1925–27, Lincoln National Life Insce. Co. 1927–46, and 1955–69 (Asst. Actuary 1928, Assoc. Actuary 1930, Actuary 1943, Second Vice-Pres. and Actuary 1945–46); Northwestern Natl. Life Insce. Co., Minneapolis 1946–51 (Vice-Pres. 1946–47; Pres. and Dir. 1947–51); Vice-Pres., Prudential Insce. of Amer. 1952–55; Vice-President and Director, Lincoln National Life Insurance Co. (Fort Wayne, Ind.) 1955–69; Director and Chairman Dominion Life Assurance Co. Waterloo Ont. 1967–69; Deputy Chairman and Director, Dominion-Lincoln (London, Eng.) 1965–69; Director, Compagnie de Réassurance Nord-Atlantique, Paris, 1967–69; former member of Board of Directors, Life Insce. Association of America, and Institute of Life Insurance; Dir. Univ. of Toronto Assoc. Inc; Past Pres. U.C. Services of Fort Wayne and Allen County; Secy. Senior Actuaries Club 1953–63; Dir. Precisioneerin Inc.; (Fort Wayne, Ind.). Independent Republican. *Clubs:* Minneapolis; Canadian (N.Y.C.); Newcomen; Fort Wayne Country; Inst. of Directors (London); Quest; Summit; Fort Wayne Chamber of Commerce. *Address:* 7011 Balmoral Drive, Fort Wayne, Ind., 46804, U.S.A.

**STAHLBRANDT, Ake Enok.** Swedish. *B.* 1914. *Educ.* Univ. of Stockholm (Business degree). *M.* 1945, Marianne Stahlbrandt. (Div.); *Dau.* Ann Cecilia. *Career:* Man. Dir., Trelleborg Aktiebolag 1949–76, Chmn. of the Bd. 1976—; Man. Dir. Tretorn Aktiebolag 1965–76, Chmn. of the Bd. 1976—. Director & Dep. Chmn., Skandinaviska Enskilda Banken 1965—, Swedish Employers Association 1965–76, Swedish Exporters Association 1963—, Swedish Chemical Industries Association 1950–76, Swedish Rubber Industry Association 1950–76, Swedish Industry Association 1966–76, Chamber of Commerce (Skåne) 1950—, and of about 10 other companies. *Address: office* Trelleborg Aktiebolag, Trelleborg, Sweden.

**STÅHLE, Anders Nils Oscar Kåse,** CBE, DLhc. Swedish administrator and diplomat. *B.* 12 July 1901. *Educ.* University of Lund (LLB). *M.* 1926, Birgit Olsson. *S.* Claes. *Daus.* Gunilla (Wenner), Cecilia (af Klint), Malin (Giddings). Swedish Foreign Service 1927–48; Envoy 1946; Director of Nobel Foundation, Stockholm 1948–72; Chmn. Bd. of Trustees Int. Fed. of Inst. for Advanced Study 1972–74; Chmn. Panel of Special Advisors 1974—; Chmn. Bd. of Trustees, Int. Inventor Award 1976—. *Clubs:* Swedish Jockey; Nya Sällskapet. *Address:* Nobel House, Sturegatan 14, 11436 Stockholm, Sweden.

**STAIRS, A. Edison.** Canadian politician. *B.* 1924. *Educ.* High School, Canterbury, New Brunswick; Meductic NB; University of New Brunswick. *M. S.* 2. *Career:* Royal Canadian Air Force 1943; Gen. Merchant at Meductic 1946; Representative, and later Manager, for Ins. Co. since 1949; Vice-Pres. Progressive Conservative Party (nat. exec.) 1960–65; Member of Legis. Assembly for Carleton County 1960 (re-elected 1963, 67 and 70); Party Whip 1967–70; Minister of Economic Growth and Agric. and Rural Development 1970–72; Minister of National Resources 1972–74; Re-elected to Legislature as member for Carleton South 1974; Minister of Finance and Chmn. of N.B. Electric Power Commission 1974–76. *President* (past) Woodstock Old Home Week Assn. *Member:* Royal Canadian Legion; Masonic Lodge, Shriners, various other Community assns. *Address:* P.O. Box 1002, Woodstock, N.B., Canada.

**STALLARD, Albert William.** MP. British politician. *B.* 1921. *Educ.* Hamilton Academy; Low Waters Public School. *M.* 1944, Sheila Murphy. *S.* 1. *Dau.* 1. *Career:* Precision Toolmaker in many Establishments 1937–55; British European Airways 1955–65; Airways Corp. Engineering Apprentice School, London Airport 1965–70; Councillor and Chmn. various Cttees. St. Pancras and Camden Borough Councils 1953–70; Member of Parliament for St. Pancras, N., 1970–74, Camden-St Pancras, N., since 1974; Parly. Private Secy. to Min. of State for Agric., Fish. & Food 1974, to Min. of State for Housing & Construction 1975; Asst. Whip. 1976. Alderman Camden Borough Council since 1971. *Member:* Inst. Training Officers; Chmn. Assn. of Mental Health; Camden Town Disablement Adv. Committee. *Award:* A.E.U. Order of Merit. *Address:* House of Commons, London, S.W.1.

**STALLARD, Sir Peter Hyla Gawne.** KCMG, CVO, MBE, KStJ. *B.* 1915. *Educ.* Bromsgrove School, and Corpus Christi College, Oxford (BA 1936; MA 1954). *M.* 1941, Mary Elizabeth Kirke, CStJ. *S.* 1. *Dau.* 1. *Career:* Entered Colonial Service, Northern Nigeria 1937; War Service West Africa and Burma 1939–45; Secretary to Prime Minister of Nigeria 1957–61; Governor and C. in C. of British Honduras 1961–66; Lieutenant-Governor, Isle of Man, 1966–74. *Club:* Athenaeum. *Address:* 18 Henley Road, Taunton, Somerset.

**STAMP, Hon. Arthur Maxwell.** British; *B.* 1915. *Educ.* Leys School, Cambridge; Clare College, Cambridge (MA; 1st

Cl. Honours Economics Tripos). *M.* 1943, Alice Mary Richards. *S.* 1. *Daus.* 2. *Career:* Barrister-at-Law, Inner Temple 1939; British Army (Lieut.-Col. Intelligence Corps) 1940–46; Financial Adviser, John Lewis Partnership 1947–50; Acting Adviser, Bank of England 1950–51; Alternate Dir. for U.K., International Monetary Fund, Washington 1951–53 (Head, Eur. Dept., Imf, 1953–54; Mem. Council International Chamber of Commerce 1961–75; Mem. Civil Aviation Authority 1976—. Adviser to the Governors, the Bank of England 1954–57. Director: Hill, Samuel & Co. Ltd. 1957–75; The De La Rue Co. Ltd. 1960—; Triplex Holdings Ltd. 1962–75; Chmn. Maxwel Stamp Associates Ltd. (Economic Consultants). *Address:* Mulberry Green Farmhouse, Copford, Essex; & 19 Clarence Gate Gardens, Glentworth Street, N.W.1. and *office* 55–63 Goswell Road ECIV 7PT.

**STANBROOK, Ivor Robert,** MP. British Lawyer & Politician. *B.* 1924. *Educ.* London & Oxford Univs.—BSc (Econ.). *M.* 1946, Joan Clement. *S.* 2. *Career:* RAF 1943–46; Colonial Admin. Service, Nigeria 1950–60; Barrister since 1960; MP (Cons.) for Orpington 1970–74; and for Bromley, Orpington since 1974. *Address:* 6 Stanbrook House, Orpington, Kent; and *office* House of Commons, London SW1A 0AA.

**STANFIELD, Robert Lorne,** PC, QC, LLD. Canadian barrister. *B.* 1914. *Educ.* Colchester Acad., Truro; Ashbury Coll., Ottawa; Dalhousie University (BA); Harvard University (LLB); appointed QC Dec. 1950. *M.* (1) 1940, Joyce Frazee (*D.*), and (2) 1957, Mary Margaret Hall. *S.* Robert Maxwell. *Daus.* Sarah, Judith, Miriam. *Career:* Law Practise, Halifax, Nova Scotia 1945–56; Pres., N.S. Progressive Conservative Assn. 1947—; Leader, N.S. Prog. Cons. Party 1948–67; Premier & Min. of Educ., N.S. 1956–67; MP for Halifax since 1968; Leader of Opposition & National Leader of Prog. Cons. Party of Canada 1967–76. Progressive Conservative. *Clubs:* The Halifax; Rideau; Saraguay. *Address:* Stornoway, Acacia Avenue, Rockcliffe Park, Ottawa, Canada.

**STANFORD, Alfred Boller.** American Publisher, Milford Citizen. *B.* 1900. *Educ.* Amherst College (BA). *M.* 1951, Berenice Langton Ladd. *S.* John, Peter. *Dau.* (step) Deborah. *Career:* Vice-Pres. and Dir., Compton Advertising 1929–42; Capt., U.S. Naval Reserve (served in World Wars I and II; Bronze Star, U.S.; Legion of Merit, U.S.; Croix de Guerre avec étoile vermille, France) 1942–44; Director, Bureau of Advertising, American Newspaper Publishers' Association 1944–46; Vice-Pres. and Director, New York Herald Tribune, 1948–50; Pres., Stanford Associates; Pres. and publisher, The Milford Citizen, Milford, Conn. *Publications:* Navigator; Ground Swell; Invitation to Danger; Man, Fish & Boats; Pleasures of Sailing; Force Mulberry; Mission in Sparrow Bush Lane. *Address:* 433 Gulf Street, Milford, Conn. 06461, U.S.A.

**STANLEY, C. Maxwell.** American consulting engineer. *B.* 1904. *Educ.* Univ. of Iowa (BS 1926; MS 1930); LHD Iowa Wesleyan Coll. 1961; Doctor of Humanities Honoris Causa, Univ. of Manila, 1970. *M.* 1927, Elizabeth M. Holthues. *S.* David M. and Richard H. *Dau.* Jane Stanley Buckles. *Career:* Structural Designer, Byllesby Engineering & Management Corp., Chicago 1926–27, and Dept. of Grounds & Buildings, State University of Iowa 1927–28; Hydraulic Engineer, Management & Engineering Corp., Chicago 1966–32; Consulting Egr., Young & Stanley, Inc. 1932–39; Partner & Pres., Stanley Engineering Co. 1939–66; Pres. 1966–71, Stanley Consultants Inc. Muscatine, Iowa Chmn. Bd. 1971—; Pres. 1944–64, Hon. Industries Inc. Chmn. Bd. since 1964; Pres. Stanley Consultants Ltd. Liberia 1959–71; Man. Dir. Stanley Consultants Ltd/Nigeria 1960–67; Pres. Atlas World Press Review 1975—. Chairman Exec. Council, World Assn. of World Federalists 1958–65; Mem. Council 1947—, World Federalists, U.S.A. (Pres. 1954–56 and 1964–66); Methodist Church Board of Christian Social Concerns 1960–68; Chmn. Strategy for Peace Conference 1962—; Chmn., Conferences on the U.N. of the Next Decade, 1965—; Pres., Stanley Foundation 1956; Bd. of Dirs of Univ. of Iowa Foundation 1966— (Pres. 1971–75). *Awards:* Distinguished Service Award, Univ. of Iowa 1967; Hancher Finkbine Medallion 1971; Alfred Noble Prize 1933, and the Collingwood Prize 1935, from American Society of Civil Engineers; John Dunlap Award 1943, Marston Award 1947, and Distinguished Service Award 1962, from Iowa Engineering Society; Hon. Membership, 1975, The 1965 Annual Award for outstanding service to the engineering profession from Natl. Socy. of Professional Engineers. Bd. of Trustees, Iowa Wesleyan Coll. 1951; Garrett Theological Semniary 1972–75. *Fellow:* Amer. Inst. of Consultant Engineers; Chmn., Fellows Ctte., Amer. Consulting Engineers Council 1974; National Socy. of Professional Engrs. Fellow: Amer. Socy. of Civil Engrs.; Inst. of Electrical and Electronics Engrs.; Amer. Socy. of Mechanical Engrs. *Publications:* Waging Peace; The Consulting Engineer (books); over 60 technical articles. *Club:* Rotary International. *Address:* 115 Sunset Drive, Muscatine, Iowa 52761; and *office* Stanley Consultants Inc., Stanley Building, Muscatine, Iowa, 52761, U.S.A.

**STANLEY, Charles Orr,** CBE. Former Chairman and Managing Director, Pye (Cambridge) Ltd., Pye Ltd., Pye (Ireland) Ltd.; Credit Finance Ltd. Chmn.: Sunbeam Wolsey Ltd., Director: Associated Television Ltd., Arts Theatre Trust Ltd.; Orr Investments Ltd.; Stanley Foundation Ltd. *B.* 1899. *Educ.* Bishop Foy School, Waterford (Ireland) and City & Guilds (Finsbury, London). *M.* (1) Elsee Florence Gibbs. *S.* John Orr; (2) 1935, Velma Dardis Price. OBE 1943; CBE 1945. Served in World War I (R.F.C.) 1917–18; Civil Engineer 1922; Hon LLD Trinity Coll. Dublin, 1960; FCGI 1961. Managing Director, Arks Publicity 1924–30. *Address:* Lisselan Clonakilty, Co. Cork, Ireland.

**STANLEY, Henry Sydney Herbert Cloete.** CMG. British diplomat. *B.* 1920. *Educ.* Eton; Balliol Coll. Oxford. *M.* 1941, Margaret Sydney Dixon. *S.* 3. *Career:* Military Service 1940–46; C'wealth Relations Office 1947; Appointed to Pakistan 1950–52; Swaziland & S. Africa 1954–57; U.S.A. 1959–61; Dep. High Commissioner Tanganyika 1961–63; Dep. High Commissioner Kenya 1963–65; Insp. & Chief Insp. Diplomatic Service 1966–70: High Commissioner to Ghana 1970–75; Assist. Under Secy. of State, F.C.O. 1975–77; High Commissioner to Trinidad & Tobago & (non-resident) to Grenada since 1977. *Award:* CMG. *Address:* c/o Foreign and Commonwealth Office, London, S.W.1.

**STANLEY, John Paul,** MP. British. *B.* 1942. *Educ.* Repton School; Lincoln Coll., Oxford—MA. *M.* 1968, Susan Elizabeth Giles. *S.* 1. *Dau.* 1. *Career:* Research Associate of the International Inst. for Strategic Studies 1968–69; Rio Tinto-Zinc Corp. Ltd. 1969–74; Conservative MP for Tonbridge & Malling since 1974; PPS to Rt. Hon. Mrs. Margaret Thatcher since 1976. *Publications:* The International Trade in Arms (1972). *Clubs:* Leander. *Address:* House of Commons, London SW1A 0AA.

**STANS, Maurice H.** American. Retired Secretary of Commerce of the U.S., 1969–72. *B.* 1908. *Educ.* Northwestern and Columbia Univs. *M.* 1933, Kathleen Carmody. *S.* 2. *Daus.* 2. *Career:* Vice-Chmn. and Dir. United California Bank 1961–63; Pres., and Dir. Western Bancorporation 1961–63; Dir., Bureau of the Budget of the U.S. March 1958–Jan. 1961; Dep. Postmaster-General of the U.S. 1955–58; Exec. Partner, Alexander Grant & Co. 1941–55. Hon. LLD Northwestern, Illinois Wesleyan and DePaul Univs.; D.P.A. Parsons College; Grove City College LLD; St. Anselm's College; Gustavus Adolphus, Rio Grande and Pomona Colleges and San Diego; elected to Accounting Hall of Fame 1960; International Salesman of the Year Award 1971. Tax Foundation Award for Distinguished Public Service 1959; Great Living American Award (U.S. Chamber of Commerce) 1961. President, Glore Forgan, Wm. R. Staats Inc. 1963–68; Former Dir. Tax Foundation; Nat. Assn. of Manufacturers. Member: American Institute Certified Public Accountants (Annual Award 1954) Pres. 1954–5; American Accounting Association (Award 1952); National Assn. of Postmasters. Republican. *Publications:* Many articles on government, business, finance and economics. *Clubs:* Shikar-Safari; Union League (Chicago); African Safari Washington; Adventurers; East African Professional Hunters (Hon. Member); Explorers; Metropolitan (N.Y.C.). *Address:* 211 South Orange Grove, Pasadena, California, U.S.A.

**STANTON, Frank (Nicholas).** *B.* 1908. *Educ.* Ohio Wesleyan Univ. (BA 1930) and Ohio State Univ. (PhD 1935). *M.* 1931, Ruth Stephenson. *Career:* Chmn. American National Red Cross; Vice-Chmn., League of Red Cross Societies (Geneva); Member, Board of Directors: CBS Inc.; American Electric Power; Atlantic Richfield Co.; Pan American World Airways Inc.; Lincoln Center for the Performing Arts Inc.: New Perspective Fund Inc.; N.Y. Life Insurance Co.; The Interpublic Group of Companies Inc.; The Observer Ltd. (London); Book Digest Co. Inc; Recorded Anthology of American Music Inc.; Municipal Art Socy. of New York; National Center for Health Education; Graduate member, The Business Council. Trustee, The Rand Corp.; Fellow: American Acad.

of Arts & Sciences, Amer. Assn. for Advancement of Science, Amer. Psychological Assn., New York Acad. of Science, Sigma Delta Chi. *Member:* Council on Foreign Relations, Institute of Electrical & Electronic Engineers; Internat. Exhibitions Cttee., Amer. Fedn. of Arts; Amer. Council on Germany Inc.; Governing Council, Rockefeller Univ. Archives Center; Radio-Television News Directors Assn.; Nat. Acad. of Television Arts & Sciences; Advisory Bd., Center for Strategic & Internat. Studies; Pres. CBS 1946–71, Vice-Chmn. 1971–73: Chmn. Center, Advanced Study in the Behavioral Sciences 1953–60; Chmn. U.S. Advis. Comm. on Information 1964–73; Trustee, The Rockefeller Foundation 1961–73; Diplomate, Amer. Bd. of Professional Psychology; Chmn., Business Cttee. for the Arts Inc. 1972–74; Hon Trustee, Amer. Crafts Council; Member, New York State Council on the Arts 1965–70; Trustee, Carnegie Inst. of Washington (Chmn.); Member, The Architectural League of New York; Chmn., Panel on International Information, Education & Cultural Relations, Georgetown Univ. Center for Strategic & International Studies 1974–75. *Clubs:* Century Assn., Links (N.Y.C.), Cosmos; Metropolitan, National Press (Washington) *Address:* 10 East 56 Street, New York, N.Y. 10022, U.S.A.

**STAREWICZ, Artur.** Polish Diplomat. *B.* 1917. *Educ.* Univ. Warsaw and Lwow; Institut Chimique de Rouen; Electrochemical Inst. of Charkov; Chem. Ing. *M.* 1946, Maria Rutkiewicz. *S.* 2. *Daus.* 2. *Career:* Party and Trade Union Official 1944–63; mem. Central Cttee Polish United Workers 1957–71, Secy 1963–71; mem. of Parlt. (SEIM) 1957–72; Polish Ambassador in United Kingdom since 1971. *Awards:* Banner of Labour 1st Class (twice), Polonia Restituta IV Class, Golden Cross of Merit. *Address:* 4 Templewood Ave., London N.W.3; and *office* 47 Portland Place, London W.C.1.

**STARK, Sir Andrew (Alexander Steel),** KCMG, CVO. British Diplomat. *B.* 1916. *Educ.* Bathgate Acad.; Univ. of Edinburgh, MA (Hons.) 1938. *M.* 1944, Rosemary Helen Oxley Parker. *S.* 2. (& 1 *dec'd.*). *Career:* Joined Foreign (now Diplomatic) Service 1948; 1st Sec., H.M. Embassy, Vienna 1951–53; Asst. Private Sec. to Sec. of State for Foreign Affairs 1953–55; Head of Chancery, H.M. Embassy, Belgrade 1956–58, & Rome 1958–60; Counsellor, Foreign Office 1960–64; Counsellor & Head of Chancery, H.M. Embassy, Bonn 1964–68; Ambassador attached to U.K. Mission to the U.N., New York 1968; Under-Sec.-Gen., U.N., New York 1968–71; H.M. Ambassador, Copenhagen 1971–76; Dep. Under-Sec., Foreign & Commonwealth Cttee since 1975. *Decorations:* Knight Commander, Order of St. Michael & St. George 1975; Companion, Victorian Order 1965; Grand Cross, Order of Dannebrog (Denmark) 1974; Grosses Verdienstkreuz (Fed. Rep. of Germany) 1965. *Address:* 41 Eaton Place, London SW1; Fambridge Hall, White Notley, Essex; and *office* Foreign & Commonwealth Office, London SW1.

**STARK, David Joseph.** Canadian. *B.* 1917. Educ. University of Oklahoma (BSc Chem Eng 1943). *M.* (1) 1945, Joan June Thomas (*Div.* 1967). *S.* David Christopher. *Dau.* Susan Glen; (2) 1968, Anna Seidel. *S.* Glen Andrew. *Dau.* Alixe Charlene. *Career:* President D. J. Stark, Associates Ltd.; Vice-Pres., Alberta Gas Ethylene Ltd. 1976; Vice-Pres., Eng. & Construction, Canadian Arctic Gas Pipeline Ltd. 1974–76; Director, Heredia Moreno S.A., Madrid, Spain 1969–73; Vice-Pres. of Operations: Intnl. Minerals & Chemicals U.S.A., and Vice-Pres. member of Board of Directors IMC of Canada 1959–64; President and Member Board of Directors, Nitrin Inc. 1961–64; Vice-Pres. Escambia Corp. 1955–59; Gen. Mgr. National Petrochemicals Corp. 1951–55; Chief Technologist Montreal Refinery, Shell Oil Co. of Canada (later Departmental Head) 1943–51. *Publications:* miscellaneous articles on management and production reviews; The President's Club. Member: Chemist's Club (N.Y.C.); Amer. Inst. Mining Engrs.; Can. Inst. of Mining. *Clubs:* Assiniboia (Regina, Sask.); Mid-America (Chicago); Skokie Country (Glencoe, Ill.); Metropolitan (N.Y.); New York Athletic Assn.; Canadian (N.Y.). *Address:* P.O. RR 3, King City, Ontario, Canada.

**STARLEY, Hubert Granville,** CBE, FIMI. *B.* 1909. *Educ.* Ermysteds, Skipton. *M.* 1933, Lilian Amy Heron. *S.* 1. *Dau.* 1. *Career:* Personal Asst. to Lord Beaverbrook, when Min. of Supply; Adv. to Air Ministry, and War Office, and on Stores packaging 1943–45; Chmn., Anglo-American Packaging Committee 1944; member, Barlow Mission to U.S.A· 1944; Hon. Chmn., Motor Industry Jubilee Cttee. 1946; Chmn., Accessory & Component Manufacturer's Section, Socy. of Motor Manufacturers and Traders 1945–46, 1953–55, 1961–62; Hon. Chmn., Inter-Services Packing Organization 1958–65. Hon. Organizer Pageant of Lord Mayor's Show, London, 1965; Vice-Pres., Aims of Freedom & Enterprise since 1942; Council Member, S.M.M.T. 1953–74, Vice-Pres. 1972–73; Vice-Chmn. Champion Sparking Plug Co. Ltd., Feltham, Middlesex. Chairman, Starley Estates Ltd.; Chmn. Starley Marine, Shepperton; Master of Company of Coachmakers and Coach Harness Makers 1966–67; President Pickwick Cycle Club 1954; President, British Cycle & Motor Cycle Industries Assn., 1969–71; Hon. Organiser SKOL 6-day Cycle Race, London 1967; President, Twickenham Conservative Assn., 1966–68, Patron 1971–77; Chmn., Fellowship of the Motor Industry, 1968. Chmn., Home Office Crime Prevention Cttee., 1968–69; Vice-Pres. Inst. of the Motor Industry; Trustee, National Motor Museum Beaulieu; Councillor Confederation British Ind. 1970–77; Councillor, College of Aeronautical & Automobile Engineering 1968–77. *Clubs:* Carlton; R.A.C.; Royal Thames Yacht; Royal Motor Yacht (Poole). *Address:* Rothesay House, London Road, Twickenham, Middlesex, TW1 1ES; and Santoy, Sandbanks, Poole, Dorset.

**STARNES, John Kennett.** Canadian. *B.* 1918. *Educ.* Trinity Coll. Schl. (Port Hope, Canada); Institut Sillig (Switzerland); Univ. of Munich (German Language Certificate) and University of Bishop's College, Canada (BA); Hon. DCL Bishop's Univ. 1975. *M.* 1941, Helen Gordon Robinson. *S.* Colin John and Patrick Barclay. *Career:* Acting Assistant Under-Secretary of State for External Affairs 1962; Ambassador to Federal Republic of Germany 1962–66; Head of Canadian Military Mission, Berlin 1962–66, Ambassador of Canada to the United Arab Republic June 1966, and concurrently to the Sudan July 1966–67; Assistant Under Secretary of State for External Affairs 1967–69. Director-General Security Service, Royal Canadian Mounted Police, 1970–73. *Club:* Turf (Cairo); Rideau (Ottawa). *Address:* Apt. 305, 333 Chapel Street, Ottawa, Canada K1N 8Y8.

**STASSEN, Harold Edward.** American lawyer, former governor, educator and government administrator. *B.* 13 April 1907. *Educ.* University of Minnesota (BA, LLB). *M.* 1929, Esther Glewwe. *S.* Glen Edward. *Dau.* Kathleen Esther. *Career:* Admitted to Minnesota Bar 1929; began practice of law in South St. Paul, Minnesota; County Attorney, Dakota County, Minnesota 1930–38; elected Governor of Minnesota Nov. 1938, re-elected 1940 and 1942; elected Chairman, National Governors' Conference 1941; re-elected 1942; resigned as Governor to enter U.S. Navy 1943; Assistant Chief of Staff to Admiral Halsey, 3rd Fleet (Legion of Merit, Bronze Star); appointed one of U.S. Delegates to San Francisco Conference of United Nations April 1945; President, University of Pennsylvania 1948–53; Director, Foreign Operations Administration 1953–55; Special Assistant to the President of U.S. 1955–58, and concurrently Deputy Representative of the U.S. on U.N. Disarmament Commission; Partner: Stassen, Kephart, Sarkis & Scullin since 1958; admitted to practice before U.S. Supreme Court 1932; Philadelphia and Pennsylvania Bar 1955; LLD, Dartmouth College, University of Pennsylvania, Princeton University, University of State of New York, Syracuse University; LHD Temple University. *Address:* Penn Towers, Philadelphia, Pa. 19103, U.S.A.

**STEEL, David Martin Scott,** PC, MP. British Politician. *B.* 1938. *Educ.* Prince of Wales Sch., Nairobi, Kenya; George Watson's Coll. & Edinburgh Univ. (MA 1960, LLB 1962). *M.* 1962, Judith Mary MacGregor. *S.* 2. *Dau.* 1. *Career:* Pres., Edinburgh Univ. Liberals 1959, Students' Representative Council 1960; Asst. Sec., Scottish Liberal Party 1962–64; MP (Liberal) for Roxburgh, Selkirk & Peebles since 1965; Liberal Chief Whip 1970–75; Leader of the Liberal Party since 1976. Mem., Parly. Delegation to UN Gen. Assembly 1967, Sponsor, Private Member's Bill to reform Law on Abortion 1966–67; Pres., Anti-Apartheid Movement of GB 1966–69; Chmn., Shelter, Scotland 1969–73. *Club:* Scottish Liberal (Edinburgh). *Address:* House of Commons, London SW1A 0AA.

**STEELE, Richard Addison.** American. Independent Oil Producer, Los Angeles. *B.* 1915. *Educ.* B.S. Petroleum Engineering, 1938. *M.* 1965, Rosa Ema Garcia. *S.* Richard A. II. *Dau.* Sandra Allison. *Career:* President, Steele Drilling Co. 1938–48, President: Utah-New Mexico Gas Co., Salt Lake City 1957–61; Falcon Oil Co., Los Angeles 1947–61; Vice-Pres. Perferaciones, Equipo y Inversiones S.A., Chilhuahua (Mexico) 1946–60. Director: Hilltop Oil Co., Carmi (Ill.) 1939–50; Mexico Minas S.A., Mexico City 1946–52, and Napo Rio Dredging Co. S.A., Quito (Ecuador) 1940–44. Secy.-Treas., Mexico Mercury Mining Co. Inc., Chilhuahua (Mexico) 1940–44; General Partner. Tesoro Oil Co., Los

Angeles 1946—; Partner, Teresa Oil Co., Los Angeles 1946—. Director: Maranon Development Co. S.A., Lima (Peru) 1956—, Pan American Land Co. S.A., Sao Paulo (Brazil) 1955—, Pacific & North Western Mining Co., Vancouver, B.C. (Canada) 1961; Dir. Advance Geophysics Inc. 1970–72; Pres. Western Oil Minerals Inc. (Dir. 1969–72); Vice-Pres. Seaboard Oil Co. Dir. since 1970. *Publications:* Real Estate in Mexico, (1963). *Member:* Independent Oil Producers Assn. of Amer.; Drilling Contractors Assn. of Amer.; Oil Producers Assn. of California. *Clubs:* Sigma Chi Fraternity 1936 (Univ. S. Calif. L.A.); Rod & Gun (Baja Calif. Ensenada, Mexico); V.F.W.; Amer. Legion (Albuq., N.M.). *Address:* 7475 Batisti Street, San Diego, Calif., 92111, U.S.A.

**STEENBERGHE, Maximilien Paul Leon.** Dutch economist. *B.* 2 May 1899. *Educ.* University of Utrecht (LLD). *M.* 1921, Catherine Theodore Marie Ausems. *S.* Paul, Amédé. *Daus.* Florentine, Elisabeth, Wilhelmine, Leontine. *Career:* Man. Dir., Dutch textile plant, 1923–34; Chairman, Catholic Employers Organization 1929–34; Minister for Economic Affairs 1934–35, 1937–42; President, Economic, Financial and Shipping Mission in Washington 1942–46; Head, Netherlands Delegation, Int. Food and Agriculture Conference, Hot Springs 1944, U.N.R.R.A. Conference, Montreal 1944, International Civil Aviation Conference, Chicago 1944; Dir. of financial and industrial companies. Knight, Order of the Netherlands Lion; Grand Officer, Order of Orange-Nassau; Cdr. St. Gregory the Great (Holy See); Grand Croix, Ordre de Léopold II (Belgium); Gran Cruz, Ordern del Mérito (Chile); Grand Cross, Order of Crown of Italy. *Address:* Goirle, Netherlands.

**STEERS, Newton I., Jr.** American. *B.* 1917. *Educ.* Yale Univ. (BA 1939; LLB 1948). *M.* 1957, Nina Gore Auchincloss. *S.* Newton Ivan III, Hugh Auchincloss, and Burr Gore. *Career:* Asst. Plant., E.I. du Pont de Nemours Co. (Parlin, N.J.) 1939–41; Asst. Supervisor, Technical Tests, same company, at Seaford, Del. 1941–43; Captain U.S.A.F. 1943–46; at Yale Law School 1946–48; Asst. Production Mgr., General Aniline & Film Corp. (Binghamton, N.Y.) 1948–51; Asst. to Branch Chief, Division Dir., Asst. Gen. Mgr., Commissioner, U.S. Atomic Energy Commission 1951–53. Republican (Maryland State Chmn.). Member. New York and D.C. Bar; Maryland State Insurance Commissioner 1967–70; Maryland State Senator 1970–76; U.S. Congress, House of Representatives since 1977. President: Atomics, Physics & Science Fund Inc., Shares in American Industry Inc., Columbian Financial Corp. Net Assets total over $60 million 1953–65. *Member:* Atomic Industrial Forum; Amer. Nuclear Socy.; National Fed. of Investment Analysts. *Clubs:* Chevy Chase; Metropolitan; Yale of N.Y.C. *Address:* 6601 River Road, Bethesda, Md. 20034, U.S.A.

**STEEVES, Winston Arnet.** Canadian executive. *B.* 1918. *Educ.* Hillsboro High School, Success Business College, Moncton. *M.* 1941, Audrey MacFarlane Brown. *S.* 2. *Dau.* 1. *Career:* Served in World War II (Gunner, 8th Field Battery). Timekeeper and Clerk, Modern Paving, Buctouche 1937; Purchasing E.G.M. Cape, St. Johns' Nfld. 1941; Sec.-Treasurer, Wheaton Bros., Moncton 1944; President: Modern Enterprises Ltd.; Modern Construction Ltd., Moncton, N.B., Imperial Equipment Ltd., Imperial Realty Ltd., Eastern Paving Ltd.; Moncton Crushed Stone Co. Ltd.; Chmn. of Bd., Steeves Pontiac Buick Ltd.; S. & G. Stores. Director, Industrial Trucking Ltd.; Past Pres. Community Chest; Moncton Rotary Club; Board of Trade; Chairman. Salvation Army Advisory Board; Past Pres., Gideons International in Canada; Vice-Chmn. Board of Governors, Acadia Univ., Wolfville, N.S. Member, A.F. & A.M.; Luxor Temple; Scottish Rite. *Clubs:* Rotary (Past President), Shriners, Golf & Country, Curling (all of Moncton). *Address:* 558 Salisbury Road, Moncton, N.B., Canada E1E 1B8.

**STEFFE, Horst-Otto,** Dr. Econ. German financial executive. *B.* 1919. *Educ.* Grammar Schools at Düren, Duisburg & Leipzig; Leipzig & Vienna Univs. *M.* Margareta Spangl. *Children:* 3. *Career:* National & military service 1937–45; Economist, Austrian Inst. for Economic Research 1948; Asst., then Dep. Section Head, Federal Ministry of Econ. Affairs, Bonn, 1952; Man. Dir., Gemeinschaft zum Schutz der deutschen Sparer 1958; Dir., National Economies & Economic Trends, EEC Commission, Brussels 1960 & Chmn., EEC Cttee. of experts for Business Cycle Analysis & of the Working Parties on Economic Budgets, Cyclical Statistics & Economic Tendency Surveys; mem., Short Term Economic Policy & Budgetary Policy Cttees.; alt. mem., Monetary Cttee.; Manager, Economic & Research Dept., European Investment Bank 1967, Vice-Chmn. since 1972. *Address:* European Investment Bank, 2 Place de Metz, Luxembourg.

**STEFFERUD, Alfred Daniel.** American editor and author; *B.* 1903. *Educ.* St. Olaf College (BA); Graduate study, Universities of Iowa, Berlin, Vienna. *M.* 1932, Doris H. Roberts (*D.* 1958). *S.* David R. and John A. *Dau.* Christine Stefferud Jacoby. Superior Service Award, U.S. Dept. of Agriculture; Distinguished Alumnus Award, St. Olaf College. *Career:* Editor and Foreign Correspondent, The Associated Press 1930–39; Bureau of Agriculture Economics 1939–42; Office of War Information 1942–45; Editor, Friends Journal, 1968–72; Contrib. editor since 1972; Publications Officer and Editor of the Yearbook of Agriculture, U.S. Department of Agriculture 1945–64. *Publications:* Editor, the Yearbooks of Agriculture: Science in Farming; Grass; Trees; Insects; Plant Diseases; Soil; Water; Crops in Peace and War; Marketing; Animal Diseases; Land; Food; Power to Produce; Seeds; After a Hundred Years; A Place to Live; Farmers' World; Consumers All. Editor-compiler, The Wonderful World of Books; (editor) Waterfowl Tomorrow; Birds in our Lives (U.S. Dept. of Int.); author: How to Know the Wild Flowers; The Wonders of Seeds; magazine and newspaper articles. *Clubs:* Cosmos (Washington); Chiltern Club of Arts; Bucks Guild of Spinners. Weavers & Dyers: Sons of Norway; Guild of Master Craftsmen. *Address:* 33 Whielden Street, Old Amersham, Bucks, HP7 0HU.

**STEIN, Erwin,** Prof. Dr. jur. German politician. *B.* 1903. *M.* 1947, Charlotte Putscher. *Career:* Public Prosecutor and Judge at various lower courts in Hessen 1932–33; removed from public service by Nazis and became Solicitor at Offenbach 1933; served in World War II, Army 1943–45; member (C.D.U.), Hessischer Landtag since Dec. 1946; Minister of Education and Public Instruction, Land Hessen 1947—; member of Synod, Evangelist Luth. Church; Bundersrat 1949–51: Vice-Pres., Standing Conference of Land Education Ministers of the Federal Republic 1949–51; Minister of Justice, Land Hessen Nov. 1949–51; Justice of the Constitutional Court of the Federal Republic 1951–71; Ehrensenator d. Universität Giessen 1957. *Awards:* Goethe Plakette d. Lande Hessen 1954; Grofin Bundes Verdienstkreug mit Stern u. Shilterband 1963; W. Leüschner-medaille 1966. *Publications:* Wege zur Volksbildung; Vorschläge zur Schulgesetzgebung in Hessen; Kommentar zur Hessischen Verfassung Elternrecht und verschiedene Aufsätze. *Address:* Bismarchstr. 5, Baden-Baden, Germany.

**STEIN, Dr. Seymour Samuel.** Consulting Engineer, Corporation President. *Educ.* City Coll. of New York (BChE); Brooklyn Polytech. Inst. (MChE); Virginia Polytech. Inst. (PhD). *M.* 1958, Lucille Richman. *Daus.* Sherry Jane, Linda Frances and Carol Ann. *Career:* Professional Engnr. (Conn., Mass., N.Y., W.Va., N.J., Idaho and Pennsylvania). Chemical Warfare Specialist, U.S.A.A.F.; Research Fellow, Virginia Polytech. Inst. Engineering Experimental Station 1951–52, Research Engineer, Process Development Section, Textile Fibers Dept., E. I. du Pont de Nemours & Co. 1952–54; Asst. Prof. of Chem. Eng. Univ. of Virginia; Ext. Div., Richmond Centre (1953–56) and Ext. Div., Fort Lee Centre (1954–56), Abstractor, Chemical Abstracts, Ohio State Univ., Columbus 1953–57; Snr. Engnr. and Project Leader, Research Div., Experiment Inc., Richmond, Va. 1954–56; Dept. Mgr. APWR Project, Section Manager, SL-1 Project, Idaho, and Supervisor of Tests and Evaluation 1959–60; Senior Nuclear Egnr. and supervisor Primary Systems, SIC Project, Naval Reactors Div., Combustion Engineering Inc., Windsor, Conn. 1956–58; Adjunct Prof. of Mechanical Engineering, Hartford Graduate Center, Rensselaer Polytechnic Inst. 1956–60. Manager, Power Plant Department, APWR Project 1958–59 of Nuclear Div., Combustion Engineering Inc., Windsor, Conn.; Astronuclear Laboratory, Westinghouse Electric Corp. Pittsburgh, Penn; Project Manager, member Research Staff 1960–61, System Research Center, N.J. Manager, NERVA Test Planning and Analysis 1961–66. Corporation president; Consulting Engineer 1966—; American nuclear engineering manager and professor of mechanical engineering. Pres. and Chairman of Board of Advanced Technology Corp., Geneva (Ohio) 1966—; Owner of Seymour S. Stein, Consulting Engineers, Geneva, Ohio and Pittsburgh, Penna since 1966. *Member:* Sigma Xi; American Association for Advancement of Science; American Chemical Society; American Institute of Chemical Engineers; National Society of Professional Engineers; American Nuclear Society; Amer. Socy. of appraisers; Member, Amer. Right of Way Assn.; American Rocket Society. *Publications:* The Effect of Operating Variables on the Performance of Packed Distillation Columns Using York Wire Mesh Pack-ings; The Design, Construction and Evaluation of a Continuous Pilot Plant Hypersorption Unit for the Vapor Phase Separation of Carbon Disulfide from Hydrogen Sulfide; contributions to technical journals. *Address:* 76 Standish Boulevard, Pittsburgh, 28, Penna, U.S.A.

**STEIN, Sidney J.** American scientist and administrator. *B.* 1921. *Educ.* Brooklyn College (AB Chem 1942); Polytechnic Inst. of Brooklyn (MS in Physical Chem 1946, and PhD in Phys Chem and Physics, 1951); L. A. Dreyfus grad. fellowship 1946–47. *M.* 1945, Bertha Weinstein. *S.* Elliot M., Michael A., and Barry D. *Dau.* Joanne R. *Career:* Silver Pin for service and contributions to the U.S. Atomic Energy programme 1943–46. Chief Chem. Operator, Amecco Chemical Co. 1942–43; Gp. Leader at Manhattan Project (instrumentation for gaseous diffusion plant; photo-electrical control systems), Kellex Corp. 1943–46; Technical Dir. and Part Owner, Maybunn Chemical Co. 1948–49; with International Resistance Co.: Asst. Dir. of Research 1949–52; Dir. of Research 1952–58; Vice-Pres. 1960–62. Dir., Process & Instruments, N.Y.C. 1960—. President, Electro-Science Laboratories, Inc., Phila. since 1962, Chief Exec. Officer (or head of its subsids. & branches) France, Germany, England, Calif. & N. Jersey; Exec. Vice-President, Apollo Industries, Pittsburgh 1963–67; President Alabama Binder Chemical Co. Tuscaloosa 1963–66; Director: Science Capital Corp., Phila. 1962–66; Taller Cooper, Inc., N.Y.C. 1963–68; Apollo-Carbon Pipe Co., Ponca City, Okla. 1963–68. *Publications:* classified publications on chemical corrosion, instrumentation, trace analysis (Atomic Energy Commn.), light scattering, high polymers and plastic; papers on high vacuum metal evaporation for preparation of a number of special resistor varieties; bonding metals to high temp.; plastics for printed wiring; new types of terminals, stand-off and feed-through insulators, hermetic seals and new forms of wire and cable; cermet and metal glaze printed coatings for hybrid microelectronics, optoelectronics, liquid crystal, light emitting chodeogas discharge, digital displays, plasma panels. Fellow: Amer. Inst. of Chemists, American Ceramic Socy., American Institution of Chemists, Amer. Ceramic Socy., Amer. Inst. of Physics, Amer. Chemical Socy. Senior Member: Inst. of Radio Engineers, Amer. Socy. for Testing Materials, Rheology Socy., Amer. Assn. for Advancement of Science, National Research Council's Conf. on Electrical Insulation, International Soc. for hybrid microelectronics, Socy. for Inf. Display, Amer. Soc. for Metals, Socy. for Glass Technology (U.K.), Philadelphia Science Council, Engineers Club of Philadelphia, Socy. of Plastic Engineers, Sigma Xi, Phi Lambda Upsilon. *Address: office* Electro-Science Laboratories Inc., 2211 Sherman Avenue, Pennsauken, New Jersey 08110, U.S.A.

**STEINER, Ludwig.** Austrian Ambassador, Dep. Secretary General, Ministry for Foreign Affairs, director of the Political Dept. *B.* 1922. *Educ.* Commercial High School (Handelsakademie) and Univ. of Innsbruck (Dr. merc. 1948). *M.* Danielle Alexander. *S.* Thomas. *Dau.* Gabrielle. *Career:* Military Service (severely wounded); resistance activities 1941–45. Previously: Press Attaché, Austrian Embassy, Paris; Secretary to Dr. Gruber, Federal Minister for Foreign Affairs; Secretary to the Federal Chancellor, Ing. Julius Raab 1953–58; Chargé d'Affairs en pied, Sofia 1958–61; Secretary of State in the Federal Ministry of Foreign Affairs, Vienna, 1961–64; Austrian Ambassador to Greece 1964–72; concurrently to Cyprus 1965–72; Dir. Political Dept. Federal Ministry, Foreign Affairs, Vienna since 1972. *Awards:* Grand Cross of the following orders: Orange-Nassau (Netherlands), Northern Star (Sweden), the Lion (Finland) and George I (Greece). Grand Silver Cross for service to the Republic of Austria; Officer, Cross for the German Order of Merit. Member, Osterreichische Volkspartei—OVP (Austrian People's Party). Commander, Cross of the Papal Order of the Holy Gregor the Great. Hon. Member Inst. for Inter. Law & Relations of Thessaloniki Greece; Vice Pres., Austrian League of Graduates. *Address:* Ballhausplatz 2, Vienna I, Austria.

**STEINHOFER, Adolf,** Prof., Dr. phil., Dr. rer. nat h.c. Senator E.h. German. *B.* 1908. *Educ.* University of Freiburg-im-Breisgau (took Degree 1933). *Career:* Assistant to Professor Dr. Hermann Staudinger, Freiburg until 1935; joined BASF 1935, manager 1951. Member of the Board, Badische Anilin- und Soda-Fabrik AG, Ludwigshafen-am-Rhein 1958–73; of funds of the chemical industry; Board of Trustees, Federal Inst. for Testing Materials; Trustees, Endowment Assn. for German Science; Council of the Deutsches Museum (Munich); Honorary Professor, University of Heidelberg, 1961. *Awards:* Oskar von Miller Medal of the Deutsches Museum 1969; Carl Engler Medal of the German Society for Mineral Oil Science and Coal Chemistry, 1966; Dr. rer. nat. h.c., Univ. of Karlsruhe, 1966; Silver Medal of the Royal Swedish Academy of Eng. Science 1967; Senator E.h. Univ., Freiburg i. Br, Ehrenmitgl des Vöch 72; Leibuiz Medal, Academy of Sciences and Literature 1973; Carl Duisberg Medal, German Chemical Socy. 1973. *Address:* D 673 Neustadt 19, Triftbrunnenweg 65, Germany.

**STEINIGER, Edward Leo.** American executive. *B.* 1902. *Educ.* Pace Coll., and New York Univ.; Hon. DComSc, Pace College; Hon. LLD Fordham University 1961. *M.* 1937, Joan V. Bergin. *Dau.* Pamela. *Career:* (Ret.) Chairman, Chief Executive Officer, Sinclair Oil Corp.; Trustee, Hanover Square Realty Investors. Knight Grand Cross of the Holy Sepulchre of Jerusalem. Dir., The Greater N.Y. Fund; Amer. Petroleum Inst. Trustee of College Mt. St. Vincent. Officer, Royal Order of the Crown (Belgium); Knight of Malta; Hon. DC, Clarkson Coll. *Clubs:* Mashomack; Links; University. *Address:* 891 Park Ave., New York City, N.Y., U.S.A.

**STEMPEL, Ernest Edward.** American. *B.* 1916. *Educ.* Manhattan College (BA); Fordham University (LLB); N.Y. University (LLM; DJrSc). *M.* 1954, Phyllis Rosa Brooks. *S.* Robert, Calvin and Neil. *Dau.* Diana. *Career:* Insurance Underwriter with Amer. Internatl. Underwriters Corp., N.Y.C. 1938–42. Lieut. U.S. Navy (Destroyers Pacific) 1942–45; Secy., Asst. to Pres., Reinsurance Mgr., Amer. Internatl. Underwriters Corp. 1945–53; Vice-Pres., Amer. Internatl. Reinsurance Co. Inc. 1953–63. Doctoral Thesis: Comparative Study of the Insurance Laws of Latin America. Pres. and Dir. American Int. Reinsurance Co. Inc. (Bermuda) 1963–; Chmn. Bd. Dirs. American International Co. Ltd. (Bermuda) 1963—; President & Director: American International Assurance Co. (Bermuda) Ltd.; American International Commercial Co. Inc., Bermuda; American International Reinsurance Co. Ltd., Bermuda; American International Reinsurance Co. Inc., Delaware. Vice-Pres., Dir. & Sec., Carmont Underwriters Ltd., Bermuda; Vice-Pres. & Dir., La Interamericana S.A., Mexico; Exec. Vice-Pres. & Dir. & Mem. of Exec. Cttee., American International Group Inc., New York. Director: Amer. Int. Assurance Co. Ltd., Hong Kong; Amer. Int. Life Assurance Co. of New York; Amer. Int. Life Insurance Co. of Puerto Rico; Amer. Int. Underwriters Japan Inc.; Amer. Int. Underwriters (Latin America) Inc., Bermuda; Amer. Int. Underwriters Mediterranean Inc., Bermuda; Amer. Int. Underwriters Overseas Ltd., Bermuda; Amer. Life Insurance Co., Wilmington, Del.; Australian Amer. Assurance Co. Ltd., Australia; C. V. Starr & Co. Inc., New York; Delaware Amer. Life Insurance Co., Wilmington, Del.; Malaysian Amer. Assurance Co. Berhad, Kuala Lumpur, Malaysia; Mt. Mansfield Co. Inc., Stowe, Vermont; Pacific Union Assurance Co., California; Philippine Amer. Insurance Co.'s, Manila, Philippines; Seguros Venezuela C. A., Venezuela; Starr Int. Co. Inc., Bermuda; Underwriters Adjustment Co., Panama; Underwriters Bank Inc., Bermuda. Mem. of Exec. Cttee., Int. Companies Div., Bermuda Chamber of Commerce since 1973. *Member:* N.Y. State Bar; Amer. Bar. Assn.; Lawyers Club of N Y. *Clubs:* Marco Polo (N.Y.); Mid-Ocean, Royal Bermuda Yacht, Coral Beach & Tennis (Bermuda). *Address:* Caliban Cove, Fairylands, Pembroke 5–56, Bermuda; and *office* P.O. Box 152, Hamilton 5, Bermuda.

**STENIUS (Kurt) Erik.** Finnish. Order of Cross of Liberty 4th Cl. (Finland). *B.* 1916. *Educ.* Univ. of Helsinki (MA) and Swedish School of Economics (Diploma). *M.* 1948, Sylvia Lilius. *S.* Thomas and Andreas. *Daus.* Micaela and Marina. *Career:* Asst. Director, Bankirfirman Ane Gyllenberg AB 1947–57; Pres. and Man. Dir., Bankirfirman Ane Gyllenberg AB, Helsinki, Jan. 1958—. Member, Board of Helsinki Stock Exchange. Member of the Bd. Oy Hartwall Ab since 1969; Oy Wärtsilä Ab since 1970; Oy Stockmann Ab and Tammerfors klädesfabriks Ab since 1974. *Club:* Stock Exchange. *Address:* 6 Kadettvagen, Helsinki; and *office* 33 N. Esplandgatan, Helsinki, Finland.

**STENNIS, John Cornelius.** American Politician. *B.* 1901. *Educ.* Mississippi State Coll.; Univ. of Virginia Law Sch. (BS, LLB). *M.* 1929, Coy H. Stennis. *S.* 1. *Dau.* 1. *Career:* Member, Miss. House of Reps. from Kemper County 1928–32; District Prosecuting Attorney, 16th Judicial District 1931 & 1935; Appointed Circuit Judge, 16th Judicial District 1937, & Elected 1938, 1946; Democratic Senator from Mississippi since 1947. *Address:* Senate Office Building, Washington, D.C. 20510, U.S.A.

**STENVALL, Arnold Ossian,** LLB. Finnish banker. *B.* 21 April 1904. *M.* 1928, Ruth Albrecht. *S.* Kurt Arnold, Henrik Gunnar Arnold. *Dau.* Carita. *Career:* Manager, Svenska Finlands Lantmannabank AB 1929; Branch Manager, AB Nordiska Föreningsbanken 1934, Asst. General Manager 1949; General Manager 1954; Knight, Order of Finnish Lion; Cross of Liberty,, 1st and 2nd Class; Knight Order of Finnish White Rose. *Address:* Pihlajatie 13, as. 8 Helsinki 27, Finland.

**STEPHEN, Harbourne Mackay,** DSO, DFC, and bar. British. *B.* 1916. *Educ.* Shrewsbury School. *M.* 1947, Sybil Erica Palmer. *Daus.* 2. *Career:* with Beaverbrook Newspapers, 1936–39 and 1945–58; Thomson Organization, 1959–63; Managing Director, Daily Telegraph Ltd., and Sunday Telegraph, 1963—. Director, Int. Newspaper and Colour Assocn. Darmstadt. Germany, 1964–69. *Clubs:* Bath Club; Royal Automobile; R.A.F. *Address:* Donnington Holt, Newbury, Berks.; and *office* Daily Telegraph Ltd., 135 Fleet Street, London, E.C.4.

**STEPHENS, Olin James II.** American naval architect. *B.* 1908. *Educ.* Massachusetts Institute of Technology; Hon. MSc Stevens Institute of Technology 1945; Hon MA Brown University 1959. *M.* 1930, Florence Reynolds. *S.* Olin James III and Sam. *Career:* Draughtsman, Henry J. Gielow, N.Y.C. 1927–28; P. L. Rhodes N.Y.C. Jan.–Apr. 1928; with Drake H. Sparkman formed the partnership of Sparkman & Stephens April 1928; incorporated 1929. President, Director & Chief Designer, Sparkman & Stephens (naval architects, marine insurance, yacht brokers), New York City 1929. Cited by both War & Navy Departments (U.S.) 'for an outstanding contribution to the work of the Office of Scientific Research and Development' 1947; awarded David W. Taylor Gold Medal by Society of Naval Architects and Marine Engineers 1959. Among outstanding yachts designed: Dorade; Stormy Weather; Ranger ('J' boat, America's Cup Winner 1937, with W. Starling Burgess); Baruna; Blitzen; Goose (6-Metre); Vim (12-Metre); Bolero; Finisterre; Dyna; Columbia (12-Metre, America's Cup Winner 1958); Constellation (America's Cup Winner 1964); Intrepid (America's Cup Winner 1967); Courageous (America's Cup Winner 1974); Clarion of Wight (Fastnet Race Winner 1963) Morning Cloud and others. Skipper and Navigator of Dorade (1931 Winner of Trans-Atlantic and Fastnet Races); Skipper of Nancy (member U.S. 6-Metre team in contests for British-American Cup, Solent 1932); Reserve helmsman on Ranger 1937 (see above); Navigator of Baruna (first to finish and winner Class A and 'Fleet' in 1938 Bermuda race); member of after-guard of Ranger & Columbia (see above). Member: U.S. Yacht Racing Union; Royal Ocean Racing Club (England); New York Yacht, Manhasset Bay (Hon.) Cruising Club of America, Royal Thames Yacht Club (London); Advisory panel of the U.S. Coast Guard Merchant Marine Council; Chairman, International Technical Cttee., Offshore Racing Council 1967–73 & 1976—; Member, Measurement Rule Cttee.; U.S. Yacht Racing Union; Pres., Amer. Boat & Yacht Council 1958–60. *Address:* Underhill Road, Scarsdale, N.Y.; and *office* 79 Madison Avenue, New York City 10016, U.S.A.

**STEPHENSON, Revis Lindsay.** *B.* 1910. *Educ.* Clarkson College of Technology (BS Mech Eng 1934). *M.* 1936, Josephine C. Papa. *S.* Revis L. Jr. *Daus.* Carol Roye and Lorne Jae. *Career:* Mech. Engineer, L. J. Wing Mfg. Co., N.Y.C. 1934–36. U.S. Hoffman Machinery Corp., 1936–61; Engineer. Field Engineer, Asst. Mgr., V.P. Dir., also Dir., Foreign & Export Operations 1957–61; President and Director, Hoffman International Corp. 1957–63; Pres., Dir., Belson Corp. N.Y.C. 1963–67; Chief Exec. Officer and Director: Clarkson Industries, Inc., N.Y.C. 1967—, President, Chief Exec. Officer & Director, Hoffman Industries of Canada Ltd. 1963—; Exec. Vice-Pres. and Dir., Stanton Foundry Inc., Solvay, N.Y. since 1963; Chairman and Dir.: Hoffman Air & Filtration Systems Ltd., Altrincham, Cheshire, England since 1964; Hoffman Air & Filtration Systems S.A.R.L., Paris, France since 1967; Hoffman Air & Filtration Systems A.G., Zug., Switzerland since 1965; Hoffman Air & Filtration Systems S.A. de C.V., Mexico since 1965; Hoffman Air & Filtration Systems, S.r.l., Milan, Italy since 1965; Hoffman Air & Filtration Systems GmbH., Dusselfdorf, Germany since 1966; Hoffman Air & Filtration Systems, Pty. Ltd., Frankston. Vict., Australia since 1972; Chmn., Atmos Engineering Co. Inc., Kenilworth, N.J. since 1971; Dir. R. McIvor & Sons (Engrs.) Ltd., Stockport, since 1972; Dir. Hoffman do Brasil de Ar e Filtragem Ltda., Brasil since 1972; Dir. Nipon-Hoffman kk, Tokyo, Japan since 1973; Trustee, Clarkson College of Technology. *Member:* American Society of Military Engineers, Amer. Ordnance Assn., Amer. Socy. Mech. Engrs., Assn. Operative Millers; Amer. Inst. Mngmt.; Amer. Mngmt. Assn., Canad. Socy. in N.Y.; Amer. C. of C. in France and London (Eng.); Mexican C. of C. of the U.S.; Sigma Delta. Mason; Tau Beta Pi. *Clubs:* Engineers, Onondaga Golf & Country, (N.Y.); Heritage Village Country (Conn.); Mission Valley Golf and Country, Florida. *Address:* 432 B Heritage Village, Southbury, Conn. 06488; and *office* 890 Ethan Allen Hwy., P.O. Box 482, Ridgefield, Conn. 06877, U.S.A.

**STERKY, Håkan Karl August.** Swedish administrator. *B.* 1900. *Educ.* Royal Institute of Technology, Stockholm (DSc, Eng); Harvard Engineering School. *M.* 1927, Kerstin Tottie. *S.* Göran, Ragnar. *Dau.* Barbro. *Career:* Chief of Design Department, Telefon AB L.M. Ericsson 1933–37; Professor of Telegraphy and Telephony (1937–42) and Vice-Principal, Royal Institute of Technology 1942; Director-General and Chief, Swedish Telecommunications Administration 1942–65; member, Swedish Atomic Research Council 1945–65, and Board of Directors, Swedish Atomic Energy Co. 1947–69; IBM Sweden 1966–71, and Scania Vabis 1966–72; President, Swedish Natnl. Cttee. of the Interntl. Scientific Radio Union 1946–69, Pres., Bd. of Trustees, Swedish Natnl. Cttee. of the Interntl. Electrotechnical Commission 1948–71, and Royal Swedish Acad. of Engineering Sciences 1963–65. Mem., Royal Swedish Academy of Sciences, Royal Swedish Academy of Military Sciences, Royal Swedish Academy of Engineering Sciences, Science Socy. of Uppsala (Sweden), and Danish Academy of Technical Sciences; Gold Medal (Polhem) and Hon. member, Swedish Association of Engineers and Architects; Gold Medal I.V.A., Medal Chalmers Technical Univ., Illis Quorum Meruere Labores 12, Knight Grand Cross, Order of North Star, Knight 1st Class, Order of White Rose of Finland, Order of St. Olav (Norway), Order of Dannebrog (Denmark), Order of the Falcon (Iceland). *Publications:* Methods of computing and improving the complex effective attenuation, load impedances and reflexion coefficients of electric wave filters; Frequency Multiplication and Division; Fernwirksbetrieb in Stromversorgungnetzen; The First Century of Swedish Telecommunications in Sweden—Present and Future; Past, Present and Future Telecommunications Standardization; A Tele-vision Community Planning and Tele-communications. *Address:* Sibyllegatan 43–45, 114 42, Stockholm, Sweden.

**STERNER, Richard Mauritz Edvard,** PhD. Swedish government official. *B.* 9 April 1901. *M.* 1931, Margareta Damereau. *S.* Tord Richard. *Career:* Statistician; took part in Carnegie-Myrdal Study of the American negro 1938–42; Under-Sec. of State 1945–52; Chief Superviser of private insurance 1952–67; Pres. State Council for the Handicapped 1965–71; National Assn. for Retarded Children 1966–72. *Publications:* Services for the Handicapped (1972): Social and Economic Conditions of the Mentally Retarded in Selected Countries (1976). *Address:* Hantverkaregaten, 32, Stockholm, 11221, Sweden.

**STEVENS, Jocelyn Edward Greville.** *B.* 1932. *Educ.* Eton and Cambridge. *M.* 1956, Jane Sheffield. *Career:* In the Rifle Brigade 1950–52; Hulton Press Ltd. 1955–56; London School of Printing 1956–57; Owner and Editor The Queen 1957–68; Dir. Beaverbook Newspapers Ltd; Evening Standard Co. Ltd.; Man. Dir. (1969–72); Man. Dir. Daily Express 1972–74; Dep. Chmn. & Man. Dir. Beaverbrook Newspapers Ltd. *Clubs:* Buck's, Beefsteak; Whites. *Address:* 121 Fleet Street, London, EC4A 2NJ.

**STEVENS, Laurence Houghton.** New Zealand company executive. *B.* 1920. *Educ.* Auckland Grammar School and Auckland Univ. (BCom). *M.* 1943, Beryl Joyce Dickson. *S.* Lynton Laurence. *Daus.* Hilary Alison and Ann Elizabeth. *Career:* Represented Auckland Univ. Tennis 1938–41 and 1947. Served in World War II (4½ years; Tonga Defence Force and 2 N.Z.E.F.; Middle East and Italy). Joined Auckland Knitting Mills 1946; Secy. 1948; Manager 1952, Man. Dir. 1962—. Pres.: N.Z. Inst. of Cost Accountants1959, N.Z. Knitting Industries Fed. 1955–60, and N.Z. Textile & Garment Manufacturers' Fed. 1959–60. Council Member, Auckland Manufacturers Association 1957–77: Pres. N.Z. Manufacturers Federation 1970–71. *Member:* Inst. of Cost Accountants (Fellow); N.Z. Socy. of Accountants (Fellow). *Club:* Professional (Foundation Member); Auckland. *Address:* Flat 1, 1 Watene Crescent, Orakei, Auckland 5; and *office* P.O. Box 18057, Glen Innes, Auckland, New Zealand.

**STEVENS, Sir Roger Bentham,** GCMG. British Foreign Service. *B.* 8 June 1906. *Educ.* Wellington; Queen's College, Oxford. *M.* (1) 1931, Constance Hallam Hipwell (*D.* 1976). *S.* 1. (2) 1977, Jane Chandler. *Career:* Vice-Consul, Buenos

Aires 1930; New York 1931; Acting Consul-General, Antwerp 1937–38; Acting Consul, Valencia 1938; Vice-Consul, Foreign Office 1939; Consul, Denver, Col. U.S.A. 1942; seconded to Secretariat, British Missions, Washington, D.C. 1944; Foreign Office 1946; Assistant Under-Secretary of State 1948; Amb. Ex. and Plen. to Sweden 1951–54; to Iran 1954–58; Deputy Under Secretary, Foreign Office 1958; seconded to Central Africa Office as Adviser to Mr. R. A. Butler June 1962; Vice Chancellor, Univ. of Leeds 1963–70. Chmn., Yorkshire & Humberside Economic Planning Council 1965–70; Member, United Nations Administration Tribunal since 1972; Chmn. Cttee. on Minerals Planning Control 1972–74. *Publications:* The Land of the Great Sophy (Persia) 1962. *Address:* Hill Farm, Thursley, Surrey.

**STEVENS, Dr. Siaka.** President of the Republic of Sierra Leone. *B.* 1905. *Educ.* Albert Academy, Freetown; Ruskin Coll. Oxford. *M.* 1940, Rebecca Stevens. *S.* 7. *Daus.* 5. *Career:* Sierra Leone Police Force; Sierra Leone Development Coy., 1st Gen. Secy. United Mines Workers Union 1931–46; Secy. Sierra Leone Trade Union Congress 1948–50; MLC 1951, 1st Minister of Mines & Labour; Depy. Leader Peoples' National Party (now dissolved) 1958–60; formed Election before Independence Movement 1960; Leader of Opposition, All Peoples' Congress 1962; Mayor of Freetown 1964; Prime Minister of Sierra Leone 1967, re-appointed 1968; (First) Exec. President of Republic of Sierra Leone since 1971. *Address:* State House, Freetown, Sierra Leone.

**STEVENS, Willy Michel.** Ambassador of Belgium. *B.* 1911. *Educ.* Doctor of Law Degree in Political Science. *M.* 1945, Lucy Vandenherreweghen. *S.* Michel and Bernard. *Dau.* Christine. *Career:* Consul-General: Lobito 1947, St. Paul de Loanda 1948, Nairobi 1949, Salisbury (S. Rhodesia) 1952; En. Ex. and Min. Plen.: Jakarta 1954, and Australia 1957; Ambassador to Australia 1959–62, to Iran 1963, Kuwait 1964 and to Ireland 1971. *Awards:* Commander, Order of Leopold; Order of the Crown; Officer, Order of Leopold II (Belgium), Grand Cross, Order of Homayoun (Iran). *Address:* c/o Ministry of Foreign Affairs, Brussels, Belgium.

**STEWARD, Stanley Feargus,** CBE, CEng, FIProdE. British. *B.* 1904. *Educ.* The Paston School, North Walsham, Norfolk. *M.* 1929, Phyllis Winifred Thurlow. *S.* 1. *Daus.* 1. *Career:* Apprentice to Bull Motors Ltd.) held positions of Chief Designer, Sales Mngr., and Dir. With Min. of Supply: Electrical Adviser to Machine Tool Control 1940; Dir. of Industrial Electrical Equipment 1941–44; Dir.-Gen. of Machine Tools 1944–45; Chmn., Mach. Tool Advisory Council 1946–47. Director, E.R. & F. Turner Ltd., Ipswich 1944–48. Chairman, South Western Electricity Board 1948–55. Managing Director, British Electrical & Allied Manufacturers Assn. 1959–71; Chairman: Wm. Steward & Co. Ltd.; George Thurlow & Sons Ltd.; Thurlow Nunn & Sons Ltd.; Thurlow Nunn International Ltd.; Dir. Elec. Res. Assoc. Ltd.; President, Executive Committee, Organisme de Liaison des Industries Metalliques Européennes 1963–66; Member Elect. Engineering Economic Dev. Cttee. 1964–71; Press Assn. Supervisory, Exec. Engineers 1971–73; Electrical & Electronic Industries Benevolent Assn. 1971–72; Member: Machine Tool Economic Dev. Cttee. since 1971; Chmn. British Electrical Development Association 1954. Managing Director, Lancashire Dynamo Holdings Ltd. 1956–59 (Chmn. 1957–58). Formerly Chairman: Lancashire Dynamo & Crypto Ltd., Lancashire Dynamo Electronics Products Ltd., and Lancashire Dynamo Group Sales. Freeman of City of London. Master, Worshipful Company of Glaziers & Painters of Glass 1964. *Club:* Athenaeum. *Address:* 41 Fairacres, Roehampton Lane, London, S.W.15; and *office* 75 Agincourt Road, London, N.W.3.

**STEWART, Alexander William.** Australian company director. *B.* 1911. *Educ.* Melbourne Church of England Grammar School, Melbourne Univ. (BAgr Sc) and Cambridge University. *M.* 1976, Margaret Morgan. *Daus.* Judith Margaret and Alexandra Beatrice. *Career:* Dir.: Broken Hill South Ltd., Metal Manufacturers Ltd., The Electrolytic Refining & Smelting Co. of Australia Pty. Ltd., Associated Pulp & Paper Mills, Commonwealth Industrial Gases Ltd., Austral Standard Cables Pty. Ltd.; Commonwealth Aircraft Corp. Ltd.; Chmn., Victorian Div., Australian Red Cross Society. *Member:* Australian Institute of Agricultural Science; Associate, Australian Institute of Mining & Metallurgy; Associate of the Royal Australian Chemical Inst.; Fellow, Inst. of Directors. *Clubs:* Royal Sydney Yacht; Royal Sydney Golf; Melbourne; Australian (Melbourne); Royal Melbourne Golf; Victorian Racing; Victoria Amateurs Turf. *Address:* 6 Kenley Court, Toorak, Victoria; and *office* 459 Collins Street, Melbourne, Vic., Australia.

**STEWART, Allan Lindsay,** BSc, BE. Australian chartered engineer. *B.* 1909. *Educ.* University of Sydney (BSc; BE). *M.* 1942, Yvonne E. Kidston. *S.* 2. *Dau.* 1. *Career:* Construction Engineer, B.H.P. Steelworks, Newcastle 1932–41; Technical Officer, Standards Assn. 1942–44 (Secretary, Southern Section 1944–46; Deputy Dir., Victoria 1946–48; Deputy Director 1948–53); Dir. since 1953. Associate Member, Institution of Engineers of Australia (AMIE Aust.). *Clubs:* Rotary, University (Sydney). *Address:* 16 Coronation Avenue, Mosman, N.S.W., Australia.

**STEWART, (Bernard Harold) Ian (Halley),** MP. British Banker & Politician. *B.* 1935. *Educ.* Haileybury Coll.; Jesus Coll., Cambridge—MA. *M.* 1966, Deborah Buchan. *S.* 1. *Daus.* 2. *Career:* Dir., Brown, Shipley & Co. Ltd., Merchant Bankers since 1971; Conservtive MP for Hitchin since 1974; Hon. Sec., Conservative Finance Cttee. 1975–76. *Member:* Fellow, Society of Antiquaries; British Academy Cttee. for Sylloge of Coins of British Isles. *Decorations:* Reserve Decoration (1972). *Publications:* The Scottish Coinage (1955; 2nd. ed. 1967). *Clubs:* MCC; Hawks; Pitt (Cambridge). *Address:* 121 St. George's Road, London SE1 6HY; & *office* Founders Court, Lothbury, London EC2.

**STEWART, D. Wallace.** Professional Engineer, Ontario. *B.* 1900. *Educ.* Queen's University (BSc). *M.* 1927, Jessie Prower Brown. *S.* Dan and Peter. *Dau.* Jane. *Career:* With Canadian Refractories Ltd. 1931–38; Basic Inc., U.S.A. 1938–43 Light Alloys Ltd., Canada 1943–50; Dir. Polyfiber Ltd. since 1950. Liberal. *Club:* National (Toronto). *Address:* *office* 14 Lochiel Street, Renfrew, Ont., Canada.

**STEWART, Donald James,** MP. Scottish Politician. *B.* 1920. *Educ.* Nicolson Inst., Stornoway. *M.* 1955, Christina Macaulay. *Career:* Company Dir. to 1970; MP (SNP) for Western Isles since 1970. *Address:* Heatherlea, Holm Road, Stornaway, Isle of Lewis.

**STEWART, Sir Dugald Leslie Lorn,** KCVO, CMG. Retired British Diplomat. *B.* 1921. *Educ.* Eton; Magdalen Coll., Oxford. *M.* 1947, Sibyl Anne Sturrock, MBE. *S.* 3. *Dau.* 1. *Career:* Entered Foreign Office 1942; 3rd Sec., Belgrade 1945–48; Control Commission, Berlin 1948–50; Consul, Amara (Iraq) 1950–51; Cairo 1951–53; London 1953–56; Belgrade 1956–59; London 1959–62; Moscow 1963–65; Imperial Defence Coll., London 1965–66; H.M. Inspector of Diplomatic Missions 1967–69; Counsellor, Cairo 1969–71; Ambassador to Yugoslavia 1971–77. *Decorations:* Knight Commander of the Royal Victorian Order 1972; Companion of St. Michael & St. George 1969; & one high Yugoslav Decoration. *Clubs:* Puffin's, Edinburgh. *Address:* Salachail, Glen Creran, Appin, Argyll.

**STEWART, Harold Douglas.** Australian printer and publisher. *B.* 1912. *Educ.* Wesley College, Melbourne. *M.* 1938, Margaret Riley Carson. *S.* Andrew Norman and Harold Bruce. *Daus.* Janet Margaret and Mary Barbara. *Career:* Chmn.: McCarron Bird Pty. Ltd. 1956—. Chmn., T. &. G. Mutual Life Soc. Ltd. Group 1956—; Dir.; Capel Court Corporation Ltd., 1969—; Wormald (Vic.) Pty. Ltd., 1966—; Gordon & Gotch (Australasia) Ltd. since 1970. *Clubs:* Australian; Athenaeum; Naval & Military; Melbourne Cricket. *Address:* 13 Raheen Drive, Kew, Vic.; and *office* 594 Lonsdale Street, Melbourne, Vic., Australia.

**STEWART, Sir Iain Maxwell,** LLD. British company director. *B.* 16 June 1916. *Educ.* Loretto School, Musselburgh; Royal Tech. Coll., Glasgow; Glasgow Univ. (BSc). *M.* 1941, Margaret Jean Walker (diss.). *S.* James Frederick Maxwell, Christopher Iain Maxwell. *Daus.* Vivien Maxwell, Margaret Anne. *Career:* Dir.: British Caledonian Airways; Beaverbrook Newspapers Ltd.; Dorchester Hotel Ltd.; Dunbar & Co. Ltd.; Eagle Star Insurance Co. Ltd. (Main Board), Lyle Shipping Co. Ltd., Heatherset Management and Advisory Services Ltd., APV Holdings Ltd., Higher Productivity (Organization & Bargaining) Ltd.; Industrial Communications Ltd. Royal Bank of Scotland Ltd., Radio Clyde Ltd., Scottish Television Ltd., West of Scotland Football Co. Ltd. *Address:* Lochbrae House, Bearsden, Dumbartonshire, Scotland.

**STEWART, James Pentland,** ME, LLD. American. *B.* 1906. *Educ.* Blair Academy; Cornell University (ME); Rider Coll. (LLD Hon.). *M.* (1) 1933, Frederica M. Stockwell (dec'd. 1974). *S.* 2. *Dau.* 1. (2) 1974, Faith Severance Hackl. *Career:*

With Elliott Co. (now Carrier Corp.) 1928–43; Borg Warner Corp., Asst. Mgr. Supercharger Div. 1943–45; De Laval Steam Turbine Co. 1946–62; De Laval Turbine Inc. 1962–66; Interim Pres. Briarcliff Coll. N.Y. 1968–69; Management Consultant, Dir. Burns and Roe Inc. N.J., Dir. several affiliated companies since 1967. Trustee: Rider Coll.; Briarcliff Coll.; James Kerney Foundation. *Member:* Amer. Socy. Mech. Engineers; Newcomen Society. *Awards:* City of Trenton, Outstanding Citizen; Town Topics, Princeton's Man of the Week. *Clubs:* Nassau; Cornell; New York Yacht; Devon Yacht. *Address:* 82 Mountain Avenue, Princeton, New Jersey 08540, U.S.A.

**STEWART, John.** American investment counsel. *B.* 1898. *Educ.* The Hill School, and Yale University (BA 1921). *M.* (1) 1924, Dorothy B. Rodgers (*Div.* 1949). *M.* (2) 1949, Frances Trenchard Leaf (*Dec.* 1964). *M.* (3) 1965, Mrs. Joseph G. B. Molten (née Gloninger). *Daus.* Mrs. Lawrence Lewis and Mrs. David B. Dorie. *Career:* With Cassatt & Co. 1921–32; Merrill Lynch Pierce Fenner and Beane 1932–40; Donner Estates (Inc.) (name changed to The Donner Corporation) 1940–49; Henry B. Warner & Co. (now out of business) 1950–54; Harrison & Co. 1954–55. President, Baxter & Stewart Inc. 1955—; Director: Chesapeake Utilities 1958—, Wellington Technical Industries, 1963—. Vice-Pres. & Bieler Inc. Dir., King Kwik Markets Inc. Republican. *Member:* Society of Sons of the Revolution (Pa.); Society of Colonial Wars (Pa.); Society of the Cincinnati (Comm. of Va.); Psi Upsilon; Skull and Bones Society of Yale University; Trustee, Chmn. Bd. Church Farm School; Dir. Bryn Mawr Hospital. *Clubs:* Racquet, Philadelphia (Member of Board 1956—); Gulph Mills Golf (Bridgeport, Pa.). *Address:* 1110 Beech Road, Rosemount, Pa. 19010; and *office* Suite 1324 Philadelphia National Bank Building, Philadelphia 7, Pa., U.S.A.

**STEWART, Rt. Hon. Michael,** CH, MP. British Politician. *B.* 1906. *Educ.* Christ's Hospital; St. John's Coll., Oxford—MA. *M.* 1941, Mary Birkinshaw (now Baroness Stewart of Alvechurch). *Career:* Labour MP for East Fulham 1945–55, & for Fulham since 1955; Under-Sec. of State for War 1947–51; Parly. Sec., Ministry of Supply Feb.–Oct. 1951; Sec. of State for Education & Science 1964–65, for Foreign Affairs 1965–66, for Economic Affairs 1966–67; First Sec. of State 1967–68; Sec. of State for Foreign & Commonwealth Affairs 1968–70; Leader, British Labour Delegation to European Parliament 1975–76; *Member:* Fabian Society; General & Municipal Workers Union. *Awards:* Honorary Freeman, London Borough of Hammersmith, 1966; Companion of Honour, 1969; Hon. Dr. of Laws, Univ. of Leeds, 1965; Hon. Dr. of Science (Econ.), Univ. of Benin, Nigeria 1972. *Publications:* The British Approach to Politics; Modern Forms of Government. *Clubs:* Reform. *Address:* 11 Felden Street, London SW6; & House of Commons, London SW1A 0AA.

**STEWART, Sir Michael (Norman Francis),** KCMG, OBE. *B.* 1911. *Educ.* Trinity Coll., Cambridge. *M.* 1951, Damaris du Boulay. *S.* 1. *Daus.* 2. Previous appointments in Washington, Peking, Ankara, Singapore and Rome. British Ambassador in Athens 1967–71; Dir. Ditchley Foundation 1971–77; Sotheby & Co. 1977. *Club:* Brooks's (London). *Address:* Combe, nr. Newbury, Berks.

**STEWART, Potter.** American. Associate Justice, Supreme Court of the United States. *B.* 1915. *Educ.* Yale Coll. (scholarship; BA *cum laude* 1937), Cambridge Univ. England (Henry Fellowship), and Yale Law School (LLB *cum laude* 1941). *M.* 1943. Mary Ann Bertles. *S.* 2. *Dau.* 1. *Career:* Member Cincinnati City Council 1950–53 (Vice-Mayor 1952–53); appt. by Pres. Eisenhower to U.S. Court of Appeals for the Sixth Circuit April 1954. Served as member of the Committee on Court Administration of the Judicial Conference of the U.S. 1955–58; Associate Justice since 1958. LLD; Yale, Kenyon Coll., Wilmington Coll., Univ. Cincinnati, Ohio State Univ. and Univ. Michigan. *Member:* Amer., Ohio. Cincinnati, City of N.Y. Bar Associations; Phi Beta Kappa; Delta Kappa Epsilon; Phi Delta Phi; Order of Coif, etc. *Clubs:* Camargo, University (Cincinnati); Chevy Chase, University (Washington, D.C.); Century (N.Y.C.); Bohemian (San Francisco). *Address:* 5136 Palisade Lane N.W., Washington, D.C. 20016; and *office* Supreme Court of the U.S., Washington, D.C. 20543, U.S.A.

**STEWART, Richard More,** BS, LLB. American Lawyer State Official and Brass Co. Exec. *B.* 1910. *Educ.* Mass. Inst. of Technology (BS); New York Law Sch. (LLB). *M.* 1934, Eleanor Noel Russell. *S.* 3. *Career:* Research Assoc. Carlton Ellis of Ellis Labs., Instructor Newark Coll. of Engineering 1932–35; Admitted to N.Y. Bar 1938; Anaconda Wire & Cable Co. 1935–49; Staff Legal Dept. The Anaconda Co., Counsel 1949–56, Dir., Industrial Relations 1956–58; Pres., Anaconda Am. Brass Co. 1958–70; Chief Exec. Officer 1959–70; Commissioner of Commerce, State of Connecticut since 1973; Vice-Pres. and Dir., Nacional de Cobre, Mexico City; Chmn. of Bd., Anaconda Am. Brass Ltd., New Toronto, Ont.; Dir., Exec. Com. Colonial Bank & Trust Co. (Waterbury, Conn.), Conn. Nuclear Corp., Hartford; Trustee, Exec. Com. Waterbury Savings Bank; Dir., Anaconda Wire & Cable Co., MacDermid Inc. (Waterbury, Conn.), Bullard Co.; Chmn. Trustees Exec. Com. Conn. Pub. Expenditures Council; Chmn., Conn. Development Authority, Conn. Council Equal Employment Opportunity; Nat. Council Boy Scouts of America; Gen. Campaign Chmn., United Council & Fund, Waterbury; Mem., Nat. Labor Mgmt. Policy Com.; Chmn., Naugatuck Valley Industrial Council; Vice-Chmn., Gov.'s Commn. on Services & Expenditures; Chmn., Gov.'s Com. against Discrimination; Former Pres., Waterbury Hosp.; Trustee Exec. Com. Westover Sch., Middlebury; Bd. of Dirs., American Shakespeare Theatre, Stratford, Conn. *Member:* N.Y. Bar; Conn. State Srs. Golf Assn.; Phi Delta Phi, Sigma Nu. *Clubs:* Highfield Waterbury Country; Veteran Motor Car of America (Vice-Pres.); Veteran Motor Car of G.B. *Address:* Central Road, Middlebury, CT 06762, U.S.A.; and *office* 210 Washington Street, Hartford CT 06106, U.S.A.

**STEWART, Samuel Bradford.** Lawyer. Banker. *B.* 1908. *Educ.* Univ. of Virginia (BA 1927) and Columbia Univ. Law School (LLB 1930); LLD Golden Gate Coll. 1965. *M.* 1934, Celeste Dorwin. *S.* James C. D. (*Dec.*). *Dau.* Linda Celeste. *Career:* Associated with Cravath, de-Gersdorff, Swaine & Wood, New York City 1930–38; Partner Blake & Voorhees (later Blake, Voorhees & Stewart), N.Y.C. 1939–47; Vice-Pres. and General Counsel, Bank of America N.T. & S.A. 1947–59; Chief Exec. Officer Trust Activities 1963–67; Senior Vice-Chmn. Bd. Bank of America N.T. & S.A. 1970–73; Special Counsel, U.S. Senate Special Committee Investigating National Defense (Truman Committee) 1943–44. Editor, The Business Lawyer (publication of Section of Corporation, Banking and Business Law of American Bar Association) 1959–60; Chairman of Section 1961–62; Pres. Sponsors S.F. Performing Arts Center, Inc. since 1973; Chmn. of Board Salk Inst. for Biological Studies since 1974. *Member:* Amer. Bar Assn.; State Bar of California; Bar Assn. of San Francisco. *Clubs:* Bohemian: San Francisco Golf; Silverado CC; Bankers. *Address:* 2288 Broadway, San Francisco, Calif. 94115; and *office* Bank of America Center, Box 37000, San Francisco, Calif. 94137, U.S.A.

**STEWART, Stanley Toft.** CMG, Singapore Citizen. *B.* 1910. *Educ.* Raffles Coll., Singapore (First Class Diploma in Arts). *M.* 1935, Therese Zelie Stewart. *Daus.* 7. *Career:* Chairman: Rural Board and District Officer, Province of Wellesley 1947–52, and of Rural Board, Singapore 1954–55. Dep. Secy., Ministry of Local Government, Lands and Housing 1955–57; Dep. Chief Secy., Singapore 1957–59; Permanent Secy., Ministry of Home Affairs 1959–63, Prime Minister's Office, Singapore 1963–66, and (concurrently) Dep. Prime Minister's Office, Singapore, 1965–66. Singapore High Commissioner in Australia 11th Aug. 1966–69; Permanent Secretary Ministry of Foreign Affairs Singapore, 1969–72; Exec. Secy. National Stadium Corp., Singapore, 1973, Co. Chmn./Dir. Private Section, 1974. *Award:* Meritorious Service Medal, Singapore, 1962. *Clubs:* Singapore Recreation. *Address:* 103, Holland Road, Singapore 10.

**STEWART-RICHARDSON, Alistair De Vere.** British. Company director several companies. *B.* 1906. *Educ.* Perth Modern School. *M.* 1944, Joan Wilson Hunt. *S.* Donald Bruce. *Career:* With Bank of New South Wales; Asst. General Manager 1950, Chief Accountant 1945, Branch Manager 1939. Deputy General Manager, Bank of New South Wales 1964–71., Gen. Mgr. 1971. *Member:* Economic Society of Australia & New Zealand. *Clubs:* Union; Australasian Pioneers. *Address:* Unit 73, 17 Wylde Street, Potts Point, N.S.W. 2011; & *office* 151 Macquarie Street, Sydney, N.S.W. Australia.

**STEWART-SMITH, Dudley Geoffrey.** British. *B.* 1933. *Educ.* Winchester College. *M.* 1956, Kay Mary Stewart-Johnston. *S.* James, Charles and David. *Career:* Regular Officer, The Black Watch, 1952–60; Journalist, Publisher, 1960—; Member of Parliament (Con.), Derbyshire, Belper 1970–74; Dir., Foreign Affairs Research Inst., Whitehall 1976—. Editor, East-West Digest; Director Foreign Affairs Circle.

*Publications:* The Defeat of Communism (1964); No Vision Here: Non-Military Warfare in Britain (1966). *Address:* Church House, Petersham, Richmond Surrey.

**STEYN, Frederick Simon.** South African judge. *B.* 1913. *Educ.* BA: LLB. *M.* 1970, Margaret Thom. *S.* 3. *Dau.* 2. *Career:* M.P.C. Transvaal 1953–58; M.E.C. Transvaal 1954–58; M.P. South Africa (Kempton Park 1958–65), appointed Senior Consultus, 1969. Ambassador of the Republic of South Africa to Belgium, Luxembourg and the E.E.C. Aug. 1965–69; Judge Supreme Court of South Africa since 1969. *Member:* South African Acad. for Arts & Sciences; Fed. of Afrikaans Cultural Assns. *Publications:* 3 dramas and 3 novels in Afrikaans language. *Club:* Constantia. *Address:* Ormonde Street, Bryanston, Transvaal; and *office* Supreme Court, Von Brands Square, Johannesburg, South Africa.

**STICKNEY Fernald Stanley.** Professional engineer. *B.* 1900. *Educ.* Univ. of Maine (BSc Mech Eng). *M.* 1946, Frances 2. Foster. *S.* Arthur Clinton and William Hampton. *Dau.* Carolyn Frances. *Career:* At Westinghouse Electrica. Engineering and Mechanical Design Schools 1923–24; Design Engineer, Westinghouse Electric & Manufacturing Co. (East Pittsburgh, Pa.) 1924–27; Instrument Design Engineer and Consulting Engineer, Newark (N.J.) plant of same company 1927–41; Vice-Pres. and Chief Engineer, Instrument Specialties Co. Inc. 1941–49 (Pres. 1949–71). Chmn. Instrument Specialities Co. Inc. (Little Falls, N.J.), *Publications:* various articles in technical journals; patents on instrument designs. *Member:* Tau Beta Pi; Kappa Phi; Amer. Socy. for Testing Materials; Amer. Socy. for Metals; Natl. Socy. of Professional Engineers; Essex County Engineering Socy. *Club:* Hamilton (Paterson, N.J.). *Address:* R.D. 2 Marlboro Ellsworth, Maine 04605; and *office* Instrument Specialities Co. Inc., Little Falls, N.J., U.S.A.

**STIKKER, Dirk Uipko.** Dutch politician and diplomat. *B.* 5 Feb. 1897. *Educ.* University of Groningen (LLD). *M.* 1922, Catherina Paulina van der Scheer. *S.* 2. *Career:* Man. Dir. Heineken's Bierbrouwerij Maatschappij N.V. 1935–48, and of N.V. Koloniale Brouwerijen; Founder and Pres., Foundation of Labour, also of Party of Freedom 1946 (People's Party for Freedom and Democracy since 1948); member of Delegation, Round Table Conferences on political status of Netherlands West Indies 1946, and with representatives of Indonesia 1948; member, First Chamber States-General 1946–48; President, Central Social Association of Employers, Labour Board; President of Board, Algemeen Handelsblad 1945–48; Board of Directors, Netherlands Bank, Nederlandse Handel Maatschappij; Minister for Foreign Affairs 1948–52; Political Conciliator, O.E.E.C. Feb. 1950; Chairman of Council, O.E.E.C. 1950–52; Amb. Ex. and Plen. to the Court of St. James's 1952–58; Ambassador, Netherlands Permanent Representative on the North Atlantic Council and to the O.E.E.C. in Paris 1958–61; Secretary-General of NATO, 1961–64. Consultant to U.N. Conf. for Trade Development. *Publications:* The role of Private Enterprise in investment and promotion of exports in developing countries; Men of Responsibility; and many articles. *Address:* Stoephout flat 66, Stoeplaan, Wassenaar, Netherlands.

**STILES, Kenneth.** Maj.-Gen. U.S.A.F. Reserve (Ret'd.). *B.* 1914. *Educ.* Columbia Coll. N.Y., and George Washington Univ. (AB 1939). *M.* 1939, Margaret Jeanne Halsey. *S.* Kenneth Halsey and Douglas Crane. *Career:* Assistant to Director of the Budget, Exec. Office of Pres. of U.S. 1949–50; Deputy to Asst. Secy. of the Army 1950–53; Vice-Pres., General Dynamics Corp. 1957–63. Certified Public Accountant 1939—. Chairman of Board: Grand Cayman Associates Ltd. Nov. 1959—; Artistic Horizons Inc. *Publications:* Capital Expenditure (1956); Accounting for Research and Development (1961). *Awards:* Victory Medal, Amer. Campaign Medal, Amer. Defense Service Medal, Asiatic-Pacific Campaign Medal with 3 battle stars, 2 Commendation Ribbons, Bronze Star Medal, Legion of Merit Medal; Award for Exceptional Civilian Service (Dept. of the Army); Socy. of the Blue Key (Columbia Coll.). *Member:* Amer. Inst. Certified Public Accountants; Air Force Assn.; Air Force Historical Foundation. *Clubs:* Army-Navy Country (Arlington, Va.); Amer. Legion. *Address:* Dame Hill Road, Orfordville, N.H. 03778; and *office* Suite 1507, 328 N, Ocean Boulevard, Pompano Beach, Fla. 33062, U.S.A.

**STIRLING, Alexander John Dickson,** CMG. British Diplomat. *B.* 1926. *Educ.* Edinburgh Acad.; Lincoln Coll., Oxford—MA. *M.* 1955, Alison Campbell. *S.* 2. *Daus.* 2. *Career:* RAFVR 1945–48; HQ, RAF Med/ME 1945–47; Adjutant, RAF Roade 1947–48; joined Foreign Office 1951; Lebanon 1952; Cairo 1952–56; Foreign Office 1956–59; Baghdad 1959–62; HM Consul, Amman 1962–64; 1st Sec., Santiago 1965–67; FCO 1967–69; Political Agent, Bahrain 1969–71, Ambassador 1971–72; Counsellor, Beirut 1972–75; Royal Coll. of Defence Studies 1976; HM Ambassador, Baghdad since 1977. *Decorations:* Companion of the Order of St. Michael & St. George, 1976. *Address:* c/o Williams & Glyn's Bank, Kirkland House, Whitehall, London SW1; and *office* Foreign & Commonwealth Office, King Charles Street, London SW1A 2AH.

**STIRLING, Duncan Alexander.** British banker. *B.* 1899. *Educ.* Harrow School and New College, Oxford (BA). *M.* 1926, Lady Marjorie Murray. *S.* Alexander Murray and Angus Duncan Æneas. *Career:* Partner, H.S. Lefevre & Co., Merchant Bankers 1929–49; Director, Westminster Bank 1935–69. Chmn., Westminster Bank; Westminster Foreign Bank, 1962–69; National Westminster Bank, 1968–69. Director: London Life Association 1935— (Pres. 1956–66); Mercantile Investment Trust Ltd. 1937–74; National Westminster Bank 1968–74. Pres., British Bankers Assn. and Chmn., Committee of London Clearing Bankers 1966–68; President, Institute of Bankers 1964–66. *Club:* Brooks' (London). *Address:* 28 St. James's Place, London, S.W.1.

**STIRLING-AIRD, Peter Douglas Miller.** British. TD; Croix de Guerre; Order of Leopold. *B.* 1915. *Educ.* Sherborne School. *M.* (1) 1945, Penelope Anne Stirling (dec'd 1971). *S.* Patrick Kenneth and Richard John. *Daus.* Meriel Frances and Laura Erica (2) 1973, Lady Margaret Boyle. *Career:* Served in World War II (52nd Lowland Div. and 7th Armoured Div. Mentioned in dispatches) 1939–45. Sales Director 1945–51, Managing Director 1951–58, R. & A. Main, and Main Water Heaters. Director, Glover & Main 1940–1962, Chairman 1959–62. Chairman, James Stott 1959–62; Man. Dir. Redfye Ltd. 1964–73; Dep. Chmn. 1974–75. *Member:* Society of British Gas Industries (Chairman 1962–63); Pres. 1976–78, Institution of Vitreous Enamellers Vice-President 1961–72); Institute of Gas Engineers (Companion). *Clubs:* Royal Thames Yacht; Hurlingham. *Address:* Kippenross, Dunblane, Perthshire; and *office* Thorncliffe Works, Chapeltown, nr. Sheffield; and 26 Sheffield Terrace, London, W.8.

**STOCK, Allen Lievesley.** British engineer. *B.* 1906. *Educ.* Charterhouse; Faraday House (Diploma); Christ's College, Cambridge (Hons Tripos Mech. Sc.). *M.* 1933, Rosemary Nancy Hopps. *S.* 2. *Dau.* 1. *Career:* Chmn., The Morgan Crucible Co. Ltd. 1959–69; London Chamber of Commerce 1958–62; Director, Universal Grinding Wheel Co. Ltd. 1959–69. *Clubs:* Junior Carlton; Hawks. *Address:* Furzefield Cottage, Bosham Hoe, West Sussex.

**STOCKDALE, Sir Edmund Villiers Minshull,** Bt, JP. Lord Mayor of London 1959–60; Partner, Read Hurst-Brown & Co., members of London Stock Exchange 1945–60; Director, Embankment Trust Ltd. and other companies. *B.* 1903. *Educ.* Wellington. *M.* 1937, Hon. Louise Fermor-Hesketh (dau. of 1st Lord Hesketh). *S.* Thomas Minshull and Frederick Minshull. *Dau.* Anne-Louise. *Career:* Entered Bank of England 1921; Asst. to Governors, Reserve Bank of India 1935; Asst. Principal, Bank of England 1937; Dep. Prin. 1941; retired 1945. Member, Court of Common Council, City of London 1946; Aldmn., War of Cornhill 1948; Commissioner of Assize; one of H.M. Lieutenants of the City of London Governor: Christ's Hospital, Royal Bethlem, Maudsley and Bridewell Hospitals 1948–63. Wellington Coll. 1955–74, United Westminster Schools 1948–54; Vice-Pres., King Edward's School, Witley 1960–63; mem. (Chmn. 1951–53) Adv. Bd. and Visiting Cttee., H.M. Prison, Holloway; Vice-Pres., The Griffins Society (formerly Holloway Discharged Prisoners Aid Soc.); Mem. Court of Assistants, Carpenters Co. (Master 1970), Glaziers Co. (Master 1973); Mem. Winchester Dioc. Bd. of Finance (Exec. Cttee.) 1963–69; Sheriff, City of London 1953; a Church Commissioner for England 1962. Junior Grand Warden, Acting Rank, Grand Lodge of England 1960–61; Grand Officer, Legion of Honour (France); Grand Cross, Order of Merit (Peru); Grand Officer, Orden de Mayo (Argentina); Kt. Cmdr., Order of the Crown (Thailand); Order of Tri Shakti Patta, Cl. II (Nepal); Gold Medal, Madrid; Comd., Order of North Star (Sweden); K.St.J. *Club:* Bucks. *Address:* Hoddington House, Basingstoke, Hants.; and Delnadamph, Strathdon, Aberdeenshire.

**STOCKIL, Sir Raymond Osborne,** KBE. Chairman, Hippo Valley Estates Ltd., Salisbury, Rhodesia. *B.* Natal, 1907. *Educ.* Heldeberg College, Cape Province; and Washington

(U.S.A.) University (BA 1929). *M.* (1). 1929, Virginia Fortner. (Dec.). *S.* 1. *Daus.* 3. (2) 1973, Margot Susan Lovett Hodgson. *Career:* Took up civil aviation and manufacturing in U.S.A. 1929–33 (obtained 5 U.S. Patents). Returned to Natal 1934; went to Fort Victoria 1936 and engaged in farming; Served in S. Rhodesia Signal Corps. 1940–45; MP for Victoria 1946–62; Leader of Opposition 1948–53 and 1956–59; resigned from Parliament 1962. *Club:* Salisbury. *Address:* 7 Addington Lane P.O., Borrowdale, Rhodesia; and *office* Hippo Valley Estates Ltd., P.O. Box 1108, Salisbury, Rhodesia.

**STOCKING, Collis.** Economist. *B.* 1900. *Educ.* Columbia Univ. (AB; MA 1925). *M.* 1929, Claudia Roberts. *Daus.* 2 Asst. Prof. of Economics, Vermont and New York Universities 1927–35. Served 26 years in Government Service, including; Asst. Dir., Bureau of Employment Security, Social Security Board 1936–41; Asst. Exec. Dir., War Manpower Commission 1941–45; Asst. Dir., Bureau of Employment Security, Dept. of Labor 1945–48; Dir., Program Div., National Security Research Board 1948–51; Dir., Production Goals, Defence Production Admin. 1951–53; Senior Economist and Admin. Officer, President's Council of Economic Advisers 1953–61; Economic Adviser, Dept. of Commerce 1962. Member of Surveys and Research Group, Statistical Advisers to Korean Government 1962—. Delegate, White House Conference on Children 1940; U.S. Rep., Commission on Employment Service, International Labour Conf., Geneva 1947, and San Francisco 1948. *Publications:* U.S. Foreign Trade (1935) Economic Principles & Problems (co-author 1936); contributor to Encyclopaedia of Social Science; Social Work Year Book; American Economic Review; Political Science Annals, and other publications. *Member:* Amer. Economic Assn.; Amer. Statistical Assn. *Clubs:* Cosmos: Washington Golf & Country. *Address:* 3225 North Glebe Road, Arlington, Va. 22207, U.S.A.

**STOCKTON, John Robert.** American college professor (business statistics). *B.* 1903. *Educ.* Maryville (Tenn.) Coll. (AB 1925); State Univ. of Iowa (MA 1927; PhD 1932). *M.* 1928, Anna Beulah Vaughn (decd. 1965). *S.* John Robert, Jr. *Daus.* Joanne Beatrice (*Dec.*), Eileen Doris. *Career:* Instructor, Coe Coll. 1927–29; Asst. Prof., Drake Univ. 1929–32; Statistician, Meredith Publishing Co. 1932–35. At The Univ. of Texas (except for leave during World War II) since 1935; Director of the Bureau of Business Research 1950–69. Principal Industrial Economist. War Production Board, Washington, D.C. 1942; Major and Lieut. Col., Ordnance Dept., Army of the U.S. 1942–46; Professor of Business Statistics, Univ. of Texas; member, Advisory Panel, Texas Aeronautics Commission, 1967–69; Technical Services Advisory Council, 1968–69. *Member:* Universities Natl. Bureau Cttee. on Economic Research (1950–54) and Governor's Oil Import Study Commission 1957–59; Texas Commission on State and Local Tax Policy 1959–62; Interim. Cttee. on State & Local Tax Policy 1963–69. Member Adv. Group to U.S. Commission of Internal Revenue 1966–67. Board of Directors, San Antonio Branch, Federal Reserve Bank of Dallas 1960–65. *Publications:* An Introduction to Business Statistics (1939 and 1947); Economics of Natural Gas in Texas (with Henshaw and Graves 1952); Business Statistics (1958 and 1962); Introduction to Business and Economic Statistics (1966, 1971 & 1975). Editor, Texas Business Review (1949–62). Hon LLD Maryville Coll. 1956. D.Litt. Texas Christian University 1971. Democrat. *Fellow:* Amer. Statistical Assn. (Cncl. member 1963–64); Amer. Economic Assn.; Amer. Marketing Assn.; Amer. Assn. of University Professors. *Clubs:* Town & Gown (Austin, Tex.). *Address:* 1010 Gaston Avenue, Austin. Tex.; and the University of Texas, Austin, Tex., U.S.A.

**STODART, James Anthony.** PC. *B.* 1916. *Educ.* Wellington College. *M.* 1940, Hazel Jean Usher. *Career:* Member of Parliament, Edinburgh West 1959–74; Under-Secy. of State for Scotland, 1963–64; Parliamentary Secy. Ministry, Agriculture, Fisheries and Food 1970–72; Minister of State, Ministry of Agriculture, Fisheries, and Food 1972–74; Chmn. Agric. Credit Corpn. Ltd. since 1975. *Publications:* Land of Abundance; Various contributions to newspapers & journals. *Clubs:* Caledonian; New (Edinburgh). *Address:* Lorimers, North Berwick, Scotland.

**STODDARD, Robert W.** American company director. *B.* 22 Jan. 1906. *Educ.* Worcester Academy; Yale University (PhB); Harvard Business School; Worcester Polytechnic Institute (D. Eng. Hon. 1952); Hon LLD, Assumption Coll. 1959, and Hon DSc Piedmont Coll. 1966; Hon. LHD Central New England Coll. of Technology 1974. *M.* 1933, Helen Estabrook. *Daus.* Judith. Valerie. *Career:* Director: First National Bank of Boston; Worcester County National Bank; International Paper Co.; L. S. Starrett Co.; Dir. and Past Pres., Associated Industries of Massachusetts; Dir., Worcester Telegram and Gazette Inc. (also Chmn. of Bd.); Dir., Raytheon Co., Worcester Community Chest; Past Pres., Worcester Y.M.C.A.; Trustee of several Worcester societies and institutions. Chmn., Wyman-Gordon Company, Worcester, Mass. *Address:* Wyman-Gordon Company, Worcester, Mass. 01601, U.S.A.

**STOECKER, Dietrich.** German Diplomat. *B.* 1915. *Educ.* Marburg/Lahn & Lausanne Univs.—Dr. Jur. *M.* 1942, Ingrid Bergemann. *S.* 4. *Career:* Asst. Judge, Hanseatic Court of Appeals, Hamburg, 1946–48; Official, High Court for Combined Econ. Area, Cologne 1948–49; Official, Fed. Ministry of Justice 1949–52; entered Diplomatic Service 1953; Ambassador to Sweden 1972–76; Ambassador to Bulgaria since 1976. *Decorations:* Grand Cross North Star (Sweden); Grand Officier St. Grégoire (Holy See); Commandeur Couronne de Chêne (Luxembourg); Commander WASA (Sweden); Grosses Bundesverdienstkreuz. *Publications:* Kommentar zum Gesetz über Ordnungswidrigkeiten (1952); Das Deutsche Obergericht für das Vereinigte Wirtschaftsgebiet in Gedächtnisschrift für Herbert Ruscheweyh (1966). *Address:* Embassy of the Federal Republic of Germany, ul. Henri-Barbusse 7, Sofia, Bulgaria.

**STOESSEL, Walter John,, Jr.** American diplomat. *B.* 1920. *Educ.* Stanford University (BA). *M.* 1946, Mary Ann Ferrandou. *Daus.* Katherine, Suzanne, Christine. *Career:* Deputy Chief of Mission, American Embassy, Moscow 1963–65; Deputy Assistant Secretary of State for European Affairs, 1965–68; Ambassador to Poland, 1968–72; Asst. Secy. of State for European Affairs 1972–74; Ambassador to U.S.S.R. 1974–76; Ambassador to Federal Republic of Germany since 1976. *Address:* American Embassy, Bonn, Federal Republic of Germany; and *office* Department of State, Washington, D.C. 20520, U.S.A.

**STOKELY, Edgar Clifford.** American. *B.* 1911. *Educ.* Houston Law School (LLB). *M.* 1943, Margaret Smallbone. *Dau.* 1. *Career:* Vice-Chmn. Radiation Advisory Board, State of Texas 1962–71. Owner. Havenwood Development Co. Director, First State Bank, Clute, Tex.; Manager, Brazos Investment Co., Brazos Land & Development Co. *Club:* Riverside Country. *Address:* 514 Circle Way, Lake Jackson, Tex.; and *office* 144 North Highway 288, Clute, Texas 77531, U.S.A.

**STOKER, Robert Burdon.** British. *B.* 1914. *Educ.* Marlborough College. *M.* 1941, Mildred. *S.* 1. *Daus.* 2. *Career:* Chmn. Manchester Liners Ltd.; British Engine Insurance Co.; Director: Furness Withy Co.; Barclays Bank (Manchester). President: Manchester Chamber of Commerce, 1966–67; Institute of Shipping & Forwarding Agents, 1964. Hon. MA (Manchester). *Publication:* The Legacy of Arthur's Chester. *Club:* St. James's, Manchester. *Address:* 23 Carrwood Road, Wilmslow, Cheshire; and *office* Manchester Liners House, Port of Manchester, Manchester M5 2XA.

**STOKES, Baron, cr. 1969 (Life Peer) of Leyland Donald Gresham, Kt. 1965**; TD, DL, C.Eng. FIMech.E, MSAE, FIMI, FCII. *B.* 1914. *Educ.* Blundell's School, and Harris Institute of Technology, Preston. *M.* 1939, Laura Elizabeth Courteney Lamb. *S.* Michael. *Career:* Export Mgr. Leyland Motors Ltd. 1946 (General Sales and Service Manager 1949; Director 1964). Dep. Chmn., Managing Dir., Leyland Motor Corp., 1963, Chmn., 1967; Member Bd. I.R.C. 1966–71; Dep. Chmn. 1969–71; Dir. London Weekend Television Ltd. 1967–71; Chmn. and Man. Dir. British Leyland Motor Corp. 1968–73; Chmn. Chief Exec. 1973–75; Pres. British Leyland Ltd. since 1975; Dir. National Westminster Bank Ltd. 1969–; Deputy Lieutenant for Lancashire; Vice-Pres. of the Engineering Employers Fed. *Member:* Society of Motor Manufacturers & Traders (Pres. 1961–62); Institution Mechanical Engineers; Pres. 1972; Univ. of Manchester Inst. of Science and Technology, Pres. 1973–76; E.D.C. for the Motor Manufacturing Industry; Worshipful Company of Carmen; Member Cttee. of Common Market Constructors. *Awards:* Hon. LLD Lancaster; Hon. DSc, Southampton; Hon. D. Tech, Loughborough; Hon. DSc, Salford, Officier de l'Ordre de la Couronne; Commandeur de l'Ordre de Leopold II (Belgium). *Clubs:* Royal Automobile; Royal Western Yacht (of England). *Address:* Nuffield House, 41–46, Piccadilly, London W1V 0BD.

**STOKES, John Heydon Romaine**, BA, MA, MP. British. *B.* 23 July 1917. *Educ.* Temple Grove; Haileybury Coll. The

Queens Coll. Oxford. *M.* 1939, Barbara Esmée Yorke. *S.* 1. *Daus.* 2. *Career:* Personnel Officer, Imperial Chemical Industries 1946–51, British Celanese 1951–59; Deputy Personnel Manager Courtaulds 1957–59; Partner, Clive and Stokes since 1959; Contested Gloucester 1964, Hitchin 1966; Member of Parliament (Con.) Oldbury and Halesowen 1970–74, Halesowen & Stourbridge since 1974. *Member:* Exec. Cttee. Oxford Socy.; Chmn. Gen. Purposes Cttee. Primrose League; Vice-Chmn. Royal Society of St. George. *Publications:* Articles on Political & Personnel Subjects. *Club:* Carlton. *Address:* Tempsford, Grove Road, Beaconsfield, Bucks.; and *office* 14 Bolton Street, London, W.1.

**STONE, Franz Theodore.** American business executive. *B.* 1907. *Educ.* Harvard Univ. (Grad. *magna cum laude* 1929); Phi Beta Kappa. *M.* 1935, Katherine Devereux Jones. *S.* Franz T. IV, T. Devereux M., and R. Courtney. *Dau.* Catherine Devereux (Diebold). *Career:* Assistant Administrator 1951–52, Deputy Administrator 1952, National Production Authority, Washington, D.C.; Consultant, Foreign Economic Administration, Washington 1944–45; Deputy Dir. Tools Div., W.P.B. 1941–43; Division Dir. Office of Strategic Services, Washington 1944–45; Pres., Columbus McKinnon Corp., Tonawanda, N.Y. 1935—. Dir. since 1935 and Chmn. sinse 1964, Columbus McKinnon Ltd., Canada; Chmn. Bd. of Dirs., McKinnon Chain (South Africa) (Pty.) Ltd. 1935–69. Director: McKinnon; Anchor Engineering Co. Pty. Ltd., Australia 1962—; Drop Forgings Pty. Ltd., South Africa 1954—; Duncan Andrew Engineers Pty. Ltd., South Africa 1954—; Germiston Bronze Products Pty. Ltd., South Africa 1954—; Pitt Waddell Bennet Chains Ltd., Australia 1962—; Wheway Watson Ltd., England 1965—; Marine Midland Western 1960—; Marine Midland Western (First Trust Office Mem. Adv. Board) 1960—; Niagara Share Corp. 1954—; Robin Industries Inc. Corp. 1964—; Utica Mutual Insurance Co. (Mem. Finance Cttee.) 1964—; Dir. & Chmn. of Bd., Midland Forge Inc., Cedar Rapids, Iowa, 1976. Active contributor to numerous social, civic and charitable organisations. *Member:* Amer. Hardware Mfrs. Assn. (Hon. Mem. Adv. Bd.; Pres. 1954–55); Amer. Management Assn.; Amer. Supply & Machinery Mfrs. Assn. (Dir.; Pres. 1950–51); Machinery & Applied Products Inst.; Natl. Assn. of Mfrs. (Mem. Industrial Problems Cttee. 1959—); Natl. Industrial Conference Board; Natl. Wholesale Hardware Assn.; Hon. Dr. of Humane Letters, Canisius Coll. Buffalo, N.Y., 1975; & Ohio State Univ. 1976. *Clubs:* Automobile, Buffalo, Buffalo Tennis, Country, Harvard (Pres. 1967), Mid-Day (all of Buffalo); Columbus Faculty (both of Columbus, Ohio); Harvard (N.Y.C.); Metropolitan (Washington); Genesee Valley Hunt; Saturn; Thursday. *Address:* "Welcome", R.R. No. 2, East Aurora, New York 14052; and *office* 1618 Marine Trust Building, Buffalo, New York 14203, U.S.A.

**STONEHOUSE, John Thomson.** British politician and banker. *B.* 1925. *Educ.* London School of Economics (BSc). *M.* 1948, Barbara. *S.* 1. *Daus.* 2. *Career:* Parliamentary Secretary, Ministry of Aviation, 1964–66; Parliamentary Under-Secretary for the Colonies, 1966–67; Minister of Aviation, Minister of State (Technology), 1967–68; Postmaster-General 1968–70; Minister Post and Telecommunications 1969–70; Mem. of Parliament 1957–76; Chmn., London Capital Securities Limited Bankers; Export Promotion and Consultancy Services Ltd. (EPACS); Global Imex Ltd. *Clubs:* Royal Automobile.

**STONER, Leland Alfred.** *B.* 1902. *Educ.* Ohio State University. *M.* 1929, Louise Durnell. *S.* Robert Leland. *Career:* With Ohio National Bank: Clerk 1923–29; Asst. Cashier 1929–30; Vice-Pres. 1930–32; Exec. Vice-Pres. 1932–39; Pres. 1939–68; Chmn. of the Board, The Ohio National Bank, Columbus, Ohio. Member, Regional Advisory Committee of Federal Reserve Bank. *Address:* 1807 Bluff Avenue, Columbus, Ohio 43212; and *office* Ohio National Bank, 51 North High Street, Columbus, U.S.A.

**STOPH, Willi.** German politician. *B.* 1914. *Career:* Member: Communist Party of Germany since 1931; Central Cttee. of Socialist Unity Party (SED) since 1950; Politbureau of SED Central Cttee. since 1953; People's Chamber since 1950; Council of State since 1963, Dep. Chmn. 1964–73, Chmn. 1973–76. Minister of the Interior 1952–55, & of Nat. Defence 1956–60; Dep. Chmn., Council of Ministers 1954–64, Chmn. 1964–73, and since 1976. *Decorations:* Patriotic Order of Merit (Gold); Hero of Labour; Order of Banner of Labour; Order of Lenin; etc. *Address:* Klosterstrasse 47, 102 Berlin, German Democratic Republic.

**STORRS, Thomas Irwin.** American. *B.* 1918. *Educ.* Univ. of Virginia (BA) and Harvard Univ. (MA; PhD). *M.* 1948, Kitty Stewart Bird. *S.* 1. *Dau.* 1. *Career:* With Federal Reserve Bank of Richmond: Runner-Clerk 1934–37, Economist 1940, Asst. Vice-Pres. 1952–56, Vice-President 1956–60. Pres., United Fund of Greater Greensboro 1965; Lecturer, The School of Banking of the South 1961–65; Vice-Chairman of Board, North Carolina National Bank 1967–69 (Pres. 1969) (Chmn. Exec. cttee. since 1974, Chmn. of the Board since 1977); Pres. N.C.N.B. Corp. 1968–73, Chmn. since 1974. Lecturer, Stonier Graduate School of Banking 1960— (Chmn. Bd. of Regents, 1969–74); Dir. The Black & Decker Manufacturing Co. Inc. Pres., North Carolina Citizens Association. *Member:* Amer. Bankers Assn.; Amer. Economic Assn.; Robert Morris Associates, Assn. of Reserve City Bankers. *Clubs:* Greenboro Country; Charlotte Country; Country Club, North Carolina; Charlotte City. *Address: office* N.C. National Bank, P.O. Box 120, Charlotte, N.C. 28255, U.S.A.

**STÖTER-TILLMANN, Rudolf.** *B.* 1901. *M.* 1937, Lieselotte Ihne. *S.* 1. Member of the Board. Member, Supervisory Board: Bicker & Co. GmbH., Essen; Rheinstahl Energie GmbH, Essen. *Club:* Rotary (Essen-Mitte). *Address:* Am Hagenbusch 28, Essen-Heisingen, Germany.

**STOW, Sir John Montague,** GCMG, KCVO. Former Governor General of Barbados. *B.* 1911. *Educ.* Harrow School and Pembroke College, Cambridge. *M.* 1939, Beatrice Tryhorne. *S.* 2. *Career:* Administrative Officer, Nigeria 1934; Secretariat, Gambia 1938; Chief Secretary, Windward Islands 1944; Administrator, St. Lucia, B.W.I. 1947; Dir. of Establishments, Kenya 1952–55; Colonial Secretary, Jamaica 1955; Governor of Barbados 1959–66; Gov. General 1966–67. *Clubs:* Caledonian; M.C.C. *Address:* 26A Tregunter Road, London, S.W.10.

**STOW HILL, Rt. Hon. Lord** (Frank Soskice), PC, QC. British. Barrister-at-Law and politician. *B.* 1902. *Educ.* St. Paul's School and Balliol Coll. Oxford. *M.* 1940, Susan Isabella Cloudesley Hunter. *S.* 2. *Career:* Barrister (Inner Temple) 1926, Bencher 1945, Treasurer 1968, K.C. 1945. Served in World War II (Oxford & Bucks Light Infantry) 1940–45. MP (Lab.) for Birkenhead (E. Div.) 1945–51, for Sheffield (Neepsend) 1951–55, for Newport, Mon. 1956–66. Solicitor-General 1945–51, Attorney-General April–Oct. 1951, Home Secretary Oct. 1964–Dec. 1965, Lord Privy Seal Dec. 1965–Apr. 1966. Created Life Peer 1966. *Address:* House of Lords, London, S.W.1.

**STRADLING THOMAS, John,** MP. British Politician. *B.* 1925. *Educ.* Rugby School. *M.* 1957, Freda Rhys Evans *S.* 1. *Daus.* 2. *Career:* Farmer; Conservative MP for Monmouth since 1970; Asst. Government Whip 1971–73; A Lord Commissioner of H.M. Treasury (Government Whip) 1973–74; Mem. of Select Cttee. on Civil List since 1971; Opposition Whip since 1974. *Member:* Council, National Farmers' Union 1963–70. *Address:* House of Commons, London SW1A 0AA.

**STRAIGHT, Whitney Willard,** CBE, MC, DFC. British company director. *B.* 6 Nov. 1912. *Educ.* Lincoln School, U.S.A.; Dartington Hall; Trinity College, Cambridge. *M.* 1935, Lady Daphne Finch-Hatton. *Daus.* Camilla Caroline and Amanda Betsy. *Career:* Served in World War II. Auxiliary Air Force 1939–45; Additional Air A.D.C. to King George VI 1944; Deputy Chairman, British European Airways Aug. 1946–June 1947; Chmn., Government Advisory Cttee. on Private Flying 1947; Managing Dir. (Chief Executive) British Overseas Airways Corporation 1947–49, Arran Trust Ltd. Chmn. 1949–55, Deputy Chmn., Post Office Corp. 1969–74; Rolls-Royce Ltd. 1957–71, Midland Bank Ltd.; Chmn., Rolls Royce Ltd. 1971–76, R-R Realisations Ltd. 1976. Fellow, Royal Socy. of Arts, Inst. of Transport, and Mem. of Council, Royal Geographical Socy. Chmn., Exec. Cttee., Alexandra Rose Day; Companion, Royal Aeronautical Socy.; mem.: British Air Line Pilots Assn.; Liveryman of the Guild of Air Pilots; Inst. of Directors; Inst. of Navigators; of the Worshipful Coy. of Goldsmiths; and of the Worshipful Company of Coachmakers and Coachharness Makers. Legion of Merit (U.S.A.); Norwegian War Cross. Fellow, Royal Society for Protection of Birds; Pres., Norwood Green Residents' Assn. *Clubs:* Bucks; Royal Yacht Squadron; Corviglia Ski; Club International des Anciens Pilotes de Grand Prix FI. *Address:* The Aviary, Windmill Lane, Southall, Middlesex.

**STRANG, Lord** (Sir William Strang), GCB, GCMG, MBE; retd. British civil servant. *B.* 2 Jan. 1893. *Educ.* Palmer's School; University College, London (BA); Sorbonne *M.* 1920, Elsie Wynne Jones. *S.* 1. *Dau.* 1. *Career:* Served in

World War I with 4th Battalion Worcestershire Regiment and H.Q. 29th Division 1914–18; entered Foreign Office and Diplomatic Service 1919; served at Belgrade 1919–22; Foreign Office 1922–30; Moscow 1930–33; Foreign Office 1933–45; Assistant Under-Secretary of State, Foreign Office 1939–43; United Kingdom Representative on European Advisory Commission 1943–45; Political Adviser to C.-in-C. of British Forces of Occupation in Germany 1945–47; Joint Permanent Under-Secretary of State, Foreign Office 1947–49; Permanent Under-Secretary of State for Foreign Affairs, Foreign Office 1949–53; Chmn., National Parks Commission 1954–66, Food Hygiene Advisory Council 1955–71; Royal Institute of International Affairs 1958–66; and Coll. Cttee., Univ. Coll., London 1963–71. *Address:* 14 Graham Park Road, Gosforth, Newcastle Upon Tyne, NE3 4BH.

**STRÄTER, Dr. jur. Artur.** German politician. *B.* 1 June 1902. *Educ.* Elementary; Grammar School; Faculty of Law. *M.* 1931, Dorita Boelitz. *S.* Christian. *Dau.* Angelika (Plange). *Career:* Formerly Advocate at Soest, newspaper publisher at Hagen, Westphalia; Minister of Justice for Northern Rhine-Westphalia 1946–47, 1948–50, and from July 1962. Deputy Prime Minister, Minister of Economy and Transport for Northern Rhine-Westphalia 1950–54; Minister for Parliamentary Affairs, Nordrhein-Westphalia at Bonn 1954–56; Deputy Prime Minister and Minister of Finance for Northern Rhine-Westphalia 1958–60; Deputy Prime Minister and Minister for Parliamentary Affairs 1960–62; Minister of Justice 1960–66. *Address:* Stadtgartenallee 4, 5800 Hagen, Germany.

**STRATFORD, Herbert R.** American. Past Chairman of the Exec. Cttee., Morton Internatl. Inc. *B.* 1905. *Educ.* Princeton Univ. (BS 1928). *M.* 1935, Margo Wyeth. *S.* Herbert R. III. *Dau.* Margo (Russell). *Clubs:* The Chicago; Casino; Commercial, Carlton (Chicago). *Address:* Lazy Bar F Ranch, Cody, Wyoming 82414; and *office* 110 North Wacker Drive, Chicago, Ill. 60606, U.S.A.

**STRATHCLYDE, Lord** (Thomas Dunlop Galbraith), PC. British Statesman. *B.* 1891. *Educ.* Glasgow Academy, and Royal Naval Colleges at Osborne and Dartmouth. *M.* 1915, Ida Jean Galloway. *S.* 5. *Daus.* 2. *Career:* Entered Royal Navy 1903, retired 1922, rejoined 1939–42; served in World War I in Audacious and Queen Elizabeth 1914–18; Flag Lieut. C.-in-C. Coast of Scotland 1919–20; Royal Naval Staff College 1920–22; Staff of C.-in-C. Coast of Scotland 1939–40; Deputy; British Admiralty Supply Representative in U.S.A. 1940–42; Chartered Accountant 1925 (Partner, Galbraith Dunlop & Co.) 1925–70; Member, Glasgow Town Council 1933–40; Magistrate 1938–40; Member of Parliament (Con.), Pollok Division of Glasgow 1940–55; Joint Parly. Under-Secretary of State for Scotland 1945 and 1951–55; Minister of State, Scottish Office 1955–58; Chmn., North of Scotland Hydro-Electric Board 1959–67. A Governor of Wellington College 1947–61; Hon. Governor Glasgow Academy. Hon. FRCP (Edin.); Hon. FRCPS (Glasgow). Received Freedom of Dingwall 1965, and of Aberdeen 1966. *Address:* Barskimming Mauchline, Ayrshire, Scotland.

**STRATHCONA, Lord Donald Ewan Palmer. (Baron Strathcona and Mount Royal).** British. *B.* 1923. *Educ.* Eton Coll.; Trinity Coll. Cambridge; McGill Univ. Montreal Canada. *M.* 1953, Lady Jane Waldegrave (*Div.* 1977). *S.* 2. *Daus.* 4. *Career:* With Royal Navy Lieut. RNVR 1942–47; Industrial Consultant Urwick Orr & Partners 1950–57; Chmn. Bath Festival Society 1966–71; Government Whip, House of Lords, Lord in Waiting 1973; Under Secretary of State, RAF Jan.–Feb. 1974; Opposition Spokesman on Energy & Defence, House of Lords 1974; Joint Dep. Leader of Opposition in the Lords 1976. *Clubs:* Brooks's; Pratt's. *Address:* Island of Colonsay, Argyll, Scotland; and *office* 89 Barkston Gardens, London, S.W.5.

**STRATTEN, T. P.** South African. *B.* 1904. *Educ.* Univ. of Cape Town, and Balliol College, Oxford (Rhodes Scholar). *M.* 1930, Mary A. Morris (of New York). *S.* 2. *Dau.* 1. *Career:* Hon. Pres. Union Corporation Ltd.; Director of War Supplies in South Africa 1940–45. Past President, Associated Scientific & Technical Societies of South Africa. Past President and Hon. Member, South African Institute of Electrical Engineers. *Clubs:* Rand; Johannesburg Country; Royal Johannesburg Golf. *Address:* 16 Pallinghurst Rd., Westcliff, 2001, Johannesburg, South Africa.

**STRATTON, Richard James,** CMG. British Diplomat. *B.* 1924. *Educ.* The King's Sch., Rochester; Merton Coll., Oxford —BA, MA. *Career:* Joined Foreign Office 1947; 1st Sec., British Embassy, Bonn 1958–60, & Abidjan 1960–62; Private Sec. to Lord Carrington, Minister without Portfolio, FCO 1963–64, & to Minister of State for Foreign Affairs, FCO 1964–66; Counsellor & Head of Chancery, British High Commission, Rawalpindi 1966–69; Imperial Defence Coll., 1970–71; Head of UN (Political) Dept., FCO 1971–72; Political Adviser to Govt. of Hong Kong 1972–74; HM Ambassador, Zaire 1974–77; Asst. Under-Sec. of State, FCO since 1977. *Decorations:* Companion of the Order of St. Michael & St. George, 1974. *Club:* Travellers' (London). *Address:* 18 Clareville Court, Clareville Grove, London SW7 5AT; and *office* Foreign & Commonwealth Office, King Charles Street, London SW1A 2AH.

**STRAUF, H. Hubert.** German. Marketing consultant. *B.* 1904. *Educ.* Univ. of Cologne. *M.* 1934, Hildegard Helf (*dec'd.*). *S.* Burkard and Hans Georg. *Dau.* Veronika. *Career:* Business education (organization, sales, advertising) 1920–24; student 1924–27; with several organizations, editor of trade and youth papers 1927–34; Marketing Consultant 1934–39; war service 1939–45. Marketing Consultant Associate, Chmn. of the Consulting Bd. Die Werbe-Euro Advertising Group, W. Germany; Member, Council of GWA. Public Expert on advertising to the Chamber of Commerce, Essen. *Member:* Christian Democratic Union; Hon. Mem. GWA & BDW (Assn. of German Advertising Consultants) & DWG (German Adv. Scient. Soc.); I.A.A.; Cav. Ord. S. Sylvestri; Medal for Merit IAA. *Publications:* Bilanz der Marke—Balance of the Brand (with Braunschweig 1948); Die moderne Werbeagentur in Deutschland—The Modern Advertising Agency in Germany; 750 Werbe-Fachwörter Deutsch-English technical expressions in advertising (with Grohmann) Stoltenbergs Werbelehre, 1965; ANA-Report, 1965 (German version 1966); German version of E. C. Eldridges Marketing Management (1969). *Club:* Haus Oefte Golf (Essen). *Address:* Elsass Strasse 27, 43 Essen 15; and *office* Brunnenstrasse 1, 43 Essen 1, F.R. Germany.

**STRAUS, Jack Isidor.** American executive. *B.* 1900. *Educ.* Westminster School (Simsbury, Conn.) and Harvard Univ. (AB 1921). *M.* (1) 1924, Margaret Hollister (*dec'd*). *S.* Kenneth Hollister. *Daus.* Patricia Harrah and Pamela McKean, (2) 1975, Virginia Megear. *Career:* Joined R. H. Macy & Co. 1921; successively Vice-Pres. 1933–39, Acting Pres. 1939–40, Pres. 1940–56, Chmn. of the Board, 1956–68; Chmn. Exec. Cttee. R. H. Macy & Co. Inc., 1968–76. *Awards:* Cross of Order of Leopold II (Belgium) 1951; Chevalier, Legion of Honour (France) 1951; and Stella della Solidarieta Italiana de 2nd Classe, 1952; Commendatore, Order of Merit of the Italian Republic, 1969. *Clubs:* Harvard (N.Y.C.); The Creek, Piping Rock (Locust Valley, L.I., N.Y.). *Address:* 19 East 72nd Street, New York City 10021; and *office* 151 West 34th Street, New York City 10001, U.S.A.

**STRAUSS, Franz Josef.** Dr. jur. h.c. German Politician. *B.* 1915. *Educ.* primary and classical grammar schools and University of Munich (Latin, Greek, History and economics); Referendar (student teacher) and Assessor (assistant teacher). *M.* 1957, Marianne Zwicknagl. *S.* 2. *Dau.* 1. *Career:* Deputy District President 1945, District President 1946–49; Counsellor, Bavarian Ministry of Culture, Ministry for Home Affairs 1948; Chmn., Youth Committee, German Parliament 1949; successively in European Security 1949, Minister for Special Affairs 1953, Minister for Atomic Affairs 1955; Federal Defence Minister 1956–62; Minister of Finance 1966–69; Member of German Parliament 1949—; President, Christian Social Union 1961—. *Publications:* numerous speeches and articles on foreign affairs, NATO European Security, East-West conflict, etc. in newspaper and periodicals. Hon. doctorates from University of Detroit 1956, Kalamazoo College 1962, Case Institute of Technology 1962, and DePaul University (Chicago). Honours and decorations from Germany, Italy, Portugal, Belgium, Greece, Netherlands, Ecuador, and the Holy See. *Address:* Lazarettstrasse 33, Munich 2, F.R.G.; & Bundeshaus, Bonn, Germany.

**STRAUSS, Rt. Hon. George Russell,** PC, MP. British politician. *B.* 18 July 1901. *Educ.* Rugby. *M.* 1932, Patricia O'Flynn. *S.* Roger Anthony, Brian Timothy. *Dau.* Hilary Jane. *Career:* L.C.C. Representative, North Lambeth 1925–41, S.E. Southwark 1932–46; MP (Lab.), North Lambeth 1929–31 and 1934–50 & for Vauxhall Div. of Lambeth since 1950; member, London and Home Counties Traffic Advisory Committee 1934–39; Vice-Chairman, Finance Committee 1934–37; L.C.C. Chairman, Highways Committee 1934–37; Chairman, Supplies Committee 1937–39; Parliamentary Private Secretary to Lord Privy Seal and later to Minister of Aircraft Production 1942–45; later Parliamentary Private

Secretary to Minister of Transport; Parliamentary Secretary to Minister of Transport 1945–47; Minister of Supply 1947–Oct. 1951. Father of House of Commons 1974. *Address:* 1 Palace Green, London, W.8.

**STREAT, Sir (Edward) Raymond,** KBE. British industrialist. *B.* Feb. 1897. *Educ.* Manchester Grammar School. *M.* 1921, Doris Davies. *S.* 2. Served in World War I, Lieut., 10th Manchester Regiment (T.A.) 1915–18; Assistant Secretary, Manchester Chamber of Commerce 1919, Director and Secretary 1920–40; Hon. Director, Lancashire Industrial Development Council 1931–40; Chairman, Cotton Board 1940–57; President, Manchester Statistical Society 1936–38; Secretary, Export Council, Board of Trade 1940; member, Advisory Council, D.S.I.R. 1942–47; President, Association of Technical Institutions 1944–45; President, Textile Institute 1946–48; Visiting Fellow, Nuffield College 1942–59, Hon. Fellow 1959; member of Council, Manchester University since 1942; Treasurer 1951–57, Chairman 1957–65. Member, General Advisory Council, B.B.C. 1947–52; Chairman, Manchester Joint Research Council 1948–51; a Vice-Pres., Lancs. and Merseyside Industrial Development Assn. 1946–75; a Trustee of John Rylands Library 1960–75. Chairman, North Western Electricity Consultative Council 1960–68, and member North Western Electricity Board. *Address:* 4 Mill Street, Eynsham, Oxford.

**STREATFEILD, Sir Geoffrey Hugh Benbow,** MC. Hon DCL (Durham). *B.* 28 July 1897. *Educ.* Rugby. *M.* 1918, Marjorie Booth. *Daus.* Yvonne Marjorie, Joan Mary, Elizabeth June. Served in World War I, Lieutenant, Durham Light Infantry and Captain, R.F.C. and R.A.F., and World War II, Major (Deputy Judge-Advocate) and Lieut.-Colonel (Assistant Judge-Advocate-General) 1940–43; called to Bar, Inner Temple, joined Northeastern Circuit 1921; K.C. 1938; Recorder, Rotherham 1932, Huddersfield 1934, Kingston-upon-Hull 1943; Solicitor-General, and Attorney-General, County Palatine of Durham 1939–47; Bencher, Inner Temple 1945; Commissioner of Assize, Western Circuit 1946; Judge, High Court of Justice, Queen's Bench Division 1947–66. Chmn., Inter-Departmental Cttee. on the business of the Criminal Courts 1958–60; Dep. Chmn., Somerset Quarter Sessions. Lay Judge of the Chancery Court of the Province of York. *Address:* Cheddon Corner, Cheddon Fitzpaine, Taunton, Somerset.

**STREET, Anthony Austin.** Australian Politician. *B.* 1926. *Educ.* Melbourne C.E.G.S. *M.* 1951, Valma Eunice. *S.* 3. *Career:* Liberal Member for Corangamite since 1966; mem., Federal Exec. Council 1971–72; Asst. Minister, Labour & National Service 1971–72; Opposition Spokesman for Social Security, Health & Welfare, Feb.–Aug. 1973; Opposition Spokesman for Primary Industry, Shipping & Transport 1973–74; Shadow Minister for Science & Technology, Shadow Minister for the A.C.T., & Special Asst. to Leader of the Opposition 1974–75; Shadow Minister for Labour 1975; Minister for Employment & Industrial Relations since Dec. 1975. *Clubs:* Melbourne; Marylebone Cricket; M.C.C.; Royal Melbourne Golf; Barwon Heads Golf. *Address:* "Eildon", Lismore, Victoria 3324; and *office* 239 Bourke Street, Melbourne, Victoria 3000, Australia.

**STREET, John Edmund Dudley,** CMG. British Civil Servant. *B.* 1918. *Educ.* Tonbridge School and Exeter College, Oxford (BA 1940). *M.* 1940, Noreen Mary Comerford. *S.* 3. *Dau.* 1. *Career:* War Service in Royal Corps of Signals 1940–46; entered Foreign Office 1947; First Secretary Oslo 1950–52, and Lisbon 1952–54; F.O. 1954–57; First Secretary Budapest 1957–60 (acted as Chargé d'Affaires from time to time); Ambassador to the Malagasy Republic 1961–62; Counsellor, Foreign Office 1963–67; Assistant Secretary, Ministry of Defence 1967–76, Asst. Under-Sec. 1976. *Address:* 162 Oatlands Drive, Weybridge, Surrey.

**STRIKE, Clifford Stewart.** American. *B.* 1902. *Educ.* University of Illinois (BS Mech. Eng. 1924). *M.* 1963, Marjorie Stanley. *S.* 2. *Daus.* 3. *Career:* With U.S. Military Government in Germany: Chief, Building Materials and Construction 1945–46, and Deputy for Reparations 1946. President: F. H. McGraw Co., U.S.A., and McGraw S.A. 1948–63. Director of various industrial and commercial companies in U.S.A. 1940–66. Director: Jamaica National Mortgage Co., Kingston, Jamaica 1962–67, and Fifth Avenue and 60th Street Corp., N.Y.C. 1963–67. President Overseas Consultants Inc. (to report on industrial capacity of Japan for reparations purposes); Chmn., Clifford S. Strike & Co., N.Y.C. 1963–70; Montego Beach Hotel Co. Ltd., and Kent Hotels Ltd. 1957–70; Superior Coatings & Chemicals 1971—; Amer. Radar Protective Devices Long Beach since 1973. *Publications:* Various articles on German and Japanese reparations. Awarded Medal of Freedom (U.S.A.); Univ. of Illinois Achievement Award; Engineering Achievement Award (Coll. of Engineering, University of Ill.). *Member:* American Socy. Mech. Eng.; Amer. Society Civil Engrs. *Clubs:* Engineers, Sky (both N.Y.C.); Rose Hall-Half Moon Golf (Montego Bay). *Address:* P.O. Box 1522 Rancho Santa Fe, Calif. 92067, U.S.A.

**STROESSNER, General Alfredo.** President of Paraguay *B,* 1913. *Educ.* Military College, Asunción. Commissioned in Paraguayan Army 1932; Chief of Staff; C.-in-C. Armed Forces 1951. Member of Partido Roja; took over governmental authority May 1954; assumed office of President Aug. 15, 1954, President for Life since 1977. *Address:* Casa Presidencial, Avenidal Mariscal López, Asunción, Paraguay.

**STROM, Harry Edwin.** Canadian. *B.* 1914. *M.* 1938. *S.* Howard, Brian and Ron. *Daus.* Faith, Beverley, Arlene. *Career:* Minister of Agriculture, 1962–68; Minister of Municipal Affairs 1968; Premier of Alberta 1968–71; Leader of Opposition since 1971. Political Party, Social Credit. Hon. Doctor of Univ. of Calgary (DUC). *Address: office* 205 Legislative Building, Edmonton, Alberta, Canada.

**STRONG, George Gordon.** Newspaper publishing executive. *B.* 1913. *Educ.* University of British Columbia (BC 1933; BA 1934); Northwestern University (MBA 1935); Graduate Study, University of California; University of Toledo (JD 1940). *M.* 1935, Jean Boyd McDougall. *S.* George Gordon, Jr. *Dau.* Jeanne Adele. *Career:* Asst. Prof., University of Toledo 1936–40; Exec. Dir., Hospital Services Assn. (Blue Cross) 1940–42; Dir. of Accounting, American Red Cross 1943–45; Business Manager-Treasurer, Toledo Blade Co. 1946–51; President Publisher & Director: Thomson-Brush-Moore Newspapers Inc. 1968—; President, San Gabriel Valley Tribune Inc. May 1960—; President & Director: Oxnard Publishing Co., Calif. 1963—; Director, Harter Bank & Trust Co. (Canton, Ohio); Great Lakes Paper Co. (Thunder Bay Ont.); Mutual Insurance Co. (Hamilton, Bermuda); Island Press (Hamilton, Bermuda); Bermuda Sun (Hamilton, Bermuda) 1969—; Clay Communications Inc., Charleston 1971—; Chmn. Bd. and Dir. Thomson Newspapers Inc. 1972—; Dir. Associated Press since 1973. *Member:* Stark County Bar Assn.; Veterans of Foreign Wars; Ohio Newspaper Assn. (Dir. and Past Pres.); Bureau of Advertising (Chmn. & Dir.) Amer. Newspaper Publishers Assn. (Dir. 1956–64); Research Inst. of ANPA 1956–64; Inland Daily Press Assn. (Dir. 1958–61). Member of Board, Aultman Hospital, Canton; Trustee: Hiram (Ohio) Coll. 1952—; Director, Ohio Broadcasting Co. (Canton, O.) 1952–68; Pres. and Dir. Salisbury Times Inc. (Md.) 1959–68; Penn-Mar Publishing Co. (Hanover, Pa.) 1958–68; Weirton Newspapers Inc. (W. Va.). 1963–68; Gen. Mgr. & Dir. 1952–54, Pres., Gen. Mgr. & Dir. 1954–64, Pres., Pub. and Dir., The Brush-Moore Newspapers, Inc. 1964–68; Vice-Pres. and Dir., Humboldt Newspapers, Inc. (Eureka, Calif.) 1966–67; Pres. and Dir. 1968—. Vice-Pres. and Trustee, Canton Police Boys Club. Member, Ohio Society of N.Y. *Clubs:* Rotary; Canton; Brookside Country; Canton Athletic; National Press (Washington); Ohio Press (Columbus); University (New York). *Address:* 2834 Demington Road, N.W., Canton, Ohio 44718; and *office* 500 South Market Avenue, Canton, Ohio 44702, U.S.A.

**STRONG, Howard William.** British. Industrial chemist. *B.* 1901. *Educ.* MSc, Melbourne; PhD, DIC London; FRACI. *M.* (1) 1926, Muriel Elizabeth Alexander (dec'd 1967). *S.* David Howard and Alexander Mark. *Dau.* Mairghread Elizabeth. (2) 1969, Mavis Olive Goldfinch (née Jonasen). *Career:* Exec. Officer, Imperial Chemical Industries of Australia and New Zealand Ltd. 1933–54; for some time Director of Brunner Mond & Co. (Aust.) Pty. Ltd., I.C.I. Alkali (Aust.) Pty. Ltd., and other associated companies of ICIANZ; Chairman, Halcyon Proteins Pty. Ltd., 1967—. *Member,* Council of Sydney Chamber of Commerce 1939–46 (Vice-Pres. 1945–46); Hon. General Secretary, Royal Australian Chemical Inst. 1948–54. Chairman and Man. Dir. of Albright & Wilson (Australia) Pty. Ltd. 1954–63. *Clubs:* Australian (Melbourne); Australian (Sydney). *Address:* "Bingara", Bullengarook, Vic., Australia.

**STROUD, Oswald Michael,** OBE, JP. British director of textile companies, and pedigree Hereford breeder and farmer. *B.* 1897. *Educ.* Bingley Grammar School, Associate, Bradford Technical Coll. (Dipl.); City and Guilds of London Institute (1st Prize and Silver Medals). *M.* 1920, Clara Morris. *S.* 1. *Daus.* 2. *Career:* Chairman, Stroud, Riley & Co.

Ltd., Bradford, 1919–72; Local Dir., Commercial Union Group Ltd. President, Bradford Rotary Club 1954–55; Chairman, Finance Committee, Bradford Hospital Management Cttee. "A" Group, 1951–69; Chmn., National Savings Local Cttee. 1956–72; Chairman, Bradford German Refugee Socy. 1933–47; Life Pres., Bradford Synagogue 1957—; Pres., Hereford Northern Breeders Socy. *Address:* Sefton Lodge, Park Drive, Bradford BD9 HDT, and Bolton Grange, Bolton Percy, Yorks.

**STROUTH, Baron Howard Steven.** American mining engineer. *B.* 1919. *Educ.* Trinity Coll., Cambridge; Univ. of Milan; Sorbonne, Pennsylvania State Univ. (BSc Eng.); PhD Rochdale-Toronto. *M.* 1951, Penelope Ann Creamer. *Career:* Asst. Manager, Drexel Bros. Ltd., New York 1941–43; U.S. Army overseas 1943–45; Liaison Officer and Military Government Official at Major War Crimes Trials, Nuremberg 1945–46; retired from army as Major, 1969. Mgr., Drexel Bros., N.Y. 1946–51; Founder & Pres., Stanleigh Uranium Mining Corp., Toronto 1954–58. President: Drexel Bros. Investments (Canada) Ltd., West Coast Petroleum Inc., Cia. Minera San Felipe, Santiago, Chile; Founding Director, Norsul Oil & Mining Ltd. (Canada); Director: La Presidenta S.A. (Salt Mine) Chile; Petromin S.A.; Minera Estero Hondo S.A., Minas y Petroleos de Ecuador S.A.; Industrial Azufrera Peruana, S.A.; Dir., Wine Estates Baron Carl Siegfried Von Strauss. *Awards:* Conspicuous Service Cross (U.S.A.); Croix du Combattant (France); Silver Lion (CSR); Commander Order Sahamatrei (Cambodia). *Publications:* Rilke, The Cornet, 1949; Mining in Mexico, 1953; Outlook for Jamaica, 1954; Canada's New Uranium Camp at Blind River, 1955; New Penn. Mine at Calaveras, 1956; Developing a Canadian Prospect, 1956; Canadian Uranium Outlook, 1958; Andacollo, 1959; South African Mining—A Time to Invest, 1959; A Window to The Morrow (1970). *Member:* A.I.M.E.; C.I.M.E.; Veterans Foreign Wars, Troa; Military Govt. Assn.; Chairman, U.S. Presidential P.T.P. Cttee., West Coast Latin America; Hon. Member, Ministry of Mines, Ecuador. *Clubs:* Chamber of Commerce, Mining (N.Y.) Engineers (Toronto); Officers (U.S.A.R.): Reserve Officers Assn. Union (San José, Costa Rica). *Address:* Villa Atalaya, Atalaya Park, Estepona, Spain.

**STRUYCKEN, Anton Arnold Marie.** Member, Netherlands Council of State. *B.* 27 Dec. 1906. *Educ.* LLD. *M.* Matthea Feldbrugge. *S.* 6. *Daus.* 2. *Career:* Practised law (solicitor) 1932–51; Alderman of Breda 1938–41; member of County Council of North Brabant 1938–40; Director of social services of H.K.I. Ltd. (Dutch Artificial Silk Industry) 1941–42; held as hostage by German military authorities during the occupation 1942–44; after the liberation Solicitor, Alderman and Deputy Burgomaster of Breda; President of various cultural and social institutions; Minister of Justice 1950–51, and Jan.–May 1959, and 1966–67. Governor of the Netherlands Antilles 1951–56; Vice Premier, Minister Home Affairs 1956–59; Member, Council of State since 1959. *Awards:* Knight of the Order of the Netherlands Lion; Grand Cross of British Empire; Grand Cordon of Simon Bolivar; Grand Officer of Orange-Nassau. *Address:* Jan. Muschlaan 54, The Hague, Netherlands.

**STUART, Spencer Raymond.** American Business Consultant. *B.* 1922. *Educ.* Haverford Coll. (BA). *M.* 1949, Eugenia Presler Birdsall. *S.* 2. *Dau.* 1. *Career:* Adv. Sales Promotion Mgs. Martin Senour Paint Co. 1947–52; Consultant Booz, Allen & Hamilton 1952–55; Principal Heidrick & Struggles 1955–56; Chmn., Chief Exec. & Dir. Esaress Int'l. Group Inc. 1956–74; Chmn., Spencer Stuart & Assoc. (Management Consultants) Westport 1956–74; Chmn. of Subsidiaries: London 1961–74, Zurich 1957–74, Frankfurt 1964–74, Paris 1964–74, Brussels 1969–74 & Dir., Sydney 1970–74; Founder Chmn. Esaress Int'l. Group Inc. ; Spencer Stuart & Assoc. Management Consultants since 1974. *Member:* Economic Club of Chicago (Past Chmn. Forums Ctte.); Assn. of Exec. Recruiting Consultants (Past Dir.); American Management Assn.; The Presidents Assn.; Newcomen Socy. in N. America; Sivermine Guild of Artists (Trustee & Vice-Pres.); Fairfield/Westchester Group (Steering Ctte.); Stowe Inst. (Trustee); Fairfield County Council, Boy Scouts of America Inc. (Council Vice-Pres. & Chmn. of Exploring Ctte.); Philo Smith Capital Corp., subsidiary of Philo Smith & Co. Inc. (Dir.); Envirodyne Inc. (Bd. of Dirs.); Ingersoll Manufacturing Consultants (Advisory Bd.); Financial Corporate Services (Bd. of Dirs.). *Clubs:* Univ. Club of Chicago, Univ. Club of New York City; Wee Burn Country Club, Darien Ct.; Landmark Club, Stamford, Ct. (Bd. of Govs.); Indian Harbor Yacht Club, Greenwich, CT; Eldorado Country Club, Calif.; Sky Club, New York City. *Awards:* Purple Heart, W.W.II; Bronze Star Medal; numerous Awards for Excellence in Graphic Design. *Address:* 60 Sunswyck Road, Darien, CT. 06820, U.S.A.

**STÜBINGER, Oskar.** German politician. *B.* 25 December 1910. *Educ.* Progymnasium Edenkoben; Gymnasium. Neustadt an der Haardt; Bonn University. *M.* 1938, Grete Hauter. *S.* Hans (*D.* 1963). *Daus.* Hilde, Ilse. *Career:* Assistant at Teaching and Research Institute for Fruit and Viticulture, Neustadt 1934–35; worked on family wine estate 1935–39; took over farm at Dreihof, Landau (Palatinate), which is well known for seed production, horse and pig breeding and wheat 1939; served in World War II 1940–41 and 1944–45; after the end of the war was active in the reconstruction of the administration, especially in the Palatinate; Hon. Director of Land Stud Farm at Zweibrücken 1946; member, Board of Administration of Provisional Land Chamber of Agriculture, Hessen-Pfalz; member (C.D.U.), Rheinland-Pfalz Landtag; Minister of Agriculture, Viticulture and Forests, Land Rheinland-Pfalz 1946–68; member German Federal Council 1949–68; Chmn. Agricultural Council of the German Federal Council 1958–68; Representative Minister President of Rheinland-Pfalz 1959–63. Senator of Honour, Univ. of Stuttgart-Hohenhein. President, Raiffeisenverband Rhein-pfalz e.v., 1968–70; and Rhein-Main e.v. 1970–74. *Address:* Raiffeisenverband Rhein-Main e.V., Neu-Isenburg/Frankfurt, Raiffeisenhaus, Germany.

**STUDHOLME, Sir Henry,** Bt, CVO, DL, *B.* 1899. *Educ.* Eton, and Oxford University (MA). *M.* 1929, Judith. *Dau.* of late Henry William Whitbread. *S.* 2. *Dau.* 1. *Career:* Member, London County Council 1931–45; served with Scots Guards 1917–19 and 1940–44; Member of Parliament (Cons.) for Tavistock Division of Devonshire 1942–66; Conservative Whip 1945–51; Vice-Chamberlain of the Household of late King George V, and of H.M. the Queen. Nov. 1951–April 1956; Joint-Treasurer of the Conservative Party 1956–62; DL (Devonshire) 1969. *Address:* Wembury House, Plymouth, Devon.

**STUHLMILLER, Henry J.** Banker. *B.* 1890. *Educ.* Graduate. Fontanelle High School. *M.* 1925, Winifred Bramble. *Dau,* Mrs. Grace Brechon. *Career:* Vice-President and Treasurer, Iowa Bankers Assn. 1940–41. Chmn. Bd. Dirs. First National Bank, Fontanelle, Iowa. *Member:* American Bankers Association; member, Fontanelle Enterprise Club; Iowa State Chairman, Gold Standard League 1951–55. *Publications:* articles on banking, economics and monetary systems. *Address:* Fontanelle, Ia. 50846, U.S.A.

**STULTS, Allen P.** American. *B.* 1913. *Educ.* University of Illinois; Loyola (N), Rutgers 1942–45 Certificate Northwestern University (N) School of Commerce 1933–41; Diploma. *M.* Elizabeth Van Horne. *S.* Laurence, John and James. *Dau.* Shirley. *Career:* With American National Bank: Discount and Credits Departments 1936–42; Asst. Cashier, Asst. Vice-President 1942–49; Vice-President, Chmn .Loan Committee 1949–56; Exec. Vice-President 1956–63; President 1963–69. Past Pres., Illinois Bankers Assn.; Pres. Walter E. Heller Int. Corp. *Member:* Executive Council, American Bankers Assn., Pres. 1972; Bankers Club of Chicago; Assn. of Reserve City Bankers. Chairman and Chief Executive, American National Bank & Trust Co. of Chicago. *Clubs:* Mid-America; Commercial; Chicago Athletic; Chicago; Economic. *Address:* 1420 Sheridan Road, Wilmette, Ill.; and *office* 33 North LaSalle Street, Chicago, Ill., U.S.A.

**STURGE, John Lewis.** British. Chairman. J. S. M. Ltd. *B.* 1928. *Educ.* Dame Alice Owen School. *M.* 1955, Diana Phoebe Vazie Simons. *S.* Edward John. *Career:* Directors: Ogilvy & Mather Ltd. 1960–66, and Ogilvy & Mather International Inc. 1966; Chmn. J. S. M. Ltd. *Address:* Tinkers, Church Farm Lane, Sidlesham, nr. Chichester, Sussex.

**STUTTAFORD, Richard Bawden.** South African. *B.* 1910. *Educ.* MA (Oxon.). *M.* 1938, Diana Emory Chubb. *S.* 1. *Daus.* 3. Department Store Exec. Chairman, Stuttaford & Co. Ltd., Cape Town; Garden Cities. *Address:* P.O. Box 69, Cape Town, South Africa.

**STYLE, Humphrey Bloomfield.** British engineer. *B.* 12 Nov. 1902. *Educ.* Marlborough College and Cambridge University (BA Eng.). *M.* 1935, Anita Dolores Brunson. *S.* Charles Humphrey. *Daus.* Ursula Anne, Ingrid Priscilla and Diana Maria. *Career:* With the International Power Co. Ltd., Montreal, as General Manager of the Bolivian Power Co. Ltd., 1930–38; with Edmundson's Electricity Corporation Ltd., as Deputy Gen. Mgr. of the Shropshire, Worcestershire and Staffordshire Power Co. 1939–42, and General Manager, The Wesser Electricity Company 1942–45; President, Rio de Janeiro Tramway Light and Power Company Ltd., The São Paulo Gas Co. Ltd., The City of Santos Improvements Co. Ltd.; Director, Brazilian Traction, Light & Power Co. Ltd., Société Anonyme du Gaz de Rio de Janeiro 1945–50; President, John Inglis Co. Ltd. 1951–64, Chairman of Board 1964–66. Executive Director, English Electric Co. of Canada Ltd. 1966—, Chmn. Bd. 1964–66 Past President: Canadian Electrical Manufacturers Assn. and Canadian Manufacturers Association. *Address:* 172 The Bridal Path, Don Mills, Ont., Canada.

**SUBANDRIO, Dr.** Indonesian diplomat. *B.* 15 Sept. 1914. *Educ.* Medical Faculty, Indonesia. *M.* 1940, Hurustiati Subandrio. *S.* Budojo. Head, Central Java Division, Ministry of Information 1945; Secretary-General, Ministry of Information 1946; Indonesian Representative in Great Britain 1947; Amb. Ex. and Plen. to the Court of St. James's 1950–54; to U.S.S.R. 1954–56; Secy.-Gen., Ministry for Foreign Affairs 1956–57; Minister for Foreign Affairs 1957–66; Second Dep. Prime Minister 1960–66; & Minister for Foreign Economic Relations 1962–66; Subsequently imprisoned for life. *Address:* Jakarta, Indonesia.

**SUBONO, Admiral Ricardus.** Indonesian Naval Officer & Diplomat. *B.* 1927. *Educ.* Nautical Sch., Indonesia; Naval Officer's Sch., Indonesia; Torpedo Anti-submarine Course, Netherlands 1952; Torpedo Control Course, Plymouth 1953; MTB Course, Portsmouth 1953; Naval Staff Coll., Indonesia 1964. *M.* 1959, Veronica Maria Umboh. *S.* 1. *Daus.* 3. *Career:* Various assignments in the Fleet, incl. Exec. Officer, destroyer *KRI Gajahmada*; Flotilla Commander, Anti-submarine Chaser; Commanding Officer, destroyer *KRI Siliwangi*; Dep. C.-in-C., Mandala Command 1962–63; Dep. to the Gov., Nat. Defence Coll. 1965; Dep. Chief of Naval Staff 1966–69; Operational Chief of Staff, Dept. of Defence 1969–73; Chief of Naval Staff 1973–74; Ambassador of Indonesia in London since 1974. *Decorations:* 21 Decorations & Medals. *Club:* Highgate Golf (London). *Address:* "Nusantara", Bishop's Grove, The Bishop's Avenue, London N2; and *office* Indonesian Embassy, 38 Grosvenor Square, London W1.

**SUBRAMANIAM, Hon. Shri C.** Indian politician. *B.* 1910. *Career:* Law Degree 1932; joined Satyagrapha Movement and imprisoned for one year; commenced law practice in Coimbatore 1936; participated in Individual Satyagrapha (and convicted for 6 months) 1941; took part in the 1942 Movement and was kept in detention 1943; associated with various movements in Coimbatore area, particularly concerning Textile labour; has held various offices in Congress organization (President, Coimbatore District Committee, Member Provincial Committee, and of All-India Congress Committee, President 1967—; member, All-India Congress Working Cttee. 1967—, Elected to Constituent Assembly 1946 and continued therein until election to Madras Legislative Assembly 1952 and 1957; Minister for Finance, Education and Law of the Govt. of Madras 1952; elected Member of Indian Parlt. 1962; Minister for Steel and Heavy Industries. Minister for Food and Agriculture, Govt. of India June 1964–67. Chairman, Aeronautics Industries Cttee., Govt. of India, 1967–69; Interim Pres. Indian National Congress July-Dec. 1969; Member, Working Cttee. National Congress, Central Parly. Bd; Chmn. National Commission, Agriculture, Govt. India 1970; Minister Planning. Science and Technology, Deputy Chmn. Planning Commission Govt. India 1971–72; Minister of Industrial Development (incl. Sc. and Technology, later Ministry of Agriculture 1972–74; Minister of Finance 1974–77. Bd. of Governors Int. Rice Research Inst. Manila. *Publications:* number of Books including, India of My Dreams; War on Poverty. *Address:* 26 Tughlek Crescent, New Delhi 110011, India.

**SUCHARITAKUL, Chitti.** Thai diplomat. *B.* 1908. *Educ.* Queen's Coll., Oxford (MA); Barrister-at-Law, Inner Temple England. *M.* 1942, Suriyanantana Suryong. *S.* Kraijit., *Career:* Joined Ministry of Justice, Thailand 1934; Judge attached to the Minister 1935; Judge of the High Court, Nakorn Rajsima 1937; Official in the Court of Appeal 1942. Transferred to the Ministry of Foreign Affairs 1949; Chief of General Services Division, Dept. of United Nations Affairs 1950. En. Ex. & Min. Plen. to the Philippines 1953, Ambassador 1956–59; Ambassador attached to the Ministry of Foreign Affairs 1958. Member of the Constituent Assembly 1959; Ambassador Ex. and Plen. to Switzerland 1959–63 (concurrently accredited to Yugoslavia from 1960–63) to India 1963. Permanent Representative of Thailand to European Office of U.N. 1963. *Awards:* Knight Grand Cross, Order of Crown of Thailand; Knight Commander, Order of the White Elephant; and Lakan, Order of Sikatuna (Philippines). *Address:* Ministry of Foreign Affairs, Bangkok, Thailand.

**SUCHARITKUL, Dr. Sompong,** MA, DPhil, LLM. Thai Diplomat. *B.* 1931. *Educ.* MA, DPhil Docteur-en-Droit (Paris); LLM (Harvard) Barrister-at-Law of the Middle Temple; Diplome de l'Academie de international de Le Hague. *M.* 1951, Thaithow Suphavamich. *S.* Somtow. *Daus.* Nadaprapai, Premika. *Career:* Lecturer in International Law 1956–57; Joined Foreign Office of Thailand as Second Secretary 1959; Secy. of National Cttee. reviewing Treaties & Covenents 1960–70; Member, Asian African Legal Consultative Cttee. 1961–66; Chief Div. Int. Organization Dept. 1963; Secy. to the Ministry Foreign Affairs 1964–67; First Secretary 1965; Dir. Gen. Economic Dept. 1967–70; Secy. Gen. NSPAC and ASEAN National Secretariat 1967–70; Ambassador of Thailand to Netherlands, Belgium and Luxembourg and concurrently Chief of Mission of Thailand to EEC, 1970–73; Ambassador to Japan since 1974. *Member:* International Law Assn.; Amer. Socy. of Int. Law; Council of World Affairs of Thailand; Bar Assn. of Thailand. *Publications:* State Immunities and Trading Activities in International Law (1959). *Clubs:* Royal Bangkok Sports. *Address:* Royal Thai Embassy, 14–6, Kami-Osaki, 3-Chome, Shinagawa-ku, Tokyo, Japan.

**SUGDEN, Allen James,** OBE. British company director. *B.* 1911. *Educ.* Shrewsbury School. *M.* 1935, Mary Bancroft. *Daus.* 2. *Career:* Former Chairman (Retd. 1968): Wm. Sugden & Sons Ltd., Wm. Sugden & Sons (Sales) Ltd., The Top Twenty Shirt Co. Ltd., and Hawksclough Mills Ltd.; Treasurer, Spen Valley Liberal Assn. 1931–35 (Chairman 1935–47); President, Spenborough Society of St. George 1947–48; President, Spen Valley Chamber of Commerce 1952–54; Chairman, Shirt, Collar and Tie Manufacturers Federation of Great Britain 1954–55; J.P., West Riding of Yorkshire 1962. Member of Clothing EDC. 1966–68. *Address:* New Royds, Gomersal, Cleckheaton, Yorks, BD19 4JQ.

**SUGGARS, Leslie Arthur.** British. *B.* 1905. *Educ.* Bancrofts School (Woodford, Essex). *M.* 1935, Lyle Sinclair Jeffrey. *S.* Jeffrey Arthur. *Daus.* Judith, Christine and Susan. *Career:* Secy., S.A. Best Pty. Ltd., Brisbane 1927–42; General Manager and Secretary, The Queensland Chamber of Manufacturers 1943–70.; Chmn. Dirs Tasman Building Socy; Past Pres. Brisbane Development Assn.; Queensland Taxpayers Assn.; Treas. Queensland Creche & Kindergarten Association. *Fellow:* Inst. of Chartered Secretaries & Administrators; and Australian Socy. of Accountants. Associate Fellow, Australian Inst. of Management. *Address:* 29 Geelong Avenue, Holland Park, Brisbane, Qld.; and *office* Manufacturers' House, 375 Wickham Terrace, Brisbane, Qld., Australia.

**SUKIRNO, Air Vice-Marshal Sujitno.** Indonesian. *B.* 1930. *Educ.* High School Indonesia; Taloa Academy Aeronautics, U.S.A.; Bomber Pilot, Jet Bomber Pilot, Air Force Staff Service Course, Royal Air Force Staff Coll. 1950–60. *M.* 1955, Mutiarawati. *S.* Timur. *Daus.* Indra, Irma, Myrna. *Career:* member, Revolutionary Armed Forces Indonesia 1945–47; Student Army 1947–50; Pilot Bomber Squadron 1. Indonesia 1953–55; Operations Officer 1955–56; Commander Squadron 1956–58; Asst. Dir. for Operations 1961; Commander Air Regional Command 1961–62. Combined Air Defence 1962, Wing Operations 1962–64, Air Defence Command 1966; Deputy II to Commander in Chief Indonesian Air Force 1966. Member, Peoples Consultative Congress 1966; Followed Mission Muljadi to U.S.S.R. 1967; Chief of Staff to Commander in Chief Indonesian Air Force 1968; Ambassador Extraordinary & Plenipotentiary of the Republic of Indonesia to the Commonwealth of Australia and New Zealand 1970–73. *Awards:* Bintang Dharma, Gerilja and Sewindu; Satya Lentjana Peristiwa Perang Kemerdekaan I and II and many others. *Address:* c/o Ministry of Foreign Affairs, Jakarta, Indonesia.

**SUKSELAINEN, V. J.,** PhD. Finnish politician. *B.* 1906. *M.* 1938, Elma Bonden. *S.* Juhani, Eljas, Tuomas. *Dau.* Marja. *Career:* M.P. (Agrarian); Leader of Agrarian Party 1945–64. President, Finnish Population Association; 1941–71; The League of Finnish Savings Banks; 1952–72; Minister of Finance 1950–51; Minister of the Interior 1951–53; Minister of Finance 1954; General Director, National Pensions Institution; 1954–71; Speaker of the Parliament 1956–57; Premier Minister 1957; Speaker 1958–9; Premier Minister

1959–61; Speaker, 1968–70 and 1972–76; Chancellor, Tampere Univ. 1969—; Pres. Nordic Council 1958, 1972 & 1977. *Address:* 02100 Tapiola, Finland.

**SUKTHANKAR, Yeshwant Narayan,** CIE. Former Governor of Orissa. *B.* 24 Aug. 1897. *Educ.* Bombay and Cambridge Universities (MA, LLB (Cantab.)); Barrister-at-Law (Lincoln's Inn). *M.* 1927. *S.* 1. *Career:* Officiating Deputy Commissioner, Central Provinces 1927, Under-Secretary to Government 1932, Officiating Revenue Secretary 1933, Deputy Indian Trade Commissioner July 1934; Acting Indian Trade Commissioner Oct. 1934 and Sept. 1935; Deputy Sec., Commerce Dept., India Gvt. July 1937, Dep. Commissioner Aug. 1937; Tea Controller for India 1939; Joint Sec., Commerce Department, Indian Government 1943, Officiating Secretary Dec. 1945 and March 1946, Additional Secretary April 1946, Secretary Aug. 1946; Secretary, Ministry of Transport, Indian Government 1947; Secy., Ministry of Commerce and Industry, Indian Government Dec. 1951; Sec. to Cabinet and Secy., Planning Commission July 1952; Sec., Min. of Commerce and Industry Oct. 1952; Special Sec. to Cabinet, and Sec. Planning Commission, Dec. 1952; Cabinet Secy. and Secy. Planning Commission 1953–57; Gov. of Orissa 1957–62; Pres., Maritime Freight Commn., Union Ministry of Transport 1963–68; Govt. Dir. on Board of Indian Shipping Companies 1964–67. *Address:* Flat 7, Silver Foil, N. Gamadia Road, Bombay 26, India.

**SULZBY, James Frederick, Jr.** American. *B.* 1905. *Educ.* Birmingham Southern College (AB 1928); LittD, Athens College. *M.* 1935, Martha Belle Hilton. *S.* James Frederick III. *Dau.* 1. *Career:* With First National Bank of Birmingham 1929–41. Partner, Sulzby Realty Co.; Chairman Birmingham (Ala.) Planning Commission 1947–60; Treasurer, Southside Baptist Church, Birmingham 1948—; Chmn., Bd. of Trustees, Alabama Academy of Science 1952—; Vice-Pres., (Fidelity) Federal Savings & Loan Association; Dir. Home Savings and Loan Assn.; Pres., Albama Real Estate Assn. (1952); Director, American Planning and Civic Association; member, Board of Directors, Birmingham Symphony Association. *Publications:* Birmingham as it was in Jackson County; Arthur W. Smith, a Birmingham Pioneer 1855–1944; Birmingham Sketches; Annals of the Southside Baptist Church, Birmingham; Ed. History of the Continental Gin Company; Historic Alabama Hotels and Resorts. *Member:* Newcomen Society of America; Secretary (Past Pres.), Albama Historical Association, Birmingham-Southern College Alumni Association (Pres.), Phi Beta Kappa, Omicron Delta Kappa, Phi Alpha Theta, Omega Tau Rho (real estate), and Delta Sigma Phi. Democrat. *Clubs:* Mountain Brook (Birmingham); University (Univ. of Albama, Tuscaloosa). *Address:* 3121 Carlisle Road, Birmingham, Ala. 35213, U.S.A.

**SUMMERFIELD, Arthur Ellsworth.** U.S. businessman. *B.* 1899. *M.* 22 July 1918, Miriam W. Graim. *S.* Arthur E., Jr. *Dau.* Gertrude (MacArthur). *Career:* Entered business 1919; established Summerfield-Chevrolet Company 1929; during World War II served as Michigan Chairman of Automobile Committee, National Automobile Dealers Association, in charge of recruitment for Ordnance Dept., U.S. Army; Michigan Director, Nat. Automobile Dealers Association 1942–49; Finance Director, Republican State Central Committee of Michigan 1943; elected Republican National Committeeman from Michigan 1944; re-elected 1948 and 1952; Vice-Chairman, Rep. Nat. Committee for North-Central States 1946; Chairman, National Committee 1952; U.S. Postmaster-General 1953–61. *Awards:* Hon. D. Business Admin., Cleary Coll., Mich.; Hon LLD, Defiance Coll., Ohio; Univ. of Mich., Ill. Inst. of Technology; Hon. D.LLD Miami Univ. Ohio; Thiel Coll. Pennsylvania. *Address:* 2952 Parkside Drive, Flint, Michigan, U.S.A.

**SUMMERSKILL, Rt. Hon. Baroness,** of Ken Wood, PC, CH, MRCS, LRCP; Hon LLD (Newfoundland). British politician. *B.* 1901. *Educ.* King's College, London; Charing Cross Hospital. *M.* 1925, E. Jeffrey Samuel. *S.* Michael. *Dau.* Shirley. *Career:* Former Medical Practitioner; MP (Lab.) for West Fulham 1938–55; for Warrington 1955–61; Parly. Secy., Ministry of Food 1945–50; Minister of National Insurance March 1950–Oct. 1951; Chmn. of Labour Party 1954–55. Life Peeress 1961. *Publications:* Babies without Tears; The Ignoble Art; Letters to My Daughter; A woman's World. *Address:* Pond House, Millfield Lane, Highgate, London, N.6.

**SUMMERSKILL Dr. The Hon. Shirley Catherine Wynne** MA, BM, BCh,, MP. British. Politician. *B.* 1931. *Educ* Somerville Coll. Oxford: St. Thomas's Hospital London. *M.* 1957, John Ryman (Diss.). *Career:* Member of Parliament for Halifax since 1964; Opposition Spokesman on Health 1970–74; Parly. Under-Sec. State at Home Office since 1974. *Address:* House of Commons, London, S.W.1.

**SUMMERVILLE, Sir (William) Alan Thompson,** Kt. (1968). Australian. *B.* 1904. *Educ.* Ipswich Grammar School and University of Queensland (DSc; Hon LLD). *M.* 1930, Ethel Barker. *Daus.* 2. *Career:* Entomological investigations 1930–36; Plant Physiology research 1937–45; studied agricultural research methods in Ceylon, Egypt, Palestine, Great Britain, U.S.A., Canada, Hawaii and New Zealand 1936–37 and 1955; Dir., Div. of Plant Industry, Dept. of Agriculture and Stock, Queensland 1950; Director-General and Under-Secretary of the Department 1958–64; Agent-General for Queensland in London 1964–73; Australian Representative on the Sugar Council since 1964; Chmn. Queensland Sugar Board 1970–73. *Publications:* Various entomological and physiological publications. Fellow, Australian Inst. of Agricultural Science. *Clubs:* Johnsonian (Brisbane); East India & Sports; Royal Automobile (London). *Address:* 25 Munro St., Indooroopilly, Queensland 4068, Australia.

**SUNAY, Cevdet.** Turkish Statesman. *B.* 1900. *Educ.* Military College and Military Academy (graduated 1930). *M.* 1929, Atifet Bakirdağ. *S.* Dr. Attila & Capt. Argun. *Dau.* Mrs. Aysel Önel. Following various military appointments, Deputy Chief of General Staff, 1958–60; Chief of General Staff, 1960–66; Senator, 1966; Pres. of Turkey 1966–73; Senator 1973—. *Award:* Hon. LLD Universities of New York, Michigan and Peshawar. *Address:* Cinnah Caddesi No. 67/12, Çankaya, Ankara, Turkey.

**SUNDSTROM, Frank L.** American. *B.* 1901. *Educ.* Cornell Univ. *M.* 1936, Jean Ross Johnstone. *S.* Frank L., Jr. *Dau.* Jean R. (Farrell). *Career:* Member, U.S. House of Representatives, from New Jersey (78–79–80th Congress) 1943–49. Formerly Vice-President, Tobacco Institute, Washington, D.C. Formerly Vice-President, Schenley Industries, New York City; Vice-President and Director, Schenley Distillers Ltd.; Partner, Burton, Dana & Co., New York. Republican. *Member:* Sigma Delta Chi; Phi Kappa Psi. *Clubs:* Touchdown (N.Y.C.); Capitol Hill (Washington, D.C.; Governor); Montclair (N.J.) Golf; Congressional Country (Washington, D.C.); Cornell (N.J.). *Address:* 19 Country Club Drive, Chatham, N.J. 07928, U.S.A.

**SUPHAMONGKHON, Konthi.** Thai diplomat. *B.* 3 Aug. 1916. *Educ.* Univ. of Moral and Political Sciences, Bangkok (LLB); Faculté de Droit, Paris (D en D). *M.* 1951, Dootsdi Atthakravi. *S.* Kanthathi, Kantadharm. *Dau.* 1. *Career:* Chief of Section, Political Div., Min. of Foreign Affairs 1940–42; Second Sec.. Tokyo 1942–44; Chief of Political Div., Western Affairs Dept., 1944–48, Dir.-Gen., 1948–50. United Nations Affairs Dept. 1950–52; Lecturer: on Public Finance, Univ. of Moral and Political Sciences, Bangkok 1944; on Public International Law, U.M.P.S., 1950 and 1952; on United Nations, 1952; on National Defence College 1960–62. Minister to Australia 1952–56. Ambassador June 1956–59, and to New Zealand Oct. 1956–59. Director-General, Department of International Organizations; Adviser to the Prime Minister on Foreign Affairs 1962–64; Secretary General, SEATO 1964–65; Ambassador to Fed. Repub. of Germany 1965–67, 1970 and concurrently Ambassador to Finland, 1967–70. Ambassador to the Court of St. James's, 1970–76. *Awards:* Kt. Grand Cordon Order of the Crown of Thailand; Kt. Grand Cordon, Order of the White Elephant; Kt. Grand Comdr., Order of Chula Chom Klao; Das Grosskreuz des Verdienstordens, Deutschland; Orden Al Merito (Argentina). GCVO. *Address:* c/o Ministry of Foreign Affairs, Bangkok, Thailand.

**SURIE, Drs. Econ. Gijsbert Anthony.** Netherlands Economist. *B.* 1913. *Educ.* Rotterdam School of Economics (Drs. Econ.). M. 1940. Gabriele Elfriede Adelheid Kobler. *S.* Gijsbert Otto. *Daus.* Susanne Clara Maria, Christiane Elisabeth Britta Jacoba. *Career:* With Handelmaatschappij H. Albert de Barv & Co. N.V., Amsterdam, 1938–45; Labouchere & Co. N.V., Amsterdam, 1947–57. *Member:* Board of Union Investment Gesellschaft, Frankfurt, Jan. 1956–Sept. 1957; Investment Council Unifonds Jan. 1956–Sept. 1957; Investment Council Uscafonds, May 1956–Sept. 1957. Nederlands Overzee Bank N.V., Amsterdam, 1957–67; Representative for Western Europe of New York Hanseatic Corpn., N.Y., 1967–69; Economic Adviser Banque de Paris et des Pays-Bas N.V. Amsterdam. *Address:* De Lairessesstraat 105, Amsterdam; and *office* Banque de Paris et des Pays-Bas N.V., Herengracht 541, Amsterdam, Netherlands.

**SUROMIHARDJO, Maj.-Gen. Suadi.** Indonesian Soldier & Diplomat. *B.* 1921. *Educ.* Pakistan Staff College (PSC). *M.* 1962, Suzanne. *S.* 1. *Daus.* 2. *Career:* Member, U.N. Commission for Indonesia in Local Joint Committee and Central Joint Board 1947–49; Deputy Chief of Staff, Diponegoro Divison in Central Java 1950; Colonel Commanding, Indonesian U.N.E.F. contingent in Egypt 1957; attended Staff College, Quetta, Pakistan, and later became Commander, Staff and Command College in Bandung, Indonesia 1958; Ambassador to Australia 1961–64, to Ethiopia 1964–69; Gov., Indonesian National Defence Council 1968. *Address:* Lembaga Pertahanan Nasional, Jalan Kebon Sirih 28, Jakarta, Indonesia.

**SUSLOV, Mikhail A.** Soviet Politician. *B.* 1902. *Educ.* Graduated from Moscow G. V. Plekhanov Inst. of National Economy. *Career:* Lecturer at Moscow Univ. and the Industrial Acad. 1928; First Sec. of Stavropol Territorial Party Cttee. 1939; Mem. of Military Council of the North-Caucasian Front 1941–45; Sec. of the CPSU Central Cttee. since 1947; Mem., Political Bureau of the CPSU Central Cttee. since 1966. Twice Hero of Socialist Labour. *Address:* Presidium of The Central Committee, Moscow, U.S.S.R.

**SUTHERLAND, Sir Gordon Brims Black McIvor,** ScD, LLD (St. Andrews), DSc (Strathclyde), FRS. British scientist. *B.* 1907. *Educ.* University of St. Andrews (MA 1928; BSc 1929) and University of Cambridge (PhD 1933; ScD 1948). *M.* 1936, Gunborg Elisabeth (dau. of Filip Wahlstrom of Gothenburg, Sweden). *Daus.* 3. *Career:* Fellow, Pembroke College, Cambridge 1936–49; Junior Proctor, Univ. of Cambridge 1943–44; Reader, Univ. of Cambridge 1947–49; Professor of Physics, Univ. of Michigan (U.S.A.) 1949–56; Director, National Physical Laboratory, 1956–64; Member, Governing Body: College of Aeronautics 1956–63, London School of Economics 1956–65, and Northampton College of Advanced Technology 1960–65, and Council for Scientific Policy 1965–68; Master of Emmanuel Coll. Cambridge 1964–77. *Member:* Société Royale des Sciences, Liège (Corresponding Member): Foreign Member, American Academy Arts & Sciences; Foreign Member, American Philosophical Society; Royal Society (Fellow, Vice-Pres. 1961–63); Inst. of Physics (Fellow) (Pres. 1964–66); Faraday Society; President, Section X of British Assn. for Advancement of Science, 1968; Hon. Fellow, Pembroke College, Cambridge 1959 & Wolfson College, Cambridge 1977; Trustee, The National Gallery since 1971. *Award:* Glazebrook Medal 1972. *Publications:* Various papers on molecular structure, spectroscopy and biophysics. *Clubs:* Royal Society. *Address:* 38 Courtyards, Little Shelford, Cambridge CB2 5ER.

**SUTTON, C. Roger.** American. Consulting engineer. *B.* 1905. *Educ.* Univ. of Detroit (BChE; MS). *M.* 1927, Catherine Adeline Donnelly. *Dau.* Erma Marie. *Career:* Chemist, Timken-Detroit Axle Co. 1926–28; Instructor, Univ. of Detroit 1927–28: Chief Metallurgist, Gemmer Mfg. Co. 1928–29; Chief Chemist, Forging & Casting Corp. 1929–30; Research Physical Chemist, Solvay Process Co. 1931; Senior Metallurgist, Chrysler Corp. 1932–41; Instructor, Chrysler Inst. of Engineering 1937–41; Dir., Engineering & Metallurgy General Alloys Co. 1941–45; Roger Sutton Associates 1945–50; Senior Metallurgist, Argonne National Laboratory 1950–55; Special Lecturer, Nuclear Materials, North Carolina State University 1956.; Supervisor Stainless Steel Development International Nickel Co. 1955; Senior Metallurgist, Nuclear Utility Services Inc. 1963; Asst. Dir. Reactor Engineering, Argonne National Laboratory 1965; Consulting Engineer since 1971. *Publications:* numerous papers on heat and corrosion-resisting alloy castings, on the effect of radiation on structural materials and on reactor core component testing and fabrication. *Address:* 1129 Central Avenue, Downers Grove, Ill. 60515, U.S.A.

**SUTTON, Glenn Wallace.** American. *B.* 1904. *Educ.* Indiana Univ. (BS 1926; AM 1927) and Ohio State Univ. (PhD 1938). *M.* 1930, Rachel Sibley. *S.* William Wallace. *Career:* Accountant, Groubs Wholesale Grocery (Seymour, Ind.) 1922, and Farmers' Co-operative Elevator Co. (Seymour) 1923; Research Assistant, Bureau of Business Research, Indiana University 1925–27; Editor, Idaho Economic Review, and Instructor of Economics, Univ. of Idaho 1927–29; at Univ. of Georgia (Prof. of Finance, Chmn. Finance Div., Editor Georgia Business Review, Dir. Bur. of Business Research, Dir. Veterans Affairs Office, Dir. Savannah Div., and Dir. Graduate Div., Coll. of Business Administration) 1929–54; Dir., Southeastern States, Urban Studies of Consumer Purchases and Income, Bur. of Labor Statistics, U.S. Dept. of Labor, Atlanta 1936; Dir., National Tabulation Office, same statistics, U.S. Dept. of Labor, Chicago 1937; Dir. Southeastern States, Survey of State, County and Municipa Employment and Payrolls, Bur. of Labor Statistics, U.S. Dept. of Labor, Atlanta, 1939–40; National Dir., same survey U.S. Dept. of Labor, Philadelphia 1941. With U.S. Navy (successively Lieut., Lieut-Comdr., Comdr. and Captain) 1942–64; U.S. Delegate to 1956 Tariff Negotiations by the Contracting Parties to GATT, Geneva; Member, U.N. Economic Committee June 1955–May 1959. Vice-Chairman, United States Tariff Commission 1966–69; Chairman, 1969–72. (Member since July 1954. During 1965; By invitation by the Secy. of the Navy, participated in 17th Annual Global Strategy Discussions, Naval War Coll.; Adviser to U.S. Deleg. to Kennedy Round of Tariff Negotiations by Contracting Parties to the GATT, Geneva; and to the U.S. Deleg. to the European Communities, and U.S. participant in trade discussions with officials of EEC, Brussels; U.S. Participant in trade discussions with British Board of Trade in London, with Economic and Foreign Ministers and State Secy. in Bonn, and with Patronat, Paris. *Publications:* some bulletins and books published by U.S. Government· Democrat. *Clubs:* Gridiron, Rotary, Taconis, Cosmos. *Address:* 649 Oglethorpe Avenue, Athens, Georgia 30601, U.S.A.

**SUTTON, Prof. William Godfrey,** K St. J, BA, BSc, FICE; Hon. LLD. South African Civil Engineer and University Principal; *B.* 28 March 1894. *Educ.* King Edward VII School Johannesburg, and Univ. of Cape Town; BA (Hon.), BSc (Eng.). *M.* 1954, Aletta McMenamin (née Wilson), *Career:* Served in German East Africa in World War I 1916–18; Asst. Engineer, Dept. of Irrigation, Un. of South Africa 1918–26; attached U.S. Reclamation Service 1921–22; Prof. Civ. Eng., Univ. of the Witwatersrand 1926–54; served in World War II (Gen. Mgr., Cent. Organization for Tech. Training Dept. of Defence 1941–44; Chief Tech. Adviser, Dept. of Commerce and Industries 1944–45); Principal and Vice-Chancellor, University of the Witwatersrand, Johannesburg 1954–62. member, Cncl., Institution of Civil Engineers, London 1951 and 1952; Pres. S.A. Institution of Engineers 1936. Civil Engineers 1945, Associa, ted Scientific & Technical Societies of S.A. 1951. Member. Smuts Memorial Cttee.; U.S.-South Africa Leader Exchange Program; Trustee, South Africa Foundation. *Address:* 48, Eastwood Road, Dunkeld, Johannesburg, South Africa.

**SUWARNASARN, Sunthorn.** Ambassador of Thailand. *B.* 1920. *Educ.* Thamasart Univ., Bangkok—LLB. *M.* 1942. Charmnarn Wasantasingh. *S.* 2. *Daus.* 2. *Career:* entered Ministry of Foreign Affairs 1940; Attaché Personal Sec. of Under-Sec. of State for Foreign Affairs 1942; Third Sec., Econ. Dept. 1944; Third/Second Sec., Royal Thai Embassy, Rangoon 1949–53; Chief of Europe & America Div., Political Dept. 1954–56; Chief Central Div. Office, Under-Sec. 1956; Consul/Acting Consul-Gen., Jeddah 1956–61; Chief of Diplomatic Privilege Div., Protocol Dept. 1961–62; First Sec., Royal Thai Embassy, Vienna & Alt. Resident Rep. of Thailand to IAEA 1962–66; Chief of Int. Conference Div., Inter.-Organisation Dept. 1966–68; Counsellor & Chargé d'Affaires, Royal Thai Embassy, Saigon 1968–72 & Colombo 1972–75; Ambassador to Arab Republic of Egypt since 1975. *Decorations:* Chaisamorabhum War Medal; Ratanaphorn—4th class; Coronation Medal H.M. King Bhumibol Aduldej of Thailand; Knight Commander of Republic of Austria; Knight Commander of The White Elephant of Thailand; Knight Grand Cross of the Crown of Thailand. *Address:* Royal Thai Embassy, 9 Bahgat Aly Street, Zamalek, Cairo, Arab Republic of Egypt.

**SVART, Anker.** Danish diplomat. *B.* 1918. *Educ.* University of Aarhus, Denmark, and Univ. of Sheffield, England. *M.* 1949, Nina Svart née Jonsson. *Career:* Attaché Danish Legation, Iceland 1944–45; Ministry of Foreign Affairs, Copenhagen 1945–52; Secy. Danish Legation Canada, 1952–55; Counsellor, Danish Embassy, Moscow 1956–60; Counsellor, Danish Embassy, Bonn 1960–62; Ambassador in Peking 1962–65; Head of Division, Econ/Political Dept, Ministry of For. Affairs 1965–66; Ambassador in Moscow (jointly accredited to Mongolia) 1966–73; Ambassador to Belgium/Luxembourg and NATO since 1973. *Address:* Royal Danish Embassy, 221 av. Louise, B 1050 Brussels, Belgium.

**SVESHNIKOV, Mefodii Naumovich.** Soviet economist and banker. *B.* 1911. *Educ.* graduated from Financial and Economic Institute. *Career:* Worked at the State Bank as Branch Manager, Regional Office Manager, Dir. of Dept., Member of Board of Directors, Deputy Chmn. of Board, 1929–69; Chmn. Bd. of Dirs. of Bank for Foreign Trade 1957–69.

Chairman of the Board of Directors of the State Bank of the USSR, 1969–76; Deputy to USSR Supreme Soviet. *Member.* C.P.S.U. *Awards:* Holder, Order of Lenin; Two Orders of the Red Banner; Order of the October Revolution. *Publications:* The System of Payments between Socialist Countries; and numerous articles. *Address:* State Bank of the USSR, 12 Neglinnaya, Moscow, U.S.S.R.

**SVOBODA, Ludvik** *B.* 1895. *Educ.* Military Academy. *M.* Irene Svobodová. *S.* 1. (*Dec.*) *Dau.* 1. *Career:* Professor Mil. Acad. Hranice 1931–34; Commander 1st Czech Army Group in U.S.S.R. 1939–45; Czech Minister of National Defence 1945–50; Commander Mil. Acad. Prague 1954–58; President Czech Socialist Republic 1968–75. *Awards:* Order of White Lion (for Victory); Order of the Republic (Czech); International Lenin Prize (for strengthening peace among nations); other Soviet, Polish & Finnish orders. *Address:* Praha-Hrad, Czechoslovakia.

**SWAIN, Robert Cuthbertson.** B. 1907. Stanford University (AB; also National Research Council Fellow); Universities of Heidelberg and Berlin (PhD). *M.* 1929, Frances Grace Johnson. *S.* Robert Johnson. *Daus.* Mary (Cole) and Nancy Elizabeth (decd.). *Career:* Research Chemist, American Cyanamid Co. 1934–43 (Director of Research Div., Stamford Laboratories 1942–45; Research Director 1945–46); Director Stanford Research Institute 1951–62 and Jefferson Chemical Co. 1947–59. Elected Executive Vice-President June 1965–71;, Director 1946–71; American Cyanamid Co. Vice-President, International Operations, and Director-General, Cyanamid International Division 1959–65; Pres., Cyanamid International Corp. 1959–65; Vice-President, Research and Development 1946–59. Director, Perkin-Elmer Corp. 1957—. *Publications:* many issued patents *Awards:* Castner Memorial Medal; James Turner Morehead Medal; Alexander Von Humbold Fellowship (Univ. of Berlin); National Research Fellow (Stanford Univ.). *Member:* Amer. Chemical Socy.; Socy. of Chemical Industry; Amer. Inst. of Chemists. *Clubs:* Greenwich (Conn.) Country; Riverside (Conn.) Yacht; Bohemian (California). *Address:* Meadow Road, Riverside, Conn. 06878, U.S.A.

**SWANN, Sir Michael.** FRS, FRSE. Chmn. BBC since 1973, Former Principal and Vice Chancellor, Univ. of Edinburgh. *Address:* Ormsacre, 41 Barnton Avenue, Edinburgh EH4 6JJ.

**SWANSON, Harold Norling.** American. President, H. N. Swanson, Inc.; President, Sunset Management Company. *B.* 1899. *Educ.* Grinnell College, Iowa. *M.* 1930, Ruth Evelyn Taylor. *Career:* Former Vice-Pres. and Editorial Dir., Collegiate World Publishing Co., Chicago; Producer, RKO Studios, Hollywood. *Publications:* Corn-Moods from Mid-America (1922); They Fell in Love (1932); Big Business Girl (1930). *Address:* 8523 Sunset Boulevard, Los Angeles Ca. 90069, U.S.A.

**SWANSON, Thomas Baikie,** CBE. Australian. *B.* 1910. *Educ.* Univ. of Adelaide (BSc; MSc). *M.* 1938, Marjorie Ella Adams. *S.* 2. *Dau.* 1. *Career:* Lecturer Pharm. Chem., Adelaide Univ, 1938–39; Foundation Lecturer in charge Chem. Dept., New England Univ. 1939–45. With I.C.I. of Australia and New Zealand Ltd.: Technical Officer 1945; General Manager, Chemical Group 1953; Group Director 1955. Director: Australian Fertilizers Ltd. 1963–71; and BALM Paints Ltd. 1963–71; Man. Dir. ICIANZ Ltd. 1964–; Chmn. Eastern Nitrogen Ltd. 1966–; Dep. Chmn. Imperial Chemical Industries of Aust, Ltd. 1968–71; Chmn. Aust. Commission, Advanced Education 1971–75 (Ret'd). *Publications:* articles to Journal of Chemical Socy.; sundry papers 1937–39. *Member:* Royal Aust. Chemical Inst. (Past Pres., Victorian Branch); Chemical Socy. of London; Royal Socy. of N.S.W.; Inst. of Directors; Aust. Inst. of Management. *Clubs:* Melbourne; Australian; Victoria Golf. *Address:* 4–112 Walsh Street, South Yarra, Vic. 3141, Australia.

**SWART, Hon. Charles Robberts.** (retd.). *B.* 1894. *Educ.* Univ. College of Orange Free State (LLD Hon. Causa); University of South Africa (BA, LLB) and Columbia Univ., New York. *M.* 1924, Nellie de Klerk. *S.* 1. *Dau:* 1. *Career:* Practised as Advocate, Supreme Ct. of South Africa 1919–48; MP (National) for Ladybrand O.F.S. 1923–38; and for Winburg O.F.S. 1941–59; Minister of Justice 1948–59; Minister of Education, Arts and Science 1949–50; Chancellor, University of Orange Free State 1950–76; Deputy Prime Minister and Leader of the House 1954–59; Governor-General of Union of S. Africa 1960–61. State President, Republic of South Africa 1961–67. *Awards:* LLD. *Hon. causa*, Rhodes Univ. and Potchefstroom Univ.; Hon. Fellow, Coll. of Physicians, Surgeons & Gynæcologists of South Africa 1963. Hon. Fdllow, Institute of S.A. Architects 1967. Hon. Member, S.A. Academy of Science and Art; Hon. President, Automobile Association, of South Africa; Life Member, Federation of Afrikaans Cultural Society; one of founders of Die Afrikaanse Handelsinstituut; Hon. Col. Regt. Oos-Vrystaat since 1953; Hon. Col. Regt. University Oranje-Vrystaat since 1962; Meritorious Service award (DMS) 1972. *Publications:* Kinders van Suid-Afrika; Die Agterryer. *Address:* "De Aap", Brandfort, O.F.S., Republic of South Africa.

**SWARTZ, Col. Hon. Sir Reginald William Colin,** KBE, MBE' ED, JP. Australian company director. *B.* 1911. *Educ.* Grammar Schools (Toowoomba and Brisbane). *M.* 1936, Hilda Robinson. *S.* 2. *Dau.* 1. *Career:* C.M.F. from 1928, Lt. 1934, Capt. 2/26 Bn. 8 Div. A.I.F. from 1940, Malaya, P.O.W., Singapore, Malaya, Thailand (Burma-Thailand Rly.); C.M.F. Darling Downs Regt., Lt.-Col. A.Q.M.G., C.M.F., N. Commd., Col. (R.L.); Hon. Colonel Army Aviation Corps 1968–74; Member, Parliament for Darling Downs 1949–72; (Parly Secy. 1951–61); Parly. Under Secy. for Commerce and Agriculture 1952–56; Commonwealth Parly. Secy. for Trade 1956–61; Minister of State for Repatriation 1961–64; Minister of Health 1964–66; Social Services 1965; Minister, Civil Aviation 1966–69; National Development 1969 and 1971–72; Leader, House of Representatives 1970–72. Chmn. of 3 Private Companies & Dir. of 5 Public Companies. Patron and/or Vice-President or member of over sixty public organizations. Liberal. *Clubs:* United Service, Australian (Melbourne), Twin Towns, RACV, RACQ, Darling Towns Aero, Southport Yacht, Surfers Paradise Bowls, No. 10, London. *Address:* 31 Furlong Street, Rio Vista 4217, Surfers Paradise, Queensland, 4217, Australia.

**SWEET, John Howard.** Chmn. Pres. and Publisher, U.S. News & World Report. *B.* 1907. *Educ.* Univ. of Manitoba. *M.* 1940, Anne Ethel Wallace. *S.* Anthony Howard. *Dau.* Elizabeth Anne. *Career:* Asst. Circulation Manager, American Medical Association 1926–29; Circulation Manager, Traffic World 1929–37; Vice-President: Poor's Publishing Co. 1937–40, and Dickie Raymond Inc. 1940–42. Lieut.-Commander, U.S. Navy 1942–45. Successively Circulation Director, 1946–51, Exec. Vice-Pres. and Publisher 1951–59, and Pres. and Publisher, U.S. News & World Report 1959–73, Chmn. Pres. & Publisher since 1973. *Clubs:* Metropolitan; International; National Press; Congressional Country (Washington); Princess Anne Country (Virginia Beach, Va). *Address:* 2124 Bancroft Place, N.W., Washington, D.C, 20008; and *office* N Street, N.W., Washington, D.C. 20037. U.S.A.

**SWEETLAND, Wilfred Wootten.** Australian Company Director. *B.* 1913. *Educ.* University of Sydney, BE. *M.* (1) 1938, Marjory Joyce Donald (*Dec.*). *S.* Jolyon, Wilfred, Nicholas. *Dau.* Sandra (Henderson), Louise. (2) 1972, Shirley Foxcroft née Waugh. *Career:* Exec. Gen. Mgr. Minerals Div. and Dir. The Broken Hill Proprietary Co. Ltd. and its subsidiaries, Australian Iron & Steel Pty. Ltd.; Australian Wire Industries Pty. Ltd.; Hematite Petroleum Pty. Ltd.; Dampier Mining Co. Ltd.; Groote Eylandt Mining Co. Pty. Ltd.; Tasmanian Electro Metallurgical Co. Pty. Ltd.; B.H.P. Nominees Pyt. Ltd.; P.T. B.H.P. Indonesia; B.H.P. Malaysia; Sdn. Berhad; Queensland Coal Mining Co. Ltd.; Mt. Newman Mining Co. Pty. Ltd.; Dir., Merchant & Miners Transport Inc., Liberia; The Adelaide Steamship Co. Ltd.; Gen. Mgr., Shipping 1959–64, Shipping and Engineering 1964–68, Engineering and Development 1968–69; Exec. Gen. Mgr. Technology 1969–71; Chmn., Mgr. Dir. Port Waratah Stevedoring Co. Pty. Ltd. 1959–68. *Publications:* Economic and Engineering Problems in the Australian Shipping Industry (1962); The Impact of Mineral Development in the Growth of Australian Ports (1969); Steel in Australia (1969). Fellow, Institute of Engineers, Australia; Member, Institute of Mining & Metallurgy, Australia. *Clubs:* The Australian (Melbourne); University, (Sydney); Newcastle (Newcastle). *Address:* 781 Orrong Road, Toorak, Victoria; and *office* B.H.P. House, William Street, Melbourne, Victoria, Australia.

**SWINBURNE, Hon. Ivan Archie,** CMG. Australian politician. *B.* 6 March 1908. *M. Dau.* 1. M.L.C. for North-Eastern Province, Victoria since 1946; Minister for Housing and Materials, Victoria June 1950–52; Leader, Country Party in Legislative Council since 1969. *Award:* Companion, Order of

Saint Michael and St. George, 1973. *Address:* P.O. Box 341, Myrtle Street, Myrtleford, Vic. 3737, Australia.

**SYED ABUL BASHER MAHMUD HUSAIN,** BA, BL. Bangladesh Judge. *B.* 1916. *Educ.* Shaistagonj High Sch., M.C. Coll., Sylhet, Dacca Univ. *M.* 1936, Sufia Begum. *S.* 3. *Daus.* 5. *Career:* Pleader, Judge's Court, Dacca 1940–42; Honorary Supdt., Darul-Ulum Govt. Aided Senior Madrassa, Dacca 1937–42; Addl. Govt. Pleader, Habiganj 1943–48; Joined as Advocate, Dacca High Court Bar 1948; enrolled as an Attorney of Fed. Court of Pakistan 1951, as an Advocate of the Court 1953 and as a Senior Advocate, Supreme Court of Pakistan 1958; Asst. Govt. Pleader, High Court of East Pakistan 1952–56 and Senior Govt. Pleader of the Court 1956–65; Acting Advocate-General, East Pakistan for some time; Judge, High Court of East Pakistan 1965; Judge, High Court of Bangladesh 1972; Judge, Appellate Div. of the High Court of Bangladesh 1972; Judge, Appellate Div. of the Supreme Court of Bangladesh 1972; Chief Justice of Bangladesh since 1975; Leader of the Hajj Delegation of Bangladesh 1975; attended the International Islamic Conference in London 1976 and presided over the Third Session of the Conference as its Chairman. *Address:* Chief Justice's House, 19 Hare Road, Dacca-2, Bangladesh.

**SYKES, Sir Richard Adam,** KCMG, MC, MA. British diplomat. *B.* 1920. *Educ.* Wellington Coll. Christ Church, Oxford. *M.* 1953, Ann Georgina Fisher. *S.* Phillip Rodney Andrew Francis. *Dau.* Eleanor Rachel. *Career:* British Army Royal Signals (retd. rank of Major) 1940–46; Foreign Office 1947–48; Second Secy. H.M. Embassy Nanking China 1948–50; Peking 1950–52; First Secy. Foreign Office 1952–56, H.M. Embassy, Brussels Belgium 1956–59, Santiago Chile 1959–62; Counsellor H.M. Embassy Athens Greece 1963–66, Foreign Office 1967–70; H.M. Ambassador, Havana Cuba 1970–72; H.M. Minister British Embassy Washington U.S.A. 1972–75; Dep. Under-Secy. FCO 1975–77; H.M. Ambassador, The Hague Netherlands since 1977. *Clubs:* Travellers, Army & Navy (London). *Address:* British Embassy, Lange Voorhout 10, The Hague, Netherlands.

**SYME, Sir Colin York,** AK. *B.* 1903. *Educ.* Scotch College, Claremont (W.A.); Universities of Perth and Melbourne (LLB). *M.* 1933, Patricia Baird. *S.* Robin, James and Martin. *Dau.* Gillian (Dahlsen). *Career:* Chairman: Broken Hill Proprietary Co. Ltd. (Director since 1937) 1952–71; President, The Walter & Eliza Hall Institute of Medical Research; Partner, Hedderwick Fookes & Alston (solicitors) 1928–67; Australian Industries Development Corp. 1971–77. *Award:* Knight of the Order of Australia; Hon DSc, Univ. of New South Wales. *Clubs:* Melbourne; Australian; Adelaide; The Links, New York. *Address:* 22 Stonnington Place, Toorak, Vic.; and *office* 140 William Street, Melbourne, Vic., Australia.

**SYMINGTON, (William) Stuart,** US Politician. *B.* 26 Jun. 1901. *Educ.* Baltimore City College: Yale University (AB). *M.* 1924, Evelyn Wadsworth. *S.* Stuart, James. *Career:* Served World War I, U.S. Army 1918; with Symington Co., Rochester, New York 1923–30; President, Colonial Radio Corporation 1930–35; President, Rustless Iron and Steel Corporation 1935–37; President and Chairman of the Board, Emerson Electric Manufacturing Co. 1938–45; Administrator, Surplus Property Board 1945; Asst. Secretary of War for Air 1946; Secretary of the Air Force 1947; Chairman, National Security Resources Board April 1950–May 1951; Administrator, Reconstruction Finance Corporation, May 1951–Feb. 1952: Senator from Missouri 1953–77. Senate Cttees., 1969, Armed Services, Foreign Relations, Joint Atomic Energy, Appropriations, Democratic Policy, Democratic Steering. *Awards:* Hon LLD: Baylor Univ., Univ. of Missouri, and William Jewell (Liberty), Park (Parkville), Rockhurst (Kansas City), Washington Univ.; and Avila (Kansas City) Colleges; Hon DLitt Coll. of Osteopathy and Surgery (Kirksville): Hon DHL, Missouri Valley Coll. *Address:* The Barclay House, 230 S. Brentwood Boulevard, St. Louis, Mo. 63105, U.S.A.

**SYMMERS, William Garth.** Lawyer. *B.* 1910. *Educ.* University of Virginia College of Arts & Sciences (BA 1933) and University of Virginia Law School (LLB 1935). *M.* (1) Marina Baruch 1936–44, and (2) Anne Hazeltine Ellis 1946. *S.* Benjamin Keith. *Daus.* Ann St. Clair, Barbara, Susan and Deborah. *Career:* Admitted to Bar of New York Court of Appeals 1937, and Supreme Court of the U.S. 1940. Associated with law firm of Bigham, Englar, Jones & Houston, N.Y. 1935–37; Counsel, U.S. Maritime Commission 1937–40. Founding member: Dow & Symmers 1940–56, and Symmers, Fish & Warner, N.Y. 1956—. Member, Supreme Court of the United States' Advisory Committee on Rules of Procedure, Judicial Conference of the United States, 1960–75. Member Titulaire, Comité Maritime International 1955—. Special Counsel, U.S. House of Representatives Committee on Naval Affairs 1942. Reserve Captain, Judge Advocate General's Dept., Army of the U.S., World War II. Lecturer on International Maritime Law and Maritime Insurance, American University Graduate School 1939–40. Practising Law Inst. 1957. *Publications:* Limitation of Shipowners' Liability (Institute of London Underwriters); various monographs in maritime and insurance journals. *Member:* Amer. Bar Assn.; Assn. of Bar of City of New York (Chmn., Cttee. on Admiralty Law 1953–56); Maritime Law Assn. of the U.S. (member, Exec. Cttee. 1959–61, First Vice-Pres. 1964–66): International Law Assn. (American Branch). *Clubs:* Down Town Association, N.Y. Yacht (N.Y.C.); University, Chevy Chase (D.C.); Field (Greenwich, Conn.). *Address:* 82 Zaccheus Mead Lane, Greenwich, Conn.; and *office* 345 Park Avenue, New York City 10022, U.S.A.

# T

**TAENI, John Ignatius.** American. Director, Member Exec. Committee, Seabrook Foods, Inc., Seabrook N.J. Vice-Chairman, Eastern Air Devices Incorporated, Luxembourg. Director: Eastern Air Devices Inc., Dover, N.H.; Peerless Fabrikkerne A/S, Copenhagen; Bretton S.A., Cluses; Director, Vice-Chmn. Member Exec. Cttee., Hygrade Food Product Corp., Detroit. Vice-Chmn. Bd. and Dir. Bernard Aronson, Taeni Incorporated Pres. Taeni Int. Division D. H. Blair & Co. Inc. *B.* 1901. *Educ.* Univ of Vienna, Austria (Dr. Sc. pol. & Ex.). *M.* 1952, Madeleine Renata Weigner. *Address:* 177 East 77th Street, New York, N.Y. 10021; and *office* 437 Madison Avenue, New York, N.Y. 10022, U.S.A.

**TAEUBER, Conrad.** American. *B.* 1906. *Educ.* Univ. of Minnesota (AB 1927; MA 1929; PhD 1931); and Univ. of Heidelberg, Germany (Student). *M.* 1929, Irene Barnes (*dec.*). *S.* Richard Conrad and Karl Ernst. *Career:* With U.S. Dept. of Agriculture in various capacities 1935–46; Chief of Statistics Branch of F.A.O. of the United Nations 1946–51; Associate Dir. Bureau of the Census U.S. 1951–73; Dir. Center for Population Research, The Joseph and Rose Kennedy Institute. *Member:* Amer. Statistical Assn. (Fellow); Amer. Sociological Assn.; Inter-Amer. Statistical Inst. (Former Pres.); Population Assn. of America: International Population Union; Int. Statistical Inst. *Awards:* Outstanding Achievement Award, Univ. of Minnesota, 1951; Exceptional Service Award, Dept. of Commerce, 1963. *Publications:* Rural Migration in the United States (with C. E. Lively 1939); The Changing Population of the United States (with Irene B. Taeuber 1958); People of the United States in the 20th Century (with Irene B. Taeuber 1971). Contributor to social science journals. *Club:* Cosmos Wash., D.C. *Address:* 4222 Sheridan Street, Hyattsville, Md. 20782; and *office* Kennedy Inst. Center for Population Research, Georgetown University, Washington, D.C. 20057, U.S.A.

**TAGAYA, Yoshio.** Japanese Master of Engineering. *B.* 1921. *Educ.* Tokyo Imperial Univ. *M.* 1948, Chieko Inaba. *S.* Osamu. *Career:* Technical Officer of Aviation in the Japanese Navy 1944–45; Technical Liaison Officer between the Civil

Aviation Bureau and the Air Force 1948–56; engaged in study of air traffic services in Europe 1956. Air Navigation Commissioner, International Civil Aviation Organization 1957–64; Councillor to the Minister of Transport, Japan (in charge of external affairs), 1964–65; Director, New York Main Office for America's Japan National Tourist Organization, 1965–69. Director, Office of General Services, United Nations, since 1969. *Publication:* Encyclopædia Japonica (Editor and one of the writers on civil aviation). ***Member:*** Japan Socy. for Aeronautical and Space Sciences. ***Address:*** 2600-31 Netherland Avenue, Bronx, New York, N.Y. 10463, U.S.A.; and 4–3, 6-chome, Sakurayama, Zushi, Kanagawa Pref., Japan 249.

**TAGGART, Joseph H.** American economist and university administrator. *B.* 1902. *Educ.* Yale (PhB), Harvard (MBA), Columbia (PhD). LLD (Hon) Long Island University, 1962; LLD (Hon) University of Lagos, Federal Republic of Nigeria 1968. *Career:* Professional staff, several U.S. univs. 1927–41; Economist. U.S. Dept. of Commerce 1941–42; Captain and Major, U.S. Army in World War II; Economic Adviser to Commissioner in Europe and Dir. of Planning, Foreign Liquidation Commission, Washington 1945–46; Econ. Adv., Chairman of Munitions Board 1947–52; U.S. Representative Western Union Military Supply Board, London 1949–50; Econ. Adv., U.S. Representative NATO Military Production and Supply Board 1950–51; Special Asst. to Dep. Administrator for International Activities, U.S. Defense Production Administration 1952; member: U.S. Delegation 9th International Conference of American States, Bogatá 1948; Professor of Economics and Finance, Rutgers University 1947–56. Professor of Finance (1956—), Associate Dean (1956–59), Dean (1959—), Graduate School of Business Administration, New York University, N.Y.C.; Executive Dean, Schools of Business, New York University (1962—). Public Governor, American Stock Exchange. Director, Allegheny Power Systems Inc., Monongahela Power Co., West Penn Power Co., James Talcott Inc., The Potomac Edison Co., J. J. Newbury Co. *Publications:* Federal Reserve Bank of Boston, Cambridge (1938); articles and reviews in professional and government journals. Independent. *Clubs:* University; Army-Navy Country; Alpha Sigma Phi; Alpha Kappa Psi; Beta Gamma Sigma; Amer. Economic Assn. *Address:* 37 Washington Square West, New York City, N.Y. 10011, U.S.A.

**TAHOURDIN, John Gabriel,** CMG. British Diplomat (Ret'd.). *B.* 1913. *Educ.* Merchant Taylors' School (London) and St. John's Coll., Oxford (BA Hons in Modern Languages). *M.* 1957, Zena Margaret Michie. *S.* Adrian John St. Clair. *Dau.* Virginia Frances. *Career:* Counsellor of Embassy, The Hague 1955–57; Foreign Office 1957–63; Minister in U.K. Delegation to the 18-nation Disarmament Conference, Geneva 1963–66; Ambassador to Senegal 1966–71; Concurrently to Mauretania 1968–71, to Mali 1969–71, to Guinea 1970–71, to Bolivia 1971–73. Member Inst. for Strategic Studies. *Clubs:* Travellers' (London). *Address:* Stone Street Farm, Aldington, Kent.

**TAIT, Sir Peter,** KBE, JP, New Zealand Share Broker, Napier, N.Z. *B.* 1915. *Educ.* Wellington (N.Z.) College. *M.* 1946, Lilian Jean Dunn. *S.* David John. *Dau.* Judith Lorraine. *Career:* Dir., Rothmans Industries Ltd.; Peros Ltd.; Municipalities Co-op. Insurance Co. Ltd.; Bowring Burgess Finance Ltd.; Mayor City of Napier 1956–74; JP 1956. MP for Napier (representing N.Z. National Party) 1951–54. Chairman: Marineland Trust Board; Princess Aleyandria Community Hospital; Exec. Hawke's Bay Medical Foundation. *Member:* Hawke's Bay Harbour Board; Chmn. Deacons; Napier Baptist Church. *Award:* OBE 1967, KBE 1975. Freeman, City of Napier. *Clubs:* Lions (Hon.); Cosmopolitan (Hon.). *Address:* 13 Simla Terrace (and P.O. Box 133), Napier; and *office* Emerson Street, Napier, New Zealand.

**TAKEUCHI, Ryuji.** Adviser to the Foreign Minister of Japan. *B.* 1903. *Educ.* Tokyo Imperial University. *M.* 1939, Yoshiko Hoshino. Grand Cordon, Order of Leopold (Belgium); Grand Cross, Order of Civil and Military Merit of Adolphe de Nassau (Luxembourg); Grosses Verdienstkreuz mit Stern und Schulterband des Verdienstordens der Bundesrepublik Deutschland; Grand Cross of Order of May of Merit (Argentina); First Class Order of the Sacred Treasure (Japan). *Career:* Entered Foreign Office 1927; after serving in Embassies in London, Shanghai, Moscow, Berlin, became 1st Sec., Moscow 1942; Chief, Russian Section, Foreign Office 1944; after the war, Chief Political Bureau, Central Liaison Office; Dir. of Sapporo and Kyoto Liaison Office; International Trade Administrator-General 1949; Chief, Govt. Overseas Agency in U.S.A. 1951; Min. Plen., U.S.A. 1952–54; Director, European and American Bureau, Foreign Office 1954; Ambassador to Belgium and Luxembourg 1955–57; Ambassador to West Germany 1957–60; Vice-Minister for Foreign Affairs of Japan 1960–63; Ambassador to the U.S.A., 1963–67; Special Adviser to the President of the Japan Air Lines. Sept. 1967—; Chmn. Bd. of Directors Nippon Roche Co. Ltd. since 1968. *Clubs:* Tokyo Country; Hodogaya Country; Chevy Chase, Burning Tree, Metropolitan (Washington). *Address:* Fuji Bldg; 2-3 3-chome Marunouchi, Chiyoda-ku, Tokyo, Japan.

**TALBOT, Phillips.** American. *B.* 1915. *Educ.* Univ. of Illinois, BA, BSJ; Univ. of London Schl. of Oriental and African Affairs; Univ. of Chicago, PhD; LLD, Mills College. *M.* Mildred A. Fisher, 1943. *S.* Bruce Kenneth, *Daus.* Susan and Nancy. *Career:* U.S. Ambassador to Greece 1965–69; U.S. Asst. Secy., of State for Near East and South Asian Affairs, 1961–65; Exec. Dir., Amer. Univs. Field Staff, Inc. 1951–61; Pres. The Asia Society N.Y. 1970—. *Member:* Assn. for Asian Studies; Royal Soc. for Asian Affairs; Council on Foreign Relations; Washington Inst. of Foreign Affairs. *Publications:* Editor, South Asia in the World Today (1950); Co-author (with S. L. Poplai), India and America (1958). *Clubs:* Century Assn., New York; Cosmos Club of Washington. *Address:* The Asia Society, 112 East 64th St., New York, N.Y. 10021, U.S.A.

**TALBOYS, Hon. Brian Edward,** PC, BA. New Zealand. *B.* 1921. *Educ.* University of Manitoba; Victoria University (BA). *M.* 1950, Patricia Floyd Adamson. *S.* 2. *Career:* Parliamentary Under Secretary to the Minister of Industries & Commerce 1961–62. Minister of Agriculture 1962–69; Minister of Science 1963–72; Minister of Education 1969–72; Minister of Industries & Commerce, Minister Overseas Trade 1972; Depy. PM 1976; Minister of Foreign Affairs & Minister of Overseas Trade 1976. Member New Zealand National Party. *Address:* 1 Hamilton Avenue, Winton, Southland, N.Z.; and *office* Parliament Buildings, Wellington, New Zealand.

**TALEGHANI, Khalil.** BSc. Iranian. *B.* 1913. *Educ.* Birmingham Univ. (BSc. Hons.). *M.* 1947, Jamileh Mohseni. *S.* 3. *Career:* Dir. Ebte Kar Co., Golpayegan Water Co. 1941–51; Minister of Agriculture & State 1951–59; Taleghani-Tashakori 1954–59; Chmn. Industrial & Mining Development Bank of Iran 1960–63. Chmn. B.F. Goodrich Iran Tyre Mfg. Co., Fellow, Amer. Socy. of Civil Engineers; Mem. Iranian Consulting Engineers Assoc. *Address:* Baghe Bank Street, Golhak, Tehran, Iran and *office:* Taleghani-Daftary Consulting Engineers, Takharestan Street, Zafar Avenue, Tehran, Iran.

**TALIAFERRO, Paul E(verett).** American. Oil corporation executive. *B.* 1905. *Educ.* North Texas State University (AB); LLB University of Tulsa 1930. Admitted to Bar 1930. *M.* 1932. Irene Winifred Warden. *S.* Bruce Owen. *Dau.* Mary Ann (Leroy Ulmer). *Career:* With Sunray Corp.: Gen. Attorney 1931, Vice-Pres. 1937, Director 1946, Vice-President and Asst. to President 1950. Exec. Vice-President 1952. Chmn. of Board and Dir., Pres. and Chief Exec. Officer, Sunray DX Oil Co. 1959–68; Deputy Chairman, Board of Directors, Sun Oil Co., 1968–70. Member, Board of Directors: Atlas Life Insurance Co. 1950—, National Bank of Tulsa 1956—61, Trustee and Treasurer, Hillcrest Medical Center. *Member:* various Associations including: Oklahoma Acad. for State Goals (Vice-Pres.); Thomas Gilcrease Institute of American History and Art. Member, Church of Christ. *Clubs:* The Tulsa. *Address:* 2735 East 57th Street South, Tulsa, Okla. 74105; and *office* Mid- Continent Building, Tulsa, Oklahoma 74103, U.S.A.

**TAN, Tan Sri. Chin Tuan,** PSM, CBE, JP. Singapore citizen. *B.* 1908. *M.* Wee Helene. *S.* 1. *Daus.* 2. *Career:* Chmn. Oversea-Chinese Banking Corp Ltd., Chmn.: Fraser & Neave Ltd., Malayan Breweries Ltd., The Straits Trading Co. Ltd., Robinson & Co. Ltd., The Great Eastern Life Assurance Co. Ltd., The Overseas Assurance Corp. Ltd., Internat. Bank of Singapore Ltd., Kinta Kellas Tin Dredging Ltd., Sime Darby Holdings Ltd., Wearne Bros. Ltd., Pres., Raffles Hotel Ltd.: Director: Gopeng Consolidated Ltd., Petaling Tin Berhad, Tronoh Mines Ltd., The United Malacca Rubber Estates Berhad, Tanjong Tin Dredging Ltd. *Member:* Singapore Municipal Commission 1939–41, Singapore Legislative Council (Deputy President 1951–55) 1948–55, and Singapore Executive Council 1948–55. *Fellow:* Institute of Bankers (London) and Australian Institute of Management. *Clubs:* Singapore Island Country. *Address:* 42 Cairnhill Road,

Singapore 9; and *office:* Oversea-Chinese Banking Corp. Ltd., P.O. Box No. 548, Singapore 1.

**TANAKA, Hideho.** Japanese Diplomat. *B.* 1919. *Educ.* Tokyo Univ. of Commerce. *M.* 1952, Sumiko Hashimoto. *Dau.* 1. *Career:* Entered Foreign Service 1943; Dir., Public Relations Div. 1961–63; Counsellor, Japanese Embassy, Nigeria 1963–64; Consul-Gen., Houston 1964–68; Dir.-Gen., General Affairs Dept., Overseas Technical Cooperation Agency 1968–70; Dir.-Gen. Middle East & African Affairs Bureau 1972–74; Counsellor, Foreign Minister's Secretariat 1974; Ambassador of Japan to New Zealand 1974–77, to Federal Republic of Nigeria since 1977. *Decorations:* from Afghanistan, Zaire & Argentina. *Publications:* Modern History of Palestine; Past & Present of River Mekong; Topography of Texas. *Club:* Ikoyi Club (Lagos). *Address:* 6 Osborne Road, Ikoyi, Lagos; and *office* Embassy of Japan, Plot 24/25 Apese Street, Victoria Island, P.M.B. 2111, Lagos, Nigeria.

**TANAKA, Kakuei.** Japanese Politician. *B.* 1918. *Educ.* Chuo Technical High Sch., Tokyo. *M.* 1942, Hanako Sakamoto. *Dau.* 1. *Career:* Building contractor, Tokyo 1940–47; Mem. House of Reps. 1947–74; Vice-Minister of Justice Oct.–Nov. 1948; Minister of Posts & Telecommunications 1957–58; Chmn., Policy Research Council of Liberal Democratic Party 1961–62; Sec.-Gen., Lib. Dem. Party 1965–66, 1968–71; Minister of Finance 1962–65; Chmn., Research Comm. on Municipal Policy, Lib. Dem. Party 1967–68; Minister of Int. Trade & Industry 1971–72; Pres., Lib. Dem. Party & Prime Minister 1972–74; re-elected to House of Reps. as Independent Member, Dec. 1976. *Publications:* A Proposal for Remodelling the Japanese Archipelago. *Address:* 12-19-12, Mezirodai, Bunkyo-ku, Tokyo, Japan.

**TANDLER, Richard Nelson.** Lieut.-Col. A.U.S. (Retd.). Bronze Star Medal (U.S.), OBE (U.K.); MID (Jan. 1945). *B.* 1900. *Educ.* Special studies, university and college level. *M.* 1920, Ida Jewell Winslow. *S.* Tyler Winslow. *Daus.* Mary (Hall) and Carolyn (Shimmon). *Career:* Served in World War I, March 1917–May 1919 (Infantry, A.E.F. in France, Belgium, Luxembourg and Germany A.O.); in World War II: Deputy Chief Intelligence Officer, M.A.A.F., to Chief Intelligence Officer Air Commodore Frank Woolley, R.A.F.; also Escape and Evasion Officer (Is-9), Africa, Italy, Southern France, etc. (total service in Mediterranean area 1942–45; also Secretary (original) J.I.C. Algiers, and C.S.D.I.C., N. Africa and Italy). Business: Mueller Furniture Co., Grand Rapids, Mich. 1926–31; Collins & Aikman Corp. N.Y.C. 1931–42; Kroehler Mfg. Co., Naperville, Ill. 1945–47; La France Industries Inc., N.Y.C. 1947–56 (Pres. and Dir.); Pres. and Dir., La France Textiles Ltd., Woodstock, Ont., Canada 1947–56; Chmn. & Dir., Pendleton (S.C.) Mfg. Co. 1947–56. With Burlington Industries Inc. (textiles N.Y.C. and N. Carolina) 1956—. Chairman and President, Smuggler's Notch Inn, Inc., Jeffersonville, Vt. 1956. *Clubs:* Bonnie Briar Country (Larchmont, N.Y.); Emerywood Country (High Point, N.C.). *Address:* (office) Smugglers' Notch Inn Inc., Jeffersonville, Vermont 05464 (also Park Road, Jeffersonville, Vt.; and One, Park Avenue, New York City 16; and Suite 2145, American Furniture Mart, Chicago, Ill.), U.S.A.

**TANFIELD, Doylah Ernst Thomas.** British company director. *B.* 1914. *Educ.* Bromsgrove School. *M.* 1939, Phoebe Phyllis Hickman. *S.* Richard Doylah and Lawrence John Bryce. *Daus.* Jennifer Bridget and Matilda Anne. *Career:* Partner, Wall & Tanfied, Chartered Accountants 1940–53; Chairman: Estate Sales & Management Ltd., 1952–57, and British Housing Corp. 1950–58. Mng. Director, J. Hickman & Son Group 1953–66. Chairman: J. B. Wilson & Sons Ltd., J. Barrett of Feckenham, Craft Centre Cymru and other company directorships. Past Chairman: Society of Friends of Bromsgrove School, and Trustee of the School Endowment. Secretary, The Bromsgrove Club 1945–49. *Publications:* articles in professional journals. *Fellow:* Inst. of Chartered Accountants, F.C.A. (Member Taxation Research Committee 1956–62; Pres. Birmingham & District Socy. of C.A.s 1962–63); President Birmingham and West Mid. C. A. Students Soc. 1968. Liberal. *Address:* Tithe Barn, Oldbury, Bridgnorth, Salop.

**TANGE, Sir Arthur Harold,** AC, CBE. Australian diplomat. *B.* 18 August 1914. *Educ.* University of Western Australia (BA). *M.* 1940, Marjorie Florence Shann. *S.* Christopher John. *Dau.* Jennifer Jane. *Career:* Economist, Bank of New South Wales 1938; Economist in various Australian Government Departments, Canberra 1942–45; First Secretary, Department of External Affairs 1945; First Secretary, Australian Mission to the United Nations, New York 1946–48; Counsellor, United Nations Division, Canberra 1948–50; Assistant Secretary, Department of External Affairs, for United Nations, Economic Relations and Economic and Technical Assistance 1951–53; member, Australian Delegation to Bretton Woods Monetary Conference and other economic and political Conferences; Minister, Washington, D.C. 1953–54; Secretary, Dept. External Affairs 1954–65; Australian High Commissioner in India and Ambassador to Nepal 1965–70; Secretary Dept. Defence since 1970. *Decorations:* Commander Order of the British Empire 1955; Companion of the Order of Australia 1977. *Address:* 32 La Perouse Street, Canberra, ACT 2603, Australia.

**TANGERMAN, Elmer John.** American. Editor, author, consulting engineer. *B.* 1907. *Educ.* Purdue University (BS, ME 1929; ME 1937). *M.* 1929, Mary M. Christopher. *S.* John Tilden (*Dec.*). *Daus.* Mary T. Salerno and Judith T. (Hickson). *Career:* Asst. Editor, American Machinist 1929–32, and Power 1932–34 (Assoc. Ed. 1934–36, Managing Ed. 1937. Consulting Ed. 1938–42); Consulting Technical Ed., Mill Supplies 1933–45; Asst. Mgr., American Machinist 1938–42; Business Manager, Power 1942–45; Technical Editor, Wings and McGraw-Hill Digest 1942–45; Managing Editor 1945–50 and Exec. Editor, American Machinist 1950–56; Gen. Manager, Nucleonics 1947–49. Editor, Product Engineering (McGraw-Hill) 1957–65, Associate Publisher 1965–66. Office of Planning & Development, McGraw-Hill Publications 1966–69. *Publications:* (books): Whittling & Woodcarving 1936 (as paperback 1962); Design & Figure Carving, 1939 (paperback, 1964); Power Operator's Guide 1939; Horizons Regained 1964; Living Tomorrow—Today (1968); The Modern Book of Whittling & Woodcarving (1973); 1001 Designs for Whittling & Woodcarving (1976). Numerous articles and editorials in technical journals. *Awards:* Freedom Foundations at Valley Forge Medal 1955; Jesse Neal Awards of Merit 1958, 1960 and 1961. *Member:* American Society Mechanical Engineers; Nat. Wood Carvers Assn. (vice-chmn.). Society Amer. Value Engineers (Hon.); Tau Beta Pi; Pi Tau Sigma; Sigma Delta Chi; Kappa Phi Sigma; Scabbard & Blade; Lambda Chi Alpha. Republican. *Address:* 111 Ivy Way, Port Washington, N.Y. 11050, U.S.A.

**TANIBAYASHI, Masatoshi.** Japanese. *B.* 1900. *Educ.* Graduated from Law Faculty of Tokyo Imperial Univ. 1924. *M.* 1951. Masuko Kadomatsu. *S.* Masanobu. *Career:* With Mitsubishi Shoji Kaishi Ltd. (Mitsubishi Corp.) 1924–47 (Dir., and Mgr., Co-ordination Dept., 1946–47); Pres. Heian Shoji Kaisha Ltd. 1947–49; Dir. Foreign Trade Bureau, Economic Stabilization Board of Japanese Govt. 1949–50; Pres. of Santo Shoji Kaisha Ltd. 1950–52; Adviser to Tokyo Boeki Kaisha Ltd. 1952–54, Auditor, Mitsubishi Shoji Kaisha 1954–72, Counsellor 1972–75. *Member:* Government and Civil Cttee. Contributor to economic and technical journals (domestic and foreign). *Award:* Blue Ribbon Medal by Japanese Govt. for meritorious services in development of foreign trade of Japan 1964. *Address:* 1-14-10 Minami-Yukigaya, Ohta-Ku-Tokyo, Japan.

**TANNER, Edward Harold,** OBE. Canadian. Vice-Pres., Tanner Brothers Ltd.; Director: Canada Permanent Trust Co. *B.* 1901. *M.* (2) Joan Fortt. *S.* William Harold Reginald. Engaged in investment security business in Toronto and Calgary 1926—. *Address:* 863 Prospect Avenue, Calgary, Alt., Canada.

**TANSLEY, Sir Eric (Crawford),** CMG. British business executive. *B.* 25 May 1901. *Educ.* Mercers School, London. *M.* 1930, Iris Richards. *S.* John. *Dau.* Jane. *Career:* Chmn. London Cocoa Terminal Market 1932; and of Cocoa Association of London 1936–37; Deputy Director, Cocoa Division, Ministry of Food 1939–40; Marketing Director, West African Produce Control Board, Colonial Office 1940–47; Managing Director, British West African Marketing Companies 1947–58; Director, Commonwealth Development Corporation, 1948–51 and 1961–68. Former Dir.: Standard & Chartered Banking Group; Standard Bank; Standard Bank of West Africa; Standard Bank Finance and Development Corporation; Gill & Duffus Ltd.; Former Chmn, Plantation and Colonial Products Ltd. *Address:* 11, Cadogan Square, London, S.W.1.

**TAPLIN, Douglas Eaton.** Chairman & Managing Director of D. E. Taplin Pty. *B.* 1910. Trained Elect. Engr. family co. 1930–45; founded D. E. Taplin Pty. Ltd. 1945, Chmn. Man. Dir. 1946; Pres. Elect. Mfrs.' Assn. N.S.W. 1957–58, Pres. Elect Mfrs.' Assn. Fed. Cl. 1959–61; Pres. Export Div.

Chambr. Manufs. since 1959; Chmn.; Aust. Manufacturers' Export Council 1959–62 and Australian General Cargo Shippers Cttee.; Exec. Councillor N.S.W. Chamber Mfrs., Member Export Development Council 1961–67. Leader and deputy Leader 3 Australian overseas Trade Missions. *Clubs:* R.A.C.A., Royal Aero N.S.W., Bowral Golf. *Address:* P.O. Box 259, Parramatta, N.S.W. 2150, Australia.

**TAPLIN, Frank Elijah.** American. Member, Order of the British Empire; Commendation Ribbon, U.S. Navy. *B.* 1915. *Educ.* Princeton Univ. (BA Hist 1937), Oxford University (MA Juris. 1939) and Yale Law School (LLB 1941). *M.* 1953, Margaret Eaton. *S.* 1. *Daus.* 5 (3 step-daughters). *Career:* Lawyer, Jones Day Cockley & Reavis, Cleveland 1946–50; Business Investor since 1950, President: Cleveland Inst. of Music 1952–56, and Cleveland Orchestra 1955–57; Asst to President of Princeton Univ. 1957–59. From Ensign to Lieut-Cmdr., U.S. Naval Reserve 1941–46. Rhodes Scholarship to Oxford University 1937–39. Chairman of the Board, Scurry-Rainbow Oil Ltd. 1961–74, (Pres. 1968–70). Director North American Coal Corp. 1940—. Member Board of Directors, Metropolitan Opera Association 1961—, Chmn. 1977—. Chmn. of Board, Marlboro. School of Music 1964–70. *Member:* Amer. Bar Assn.; Assn. of American Rhodes Scholars; Phi Beta Kappa (Princeton); Pres. Chamber Music Society of Lincoln Center. Pres. 1968–73, Vice-Pres. since 1973; Trustee: Sarah Lawrence College 1969–77, Chmn. of the Board 1973–77; Institute for Advanced Study. Amer. Fed. of Musicians (Local 4). Princeton University Council for Univ. Resources; Trustee Lincoln Centre for Performing Arts; Vice-Chmn. Woodrow Wilson Nat. F'ship. Foundation: Former Chmn. U.S. Comm. for United World Colleges. *Clubs:* University; Union Tavern (Cleveland); Nassau, Pretty Brook (Princeton); Ranchmen's (Calgary, Canada). *Address:* 55 Armour Road, Princeton, N.J.; and *office* 1 Palmer Square, Princeton, N.J. 08540, U.S.A.

**TAPSELL, Peter,** MP. British Politician & Stockbroker. *B.* 1930. *Educ.* Oxford Univ.—MA, 1st Class Hons. *M.* 1974, Gabrielle Mahieu. *S.* 1. *Career:* Conservative Research Dept. 1954–57; Personal Asst. to PM (Sir Anthony Eden), General Election Campaign of 1955; mem., James Capel & Co. (Stockbrokers); Chmn., Coningsby Club 1957–58; MP (Cons.) for Nottingham West 1959–64, & for Horncastle (Lincs.) since 1966: Jt. Chmn., British Caribbean Assoc. 1963–64; Cons. Parly. Front Bench Spokesman on Foreign & Commonwealth Affairs. *Member:* London Stock Exchange; Court of Univs. of Nottingham & Hull; Hon. mem., Brunei Govt. Investment Adv. Bd. 1976. *Decoration:* Brunei Dato (Datuk), 1971. *Clubs:* Carlton; Hurlingham. *Address:* House of Commons, London SW1A 0AA.

**TARAKANOV, Nikolai Y.** Soviet Diplomat. *B.* 1913. *Educ.* Moscow State University, History Department. *M.* 1940, Tamara I. Bakeeva. *S.* Vladmir. *Career:* Joined U.S.S.R. Min. of Foreign Affairs 1950; Counsellor, Embassy, Czechoslovakia 1950–55; Min. of Foreign Affairs 1955–58; Consul-General, Bombay, 1958–60; Ambassador, Ceylon. 1960–65; Deputy Head, Branch for S. Asia in Min. of Foreign Affairs 1965–67; Ambassador in Australia 1967–72. *Awards:* Order of Red Star; Badge of Honour for dist. work in field of foreign policy. *Address:* c/o Ministry of Foreign Affairs, 32–34 Smolenskaya-Sennaya Ploshchad, Moscow, U.S.S.R.

**TARJANNE, P. K.** Finnish diplomat. *B.* 4 May 1903. *Educ.* University of Helsinki and Paris. *M.* 1932, Anna-Kerttu Ritavuori. *S.* Heikki, Pekka, Jukka. *Career:* Entered Diplomatic Service 1928; First Secretary, Permanent Delegation to League of Nations, Geneva 1932–34; Counsellor, Stockholm 1934–38; Chief of Administrative Department, Ministry of Foreign Affairs 1939–45; En. Ex. and Min. Plen. since 1942, to Norway 1945–50, to Iceland 1947–50; Secretary-General, Ministry of Foreign Affairs1950–53; Env. Ex. and Min. Plen. to Denmark 1953–54, Ambassador 1954–56; Ambassador to Sweden 1956–61; to Denmark 1961–70. Member, The Chapter the Orders of the White Rose of Finland and the Lion of Finland 1970. *Awards:* Grand Cross, Order of the Lion of Finland, Commander 1st Class, Order of the White Rose of Finland; Grand Cross of following Orders: Dannebrog (Denmark), (Grand Star with brilliants), Falcon (Iceland), St. Olav (Norway), North Star (Sweden). *Address:* Kuhatie 21 A 02170, Espoo 17, Finland.

**TARNEJA, Dr. Ram S.** PhD. Indian. *B.* 1931. *Educ.* University of Delhi (BA (Hons); MA); University of Virginia (MA); Cornell University (PhD) Gold Medallist. *M.* 1958. *Daus.* 2. *Career:* Research Assistant, University of Virginia 1953–55; Graduate Research Assistant, Cornell University 1955–57; Assistant Professor of Management, Duquesne University 1957–60; Director, Graduate Department of Business Administration, Duquesne 1958—61; Assoc. Prof. of Management, same Univ. 1960—; Dir. of Personnel Sahujain Group of Industries, Calcutta 1961–70; Exec. Dir. Dehri-Rohtas Light Railway Co. Ltd. 1965–70; Deputy Gen. Manager Bennett, Coleman & Co. Ltd. (Times of India Group of Publications) Bombay 1970–73; Assoc. Gen. Mgr. since 1973; Dir. Arim Metal Industries Private Ltd. United News of India, Welcast Steels Ltd., Bombay Wire Ropes Ltd., Maharashtra Tourism Devel. Corp. Ltd., Audit Bureau of Circulations Ltd. Pres. All India Mgmt. Assn.; Fellow Inst. Dirs. London; Member, All India Bd. Technical Studies in Management; Ministry of Education, Govt. of India; Academy of Management U.S.A.; India Inst. of Public Admin.; Cttee. member Indian & Eastern Newspaper Society; Former Pres. Indian Inst. Personnel Management Calcutta; ex Bombay Chamber of Comm. & Industry. *Publications:* Profit Sharing and Technological Change (1964); Developing Better Managers; Chapter in India (with Dr. Kamla Chowdhury, 1961); articles and papers in the field of business management. Personnel and Industrial Relations etc. *Club:* Saturday (Calcutta); Bengal; Calcutta; Royal Calcutta Golf Club; Chelmsford (Delhi); Bombay Gymkhana; Rotary (Bombay). *Address:* 3C Woodlands, 67, Pedder Road, Bombay 26; and *office* Times of India, Fort Bombay 1, India.

**TARNELL, Edward Joseph.** BS. American. *B.* 1919. *Educ.* Polytech. Inst. of Brooklyn (BS). *Career:* Research Chemist, Koppers Co. 1946–51; Pres. Dir. Roger Williams Technical & Economic Services Inc. *Member:* American Management Assn.; Chemical Marketing Research Association. *Address:* 330 East 70th Street, New York, N.Y. 10021 and *office:* Box 426, Princeton, N.J. 08540, U.S.A.

**TARZIAN, Mary Mangigian.** American. BS, MA, PhD. *Educ.* Univ. of Pennsylvania (BS, MA, PhD); Postgrad. Inst. Higher Int. Studies, Geneva; Bryn Mawr College. *M.* Sarkes Tarzian. *S.* 1. *Dau.* 1. *Career:* Former Vice Pres. Bynum Supply Co.; Dir. Dean Brothers Pump Co.; Vice Pres. Television Stations WPTA-WTTV Radio Stations WTTS-WATI-FM, Stations WTTV-WPTH; Vice-Chmn. of the Bd., Sarkes Tarzian Inc. Involved in manufacture of television parts, patents, connections in South America, Japan, Taiwan & India. *Member:* U.K. Colony Civic N.Y. Welcome to Washington; Nat. Council Metropolitan Opera (mem. Exec. Cttee. 1977–81); Amer. Nat. Opera Co.; Amer. Assn. University Women; Civic Ballet Socy.; Civic Theatre Group; Chmn. Friends of John F. Kennedy Center, Performing Arts (President Nixon's appointee Adv. Bd.); Bd. member Int. Platform Assn.; Founder, Bd. member Eisenhower Scholarship Foundation. *Awards:* Eisenhower Distinguished American; Distinguished Women of Northwood Institute; Indiana Mother of the Year 1976. *Address: office* East Hillside Drive, Bloomington, Ind. U.S.A.

**TASNING, Haerudden.** Indonesian diplomat. *B.* 1922. *Educ.* Agricultural College (degree); Agric. Faculty, Gaja Mada Univ.; Command and General Staff College in Bandung (Indonesia) and Ft. Leavenworth (U.S.A.). *M.* 1949. R. Madahera Purwosiswoyo. *S.* 3. *Dau.* 1. *Career:* Asst. to Chief of Staff 3rd Div. 1949; C.O. Mil. Police Detachment 1950–53; Asst. to C.O. Mil. Police Training Centre 1954–56; 2nd in Command 7th Mil. Police Battalion 1956–57; Chief of Staff 14th Div. 1957–59; Mil. Attaché in Egypt 1959–62; Chief Army Foreign Relations 1963–66; Dir.-Gen. Research, Security and Communication, Dept. of For. Affairs 1966–73; Ambassador of Indonesia in Australia since 1973. *Decorations:* 15 national and 2 foreign. *Clubs:* Jakanta Golf; Royal Canberra Golf. *Address:* 16 Monano Crescent, Red Hill, Canberra ACT, Australia; and *office* 8 Darwin Ave., Yarralambla, Canberra ACT, Australia.

**TASWELL, Harold Langmead Taylor.** South African *B.* 1910. *Educ.* MCom (Cape Town). *M.* 1940, Vera Blytt. *Daus.* 3. *Career:* Joined Dept. of Foreign Affairs, Pretoria 1935; Attaché, South African Legation, Berlin 1937–39; S.A. High Commissioner's Office, London 1939; Attaché Legation, The Hague 1940; Vice-Consul, New York 1940–46; Consul, Elisabethville, Belgian Congo 1946–49; Internatl. Trade and Economic Section, Dept. of Foreign Affairs, Pretoria 1949–51; First Secretary, Embassy, Washington 1951–56; Consul General, Luanda, Angola 1956–59; Accredited Diplomatic Representative Salisbury, Federation of Rhodesia and Nyasaland 1960–64; Under-Secretary, and

Head of African Division, Dept. of Foreign Affairs, Pretoria 1964–65. Ambassador to U.S.A. 1965–71; Permanent Representative, United Nations, Geneva 1971–75; Council Mem., Africa Inst. of South Africa since 1976. *Address:* 39 Simonstown, 7975 Fish Hoek, South Africa.

**TATA, J. R. D.** Industrialist. *B.* 1904. *Educ.* India, France, Japan. DSc (Hon. Causa), Allahabad Univ. 1947. *M.* 1930, Thelma Vicaji. *Career:* Chairman: Tata Sons Ltd.; Tata Industries Ltd.; Tata Iron & Steel Co. Ltd.; Tata Oil Mills Co. Ltd.; Tata Chemicals Ltd., The Indian Hotels Co. Ltd.; Air India. Vice-Chairman: Investment Corporation of India Ltd.; Chairman: Tata Inst. Fundamental Research; Lady Tata Memorial Trust; J. R. D. Tata Trust; J. N. Tata Endowment for Higher Edn. Indians; Sir Dorabji Tata Trust; Managing Council, National Centre for the Performing Arts; Dir. Tata Engineering and Locomotive Co. Ltd. *Member:* Indian Inst. Sci. (pres., court). Founder, Tata Airlines, 1932. *Awards:* Officer, Legion of Honour; Knight Comdr., Order of St. Gregory the Great; Hon. Air Vice Marshal, Indian Air Force. *Address:* The Cairn, Altamount Rd., Cumballa Hill, Bombay 400 026; and *office* Bombay House, Homi Mody Street, Fort Bombay 400 023.

**TATA, Naval H.** Indian company director. *B.* 30 Aug., 1904. *Educ.* Elphinstone College, Bombay and England. *Career:* Chairman, Tata Group of Electric and Textile Mill Companies. Deputy Chairman, Tata Sons and Tata Ind., President, The Employers' Federation of India; Indian Cancer Society; The National Institute of Labour Management; member, Governing Body, I.L.O.; Cttee.: Indian Cotton Mills Federation. *Address: office* Bombay House, Homi Mody Street, Fort Bombay, India.

**TAUSK, Prof. Marius.** Dutch endocrinologist. *B.* 1902. *Educ.* MD (Graz, Austria) 1926, and Privat Docent (reader), Univ. of Utrecht 1937; Hon. degree MD, Graz 1972. *M.* 1928, Norah Gladys Hellmer. *S.* Hein and Robert. *Daus.* Susanne and Anna Beata. *Career:* Head of factory 1926 and subsequently Managing Director of N.V. Organon, Oss, Netherlands (pharmaceutics) 1929, and later international research coordinator. Retired 1967. Former Professor (endocrinology), Faculty of Medicine, University of Utrecht. *Publications:* De Hormonen (4th edn. 1961); Farmacologie van de Hormonen (4th edn. 1976; German edition 1973, English edition 1975); articles in medical journals, including Hormones (publ. Organon). Hon. Member, European Socy. of toxicology; Deutsche Gesellschaft für Endokrinologie; Gold Medal Hoogewerff Fonds, 1963. *Member:* Endocrine Socy. (U.S.A.); Nederlandse Verening voor Endocrinologie. *Address:* Bergweg 6, Nijmegen, Netherlands.

**TAVALLALI, Dr. Djamchid.** Iranian Diplomat. *B.* 1927 *Educ.* Univ. of Lausanne—Doctorate in Political Science, *M.* 1956, Mrs. Nini Chaicar. *S.* 2. *Career:* Third/Second Sec., Imperial Embassy of Iran, Madrid 1961–65; Protocol Dept., Ministry of Foreign Affairs, Tehran 1965–67; Dir.-Gen., Ministry of Information, Tehran 1967–68; First Sec. & Counsellor, Imperial Embassy of Iran, London 1969–72; Minister-Counsellor, Islamabad 1973–74; Head of Fifth Political Dept., Ministry of Foreign Affairs, Tehran 1975; Minister-Counsellor, Imperial Embassy of Iran, Washington, D.C. since Oct. 1975. *Decorations:* Taj (Iran); and decorations from Spain, Rumania & Yugoslavia. *Publications:* Le Parlement Iranian (French); translations from French into Farsi: L'Engrenage by Jean Paul Sartre; Les Lettres de Mon Moulin by Alfonse Daudet. *Clubs:* Ministry of Foreign Affairs Club, Tehran: Pisces Club, Washington, D.C. *Address:* Imperial Embassy of Iran, 3005 Massachusetts Avenue, N.W., Washington, D.C. 20008, U.S.A.

**TAVERNE, Dick,** QC. *B.* 1928. *Educ.* Balliol College, Oxford (First Class Honours Literae Humaniores—'Greats'). *M.* 1955, Janice Hennessey. *Daus.* Suzanna and Caroline. *Career:* Called to the Bar 1954; Queen's Counsel 1965. Parliamentary Under Secretary, Home Office 1966–68; Minister of State, Treasury, April 1968–69; Financial Secy. to the Treasury 1969–70; Elected MP Lab. for Lincoln, Mar. 1962; re-elected October 1964, Mar. 1966 and June 1970, Resigned October 1972; Re-elected Independent Democratic Labour MP for Lincoln 1973, & Feb.–Oct. 1974; Mem. Europ. Parlt. 1973–74; The Dir. Institute for Fiscal Studies; Dir. BOC International Ltd; Dir. Equity and Law Life Ass. Soc. *Publication:* The Future of the Left (1974). *Address:* 60 Cambridge St., London SW1V 4QQ.

**TAXELL, Lars Erik.** Professor (private law and general theory of law), The Abo Swedish University since 1948; Rector 1950–57. *B.* 1913. *Educ.* LLD. *M.* 1942, Hillevi Taxell. *S.* Björn and Christofer. *Dau.* Helena. *Publications:* On Board of Directors of the Company; Rights of Shareholders; The Managing Director of the Company; on Bonds; Law and Humanity; On Contracts; Law & Democracy. Other publications in the field of private law, especially law of the merchant law of contracts and the general theory of law. Member, The Swedish People's Party in Finland (Svenska folkpartiet i Finland); Chairman of the Party 1956–66. *Address:* Tavastg 5C, Abo, Finland.

**TAYLOR, Ann,** MP. British Politician. *B.* 1947. *Educ.* Bolton Sch., Sheffield Univ.; Bradford Univ.—BSc (Hons.), MA. *M.* 1966, David Taylor. *Career:* MP (Lab.) for Bolton West since 1974; PPS, Dept. of Agriculture, Fisheries & Food, Jan.–Nov. 1975; PPS, Dept. of Education & Science 1975–76; PPS, Dept. of Defence 1976–77; Government Whip since 1977. *Address:* 7 Bellgreave Avenue, New Mills, Huddersfield; and *office* House of Commons, London SW1A 0AA.

**TAYLOR, Arthur Grahame.** Australian. *B.* 1922. *Educ.* Malvern Grammar School. *M.* 1949, Marjorie Jean Scott. *S.* 2. *Daus.* 2. *Career:* Partner, Irish, Young & Outhwaite, Chartered Accountants, Melbourne, Vice-Chmn. Victorian Div., Australian Red Cross Socy. 1962—, Aberfoyle Ltd. 1964—, and Cleveland Tin N.L. 1965—, Director: Ardlethan Tin N.L. 1965—, Beacon Investment Ltd. 1966—, Bryant & May Pty. Ltd. 1965—, Wm. Haughton & Co. Ltd., 1967—; Palladium Investment Ltd. 1966—. Dir.: Birmid Auto Castings Pty. Ltd. 1969—, Chatham Investment Co. Ltd. since 1973. Fellow, Inst. of Chartered Accountants in Australia (Vic. Branch); Chmn. 1964–66; Member, Institute of Directors. Patriotic Funds Council of Victoria 1967—. *Clubs:* Melbourne, Australian; Athenaeum, Royal Automobile of Victoria; Metropolitan Golf, Frankston Golf; Lawn Tennis Assn. of Victoria; Victoria Amateur Turf; Melbourne Cricket; Somers Yacht. *Address:* 39 Ranfurlie Crescent, Glen Iris, Vic.; and *office* Irish, Young & Outhwaite, Chartered Accountants, 535 Bourke Street, Melbourne, Vic., 3001, Australia.

**TAYLOR, Sir Charles (Stuart),** Kt. 1954, TD, MA Cantab., DL. *B.* 1910. *Educ.* Epsom Coll.; Trinity Coll., Cambridge (BA 1932); Hons. Law Degree Tripos. *M.* 1936, Constance Ada Shotter. *S.* 3. *Dau.* 1. *Career:* Chmn., Onyx Country Estates Co. Ltd. & other companies; formerly: Man. Dir., Unigate and Cow & Gate Ltd.; Dir., Trust House Ltd.; Chmn., later Pres., Grosvenor House (Park Lane) Ltd. Pres., Residential Hotels Assn. of Great Britain until 1948 & Vice-Chmn. of Council of British Hotels & Restaurants Assn. until 1951; Mem. of Honour, Internat. Hotels Assn.; Vice-Pres., Building Societies Assn. MP (Cons.) for Eastbourne, March 1935–Feb. 1974; Leader of Parly. Delegations to Germany, Ethiopia, Mauritius; Mem., Parly. Delegation to Romania. Joined TA 1937 (Royal Artillery), Capt., August 1939; DAAG & Temp. Major Jan. 1941; attended Staff Col. June 1941 (war course) graduated sc. Hon. Colonel. DL Sussex 1948. Serving Brother, Order of St. John. Hon. Freeman, Co. Borough of Eastbourne 1971. Paduka Seri Laila Jasa (Dato), Brunei 1971. Under Warden, The Worshipful Company of Bakers. *Clubs:* 1900; Buck's; MCC; Royal Thames Yacht; Ski Club of Great Britain (Hon. Life Mem.). *Address:* 4 Reeves House, Reeves Mews, London W.1.

**TAYLOR, Edward Macmillan,** MP. British Politician. *B.* 1937. *Educ.* Glasgow High School; Glasgow Univ.—MA (Hons.). *M.* 1970, Sheila Duncan. *S.* 2. *Career:* Industrial Relations Officer, Clyde Shipyard 1959–64; Conservative MP for Cathcart Div. of Glasgow since 1964; Journalist. *Publications:* Hearts of Stone (Novel). *Clubs:* St. Stephen's Club, London. *Address:* 77 Newlands Road, Glasgow G43 2JP.

**TAYLOR, Edward Plunket,** CMG. Canadian. *B.* 1901. *Educ.* McGill University (BSc Mech Eng). *M.* 1927, Winifred Thornton Duguid. *S.* Charles P. B. *Daus.* Mrs. John N. Mappin and Mrs. Alan Edwards. *Career:* Dir. The Brading Breweries 1923; also entered the investment house of McLeod, Young, Weir & Co., Ottawa 1923 (Dir. Jan. 1929; resigned Sept. 1930); Pres., Canadian Breweries 1930; Chmn. of Bd. 1944. Member, Exec. Cttee., Dept. of Munitions & Supply April 1940; Joint Dir.-Gen. of Munitions Production Nov. 1940; Exec. Asst. to Minister of Munitions & Supply Feb. 1941 President. War Supplies Ltd., Washington April 1941; appointed (by Mr.

Winston Churchill) President and Vice-Chairman, British Supply Council in North America Sept. 1941; Director-General, British Ministry of Supply Mission Feb. 1942; Canadian Deputy Member on Combined Production and Resources Board Nov. 1942; also Canadian Chmn., Joint War Aid Cttee., U.S.-Canada Sept. 1943; Chmn. International Housing Ltd. The New Province Development Co. Ltd., Nassau (to conserve space the term 'Limited' has been ignored in the case of the following concerns): President: The Lyford Cay Co., Nassau, Bahamas; Windfields Farm, Willowdale, Ont. Hon. Chairman of Board. The Jockey Club, Toronto, Ont.; Chmn. & Chief Steward Jockey Club of Canada; Trust Corp. of Bahamas, Nassau; Roy West Banking Corp., Nassau: Dir., Royal Bank of Canada International, Nassau, Bahamas. *Member:* Jockey Club, N.Y.; Governor: Trinity Coll., Sch., Ashbury Coll. *Award:* Companion of the Most Distinguished Order of St. Michael and St. George, July 1946. *Clubs:* Toronto, York; Royal Yacht Squadron (Cowes); Turf, Buck's (London, Eng.); Rideau; Metropolitan; Lyford Cay, Nassau. *Address:* Lyford Cay, New Providence, Bahama Islands.

**TAYLOR, Sir Frank.** British. DSc (Hon.). Founder and Managing Director, Taylor Woodrow Group (building, civil and mechanical engineering contractors). *B.* 1905. *M.* 1956, Christine Enid Hughes. *Daus.* 3 (2 by prev. marriage). *Career:* Member, Adv. Cncl. to Minister of State, 1954–55; Chmn., Export Group for Constructional Industries, 1954–55, and International Road Federation 1954; Pres., Provident Inst. of Builders Foremen & Clerks of Works 1950; Member, Adv. Cncl. on Middle East Trade. Dir., B.O.A.C., 1958–60; Created Knight 1974; Govnr., Queenswood School for Girls; London Grad. School, Business Studies. Mem., Cncl., Export Group for Constructional Industries; Dir. Freedom Federal Savings and Loan Assn., Worcester, Mass., since 1972. Fellow Inst. of Builders. *Clubs:* R.A.C.; Queen's; Hurlingham; All England. *Address:* 10 Park Street, London, W1Y 4DD.

**TAYLOR, George Edward.** American. Programme Administrator. *B.* 1931. *Educ.* State University of Iowa (BSc, MA); Carnegie Institute of Technology. *M.* 1961, Joanne Marie Bauer. *S.* Michael Edward, Matthew Alan. *Dau.* Mary Elizabeth, Marcia Anne Marie. *Career:* Financial Planning Manager, Research Laboratory, Aeronutronic Division, Ford/Philco Corp., 1960–62; Minutemen Research & Dev. Programme 1969–70; Group Controller, Electronic Memories & Magnetics 1970–71; Man. Financial Planning & Control, California Computer Products since 1971. *Member:* Technical Staff, Aerospace Ground Equipment Engineering; Senior Staff Engineer Autonetics Division, North American Rockwell Corporation, 1966–69. American Economics Assoc.; National Management Assoc; Financial Executives Institute. Republican. *Publication:* Editor, Lectures in Financial Management (1959), Ford Foundation Fellowship, Bus. Economics, 1959–60. *Address: office* 2411 W. La Palma, Anaheim, California, U.S.A. 92801.

**TAYLOR, Gordon Edward,** P Eng, MLA. Canadian. Former Minister with Alberta Government. *B.* 1910. *Educ.* Schoolmaster (First Class). *Career:* Minister of Railways & Telephones 1950–59; Minister, Highways & Transportation 1951–71; Chairman, Alberta Research Council 1955–59; House Leader, Her Majesty's Loyal Opposition 1972. Pres. Canadian Goods Roads Assn. 1953–54 and 1965; Chmn. Canadian Highway Safety Conference 1958; Pres. Camp Gordon Socy. 1931–77. *Clubs:* Canadian; Royal Glencora; Camp Gordon. *Address:* 7618–110th Street, Edmonton, Alta.; and *office* Legislative Building, Edmonton, Alta. T5K 2B6, Canada.

**TAYLOR, John Paul.** Publisher and editor. *B.* 1918. *Educ.* Purdue University (BSc Mech Eng 1939). *M.* 1939, Dorothea Justin (*Dec.* 1961). (2) 1964, Mary Elizabeth Timm. *S.* Paul Adam. *Daus.* Jessica, Lucinda and Karen. *Career:* Asst. and then Assoc. Editor, Industry & Power magazine 1939–42; Pres. The John Paul Taylor Co. (founded in 1942); First Private then 2nd Lieut., Corps of Engineers, Army of the U.S. 1944–46; Exec. Dir. Industrial Marketing Assoc. Inc. 1947—; Co-founder and Secy-Treasurer, Proebsting, Taylor Inc. 1948–55; Secretary-Treasurer, Work-at-Ease Chair Co. 1948–61; Owner, Runyan, Taylor Advertising 1961—; Exec. Dir. Materials Marketing Associates Inc. 1963—; Cormac Inc. 1971—; Parmar Inc. since 1972. *Awards:* Liberty Bell Award for 1962, from Young Lawyers Section, State Bar of Michigan. *Member:* Amer. Socy. of Mechanical Engineers, Amer. Marketing Assn.; Sigma Delta Chi (journalism): Instrument Society of America. President, Economic Club of Southwestern Michigan 1953—, and Fort Miami Heritage Society Inc. 1965–67; President, Board of Trustees, Public Library of St. Joseph Michigan. Republican. *Publications:* technical articles in U.S.A. engineering and sales magazines. *Clubs:* Economic (Southwestern Michigan); Rotary; Lake Shore (Chicago); Berrien Hills Country. *Address:* 2618 Lakeview Avenue, St. Joseph, Mich.; and *office* Shepard-Benning Building, St. Joseph, Mich., U.S.A.

**TAYLOR, Sir Robert Mackinlay,** CBE. British. *B.* 1912. *Educ.* Plymouth Coll., Hele's School, Exeter, and Exeter University; MSc (Econ) London. *M.* 1944, Alda Lorenzino. *Dau.* Valerie Anne. *Career:* Secretary to Transport and Communications, Fed. of Rhod. & Nyasaland 1953; Financial Secy., Northern Rhodesia 1952; Fin. Secy., Fiji 1947; Military Service (Colonel) 1939–47. Secy. to Treasury. Fed. of Rhodesia and Nyasaland 1954–58. Retired from Government service at end of 1958; Chmn. Richard Costain Ltd. 1969–73; Deputy Chmn., Standard Chartered Bank Ltd. since 1974; Chmn. Thomas Tilling Ltd. since 1976. *Publications:* A Social Survey of Plymouth (1938). *Clubs:* Athenaeum Naval & Military; M.C.C. (London); Salisbury (Rhodesia). *Address:* 10 Clements Lane, London EC4N 7AB.

**TAYLOR-SMITH, Dr. Ralph Emeric Kasope.** Sierra Leonean diplomat. *B.* 1924. *Educ.* Univ. of London, BSc., PhD. *M.* 1953, Sarian Dorothea. *S.* 5. *Career:* Analytical chemist 1954; Demonstrator, Woolwich Polytechnic 1956–59; Lecturer Fourah Bay College, Sierra Leone 1959–60, and 1963; Post-Doctoral Fellow, Weizmann Inst. of Science, Israel, 1962–63; Research Assoc., N. Jersey, Princeton Univ. 1965–69; Sen. Lecturer, Fourah Bay, S.L., 1965, Dean of Faculty of Pure and Applied Science 1967, Assoc. Professor 1968; Visiting Professor of Chemistry (Sabbatical year) 1969; Assoc. Prof., Fourah Bay, S.L.; Ambassador Extraordinary and Plenip., Sierra Leone, PRC Peking 1971; High Commissioner of Sierra Leone in London since 1974. *Member:* numerous Committees, Councils at Fourah Bay College, Univ. of S.L. 1963–68; Chmn. Board of Directors, S.L. Petroleum Refinery Co. 1970; Mem. Board of Education, Sierra Leone 1970; President, Teaching Staff Assn. Fourah Bay College 1971. *Publications:* Presented Papers to Science Assns. in various parts of the world on Science and Chemistry in own specialised fields; Numerous papers and reports of investigations on West African Plants and Synthesis of optical-active allenec matters (chemistry). Also several papers on West African plants in preparation. *Associate* Royal Inst. of Chemistry (1960). *Fellow:* Royal Inst. of Chemistry (1969). *Address:* 33 Portland Place, London W.1.

**TAZI, Dr. Abdelhadi.** Moroccan diplomat. *B.* 1921. *Educ.* Univ. of Qaraouiyin, Fez; Dr., Univ. of Alexandria, Egypt. *Career:* Prof. Emeritus at the Univ. Mohammed V; Gen. Secy., Co-ordinating body between UNESCO & Arab countries; Ambassador to several Arab countries; Dir. of Research, Scientific Inst., Rabat. *Member:* Academies of Baghdad & Cairo. *Decoration:* Awarded the Medal of Intellectual Merit, First Class, by His Majesty the King. *Address:* Souissi, Aît Ourir, Villa Baghdad, Rabat, Morocco.

**TCHKOTOUA, Prince Nicolas.** Ambassador of the Sovereign and Military Order of Malta. *B.* 1909. *Educ.* German private school, Tiflis; University of Geneva. *M.* Carol Carpenter Marmon. *Children* 6. *Career:* Diplomat, Chargé d'affaires, Lima, Peru 1954–56; Envoy Extra. Minister Pleny. San Jose, Costa Rica 1958–61; Ambassador Extra. Pleny. Chile 1968–70; Ambassador, Minister Pleny., Spain 1970–71; Ambassador Extra. Pleny. in Spain 1972. *Awards:* Bailiff Grand Cross of Honor, Devotion of the Sovereign and Military Order of Malta; Grand Cross, Merit; Grand Cross, National Order Bernardo O'Higgins, Chile; Grand Cross, Dynastic Russia Order, St. Anne; Knight of Justice of Constantinian; Order of St. George; Commander, Order of Condor, Los Andes of Bolivia etc. *Publications:* Timeless, The Thomas More Book Club. *Clubs:* Cercle de l'Union (Paris). *Address:* 7 Chemin de Mornex, Lausanne, Switzerland.

**TEASDALE, Joseph Patrick.** American State Governor. *B.* 1936. *Educ.* St. Benedict's Coll., Atchison, Ka.; Rockhurst Coll., Kansas City—BS; St. Louis Univ. Law Sch. *M.* 1973, Mary Theresa Ferkenhoff. *S.* 1. *Career:* Asst. U.S. Attorney 1962–66; Jackson County Prosecuting Attorney 1967–72; Governor of the State of Missouri since 1977. *Member:* National District Attorney Assoc.; Kansas City Bar Assoc.; Missouri Bar Assoc. *Awards:* Named Outstanding Man of the Year, Kansas City Junior Chamber of Commerce 1969. *Address:* Governor's Mansion, 100 Madison,

Jefferson City, Mo. 65101; and *office* Governor's Office, Capitol Building, Jefferson City, Mo. 65101, U.S.A.

**TEBBIT, Norman Beresford.** British politician. *B.* 1931. *Educ.* Grammar School, London Matriculation. *M.* 1956, Margaret Elizabeth Daines. *S.* John, Beresford, William Mark. *Dau.* Alison Mary. *Career:* Junior Journalist Financial Times 1947–49; R.A.F. Commissioned General Duties Branch 1949–51; Advertisement Manager Golfing & Malaya Magazine 1951–53; Airline Pilot with B.O.A.C. 1953–70; Member of Parliament for Epping 1970–74, MP for Waltham Forest (Chingford) since 1974; Member Select Cttee on Science & Technology; Former Secy. and Vice-Chmn. Conservative Members Housing Cttee.; Former Secy. New Town Members Cttee.. Former Party Private Secy. Minister of State. Dept. of Employment. *Member:* Chmn. Cons. Members Aviation Cttee. *Address:* House of Commons, Westminster, London, S.W.1.

**TEES, Ralph C.** Canadian. *B.* 1907. *Educ.* Commercial High School (Montreal); McGill University (B Comm). Fellow, Chartered Institute of Secretaries; Fellow, Socy. of Commercial Accountants. *M.* 1937, Winnifrede Helen Chisholm. *S.* Richard Chisholm. *Dau.* Kathryn Vaughn Victoria. *Career:* Chairman and President, Guardian Trust Co. (618 St. James Street W., Montreal) since 1956; Vice-Pres., Secretary & Director: Canadian Devices Ltd.; Chmn. & Dir., Robert Mitchell Co. Ltd.; Asst. Secy., Treas. & Dir., Eberhard Faber (Canada) Ltd.; Secy. & Dir., Gama Toy Co. Ltd.; Hemmingford Overseas Trading Co. Ltd.; Hunt & Moscrop (Canada) Ltd.; President & Dir., Morgan & Dilworth Inc.; Secy. & Dir., Transcom Electronics Manufacturing Ltd.; Shortall Electric Ltd.; Vice-Pres. and Director, The Agro Company of Canada Ltd.; Greenbank Hoods & Drying Co. Ltd.; President and Director, Victoria Square Corp.; Dir., Canada Fans Ltd. Chmn., Secy. Treas. & Dir., Rudel Export Ltd.; Secy. Treas. & Dir., VDF Machine Tools (Canada) Ltd.; Asst. Secy. & Dir., Napierville Junction Rlwy. Co.; Director: Douglas Bros. Ltd.; Garth Co .Ltd.; Kindermann (Canada) Ltd.; Paul H. Knowlton Ltd.; Prowse Ltd.; Renouf Publishing Co. Ltd. Secy. Treas., Choate School Canadian Fund Inc.; Life Governor, Montreal General Hospital; Newcomen Society. *Clubs:* Engineers, Royal Montreal Curling (Montreal); Canadian (Montreal); Canadian (New York); Knowlton Golf. *Address:* 33 Renfrew Avenue, Westmount, P.Q., Canada.

**TEETOR, Ralph R.** American engineer. *B.* 1890. *Educ.* Grade School, High School, University of Pennsylvania; BS in ME 1912; ME 1930. *M.* 1922, Nellie Van Antwerp. *Dau.* Marjorie. General Engineering, Research and administration, Teetor-Hartley Motor Co. 1912–18; New York Shipbuilding Corp., Camden, N.J. (developing methods for balancing high speed turbine rotors for torpedo boat destroyers) 1918–19; Director and Chief Engineer, Perfect Circle 1919–38 (Vice-Pres. 1938–46; Pres. 1946–57; Director and Consultant 1957–64). President, Perfect Circle Corporation 1946–57. Director 1957–64. Fellow Member, American Soc. Mechanical Engineers, 1965; Soc. Automotive Engineers, National, 1976; Soc. Automotive Engineers, State, 1976; Masonic 33rd, 1976. Hon. D. Eng. Indiana Inst. of Technology, 1965. Hon. LLD Earlham Coll. 1965. (Richmond, Ind.). Republican. *Address:* 300 West Main Street, Hagerstown, Ind. 47346, U.S.A.

**TEILLET, Hon. Roger,** PC. Canadian. *B.* 1912. *Educ.* St. Boniface Coll., Manitoba. *M.* Jeanne Boux. *S.* 2. *Career:* Served overseas with R.C.A.F. in World War II. Member, Manitoba Legislative Assembly 1953–59. Member Canadian House of Commons 1962–68; Minister of Veterans Affairs 1963–68; Member, Canadian Pension Commission since 1968. *Address:* Veteran's Affairs Building, Ottawa, Ont., Canada.

**TEIR, Grels Olof.** Finnish Politician. *B.* 1916. *Educ.* LLB, 1944. *M.* 1950, Doris Häggblom. *S.* Mans Olof. *Daus.* Gun Louise and Carola Margareta. *Career:* Attorney-at-Law 1945–59; Town Councillor of Gamlakarleby 1948–51, MP 1951; President, Swedish People's Youth Union 1953–56, Vice-Pres. Swedish Peoples' Party in Finland 1956–70; Chmn. of Swedish Group in Parlt. 1963–64, 66–68, and 1971–72; Dir. Gamlakarleby office of Helsingfors Aktiebank 1959–71; Minister for Communications and Public Works 1964–66; Minister for Trade and Industry 1968–70 and 1972; Dir. Gen. of State Treasury since 1973. Director of companies, chairman and member of several cultural, economic and social societies. *Publications:* Political Chronicles from 1954. *Awards:* Commander of Finnish Lion order; Grand cross of Belgian Crown; Grand Cross Brasilian Rio Branco order; Knight of the White Rose of Finland; Commander 1st Class Swedish North Star Order. *Clubs:* Commercial, Sällskapsklubben (both in Gamlakarleby). *Address:* Parksvangen 13 D 44, 00200 Helsinki 20, Finland.

**TEJERA PARIS, Dr. Enrique.** Venezuelan lawyer, banker and Senator. *Educ.* Central University of Venezuela (Lic. in Econ. *summa cum laude*, D. Pol. Sc. *summa cum laude*). *M.* 1957, Josefina Coto. *S.* Enrique, Carlos, Alvaro and Gonzalo. *Daus.* Diana and Mariela. *Career:* Professor of Public Administration and Econ., Central University of Venezuela, 1942–65; Hon. Vice-Pres., Univ. de Oriente, 1959–64; Foundr., Dir., Adv., School of Public Admin. Central America 1953–55; Adm. Dir. Min. of Agriculture 1945–46; Founder, Chief, Central Office for Coordination and Planning 1958–59; Governor of State Sucre 1959–61; Alt. Pres., Venezuelan Petroleum Corp., 1961–63; Chief of Mission, Min. Counsellor for Immigration matters in Italy 1946–47; Chmn., Immigration Commn. 1945–48; U.N. Secretariat, Tech. Asst., 1951–57; Ambassador to the OAS 1963–66; Exec. Dir. Int. Monetary Fund 1964–66; Dir., French & Italian Bank 1951; Banco del Caribe 1970—; Pres. Industrial Bank 1962–63. Ambassador to the United States 1963–68; Elected Senator 1968—; Senior partner Lares, Tejera Asociados; Pres. Sociedad Financiera Atlantica. Entepar (Electronics). *Awards:* Orden del Libertador, grado de Gran cordon; Orden Andres Bello; Ordine Repubblica Italiana. *Publications:* Public Administration. Theory of Development Structures, Caracas (1953); Problems of Installation, San Jose (1954); Two Elements of Government, Caracas (1960). *Address:* Apartado 31, Caracas, Venezuela.

**TELLEFSEN, Jens Aage.** Norwegian. Chairman, International Business Machines A.S., Norway since 1935. *B.* 1903. *Educ.* Matriculated, Commercial College of Oslo (Degree); Princeton University (BA Degree). *M.* 1936, Gunvor Margrethe Bull. *S.* Jens Aage, Jr. and Dag. *Address:* 6 Dronning Maudsgate 10, Oslo, Norway.

**TELLER, Edward.** American scientist *B.* 1908. *Educ.* Karlsruhe Technical Institute, University of Munich and University of Leipzig (PhD 1930). *M.* 1934, Augusta Harkanyi. *S.* Paul. *Dau.* Susan Wendy. *Career:* Research Associate, Leipzig 1929–31, and Gottingen 1931–33; Rockefeller Fellow, Copenhagen (with Niels Bohr) 1934; Lecturer, University of London 1934–35; Prof. of Physics, George Washington University (Washington, D.C.) 1935–41, Columbia Univ. 1941–42, Univ. of Chicago 1946–52, and Univ. of California 1953–60; Physicist, Manhattan Engineer District 1942–46, Univ. of Chicago 1946–52, and Los Alamos Scientific Laboratory 1943–46; Asst. Dir., Los Alamos (on leave, Univ. of Chicago) 1949–52; successively Consultant, Asst. Dir. 1952–53, Assoc. Dir. 1954—, and Dir. 1958–60, Lawrence Radiation Laboratory, Livermore Branch; Professor of Physics at-Large, July 1960–70; Chmn., Dept. of Applied Science, 1963–66, and Assoc. Director 1954—, Lawrence Livermore Laboratory, Univ. of California; Dir. Thermo Electron Corporation. University Professor sinse 1970; Professor Emeritus, Dir. at large Emeritus Sap. Research Fellow (Hoover Inst., Stanford Univ.). *Member:* National Acad. of Sciences: Amer. Nuclear Socy. (Fellow); Amer. Physical Socy.; Amer. Acad. of Arts & Sciences; Scientific Adv. Bd., Air Force; President's Foreign Intelligence Adv. Board 1971. Formerly, General Adv. Cttee., Federal Union; Atlantic Union; Atomic Energy Commn.; Amer. Defense Preparedness Assn. *Awards:* Hon. DSc Yale University, University of Alaska, Fordham Univ., The George Washington Univ., Univ. of Southern California, St. Louis Univ., Rochester Inst. of Technology, Clemson Univ.; Univ. of Detroit, Hon. Dr of Laws, Boston Coll., Seattle Univ., Univ. of Cincinnati, Univ. of Pittsburgh DrLittHum, Mount Mary Coll., Clarkson 1969; Joseph Priestly Memorial Award, Dickinson Coll., Carlisle, Pa. 1957; Albert Einstein Award 1958; Gen. Donovan Memorial Award 1959; Midwest Research Inst. Award & Living History Award 1960; Thomas E. White and Enrico Fermi Awards 1962; Leslie R. Groves Gold Medal (1974); Harvey Prize 1975. *Address:* Stanford, Calif. 94305; and Lawrence Livermore Laboratory, University of Calif., Livermore 94550, Calif., U.S.A.

**TEMPLE, Arthur.** American. Lumberman, Corporate executive. *B.* 1920. *Educ.* Univ. of Texas 1938. *M.* 1939, Mary MacQuiston (Div.). *S.* Arthur Temple III. *Dau.* Charlotte Ann (Spencer). (2) 1963, Charlotte Dean. *Career:* Bookkeeper, Asst. Mgr. of Retail Yard, Mgr. Retail Yard, Temple Lumber Co. 1938–48; joined Southern Pine Lumber Co. (now Temple Ind. Inc.), Diboll Texas 1948, Exec. Vice-Pres. until 1951, Pres. & Chief Exec. Officer 1951–72, Chmn. of the Board 1972—; Chmn. Bd., Pres. & Chief Exec. Officer,

Temple-Eastex Inc. 1975—; Chmn. Planning & Dev. Cttee., Time Inc. 1973—; Exec. Cttee. Time Inc. 1973—; Bd. of Dirs., Time Inc. 1973—; Group Vice-Pres., Time Inc. 1975—. Director: Contractors' Supplies (Lufkin); Wheelabrator-Frye Inc. (New York); Madison Fund (New York) (Dir. & Exec. Cttee. mem. 1975—); Coppee-Rust (Brussels, Belgium); Gulf States Utilities (Beaumont); Republic of Texas (Dallas) (Dir. & Exec. Cttee. mem. 1976—). Advisory Director: First Bank & Trust (Lufkin); Pineland State Bank (Pineland). Mem. & Past Pres., Economic Council of Forest Products Industries. Dir., American Paper Inst. Mem., Adv. Cttee. on Multiple Use of the National Forests. Mem., Delta Kappa Epsilon; Confrerie des Chevaliers du Tastevin. *Awards:* One of Five Outstanding Young Men of Texas of 1948, Texas Junior Chamber of Commerce; Medal of Merit, Veterans of Foreign Wars; Lone Star Farmers Degree, Future Farmers of America; Forest Farmer Annual Award 1965, Forest Farmers Assn., Atlanta, Ga. *Address:* Diboll, Texas and *office* Temple Industries, Inc., Diboll, Texas, U.S.A.

**TEMPLE-MORRIS, Peter,** MP. British Barrister & Politician. *B.* 1938. *Educ.* Hillstone School, Malvern; Malvern Coll.; St. Catharines Coll., Cambridge—BA (Hons.), MA; called to the Bar (Inner Temple) 1962. *M.* 1964, Tahere Alam. *S.* 2. *Daus.* 2. *Career:* Judge's Marshal to the Hon. Mr. Justice Finnemore on Midland Circuit 1958; Chmn., Cambridge Univ. Conservative Assoc. 1961; mem., Cambridge Afro-Asian Expedition 1961; mem., Young Barristers' Cttee., Bar Council 1962–63; in practice on Wales & Chester Circuit 1963–66; contested Newport (Mon.) in General Elections of 1964 & 1966 as Conservative: in practice in London and on South-Eastern Circuit 1966–76; contested 1970 General Election at Norwood (Lambeth); Second Prosecuting Counsel to Inland Revenue on South-Eastern Circuit 1971–74; Conservative MP for Leominster since 1974; appointed a Governor of Malvern College 1975. *Member:* Exec. Cttee., Soc. of Conservative Lawyers 1968–71; Chmn., Hampstead Conservative Political Centre 1971–73; Council, Iran Society since 1968; Sec., Anglo-Iranian Parly. Group & Anglo-Lebanese Parly. Group; Sec., Cons. Parly. Transport Cttee. 1976—; Exec. of the British Branch of the Inter-Parliamentary Union; Royal Inst. of International Affairs; Freeman of the City of London & Liveryman of the Worshipful Company of Basketmakers. *Clubs:* Carlton. *Address:* 7 Redington Road, London NW3; and Huntington Court, Huntingdon, Hereford HR4 7RA; and House of Commons, London SW1A 0AA.

**TEMPLER, Field Marshal, Sir Gerald Walter Robert,** KG, GCB, GCMG, KBE, DSO, Hon. DCL (Oxon), Hon. LLD (St. Andrews). *B.* 1898. *Educ.* Wellington Coll.; Royal Military Coll., Sandhurst. *M.* 1926, Ethel Margery Davie. *S.* 1. *Dau.* 1. *Career:* Served in World War I, Royal Irish Fusiliers 1916–18; took part in operations in N.W. Persia and Mesopotamia 1919–20; Brevet Major 1935; took part in operations in Palestine (dispatches) 1936; Brevet Lieut.-Col. 1938; Commanded, 2nd Corps, 47th (London) Div., 1st Div., 56th (London) Div., and 6th Armoured Div. between 1942–44; Dir. of Military Govt., 21st Army Group 1945–46; Director of Military Intelligence, War Office 1946–48; Vice-Chief of the Imperial General Staff 1948–50; G.O.C.-in-C., Eastern Command 1950–52; High Commissioner and Director of Operation for the Federation of Malaya 1952–54; Chief Imperial General Staff 1955–58; Col., The Royal Irish Fusiliers 1946–60; The Fed. Regiment of Malaya 1954–9 ; 7th Duke of Edinburgh's Own Gurkha Rifles 1956–64; Royal Horse Guards (The Blues) 1963–69, The Blues and Royals (Royal Horse Guards and 1st Dragoons) since 1969; and Gold Stick to H.M. The Queen 1963. H.M. Lieutenant for Greater London 1967–73; Trustee Nat. Portrait Gallery 1958–72; Member of Council, National Army Museum since 1960, V.S.O. since 1961, Scout Assoc. since 1968; Pres., Socy. Army Historical Research since 1965; Trustee, Imperial War Museum 1959–66; Historic Churches Preservation Trust 1963—; Council, Outward Bound Trust 1954–76; National Trust 1959–74; Pres., British Horse Society 1968–70; Comr., Royal Hosp. Chelsea since 1969, Hon. Freeman, Armourers' & Brasiers' Co. 1965. *Clubs:* Boodles'; Buck's. *Address:* Flat 7, 31 Sloane Court West, London SW3.

**TEMPLETON, John Marks.** British. *B.* 1912. *Educ.* Yale University (BA 1934) and Oxford University (Balliol College; MA 1936). *M.* 1958, Irene Reynolds. *S.* John. M. Jr. and Christopher W. *Dau.* Anne Dudley. *Career:* President: Lexington Research & Management Corp. 1959–62; Research Investing Corp. 1955–65; Corporate Leaders of America Inc. 1959–62. President and Director: Templeton Growth Fund Ltd. (Toronto); First Trust Bank Ltd. (Nassau). Member, Council on Theological Education of United Presbyterian Church. Trustee & Former Chmn. Princeton (N.J.) Theological Seminary. President, Chief Executives Forum of U.S.A. 1968. Director Chase Manhattan Trust Co. (Bahamas); Magic Chef Inc. & Templeton Foundation Inc.; British American Insurance Co. (Bahamas); Bahamas National Trust. *Member:* Chartered Financial Analysts (himself a Chartered Financial Analyst); Phi Beta Kappa; Investment Counsel Assn. of America. *Award:* Hon LLD Beaver Coll. 1965, Wilson Coll. Penn 1974. *Clubs:* Yale (N.Y.C.); University (N.Y.C.); Lyford Cay (Nassau); Elihu (New Haven Conn.); Lansdowne (London). *Address:* Box N 7776 Lyford Cay, Nassau, Bahamas; and *office* 145 King Street W., Toronto, Canada.

**TEPER, Lazare,** Economist. *B.* 1908. *Educ.* Johns Hopkins Univ. (PhD 1931). *Career:* Student Assistant, Johns Hopkins 1929–31; Research Asst., Walter Hines Page School of International Relations 1931–34; Instructure, Economics, Brookwood Inc. 1934–36; Dir. of Research, Joint Board of Dressmakers' Union 1935–37, Int. Ladies Garment Workers Union 1937—. Consultant to Research Div., Social Security Board 1938–43; member, Committee on Seasonality in Industry, N.Y. Dept. of Labour 1939–40; U.S. Delegate to World Statistical Congress 1947; AFL and ICFTU representative at U.N. Statistical Commission 1947—; member, Intensive Review Committee, Bureau of the Census 1955, and of Special Committee on Employment Statistics 1954; Consultant to U.S. Delegation on Textiles Negotiations 1961—; member, A.S.A. Census Advisory Committee 1955–68 & Management-Labor Textile Advisory Committee 1962—; Member Metropolitan Economic Assn. (Pres. 1975); Dir. National Bureau of Economic Research 1970—; Mem. Bd. of Dirs., Federation Employment & Guidance Service; Trustee, Federal Statistics Users' Conference 1963—. *Publications:* Hours of Labor; Women's Garment Industry; numerous articles in professional journals. *Fellow:* Amer. Statistical Assn., and Amer. Assn. for Advancement of Science. *Member:* Amer. Economic Assn.; Econometric Socy.; Amer. Marketing Assn.; Industrial Relations Research Assn.; Acad. of Political Science. *Address:* 650 West End Avenue, New York City 10025; and *office* 1710 Broadway, New York City 10019, U.S.A.

**TERENCE, Nsanze.** *B.* 2 Feb. 1937. *Educ.* Primary Secondary Schools and College Burundi; Georgetown Univ. American Univ. Washington D.C.; City Univ. New York; Brooklyn Coll. New York. Master's Degree Political Sciences; Diploma Social, Theological Sciences and Philosophy. *Married. Children:* 2. *Career:* Manager, Editor in Chief, National Leading Newspapers Ndongozi, The Guide 1961; Sec. Gen. Union, Burundere Students UNEBA 1961; Pres. Panafrican Student Organization in the Americas 1962–63; African Catholic Students; East African Student Union all Washington D.C. 1962–63; Del. Gen. Assembly U.N. 1962; Summit Conference Heads of State, and Govt. Cairo 1964; Perm. Secy. Organization, Africa Unity, U.N. 1965; Head Burundese Del. 21st Session U.N. 1966; Head Special Mission, Dir. Gen. of the Int. Labor Office 1966; Chmn. Cttee. Agric. Affairs 1967; Del. Conference of Pacem in Terris 11, Geneva 1967; Head of many Delegations U. Nations 1967–71, Vice-Pres. Gen. Assembly 1971; Former Ambassador Extraordinary and Plenipotentiary & Perm. Representative to United Nations, United States and Canada. *Publications:* many Books and Articles 1964–71. *Address:* c/o Ministry of Foreign Affairs, Bujumbura, Republic of Burundi.

**TESH, Robert Mathieson,** CMG. British diplomat. *B.* 1922. *Educ.* Queen Elizabeth's Wakefield; Queen's Coll. Oxford, MA. *M.* 1950, Jean Bowker. *S.* 2. *Dau.* 1. *Career:* British Army 1942–45; British Embassy, Delhi 1948–50; Foreign Office 1950–53; NATO 1953–55; British Embassy, Beirut 1955–57; Foreign Office 1957–60; British Embassy, Bangkok 1960–64; Commonwealth Relations Office 1964–65; Depy. High Commissioner Accra, and Lusaka, 1965 and 1966; British Embassy Cairo 1966–69; Imperial Defence College 1969–70; Foreign and C'wealth Office 1970–72; British Amb., Bahrain 1972–75; British Amb., Hanoi since 1976. *Decoration:* Companion of the Order of St. Michael and St. George. *Club:* Travellers. *Address:* Ashenden, 10 Albany Close, Blackhills, Esher, Surrey; and *office* c/o Foreign and Commonwealth Office, King Charles Street, London S.W.1.

**TESTORI, Edoardo. Italian textile executive.** *B.* 1901. *Educ.* School of Textiles and Technical School. *S.* Ruggero, Giovanni. *Dau.* Anna. Owner, with his brother Cesare, of the firm Figli di G. Testori (technical school for the Textile

Industry and Representatives; established 1904; owner 1918—); Director, Board of Management, Ente Fiera di Milano, Jan. 1959—, member, Advisory Council of Commercial Union of Milan 1947—. Director, Society Grob, Italiana di Milano; President, National Association of Businessmen and Representatives in the Textile Industry for Sewing and Hosiery, CUMATEX, Milan 1947—; Vice-President, Friends of the Soldier (Amici del Soldato), Milan 1956—. Commander, Order of St. Sepulchre; Chevalier, Crown of Italy; Grand Off. of the Republic of Italy. *Address:* Via Melzi d'Eril 20, Milan and *office* Via Melzi d'Eril 18, Milan, 20154 Italy.

**TETLEY, Sir Herbert,** KBE, CB. British. *B.* 1908. *Educ.* Leeds Grammar School; The Queen's College, Oxford: MA 1st Class Hons. Mods. (Mathematics) 1928; 1st Class Final Hons., School of Mathematics 1930. *M.* 1941, Agnes Maclean Macfarlane Macphee. *S.* Andrew David Rycroft. *Career:* Principal Actuary, Government Actuary's Dept. 1950; Deputy Govt. Actuary 1953; The Government Actuary 1958–73. *Publications:* Actuarial Statistics (Vol. 1, 1946), and (jointly) Statistics—An Intermediate Text-Book (Vol. 1, 1949; Vol. 2, 1950). *Fellow:* Inst. of Actuaries (Pres. 1964–66), and Royal Statistical Society. *Address:* 8B Langley Avenue, Surbiton, Surrey.

**TETLOW, Norman.** British consulting engineer. Specialist in design of and application of centrifugal reciprocating and hydraulic pumps, prime movers, crude oil pipelines and pumping stations. *B.* 1899. *Educ.* Manchester Univ. (BSc Hons); FIMechE; FIEE; FRAer Socy.; member ASME. With Mather & Platt Ltd., Manchester 1923–45; *Publications:* MechE. Water Arbitration Prize (1940); IEE Crompton Premium (1943); and other technical papers. *Address:* 41 New Road, Blakeney, Norfolk.

**TEVETOGLU, C. Fethi,** MD. Turkish doctor, politician and author. *B.* 1916. *Educ.* Faculty of Medicine, Univ. of Istanbul; post graduate studies at Texas and Baylor Universities for six years (U.S.A.). *M.* 1941 Gulcan Krimsamhal. *Daus.* Filiz, Nur, Aliye, Tolunay and Tomris. *Career:* Served 20 years in the regular Turkish army. Active in politics since 1957 and a wellknown fighter of communism since 1934 when his first book and monthly journal (Kopuz) were published. President, Committee for Foreign Affairs in the Senate. President of the Turkish NATO Parliamentarians' Group, and a member of their Standing & Economic Cttees. (1962–64). Chairman of the Justice Party Group in the Senate 1966–67 and 1972–73. President of The Turkish Parliamentary Group in the Common Market 1965–70. Member of the Directing Committee of the Justice Party. Senator (Justice Party) for Samsun 1961–73; Chief, Turkish Parliamentary Delegations at U.N. (1968); Chief Delegate, Asian People's Anti-Communist League's & World Anti-Communist League's Conferences since 1963; Member, WACL Executive Cttee. since 1967; Sec.-Gen. of the Middle East Solidarity Conference 1975—, & Dep. Sec.-Gen. of the Islamic Conference for Political Affairs since 1976. Editor in Chief, Turkish Encyclopaedia. *Publications:* Rabindranath Tagore, his life and works (1938); Muftuoglu Ahmed Hikmet (1951); Enis Behic Koryurek (1951); No Fascist, but Communist (1962); Our Views on Foreign Policy (in four languages) (1963); Two Declarations (The Declaration of Independence and La Déclaration des droits de l'homme et du citoyen) (1963); The Shamewall (Berlin 1964); I am disclosing (1965); The Holy Lands (1965); Cyprus and Communism (1966); The Socialist and Communist Activities in Turkey (1910–1960) (1967); The Russia I Saw of Today (1968); Those who went ashore at Samsun with Ataturk (1971); Ömer Naci (1973). *Address:* Bakanliklar, P.K. 250, Ankara, Turkey; and P.O. Box 178, Jeddah, Saudi Arabia.

**TEVOEDJRE, Virgile-Octave.** *B.* 1931. *Educ.* Lycée Victor Ballot 1946–49; Lycée Van Hollen Haven 1949–53; Univ. Dakar 1953–55; Univ. Bordeaux 1955–59; Diploma Inst. of Political Studies (1959); Licence Es-Lettres (non-teaching BA) 1958. *M.* Mireille Gabriel. *S.* 1. *Dau.* 1. *Career:* Tutor Delafosse Tech. College Dakar 1954–55; Assist-Prof. of Lit. at Classical and Modern College of Nerae & Lycée Montesquieu de Bordeaux 1958–59; mem. foreign ministry at Accra, interpreter and programme writer 1959–60; Tech. Adviser and Secy. Min. of Foreign Affairs 1960–61; Counsellor of Dahomey in Washington 1962 (res. in NY); Internat. Civil Servant F.A.O. 1962–66; Min-Counsellor of Dahomey in Washington, also chargé d'affaires there and in Canada 1967–70; Dir. Internat. Orgs and Tech. Assist. at Foreign Ministry 1970–71; Ambassador of Dahomey to Republic of Zaire 1971–73; Ambass. of Dahomey to Fed. Rep. of Germany, and accredited Ambass. to Austria. Sweden, Norway, Denmark and the Vatican 1973 and Ambass. to Swiss Confed. 1973; Ambassador of Benin to Benelux, Representative to EEC & Perm. Rep. to UN in Geneva 1975–77. *Delegate:* for Dahomey at UNO, WHO, ICAO, FAO, AMU, OAU, World Bank. *Publications:* former publ. dir. Jeunesse d'Afrique; La Crise du Rassemblement Democratique Africain (1959); Visage d'Afrique and other contr. to newspapers. *Decorations:* Knight of National Order of Dahomey; Commander of the Order of the Leopard of Rep. of Zaire; Grand Officer of the Order of Merit, Federal Republic of Germany. *Address:* c/o Ministry of Foreign Affairs, Cotonou, Benin; & Voteland la Canoire, Houinme, Porto-Novo, Benin.

**THALMANN, Dr. Ernesto.** Swiss Diplomat. *B.* 1914. *Educ.* Gynasium (Grammar School), Berne & Zurich; Univ. of Zurich—Doctor of Law. *M.* 1943, Paula Degen. *S.* 2. *Dau.* 1. *Career:* Minister-Counsellor & Dep. Head of Mission, Swiss Embassy, Washington, 1957–61; Perm. Observer to UN, New York (Amb. Extraordinary & Plenipotentiary) 1961–66; Head of International Organizations Div., Fed. Political Dept., Berne 1966–71; Special Mission in Jerusalem, after Six-day War, as Personal Rep. of the UN Sec.-Gen., U Thant 1967; Sec.-Gen. of Fed. Political Dept. & Dir. of Political Affairs 1971–75; Swiss Amb. to the Court of St. James's since 1976. *Address:* 21 Bryanston Square, London W1H 7FG; and *office* 16–18 Montagu Place, London W1H 2BQ.

**THATCHER, Rt. Hon. Margaret Hilda,** MA, BSc, MP. British politician. *B.* 1925. *Educ.* Kesteven and Grantham Girls' School; Somerville Coll. Oxford. Master of Arts, Bachelor of Science. *M.* 1951, Denis Thatcher. *S.* 1. *Dau.* 1. *Career:* Research Chemist 1947–51; Barrister, Lincoln's Inn since 1953; Member of Parliament for Finchley since 1959; Joint Parly. Secy. Ministry, Pensions & National Insurance 1961–64; Secy. of State for Education and Science 1970–74; Shadow Minister for Environment and Housing, and later shadow minister with special responsibility for finance and public expenditure 1974–75; Leader of the Opposition since 1975. *Address:* House of Commons, London, S.W.1.

**THEDIECK, Franz.** German government official. *B.* 1900. *Educ.* University. *M.* 1941, Hilde Bömer. Civil Servant Official in Köln since 1923; Secretary of State 1949–63. Intendant, Deutschlandfunk Köln Marienburg 1966–72. *Address:* Haager Weg 7, 53 Bonn-Venusberg, Germany.

**THEED, William Denis Learoyd.** British company director. *B.* 1906. *Educ.* Westminster School, London. *M.* 1933, Elizabeth P. Pounsford. *S.* 1. *Daus.* 3. *Career:* Dir., Godfrey Engineering Ltd. *Clubs:* Oriental; Royal Thames Yacht; Phyllis Court (Henley-on-Thames). *Address:* Ferry House, Wargrave, Berks.

**THEODORE, Normsby Basil** (John). Australian industrialist. *B.* 1912. *Educ.* St. Ignatius College, Riverview, N.S.W.; Sydney University. *M.* 1937, Violet Kathleen Hegarty. *Career:* Chmn. Loloma Mining Corp.; Secretary, Associated Gold Mining Companies, Fiji 1933–35; Chairman of Directors. Sydney Newspapers Pty. Ltd. 1945–47; Consolidated Press Ltd. 1948–57; N.L. 1950—; Dir. Emperor Gold Mining Co. Ltd. (Fiji); Tavua Power Pty. Ltd.; Emperor Mines Ltd. 1950–70; Chmn. Man. Dir. Dolphin Mines Ltd. (Fiji) 1953–69. Managing Director Television Corporation Ltd. (Channel 9, Sydney) from inception to 1957; Director, Great Boulder Gold Mines Ltd. since 1962. *Address:* P.O. Box 228, North Sydney, N.S.W., Australia.

**THERIAULT, Leon Norbert.** Canadian. *B.* 1921. *Educ.* Baie Ste. Anne Secondary School (Graduated) and The Little Seminary of Rimouski, St. Francis Xavier Univ. *M.* 1941, Josephine Martin. *S.* 6 (one adopted). *Daus.* 4. *Career:* Appointed Manager of W. S. Loggie Co. Ltd. 1941; established his own business as a General Merchant 1945. Elected Counsellor for the municipality of Northumberland 1959; elected Deputy Prefect of the same countty 1961, and Prefect 1963; Representative, Northumberland 1960— (re-elected 1963—); Minister, Municipal Affairs in Legislative Assembly of New Brunswick 1965; Minister, Health and Welfare 1967. Member of the Liberal Party. *Clubs:* Newcastle Curling; Chatham Council, Knights of Columbus. *Address:* c/o Legislative Building, Fredericton, New Brunswick, Canada.

**THESIGER, Sir Gerald Alfred,** MBE. Hon. Mr. Justice Thesiger; Judge of the Queen's Bench Division of the High Court of Justice. *B.* 1902. *Educ.* Gresham's School, Holt, and Magdalen College, Oxford (MA). *M.* 1932, Marjorie Eileen Guille (*D.* 1972). *Daus.* Oonah Caroline (Vincent

Vine), Virginia Mary (Pinckney) (*D.* 972), Juliet Elizabeth (Neville). *Career:* Called to the Bar (Inner Temple) 1926; KC 1948; Bencher 1956. Member: Fulham Boro. Council 1934–37; and of Chelsea Borough Council (Mayor 1944–46) 1937–38; Freeman 1964. Recorder of Rye 1936–42, Hastings 1942–57, and Southend-on-Sea 1957–58; Chairman, West Kent Quarter Sessions 1947–58; Judge, High Court of Justice since 1958. *Member:* International Commission of Arbitration on Ambatielos Claim 1955–56; Chairman, Departmental Committee on Licensing of Road Passenger Transport 1952–53; Chairman Governors, United Westminster Schools 1947–58; member, General Council of the Bar 1957–58; Dep. Chairman Boundary Commission for England 1963–74. *Club:* Hurlingham. *Address:* Royal Courts of Justice, Strand, London, W.C.2.

**THIBAUT de MAISIERES, Robert.** Belgian engineer specialist in organization. *B.* 1901. *Educ.* Ingénieur electro-mécanicien—It.P.Lg. *M.* 1907, Marthe Van den Bosch Sanchez de Aguliar. *S.* Xavier. *Career:* (engineer with Solvay Co.). Engineer, Sté. Foraj Lemoine (oil exploitation in Rumania) 1925–27, and Etablissement Sandelin (surveys, reports). Brussels 1928. Chief Engineer, Société Solvay et Cie. (chemical products; 17 plants in Europe). Brussels 1929—Order of Léopold; Order of the Crown. *Member:* Société belge d'Etudes et d'Expansion (Liége); Association des Patrons et ingénieurs catholiques (Assn. of Catholic Employers and Engineers), Brussels. *Clubs:* Royal Automobile; Royal Touring (Belgium). *Address:* 25 Rue Village, Couture St. Germain, Belgium, 1482.

**THIESS, Sir Leslie Charles,** CBE, JP, FCIT. Australian. *B.* 1909. *M.* 1929, Christina Mary Erbacher. *S.* Geoffrey Leslie and Alan Charles. *Daus.* Esmay (married), Thelma (married) and Margaret Kay (married). *Career:* Chairman of Directors, Thiess Holdings Ltd. Thiess Bros. Pty. Ltd.; Thiess Toyota Pty. Ltd.; Thiess Peabody Mitsui Coal Pty. Ltd. *Awards:* Created Knight Bachelor 1971; The Third Class, Imperial Order of the Sacred Treasure Japanese Government. *Clubs:* Brisbane; Tattersalls; N.S.W. Sports; Huntington; Royal Queensland Yacht; The Mining (Sydney); Royal Queensland Aero (Brisbane). *Address:* 121 King Arthur Terrace, Tennyson, Brisbane; and *office* Thiess Holdings Pty. Ltd., Kerry Road, Archerfield, Brisbane, Qld., 4105, Australia.

**THOLSTRUP, Knud R.,** pp. Danish. Businessman and shipowner. *B.* 12 July 1904. *Educ.* Public and Agricultural school. *M.* Signi Grenness. *S.* Ole Knud, Svend Knud. *Dau.* Inga. MP (League of Justice) 1946–58; Managing Director, Kosan Tankers a/s, Chmn. Kosan a/s, Vester Farimagsgade 1, 1648 Copenhagen v. *Address:* Osterstrand, 2950 Vedbaek, Denmark.

**THOMAS, Charles Allen.** American chemist and executive. *B.* 15 Feb. 1900. *Educ.* Transylvania College (AB, DSc), Massachusetts Institute of Technology (MS). *M.* 1926, Margaret Stoddard Talbott. *S.* Charles Allen. *Daus.* Margaret Talbott, Frances Carrick, Katharine Tudor. *Career:* Research chemist, General Motors Research Corporation 1923–24; Ethyl Gasoline Corp. 1924–25; Pres., Thomas & Hochwalt Labs. 1926–36. Dir., Central Research Dept., Monsanto Company 1936–45; Vice-President and Technical Director 1945, Exec. Vice-President 1947, President 1951, Chairman of Board 1960, of Finance Committees 1965–68. U.S. Medal for Merit, Industrial Research Institute Medal, American Institute of Chemists' Gold Medal 1948, Perkin Medal 1953. Priestley Medal 1955; Hon DSc, Washington University, Kenyon College, Princeton, Ohio Wesleyan, Brown University, Brooklyn Polytechnic, University of Alabama, St. Louis University, Simpson Coll. Hon D Eng, Univ. of Missouri. Hon LLD Hobart Coll., Lehigh Univ., Westminster College. *Address:* 7701 Forsyth Boulevard, St. Louis 63105, Mo., U.S.A.

**THOMAS, H. Emerson.** American business executive. *B.* 1902. *Educ.* University of Illinois and Oklahoma City University, First Distinguished Alumni Award; AB Magna *cum laude*. *M.* 1928, Helen Hefferline. *S.* H. Emerson, Jr., and Gordon B. *Career:* Eastern Representative, Philips Petroleum Company 1929–42; Formerly Pres. and Owner, Fuelite Natural Gas Corp. 1935–54; Yankee Bottled Gas Corp. 1944–54; Eastern Bottle Gas Co. 1950–54; Jersey Shore Gas & Heating Co.; Valley Cities Gas Co.; Berwick Gas Co.; Williamstown Gas Co.; Martinburg Gas & Heating Co.; Elkton Gas Co.; Elizabeth & Suburban Gas Co.; N. Carolina Gas Corp.; Rock Hill Gas Co.; Hudson Valley Gas Co.; Former Pres. Liquefied Petroleum Service Co.; Trustee (former Pres. & Dir.) Westfield YMCA, First Golden Man Award; Former Pres. & Dir. Petroleum Gas Service, Inc., and Superior Gas Co. Former Dir., The Leasing Corp. and Junior Chamber of Commerce of U.S. Consultant to Government and private business; Owner and President, Thomas Associates Inc. Pres., United Transportation Inc. Pres. and Dir. Suburban Fuel Tank Car Co.; Pressure Tank Car Co. President and Director, Thomas Building Ltd.; Westfield Corp.; Continental Tank Car Corp.; Thomas Investment Co.; Federal Rail Car Corp.; Pres., Hetsons Ltd.; Partner Woodbridge Co. Ltd.; Director and Exec. Com. Central Jersey Bank & Trust Co. & Instogas Corporation; Dir. Gilco Marine; Waywick Corp.; Dir. and Vice-Pres. Frost Valley Assn. Dist. Service Award; Dir. (former Vice-Pres.), Westfield Historical Society. Trustee, United Campaign Bd. Director Children's Specialized Hosp. Member, Natl. Fire Protection Assn. (Award); Amer. Gas Assn. (Award of Merit); member, Dir. and Past Pres., a National Liquefied Petroleum Gas Assn. (which Assn. awarded him Distinguished Service Award and Seley Award for outstanding services to the industry); Dir. (and Past Pres.), Compressed Gas Assn. Sigma Chi member; former Mayor and council man, Westfield. Dir., United Fund Inc. *Publications:* various articles on liquefied petroleum gas in trade magazines and gas handbooks. *Clubs:* N.Y. Engineers; N.Y. Advertising; Rotary; Echo Lake Country (Past Pres. and Dir.). *Address:* 34 Cowperthwaite Place, Westfield, N.J. 07090, U.S.A.

**THOMAS, Jeffrey.** QC, MP. British barrister. *B.* 1933. *Educ.* King's Coll., London and Grays Inn. *M.* 1960, Margaret Jenkins. *Career:* Pres. Univ. of London Union 1955–56; Commissioned Royal Corps of Transport, Deputy Asst. Dir. Army Legal Services (Major) 1960; Gen. Election candidate for Barry 1966; Labour Member of Parliament for Abertillery, Gwent since 1970; Queen's Counsel since 1974; Recorder of the Crown Court since 1975. *Member:* Council of Justice British Section International Commission of Jurists; Chmn. Council of the British Caribbean Assn.; Socy. of Labour Lawyers; Fabian Society; Exec. Cttee., British Group Inter-Parly. Union. *Clubs:* Reform; Aber Rugby Football. *Address:* 60 Lamont Road, London, S.W.10; and *Chambers* 3 Temple Gardens, Temple, E.C.4.

**THOMAS, Lee Baldwin.** American executive. *B.* 1900. *Educ.* Univ. of Washington (BBA). *M.* (1) 1924, Margaret T. Thomas (*Dec.*). *S.* Lee B., Jr. *Daus.* Susan Jane and Margaret Ellen. (2) Elizabeth Cawthorne Thomas. *Career:* Advertising Manager, Ernst Hardware Co., Seattle, Wash. 1923–24; Buyer, R. H. Macy & Co., New York City 1924–25; Sales Manager, Ernst Hardware Co. 1926–29; Director, Home Goods Merchandising, Butler Bros., Chicago 1929–41; President, Ekco Products Co., Chicago (1941–47), and American Elevator & Machine Co., Louisville 1947–48. Chairman of Board: Vermont American Corp., and subsidiaries, Electric Sprayit Foundation (Sheboygan, Wis.); Chmn. Exec. Cttee. Thomas Industries and subsidiaries; Director: Honey Locust Foundation (Louisville), *Clubs:* Union League, Mid-Day (Chicago); Pendennis (Louisville); Owl Greek Country (Anchorage, Ky.); Harmony Landing Country (Prospect, Ky.); Mountain Lake; Lake Wales; Lake Region Country; Winter Haven (Florida). *Address:* 401 Vermont American Building, 100 East Liberty Street, P.O. Box 1523, Louisville, Ky., U.S.A.

**THOMAS, Michael Stuart (Mike),** MP. British. *B.* 1944. *Educ.* King's School, Macclesfield; Liverpool Univ.—BA. *M.* 1976. *Career:* Pres., Liverpool Univ. Guild of Undergraduates & Mem. of National Exec. of National Union of Students 1965–68; Head of Research Dept., Cooperative Party 1966–68; Senior Research Officer, PEP (Political & Economic Planning) 1968–73; Dir., National Volunteer Centre 1973–74; Labour & Co-op. MP for Newcastle upon Tyne East since 1974; PPS to Rt. Hon. Roy Hattersley MP 1975–76; Member, Select Cttee. on Nationalised Industries 1975—; Founder of Parliament's own journal *The House Magazine*. *Member:* Union of Shop, Distributive & Allied Workers. *Publications:* various for Cooperative Party & PEP; reviews, articles etc. *Clubs:* Walker Social, Newcastle upon Tyne. *Address:* House of Commons, London SW1A 0AA.

**THOMAS, Rt. Hon. Peter John Mitchell,** PC, QC, MP, *B.* 1920. *Educ.* Jesus College, Oxford (MA), and Middle Temple, London. *M.* 1947, Frances Elizabeth Tessa Dean. *S.* 2. *Daus.* 2. *Career:* With R.A.F. 1939–45; Barrister-at-Law, Middle Temple 1947; QC 1965; Member, Parliament (Con.) Conway Div. Caernarvonshire 1951–66, for Hendon South 1970–74, for Barnet, Hendon South since 1974; Parliamentary Private Secretary to the Solicitor-General 1954–59; Parliamentary Secretary, Ministry of Labour 1959–61;

Parly. Under-Secy. of State for Foreign Affairs, June 1961–63; Minister of State for Foreign Affairs 1963–64; Secy. State for Wales 1970–74; Chmn. Conservative Party 1970–72; Pres. Nat. Union of Conservatives and Unionists Assn. 1973–75; Master of the Bench, Middle Temple, London. Conservative. *Club:* Carlton; Cardiff & County. *Address:* 145 Kennington Road, London, S.E.11; Bath, Llanbedr-y-Cennin, Conway, North Wales; and House of Commons, London, S.W.1.

**THOMAS, Ralph, Sr.** American. *B.* 1896. *Educ.* Virginia Military Institute (BA 1919). *M.* 1922, Helen Hines. *S.* Edward W. and Ralph, Jr. *Dau.* Sarah Jane. *Career:* Foundry Executive, Maxwell-Chalmers Motor Car Co. 1919–21; Lincoln Motor Co. 1922–23; joined Speaker-Hines Printing Co. 1924; member of firm 1928 (firm established 1884). President, Speaker-Hines & Thomas, Inc. (printers and lithographers, Detroit and Lansing) since 1938; Secretary, Automobile Club of Michigan. Past Pres.: American Automobile Assn.; Detroit Rotary Club, Detroit Executives Assn.; one of the founders, Printing Industry of America, National Trade Assn.; Past Pres.: Graphic Arts Assn. of Michigan, and Automobile Club of Michigan (member, Board of Directors); Director, Detroit Auto Inter-Ins Exchange, Trustee, The Arnold Home, Cleary College. *Clubs:* Detroit Athletic; Country; The Automobile; Lansing. *Address:* 222 Merriweather Road, Grosse Pointe Farms, Michigan 48236, U.S.A.

**THOMAS, Ralph L.** American. Professor of Economics, *B.* 1905. *Educ.* Dartmouth Coll. (1922); Univ. of Pittsburgh (1925); BS Lafayette College (1926); Rutgers University Graduate School of Banking (1937); MLitt, University of Pittsburgh (1955); PhD, Univ. of Pittsburgh (1961); Pembroke College, Cambridge (1962). *M.* 1936, Elizabeth M. Heidenkamp. *Career:* With First National Bank, Pittsburgh, 1926–34; assistant cashier, 1934–42; Lt. Col. Finance Dept. AUS, 1942–45; grad. Army Finance School, 1942; asst. v.p. Peoples First National Bank & Trust Co., Pgh., 1946–48; v.p. 1948–56; instructor; Department of Economics, University of Pittsburgh, 1957–60; Chairman, Department of Economics, Ohio Northern University, Ada, Ohio, 1961–64; Professor of Economics, Edinboro State College, Edinboro, Pa. 1964–66; Professor of Economics, California State Coll., California, Pa. 1966–70. Director of Coe-American Studies Program at Calif. State College, California, Pa.1968. Member Tri-State Graduate School of Banking Alumni Assn. (Pres. 1937–57). Life Member, Military Order of World Wars and Sigma Chi. *Clubs:* Duquesne, Longue Vue, Bankers. Contributor, Articles to Banking publications. *Publication:* Policies Underlying Corporate Giving, 1966 Edition. *Address:* 5023 Frew Ave., The Park Mansions, Pittsburgh, Pennsylvania 15213, U.S.A.

**THOMAS, Robert E.** American. *B.* 1914. *Educ.* Wharton School of Finance of University of Pennsylvania (BSEcon 1936). *M.* 1949, Barbara Darcey. *S.* Robert E., Jr. *Dau.* Barbara Ann. *Career:* Chairman Executive Committee and Director, Missouri-Kansas-Texas Railroad, Sept. 1955–Mar 1965; Vice-President Pennroad Corp. (now Madison Fund Inc.) June 1953–59; Executive, Keystone Custodian Funds Inc., June 1936–53. Chmn. & Pres., Dir., Member Exec. Cttee., and Chief Exec. Officer, (Chief Exec. Officer Subsidiary Comps.) Mapco Inc. (Tulsa, Okla.) 1960—. Director and Member Executive Committee, Perkin-Elmer Corp. 1955—, Director, National Bank of Tulsa Jan. 1962—; Dir. & Member Exec. Cttee. Founders Financial Corp. (Tampa, Fla.); Dir. Amer. Petroleum Inst.; Dir. Independent Petroleum Assn. of America; Dir. Transportation Assn. of America. *Member:* National Petroleum Council; Newcomen Society. *Clubs:* Southern Hills Country, Summit, Tulsa (Tulsa, Okla.); N.Y. Yacht; Links (N.Y.C.); Metropolitan (N.Y.C.); The Chicago; The Kansas City; Ocean Reef; Key Largo (Fla.); Cat Cay (Bahamas). *Address:* 2870 East 33rd Street, Tulsa, Okla. 74105; and *office* 1437 South Boulder Avenue, Tulsa, Okla. 74119, U.S.A.

**THOMAS, Rt. Hon. Thomas George,** PC, MP. British. Politician. *B.* 1909. *Educ.* Southampton Univ. *Career:* Member of Parliament since 1945; Parly. Under Secy. of State 1964–66; Minister of State, Welsh Office 1966–67; Min. of State Commonwealth Office 1967–68; Secretary of State Welsh Office 1968–70; Deputy Speaker & Chmn. of Ways & Means 1974–76; Speaker since 1976. *Member:* Hon. Life G.T. Mem., National Union of Teachers. *Awards:* Freeman of Borough of Rhondda; Dato Setia Negara Brunei 1971; Life Member, Cardiff National Union of Teachers; Fellow Univ. Coll. Cardiff 1972; Hon. Dr. of Civil Laws, Ashbery Coll., Kentucky, U.S.A.; Hon. LLD (DL), Univ. of Southampton 1977; Hon. Dr. of Law, Univ. of Wales 1977. Vice-Pres. Methodist Church 1960–61; Freeman of City of Cardiff March 1975. *Publications:* The Christian Heritage in Politics. *Address:* 173 King George V Drive, Cardiff; and *office* House of Commons, London, S.W.1.

**THOMAS, of Remenham, Rt. Hon. Lord, (William Miles Webster),** DFC, MIMechE, MSAE. British company director. *B.* 2 Mar. 1897. *Educ.* Bromsgrove School and Birmingham University. *M.* 1924, Hylda Nora Church. *S.* 1. *Dau.* 1 *Career:* Served World War I, with armoured car squads in German East Africa, R.F.C. and R.A.F. in Mesopotamia, Persia and Southern Russia 1914–18; founded Morris-Oxford Press in 1926; Dir. and Gen. Sales Mgr. of Morris Motors Ltd. 1927; Director and General Manager, Morris Commercial Cars Ltd., Birmingham 1934, and Wolseley Motors Ltd., Birmingham 1935; Managing Director, Wolseley Motors Ltd. 1937; Chairman, Cruiser Tank Production Group and member of Advisory Panel on Tank Production 1941, British Tank Engine Mission to U.S.A. 1942, Government of Southern Rhodesia Development Co-ordinating Commission 1947, Oxfordshire Council, Order of St. John 1947: President, Society of Motor Manufacturers 1947–48; Director, Colonial Development Corporation 1948–50; President, Advertising Association 1949–52. International Air Transport Association 1951–52; Chairman, B.O.A.C. 1949–56; Chairman: Monsanto Chemicals Ltd. 1956–63, National Savings Committee 1965–70, Agricultural Central Trading Ltd. 1962–67, Development Corporation for Wales 1958–67, and British Productivity Council 1959–60. *Address:* 7 Cleveland Row, St. James's, London, S.W.1.

**THOMPSON, Cecil Harry,** O.B.E. British economist. *B.* 1918. *Educ.* Birmingham University (BCom (Hons); MCom). *M.* 1946, Joan Berry. *Daus.* 2. *Career:* British Army (R.A.S.C.; Major; despatches) 1940–45; seconded from R.A.S.C. and appointed Economist with military and (later) civil government in Malaya 1945–46; Lecturer in Economics, University of Leeds and member, Colonial Primary Products Committee, U.K. Govt. 1946–48; Senior Lecturer, Univ. of the Witwatersrand 1948; Economost with Govt. of S. Rhodesia 1949–53; Chief Economist, Government of the Federation of Rhodesia and Nyasaland 1954–60; Economic Adviser, Europe and Middle East Dept. of International Bank for Reconstruction & Development 1961–73; Deputy Dir. World Bank Resident Staff in Indonesia since 1973. *Publications:* Economic Development in Rhodesia and Nyasaland (with H. W. Woodruff 1955); numerous articles and reviews on economic subjects, particularly the development of backward areas. Member Salisbury Club. *Address:* c/o International Bank for Reconstruction & Development Resident Staff in Indonesia, P.O. Box 324 DKT, Jakarta, Indonesia.

**THOMPSON, Sir Edward Hugh Dudley,** MBE, TD. *B.* 1907. *Educ.* Uppingham and Lincoln Coll., Oxford. *M.* (1) 1931. Ruth Monica Wainwright; (2) 1947, Doreen Maud Tibbitt, *S.* John Robin Neale, Martin Charles Neale, and Simon Christopher Neale. *Dau.* Merelyn Neale. *Career:* Practising Solicitor 1931–36; Asst. Man. Dir. Ind Coope & Allsopp Ltd. 1936–39, Man. Dir. 1939; Chmn. Ind Coope Ltd. 1955–62; Chmn. Allied Breweries Ltd. (formerly Ind Coope, Tetley, Ansell) 1961–68; Trustee, The World Security Trust. Mem. Northumberland Cttee. for Foot and Mouth. *Club:* Boodle's. *Address:* Culland Hall, Brailsford, Derby; and *office* Allied Breweries Ltd., St. John Street, Clerkenwell, London, E.C.1.

**THOMPSON, Elwood N.** American. President, Cooper Foundation. *B.* 1913. *Educ.* University of Nebraska (AB 1933); School of Law; School of Journalism, Columbia University (BS 1935; Pulitzer Scholarship); New York University (LLB 1943); member, Phi Beta Kappa. *M.* 1935, Katherine Clarke. *S.* Elwood Arthur. *Dau.* Karen Katherine. *Career:* Institute of Public Administration, N.Y. City 1935; State Tax Commission 1935; volunteer reporter, Associated Press Bureaus, London, Geneva, Berlin 1935–36; Des Moines Register and Tribune 1936–37; Hearst Corp., Washington 1937; Associated Press, Washington 1937–39; Field Representative and Asst. Secy., National Municipal League, N.Y. City 1939–43; Bureau of the Budget 1943–45; Dept. of State 1945–47; Dep. Dir., Office of U.N. Affairs 1947; Secy., Carnegie Endowment for International Peace 1948–50; Secy., First Trust Co. of Lincoln 1950–53, Exec. Vice-Pres. 1953–54; Dir. 1951–61; Pres. 1954–61. Pres., Lincoln Community Chest 1958. Member of Board, Woodmen Accident and Life Co. Member, Bd. & Exec. Cttee., National Assn. of Theatre Owners; Trustee, Cooper Foundation; Trustee &

Member Bd. Univ. of Nebraska Foundation; Lincoln Industrial Development Corp. (President 1958–73); Member Bd. of Trustees, Nebraska Arts Council & Nebraska Art Association. Chairman University of Nebraska Centennial Committee; Univ. of Nebr. Builder Award, 1969; U. of N. Alumni Distinguished Service Award. Pres., Lincoln Chamber of Commerce 1960–61. Republican. *Address:* 2900 Sheridan Boulevard, Lincoln, Neb., U.S.A.

**THOMPSON, Jack Burn.** American. *B.* 1905. *Educ.* Swarthmore Coll. (BA); Johns Hopkins Univ.; American Press Inst.; Columbia University. *M.* 1930, Lois Thompson. *Daus.* Marlen Ruth (Gaskill), Deborah Knight (Lewis) and Lois (Murray). *Career:* Editor, Chester Times, Chester, Pa., 1942–53. President, Treasurer, Director, The Clifton Forge Review, Inc.; Editor and Publisher, The Daily Review, Clifton Forge, Va., 1953–72. *Member:* Board of Manager, Swarthmore Coll. 1952–56; Swarthmore College Alumni Assn. (past President); American Society of Newspaper Editors; Newcomen Society of North America, etc. Dist. Service Award, War Finance Program, U.S. Treasury 1945; Legion of Honour Degree; Order of DeMolay. Independent Republican. *Club:* Cliftondale Country. *Address:* 909 Linden Avenue, Clifton Forge, Va. 24422, U.S.A.

**THOMPSON, John Kenneth,** CMG. British. *B.* 1913. *Educ.* King's College, London (BA, AKC) and Lausanne Univ. *M.* 1937, Janet More. *S.* John More and Kenneth Robin More. *Career:* Assistant Master, Queen's Royal Coll., Trinidad, B.W.I. 1935–39; War Service, West Indies and London 1939–45; West African and International Relations Department Colonial Office 1945–49; Colonial Attaché, British Embassy, Washington 1950–52; Head, Social Services Department, Colonial Office 1953–59; Director, Colombo Plan Bureau June 1959–62; Asst. Secretary, Department of Technical Co-operation, London 1962–64. Director, Overseas Appointments, Ministry of Overseas Development, London 1964–69. Chairman, Exec. Cttee., Royal Commonwealth Society for the Blind since 1952; Director, Commonwealth Inst. London since 1969. *Address:* Commonwealth Institute, Kensington High Street, London, W.8.

**THOMPSON, Lee Bennett.** American lawyer. *B.* 1902. *Educ.* Univ. of Oklahoma (BA 1925; LLB 1927). *M.* 1928, Elaine Bizzell. *S.* Lee Bennett Jr. and Ralph Gordon. *Dau.* Carolyn Elaine. *Career:* Vice-Pres. and General Counsel of several business corporations; Pres. Bd. of Trustees, Oklahoma Memorial Union Inc; Deacon and Former Elder, First Christian Church; Vice-Pres. U.S. Junior Chamber of Commerce 1930–31; Dir. Okalhoma City Chamber of Commerce 1931–32 and 1955–56; served in World War II (Captain, Major, Lieutenant-Colonel and Colonel; 33 months in South Pacific; 5 Campaign Stars and Legion of Merit) Sept. 1940–May 1946; Pres. Beta Theta Pi National Convention 1942; Vice-Pres. Trustee Beta Theta Pi Fraternity 1945–48; Pres. Oklahoma Assn. of Phi Beta Kappa; Chmn. Oklahoma County Chapter, American National Red Cross 1951–52; 1952–53; Pres. Oklahoma County Bar Assn. 1955–56; Oklahoma City Rotary Club 1955–56; Special Justice, Oklahoma Supreme Court 1967–68; Pres. Elect Oklahoma Bar Association 1971, Pres. 1972; Member House of Delegates 1972. *Awards:* Distinguished Service Citation, The Univ. of Oklahoma 1971; Fellow: American Bar Foundation; Fellow American Coll. of Trial Lawyers; Amer. Judicature Society. Mason 33rd; Shriner; Royal Order of Jesters. *Member:* Oklahoma County Bar Assn.; Oklahoma Bar Assn.; American Bar Assn.; House of Delegates 1972. Democrat. *Clubs:* Men's Dinner; 75; Beacon; Oklahoma City Golf & Country. *Address:* 539 N.W. 38th Street, Oklahoma City, Okla. 73118 and *office* Thompson, Nance, Harbour & Selph, 2120 First National Building, Oklahoma City 73102, U.S.A.

**THOMPSON, Leslie James.** Australian. *B.* 1888. *M.* 1913, Vera Annie Elizabeth Andrews. *Dau.* Ailsa Marie. *Career:* Chmn. of Dirs. Australian Provincial Assurance Ltd., 1950; A. P. A. Fixed Investment Trust Ltd., 1950; A. P. A. Fire & General Insurance Co. Ltd. 1956; A. P. A. Holdings Ltd. Fellow, The Institute of Chartered Accountants in Australia. The Chartered Institute of Secretaries. Past President, Institute of Directors (Aust. Div.). Hon. member, The Pharmaceutical Society of New South Wales. *Address:* 156 Copeland Road, Beecroft, N.S.W., Australia.

**THOMPSON, Hon. Lindsay Hamilton Simpson,** CMG, MP, BA (Hons.), BEd, MACE. Australian. *B.* 1923. *Educ.* Honours Arts Degree in Hist. and Political Science; BA BEd (1st place in Hist. of Education); Capt. and Dux of Caulfield Grammar Schl. *M.* 1950, Joan Margaret Poynder. *S.* 2. *Dau.* 1 *Career:* Member, Higinbotham Province in Legistlative Council 1955–67 (youngest member ever elected at that date); State Government Representative on Melbourne Univ. 1955–59; Parliamentary Secy. to the Cabinet 1956–58; Asst. Chief Secy. and Asst. Attorney-General 1958–61; Asst. Minister, Transport 1960–61; Min. of Housing and Forests 1961–67; Deputy Leader, Government in Legislative Council, Victoria 1962–70; Minister i/c Aboriginal Welfare 1965–67; Member for Monash Province, 1967–70 and for Malvern since 1970. Min. of Education 1967; Leader of Legislative Assembly sinse 1972; Deputy Premier of Victoria since 1972. *Publications:* Australian Housing Today and Tomorrow (1965); Looking Ahead in Education (1969). Mem. Melbourne Univ. Graduates Assn. Liberal Party; Pres. Royal Life Saving Socy. (Vict.) since 1970. *Awards:* Bronze Medal, Royal Humane Socy. 1974; Companion of Order of St. Michael & St. George, Queen's Birthday Hons. 1975. *Clubs:* Melbourne; Kingston Health Golf; Melbourne Cricket Ground (Trustee). *Address:* Kinleath, 19 Allenby Avenue, Glen Iris, Vic.; and *office* Department of Education, Treasury Buildings, Melbourne, Vic., Australia.

**THOMPSON, Sir Richard Hilton Marler,** Bt., *B.* 1912. *Educ.* Malvern College. *M.* 1939, Anne Christabel de Vere Annesley. *S.* 1. *Career:* In business in India, Ceylon and Burma, 1930–40; served in World War II (Royal Navy; dispatches 1942). MP for Croydon West, 1950–55; for South Croydon, 1955–66. Asst. Government Whip, 1952; Lord Commissioner of the Treasury 1954; Vice-Chamberlain of H.M. Household 1956; Parliamentary Secretary, Ministry of Health 1957–59; Parliamentary Under-Secretary of State, Commonwealth Relations Office, 1959–60; Parliamentary Secretary, Ministry of Works 1960–62; Member Parliament S. Croydon 1970–74; Chairman Overseas Migration Board 1959; led U.K. Government delegation to ECAFE, Bangkok 1960; Member. Public Accounts Cttee 1973. Chmn., Capital & Countries Property Co. Ltd. 1971–76; Pres., British Property Federation 1976–77. Trustee of the British Museum. *Club:* Carlton. *Address:* Rhodes House, Sellindge, Ashford, Kent.

**THOMSON, Alexander Stuart,** BSc. British electrical engineer and company director. *B.* 1900. *Educ.* Strathallan School, Forgandenny, Perthshire, and King's College, University of London (BSc Eng). *M.* 1933, Eileen Catherine Macgregor. *S.* 3. *Dau.* 1. *Career:* Former Dir. Contropanels Ltd.; James Scott & Co. (Electrical Engineers) Ltd.; James Scott & Co. (Electricity Service Centres) Ltd.; James Scott (Electronic Engineering) Ltd.; Malcolm & Allan Ltd. Served apprenticeship with Bruce Peebles & Co. Ltd.; joined James Scott & Co. (Electrical Engineers) Ltd., Perth, as Contracts Manager 1927 (Partner 1931; Joint Managing Director 1948). Director, James Scott Engineering Group Ltd. 1947–74, Consultant 1974–77 (Ret'd.). *Address:* Auchraw of Mailer, Craigend, by Perth, Scotland.

**THOMSON OF MONIFIETH, Rt. Hon. Lord** (George Morgan), PC, LLD. *B.* 1921. *Educ.* Grove Acad., Dundee. *M.* 1948, Grace Jenkins. *Daus.* 2. *Career:* Editor, Forward 1948–53; Labour MP for Dundee, 1952–72; Jt. Chmn., Council for Education in the Commonwealth 1959–64; Adviser to the Educational Institute of Scotland, 1960–64; Minister of State, Foreign Office, 1967; Secy. of State for Commonwealth Affairs, 1967–68; Minister without Portfolio, Oct. 1968–Oct. 1969; Chancellor of the Duchy of Lancaster and Minister for European Affairs, 1969–70; Shadow Defence Secretary 1970–72; Chmn., David Davies Inst. International Affairs; Chmn. Labour Cttee. for Europe 1971–72; Commissioner European Economic Community 1972–76. Chmn., European Movement in the U.K. since 1976, Advertising Standards Authority since 1977. *Awards:* Hon. LL.D., University of Dundee, 1967; D. Litt. Univ. Edinburgh 1973; Hon. Dr. of Science, Univ. of Aston in Birmingham 1976; Created Life Peer 1977. Member of the Labour Party. *Clubs:* Brooks's (London), Union (Brussels). *Address:* The Rowans, Invergowrie, Dundee.

**THOMSON, Jack,** CBE (OBE 1945), C Eng FIMechE, FIMM, M(SA)IE. British. *B.* 1903. *Educ.* Sciennes and Boroughmuir Secondary Schools, Edinburgh, Heriot Watt College (Dipl Eng). *M.* 1930, Elaine Cawood. *S.* 1. *Dau.* 1. *Career:* Retired March 1965 from being a Vice-President of RST Group of Companies in Lusaka, Zambia, was a Member of the London Advisory Committee of Roan Selection Trust Ltd. 1965–70; Director, African Selection Trust Exploration; Alt. Dir., Unisel Gold Mines Ltd. Served pupil apprenticeship with Bertrams Ltd., Engineers, Edinburgh (some experience in coal and shale mines in Scotland). Joined engineering staff of Wankie Colliery Co. Ltd., S. Rhodesia 1925–29; Roan Antelope Copper Mines Ltd., successively Engineering Assistant, Workshops Supt., Mech. Engineer, Resident Engineer, Asst. Manager 1945, Manager 1946, General Manager 1951–57. Head of Rhodesian Dept. of Selection Trust Ltd., London, 1957–60. Returned to Zambia as Resident Director and later Vice-President for Special Duties, Lusaka, RST Group of Companies 1960–65. *Awards:* Queen's Coronation Medal; Hon. Member Engineering Institution of Zambia. *Address:* Lundie Cottage, 19 Horne Drive, Leisure Isle, Knysna, Cape Province, Republic of South Africa.

**THOMSON, Brevet Col. Sir John,** KBE, TD. British. *B.* 1908. *Educ.* Winchester College; Magdalen College, Oxford; MA. *M.* 1935, Elizabeth Brotherhood (JP 1957) (*D.* 1977). *Career:* Joined staff of Barclays Bank Ltd. 1929; Local Dir., Oxford (1935—). Dir., Barclays Bank Ltd. 1947—, Dep. Chairman (1958), Chairman, 1962–73; Deputy Steward, Oxford University, 1951—. A curator of the Oxford Univ. Chest 1949–74; Chmn., Nuffield Medical Trustees; Treasurer or Trustee of other local organizations; Member, Royal Commission on Trade Unions & Employers' Associations, 1965–68. Joined Oxfordshire Yeomanry 1927; commanded them 1942–44 and 1947–50; High Sheriff, Oxfordshire 1957; Vice-Lieutenant, Oxfordshire 1957; Lord Lieutenant, Oxfordshire 1963—; Honorary DCL, Oxford 1957; President British Bankers Association, 1964–66; Chairman Committee of London Clearing Bankers 1964–66; Hon. Col. 299 Field R.A. (T.A.) 1965–67. Hon. Col. Oxfordshire T.A. 1967–69. Hon. Col. Oxfordshire Territorial Cadre, 1969–74; Pres., East Wessex TAVR 1974–76. *Club:* Cavalry. *Address:* Manor Farm House, Spelsbury, Oxford; & Achnaba, Lochgilphead, Argyll.

**THOMSON, Sir John Adam,** KCMG. British Diplomat. *B.* 1927. *Educ.* Phillipe Exeter Academy. N.H., U.S.A.; Aberdeen Univ.—MA; Trinity Coll., Cambridge—MA. *M.* 1953, Elizabeth Anne McClure. *S.* 3. *Dau.* 1. *Career:* Foreign Office 1950–51; Jedda 1951–53; Damascus 1954–55; Foreign Office 1955–58; Private Sec. to Perm. Under-Sec. 1958–60; Washington 1960–64; Foreign Office 1964–66; Head of Planning Staff 1966–68; Chief of Assessments Staff, Cabinet Office 1968–71; Minister & Dep. Perm. Rep., NATO 1972–73; Asst. Under-Sec. of State, FCO 1973–76; High Commissioner in New Delhi since 1976. *Decorations:* Knight Commander of St. Michael & St. George (1978) (Companion 1972). *Publications:* (with Robin Fedden) Crusader Castles. *Clubs:* Athenaeum. *Address:* Lochpatrick Mill, Kirkpatrick Durham, Castle Douglas, Kirkcudbrightshire; and *office* Foreign & Commonwealth Office, Downing Street, London SW1.

**THORN, William.** Australian engineer. *B.* 1902. *Educ.* Master of Electrical Engineering (Melbourne Univ.). *M.* 1931, Joan Darbyshire. *S.* 3. *Career:* Electrical Engineer, State Electricity Comm. of Victoria 1939–61, Engineer for Production 1949–61; Ministry of Munitions, Asst. Controller, Material Supplies Directorate 1941–45; Dir. Bruce Peebles (Aust.) Pty. Ltd. 1962–68; Consulting Engineer, Anderson Connell Consultants since 1968. Mem., Graduate Ctte., Building Ctte and Faculty of Engineering, Melbourne Univ. *Publications:* Capacitors in Distribution Systems (awarded IEA Electrical Premium), 1940; Low Load Factor Hydroelectric Schemes (1952). *Member:* FIEE; FIE (Aust.). *Club:* Savage. *Address:* 9 Florence Avenue, Kew, Vic. 3101; and *office* Anderson Connell Consultants Pty. Ltd., 60 Albert Road, South Melbourne 3205, Australia.

**THORNBROUGH, Albert A.** American. *B.* 1912. *Educ.* Kansas State Coll. (MA) and Harvard Univ. *M.* Virginia Dole. *S.* Wayne and Grant. *Dau.* Susan. *Career:* Lectured at Harvard Univ. for two years before joining U.S. Dept. of Agriculture; appointed Chief of Farm Machinery and Tractor Branch, Office of Price Administration 1942. With U.S. Army (gaining rank of Lieut.-Colonel 1942–46. Joined Harry Ferguson Inc. (Detroit) 1946, rising to Vice-President and Director; appointed Executive Vice-President, Massey-Harris-Ferguson Ltd. (Toronto) 1955 (Director July 1956; President Dec. 1956; Chief Exec. Officer 1965). *Member,* Farm & Industrial Equipment Inst. (President 1963; Chairman of Board 1964). *Clubs:* Detroit Athletic; Lampton; York; The Toronto. *Address:* 200 University Avenue, Toronto, Ont. M5H 3E4, Canada.

**THORNEYCROFT, Rt. Hon. Lord,** PC (George Edward Peter Thorneycroft); (cr. Life Peer 1967; Baron of Dunston). British. *B.* 1909. *Educ.* Eton; Royal Military Acad., Woolwich. *M.* (1) 1938, Sheila Wells Page (marriage dissolved 1949). *S.* John; (2) 1949, Countess Carla Roberti. *Dau.* Victoria Elizabeth Anne. *Career:* Commissioned in Royal Artillery 1930; resigned commission 1933; called to the Bar, Inner Temple 1935; MP (Cons.) for Stafford 1938–45, for Monmouth 1945–66; Parliamentary Secretary, Ministry of War Transport 1945; President of the Board of Trade 1951–57; Chancellor of the Exchequer 1957–58; Minister of Aviation, July 1960–62. Minister of Defence, 1962–64; Secy. of State for Defence, 1964. Dir., Securicor Ltd.; Chairman: Pye Holdings Ltd., 1967—; Pye of Cambridge Ltd., 1967; Pirelli General Cable Works Ltd., 1966—; Simplification of International Trade Procedures 1968–75; Pirelli Ltd., 1969—; Trust Houses Forte 1971; British Overseas Trade Board 1972–75. Chmn., Conservative Party 1975—. *Club:* Army & Navy. *Address:* House of Lords, London, S.W.1.

**THORNLEY, Sir Colin Hardwick,** KCMG, CVO. *B.* 1907. *Educ.* Bramcote School, Scarborough; Uppingham; Brasenose College, Oxford (MA in the Honour School of Jurisprudence). *M.* 1940, Muriel Betty Hobson. *S.* 1. *Daus.* 2. *Career:* Served in Colonial Administrative Service (now merged in H.M. Overseas Civil Service) in the Tanganyika Terriroty 1930–39; seconded to Colonial Office 1939–45; Principal Private Secy. to Secy. of State for the Colonies 1941-45; Administrative Secretary, Govt. of Kenya 1945–47; Depty. Chief Secretary, Kenya 1947–52; Chief Secretary, Uganda 1952–55; Governor and C.-in-C. British Honduras 1955–61; Director-General, Save the Children Fund 1965–74. *Address:* Spinaway Cottage, Church Lane, Slindon, Nr. Arundel, Sussex.

**THORNLEY, Dr. David Andrew.** Irish Politician. *B.* 1935. *Educ.* Homefield School, Sutton, Surrey; St. Paul's School, London; Trinity Coll., Dublin—MA, PhD. *M.* 1958, Petria Hughes. *S.* 1. *Dau.* 1. *Career:* Fellow, Trinity Coll., Dublin 1964; Associate Prof. of Political Science, Trinity Coll., Dublin since 1968. *Publications:* Isaac Butt & Home Rule (1964). *Clubs:* Dublin University. *Address:* 17 Serpentine Terrace, Dublin 4, Ireland; and *office* Trinity College, Dublin 2; and Dail Eireann, Dublin 2.

**THORNLEY, Ronald Howe.** British company director. *B.* 5 Dec. 1909. *Educ.* Bramcote School, Scarborough; Winchester College; Clare College, Cambridge (BA). *M.* 1952, Isabel Marjorie Johnson. *Career:* Joined Auditing Staff of Foreign Division of the American Radiator Co. 1931; served in World War II (Lt.-Col.) 1939–45; Secretary, Ideal Boilers & Radiators Ltd. Dec. 1945, Man. Dir. Sept. 1951— (company name changed to Ideal-Standard Ltd. Sept. 1961); Director National Radiator Co. Ltd., Standard Sanitary & Bath Co. Ltd., Ideal Warming Investment Co. Ltd., Ideal Bath Co. Ltd., since Nov. 1951, and Ideal Boilers & Radiators Ltd. since Sept. 1961 (when company was formed). *Address:* Cherry Garth, Cherry Burton, Beverley, E. Yorks.

**THORNTON, Douglas Cruse.** Australian insurance attorney *B.* 1919 *Educ.* Caulfield Grammar School *M.* 1943, Madeleine Seymer Paulsen-Forster. *S.* Keith Ross. *Dau.* Yvonne Madeleine. *Career:* War service, Flying Officer (Air Crew) R.A.A.F. 1940–45; Manager for N.S.W., Law Union & Rock Insurance Co. Ltd. 1949–55; Managing Director: Commonwealth Underwriters Pty. Ltd. and Commonwealth Underwriters (Vic.) Pty. Ltd. 1955–61. Managing Director: D. C. Thornton Pty. Ltd.; D.C. Thornton (Vic.) Pty. Ltd; D. C. Thornton (S.A.) Pty. Ltd.; D. C. Thornton (W.A.) Pty. Ltd. Dir. K. R. Thornton Pty. Ltd. Attorney in Australia for Baltica-Skandinavia Insurance Co. Ltd. *Clubs:* Australian; Royal Automobile (Australia); Melbourne Cricket; Sydney Cricket; Roseville Tennis. *Address: office* 82 Pitt Street, Sydney, N.S.W., Australia.

**THORNTON, Sir Ronald George.** British. *B.* 1901. *Educ.* St. Dunstan's Coll., Catford. *M.* 1927, Agnes Margaret Masson. *S.* Geoffrey Ronald. *Dau.* Margery Janet. *Career:* Entered Barclays Bank Ltd. 1919; Gen. Mgr. 1946. Vice-Chairman, Barclays Bank Ltd. 1962–66. Chairman, Barclays Export Finance Co. Ltd. 1964–66. Director: Bank of England 1966–70. Director: Friends Provident & Century Life Office, Century Insurance Co. Ltd., and Utd. Dominions Trust Ltd. 1962–71; Chmn. Exec. Cttee. Banking Information Service 1962–66; Bank Education Service 1964–66. Fellow Royal Society of Arts. Member: Export Council for Europe 1960–64, and Decimal Currency Committee 1962–63. *Member:* Governing Body St. Dunstans Educ. Foundation 1966–73; Institute of Bankers (Fellow). *Address:* South Bank, Rectory Lane, Brasted, Westerham, Kent.

**THORNYCROFT, John Ward,** CBE. British. *B.* 1899. *Educ.* Royal Naval Colleges, Osbourne Dartmouth and Keyham;

and Trinity College, Cambridge. *M.* 1930, Esther Katherine Pritchard. *S.* Timothy Edward. *Dau.* Jill Elizabeth. *Career:* Officer in the Royal Navy 1912–20, Hon. President, John I. Thornycroft & Co. Ltd. Director, Southampton, Isle of Wight & South of England Royal Mail Steam Packet Co. 1961—; Hon. Vice-Pres. of R.I.N.A.; Royal Institution of Naval Architects; Fellow Institution of Mechanical Engineers. Chartered Engineer; Fellow Royal Society of Arts. *Clubs:* Naval & Military; Royal Yachting Assn.; Bembridge Sailing; Farmer (Meat). *Address:* Steyne, Bembridge, Isle of Wight.

**THORPE, Rt. Hon. John Jeremy,** PC, MP. Leader of the Liberal Party 1967–76. *B.* 1929. *Educ.* Rectory School, Pomfret, Connecticut, U.S.A.; Eton; Trinity College, Oxford (Hons. Degree, Jurisprudence). *M.* (1) 1968, Caroline Allpass (*Dec'd.*). *S.* Rupert Jeremy. (2) 1973, Marion Stein. *Career:* President, Oxford Union 1951; Barrister-at-Law, Inner Temple; Contested N. Devon in General Election, 1955; elected Member for N. Devon 1959; Re-elected 1964, 1966, 1970 and 1974; Liberal Party, Hon. Treasurer, 1965–67; Privy Councillor, 1967; Leader, Liberal Party 1967–76. Chmn. National Executive, UN Association. Formerly President Oxford University Liberal Club; President Oxford Univ. Law Society; Pres., Russell and Palmerston Club; Vice-Chmn. Electoral Reform Society; founder Member, National Benevolent Fund for the Aged; former Hon. Treasurer, United Nations Parliamentary Group; former member, BBC General Advisory Committee; former Secretary of World Campaign for Release of South Africa Political Prisoners. Hon. Pres. UNA of GB and NI.; Hon. Fellow Trinity Coll. Oxford; Hon. LLD Exeter Univ. *Publications:* To All Who are Interested in Democracy. *Clubs:* Reform; National Liberal. *Address:* House of Commons, London, S.W.1.

**THORPE, Stuart Walter,** FCIS, FASA. Australian. *B.* 1911. *Educ.* Secretarial, Costing and Accountancy Inst. Degrees. *M.* 1933, Joyce Poynton Thorpe (née Le Lievre). *S.* Ian Stuart and Robert James. *Daus.* Phyliss and Wendy Joan. *Career:* Company Secretary, Australian Motor Petrol Co. Ltd. (now Ampol) 1937–51; during World War II, on loan as Asst. Sec., Dept. of the Army and Asst. Business Adviser Min. Army and Commander-in-Chief; Chmn. & Director, Fire Fighting Enterprises Ltd. Chmn. Protector Safety Industries Ltd; Sydney, N.S.W.; Director: Ampol Exploration Ltd.; Ampol Petroleum Ltd.; Australia Reliance Fire Fighting Equipment Pty. Ltd.; Auckland N.Z. Life Member, Royal Life Saving Society, S A.; President, Royal Life Saving Society N.S.W. 1949–56. *Address:* 10 Burrawong Avenue, Clifton Gardens, N.S.W., Australia.

**THORSON, Reuben.** Investment banker and stock broker. *B.* 1901. *Educ.* Univ. of Minnesota (BS 1924). *M.* 1930. Dorothy DeVry Whalen. *S.* Robert Douglas and Donald Richard. *Daus.* Dorothy Jeanne (Foord) and Virginia Luise (Goodall, Jr.). *Career:* Registered Representative with Paul H. Davis & Co. 1924–31; Resident Manager, Paine, Webber, Jackson & Curtis 1931–36. General Partner 1936—, Chairman of the Policy Committee 1955—, Paine, Webber, Jackson & Curtis, Chicago. Director: Booth Fisheries Corp. 1958—, Growth Industry Shares Inc. 1955—, The Hallicrafters Co. 1959—, Illinois Mic-Continent Life Insurance Co. 1957—, United Electric Coal Companies 1959—, and Wilson Jones Co. 1955–58 and 1960—. *Member:* Advisory Board of Junion Achievement, Chicago; Scandinavian Foundation (Dir.); Cook County School of Nursing (Dir. and Past Pres.); Citizens' Board, University of Chicago; Loyola University Citizens' Board; Art Institute of Chicago (Life); Auditorium Theater Council. Member: Chicago Stock Exchange (former Governor and Chairman of the Exec. Cttee. This exchange is now called Midwest Stock Exchange—Member 1953–55 and former chmn. Bd. of Governors); Chicago Board of Trade; Mercantile Exchange; Winnipeg Grain Exchange; Chicago Assn. of Stock Exchange Firms (former Chmn. of Board). *Clubs:* Attic; Executives (Chicago); Edgewater Golf; The Chicago; Chicago Athletic Association Bond (Chicago); Brook (N.Y.C.); Racquet (Chicago); Saddle & Cycle; Sigma Nu. *Address:* 399 Fullerton Parkway, Chicago, Ill. 60614; and *office* 209 South La Salle Street, Chicago 4, Ill., U.S.A.

**THORSTEINSSON, Pétur.** Icelandic diplomat. Special adviser to the Ministry for Foreign Affairs & since late 1976 Ambassador to China, Japan, India, Pakistan & Iran with residence in Reykjavik, Iceland. *B.* 1917. *Educ.* Univ. of Iceland (grad. economics 1941 and law degree 1944). *M.* 1948, Oddny Stefansson. *S.* Pétur, Bjoergolfur, and Eirikur. *Career:* Entered Ministry for Foreign Affairs 1944; Attaché 1944, Secretary, Moscow, Oct. 1946; Ministry for Foreign Affairs, Dec. 1947; Delegate, F.A.O. Assembly, Washington 1949; Sec. Icelandic F.A.O. Cttee. 1948–51; Chief of Division, Ministry for Foreign Affairs 1950–51; Chairman, Inter-Bank Committee on Foreign Exchange Oct. 1952; member, various trade delegations, *i.a.* to U.S.S.R. (chairman) 1946 and 1947, Czechoslovakia 1947, Poland and Hungary (chairman) 1953, U.S.S.R. (chairman) 1953, En. Ex. and Min. Plen. to Moscow 1953–56; Ambassador 1956–61 (concurrently to Rumania and Hungary); Ambassador to Bonn and Greece, and Minister to Switzerland and Yugoslavia 1961–61. Delegate to U.N. General Assembly, N.Y., Sept.–Dec. 1958; Ambassador to France, Permanent Representative to N.A.T.O. and O.E.C.D. 1962; concurrently Ambassador to Belgium 1963; to Luxembourg 1962; and Chief of Icelandic Mission to the E.E.C. 1963. Ambassador to U.S.A., and concurrently to Canada, Mexico, Brazil and Argentina, and Minister to Cuba 1965–69; Secy. General of the Ministry for Foreign Affairs 1969–76. *Awards:* Cmdr., Order of the Icelandic Falcon with Star, Grand Cross, Order of the Crown, and of the Oak Crown; Grand Officer, Order of Merit; Grand Cross, Order of St. Olaf; Grand Cross, Order of Danebrog; Grand Cross Order of the North Star; Grand Cross Order of the Lion (Finland); Grand Officier, Legion of Honour. *Address:* Ministry for Foreign Affairs, Reyjkavik, Iceland.

**THORVALDSON, Hon. Gunnar S.,** QC. Senator of the Dominion of Canada. *B.* 1901. *Educ.* Univ. of Saskatchewan (BA 1922) and University of Manitoba (LLB 1925). *M.* 1926, Edna E. Schwitzer. *Daus.* 3. *Career:* Life Bencher, Law Society of Manitoba. Senior Partner in legal firm of Thorvaldson & Company, 209 Bank of Nova Scotia Building, Winnipeg. Director: Western Gypsum Ltd., Winnipeg; The North Canadian Trust Co.; Gamble MacLeod Ltd.; Anthes-Imperial Ltd.; Canadian Aviation Electronics Ltd.; Canadian Premier Life Insurance Co.; Canada Security Assurance Co. Past President: Winnipeg (1952–53) and Canadian (1954–55) Chambers of Commerce. Member, Canadian Delegation to U.N. in New York 1958; Head, Canadian Parliamentary Delegation to Inter-Parliamentary Union, Tokyo 1960, Brussels 1961, Brasilia 1962; Member of Council, I.P.U. 1960–61–62. *Member:* Canadian and Manitoba Bar Associations. Progressive Conservative. Member, Zeta Psi Fraternity. *Clubs:* Manitoba; St. Charles Country; Winnipeg Conservative; Winnipeg Winter; Optimist (Winnipeg); Rideau (Ottawa); Seigniory (Montebello, P.Q.). *Address:* 1009–99 Wellington Crescent. Winnipeg, Man., Canada.

**THRAP-MEYER, Carl Oscar Herman von Tangen.** Norwegian director of companies. President, Norwegian Shipbuilders' Association 1954–59. *B.* 1903. *Educ.* Glasgow University (BSc). *M.* 1936, Senta Forshell. *S.* Herman von Tangen. *Award:* Knight, Order of St. Olav. *Address:* Kaldnes mek Verksted, Tönsberg, Norway.

**THRAY SITHU KYAW NYUN.** Burmese. *B.* 1916. *Educ.* BSc (Hons) 1937. *M.* 1939, Daw Khin San Aye. *S.* 3. *Daus.* 6. *Career:* Under Sec., Min. of Defence & External Affairs 1946–47; Dep. Commissioner, General Administration 1947–49; Sec., Min. of Finance & Revenue 1950–67; Sec., Min. of National Planning 1968–69; Chmn., Union Bank of Burma 1970–75; Mem. of Burmese Delegations to Annual Meetings of World Bank & Int'l Monetary Fund; Alternate Gov. of World Bank & Gov. of Int'l Monetary Fund 1955–67 & 1970–75. *Address* and *office:* Royal Trust Building, 116 Albert Street, Ottawa, Ont., Canada.

**THUNE, Erik.** American cement and machinery executive. *B.* 1893. *Educ.* Frederiksberg Gymnasium 1909; Commercial College, Copenhagen 1912–13. *M.* 1923, Anne Marie Thomsen (*Div.* 1936). *Dau.* Emma (Riggs Parker). Commander, Order of Dannebrog (Denmark); Comdr., Order of the White Elephant (Thailand); Knight 1st Class, Order of White Rose (Finland). *Career:* Finnish Consul General 1931; Trustee, American Scandinavian Foundation, N.Y.; Hon. Chairman, Danish-American Society N.Y. Commercial Education, Scandinavian Oil Co., Copenhagen 1909–14; Student, Tunnel Portland Cement Co. Ltd., London 1914; with the Siam Cement Co. Ltd., Bangkok, Thailand 1914 (successively Chief Accountant and Secretary 1914–23; Vice Manager 1923–26; Gen. Mgr. 1926–35). Pres., Danish Society in Siam 1926; National Portland Cement Co. (1936 Comptroller 1936–37; 1st Vice-Pres. 1937–42; Pres. 1942–63); member, Board of Directors, Rajah Hitam Coconut Estate Ltd., Thailand 1923–26; Bangnara Rubber Co. Ltd., Thailand 1926–36: Aalborg Portland Cement Co., Copenhagen 1946–58; Nordisk Industri Holding Co. 1946–58. President F. L. Smidth & Co., New York 1940–61, (Chairman 1940–70) Managing Director, F. L. Smidth & Co., Copenhagen, 1946–48; Nordiske Kabeland Traadfabriker; Chmn. Bd. Carlsberg Agency Inc. New York. Chairman: National Portland Cement Co. (Philadelphia) 1942–67; F. L. Smidth & Co. (Del.) and F. L. Smidth & Co. (Canada); 1940–49; Bd. of Directors: F. L. Smidth & Co., A/S Copenhagen; 1946–69; F.L.S. Overseas A/S 1962–69. *Clubs:* Peale Club. *Address:* 220 West Rittenhouse Square, Philadelphia, Pa. 19103, U.S.A.

**THUNHOLM, Lars-Erik**, Ph.D.hon, CBE, Grand Cross, Order of the North Star, Knight Commander of the Order of Vasa. Chairman. *B.* 1914. *Educ.* Graduated from the Stockholm School of Economics, Master of Political Science at the University of Stockholm. *M.* 1939, May Bruzelli. *Daus.* Görel and Eva. *Career:* Economic Adviser, Svenska Handelsbanken 1938–55; Man. Dir., Swedish Federation of Industries 1955–57; Man. Dir. of Skandinaviska Banken 1957–1965, Chief Man. Dir. 1965–1971; Man. Dir. and Chief Exec. Officer of Skandinaviska Enskilda Banken 1972–76; Chairman of the Board 1976. Chmn.: Billeruds AB, Säffle, Kockums Shipyard, Malmoe, Swedish Match; Vice-Chmn.: AB Bofors; Dir.: Custos AB, Euroc AB, Skandia Insurance, Gränges AB; Chmn.: Banque Scandinave en Suisse, Geneva, Scandinavian Bank Ltd. London; Dir.: ADELA, Peru, Deutsch-Skandinavische Bank, Frankfurt/Main.—Chmn.: Swedish-British Society; Vice-Chmn.: Swedish National Committee of the ICC; Director: Nobel Foundation, Swedish Bankers Association; The Atlantic Institute for International Affairs, International Center for Monetary and Banking Studies. *Address:* Skeppsbron 24, 111 30 Stockholm; and *office* Skandinaviska Enskilda Banken, S-103 22 Stockholm 16, Sweden.

**THURLOW, 8th Baron, Francis Edward Hovell-Thurlow Cumming Bruce.** KCMG. *B.* 1912. *Educ.* Shrewsbury and Trinity Coll., Cambridge. *M.* 1949, Yvonne Diana Aubyn Wilson. *S.* 2. *Dau.* 2. *Career:* Asst. Principal, Dept. of Agriculture for Scotland 1935; Dominions Office 1935; Asst. Secy., Office of U.K. High Commissioner in N.Z. 1939, and in Canada 1944; Member, Secretariat of Meeting of Commonwealth Prime Ministers in London 1946; U.K. Delegation at Peace Conf., Paris 1946; and General Assembly of U.N. 1946 and 1948; Principal Private Secy. to Secy. of State 1946; Asst. Secy., Commonwealth Relations Office (C.R.O.) 1948; Head, Political Div., Office of U.K. High Commissioner in India 1949; Establishment Officer (1952), Head of Commodities Dept. (1954), C.R.O. Adviser to Governor of Gold Coast 1955; Deputy High Commissioner for U.K. in Ghana 1957; in Canada 1958; High Commissioner in New Zealand 1960–63, and Nigeria 1963–67; Gov. of the Bahamas 1968–72. *Club:* Travellers. *Address:* 16 Warwick Ave., London W.2.

**THURMOND, Strom.** U.S. Senator, lawyer and farmer. *B.* 5 Dec. 1902. *Educ.* Clemson College (BS). *M.* (1) 1947, Jean Crouch (*Dec.* 1960). *M.* (2) 1968, Nancy Moore. *S.* 2. *Dau.* 2. *Career:* Teacher, South Carolina Schools 1925–29; admitted to South Carolina Bar 1930; County Superintendent of Education 1929–33; City Attorney and County Attorney; State Senator 1933–38; Circuit Judge 1938–46; Governor of S.C. 1947–51, serving as Chairman, Southern Governors' Conference 1950; practiced law in Aiken as partner of Thurmond Lybrand & Simons Law firm 1951–55; volunteered for World War II active duty, served 1942–46, European and Pacific Theatres, participated in Normandy invasion with 82nd Airborne Division; Maj.-Gen in Army Reserve; Past National Pres., Military Government Association, and Past National Pres., of Reserve Officers Assn.; member, Baptist Church, American Bar Assn., and numerous defense, veterans, civic, and fraternal organizations; delegate to Democratic National Conventions in 1932, 1936, 1948, 1952, 1956 and 1960 (Chairman S.C. delegation and national committeeman in 1948); States' Rights Democratic candidate for President in 1948, winning four states and 39 electoral votes; Delegate to Republican National Convention, 1968, 1972 & 1976; elected to U.S. Senate from South Carolina, 2 Nov. 1954, as write-in candidate for term ending 3 Jan. 1961; resigned 4 Apr. 1956, in keeping with a promise made to the people of S.C. during 1954 campaign; re-elected without opposition 1956; re-elected 1960; changed to Republican Party 1964. Re-elected 1966 and 1972. *Awards:* 18 decorations, medals, and awards, including Legion of Merit with Oak Leaf Cluster, Bronze Star with 'V,' Purple Heart, Army Commendation Ribbon, Presidential Unit Citation, French Croix de Guerre, Belgian Order of the Crown; Congressional Medal of Honor Socy's Patriot's Award, 1974. *Address:* Aiken, South Carolina, U.S.A.

**THYGESEN, Jacob Christoffer.** MA. Danish. *B.* 1901. *Educ.* Univ. of Copenhagen (MA. Law); Danish Foreign Office Service 1926–30. *M.* 1932, Rigmor. *S.* 1. *Career:* Dir. United Paper Mills Ltd.; Scandinavian Tobacco Ltd.; Synthetic Ltd. other industrial companies; Chmn. The National Bank of Denmark; Superfos Ltd.; The Royal Chartered General Fire Insurance Co. Ltd.; Otto Mønsted A/S; Man. Dir. Aktieselskabet De Danske Spritfabrikker (Danish Distilleries Ltd.). 1953–71. *Member:* Atomic Energy Comms. 1964–68; Academy, Technical Sciences. Vice-Pres. Business & Industry Adv. Cttee. to O.E.C.D.; Former Chmn. Fed. Danish Industries; Danish Nat. Cttee. International Chamber, Commerce. *Awards:* Cdr. 1st Class, Order of Dannebrog (Denmark); Knight Order, Oranien-Nassau (Netherlands); Grand Officier, Order of the Crown Belgium. *Address:* Amaliegade 22, 1256 Copenhagen K., Denmark.

**THYGESEN, Johannes Valdemar.** Danish. *B.* 1908. *Educ.* University of Copenhagen (LLM 1932). *M.* 1934, Helga Callø. *S.* Jesper and Lars. *Dau.* Charlotte. *Career:* Government Bank Supervisor 1932–39; with Ministry of Commerce 1939–54 (Head of dept. 1945–48; Under-Secy. 1948–54); Man. Dir. Privatbanken i Kjøbenhavn 1954–74; Chmn. Federation of Danish Banks 1970–74. Member, Board of Directors: The Housing Mortgage Fund of Denmark 1964–72; (Chmn. 1965–72), and The Ship Credit Fund of Denmark 1961–74; Vice-Pres. Féd. Bancaire de la Communaute Economique Européenne 1972–74; Chmn. Export Credit Board of Denmark since 1974; Mem. Bd. of Dirs. Berlingske Tidende 1974, Chmn. 1975. *Award:* Comdr. Icelandic Order of the Falcon; Comdr., Order of Dannebrog (Denmark); Comdr. Order of North Star (Sweden); Comdr. Italian Order of Merit. *Address: office* Privatbanken 4, Boersgade, Copenhagen K, Denmark.

**THYGESEN, Major-General Thyge Karl.** Danish Officer. *B.* 30 Aug. 1895. *Educ.* University of Copenhagen. *M.* 1934, Edith Ingeborg von Mehren. *S.* Erik Thyge. *Career:* Second Lieutenant 1917; First Lieutenant 1919; Captain 1932; member, General Staff 1928; Head of Dept., Ministry of War 1937–42; Chief of Regiment and member of Supreme Staff of the Danish Resistance Movement 1940–45; Lieutenant-Colonel 1945; Colonel 1946; Director-General, Ministry of War 1946–51; Major-General 1951; Commander in Chief of Western Command and Western Corps 1951–60; Cmdr., 1st Cl., Order of St. Olav (Norway); Commander 1st Class Order of the Sword (Sweden); Commander 1st Class and Silver Cross, Order of Dannebrog; Commander 2nd Class (Finland); Commander 1st Class, de la Légion d'Honneur (France); Commander Order of Merit, 1st Class (Italy); Distinguished Service Medal (Denmark); Medals of Honour from Royal Reserve Officers' Association and Royal Rifle Shooting Assocn. (both of Denmark); Danish Red Cross Medal. *Address:* Maltegaardsvej 27, 2820 Gentofte, Denmark.

**TICKELL, Crispin.** British Diplomat. *B.* 1930. *Educ.* Westminster School (King's Scholar); Christ Church, Oxford (Hinchcliffe & Hon. Scholar)—MA. *M.* (1) 1954, Chloe Marya Gunn (*diss.* 1976). *S.* 2. *Dau.* 1. (2) 1977, Penelope Thorne Thorne. *Career:* Coldstream Guards 1952–54; Foreign Office 1954–55; British Embassy, The Hague 1955–58, Mexico 1958–61; Foreign Office, Planning Staff 1961–64; British Embassy, Paris 1964–70; Private Sec. to successive Chancellors of the Duchy of Lancaster 1970–72; Foreign & Commonwealth Office 1972–75; Fellow in the Center for International Affairs, Harvard Univ. 1975–76; Chef de Cabinet to Pres. of the European Commission since 1977. *Decorations:* MVO (1958); Officer Order of Orange Nassau (1958). *Publications:* Climatic Change & World Affairs (1977); contributor to The Evacuees (1968); Life After Death (1976). *Clubs:* Brooks's. *Address:* 51 Blomfield Road, London W.9; and *office* 1 Avenue des Gaulois, 1040 Brussels, Belgium.

**TIFFANY, Kenneth Carl.** American. *B.* 1908. *Educ.* University of Detroit and Detroit College of Law; Certified Public Accountant. *M.* 1957, Wilda Catherine King. *Career:* With Price Waterhouse & Co. 1931–42; U.S. Army 1942–44; Exec. Office of the President of U.S.A., Office of Contract Settlement 1944–45; Price Waterhouse & Co. 1946–48; Vice-Pres. of Finance and Director, Burroughs Corp. 1948–60. Vice-President and Director, Massey-Ferguson Ltd., Toronto, Ont., Canada, 1960–68; Dir. several financial and Industrial Organizations; Advisor, several International Companies, Domestic Financial Institutions since 1969; Senior Partner Wilkin & Company; Member Int. Council Amer. Management Association. Author of several articles in business and professional publications. *Member:* Michigan

Assn. of C.P.A.s; Natl. Assn. of Accountants; Natl. Assn. of Credit Men.; Amer. Inst. of Accountants; Inst. of Chartered Accountants of Ontario; Financial Executives Inst. *Clubs:* Detroit, Bloomfield Hills Country. *Address:* 2080 W. Valley Road, Bloomfield Hills, Mich., U.S.A.

**TIIVOLA, Carl Mikael (Mika).** Finnish banker. *B.* 1922. *Educ.* University of Helsinki (qualified in law, political science and economics). *M.* 1975, Satu Vuoristo. Children by previous marriage: Irmeli, Anna-Maija, Ilkka. Admitted to bar, 1954; practiced law 1954–61; Union Bank of Finland Ltd. since 1961; Chief General Manager 1966–70; Chairman and President since 1970; Chairman Kymi Kymmene Oy, Ovako Oy, Oy Strömberg Ab; Vice-Chairman Industrial Bank of Finland Ltd., Oy Nokia Ab; Chairman, Joint Delegation of the Banking Institutions, Finnish Foreign Trade Association. Stock Exchange Committee; Member of Board Finnish Bankers Association. *Address:* Punjo, 02820 Espoo 82, Finland; and *office* Union Bank of Finland Ltd., Aleksanterinkatu 30, 00101 Helsinki 10, Finland.

**TIKANVARRA, Karl Torsten.** Finnish diplomat. *B.* 1909, *Educ.* University of Helsinki (Higher Law Degrees). *M.* 1944, Marita Linnea Sergelius. *S.* Kaarlo Axel Mikael. *Dau.* Laura Anneli Noëlle. *Career:* Attaché, Paris 1939; Second Secretary (same Legation) 1943; Secretary of Bureau, Ministry for foreign Affairs 1944; First Secretary, Buenos Aires 1947; Chief of Bureau, Min. for Foreign Affairs 1952; Asst. Chief of Department, Min. for Foreign Affairs 1954; Permanent Delegate to U.N.O., Geneva 1955, Chief of Department, Min. for Foreign Affairs 1959; Head of Commercial Representation of Finland in Federal Republic of Germany, Cologne 1961; Ambassador of Finland to Canada, 1964–67, to Peru, Bolivia, Columbia, Ecuador and Venezuela 1967–76. *Awards:* Commander, Order of the Lion 1st class (Finland); Grosse Verdienstkreuz mit Stern des Verdienstordens der Bundesrepublik Deutschland; Chevalier de la Légion d'Honneur; Order of the White Rose, 1st Class (Finland); Orden de Boyacá en el Grado de Gran Cruz de Colombia; Orden del Libertador Gran Cordón de Venezuela; Orden del Sol Del Peru Gran Cruz. *Address:* c/o Ministry of Foreign Affairs, Helsinki, Finland.

**TILGNER, Charles, Jr.** American. *B.* 1905. *Educ.* Princeton Univ. (BS 1925; CE 1926). *M.* 1930, Edna Doscher. *S.* Charles III. *Dau.* Margaret. *Career:* Stress Analyst, Loening Aero. Eng. Corp. 1928–29; Instructor, Pratt Institute 1929–31; joined Grumman 1931 (successively Chief of Structures, of Aerodynamics and Flight Test, and Chief Aeronautical Engineer); Dir. of Professional Activities, Grumman Aircraft Engineering Corp. 1955–71; Senior Associate R. Dixon Speas Associates since 1971. Member: U.S. Naval Technical Mission, Europe 1945; Aerodynamics Cttee., NACA 1944–45, 1954–57; Natl. Adv. Cttee. for Aeronautics, Sub-cttee. on Stability and Control 1947–54. Member and Past Secy., Cornell Aero Lab. Technical Adv. Cttee. 1946–56. Member Adv. Cncl., Dept. of Aero. Eng. and Mech. Sciences, Princeton Univ. 1957—, and of Alumni Cncl. of the Univ. 1960—. *Member:* Amer. Inst. Aeronautics P Astronautics (Fellow); Royal Aeronautical Socy. (Fellow); Canadian Aeronautics & Space Inst. (Fellow); British Interplanetary Socy. (Fellow); Amer. Assn. Advancement of Science (Fellow); Amer. Astronautical Socy. Fellow, Princeton Engineering Assn. *Clubs:* Princeton (N.Y.C.); Idle Hour Tennis. *Address: office* R. Dixon Speas Associates, Manhasset, New York, U.S.A.

**TILLI, Kalevi.** Finnish banker. *B.* 1918. *Educ.* MA and MSc (Econ.). *M.* 1944, Marita Inger Linnea af Björksten. *S.* Harri and Henri. *Career:* Member, Board of Management, Post Office Savings Bank (Finland) 1950–58. Member, Board of Management, Suomen Yhdyspankki Oy (Union Bank of Finland Ltd.) 1958—. Member, Board of Confederation of Commercial Employers 1963–75; Member. Bd. Dirs. Bank Employers Assn. 1973–75; Chmn. Finnish Assn. Non-Commissioned Officers in the Reserve, since 1973. Member, Finnish Conservative Party. *Awards:* Commander of the Order of the Lion (Finland) 1974. *Clubs:* Lions Helsinki-Munkkivuori (Charter Member). *Address:* Perustie 13 A 16, Helsinki 33; and *office* Aleksanterinkatu 30, Helsinki 10, Finland.

**TILLINGHAST, Charles Carpenter, Jr.** American. *B.* 1911. *Educ.* PhB Brown University 1932; JD Columbia Univ. 1935; LHD S. Dakota School of Mines and Technology 1959; LLD Franklin College 1963; University of Redlands 1964; Brown Univ. 1967; Drury College 1967; William Jewell Coll. 1973· *M.* 1935, Lisette Judd Micoleau. *S.* Charles Carpenter III. *Daus.* Elizabeth, Jane and Anne Shaw. *Career:* Admitted New York Bar 1935, Michigan Bar, 1943, Assoc. Hughes, Schurman & Dwight 1935–37; Dep. Asst. District Attorney, N.Y. County 1938–40; Assoc. Hughes, Richards, Hubbard & Ewing 1940–42; Partner, Hughes, Hubbard & Ewing and successor firm, Hughes, Hubbard, Blair & Reed 1942–57. Vice-President and Director, The Bendix Corp., New York and Director various subsidiaries and affiliates 1957–61. Chairman & chief executive officer, Trans-World Airlines, 1969—; Pres. & Dir., 1961–69. Director: Amstar Corporation 1964—, and Merck & Co. 1962—; Yonkers Savings Bank N.Y. 1956–62; Trustee. Brown Univ. 1954–61. Chancellor 1968—; Midwest Research Inst. 1963—; The Conference Board Inc. 1965—; Nominating Comm. 1974—; Luce Foundation 1974; People to People Program 1961–70; USO of N.Y. City 1965–69, Hon. Mem. 1969—; Seaboard Surety Co. 1956–66; Wilcox & Gibbs Sewing Machine Co. 1953–57; Mutual Life Insurance Co. of New York 1966—; Cttee. for Economic Development 1967—; Dir. Air Transport Assn. 1961–72; Columbia Law Review Assn. 1967—; Member IATA Exec. Cttee. 1969—; U.S. Dept. of Commerce NIPCC 1970–73; Chmn.: Secy's. Adv. Cttee. on International Business Problems 1968—; Airlines and Aircraft Subcouncil 1970–73; Canteen Corp. Chmn. Exec. Cttee. 1973—; Hilton Int'l. 1967; Economic Club of New York 1972, Chmn. 1974; Int'l. Exec. Service Corps. 1972—; Travel Program for Foreign Diplomats 1972–73; Board of Visitors, School of Law, Columbia Univ. 1962; Amer. Bar Assn.; Association of the Bar of New York; Former Gov. Lawrence Hospital Bronxville; Republican. *Clubs:* Blink Brook; The Economic Club of New York; Hope; Brown University (N.Y.); Consilium; Conquistadoves del Cielo; The Presidents; Sakonnet Golf; Siwanoy Country; Sky. *Address:* 56 Oakledge Road, Bronxville, N.Y. 10708; and *office* 605 Third Avenue, 42nd Floor, New York, N.Y. 10016, U.S.A.

**TILSTON, Frederick A.,** VC. Canadian. *B.* 1906. *Educ.* Ontario Coll. of Pharmacy, and Univ. of Toronto (PhmB 1929). *M.* 1946, Elizabeth Ellen Adamson. *S.* Michael Anthony. *Career:* With Sterling Drug Ltd.: Salesman 1930–36; Sales Mngr. 1937–40; Vice-Pres. Sales 1946–57. Chairman of the Board & Chief executive officer, Sterling Drug Ltd. (Aurora, Ont.) 1957–71. Hon. Col., Essex & Kent Scottish R.C. and C. (Windsor, Ont.) 1963. Served in Canadian Army (Victoria Cross) 1941–45. Mem.: Ont. Coll. of Pharmacy; Canadian Socy. of Industrial Pharmacists; Canadian Foundtn. for Advancement of Pharmacy. *Awards:* Commander, Order of Hosp. of St. John of Jerusalem 1976; LLD (h.c.) Univ. of Windsor 1977. *Clubs:* The Windsor, The Press, Essex County Golf (all of Windsor), Royal Canadian Military Inst. (Toronto); Utd. Services (Montreal); Summit Golf & Country (Oak Ridge, Ont.). *Address:* Wellington Street West, Box 35, Aurora, Ont.

**TIMBERG, Sigmund.** American lawyer. *B.* 1911. *Educ.* Columbia College (AB 1930), Columbia Univ. (MA 1930) and Columbia Univ. Law School (LLB 1933). *M.* 1940, Eleanor Ernst. *S.* Thomas Arnold, Bernard Mahler and Richard Ernst. *Dau.* Rosamund. *Career:* Senior Attorney, Office of Solicitor, Dept. of Agriculture 1933–38, and the Securities & Exchange Commission 1938–42; Chief, Industrial Organization Div., Board of Economic Warfare & Foreign Economic Administration 1942–44; Special Assistant to the Attorney-General and Chief, Judgments and Judgment Enforcement Section, Anti-trust Division 1944–52; Secretary, United Nations *ad hoc* Committee on Restrictive Business Practices 1952–54; Special Counsel, Senate Military Affairs Sub-committee on Surplus Property Legislation 1944; member, Mission for Economic Affairs, American Embassy, London 1945; Delegate: Anglo-American Telecommunications Conference, Bermuda 1945, and Universal Copyright Convention, Geneva 1952; Faculty George town Univ. Law School 1951–53; Parker School, Foreign and Comparative Law Columbia Univ. since 1967. *Publications:* has written extensively in the fields of anti-trust and international law, and has also published articles relating to the law of industrial property, corporation law and administrative law. *Member:* American, D.C., New York State, Federal and International Bar Associations; International Law Assn.; Amer. Foreign Law Assn.; Assn. of the Bar of the City of New York; Washington Foreign Law Socy.; Copyright Socy. of America; Amer. Law Institute. *Clubs:* Cosmos, Philosophy (Washington); Torch; National Lawyers; The Scribes. *Address:* 3519 Porter Street, N.W., Washington, D.C. 20016 and *office* 1700 K Street, N.W., Washington, D.C. 20006, U.S.A.

**TIMM, Prof. Bernhard,** Dr phil nat. German. *B.* 1909. *Educ.* Reform High School, Altona; and University of Heidelberg (astronomy, physics, maths and chemistry: took degree 1934). *Career:* Assistant in private laboratory of Prof. Dr. Carl Bosch, Heidelberg 1934–36; joined BASF 1936 (Director 1950, Vice-Chairman of Board 1952; Chairman 1965–74). Chairman of the Supervisory Board, BASF Aktiengesellschaft, Ludwigshafen-am-Rhein. Deputy-Chairman Mannheimer Versicherungsgesellschaft, Mannheim (insurance); Deutsche Shell AG, Hamburg; Member of the Boards of Allgemeine Elektricitäts-Gesellschaft AEG Telefunken, Berlin-Frankfurt (electrical); Continental Gummi-Werke AG, Hannover (tyres); Preussag AG, Hannover; Hugo Stinnes AG, Mulheim; Rhenus AG, Mannheim. Chairman: Association for Encouragement of Cancer Research in Germany Heidelberg. Member of the Council, Association of the Chemical Industry. Frankfurt/Main. Board of Trustees, 'Deutsche Sporthilfe', Frankfurt; Vorstandsrat des Deutschen Museums, Munich. Hon. Professor in University of Heidelberg, 1966; Dr-Ing E.h Univ. Stuttgart 1969; Dr rer nat h.c. Univ. Mainz 1969; Senator E.h Univ. Heidelberg 1969; Grosses Bundesverdienstkreuz mit Stern 1969; Castner-Medaille Socy. Chemical Industry, London 1970; Chmn. Supervisory Board BASF since 1974. *Address:* 69 Heidelberg, Am Rosenbusch 1, Germany; and *office* c/o BASF Aktiengesellschaft, Ludwigshafen-am-Rheim, Germany.

**TIMPSON, Robert Clermont Livingston.** American merchant banker. *B.* 1908. *Educ.* Eton College (England) and Harvard University (AB *magna cum laude* 1931). *M.* (1) 1937, Elizabeth Johnson Hutton. *S.* Lawrence Livingston and Robert Clermont Livingston. *Dau.* Sarah Livingston; (2) 1954, Louise Morris Clews; (3) 1966, Hilles Morris. *Career:* With White Weld & Co., New York City 1931–38; W. E. Hutton & Co., New York City 1938–53 (Partner 1941–53); Managing Partner, Robert Timpson & Co. 1954–62; Hill, Samuel (S.A.) Ltd., Durban (Manager). 1963–70; Served with Air Corps, U.S. Army 1942–45; Lieut. to Major 1943; radar officer First Fighter Command and First Air Force; Army representative, special mission of the Joint Chiefs of Staff to Southwest Pacific Theatre; two battle stars. *Member:* Colonial Lords of Manors Society. *Clubs:* Brook (N.Y.C.); Fly, Hasty Pudding, Phi Beta Kappa (Harvard), Eton Vikings (London); Durban (Durban). *Address:* 12 Insala Rd., Kloof, Natal, 3600 South Africa and Millstone Brook Road, Southampton. N.Y. 11968. U.S.A.

**TINBERGEN, Dr. Jan.** Dutch. Professor Emeritus, Erasmus Univ., Rotterdam. *B.* 1903. *Educ.* University of Leyden (DSc). *M.* 1929, Tine Johanna de Wit. *Daus.* 3. *Career:* Dir. Central Planning Bureau 1945–55. Dr *honoris causa* of 15 European universities.; Nobel prize for Econ. 1969. Knight of the Netherlands Lion, Commander, Order of Orange Nassau. *Member:* Econometric Society. Member Labour Party. *Publications:* Shaping the World Economy, (1962); Lessons from the Past, (1963); and several others on planning. *Address:* Haviklaan 31, The Hague, Netherlands.

**TINDEMANS, Leo.** Belgian politician. *B.* 1922. *Educ.* State Univ. of Ghent; Catholic Univ. of Louvain. *M.* 1960, Rosa Naesens. *S.* 2. *Daus.* 2. *Career:* Mem., Chamber of Deputies since 1961; Mayor of Edegem since 1965; Minister of Community Affairs 1968–71, of Agriculture & Middle Class Affairs 1972–73; Dep. Prime Minister & Minister for the Budget & Institutional Problems 1973–74; Prime Minister since 1974; Pres., European People's Party; Vice-Pres., European Union of Christian Democrats; Visiting Prof. in the Faculty of Social Sciences, Catholic Univ. of Louvain. *Awards:* Charlemagne Prize 1976; Hon. DLitt, City Univ. 1976. *Address:* Jan Verbertlei 24, B-2520 Edegem, Belgium; and *office* Prime Minister's Office, Wetstraat 16, B-1000 Brussels, Belgium.

**TINÉ, Jacques Wilfrid Jean Francis.** French Diplomat. *B.* 1914. *Educ.* Lycée d'Alger; Faculté de Droit, Paris—Licence en Droit, Diplome Sciences Politiques. *M.* 1948, Héléna Terry. *S.* 1. *Dau.* 1. *Career:* entered Diplomatic Service 1938; Counsellor, French Embassy, Copenhagen 1949–50, UN 1950–55, London 1955–61; Minister Plenipotentiary, Rabat, Morocco 1961; Dep. Perm. Rep. to UN 1963–67; Amb. to Portugal 1969–73; Amb. & Perm. Rep. to North Atlantic Council since 1975. *Decorations:* Officier, Légion d'Honneur; Croix de Guerre; Commandeur de l'Ordre du Merite; Commandeur des Arts et Lettres. *Clubs:* Nouveau Cercle, Paris. *Address:* 120 Rue du Bac, Paris, France; and *office* French Delegation, Boulevard Léopold III, Brussels, Belgium.

**TISHLER, Max.** American organic and biochemical chemist. Professor Chemistry Wesleyan Univ., Connecticut. *B.* 1906. *Educ.* Tufts Univ. (BS); Harvard Univ. (MA; PhD); Hon. DSc: Tufts Univ. 1956, Bucknell Univ. 1962; Phila. Coll. of Pharmacy, 1966; Rider College 1970. Univ. of Strathclyde, 1969; Fairfield Univ. and Upsala Coll. 1972; Hon. DEng, Stevens Institute of Technology, 1966. Merck & Co. Inc., Board of Dirs. Scientific Award, resulting in establishing Max Tishler Visit. Lectureship, Harvard Univ. and Scholarship Tufts Univ.; Phi Beta Kappa; Sigma Xi. *M.* 1934, Elizabeth M. Verveer. *S.* Peter V. and Carl L. *Career:* Austin. Teaching Fellow, Harvard 1930–34; Research Assoc., Harvard 1934–36; Instr. in Chem., Harvard 1936–37; Research Chem., Merck & Co. Inc. 1937–41; and successively in the same firm: Section Head (1941–44), Director Developmental Research (1944–53), Director of Process Research and Development 1953, and Vice-Pres. Scientific Activities Chemical Div. 1954. Vice-Pres. and Exec. Dir., Merck, Sharp & Dohme Research Laboratories 1956–57. President, Merck Sharp & Dohme Research Laboratories, Merck & Co. Inc. U.S.A., 1957–70. Member Board of Directors, Merck & Co. Inc. 1962–70. *Member:* Socy. Chem. Industry, Hon. Vice-Pres., 1968 (Chmn. Amer. Section 1966–67); Industrial Research Inst. (recipient 1961 Medal); Soc. Chem. Industry American Section Medalist 1963; Rennbohn Lecturer, Univ. Wisconsin 1963; Julius W. Sturmer Lecture Award, Philadelphia College of Pharmacy 1964; Swedish Royal Academy of Engineering Science Lecture Award 1964; Kauffman Mem. Lecturer, Ohio State Univ. 1967; Chemical Pioneer Award, American Institute of chemists 1968; Priestley Medalist of Amer. Soc. Microbiol. 1974; Eli Whitney Award of Conn. Patent Law Assn. 1974; Swiss Chemical Society; National Defense Reserve Cttee.; Assn. of Harvard Chemists (Pres. 1946); Natl. Academy of Sciences; American Academy of Arts & Sciences; New York Academy of Science (Fellow); Hon. Member, Amer. Pharmaceutical Assn., Chemist Club of N.Y.C., Société Chimique de France; Fellow, Acad. of Pharmaceutical Sciences; Mem. Connecticut Acad. of Science & Engineering; American Chemical Society (Chairman, Organic Div. 1951); Pres. 1972; American Association for the Advancement of Science; American Institute of Chemists (Councillor; Honor Scroll; Gold Medal 1977; Life Fellow, 1977); The Chemical Society of London (Eng.); Royal Society of Medicine Foundation (Dir.). Board of Trustees. Tufts Univ.; Chmn. Visiting Cttee. Chemistry Admin. Board, Tufts New England Medical Center 1963—; Visiting Cttee. (Chemistry and School of Public Health) Harvard Univ. Associated Trustee, Univ. of Pennsylvania 1961–65. Member, Board of Trustees, Union College, N.J. Member, Board of Governors. Weizmann Institute, Israel. Member, Board of Visitors, Fac. Health Sciences, State Univ. of New York, Buffalo; Pres. Amer. Chem. Socy. 1971; Councillor Amer. Chem. Inst. 1955–58. *Publications:* Books: Chemistry of Organic Compounds (with J. B. Conant, 1937); Streptomycin (with S. A. Waksman, 1949); scientific articles (about 120) in scientific journals, covering amino acids, vitamins alkaloids, steroids, hormones, organic reaction mechanism, antibiotics, drugs, etc.; Editor-in-Chief, Organic Syntheses, vol. 39. *Address:* 6 Red Orange Road, Middletown, Conn., 06457, U.S.A.

**TITO, President (Josip Broz).** Marshal of Yugoslavia. Prime Minister and Minister of National Defence since 1945; President of Yugoslavia since 1953, Life President since 1974; Secretary General of the League of Communists of Yugoslavia; Supreme Commander of the Yugoslav Army. *B.* 1892. *M.* Jovanka Budisavljević, 1952. Served in Austro-Hungarian Army 1913–15; war prisoner, Russia 1915–17; fought with International Red Guard; returned to Yugoslavia 1920, worked as machinist and mechanic, and became Croatian Labour leader working with Metal Workers' Union; imprisoned in 1928 for five years for conspiracy after taking part in illegal communist activities; left the country on release and recruited Yugoslavs for the InternationalBrigades in Spanish Civil War. Became member of Central Committee, 1934; Secretary-General of the Yugoslav Communist Party, 1937; returned to Yugoslavia before War of 1939–45; during Second World War, at the head of Yugoslav Communist Party led the general people's uprising and revolution in occupied Yugoslavia; Supreme Commander of the Yugoslav National Liberation Army. Elected Marshal of Yugoslavia and President of the National Liberation Committee, 1943: President of the Yugoslav Government 1945; President of the Republic 1953 (re-elected 1954, 1958 and 1963). *Awards:* Grand Star of Yugoslavia; Order of Liberty; National Hero; Hero of Socialist Work; National Liberation; War Flag; Great Cordon of Yugoslav Flag; Partisan Star with Golden Wreath; Merit for the People with Golden Star; Fraternity and Unity with Golden Wreath; Outstanding Courage; Order of the October Revolution (USSR). *Publications:* sixteen volumes of articles, speeches and other documents covering the period 1941–61. *Address:* Uzička 15, Belgrade, Yugoslavia.

**TITTERTON, Sir Ernest William,** Kt Bach CMG, FAA, FRSA. British. *B.* 1916. *Educ.* BSc. MSc. PhD. Diploma in Education. *M.* 1942, Peggy Eileen Johnson. *S.* Andrew Brian. *Daus.* Elizabeth Jennifer and Ashley Clare. *Career:* Research Officer, Admiralty, London 1939–43, member, British Mission to U.S.A. on Atomic Bomb Development 1943–47; Senior Member, Timing Group, First Atomic Bomb Test 1945; Adviser on Instrumentation, Bikini Weapon Tests 1946; Head, Electronics Div., Los Alamos Laboratory 1946–47; Group Leader, i/c Research Team AERE, Harwell 1947–50; Prof. of Nuclear Physics 1950—, Dean of the Research School of Physical Sciences 1966–68, Director, Research School of Physical Sciences, 1968–73; Australian National University, the Research School of Physical Sciences; Dep. Chmn. Aust. Atomic Weapons Safety Cttee. 1954–56; Chairman, Australian Atomic Weapons Test Safety Committee 1957–73. Member: Defence Research & Development Policy Committee 1958–74, and National Radiation Adv. Cttee. 1957–73. Member Scientific Adv. Cttee. to Australian Atomic Energy Commission 1955–64; Advisory Cttee. of Strategic and Defence Studies Centre, A.N.U. since 1967. *Publications:* some 190 papers mainly in nuclear physics, electronics and atomic anergy, in technical journals; book: Facing the Atomic Future (Macmillan, London and N.Y.; and Cheshire & Co., Melbourne) 1956. Fellow, Royal Socy. of Arts & Sciences of London, 1952; Fellow, Australian Acad. of Science (Vice-Pres. 1964–67); Fellow, Australian Inst. of Nuclear Science and Engineering Vice-Pres. 1965–72, Pres. 1973–75. Fellow, American Physical Society. *Address:* 8 Somers Crescent, Forrest, Canberra, A.C.T.; and *office* Research School of Physical Sciences, Australian National University, Canberra, A.C.T., Australia.

**TOCAO, Sergio F.** Lawyer-Parliamentarian. *B.* 1911. *Educ.* AB; LL.B; (PhD hon). *M.* Angeles D. Labata. *Career:* Presidential co-ordinator for Presidents Magsaysay and Garcia; Head presidential task force (Pecafe Malacanang) graft and corruption and distribution of land; Student leader, Debater, Orator; Delegate Constitutional Convention 1971; Pres. Mindanao-Sulu-Palaway Del. Assn.; Rep. Sponsorship Council Citizenship Cttee.; Vice-Chmn. Sub-Council Internal and External Relations; Vice-Pres. Mindanao, Philippine Constitution Assn., Philconsa since 1973. *Awards:* Nations Press, Radio, TV Merit Plaque; Rizal Press Club of Honor; Ginatilan Professional League, of Distinction; Writers Guild and Greater Manila Radio TV Distinction; Univ. of the Visayas Trophy; Outstanding Visayan in Public Service; Labor Inst. Leadership; Mass Media Research Council, most Valuable Constitutional Delegate; N.C. Judicial Reports Bd. Dirs. plaque of Distinction; Nat. Reporters Assn. Outstanding Citizen. *Address: office* 3rd Floor, Madrigal Bldg., Escolta, Manila, Philippines.

**TODA y TOLEDO, Benigno.** Filipino. *B.* 1901. *Educ.* College of St. Juan de Letran (AB 1916) and Univ. of Santo Tomas (studies medicine 1921–23). *M.* 1924, Elisa Pintado. *S.* 3. *Daus.* 2. *Career:* Sugar planter and businessman since 1923. Director: Philippine Aiir Lines (PAL), Benison Equipment Corporation, Fortuna Offshore Corporation; Chairman Sales Committee, Association of Sugar Planters, Pampanga Sugar Mills 1936–41; President International Stock Exchange, Manila 1938–39. Philippine Ambassador to the Holy See, Apr. 1962–June 1966. First Filipino Minister to Sovereign Military Order of Malta in Rome 1965–66. Philippine Association of the Pontifical Decorees. Chairman, Cibeles Insurance Corp. Chairman Official and Special Missions: Opening of Vatican Ecumenical Council 1962; Funeral Ceremonies of Pope John XXIII 1963; Coronation of Pope Paul VI 1963; Closing Ceremonies of Ecumenical Council 1965. Outstanding Alumnus of San Juan de Letran College 1963. Knight of Grand Cross of Magistral Grade with ribbon of the Sovereign Military Order of Malta. Recipient of Grand Cross of the Orders of Knights of Pius IX (Ist. Cl.); Pro Mérito Melitensi (Military Order of Malta); Civil Merit (Spain); Faithful Service (Knights of Columbus); Member, Knights of Columbus (4th degree). *Clubs:* Hunters' (Vice-President), Casino Español, Army & Navy (all of Manila); Baguio Country (Baguio). *Address:* 69, Real Street, Urdaneta Village, Makati, Rizal, Philippines.

**TODD, Hon. (Reginald Stephen) Garfield.** Managing Director, Hokonui Ranching Co. (Pvt.) Ltd. *B.* New Zealand 1908. *Educ.* Glenleith Theological Coll., Univ. of Otago and Univ. of Witwatersrand; DD (Hon.), Butler Univ., and LLD (Hon.) Milligan Coll. (U.S.). *M.* 1932, Jean Grace Wilson. *Daus.* Alycen, Judith and Cynthia. *Career:* Ordained to Ministry 1931; appointed Superintendent, Dadaya Mission, S. Rhodesia 1934. Elected to Parliament of S. Rhodesia 1946 (but remained as Hon. Superintendent & Principal of Dadaya Mission until 1953); Prime Minister of S. Rhodesia 1953–58; MP for Shabani 1946–58. First Vice-Pres., World Convention of Churches of Christ 1955–60. At Declaration of Independence, Nov. 1965, was arrested & detained on Hokonui Ranch for 12 months. At time of Smith–Home negotiations was arrested, imprisoned without charge or trial for 5 weeks & then detained at Hokonui Ranch from Jan. 1972–June 1976. Mem. Exec. Cttee., United Coll. of Education 1965—; Chmn. Dadaya Governing Bd. Recipient of Citation from World Convention of Churches of Christ, 1960, for Political & Christian leadership. *Address:* Hokonui Ranch, Dadaya, Rhodesia.

**TOGNI, Giuseppe,** Dr sc pol. Italian politician. *B.* 5 Dec. 1903. *M.* 1930. Bianca Corbin. *S.* Ettore, Paolo, Pietro. *Dau.* Tatiana. *Career:* Member of the C.N.L. (Rome) 1943–44; Member, Consulta Nazionale 1945; member (Christian Democrat), Constituent Assembly 1946–48; Under-Secretary, Ministry of Labour 1947; Minister for Economic Coordination 1948; Minister of Industry and Commerce 1950–51; member (C.D.), Chamber of Deputies Apr. 1948—, re-elected 1953, '58, '63; member (C.D.) Senate 1968, re-elected 1972; Minister of Transport 1953; of State Participation 1957; of Public Works 1957–60 of Industry & Commerce 1963; Post and Telecommunication 1973–74. Professor, Univ. of Rome. *Awards:* Grand Cdr., Legion of Honour; Grand Cross (with Stars) for Merit (Fed. Germany); Grand Cross, Equestrian Order of Holy Sepulchre of Jerusalem; Grand Cross of St. Sylvester (Holy See); Magisterial Grand Cross of Honour and Devotion, Sovereign Military Order of Malta; Grand Cross: St. Gregorio Magno; del Sol (Peru); of the Argentine Republic; Iran; Greece; San Marino. President: Confederazione Italiana Dirienti di Azienda 1945–70, and Confederation Internationale des Cadres 1951–70; Instituto Superiore per la Direzione Aziendale; Associazione Italiana Relazioni Pubbliche; Istituto Nazionale Commercio Estero 1949. *Address:* Via G. Paisiello, No. 53, Rome, Italy.

**TOH CHIN CHYE, Dr.** Singapore Physiologist and Politician. *B.* Perak, 1921. *Educ.* Raffles College, Singapore; Univ. of London (BSc); Nat. Institute of Medical Research, London (PhD). *Career:* Chairman, People's Action Party 1954—; Reader in Physiology, University of Singapore 1958–64; Mem., Singapore Parliament 1959—; Deputy Prime Minister of Singapore 1959–68; Minister for Science and Technology 1968–75; Chmn. Bd. Governors, Regional Institute of Higher Education and Development 1970–74; Founder Member, People's Action Party; Member Parl., Singapore 1959–74. Research Associate in Physiology in Univ. of Singapore. Chairman, Bd. of Governors, Singapore Polytechnic 1959–75; Mem. Admin. Bd. Assoc. of S.E. Asian Insts. of Higher Learning 1968–75; Vice-Chancellor, Univ. of Singapore 1968–75; Minister for Health since 1975. *Awards:* Hon. D.Litt., Univ. of Singapore 1976. *Address:* The Parliament, Singapore.

**TOIVANEN, Toivo Adrian.** Finnish. *B.* 1913. *Educ.* Abo Academy (Dipl Eng). *M.* 1940, Mirjam Saikkonen. *S.* Markku, Mauri and Esko. *Dau.* Eva. *Career:* Smelter Superintendent 1940; General Superintendent 1957. Consultant Engineer in Japan 1956, U.S.A. 1957, and South Africa 1963. Manager, Cooper and Nickel Smelter and Nickel Refinery, Harjavalta, Finland 1960—. *Member:* American Inst. of Mining & Metallurgical Engineers; Canadian Inst. of Mining & Metallurgical Engineers; Finnish Mining Institute. *Club:* Finnish. *Address:* Harjavalta, Finland.

**TOLBERT, William R., Jr.** President of Liberia. *B.* 1913. *Educ.* Univ. of Liberia. BA (*cum laude* 1934); DCL (1952). *M.* 1936, Victoria David. *S.* 2. *Daus.* 5. *Career:* Clerk in Bureau of Supplies, Govt. Treasury, and later Disbursing Officer 1935–43; Elected to House of Representatives (Montserrado County) 1943–51; Elected Vice-President 1951–71; President of the Republic of Liberia since 1971. Has represented his country in many parts of the world since 1949 and as President of Liberian Baptist Mission since 1965 and as Baptist World Alliance President has visited many areas 1968–71. *Honours.* DD (Hon. Causa); Dr. of Sacred Literature (Switz.); Emeritus mem. Humanist Inst. (France). *Decorations:* Grand Band of Humane Order of African Redemption and of the Order of Star of Africa, Grand Cordon of Most Venerable Order of Knighthood of Pioneers (Liberia); Commander with Plaque and Grand Cross of L'Ordre de L'Etoile, Knight

Cmmdr. of Legion of Honour (France); Grand Cordon of the National Order of the Cedar; Grand Cordon of Order of Merit of Lebanon (Lebanon); National Onayyad Decoration with star (Syria); Grand Croix (Silver Plaque) of Order Honour and Merit (Haiti); Grand Band of the Order of St. Gregory Magnus; Grand Cross (1st Class) The Equestrian Cavalier Order of Pope Pius X (Holy See); Hon. KCMG (England); Hon. Mem. Grand Cross of Italy; Cavaliere di crau croce Orderedi Merit (Italy); Grand Cross of Order of Merit (FDR); Hon. Life Member (Fellow) American International Acad.; Dist. Service Award, Nat. Med. Assn. (U.S.A.); Grand Cross of Order of Orange Nassau (Neth.) Grand Cross of Order of Polar Star (Sweden); Great Cordon of Yugoslav Flag (Yugoslavia) Grand Cordon of National Order of Tunisia: Grand Cordon of Order National of Zaire and decorations from the Dominican Republic, Cameroon, Senegal, Togo, Malagasy Republic, Ivory Coast, Upper Volta, Guinea, United Arab Republic and Haiti. *Address:* The Executive Mansion, Monrovia, Liberia, West Africa.

**TOMKINS. Sir Edward.** GCMG. CVO. *B.* 1915. *Educ.* Ampleforth Coll., Trinity Coll. Cambridge. *M.* 1955, Gillian Benson. *S.* 1. *Daus.* 2. *Career:* H.M. Embassy Moscow 1944–46; For. Office 1946–51; H.M. Embassy Washington 1951–54; H.M. Embassy Paris 1954–59; For. Office 1959–63; Min. H.M. Embassy Bonn, 1963–67; Min. H.M. Embassy Washington; Ambassador to Netherlands 1970–72; Ambassador to France 1972–75. Member, Buckinghamshire County Council 1977. Chmn., The Friends of University College at Buckingham. *Address:* Winslow Hall, Winslow, Bucks and *office* 17 Thurloe Place Mews, London S.W.7.

**TOMKINS, The Rt. Rev. Oliver Stratford.** British. *B.* 1908. *Educ.* Trent Coll.; Christ's Coll.; Cambridge BA, MA; Westcott House Cambridge; DD honoris causa, Edinburgh; Hon. LLD Bristol 1975. *M.* 1939, Ursula Mary Dunn. *S.* Stephen Portal. *Daus:* Monica Mary, Catherine Ruth and Deborah Clare. *Career:* Asst. Gen. Secy. Student Christian Movement of Gt. Britain and Ireland 1935–40; Vicar Holy Trinity Church Millhouse Sheffield 1940–45; Asst. Gen. Secy. World Council of Churches 1945–48; Assoc. Gen. Secy. 1948–52; Secy. Commission Faith and Order, W.C.C. 1945–52; Warden, Theological Coll. Lincoln and Canon Lincoln Cathedral 1953–59; Bishop of Bristol 1959–75. Central Cttee. World Council of Churches 1968–75. *Publications:* The Wholeness of the Church (1949); The Church in the Purpose of God (1951); Life of Edward Woods, Bishop of Lichfield (1957); A Time for Unity (1964); Guarded by Faith (1971). *Address:* 14 St. George's Square, Worcester.

**TOMLINSON, John Edward,** MP. British Politician. *B.* 1939. *Educ.* Westminster City Sch.; Co-operative Coll.; Brunel Univ. *M.* 1963, Marianne Sommar. *S.* 3. *Career:* Sec., Sheffield Co-operative Party 1962–68; Head of Research Dept., Amalgamated Union of Engineering Workers 1968–70; Lecturer in Industrial Relations 1970–74; MP (Lab.) for Meriden since 1974; PPS to the Prime Minister 1975–76; Parly. Under-Sec. of State, FCO since 1976 & concurrently Parly. Sec., Ministry of Overseas Development since 1977. *Member:* British Inst. of Management. *Address:* House of Commons, London SW1A 0AA.

**TONČIĆ-SORINJ, Lujo.** Austrian. *B.* 1915. *Educ.* Studies of Law and Philosophy at Vienna and Agram (graduated with degree of LLD); studies of law and political science at Institute d'Etudes Politiques, Paris. *M.* 1956, Renate Trenker. *S.* 1. *Daus.* 4. *Career:* University Assistant, Austrian Research Institute for Economics and Politics, Salzburg 1946–49; Editor and journalist Berichte und Informationen 1946–49; elected Member People's Party in Parliament 1949–66 (Chairman, Legal Cttee. 1953–56, and of Foreign Relations Cttee. 1956–59; Spokesman on Foreign Affairs of the Party 1959–66); Parliamentary Observer at Consultative Assembly of Council of Europe 1952–66 (Vice-Pres. of the Assembly 1961 and 1962, and of the Political Cttee. of the Council). Austrian Federal Minister of Foreign Affairs, Apr. 1966–68. Secretary General, Council of Europe, 1969–74. *Publications:* periodical Blick nach dem Osten: Politische Sonderformen im Südosten; Der rechtliche Status Österreichs; and about 300 treatises on political and scientific questions. Certificate of Academy for International Law, The Hague. Grosses Goldenes Enrenzeichen am Bande (Austria) GCMG (UK) and other decorations. *Address:* Schloss Fürberg, Pausingerstrasse 11, Salzburg, Austria.

**TONKIN, Hon. John Trezise,** A.C. Retired Western Australian Politician. *B.* 1902. *Educ.* Eastern Goldfields High School and Teachers Training College Claremont. *M.* (1) 1929–69 Rosalie Cleghorn; (2) 1971 (Mrs.) Joan West. *S.* 1. *Dau.* 2. *Career:* School Teacher and 1st Asst. at North Fremantle State School until 1933: Member of Parliament 1933–77; Leader of Opposition 1967–71, 1974–76; Premier and Treasurer 1971–74; Fellow Australian Institute of Accountants. *Clubs:* East Fremantle Football, Rhein Donau. *Address:* 174 Preston Point Road, East Fremantle, Western Australia.

**TOOLE, George Henry.** American Lawyer and Foreign Service Lawyer. *B.* 1903. *Educ.* Suffolk Univ. (LLB 1929) Calvin Coolidge Law School (LLM 1942) Benjamin Franklin Univ. (BCS 1945); BS in transportation, Southeastern Univ. 1957 (MS 1958); Suffolk Univ. Law School, (JD 1969); BSc (Econ), Univ. of London, 1970. *M.* 1940 Kathleen Virginia Gibbons. *Career:* Admitted to practice of law, Supreme Judicial Court of Massachusetts (1929), Supreme Court of U.S. (1933), and U.S. Court of Appeals for D.C. (1939); High Court for American Samoa 1971. Legal Adviser, Spanish Consulate, Boston 1929–39; Consul for Belgium and Acting Consul of Luxembourg, Boston 1932–43; Shipping Co-ordinator, U.S. Naval Air Station, Quonset Point (R.I.) 1941–42; Transportation Consultant, War Department 1943–45; engaged in ocean shipping business, N.Y.C. 1946–50; Transportation Specialist, Dept. of the Army 1950–51; Member, Export Control Investigation Staff, Office of International Trade, Washington 1951–53; Traffic Control Supervisor (with HQ at La Rochelle, France), U.S. Army, Europe 1953–54; Chief, Foreign Shipping Branch, General Services Admin. 1954–56. Examiner, U.S. Maritime Administration 1956–62; Professor of Transportation, Southeastern Univ. 1957–63; Assistant Dean, School of Transportation, Southeastern Univ. 1958–63; Lecturer in International Transportation, School of Foreign Service, Georgetown Univ. 1960–64; Chief, Division of Economic Analysis, Federal Maritime Commission, U.S.; Professor, Economics Benjamin Franklin Univ. 1971–72. Member, Inter-agency Cttee. on Foreign Trade Statistics, Office of the President, 1963–72. Prof. Social Sciences Mass. Maritime Academy 1972–74; Consul of Tunisia at Boston since 1975. *Member:* American Society of International Law, Institute of Transport (London), Ocean Shipping Management Institute Planning Cttee., American University 1961–67. Fellow: Royal Economic Society; American Economic Assn.; Economic History Assn.; Economic History Socy.; National Aviation; Royal Geographical and American Geographical Societies. *Address:* 60 Old Colony Drive, Weymouth, Massachusetts 02188, U.S.A.

**TOOLE, John L.** Canadian. *B.* 1913. *Educ.* Univ. of Toronto (BA Comm. and Finance); Chartered Accountant. *M.* 1943, Elaine Patricia Callen. *Career:* Auditor with Sholto Scott, C.A. 1938–40; Assistant to Group Accountant, Canadian Industries Ltd. 1940–42; Assistant Controller and later Control Manager, Dominion Rubber Co. Ltd. 1942–49; Asst. Controller, Ford Motor Co. of Canada 1949–54; and Asst. Comptroller Canadian National Railways 1954–57, Comptroller, 1957–59; Vice-President, Accounting & Finance, 1959–68. Chairman, CN Investment Division 1968 and Vice-Pres. C.N.R. (Ret'd. 1977). Director: Toronto College Street Centre Ltd.; Seachel Accommodations Ltd.; The Mortgage Insurance Co. of Canada; Markborough Properties Ltd.; MICC Investments Ltd.; Morguard Mortgage Investment Co. of Canada; Canadian Commercial & Industrial Bank. *Member:* Institute Chartered Accountants of Ontario, and of Quebec; Treasury Division of Assn. of American Railroads. *Clubs:* (Montreal) Canadian Railway; Summerlea Golf & Country (Past Pres.); Saint James's Club. *Address: office* Place Bonaventure, Montreal, Quebec, H5A IA8, Canada.

**TOOLEY, James Francis.** Canadian. *B.* 1915. *Educ.* chartered accountant. *M.* 1939, Dorothy Bernice Yates. *S.* James A., George. *Dau.* Heather Jane Kittredge. *Career:* Vice-Pres. and Comptroller, Canadair Ltd., 1947–57; Pres., C.A.E. Industries Ltd., 1957–67. Chairman, Nordair Ltd. Director: Mitchell Holland Ltd.; Marine Transport Ltd.; Selkirk Navigation Ltd. *Clubs:* Mount Royal, Montreal. *Address:* 3185 Delavigne Road, Montreal 218; and *office* Nordair Ltd., Montreal International Airport, Dorval, Quebec, Canada.

**TOON, Malcolm.** American Diplomat. *B.* 1916. *Educ.* Tufts Univ., Medford, Mass.—AB; Fletcher School of Law & Diplomacy—MA; Harvard Univ. *M.* 1943, Elizabeth Taylor. *S.* 1. *Daus.* 2. *Career:* National Resources Planning Bd. 1939–41; Ensign–Lt. Cmdr., US Naval Reserve 1942–46; joined US Foreign Service 1946; Amb. to Czechoslovakia 1969–71; Amb. to Yugoslavia 1971–75; Amb to Israel 1975; Amb. to the U.S.S.R. 1976. *Decorations:* Superior Honor Award, Dept. of State (1965); Bronze Star Medal

(Combat); Hon. LLD Tufts Univ. 1977. *Clubs:* Kenwood Golf & Country Club, Washington D.C.; Royal Automobile Club, London; Ceasarea Golf Club, Israel; Pinehurst Country Club, Pinehurst N.C. *Address:* Dept. of State, Washington, D.C. 20520, U.S.A.

**TOOTH, Hon. Sir (Seymour) Douglas.** Australian. *B.* 1904. *Educ.* Teacher Training, Queensland Dept. of Education: University of Queensland (Class 1 Teaching Certificate). *M.* 1937, Eileen Mary O'Connor. *Dau.* 1. Member Legislative Assembly of Queensland 1957–74, Minister for Health & Member of the Exec. Council of Queensland 1964–74. Member Liberal Party of Australia. *Address:* Parmelia Close, 61 Bellevue Terrace, Clayfield, Qld., Australia.

**TOOTHILL, Sir John Norman,** CBE. British company director. *B.* 1908. *Educ.* Beaminster Grammar School; FCWA. *M.* 1935, Ethel Amelia Stannard. *Career:* Chief Cost Accountant, Ferranti Ltd., Hollinwood, 1935–43; Gen. Manager, Ferranti Ltd., Edinburgh, 1943–68. Director: Edinburgh Investment Trust, 1963—; A. I. Welders Ltd. 1963—: R. W. Toothill Ltd., 1968—: W. A. Baxter & Sons Ltd. since 1970; Brand-Rex Ltd. 1975—. *Awards:* Comp. IEE; Comp. IERE; Hon. Comp. RAeS; LL.D (Aberdeen); DSc (Heriot-Watt, Edinburgh); Fellow, Royal Society of Edinburgh. *Member:* Institute of Cost & Works Accountants; Vice-President, Scottish Council Development & Industry; N.I.E.S.R. *Publications:* Toothill Report on the Scottish Economy. *Club:* Caledonian. *Address:* St. Germains, Longmiddry, East Lothian.

**TOPPING, Charles Hinchman.** American. Civil Engineer, Borough Manager, Swarthmore Pa., U.S.A. *B.* 1904. *Educ.* Massachusetts Institute of Technology (BSc 1928). *M.* Elise Gene Walker. *S.* Thomas Stirling Reid. *Daus.* Carol Hinchman (Baum) and Cynthia Bowen. *Career:* Civil Engineer, Pan American Petroleum Corporation and subsidiaries, Venezuela and U.S.A. 1928–30, 1931–32, 1935–38; Superintendent of Construction, South Persia State Railways 1932–33; Cartographer, University of Penna. Archaeological Expedition to Persia 1933–34; Project Engineer, City of Houston Water Dept. 1938–39, and Lockwood & Andrews, Houston 1940–42; Civil Engineer, E. I. du Pont de Nemours & Co. 1942–45; Principal Architectural and Civil Engineer 1945–54; Senior Architectural and Civil Consultant 1954–63, Building Products Development Manager for Development Dept., 1963–69. Member: Building Research Adv. Bd. 1952–57, Building Research Inst. (Vice-Pres. 1955–57, Pres. 1957–59, Research Cttee. 1959–62, Chmn. Documentation Cttee. 1959–60). Assoc. Mem., Highway Research Bd. 1952–63. Member: Delaware Highway Research Council 1950–64 (Chairman 1961–64); Advisory Group for Institute of Building Research, Penna. State University, 1964–68; Advisory Panel to Bldg. Research Division Natl. Bureau of Standards, 1963–70; Representative, Supporting Organization of International Council, Building Research and Documentation Studies, 1963–70. American Socy. of Civil Engrs. (Fellow; Cttee. on Building Systems, President Delaware Section 1953–54); Delaware Engineering Association (President 1950–51); American Institute of Architects-Engineers Joint Council Co-operative Committee (Co-Chairman 1958–59); Plastics-in-Building Committee of Manufacturing Chemists Assn. 1958–64; Code Adv. Committee Society of Plastics Industry 1958–66; Chairman, Joint MCA-SPI Committee on Identification of Plastics and Elastomers; 1962–65; Chairman, SPI Code Sub-Committee; 1964–66; Producers' Council (Board of Directors, Executive Committee, Treasurer 1967, 1969) Franklin Inst. Cttee. on Science and the Arts 1953— (Chairman 1962, and Chairman Brown Medal Committee 1957–58, 1964–65, 1967–68, Chairman Committee on Frequency of Awards and New Fields of Interest); Chmn. Sub-Cttee. on Award Liaison. *Member:* New Cities Panel, (Penna.) Governor's Science Advisory Cttee 1969; Newcomen Society in North America 1963–70. Engineer, Board of Health, New-Castle, Delaware 1947–49; Borough Councilman, Swarthmore, Pa. 1957; Pres., of Board, Swarthmore Public Library; 1968–73; Bd. of Directors, Member Central Delaware County Authority; Underwriters Laboratories Panel on Building Materials; Rotary, Phi Gamma Delta, Theta Tau. Mason. *Publications:* Eleven articles in technical and trade journals; licensed professional engineer. *Address:* 323 N. Princeton Avenue, Swarthmore, Pa., 19081; and *office* 121, Park Avenue, Swarthmore, Pa. 19081, U.S.A.

**TOPSØE, Haldor,** MSc, DPhil, DtechSc. Danish civil engineer. *B.* 1913. *Educ.* Frederiksberg Grammar School; Technical Univ. of Denmark (grad. 1936). *M.* 1936, Inger Kunst. *Career:* Engineer Aarhus Oliefabrik A/S 1936–39; Consulting Engineer Copenhagen 1940–72; Chmn. of the Board, Haldor Topsoe AS since 1972; Member Bds. Kansax AS, AS Jens Villadesens Fabrikker; Chmn. Danish Air Lines Ltd. (alternating) Scandinavian Airlines System since 1968. *Member:* Danish Academy, Technical Science; Danish Atomic Energy Commission's Research Establishment Risø; Swedish Academy, Technical Science. *Awards:* DPhil. Univ. of Aarhus; DtechSc Technical Univ. of Denmark; Order of Dannebrog; G.A. Hagemann Medal. *Publications:* Danmarks Produktionsliv omkring (1935). *Address:* Frydenlund, Frydenlundsvej DK2950 Vedbaek, Denmark.

**TOREM, Charles.** International lawyer. *B.* 1914. *Educ.* Amherst (BA *magna cum laude* 1935 and Harvard Law School (LLB 1938)). *S.* Christopher. *Career:* Admitted New York Bar 1939, Florida Bar 1941, U.S. District Court, Southern District of Florida 1942, U.S. Supreme Court 1957. Lecturer, Practising Law Institute. Senior partner, law firm of Coudert Frères, Paris. *Director:* Ashland Chemical (France) S.A.; Mallory Batteries S.A.; Procter & Gamble France; Permanent Board Representative: Hertz France; Reece Machinery Company (France); General Radio France. Phi Beta Kappa and Delta Sigma Rho. Special U.S. Navy Commendation (issued at COM NOB, Oran 1945). Member, Court of Arbitration of International Chamber of Commerce in France since 1960, Vice Chairman 1968—. American Chamber of Commerce in France: Director 1958—; President 1966–69. Hon. Chmn., Council of American Chambers of Commerce in Europe 1969. *Member:* American, New York City, Federal, International, Inter-American Bar Associations; American Foreign Law Association; American Society of International Law. Governor. American Hospital in Paris. National Vice-Pres. & Past-President, Harvard Law School Association of France; Vice-President, Harvard Club of France. Past-President, Amherst Club of France. *Award:* Chevalier de la Légion d'Honneur. *Publications:* Minority Stockholders' Rights under French Law (The Business Lawyer, Jan. 1960); Corporation and Tax Laws Monaco (The Business Lawyer, July 1961); Control of Foreign Investment in France (Michigan Law Review, Feb. 1968); Denigration and Disparagement—A Franco-American Comparative Analysis (Texas International Law Journal, Winter 1972); The Subsidiary in France: Problems of Control under French Law (Texas International Law Journal, Spring 1973). *Clubs:* The Travellers, Automobile, Polo, Cercle Interallié, American, Le Cercle du 33 Avenue Foch (Paris); American (London); Harvard (New York). *Address:* 4, rue Marbeuf, Paris 8e; and *office* Coudert Frères, 52 Champs Elysées, Paris 8e, France.

**TORNO, Noah,** MBE. Canadian. *B.* 1910. *M.* 1950, Rose Rein (Laine). *Stepson,* Michael Laine. *Career:* Served in World War II with R.C.N. with rank of Lieutenant 1942–45; Chmn. Bd. Chief Exec. Officer; Jordan Wines Ltd.; Director: Canada Trust—Huron & Erie, Consumers' Gas Co. Ltd.; Cygnus Corporation Ltd.; Chmn. Bd. Trustees, Royal Ont. Museum; Mem. Board of Management O'Keefe Centre for the Performing Arts; Board of Governors Toronto Arts Foundation. Dir., Hon. Secy. Mount Sinai Hospital, Toronto. *Address: office* P.O. Box No. 3 Toronto-Dominion Centre, Toronto, Ontario, Canada.

**TÖRNQVIST, Erik Olof.** Finnish civil administrator. *B.* 20 July 1915. *Educ.* Cand pol sc; MA. *M.* 1939, Liddy Emilia Backman. *S.* 2. *Career:* Registrar, Board of Customs Statistical Bureau 1939–40; Research Official, Bank of Finland 1940–42; Secretary, Price Regulation Board 1942–46; Secretary-General, Economic Council 1946–47; Director, War Reparations Board 1947–49; Director in Chief of Economic Dept., Min. of Finance since 1949; Chairman, Finance Commission 1949–61. Secretary General, Economic Planning Council 1951–53; Secretary to Prime Minister 1953; Chairman, Finnish Group of Nordic Economic Co-operation Committee 1956–57 and 1968–70; Chief of Section, U.N.E.C.E. 1957–59; U.N.E.C.L.A. 1959–61; U.N.T.A.B. expert 1962–63; Exec. Dir. of the IBRD 1970–72; Ambassador of Finland to Mexico 1972. *Award:* Comdr. Order of the Lion & Order of the White Rose (Finland). *Publications:* articles on economics in various journals and periodicals. *Address:* Ministry for Foreign Affairs, Helsinki, Finland.

**TORRANCE, Alexander Edward,** PrEng., CEng., FIEE, FSAIEE, Sen. Life MIEEE. South African. Professional Engineer, Chartered Engineer, retired director of companies, Chairman Commercial Exchange of Southern Africa 1953/57/58/66/67 & elected Hon. Life Member in 1976. *B.* 26 Aug. 1907. *Educ.* Newton Heath Technical School and Manchester

College of Technology. *M.* 1936, Allison Welsh Rennie. *Address:* B208 Empire Gardens, Empire Road, Parktown, Johannesburg, South Africa.

**TORRIJOS HERRERA, Gen. Omar.** Panamanian Army Officer. *B.* 1929. *Career:* Commander, Panama National Guard since 1968; Leader of the Panamanian Revolution since 1972. *Address:* Palacio de las Garzas, Panama City, Panama.

**TORY, Sir Geofroy William,** KCMG. British. *B.* 1912. *Educ.* King Edward VII Schl., Sheffield, and Queens' Coll., Cambridge (BA). *M.* (1) 1938, Emilia Strickland. *S.* 2. *Dau.* 1. *M.* (2) 1950, Hazel Winfield. *Career:* Joined Dominions Office 1935; served in World War II, 1939–43; Principal Private Secretary to Secretary of State for Dominion Affairs 1945; Senior Secretary, office of U.K. High Commissioner, Canada, 1946–49; Principal Secretary, and later Counsellor, British Embassy, Dublin, 1949–52; Imperial Defence College 1952; Deputy High Commissioner for U.K. in Pakistan (Peshawar) 1953–54, and in Australia 1954–57; British High Commsnr., Federation of Malaya (later Malaysia) 1957–63. Ambassador to the Republic of Ireland 1964–67. British High Commissioner in Malta 1967–70. *Address:* Rathclaren, Kilbrittain, Co. Cork.

**TOSHIMA, Kenkichi.** Japanese. *B.* 1902. *Educ.* Kyoto Imperial Univ. (Graduate in Mining and Metallurgy). *M.* 1933, Michiko Tamiya. *Daus.* Mrs. Masa Toshima, Mrs. Yoshi Fujisaka and Mrs Hisa Ikeda. *Career:* With Kobe Steel Ltd.: Elected a Director Aug. 1949, re-elected a Director and appointed Executive Officer Nov. 1953, re-elected a Director and appointed Executive Vice-President Nov. 1956; President 1958 & Senior Counsellor 1975; Director: Kobe Commercial & Industrial Trade Centre 1967—. *Award:* Blue Ribbon Medal, May 1961, Director: Japan Machinery Fed. *Clubs:* Fuji Lake Side Country; One Golf; Asuka Country. *Address:* 15–17 Roku, Rokusou, Ashiya City, Hyogo Prefecture, Japan; and *office* No. 36, 1-chome, Wakinohama, Fukiai-ku, Kobe, Japan.

**TOTSUKA G.** Japanese. *B.* 1914. *Educ.* Tokyo Univ. of Commerce. *M.* Yoshiko. *S.* 2. *Daus.* 2. *Career:* Dir. Hokkai Unyu Co. Ltd.; The Japan Shipping Exchange Inc.; Pres. Ilno Kaiun Ltd. *Member:* Maritime Arbitration Comm; The Japanese Shipowner's Assn. *Address:* 797 Kugahara-cho, Ota-Ku, Tokyo, Japan and *office* IINO Building, 2-1-1 Uchisaiwai-Cho Chiyoda-Ku, Tokyo, Japan.

**TÖTTERMAN, Richard Evert Björnson.** Finnish diplomat. *B.* 1926. *Educ.* Univ. of Helsinki, LLB (1948); LLM (1949); Univ. of Oxford, Brasenose Coll. D.Phil (1951). *M.* 1953, Camilla Susanna Veronica Huber, *S.* 1. *Dau.* 1. *Career:* Entered Diplomatic service 1952; posted to Stockholm 1954–56, Moscow 1956–58; Min. for For. Affairs 1958–62; 1st Secy. Berne 1962–63; Counsellor, Paris 1963–66; Deputy Dir. Min. for Foreign Affairs 1966; Secy. Gen. Office of President of Finland 1966–70; Secy. Gen. Min. for Foreign Affairs 1970–75; Finnish Ambassador at the Court of St. James's since 1975. *Decorations:* Kt-Comm. Order of White Rose of Finland; Officer of the Order of Lion of Finland; GCVO, OBE; Grand Silver Cross of Merit (Austria); Grand Cross, Order of Dannebrog, (Denmark), Hamayoun (Iran), of the Falcon (Iceland), of Orange-Nassau (Neths.) of North Star (Sweden): Kt-Comm. of Order of the Crown (Belg.), of St. Olav (Norway), of Merit (Poland), of the Lion (Senegal); Order of the Banner (Hungary), of Star (Romania); Comm. of Nat. Order of Merit (France). *Clubs:* White's; Hurlingham; Travellers. *Address:* 14 Kensington Palace Gardens, London, W.8; and *office* 38 Chesham Place, London, S.W.1.

**TOURE, Sekou.** President of the Republic of Guinea. *B.* 1922. *Educ.* Ecole Professionnelle Georges Poiret, Conakry. Entered Posts and Telecommunications Service, French Guinea 1961; Secy.-Gen. Syndicat du Personnel des P.T.T. 1945; Member, Federal Consultative Commission for Labour 1945; Territorial Consultative Commission, Guinea 1945; Parliamentary and Administrative Commissions 1945; Secy.-Gen., Union of Treasury Employees 1946; founder-member, Rassemblement Démocratique Africain (R.D.A.) 1946. Secretary-General: Territorial Union, Confédération Générale du Travail (C.G.T.) 1948; Co-ordination Committee, French West Africa and Togoland 1950, and Guinea Democratic Party 1952; Territorial Councillor 1953; Pres., Confédération Générale des Travailleurs d'Afrique Noire (C.G.T.A.) 1956; Mayor of Conakry; Deputy for Guinea in French National Assembly 1956; Grand Councillor, French West Africa; Vice-Pres. of Council, Govt. of Guinea 1957, and of R.D.A. 1957; Head of State since 1958; Prime Minister 1968–72. Received Lenin Peace Prize 1960. *Address:* Présidence de la République, Conakry, Republic of Guinea.

**TOUZARD, Paul.** Chevalier du Mérite Industriel et Commercial. French. *B.* 1912. *Educ.* Ecol Supéricure Nationale des Arts et Métiers; Ecol Superieure du Froid Industriel. *M.* 1937, Yvonne. *Career:* Administrator, Dir. Gen. Air Industrie; Pres. Syndicat des Constructeurs et Constructeurs Installateurs de Matériel Aeraulique. Vice-Pres. Honoraire de l'Assoc. des Ingénieurs en Chauffage et Ventilation de France; Pres. Centre Technique des Industries Aerauliques et Termiques. *Address: office* 19 Avenue Dubonnet, 92401 Courbevoie, France.

**TOVAZZI, Gino.** Italian. Permanent Delegate of the Mexican Consular Corps. *B.* 1922. *Educ.* Doctor of Political Science; Doctor of Engineering; Professor of Engineering. *M.* Amelia Rigodanza, 1956. *S.* 4. *Dau.* 1. *Career:* Consul of Panama to Bolzano, 1953–55; Consul-General of Guatemala to Venecia, 1955–59; Consul-General of Bolivia to Venecia, 1964; Co-Ordinator of the Industrial Cttee. of Tlaxcala, Mexico, to Europe, 1966; Delegate of the Red Cross (Mexican) to Italy; Hon. Member, State Senate & Co-ordinator of Industrial Cttee., Louisiana Dept., of Commerce & Industry. Hon. Rector, Potosi University, Bolivia; Dean & Professor of Engineering, Potosi University; Professor of Geodosy, St. Andrew's Univ., La Paz, Bolivia; Professor, Military Engineering School, Bolivia; Military College, Bolivia; Visiting Professor, Nicaragua Univ., Leon; San Carlos Univ., Guatemala; Setton Hall Univ., New Jersey; Mackenzie Univ., S. Paul, Brasil; Univ., of Florida Gainesville; Ph. College, London, Canada; Ambassador of the Order of St. John to the U.N., Bolivia, Peru & Brazil; Delegate & Representative (Mexican Government) to Europe; Consul of Honduras to Venice, Ambassador Extra. and Pleny. to Europe. *Awards:* Hon. Secretary of State, U.S.A. 1977; Count of Vipiteno; Order of the Golden Fleece; Knight of the Grand Cross; Order of St. John; Order of St. Maurice & Lazarus & Order of Italian Crown; Order of the Consular Merit; Order of Merit of Tunisia; Order of the White Lion (Czechoslovakia); Order of the White Eagle (Poland); Order of the S. Agatha (San Marino); Order of 'Honour & Merit', Red Cross (Mexico & Cuba); Order of the 'Quetzal' (Guatemala); Order of the Condor, (Bolivia); Civil Merit, Bulgaria; Bolivar Merit, U.S.A.; 'Polonia Restituita' Poland; Member, Merit, Cuba; S. Victimas 2 de Mayo, Spain; War Medal, Gen. D. Eisenhower, U.S.A.; Gold Medal of Academic honour, France & U.S.A.; Academia Prize & Hon. Mem. Japan Univ. Al. Assn.; Eloy Alfara, Panama; Great Star of the Voilinia Legion, and Haute Silesie; Hon. Citizen, New Orleans, Louisiana; Miami, Florida; Montgomery, Alabama; Santa Fe, New Mexico; State of Tennessee; State of Kentucky. Hon. Mayor, City of Bellefontaine, Ohio, and many other awards. Doctor (hc): Andhra University (India); Tomas Frias Univ. (Bolivia); St. Andrew's Univ. (Bolivia); S. Univ. (Calif.); Dr. of Jurisprudence, Boston; Hon. Pres. Military Organization, Bolivia; Major-Gen. SAME. Logistic Div. Headquarters Allied Forces Southern Europe, Naples. *Member:* Academia Nacional de la Historia; Academia Nacional de Ciencias (both Bolivia); Real Academia de Cordoba, de Barcelona, de Cadiz; The American Chemical Soc.; The American Military Engineers; Consular Law Soc., The American Military Engineers; Consular Law Socy., U.S.A.; The Academy of Political Science; Academia de Ciencias Penales; Ateneo de Cienciasy Artes. Academia Nacional de la Historia, Mexico; Academia degli Euteleti, Consular Law Society, New York; Fellow Consular Corps Coll. & Internat. Consular Acad (U.S.A.); Hon. men. Supreme Council 33 degree Scottish Rite. *Publications:* Theoretical Chemistry (2. Vols. 1955). *Clubs:* The Union League; Country (Both Philadelphia, Pa.); Rotary (Bolivia); University (Washington); Army & Navy (New Orleans); Circolo Militar (Bolivia, Italy, Mexico); The American Legion, Post n.1 Alianza Inter-americana (Hon. Member), U.S.A. *Address:* Villa Olanda 30030, Mira-Porte, Venice, Italy.

**TOWBIN, Belmont.** American. Partner, C.E. Unterberg Towbin Co., Investment Bankers, New York City. Director, various companies. *B.* 1910. *Educ.* Johns HopkinsUniv. (BA 1931) and Harvard Graduate School of Business Administration (MBA 1933). *M.* 1941, Phoebe Jacobs. *Clubs:* Harvard (N.Y.C.). *Address: office* 61 Broadway, New York N.Y., U.S.A.

**TOWERS, George Harold Readhead,** JP. British. *B.* 1910. *Educ.* Leighton Park School, Reading. *M.* 1936, Aileen

Mary Glass. *S.* Rodney Harold and Nicholas James. *Daus.* Angela Mary and Carol Jane. *Career:* Managing Director (1940— Chmn. 1957–70), John Readhead & Sons Ltd. (shipbuilders, marine engineers and dry dock owners), South Shields; Charles W. Taylor & Son Ltd.; Lawson Batey Tugs Ltd.; Blyth Tug Co. Ltd.; Laygate Investments Ltd.; Donkin & Co. Ltd.; Tyne Tugs Ltd. Past President, Shipbuilding Employers' Federation; Twice Chairman, Tyne Shipbuilders' Assn.; Liveryman, Worshipful Company of Shipwrights. Freeman, City of London and South Shields. Fellow, North East Coast Institution of Engineers and Shipbuilders (President 1962–64). Member, Royal Institution of Naval Architects. *Address:* 50 Greenfield Road, Brunton Park, Gosforth, Newcastle upon Tyne NE3 5TP.

**TOWLER, Eric William,** CBE Hon. MA Oxon. British company director and farmer. *B.* 28 Apr. 1900. *Educ.* Morley Grammar Schl. *M.* (1) 1921, Isabel Edith Ina Hemsworth. *S.* 2. *M.* (2) 1948, Gwendolin Betty Bateman. *Career:* Farms 2,000 acres. M.F.H. Badsworth Hunt 1938–43; M.F.H. South Shropshire 1951–56; Mining Dir., Dorman Long & Co. Ltd., 1937 until nationalisation of Iron & Steel; Chmn. Cawoods Holdings Ltd. 1961–72; Founder, Cawood Wharton & Co. Ltd. Managing Director 1931–42; Chairman 1942–72; Chmn., Bd. Governors, Untd. Oxford Hosps., 1964–72. *Address:* Glympton Park, nr. Woodstock, Oxon and Willett House, Lydeard St. Lawrence, Somerset.

**TOWNSEND, Cyril David,** MP. British Politician. *B.* 1937. *Educ.* Bradfield Coll., Berks.; Royal Military Acad., Sandhurst. *M.* 1976, Anita Walshe. *Career:* Officer in British Army until 1966; Personal Asst. to Leader of the Greater London Council 1966–68; Personal Asst. to Rt. Hon. Edward Heath (then Leader of the Opposition) 1968–70; Conservative Research Dept. 1970–74; MP (Cons.) for Bexleyheath since 1974. *Member:* Exec. Cttee., S.E. London Industrial Consultative Group; Council Mem., St. Christopher's Fellowship; Friends of Cyprus. *Address:* 30 Maunsel Street, London SW1; and *office* House of Commons, London SW1A 0AA.

**TOWNSEND, Lynn Alfred.** American. *B.* 1919. *Educ.* Univ. of Michigan (AB 1940; MBA 1941). *M.* 1940, Ruth M. Laing. *S.* James L., Charles S., and Richard J. *Career:* Accountant: Briggs & Icerman, Ann Arbor, Mich. (part-time) 1939–41, and Ernst & Ernst, Detroit 1941–44 and 1946–47. Supervising Accountant: George Bailey & Co., Detroit 1947, and Touche, Niven, Bailey & Smart (also Partner) 1947–57. Chairman of the Board, Chrysler Corporation 1967–75 (Comptroller 1957–58, Group Vice-President International Operations 1958–60, Admin. Vice-Pres. 1960–61, Pres. 1961–66, Chief Exec. Officer 1966–75). Director Manufacturers Hanover Corpn.; Manufacturers Hanover Trust Co.; Dir. National Alliance of Businessmen Chmn. 1970; Trustee, New Detroit Inc. Chmn. 1972; Dir. Project Hope; Detroit Renaissance. *Member:* Motor Vehicle Manufacturers Assn. (Chairman 1966–68. Member Board Dirs.) Automotive Safety Foundation (Trustee); United Foundation of Detroit Dir.; Economic Club of Detroit; American Accounting Assn.; Society of Automotive Engineers; American Institute of Accountants; Beta Gamma Sigma; Phi Kappa Phi; Beta Alpha Psi; Alpha Kappa Psi; Beta Theta Pi. Businessman Award of the Year (Univ. of Michigan, May 1963). Hon. LLD Bucknell, Michigan Delaware Alma and Rider College. *Awards:* Hon. Degree 1968. Doctor of Business Administration, Univ. of Evansville (Indiana), Communicator of the Year Award (International Cncl. Industrial Editors) 1965; Marketing Statesman of Year (Sales & Exec. Club, N.Y.) 1966; Distinguished Service to the Nation, National Chmn. U.S. Ind. Payroll Cttee. 1966; Presidential Citation, Exemplary Service to Nation 1971; Chevalier de la Legion d'Honneur 1972. *Clubs:* Detroit Athletic (Dir. and Pres. 1969); Bloomfield Hills Country; Detroit; Detroit Press; Recess (Detroit); Sky, Economic; Links (N.Y.C.). *Address:* Bloomfield Hills, Michigan 48013, U.S.A.

**TOXOPEUS, Edzo Hendrik.** Dutch statesman. *B.* 1918. *Educ.* LLD. *M.* 1944, H. A. Ufkes. *S.* Menno. *Dau.* Ernestine. *Career:* Attorney 1942–59. Member of Community Council of Breda (North Brabant) Sept. 1949–May 1959. Member of the Second Chamber of the States-General (IIe Kamer der Staten-Generaal) 1956–59; Min. of Home Affairs, Netherlands, 1959–63 & 1963–65; Mem. 2nd Chamber of States General 1965–69; Leader of Parly. Group of Liberal Democ. Party, 1966–69; Queen's Comm. in province of Groningen since 1970. Member, Liberal Democratic Party (Volkspartij voor Vrjheid en Democratie). *Address:* Markstraat 17, Groningen, Netherlands.

**TRACY, Osgood Vose.** *B.* 1902. *Educ.* U.S. Naval Acad. (BS 1924); Clarkson Coll. of Technology (Hon. DSc 1958). *M.* 1926, Pauline Crawford. *Daus.* Sarah O. (Mrs. F. G. Sigler III), Mary M., and Susan C. (Mrs. Timothy Mellon). *Career:* With Esso Standard Oil Co. (now Esso Standard Division of Humble Oil & Refining Co.) 1930–60 (Director 1954–60, Vice-Pres. 1956–59; President 1959–60; retired Aug. 1960); General Manager, Chemical Products Dept. 1940–56; ENJAY Co. (now Enjay Chemical Co.), 1948–58 (Pres. 1952–58; Director 1948–60). Consultant & Director Emeritus, W. R. Grace & Co., New York, 1967—, (Exec. Vice-Pres. & Dir., 1960–67); Dir., Crouse-Hinds Co., RAC Corp. and Inexco Oil Co. *Member:* Amer. Chemical Socy.; Amer. Petroleum Inst.; Manufacturing Chemists' Assn.; Socy. of Chemical Industry (Amer. Section); Chamber of Commerce of the U.S. Trustee; Newark (N.J.) College of Engineering Research Foundation. *Clubs:* New York Yacht (N.Y.C.); Metropolitan (Washington); The Army & Navy. *Address: office* 7 Hanover Square, New York City 5, U.S.A.

**TRANMIRE, Baron (Robert Hugh).** PC, KBE, MC, DL, JP. *B.* 8 Aug. 1903. *Educ.* Eton Coll. and Balliol Coll., Oxford. *M.* 1928, Ruby Christian Scott. *S.* 3. *Dau.* 1. Member (C.) for Thirsk and Malton 1929–74; Called to Bar (Inner Temple) 1926; served in World War II (as DAAG 50th (N) Div., A.A.G., G.H.Q., M.E.F.); Parliamentary Secretary, Minister of Nat. Insurance 1951–53; Parliamentary Secretary, Minister of Pensions and National Insurance 1953–54; Parliamentary Under-Sec. Foreign Office Oct. 1954: Minister of Health Dec. 1955–Jan. 1957; Chmn., Select Cttee. on Procedure 1970–73; Chmn., Commonwealth Industries Assn. 1963–73. *Address:* Upsall Castle, Thirsk, Yorks.; 15 Greycoat Gardens, London, S.W.1.

**TRASK, Frederick Kingsbury, Jr.** Lieut.-Col., FD, AUS (Retd. 1946); private investing. *B.* 1907. *Educ.* Groton School (Certificate *cum laude* 1926) and Harvard College (AB 1930). *M.* 1930, Margaret Moulton Pope. *S.* Frederick Kingsbury III. *Daus.* Jane Bicker Shaw (Freund), Margaret Jacquelin (Duffek), and Frances Pope (Wozencraft). *Career:* With New York Trust Co. 1930–35; Farmers Deposit National Bank, Pittsburgh, Pa. 1935–46 (Asst. Cashier 1940–43, Asst. Vice-Pres. 1943–44, Vice-Pres. 1944–46). Served as Major, Army Service Forces and Finance Department, 1942–43, Lieut.-Col. 1943–44; Asst. Director, Office of Contract Settlement, Washington, D.C. 1944–45; Managing Partner, Payson & Trask, New York City 1947—; Director and member of Executive Committee General Reinsurance Corp. 1950—; United States Trust Co. of New York 1949—; Great Northern Nekoosa Corp. 1949—; Director: Guaranty Reinsurance Co. Ltd. 1959–72, and Vitro Corp. of America 1960–68. Pres. 1961–65, and Governor 1954—; Society of the New York Hospital; 1961—; Joint Administrative Board of New York Hospital—Cornell Medical Center; Director, China Medical Board of New York 1956–76; Allied Building Credits Inc. 1959–63; General Reassurance (Life) Corp. 1962—; N.Y. Metropolitan Baseball Club 1962—. *Award:* Gold Heart Award of the American Heart Association; Captain's Chair, Society of the New York Hospital. Republican. *Clubs:* Links, Harvard (N.Y.C.); Round Hill (Greenwich, Conn.); Union (N.Y.C.). *Address:* Marsh Drive, Hilton Head, S.C. 29928; and *office* 748 Madison Avenue, New York City 10021, U.S.A.

**TRAVERS, William Holmes.** British. *B.* 1915. *Educ.* Sydney University (BEcon); Shore School North Sydney (ABS White Scholar). *M.* 1948, Kathleen Clayton. *S.* 2. *Daus.* 2. *Career:* Captain, Australian Imperial Force, 1939–45; Fellow, Sydney University Senate (representing undergraduates), 1946–48; Australian Consolidated Press Ltd.: Circulation Mgr., 1955; Administration Mgr., 1958.; Asst. Gen. Mgr. 1969–72; Joint Man. Dir. T. B. Clarke (Overseas) Pty. Ltd. since 1972. *Member:* Synod of the Diocese of Sydney 1963–69; Australian Administrative Staff College Assoc.; Assoc. Aust. Inst. of Graphic Arts Management. *Publication:* The Crete Affair (private circulation). *Clubs:* Australian; Royal Sydney Yacht Squadron. *Address: office* P.O. Box 2 Woollahra, N.S.W. 2025, Australia.

**TRAVIS, Norman John.** British *B.* 1913. *Educ.* Clifton College and Trinity Coll. Oxford (MA; BSc). *M.* 1939, Mary Elizabeth Dale-Harris. *S.* Rupert, Julian, Michael and Mark. *Career:* With Imperial Chemical Industries Ltd. 1937–58; Managing Director of ICI's subsidiary company, British Visqueen Ltd. 1953–58; Director Rio Tinto Zinc Corp., Ltd. Chairman, Borax (Holdings) Ltd., 1969—; Dir., 1958—; Chmn., United States Borax & Chem. Corp. 1966—. Chmn. Council of Clifton College. *Clubs:* Bath; M.C.C. (both of London); California and Los Angeles Country. *Address:*

Howe Green Hall nr. Hertford; and *office* Borax House, Carlisle Place, London, S.W.1.

**TRAXLER, Arthur Edwin.** *B.* 1900. *Educ.* Kansas State Teachers Coll. (BSEd 1920); Univ. of Chicago (MA 1924; PhD 1932). *M.* 1924, Bobbi Yearout. *Dau.* Karen. *Career:* Superintendent of Schools: Holyrood (Kan.), Quincy (Kan.), Derby (Kan.), Wakefield 1918–28; Fellow, Univ. of Chicago 1929–31; Psychologist, Univ. of Chicago High School 1931–36. Summer and part-time teaching in following universities: Arkansas, Alabama, Columbia, Temple, Syracuse, New York State, California 1935–59. Lecturer in Education. University of Miami (U.S.A.) 1965; Prof. of Education since 1972. Executive Director Emeritus, Educational Records Bureau, New York. *Publications:* The Measurement & Improvement of Silent Reading at Junior High School Level, (1932); The Teaching of Reading in Junior & Senior High Schools, (1934); Silent Reading Test, (1934); Read & Comprehend (co-author, 1937 rev. 1949); High School Reading Test, (1938); Guidance in Public Secondary Schools (editor, 1939); Ten Years of Research in Reading, (1941); International Transport policy for the U.S., (1943); Develop Your Reading (co-author, 1941); Techniques of Guidance, (1945 rev. 1966); Another Five Years of Research in Reading, (1946); Problem in the Improvement of Reading, (1946 rev. 1955, 1967); Introduction to Testing and the Use of Test Results in Public Schools, (1952); Guidance Services, (1953 rev. 1967); Eight More Years of Research in Reading, (1955); Research in Reading during Another Four Years, (1960); editor of reports on annual educational conferences and contributor to educational and psychological journals. *Address:* 6825 S.W. 59th Street, Miami, Fla. 33143, U.S.A.

**TREADWAY, Lyman H.** American Banker. *Educ.* Yale Univ —BA; Case Western Reserve Univ.—LLB. *M.* Nancy. *S.* 1 *Daus.* 2. *Career:* US Army, Military Intelligence 1952–55; Exec. Vice Pres., Dir. & Chmn. of Exec. Cttee., Western Reserve Life Assurance Co. of Ohio (& Pioneer Western, its Parent Corp.) 1959–68; Chmn. of Bd. & Chief Exec., First National Bank of Ashland, Ohio, 1969–74; Chmn. of Bd. & Chief Exec., First Citizens Bank of Greencastle, Indiana 1969–74; Chmn. of Bd. & Chief Exec. Officer, Union Commerce Bank, Cleveland, Ohio since 1974. Other business affiliations: Dir. & Mem. of Exec. & Audit Cttees., Union Commerce Bank since 1970; Dir., & Mem. of Exec. Cttee., Union Commerce Corp. since 1974; Dir., Forest City Enterprises since 1974; Dir., Merriman Construction Co., since 1962. *Member:* Ohio Bar Association; Cleveland Bar Association; Reserve City Bankers Association; Young Presidents' Organization (YPO). *Clubs:* Cleveland Racquet Club; Kirtland Country Club; Pepper Pike Club; Tavern Club; Union Club. *Address:* 18928 Shelburne Road, Shaker Heights, Ohio 44118, U.S.A.

**TREADWELL, Charles James,** CMG. British diplomat. *B.* 1920. *Educ.* Wellington Coll. N.Z.; Univ. of New Zealand (LLB). *M.* 1946, Philippa Perkins. *S.* 3. *Career:* served with H.M. Forces 1939–45; Sudan Political Service, Sudan Judiciary 1945–55; Foreign Office 1955–57; British High Commission Lahore 1957–60; H.M. Embassy Ankara 1960–62, Jedda 1963–64; British Political Agent Abu Dhabi 1968–71; Ambassador to the United Arab Emirates 1971–73; British High Commissioner Bahamas 1973–75; Ambassador to the Sultanate of Oman since 1975. *Address:* Lindfield Gardens, London Road, Guildford, Surrey; and *office* c/o Foreign and Commonwealth Office, London, S.W.1.

**TREBECK, Norman Bruce.** Australian company director and woolbuyer. *B.* 1917. *Educ.* Sydney Church of England Grammar School, followed by Sheep and Wool course at Sydney Technical College. *M.* 1943, Jean Vearing. *S.* David Bruce and Peter Charles. *Career:* On completion of education, joined Frederick H. Booth & Son Pty. Ltd. 1935, and has remained with the firm until merger with Sir James Hill & Sons (Aust.) Pty. Ltd., Man. Dir. and Director 1968. Served in World War II (Lieut., 2/17 Australian Infantry Bn., 2nd A.I.F., serving in Middle East and throughout Tobruk); after attending Middle East Staff School (1942) returned to Pacific area and served in various staff appointments until early in 1945; rejoined 2/17 Bn. prior to final campaign in Borneo (promoted Captain 1942 and Major 1943) 1940–45; since the war, active in Wool Trade affairs, serving on Committee of N.S.W. and Queensland Woolbuyers Assn. in 1956; Chairman, Australian Council of Wool Buyers, 1969–70; Member, Australian Wool Corp. Advisory Cttee. on Objective Measurement since 1969; Member, Australian Wool Corp. Distribution Research Advisory Cttee. since 1973; Chairman, Australian Wool Shipper Cttee. 1964–70; Member, FEOTC and Management Cttee., Sydney Greasy Wool Futures Exchange. *Address:* c/o Messrs. Booth Hill & Sons Pty. Ltd., 44 Young Street, Sydney, N.S.W., Australia.

**TRECKER, Francis J.** American. *B.* 1909. *Educ.* Marquette Univ. School of Business Administration, and Cornell University (BS MechEng and Administrative Engineering). *M.* 1968, Dorothy G. Knowles. *Career:* President and Director: Kearney & Trecker Corp. 1947–68, and Cleereman Machine Tool Corp. Green Bay, Wis. Dir.: 1967–70, Kearney & Trecker Ltd. (London, Eng.) 1957–74; Gorton Machine Corp., Council for Technological Advancement, Washington, D.C. Trustee: Amer. Heritage Foundation, N.Y. and Ripon Coll., Wis. 1952–71, Presidential Adviser, North Central Airlines, Minneapolis 1956—. Director, Aircraft Advisory Board, Rockwell-Standard Corp., Pittsburgh 1965–68. Expert Consultant: to Secy. of War on Sub-contracting & Facilities Procurement, and of Asst. Secy. Air Force for Material 1963–66; Chmn. Ad Hoc Machine Tool Adv. Cttee. to the Air Force 1965; Pres. Natl. Machine Tool Builders 1961–62; Dir. Natl. Assn. of Manufacturers 1955–58; Chmn. Wisconsin Legislative Cttee., Aeronautics Adv. Board 1944; Vice-Pres. Tools for Freedom, Headquarters N.Y.C. 1962–63. Fellow-in-Perpetuity, Metropolitan Museum of Art; Life Member, Natl. Aeronautic Assn. (for outstanding contribution to private aviation); Trustee Ducks Unlimited since 1970. *Member:* Amer. Socy. Mech. Engineers; Amer. Socy. Tool Engineers. Republican. *Clubs:* University, Milwaukee, Country (all of Milwaukee); Bark River Game Preserve (Sullivan, Wis.), Paradise Valley Country (Phoenix, Ariz.). *Address:* 7100 Mummy Mountain Road, Scottsdale, Arizona, U.S.A.

**TREFETHEN, Eugene E., Jr.** American industrialist. *B.* 1909. *Educ.* Univ. of California (BA) and Harvard School of Business Administration. *M.* 1937, Catherine Morgan. *S.* John Vance. *Dau.* Carla Jean. *Career:* President, Kaiser Industries Corp. Retd.; Vice-Chairman of the Board, Kaiser Foundation Health Plan Inc.; Kaiser Foundation Hospitals; Dir. Kaiser Industries Corp.; Kaiser Cement & Gypsum Corp.; Kaiser Aluminium & Chemical Corp.; Kaiser Steel Corp.; Life-time Member Board of Trustees, Mills Coll. President, University of California, Berkeley Foundation; Vice-Chairman, Board of Trustees, The UC Santa Cruz Foundation; President, San Francisco Museum of Art; Member of Exec. Cttee and Past President, Bay Area Council. *Member:* Chi Psi. Hon. Doctorate Degrees: Univ. of Portland, Mills Coll., Golden Gate Univ.; Hon. Alumnus of the Coll. of Engineering, Univ. of California, Berkeley. *Club:* Pacific Union. *Address:* 300 Lakeside Drive, Oakland 94666, Calif., U.S.A.

**TREHOLT, Thorstein.** Norwegian. *B.* 1911. *M.* 1939, Olga Lyngstad. *S.* Einar, Arne Thor. *Dau.* Kari. *Career:* Secy. for County head of Agriculture Oppland 1935–38; Municipal Agronom at Brandbu 1939–49; Teacher Agricultural Affairs, Valdres Jordbruksskole 1949–50; Prorector, Valdres Jordbruksskole 1950–60; Secy. of State, Ministry Agriculture 1954–57; Member of Parliament, Oppland Labour Party since 1957; Chmn. Bd. Norwegian State Bank of Agriculture since 1965; Chmn. Cttee. for Agriculture in Parliament 1961–65, Vice Chmn. 1965–71. Member Cttee. Foreign Relations in Parliament; Member Nordic Council; Minister of Agriculture 1971–72, and 1973–76. *Address:* 2760 Brandbu, Norway.

**TREIBER, William Frederick.** Banker. *B.* 1908. *Educ.* Columbia University (AB 1927; LLB 1929). *M.* 1936, Elizabeth Stewart. *S.* William F., Jr. *Dau.* Betty Jane. *Career:* With Sullivan & Cromwell 1929–31, and Robb, Clark & Bennitt 1931–34. With Federal Reserve Bank of New York; Assistant Counsel, Sept. 1934; Secretary Apr. 1942–Oct. 1949; Asst. Vice-Pres. July 1945–May 1950; Vice-Pres. May 1950–Mar. 1952; First Vice-President, Federal Reserve Bank of New York, 1952–73, Consultant since 1973. *Member:* American Bar Association, and Bar Association of City of New York. *Address:* Winchester Center, Connecticut 06094, U.S.A.

**TREMBLAY, Hon. Lucien.** Canadian. *B.* 1912. *Educ.* Classical studies and Faculty of Law (BA and LLD). *M.* 1939, Jeannine Martin. *S.* Pierre-Jean-François. *Dau.* Monique. *Career:* Practised law in Montreal 1936–61. Chief Justice of Quebec, since 1961. Chancellor, University of Montreal, Nov. 1967–70. *Publications:* Les biens réservés de la Femme mariée (thesis). Hon. LLD hc, Laval University; Doctor hc, Montreal University; Professor Emeritus of Montreal University. *Clubs:* Quebec Garrison; Le Cercle Universitaire de Montreal; Chapleau Fish & Game. *Address: office* Court House, Montreal, P.Q., Canada.

**TREMBLAY, Paul.** Canadian diplomat. *B.* 1914. *Educ.* Univ. of Montreal (BA; LLB; LScSoc) and McGill Univ. (student of constitutional law). *M.* 1943, Gertrude Nadeau. *S.* Pierre. *Daus.* Michèle and Helène. *Career:* Practised law 1939–40; joined Canadian Foreign Service 1940; 2nd Secy. Washington 1943–46; Chargé d'Affaires, Santiago (Chile) 1946–47; Counsellor, The Hague 1951–54; Minister-Counsellor, Canadian Permanent Delegation to NATO, Paris 1954–57; Head, Liaison Div., Dept. of External Affairs, Ottawa 1957; Ambassador to Chile 1959–62; Amb. and Permanent Representative to the U.N. 1962–66; Ambassador to Belgium, Luxembourg and to the European Communities, 1966–73; Associate Under Secretary of State for External Affairs, 1970–73; Ambassador to the Holy See since 1973. *Address:* Department of External Affairs, Ottawa, Ont., Canada.

**TREMELLONI, Dr. Roberto.** Italian politician. *B.* 30 Oct. 1900. *Educ.* Univ. of Turin (DSc Econ and Laur). *M. Dau* 1. *Career:* Prof., Milan Polytechnic since 1953; previously: Commsnr, Min. of Industrial Production, and President C.I.A.I. until 1946; Under-Secretary of State for Industry until 1947; Delegate to Marshall Plan Conference, Paris; President, F.I.M. since 1947; member of Constituent Assembly since 1946; Minister for Industry since 1947; Deputy of Parliament since May 1948; Minister-Vice President of Interministerial Economic Committee since May 1948; Delegate to Council of Ministers of O.E.E.C. since Mar. 1949; President, Parliamentary Commission of Enquiry on Unemployment 1952; Minister of Finance 1954–55. Deputy of Parliament 1946—; Chmn., Parliamentary Commission on Enquiry on Workable Competition 1961; Ministry of Treasury 1962–63; Minister of Finance 1964–65; Minister of Defence 1966–68; Pres., Budget Cttee., Chamber of Deputies 1969–70. Member, Social Democratic Party. *Publications:* Storia dell'Industria Italiana contemporanea; L'Industria Tessile Italiana; L'Italia in un'economia aperta; Il danaro pubblico. *Address:* Camera dei Deputati, Roma, Italy.

**TREMPONT, Jacques.** Belgian economist. *B.* 1925. *Educ.* LLD; Lic Sc Pol and Dipl; BPhil; BSc Econ; studied at Louvain, The Hague, Valladolid and Oxford Universities; Lauréat du Concours international interuniversitaire du Conseil de l'Europe, 1953. Lauréat du Grand Prix International Emile Bernheim 1956. *M.* 1953, Nadine Masoin. *S.* Dominique. *Daus.* Anne-Isabelle and Catherine. *Career:* With Military Government in Germany 1945–49; with Division for Economics and Finance of NATO, Paris, 1952–54; with Dept. of Operations in Europe, Africa and Australasia of World Bank, Washington, D.C. 1955–56. In private business 1956—; University Professor; Hon. Consul-General Chmn.; S.C. de Peintures et Vernis; S.A. Molimex et Vanandel. *Publications:* L'organisation des paiements intraeuropéens; Le potential économique de l'URSS et pays de l'OTAN; L'Unification de l'Europe Conditions et Limites (honoured by the Council of Europe); Ententes et concentrations dans la C.E.E.; De la Defense a la Detente; Ou va le Tiers-Monde?; etc. *Address:* 15 Ave de la Folle Chanson, B-1050 Brussels, Belgium.

**TRENCH, Sir David Clive Crosbie,** GCMG, MC. *B.* 1915. *Educ.* Tonbridge and Jesus Coll., Cambridge. *M.* 1944, Margaret Gould (of New York). *Dau.* 1. *Career:* Entered Colonial Service 1938; Joint Services Staff Coll. 1949; Asst. Secy., Hong Kong 1950; Imperial Defence Coll., 1958; Dep. Colonial Secy., Hong Kong 1959–60; High Commissioner for Western Pacific 1961–64; Governor and Commander-in-Chief, Hong Kong 1964–71, Vice-Chmn. Adv. Cttee. on Distinction Wards. Dept. Health & Social Security since 1972; Chmn. Dorset Area Health Authority since 1973; A Deputy Lieutenant for Dorset 1977. Served in World War II (Solomon Islands Defence Force; Lieut.-Col. 1945) 1942–46. *Member:* Dorset County Council since 1974, U.S. Legion of Merit; MA; LLD (Hon). *Address:* Church House, Church Road, Shillingstone, Blandford, Dorset.

**TRENCH, Sir Nigel Clive Cosby,** KCMG. *B.* 1916. *Educ.* Eton; Cambridge, BA (Hons.). *M.* 1939, Marcelle Catherine Clotterbooke Patyn. *S.* Roderick Nigel Godolphin. *Career:* Counsellor, Tokyo, 1961–63; Washington, 1963–67; Cabinet Office, 1967–69. British Ambassador to Republic of Korea, Mar. 1969–71; Civil Service Selection Board 1971–73; Brit. Ambassador to Portugal 1974–76. *Club:* Bath Club. *Address:* 4 Kensington Court Gardens, Kensington Court Place, London W8 5QE.

**TREVASKIS, Sir (Gerald) Kennedy (Nicholas),** KCMG, OBE. *B.* 1915. *Educ.* Marlborough College and King's College, Cambridge (BA History; Hons.). *M.* 1945, Sheila James Harrington. *S.* Jeremy Hugh Kennedy and Nicholas James Kennedy. *Dau.* Jennifer Patricia. *Career:* Entered Colonial Service 1938; District Officer, N. Rhodesia 1938. Served in N. Rhodesian Regt. 1939; taken P.O.W. in British Somaliland 1940; British Military Administration, Eritrea 1941–50; District Commissioner, Ndola, N. Rhodesia 1950–51; Political Officer, Western Aden Protectorate 1951, Deputy British Agent 1952–53, Adviser and British Agent 1953–62, and Deputy High Commissioner 1963. British High Commissioner in Aden and Protectorate of Southern Arabia 1963–65; Dir. Sunningdale Oils Ltd. since 1971. *Member:* Royal Institute of International Affairs. *Publications:* Eritrea: a Colony in Transition, 1941–52 (Oxford U.P.); Shades of Amber: a South Arabian Episode (Hutchinson). *Club:* Bath (London). *Address:* The Old Vicarage, Chaddleworth, Berks.

**TREVELYAN, Lord (Humphrey),** KG, GCMG, CIE, OBE. Retired British Diplomat. *B.* 1905. *Educ.* Lancing; Jesus Coll. Cambridge (Hon. Fellow) MA. *M.* 1937, Violet Margaret Bartholomew. *Daus.* 2. *Career:* Indian Civil and Political Services 1929–47; Jr. Secy. External Affairs Dept. Govt. of India 1946–47; Economic adviser to High Commiss. in Germany 1951–53; Chargé d'Affairs Peking 1953–55; Ambassador in Egypt 1955–56; Under-Secy. United Nations 1958; Ambassador in Iraq 1958–61; Deputy-Secy. Foreign Office 1962; Ambassador in the Soviet Union 1962–65; High Commissioner in South Arabia 1967; Chmn. Bd. of Trustees British Museum since 1970; Chmn. Royal Inst. of International Affairs 1970–77. *Director:* British Petroleum Co. Ltd. 1965–75. British Bank of Middle East 1965–77; General Electric Co. Ltd. 1965–76; *President:* Council of Foreign Bondholders. *Decorations:* Knight of the Garter; Grand Cross of St. Michael and St George, Commander of the Indian Empire; Officer of the Order of the British Empire. *Awards:* Hon. Degrees, LLD (Cambridge), DCL (Durham), D.Litt (Leeds). *Publications:* The Middle East in Revolution (1970); Worlds Apart (1971); The India We Left (1972); Diplomatic Channels (1973). *Clubs:* Beefsteak; Pratts. *Address:* 13 Wilton Street, London, S.W.1.

**TREW, Peter John Edward.** MICE, ACIS. British *B.* 1932. *Educ.* Diocesan Coll. of Rondebosch, Cape, South Africa; R.N. Coll. Dartmouth. *M.* 1955, Angela Margaret Rush. *S.* Robin, Martin. *Dau.* Sarah. *Career:* Royal Navy 1950–54; Mining Industry, South Africa 1954–57; Construction Industry, South Africa 1957–60; Construction Industry Britain 1960–70; Member of Parliament for Dartford 1970–74; Dir., Rush & Tompkins Group Ltd. since 1973. *Member:* Institution Civil Engineers. *Clubs:* Naval and Military. *Address:* Great Oaks, Shipbourne, Nr. Tonbridge, Kent.

**TRHLÍK, Zdenek.** Ambassador of the Czechoslovak Socialist Republic. *B.* 1923. *Educ.* Faculty of Law, Charles University, Prague. *M.* 1950, Magda Trhlíková. *Daus.* Lenka and Eva. *Career:* Lecturer in International Law, Charles University 1949. Joined Ministry of Foreign Affairs 1950; Head of Department for Internatl. Organization 1956–61; took part in 7th–16th Sessions of General Assembly of U.N. 1952–62; Ambassador to London 1961; Ambassador to New Delhi, also accredited to Kuala Lumpur. *Address:* 50-M Niti Marg, Chanakyapuri, New Delhi 110021, India.

**TRIGG, Frank Elliot,** OBE, AUA, FCA, ACIS. *B.* 1906. *Educ:* Univ of Adelaide. *M.* 1938, Margaret Waterhouse. *S.* 2. *Career:* Partner, Price Waterhouse & Co. (Internation) & Snr. Partner Price Waterhouse & Co. (Australia) 1961–71; former Trustee (Policyholders) Mutual Life and Citizen's Assurance Co. Ltd., Deputy-chmn. Bd. of Governors N.S.W. State Conservatorium of Music; Chmn. Church Property Trust, Diocese of Sydney; Fellow, Bursar and Trustee of St. Paul's College (Univ of Sydney); Lay Canon St. Andrew's Cathedral. *Address: office* Royal Exchange Bldg., Gresham St., Sydney, N.S.W., Australia.

**TRIMMEL, Rudolf,** Dipl. Ing. Generaldirektor a.D., Austria. *B.* 1906. *Educ.* High School, Technical Univ., Commercial Coll., and Graphic Trades School; Dipl. Ing. Engineer in steam power plant 1927. *Career:* Production Manager in manuf. of aircraft engines during World War II, 1939; Public Administrator, Automotive Industry (Trucks) 1945; Traffic Dept., Municipality of Vienna 1946; Member, Board of Directors, Gebr. Böhler A.G., Vienna 1949–65. Director-General, Rolling Stock Industry (SGP), Vienna and Graz 1950; Reparations Committee, Federal Chancellory 1956; Director-General, Austrian Airways (ASA) 1955; Manager, Austrian Airlines (AUA) 1958. Director, Vöest Vereinigte Österr.Eisen-Stahl werke A.G., Linz 1960. *Publications:*

numerous articles and patents. Socialist. Officer and/or member of technical, scientific and general societies. *Address:* Breitenfurterstrasse 589, A-1237 Vienna, Austria.

**TRIPP, Dermot Alker.** British. *B.* 1913. *Educ.* Aldenham Schl., Elstree. *M.* 1939, Iona Nancy Charlotte Thomson. *S.* Michael John Dermot Alker and Anthony Patrick. *Career:* Joined Thorne, Lancaster & Co. (Chartered Accountants) 1932; Qualified as Chartered Accountant 1937. Army service with D.C.L.I. and R.A.O.C., with rank of Major, 1940–46, Made Partner of Thorne, Lancaster & Co. 1946. Joined S. H. Benson Ltd. July 1958. Director: S. H. Benson International Ltd., Dome Stores Ltd., News Features Ltd., S.H. Benson (India) Ltd., Saviles Private Ltd., S. H. Benson(Nigeria) Ltd., S. H. Benson (Singapore) Ltd., S. H. Benson (E. Africa) Ltd., Media Computer Service Ltd. *Member:* Inst. of Chartered Accountants in England and Wales (Fellow); Inst. of Dirs. (Fellow); Inst. of Practitioners in Advertising (Associate Member). *Clubs:* Eccentric; Royal Thames Yacht; The Arts. *Address:* Beech Cottage, 21 Woodside Avenue, Walton-on-Thames, Surrey.

**TRIPP, Edwin Cooke, III.** American aeronautical engineer. *B.* 1915. *Educ.* University of California (BSME 1938). *M.* (1) 1943, Olga Glidden (*D.* 1970). *S.* John Glidden. *Dau.* Wendy Monica, (2) 1975, Irene Wiessner Dixon. *Career:* Design Engineer, Air Conditioning, Douglas Aircraft 1953–58; Service Engineer, Lockheed Aircraft (1951–53) and Boeing Airplane Co. (1950); Engineering Superintendant, Pan American-Grace Airways 1945–49; Aircraft Engineer, same Company 1940–45; Supervisor, Space Mechanical Section (Saturn) 1962–63; Design Specialist, Douglas Aircraft Co. Inc., Santa Monica, California 1958–62, Branch Chief, Saturn Structural-Mechanical Department 1965–66; Branch Manager, Mol Systems Development 1966–70. Chief Operations Branch 1966—. Principal Engineer Saturn Systems Engineering 1970–73. Member of Technical Staff, Shuttle, Rockwell International Space Division, Downey, Calif. since 1973. *Member:* Amer. Inst. of Aeronautics & Astronautics; Society of Automotive Engineers. *Address:* 17503 Berendo Gardena, Calif., U.S.A.

**TRIPP, John Peter,** CMG. British diplomat. *B.* 1921. *M.* 1948, Rosemary Rees Jones. *S.* 1. *Dau.* 1. *Career:* War Service with Royal Marines; Sudan Political Service 1946–54; Foreign, later Diplomatic Service 1954—; H.M. Ambassador to Libya 1970–74: Brit. High Commissioner Singapore 1974–77. *Award:* Companion, Order St. Michael and St. George. *Address:* 30 Ormonde Gate, London, S.W.3.

**TRITES, Evan Allison,** MBE. Canadian. *B.* 1912. *Educ.* Mount Allison Univ. (BSc Hon.-Chemistry, 1933). *M.* 1939, Jean Biden Conley. *S.* Michael Allison (BA) and Stephen Andrew. *Career:* Joined present company 1933 as office junior; apprenticed taster; employed as such and also production management until 1949, when he was appointed General Manager, St. John, N.B., branch; successively Director1951; Director and Acting President, Blue Ribbon Ltd. 1953; N. A. Sales Director 1953–62. Resident Director, Brooke Bond Canada Ltd. 1962—. Vice-President, T. H. Estabrooks Co. (1959) Ltd. 1959—. Director, Stanway Hutchins Ltd. 1960—. Served in Canadian Army (CIC) from ranks to Major (several staff appointments) 1940–46. Hon. JSC, Royal Military College 1945. Director, Tea Council of Canada. Conservative. *Clubs:* Union (St. John, N.B.); Town of Mount Royal Curling; Riverside; St. Andrews Curling; Riverside Country. *Address:* 3 Sunset Lane, Kennebecasis, Saint John; and *office* 49 Mill Street, Saint John, N.B., Canada.

**TRIVEDI, Vishnuprasad Chunilal.** Secretary, Ministry of External Affairs New Delhi. *B.* 1916. *Educ.* Bombay University (BA); Cambridge University (BA). *M.* Devika. *Career:* Joined service with Govt. of Bombay 1940 and Govt. of India 1944; Under Secy., Deputy Secy. and Joint Secy. in the Ministries of Commerce and External Affairs 1945–64; Counsellor, India High Commission, London 1955–59; High Commissioner in Karachi 1960–61; Alternate Representative and Representative of India to the Economic and Social Council 1962–63–65–67; Representative to U.N. General Assembly 1963–65–67. Ambassador to Switzerland and concurrently to the Holy See 1964–67; Leader of the Indian Delegation to the Conference of the Eighteen Nation Committee, on Disarmament 1964–67; Ambassador of India to Austria; Governor, on the Board of the Int. Atomic Energy Agency 1967–72; Chmn. Bd. of Governors 1971–72. Fellow, Gujerat College, University of Bombay 1936. *Address:* Secretary, Ministry of External Affairs, New Delhi, India.

**TROFIN, Virgil.** E. Econ. Romanian politician. *B.* 1926. *Educ.* Bucharest Acad. of Economics. *Career:* member Communist Party 1945—; Central Cttee. revolutionary youth org. 1945–47; Bureau, Central Cttee. Union Comm. youth 1945–47; First Secy. Central Cttee. 1956–64; Secy. Central Cttee. 1965–71; Member Exec. Cttee. 1968—, and Standing Presidium Central Cttee. 1968–74; Chmn. Nat. Union Agric. Production Cooperatives 1969–71; Chmn., Gen. Trade Confederation 1971–72; Vice-Chmn. Council of Ministers & Minister of Home Trade 1972–74. Hero of Socialist Labour. *Address:* Central Committee of the Romanian Communist Party, Bucharest, Romania.

**TROTTER, Neville Guthrie,** MP. British Chartered Accountant & Politician. *B.* 1932. *Educ.* Shrewsbury Sch.; Durham Univ.—B.Com. *Career:* Partner, Thornton Baker & Co. (Chartered Accountants) 1962–74, Consultant since 1974; mem., Newcastle City Council 1963–74 (Alderman 1970, Chmn. of Finance, Transport & other Cttees., Vice-Chmn. Northumberland Police Authority, mem. of Port of Tyne Authority); mem., Northern Economic Planning Council 1968–74; mem., Civil Aviation Authority Airline Users Consultative Cttee.; Justice of the Peace; MP (Cons.) for Tynemouth since 1974. *Member:* Inst. of Chartered Accountants in England & Wales; Council of the Royal United Services Inst. *Club:* Junior Carlton. *Address:* Granville House, 12 Granville Road, Jesmond, Newcastle upon Tyne; and *office* c/o Thornton Baker & Co., Alliance House, Hood Street, Newcastle upon Tyne NE1 6LB.

**TROUGHTON, Sir Charles Hugh Willis,** CBE, MC, TD. British. *B.* 1916. *Educ.* Haileybury Coll.; Trinity Coll., Cambridge (BA 1938). *M.* 1947, Constance Gillean Mitford. *S.* 3. *Dau.* 1. *Career:* War Service 1939–45 (POW 1940–45); called to the Bar 1945; Mem., Bd. of Management, NAAFI 1953–73; Chmn., W. H. Smith & Son (Holdings) Ltd. 1972–77 (Dir. since 1949); Dir., Equity & Law Life Assurance Soc. Ltd., Electric & General Investment Co. Ltd., Barclays Bank UK Management Ltd., Thomas Tilling Ltd.; Chmn., British Council since 1977. Knight Bachelor 1977. *Clubs:* M.C.C.; Boodles. *Address:* Woolleys, Hambleden, Henley-on-Thames, Oxfordshire.

**TROUT, Sir (Herbert) Leon,** Kt. 1959. FASA. Australian solicitor. Director of several companies. *B.* 1906. *Educ.* Brisbane Grammar School. *M.* 1936, Peggy Elaine Hyland. *Career:* Active service overseas (War of 1939–45; Commissioned rank, Queensland Cameron Highlanders). Federal Pres., Australian Automobile Assn. 1946; Pres. Brisbane Chamber of Commerce 1953–56; Fed. Pres. Associated Chambers of Commerce of Australia 1956–59; Member Exports Payment Insurance Corp. 1958, and Manufacturers' Industries Advisory Council 1958. Pres. Liberal Party of Queensland 1953–57. Pres. Queensland National Art Gallery Socy. 1951–54; Chmn. of Trustees, Queensland Art Gallery; Pres. Queensland Musical Literary Self-Aid Socy. for the Blind 1938–45. *Clubs:* Brisbane (Pres. 1955–56); Royal Queensland Yacht (Hon. Life Member); Royal Automobile, Queensland (Pres. 1946–47–48). *Address:* Everton House, Dargie Street, Everton Park, 4053 Brisbane, Qld., Australia.

**TROYANOVSKY, Oleg Aleksandrovich.** USSR Diplomat. *B.* 1919. *Educ.* Moscow Inst. for Foreign Languages; Moscow State Inst. for Philosophy, Literature & History. *M.* 1953, Tatiana Popova. *Dau.* 1. *Career:* TASS 1941; Soviet Army 1941–42; Soviet Information Bureau 1942–44; Soviet Embassy, London 1944–46; Ministry of Foreign Affairs, Moscow 1946–58; Asst. to the Chmn. of the Council of Ministers of the USSR 1958–67; Soviet Ambassador to Japan1967–76; mem., Collegium of the Ministry of Foreign Affairs of the USSR & Head of the 2nd Far Eastern Dept. 1976; Perm. Rep. of the USSR to the UN since 1976. *Decorations:* Order of Lenin; Order of the Red Banner of Labour (twice); Order of Merit. *Address:* Permanent Mission of the USSR to the UN, 136 East 67th Street, New York, N.Y. 10021, U.S.A.

**TRUDEAU, Rt. Hon. Pierre Elliott,** PC, FRSC, QC, MP. Prime Minister of Canada. *B.* 1919. *Educ.* Jean-de-Brébeuf Coll., Montreal; Univ. of Montreal; Harvard Univ.; Ecole des Sciences Politiques, Paris; London School of Economics. *M.* 1971, Margaret Sinclair. *S.* 3. *Career:* Called to Bar, Quebec 1943; practised law, Province of Quebec; co-founder of Review Cité Libre; Assoc. Prof. of Law, Univ. of Montreal 1961–65; mem. of House of Commons since 1965; Parly. Sec. to Prime Minister Jan. 1966–April 1967; Minister of Justice & Attorney General April 1967–July 1968; Leader of Liberal Party & Prime Minister of Canada since April 1968. *Member:* Bars of Provinces of Quebec & Ontario; founding mem.,

Montreal Civil Liberties Union. *Awards:* Hon. Dr. of Laws, Univ. of Alberta 1968; Dr. h.c., Duke Univ. 1974; Hon. Fellow, LSE 1969; Freeman of City of London 1975. *Publications:* La Grève de l'Amiante (1956); (with Jacques Hébert) Deux Innocents en Chine Rouge (1961); Le Fédéralisme et la Société canadienne–française (1968); Reponses (1968). *Address:* Prime Minister's Residence, 24 Sussex Drive, Ottawa, Canada.

**TRUE, Henry Alfonso (Dave), Jr.** American. Oil producer, drilling contractor and rancher. *B.* 1915. *Educ.* Montana State Coll. (BS Indus Eng 1937). *M.* 1938, Jean Durland. *S.* Henry A III, Diemer D. and David L. *Dau.* Tamma Jean (Hatten). *Career:* The Texas Co. Roustabout Pumper, Foreman 1937–45; Supt. Drilling & Production State, Wyoming 1945–48; Manager Reserve Drilling Co. Inc. 1948–51, Pres. 1951–59; Partner True Drilling Co. since 1951; True Oil Co. since 1951; Vice-Pres. 1953–70 Pres. 1954–70 True Service Co.; Vice-Pres. & Secy. 1952 Toolpushers Supply Co. Pres. since 1954; Pres. True Building Corp. 1956–67; Little Smokey Oil Co. 1956–68; Pres. Belle Fourche Pipeline Co. since 1957; Owner True Ranches since 1957; Dir. First Nat. Bank Casper since 1962; Chmn. Bd. Powder River Oil Shippers Service Inc. 1963–67; Pres. Camp Creek Gas Co. since 1964; Vice-Pres. George Mancini Feed Lots, 1964–72; Vice-Pres. 1965–69 Black Hills Oil Marketeers, Inc. Pres. since 1969; Dir. since 1965 Reserve Oil Purchasing Co. Vice-Pres. 1966–72; Pres. 1973—; Vice-Pres. White Stallion Ranch Inc. since 1965; Mountain Bell Wyoming Bd. Advisors since 1965 and Bd. of Dirs. since 1974; Federal Energy Office, Rocky Moutain Petroleum Industry Advisory Cttee since 1973. *Member:* Amer. Assn. Oilwell Drilling Contractors (Dir. 1950—)Amer. Petroleum Inst. (Bd. of Dirs. 1960—, Exec. Cttee. since 1970; Business-Industry Political Action Cttee. Reg. Vice-Chmn. 1966–69, Bd. Dir. since 1964; Boys' Clubs of America, Nat. Assoc. 1964–69, Hon. Chmn. Local Chapter 1971; Casper Air Terminal Bd. Trustees 1961–71, Pres. 1964–65, 67–68); Casper Petroleum Club (Dir. 1954—); Federal Power Commission, Natural Gas Adv. Council 1964–65, Federal Power Exec. Ad. Cttee since 1971; Gas Supply Cttee. 1965–69, Vice-Chmn. 1967–73; Int. Oil & Gas Educ. Center (Adv. Bd. 1964—, Vice-Chmn. 1969–73); Rocky Mountain Oil & Gas Assn. Pres 1962–63 (Dir. 1950—, Exec. Cttee. 1954, Vice-Pres. 1956–58); Wyoming Stock Growers Assn. 1957—; Independent Petroleum Assn. of Amer. (Vice-Pres. 1960–61, Exec. Cttee. 1962, Pres. 1964–65); Natl. Assn. of Manufacturers; State Chmn. Membership Cttee. for Wyoming since 1965, Education Cttee. 1970–71; Chmn. 1972–74; Natl. Petroleum Cncl. Member since 1962; Appointment Cttee. 1964–65, Policy Cttee, since 1965, Vice-Chmn. 1970–71; Chmn. since 1972; Wyo. Oil Industry Cttee., Exec. Cttee. 1958–74; Treas. 1958–59, Pres. 1960–62, now Petroleum Assn. of Wyoming, Bd. of Directors since 1974; Public Land Law Review Commission (Adv. Cncl. 1965–70); Dir. U.S. Industrial Council (formerly Southern States Industrial Council) since 1971, Exec. Cttee, since 1974; Southwestern Legal Foundation, Member Research Fellows since 1968; U.S. Chamber of Commerce Policy Cttee. since 1966 and Dir since 1975. Mem. Independent Petroleum Assocn. of Rocky Mountain States since 1972 and Rocky Mountain Pioneers since 1968; Mem. 25 Year Club of Petroleum Industry since 1973; Pres. Bd. Trustees Univ. of Wyoming. 1971–73; member adult Educ. Comm. Service Council 1961–64, Bd. Trustees since 1965; member, All Amer. Wildcatters; Hon. member, Alpha Chapter Wyoming; Beta Gamma Sigma 1972. *Awards:* C. of C. Award, State of Wyoming; Oil Man of the Year, 1959; Honoured Citizen Award (City of Casper, Wyo.), 1964; Kentucky Colonel, 1955; Chief Roughneck of the Year, Lone Star Steel Award, 1965; 1965 Annual Industrial Award Wyoming Association of Realtors; Distinguished Businessman of 1966–67 (Coll. of Comm. and Industry, Univ. of Wyo. Award); Dir and Trustee National Cowboy Hall of Fame and Western Heritage Center since 1975; Dist. Service Award Independent Oil operator. Texas Oil & Gas Assn. 1971. National Council for Small Business Management Development Awards, Outstanding National Small Businessmen for 1967 and Western Region National Small Businessman of the Year for 1967; The John Rogers Award. Southwestern Legal Foundation 1975; Russell B. Brown Memorial Award. Independent Petroleum Assocn. of America 1975. *Address:* Box 2360 Casper, Wyoming, U.S.A. and 6000 So Poplar Street, Casper, Wyo., and Lak Ranch, Newcastle, Wyoming, U.S.A.

**TRUSCOTT, Sir Denis (Henry), GBE, TD. British.** Master-printer. *B.* 1908. *Educ.* Rugby School and Magdalene College, Cambridge. *M.* 1932, Ethel Margaret Lyell. *Daus.* 4. *Career:* Elected Court of Common Council, City of London 1938; Alderman from 1947· Sheriff 1951–52; Lord Mayor of London 1957–58; one of H.M. Lieutenants for the City of London; Court of Assistants, Worshipful Company of Vintners (Master 1955–56); Worshipful Company of Stationers and Newspaper Makers (Master 1959–60); Worshipful Company of Musicians (Master 1957 and 1971); Guild of Freemen of the City of London (Master 1957–58); member of Cttee., Automobile Assn 1952—; Board of Governors, St. Bartholomew's Hospital 1949–69; Board of Royal Hospital and Home for Incurables, Putney, 1938—; Council, Royal Holloway College, Egham, 1947–69; member, Darenth and Stone Hospital Management Cttee 1952–70; (Chairman 1957–70;) Trustee Rowland Hill Benevolent Fund, Chairman 1954—· Director, Bedford General Insurance Co.: Chmn Zurich Life Assurance Soc. Ltd. since 1974. Vice-Pres. Squash Rackets Assn. of England; Pres., Brown Knight and Truscott Ltd. (printers, etc.); Pres., Printing and Allied Trades Research Assn. 1956–64; Institute of Printing 1961–63. Grand Cross of Merit (Fed. Republic of Germany); Grand Officer. Order of Merit (Republic of Italy). *Address:* Invermark, 30 Drax Avenue, Wimbledon, London, S.W.20.

**TRYPANIS, Constantine Athanasius,** MA, DLitt, DPhil, FRSL. Greek University Professor. *B.* 1909. *Educ.* Chios Gymnasium; Univs. of Athens, Berlin & Munich. *M.* 1942, Alice Macri. *Dau.* 1. *Career:* Classical Lect., Athens Univ. 1939–47; Bywater & Sotheby Prof. of Byzantine & Modern Greek Language & Literature, & Fellow, Exeter Coll., Oxford 1947–68; Emeritus Fellow since 1968; Univ. Prof. of Classics, Chicago Univ. 1968–74; Minister of Culture & Science, Govt. of Greece since 1974. *Member:* FRSL 1958; Life Fellow, Internat. Inst. of Arts & Letters 1958; Inst. for Advanced Study, Princeton, U.S.A. 1959–60; Visiting Prof.: Hunter Coll., N.Y. 1963, Harvard Univ. 1963, 1964; Univ. of Chicago 1965–66; Univ. of Cape Town 1969. Corresponding Mem., Inst. for Balkan Studies (Greece); Athens Acad. 1974 (Corresp. Mem. 1971); Medieval Acad. of America. Archon Megas Hieromnemon of the Oekumenical Patriarch. Dr. of Humane Letters (h.c.), MacMurray Coll., U.S.A. 1974; Dr. of Humane Letters, Assumption Coll., U.S.A. 1977. Hon. Fellow, The International Poetry Society 1977. *Address:* Ministry of Culture & Science, Athens, Greece.

**TRYSTRAM, Emile (Jean Louis Roger).** French civil mining engineer. Knight Legion of Honour. *B.* 1911. *Educ.* Ecoles des Mines de Paris; BA (Law). *M.* 1938, Odile Bedel. *S.* Didier and Jean-Paul. *Daus.* Florence Gandilhon, Isabelle and Helene. *Career:* Mining Director at Zellidja 1953; Chief Director, Compagnie des Freins et Signaux, Westinghouse 1953–61; Dir. Etablissements Boussac 1961–68; Pres. Bedel et Cie 1969—; Expert Tribunal Commerce Paris since 1972. *Member:* AIME; Civil Engineers of France. *Club:* Automobile (France). *Address: office* 47 Rue de la Haie, 93300 Aubervilliers, France.

**TSARAPKIN, Semen K.** Soviet diplomat. *B.* 1906. *Educ.* Institute of Oriental Studies; Moscow University; former Chief of 2nd Far Eastern Department, P.C.F.A. and Head of American Department, P.C.F.A.; Delegate, Dumbarton Oaks Conference 1944; Delegate, U.N.C.I.O. 1945; Delegate, 1st General Assembly 1947; member, 2nd Special Session, General Assembly 1948; member of Trusteeship Council 1948; member, Collegium, Ministry of Foreign Affairs, U.S.S.R. 1948; Chargé d'Affaires, Washington 1948; former Alternate Representative to U.N. Security Council (with rank of Minister and Deputy Permanent Representative, U.N.) 1949–54; Head of Div. for Int. Orgs., Moscow 1954–66; Head of Soviet Del. to Geneva Disarmament Talks 1961–66; Ambassador to Fed. Republic of Germany 1966–71; Ambassador at Large since 1971. *Address:* Ministry of Foreign Affairs, Smolenskaya-Sennaya Ploshchad 32-34, Moscow, U.S.S.R.

**TSATSOS, Alexander George.** Greek civil engineer and company director. *B.* 8 July 1905. *Educ.* Federal Polytechnic School, Zurich. *M.* 1936, Despina Hadjikyriacos. *S.* George, Andreas. *Career:* Designer and Construction Engineer on Struma Works 1929–35; Chief Engineer, Ertha Co. of Athens 1936–38; Partner George J. Tsatsos & Sons 1938–73; Managing Director (1939–59) and Chairman of the Board 1959—, HERACLES General Cement Co., Athens; Dir. Deputy Chmn. Chemical Industries Co. 1940–76; Astir Insurance Co. 1947–74; Chairman of the Board and Managing Director, Industrial Development Corp., Athens 1960–62; Chmn. AIGIS Industry for Packaging Materials 1971–76; HERACLES Shipping Co. S.A. 1971—; Gov. Hellenic Industrial Development Bank S.A.; Dir. and Chmn. Greek Exports S.A. 1973; Deputy Chmn. Assoc. of Greek Industrial

Product Exporters 1970—. *Member:* Various Government Adv. Cttees. 1946–62; Greek Del. Int. Conferences, I.L.O. and I.M.F., etc.; Vice-Pres., Fed. of Greek Industries 1945–52 (Pres. 1952–53 and 1954–55); Chmn. National Welfare Organization, Greece 1968–73; Cttee. Drafting of the Perspective Plan of Greece 1971–72; Member, Deputy Speaker Adv. Council, Drafting of Laws and Decrees, 1970–73; For. Corresp. (Greece) of Conference Bd. N.Y. 1957—; For. Corresp. of Stanford Research Inst., Calif. 1957—. *Member:* Société des Ingénieurs Civils de France; Int. Panel, Arbitrators, Amer. Arbitration Assn.; Life member, American Society of Civil Engineers, A.S.T.M., Greek Technical Chamber of Engineers. *Address:* HERACLES General Cement Co., S.A., P.O. Box 500, Athens, Greece.

**TSENG, Hsu-pai.** Chinese journalist. *B.* 1894. *Educ.* St. John's University (BA). *Career:* Man. Dir. and Editor-in-Chief, China Evening News, Shanghai 1932–36; Counsellor, National Military Council 1935–37; Director, International Department, Ministry of Information 1938–47; Vice-President, Post-Graduate School of Journalism, Central Political Institute 1943–46; Deputy Director, Government Information Office 1947–48; Director, Fourth Department of Kuomintang Central Reform Committee 1950–51; member of Kuomintang Central Reform Committee 1950–52; Director, Central News Agency 1950–64; Associate Manager and News Commentator, Broadcasting Corporation of China 1950–53; Special Column Writer, Central Daily News and Sin Shen Pao since 1950; President, Taipei Press Association 1951–57, 1968–69 and 1971–72; President, Taipei Chapter of Lions International 1955–56; Dean, Graduate School of Journalism, National Chengchi Univ., Formosa 1954–71; Member of the Executive Committee to the China Chapter, Asia Anti-Communist League since 1955; member, Exec. Committee P.E.N. Club (China Chapter) 1958; invited by UNESCO as an expert to participate in the Meeting on Development of Information Media in South East Asia, Bangkok 1960. Member, Standing Cttee., The Chinese 4-H Club 1960—; President, Natl. Assn. of News Agencies 1963–65; Governor, District 300, Lions International 1964, International Councillor 1966—. Chairman, Board of Directors. Board Member, Central News Agency 1965–72; Chairman, Program Study Committee, National Television Research Institute China, 1970—; Dean and Prof. The Sun-Yat-Sen Research Institute, Chinese Cultural College 1974. *Publications:* American Literature A.B.C.; English Literature A.B.C.; The Theory and Practice of Democratic Industrial System; Comment on World Affairs; New Interpretation of Party Principles; My American Travelogue; History of Chinese Journalism; The Current Contribution of Dr. Sun Yat-sen's Philosophy; World Crisis and Comments, Principle of Public Opinion. *Address:* Central News Agency, Inc. Taipeh, Taiwan.

**TSHINGOMBA, Kaninda Mpumbua.** Zaire diplomat. Ambassador of Zaire in London. *Address:* 26 Chesham Place, London SW1X 8HH.

**TSUR, Jacob.** Israeli diplomat. *B.* 1906. *Educ.* Hebrew College, Jerusalem; University of Florence; Sorbonne Faculty of Letters. *M.* 1928, Vera Gotlib. *S.* 1. *Dau.* 1. *Career:* On editorial staff of 'Haolam' Paris 1926–29; Haaretz, Tel-Aviv 1929; Press Officer, Jewish National Fund, Jerusalem 1930–48; on missions on behalf of the Jewish Agency (Belgium, Greece, Bulgaria) 1933–40; Liaison Officer, H.Q. British Forces in Egypt 1943–44; Chmn., Recruiting Cttee. Jerusalem, during war of independence 1948; first envoy of Israel in S. America; Minister to Uruguay (1949). Argentina (1950), Chile (1951), Paraguay (1951); Amb. Ex. and Plen. to France 1953–59; Actg. Director-General, Foreign Ministry 1959. Chmn. Jewish National Fund, and President, Israel's Ibero-American Institute. Grand Officer, Legion of Honour. *Publications:* Sunrise in Zion (Hebrew, French, English editions 1965); An Ambassador's Diary in Paris, (Hebrew, French 1967); La Révolte Juive (French 1970, Italian, Spanish 1972); Portrait of the Diaspora (Hebrew, 1975); L'Epopée du Sionisme (French, English, German, Italian, 1975). *Address:* Mevo Yoram 5, Jerusalem, Israel.

**TUCK, Raphael,** MP. British Politician & Barrister at Law. *B.* 1910. *Educ.* St. Paul's Sch., London Univ.—BSc (Econ.); Cambridge Univ.—MA; Harvard Univ.—LLM. *M.* 1959, Monica Ley-Greaves. *Career:* British Embassy, Washington D.C. 1940–41; Lecturer in Law, Univ. of Saskatchewan 1941–44; Constitutional Adviser to Premier of Manitoba 1943; Prof. of Law, Univ. of Saskatchewan 1944–45; Special Research work, Dept. of Labour, Ottawa 1944; Prof. of Political Science, McGill Univ., Montreal 1945–46, & Tulane Univ., New Orleans 1947–49; Barrister at Law since 1951; MP (Lab.) for Watford since 1964. *Member:* Harvard Law Assoc. of the UK; Soc. of Labour Lawyers; Harvard Club of London; Hertfordshire Soc., Watford Philharmonic Assoc. *Awards:* Lord Justice Holker (Holt) Scholarship, Gray's Inn 1937; Exhibitioner, Trinity Hall, Cambridge 1938 (1st Class Hons.). *Publications:* Articles in *Univ. of Toronto Law Journal, Canadian Journal of Economics & Political Science, Canadian Bar Review, Public Affairs* (Canada), *Solicitor's Law Journal. Address:* 17 Vicarage Lane, East Preston, Sussex; and *offices* 10 King's Bench Walk, Temple, London EC4.

**TUCKER, Sir Henry James,** CBE. First Government Leader under the new constitution of Bermuda, 1968–71. *B.* 1903. *Educ.* Saltus Grammar School, Bermuda; Sherborne School, Dorset, England. *M.* 1925, Catherine Newbold Barstow. *S.* Henry James III, Robert Newbold. *Dau.* Judith Trott. *Career:* General Mgr. Bank of Bermuda 1938—; Government Leader 1968–71. *Member:* Bermuda House of Assembly, 1938—; United Bermuda Party. *Clubs:* Royal Bermuda Yacht; Royal Hamilton Amateur Dinghy; Mid-Ocean. *Address:* The Lagoon, Paget East, Bermuda; and *office* Bank of Bermuda Ltd., Hamilton, Bermuda.

**TUCKER, Morrison Graham.** American banker. *B.* 1911. *Educ.* Dartmouth College (AB). *M.* 1944, Gladys Mae Hartz. *S.* John Graham. *Dau.* Suzanne. *Career:* Assistant National Bank Examiner 1932, Federal Bank Examiner 1936, Assistant Chief Examiner for the U.S. with the Federal Deposit Insurance Corp. 1939. Lieut. in U.S. Navy, 1942–44. Banking Adviser to President of the Philippines 1944–47; Manager of certain interests in Latin America of the Rockefeller family 1947–51; Owner Morrison G. Tucker & Co., Banking & Investments. Director: American General Life Insurance Co., Capitol Steel & Iron Co.; Anta Corp.; Trustee Okla. City University; Chmn. Union Bank & Trust Co., First Security Bank & Trust Co., Southwestern Bank & Trust Co., United Oklahoma Bank; Will Rogers Bank & Trust Co.; Chairman, Exec., Cttee., Liberty National Bank & Trust Co. to 1969; Member Amer. Economic Assn. *Clubs:* Metropolitan (Washington, D.C.); University (N.Y.C.); Men's Dinner, Okla., City Golf & Country, Petroleum (all of Oklahoma City). *Address:* 2403 N.W. Grand Blvd., Oklahoma City, Okla. 73116; and *office* 2900 Liberty Tower, Oklahoma City, Okla. 73102, U.S.A.

**TUGENDHAT, Christopher Samuel.** British Politician & Author. *B.* 1937. *Educ.* Cambridge Univ.—MA. *M.* 1967, Julia Lissant Dobson. *S.* 2. *Career:* Leader & Feature Writer on The Financial Times 1960–70; Conservative MP for Cities of London & Westminster 1970–74, & for City of London & Westminster South 1974–76; Member, Commission of the European Communities since 1977. *Publications:* Oil, The Biggest Business (1968); The Multinationals (1971—McKinsey Foundation Book Award). *Address:* Commission of the European Communities, 200 rue de la Loi, 1049 Brussels, Belgium.

**TULLIS, John Ledbetter.** *B.* 1911. *Educ.* University of Texas (BSEE 1933). *M.* 1954, Jeanne Allen Perkins. *S.* John L. III. *Career:* With AMF Beaird Inc.: Sales Engineer, Sales Manager 1947–54; Vice-President Sales 1954–57; Executive Vice-President 1957–58; Pres. and General Manager 1959–62; President and Chairman 1962–68; Vice-Pres. AMF 1963, Group Exec. AMF's Ind. Products Group 1963–68; Exec. Vice-Pres. 1968, Pres. since 1970; Pres. Chief Operating Officer, Dir. AMF Inc. 1970–73; Consultant, Interstate Electric of Shreveport, Dir. Interstate. *Awards:* Distinguished Engineering Graduate Award, College of Engineering, Univ. of Texas, 1963. Registered Professional Engineer, State of Texas. *Clubs:* Shreveport; Shreveport La.; Shreveport Country. *Address:* 3008 Country Club Drive, Shreveport, Louisiana, 71109 and *office* 1419 Culpepper, Shreveport, La. 71130, U.S.A.

**TULLIS, Richard Barclay.** American. *B.* 1913. *Educ.* Principia College, Elsah, Ill. (AB). *M.* 1935, Chaillé Handy. *S.* Barclay J., Garner H. *Dau.* Sarah (de Barcza). *Career:* Pres., Miller Printing Machine Co., 1952–56; Chmn. and Dir., Harris-Intertype Corporation now Harris Corp. (since 1974); Director: Cleveland Electric Illuminating Co.; National City Bank of Cleveland. Trustee First Union Real Estate Investment Trust; Trustee, Principia College; Trustee, Case Western Reserve Univ., Cleveland. *Address:* 13515 Shaker Boulevard, Cleveland, Ohio 44120; and *office* 55 Public Square, Cleveland, Ohio 44113, U.S.A.

**TUNGELER, Johannes.** German banker. *B.* 23 Nov. 1907. *M.* 1939, Margarete Uebel. *Career:* Served with the Reichsbank 1922–25; apprentice and clerk in private bank 1925–31; with Reichsbank 1931–39; with Trade Dept., Ministry of Economic Affairs, 1939–45; engaged in organization and direction of the foreign department of Bank deutscher Länder 1946–53; member of the Board of Directors of the bank now named Deutsche Bundesbank 1953—. *Address:* Wilhelm-Epstein-Strasse 14, 6, Frankfurt/Main, Germany.

**TUNHAMMAR, Elam Wihlgott.** Swedish. *B.* 1903. *Educ.* Univ. of Lund (LLB). *M.* 1940, Margaretha Mathiasson. *S.* 1. *Daus.* 2. *Career:* Solicitor, Hellefors Bruks AB 1929–36; Director Swedish Iron & Steel Works Employers Association 1936–41; Dir. Fed. of Swedish Industries 1942–47, and of AB Electrolux 1947–51. Managing Director, Swedish Tobacco Monopoly 1951–57; Managing Dir., Skãnska Cement AB & AB Ifoverken 1957–68; Chairman Industri AB EUROC (formerly AB Cementa & AB Ifoverken) 1968–75; Chmn. of Board; Holmens Bruk AB; Mem. of Board Nitro Nobel AB 1945–76: Kockums Mek; Verkstads AB 1963–73; Chmn. of Board Trygg-Hansa, group of insurance companies 1971–73; AB Atomenergi (Vice-Chmn. of Board) 1947–76; MEA A.B. (Chmn. of Bd.) 1954–76. Member of Board: Swedish Employers Federation 1959–75; Assn. Swedish Chemical Industries 1951–75; Fed. of Swedish Industries 1960–75; Swedish Petroleum Inst. (Hon. Chmn. of Bd.). *Awards:* Commander of Order of Vasa (1st Cl.); Commander Grand Cross Order of Northern Star; Knight, Finnish Order of the Lion (1st Cl.); Order of Service (in gold) of Greek Red Cross; French Merite Civique and Order of Service (in gold) of Swedish Mine Owners Association. *Address:* Annebergsgatan 15A, 214 66 Malmo, Sweden.

**TUOMINEN, Leo Olavi,** KBE. *B.* 1911. *Educ.* Univ. of Turku (MA 1932); Dr. of Humanities (h.c.) 1974, Marquette, U.S.A.; Officer of Reserve 1934. *M.* 1938, Helene Johanna Habert. *S.* 1. *Daus.* 3. *Career:* Entered diplomatic service 1934; Attaché, Paris (1934–38), Riga (1938–39), Warsaw (1939) and Min. for Foreign Affairs (1940); Secy., 1941–43; Head of Section, 1943–46; Consul, Antwerp, 1946–47; First Secy., Brussels, 1947–48; Asst. Dir., Commercial Div., Min. for Foreign Affairs, 1948–50; Permanent Delegate to the International Organizations in Geneva, 1950–52; Min. to Argentina, Uruguay and Chile, 1952–55; Director, Commercial Division, Ministry for Foreign Affairs, 1955; Secretary of State in same Ministry 1956–57, Head of delegation for commercial negotiations with Germany, Belgium, France, Greece, Italy, the Netherlands, Poland, Spain, United Kingdom, U.S.A., U.S.S.R., etc. 1945–56, Vice-President of Finnish delegation, Conference on Tariffs and Trade (GATT) Annecy, 1949, and Pres. of the delegation at GATT Conference, Torquay, 1950. Ambassador to the Court of St. James's, 1957–68 and to Italy, 1968; Appointed Ambassador of Finland to Sweden, 1969 and Washington 1972. *Awards:* Cdr. 1st Cl., Order of the White Rose of Finland; Grand Cross of Lion of Finland; Grand Cross of North Star of Sweden; Grand Cross, Order of the Falcon (Iceland); KBE; Comm. of the following Orders: Leopold II (Belgium); Crown of Italy; Oak Crown of Luxembourg; Orange-Nassau of the Netherlands; Grand Officer, Order of Merit (Argentina); Officer, Legion of Honour (France); Silver Medal of Physical Education (France); Medal of Merit of Physical Education (Finland). *Address:* Finnish Embassy, 1900 Twenty-Fourth Street, N.W., Washington D.C. 20008, U.S.A.

**TURCOTTE, Lawson Phillippe.** Executive. Vice-President: Georgia Pacific Corp. 1950–63, and Pres., Ketchikan Pulp Co., Ketchikan, Alaska 1952—. *B.* 1896. *Educ.* Sacred Heart Coll., Grand Mere, Que., Canada, and Garbutt Business Coll., Alberta. *M.* 1923, Eva A. Pearson. *S.* Donald Lawson. Accnt., Stacey Lumber Co., Lethbridge, Alberta 1913–15; with Canadian Army (Canada, England, France) 1915–19; Secy., Great War Veterans Association, Lethbridge 1920–26; successively Accountant, Treasurer, Executive President, Puget Sound Pulp & Timber Co. 1926–63. *Publications:* various articles on the pulp and paper industry in home and foreign journals. *Member:* National Assn. of Manufacturers (Dir.); National Chamber of Commerce (Washington, D.C.). Republican. *Clubs:* Rainier, Washington Athletic, Golf; Harbor (all of Seattle); Golf, Yacht (Bellingham). *Address:* Georgia Pacific Corporation, Bellingham, Wash., U.S.A.

**TURK, Dr. Fouad.** Lebanese Diplomat. *B.* 1931. *Educ.* Zahle Oriental Coll.; Colegio de la Sagesse, Beirut; Univ. of the Lebanon; Univ. of Ottawa, Canada—Lic. en Letras, Doctor of History. *Career:* Prof. of History 1956; joined Ministry of Foreign Affairs 1957; Attaché, Lebanese Embassy Ottawa 1959–64; 1st Sec., Lebanese Embassy, Bogota 1964–66; Lebanese Chargé d'Affaires to the Govt. of Colombia 1966–69; Head of International Section, Central Admin. of the Ministry of Foreign Affairs 1969; various appointments, incl. mem. of the Presidential Goodwill Mission in 9 East African countries 1970–71; Consul-Gen. of Lebanon in New York, & Minister Counsellor to the Perm. Mission of the Lebanon to the UN 1971; Lebanese Ambassador to the Republic of Argentina since 1972. *Decorations:* Knight of the National Order of the Cedar; Order of Merit of the Lebanese Worldwide Cultural Union; Commander, Order of Colombia, of the Ivory Coast, & of Chad. Said AKL Prize, 1968. *Address:* Embassy of the Lebanon, Av. del Libertador 2354, Buenos Aires, Argentina.

**TURNER, Rt. Hon. Sir Alexander Kingcome,** KBE, PC. New Zealand. *B.* 1901. *Educ.* Auckland (N.Z.) Grammar School and Univ. of Auckland (MA; LLB); LLD Univ. of Auckland 1965. *M.* 1934, Dorothea Frances Mulgan. *S.* Richard Nicholas and Joseph Patrick Franklin. *Dau.* Cecilia. *Career:* Called to N.Z. Bar 1923; practised as Barrister and Solicitor at Auckland 1927–51; Queen's Counsel 1952; Judge of Supreme Court 1953; Judge of the New Zealand Court of Appeal 1962–72; President 1972–73; Gen. Editor Commentary on the 4th Ed. of Halsbury since 1973. Member, Auckland University Council 1934–50; Vice- President, Auckland University 1949–50; Governor, Massey Agricultural College and Chairman of its Research Committee 1944–53, Carnegie Fellowship 1949. Served with N.Z. Army in New Zealand 1941–42. *Publications:* Spencer Bower and Turner on the Law of Estoppel by Representation (1966); Spencer Bower and Turner on Res Judicata (1969); Spencer Bower & Turner on Actionable Misrepresentation (1974). *Clubs:* Auckland; Wellington. *Address:* 14 St. Michaels Crescent, Wellington 5; and P.O. Box 10223, The Terrace, Wellington 1, New Zealand.

**TURNER, Colin William Carstairs.** DFC. British International Media representative and politician. *B.* 1922. *Educ.* St. Johns Coll., Manor House; Highgate School. *M.* 1949. *S.* 3. *Daus.* 1. *Career:* Member, National Exec. Cons. Party 1947–53, 1968–73, 1976–77; Nat. Exec. G. P. Cttee. 1949–53; Chmn., Far East Sub Cttee. of Commonwealth Affairs 1959–64; Member Parliament, Woolwich West 1959–64; Chmn., S.E. Asia Cttee., Commonwealth & Overseas Council 1964–75; Deputy Chmn. Conservative Commonwealth & Overseas Council 1975–76, Chmn. 1976–77; Member, Nat. Exec. Publicity Cttee. 1969–73; Member, West India Cttee., Inst. of Directors; Assoc. member, Comm. Press Union; Pres. Overseas Press Media Assn. 1967–68; Editor Overseas Media Guide 1968–74, Hon. Treas. since 1974; Chmn. P.R. Cttee. CPU since 1971. *Clubs:* Royal Overseas League; R.A.F. Reserves; No. 10 Club; North Enfield, Enfield Highway & Eltham Conservative. *Address:* 55 Rowantree Road, Enfield, Middlesex and *office* 122 Shaftesbury Avenue, London, W.1.

**TURNER, Sir Harvey,** CBE. New Zealand company director. *B.* 11 Sept. 1889. *M.* Margaret Ethel. *S.* John Penman, David Ross, Grahame Harvey. *Daus.* Marjorie Ethel, Audrey Maude. *Career:* Advisory Director, Turners & Growers Ltd. Auckland, and Director or Advisory Director of associate companies, at Whangarei, Hamilton, Tauranga, Rotorua, Palmerston North, Wanganui, Hastings/Napier, Wellington & Christchurch. Past Chmn. of the Auckland Harbour Board; Past President, Auckland Chamber of Commerce; Sen. Active member, Auckland Rotary Club. *Address:* P.O. Box 56, Auckland, 1, New Zealand.

**TURNER, John H. F.,** OBE. *B.* 1900. *Educ.* Andover (N.B.- Grammar School. *M.* 1931, Jean McIlwraith. *S.* John Doug) las. *Career:* Entered Bank at Perth 1916; served in London (Eng.) and Paris 1925–29; Asst. Manager, Hamilton 1931, and Montreal 1938; Asst. Superintendent, Foreign Dept., Head Office 1945; Superintendent 1946; Asst. General Manager 1952–56; General Manager for Europe, London 1961–64. In 1942 services loaned to Canadian Government and appointed Cotton Administrator, War Time Prices and Trade Board. Member: Canadian Trade Mission to U.K., Nov.–Dec. 1957; Canadian Delegation to Congress of Chambers of Commerce of the British Commonwealth and Empire, London 1957, 1962 and 1968; and International Chamber of Commerce, Naples 1957; Washington, D.C. 1959; Copenhagen 1961; New Delhi 1965; and Montreal 1967, City of London Society; Freeman, City of London; and member, Worshipful Company of Loriners. General Chairman, Welfare Federation of Montreal (Red Feather Campaign) 1958. Vice-Pres. (Treas. 1964–69), Federation of Commonwealth Chambers of Commerce;

Governor Canadian Council International Chamber of Commerce. *Member:* Royal Commonwealth Society; Royal Institute of Internl. Affairs; McGill **Assocs.; English-Speaking** Union; Greater **Victoria Chamber** of Commerce, Victoria; Canada Club; Vancouver Bd. of Trade. *Clubs:* Union; Victoria Golf (Vic. B.C.); Royal Automobile; Overseas Bankers (London). *Address:* **201-1400 Newport Avenue,** Victoria, B.C., Canada.

**TURNER, Sir Michael (William),** Kt (1961) CBE (1957). *B.* 1905. *Educ.* Marlborough Coll. and Univ. Coll., Oxford; Ma (Oxon); Hon. LLD, Hong Kong 1959. *M.* 1938, Wendy Spencer Stranack. *S.* 3. *Career:* Formerly Chairman and Chief Manager of The Hongkong and Shanghai Banking Corp., Hong Kong (retd. 1962). Member of London Cttee., The Hongkong and Shanghai Banking Corp. *Awards:* Colonial Police Medal 1956; CStJ, 1960; Comdr., Order of Prince Henry the Navigator (Portugal) 1963. Skinner and Citizen of the City of London; Fellow, Zoological Socy., London. *Clubs:* Vincent's (Oxford); Hong Kong (Hong Kong). *Address:* Kirawin, Cliveden Mead, Maidenhead, Berks.

**TURNER, Norfleet.** Banking. *B.* 1902. *Educ.* Washington and Lee Univ., Lexington, Va. *M.* 1927, Elinor Ragland. *S.* Norfleet Ragland. *Dau.* Mrs. Edward Giobbi. *Career:* Chmn. Emeritus, The First National Bank of Memphis 1970—. Past Dir. Chamber of Commerce of the U.S. *Member:* American Bankers Assn.; Assn. of Reserve City Bankers (Past Vice-Pres.); A.B.A. Govt. Bor. Cttee.; Past member, Federal Advisory Council, Fed. Res. Bd. *Clubs:* Country, Lost Tree, N. Palm Beach, Fla., & Augusta National Golf Club, Augusta, Ga.; Petroleum, Hunt & Polo; Farmington C.C. *Address:* 247 Baronne Place, Memphis 38117; and *office* 165 Madison Avenue, Memphis, Tenn. 38109, U.S.A.

**TURNER, Sir Ralph Lilley,** MC. Nepalese Order of Gurkga Dakshina Bahu (1st Cl.). *B.* 5 Oct. 1888. *Educ.* Christ's College, University of Cambridge (MA, LittD); Hon. DLit London, Hon. DLitt Benares, Hon. LitD Ceylon; Hon.D. Litt Shantiniketan. *M.* 1920, Dorothy Rivers Goutly. *S.* John Nelson. *Daus.* Kathleen Lilley, Audrey Rivers, Mary Elizabeth. *Career:* Fellow, Christ's College, Cambridge 1912; Indian Educational Service 1913–22; Professor of Indian Linguistics, Hindu University of Benares 1920–22; Indian Army Reserve of Officers, attached 3rd Gurkha Rifles 1915–19; Pres. Philological Society 1939–43; and of Royal Asiatic Soc. 1952–55; Fellow, British Academy 1942; Hon. Fellow, Christ's Coll., Cambridge 1950; Hon. Fellow, School of Oriental and African Studies 1957, and Deccan College, Poona. Corres. member, Académie des Inscriptions et Belles Lettres, Institut de France, and Czechoslovakian Oriental Institute of Prague; Hon. member, Norwegian Academy of Science and Letters; Société Asiatique, Paris; Deutsche Morgenländische Gesellschaft; American Oriental Soc.; Linguistic Society of America; Linguistic Society of India; Bihar Research Soc.; Bhandarkar Oriental Research Institute; Ceylon Linguistic Socy.; Ceylon Branch of the Royal Asiatic Soc.; Ceylon Academy; Nagaripracarini Sabha, Benares; Vishvesharanand Vedic Research Inst.; Gangenatha Jha Research Inst.; Dir., School of Oriental and African Studies, Univ. of London 1937–57; Prof. of Sanskrit Univ. of London 1922–54; Prof. Emeritus 1954. *Publications:* Gujarati Pholnology; The Position of Romani in Indo-Aryan; A Comparative and Etymological Dictionary of the Nepali Language. The Gavimath and Palkigundu Inscriptions of Asoka; Edited Indian Studies presented to Prof. E. J. Rapson; Indian and Iranian Studies presented to Sir G. A. Grierson; part author of Report to Nuffield Foundation on a visit to Nigeria; Some Problems of Sound Change in Indo-Aryan; A Comparative Dictionary of the Indo-Aryan Languages; Collected Papers 1912–73; articles in various journals, etc. *Address:* Haverbrack, Bishop's Stortford, Herts.

**TURNER, Sir (Ronald) Mark (Cunliffe).** British banker. *B.* 29 Mar. 1906. *Educ.* Wellington College, Berks. *M.* (1) 1931, Elizabeth Sutton (*Diss.* 1936). *Dau.* 1; and (2) 1939, Margaret Wake. *S.* Christopher, Richard, Roger. *Daus.* Catherine, Margaret. *Career:* Chmn. & Chief Exec., Rio Tinto-Zinc Corp. Ltd.; Dep. Chmn., Kleinwort, Benson, Lonsdale Ltd.; Director: Sotheby Parke Bernet Group Ltd., Whitbread Investment Co. Ltd.; joined M. Samuel & Co. Ltd. 1924; with Robert Benson & Co. Ltd. 1934–39; with Min. of Economic Warfare 1939–44, and Foreign Office 1944–45; Under-Secretary, Control Office for Germany and Austria 1945–46. *Address:* 3 The Grove, Highgate, London, N.6.

**TURNER, Admiral Stansfield.** US Naval Officer. *B.* 1923. *Educ.* Amherst Coll.; US Naval Acad.—BS; Oxford Univ. (Rhodes Scholar)—MA. *M.* 1953, Patricia Busby Whitney. *S.* 1. *Dau.* 1. *Career:* Entered US Navy as Ensign in 1946; Shore assignments: Politico-Military Policy Div. in Office of Chief of Naval Operations; Office of the Asst. Sec. of Defence for Systems Analysis; & Advanced Management Program, Harvard Business Sch.; Commander, *USS Horne* 1967; Exec. Asst. & Aide to Sec. of Navy 1968–70; Commanded Carrier Task Group of 6th Fleet 1970–71; Dir., Systems Analysis Div., Office of Chief of Naval Ops. 1971–72; Pres., Naval War Coll. 1972–74; Commander, US 2nd Fleet 1974–75; C-in-C, Allied Forces Southern Europe 1975–77; Dir. of Central Intelligence since 1977. *Decorations:* Distinguished Service Medal; Legion of Merit (2 awards); Bronze Star. *Publications:* various professional articles in *Naval Institute Proceedings & Foreign Affairs. Address:* Central Intelligence Agency, Washington, D.C. 20505, U.S.A.

**TURNER, Wilfred,** CMG. British Diplomat. *B.* 1921. *Educ.* Heywood Grammar Sch., Lancs.; BSc (London). *M.* 1947, June Gladys Tite. *S.* 2. *Dau.* 1. *Career:* Ministry of Labour 1938–55 (HM Forces 1942–47); Asst. Labour Adviser, British High Comm., New Delhi 1955–59; Snr. Wages Inspector, Ministry of Labour 1959–60; Principal, Ministry of Health 1960–66 (Sec., Cttee. on Safety of Drugs 1963–66); 1st Sec., Commonwealth Office, Kaduna & Kuala Lumpur 1966–73; Dep. British High Commissioner, Accra 1973–77; British High Commissioner, Gaborone since 1977. *Decorations* Companion, Order of St. Michael & St. George, 1977. *Club:* Royal Commonwealth Soc. *Address:* 44 Tower Road, Twickenham TW1 4PE; and *office* British High Commission, P.O.B. 0023, Gaborone, Botswana.

**TURNER, William Ian MacKenzie.** Canadian professional engineer. *B.* 1903. *Educ.* Univ. of Toronto (BASc 1925), and Univ. of Western Ontario (Business Management Diploma 1948). *M.* 1928, Marjorie Hilda Merrick. *S.* William Ian MacKenzie, Jr. and Peter Merrick. *Career:* Member of Senate, Univ. of Toronto 1960–68; President, Engineering Alumni Assn., Univ. of Toronto 1960–62; Pres. St. Andrew's Socy. of Toronto 1965–67. Associated with Westinghouse Electric & Mfg. Corp., Pittsburgh, Pa., in graduate student course 1925–26; Sales Engineer, Power Transformer Section, Sharon, Pa. 1926–30; joined Railway & Power Engineering Corp. Ltd., Toronto, sales engineer 1930–34; Manager, Control Apparatus Div. 1934–46; elected a director 1944; Asst. Gen. Mgr. 1946–49; Dir., Railway & Power Engineering Corp. Ltd., Montreal; Vice-Pres. and Gen. Mgr., Canadian Controllers Ltd., Toronto 1949–53 (Pres. & Gen. Mgr. 1953–68); Hon. Dir., Canadian Controllers Ltd. *Member:* Assn. Professional Engineers of Ontario; Royal Canadian Institute; Canadian Electrical Manufacturers Assn. (Pres. 1958–59); Electric Club of Toronto (Pres. 1949–50); Toronto Industrial Commission. *Clubs:* Engineers; Granite; Hart House; Phi Kappa Pi (all of Toronto). *Address:* 57 Mason Boulevard, Toronto, Ont. M5M 3C6, Canada. and *office* 1550 Birchmond Road, Scarborough, Ont., Canada.

**TURPIN, James Alexander,** CMG. British diplomat. *B.* 1917. *Educ.* The King's Hospital, Dublin; Trinity College, Dublin, MA. *M.* 1942, Kathleen Iris Eadie. *Dau.* 1. *Career:* Asst. Lectr. Trinity Coll. Dublin 1940–42; Captain, Royal Irish Fusiliers 1942–46; Joined H.M. Foreign (later Diplomatic) service 1947. Asst. Under-Sec. of State, FCO 1971–72; Ambassador to The Philippines 1972–76. *Decoration:* Companion of St. Michael and St. George. *Club:* Travellers. *Address:* c/o Foreign & Commonwealth Office, London SW1.

**TUTHILL, John Wills.** American Diplomat. *B.* 1910. *Educ.* College of William and Mary (SB); New York University (MBA); Harvard University (MA). *M.* 1937, Erna Margaret Lüders. *S.* David Wills. *Dau.* Carol (Battleson). *Career:* U.S. Ambassador: O.E.C.D., 1960–62; European Communities 1962–66; Brazil 1966–69. Professor, International Politics, John Hopkins Univ. 1969; Dir.-Gen. & Gov., Atlantic Inst. for International Affairs, Paris 1969–76; Pres., Salzburg Seminar in American Studies 1977. Hon. LLD McMurray College; International Award, 1968, International Neurological Organization. *Member:* American Economic Assn.; N.Y. Council on Foreign Relations; American Foreign Service Assn.; Century Assocn. New York, N.Y. *Clubs:* Union Interalliee, (Paris) & Polo de Paris. *Address:* 2801 New Mexico Avenue, N.W., Washington, D.C. 20009, U.S.A.

**TWAITS, William Osborn,** CC, BComm, DCL, DBA. Canadian. *B.* 1910. *Educ.* University of Toronto (BCom). *M.* 1937, Frances H. Begg. *Daus.* 2. *Career:* Pres., Sarcalto Ltd.; Vice-Pres. & Dir., The Royal Bank of Canada; *Director:* Abitibi Paper Company Ltd., Alcan Aluminium Ltd., Ford Motor

Company of Canada Ltd., New York Life Insurance Company, Norcen Energy Resources Ltd., TRI Ltd. Hon. Pres., The Arthritis Society; Gov., Olympic Trust of Canada; Councillor, The Conference Board Inc. *Member:* The Conference Board in Canada, the C.D. Howe Research Inst., the British-North American Cttee., The Canadian-American Cttee., Council of Honor Stanford Research Inst. *Address:* 17 Old Forest Hill Road, Toronto, Ontario M5P 2P6; and *office* Suite 300, 1235 Bay Street, Toronto, Ontario M5R 3K4, Canada.

**TWEEDLE, Charles Earl.** American executive. *B.* 1905. *Educ.* BSc Elec Engineering. *M.* 1947, Barbara Bryant. *Dau.* Barbara Anne. *Career:* Exec. Vice Pres. Askania Regulator Co. Chicago 1945; Works Mgr. Georgia Kaolin Co. Elizabeth N.J. 1950; Exec. Vice Pres. Birdsey Flour Mills, Macon Ga. 1955; Managing Director General Grain of Jamaica Ltd. 1960; Industrial Consultant Crown Continental Merchant Bank Kingston; Dir. Realco Ltd.; Uni-Print Ltd.; Ruel Samuels Mfg. Co. Ltd.; Project Managers Ltd. (all Jamaica). *Member:* Nat. Socy. of Prof. Engineers; Inst. of Engrs. Jamaica; Assn. of Consulting Engrs. etc. *Clubs:* Liguaea Golf & Country; Constant Spring Golf; (all Jamaica). *Address:* P.O. Box 1418, Grand Cayman, British West Indies.

**TWEEDSMUIR OF BELHELVIE,** Baroness of Potterton, Aberdeen. (Priscilla Jean Fortescue Buchan). *B.* 1915. *Educ.* England, Germany and France. *M.* (1) 1934, Major Sir Arthur Lindsay Grant 11th Bt. Grenadier Guards (D. 1944). *Daus.* 2. (2) 1948, 2nd Baron Tweedsmuir. *Dau.* 1. *Career:* MP for South Div. of Aberdeen 1946–66; Created Life Peer 1970; Chmn. Scottish Panel, British Council, Delegate Council of Europe 1950–53; Member Commonwealth Parly. Del. West Indies 1955; Delegate to United Nations 1960–62; Joint Parly. Under Secy. of State Scottish Office 1962–64; Min. of State for Scotland 1970–72; Min. of State For. & C'wealth Office 1972–74; Chmn. Select Cttee. on European Communities & a Principal Dep. Chmn. of Cttees. 1974–77. A Deputy Speaker. Privy Council 1974. *Publications:* for TV and newspapers. *Address:* 40 Tufton Court, Westminster, London, S.W.1 and Potterton House, Balmedie, Aberdeenshire.

**TYABJI BADR-UD-DIN, Faiz Hasan Badr-ud-din.** Former Indian diplomat. *B.* 12 Nov. 1907. *Educ.* Balliol College, Oxford (BA). *M.* 1939, Surayya Aamir Ali. *S.* 3. *Dau.* 1. *Career:* Served in Punjab as Assistant Commissioner, Under-Secretary, Finance, Home and Political 1932–38; Under-Secretary, Government of India, Defence Department 1938–39; Deputy Commissioner, Punjab 1940–42; Controller of Supplies, Government of India, Karachi and Bombay 1942–44; Deputy Secretary, Government of India, Planning and Development 1944–46; Joint Secretary, Constituent Assembly Secretariat and Ministry of External Affairs and Commonwealth Relations 1946–48; Minister-Chargé d'Affaires of India in Belgium and Luxembourg 1948–50; Joint Secretary, Ministry of External Affairs, New Delhi 1950–52; Commonwealth Secy., 1952–53; Ambassador to Indonesia 1954–56; to Iran Nov. 1957–May 1958; to Federal Germany July 1958–Dec. 1960; Secretary, Ministry of External Affairs 1961–62. Vice-Chancellor, Aligarh Muslim University 1962–65; Ambassador to Japan, Mar. 1965–67. After retirement engaged in public life—politics, education, social affairs, & literary activities. *Publications:* Chaff and Grain (1962); Self in Secularism (1971); Indian Policies & Practice (1972). *Address:* 23 First Street, Shantiniketan, New Delhi-110021, India.

**TYARKS, Fredic Ewald.** Publisher. *B.* 1908. *Educ.* New York Univ. (BCS). *M.* 1932, Charlotte Blum. *Daus.* Linda Catherine Dughi and Peggy Valerie Drouet. *Career:* Partner, Harian Publications, Greenlawn, N.Y. 1937—. Director, Sports Car Press 1958—. Partner, Yorkshire Press 1936, and Viking Voyages 1935; Director, The Record Press 1958–62. *Publications:* Europe on a Shoestring (published annually 1939–74); Travel Routes Around the World (published annually since 1935); Today's Best Buys in Travel Around the World; Where to Find the Best in the U.S., Canada and Mexico; Vagabond Voyaging; Two Days to Two Weeks; Harian's Favourite Travel Finds; Foreign Lands at Stay-at-Home Prices; Plan for Independence, and others. Charter Member, Society of American Travel Writers. Democrat. *Address:* P.O. Box 536, San Juan Capistrano, Calif. 92675, U.S.A, *office* Harian Publications, Greenlawn, New York 11740. U.S.A.

**TYLER, William Royall.** American. *B.* 1910. *Educ.* Ballio College, Oxford; Harvard University (MA); Hon. DLitt, Marlboro College, Vermont. *M.* 1934, Bettine Mary Fisher-Rowe. *S.* Royall. *Dau.* Matilda Eve. *Career:* Director, Office of Western European Affairs, Department of State, 1957–58; Counsellor, U.S. Embassy, Bonn 1958–61; Assistant Secretary of State for European Affairs, Dept. of State. 1962–65; Ambassador to the Netherlands, 1965–69. Director, Dumbarton Oaks Research Library & Collection, Washington 1969–77. *Awards:* Kt., Order of the Legion of Honour (France). Corresponding mem. Academie des Arts, Sciences et Belles Lettres, Dijon; Assoc. mem., Mass. Hist. Soc.; Fellow, The Royal Society of Arts. *Member:* Phi Beta Kappa; Colonial Society of Massachusetts; American Academy of Arts & Sciences; Royal Antiquarian Society of the Netherlands. *Clubs:* Cosmos (Washington); Tavern (Boston). *Address:* Antigny-le-Château, 21230 Arnay-le-Duc, France.

**TYRRELL, Sir Murray Louis,** KCVO, CBE, CStJ, JP. Australian. *B.* 1913. *Educ.* Melbourne Boys' High School. *M.* 1939, Ellen St. C. Greig. *S.* Michael. *Daus.* Leonie and Margot. *Career:* Private Secretary to various Ministers of the Commonwealth of Australia 1940–47; Comptroller to the Governor-General of Australia 1947–53. Official Secretary to the Governor-General of Australia 1947–73. Alderman, Queanbeyan City Council, N.S.W. 1974—; Mem., Southern Tablelands County Council 1974—; Registrar, Ven. Order of St. John of Jerusalem in Australia 1976—. Member of several clubs. *Address:* 11 Blundell Street, Queanbeyan 2620, N.S.W., Australia.

# U

**UBERTALLI, Pier-Carlo.** Knight-Cmdr. Order of the Italian Republic. *B.* 1911. *Educ.* Doctor of Economics and Commerce. *M.* 1942, Marcella Ferrero Ventimiglia de Gubernatis. *S.* Marco. *Dau.* Carla. *Career:* Company Director. Managing CEAT, Turin. Dir.: CEAT International, Lausanne; CEAT, Poissy. Has been with CEAT for 42 years. Member: Association of Commerce. Graduates, Turin; Fed. of Company Directors Rome. *Clubs:* Whist Club; Philharmonic Society; Golf Club, all of Turin. *Address:* Via Cavour 41, Turin; and *office* CEAT, Corso Palermo, Turin, Italy.

**UDALL, Stewart.** B. 1920. *Educ.* Eastern Arizona Coll. (Thatcher) and Univ. of Arizona (LLB 1948). *M.* 1947, Ermalee Webb; six children. *Career:* Admitted to Arizona Bar 1948; practised in Tucson 1948–54. Represented 2nd District of Arizona at the 84th-85th-86th-87th Congresses (Democrat); member of Congressional Committee on Interior and Insular Affairs, and of the Labour and Education Cttee.; Secretary of the Interior of the U.S., Jan. 1961–69; Chmn. of the Bd., Overview Group; Visiting Prof. in Environmental Humanism, Yale Sch. of Forestry. *Member:* Amer. Bar Assn. *Address:* 1311A Dolley Madison Boulevard, McLean, Va. 22101, U.S.A.

**UEDA, Kazuo.** Japanese. Counsellor, Sanwa Bank Ltd., Osaka since 1971. *B.* 1903. *Educ.* Tokyo University Faculty of Law (BA 1925). *M.* Shizuko Ayata. *S.* Mikio, Shozo and Saburo. *Dau.* Kazuko. With Sanwa Bank: Managing Director 1947–56, Senior Managing Director 1956–57, Deputy President 1957–60, President 1960–71. *Member:* Kansai Economics Federation (Vice-President). *Club:* Rotary (Osaka). *Address:* (14–7 Midorigaokach-Ashiya-shi) 4–6–11 Akasaba, Minato-Ku, Tokyo; and *office* 10 Fushimimachi 4, Higashi-ku, Osaka, Japan

**UGELSTAD, Samuel.** Norwegian shipowner; Managing Director, S. Ugelstads Rederi A/S. *B.* 1907. *Educ.* Norwegian Commercial High School. *M.* 1953, Elizabeth Wexelsen Freihow. *Address:* Haakon VII, Gate 1, Oslo, Norway.

**ULLERY, Lowell Emerson.** American; financial consultant to petroleum industry. *B.* 1903. *Educ.* Ohio State University (Bachelor of Business Administration 1927). *M.* 1933, Florence Stilwell. *S* Thomas. *Dau.* Susan. *Career:* Public Accountant Wiegner, Rockey & Co. 1927–29; clerk, The Chase National Bank, N.Y. 1929–32; Assistant Manager Credit Dept. 1939–42; Assistant Cashier 1942–45; 2nd Vice-Pres. 1945–48; Vice-Pres. 1948–55; Vice-President, Chase Manhattan Bank 1955–61 (Executive Head, Petroleum Dept. 1950–61). *Address:* 1404 Green Cove Road, Winter Park, Florida 32789, U.S.A.

**ULMER, Alfred Conrad, Jr.** American; diplomat and investment banker. *B.* 1916. *Educ.* Princeton Univ. (AB Honours). *M.* 1942, Doris Lee Bridges (*Div.*). *S.* Alfred 3rd, Nicholas. *Dau.* Doris Marguerite. *Career:* Lieut-Comdr., U.S.N.R. 1941–45; First Secy. Embassy, Athens, Greece 1952–55; Consultant on Far Eastern Affairs, Dept. of State, Washington, D.C. 1955–58; Special Asst. to Ambassador, American Embassy Paris 1958–62; previous diplomatic assignments Madrid and Vienna; Vice Pres. member Exec. Cttee, Jesup and Lamont Inc. Investment bankers and brokers; since 1975 with Lombard, Odier et Cie, Private Bankers, Geneva. *Awards:* Bronze Star (U.S.A.), and Order of the Phoenix (Greece); Member: Council on Foreign Relations (U.S.A.); Inst. for Strategic Studies (U.K.). *Clubs:* Boodle's, Bucks.; Pilgrims (London); Knickerbocker and Links (N.Y.C.). *Address:* 11 Rue de la Corraterie, 1204 Geneva, Switzerland; & 2 East 62nd St., New York City, U.S.A.

**ULRICH, Franz Heinrich.** *B.* 1910. Chmn. of the Supervisory Board of the Deutsche Bank AG; Chairman of Supervisory Board, Deputy Chmn., and member of Supervisory Board of several major companies. *Address:* Königsallee 45–47 Düsseldorf, Germany.

**UNDERWOOD, James Martin.** American company executive. *B.* 1909. *Educ.* Univ. of Pittsburgh (BS in Business Admin. 1930) and Harvard Univ. (MBA 1932). *M.* (1) 1930, Ann E. W. Saxman (*D.* 1974). *S.* 3. *Dau.* 1. (2) 1977, Alice A. Clemers. *Career:* Partner, Morgan, Underwood & Butler (investment counsel) Pittsburgh 1932–35; Prof. Business Admin., St. Vincent Coll., Latrobe 1932–36; Asst. Secy.-Treas., later Asst. to Pres., Vulcan Mold & Iron Co. 1935–40; Gen. Mgr. and Pres., The Halund Co., Latrobe 1940–44; Gen. Sales Mgr. Latrobe Steel Co. 1944–46; Director, Chairman, Chief Exec. officer, Vulcan Inc., Latrobe, Pa, 1946—, and Director, Latrobe Steel Co. 1948–75. Dir.: Latrobe Hosp. Assn. (Pres. 1963–70; Chmn. Building Fund Drive 1959); Latrobe Community Chest (also Trustee); Defense Orientation Conf. Assn., Washington, D.C.; Univ. of Pittsburgh (Trustee 1963–70; Tri-City Municipal Authority of Westmorland County Chmn. and Dir. 1951—); Western Pennsylvania Safety Council. Civic Affairs; Councilman, city govt. of Latrobe 1943–70; (Pres. 1948–56 and 1962–70); Chmn. Young Republicans of Westmoreland County 1939–40 (unsuccessful nominee to U.S. Congress 1940); Deleg. to Republic Natl. Convention 1960 and 1968. *Member:* Phi Delta Theta; Young Presidents' Org. (founder); American Iron & Steel Inst.; American Foundrymen's Assn.; Amer. Inst. Mining & Metallurgical Engineers. Mason. *Clubs:* Latrobe Country (Dir. 1944—); University, Duquesne, Harvard-Yale-Princeton (all in Pittsburgh); Oakmount Country, Rolling Rock. *Address:* (summer) P.O. Box 70, Latrobe, Pa. 15650; & (winter) Sea Island, Georgia, U.S.A.

**UNGER, Stig (Magnus Abraham).** Swedish diplomat. *B.* 1910. *Educ.* LLB and admitted to the Bar 1933 after studies at the University of Uppsala. *M.* 1948, Margaret Lagerlöf. *S.* Johan. *Daus.* Cecilia and Kerstin. *Career:* Entered Swedish Foreign Service 3 Dec., 1934; Attaché at Washington, New York, Copenhagen, Ministry for Foreign Affairs 1935–39; Second Secretary 1939; First Secretary 1941; Consul, Berlin 1946–47; Chief of Section, Ministry for Foreign Affairs 1947–49; Counsellor, London 1949–53; Deputy Head of Division, Ministry of Foreign Affairs 1953; Minister at Belgrade 1956 (Ambassador 1956–61); Ambassador of Sweden to Belgium and Luxembourg 1961–65. *Address:* c/o Atlas Copco AB, Stockholm, Sweden.

**UNGER, Leonard.** American diplomat. Ambassador of the United States to the Republic of China. *B.* 1917. *Educ.* Harvard University (AB in Geography). *M.*1944, Anne Axon. *S.* Philip, Andrew, Daniel. *Daus.* Deborah (Mackintosh), Anne Thomas. *Career:* Joined U.S. Department of State, 1941; Political Advisor to the AMG, Trieste, then to Commander of NATO Southern Region, Naples, 1950–54; U.S. Representative at the Trieste Negotiations in London 1954; Officer-in-Charge, Politico-Military Affairs, European Bureau, Department of State, 1954–57; Detailed to the National War College, Washington, D.C., 1957–58; Deputy Chief of Mission (U.S. Embassy), Thailand, 1958–62; U.S. Ambassador to Laos, 1962–64; Deputy Assistant Secretary of State for East Asian and Pacific Affairs, 1956–67; US Ambassador to Thailand 1967–73, to Taiwan since 1974. *Award:* Distinguished Honour Award, Department of State, 1965. *Member:* Assn. of American Geographers; American Foreign Service Assn.; The Siam Society; Phi Beta Kappa. *Publications:* Focus on South East Asia (2 Chapters); Focus (a monograph on Laos, 1964; Thailand 1970) and articles in the Geographical Review on Trieste, The Campania, and the Chinese in Southeast Asia. *Address:* American Embassy, 2 Chung Hsiao E. Road, Sec. 2, Taipei, Taiwan.

**UNWIN, Sir Keith,** KBE, CMG, MA. British. Former member Diplomatic Service. *B.* 1909. *Educ.* Merchant Taylors School; St. John's College, Oxford (BA 1927). *M.* 1935, Linda Giersé. *S.* 1. *Daus.* 2. *Career:* Minister (Commercial): Buenos Aires 1950–55, and Rome 1955–59; U.K. Representative on Economic & Social Council of U.N. 1962–66; British Ambassador to Uruguay, Sept. 1966–69; Member of Human Rights Commission of U.N. since 1970. *Club:* Canning (London). *Address:* Wildacres, Fleet, Hants.

**UPADHYAY, Shailendra Kumar.** Nepali Diplomat. *B.* 1929. *Educ.* Nepal & India; Arts Graduate, Benares Hindu Univ. *M.* 1967, Beena Upadhyay. *S.* 3. *Dau.* 1. *Career:* Mem., Rastriya Panchayat (Nat. Parliament), representing Nepal Youth Org. 1962–71; Asst. Minister for Forests, Food & Agriculture 1962–64; promoted Minister of cabinet rank & Minister of Panchayat 1964–65; Vice-Chmn., Nat. Planning Comm. 1968–70; reappointed as Minister for Home & Panchayat, Land Reforms & Information 1970–71; Perm. Rep. of the Kingdom of Nepal to the UN since 1972. *Decorations:* Order of Gorkha Dakshin Bahu (Order of the Right Hand of the Gurkhas) Class 1; Bishes Seva Padak (Medal for Special Service); Coronation Medal. *Publications:* Articles in Nepali & English newspapers & magazines. *Club:* Royal Nepali Golf. *Address:* 500 East 77th Street, # 430, New York, N.Y. 10021; and *office* 711 Third Avenue, Room 1806, New York, N.Y. 10017, U.S.A.

**UPCHURCH, Walter McGowan, Jr.** American. *B.* 1909. *Educ.* Duke Univ. (AB; LLB). *Career:* Director of Appointments, Duke University, 1940–42; Personnel Director, Shell Development Co., Emeryville, Calif., 1942–50; Asst. Personnel Director, Shell Oil Co. (U.S.A.) 1950; Manager, Employee Publications, 1950–54; Senior Staff Officer, Shell Companies Foundation Inc., New York, 1954— (Senior Vice-President, 1962—); Trustee, Duke University, Durham, North Carolina, 1960—; Senior advisor to managements, Shell companies (U.S.A.) on donations, 1954—. Member, Council of Executives on Company Contributions, National Industrial Conference Board; Senior Consultant, Foundation Library Center, New York City. *Clubs:* Omicron Delta Kappa; Pi Kappa Alpha; Rockefeller Center, New York. *Address: office* 50 West 50th Street, New York City 10020, U.S.A.

**UPTON, Geoffrey Thomson,** DSO; Bronze Star (U.S.A.) New Zealand. *B.* 1912. *Educ.* MA (Cantab.). *M.* (1) 1935, Margaret Galbraith (*D.* 1953), and (2) 1954, Heather McDonald Paterson. *S.* John Selwyn and Bruce McDonald; *Dau.* Winifred Anne. *Career:* Reporter Christchurch Star-Sun 1934; Sub-editor, Auckland Star 1937 (Commercial Editor 1938–39; Asst. Editor 1945–54; Editor, 1954–64). War service with Fiji Military Forces (Lieut.-Col. Commanding 1st Battalion Fiji Infantry Regt.) 1940–45; Col. 1967—. Editor-in-Chief Auckland Star 1964–67, (Editor 1954–64); Editor-in-Chief and Dir. New Zealand Newspapers Ltd. 1968–76, Chmn. of Dirs. 1976—; Chmn. Napier Daily Telegraph since 1970. *Clubs:* Northern; Royal New Zealand Yacht Squadron. *Address:* 89 St Stephens Ave., Parnell, Auckland, 1; and *office* Auckland Star, Box 1409, Auckland, New Zealand.

**URE, John Burns.** MVO, MA. British diplomat. *B.* 1931. *Educ.* Uppingham School; Magdalene Coll. Cambridge; Harvard Business School, (AMP). *M.* 1972, Caroline Allan. *Career:* Third Secretary, British Embassy Moscow, Private Secy. H.M. Ambassador 1957–59; Resident Clerk, Foreign Office 1960–61; Second Secy. Leopoldville 1962–63; Foreign Office 1964–66; First Secy. Santiago Chile 1967–70; Foreign & Commonwealth Office 1971–72; Counsellor, Lisbon 1972–77; Head of the South America Dept. of the Foreign & Commonwealth Office since 1977. *Awards:* Fellow Royal Geographical Socy; Member, Royal Victorian Order; Commander Military Order of Christ (Portugal); Master of Arts, Cambridge. *Publications:* Cucumber Sandwiches in the Andes (1973); Prince Henry the Navigator (1977); articles on geographical and Historical subjects. *Clubs:* Travellers, White's, Beefsteak (London). *Address:* c/o Foreign & Commonwealth Office, London, S.W.1.

**URE SMITH, Sydney George** (Sam). Australian. *B.* 1922. *Educ.* Knox Grammar School (post intermediate). *M.* 1949. Heather Isobel Elder. *Daus.* Susan and Anne. *Career:* Served in World War II; 30th Australian Infantry Battalion, Australia and New Guinea 1945–46, Captain and Adjutant. Managing Director & Publisher, Ure Smith Pty. Ltd. 1956–75; Dir. IPC Books (The Hamlyn Group) Australia 1972–75; Managing Dir. & Publisher, The Fine Arts Press Pty. Ltd. 1976—; Publisher of "Art & Australia" quarterly journal & books on Australia & Fine Arts. *Clubs:* Avondale Golf, Pymble; Australian Journalists. Member, Australian Book Publishers Assn. (Pres. 1963–65). *Address:* The Fine Arts Press Pty. Ltd., 34 Glenview Street, Gordon, N.S.W. 2072, Australia.

**UREN, Thomas Hunter,** FCA. Australian company executive. *B* .28 Jan. 1914. *Educ.* Wesley College, Melbourne. *M.* 1946, Florence Winifred Spicer. *S.* 1. Asst. Gen. Mgr. (Finance), The Australian Estates Co. Ltd. *Club:* Savage (Melbourne). *Address:* 45 Yeneda Street, North Balwyn, Vic., Australia.

**ÜRGÜPLÜ, Ali Suat Hayri.** Turkish diplomat & Politician. *B.* 1903. *Educ.* Galatasaray Lycée and Faculty of Law, Istanbul University. *M.* 1932, Niger Urgüplü. *S.* 1. *Career:* Turkish Secretary, Mixed Courts of Arbitration established by Treaty of Lausanne 1926–29; Magistrate, Supreme Commercial Court, Istanbul 1929–32; Lawyer at Istanbul Courts and member of Administrative Council 1932–39; MP for Kayseri 1939–43; Minister of Customs & Monopolies 1943–46; re-elected MP for Kayseri 1950; in following years Turkish representative and President of Delegation to Consultative Assembly, Council of Europe, Strasbourg (elected Vice-Pres. 1950, and re-elected 1951 and 1952); Representative at Conference of Inter-Parliamentary Union in Dublin and Istanbul 1950–51; while still member of 9th Legislative Period was appointed Ambassador to Fed. Republic of Germany (Bonn) 1952–55; participated in Tripartite Conf. on Eastern Mediterranean and Cyprus, London, Aug. 1955; Ambassador to Court of St. James's 1955–57; to U.S. 1957; to Spain 1960. Elected Member of Senate, and Speaker 1961–63. Member, Turkish Delegation to Ministerial meeting of the North Atlantic Council, Washington, Apr. 1959; Pres., Turkish Parliamentary Delegation to U.S.S.R. 1963; Prime Minister, 1965 and 1972; Chairman, Foreign Affairs Cttee. o.c. Senate, 1966–68. *Member:* Culture & Art Foundation, Istanbul (Chmn.); Europ. League for Econ. Co-op. (Pres. Turkish Section). *Award:* Hon. Member, Mark Twain Society; Dr. Hon. Causa, World Organization of International Law; Federal Grand Cross of Merit with Star and Sash; Grand Cross, Order of Merit of Fed. Republic of Germany. *Publications:* articles & studies in various judicial reviews. *Address:* Sahil Cad 19, Yesilyurt, Istanbul, Turkey and *office:* Yapi re Kredi Bankasi, Istanbul, Turkey.

**URQUHART, Alastair Hugh,** CBE, FSIA, FAIM. Australian. *B.* 1919. *Educ.* Syd. C.E.G.S. *M.* 1947, Joyce Muriel Oswald. *Daus.* Virginia Anne and Amanda Helen. *Career:* 2nd A.I.F. 1940–45; (7 Div., later 9 Div.) M.E. Tobruk 1942; P.O.W. Rehab. Work U.K. 1944–45; Member Syd. Stock Exchange since 1949, Chmn. 1959–66; Vice-Chmn. 1956, 1958–59; Pres. Aust. Assoc. Stock Exchanges 1959, 1964–66, Vice-Pres. 1960–63; Sen. Partner Mullens & Co.; Chmn. Chubbs Australian Co. Ltd.; Chmn. Hogg Robinson CCL Pty Ltd.; NSW Permanent Bld. Soc. Ltd.; Chmn. Swedex Clothing Pty. Ltd.: Oswalds Bonded & Free Stores Ltd., *Member:* Executive Council of Australian Red Cross Society (N.S.W. Div.) 1959—; Council of Sydney Chamber of Commerce 1959—74; and Development Corp. of N.S.W. 1966–75. N.S.W. Industries Promotion Advisory Council 1962–65; Commonwealth Immigration Planning Council 1962–68; Chmn. Nat. Cttee. Nat. Heart Appeal 1969; Cttee. N.S.W. Br. Inst. of Directors, Fellow, Inst. of Directors 1962—; Council National Roads & Motorists Association. *Clubs:* Rotary, Union, Royal Sydney Yacht Squadron, Elanora Country; Royal Sydney Golf; Imperial Services. *Address:* 4 Wentworth Place, Point Piper, N.S.W. 2027, Australia.

**URWIN, Thomas William.** British Labour Party politician. *B.* 1912. *M.* 1934, Edith Scott. *S.* 3. *Dau.* 1. *Career:* Minister of State, Department of Economic Affairs. 1968–69; Minister of State, Local Government and Regional Planning, with Special Responsibility for the Northern Region, October 1969–June 1970; Leader of British Parly. Del. to Council of Europe, April 1976. *Address:* 28 Stanhope Close, Houghton-le-Spring, Co. Durham.

**USAMI, Makoto.** Japanese banker. *B.* 1901. *Educ.* Keio University (Economics). *M.* 1937, Hiroko Nakamura. *Career:* Joined Mitsubishi Bank, 1924; Manager: Economic Research Dept., 1947; General Affairs Dept., 1949; Dir. 1950; Dir. & Manager, Head Office, 1951–54; Man. Dir., 1954–59; Deputy Pres., 1959–61; Pres., 1961–64. Chmn. Policy Board, & Governor, Bank of Japan, 1964–69; Alternate Governor: I.M.F. & I.B.R.D., 1964; Asian Development Bank, 1966. Chairman, Board of Counsellors, Keio University, 1966. Chmn., Federation of the Bankers' Assn. of Japan, 1962–63. Adviser, Federation of Economic Organizations. *Address:* Room 524, Marunouchi Yaesi Building 6-2, 2 Marunouchi, Chiyoda-ku, Tokyo 100, Japan.

**USHER, Arsène Assouan.** Citizen of Ivory Coast. Lawyer. *B.* 1930. *Educ.* Lic. en Droit of Faculties of Bordeaux and Poitiers; C.A.P.A., Faculty of Law, Poitiers. *M.* 1955, Cécile Laga. *S.* Sylvain, Daniel Félix. *Daus.* Melanie, Mari-José, and Georgette. Practised law at Poitiers. *Career:* Was attached to the cabinet of M. Felix Houphouet-Boigny, a Minister in the Guy Mollet government; in 1957 was Asst. Mgr. of the Ivory Coast Caisse de Compensation des Prestations, Familiales; in the same year was Gen. Counsel to the Territorial Assembly; in 1959 he became a Deputy in the Legislative Assembly and in the National Assembly, of which he was Vice-Pres.; Head of Ivory Coast Permanent Mission and Ambassador to United Nations Dec. 1960–66. Chief Delegate to 16th Session of U.N. General Assembly Sept. 1961–67; Foreign Minister since 1966. Member of the African Democratic Assembly (R.D.A.), and of the Association of Advocates of France. Representative of Ivory Coast to Security Council 1964–65. *Address:* c/o Ministry of Foreign Affairs, Abidjan, Ivory Coast.

**USHIBA, Nobuhiko.** Japanese statesman & diplomat. *B.* 1909. *Educ.* Tokyo Imperial University (LLB). *M.* Fujiko Kobayashi. *S.* Akihiko. *Daus.* Yasuko, Noriko and Reiko. *Career:* Second Secretary of Embassy, Germany 1943; Chief, 1st Section, 4th Division, General Liaison Office, Ministry of Foreign Affairs 1945; Dir., Secretariat Foreign Exchange Control Board, Prime Minister's Office 1949, and of Trade Bureau, Ministry of International Trade and Industry 1951; Counsellor of Embassy, Burma 1954; Dir. Economic Affairs Bureau, Ministry of Foreign Affairs 1957; Ambassador to Canada 1961; Deputy Vice-Minister, Ministry of Foreign Affairs 1964–67; Vice-Minister, Ministry of Foreign Affairs 1967–70. Ambassador to USA 1970–73; Adv. to Min. of Foreign Affairs 1973–77; State Minister for External Economic Affairs since Nov. 1977. *Clubs:* Tokyo; Hodogaya Country. *Address: office:* Ministry of Foreign Affairs, 2 Kasumigaseki, Chiyoda-ku, Tokyo, Japan.

# V

**VAES, Robert R.** Belgian diplomat. *B.* 1919. *Educ.* Doctor of Laws. *M.* 1947, Anne Albers. *D.* 1. *Career:* Barrister 1942–46; Diplomatic Executive 1946; Washington D.C. 1947–49; Paris 1949–54; Hong Kong 1954–56; London 1956–58; Assist. to Minister of Foreign Trade, Brussels 1958–60; Rome 1960–64; Dir. Gen. Political Affairs 1964–66; Secy. Gen. Foreign Affairs, Belgium (Foreign Trade and Development Co-operation) 1966–72; Belgian Ambassador in Madrid 1972–76; & in London since 1977. *Decorations:* KCMG; Grand Officer Legion D'Honneur and others. *Clubs:* Royal Yacht (Belgium): Real Club (Puerto De Hierro, Madrid); Foundation Universitaire (Brussels); White's, Beefsteak (London). *Address:* 103 Eaton Square, London SW1.

**VAHERVUORI, Torsten Oskar.** Finnish diplomat; *B.* Jan. 1901. *Educ.* University of Helsinki (MA). *M.* (1) 1926, Rauna Schroderus (*D.* 1958). *Daus.* 2. *M.* (2) Pirkko Greis, 1964. *S.* 1. *Career:* Attaché, For. Min. 1926; Secy. of Legation, Rio de Janeiro 1929–32; Chargé d'Affaires a.i. Buenos Aires1932–34; Head of Bureau of Commercial Treaties, Min. of Foreign Affairs 1935–39; Finnish Representative at Commercial Conferences of the Oslo Powers 1936–38; Consul General, New York 1939–43; Council of Legation, Washington 1943–44; Director of Administrative Affairs, Foreign Ministry 1946–48; Dir. of Political Affairs 1948–51; En. Ex. and Min. Plen. to Brazil 1951–56; Ambassador to Denmark 1956–57; State Secretary, Ministry of Foreign Affairs 1957–61; Ambassador to Italy 1961–68. *Address:* Tehtaankatu 7 B, Helsinki, Finland.

**VAILE, Horace Snyder.** American management consultant. Own business since 1937. *B.* 1896. *Educ.* Purdue Univ. (BS 1920; EE 1926). *M.* 1928, Jeanne Scott. *S.* Horace Snyder, Jr., and Edward Scott. *Career:* With Marshal Field & Co. (as Comptroller) 1936–37; Asst. Vice-Pres., United States Steel Corp. 1928–36; Manager, McGraw-Hill Publishing Co. 1920–28. Member: Society of Colonial Wars; Sons of American Revolution. *Clubs:* Exmoor Country; Ephraim Yacht; Chicago Curling; Mid-Day. *Address:* 112 Maple Avenue, Highland Park, Ill. 60035, and *office* 11 South La Salle Street, Chicago 60603, Ill., U.S.A.

**VALDAR, Colin Gordon.** British journalist. *B.* 1918. *M.* (1) 1940, Evelyn Barriff. *S.* Richard and Peter (2) Jill Davis. *Career:* Royal Engineers 1939–42; Executive Sunday Pictorial 1942–46; Features Editor and Assistant Editor, Daily Express, London 1946–53; Editor Daily Sketch 1959–62; Director Daily Sketch and Daily Graphic Ltd., 1959. Editor Sunday Pictorial London 1953–59; Director, Sunday Pictorial Newspapers (1920) Ltd. 1957–59; Council Member, Commonwealth Press Union 1955–59; Chmn. Bouverie Publishing Co. Ltd. since 1964. *Address:* 94 Clifford's Inn, Fleet Street, London, E.C.4.

**VALDÉS LARRANAGA, Manuel, Marqués de Avella.** Spanish diplomat. *B.* 16 April 1909. *Educ.* Jesuit Colleges, Universities of Madrid and Barcelona; Higher School of Architects, Madrid. *M.* 1939, Piedad Colón de Carvajal y Hurtado de Mendoza. *S.* Manuel, Luis. *Daus.* María Pilar, María Cristina and Ana Teresa. *Career:* Formerly Under-Secretary for Labour; Head of Spanish National Syndicates; Attorney in the Cortes; National Counsellor; member of the Political Junta; Dean and President, Colegio Superior de Arquitectos de Madrid; Amb. Ex. and Plen. to the Dominican Republic 1952; to Venezuela; again to Dominican Republic; to the United Arab Republic; to Lebanon and Kuwait. *Awards:* Gran Cruz, Ordem del Mérito Civil; Orden de Cisneros; Gra Cruz, Ordem de la Benemerencia (Portugal); Gran Cruz, Orden de Cristóbal Colón; Gran Cruz, Orden de Trujillo; Gran Cruz, Orden del Mérito Juan Pablo Duarte (all of Dominican Republic) and Enrique el Navigante (Portugal). Knight of Malta. *Address:* c/o Ministry of Foreign Affairs, Madrid, Spain.

**VALENTINE, Alan.** American university president, government official and author. *B.* 1901. *Educ.* Swarthmore College (BA); University of Pennsylvania (MA); Oxford University (BA Honours and MA). *M.* 1928, Lucia Garrison Norton. *S.* Garrison N. (Captain, U.S. Air Force). *Daus.* Annie Laurie (Mrs. John Buffinton) and Sarah McKim. Dean and Professor, Swarthmore and Yale; President, University of Rochester 1935–50. Director of various companies and trustee of various foundations 1935–50; Chief, Netherlands Mission of E.C.A. 1948–49. Administrator, Economic Stabilization Agency, Washington 1950–51; President, Committee for a Free Asia 1951–52. Withdrew from activities in 1952 to devote time to writing and travel. Several honorary degrees. Fellow International Institute of Arts and Letters. *Publications:* The English Novel; Biography; Dusty Answers; The Age of Conformity; Vigilante Jutsice: Lord North (2 vols.); The British Establishment 1760–1784, (2 vols.); Lord Stirling; Trial Balance; Between Two Worlds, 1913; Lord George Germain; Fathers to Sons, and articles. *Address:* 7 Lafayette Road, Princeton, N.J. 08540, U.S.A.

**VALENTINE, Kenneth Franklin.** American. Major, U.S.A.F. (honourably discharged). Vice-Chairman Pres. and Director, American Fletcher National Bank 1964—. Director, Federal Home Loan Bank 1961–69, Haag Drug Co. Inc. 1966. *B.* 1906. *Educ.* Univ. of Wisconsin School of Pharmacy. *M.* 1929, Mary Weber. Immediate Past-Pres., Pitman-Moore Division, The Dow Chemical Co. 1947–63; Vice-Pres., Mem. Adv. Bd., American Fletcher National Bank & Trust Co. 1963–64; Dir. and Vice-Pres., Allied Laboratories Inc., 1952–63; Chmn. United Fund of Indianapolis 1963–64; Pres., Health News Institute 1956–60; Dir., Health Information Foundation 1954–60. Dir. and Vice-Pres., Allied Laboratories Inc. (Kansas City, Mo.) 1952–63 Pres. and Dir., Pitman-Moore of Canada 1947–61. Director: National Pharmaceutical Council 1960–61–62; Indiana National Bank 1956–63; Indianapolis Hospital Development Board 1962 (President 1967); and Columbia Club 1960. Trustee, National Fund for Graduate Nursing Education 1961. Director: American Red Cross, 1966—; Central Indiana Health Facilities & Program Planning Council, Inc., 1967—; Indianapolis-Marion County Building Authority, 1967—; President Indianapolis Hospital Development Association, 1967—; Member: Central Indiana Council, Boy Scouts of America, 1966—; Lay Adv. Board, St. Vincents Hospital, 1963—; Trustee: Indianapolis-Marion County Building Authority, 1967—; YWCA, 1965—; Vice-Chairman, American Overseas Banking Corp., 1968—; Mem., President's Adv. Cncl., Franklin Coll.; Dir., Indiana State Symphony Society, 1966—; Member: Assn. of Reserve City Bankers; Pharmaceutical Manfs. Assn. (Vice-President 1961–62–63; President 1952–53); American Bankers' Assn.; Sigma Alpha Epsilon; Scottish Rite; American Legion Air Service Post. Republican. *Clubs:* Meridian Hills Country (Dir. 1960–61); Indianapolis Athletic; Murat Shrine; Rotary; The Hundred (Pres. 1967); University; 702; Crooked Stick Golf. *Address: office* American Fletcher National Bank, 101 Monument Circle, Indianapolis, Ind., U.S.A.

**VALERIO, Dr. Ing. Giorgio.** Italian executive. *Educ.* Milan Engineering University (1926). *M.* 1935, Viviane Talan. *S.* Guido and Claudio. *Dau.* Olga (*M.* to Dr. Ing. Emilio Casnedi). Former Chairman and Managing Director, Montecatini Edison S.p.A. Director: Riunione Adriatica di Sicurtà (R.A.S.). *Address:* Foro Bonaparte 31, Milan, Italy.

**VALLAT, Eugene Hopson.** American geologist, geophysicist, and petroleum engineer. Director, Vallat Ranches Inc. *B.* 1904. *Educ.* Stanford University (ABGeol 1926). *M.* 1931, Marion Meek Miller (*Div.* 1964). *S.* Robert Eugene. *Dau.* Ann (Mrs. Terry Sparks). *M.* (2) Georgia Snook. *Career:* Geologist and Div. Geophysicist 1929–44; Continental District Geologist 1944–52; The Ohio Oil Co., Los Angeles; Vice-Pres., Triad Oil Co. Ltd., Calgary, Canada 1952–55; Oil Industry Consultant 1955—, Oil Producer 1957–63. *Publications:* Geology, Wasco Field, Kern County, Calif.; California Oil & Gas Exploration & Development 1940. *Member:* Canadian Petroleum Assn. (Dir. 1952–55); Member Amer. Assn. of Petroleum Geologists; Socy. of Exploring Geophysicists; Alberta Socy. of Petroleum Geologists.

*Clubs:* Petroleum (Dir. 1955–58), The Ranchmen's (of Calgary). *Address:* P.O. Box 2026, Port Angeles, Washington 98362 U.S.A.

**VAN AGT, Andreas Antonius Maria.** Netherlands Politician. *B.* 1931. *Educ.* Gymnasium, (Classical Grammar School); Catholic University Nijmegen, Degree in Law (cum laude) 1955. *M.* 1958, Dr. Eugenie J. Th. Krekelberg. *S.* 1. *Daus.* 2. *Career:* Law Practice, Eindhoven (2 years); Ministry of Ag. and Fisheries (Legal and Indust. Org. Directorate) 1958–63; Ministry of Justice (Public Law Legis. Div.) 1963–68; Sen. Lectr. Faculty of Law, Cath. Univ. Nijmegen 1968; Professor of Criminal Law and Criminal Procedure Nijmegen 1968–71; Minister of Justice 1971–77; Minister of Justice and Dep. Prime Minister 1973–77; Prime Minister since 1978. *Decorations:* Several foreign decorations; Hon. medal, Order of House of Orange. *Publications:* Report for Agrarian Law Society on forms of co-operation in Agriculture; Report for Thym Society (Assn. of Cath. Univ. Graduates) on legislator's role; Toward Extrovert Criminal Law, inaugural lecture 1969; Report for Netherlands Jurists Assn. on disciplinary law, (1971). *Address:* Office of the Prime Minister, The Hague, Netherlands.

**VANAMO, Jorma Jaakko.** Finnish diplomat. *B.* 1913. *Educ.* Licentiate of Law. *M.* 1938, Hanna Hongisto. *S.* 2. *Dau.* 1. *Career:* Attaché Stockholm and Moscow 1940; Secy. Bureau of Ministry for Foreign Affairs 1941–45, Chief Secy. from 1949–50; 1st Secy. Finnish legation Moscow 1945–48; Counsellor legation, Stockholm, Washington 1951–56; Chief of admin. div. Ministry for Foreign Affairs, Finland 1956–58; Ambassador to Poland (Warsaw) also envoy to Bucharest (Romania) and Sofia (Bulgaria) 1958–63; Ambassador to USSR (Moscow) and envoy to Kabul and Ulan Bator (Mongolia) 1963–67; Ambassador in Mongolia 1966–67; Secy.-Gen. Ministry of Foreign Affairs, Helsinki 1967–70; Ambassador to Italy (Rome), also ambassador to Nicosia (Cyprus) and Valletta (Malta) 1970–75; Finnish ambassador to Stockholm (Sweden) since 1975. *Decorations:* 2nd War and other medals and Knight Commander, Order Lion, Finland; Commdr. 1st Class Order White Rose of Finland; Grand Knight with Star (Icelandic Order Falcon), Comdr. 1st Degree (Order Dannebrog); Comdr. with star (Order Polonia Restituta); Grand Cross (Order Republic Tunisia); Order Leopold II (Belgium); Order of Merit (Italian Republic); Royal Order of the Polar Star (Sweden). *Address:* 13 Västra Trädgårdsgatan, S-111 53 Stockholm, Sweden; and *office:* Embassy of Finland, Box 7096, S-103 82 Stockholm 7, Sweden.

**van ARKEL, Hubertus.** *B.* 1913. *Educ.* Technical University, Delft, Netherlands (MSc in Mining and Metallurgical Engineering 1939). *M.* 1947, Petronella Guldemond. *S.* Hendrik Jaap. *Dau.* Catharina Geertruida. *Career:* With Billiton Company: successively underground Superintendent, Chief, geological dept., Plant Manager Billiton Bauxite Mines (Surinam), Chief, nickel exploration (Celebes), Chief, ore dressing research (Banka), and Chief, dredging operations, Sungailiat Tin Belt (Banka) 1939–51. With Alcoa: plant manager, Moengo Works, Surinam S.A. 1952–54; Consulting Engineer, Hugo Neu Corp. 1955; with Naarden Chemical Works; Technical Secretary of Managing Director, factory comptroller 1955–61; Principal, Berenschot Management Consultants 1962; Vice-Pres., Chemical and Process Div., Berenschot Consultants 1964–68; Delegate of the Board of André van Spaandonck Wool Textile Manufacturers 1969; Secy-Gen., and Dir., Bureau of IUC (Internat. Univ. Contact for Management Education) 1970–71; co-founder and Sec. Gen. EFMD (European Foundation for Management Development) 1972–73; owner-exec. Mgmt. Clinical Hour since 1974. *Publications:* translation of Bo Casten Carlberg's Management of the Growing Enterprise (from Swedish into Dutch), translation of John W. Humble's Improving Business Results (into Dutch); paper on Quantifying the task of the operator, XXXVI Congress of Chemistry. *Member:* (Senior) Amer. Inst. Mining, Metallurgical and Petroleum Engineers; (founding) member EFMD & DMG(Deutche Mgmt. Gesellschaft). *Address:* Nwe Bussumerweg 34, Huizen (N.H.), Netherlands.

**van BEEK, Hzn. A. L.** Netherlands leaf tobacco dealer and company director. *B.* 1913. *M.* 1942, Hubertine Johanna Bonjer. *S.* 3. *Dau.* 1. *Career:* Man. Dir., A. L. van Beek N.V., Dir. Amsterdam-Rotterdam Bank, N.V., Holland Amerika Lijn, N.V. Maatschappij Zeevaart; Autom. Ind. Rotterdam N.V. *Address:* Eendrachtsweg 71, Rotterdam 3002, Netherlands.

**van CAUWENBERG, Willy.** Belgian. *B.* 1914. *Educ.* University of Ghent (Dr. Econ.). *M.* 1940, Nini Wenger. *Career:* Joined the Department 1938; Vice-Consul New York 1945 (Consul 1946); Consul General: Kansas City 1952, San Francisco 1954; Economic Minister, Washington 1958. Ambassador to the Commonwealth of Australia 1963–66. Ambassador to the Netherlands 1966–74; Ambassador to USA since 1974. *Awards:* Grand Officer, Order of the Crown, Order of Leopold II & Order of Leopold (Belgium); Grand Cross Order Orange Nassau (Netherlands); Grand Officer, Order of Merit (Luxembourg). *Address:* 3330 Garfield St., NW., Washington, DC 2008, U.S.A.

**VANCE, Cyrus Roberts.** U.S. Secretary of State. *B.* 1917. *Educ.* Kent School; Yale Univ.—BA 1939; Yale Univ. Law School—LLB 1942. *M.* 1947, Grace Elsie Sloane. *S.* 1. *Daus.* 4. *Career:* Served to Lieut. (s.g.) USNR 1942–46; admitted to New York Bar 1947; Asst. to Pres. of The Mead Corp. 1946–47; Associate & Partner of Simpson Thacher & Bartlett 1947–60 and 1967–77; Special Counsel, Preparedness Investigation Subcttee. of the Senate Armed Services Cttee. 1957–60; Consulting Counsel, Special Cttee. on Space & Astronautics, U.S. Senate 1958; General Counsel, Dept. of Defense 1961–62; Secretary of the Army 1962–64; The Dep. Secretary of Defense 1964–67; Special Rep. of the President in Civil Disturbances in Detroit Jul.–Aug. 1967; Special Rep. of the President in the Cyprus Crisis Nov.–Dec. 1967; Special Rep. of the President in Korea Feb. 1968; one of the two U.S. Negotiators, Paris Peace Conference on Viet-Nam May 1968–Feb. 1969; Member of the Commission to Investigate Alleged Police Corruption in New York City May 1970–Aug. 1972; Pres., Assn. of the Bar of the City of New York 1974–76; Secretary of State since Jan. 1977. Director: IBM Corp.; Pan American World Airways Inc.; One William Street Fund Inc.; The New York Times Company. Trustee: Rockefeller Foundation; Columbia-Presbyterian Hospital; Urban Inst.; Yale Univ. *Awards:* Medal of Freedom 1969. Hon. Degrees from Marshall Univ. 1963, Trinity Coll. 1966, Yale Univ. 1968, West Virginia Univ. 1969, Brandeis Univ. 1971. *Address:* Department of State, 2201 C Street, N.W., Washington, D.C. 20520, U.S.A.

**VANCE, Sheldon Baird.** American lawyer & former diplomat. Washington, DC. *B.* 1917. *Educ.* Carleton College (AB); Harvard Law School (JD). *M.* 1939, Jean Chambers. *S.* Robert Clarke, Stephen Baird. *Career:* After law practice with Ropes, Gray, Best, Coolidge & Rugg, Boston, Mass., joined Foreign Service, 1942; served Rio de Janeiro, Nice, and Martinique, 1942–51; Belgium-Luxembourg Desk Officer, Dept. of State, Washington, 1951–54; First Secretary, Embassy, Brussels, 1954–58; Chief, Personnel Placement Branch, for Africa, Middle East & South Asia, 1958–60; Student, Senior Seminar in Foreign Relations, 1960–61; Director, Office of Central African Affairs, 1961–62; Deputy Chief of Mission, Addis Ababa, 1962–66; Senior Foreign Service Inspector, Dept. of State, 1966–67; Ambassador to Chad, 1967–69, to Republic of Zaire 1969–74; Snr. Advisor to the Sec. of State (Internat. Narcotics) 1974–77; currently practising international private & public law with Vance & Joyce, Washington, D.C. *Member:* Federal & American Bar Assns.; Massachusetts Bar; Foreign Service Association, Dept. of State, Washington. *Club:* National Lawyers, Washington. *Address:* 8510 Lynwood Place, Chevy Chase, Maryland 20015, U.S.A.; and *office* 1701 Pennsylvania Avenue, N.W., Washington D.C. 20006, U.S.A.

**VAN DEN BERG, Pieter.** American. *B.* 1903. *Educ.* Business School, Rotterdam. *M.* Cornelia Beets. *S.* Jan. B. and Willem H. *Dau.* Johanna Engel (Mrs. F.). *Career:* With Management N.V. Philips, Holland 1926–48, Chairman, North American Philips Corp. 1948—; Philips Industries Inc., 1948—; Pres. and Dir. U.S. Philips Corp. 1969—; Director, P.E.P.I. Inc., Alliance Mfg. Co., Rexham Corp. *Awards:* Knight-Comm. Royal Order of Orange-Nassau. Half Moon Award, Netherlands Club, N.Y.C.; Gov. Pieter Stuyvesant Award, 1969. Director: Netherlands-American Chamber of Commerce and Netherlands-American Foundation; Chmn., Governing Cttee., U.S. Philips Trust. Member, Advisory Board Bankers Trust. *Clubs:* Sky, Netherlands (both of N.Y.C.); Bonnie Briar Country (Larchmont, N.Y.). *Address: office* 100 East 42nd Street, New York City, U.S.A.

**van den BERGHE, Leon Arthur.** *B.* 1913. *Educ.* Bruges and Ghent; Univ. of Louvain (Lic.-en Sc. Com. and Con. and Cand.-en-Sc. Pol. and Diplomacy). *M.* Marie Josée De Backere. *Career:* At Foreign Office, Brussels 1935–36; Vice-Consul Cologne 1937–40; Flying duties with R.A.F. 1940–44; Secy. then Counsellor of Embassy, Washington 1945–49; Consul-General Kansas City 1949–50; External Affairs

Brussels, American Aid Programme 1951–52; Originator and General Manager of Belgian Trade Promotion, in U.S.A. Chicago 1953–56; Consul-General Hamburg 1956–60; Min. Plen. to Indonesia 1960–62; Ambassador Plen. to New Zealand 1962. Consul-General of Belgium in the Fiji Islands and other British possessions, and in French Polynesia 1962–68. Ambassador Plen. to New Zealand, 1962–68; Ambassador to Norway and Iceland 1968; General Adviser, External Trade Relations, Brussels 1977. *Awards:* Grand Cross, Royal Order, St. Olav and Icelandic Order of the Falcon; Grand Officer, Order of Leopold II; Cmdr. Order of Leopold, and of the Order of the Crown; Commemorative Medal of Reign of King Albert I; Croix Civique (1st class); War Medal with Crossed Swords 1940–45; France and Germany Star; etc. Lt.-Col. d'Aviation Re's. *Club:* Caterpillar. *Address:* 52 Avenue George Bergmann, Brussels 1050, Belgium.

**van den BOEYNANTS, Paul.** Belgian politician. *B.* 1919. *Educ.* College of St. Michael, Brussels (Humanities). *M.* 1942, Lucienne Deurinck. *S.* 1. *Daus.* 2. *Career:* Prisoner-of-war in Germany 1940; President, Brussels Corporation of Butchers 1945; Founder of the School of Butchery 1945; Deputy at the age of 29 years, 1949; National Federation of Butchers and Pork Butchers of Belgium 1952; Alderman of Brussels 1953; Deputy Administrator, Universale Exhibition, Brussels 1958; President, Christian-Social Party 1961; Alderman for Public Works 1965; Prime Minister of Belgium 1966–69; Min. of State 1969–72; Min. of National Defence since 1972 & Dep. Prime Minister since 1977. *Awards:* Belgian: Cmdr. Order of Leopold; Commemorative Medal 1940–45 (two crossed swords with cap); foreign: Grand Cross, Orders of du Sud, de Niger, Liberator San Martin (Argentina), Merit (Austria), Merit (Camerouns), Pius IX (Hoy See), Orange-Nassau (Netherlands), St. Sylvester (Holy See), St. Michael and St. George (U.K.), Polar Star (Sweden), Republic (Tunis). Grand Officer, Order of Merit (Italy); Cmdr. Order of French National Economy; Order of Merit (Chile); Orders from Luxembourg, Congo & Finland; Grand Off. Legion of Honour. *Address: office* 8 rue Lambermont, 1000 Brussels, Belgium.

**van den BOSCH, Baron Jean,** GCVO, Belgian ambassador. *B.* 1910. *Educ.* Louvain Univ. (Dr. of Laws 1931; Bach. Historical Sciences 1932; Bach. Pol. and Diplo. Sciences 1932). *M.* 1944 Helene Cloquet. *Daus.* Sophie and M. Caroline. *Career:* Entered Min. Foreign Affairs Jan. 1934; Att. London, Paris, 1934; Secy. Peking 1937, Ottawa, 1940; Chargé d'Affaires to Luxembourg Govt. in London, 1943; Deputy to the Cabinet Office of the Prince Regent of Belgium, 1944; Counsellor and Chargé d'Affaires a.i., Cairo, 1948; Counsellor, Paris, 1949; Minister, Paris, 1953; Consul-General Hong Kong, Singapore and Saigon, 1954; Ambassador Cairo, 1955 concurrently Minister Libya, 1956; Secy.-General, Ministry of Foreign Affairs and External Trade, 1959; Ambassador to Leopoldville 1960; re-appointed Secretary-General, 1960—. Ambassador to the Court of St. James's and Belgian Permanent Representative to the Council of Western European Union, 1966; Dir. LBI Ltd.; Lloyds Bank International (Belgium) 1972—; Chmn. Lloyds Bank International (Belgium) since 1973. *Awards:* Grand Officer, Order of Leopold, Order of the Crown, Order of Leopold II (Belgium); Foreign Orders from Austria, Brazil, China, Ethiopia, France, Greece, Holy See, Iran, Ivory Coast, Luxembourg, Netherlands, Norway, Peru, Portugal, Sweden, Thailand, United Arab Republic and U.K. *Clubs:* Anglo-Belgian; Beefsteak; White's. *Address:* 1 Avenue de l'Hippodrome, 1050 Brussels, Belgium.

**van den BOSCH, Count Johannes Hendrik Otto,** LLD. Dutch banker. *B.* 12 April 1906. *M.* 1937, Benudina Maria Royaards. *S.* 1. *Daus.* 3. *Career:* With Twentsche Bank 1932–34, Director of Branch Office, Utrecht 1941–45; with Nederlandsche Bank 1934–39, Head of Foreign Department 1939–41; Deputy Director 1945–47, Director 1947–71; Dir. Albert de Bary; Chmn. Enschede. *Awards:* Commander 2nd Class, Order of Vasa (Sweden), Kt., Order of the Lion (Netherlands); Commander Order Orange-Nassau. *Address:* Koningin Wilhelminalaan 4, Amersfoort, Netherlands.

**van den BRINK, J. R. M.** Dutch banker. *B.* 12 April 1915. *Educ.* Catholic Economic High School, Tilburg. *Career:* with Ministry of Commerce and Industry 1940–42; Professor, Roman Catholic University, Nijmegen 1945–48; member (R.C.P.P.), First Chamber 1945–48; Minister of Economic Affairs 1948–52; General Adviser, Amsterdamsche Bank N.V. and Incasso-Bank N.V. 1952–53; Gen. Mgr. Amsterdamsche Bank N.V. 1953–64; Managing Dir., Amsterdam-Rotterdam Bank N.V. since 1964. *Address:* Herengracht 595, Amsterdam, Netherlands.

**van den Wall BAKE, Herman Willem Alexander,** BSc. Dutch company director. *B.* 5 Nov. 1906. *M.* 1932, Louise Hillegonda van Dorp. *Daus.* Anna Agatha, Eulalie Hermance, Louise Hillegonda, Elisabeth Margaretha. *Career:* With Shell Co., Amsterdam, The Hague, London, Dutch East Indies 1929–45; Man.-Dir., Inst. for Netherlands-American Industrial Co-operation 1945–49; Netherlands Participation Co. 1948–49; Industrial Adviser, Nederlandsche Handel-Maatschappij 1949–50, Man.-Dir. since 1950 (President since May 1962); former Pres. now Vice-Chmn. Algemene Bank Nederland N.V. (merger between Nederlandsche Handel-Maatschappij N.V. and De Twentsche Bank N.V.) merged Feb. 1968 with Hollandsche Bank-Unie; Chairman 'Naarden' International; Koninklijke Nederlandsche Vliegtuigenfabriek Fokker N.V.; V.F.W. Fokker m.b.H., Koniklijke Ned. Stoomboot-Mij; Koninklijke Nederlandsche Hoogovens en Staalfabrieken. Koninklijke Drukkeri en Uitgeveri v/hc. de Boer Jr. N.V. Hilversum. *Address:* Flevolaan 3, Huizen N.H., Netherlands.

**VANDEPUTTE, Robert M. A. C.** D.en D. D.en sc pol. et soc. Belgian banker and University professor. *B.* 1908. *Educ.* Univs. of Louvain, Nijmegen, Paris, Berlin and Berne. *M.* 1938, Marie-Louise Cauwe. *S.* 2. *Dau.* 1. *Career:* Lawyer at Bar of Antwerp 1930–40; Prof. Univ. of Louvain 1936; Cabinet Chief, Ministry of Economic Affairs 1939–40; Secy. Gen. Assoc. Belge des Banques 1940–42; Dir. Nat. Banque of Belgium 1943–44; Governor 1971–75; Man. Dir. Socy. Nat. de Crédit of Industry 1944–48, Pres. 1948–71; Nat. Regent Banque 1954–71: member Caisse Générale d'Epargne et de Retraite 1958–75; Dir. and member Directing Cttee. Société Nat. d'Investment 1962–71; Pres. Inst. de Réescompte et de Garantie since 1973; Admin. Palais des Beaux-Arts de Belgique since 1966; Member Conseil Sup. des Finances 1969–71; Pres. Hoger Inst. voor Bestuurs-en Handelswetenschappen since 1959. *Decorations: (Belgian):* Hon. Deacon of Labour 1953; Civil Cross, 1st class (1940–45) 1953; Commander, Order of the Crown (with gold bar) 1954 (Commander 1945); Commander, Order of Leopold 1962 (Knight 1939); Civil Cross, 1st class (service decoration) 1969 (Civil Medal, 1st class 1959); Grand Commander, Order of Leopold II 1969; Grand Commander, Order of Leopold 1974. *(Foreign):* Commander, Order of St. Gregory the Great 1949; Office, Order "Al Merito della Repubblica Italiana" 1955; Grand Commander, Order of the Crown of Oak (Luxembourg) 1972; Commander, National Order of the Leopard (Zaire) 1972; Grand Cross, Order of Merit of the Grand Duchy of Luxembourg 1975; Grand Cross of Orange Nassau (Netherlands) 1975; Grand Cross, Order of Service with Star of the Federal Republic of Germany 1975. *Publications:* in Dutch, Beginselen van Nijverheidsrecht, Handboek voor Verzekeringen en Verzekeringsrecht, Wat ik rondom mij zag, De Overeenkomst; in French. Quelques aspects de l'Activité de la Société Nationale de Crédit à l'Industrie; Le Statut de l'Entreprise. *Address:* Avenue de Tervueren 282, 1150 Brussels, Belgium.

**van der BYL, Pieter Kenyon Fleming-Voltelyn.** Rhodesian Politician. *B.* 1923. *Educ.* Cape Town, Cambridge & Harvard Univs. *Career:* Tobacco farmer in Rhodesia since 1946; mem. of Parl. since 1962; Dep. Minister of Information 1964–68; Minister of Information, Immigration & Tourism 1968–74, of Defense 1974–76, of Foreign Affairs since 1974. *Address:* Ministry of Foreign Affairs, Salisbury, Rhodesia.

**VAN DER HEK, Arie.** Netherlands politician. *B.* 1938. *Educ.* Doctorandus Political Science. *M.* 1963, Elisabeth Margaretha Maria Haster. *Daus.* 2. *Career:* Assist. Internat. Secy. Netherlands Labour Party 1968–70; Civil Servant, Neth. Ministry of Foreign Affairs 1970–72; Civil Servant, Neth. Ministry of Economic Affairs 1972–73; M.P. 2nd Chamber since 1973; Member of European Parlt. since 1973; Member Party Exec. Board since 1975; Chmn., Economic & Monetary Commission, European Parliament 1976–77. *Publications:* Scientific periodicals on trade matters, energy problems and development co-operation. *Address:* Schweitzerplein 2, Gouda, Netherlands; and *office* Binnenhof 1A, The Hague, Netherlands.

**VAN DER MEULEN, Jozef Vital Marie.** Belgian Diplomat. *B.* 1914. *Educ.* Licencié in Political & Social Sciences. *Career:* Inspector of Finances; Dir. Gen. (non-exec.) at the Ministry of Economic Affairs; Hon. Sec. of the Council of Ministers; Hon. Chief of Cabinet of the Prime Minister & the Minister of Economic Affairs; Member of the Management Cttee. of the Agence Européene pour l'Energie Nucléaire, Paris; Pres. of the Board of Dirs. of the Fondation Francqui; Capitaine-Commandant de Réserve Honoraire; Amb. & Perm. Rep. of Belgium to the European Community. *Decorations:* Cadet d'Honneur du Travail de Belgique; Médaille Commémorative 1940–55; Médaille du Prisonnier de Guerre: Grand Officier de l'Ordre de la Couronne; Grand Officier de l'Ordre de Léopold II; Grand Officier de l'Ordre de Léopold; Médaille Civique de lère classe; & 11 foreign decorations. *Address:* Permanent Representation of Belgium to the EEC, 62, Belliardstraat, 1040 Brussels, Belgium.

**van der SPEK, Jean Hector.** Belgian engineer and Doctor in Applied Science. *B.* 1916. *Educ.* Brussels Univ., Liège Univ. (Dr. in Applied Science), and Harvard Univ. (Adv. Management Programme). *M.* 1951, Marianne de Sivers. *S.* Jean. *Daus.* Veronica, Ingrid and Anne. *Career:* Engineer, Electric and Rolling Stock Departments of Brussels Tramways 1939–47; interruption from 1945 to 1946, when appointed personal assistant to the Minister of Economic Affairs; Engineer, Union Minière du Haut-Katanga 1948–66, then consultant in Atomic Energy, Detroit Edison Company 1965. Member 26th AMP, Harvard BS; Pres. Syndicat d'Etude de Industrie Atomiques.; Director, Belgonucléaire 1957; Sivers & Neame 1960; Patino NV 1975; Société Anglo-Belge Vulcain 1963; Managing Director Concours Musical International Reine Elisabeth, Chapelle Musicale Reine Elisabeth. *Publications:* Redresseurs à Vapeur de Mercure; Notes sur la Traction Electrique; various articles on nuclear energy and on Einstein's theories of Relativity. *Member:* Société Royale Belge des Ingénieurs et des Industriels; Société Belge des Electriciens; American Nuclear Socy. *Clubs:* Cercle Gaulois; Cercle Royal Africain; Cercle de la Fondation Universitaire, Royal Golf de Belgique; Royal Léopold Club; Harvard Alumńi Association. *Address:* Avenue de l'Observatoire 9, 1180 Brussels, Belgium.

**VAN DER STOEL, Max.** Netherlands politician. *B.* 1924. *Educ.* Municipal Gymnasium Leyden; Leyden Univ. Law degree; Law degree (2nd) sociology (1953). *M.* Maria Johanna Aritia De Kanter. *S.* 1. *Daus.* 4. *Career:* Staff member Dr. Wiardi Beckman Inst. 1953–58; Member 1st Chamber of States-Gen. 1960–63; 2nd Chamber 1963–65; State Secy. Foreign Affairs in Cals. Govt. 1965; Mem. of 2nd Chamber 1967; Mem. of Council of Europe Consultative Assembly 1967–72; Chmn. of Board of Neth. Inst. for Peace Problems since 1970; Chmn. of Bd. of Trustees of Inst. of Social Studies since 1969; Member of European Parlt. since 1972, Member of North Atlantic Assembly; Chmn. of Standing Cttee. for For. Affairs (2nd Chamber) 1971–73; Minister for Foreign Affairs, Netherlands since 1973. *Member:* Bureau Socialist International 1958–65; Former Intern. Secy. of Dutch Labour Party (1958–65;) Verdam State Commission for revision of company law. *Publications:* Hulp aan Ontwikkelingslanden (Aid for Developing Countries) 1963; Politiek voor vrede (A Policy for Peace) (written with Labour Party Cttee.). *Decorations:* Knight, Order of Netherlands Lion; Grand Cross, Order of the Crown of Belgium; Grand Cross, Order of Merit (Ivory Coast); Grand Cross, Order of the Dannebrog of Denmark; Grand Cross, Order of Merit (Italy); Grand Cross, Order of the Republic of Tunisia; Grand Cross, Order of Star of Africa (Liberia); Grand Cross, Order of White Rose of Finland; Grand Cross, Order of the Oak Wreath (Luxembourg); Grand Cross, Order of Merit (Senegal); Grand Cross, Order of the Liberator (Venezuela). *Address:* Ministry of Foreign Affairs, The Hague, Netherlands.

**van der STRATEN-WAILLET, Baron Francois Xavier.** Belgian politician and diplomat; Ret. *B.* 1910. *M.* 1935, Marie Thérèse Moretus-Plantin. *S.* Paul, Emmanuel, Arnould. *Daus.* Suzanne, Régine, Brigitte. *Career:* Min. of Overseas Trade 1947–48; Min. of Public Health 1948–49; National Pres., Social Christian Party 1949–50; member, Chamber of Representatives; Ambassador to the Argentine 1952–55; to the Netherlands June 1955. Dir. Gen. Min. of Foreign Affairs; Ambassador to Italy 1970–75 (Ret'd.). *Awards:* Grand Officer: Order of Leopold; Order of Leopold II, Cmdr., Order of the Crown (Belgium); Grand Cross Nederlandse Leeuw; Grand Cross Order of Orange-Nassau; Grand Cross Order of the House of Orange; Grand Cross of Merit (Argentina); St. Sylvester (Vatican). *Address:* Duindak, D-Logo Strabroek, Belgium.

**VAN DER VELDEN, Jan.** Dutch. *B.* 1909. *M.* 1936, Cornelia Maria Van den Broek. *S.* 1. *Dau.* 2. *Career:* Past-Pres. Exec. Bd. Nationale-Nederlanden N.V.; Presently: Vice-Chairman Central Organization for Applied Scientific Research in the Netherlands TNO; Chairman Verenigde Bedrijven Bredero N.V.; Chairman "CETECO" Trading and Industrial Corporation; Chairman Netherlands Reinsurance Group; Chairman N.V. Stadsherstel Den Haag en Omgeving; Dir. AHOLD N.V.; Dir. Nationale-Nederlanden N.V.; Dir. Netherlands-Canada Chamber of Commerce; Dir. Vereeniging Z.A.S.M. (Zuid-Afrikaansche Stichting Moederland); Chairman Jan van Riebeeck Foundation; Chairman Campagne Committee Netherlands Red Cross. *Address:* Jagerslaan 1, Wassenaar, Netherlands; and *office* Juliana van Stolberglaan 148, The Hague, Netherlands.

**VANDERVELL, Charles Anthony.** British. *B.* 1927. *Educ* Stowe School; Univ. Coll. London. *M.* 1959, Audrey J. McCall. *Daus.* 2. *Career:* Dir. Vandervell Products Ltd. 1955–58; Man. Dir. Polypenco Ltd. 1963–72; Vice Pres, European Operations, Poymer Corp. Pa. 1972—; Dir. Clark & Fenn (Holdings) Ltd. 1972–77; ACF Industries (U.K.) Ltd.; ACF (Great Britain) Ltd.; Polypenco Ltd.; Eng. Industrial Plastics Ltd.; Man. Dir. Bucklersbury Industrial Holdings Ltd. *Member:* The Game Conservancy (Vice-Chmn); Inst. of Marketing; Inst. of Directors; American Chamber of Commerce. *Clubs:* Royal Thames Yacht; Royal London Yacht. *Address:* Horseshoe Hill House, Burnham, Bucks. and *office:* 60–62 London Road, Kingston, Surrey.

**VAN DEVENTER, William F.** Retired, formerly general partner, Laidlaw & Co., New York City; Director, ACF Industries Inc. *B.* 1905. *Educ.* Princeton Univ. (BS 1928). *M.* 1969, Virginia Jones Lee (widow). *Daus.* Adelaide Chapman (Gibson) and Sandra Blackwell (Eaton). *Member:* The Holland Society of New York; New Jersey Historical Society; Society of Colonial Wars in the State of New Jersey; Assn. of Ex-Members of Squadron 'A'. *Clubs:* Princeton, Anglers (N.Y.C.); Somerset Hills Country (Bernardsville, N.J.). *Address:* Windy Ridge Farm, Far Hills, N.J. 07931; and Summer: Harborside, Biddeford Pool, Maine 04006, U.S.A.

**VAN DIJKE, Pieter,** Dutch; Secretary-General of the Ministry of the Interior. *B.* 1920. *Educ.* LLM. *M.* 1947, Elisabeth Antonia Johanna de Bruijn. *S.* Hans, Kees; *Daus.* Karin, Josje. *Career:* Public Relations Officer Municipality of Utrecht 1951; Director Dutch–German Chamber of Commerce Hamburg 1955; Chief Administrator Municipality of Utrecht 1956; Town Clerk Utrecht 1964; Mayor of Gouda 1969. Sec-Gen. Min. of Interior, Netherlands, 1973. *Publications:* numerous acticles on administrative law, on public relations and on management training in Netherlands professional journals. *Address:* 68 Lange Kerkdam, Wassenaar; office Ministry of the Interior, 19 Binnenhof, The Hague.

**VANDIVIERE, Horace Mac,** MD. *B.* 1921. *Educ.* Mercer Univ. (AB 1943, MA 1944), Univ. of Michigan (Grad. work, bacteriology and neuroanatomy, 1944–46) and Univ, of North Carolina School of Medicine (MD 1960). *M.* 1941. Margaret Reynolds (*D.*); and (2) 1968, Irene Melvin. *S.* Christopher Reynolds and Martin Mac. *Career:* Instructor 1942–44, and Ast. Professor 1946–48, Department of Biology, Mercer University; Instructor, Univ. of Michigan 1944–46; Director of Special Service Unit, Georgia Dept. of Public Health 1948–51; Research Bacteriologist, North Carolina Sanatorium, McCain, N.C. 1951–53; Director of Research, North Carolina Sanatorium System, Gravely Sanatorium, Chapel Hill, N.C. 1953–67. Lecturer in Tuberculosis, School of Public Health, University of N.C. 1959; Dir. and Organizer, Haitian-Amer. Tuberculosis Inst. 1961; Dir., Div. of Tuberculosis and Fungal Diseases, Kentucky Dept. of Health 1972–74; Dir., Div. Remedial Health Service (M.H., Resp. Dis., Forensic Med.), Kentucky Dept. of Human Resources 1974–77; Assoc. Professor, Dept. Comm. Med. Univ., Kentucky Coll. of Medicine 1967–72; Professor since 1972; *Member:* American Medical Assn.; Amer. Thoracic Socy., Cttee. on Antigens 1961–62; Cttee. on Diagnostic Skin Testing 1962–63. *Publications:* numerous scientific publications, many in the field of anti-tuberculosis vaccination and skin testing involving techniques of standardization and production of vaccines and evaluation of vaccines and skin testing materials. *Clubs:* Exchange, Knights of Pythias. *Address:* Dept. Comm. Med., U.K. College of Med., Lexington, Ky. 40506, U.S.A. (and H.A.T.I. Jeremie, Haiti, W.I.).

**VAN DUSEN, Richard C. BS, LLB.** American. Attorney, Former Government Official. *B.* 1925. *Educ.* Deerfield Academy; Univ. of Minnesota; Harvard Law School. *M.* 1949, Barbara Congdon. *Daus.* Amanda, Lisa and Katherine. *Career:* Associate, Dickinson, Wright, McKean, Cudlip & Moon, Detroit 1949–57; Partner 1958–62, 1964–68, & since

1973; Member, Michigan House of Representatives 1954–56; Legal Advisor to Governor of Michigan 1963; Under Secy. United States Dept. of Housing & Urban Development 1969–72. Member, Council of Administrative Conference of the United States since 1969. *Member:* Amer. Bar Assn.; State Bar of Michigan, Federal Bar Assn.; Detroit Bar Assn.; Economic Club of Detroit. *Address:* 32205 Bingham Road, Birmingham, Michigan 48010 and *office* 800 First National Building, Detroit, Michigan 48226, U.S.A.

**van ECK, Johan Herman Isaac.** Netherlands. *B.* 1915. *Educ.* Public Schools. *M.* 1948, Sonja Jepsen. *S.* Juan. *Dau.* Fleur. *Career:* With Bührmann (paper dealers) in Amsterdam, Sweden and United Kingdom 1932–36; Nationale Handelsbank in Shanghai, Manila, Djakarta and Singapore 1936–47. With Labouchere & Co. N.V. (Commercial and Investment Bank) Amsterdam: Secretary to Management 1947, Deputy Managing Director 1952, Managing Director 1954–76; Chairman and Delegate Member of the Board of Supervisory Directors of Bank Morgan Labouchere N.V. 1976—. Supervisory Director of N.V. Verto, Rotterdam, since 1964; N.V. Zwolsche Algemeene, Utrecht, since 1970; Iduna Corset Industrie N.V., Uden, since 1954; Leaseco Nederland B.V., Amsterdam, since 1963; Papier en Karton Holding Kappa N.V., Haren, since 1972. Member of Amsterdam Stock Exchange, Nederlandse Bankiers-vereniging (Netherlands Bankers' Association). *Clubs:* Industrieele Groote Club, Amsterdam; Hilversumse Golf club. *Address:* Standelkruid 6, Laren N.H., Netherlands; and *office:* Tesselschadestraat 12, P.O. Box 154, Amsterdam, Netherlands.

**van EEGHEN, Henri Louis.** Dutch banker. *B.* 1 Dec. 1887. *Educ.* Commercial School, Amsterdam; University of the Sorbonne, Paris. *M.* 1918, C. M. Boreel. *S.* 4. *Daus.* 2. *Address:* Noordhout, Driebergen, Netherlands.

**VAN ELSLANDE, Renaat.** Belgian Politician. *B.* 1916. *Educ.* Classical sec. ed. (Greek-Latin humanities and study of philosophy); Doctor of Laws and Bachelor of Political and Social Science. *M.* 1945, Ghislaine Van Acker. *S.* 1. *Daus.* 3. *Career:* Lawyer 1942–45; Professor University Louvain 1947; Burgomaster of Lot 1947; Member of Chamber of Representatives 1949; Minister-under-Secy. of State for Culture 1960–61; Deputy-Min. of Nat. Educ. and Culture 1961–63; Minister of Culture, deputy Min. of Educ. 1963–65; Min. for European Affairs and Flemish Culture 1966–68; Min. of Home Affairs 1972; Min. of Foreign Affairs 1973–77; Min. of Justice since 1977. *Publications:* Europa's toekomst (1975); Belgié en der Derde Wereld (1977). *Address:* Ministry of Justice, Place Poelaert 4, 1000 Bruxelles, Belgium.

**VAN GARSSE, Yvan.** Belgian. Editor, Studies in Genocide and War Crimes. *B.* 1944. *Educ.* PhD. *Publications:* La recherche sociale en Europe (1967); Etude sur l'ethnocentrisme en Afrique tropicale (1968); The international Organisation of Criminology (1969); Bibliography on genocide, Crimes against humanity and War Crimes (1970); Aggression in Animals (1970); Pamphlet literature of the radical left in the United States (1971); Los indios norteamericanos (1971). Doctor honoris causa in Psychology; Grand Prix Humanitaire de France. *Address:* Patotterijstraat 12, B–9170, Belgium; and *office:* Parklaan 2, Sint Niklaas Wass, Belgium.

**VAN HORN, Kent Robertson.** Metallurgist. *B.* 1905. *Educ.* Case Institute of Technology (BS 1926) and Yale Univ. (MS 1928; PhD 1929). *M.* 1932, Estelle V. Yost. *S.* Karl Robertson and Neil Yost. *Career:* Research Metallurgist, Alcoa Research Laboratories, Aluminum Co. of America 1929–44: Chief, Cleveland Research Div. 1945–47; Asst. Dir. of Research 1948–50; Associate Director of Research 1950–51; Director of Research 1951–62. Vice-President, Research & Development, Aluminium Company of America 1962—. *Awards:* Honours: DSc, Case Inst. of Technology; Inst. of Metals Lecture, 1952; Campbell Memorial Lecture, A.S.M. 1954; Honor Lecture, Socy. of Nondestructive Testing, 1957 (is Hon. Member & Fellow of the Socy.). Sainte Claire-Deville Medal, Sté Française de Métallurgie. *Member:* Amer. Socy. for Metals (President 1944; Honorary Member 1963); Fellow 1970. Gold Medal, 1970, Society for Nondestructive Testing (President 1945); American Institute of Mining & Metallurgical Engineers (Fellow); British Inst. of Metals; American Society for Testing Materials; Inst of Metals (London) Platinum Medal 1973. *Publications:* three books: Practical Metallurgy (with George Sachs), Alumium, and Aluminium in Iron Steel (with Samuel Case); 40 original articles in scientific journals. *Clubs:* Duquesne; Fox Chapel Golf. *Address:* 373 Fox Chapel Road, Pittsburgh, 38, Pa.; and *office* Aloca Building, Pittsburgh, Pa., U.S.A.

**van HOUTEN, Hans Rudolf.** Dutch. *B.* 13 Aug. 1907. *Educ.* Gymnasium, The Hague; University of Leyden. *Career:* Attaché, Copenhagen and Stockholm 1932–34; Secretary of Legation, Berlin 1935–40; Counsellor of Embassy, Washington 1940–45, Brussels 1945–48; Dir., Foreign Service 1948; En. Ex. and Min. Plen. to Mexico 1951–54; Amb. 1954–58; Dir. Gen. for Political Affairs 1958–59; Under-Secy. of State for Foreign Affairs 1959–63: Ambassador to Austria 1964–68 (Ret'd.). *Address:* Ministry of Foreign Affairs, Plein 23, The Hague, Netherlands.

**van HOUTTE, Jean (Baron).** D. en D.; Belgian politician. *B.* 17 Mar. 1907. *M.* 1932, Cécile de Stella. *S.* Hubert. *Daus.* Marie Louise (Mrs. J. C. Velge), Thérèse (Mrs. P. M. De Smet), Anne Elisabeth (Mrs. J. P. De Bandt). *Career:* Barrister-at-Law 1928; Professor of civil law and taxation law in the Universities of Liège 1931 and Ghent 1937; Chef de Cabinet to the Minister of the Interior and Information 1944–45; Assesseur au Conseil d'Etat 1948–49; Co-opted Senator 1949–68; Min. of Finance 1950–Jan. 1952; Prime Minister Jan. 1952–April 1954; Min. of Finance 1958–61; Min. of State 1966. Grand Croix, Ordre de la Couronne. *Publications:* La responsabilité dans les transports aériens; Formulierboek voor Notarissen; La réparation des dommages de guerre aux biens privés; Traité des sociétés de personnes à responsabilité limitée; Principes de droit fiscal belge. *Address:* 54 Boulevard St. Michel, Brussels 4, Belgium.

**van KARNEBEEK, Jonkheer Maurits Peter Marie;** Dutch diplomat. *B.* 8 Dec. 1908. *Educ.* Utrecht University. *M.* 1933, Dorothée Baroness van Wijnbergen van Bussloo. *S.* Herman Adriaan. *Dau.* Dorothée Odette Civile. *Career:* Burgomaster of Zuidlaren and later Zwolle; entered Diplomatic Service after World War II; member, Delegation, Preparatory Commission of United Nations, and First and Second General Assemblies; Head (with rank of Major-General) Military Mission in Austria 1946; for some time Counsellor and Chargé d'Affaires, Embassy, Moscow; Chargé d'Affaires, Embassy, Karachi; En. Ex. and Min. Plen. to Israel; En. Ex. and Min. Plen. then Ambassador to Norway until May 1958; Director-General, Commission of European Economic Community in Brussels 1958–61; Adviser, Foreign Relations Dept., KLM Royal Dutch Airlines 1961—; Manager Algemene Bank Nederland N.V. 1964. Knight, Order of the Lion (Netherlands); Grand Cross, Order of St. Olav (Norway); Grand Cross of Adolphe de Nassau (Luxembourg). *Address:* Van Trigtstraat 49, The Hague, Netherlands.

**van KLEFFENS, Eelco Nicolaas.** Netherlands diplomat. *B.* 1894. *Educ.* University of Leyden (LLD); various honorary degrees. *M.* 1935, Margaret Helen Horstman. *Career:* adjusted shipping questions affecting Netherlands arising from World War I 1919; member of Secretariat, League of Nations 1919–21; Secretary to Board of Royal Dutch Petroleum Co. 1921–23; Deputy Chief, Legal Division, Netherlands Ministry for Foreign Affairs 1923–27; registrar of Arbitral Tribunal under Dawes and Young Plan; Deputy Chief, Diplomatic Division 1927–29; Chief 1929–39; Minister to Switzerland, and Netherlands representative at League of Nations 1939; Minister for Foreign Affairs 1939–46; Minister without portfolio and Netherlands representative on Security Council and Economic and Social Council of U.N. 1946–47; Ambassador to U.S.A. 1947–50; member, Curatorium of Hague Academy of International Law (1946–68); Pres. 9th Gen. Assembly, U.N.; Minister to Portugal 1950–56; Netherlands Minister of State (Life Appt.) since 1950. Permanent Netherlands Representative on N. Atlantic Council 1956–58; Chief Representative in U.K. of the European Coal and Steel Community 1958–67; Pres., American-British-French-German Arbitration Tribunal, 1957–70. *Awards:* Grand Cross, Order of Orange-Nassau (Netherlands); Grand Cross, Legion of Honour (France), and other decorations. *Publications:* Relations between the Netherlands and Japan—1605–1917 (Leiden 1918); The Rape of the Netherlands (London 1940); translations were published in Switzerland and Mexico; Amer. edition, New York (1941); numerous clandestine editions circulated in the Netherlands during the German occupation; Sovereignty in International Law (1953). Hispanic Law until the end of the Middle Ages (1968). *Address:* Casal de Sta. Filomena, Almoçageme, Colares, Portugal.

**VAN KREVELEN, Dirk Willem.** Dutch. *B.* 1914. *Educ.* Rotterdam Grammar School; Univ. of Leiden. *M.* 1939, E.L.J.M. Kreisel. *S.* 3. *Dau.* 1. *Career:* Exec. Vice-Pres. AKZO E.Y.; Chmn. N.V. AHZO Research & Engineering, Dir. Aerican: Enka Corp. Nor it N.Y.; Elsevier Publishing Co. *Addrses:* Bakeubergseweg 85, Arnhem, The Netherlands.

**van LANSCHOT, Willem Charles Jean Marie.** Dutch executive. Partner van Lanschot Bank's-Hertogenbosch. *B.* 1914. *Educ.* Royal Military Academy Breda and Leiden Univ. *M.* 1946, Jonkvrouwe L. M. van Meeuwen. *S.* 1. *Dau.* 1. *Career:* Joined N.V. Philips Gloeilampenfabrieken, Eindhoven 1949, became Secretary in General Service and Head of Public Relations Dept. and finally Managing Director for N. Africa and the Middle East; assumed present position 1966. Became a regular army officer in 1935. During the war was charged with special missions; captured by the Germans in 1942; subjected to third degree interrogations for 100 hours on end; finally taken to Natzweiler Concentration Camp, and thence to Dachau, whence he was liberated by the American Rainbow Division in 1945. For his conduct during the war he was created Knight of the Militaire Willems-Orde by H.M. Queen Juliana personally; Appointed Head of the Dutch Military Mission for Tracing Missing Persons; retired with rank of Colonel in 1949. Appointed Member of Bd. of Netherlands division of Intern. Chamber of Commerce, 1975. Elected Lieutenant for the Netherlands, Equestrian Order of the Holy Sepulchre of Jerusalem 1975. *Member:* World Veterans Federation (Pres.); Assn. of Dutch Military War Victims—BNMO (Pres.); Board of the Netherlands War Graves Foundations; Board of Netherlands Assn. for International Legal Order—VIRO; Board of the Lamp of Brotherhood (Counsellor). *Awards:* Knight, Militaire Willems-Orde; Officer, Orange-Nassau, Knight, Order of the Dutch Lion; Chevalier Legion of Honour; Officer of Crown of Belgium; Cmdr. of Yugoslavian Flag; Knight of Gregorious the Great; Comdr. in the Order of Merit of the Federal Republic of Germany and many others. *Publications:* Various articles on veterans affairs, and the Middle East. *Address:* Leeuweriklaan 9, Eindhoven, Netherlands.

**VAN MELL, Herman Teufel.** American lawyer. *B.* 1911. *Educ.* University of Wisconsin (BA; MA 1935); Harvard Law School (JD 1938). *M.* 1952, Helen Strotz. *S.* Robert Hendrik and Derrick Herman. *S.* (by former marriage) Richard. *Career:* Partner law firm of Finn, Van Mell & Penney, Chicago: admitted Illinois Bar 1939; admitted to Bar of the United States Supreme Court 1951; Dir., The Parker Pen Co. Retired as Snr. Vice-President, Law, Secretary and General Counsel, Sunbeam Corporation, Chicago on June 30, 1977. *Publication:* The Case for Fair Trade (Illinois Bar Journal 1956). *Clubs:* Chicago Yacht (Past Commodore); New York Yacht; Chicago Athletic Assn. *Address:* 180 N. La Salle Street, Chicago, Ill. 60601, U.S.A.

**VAN NUYS, Francis.** American. *B.* 1912. *Educ.* Harvard College (AB) and Harvard Law School (LLB). *M.* 1935, Anne G. Chute. *S.* Francis B. and Peter. *Career:* Appointed New York Bar 1939; Vice-President, Law 1967—, and General Counsel, Bethlehem Steel Corporation. Member: N.Y. State, Penna State Northampton County (Pa.) and American Bar Associations; American Inst. of Amer. Iron & Steel Inst.; Asia Society; American Law Institute. *Clubs:* Saucon Valley Country, Bethlehem (both of Bethlehem); The Canadian Club of New York. *Address:* Bethlehem Steel Corporation, Martin Tower, Bethlehem, Pa. 18016, U.S.A.

**van RAALTE, Felix.** Netherlands Diplomat. *B.* 1915. *Educ.* Gymnasium A; Theology & Law Studies, Univ. of Leiden. *M.* 1970, Brigitte. *S.* 2. *Daus.* 2. *Career:* Netherlands Foreign Service: London 1946–47, Paris 1947–48, Athens 1949, Bonn 1950, Sofia 1950, Bucharest 1950, Wellington 1951–55, Warsaw 1955–59, Singapore 1959–61, Copenhagen 1961–63, Lusaka 1965–66, Berlin 1967–71, Monrovia 1971–74, & Ambassador, Dublin since 1974. *Decorations:* Grand Cross, African Star; Grand Cross, African Redemption; Commander, Order of Dannebrog; Officer, Order of Orange-Nassau. *Address:* Royal Netherlands Embassy, 160 Merrion Road, Dublin 4, Eire.

**van RHIJN, Arie Adriaan.** Dutch government official, *B.* 23 Oct. 1892. *Educ.* Universities of Groningen (JD. DSc, LLD) and Utrecht (PhD). *M.* 1919, E. M. E. van Dijk. *S.* S. *Daus.* 2. *Career:* Deputy-Secretary, Court of Arbitration for Railway Personnel 1917–18; Secy., Master Printers Union 1919–27; Head of Department, Ministry of Social Affairs 1928–32; Secretary-General, Ministry of Economic Affairs 1933–39; Minister of Agriculture and Fisheries 1940–41; Chairman, Netherlands Financial Control Board 1941–45; Secretary-General, Ministry of Social Affairs 1945–50; Secretary of State for Social Affairs 1950–58; Member, Council of State 1960–67. Knight, Order of Netherlands Lion; Grand Commander, Order of Star of Rumania; Grand Officier, Ordre de la Couronne (Belgium); Comdr., Order of Orange-Nassau (Netherlands). *Publications:* Free Competition and Collective Labour Agreement; Social Security; Planning Worker or Co-worker; New Ideas on Participation in Management in Industry. *Address:* Wassenaarseweg 76, Flat 401, The Hague, Netherlands.

**van ROIJEN, Jan Herman.** Dutch diplomat. *B.* 10 April 1905. *Educ.* University of Utrecht (PhD). *M.* 1934, Anne Snouck Hurgronje. *S.* Jan Herman, Willem. *Daus.* Henriette Albertina, Digna. *Career:* Attaché, Legation, Washington, D.C. 1930–33; recalled to Ministry of Foreign Affairs 1933; Secretary of Legation, Tokyo 1936; Chief, Political Dept. Ministry of Foreign Affairs 1939; during occupation of the Netherlands by the Germans, was jailed three times for resistance movement activities, escaping to London 1944; Minister without Portfolio 1945; Minister of Foreign Affairs Mar.–June 1946; Assistant Delegate, Netherlands Delegation to United Nations Conferences San Francisco, London and New York 1945–48; Assistant Delegate, Economic and Social Council 1947; Amb. Ex. and Plen. to Canada Mar. 1947–June 1950; to U.S.A. Sept. 1950–64; to The Court of St. James's 1964–70; and to the Republic of Iceland. Grand Cross, Order of Orange-Nassau; Commander, Order of Netherlands Lion; Commander, Order of the British Empire; Grand Cross, Order of Oak Crown (Luxembourg); Commander, Order of Holy Treasure (Japan). *Address:* Stoeplaan 11, Stoephoutflat 15, Wassenaar, Netherlands.

**van ROOY, Charles Joan Marie Adriaan.** Netherlands *B.* 1912. *Educ.* Roman Catholic lyceum at Overveen; and Universities of Amsterdam and Utrecht; Doctor of Law. *M.* 1939, M. J. Müller. *Daus.* Paula, Irene and Yvonne. *Career:* Burgomaster: Hontenisse 1939–45, Etten-Leur 1945–52, Venlo 1952–57, Eindhoven 1957–59; Heerlen 1962–64; Minister of Social Affairs and Public Health, 1959–61. Queen's Commissioner for Province of Limburg 1964–77. *Awards:* Knight, Order of Netherlands Lion; Grand Officer, Order of Orange-Nassau; Cross of Merit, Netherlands Red Cross; Commander, Order of St. Gregory; Grand Cross, Order of Mayo (Argentina); Grand Cross, Order of Danëil A. Carrion (Peru); Grand Officer, Order of the Crown (Belgium); Grand Officer, Order of Merit (Federal Republic of Germany). Member, Roman-Catholic People's Party. *Address:*Bomanshof 245, Eindhoven, Netherlands.

**van STRAUBENZEE, William Radcliffe,** MBE, MP. (Cons. Wokingham 1959—). *B.* 1924. *Educ.* Westminster School. Parliamentary Secretary to the Minister of Education 1960–62. Joint Parly. Under Secy. of State for Education & Science 1970–72; Minister of State for N. Ireland 1972–74; Chmn. Select Cttee. on Assistance to Private Members 1975. *Member:* The Law Society of London. *Club:* Carlton (London). *Address:* 199 Westminster Bridge Road, London, S.E.1.

**Van WALT Van PRAAG, Hendrik Maurits.** Dutch diplomat. *B.* 1912. *Educ.* Kennemer Lyceum, Holland; Reimann Schule, Berlin; Ecole des Sciences Politiques, Paris (Dip Pol Sc). *M.* 1937, Odette van der Elst. *S.* Michael and Vincent. *Daus* Theodora and Djellah. *Career:* during German occupation of the Netherlands arrested for resistence movement activities, escaping to London 1943; Repatriation Commn., London, 1943–44; Liaison Officer, SHAEF, 1944–45; Diplomatic appointments in Belgium, Netherlands, Germany; Netherlands Military Mission, Berlin 1946–50; Min. Foreign Affairs, The Hague 1950–51; Secy. of Embassy, Brussels 1951–54; Karachi 1954–57; Counsellor of Embassy, Rome 1957–62; Consul Gen., Hong Kong and Macao 1962–66; Ambassador Extra. and Plen. to New Zealand 1967–70 and to Luxemburg 1972–74. *Awards:* Officer Ord. Orange Nassau; Cross of Merit, War Commemoration Cross, Cdr., Order of Merit (Italy); Officer, Order of the Crown (Belgium); Grand Cross, Order of Merit (Luxemburg). *Address:* Refelingse Heide 3, Nuenen, Netherlands.

**van WELL, Günther.** German Diplomat. *B.* 1922. *Educ.* Bonn Univ., economics degree; First State Law exam. *M.* 1957, Carolyn Bradley. *S.* 1. *Dau.* 1. *Career:* Office of the Perm. Observer of the Federal Republic of Germany at the UN, New York 1954–59; Fed. Foreign Office, Bonn 1959–62; Fellow at the Center for Internat. Affairs, Harvard Univ. 1962–63; Counsellor (Political Affairs), German Embassy, Tokyo 1963–67; Head of Section (foreign policy questions concerning Berlin & Germany as a whole), Fed. Foreign Office, Bonn 1967–71; Dep. Dir. of Political Affairs, Bonn 1971–72; Dir. of Political Affairs (Div. 3), Bonn 1972–73; Dir. of Political Affairs (Div. 2), Bonn 1973–77; Sec. of State, Fed. Foreign Office, Bonn since 1977. *Member:* Deutsche Gesellschaft für Auswärtige Politik, Bonn. *Decorations:* Bundesverdienstkreuz 1 Klasse (FRG); Order of the Rising

Sun, 3rd Class (Japan); Grand Croix d'Honneur avec plaque; & Ordre de la Maison d'Orange (Netherlands); Komturkreuz 1 Klasse des Königlich Schwedischen Nordsternordens (Sweden); Grosses Goldenes Ehrenzeichen mit dem Stern (Austria); Komturkreuz mit Stern des St. Olafs Orden (Norway); Tudor Vladimirescu III (Romania); Grossoffizierkreuz des Verdienstordens des Grossherzogtums Luxembourg; & Grossoffizier/Eichenkrome (Luxembourg); Commandeur de 1er Grade de l'Ordre du Dannebrog (Denmark); Grande Ufficiale dell'Ordine Al Merito della Repubblica Italiana (Italy); Isabel La Catolica Grad: Encomienda de Numero (Spain). *Publications:* The European political cooperation as seen by the Federal Republic of Germany under foreign policy perspectives (1973); Structural elements of a new political state system in Europe under discussion (1974); The Development of a common Middle East Policy of the Nine (1976); The participation of Berlin in international activities: an urgent item on the East–West agenda (1976). *Address:* Steinstrasse 52, 5300 Bonn-Bad Godesberg; and *office* Auswärtiges Amt, Adenauerallee, 5300 Bonn, Federal Republic of Germany.

**van YPERSELE de STRIHOU, Baron Adelin Charles Léonce Marie.** Administrator of several companies. *B.* 1911. *Educ.* Agronomy. *M.* 1932. Marie-Thérèse Wauters-van Put. *S.* Hervé. *Daus.* Mireille, Francine, Claude. *Awards:* Cdr. Order of Leopold II; Officer, Order of Leopold; Order of la Couronne (Belgium); Officer, Order of Al Merito Civil (Spain); Officer Al Merito (Italy); Cmdr. Ordre Equestre St. Gregoire le Grand; Order of St. Silvester; Commander of the Polonia Restituta; Cdr. Order of l'Etoile Brillante (Formose); Grand Officier de l'Ordre d'Isabelle la Catholique; Chevalier de l'Odre Souverain et Militaire de Malte; Administrator, Royal Belg. Auto. Club, and Nobility Assoc. of Belgium; Counsellor to the Belgian Foreign Trade Office, and the Board of the Belgian Red Cross. President, A.E.A.; Pres,. Spain–Belgium Assn. *Address:* 194 Avenue Montjoie, Brussels, 1180, Belgium.

**VARMA, Paripurnanand.** Indian journalist. *B.* 2 Feb. 1907. *Educ.* Kashi Vidyapith, Varanasi. *Career:* Formerly Professor of English; editor and chief editor of several dailies and weeklies; noteworthy criminologist of Asia. Past-Chmn., U.P. and Rajasthan Jail Reforms Enquiry Commissions; member, Social Welfare Evaluation Committee, and Committee for Investigation of Corruption in Courts, U.P. Govt.; President, All-India Crime Prevention Society, Hindustani Biradari, Rentpayers' Association; Exec. Councillor, Agra University. Member, Police Research Committee. *Publications:* author of 32 books, including Science of Symbols; History of Oudh; Definition of Human Lapses; Capital Punishment; Pathology of Crime and Delinquency, Crime, Criminal & Convict; She was not Ashamed; Suicide in India & Abroad. *Address:* 4 L.R. Bungalows, Kalpi Road, Kanpur 208 012, India.

**VASCONCELLOS, Arnaldo,** Brazilian diplomat. *B.* 1912. *Educ.* Faculty of Law, Federal Univ. of Rio de Janeiro (legal and social sciences). *Career:* Advanced war course 1966; Consul (3rd class) Min. of Foreign Relations 1938–40; vice-consul at New Orleans and Philadelphia 1941–43; Consul (2nd class), deputy consul Montreal 1944–46; Min. Foreign Relations 1946–47; dep.-consul New York 1948–49; Consul (1st class) 1st Secy. Embassy in Mexico 1949–51; Chargé d'Affaires 1950 and 1951, 1st Secy. Washington (Embassy) 1951–52, Caracas (Embassy) 1952–54; Counsellor to Embassy at Caracas 1954, Chargé d'Affaires 1952, 53, 54, and deputy-head (Economic Division) Ministry of Foreign Relations 1955; Minister (2nd class) Head of Economic Divison (Min. of For. Rel.) 1956–57; Deputy Head of Economic and Cons. dept. (Min. of For. Rel.) 1957; Minister Counsellor to Embassy at Bonn 1958–62, Chargé d'Affaire 1958, 1961, & 1962; Min.-Couns to Embassy in Washington & Chargé d'Affaires 1962; Minister (1st class) Ambassador in La Paz 1962–64; Assist secy.-gen. for American affairs 1964–66; Replacement for secy.-gen. to Min. of For. Relations 1965; Ambassador in Cairo 1968–71 (also Khartoum and Kuwait, 1969–71); Ambassador in Montevideo 1971–74; Ambassador to European Communities since 1974. *Delegate:* for Brazil to Washington (Tungsten and Molybdene Cttee.) 1951, 3rd Session Inter-American Econ. & Social Council Washington 1959, FAO conference Rome 1955, 1956, 1957 & 1959; FAO council Madrid 1957, 1958, 1959, 1960, Conference for internat. cocoa agreement, Geneva (1962), Renewal of Wheat agreement with Argentina (1964); conf. of Montevideo Treaty (1965), Inter-American Conference (Rio de Janeiro) 1965, U.N. Gen. Assembly N.Y. 1967, Rio Plata meeting (Punte del Este) 1972; also member of numerous international commissions and conferences. *Address:* 51 rue de la Loi, 1040 Brussels, Belgium.

**VASSILION, Arthur E.** President, Vassilion Graphic Arts Services (formed the Services to expand consultation services, which offer creative copywriting; editing and re-writing; offset composition and display type; art preparation and publishing services). Editor, Home Building News since 1973. *B.* 1920. *Educ.* Syracuse Univ. (AB *magna cum laude* 1948); Maxwell School of Citizenship (MA); attended courses in University of Algiers and American Academy in Rome (Italy) during the war; accomplished work on doctoral programme—humanities. *M.* 1948, Amelia Antoinette Andriello. *Career:* Served in World War II (U.S. Army Signal Corps in cryptography and communications, primarily with Allied Force H.Q. in Africa and Italy); recalled to active service during Korean war, as project editor and liaison with Monmouth Technical Publishing Agency; completed two large projects which received Presidential commendation; discharged from reserve. Worked 38 years on and off as writer, editor, designer and publishing executive; textbook writer and editor with Iroquois Publishing Co. (served as Exec. Editor and Production Manager until 1958). *Publications & awards:* Platonic Theory of Inspiration; many articles of various sorts, poetry, etc.; Assoc. Editor of Beacon Lights of Literature series: Action, Flights in Friendship, and teachers' manuals for series; Editor of Rough Proofs, which twice won competitive award gold cups in I.A.P.H.C. competition (2nd place 1957, 1st place 1958); member of four-men executive editorial board which produced Printing Progress, a commemorative limited volume published by International Association of Printing House Craftsmen (IAPHC) in 1959; publisher-producer of several publications, e.g., Records Retention, Rochester's Story, Sung Under the Breath, and others. Received Pres. Citation as Craftsman of the Year (Interl. Assn. of Printing House Craftsmen) 1967; Intern. District Craftsman of the year (IAPHC) 1974. *Member:* Phi Beta Kappa; Theta Beta Phi; Rho Delta Phi; Academy of Political Science; Columbia Council of Learned Societies; National Council of Teachers of English; N.Y. State English Council; Advisory Committee on Graphic Arts (for Syracuse Board of Education); Rochester Board of Education (publications consultant); IAPHC Bulletin Committee; Syracuse Club of the IAPHC (successively editor, secy., treas., chmn. of Bd., 2nd Vice, 1st Vice, and President); Int. Governor, 2nd District, Int. Assn. of Printing House Craftsmen 1973–75. *Address:* 111 Eloise Terrace, Syracuse 7, N.Y.; and all mail: P.O. Box 116, Elmwood Station, Syracuse, N.Y. 13207, U.S.A.

**VATIDIS, Andrew E.** Greek. *B.* 1912. *Educ.* High Commercial School, Neuchâtel Switzerland. *M.* 1943, Helen Moulas. *S.* 2. *Career:* Gen. Mgr. C.M. Salvago & Co. Alexandria 1942–61; Man. Dir. S. A. Nett & Pressage Coton 1954–61; Dir. Alexandria Insurance (Life) Co. 1955–61; Member Bd. Dirs. Bodossaki Foundation, Laiki Insurance Co. S.A.; Lainerie Hellenique S.A.; Hellenic Eleusis Owens Glass Factory S.A.; Man. Dir. Greek Powder & Cartridge Co. S.A.; Mem. Bd. Dirs., S.A. Hellénique de Vins et Spiritueux; Vice-Chmn. Grecamer S.A.; Vice Chmn. Amfion S.A.; Chmn. National Org. Systems S.A. *Address:* Heliopoleos Avenue 1, Athens 455a, Greece and *office:* Amalias Avenue, 20 Athens 118.

**VAUBEL, Ludwig,** Dr jur. *B.* 1908. *Educ.* Giessen and Hamburg Universities (law); and Harvard University (Advanced Management Program 1950). *M.* Inge Fock. *S.* 2. *Dau.* 1. *Career:* Attorney in legal department of Vereinigte Glanzstoff-Fabriken AG (manmade fibres), Wuppertal-Elberfeld 1934, Exec. Secretary 1941; Member Bd. 1953–69, Glanzstoff AG. Pres. 1969–72; Member Supervisory Bd., AKZO N.V. Arnheim; Enka Glanzstoff AG, Wuppertal. International Academy of Management (C10S); Pres. *Publications:* Unternehmer gehen zur Schule (1952). *Clubs:* Rotary; Harvard Alumni Assn. *Address:* Spessartweg 25, Wuppertal-Küllenhahn; and *office* Glanzstoff-Haus, Wuppertal, Germany.

**VAUGHAN, Sir (George) Edgar,** KBE. British diplomat *B.* 1907. *Educ.* Jesus College, Oxford; BA, 1928; BA, 1929; MA, 1937. *M.* 1933, Elsie Winifred Deubert. *S.* 1. *Daus.* 2. *Career:* Member, British Foreign Service 1931–66, serving in Consular and Diplomatic posts in Europe, Africa, North America and Latin America. British Ambassador to Panama 1960–64, and to Colombia 1964–66; Professor of History 1967–74, Dean of Arts and Science 1969–73, University of Saskatchewan, Regina Campus, Canada. *Awards:* Hon. Fellow, Jesus College, Oxford, 1966; Fellow, Royal Historical Socy., London, 1965. OBE 1937; CBE 1956; KBE 1963. *Club:* Travellers' London. *Address:* 27 Birch Grove, London W3 9SP.

**VAUGHAN, Dr. Gerard Folliott, MP.** British Politician. *B* 1923. *Educ.* Privately, East Africa; London Univ.; Fellow of the Royal College of Physicians (FRCP); Fellow of the Royal College of Psychiatrists (FRCPsych.). *M.* 1955, Thurle Joyce (née Laver). *S.* 1. *Dau.* 1. *Career:* Alderman, London County Council 1955–70; Alderman, Greater London Council 1970–72; Chmn., Strategic Planning Cttee., GLC 1968–71; Conservative MP for Reading 1970–74, for Reading South since 1974; PPS to Sec. of State for Northern Ireland 1974; Opposition Whip 1974–75; Opposition Front Bench Spokesman for Health since 1975. *Member:* Former Governor, University Coll., London; Council Member, Medical Research Council; Chmn. of Panel set up to help Thalidomide Children. *Publications:* various professional & general literary publications. *Clubs:* Carlton. *Address:* 14 Tufton Court, Tufton Street, London SW1; and House of Commons, London SW1A 0AA.

**VAUGHAN-LEE, Charles Guy,** DSC. *B.* 1913. *Educ.* Eton College and Christ Church, Oxford. *M.* (1) 1940, Agnes, Celestria King (*Dec.*). (2) 1949, Barbara, Bateman (*Div.*). *S.* 2 (and one adopted). *Daus.* 3. *Career:* Served in Royal Naval Volunteer Reserve (DSC; mentioned in dispatches) 1939–45. Member of the London Stock Exchange. Chmn., J. & A. Scrimgour. Ltd.; Commissioner Public Works Loan Board; Director, Hume Holdings Ltd. Hon. Treas. of Royal Hospital for Incurables, Putney; Chairman, Mental After-Care Assoc. Member, Royal Institute of International Affairs. *Address:* 25 Porchester Place, London, W.2; and Somerton Randle, Somerton, Somerset; and *office* The Stock Exchange, London EC2N 1HD.

**VAUGHN, George Augustus, Jr.** American Lieut.-Col. (Retd.); DSC (U.S.), DFC (Brit.), Silver Star (U.S.). *B.* 1897. *Educ.* Princeton Univ. (BS). *M.* 1925, Marion Perkins. *S.* George A. III and James W. *Dau.* Jane (Love). *Career:* President Eastern Aeronautical Corp. 1927–32. Vice-President: Casey Jones School of Aeronautics 1932–60, and Academy of Aeronautics 1941–64. Partner, J. V. W. & Co. 1932–64. Director, First National State Bank of New Jersey 1943–63. Member, N.Y. State Aviation Commission. Military service: U.S. Army Aviation Service, World War I (second ranking 'Ace' to survive); Commanding Officer 27 Div. Aviation N.Y.N.G. 1922–39. Member: Inst. of Aerospace Sciences; National Aeronautic Assn.; Veteran Air Pilots Assn.; Order of Daedalians 'Q.B.'. Chmn. Bd. of Trustees, Academy of Aeronautics, New York. Director: Atlantic Casting & Engineering Corp., and of MAARK Corp. *Clubs:* Union, Princeton, Wings (all of N.Y.C.); Richmond County Country; Coral Beach (Bermuda); Cotton Bay (Eleuthera). *Address:* 2 Helen Road, Dongan Hills, Staten Island, N.Y. 10304; and *office* Academy of Aeronautics Building, Flushing N.Y. 11371, U.S.A.

**VAUGHN, Dr. James Abbott.** American former economist, corporation executive and educator. *B.* 1909. *Educ.* Cushing Acad. (Dipl.); Boston Univ. (BBA; MBA; PhD); Suffolk Univ. (LLB); Blackstone College of Law (JD; LLD); Harvard and New York Univs. (graduate work); Portia Law School, Ed. D. degree. *M.* 1936, Thelma Louise Fisher. *Career:* Teacher of History, Lexington High Schl. 1941–42, and Vermont Acad. 1942–43; Faculty mem., Boston Univ. 1943–44 and Simmons Coll. 1944–50 (also Dir. of Public Relations and Exec. Dir. of the Coll. Fund Drive $3,500,000); New England Manager, James Flett Organization Inc. 1950–56; Pres. New England Management Corporation June 1956—; Trustee: Bowman Trust 1954, Harcourt Trust 1954—, and Hargreaves Trust 1955—. Fellow, Royal Economic Socy. (Eng.); Amer. Economic Assn.; Amer. Assn. of University Professors; Fellow, Corporation of Secretaries (England); Delta Sigma Pi; Pi Gamma Mu; Delta Pi Epsilon; Rotary International; 32° Mason; Shriner. *Publications:* The Business Trust; Political Influence of Unions; This Business of Fund Raising. Independent. *Clubs:* Harvard University Faculty; Boston University Faculty. *Address:* 581 Cambridge Street, Allston, Mass., U.S.A. 02134.

**VAUGHN, William Scott.** American. *B.* 1902. *Educ.* Vanderbilt Univ. (AB), Rice Univ. (MA) and Oxford Univ. (BA Hons MA); Rochester Inst. of Technology (LLD). *M.* 1928, Elizabeth Harper. *Daus.* Janice H. (Middlebrook) and Helen S. (Meyer Jr.). *Career:* Vice-Pres. and Asst. Gen. Mgr., Eastman Kodak Co. 1950–52, Vice-Pres. and General Manager 1959; First Vice-Pres., Tennessee Eastman Co. and Texas Eastman Co. 1952–59; Pres. Eastman Chemical Products Inc. 1956–58; Director, Eastman Kodak Co. 1959–73; Chairman, 1967–70; Executive Cttee., 1960–67; Chmn., 1969–70; President, 1960–66. Director: Procter & Gamble Co. 1960–74; Lincoln Rochester Trust Co. 1960–71; Lincoln First Banks Inc. 1967–77, Rochester Gas & Electric Corp. 1962—, Eastman Gelatine Corp., Canadian Kodak Co. Ltd. 1960–70, Kodak-Pathé, Kodak Ltd. 1962–71; and Kodak A.G. 1966–70. Trustee: Rochester Savings Bank 1959–77; Univ. of Rochester 1959–77, Colgate Rochester Divinity School, Vanderbilt University, International Museum of Photography at George Eastman House, and Rochester Museum and Science Center (Hon.). *Member:* Phi Beta Kappa; Rhodes Scholar, Oxford Univ.; Poor Richard Award. *Clubs:* Rochester Country; Pundit. *Address:* 170 Sandringham Road, Rochester, N.Y. 14610, U.S.A.; and *office* 343 State Street, Rochester, N.Y. 14650, U.S.A.

**VAXELAIRE, Baron Francois Georges Raymond Marie Joseph.** Belgian company director. *B.* 6 Aug. 1921. *M.* 1945, Nadine Regout. *S.* Raymond, Emmanuel Roland, Patrick. *Dau.* Françoise, Ariene. *Career:* Exec. Man. Dir., S.A. GB-INNO-BM; Dir., Banque de Bruxelles; Chevalier, Order of Leopold; Chevalier Legion of Honour, Cmdr. Order of the Phoenix (Greece); Croix de Guerre with Palms; Bronze Star (U.S.A.); Officer Order de la Couronne. *Address:* 11 Avenue de l'Astronomie, Brussels 3, Belgium.

**VAZQUEZ-CARRIZOSA, Alfredo.** Colombian Diplomat. *B.* 1909. *Educ.* Gimnasio Moderno de Bogotá; Institut de Philosophie, Univ. of Louvaine, Belgium—Degree in Law, specialising in Economic & Diplomatic Science; Post Graduate Studies at Univ. of Paris. *M.* 1960, Lucía Holguín. *Career:* Lawyer & Prof. of International Law in the Colegio Mayor de Nuesta Senora del Rosario de Bogotá since 1950; Prof. of International Labour Law, Faculty of Law, University Nacional, Bogotá; Prof. of International Public Law, Inst. of Diplomatic Studies, University Jorge Tadeo Lozano, Bogotá; Prof., School of International Officials, Univ. of Madrid 1959; Diplomatic Div., International Labour Office, Geneva; Member of the UN Staff; Rep. of the International Labour Office in Colombia; Member of Permanent Court of Arbitration, The Hague. Has held many Diplomatic Appointments, incl.—Member, Advising Commission of Ministry for Foreign Affairs; Head of Dept. of International Orgs. & Sec.-Gen. of Ministry for Foreign Affairs; Sec.-Gen. of the Presidency of the Republic; Amb. Ex. & Plen. to General Assembly of UN & mem. of Colombian delegation on several occasions; Amb. Plen. to the VIII, IX, X and XI Meetings of Consultation of Ministers for Foreign Affairs of the American States; Amb. to Belgium; Pres. of the General Assembly of American States etc. Mem. of House of Representatives for Cundinamarca; Rep. to the National Congress; Mem. of Conservative Governing Body of Cundinamarca; Sec.-Gen. of the Conservative Party; Dir. of weekly "El Nuevo Tiempo"; Subdir. & Dir. of Newspaper "La Republica", Bogotá; Minister for Foreign Affairs 1970–74; Amb. to the Court of St. James's 1975–77. *Member:* Colombian Acad. of History; Colombian Acad. of Language. *Decorations,* Decorations from 17 countries, inc.—Gran Cruz de la Ordr: de Boyacá, Colombia; Grand Croix de l'Ordre de la Couronnee Belgium; Grand Cross of the Order of Merit, Germany; Commander of the Legion of Honour, France; Commander of the Order of Orange Nassau, Holland etc. *Publications:* Constitutional Law (Spanish); International Law (Spanish, 2 vols. 1950); Colombia & the Problems of the Sea (Spanish, 1973); El Concordato (1973); Quitasueño, Roncador y Serrana (1974): The New Law of the Sea (Spanish, 1976). *Address:* c/o Colombian Embassy, 3 Hans Crescent, London SW1.

**VEDEL, Vice-Admiral A. H.,** DSc (hc). Danish officer. *B.* 1 Sept. 1894. *M.* 1921, Kirsten Vedel. *S.* Helge, Erik. *Daus.* Thyra, Inger. *Career:* Sub-Lieutenant 1916; Commander 1932; Captain 1939; Vice-Admiral 1947; C.-in-C. Royal Danish Navy (retd. 1958); Chmn.: Danish Delegation to Scandinavian Defence Cttee., 1948–49; Cttee. for Pearlyland Expedition 1947; member, Cttee, for Galathea Expedition 1948; Vice-President, Danish Royal Geographical Society 1946–74; Pres., Danish Arctic Institute 1955—; member of Board, East Asiatic Co. Ltd. 1955–72; Chmn., Government Cttee. for Navigation in Greenland Waters 1959; President, UNESCO Inter-governmental Conference on Oceanography 1960. Member, Board, Danish Seamen Mission in Foreign Ports, 1956–71; *Awards:* Grand Cross, Order of Dannebrog; Knight Commander, Order of the Bath (Great Britain); Grand Cross, Order of Sword (Sweden); Grand Cross, Order of St. Olav (Norway); Grand Cross, Order of Falcon (Iceland) Grand Officer de la Légion d'Honneur; Legion of Merit (U.S.A.). *Address:* Rypevej 13, Hellerup, Denmark.

**VEIT, Otto.** Dr. phil; German economist and banker. *B.* 1898. *Educ.* Frankfurt am Main. *M.* 1935, Victoria von Leyden. *Career:* Reichsstelle für Aussenhandel until 1934, when was removed for political reasons; Economic Adviser and Managing Director, Hardy & Co. G.m.b.H., Berlin until 1945; Managing Director, Nassauische Landesbank, Wiesbaden 1946; President, Landeszentralbank von Hessen 1947–52; Board of Directors Bank deutscher Länder 1948–52; Chairman, Board of Directors, Landeszentralbank von Hessen 1952–53; Board of Directors, Frankfurter Bank 1953–73; Professor, University of Frankfurt am Main; Director, Institut für das Kreditwesen, since 1952. *Award:* Grand BVK. *Publications:* Gefühl und Vernunft in der Wirtschaft; Die Tragik des technischen Zeitalters; Die Zukunft des Goldes; Die Flucht vor der Freiheit; Volkswirtschaftliche Theorie der Liquidität; Deutsche Geldpolitik; Soziologie der Freiheit; Die veränderte Währungspolitik und ihre Folgen; Der Wert unseres Geldes; Reale Theorie des Geldes; Währungspolitik als Kunst des Unmöglichen; Grundriss der Währungspolitik 3. Ed. Christlich-jüdische Koexistenz 2. Edition. *Address:* Abegg Str. 14, Wiesbaden, Germany.

**VENEGAS, Dominador N.,** Filipino industrialist. *B.* 1925. *Educ.* Bataan and Manila public schools; Lacson college of Law, Manila. *M.* 1950. Nenita Mendoza, *S.* 2. *Daus.* 2. *Career:* President, D. N. Venegas Company, Inc.; Gen. Mgr. Venlay Plywood Company; President Far Eastern Diesel Supply Company, Inc.; Dir. Integrated Wood Processing Co., Inc.; Treas. Veramil Enterprises. *Member:* President, Lions International, Dist. 301-D (1971–72); Life member, YMCA of the Philippines; Cabinet Secretary, Lions International, Dist. 301-D, (1973–74); Rector & lecturer, Orion Cursillo House; Life member, Lions Presidents League. *Clubs:* Valley Golf & Country Club. *Address: office* D. N. Venegas Co., Inc., 664 Ronquillo, Manila, Philippines.

**VENEMA, Maynard Peter,** Petroleum executive. *B.* 16 Sept. 1910. *Educ.* Armour Institute of Technology (BS; ChE 1932) (now Illinois Inst. of Technology); De Paul Univ.; and Georgetown Univ. (JD 1943). *M.* 1935, Hazel Kasten. *S.* Maynard Peter. *Dau.* Carol Ann. *Career:* With Universal Oil Products Co. since 1935; successively Engineer 1935–38, Patent Department 1938–44 (Manager of the Dept. 1944–49), Vice Pres. 1949–52, Exec. Vice-Pres. 1952–55, President 1955–61; Chmn. Pres. and Chief Exec. Officer 1961–64; Chmn. Chief Exec. Officer 1964–71; Chmn. Bd. 1972–74, Chmn. Exec. Cttee. 1974; Pres. Mid-America Legal Foundation 1975—; Chmn. of the All-Illinois Action Cttee. on Internat. Trade; Pres. of the Midwest U.S./France Assocn.; Dir. Universal Oil Products Co.; The Trane Company; Chicago Theological Seminary; Adlai Stevenson Institute of Internat. Affairs; Past Chmn. of Bd., Past Chmn. of Exec. Cttee., now Hon. Vice-Pres. and Dir. Nat. Association of Manufacturers; Past Chmn. of Bd. Mid-Amer. Chapter, Amer. Red Cross; Japan Amer. Socy. of Chicago; Past Pres. Lay Adv. Bd. (now a mem.) Resurrection Hospital; Chmn. Bd. Trustees Illinois Institute Technology. *Member:* Past, Pres., Chicago Assn. of Commerce & Industry, mem. Snr. Council & Chmn. to Public Transp. & Energy Cttees.; Amer. and Chicago Bar. Assns.; Amer. Chemical Socy.; Amer. Inst. of Chemical Engineers; Patent Lawyers Assn. (Chicago); Amer. Patent Law Assn.; Business Leader's Foundation and Northfield, Illinois Community Church; Mem. Council, Grad. Sch. of Business, Chicago Univ.; Dir. Chicago Council Foreign Relations; Chmn. Bd. of Govs., Ill. Council Economic Education; Adv. Cttee. Transportation Center Northwestern Univ.; Northwestern Univ. Assoc.; De Paul Univ. Bd. of Assoc.; Trustee, Goodwill Industries and National Jewish Hospital (Denver); Mem. Bd. Trustees, Bensenville Home Soc.; Protestant Business Leaders' Foundation; Dir. Max McGraw Wildlife Foundation. *Awards:* Alumni Medal 1973; Research Award 1975. *Clubs:* The Chicago, University, Sunset Ridge Country, The Economic; The Economic Commercial Executives 25 Year Club of the Petroleum Industry (all of Chicago). *Address:* 536 Somerset Lane, Northfield, Illinois 60093; and *office* 20 North Wacker, Chicago, Ill. 60606, U.S.A.

**VENIOT, Hon. Harvey Alfred,** QC, BA, LLB. Canadian lawyer & politician. *B.* 1916. *Educ.* Pictou Academy; St. Francis Xavier University Antigonish; Dalhousie University, Halifax; University of Saskatchewan. *M.* 1944, Rhoda Marion MacLeod. *S.* James Stewart. *Dau.* Susan. *Career:* Elected to Nova Scotia Legislature, 1956; Speaker, 1961–68; Member Legislative Assembly (N.S.) for Pictou West. *Clubs:* Pictou Lions; Pictou Golf and Country; New Caledonia Curling. *Address: office* Johnstone Building, Halifax, Nova Scotia, Canada.

**VENNAMO, Veikko E. A.** Finnish civil administrator. *B.* 1913. *Educ.* Jur. Lic.; solicitor. *M.* 1944, Sirkka Tuominen. *S.* 1. *Daus.* 2. *Career:* Member of Parliament 1945–61 and 1966—. Minister of Finance 1954–56; Dir. in Chief, Ministry of Agriculture Colonizing Dept. 1944–59; Customs Councillor 1960—; Member, Helsinki City Council, 1969–76; has served in Inst. of Justice and governmental offices from 1936, including the House of Commons (as MP) in State Finance Dept.; Chmn., Grand Division of Parliament; Leader, Rural Party, Finland; Chmn. Bd. Dirs. Party headorgan Suomen Uutiset; Member Parly. Constitutional, Defence Cttee. Representing Finland in Interparliamentary Union and Nordiska Rådet, 1959–75. *Publications:* Maanhankintalaki; various social-political articles in press and journals; Commander, Order of White Rose (Finland); Cross of Freedom with Swords, 4th Cl. (Finland). *Address:* Ritokalliontie 1, Helsinki, Finland.

**VERDET, Ilie.** Romanian politician. *B.* 1925. *Educ.* Acad. of Econ. Studies, Bucharest. *Career:* member C.P. 1945—; Local Party Organizations of Banat Region 1948–54; Head of Section, Central Cttee. Romanian C.P. 1954–55; First Secy. Hunedoara Regional Party Cttee.; 1954–65; Central Cttee. member 1960—; Deputy to Grand Nat. Assembly 1961—; Alt. member Exec. Cttee. Central Cttee. R.C.P. 1965–66; member Permanent Presidium 1966–74; First Deputy Chmn. Council. Ministers of Socialist Republic 1966–74; Secy of Central Cttee RCP 1974—; Pres. of the Central Council for the Workers' Control of the Economic & Social Activity 1974—; Hero of Socialist Labour 1971. *Address:* Central Cttee of the RCP, Bucharest, Romania.

**VERDON-SMITH, Sir (William) Reginald,** Kt Bach, DL. British. Barrister-at-law and company director. *B.* 5 Nov. 1912. *Educ.* Repton School and Brasenose College, Oxford (First-Class Jurisprudence and BCL and Vinerian Scholar); Hon. LLD Bristol Univ. 1959; Hon Fellow Brasenose Coll. Oxford 1965; Hon. D.Sc. Cranfield Inst. Technology 1971. *M.* 1 Nov. 1946, Jane Margaret (née Hobbs). *S.* William George. *Dau.* Elizabeth Jane. *Career:* Chmn. Lloyds Bank International Ltd.; Dep-Chmn. Lloyds Bank Ltd.; Dir. Lloyds Bank, California; Pro-Chancellor Univ. of Bristol. Deputy Lieutenant, County of Avon 1974. *Address:* 13 Redcliffe Parade, Bristol BS1 6SP.

**VERHAGEN, Jacobus.** Belgian banker. *B.* 5 Oct. 1896. *M.* 1922, Martha Goossens (*Dec.*). *S.* 2. Hon. Chmn. Société Belge de Banque S.A., Brussels 1965. Hon. Mng. Dir. Sté. Générale de Banque S.A., Brussels 1967. Order of Orange-Nassau; Commander, Ordre de la Couronne, and Officer, Order of Léopold (Belgium). *Address:* 178 Avenue Winston Churchill, Box 2, 1180 Brussels, Belgium.

**VERINGA, Professor G. H.** *B.* 13 April 1924. *Educ.* State Modern Grammar School, Groningen; Studied Law, Univ. of Groningen; Faculty of Political & Social Sciences of Fordham Univ. New York; Graduated Master of Arts, 1947; Doctor of Philosophy 1949. *Career:* Lecturer in the sociology of crime and punishment Manhatten Coll. 1949; Research Asst. to Prof. P. J. Bouman, Groningen 1950; Prisons Department of the Ministry of Justice 1952–53; Seconded by Ministry to act as Governor special prison for young men in Zutphen; Head, Central Training Institute for Prison Officers at the Hague 1955–62, Research Supervisor from 1959; Ministry of Justice and Deputy Head, Prisons Department 1961; Prof. Ext. of Plen. Law, Roman Catholic Univ. of Nijmegen 1965; Director of Applied Penology 1966; Minister of Education and Sciences 1967–71; Member Council of State since 1972. *Address:* Frans Halskade 95, Rijswijk Z.H. Netherlands.

**VERITY, Conrad Edward Howe,** OBE, JP. Legion of Merit (U.S.A.). *B* .1901. *Educ.* Wellingborough School. *M.* 1931, Doreen Bishop. *S.* John Conrad. *Dau.* Anna Doreen. *Career:* Contract Engineer, W. H. Allen Sons & Co., Bedford 1922; Technical Engineer and Asst. to Gen. Mgr., Contraflo Eng. Co. 1924; Technical Engr. (Mechanical Eng.), London Power Co. 1927. War Service R.A.F. 1940–46. Head, Technical and Development Dept., London Power Co. 1946; Generating Engineer (Construction), British Electricity Authority, London 1948; Dep. Chief Engineer (Construction), Central Elect. Auth. 1951, Dir. 1955–60. Mng. Dir. 1960–62, Chmn. 1962–66. Dir. 1966–67, Foster Wheeler Ltd. London. Dep. Chmn., Foster Wheeler, John Brown Boilers Ltd. 1966–67. Dir., Foster Wheeler Corp., N.Y. 1960–66. Dir.: Foster Wheeler International Corp., New York 1960–66, Rolls Royce & Associates, Derby 1959–67, and Vickers Nuclear Engineering Ltd. 1963–66. Co-Chairman. Committee of

Foster Wheeler/John Brown Land Boilers Consortium 1960–67. FICE; FIMechE; FIEE; MIMarE; FInstF. FASME. *Publications:* Paper before Institution of Civil Engrs. on the Deptford West Power Stat. 1931 (awarded Telford Premium). BEAIRA Tech. Report H/T34, on Use of Steel Condenser Tubes 1941; and Paper before Electrical Power Engineers Assn. on Efficiency Testing of Power House Plant; sundry articles in technical press. *Club:* Naval and Military. *Address:* Farthings, Earleydene, Sunninghill, Berks.

**VERNON, Sir James,** Kt, CBE. Australian. *B.* 1910. *Educ.* Sydney University (BSc); University College, London (PhD). *M.* 1935, Mavis Lonsdale Smith. *Daus.* 2. *Career:* with C.S.R. Ltd.: Chief Chemist, 1938–51; Senior Executive Officer, 1951–56; Assistant General Manager, 1956–57, Gen. Mgr. 1958–72; Chairman, Commonwealth Cttee. of Economic Inquiry, 1963–65; Chmn. Australian PO Commission of Inquiry 1973–74; Director, CSR Ltd.: West Ham Dredging Co. Pty. Ltd.; United Telecasters Sydney Ltd.; MLC Ltd.; Comm. Banking Co. of Sydney Ltd.; Chmn. Martin Corp. Ltd.; Chmn. Aust. Japan Business Co-operation Cttee.; Pres. Aust. National Cttee., Pacific Basin Economic Council; Mem. Chase Manhattan Bank Internat. Advisory Cttee. Hon. DSc, Sydney and Newcastle; Leighton Medal, Royal Australian Chemical Institute 1965; John Storey Medal, Aust. Institute of Management 1971. *Clubs:* Australian; Union; Royal Sydney Golf. *Address:* 27 Manning Road, Double Bay, N.S.W. 2028; and *office* 16 O'Connell Street, Sydney, N.S.W. 2000, Australia.

**VERONESE, Vittorino.** Italian lawyer. *B.* 1 Mar. 1910. *M.* 1939, Maria Petrarca. *S.* 4. *Daus.* 3. *Career:* Chmn. Bd. of Directors, Banco di Roma, Nov. 1961 (Auditor 1945–53, Director 1953–57); Vice-Chmn. Banco di Roma (France), Paris; Banco di Roma (Belgique) Bruxelles; Italian Catholic Action 1944–46 (Pres. 1946–52); Vice-Pres., Banca Cattolica del Veneto; President, Consorzio di Credito per le Opere Pubbliche 1957–58, and of the Instituto per le Imprese di Pubblica Utilità; Italian Delegate to Gen. Conference of UNESCO, Beirut 1950; Paris 1952–53; member, Italian Natl. Commission 1953–58; Vice-Pres., Exec. Board since 1954, Pres. 1956–58; Vice-Pres., International Movement of Catholic Intellectuals of Pax Romana 1947–55; formerly member, Executive Board of U.A.I. (Union des Associations Internationales), Bruxelles; Groupe des Vingt du Centre Européen de la Culture, Geneva; Pres., Intellectual Refugees in Italy Organization, Peregrinatio Romana ad Petri Sedem, Pius XII Foundation for Apostolate of the Laity, Institute of Liturgical Art; Secretary, Permanent Committee of International Congresses Lay Apostolate in Rome; appointed Director-General of UNESCO, Nov. 1958 (resigned Nov. 1961). Vice-Pres. Comité Consultatif International pour la Sauvegarde de Venise (UNESCO). President. Italian Consultative Cttee. for Human Rights; Mem. Pontifscal Commission for Justice & Peace. Cameriere d'Onore Soprannumerario di Cappa e Spada di Sua Santità Giovanni XXIII, e di Sua Santità Papa Paolo VI, Knight, Grand Cross of Order of St. Silvester; Grand Croix of Leopold II; lay Auditor of the Ecumenical Council Vatican II. Commendatoredell' Ordine Piano; Cavaliere di Gran Croce della Repubblica Italiana; Chevalier de la Légion d'Honneur; Gran Oficial Orden de Isabella Catolica; Gran Cruz, Orden Civil de Alfonso X, el Sabio; Gold Medal awarded for Culture (It. Rep.). LLD *honoris causa.* Laval Univ. Quebec. *Address:* Banco di Roma, Via del Corso 307, Rome, Italy.

**VERSAN, Vakur,** MA. DCLS, LLD. Turkish lawyer; Professor of Administrative Law and Government & Director of the Institute of Administrative Law & Administrative Sciences, University of Istanbul, Bosphorus Univ.; Academy of Economic & Social Sciences. *B.* 1918. *Educ.* Downing College, Cambridge, and Faculty of Law, Istanbul University. *M.* 1950, Seyda. *S.* Rauf. *Career:* Visiting Professor of Government in Columbia University, New York 1955–56 and 1961–62; Lectured on Political and legal problems of Turkey in various countries including Western Europe, U.S.A., Iran, Pakistan and India. Member Cttee. of Jurists who prepared the present Turkish Constitution; Istanbul Bar Assn.; Couns. to Mobil Oil in Turkey; Trustee, Turkish Wildlife Fund; Pres. Istanbul Turco-British Cultural Assocn.; Past Pres. and mem. Turkish-American University Assocn.; Hon. Life mem., Turkish Touring & Automobile Assn. *Publications:* Public Administration (6th ed.), Political and Administrative Institutions of Turkey, Economic Provisions of the Turkish Constitution, Economic Doctrines of the Turkish Political Parties, Local Government and various other books and articles. *Clubs:* Turkish-American University Association; Propeller; Moda Yachting. *Address:* Vali Konak Caddesi 161, Nisantas, Istanbul, Turkey, and Faculty of Law, Istanbul University, Istanbul, Turkey.

**VERULAM, The Rt. Hon. The Earl of (John Duncan Grimston).** British Company director. *B.* 1951. *Educ.* Eton and Christ Church Oxford, (BA Hons Oxon.); Hon. degree Engineering and Economics Oxford University. *Clubs:* Beefsteak; Turf; Bath. *Address:* Gorhambury, St. Albans, Herts.

**VETTER, Herbert.** Austrian physician. *B.* 1920. *Educ.* Univ. of Vienna (MD 1948). *M.* (1) 1946, Eleonore von Hacklaender (*Div.* 1969). *Dau.* 1. (2) 1973 Brigitte Frei. *Career:* Physician, Allgemeines Krankenhaus, Vienna, Austria 1948–60; British Council research fellow 1951; research fellow Sloan-Kettering Inst. Cancer Research N.Y.C. 154; head radio-isotopes Lab. 2nd Med. Univ. Clinic, Vienna 1951–60; assoc. prof. medicine U. Vienna 1959–67, and prof. medicine 1967—; senior officer, Internat. Atomic Energy Agy. 1958—. Chairman, Planning Board I-B, Internat. Commission on Radiation Units and Measurements 1962–69; Consultant to Commission since 1969. *Publications:* (with N. Veall): Radioisotope Techniques in Clinical Research and Diagnosis, 1958 (German transl. 1960, Spanish transl. 1964). Editor: Radioaktive Isotope in Klinik und Forschung (Vol. I, II, III), 1955, 1956, 1958; journal 'Nuclear Medicine,' 1959—. Radioisotopes in Medical Diagnosis 1971, Fed. Pres. Republic of Austria Prize for Art and Science, 1956; Affiliate, Royal Society of Medicine. Soci-für Innere Medizin. Vienna 1954—; Osterreichische Röntgengesellschaft, Vienna 1956—. *Club:* Rotary-Wien. *Address:* Landesgerichtsstrasse 18, Vienna 1010; and *office* International Atomic Energy Agency, Kärtnerring 11, Vienna 1010, Austria.

**VICCHI, Adolfo Angel.** *B.* 1900. *Educ.* Lawyer, University Professor. *M.* 1927, Maria Eugenia Arroyo Benegas. *S.* Adolfo, Eduardo, and Julio Alberto. *Daus.* Raquel (de la Reta) and Maria Eugenia. *Career:* Member Deliberative Council of City of Mendoza 1932–38; National Representative for Mendoza 1932–38; Government Minister and Minister of Public Welfare of Mendoza; Governor of Mendoza 1941–43; Ambassador to United States of America 1956–57; Representative of Province of Mendoza to National Constituent Convention at Santa Fe 1957; National Senator for Province of Mendoza 1961–62. Ambassador of the Argentine Republic to the Court of St. James's, April 1964–65. *Publications:* Politica Econonómica: Federalismo y Libertad; Servidumbres Administrativas: La Revolución de (1955): antecedentes y consecuencias. *Member:* Federation of the Colleges of Argentine Lawyers; Institute of Administrative Law, Liège. Conservative. *Clubs:* Círculo de Armas (Buenos Aires); El Círculo (Mendoza). *Address:* Colón 460 Mendoza, Republic of Argentina.

**VICK, Sir (Francis) Arthur.** OBE. Kt. British physicist. *B.* 1911. *Educ.* Birmingham University; BSc (hons. physics). PhD., Hon. DSc. (Keele & NUI); Hon. LLD(Dublin & Belfast); Hon DCL(Kent). *M.* 1943, Elizabeth Dorothy Story. *Dau.* 1. *Career:* Asst. Lecturer in Physics, Univ. Coll. London 1936 (Lecturer 1939–44); Asst. Director of Scientific Research, Ministry of Supply 1939–44; Lecturer in Physics, Manchester Univ. 1944 (Senior Lecturer 1947–50); Professor of Physics, Univ. Coll. of North Staffordshire 1950–59 (Vice-Principal of the College 1950–54, Acting Principal 1952–53); Deputy Director, A.E.R.E., Harwell 1959–60, Director, 1960–64, and U.K.A.E.A. Research Group 1961–64 (Member for Research 1964–66); President and Vice-Chancellor, Queen's University, Belfast 1966–76; Pro-Chancellor & Chmn. of Council, Univ. of Warwick 1977—. *Member:* University Grants Committee 1959–66. Advisory Council on Research and Development, Ministry of Power, 1960–63; Scientific Adv. Council, Min. of Supply 1956–59; Nuclear Safety Advisory Committee, Ministry of Power 1960–66. Chmn., Acad. Adv. Cttee., Min. of Defence 1969; Member: F.I.E.E.; F.Inst. P.; MIRA. *Awards:* OBE, 1945; knighted 1973. *Clubs:* Savile, Athenaeum. (London). *Publications:* various papers and contributions to books on physics and education. *Address:* Fieldhead Cottage, Fieldhead Lane, Myton Road, Warwick CV34 6QF.

**VICKERS, Sir (Charles) Geoffrey),** VC. British solicitor. Administrator and author. *B.* 13 Oct. 1894. *Educ.* Oundle School; Merton College, Oxford (MA). *M.* (1) 1918. Helen Tregoning Newton (marriage dissolved 1934). *S.* Douglas Burnell Horsey. *Dau.* Pamela Tregoning (2) 1935, Ethel Ellen Tweed. *S.* Hugh. *Career:* Served in World War I, Major, Sherwood Foresters, France and Belgium 1915–18, World War II, Colonel; practised as Solicitor 1923–46, Partner, Slaughter and May 1926–46; member, Council of the Law

Society 1942–1946; member, London Passenger Transport Board 1941–46; seconded as deputy dir. general i/c economic intelligence Min., of Economic Warfare and member Joint Intelligence cttee. of the Chiefs of Staff 1941–46. Legal Adviser, National Coal Board 1946–48, member of Board 1948–55; member, Medical Research Council 1952–60; Chairman, Research Committee, Mental Health Research Fund 1952–67; Hon. Fellow Royal Coll. of Phychiatrists. *Publications:* of many papers and six books on government, management and medical subjects including, The Art of Judgment (1965), Value Systems and Social Process (1968) and Freedom in a Rocking Boat (1970); Making Institutions Work (1973). *Award:* Medal of Freedom; Croix de Guerre. *Address:* Little Mead, Goring-on-Thames, Oxon.

**VIDAL ZAGLIO, Luis J.** *B.* 1913. *Educ.* Faculty of Law and Social Sciences. *M.* Dona Nelly Amodeo. *S.* Julio Alberto. *Dau.* Martha Susana (his private secretary). *Career:* On leaving the Faculty he took up journalism with La Tribuna Popular and El Debate. An associate of the National Party Chief, Dr. Luis Alberto de Herrera, he took an active part in politics. He was a civil servant in the Departments of Superannuation Benefits and Pensions, and in Industry and Commerce; he specialised in problems relating to Social Security. He became a director in 1948. He entered the Chamber of Deputies in 1950, and was three times elected (1954–58–62). In 1963 he was a member of the Uruguayan delegation to the U.N., and in 1965 he represented Uruguay in the Security Council. In 1965 he was elected one of the Commissioners on Social Security in the Chamber of Representatives; was also a member of several important commissions on the Law of Property Hiring, and on Land; he also took part in the Budget Commission; Minister, Foreign Affairs 1965–67. *Address:* Ministerio de Relaciones Exteriores, Montevideo, Uruguay.

**VIDELA, Jorge Rafael.** President of Argentina. *B.* 1925. *Educ.* Army Staff Coll. *M.* Alicia Raquel Hartridge. *S.* 4. *Daus.* 2. *Career:* Cadet at National Military Coll. 1942–44; Sub-Lieutenant 1944–46; Lieutenant 1946–48; 1st Lieutenant 1948–51; Captain 1951–56; Major 1956–60; Lieutenant Colonel 1960–65; Colonel 1965–71; Brigade General 1971–75; Divisional General 1975; Lieutenant General since 1975; President of Argentina since 1976. *Decorations:* Grand Officer of the Order of Guerrillero Jose Miguel Lanza (Bolivia); Grand Cross, Order of Guerrillero Jose Miguel Lanza (Bolivia); Venezuelan Land Forces Cross, 1st class (Venezuela). *Address:* Oficina del Presidente, Casa Rosada, Buenos Aires, Argentina.

**VIDOVIC, Uros.** Yugoslav diplomat. *B.* 1914. *Educ.* Belgrade Univ. Grad. Law; Doctor's degree course and High Political School. *M.* 1945, Ljiljana Dikic. *S.* 1. *Dau.* 1. *Career:* joined Nat. Lib. Army 1941; Secy. Economic Council, Govt. Bosnia-Hercegovina and Vice-Pres. Planning Commission; Professor, Law School, Economic School Univ. Sarajevo; Asst. Chmn. Economic Council, Govt. Bosnia Hercegovina; Dir. Statistical Office, Counsellor Fed. Inst. Economic Planning. Deputy Secy. State Secretariat, Economic Affairs Yugoslav Govt.; Special Counsellor, Economic Affairs, Govt. Tanzania; Dir. Fed. Fund, Crediting Economic Progress, Less Developed Republic's and Provinces in Yugoslavia: Ambassador, Socialist Fed. Republic of Yugoslavia to Australia 1971–76. *Address:* c/o Ministry of Foreign Affairs, Belgrade, Yugoslavia.

**VIESER, Milford August.** American. *B.* 1903. *Educ.* Pace Univ. (N.Y.C.). *M.* 1928, Vera Kniep. *S.* William Milford. *Career:* U.S. Delegate to Economic Commission for Europe, Geneva, Nov. 1957; Appointed by President Eisenhower to Federal New Jersey Tercentenary Celebrations Commission, Dec. 1960; Hon. Director, The Mutual Benefit Life Insurance Co., Chmn. Finance Cttee. 1960–67; First National State Bancorporation; First National State Bank of New Jersey, Triangle Industries Inc.. (all the above are located in Newark, N.J.); American General Bond Inc. (Houston, Texas); Dir., American General Convertible Securities Inc. (Houston, Texas); 545 Corp. (Union, N.J.). Dir. & Vice-Pres., 200 Club of Essex County. Hon. Co-Chairman, Newark's (N.J.) 300th Anniversary Corporation May 1965. Chmn., New Jersey Historical Society; Mem., N.J. Bicen. Revol. Celeb. Cttee. (Fmr. Chmn.); Dir. Emeritus, Regional Plan Assn. Trustee & Vice-Pres. St. Barnabas Medical Center; Trustee, Milford Reservation; Newark Museum; New Jersey Symphony Orchestra. *Publications:* various articles and speeches throughout the U.S. and Europe on the American Economic System and on urban renewal in America, Hon. LLD Fairleigh-Dickinson University, Rutherford, N.J. *Member:* Amer. Chapter, International Real Estate Fed.; Amer. Inst. of Real Estate Appraisers; Mortgage Bankers Assn. of America; Greater Newark Chamber of Commerce (Dir. and Past Pres.). Fellow, Royal Academy of the Arts. Republican. *Clubs:* Advertising Club of N.J. (Past Pres.); Baltusrol Golf (Springfield, N.J.); Essex (Newark, N.J.); Tarratine Yacht (Dark Harbor, Maine). *Address:* 8 Shore Edge Lane, Short Hills, N.J., U.S.A.

**VIGER, David N.**, OBE. American executive. *B.* 1912. *Educ.* Brown Univ. (PhB 1934) and Harvard Law School 1935. *M.* 1941, Mary Louise Kern. *S.* David N., Jr. and Peter Edward. *Daus.* Mary Katherine Hester and Susan Rebecca Lambrecht. *Career:* Director and Secretary, Ernst Kern Co. 1947–59; Director and Vice-Pres., Kern Realty Corp. 1947–59. Major U.S. Army 1942–46; Pres. American Diesel Corp. 1959—; Pres. and Treas. The Woodlea Corp. 1961–68; Vice-Pres. G.K.N. International since 1968. *Publications:* The Use of Diesel Power in Taxicab Operation. *Awards:* Amer. Theatre Ribbon; Asiatic-Pacific Theatre Bronze Battle Star; Philippine Liberation Ribbon Bronze Battle Star; Victory Medal—2 Overseas Bars; Officer Order of the British Empire, 1976. Member, Society of Automotive Engineers. Republican. *Clubs:* Detroit, County (Detroit); Mackinac Island Yacht; U.S. Coast Guard Auxiliary; U.S. Power Squadron. *Address:* 356 Moross Road, Grosse Pointe Farms 36, Mich.; and *office* 1959 E. Jefferson Avenue, Detroit, Mich., 48207 U.S.A.

**VIGGERS, Peter John.** MP. British. *B.* 1938. *Educ.* Alverstoke Primary School, Gosport; Portsmouth Grammar School; Trinity Hall, Cambridge—MA. *M.* 1968, Dr. Jennifer Mary McMillan. *S.* 2. *Dau.* 1. *Career:* Pilot, R.A.F. 1956–58; Solicitor with Chrysler (UK) Ltd. 1968–70; Dir. of several companies, incl. Energy, Finance & General Trust Ltd., Premier Consolidated Oilfields Ltd. & The Sangers Group Ltd. Underwriting member of Lloyds; Conservative MP for Gosport since 1974. *Address:* House of Commons, London SW1A 0AA.

**VIGNON, Robert**, L en D, L ès L. French administrator. *B.* 17 Nov. 1910. *M.* Michèle Casaux. *Dau.* Arlette. *Career:* Chef Adjoint du Cabinet of Prefect of Tarn Sept. 1934, Chef de Cabinet June 1936; Chef de Cabinet of Prefect of Haute-Vienne July 1939; served in World War II, Captain of the Reserve 1939–Jan. 1941; Secretary-General of the Vendée Nov. 1940; Directeur du Cabinet of Regional Prefect of Orleans Jan. 1942; Secy. Gen. of Loir-et-Cher Feb. 1944; Chef Adjoint du Cabinet of Minister of Agriculture Dec. 1946; Prefect of French Guiana 1947–55; Prefect of Allier 1935–56; Prefect of Great Kabylie (Algeria) 1956; Minister of the Interior, May 1958 and 1959. Head of Atomic Energy Mission 1959–62. Senator of the Guyane 1962—. Officer de la Legion d'Honneur; Croix de Guerre avec palme (2 citations); Palmes Académiques; Ordre de Mérite Agricole; Médaille des Blessés; Chevalier, Ordre de la Santé Publique; Médaille d'Argent de la Reconnaissance Française; Commandeur du Nichan Iftikar, du Ouissam Alaouite (Tunis); Commandeur, Ordre of Orange-Nassau (Netherlands); Officer, Order of Southern Cross (Brazil); Officer, Order of the Black Star of Benin; Officer, Order of Nigral of Sahametril; member of various learned societies. *Address:* 108 Résidence Elysee II, 78 Lacelle St Cloud, France.

**VIGODNY, Andrew.** British. *B.* 1913. *Educ.* Commercial Academy, Budapest, and Technical College, Freiberg (Germany). *M.* (Divorced) *S.* David. *Daus.* Andrea and Gabrielle. *Career:* Dir.: West Coast Associated Tanneries Ltd. T. H. Leathers Ltd., Hamilton Palmer Ltd., West Coast Distributors Ltd., and West Coast Tanneries Ltd. *Address:* The Oaks, The Green, Millom, Cumberland; and *office* The Tannery, Millom, Cumberland.

**VIIG, Sven.** Norwegian banker. *B.* 26 Sept. 1910. *Educ.* University of Oslo (Graduate in Economics 1932, and in Law 1937). *M.* 1935, Astri Reime Reinertsen. *Daus.* Anne, Berit. *Career:* Manager, Bodo Branch, Bank of Norway 1941 (Dir. 1942); Secretary, Head Office 1946; Sub-Dir. 1950; Acting Deputy-Governor 1952; Deputy Governor 1953; Vice-Chairman, Board of Directors, Bank of Norway 1953–58; Executive Director, International Bank for Reconstruction and Development. Washington 1956–58; Managing Director, Christiana Bank og Kreditkasse 1958—. *Address:* Dalsnaret 6, Ljan, Norway.

**VILA, George Raymond.** American rubber industry executive. *B.* 1909. *Educ.* Wesleyan University (AB 1932) and Massachusetts Institute of Technology. (S. M. 1933), Hon. Doc. Eng. Clarkson College of Technology. *Career:* Prod. Engineer, Boston Woven Hose & Rubber Co. 1933–36; with U.S.

Rubber Co. (now Uniroyal Inc.) since 1936; Research chemist, Dir. Synthetic rubber development; Gen. Sales Manager, Asst. Gen. Mgr. 1936–57; Gen. Mgr. Vice-Pres. Co. 1957; Group Exec. Vice-Pres. 1957–60; Member Exec. Cttee. and Dir. 1960–77; Chief Exec. Officer 1962–75; Chmn. Bd. Exec. Cttee. 1964–75; Former Chmn. Bd. Uniroyal Ltd.; Dir. The Bendix Corp.; Church & Dwight Co. Inc.; Chemical Bank. Member Technical Industrial Intelligence Cttee. Joint Chiefs of Staff, World War II; Mfg. Chemists Assn.; Amer Chem. Socy.; Mass Inst. Tech. Corp.; Nat. Agric. Chem. Assn. (Past Dir.); Newcomen Socy. N. Amer.; Socy. of Automotive Engineers; Psi Upsilon; Trustee Wesleyan U, Center for Information on America; The Kent School; The Institute for the Future; Foreign Policy Assn; *Publications:* Critical Analysis of T-50 Test, (1939); Action of Organic Acceleration in Buna S, (1942); Plastication & Processing of GR-S, (1943); Approach of Statistical Methods to Manufacture of Synthetic Rubber, (1944); A New Era in Synthetics in Rubber to Match Plastics, (1955); Tires: An Expanding Market for Chemicals, (1956); 1960 Outlook for In-Process Materials, (1959); Economics and Trends in Rubber and the New Rubber-Like Materials, (1959); The Stereo Rubbers, (1962); Who Pays the Profit? (1965). Republican. *Clubs:* University, Economic. *Address:* Sharon. Conn.; and *office* 1230 Av. of Americas New York City, N.Y. 10020, U.S.A.

**VILJOEN, Hon. Marais.** South African. *B.* 1915. *Educ.* Univ. of Cape Town. *M.* Dorothea Maria Brink. *Dau.* Elizabeth Magdelena. *Career:* Previously Deputy Minister of Labour, Immigration, Education, Arts and Science, and of the Interior. Deputy Minister of Labour and of Mines, 1958. Minister of Labour and Coloured Affairs, 1966–70; Minister of Labour and of Post and Telegraphs, 1970–72; Pres. of the Senate 1976. Member S.A. National Party. *Address:* 188 Pine Street, Pretoria, South Africa.

**VILLERS, Dr. Raymond.** American consultant in industrial management. *B.* 1911. *Educ.* Columbia University (M.B.A.); University of Leipzig (JD); University of Paris (BS and DES); recipient Du Pont de Nemours-General Motors Joint Fellowship of Research 1946). *M.* Garda Graaff Schmidt. *S.* Philippe. *Career:* Associate Professor of Industrial Engineering, Stevens Institute of Technology 1952–57; Asst. Professor of Industrial Engineering, Columbia Univ. 1947–52. Lecturer in Industrial Engineering, Columbia Univ. 1952–65. Served in World War II (French Army; Free French Naval Staff 1939–43; U.S. Navy 1944–45; Partner, Rautenstrauch & Villers 1947—; Professor of Industrial Engineering, Syracuse University and Consultant U.S. Army 1965–66; Professor, Graduate School of Business Administration, Pace College 1966–73. *Publications:* Dynamic Management in Industry (Prentice Hall, 1960, 1961; Spanish translation, Herrero Hermanos S.A. Mexico, 1962; Japanese translation, Maruzen Co., Tokyo 1964); The Dynamics of Industrial Management (Funk & Wagnalls, 1954—German translation, Deutsche Volkswirtschaftliche Gesellschaft, 1960); Industrial Budgeting (in Handbook of Industrial Engineering and Management, Prentice-Hall, 1955); Economics of Industrial Management (Funk & Wagnalls, 1949; revised edition, 1957; Spanish translation, Fondo de Cultura Economica—Mexico, 1953); Budgetary Control (Funk & Wagnalls, 1950—, revised edition 1968; Spanish translation, Fondo de Cultura Economica—Mexico, 1955); Research and Development—Planning and Control (Financial Executives Research Foundation 1964); Research Management (in Handbook of Business Administration, McGraw Hill, 1967); Organization of the R.D. Function; A.M.A. Management Handbook, American Management Association (1970); articles in Harvard Business Review, Dun's Review & Modern Industry The Controller, Journal of Industrial Engineering, Financial Executive. Member, Board of Trustees, Marlboro College 1952–67. *Member:* American Society of Mechanical Engineers; American Institute of Industrial Engineers (Vice-Pres. 1952); Amer. Association of University Professors; Amer. Society for Engineering Education; Newcomen Society; Amer. Management Assn. *Address:* Villers Farm, R.F.D., No. 1, Bellows Falls, Vt. 05101; and *office* 185 East 85th Street, New York, N.Y. 10028, U.S.A.

**VILLIERS, Sir Charles.** MC. Chairman, British Steel Corporation, 1976; Member, National Economic Development Council 1976. *B.* 1912. *Educ.* Eton and New College Oxford. *M.* 1946, Marie José de la Barre d'Erquelinnes. *S.* 1. *Daus.* 2. *Career:* Glyn Mills and Co. 1931; Grenadier Guards, Dunkirk and special operations exec. in Jugoslavia 1939–45; Partner in Helbert Wagg (1948); Man. Director of Schroder Wagg 1960–68; Man. Director Industrial Reorganisation Corp. 1968–71; Chairman Guinness Mahon and Co. Ltd. 1971–76; Exec. Deputy Chairman Guinness Peat Group Ltd. 1973–76; Director Sun Life Assurance Socy. Ltd. 1955–76; Courtaulds Ltd. 1971–76; Belgian and General Investments Ltd. 1961–1976; Finacor S.A. 1971–76; Chairman The Windsor Theatre Co. since 1964; Trustee Royal Opera House since 1974; Pres. International Institute of Banking Studies 1957–76; Chairman Federal Trust Group on European Monetary Integration 1972; Chairman Northern Ireland Finance Corp. 1972–73; Co. Chairman Europalia 73 Festival (Brussels) 1973. *Fellow:* Royal Society of Arts; British Institute of Management. *Member:* Institute of Directors. *Decorations:* Military Cross; Order of the People, Jugoslavia (1970); Grand Officer of Order of Léopold II (1974); Gold Medal of IRI (Italy) 1970. *Publication:* Tomorrow's Management (Maurice Lubbock Memorial Lecture, Oxford, 1971). *Address:* Blacknest House, Sunninghill, Berks; and 54, Eaton Square, SW1; and *office* 33 Grosvenor Place, SW1.

**VILLONCO, Romeo S.** Filipino. *B.* 1915. *Educ.* La Salle Coll (BScCom 1935). *M.* 1944, Thelma Gallego. *S.* 3. *Daus.* 2 *Career:* Pres. Villonco Realty Co.; Gen. Mgr., Mas-Arabica Coffee Plantation; Chmn., Teoville Development Corp., Motion Picture Laboratories (Phil.) Inc.; Pres. & Gen. Mgr., Life Theatre Inc.; Pres. & Dir., Travel Wide Associated Sales Phil. Inc., Rural Bank of Atimonan; Pres., Pioneer Natural Resources Exploration Co. Inc.; Vice-Pres., Liberty Insurance Corp.; Vice-Pres. & Treas., H. I. Development Corp.; Vice-Pres. & Dir., United Housing Corp.; Treas. & Dir., Bataan Pulp & Paper Mills Inc., Phil. Express Travel & Tours Inc.; Director: American Asiatic Oil Corp., Filipinas Mutual Finance Inc., Republic Real Estate Corp., Philippine Reclamation Corp., Holiday Hills Inc., United General Industries, Industrial Finance Corp., Mutual Realty Corp., Investment Planning Corp. of the Philippines, Phil. Oil & Geothermal Energy Inc., Philippine Village Resort Corp., Tradewinds International Resort & Country Club. *Member:* Columbian Farmers Assn.; Rotary Club of Manila (Dir. 1967–68); Chamber of Commerce of the Philippines (Dir. 1966–67); Bd. of Govs., Phil. National Red Cross 1967–73, 1974—; Chmn., Quezon City Red Cross Chapter; Dir., Petroleum Assn. of the Philippines. *Awards:* From Homeowners' Assn. of the Philippines, Quezon City Red Cross Chapter, Immaculate Conception Church Fund Campaign, Phil. Eye Bank, Manila Bd. of Realtors, Anti-TB Educational & Fund Campaign, Phil. National Red Cross, Rotary Club. *Clubs:* Wack Wack Golf & Country; Manila Overseas Press; John Hay Air Base (Baguio); Manila Polo. *Address:* 508 Buendia Avenue Ext., North Forbes Park, Makati, Rizal; & VRC Building, 219 Buendia Avenue, Makati, Rizal, Philippines.

**VINCENT, Ivor Francis Sutherland.** CMG, MBE, MA. British diplomat (Ret'd.). *B.* 1916. *Educ.* St. Peter's Coll. Radley; Christ Church Oxford. *M.* 1949, Patricia Mayne. *Daus.* Frances, Katharine, Nicola, Sarah. *Career:* Indian Army, Royal Garhwal Rifles, Major, 1941–46; Second Secy. Foreign Office 1946–48; First Secy. Buenos Aires 1948–51, U.K. Delegation N.A.T.O. Paris 1951–53, Foreign Office 1954–57, Rabat 1957–59; U.K. Disarmament Del. Geneva 1960, U.K. Del. O.E.C.D. Paris 1960–62; Counsellor Foreign Office 1962–66, Baghdad Jan-June 1967, Caracas 1967–70; H.M. Ambassador, Managua 1970–73; Consul-Gen. Melbourne 1973–76. *Clubs:* Travellers. *Address:* 101 Barkston Gardens, London, S.W.5.

**VINCENTI MARERI, Count Francesco.** Italian diplomat. *B.* 30 July 1911. *Educ.* Istituto Universitario Orientale. Naples. *M.* 1934, Giuseppina dei Marchesi Cittadin Cesi. *S.* Ippolito. *Dau.* Lavinia. *Career:* Acting Chinese Secretary, Italian Legation, China 1933–36; Second Chinese Secretary, in charge Pekin Office of Embassy 1936–42; Consul, Saigon 1942–49; Chargé d'Affaires, Vietnam, Cambodia and Laos 1949–51; Chargé d'Affaires, Rangoon 1953; Consul-General Port Said 1955–56; Ceremonial, Ministry of Foreign Affairs 1957–58; Consul-General, Casablanca 1959–60; Chief of Section, Cultural Affairs Division, Ministry of Foreign Affairs 1961–62; Consul-General, Johannesburg July 1962, Minister Plenipotentiary 1964; Cultural Affairs Div. Min. of Foreign Affairs 1965–66; Ambassador, Baghdad (Iraq) 1966–70; Consul General Nice since 1971; Ambassador (Ret.'d) 1973. *Address:* 4 Via Monti Parioli, Rome, Italy.

**VINCI, Piero.** Italian diplomat. *B.* 1912. *Educ.* Univ. of Rome—law degree. *M.* Maria Laura Annibaldi. *Career:* Vice-Consul, Zurich 1939–40; 1st Sec., then Chargé d'Affaires, Sofia 1943–46; Head of Press Section, Ministry of Foreign Affairs, Rome 1948–49; 1st Sec., Beirut 1949–53; Consul-Gen., London 1953–55; Head of UN Div., Ministry of

Foreign Affairs, Rome 1955–59; Chef de Cabinet of Dep. Prime Minister, Signor A. Piccioni 1960–63; Perm. Rep. to UN 1964–73; Ambassador to Moscow 1973–75; Perm. Rep. to UN since 1975; Pres. of UN Security Council, Aug. 1971 & July 1976. *Member:* Bd. of Trustees, UN Inst. for Training & Research (UNITAR) since July 1973; International Cttee. of the Inst. on Man & Science. *Decorations:* Knight Grand Cross of the Order of Merit of the Republic of Italy. *Club:* Circolo della Caccia (Rome). *Address:* 925 Fifth Avenue, New York, N.Y. 10021; and *office* 747 Third Avenue, New York, N.Y. 10017, U.S.A.

**VINES, Sir William Joshua,** CMG, AASA, ACIS. Australian. *B.* 1916. *Educ.* Haileybury Coll. Victoria, Australia. *M.* 1939, Thelma Jean Ogden. *S.* 1. *Daus.* 2. *Career:* Chmn. Dalgety Australia Ltd.; Chmn. Carbonless Papers (Wiggins Teape) Ltd.; Deputy Chmn., Tubemakers of Australia Ltd.; Dir., Associated Pulp & Paper Mills Ltd.; Conzinc Rio Tinto of Australia Ltd.; Commercial Union Assurance Co. of Australia Ltd.; Port Phillip Mills Pty. Ltd.; Dalgety Ltd. (London); Dalgety New Zealand Ltd. (New Zealand); Wiggins Teape Ltd. (London). *Member:* Board of International Wool Secretariat; Executive, CSIRO. *Clubs:* RAC; Junior Carlton; Melbourne; Royal Sydney Union (Aust.). *Address:* 73 Yarranabbe Rd., Darling Pt., Sydney, Australia; Old Southwood, Tara, Queensland, Australia.

**VINICCHAYAKUL, Serm.** Thai politician. *B.* 1908. *Educ.* Barrister at Law, Law School; Ministry of Justice, Docteur En Droit and Higher Certificate in Private Law and Economic, Univ. of Paris. *M.* 1941, Chomsri Pashyananda. *S.* 2. *Daus.* 2. *Career:* Joined Juridical Council 1932; Secy. Gen. of the Juridical Council 1946; Governor Bank of Thailand 1946–47, 1952–54; Governor for Thailand in the Boards of Governors of Ibrid & IFC 1952–59; Under Secy. of State for Finance 1945–65; Professor, Faculty of Law Thammasat Univ. 1954; Minister of Finance also Under Secy. of State for Finance 1957–58; Minister of Finance 1965–73; Governor for Thailand in the Boards of Governors of Ibrid, IFC and IDA 1965–73; Chmn. Exec. Cttee. of National Economic & Socia lCouncil since 1972; Pres., Royal Institute of Thailand since 1976. *Awards:* Knight Grand Cordon of the Most Noble Order, Crown of Thailand; Knight Grand Cordon, Most Exalted Order of the White Elephant; Exalted Order of the White Elephant; Knight Grand Cross (First Class) Most Illustrious Order of Chulo Chom Klao. Doctor of Law Thammasat University. *Address:* 159 Soi Asoke, Sukhumvit Road, Bangkok; and *office:* Nat. Economic & Social Council, Bangkok, Thailand.

**VINSON, Gerald Loring** (Jerry); American. *B.* 1905. *Educ.* Midwestern University. *M.* 1928, Helen Lorene Howard. S. Robert Emerson. *Daus.* Joan (Miller) and Ann (Inman). *Career:* One of the founders and President of Industrial Supply Co. 1933–62; independent oil and gas producer 1962—; Dir. City National Bank (Wichita Falls, Tex.) 1962—, Missouri-Kansas-Texas Railroad 1954–69; Panhandle Steel Products 1958–68; Beaumont Broadcasting Corp. 1948–71; Midwestern University Foundation 1960—. Vinson & Clark 1950—. Owner-Manager, G. L. Jerry Vinson Oil & Gas. Operator, Vinson Ranch. President: Vinson Petroleum Co.; Vinson Petroleum Co. of Canada; Pres. Bison Oil Co. since 1973; Partner Tenntex Oil Co. since 1970; Pres. Cumberland Petroleum Corp. since 1971. Vice-Pres. & Dir., Game Conservation International. Past member Adv. Committee, U.S. Dept. of Commerce; Adv. Board, Wichita Falls Museum and Art Center; Past President Wichita Falls Chamber of Commerce, and of Wichita Falls Junior Chamber of Commerce: Past Director of U.S. and Past Vice-President, Texas Junior Chamber of Commerce; Past member, Adv. Committee, Petroleum Administration for War. Member: Texas Independent Producers & Royalty Owners Assn. (District Director and member Imports Cttee. 1964–65); North Texas Oil & Gas Assn. (Past Pres. and member Executive Committee); Independent Petroleum Assn. of America (Director); American Petroleum Inst; Nat. Petroleum Council since 1973. *Clubs:* The Wichita; Wichita Falls Country; Cipango (Dallas Tex.); Shikar-Safari International. (President). *Address:* 2209 Clarinda, Wichita Falls, Tex. 76308; and *office* 200 City National Building, Wichita Falls, Tex. 76301, U.S.A.

**VIRTUE, Hon. Sir John Evenden.** KBE. Judge of the Supreme Court of Western Australia 1951–75. *B.* 1905. *Educ.* Univs. of Melbourne and Western Australia (BA; LLM). *M.* 1938, Mary Joan Lloyd. *Career:* Barrister and Solicitor of Supreme Court of W.A. 1928–50; Appointed King's Counsel 1950. Pres., Law Society of W.A. 1950. Served in World War II (A.I.F.; 16 Inf. Bn.; attained rank of Major). *Clubs:* Weld (Perth); Royal Perth Yacht. *Address:* 74 Kingsway, Nedlands, W.A., Australia.

**VISSE, Jan Hendrick.** South African Diplomat. *B.* 1913. *Educ.* Lawyer, Pretoria Univ. *M.* 1941, Perpetua Wolhuter. *S.* 1. *Dau.* 1. *Career:* Mayor, Pretoria 1950–53; Member of Parliament 1953–73; Deputy Speaker, S. African Parliament, 1966–73; South African Ambassador in Switzerland since 1973. *Director:* SAN Lam (SA); SATBEL (SA); SANKOR (SA). *Member:* S. African Law Socy. Pretoria. *Address:* Kirchenfeldstr, 60 Berne, Switzerland; and *office* Jungfraustr 1, 3005, Berne, Switzerland.

**VITA-FINZI, Paolo.** Italian diplomat. *B.* 31 March 1899. *Educ.* Turin University (LLD). *M.* 1935, Nadia Touchmalova (*D.* 1952). *S.* Ennio, Claudio. *Career:* Served World War I 1917–18; Bronze Medal for Bravery; Assistant at Institute of Economics, Bocconi University, Milan 1920–21; entered Diplomatic Service 1924; Secretary, Foreign Office Press Bureau 1924–26;in charge of Consulate-General, Düsseldorf 1926–27; Vice-Consul, Sfax 1927; Consul, Tiflis 1928–30; Secretary, Direction for Political Affairs 1931–33; Expert, Stresa Conference for Central and East Europe 1932; Consul-General, Rosario 1934, Sydney 1935–36; Head of North American Bureau, Direction of Transoceanic Affairs 1937–38; Dismissed after Hitler-Mussolini Pact, emigrated to Argentina and worked at the Instituto Argentino de Investigaciones Economicas; contributed to newspaper La Nación 1939–46; founded political and literary review Domani, Buenos Aires 1943–45; reinstated and appointed Consul-General, London 1946–50; En. Ex. and Min. Plen. to Finland, March 1951–53; Ambassador to Norway 1955–58, and to Hungary 1961–65. Delegate to U.N. General Assembly 1959, and U.N. Economic & Social Council 1961; Contributor, newspaper Corriere della Sera 1968–72. *Awards:* Knight Commander, Order of the Crown of Italy; Grand Cross, Order of Merit of the Republic (Italy); Knight, Order of St. Maurice and St. Lazarus; Knight, Order of the Redeemer (Greece); Grand Cross, Order of the Lion (Finland); Grand Cross, Order of St. Olav (Norway). *Publications:* Terra e Liberta in Russia; Peron mito e realtà. Le Delusioni della libertà; Diario Caucasico. *Address:* Via Crescenzio 91, Rome 00193, Italy.

**VITSAXIS, Vassilis.** Greek Diplomat. *B.* 1920. *Educ.* PhD Law & Philosophy. *M.* Zoe-Kety Ioannidou. *Career:* Entered Greek Diplomatic Service 1946; served in Paris, Belgium & New York & as mem. of delegations to the Council of Europe & the UNO; First Vice-Pres., Soc. of Foreign Consuls in New York 1963; Counsellor 1964, then Minister Counsellor & Chargé d'Affaires 1965–66, Greek Embassy, Ankara; Ambassador Ex. & Plen. & Perm. Delegate to the Council of Europe 1966; Ambassador Ex. & Plen. to the USA 1969; Ambassador Ex. & Plen. to India, concurrently to Nepal, Sri Lanka, Burma, Thailand, Malaysia, Singapore, Indonesia & Vietnam since 1973, also first Greek Ambassador to Bangladesh. *Member:* Associate, Inst. of International & Private Law; Indian PEN Club. *Decorations:* Golden Cross of the Belgian Crown; Cross of the Grand Commander of the Royal Order of the Phoenix; Grand Commander, Royal Order of King George; Cross of the Commander of the Holy Sepulchre. *Publications:* Author, poet & translator; received French Academy Award for poetry, 1969. *Address:* Embassy of Greece, 188 Jor Bagh, New Delhi 110003, India.

**VOGEL, Karl Theodor.** German publisher. Co-proprietor of Vogel-Verlag Würzburg, Western Germany. *B.* 1914. *Educ.* Cornell Univ. (U.S.A.) and Empire State School of Printing, Ithaca, N.Y., U.S.A. *M.* 1940. Gisela Bormann. *Daus.* Kathrin, Gabriele and Jutta. Executive member: Landesverband Bayer. Zeitschriftenverleger e.V., Munich; Fachgruppe Fachzeitschriften im Verband Deutscher Zeitschriftenverleger e.V., Bonn. Committee member: Verband Deutscher Zeitschriftenverleger e.V.; Fédération Internationale de la Press Périodique (FIPP) London, Deutscher Presserat, and Borsenverein des deutschen Buchhandels e.V. *Address:* Judenbühlweg 17, Würzburg; and *office* Max Planck-Strasse 7/9 Würzburg, Germany.

**VOGT, Hersleb.** Norwegian Diplomat. *B.* 1912. *Educ.* Univ. of Oslo. *M.* 1947, Inger Hansen. *Career:* Joined Diplomatic Service & served Ministry of Foreign Affairs 1936; Paris & Luxembourg 1937; Rome 1938; Ministry of Foreign Affairs, London 1944; Oslo 1945; Brussels & Luxembourg 1948; London & Dublin 1949; Minister to Japan 1953–58, Ambassador 1958; Amb. to German Fed. Republic 1958–63, to Denmark 1963–67, to France 1967–73, to Sweden 1973–77, to France since 1977. *Decorations:* Commdr. Order of St. Olav; Norwegian War Participation Medal (with Star); CVO; Commdr. Order of Phoenix, Greece; Grand Cross, Order of Rising Sun, Japan; Grand Cross (1st class), Order of Merit, Fed. Republic of Germany; Grand Cross, Order of Dannebrog, Denmark; Grand Commdr., French Legion of Honour; Grand Cross, Order of Nordstjärna, Sweden. *Address:* Ambassade Royale de Norvège, 28 rue Bayard, 75008 Paris, France.

**VOKEY, Richard Snow.** American. *B.* 1928. *Educ.* Bowdoin Coll. (BA); Harvard School, Business Admin. (MBA). *M.* 1961, Maureen Wright. *S.* 3. *Dau.* 1. *Career:* First National City Bank, N.Y.C. 1957; Mem. Foreign Inspection Staff, Europe & Far East 1959—60; Asst. Man. Beirut, Lebanon. 1960–62; Man. Jeddah, Saudi Arabia 1962–65; Vice-Pres. London 1965–69; Senior Vice Pres. 1969–72; Vice Chmn of Hill Samuel & Co. Ltd. 1972 and Dep. Chmn. 1974–76; Chmn. Exec. Cttee., State Street Bank & Trust Co., Boston, Mass. since 1977. *Member:* American Ditchley. *Clubs:* Hankley Common Golf, R.A.C. *Address:* 675 Monument Street, Concord, Massachusetts, U.S.A.

**VOLK, Harry J.** Banking and insurance. *B.* 1905. *Educ.* Rutgers Univ. (AB 1927; LLB 1930). *M.* (1) 1931, Marion Waters (*D.* 1972). *S.* Robert H. and Richard R. *Dau.* Carolyn E. (Jacques). (2) 1976, Marjorie Lord. *Career:* Vice-Pres. in charge of Western Operations, Prudential Insurance Co. of America, Los Angeles 1947–57. Divisional Chief, U.S. Strategic Bombing Survey 1945. President and Director, Union Bank, Los Angeles 1957–69; Chmn. Dir. Union Bancorp 1969–73; Chmn., Union Bancorp since 1974; Union Bank 1969—; Dir. Pacific Lighting Corp.; Union Bank; Union Bancorp; Western Air Lines Inc. *Member:* Los Angeles Clearing House Assn.; The Assocs. Calif. Inst. of Technology; Founding Benefactor Los Angeles County Museum of Art. Trustee, Calif. Inst. of Technology; The Hospital, Good Samaritan (Los Angeles). Hon. LHD Rutgers Univ. 1958. *Clubs:* California (Los Angeles); Los Angeles Country; Bohemian (San Francisco). *Address:* 1110 Maytor Place, Beverly Hills, Calif. 90210; and *office* c/o Union Bank, 445 South Figuerra Street, Los Angeles, Calif. 90071, U.S.A.

**von BRAUN, Baron Sigismund** (Maximilian Wernher Gustav Magnus). German diplomat. *B.* 1911. *Educ.* College Français, Berlin; Univs of Hamburg and Berlin (law); apprenticeship in banking; exchange student Univ. Cincinnati/Ohio. *M.* 1940, Hildegard Beck-Margis. *S.* 1. *Daus.* 4. *Career.* Foreign Service 1936; Counsellor, German Embassy London 1953–58; Chief of Protocol (Ambassador) Foreign Office, Bonn 1958–62, Observer (Ambassador) FRG to UN, New York 1962–68; Ambassador FRG in Paris 1968–70; State Secy. Federal Foreign Office 1970–72; Again Ambassador FRG in Paris 1972–76 (Ret'd.). *Member:* German-French Circle, German Academic Exchange Office; German Assn. for Foreign Policy. *Decorations:* numerous. *Address:* Graf Stauffenbergstr. 21, D-5300 Bonn 1, Federal Republic of Germany.

**VON DER HUDE, Preben Arthur.** Danish diplomat. *B.* 1913. *Educ.* Univ. of Copenhagen, LLB. *M.* Inge Kaehler. *Daus.* 3. *Career:* Entered Danish foreign service 1940; Attaché Berlin 1941–44; Private Secy. to Foreign Minister 1946–48; 1st Secy. Danish Legation in Brussels 1950–54; Head of Div., Ministry of For. Affairs 1958–62; Consul-General in San Francisco 1962–70; Ambassador to New Zealand 1970–74; Danish Ambassador in Australia 1973–75; Perm. Rep. to the Council of Europe, Strasbourg since 1975. *Decorations:* Officer of Order of Dannebrog; Decorations from Belgium, Finland, France, Iran and Sweden. *Clubs:* Bohemian (San Francisco); Wellington (N.Z.); Commonwealth (Canberra). *Address:* c/o Ministry of Foreign Affairs, Christiansborg, Copenhagen, Denmark.

**von FALKENHAUSEN, Freiherr Gotthard.** Dr. jur. German banker. *B.* 1899. *Educ.* Universities of Göttingen, Halle and Berlin; Doctor of Law. *M.* 1926, Annemarie Körte. *S.* Bernhard and Hasso. *Daus.* Gabriele, Angelika, Vera and Andrea. *Career:* Admitted to German Bar 1926; private practice of law 1926–28; with Legal Department, Deutsche Bank, Berlin 1929–34; Manager at Essen 1936–38; Chmn. Bd. of Admin., Bankaus Burkhardt & Co., Essen. Chmn. of Bd., Kundenkreditbank KGaA, Düsseldorf 1948—; Director, Klöckner Werke AG; Pres., Chambers of Comm. of Essen 1960–70; Hon. Pres., German-French Chamber of Comm., Paris; Vice-Pres., Chamber of Commerce, Essen. Member, German Social Foreign Policy. *Address:* 21 Brachtstrasse, Essen; and *office* 7/9 Linden-nallee, Essen, Germany.

**von FRENCKELL, Gustaf Christoffer.** Finnish. *B.* 20 May 1912. *Educ.* University of Helsinki. *M.* 1960, Ritva Lohi. *S.* Johan, Mikael, Otto, Wilhelm, Hubertus. *Daus.* Christina, Helena. *Career:* Director, Finnish Sugar Co. 1941–49; Helsingfors Aktiebank 1949; Deputy Chief General Manager 1956–67; Chairman of the Board, W. Rosenlew Ltd. 1967–77. *Address:* Parkgatan 3, Helsinki 14, Finland.

**von HASE, Karl Gunther.** GCVO, KCMG. German diplomat. *B.* 1917. *Educ.* Military Service, German Foreign Service. *M.* 1945, Renate Stumpff. *Daus.* 5. *Career:* entered German Foreign Service Bonn 1950; Final Examination, Senior Foreign Service Officials 1951; Studies, Georgetown Univ. Washington 1952; Counsellor, Legation German Embassy Ottawa 1953–56; Press Section Fed. Foreign Office Bonn 1956–58; Head, Press Section 1958–61; Appointed Ministerial Counsellor 1959; Min. Dir. Head Western Dept. 1961; State Secy. Head Press & Information Office of Fed. Govt. 1962; State Secy. Fed. Ministry of Defence Bonn 1968–69; Ambassador to United Kingdom 1970–77; Dir.-Gen. of German TV second channel (ZDF) since 1977. *Awards:* Knight Grand Cross, Royal Victorian Order; Knight Commander, St. Michael and St. George. *Address:* ZDF, 6500 Mainz 1, Postfach 40 40, Federal Republic of Germany.

**von HASSEL, Kai-Uwe.** German politician. *B.* 1913. *Educ.* Gymnasium, Abitur. *M.* (1) Deceased. (2) 1936, Dr. Monika Weichert. *S.* 1. *Dau.* 1. *Career:* Hon. Mayor 1947–63; Mem. County Council 1948–55; mem. State Parliament Schleswig-Holstein 1950–65; Prime Minister Schleswig-Holstein 1954–63; Fed. Minister of Defence 1963–66; Min. for refugees, expellees 1966–69; MP 1953–54 and since 1965; Speaker of Federal Parlt. 1969–72; Deputy Speaker since 1972; Deputy Chmn. CDU 1956–69; mem. presidium CDU since 1969. *President* Hermann-Ehler's Foundation since 1968, European Union of Christian Democrats since 1973. *Chairman.* Board of DOAG. *Decorations:* 22 including Grand Cross of Merit Fed. Rep. of Germany; hon OBE. *Publications:* Verantwortung für die Freiheit; Waafrika Wa Leo (Swahili). *Address:* 2392 Glücksburg, Fordestraße 11, Haus Belmar, Federal Republic of Germany; and *office* 53 Bonn, Bundeshaus, Federal Republic of Germany.

**von HAYEK, Friedrich August.** British. (retired) Univ. Professor. *B.* 1899. *Educ.* Gymnasium and University, Vienna; Dr. Jur and Dr. rer. pol. *M.* (1) 1926, Helene Berta Maria von Fritsch; (2) 1950, Helene Anna Elisabeth Bitterlich. *S.* 1. *Dau.* 1. *Career:* Austrian Civil Servant (Legal Consultant 1921–26; Dir. Austrian Inst. for Business Cycle Research 1927–31, also Lectr. Univ. of Vienna 1929–31; Professor of Economics and Statistics, Univ. of London (LSE) 1931–50; Professor of Social and Moral Science, Univ. of Chicago 1950–1962; Professor of Political Economy, Univ. of Freiburg-im-Breisgau; 1962–69; Visiting Prof. Univ. of Salzburg 1970–74. *Fellow:* British Academy. *Award* Nobel Prize in Economics, 1974. *Publications:* Prices and Productions (1931); The Pure Theory of Capital (1941); The Road to Serfdom (1944); Individualism and Economic Order (1949); The Counter-Revolution of Science (1951); The Sensory Order (1952); The Constitution of Liberty (1960); Law Legislation and Liberty, vol. I (1973), vol. II (1976). *Club:* Reform (London). *Address:* Urachstrasse 27, D-7800 Freiburg: Brg., Federal Republic of Germany.

**von HOFSTEN, Gerhard Sixtensson.** Swedish. *B.* 1916. *Educ.* Studentexamen, Stockholm 1935, Royal Inst. of Technology, Stockholm, 1942, and Mass. Inst. of Technology (U.S.A.); MSc 1950. *M.* 1948, Anna Viveka Lagercrantz. *Daus.* Elisabeth, Viveka, and Isabella. *Career:* Assistant to Chief of Jernkontorets Research Assn. 1943–45; Leader, Swedish Steelworks Joint Project for magnetizing roasting of Iron Ore, Striberg, 1945–48; Assistant to General Manager of AB Ferrolegeringar, Stockholm, 1948–49; Swedish-American Association award for studies in U.S.A. 1949–50; Ferrochrome Plant Manager of AB Ferrolegeringar, Trollhättan 1950–53 (Director of Research 1954–59; Director of Research & Manager of Product Control 1960–61). Director of Metallurgical Research, Höganäs AB, Höganäs, Sweden 1961–67. Director, Patents and Licenses 1967–69. President & Managing Director, AB Carbox, Ystad, 1969–71. *Publications:* Svikta grundvalarna för vårt välstånd? also many articles in technical journals. Member: Jernkontorets Powder Metallurgy Research Committee (Chairman 1964–67); Sällskapet Riksdagsmän och Forskare (RIFO); Svenska Bergsmannaföreningen; American Society for Metals; American Inst. of Metallurgical Engineers; Verein Deutscher Eisenhüttenleute; Plansee International Powder Metallurgy Society. *Address:* Neptunivägen 7. 181 63 Lidingö, Sweden;

and *office* Svenska Utveckkeings AB, Fack, 103 40 Stockholm. Sweden.

**von HORN, Knut (Raoul Leopold Robert).** Swedish. Comdr. Order of Wasa and of the Polar Star (Sweden) and of Order of Dannebrog (Denmark). *B.* 1907. *Educ.* University of Stockholm (BA 1930; LLB 1934); study of Economics, Cambridge University (1926–27). *M.* 1940, Birgitta von Horn. *S.* Johan and Edward. *Dau.* Michaëla. *Career:* Secretary, Swedish State Commission of Trade 1939–41; Chief of Section, Ministry of Supply 1942–46, and Ministry of Commerce 1946–48; Chamberlain to the King 1946; Deputy Marshal of the Diplomatic Corps 1950–59; Hon. Keeper of the King's Privy Purse 1956—; Chairman, Swedish Milling Association 1973—; Member, Board of Directors: Korsnœs-Marma AB, Investments AB Kinnevik. AB Swedish Lithographic Industries; Vice-Chmn, Svenska Handelsbanken; Chmn, Swedish Royal Academy of Agriculture & Forestry 1972–75. Swedish delegate at GATT and ECE international economic conferences 1946–55. Member, State Commission for Agriculture 1950–56. *Address:* Hjelmarsnaes, Stora Mellösa, Sweden.

**von MOOS, Ludwig.** Dr. hc Swiss. *B.* 1910. *Educ.* University of Fribourg. Secretary, Municipal Council of Sachseln 1933 (Mayor 1941–46); Councillor of State 1943; Cantonal Judge 1943–46; State Councillor, Obwalden 1946; elected Federal Councillor Dec. 1959; Minister of Justice and Police; Federal Councillor 1960–71. *Address:* Luternauweg 6, Berne, Switzerland.

**von MURALT, Alexander.** Swiss. *B.* 1903. *Educ.* Dr. med (Univ. of Heidelberg), Dr. phil (Univ. of Zürich). *M.* 1927, Alice Baumann. *Daus.* 3. Research Associate, Harvard Medical School (U.S.A.) 1928–30; Research Assistant, Kaiser Wilhelm Inst., Heidelberg 1930–35. Professor of Physiology and Director of Physiological Institute, Univ. Berne 1935–68. President: Scientific Station on Jungfraujoch 1936–73; Theodor Kocher Institute 1950—, and National Research Council 1952–68. *Publications:* works in field of muscle physiology, physiology of high altitudes, and neurophysiology. Dr. hc: Basle, Berne, Lausanne, Geneva, Zürich, Cologne, Brussels, Manchester, Rio de Janeiro. *Awards:* Kocher Prize; Marcel Benoist Prize. Hon. member or corresponding member of many academies in Europe and America. *Address:* Freiestrasse 1, Berne, Switzerland.

**von NUMERS, Sigurd Waldemar.** Finnish diplomat. *B.* 1903. *Educ.* LLD Helsinki. *M.* 1928, Eleni Sundwall. *S.* Sigurd Johan. *Dau.* Helena Cecilia. *Career:* Attaché and Secretary of Bureau, Ministry for Foreign Affairs, 1927–29; Attaché Berlin 1929–31 and Stockholm 1931–33; Secretary of Bureau, Ministry 1933–34; Washington 1934–39; Chief of Bureau and Asst. Chief of Division, Ministry 1939–45; Counsellor, Washington, 1945–49; Chief of Legal Division; Ministry, 1949–54; Chargé d'Affaires. Ottawa, 1954–59; Ambassador at New Delhi (and concurrently Minister Bangkok, Colombo, Djakarta, Rangoon) 1959–61; Consultative Counsellor, Ministry of Foreign Affairs 1961; Chief of Legal Division Ministry of Foreign Affairs 1961–64. Ambassador at The Hague 1964–70 (concurrently to Eire). *Publications:* Kampmedel i Sjökrig; and various articles in periodicals. *Awards:* Liberty Cross, 4th Class (Finland); Commander 1st Cl.: Lion of Finland, and of White Rose (Finland); Commemoration Medal of the 1939–40 War (Finland); St. Olav (Norway); Commander 1st Cl., North Star (Sweden); Knight 1st Cl., Vasa (Sweden); Delaware Medal (Sweden); Grand Officer, Order of the Tunisian Republic; Commander 1st Cl. Flag of Yugoslavia, Grand Cross Order Nassau. *Address:* Topeliusgaten 9 A 10, 00250 Helsingfors 25, Finland.

**v. RANTZAU (nee Essberger), Mrs. Liselotte.** German. Partner, John T. Essberger; Chmn., DAL Deutsche Afrika-Linien GmbH & Co., *B.* 1918. *S.* Roland v. Rantzau, Heinrich v. Rantzau and Eberhart v. Rantzau. *Address:* 2 Hamburg 55—Blankenese, Muehlenberger Weg 34; and *office* 2 Hamburg 50-Altona, Palmaille 45, Federal Republic of Germany.

**von SCHIRNDING, Kurt Robert Samuel.** South African Diplomat. *B.* 1930. *Educ.* Univ. of Cape Town—BA (political philosophy). *M.* 1954, Gisela Westphal. *S.* 2. *Daus.* 2. *Career:* Ministry of Foreign Affairs, Pretoria 1952–56; S.A. Embassy. London 1956–60; S.A. Consulate-General, New York 1960–64; Ministry of Foreign Affairs, Pretoria (Africa Div.) 1964–68; Resident S.A. Rep. to the International Atomic Energy Agency, Vienna 1968–77; S.A. Governor on the Bd. of Govs., IAEA, Vienna 1973–77; S.A. Ambassador to Austria 1973–77; S.A. Ambassador to the Federal Republic of Germany since 1977. *Clubs:* Pretoria Country Club; Kelvin Grove (Cape Town). *Address:* 53 Bonn-Bad Godesberg, Rüdigerstrasse 20–22; and *office* 53 Bonn-Bad Godesberg, Auf der Hostert 3, Federal Republic of Germany.

**von STEIN, Johann Heinrich.** German banker. Hon. Consul of Belgium. Holds directorships in about twenty firms in the textile industry and in insurance, banking, machinery, technical instrument production. Member of the Board of the University of Cologne. *B.* 1899. *Educ.* training in the banking house of Delbrück, Schickler & Co., Berlin; in the coal and iron industry in the Siegerland, Cologne and Ruhr District; short training in London and Paris; and almost two years in U.S. banking and industry in New York, Detroit, San Francisco. Partner with J. H. Stein since 1926. *M.* 1933, Marion de Weerth. *S.* 1. *Dau.* 1. *Club:* Cologne Rotary and others. *Address:* Auf dem Römerberg 29, 5 Köln-Marienburg; and *office* Unter Sachsenhausen 10–26, 5 Köln, Germany.

**von SYDOW, Erik.** Swedish Diplomat. *B.* 1912. *Educ.* Uppsala Univ.—Bachelor of Law. *M.* 1940, Lia Akel. *S.* 1. *Dau.* 1. *Career:* Ministry of Foreign Affairs 1936; early service, Germany & Baltic States 1937–39; Sec., Legation to Japan 1940; Chargé d'Affaires 1945–46; Head of Div., Min. of Foreign Affairs 1947–49; Perm. Rep. to OEEC 1949–53; Counsellor, U.S.A. 1954–56; Asst. Under Sec., Commercial & Econ. Affairs, Min. of Foreign Affairs 1959–63; Amb. & Perm. Rep. to EFTA & other International Orgs. in Geneva 1964–71; Amb. to EEC, Brussels since 1972; Chmn., numerous bilateral & multilateral trade negotiations. *Decorations:* Swedish & numerous foreign decorations. *Address:* 28, Avenue du Prince d'Orange, 1180 Brussels, Belgium; and *office* Délégation de Suède auprès des Communautés Européennes, 6 Rond-Point Robert Schuman, 1040 Brussels, Belgium.

**von SYDOW, (Gustav Karl Oskar) Kristian.** Swedish. *B.* 1917. *Educ.* Matric. 1935; Grad. Gothenburg School of Economics 1938. *M.* 1948, Marie-Christine J. Brostöm. *S.* Oscar and Henrik. *Dau.* Emily. *Career:* With Swedish Orient Line, Gothenburg 1939–45; Swedish Shipowners' representative-adviser to Swedish Embassy, Washington 1945–46 and 1948–49; Asst. Dir., Swedish East Asia Co. Ltd., Gothenburg 1950–57. Managing Director: Swedish East Asia Co. Ltd., Gothenburg 1966–76; Tirfing Steamship Co., Gothenburg, 1969–75. Deputy Chairman: Götabanken, Swedish Shipowners Assn., Atlantica. Chmn.: Broström Shipping Co. (formerly Tirfing Steamship Co.), Swedish East Asia Co. Ltd., Gothenburg, Member of Bd. Custos, SILA. *Address:* Prästgårdsgatan. 58, S-412 71 Gothenburg; and *office* Broströms Rederi AB, S-403 30 Gothenburg, Sweden.

**von WALTHER, Gebhardt R. E. A.** German diplomat. *B.* 1902. *Educ.* Dr. jur. *M.* 1954, Anneliese Gierlichs. *Career:* Attaché, Foreign Office 1929–32; Attaché, Consulate, Beirut 1932–34; Attaché, Consulate-General, Memel 1934–36; Secretary of Legation, Moscow (and Private Secy. to the Ambassador, Graf von der Schulenburg) 1936–41; Consul, Tripoli 1941–43; Counsellor of Embassy, Ankara 1943–44; interned in Turkey 1944–45; industrial appointment with Malmedie & Co., A. G., Düsseldorf 1945–51; Minister-Counsellor of Embassy, Paris 1951–55; Amb. to Mexico 1956–58; to Brazil 1958–59. Ambassador, Permanent Representative of Fed. Republic of Germany to NATO 1959–62. Ambassador to Turkey 1962–66; to U.S.S.R. 1966–68; Acting Vice-Pres. German Society for Foreign Affairs, Bonn since 1968. Commander, Crown of Italy; Commander, Legion of Honour. *Publication:* Convertible Bonds im Amerikanischen Recht und ihre Einführbarkeit in Deutschland. *Address:* Oberbuschweg 214, 5000 Köln 50, Federal Republic of Germany

**VON WINCKLER, Karl.** Dr. rer. pol. German & Austrian. *B.* 1912. *Educ.* Vienna and Rome Universities. *M.* (1) Gertrud Dangl. (D. 1967). *S.* 1. *Dau.* 1. (2) 1968, Ruth Fehling. *Career:* Eldelstahlwerke Buderus AG, Wetzlar; Deputy Chmn. Adv. Bd. Tiroler Röhren-und Metallwerke AG, Solbad Hall; Member Adv. Bd. GHWGes f. Huttenwerksanlagen mbH; Pres. Admin. Bd. Giessener Hochschules. e.V; Deutsche Handelskammer in Österreich. *Awards:* Ehrensenator of Hochschule f. Welthandel, Vienna and Univ. of Giessen; Grosses Goldenes Ehrenzeichen d. Landes Steiermark; Grand Officer Merit of Sovereign Mil. Order of Malta; Cdr. Merit of the Fed. Republic of Germany. *Club:* Companion Teutonic Order; Lions. *Address:* Rohrmoos 79, A8970 Schladming, Austria and Am Birkengarten 32, D 8012 Ottobrunn, Federal Republic of Germany.

**von WUNSCHHEIM,** Alfons. Austrian executive. *B.* 1904. *Educ.* Dr. juris. *M.* 1930, Eva Seidl von Hohenveldern. *S.* Johannes and Alfons. *Daus.* Marie Elisabeth Freifrau von Haerdtl, and Katharina von Kleemann. *Career:* With Austrian Siemens Schuckert Werke A.G., Vienna 1927–45. Kommerzialrat Director, Sprecher & Schuh Ltd., Linz 1946–75; Member of the Bd. Upper Austrian Association of Austrian Industrialists. Vice-Chairman of Board of Directors, Vöslauer Kammgarnfabrik A. G., Bad Vöslau. Member of honour, Gesellschaft für Social und Wirtschaftspolitik, Linz; Chmn., Austrian Delegation to Conseil International de la Chasse, Paris; Aust Employers Del., Int. Labor Conference, Geneva; Member, Gesellschaft der Museumsfreunde, Vienna, Knight, Sovereign Order of Malta. *Club:* Rotary (Linz). *Address:* Leonding, Upper Austria.

**VOORST tot VOORST, Baron van Sweder Godfried Maria.** Former Dutch ambassador. *B.* 1910. *Educ.* LLD. *M.* 1945, Jkvr. A.M.E.L. van Bönninghausen tot Herinckhave. *Career:* Entered Department of Foreign Affairs 1934; Attaché 1934–39, 2nd Secretary 1939–40, Brussels and Paris, May—June 1940; At Ministry of Foreign Affairs of Netherlands Govt. in London 1940–44; 1st Secy. Brussels 1944–46; Chargé d'Affaires, Madrid 1946–48; Deputy Head, Netherlands Military Mission, Berlin 1948–50; Director of European Affairs Foreign Ministry 1950–52; Permanent Representative at Council of Europe, Strasbourg 1952–54; Minister, Washington 1954–59; Ambassador: Belgrade 1959–64; Luxembourg 1964–67 to the Holy See 1968–75. *Awards:* Knight, Order of Netherlands Lion; Officer, Order of Orange-Nassau; Grand Cross Order of Flag (Yugoslavia): of Oak Crown (Luxembourg) and of Pius (Holy See); Cmdr., Order of Belgian Crown; Star 2nd Cl. of Italian Solidarity; Knight, 1st Cl. St. Olav (Norway); Officer, Order of Leopold II (Belgium); Knight of Malta. *Club:* Haagsche (The Hague). *Address:* Eton Residence, Ave. Messidor 205, 1180 Brussels, Belgium.

**VORSTER, Hon. Balthazar Johannes,** BA, LLB, DPhil(hc) LLD(hc). Prime Minister of South Africa. *B.* 1915. *Educ.* University of Stellenbosch, BA, LLB, 1938; D.Phil (*honoris causa*) 1966, University of O.F.S., LLD, (*honoris causa*) 1967 University of Pretoria, LLD (*honoris causa*) 1967. *M.* 1941 Martini Steyn. *S.* 2. *Dau.* 1. *Career:* MP for Nigel 1953 (re elected 1958–61–66 70 & 74; Dep. Min. Education, Arts and Science, Social Welfare and Pensions 1958–61; Min. of Justice of Ed. Arts and Science Aug.–Nov. 1961; Min. of Justice 1961–66; Min. of Justice Police and Prisons April–Sept 1966; Prime Minister Min. of Police. Leader National Party 1966–68; Prime Minister and Leader National Party since 1968. *Clubs:* Zwartkop and Rondebosch Golf. *Address:* Union Buildings, Libertas Bryntirion, Pretoria and Groote Schuur, Cape Town, South Africa.

**VOS, Arthur, Jr.** American business executive and consultant. *B.* 1908. *Educ.* Univ. of Colorado 1930. *M.* 1932, Ruth Louise Knight. *S.* Arthur III. *Daus.* Marcia Ann (Moss) and Diana Louise. *Career:* Chairman, Pikes Peak Greenhouses Inc. and Burgyard Floral Co., Colorado Springs 1954–72; Director: 1958–61; Chairman of Board, Amer. Inst. of Baking, Chicago 1960–61; Life Gov. and Mem. Exec. Comm., American Bakers Assn., Chicago. *Member,* Sigma Chi Fraternity 1927; Co-editor, Norman Shield (manual of the Fraternity) 1929–38; Treasurer, Sigma Chi House Corp. 1938–52; Business Mgr. The Tilden Health School Assn., Denver, 1930–32; Treasurer 1932–35; Asst. Gen. Mgr. (1939–41), Treasurer and Director (1941–43), President (since 1943), The Macklem Baking Co., Denver; Pres. Pikes Peak Greenhouses, Inc. since 1953; Pres. and Governor, Rocky Mountain Bakers Assn. 1939–43; Pres. American Bakers Assn. 1948–49; member Exec. Cttee. 1946–60; Director, American Institute of Baking, Chicago, since 1952; Colorado Flower Growers Association Inc., since 1956 (Treasurer 1958); *Publications:* contributor to various journals of the baking industry. Member, Board of Health and Hospitals, City and County of Denver 1956–65. Chairman, Board of Health and Hospitals 1962–64. President, Inter-continental Coffee Corp., Denver 1962–63 and Tocumen Development Corp. S.A., Panama City 1962–63; Mason Shriner Potentate, 1955; Jester Director; 1959, Sec. Treas., Central Shrine Assoc., Red Cross of Constantine-Sovereign, 1970; Intendent General 1977. *Club:* Denver Country. *Address:* 930 Bonnie Brae Boulevard, Denver, Colo., 80209, U.S.A.

**VUM KO HAU, U.** PhD. Burmese (Siyin Chin) diplomat. *B.* 1917. *Educ.* Government High School, Sagaing; Research Student, PhD (Sociology, Ethnography, History of Philosophy), Charles Univ. Prague 1974. *M.* Tina Mang Ko Tiin. *Career:* Resistance leader in Chin Hills during World War II; served as Chief-of-Staff of the Siyin Resistance Army and the Chinwag Forces 1942–45; District Commissioner, Chin Hills-Manipur Division of the N.W. Frontier Province of Burma 1944; Chmn. Chin Leader's Freedom League 1944; member, Burma Defence and Financial Commission, London 1947; Delegate, Conference on the Anglo-Burmese Treaty signed in London, Oct. 1947; Member, Burma Constituent Assembly 1947–48; Minister for Frontier Areas in General Aung San's Cabinet; Counsellor to the Govenor of Burma 1947–48 and continued to serve in Premier U. Nu's Cabinet after Aung San's assassination until 1948; member, Burma Constituent Assembly, Select Committee of Seventeen to draft the Constitution of Burma; Rees-Williams Frontier Areas Enquiry Commission; Leader of Chin Hills delegation to the Panglong Conference (where he played an important part in bringing the Frontier States into the Union of Burma); Vice-Pres., Supreme Council of United Hill Peoples League 1947–48; member, Goodwill Mission to Pakistan, Feb. 1948; Delegate to International Rice Commission 1950; Representative 1953 and Acting Deputy Leader of Burmese delegation to the 20th U.N. General Assembly, New York 1965; Delegate F.A.O. Special Technical Meeting on the Economic Aspects of the Rice Industry 1954; an author of the Panglong Agreement, 1947; Cabinet Delegate to the Nu-Attlee Treaty, London, 1947; co-founder and Secretary of the Chin Hills Educational Uplift Society, Falam, 1938; Chief Burmese Delegate to the 10th anniversary of Bandung Conference, Jakarta, 1965; Delegate to ECAFE, held in Jogjakarta, 1959; Panel Chairman, Burma Constituent Assembly, 1947–48; Member of Staff in Charge of Guerrilla organizations under Admiral Lord Mountbatten in the Chin Hills, 1943–44. Deputy Secretary-General in the Foreign Office Feb. 1948; in charge of Protocol, United Nations and Political divisions; Minister to France and Netherlands 1955–59; Director of the Burma Y.M.C.A., Rangoon; founder Siyin Valley National High School 1944 and of Sagaing Old Students Assn., Rangoon; Chmn., Foreign Office Co-operative Credit Soc. Ltd., Rangoon; Leader of Burmese delegation at 10th anniversary of World Fed. of U.N. Associations, Geneva 1956; Chief delegate, International Atomic Energy Conf., Vienna 1957 and 1971; 10th anniversary of W.H.O., Geneva 1958; Ambassador to Indonesia 1960–65; to Cambodia and Laos 1966–71; to Czechoslovakia, Austria & Hungary 1971. Life member, Burma Research Society, Rangoon; Member: Executive Cttee., World Vetarans Assoc. 1953; Sub-cttee. to compose Burma's national song, and design national flag and State Seal, 1947; Member, Standard Athletic Club, Paris. *Awards:* Order of Sithu (Burma); Order of Banner (Yugoslavia); Burma Star and other World War II British medals; F.R.G.S., F.R.A.I. Staff-Major, Chinwags Guerilla Force, XIV Army, SEAC 1943–44; Fellow, Royal Anthropological Inst. Gt. Britain (Life Fellow since 1958). *Publications:* (co-author) Bogyoke Aung San's biography; The Oldest Burmese Printed Book; Profile of a Burma Frontier Man, (1963); broadcaster; lecturer; articles to Guardian (monthly English magazine, of which Vum Ko Hau was co-founder in 1953), daily newspapers and Burma; *Address:* c/o The Foreign Ministry, Prome Court, Rangoon, Burma.

# W

**WÄCHTER, Adolf.** German. Permanent Member of Board, Bayerische Hypotheken und Wechsel Bank, Munich. *B.* 1917. *Educ.* Univ. of Munich (law studies). *M.* 1951, Dr. med Eva Maria Schattenfroh. *S.* Stephan and Christian. *Daus.* Gabriele and Barbara. *Career:* Studied for Bar 1948–51. Successively Directorial Asst. 1951–61, Acting Member of Board 1961–64, Permanent Member 1964—, Bayerische Hypotheken und Wechsel Bank. Hon. Senator, University of Munich. Commercial Magistrate in Fifth Chamber of Bavarian High Court; Chmn. Bd. Heimstatt Bauspar AG, München; Württembergischen Hypothekenbank, Stuttgart; Gesellschaft für Kraftwerksbauten, Ensdorf/Saar; Member Bd. Isar-Amperwerke AG, Munchen, Bayerische Landessiedlung München, Pfälz Hypothekenbank, Ludwigshafen; Adv. Cttee., Wesdt. Bauvereinsbank, Dortmund; Treas. Univ. Society; Member Exec. Bd. Deutscher Paritätischer Wohlfahrtsverband; Central Cttee. Conféderation Internationale du Crédit Agricol; Bd. Trustees Pfennigparade e.V. Munchen; Socy. Christian-Jewish Co-operation e.V.; Admin. Bd. Kath. Zentralgesellenhausstiftung, Munchen. *Clubs:* KStV Ottonia; Wettsegelvereinigung Gollenhausen. *Address:* Kardinal Faulhaber Strasse 10, 8 München 1, Germany.

**WACKER, Alfred.** Swiss Diplomat. *B.* 1918. *Educ.* Univ. of Berne; Lawyer. *M.* 1950, Chantal Thormann. *S.* 1. *Daus.* 2. *Career:* Diplomatic Service, Berne 1945–50; Bonn 1950–54; Budapest 1955–57; Berne 1958–60; Mexico City 1961–64; Deputy-Head of Swiss Mission to the European Communities, Brussels 1964–66; Deputy Sec.-Gen. of EFTA, Geneva 1966–73; Ambassador, Perm. Rep. of Switzerland to the Council of Europe, Strasbourg since 1973. *Address:* CH-1787 Mur, Switzerland; and *office* F-67000 Strasbourg, 7 Rue Schiller, France.

**WADDELL, Sir Alexander Nicol Anton,** KCMG, DSC; U.K. Commissioner, British Phosphate Commissioners *B.* 1913. *Educ.* Edinburgh Univ. (MA) and Gonville and Caius Coll., Cambridge. *M.* 1949, Jean Margot Lesbia Masters. *Career:* Entered Colonial Administrative Service 1937; successively Cadet, Dist. Officer, Dist. Commissioner, Acting Resident Commissioner, British Solomon Islands Protectorate 1937–45; Malayan Civil Service 1946; Princ. Asst. Secy., North Borneo 1947–52; Colonial Secy., Gambia 1952–56; Sierra Leone 1956–58; Deputy Governor 1958–59; Governor and C.-in-C. Sarawak 1960–63; Commissioner British Phosphate since 1965. Served in World War II (Lieut. R.A.N.V.R. Military Service 1945–47; Lieut.-Col. General List), Member Royal Commonwealth Society. *Clubs:* R.N.V.R.; East India & Sports. *Address:* Pilgrim Cottage, Ashton Keynes, Wilts.

**WADE, Robert Hunter.** New Zealander diplomat. *B.* 1916. *Educ.* Waitaki School & Univ. of Otago (MA). *M.* 1941, Avelda Grace Petersen. *S.* Robert H. and Peter B. *Daus.* E. Judith and Kristin A. *Career:* Entered New Zealand Public Service (Treas. & Marketing Depts.) 1939; Official Secy., N.Z. Deleg., Eastern Group Supply Council, Delhi and Simla, 1941–43; N.Z. Govt. Offices, Sydney, 1943–47; Interim Secretariat, South Pacific Commission, Sydney, 1947; Assistant-Secretary, N.Z. High Commissioner's Office, Canberra, 1947–49; Head, Eastern Section, Dept. of External Affairs, Wellington, 1949–51; First Secretary, N.Z. Embassy, Washington, D.C., 1951–56; First Secretary N.Z. High Comn., Ottawa 1956–57; Dir., Colombo Plan Bureau, Colombo 1957–59; Head of External Aid Div. Dept. of External Affairs, Wellington 1959–62. New Zealand Commissioner in Singapore, Sarawak & North Borneo 1962–63; High Commissioner in Malaysia 1963–67. Deputy High Commissioner for New Zealand in U.K. 1967–69. Ambassador to Japan and Republic of Korea 1969–71; Commonwealth Deputy Secy. General, London, 1972–74; Ambassador in FR of Germany and Switzerland since 1975; Represented N.Z. at Uganda 1962, Botswana 1966, and Lesotho 1966, Independence celebrations; and at various international conferences. *Address:* New Zealand Embassy, 53 Bonn, Bonn-Center, Germany.

**WADIA, Neville Ness.** Company director. *B.* 22 Aug. 1911. *Educ.* Malvern Coll.; Trinity Coll., Cambridge. *M.* 1938, Dina Jinnah, *S.* Nusli Neville. *Dau.* Diana Clare. *Career:* Dir.: Nowrosjee Wadia & Sons (Private) Ltd.; Bombay Dyeing & Mfg. Co. Ltd.; Natl. & Grindlays Bank Ltd.; The Bombay Burmah Trading Corp. Ltd.; Tata Iron & Steel Co. Ltd.; Natl. Peroxide Ltd.; Chemicals & Fibres of India Ltd.; Sturdia Chemicals Ltd.; Botanium Ltd.; Tata Engineering & Locomotive Co. Ltd.; Herdillia Chemicals Ltd.; National Machinery Manufacturers Ltd.; Formica Ltd. *Address:* c/o Bombay House, Homi Mody Street, Fort Bombay 400 023, India.

**WADLEY, Douglas.** British solicitor and company director. *B.* 1904. *Educ.* Central Technical College High School. *M.* 1928, Vera Joyce Bodman. *S.* Douglas John and Peter Frank. *Daus.* Honora Rose and Patricia Vera Irene. *Career:* Chairman of Directors, Carlton and United Breweries (Queensland) Ltd., Queensland Television Ltd.. and Western Drive-in Pty. Ltd. Director: Mercer Pty. Ltd.; Member and Pres., Royal Natl Agricultural and Industrial Assn. of Queensland; Member & Chmn. Queensland Turf Club. *Address:* Nindethana, Nindethana Street, Indooroopilly, Brisbane, Qld. 4068, Australia.

**WADSWORTH, George.** British industrialist. *B.* 1902. *Educ.* Heath Grammar School (Halifax) and Willaston College (Nantwich). *M.* 1930. Gwinevere Shepherd. *Dau.* Rosemary. *Career:* Member of Parliament 1945–50 (served on Public Accounts Cttee. 1945–50). Member Halifax Town Council 1938–45. Dir., G. Wadsworth & Son Ltd., Halifax 1926—, and 10 other companies. Member: Commonwealth Parliamentary Assn., and Inter-parliamentary Assn. 1945. Conservative (Chmn., Vice-Pres. Howden Conservative Assn.). Exec. Member, British Atlantic Cttee. (NATO). *Address:* Kingston Grange, Halifax, West Yorks.

**WAGENHÖFER, Carl Friedrich.** German banker, *B.* 1910. *Educ.* Universities of Erlangen, Vienna, Kiel and Munich; Dipl. rer. pol. 1932; Assessor 1936. *M.* 1937, Gretl Hofmann. *S.* Gert. *Dau.* Erika. *Career:* Previously: Assessor, Economic Section, Government of Ansbach; Regierungsassessor, Department of Finance of Bavaria 1937; Regierungsrat (Head government official) 1939; Army Service (six years; successively gun and then Battery Commander, Adjutant and First Lieutenant); Chief of Section for inter-ministerial and super-regional questions at the Department of Finance of Bavaria; financial expert of the Länder at the Finance Committee of the Deutsche Bundesrat; member of the Conference of Ministers of Finance of the Länder 8½ years, 1947; Ministerialrat 1950; appointed to the Senate as Councillor of State, leading official of the Finance Authorities, and adviser of the Senate in financial affairs of the Free and Hanseatic State of Hamburg 1952; appointed President of the Landeszentralbank of Bavaria by the Prime Minister of Bavaria 1956; President, Landeszentralbank of Bavaria 1956—; Member, Central Bank Council of the German Bundesbank. *Publications:* a series of publications in professional journals and newspapers (dealing with financial problems, especially financial equalization between the Länder and the Bund); Der Föderalismus und die Notenbankverfassung (Richard Pflaum Verlag, Munich 1957); Währungspolitik in der Sozialen Markwirtschaft, (1961). Member, Managing Committee: Deutsches Museum; IFO—Institut für Wirtschaftsforschung; Bd. of Trustees, Gesellschaft der Freunde Haus der Kunst München. Manager, Gesellschaft zur Förderung der Münchner Opernfestspiele e.V. *Club:* Rotary (München Mitte). *Address:* Hermine-Bland-Str. 1, 8 München 90; and *office* Ludwigstr. 13, 8 Munich 22, Germany.

**WAGEUS, Olle,** MS. Swedish. *B.* 1913. *Educ.* Royal Tech. Univ. Stockholm (MS. Eng.). *M.* 1945, Kerstin Alexanderson *S.* 1. *Career:* Sales Mgr. AB Standard Radiofabrik (ITT group) 1939–52; Dir. AB Navigatorservice; Chmn. CGR Svenska AB, Thomson-CSF Elektronrör AB, & Decca Survey Sweden AB; Man. Dir. Decca Navigator och Radar AB. *Member:* Swedish Assn. Engineers & Architects; Rotary International. *Award:* Order of Vasa. *Address:* Karlaplan 12, Stockholm NO, Sweden; and *office:* Sandhamnsgatan 65, Stockholm.

**WAGNER, Charles Abraham.** American poet and journalist. *B.* 1901. *Educ.* Columbia College, Columbia Univ. (AB.), Nieman Fellow Harvard University. *M.* 1930, Celia B. Wagner. *S.* Carl. *Dau.* Carol Fern. *Career:* Book Reviewer, Brooklyn (N.Y.) Times-Union (1932–35), and New York World 1928–30; Drama Reviewer, N.Y. Morning Telegraph 1926–27; Sunday Editor, late N.Y. Daily Mirror 1933–57; Art and Book Critic to both daily and Sunday editions 1933–64; Exec. Secretary, Poetry Society of America 1964. Editor-in-Chief, New York Mirror Sunday Magazine. *Publications:* Poems of the Soil and Sea; Nearer the Bone—later poems; Prize Poems—an anthology (Editor); City and Country Cantos (in preparation); Harvard: Four Centuries and Freedoms—a popular history. Democrat. *Member:* American Philosophical Society. *Clubs:* Harvard (N.Y.C.); Nat. Arts. *Address:* 106 Morningside Drive, New York, N.Y. 10027; and *office* Poetry Society of America, 15 Gramercy Park, New York, N.Y. 10003, U.S.A.

**WAGNER, Chris (Emil Christian III).** American manufacturer and consultant. *B.* 1911. *Educ.* Chester (Pa.) public schools. *M.* (1) 1936, Ruth Olive Miller (*Dec.* March 1956), and (2) 1957, Esther Althea (Hossler) Weaver. *S.* Charles Valiant Wagner and (Rev.) Sherman Douglas Weaver. *Career:* Head, Mechanical Research, Frank Rieber Inc., West Los Angeles 1939–41; Head, Watch Gear Dept., Technical Oil Tool Corp., Hollywood 1942–43; Foreman, Camera Shop, Berndt-Bach Inc., Hollywood 1943–46; Owner, Watchmakers' Tools, Industrial Sapphire Products, El Monte, Calif. 1946–51; Owner, Scientific Instruments, Hemet 1951–54; Owner, Chris Wagner Co., Hemet, Calif. (specializing in spherical cavity bearing systems, gas lubricated bearings, valves, research in spherics) 1946—. Sponsor, Hour of Amazing Grace, Radio KHSJ, 1961–73. Republican. *Member:* Amer. Inst. of Physics; Optical Socy. of Amer.; Amer. Socy. of Lubrication Engineers; Instrument Socy. of Amer.; Socy. of Motion Picture and Television Engineers; Soc. of Manufacturing Engineers; American Watchmakers' Inst.; Christian Business Men's Cttee. International. Chmn.: Missionary Cttee., First Baptist Church of Hemet; Projectionist-Teacher, The Bible Visualized Classes 1973—. *Publications:* The Watchmakers' Lathe (Amer. Horologist, Oct. 1945); Industrial Sapphire in Motion Picture Equipment (with Walter Bach) (Journ. Socy. Motion Picture and TV Engineers, Jan. 1950). *Address:* Post Office Drawer 1317, 25124 Santa Fe Avenue, Hemet, Calif., 92343, U.S.A.

**WAGNER, George Corydon.** American lumberman. *B.* 1895. *Educ.* Yale University (PhB 1916) and Yale School of Forestry. *M.* 1924, Eulalie Merrill. *S.* George Corydon III. *Daus.* Wendy (Weyerhaeuser) and Merrill. (Ryman). *Career:* Vice Pres. and Treas. St Paul & Tacoma Lumber Co. 1933–60; Vice Pres. Winthrop Hotel Corp. 1949—; Formerly Pres., C. W. Griggs Investment Co. 1937–57, Douglas Fir Export Co. 1945–50, and Director, Griggs Cooper Co. 1938–52; Pres., The Wilkeson Co. 1939–60, Merrill & Wagner Ltd. 1961—; Chairman, Cariboo-Pacific Corp., Tacoma, 1961—, Merrill Canadian Properties, Vancouver, B.C., 1965—; Fellow, Oberlaender Foundation. Chmm., U.S. deleg. to 16th sess. of E.C.E. Timber Cttee. 1958 and 1959; Advisor to U.S. delegation, 3rd World Forestry Cong., Helsinki 1949; deleg. to 4th Cong., Dehra Dun 1954. President Tacoma General Hospital 1957–60; President, Western Forestry & Conservation Assn. 1955–60; Chmm. Finance Cttee., and Vice-Chairman, U.S. Delegation to Fifth World Forestry Congress (1958–60); Chairman, Cariboo Pacific Corp. 1961. Director: Booth Kelly Lumber Co. 1948–59, Merrill Ring Western Lumber Co., and Puget Sound National Bank, Republican. Member: International Dendrology Socy., London, 1967—, U.S. Chamb. of Com. (Dir.), Tacoma Consumers Heating (Co. Dir.), Natnl. Lumber Manufacturers Assn. (Dir., Chmn. and Pres. 1950–51), West Coast Lumbermen's Assn. (Dir. Pres. 1940–41), American Forest Products Industries (Pres. 1945–47), Tacoma Chamber of Commerce (Pres. 1935), Assn. of Washington Industries (Vice-Pres), Industrial Forestry Assn. (Dir.), Forest History Foundation (Dir.), Annie Wright Seminary Foundation (Dir.), U.S. Golf Assn., N.Y. (Exec. Cttee.), Aurelian Honor Socy., Socy. of Sigma Xi, Yale Univ. 1916; Delta Phi, St. Elmo. *Clubs:* Valley Club, Montecito, Calif.; Union Club, Victoria, B.C., Canada; Yale (N.Y.); University (Seattle); The '487': Tacoma Country & Golf; The Tacoma. *Address:* P.O. Box 99906, Tacoma, Wash. 98499, U.S.A.

**WAGNER, Jean.** Luxembourger diplomat. *B.* 1924. *Educ.* Univ. of Basle, Lausanne and Paris; Coll. of Europe Bruges LLD. *M.* 1957, Laura Wissiak. *S.* Antoine. *Daus.* Beatrice and Federica. *Career:* Practiced law in Luxembourg 1951–53; Federation des Industriels 1953–54; Attaché of Legation, Min of Foreign Affairs 1954–57; Secy. of Legation 1957–63; Luxembourg Embassy. Paris, 1959–64; Counsellor of Legation 1963–65; Rep. of Luxembourg, The Council of Europe 1964–69; Dir. Political Affairs, Ministry Foreign Affairs 1965–69; Ambassador of Luxembourg to Washington since 1969; to Mexico 1970–74; to Ottawa 1970–74. Amb. of Luxembourg in Rome since 1974. *Awards:* Officier des Ordres Nationaux de la Couronne de Chêne et du Mérite; Grand Officer of Orange-Nassau; Grand Officer, order of Leopold II; Legion of Honor Official (France); Commander, Order of Merit (France); Commander, Order of Merit (Italy). *Address:* Luxembourg Embassy, Via Guerrieri 3 (Aventino), Rome 00153, Italy.

**WAGNER, Robert F., Jr.** *B.* 1910. *Educ.* Yale Univ. (AB 1933; LLB 1937); Harvard School of Business Administration. *M.* Susan Edwards (*Dec.* 1964). *S.* 2. *Career:* Member of New York State Assembly 1938–41; Tax Commnr., N.Y.C. 1946; Commr. for Housing and Buildings 1947; Chmn. City Planning Commission 1948; Pres. Borough of Manhattan, Greater New York City 1949–53; Mayor of the City of New York 1954–65; Partner in law firm of Finley, Kumble, Wagner, Heine & Underberg, N.Y.C. First Vice-President of N.Y. State Constitutional Convention; U.S. Ambassador to Spain 1968–69. Served in World War II (8th Air Force; discharged as Lieut.-Col.) 1942–45. *Address: office* 425 Park Avenue, New York, N.Y. 10022, U.S.A.

**WAGNSSON, Ruben.** Swedish administrator. *B.* 8 Sept. 1891. *Educ.* University of Lung (BA). *M.* 1915, Helga Nilsson. *S.* Torgny, Bjorn. *Dau.* Ingrid. *Career:* Member, Second Chamber, Riksdag 1921–27, First Chamber 1928–47; member. Royal Board of Education 1935–47; Pres. T.C.O. 1937–47; Chmn. Swedish-Norwegian Relief Work 1942–45; President, Swedish European Relief 1946–48; President, I.O.G.T. 1947–66; Governor, Provinces of Kalmar and Oland, Stateholder of Kalmar Castle 1947–58; Pres., State Commussion for Air Purification 1963–68; President, International Council on Alcohol & Addicts 1960—. *Publications:* Kommunernas skoluppgifter; Folkskolestadgan; Svenska folkskolan i ord och bild; Var folkundervisning fran medeltid till enbetskola; Democracy in Development. Memoirs. *Address:* Burtraskgatan 61, 16221 Vällingby, Sweden.

**WAGSTAFF, Robert W.** American. *B.* 1909. *Educ.* Kansas Univ. (AB 1930); Harvard University (LLB 1933). *M.* 1936, Katherine Hall. *S.* Robert Hall and Thomas Walton. *Dau.* Katherine Hall Tinsman. *Career:* Admitted to Kansas Bar 1933; general law practice 1933–34; Attorney, Sinclair Refining Co., Kansas City 1935–45; General Counsel, The Vendo Company, Vice-Chmn. Chief Exec. Officer 1945–61; Chairman & President, The Coca-Cola Bottling Co. of Mid America Inc., Lenexa, Kansas; Pres., Mid America Container Corp. Lenexa; Former Chmn., Fed. Reserve Board of Kansas City, Mo. *Address:* 9000 Marshall Drive, P.O. Box 500, Shawnee Mission, Kansas 66201, U.S.A.

**WAINWRIGHT, Richard Scurrah,** M.P. British. *B.* 1918. *Educ.* Open Scholarship to Clare Coll., Cambridge—BA (Hons.) in History. *M.* 1948, Joyce Mary Hollis. *S.* 1. *Daus.* 2. *Career:* Liberal MP for Colne Valley 1966–70 & since 1974; Chmn., Liberal Party 1971–73; Liberal Spokesman on Industry & Trade since 1974. *Member:* Pres., West Yorkshire Society of Chartered Accountants, 1966. *Publications:* Own As You Earn (1960). *Clubs:* Reform; National Liberal. *Address:* The Heath, Adel, Leeds LS16 8EG.

**WAKEFIELD, Sir Peter George Arthur,** KBE, CMG. British Diplomat. *B.* 1922. *Educ.* Cranleigh Sch.; Corpus Christi Coll., Oxford. *M.* 1951, Felicity Maurice-Jones. *S.* 4. *Dau.* 1. *Career:* Army Service 1942–47; Military Govt., Eritrea 1946–47; Hulton Press 1947–49; entered Diplomatic Service 1949; Middle East Centre for Arab Studies 1950; 2nd Sec., Amman 1950–52; Foreign Office 1953–55; 1st Sec., Brit. Middle East Office, Nicosia 1955–56; 1st Sec. (Commercial), Cairo 1956; Admin. Staff Coll., Henley 1957; 1st Sec. (Commercial), Vienna 1957–60, Tokyo 1960–63; Foreign Office 1964–66; Consul-Gen. & Counsellor, Benghazi 1966–69; Econ. & Commercial Counsellor 1970–72, then Minister 1973, Tokyo; Seconded as Special Adviser on the Japanese Market, Brit. Overseas Trade Bd. 1973–75; HM Ambassador to the Lebanon since 1975. *Decorations:* Knight Commander, Order of the British Empire, 1977; Companion, Order of St. Michael & St. George. *Club:* Travellers'. *Address:* Lincoln House, Montpelier Row, Twickenham, Middx.; and *office* c/o Foreign & Commonwealth Office, King Charles Street, London SW1A 2AH.

**WAKEFIELD OF KENDAL, Lord.** British politician. *B.* 10 March 1898. *Educ.* Sedbergh School; Pembroke College, Cambridge (MA). *M.* 1919, Rowena Doris Lewis. *Daus.* 3. *Career:* Served World War I, R.N.A.S. and R.A.F. (dispatches) 1914–18, World War II, Director, Air Training Corps 1942–44; captained English Rugby football team; MP (Nat. Cons.) for Swindon 1935–45, (Cons.) for St. Marylebone, London 1945–63; Past-President, Rugby Football Union; Chairman, Parliamentary and Scientific Committee 1952–55; member, Exec. Cttee. and Council, National Playing Fields Association. President: British Sub-Aqua Club 1967–71; British Water Ski Federation; Metropolitan Association of Building Societies. Director: Portman Building Society; and other companies. *Address:* 71 Park Street, London, W.1.

**WAKEHAM, John,** FCA, JP, MP. British Politician & Chartered Accountant. *B.* 1932. *Educ.* Charterhouse. *M.* 1965, Anne Roberta Bailey. *S.* 2. *Career:* 2nd Lieutenant, Royal Artillery 1955–57; Chartered Accountant & Company Dir. since 1957; Justice of the Peace since 1972; Conservative Candidate, Coventry 1966, Putney 1970; Conservative MP for Maldon (Essex) since 1974. *Member:* Inst. of Chartered Accountants since 1955. *Publications:* various pamphlets & articles. *Clubs:* St. Stephen's. *Address:* House of Commons, London SW1A 0AA.

**WAKELY, Leonard John Dean,** CMG, OBE. *B.* 1909. *Educ.* Westminster School and Christ Church, Oxford (MA). *M.* 1938, Margaret Houssemayne Tinson. *S.* 2. British Deputy High Commissioner in Canada 1962–65. British Ambassador at Rangoon 1965–67. *Address:* Long Meadow, Forest Road, East Horsley, Surrey.

**WAKEMAN, Arthur G.** American paper manufacturer. *B.* 1898. *Educ.* Massachusetts Inst. of Technology (BSc). *M.* 1928, Loraine Cheeseman. *Dau.* Frances N. (Parker). *Career:* U.S. Army 1918; Kimberly-Clark Corp. 1924; Fox River Paper Co. 1928–40; War Production Board 1941–44; Mission on Economic Affairs, London 1944; Survey of Paper Industry for U.S. Army in Europe 1945; Director, Kimberley-Clark Corp. 1957—; Royal Crown Cola Co. 1958; Green Bay Packaging Inc. 1964. For U.S. Dept. of State in Republic of China 1963–64. Publisher, Paper Industry News Summary 1963—; for U.S. Dept. to Tunisia 1965; Listas Telefonicas, Braseleiras, Brazil 1967; U.S. State Dept. to Chile 1968; John Hoad Assoc. to Argentine 1969; Int. Exec. Corps to Turkey 1970; Internal Revenue to France & Sweden 1970; Ecuadorian Govt. to Ecuador 1970; Int. Exec. Service Corps to Philippines 1971; Development Consultants Ltd. to India 1971; Diversified Service to Puerto Rico 1972; Int. Exec. Service Corps. to Argentina 1973. Republican. *Clubs:* University (Chicago); North Shore Golf (Menasha, Wis.); The Country; Delray Beach (Florida). *Address:* 130 Limekiln, Neenah, Wis. 54956 and (Winter) 2075 So. Ocean Drive, Delray Beach, Florida, U.S.A.

**WALCH, Richard Fleming,** FAIM. psc. British. *B.* 1923. *Educ.* Hutchins School (Hobart); Royal Military College; Duntroon A.C.T.; Australian Staff College (p.s.c.). *M.* 1947. Elizabeth Mary Downie. *S.* Geoffrey Richard Arthur. *Daus.* Elizabeth Anne Gillian Margaret, Prudence Mary and Deborah Jane. *Career:* Adjutant 2/7 Inf. Battalion 1944–45; Staff Capt. 34 Inf. Brigade BCOF 1945–46; DAA and QMG, Kobe, Sub Area, BCOF, Japan 1946–47; Brigade Major, 11 Aust. Inf. Brigade 1949–50; Instructor, Tactics, Royal Military Coll., Duntroon 1951–54; Dir.: J. C. McPhee Pty. Ltd. 1956–72; O. B. M. Pty. Ltd. 1956–72; Platypus Publications Pty. Ltd. 1964—; Chas. Davis Ltd. 1965—; Cooperative Motors 1970—; Mercury-Walch Pty. Ltd. 1970–74; Man. Dir. J. Walch & Sons Pty. Ltd.; Hobart Tasmania 1963; (all firms located in Hobart); Dir., Investment & Merchant Finance Corp. Ltd., Adelaide 1976—. Member: Hutchins School Board of Management 1959–69; Council Fahan Presbyterian Girls' College, 1969–75; Executive Councillor, Printing & Allied Trades Employers Federation of Australia 1965–73. Member, General Cttee., Hobart Savings Bank 1960–64; Pres. Hobart Chamber of Commerce 1962–64; Hutchins School Board of Management 1965–66; Tasmanian Branch, Australian Forces Overseas Fund 1968–69 *Club:* Tasmanian (Hobart); Kingston Beach Golf; Royal Yacht; Royal Tennis (Hobart). *Address:* 17 Taroona Crescent, Taroona, Tasmania; and *office* 130 Macquarie Street, Hobart, Tasmania.

**WALCUTT, Lester O.** American mechanical engineer (ret.). *B.* 1914. *Educ.* Ohio State Univ. (BME 1936); Reg. Prof. Eng. of W. Virginia and Kentucky. *M.* 1936, Gertrude Reeves. *Daus.* Trudy Louise and Billie Jeane. *Career:* With Borden Milk Co. 1936; Norfolk & Western Railway Co. 1936–41; Engineering and Maintenance Dir., Huntington Alloy Products Div., The International Nickel Co. Inc., Huntington, W. Virginia 1964 (Works Engineer 1952–64–72). *Member:* Amer. Socy. of Mechanical Engineers. Mason. *Club:* Engineers' (Huntington). *Address:* 652 Boca Ciega Point, Boulevard North, St Petersburg, Florida 33708, U.S.A.

**WALDBRUNNER, Karl.** Austrian politician. *B.* 25 Nov. 1906 *Educ.* Technische Hochschule, Vienna (Dipl Ing). *M.* 1969 Friedl Sinkovc. *S.* Karl. *Dau.* Martha. *Career:* After completion of studies went to Soviet Russia to work on the reconstruction of industry; took part in building of power plants in the Ural Mountains. After returning to Austria in 1937 became a leading engineer at Schoeller-Bleckmann Steel Works, Ternitz. During German occupation of Austria worked illegally for Socialist Party; Under-Secretary of State for Commerce, Industry and Transport in provisional Government 1945; Secretary of State for Protection of Property and Economic Planning 1945–46; En. Ex. and Min. Plen. to U.S.S.R. 1946; Central Secretary. Socialist Party 1946–57; Minister of Transport and Nationalized Industries 1949–56; Minister of Communications and of Electric Power Development 1956–62. Member (Soc.) Nationalrat 1945–71. Second President of Parliament, 1962–70. President of Parliament, 1970–71; Vice-Pres. Oesterreichischen National bank since 1972. *Awards:* Grosses Goldenes Ehrenzeichen am Bande für Verdienste um die Republik Österreich. *Address:* Postfach 61, A-1011 Wien, Austria.

**WALDENSTRÖM, Erland.** Swedish. *B.* 1911. *Educ.* Royal Inst. of Technology. *M.* 1945, Dorothy Ethel Boleyn Drewry. *S.* Martin. *Daus.* Hedda and Cecilia. *Career:* Engineer, Kornäs Sågverks AB, Gävle 1934, 1936–40; Chief, Technical Office, Svenska Cellulosa AB, Sundsvall 1942–46 (Chief Engineer 1947–49); Pres. 1950–71, Board of Gränges AB. Chmn. since 1971; Chmn. of the Concert Assocn. of Stockholm 1973—; Lamco Joint Venture 1960–75; Dir. 1958–70, Liberian Iron Ore Ltd. (Toronto), Chmn. and Pres. since 1971; Chmn. Gränges American Corp.; Dir. Luossavaara AB 1950—; (Pres. 1950–57); Liberian Amer-Swedish Minerals Co. (LAMCO) Monrovia 1955–75, Chmn. since 1975; Chmn. Swedish Lance Syndicate 1963—; Skandinaviska Enskilda Banken 1957—, Vice-Chmn. 1968—; AB Bofors (Bofors) 1960—; The Swedish Lamco Syndicate 1963—; S.A. Cockerill-Ougrée-Providence et Espérance—Longdoz (Seraing) since 1970—. *Member:* Export Technical research development, Swedish Fed. of Industries 1940–46; Official Expert and Secy. State Cttee. on Technical Research 1941–42; Industrial Counsellor, U.N. Economic Commission for Europe (ECE) Geneva 1948; Royal Swedish Academy of Engineering Sciences 1948—, Pres. since 1977; Gen. Export Assn. of Sweden 1951–59; Swedish Employers Confederation 1951–72; The Royal Swedish Opera 1961–72; Chmn. Swedish Mining Assn. 1957–59; The Thiel Art Gallery 1961—; Swedish Export Assn. 1971—. Dir. Ironmasters Fed. 1944—; Concert Assn. 1956—; Chmn., Industrial Inst. for Economic & Social Research 1975—. *Awards:* Comdr. Royal Order of Vasa, and Knight 1st Class Royal Order of North Star; Grand Banner of the African Star; Fellow, Royal Society of Arts. *Publications:* On Industrial Progress in Sweden (1942); Waste and Residual Products in Forestry (1942); Development Trends in Forestry (1946). The Lamco Project—a Commercial Contribution to African Economic Development (1961); several essays on technical and economic questions; Industrial Democracy in Theory and Practice (1968); Competitive Power and Profitability in Swedish Industry (1971); Economic Policy & the Future of Industry (1973); Investments in Developing Countries—Hopes & Disappointments (1974); Structural Problems in Diversified Companies (1974). *Address:* Villa Gröndal, Manillavägen 17, Djurgarden, S-115 25 Stockholm; and *office* Gränges, Fack, S-103 26 Stockholm 16, Sweden.

**WALDER, (Alan) David,** ERD, MP. British Politician & Author. *B.* 1928. *Educ.* Latymer Upper Sch., London; Christ Church, Oxford—MA (History). *M.* 1956, Elspeth Milligan. *S.* 1. *Daus.* 3. *Career:* National Service & Reserve with Queen's Royal Irish Hussars; Called to the Bar, Inner Temple 1956–66; Conservative MP for High Peak of Derbyshire 1961–66, & for Clitheroe Div. of Lancashire since 1970; Asst. Government Whip 1973–74; Mem. of Executive of the 1922 Cttee. since 1975. *Member:* Executive of National Book League; Royal United Services Inst. *Decorations:*

Emergency Reserve Decoration. *Publications:* Stability & Survival (with Julian Critchley) (1961); Fiction: Bags of Swank (1963); The Short List (1964); The House Party (1966); The Fair Ladies of Salamanca (1967); Non-Fiction: The Chanak Affair (1968); The Short Victorious War (1972); Nelson (1978). *Clubs:* Cavalry & Guards. *Address:* The White House, Grimsargh, nr. Preston, Lancashire; and 45 Courtenay Street, London SE11.

**WALDHEIM, Kurt.** Secretary General United Nations. *B.* 1918. *Educ.* High School. Consular Acad. of Vienna; University of Vienna (LLD 1944). *M.* 1944, Elisabeth Ritschel. *S.* 1. *Dau.* 2. *Career:* Entered Foreign Service 1945; Political Division of Foreign Office, Vienna, Office of For. Minister; member of Austrian delegation to Paris, London and Moscow for negotiations on Austrian State Treaty, 1945–47; 1st Secy. Embassy, Paris 1948–51; Counsellor, head of Personnal Div., Foreign Office, Vienna 1951–55; Permanent Austrian Observer UN 1955–56; Min. Plen. to Canada 1956–58, Ambassador 1958–60. Dir.-Gen., Political Affairs Dept., Ministry of Foreign Affairs, Vienna 1960–64; Permanent Representative of Austria to the UN New York 1964–68; Chmn. Outer Space Cttee. UN 1958–60 & 1970–71; Federal Min., For Foreign Affairs Republic of Austria 1968–70; Candidate for President of Austria 1971; Permanent Representative UN 1970–71; App. Sec. Gen. 1971. *Awards:* LLD from following: Univ. of Chile, Carleton Univ. (Ottawa), Jawarharal Nehru Univ. (New Delhi), Fordham Univ., Univ. of Bucharest, Wagner Coll. (N.Y), Catholic Univ. of America (Washington, D.C.), Wilfrid Laurier Univ. (Waterloo, Canada), Catholic Univ. of Leuven (Belgium), Charles Univ. (Prague), Hamilton Coll. (N.Y.), Univ. of Denver (Colorado), Univ. of the Philippines (Manila), Univ. of Nice (France), American Univ. (Washington, D.C.), Kent State Univ. (Ohio), Univ. of Warsaw (Poland). *Publications:* The Austrian Example, (1971/73). *Address:* United Nations, New York, N.Y. 10017, U.S.A.

**WALDOCK, Sir (Claud) Humphrey (Meredith),** CMG, OBE. QC. International lawyer. *B.* 1904. *Educ.* Uppingham Sch; Brasenose College, Oxford; BA 1927; BCL 1928; DCL 1952. *M.* 1934, Ethel Beatrice Williams. *S.* 1. *Dau.* 1. *Career:* Barrister-at-Law, Gray's Inn 1928–30 (Bencher 1957—); Treas. 1971. Fellow and Lecturer in Law, Brasenose College 1930–47; Chichele Professor of International Law. and Fellow of All Souls College, Oxford 1947–72; Assessor in Chancellor's Court 1947–72; Judge International Court of Justice, The Hague since 1973; Member of Curatorium of the Hague Academy since 1977. *Member:* European Commission on Human Rights 1954–61 (Pres. 1955–61). Judge, European Court of Human Rights 1966–74; Vice-Pres. 1968, Pres. 1971–74; Member International Law Commission 1961–73; (Special Rapporteur on Law of Treaties 1962–66; On Succession of States in respect of Treaties, 1968–72; Pres. 1967) and of Perm. Ct. of Arb. 1965—; Chmn., Cttee., Inquiry into Oxford Univ. Press 1967–70. Temporary Principal, Admiralty 1940 (Asst. Secretary 1943, Principal Asst. Secy. 1944); United Kingdom Commissioner on the Italo-Yugoslav Boundary Commission and Free Territory of Trieste 1946; member, Hebdomadal Council, Oxford Univ. 1949–61; Queen's Counsel 1951; Member: Swedish-Finnish, Swedish-Swiss, Swedish-Turkish, Swedish-Spanish, German-Swiss, U.S.-Danish, Chilean-Italian and Danish-Norwegian Cncl. Comm. *Publications:* International Law: The Regulation of the Use of Force, (1952); General Course on Public International Law, (1962); Editor, 6th edition, Brierly's Law of Nations, (1963); articles in the British Yearbook of International Law and other journals on the Plea of Domestic Jurisdiction; Decline of the Optional Clause; Altmark Incident; Anglo-Norwegian Fisheries Case; Continental Shelf, etc.; English Law: The Law of Mortgages. Hon. Fellow, Brasenose College 1960—; Associate Member, Institute of International Law 1950—, Member 1961. *Club:* United Oxford & Cambridge University. *Address:* 6 Lathbury Road, Oxford; and All Souls College, Oxford.

**WALE, Laurence Sydney.** South African company director. Hon. Consul for Mexico in South Africa 1952–74. *B.* 1916. *Educ.* Diocesan College and University of Cape Town. *M.* 1952, Stephanie Brink Bester. *S.* Peter Laurence. *Dau.* Cheryl Ann. *Career:* Served in World War II (Officer HQ. 6th S.A. Armoured Div. in Egypt and Italy); after the war appointed editor of Spotlight, national weekly journal for S.A.; founded Architect & Builder (monthly journal for architects in S.A. and Rhodesia) 1951; founded building centres in Cape Town, Johannesburg, Durban, Salisbury and Bulawayo; Hon. Governor, Wedgeport International Tuna Tournament in Nova Scotia; captained Springbok game fishing team, New Zealand 1960; Pres., Western Province Clay Pigeon Shooting Assn.; Crew of Sayula II, winner of Round-the-World Yacht race 1974. *Address:* Primrose Avenue, Claremont, Cape Town, South Africa.

**WALES-WALDES, Alexander Peter.** International trade fair consultant and organiser. *B.* 1904. *Educ.* Vienna. *M.* 1940, Mary Theresa Chlupova. *Dau.* Yvonne. *Career:* Journalist; Publisher Economics and Modern Architecture (Vienna and European branches) 1926–38; British Army, 1939–45; founder and editor, Scottish Industrial Estates News 1945–49; organised Made in Scotland exhibits, Canadian International Trade Fair, Toronto, 1949; Director for Britain of the Chicago International Trade Fair 1950; promoted International Gift and Fancy Goods Show, New York (concurrently European Director of the Fair) 1953–54–55; European Director, New York Motor Show 1953–54–55; Consultant and Chief Planner, U.S. World Trade Fair, New York, 1955; Director, British & Commonwealth Office of same Fair 1956–57–58; Consultant, Planner, and Executive Director, U.S.A. International Book Exhibitions 1956–69; President, Tokyo International Book Exhibitions 1958–65. Publisher, Publisher's International Year Book and World Library Directory. *Publications:* numerous contributions to newspapers on international trade fairs and exhibitions. *Address:* 34 Hamlet Gardens, London, W.6.

**WALEY-COHEN, Sir Bernard Nathaniel,** Bt. *B.* 1914. *Educ.* H.M.S. Britannia; (Royal Naval College, Dartmouth); Clifton and Magdalene College Cambridge; MA. *M.* 1943, Hon. Joyce Constance Ina, MA, JP. *S.* Stephen Harry and Robert Bernard. *Daus.* Rosalind Alice (Burdon) and Eleanor Joanna. *Career:* Gunner. H.A.C. 1937–38. underwriting member of Lloyd's (London) 1939—; Dir. Matthews Wrightson Pulbrook Ltd.; Bray Gibb (Agencies) Ltd.; Lloyd's Bank Ltd. Central London Region; Kleeman Industrial Holdings Ltd. and other Companies. Chmn., Public Works Loan Board since 1972. Liveryman Clothworkers' Co. 1936; Court 1966, Master 1975–76; Principal, Ministry of Fuel & Power 1940–47; Vice-Chmn., Chmn. Palestine Corporation, Union Bank of Israel 1947–54; Chmn., Simo Securities Trust Ltd. 1955–70. Alderman City of London (Portsoken Ward) 1949; one of H.M. Lieutenants for City of London 1949; Sheriff of London 1955, Lord Mayor of London 1960–61; Gov. the Hon. the Irish Society 1973–76. *Member:* of Council and Board of Govs., Clifton Coll. 1952—; Hon. Treas. Jewish Welfare Board 1948–53; Vice-Pres. United Synagogue 1952–61; Pres., Jewish Museum 1964—; Member of College and Finance Cttees. Univ. Coll. London 1953, Treas. 1962–70; Vice Chmn. Coll. Cttee. 1970. Chmn. 1971; Chmn. Devon & Somerset Staghounds 1953—; Member Marshall Aid Commemoration Cttee. 1957–60; Member of Court (since 1966), and Senate (since 1962), London Univ.; Vice-Pres. Anglo-Jewish Association 1962—; Pres. Bath & West Show 1962–63; Devon Cattle Breeders' Society 1963; Member, Nat. Corp. for Care of Old People 1965—; Central Council of Probation 1965–69; Chmn. Wellesley House Preparatory School 1965–77; Treas., British Field Sports Society 1965—. *Awards:* Kt. Bach. 1957; Baronet 1961; Hon. LLD, London University 1963; KStJ 1961. Honorary Liveryman Farmers' Company 1961; Fellow Univ. Coll. London 1963. *Clubs:* Boodles; Pratts; City Livery; Univ. Pitt (Cambridge); M.C.C.; Harlequins R.F.C.; Jockey Club Rooms (Newmarket). *Address:* 11 Little St. James's Street, London, SW1A 1DP; and Honeymead, Simonsbath, Minehead, Somerset, TA24 7JX.

**WALFORD, A. Ernest.** Canadian corporation executive. *B.* 1896. *Educ.* grad. Westmount (Que.) Academy 1915. *M.* 1922, Olive M. Dyke. *S.* A. Harvie. D. *Career:* Partner, Alfred Walford & Sons, Chartered Accountants, Montreal 1920–29; Dir. Treasurer & Secretary, Jas. A. Ogilvy's Ltd., 1929–39; Director and Secretary-Treasurer, Henry Morgan & Company 1946–61; President and Director, Morgan Trust Co. 1948–63; Chairman of Board, Canadian Vickers Ltd., Montreal 1959–67; Hon. Dir. and Chmn. Montreal Adv. Bd. Canada Trust Co. 1961–72; Chmn. E.G.M. Cape & Company Ltd. 1965–68; Vice-Pres. & Dir., Mercantile Bank of Canada 1961–70. Fellow & National Dir., Canadian Chartered Inst. of Secretaries and Administrators. *Member:* Order of Chartered Accountants of Quebec; Institute of Directors. Past President: Federation of Commonwealth Chambers of Commerce Montreal Board of Trade, Executive Development Institute. Hon. Chairman English Speaking Union in Canada, Member, Met. Advisory Board, Montreal Y.M.C.A.; National Adv. Board, Salvation Army. Canadian Army 1914–19 and 1939–46; Adj.-General Canadian Forces 1944–46. *Clubs:* St James's; Forest and Stream. *Address:* Apt.

E 90, The Chateau, 1321 Sherbrooke St. West, Montreal H3G 1J4; and *office:* Suite 1400, 635 Dorchester Blvd. West, Montreal H3B 1S3, Quebec, Canada.

**WALFORD, Michael Arthur Howard**, FIMech, MIEE, FI Marine E. British. *B.* 1924. *Educ.* Cheltenham Coll.; Cambridge Univ. (MA Hons.). *M.* 1954, Jill Adrienne Gluckstein. *S.* 2. *Daus.* 2. *Career:* Asst. Engineer Wm. Cory & Son Ltd. 1948–51; Tech. Engineer Philips Elec. Ltd. 1951–53; Deputy-Man. Dir. Plenty & Son Ltd. 1954–69; Man. Dir. Leadenhall-Sterling Investments Ltd. 1969–70; Consulting Engineer, Dir. Shoosmith Howe Consultants Ltd. 1971–75; Man. Dir. Saunderson & Costin Ltd. *Clubs:* O. & C. Univ. *Address:* Baughurst House, Ramsdell, Basingstoke, Hants.; and *office* Andover Road, Highclere, nr. Newbury, Berks.

**WALG, Lorenz Friedrich Andreas.** Dipl. Kfm.; Dr. rer. pol. German economist consultant and lecturer. *B.* 1920. *Educ.* J. W. Goethe University (Frankfurt/M.); Economic and Social Sciences, French and English. *M.* 1952, Anna Margareta Nassenstein. *Dau.* Anna Karolina. *Career:* Assistant, Goethe University 1948–50; with DEMAG A.G., Duisburg 1950–51; Dozent f. Betriebswirtschaftslehre, Akademie der Arbeit i.d. Universität, Frankfurt 1952–67; Member of Managing Board, German Rubber Manufacturers Assn., Frankfurt 1953–64; Government Missions to Cameroons, Liberia, Senegal, Upper Volta Netherlands Antilles and East Africa 1964–65; Lecturer U.N.-African Inst. for Economic Development & Planning, Dakar, 1967–68. Head, Bureau Führ. Kräfte zu Int. Organisation in der ZAV, Bundesanstalt für Arbeit, Frankfurt, 1969—. Previously Chairman of several committees of the German rubber industry 1954–64, and of the Taxation Committee of the Bureau de Liaison des Industries du Caoutchouc de la C.C.E. (Brussels) 1958–64. *Publications:* Richtlinien für die Buchführung in der Kautschukindustrie; and other publications. *Address:* Wiesenstrasse 48, Offenbach am Main, Germany.

**WALGREEN, Charles R., Jr.** Registered Pharmacist. *B.* 1906. *Educ.* University of Michigan (PhC 1928). *M.* 1933, Mary Ann Leslie. *S.* Charles R. III, and James Alan. *Dau.* Leslie Ann (Pratt). *Career:* Pres. 1939–63, Chmn. of Board 1963–71, and Dir. 1934–77; Walgreen Co. Dir.: Sanborn Hnos., Mexico City 1946–77; The First Chicago Corporation 1970–71; The First National Bank of Chicago, 1969–71; King-Stevenson Gas & Oil Co. 1961–63. Director: Evanston Hospital Assn. 1955–64 & 1968— (Vice-Pres. 1961–62); Univ. of Michigan Development Council 1957–63; American Foundation for Pharmaceutical Education (Past Pres.); International Museum of Surgical Science & Hall of Fame (Past Sec.); National Assn. of Chain Drug Stores 1941–69 (Past Pres.). Hon. MSc Univ. of Michigan 1951; Hon. DSc North Dakota State Univ. 1968; Rho Chi Member; Past Vice-Pres., Chicago Assoc. of Commerce & Industry. *Clubs:* Commercial; Executives; Rotary: Chicago Yacht; North Shore Country; Dixon Country; Key Largo Anglers; Chub Cay (Bahamas); Tavern; Adventurers; Tau Kappa Epsilon; Chicago. *Address:* 200 Wilmot Road, Deerfield, Illinois 60015, U.S.A.

**WALKER, Brooks Jr.**, BA, MBS. American. *B.* 1928. Educ. Univ. of California (BA, Econ.); Harvard Grad. School, Business Admin. (MBS, Finance). *M.* 1955, Margaret Kirby. *S.* 1. *Daus.* 2. *Career:* various previous appointments, United States Leasing Corp.; Dir. Bank of California, N.A.; Dillingham Corp.; Fibreboard Corp.; The Gap Stores Inc.: System Development Corp.; Canadian Dominion Leasing Co. Ltd. Chmn. San Francisco Real Estate Investors; Chmn. United States Leasing International Inc. *Clubs:* Burlingame County; Pacific Union; River Club of New York. *Address:* 2930 Broadway, San Francisco, Cal.; and *office:* 633 Battery Street, San Francisco, Cal., U.S.A.

**WALKER, Sir Charles Michael**, GCMG. British. *B.* 1916. *Educ.* Charterhouse and New College, Oxford (2nd Class Honours Degree PPE). *M.* 1945, Enid Dorothy McAdam. *S.* Peter Graham. *Dau.* Katrina Frances. *Career:* Enlisted Oct. 1939; commissioned in R.A. March 1940; service in India and Iraq 1940–44; British Army Staff, Washington 1944–45; released with rank of Lieut-Col. 1946. Principal, Dominions Office 1947; on secondment to Foreign Service as First Secretary, British Embassy, Washington 1949–51; Assistant Secretary in offices in Calcutta and Delhi of British High Commission in India 1952–55; Establishment Officer, Commonwealth Relations Office 1955–57; Imperial Defence College 1958; Director of Establishment and Organization, Commonwealth Relations Office 1959; High Commissioner to Ceylon 1962–65; to Malaysia 1966–71; Secy. Overseas Development Admin. Foreign and Commonwealth Office 1971–73; High Commissioner to India 1974–76. *Clubs:* Travellers', Oriental (London). *Address:* 40 Bourne Street London, S.W.1.

**WALKER, Sir (Edward) Ronald**, CBE. Australian economist and diplomat. *B* 26 Jan. 1907. *Educ.* University of Sydney (MA), DSc. (Econ); Cambridge University (PhD, LittD). *M.* 1933, Louise Donckers. *S.* Ronald Alfred. *Dau.* Denise. *Career:* Lecturer in Economics, University of Sydney 1927–38; Economic Adviser, State Treasurery, New South Wales 1938–39; Professor of Economics, University of Tasmania and Economic Adviser to Tasmanian Government 1939–41; Chief Economic Adviser and Deputy Dir.-Gen., Department of War Organization of Industry, Australia1941–45; attached H.Q., UNRRA. 1945; Counsellor and intermittently Chargé d'Affairs, Embassy, Paris 1945–50; Economic Counsellor for Europe, 1946–50; Member, Executive Board, UNESCO 1946–50; Australian Representative, Governing Body, I.L.O. 1947–49. Economic and Social Council, United Nations 1948–50, 1962–64, President 1964; at UN General Assembly 1946, 48, 50, 55–58; UN Adv. Cttee. on Science and Technology 1964–74; UN Economic Commission for Asia and Far East 1955, and UN Commission for Unification and Rehabilitation of Korea 1955; Exec. member, Australian National Security Resources Board 1950–52; Ambassador to Japan 1952–55; Permanent Rep. to UN 1956–59; Representative on Security Council 1956–57; Ambassador to France 1959–68. Ambassador to Federal Republic of Germany 1968–71; Amb. to OECD Paris 1971–73. *Publications:* An Outline of Australian Economics; Australia in the World Depression; Money; Unemployment Policy; War-time Economics; From Economic Theory to Policy; Australian Economy in War and Reconstruction. *Address:* 1 rue de Longchamp, Paris 16e, France.

**WALKER, Harold.** MP. *B.* 1927. *Educ.* Manchester College of Technology. *M.* 1956, Barbara. *Dau.* Lyn. *Career:* Member of Parliament for Doncaster; Government Whip 1967–68, Parly. Under-Secy. of State at Dept. of Employment & Productivity 1968–70; Front Bench (opposition) Spokesman on Industrial Relations 1970–74; Parly. Under-Secy. of State, Dept. of Employment 1974–76, & Minister of State since 1976. *Address:* 25 Grange Road, Bessacarr, Doncaster, Yorks.

**WALKER, James Herron.** American. *B.* 1907. *Educ.* University of Kansas (AB 1929) and Harvard Graduate School (MBA 1931). *M.* 1939, Louise McKelvy. *S.* Graham McKelvy, James Addison and Douglas Corwin. *Career:* Vice-Pres., Finance, Trustee Pension Fund, and Member Finance Committee, Bathlehem Steel Corporation, June 1955—. *Member:* Phi Beta Kappa; Beta Theta Pi; Council of Financial Executives; National Industrial Conference Board; N.Y. Society of Security Analysts. *Clubs:* Blooming Grove Hunting & Fishing (Hawley, Pa.); The Leash, Anglers, and University (all N.Y.C.); Jupiter Island (Hobe Sound, Fla.); Saucon Valley Country (Bethlehem, Pa.). *Address: office:* Bethlehem Steel Corporation, Bethlehem, Pa. 18016, U.S.A.

**WALKER, Rt. Hon. Peter Edward**, PC, MBE, MP. *B.* 1932. *Educ.* Latymer Upper School. *M.* 1969, Tessa Pout. *S.* 2. *Dau.* 1. *Career:* Member of Parliament (Cons.) for Worcester 1961—; PPS. to Leader of House of Commons 1963–64; Opposition Front Bench Spokesman, Finance and Economics 1964–66; Shadow Minister, Transport 1966–68; Local Government, Housing and Land 1968–70; Minister, Housing and Local Govt. June–Oct. 1970; Secretary of State for Environment 1970–72; Secy. of State for Trade and Industry since 1972–74; Shadow Min. for Trade, Industry & Consumer Affairs Feb–June 1974; Shadow Min. for Defence June 1974–75. *Address:* Deer Park, Droitwich, Worcestershire.

**WALKER, Philip Gordon**, FCA. British company director. *B.* 1912. *Career:* Chmn. and Chief Exec., Sun Life Assurance Society Ltd., Sun Life Pensions Management Ltd.; Chmn., Chapman & Co. (Balham) Ltd., Chapman & Co. Engineers (Balham) Ltd., The New Waterside Paper Mills Ltd., Weir Waste Paper Co. Ltd., Solar Life Assurance Ltd., Artagen Properties Ltd., Chapman Cartons Ltd., Chapman Envelopes Ltd. *Member:* Performing Right Tribunal; Restrictive Practices Court. *Address:* 'Dunwood', East Drive, Wentworth, Virginia Water, Surrey.

**WALKER, Robert Alexander, QC.** (1956). Canadian barrister and solicitor. *B.* 1916. *Educ.* Univ. of Saskatchewan (LLB). *M.* 1941, Rosa Nagel. *S.* Robert Douglas, Kenneth George and James Donald. *Dau.* Eileen Joan. *Career:* Served in R.C.A.F. 1942–45; student, University of Saskatchewan 1945–49; engaged in private practice in Saskatoon 1951—.

Attorney-General of Saskatchewan July 1956–May 1964; assumed the additional portfolio of Provincial Secretary, August 1957; Member of Legislative Assembly of Saskatchewan 1948–67. *Member*. Bd. Governors Univ. of Saskatchewan. Member of New Democratic Party. *Address:* Box 3007, Saskatoon, Sask., Canada.

**WALKER, Col. Sir William Giles Newsom**, TD, DL. Manufacturer and director of companies. *B.* 1905. *Educ.* Shrewsbury School, and Jesus College, Cambridge (BA). *M.* Mildred Brenda Nairn. *S.* Michael Giles Neish. *Daus.* Margaret Elizabeth Bluebell, Angela Rachel. *Career:* Joined Jute Industries Ltd. 1927; on production side of Company's business until 1939; mobilized with T.A. Aug. 1939 as Major (1st Fife and Forfar Yeomanry); commanded Regiment as Lt.-Col. 1943–45; saw service with B.E.F. 1940, and in N.W. Europe 1944–45; rejoined Jute Industries and appointed Director 1946; Chairman and Managing Director 1948–69. Dundee, Perth & London Shipping Co. Ltd. 1946–71; Clydesdale Bank Ltd. 1961; Nairn Williamson Ltd. (formerly Nairn and Williamson (Holdings) Ltd.) 1954–75; Scottish Television Ltd. 1964–74; Alliance Trust Co. Ltd.; Second Alliance Trust Co. Ltd. 1964–76. Chmn. Jute Industries (Holdings) Ltd. 1969–70. *Address:* Pitlair, Cupar, Fife, Scotland.

**WALKER, Winthrop Brooks.** American. *B.* 1914. *Educ.* Bowdoin Coll. (AB 1936), Harvard Law School (LLB 1939) and Rutgers School of Banking 1953. *M.* 1944, Sidney Anne Smith. *Daus.* Margaret V. and Sidney L. *Career:* Trustee and Member Investment Cttee, Portland Savings Bank 1956–59; Dir. Cumberland Savings & Loan Association 1955–59; Dir., Treas. and Member Exec. Cttee., Greater Portland Chamber of Commerce 1957–59; Vice-Pres. Canal National Bank, Portland, Me. 1946–59. First Vice-President, State Street Bank & Trust Co., Boston, Mass. Director, Biddeford & Saco Bus Lines Inc. Trustee, Boston Hospital for Women. Member of the Corporation, Maine Medical Center. Trustee, Maine Eye and Ear Infirmary. Director, Home for Aged Women of Portland. *Publications:* A Re-examination of Common Stocks as Long-Term Investments, (1954). *Awards:* Amer. Defense Service Medal; Amer. Campaign Medal; European Theatre Medal; World War II Victory Medal. *Member:* Amer. Inst. of Banking, Harvard Law School Assn. of Massachusetts. *Clubs:* Algonquinn; The Knockers. *Address:* Baker Bridge Road, Lincoln, Mass. and *office* State Street Bank & Trust Co., 225 Franklin Street, Boston, Mass., U.S.A.

**WALKER-SMITH, Rt. Hon. Sir Derek Colclough**, Bt, PC, QC, TD, MP. *B.* 1910. *Educ.* Rossall School; Christ Church, Oxford. *M.* 1938, Dorothy Etherton. *S.* 1. *Daus.* 2. Called to Bar 1934 (QC 1955, Bencher 1963); Member of Parliament (Con.) East Div. of Hertfordshire since 1955 (Herts. Div. 1945–55); Parly. Secretary to Board of Trade 1955–57; Economic Secretary to the Treasury 1956–57; Minister of State, Board of Trade 1957; Minister of Health, Sept. 1957–60; Mem., British Delegation to European Parliament since 1973; Chmn. Cons. Adv. Cttee. on Local Govt. 1954–55; Chmn. Conservative Members (1922) Cttee. 1951–55; Chmn. Soc. of Conservative Lawyers 1969–75. Legion of Honour; F.R.S.A. *Club:* Carlton. *Address:* 25 Cavendish Close, St. Johns Wood, London, N.W.8.

**WALL, Baron** cr. 1976 (Life Peer), of Coombe in Greater London, OBE (John Edward Wall). British. *B.* 1913. *Educ.* London School of Economics (B. Com. 1933). *M.* 1939, Gladys Evelyn Wright. *S.* 2. *Dau.* 1. *Career:* Under Secy. Ministry of Food 1939–52; Head of Organization Division, Unilever Ltd. 1956–58 (Dep. Head Finance Dept. 1952–56); Dep. Chmn. of the Post Office, Oct. 1966–68; Chairman, International Computers (Holdings) Ltd., and International Computers Ltd., 1968–72; Dir. Laporte Industries Holdings Ltd.; Man. Dir., Electric & Musical Industries Ltd. 1960–66 (Dir. of Group Services 1958–60); Dir. Exchange Telegraph Co. 1972—; Chmn. Burrup Mathieson 1973–76; Dir. Grundy (Teddington) since 1972; Chmn. Charterhouse Development Capital Ltd. since 1976; Dir., Nurdin & Peacock since 1977. *Awards:* Life Peer 1976; Kt 1968; OBE 1942; Officer, Order of Orange-Nassau (Netherlands). Hon. Fellow, London School of Economics; Fellow, Royal Statistical Society; *Associate Member:* Operational Research Society; Fellow, British Institute of Management; Companion: Inst. of Electronic and Radio Engrs.; Inst. of Electrical Engrs. *Club:* Royal Automobile. *Address:* Wychwood, Coombe End, Kingston-upon-Thames, Surrey.

**WALLACE, Harold Anthony.** American. *B.* 1909. *Educ.* Univ. of Illinois (BC) and Harvard Business School, (A.M.P.). *M.* 1941, Ruby Harmon. *S.* Daniel, Leon, Lindsay. *Career:* Vice-Pres. Manufacturing and Dir., Ethicon Inc. 1947–56; Vice-Pres. Manufacturing 1956–70; and Dir. 1960–70; Massey-Ferguson Ltd., Toronto. *Member:* Amer. Management Assn. *Clubs:* Union League (Chicago); Detroit Athletic; Granite, The Newcomen Society, North America St. George's Golf, Country (Toronto); Coventry Golf (England). *Address:* P.O. Box 1047 Pinehurst, North Carolina 28374, U.S.A.

**WALLACE, Henry James.** American. *B.* 1914. *Educ.* Northeastern State College. (Tahlequah, Oklahoma) and Oklahoma State University. *M.* 1937 Barbara Ellis Denton; Henry James. *Career:* Jr. Teacher, Oklahoma Rural Schools 1933–42. From Private to 1st Lieut., Army of the U.S. 1942–46. Reg. Representative, N.Y. Stock Exchange 1946–48; Asst. Office Manager, Merrill Lynch, Pierce, Fenner & Smith Inc. 1948–53 (except 1951–52). 1st Lieut. Army of U.S., Korea 1951–52; President: Mid-West Cemen Pipe Lining Co. Inc. 1953—, and B & W Testing Service Inc. 1958—. Partner Just Right Enterprises 1966—. Dir., Superior Spray Builders, Inc. since 1968. *Publications:* Corrosion—What It Is—What To Do About It. (1961); The Wabash Valley—A Sleeping Paradise, (1966); Historic Morrison Mill (5,000 copies, 1969). Life Member, Wabash Valley Association, and Buffalo Trace Council, Boy Scouts of America. Council Representative B.S.A. Member: Veterans of Foreign Wars, American Legion, Illinois Oil & Gas Assn. *Address:* Eastmain Wallace Street, Crossville, Ill. 62827, U.S.A.

**WALLACE, John McChrystal.** Retired banker. *B.* 1893. *Educ.* University of Utah (BA 1916) and Harvard (MBA 1921). *M.* 1920, Glenn Walker. *S.* Mathew Walker and John McChrystal, Jr. *Career:* Dir.: Walker Bank & Trust Co., 1923–67, Banner Mining Co. March 1953–71; Western Bancorporation March 1961–68. Director Emeritus Western Air Lines, Inc. 1966—. Pres., Walker Bank & Trust Co. 1944–57, Chmn. 1957–66; Mayor of Salt Lake City 1938–39; Civilian Aide to Secretary of the Army 1955–59; Pres. and Dir. United Park City Mines Co. Feb. 1955–64; Dir. Western Air Lines Inc. Feb. 1950–66; Transamerica Corp. 1957–58; and Firstamerica Corp. 1958–61. Honorary Colonel Utah National Guard; Commander of the Most Venerable Order of St. John of Jerusalem; Mason 33°; Member Co-ordinating Council of Higher Education 1959–61. *Clubs:* Alta, Country (Salt Lake City); Los Angeles Country. *Address:* 2520 Walker Lane, Salt Lake City, Utah; and *office* 1600 Walker Bank Bldg., Salt Lake City, Utah, U.S.A.

**WALLACE OF COSLANY, Lord (George Douglas).** British Statesman. *B.* 1906. *Educ.* Secondary Sch. Cheltenham. *M.* 1932, Vera. *S.* 1. *Dau.* 1. *Career:* Member of Parliament (Chislehurst) 1945–50; Mem. Kent County Council 1952–57; Member of Parliament Norwich (North) 1964–74; P.P Secy. to Lord President of Council 1964–66; P.P. Secy. to Secy. of State for C'wealth Affairs 1966–67; P.P. Secy. to Min. of State, Housing and Local Govt. 1967–68; Commissioner C'wealth War Graves Comm. since 1970; Chairman's Panel H. of C. 1970–74; Vice-Chmn. Area Health Authority since 1974; Lord in Waiting since 1977. *Member:* C'wealth Parly. Assn.; Inter-Parliamentary Union. *Awards:* Defence and War medals; Created Life Peer Dec. 1974, taking title Baron Wallace of Coslany (in the city of Norwich). *Address:* 44 Shuttle Close, Sidcup, Kent.

**WALLACH, Frederick.** Oberlandesgerichtsrat a.D., Dr. jur. Attorney and Counselor-at-Law, in practice in New York City since 1952. *B.* 1907. *Educ.* Referendar, Bonn 1929, Assessor, Berlin 1934, Dr. jur., Bonn 1935, LLB Columbia 1949, MBA Graduate School of Business Administration, N.Y. University 1952; J.D. Columbia 1969; Graduate, Command & General Staff College, Fort Leavenworth 1962; Alumnus, Industrial Coll. of the Armed Forces, Washington, D.C. 1963. *M.* 1940, Dr. Elisabeth Dannheisser (*Dec.* 1976). *S.* Dr. Donald F. *Career:* In German legal service until 1934; dismissed by Hitler; interned in Dachau concentration camp 1938; exiled 1939. Emigrated to U.S.A. 1940; drafted into U.S. Army 1941; discharged Nov. 1945 (served overseas with General Staffs, U.S. VII Corps until capture of Cherbourg, then First U.S. Army until V.E. Day). Public safety official of OMGUS 1946–47. Now Major, U.S. Army Reserve. Awarded Bronze Star (U.S.) and five campaign stars. *Publications:* The Western German Banking System, (1952); Introduction to European Commercial Law, (1953); contributions to professional journals. *Member:* Amer. Security Council; Amer. Bar. Assn.; Amer. Judicature Socy.; World Peace Through Law Center, Geneva; Elected, Wisdom Hall of Fame. Republican. *Club:* Bayside Yacht. *Address:* 64-48 Bell Boulevard, Bayside, L1, N.Y. 11364, U.S.A.

**WALLENBERG, Jacob.** Swedish banker and company director. *B.* 1892. *Educ.* School of Economics, Stockholm; DEcon, hc 1956; MD, hc 1960. *Career:* Asst. Mgr., Stockholms Enskilda Bank 1918, Vice-Managing Director and member of the Board 1920; Managing Director 1927–46, Vice-Chairman of the Board 1946–50. Chairman 1950–69; Chairman of Boards: Förvaltnings AB Providentia, AB Investor, Knut & Alice Wallenberg Foundation, 1966. Member of Bd. of Nobel Foundation 1952–68, Swedish deleg. to trade negotiations with Germany 1934–44. Commander, Grand Cross, Order of Polar Star; Commander Grand Cross, Order of Vasa; Commander 1st Class, Order of Dannebrog (Denmark); Commander of White Rose of Finland; Knight, Legion of Honour. *Address:* Knut och Alice Wallenaergs Stiftelse, Kungsträdgärdsgatan 8, III4 7. Stockholm, Sweden.

**WALLENBERG, Marcus.** Dr. Techn hc. Dr. Econ. h.c. Swedish banker and industrialist. *B.* 5 Oct. 1899. *Educ.* Stockholm School of Economics. *M.* (1) 1923, Dorothy Helen Mackay. *S.* Peter. *Dau.* Ann-Mari; (2) 1936, Baroness Marianne de Geer af Leufsta. *Career:* Asst. Manager, Stockholms Enskilda Bank 1925, Vice-Mng. Dir. 1927, Mng. Dir. 1946–58; Vice-Chmn. of Board 1958–69. Chmn., 1969–71; Chmn. Skandinaviska Enskilda Banken 1972–76, Hon. Chmn. of the Board since 1976; Hon. Chmn. of the Board of ASEA & LM Ericsson; Chmn. and Dir. many Swedish and foreign companies, i.a. Atlas Copco (Hon. Chmn.), Incentive, Kopparfors, Saab-Scania, Stora Kopparbergs Bergslags and The Liberian Swedish-American Minerals Co. LAMCO Chmn. emeritus; Chmn. Swedish Banks Assn. 1949–51 and 1955–57; Pres. Institut International d'Etudes Baneaires 1955–56; Vice-Chmn. and Chmn. Fed. of Swedish Industries 1959–64; Chmn., Council of European Indust. Feds. 1960–63; Business and Industry Advisory Cttee. to OECD 1962–64; Swedish delegate to trade negotiations with G.B. 1939–43, Great Britain and U.S. 1943–45 and Finland 1940–44; Chairman, Swedish National Committee of International Chamber of Commerce 1951–64. Hon. Chmn., 1964—; Pres. International Chamber of Commerce 1965–67; Co-Chmn. ICC-UN/GATT Economic Consultative Cttee. 1969–71; Member, Swedish Govt. Stabilization Council 1955–57; Economic Planning Council 1962–64; Bd. Member Knut and Alice Wallenberg Foundation. *Awards:* K.B.E.; Order of Seraphim; Grand Cross, Order of Vasa; Grand Cross, Order of Polar Star; Grand Cross, Lion of Finland; Grand Cross, Order of Merit (Italy); Grand Band, Order of the Star of Africa (Liberia); Knighthood of Légion d'Honneur; Commander: Order of Cruzeiro do Sul (Brazil); Order of White Rose of Finland; 1st Class of Order of Dannebrog (Denmark); 1st Class of Order of St. Olav (Norway); 1st Class of Order of Mexican Eagle; Order of Falcon of Iceland. *Clubs:* Swedish Lawn Tennis Assn. Chmn. 1934–53, Hon. Chmn. since 1953; Royal Lawn Tennis Club. Chmn. since 1953. *Address: office* Kungsträrdsgatan 8, Stockholm 16, Sweden.

**WALLER, Sir (John) Keith,** CBE. Retired Australian diplomat. *B.* 19 Feb. 1914. *Educ.* University of Melbourne (MA). *M.* 1943, Alison Irwin Dent. *Daus.* Anne, Gillian. *Career:* Entered Diplomatic Service 1936; Private Secy. to Minister for External Affairs 1937–40; Diplomatic Adviser to Ministry of Information 1940; Second Secy., Australian Legation Chungking 1941–44; Chief of Political Intelligence Division, Department of External Affairs, Canberra 1944–45; Secretary-General, Australian Delegation, U.N.C.I.O. Conference, San Francisco 1945; First Secretary, Australian Legation, Rio de Janeiro 1945–47; Australian Embassy Washington 1947–48; Consul-General, Manila 1948–50; Chargé d'Affaires, Legation, Manila 1950; Counsellor, London 1951; Asst. Secretary, Dept. of External Affairs, Canberra, 1953; Ambassador to Thailand, and Australian Representative on Council of SEATO 1957–60; Ambassador to U.S.S.R. July 1960–62. First Asst. Secy., Department of External Affairs. Ambassador to Washington 1964–70; Secy., Dept. of Foreign Affairs, Canberra, 1970–74. *Address:* 17 Canterbury Cres., Deakin, ACT 2600, Australia.

**WALLICH, Henry C.** American. *B.* 1914. *Educ.* Oxford University 1932–33 and Harvard Univ. (MA 1941; PhD 1944). *M.* 1950, Mable Inness Brown. *S.* Paul I. *Daus.* Christine and Anna. *Career:* Professor of Economics, Yale University 1951–74; Assistant to the Secretary of the U.S. Treasury 1958–59; Member President's Council on Economic Advisers 1959–61; Senior Consultant, Secretary of the Treasury 1969–74; Mem. Bd. of Governors of Federal Reserve System since 1974. *Publications:* Monetary Problems of an Export Economy; Public Finances of a Developing Country (with John Adler); Mainsprings of the German Revival; The Cost of Freedom. Editorial writer Washington Post 1961–63; columnist Newsweek 1965–74. *Member:* American Economic Association; American Finance Association. *Club:* Harvard (N.Y.C.). *Address:* 1300 Ranleigh Rd., McLean, Va. 22101, U.S.A.; and *office:* B-2004 Federal Reserve Bldg., Washington, DC 20551, U.S.A.

**WALLINGER, Sir Geoffrey Arnold,** GBE, KCMG. Former British diplomat. *B.* 1903. *Educ.* Sherborne School; Clare College, Cambridge (BA). *M.* (1) 1939, Diana Peel Nelson (marriage dissolved 1949). *S.* John Arnold; (2) Alix de la Faye (*D.* 1956); (3) 1958, Stella Zilliacus. *Career:* Entered Diplomatic Service 1926; Third Secretary, Cairo 1926, Vienna 1929, Foreign Office 1931; Second Secretary 1931; Political Secretary to United Kingdom High Commissioner in South Africa 1935; First Secretary 1938; Head of Chancery, Buenos Aires 1938; Foreign Office 1942–43; Acting Counsellor later Chargé d'Affaires, Chungking 1943; Counsellor with local rank of Minister, Nanking 1945–47; Foreign Office 1947–49; En. Ex. and Min. Plen. to Hungary April 1949–51; Amb. Ex. and Plen. to Thailand 1951–54; to Austria 1954–58; to Brazil 1958–63; retired from Foreign Service 1963. *Club:* Brooks's. *Address:* 10 Baskerville Road, London SW18.

**WALMSLEY, Hon. William Arthur,** MLC. *B.* 1892. *M.* Adelaid Helena Frith. *Daus.* 2. *Career:* Foundation Member, Lismore Rotary Club, 1932. Alderman, Lismore City Council 1947–53, Deputy-Mayor 1951; Executive, Local Government Association, N.S.W. 1951–53. Member, Legislative Council of New South Wales 1951–64; Chairman and Managing Dir., Car Owners Mutual Insurance Co. until 1964; Chairman, Group I, Agricultural Shows Assn. of N.S.W. 1955–58; Chmn. of Directors, Lismore Telecasters 1959—. President, N. Coast, National Show Society 1949–58. Member, Australian Country Party. Life Honorary Member, Australian County Party, N.S. Wales, 1970; Australian Mlawarra Dairy Cattle Society, 1970. *Address:* 92 Dalley Street, Lismore, N.S.W. Australia.

**WALSH, Cornelius Stephen.** American steamship executive. *B.* 1907. *Educ.* Eastman-Gaines School. *M.* 1930, Edwyna Lois Senter. *S.* Richard Stephen. *Daus.* Jane Linda and Suzanne Patricia. *Career:* With Dyson Shipping Co. Inc. 1924–27; Interocean Steamship Corp. 1928–30; States Marine Corporation. Secretary 1931, Vice-Pres. 1938–53, Dir. 1950–64; Pres. 1953–64; Pres. & Dir. States Marine Lines 1946–64; Chmn. Bd. Dirs. Waterman Steamship Corp. 1965—; Waterman Industries Corp. 1965—; Hammond Leasing Corp. since 1967; Oliver Corp since 1974; Hon. Director, Japan Soc. N.Y.C.; Dir. Far East Amer. Council, Commerce Industry. Member of syndicate which built 12-metre yacht Weatherly to compete for the defence of the America's Cup 1958, and which successfully defended the Cup in 1962. Member; American Bureau of Shipping N.Y.C. Society of Naval Architects & Marine Engineers (N.Y.C.); Society of Four Arts (Palm Beach, Fla.); Advisory Board, Manufacturers Hanover Trust Co. *Clubs:* Wall Street; New York Yacht; Metropolitan Opera. (N.Y.C.); Everglades, Bath and Tennis; Seminole Golf, Sailfish Club of Florida (Palm Beach); Seawankaha Corinthian Yacht (Oyster Bay, N.Y.); Pine Valley Golf (Clementon, N.J.). *Address:* 220 El Bravo Way, Palm Beach, Fla.; and 120 Wall Street, N.Y.C., U.S.A.

**WALSH, William L.** Chemist. *B.* 1910. *Educ.* Boston College (AB) and Massachusetts Inst. of Technology (MS; PhD). *M.* 1937, Grace Croshaw. *Daus.* Sheila and Susan. *Career:* Successively Research Chemist, Production Manager, Plant Manager, and Director of Manufacturing, General Aniline & Film Corp. 1936–55. With Quebec Iron & Titanium Corp. 1955—; Pres. 1955–73, Chmn. Bd. since 1973. *Member:* Sigma Xi; Amer. Chemical Socy.; A.I.M.E.; Socy. of the Chemical Industry. *Publications:* Catalytic Oxidation in Vapor Phase et alia. *Clubs:* Canadian (N.Y.C.); Mining; M.I.T. *Address: office* 161 East 42nd Street, New York, New York 10017, U.S.A.

**WALTERS, Dennis,** MBE, MP. British politician. *B.* 1928. *Educ.* Downside; St. Catharine's Coll. Cambridge. Cambridge (MA). *M.* (1) 1955, Vanora McIndoe (*Div.*). *S.* Nicholas *Dau.* Lorian. (2) 1970, Celia Kennedy. *S.* Dominic. *Career:* Chmn. Federation Univ. Conservative Assn. 1949–50; Personal Asst. to Lord Hailsham, Chmn. Conservative Party 1957–59; Chmn. Coningsby Club 1959; Secy. Conservative Party Foreign Affairs Cttee, 1965–71; Vice Chmn Conservative Parly. Foreign Affairs Cttee 1974—; Member of Parliament for Westbury. Chmn. Asthma Research Council; Chmn. Council, Advancement of Arab-British Understanding since 1970. *Awards:* Commander, Order of the Cedars (Lebanon). *Clubs:* Boodles. *Address:* 63 Warwick Square, London. S.W.1.; and *office* House of Commons, London S.W.1,

**WALTINGTON, John Francis, Jr.** American. *B.* 1911. *Educ.* Washington & Lee University (AB 1933; Valedictorian, Phi Beta Kappa) and Graduate School of Banking, Rutgers University. *M.* Margaret Jones. *S.* John F. III. *Dau.* Anne. *Career:* With Wachovia Bank & Trust Co.: Asst. Treas. (W-S) 1938, Asst. Vice-Pres. and Head of Charlotte Office 1939, Vice-Pres. (Charlotte) 1942, Snr. Vice-Pres. and Chmn. Charlotte Board 1946, Pres. and Chief Exec. Officer (W-S) 1956; President, Wachovia Bank & Trust Co., Winston-Salem, N.C. Director: Colonial Stores, Piedmont Natural Gas Co., Bank of Reidsville, Piedmont Aviation, American Enka Corp., Georgia-Pacific Corporation, and Massachusetts Mutual Life Insurance Co. *Member:* Winston-Salem Chamber of Commerce; Assn. City Reserve Bankers; Amer. Bankers Assn.; National Municipal League (Vice-Pres.); North Carolina Citizens Assn. (Dir. and Past Pres.); Newcomen Society of North America (N.C. Chmn. 1959—). Named Charlotte's Man of the Year 1951. *Clubs:* Rotary; Forsyth Country; Old Town; Country (N.C.); Biltmore Forest Country; Twin City. *Address:* Wachovia Bank & Trust Co., Winston-Salem, N.C. 27102, U.S.A.

**WALTNER, Harry George, Jr.** American lawyer-executive. *B.* 1906. *Educ.* Univ. of Missouri; Kansas City Law School. Univ. of Kansas City. *M.* 1927, Ruth Anna Laitner. *S,* Harry George III. *Daus.* Barbara Adams, Beverly Ruland, Lillian LeRoyce (Bascome). *Career:* Admitted to Missouri State Bar 1928; general law practice, Waltner & Waltner, Kansas City 1928–32; Asst. Attorney-General, State of Missouri 1933–37; Chief Counsel, Unemployment Compensation Commission, State of Missouri 1937–39 (Dir. 1939–44); Social Security specialist, Insurance and Social Security Dept., Standard Oil Co. (N.J.), N.Y.C. 1944–50 (Asst. Mgr. 1950–55); Consultant: N.Y. State Joint Legislative Cttee. on Unemployment 1948, and N.Y. State Joint Legislative Cttee. on Labor & Industrial Conditions 1949; member, Disability Benefits Adv. Council to Chmn. N.Y. Workmen's Compensation Bd. 1949–60; Participant, American Assembly on Economic Security, Arden House 1953; Fed. Adv. Council on Employment Security to U.S. Secy. of Labor 1954–58; Social Security Adv. to Standard Oil Co. (N.J.) 1955–58; Participant, President's Conference on Occupational Safety 1958; Latin Amer. Adviser, Insurance and Social Security Dept. Standard Oil Co. (N.J.) 1958–62; Benefits Adviser, Latin Amer. Employee Relations Dept. 1963–66; Senior Plans Adv. Employee Relations Dept. Esso Inter-America Inc. 1966–71; Consultant, Employee Benefit and Insurance since 1971. *Member:* Phi Alpha Delta Law Fraternity; American, Missouri State and Kansas City Bar Associations; American Bar Assn. Cttees. on Pensions and Other Deferred Compensations; Employee Benefits; Social Security and Unemployment 1944–58; Nat. Assoc. of Manufacturers Cttee. on Employee Health and Benefits (Vice-Chairman 1954–59). Member, Legislative and Executive Committees, Interstate Conf. on Employment Security Administrators; U.S. Chamber of Commerce Cttee. on Economic Security; American Marine Institute, Maritime Unemployment Insurance Cttee. (Chmn. 1947–51); National Federation of America Shipping Cttee. on Unemployment Insurance for Seamen; Exec. Cttee., N.Y. State Employers Conference; National Association of Employment Security Administrators; Council of State Chambers of Commerce Social Security Cttee.; Chmn., American Petroleum Industries Advisory Cttee. on Social Security, and Commerce and Industry of New York, Inc. Cttee. on Social Security; member, International Socy. for Labor and Social Legislation 1961—; American Judicature Society since 1961. *Publications:* New Jersey Cash Sickness Law (1948); The New York Disability Law, The First Five Years (1955). *Clubs:* Delta Tau Delta; Orienta Beach Yacht (Commodore 1962–64) (Mamaroneck, N.Y.); Pan-American Society; Rotary (Coral Gables); Yacht Racing Assn. of Long Island Sound; North American Yacht-Racing Union; Country Club of Coral Gables. *Address:* 1039 Hardee Road, Coral Gables, Fla. 33146, U.S.A.

**WALTON, Cecil Robert.** Canadian. *B.* 1908. *Educ.* Sault Ste. Marie Collegiate Institute. *M.* 1936, Alice May Merrett. *Daus.* Sharon Joan (Burns, R.N.) and Dorothy Wenda (Beilhartz). *Career:* In Electrical Dept., Algoma Steel Corp. 1927–33; Manager, Soo Dairies Ltd. 1934–40 (Dir., 1951; Pres. 1966–69); Electrical and Construction 1940–49, and Assistant Secretary and Assistant Treasurer 1949–50, Great Lakes Power Co. Ltd; Secretary: Great Lakes Power Corp. Ltd., May 1950—, and Great Lakes Power Co. Ltd., May 1950— (Vice-Pres. 1969—). Director and Secretary, Lake Superior Power Co., since 1950. Fellow Chartered Institute of Secretaries (F.C.I.S.). *Club:* Sault Ste. Marie Rotary. *Address:* 110 Bishop's Court, Sault Ste. Marie, Ont.; and *office* 122 East Street (P.O. Box 100), Sault St. Marie, Ont., Canada. P6A 5L4.

**WALZ, Hanna.** German politician. *B.* 1918. *Educ.* Grammar school; Law Study at Tubingen and Berlin. Dr. of Law 1948. *M.* 1941, Dr. Hans-Hermann. *S.* 2. *Dau.* 1. *Career:* Asst. at Univ. of Berlin (law of labor) 1941–43; Licence-bearer for Deutsches Allgemeines Sonntagsblatt, until 1948; Bibliothecarian at World Council of Churches in Geneva 1950–54; Member of town council of Fulda until 1958; Member of Diet of Hessen 1958–69; Member of Deutscher Bundestag, since 1969; Member of European Council and Western European Union 1969–72; Member of European Parlt. since 1973. Member of Evangelischer Arbeitskreis der CDU/CSU; representative Chairman of CDU-Hesse; Pres., Parly. Comm. for Energy Research & Technology of the European Parliament. *Decoration:* Bundesverdienstkreuz I klasse (1974); Gold Medal des Arbeitskreises Korrektes Fernlehrwesen (1974). *Publications:* Co-worker of Weltkirchenlexicon (1960); Protestantische Kulturpolitik (1964); Protestantische Perspektiven (1972); articles and essays. *Club:* IPA. *Address:* C-64 Fulda, Magdeburger Str. 72 GFR; and *office* D53 Bonn, Bundeshaus, G.F.R.

**WANGEMAN, Frank George.** American. *B.* 1912. *Educ.* Univ. of Zaragosa (Spain), Sorbonne, L'Ecole Hotelière (Lausanne) and Advanced Management Programme, Harvard Business School, Harvard Univ. *M.* 1946, Marie Moyle. *S.* Henry Moyle and Conrad Moyle. *Daus.* Alberta Ann and Marie Ellen. *Career:* Asst. Mgr., Waldorf-Astoria, N.Y.C. 1933–43; Operating Manager, Plaza Hotel, N.Y.C. 1943–45; General Manager; The Town House, Los Angeles 1945–47, and Plaza Hotel, N.Y.C. 1947–49; Vice-Pres. and Gen. Manager, The Caribe Hilton, San Juan, Puerto Rico 1949–51, and the Roosevelt Hotel, N.Y.C. 1951–53; Gen. Manager, Hotel New Yorker, N.Y.C. 1954–56; Senior Vice-President, Hilton Hotels Corporation, (Vice-President 1955—, Senior Vice-President, 1962—). Executive Vice-President, General Manager, Vice-Chairman of Bd. & Director, The Hotel Waldorf-Astoria Corp., Jan. 1961; Dir., Hotel Utah Co., Salt Lake City; member, Operating Cttee., and Bd. Dirs. Hilton Hotels Corp. Director: New York Convention & Visitors Bureau (Mem. Exec. Cttee.); Better Business Bureau of Metropolitan N.Y.; Wine & Food Socy. of N.Y. Trustee: N.Y.C. Hotel Trades Council Union Pension Fund; Hotel Assn. of New York City, Inc.; Fifth Avenue Assn.; Mem. Comite de Patronage, L'Ecole Hoteliere, Lausanne; Confrerie des Chevaliers du Tastevin (Officier Comdr.); La Chaine des Rotisseurs, Chancellier du Bailiage National des U.S.A.; Bryant College, Hon. Trustee. Awarded degree of Dr. of Science in Business Administration *honoris causa* by Bryant College, Providence, Rhode Island, June 1968. *Publications:* contributions to various trade publications. *Clubs:* Bohemian, San Francisco; Quaker Hill Country (New York). *Address:* The Hotel Waldorf-Astoria, New York City, N.Y. 10022, U.S.A.

**WANSBROUGH, George.** British company director (Ret'd.). *B.* 23 April 1904. *Educ.* Eton (King's Scholar) and King's College, Cambridge (Mathematical Scholar; 1st Class Maths. Tripos Part I; 2nd Class Economics Tripos Part II). *M.* (1) 1928, Elizabeth, (2) 1939, Barbara, (3) Nancy. *S.* Joseph Alonzo and David George Rawdon. *Dau.* Miriam Beatriz. *Career:* With Selfridge & Co. Ltd. 1923–27; Robert Benson & Co. (Director 1932–35) 1927–35; Director, A. Reyrolle & Co., Ltd. (Chairman 1945–49) 1936–49; Director, Bank of England 1946–49; Chmn. Jowett Cars Ltd. 1946–49; Chairman, Morphy-Richards Ltd., 1943–54; Director, Mercantile Credit Co., Ltd., 1934–75; Dir., Gordon-Keeble Cars Ltd. 1960–65; Member of Committees to advise Government on the purchase of aircraft for Airways Corporations 1948, and sundry other Government Committees; member, Council BEAMA (British Electrical and Allied Manfct. Assn.) 1939–49; Council, Institution of Electrical Engineers 1947–50; Council, Assn. of Electric Power Cos. 1939–48; Companion, Institute of Electrical Engineers; Member, Socy. of Automotive Engineers 1966; Governor, Bedales School 1966–74. *Publications:* various articles, reviews, etc., signed and unsigned, in The Times, The Economist, The Economic Journal, and motoring and yachting press. *Address:* Udimore Cottage, Otterbourne Hill, Winchester, Hants.

**WANSBROUGH-JONES, Sir Owen Haddon,** KBE, CB, British scientist. *B.* 1905. *Educ.* Greshams School, Holt. and Trinity Hall, Cambridge; MA (Cantab.); PhD, FRIC, Natural Sciences Tripos Pts. 1 and 2: Chemistry 1st Class

Hons.; Open Scholar and sometime Fellow Trinity Hall Cambridge, Hon. Fellow, Trinity Hall 1957; Goldsmiths Exhibitioner; Salters Company Student; Ramsay Memorial Fellow. *Career:* Tutor Trinity Hall 1935–39; Military Service 1939–45 (demobilized as Brigadier 1946); Scientific Adviser to Army Council 1946–50; Principal Director of Scientific Research (Defence) Ministry of Supply 1951–53; Chief Scientist ,Ministry of Supply 1953–59; Director, Albright & Wilson 1959–69. Exec. Vice-Chmn. 1965–67. Chmn. 1967–69. *Publications:* various in scientific journals. *Address:* 7 King Street, St. James's, London, S.W.1; and Orchard Leigh, Long Stratton, Norfolk.

**WANSTALL, Hon. Sir Charles Gray.** Senior Puisne Judge of the Supreme Court of Queensland. *B.* 17 Feb. 1912. *M.* 1938, Olwyn Mabel John. *Dau.* 1. *Career:* Called to Bar, Nov. 1933; QC 1956; member (Lib.), Queensland Legislative Assembly, April 1944–April 1950; Deputy Leader of Liberal Party in Queensland Parliament 1947–50; President, Liberal Party of Australia (Queensland Division) 1950–53. *Address:* Judge's Chambers, Supreme Court, Brisbane, Australia.

**WARBERG, Mogens.** Danish Diplomat. *B.* 1916. *Educ.* Univ. of Copenhagen—Master of Law. *M.* 1944, Vibeke le Sage de Fontenay. *S.* 3. *Career:* Attaché, Royal Danish Embassy, London 1947–49; Dept. Head, Foreign Office, Copenhagen 1949–55; Consul, Danish Consulate-Gen., New York 1955–61 (Acting Consul-Gen. 1956–57); Dept. Head, Foreign Office, Copenhagen 1961–69; Ambassador of Denmark, Beirut 1969–75, currently to Amman & Damascus 1969–75, Riyadh & Kuwait 1970–75, & Nicosia 1969–75; Ambassador of Denmark to Australia & New Zealand since 1975. Denmark's Perm. Rep. to Council of Europe in Strasbourg, Minister Ex. & Plen. 1965. *Decorations:* Knight of the Order of Dannebrog, 1st Degree; Independence Order of Jordan, 1st Class; Commander, Order of the Lion of Finland, 1st Degree; Grand Honour for Services of Austria; Knight of the Phoenix Order of Greece. *Address:* 9 Baudin Street, Forrest, A.C.T. 2603; and *office* Royal Danish Embassy, 24 Beagle Street, Red Hill, A.C.T. 2603, Australia.

**WARBURG, Sir Siegmund George.** British. *B.* 1902. *Educ.* Gymnasium, Reutlingen, Germany; and Humanistic Seminary, Urach, Germany. *M.* 1926, Eva Maria Philipson. *S.* George S. *Dau.* Mrs. Anna Biegun. With S. G. Warburg & Co. Ltd., London 1946—. Pres. since 1970. *Address:* 30 Gresham Street, London, E.C.2.

**WARBURTON, Eric John Newnham,** CBE. British. *B.* 1904. *Educ.* Eastbourne Grammar Sch. *M.* 1933, Louise Rachel Martin. *S.* 1. *Dau.* 1. *Career:* With Lloyds Bank: Jt. General Manager 1953, Deputy Chief General Manager 1958, Chief General Manager 1959, Dir. and Chief General Manager 1965. Vice-Chairman, Lloyds Bank Ltd. 1967–75; Deputy Chmn. Lloyds Bank International Ltd. 1971–75; Director: Lloyds Bank Europe 1962–71, Lloyds Bank Unit Trust Managers Ltd. 1967–75, Bank of London & South America (Dep. Chmn. 1968; Dir. 1965–71), Lewis's Bank Ltd. 1967–75, and Bowmaker Ltd. 1967–70; Chairman: Executive Cttee., Banking Information Service 1965–71, and Bank Education Service 1966–71. Member: Exports Credits Guarantee Dept. Advisory Council 1966–70; Decimal Currency Board 1967–71; National Savings Cttee. 1962–74; and City of London Savings Cttee 1962–74, Vice-Pres. since 1974. *Awards:* Hon. FTCL, FRSA. Fellow Institute of Bankers. *Club:* Bath (London). *Address:* 9 Denmans Close, Lindfield, Haywards Heath, Sussex RH16 2JX.

**WARD, Edward Peter,** MA. CEng, FIMechE. British. Industrial Consultant & Founder of Company Specialising in Techno-economic Research—Worldwide. *B.* 1926. *Educ.* Mitcham Co. School; Trinity Coll. Cambridge (MA Hons., Mech. Sc.). *M.* 1953, Brenda Eva. *S.* 3. *Dau.* 1. *Career:* Dir., Deputy- Editor Engineering Ltd. 1953–61; Dir. Martech Consultants Ltd. 1962–65; Man. Dir. Product Planning Ltd. 1965–67. Man. Dir., Peter Ward Associates (Interplan) Ltd. 1967–76; Chmn. Interplan Div., Metra Consulting Group Ltd. *Publication:* Dynamics of Planning. *Address:* Trio, Carlton Road, South Godstone, Surrey RH9 8LE and *office:* 22 Lower Belgrave Street, London SW1W 0NS.

**WARD, Michael John,** MP. British. *B.* 1931. *Educ.* State Elementary and Grammar Schools; Univ. of Manchester—BA (Admin.). *M.* 1953, Lilian Lomas. *Daus.* 2. *Career:* Commissioned in RAF 1953–57; Councillor, Romford Borough Council (now London Borough of Havering) since 1958 and Leader of Council 1971–74; Registrar, The Chartered Inst. of Secretaries 1958–60: O & M consultant to local authorities 1960–61: Local Government Officer to Labour Party 1961–65; local government public relations consultant 1965–70; Press Officer, ILEA 1970–74; Labour MP for Peterborough since 1974; PPS to Minister for Overseas Development 1975–76, & to Minister of State, FCO since 1976. *Member:* Inst. of Public Relations; National Union of Journalists. Pres., London Government Public Relations Assn. since 1977. *Address:* House of Commons, London SW1A 0AA.

**WARD, Murray.** American consultant. *B.* 1901. *Educ.* Stanford University (AB). *M.* 1942, Virginia Ducommun. *S.* Anthony Converse. *Career:* Senior Vice-President, E. F. Hutton & Co. Inc. 1960–66; President, Hill Richards & Co. 1946–54; Chmn., California Investment Bankers Assn. 1960; Vice-Chmn., Board of Directors, Natl. Assn. of Securities Dealers; Member, U.S. Surrender Party, Tokyo Bay, 2 Sept. 1945. Fleet Chief Censor, U.S. Pacific Fleet 1943–45; Advisory Dir. Ducommun Inc. Los Angeles 1945—. Senior Consultant, E. F. Hutton & Co. Inc., since 1966. *Awards:* Legion of Merit with Combat V. (U.S.A.). Grand Officer Confrerie des Chevaliers du Tastevins; Commanderie Bordeaux. *Clubs:* California; Los Angeles Country; Tran-Pacific Yacht; Outrigger Canoe (Honolulu); Eldorado Country; Birnam Wood Country. *Address:* 10464 Bellagio Road, Bel-Air, Los Angeles, Calif. 90024; and *office* 9797 Wilshire Boulevard, Beverly Hills, Calif. 90212, U.S.A.

**WARD, of North Tyneside,** baroness (Cr. 1974) (Irene Mary Bewick Ward), CH, DBE, JP. British. *Publications:* 'F.A.N.Y. Invicta'; member of Conservative Party. *Address:* 4 Roseworth Terrace, Gosforth, Newcastle-on-Tyne.

**WAREHAM, Arthur George.** British journalist. Editor: Daily Mail. London 1955–59: Chmn., Arthur Wareham Associates Ltd. 1961–77. *B.* 1908. *Educ.* Queen's College, Taunton. *M.* 1936, Kathleen Mary Tapley. *S.* 1. *Dau.* 1. Western Morning News 1926–35; Daily Mail 1935–60. *Address:* Three Corners, Forest Ridge, Keston, Kent.

**WARES, James Dallas.** South African. *B.* 1905. *Educ.* Watson's College, Edinburgh, and Edinburgh University; Fellow, Faculty of Actuaries (FFA). *M.* 1938, Moira Kirkland. *S.* 3. *Dau.* 1. *Career:* Dir.: Colonial Mutual Life Assurance Socy.; Cape of Good Hope Savings Bank; Garden Cities Western Province Sports Club. *Address:* Crannoch, Peninsula Road, Zeekoevlei, Cape Province, South Africa.

**WARING, Sir Douglas (Tremayne),** CBE (Ret.). British. *B.* 1904. *Educ.* Rossall School. *Career:* Chairman: London Tin Corporation Ltd. 1961–73; and other tin mining companies in Malaysia, Thailand and Nigeria. Chairman, The Malayan Chamber of Mines 1963–73. Member, Legislative Council, Fedn. of Malaya, 1948–59; President, F.M.S. Chamber of Mines, Malaya; Chairman, Anglo-Oriental (Malaya) Ltd. 1952–59, and of other tin mining companies registered in Malaya. Hon. Panglima Mangku Negara (Malaysia). Fellow Inst. of Chartered Accountants in England and Wales; Member, Inst. of Directors. *Clubs:* City of London; East India and Sports. *Address:* 93 Whitehall Court, London, S.W.1.; and *office* 55/61 Moorgate, London, E.C.2.

**WARING, Hon. Frank Walter.** South African. Former Minister of Information, Forestry, Tourism, Sport and Recreation and Indian Affairs. *B.* 1908. *Educ.* BA and BCom. *M.* 1934, Joyce Brereton Barlow. *S.* 1. *Daus.* 2. *Career:* Minister of Information 1961–66. Member of the National Party. *Clubs:* various sporting and cultural. *Address:* 252 Ocean View Drive, Fresnaye Sea Point, Cape Town, and *office:* c/o F. R. Waring Pty. Ltd., Packer Avenue, Epping No. 2 Cape Town, South Africa.

**WARIS, Klaus Henrik,** PhD. Finnish economist. *B.* 17 March 1914. *M.* 1939, Elina Leppänen. *S.* Hannu, Juha. *Dau.* Riitta. Governor, Bank of Finland 1957–67. Chancellor, Helsinki School of Economics. *Address:* Kartanontie 12, Helsinki, Finland.

**WARK, Sir Ian William,** Kt. Bach., CMG., CBE Australian. *B.* 1899. *Educ.* University of Melbourne (MSc 1921; DSc 1924); University of London (PhD 1923); University of California at Berkeley (post-graduate 1925); Exhibition of 1851 Science Research Scholarship 1921–24. *M.* 1927, Elsie E. Booth. *Dau.* 1. *Career:* Lecturer in Chemistry, Sydney University 1925; Research Chemist, Electrolytic Zinc Co. of Australasia Ltd. 1926–39. With C.S.I.R.O.: Chief, Division of Industrial Chemistry 1940–58, and Director, Chemical Research Laboratories 1958–60, Member

Executive 1961–65; Chairman, Commonwealth Advisory Committee on Advanced Education 1965–71; Hon. Consultant CSIRO Minerals Research Laboratories since 1971. Created Knight Bachelor 1969. Governor of the Ian Potter Foundation 1964—. Hon. Member, Australasian Inst. of Mining & Metallurgy. Fellow: University College, London; Australian Academy of Science (Treasurer 1959–63); Australian Academy of Technological Sciences; and Royal Australian Chemical Institute President 1957–58. *Publications:* Principles of Flotation (1938 revised with K. L. Sutherland, 1955); Why Research? (1968). *Club:* Sciences. *Address:* 31 Linum Street, Blackburn, Victoria 3130, Australia.

**WARMKE, Leon Eugene.** American Attorney-at-Law; practising lawyer in Stockton, California. *B.* 1911. *Educ.* Stanford University (LLB, JD 1936); Stanford Law School (Honour Graduate), California State Univ., San Jose (BA 1933). *M.* 1941, Jane Elizabeth Carter. *S.* Ralph Carter. *Dau.* Nancy Lee. *Career:* Practising attorney in San Francisco and San Jose 1936–38); Professor College of Law Santa Clara Univ. 1938–39; Exec. Secretary of Committee of Bar Examiners of the State Bar of California 1942–45; Aide and Flag Sec. to Deputy Commander in Chief, U.S. Fleet and Chief Naval Operations 1941–46; general practice in civil law since 1946. Pres., Community Chests Councils and United Funds of Central and Northern California 1958–59; Stockton United Crusade 1958–59; Advisory Council of United Community Funds and Councils of America 1958–59; Dir., Community Youth and Welfare Council, Y.M.C.A., Stanford Fund, Northern California Stanford Lawyers' Assn.; Pres., San Joaquin Health Association; Redevelopment Agency of City of Stockton; Bd. of Trustees of Stockton Unified School District; Law Institute, American Bar Association, State Commonwealth Club of California, Rotary International, Shrine, Elks, Yosemite Club, Stockton Golf and Country Club. *Awards:* Letter of Commendation, with authority to wear the Commendation Ribbon, from Secretary of the Navy, James Forrestal, for service as a Lieutenant-Commander, U.S.N.R., during World War II member, Order of the Coif. *Publications:* Constitutional Law (in Vol. 1 of Survey of California Law); The Long Pull, The Strong Pull, and the Pull Altogether (in the Bar Examiner); various legal articles in the California State Bar Journal, and Continuing Education of the State Bar of California. *Address:* Suite 21, 4545 Georgetown Place, Stockton, Calif., U.S.A.

**WARNER, Bradford Arnold.** American. *B.* 1910. *Educ.* Yale (AB 1932) and Columbia (MS 1935). *M.* 1932, Nancy Hill. *S.* Bradford A., Jr. and Miner Hill. *Career:* Trainee, Manufacturers Trust Co. 1932–35; President's Staff, General Motors Overseas Operations 1935–40; Rep. Fortune Magazine 1940–54; Vice-Pres. & Dir. Manufacturers Hanover Trust Co. 1954–62; Senior Vice-Pres. Belgian-American Bank & Trust Co. 1962–68; Belgian American Banking Corp. 1962–68. Director: Fantus Co. 1964–66; International Recreation Assn. 1965–67; Senior Vice-Pres. & Dir. European-American Bank & Trust Co. 1968–75; European-American Banking Corporation 1968–75; Dir. of Corporate Communications, Instrument Systems Corp. 1975–76; Vice-Pres. Corporate Planning, Gilman Paper Co. since 1976. *Director:* First Realty Investment Corporation 1969–71; Friedlich. Fearson & Strohmeier Inc., 1969–74; John Lowry Inc. 1970—; Buildex Incorporated 1972—; Commercial Alliance Corporation since 1972; Albert Frank-Guenther Law 1975–76; Bishop's Services Inc. 1976—; Applied Devices Corp.; Colonial Surety Co.; Datatrol Inc.; Morningside House Gerontological Center; Inst. for Crippled & Disabled. Consultant Cumberland Associates. *Member:* Mayflower Socy. Lay Cncl., International Cardiology Foundation; Trustee, Woodlawn Cemetery; Chmn., Natl. Socy. for Prevention of Blindness; Trustee, Allen-Stevenson School; Dir., Franki Foundation Company 1965–76; Trustee, Knickerbocker Hosp. 1955–58; First Mortgage Investors 1967; Central Savings Bank 1971—; American Foundation for the Blind; American Red Cross of New York. Treas. & Chmn. Finance Cttee., New York Public Library. Mem., Economic Club of New York. *Clubs:* Piping Rock, Links, Anglers, The Pilgrims, Yale (all of N.Y.C.); Flyfishers (London). *Address:* 116 East 68th Street, New York, N.Y. 10021; and *office* Gilman Paper Company, 111 West 50th Street, New York, N.Y. 10020, U.S.A.

**WARNER, Sir Frederick Archibald,** GCVO, KCMG. *B.* 1918. *Educ.* Royal Naval College, Dartmouth and Magdalen College, Oxford; MA (Oxon). *M.* 1971, Simone de Ferranti. *S.* 2. *Career:* Head of S.E. Asia Department, Foreign Office 1960–63. British Ambassador to Laos, May 1965–68. Minister to N.A.T.O. 1968–69; Deputy Permanent Representative to United Nations and Security Council with rank of Ambassador 1969–71; Ambassador to Japan 1972–75; Chmn., Guinness Peat (Overseas) Ltd. *Member:* Roya Institution; National Farmers Union. *Clubs:* Beefsteak; Puffins; Turf. *Address:* Laverstock, Bridport, Dorset; and L.6 Albany, Piccadilly, London, W.1.

**WARNER, James Prince.** American. *B.* 1904. *Educ.* Massachusetts Inst. of Technology (BSChem Eng 1926; MSChem Eng 1927), and Harvard Univ. (Advanced Management Programme 1949). *M.* 1928, Ruth Elise Griffin. *S.* James Prince III. *Dau.* Mary Elizabeth (Harvey, Jr.). *Career:* General Manager, Manufacturing, Esso Standard Oil Co. 1956–59 (Vice-Pres. and General Manager 1959–60); Vice-Pres. and General Manager, Manufacturing, Esso Standard Div. of Humble Oil & Refining Co. 1960–61. Vice-President, Refining, Humble Oil & Refining Co. 1961–69; Bd. Member Pennsylvania Industrial Chemical Corp.; Devonshire Investment Co. *Member:* Amer. Petroleum Inst.; Alpha Chi Sigma; Trustee Mount Holyoke College. *Clubs:* University; Lakeside Country (all of Houston). *Address: office* P.O. Box 2180, Houston, Tex. 77001, U.S.A.

**WARNOCK, Maurice John.** American. *B.* 1902. *Educ.* University of Oregon (BS 1926). *M.* (1) 1930, Isabel Cherry (dec'd). *S.* Thomas Clark and John H. Bair. (2) 1975, Gertrude Baur. *Career:* Joined Armstrong Co. 1926; Assistant Sales Manager, Floor Division 1930; Director, Advertising and Promotion 1941; Treasurer 1943; Vice-President and Treasurer and Vice-Pres. in Charge of Munitions Division 1950; assigned responsibility as Vice-President in charge of Finance, Employee Relations, Advertising-Promotion and Public Relations, Munitions Operations, 1954; 1st Senior Vice-Pres. 1961, Pres. 1962; Chairman of the Board 1968–76; member Board Dirs., 1959–76. Dir., Pennsylvania Power and Light Co. 1964–75. Member board Dirs.: Selas Corp. of America; Pennsylvania Chamber of Commerce 1961–77; Lancaster Lebanon Boy Scout Council; Natl. Assn. of Manufacturers, 1966–73, Hon. Vice-Pres. for Life; Home Capital Funds Inc. 1967–76; Dir. Lancaster General Hospital 1941–77, Hon. Trustee 1977—; Dir. Lancaster Chapter A.R.C. 1942–52; Community Chest 1945–52 (general campaign Chairman 1946, President 1947); Director and member Executive Committee Pennsylvania Economy League 1963–77; Trustee: Natl. Safety Cncl. 1970–76; Chmn. Foundation for Independent Colleges, Inc. U.S. Council International Chamber of Commerce; Denison Univ. 1965–77, Life Trustee 1977—; Franklin and Marshall Coll., Hon. Trustee 1977—; Linden Hall School for Girls 1946–77; Trustee Emeritus Lancaster Country Day School (Treasurer 1953–58). *Member:* Conf. Bd.; U.S. Chamber of Commerce; Newcomen Socy., Pa. Socy. N.Y.; Cliosophic Socy.; Phi Kappa Psi; (Trustee Endowment Fund 1970–76); Beta Gamma Sigma; Alpha Kappa Psi; Republican. *Clubs:* Lyford Cay (Bahamas); Lancaster Country Club, Hamilton Club; Bald Peak Colony (N.H.); Union League (Philadelphia); Old Baldy (Wyoming). *Address:* 191 Eshelman Road, Lancaster, Pa., 17601, U.S.A.

**WARNOCK, William,** BA; LLD. Irish diplomat. *B.* 22 Sept. 1911. *Educ.* High School; Trinity College, Dublin. *M.* Dorothy Murray. *S.* 2. *Dau.* 2. *Career:* Entered Department of External Affairs 1935; Secy., Berlin 1938 (Chargé d'Affaires a.i. Aug. 1939–Feb. 1944); 1st Secy., Dept. of External Affairs 1944–47; Chargé d'Affaires en titre, Stockholm 1947–50; En. Ex. and Min. Plen. to Switzerland 1950–52 and concurrently to Austria 1952–54; Assistant Secretary, Department of External Affairs 1954–56; En. Ex. and Min. Plen. to Federal Rep. of Germany, Oct. 1956–59, Ambassador 1959–62; Ambassador to Switzerland 1962, and concurrently to Austria 1963; Ambassador to India 1964–67 and to Canada, 1967–70, to United States of America 1970–73, to Austria 1973–74; Ambassador to Switzerland 1973–76 and concurrently to Israel 1975–76. *Address:* 1 Castle Court, Booterstown, Co. Dublin, Eire.

**WARP, Harold.** Plastics manufacturer. *B.* 1903. *Educ.* High School; Hon. Degree, Nebraska Wesleyan University. *M.* 1945, Anita Krauspe. *S.* Harold G. *Career:* Developed first practical window material for admitting ultra-violet rays 1924—; President and Founder, Flex-O-Glass Inc. 1924—; developed shade screen, now made by Kaiser under royalty, many 'Warps' plastics. Co-Founder and Vice-President, Trico Feed Mills, Minden, Neb. 1941. Developed Pioneer Village, Minden (opened June 1953), consisting of 30,000 historic items in 22 buildings on 20-acre tract. *Publications:* Russia As I Saw It; History of Man's Progress; Over the Hill and Past Our Place. Awards by Trustees of Neb. State Coll. American Pioneers, Native Sons and Daughters of Nebraska, and Nebraska Historical Society. Founding Director, Old West Trails. *Member:* Society of the Plastics Industries; U.S. Chamber of Commerce; Better Business Bureau; Illinois Manufacturers Assn. *Clubs:* Chicago Yacht, Svithiod, and others. *Address:* 1100 Cicero Avenue, Chicago 51, Ill., U.S.A.

**WARR, George Michael,** CBE. British. *B.* 1915. *Educ.* Oxford University (2nd class Modern History 1936). *M.* 1950, Gillian Dearmer. *S.* 1. *Stepson* 1. *Daus.* 2. *Career:* Joined Diplomatic Service 1938; served in Brussels, Bonn, Moscow, Montevideo, Santiago and the Foreign Office; Ambassador to Nicaragua, July 1967–70 (Ret.). *Address:* Woodside, Frant, Tunbridge Wells TN3 9HW; and 48 Jubilee Place, London SW3 3TQ.

**WARREN, Hon. Sir Edward Emerton,** KCMG, KBE, MSM. Australian. *Educ.* Broken Hill, N.S.W. *M.* 1926, Doris Schultz. *S.* 2. *Career:* Served in 18 Bn. A.I.F. (Gallipoli and France) in World War I. Member: Legislative Council, N.S.W. Parliament 1954—. Member of Council, Univ. of N.S.W. Vice-Chmn., International Exec. Council and of Australian National Committee, World Power Conference. Pres., Australia-Japan Business Co-operation Committee. Chmn. Australian Coal Association and Australian Coal Association (Research) Ltd. since foundation; and of N.S.W. Combined Colliery Proprietors' Association 1949—, Northern Colliery Proprietors' Association. Chairman of Directors, Brown's Coal Pty. Ltd. (Melbourne); Coal & Allied (Sales) Pty. Ltd.; Dowsett Engineering (Australia) Pty. Ltd.; Managing Director, Wallarah Coal Co. Ltd. Governing Director, Thomas Brown Ltd. (N.Z.); Man. Dir., Coal & Allied Industries Ltd., J. & A. Brown & Abermain Seaham Collieries Ltd.; Caledonian Collieries; Cessnock Collieries; Liddell Collieries Pty. Ltd.; Durham Mines Pty. Ltd.; Jones Bros. Coal Pty. Ltd. Director: South Maitland Railways Pty. Ltd.; Westinghouse Brake (A/sia) Pty. Ltd.; McKenzie & Holland (Australia) Pty. Ltd., Hexham Engineering Pty. Ltd.; Coal & Allied Industries K.K. (Tokyo). President, Australia/Korea Business Co-operation Cttee.; International Pres. Pacific Basin Economic Cooperation Council 1969. *Clubs:* American, Newcastle, New South Wales, R.A.A.C., N.S.W. Sports, Manly Golf, Tattersall's. *Address:* 16 Morella Road, Clifton Gardens, N.S.W. 2088, Australia.

**WARREN, Jack Hamilton.** Canadian Coordinator for the Multilateral trade negotiations. *B.* 1921. *Educ.* Queen's Univ. Kingston Ont. Canada (BA). *M.* 1953, Hilary Joan Titterington. *S.* 2. *Daus.* 2. *Career:* served with Royal Canadian Navy (VR) as Lieut. (Exec.) 1941–45; with Dept. External Affairs 1945; Financial Counsellor, Canadian Embassy, Washington 1954–57; Chmn. GATT Contracting Parties 1962–65; Dept. Minister, Trade and Commerce 1964; Dept. Minister Industry, Trade and Commerce 1968; High Commissioner to the U.K. 1970–74; Ambassador to the U.S.A. 1975–77. *Awards:* Hon. LLD Queen's, Ont. 1974; Outstanding Achievement Award, Public Service of Canada 1975. *Address:* Canadian Coordinator for the MTN, 4th Floor West, 240 Sparks Street, Ottawa, Ontario K1A 0H5, Canada.

**WARREN, Louis Bancel.** American lawyer. *B.* 1905. *Educ.* Oxford University (Trinity College), AB 1927, MA (Hons. Jurisprudence); Columbia University, DJ 1930. *M.* 1934, Rosalie Watson. *S.* Louis B. Jr. *Daus.* Hope Wilberforce (Shaw) and Rosalie Starr (Byard). *Career:* Associate of firm of Larkin, Rathbone & Perry (now Kelley Drye & Warren) 1930–40. Member of firm of Kelley Drye & Warren 1940— Dir. (and member Compensation Cttee.) Chrysler Corporation, Sept. 1957–76; Chrysler France; Chrysler United Kingdom; Chrysler Espana; Hammerson Holdings (U.S.A.) Inc.; American European Associates Inc.; Trustee, Homeland Foundation Inc.; Pres. & Dir. American Ditchley Foundation 1962–72; Dir. France-American Socy.; Member Exec. Cttee. Correctional Assn. of N.Y.; Fellow Pierpont Morgan Library; member, Board of Visitors, Columbia Law School. *Awards:* Kt. Cdr., Order of St. Gregory the Great (Holy See 1957); Officer's Cross of Merit, Sovereign Order of Malta 1968; Chevalier Legion of Honour (France 1971); Commander, Order of the British Empire 1972; Hon. LLD, Holy Cross 1973. Republican. *Member:* St. Nicholas Socy., Pilgrims Society, St. George's Society, The French Institute, Alliance Française, English-Speaking Union, Association of the Bar of the City of New York, New York State Bar Assn., American Bar Assn. and American Judicature Society; The American Society of International Law and International Bar Assn. *Clubs:* Century Association; Racquet & Tennis; Knickerbocker (N.Y.C.); Detroit; Somerset Hills Country; Somerset Lake & Game. *Address:* Ballantine Road, Bernardsville N.J.; and *office* 350 Park Avenue, New York 10022, N.Y., U.S.A.

**WARTIOVAARA, Otso U.** (GCVO) Finnish diplomat. *B.* 1908. *Educ.* Helsinki Univ. (Master of Law). *M.* 1936. Maine Alanen. *S.* 3. *Career:* Entered Foreign Service 1934; Attaché, Paris 1936–39; Secretary and Head of Section, Min. of Foreign Affairs 1939–42; Counsellor of Embassy, Stockholm 1942–44; Consul, Haaparanta, Sweden 1944–45; Head of Section, Min. of Foreign Affairs 1945–49; Counsellor of Embassy, Washington 1949–52; Head, Administrative Dept., Min. of Foreign Affairs 1952–54; Head, Legal Dept. 1954–56; Envoy Extraordinary & Minister Plenipotentiary to Belgrade & Athens 1956–58; Ambassador to Belgrade 1958–61; to Vienna & Perm. Rep. to I.A.E.A. 1961–68; to Holy See 1966–68; to Court of St. James's 1968–74. *Awards:* Cmdr. 1st Class Order of the White Rose; Cmdr. 1st Class Order of the Lion (Finland); Cross of Freedom 4th Class; Grand Gold Cross (Austria); Grand Cross: Order of the Phoenix (Greece), Order of Pius IX, Order of the Flag (Yugoslavia); Cmdr. 1st Class, Order of the Northern Star (Sweden); Cmdr.: Order of St. Olav (Norway), Order of Vasa (Sweden). *Address:* Lutherinkatu 6A, 00100 Helsinki 10, Finland.

**WARWICK, Cyril Walter.** *B.* 1899. *Educ.* Tollington School; King's College, University of London. *M.* 1925, Dorothy Miller. *S.* Peter John. *Dau.* Angela Mary. *Career:* President, Houlder Bros. & Co. Ltd.; Chmn., Hadley Shipping Co. Ltd., and Warwick Tanker Co. Ltd.; Dir., Warwick & Esplen Ltd., Chmn. since 1973; Dir. United Demurrage & Protective Assn. Ltd. Fellow, Institute of Chartered Shipbrokers; Worshipful Company of Shipwrights; Hon. Member, Baltic Exchange. *Clubs:* Bath; Canning; Hadley Wood Golf Club. *Address:* Witley Court, Wormley, Goldaming, Surrey, and *office* 53 Leadenhall Street, London, E.C.3.

**WASSERMAN, William Stix.** American investment banker. *B.* 24 Mar. 1901. *Educ.* Princeton University (AB). *M.* 1923, Marian Fleischer. *S.* William, Joseph. *Dau.* Marie. *Career:* American Delegate to World Economic Congress, Berlin 1931; Adviser to U.S. Delegation to International Labour Conference, Geneva 1937; Chief, U.S. Lend-Lease Mission to Australia 1942; Represented the Office of Economic Warfare (now Foreign Economic Administration) on two special missions to England 1943; Special adviser to Mr. Maury Maverick, Chmn., Smaller War Plants Corp. 1944. Pres.: Investment Corporation of Philadelphia; and Sky Line Ranch Inc., La Honda, Calif. Director and member of the Executive Committee, American Bosch Corporation. Director, Alexander's Dept. Stores; Dir. Hydron Pacific Corp.; Pres. Wm. Stix Wasserman Co. *Address:* Barrytown, N.Y. 12507, U.S.A.

**WATANABE, Seibi Masami.** Japanese. *B.* 1919. *Educ.* Keio University (Grad in Econ). *M.* 1951, Eiko Maruyama. *S.* Chiharu and Chifuyu. *Career:* With N.Y.K. Line 1943; Maritime Bureau of the Japanese Government 1946; Reconversion Finance Bank 1948; The Japan Development Bank 1951; Senior Man. Dir. Shinwa Kaiun Kaisha Ltd. since 1976 *Clubs:* Musashi Country. *Address:* 2–45–1 Utsukushigaoka Midori-Ku, Yokohama, and *office* Shin-Yaesu Bldg., No. 3. 1-Chome Kyobashi, Chuo-Ku, Tokyo, Japan.

**WATERFIELD. John Percival.** British civil servant. *B.* 1921. *Educ.* Charterhouse (Scholar) and Christ Church, Oxford (Scholar). *M.* 1950, Margaret Lee Thomas. *S.* 2. *Dau.* 1. *Career:* Served with the King's Royal Rifle Corps in Western Desert, North Africa, Italy and Austria (mentioned in dispatches). Entered Foreign Office 1946; 3rd Secy. Moscow 1947, 2nd Secy. Tokyo 1950. Returned to Foreign Office 1952; 1st Secy. Santiago (Chile) 1954; Consul (Commercial) New York 1957; returned to Foreign Office 1960. Ambassador to Mali Republic 1964 and to Republic of Guinea concurrently 1965. Returned to U.K. on rupture of diplomatic relations by both countries. Employed on duties connected with NATO 1966; Counsellor & Head of Chancery, U.K. High Commission Delhi, 1966–68. Counsellor: Head of Western Organizations Department, Foreign & Commonwealth Office 1969; Man. Dir. British Electrical and Allied Manufacturers Assn. 1970–73; Principal Finance & Establishments Officer, Northern Ireland Office since 1973. *Club:* Boodle's. *Address:* 30 Kelso Place, London, W.8; and 5 North Street, Somerton, Somerset.

**WATERMAN, Sir Ewen McIntyre,** Kt Bach. Australian grazier and company director. *B.* 1901. *Educ.* Woodville High School, and South Australian School of Mines &

Industries (now South Australian Institute of Technology). *M.* 1928, Vera Jessie Gibb. *Dau.* 1. *Career:* Dir. Elder Smith Goldsborough Mort Ltd.; F. & T. Industries Ltd.; Waterman Bros. Holdings Pty. Ltd.; B.E.A. Motors Pty. Ltd.; Chmn, Onkaparinga Textiles Ltd.; Australian Member 1948–55. and Chairman 1952–54 International Wool Secretariat, London; Chmn. Exec. Cttee., Wool Secretariat, London; Chairman of Executive Committee, Wool Bureau Inc., U.S.A. 1952–54; Pres. South Aust. Adult Deaf Socy. since 1947; Commonwealth Member, Australian Wool Bd. 1955–63; Pres. Royal Flying Doctor Service (South Aust. Section) 1960–62; Member Bd. of Governors, Adelaide Festival of Arts; Hon. Governor, Postgraduate Foundation in Medicine (Univ. of Adelaide). Australian-American Association (Past Pres.); Council South Australian Institute of Technology 1962–69; Served as Consultant on Food & Agricultural Organization, United Nation Livestock Survey in East Africa 1965; Chmn. Aust. Wool Industry Conference since 1966. *Clubs:* Adelaide; Oriental (London). *Address:* Blackwood Park, Strathalbyn, S.A. 5255; and *office* Da Costa Building, 68 Grenfell Street, Adelaide, S.A., Australia.

**WATERS, Norman D.** American. President, Norman D. Waters & Associates, Inc., and Compass Advertising Inc. *B.* 1905. *Educ.* Columbia University (BA). *M.* 1928, Elaine Charlotte Lion. *S.* Lion Sandford. *Dau.* Elizabeth Raiff. *Career:* Founded own advertising agency 1927; in addition, established Art & Design Workshop, Inc. 1952; former President, American Television Society (1940–44). *Publications:* books and articles on advertising and television. *Address:* Greacen Point Road, Mamaroneck, N.Y., U.S.A.

**WATKINS, Daniel Anthony.** New Zealand executive. *B.* 1918. *Educ.* New Plymouth Boys' High School. *M.* 1942, Betty Eileen Whitcombe. *Daus.* Shirley and Margaret. *Career:* Own business and farming 1936; business partnership 1942–44; Chairman of Directors Ivon Watkins Dow Ltd. since 1971 (agricultural chemical manufacturers), and Director of subsidiary companies; United Chemicals Ltd., Vegetation Control Ltd. Director: Farmers Industries Ltd. (New Zealand); Mollers Holdings Ltd. *Member:* National Chairman, Pacific Basin Economic Council; Council of N.Z. Manufacturers' Federation; N.Z. Institute of Management; Weeds Society of America (charter member); Life member N.Z. Weed & Pest Control Conference; Fellow, N.Z. Institute of Agric. Science; Business Advisory Cttee., Victoria Univ.; Trustee, N.Z. Inst. of Economic Research. *Clubs:* Wellington; Returned Services Assn.; Rotary, New Plymouth, New Zealand. *Address:* Ivon Watkins-Dow Ltd., P.O. Box 144, New Plymouth, New Zealand.

**WATKINS, John Chester Anderson.** Lt.-Col. U.S.A.F. (Reserve). (Ret.). *B.* 1912. *Educ.* private schools in U.S., Mexico and Philippine Islands. *M.* (1) Helen M. Danforth (*Div.* 1959), (2) 1960, Izetta J. Smith. *S.* Robert Danforth and Stephen Danforth (stepson R. W. D. Smith). *Daus.* Fanchon Metcalf (Burnham), Jane Pierce (stepdaughter Izetta J. Smith: Mrs. Richard J. Nesbitt). *Career:* Ops. Officer 325th Fighter Gp., MTO, Exec. Officer Asiatic Theatre Branch, Asst. Chief Air-Staff Plans U.S.A.F., Washington; Executive Officer to Dep. Chief of Staff, U.S.A.F. (all in World War II); Cmdr. R. I. Air National Guard through 1948; First Cmdr., R. I. Wing, Air Force Assn.; Chairman of the Board, Providence Gravure Inc. Chmn. & Director: Providence Journal Co. (publisher Providence Journal and Evening Bulletin), and Providence Gravure Inc. and Rhode Island Hospital Trust Corporation. *Awards:* LittD, Bryant College 1966; DFC, Air Medal (9 Oak Leaf clusters); Dist. Unit Citation (2 Bronze Stars); Defense Department Commendation Medal; Knight Comdr., (Cavaliere Officiale) Order of Merit, Italy. President (1971–72), Director, and member exect. Committee, Inter-American Press Association. *Clubs:* Hope, Agawam Hunt Squantum Association (Providence): The Brook, N.Y. Yacht (N.Y. City) Army-Navy Country (Washington); New Bedford Yacht (Padanarum, Mass.); Cruising Club of America. *Address:* Post Office Box 1085, Providence, R.I. 02901; and *office* Providence Journal Co., 75 Fountain Street, Providence, R.I. 02902, U.S.A.

**WATKINSON, Rt. Hon. Viscount** (Harold Arthur Watkinson), PC, CH. British politician. *B.* 25 Jan. 1910. *Educ.* Queen's College, Taunton; King's College, London. *M.* 1939, Vera Langmead. *Daus.* 2. *Career:* With family business 1929–35; journalism 1935–39; served in World War II (active service R.N.V.R.) 1940–46. MP (Con.) Woking Division of Surrey 1950–64; Parly. Secy. to Ministry of Labour & National Service 1952–55; Minister of Transport & Civil Aviation 1955–59; of Defence Oct. 1959–62. Schweppes Ltd., Group Man. Dir. 1962–68. Pres. C.B.I.; Chairman: Cadbury Schweppes Ltd., 1969–74; British Institute of Management 1968–70; Dir., Midland Bank Ltd.; Dir. British Insulated Callenders' Cables Ltd. Chairman: Committee for Exports to U.S.A. 1964–67; Pres. Grocers Institute 1970–71; Pres. Institute, Grocery Distribution 1972–73; Pres. RNVR Officers Association 1973–76. *Member:* British National Export Council 1964–70. *Address:* Dibbles, West Clandon, Surrey.

**WATKINSON, John Taylor,** MP. British Politician. *B.* 1941. *Educ.* Bristol Grammar Sch.; Worcester Coll., Oxford—BA. *M.* 1970, Jane Elizabeth Miller. *S.* 2. *Career:* Schoolmaster 1964–70; Barrister 1970–74; Labour MP for Gloucestershire West since 1974; PPS, Home Office 1975; Member, Council of Europe, Western European Union and Public Accounts Cttee. of House of Commons since 1975. *Member:* Transport & General Workers Union; Fabian Soc.; Labour Lawyers; Middle Temple. *Address:* House of Commons, London SW1A 0AA.

**WATLEY, Eric John Arthur.** Canadian executive. *B.* 1916. *Educ.* St. Lawrence College, Kent, England; London University Extension (Senior Oxford); Toronto University (Business Administration). *M.* 1944, Eleanor I. White (author: Food Glorious Food. Cookbook). *S.* Brian John Arthur. *Daus.* Jennifer, Andrea and Robin. *Career:* Engaged in special intelligence work with Palestine P.F. and 7th Army (Palestine Medal); Director of Civil Defence, Jerusalem 1943; Information Officer, P.I.O., Jerusalem 1945. President & General Manager, Ronson Products of Canada 1950—; Vice-Pres., General Manager & Director, Ekco Products of Canada 1956—; Director of Marketing, International Latex Co. of Canada 1959—; and H. Corby Distillery Co., Canada 1960—; Watleys Ltd. 1965—. Director, Central Neighbourhood House. *Publications:* various articles in the press, dealing with business management and marketing. Recipient of special military commendation. Conservative. *Club:* Granite, RCYC (Toronto). *Address:* 553 Church Street, Toronto, Ont., Canada.

**WATSON, Alfred Nelson.** American. Attorney, Financial consultant, Bronxville, New York. *B.* 1910. *Educ.* AB; MSc; PhD; JD. *M.* 1934, Elizabeth Dixon. *S.* Keith Stuart and Andrew Graham. *Career:* Professor of Business, Graduate School of Business, Columbia University, N.Y. 1963–65; Senior Vice-President, United States Rubber Co. 1961–63; Pres. Greater N.Y. Chapter Epilepsy Foundation of America; Chmn. Living Care Centres of America. Honours from Social Science Research Council, Fellow in Statistics, University of London (Eng.) 1937–38. Fellow: American Assn. for Advancement in Science; Operations Research Society of America; American Statistical Association. *Club:* Siwanoy (Bronxville, N.Y.). *Address:* 54 Hereford Road, Bronxville, N.Y. U.S.A.

**WATSON, (James) Kingston.** Australian journalist. *B.* 1908. *Educ.* University High School, Melbourne. *M.* 1938, Eleanore Macfarlane. *Dau.* Sharon. *Career:* Cadet journalist, The Herald, Melbourne 1927; Sub-Editor, The Star, Melbourne 1933–36, The Herald, Melbourne 1936–37, and Daily Telegraph, Sydney 1938; News Editor, Sunday Telegraph, Sydney 1939–43; Deputy Chief of London Office, Australian Consolidated Press 1943; war correspondent, Supreme Headquarters Allied Expeditionary Forces (SHAEF) 1944–45; established Australian Consolidated Press, Paris Office 1945–46; reported Paris Peace Conference 1946–47; Deputy News Editor, Daily Telegraph, Sydney 1948 (News Editor 1951–53). Editor 1953–70; Editor Sunday Telegraph 1971–72; Founding Editor, merged Sunday Telegraph, Sunday Australian 1972–74; London Editor Australian Consolidated Press since 1974; Original Member interviewing panel 'Meet the Press' TCN9, Sydney 1957. Producer and Panellist since 1971. Australian delegate, Commonwealth Press Union quinquennial conferences: India-Pakistan 1961, West Indies 1965. Scotland & Mediterranean 1970 (leader). *Address: office:* Australian Consolidated Press, 107 Fleet St., London E.C.4; and 1 Madeline Street, Hunter's Hill, N.S.W., Australia.

**WATSON, John Hugh Adam,** CMG. British. *B.* 1914. *Educ.* Rugby, and King's College, Cambridge (MA). *M.* 1950, Katharine Anne Campbell. *S.* Douglas Charlton and Alaric. *Dau.* Katharine Alice, *Career:* Entered Diplomatic Service 1937; served Bucharest 1939, Cairo 1940, Moscow 1944, Foreign Office 1947, Washington 1950; Head of African Dept., Foreign Office 1956–59; Consul-General, Dakar 1959; Ambassador to Mali Federation 1960; to Togo, Senegal and

Mauritania 1960–62. Ambassador to Cuba. 1963–66; Assistant Under-Secretary of State, Foreign Office 1966–68; Senior Executive, British Leyland Motor Corp. 1968; Dir.-Gen. International Assn. for Cultural Freedom since 1974. *Club:* Brooks's. Gwilym Gibbon Fellow, Nuffield College, Oxford 1962–63. *Address:* Sharnden Old Manor, Mayfield, Sussex; 53 Hamilton Terrace, London, N.W.8.

**WATSON, Laurence Roy.** British. *B.* 1918. *Educ.* Murray Bridge High School; AAIA (Dip). *M.* 1941, Gwenllian Elizabeth Robinson. *Career:* Publicity Mgr., S. Australian Govt. Tourist Bureau 1951–58; U.K. Mgr. (London), Australian National Travel Assn. 1958–64; Director of Tourism, Aust. Capital Territory Government Tourist Bureau since 1965. Member: ACT Advisory Bd. on Tourism since 1966; ACT Liquor Licencing Bd. since 1975; ACT Poker Machine Licencing Bd. since 1976. First President, Adelaide Branch of Air Force Assn. 1946–48; Pres., Travel League of S. Australia 1956. National Pres., Associated Travel Leagues of Australia 1957; Producer of 31 documentary films for the S. Australian Govt. Recipient King's Air Force Commendation. *Clubs:* Naval & Military (Melb.); Assn. International des Skal Clubs (Canberra); Rotary International (Canberra). *Address:* 46 Lynch Street, Hughes, A.C.T.; and *office* Government Tourist Bureau, London Circuit, P.O. Box 744, Canberra City, A.C.T., 2601, Australia.

**WATSON, Sir (Noel) Duncan,** KCMG. British. HM Diplomatic Service (retired). *B.* 1915. *Educ.* Bradford Grammar School and New College, Oxford (BA Oxon 1938; MA 1967). *M.* 1951, Aileen Bryans Henry (née Bell). *Career:* Administrative Officer, Govt. of Cyprus 1938–43; Asst. Colonial Secy., Trinidad 1943–45; Principal, Colonial Office 1946; Principal Private Secy. to Secy. of State for the Colonies 1947–50; Asst. Secy., Colonial Office and Central Africa Office 1950–62; Under-Secy., Central Africa Office 1963; Asst. Under Secy. of State, Commonwealth Office 1964–67. Political Adviser to the Commander-in-Chief, Far East, Singapore, 1967–70; High Commissioner to Malta, 1970–72; Deputy Under Secretary of State, Foreign and Commonwealth Office 1972–75. *Clubs:* Travellers; Royal Commonwealth Society (London); Leander (Henley-on-Thames). *Address:* Sconce, Steels Lane, Oxshott, Surrey.

**WATSON, Thomas John, Jr.** American business executive. *B.* 1914. *Educ.* Brown Univ. (BA). *M.* 1941, Olive Field Cawley. *S.* Thomas John III. *Daus.* Jeannette, Olive, Lucinda, Susan and Helen. *Career:* International Business Machines Corp. 1937–40, 1946—: Pres. 1952–71, Chmn. 1961–71, Chmn. Exec. Cttee. IBM since 1971; Dir., Pan American World Airways Inc., Time Inc.; Citizen Regent of the Smithsonian Institution. *Member:* Nat. Advisory Council Boy Scouts of America, the Business Council (Graduate mem.), Council on Foreign Relations. Senior Fellow, Woodrow Wilson Nat. Fellowship Foundation. *Trustee:* The American Museum of Natural History, Brown Univ., California Inst. of Technology, the John F. Kennedy Library, Mayo Foundation, Mystic Seaport Inc. *Awards:* Presidential Medal of Freedom, Air Medal, Army Commendation Ribbon. Hon. degrees from Brown, Columbia, Harvard, Oxford, Yale and a number of other Universities. *Address: office:* IBM, Old Orchard Road, Armonk, N.Y. 10504, U.S.A.

**WATT, Sir Alan (Stewart),** CBE. Australian diplomat. *B.* 13 Apr. 1901. *Educ.* Sydney University (BA) and Oxford University (MA); Rhodes Scholar for New South Wales 1921; Barrister-at-Law (N.S.W.). *M.* 1927, Mildred Mary Wait. *S.* 3. *Dau.* 1. *Career:* Practised at law, Sydney; appointed to Dept. External Affairs, Canberra 1937; First Secretary, Legation, Washington 1940–45; Asst. Secretary (Political), Dept. External Affairs 1946; Minister to U.S.S.R. 1947–48 (Ambassador 1948–50); Sec., Dept. External Affairs 1950–53; member, Australian Delegation to U.N. Conf., San Francisco 1945; to U.N. Assemblies 1946 to 1948; Leader, Australian Delegation to Conf. on Freedom of Information and the Press, Geneva, 1948; Alternate Leader, Australian Delegation to Conf. on Korea and Indo-China, Geneva 1954; member, Austr. Delg. to ANZUS Council Meetings (Honolulu 1952, Geneva 1954); member, Delegation accompanying Prime Minister to Commonwealth Prime Ministers' Conf., London 1951 and 1953; Australian Commissioner (personal rank of Ambassador) in S.E. Asia 1954–56; Ambassador to Japan 1956–59; to Fed. Repub. of Germany, April 1960–62. Dir., Australian Inst. of International Affairs 1963–69. Hon. Fellow, Department of International Relations, Australian National University, Canberra. *Publications:* Memoirs. Australian Foreign Policy 1938–65. Vietnam, United Nations. *Address:* 1 Mermaid Street, Red Hill, Canberra, A.C.T. 2603, Australia.

**WATT, Rt. Hon. Hugh,** MP, JP. New Zealand Politician. *B.* 1912. *Educ.* Secondary School. *M.* Irene Frances Ray. *S.* 2. *Daus.* 2. *Career:* Minister of Works and Development; Minister in Charge of, the Earthquake & War Damage Commission in the Govt. of New Zealand; Chmn. National Roads, Board and National Water & Soils Conservation Authority; N.Z. High Commissioner in London 1975–76; Commissioner, Accident Compensation Comm. *Address:* Commissioner to the Accident Compensation Commission, Private Bag, Wellington, New Zealand.

**WATT, Ian Buchanan,** CMG. HM Diplomatic Service (Ret'd.). *B.* 1916. *Educ.* Perth Academy and St. Andrews University (MA). *M.* 1963, Diana Susan Villiers. *S.* James Alexander McDonald. *Career:* In Colonial Office 1946–62; Deputy-U.K. Commissioner. Malta 1962–64, Deputy-High Commissioner 1964–65; Commonwealth Office 1965–66. High Commissioner, Lesotho 1966–70; Counsellor, FCO 1970–72; High Comm. to Sierra Leone 1972–76. *Club:* Travellers'. *Address:* Rosewood House, Weston Park, Thames Ditton, Surrey.

**WATT, Prof. John Mitchell,** ED, MB, ChB. South African. Professor Emeritus of Pharmacology & Therapeutics. Univ. of the Witwatersrand. *B.* 1892. *Educ.* Univ. of Edinburgh (MB, ChB 1916); FRCPE, FRSE, FRSSAf. *M.* 1942, Betty Gwendoline Watt. *S.* 1. *Dau.* 1. *Career:* Served in World War I (40th Field Ambulance 13th Div. and 23rd Stationary Hospital in Mesopotamia, Persia and the Caucasus) 1916–19; in World War II as M3 General H.Q. in Pretoria of the Union Defence Forces 1941–45; Asst. to the Prof. of Materia Medica., Univ. of Edinburgh 1920–21; on two occasions Dean of the Faculty of Medicine. Hon. LLD. (Witwatersrand). *Publications:* Medicinal and Poisonous Plants of Southern and Eastern Africa; several works and numerous contributions to scientific and medical journals. *Address:* 36 Ludlow Street, Chapel Hill, Qld. 4069, Australia.

**WATT, John Norman.** Australian executive. *B.* 1918. *Educ.* Mont Albert Central and University High School, Melbourne. *M.* 1946, Charlotte King Davies. *S.* Roy. *Daus.* Faye and Julie. *Career:* With Commonwealth Bank until 1939. On Active Service (2nd A.I.F.; Commissioned Officer rising to rank of Major; Mentioned in Despatches) 1939–46. Accountant 1946–49, Deputy General Manager 1949–55, Cox Brothers (Aust.) Ltd.; Deputy General Manager, Foy & Gibson Ltd. 1955–58; Managing Director, Foy & Gibson Ltd. 1958–65 Executive Director Industrial Design Council of Australia 1966; Property Development Manager, Victoria & Tasmania, for Woolworths Ltd. 1968—; Retail Consultant since 1970. *Clubs:* Melbourne Cricket; Royal South Yarra Lawn Tennis; Sorrento Golf. *Address:* 763 High St. Rd., Glen Waverley, Vic., Australia.

**WATTS, Colin Arthur.** Australian. Company Exec. Dir. *B.* 1921. *Educ.* Degrees from ASA; CIS; AICA. *M.* 1944. Peggy Joy Selth. *S.* 2. *Dau.* 1. *Career:* Director, Deputy Managing Director, Controller and Secretary, Massey-Ferguson (Australia) Ltd. 1958–63; Man. Dir. Pak Pacific Corporation Group 1963–70; Controller Conzinc Riotinto of Australia Ltd. Fellow: Aust. Socy of Accountants; Chartered Inst. of Secretaries; Aust. Inst. of Cost Accountants; Aust. Inst. of Management; Inst. of Directors (U.K.). *Clubs:* Royal Automobile (Victoria); Eastern Golf. *Address:* 2 McDonald Avenue, Templestone, Vic.; and *office* c/o Conzinc Riotinto of Australia Ltd., 95 Collins Street, Melbourne, Vic., Australia.

**WATTS, David Rowland Wallace,** CBE. British. Director, George Wimpey & Co. Ltd. *B.* 1911. *Educ.* King's College, London University (BScEng). *M.* 1938, Josephine Mary Jarvis. *S.* Michael David. *Dau.* Carole Ann. With George Wimpey; Civil Engineer 1934, Departmental Manager 1947, Director 1953. Mem. Council of the Export Group for the Constructional Industries 1964–75; Pres. The Federation of Civil Engineering Contractors. Fellow, Institution of Civil Engineers (FICE). *Address:* George Wimpey & Co. Ltd., Hammersmith Grove, London, W.6 and Lakeview Court, Wimbledon Park Road, London, S.W.19.

**WATTS, Ernest Alfred,** FAIB. FIBA. Australian. Master builder and contractor, and company director. *B.* 1893. *Educ.* State School, Northcote, Victoria; Apprenticeship Building Trade; Building Diploma, Int. Correspondence School, London. *M.* 1914, Mabel Courtis (D.). *Daus.* 5. *Career:* Dir. Melbourne Builders Lime & Cement Co. Pty. Ltd. 1937–58· Aust. Alliance Assurance Co. 1944–51;

Governing Dir. Mecho Constructions Pty Ltd. (Civil Engineers) 1951—; Man. Dir. and Chmn. E. A. Watts Pty. Ltd. 1953–65, E. A. Watts Holdings Ltd. 1964–65; Man. Dir. & Chmn. Wet Mix & Pre-Cast Concrete Pty. Ltd. 1954–59; Collingwood Timber Joinery & Trading Co. Pty. Ltd. 1953–65; Gov. Dir. & Chmn. Mecho Plant Hire since 1973. *Member:* Aust. Inst. of Chartered Master Builders; Building Industry Congress; Chamber of Manufacturers; Company Directors Assn. of Australia; Intercontinental Biog. Assn. (1970); Master Builders' Assn.; Royal Agric. Socy. Life Gov.: Austin Hospital; Victorian Institute of Blind, and Freemasons Hospital; Royal Children's Hospital; Melbourne District Nursing Society and After Care Hospital. *Awards:* Citation Award I.C.S. for Home Study Man of the Year 1965; Australian Inst. Builders Bronze Medal, Service to Industry. Certificate of Merit, Dictionary of International Biography for Distinguished Service to the Construction Industry 1967; Certificate National Register Prominent Americans and International Noteables Research Centre, 1970. Diploma for Distinguished Achievement in the Two Thousand Men of Achievement. *Clubs:* Melbourne Cricket; Kew Golf; Victoria Racing; Royal Automobile; R.A.C.V. Country: Australian-American; Catalina Golf; Batemans Bay. *Address:* 377 The Boulevard, East Ivanhoe, Melbourne, Vic., Australia.

**WAYNE, Albert Rodney.** American. *B.* 1911. *Educ.* Rutgers Univ. (BA Bus Admin). *M.* 1945. Lorraine A. Shock. *S.* Collin Stuart. *Daus.* Hollis Leslie and Loren Christopher. *Career:* Vice-Pres., Air Reduction Co. 1932–46; Management Consultant, Booz, Allen & Hamilton 1946–51; Vice-Pres. Acme Steel Co. 1951–54; Pres. Mead Johnson International and Vice-Pres., Mead Johnson Laboratories 1955–60. Pres., Abbott Universal Ltd. Exec. Vice-Pres. and Direc., Abbott Laboratories. Dir. National Foreign Trade Council. *Address: office* 14th Street and Sheridan Road, North Chicago, Ill., U.S.A.

**WAZIR, Hon. Mr. Justice Janki Nath.** Indian judge. *B.* 6 Dec. 1905. *Educ.* Punjab University (BA); London University (LLB). *M.* 1933, Champa Rani Sawhney. *S.* Aman Kumar, Vinod Kumar, Vidhur Kumar. *Daus.* Urmila Rani, Ambika Rani. *Career:* Called to the Bar, Middle Temple; enrolled as an Advocate of Lahore High Court 1931; part-time Law Lecturer, Law College, Lahore 1933–36; Judge, High Court Jammu and Kashmir State Dec. 1936, Chief Justice 1948–67; Vice Chancellor J & K University 1950–57; Vice-Chancellor, University of Jammu and Kashmir 1950–57; Acting Governor Jammu and Kashmir 1967; Chmn. Backward Classes Commission 1969; Chmn. Anti-Corruption Comm. Jammu & Kashmir 1969; Chmn. Enquiry Comm., Kishtwar Firing 1975; currently Chmn., Appellate Tribunal for Forfeited Property, New Delhi since Jan. 1977. *Address:* Chief Justice (retired), Gupkar Road, Srinagar, Kashmir, India.

**WEATHERILL, (Bruce) Bernard,** MP. British Politician. *B.* 1920. *M.* 1949, Lyn Eatwell. *S.* 2. *Dau.* 1. *Career:* Indian Army (19th King George V's Own Lancers) 1940–45; Man. Dir., Bernard Weatherill Ltd. (Tailors) 1958–70; Conservative MP for Croydon North-East since 1964; appointed Opposition Whip 1967–70; Lord Commissioner of the Treasury 1970–71; Vice Chamberlain of HM Household 1971–72; Comptroller of HM Household 1972–73; Treasurer of HM Household & Govt. Dep. Chief Whip 1973–74; Opposition Dep. Chief Whip since 1974. *Publications:* Acorns to Oaks: The Future for Small Business in Britain. *Address:* 98 Lupus Street, London SW1; and House of Commons, London SW1A 0AA.

**WEAVER, Robert C.** American. *B.* 1907. *Educ.* Harvard Coll. (BS *cum laude* 1929) and Harvard Univ. (MA 1931; PhD 1934). *M.* 1935, Ella Haith. *S.* 1 (*Dec'd*). *Career:* Visiting Prof. N.Y. Univ. School of Education 1948–50; Dir. Opportunity Fellowships, John Hay Whitney Foundation 1950–55; Deputy Commissioner, N.Y. State Div. of Housing, Jan.–Dec. 1955; Administrator, N.Y. State Rent Commission 1955–58; Consultant, Ford Foundation 1959–60; Vice-Chmn. Housing and Re-development Board, N.Y.C. 1960–61; Administrator, Housing and Home Finance Agency 1961–66. Secretary, Department of Housing and Urban Development, Washington, Jan. 1966–68. President, Bernard Baruch College, City University of New York 1969–70; Distinguished Professor of Urban Affairs, Hunter College. *Publications:* Negro Labour—a National Problem (1946); The Negro Ghetto (1948); The Urban Complex (1964); Dilemmas of Urban America (1965). *Award:* Honorary Degrees from 29 colleges and universities; Spingarn Medal; Shepard Memorial Lecturer at Ohio State Univ.; Herman G. James Memorial Lecture at Univ. of Ohio; Sidney Hillman Lecturer at Univ. of Rochester; Lorado Taft Lecturer at Univ. of Illinois; Godkin Lectures at Harvard Univ. Fellow, Amer. Acad. of Arts & Sciences. Member of Lambda Alpha. Democrat. *Address:* 215 East 68th Street, New York, N.Y. 10021, U.S.A.

**WEAVER, William Merritt, Jr.** American investment banker. *B.* 1912. *Educ.* Princeton (BA 1934). *M.* (1) Shirley Fetterolf. (2) Solveig Eklund. (3) Rosemary Fine. *Daus.* 4. *Career:* Partner, Nathan Trotter & Co. Inc., Phila, 1934–40; Pres. and Dir., Frank Samuel & Co. Inc., Phila. 1945–59; Haile Mines, N.Y.C. 1957–58; President, Howmet Corp., N.Y.C. 1958–65 (Chmn. of Bd. 1965–66); Partner, Alex Brown & Sons 1966—. Director: U.M.C. Corporation; Allen Group; Marathon MFG; I.U. International; Columbus Dental Co. Served as Colonel, AUS 1941–45; Legion of Merit, Bronze Star (U.S.); Croix de Guerre (France and Belgium). Member, Downtown Association. *Clubs:* River, Downtown Assn (N.Y.C.), Ekwanok Country (Manchester, Vt.), Lyford Cay (Nassau). *Address:* Smith, Nevada, U.S.A.

**WEBB, David Evan.** British Chartered Accountant. *B.* 1910. *Educ.* Uppingham and Brasenose College, Oxford (BA Law). *M.* 1945, Mary Charlotte Andreae. *S.* 1. *Daus.* 3. *Career:* Senior Partner of Hays, Allan. Dir.: Calcutta Tramways Co. Ltd. (Chmn.); Beecham Group Ltd.; Artagen Properties Ltd.; Hovertravel Ltd.; Chmn. Intercobra Ltd.; Clubmaster of Scotland Ltd.; Thermaplex Ltd.; Coldfall Securities Ltd.; Straker Bros. Ltd.; Artagen Investments Property Ltd., (Australia); Vice-Chairman, Board of Governors of the Royal Free Hospital. *Clubs:* Boodles; St. George's Hill Golf. *Address:* Shandon, Cavendish Road, St. George's Hill, Weybridge, Surrey; and *office* Hays Allan, 317 High Holborn, London WC1V 7NL.

**WEBB, James E(dwin).** *B.* 7 Oct. 1906. *Educ.* AB, North Carolina; Hon. LL.D. 1949; Syracuse 1950; Colo. Coll. 1957; George Washington 1961; Duke 1966; New Mexico 1966; Brown 1976; Hon. Sc.D Notre Dame 1961; Washington (St. Louis) 1962; Washington Univ. 1962; N.Y. Univ. 1967; Wake Forrest 1969; Hon. D.C.L. Pittsburgh 1963; and many other honorary degrees. *Married:* Children 2. *Career:* From Personnel Dir. & Asst. to Pres. to Vice Pres. Sperry Gyroscope Co. 1936–43; Practicing Attorney 1945–46; Exec. Asst. Under Secy. Treas. 1946; Dir. U.S. Bur. Budget 1946–49; Under Secy. State, U.S. Dept. State 1949–52; Pres. Gen. Mgr. and Dir. Republic Supply Co. 1953–58; Admin. NASA 1961–68; Dir. Asst. to Pres. Kerr-McGee Oil Industries Inc. Okla 1952–61, 1969—; Dir. McDonnell Aircraft Corp. Mo. 1952–61; Oak Ridge Inst. Nuclear Studies Inc. 1956–60; Gannett Co. 1969—; Sperry Road Corp. 1969—; McGraw-Hill, Inc. since 1972. Trustee George Washington 1951–63; Meridian House Found. 1962–73 (Chmn. 1962–70); Cttee. Economic Dev. 1952–73; Nat. Geographic Socy. 1966—; Inst. for Court Management 1970–75; Regent Smithsonian Inst. 1970—. *Member:* Govt. Procurement Commission 1972–73; U.S.M.C.R. (Ret.); Lt. Colonel. Political Science Assn.; Bar Assn.; Socy. Pub. Admin. (Pres. 1966–67); Academy Political & Social Science; National Space Club; American Astronautical Soc. (Fellow); National Acad. of Public Admin. *Awards:* numerous, incl. Collier Trophy; Oklahoma Hall of Fame; Silver Buffalo; Boy Scouts of America; NASA Distinguished Service Medal; Pres. Medal of Freedom; Goddard Mem. Trophy; N.C. Public Service Award; Henry G. Bennett Distinguished Service Award (1973); Langley Gold Medal of the Smithsonian (1976). *Publications:* Governmental Manpower for Tomorrow's Cities (1962); Space Age Management (1968); NASA as an Adaptive Organization (1968); Leadership Evaluation in Large-Scale Efforts (1972); Management Leadership and Relationship (1972). *Address:* 1707 H Street, N.W., Washington, D.C. 20006, U.S.A.

**WEBB, Jervis Campbell.** American Engineer. *B.* 1915. *Educ.* M.I.T. (BS 1937). *M.* 1977, Patricia D. Webb. *Career:* Entered Jervis B. Webb Company in 1937 (in engineering and sales department). President and Chairman of the Board: Jervis B. Webb Company, Farmington Hills, Michigan; Spider Installations Limited, Hamilton, Ontario. Chairman of the Board: Jervis B. Webb Limited, London, England. President and Director: Control Engineering Company, Farmington Hills, Michigan; Webb Electric Company, Farmington Hills, Michigan; Webb Forging Company, Belleville, Michigan; Jervis B. Webb International Company, Farmington Hills, Michigan; Jervis B. Webb Continental Company, Farmington Hills, Michigan; Campbell, Henry & Calvin, Incorporated, Farmington Hills, Michigan; Ann Arbor Computer Corporation, Ann Arbor, Michigan; Jervis B. Webb Company of California, Los Angeles, California; Jervis

B. Webb Company of Georgia, Atlanta, Georgia; Jervis B. Webb Company of Canada, Limited, Hamilton, Ontario. Director: First Federal Savings and Loan Association, Detroit, Michigan; Huron Forge and Machine Company, Detroit, Michigan. *Member:* National Sanitation Fund; Traffic Safety for Michigan; American Materials Handling Society; American Ordnance Association; Greater Detroit Board of Commerce; American Society of Mechanical Engineers; Conveyor Equipment Manufacturers Association (past president); Detroit Area Council of Boy Scouts of America (Council Member at Large); Detroit Chapter Circumnavigators; Employers Association of Detroit (past director); Engineering Society of Detroit; Foundry Equipment Manufacturers Association (past director); Machinery and Allied Products Institute; Material Handling Institute; Michigan Manufacturers Association (past director); National Association of Manufacturers (director); Newcomen Society of North America; United States Chamber of Commerce. *Clubs:* Economic Club of Detroit (director); Detroit Athletic Club (past president); Detroit Golf Club; Detroit Rotary Club (past president); Engineers (N.Y.C.); Huron River Hunting and Fishing Club; Lake Shore Club; Bloomfield Hills Open Hunt Club; Oakland Hills Country Club. Author: many articles on materials handling, automation, and management philosophy. *Address:* 1436 Kirkway, Bloomfield Hills, Michigan 48013; and *office:* World Headquarters, Webb Drive, Farmington Hills, Michigan 48018, U.S.A.

**WEBB, John Percival**, OBE, JP. Australian. *Educ.* Marist Brothers' College, Bendigo, Victoria; Fellow, Chartered Institute of Secretaries. *M.* 1927, Vera E. Stokes. *S.* John B. (MB, BS). *Career:* Chmn. and Man. Dir., Victorian Producers' Co-operative Co. Ltd. (since 1947); Commissioner, Melbourne Harbour Trust (1941); Chairman of Directors: Group Warehouse Ltd. (1947). Director: The Producers & Citizens Co-op. Assurance Co. Ltd. (1939); United Holdings Ltd. (1939); P & C. Fire & General Insurance Co. Ltd. (1960); U.H. Investments Ltd. (1962); Lacy Pty. Lt. (1962); Associated Properties Ltd. 1967—. Mem.: State Wool Committee (when wool was under Commonwealth Government control) 1943–46; Commonwealth Government Dairy Industry Committee of Enquiry 1959–60. Councillor, Melbourne Chamber of Commerce 1942–51. *Address:* 16 Heyington Place, Toorak, Victoria, Australia.

**WEBER, Carl Nicholas.** Canadian. *B.* 1899. *Educ.* Kitchener and Waterloo. *M.* 1925, Irene Wittig. *S.* Carl J., Paul, Eric, John G., Bruce. *Daus.* Ilene (Torode) and Jene (Good). *Career:* Chmn. C. N. Weber Ltd. 1937 (wholesalers and distributors of industrial equipment, building materials and hardware); President: Kitchener-Waterloo Hospital 1934–54; Ontario Hospital Assn. 1952–53; Ontario Assn. Boards of Trade and Chamber of Commerce 1945–46. Governor, Univ. of Waterloo. *Address:* 340 Long-fellow Drive, Waterloo, Ont.; and *office* 675 Queen Street South, Kitchener, Canada.

**WEBSTER, Sir Robert Joseph**, CMG, CBE, MC, Hon DSc. Univ. of N.S.W. and Univ. of Wollongong. *B.* 1891. *Educ.* Charters Towers Public School. Queensland. *M.* (1) 1921, May Twigg (*D.* 1949), and (2) 1954, Daphne Kingcott. *S.* 2 (1 Dec.). *Daus.* 3. *Career:* In Commonwealth Public Service 1906–19; Rural Pursuits, Murgon, Qld. 1919–26; Director, South Burnett Dairy Co. Member Cncl. of Agriculture; General Manager, Queensland Cotton Board 1926–36. Served in World War I with Australian Imperial Forces; Staff Capt. (first Australian to be appointed to Staff at General HQ. France) in Egypt, Gallipoli and France (despatches; MC). President, N.S.W. Chamber of Manufacturers 1950–51 and Associated Chambers of Manufacturers of Australia 1951. Member, Australian National Airlines Commission 1952–55. Commonwealth Controller of Cottons 1942–46; a Trustee of N.S.W. Museum of Applied Arts & Sciences 1946–61 (Pres. 1950–61); Chairman. Bradmill Industries 1939–40 & 1960–76, Gen. Mgr. 1936–40, Man. Dir. 1940–67; Mem. of Council, Univ. of New South Wales 1947–76, Chancellor 1970–76, Chancellor Emeritus; Councillor, Design Council of Australia; Federal President, Australian Inst. of Mgmt. 1962–65; Pres. Textile Cncl. of Australia, 1960–73; Men.: Australia–Japan Business Co-operation Cttee. Fellow, Australian Society of Accountants; Int. Academy of Management, and of Australian Institute of Management (Pres.. Sydney Div., 1947–50 and 1958–62, Federal Pres. 1962–64). Companion, British Textile Institute. *Clubs:* The Australian Golf; Union; Imperial Service; American National. *Address:* 2 Buena Vista Avenue, Mosman, Sydney, N.S.W.; and *office* Bradmill Industries Ltd., 39–65 Parramatta Road, Camperdown, N.S.W., Australia.

**WEDELL-WEDELLSBORG, Baron Gustav.** Danish executive. *B.* 1905. *Educ.* Graduated from Stenhus, Holbaek (Denmark) 1925; practical business training at Vejen and Kolding, Jutland (Denmark). *M.* 1938, Kathryn Maxine Alcott. *S.* Henri. *Dau.* Louisa. *Career:* Joined The East Asiatic Co., Copenhagen 1928. President and Member of Board of Directors: The East Asiatic Co. (P.Q.) Ltd., The East Asiatic Co. Inc., The American Transpacific Corp. Member: Board of Dirs., Scandinavian Airlines System Inc. New York (rotating Chmn.), The Constitution Insurance Corp. N.Y.; The West Indian Co. Ltd., Virgin Island, U.S.A., and Carlsberg Agency Inc.; Danish-American Trade Council Inc., U.S.A. (Hon. Chmn.); Commissioner-General for Denmark Pavilion, N.Y. World Fair 1965. Mem., Bd. of Trustees and Treas., The American Scandinavian Foundation, New York. Co-founder of H. Rudebeck & Co. Ltd., London, Eng. Mem.: Bd. of Trade of Chicago and Memphis, Foreign Policy Assn. of U.S.A., New York Produce Exchange, New York Cocoa Exchange, New York Coffee and Sugar Exchange Inc. (Member, Bd. of Managers), and Board of Directors, Natl. Coffee Assn. of U.S.A. *Award:* Knight, Order of Dannebrog, and First Knight of Dannebrog (Denmark) and received Freedom Medal of King Christian X. *Clubs:* Explorers; India House (New York); Royal Danish Yacht (Life Member); Ocean Club of Florida; Siwanoy Country, Bronxville. *Address:* Winter: 3 Sabal Island Drive, Delray Beach, Florida, U.S.A.

**WEEKS, Charles Carson.** Canadian. *B.* 1914. *Educ.* Graduated High School. *M.* 1936, Mildred Frances See. *Dau.* Mildred Sharon. *Career:* With Algoma Steel since 1937; Manager of Sales 1948–57; Vice-Pres. Sales 1957; Senior Vice Pres. 1973. *Member:* Amer. Iron & Steel Inst.; International Iron & Steel Institute. *Address:* 8 Summit Avenue, Sault Ste. Marie, Ont.; and *office* Algoma Steel Corporation, Queen Street East, Sault Ste. Marie, Ont., Canada.

**WEEKS, Sir Hugh**, CMG. British. *B.* 1904. *Educ.* Cambridge University (MA). *M.* 1949, Constance Tomkinson. *S.* 1. *Daus.* 2. *Career:* Director General of Statistics & Programmes, Ministry of Supply 1941–43; Ministry of Production 1942–45; Director, J. S. Fry & Sons 1945–47; Member Economic Planning Board 1947–48 and 1959–61; Joint Controller, Colonial Development Corp. 1948–51; Deputy Chairman, Truscon Ltd. 1951–60; Dep. Chmn. Richard Thomas Baldwin 1965–68; Director: Industrial and Commercial Finance Corp. Ltd. 1959–74; Black and Decker European Board; Chmn. Leopold Joseph Holdings Ltd.; Chmn., London American Finance Corp. Ltd.; Chmn. Electrical & Industrial Securities 1970–77; Chmn., Economic Cttee., Confederation of British Industries 1957–72; Pres. British Export Houses Association, 1972–74. *Award:* U.S. Medal of Freedom with Silver Palm. *Publications:* (with Paul Redmayne) Market Research. *Clubs:* United Oxford and Cambridge University (London). *Address:* 8 The Grove, Highgate Village, London, N.6; and *office:* 31–45 Gresham Street, London, E.C.2.

**WEERASINGE, Oliver**, OBE. Ceylonese. UN Consultant. *B.* 1907. *Educ.* Royal College, Colombo, Ceylon; Liverpool University, England. *M.* 1942, Christobel Beatrice Kotelwela. *S.* Rohan Senka. *Dau.* Dharmini Menakka McDougal. *Career:* Head, Town & Country Planning Dept., Ceylon 1947–56; Chmn. Bd. of Improvement Commissioners 1953–56; Chief Planning & Urbanization Section, Dept. of Economic & Social Affairs, United Nations, New York, 1956–64; Ambassador to the United States of America 1965–70. Concurrently Ambassador to Mexico 1967–70. Exec. Secy. U.N. Seminar on Regional Planning, Tokyo 1958; U.N. Expert Group on Metropolitan Planning, Stockholm, 1961; U.N. Symposium on New Towns, Moscow 1964; Deputy Director, Centre for Housing, Building & Planning, U.N., N.Y. 1965; United Nations Consultant in Urban Dev. Policy. Delegate to 20th Session, U.N. General Assembly 1965. Fellow: Royal Institute of British Architects, and Royal Town Planning Institute of England. *Address:* 94 Barnes Place, Colombo 7, Sri Lanka.

**WEGENER-CLAUSEN, Thorkild.** Danish diplomat. *B.* 1908. *Educ.* Candidatus juris 1934. *M.* 1955, Agnethe Boserup. (*dec'd*). *Career:* Entered Danish Foreign Service, May 1935; Vice-Consul, Hamburg, April 1938; Secy., Ministry of Foreign Affairs, Copenhagen, April 1941; Assistant Head of Section, April 1944; Commercial Secy., London, June 1945; Asst. Head of Section, Oct. 1949, Head of Legal Dept., Aug. 1951, Min. of For. Affs.; Deputy Consul-General, New York, Aug. 1953; Counsellor, Embassy, Oslo, Aug. 1955; Chargé d'Affaires e.p. in New Zealand and Consul General in New

Zealand and for Fiji Islands, Mar. 1958–Aug. 1962. Consul General in Hamburg, Aug. 1962–Sept. 1968. From Sept. 1969, at the disposal of the Foreign Ministry; Envoy Extraordinary and Minister Plentipotentiary 1972. *Awards:* Cross of Knight of Order of Dannebrog 1st Class, and of Commander of Norwegian Order of St. Olav 2nd Class; Grand Cross of Merit, The Order of Merit Federal Republic of Germany. *Address:* Le Mas Né, Le Cannet des Maures, Var, France.

**WEGHSTEEN-COURTOY, Pierre J. M. G.** *B.* 1921. *Educ.* Docteur en droit (UCL). *M.* (1) 1946, Denise Courtoy (*D.* 1974). *Daus.* 3. (2) 1975, Janyne Herkens. *Career:* Sec.-Gen., Caisse Privée 1947–59; Man. Dir., Banque d'Investissements Privés, Geneva 1959–76, Dir. & Adviser 1976; Dir. (1951–65) & Pres. (since 1965), S.A. Bureau Courtnoy N.V. (Office of Industrial & Agricultural Studies), Brussels; *Director:* Union Generale Belge d'Electricité, Brussels 1951–66; Construction et Entreprises Industrielles, Brussels 1952–65; Financière Privée, Brussels 1955; Comptoir Mobilier et Financier, Brussels 1976; Sté de contrôle et d'Investissements Financiers, Geneva 1962—. Pres., Commodity Investment Corp. Ltd. Fribourg 1977—. *Member:* Assn. of Swiss Bankers; Academic Soc. of Geneva. Fellow, International Bankers Assn. Inc., Washington D.C. *Award:* Chevalier, Order of Leopold (Switzerland). *Clubs:* Touring Club of Switzerland; Fédération Suisse de Ski; Amis des Beaux-Arts. *Address:* Mars A.V. 4, App. 103, 1972 Anzère; and *office* 7 Place de l'Université, P.O. Box 138, 1211 Geneva 11, Switzerland.

**WEHENKEL, Antoine (Louis Nicolas).** Luxembourger. *B.* 1907. *Educ.* Ecole Centrale de Paris (Engineer of Arts and Manufactures). *M.* 1930, Marie-Louise Guillier. *S.* 4. *Dau.* 1. *Career:* Engineer with the French Railways 1935; Chief Engineer, National Company of Luxembourg Railways 1948 (Director-General 1962–64); Deputy Manager, Our Department Electric Co. 1957–64; Vice-Pres., International Co. of Canalization from the Moselle 1957–64. Member: Chamber of Deputies 1951–62 and 1969—; Commune Council of the city of Luxembourg 1951–64; Minister of the Budget, the National Economy, and of Power, July 1964–69. *Publication:* Etude sur l'éctrification des Chemins de Fer Luxembourgeois (Survey of the Electrification of the Luxembourg Railways). *Awards:* Commander, Order of the Oak Crown (Luxembourg); Officer, Order of Merit (Luxembourg); Comdr., Order of the Crown (Belgium); Comdr. Legion of Honour (France); Grand Cross, Order of Merit with Star (Germany); Grand Cross, Order of St. Olav (Norway); Grand Officer, Order of Liberation (Central Africa); Grand Officer, Order of Adolf de Nassau; Grand Cross, Order of the Liberation, Tunisia. Corresponding Member of the Grand Ducal Institute of Sciences. *Member:* Luxembourg Association of Graduate Engineers; Civil Engineers of France; Pres. Luxembourg Socialist Workers' Party. *Address:* 11 Bd. Grande de cheme, Charlotte, Luxembourg.

**WEICKER, Lowell Palmer.** American industrialist. *B.* 14 Oct. 1903. *Educ.* Yale University (BS). *M.* (1) Mary Hastings Bickford (*Div.* 1951); (2) 1953, Beverly Kraft (*Div.* 1965); (3) Antoinette Littell. *S.* Theodore Martin, Lowell Palmer, Harold Hastings. *Dau.* Mary-Audrey. *Career:* Joined the U.S. Army Air Force June 1942 and was commissioned Major; went overseas immediately as Asst. A-5, 8th Air Force; appointed Exec. A-2 of the 8th Air Force Dec. 1942; Acting A-2 of the 8th Air Force 1943; Dep. Dir. of Intelligence, U.S. Strategic Air Forces in Europe 1944–45; Asst. Sec. Gen., N.A.T.O. for Production and Logistics (1953–55); member of the Corp., Presbyterian Hospital, New York; member of Bd. of Directors, New York Heart Association; mem. Midtown Advisory Cttee. Chase Manhattan Bank. Former Chmn., Pres., Chief Exec. Officer & Dir., Bigelow-Sanford Inc., N.Y.C.; former Dir., Bigelow-Sanford AG (Switzerland); former Dir. & mem. Exec. Cttee., Sperry & Hutchinson Co.; Pres. & Dir., Northco Corp. of Panama; former Chmn. of the Bd., Jesup & Lamont International Securities Ltd., London. Prior to entrance into diplomatic service was President and a Director of E. R. Squibb & Sons; Director: E. R. Squibb & Sons Ltd. (England); Vice-Chmn. of the Board, Compania Squibb De Fomenta, S.A.; Vice-Pres. and a Director of Jones Estate Corporation; Chairman of the Board and a Director of Lentheric Inc.; Chairman of the Board and a Director of Lentheric of Canada Ltd.; Chairman and a Director of Lentheric Ltd. (England); Managing Director of Parfums Lentheric, G.M.B.H.; Director of Lentheric, S.A. (France); Chmn. Bd. Jesup & Lamont International Ltd., London. *Awards:* Legion of Merit; Bronze Star; U.S. Army Commendation Medal; Order of the British Empire; Légion d'Honneur; Croix de Guerre avec Palme; Grand Ufficiale al Merito della Republica (Italy); Star of Solidarity (Italy). *Address:* 330 Madison Avenue, New York 10017, U.S.A.

**WEIDEN, Paul L.** Attorney-at-Law. *B.* 1908. *Educ.* Doctor of Law, Univ. of Frankfurt, Germany 1931; and Master of Law, Univ. of London, England 1936. *S.* Dr. Paul Weiden, resident internal Medicine, Univ. of Washington Seattle Wash. (of first marriage), Peter and Michael. *Career:* Chief of Legal Section, Liberated Area Branch. Foreign Economic Administration, U.S. Government 1942–43; specializing in International Law, New York 1947—; Member of the Bar of the State of New York and of the Supreme Court of the U.S. 1942—. Member of the English bar 1936—, and of the German Bar; Attorney, Securities and Exchange Commission, U.S. Government 1944–55. Barrister-at-Law, London 1936—, and Attorney-at-Law, U.S.A. 1938—. Chairman, Board of Directors, various European and American corporations. *Publications:* miscellaneous publications in American, British and German legal periodicals. *Member:* Association of the Bar of the City of New York; County Association. *Address:* 800 Third Avenue, New York, N.Y. 10022; and *office* 660 Madison Avenue, New York, N.Y. 10021, U.S.A. and Bockenheimer Anlage 38, Frankfurt/Main, Germany.

**WEIKOP, Ove Vilhelm.** Danish politician. *B.* 21 April 1897. *M.* 1918, Emmy Hansen. President, Danish Textile Union 1936–37 and 1938–50; member, Copenhagen Town Council 1933–50, Maritime and Commercial Court, Copenhagen 1940–51; MP (Cons.) 1947–68; Formerly Minister of Commerce, Industry and Shipping; Burgomaster of Copenhagen 1951–70. Cmdr., Order of Dannebrog; KCV; Grand Officer, Order of Orange-Nassau: Cmdr., Crown of Thailand. *Address:* 22 Borgmester Jensens Alle, 2100 Copenhagen, Denmark.

**WEINSTOCK, Sir Arnold.** British. Managing Director, The General Electric Company Ltd., 1963—. *B.* 1924. *Educ.* London School of Economics, BSc (Econ). *M.* Netta Sobell. *S.* 1. *Dau.* 1. Fellow, Royal Statistical Society. Hon. LLD, Leeds 1977; Hon. DSc. *Address:* 1 Stanhope Gate, London W1A 1EH.

**WEIR, James Harrison.** New Zealand Diplomat. *B.* 1922. *Educ.* Christchurch (N.Z.) Boys' High School, and Canterbury University (MA). *M.* 1947, Mary Helen de Muth. *S.* 1. *Daus.* 3. *Career:* Joined N.Z. Dept. of External Affairs 1947; Third Secy. and Vice-Consul, New York 1949–51; Second Secy., Ottawa 1951–52; Dept. of External Affairs, Wellington 1952–56; First Secy., Canberra 1956–59; Counsellor, 1959–61; Dept. of External Affairs, Wellington, 1961–61; Counsellor, Washington 1963–64; Minister 1965. New Zealand High Commissioner at Singapore 1966–70; Asst. Secy. Ministry, Foreign Affairs Wellington 1970–73; N.Z. High Commissioner Kuala Lumpur 1973–76, and concurrently Amb. to Burma & Commissioner to Brunei 1974–76; Ambassador Moscow & concurrently to Finland & Outer Mongolia since 1977. *Address:* New Zealand Embassy, Moscow, U.S.S.R.

**WEISBROD, Maxfeld.** American attorney specializing in trials and appeals. *B.* 1894. *Educ.* George Washington University Law School (LLB). *M.* 1931, Rose Anna Pusheck. *S.* Charles Albert. *Dau.* Anita Elizabeth. *Career:* Asst. to Manager of Patent Department, General Electric Company, Washington, D.C. 1915–23; admitted to practice before the courts of District of Columbia, United States Patent Office, and courts of Illinois; servee in World War I (France; Engineers). *Publications:* contributions to various legal journals. *Address:* 4182 Clarendon Avenue, Chicago, Ill., 60613 U.S.A.

**WEISSKOPF, Victor Frederick.** American (Austrian born) scientist. *B.* 1908. *Educ.* University, of Göttingen (PhD). *M.* 1934, Ellen Tvede. *S.* Tom. *Dau.* Karen. *Career:* Research Associate, Berlin 1932–32, Zürich Institute of Technology 1933–36; Rockefeller Foundation Fellow, Copenhagen and Cambridge 1936–37; Instructor in Physics, University of Rochester (U.S.A.) 1937–40, Asst. Professor 1940–43; Group Leader, Los Alamos Scientific Laboratory 1943–45; Prof. of Physics, Massachusetts Inst. of Technology 1945–61; Member Directorate, CERN 1960–61: Dir.-Gen. of CERN (European Organization for Nuclear Research) 1961–65; Chairman, Dept. of Physics, Massachusetts Institute of Technology 1967—. *Award:* Max Planck Medal 1956; Hon. Fellow; Société Française de Physique, and Weizmann Inst. Corresponding Member, Acad. of Sciences, Munich, Royal

Society, Edinburgh. Hon. DSc: Manchester, Lyons, Basle, Uppsala, Geneva, Yale, Oxford, Copenhagen, Vienna Rehovoth, Israel, Paris and Chicago, Turin. *Member:* American and Italian Physical Societies; Academie des Sciences; and National, Royal Danish, Bavarian, Scottish and Austrian Academies of Sciences. *Publications:* Theoretical Nuclear Physics (Wiley, 1952); Knowledge & Wonder (Doubleday, 1962). Physics in the XX Century (M.I.T. Press 1972). Chevalier, Legion of Honour (France). *Address:* 36 Arlington Street, Cambridge, Mass. 02140; and *office* M.I.T., Cambridge, Mass., U.S.A.

**WEISSMAN, George.** American. Commander of the Order of Merit of the Italian Republic. *B.* 1919. *Educ.* B.B.A. City Coll., N.Y.; graduate work at N.Y. Univ. and Univ. of Illinois. *M.* 1944, Mildred Stregack. *S.* Paul Jonathan and Daniel Mark. *Dau.* Ellen Victoria. *Career:* With Philip Morris. Asst. to the Pres. and Dir. of Pub. Relations 1952-53; Vice-Pres. 1953–57; Vice-Pres., Dir. of Marketing 1957–59; Exec. Vice Pres. Marketing of Philip Morris Inc. 1959; Chmn. Bd. Chief Exec. Officer Philip Morris International 1960; Exec. Cttee. Bd. Philip Morris Incorporated 1964; Bd. Dirs. Benson & Hedges( Canada) Ltd. 1958–70; Miller Brewing Co. since 1969. With U.S. Navy 1942–46; Lieut. (SG), Capt. of U.S.S. SC 497; Exec. Officer, U.S.S. Horace A. Bass. Named 'Exec. of the Year' by National Assn. of Tobacco Distributors, 1954. Trustee. Associated YM-YWHA's of Greater New York; Bd. of Dirs. Lincoln Center. Member Bd. Managers, Swarthmore College; National Citizens Committee of the United Community Campaign of America; Business Cttee. for the Arts. Dir. of Avret Incorporated. *Clubs:* Sky; National Press. *Address:* 100 Park Avenue, New York, N.Y. 10017, U.S.A.

**WEITNAUER, Dr. Albert.** Swiss diplomat. *B.* 1916. *Educ.* Basle Classical Gymnasium; Basle Univ. (Dr. of Laws). *Career:* entered Swiss Government Service 1941; Legal Adv. Central Office, War Economy 1941–46; Div. Foreign Trade 1946; 1st Head of Section 1951; Counsellor, in charge Economic Affairs Swiss Legation, London 1953–54; Embassy in Washington 1954–58; Swiss Govt. Delegate, Trade Agreements, Head Swiss Del. to GATT 1959–71; Min. Plenipotentiary 1961, Ambassador 1966, Del. Special Missions 1966–71; Ambassador to the Court of St James's 1971–75; Sec.-Gen. of the Swiss Foreign Ministry since 1976. *Publications:* articles, problems Swiss Foreign policy, European Integration and World Trade. *Address:* Ministry of Foreign Affairs, Berne, Switzerland.

**WEITZMAN, David, QC, MP.** British. *B.* 1898. *Educ.* Hutcheson's Grammar School, Glasgow; Manchester Central School; Manchester Univ. (BA) History Honours. *M.* Vivienne Hammond. *S.* Peter. *Dau.* Ruth Marion. *Career:* MP, Stoke Newington 1945–50; Appointed Queen's Counsel 1951; Member of Parliament for Stoke Newington & Hackney North since 1951. *Address:* Devereux Chambers, Devereux Court, Temple, London WC2R 3JJ.

**WELCH, Alexander Walker.** Australian company executive. *B.* 1905. *Educ.* University of Sydney (BA). *M.* 1935, Kathleen Jean Clark. *S.* Peter Alexander Lawson. *Dau.* Robyn Marjorie Elliott. *Career:* Clerk, Police Department 1921–30; Minute Secretary, Metropolitan Transport Trust, Sydney 1930–32; Private Secretary to Premier of N.S.W. 1932–35; Clerk, Premier's Department 1935–37 (Chief Clerk 1938); Asst. Under Secretary, Premier's Department 1938–41; Assistant-Secretary Department of Defence Co-ordination, Melbourne 1941; Secretary, Department of Home Security, Canberra 1941–44; Commonwealth Director of Housing, 1944–51; Managing Director, N.S.W. Mining Co. Pty. Ltd. 1952–58; Director, Newstan Colliery Pty. Ltd. 1951–58. Huntley Colliery Pty. Ltd. 1951–58, Newcom Colliery Pty. Ltd. 1951–58, Associated Plywoods Pty. Ltd. 1959–65, Australian Coal Assn. Research Ltd. 1958–65; Director and Sydney Secretary, Bulolo Gold Dredging Ltd. 1961–65, Director IDAC Pty. Ltd. 1963–65, Sydney Secretary Placer Development Ltd. 1961–65; Director, Clutha Development Pty. Ltd. 1960—; Wollclift Pty. 1965—; S. & M. Fox Pty. Ltd. 1965—; Burragorang Collieries Pty. Ltd. 1965—; Coal Right Pty. Ltd. 1965—; South Clifton Colliery Pty. Ltd. 1965—; Excelsior Collieries and Coke Works Pty. Ltd. 1965—; Owen's Tongarra Colliery Pty. Ltd. 1965—; S. & M. Fox Industries Pty. Ltd. 1965—; William Fox Pty. Ltd. 1960—; Fox Holdings Pty. Ltd. 1965—; Fox and Co. Pty. 1960—; Clintons Transports Pty. Ltd. 1965—; Clintons Nattai Collieries (Pty.) Ltd. 1965—; Western Main Collieries Pty. Ltd. 1965—; Lidsdale Real Estate Pty. Ltd. 1965—; The Nattai-Bulli Coal Co. Pty. Ltd. 1965—; Valley Coal Co. Pty. Ltd. 1965—. *Address:* 21 Kimbarra Road, Pymble, N.S.W., Australia.

**WELDON, Lt.-Col. Douglas Black, MC, ED, LLD.** Canadian investment dealer. *B.* 1895. *M.* 1923, Laura Margaret, dau. of Hon. F. B. Black. *S.* David Black. *Daus.* Marcia (Gould) and Ann (Lowry). *Career:* Chmn., Emeritus Bd. of Governors, University of Western Ontario. *Member,* London YM-YWCA; Director, The Royal Winter Fair. Dir., Citizens Research Inst. of Canada; member, National Finance Committee, Canadian Inst. of International Affairs. Served in World War I (47th Bn.; awarded Military Cross; Staff Capt. 10th Inf. Brigade). After the war with F. B. McCurdy Co., Halifax; opened branch office in Moncton, N.B., and later in London (Ont.) opened branch for Johnson & Ward. Organized Midland Securities Corpn. Ltd. in 1925. Member, the Military & Hospitaller Order of St. Lazarus, Jerusalem. LLD, Univ. of New Brunswick; LLD, University of Western Ontario. Conservative. *Clubs:* The Links (N.Y.C.); Toronto, York (Toronto); Ristigouche Salmon; Caledon (Inglewood, Ontario); Royal & Ancient Golf (St. Andrews); London; London Hunt & Country (London, Ontario). *Address: office* 220 Dundas Street, 801 Canada Trust Building, London, Ontario, Canada.

**WELENSKY, Rt. Hon. Sir Roy, PC, KCMG.** Former Prime Minister of Fed. of Rhodesia and Nyasaland. *B.* 1907. *Educ.* Salisbury, S. Rhodesia. *M.* (1) 1928, Elizabeth Henderson, (*Dec.*). *S.* 1. *Dau.* 1. (2) 1972, Miriam Valerie Scott. *Dau.* 1. *Career:* Joined Railway Service 1924; member National Council of Railroad Workers Union; Director, Manpower, N. Rhodesia 1941–46; formed N. Rhodesia Labour Party 1941; member: Foster Commission to investigate 1940 Copperbelt riot, Strauss (1943) and Grant (1946) Railway Arbitration Tribunals, of deleg. to London to discuss mining royalties 1949, and of deleg. to discuss Constitution 1950 and 1951; N. Rhodesia deleg. to Closer Association Conf., Victoria Falls 1951; M.L.C. N. Rhodeisa 1938; M.E.C. 1940–53; Chmn., Unofficial Members Assn. 1946–53; member, Interim Fed. Govt. Sept.–Dec. 1953; Fed. Min. Transport, Communications and Posts 1954–56; Deputy Prime Minister Mar. 1955–Oct. 1956; Prime Minister 1956–63; Fed. Min. Defence 1956–59. *Address:* P.O. Box 804, Salisbury, Rhodesia.

**WELLS, Harold Donald, Jr.** American consulting engineer, Director and Vice-President: A.P.M.E.W. Inc. 1950—. American Paper Machinery & Engineering Works 1940—, Harold D. Wells Inc. 1951—, Adirondack Fibre Corp. 1951—; Consulting Engineer, Rist, Bright and Frost 1962–63; Design Engineer, Kanryn Inc. 1963–64. *B.* 1918. *Educ.* Union College (Schenectady, N.Y.) and General Electric Co. (Advanced Course in Engineering). *M.* 1967, Victoria Basuk Wells. *S.* Thomas Rehn and Donald Rehn. Design Engineer, General Electric Co., Schenectady 1942–48. Author of magazine articles and technical papers. Awarded First Place, Class A.P., National Drawing Competition. *Member:* Technical Assn. of the Pulp & Paper Industry; Canadian Pulp & Paper Assn.; National Socy. of Professional Engineers; Amer. Socy. of Heating, Refrigerating and Air-Conditioning Engineers; Illuminating Engineering Socy.; Chamber of Commerce; Inst. of Electrical & Electronics Engineers; Paper Industry Management Assn.; Delta Phi; Lamplighters Assn.; Glen Falls Aero Club Inc. *Address:* 73 Chestnut Ridge Road, Glen Falls, N.Y., U.S.A.

**WELLS, James Doring.** American. *B.* 1920. *Educ.* Dartmouth Coll. (AB); Amos Tuck School of Business Admin. (MCS). *M.* 1944, Jane A. Page. *Daus.* 2. *Career:* Pres. Columbus & Sons Creamery Assn. Ltd. *Clubs:* Weston Golf; Union Club of Boston; Harvard (Boston). *Address: office* 1 Red Devil Lane, Watertown, Mass. 02172, U.S.A.

**WELLS, John Julius, MP.** *B.* 1925, *Educ.* Eton College and Corpus Christi College, Oxford (MA). *M.* 1948, Lucinda Meath-Baker. *S.* W. A. Andrew and Oliver. *Daus.* Julia J. and Henrietta F. *Career:* World War II in R.N.V.R. as Lieutenant. Submarines 1942–46; Borough Councillor Leamington Spa 1953–55; Dir. City Marine Finance Ltd. 1957–72; South Western Consultants Ltd. 1957—; ESAB Ltd. 1962—; Rotary Photographic Co. Ltd. 1962—; Member, Parliament Con. Maidstone since 1959; Opposition Spokesman, Horiculture 1964–70; Chmn. Parly. Select Cttee. on Horticulture 1966–68; Member of Speaker's Panel of Chmn.; Vice-Chmn. Cons. Party Agric. Cttee. 1970–73; Assn. Cons. Clubs 1970. *Member:* of Court, Kent Univ. 1965—. *Awards:* Knight Comdre. of Order of Civil Merit (Spain); Master, Worshipful Company of Fruiterers 1977. *Address:* Mere

House, Mereworth, Kent; and *office:* 6 Acre Road, Kingston, upon-Thames, Surrey.

**WELSH, Andrew,** MP. Scots Politician. *B.* 1944. *Educ.* Govan High Sch.; Univ. of Glasgow—MA (Hons) History & Politics. *M.* 1971, Sheena Margaret Cannon. *Career:* Scottish Nationalist MP for South Angus since 1974. *Member:* Educational Inst. of Scotland; General Teaching Council. *Clubs:* Univ. of Glasgow Union. *Address:* Olympia Buildings, Market Place, Arbroath, Scotland; and House of Commons, London SW1A 0AA.

**WELSH, Robert James,** WhEx, CEng, FIMechE, FIMarE, MNEC Inst. British. Mechanical Engineering Consultant. *B.* 1902. *Educ.* Spiers School Beith; Rutherford Tech. Coll., Newcastle-upon-Tyne; Sunderland Tech. College. *M.* 1935, Joan Monica Oakford. *S.* 1. *Daus.* 2. *Career:* Gen. Sales Mgr. Petters Ltd. 1935, Gen. Mgr. Gas Turbines Div. English Electric Co. Ltd. 1946–54; Dir. Glacier Metal Co. Ltd. 1955–60; Chmn. Man. Dir. Herbert Hunt & Sons Ltd. 1960–64; Man. Dir. Churchill Machine Tool Co. Ltd. 1964–65; Chmn. Assoc. British Machine Tool Makers Ltd. 1965–70. *Member:* Inst. of Directors; Shipwrights Co.; F.R.S.A.; M.B.I.M. *Clubs:* R.A.C.; E.E. O'seas. *Address:* 89 Brantingham Road, Manchester M16 8LX.

**WERNER, Dr. Jesse.** Chemical executive. *B.* 1916. *Educ.* Brooklyn Coll. (BS *cum laude* 1935) and Columbia University (MA 1936, PhD 1938—Organic Chemistry). *M.* 1943, Edna Lesser. *S.* Kenneth Mark. *Dau.* Nancy Ellen. *Career:* Assistant in Chemistry, Columbia University 1936–38; GAF Corp. 1938—; successively Research Chemist, Group Leader, Section Leader; Asst. Manager, Process Development; Technical Asst. to Vice-President Operations; Director of Commercial Development; Vice-Pres. Chmn. and Pres., GAF Corp., Chairman 1964, Pres. 1962; Dir. Curtis-Wright Corp. Director of many domestic and foreign subsidiaries and affiliates. *Award:* Alumni Award of Honor and Medal, Brooklyn College, 1962; Honor Award, Commercial Development Assn., 1963; Chemical Marketing Research Assn. Memorial Award, 1967; Chemical Industry Medal (Soc.CI, Am. Sect.) 1972. *Member:* American Assn. for Advancement of Science (Fellow); American Chemical Society; American Institute of Chemists (Fellow); Amer. Inst. of Chemical Engineers; Chemical Market Research Assn.; Com. Development Assn.; N.Y. Acad. of Sciences; Socy. of the Chemical Industry; Pi Mu Epsilon; Phi Lambda Upsilon; Sigma Xi. *Publications:* over sixty publications and patents on various phases of organic chemistry and chemical engineering. These include the Amination by Reduction section of the Annual Unit Process Review of Industrial and Engineering Chemistry which he wrote from 1948 to 1961, and numerous articles which he has contributed to the Encyclopedia of Chemical Technology, as well as chapters in the books Practical Emulsions and Commercial Waxes. Co-author of the chapter on Amination by Reduction in Groggins' Unit Processes in Organic Synthesis (5th Edn.). *Clubs:* Economic (N.Y.C.) (Pres. 1968–69); Hemisphere. *Address:* 140 West 51st Street, New York City, U.S.A.

**WERNER, Pierre.** Luxembourg Lawyer and Politician. *B.* 1913. *Educ.* Cours Supérieurs, Luxembourg; Faculty of Law, Univ. of Paris (Dr in Law); Independent School of Political Sciences, Paris (Diplome fin d'études). *M.* 1939, Henriette Pescatore. *S.* Jean, Charles, Henri. *Daus.* Marianne, Elisabeth. *Career:* Lawyer 1938, Banque Générale du Luxembourg 1938–44; Commissioner of the Contrôle Bancaire 1945, and Counsellor of the Government 1949–53; Minister of Finance and the Armed Forces 1954–58; Prime Minister and Min. of Finance 1959–64; Prime Minister, Min. Foreign Affairs, of Treasury and Justice 1964–66; Prime Minister Min. Treasury and Public Function 1967–69; Prime Minister and Minister of Finance 1969–74; Chmn. EEC Study Group for Economic and Monetary Union (Werner Report) 1970; Hon. Minister of State (and MP) since 1974. *Awards:* Grand Cross of the Orders of Leopold (Belgium), Orange-Nassau (Netherlands), Couronne de Chêne (Luxembourg); Mérite Civil (Luxembourg); Légion d'Honneur (France); Icelandic Falcon (Islande). Merit (Italy), Merit (Germany), White Elephant (Thailand), King George I (Greece); Pius IX (Vatican), Grosse goldene Ehrenzeichen am Bande (Austria), St. Olav (Norway), South (Brazil), Republic (Tunisia). *Member:* Christian-Social Party; Vice-President: *Pax Romania* 1937; President: Association des Universitaires Catholiques 1936–37. *Publications:* include reports on financial problems. *Address:* 2 rondpoint Robert-Schuman, Luxembourg.

**WERRING, Niels.** *B.* 1897. *M.* Else Wilhelmsen in 1926. *Career:* Former Snr. Partner Wilh. Wilhemsen, shipowners (Oslo); former chmn. of Bd. all Wilhemsen group of shipping companies. *Awards:* Member of Académie de Marine, Paris; Commander Order of St. Olav (Norway); Commander, Order of Dannebrog (Denmark); Commander, Order of Vasa (Sweden); Commander, Order of The Crown of Thailand, and Order of Aguila Azteca (Mexico); Officer, Legion of Honour (France) and Order of Leopold (Belgium). *Address:* Wilh. Wilhelmsen, Roald Amundsens Gate 5, P.O. Box 1359, Vika Oslo 1, Norway.

**WESSNER, Hans Otto.** Swiss industrialist. *B.* 1901. *Educ.* Univ. of St. Gall (Comm.) and King's Coll., Cambridge (Econ. and History). *M.* 1924, Alice Boskovits. *Career:* Managing Director (1925—), President, Board of Directors (1936—), and President, Managing Committee (1939–56), Zellulose Fabriks A.G., St. Michael, Vienna; Director, Board of Association of Austrian Paper & Cellulose Industry; member, Board of Directors, Zellstoff-Vertriebs G.m.b.H., Vienna; Proprietor, O. Wessner & Co. Ltd., Manufacturers and Merchants of Swiss Embroideries and Laces, 31 Vadianstrasse Gall 1961. *Member:* Bd. of Dirs. Swiss Chamber of Commerce. *Address:* Bartensteingasse 9, Vienna I; and Dierauerstrasse 14, St. Gall, Switzerland.

**WEST, Rt. Hon. Henry William,** PC. *B.* 1917. *Educ.* Portora Royal School. *M.* 1956, Maureen Elizabeth Hall. *S.* 4. *Daus.* 3. *Career:* Farmer. Northern Ireland Representative on British Wool Marketing Board 1950–58; High Sheriff, Co. Fermanagh 1954; Pres., Ulster Farmers' Union 1955–56. MP (U.) Enniskillen 1954–72; Parly. Secy. Minister of Agriculture 1958; Minister of Agriculture in Parliament of Northern Ireland 1960–67 and 1971–72; Mem. N. Ireland Assembly for Fermanagh & S. Tyrone 1973–75; MP at Westminster for Fermanagh & S. Tyrone Feb.-Sept. 1974, at N. Ireland Constitutional Convention 1975. *Address:* Rossahilly House, Enniskillen, Co. Fermanagh, Northern Ireland.

**WEST, John Cristy.** American banker. *B.* 1908. *Educ.* Yale Univ. (AB). *M.* 1943, Barbara Robinson. *S.* John Robinson. *Dau.* Cristy. *Career:* With J. P. Morgan & Co. 1930–34; with Brown Brothers, Harriman & Co. since 1934; Partner, Private Bank, Brown Brothers, Harriman & Co., 59 Wall Street, New York City; Director: Philadelphia Life Insurance Co., Transatlantic Fund Inc., Howmet Corporation, American Bank Note Co., Vice-President, Seamen's Church Institute, Philadelphia. *Address: office* 59 Wall Street, New York City, U.S.A.

**WEST LAU, John Anthony.** Australian company director *B.* 1919. *Educ.* Gordon Institute of Technology, Geelong, Vic. *M.* 1945, Fay Thelma Shepherd. *S.* John Frederick. *Career:* Fifteen years with Ansett Transport Industries companies; General Manager, Ansett Travel Service Pty. Ltd.; Gen. Mgr., Ansett Airways Pty. Ltd.; Asst. Gen. Mgr., Ansett-Australian National Airways Pty. Ltd. (after merger of the companies); Director & Gen. Mgr., Ansett-Ana Pty. Ltd.; Asst. to Managing Director, Ansett Transport Industries Ltd.; thence transfer as Gen. Mgr., John D. Harris & Co., Printers & Publishers. *Member:* Institute of Transport. *Clubs:* Royal Yacht (Tasmania and Victoria); Sportsmen's Assn. of Australia. *Address: office* 1–9 Gold Street, Collingwood, Vic., Australia.

**WESTACOTT, John Dudley.** British Chartered surveyor *B.* 1904. *Educ.* City of London School. *M.* 1929, Kathleen Liliann Johnson. *S.* John Bentley. *Career:* Director: Cosby Properties Ltd.; Bentley Estates Ltd. Fellow, Chart. Surveyors Institute. Conservative. *Clubs:* London Golf Captains; Royal Motor Yacht. *Address:* 11 Minterne Grange, Crichel Mount Road, Poole, Dorset, BH14 8LU.

**WESTERMAN, Sir (Wilfred) Alan,** CBE. Australian. *B.* 1913. *Educ.* Universities of Tasmania, Melbourne and Columbia (N.Y.); EdD; MA (Econ). *M.* 1969, Margaret White. *Career:* Chairman: Commonwealth Tariff Board 1958–60; Secy. Dept. of Trade & Industry, Commonwealth of Australia 1960–71; Exec. Chmn. Australian Industry Development Corp. 1971—. *Clubs:* Union (Sydney); Atheneum (Melbourne); Commonwealth (Canberra); Royal Canberra Golf. *Address:* 47 Tasmania Circle, Forrest, Canberra, A.C.T.; and *office* A.I.D.C. Northbourne Avenue, Canberra, A.C.T., Australia.

**WESTON, (Willard) Garfield.** Chairman, George Weston Holdings Ltd., and associated companies, Allied Bakeries Ltd. and Weston Foods Ltd.; Chairman, George Weston

Ltd., Toronto (and associated companies) and of Weston Bakeries Ltd., Toronto; William Paterson Ltd. (Brantford, Ont.) and Weston Biscuit Co. (Passaic, N.J.); Chairman, Fortnum & Mason Ltd. (London). *B.* 1898. *Educ.* Harbord Collegiate Inst., Toronto. *M.* 1921, Reta Lila Howard. *S.* 3. *Daus.* 6. Served in World War I (Canadian Engineers in France). With George Weston Ltd., Toronto since 1919 (Vice-Pres. 1921; Manager 1922); went to U.K. 1934; founded Weston Biscuit companies and Allied Bakeries Ltd.; erected new plants in many parts of the country. MP (National Unionist) for Macclesfield 1939–45. *Club:* Carlton. *Address:* Weston Centre, 40 Berkeley Square, London, W.1.

**WESTOVER, Russell Channing.** American attorney. *B.* 1910. *Educ.* University of Virginia (LLB) 1971 (JD). *M.* 1935, Ruth Vander Veer. *S.* Russell C. III, and Garrett V. *Dau.* Gail DeLancey. *Career:* Pres. Dir., Ray Oil Burner Co. Director: President and Director, Civic Federal Savings & Loan; Ray Oöl Brener G.M.B.N. *Address: office* Ray Oil Burner Co., 1301 San Jose Avenue, San Francisco, U.S.A.

**WESTPHAL, William Henry,** OBE. American, International Management. *B.* 1907. *Educ.* University of Pennsylvania (BSEcon). *M.* 1942, Eleanor L. Smith. *S.* Stuart William. *Career:* With Eastman Kodak Co. 1930–41; U.S. Army, Lieut-Col. 1942–45; Honeywell Inc. 1946–52; W. J. German Inc. 1952–56; Daystrom Inc. 1956–63; Vice-President, Rockwell Manufacturing Co. (Pittsburgh, Pa.) Nov. 1963–70; Consultant since 1970. *Address:* 3645 White Sulphur Place, Sarasota, Fla. 33580, U.S.A.

**WESTWOOD, Bryan Percy,** FRIBA, AADip (Hons). British Chartered Architect; Consultant (former Partner), Westwood, Piet, Poole & Smart, 21 Suffolk Street, London, S.W.1. Past President, Architectural Association. *B.* 1909. *Educ.* Sidcot School and Architectural Association School (Hons Diploma). *M.* 1943, Lavender Mary Bruce. *S.* 1. *Daus.* 2. *Career:* Partner, P. J. Westwood, Sons & Partners 1934–40; served in World War II (R.N.V.R.; Sub.-Lt. 1940; Lieut. 1941; Lt.-Cmdr. 1944); member, Architects Registration Council 1938–40 and 1948–52; member, Council of Royal Institute of British Architects 1954–56 and 1962–64; member, Council of Architectural Association 1936–39 and 1947–56 (Hon. Treas. 1951–53; Vice-Pres. 1953–54; Pres. 1956); Won Architectural Competition for Goldalming Civic Centre 1939. *Publications:* The Modern Shop (Architectural Press); various technical articles on architecture and photography; photographic illustrations for Country Notes, V. Sackville-West (1939). *Address:* The River House, by Loddon, Wargrave, Berks.

**WETTERLUNDH, Sune Charles Gustaf.** Swedish executive. *B.* 1904. *Educ.* University of Lund (ML). *M.* 1933, Gunborg (Ickan) Lundström. *S.* Göran and Einar. *Dau.* Inger. *Career:* Vice-Governor of Malmöhus Province 1949–55; Managing Director of Sydsvenska Kraftaktiebolaget 1956–70; Chairman of Norrlandskraft AB 1959–69; Oskarshamnsverkets Kraftgrupp AB 1965–72; Atomkraftkonsortiet 1960–76; Angpanneforeningen, 1970–76; and of Svenska Kraft verksföreningen 1968–72; Member of Boards of Skandinaviska Enskilda Banken 1962–73. *Awards:* KVO 1st Class; KNO; KDI 1st Class; OffEtSO; HvGm. *Member:* Royal Physiographic Society, Royal Society of Letters, and The New Society of Letters (all of Lund). *Clubs:* Rotary; Travellers'. *Address:* Fersens Väg 12, 21142 Malmo, Sweden.

**WEYBRIGHT, Victor (Royer).** Book publisher, editor, author. *B.* 1903. *Educ.* Universities of Pennsylvania and Chicago. *M.* 1950, Helen Macdonald Talley (2nd). *Stepson:* Truman Macdonald Talley. *Stepdaughter,* Mrs. Helen Haskell Sampson. *Career:* Sec. to Jane Addams, Chicago 1924–26; Travelling newspaper correspondent 1926–27; Associate Editor, Butterick Publishing Co., N.Y.C. 1927–34; Freelance writer 1934–35; Managing Editor, Survey Associates 1935–42; Consultant, Reader's Digest 1935–42; Executive, Office of War Information, Special Assistant to U.S. Ambassador, London 1942–45; Founder and chairman of the Board, New American Library Inc., publishers of Signet, Mentor Books and NAL Books, N.Y.C. 1945–66 (Chairman of Executive Committee 1960–64); Director: Times-Mirror Co., Los Angeles 1961–64, and New English Library (Holdings) Ltd., London, England 1961–66; Independent Publishing (books and magazines) since 1966. Mem. of Bd., American Book Publishers Council 1954–57. *Awards:* Hon. LHD, Wagner College, 1961; Hon. LL.D Univ. of Wyoming 1972; Hon. LHD Univ. of Syracuse 1974; Hon. LittD Western Maryland Coll. 1976. *Member:* Author's League (U.S.A.); P.E.N. (member Bd.); Society of Authors (England). Democrat. *Publications:* Spangled Banner. The Story of Francis Scott Key (1935); Buffalo Bill and the Wild West (with Henry B. Sell, 1955); The Americans—South and North (1941); The Making of a Publisher (1967); Contributions to magazines. *Clubs:* Century Association, Overseas Press, Players, National Beagle (N.Y.C.); Cosmos (Washington); Timber Ridge Hunt (Md.); Hamilton (Baltimore, Md.); Savile (London). *Address:* 50 East 77th Street, New York City 10021; and *office* 516 Fifth Avenue, New York, 10036, U.S.A.

**WHALLEY, Wilfrid Barrett.** American research engineer and professor. *B.* 1908. *Educ.* Univ. of Toronto (BASc Hons 1932; MASc 1935). *M.* 1941, Dorothy Ermyn Hill. *S.* Lawrence Reginald. *Dau.* Alison Brenda. *Career:* Instructor, Dept. of Electrical Engineering, Univ. of Toronto 1931–36; Research Engineer, Radio Corp. of America 1937–40; Research Physicist, National Research Council, Ottawa 1940–41; Research Engineer, Research Enterprises Ltd., Toronto 1941–43, and Radar and Television, R.C.A. Laboratories, Princeton, N.J. 1943–47; Asst. Professor Engineering Physics, Cornell Univ. 1947–48; Head, Applications Research Laboratory, Sylvania Electric, Bayside, N.Y. 1948–53. Senior Television Engineer, Columbia Broadcasting System, New York 1954–62; Adjunct Professor, Electrical Engineering, Polytechnic Institute of Brooklyn, N.Y., 1951–62; Senior Technical Specialist, Navigation, Systems Division, Autonetics, a Division of North American Rockwell, Anaheim, California 1962–69; Senior Engineering Specialist Div. Staff, Western Development Laboratories, Philco-Ford, Palo Alto, California 1969–73; Electronic Systems Consultant since 1973. *Publications:* Forty-nine technical papers published to date, including, Panoramic Mass Spectrometer Observation (1946); Developmental Television Transmitter for 500–800 Megacycles (1948); The Simplification of Television Receivers (1950); Television Picture Quality (1952); The Germanium Diode as Video Detector (1963); Compact Color Video Equipment (1956). Senior Member: Institute of Electrical and Electronics Engineers. *Member:* Sigma Xi, American Association of University Professors, American Physical Society. *Address:* 891 Loma Verde, Palo Alto, California 94303, U.S.A.

**WHEATLEY, Rt. Hon. Lord,** PC, QC. created Baron Wheatley of Shettleston, Glasgow, 1970. Lord Justice-Clerk & Senator of the College of Justice in Scotland. *B.* 17 Jan. 1908. *Educ.* St. Aloysius College, Glasgow; Mount St. Mary College, Sheffield; Glasgow University (MA, LLB, LLD); D.Univ. (Stirling University); FEIS (Hon). *M.* 1935, Agnes Nichol. *S.* 4. *Dau.* 1. *Career:* Called to Scottish Bar 1932; served in World War II in Field Artillery and later in Judge Advocate-General's Department 1939–45; Solicitor-General for Scotland Mar.–Oct. 1947; Lord Advocate Oct. 1947–Oct. 1951; MP (Lab.) for East Edinburgh 1947–54; Judge of the Court of Session in Scotland 1954–72; Lord Justice Clerk since 1972. *Address:* 3 White House Terrace, Edinburgh EH9 2EU.

**WHEATLEY, Eric Howard,** FCA, FCIS. *B.* 1918. Fellow of The Inst. of Chartered Accountants in Australia (FCA); Fellow, The Chartered Institute of Secretaries (FCIS). *M.* 1941, Sylvia Daisy Driver. *S.* 3. *Dau.* 1. *Career:* After qualifying as Chartered Accountant (1941), joined R.A.A.F. and served as pilot in New Guinea and other areas until end of 1944; civil airline pilot with Airlines W.A. Ltd. 1945; joined E. S. Saw in partnership in firm Saw, Wheatley & Co. as from 1 Jan. 1946; Dir.: Perth Arcade Co. Ltd.: Midland Brick Co. Pty. Ltd.; Floreat Close Ltd.; Atkins Carlyle Ltd.; Dir. AMP Socy.; Dir. Swan Portland Cement Ltd.; Chmn. W.A. Meat Commission (Midland & Robb Jetty); Hill 50 Gold Mine No Liability; W.A. Trustee Executor & Agency Co. W.A. Ltd.; Member, Valuation Bd. No. 13 (Taxation Administration); Partner, Binder Hamlyn & Co. (Ret.), Consultant since 1973. Partner, Binalong Grazing Co. Denmark, W.A. since 1973. *Address:* Strathearn, 16, King's Park Avenue, Crawley, W.A.; and *office:* 12 St. George's Terrace, Perth, Western Australia.

**WHEATON, Elmer Paul. American.** Vice-President, Lockheed Aircraft Corp. *B.* 1909. *Educ.* Pomona College (BA Physics 1933); Graduate, Executive Management Program, Graduate School of Business Administration, University of California at Los Angeles; Registered Professional Engineer, California. *M.* 1933, Martha Elizabeth Davis. *S.* Markeley Paul. *Dau.* Sara Elizabeth. *Career:* Vice Pres. & General Manager, Research & Development Division, Lockheed Missiles & Space Co. Inc.; Pres. 1969–72, Member Bd. 1972; Member Eng. Adv. Council UC Berkeley 1973; Nat. Adv. Cttee. Oceans and Atmosphere 1973–76. Lockheed Petroleum

Services Ltd. With Lockheed Missiles & Space Co. 1962–74; (Vice-President & General Manager Space Programs Div. 1962–63; Assistant to President 1962). With Douglas Aircraft Co. 1934–61; Director Astropower Inc. (subsidiary of Douglas Aircraft) 1961. Vice-Pres.; Engineering, Douglas Aircraft (i/c all engineering 1961; all technical engineering 1960–61, missiles and space systems 1958–61); Director Missiles & Space Systems 1958; Chief Missiles Engineer 1955–58; Chief, Missile Projects (Nike Ajax, Nike Hercules, Sparrow I, II and III, Genie, Bumper, and other projects) 1945–55; Chief, Dynamics and Sound Control 1945; Manager Applied Physics Lab. 1945. On loan to RAND Corp. to project writing of first earth satellite report for the Air Force 1945, and to MIT Radiation Lab. to work on development of airborne radar bombing systems 1944; Assistant Chief, Engineering Labs. 1943, and Research Section 1940–43; Research Engineer 1936–40. Special activities: *Member*, Aerospace Industries Assn. Guided Missile Committee (Chairman 1953–54); Guided Missile Council (Chairman 1959–60); and Aircraft Technical Committee. Consultant, Adv. Panel for Aeronautics, Office of Dir. of Defense for Research Engineering 1957–59; Member, Special Industry Committee on Missiles, Office of Secretary of the Air Force for Research & Development 1954; National Academy, Engineering and NAE Marine Bd.; National Science Foundation's advisory panel on the International Decade of Ocean Exploration; Patron, Member and Past Pres. Marine Technology Society; Member Sea Grant Coordinating Council, Univ. of California. Lecturer on vibration, sound control and missile design, Guggenheim Aeronautical Lab. Calif., Institute of Technology, 1941–54. National Director, American Ordnance Association. Member: National Council on Marine Resources & Engr. Dev. (Consultant & Member of Panel on Ocean Engineering), 1968–69. Commission on Marine Science, Engr. & Resources (Consultant Nov. 1967–Jan. 1969), American Association for Advancement of Sciences; American Oceanic Organization. Advisory Council; State Calif. Marine Research Cttee. since 1972. *Awards:* Certificate of Merit for Outstanding Contribution: War & Navy Dept. 1947, and office of Scientific Research & Development; Robert M. Thompson Award for Outstanding Civilian Leadership, Navy League of the U.S. Fellow American Institute Aeronautics & Astronautics. Fellow: Royal Aeronautical Society; American Astr nautical Society. *Publications:* Designing Missiles to Fly (1951); The Penalty of Payoff of a Changing Technology in Aircraft and Missiles (1958); Human Factors in Engineering Design (1959); What Will the Future Hold? (1959); Fundamental Limitations of Space Flight (1960); The Expanding Role of Research in the Aerospace Industry (1963), etc. *Address:* 127 Solana Road, Portola Valley, Calif. 94025, U.S.A.

**WHEELER, Hon. Asher Louis.** American attorney. *B.* 1919. *Educ.* Univ. of Georgia (AB 1940); Harvard (LLB 1944), JD 1969. *M.* 1950, Ann Naoma Smith. *S.* James Julian and Thomas Smith. *Dau.* Anita Margaret. *Career:* Practised law in Washington, D.C. since 1945; President and Director: Vega Investment Corp.; Pres. & Director, Pennsylvania Telephone Co.; Pres. Pioneer Industries Inc.; Former Dir.: Foundation for Better Government 1954; Pioneer Communications Inc.; Counsel and Clerk, District of Columbia Cttee., of the U.S. Senate 1949–50; General Vice-Chmn., President's Inaugural Cttee. 1949; Amer. Bar Assn.; D.C. Bar Assn.; Chmn. of a number of various Cttees. of D.C.; Phi Beta Kappa; Omicron Delta Kappa; Blue Key; Newcomen Society of North America. Mbr. of Democratic Central Committee 1946–60 (Chairman 1948–60); Executive Vice-Pres., Truman-Barkley Club of the District of Columbia 1948; Hon. Pres., Stevenson-Sprakman Club of D.C. 1952; Hon. Chmn., Stevenson-Kefauver Club of D.C. 1956; Delegate to Democratic National Convention 1948–52–56. *Address:* 3030 West Lane Keys, N.W., Washington, D.C.; and *office* 1522 Wisconsin Avenue, N.W. Washington 7, D.C., U.S.A.

**WHEELER, Sir Frederick Henry,** CBE. British. *B.* 1914. *Educ.* Trinity Grammar School; Scotch College (Melbourne) and Melbourne University (BCom). *M.* 1939, Peggy Hilda Bell (*Dec.* 1975). *S.* Philip John. *Daus.* Pamela and Elizabeth. *Career:* Member: Australian Delegations Bretton Woods Monetary Conference and various British Commonwealth Finance Ministers Conferences, Asst. Secretary, Department of the Treasury 1946 (First Asst. Secy. (1949); Treasurer-Comptroller, International Labour Organization, Geneva 1952–60; Chmn. Commonwealth Public Service Board Canberra 1961–71; Member United Nations Civil Service Adv. Bd. 1969–72; Secretary to the Treasury since 1971. *Clubs:* Commonwealth (Canberra; Pres. 1966–69); Royal Canberra Golf. *Address:* 9 Charlotte Street, Red Hill, A.C.T. 2600; and *office* The Treasury, Canberra A.C.T. 2600, Australia.

**WHEELER, Maynard Clifford.** Retired corporate executive. *B.* 1900. *Educ.* Purdue University (BS Chemical Engineering; PhD (Hon) Engineering). *M.* 1923, Mary Wilbie McDaniel. *S.* Maynard C., Jr. *Dau.* Marilyn (Pendergast). *Career:* with Commercial Solvents Corp., in 1923: successively Production Manager 1940–45, Vice-Pres., Production & Engineering 1945–55, and of Research, Development & Engineering 1954–57; Senior Vice-Pres. 1957–58; Chmn. Bd. 1966–68; President Executive Officer 1959–66. Dir. Foundation for American Agriculture; Purdue Research Foundation. Dir. and Member of Exec. Committee: Grain Drying Equipment Company. Member of Board of Directors: Goodwill Industries; Indiana State University Foundation; Sheldon Swope Art Gallery; Terre Haute Committee for Area Progress; Vigo County Extension Board. Member of Board of Managers: Rose Polytechnic Institute. Former Director and Chairman of Research Committee of National Association of Manufacturers. *Member:* American Chemical Society, American Inst. of Chemical Engineers; Newcomen Society of North America: Tau Beta Phi (Fraternity): and Delta Chi. *Clubs:* Columbia (Indianapolis, Ind.); Country (Terre Haute); Leland Country; Rotary. *Address:* 1331, So. First St., Terre Haute, Indiana, U.S.A.

**WHEELER, Towson Ames.** Treasurer Smithsonian Institution 1968—. *B.* 1911. *Educ.* Harvard Univ. (AB 1932); Harvard Graduate School of Business Administration (MS 1934). *M.* 1937, Alma Lackey Wilson. *Daus.* Sue Elizabeth (Mrs. Dwight N. Mason), Sara Ames (Dieter Forster) and Laurie Wilson (Fayette Brown III). *Career:* Field of Engineering, Chrysler Corp. 1934–35; Securities Analyst, Investment Counsel Inc. 1935–38; Investment Dept., The Detroit Bank 1939–42; Staff Asst., Financial Dept., U.S. Steel Corp. of Delaware 1942–46, successively Statistician 1946–49, Manager, Costs and Statistics 1949, Controller 1950–60, Allegheny Ludlum Steel Corporation, Vice-Pres. in charge of Planning 1960–63; International & Sect., 1964–68. Director, Allegheny-Longdoz S.A. Brussels, Allegheny Ludlum International S.A., Geneva, now resigned from all these positions. *Member* Tau Beta Pi; Phi Beta Kappa. Pres. Com. Chest of Allegheny County 1965–66. *Member:* Harvard Business School Club of Washington. *Clubs:* Allegheny Country (Pittsburgh) Burning Tree; Chevy Chase; Metrop. (Wash.); Mid-Ocean (Bermuda). *Address:* 4645 Hawthorne Lane NW, Washington D.C. 20016; and *office* Smithsonian Institution, Washington, D.C. 20560, U.S.A.

**WHEELER, William Henry,** CMG, PhD, BA, CEng. British. *B.* 1907. *Educ.* St. Catherine's Coll. Cambridge (BA); Imperial Coll. of Science (PhD). *M.* 1937, Mary Inkpen. *Career:* Dir. Guided Weapons 1950–55; Scientific Adviser to High Commisssioner Australia 1955–59. Chief Exec. and Deputy-Chmn., Urquhart Engineering Co. Ltd., Dep. Chmn. Steam & Combustion Engineering Ltd.; Chmn. Mark Laboratories Ltd.; Process Combustion Corp. (U.S.A.) & Urquhart Engineering GmbH. *Address:* Mark House, Ashmead Lane, Denham Village, Bucks; and *office:* 5 Wadsworth Road, Perivale, Middlesex.

**WHITAKER, Horatio Nelson,** MBE. British. *B.* 1905. *Educ.* FASA; ACIS. *M.* 1930, Marie Doris Ruddell. *S.* Dr. Alan Whitaker. *Career:* Public Service (Taxation Dept.) 1921–25; Secretary, A. J. Draper Pty. Ltd. 1925–38; Manager-Secretary, Babinda Central Mill Co. Ltd. 1938–39; Gen. Mgr. Mullgrave Central Mill Co. Ltd. 1939–71; Director: Australian Sugar Producers Assoc. Ltd.; Sugar Research Ltd. Chairman: Australian Molasses Pool Committee; Member, Cairns Harbour Board; Bulk Sugar Terminal Organization. *Address:* 4 Trident Street, Mansfield, Q. 4122, Australia.

**WHITAKER, Howard Edwards.** American. *B.* 1903. *Educ.* Mass. Inst. of Technology (ScB; ScM, in Chm Eng). *M.* 1930. Patricia Jones. *S.* Michael. *Dau.* Catherine. *Career:* Joined Mead Corporation 1925; various technical and operating positions; Vice-President Operations 1949, Exec. Vice-Pres. 1951, Pres. 1952. Chairman 1957–68; former Chairman Georgia Kraft Co. and Brunswick Pulp & Paper Co.; Vice-Pres. and Past Pres., American Paper & Pulp Assn.; Hon LLD, Miami University (Ohio). *Address:* 132 West Second Street, Chillicothe, Ohio, U.S.A.

**WHITAKER, Thomas Kenneth,** DEconSc, LLD. *B.* 1916. *Educ.* Christian Brothers School, Drogheda, Co. Louth. *M.* 1941, Nora Fogarty. *S.* 5. *Dau.* 1. *Career:* Irish Civil Service 1934–69; Secy. Dept. of Finance (Head of Civil

Service) 1956–69; Governor, Central Bank of Ireland 1969–76; Chancellor, National Univ. of Ireland; Chmn., Bord na Gaeilge and Agency for Personal Service Overseas. *Member:* Royal Irish Academy; Governing Body, School of Celtic Studies; Council, Statistical and Social Inquiry Socy. of Ireland. Pres., Economic and Social Research Institute. Commandeur de la Légion d'Honneur. *Publication:* Financing by Credit Creation. *Club:* Royal Dublin Society. *Address:* 148 Stillorgan Road, Donnybrook, Dublin, 4, Eire.

**WHITE, Hon. Sir Alfred,** Kt. Australian politician. *B.* 2 Feb. 1902. *M.* 1939, Veronica Punch. *S.* 2. *Daus.* 2. M.H.A. for Denison, Tasmania 1941–59. Agent-General for Tasmania in London Feb. 1959–71. *Address:* 18 Clarke Avenue, Battery Point, Hobart, Tasmania 7000, Australia.

**WHITE, Byron R.** Associate Justice, Supreme Court of U.S.A., Apr. 1962—; Deputy Attorney-General of the U.S. Jan. 1961–62. *B.* 1917. *Educ.* Univ. of Colorado, Oxford Univ. (Rhodes Scholar) and Yale Univ. (Law Degree). *M.* Marion Stearns. *S.* Charles. *Dau.* Nancy. *Career:* Served as U.S. Naval Intelligence Officer in South Pacific area. Clerk to the Chief Justice of the U.S. Supreme Court, Mr. Fred M. Vinson, 1946–47; later, Chmn. National Citizens-for-Kennedy Movement during the Presidential election campaign; with law firm of Lewis, Grant, Newton, Davis & Henry (now Davis, Graham & Stubbs), Denver 1947–61. *Address:* Supreme Court of the U.S., Washington, D.C., U.S.A.

**WHITE, Sir Dennis Charles,** KBE, CMG. *B.* 1910. *Educ.* Bradfield College. *Career:* Joined Sarawak Civil Service 1932; Civilian prisoner-of-war Dec. 1941–Sept. 1945; Colonial Service 1946; Secy. Native Affairs, Sarawak 1946; Senior Resident, Sarawak 1956; British Resident, Brunei 1958; High Commissioner for the United Kingdom in Brunei, Sept. 1959–63; Brunei Govt. Agent in United Kingdom 1967—. Holds Family Order of Brunei (1st Class), Star of Sarawak (3rd Class). *Clubs:* Travellers; Royal Overseas League; Sarawak Club. *Address:* Virginia Cottage, Emery Down, Lyndhurst, Hants.

**WHITE, the Rt. Hon. the Baroness (Eirene White),** cr. life Baroness of Rhymney 1970. *B.* 1909. *Educ.* St. Paul's Girls' School, London, and Somerville Coll., Oxford (MA). *M.* 1948, John Cameron White (*D.* 1968). *Career:* Member of Parliament East Flintshire 1950–70; Minister of State, Foreign Office London 1966–67; Minister of State for Wales 1967–70; Chairman, Labour Party 1968–69; Mem. Royal Commission on Environmental Pollution 1974—; University Grants Cttee. 1977—; Chmn., Land Authority for Wales 1975—. *Address:* 36 Westminster Gardens, Marsham St., London, S.W.1.

**WHITE, Sir Frederick (William George),** KBE, FRS, FAA. Australian. *B.* 1905. *Educ.* Victoria Univ. Coll., Univ. of New Zealand (MSc 1928); Cambridge Univ. (PhD 1932). *M.* 1932, Elizabeth Cooper. *S.* Peter. *Dau.* Jane Elizabeth. *Career:* Research in Physics, Cavendish Laboratory 1929–31; Asst. Lecturer in Physics, King's Coll., Univ. of London 1931–36; Prof. of Physics, Canterbury Univ. Coll., New Zealand 1937; seconded to Australian Council for Scientific and Industrial Research 1941; Chairman, Radiophysics Advisory Board 1941; Chief, Div. of Radiophysics 1942, Executive Officer 1945, member of Exec. Cttee. 1946, Chief Executive Officer 1949–57, Deputy Chairman 1957, of C.S.I.R.O., Chmn. 1959–70. *Awards:* Hon. DSc, Monash Univ. Melbourne; Australian National Univ. Canberra; Univ. Papua, New Guinea. *Publications:* various scientific papers on the nature of the ionosphere over New Zealand, and in the propagation of radio waves; Electromagnetic Waves, 1934. *Club:* Melbourne. *Address:* 57 Investigator St., Red Hill, Canberra, A.C.T. 2603, Australia.

**WHITE, George David Lloyd,** MVO. New Zealand diplomat. *B.* 1918. *Educ.* Univ. of New Zealand (MA Econ 1940). *M.* 1946, Miranda Daisy Turnbull. *S.* Anthony Paul. *Career:* With N.Z. Army in Middle East 1941–45. Joined N.Z. Government Service 1945, External Affairs Dept. 1949, Economic Counsellor, London 1954–55; Counsellor, Washington 1956–58; Chargé d'Affaires, N.Z. Embassy, Washington 1958–61; Deputy High Commissioner for New Zealand in U.K. 1961–64; Deputy Secy. Ministry of Foreign Affairs Wellington 1964–72; Ambassador to Washington D.C. since 1972. *Club:* Wellington. *Address:* New Zealand Embassy, 19 Observatory Circle, NW, Washington, D.C., 20008, U.S.A.

**WHITE, Sir George Stanley Midelton.** Bt. British. *B.* 1913. *Educ.* Harrow and Magdalene College, Cambridge. Member of firm of George White, Evans, Tribe & Co. (Stockbrokers), Bristol. *Address:* Pypers, Rudgeway, near Bristol.

**WHITEHEAD, J. (James) Ralph.** Canadian. *B.* 1918. *Educ.* McGill University. *M.* 1941, Margaret Wistar Brooks (*D.* 1970). *S.* Peter George. *Dau.* Elizabeth Jeanne. *Career:* Served with Hastings & Prince Edward Regiment 1941. Former President: Lally-Munro Fuels Ltd. 1947–71; Universal Terminals Ltd. 1957–71, Cornwall Storage & Warehousing Ltd. 1960–71; and Hydra-Clene Corp. of Canada Ltd. Director: Fiberez of Canada Ltd., DuVerre Ltd., Metro Oil Carriers, Kirk Hill Developments Ltd., and Blanchard Fuels Ltd. *Member:* Board of Trade; Young Presidents Organization (President Montreal Chapter 1956–58); Shriners; Mason (32 degree). *Clubs:* Mount Stephen, Seigniory. *Address:* 2445 Sunset Road, Town of Mount Royal, Que.; and *office:* 4826 Sherbrooke Street W., Westmount, Que. H3Z 1G8, Canada.

**WHITEHEAD, Phillip,** BA, MP. British politician. *B.* 1937. *Educ.* Lady Manners School, Bakewell (Foundation Scholar); Exeter Coll., Oxford (Exhibitioner). *M.* 1967, Christine Hilary Usborne. *S.* Richard Joshua, Robert Francis. *Dau.* Lucy Victoria. *Career:* Lieut. Sherwood Foresters & Royal West African Frontier Force 1956–58; Oxford Univ. 1958 61; Producer B.B.C. Overseas 1961–62, Television Gallery Panorama 1962–67; Editor This Week, Thames T.V. 1967–71; Member of Parliament for Derby North since 1970. *Member:* Nat. Union of Journalists; Free Communications Group; Co-operative Party; Fabian Society; Mem. Annan Cttee on the Future of Broadcasting 1974–77; Council of Europe 1975—. *Awards:* Guild of Television Producers Best Factual Programme 1968; Chmn. E.U.R.N.A.C. Task Force, Brussels, 1971. *Publications:* Strangers Within (1965); Contributor, More Power To The People (1967). *Address: office* House of Commons, London, S.W.1.

**WHITELAW, Rt. Hon. William Stephen Ian,** PC, CH, MC, MP. British politician, farmer and landowner. *B.* 1918. *Educ.* Winchester and Trinity College, Cambridge. *M.* 1943, Cecilia Doriel Sport. *Daus.* 4. *Career:* MP (Con.) for Penrith and the Border 1955—. Formerly Regular officer, Scots Guards (resigned 1947); P.P.S. to President of Board of Trade 1956–57, and to Chancellor of the Exchequer 1957. Lrd Commissioner of the Treasury, Mar. 1961–62; Parliamentary Secretary, Ministry of Labour, July 1962–64; Assistant Whip Jan. 1959. Opposition Chief Whip 1964–70; Lord Pres. of the Council and Leader of the House of Commons, 1970–72; Secy. of State for Northern Ireland 1972–73; Secy. State for Employment 1974. Chmn. of Conservative Party June 1974–Feb. 1975; Dep. Leader Feb. 1975. *Clubs:* Carlton; Guards (London). *Address:* House of Commons, London, S.W.1, and Ennim, Penrith, Cumbria.

**WHITELEY, Ernest Alfred,** CBE, DFC. Australian. Group Capt. R.A.F. (Retd.). *B.* 1914. *Educ.* BA. LLB. CEng, FRAeS. *M.* 1949, Yvonne Dewez. *Daus.* 3. *Career:* R.A.F. General Duties Officer 1936–56 (HQ Research and Development Command U.S.A.F. 1949–51; Director of Plans, HQ Far East Air Force, Singapore 1952–55); Director and General Manager, Bristol Aeroplane Co. (Aust.) Pty. Ltd. 1956–58 (Managing Director 1958–61). Manager for Victoria, Australian Broadcasting Commission since 1961. *Award:* Taylor Gold Medal, RAeS 1952. *Clubs:* Naval & Military (Melbourne). *Address:* 40 Alto Avenue, Croydon, Vic. 3136; and *office* c/o ABC St. James Building, 121 William Street, Melbourne, Vic., Australia.

**WHITING, Macauley.** American company director. *B,* 1925. *Educ.* Yale University (BE 1945; ME 1948). *M.* 1945, Helen A. Dow *S.* Henry and Macauley, Jr. *Daus.* Susan. Martha, Helen and Mary. *Career.* Dir.: The Dow Chemical Co., U.S.A. 1959—. Gen. Man. Petroleum Production and Service, Dow Chemical, U.S.A. 1973–75; Dir., Dowell Schlumberger Ltd. 1971–75. Trustee, Northwood Institute, U.S.A., since 1963; Gen. Man. Hydrocarbons Dept., Dow Chemical, U.S.A. 1971–73; Dir., Dow Chemical of Canada Ltd. 1966–73; Dir., Asahi Dow Ltd., Japan 1962–71; Dir., Basic resources, The Dow Chemical Co. 1968–71; Dir. Lepetit S.p.A., Italy 1964–69; Ivon Watkins-Dow Ltd. 1962–69; Dir. of Planning and Gen. Man. Hydrocarbons and Energy, The Dow Chemical Co. 1966–68; Pres., Dow Chemical International, S.A. 1962–66; Dir., Dow Unquinesa S.A., Spain 1962–66; Distrene Ltd., England 1959–62. LLD Sioux Falls Coll. 1967; Dr Eng Michigan Tech. Univ. 1960; Registered Professional Engineer 1955; Tau Beta Pi 1944. *Member:* Inst. of Management Science; Amer. Socy. of

**Mechanical Engineers; Michigan Socy.** of Professional Engineers. *Address:* 2203 Eastman Road, Midland, Mich. 48640; and *office:* The Dow Chemical Co., Midland, Mich. 48640, U.S.A.

**WHITINGTON, Alexander Peter,** (Ret.) *B.* 1905. *Educ.* St. Peter's College, Adelaide, S.A. *M.* (1) 1925, Irene Helene Best and (2) 1948 Janet Lindsay Richardson. *Daus.* 3. *Career:* National Bank of Australasia Ltd. 1920; Accountant, Bunge (Australia) Pty. Ltd. 1933–36; Assistant Manager 1936–46, Manager 1946–1970; Dir. Australian Bd. 1957–70; R.A.A.F. 1942, Admin, Section Aust. Air Training Corps. 1943–44 Wing Co-ordinating Officer; Hon. Flight Lt; Chmn. Corn Trade Section Adelaide Chamber Commerce 1947–51; Pres. Adelaide Corn and Produce Exchange 1949–51; Vice-Pres. Adelaide Chamber Commerce 1952–53, 53–54, Pres. 1954–56; Pres. Amateur Sports Club S.A. 1954; Pres. Australian Chamber of Commerce Export Council 1959–61; Chmn. Government Consultative Economic Cttee. Adelaide Chamber Commerce 1963–70; Mem. Exec. & Council, S.A. Chamber of Commerce & Industry 1973—. *Clubs:* Stock Exchange *Address:* la Victoria Avenue, Unley Park, S.A., Australia.

**WHITLAM, Hon. Edward Gough,** QC, MP. Australian Politician. *B.* 1916. *Educ.* Univ. of Sydney. BA. 1938, LLB. 1946, *M.* 1942, Margaret Elaine. *S.* 3. *Dau.* 1. *Career:* R.A.A.F., Flight Lieut. 1941–45; Barrister 1947; Deputy-Leader, Aust. Labour Party 1960, Leader 1967–77; Prime Minister 1972–75; Leader of Opposition 1975–77. *Address:* Parliament House, Canberra ACT 2600, Australia.

**WHITLOCK, Albert N(ickerson).** Manufacturing executive. *B.* 1911. *Educ.* Univ. of Illinois (BS). *M.* 1936, Bonita Matthews. *S.* Scott Nickerson. *Career:* Junior Partner, A. T. Kearney & Co. 1943–48. With Caterpillar: Assistant Controller 1948–52, Controller 1952–56, Manager, Aurora Plant 1956—; Manager, Caterpillar Tractor Co., Aurora, Ill. 1956—; Director, Aurora National Bank 1960—; member, Board of Governors, Copley Memorial Hospital 1961—. *Member:* Fox Valley Industrial Assn. (Vice-Pres. and Dir.); Illinois Manufacturers' Assn.; Illinois and Aurora Chambers of Commerce; Amer. Management Assn.; Kappa Delta Rho. *Clubs:* Aurora Country; Union League (Aurora). *Address: office* P.O. Box 348, Aurora, Ill., U.S.A.

**WHITNEY, George Kirkpatrick.** American consultant. *B.* 1907. *Educ.* Harvard (AB); Harvard Grad. School of Business Admin. (MBA). *M.* 1951, Una Rogers King. *S.* Robert Hayden. *Daus.* Sarah Minot and Faith (Newcomb). *Career:* With Trust Invest. Div. of First Nat. Bank of Chicago 1931–34; Invest. Dept., Connecticut Bank & Trust Co. 1934–43; Investment Research Department, Massachusetts Investors Trust 1943–47. Trustee, Massachusetts Investors Trust 1947–70; Director: Associated Harvard Alumni 1968–70; Massachusetts Investors Growth Stock Fund 1945–70; Director, Transportation Association of America 1947—; (Chairman 1968–70, Hon. Chmn. 1971–73); Harvard Business School (Visiting Cttee 1968–74); Partner, Massachusetts Financial Services; Dir. Pennsylvania Co.; Dir. World Affairs, Council of Boston; Chairman, Harvard Business School Fund 1963–66; Harvard Business School Association Executive Council 1966–73 (President 1967–68). President, National Association of Investment Companies 1960–61; Investment Company Institute Governor and member of Executive Committee 1961–63). Distinguished Service Award, Harvard Business School Association, 1969. Life Member: American Forestry Association; Bostonian Society; National Trust for Historic Preservation. Republican. *Award:* TAA Dist. Service Medal. *Member:* Massachusetts Historical Society (Member of Council 1970–77); Society of Colonial Wars. *Publications:* articles on investments in various periodicals, including Analysts Journal, Commercial & Financial Chronicle, Journal of Babson Institute, etc. *Clubs:* Union (Boston); Metropolitan (Washington); The Country (Brookline Mass.); Harvard (N.Y.C.); Concord Country (Concord, Mass.); Ekwanok Country (Manchester, Vt.); Mid-Ocean (Bermuda); Harvard Varsity (Cambridge); Boston Economic. *Address:* 207 Muske taquid Road, Concord, Mass. 01742, U.S.A.

**WHITNEY, John Hay.** American publisher. *B.* 1904. *Educ.* Yale University (BA 1926) and Oxford University. *M.* 1942, Betsey Cushing. *Career:* Partner J. H. Whitney & Co., New York City; Editor-in-Chief and Publisher of New York Herald Tribune (1961–66); Chairman, The International Herald Tribune( Paris). Chmn. of Bd., Whitney Communications Corp.; Chairman, John Hay Whitney Found.; Ambassador of the United States to the Court of St. James's 1957–61. Served as Colonel, A.A.F. in World War II. Appointed special adviser and counsellor on public affairs by Department of State; Graduate member, Business Council; Fellow, Corporation of Yale University 1955–70, Senior Fellow 1970–73. *Member,* American Friends of the Tate Gallery; member, Commission on Foreign Economic Policy 1954; Saratoga Springs Commission 1971–74; Corporation for Public Broadcasting, 1970–72; Secretary of State's Public Committee on Personnel 1954; Board of Governors, N.Y. Hospital; Museum of Modern Art; Saratoga Performing Arts Center. Vice-President, National Gallery of Art, Washington, D.C. Steward Jockey Club. *Clubs:* Augusta National Golf; Yacht; Racquet & Tennis; Scroll & Key. *Address:* Manhasset, L.I.; and *office* 110 West 51st Street, New York 10020, N.Y., U.S.A.

**WHITWELL, Stephen John,** CMG, MC (Ret.). British diplomat. H.M. Ambassador to Somali Republic 1968–70. *B.* 1920. *Educ.* Stowe School; Christ Church, Oxford (MA). Served in Tehran, Belgrade, New Delhi, Seoul, 1947–63; Political adviser to C.-in-C. Middle East. Aden, 1964; Counsellor, British Embassy, Belgrade, 1965. *Clubs:* Travellers. *Address:* Jervis Cottage, Aston Tirrold, Oxon.

**WHYTE, David Gosman.** Australian. Dir., West Australian Newspapers Ltd. *B.* 1908. *Educ.* Christian Brothers' College, Perth, W.A. *M.* 1933, Kathleen Jean Askew. *Daus.* 3 Manager, Perth Daily News, 1951–54; Bus. Man. and Secy., W. Aust. Newspapers Ltd. 1954–63, Gen. Man. 1963–69, Dir. since 1969. *Address:* 17 Lookout Road, Kalamunda, W.A., Australia.

**WHYTE, Joseph Lawrence.** Banker. *B.* 1912. *Educ.* New York University (BS in Banking and Finance 1936), George Washington University School of Law (LLB 1944), and Graduate School of Banking 1953. *M.* 1943, Charlotte E. Morris. *S.* Joseph L. P., Robert E. W. *Daus.* Barbara W. Brereton and Diane W. Warin. *Career:* With Bank of New York 1929–41, Administrative Asst. to Vice-Pres. and Secretary in Trust Dept. 1945–46. Joined present company, American Security Bank, N. A. 1946; Asst. Trust Officer 1948–51; Trust Officer 1951–56; Senior Vice President and Trust Officer in charge of Trust Department 1968; Executive Vice President and Trust Officer in charge of Trust Department 1973—; Adjunct Professor of Law on Estate Planning, 1956—. Contributes regularly articles to estate planning publications. President, Elizabeth R. Shoemaker Home for ladies; President, Mary and Daniel Loughran Foundation; President, the John Dickson Home; Vice Chairman of the D. C. Chapter of the American National Red Cross; National Treasurer of the Reserve Officers Association of the United States; Director: General Services Life Insurance Company, Acacia Investment Management Corporation; Chairman of Endowment Committee and Member of the Board of Metropolitan Police Boys' Club; Member: District of Columbia Bar; Federal Legislative Council, American Bankers Association, Trust Division; Past President and Member of The University Club of Washington, D.C.; Member, the Metropolitan Club, Congressional Country Club, Rehoboth Beach Country Club, and Henlopen Acres Beach Club. *Address:* Trust Department, American Security & Trust Co., Washington, D.C. 20013, U.S.A.

**WHYTE, Quintin Alexander.** South African. Former Director, South African Inst. of Race Relations. *B.* 7 Mar. 1909. *Educ.* MA (Hons); LLD (Hon) Univ. of the Watersrand, Union Education Diploma. *M.* 1939, Margaret Elizabeth Campbell. *Career:* Dir., S.A. Inst. of Race Relations 1948–70. Trustee of a number of Trusts concerned with African Coloured & Indian welfare and education; previously Asst. Magistrate and Collector, United Provinces, India 1934; Teacher, Healdtown and Lovedale Missionary Institutions; Asst. Director, S.A.I. R.R. 1946; Carnegie Travelling Fellowship 1950. *Address:* P.O. Box 290, Somerset West, South Africa.

**WIBAUX, Fernand.** French Ambassador. *B.* 1921. *Educ* Faculté de Droit, Paris—Diploma: Doctor. *M.* 1973, Jeanine Petrequin. *S.* 1. *Daus.* 2. *Career:* Civil Service Admin., Algeria 1944–49; Attaché to Sec. of State for Overseas Territories, Paris 1949–50; Attaché to Minister for Merchant Marine, Paris 1950–51; Attaché to High Commissioner French West Africa 1952–55; Chief Asst. to Ministers for Overseas Territories 1956; Dir.-Gen. of Niger Office, Paris 1956–60; Consul-Gen. Bamako 1960–61; Amb. to Mali 1961–64; Dir., Office de Coopération et d'Accueil Universitaire, Paris 1964; Amb. to Chad, Fort-Lamy 1968–74;

Plenipotentiary Minister & Dir. of Cultural & Social Affairs in Ministry of Cooperation 1974–76; Cabinet Dir. of Ministry of Cooperation 1976; Amb. to Senegal 1977. *Decorations:* Croix de Guerre; Officier de la Légion d'Honneur. *Address:* 6, rue du Hêtre—94170 Le Perreux, France; and *office* French Embassy, Dakar, Senegal.

**WICKSTRÖM, Hugo.** Swedish judge. *B.* 1892. *Educ.* Univ. of Lund (cand jur). Dep. Judge 1918; Judge of Mixed Courts of Egypt 1926–47 (Pres. Trib. Alexandria 1946–47); Judge, Court of Appeal of Sweden 1930–51 (Pres. of Div. 1948–51); President, Arbitral Commission on Property, Rights and Interests in Germany 1956–69; President, Arbitration Tribunal under the Convention on Relations between the Three Powers & Federal Republic of Germany, 1970—. Vice-President, International Arbitration Tribunal and Mixed Commission for the London Agreement on German External Debts 1967—. Member, United Nations Tribunal in Libya 1951–56, and in Eritrea 1952–54. *Address:* Postfach 2005, Koblenz, Germany.

**WIDGERY, The Rt. Hon. Lord John Passmore** (Baron Widgery of South Molton, Devon), PC, OBE, TD. British. Lord Chief Justice of England. *B.* 1911. *Educ.* Queens Coll., Taunton. *M.* 1948, Anne Edith Kermode. *Career:* Solicitor of the Supreme Court, 1933–39; Service, Royal Artillery Lt.-Col. 1939–45; Barrister, 1946–58; Queens Counsel, 1958–61; Judge Queens Bench Div. 1961–68; Lord Justice of Appeal, 1968–71; Lord Chief Justice since 1971. *Address:* Royal Courts of Justice, Strand, London, W.C.2.

**WIERBLOWSKI, Stefan.** Polish diplomat. *B.* 17 Mar. 1904. Under-Secretary of State, Ministry of Propaganda and Information 1945; En. Ex. and Min. Plen. to Czechoslovakia 1945; Amb. Ex. and Plen. to Czechoslovakia 1947; Secretary-General, Ministry of Foreign Affairs 1948–51; Under-Secretary of State since May 1951; Professor of History, Inst. of Social Sciences, Warsaw, since 1954; Chmn., Publications Cttee., Polish Academy of Sciences since 1954; Chmn., Polish Natl. Cttee. for U.N.E.S.C.O. since 1954; member, Exec. Cttee. of U.N.E.S.C.O. 1956–64. *Address:* Polish National Committee for Unesco, Palace of Culture, Warsaw, Poland.

**WIETHOFF, Paul.** German manufacturer. *B.* 1919. *M.* 1945. Margit Kaiser. *S.* Horst-Peter. *Dau.* Stefanie. *Career:* Owner, Veltins, Wiethoff & Co. Schmallenberg, Sauerland; Grundverwaltung Schmallenberg GmbH, Schmallenburg; & Eifeler Strumpfwarenfabrik GmbH, Bitburg/Eifel. Pres., GfK Nürnberg (Ges. für Konsum-, Markt- u. Absatzforschung). Pres., ZAW-Zentralausschuss der Deutschen Werbewirtschaft, Bonn-Bad Godesberg; Presidential mem., DIN—Deutsches Institut für Normung, Berlin. Mem. Exec. Cttee., Schuchtermann-Schiller'sche Familienstiftung im DIN. Mem. Bd. of Dirs., Rothenfelder Solbad und Saline AG, Bad Rothenfelde; Rechenzentrum Sauerland GmbH, Attendorn; Beirat Dresdner Bank AG; Schüchtermann-Schiller'sche Verwaltung GmbH. Dortmund; Lehmann KG—Kurkliniken Rothenfelde—G. & I. Forschungsgemeinschaft, Nürnberg/München; Textilnorm, Berlin; Industrie-und Handelskammer für das Südöstliche Westfalen zu Arnsberg. *Publication:* Geschichte des Strumpfes (History of the Stocking). *Member:* Verband der Textilindustrie Westfalen Münster; BDI—Bundesverband der Deutschen Industrie. *Club:* Lions (Neheim-Hüsten). *Address:* Haus am Aberg, D-5948 Schmallenberg, Federal Republic of Germany.

**WIGAN, Arthur Cleveland,** CBE. Australian. *B.* 1902. *Educ.* St. Peter's College, Adelaide. *M.* 1925, Gwenyth Matters, *Dau.* Averil Cleveland Derham. *Career:* with General Motors-Holden's Pty. Ltd., Australia, 1931–67 (Dir.); Director: Overseas Corp. (Australia) Ltd., Chairman, Ensign Holdings Ltd.; Russell Armstrong Pty. Ltd. 1953. Fellow, Australian Institute of Management (Victorian Div.), and Institute of Directors (London). Company Executive, Holden's Motor Body Builders, Adelaide 1924. *Address:* 3 McMaster Court, Toorak, Vic., Australia.

**WIGLEY, Dafydd,** MP. Welsh Politician. *B.* 1943. *Educ* Caernarfon Grammar Sch; Rydal Sch.; Manchester Univ.—BSc. *M.* 1967, Elinor Bennett Owen. *S.* 3. *Dau.* 1. *Career:* Finance Staff, Ford Motor Co. 1964–67; Chief Cost Accountant & Financial Planning Mgr., Mars Ltd. 1967–71; Financial Controller, Hoover Ltd. 1971–74; Plaid Cymru MP for Caernarfon since 1974; Party Spokesman on Economic & Industrial Affairs. *Member:* Inst. of Cost & Management Accountants. ***Publications:*** An Economic Plan for Wales (1970); regular Columnist in Liverpool Daily Post & Welsh Nation. *Address:* Hen Efail, Bontnewydd, Caernarfon, Gwynedd, Wales; and *office* Swyddfa'r Blaid, 21 Penllyn, Caernarfon, Gwynedd, Wales.

**WIGNY, Baron L. J. J.** Belgian politician. *B.* 18 April 1905. *Educ.* Liège Univ. (A en D); Harvard Univ. (SJD). *M.* 1929, Juliette Borboux. *S.* Pierre Henry, Damien. *Dau.* Jacqueline. *Career:* Sécrétaire-Général, Centre d'Études pour la Réforme de l'État 1936–40; Pres., P.S.C. Studies Centre 1945–46; Minister of the Colonies 1947–50; member (P.S.C.) Chamber of Representatives 1949–71, (Vice-Pres. 1968–71); Secy.-Gen. Inst. Inst. of Differing Civilizations (Incidi) 1952–58;; Pres. Political Economic Socy. of Belgium 1954–58; Member European Parly. Assembly and ECSC Common Assembly 1952–58; Pres. Christian-Dem. Group 1958; Belgian Minister of Foreign Affairs 1958–61, of Justice 1965–66, of Justice and of French Culture 1966–68; Professor of Law, Louvain Univ. and Faculty of Namur. Member: Académie Royale de Belgique, des Sciences d'Outre-Mer Brussels; des Sciences d'Outre-Mer Paris. Past Pres.: Commission Royale des Monuments et des Sites, and Caisse Nationale de Credit Professionnel. *Address:* 5920 Perwez, Brabant, Belgium.

**WIJEYEWARDENE, Sir Edwin Arthur Lewis,** QC. Ceylonese advocate. *B.* 21 Mar. 1887. *Educ.* Ananda College; St. Thomas' College, Ceylon. *M.* 1921, Lilian Beatrice Perera. *S.* Leslie Arthur. *Career:* Advocate 1911; Public Trustee 1935; Solicitor-General 1936; Acting Attorney-General 1938; Judge, Supreme Court 1938; Officer Administering the Government 1949; Chief Justice 1949–50; Chairman, Service Tenure 1953, Delimitation Commission 1953, Official Languages Commission 1951, Commn. on Higher Education, 1954, Land Commission 1955; Crown Arbitrator, 1955; Pres., Arts Council of Ceylon, 1956. *Address:* Lulworth, Vajira Road, Colombo; and Polhengoda Walawwa, Nugegoda, Sri Lanka.

**WILAIRAT, Nibhon.** Former Ambassador of Thailand. *B.* 1916. *Educ.* Thamasart Univ. Bangkok (LL.B); London Inst. of World Affairs. *M.* 1940, Sadappin Chandhanasiri. *S.* 4. *Career:* Deputy District Officer, Ministry of Interior 1934; Member of Section, Office of Royal Household 1936, of Prime Minister 1938, of Dept. Public Relations 1940, Chief of Section 1941; Ministry, Foreign Affairs 1947; Third Secy. Protocol Dept. 1949; Chief of Section, Office Under-Secy. of State Foreign Affairs 1950; Third Secy. Royal Thai Embassy, London 1950, Second Secy. 1954; Chief Central Div. Office, Under-Secy. State for Foreign Affairs, Reception Div. Protocol Dept. Acting Dir.-General 1955; Consul General Singapore 1956; Chief, South, Near & Far East, Africa Div. Political Dept. 1961; First Secy. Royal Thai Embassy, Washington D.C. 1963, Counsellor 1965; Ambassador to the Republic of Singapore 1967, to Arab Republic of Egypt and Lebanon 1973; to Italy, Greece and Israel 1975–76. *Awards:* Knight Grand Cross of Order of the Crown & Knight Commander of Order of the White Elephant of Thailand; Order First Class of Arab Republic of Egypt; Commanders of the Order Phoenin (Greece); Order of Merit (Italy); Brilliant Stars (Republic of China); Coronation Medals, H.M. King Bhumibol Aduldej of Thailand; Queen Elizabeth II, Great Britain. *Address:* c/o Ministry of Foreign Affairs, Saranrom Palace, Bangkok, Thailand.

**WILBUR, John Smith.** American. *B.* 1911. *Educ.* Yale Univ. (BA 1933). *M.* 1934, Atheline Miller. *S.* John Smith, Jr. *Daus.* Atheline (Nixon), Andrea (de Chiara) and Maren Spencer. *Career:* Vice-Chmn. and Director, The Cleveland-Cliff Iron Co., Cleveland, Ohio (employed by firm since 1940). Director Lamson & Sessions Co., Cleveland; Society National Bank, Cleveland. *Member:* Amer. Iron & Steel Inst.; Amer. Iron Ore Assn.; Cleveland Chamber of Commerce; Lake Carriers Assn.; Wheeling Steel Pittsburgh. *Clubs:* Chicago; Duquesne; The Fifty; Union (Cleveland); Kirtland Country; Pepper Pike Country; Seminole Golf; Tavern; Yale (N.Y.C.); Yale Alumni Assn. (Cleveland). *Address: office* 1460 Union Commerce Building, Cleveland Ohio 44115, U.S.A.

**WILCKENS, Henry.** Australian. *B.* 1916. *Educ.* Adelaide High School and University of Adelaide. *M.* 1940, Joy Grace Stacy. *S.* John Leonard and David Edward. *Dau.* Helen Elizabeth. *Career:* Member of Board, Commonwealth Government Housing Loans Insurance Corp. 1964–70. Board Member, Municipal Tramways Trust of South Australia 1962–71. Pres., International Federation of Asian & Western Pacific Contractors Assn. 1968–69; Federal Pres., Master Builders Fed. of Australia 1961–62, and of Australian Inst. of

Builders 1963–64; State Member, Commonwealth Council of Scientific & Industrial Research Organization 1963–75; Member, Exec. Board, South Australian Chamber of Manufacturers 1965–69, Board of Salvation Army Board of Advice 1965–75, Commonwealth Govt. Building Research Adv. Council 1962—. *Clubs:* Cruising Yacht Club of Australia. *Address:* 117 Kingston Terrace, North Adelaide, S.A. 5000; and *office* 309 Angas Street, Adelaide. S.A. 5000, Australia.

**WILCOCK, William Howard,** CBE. (Honorary Tan Sri-Panglima Mangku Negara, Federation of Malaysia); Ret. Australian banker. *B.* 1904. *Educ.* Ballarat. *M.* 1931, Dulcie O. Saunders (*D.* 1956). *Dau.* 1. *M.* (2) 1956, Barbara P. Barkas. *Career:* Chairman, Administrative Committee, Bankers Administrative Staff College, Australia 1954–55; Assistant Governor (Administration) Commonwealth Bank of Australia, Sydney 1955–58; Banking Adviser, Government of the Federation of Malaya 1958; first Governor and Chairman of the Board, Bank Negara Malaysia (Central Bank of Malaysia) 1959–62; Adviser, Reserve Bank of Australia and Gen. Mgr. Note Issue Dept. 1963–69; Chmn. Aust. Apple and Pear Board 1970–74. *Address:* 6 Heron Street, Mount Eliza, Vic. 3930, Australia.

**WILD, Major Hon. Gerald Percy,** MBE, JP. Australian legislator and company director. *B.* 2 Jan. 1909. *Educ.* Shoreham Grammar School, Sussex, and Chivers Academy, Portsmouth, Hants. *M.* 1944, Virginia Mary Baxter. *S.* Colin Robert, Gerald Keith. *Dau.* Heather Joan. *Career:* Served in World War II, Nov. 1939–Nov. 1945, in Middle-East, Greece, Crete, Syria, New Guinea, and Moratai, Netherlands East Indies (Major; despatches and MBE for service in the Desert 1940); elected member, Legislative Assembly for Western Australia, April 1947; Minister for Housing and Forests, 1950–53; Minister for Works and Water Supplies (W.A.) April 1959, and for Water Supplies and Labour 1962–65; Agent General for Western Australia 1965–71; Appt. Justice of the Peace (Perth) 1953. *Address:* 2/41 Park Street, Como, Western Australia 6152.

**WILD, Hermann.** Swiss. General Manager, Handelsbank in Zurich, Talstrasse 59, Zurich. *B.* 1913. *Educ.* Certificate of Maturity of Kantonsschule. St. Gallen. *M.* 1940, Helene Schenkermayr. *S.* Ruedi. *Daus.* Ursula and Helen. *Career:* Previously: Eidg. Bank, St. Gail; Verwaltungsesselschaft Affida, Zürich; Hendelsbank in Zürich. Member Board of Directors: Atlantic Finanzierungs AG, Zurich; Compania de Fomento e Inversiones SA (Peruinvest), Lima; Basler Handelsbank, Basle; Banque Hypothécaire Européenne, Paris; Société Parisienne des Participations, Paris; Crédit Immobilier Européen, Paris; Wien; Dow Banking Corp. Zurich; C. G. Trinkaus & Burkhardt, Dusseldorf; Handelsbank in Zurich (Overseas) Ltd. Nassau; Vowerk & Co.; Banque Louis-Dreyfus en Suisse SA, Zurich. *Clubs:* Golf & Country (Zürich). *Address:* c/o Talstrasse 59, Zurich, Switzerland.

**WILD, John Leslie.** Canadian. *B.* 1917. *Educ.* Univ. of Western Ontario (BA 1941); Univ. of Michigan (MA Pol Sc 1958). *M.* 1950, Audrey Elizabeth Stevens. *S.* Stevens John Leslie. *Dau.* Laura Suzanne Elizabeth. *Career:* Reporter: London (Ont.) Advertiser (1932–36) and London (Ont.) Free Press 1936–41; Editor, Wings Abroad, R.C.A.F. official newspaper, published in London (Eng.) 1943–45; Financial Editor, London (Ont.) Free Press 1945–47; adviser on Canadian Economy, Fortune, N.Y. (summer) 1948; Professor and Head, Department of Journalism, Univ. of Western Ontario 1952 (appointed to the Faculty 1947); Western Ontario correspondent for Time and Life 1948–68; Project Officer, Royal Commission on Government Organization 1961–62. Liberal. *Member:* Baconian Club of London (Ont.); Canadian Institute of International Affairs. *Club:* City Press (London, Ont.). *Address:* 6 Rollingwood Circle, Orchard Park, London, Ont., Canada.

**WILD, Rt. Hon. Sir Richard,** KCMG. Chief Justice of New Zealand 1966—. *B.* 1912. *M.* 1940, Janet Grainger. *S.* 2. *Daus.* 2. *Club:* Wellington. *Address:* 10 Homewood Avenue, Karori, Wellington, N.Z.; and *office* Chief Justice's Chambers Supreme Court, Wellington, New Zealand.

**WILDER, William Price,** BCom, MBA. Canadian company executive. *B.* 1922. *Educ.* Upper Canada Coll.; McGill Univ. (BCom); Graduate School, Business Admin.; Harvard Univ. (MBA). *M.* 1953, Judith Ryrie Bickle. *S.* 3. *Dau.* 1. *Career:* Dir. Allstate Insurance Company of Canada; John Labatt Ltd.; Noranda Mines Ltd.; Simpsons Ltd.; Simpsons-Sears Ltd.; Lever Bros. Ltd.; Chmn. Chief Exec. Officer Canadian Arctic Gas Pipeline Ltd. Trustee, Hospital for Sick Children. *Clubs:* Badminton & Racquet; Toronto Golf; University (Toronto); Saint James's Montreal; Queen's (Toronto); Rideau (Ottawa); Brooks's (London); The Vancouver. *Address:* 179 Warren Road, Toronto, Ontario M4V 2S4; and *office:* Box 139, Commerce Court Postal Station, Toronto, Ontario M5L 1E2 Canada.

**WILEY, W. Bradford.** American. *B.* 1910. *Educ.* Colgate University (AB). *M.* 1936, Esther T. Booth. *S.* William Bradford II and Peter Booth. *Dau.* Deborah Elizabeth. *Career:* Chmn., Chief Exec. (1970—) and Director (1942—), John Wiley & Sons Inc., N.Y.C.; John Wiley, Canada. Chmn., Dir.: John Wiley & Sons Ltd., London, and John Wiley & Sons Australasia Pty. Ltd. Sydney. Hon. LLD Colgate University 1966. *Member:* Association of American Publishers (Chmn. 1970–72); Trustee, Drew University 1976—. *Clubs:* The Players, University (N.Y.C.); Sakonnet Golf, Sakonnet Yacht (R.I.); Baltustol Golf (N.J.); Beacon Hill (N.J.). *Address:* 57 Prospect Hill Avenue, Summit, N.N. 07901; and *office:* 605 Third Avenue, New York, N.Y. 10016, U.S.A.

**WILHELMSEN, Morten Wilhelm.** Norwegian shipowner. Partner, Wilh. Wilhelmsen; Chmn., The Ship Research Inst. of Norway; Vice-Chmn., Saga Petroleum A/S & Co. *B.* 1937. *Educ.* Examen Artium Commercial College. *M.* 1967, Inger Helene Musaeus. *Address:* Hoffsjef Løvenskiolds vei 47, Oslo 3; and *office* Roald Amundsens gt. 5, Oslo 1, Norway.

**WILHELMSEN, Tom.** Norwegian shipowner. *B.* 18 Aug. 1911. Partner, Wilh Wilhelmsen, Oslo. Honours, Knight first class, Danish Royal Order. Dannebrog; Finnish White Rose Order; Chevalier, l'Ordre National de la Légion d'Honneur; Comdr., Norwegian Royal Order St. Olav; Comdr., Swedish Royal Order Vasa; Comdr., Mexican Order of Aguila Azteca; Officier de l'Ordre de la Couronne (Belgium). *Address:* Roald Amundsen gt. 5, Oslo, Norway.

**WILKE, Prof. Charles R.** American. Chemical engineer. *B.* 1917. *Educ.* Univ. of Wisconsin (PhD 1944), Univ. of Dayton (BChE 1940) and State Coll. of Washington (MS 1942). *M.* 1946, Bernice L. Arnett. *Career:* Chem. Eng., Union Oil Co. of Calif. 1944–45; Instructor in Chm. Engineering, State College of Washington; Professor of Chemical Engineering, Department Chairman, Univ. of California (Berkeley) 1953–63. Chemical Engineering Consultant. Member, Californian State Board of Registration for Professional Engineers 1964—. Author of approx. 70 publications in scientific journals in the field of chemical engineering. *Awards:* Colburn Award 1951; Inst. Lecturer 1957; William H. Walker Award, 1965; Director 1960–62, Amer. Inst. of Chem. Engineers. Fellow Amer. Inst. of Chemists. Elected to National Academy of Engineering 1975. *Member:* Amer. Inst. of Chem. Engineers; Amer. Chemical Socy.; Amer. Socy. for Engineering Education; Amer. Socy. for Microbiology; Socy. Applied Bacteriology. Adv. Board, Petroleum Research Fund 1964–67, Int. Chemical Engineering 1961—. *Member:* Sigma Xi; Tau Beta Pi. *Address:* 1327 Contra Costa Drive, El Cerrito, Calif.; and *office* Department of Chemical Engineering, University of California, Berkeley, Calif., 94720 U.S.A.

**WILKINS, Charles Timothy,** OBE, CEng, FRAeS. British. *B.* 1905. *Educ.* Brighton College; Course of aeronautical engineering with Vickers Aircraft. *M.* 1940, Gladys Alexander. *S.* Nicholas Alexander. *Dau.* Amanda Jean. *Career:* With de Havilland Aircraft Co. Ltd. 1928–30; Cierva Autogiro Co. 1930–31; Handley Page Ltd. 1931–32. Rejoined de Havilland Aircraft Co. Ltd. 1932; appointed to the Board 1958; appointed Technical Director 1960. Dir., Space, Hawker Siddeley Dynamics Ltd., Stevenage, Herts., 1963–70. Fellow, Royal Aeronautical Society. *Address:* Brook Hill Cottage, Brook Hill, Woodstock, Oxon.

**WILKINS, Hon. Mr. Justice Raymond Sanger.** American. Chief Justice, Supreme Judicial Court of Massachusetts Sept. 1956–70. Resigned. *B.* 1891. *Educ.* Harvard Univ. (AB 1912; LLB 1915). *M.* 1965, Georgie E. Hebbard. *S.* Raymond S., Jr. and Herbert P. Admitted to Massachusetts Bar 1915; practised law in Boston 1915–44; Associate Justice, Supreme Judicial Court 1944–56. *Address:* c/o 1300 Court House, Boston 02108, Mass., U.S.A.

**WILKINSON, John Arbuthnot Ducane,** MA. British. Senior Sales Exec., Eagle Aircraft Services Ltd. *B.* 1940. *Educ.* Eton Coll. King's Scholar); RAF Coll. Cranwell (Philip Sassoon Memorial Prize): Churchill Coll. Cambridge Hons. Modern History. *M.* 1969. Paula Adey. *Career:* Cadet RAF

Coll. Cranwell, Commissioned & Qualified Pilot 1959–61; Flying Inst. 8, F.T.S. Swinderby 1962; Trooper, 21st. SAS Regt. (Artists) T.A. 1963–65; Flying Instructor, RAF Coll. Cranwell 1966–67; A.D.C. to Commander 2nd. Allied Tactical Air Force 1967; Tutor Stanford Univ. 1967; Head, Univ. Dept. Conservative Office 1967–68; Aviation Specialist Cons. Research Dept. 1969; Sen. Admin. Officer Anglo French Jaguar Project 1969–70; Preston Div. B.A.C.; Chief Flying Instructor. Skywork Ltd., 1974–75; Gen. Man. G.A. Divn., Brooklands Aviation Ltd. 1975; P.A. to Chmn. of British Aircraft Corp. 1976–77. Member, Parliament (Cons.) Bradford West 1970–74; Secy. Conservative Defence Cttee., 1972–74; Jt. Secy. Conservative Aviation Cttee. 1972–74; Prospective Conservative Parly. Candidate for Ruislip/Northwood since 1975. *Publications:* Several pamphlets on Politics & Defence. *Club:* Royal Air Force. *Address:* c/o Lloyds Bank Ltd., 36 Trinity Street, Cambridge.

**WILKINSON, Keith Charles.** Australian. *B.* 1907. *Educ.* Perth Boys' School. *M.* 1932, Florence Annie Butt. *S.* Roger Charles and Murray Keith. *Dau.* Julia Florence. *Career:* State Manager, Humes Ltd.: Western Australia 1938–45; New South Wales 1945–53; Asst. General Manager 1953–59. General Manager, Humes Ltd., Melbourne 1959–70; Director: Humes Ltd.; Qantas Airways Ltd. 1966–72. Chmn. Skinner Manufacturing Pty. Ltd. and Associated Companies. *Member:* Associate Australian Socy. of Accountants; Associate Chartered Inst. Secretaries. *Clubs:* Athenaeum; Savage; Rotary (Melbourne); Glenferrie Hill Bowls. *Address:* 19 Chelmsford Street, North Balwyn, Vic. 3104, Australia.

**WILLAN, Edward Gervase.** CMG. MA. British diplomat. *B.* 1917. *Educ.* Radley Pembroke Coll. Cambridge. *M.* 1944, Mary Bickley Joy. *Career:* Indian Civil Service 1940–47; H.M. Foreign (Later H.M. Diplomatic) Service 1948–77. 2nd, Later 1st Secy. New Delhi 1947–49; Foreign Office 1949–51; 1st Secy. The Hague 1952–55; 1st Secy. Bucharest 1956–58; Head, Communications Dept. Foreign Office 1958–62; Political Adviser, Hong Kong 1962–65; Head Scientific Relations Dept. Foreign Office 1966–68; Minister, Lagos 1968–70; H.M. Ambassador Rangoon 1970–74; H.M. Ambassador to Prague 1974–77. *Clubs:* United Oxford and Cambridge University. Hong Kong. *Address:* 14 Markham Street, London SW3.

**WILLESEE, Donald Robert.** Australian politician. *B.* 1916. *Educ.* State Schools, Carnavon, W. Australia. *M.* 1940, Gwendoline C. Clarke. *S.* 4. *Daus.* 2. *Career:* Leader of Opposition in Senate 1966–67; Deputy Leader of Opposition in Senate 1969–72; Member Federal Exec., Australian Labour Party since 1969; Deputy Leader of Govt. in Senate 1972–75; Minister Assisting the Min. for Foreign Affairs, and special Minister of State 1972–73; Vice-Pres. of Exec. Council 1972–73; Australian Minister for Foreign Affairs 1973–75. *Address:* 25 Walton Place, Quinns Rock, W.A. 6065, Australia; and *office* Parliament House, Canberra, ACT, Australia.

**WILLEY, George Tom.** Management Consultant. *B.* 1901. *Educ.* Merchant Venturers Technical College, Bristol, England (Mech Eng Deg). *M.* 1932, Elizabeth Virginia Kelley. *S.* Robert (*Dec.*). *Career:* Apprentice, Bristol Airplane Co. 1918–23; Layout draughtsman, Westland Aircraft Co., Bristol 1923–24, and Sir W. G. Armstrong-Whitworth, England 1924–25; Design Engineer, Gloucester Aircraft Co., England 1925–28, and Canadian-Vickers Co., Montreal 1928–29; successively Group, Project, and Executive Engineer, and Quality Manager, The Glenn L. Martin Co., Baltimore 1929–43; Vice-Pres. and Gen. Manager, The Glenn L. Martin-Nebraska Co., Omaha 1943–45; Vice-Pres., Manufacturing, The Martin-Baltimore Div. 1945–57; Corporate Vice-Pres., Manufacturing The Martin Co. 1957–58; Vice-Pres. and Gen. Manager, Cocoa (Fla.) Div. 1958–59, and Aerospace Div. of Martin-Marietta Corp., Orlando 1959; Chmn. Bd. Nat. STD Life Insurance Co; Former Vice-Pres. and General Manager, Aerospace Division, Martin Co. Former Director First National Bank of Orlando; Winter Park Telephone Co., R. C. Le Tournear Corp. (Longview, Tex.); United Appeal of Orange County; and Florida State Chamber of Commerce. Former Vice-Pres., Central Florida Development Cttee. International Chairman, Christian Businessmen's Committee, 1965–. *Member:* Inst. of Aeronautical Sciences; Socy. of Automotive Engineers; Royal Aeronautical Sciences (Assoc.); Aerospace Industries Assn.; Assn. of U.S. Army; Rotary Club of Orlando. Hon. LLD, Hon. DSc. *Address: office* Martin Co., Orlando, Fla., U.S.A.

**WILLIAMS, Alan John,** PC, BA, BSc, MP. British. *B.* 1930. *Educ.* Politics, Philosophy & Economics Oxon.; Economics London. *M.* 1957, Mary Patricia Rees. *S.* Ian, Robin. *Dau.* Sian. *Career:* Lecturer, Welsh Coll. of Advanced Technology 1964; Member of Parliament for Swansea West since 1964; PPS to PMG 1966–67; Parly. Under-Secy. of State Dept. of Economic Affairs 1967–69; Parly. Secy. Ministry of Technology 1969–70; Shadow Spokesman on Higher Education 1970–72; Shadow Spokesman on Minerals, Private Industry and Consumer Protection 1972–74; Minister of State, Dept. of Prices & Consumer Protection 1974–76; Minister of State, Dept. of Industry since 1976. *Clubs:* Clyne Golf. *Address: office* House of Commons, London, S.W.1.

**WILLIAMS, Albert Lynn.** American. *B.* 1911. *Educ.* Beckley Coll. 1928–30. *M.* (1) 1931, Ruth Bloom (*Nov.* 1964). *S.* A. Lynn, Jr. *Dau.* Gail B.; (2) 1966, Katherine Y. Carson. *Career:* Accountant, Commonwealth Pa., Harrisburg 1930–36; Student Sales Rep. IBM, N.Y.C. 1936, Sales Rep. 1937 (Controller 1942, Treas. 1947; V.P. Treas., 1948; exec., V.P. 1954–61, Pres. 1961–66, Chmn. Exec. Cttee. Bd. 1966–71. Chairman of the Finance Committee of the Board of Directors 1971—; Member of the Boards of Directors, International Business Machines Corp. 1951—: Director: Mobil Corp.; Citibank (N.Y.C.); Eli Lilly and Company; Chairman, Commission, International Trade & Investment Policy 1970. *Member:* American Institute of C.P.A.s. *Clubs:* Links (N.Y.C.); Siwanoy Country (Bronxville, N.Y.); Country Club, Ocean, Delray Beach Yacht, Gulf Stream Golf, and Gulf Stream Bath & Tennis (Florida). *Address:* Old Orchard Road, Armonk, New York 10504, U.S.A.

**WILLIAMS, Anthony James.** CMG. British diplomat. *B.* 1923. *Educ.* Oundle & Oxford, Trinity College. *M.* 1955. Hedwig Gräfin Neipperg. *S.* 2. *Daus.* 2. *Career:* entered H.M. Foreign (later Diplomatic) Service 1945; Counsellor H.M. Embassy Moscow 1965–67, Washington 1968–70; H.M. Ambassador Phnom Penh, Khmer Republic Cambodia 1970–73; British Minister, Rome Italy 1973–76; H.M. Ambassador Tripoli, Libyan Arab Republic since 1977. *Clubs:* Beefsteak (London). *Address:* Jollys Farm House. Salehurst, E. Sussex; and *office* H.M. Embassy, Tripoli. Libyan Arab Republic.

**WILLIAMS, Bruce Macgillivray.** Canadian diplomat. *B.* 1918. *Educ.* Univ. of Toronto. *Career:* Joined Dept. of External Affairs, Canada, Aug. 1946; served with Canadian Delegation to U.N., New York 1946–48; Deputy Permanent Delegate to European Office of the U.N., Geneva 1952–53; Counsellor, Office of the High Commissioner for Canada in India 1953–56; Canadian Commissioner, International Supervisory Commission for Viet-Nam 1956–57; High Commissioner for Canada in Ghana June 1959–62; Ambassador to Turkey 1962–64; Asst. Under-Secretary of State for External Affairs, Ottawa 1964–67; Ambassador to Yugoslavia, Rumania and Bulgaria 1967–72; High Commissioner to India and concurrently Canadian Ambassador to Nepal 1972–74; Dir. Gen. Bureau of Public Affairs, Dept. of Public Affairs, Ottawa 1974; Exec. Vice-Pres. Canadian International Devel. Agency since 1974. *Address:* Canadian International Development Agency, 122 Bank St., Ottawa, Ontario K1A 0G4, Canada.

**WILLIAMS, Cecil Beaumont,** OBE. Barbadian Diplomat. *B.* 1926. *Educ.* Harrison Coll.; Codrington Coll., Barbados; King's Coll., Newcastle-upon-Tyne; Durham Univ.—BA, Dip. Ed.; New Coll., Oxford; Economic Development Inst., Interoational Bank for Reconstruction & Development (IRBD). *M.* Dorothy Williams. *S.* 2. *Dau.* 1. *Career:* Asst. Master, Harrison Coll. 1948–54; Asst. Sec., Government Personnel Dept. & Ministry of Trade, Industry & Labour 1954–56; Perm. Sec., Ministry of Education 1958; Perm. Sec., Ministry of Trade, Industry & Labour 1958–63; Dir., Economic Planning Unit 1964–65; Mgr., Industrial Development Corp. 1966–67; High Commissioner to Canada 1967–70; Perm. Sec., Ministry of External Affairs 1971–74; Ambassador to U.S.A. & Perm. Rep. to the OAS 1974–75; High Commissioner for Barbados in the U.K. since 1976. *Decorations:* Officer Order of the British Empire. *Clubs:* Senior Vice-Pres., Carlton Sports Club. *Address:* "Iverta", Burtenshaw Road, Thames Ditton, Surrey; and *office* Barbados High Commission, 6 Upper Belgrave Street, London SW1.

**WILLIAMS, Dr. Clyde E.** *B.* 1893. *Educ.* University of Utah (BSc Chem Eng 1915); DSc, Case Institute of Technology, University of Utah, Ohio State University: LLD.

Marietta College; DEng, Michigan Coll. of Mining & Techny.; Presidential Citation and Medal for Merit for wartime direction of research activities. *M.* 1919, Martha Barlow. *S.* Clyde E., Jr., Samuel B. and Thomas J. *Career:* Successively Chem., U.S. Smelting Co.; Grad. Fellow, U.S. Bureau of Mines and Univ. of Utah; Chem., Santa Fé Copper Co., and U.S.B.M. (Cornell Univ. Stn.), Research Chem., Hooker Electrochem. Co.; Supt., North-west Experimt. Stn., U.S.B.M.; Metallurgist, Govt. of Argentine (Commission to study iron, steel and fuel resources of Argentina); Chief Metallurgist, Columbia Steel Corp. 1925–29; Asst. Dir. (1929–34), Dir. (1934–56), Pres. (1953–58), Battelle Memorial Inst.; President, Clyde Williams & Co. (industrial advisers), since 1958; Chmn. Clyde Williams Enterprises Inc. 1966—; Applied Computer Technology Corp. 1968–71; Dir. The Claycraft Co. 1950—; Gammatronix Inc.; Jaccard Corp.; Ohio Chamber of Commerce; Solidstate Controls Inc.; Trustee, Finance Cttee. *Member:* Int. Platform Assn. Franklin County Historical Socy.; Steering Cttee. Greater Columbus Development Cttee.; Editorial Adv. Bd. Industrial Research; North America; Ohio Information Cttee.; City Columbus Welcoming Cttee.; Research Councillor, The Columbus Area Chamber of Commerce. Battelle Memorial Institute. Dir. Ohio Chamber of Commerce; Columbus Area Chamber of Commerce. Wartime: held various appointments with Office of Scientific Research and Development, War Production Board, National Acad. of Sciences, Nat. Research Coun., Army & Navy Munitions Bd., Coun. of Nat. Defense, National Advisory Committee for Aeronautics; Member, National Engineering Committee (which prepared for U.S. Govt. a plan for disarmament of aggressor states), and Technical Industrial Intelligence Commission, U.S. Dept. of Commerce (to organize technical missions to Germany). Mem. Endowments Cttee, AIME 1972–75. *Publications:* more than 100 articles on scientific, metallurgical, industrial, commercial and national subjects. *Clubs:* Rotary (Dir., Internatl. Service 1955–56), Research Directors', Cosmos, Columbus, Mining, Faculty, Scioto Country, Columbus Gallery of the Fine Arts. Life Member Sigma Chi; Sigma Xi; Tau Beta Pi; Sigma Delta Chi. *Clubs:* Rotary; Cosmos; Columbus; Engineers; Mining; Scioto Country. *Address:* Clyde Williams & Co., 150 East Broad Street, Columbus, Ohio 43215, U.S.A.

**WILLIAMS, David Benton.** *B.* 1920. *Educ.* Harvard (AB *magna cum laude* 1942—with highest honours in field). *M.* 1944, Edith Chapin Huntington. *S.* David Huntingdon and Howard Chapin. *Dau.* Deborah Benton. *Career:* With U.S. Army-Counter Intelligence Corps 1942–45; Erwin Wasey & Co. 1945 (President 1956); Dir. Sen. Vice-Pres. The Interpublic Group of Cos. 1963–68. President, Wilson Haight & Welch Inc since 1974; Pres. 1035 5th Av. Corp. *Member:* Phi Beta Kappa. *Clubs:* University (N.Y.); Preston Mountain (Kent, Conn.); Harvard Boston; American (London, Eng.). *Address:* 1035 Fifth Avenue, New York City 28; and *office* 65 East 55th Street, New York City, NY 10022, U.S.A.

**WILLIAMS, David Rogerson, Jr.** American engineer and executive. *B.* 1921. *Educ.* Yale Univ. (BEng). *M.* 1944, Pauline Wilson Bolton. *S.* David R., III. *Daus.* Pauline B. (G. d'Aquin) and Rachel K. *Career:* Construction Engineer and Superintendent of Williams Brothers Corp. 1939–1949; a co-founder of The Williams Companies (formerly Williams Brothers Co.) 1949; Vice-Pres. 1949–66; Chmn. Exec. Cttee. 1966–70. Chairman: The Resource Sciences Corp. (Tulsa), Williams Bros. Engineering Co. (Tulsa), Williams Bros. Process Services Inc. (Tulsa), Williams Bros. Urban Ore Inc. (Tulsa), Datap Systems Ltd. (Calgary), Williams Bros Canada Ltd. (Calgary). Director: Alaskan Resource Sciences Corp. (Anchorage), Filtrol Corp. (Los Angeles), Great Western Bank & Trust (Phoenix), Holmes & Narver Inc. (Anaheim), Northern Engineering Services Co. Ltd. (Calgary), Patagonia Corp. (Tucson), Pima Savings & Loan Assn. (Tucson), U.S. Filter Corp. (New York), Western American Mortgage Co. (Phoenix), Williams Bros. Engineering Ltd. (London), Williams Bros. Engineering Malaysia Sdn. Bhd. (Tulsa). *Member:* Amer. Petrol Inst.; Alberta Assn. of Professional Engineers; Amer. Gas Assn.; Independent Natural Gas Assn.; Yale Engineering Association; The Royal Society of Arts (London). Fellow, American Society of Civil Engineers. *Clubs:* Ranchmen's (Calgary); Toronto (Toronto); Union (Cleveland, Ohio); Racquet & Tennis (N.Y.C.); Springdale Hall (Camden, S.C.); Chagrin Valley Hunt (Ohio); Rolling Rock (Pennsylvania); Sky; Yale (N.Y.C.); Petroleum, Southern Hills Country, Summit (Oklahoma). *Address:* Resource Sciences Center, 6600 South Yale, Tulsa, Oklahoma 74136, U.S.A.; & Williams Brothers Engineering Ltd., 140 Park Lane, London W1Y 3AA.

**WILLIAMS, Douglas.** Management consultant. *B.* 1912. *Educ.* Cornell Univ. (AB) and Harvard Business School (MBA). *M.* 1936, Esther Jane Grant. *S.* Grant Tuthill. *Dau.* Penelope Grant. *Career:* Associated with Dr. Gallup's American Institute of Public Opinion, 1939; Elmo Roper and Associates 1939–40; and National Opinion Research Center 1940–41. Pres., Douglas Williams Associates Inc. 1947—. During World War II acted as chief of the Army Research Branch, in U.S.A. and overseas, with the mission of conducting morale surveys among troops; discharged with rank of Lieut.-Col. *Publications:* Management Education For Its Employees; The New Era In Medical Research. *Clubs:* Winged Foot Golf; Larchmont University; Larchmont Yacht; Cornell; Harvard; Union League. *Address: office:* 6 East 43rd Street, New York City 10017, U.S.A.

**WILLIAMS, Dudley Cadelle Leslie,** CBE. Australian. *B.* 1909. *Educ.* Wesley Coll. Melbourne; Queen's Coll. Melbourne Univ. (LLB). *M.* 1966, Margaret Crofton Harper. *Career:* Commerce Department 1934–42; Department of Supply and Shipping 1943–48; Asst. Secy., Shipping Dept. of Shipping and Fuel 1948–50; 1st Asst. Secy. Dept. of Shipping and Transport 1950–57; Secretary Department of Shipping and Transport 1957–69; Commissioner of Australian Coastal Shipping Commission 1956–70; Chairman, Australian Shipping Board 1957–61. Chmn., Commonwealth Explosives Transport Committees and Commonwealth Explosives Port Facilities Committee 1953–57: Dep. Chmn., Australian Shipbuilding Board 1951–58. *Address:* 5 Bramley Court, Kew, Victoria, Australia.

**WILLIAMS, Rt. Hon. Eric,** PC, CH. Prime Minister of Trinidad and Tobago since 1961. *B.* 1911. *Educ.* Queen's Royal Coll., Trinidad and St. Catherine's Society, Oxford (BA 1932, Class I Hist., DPhil 1938). At Howard Univ., Washington, D.C.; Asst. Prof. Social and Political Science 1939 (Assoc. Prof. 1944, Prof. 1947). With Caribbean Commission, and Research Council (Dep. Chmn. of latter 1948–55). Founder and Political Leader, People's National Movement 1956. First Chief Minister and Minister of Finance 1956; first Premier 1959: Minister of External Affairs 1961–67; Minister of Finance Planning and Development 1967–70. Led Trinidad and Tobago Delegations to London: U.S. Bases 1960, West Indian Federation Conf. 1961, Independence Conf. 1961, Commonwealth Prime Ministers' Conf. 1962; and to E.E.C., Brussels 1962, Pro. Chancellor, Univ. of West Indies & Hon. LLD (Univ. of New Brunswick); Hon DCL (Oxford). *Publications:* The Negro in the Caribbean (1942); The Economic Future of the Caribbean (1943); Capitalism and Slavery (1944); Education in the British West Indies (1950); History of the People of Trinidad and Tobago (1962); Documents of West Indian History (Vol. I—1492–1655); Inward Hunger (1969); From Columbus to Castro, (1970). *Address:* Prime Minister's Residence, La Fantasie Road, St. Anns, Port of Spain, Trinidad.

**WILLIAMS, Eric Charles.** British. *B.* 1915. *Educ.* University of Birmingham (MSc; BSc Hons. 1st Class). *M.* 1946, Elisabeth Bryan. *S.* Charles Timothy. *Dau.* Angela Elisabeth. *Career:* Hon. Wing-Comdr. R.A.F. 1942–45. At Imperial Defence Coll. 1947; Asst. Scientific Adviser, Air Ministry 1947–49; Director of Operational Research, Admiralty 1949–54; Scientific Adviser, Intelligence, Ministry of Defence 1954–60; Director, Technical Centre, Supreme Headquarters, Allied Powers Europe 1960–64. Chief Scientific Adviser, Ministry of Transport (U.K.), Sept. 1964–68. Chief Scientist, Ministry of Power (U.K.) 1968–71; Chief Scientific Adviser, (Energy), Dept. Trade & Industry 1971–74: Chief Inspector of Nuclear Installations 1971–76 (Ret'd.). *Club:* Athenaeum. *Address:* 4 Sandringham Drive, Bangor, Co. Down, N. Ireland.

**WILLIAMS, Chief Frederick Rotimi Alade,** QC. *B.* 1920. *Educ.* Cambridge Univ. (MA); Barrister-at-Law. Member Western Nigeria Committee (on new Regional Legislation) which visited U.K., U.S.A. and Australia 1954. Chairman, Provisional Council, University of Ife, Western Nigeria, 1961–63. Chmn., National Universities Commission 1968–70; Chmn. Council Univ. of Nigeria NSUKKA since 1974; Chmn. of the Cttee. appointed by the Federal Military Government in Nigeria to prepare a Draft Constitution for return to civilian government in Nigeria 1975–76. Member: Council of Legal Education 1962–68. President Nigerian Bar Assoc. 1959–68. *Address:* 26 Moloney Street, P.O. Box 3426, Lagos; and *office* Palm Grove House, 1 Shagamu Avenue, Ikorodu Road, Yaba, Lagos, Nigeria.

**WILLIAMS, Glenn Carber.** Chemical engineer. *B.* 1914. *Educ.* Univ. of Illinois (BS 1937, MS 1938), and Mass. Inst of Technology (ScD 1942). *M.* 1939, Dorothy Cleo Bryan. *S.* Glenn L. *Dau.* Cheryl Anne. *Career:* With M.I.T.: Instructor 1940–42; Asst. Prof. 1942–46, Assoc. Prof. 1946–54. Director, Torpedo Fuel Laboratory 1944–46; Assoc. Director, Hydrogen Peroxide Laboratory 1946–50; Project Meteor Research Committee 1945–50. Government Activities: Jet-Propelled Missiles Panel, O.S.R.D. 1945; Joint Chiefs of Staff Guided Missiles Committee 1946—; Sub-Committee on Combustion, N.A.C.A. 1946–58 (Chmn. 1950); Panel on Propulsion, Committee on Undersea Warfare, National Academy of Sciences 1949–52; Professor of Chemical Engineering, Massachusetts Institute of Technology 1954—. Member: Research Advisory Committee on Chemical Energy Processes, National Aeronautics & Space Agency; Scientific Advisory Committee, Ordnance Corp., Department of the Army; Research Advisory Panel, National Bureau of Standards; Advisory Committee for Army Ordnance Research & Development 1951—. Associate Director, Fuels Research Laboratory 1942–68, Dir. since 1968. *Publications:* Absorption by Spray Droplets (with H. F. Johnstone); Charts of Thermodynamic Properties of Fluids Encountered in Internal Combustion Engines (with A. C. Hottel); Flame Stabilization & Propagation in High Velocity Gas Streams (with Hottel and H. C. Scurlock); Generalized Thermodynamics of High Temperature Combustion (with Hottel and C. N. Satterfield); Basic Studies on Flame Stabilization; Graduate-Level Studies for Chemical Engineers (1957); Thermodynamic Charts for Combustion Processes (joint author), 1949; and other titles. *Member:* The Combustion Inst. (Secy. and Dir. 1954—, Vice-Pres. 1964–70, Pres. since 1970); Amer. Inst. of Chemical Engineers; Amer. Chemical Socy.; Inst. of Aeronautical Sciences; Amer. Acad. of Arts & Sciences; Sigma Xi; Tau Beta Pi. *Address:* 20 Barberry Road, Lexington, Mass. 02173; and *office* Room 66–366, Massachusetts Institute of Technology, Cambridge 02139, Mass., U.S.A.

**WILLIAMS, Harrison Arlington, Jr.** American Lawyer & Politician. *B.* 1919. *Educ.* Oberlin Coll., Ohio; Columbia Univ. Law Sch. & Georgetown Univ. Foreign Service Sch. (BA, LLD). *Career:* Served with U.S. Navy during W.W. II; Mem., House of Reps. 1953–56; Democratic Senator from New Jersey since 1959; Chmn., U.S. Senate Cttee. on Human Resources 1971. *Address:* Senate Office Building, Washington, D.C. 20510, U.S.A.

**WILLIAMS, Harvey Ladew.** American. Chevalier Légion d'Honneur, Intl. Business Consultant. *B.* 1900. *Educ.* Harvard Univ. and Massachusetts Inst. of Technology. *M.* (1) 1927, Gertrude Elizabeth Hoxie; (2) 1943, Brenda Hedstrom Boocock. *S.* Harvey Ladew III. *Daus.* Eleanor Ladew (Dowd), Sheila (Stewart Scott), Hannah Hooker (Ackerman, *Dec.*). *Career:* President and Director, Air Investors Inc. and other air transport and aeronautical companies, 1928–34; Manager, New Properties Department, Stone & Webster Inc., N.Y. and Boston 1922–28; Management Consultant, Harvey Williams & Associates, 1933—; Pres. and Dir., Philco International Corp. (and subsidiaries and affiliates) 1957–62, Vice-President: International Operations, Avco Corp. 1953–57; Chmn. Connecticut Aeronautical Development Commission 1939–43; U.S. Army 1943–46; Vice-Pres. Overseas Operations, Dir. and Member Exec. Cttee. H. J. Heinz Co. (and Subsidiaries) 1946–53); Pres. & Director, The Company for Investing Abroad, Philadelphia; Director, The Fidelity International Corporation, 1963–72; Chmn., Comm. on the Expansion of Intl. Trade, Intl. Chamber of Commerce; Member Exec. Cttee. and Chmn., Cttee. Commercial Policy, U.S. Council of the I.C.C.; Pres. United States Council, International Chamber Commerce 1973–77, Hon. Life Pres. & Senior Trustee 1977—; Treas.-Secy. U.S.A. Business and Industry Adv. Council of the OECD (Paris) since 1973. *Member:* General Soc. of Colonial Wars. Vice-Chairman and Life-Trustee, Board of Trustees. Tabor Academy, Marion, Mass. *Member:* Commerce and Industry Council, C. of C. of Greater Philadelphia (Dir.); American-Australian Association (Director); International House, Philadelphia; Member of the Athenaeum of Philadelphia; Institute of Directors, London (Life Fellow); English-Speaking Union of the Commonwealth (Life Member); Amer. Ordnance Association, Navy League of the U.S. (Life Member of each); Newcomen Socy. of N.A.; President's Assn. N.Y.; Phila. Committee on Foreign Relations; English-Speaking Union in U.S. Amer. Socy. of Legion of Honour, N.Y.; Amer. Socy. in London; Stewards' Enclosure, Henley (Eng.); Amer. Legion, Greenwich, Conn.; *Publications:* Magazine articles and addresses on international economics. *Clubs:* Racquet; Orpheus; Athenaeum (Phila.); Harvard, India House; University; Wings (N.Y.C.); Kittansett, Beverley Yacht (Marion, Mass.); Ocean Reef Keylargo, Florida; Bucks. (London); Travellers (Paris); Melbourne, (Melbourne, Australia). *Address:* 37 Island Drive, Ocean Reef, Key Largo, Florida 33037, U.S.A.

**WILLIAMS, Sir John Protheroe,** CMG, OBE. Australian. *B.* 1896. *Educ.* Queen Elizabeth's Grammar School, Carmarthen. *M.* 1921, Gladys Grieves (*Dec.*). *S.* 1. *Daus.* 3. *M.* (2) 1964, Althea Carr (widow). *Career:* Officer in command of salvage operations of R.M.S. Niagara on behalf of the Bank of England in 1942, when £2,396,000 worth of bullion was recovered from depth of 438 feet of water. Chairman: Australian Coastal Shipping Commission 1956–71; City Ice & Cold Storage Pty. Ltd., Underwriting Member of Lloyd's; Master Mariner; Chmn. United Salvage Pty. Ltd. *Clubs:* Australian (Melbourne and Sydney); Savage, Melbourne (Melbourne). *Address:* 77 St. George's Road, Toorak, Vic. 3142; and *office* Union Steamships Bldgs., Sideley Street, Melbourne, Australia.

**WILLIAMS, John Robert,** CMG. British diplomat. *B.* 1922. *Educ.* Sheen County School; Fitzwilliam House, Cambridge. *M.* 1938, Helgebeth Konow Lund. *S.* 2. *Daus.* 2. *Career:* with Colonial Office 1949–56; First Secretary British High Commission New Delhi 1956–58; Commonwealth Relations Office London 1958–59; Deputy-High Commissioner, Penang Malaya 1959–62; Counsellor British High Commission, New Delhi 1963–66; Foreign & Commonwealth Office, London 1966–70; High Commissioner in Fiji 1970–74; Minister, British High Commission, Lagos since Nov. 1974. *Award:* Companion, Most Excellent Order, St. Michael and St. George. *Clubs:* Royal Commonwealth Socy. Roehampton. *Address:* Foreign & Commonwealth Office, King Charles Street, London, S.W.1.

**WILLIAMS, Langbourne Meade.** American business executive. *B.* 1903. *Educ.* University of Virginia (AB 1924) and Graduate School of Business Administration, Harvard Univ. (MBA 1926). *M.* (1) 1930, Elizabeth Goodrich Stillman (*D.* 1956), and (2) 1959, Frances Pinckney (Breckinridge). *Career:* With Lee Higginson & Co., N.Y.C. 1926–27; with family banking firm of John L. Williams & Sons, Richmond, Va. 1927–30, Vice-President and Treas. (1930–33) and Pres. (1933–58), Chmn. 1957–69 Freeport Minerals Co.; First Director, Industry Div., Economic Co-operation Administration (Marshall Plan), Paris 1948. Director and Member Exec. Cttee., Texaco Inc. Chairman Exec. Cttee., Freeport Minerals Co. 1957–73. Councillor and former Chmn., The Conference Board. Hon. Member, Board of Governors, Society of N.Y. Hospital; Trustee George C. Marshall Research Foundation. *Member:* The Business Council, Washington, D.C.; Virginia Historical Society; Delta Psi, Phi Beta Kappa. *Clubs:* Century, Union (N.Y.C.); Metropolitan (Washington); Commonwealth (Richmond, Va.). *Address:* Retreat, Rapidan, Va. 22733; and *office* Rapidan, Virginia, 22733, U.S.A.

**WILLIAMS, Leslie Henry.** British. *B.* 1903. *Educ.* Highbury County School and London Univ. (BSc; C.Chem; FRIC); Hon. DSc. Salford. *M.* 1930, Alice, dau. of late Henry Oliver Harrison. *S.* 1. *Career:* Joined I.C.I. Paints Div., 1929; subs. Dir. 1943, Managing Dir. 1946, Chmn. 1949, Dir. I.C.I. 1957, and Dep. Chmn. 1960. Director: British Nylon Spinners Ltd. 1957–64; Ilford Ltd. 1958–67; Deputy Chmn. I.C.I. Ltd. 1960–67; Chmn. I.C.I. Fibres Ltd. 1965–67. Pres. Royal Inst. of Chemistry, 1967–70, Hon. Fellow 1977; Member, Monopolies Commission 1967–73. *Address:* Penny Green, Stoke Poges, Bucks.

**WILLIAMS, Sir Michael Sanigear,** KCMG. *B.* 1911. *Educ.* Rugby School and Trinity College, Cambridge (BA). *M.* (1) 1942, Joy Holdsworth Hunt (*Dec.* 1964). *Daus.* 2; (2) 1965, Mary Grace Lindon (née Harding). *Career:* Entered British Diplomatic Service 1935; Embassy Spain 1938–39; Foreign Office 1939–47; Embassy Rome 1947–50, and Rio de Janeiro 1950–52; Foreign Office 1952–56; Minister at Bonn 1956–60; to Guatemala 1960–62; Ambassador to Guatemala 1962–63; Foreign Office 1963–65. British diplomat. Minister to the Holy See, 1965–70. *Address:* Wentways, Waldron, Sussex.

**WILLIAMS, Peter Gordon,** OBE, JP, BSc. British. *B.* 1920. *Educ.* Whitgift School; London Univ. (BSc Econ). *M.* 1947, Anne Catherine Newmarch. *S.* 2. *Career:* Vice-Chairman, Dodwell & Company Ltd.; Chairman: The Hongkong Electric Co. Ltd; Auto Electric Co. Ltd.; Great China Hardware Co. Ltd.; Engineering Equipment Co. Ltd.; Lab. Test Ltd.; Prodev Ltd.; Director: Metro-Dodwell Motors Ltd.; Burmah Castrol (Far East) Ltd.; Dairy Farm, Ice &

Cold Storage Co. Ltd.; Hongkong Shanghai Banking Corporation; The Hong Kong & Kowloon Wharf & Godown Co. Ltd.; Star Ferry Co. Ltd.; Union Insurance Society of Canton Ltd.; British Traders Insurance Co. Ltd.; North Pacific Insurance Co. Ltd.; Nanyang Cotton Mill Ltd.; Hong Kong Telephone Co. Ltd.; Mercantile Bank Ltd.; Island Dyeing & Printing Co. Ltd.; Commonwealth Garments Ltd.; Ocean Park Ltd.; Dodwell Travel Ltd.; Inchcape Far East Ltd. *Member:* Hong Kong General Chamber of Commerce; Community Chest; Board of Education; Hongkong Management; Board of Governors of Hong Kong Polytechnic; English Schools Foundation; Council of the Chinese University of Hong Kong; (Hon. Vice President) Economic Society, University of Hong Kong. *President:* Hong Kong Amateur Fencing Association; Chairman of the Stewards, The Royal Hong Kong Jockey Club. *Address:* 35 Magazine Gap Road, The Peak, Hong Kong; and *office:* P.O. Box 36, Hong Kong.

**WILLIAMS, Roger, Jr.** Chemical engineering economist. *B.* 1920. *Educ.* Amherst College (AB) and Massachusetts Inst. of Technology. *M.* 1950, Anna Given. *S.* Roger III. *Daus.* Lynn Adair, Jan Carol and Valerie Anne. *Career:* With Dupont: Ammonia Department, West Virginia 1941–46; Research Staff Asst., Plastics Department 1946–48; McGraw-Hill Publishing Co. 1948–50. Chairman, Roger Williams Technical & Economic Services Inc. 1950—. *Publications:* Technical Market Research—A Bird's Eye View; contributing Editor to Encyclopedia of Chemical Technology, Chemical Engineering Economics, and Chemical Market Research in Practice; The Petrochemical Industry, Markets & Economics; contributor of articles to Chemical Engineering, Chemical Week, Chemical Engineering Progress, Chemical & Engineering News; Chimie Industrielle, Poliplasti, Anglo-American Trade News, Journal of Commerce, Financial Analyst's Journal. Fellow A.A.A.S., Amer. Inst. of Chemists. *Member:* Amer. Chemical Socy.; Chemical Market Research Assn.; Socy. of Chemical Industry; Amer. Physics Socy.; Socy. of the Plastics Industry; Amer. Inst. of Chemical Engineers, Assn. of Consulting Chemists and Chemical Engineers; Société de Chimie Industrielle Phi Gamma Delta. *Clubs:* Chemists (N.Y.C.); American (London). *Address:* 'Gladacres', Box 167, RD2 New Hope, Pa. 18938; and *office* Box 426, Princeton, N.J. 08540, U.S.A.

**WILLIAMS (Mrs.), Shirley Vivian Brittain,** MP. *B.* 1930. *Educ.* MA (Oxon), Smith-Mundt Visiting Scholar, Columbia University. *M.* 1955, Professor Bernard Williams (*div.*). *Dau.* Rebecca Clare. *Career:* Labour MP for Hitchin Herts., later Hertford & Stevenage; General Secy. Fabian Socy. 1960–64; Parly. Private Sec. to Minister of Health 1964–66; Parliamentary Secretary Minister of Labour 1966–67. Minister of State, Education and Science 1967–69; Minister of State Home Office, 1969–70; Opposition Shadow Spokesman on Home Affairs 1970–71; Shadow Home Secretary 1971–73; Opposition Spokesman on Prices and Consumer Affairs 1973–74; Secy. of State for Prices & Consumer Protection 1974–76; and additionally appointed Paymaster-General April 1976; Sec. of State for Education & Science since Sept. 1976. *Publications:* The Common Market and its Forerunners (1958); The Free Trade Area: Central Africa—the Economics of Inequality; chapter on Christian Order and World Poverty (1960). *Member:* Royal Institute of International Affairs; Past Visiting Fellow, Nuffield College, Oxford. Hon. Doctor of Edn., C.N.A.A.; Hon. Doctor of Political Economy, Univ. of Leuven. *Address:* House of Commons, London, S.W.1.

**WILLIAMS, Walter Joseph.** American. Lawyer. *B.* 1918. *Educ.* Ohio State University (BS Bus Admin 1940) and University of Detroit (JD 1942). *M.* 1944, Maureen June Kay. *S.* John Bryan. *Career:* Captain, U.S. Army 1942–46. Title Attorney, Abstract & Title Guaranty 1946–47; Corporate Attorney Ford Motor Co. 1947–51; Studebaker-Packard Corp. 1951–56. Corporate Secretary and House Councel: American Motors Corp.; American Motors Sales Corp.; American Motors Pan-Americ. Corporation; Evart Products Co.; Jeep Corporation; Jeep-Sales Corporation. Jeep Int. Corporation, AM General Corporation. Director: Evart Products Co., Detroit; Metropolitan Industrial Development Corp.; Amer. Motors (Canada) Ltd. Assistant Secretary, American Motors (Canada) Ltd.; AM Data Systems Corporation, 1956–72; Partner Gilman and Williams Law Firm 1972–74; Corporate Attorney, Detroit Edison Co. 1974–75; Senior Staff Attorney, Burroughs Corp. since 1975; Asst. Sec., Burroughs Corp. & International Subsidiaries since 1974. *Member:* Michigan State, Federal, American, and Detroit Bar Assns.; Delta Theta Phi Law Fraternity; Ohio State University; Alumni Assn.; University of Detroit Alumni Association. *Publications:* General Aspects of Dealer Franchising (1964). *Club:* Oakland Hills Country. *Address:* 3644 Darcy Drive, Birmingham, Michigan 48010; and *office* Burroughs Place, Detroit, Michigan 48232, U.S.A.

**WILLIAMS, Sir William Thomas,** QC, MP. British lawyer politician. *B.* 1915. *Educ.* Univ. of Wales; Univ. of Oxford; Lincoln's Inn. *M.* 1942, Gwyneth. *S.* 1. *Dau.* 1. *Career:* Baptist Minister Chaplain Royal Air Force 1941–46; Lecturer, History of the Reformation, Oxford Univ. 1946–49; MP Hammersmith South 1949–55; Parly. Private Secy. Minister of Pensions 1949–50, Minister of Health 1950–51; Barrister at Law since 1952; MP Barons Court 1955–59; Member of Parliament for Warrington since 1961; Parly. Private Secy. Attorney General 1964–67; Queen's Counsel since 1964; Bencher Lincolns Inn since 1972. *Member:* Lord Chancellor's Cttee. on Statute Law; Lord Chancellor's Cttee. on Public Records; Select Cttee. on the Parly. Commissioner for Admin.; Select Cttee. on Parly. Procedure (Chmn.); Exec. of the Inter-Parly. Union (Chmn. 1974) & Pres. World Council of the Inter Parly. Union. *Publications:* Return to Reality, the Social Teaching of the Bible (1946). *Clubs:* Royal Automobile; London Welsh; Liverpool Raquet. *Address:* 17 Ashley Court, London SW1; and *office* Lamb Building, Temple, London, E.C.4.

**WILLIAMSON, Lord** (Thomas Williamson), CBE, JP. *B.* 1897. *Educ.* Knowsley Road School, St. Helens and Workers' Educational Association, Liverpool University; Hon. LLD, Cambridge Univ. 1959. *M.* 1925, Hilda Hartley. *Dau.* 1. *Career:* Gen. Secy., National Union of General and Municipal Workers 1946–61; Chairman, British Trades Union Congress 1956; member, T.U.C. General Council 1947–61; Vice-President, British Productivity Council 1956; member 1953–60; member, National Production Advisory Council on Industry 1948–60; Chmn., Trade Union Side of Minister of Labour's National Joint Advisory Council 1949–61; Pres., Public Services International 1938–56; member, National Council of Labour 1954–61; Hon. Associate, College of Technology, Birmingham 1955; Director: Daily Herald 1953–62. *Member:* Liverpool City Council 1929–35; member, National Executive of Labour Party and Chairman Finance Committee 1940–47; Member of Parliament (Lab.) for Brigg Division of Lincoln and Rutland 1945–48; Chairman, British Productivity Council 1954. *Address:* 13 Hurst Lea Court, Brook Lane, Alderley Edge, Cheshire SK9 7QF.

**WILLIS, Charles Reginald.** British journalist. *B.* 1906. *Educ.* Tiverton Grammar School. *M.* 1929, Violet Stubbs. *Dau.* 1. *Career:* Five years' apprenticeship on the Gazette series, Tiverton; then to N.W. Daily Mail (Barrow-in-Furness), Evening Chronicle (Newcastle-on-Tyne), Evening Chronicle (Manchester), Empire News (London); Editorial Director, Harmsworth Publications; former Editor, Evening News, London; Director, Assoc. Newspapers Ltd. 1961–71; Director, Tiverton Gazette series, Devon since 1971. *Address:* Howden Heyes, Ashley, Tiverton, Devon.

**WILLIS, Hon. Sir Eric Archibald,** KBE, CMG, MLA. Australian. *B.* 1922. *Educ.* BA (Hons.). *M.* Norma Dorothy Knight. *S.* 2. *Dau.* 1. *Career:* Deputy Leader of the Opposition, N.S.W. Legislative Assembly 1959–65. N.S.W. Minister for Labour and Industry 1965–71; Chief Secretary and Minister for Tourism and Sport 1965–72; Minister for Education 1972–76; Premier and Treasurer 1976; Leader of the Opposition since 1976; Deputy Leader, N.S.W. Parliamentary Liberal Party 1959–75, Leader since 1976. Member, N.S.W. Legislative Assembly 1950—. *Clubs:* National; Earlwood Bowling; St. George Leagues; Earlwood-Bardwell Park R.S.L. *Address:* 16 Crewe Street, Bardwell Park, N.S.W.; and *office* Parliament House, Macquarie Street, Sydney, N.S.W., Australia.

**WILLIS, Rt. Hon. Eustace George,** PC. Politician. *B.* 1903. *Educ.* Secondary School. *M.* 1929, Mary Swan Nisbet. *Dau.* Elizabeth Rose. *Career:* Member Parliament for NorthEdinburgh 1945–50; Elected MP for East Edinburgh 1954. Re-elected 1955 and 1959, 1964–66; Minister of State for Scotland 1964–67. *Address:* 31 Great King Street, Edinburgh 3.

**WILLIS, Hector Ford,** CB. U.S. Medal of Freedom (Silver Palm). British Civil Servant. Scientific Adviser, Ministry of Defence, Retired 1970. *B.* 1909. *Educ.* University of Wales (BSc 1930; MSc 1932) and Cambridge University (PhD 1935). *M.* 1936, Marie Iddon Renwick. *Career:* Scientist with British Cotton Industry Research Assoc., Manchester 1935–38;

Scientist with Admiralty 1938–62 (Superintendent, Admiralty Research Laboratory 1953–54; Chief, Royal Naval Scientific Service 1954–62). *Publications:* various papers in Proceedings of Royal Society, Philosophical Magazine, and Proceedings of Faraday Society. Member of Royal Institution. *Address:* Fulwood, Eaton Park, Cobham, Surrey.

**WILLISTON, Ray Gillis,** BA. Canadian. *B.* 1914. *Educ.* Victoria, University of British Columbia (BA). M. 1939, Gladys Edna McInnes. *S.* Hubert Neil. *Daus.* Dianne Elaine and Sandra Raye. *Career:* R.C.A.F., Armament Instructor, Pilot, 1941–45; Supervising Principal Prince George Schools, 1945–49; Inspector of Schools, 1949–53; Elected M.L.A., (Fort George), 1953; Minister of Education, 1954; Minister of Lands and Forests, 1956; Minister of Lands, Forests and Water Resources, 1962–72; Director, Pacific Great Eastern Railway, 1957–72; B.C. Hydro and Power Authority, 1962–72; Y.M.C.A. and Y.W.C.A., Victoria; Chmn. Canadian Entity Columbia River Development 1970–72; British Columbia Environment and Land Use Cttee. 1971–72; Forest Consultant, Govt. New Brunswick, United Nations Dev. Programme, Canadian International Development Agency 1972–73; Gen. Man. New Brunswick Forest Authority 1973; Pres., British Columbia Cellulose Co. since June 1976. *Awards:* Named British Columbian of the Year by Newsmen's Club of B.C., 1964; special award for distinguished current achievement in forestry (Western Forestry and Conservation Assn.). *Address: office* 2659 Douglas Street, Victoria, B.C. V8T 4M3, Canada.

**WILLOUGHBY, John Lucas,** OBE. British Barrister-at-Law. *B.* 11 Oct. 1901. *Educ.* Ovingdean Hall and Westminster School (King's Scholar). *M.* 1932, Hilary W. T. Tait. *S.* 3. *Dau.* 1. *Career:* F.C.I.T.; Port Man., Port Sudan 1937–44 (rep. Min. of War Tran. in Sudan and was Chairman of Local War Transport Committee 1941–44); Traffic Manager, Sudan Railways 1944–46; Deputy General Manager 1946–48; transferred to British Road Services 1948; Deputy Secy. 1949–53; Secretary 1953–57; mentioned in despatches 1941. Member of Council, Inst. of Transport 1959–62. *Address:* 2 The Grange, Mere, Warminster, Wilts.

**WILLS, Charles Henry.** Canadian barrister and solicitor. *B.* 1924. *Educ.* University of British Columbia (BA; LLB). *M.* 1950, Marion Capelle Hebb. *S.* Charles Hebb. *Daus.* Allyson Hayden, Lindsay Anne, Christie Capelle and Elizabeth Sewell. *Career:* Served in Royal Canadian Volunteer Naval Reserve 1943–45; Partner, Farris, Vaughan, Wills and Murphy, Vancouver B.C. Dir.: Canfor Investments Ltd.; Yorkshire Trust Co.; Alberta Distillers Ltd.; Kelly Douglas & Co. Ltd.; Cyprus Anvill Mining Corporation Ltd. Trustee, B.C. Sports Hall of Fame. *Member:* Health Centre for Children (Past Pres.).; Naval Officers Assns. of Canada; Canadian and Vancouver Bar Assns.; British Columbia Law Society; Hon Consul for Thailand with jurisdiction for the Provinces of British Columbia, Alberta, Saskatchewan, Manitoba, Northwest Territories and the Yukon Territory. *Clubs:* Vancouver, University (Vancouver), Past president. *Address:* 1789 Matthews Avenue, Vancouver 9, B.C., Canada.

**WILLS, Philip Aubrey,** CBE. British *B.* 1907. *Educ.* Harrow. *M.* 1931, Katharine Fisher. *S.* Christopher, Stephen and Justin. *Dau.* Vanessa. *Career:* Joined George Wills & Sons Ltd. 1928; Managing Director 1931. War career: Director of Operations and Second in Command Air Transport Auxiliary 1939–46; General Manager (Technical), British European Airways 1945–47; returned to family business 1948; Pres., George Wills & Sons (Holdings) Ltd. 1977—. President: British Gliding Association 1968—. Vice-Pres., Royal Aero Club 1977. *Awards:* World Gliding Champion 1952; Lillienthal Medal 1954; five times British Gliding Champion; Britannia Trophy 1953; numerous other awards and records for gliding. Coronation Medal. Member, Royal Aeronautical Society. *Publications:* On Being a Bird (1953); Beauty of Gliding (1960); Where No Birds Fly (1962); Free as a Bird (1973); The Inevitability of Confrontation: a Structural Solution to Britain's Problems (1974). *Club:* Royal Aero. *Deceased* 16*th January* 1978.

**WILMOT, Anthony Talbot de Burgh,** MA. British. *B.* 1915. *Educ.* Tonbridge School; Oxford Univ. (MA, Hons.). *M.* 1946, Alice Eva Stanley Smith. *S.* 5. *Daus.* 2. *Career:* Former Chmn.; Omo Sawmills of Nigeria Ltd.; Coast Construction (Nigeria) Ltd.; Coast Engineering Ltd.; Coast Construction Ltd., Ghana; Development Corp. (W.A.) Ltd.; Industrial & Agricultural Co. Ltd.; Northern Developments (Nig.) Ltd.; Sierra Leone Investments Ltd.; Nigeria Building Society; Nigeria Hotels Ltd.; Lagos Hotel Ltd.; Freetown Hotel Ltd.; Brandler & Rylke Ltd.; Brandler & Rylke (Cameroons) Ltd.; Magic-Pak Ltd.; Former Dir.: Malaya Borneo Building Society; Central Electrical Board Malaya; Borneo Abaca Ltd.; Nigeria Cement Co. Ltd.; Ilushin Estates Ltd.; Northern Housing Estate Ltd.; Dorman Long (Ghana) Ltd., and (Nigeria) Ltd.; Investment Co. of Nigeria Ltd.; Brandler & Rylke (Liberia) Inc.; Kajola House (B & R) Ltd.; Maryland Logging Corp.; Mandilas Ltd. Former Man. Dir. Cornerstone Organisation Ltd.; Checchi & Co.; Phoenix of Nigeria Ltd. Currently Dir.: Baraka Press Ltd.; Eye Centres (Nigeria) Ltd.; Health Foods (Nigeria) Ltd.; Consultant to ECWA, ECWA Productions Ltd., United Bible Societies & others. *Member:* Council, Scripture Union of Nigeria; Socy. Int. Development. Fellow, Chmn. Bd., Nigerian Inst. of Management. *Clubs:* Number Ten; Royal Commonwealth; Metropolitan Lagos. *Address:* Stone House, Stone Street, nr. Sevenoaks, Kent. and *office* P.O. Box 3181, Lagos, Nigeria; and PMB 2009, Jos, Nigeria.

**WILSON OF RADCLIFFE, Lord (Alfred).** British Retired Company Exec. *B.* 1909. *Educ.* Newcastle upon Tyne Tech. School. *M.* (1) Elsie Hulton (dec'd). *D.* 1. (2) Freda Mather. *Career:* Deputy-Secy. and Exec. Officer Co-op Wholesale Socy. Ltd. 1953–65, Secy. 1965–69; Chief Exec. Officer C.W.S. Ltd. 1969–74; Chmn. Co-op Bank Ltd. 1971–74; Chmn. Co-op Commercial Bank Ltd. 1969–74; Jt. Deputy Chmn. Spillers-French Holdings Ltd. 1972–74; Jt. Chmn. J. W. French (Milling and Baking Holdings) Ltd. 1971–74; Chmn. F. C. Finance Ltd. 1969–74. *Fellow:* Chartered Inst. of Secretaries; Brit. Inst. Mgmt. (until retiring). *Award:* Created Life Peer 1974. *Address:* 58 Ringley Rd., Whitfield, Manchester M25 7LN.

**WILSON, Sir Alan Herries.** FRS, Hon. DSc, Oxon. & Edin. British. *B.* 1906. *Educ.* Wallasey Grammar School; Emmanuel College, Cambridge (MA). *M.* 1934, Margaret Constance Monks (*Dec.* 1961). *S.* Peter Robert, John Richard. *Career:* Lecturer in Mathematics, Univ. of Cambridge, 1933–45; with Courtaulds Ltd., 1945–62 (Man. Dir. 1954; Dep. Chmn. 1957); Dir. International Computers Holdings Ltd. 1962–72; Chairman, Glaxo Group Ltd. 1963–73; Deputy Chairman: Electricity Council 1966–76. *Member:* Iron & Steel Board 1960–67. Past Pres.: Institute of Physics; The Physical Society. *Publications:* Semi-conductors & Metals; Theory of Metals; Thermodynamics & Statistical Mechanics. Hon. Fellow: Emmanuel College, Cambridge, St. Catherine's College, Oxford. *Club:* Athenaeum. *Address:* 65 Oakleigh Park South, Whetstone, London, N.20.

**WILSON, Earl Boden.** American sugar refiner. *B.* 30 May 1891. *M.* 1920, Margaret Eileen Pew. *S.* Earl Boden. *Daus.* Pleasantine Cushman (Drake), Margaret Pew (Kershaw). *Career:* With U.S. General Land Office, surveying New Mexico and Alaska 1910–15; served World War I, U.S. Army, Major of Cavalry 1916–19; in sugar business since 1919; Vice-President, The National Sugar Refining Company, New York 1940–43; Principal Industrial Specialist, War Production Board and Consultant, Office of Economic Warfare, Washington, D.C. 1942; Dir.: Sugar Division, Commodity Credit, Corporation, U.S. Department of Agriculture, Washington, D.C. 1943–45; Sugar Branch, Production & Marketing Administration, U.S. Department of Agriculture 1945–46; President and Director, California and Hawaiian Sugar Refining Corporation Ltd. 1946–51; Chairman, Board of Directors, Sterling Sugars, Inc. since 1952; Director, Commercial Bank & Trust Co., Franklin, Louisiana. *Publication:* Sugar and its Wartime Controls 1941–47. *Address:* Sterling Plantation, Franklin, Louisiana, U.S.A.

**WILSON, Forbes Kingsbury.** American. *B.* 1910. *Educ.* Yale University (BS). *Married. Daus.* Barbara, Jacqueline. Sally, Nancy and Jean. *Career:* Gen. Mgr. Timmins Ochali Mining Co. 1936–42; Nicaro Nickel Co. 1945–47; Vice-Pres. Freeport Minerals Co. 1957–71, Senior Vice-Pres. 1972–74, Consultant since 1974; Pres. Freeport Indonesia Inc. 1967–74, Dir. since 1967. *Publications:* numerous technical articles on gold mining in Columbia, lateritic nickel deposits in Cuba, and mineral exploration activities in Australia. *Member:* A.I.M.E.; Mining & Metallurgical Socy. of America; Explorers. *Awards:* Jackling Award 1977 & Distinguished Member Award, Society of Mining Engineers of A.I.M.E. *Clubs:* Yale (N.Y.C.); Mining; Country Club, Darien (Conn.); Pinehurst, Country (N.C.). *Address:* 167 Organug Rd., York, Maine 03909; and *office:* 161 East 42nd Street, New York, N.Y. 10017, U.S.A.

**WILSON, Sir Geoffrey Masterman,** KCB, CMG. British. *B.* 1910. *Educ.* Oxford Univ. (MA). *M.* 1946, Julie Stafford Trowbridge. *S.* Peter and John. *Daus.* Susan and Catherine. *Career:* Served in British Embassy, Moscow, and Russian Dept. of Foreign Office 1940–45; Cabinet Office 1947; Treasury 1948. Director, Colombo Plan Tech. Co-op. Bureau 1951–53; Under-Secy., Treasury 1956–58; Dep. Head of U.K. Treasury Deleg. and Alternate Exec. Dir. for U.K. Intl. Bank for Recon. and Development, Washington 1958–61; Vice-Pres., Intl. Bank for Reconstruction and Development 1962–66; Ministry of Overseas Development, 1966–71; Chmn. Race Relations Board 1971–76; Chmn. Oxfam since 1976. *Address:* Hansteads, East Hanney, Oxon.

**WILSON, of LANGSIDE, Baron (Rt. Hon. Henry Stephen Wilson),** PC, QC. British. *B.* 1916. *Educ.* High School of Glasgow and Univ. of Glasgow (MA; LLB). *M.* 1942, Jessie Forrester Waters. *Career:* Admitted Member of Faculty of Advocates 1946; Sheriff Substitute of Lanarkshire at Glasgow 1956–65; Solicitor General for Scotland 1966–67; Lord Advocate 1967–70; Dir. Scottish Courts Administration 1971–74; Sheriff of Glasgow 1971–75; Sheriff Principal of Glasgow & Strathkelvin 1975–77. *Club:* Western, Glasgow. *Address:* Dunallan, Kippen, Stirlingshire.

**WILSON, J. Russell.** Consultant. *B.* 1904. *Educ.* Alabama Polytec. Inst. (BS ChemEng 1926); George Washington Univ. (MS Org Chem 1927); Chicago-Kent Coll. (LLB 1932). *M.* 1931, Elizabeth Ebert. *S.* Robert G. and David R. *Career:* With Monsanto Co.; Vice-Pres. & Gen. Manager, Domestic Subsidiaries & Affiliates Div., and Director, Patent Dept. April 1956; Vice-Pres. & Gen. Mgr., Research & Engineering Division, Jan. 1954; Director, Patent Dept. and Director, Gen. Development Dept. 1952; Patent Dept. 1938–46. Attorney, Standard Oil Co. of Indiana 1931–38; Examiner, U.S. Patent Office 1929–31; Chemist, U.S. Dept. of Agriculture 1928–29. *Member:* Amer. and Missouri Bar Assns.; St. Louis Patent Bar Assn.; Amer. Chemical Socy.; Amer. Patent Law Assn.; Amer. Arbitration Socy.; Internatl. Patent & Trademark Assn.; Socy. of Chemical Industry. *Clubs:* Algonquin Golf (St. Louis). *Address:* 3 Robin Hill Lane, Ladue 24, Mo.; and *office* 7733 Forsyth Boulevard, Suite 2162, St. Louis, Mo. 63105, U.S.A.

**WILSON, Rt. Hon. Sir (James) Harold,** KG, PC, OBE, FRS. MP. *B.* 11 March, 1916. *Educ.* Wirral Grammar School; Jesus Coll., Oxford. *M.* 1940, Gladys Mary Baldwin. *S.* Robin James; Giles Daniel John. *Career:* Lecturer in Economics, New Coll., Oxford 1937–45, Fellow of University Coll. 1938–39, Praelector in Economics and Domestic Bursar; Director of Economics and Statistics Min. of Fuel and Power 1943–44; MP (Lab.), Ormskirk 1945–50, Huyton since 1950; Parliamentary Secretary, Ministry of Works 1945; Leader of Delegation to World Food Conference, Washington 1946, 1947, 1949, World Trade Conference, Geneva 1947 and Trade Missions to U.S.S.R. 1947, Canada 1949, U.S.A. 1949; Secretary for Overseas Trade 1947; President of Board of Trade 1947–April 1951; Chairman, Public Accounts Committee 1959–63; Leader of Labour Party 1963–76; Leader of Opposition, 1963–64; Prime Minister, First Lord of the Treasury 1964–70; Leader of the Opposition 1970–74; Prime Minister, First Lord of the Treasury 1974–76; Chmn., Cttee. to review the functioning of Financial Insts. 1977. Pres. Royal Statistical Socy. 1972–73. *Publications:* New Deal for Coal (1945); In place of Dollars (1952); The War on World Poverty (1953); Purpose in Politics (1964), The Relevance of British Socialism (1964); The New Britain (1964); Purpose in Power (1966); The Labour Government 1964–70, A Personal Record (1971); The Governance of Britain (1976). *Address:* House of Commons, London SW1A 0AA.

**WILSON, John Donald,** JP, FISM, FAIM, FID. British. Model Proprietor. *B.* 1925. *Educ.* Beechworth Bairnsdale. *M.* 1974, Carole Ann Friend. *Career:* Gen. Sales Mgr. Blyth Chemicals Ltd. 1956–59; Man. Dir. Olims Industries Ltd. 1959–61; Chmn., Man. Dir. Amalgamated Chemicals Ltd. 1961–69; Dir. Dairy Farmers Co-op Ltd. *Club:* R.S.L. *Address:* Marlborough Motel, Monaro Highway, Cooma, N.S.W., Australia.

**WILSON, John Gardiner,** CBE. Australian. *B.* 1913. *Educ.* MA Cantab Mech Sci Tripos; Harvard School of Business Admin. AMP. *M.* Margaret Louise De Ravin. *Daus.* 3. *Career:* Stock Exchange, Melbourne, J. S. Wilson & Co. 1933–39 and 1946; Served in World War II (Col. Royal Australian Engineers) 1939–46; Australian Paper Manufacturers Ltd. 1947; Dep. Chmn., Australian Paper Manufacturers Ltd. 1977. Director: The British Petroleum Co. of Australia Ltd.; Vickers Australia Ltd.; Qantas Airways Ltd.; Australian Associated Stock Exchanges Ltd. *Member:* Australian Science & Technology Council. *Address:* 6 Woorigoleen Road, Toorak, Vic. 3142, Australia.

**WILSON, John Joseph,** MS. American *B.* 1907. *Educ.* Mass. Inst. of Technology (BS, MS). *M.* 1947, Dorothy Ann Simpson. *S.* 1. *Daus.* 3. *Career:* Pres., Chmn. Doelcam Corp. 1946–55; Vice-Pres. Honeywell Inc. 1954–57, Dir. 1954–72; Dir.: Delta Engineering Corp.; National Instrument Corp.; and State Street Bank & Trust Co. *Member:* Cruising Assn. (U.K.). *Trustee:* Museum of Fine Arts; Peter Bent Brigham Hospital. Life Member, Secy. Corp., Mass. Inst. of Technology. *Clubs:* Union; Country; Brookline; St. Botolph; Boston; Skating Commercial (all Boston); Eastern Yacht (Commodore); Cruising Club of America; Storm Trysail. *Address:* 99 Sargent Road, Brookline, Mass., U.S.A.; and *office* 53 State Street, Boston, Mass. 02109, U.S.A.

**WILSON, John Lohner.** American. *B.* 1902. *Educ.* Wittenberg Coll. and Wittenberg Univ. (LLD 1962). *Daus,* Mary John (Siphron) and Kay Lohner (Strickler). *Career:* With Mack Truck Co. 1922–44 (successively salesman, branch manager Oklahoma City, sales manager national accounts, district manager S.W. territory and Old Mexico, Dallas (Tex.), and manager bus division, Chicago). President: St. Louis Public Service Co. (also Director) 1944–51. Dir. Anheuser-Busch Inc. (Chmn. Finance Cttee.; mem. Exec. Cttee.; Exec. Vice-Pres. 1951–59); General American Life Insurance Co.; Liberty Loan Corp.; St. Louis National Baseball Club Inc. Pres. and Chief Exec. Officer, Universal Match Corp., St. Louis 1959–60 (Chmn. of Board, Pres. and Chief Exec. Officer 1960–62). Secy., Treas. and Dir., St. Louis Research Council; Bd. of Trustees, Rankin Technical Inst., St. Louis (1965—), Pres. 1972—. *Clubs:* Log Cabin; Missouri Athletic; Old Warson Country; Racquet; St. Louis. *Address:* 29 Trent Drive, St. Louis 24, Mo.; and *office* 515 Olive Street, St. Louis 1, Mo., U.S.A.

**WILSON, Sir Keith Cameron.** Australian. *B.* 1900. *Educ.* Collegiate School of St. Peter; Univ. of Adelaide (LLB). *M.* 1930, Elizabeth, dau. of Sir Lavington Bonython. *S.* Ian Bonython Cameron and Andrew Bray Cameron. *Dau.* Elizabeth Cameron. *Career:* Member of House of Representatives, Australia 1949–54 and 1955–66. Member of the Senate 1938–44. Former Chairman: Aged Cottage Homes Inc.; Chmn. War Blinded Welfare Fund; former Chairman, Commonwealth Immigration Adv. Council; Past Pres. Good Neighbour Council, South Aust.; Pres. Queen Elizabeth Hospital Research Foundation. *Publication:* (with Uppill) Wheat Equalization Scheme. Member Liberal Party of Australia. *Club:* Adelaide. *Address:* 79 Tusmore Avenue, Tusmore, S.A. 5065; and *office* 123 Waymouth Street, Adelaide, S.A., Australia.

**WILSON, Norman George,** CMG. Australian company director. *B.* 1911. *Educ.* Melbourne Univ., (BCE). *M.* 1939, Dorothy Gwen, dau. of late Sir W. Lennon Raws. *S.* 1. *Daus.* 2. *Career:* Joined ICI Australia Ltd. 1935; Executive positions 1936–48; Controller, Dyes and Plastics Group 1949–54; Managing Director, Dulux Pty. Ltd., 1954–62; Dir. ICI Australia Ltd. since 1959. Managing Director, Fibremakers Ltd. 1962–72; Commercial Dir. ICI Australia Ltd. 1972–73; Dpty. Chmn. Fibremakers Ltd.; Business Adviser to the Dept. of Air, and Member Defence Business Board, Commonwealth Govt. 1957—. Chairman, Production Board. Dept. of Supply, Commonwealth Govt. 1960. *Member:* Victorian Railways Board; Victoria Conservation Trust1973. Fellow: Inst. of Dir.; Royal Australian Chemical Inst., Australian Inst. of Management. *Clubs:* Australian (Melbourne); Royal Melbourne Golf; Melbourne Cricket; Frankston Golf; Victoria Racing. *Address:* Apt. 14, 18 Lansell Road, Toorak, Vic. 3142, Australia.

**WILSON, Raymond.** British. *B.* 1915. *Educ.* New Mills Grammar School; RAF Technical College. *M.* 1940, Hazel Joan. *Dau.* 1. *Career:* Dep. Chmn. Union Carbide Europe Sa. Geneva; *Director:* Union Carbide France, S.A. Rungis; Union Carbide Iberica S.A., Madrid; Argon S.A. Madrid; Bakelite Xylonite Ltd. London; A's Meraker Smelteverk, Norway; Union Carbide Belgium N.V. Antwerp; Union Carbide Hellas, S.A. Athens; Union Carbide Europe Inc. Delaware; Dir. Wimpey Unox Ltd.; Chmn. British Acheson Electrodes Ltd. Sheffield; Union Carbide U.K. Ltd. London; Kemet Products Ltd. London; Union Carbide Italia S.p.A. Milano; Elettrografite Meridionale, S.p.A. Milano; *Chairman:* Wimpey-Unox Ltd. Brentford, Middx. *Member:* Inst. of Directors; Inst. British Foundrymen; Iron & Steel Inst.;

Assn. Inst. Marketing & Sales Management. *Clubs:* American. *Address:* 10A Chemin de la Haute Belotte 1222, Vesenaz/Geneva; and *office* 5 rue Pedro Meylan, Geneva, Switzerland.

**WILSON, Sir Reginald Holmes.** British. Scottish Chartered Accountant. Chairman of various business and finance companies. *B.* 1905. *Career:* Partner in Whinney Murray & Co. 1937–72; H.M. Treasury 1940; Principal Assistant Secretary, Ministry of Shipping 1941; Director of Finance, Ministry of War Transport 1941; Under Secy. Ministry of Transport 1945; returned to City 1946; Joint Financial Adviser, Ministry of Transport 1946; Member: Royal Commission on Press 1946; Vice-Chairman: Hemel Hempstead Development Corporation 1946–56; Adviser on Special Matters to Control Commission for Germany 1947; Comptroller, British Transport Commission 1947; Chairman, Eastern Area Board B.T.C. 1955–60; Chairman, London Midland Area Board 1960–62; Dep. Chmn. Transport Holding Co. 1962–67; Chmn. 1967–70; Chmn. National Freight Corp. 1969–70; Chmn. Transport Development Group Ltd. 1970–75; Chmn. Thos. Cook & Son Ltd. 1966–76; Chmn. Board for Simplification of International Trade Procedures 1976—. Award of Merit, Inst. of Transport 1953. Pres. Railway Students Assn. 1955–56; Inst. of Transport 1957–58. *Member:* Cttee. of Enquiry into Civil Air Transport 1967–69. Chmn. Bd. of Governors National Heart and Chest Hospitals; UK Representative, Council of Management, International Hospital Federation. *Publications:* Papers on transport matters, etc. *Address:* 13 Gloucester Square, London, W.2.

**WILSON, Sir Roland,** KBE. Australian. *B.* 7 April 1904. *Educ.* Univ. of Tasmania (BCom) and Chicago Univ. (PhD); Oriel Coll., Oxford (DPhil); Hon LLD, Univ. of Tasmania, 1969. *M.* 1930, Valeska Thompson (*Dec.*) *M.* 1975, Joyce Chivers. *Career:* Pitt-Cobbett. Lecturer in Economics, University of Tasmania 1930–32; Assistant Commonwealth Statistician and Economist 1932–35; Commonwealth Statistician and Economic Adviser to Treasury 1936–51; Permanent Head, Department of Labour and National Service 1941–46; Economic Counsellor, Embassy, Washington and Alternate Director, International Monetary Fund and International Bank for Reconstruction and Development 1948–49; Secretary to the Treasury 1951–66. Member, Economic and Employment Commission, United Nations 1947–51, Chairman 1948–51; member, Advisory Council, Commonwealth Bank of Australia 1949–51; member, Commonwealth Bank Board 1951–59; member, Reserve Bank Board 1960–66, and of Commonwealth Banking Corp. 1960–75; Director Qantas Airways 1954–73; Chmn. Bd.; Qantas Airways Ltd. 1966–73; Wentworth Hotel Ltd. 1966–73; Commonwealth Banking Corporation 1966–75. Director: M.L.C. Ltd.; Wentworth Hotel Ltd.; *Publications:* Capital Imports and the Terms of Trade; Public and Private Investment in Australia; Facts and Fancies of Productivity. *Address:* 64 Empire Circuit, Forrest, Canberra, A.C.T., Australia.

**WILSON, Sir (Thomas) George,** KBE. British argriculturist and company director. *B.* 24 Nov. 1900. *Educ.* Harrow School; Cambridge University (MA). Chairman, Scottish Milk Marketing Board 1934–50; member, Balfour of Burleigh Committee on Hill Sheep Farming in Scotland; member, Stirling County Council 1930–75; Chairman of Governors West of Scotland Agricultural College 1942–71. Hon LLD, Glasgow University, Hon D. Stirling University. *Address:* King's Mile, Killearn, by Glasgow, Scotland.

**WILSON, Thornton Arnold.** American. *B.* 1921. *Educ.* Iowa State University (BS Aeronautical Engineering), California Inst. of Technology (MS Aeronautical Engineering); Sloan Fellow in Industrial Management, Mass. Inst. of Technology. *M.* 1944, Grace Louise Miller. *S.* Thornton Arnold III and Daniel Allen. *Dau.* Sarah Louise. *Career:* Vice-Pres.: Operations & Planning, The Boeing Co. 1964; Vice-Pres.-Manager, Minuteman 1962, Exec. Vice-Pres. 1966, Pres. & Chief Exec. Officer 1969–72, Chmn. of the Bd. & Chief Exec. Officer 1972—, the Boeing Company. *Awards:* U.S.A.F. Commander's Award; Univ. of Missouri Honor Award for Distinguished Service in Engineering. Fellow: Amer. Inst. of Aeronautics & Astronautics. *Club:* The Rainier. *Address: office* The Boeing Co., P.O. Box 3707, Seattle, Wash. 98124, U.S.A.

**WILSON, William Douglas.** South African director of companies. *B.* 1915. *Educ.* Cambridge University; Middle Temple, London; Advocate of the Supreme Court of South Africa. *M.* 1947, Beatrice Helen Buchanan. *S.* 1. *Daus.* 3. In practice at Johannesburg Bar 1938–40. *Career:* Served in World War II (1st S.A. Div. Abyssinia and Western Desert; British Military Mission to Jugoslavia; despatches; rank Lieut.-Col.) 1940–45; returned to practice at Johannesburg Bar until Aug. 1946; joined Anglo-American Corp. of S.A. Ltd.; Director, Anglo-American Corporation of South Africa since 1958. *Address:* 44 Main Street, Johannesburg, South Africa.

**WILSON, William Garrick,** BEc, AASA. Australian. *B.* 1904. *Educ.* Sydney Gr. School; St. Andrew's Coll. Univ. of Sydney. *M.* 1942, Rosemary Margaret Wright. *S.* 1. *Dau.* 1. *Career:* Chmn. Gillespie Bros. Holdings Ltd. *Clubs:* Australian; Elanora Country. *Address:* 3 Garnet St., Killara, Sydney, N.S.W., Australia; *office:* G.P.O. Box 2518, Sydney, N.S.W.

**WILSON SMITH, Sir Henry,** KCB, KBE. British company director and former civil servant. *B.* 30 Dec. 1904. *Educ.* Peterhouse, Cambridge University. *M.* 1931, Molly Dyson. *S.* 2. *Career:* Administrative Class, Home Civil Service 1927; with Secretary's Office, G.P.O. 1927–29; joined M.M. Treasury 1930; Assistant Private Secretary to Chancellor of Exchequer 1932, Principal Private Secretary 1940–42; Under-Secretary, H.M. Treasury 1942–46; Permanent Secretary, Ministry of Defence 1947–48; Additional Second Secretary in charge of overseas finance, H.M. Treasury 1948–51; resigned Jan. 1951; Director: Guest Keen & Nettlefolds Ltd. 1951–72 (Dep. Chmn. 1962–72), Doxford & Sunderland Ltd. 1961–72, H.A.T. Group Ltd., and member (part-time), National Coal Board until Nov. 1959. *Address:* 68 Colinas Verdes, Bensafrim, Lagos, Algarve, Portugal.

**WILTON, Arthur John,** CMG, MC. British diplomat. *B.* 1921. *Educ.* Wanstead County High School; St. John's Coll. Oxford (Scholar). *M.* 1950, Maureen Elizabeth Alison Meaker. *S.* 4. *Dau.* 1. *Career:* Served with Royal Ulster Rifles and Irish Brigade 1942–46; Diplomatic Service in Arab and Balkan countries 1947—; H.M. Ambassador to Kuwait 1970–74; Asst. Under-Secy. State, For. & C'wealth Office 1974–76; H.M. Ambassador to Saudi Arabia since 1976. *Awards:* Military Cross: Companion Order of St. Michael and St. George. *Address:* c/o Lloyds Bank, Chichester; and *office* c/o Foreign and Commonwealth Office, London, S.W.1.; & British Embassy, Jedda, Saudi Arabia.

**WILTON, Clifford William,** TD. British. *B.* 1916. *Educ.* Fettes College, and Gonville & Caius College, Cambridge (MA); Barrister-at-Law, Gray's Inn. *M.* 1939, Alice Linda Travers. *Daus.* 3. *Career:* Chmn. The Renwick Group Ltd.; Western Fuel Co. *Clubs:* British Sportsman's City Livery; Constitutional; East India & Sports. *Address:* 86 Lexham Gardens, Kensington, London, W8 5JB; and *office* 151 Great Portland Street, London W1N 5FB.

**WINDEYER, Rt. Hon. Sir (William John) Victor,** KBE, CB, DSO, ED. *B.* 1900. *Educ.* University of Sydney (MA; LLB). *M.* 1934, Margaret M. Vicars. *S.* 3. *Dau.* 1. *Career:* Admitted to Bar of N.S.W. 1925; Officer in Australian Military Forces (Militia) from 1922; Active Service 1940–45 (Tobruk, El Alamein, New Guinea, Borneo; Lt.-Col. and Brigadier; CBE, DSO and Bar). Renewed practice of law after the war. KC 1949. Fellow of Senate, Univ. of Sydney 1949–59, Dep. Chancellor 1955–58. Member, Australian Military Board 1950–53. Retired from Citizen Military Forces 1957, rank of Major-General; Justice of the High Court of Australia 1958–72; Member of the Privy Council 1963—. Hon. LLD Sydney 1975. Hon. Bencher, Middle Temple 1972. *Publications:* include Lectures on Legal History and articles on legal and historical subjects. *Clubs:* Australian, Pioneers (Sydney). *Address:* Peroomba, Turramurra, N.S.W., Australia.

**WINDHAM, Sir Ralph.** British. Order of the Brilliant Star of Zanzibar (2nd class); Grand Commander, Star of Africa (Liberia). *B.* 1905. *Educ.* Wellington College; Trinity College, Cambridge (MA. LLB). *M.* 1946, Kathleen Mary FitzHerbert. *S.* 2. *Daus.* 2. *Career:* Legal Draftsman, Palestine 1935; District Court Judge, Palestine 1942; Puisne Judge Supreme Court, Ceylon 1947; Puisne Judge, Supreme Court, Kenya 1950; Chief Justice, Zanzibar 1955; Justice of Appeal, Court of Appeal for Eastern Africa 1959; Chief Justice, Tanganyika (now Tanzania) 1960–65; Commissioner, Foreign Compensation Commission 1965—, Chmn. since 1972. *Club:* Landsdowne. *Address:* Hook's Cottage, Kingscote, nr. Tetbury, Gloucestershire; and *office* Foreign Compensation Commission, Alexandra House, Kingsway, London, W.C.2.

**WINDLESHAM, Lord.** (**3rd Baron. David James George Hennessy**), PC. *B.* 1932. *Educ.* Ampleforth; Trinity Coll. Oxford (MA). *M.* 1965, Prudence Glynn. *S.* 1. *Dau.* 1. *Career:* Member, Westminster City Council 1958–62; Dir. Rediffusion Television 1965–67; Man. Dir. Grampian Television 1967–70; Minister of State Home Office 1970–72; Minister of State N. Ireland 1972–73; Lord Privy Seal, Leader of House of Lords 1973–74; Jt. Man. Dir. ATV Network 1974–75, Man. Dir. since 1975. *Address:* House of Lords, London, S.W.1.

**WINGATE, Henry Smith.** *B.* 1905. *Educ.* Northfield High School; Carleton College (BA), and University of Michigan Law School (Juris Doctor). *M.* 1929, Ardis A. Swenson. *S.* Henry Knowles and William Peter. *Career:* Joined International Nickel Canada as Assistant Secretary 1936, and its U.S. subsidiary, International Nickel Inc. as Assistant to the President 1935; Chairman & Chief Officer (until retirement as an Officer in 1972): International Nickel Co. of Canada Ltd. Director: United States Steel Corporation, American Standard Inc.; Mem. Advisory Council, Morgan Guaranty Trust Co. *Awards:* Alumni Achievement Award, Carleton College 1956; Hon. LLD, University of Manitoba 1957, Sesquicentennial Award, University of Michigan 1967; Hon. LLD Marshall University; York University, 1967; Laurentian University, 1968; Colby College, 1970; Hon. L.H.D. Carleton Coll.1973. *Member:* Can. Amer. Cttee. of National Planning Assn. (Washington, D.C.) and C. D. Howe Research Inst. Montreal; Canadian Institute Mining & Metallurgy; American Institute Mining, Metallurgical & Petroleum Engineers; Mining & Metallurgical Society of America; Association of Bar of City of New York; Newcomen Society of N. America: The Business Council (Washington, D.C.). Former, Dir. Bank of Montreal, Canadian Pacific Ltd., Morgan Guaranty Trust Co., J.P. Morgan & Co. Inc. &, Inco Ltd.; Trustee, Legal Aid Socy. of N.Y.; Public Health Inst. City of N.Y.; Manhattan Eye, Ear and Throat Hospital; U.S. Council, Int. Chamber of Commerce; Annuity Fund for Congl; Ministers and Retirement Fund, Lay Workers. *Clubs:* Unversity, Union, Recess (N.Y.C.), Cold Spring Harbor Beach & Huntingdon Country Golf (L.I., N.Y.). *Address:* 520 East 86th Street, New York City 10028; and Lloyd Neck, L.I., N.Y.; and *office* 1 New York Plaza, New York 10004, U.S.A.

**WINGER, Maurice, Jr.** American lawyer. *B.* 1917. *Educ.* William Jewell College (Liberty, Mo.) AB; Duke University School of Law; LLB. *M.* 1940, Virginia McNabb. *S.* Eric and Stephen. *Career:* With Sullivan & Cromwell (N.Y.) 1942; Export-Import Bank of Washington, D.C. 1943–44; First Lieutenant, U.S. Marine Corps 1944–46; General Corporate Practice, Douglas, Proctor, MacIntyre & Gates, Washington, D.C. 1946–48; General Corporate Practice, Debevoise, Plimpton & McLean (N.Y.) 1948–50; Secy. and Asst. Gen. Counsel to American Enka 1950–60, Gen. Mgr. Rex Div. 1960–64. Vice-Pres. and General Manager, Nylon Division, American Enka Corporation (Enka, N.C.) Jan. 1965–70; Pres. American Enka Company since 1970. Distinguished Service Award as Man of the Year, Junior Chamber of Commerce, Asheville, N.C. 1953; Captain, All-American team sent to England to debate with Universities of Oxford, Cambridge, London, etc. 1939. *Address:* c/o American Enka Co, Enka, N.C., 28728, U.S.A.

**WINNACKER, Karl.** German executive. *B.* 1903. *Educ.* Matriculated, Barmen 1922; studied chemistry Technische Hochschule, Braunschweig 1925, and at Techn. Hochschule, Darmstadt 1930; Degree 1928, promoted to Dr.-Ing. 1930. *M.* 1936, Gertrud Deitenbeck. *S.* Ernst-Ludwig and Albrecht. *Dau.* Lotte. *Career:* Chairman of Advisory Board, Hoechst AG. Chairman and/or Member of Boards of numerous companies. Hon. Chairman DECHEMA (German Association for Chemical Apparatus Research), Frankfurt; Hon. President, German Atomic Forum. *Awards:* Dr.rer.nat.h.c., TH-Braunschweig 1953, and Univ. of Mainz 1961; Dr.phil.h.c., Univ. of Marburg 1963; Dr. Ciencias Quimicas h.c., Universidad Complutense, Madrid 1977; Dr. technologiae h. c., Universitet Lund, Sweden 1977; Silver Medal of the City of Paris 1957; Gauss-Weber Medal, Univ. of Göttingen 1962; Order of Merit of Bavaria 1961; Grand Cross of Merit with Star & Sash of the Order of Merit of the Fed. Rep. of Germany 1963; Officier dans l'ordre Nationale du Mérit, France 1966; Cavaliere di Gran Croce dell ordine al Merito della rep. Italiana 1973; Hon. Commander of the Civil Div. of the Most Excellent Order of the British Empire (CBE) 1974. *Publications:* Chemische Technologie (with Küchler); Challenging Years, My Life in Chemistry; Grundzüge der Chemischen Technik (with Biener); Das unverstandene Wunder (with Wirtz). *Address:* Ölmühlweg 31a, 6240 Königstein/Ts.; and *office* Hoechst AG, 6230 Frankfurt/M, Germany.

**WINNEKE, H.E. the Hon. Sir Henry Arthur,** KCMG 1966 KCVO 1977, OBE, QC. Governor of Victoria. *B.* 1908. *Educ.* Scotch College, Melbourne and Melbourne University (LLM). *M.* 1933, Nancy Wilkinson. *S.* 2. *Career:* Senior Counsel to Attorney-General, Victoria, and Crown Prosecutor 1950–51; Solicitor-General, Victoria 1951–64, Chief Justice 1964–74; President Library Council of Victoria 1966–67. Appointed KC 1949. Member: Victoria Bar Council 1948–50. President Victorian Council of Legal Education; Scotch College Council 1946–55; Chief Scout, Victoria; Victoria Law Foundation. *Clubs:* Athenaeum; M.C.C.; R.A.C.V. Moonee Valley Racing; Metropolitan Golf. *Address:* Government House, Melbourne, Vic., Australia.

**WINSETT, Marvin Davis.** Hon. Dr. of Humane Letters, FIAL, FRSA. American advertising executive, poet and writer. *B.* 1902. *Educ.* Austin Col. Preparatory Dept. and Southern Methodist Univ. *M.* 1925, Hettie Lee Bryant. *Daus.* Betty Lee (Mrs. Wilbur Ausphera Richerson, Jr.) and Janis Sue (Mrs. Roger LeRoy Swain). *Career:* Buyer, Sanger Bros., Dallas 1925–28; Manager, El Paso and Abilene Sears Roebuck Co. Stores 1928–30; established Marvin Winsett Advertising Agency (owner) 1930–47; Partner, Winsett, Gidley & Darley Advertising Agency 1947–52; Owner, Marvin Winsett Advertising Agency, Dallas, Tex. 1952–69. Member: Editorial Committees: International Who's Who in Poetry 1969— and Royal Blue Book 1968. Decorated, Pres. Diosdado Macapagal Gold Medal 1965; Pres. Marcos Gold Medal 1968; Citation, Poetry Socy. of Texas 1966; Associé Étranger, Académie Française de la Poésie, 1973. Member: National Fed. of State Poetry Societies (Vice-President 1963, President 1964–66); Vachel Lindsay Association (Member Adv. Board); Academy of American Poets; Hon. Member: Honorary Life Member, Poetry Society of Texas (Treasurer 1956–61; President 1962–66); Amer. Poetry League (Advisory Board 1962–64). Appointed Poet Laureate of Texas for 1962, by the Texas Legislature. *Awards:* the Deanne Settoon Mernagh Award for the best sonnet published in Kaleidograph Magazine during the year. Winner of many poetry awards, including International Gold Medal and Laurel Wreath from United Poets Laureate International. Member Editorial Bd. Dictionary of International Biography; Originator of the Cylus verse form; Chmn. Texas Council for the Promotion of Poetry. Citation of Merit for distinguished service to poetry) South & West Inc.; Hon. Poet Laureate Leader 1965. Fellow: International Institute of Arts and Letters. Royal Society of Arts. Mason (32 deg. Scottish Rite), Royal Arch Chapter and Council, Hella Temple Shrine; Lambda Chi Alpha Sigma Delta Chi (professional journalist fraternity); S.M.U. Alumni Association. Presbyterian. *Publications:* Winding Stairway—A Book of Verse (1953); Basic Ad Writing (1954); April Always (poetry, 1965); Remembered Earth (poetry, 1962); contributor to national and international poetry journals and other publications. *Club:* Dallas Coin. *Address:* 3936 Colgate Street, Dallas, Texas 75225, U.S.A.

**WINSLOW, Richard Sears.** American. *B.* 1908. *Educ,* Harvard Coll. (AB) and Harvard Univ. (AM). *M.* 1941. Lucy Prescott. *S.* Richard S. Jr. and Charles Prescott. *Dau.* Lucy Bennett. Vice-Pres., Foreign Policy Assn., New York City, and Director of its World Affairs Center 1958–64; Exec. Asst., Human Resources Admin., City Govt. of New York 1966; Consultant, Bureau of Corruption Analysis & Prevention, Dept. of Investigation of the City of New York since 1976. Secy.-General, Permanent U.S. Mission to U.N. 1946–54; Executive Dir., South End Settlement House, Boston, Mass. 1938–43. Hon. LLD Eastern Michigan Univ. Member Council on Foreign Relations. *Address:* 51 Barry Road, Scarsdale, N.Y. 10583; and *office* Bureau of Corruption Analysis & Prevention, 130 John Street, Room 1016, New York, N.Y. 10038, U.S.A.

**WINSPEAR, Francis George,** OC, FCA, RIA, LLD, FRSA. Canadian Chartered accountant & company director. *B.* 1903. *Educ.* CA (Alberta); Hon. LLD University of Alberta. *M.* 1927, Bessie Brooks Watchorn. *S.* Claude Willan and William Watchorn. *Career:* Founding Partner, Winspear, Hamilton, Anderson & Company, Chartered Accountants, Edmonton Alberta (Ret. as partner); Chairman of the Board, Coutts Machiner Company Ltd.; Pres. The Winspear Foundation; Dir., Lake Ontario Steel Co. Ltd.; Corod Manufacturing Ltd.; Co-Steel International Ltd.; Sheerness Steel Co. Ltd. *Member:* Institutes of Chartered Accountants of Alberta, British Columbia & Manitoba; Society, Industrial Accnts., of Alberta; Canadian-American and British–North American Committee of C. D. Howe Research Institute; Nat. Advs. Y.M.C.A.; Hon. Dir. Care of Canada; member

Canadian Chamber of Commerce (Past Pres.); Edmonton Chamber of Commerce (Past Pres.); Bd. Governors, The Edmonton Opera Association: Fellow, Royal Society for the Encouragement of Arts, Manufacturers and Commerce London. *Clubs:* Edmonton, Mayfair Golf & Country. *Address:* Apartment 701, Valleyview Manor, Edmonton, Alta.; Summer Residence: 687 Ardmore Drive, Sidney, B.C., Canada, and *office:* 5th Floor Bental Building, Edmonton, Alberta T5J OW7.

**WINTER, Elmer Louis**, BA, LLB. American. *B.* 1912. *Educ.* Univ. of Wisconsin (BA); Univ. of Wisconsin Law School LLB. *M.* 1936, Nannette Rosenberg. *Daus.* 3. *Career:* Past Pres., Manpower Inc.; Dir., Jack Winter Inc. Metro. Dir 1968–70, National Alliance of Businessmen Jobs Programme; Hon. Nat. Pres. Amer. Jewish Cttee.; Dir. Greater Milwaukee Cttee.; Univ. of Wisconsin Foundation; Chmn. Co-Founder, Milwaukee Voluntary Equal Employment Opportunity Council; Trustee, Citizens Governmental Research Bureau. *Member:* Exec. Cttee. Pres. Johnson's Nat. Citizens Council, Community Relations; Adv. Cttee. Vice-Pres. Humphrey's Youth Opportunity Campaign; Equal Business Opportunity Councils; Chambers of Commerce of U.S.A. *Award:* Hon. Doctor of Laws Degree, Univ. of Wisconsin 1970. *Address:* 8014 N. Lake Drive, Milwaukee, Wis., U.S.A.; and *office:* 5301 North Ironwood Road, Milwaukee, Wis. 53217, U.S.A.

**WINTER, George.** Class of 1912 Professor of Engineering Cornell University, Ithaca, N.Y. 1948; Consultant to American Iron and Steel Institute and other bodies. *B.* 1907. *Educ.* Cornell University (PhD) and Munich Technical University (Dipl Ing). *M.* 1931, Anne Singer. *S.* Peter Michael. *Career:* Designer, Rella and Neffe, Vienna 1931–32; Foreign Technical Consultant, Sverdlovsk, U.S.S.R. 1932–38; successively research associate, instructor, assistant and Associate Prof., Cornell Univ. 1938–48; Visiting Professor, California Institute of Technology 1950; Univ. of California, Berkeley, 1969; Visiting Lecturer, Univ. of Liège, Belgium 1956; Director of Research on cold-formed, thin-walled steel structures at Cornell University for American Iron and Steel Institute since 1939. *Awards:* L. S. Moisseiff Award (Amer. Socy. Civil Engrs.) 1948; Guggenheim Memorial Fellowship, 1956; Technical Meetings Award (Amer. Iron & Steel Inst.) 1960; J. J. Croes Medal (Amer. Socy. Civil Engineers) 1961; Wason Medal (Amer. Concrete Inst.) 1965; Turner Medal (Amer. Concrete Inst. 1972); Hon. member, Amer. Socy. of Civil Engineers. Dr.Ing.hc, Tech. Univ. Munich 1969. Member: Nat. Acad. of Eng'g. 1970; Amer. Acad. of Arts & Sciences 1976; International Assn. for Bridge & Structural Engineering (member Permanent Cttee.); Column Research Council Chmn., etc. *Publications:* Design of Concrete Structures, 8th edition 1972 (with Nilson); Commentary to Light Gage Steel Design Manual, 4th edition 1968; more than 80 research papers in American and other engineering journals; contributor to Encyclopaedia Britannica, American Civil Engineering Practice; Structural Eng. Handbook, etc. *Clubs:* Cornell Research; Statler; Cornell (N.Y.C.). *Address:* 1010 Highland Road, Ithaca, N.Y. 14850, U.S.A.

**WINTER, Hon. Gordon Arnaud**, OC, LLD. Lieutenant Governor of Newfoundland. *B.* 1912. *Educ.* Bishop Field College, St. John's, Newfoundland, and Loretto School, Scotland. *M.* 1937, Millicent Anderson. *Daus.* Linda, Valda. *Career:* Chm.: T. & M. Winter, Ltd. (established 1878); Standard Manufacturing Co. Ltd. Bd. of Regents, Memorial Univ. of Newfoundland 1968–74. Pres., Newfoundland Bd. of Trade 1946; Chmn., St. John's Housing Corp. 1949–50; Mem. Advisory Bd., Newfoundland Savings Bank 1959–62; Governor, Canadian Broadcasting Corporation 1952–58; appointed by His Excellency, The Governor in Commission, Member of the Newfoundland Delegation which negotiated and signed (11 Dec. 1948) terms of Union between Newfoundland and Canada; appointed Minister of Finance in the first Provincial Government of Newfoundland, 1 April 1949. Anglican. *Clubs:* Bally Haly Golf and Country; Murray's Pond Fishing. *Address:* Government House, St. John's, Newfoundland, Canada.

**WINTERTON, Nicholas Raymond**, MP. British. *B.* 1938. *Educ.* Bilton Grange Prep. Sch.; Rugby Sch. *M.* 1960, Jane Ann Hodgson. *S.* 2. *Dau.* 1. *Career:* 2nd Lieutenant, 14th/20th King's Hussars 1957–59; Sales Exec. Trainee, Shell-Mex & BP Ltd. 1959–60; Sales & Gen. Mgr., Stevens & Hodgson Ltd., Birmingham 1960–71; County Councillor, Atherstone Div. of Warwickshire CC 1967–72; Conservative MP for Macclesfield since 1971; Chmn., Camra (Real Ale) Investments Ltd. since 1974. *Member:* Hon. Mem., Midland Branch, Contractors' Mechanical Plant Engineers Association. *Clubs:* Lighthouse Club; Eccentric Club. *Address:* Whitehall Farm, Newbold Astbury, Congleton, Cheshire; & House of Commons, London SW1A 0AA.

**WINTERTON, Hon. W. A. E.**, JP. Rhodesian politician. *B.* 16 Jan. 1902. *Educ.* St. Andrew's College, Grahamstown, C.P. *Career:* Attorney, notary and conveyancer; senior partner in firm, Winterton, Holmes & Hill; Justice of the Peace; served World War II, Abyssinia and Burma, Major (despatches) 1939–45; MP 1933–65; Minister of Native Affairs and Minister of Health 1949–51; Minister of Trade and Industrial Development 1951–53; elected to Federal Assembly (Federation of Rhodesia and Nyasaland) Nov. 1953; Elected to Southern Rhodesia Legislative Assembly 1962. *Address:* P.O. Box 452, Salisbury, Rhodesia.

**WINTHROP, Robert.** American banker. *B.* 21 Jan. 1904. *Educ.* Harvard (BA). *M.* (1) 1928, Theodora Ayer. *Daus.* Theodora (Higginson), Elizabeth Amory (Ripley), Cornelia Beekman (Bonnie). *M.* (2) 1942, Margaret Stone. *Career:* Served World War II, U.S. Naval Reserve, rank of Commander. Honorary Chairman, Wood ,Struthers, & Winthrop. Inc.; Former Member Bd. Dirs.; First National City Bank of New York 1939–64. Republican. *Address:* Village of Old Westbury, Long Island, N.Y., U.S.A.

**WIRLANDNER, Stefan.** Austrian economist. *B.* 11 Dec. 1905. *Educ.* Vienna University (Dipl. Volkswirt, Dr.rer.pol.). *M.* 1970, Elfriede Langer. *Daus.* Doris, Suse. Petra. *Career:* Member, Bd. of Dirs., Österreichische Investitionskredit AG, Kreditlenlungskommission, Vienna. Staatswissenschaftliche Prüfungskommission; Kartellobergericht beim Obersten Gerichtshof. *Address:* Linzerstrasse 428, Vienna XIV, Austria.

**WISE, Jack.** British. *B.* 1930. *Educ.* Queen Elizabeth Grammar School (Penrith, Cumberland); qualified as a chartered accountant (now F.C.A.). *M.* 1963, Ann Barbara Jon, Brewin (of Doncaster, Yorks.). *Daus.* Melanie Jane and Louise Rachel. *Career:* Senior Partner in F. F. Sharles & Co., Chartered Accountants, of London and Glasgow. Director of a number of companies. Member: Inst. of Chartered Accountants and Inst. of Directors. *Club:* Royal Automobile (Full Member). *Address: office* Portland House, 4 Great Portland Street, London, W.1.

**WISHART, Hon. Arthur Allison**, QC. Canadian. *B.* 1903. *Educ.* Univ. of New Brunswick (BA); Law degree Osgoode Hall 1930; Barrister-at-Law. *M.* 1936, Mary Ellen Anne Lidstone. *S.* John Charles Gordon. *Daus.* Alison Anne, Margaret Ellen, Rosalind Jean, Marion Joyce and Pamela Joan. *Career:* Minister of Justice and Attorney General of Ontario 1964–71; Minister Financial and Commercial Affairs Mar. to Dec. 1971; Chmn. Criminal Injuries Compensation Board 1972. *Member:* Sault Ste. Marie Law Assn.; and Canadian Bar Assn. Progressive Conservative. *Clubs:* The Albany; University (Toronto); Algoma Steel Men's; Officers (of 49th Sault Ste. Marie Regiment); Royal Canadian Military Inst; The Empire. *Address: office* 481 University Avenue, Toronto, Ont., Canada.

**WITHERS, Rt. Hon. Reginald Greive.** Australian Senator & Minister of State. *B.* 1924. *Educ.* Bunbury; Univ. of Western Australia—LLB. *M.* 1953, Shirley Lloyd-Jones. *S.* 2. *Dau.* 1. *Career:* Councillor, Bunbury Municipal Council 1954–56; mem., Bunbury Diocesan Council 1958–59, Treas. 1961–68; Sec., S.W. Law Soc. 1955–68; State Vice-Pres., Liberal & Country League of W.A. 1958–61, Pres. 1961–65; mem., Fed. Exec. of the Liberal Party 1961–65 (Fed. Vice-Pres. 1962–65); Senator (Lib.) for W.A. 1966, & since 1967; Govt. Whip in the Senate 1969–71; Leader of Opposition in the Senate 1972–75; Special Minister of State, Min. for the Capital Territory, Min. for the Media & Min. for Tourism & Recreation, Nov.–Dec. 1975; Vice-Pres. of the Exec. Council since Nov. 1975; Leader of the Govt. in the Senate & Min. for Admin. Services since Dec. 1975. Privy Councillor. *Address:* 23 Malcolm Street, West Perth, W.A. 6005; and *office* Parliament House, Canberra, A.C.T. 2600, Australia.

**WITTEVEEN, H. Johannes.** Dutch Economist & Politician. *B.* 1921. *Educ.* Gymnasium Erasmianum; Netherlands Sch. of Economics, Rotterdam—PhD. *M.* 1949, Lysbeth de Vries Feyens. *S.* 3. *Dau.* 1. *Career:* Netherlands Central Planning Bureau 1945–48; Lect., Netherlands Sch. of Economics, Rotterdam 1946–48, & Professor 1948–63; Libera

Party Member, First Chamber of Parliament 1958–63; Minister of Finance, Netherlands 1963–65; Liberal Party Member, Second Chamber of Parliament 1965–67; First Dep. Prime Minister & Minister of Finance 1967–71; Advisor & Mem. of Board, Robeco NV & Member of Boards of Royal Dutch Petroleum NV, Unilever NV, Daiwa Europe NV, Rommenhöller NV, Zaanen & Verstoep NV, Bank der Bonspaarbanken NV. 1971–73: Man. Dir., International Monetary Fund 1973–78. *Decorations:* Grand Cross, Order of Crown (Belgium); Grand Cross, Order of Oak Wreath (Luxembourg); Grand Cross, Order of Merit (Fed. Rep. of Germany); Knight, Order Netherlands Lion; Commander, Order Orange Nassau (Netherlands); Bintang Republik Indonesia; Order of the Yugoslav Flag; Knight Grand Cross, Order of Merit (Italy). *Publications:* Loonshoogte en Werkgelegenheid (Wage Level & Employment—Doctoral Dissertation, 1947); Growth & Business Cycles (1954); Articles in Economisch-Statistische Berichten, reprinted in Monetaire Uiteenzettingen (Monetary Explanations) (1954–57); Economic Growth & the Share of Profits (1961); Financing Oil (Article in Euromoney, 1974). *Address:* 2335 49th Street, N.W., Washington, D.C. 20007, U.S.A.; & *office* International Monetary Fund, Washington, D.C. 20431, U.S.A.

**WOLCOTT, Samuel Huntington, Jr.** Professional Trustee. *B.* 1910. *Educ.* St. Paul's School, and Harvard College (AB 1933). *M.* 1934, Mary E. Weld. *S.* Samuel H. III, Philip W. and William Prescott. *Dau.* Pamela. *Career:* With First National Bank of Boston 1933–37; President & Trustee, Consolidated Investment Trust. Director and member of Exec. Cttee., State Street Bank & Trust Co.; Dir.: Big Sandy Co., Essex Co.; Dir. & mem. Exec. Cttee., State Street. (Boston) Financial Corp.; Trustee: Penn Mutual Life Insce. Co. Provident Inst. for Savings, Harvard Mutual Foundation, Mt. Auburn Cemetery (Mem. Finance Cttee.), and Sailors' Snug Harbor. *Clubs:* The Country (Brookline). *Address:* 35 Congress Street, Boston, Mass., U.S.A.

**WOLD, Knut Getz.** Norwegian economist. *B.* 3 Aug. 1915. *Educ.* Oslo University. *M.* 1948, Astrid Margit Graver. *S.* Bjorn Kjetil. *Daus.* Marit, Ellen. *Career:* Researcher, Oslo University Institute of Economics 1939–40; Adviser to Norwegian Ministry of Finance. in London and Oslo 1941–46; Under-Secretary, Ministry of Social Affairs, Oslo 1946–48; Adviser in Economics to Nobel Institute, Oslo 1946–58; Director, Foreign Trade Division, Ministry of Commerce 1948–58; Dep. Governor, Bank of Norway 1958; Governor 1970; member of the Board of Management, European Payments Union and Monetary Agreement, 1951–69. Chairman, EFTA Economic Committee 1967–71. Director: Alcan Aluminium Ltd. 1967–71; Governor for Norway Int. Monetary Fund since 1970. *Publications:* Kosthold og levestandard; Plan for velstand. T.V.A. og Norge; Levestandardens ekonomi; Okonomisk Styring i et fritt Samfunn. *Address:* Fougstadgt 7, Oslo 1, Norway.

**WOLF, Alfred L.** American. *B.* 1904. *Educ.* BS Princeton; BA Oxford (Hon. Juris). *M.* 1931, Constance Cann. *Career:* Brig. Gen. U.S.A.F. (Ret.); 5 Battle Ribbons in World War II. Partner, Law firm of Wolf, Block, Schorr & Solis-Cohen. General Counsel of International Council of Aircraft Owner and Pilot Association (IAOPA), and of Americam Helicopter Society. *Publications:* sundry aviation law articles. *Clubs:* Wings (N.Y.C.), Royal Aero (U.K.), Aero de France, Phila Aviation C.C., and National Aviation. *Address:* Blue Bell, Penna. 19422, U.S.A.

**WOLFE, Stewart James.** District Manager, National Federation of Independent Business. *B.* 1920. *Educ.* Purdue Univ. (B.S.E.E.). *M.* 1943, Lorraine Roebuck. *Career:* Mgr., Mercury Sales Cncl., Mercury Div., Ford Motor Co. 1955–57; Mgr., Publications Dept., Hudson Motor Div., American Motors Corp., Detroit 1949–55; Supervisor of Publicity, Parke Davis & Co., Detroit 1946–49; Fisher Body Div., Gen. Motors Corp., Detroit 1943–45; radio newscaster and variety director, W.B.A.A. 1941–43, and United Press Assn., Indianapolis 1941—43. Former editor: Mercury Messenger (dealers), Mercury Sales Councillor (salesman), Hudson Dealer News, and Hudson Family Magazine. Director: Marketing, Palace Corporation, Williamston, Mich.; Advertising and Public Relations, De Luxe Laboratories, Hollywood 1968. Sales Training Specialist, Jam Handy Organization, Detroit. Marketing Director, Palace Manufacturing Corporation, Williamston, Mich. 1969; Field Rep., Nation's Business, U.S. Chamber of Commerce 1970; Editor, Reporting Magazine, International Council of Industrial Editors (I.C.I.E.) since July 1957 (President 1954–55). *Address:* 905 Flint Rock Circle, Alabaster, Ala. 35007, U.S.A.

**WOLFENDEN, Lord (baron 1974, UK, Life Peer), Sir John Frederick Wolfenden,** CBE, MA. *B.* 1906. *Educ.* Oxford University (MA). *M.* 1932, Eileen Spilsbury. *S.* 1 *Daus.* 2. *Career:* Fellow, Magdalen College, Oxford 1929–34; Headmaster, Uppingham School (1934–44) and Shrewsbury School (1944–50); Vice-Chancellor of the University of Reading 1950–63; Chmn., University Grants Committee 1963–68. Director and Principal Librarian, British Museum 1969–73. *Publications:* The Approach to Philosophy. How to Choose your School; The Public Schools Today; Turning Points. *Address:* The White House, Westcott, Nr. Dorking, Surrey.

**WOLFF, Hon. Sir Albert,** KCMG. *B.* 30 April 1899. *M.* (1) 1924, Ida Jackson (deceased). *S.* 1. *Dau.* 1. (2) 1956, Mary Godwin (deceased). *Career:* Called to the Bar 1921; Crown Prosecutor. Western Australia 1926; Crown Solicitor and Parliamentary Draftsman 1929; King's Counsel 1936; Judge, Supreme Court of Western Australia 1938–69. Senior Puisne Judge 1945. K.C.M.G. 1959. Former Chief Justice Western Australia March 1959–69; Lieutenant Governor of Western Australia 1968–75. *Club:* Weld, Perth. *Address:* Tralee, 151 The Esplanade, Mt. Pleasant, W.A. 6153, Australia.

**WOLFF, Miles Hoffman.** Editor (retired). *B.* 1899. *Educ.* Roanoke College (AB) and Univ. of N. Carolina (MA). *M.* (1) 1940, Anna S. Webster (*D.* 1974). *S.* Miles H., Jr. *Daus.* Anna W. (Mrs. R. B. Dixon) and Eliza McCormick. (2) 1977, Elizabeth S. Cheatham. *Career:* Reporter, Charlotte (N.C.) Observer 1926–28; Associated Press reporter, 1928–32; Chief, Associated Press Bureau, Baltimore 1932–34; with Baltimore Sun (of which Managing Editor, The Evening Sun 1941–49) 1934–49; Exec. Editor, Greensboro (N.C.) Daily News 1949–65; Pres., Greensboro Rotary Club 1957–58; elected Bd. of Dir., Amer. Socy. of Newspaper Editors 1958 (Treas. 1961–62), Second Vice-Pres. 1962–63; First Vice-Pres. 1963–64 (Pres. 1964–65). American Consultant to Nationl Aeronautics and Space Administration, Washington, D.C. 1965–67; Exec. Dir. Greensboro (N.C.) Arts Council 1967–73; Board of Associated Press Managing Editors Assn. 1953–58. Member, Pulitzer Prize Jury 1951—55, 1959–60 and 1964–65. President: Greater Greensboro United Fund 1960; Greater Greensboro Chamber of Commerce 1962. *Award:* Distinguished Citizen (1974). *Address:* 833 North Elm Street, Greensboro, N.C. 27401, U.S.A.

**WOLFSON, Sir Isaac,** Bt, FRS. British. Chairman 1946—, The Great Universal Stores Ltd. (which he joined in 1932). *B.* 1897. *Educ.* Queen's Park School, Glasgow. *M.* 1926, Edith Specterman. *S.* Leonard. Hon LLD (London), Glasgow, Cambridge, Manchester, Strathclyde, Brandeis University, U.S. Hon. FRCP, Hon DCL (Oxon); Hon. F.R.C.P. & S. Glasgow; Hon Fellow (and Hon President), Weizmann Inst. of Science, Israel, and St. Edmund Hall, Oxford; Churchill College. *Awards:* Einstein Award (U.S.) 1967; Herbert Lehmann Award, 1968; Cambridge; Founder Fell., Wolfson College, Oxford; Freeman of the City of Glasgow; Hon LLD (Nott.); Hon PhD (Jerusalem); Hon FRCS; Hon Fellow Jews' College. Member: Worshipful Coy. of Pattern-makers, and of Grand Council, British Empire Cancer Campaign. Trustee: Religious Centre, Jerusalem. Patron, Royal College of Surgeons; Founder Chairman and Trustee, Wolfson Foundation, created 1955. *Address:* 74 Portland Place, London, W.1.

**WOLSTENHOLME, Sir Gordon (Ethelbert Ward),** OBE. English. Director, The Ciba Foundation, London, 1949—; Chmn. Genetic Manip. Adv. Group 1976—; Pres. Royal Soc. of Medicine, 1975; Mem. Gen. Medical Council 1973. *B.* 1913. *Educ.* MA, MB, B Chir (Cambridge), FRCP, FI Biol. *M.* 1948, Dushanka Messinger. *Daus.* Margaret Olivia and Sarah Felicia. Lt.-Col. R.A.M.C. (Adviser on Resuscitation and Transfusion); Dermatological Registrar, Middlesex Hospital. *Publications:* Editor: Ciba Foundation Symposia (over 200 vols.); Royal College of Physicians, Portraits; *author,* numerous papers on World Health, medical education, medical ethics. Hon. LLD (Cambridge); Hon. Member: Society for Endocrinology; Swedish Endocrine Society; Swiss Academy of Medicine; Foreign Member Swedish Medical Society. *Awards:* Chev. Leg. d'Honneur; Star of Ethiopia; Gold medal Italian Min. of Educ.; Gold Medal Perugia Univ. *Club:* Athenaeum. *Address:* The Dutch House, 77A Fitzjohn's Avenue, London, NW3 6NY; and *office* The Ciba Foundation, 41 Portland Place, London, W1N 4BN.

**WOLTERS, Baron Laurent B.** Belgian. Officer Ordre de Léopold; Officer, Ordre de la Couronne (Belgium). *B.* 1901. *Educ.* School for Higher Commercial Studies, Paris. *M.* 1925, Olga Bogdanova (*D.* 1970). *S.* André (*D.* 1972), Adrien. *Dau.* Mrs. Malcolm Subhan. *Career:* With Petrofina since 1924; Honorary Chmn. Petrofina S.A. *Address:* 'Le Bisdom' 1900 Overijse (Bt.), Belgium; and *office* rue de la Loi 33, 1040, Brussels.

**WOOD, Edward Cabell.** Canadian. *B.* 1899. *Educ.* Public and High Schools. *Career:* Engaged in tobacco business in Richmond, Va. 1917, New York City 1920, China 1921; with Imperial Tobacco Co. of Canada (Director 1937, Vice-Pres. 1945, Exec. Vice-President 1948, President 1950, Chairman of Board 1963; retired December 1964); Dir. & member Exec. Cttee. Dominion Fabrics Ltd.—; Wabasso Ltd. (member Executive Committee 1963—); Life Governor, Montreal Gen. Hospital. *Clubs:* Mount Royal; St. James's. Forest & Stream; Ste. Marguerite; Salmon. *Address:* 1455 Sherbrooke Street West, Montreal H3G 1L2; and *office* 1455 Sherbrooke Street West, Montreal, P.Q., H3G 1L2, Canada.

**WOOD, Harleston Read.** American. *B.* 1913. *Educ.* Haverford School and Princeton Univ. (AB). *M.* 1942, Emily Newbold Campbell. *S.* Harleston R., Alan IV, Ross G., Morrow and Anthony. *Career:* Sales Development Engineer 1946–50; Manager of Planning and Development 1950–52; Asst. Vice-Pres. 1952–54, Alan Wood Steel Co; Chairman (Sept. 1962—) and President (Aug. 1955–72), Alan Wood Steel Co., Conshohocken, Pa., U.S.A. Director: The Budd Co.; Fidelity-Mutual Life Insurance Co. *Member:* Amer. Iron & Steel Inst. (Director); Amer. Management Assn. Republican. *Clubs:* Philadelphia Country; Racquet; Gulph Mills Golf; Duquesne. *Address: office* Conshohocken, Pa., U.S.A.

**WOOD, J. Howard.** American. *B.* 1901. *Educ.* Lake Forest Coll. (AB) and Harvard Univ. (Grad.). *M.* (1) 1928, M. Ruth Hendrickson (*Dec.*). *S.* John H. and Robert E. *Daus.* Janet B. (Diederichs) and Ann E. (2) 1972, Barbara Johnston. *Career:* Chmn. Exec. Cttee. and Dir. Tribune Company; Chmn. Bd. Dir. and Chief Exec. Officer W.G.N. Continental Broadcasting Co.; Dir. The Chicago Tribune Co.; New York News Inc.; Gore Newspapers Co.; Sentinal-Star Co.; Manicouagan Power Co.; Associated Press and Lake Shore National Bank. Trustee, Lake Forest Coll. Univ. of Chicago. *Clubs:* Commercial (Chicago); Knollwood; Lake Zurich Golf; Old Elm; The Brook (N.Y.C.); and Glen View. *Address:* Tribune Tower, 435 North Michigan Avenue, Chicago, Ill. 60611, U.S.A.

**WOOD, Rt. Hon. Richard Frederick,** PC, MP. *B.* 1920 (Younger son of 1st Earl of Halifax, KG, OM, GCIE). *Educ.* Eton and New College, Oxford. *M.* 1947, Diana, daughter of Col. E. O. Kellett, DSO, MP. *S.* 1. *Dau.* 1. *Career:* Attaché, British Embassy, Rome 1940. Lieut. K.R.R.C. 1941–43 (retired, wounded). Toured U.S. Army hospitals 1943–45; Oxford 1945–47; Member of Parliament (Cons.) Bridlington Div. of Yorks. 1950—; Joint Parliamentary Secretary, Ministry of Pensions and Nat. Insurance 1955–58, and Parly. Sec., Ministry of Labour 1958–59; Minister of Power 1959–63; Minister of Pensions & National Insurance 1963–64; Minister for Overseas Development 1970–74; Hon. Col. 4th Bn., Royal Green Jackets; Hon. LLD Sheffield Univ. & Leeds Univ. Dep. Lieut (Humberside). Dir. Hargreaves Group of Companies. *Address:* Flat Top House, Bishop Wilton, York YO4 1RY; and 49 Cadogan Place, London, SW1 9RT.

**WOOD, Thomas Alwyn, Jr.** President of Wood's Index, Inc., (a Philadelphia Investment Strategy Group). Lecturer on economics. *B.* 1923. *Educ.* Westminster College, Buenos Aires; The Haverford School, Haverford, Pa.; and Harvard College (BS). *M.* 1967, Virginia Alden Weis. *Career:* Founded Wood's Index 1973; Strategy Consultant, Drexel Firestone 1971–73; President, Woodcock, Moyer, Fricke, and French, Inc. 1970–71; Vice President, Woodcock, Moyer, Fricke, and French, Inc. 1965–70; Director of Research, Woodcock, Moyer, Fricke, and French, Inc. 1961–70; Vice President, South American Wools Co. 1950–61; Served in the U.S. Navy 1944–46. *Member:* Past Director, Nationalities Service Center, Philadelphia; Director, Americans for Competitive Enterprise System; Council Member, Colonial Society of Pennsylvania; Past Director, Y.M.C.A.; Director, Cystic Fibrosis Foundation, Director, Academy of Vocal Arts. *Clubs:* Merion Cricket, The Racquet, Union League of Philadelphia, Harvard (Phila.), Harvard (N.Y.). *Address:* 324 Keller Road, Berwyn, Pa. 19312, U.S.A.

**WOODBRIDGE, Henry Sewall.** American. *B.* 1906. *Educ.* Middlesey School, Rivers Country Day School, and Harvard College. *M.* 1928, Dorothy White. *S.* Henry Sewall, Jr. *Daus.* Anne (Pickford) and Victoria (Hall). *Career:* Industry Representative at War Labor Board 1942–46; War Production Board Safety Committee 1947–46. Commissioner, State of Connecticut Development Commission 1946–51. Director: E. T. Barwick Industries, Inc., Hambro Amer. Corp; First Empire Bank-New York; American Optical Co. Hillwood Corp. (Mng. Dir.), Logetronics Inc., Metritape Inc., VCR Hardware Inc., Reeves Industries Inc., Tudor Capital Fund; Tudor Hedge Fund; Union Labor Life Insurance Co. Trustee: American Institute for Free Labor Development, Day-Kimball Hospital (Putnam, Conn.), Middlesex School (Concord, Mass.), and Old Sturbridge Village (Mass.). *Member:* Council of Foreign Relations; Industrial Relations Research Assn.; National Industrial Conference Board. *Clubs:* Union, India House, The Coffee House, Harvard (all of N.Y.C.); Metropolitan, Cosmos (Washington); Harvard (Boston). *Address:* P.O. Box 156, Pomfret, Conn. 06258, U.S.A.

**WOODBURN, Rt. Hon. Arthur,** PC, DLtt. British politician. *B.* 25 October 1890. *Educ.* Public Schools; Heriot-Watt College, Edinburgh. *M.* 1919. Barbara Halliday. *Career:* Scottish Secretary, Labour Party 1932–39; member, Select Cttee. on National Expenditure 1939–45; Administrative Committee, Parliamentary Labour Party 1943–45; Speaker's Conference on Electoral Reform 1944; Parliamentary Secretary to Ministry of Aircraft Production 1945–46, to Ministry of Supply 1946–47; Secretary of State for Scotland 1947–50. Member of Select Committees on Electoral Laws for clergy and delegated legislation; led first Parliamentary Delegation to the West German Parliament, and to Uruguay; member of first Parly. Delegation to the Spanish Cortes 1960. Delegate to Uganda to present Mace 1964; led deleg. to Kenya Parliament 1966. Has visited Russia, Germany, France, Belgium, Austria, Italy, Switzerland, Spain, Argentina and Brazil. Pres., U.K. Council for Europe. MP (Lab.) for Clackmannan and East Stirlingshire 1939–70. President, National Council of Labour Colleges. Trustee, National Library of Scotland 1961—. Mem., Historical Buildings Council for Scotland. *Publications:* Mystery of Money; Outline of Finance; Guide to Nationalization. *Address:* 83 Orchard Road, Edinburgh, Scotland.

**WOODCOCK, Rt. Hon. George,** PC, CBE. British. *B.* 20 Oct. 1904. *Educ.* Brownedge Elementary School, Ruskin College, Oxford, New College, Oxford (Dip Econ and Political Science 1931); First-Class Hons PPE 1933; Jessie Theresa Rowden Scholar 1933, and Manchester Univ. (Post-Graduate); Hon Fellow: New College 1963; London School of Economics 1965; Hon LLD Sussex 1963, Hon DCL Oxon 1964, and Hon DSc Aston 1967; Hon LLD Manchester 1968; Hon DCL Kent 1968; Hon LLD Lancaster 1970; Hon LLD London 1970. *M.* 1933, Laura Mary McKernan. *S.* Peter Anthony. *Dau.* Vilja Teresa. *Career:* Commenced as cotton weaver 1916–27 Civil Servant 1934–36; Secretary Trades Union Congress Research and Economic Dept. 1936–47 Assistant General Secretary, Trades Union Congress 1947–60. General Secretary, Trades Union Congress 1960–69. Member: Royal Commission on Taxation of Profits and Income 1955 British Guiana Constitutional Commission 1954. Vice-Chairman, National Savings Cttee. Member: Committee on Working of the Monetary System 1957; Royal Commission on Trade Unions 1965; National Economic Development Council 1961–69; Chmn. Commission on Industrial Relations 1969–71. *Address:* 24 Lower Hill Road, Epsom, Surrey.

**WOODCOCK, Leonard.** American Union Leader. *B.* 1911. *Educ.* St. Wilfred's Coll., Oakmore; Northampton Town & Country Sch., U.K.; courses at Wayne State Univ. *M.* 1941, Loula Martin, *S.* 1. *Daus.* 2. *Career:* Regional Dir., UAW 1947–55; Vice-Pres., UAW 1955–70; Pres. Int. Union, United Automobile Aerospace & Agricultural Implement Workers of America (UAW) 1970–77, Pres. Emeritus 1977; appointed by President Carter as Chief of Mission, U.S. Liaison Office, People's Republic of China 1977. *Address:* 8000 E. Jefferson Street, Detroit, Mich. 48214, U.S.A.

**WOODROOFE, Sir Ernest (George),** Kt. 1973. FI Chem E, FInstP. British. *B.* 1912. *Educ.* Leeds University (BSc, PhD). *M.* (1) 1938, Margaret Downes (*D.* 1961). *Dau.* Susan Margaret; (2) 1962, Enid Grace Hutchinson Arnold. *Career:* Director, British Oil & Cake Mills Ltd. 1951–55; Head, Research Division, Unilever Ltd. 1955–61; Dir. Unilever

Ltd. and N.V. 1956–74; United Africa Co. Ltd. 1961–63; President, International Society for Fat Research 1962; Chairman, Research Cttee., Confederation of British Industry 1965–69. Chairman, Unilever Ltd. Vice-Chairman Unilever N.V. 1970–74; Dir. British Gas Corp. 1973—; Dir. Commonwealth Development Finance Co. Ltd. 1970–75; Dir. Schroder Ltd. since 1974; Dir. Burton Group Ltd. since 1974; Dir. The Guthrie Corp. since 1974. Governor, London Graduate School of Business Studies & Administrative Staff College Henley 1970–75. *Member:* Govt. Committee of Enquiry into the organization of Civil Science 1962–63; Council for National Academic Awards 1964–67. Member: Royal Commission for the Exhibition of 1851 1968—; Tropical Products Institute 1964–69; Chmn., Review Body on Doctors' & Dentists' Remuneration since 1975. *Awards:* Hon. Assoc. Liverpool Coll. of Technology; Hon. Fellow, Univ. of Manchester Inst. of Science & Technology; Hon LLD, Leeds Univ.; Hon. D. Univ. Surrey Univ.; Visiting Fellow, Nuffield Coll. Oxford; Commander in the Order of Orange Nassau Netherlands 1972. *Club:* Athenaeum. *Address:* The Crest, Berry Lane, Worplesdon, Guildford, Surrey.

**WOODRUFF, Joseph F.** American. *B.* 1913. *Educ.* Captial University (BS 1935); Ohio State University (1935–36). *M.* 1939, Marie M. Miller. *Daus.* Joanne Marie and Carolyn Jeanette. *Career:* Instructor: Kings Mills High School (1936–38), Greenhills High School (1938–39); McCain High School 1939–41; Armco Research Laboratories, Armco Steel Corp. 1941—. Research Manager, 1968— of spectroscopy, X-ray and electron diffraction; X-ray emissar, Auger Spectroprosy and microprobe; Pres. Board of Education 1954–63; Chmn. Finance Cttee. (1959–62) Ohio School Boards Association 1962–64 (Policy Committee 1963); member, Adv. Board of Special Service Bureau of Miami Univ. 1956–64; Board of Dir., Butler County Heart Assn. 1954; Chmn., Cttee. E-2, American Society for Testing Materials; elected to Board of Education 1951–63. *Member:* Amer. Socy. for Testing Materials; National Education Socy.; Capital University Alumni Association; Middletown Chamber of Commerce; American Management Association 1969–71. Consulting member ANSI Exec. Committee, N.II. Standard Committee, Basic Materials, Nuclear Applications, 1965; Spectroscopy Socy. of Canada 1967–73; Life Member, Junior Chamber of Commerce. *Award:* National Distinguished Service Award of Junior Chamber of Commerce 1964. Award of Merit of American Society for Testing Materials, 1968; Fellow by ASTM 1970; Hon. Life Mem. ASTM 1975; ASTM E2; Distinguished Service Middleton City Schools; (ASTM) H. V. Churchill Award 1974; Hon. Southwest Reg. School Board, since 1974. *Publications:* The Influence of Varying Amounts of Elements in Steel and Cast Irons on Spectral Intensity (Journal of the Optical Society of America, Feb. 1953); A Spectrochemical Method for the Determination of Trace Amounts of Silver in Stainless Type Steels (Applied Spectroscopy); The Use of Briquetted Samples in the Spectrochemical Analysis of Carbon and Alloy Steels and Other Metals (Journal of the Optical Society of America, April 1950); A Rapid Spectrographic Control Method for the Determination of Lime-Silica Ratios in Open Hearth Slags (Open Hearth Proceedings of American Institute of Mining & Metallurgical Engineers, 1947); Quality Control of Steel Using Clock and Chart Recording Photoelectric Spectrometer (Applied Spectroscopy, 1962); Education for the American Way of Life (Ohio School Boards Assn. Journal, 1962); Rapid Spectrochemical Analysis for Control of Basic Oxygen and Open Hearth Shops (Open Hearth Proceedings, 1964); Methods for Spectrochemical Analysis 1971. *Clubs:* Forest Hills Country; Armco Association. *Address:* 3437 Central Avenue, Middletown, Ohio, U.S.A.

**WOODRUFF, Robert Winship.** American businessman. *B.* 6 Dec. 1889. *M.* 1912, Nell Hodgson. Chairman, Finance Committee, The Coca-Cola Company; Member, Directors Advisory Council, Morgan Guaranty Trust Company of New York; Directors Advisory Council, Trust Company of Georgia. *Address:* P.O. Drawer 1734, Atlanta, Georgia, U.S.A.

**WOODS, Sir Colin Philip Joseph,** KCVO, CBE. British Police Officer. *B.* 1920. *Educ.* LCC Primary & Secondary Schools; Finchley Grammar Sch., *M.* 1941, Gladys Ella May Howell. *Dau.* 1. *Career:* War Service in 60th Rifles & Royal Ulster Rifles 1939–46; joined Metropolitan Police 1946 & served through the ranks; Commandant, Nat. Police Coll. 1969–70; Asst. Commissioner (Traffic) 1970–72, Asst. Commissioner (Crime) 1972–75, Dep. Commissioner 1975–77, Metropolitan Police; HM Chief Inspector of Constabulary since 1977. *Decorations:* Knight Commander of the Royal Victorian Order, 1977; Commander of the British Empire, 1973. *Address:* Home Office, 50 Queen Anne's Gate, London SW1.

**WOODS, George David.** American banker. *B.* 1901. *Educ.* American Institute of Banking and New York Univ. *M.* 1935, Louise Taraldson. *Career:* With Harris, Forbes & Co., N.Y.C. 1918–31; Chase, Harris Forbes Co. 1931–34, and The First Boston Corp., N.Y.C. 1934–62 (Chmn. of Board 1951–61); Chmn of Bd. and Pres. International Finance Corp. 1963–68; President and Chairman of Executive Directors, International Bank for Reconstruction and Development (World Bank) and International Development Association, Washington 1963–68. Chairman and Trustee: Henry J. Kaiser Family Foundation, 1968—. Dir.: The First Boston Corp. 1968–76, First Boston Inc. since 1976; Chmn, International Executive Service Corps., 1968–74, Chmn. of Exec. Cttee. 1974. Served from Major to Colonel, General Staff Corps, U.S. Army 1942–45. *Clubs:* Links, Pinnacle, Players, Racquet & Tennis, The Club at World Trade Center (N.Y.C.); Duquesne (Pittsburgh); Federal City (Washington, D.C.). *Address:* 825 Fifth Avenue, New York City 10021; and *office* 277 Park Avenue, N.Y. City 10017, U.S.A.

**WOODS, John Lucius.** American Mgmt. Consultant. *B.* 1912. *Educ.* Northwestern University (BS Com); C.P.A. District of Columbia and Illinois. *M.* 1938, Mary Torkilson. *S.* Thomas George and John Franklin. *Daus.* Jean Katherine and Judith Anne (Ruff). *Career:* Senior Accountant, Arthur Anderson & Co. 1934–42; office Manager and Asst. Controller, Bauer & Black 1942–44. With Amphenol Corp.: Controller 1944: Vice-Pres.-Controller and Director 1955; Vice-Pres. Finance 1958; Vice-Pres. Finance and Administration 1961; Member, Exec. Cttee. of Bd. of Dirs., 1956–68. Dir.: Valuation Counselors Inc.; Chicago District Golf Assn.; Vision Wrap Industries; Vice-Pres., Finance Bunker-Ramo Corporation. President & Director, Borg Investment Co. *Member:* Financial Executives Inst.; Amer. Inst. of C.P.A.'s; Am. Mymt. Assn; Illinois Secy. of C.P.A.s. *Clubs:* Economic (Chicago); Knollwood; Mid-day; Union League; Executive; Wall St. (New York). *Address:* 5 Court of Bucks County, Lincolnshire, Ill. 60015; and *office* Suite 556, 230 W. Monroe Street, Chicago, Ill. 60606, U.S.A.

**WOODS, John Russell.** Canadian mining executive. *B.* 1930. *Educ.* Ashbury College, Trinity College School. *M.* 1953, Nancy Elizabeth Braden. *S.* James Braden. *Dau.* Jennifer. *Career:* Served with Canadian Army; Korea with 2nd Royal Canadian Regt., H.Q., 25th, Canadian Inf. Bde.; retired from Army 1954; Former Nat. Dir. of Finance, Liberal Party of Canada; former Pres. and Chmn. Bd. The Holden Manufacturing Co. Ltd. and S. E. Woods Ltd.; Dir. Columbia Lime Products Ltd; ETS Tool Corp. Ltd.; Touratrax Ltd.; Eaglet Mines Ltd.; Lynx Canada Explorations Ltd.; Cogper Ltd.; Chmn. of the Board Columbia Lime Products Ltd. *Clubs:* Ottawa Valley Hunt; The Country; Rideau; Maganassippi Fish & Game. *Award:* Knight Commander of the Military, Hospitaler Order, St. Lazarus of Jerusalem. *Address:* Suite 904, 140 Wellington Street, Ottawa, K1P 5A2, Ontario, Canada.

**WOODS, Richard Ainsa.** American. *B.* 1907. *Educ.* Princeton Univ. *M.* 1935, Frances Stent. *S.* Richard M. *Dau.* Frances S. *Career:* With Merrill Lynch since 1931. Lt.-Cmdr. U.S.N.R. (Pacific Area) in World War II, 1942–45; Partner 1954—, Vice-President 1959—, Merrill, Lynch Pierce, Fenner & Smith, New York City. *Member:* N.Y. Stock Exchange; Bond Club (N.Y.C.); Boys Club of Greenwich, Conn. (Dir.). *Clubs:* Princeton, Stock Exchange Lunch (both N.Y.C.); Field, Indian Harbor Yacht (both of Greenwich). *Address:* *office* 70 Pine Street, New York, N.Y. 10005, U.S.A.

**WOODS, Thomas Cochrane, Jr.** American corporation executive. *B.* 1920. *Educ.* University of Nebraska (BA 1943). *M.* 1943, Marjorie Jane Jones. *S.* Thomas Cochrane III. *Daus.* Avery Ladd. *Career:* Served from Pvt. to 1st Lt. U.S.F.A. (Parachute Tr.) 1943–46; Asst. Adv. Mgr. Addressograph Multigraph Corp. Cleveland Ohio 1947–58; Pres. and Chmn. Exec. Cttee. The Lincoln (Nebraska) Telephone and Telegraph Company 1958; Pres. Nellewood Corp. 1961; Vice-Pres. Lincoln Development Co. 1958; W-K Realty Co. Lincoln 1958; Dir. Sahara Coal Co. Inc. Chicago 1958; Woodmen Accident & Life Co. Lincoln 1959; Dir. & Mem. of the Exec. Cttee., First National Bank & Trust Co. 1961. Trustee Nebraska Human Resources Research Foundation 1968; Univ. of Nebraska Foundation 1961; Hon. Trustee, Joslyn Liberal Arts Socy. 1964; Founding Trustee, Univ. of Nebraska Regents Endowment for Distinguished Teaching

1961. Commissioner, Nebraska State Building Comm. 1966. *Member:* Lincoln Foundation 1966; Chamber of Commerce of the U.S. 1962; Lincoln Chamber of Commerce; Council on Foundations; Univ. of Nebraska Alumni Assn. 1961; Lincoln Center Development Assn. 1967; SAR; Ak-Sar-Ben; YMCA; First Plymouth Congregational Church; Past Member Bryan Memorial Hospital Exec. Cttee; Lincoln City Park & Recreation Adv. Bd.; Young President's Org.; Past Trustee, Nebraska State Historical Soc.; Nebraska Independent College Foundation; Past Dir. Nebraska Assn. of Commerce & Industry; Nebraska Mangt. Analysis Study Cttee.; United Arts Fund; Nebraska State Historical Soc.; Lincoln Community Chest; Lincoln Community Council; Past Pres. Nebraska Human Resources Research Foundation; TV Transmission Inc. *Clubs:* Lincoln Country; Lincoln University; Nebraska Club. *Address:* 2540 Woodcrest Avenue, Lincoln, Nebraska 68502 and *office* 1440 M Street, P.O. Box 81309, Lincoln, Nebraska 68501, U.S.A.

**WOODWORTH, Alfred Skinner.** *B.* 1907. *Educ.* Harvard University (BA) and Harvard Business School (MBA). *M.* 1947, Beatrice Hardon. *S.* Alfred S., Jr. and Charles Kennard. *Dau.* Virginia. *Career:* Dir., State Street Bank & Trust Co., Boston, Mass., Chmn. of Board, Federal St. Capital Corp.; Director, Codex Book Co. Inc.; Dir. White Consolidated Industries; Incoterm Corp.; Albert Trostel & Sons. *Clubs:* The Country (Brookline, Mass.); Harvard. *Address: office* 225 Franklin Street, Boston, Mass., U.S.A.

**WOODYATT, James B.,** BSc, DCL. Canadian industrialist. *B.* 1886. *Educ.* McGill Univ. (BSc Elec Eng). *M.* Mary Davidson. *Dau.* Betty (Mrs. H. J. L. Petersson). *Career:* Pres. and Director: The Winisk Co. Ltd.; Honorary Director: Power Corporation of Canada; Bathurst Paper Co. Chainman, Niagara & Welland Power Co. 1904; Topographer, Toronto & Hamilton Railway 1905; Apprentice, Canadian Westinghouse Co. 1906–08; investigating ice conditions in the Gulf and River St. Lawrence under direction of Dr. Barnes for the Dominion Govt. 1908–09; Salesman, Allis-Chalmers-Bullock Co. 1909–10; Supt., Sherbrooke Railway & Power Co. 1910–13; General Supt., Southern Canada Power Co. 1913–16 (Gen. Mgr. 1916–20; Vice-Pres. and General Mgr. 1920–25; Pres. and Gen. Mgr. 1925–52; Pres. 1952–56; Chmn. 1956–63). Member: Engineering Inst. of Canada; Corporation of Professional Engineers of the Province of Quebec; Canadian Electrical Assn.; Inst. of Electric and Electrical Engineers; Delta Upsilon Fraternity. Freemason. *Clubs:* Royal Automobile, Royal Montreal Curling, Royal Montreal Golf, St. James's, University, St. George's (Sherbrooke), Montreal Amateur Athletic Association. *Address: office:* c/o Montreal Trust Co., Estates & Trusts Division, 1 Place Ville-Marie, Montreal, Quebec, H3B 4A5, Canada.

**WOOLDRIDGE, Dean Everett.** American scientist, executive. *B.* 1913. *Educ.* University of Oklahoma (AB 1932; MS 1933), and California Institute of Technology (PhD 1936). *M.* 1936, Helene Detweiler. *S.* Dean Edgar and James Allan. *Dau.* Anna Lou. *Career:* Member of Technical Staff, Head of Physical Electronics Research, Bell Telephone Laboratories, N.Y.C. 1936–46; Co-Director, then Director, Research and Development Laboratories, then Vice-Pres., Research and Development Hughes Aircraft Co., Culver City, Calif. 1946–53; Pres. and member, Bd. of Dirs., The Ramo-Wooldridge Corp., Los Angeles 1953–58; Pres., Thompson Ramo Wooldridge Inc. 1958–62; Research Associate, California Institute of Technology 1962—. *Awards:* 1950 Air Force Association Citation of Honour for outstanding achievement in the field of electronic research and development. 1954 Raymond E. Hackett Award for outstanding achievements in the field of electronic science, 1960 Distinguished Service Citation, Univ. of Oklahoma; AAAS-Westinghouse Award for Science Writing, 1963. *Publications:* The Machinery of the Brain (1963); The Machinery of Life (1966); Mechanical Man (1968); numerous technical publications. Trustee: Harvey Mudd College 1960—; Trustee, Calif. Inst. of Technology, 1974. *Member:* Phi Beta Kappa, Tau Beta Pi, Eta Kappa Nu, Sigma Xi, Amer. Physical Socy. (Fellow), Inst. of Electrical & Electronic Engineers (Fellow), Amer. Inst. of Aeronautics & Astronautics (Fellow), Amer. Acad. of Arts & Sciences (Fellow), Amer. Inst. of Physics, Amer. Assn. for Advancement of Science; National Academy of Sciences. *Address:* 4545 Via Esperanza, Santa Barbara, Calif. 93110, U.S.A.

**WOOLLEY, Lord** (Harold Woolley), CBE. British farmer. *B.* 1905. *Educ.* Blackburn Grammar School, Woodhouse Grove School (nr. Bradford, Yorks.) and Lancashire School of Agriculture. *M.* (1) 1926, Martha Annie Jeffs *S.* 4; and (2) 1937, Hazel Eileen Archer Jones. *Daus.* 2. *Career:* Vice-President 1948 and 1955, and Deputy President 1949–50 & 1956, The National Farmers' Union; President of The National Farmers' Union, 1960–66. Director: N.F.U. National Insurance Society Ltd.; D.L. County of Cheshire. *Member:* Abbey National Building Soc., Regional Board; Member of Council, National Farmers Union. *Clubs:* Farmers (London); MCC. *Address:* Hatton House Farm, Hatton Heath, Chester, Cheshire.

**WOOLLEY, Knight.** American banker. *B.* 1 May 1895. *Educ.* Yale University (BA). *M.* 1934, Sarah Currier (*D.* (1954)). *M.* (2) 1957, Marjorie Fleming. *Career:* Served World War I for two years as Captain and later as Major of the 308th Field Artillery, 78th Division, both in U.S.A. and in France; on staff of Guaranty Trust Co. 1919–20; Assistant Cashier and later Asst. Vice-Pres. American Exchange National Bank 1920–27; joined Harriman Brothers & Co. later merged with Brown Brothers as Brown Brothers Harriman & Co. 1931; Partner, Brown Brothers Harriman & Co. since 1931. *Address:* 59 Wall Street, New York 10005, N.Y., U.S.A.

**WOOLLEY, Sir Richard van der Riet,** OBE, FRS. British Astronomer. *B.* 1906. *Educ.* University of Cape Town (MSc) and Gonville and Caius College, Cambridge (MA; ScD); Hon LLD Melbourne; Hon DSc Capetown; Hon DSc Sussex. *M.* 1932, Gwyneth Jane Margaret Meyler. *Career:* Commonwealth Fund Fellow at Mount Wilson Observatory, California 1929–31; Isaac Newton Student, Cambridge Univ. 1931–33; Chief Assistant, Royal Observatory, Greenwich 1933–37; John Couch Adams Astronomer, Cambridge 1937–39; Commonwealth Astronomer 1939–55; Hon Professor of Astronomy, Australian National Univ. 1950–55; Vice-Pres., International Astronomical Union 1952; Pres., Australian and New Zealand Assn. for Advancement of Science (Melbourne meeting) 1955; Astronomer Royal 1956–71; Visiting Prof. of Astronomy, Univ. of Sussex 1966—. Dir South African Astronomical Observatory 1972–77. *Awards:* Hon Fellow of University House, Australian National University since 1955, and of Gonville and Caius College since 1956. Hon Dr Phil, Uppsala; corresponding member, Royal Society of Sciences of Liège 1956; Master, the Worshipful Company of Clockmakers 1969; Gold Medal Royal Astronomical Society. *Publications:* (with Sir Frank Dyson) Eclipses of the Sun and Moon. 1937; (with D. W. N. Stibbs) The Outer Layers of a Star (1953). *Address:* Magnolia House, Hankham, Sussex.

**WORDEN, Edwin Sheldon.** American. *B.* 1908. *Educ.* Massachusetts Inst. of Technology (BS 1931) and New York Univ. (MBA 1940). *M.* (1) 1934, Julia Louis Storey (*D.*). *Daus.* 1. (2) 1972, Sara Reynolds Harshbarger. *Career:* Technical Sales Training Supervisor, Worthington Corp. 1934–36; Purchasing Engineer, Pacific Commercial Co. 1936–37; Research Engineer, Edgar Steiner & Co. 1937–42; Office of Quarter-master-General of U.S.A. War Department 1942–47 Vice-Pres. Container Laboratories Inc. 1947–51; Partner, Koehler & Worden 1951–55; Pres., Edwin S. Worden & Associates 1955–60. Pres. and Dir., Raymond Eisenhardt & Son, Oakland, New Jersey (formerly Edgar Steiner & Co., New York) 1960–73, Vice Chmn. since 1973 (ret'd). *Award:* U.S.A. War Dept. Commendation for Meritorious Civilian Service. *Member:* Mass. Inst. of Technology, Educational Cncl.; Amer. Socy. for Testing Materials; Technical Assn. Pulp & Paper Industry; U.S.A. Packaging Inst.; U.S. Naval Inst.; U.S. Power Squadron, etc. *Publications:* several technical articles on plastics and packaging. *Clubs:* Mount Dora Yacht; M.I.T. (N.Y.C.); N.Y. Univ. Alumni Assn. *Address:* P.O. Box 1241, Mt. Dora, Fla. 32757, U.S.A.

**WORMLEY, Lorentz Englehart, Sr.** American civil engineer and educational administrator. *B.* 1899. *Educ.* Univ. of Illinois (BS in Mining Engineering); extension work, Univs. of Chicago, Purdue and Stanford; Special Graduate Work in educational administration, Univ. of Calif. 1930–40. *M.* 1921, Geneva A. Stillman. *S.* Dr. Lorentz E. *Dau.* Mrs. Phyllis Jeanne Adams. *Career:* Departmental Supervisor of Education, Dept. of Corrections, Sacramento, Calif, 1947–69; Training Officer, Veterans Admin., S. Francisco 1946–47; Area Training Specialist, Office of Secy. of War, S. Francisco 1943–46; Supervising Engineer, Defense Plant Corp.1942–43; Dir. (trade and industrial training) Unified School District, S. Francisco 1941–42; Asst. State Supervisor (trade and industrial education), Sacramento 1940–41; Director of Adult Education, Monterey (Calif.) Union High School 1930–40; Construction Engineer, Asst. to Mgr., Austin Co. 1930; Asst. Bridge Engineer and Resident Engineer, State Highway Dept., Sacramento 1929–30; Construction and Plant Engineer (field engineering unit) Columbia Steel Corp. 1928–29; Instructor, Departmental Head, Hammond (Ind.) Technical High School 1926–28, and Du Quoin TWP High School 1923–26; Resident Engineer, Illinois Div. Highways, East St. Louis 1923–24; Mining Engineer, Roane Iron Co. 1922–23. Author of magazine and newspaper articles on professional subjects. *Member:* Pi Kappa Phi; Calif. Assn. of Adult Education Administrators, Vice-Pres., 1937; Sec., Treas. 1940–42. Correctional Education Association (President 1958–60); California Retired Teachers Association, National Retired Teachers Association, Veterans of World War 1, University of Illinois Alumni Association; International Platform Assn.; Republican. Mason. Secretary, State of California Interagency Committee for Correctional Inmate Training and Placements 1955–68. Member: Comstock Club, The Sons of the American Revolution, Retired State Govt. Employees Assoc.; California Statewide Cttee. for Equal Opportunity in Apprenticeship & Training for Minority Groups 1961–68. *Address:* 2360 Purinton Drive, Sacramento, Calif. 95821, U.S.A.

**WORNER, Howard Knox.** British-Australian. *B.* 1913. *Educ.* Melbourne Univ. (BSc 1934; MSc 1936, DSc 1942); Hon DSc (Newcastle) 1966; Assoc. of Bendigo School of Mines (ABSM) 1933; Fellow, Aust. Academy of Science 1973; Foundation Fellow & Sec., Aust. Acad. of Technological Sciences 1975: Silver Medallist, Australian Inst. of Metals, 1974; Kernot Medallist, Univ. of Melbourne, 1976; Kent Medallist, Inst. of Fuel, 1976. *M.* 1937, Rilda Beryl Muller. *S.* 2. *Dau.* 1. *Career:* Senior Demonstrator in Metallurgy, University of Melbourne 1935–36 (Lecturer 1937–38); Res. Fellow, National Health and Medical Res. Council of Australia and Hon. Scientific Consultant to Medical Equipment Control Committee of Australia 1939–46; Professor of Metallurgy, Univ. of Melbourne 1947–55; Dean, Faculty of Engineering, Univ. of Melbourne 1953–55; Member of Council, Newcastle Univ. 1962–66. Director of Research, The Broken Hill Proprietary Co., Ltd., and Associated Companies 1956–62; International Consultant 1963. Director, New Process Development, Conzinc Riotinto of Australia Ltd. 1964–75; Council Mem. National Museum of Victoria since 1973; Chmn. Victoria Govt. Brown Coal Research Cttee. since 1975; Metallurgical Consultant since 1975; Chmn., National Energy Adv. Cttee. since 1977. *Publications:* some 125 papers on the properties of lead and its alloys, the properties of dental and surgical materials, extraction of titanium, iron and steel production, continuous smelting and refining of metals, energy & coal conversion; Inventor, Worcra processes for metal production. *Address:* 18 The Boulevard, North Balwyn, Vic., Australia.

**WORTHAM, Gus Sessions.** *B.* 1891. *Educ.* University of Texas. *M.* 1926, Lyndall Finley. *Daus.* Lyndall Finley and Diana. *Career:* Enlisted in Air Service of U.S. Army 1917, and was C.O. 800th Aerial Sqdn. during World War I. With State Board of Insce., Austin, Tex. 1915–17. Retired Chairman of Board and Director, American General Insurance Co.; Director: Houston Symphony Orchestra, Texas Children's Hospital, Houston Livestock Show and Rodeo. *Awards:* Insurance Man of the Year Award for 1958, by Fed. of Insce. Counsel; Bd. of Dirs. Museum of Fine Arts; Recipient Distinguished Alumnus Award (Univ. of Texas) 1962; Coronat Medal (St. Edward's Univ., Austin) 1963. *Member:* Beta Gamma Sigma (Hon. Fraternity); Alpha Chapter, University of Texas; Sigma Nu. *Clubs:* Houston; Allegro; Metropolitan. *Address:* 1505 South Boulevard, Houston 6; and *office* 2727 Allen Parkway, Houston, Tex., U.S.A. 77019.

**WORTHEN, Charles Rexford.** Canadian banker. *B.* 1921. *Educ.* Bishop's Univ. (BA 1949) and Queen's Univ. School of Industrial Relations 1949–50. *M.* Mary Ward. *Daus.* Nancy and Ann. *Career:* Joined Canadian Bank Note Co. in 1955; Asst. to the Pres. 1956, Vice-Pres. 1964, Pres. since 1965. *Clubs:* Royal Ottawa Golf, Country (all in Ottawa); Seigniory (Montebello, Que.). *Address:* Apt. 2408, 400 Stewart Street, Ottawa, Ont. K1N 6L2; and *office* 145 Richmond Road, Ottawa K1G 3H8, Ont., Canada.

**WORTHY, James C.** Educator. *B.* 1910. *Educ.* Northwestern Univ. Lake Forest College (BA). *M.* 1934, Mildred Leritz. *Dau.* Joan (Barr). *Career:* Assistant Deputy Administrator, National Recovery Administration, Washington, D.C. 1933–36; Employment Manager, Schuster & Co., Milwaukee 1936–38; Personnel Staff, Sears, Roebuck & Co., Chicago 1938–53; Asst. Secretary of Commerce, Washington 1953–55; Vice-Pres., Sears, Roebuck & Co., Chicago 1955–61. Vice-President Cresap, McCormick & Paget Inc., 1962–72; Professor Public Affairs and Management, Sangamon State Univ. since 1972. *Publication:* Big Business and Free Men (Harper's 1959). Hon. LLD: Lake Forest College 1959, and Chicago Theological Seminary 1960. Fellow, Acad. of Management. *Member:* Amer. Socy. for Public Administration. Republican. *Clubs:* Chicago; University; Commercial; Sangamo. *Address:* 4 Country Place, Springfield, Ill. 62701, U.S.A.

**WRAIGHT, Sir John Richard,** KBE, CMG. British diplomat (Ret'd.). *B.* 1916. *M.* 1947, Marquita Elliott. *Career:* served with HAC, RHA Western Desert Libya. Ministry, Economic Warfare Mission, Middle East Cairo; Economic Warfare Adviser H.Q. Mediterranian Allied Air Forces Italy 1940–44; Foreign Office 1945; Special Asst. to Chief of UNRRA operations, Europe 1946; Entered Foreign (subsequently Diplomatic) Service 1947; British Embassy Athens 1948–50. Tel Aviv 1950–53, Washington 1953–57; Foreign Office 1957–59; British Embassy Cairo 1959–62, Brussels and Luxembourg 1962–68; Minister & Consul-Gen. Milan 1968–73; H.M. Ambassador to Switzerland 1973–76. Retired 1976. Now International Company Consultant & Company Director. *Member:* Royal Institute International Affairs; Hon. Artillery Company. *Awards:* Knight Commander, Order of the British Empire; Companion, Order St. Michael and St. George; Commander, Order of the Crown Belgium. *Address:* 35 Jameson Street, London W8 7SH.

**WRATHER, J. Devereaux, Jr.** American oil producer, motion-picture producer, and financier. *B.* 1918. *Educ.* University of Texas (BA). *M.* 1947, Bonita Granville. *S.* Jack and Christopher. *Daus.* Molly and Linda. *Career:* Served as Major U.S.M.C. Reserve 1942–53. Pres.: Evansville (Ind.) Refining Co. 1938–40; Overton Refining Co., and Amarillo Producers & Refiners Corp., Dallas 1940–49; Jack Wrather Pictures Inc. 1947–49; Freedom Productions Inc. 1949—; Western States Investment Corp., Dallas 1949—; Wrather TV Productions Inc. 1951—; Wrather-Alvarez Broadcasting Inc., The Lone Ranger Inc., Lassie Inc., The Disneyland Hotel (Anaheim, Calif.), Sergeant Preston of the Yukon Inc.; L'Horizon Hotel, Palm Springs, Calif.; Director, Teleprompter Corp. Owner: KFMB, KERO and KFMB-TV, San Diego, Calif.; KOTV-TV, Tulsa. Part-owner: WNEW, New York City. Chairman of the Board; Muzak Inc., and Independent Television Inc. Chairman of the Board, A. C. Gilbert Co.; President, Balboa Bay Club Inc. and Kona Kai Inc., Oct. 1959—; Director: Capitol Records Inc., and Transcontinent Television Corp.; President and Chairman of the Board, Wrather Corp. *Member* of Board of Directors, American Foundation of Religion & Psychiatry; Development Board of University of Texas, Vice-Chairman of the Chancellor's Council University of Texas; International Radio and T.V. Society; National Petroleum Council; Board of Directors Corporation for Public Broadcasting. *Clubs:* Athletic Petroleum (Dallas); The Players (N.Y.C.); Cat Cay (British Bahamas). *Address:* 270 North Canon Drive, Beverly Hills, Calif.; and 375 Park Avenue, New York City 22, U.S.A.

**WREDEN, William Paul.** American rare bookseller and publisher, *B.* 1910. *Educ.* Stanford University (AB 1934). *M.* 1936, Byra Jean Smith. *S.* William Paul III, Douglas Victor, Phillip Roderick. *Daus.* Paula Jean (Campbell) and Denise Victoria Byra. *Career-* Owner, Pinole Land & Cattle Company, California, since 1941; entered rare-book business 1937; Statistician, Anglo-Californian National Bank 1935–37. *Publication:* Bibliography of Valentine Greatrakes. *Address:* 60 Parkwood Drive, Atherton, California 94025; and *office* 200 Hamilton Avenue, Palo Alto, Calif 94301, U.S.A.

**WREFORD, Peter Graham.** British company executive. *B.* 1918. *Educ.* University College School, Frognal; and London School of Economics (BSc Econ 1948). *M.* 1949, Rosemary Billie Brass. *S.* Anthony William. *Daus.* Diana Elizabeth, Alison Rosemary, and Jacqueline Mary. *Career:* Secretary, Ship Mortgage Finance Co. Ltd. 1950–55; Manager, Estate Duties Investment Trust Ltd. 1955–58; Chmn.: Gresham Trust Ltd. 1958—, Gresham Investment Trust Ltd. 1965—. Director: Robert Moss Ltd.; Marshall Cavendish Ltd.; Crown House Limited; R. Green Properties Ltd.; Chamberlain Phipps Ltd.; Dep. Chmn. Clive Discount Co. Ltd.; Sterling Credit Ltd. All or part of the share and loan capital of these concerns are quoted on the London Stock Exchange. *Member:* Chartered Inst. of Secretaries; Inst. of Bankers. *Club:* Marylebone Cricket. *Address:* Winters Grace, Shamley Green, nr. Guildford, Surrey; and *office:* Barrington House, Gresham Street, London EC2V 7HE.

**WRIGGLESWORTH, Ian.** MP. British Politician. *B.* 1939. *Educ.* Stockton Grammar Sch.; Stockton-Billingham Tech. Coll.; Coll. of St. Mark & St. John, Chelsea. *M.* 1967, Patricia Truscott. *S.* 2. *Career:* Clerk, Midland Bank Ltd., Middlesbrough 1957–60; Personal Asst. to Sir Ronald Gould, Gen. Sec. of the Nat. Union of Teachers 1966–68; Head of Research, Cooperative Party 1968–70; Pres. & Public Affairs Mgr., National Giro 1970–74; MP (Lab. & Co-op.) for Teeside, Thornaby since 1974. *Address:* House of Commons, London SW1A 0AA.

**WRIGHT, Sir Denis Arthur Hepworth.** GCMG. British. *B.* 1911. *Educ.* Brentwood School, St. Edmund Hall, Oxford. *M.* 1939, Iona Craig. *Career:* Vice-Consul Constanza, Rumania 1939–41, Trebizond 1941–43, and Mersin (Turkey) 1943–45; First Secy. (Commercial), Belgrade 1946–48; Superintending Trade Consul, Chicago 1949–51; Head, Econ. Relations Dept., Foreign Office 1951–53; Chargé d'Affaires Dec. 1953 (on resumption of diplomatic relations with Iran); Counsellor of Embassy, Teheran 1954–55; Asst. Under-Secy., Foreign Office 1955–59; Ambassador to Ethiopia Dec. 1959–62; Asst. Under-Secy., Foreign Office Aug. 1962. Ambassador to Iran April 1963–71; Dir. Mitchell Cotts Group; Standard Chartered Bank Ltd.: Shell Transport & Trading Co.; Hon. Fellow, St. Edmund Hall 1972; St. Antony's Coll. 1976. Gov., International Briefing Centre, Farnham Castle; Chmn., Iran Society; mem. of Council, British Inst. of Persian Studies. *Address:* Duck Bottom, Haddenham, Aylesbury.

**WRIGHT, James Otis.** *B.* 1912. *Educ.* North Carolina State Univ. (BS 1934) and The George Washington Univ. Law School, Washington, D.C. (JD 1938); Admitted to District of Columbia (1938) and Virginia (1943) Bars. *M.* 1938, Alice Dickinson Croom. *S.* James O., Jr. *Dau.* Alice (Jacobus). *Career:* Statistician and Attorney, U.S. Housing Authority 1937–42. With Ford Motor Co. beginning in 1946, successively as Manager, Organization Dept.; Assistant to the Vice-President Finance; Assistant to Vice-President and General Manager, Ford Div.; Assistant General Manufacturing Manager, Ford Div.; Asst. General Purchasing Agent, Ford Div.; Director of Purchasing, Ford Motor Co.; Asst. Gen. Manager, Ford Div.; Gen. Manager of Ford Div. and Vice-Pres., Ford Motor Co. 1957; Vice-President, Car and Truck Group, and Director, 1960; President, Federal-Mogul Corp. 1963–68; Pres. Wright Enterprises Inc. & Cepco Inc. *Member:* Kappa Sigma; Phi Kappa Phi; Air Force Assn.; Dir., Litton Industries Inc., Wallace-Murray Corp., Cepco Inc.; First Nat. Bank of Brunswick; Wright Enterprises, Inc. Trustee; The George Washington Univ.; Brunswick Junior Coll. Foundation; Advisory Board, MacArthur Memorial Foundation. *Clubs:* Detroit, Bloomfield Hills Country, (Michigan); Princess Anne Country; Norfolk Yacht and Country; Harbor (Virginia); Sea Island Golf, Sea Palms Country (Ga.); Ocean Reef (Fla.). Lt.-Col., U.S.A.A.F. 1942–45 (Legion of Merit); Col., U.S.A.F. Res. *Address:* Sea Island, Ga. 31561, U.S.A.

**WRIGHT, John Bernard.** Australian bank officer (Ret'd). *B.* 1913. *Educ.* De La Salle Coll. (Ashfield, N.S.W.) and Sydney Univ. (BEcon); Associate, Bankers' Inst. of Australia. *M.* 1937, Gladys Nance Johnstone. *S.* Robert John and William Joseph. *Dau.* Patricia Mary. *Career:* Commercial banking, Commonwealth Bank of Australia 1929–39; Exchange Control Administration 1940–48; member, delegation to Commonwealth Finance Ministers Conference, London 1949; member, Australian delegation to GATT, Torquay 1950; seconded to Washington as Actg. Chief, Exchange Control Div., International Monetary Fund 1951–53; Actg. Secretary 1953, and Secretary 1954–57, Commonwealth Bank of Australia; Manager, Banking Dept. 1958; Adviser to the Governor, Reserve Bank of Australia 1960–64. Manager, London Branch 1962–64. Dir.. Australian Mutual Provident Soc. (N.S.W.). *Address:* 10/21 Woods Parade, Fairlight, N.S.W., Australia.

**WRIGHT, John Charles Young.** American oil and gas executive. *B.* 1925. *Educ.* Denison University (BA 1947) and Ohio State University (BS Min Eng 1949; MSc Petroleum Eng 1950). *M.* 1951, Becky Bell Lewis. *S.* John Charles Young, Jr. and William Lewis. *Dau.* Mary Carolyn. *Career:* Pres., The Ohio and Gas Association 1968—. Pres. Treasurer and Director, The Wiser Oil Company, 1961— (Vice-President 1953–61). Director, First Tyler Bank; Vice-Pres. and Dir. Kentucky Oil & Gas Assns. 1974—. *Awards:* Texnokoi—Outstanding Alumnus Award from Ohio State Univ. 1957; West Virginia Oil & Gas Man of the Year 1976. *Member:* Sigma Gamma Epsilon; Sigma Chi; Ohio Oil & Gas Assn. (Treas. and Trustee); Independent Petroleum Association of America (Director and Vice-Pres. for W.Va.); Amer. Inst. for Mining & Metallurgical Engineering; Vice Pres., W.Va. Chamber of Commerce (Northern reg.); Engineers' Cttee. for 100 from Ohio State Univ.; Ohio State Univ. Assn.; Amer. Legion; Blue Lodge Mason and member of the Shrine. *Club:* Sistersville Country. *Address:* 252 Oxford Street, Sistersville, West Va.; and *office:* Box 192 Sistersville, West Va., U.S.A.

**WRIGHT, John David.** American business executive. Chairman of Board, TRW Inc. Oct. 1958–70. Dir. 1939—. *B.* 1905. *Educ.* Western Reserve Univ., Cleveland, Ohio (BA 1927) and Western Reserve Univ. School of Law (LLB 1929). *M.* 1932, Ethel Husselman (*Dec.* 1964). *M.* (2) 1965, Bernadine Mohler. *S.* John David, Jr. *Dau.* Maude Ann (Trenholme). *Award:* Order of the Coif. With law firm of Garfield, Cross, MacGregor Daoust & Baldwin, Cleveland 1926–33. Asst. to Pres. TRW 1933–35, Secy. 1937, Secy.-Treas. 1941–43, Vice-Pres. 1943–49, General Manager 1949–53, President 1953–58. *Clubs:* Kirtland Country, Pepper Pike, Union, Country (all of Cleveland); Everglades, Bath & Tennis (Florida). *Address:* Kirkland House, Apt. 4a, 101 Worth Avenue, Palm Beach, Fla. 33480; and *office* 23555 Euclid Avenue, Cleveland, Ohio 44117, U.S.A.

**WRIGHT, Sir John Oliver,** KCMG, DSC. *B.* 1921. *Educ.* Cambridge University (MA). *M.* 1942, Marjory Osborne. *S.* 3. *Career:* Private Secretary to the Prime Minister 1963–66; to the Secretary of State for Foreign Affairs 1960–63; British Ambassador to Denmark Oct. 1966–69; United Kingdom Government Representative to the Government of Northern Ireland, 1969–70; Deputy-Under-Secretary of State and Chief Clerk Foreign & Commonwealth Office 1970–75; British Ambassador to the Federal Republic of Germany since 1975. *Club:* Travellers. *Address:* Burstow Hall, Horley, Surrey; and British Embassy, Bonn.

**WRIGHT, Sir Rowland,** CBE. British chemist and Director. *B.* 1915. *Educ.* High Pavement, Nottingham; Univ. Coll. Nottingham, BSc. (chem.), FRIC, Hon FIChemE. *M.* 1940, Kathleen Mary Hodgkinson. *S.* 2. *Dau.* 1. *Career:* Joined ICI (Dyestuffs Div.) 1937; Prod. Dir. Imperial Chemical (Pharms) Ltd. 1955–57, (Dyestuffs Div.) ICI Ltd. 1957–58; Research Dir. (Dyestuffs Div.) ICI 1958–61; Joint Man. Dir. Agricultural Div. 1961–63, Chairman 1964–65; Dir. ICI Ltd. from 1966; Personnel Dir. ICI Ltd. 1966–70, Deputy Chmn. 1971–75; Chmn. ICI 1975–78; Dir. Royal Insurance Co. from 1973, Barclays Bank Ltd. from 1977. *Fellow:* RSA 1970, BIM 1975, Inst. of Chem. Engineers (Hon.) 1975; *Pres.* Inst. of Manpower Studies 1971–77, Hon. Pres. from 1977. *Vice-Pres.* Soc. of Chem. Ind. 1971–74; *Trustee:* Civic Trust 1975; *Member:* Royal Institution 1971, Council CIA 1968–73. *Address:* ICI Ltd., Millbank, London SW1.

**WRIGLEY, William.** American. *B.* 1933. *Educ.* Yale University (BA). *M.* (1) 1957, Alison Hunter (*div.*). *S.* Philip Knight and William Jr. *Dau.* Alison Elizabeth. (2) 1970, Joan Fischer. *Career.* With Wm. Wrigley Jr. Co., Chicago, 1956— Dir. 1960—; Vice-Pres. 1960–61, Pres. and Chief Exec, Officer 1961—, Pres. and Dir. Wrigley Espana S.A., Spain, 1969—; Dir. Wm. Wrigley Jr. Co. Ltd., (Canada), 1959—; Wrigley Co. Ltd. (United Kingdom), 1959—; Wrigley Co. (New Zealand), 1960—; Wrigley Co. Pty. Ltd. (Australia), 1960—; Wrigley N.V. (The Netherland), 1962—; Wrigley Philippines, Inc., 1963—; Wrigley S.A. (France), 1963—; Wrigley Co. (H.K.) Ltd. (Hong Kong), 1969—; The Wrigley Company (East Africa) Ltd., (Kenya) 1969—; Wrigley & Company Ltd., Japan, 1970—; Dir., Chicago National League Ball Club, 1956—, Chmn. Exec. Comm. 1976—; Texaco, Inc., 1974—; National Boulevard Bank of Chicago; Dir. 1958—, mem, Exec. Comm. 1961; Dir. 1956—, Vice-Pres. and mem. Exec. Cttee. 1964—, Santa Catalina Island Co.; Dir. 1958—, Member and Dir., Wrigley Memorial Garden Foundation, 1972. Benefactor Member, Santa Catalina Island Conservancy, 1975. Dir., Northwestern Memorial Hospital, 1962—; Mem., National League of Professional Baseball Clubs 1974—. Served from Ensign to Lt. (j.-g.) U.S.N.R. on active duty in the Pacific, 1954–56; now Lt. Cdr. in Ready Reserve. *Member:* Chicago Historical Soc., Field Museum of Natural History, Art Institute of Chicago., Navy League of the United States. Wolf's Head Soc.. Delta Kappa Epsilon. *Clubs:* Chicago Yacht; Saddle and Cycle; Racquet; Tavern; Commerical (all of Chicago); Lake Geneva Country and Lake Geneva Yacht (Wis.); The Brook (N.Y.). *Address* and *office:* 410 North Michigan Avenue, Chicago, Ill. 60611, U.S.A.

**WRISTON, Walter B.** American. *B.* 1919. *Educ.* Wesleyan University (BA 1941), The Fletcher School of Law and Diplomacy (MA 1942), and Special Courses at American Institute of Banking 1946. *M.* 1942, Barbara Brengle (*Dec.*). *Dau.* Catherine B. *M.* (2) 1968, Kathryn Ann Dineen. *Career:* With Citibank: Vice-Pres. 1954, Senior Vice-Pres. 1958, Exec. Vice-Pres. 1960, Pres. 1967, Chmn. 1970; Dir. General Mills Inc. (1960–67). Director; Citibank 1967—; Pres. and Dir. Citicorp 1968; Chmn. & Dir. 1970; General Electric Co., and J. C. Penney Co.; The Chubb Corporation; Board of Visitors, Fletcher School of Law and Diplomacy; Board of Governors, New York Hospital; D.C.S.-Pace College, St. John's University; D.H.L.-Lafayette College. *Member:* Council on Foreign Relations; The Business Council, Trustee, Rand Corporation, Visiting Cttee. Harvard Univ. Graduate School of Business Administration. *Awards:* LLD Lawrence Coll; Brown Univ; Tufts Univ; Columbia University. *Clubs:* Links; River; Metropolitan (Washington, D.C.); Sky. *Address:* 870 United Nations Plaza, New York; and *office* 399 Park Avenue, New York, N.Y. 10022, U.S.A.

**WUNNERLICH, Gerhardt,** Dipl Ing. German civil engineer. *B.* 1929. *Educ.* Grammar School and Stuttgart Technical Univ. *M.* 1956, Karin Schulz zur Wiesch. *S.* 3. *Dau.* 1. *Career:* Previously: one year in practical work in Germany, and another year in the U.S.A.; Procurist Vogtlaendische Baumwollspinnerei Hof 1956–62; Mgr. Inovan-Stroebe KG Birkenfeld 1962–71; Manager Technisches Büro since 1972. *Member:* Reuchlingesellschaft Pforzheim. *Club:* Tennis (Birkenfeld). *Address:* Hegelstrasse 19, D7534 Birkenfeld. Germany.

**WURFBAIN, Johan Cornelis.** Netherlands. *B.* 1907. Former President of the Presidium of the Managing Board, Algemene Bank Nederland N.V. (General Bank of the Netherlands); Member, Supervision Bd. since 1972. *Address:* De Lairessestraat 96, Amsterdam, Netherlands.

**WYLIE, Frank Winston.** *B.* 1924. *Educ.* Harvard University (AB 1948). *M.* 1948, Martha Rockwood. *Dau.* Deborah. *Career:* With Harris Mann Associates 1946–48; Technical writer, Display Manager, Chrysler Corp. 1948–52 (Manager, New Worlds in Engineering 1953–54; Manager, Special Events, Dodge Div. 1955; Manager, Public Relations, Dodge Div. 1956–58); Director, Public Relations, Dodge Division of Chrysler Corp. 1958–71; Dir. Public Relations, U.S. Auto Sales Service, Chrysler Motor Corp, since 1975. President-elect, Public Relations Socy. of America. *Clubs:* Harvard; Detroit Press. *Address:* 390 Washington Road, Grosse Pointe, Mich. 48230; and *office* P.O. Box 1919, Detroit 31, Mich. 48288, U.S.A.

**WYLIE, Matthew John Graham,** MBE. British. *B.* 1919. *Educ.* Warriston School Moffat; Loretto School Musselburgh. *M.* Elspeth Hutton Lamberton. *S.* 2. *Dau.* 1. *Career:* Director: Anglo American Asphalt Co. Ltd., Metrotect Ltd., Ventek Ltd., Fordcombe Holdings Ltd., Tomey Industries Ltd. Dep. Chmn., Aims for Freedom & Enterprise Scottish Cttee.; Chmn., Post Office Users' Council for Scotland, Prestwick Airport Consultative Cttee. *Member:* Economic & Social Cttee. to the EEC; VAT Tribunal for Scotland; Transport Action Group; Past Chmn., CBI Council Scotland & Design Council Scottish Cttee. *Address:* Landale, Troon, Ayrshire KA10 6HD.

**WYLIE, Rt. Hon. Lord Norman Russell,** VRD, PC, QC. British. Senator of College of Justice. *B.* 1923. *Educ.* St. Edmund Hall, Oxford (Hon. Fellow 1975); and Universities of Glasgow and Edinburgh; BA (Oxon), LLB (Glas.). *M.* 1963, Gillian Mary Verney. *S.* Julian Richard, Russell Neville, Philip Verney. *Career:* Solicitor-General for Scotland April-Oct. 1964; Member of Parliament (Con.) for Pentlands 1964-74; Lord Advocate 1970-74; Privy Councillor since 1970; Senator of the College of Justice in Scotland since 1974; Member, Faculty of Advocates (1952). *Clubs:* New (Edinburgh); Royal Highland Y.C. *Address:* 30 Lauder Road, Edinburgh 9.

**WYLLIE, Robert Lyon,** CBE, DL, JP. British Chartered Accountant. *B.* 1897. *Educ.* Hermitage School (Helensburgh) and Queen's Park School (Glasgow); Fellow, Institute of Chartered Accountants. *M.* 1924, Anne Rutherford. *Daus.* Margaret Rutherford (Ross), and Anne Lyon (Sutcliffe). *Career:* Served in World War I( Yeomanry; France) 1915–18. Director: West Coast Tanneries Ltd.; Ashley Accessories Ltd.; Perm. Vice-Pres., Cumberland Development Council Ltd. *Address:* The Cottage, Papcastle, Cockermouth, Cumberland.

**WYNDHAM WHITE, Sir Eric,** KCMG. British. *B.* 1914. *Educ.* LLB University of London; member of the English Bar. *M.* 1947, Tina Gibson Thayer. *Daus.* Ann and Carolyn. *Career:* Member Law & Commerce Faculty, London School of Economics 1936–39; varied service with U.K. Govt. 1940–45; Special Assistant to European Director of UNRRA 1945; Secy.-Gen., Emergency Economic Committee for Europe 1946; Exec. Secy., Preparatory Committee for the International Trade Organization 1946, of UN Conference on Trade and Employment 1947, and of General Agreement on Tariffs and Trade 1948–65, Director-General 1965–68. LDL University of California; LLD (h.c) Dartmouth College; Doctor rerum publicarum, School of Economics, Business & Public Administration, St. Gall, Switzerland. Member Société Royale d'Economie Politique de Belgique. *Club:* Reform (London). *Address:* Case Postale 470, 1200 Geneva 3 Rive, Switzerland.

**WYNER, Justin Lawrence.** American executive. President Shawmut Mills, Division of R. H. Wyner Associates, Inc., Stoughton, Mass. *B.* 1925. *Educ:* Tufts Univ. (BS *cum laude*) and Harvard Graduate School of Business Administration (MBA). *M.* 1955, Genevieve Gloria Geller. *S.* George Michael, Daniel Mark, and James Henry. *Career:* Has been with present manufacturing organizations since graduating from Harvard Business School in 1948. Elected member of Town meeting, Brookline, Mass., 1950–70; Elected Moderator Town of Brookline, 1970—. Hon. Director, Underwear Institute. Past Chairman, Advisory Committee of Thirty (Finance Committee), Brookline; Chairman, Brookline United Fund 1960 Campaign; Mem., Amer. Assn. of Textile Technologists; Trustee: Combined Jewish Philanthropies; Temple Israel, Boston, Mass.; Hebrew Teachers College; Beth Israel Hospital; Temple Kehillath, Israel, Past Pres. President, Harvard-Radcliffe Hillel; Hillel Council of Metropolitan Boston; Past Pres. Jewish Comm. Council of Metropolitan Boston. *Member:* American Radio Relay League. *Clubs:* Belmont Country; Harvard (Boston and N.Y.C.) Rising Star Lodge (A.F. & A.M.). *Address:* 33 Martha's Lane, Chestnut Hill, Mass. 02167, U.S.A.

# Y

**YALE, Harry Louis.** American. Research chemist in field of medicinal chemistry. *B.* 1913. *Educ.* Univ. of Illinois (BSc Chem 1937), and Iowa State Univ. (PhD Organic Chem. 1940). *M.* 1948, Minnie Panter. *Daus.* Louise, Arlene Dina and Suzanne Iva. *Career:* With National Defense Research Cttee., Manhattan Project 1940–42; Shell Development Co., Emeryville, Calif. 1942–46; Squibb Inst. of Medical Research 1946—. Senior Research Fellow, Squibb Institute for Medical Research, New Brunswick, N.J. since 1959. *Publications:* approximately 125 scientific publications in Journal of the American Society, American Review of Tuberculosis, Journal of Medicinal & Pharmaceutical Chemistry. Member, Editorial Board, Organic Chemistry; three chapters in Pyridine (Interscience Series on Heterocyclic Compounds); article on Drugs Affecting the Mental State in Encyclopedia of Chemistry. Inventor or co-inventor of about 180 U.S. patents, and many foreign patents. Member of group at Squibb Institute responsible for discovery of Isoniazid for treatment of tuberculosis. *Award:* The Lasker Award for the discovery. *Member:* Sigma Xi; Phi Lambda Upsilon; Amer. Chemical Socy.; Swiss Chemical Society; Sigma X; New York Academy of Sciences. *Address:* 4 New York Avenue, New Brunswick, N.J.; and *office* Squibb Institute for Medical Research, Lawrenceville, N.J. 08540, U.S.A.

**YAMANI, Ahmed Zaki.** Saudi Arabian politician. *B.* 1930. *Educ.* Cairo Univ.; New York and Harvard University. *M.* Laila Sulleiman Faidhi. *S.* Hani. *Daus.* Mai and Maha. *Career:* Saudi Arabian Govt. Service, Private Law Practice; Legal Adviser to Council of Ministers 1958–60; Minister of State 1960–62; Minister, Petroleum and Mineral Resources since 1962; Dir. Arabian American Oil Co. since 1962; Chmn. Bd. Dirs. General Petroleum and Mineral Organization since 1963; Chmn. Bd. of Trustees, Coll. of Petroleum and Minerals, Dhahran since 1963; Saudi Arabian Fertiliser Co. (SAFCO) since 1966; Sec. Gen. Arab Petroleum Exporting Countries (OAPEC) 1968–69, Chmn. 1974–75. *Publications:* Islamic Law and Contemporary Issues. *Address:* Ministry of Petroleum and Mineral Resources, Riyadh, Saudi Arabia.

**YAMAOKA, George.** American lawyer. *B.* 1903. *Educ.* University of Washington, and Georgetown University (JD). *M.* 1933, Henriette d'Auriac. *Dau.* Colette Miyoko (Sonderegger). *Career:* Japanese Government Commission, Philadelphia Sesquicentennial Exposition 1926; Adviser, Japanese Consulate-General 1928–30; Adviser, Japanese Delegation, London Naval Conferences 1929–30. Admitted N.Y. Bar 1931, and Japanese Bar 1949. Associate, Hunt Hill & Betts 1930–40 (Partner 1940–56); Senior Partner: Hill, Betts, Yamaoka & Logan, Tokyo 1956–60, and Hill, Betts & Nash 1956–60. Chairman of American Defence, Supreme Commander Allied Powers, International Military Tribunal for Far East (Tojo and other Class A War Crimes) 1946–49. Adv. Panel Int. Law, U.S. Dept. of State; Senior Partner, Hill, Betts, Yamaoka, Freehill & Longcope, New York and Tokyo, 1960–70; Hill Betts & Nash since 1970. Secy. and Dir., Bank of Tokyo Trust Co., New York City; Pres. and Dir., Nippon Kogaku (U.S.A.) Inc. Director: Okura & Co., New York Inc.; Chairman Board of Directors, Yasuda Fire & Marine Insurance Co. Dir. Japan Society Inc., N.Y.; and Japanese Chamber of Commerce Inc., N.Y.C. *Award:* Third Order of Sacred Treasure, Japanese Government, 1968. *Member:* American and Federal Bar Associations; Association of Bar of City of N.Y.; N.Y. County Lawyers Association; N.Y. State Bar Association; American Bar Association; Consular Law Society; American Foreign Law Assn.; Intl. Law Assn.; World Law Center; Maritime Law Assn. U.S.; Federal Bar Assn.; First Bar Assn., Tokyo. *Clubs:* Bankers, Marco Polo, World Trade Center Club, Downtown Athletic; American (Tokyo); Hodogaya Country, Kasumigaseki Country (Japan). *Address:* 24 Gramercy Park, New York, N.Y. 10003; and *office* World Trade Center, New York, N.Y. 10048, U.S.A.

**YAMÉOGO, Maurice.** Upper Voltan Politician. *B.* 1921. Member of the Grand Council of French West Africa 1948– 52; Minister of Agriculture, Upper Volta 1957–58, of the Interior 1958; Prime Minister 1958–60; President. Council of Ministers 1959–66 & Pres. of the Republic 1960–66; Minister of Defence 1965–66; Imprisoned 1969, released 1970. *Address:* c/o Rassemblement Démocratique Africain, Ouagadougou, Republic of Upper Volta.

**YANCEY, Robert Earl.** American. *B.* 1921. *Educ.* Marshall University, Huntington, West Virginia (BES). *M.* 1941, Mary Estelline Tackett. *S.* Robert Earl. Jr. *Dau.* Mrs. Susan Yancey Farmer. *Career:* Pres. Ashland Oil, the parent Co. of, Ashland Petroleum, Ashland Chemical, Ashland Resources, Ashland Exploration, Ashland Oil Canada, Ashland Oil International. Past Pres., National Petroleum Refiners Assn., member Bd. 1972; Bd. of Dirs. American Petroleum Institute; Pres. member Bd. Dirs. Ashland Oil Incoroorated since 1972. *Address: office* Ashland Oil Inc., P.O. Box 391, Ashland, Kentucky 41101, U.S.A.

**YANKOV, Alexander.** Bulgarian diplomat. *B.* 1924. *Educ* Sofia Univ. Law School; Hague Academy of International Law. *M.* 1949, Elza Vartanova. *S.* 1. *Dau.* 1. *Career:* Asst· Professor, Int. Law Sofia Univ. 1951–54; Secy. Int. Union, Students (Prague) 1954–57; Senior Asst. Prof. International Law 1957–64; Attended Hague Academy, Int. Law 1961; Assoc. Prof. Int. Law Sofia Univ. 1964; Counsellor Bulgaria's Mission to U.N.A. 1965–68; Prof. Int. Law Sofia Univ. 1968—; Ambassador of the People's Republic of Bulgaria to the United Kingdom 1972–76; Pres. 8th Session, Assembly of IMCO 1973; Chmn. Third Main Cttee. UN Conference, Law of the Sea. Caracas 1974, Geneva 1975; Ambassador & Perm. Rep. to the UN since 1976. *Member:* Court of Arbitration Bulgarian Chamber, Commerce; Permanent Court, Arbitration, The Hague; Vice Chmn. U.N. Cttee. Peaceful Uses of the Sea-bed; member, Nat. Union, Bulgarian Lawyers; Int. Law Assn.; Amer. Socy. Int. Law. *Publications:* The European Collective Security System (1958); The United Nations, Legal Status and International Personality (1965); Exploration and Uses of the Sea-bed, A new Legal Framework (1970); The United Nations and the development of the International Trade Law (1971); The United Nations Declarations on the Principles of Friendly Relations and the Progressive Development of International Law (1971), and many others. *Address:* 11 East 84th Street, New York, N.Y. 10028, U.S.A.

**YANO, Ichiro.** Japanese. *B.* 1899. *Educ.* Tokyo Imperial University (BS). *M.* 1924, Hatsuko Ikuta. *Daus.* Mariko Akiguchi, Teiko Takashima and Yuko Sato. *Career:* With Mitsubishi Bank Ltd. 1924–32; Dai-ichi Mutual Life Ins. Co. 1932— (Dir. 1941. Pres. 1947, Chmn. of Bd. 1959, Dir. and Advisor 1970, Advisor 1977—). Chmn. of Board of Governors, N.H.K. (Japan Broadcasting Corp.) 1950–56; Dir. Odakyu Electric Railway, Co. 1951—; Kyowa Hakko Kogyo Co. 1952—; Imperial Hotel 1956—; Tokyu Corporation 1960—; Tokyo Electric Power Co. 1975—; (Dir. 1951–62; Auditor 1962–75); Hon. member, Fed. of Economic Organizations (Dir. 1948–70). Hon. Adviser: Life Insurance Assn. of Japan (Chmn. 1951–59); N.H.K. Welfare Cultural Center (social work) (Chmn.); Japan-Sweden Socy. (Hon. mem., Pres. 1965–74); American Studies Foundation (Dir., Chmn. 1964–74); Cardiovascular Research Inst. (Hon. Counsellor, Chmn. 1959–74, Dir. 1974–77); Community Study Foundation (Chmn.); Japan Inst. of Human Posture Research (Chmn.); *Publications:* Dongri Cho (essays); The Beginners Book of the Bushido (edited). *Clubs:* Nippon (Vice-Pres. & Director), Japan Industrial (auditor), University (auditor); Rotary (Tokyo). *Address:* 39–3, 3-chome, Denenchofu, Ota-ku, Tokyo 145; and *office* 1-chome, Yurakucho, Chioda-ku, Tokyo, 100, Japan.

**YANO, Prof. Kentaro.** Japanese. *B.* 1912. *Educ.* Tokyo Univ. (DSc) and Univ. of Paris (Doctor). *M.* Yukako. *S.* Teiichi and Junji; Prof. Emeritus Department of Mathematics, Tokyo Institute of Technology. *Member:* Mathematical Society of Japan; American Mathematical Society. *Publications:* Curvature and Betti numbers; The theory of Lie derivatives and its applications; Differential geometry on complex and almost complex spaces; Iotegral formulas in Riemannian geometry; Tangent and cotangent bundles; Differential geometry; Anti-invariant submanifolds. *Address:* 1-31-10, Kaminakazato, Kita-ku, Tokyo, 114; and *office* Department of Mathematics, Tokyo Institute of Technology, Ohokayama, Meguro-ku, Tokyo, 152, Japan.

**YAP, Dr. Diosdado Maurillo.** Philippines. Lecturer, editor, publisher, professor, economist and business executive; *B.* 1907. *Educ.* AA; AB; BS; MA; MS; LLB; LLD; PhD; EdD. *M.* 1934, Margaret Mitchell. *S.* Diosdado Jr. *Career:* Expert Consultant, U.S. Secretary of War; Publicity Director, Philippine Government, and Director, Philippine Information Bureau; Chairman, Philippine Chamber of Commerce (Bd. of Directors); President, Bataan Foundation Inc., and Capital Publishers Inc.; Editor and Publisher: Know Your Congress; Know the United States of America; Know Your Country; Congressional Club Directory; Facts About Our Presidents; The Flags of Our 50 States; The Constitution and Its Framers; What Now for Free China?; How The President is Elected; Congress Illustrated; Pledge of Allegiance To The Flag; Our Nation's Capital; Congress At Work; Pictorial Guide of the United States Capitol; Editor and Publisher, The Asian World; Chief, Washington Bureau, The Manila Chronicle; feature writer, The Evening News and The Weekly Nation of Manila; Congress Speaks On Nixons Visit to China. *Publications:* The Asian World; Philippine-American Affairs; History of Higher Education in the Philippines, etc. *Member:* Golf Writers Assn.; Congressional Press Gallery; White House Correspondents Association. *Club:* Bethesda Golf & Country (Mem. Board Dirs. and Exec. Cttee.); National Pres; Variety. *Address:* 5306 Belt Road, Chevy Chase, E. Washington, D.C. 20015, U.S.A.

**YARBOROUGH, Hon. Ralph Webster.** American Attorney-at-Law. *B.* 1903. *Educ.* Univ. of Texas Law School (LLB with highest honours). *M.* 1928, Opal Warren. *S.* Richard Warren. *Career:* Asst. Attorney-General of Texas 1931–34; Member: Original Board of Directors of Lower Colorado River Authority 1935–36; District Judge of 53rd Judicial District of Texas 1936–41 (and for three years Presiding Judge, 3rd Administrative Judicial District of Texas).

Member, Board of Law Examiners 1947–51. Former Senator from Texas (elected April 1957–71); Commissioner Texas Constitution Revision since 1973. *Awards:* Hon. DHL, Lincoln College; Hon. Fellow, Post-Graduate Centre for Mental Health, N.Y. City; Order of the Coif; Hon. Doctor of Laws, St. Edwards Univ. Austin Texas. *Member:* Senate Committee on Appropriations; Chairman, Senate Labor and Public Welfare Committee. Labour Sub-Committee; Health Sub-Committee Senate Office and Civil Service Committee. Member: Travis County, El Paso and American Bar Associations; State Bar of Texas (former Director); American Law Institute. Democrat. *Publications:* Lincoln as Liberal Statesman (essay in Lincoln for the Ages, 1959); Sam Houston—Giant on a Postage Stamp (speech in Texas Avenue at Main Street, 1964); foreword to Three Men in Texas (1967); Frank Dobie: Man and Friend, The Great Western Series, No. 1, Potomac Corral, The Westerners, Washington D.C. (1967). *Clubs:* Town and Gown; Phi Del Phi. Delegate, Interparliamentary Union Conferences: Brazil, 1962; Ireland, 1965; Australia, 1966; Iran, 1966; Spain, 1967; Peru, 1968; Austria, 1969; India, 1969; The Hague Netherlands, 1970. *Address:* 2527 Jarratt Avenue, Austin, Texas 78703; and *office* 721 Brown Building, Austin, Texas, U.S.A.

**YAREMKO, John.** Canadian, *B.* 1918. *Educ.* University of Toronto (BA), called to Bar, Osgoode Hall Law School. *M.* 1945, Mary A. Materyn. *Career:* Minister without portfolio 1958; Minister of Transport 1958; Provincial Secretary 1960; Provincial Secretary and Minister of Citizenship 1961; Minister of Public Welfare 1966 (re-named Social & Family Services in 1967); Solicitor General 1972–74; Government of the Province of Ontario, Canada Q.C; Hon LLD: Chmn., Liquor Licence Appeal Tribunal. *Member:* York County Bar Assn.; Toronto Lawyers Club; Canadian Bar Assn. *Clubs:* Canadian; Empire; Commonwealth. *Address:* 1 Connable Drive, Toronto 4, Ontario, Canada; and *office* 1 St. Clair Avenue W., Toronto, Ont., Canada.

**YARROW, Sir Eric G.,** Bt, MBE. British. *B.* 1920. *Educ.* Marlborough College and Glasgow University. *M.* (1) 1951, Rosemary Ann Young (*D.* 1957) and (2) 1959, Annette Elizabeth Françoise Steven (*Div.* 1975). *S.* Richard Grant, Norman Murray, Peter Harold (twin) and David Eric. *Career:* Asst. Mgr. 1946, Dir. 1948, Man. Dir. 1958–67, Yarrow & Co. Ltd. Chairman, Yarrow & Co. Ltd., Scotstoun, Glasgow 1962—Yarrow (Shipbuilders) Ltd. 1967—; Director: Yarrow (Africa) (Holdings) (Pty.) Ltd. 1949—, Clydesdale Bank Ltd. since 1962 & Dpty Jt. Chmn. since 1975, Standard Life Assurance Co. 1958—, Croftinloan (Holdings) Ltd., 1959—; Chairman, Y-ARD (Australia) Pty. Ltd., 1968—. Yarrow Engineers (Glasgow) Ltd., 1969—; Yarrow Admiralty Research Dept. Ltd., since 1969; Hon. Vice-Pres. Royal Institution of Naval Architects. *Member:* General Cttee. of Lloyd's Register of Shipping; Court of Worshipful Company of Shipwrights; Merchants House; Incorporation of Hammermen (Past Deacon) retired Member of Council of Institution of Engineers & Shipbuilders in Scotland; Prime Warden of Worshipful Co. of Shipwrights 1970—71. *Clubs:* Army & Navy; Royal Scottish Automobile. *Address:* Cloak, Kilmacolm, Renfrewshire; and *office* Yarrow & Co. Ltd., Scotstoun, Glasgow, G14 0XD.

**YASSEIN, Mohamed Osman.** Sudanese International Government Official *B.* 1915. *Educ.* Khartoum Sch. of Admin.; London Sch. of Economics. *Career:* Joined Sudanese Government Service 1933; Administrative & Political Service 1942; Liaison Officer, Ethiopia 1951–52; Governor, Upper Nile Province 1953–55; Perm. Under. Sec. for Foreign Affairs 1956–65; UN cons. with ECA 1966; UN Special Adviser to the Govt. of Zambia on Civil Service Structure 1966–67; UN Special Adviser on Public Administration, S. Yemen 1968–69, Yemen Arab Republic 1969; Resident Rep., UN Development Program, Amman, Jordan 1969, Chmn., Bd. of Dirs., Sudan Commercial Bank 1975; Delegate to numerous Public Administration Conferences in Africa; Near East etc. *Decorations:* Knight Gt. Band of Human, Order African Redemption (Liberia); Grand Officer, Order of Menelik II; Republican Order of Egypt; Star of Yugoslavia, Independence Order (Jordan). *Publications:* numerous Books & Articles on Social & Economic Development. *Address:* P.O. Box 2201, Khartoum, Sudan; & *office* Sudan Commercial Bank, P.O. Box 1116, Khartoum, Sudan.

**YEH, George Kung-chao.** Chinese statesman and diplomat. *B.* 20 Oct. 1904. *Educ.* Amherst College, Massachusetts (BA), LLD and Cambridge Univ. (MA). *M.* 1930, Edna Yun-hsi Yuan. *S.* Max Wei. *Dau.* Marian T'ung. *Career:* Professor of English, National Peking Univ. 1926–27. National Chinan University 1927–29, National Tsing Hua University 1929–35; National Peking University 1935–39; Dir., British Malaya Office (1940–41) and United Kingdom Office, Chinese Ministry of Information 1942–46; Counsellor and concurrently Director of European Affairs Department, Ministry of Foreign Affairs 1946–47; Administrative Vice-Minister for Foreign Affairs 1947–49; Amb. Ex. on special mission to Burma Dec. 1947; Political Vice-Minister of Foreign Affairs 1949; Minister of Foreign Affairs 1949–58; Ambassador to U.S.A. 1958–61; Cabinet Minister without portfolio 1961—; Chmn., Chinese Delegation to several Sessions of U.N. Gen. Assembly, and to the Commemorative Session of 10th Anniversary of U.N. 1955; member, Royal Asiatic Society, London. *Awards:* Special Grand Cordon, Order of Brilliant Star, and of Propitious Clouds (China); Caballero, Grand Cross of Civil Merits (Spain), Grand Cordon of Liberator (Venezuela); Grand Cross of Civil Merits, Manuel de Cespedes (Cuba); Grand Officer of Merits (Chile); Grand Cross of Merit (Ecuador); Knight, Grand Cross 1st Class of the White Elephant (Thailand), etc., LLD (Hon) Seoul University. *Publications:* Social Forces in English Literature; Introducing China; The Concept of Jen, etc. *Address:* The Executive Yuan, Tapei, Taiwan.

**YENKO, Mariano A., Jr.** Filipino. Colonel, Judge Advocate General Service, Armed Forces of the Philippines (Res.). *B.* 1917. *Educ.* AB; LLB. *M.* 1943, Josefa Filart. *S.* José, Ignatius, Robert and Francis. *Daus.* Luisa, Milagros. Lourdes, Dulce and Marie. *Career:* Chief, National War Crimes Office, July 1948; Asst. Exec. Secretary, Office of the President of the Philippines, Dec. 1953; Under-Secy. of National Defence, Aug. 1957. Vice-President and Corporate Secretary, Philippine Lines Inc., since 1962. Served in World War II (all decorations and awards to USAFFE Personnel in Pacific Theatre). *Member:* Philippine Bar; Philippine Assn. of Judge Advocates: Bd. of Trustees, R. Magsaysay Memorial Soc., Mother Rosa Memorial Soc., Atteneo Alumni Assn. (Past Pres.). *Club:* Kiwanis, Makati (Past Pres.). *Address:* 28 Eisenhower Street, Green Hills, San Juan, Rizal; and *office* PAL Building, Ayala Avenue, Makati, Rizal, Philippines.

**YNTEMA, Theodore Otte.** American. Visiting professor, Oakland University; Business consultant; Xenex Corp. *B.* 1900. *Educ.* Hope College, Holland, Mich. (AB *summa cum laude* 1921; Hon ScD 1960); University of Illinois (AMChem 1922), University of Chicago (AM 1924; PhDEcon 1929); Harvard (economic studies 1926–27). *M.* 1923, Kathryn Elizabeth van der Veen. *S.* John Arend. *Dau.* Elizabeth Yntema Alfvin. *M.* (2) 1939, Mrs. Virginia Heigho Payne. *S.* Theodore Otte, Jr. *Dau.* Virginia Gwin. CPA Illinois 1924, Hon LLD: Grinnell Coll., Franklin, Marshall College, Central Michigan University. *Career:* Successively Instructor in accounting, Prof. Statistics, Prof. Business and Economic Policy 1923–49, Univ. of Chicago. Dir. Research, Cowles Commission 1939–42; Actg. Assoc. Prof. Statistics, Stanford Univ. 1929–30; Economic Consultant N.R.A. 1934–35; Economist, Chief Statistician, Div. Industrial Materials, Defense Commission 1940; Special Consultant, War Shipping Admin. 1942, and E.S.A. 1951; Consulting Economist various companies 1933–49 and 1965—; Research Director CED 1942–49; Vice-Pres., 1949–65, and Director 1950–65, Ford Motor Company. Trustee: Committee for Economic Development. Director, National Bureau of Economic Research; National Industrial Conference Board. Fellow: American Academy of Arts and Sciences; American Assn. for Advancement of Science; Amer. Statistical Assn.; Econometric Socy. *Member:* Amer. Economic Assn.; Amer. Inst. of C.P.A.s; Council on Foreign Relations; Inst. of Mathematical Statistics; Mont Pelerin Socy. *Publications:* A Mathematical Re-formulation of the General Theory of International Trade (1932); co-author: Jobs and Markets (1946). *Clubs:* The Detroit; Detroit Athletic; Bloomfield Hills Country; Bloomfield Open Hunt; Recess. *Address: office* Dept. of Economics, Oakland Univ. Rochester, Mich. 48063, U.S.A.

**YOCOM, John Henry.** Canadian. *B.* 1911. *Educ.* Univ. of Toronto (BA—Hons English and History) and Univ. of Ottawa (MA; PhD); York University (MBA). *M.* 1940, Helen Doris Dolan. *S.* John J. and Paul A. *Dau.* Mary Anne. *Career:* On Staff, Ottawa Collegiate 1934–39, Malvern Collegiate, Toronto 1939–41; freelance writer. With R.C.A.F., Canada, U.K. and Europe (discharged with rank of Flt. Lieut.) 1941–45. Assoc. Editor and Asst. Managing Editor, Saturday Night 1945–49, Managing Editor 1949–53. Manager, Public Relations, Gulf Oil Canada Ltd. 1953–76; Director, Ontario Chamber of Commerce 1961, and Canadian Public Relations Society 1959; 1st Vice-President 1964. National

President 1965–66) .Member: Public Relations Committee, Canadian Manufacturers' Association 1957; Judging Committee, National Newspaper Awards 1950. *Member:* American Petroleum Institute; Canadian Public Relations Society Toronto (Pres. 1959–60); Public Relations Society of America (Assemblyman 1969—); Canadian Legion; Royal Canadian Military Inst. Progressive Conservative. *Publications:* articles in Canadian magazines; and (book) Music Appreciation and Enjoyment (Ryerson Press, 2 vols.). Director, Toronto Symphony Orchestra Association since 1966; Director, National Youth Orchestra, 1975; Vice-Chairman, Metro Toronto United Appeal (1968). *Clubs:* Arts & Letters Club (Pres. 1967–69); Toronto Men's Press; University (Toronto); Canadian Club of Toronto, Dir. since 1969; Pres. 1976–77. *Address:* 25 Munro Boulevard, Willowdale, Ontario; and *office* 800 Bay Street, Toronto, Ontario, Canada.

**YOH, Harold Lionel.** American. *B.* 1907. *Educ.* Wharton School, University of Penn. (BScEcon 1929); Doctor of Engineering (Honorary) PMC Colleges Chester Pa., 1969. *M.* (1) 1934, Katherine Hulme, and (2) 1949, Margaret Krieble (both *Dec.*). *S.* 3. *Daus.* 2; (3) 1967, Mary Catherine O'Hey Pickering. *Career:* Mr. Yoh founded H. L. Yoh Co. 1943, and has directed its development to its present staff of over 1000 engineers and technicians in the electrical, mechanical, civil, structural and architectural fields, and has completed projects for over 500 companies and government agencies. In 1961 he acquired Day & Zimmermann Inc. and later Barrington & Co. His interests now employ approximately 8000 personnel; Former Chmn. of Board, Pres. and Chief Exec. Officer, Day & Zimmermann Inc. (International Engineers Constructors and Consultants to Management). Philadelphia, and its Divisions: Engineering and Construction Division; H. L. Yoh Company Division; Consulting Services Division; Plant Operations Division; Electric Line Construction Division; Real Estate Services Division. Member: Board of Directors, Continental Bank & Trust Co. *Member:* Alpha Tau Omega; Navy League U.S.; Amer. Socy. Military Engineers; American Defense Preparedness Assn.; Amer. Air Force Association. *Clubs:* Metropolitan (Washington and N.Y.C.); Merion Golf (Ardmore, Pa.); Radnor Hunt (Malvern, Pa.); Everglades, Bath & Tennis (Palm Beach, Fla); Netherlands Society of Philadelphia; Beach (Palm Beach. Fla.); The Philadelphia Country (Gladwyn, Pa.). *Address:* 341 Peruvian Avenue, Palm Beach, Florida, U.S.A.

**YORAN, Calvin S.** American chemist. *B.* 1908. *Educ.* University of Chicago (BS 1930; PhD 1933). *M.* 1935, Isabel Lange. *Career:* Chief Chemist, Featheridge Rubber Co., Chicago 1933–43, and Witco Chemical Co., Chicago (in charge of Research & Development Laboratory for supply of raw materials to rubber, paint, ink and plastics industries) 1942–44; Research Director, Director of Corp., Vice-President, Sponge Rubber & Plastic Foams, Brown Rubber Co., Lafayette, Inc. 1944–58; Technical Director, Dryden Rubber Division, Sheller Manufacturing Corp., Keokuk, Iowa 1958; Vice-President, Research and Development, American Rubber & Plastics Corp., La Porte Ind., July 1960–62. (Research and Development Manager, Brown Rubber Works, Thermoid Division H. K. Porter Co., Inc. (Ret. 1971). Vice-President and Technical Director, Brown Rubber Co. Lafayette, Indiana. *Publications:* Engineering with Sponge Rubber (1948); Vinyl Foam (with Robert J. Stockman, 1959); Tall Oil Esters as Plasticizers for GR-S (with W. I. Harber, 1945); Witcogum—A New Chemurgic Elastomer (with W. I. Harber, H. F. Schwartz and S. G. Armato, 1943). *Member:* Amer. Chemical Society; American Society for Testing Materials; Society of Automotive Engineers. *Club:* Elks; Rotary; Lafayette Country. *Address:* 1110 Eton Street, West Lafayette, Indiana 47906. U.S.A.

**YORK, Archbishop of,** Most Rev. and Rt. Hon. Stuart Yarworth Blanch. PC. British. *B.* 1918. *Educ.* Alleyn's School, Dulwich; St. Catherine's Coll. Oxford, BA (1st Cl Th.) MA; Wycliffe Hall, Oxford. *M.* 1943, Brenda Coyte. *S.* 1. *Daus.* 4. *Career:* Curate at Highfield 1949–52; Vicar at Eynsham 1952–57; Tutor and Vice-Principal, Wycliffe Hall Theological College 1957–60; Oriel Canon of Rochester Cathedral 1960–66; Warden, Rochester Theological College 1960–66; Bishop of Liverpool 1966–75; Archbishop of York since 1975; Pro-Chancellor Hull Univ. since 1975. *Chairman:* Wycliffe Hall Theological College; Standing Conference of Theol. Colls. and of Post-ordination training Cttee. of Advisory Council for the Church's Ministry. *Member:* Council of Liverpool University 1966–75; Council of York Univ. 1976—. *Awards:* Privy Councillor; Hon. LLD Liverpool Univ. 1975; Hon. DD Hull Univ. 1977. *Publications:* The World our Orphanage (1972); For All Mankind (1976). *Club:* Royal C'wealth Socy. *Address:* Bishopthorpe, York YO2 1QE.

**YORSTON, Sir Keith,** CBE, OBE, BComm, FCA, FASA, FCIS, Hon.FAIM. *B.* 1902. *Career:* in practice Chartered Accountant, Sydney 1933–70; Principal Australian Accountancy Coll. 1933–66; Chmn. Presbyterian Property Trust (NSW) 1964–75; Pres. (NSW) Australian-America Assn. 1957–63, 1965–75; Fellow, Inst. Chartered Accountants in Australia; Aust. Socy. of Accountants; Aust. Inst. of Management; Chartered Inst. Secretaries. Delivered Annual Research Lecure Aust. Socy. Accounts, at Universities of Sydney 1951, Western Aust. 1952, Tasmania 1953, Melbourne 1959. Represented Aust. 7th Int. Congress of Accounts. Amsterdam 1957; 11th Int. Congress Inst. of Management Paris 1957; 8th Int. Congress Accounts. New York 1962. Founded, Junior Aust. Amer. Assn. Sydney 1958, founded Aust-Amer. Assn. Canberra 1962, Hobart 1963. Guest Lect. 1960 Jubilee Convention N.Z. Society 1959. *Member:* Bd. Scottish Hospital Sydney; Adv. Bd. Presbyterian Foundation. *Publications:* Australian Mercantile Law; Advanced Accounting; Australian Company Director: Australian Commercial Dictionary; Australian Shareholders' Guide; Company Law; Twentieth Century Commerce and Bookkeeping; Accounting Fundamentals; Company Secretary's Guide (N.S.W.); Proprietary and Private Companies in Australia and many others. *Address:* 29 Trafalgar Avenue, Roseville, N.S.W., Australia.

**YOUDE, Sir Edward,** KCMG, MBE. British Diplomat. *B.* 1924. *Educ.* Penarth County Sch.; Sch. of Oriental & African Studies, Univ. of London. *M.* 1951, Pamela Fitt. *Daus.* 2. *Career:* RNVR 1943–46; entered Foreign Office 1947; 3rd Sec., Nanking & Peking 1948–51; Foreign Office 1951; 2nd Sec., Peking 1953–55; 1st Sec., Washington 1956–59; Peking 1960–61; Foreign Office 1962–65; Counsellor & Head of Chancery, UK Mission to UN, New York 1965–69; Private Sec. (Overseas Affairs) to Prime Minister 1969–70; Imperial Defence Coll. 1970–71; Head of Personnel Services Dept., FCO 1971; Asst. Under-Sec. of State, FCO 1973–74; HM Ambassador to People's Republic of China since 1974. *Decorations:* Knight Commander, Order of St. Michael & St. George, 1977; Member of the British Empire, 1949. *Club:* Travellers'. *Address:* 35 Edge Hill, Wimbledon Common, London SW19; and *office* c/o Foreign & Commonwealth Office, King Charles Street, London, SW1A 2AH.

**YOUNG, Andrew.** American politician. *B.* 1932. *Educ.* Howard Univ.; Hartford Theological Seminary. *M.* 1954, Jean Childs. *S.* 1. *Daus.* 3. *Career:* Ordained to ministry, Congregational Church 1955, pastor in Thomasville, Georgia 1955–57; Assoc. Dir. for Youth Work, Nat. Council of Churches 1957–61; organiser for civil rights movement; Administrator, Christian Education Program , United Church of Christ 1961–64; Staff, Southern Christian Leadership Conf. 1961–70, Exec. Dir. 1964–70, Exec. Vice-Pres. 1967–70, currently Dir.; mem. U.S. House of Reps. 1972, re-elected 1974, 1976; appointed U.S. Perm. Rep. to the U.N. Jan. 1977. *Address:* Permanent Mission of the United States to the U.N., 799 U.N. Plaza, New York, N.Y. 10017, U.S.A.

**YOUNG, Douglas M.** Canadian. *B.* 1912. *M.* 1935, Phyllis Elizabeth Brett. *Career:* Chief of Personnel, I.L.O., Geneva, Jan. 1953–Aug. 1957 (Director, Canada Branch, Sept. 1957–60). Previously in industrial relations in Canadian industry; Chmn., Hay Associates Canada Limited, Management Consultants, Toronto; Partner, Hay Associates, Philadelphia. *Address:* The Toronto Dominion Centre, P.O. Box 13, Toronto M5K 1A1, Ont., Canada.

**YOUNG, Sir George,** MP. British Politician. *B.* 1941. *Educ.* Eton; Christ Church, Oxford. *M.* 1964, Aurelia Nemon-Stuart. *S.* 2. *Daus.* 2. *Career:* Economist, National Economic Development Office 1966–67; Kobler Research Fellow, Univ. of Surrey 1967–69; Councillor, Lambeth Borough Council 1968–71; Economic Adviser, Post Office Corp. 1969–74; Mem., Greater London Council 1970–73; Chmn., Acton Housing Assn. 1972—; Conservative MP for Ealing, Acton since 1974. *Publications:* Accommodation Services in the UK 1970–80 (1970); Tourism, Blessing or Blight ? (1973). *Address:* Formosa Place, Cookham, Berks. SL6 9QT; and House of Commons, London SW1A 0AA.

**YOUNG, George Berkeley.** American. *B.* 1913. *Educ.* Yale (BA 1934; MA 1937; PhD 1939) and Northwestern University Law School (JD 1948). *M.* 1944, Mary Seymour Adams. *S.* George A. *Dau.* Mary B. *Career:* Chmn. Field Enterprises

Inc. 1964–68: Member Bd. of Dirs. Chrysler Corporation CNA Income Shares Inc. & Industrial Nucleonics Corp. *Member:* Chicago Bar Assn. *Publications:* Politics, Strategy and American Diplomacy—Studies in Foreign Policy 1873–1917 (with J. A. S. Grenville). Hon DHL (MacMurray Coll.); 1966; Hon. LLD (Lake Forest Coll.) 1967. *Clubs:* Brook, Century, Yale (N.Y.C.); The Chicago (Chicago). *Address:* 2430 Lakeview Avenue, Chicago, Ill. 60614; and *office* 410 North Michigan Avenue, Chicago, Ill. 60611, U.S.A.

**YOUNG, John Donald.** Assistant Secretary Management & Budget, Dept. of Health, Education & Welfare 1977. *B.* 1919. *Educ.* Colgate Univ. (BA Soc Sc—Hons); Syracuse University (MS Publ Admin); American Univ. (PhD). *M.* Laura Virginia Gwathmey. *S.* John Hardin. *Dau.* Becky Ann. *Career:* Member President's Task Force on Cost Reduction 1964. Dir of Management Analysis, Office of Admin., NASA 1960–61; Adviser to the Director, Peace Corps; Associate, Senior Consultant, Principal, McKinsey & Co. 1954–60; Exec. Officer, Office of Defense Mobilization 1953–54 (Exec. Secy. 1951–53; also served as one of three staff members, President's Advisory Cttee. on Government Organization; Asst. to Chmn., Cttee. on Reorganization of Dept. of Defense; Staff of Appropriations Committee, U.S. House of Representatives); Special Asst. to Administrator, Federal Civil Defense Admin. Jan.–July 1951; Admin. Asst. Office of Chairman, National Security Resources Board 1949–51 (Organization & Methods Examiner 1947–49); Budget Examiner, U.S. Bureau of the Budget 1946–47. Served in Marine Corps 1943–45. Assistant to Director, U.S. Bureau of the Budget 1966–67. Dir., Economics, Science & Technology Div., U.S. Bureau of the Budget 1968. Assistant Administrator for Administration, National Aeronautics and Space Administration (NASA) 1963–66. Dpty Associate Director, Science & Energy Division, Office of Budget & Management 1973; Asst. Secy. (Comptroller), Dept. of Health, Education, Welfare 1973–77; Asst. Sec., Management & Budget, Dept. of Health, Education & Welfare 1977. *Publications:* various articles on management. *Award:* William A. Jump Memorial Award. 1954. NASA Award for Outstanding Leadership 1966, *Member:* Amer. Socy. for Public Admin.; Amer. Political Science Assn.; Amer. Assn. for Advancement of Science. *Address:* 3028 Cedarwood Lane, Falls Church, Va.; and *office* U.S. Bureau of the Budget, Washington 25, D.C., U.S.A.

**YOUNG, John M.** American investment banker. *B.* 1901. *Educ.* Virginia Military Institute, and Harvard Business School (MBA 1924). *M.* 1933, Marian Hillyer Wolff. *S.* Jonathan McLain and Hillyer McDowell. *Dau.* Meredith Young Wood. *Career:* Student worker, J. P. Morgan & Co., N.Y. 1924, advancing to position of Manager of the Bond Dept. Resigned 1935. One of the original organizers and Director of Morgan Stanley & Co. Inc. (underwriting and wholesaling investment securities) 1935–41; General Partner 1941–72; Limited Partner 1972–75; Advisory Director 1975. Served as Comdr., U.S.N.R. on active duty Navy Dept., Washington, D.C. 1942–45; assigned to Joint Army and Navy Munitions Board 1942–43; Deputy Chief, Industrial Readjustment Branch, Office of Procurement and Material, Navy Dept. 1943–45. Director, 825 Fifth Avenue Corp. American-Australian Association & Chamber of Commerce Inc. *Award:* Legion of Merit, U.S.N. *Member:* Council on Foreign Relations; France-America Society; The Pilgrims. *Clubs:* Links, Bedford (N.Y.); Golf & Tennis. *Address:* 825 5th Avenue, New York, NYC 10021, U.S.A.

**YOUNG, John Percival,** OBE. Australian. *B.* 1917. *Educ.* Dubbo High School; Armidale Teachers' Coll., University of Sydney (BA, Dip Ed); University of Melbourne (post Grad.) *M.* 1949, Dulcie Wingrove Whittaker. *S.* Colin Maxwell. *Daus.* Susan April and Janet Ann. *Career:* Aust. Govt. Colombo Plan Adviser to Indian Govt. on woollen textile industry 1963; Member, Aust. Trade Mission to S. America 1962; Chairman, John P. Young & Associates Pty. Ltd. Management Consultants. *Publications:* Practical Techniques of Executive Development. Hon. Consultant to Royal Melbourne Hospital 1950—; Australian Representative at Davis Cup Nations Meetings in London and International Lawn Tennis Fedn., Europe, for 6 years. *Member:* L.T.A. of Australia; Fellow: Aust. Inst. of Management; Sales and Marketing Executives; Lawn Tennis Assn. of Victoria (Pres. since 1974). *Clubs:* Athenaeum; Melbourne Cricket; Victorian Racing; R.A.C. of Victoria; Victoria Amateur Turf; Australian American Assn. (Director): Riversdale Golf; Davey's Bay Yacht; Ranelagh Country; Naval & Military. *Address:* 2 Fordholm Road, Hawthorn, Vic. 3122; and *office* 2 Glen Street, Hawthorn, Victoria 3122, Australia.

**YOUNG, Milton R.** American politician. *B.* 6 Dec. 1897. *Educ.* LaMoure County Public Schools; North Dakota State Agricultural College; Graceland College, Lamoni, Iowa. *M.* 1969, Patrica M. Byrne. *Career:* Activity engaged in the operation of his farm near Berlin, North Dakota, until appointed to the United States Senate; member of school, township and County A.A.A. Boards; member, House of Representatives of North Dakota 1932–34; State Senator 1935–45; majority floor leader 1943; Republican State campaign manager 1940 and 1944; U.S. Senator from North Dakota since 1945; Secy., Republican Conference 1948–71; Member, Senate Appropriations and Agriculture Committees. *Address:* LaMoure, North Dakota, U.S.A.

**YOUNG, Richard Allen.** American. *B.* 1915. *Educ.* Washington Univ., St. Louis (BS Chem Eng); Harvard Graduate School of Bus. Admin. (MBA). *M.* 1945, Janice Westmoreland. *S.* Richard Allen and Alfred Westmoreland. *Dau.* Harriette Louise. *Career:* Vice-President, American Zinc Co. 1950–62 and Executive Vice-President 1963–64; Executive Vice-President Uranium Reduction Co. 1955–62. Directorships: Consolidated Gold Fields Ltd. (London), Gold Fields American Corp. and other companies; Former Chmn. Bd: and Chief Exec. Officer, American Zinc Co. St. Louis; Dir. since 1964 Bemis Company Inc.; Pres. since 1971 & Chief Exec. Officer since 1976. Dir. First Nat. Bank, Minneapolis; Dir. Soo Line Railroad Co. *Member:* Amer. Zinc Inst., Amer. Mining Congress, Mining and Metall. Socy. of Amer., etc.; Dir. Greater Minneapolis Chamber of Commerce; Dir. National Assn. of Manufacturers, N.Y.; Trustee, Twin City Area Educational TV Corp. *Awards:* Washington University Annual Alumni Award for Outstanding Contribution to Chem. Engng. Profession, 1960. Republican. *Clubs:* Old Warson Country; Bogey; St. Louis; Clayton; Mining; Sky (N.Y.); Minneapolis; Minikahda; Woodhill Country. *Address:* 950 Sixth Avenue, North Road, Wayzata, Minn. 55391; and *office* 800 Northstar Center Minneapolis Minn. 55402, U.S.A.

**YOUNG, Sir Richard Dilworth,** Kt 1970. British. *Educ.* University of Bristol (BSc). *M.* 1951, Jean B. P. Lockwood. *S.* 4. *Career:* Chairman, Alfred Herbert, Ltd. Director: Rugby Portland Cement Co. Ltd.; Boosey & Hawkes Ltd.; Commonwealth Finance Development Corporation Ltd.; Man. Dir. Tube Investments Ltd. Member Social Science Research Council 1973. *Member:* Central Advisory Council on Science & Technology; Council, University of Warwick. Council of Institution of Mechanical Engineers, London. *Address:* Bearley Manor, Nr. Stratford-on-Avon, Warwickshire.

**YOUNG, Thomas.** South African advertising Practitioner. *B.* 1914. *M.* 1943, Ivy Doris Jacobsen. *S.* 1. *Dau.* 1. *Career:* Elected President. Association of Accredited Practitioners in Advertising 1954–58–66. Chmn., Marchant Young (Pty.) Ltd., & Man. Dir., Horak Stereos (Pty.) Ltd., Johannesburg. Executive Member, Audit Bureau of Circulations of South Africa, South African National Tuberculosis Association, Johannesburg Chamber of Commerce: Past Pres. Advertising Club of South Africa; Founder, Pres. Adv. Benevolent Fund, South Africa; Founder, Pres. S. African Chapter, International Adv. Association. *Address:* 26 Upper Park Drive, Forest Town, Johannesburg, South Africa.

**YOUNG, William Hilary,** CMG. British. *B.* 1913. *Educ.* Marlborough Coll. and Emmanuel Coll. Cambridge (BA 1934; MA 1938). *M.* 1946, Barbara Gordon Richmond. *S.* 1. *Dau.* 1. *Career:* Diplomatic appointments in Iran 1935–41, Berlin 1945–48, Budapest 1948–50, Delhi 1952–54, Foreign Office (Counsellor) 1954–57, Moscow (Minister) 1957–60. Senior Civilian Instructor, Imperial Defence College 1960–62; Minister, Pretoria/Cape Town 1962–64; Visiting Fellow, Harvard University Centre for International Affairs 1965–66. Ambassador to Colombia, Sept. 1966–70. *Address:* Blackmoor, Four Elms, Edenbridge, Kent.

**YOUNG-HERRIES, Sir Michael Alexander Robert,** OBE, MC, LLD. British. Chairman, Royal Bank of Scotland. *B.* 1923. *Educ.* Eton and Trinity College, Cambridge (MA Cantab). *M.* 1949, Elizabeth Hilary Russell Smith. *S.* William and Robert. *Dau.* Julia. *Career:* Served with King's Own Scottish Borderers 1942–49; Captain T.A. (Reserve of Officers) 1949—. Joined Jardine Matheson in same year and served in the Far East. Chairman and Managing Director, Jardine Matheson & Co. Ltd., Hong Kong 1963–70; Chmn. Matheson & Co. Ltd. London 1971–75; Dir. Jardine Matheson & Co. Ltd.; Chmn. Royal Bank of Scotland since 1976; Dir., Scottish Widows Fund & Scottish Mortgage & Trust Co.; Dep. Chmn., National & Commercial Banking Group. *Clubs:* New Club (Edinburgh); Caledonian; Farmers' (London); City of

London; Member, Royal Company of Archers. *Address:* Spottes, Castle Douglas, Scotland; and *office* Royal Bank of Scotland Ltd., 42 St. Andrew Sq., Edinburgh.

**YOUNGER, The Hon. George Kenneth Hotson,** TD, DL, MP. *B.* 1931. *Educ.* Cargilfield School Edinburgh; Winchester, New College Oxford (Hons degree Modern History). *M.* 1954, Diana Rhona Tuck. *S.* 3. *Dau.* 1. *Career:* Served Argyll & Sutherland Highlanders 1950–65. Adopted as candidate for Kinross & N. Perth, but stood down for Sir Alec Douglas-Home (1963); Member of Parliament for Ayr since 1964; Scottish Conservative Whip 1965–67; Deputy Chmn. of Conservative Party in Scotland 1967–70; Parly. U-Secy. of State for Development, Scottish Office 1970–74; Minister of State for Defence Jan-Feb 1974; Chmn. of Conservative Party in Scotland 1974; Shadow Secy. of State for Defence 1975–76. *Director:* George Younger and Son Ltd. 1958–68; J. G. Thomson and Co. Ltd., Leith, 1962–66; Maclachlans Ltd. 1968–70; J. G. Thompson and Co. Ltd. 1974; Tennent Caledonian Breweries Ltd. 1977. *Member:* Queen's Body Guard for Scotland (R. Co. of Archers). Appointed Deputy Lieutenant for Stirlingshire 1968. *Clubs:* Caledonian; Highland Brigade. *Address:* House of Commons, London SW1A 0AA.

**YOUNGMAN, William Sterling.** Lawyer. *B.* 1907. *Educ.* Harvard (AB *magna cum laude* 1929) and Harvard Law School (LLB *magna cum laude* 1932). *M.* 1937, Elsie Hooper Perkins. *S.* William S., III, Robert P. *Dau.* Elsie Forbes. *Career:* Law Secretary to Judge Learned Hand, N.Y.C. 1932–33; associated with law firm of Storey, Thorndike, Palmer and Dodge (later Palmer, Dodge, Barstow, Wilkins and Davis), Boston 1933–38; Counsel, National Power Policy Cttee., and Chief Counsel Power Division, Public Works Administration, Washington 1939–40; General Counsel and liaison officer for the Federal Power Commission for National Defence Work in co-operation with other governmental agencies, Washington 1940–41; Exec. Vice-President and Director 1941–42, President 1942–45, China Defense Supplies (Chinese Government Lend-Lease Agency in U.S.) and General Counsel in U.S.A. of the Natural Resources Commission of China, Washington 1944–47. Associated with Corcoran & Youngman (later Corcoran, Youngman & Rowe), Washington 1941–49. Trustee, Middlebury College, Middlebury, Vt. Chairman of the Board: American International Underwriters Corp. 1959—, American Home Assurance Co. 1952—, The Insurance Co. of the State of Pennsylvania 1953—, American International Marine Agency of New York, Inc., 1965—. Chairman of Board, American International Reinsurance Co. 1965—. Director: American International Enterprises Inc., American International Marine Agency of Louisiana Inc., American International Reinsurance Co., American Life Insurance Co., American International Underwriters Agency Inc. (N.J.), Mt. Mansfield Co. Inc. *Member:* N.Y. State and Massachusetts Bars; U.S. Supreme Court; U.S. District Court for the District of Columbia. Vice-Chairman Council for Latin America. Member: Council on Foreign Relations; Foreign Policy Assn. *Clubs:* Badminton & Tennis, Longwood Cricket, St. Botolph, Bostonian Society (Boston); Down Town, Harvard, River (N.Y.C.); Chevy Chase, Metropolitan (Washington); Essex County, Manchester Yacht, Singing Beach (Manchester, Mass.). *Address: office* 102 Maiden Lane, New York City, 10005, U.S.A.

**YOUSUF, Lt.-Gen. Mohammed.** Pakistan. *B.* 1908. *Educ.* Royal Military College, Sandhurst (later attached to Yorks. and Lancs. Regt.; subsequently posted to 7th Light Cavalry). *M.* 1936, Zubeida Begum. *Career:* Served in World War II in Arakan and Assam on the Burma front. In 1947, during the partition of the sub-continent, he was appointed to supervise the task of evacuating refugees from across the Indian borders. Served on the Pakistan Nationalization Committee and appointed to command a Brigade, Jan. 1948; later promoted to rank of Major-General; G.O.C. Pakistan 1950–51; later Chief of General Staff; promoted Lieut.-Gen. 1954; retired from the army 1956; Pakistan High Commissioner in Australia and New Zealand 1956–59; London 1959–63; Kabul (Afghanistan) 1963–68; High Commissioner Ambassador London 1971–72; Ambassador in Switzerland and Holy See since 1972. *Award:* Sitara-i-Pakistan *Address:* Embassy of Pakistan, 47 Bernastrasse, 3000 Berne, Switzerland.

**YOXALL, Harry Waldo,** OBE, MC, JP. British publisher. *B.* 1896. *Educ.* St. Paul's School, London (Scholar) and Balliol College, Oxford (Classical Scholar). *M.* 1918, Josephine Baldwin. *S.* Nicholas Baldwin. *Dau.* Lindsey Elizabeth (Pietrzak). *Career:* Served in World War I (Capt.; MC and Bar 1915–19); foreign advertising department, Burroughs Adding Machine Co. Inc., Detroit, U.S.A. 1919–21; The Condé Nast Publications Inc., New York 1921–24; Director, The Condé Nast Publications Ltd., London 1924–35; Managing Director 1935–56, Chairman 1957–64; Pres., Periodical Proprietors' Assn. 1956–59, Vice-Pres. 1959–65. Vice-Pres., International Federation of the Periodical Press 1961–65. Magistrate, Richmond (Surrey) Bench 1941— (Chairman 1952–54, and 1962–64); Governor, Star & Garter Home for Disabled Ex-Servicemen 1941–76, Vice-Pres. 1976—. (Chairman Finance Committee 1964–68). Former Commissioner of Income Tax for the Elmbridge Division of Surrey; former member, Council of the Royal College of Art. Chmn. International Wine & Food Society 1972–75, Vice-Pres. 1975—. Grand Officier, Confrérie des Chevaliers du Tastevin. *Publications:* Modern Love; All Abroad; A Respectable Man; Journey into Faith; Forty Years in Management; A Fashion of Life; The Wines of Burgundy; Retirement a Pleasure; The Enjoyment of Wine. *Address:* Campden House Court, Gloucester Walk, London, W8 4HU.

**YU KUO-HUA.** Chinese banker. *B.* 1914. *Educ.* Tsinghua Univ.; Harvard Univ. Graduate Sch.; London School of Economics. *Career:* Sec. to Pres. of Nat. Mil. Council 1936–44; Alt. Exec. Dir., Int. Bank for Reconstruction & Development (IBRD) 1947–50; Pres., Central Trust of China 1955–61; Man. Dir., China Development Corp. 1959–67; Chmn. Bd. of Dirs., Bank of China 1961–67, China Insurance Co. Ltd. 1961–67; Alt. Gov., IBRD 1964–67, Gov. for Republic of China 1967–69; Minister of Finance 1967–69; Gov., Central Bank of China since 1969; Minister without Portfolio since 1969; Gov., Int. Monetary Fund since 1969, Asian Development Bank since 1969. Dr. (h.c.), St. John's Univ., Jamaica, N.Y. *Address:* Central Bank of China, Paoching Road, Taipei, Taiwan.

**YUKAWA, Morio.** Japanese diplomat. *B.* 1908. *Educ.* Tokyo Imperial University (Law Dept.). *M.* 1940, Teiko Kohiyama. *S.* Masao and Tomoo. *Career:* Joined Diplomatic Service and appointed Attaché London 1933. Vice-Consul, Geneva 1934; Head of Personnel Division (Foreign Ministry) 1945; Dir.: Foreign Trade Bureau of Economic Stabilization Board. (Cabinet) 1950; Director, Economic Affairs Bureau (Foreign Ministry) 1951; Counsellor of Embassy, Paris, 1952; Dir. of International Co-operation Bureau (Foreign Ministry) 1954; again Director of Economic Affairs Bureau 1955; Ambassador to the Philippines 1957–61; Deputy Vice-Minister of the Foreign Ministry 1961–63; Ambassador to Belgium 1963–68, concurrently to Luxembourg and also Chief of Japanese Mission to European Economic Community 1964–68; Ambassador to Court of St. James's 1968–72; Grand Master of the Ceremonies, Imperial Household, since 1973. *Awards:* Knight Grand Cross of the Royal Victorian Order (UK); Grand Cordon de l'Ordre de Leopold; Grand Croix de l'Ordre de la Couranne (Belgium); Grand Croix de la Couronne de Chene (Luxembourg); Laken of the Order of Sikatuna (Philippines); Gran Oficial de la Orden de Mayo Al Merito (Argentina); Officer de la Legion d'Honneur (France). *Member:* Society of International Law and Diplomacy. *Publications:* articles and brochures, mainly on economics. *Clubs:* Gakushikai; Hodogaya Country; Tokyo; Nihon. *Address:* 5-10-502, Sanbancho, Chiyoda-ku, Tokyo, Japan.

**YUN, Suk Heun.** Korean Diplomat. *B.* 1922. *Educ.* Seoul National University (BA, major, Pol Sc). *M.* 1949, Young June Choi, *S.* Seh Jung and Seh Wook. *Daus.* Seh Wha and Seh Ra. *Career:* Min. of For. Affairs 1954–56; Korean Embassy, Washington 1957–59; Dir. Bureau of Intern. Relations 1959–60; Dir., Political Affairs, Min. of Foreign Affairs, 1960; Counsellor, Korean Embassy in Bonn, 1961; Consul Gen., Cairo, 1962; Minister, Embassy, Washington, D.C., 1963–65; Director General, Foreign Affairs Inst., Seoul, 1966; Ambassador Eytraordinary and Plenipotentiary of the Republic of Korea to the Republic of the Philippines 1967–69; Vice Min. Foreign Affairs 1969–74; Ambassador of Republic of Korea in Paris since 1974. *Awards:* Republic of Korea, Order of Diplomatic Achievements Heung-In, Soong-Rye & Kwang-Wha; Order of Service Merit, Yellow. *Address:* 52-10 Chung Woon Dong, Chong No Koo, Seoul, Korea.

**YUVAL, Moshe.** Israeli Diplomat. *B.* 1913. *Educ.* Elementary and secondary education in Latvia and the Hebrew Univ., Jerusalem. *M.* 1952, Tamar Fay Roos. *S.* Boaz. *Dau.* Naomi Hava. Secretary of Defence Section, Political Dept., Jewish Agency for Palestine, Jerusalem 1936; Sec., Central Mobilization Board, Jerusalem 1939; Military Sec. to Head of Political Dept., Jewish Agency 1940; member, Jewish Agency deleg. to U.N. 1947; Consul and Passport Control Officer, New York 1948; Consul, Shanghai 1948; First Sec., Washington 1949; Consul and Act. Consul-General, Montreal 1950; Consul, Nicosia 1952. Director (with rank of Counsellor), Research Division, Min. for Foreign Affairs 1953. Director, Dept. of Information, Ministry for Foreign Affairs, Israel 1965–67. Ambassador of Israel to Australia and New Zealand Oct. 1958–63. Dep. Commandant, Israel National Defence College 1964–65; Ambassador to Peru and Bolivia 1968–71: Political Advisor to Minister of Foreign Affairs since 1971; Member, Exec. Cttee. of Yad Vashem (Holocaust Memorial Authority). Member Israel Labour Party. *Address:* Ministry of Foreign Affairs, Jerusalem, Israel.

# Z

**ZACHAROFF, Lucien.** American publishing executive, writer and editor. *B.* 1907. *M.* 1929, Stella Dubin. *S.* Zane Paul. *Career:* Went from Russia to U.S. 1922; naturalized 1929. Eye-witness of Russian revolution and civil war 1917–22; post-war traveller in Germany and Baltic States; in 1929, with wife, covered 9,000 miles in 6-week airplane hitch-hiking tour, writing daily despatches to sponsoring newspapers and periodicals; reporter, analyst of aero developments, adviser on air cargo problems; commentator on military and diplomatic phases of world affairs for numerous American and European periodicals; lecturer War Dept. Orientation Course 1942; founder, editor and publisher, Payload & The Air Shipper since 1947; combined with Shipping Management 1955, retained as editor and general manager till 1958; head, economic research, analysis and planning work, International Air Transport Division, Board of Economic Warfare and Foreign Economic Administration, World War II (detailed to Civil Aeronautics Board as editor, Foreign Air News Digest and Foreign Airlines Manuals); U.N. Correspondent, International Travel Digest. *Member:* International Society of Aviation Writers (accredited as its U.N. Observer 1957–60); Authors League of America; International Platform Association; National Writers Club (Board of Directors, President New York Metropolitan Chapter; accredited U.N. Observer 1960–64). *Publications:* What Every High School Editor Should Know (1927); Radio is Censored (in collaboration, 1936); This is War! (1939); 'We Made a Mistake'—Hitler (1941); The Voice of Fighting Russia (1942); The World's Wings (1946); Chinese Traditional Medicine (1967, in collaboration); Editor, Vital Problems of Air Commerce (1946); winner, T.W.A. annual award for best aviation journalism, 1945; translator of books and other materials from the Russian and other Slavic languages into English; consultant on East-West trade and cultural affairs; many contributions to U.S. and foreign publications. *Address:* G.P.O. Box 775, Brooklyn, N.Y. 11202, U.S.A.

**ZAFRULLAH KHAN, Hon. Chaudhri Sir Muhammad,** KCSI. Pakistani statesman. *B.* 6 Feb. 1893. *Educ.* Government College, Lahore (BA Hons); King's College, London (LLB Hons) and Lincoln's Inn. *M.* Bushra Rabbani, eldest dau. of the late S. S. Rabbani. *Career:* Advocate, Sialkot, Punjab 1914–16; practised in the Lahore High Court 1916–35; Editor, Indian Cases 1916–32; member, Punjab Legislative Council 1926–35; Delegate to the Indian Round Table Conference 1930, 1931 and 1932; Delegate to the Joint Selected Committee on Indian Parliamentary Reforms 1933; President, All-India Muslim League 1931; member, Viceroy's Executive Council 1935–41; Agent-General to the Government of India in China 1942; Judge, Indian Federal Court Oct. 1941–May 1947; Constitutional Adviser to the Nawab of Bhopal June–Dec. 1947; Leader of the Pakistan Delegation to the Annual Session of the General Assembly of the United Nations 1947–54; Leader, Pakistan Delegation to the Security Council of the U.N. on India-Pakistan dispute 1948–54; Minister of Foreign Affairs and Commonwealth Relations, Government of Pakistan 1947–54; Judge, International Court of Justice, The Hague, Oct. 1954–61 (Vice-Pres. 1958–61); Permanent Representative of Pakistan to U.N. 1961. President, 17th Session, U.N. General Assembly 1962; Judge, International Court of Justice, The Hague 1964–73; Pres. Int. Court of Justice 1970–73. *Awards:* Hon. LLD, Cambridge; Hon LLD, Columbia Univ.; Hon. Fellow of King's College, London; Hon. Fellow, London School of Economics; Hon. Bencher of Lincoln's Inn London. *Address:* 16 Gressenhall Road, London, S.W.18.

**ZAHEDI, Ardeshir.** Iranian diplomat. *B.* 1928. *Educ.* American Coll. of Beirut; Utah State Univ.—BSc 1950. *M.* 1957, Her Imperial Highness, Princess Shahnaz Pahlavi (*Diss.* 1964). *Dau.* Princess Mahnaz. *Career:* Treas., Joint Iran-American Comm. & Asst. to the Dir. of Point IV Program, 1950; participated in the revolution led by his father, General Zahedi, which overthrew Prime Minister Mossadegh, 1953; Special Advisor to the Prime Minister, 1953; Chamberlain to His Imperial Majesty, the Shahanshah Aryamehr of Iran, 1954—; Head of the Iranian Students' Program, 1959–60; Ambassador of Iran to the U.S. 1959–61; Head of Mission representing Iran at the 150th Anniversary Celebration in Argentina 1960; Ambassador of Iran to Great Britain, 1962–66; Rep. of Iran at signing of the treaty banning nuclear tests, London 1963; Foreign Minister of Iran, 1967–71; Rep. of Iran at Independence Celebrations of the Commonwealth of the Bahamas, 1973; Ambassador of Iran to the U.S. since 1973, & concurrently to Mexico 1973–76; Head of Iranian delegation to inauguration of the President of Brazil, 1974 & the President of Mexico 1976. *Awards:* Decorations from Iran & 23 other countries, incl. Iranian Taj with Grand Cordon First Class, 1975; Hon. Doctorates in Law from Utah Univ. 1960, Chungang Univ. of Seoul 1969, East Texas State Univ. 1973, Kent State Univ. 1974, & St. Louis Univ. 1975. *Address:* Imperial Embassy of Iran, 3005 Massachusetts Avenue, N.W., Washington, D.C. 20008, U.S.A.

**ZAHN, Eberhard Detloff,** Dr rer oec. *B.* 1910, *Educ.* Univs. of Frankfurt and Cologne; Berlin and Leipzig. Comm. Colls.; Dipl. Kaufmann 1931; Grad. 1933. *M.* 1943 to the late Ruth Poensgen. *S.* Eberhard, Joachim & Andreas. *Daus.* Ellen, Stephanie & Susanne. *Career:* IG Farbenind AG, Frankfurt/Main 1929–35; Thür. Gasgesellschaft, Leipzig 1936–38; Fendel Schiffahrts AG (member Bd. of Directors), Mannheim 1938–45; Zellstoff-fabrik Waldhof; Mannheim u. Wiesbaden (member Bd. of Directors) 1946–56. President of Board of Directors, Ruhr-Stickstoff Aktienges. 1957–1974, and of Ruhr-Schwefelsaeure GmbH, Bochum. *Member:* Supervisory Board Ruhr-Stickstoff AG, Bochum; Fincell GmbH, Wiesbaden; Advisory Committees Gerling Konzern, Cologne and Stuwadoors Maatschappij AEGIR NV, Rotterdam. *Club:* Cotary (Bochum). *Address:* St. Wolfgang-Ried Nr. 3, Austria.

**ZAHN, Johannes C. D.** Professor, Consul of the Norwegian Kingdom, German banker. *B.* 1907. *Educ.* Univ. of Bonn (*Dr jur*) and Harvard (SJD 1930). *M.* 1938, Victoria Brandeis. *S.* 1. *Daus.* 3. *Career:* Chmn. of the Bd. Bank Trinkaus & Burkhardt, Düsseldorf; President, NRW Stock Exchange, Düsseldorf; German-Belgian-Luxembourg Chamber of Commerce; President or member of supervisory councils of numerous leading German industrial concerns. Arbitration judge, German Arbitration Commission on Industry and Commerce since 1951; member, International Chamber of Commerce, Paris, since 1955; Executive Director, International Bank for Reconstruction and Development, Washington 1952–54. *Publications:* Bank Inspection Laws of the World (1938); Ethics of Administration and Contract in Stock and Share Legislation (1934); Banktechnik des Aussenhandels (1956) 6th Ed. 1974; Zahlung und Zahlungssicherung im Aussenhandel (1958), 5th Ed. 1975; Der Privatbankier (3rd Ed. 1972). *Address:* Königsallee 21/23 Dusseldorf, Germany.

**ZAHN, Louis.** American. *B.* 1909. *Educ.* High School. *M.* 1934, Frieda Kaplan. *S.* Melvyn. *Dau.* Barbara (Gunther). *Career:* Chmn. Bd. and Owner, Louis Zahn Drug Co. 1932—. Dir. Sears Bank & Trust Co; Bd. Gov. Gottlieb Memorial Hospital; Bd. Trustees Shimer Coll; Past member Ill. Parole & Pardon Bd; Past Pres. Midwest Bd. Amer. Med.

Center; West Towns Hospital; Edgewater Beach Playhouse; Bd. Dirs. Eleanor Roosevelt Inst. Cancer Research, Cancer Prevention Center; Bd. Assoc. De Paul Univ; Chmn. Greater Chicago Israel Bond Drive; Bd. of Trustees, Ed. Foundation of Am. Soc. of Oral Surgeons; 1965 Chmn. of City of Hope Medical Research dinner; Past Chmn. UJA Drug Div.; Past Pres. Dr. Jerome Solomon Research Foundation *Member:* National Wholesale Druggists Association; Chicago Retail Druggist Association; Chicago Drug Club; Chicago Drug and Chemical Club; Bd. Gastro-Intest. Res; Bd. Friends of Hebrew Univ., Hon. Doctorate Liberal Arts, Shimer College. *Award:* Horatio Alger Award, 1957; John Fitzgerald Kennedy Peace Award, 1964; 1971 Israel Bond Man of the Year. Man of the Year Shromrim Socy.; Traveler of Year award (Ill Pahrm. Assn.) *Clubs:* Standard; Bryn Mawr Country; Covenant (Chgo.). *Address:* 1930 George Street, Melrose Park, Illinois 60160, U.S.A.

**ZAHNER, Victor Henry.** American. Investment banker *B.* 1910. *Educ.* Rockhurst College (BA 1929; also Hon. Dir.) *M.* (1) 1931, Lorene A. Soden (*Dec.*). *S.* 1. *Daus.* 3. *M.* (2) 1959, Kathryn Cannon (*Div.* 1977.). Step-children 2. *Career:* With Bond Dept., City National Bank, Kansas City 1930–39; organizer, officer and director, Soden & Co., Kansas City 1939–43; Asst. to factory manager, Aircraft Div., Pratt & Whitney Co. 1943–45; President Zahner & Co., Kansas City 1945—. *Member:* Investment Bankers Assn. (Chairman S.W. Group 1950, Board of Governors 1960–63); Mission Hills Country; Kansas City Society of Financial Analysts. *Member:* Native Sons of Kansas City. *Club:* Mission Hills Country. Rotarian. *Address:* 1001 West 57th Street, Kansas City 64113; and *office* 127 West Tenth Street, Kansas City 64105, Mo., U.S.A.

**ZAISER, John Donald.** President and General Manager, Hydro-Thermal Corporation Milwaukee, Wisconsin, 1970—. *B.* 1910. *Educ.* Purdue University (BSc in Mech Eng 1932). *M.* 1934. Betty Strauss. *S.* Gary Carl. *Career:* President, Ampco Foundation 1956–64; Vice-President, Fire & Police Commission of Wauwatosa, Wisconsin 1952–62; Trustee, St. Luke's Medical Library Foundation; Director, Wisconsin Chapter of American Foundrymen's Society 1961–64; Steering Committee Production Techniques Section of American Ordnance Association 1958–64; member, Advisory Committee, War Production Board 1943–45; Director, Milwaukee Association of Commerce 1947–48; American State Bank 1948–58; National President, Non-Ferrous Founders' Society 1950–52; President, Wisonsin Chapter, Young Presidents Organization 1957–58. With Ampco Metal Inc.: Production Department 1933–64. Sales Engineer 1934, Field Sales Manager 1936, General Sales Manager 1938, Assistant General Manager 1944, General Manager 1945, President and General Manager 1946, Pres., Director, General Manager, 1946–64. Consultant to General Management, Ampco Metal Inc., Milwaukee. 1964–69; Consultative capacity, 1964–70. *Publications:* various technical papers pertaining to the non-ferrous industry. Republican. *Clubs:* Wisconsin; Milwaukee Press; Bluemound Golf and Country; various Masonic. *Address:* 1040 North Perry Court, Wauwatosa 53213, Wis., U.S.A.

**ZAVALA ORTIZ, Dr. Miguel Angel.** Argentine Lawyer & Politician. *B.* 1906. *Educ.* University of Buenos Aires (Law degree 1927). *M.* Lidia Olmos. *Career:* Has been an active member of the Radical Party since 1934, and as such takes a keen interest in social economics. In the Province of Córdoba the originator of a movement to awaken an interest in regional packing houses and power co-operatives; in 1936 he was chosen to represent Córdoba at the first National Power Co-operatives Congress. He has held various important positions within the Radical Party; in 1948 he was returned as a National Deputy, and as a member of the Chamber of Deputies he has concentrated on economic and international matters, and the claims of the farmers. In 1951, following the events of 28 Sept., he was deprived of his parliamentary privileges, tried at law and subsequently imprisoned; shortly after his release he was re-arrested and tried for contempt of the law. He took an active part in the revolutionary movement of 1955 and was subsequently appointed to the National Consultative Board; Minister of Foreign Affairs 1963–66. *Publications:* La Crisis Social Contemporànea y el Radicalismo; La Reforma Agraria; Conciencia Nacional y Social del Empressario; Por una Argentina Social; La No-Intervención y la Realidad Internacional de Argentina. He is also the author of the draft for a Civil Aeronautics Code which was approved by the II National Air Conference held in Mendoza in 1934, and of an Administrative Litigation Code. With other political leaders he visited Germany, Great Britain and the EE.UU, as a guest of the resgective governments. On his return to Argentina he delivered a series of lectures commending Western Europe's social democracy. *Address:* c/o Ministry of Foreign Affairs, Arenales 761, Buenos Aires, Argentina.

**ZELLERBACH, Harold Lionel.** American. *B.* 1894. *Educ.* Univ. of Pennsylvania (BSc). *M.* 1917, Doris Joseph. *S.* William Joseph and Stephen Anthony. *Dau.* Rolinde (Loew, Jr.). *Career:* Consultant & Director Emeritus, Crown Zellerbach Corporation. Hon. Director: Zellerbach Paper Co. President Emeritus, San Francisco Art Commission; Past Pres., Dir. Emeritus Newhouse Foundation. Pres. & Dir. Zellerbach Family Fund; Dir. Emeritus, San Francisco Ballet Assn.; Hon. Dir., Laguna Honda Hospital Volunteers Inc.; Director San Francisco Art Institute, San Francisco Opera Assn.; Pres. Harold and Doris Zellerbach Fund. Trustee: Emeritus University of Pennsylvania; Trustee: Fine Arts Museums of San Francisco. Vice-President, Member Board of Governors & Exec. Cttee. San Francisco Symphony Association. *Address:* One Bush Street, San Francisco 94119, Calif., U.S.A.

**ZELLERBACH, William Joseph.** American. *B.* 1920. *Educ.* Wharton School of University of Pennsylvania (BS Econ 1942), and Harvard Advanced Management Program 1958. *M.* 1946, Margery Haber. *S.* John W., Thomas H. and Charles R. *Dau.* Nancy. *Career:* President, Zellerbach Paper Co., San Francisco, Calif. 1961—; Board of Directors, Crown Zellerbach Corp., San Francisco 1960—; Lloyds Bank Cal., Los Angeles 1963—; Purex Corp., Lakewood, Calif. 1973—; Van Gelder Papier, Amsterdam, The Netherlands 1974—; Zellerbach Family Fund; San Francisco Chamber of Commerce, San Francisco; Bay Area Sports Enterprises, San Francisco; Trustee University of Pennsylvania, Philadelphia. *Clubs:* San Francisco Yacht, Concordia, Stock Exchange, Commercial, Commonwealth, Villa Taverna, Presidio Golf (all of S.F.); Peninsula Golf Club (San Mateo, Calif.). *Address:* 3540 Jackson Street, San Francisco, Calif.; and *office* 55 Hawthorne Street, San Francisco, Calif., U.S.A.

**ZELLI, Manoutchehr.** Iranian. Under-Secretary of State for Political & Parliamentary Affairs, July 1977. *B.* 1920. *Educ.* Bachelor of Science, Political Science, Law College, Tehran University. *M.* 1951, Nicou. *Dau.* Soheila. *Career:* Entered Government service 1942; joined Iranian Foreign Service 1945; Attaché and Third Secretary London 1950–52; Deputy Director of Information, Ministry of Foreign Affairs 1953; Second and First Secretary London 1954–57; Dep. Dir., Dept. of Economic Affairs 1958; Dep. Chief of Protocol; Acting Dir., Second Political Dept. 1959; Member Iranian Delegation to 14th Session of U.N. General Assembly 1959; Counsellor and Minister at New Delhi 1960–63; Dir., First Political Dept. 1963. Minister at the Iranian Embassy in London, Mar. 1964–Feb. 1967; Ambassador to Lebanon 1967–69; Dir. General Political Affairs for Europe and America May 1969; Delegate, 24th Session of U.N. Gen. Assembly May 1969; Under Secy. of State for Political Affairs, Ministry of Foreign Affairs 1970–72; Ambassador of Iran to Pakistan 1972–77, concurrently accredited to the Republic of Sri Lanka 1973–75. *Member:* International Law Assn., Iranian Branch. *Awards:* Grand Cordon of the Order of Homayoun (Iran), Commander of the Orders of Taj (Iran), Orange-Nassau (Netherlands), Rising Sun (Japan) and Dannebrog (Denmark); Knight Grand Cross of the Order of Polar Star (Sweden). *Address:* Imperial Ministry for Foreign Affairs, Tehran, Iran.

**ZEMLA, Dr. M.** Czechoslovak diplomat. *B.* 1925. *Educ.* Faculty of Law, Charles University, Prague. *M.* 1954, Libuse. *Dau.* Hana. *Career:* Chmn. Chargé d'Affaires, Kabul, 1950–52; Dep. Head, Czechoslovak Delegation, Neutral Nations Supervisory Commission in Korea, 1954–55; First Secretary, Peking, 1955–58; Chargé d'Affaires, Hanoi, 1956–57; Advisor (and alternate member) Czech Delegations to 14th, 15th, 16th and 17th Sessions, U.N. General Assembly; Member: Czech Delegations to the Disarmament Conferences, Geneva, 1958–64. Ambassador to Canada 1964–68. Head of the Department of Analysis and Programme 1968. Secretary General of the Ministry of Foreign Affairs, Prague, 1969–71; Deputy Head, Czechoslovak Delegation to the 25th Session. U.N. General Assembly; Ambassador to Great Britain 1971–74: Ambassador, Dep. Head of Legal Dept., Min. of Foreign Affairs, Prague; Chmn., Czechoslovak Delegation to U.N. Conference on Territorial Asylum, Geneva Jan.–Feb. 1977. *Club:* Rideau, Ottawa. *Address:* c/o Ministry of Foreign Affairs, Prague, Czechoslovakia.

**ZHIVKOV, Todor.** Bulgarian Politician. *B.* 1911. *Educ.* Secondary Graphical School and High School, Sofia. *Career:* Printer. Joined the Young Communist League 1928 and the Communist Party 1932. Active organizer of the partisan movement in Sofia District during the anti-Fascist struggle in Bulgaria. Candidate Member of the Central Committee of the Bulgarian Communist Party 1944 (full member 1948), First Secretary 1954—. Member of the National Assembly 1945— and member of the Presidium of the National Assembly 1956–62; Prime Minister 1962–71; Chmn. of State Council since 1971. *Publications:* For the Youth (1963); Speeches, Reports. Articles (1942–64); Science and Art in the Service of the People (1965). *Address:* Durzhaven Suvet, Sofia, Bulgaria.

**ZIEGLER, Vincent Charles.** American. *B.* 1910. *Educ.* College of the City of Detroit 1927–29. *M.* 1933, Marian Louise Hahn. *S.* Robert Earl. *Dau.* Mary Ann. *Career:* With Chrysler Corp., Detroit 1927–34, and Hiram Walter, Detroit 1935–42. Major, U.S. Army Ordance 1942–46. Exec. Asst. to Vice-Pres. Charge of Sales, Gillette Safety Razor Co., Boston 1946; Eastern Div. Sales Mgr. in N.Y.C. 1949; Assistsnt Sales Mgr. Boston 1951; General Sales Mgr. 1952; Vice-Pres. i/c Sales 1953; Pres. Safety Razor Co. 1958; Exec. Vice-Pres. The Gillette Co. 1964; Pres. The Gillette Co. 1965. Chairman of the Board, The Gillette Co., Boston 1966–75, Dir. 1976. Director: National Shawmut Bank 1963—; Reed & Barton Corporation; New England Mutual Life Insurance Co.; Zayre Corporation. *Member:* American Chapter, Knights of Malta 1965—; Bd. of Overseers, Boys' Club of Boston 1959—; Simmons College Business Advisory Committee 1960—. Member, Corporation, Northeastern Univ., 1966; Cypress Point Club (Calif.). Fellow, Brandeis Univ., 1968. *Member:* National Sales Executives Inc.; Boston Chamber of Commerce. *Clubs:* Algonquin (Boston); Brae Burn Country (W. Newton, Mass.). *Address:* 21 Allen Road, Wellesley Hills, Mass.; and *office* Prudential Tower Building, Boston, Mass. 02199, U.S.A.

**ZIEGLER, William Smith,** CBE, DSO, ED. Canadian. *B.* 1911. *Educ.* Schools of Calgary and Edmonton; Univ. of Alberta (Civil Engineering). *M.* 1940, Mildred Elizabeth Dean. *S.* Rodney Christopher. *Career:* Served in World War II with Canadian Army from 1939; overseas in various theatres in Europe; gazetted Brigadier at age of 32; after hostilities served in senior administrative posts with British Foreign Office (German Section) with Control Commission in Germany. Joined Canadian National Railways 1951 as Assistant to Vice-President Research and Development, and then various posts to Assistant Vice-President Personnel, Montreal 1955, Inland Cement Industries Ltd. 1956–73; Director: Genstar Ltd.; Alberta & Northwest Chamber of Mines, Oils, Resources. Canadian Executive Service Overseas. *Member:* Advisory Bd. The Salvation Army; Assn. of Professional Engineers of Alberta. *Clubs:* Edmonton Petroleum; Mayfair Golf & Country. *Address:* 13834 Ravine Drive, Edmonton, T5N 3ML, Canada.

**ZIEMER, Gerhard,** Dr jur. German banker. *B.* 1904. *Educ.* Dr jur; Barrister and Junior Judge. *M.* 1928, Gerda Holste. *S.* 4. *Daus.* 2. *Career:* Managing Director, Lastenausgleichsbank, Bad Godesberg. Member of the Board: Wirtschaftsaufbaukasse Schleswig-Holstein AG, Kiel; and of J. Gollnow & Sohn, Karlsruhe; Trustee for the property of the Eastern Counties. *Address: office* Kronprinzenstr. 8, Bad Godesberg Germany.

**ZIJLSTRA, Jelle,** Dr Econ Sc. Netherlands professor of economics, politician and banker. *B.* 27 Aug. 1918. *Educ.* School of Economics, Rotterdam. *M.* 1946, Hetty Bloksma. *S.* Ane Jelle, Sjoerd. *Daus.* Irene, Anne Elizabeth, Nynke T. *Career:* Assistant, Netherlands School of Economics, 1945–46; Lecturer, 1947; Professor of Economics, Free Univ. of Amsterdam; Minister of Economic Affairs 1952–59, of Finance May 1959–63; President: Board of Governors, European Investment Bank, 1962–63; Professor of Public Finance and Senator 1963–67. Prime Minister, 1966–67. President: Netherlands Bank, 1967—; Bank for International Settlements, 1967—; Governor, International Monetary Fund, Washington, since 1967. *Publications:* On the Velocity of Circulation of Money. *Address:* Bavoylaan 14, The Hague; and *office* De Nederlandsche Bank N.V., Westeinde 1, Amsterdam, Netherlands.

**ZILKHA, Abdulla Khedouri.** Italian. *B.* 1913. *Educ.* American Univ., Beirut (Lebanon). *M.* 1935, Zmira Many. *S.* Elie and Daniel. *Dau.* Ruth. *Career:* Managing Director, Banque Zilkha, SAE, Cairo and Alexandria 1929–48; Director, THALASSA S.A., Paris, 1949–55; Dir. Ufitec S.A. Zurich 1949—. *Clubs:* Polo de Paris; Golf de Saint-Nom-La-Breteche; Union Interalliée (Paris); du Chateau (Castelleras A/M). *Address:* 11 *bis*, Avenue du Maréchal Maunoury, Paris XVI, France.

**ZILKHA, Ezra Khedouri.** American banker. *B.* 1925. *Educ.* Hill School, Pottstown, Pa.; Wesleyan Univ., Middletown Conn.—BA 1947. *M.* 1950, Cecile Iny. *S.* 1. *Daus.* 2. *Career:* Came to U.S. 1941, naturalized 1950. Chmn. Bd. Fidelity International Bank, New York 1968; Pres. Zilkha & Sons Inc., 1956; Director: Hudson General Corp.; Handy & Harman, N.Y.C.; Mothercare Ltd., London; Mothercare Stores Inc., N.Y.C.; INA Corp., Phila.; INA Life Insurance Co. of New York; Blyth Eastman Dillon, N.Y.C.; Fidelity Bank (France), Paris, ICD Rehab. & Research Center, N.Y.C. Bd. Dirs., Chmn. Investment Comm., Wesleyan Univ.; Trustee, Lycee Francais de N.Y., Spence School, N.Y.C. Member, Council on Foreign Relations. *Decorations:* Chevalier de la Legion d'Honneur (France). *Clubs:* University; Bankers; Down Town Assn. of N.Y.C.; The Knickerbocker; The Meadow (Southampton, N.Y.); Brooks's (London); Polo (Paris); The Travellers' (Paris). *Address:* 927 Fifth Avenue, New York, N.Y. 10021; and *office* 99 William Street, New York, N.Y. 10038, U.S.A.

**ZILKHA, Selim Khedoury.** American. Chairman and Managing Director, Mothercare Ltd. *B.* 1927. *Educ.* Williams College, Williamstown, Mass. (BA). *S.* Michael. *Dau.* Nadia. *Clubs:* Brooks's (London); Sunningdale Golf; Portland (London); Travellers' (Paris). *Address:* 74 Portland Place, London, W.1; and *office* Cherry Tree Road, Watford, Herts.

**ZIMMERMAN, Charles J.** *B.* 1902. *Educ.* Dartmouth College (BS 1923); Amos Tuck School of Business Administration (Dartmouth College), MBA 1924; American College of Life Underwriters (CLU Deg. 1931); Hon MA Dartmouth College 1952; Hon LLD (Univ. of Hartford) 1967; Hon. LLD (Dartmouth) 1973; John Newton Russell Memorial Award 1951; Insurance Hall of Fame, 1969. *M.* 1942, Opal Marie Smith. *Career:* Trustee & Hon. Chmn., American College of Life Underwriters; Dir. (Pres. 1968–72) Inst. of Living; Trustee, Hartford Easter Seal Rehabilitation Center; Trustee, Combined Hospitals Fund; Trustee, National Conf. of Christians & Jews Inc.; Hon. Trustee, Lawrence Acad.; Dir., Hartford Council, Navy League of the U.S.; Trustee, Dartmouth Coll. (1952–72); Founder, Univ. of Hartford; Pres., Nat. Assn. of Life Underwriters (1939–40); Pres., American Life Convention (1969–70); Dir., Conn. Bank & Trust Co. (1960–72); Dir., Conn. Natural Gas Corp. (1960–72). Executive Manager, N.Y. Life Underwriters Association 1924–26. Agent, The Connecticut Mutual Life Insce. Co. 1926–31 (General Agent 1931–41); Assistant and Associate Managing Director, Life Insurance Agency Management Association, 1946–51 (Managing Director 1951–56). Director, The Connecticut Mutual Life Insurance Co. 1956–72 (Pres. 1956–67, Chmn. 1967–72); Republican. *Clubs:* Hartford; Hartford Golf; Country Club of Florida; Ocean of Florida. *Address:* 70 Mohawk Drive, West Hartford, Conn. 06117; and *office* 140 Garden Street, Hartford, Conn. 06115, U.S.A

**ZIMMERMAN, Joseph.** American business executive and lawyer. *B.* 1891. *Educ.* City College (BA); Columbia Univ. (MA); New York Univ. (JD). *M.* 1918, Anna R. Cohn (*Dec.*). *Daus.* Phyllis Winifred (Seton) and Mimi Z. (Gordon). *Career:* Asst. Dir. Educational Clinic 1915–18; College Instructor-Education 1915–18. Vice-Pres. in Charge of Corporate Development 1961—; Miles Metal Co. (NY); Editor-in-Chief, Daily Metal Reporter 1920–61. *Publications:* metal economist; business and market analyst; lecturer. *Member:* Phi Beta Kappa; Mining and Metallurgical Society of America; American Institute of Mining and Metallurgical Engineers; Academy of Political Science; American Association for the Advancement of Science. *Club:* Mining. *Address:* 6 Peter Cooper Rd., New York; and *office* 250 Park Ave., New York, N.Y., U.S.A.

**ZODDA, Alfred Travis.** American. *B.* 1920. *Educ.* BA (*cum laude*) and MA (Fellow). *M.* 1942, Jean Maydan. *S.* Alfred T. Jr., Deni Michael. *Dau.* Christie Ann. *Career:* Vice-Pres., Olin Mathieson Chemical Corp. 1961—, and of Olin Mathieson International Operations 1957. With E. R. Squibb & Sons International; General Manager 1955, Director of Marketing 1954, and Advertising Manager 1952; President, Conat International Corp. 1963—. President and Chief Executive Officer, Mart Rubber Corp. 1966—; Vice Pres. (Corporate) Damon Corp. since 1971. *Awards:* Downer Scholarship for Study Abroad; Rev. Dumas Scholarship. Fordham University;

Spanish Honors Diploma, C.C. New York. *Member:* Ethical Export Executives; Pharmaceutical Advertising Club; International Advertising Assn. *Clubs:* New York Athletic; Huntington Crescent. *Address: office* 54 Highland Circle, Wayland, Mass. 01778, U.S.A.

**ZOPPI, Rolando.** Swiss banker. *B.* 1932. *Educ.* University of Geneva (Licencie en Sciences Sociales). *M.* 1957. *S.* Luca. *Dau.* Roberta. *Career:* Man. Dir. Weisscredit Trade & Investment Bank 1955—. With Swiss Credit Bank, Zurich 1955–57; with Banca Weiss since 1957 (now Weisscredit Trade & Investment Bank). *Address:* Morcote; and *office* Via Motta 10, Chiasso, Switzerland; Via Pioda 9, Lugano, Switzerland.

**ZORIN, Valerian Alexandrovitch.** Soviet government official. *B.* 1902. Organizer on Central Committee of Komsomol (Communist Youth League) 1922–32; Research Student at Higher Communist Institute of Education 1933; Communist Party and teaching work 1935–41; Assistant General Secretary, Commissariat of Foreign Affairs 1941; Head of 4th European Department 1943–45; Amb. Ex. and Plen. to Czechoslovakia 1945–47; Dep. Min. of Foreign Affairs 1947–55, 1956–57 & concurrently Perm. Rep. to UN Security Council 1952–53; Amb. to Fed. Rep. of Germany 1955–60; Perm. Rep. to UN 1960–62; Alt. Mem. Central Cttee. of C.P.S.U. 1956–61, Mem. 1961—; Amb. to France 1965–70. Order of Lenin (twice); Order of Red Banner of Labour (twice); Medal for Valorous Services in 1941–45 War. *Address:* c/o Ministry of Foreign Affairs, 32–34 Smolenskaya-Sennaya Ploschchad, Moscow, U.S.S.R.

**ZUCKERMAN, Lord, of Burnham Thorpe Norfolk.** (Solly Zuckerman). OM, KCB, FRS, MA, MD, DSc. MRCS. FRCP. British. *B.* 1904. *Educ.* South African College School and Univs. of Cape Town, London, Oxford, and Yale; MA (Oxford and Cape Town); MD (Birmingham); DSc (London); FRCP (London); Hon FRCS (London). *M.* 1939, Lady Joan Rufus Isaacs. *S.* Paul Sebastian. *Dau.* Stella Maria. *Career:* Demonstrator, Univ. of Cape Town 1923–25; Union Research Scholar 1925; Research Anatomist to Zoological Socy. of London; Demonstrator, University College London 1928–32; Research Associate and Rockefeller Research Fellow, Yale Univ. 1933–34; University Demonstrator and Lecturer, Oxford 1935–45. William Julius Mickle Fellow, Univ. of London 1935; Beit Memorial Research Fellow 1934–37; Hunterian Prof., Royal College of Surgeons 1937; Prof. of Anatomy, Univ. of Birmingham 1943–68. now Prof. Emeritus; Hon. Secy., Zoological Society of London 1955–77, Pres since 1977; Chief Scientific Adviser to the Secy. of State for Defence 1960–66; to the British Government 1964–71; Prof.-at-large, Univ. of E. Anglia 1969–74; Prof.-Emeritus since 1974. *Member:* Royal Society of London and various other scientific societies. Fellow, Inst. of Biology; Hon. Fellow, Pharmaceutical Society; Trustee, British Museum (Natural History). Visitor of Bedford College and Fellow of Univ. College, Univ. of London; Pres. Parly. and Scientific Cttee. 1973–76; Pres. Fauna Preservation Socy. since 1974. *Awards:* Hon. Member Academia das Ciencias de Lisboa; Fellow Commoner, Christ's Col. Cambridge; Dr (hc) University of Bordeaux; Hon DSc Univ. of Sussex, Jacksonville Univ. (U.S.A.) and Univ. of Bradford; Hon. LLD. Birmingham; Hon. FRCS; Foreign Member, American Philosophical Socy. Medal of Freedom with Silver Palm (US); Chevalier, Legion of Honour (France); Created Life Peer 1971. *Publications:* The Social Life of Monkeys and Apes: Functional Affinities of Man, Monkeys and Apes; A New System of Anatomy; Scientists and War; Beyond the Ivory Tower; From Apes to Warlords: 1904–46. Editor, The Ovary (Vols. I and II); contributions to scientific journals. *Clubs:* Beefsteak, Brooks's. *Address:* House of Lords, Westminster, S.W.1.

**ZULUETA, Sir Philip (Francis de).** British banker. *B.* 1925. *Educ.* Beaumont; New College, Oxford (MA). *M.* 1955, Hon. Marie Louise Hennessy. *S.* 1. *Dau.* 1. *Career:* Private Secretary to the Prime Minister (Lord Avon, Mr. Macmillan. Sir A. Douglas-Home) 1955–64; Director, Hill Samuel & Co, Ltd. 1965–73; Tanganyika Concessions Ltd.; Union Minière and of other companies. Chief Exec. Antony Gibbs Holdings Ltd. 1973–76, Chmn. 1976. *Clubs:* Beefsteak; Pratt's; Whites: Jockey Paris. *Address:* 11, Vicarage Gardens, W.8; and *office* 23 Blomfield Street, London EC2M 7NL.

**ZUMWALT, Admiral Elmo Russell, Jr.** American Naval Officer. *B.* 1920. *Educ.* U.S. Naval Acad., Naval War Coll., Nat. War Coll. *M.* 1945, Mouza Coutelais-du-Roche. *S.* 2. *Daus.* 2. *Career:* Commissioned Ensign, U.S. Navy 1942, & advanced through the ranks to Admiral 1970; service on USS Phelps 1942–43, USS Robinson 1943–45, USS Saufley 1945–46, USS Zellars 1947–48; Asst. Prof., Naval Science 1948–50; Commanding Officer, USS Tills 1950–51; Navigator, USS Wisconsin 1951–52; Head, Shore & Overseas Bases Section, Naval Personnel, Washington 1953–55; Commanding Officer, USS Arnold J. Isbell 1955–57; LT Detailer, Naval Personnel 1957; Special Asst. for Naval Personnel, Office of Asst. Sec. of the Navy, Washington 1957–58, Exec. Asst., Snr. Aide 1958–59; Commanding Officer, USS Dewey 1959–61; Desk Officer for France, Spain & Portugal, Office of Asst. Sec. of Defense for Int. Security Affairs 1962–63; Dir., Arms Control & Contingency Planning for Cuba 1963; Exec. Asst., Snr. Aide, Sec. of Navy 1963–65; Commanding Officer, Cruiser-Destroyer Flotilla Seven 1965–66; Dir., Chief Naval Operations Systems Analysis Group, Washington 1966–68; Commander, US Naval Forces, Vietnam, & Chief Naval Advisory Group Vietnam 1968–70; Chief of Naval Operations 1970–74; ran for Senator from Virginia 1976. *Awards:* Distinguished Service Medal with Gold Star; Legion of Merit with Gold Star; Bronze Star Medal with Combat V; Navy Commendation Medal with Combat V; & many others: Hon. LLD, Villanova Univ.; Hon. D. Hum. Litt., U.S. Int. Univ. *Address:* 1500 Wilson Boulevard, Suite 1700, Arlington, Va. 22209, U.S.A.

**ZURAYK, Constantine Kaysar.** Professor, American University of Beirut. *B.* 18 Apr. 1909. *Educ.* American University of Beirut (BA), University of Chicago (MA), and Princeton University (PhD); Litt Dhc Univ. of Michigan. *M.* 1940, Najla Cortas. *Daus.* Ilham, Huda, Afaf, Hanan. *Career:* Asst. Professor of History, Beirut 1930–42; Associate Professor 1942–45; First Counsellor, Syrian Legation, Washington 1945–46; Minister, Delegate to U.N. Gen. Assembly, and Alternate Delegate to Security Council, 1946–47; Vice-Pres. and Prof. of Hist., Am. U. of Beirut 1947–49; Rector, Syrian University 1949–52; Vice-Pres., and Prof. Beirut 1952–54; Acting President 1954–57; Distinguished Prof. of History Apr. 1956—; member, International Commission for a Scientific and Cultural History of Mankind; President, Int. Assn. of Universities 1965–70, Hon. Pres. 1970—; Corresponding member, Arab Academie, Damascus and Iraqi Academie, Baghdad; Hon. Life member, Amer. Historical Association; Lebanese Education Medal, First Class; Commander, Order of the Cedar; Order of Merit, Distinguished Class, Syria. *Publications:* Editor (with Najla Izzeddin) The History of Ibn al-Furat; Ismail Beg Chol, al Yazidiyyah qadiman wa hadithan; Miskawayh's Tahdhib al-Akhlaq; author of (in Arabic) National Consciousness; The Meaning of the Disaster; Whither Tomorrow; Facing History; This Explosive Age; The Battle for Culture; The Meaning of the Disaster Again; More than Conquerors (in English); articles in Arabic and in Western journals; Trans. Miskawayh's Tahdhib al-Akhlaq. *Address:* c/o American University of Beirut, Beirut, Lebanon.

# GENERAL INDEX

## FOR BIOGRAPHICAL ENTRIES ONLY

If you have an entry in the Biographical Section of this reference book, you may care to suggest the names of individuals who do not at present appear but whom you consider worthy to be included. Please insert your own name in this space [                    ] and add below the name and address of any suitable person or persons to whom we will be pleased to send a questionnaire. Please detach this form and return to THE INTERNATIONAL YEAR BOOK AND STATESMEN'S WHO'S WHO, Tudor House, 26, Upper Teddington Road, Hampton Wick, Kingston upon Thames, Surrey, England.

Name..............................................................................................

Profession.......................................................................................

Address ..........................................................................................

.......................................................................................................

Name ..............................................................................................

Profession.......................................................................................

Address ..........................................................................................

.......................................................................................................

Name ..............................................................................................

Profession .......................................................................................

Address ..........................................................................................

.......................................................................................................

(BLOCK LETTERS, PLEASE)